This dictionary is not published by the original publishers of Webster's Dictionary or by their successors

WEBSTER'S UNIVERSAL DICTIONARY

OF THE ENGLISH LANGUAGE

with

A Comprehensive Addenda of Newest Words

Compiled by Joseph Devlin, M. A.

Profusely Illustrated

BEING THE UNABRIDGED DICTIONARY

By

NOAH WEBSTER, LL. D.

Edited under the supervision of

Thomas H. Russell, LL. D.; A. C. Bean, M. E., LL. B.; and L. B. Vaughan, Ph. B. and a staff of eminent scholars, educators, and specialists

VOLUME I

A — LITHISTID

THE WORLD SYNDICATE PUBLISHING COMPANY

CLEVELAND, O. NEW YORK, N. Y.

Made in U. S. A.

1936

CONTENTS

INTRODUCTORY

VOCABULARIES

INTRODUCTION

A LIVING LANGUAGE is not today what it was fifty years ago, or even what it was one year ago. Old words pass into the ocean of oblivion, new words flow in from the fountain of popular talk. Moreover, the philologist learns more from year to year. The study of language as a science is comparatively modern. Before the discovery of Sanskrit in the closing years of the Eighteenth Century there had been many accomplished linguists, there had been many guessers at philological truth. Words are a fascinating subject; they are men's tools to work with and to play with, and men have always been interested in speculation about them. The discovery of Sanskrit opened up a new world to the lover of language. It laid the foundation for the study of comparative philology, and each generation, since its introduction to European scholars, has made great advances. Dictionaries have been written, embodying the results of the greater knowledge, and new dictionaries and revisions of old dictionaries continually appear to record the result of scholarly investigation as it reaches further and further into the history of language

But this is after all but a minor reason for the work of the lexicographer. He seeks first and foremost to supply a popular need. With the diffusion of education comes a demand for standards, for correct information as to the meaning and proper use of words, as to the pronunciation and the spelling, preferred by men of culture and judgment. These standards themselves change from year to year. We do not speak English, we do not spell English, we do not use English words as our grandfathers did.

And this is because the English speaking people, as well as the philologist, have been learning something. Our pronunciation changes so that our words may be easier to pronounce. We drop the *p* and *l* of *psalm*, the *ugh* of *though*; *boatswain* becomes *bos'n; fourteen-night* becomes *fortnit.* We save time and labor for our organs of speech.

With change of pronunciation comes a change of spelling. Our spellings change slowly, it is true; not so fast as our sounds, and so pronunciation and spelling grow apart. Then comes the philologist, the lover of words, and urges reform; and in our spelling, *music* is no longer spelled with a *k*, and *honour* gradually loses its *u*. Our people begin to write *tho, thru* and *catalog*, and save time and money. Such changes the new dictionaries must record, and they must record the new meanings given to words; for new inventions and new discoveries, not only add new words to the language, but they borrow old words to use with a new signification. *Ace* is an old word, but its significance as descriptive of a hero in air fighting is new.

Most of all, our dictionaries must record the new words that come into our language almost every day. A language reflects the mind and soul of a people. The languages of savage tribes are rich in words which proclaim their degradation and debasement. But when a nation is thinking new thoughts and learning new facts, its language will be advancing too. Every new thought, every new fact, becomes fixed in words.

Some of these new words come into being as the result of men's conscious endeavor. The scientist discovering a new truth, the botanist a new plant, the inventor constructing a new machine may invent the word which names it. But there are also hundreds of words in every generation that seem to come from the heart of the people. They, too, must have been first spoken by some single man. But neither technical terms, selected by a great scientist, nor popular form blurted out without thought by some unknown poet of the people can become a part of the language unless it is approved by the community, and the community will only approve if the word supplies a perceived want, and fits in with the principles which are at the base of their language structure. And it is this necessity for words to represent the human mind of the community which makes impossible a successful use of the artificial languages which are invented from time to time by pseudo-scientists. "These", says Professor W. D. Whitney, (Language and the Study of Language, p. 51) "are indeed artful devices in which the character and bearing of each part is painfully weighed and determined in advance; compared with them language is a real growth; and human thought will as readily exchange its natural covering for one of them as the growing crustacean will give up its shell for a casing of silver wrought by the most skillful hands."

So it is that without the approval of those who use it no new word can come into the language, and language history is full of the records of technical words suggested by scientists which have never been accepted, and of nonce-words suggested by poets or philosophers which have never made their way. Such words often present a difficult problem to the lexicographer. They may seem to be reasonable, they may seem to be needed, and yet they must be excluded from his vocabulary, for only words belong to a language which are accepted by usage—reputable, present, national usage. Many words, on the other hand, may seem unnecessary, in bad taste, badly constructed, and yet they are universally accepted. Some lexicographers inspired by a laudable desire to improve their language have endeavored to exclude certain words which they regarded as unfit. The French Academy, including the most distinguished writers of France, made such an attempt, but when the words were accepted by the people, the dictionary of the Academy was compelled to give way. It learned the truth of Montaigne's saying, "They that will fight custom with grammar are fools." Still greater fools are they who will fight usage with a dictionary.

In the days of Queen Anne it was common to think of the English language as having reached perfection. It was the Augustan age of English literature, and Dr. Johnson's dictionary was the arbiter of elegance. To use a word not included in that sacred volume was a deadly sin. Even in modern times public discussions have taken place over words, in which authors and poets have declared a word not English because it was not found in the current standard dictionaries. Such a view of the power of dictionaries strays far from the truth. The record in the dictionary is only one form of evidence, the opinion of one man or of one group of men. Other dictionaries may differ, and in many cases other dictionaries do differ. In doubtful questions of language each man must decide for himself, as best he can.

But though the dictionary may not decide, it may indicate its preferences. Its great influence should be used for sound scholarship and good taste. It is one of the great forces which make language what it is. It is powerful, though not all powerful, and it should use its power wisely and well.

The changes that take place from period to period in any language take place at greater or at less speed according to the influences which are brought to bear upon the people who speak it. Some languages are very slow to change. The language of Iceland, a land comparatively isolated and little in touch with advances, political or cultural, has changed but slowly, and it differs but little from the language spoken by the Danes in the time of Alfred. But the Anglo-Saxon of Alfred's day is hardly recognizable in our modern English. The influence of the Danes and the Norman Conquest made it almost a new speech. Political convulsions, great wars, great advances in scientific knowledge hasten enormously the natural rate of change in any language. But a period of peace where people reflect and criticise is a period of slow change. A people that think of their speech alter it slowly.

Even in peaceful times there may be a difference in the rate of language change according to the character of the people. A people controlled by their aristocracy and by their cultured classes move but slowly. New words meet a cold reception. In a democracy where the cultured class is not so powerful the people will act for themselves. No effort on the part of scholars will be able to prevent the American people from changing the English language according to its own taste. So it is that from year to year the language spoken in England and the language spoken in America grow apart. We have not yet what may truly be called an American language, yet in America we use many words not known in the Mother country or with meanings unfamiliar to our English cousins.

The English language adopts words of foreign origin with great ease. This is mainly because it is a composite language. Its historical elements include languages of widely different characteristics. Words like German are found in its words of Anglo-Saxon origin, and the Norman Conquest made more than half our English words like those of a Romance language. The English, too, have been a great seafaring people. They have sent their commerce over all the world and brought back from their colonies words from many aboriginal languages. Hardly a language in the world but has given some words to the English vocabulary. So when the English language goes out to borrow, the new word does not find itself alone, awkward and unnatural, but it meets in the English vocabulary with plenty of its old friends. It is quickly assimilated and soon becomes as to the manor born.

During the last half century an immense number of new words and phrases have been introduced into the English language. Great wars—the American Civil War, the War with Spain, the British War in South Africa, have each introduced its hundreds of words. The wonderful new inventions and discoveries in science have added thousands of others, and the Great World War enormously stimulated the appetite for change. It is not alone that the English language borrowed from the French such words as *boche, poilu, aileron, barrage, escadrille, fuselage,* and a hundred other war terms; adopted *Bolsheviki, Soviet* and other Russian forms, consented to the *slacker,* and the *Anzac* and the *blimp* of the English, and the *kultur* and the *Taube* and the *pickelhaube* of the German, but the tremendous advances in the art of war, especially on its scientific side, almost revolutionized certain phases of the language of science. When the United States entered the war, and the Ordnance Department undertook to fit out the American armies with modern munitions, it was found that hundreds of forms of military equipment necessary for a modern army had been invented since the war began, forms which no factories in America had ever manufactured, or knew how to manufacture. The art of aviation, for instance, was a new thing. When the war began the airplane was in existence, but almost worthless as a means of warfare. The aviators were unarmed and made no attempt to fight either each other or the enemy upon the land. Today, the aviator is a knight of the air, armed with wonderful weapons, equipped with the utmost skill of science.

In peace, as in war, our language grows to encompass the new developments in our march toward a greater civilization. The engineer, the physicist, the biologist, each does his part in this great endeavor. All have added words to our vocabulary. There is need for a dictionary to record these terms, to make clear to those who live in this age of invention and discovery what is going on about them. This new Unabridged Dictionary has endeavored to collect a very complete vocabulary of such words as well as of those which have made up the body of our language for many centuries, to aid in interpreting the past as well as contemporary civilization.

The English language is a very large one. The ordinary man uses only a few thousand of its words. Shakespeare himself used but 15,000, and Milton half as many. Yet each man understands many times more words than he has at his tongue's end, and the man who reads meets with dozens every day that he does not clearly understand. It is wise to read with a dictionary by one's side, it is wise to write with a dictionary as one's aid, and never more than now.

Francis A. March, Jr.,
Lafayette College

PREFACE

Webster's Universal Unabridged Dictionary of the English Language, prepared by eminent scholars and published by an organization long devoted to the making of dictionaries, marks a new era in lexicography. It is the concrete expression of modern literary enterprise, a representative practical result of modern methods. As such it is that this work will be welcomed by English-speaking people in all parts of the world, who will be quick to recognize and appreciate its practical points of advantage.

Of many good and sufficient reasons for the publication of this work, one stands preeminent: the sincere belief of the editors and the publisher that a good working dictionary of the English language, complete in all departments, should be brought within the reach of the general public. They felt that a volume as indispensable to an understanding of modern progress in science and culture should be available to every reader.

It has been said that dictionaries should be revised at least once in every seven years. No one can be unaware of the necessity for accommodating them to the growth of the language especially in this period of its most remarkable increase. Never before, probably, in the history of speech has the vocabulary of a language grown by accretion so rapidly as that of the English language during the past few decades. Never before was there greater necessity than during that period for the lexicographer to busy himself; never has there been greater need than now for a new dictionary.

The unrivaled elasticity of our language has combined with recent remarkable scientific and political events, especially those of the last two decades, to add to its vocabulary thousands of new words and phrases, some of which are formally defined for the first time in this dictionary.

In all the fields of science investigators have been busy achieving results of marvelous character, demanding original and novel nomenclature, as well as the wide extension and expansion of that already in use. The discoveries in the field of endocrinology, for example, are a good illustration of the results of recent scientific research which has enriched and expanded a language capable of infinite expansion.

From the laboratories on both sides of the Atlantic a constant stream of new words and phrases has issued, together with new applications of old words and countless derivatives that make their first bid for public notice and permanent adoption in the pages of the newspapers and the scientific journals. Many of these new words, phrases, derivatives, and specific significations deserve prompt recognition and a speedy place in a complete standard dictionary of the English language, and in this respect this Dictionary will be found to have reflected faithfully the scientific progress of the language of English-speaking peoples the world over.

In illustration of the expansion of the language resulting from scientific research and the widened application of scientific methods to everyday needs, the experience of the officials of the United States Geological Survey may be cited. In the prosecution of their important work new terminology became necessary and often indeed was freely imposed upon them, to such an extent that regulation was required and a set of rules was formulated to govern the admission of new words and new uses of old ones.

The experience of the Geological Survey has been that of all bodies of men engaged in the fields of scientific research and accomplishment, where new nomenclature arises and must be either recognized or ignored. The duty of the lexicographer is, not to decide, but to record the decision.

It is not only in scientific terminology, however, that the English vocabulary has expanded during the past decades. Men and women have been busy as never before, along all lines of human effort, with one uniform and inevitable result—new words and new uses of old ones. Peace and war alike have contributed their quota, and in the case of the United States (ever a free-flowing fount of vigorous English) expansion of territory has been followed by correlative expansion of vocabulary. As the frontier pushed steadily westward the hardy pioneers added new words to our language, giving it a freshness and vigour that makes it distinctly American, and distinguishes it from the Mother tongue, English. After the acquisition in 1898 of territories formerly held by Spain, many Spanish words came into general use in the United States, some of which became a permanent part of the language. The World War and subsequent upheaval in military science, economics and geography, played a great part in adding words to our vocabularys that had never been used before, and in giving new meanings to old words.

Throughout the preparation of this Dictionary the greatest care has been taken in all cases to include in the vocabulary only such new words as are likely to find permanent place in the usage of English-speaking people. No attempt has been made to force new words into the word-list, for the mere purpose of increasing its size, and on the other hand no well-accredited or properly-introduced stranger has been denied admission.

Briefly, the object of this publication is to place in the hands of the English-speaking public a complete working dictionary, practical, comprehensive, and correct, sufficiently technical in its treatment of technical terms to satisfy the requirements of the specialist, and yet not too technical to afford enlightenment to the average reader; arranged upon a plan which shall make desired information easy to obtain, and devised to be a friend in need in the offices, stores, workshops, and homes where a complete dictionary of the English language is indispensable to an understanding of the changes that are taking place so rapidly in the world today. The intelligent person must read constantly to keep informed of these new developments in the world in which he lives, and he can have no greater aid in his reading than a dictionary that itself has kept pace with modern progress.

Origin of the Work. The idea which has found embodiment and expression in this new Dictionary was conceived by Mr. George W. Ogilvie ten years ago. By way of practical equipment for the task, he had many years' experience as a publisher of works of reference, the names of several of which are household words in America. Recognizing the opportunity for literary and commercial enterprise in a field wholly unoccupied, and at the same time realizing the vastness and importance of the project, he made arrangements with a view to the completion of the editorial work within as brief a space of time as was consistent with the requisite care and accuracy, the object being to secure uniformity throughout the entire work and to obviate a difficulty often experienced by lexicographers—that of finding the early portions of their work practically out of date before the end was ready for the printer. Thus the final literary labors of preparing this work for the press were compressed into a period of three years, during which comparatively brief time, however, its extensive corps of editors were compelled to strive without ceasing and with the expenditure of much midnight oil.

Plan and Scope. The plan of the Dictionary, as evolved by the publisher, contemplated a book that should be a practical and useful work of reference for all English-speaking people, but as the project grew and assumed definite shape, the original plan broadened and a still more important achievement was aimed at, namely, the preparation of a dictionary that, from the standpoint of the general public, should surpass all of its predecessors in every essential particular. To accomplish this end required a much greater expenditure of time, labor, and money than was originally contemplated, but the aim was a high one and the end justified the effort. It is not merely a good working dictionary, therefore, that is presented to the public in this work, but a complete dictionary of the English language that stands upon as high a plane as any of its predecessors, and will be found to excel them in many important particulars.

In aiming to produce a practical book of reference the editors have ever kept before them a high ideal, namely, to ascertain the true principles of the language, in its orthography and structure; to purify it from palpable errors and reduce the number of its anomalies, thus giving it more regularity and consistency in its forms, both of words and sentences, and in this manner to furnish a standard of our vernacular tongue. They have endeavored to make and keep the work free from eccentricities of any and every kind, and to maintain a conservative level by including among the compounded words only such as the best usage requires to be placed in that category, while the spellings adopted are those decided upon by a well-qualified Committee on Orthography. In short, they have made a dictionary of the English language as it is.

The Editorial Staff. Much of the editorial work upon this Dictionary has been performed, as in the case of all its predecessors, by an office staff gathered by a process of selection and with infinite pains. These office editors have been aided by many well-known educators and scientific specialists, from whom a vast quantity of new material has been obtained. Among these special editorial contributors to the pages of this work are included presidents and professors of college faculties from the Atlantic to the Pacific, and their practical assistance and kindly suggestions have been invaluable. The various departments of the Government at Washington have also been drawn upon freely for information, and a most obliging and helpful spirit has been found to prevail among the officials generally. Many of them have been at considerable pains to respond at length to the queries showered upon them by the editors, and especial thanks are due to the officials of the State and War departments for the care and thoroughness with which they have afforded information upon questions connected with the English vocabulary arising from our more intimate relationship in the family of nations and our broadened international interests.

In the prosecution of their work the editors have used a large and carefully-selected office library of works of reference covering all the important branches of human knowledge. The world's greatest libraries, including that of the British Museum and the Congressional Library at Washington, have been laid under constant contribution for aid in the work, and special facilities for research were afforded the editors at many libraries. For instance, they had at their immediate command the thousands of scientific books contained in the Crerar Library, only a stone's throw from the editorial headquarters; the large library of reference works in the Newberry Library, also close at hand; the vast resources of the Chicago Public Library; the library of the Field Columbian Museum, with many valuable references on anthropology, botany, geology and zoology, and including the Ayer collection of ornithological works; the Ryerson Library of the Chicago Art Institute, containing a large collection of works on the fine arts; the splendid library of the University of Chicago; and the huge collection contained in the New York Public Library. From the librarians and other officials of these libraries much assistance has been received, and thanks for their valuable aid is here sincerely tendered.

Upon the regular editorial staff there have been engaged constantly representative graduates from the great American universities, while those of Oxford, Cambridge, Dublin, and Aberdeen, and King's College, London, have also been represented by graduates and former members of their faculties. Canada, India, and Australia have likewise contributed of their scholarship to the personnel of the staff. Writers of great and varied experience, lawyers, doctors, and clergymen have been actively engaged in the work, together with men whose labors in the field of education have been lifelong, and from this varied material there was evolved a homogeneous working force, the result of whose labors it required only the work of the printer and of expert proofreaders to transform into the most complete modern dictionary.

Some Special Advantages. Regarded from any standpoint the making of a new dictionary of the English language is an important event in the world of letters. It means to the scholar an additional source of information, to the student a new friend and guide, to the teacher a time-saving help and frequently a timely prop, to the writer an indispensable companion, and to the general public a boon that speedily finds recognition. The reason is obvious. The makers of a new dictionary no longer have to blaze their way in a primeval forest, even though they tread no well-worn path. They have had predecessors—a few of them—and can profit to a large extent by the experience of those who have gone before, to the ultimate advantage of the public, which justly expects in a new dictionary great improvement upon the books of the past.

Some of the advantages offered by this Dictionary may be enumerated briefly as follows:

1. The vocabulary and definitions have been designed primarily for the average reader. The definitions are couched in simple, easily understandable language so that the person with no previous knowledge of his subject can comprehend them. Quotations showing how the defined word is used are frequent, and synonyms add to the clarity of the definition. Technical and scientific terms are explained to the layman in familiar words that draw a vivid and accurate picture for him, while profuse illustrations throughout the volume help to fix this picture and make it concrete.

2. The only words capitalized in the vocabulary of this Dictionary are those which should be written or printed with a capital initial. Words ordinarily appearing with a lower-case initial are so printed in the vocabulary, and it is believed that this point will be appreciated by many to whom the plan of beginning all vocabulary entries with a capital letter did not solve that which was a most perplexing problem.

3. The pronunciation of every word in the Dictionary is plainly indicated by a system of diacritical markings, the signification of which is exemplified at the bottom of each page.

4. Words are only respelled for pronunciation in isolated instances, when the correct pronunciation cannot be closely indicated by diacritics, and thus the average reader is not confused by two apparent spellings of the same word.

5. The typographical appearance, arrangement, and style of the work are such as to assist the reader in his search for the information desired. The type is clear and easy to read. The make-up of the page renders it possible to find the word desired with a minimum of trouble.

6. The compound words require no additional effort for their finding, being treated as all other words and placed alphabetically in the vocabulary. The plan followed in compounding is plainly treated of hereafter in the section entitled "Compound Words."

7. This Dictionary having been made complete as a wordbook of the English language, it will be equally valuable on both sides of the Atlantic and wherever English-speaking people are found.

The Vocabulary. The word-list of this Dictionary has been compiled from many sources, and may reasonably be regarded as a complete vocabulary of English speech. It is comprehensive to a degree that will cause welcome surprise, being rich in word-forms that perhaps might not be expected in its columns, but are nevertheless included as being legitimate ramifications of the English language. The vocabulary is based upon that of the Dictionary of Noah Webster, LL.D., which, however, comprehensive as it appeared in his day, was but a mere foundation upon which to build the structure of a complete modern vocabulary. The never-ceasing growth, expansion, and change of the English language, which have gone on to a greater degree than ever during the recent unparalleled period of world-wide intellectual activity, have added to the vocabulary hosts of new words and terms connected with all departments of human thought and endeavor.

The recent additions made to the English language consist largely of terms belonging to science, technology, and the arts in general; but besides these there have been inserted in this Dictionary many new terms employed by modern writers of prose and poetry, as well as by writers of general literature from the days of Chaucer. Other additions that may be mentioned are those of Scottish words used by Sir Walter Scott, Burns, and others, together with numerous words of local meaning. Numbers of words from modern languages that are frequently met with in English literature have also been included for the benefit of the general reader, and it was essential that many of the colloquialisms inevitably invented and adopted by a live progressive people should be included.

Obsolete and Rare Words. Many so-called obsolete words will be found defined in the pages of this work, as in all dictionaries aiming to present a complete view of the English language, and for good reason. As one well-known authority has said: "The first end sought in making a dictionary should be the inclusion of all simple English words used by writers of repute since the formation of the language, at about A. D. 1250, beginning with the works of Wyclif, Chaucer, and Gower. The omission of any such word would be a defect in the dictionary. The plea of obsoleteness is no justification for such an omission. There is no obsoleteness in literature." Writing upon the same point Archbishop Trench said:

> In regard of obsolete words our dictionaries have no certain rule of omission or exclusion. But how, it may be asked, ought they to hold themselves in regard of these? Their character should be all-comprehensive. There are some, indeed, who, taking up a position a little different from theirs who would have them contain only the standard words of the language, yet proceeding on the same inadequate view of their object and intention, count that they should aim at presenting the body of the language as now existing; this and no more; leaving to archaic glossaries the gathering in of words that are current no longer. But a little reflection will show how untenable is this position; how this rule, consistently carried out, would deprive a dictionary of a large part of its usefulness. . . . It is quite impossible, with any consistency, to make a stand anywhere, or to admit any words now obsolete without including, or at least attempting to include, all.

"A professed dictionary of the English language which does not contain all the simple words and their compounds of deflected meaning which are used by an English poet of such eminence as Chaucer, is not what its name pretends it to be," says the well-known authority quoted above, and in compiling the vocabulary of this Dictionary the editors have aimed to include all words found in English literature for which a definition is likely to be sought.

In summing up a discussion of the principles that should govern the admissibility of words into a vocabulary, in his work "On Some Deficiencies of Our English Dictionaries," Archbishop Trench well said:

> A dictionary, according to that idea of it which seems to me alone capable of being logically maintained, is an inventory of the language; much more indeed, but this primarily. . . . It is no task of the maker of it to select the *good* words of language. If he fancies that it is so, and begins to pick and choose, to leave this and to take that, he will at once go astray. The business which he has undertaken is to collect and arrange all words, whether good or bad, whether they commend themselves to his judgment or otherwise, which, with certain exceptions, those writing in the language have employed. He is a historian of it, not a critic.

In general, the policy adopted in making up the vocabulary of this Dictionary has been one of liberal conservatism, with due observance of the wise injunction of Pope in his "Essay on Criticism":

> In words, as fashions, the same rule will hold,
> Alike fantastic if too new or old.
> Be not the first by whom the new are tried,
> Nor yet the last to lay the old aside.

The Definitions. The definitions in this Dictionary are based upon the consideration of practical utility. No strenuous attempt has been made to follow what is known as the historical method of definition, which consists in arranging the definitions of a word chronologically in the order of their becoming obsolete or obsolescent, leaving the present, practical definition to the end; nor has the contrary policy been adopted in all cases, of giving the present-day definition first, since the etymology, which naturally precedes the definitions, is frequently aided, completed, and rounded out by the insertion of original or former meanings of the vocabulary word prior to its common present definition. Judgment has been exercised in this matter, as in all others, with the object of assisting the reader to a clear understanding of the vocabulary word.

It has been said that the definitions in a model dictionary should be formed upon the principle that a word can have but one meaning, all others being subsidiary modifications of it. But no modern dictionary would be considered complete without the definitions that convey to the mind a clear view of all the senses in which a word is used, as well as its primary or most important sense. New uses of old words are as worthy of a place in a dictionary as new words themselves, and the editors of this work have been ever on the watch for them, as well as careful to include all important specific definitions sanctioned by usage in literature or speech.

The definitions consist of direct statements followed by synonyms, the form preferred by the best authorities. Much additional matter of an explanatory character has been inserted, to the advantage of the seeker after information. Thus, under the word *board* the important phrase *board of trade* is defined in detail, and for the first time the reader of a dictionary is enabled to discover just what a board of trade really is. Similarly, under the word *trust* the various forms of trust are defined at length in a valuable special article, the insertion of which is completely justified by the importance of the word in present usage. In a so-called Webster's dictionary published fifteen years ago, this important word *trust* was classed as *cant* and dismissed cavalierly with a three-line definition as follows:

> **Trust,** *n.* An organization formed mainly for the purpose of regulating the supply and price of commodities, etc.; as a sugar *trust.* [Cant.]

Compare with this the 150-line definition of the same word in this Dictionary, including the special article classifying the trusts, and giving the decisions of the United States Supreme Court in regard to them. This word has attained an added significance which demands new and extended treatment by the lexicographer. In like manner many other words, of which *law* and *ray* may be mentioned as examples, have received the exhaustive treatment that their importance in the language of the present day demands.

The Cross-Reference System. By a system of cross-references which has been carefully guarded against all possible error, much unnecessary repetition of definitions has been avoided, and at the same time the preferred forms of words possessing variants have been indicated. The references are invariably direct; that is, the definition required will be found under the first word to which reference is made.

Illustrative Quotations. The quotations from classic and current English literature used in this Dictionary have been carefully selected with the object of illustrating English as it is rather than as it was, and free use has been made of the editorial columns of the daily newspapers, which reflect so faithfully the current speech of English-speaking people.

It is fully recognized that there are diverse opinions as to the value of this class of illustrations. According to one writer, "the maker of a dictionary for general use—that is, a hand wordbook—is not called upon to give a brief history and epitome of his language, with the purpose of illuminating his pages or justifying his vocabulary." But against this author may be cited the needs of the thousands to whom the significance of a definition is made vastly more clear by an example of the use of the word or an illustrative quotation; hence, the judicious use of quotations has been the rule throughout the preparation of this work.

The Illustrations and Tables. Several thousand pictorial illustrations have been inserted to aid and illuminate the definitions, and many plates of a valuable character are scattered through the Dictionary. Particular attention is directed to the frequent use of tabular matter in the body of the work, including the tables of the chemical elements, of the solar system, of foreign coin values, of standard units, of state names, of the decimal system, and many others of useful and unique character.

The Etymology. The etymological department of this work will be found to be unusually valuable and complete. Those who have had the work in charge have indicated the origin and derivation of every important word. They have tried to avoid the pitfalls into which their predecessors have fallen, and have refrained from giving unnecessary foreign equivalents, striving primarily and mainly to give word-derivations in the simplest manner possible. Their object has been to give a clear, logical etymology of every vocabulary word, and only such words and forms have been used as will tend to show the history of the word. In the more important cases an effort has been made to trace the word to its ultimate source whenever possible. The use of doubtful forms has been studiously avoided, and hypothetical words have been entirely omitted from the etymology. In this portion of the work the valuable "Etymological Dictionary of the English Language," by the Rev. Walter W. Skeat, Litt.D., Elrington and Bosworth professor of Anglo-Saxon in the University of Cambridge, has been found extremely useful, but was not absolutely relied upon. Nothing was blindly accepted from any source as correct, independent research being made in all cases.

Modern philology will in future turn more and more upon phonetics, and the truth now confined to a very few will at last become general, that the vowel is commonly the very life, the most essential part of the word, and that, just as pre-scientific etymologists frequently went wrong because they considered the consonants as being of small consequence and the vowels of none at all, the scientific student of the present day may hope to go right, if he considers the consonants as being of great consequence and the vowels as all important.

The views of the men most eminent in their respective branches of science have had due weight with the editors of this Dictionary, and the opinions of those who have worthily attained eminence in philological science have been accepted with some confidence.

In presenting the etymologies in this book, as a rule the word is first given which is nearest the vocabulary word in time and form. In many cases, it is doubtful whether the English word came, say, from the Latin directly or from the Latin through the French. In such cases of doubt the preference has been given to the word closest in resemblance to the vocabulary word.

It has been found convenient to use a combining form in the etymology in many cases where the first element of a word is composed of another word. This occurs especially in scientific names and terms, and the use of combining forms in such cases has prevented much unnecessary repetition. An unusually large number of the combining forms will be found entered in the vocabulary in their due alphabetical order, traced to their sources, defined, and exemplified in use.

Etymologies of obsolete words have been omitted as a rule, exceptions being made in cases of words of common occurrence in classical literature, especially when in such cases an etymology helps to elucidate the meaning of the word.

In the case of a group of words formed from one root and appearing in close proximity to one another in the vocabulary, the etymological treatment has often been confined to the most important word, the derivation of which being given leaves that of the others practically self-evident.

Many scientific terms of recent origin commonly classed as "New Latin" are followed in this work by the simple abbreviation [L.] to signify that they are Latinized forms. The forms of other words, especially new terms and compounds in chemistry, are explained by the insertion of the separate words from which they are derived, the portions of such words actually used being italicized.

It will be noticed that no cross-references have been made in the etymologies, and much confusion and vexation have thus been avoided. The aim has been to give in close proximity to each vocabulary word all the essential etymological facts and forms connected with it.

Incidentally, etymologies have been inserted for many new words herein defined for the first time in a standard dictionary. Transliteration has been employed in the case of Greek, Hebrew, Sanskrit, etc., for the sake of simplicity and for the benefit of the reader unfamiliar with the written characters of these languages

Synonyms and Comparative Treatments.

Throughout this work there will be found lists of synonyms of the vocabulary words, carefully selected from the best authorities. These lists are frequently accompanied by comparative treatments, in which the uses of the vocabulary word and its so-called synonyms are clearly differentiated. Certain words are followed by a comparison of their meaning and usage with those of other words, not synonyms, with which they are in some degree related or may possibly be confused; thus, the definitions of *politician* are followed by an interesting comparison of *politician statesman, diplomat.* This feature of the Dictionary will be found extremely helpful in many cases.

Pronunciation.

To attempt to indicate the proper pronunciation of all the words in a complete lexicon of the English language is a task of self-evident magnitude, and many curious anomalies have invariably crept in whenever the attempt has been made. For who shall say what proper pronunciation is? Who or what is the authority? Who fixes the canons? Every dictionary-maker that ever deliberately assumed the task has been assailed by a storm of criticism; some have aroused the enmity of a whole people, as when, for instance, Webster's strictures upon some local pronunciations incensed the people of Philadelphia, who condemned what one writer has been pleased to call "his offensive egotism."

"In matters of pronunciation," says Thomas R. Lounsbury, the eminent professor of English in Yale University, "one thoroughly-educated man is as good an authority as another, and nobody is any authority at all." This dictum seems somewhat iconoclastic to people who are accustomed to appeal to their favorite dictionary as a court of last resort, but, as a writer in the periodical *Current Literature* pointed out, "when one remembers that one of our great dictionaries devotes a score of pages in small type to exhibiting the varied pronunciations of English words preferred by a representative group of scholars, he is inclined to accept the dictum, and to add to it that when the 'thoroughly-educated' doctors disagree in matters of pronunciation, the common people often step in and settle the dispute themselves." In his scholarly work, "The Standard of Pronunciation in English," Prof. Lounsbury cites many examples of words whose pronunciation has been changed in spite of the "authorities." Thus nearly all eighteenth-century orthoepists pronounced "yes" as if it were spelled "yis"; "bal-co′ny" has become "bal′-cony," "goff" has become "golf," and Ju-ly′ has been changed from Ju′ly.

For speech itselfe is artificiall and made by man, and the more pleasing it is the more it prevaileth to such purpose as it is intended for. —Puttenham.

It has been said that in matters of English pronunciation, generally speaking, the usage of the most cultivated people of English blood and speech is absolute, as far as their usage itself is fixed. But, as Richard Grant White says, "pronunciation is the most arbitrary, varying, and evanescent trait of language; and it is so exceedingly difficult to express sound by written character that to convey it upon paper with certainty in one neighborhood for ten years, and to the world at large for one year, is practically impossible."

There is, however, an imperative demand for the indication of pronunciation in every complete dictionary, and the editors of this work conscientiously addressed themselves to the task, with full knowledge of its difficulties. The demand for pronouncing dictionaries came originally from those who did not care to exercise the right of private judgment and consequently desired authority. It was created, according to Prof. Lounsbury and other able writers, "by a desire on the part of the imperfectly-educated middle class to know what to say and how to say it." This desire became all the stronger as the members of this class of society gradually rose into prominence, and two desirable results have followed in the wake of the pronouncing dictionary: increasing uniformity of pronunciation and greater conformity of spoken speech to the written word.

The system of diacritical markings in this work is founded on that used by Webster and plainly indicates the pronunciation of the great bulk of the vocabulary. Being designed to avoid the necessity of respelling for pronunciation, while of the simplest character consistent with the completeness of all other parts of the work, some of the diacritics have been rendered elastic in use, as is indicated in the Key preceding the vocabulary.

Compound Words. The use of the hyphen with proper discrimination in compounding words is and long has been a difficulty common to all writers of English. As in matters of pronunciation there is no authority of universal recognition, and can be none, so in the matter of making compound words there are no fixed rules, and can be none. No one can say, in regard to compounds, this is right or that is wrong, and a recollection of this undoubted fact should underlie every critical review of the work of others in this particular department of dictionary-making. Just what words or classes of words shall be chosen for compounding is one of the prime difficulties experienced by the modern lexicographer. The usage of authors and journalists is individually arbitrary. Two daily newspapers published in the same city may differ entirely, on every possible point, in their style of making compounds or not making them. There is none to make rules that will receive universal or even general acceptance. There is none to fix canons, and individual preference reigns supreme.

The general plan followed in compounding words throughout this work is as follows: first, those words are compounded which in combination have acquired a meaning different from that of the mere union of their elements; thus, *walking-stick* becomes a compound, since the stick does not walk but is used in walking; second, nouns are compounded when used together as one term, with unification of sense. Adjectives and nouns in regular use are seldom joined by the hyphen, though in arbitrary usage they frequently become one word; thus, *blue coat*, used for the garment itself, becomes *bluecoat* when applied to the man who wears it. Terms consisting of two or more elements, which have been found as one word in respectable usage in current or classic literature, are generally made one word in this work. Current usage has been closely studied and made the principal guide of the editors in this respect. They have been inclined to let the majority rule and to form compounds or not to form them according to the usage of the greater number of recognized writers. At the same time an effort has been made to secure uniformity of treatment of groups of words having one element in common, and the result, it is confidently believed, will be of practical assistance and value to many who have sought in vain in other dictionaries for help and guidance in the making of compounds. The German hyphen (-) has been used throughout the vocabulary between the elements of compound words, the ordinary hyphen (-) indicating syllabication.

Words Excluded. In making up the vocabulary the object has been not merely to make a word-list greater than that of any other dictionary, but to make a better word-list, and one in which the word desired may be more easily found than elsewhere. There has been no attempt to extend the vocabulary unduly merely to give an appearance of copiousness. Some words have been excluded for reasons that vary but are satisfactory. The smart unusual words often manufactured for the purposes of lighter literature have been generally ignored. The unlimited list of self-evident compounds has not been drawn upon for vocabulary entries. Participles have not been inserted as separate words when they are merely forms of verbs, and when there is no irregularity in their formation, except in some cases when they also form adjectives and are used in senses diverging from those of their verbs. Thus, *loving* is inserted as an adjective, because we speak of *loving* looks, *loving* words, etc. So verbal nouns in *-ing* have not often been entered in the vocabulary when they express nothing more than the mere act expressed by their primitive verb, but when they have a concrete meaning or denote important operations, they are separately defined, the word *engraving* being an example.

Special Contributors. As the work of preparing this Dictionary progressed, great interest in the undertaking was manifested by leading educators, scholars, specialists, and others on both sides of the Atlantic, and much practical assistance was received from such sources, together with numerous suggestions of inestimable value. The names of those who furnished such editorial assistance and from or through whom valuable information was obtained are legion.

To those who thus aided and also to the numerous authors and publishers of books on special subjects who freely gave permission for the use of their works in the preparation of this Dictionary, cordial thanks are hereby extended.

A Special Acknowledgement. During the course of their work the editors have enjoyed the inestimable advantage of consulting and obtaining much valuable information from Dr. James A. H. Murray's "New English Dictionary," published at Oxford University. This monumental work which was begun by Dr. Murray and his associates in 1857 and completed in 1928 after 70 years of painstaking labor, is characterized by the completeness of its vocabulary and the application of the historical method to the life and use of words. A point made by Dr. Murray in introducing his truly remarkable work is of general application, and may well be repeated here. "It has to be borne in mind," says the learned lexicographer, "that a dictionary of the English language is not a cyclopedia; the cyclopedia *describes* things, the dictionary *explains words*, and deals with the description of things only so far as is necessary in order to fix the exact signification and use of words."

A Final Word. In conclusion, it need only be said that this Dictionary will fill a place hitherto unoccupied in the book-world; that it is qualified to stand upon its merits, and that the favorable judgment of the English-speaking public upon those merits is awaited with confidence. To have brought a complete dictionary of the English language within the reach of those to whom such a work has been hitherto unattainable is in itself no mean achievement; to present under such conditions an entirely new and modernized work, superior to all predecessors in its vocabulary and other essential features, is little short of a literary miracle. The contents of this book will speak for themselves; in accuracy they will be found to compare more than favorably with those of any dictionary extant, but it should ever be borne in mind that "labor with what zeal we will, something still remains undone" and, as was written by the publishers of a highly-lauded lexicon to a friendly critic who had called attention to errors in their book, "only Omnipotence can make a *perfect* dictionary."

Beyond a doubt this Dictionary represents an honest endeavor to unite broad-minded scholarship and practical twentieth-century methods in the preparation of a standard lexicon of the English tongue as it is *to-day*. The Editors believe that the endeavor was not misdirected, when the result is a volume as useful as they believe this to be. Its fruition has been accomplished only after prolonged labor, and in spite of seemingly insuperable difficulties, but when the finished work finds its way into every home, study and office, and aids in realizing the high ideal of its editors by bringing a standard of our vernacular tongue within the reach of all, the time and effort expended in its preparation will not have been in vain.

THOMAS H. RUSSELL.

MEMOIR OF NOAH WEBSTER.

It is natural for those who make frequent use of Webster's dictionaries to desire some knowledge of the life of that great lexicographer. To gratify this desire is the object of this memoir.

NOAH WEBSTER was born in Hartford, Connecticut, October 16, 1758. His father was a descendant of John Webster, one of the first settlers of Hartford, who, at a subsequent period, became governor of Connecticut. His mother was a descendant of William Bradford, the second governor of the Plymouth colony.

Mr. Webster commenced the study of the classics in the year 1772, and in 1774 was admitted a member of Yale College, from which he was graduated in 1778. After publishing numerous works of a literary and educational character, Mr. Webster entered (1807) on the great work of his life—that of preparing a new and complete dictionary of the English language. As preliminary to this, he had published, in 1806, a smaller dictionary containing a large number of words not to be found in any similar work. From this time, his reading turned more or less directly to this object. A number of years were spent in collecting words which had not been introduced into the English dictionaries, in discriminating with exactness the various senses of all the words in our language, and adding those significations which they had recently received. The story of Webster's work can be best told in his own language, by quoting from the author's preface to his complete dictionary, as follows :

"In the year 1783, just at the close of the Revolution, I published an elementary book for facilitating the acquisition of our vernacular tongue, and for correcting a vicious pronunciation, which prevailed extensively among the common people of this country. Soon after the publication of that work, Dr. Goodrich, one of the trustees of Yale College, suggested to me the propriety and expediency of my compiling a dictionary, which should complete a system for the instruction of the citizens of this country in the language. At that time, I could not indulge the thought, much less the hope, of undertaking such a work, as I was neither qualified by research, nor had I the means of support, during the execution of the work, had I been disposed to undertake it. For many years, therefore, though I considered such a work as very desirable, yet it appeared to me impracticable, as I was under the necessity of devoting my time to other occupations for obtaining subsistence.

"About thirty-five years ago, I began to think of attempting the compilation of a Dictionary. I was induced to this undertaking, not more by the suggestion of friends, than by my own experience of the want of such a work, while reading modern books of science. In this pursuit I found almost insuperable difficulties, from the want of a dictionary, for explaining many new words, which recent discoveries in the physical sciences had introduced into use. To remedy this defect in part, I published my *Compendious Dictionary* in 1806 ; and soon after made preparations for undertaking a larger work. . . .

"It has been my aim in this larger work, now offered to my fellow-citizens, to ascertain the true principles of the language, in its orthography and structure ; to purify it from some palpable errors, and reduce the number of its anomalies, thus giving it more regularity and consistency in its forms, both of words and sentences ; and in this manner to furnish a standard which we shall not be ashamed to bequeath to *five hundred millions of people*, who are destined to occupy, and I hope to adorn, the vast territory within our jurisdiction.

"If the language can be improved in regularity, so as to be more easily acquired by our own citizens and by foreigners, and thus be rendered a more useful instrument for the propagation of science, arts, civilization, and Christianity;—if it can be rescued from the mischievous influence of sciolists, and that dabbling spirit of innovation, which is perpetually disturbing its settled usages and filling it with anomalies;—if in short, our vernacular language can be redeemed from corruptions, and our philology and literature from degradation, it would be a source of great satisfaction to me to be one among the instruments of promoting these valuable objects. If this object cannot be effected, and my wishes and hopes are to be frustrated, my labor will be lost, and this work must sink into oblivion.

"This Dictionary, like all others of the kind, must be left, in some degree, imperfect; for what individual is competent to trace to their source, and define in all their various applications, popular, scientific and technical, *seventy* or *eighty thousand* words! It satisfies my mind that I have done all that my health, my talents, and my pecuniary means would enable me to accomplish. I present it to my fellow-citizens, not with frigid indifference, but with my ardent wishes for their improvement and their happiness; and for the continued increase of the wealth, the learning, the moral and religious elevation of character, and the glory of my country.

"To that great and benevolent Being, who, during the preparation of this work, has sustained a feeble constitution, amidst obstacles and toils, disappointments, infirmities, and depression; who has borne me and my manuscripts in safety across the Atlantic, and given me strength and resolution to bring the work to a close, I would present the tribute of my most grateful acknowledgments. And if the talent which He intrusted to my care has not been put to the most profitable use in His service, I hope it has not been 'kept laid up in a napkin,' and that any misapplication of it may be graciously forgiven."

Energy, self-reliance, fearlessness, the resolute defense of whatever he thought right and useful, the strong hope of ultimate success,—these became the great elements of Dr. Webster's intellectual character. He carried them with him into all his literary pursuits, and they sustained him under the pressure of difficulties which would have crushed the spirit of almost any other man.

One of the habits which Dr. Webster formed was that of arranging all his acquired knowledge in exact order, and keeping the elements of progressive thought continually within his reach. Although his memory was uncommonly quick and tenacious, he saw how unsafe it was to rely on mere recollection for the immense mass of materials which a writer must have ever at command. All that he had ever written, everything that he met with which seemed likely to be of use at any future period, was carefully laid aside in its appropriate place. He had also a mark by which he denoted, in every work he read, all the new words, or new senses of words, which came under his observation. He filled the margin of his books with notes and comments containing corrections of errors, a comparison of dates, or references to corresponding passages in other works, until his whole library became a kind of *Index Rerum*, to which he could refer at once for everything he had read.

Another habit, which resulted in part from his early pursuits, was that of carrying on numerous and diversified employments at the same time. To men of the present generation, Dr. Webster is known chiefly as a learned philologist; and the natural inference would be, that he spent his whole life among his books, and chiefly in devotion to a single class of studies. The fact, however, was far otherwise. Though he was always a close student,—reading. thinking, and writing at every period of his life,—he never withdrew himself from the active employments of society. He entered politics and became a judge of one of the state courts, and subsequently a member of the legislature. He gave freely of his time, his counsel, and the efforts of his pen, for the promotion of every kind of improvement. Equally large and diversified was the range of his intellectual pursuits. There was hardly any department of literature which he had not explored with lively interest. He wrote on a greater variety of topics than perhaps any other author in the United States;—on the foundations of government, the laws of nations, the rights of neutrals, the science of banking, the history of his country, the progress of diseases, and the variations of climate; on agriculture, commerce, education, morals, religion, and the great means of national advancement, in addition to the principal theme of his life, philology. Such was the activity of his mind, and the delight he found in new acquisitions, that a *change* of employment was all the relief he needed from the weariness of protracted study. The refreshment which others seek in journeys, or the entire suspension of intellectual effort, he found, during most of his life, in the stimulus afforded by some new and exciting object of pursuit. Mental exertion was the native element of his soul; and it is not too much to say, that another instance of such long-continued literary toil, such steady, unfaltering industry, can hardly be found in the annals of our country. It is unnecessary to say how perfectly these habits were adapted to prepare Dr. Webster for the leading employment of his life, the production of the complete dictionary. Nothing but his eager pursuit of every kind of knowledge, and his exact system in bringing all that he had ever read completely under his command, could have enabled him to give in his first edition more than twelve thousand words and forty thousand definitions, which could then be found in no other similar work. He was aware that there must be many things in a book like this which would not stand the test of time. But he never doubted, even in the darkest seasons of discouragement, that he could produce such a work, that the world "should not willingly let it die." The decision of the public verified his anticipations. The demand has ever increased wherever English is spoken; and the author might well have been gratified to learn, that a gentleman who asked at one of the principal bookselling establishments of London, for the best English dictionary on their shelves, had Webster's handed to him, with the remark, "That, sir, is the only *real* dictionary which we have of our language, though it was prepared by an American."

When Dr. Webster's work appeared seventy years had elapsed since the first publication of Johnson's Dictionary; and scarcely a single improvement had been attempted in the various editions through which it had passed, or the numerous compilations to which it had given rise, except by the addition of a few words to the vocabulary. Yet in this period the English-speaking peoples were exerting themselves in every direction, with an accuracy of research and a fertility of invention which were without a parallel in any previous stage of history. Then, as now, a complete revolution had taken place in almost every branch of physical science; new departments had been created, new principles developed, new modes of classification and description adopted. The political changes which so signally marked that period, the excitement of feeling and conflict of opinion resulting from the American and French revolutions, and the numerous modifications which followed, had also left a deep impress on the language of politics, law, and general literature. Under these circumstances, to make a defining dictionary adapted to the state of the language, was to produce an entirely *new work*; and how well Dr. Webster executed the task appeared from the decision of men best qualified to judge, both in this country and in Europe, who declared that his improvements upon Johnson were even greater than Johnson himself made on those who preceded him, just as this new WEBSTER'S DICTIONARY is an improvement upon other Websters so vast that only by comparison with them can a just estimate of its superiority be made.

In his social habits, Dr. Webster was distinguished by dignified ease, affability, and politeness. He was punctilious in his observance of all the nicer proprieties of life, and had an uncommon degree of refinement in all his thoughts and feelings. In his pecuniary transactions, he was not only just, but liberal. It was a principle with him, for life, never to be in debt. Everything was paid for at the time of purchase. In all his dealings and social intercourse, he was remarkably direct, frank, and open. He had but one character, and that was "known and read of all men." No one ever suspected him of double dealing; no one ever thought he was capable of a mean or dishonorable action. After the completion of his dictionary he felt that the labors of his life were ended, and that little else remained but to prepare for death. With a grateful sense of past mercies, a cheering consciousness of present support, and an animating hope of future blessedness, he waited with patience until his appointed change should come. The revision during the spring of 1843, by Dr. Webster of the appendix of his dictionary, was the closing work of his life. His hand rested, in its last labors, on the volume which he had commenced thirty-six years before, and after an illness of but a few days, without one doubt, one fear, he resigned his soul into the hands of his Maker, and died on the 28th day of May, 1843, in the eighty-fifth year of his age.

In his person, Dr. Webster was tall and somewhat slender, remarkably erect throughout life, and moving, even in his advanced years, with a light and elastic step. In conclusion, it may be said that the name of NOAH WEBSTER, from the wide circulation of his works, is known familiarly to a greater number of the English-speaking people than the name, probably, of any other individual. Whatever influence he acquired was used at all times to promote the best interests of his fellow-men. His books, though read by millions, have made no man worse. To multitudes they have been of lasting benefit, not only by the course of training they have furnished, but by that wisdom with which almost every page is stored.

PARTIAL LIST OF REFERENCE WORKS

and other Publications Consulted or Used in the Preparation of this Dictionary.

Absolute Measurements in Electricity and Magnetism .... Andrew Gray
Aerial Navigation .... Frederick Walker
Aerial or Wire-Rope Tramways. A. J. Wallis-Tayler
Aids in Practical Geology .... G. A. J. Cole
Algebra .... J. Todhunter
Allgemeine Deütsche Biographie. Duncker & Humblot
American and English Encyclopedia of Law. Pub. by The Edward Thompson Co.
American Constitutional Law .... J. C. Hare
American Electro-Therapeutic and X-Ray Era. Pub. by R. Friedlander
American Illustrated Medical Dictionary. W. A. N. Dorland
American Mechanical Dictionary. E. H. Knight
Analytical Statics .... E. J. Routh
Analytical Statics .... J. Todhunter
Analytic Geometry .... Bailey & Woods
Analytic Geometry .... P. H. Lambert
Anarchism .... E. V. Zenker
Anderson's Dictionary of Law. W. C. Anderson
Auorganischen Chemie .... Dr. A. Michaelis
A. O. U. Check List of North American Birds, The. Pub. by American Ornithologists' Union
Applied Mechanics .... J. H. Cotterill
Applied Mechanics .... Gaetano Lanza
Applied Mechanics .... John Perry
Applied Mechanics .... Professor Rankine
Architectural Perspective ...... F O. Ferguson
Art and Science of Sailmaking .... S. B. Sadler
Asbestos and Asbestic .... R. H. Jones
Astronomical Glossary, An .... J. E. Gore
Astronomie .... J. LeF. deLalande
Astronomy .... G. F. Chambers
Astronomy .... Sir John Herschel
Audubon and His Journals ..... M. R. Audubon
Aurora Borealis, The .... Alfred Angot

Bacterial Purification of Sewage. Sidney Barwise
Bartlett's Dictionary of Americanisms. Little, Brown & Co.
Beckmann's History of Inventions. John Beckmann
Bimetallism .... Leonard Darwin
Biographie Universelle .... Nuchaud
Birds .... A. H. Evans
Book of Type. Pub. by Barnhart Bros. & Spindler
Botany .... Sir Joseph Hooker
Botany .... Alexander Johnstone
Botany All the Year Round ..... E. F. Andrews
Botany Key and Flora .... J. Y. Bergen
Brehm's Tierleben .... Pechuel & Loesche
Burke's Peerage.

Calmet's Dictionary of the Holy Bible. Pub. by Crocker & Brewster
Cambridge Modern History, The. Pub. by The Macmillan Co.
Cambridge Natural History, The. Harmer & Shipley
Capital .... Karl Marx
Cassell's Cyclopedia of Mechanics. Paul N. Hasluck
Catalogue of Minerals and Synonyms. Thos. Eggleston
Catholic Socialism .... F. S. Nitti
Celebrities of the Century .... Lloyd C. Sanders
Celestial Mechanics .... F. R. Moulton
Century Dictionary, The. Pub. by The Century Co.
Century of Electricity, A ..... T. C. Mendenhall
Chain Cables and Chains .... T. W. Traill
Characteristics of Volcanoes .... J. D. Dana
Chemical Analysis of Iron, The ..... A. A. Blair
Chemisch-Technische Analyse .... Jul. Post
Chemisch-Technische Untersuchungs-Methoden .... Friedrich Böckmann
Chemistry; General, Medical, and Pharmaceutical .... John Attfield
Chinese Biographical Dictionary, A.. H. A. Giles
Civil Engineering .... Professor Rankine
Civil Engineering as Applied in Construction. Vernon & Harcourt
Coal and Coal Mining .... Sir Warington Smyth
College Algebra .... Webster Wells
College Chemistry .... Ira Remsen
Commercial Organic Analysis ...... A. H. Allen
Communist Societies of the United States, The .... C. Nordhoff
Compend of Geology, A .... Joseph Le Conte
Complete Geography .... Tarr & McMurry
Concrete; Its Nature and Uses .. G. L. Sutcliffe
Condensed Mechanics .... W. G. C. Hughes
Congressional Currency .... A. C. Gordon
Conklin's Familiar Quotations .. G. W. Conklin
Conklin's Peerless Manual of Useful Information and World's Atlas .... G. W. Conklin
Constitutional Limitations .. Thomas M. Cooley
Construction of Oblique Arches, The. John Hart
Contemporary History of the World. E. A. Grosvenor
Contemporary Socialism .... John Rae
Continuous Current Dynamos. J. Fisher-Hinnen
Continuous Railway Brakes .. Michael Reynolds
Contributions to the Physical History of the British Isles .... Edward Hull
Cook's Otto's German Grammar. William Cook
Coöperative Commonwealth, The. Laurence Gronlund
Coördinate Geometry .... S. L. Loney
Cours de Mécanique Analytique. Ernest Posquier
Crabb's English Synonyms ...... George Crabb
Crystallography .... W. J. Lewis
Cyclopedia of American Horticulture. Pub. by The Macmillan Co.
Cyclopedia of Engineering. Pub. by American Technical Society
Cyclopedia of the Manufactures and Products of the United States. Industrial Publishing Co.

Dana's System of Mineralogy .... E. S. Dana
Dawn of Astronomy, The .... J. N. Lockyer
Decline and Fall of the Roman Empire, The. Edward Gibbon
De l'Optic des Rayons de Röntgen et des Rayons Secondaires qui en Dérivent. Georges Sagnac
Deschanel's Natural Philosophy .. J. D. Everett
Dictionary of Biographical Reference. L. B. Phillips
Dictionary of Birds, A .... Alfred Newton
Dictionary of Chemical Solubilities, A. A. M. Comey
Dictionary of General Biography. W. L. R. Cates
Dictionary of Greek and Roman Biography and Mythology .... Wm. Smith
Dictionary of Hygiene and Public Health. Blyth & Tardieu
Dictionary of National Biography. Pub. by The Macmillan Co.
Dictionary of Terms, A .... Weale and Hunt
Dictionary of Terms Used in Architecture, Building, Etc .... John Weale
Dictionary of the Names of Minerals. A. H. Chester
Dictionary of Topographic Forms. H. M. Wilson
Dictionnaire de Chemie .... Ad. Wurtz
Dictionnaire des Contemporaines. G. Vapereau
Dictionnaire d'Histoire .... M. N. Bouillet
Differential and Integral Calculus. A. G. Greenhill
Differential Calculus ...... W. S. B. Woolhouse
Differential Equations .... A. R. Forsyth
Discourses, Biological and Geological. T. H. Huxley
Discoveries and Inventions of the Nineteenth Century .... Robert Routledge
Distribution of Income, The .... Wm. Smart
Dynamic Electricity and Magnetism. Philip Atkinson
Dynamic Electric Machinery .. S. P. Thompson
Dynamics .... Williamson & Tarleton
Dynamo and Electric Machinery. Samuel Sheldon
Dynamo Construction .... J. W. Urquhart

Earth and Its Inhabitants, The .. Elisée Réclus
Economic History .... W. J. Ashley
Electrical Conductors .... F. A. C. Perrine
Electrical Dictionary .... E. J. Houston
Electrical Engineering .... Slingo & Brooker
Electrical Science .... G. J. Burch
Electricity and Magnetism .... J. C. Maxwell
Electricity in the Service of Man. R. Wormwell
Electricity, Magnetism, and Acoustics. Dr Lardner
Electric Light .... J. W. Urquhart
Electric Power Transmission .... Louis Bell
Electro-Deposition .... Alexander Watt
Electro-Metallurgy .... Alexander Watt
Elektrochemie .... W. Ostwald
Elektrostatische Ablenkung der Radiumstrahlen .... Ernst Dom
Elementary Lessons in Electricity and Magnetism .... Sylvanus Thompson
Elementary Magnetism and Electricity. Balfour Stewart
Elementary Rigid Dynamics .... E. J. Routh
Elementary Treatise on Analytic Mechanics, An .... E. A. Bowser
Elementary Treatise on Heat, An. Balfour Stewart
Elementary Treatise on the Calculus for Engineering Students, An .... John Graham
Elemente der Reinen Meckanik ... Josef Finger
Elements de Cinématique et de Mécanique. Maurice Lévy
Elements of Astronomy, The ... Sir Robert Ball
Elements of Astronomy ...... Simon Newcomb
Elements of Botany .... Francis Darwin
Elements of Descriptive Astronomy. H. A. Howe
Elements of Determinants ..... Paul H. Hanus
Elements of Electrical Engineering. Tyson Sewell
Elements of Electricity and Magnetism. J. J. Thomson
Elements of Euclid .... Todhunter & Loney
Elements of Forestry, The .... F. B. Hough
Elements of Geology .... Joseph Le Conte
Elements of Geometry .... Phillips & Fisher
Elements of International Law .... G. B. Davis
Elements of Ornithology, The. St. George Mivart
Elements of Practical Astronomy. W. W. Campbell
Elements of Statics and Dynamics, The. S. L. Loney
Elements of Theoretical and Descriptive Astronomy, The .... C. J. White
Encyclopedic Dictionary, The. Pub. by Syndicate Publishing Co.
Encyclopedic Medical Dictionary .. F. P. Foster
Engineering Chemistry .... T. B. Stillman
English Associations of Working Men. J. M. Baernreither
English Dialect Dictionary, The. Joseph Wright
Essay on Oblique Bridges .... G. W. Buck
Essays on Taxation .... E. R. A. Seligman
Essentials of Botany, The .... C. E. Bessey
Etymological Dictionary, An ..... W. W. Skeat
Euclid .... Rupert Deakin
Evolution of Industry, The .... Henry Dyer
Examination of Medical Chemicals. Hoffman & Power
Experimental Mechanics .... Sir Robert Ball

Face de le Terre, La .... Edward Suess
Familiar Quotations .... John Bartlett
Field Engineering .... W. H. Searles
Field, Forest, and Garden Botany .... Asa Gray
Field Testing for Gold and Silver. W. H. Merritt
Finance .... H. C. Adams
Fires, Fire-Engines and Fire Brigades. C. F. T. Young
First Steps in International Law. Sir Sherston Baker
First Studies of Plant Life ..... G. F. Atkinson
Foods, Their Composition and Analysis. Blyth & Blyth
Foundations of Botany .... J. Y. Bergen
Foundations of Zoölogy, The. Wm. Keith Brooks
Fourier's Series and Harmonies. W. E. Ryerly
Free Trade and Protection ..... Henry Fawcett
French Dictionary .... J. E. Wessely
Fuels: Solid, Liquid, and Gaseous. H. J. Phillips

Gaelic Names of Plants .... John Cameron
Gas-Engine Handbook, The ..... E. W. Roberts
Gas Engines, On .... F. M. Goodeve
Geodesy .... J. H. Core
Geographical Sketches .... Louis Agassiz
Geological History .... Arthur Nichols
Geologie et Mineralogie Appliquées. Henri Charpentier
Geologie Générale, La .... Stanislas Meunier
Géologie pratique et petit Dictionnaire Technique des Termes Geologique Les plus Usuels. L. de Launey
Geometry of Position .... Theodor Reye
Gillespie's Surveying .... Cady Staley
Glacial Nightmare and the Flood, The. Sir Henry Howorth
Glossary of Botanic Terms .... B. D. Jackson
Grammar and Composition .. Reed and Kellogg
Granites .... G. F. Harris

Graphic and Analytic Statics...R. H. Graham
Gray's Anatomy.......................T. P. Pick
Great Astronomers.............Sir Robert Ball
Great Ice Age.....................James Geikie
Greek English Lexicon..........Liddell & Scott
Growth of the Brain, The.....H. H. Donaldson
Grundzüge der Geographischmorphologischen Methode der Pflanzensystematik. Richard von Wettstein
Guide to the Study of Common Plants. V. M. Spaulding

Handbook of American Constitutional Law. H. C. Black
Handbook of Field Fortification. Major W. W. Knollys
Handbook of Geological Terms....David Page
Handbook of Plant Dissection. Barnes & Coulter
Handbook of Systematic Botany. E. Knoblauch
Handbook on the Steam Engine, A. Herman Haeder
Handbuch der Anorganischen Chemie. O. Dammer
Handbuch der Hygiene.............M. F. Weyl
Handbuch der Ingenieurwissenschaften. Meyer und Willmann
Handbuch der Organischen Chemie. F. Beilstein
Harper's Cyclopedia of United States History. Pub. by Harper & Bros.
Heat, a Mode of Motion..........John Tyndall
High School Arithmetic.....Wentworth & Hill
Historical Jurisprudence.........Guy Carleton
Historical Reference Book.....Louis Heilprin
History for Ready Reference. Compiled by J. N. Larned
History of Astronomy............Arthur Berry
History of Astronomy.............A. M. Clerke
History of Banking in All Leading Nations, A. Pub. by The Journal of Commerce and Commercial Bulletin.
History of Banking in All Nations, A. Pierre des Essars
History of Bimetallism in the United States. J. Laurence Laughlin
History of Chemistry.........Ernst von Meyer
History of Germany.........Wolfgang Menzel
History of Lawyers, Ancient and Modern, The. Wm. Forsyth
History of Modern Europe..........C. A. Fyffe
History of Physics.........................F. Cajori
History of Socialism................Thos. Kirkup
History of the English People......J. R. Green
History of the World...........H. F. Helmholt
History of Trade Unionism, The. S. & B. Webb
Household Dictionary of Medicine, A. F. R. Walters
How to Make a Dynamo...........Alfred Crofts
Human Physiology.................A. D. Waller
Humber's Modern Engineering. William Humber
Hydraulic Power Engineering.....G. C. Marks
Hydrostatics and Elementary Hydrokinetics. G. M. Minchin

Illustrated Dictionary of Gardening. Pub. by L. N. Gill
Imperial Dictionary The. Pub. by Blackie & Son
Industrial Democracy............S. & B. Webb
Infinitesimal Calculus..............Horace Lamb
Inflammable Gas and Vapour in the Air. Frank Clowes
International Law...................W. E. Hall
International Law................G. G. Wilson
International Monetary Conferences. H. B. Russell
Introduction to Analytic Functions, An. Harkness & Morley
Introduction to Botany...........W. C. Stevens
Introduction to Chemical Theory. Alexander Scott
Introduction to Geology, An.......W. B. Scott
Introduction to Physical Chemistry. James Walker
Introduction to Quaternions...Kelland & Tait
Introduction to the Study of Botany, An. Edward Aveling
Introduction to the Study of Political Economy..............................Luigi Cossa
Iron Ores of Great Britain and Ireland. J. D. Kendall
Italian Dictionary..................J. E. Wessely
Italian-English Dictionary, Hill's. Pub. by Geo. W. Ogilvie & Co.

Judicial Dictionary of Words and Phrases, The. F. Stroud

Key to Algebra......................I. Todhunter
Konstruktion, Ban und Betreib von Funkeninduktoren.......................Ernst Ruhmer
Kosmos...................Alexander Humboldt
Kräuterbuch...............................F. Losch

Labberton's Universal History. R. H. Labberton
Laboratory Arts, On.........Richard Threlfall
Laboratory Manual of Botany, A. O. W. Caldwell
Lamb's Biographical Dictionary of the United States............Pub. by James H. Lamb Co.
Land and Marine Surveying....W. D. Haskoll
Lathe-Work..........................P. N. Hasluck
Law Dictionary.............Wm. C. Anderson
Lectures on the Evolution of Plants. D. H. Campbell
Lehrbuch der Botanik.................Max Reess
Lehrbuch der Organischen Chemie. Meyer und Jacobson
Lehrbuch der Technischen Mechanik. August Ritter
Lehr-und Handbuch der Weltgeschichte. Georg Weber
Lessons in Astronomy.............C. A. Young
Lexikon der Gesamten Technik..Otto Luegers
Life and Labour of the People..Charles Booth
Life in Ponds and Streams.......W. Furneaux
Light.............................Lewis Wright
Light, On........................John Tyndall
Lightning Conductors and Lightning Guards. O. J. Lodge
Lippincott's Pronouncing Biographical Dictionary.............Pub. by Lippincott & Co.
Liquid Air........................T. O'C. Sloane
Lockwood's Dictionary of Mechanical Terms. Pub. by Crosby Lockwood & Son
Locomotive Engine, The. Robert Weatherburn
Locomotive Engine and its Development, The. C. E. Stretton
Locomotive Engine Driving. Michael Reynolds
Logarithmic Tables..........Baron von Vega

Magnets and Electric Currents..J. A. Fleming
Management of Dynamos, The. G. W. Lummis-Paterson
Mantissa in Volumen Primum Systematis Vegetabilium......................Carl von Linné
Manual and Dictionary of the Flowering Plants and Ferns, A...............J. C. Willis
Manual of Botany, A..................J. R. Green
Manual of Descriptive Mineralogy. Geo. J. Brush
Manual of Geology......................J. D. Dana
Manual of Mechanics, A.........T. M. Goodeve
Manual of Printing. Pub. by The Inland Printer
Manual of the Mollusca........S. P. Woodward
Manuel d'Histoire...........A. M. H. J. Stokvis
Marine Engineers' Pocket-Book. Frank Proctor
Marine Engines and Steam Vessels. J. S. Brewer
Mars..........................Percival Lowell
Masonry Dams from Inception to Completion. C. F. Courtney
Materials of Construction, The..J. B. Johnson
Mathematical Dictionary.....Davies and Peck
Matter and Motion...............J. C. Maxwell
Matter, Energy, Force, and Work. S. W. Holman
Measures, Weights, and Moneys of all Nations. W. S. B. Woolhouse
Mechanical Engineer's Reference Book, The. Nelson Foley
Mechanics and Hydrostatics..R. T. Glazebrook
Mechanics Applied to Engineering. John Goodman
Mechanics of Engineering.........J. P. Church
Mechanics of Engineering, The...A. J. DuBois
Mechanics, Theoretical, Applied, and Experimental...........W. W. F. Pullen
Mécanique, Hydraulique, Thermodynamique. Georges Dariès
Medical Chemistry............Elias H. Bartley
Medical Dictionary.................G. M. Gould
Memoires Röntgen, Stokes, and J. J. Thomson
Men and Women of the Times......V. G. Plarr
Metalliferous Minerals and Mining. D. C. Davies
Metallurgy of Gold, The.............M. Eissler
Metallurgy of Silver, The...........M. Eissler
Meteoritic Hypothesis, The......J. N. Lockyer
Method of Conducting a Trigonometrical Survey, The...............Lieut.-General Frome
Meyer's Modern Theories of Chemistry. Lothar Meyer
Microscope........................W. E. Baxter
Military Dictionary and Gazetteer. Thomas Wilhelm
Milling Machines and Processes. P. N. Hasluck
Miscellaneous Papers connected with Physical Science..............Humphrey Lloyd
Modern Analytical Geometry.......C. A. Scott
Modern Chromatics.................O. W. Rood
Modern Engineering.................W. H. Burr
Modern English Biography...........F. Boase
Modern Factory System..........W. C. Taylor
Modern Views of Electricity.......O. J. Lodge
Money....................Francis A. Walker
Moon, The..................Nasmyth-Carpenter
Motor Cars or Power-Carriages for Common Roads.....................A. J. Wallis-Tayler
Movements of the World's Crust, On the. Axel Blytt
Natural History of Plants......A. K. Marilaun
Nature and Work of Plants, The. D. S. MacDougal
Naval Architects' and Shipbuilders' Pocket-Book, The.
Neues Handwörterbuch der Chemie. Pub. by Friedrich, Vieweg und Sohn
New Physical Geography, A.....Elisée Réclus
Nineteenth Century, The....Robert Mackenzie
Nineteenth Century Series...Justin McCarthy
Nitro-Explosives...................P. G. Sanford
Nomenclator Botanicus....Ludovicus Pfeiffer
North American Geology and Palæontology. S. A. Miller
Nouvelle Biographie Générale. Mme. Firmin-Didot et Cie.
Nouvelle Nomenclature des Êtres Organisées et des Mineraux..........Alfonso L. Herrera
Nuttall's Ornithology..Montague Chamberlain

Optical Projection.................Lewis Wright
Organic Chemistry.................R. Anschütz
Organic Chemistry................A. Bernthsen
Organischen Chemie.............Hermann Kolbe
Origin and Growth of the Healing Art. Edward Berdoe
Outlines of Botany..................R. G. Leavitt
Outlines of Field Geology. Sir Archibald Geikie
Outlines of Universal History.....G. P. Fisher
Organography of Plants...........Carl Goebel

Pattern Making.....................J. G. Horner
People of the Period.............A. T. C. Pratt
People's Banks........................H. W. Wolf
Pflanzennamen....................Hermann Prahn
Pflanzenreich, Das.....Pub. by W. Engelmann
Philosophy and Political Economy. James Bonar
Physical Geography................Arnold Guyot
Physical Properties of Gases, The. Arthur L. Kimball
Physics.............................G. F. Barker
Physikalischen und Theoretischen Chemie. Harstmann und Landolt
Physiography.....................T. H. Huxley
Physiological and Pathological Chemistry. G. Bunge
Physiological Chemistry. Hammarsten and Mandel
Plane Trigonometry.............E. W. Hobson
Plane Trigonometry...............I. Todhunter
Plantes des Champs et des Bois, Les Gaston Bonnier
Plant Structures...................J. M. Coulter
Plating and Boiler Making.......J. G. Horner
Plattner's Qualitative and Quantitative Analysis with the Blowpipe. Trans. by H. C. Cornwall
Pocket Glossary of Technical Terms. J. J. Fletcher
Political Economy in England......L. L. Price
Portable Engine, The......W. D. Wansbrough
Power Transmitted by Electricity. P. Atkinson
Practical Electro-Chemistry..Bertram Blount
Practical Engineer's Handbook, The. W. S. Hutton
Practical Forestry.................C. E. Curtis
Practical Masonry.............W. R. Purchase
Practical Mechanics..............S. H. Wells
Practical Navigation..............Henry Law
Practical Physiology............A. F. Blaisdell
Practical Surveying..............G. W. Usill
Practical Treatise on Handrailing. George Collins
Practical Tunnelling..............F. W. Simms
Primer and Vocabulary of the Moro Dialect. R. S. Porter
Primer of Astronomy, A........Sir Robert Ball
Principles and Practice of Levelling. F. W. Simms
Principles of Chemistry.....................P. Muir
Principles of Elementary Mechanics, The. DeVolson Wood
Profit Sharing......................N. P. Gilman
Progress of Invention in the 19th Century. E. W. Byrn
Pronouncing Gazetteer and Geographical Dictionary of the Philippine Islands. U. S. Printing Office
Properties of Matter..................P. G. Tait
Properties of the Field Surrounding a Crookes Tube, On the...............A. W. Goodspeed
Psychology..........................John Dewey
Public Debts.........................H. C. Adams
Public Finance....................C. F. Bastable
Public School Arithmetic...McClellan & Ames
Pumps and Pumping.................M. P. Ball

Qualitative Chemical Analysis. C. R. Frasenius
Quantitative Chemical Analysis...F. A. Cairns
Quaternions..........................P. G. Tait

Recent Economic Changes.........D. A. Wells
Refrigerating and Ice-Making Machinery. A. J. Wallis-Tayler
Refrigeration, Cold Storage, and Ice-Making. A. J. Wallis-Tayler
Report of the Monetary Commission of the Indianapolis Convention.

Report of the Philippine Commission, 1902.
Rights of War and Peace, The...Hugo Grotius
River Bars ....I. J. Mann
Rocks, Rock-weathering, and Soils. G. P. Merrill.
Rural Water Supply...........Allan Greenwell

Scheiner's Astronomical Spectroscopy. E. B. Frost
School Physics.....................E. M. Avery
Science of Mechanics, The..........Ernst Mach
Scientific American Cyclopedia of Receipts, Notes, and Queries....Ed. by Albert Hopkins
Scope and Method of Political Economy. J. N. Keynes
Screw-Threads...................P. N. Hasluck
Sea Coast, The..................W. H. Wheeler
Sea Terms, Phrases and Words......W. Pirrie
Select Methods in Chemical Analysis. W. Crookes
Sensations of Tone, On the. H. L. F. Helmholtz
7,000 Words Often Mispronounced. W. H. P. Phyfe
Short History of Mathematics, A. W. W. R. Ball
Sight.......................Joseph Le Conte
Smith's English-Latin Dictionary. William Smith
Smith's Financial Dictionary......H. J. Smith
Socialism.......................Robert Flint
Socialism and Social Reform.........R. T. Ely
Sound, On.......................John Tyndall
Sound and Music...................J. A. Zahm
Spectrum Analysis.............John Landauer
Spons' Dictionary of Engineering. Ernest Spons
Standard Dictionary.........Funk & Wagnalls
Standard Electrical Dictionary..T. O'C. Sloane
Stargazing.....................J. N. Lockyer
Stars, The.....................Simon Newcomb
Stars and Telescopes...........David P. Todd
Stationary Steam Engines......Charles Hurst
Steam Boiler Construction.......W. S. Hutton
Stone-Working Machinery...........M. P. Bale
Storage Battery, The.....Augustus Treadwell
Story of Our Planet, The..........T. G. Bonney
Strength of Materials, The.......J. B. Johnson
Structural Botany......................Asa Gray
Student's Lyell, The..........Sir Charles Lyell
Studies in Economics...............Wm. Smart
Studies in History and Jurisprudence. James Bryce
Submarine Telegraphs...........Charles Bright
Subterranean World, The......Georg Hartwig
Sun, The.........................C. A. Young
Surveying as Practised by Civil Engineers and Surveyors...................John Whitelaw
Synonyms Discriminated...........C. J. Smith
System of Geology, Popular and Scientific, A. James Bell
System of Inorganic Chemistry, A. Wm. Ramsay

System of the Stars, The..........A. M. Clerke

Tariff History of the United States. F. W. Taussig
Taxation in American States and Cities. R. T. Ely
Tea Machinery and Tea Factories. A. J. Wallis-Tayler
Technical Mechanics.............E. R. Maurer
Technologisches Wörterbuch. Dr. Ernst Röhrig
Technologisches Wörterbuch..M. A. Tolhausen
Tests and Reagents..................A. I. Cohn
Technische Mechanik.....Edmund Autenrieth
Text-book of Electricity, A.........H. M. Noad
Text-book of Geology...........A. P. Brigham
Text-book of Histology, A....Böhm & Davidoff
Text-book of Histology............Philip Stöhr
Text-book of Mineralogy, A..........E. S. Dana
Text-book of Physiology, A..........M. Foster
Text-book of the Principles of Physics. J. S. Ames
Text-book of Zoölogy........Claus & Sedgwick
Text-book of Zoölogy........Parker & Haswell
Text-book on the Steam Engine. T. M. Goodeve
Theoretical and Practical Graphics. F. N. Willson
Theoretical Mechanics.........W. W. Johnson
Theoretical Mechanics.......Arthur Thornton
Theory and Practice of Hygiene. Notter & Firth
Theory and Practice of Modern Framed Structures, The......................J. B. Johnson
Theory and Practice of Surveying. J. B. Johnson
Theory of Equations.................H. B. Fine
Theory of Equations..............I. Todhunter
Theory of Heat................Thomas Preston
Theory of Light, The...................C. E. Joly
Theory of Optics, The..............Paul Drude
Thermochimie....................M. Berthelot
Thesaurus Dictionary of the English Language, A..........................F. A. March
Thesaurus of English Words and Phrases. P. M. Roget
Thirty Years of American Finance. A. D. Noyes
Topographical Atlas of the United States. U. S. Printing Office
Topographic Surveying..........H. M. Wilson
Traité d'Analyse des Substances Minérales. Adolphe Carnot
Traité de Botanique................L. Courchet
Traité de Mécanique..............S. D. Poisson
Traité de Mécanique Rationnelle..P. E. Appell
Trautwine's Engineer s Pocket Book. J. C. Trautwine
Treatise on Chemistry..Roscoe & Schorlemmer
Treatise on Dynamics of a Particle. Tait & Steele

Treatise on Hydraulics, A. Mansfield Merriman
Treatise on Hygiene and Health. Ed. by Stevenson & Murphy
Treatise on International Public Law. Hannis Taylor
Treatise on Natural Philosophy. Thomson & Tait
Treatise on Ore Deposits, A...Phillips & Louis
Treatise on Practical, Plane, and Solid Geometry..........................Evans & Pullen
Treatise on Steam Boilers, A........R. Wilson
Treatise on the Strength of Materials, The. Peter Barlow
Treatise Upon the Law of Copyright, A. E. J. MacGillivray
Trusses of Wood and Iron....William Griffiths
Tunnelling.......................Charles Prelini
Tutorical Trigonometry.......Briggs & Bryan

Universal Encyclopedia.....L. Brent Vaughan
University Text-book of Botany, A. D. H. Campbell

Ventilation.......................W. P. Buchan
Volcanoes of North America.....J. C. Russell
Volumetric Analysis............Francis Sutton

Wannan's Marine Engineers' Guide. A. C. Wannan
Wasser, Das.........................H. Blücher
Water Analysis..........Wanklyn & Chapman
Water and its Purification............S. Rideal
Water Engineering......................C. Slagg
Water Supply of Cities and Towns. William Humber
Water Supply of Towns and the Construction of Water-Works, The...........W. K. Burton
Watt's Dictionary of Chemistry. Morley & Muir
Webster's International Dictionary. G. & C. Merriam Co.
Webster's Unabridged Dictionary, The Original.....................Geo. W. Ogilvie & Co.
What is Electricity?..........John Trowbridge
Who's Who?...........Pub. by A. & C. Black
Who's Who in America? Pub. by A. N. Marquis & Co.
Woman's Universal Cambist....J. H. Norman
Wood's Natural History............J. G. Wood
Worcester's Dictionary. Pub. by J. B. Lippincott & Co.
Words and Their Uses..............R. G. White
Wurtz's Elements of Chemistry. Greene & Keller

X-Ray Manual..................M. K. Kassabian

Zoölogy..............................A. S. Packard
Zoölogy....................Shipley & MacBride

MARKS USED IN PROOFREADING.

1. Original Proof. 2. Marked Proof. 3. Corrected Matter.

By RALPH E. RUSSELL, LL.B.

(1.)

Essay on Burns.—Thom. Carlisle.

Burn's first came upon the World as a prodigee; and was, in that character, entertained by it, in the usual fashion, with vague, loud, tumultuous wonder, spedily subsiding into sencure and neglect; till his early and most mournful death again awakened an enthu siasm for him, which, especially as there was now nuthing to be done, and much to be spken, has prolonged itself even to our own time,

it is true, the 9 days have long since elapsed; and the very continuance of this clamour proves that Rurns was no vulgur wonder. Accordingly, He has come to rest more & more exclusively on his own intrinsic merits, ane may now be wellnigh shorn of that causal radiance he appears not only as a true English poet, but as one of the most considerable British men of the 18th century. Let it not be objected that he did little. He did very much, if we consider how where and. . . . we must recollect that he had his every materials to discover; fore the for the metal He worked in lay hid under the desert, whre no eye but his had guesst its existence; and wemay almost say that with his own hands he had to construct the tools for fashioning it. For he found himself in deepest security—without help, instruction, without model; or with models only of the meanest sort. An educated man stands, as it were, in the midst of a boundless arsenal and magazine, filled with all the weapon sand engines which mans' skill has been able to devize from the earliest rowed from all Past ages. How different is his state time; and he works, accordingly, with a strength bor- who stands on the outsid of that storehouse, and feels that its gates must be stormed, or remain *forever* shut against him? * * * a dwarf back his steamengene may remove mountains; but no dwarf will hue them down with a pickax; and he must be a Titan who hurls them abroad with his arms.

(2.)

Essay on Burns.—Thom. Carlisle.

Burn's first came upon the World as a prodigea; and was, in that character, entertained by it, in the usual fashion, with vague, loud, tumultuous wonder, spe-dily subsiding into sencure and neglect; till his early and most mournful death again awakened an enthu siasm for him, which, especially as there was now nything to be done, and much to be spken, has prolonged itself even to our own time,

it is true, the 9 days have long since elapsed; and the very continuance of this clamour proves that Kurns was no vulgr wonder Accordingly, He has come to rest more & more exclusively on his own intrinsic merits, and may now be wellnigh shorn of that causal radiance he appears not only as a true English poet, but as one of the most considerable British men of the 18th century. Let it not be ob jected that he did little. He did very much, if we consider how where and. . . . we must recollect that he had his every materials to discover; fore the for the metal He worked in lay hid under the desert, whre no eye but his had guesst its existence; and wemay almost say that with his own hands he had to construct the tools for fashioning it. For he found himself in deepest security—without help, instruction, without model; or with models only of the meanest sort. An educated man stands, as it were, in the midst of a boundlss arsenal and mag. azine, filled with all the weapon sand engines which mans' skill has been able to devize from the earliest rowed from all Past ages. How different is his state time; and he works, accordingly, with a strength bor- who stands on the outsid of that storehouse, and feels that its gates must be stormed, or remain *forever* shut against him? * * * a dwarf back his steamengene may remove mountains; but no dwarf will hue them down with a pickax; and he must be a Titan who hurls them abroad with his arms.

(3.)

ESSAY ON BURNS.—*Thomas Carlyle.*

Burns first came upon the world as a prodigy; and was, in that character, entertained by it, in the usual fashion, with loud, vague, tumultuous wonder, speedily subsiding into censure and neglect; till his early and most mournful death again awakened an enthusiasm for him, which, especially as there was now nothing to be done, and much to be spoken, has prolonged itself even to our own time. It is true, the "nine days" have long since elapsed; and the very continuance of this clamour proves that Burns was no vulgar wonder. Accordingly, even in sober judgments, where, as years passed by, he has come to rest more and more exclusively on his own intrinsic merits, and may now be well-nigh shorn of that casual radiance, he appears not only as a true British poet, but as one of the most considerable British men of the eighteenth century. Let it not be objected that he did little. He did much, if we consider where and how. . . We must remember that he had his very materials to discover; for the metal he worked in lay hid under the desert, where no eye but his had guessed its existence; and we may almost say that with his own hand he had to construct the tools for fashioning it. For he found himself in deepest obscurity, without help, without instruction, without model; or with models only of the meanest sort.

An educated man stands, as it were, in the midst of a boundless arsenal and magazine, filled with all the weapons and engines which man's skill has been able to devise from the earliest time; and he works, accordingly, with a strength borrowed from all past ages. How different is *his* state who stands on the outside of that storehouse, and feels that its gates must be stormed, or remain forever shut against him! . . . A dwarf behind his steam-engine may remove mountains; but no dwarf will hew them down with a pickaxe: and he must be a Titan who hurls them abroad with his arms.

Explanation of Marks.

The alterations to be made in the type are indicated by the marks on the margin of the proof, and as nearly opposite the specified error as possible. The marks customarily used are as follows: δ, delete (L. *delere*, destroy), or expunge; #, insert space as indicated by caret (^); ⊥, push down space; ϱ, turn inverted letter; *stet*, (L. *stare*, let it stand), matter inadvertently altered to remain as originally set, dots (. . .) being placed under the matter; *tr.*, transpose letters, characters, lines, leads, etc.; *center*, bring line to point indicated by [; □, indent line an em of its own measure; a cross (×) denotes a broken or worn letter; ⊙, insert period; ⁀, close up letters or parts of words; δ⁀, a combination of δ, and ⁀, indicates take out intervening space or character and close up; ═, straighten lines; ||, line up or justify correctly; [, bring matter to the left;], bring matter to the right; ⌐¬, raise word or letter; └┘, lower word or letter; *w.f.*, wrong-font letter; *ital.*, change roman to italic; *rom.*, change italic to roman; if necessary to alter the style in which letters or words are set, it may be done by the use of parallel lines. for capitals, *three lines* (≡); for small capitals, *two lines* (=); and for italic, *one line* (—); *l.c.*, indicates lower case; if matter has been omitted it may be written in on the margin of the proof, or if too lengthy, the words *"out see-copy"* are used; where more than two words are to be transposed, the same should be numbered in body of the type matter, and marked *"tr. as numbered"*; *sp.*, indicates spell out figure or abbreviated word; ¶, indicates a new paragraph; *no* ¶, indicates that matter is to be run in; certain letters when appearing in combination, as *fi, ff, ffl*, and diphthongs. as æ, œ, etc., cast as one character, are called logotype, and are indicated by a tie, ⁀; *eq.#*, indicates equal spacing, that is, make the space between each word as uniform as possible. Leaders or dots (. . .) are used to show an ellipsis.

SIGNS AND SYMBOLS

USED IN WRITING AND PRINTING.

ASTRONOMICAL.

1. GREATER PLANETS, ETC.

☉	The Sun; Sun's Longitude.	✳, *or* ✳	Fixed Star.
●	New Moon.	⊕, ⊖ *or* ♁	The Earth.
☽	First Quarter; Moon's Longitude.	♂	Mars.
○, *or* ☺	Full Moon.	♃	Jupiter
☾	Last Quarter.	♄	Saturn.
☿	Mercury.	♅, *or* ⛢	Uranus.
♀	Venus.	♆	Neptune.

The sign ☉ is derived from a buckler with its umbo; ☿ is the caduceus of Mercury, or his head and winged cap; ♀, a looking-glass, appropriately refers to the vanity of Venus; ⊖, the earth and its equator; ⊕ indicates the four quarters of the globe; the sign ♁ indicates the globe and cross of sovereigns, a symbol of dominion; ♂, the symbol of Mars, is derived from the head, helmet, and nodding plume of a warrior, or a shield and spear; ♃, a representation of an eagle, with expanded wings, or the initial letter of the Greek name of Jupiter, with a line through it as a mark of abbreviation; ♄, a sickle, the emblem of the god of time; ♅, the initial letter of *Herschel*, the discoverer of Uranus (by whose name the planet was formerly known), with a planet suspended from the crossbar; ⛢, the sign derived from that for the sun [☉], together with a part of that for Mars [♂]; ♆, a trident, the emblem of Neptune, the god of the sea.

2. MINOR PLANETS.

These planets were formerly designated by signs, but latterly they are all commonly designated by numbers indicating the order of their discovery, and their symbol is a small circle or oval inclosing this number. Sometimes letters of the Greek alphabet are used in connection with the name of the constellation in which the star or planet is situated.

3. ZODIACAL SIGNS.

1.	♈ Aries, *the Ram.*	7.	♎ Libra, *the Balance.*
2.	♉ Taurus, *the Bull.*	8.	♏ Scorpio, *the Scorpion.*
3.	♊, ◻ Gemini, *the Twins.*	9.	♐ Sagittarius, *the Archer.*
4.	♋ Cancer, *the Crab.*	10.	♑ Capricornus, *the Goat.*
5.	♌ Leo, *the Lion.*	11.	♒ Aquarius, *the Waterman.*
6.	♍ Virgo, *the Virgin.*	12.	♓ Pisces, *the Fishes.*

These twelve signs are divided into four groups of three each—representing the spring, summer, autumn, and winter seasons.

☞ The sign ♈ is derived from the horns of a ram; ♉, the head and horns of a bull; ♊, the statues of Castor and Pollux; ♋, the claws of a crab; ♌, a corruption of the Greek letter Lambda, the initial of Leōn, a lion, or else a representation of a lion's tail; ♍, a corruption of *par*, the first syllable of the Greek word for *virgin*; ♎, a balance; ♏, the legs and tail of a scorpion; ♐, an arrow and a small portion of the bow, which is to be seen at the bottom of the character; ♑, a character combining the letters of the Greek word *tragos*=a goat; ♒, waves of water; ♓, two fishes tied together.

4. ASPECTS AND NODES.

☌ Conjunction;—the bodies having the same longitude, or right ascension.

✳ Sextile;—a difference of 60° or ⅙ of the circle in longitude, or right ascension.

☾, *or* ☉ Quintile;—a difference of 72° or ⅕ of the circle in longitude, or right ascension.

◻ Quadrature;—a difference of 90° or ¼ of the circle in longitude, or right ascension.

△ Trine;—a difference of 120° or ⅓ of the circle in longitude, or right ascension.

☍ Opposition;—a difference of 180° or ½ of the circle in longitude, or right ascension.

☊ Ascending Node.

☋ Descending Node.

5. SIGNS AND ABBREVIATIONS USED IN ASTRONOMICAL CALCULATIONS AND FORMULÆ.

a. Mean distance.
A. R. Right ascension.
β Celestial latitude.
D. Diameter.
δ Declination.
△ Distance.
E. East.
e Eccentricity.
h., *or* h Hours; as 5h., or 5h.
i Inclination to the ecliptic.
L, *l*, *or* *ε* Mean longitude in orbit.
λ Longitude.
M. Mass.
m., *or* m Minutes of time; as 5m., 5m.
μ, *or* *n* Mean daily motion.
+ *or* N. North.
N. P. D. North polar distance.
v, ☊, *or* L. Longitude of ascending node.
π *or* *ω* Longitude of perihelion.
q. Perihelion distance.
ρ, *or* R. Radius, or radius vector.
—, *or* S. South.
s, *or* s. Seconds of time; as, 16s., or 16s.
T. Periodic time.
W. West.
φ Angle of eccentricity; also, geographical latitude.
° Degrees.
′ Minutes of arc.
″ Seconds of arc.

BOTANICAL.

These signs are used to designate the peculiarities of different species and varieties of plants, and are usually written without any accompanying verbal description. The signs are borrowed mainly from astronomy and chemistry.

◐, ☉, ○ Annual.
♂, ☉, ☉, ☽ Biennial.
♃ Perennial.
△ Evergreen.
☉ Monocarpous plant; flowers but once.
♂, *or* ♂ A staminate or male flower.
♀ Pistillate, fertile, or female.
☿ Perfect or hermaphrodite.
♂ ♀ Unisexual; male and female flowers separate.
♂ – ♀ Monœcious; male and female flowers on the same plant.
♂ : ♀ Diœcious; male and female flowers on separate plants.
☿ ♂ ♀ Polygamous; having hermaphrodite and unisexual flowers on the same or different plants.
⌒ A climbing plant.
) Turning to the left.
(Turning to the right.
○= Cotyledons accumbent, and radicle lateral.
○‖ Cotyledons incumbent, and radicle dorsal.
○» Cotyledons conduplicate, and radicle dorsal.
○‖‖ Cotyledons folded twice, and radicle dorsal.
○‖‖‖ Cotyledons folded three times, and radicle dorsal.
∞, *or* 00 Indefinite number; applied to stamens, more than twenty.
0 Wanting; showing the absence of a part.
° Feet.
′ Inches. ″ Lines. [With some writers the signs for feet, inches, and lines are ′, ″, ‴.]
! indicates certainty. Appended to the name of an author, it indicates that he has examined an authentic specimen; appended to the name of a locality, that the writer has seen or collected specimens from that locality.
† *or* ? Doubt or uncertainty.

CHEMICAL.

˙ One equivalent of oxygen;—when written above an elemental symbol the number of repetitions indicates the number of equivalents of oxygen entering into a composition; as, $\dddot{S}=SO_3$.

′ One atom or equivalent of sulphur; thus, $\overset{\prime\prime}{Fe}$=bisulphid of iron.

A dash drawn across a symbol having either of the foregoing signs above it multiplies the atoms of the symbol by 2; thus, $\dddot{Fe}$ with a dash across it$=Fe_2O_3$=sesquioxid of iron.

\+ is used between the symbols of substances brought together for a reaction or produced by reaction. In organic chemistry it=a base or alkaloid if written above the initial letter of the name of the substance; as, $\overset{+}{M}$, morphine; $\overset{+}{Q}$, quinine.

— signifies a single unit of affinity; in organic chemistry, an acid, when written above the initial letter of the name of the acid; as, $\bar{S}$=sulphuric acid; sometimes used as a sign of subtraction.

For table of symbols and atomic weights of chemical elements see page 545 of the Dictionary.

By means of chemical symbols, or formulas, the composition of the most complicated substances can be very easily expressed, and that, too, in a very small compass. An abbreviated expression of this kind often gives, in a single line, more information as to details than could be given in many lines of letterpress.

When any of the chemical symbols stands by itself it indicates one atom of the element it represents. Thus H stands for one atom of hydrogen, O for one atom of oxygen, and Cl for one atom of chlorin.

When a symbol has a small figure or number underwritten, and to the right of it, such figure or number indicates the number of atoms of the element. Thus O_2 signifies two atoms of oxygen, S_5 five atoms of sulphur, and C_{10} ten atoms of carbon.

When two or more elements are united to form a chemical compound, their symbols are written one after the other, to indicate the compound. Thus H_2O means water, a compound of two atoms of hydrogen and one of oxygen; $C_{12}H_{22}O_{11}$ indicates cane-sugar, a compound of twelve atoms of carbon, twenty-two of hydrogen, and eleven of oxygen.

These two expressions as they stand denote respectively a molecule of the substance they represent, that is, the smallest possible quantity of it capable of existing in the free state. To express several molecules a large figure is prefixed; thus, $2H_2O$ represents two molecules of water, $4(C_{12}H_{22}O_{11})$ four molecules of cane-sugar.

When a compound is formed of two or more compounds the symbolical expressions for the compound are usually connected together by a comma; thus, the crystallized magnesic sulphate is $M_gSO_4, 7H_2O$. The symbols may also be used to express the changes which occur during chemical action, and they are then written in the form of an equation, of which one side represents the substances as they exist before the change, the other the result of the reaction. Thus, $2H_2+O_2=2H_2O$ expresses the fact that two molecules of hydrogen, each containing two atoms, and one of oxygen, also containing two atoms, combine to give two molecules of water, each of them containing two atoms of hydrogen and one of oxygen.

MATHEMATICAL.

1. NUMERATION.

Arabic.	*Greek.*	*Roman.*	*Arabic.*	*Greek.*	*Roman.*
0	...		20	κ	XX.
1	α	I.	30	λ	XXX.
2	β	II.	40	μ	XL, *or* XXXX.
3	γ	III.	50	ν	L.
4	δ	IV, *or* IIII.	60	ξ	LX.
5	ε	V.	70	ο	LXX.
6	ϛ	VI.	80	π	LXXX, *or* XXC.
7	ζ	VII.	90	ϟ	XC, *or* LXXXX.
8	η	VIII, *or* IIX.	100	ρ	C.
9	θ	IX, *or* VIIII.	200	σ	CC.
10	ι	X.	300	τ	CCC.
11	ια	XI.	400	υ	CCCC.
12	ιβ	XII.	500	φ	D. *or* IↃ.
13	ιγ	XIII, *or* XIIV.	600	χ	DC, *or* IↃC.
14	ιδ	XIV, *or* XIIII.	700	ψ	DCC, *or* IↃCC.
15	ιε	XV.	800	ω	DCCC, *or* IↃCCC.
16	ιϛ	XVI.	900		DCCCC, IↃCCCC, *or* CM.
17	ιζ	XVII.	1,000		M. *or* CIↃ.
18	ιη	XVIII, *or* XIIX.	2,000		MM, *or* CIↃCIↃ.
19	ιθ	XIX, *or* XVIIII.			

In the Roman notation, a character at the right hand of a larger numeral is added to that of such numeral; as, VI=V+I=6. I, X, and sometimes C, are also placed at the left hand of larger numerals, and when so situated their value is subtracted from that of such numerals; as, IV, that is, V—I=4. After the sign IↃ for D, when the character Ↄ was repeated, each repetition had the effect to multiply D by ten; as, IↃↃ, 5,000; IↃↃↃ, 50,000; and the like. In writing numbers twice as great as these, C was placed as many times before the stroke I, as the Ↄ was written after it.

2. CALCULATION.

+ Plus, the sign of addition; used also to indicate that figures are only approximately exact.

− Minus, the sign of subtraction; used also to indicate that figures have been left off from the end of a number, and that the last figure has been increased by one.

±, *or* ∓ Plus or minus; indicating that either of the signs + or − may properly be used.

× Multiplied by; 5×4=20.

Multiplication is sometimes indicated by placing a dot between the factors; 2 . 3 . 5=30.

÷ The sign of division; division is also indicated by the sign : ; as $x \div y$, $x : y$. It is also indicated when two numbers have a straight line drawn between them, as $\frac{a}{b}$; or an oblique line, as a/b. Yet another sign is the character ⊥; thus 8 ⊥ 4=2.

= Is equal to; equals.

> Is more than; as, $x > y$; that is, x is greater than y.

< Is less than; as, $x < y$; that is, x is less than y.

The above signs reversed have a contrary meaning and express the fact that numbers may be equal or greater or less than the number at the apex of the angle.

≏ Is equivalent to; applied to magnitudes or quantities which are equal in area or volume, but are not of the same form.

∽ The difference between; used to designate the difference between two quantities without indicating which is the greater.

−: The same as ∞.

∝ Varies as; as, $x \propto y$; that is, x varies as y.

∺ Geometrical proportion; as, ∺ $x : y :: a : b$, that is, the geometrical proportion of those quantities.

: Is to; the ratio of.

:: As; equals.

.. Minus; also used to express the arithmetical ratio of numbers.

:: Equals.

∞ Indefinitely great; greater than any finite or assignable quantity.

0 Indefinitely small; less than any assignable quantity.

! *or* ∟ The continued product of numbers from one upward; as, 5 !=5×4×3×2×1.

∴ Therefore.

∵ Since or because.

. . . And so on.

≡ Is the same as; as 2×4≡6+2.

∠ Angle; frequently written > or ∠.

The angle between two lines is also indicated by placing one of the letters denoting the inclosing lines over the other.

∟ Right angle.

⊥ The perpendicular; as EF ⊥ MN=EF drawn perpendicularly to MN.

∥ Parallel; parallel to.

$\underline{\vee}$ Is equiangular to.

$\underline{\|}$ Is equilateral to.

○ Circle; circumference; 360°.

⌒ Arc of a circle.

△ Triangle.

□ Square.

▭ Rectangle.

√, *or* √‾ Root, indicating, when used without a figure placed above it, the square root. When any other than the square root is meant a figure (called the *index*) expressing the degree of the required root, is placed above the sign; as, $\sqrt[3]{a}$, $\sqrt[4]{a}$.

This sign is a modification of the letter *r*, which was used as an abbreviation of the Latin word *radix*. Sometimes a root is denoted by index in fractional form at the right-hand side of the quantity and above it, the denominator of the index expressing the degree of the root; as, $x^{\frac{1}{2}}$, $x^{\frac{1}{3}}$, $x^{\frac{1}{4}}$.

—— Vinculum *or* ( ) Parentheses, [ ] Brackets, *or* { }, Braces, } These signs denote that the quantities to which they are applied are to be taken together.

f, *or* F Function; other letters or signs are frequently used to indicate functions. Some are used without the parentheses.

d Differential.

δ Variation.

Δ Finite difference.

D Differential coefficient.

· Fluxion; differential; written above the quantity, as, $\dot{x}$.

∫ [An old-fashioned long *s* (the initial of the word *summa*).] Integral. It is repeated to indicate that the operation of integration is to be performed twice, or three or more times, as, ∫∫, ∫∫∫, etc. For a number of times greater than three, an index is written at the right hand above; as, ∫*m xyzm*; that is, the *m*th integral, or the result of *m* integrations of *xyzm*.

$\int_y^x$ Indicates that the integral is to be taken between the value *y* of the variable and its value *x*. ∫*x* denotes that the integral ends at the value *x* of the variable, and ∫*y* that it begins at the value *y*.

Σ Sum; algebraic sum; when used to indicate the summation of finite differences, it has a sense similar to that of the symbol ∫.

Π The continued product of all terms such as [those indicated].

π [The Greek letter *pi*.] The number 3.14159265+; the ratio of the circumference of a circle to its diameter, of a semicircle to its radius, and of the area of a circle to the square of its radius.

ε, *or* *e* The number 2.7182818+; the base of the Napierian system of logarithms; also the eccentricity of a conic section.

M The modulus of a system of logarithms; especially of the common system of logarithms. In this system it is equal to 0.4342944819+.
g The force of gravity.
° Degrees.
′ Minutes of arc.
″ Seconds of arc.
^{h} Hours.
^{m} Minutes.
^{s} Seconds.
R° Radius of a circle in degrees of arc.
R′ Radius in minutes of arc.
R″ Radius in seconds of arc.
′, ″, ‴, etc. Used to mark quantities of the same kind which are to be distinguished.

When the number of accents would be greater than three, the corresponding Roman numerals are used instead of them.

^{1}, ^{2}, ^{3}, etc. Exponents placed above and at the right hand of quantities to indicate that they are raised to powers whose degree is indicated by the figure.
sin.=sine of; cos., tan., cot., sec., cosec, versin., and covers., denote respectively cosine, tangent, cotangent, secant, cosecant, versed sine, and coversed sine of an arc.
sinh. The hyperbolic sine.
cosh. The hyperbolic cosine.

MEDICAL.

āā (Gr. ἀνα.) Of each.
Ad=add.
Ad. lib.=at pleasure.
Aliquot=several, some.
B. d.=*Bis in die*=twice a day.
Chart.=*chartula*=a small paper.
Coch.=spoonful.
Coch. umplum or *magnum*=tablespoonful.
Coch. medium=dessert-spoonful.
Coch. minimum=teaspoonful.
Cochleatim=by the spoonful.
Cyanth.=wineglassful.
Haus.=a draught.
Log.=a bottle.
M.=mix.
Q.S.=a sufficient quantity.
Q. V. *or* Q. P.=as much as you please.
℞ (L. *Recipe.*) Take. Said to have been originally the same as ♃, the symbol of Jupiter, placed at the top of a formula to invoke the king of the gods, that the compound might act favorably.
S. (L. *Signa.*) Write; used in a prescription to indicate directions to be put on the label of the package.
C (L. *Congius.*) Gallon.
O, or O. (L. *Octarius.*) Pint.
℥ Ounce; ℥i, one ounce; ℥ij, two ounces; ℥ss, half an ounce; ℥iss, an ounce and a half. *f*℥ Fluid ounce.
℈ Scruple; ℈i, one scruple; ℈ij, two scruples; ℈ss, half a scruple; ℈iss, a scruple and a half.
ʒ Dram or drachm; ʒi, one dram; ʒij, two drams; ʒss, half a dram; ʒiss, dram and a half; *f*ʒ Fluid drachm.
♏ *or* ♍ Minim; a drop.
gtt=drops; *guttatim*=drop by drop.

MISCELLANEOUS.

&, &, &. And.
&c. (*Et cætera*); and so forth.
Church-Service Book marks.
- ℟ Response.
- * Used to divide each verse of a psalm into two parts, and show where the response begins.
- ✠ *or* + A sign of the cross used by the pope, and by Roman Catholic bishops and archbishops, immediately before the subscription of their names. In service-books, used in those places in the prayers and benediction where the sign of the cross is to be made.

× *or* + A character made by persons unable to write, when they are required to sign their names. The name of the party is added by some one who can write; as, John × Doe (his / mark).
☿ ♂ Male;—used in zoölogy.
♀ Female;—used in zoölogy.
< Derived from;—used in giving etymologies.
> Whence is derived;—used in giving etymologies.
\+ And;—used in giving etymologies.
* Assumed or supposed, but not found or verified; used in giving etymologies.
† Died;—used in genealogies, etc.

MONETARY AND COMMERCIAL.

$ Dollar or dollars; as, $100.
¢ Cent.
£ Pound or pounds sterling; as, £100.
/ Shilling or shillings; as, 2/6, two shillings and sixpence.
℔ Pound (in weight).
@ At; as, 200 @ $1 each.
℘ Per.
% Per cent; as, 5%.
a/c Account.
B/L Bill of Lading.
c/o Care of.
d/a Days after acceptance.
d/s Days after sight.
L/C Letter of Credit.
A1 The rating of a first-class vessel; the letter denoting that the hull is seaworthy, and the figure the efficient state of her equipment, etc. The figure 2 would imply that the equipment is of an inferior quality. When a vessel is too old for the character A (four to fifteen years), it is registered A in red.
Æ The rating of a vessel of the third class, fit to convey perishable goods on short voyages only.
E The rating of a vessel fit for carrying on a voyage of any length such goods only as are not liable to sea damage.
I The rating of a vessel fit for carrying goods of the same sort on shorter voyages only.
MC Indicate that the boiler and machinery of a steam-vessel are in good order and safe working condition.
XX Ale or other liquor of double strength.
XXX Ale or other liquor of triple strength.
4to, 4° Quarto; with four leaves or eight pages to the sheet.
8vo or 8° Octavo; with eight leaves or sixteen pages to the sheet.
12mo or 12° Duodecimo or twelvemo; with twelve leaves or twenty-four pages to the sheet.
16mo or 16° Sextodecimo or sixteenmo; with sixteen leaves or thirty-two pages to the sheet. Similarly 18mo, 24mo, etc.

TYPOGRAPHICAL.

MARKS OF PUNCTUATION.

, Comma.
; Semicolon.
: Colon.
. Period.
— Dash.
? Interrogation.
! Exclamation.
() Parentheses.
[] Brackets.
' Apostrophe.
- Hyphen.

´ Acute Accent.
` Grave Accent.
ˆ Broad *or* Circumflex Accent.
˜ *or* ⌒ Circumflex *or* Tilde.
¯ Long Accent, *or* Macron.
˘ Short, *or* Breve.
¨ Diæresis.
¸ (ç) Cedilla.
‸ Caret.
“ ” Quotation marks.
} Brace.

*** Omission.
. . . Omission; *also* Leaders.
—— Omission.
* Asterisk.
† Dagger, *or* Obelisk.
‡ Double Dagger.
§ Section.
‖ Parallels.
¶ Paragraph.
☞ Index.
⁂, *or* ⁂ Asterism

A DICTIONARY
OF THE
ENGLISH LANGUAGE

LIST OF ABBREVIATIONS

USED IN THIS DICTIONARY.

a. or adj. stands for adjective.
abbrev. .. abbreviation, abbreviated.
acc. .. accusative.
act. .. active.
adv. .. adverb.
Afr. .. African.
Am. .. America *or* American.
Am. Ind. .. American Indian.
anat. .. anatomy.
anc. .. ancient.
Anglo-Ind. .. Anglo-Indian.
aor. .. aorist, aoristic.
Ar. .. Arabic.
arch. .. architecture.
archæol. .. archæology.
arith. .. arithmetic.
Arm. .. Armoric.
art. .. article.
AS. .. Anglo Saxon.
at. wt. .. atomic weight.
aug. .. augmentative.

biol. .. biology.
Bohem. .. Bohemian.
bot. .. botany.
Braz. .. Brazilian.
Bulg. .. Bulgarian.

Catal. .. Catalonian.
caus. .. causative.
Celt. .. Celtic.
Ch. .. Chaldee.
chron. .. chronology.
colloq. .. colloquial.
comp. .. comparative, compound, *or* composition.
conch. .. conchology.
conj. .. conjunction.
contr. .. contraction, contracted.
Corn. .. Cornish.
cub. .. cubic.
Cym. .. Cymric.

D. .. Dutch *or* Belgic.
Dan. .. Danish.
dat. .. dative.
def. .. definite.
deriv. .. derivation.
dial. .. dialect, dialectal.
dict. .. dictionary.
dim. .. diminutive.
distrib. .. distributive.
dyn. .. dynamics.

E., Eng. stands for English.
eccles. .. ecclesiastical.
Egypt. .. Egyptian.
E. Ind. .. East Indian.
Eth. .. Ethiopic.
ethn. .. ethnography, ethnology.
etym. .. etymology.
Eur. .. European.
exclam. .. exclamation.

F., Fahr. .. Fahrenheit.
f. .. feminine.
fig. .. figuratively.
Fl. .. Flemish.
Fr. .. French.
freq. .. frequentative.
fut. .. future.

G. .. German.
Gael. .. Gaelic.
genit. .. genitive.
Goth. .. Gothic.
Gr. .. Greek.
gram. .. grammar.

Heb. .. Hebrew.
her. .. heraldry.
Hind. .. Hindustani, Hindu, *or* Hindi.
hist. .. history.
hort. .. horticulture.
Hung. .. Hungarian.

Ice. .. Icelandic.
imper. .. imperative.
imperf. .. imperfect.
impers. .. impersonal.
incept. .. inceptive.
ind. .. indicative.
indef. .. indefinite.
Indo-Eur. .. Indo-European.
inf. .. infinitive
intens. .. intensive.
interj. .. interjection.
Ir. .. Irish.
Iran. .. Iranian.
It. .. Italian.

Japan. .. Japanese.

L. .. Latin.
L.G. .. Low German.
L.Gr. .. Low Greek.
lit. .. literal, literally.

Lith. stands for Lithuanian.
LL. .. Low *or* late Latin.

masc. .. masculine.
math. .. mathematics.
M.D. .. Middle Dutch.
ME. .. Middle English.
mech. .. mechanics.
med. .. medicine.
metal. .. metallurgy.
Mex. .. Mexican.
M.H.G. .. Middle High German.
milit. .. military.
mineral. .. mineralogy.
myth. .. mythology.

n. .. noun.
N. Am. .. North American.
nat. ord. .. natural order.
nat. phil. .. natural philosophy.
neg. .. negative.
neut. .. neuter.
nom. .. nominative.
Norm. .. Norman.
Norw. .. Norwegian.

obj. .. objective.
obs. .. obsolete.
O.D. .. Old Dutch.
OE. .. Old English.
OFr. .. Old French.
O.H.G. .. Old High German.
O.Per. .. Old Persian.
ornith. .. ornithology.
OS. .. Old Saxon.
O.Sp. .. Old Spanish.

p. .. participle.
part. .. participle.
pass. .. passive.
Per. .. Persic or Persian.
perf. .. perfect.
pers. .. person.
Peruv. .. Peruvian.
Port. .. Portuguese.
philol. .. philology.
philos. .. philosophy.
Phen. .. Phenician.
phys. geog. .. physical geography
pl. .. plural.
poet. .. poetical.
Pol. .. Polish.
pol. econ. .. political economy.
poss. .. possessive.
pp. .. past participle.

ppr. stands for present participle.
Pr. .. Provençal.
prep. .. preposition.
pres. .. present.
priv. .. privative.
prob. .. probably.
pron. .. pronoun, pronunciation, pronounced.
pros. .. prosody.
prov. .. provincial.
psychol. .. psychology.
pt. .. past tense.

R. C. .. Roman Catholic.
rhet. .. rhetoric.
Rom. .. Roman.
Russ. .. Russian.

S. Afr. .. South African.
S. Am. .. South American.
Sam. .. Samaritan.
Sans. .. Sanskrit.
Scand. .. Scandinavian.
Scot. .. Scotch or Scottish.
Scrip. .. Scripture.
Sem. .. Semitic.
Serv. .. Servian.
sing. .. singular.
Slav. .. Slavonic, Slavic.
Sp. .. Spanish.
sp. gr. .. specific gravity.
subj. .. subjunctive.
superl. .. superlative.
Sw. .. Swedish.
sym. .. symbol.
syn. .. synonym.
Syr. .. Syriac.

Tart. .. Tartar.
Tat. .. Tatar.
term. .. termination.
Teut. .. Teutonic.
theol. .. theology.
trans. .. translation.
Turk. .. Turkish.
typog. .. typography.

U.S. .. United States.

var. .. variety (of species).
v.i. .. verb intransitive.
v.t. .. verb transitive.

W. .. Welsh.
W. Ind. .. West Indian.

KEY TO PRONUNCIATION.

The accents are indicated thus: primary ′, secondary ″. The mark of the secondary accent or subordinate stress is only used when it falls at an irregular interval from the primary or main stress, i. e., at an interval other than two syllables.

ā..as in fāte, āle; also as in senāte.
ä.. " " fär, fäther; also as in whät.
ȧ.. " " fȧst, glȧss, sodȧ, Americȧ.
a̤.. " " fa̤ll, pa̤w.
ă.. " " fināl, seamăn, solăr.
â.. " " câre, âir.
a.. " " at.

ē..as in mēte, hē.
e̤.. " " pre̤y, e̤ight.
ẽ.. " " hẽr, vẽrse.
e.. " " met, ebb.

ī..as in pīne, īdea.
ï.. " " marïne.
ĩ.. " " bĩrd, fĩr.
i.. " " pin, it.

ō..as in nōte, ōat, sō; also as in renōvate.
ö..as in möve, pröve.
o̤.. " " fo̤r, o̤r, lo̤ng, cro̤ss, o̤ff.
ŏ.. " " atŏm, plŏver; also as in actŏr, wŏrd, wŏrk; also as in buttŏn.
o.. " " not.
o͞o.. " " mo͞on, co͞o.
oo.. " " book, hood, foot.

ū..as in ūse; also as in fūtūre.
u̇.. " " bu̇ll, pu̇t.
ü.. " " brüte, jüry; also used for the German ü.
ũ.. " " tũrn, fũr.
u.. " " up, tub.

ȳ..as in crȳ, eȳe.
y.. " " myth, city.

ç..as in çat, tobaçço.
ç.. " " maçhine.

c..as in ace, cedar.
ch..as in church.
ḡh.. " " ḡhord, loḡh.
ġ..as in ġem.
ñ..as in añger, sphiñx.
ṅ.. " " boṅ [Fr.].
ng..as in ring.
ş..as in mişer, aş.
th..as in this.
th.. " " thin.
ẓ..as in aẓure.
ou..as in out.
au..as in umlaut.
oi..as in oil.
oy.. " " boy.

ew..as ū.
ow..as in now.
-tion ...... } as -shun.
-sion ...... }
-tian ..... } as -shun.
-sian ..... }
-liŏn .... as -lyun *or* -yun.
-ceous .... } as -shus.
-(s)cious. }
-ous .... as -us.
ph-.......... as f- (in phone, etc.).
-le.......... as -l (at end of syllable, as in able, cycle, etc.).
-iȧ .... as -yȧ.
wh-.......... as hw- in whale, etc.

NOTE.—In the vowels ordinary or "short" quality is unmarked. The "avowedly ambiguous" a, as in bath, pass, etc., is usually marked ȧ. The modified e, as in the second syllable of recent, is unmarked, as is the a in apply, annul, etc. When two vowels stand together and only one is marked, the word is pronounced as indicated by the diacritic. The digraphs æ and œ ending a syllable are pronounced as long ē; when followed by a consonant in the same syllable they are pronounced as e in met.

ADDENDA
TO A
DICTIONARY OF THE ENGLISH LANGUAGE

abasia (ȧ-bā'zhi-ȧ), *n.* inability to walk properly, due to lack of coördination of the leg muscles.

abiosis (ab-i-ō'sis), *n.* a state of lifelessness; absence of life.

Academic City (ak-ȧ-dem'ik), a name given to Worcester, Mass. on account of its numerous educational institutions.

according to Hoyle (ă-kôrd'ing, hoil), playing any kind of game fair, according to recognized rules; doing what one conscientiously believes is right and proper under the circumstances: after Edmond Hoyle (1672-1769) an English writer on games, especially whist and other card games, who was considered an authority in his day.

achromasia (ăk-rō-mā'shi-ȧ), *n.* lack of pigment in the skin.

acidophilous (ăs-id-of'i-lŭs), *adj.* disposed to acid stains; readily staining with such.

acidosis (ăs-i-dō'sis), *n.* excess of acid in the blood or urine.

acroanaesthesia (ăk-rō-ăn-ĕs-thē'si-ȧ), *n.* loss of feeling or sensation in the extremities.

acrocyanosis (ak'rō-sī'a-nō-sis), *n.* a state characterized by blueness of hands and feet.

acroma (ȧ-krō'mȧ), *n.* paleness of skin, due to lack of normal pigment.

acromania (-mā'ni-ȧ), *n.* a violent form of mania; incurable insanity.

acrotism (ăk'rō-tizm), *n.* weakness of the pulse beats; cessation of pulsation.

actinomycosis (ăk-tĭn-ō-mī-kō'sĭs), *n.* a chronic and infectious disease of both humans and animals; said to be due to the presence of a certain species of fungus.

activist (ăk-tĭv'ist), *n.* an individual who favors, incites, or demands intensified activities, especially in time of war.

adactylia, *n.* see *adactylism* main vocabulary.

addressograph (a-dres'o-grăf), *n.* trade name of a mechanical device designed for addressing letters by printing each address separately from raised letters on a plate within the machine.

adenectomy (ăd-ĕ-nĕk'tō-mĭ), *n.* excision of a gland.

adenoids (ad'e-noidz), *n.pl.* diseased growths within the upper throat; hypertrophy of the pharyngeal glands.

Adirondacks (ăd-i-rŏn'dăks), *n.* a group of the Appalachian mountain system in New York State: the name is that which an Iroquois Indian applied to an Algonquian, and means "he eats bark."

adnexa (ăd-nĕk'sȧ), *n.pl.* in anatomy, parts that are conjoined; appendages.

adrenalin (ad-rē'nal-in), *n.* extract from a suprarenal gland, of which it is the active principle: it is a crystalline substance, known in chemistry as $C_9H_{13}O_3N$, and is used in medicine as a stimulant to raise blood pressure, and to stop hemorrhage or loss of blood.

aërodonetics (ā-ĕr-dŏ-nĕt'iks), *n.* the science of soaring or gliding flight.

aërophagy (ā-rŏf'ȧ-ji), *n.* the swallowing or gulping of air.

aërophotography (-fō-tŏg'rȧ-fĭ), *n.* the art or practice of taking photographs or pictures from aëroplanes or airships.

aerotravel (ā'ĕr-ō-trav"l), *n.* travel through the air by aeroplane or dirigible; travel in any kind of flying machine.

agenesia (ȧ-jĕn-ē'shi-ȧ), *n.* in anatomy, absence, or undevelopment, of parts; sterility; agenesis.

ageusia (ȧ-gū'si-ȧ), *n.* loss or impairment of the sense of taste.

agent provocateur (ā'zhăn prō-vŏk'ȧ-tūr), [Fr.], one who associates with suspected persons and plays on their sympathies in order to learn secrets to incriminate them.

Aglipayan (ȧ-glĭ-pī'an), *adj.* referring to, or denoting a movement started in the Philippines in 1902 by the Rev. Gregorio Aglipay, a Filipino priest, to establish a "Philippine Independent Catholic Apostolic Church."

agrimotor (ag'ri-mō'tĕr), *n.* a field tractor chiefly used by farmers for hauling harvesters or reaping machines.

ahypnia (ȧ-hip'ni-ȧ), *n.* insomnia; sleeplessness.

air condenser (kon-dens'ĕr), a condenser in which air is the principal conductor.

air conditioning (-dĭsh'ŭn-ĭng), a process of washing and humidifying air before it enters a room.

airplane (âr'plān), *n.* any mechanically operated machine or contrivance, heavier than air, used for the purpose of air travel.

air pocket (pok'et), a part of the atmosphere different from surrounding strata, in which an aeroplane dips from its course.

air raid (rād), an attack from the air by a force of hostile aeroplanes.

Alabama (al-ȧ-bä'mȧ), *n.* a State of the U.S., the Cotton State: the name is Indian, meaning "Here we rest"; a privateer vessel built in England which did much damage to American shipping during the Civil War: sunk by the Kearsage off Cherbourg, France, June 19, 1864.

Alabama claims (klāmz), claims made upon England by the United States for damages to American shipping during the Civil War by privateers, especially the Alabama: a tribunal of arbitration, sitting at Geneva, 1872 awarded $15,000,000 to the United States: also known as the Geneva award.

Aladdin (ȧ-lăd'ĭn), *n.* the young man in the "Arabian Nights" who obtains a magic lamp and ring, the rubbing of which causes two horrible genii to appear, who do the bidding, or fulfil the wish, of the one who has the lamp and ring in his possession at the time.

Al Araf (ăl ä'răf), in Mohammedan belief, the wall that separates heaven from hell, as described in the Koran.

Aleut (al'e-ōōt), *n.* one of a tribe of Eskimos inhabiting Alaska and the Aleutian Islands.

alganesthesia (ăl-găn-ĕs-thē'shi-ȧ), *n.* complete insensitiveness to pain.

alginuresis (ăl-ji-nū-rē'sĭs), *n.* painful urination.

algivorous (ăl-jĭv'ō-rus), *adj.* feeding on algæ or seaweeds.

alkalosis (ăl-kă-lō'sĭs), *n.* a condition in which there is not a sufficiency of alkalinity in the blood.

allantiasis, *n.* see *botulism* main vocabulary.

Allies (ă-līz'), *n.pl.* specifically, the group of nations that joined in alliance to wage combat against the Central Powers in the World War—with *the*; [a-], any group of nations allied against some nation or group of nations.

allergy (ăl'ĕr-ji), *n.* acquired immunity through which a person reinfected by a germ reacts differently from the way he reacted to the primary infection.

aloha (ä-lō'hä), *interj.* hail! also, farewell! *n.* in the Hawaiian Islands, a salutation given to those either coming or going, simply meaning *love to you.*

alpha particle (al'fȧ pär'ti-k'l), a positively charged particle of four protons and two electrons, forming a constituent of the nuclei of many atoms.

alpha rays (rāz), rays emitted by radioactive substances, as radium, consisting of positively charged particles, probably, of helium: they are small in mass, are of great velocity, but very low in penetrating power.

alter ego (ôl'tĕr ē'gō), [L.], literally, other I; specifically, a bosom friend; a close pal; often applied to a friend who speaks or acts for another.

altricial, *adj.* see *altrical* main vocabulary.

Amadis (am'ȧ-dis), *n.* [Sp.], a constant or faithful lover.

Amadis of Gaul (gawl), a faithful lover, much celebrated as a hero in a series of prose romances of the 16th century; he was a love-child whose mother put the infant into a box and cast it into the sea: the child was rescued and brought up at the Scottish Court.

ambivalence (ăm-bĭv'ȧ-lĕns), *n.* in psychology the quality of possessing conflicting mental forces, as of love and hatred for the same person.

Americana (ȧ-mer'i-kā'nȧ), *n.pl.* matter relating to America, as in history, ethnography, description, development, social and material advancement, general literature, etc.

American Expeditionary Forces (ĕks-pĕ-dĭsh'ŭn-ȧ-rĭ fōrs'ĕs), [A.E.F.], the U.S. troops who served overseas in the World War.

American Federation of Labor (fed-ĕr-ā'shun, lā'bĕr), [A.F. of L.], an American organization of industrial unions, chiefly composed of skilled laborers, the principal activities of which consist in establishing self-governing unions in every legitimate trade and occupation, the improvement and safeguarding of working conditions, the maintenance of a decent living wage, and the gaining of the sympathy and support of the public, by means of press and platform, to any legislative measures that may be brought forward in its behalf.

American Legion (lē-jŭn), a nonpartisan, nonpolitical patriotic organization composed of veterans of the World War, incorporated by Act of Congress, September 16, 1919: all soldiers, sailors, or marines who served honorably between April 6, 1917 and November 11, 1918 are eligible to membership; also, women, engaged in either branch of the service during the same period.

Amerind (ăm'ĕr-ind), *n.* one of the native races of America, such as the Indians and Esquimaux.

Ananias (ăn-ȧ-nī'ăs), *n.* a disciple of the first Apostles whom Peter censured for lying and hypocrisy (*Acts v.*); hence, any liar, cheat, or hypocrite.

anaphylaxis (ăn-ȧ-fĭ-lĕk'sĭs), *n.* increased susceptibility to infectious diseases; decrease of resistance to disease, due to the effects of former attacks of illness.

anergy (ăn'ĕr-ji), *n.* a weak condition in which there is little resistance to the infection of disease; lack of energy; inactivity.

anolyte (ăn'ō-līt), *n.* that portion of an electrolyte surrounding the anode in an electrolytic cell.

antibody (-bŏd'i), *n.* a substance that lessens or counteracts the bacteria of toxins; an antitoxin.

antidisestablishmentarianism (ăn'tĭ-dĭs-ĕs-tăb'-lĭsh-mĕn-tā'rĭ-ăn-ĭzm), opposition to the disestablishment of a church or religious body; specifically, strong opposition to the disestablishment of a State Church, as was manifested in Ireland in 1869, when Gladstone disestablished the Irish Church (Protestant) to which all the people, including Roman Catholics, had been compelled to pay tithes.

Antietam (ăn-tē'tam), *n.* a deep river in Maryland, falling into the Potomac, seven miles above Harper's Ferry: on its banks, near Sharpsburg, was fought one of the fiercest battles of the Civil War, in which the Union troops under McClellan defeated the Confederates under Lee: the former lost 13,000 men.

antigen (ăn'tĭ-jĕn), *n.* anything that causes the formation of antibodies.

Anti-Saloon League (ăn-tĭ-sȧ-lōōn' lēg), an organization founded at Washington, D.C., December 18, 1895, and originally known as the Anti-Saloon League of America, having for its objective the suppression of the liquor traffic, first, throughout the U.S. and next, over the whole world: it was the principal agency in bringing about the 18th or Prohibition amendment to the Constitution of the U.S., which was repealed under President Franklin D. Roosevelt in 1933.

apeman (āp'man), *n.* one of a hypothetical genus of primates intermediate between man and the anthropoid apes; specifically, the *Java man*, living about 500,000 years ago, some of whose bones were unearthed in that island in 1891.

aphagia (ȧ-fā'ji-ȧ), *n.* loss of power to swallow.

apnea (ap-nē'ȧ), *n.* weakness of respiration; temporary suspension of breathing.

Apostle of the Indians (ȧ-pos"l, in'di-ans), appelation of the Rev. John Eliot (1604-1690), the first missionary to the Indians of Massachusetts Bay.

applesauce (ăp"l-sôs), *n.* a relish made up of stewed or boiled apples, sweetened and flavored: usually served as a dessert; [Slang], piffle; buncombe; blah; flapdoodle; nonsense; exaggeration; lying.

argyrol (är'jir-ol), *n.* a compound of silver, used as an antiseptic.

Arizona (ăr-ĭ-zō'nȧ), *n.* a State of the U.S., the Copper State; from a Papago Indian word, meaning "Place of Little Springs."

Arizona gourd (gōrd), a wild squash having a large root from the pulp of which the natives make soap: also used to ease hemorrhoids.

Arkansas (är'kan-saw), *n.* a State of the U.S., the Bear State; from arc, a bow—prefixed to Kansas.

Arkansas toothpick (tōōth'pik), [Slang], a Bowie knife.

Armistice Day (är'mĭs-tĭs), November 11, the day on which a general armistice was declared between the Allies and the Central Powers in the World War in 1918.

asexualization (ȧ-sĕk'shū-ăl-i-zā'shŭn), *n.* sterilization of a human, or of an animal.

Aspasia (as-pā'shi-ȧ), a famous hetæra of Ancient Greece (470-410 B.C.), and consort of Pericles: she was highly gifted as well as beautiful, and many of the well-known men of Athens frequently visited her, including Socrates and Alcibiades.

asynesia (as-i-nē'zhi-ȧ), *n.* dullness of intellect; stupidity.

Athens of America (ath'enz, ȧ-mer'i-kȧ), name given to Boston, on account of its culture.

atrichia (ȧ-trik'i-ȧ), *n.* loss of the hair, especially of the head; baldness.

atta boy (ăt'ȧ boi), [Slang], a distinctively American exclamatory phrase expressing approval or encouragement.

audion (aw'di-on), *n.* trade name for a three-electrode electron tube used in radio, in which a small amount of gas helps in the functioning as detector.

authoritarian (aw-thor-i-tā'ri-an), *n.* one who is given, or exercises, arbitrary power in a state or community: *adj.* referring to such person.

autoanalysis (aw-tō-a-nal'i-sis), *n.* in psychology, self-analysis by psychoanalytic method.

autobus (ô'tō-bus), *n.* a motor omnibus; any self-propelled four-wheeled vehicle.

autochrome (aw'tō-krōm), *n.* a specially prepared panchromatic plate used in the Lumière process of color photography; a positive plate or print obtained from such negative: *adj.* pertaining to the Lumière process of color photography.

A. W. O. L., in military service, the official abbreviation of *Absent Without Leave*: as there is no O among these initials, many believe the abbreviation represents Absent Without Official Leave, but the O does not stand for Official: it was inserted simply to prevent confusion with *A. W. L.*, the abbreviation for *Absent With Leave.*

B

bacterin (băk'tē-rĭn), *n.* a bacterial vaccine.

bacteremia (băk-tē-rē'mĭ-å), *n.* presence of bacteria in the blood.

bacteriuria (băk-tēr-i-ū'rĭ-å), *n.* passage of bacteria in the urine.

Badger State (baj'ēr), nickname for Wisconsin, on account of its numerous badgers.

Bahaism (bå-hā'izm), *n.* a creed or division of Babism: named after Mirza Hussein Ali, commonly known as Bahá-ullâh.

Bahaist (bå-hā'ist), *n.* one who professes, or believes in Bahaism.

bakelite (bā'ke-līt), *n.* synthetic resin; trade name for a condensed product of phenols and formaldehyde, used in the manner of hard rubber and celluloid: of high electrical and chemical resistance: named after L. H. Baekeland.

Balinese, (bäll-nēz'), *adj.* of or pertaining to the island of Bali, or its inhabitants.

balloon tire (ba-lōōn'tīr), a pneumatic cord tire containing a large volume of air at low pressure: it has a light flexible frame with wide cross section: designed for cushioning purposes.

Barbarossa (bär'bå-rŏs-å), *n.* literally, red beard, surname of Frederick I. (1121-1190), Emperor of Germany: it is said he never died, but is still sleeping in Kyffhäuserberg in Thuringia.

Barkis (bär'kĭs), *n.* an eccentric character in Dickens' "David Copperfield," whose proposal of marriage (often quoted) took the form of "Barkis is willin'."

Basedow's disease (bä'zĕ-dōz dĭ-zēz'), exophthalmic goiter, a disease in which the thyroid gland swells, the eyeballs become very prominent, and the heart-beats irregular: after Johann Basedow, a German physician: sometimes called Graves's disease.

batty (bat'i), *adj.* [Slang], half-witted; silly; rambling in talk.

Baumes laws (baw'mes), a series of amendments to the criminal code of New York, drafted by a joint-committee of the legislature headed by State Senator Caleb H. Baumes, and put into effect July 1, 1926; their object was to check the crime wave by prompt prosecution and stricter punishment. Under these laws, persons convicted of a felony for the fourth time are automatically sentenced to life imprisonment, and are not subject to pardon or executive clemency.

Bay State, popular name for Massachusetts, because it was originally the colony of Massachusetts Bay.

Bayou State (bī'ōō), nickname for Mississippi, on account of its many bayous or water courses.

bean, *n.* see main vocabulary.

bean (bēn), *n.* [Slang], the head.

beanery (bēn'rĭ), *n.* [Slang], a low-class lunch room; a cheap cafeteria.

Bear State, nickname for Arkansas, because of the large number of bears that formerly roamed over it.

beat it, [Slang], depart: go away; get out; used imperatively.

beautician (bū-tish'ăn), *n.* one skilled in beautifying the person, especially the hair and face; manager of, or operator in, a beauty parlor.

beauty parlor (pär'lēr), a shop or place, especially for women and girls, where aids to physical attractiveness are given, as hairwaving, facial treatment, massage, manicuring, etc.

behaviorism (bē-hāv'yēr-izm), *n.* in psychology, the reaction or response of an individual to some stimulus or suggestion: it is based upon the conception that conduct is dependent upon objective rather than subjective forces.

beetleware (bē't'l-wâr), *n.* an odorless, shatter-proof, water-proof, non-inflammable material, from which are formed various domestic and commercial articles: the material originates in a phenolic type of the molding powders, placed in a steel mold, and put under a pressure of 3,000 lbs. to the square inch, which causes the powder to fuse and flow.

benevolent assimilation (be-nev'o-lent a-sim-i-lā'shun), a phrase used by President William McKinley to describe the American policy in taking over the Philippine Islands from Spain in 1898. In a letter of instructions to Secretary of War Russell Alger he wrote "the mission of the United States is one of *benevolent assimilation*, substituting the mild sway of justice and right for arbitrary rule."

Ben Hur, the Jewish hero in General Lew Wallace's popular novel of "Ben Hur."

beta particle (bē'tå pär'ti-k'l), an electron: so called from its presence in beta rays.

beta rays (rāz), emanations of radium.

biff (bif), *v.t.* [Slang], to strike or punch suddenly.

Big Ben, the large deep-toned bell of the famous Westminster clock in the tower of Parliament, in London.

Big Bend State, nickname for Tennessee, on account of the big bend in its river.

Big Bertha (bürtha), one of the big German field guns in the World War of most destructive power and far-carrying range: after Bertha Krupp.

big wind (wĭnd), a violent wind storm that raged round the coasts of Ireland for two days and nights beginning on the evening of January 6, 1839: the Irish Sea was strewn with the wrecks of many ships and hundreds lost their lives: thousands of houses were blown down in cities and towns, including Dublin, Belfast, Cork, Galway, Limerick, and Athlone: most devasting storm Ireland has ever experienced.

billfold (bĭl'fōld), *n.* a form of wallet, having a compartment fitted for uncreased dollar bills.

bimbo (bĭm'bō), *n.* [Slang], a young man.

biparental (bī'på-ren'tal), *adj.* derived from both parents.

birth control (bērth kŏn-trōl'), regulation of childbearing, especially by contraceptives or means of preventing conception, or by lessening the frequency of impregnation, or by sterilizing those not deemed fit for propagation.

birth-rate ('rāt), *n.* the increase of population as shown by the percentage of registered births to the number of inhabitants in a district within a specified period.

Black Jack (blak jak), nickname given to John Alexander Logan (1826-1886), American general and political leader, on account of his dark complexion; sobriquet also applied to General John J. Pershing, Commander of the American forces in the World War.

black man, designation for the devil in witchcraft days in New England.

Black Shirts (shērtz), popular name for the Italian Facisti, the followers of Benito Mussolini.

Black Thursday (thērz'dā), February 6, 1851 when the most terrible bush fire recorded in the annals of Australia occurred in the Colony of Victoria: it raged over thousands of square miles, destroying all animal life within its range, even birds on the decks of coasting vessels fell dead.

Black Watch (wŏch), a famous Scottish regiment in the British Service, the 42nd Infantry: so called from their black tartans.

blah (blä), *interj.*, an exclamation of disgust: *n.* buncombe; nonsense; idle or foolish talk.

blastomycetes (blas-tō-mī-sē'tēs), *n. pl.* the yeasts: these fungi reproduce vegetatively by gemmation.

blepharism (blef'å-rism), *n.* spasmodic twitching of the eyelids.

blighter (blīt'ēr), *n.* a worthless fellow; a loafer; one who shirks responsibility.

blighty (blīt'i), *n.* [Slang], home, England, to the British soldier in the World War: *adj.* pertaining to the cause of return, as a *blighty* wound, or to the train or ship on which return was made.

Blind President (prez'i-dent), Theodore Roosevelt (1885-1919), who was blind in one eye during the last few years of his life the result of a boxing bout in the White House.

blind-tiger (blīnd-tī'gēr), *n.* a place where illicit liquor is sold.

blither (blith'ēr), *v.i.* to talk at random; speak foolishly or nonsensically.

Blue Eagle (blōō ē'gl), picture or representation of an eagle, done in blue coloring, and used as a symbol for the National Industrial Recovery Act of the F. D. Roosevelt administration, which was declared unconstitutional by the U. S. Supreme Court, June, 1935.

Blue Hen State, cant name for state of Delaware: Captain Jonathan Caldwell of Haslet's Delaware regiment in 1776 raised game cocks and claimed none of the birds could have good fighting quality, unless the mother was a blue hen.

blue lights, a system of blue lights used by certain Federalists in the War of 1812 for secretly signaling British vessels.

blue lodge (blū loj), in Freemasonry, a symbolic lodge in which the first three degrees of Masonry are conferred: so called from the blue color of its decorations.

blurb, *n.* a brief laudatory description of a book printed on the jacket or outside cover; also, a short personal notice of the author.

bohunk (bō'hŭnk), *n.* a dull stupid fellow; a boob; a clown.

bomb calorimeter (kăl-ŏ-rĭm'ĕ-tēr), a special form of calorimeter to measure the heat of combustion, as of coal.

bonehead (bōn'hĕd), *n.* [Slang], a stupid person.

bonzer (bon'zēr), *adj.* a distinctively Australian word, signifying the superlative of excellent; denoting anything extraordinarily good or fine.

boob, see *booby* (1) main vocabulary.

bookie, see *booky* main vocabulary.

boon-doggling (bōōn-dŏg'lĭng), *n.* [Western U.S. Slang], the forming or fashioning of various gadgets or contrivances from old discarded material, as rags, ropes, pieces of leather, etc.

bootleg (bōōt'lĕg), *adj.* denoting alcoholic liquor manufactured, or obtained, illicitly: *v.t.* to sell or dispose of alcoholic liquor contrary to law; *v.i.* to sell or transport anything illegally; also, to import illegally: *n.* alcoholic liquor manufactured, or procured, illegally.

bootlegger ('ēr), *n.* one who sells, transports, or imports illegally, especially alcoholic liquors.

Boston massacre (bos'tŭn măs'a-kēr), an attack made by a British garrison upon a street crowd in Boston, March 5, 1770, in which many were killed.

botulism (bot'ū-lizm), *n.* poisoning from meats, fish, vegetables, etc. in which specific bacilli have developed; sausage poisoning.

boulimia (bōō-lim'i-å), *n.* voracious appetite.

brachialgia (brăk-ĭ-ăl'ji-å), *n.* pain or neuralgia in the arm.

brachiotomy (-ŏt'ŏ-mĭ), *n.* amputation of an arm.

brachydactylia, (-dăk-tĭl'ĭ-å, **brachydactylism** -dak'til-izm), *n.* abnormal shortness of fingers or toes.

brachysm (brăk'izm), *n.* a state or condition in which the body is subnormal; a state or condition of dwarfishness, in which the arms are extremely short.

brain storm (brān stôrm), a temporary violent mental derangement.

bravest of the brave (brāv'est, brāv), a title applied to Michel Ney, Duke of Elchingen, Prince of the Moskva, and Marshal of France, born 1769 and executed 1815.

bread line, a line of persons waiting to receive bread, or other food, given as charity.

Breeches Bible (brich'ez bī'b'l), an English translation of the Bible printed in Geneva, Switzerland (1557-1560) in which a part of *Genesis* 3:7 was translated as: "they sewed figge-tree leaves together and made themselves breeches."

bridge (brij), *n.* a card game derived from whist, which has been superseded by *auction bridge* and *contract bridge.* In original bridge the trump was always named by the dealer or his partner, and the dealer always played the dummy no matter which partner made the trump. In *auction bridge* the players bid for the privilege of naming the suit that will be trump, or they play without a trump. *Contract bridge* is a variation of *auction bridge*, in which one side or other can score only the number of tricks named in the contract, additional tricks being scored as honors: slams get a bonus only when bid; the scoring in the game is complex.

brilliant madman (brĭl'yant mad'man), Charles XII. of Sweden, born 1682, reigned from 1697 until 1718.

bronchoscope (brŏnk'ŏ-skōp), *n.* an instrument for examination of the windpipe.

Bronx cheer (bronks chēr), [Slang], a derisive cheer; a sound of contempt made by hissing through the lips.

brunch (brŭnsh), *n.* [Slang], in England, breakfast taken so late that it serves for midday lunch.

Buckingham Palace (bŭk'ing-hăm păl'ās), one of the ornate residences of the British Royal Family, opposite St. James's Park in London: built in the reign of George IV.

Buffalo Bill (bŭf'å-lō), nickname of William Frederick Cody (1846-1917), American scout, guide, tracker, trapper, Indian fighter, and showman.

bull, *n.* see main vocabulary.

bull, *n.* [Slang], boastful or bombastic talk; exaggeration; lying in order to deceive: *throwing the bull*, talking wildly, boastfully, or proclaiming self-praise: *harness bull*, a uniformed policeman, as distinguished from a detective in mufti.

Buridan's ass (bŭr'i-dănz), the hypothetical ass of Buridan, Greek sophist philosopher, who maintained that "if an ass could be placed between two hay-stacks in such a way that its choice was evenly balanced, it would

ndeavoring to make personal appearance more attractive, especially in reference to the application of cosmetics.

mic rays (kos'mik rāz), rays of extremely high frequency and penetrating power, supposed by some scientists, produced above or beyond our atmosphere by the continual transmutations of atoms through interstellar space: they are constantly bombarding the earth in all directions; many scientists regard them simply as charged particles in very rapid motion, while some claim they are waves; if waves, their length is shorter than that of any known, while their frequency is more than a thousand times that of X-rays.

ovent Garden (kŭv'ĕnt gär'd'n), a large square in London, formerly the garden of a monastery or convent, now used as a fruit, flower, and vegetable market.

Coverdale Bible (kŭv'ĕr-dāl bī'b'l), a translation of the Bible by Miles Coverdale, afterwards Bishop of Exeter, issued in 1535, and dedicated to Henry VIII: it was the first Bible sanctioned by royal authority.

Cradle of Liberty (krā'd'l), popular designation of Faneuil Hall, Boston, as the place where the Revolutionary leaders often met and spoke.

Creole State (krē'ōl), nickname for the State of Louisiana, because of its many descendants of Spanish and French settlers.

Cro-Magnon (krō-mȧ-nyong'), *adj.* relating to the Cro-Magnon race: *n.* one of an early race of men, supposed to belong to the Magdalenian period, remains of which were found in the Cro-Magnon cave in Dordogne, France: they were of dark complexion, had long narrow heads, low foreheads, and deep-set eyes.

croquignole (krō'kwi-nōl), *n.* a French method of hair waving from forehead up; the machine used in forming this wave.

cross kisses (krôs kĭs'es), a number of small marks or characters, each in the form of a St. Andrew's cross, put at the end of a letter to suggest kisses: in medieval times, the signer of a document marked it by drawing a cross at the end, which he kissed as a pledge of his fidelity, truth, and honor; hence, the modern custom.

crossword puzzle (krôs'wẽrd puz''l), a form of word puzzle based on a printed diagram, divided into squares, each row of which, horizontal and vertical, is to be filled, or partly filled, with a word or words, the clue to which is given in corresponding definitions which accompany the diagram: this form of puzzle was very popular in the U. S. a few years ago, and is still a feature of many newspapers and periodicals.

crown colonies (kroun kŏl'ō-nĭz), foreign possessions in which the British Government retains control of legislation, comprising Gibraltar, Malta, Cyprus, Mauritius, Bermuda, Newfoundland, Labrador, Sierra Leone, Nigeria, Fiji, the Straits Settlements and Hongkong.

cryalgesia (krī'al-jē'si-ȧ), *n.* pain due to any cold application.

cryesthesia ('es-thē'si-ȧ), *n.* sensitiveness to cold.

crying bird (krī'ing bẽrd), a tropical American rail-like bird, noted for its cry; the courlan.

cystalgia (sis-tăl'ji-ȧ), *n.* pain in the bladder.

cystectomy (-tek'tō-mi), *n.* excision of the gall bladder or urinary bladder.

cystodynia (-din'ĭ-ȧ), *n.* same as cystalgia.

cystoplegia (-plē'ji-ȧ) *n.*, paralysis of the bladder.

D

dacmonomania (dăk-mŏn-ō-mā'ni-ȧ), *n.* a belief in one's self being possessed by devils.

dactylogram (dak-til'ō-grăm), *n.* a fingerprint.

dactylomegaly (dak'til-ō-mĕg'ȧ-lĭ), *n.* abnormal largeness of the fingers.

dactylospasm (-tĭl'o-spasm), *n.* spasmodic contraction of the fingers.

Dadaism (dȧ-dä'izm), *n.* extreme radicalism in art or literature.

daghestan (dä-gĕs-tän'), *n.* a certain weave of heavy carpet: after Daghestan, a government of the U. S. S. R. on the north side of the Caucasus mountains.

Dail Eireann (däl âr'in), the Chamber of Deputies or Lower House of the Irish Free State Legislature in Dublin, the members of which are elected for four years on a population basis: the membership at present (1935) numbers 155.

Dakin's solution (dā'kinz sō-lū'shŭn), a combination of sodium carbonate, chlorinated lime, and boric acid, much used as an antiseptic in the treatment of wounds: after Henry Drysdale Dakin, chemist.

Dalai Lama (dä-lī' lä'mȧ), the Grand Lama or spiritual head of Lamaism, a form of Buddhism, peculiar to Tibet and Mongolia, an elaborate hierarchal organization, characterized by much ritual in which prayer flags, prayer wheels, rosaries and bells are important accessories.

Daltonism (dōl'tŭn-izm), *n.* a form of color blindness in which objects appear more or less red: after John Dalton, an English chemist who suffered from the infirmity and described it.

dandy dinmont (dăn'dĭ dĭn'mŏnt), one of a breed of Scotch terriers, characterized by a rough coat, long body, and short legs.

dark and bloody ground (därk, blŭd'ĭ, ground), nickname for Kentucky, on account of the many fierce contests formerly waged there by whites and the Indians.

Darling (där'ling), *n.* a well-known river of Australia, about 1200 miles long, having its rise in Queensland, and flowing through New South Wales until it joins the Murray at Wentworth: its watershed is a great pastoral tract of country, over 50,000 sq. m. in area: the Darling and Murray form the longest river system in the world.

Darling Downs (dounz), a tableland of about 6,000 sq. m. in southern Queensland, Australia, noted for its large sheep farms: the soil is black and exceedingly fertile.

d'Artagnan (där-tăn-yăng'), *n.* the hero of Dumas's "Three Musketeers," a dashing Gascon youth who by his sword, and his daring, and intrigue, and with the aid of his three friends, makes his way to fame and fortune; hence, any soldier of fortune; an adventurer.

dasheen (dăsh-ēn'), *n.* a tropical American plant of the Arum family, having a farinacaous root, resembling that of the taro, which is cooked and eaten like the potato.

dasetherapy (dăz'e-thĕr'ȧ-pĭ), *n.* the pine-tree cure; treatment of ills, especially of consumption, by sojourning for a time in a forest of pines.

daylight saving (dā'līt sāv'ing), a method of regulating working hours in the summer months by keeping clocks, watches, and time-indicators one hour ahead, so that those engaged begin an hour earlier and stop an hour earlier than during the period regulated by standard time: the objective is to gain more of daylight for rest, relaxation, or recreation.

dazzle painting (dăz''l pānt'ing), a style or system of painting ships during the World War by which the lines of the vessels were distorted in a way that gave observers a wrong idea of their course: done to dodge submarine attacks.

dead load (lōd), the weight of a structure in itself.

dead man, the part of a log or beam sunk in the ground, when the log is used as an anchor for guy ropes, or the like.

Dead Sea, a lake in Palestine about 50 miles long, and from 5 to 10 miles wide, 1300 feet below the level of the Mediterranean, fed principally by the Jordan river: its water is rich in salt and potash.

dead storage (stō'rāj), the storage in one place of articles that are not subject to removal for some specified time.

dead wall, a blank wall in which there is no ingress, or outlet.

Death Valley (val'ĭ), a valley, notorious as fatal to life, in Inyo County, California, between Armagosa and Panamint Mountains.

decalvant (dē-kăl'vănt), *adj.* hair-removing; denoting that which destroys hair roots.

decathlon (-kăth'lŏn), *n.* a combination contest in the Olympian games, consisting of 100-, 400-, and 1500-meter runs, broad jump, running high jump, putting the shot, throwing the discus, throwing the javelin, pole-vaulting, and a 100-meter hurdle race.

decelerate (dē-sĕl'ĕr-āt), *v.i.* to move with decreased pace or velocity.

decode (dē-kōd'), *v.i.* to translate a message or communication into words easy of comprehension.

defeatist (dē-fēt'ist), *n.* one who in time of war advocates peace without victory.

Defender of the Faith (de-fĕn'dẽr, fāth), a title conferred on Henry VIII. by Pope Leo X (1521), for the former's tract against Luther, entitled "Assertion of the Seven Sacraments": the title is still retained by the English sovereign and appears on British coins.

deficiency disease (dē-fish'en-si di-zēz), a disease, as scurvy, due to a deficiency of proper vitamins in the food.

Delaware (dĕl'ȧ-wẽr), *n.* a State of the U. S., the Blue Hen State; named in honor of Lord de la War, Governor of Virginia: first of the original 13 States to ratify the Constitution, December 7, 1787.

dementia praecox (de-men'shi-ȧ prē'koks), a form of adolescent insanity: a collective term for mental disorders that begin at puberty, or shortly after, and gradually progress in degeneration until finally all the mental faculties break down.

dentalgia (den-tal'ji-ȧ), *n.* toothache.

depth bomb (dĕpth bŏm), an explosive bomb designed for the destruction of submarines.

desert-rat (dez'ẽrt-rat), *n.* a prospector living in a desert.

detectaphone (-tek'tȧ-fōn), *n.* a telephonic contrivance, having a microphone transmitter attached, by which conversations can be overheard by a listener: chiefly used for the detection of criminals.

Deutschland über Alles (doich'lant ē'bẽr ăl'ĕs), [G.], Germany over or above all: slogan of German soldiers in the World War.

Devil Dog, English of *Teufel Hund*, a name applied by the Germans in the World War to a U. S. marine.

Devil's Tower (tou'ẽr), a lofty isolated rock in Wyoming: it is a striking example of the effects of erosion in the higher mountains.

dextrophobia (deks'trō-fō'bi-ȧ), *n.* morbid fear or dread of objects on the right-hand side.

dhamnoo (dam'nōō), *n*, a tree of the Himalayan slopes which yields a very pliable wood, used by the natives for various purposes.

Diamond State (dī'ȧ-mŭnd), a nickname for the State of Delaware, on account of it being diamond-shaped.

Diesel engine (dē'sel en'jin), an internal combustion engine which operates by burning liquid fuel, injected in the form of a spray, directly into the combustion space, with ignition obtained solely through heat of compression: air only is compressed, the liquid fuel being sprayed into the clearance space as the piston approaches top center.

Dies Irae (dī'ēz ī'rē), [L.], literally, Day of Wrath or Anger, a famous Latin hymn about the Day of Judgment: said to have been written by a Franciscan monk in 1250.

dilly (dĭl'ĭ), *adj.* foolish; half-witted.

dinkum (din'ŭm), *adj.* [Australian Slang], good; true; genuine; dependable; honest.

diplocephaly (dĭp-lō-sĕf'ȧ-lĭ), *n.* the presence of two heads on one body.

Diplodocus (dĭp-lŏd'ō-kŭs), *n.* a genus of long-necked, long-tailed, gigantic herbivorous dinosaurs of the order Sauropoda, of the Upper Jurassic of Colorado and Wyoming: they were about sixty-five feet tall, and had very small heads.

dipsesis (dĭp-sē'sis), *n.* abnormal thirst.

dirt farmer (dẽrt färm'ẽr), one who, for political purposes, claims to be a practical farmer, though he may know little or nothing about farming.

Dismal Swamp (dĭz'măl swŏmp), a swamp on the border of Virginia and North Carolina, with a lake (Drummond) in the middle, about six miles wide: apart from this, it is covered with a dense growth of cedar and cypress trees, and presents a very *dismal* appearance: a canal connects it with Chesapeake Bay.

Distinguished Service Cross (dĭs-ting'gwĭsh'd sẽr'vis krôs), a bronze cross awarded since the entrance of the U. S. into the World War, to Americans who displayed great heroism or valor in connection with any military operation or movement made against an armed enemy of their country; in England, a silver cross, instituted 1901, awarded to naval men below the rank of lieutenant-commander for "distinguished service before the enemy."

Distinguished Service Medal (mĕd'ăl), a bronze medal awarded to Americans since April, 1917, who distinguished themselves in time of war by rendering meritorious service while discharging responsible and important duties; in England, a bronze medal, instituted, 1914, awarded to marines and men in the Royal Navy for gallantry in time of war.

Distinguished Service Order (or'dẽr), in England, a gold cross and ribbon, instituted, 1886, awarded to officers in the Army, Navy, and Royal Air Force for distinguished service in their own particular line of duty.

dollar diplomacy (dŏl'ẽr dĭ-plō'mȧ-si), negotiations or representations made by those who seek to establish good will and friendly relations with foreign countries, with a view to promoting the commercial and financial interests abroad of their own country.

domatophobia (dō-mat'o-fō'bi-ȧ), *n.* morbid dread or fear of being confined in a house.

Donnybrook Fair (dŏn'ĭ-brōōk), a fair formerly held once a year in August at Donnybrook, a village near Dublin, Ireland, which became so notorious for fighting and bloodshed that it was discontinued in 1855; hence, any place where fighting and rowdyism are carried on: Donnybrook is now incorporated in the city of Dublin, Irish Free State.

doodle-bug (dōō'd'l-bŭg), *n.* the ant-lion, a rapacious insect resembling the dragon-fly, of the order, *Neuoptera*, which constructs a sort of trap in the earth to catch other smaller insects.

Dora (dō'rä), *n.* the British Act of Parliament known as Defense of the Realm Act, passed in November, 1914, giving the government control over all means of communication: two amendments were added during the World War, one placing all factories manufacturing munitions under government supervision, the other authorizing state control over the sale of liquor in certain specified areas: the Act

starve to death, for there would be no motive why it should choose the one in preference to the other"; hence, the term is applied to a person of indecision who cannot make up his mind to pursue a definite course; one afraid to decide for himself.

burley (bẽr'li), *n.* a kind of tobacco, coarse and strong.

butternuts (bŭt'ẽr-nŭtz), *n. pl.* nickname given to the Confederates in the Civil War, from the color of their clothing which resembled that of butternuts.

B.V.D.'s (bē-vē-dēz'), *n.* trade name of a type of athletic underwear for men, each suit consisting of a combination of shirt and shorts: from the initials of the firm of Bradley, Voorhees & Day of New York, which manufactured them for many years.

Byng boys (bĭng bois), Canadian soldiers in the World War: after Gen. Julian H. Byng who commanded the Canadian Army Corps, and made the famous tank surprise attack on the Cambrai front.

C

cacogenics (kă-kō-jĕn'iks), *n.* the science that treats of the causes and influences which tend to deteriorate the race: opposite of *eugenics.*

cacogenesis (-jĕn'ĕ-sis), **cacogensia** (-jĕn'shĭ-ȧ), *n.* race deterioration; monstrosity; abnormal formation.

Cagliostro (käl-yôs'trō), *n.* Guiseppe Balsamo, an infamous charlatan, impostor, faker, and literary thief, who assumed the title and name, Count Alessandro *Cagliostro*, and toured Europe towards the close of the 18th Century, posing as a miracle man: he was born in Palermo, Sicily, in 1743 and died in jail at St. Leon, in 1795; hence the name, *Cagliostro*, is applied to any literary cheat, faker, forger, or humbug.

California (kăl-ĭ-fôr'nĭ-ȧ), a State of the U.S., the Golden State; name derived from an imaginary island in old Spanish romance.

California coffee (kŏf'ĭ), the cascara buckthorn which yields Cascara sagrada.

California condor (kŏn'dôr), the largest bird of prey on the North American continent, now almost extinct: is of a dull black color, the head and neck bare of feathers: it is really a vulture resembling a condor.

California Jack, in card-playing, a variation of seven-up, played by two: after each trick the hands are replenished by drawing a card from the top of the pack, with face up.

campcraft (kămp'krȧft), *n.* skill in the art of laying out, and conducting, a camp.

Campfire Girls (gẽrlz), an organization of young girls, ranging from 12 to 20 years old, corresponding to the Boy Scouts, founded in 1911 and incorporated in 1914; it aims to develop strong physical bodies by fresh air and outdoor exercise, to instil a spirit of coöperation, and inculcate sound moral principles in the formation of character: each local branch or chapter is known as a *Camp Fire*, and the attendant girls are of three ranks, *viz.*: *wood gatherers, fire makers*, and *torch bearers.*

canape (kȧ-nȧ-pā'), *n.* [Fr.] a delicatessen consisting of sliced bread fried, usually, in butter, but frequently in rendered beef fat, immediately after which it is served with a fish dressing, generally anchovies or sardines, and sometimes with a spread of mushrooms: the original meaning was a bed or couch with a *canopy* over it.

Canberra (kăn-bẽr'ȧ), *n.* the recently constructed Federal Capital of the Commonwealth of Australia, situated in Federal Territory in New South Wales, 204 miles southwest of Sydney, and 430 miles north-east of Melbourne: the city was built from designs of an American architect, W. B. Griffin, Chicago, and has a population of 10,200 (1935): several Federal buildings are in course of construction, also a University: the Territory, set apart for the government buildings and grounds, covers 940 sq. m.

canities (kȧ-nish'ĭ-ēz), *n.* grayness of the hair.

carabineers (kăr-ȧ-bĭ-nērz'), *n.pl.* the soldiers of a crack British regiment, the 6th Dragoon Guards.

carabiniere (kä-rä-bē'nyĕ'rā), *n.* [*It. pl.* carabinieri], a member of the Italian military police.

caranga (kȧ-rang'gȧ), *n.* a modified form of Spanish dance, recently introduced in the U. S.

cardiataxia (kär-dĭ-ă-tĕk'shĭ-ȧ), *n.* extreme irregularity of the heart beats.

cardiectasis (-ek'tȧ-sis), *n.* dilatation of the heart.

Cardiff giant (kär'dif jī'ănt), a gypsum statue of a man, 10½ feet high, said to have been unearthed near Cardiff, Onondaga County, New York in 1869: it was exhibited for a time as a petrified human, but, finally, the hoax was discovered and the perpetrators confessed.

cardiodynia (kär-di-o-din'ĭ-ȧ), *n.* pain in the heart.

cardiomegaly (-mĕg'ȧ-li), *n.* hypertrophy or excessive development of the heart.

cardiopathy (-ŏp'ȧ-thĭ), *n.* any diseased condition of the heart.

carditis (kär-dī'tis), *n.* inflammation of the heart.

Carolina gamecock (kăr-ō-lī'nȧ gām'kŏk), nickname of Gen. Thomas Sumter, of South Carolina, because of his pluck and courage in resisting the British after the fall of Charleston in 1780: Lord Cornwallis said of him, "he's our greatest plague in this country."

Carranzista (kȧ-răn-zis'tȧ), *n.* member of a Mexican political group; an adherent of Venustiano Carranza, former Mexican president, who got control of the government and the army in 1913 after the fall of Madero. In April 1910 a revolution drove Carranza from the capital, and he was slain in his camp.

Castle Garden (kȧs''l gär'd'n), Battery Park, at the southern extremity of Manhattan Borough, New York City: laid out in 1807 and originally called Castle Clinton: successively, a fort, place of entertainment, and landing place for immigrants: now, the chief building is an aquarium.

catharsis, *n.* see main vocabulary.

catharsis (ka-thär'sis), *n.* in psychology, a purging or cleansing of the mind or soul of base, sordid, disagreeable thoughts, ideas, and images by recalling the emotions which caused them, and endeavoring to eliminate such emotions by complete expression; simply, a mental or physical cathartic.

Catholic chaplain (kăth'ō-lik chăp'lĭn), the Rev. Constantine Pise, the one and only Catholic priest who served as chaplain of the U. S. Congress, appointed December 11, 1832, during the first administration of Andrew Jackson: he was proposed by Henry Clay.

cedars of Lebanon (sē'dẽrz, leb'ȧ-non), famous pinaceous trees of which there were many groves on the slopes of the Lebanon mountain range in Western Syria, but very few now remain: cedars of this kind are very handsome, attain a great height, and are long-lived.

ceiling, *n.* see main vocabulary.

ceiling (sē'ling), *n.* the height above sea level at which an aircraft is not supposed to ascend further at a speed greater than a fixed rate, which, in the U. S., is 100 feet per minute—this ceiling is called the *service* ceiling; the maximum height above sea level to which an aircraft can approach under standard rules—this is called the *absolute* ceiling.

celiotomy (sē-lĭ-ŏt'ō-mĭ), *n.* incision into the abdominal cavity.

cellophane (sel'o-fān), *n.* trade name for viscose solidified in thin, transparent, waterproof sheets; the finished product, as used for wrapping cigars, candies, cakes, bread, groceries, and sundry other commodities, chiefly to protect them from germs.

Centennial State (sĕn-tĕn'ĭ-ăl), Colorado, because admitted to the Union in 1876.

cephalgia (sĕf-ăl'ji-ȧ), *n.* headache: **cephalalgia, cephalalgy.**

chalcosis (kăl'kō'sis), *n.* chronic copper poisoning.

chalmoogra, see *chaulmugra* main vocabulary.

Château-Thierry (shä-tō'tē-ẽr-ē'), a town on the Marne, in the Department of Aisne, France, 60 m. north-east of Paris, where the American troops won their first success against the Germans in the World War: pop (1930) 7,750.

chatookee (shä-tōō'kĭ), *n.* an East Indian bird that never drinks from a stream, but catches the rain-drops in falling: mentioned by Southey in his "Curse of Kehama."

Cheka (chĕ'kȧ), *n.* the secret service of Soviet Russia.

chemurgy (kĕm'ẽr-jĭ, kē-mŭr'jĭ), the application of a scientific knowledge of chemistry to the cultivation of the soil, so as to secure from it, not only food, but clothing, shelter, heat, power, and other possibilities.

Cheshire cat (chĕsh'ẽr), a grinning cat in "Alice's Adventures in Wonderland" that gives Alice advice, and then disappears.

Cheshire cheese (chēs), a hard kind of cheese made in Cheshire county, England; [C-C-] a celebrated inn on Wine Office Court, off Fleet street, London, where Dr. Samuel Johnson, lexicographer, was accustomed to dine with favorite companions, and where a copy of his first dictionary is still preserved and shown to visitors.

chiloschisis (kī-lŏs'kĭ-sĭs), *n.* harelip.

China's Sorrow (chī'nȧs sŏr'ō), the Hwang-Ho or Yellow River which frequently overflows, devastating large areas, destroying crops, and causing famine.

chiragra (kī-rā'grȧ), *n.* gout in the hand.

chiromegaly (kī-rō-mĕg'ȧ-lĭ), *n.* abnormal size of one or both hands.

chirospasm (kī'rō-spȧzm), *n.* writer's cramp.

chisel (chĭz''l), *v.t.* to take unfair advantage; to obtain through misrepresentation.

chiseler (''l'r), *n.* one who chisels; specifically, a person who, while not in need, applies for, and obtains, a share of pub priated for those in real distre

chiseling (-ing), *n.* obtaining of under false pretense or misr

cholecystectomy (kŏl-ē-sis-tek operation of removing the gall

Christ of the Andes (krīst, ăn' bronze statue of the Savior, u at Cambre Pass, a lonely mou 13,000 feet above sea level, betw the Argentine: erected to com settlement of a dispute over bo would have precipitated a war two countries.

chromotherapy (krō-mō-ther'ă-pi), ment of diseases by colored lights

Cincinnati (sĭn-sĭ-nä'tĭ), an order founded in 1783 to perpetuate th of officers in the Revolutionary relieve the widows and orphans of it still continues, the membership of only the oldest living male linea ants of the original members.

Cinderella (sĭn-dẽr-ĕl'ȧ), *n.* the heroin tale, originally a drudge, despised a treated by a stepmother and step fairy godmother equips her to atten ball given by a prince, where she los slipper—the prince finds the slipper means of it discovers Cinderella, w marries, to the great discomfiture of mistresses; hence, a scullery maid; drudge; a cinder-woman or sweeper o

City of Brotherly Love (brŭth'ẽr-li), Phila Pennsylvania: so called from the litera pretation of its name.

City of Churches (chẽrch'ĕz), Brooklyn, Borough of New York City: so called b of its numerous churches.

City of Elms, popular name for New H Connecticut, on account of the rows o trees which shade its principal streets.

City of Magnificent Distances (măg-nĭf'ĭ dis'tans-es), popular name of Washin D. C., because it is laid out on an elab scale, providing wide and magnificent vist its surroundings.

city manager (măn'ā-jẽr), a municipal, n partisan executive chosen by a Commiss to direct the affairs of a city.

City of Spindles (spĭn'd'lz), popular name Lowell, Massachusetts, because of its ma cotton factories.

claustrophobia (klaws-trō-fō'bi-ȧ), *n.* morbi dread of being confined, as in a room or sma space.

Clayton-Bulwer treaty (klāy-tun-bool'wẽr trēt'ĭ), a treaty arranged July 4, 1850 between the U. S. and Gt. Britain, providing that "neither country shall have exclusive control of any inter-oceanic canal in Central America, or erect fortifications in the country."

cliner (klī'nẽr), *n.* [Australian Slang], a young unmarried female: a bold, forward girl.

clobber (klŏb'ẽr), *n.* [Australian Slang], clothing; raiment; vesture.

cockeyed (kŏk'īd), *adj.* having a squinting eye; [Slang] denoting a person who talks foolishly, or expresses a wrong opinion, or arrives at a false conclusion; also, applied to a tipsy individual.

cockpit of Europe (kŏk'pit, ū'rŏp), Belgium.

cold shoulder (shōl'dẽr), indifference; non-receptiveness; unfriendly attitude: said to have derived from a custom in hotels of medieval France of serving hot roasts to welcome guests, and *cold shoulders* to unwelcome ones.

colectomy (kō-lĕk'tō-mĭ), *n.* excision of a part of the colon.

Colorado (kŏl-ō-rä'dō), *n.* a state of the U. S., the Centennial State; from the Spanish, red or colored.

columnist (kŏl'ŭm-nĭst), *n.* the writer of a column in a newspaper or periodical in which he puts forth his views on public affairs and current events.

commissar (kŏm'ĭ-sär), *n.* a commissioner; specifically, a chief or head of government in any of the separate states that make up the Union of Socialist Soviet Republics.

conk (kŏnk), *n.* [Australian Slang], the nose.

Connecticut (kŏ-net'ĭ-kŭt), *n.* a State of the U. S., the Nutmeg State; from the Indian word, *quonektacut*, meaning "Long River."

contraception (kŏn-trȧ-sĕp'shŭn), *n.* the prevention of impregnation or conception; birth control.

contraceptive (-sĕp'tĭv), *adj.* preventing conception; rendering impregnation ineffective: *n.* a drug or preparation for causing misconception, miscarriage or abortion.

Corn Belt (kôrn belt), the Upper Mississippi Valley, or that portion of the United States which includes the States Illinois, Iowa, Indiana, Kansas, and Missouri, in all of which large harvests of grain are reaped.

cosmetician (kŏs-mĭ-tĭsh'ăn), *n.* one skilled in the use of cosmetics as an aid to personal attractiveness.

cosmetologist (-tŏl'ō-jist), *n.* a person having knowledge of the art and practice used in

became inoperative on the legal termination of the War, August 31, 1921.
dorsalgia (dôr-săl'ji-å), *n.* pain in the back.
Doukhobors, see *Dukhoboretsi* main vocabulary.
Downing Street (down'ing strēt), a short street in Whitehall, London, in which are located the Home, Colonial, and Foreign Offices, also the official residences of the Prime Minister and the Chancellor of the Exchequer; hence, the words are frequently used as a synonym for the British Government.
drango (drång'o), *n.* an American bird somewhat resembling a crow, but having a forked tail.
dry, *adj.* & *v.* see main vocabulary.
Dry, *n.* in the U. S., one who favors, or advocates the suppression of any and all alcoholic or intoxicating liquors; a Prohibitionist.
dry farming (färm'ing), the raising of crops without irrigation in dry areas by a manner of tillage which conserves soil moisture, and by cultivating crops that are drought-resisting.
dud, *n.* see main vocabulary.
dud (dŭd), *n.* a person without energy or initiative; a slow-witted individual; a shell or bomb that fails to explode when thrown.
duograph (dū'o-grăf), *n.* in photo-engraving, a picture in two shades of the same color, made from two half-tone plates produced by setting the screen at different angles.
duotype (-tīp), *n.* in photo-engraving, a print produced from two half-tone plates made from the same negative, but etched differently.
duplex dwelling (dū'pleks dwel'ing), a two-family house in which the occupants of the street floor, also have two rooms on the second floor, reached by a private stairway, and partitioned off from the other rooms on this floor which, with all the rooms on the third or top floor, are occupied by the second family.
duplex process (pros'es), a process for making steel by using two different types of furnace: a Bessemer converter is used for the first stage, and an open hearth furnace for the finishing stage.
duralumin (dū-rȧ-lū'min), *n.* trade name of an alloy of aluminum, consisting of 95.5 parts of aluminum, 3 parts of copper, 1 of manganese, and 0.5 of magnesium: it is equal to soft steel in strength and hardness.
Dutch uncle (dŭch ŭng'k'l), a person who scolds or reproves another bluntly and sharply, yet with a certain degree of kindness; one who aids another in difficulty, though seemingly reluctant to do so.
Dutch treat (trēt), a dinner, luncheon, or entertainment at which each guest pays his own individual score or reckoning.
duvetyn (dōō-vē-tēn'), *n.* any of several wool or silk fabrics having a nap resembling plush.
dysbasia (dis-bā'shi-å), *n.* difficulty in walking.
dyschromatopsia (dis-krō-mȧ-top'shi-å), *n.* defective color vision; difficulty in distinguishing colors.
dysesthesia (dĭs-ĕs-thē'sĭ-å), *n.* impairment of any of the senses.
dysgenic (-jĕn'ĭk), *adj.* harmful to the race; detrimental to racial improvement, owing to degenerative influence in the propagation of the species.
dysgeusia (-gū'shi-å), *n.* abnormal sense of taste.
dysidrosis (-ĭ-drō'sis), *n.* abnormal secretion of sweat; a condition in which vesicles form on the palms of the hands and soles of the feet.
dyslalia (-lā-li-å), *n.* difficulty in articulation.
dyslogia (-lō'ji-å), *n.* difficulty in speech; impairment in the faculty of reasoning.
dysosmia (-ŏz'-mi-å,) *n.* impairment of the sense of smell.
dyspathy (dis'pȧ'thĭ), *n.* lack of fellow feeling: the opposite of *sympathy.*
dyspituitarism (dĭs-pĭ-tū'ĭ-tā-riz'm), *n.* a morbid condition due to disordered functioning of the pituitary gland.
dysuria (dis-ū'rĭ-å), *n.* painful urination.

E

echokinesia (ĕk-o-kĭn'ē-shĭ-å), *n.* meaningless mimicry of the actions of others.
echokinesis ('ē-sis), *n.* same as echokinesia.
echopathy (ĕ-kŏp'å-thi), *n.* meaningless repetition of speech ,and mimicry of actions.
echophrasia (ĕk-ŏ-frā'shi-å), *n.* see *echolalia* main vocabulary.
ecolalia (ĕk-ŏ-lā'li-å), *n.* a meaningless repetition.
Ecole des beaux-arts (ā-kōl'dā-bō-zär'), [Fr.], a famous endowed school in Paris, France, where the fine arts are taught free.
ecomania (mā'ni-å), *n.* uncontrollable passion; unrestrained temper.
ecrasons' l'infâme' (ā-krā-zong' lang-fäm'), [Fr.], let us crush the infamous, the vile: this was the famous slogan of Voltaire, that rang throughout Europe, by which he referred to clerical domination, intolerance, fanaticism, and superstition.
ectromelia (ĕk-trŏ-mē'li-å), *n.* absence of a limb or limbs.
egomania (ē-go-mā'ni-å), *n.* morbid self-esteem; a state in which one regards himself great and imagines others look up to him as such.
egomaniac (-ak), one who regards himself superior; a person who boasts of his own qualities with a view to getting others to admire him.
Eiffel Tower (ĕf-ĕl' tou'ĕr), a huge iron tower, 985 ft. high, in the Champ de Mars, Paris, built for the Exposition of 1889 by the engineer who designed the framework of the Statue of Liberty, in New York Harbor, Alexander Gustave Eiffel (1832-1923).
Einsteiniam (īn-stīn'ĭ-ăn), *adj.* pertaining or relating to Albert Einstein (1879-), German-Swiss physicist, or to his theory of relativity.
Einstein theory (īn'stīn thē'o-ri), a theory put forward, and defended by Albert Einstein, German physicist, usually called the *theory of relativity.* See **relativity.**
Emden (ĕm'dĕn), *n.* a large white goose, with orange legs and feet, and a flesh-colored bill: so called from Emden, Westphalia, where the breed originated; the name of a German raiding cruiser in the World War, which, in three months, sank over seventy ships of the allied nations: she was destroyed by the Australian cruiser, *Sydney,* off North Keeling Island on Nov. 9, 1914.
Emma Gee (em'å jē), in the World War, a machine gun or machine gunner: from the letters, M. G., used in signal telephoning.
empathy (em'pȧ-thi), *n.* in psychology, the feeling one experiences when hearing or reading of some remarkable event or happening, which causes him to conjure up or imagine the scene and have the same sensation as those actually participating in it.
Empire State (em'pīr stāt), the State of New York: so called because it is the first State in the Union in both population and wealth.
Empire State Building (em'pīr stāt bild'ing), the highest building in the world, 1248 ft., standing on the former site of the Waldorf-Astoria hotel, on the south-west corner of 34th street and Fifth Avenue, New York City: it is devoted to offices, accommodating some 25,000 tenants, and has 63 express elevators: there are observation platforms on the 80th and 102nd floors, which are daily crowded with visitors and sightseers.
Empire State of the South, the State of Georgia, so called from its eminence among Southern States.
encephalitis lethargica (ĕn-sĕf'å-lī'tis lĕ-thär'ji-kå), sleeping sickness; specifically, epidemic inflammation of the brain which causes somnolence, brings on general debility and finally, complete paralyzation of the cranial nerves.
endocrine (ĕn'dŏ-krīn), *n.* one of the internal secretions found in the blood, and which come from certain organs whose only known functions seem to be the supply of this substance, which acts chemically on certain glands, as the thyroid, and parathyroid, the pituitary and the pineal: *adj.* pertaining to internal secretions; secreting internally; denoting the ductless glands.
endocrinology (-krĭ-nŏl'ŏ-jĭ), *n.* the science or study of internal secretions from the ductless glands, as the thyroid and pituitary.
endotoxin (-tok'sĭn), *n.* toxin retained within the producing cell.
enlargement, *n.* see main vocabulary.
enlargement (ĕn-lärj'mĕnt), *n.* in photography, a print larger than the negative.
Entente Cordiale (äng-tängt' kŏr-dyål'), [Fr.], an alliance entered into by Great Britain and France, and signed April 8, 1904.
enterodynia (ĕn-tĕr-o-din'ĭ-å), *n.* pain in the intestines.
enterogastritis (-găs-trī'tĭs), *n.* inflammation of the stomach and intestines.
enteromycosis (-mī-kō'sĭs), *n.* disease of the intestines caused by fungi.
enteroplegia (-plē'ji-å), *n.* paralysis of the intestines.
enterorrhagia (ĕn-tĕr-ŏ-rā'ji-å), *n.* hemorrhage from the intestines.
enterorrhaphy, see *enterorrhaphia* main vocabulary.
entheomania (ĕn-thē'ŏ-mā'nĭ-å), *n.* religious insanity.
Eoanthropus (ē-o-an-thrō'pŭs), *n.* the genus which is constituted by the Piltdown man, supposed to be representative of a race of primitive humans: the belief in such a being rests upon the basis of parts of a skull found at Piltdown, Sussex, England, in 1911, in strata apparently of the early Pleistocene.
Eohyus (ē-ō-hī'us), *n.* the Eocene ancestor of pigs.
Eoliths (ē-o-līths), *n.pl.* the most primitive stone tools supposedly made by man.
epidiascope (ĕ-pĭd'ĭ-å-skōp), *n.* a device for projecting images of opaque objects upon a screen.
Epihippus (ĕp-ĭ-hĭp'ŭs), *n.* a genus of ancestral horses of the upper Eocene, having a prominent, middle toe on each foot.
epilation (lā'shŭn), *n.* the process of removing hair by the roots.
epilatory (ĕ-pil'å-tŏ-rĭ), *adj.* hair-removing: *n.* a substance or preparation for removing hair; a depilatory.
epilobium (-lō'bi-ŭm), *n.* a strong-smelling plant that flourishes on ground that has been burned, as by bush fire; fireweed.
E pluribus unum (plōō'rĭ-bus ū'nŭm), [L.], one out of many: motto of the U. S.
Epworth League (ep'wẽrth lēg), an American organization of young people of the Methodist Episcopal Church, founded at Cleveland, Ohio, in 1889, to promote personal evangelism, and intelligent Bible study.
Equisetum (ĕk-wĭ-sē'tŭm), *n.* a genus of bristly herbaceous plants—the horsetails.
eremophobia (ĕr-ĕ-mŏ-fō'bĭ-å), *n.* a morbid dread of solitude.
ergatocracy (ĕr-gȧ-tŏk'rȧ-si), *n.* rule of the workers; dominion of the toilers.
ergosterol (ĕr-gŏs'tĕr-ol), *n.* a sterol now obtained from yeasts and mushrooms,but formerly from ergot, hence its name. Some claim it as the pro-vitamin or principle in foods and identify it, at present, with Vitamin D. When exposed to ultra-violet rays, it is said to cure rickets: thus irradiated it performs the functions of Vitamin D. The Board of Pharmacy of the American Medical Association recognizes it as a remedy under the name *viosterol.*
Erin go bragh (brāh), Erin (Ireland) forever—the war cry of the ancient Irish.
erithropia (ĕr-ĭ-thrō'pi-å), *n.* a condition in which nearly all objects appear to have a red tinge to the affected.
Esperantido (ĕs-pĕ-rān-tē'dō), *n.* a modified form of Esperanto, intended for universal usage.
Ethiopian lily (ē-thĭ-ō'pi-ăn lĭl'ĭ), the calla lily.
Ethiopian wood (wŏŏd), ebony.
eugenism (ū'je-nizm), *n.* the collective or combined influences that are best adapted to improve the native qualities of a people.
eugenist (-nist), *n.* one well versed in the study of eugenics, or the betterment of the race.
Eumycetes (ū-mī-sē'tēz), *n.pl.* a class of the Thallophyta, in which are included all the true fungi, as distinguished from seaweeds or algae.
eunoia (ū-noi'å), *n.* alertness or quickness of mind and will.
euonym (ū'ŏ-nĭm), *n.* a good name; a name that is suitable.
euphagia (ū-fā'ji-å), *n.* normal or natural and correct manner of eating.
eurythymic (ū-rith'mĭk), *adj.* pertaining to the harmony or sympathy of motion, especially, the motion of dancing.
eutocia (ū-tō'shĭ-å), *n.* easy parturition; natural birth.
eutony (ū'tŏ-ni), *n.* agreeableness or harmony of sound.
Everglade State (ĕv'ĕr-glād), the State of Florida on account of its many marshes.
Excalibur (ĕks-kăl'i-bŭr), *n.* the mystic sword of King Arthur, sheathed in stone, from which none could withdraw it save the king—given to him by the Lady of the Lake.
Excelsior State (ĕks-sĕl'si-ŏr), the State of New York; so called from the motto "Excelsior" on its coat-of-arms.
exocardia (ĕks-ŏ-kär'dĭ-å), *n.* abnormal position of the heart.
Expounder of the Constitution (ĕks-pound'ĕr, kŏn-sti-tū-shŭn), Daniel Webster (1782-1852), because of his eloquent and elaborate exposition of the Federal Constitution.
expressionism (-prĕsh'ŭn-ĭzm), *n.* self-expression; the theory that in any department of art, as in painting or sculpture, one shows his individuality in the work he produces, which expresses, as it were, his feelings, sensations, and emotions while engaged upon it.
Eye of Greece (ī, grēs), Athens.
eye-opener (ī-ōp'nĕr), *n.* something that causes the eyes to open widely, or stare, as a striking occurrence or event, or the hearing or reading of startling news; [Slang], a drink of liquor taken in the morning after awakening to offset the effects of "the night before."
eye of the storm (stôrm), the calm region in the center of a tropical cyclone.
Ezekiel (ĕ-zē'ki-ĕl), *n.* a Hebrew prophet who lived among the exiled Jews of Babylonia, about 560 years B. C.; a Book of the Old Testament.
Ezra (ĕz'rå), *n.* one of the Hebrew prophets of the 5th century B. C.; the Book of *Ezra* in the Old Testament, following Chronicles II.

Fagin (fā'gin), *n.* a thief; swindler; cheat; especially, a fence or receiver of stolen goods: after a character in Dickens' "Oliver Twist."

fabrikoid (făb'rĭ-koid), *n.* trade name for a leather-like, impervious fabric, having a cloth base covered with a coating of pyroxylin: used in upholstery, book-binding, and for handbags, pocketbooks, etc.

fall guy (fawl gī), [Slang], one tricked into some criminal action for which he alone will be held responsible, while his deceiver takes no risk at all, and gets whatever gain accrues from the deed.

farmerette (fär-mēr-et'), *n.* [Colloq.], a woman who owns, works on, or has charge of a farm.

Fascism (făs'izm or făsh''izm), *n.* the principles, propaganda, teachings, or work of the Fascisti.

Fascista (fä-shē'stä), *n. pl.* Fascisti ('stē), [It.], a member of an Italian organization, founded at Milan, in 1919, by Benito Mussolini for the purpose of opposing, and downing by force, if necessary, all radical movements in Italy; it quickly spread and in 1922, the "Black Shirts", as the members were styled, made their famous march to Rome, where headquarters was established. Premier Facta resigned, and at the request of King Victor Emmanuel III., Mussolini formed a new government, with himself as prime minister, since when he has been virtually the Dictator of Italy, holding several portfolios in the government, as well as that of prime minister.

Father of His Country (fäthēr, kŭn'trĭ), a title conferred on George Washington (1732-1799), as "defender and paternal counselor of the American States."

Father of History (his'tō-ri), Herodotus (B. C. 484-425), the Greek historian, born at Halicarnassus, Asia Minor: wrote, in Ionian dialect, the history, geography, manners and customs of the peoples of Eqypt, Lyria, Scythia, Media, Assyria, and also, a history of the Graeco-Persian Wars.

Father of Medicine (mĕd'i-sĭn), Hippocrates (B. C. 460-377), a Greek physician who had wonderful skill in diagnosis and in detecting morbid symptoms: wrote a treatise, "On Epidemics": the *Hippocratic Oath*, taken by physicians, was so named in honor of this early scientist.

Father of Waters (waw'tērz), a popular name for the Mississippi River, on account of its great length, and the numerous tributaries that flow into it.

Fathers of the Church (fä'thērz, chērch), the great writers, teachers, and theologians who succeeded the Apostles from the second to the sixth century, such as St. Augustine, St. Athanasius, etc.

Federal Land Banks (fĕd'ēr-ăl), twelve banks established in various opportune localities throughout the U. S., under the Farm Loan Act of 1916, to enable farmers to capitalize their holdings through long-time mortgage loans.

Federal Prisons (prĭz'nz), detention institutions for those convicted of federal transgressions, located at Leavenworth, Kans., Atlanta, Ga., and McNeil Island, Wash., in addition to which there is a Reformatory for men at Chillicothe, O., and one for women at Alderson, W. Va., also, a House of Detention in N.Y. Since 1934, the most notorious of federal offenders have been sent to an institution on Alcatraz Island, in San Francisco Bay.

Federal Reserve System (rē-zērv' sĭs'tĕm), a national banking system, established by Act of Congress in 1913, having for its object the concentration of all the banking resources of the country, so as to provide an elastic currency with a view to displacing national bank notes: twelve regional banks, with their branches, formed the original system, which was coördinated under the supervision of a central board at Washington.

Federal Trade Commission (kō-mish'ŭn), a U. S. commission of five members appointed by the President, and empowered to prevent merchants, traders, corporations, partnerships, and individuals from using underhand or unfair methods of competition in business or commerce: it also acts in connection with contracts, acquisition of stocks, price-fixing, etc.

feminism (fĕm'ĭ-nĭzm), *n.* a theory, cult, or movement on the part of those who assert and advocate what they consider the rights of women, and who favor doing away with all social, economic, and political restrictions on the sex.

fence-sitter (fĕns-sĭt'ēr), *n.* in track parlance, one who sits upon a fence or railing, watching the exercising of horses booked for a race, so that he can get knowledge of their speed and racing points, in order to profit by this knowledge in giving 'tips' and placing bets.

ferrates (fĕr'ātz), *n.pl.* compounds containing iron.

Field Museum (fēld mū-zē'ŭm), a celebrated museum in Grant Park, Chicago, fronting Lake Michigan, very rich in specimens representing the fields of anthropology, zoölogy, botany, and geology; it has an unique possession in sculptures, depicting the story of man from a million years ago to the dawn of history: the Museum gets its name from Marshall Field (1835-1906), merchant prince who was the chief contributor to its establishment.

Field of Blood (blŭd), Aceldama, the plot of land bought with the thirty pieces of silver that Judas received for betraying Christ, and which the former threw down in the temple. See *Matt.* xxvi:5.

Field of Honor (on'ēr), the scene where a duel takes place.

fiery cross (fī'ēr-i krôs), a large wooden cross borne by members of the Ku Klux Klan, around the arms and standard of which is wrapped inflammable material, generally saturated with oil; at the close of meetings, this cross is set up and ignited, as a blazing defiance to all who see it and who differ from the Klansmen in principles and practices: the Klan has been quiescent since the Presidential Election of 1928; also, see *Fiery Cross* main vocabulary.

Fighting Joe (fīt'ing jō), sobriquet of Joseph Wheeler (1836-1906), Confederate General in the Civil War.

fire-damp (fīr'damp), *n.* an explosive gas that sometimes arises in coal mines and is much dreaded by miners.

firing line (fīr'ing līn), the main body of soldiers engaged in action within range of the enemy.

firing squad (fīr'ing skwad), a detail of soldiers who fire a farewell salute when a brother soldier or officer is buried; a number of soldiers assigned to carry out the sentence of a military court by shooting the condemned.

First Lady of the Land, the wife of the President of the U. S., since the establishment of the Federal Government.

Fisher (fĭsh'ēr), *n.* [Slang], in England, a treasury note, bearing the signature of Sir Warren Fisher: this note, first issued in 1919, replaced the one known as "a Bradbury" during the World War, after the then Secretary of the Treasury.

fit to a T, fit in everyway: fitting exactly: in allusion to the T-square used by carpenters.

Flag Day, in the U. S., June 14, the anniversary of the day in 1777, when Congress adopted the Stars and Stripes as the flag of the new nation.

Flag Pledge (plej), the pledge of allegiance, accompanied by salute, to the Stars and Stripes: this pledge was written in 1892 by Francis Bellamy, of the editorial staff of *The Youth's Companion*, and reads: "I pledge allegiance to the Flag of the United States of America and the Republic for which it stands, one Nation indivisible, with liberty and justice for all.": widely recited, especially in the public schools.

flame chair (flām chār), [Slang], the electric chair, in which condemned murderers are put to death.

flapdoodle (flăp-dōō'd'l), *n.* the food of fools; hence, boastful, silly, or nonsensical talk; piffle; twaddle; buncombe.

flash, *n.* see main vocabulary.

flash (flash), *n.* in moving pictures, a view injected on the screen, incidental to, or illustrative of, a part or the whole of the main feature being shown; in radio, news of some startling occurrence or important event heard over a receiving set at a transmitting station and immediately re-broadcasted to listeners.

flat tire, [Slang], an unattractive person; one without personal magnetism.

Flickertail State (flik'ēr-tāl), the State of North Dakota, because of its great abundance of ground squirrels, popularly called *flickertails*, from their habit of flicking or flipping their tails: some confound these animals with prairie dogs, others with gophers, but they are distinct from both.

flivver (fliv'ēr), *n.* any small cheap autocar, though usually applied to a Ford; hence, anything small and cheap of its kind; something of little importance or consequence, or that does not fulfil expectation.

flivverboob (-bōōb), *n.* [Slang], the driver of a flivver; hence, a reckless or careless driver.

floccinaucinihilipilification (flŏk'sĭ-nô''sĭ-nĭ'hĭl-ĭ-pĭl''ĭ-fĭ-kā'shŭn), *n.* [L.] the habit or custom of judging or pronouncing as worthless or of no value.

Florida (flŏr'ĭ-dȧ), *n.* a State of the U. S., the Peninsula State; after the Spanish, *Pascua Florida*, Easter Sunday.

flubdubbery (flŭb'dŭb-ēr-ĭ), *n.* [Slang], foolish talk; nonsence; buncombe.

Flying Dutchman (flī'ing dŭch'man), a phantom ship, supposedly seen in stormy weather off the Cape of Good Hope, and said to forebode bad luck. Legend says it was a vessel laden with gold and precious stones on which a horrible murder had been committed, whereupon a plague broke out and no port would permit the ship to enter, so it was doomed to sail on forever without rest.

Foreign Legion (fôr'en lē'jun), any volunteer corps of foreign sympathizers who serve a country in time of war; especially the outsiders, mostly adventurers, who serve France, chiefly in her colonial campaigns.

forgotten man (fŏr-gŏt'en), a hypothetical individual, symbolic of a large number of poverty-striken and depressed U. S. citizens who seem to have been forgotten by those in power to assist or relieve; an assumed representative of a numerous class of persons believed to be in real distress and too proud to seek public relief, or make their wants known, and who are ignored by scheming statesmen and sordid politicians, save when the latter are seeking votes at election time: term coined in the U. S. at the beginning of the F. D. Roosevelt administration.

Four Horsemen of the Apocalypse (hôrs'mĕn, ȧ-pok'ȧ-lips), the symbols of War, Conquest, Famine, and Death, as described by the late Vicente Blasco Ibanez in his German-hating novel, "The Four Horsemen of the Apocalypse."

Four Hundred (fōr hŭn'drĕd), the number of persons who belong to the exclusive set of society in any city or place; specifically, the higher class of society in New York City—the *bon-ton*: phrase coined by Ward McAllister, New York society leader, in 1889.

Fourteen Points (fōr'tēn pointz), fourteen conditions set forth by President Wilson in January, 1918, as the basis of a post-war world peace.

frail, *n.* see main vocabulary.

frail (frāl), *n.* a woman of questionable virtue.

frame, *v.t.*, *v.i.* and *n.* see main vocabulary.

frame (frām), *v.t.* [Slang], to make one the victim of a plot for a sinister or evil purpose; to accuse a person wrongfully and endeavor to prove him guilty by false testimony.

frame-up (frām'ŭp), *n.* [Slang], a plot or a conspiracy to incriminate a person by false evidence or testimony.

Franco-Prussian War (frangk'kō prŭsh'an), the conflict (1870-71) between France and Prussia that resulted in the defeat of France, the loss of Alsace-Lorraine to that country, the formation of the Third French Republic, and the establishment of the German Empire under Prussian sway.

fraud pledge (frôd plej), the system in Anglo Saxon times by which communities were divided into tithings of ten houses, the holders of which were responsible for faults or crimes committed by any of them.

free love, the doctrine of living openly with a person of the opposite sex, without marriage, for the sake of the pleasures and conveniences derived from the arrangement.

freezing-point (frēz'ing-point), *n.* the temperature at which water freezes: indicated on Fahrenheit thermometer at 32° above zero, on the Rèaumur thermometer at 0°.

Freudian (froi'di-an), *adj.* pertaining to Sigmund Freud, or his theories, especially to the cause of dreams and psychopathic phenomena; relating or referring to pyschoanalysis.

Freudianism ('di-ȧ-nizm), *n.* investigation or study of the causes of mental phenomena, based on the theories put forward by Sigmund Freud, Viennese psychologist, especially in regard to the causes and treatment of hysteria, and other psychopathic manifestations, to the interpretation of dreams, and to various mental disturbances, based on a psychology of the sex impulses, and of the unconscious.

frightfulness (frīt'fŭl-nes), *n.* violent actions and outrages in warfare intended to terrorize the enemy: English translation of the German *schrecklichkeit*.

frigidaire (frij'ĭ-dār), *n.* trade name for an electric air-conditioned refrigerator and water cooler for domestic and commercial use.

frisk, *v.t.* see main vocabulary.

frisk (frĭsk), *v.t.* [Slang], to search a person suspected, or accused, of crime to determine if he has concealed weapons or other contraband articles in his possession; also, to steal by searching the person.

Fritz (fritz), *n.* a German, especially a German soldier in the World War: the word is an abbreviation or nickname for *Friedrich* (Eng. Frederick).

frozen credit (frō'z'n kred'it), credit given, as to farmers or merchants, on goods or commodities that have no ready sale and may not be disposed of for a considerable time.

fuehrer (fū'rēr), *n.* [G.], leader; title conferred on Adolf Hitler as Chancellor of the modern Germany.

fundamentalist (fŭn-dȧ-men'tal-ist), *n.* a person, especially a clergyman, who implicitly believes in the teachings and literal interpretation of the Bible.

futurism (fūtūr-izm), *n.* a form or phase of postimpressionism, which see below.

gabble, *n.* see main vocabulary.
gabble (gab''l), *n.* weird cries like the whining of hounds, heard at night, supposed to forebode trouble: superstitiously believed to be the wailings of unbaptized infants wandering through the air to the day of judgment: word is often extended to read *gabbleretchet.*
Gadarene (găd-ă-rēn'), *v.i.* to act or behave as did the Gadarene swine when possessed of devils: see *Matt.* viii. 28-34.
gaduol (găd'ū-ōl), *n.* an alcoholic extract of cod liver oil.
Gainsborough (gānz'b'rō), *n.* any painting by Thomas Gainsborough (1727-1788), considered the foremost of English portrait and landscape artists: his most famous picture is "Blue Boy," now owned by H. Huntingdon, New York City.
Gainsborough hat, a woman's hat with a very wide brim and, usually, ornamented with two or three large feathers: patterned after those represented by Gainsborough in his portraits of ladies.
galah (gȧ-lä'), *n.* in Australia, native name for the pink-breasted cockatoo, and also for one of the red variety of parrots, of which there are many: the second syllable is strongly accented, as if spelt *lar.*
galeropia (găl-ēr-ō'pi-ȧ), *n.* abnormal acuteness of vision.
gamma lines (gam'ȧ-līnz), lines of extremely high frequency in the X-ray spectrum of an element, having their wave-lengths definitely related to the atomic number of the element.
Gandhiism (gän'di-izm), *n.* the theory, doctrine, teachings, belief, or movement of Mohandas K. Gandhi, Hindu seer, reformer and leader, who strongly stresses the efficacy of passive resistance in the struggle for native independence in India: though Gandhi preaches non-resistance and peace he is accused of being the cause of all the strife and disturbances.
gangster (gang'stēr), *n.* member of a gang banded together for sinister or unlawful purposes; an underworld character who preys upon society for a living; desperado; ruffian; crook.
garambullo (gä-räm-bōōl'yō), *n.* the berry or fruit of a cactus-like plant that flourishes on the high tablelands of Mexico.
Garden City (gär'd'n sit'i), popular name for Chicago: from the motto on its seal, "Urbs in Horto," Latin, for City in a Garden.
Garden of the Gods, a valley in El Paso County, Colorado, interspersed with isolated rocks, eroded into curious imitative forms.
Garden of the West, the State of Illinois, on account of its richness and fertility.
Garden of the World (wērld), the region drained by the middle course of the Mississippi River, on account of its productiveness.
Gardens of the Sun (gär'd'nz), the East Indian or Malayan archipelago.
Garden State, the State of New Jersey.
Garraway's (gär'ă-wāz), *n.* a famous coffee-house in Exchange Alley, London, which continued for almost 220 years. In 1657 tea was sold here for 50 shillings (about $12) per lb.
Gary school system (gā'ri skōōl sis'tĕm), a system of school management by which a specified time is devoted to study, to manual training, and to play, with special teachers or supervisors for each division: after Gary, Ind., where first tried.
gastrin (găs'trĭn), *n.* in chemistry, a hormone that causes secretion of gastric juice.
gastromegaly (găs-trō-mĕg'ȧ-li), *n.* enlargement of the stomach.
gastroplegia (găs-trō-plē'ji-ȧ), *n.* acute dilatation of the stomach.
gastrorrhagia (-rā'ji-ȧ), *n.* hemorrhage from the stomach.
gate of tears (gāt, terz), the strait of Babelmandeb, the passage from the Indian Ocean into the Red Sea: so called by Moore in "Lalla Rookh."
gene (jēn), *n.* in biology, a factor or determiner; an entity believed to have an important part in the transmission, development, and determination of hereditary character; an element of the germ plasm which some scientists regard as part of a chromosome.
genotype (jen'o-tīp), *n.* in biology, a type showing a combination of the hereditary qualities peculiar to an organism or race; a group of organisms showing the same combination of hereditary characters.
gentlemen's agreement (jĕn't'l-mĕnz ȧ-grē'mĕnt), a compact which is binding on the parties to it only as a matter of honor: it has no legal standing and cannot be enforced in a court of law.
geophagia (jē-o-fā'ji-ȧ), *n.* the eating of earth or dirt.
geophone (jē'ŏ-fōn), *n.* a device for detecting sounds coming through earth escarpments or embankments, or from ground underneath: much used by both sides in the World War.
georgette (jor-jet'), *n.* a very thin silk crepe of fine texture, and almost transparent: after Mme. *Georgette* de la Plante, French Modiste.
Georgia (jôr'ji-ȧ), *n.* a State of the U. S., the Cracker State; named in honor of King George II, of England.
geriatrics (jĕ-rĭ'ȧ-triks), *n.* treatment of diseases and ills peculiar to old age.
Germanophile (jĕr'mȧ-nō-fīl), *adj.* favoring, or approving, Germany and the German people in their activities and relations, as political, social, economic, religious, etc.; *n.* one who loves Germany and its people and approves of all the activities of the latter.
Gesta Romanorum (jes'tȧ rŏ-mȧ-nō'rŭm), literally, the deeds of the Romans, a collection of stories and legends in Latin, which were widely read during the Middle Ages: the author is unknown: the stories are of a moral character and uplifting: they were a source from which many later writers drew inspiration.
Gethsemane (geth-sem'ȧ-ne), *n.* the garden on the outskirts of Jerusalem, wherein Christ wept, and prayed, and was arrested (*Matt.* xxvi: 36-50).
Gettysburg Address (get'iz-bûrg ă-drĕs'), the famous oration delivered by President Abraham Lincoln at the dedication of the national cemetery at Gettysburg, Pa., November 19, 1863, beginning—"Four score and seven years ago our fathers brought forth on this continent a new nation, conceived in liberty, and dedicated to the proposition that all men are created equal."
giant panda (ji'ȧnt pän'dȧ), a large bearlike mammal of Tibet, of a black-and-white color: it is very rare, almost extinct.
Giants' Causeway (jī'antz kôs'wā), a great basaltic promontory on the coast of Antrim, Northern Ireland: there are thousands of vertical columns, most of them six-sided, but many have nine regularly formed sides: the formation is ascribed to a large flow of lava in the Tertiany period: there has been much erosion since then which has exposed many great cliffs, some of which stand over 500 ft. above sea-level. Legend says the Causeway was "the work of giants in the old days, trying to build a bridge over to Scotland." It attracts many sightseers from foreign countries, especially Americans, during the summer months.
Gibraltar of America (ji-brôl'tēr, ȧ-mer'i-kȧ), the narrow promontory on the north bank of the St. Lawrence River, Province of Quebec, Canada, whereon the City of Quebec is located.
gigolo (jig'o-lō), *n.* [Slang] a professional dancer in a dance hall, paid for acting as partner to a female patron or visitor; a lounge-lizard; an idle or worthless fellow.
Gilderoy (gil'de-roi), *n.* nickname of a famous Scottish robber of the 17th century, who "had the honor" of robbing Cardinal Richelieu and Oliver Cromwell: he was hanged at Edinburgh: his real name was Patrick MacGregor
Gilderoy's kite (kīt), *n.* a fanciful nickname for the gibbet or scaffold on which Gilderoy was hanged: as the robber was a tall man, the scaffold was built very high, so high that it was likened to "a kite in the air": some claim that it was the robber's body, not the gibbet, that was likened to a kite.
gimper (gim'pēr), *n.* [Slang], in the World War, a close buddy; a true pal; one who proved friend and helper in difficulty, or danger.
ginkgo (gink'gō), *n.* a tree of remote antiquity, said to have originated in ancient China: ginkgo trees have recently been transplanted in the United States: they serve well for street borders and lawns, and are immune to the attacks of insects.
girl guide (gērl gīd), one of an English organization of girls formed during the World War for active service, as nursing, general hospital work, cleaning, and in signalling and telegraphy.
girl scout (skout), member of an American national organization of girls, originally founded at Savannah, Ga., 1912, as "Girl Guides", but was changed the following year to that of "Girl Scouts": the object is about the same as that of the Boy Scouts—to be kind and considerate to all, and do as much good in the world as one can possibly accomplish.
Glacier National Park (glā'shēr năsh'ŭn-ăl pärk), a public park in Montana, just south of the Canadian border; it is 45 miles long and covers an area of 1534 sq. m.; it has some 60 glaciers and 250 small lakes.
glide (glīd), *v.i.* in aviation, to descend at a normal angle of attack without engine power sufficient for level flight: *n.* the action of thus descending.
Glorious Fourth (glō'ri-ŭs fōrth), July 4th, the anniversary of the signing of the Declaration of Independence, at Philadelphia, July 4, 1776, observed as the leading national holiday throughout the U. S., its territories and dependencies.
Glorious Preacher (prēch'ēr), St. John Chrysostom (354-407): the name is from the Greek; *chrusos stoma*, meaning "gold mouth" in English, hence, the preacher was often called John Goldmouth or Goldenmouth.
glossalgia (glo-săl'ji-ȧ), *n.* pain in the tongue.
glyptolith (glip'tō-lith), *n.* a pebble or stone having façets that have been formed and polished by the action of the weather.
G-men, *n.pl.* officers of the Federal Bureau of Investigation of the Department of Justice; government detectives; also called F.B.I. men.
goat (gōt), *n.* [Slang] a scapegoat; one who voluntarily, or under compulsion, bears blame for another: *getting his goat*, causing a person to become angry or indignant.
Gog (gŏg), *n.* Antichrist: see *Rev.* xx:7-9.
Gog and Magog (mā'gŏg), in conjunction, a symbolism for all the princes of the earth who are enemies of the Christian Church; two colossal wooden statues in the Guildhall, London, constructed 1708 to replace effigies burned in the Great Fire of 1666.
Golden Horn (hôrn), the inlet of the Bosphorus on which the City of Istanbul (formerly Constantinople) stands: so called from its shape and beauty.
Golden Vale (vāl), a fertile tract of country in the center of the Irish Free State, midway between Dublin and Galway, including parts of Kings County, Queens County, Meath, Westmeath, and Tipperary.
gold digger (dig'ēr), *n.* one engaged in placer-mining for gold: [Slang] a female who inveigles or entices rich men for purposes of gain.
gonadectomy (gŏn-ăd-ĕk-tō-mĭ), *n.* the excision of a gonad, or sexual gland.
Good Gray Poet, a title bestowed by his admirers on Walt Whitman (1819-1892), American poet.
goof (gōōf), *n.* [Slang] a slow-witted person; a dullard; a blockhead.
Goorkha, see *Gurkha* main vocabulary.
Gopher State (gō'fēr), a nickname for the State of Minnesota, on account of its numerous gophers.
goshenite (gō'shen-īt), *n.* a colorless kind of beryl: after Goshen, Mass., where found.
gowk storm (gouk stôrm), in Scotland, a stiff but short storm, that generally comes about the middle of April when the gowk or cuckoo arrives.
Grand Cathedral (kȧ-thē'drăl), St. Peter's in Rome, built in the form of a Latin cross; length of interior, 613 ft.; of transept, 447 ft.; height of nave, 153 ft.; diameter of cupola, 193 ft.; height of dome from pavement to top of cross, 448 ft.; the great bell alone, without hammer or clapper, weighs 18,600 lbs. The structure was begun in 1450 and not entirely finished until 1880; it cost $75,000,000: it is the largest and grandest temple of worship in the world.
grandfather clause (grănd'fä-thēr klôz), a provision in a state constitution by which a person's right to vote was based on his descent from a voter; in effect, it read: "No person shall vote in this State if he is unable to read and write, unless his father or *grandfather* was a voter before 1867." Its object was to prevent Negroes from voting in some of the Southern States.
grand old gardener (gär'd'n-ēr), a poetical title for Adam, the first man, according to the Bible.
Granite State (grăn'ĭt), popular name for the State of New Hampshire, on account of its granite hills.
granolith (grăn'ō-lĭth), *n.* artificial stone made up of crushed granite and cement.
Great Dane, see *Danish dog* under *Danish* in main vocabulary.
great unwashed (ŭn-wôsht), the term of contempt which Edmund Burke (1729-1797), Irish Statesman and orator, applied to the working and artisan classes: afterwards, popularized by Sir Walter Scott.
Great Wall (wôl), the defensive wall between Mongolia and China proper, built by the Chinese to keep out the Tartars; it is 35 feet high, 21 feet thick, and extends for 1250 miles. The Japs made several breaches in it during the disturbances of 1933-34.
Grevillea (grĕ-vĭl'ĕ-ȧ), *n.* a large genus of Australian trees, with tetramerous flowers and handsome silky leaves, on account of which they are popularly called *silk oaks*; [g-], a tree of this genus.
griffawn (grif'ăn), *n.* in Ireland, a turf spade, an implement like an ordinary spade, but having an iron wing on one side of the blade to shape the soft peat, as it is dug from the mass, into square form before drying.
griffon (grĭf'ŏn), *n.* one of a breed of rough-coated European dogs, usually of a grayish color, used in hunting game birds.
grifter (grif'tēr), *n.* [Slang] a cheap crook; a petty thief.
grocetaria (grō-se-tā'ri-ȧ), *n.* a cheap grocery store in which the customers wait upon themselves and pay the cashier when leaving.

guanahan (gwä-nä-hä'nĭ), *n.* native name of the first American island (San Salvador) on which Columbus landed: called Watling Island by the British.

guanches (gwän'kēz), *n.pl.* the aborigines of the Canary Islands.

guao (gwä'ō), *n.* a West Indian tree which poisons by contact.

guarapo (gwä-rä'pō), *n.* in the West Indies, a fermented drink made from the juice of the sugar cane.

Gudrun (gōōd'rōōn), *n.* an old German saga; the heroine of this saga, rescued by her lover after many years of suffering; in the Volsunga Saga, the sister of Gunnar, who wins Sigurd by a magic draft.

guenon (gē-nông'), *n.* a small, long-tailed monkey of equatorial Africa, very active in its habits.

Guesdism (gĕd'izm), *n.* a form of Socialism similar to that of Karl Marx, put forward and advocated by the late Jules Basile Guesde (ged), French political leader.

guff (gŭf), *n.* [Slang], nonsense; idle or foolish talk; sometimes, impudence or impertinence.

gums (gumz), *n.pl.* collectively, the gum-trees of Australia, of the genus *Eucalyptus*.

gum-shoe ('shōō), *n.* a rubber overshoe; [Slang], *adj.* denoting some action or movement carried on surreptitiously, secretly, or deceptively, as a *gum-shoe* conference.

gun-moll (gun'mawl), *n.* [Slang] a female desperado who carries a pistol and assists male companions in hold-ups, burglaries, and other criminal acts.

Gutenberg Bible (gōō'tĕn-berch bī'b'l), the earliest book printed in movable metal type, date about 1450; very rare now, only a few copies in existence, a good one being worth, probably, $50,000: also, called the Mazarine Bible because the first copy was placed in the Bibliothèque Mazarine, a library named after Cardinal Mazarine.

Guy's Hospital (gīz hŏs'pi-tăl), a well-known hospital in London, founded in 1721 by Thomas Guy (1644-1724), a wealthy printer of the period.

gyromitra (gī-rom'i-trâ), *n.* a species of poisonous fungus.

H

Hadrian's wall (hā'drĭ-anz wôl), ruins of an ancient wall in the north of England, built by order of the Roman Emperor, Hadrian, about 125 A. D.; it was 75 miles long from 7 to 10 ft. high, and extended between the Solway and the Tyne.

hafnium (haf'ni-um), *n.* a rare earth group element, recently discovered in zirconium minerals.

Hague Tribunal (hāg trī-bū'nâl), a permanent court of arbitration created by the "International Convention for the Pacific Settlement of International Disputes," founded in 1899 by the International Peace Conference.

hag-fish, *n.* a kind of lamprey with strong suctorial mouth, but jawless, that bores into the bodies of fish and devours their viscera: it is one of the Cyclostomi, the lowest of the craniate vertebrates.

Haile Sellassie I (hăl'i sĭ-lâs'ĭ), Emperor of Abyssinia, born 1891: he was crowned Negus (King) Tafari, in 1928, and two years later was proclaimed emperor with the above title.

halitosis (hal-ĭ-tō'sĭs), *n.* an offensive odor from the mouth; foul breath.

halisteresis (hâ-lĭs-tĕr-ē'sĭs), *n.* a chronic progressive disease during which the bones gradually soften, often resulting in great deformity; osteomalacia: pregnant women are especially prone to it.

Halley's comet (hal'ĕz kŏm'ĕt), a periodic comet that appears about every 77 years; first observed 11 B. C.; last appearance, 1910; next expected 1987; named after Edmund Halley (1656-1742), English astronomer who computed its orbit, and accurately foretold when it would be seen again in the northern heavens.

Hall of Fame, a national institution founded in 1900 by the Council of N. Y. University for a memorial of famous U. S. Americans: places were arranged for 150 commemorative tablets, about 70 of which have been filled to date (1935): the names of five distinguished Americans to be thus honored are chosen every five years.

hallucinosis (hâ-lū-sĭ-nō'sĭs), *n.* a state of mental affliction in which one is subject to hallucinations; a morbid condition characterized by weird imaginings.

Hammurabi (hăm-ōō-rä'bĭ), *n.* king of Babylon who flourished about 2,000 B. C. He promulgated a set of laws known as the *Code of Hammurabi*, afterwards termed the *Judgment of Righteousness*.

Hampstead Heath (hămp'stĕd hēth), a natural park of about 300 acres on the border of London, containing an eminence called *Hampstead Hill*: formerly, the scene of many robberies, and several murders.

handwriting expert (hand-rīt'ing ĕks'pert), one skilled in the differentiation of various types of handwriting; one who, by comparing the acknowledged script of an individual with a writing which he denies, claims he can tell whether both specimens were, or were not, written by the same hand.

hangout (hang'out), *n.* [Slang] an undercover rendezvous for underworld law breakers; resort for criminals; retreat for gangsters.

hangover (hăng-ō'vĕr), *n.* [Slang], a sickly or drowsy morning feeling, the result of overindulgence the night before.

haphephobia (hăf-ē-fō'bĭ-â), *n.* a morbid dread of being touched.

hard-boiled (härd-boil'd), *adj.* [Slang] tough; shrewd; experienced in worldly ways.

hard labor (lā'b'r), compulsory, and usually, hard work, imposed upon criminals during a term in jail.

haricot, *n.* see main vocabulary.

haricot, *n.* red copper oxide.

Hathor (hä'thôr), *n.* in Egyptian mythology, the goddess of love, mirth and joy: usually, represented with the head of a cow.

health insurance (ĭn-shōōr'âns), insurance against loss by sickness, the loss being of two kinds, that of earning capacity, and the cost of medical attendance.

hebephrenia (hē-bē-frē'nĭ-â), *n.* a mental derangement frequently occurring at puberty: in young women, generally due to chlorosis or green sickness.

hedonol (hē'dō-nōl), *n.* a white crystalline powder which, dissolved in water, is used for a sleeping draught—$C_6 H_{13} O_2 N$.

heeby-jeebys (hēb'i-jēb'ez), *n.* [Slang] dull feeling as from a hangover; the blues; the creeps: sometimes applied to delirium tremens.

Heidelberg Man (hī'dĕl-bergh), representative of an ancient race of humans, supposed to have lived 350,000 years ago: from a few fossil bones found near Heidelberg, Germany.

Heights of Abraham (hītz, ā'brâ-hăm), another name for the *Plains of Abraham*, near Quebec Canada: after Abraham Marten, a Canadian pioneer of Scotch descent, a pilot on the St. Lawrence River in the time of Samuel de Champlain.

Heinie (hī'nĕ), *n.* [Slang], a German, especially a German soldier; also derisively used for things of German manufacture, as airships, boats, guns, etc.: the word is a nickname for *Heinrich*, the German form of Henry.

heliotherapy (hē-lĭ-o-thĕr'â-pi), *n.* the sun cure; the treatment of diseases by sun baths or exposing the naked body to the rays of the sun at intervals during the day.

hell-for-leather (-lĕth'ĕr), *adj.* [Slang], denoting or referring to something done with great speed or quickness, as a *hell-for-leather* race.

Hell Gate (gāt), a narrow channel in the East River, New York City, formerly regarded as dangerous on account of a big rock which was blown up in 1885.

hell-raker (-rā'kĕr), *n.* [Slang, Eng.], a wild, reckless fellow.

hell's half acre (ā'kĕr), [Colloq.], a neighborhood or locality, usually in a big city, of evil reputation.

heloma (hē-lō'mâ), *n.* a corn or callosity on hand, or foot.

hemafecia (hĕm-â-fā'shĭ-â), *n.* the presence of blood in the feces.

hemaphobia (hĕm'â-fō'bĭ-â), *n.* morbid dread of the sight of blood.

hematocyte (hem'â-tō-sīt), *n.* any blood corpuscle.

hematocyturia (hĕm-â-tō-sī-tū'rĭ-â), *n.* the presence of blood corpuscles in the urine.

hematolysis (-tŏl'ĭ-sĭs), *n.* dissolution of red corpuscles in the blood, as a result of which it fails to coagulate.

hematorrhea (hĕm-â-tō-rē'â), *n.* a bloody discharge from the bowels.

hemialgia (hĕm-ĭ-âl'jĭ-â), *n.* neuralgia on one side only.

hemolysis, same as hematolysis.

hemothymia (hĕm-ō-thĭm'ĭ-â), *n.* an insane tendency to murder.

hempy (hĕm'pĭ), *n.* [Colloq.], in Scotland, a young person, especially, a bold, forward, or impudent young girl.

henbill (hĕn'bĭl), *n.* the American coot; the dabchick.

Hengist and Horsa (hĕng'gĭst, hôr-sa), two brothers (Jutes) who led the first Germanic invasion of Britain, about 450 A. D.

henism (hĕn'izm), *n.* in philosophy, the doctrine that everything,—the whole universe, is reducible to a single form or principle.

henosis (hĕ-nō'sĭs), *n.* the operation of uniting two parts naturally separated.

hepatocirrhosis (hĕp-â-tō-sĭ-rō'sĭs), *n.* cirrhosis of the liver.

hepatodynia (-dĭn'ĭ-â), *n.* pain in the liver.

hepatoid (hĕp'â-toid), *adj.* resembling the liver, as in tissue.

hepatoma (hĕp-â-tō'mâ), *n.* tumor of the liver.

hepatomalacia (-mâ-lā'shĭ-â), *n.* morbid softening of the liver.

hepatopexy (hep'â-tō-pek-si), *n.* the operation of putting a prolapsed liver into proper place.

herepetology (hē-rĕp-ē-tŏl'ŏ'ji), *n.* the study of reptiles.

Herodias (he-rō'di-âs), *n.* in Biblical literature, the wife of Herod Antipas, and mother of Salome, whom she instigated to ask Herod for the head of John the Baptist, as a reward for her dancing. See *Matt.* xiv:3-12, and *Mark* vi:17-29.; hence, *Herodias* is used as a synonym for a bad, designing woman.

Herodotus (hē-rŏd'ō-tŭs), *n.* a Greek historian, called "the father of history," born at Halicarnassus, in Asia Minor about 484 B. C.; he traveled over most of the then known world and wrote, in Ionian dialect, histories of Egypt, Lydia, Scythia, Media, and Assyria: he died about 425 B. C.

heroin (her'ō-ĭn), *n.* a white crystalline, odorless, bitter powder, $C_{17}H_{17}O_3N$, derived from morphine, used in medicine as an anodyne and sedative, and to relieve bronchitis and allay coughing: it is a dangerous, habit-forming drug, to which many are addicted, especially in the underworld, who either sniff it as 'snow', or inject it in solution, as it is soluble in both water and alcohol.

heroinism (-izm), *n.* the heroin habit.

Hertzian waves (hĕrt'sĭ-ăn wāvz), electric waves: after Heinrich Rudolph Hertz (1857-1894), a German physicist who discovered that electricity can be manifested in waves, similar to light waves: the *Hertzian waves* are the basis of radio broadcasting.

Hester Prynne (hĕs'tĕr prĭn), the unfortunate woman of Nathanial Hawthorne's "The Scarlet Letter," who bore the badge of shame, a crimson 'A', signifying Adulteress.

Hetepheres (hĕ-tef'e-rēz), *n.* an Egyptian queen whose son, Cheops, built the pyramid at Gizeh; in 1927 her tomb was opened in which many gold and alabaster articles were found, but no mummy.

heterochrosome (hĕt-ĕr-ō-krō'mō-sōm), *n.* a chromosome, the functioning of which, it is believed, determines the sex.

heterodyne (het'ĕr-ō-dīn), *adj.* in radio, pertaining to a receiving method by which oscillations occur in the receiving set nearly identical in frequency and strength with the transmitted waves: *n.* an auxiliary generator of radio-frequency voltage used in heterodyne reception.

heterosexuality (sĕk-shū-al'i-ti), *n.* morbid sexual passion of the male for the female, or of the female for the male.

heterosis (het-ĕr-ō'sĭs), *n.* abnormal development and size of animals, or plants, produced by cross-breeding.

hexathlon (hĕk-săth'lŏn), *n.* in indoor sports, a composite contest consisting of running high jump, standing broad jump, fence-vaulting, shot-putting, and 60- and 160-yard potato races: instituted by the Y. M. C. A.

Hezekiah (hez-e-kī'â), *n.* the twelfth King of Judah who flourished about 750 B. C.: he tried to put down idolatrous worship among the Jews, and destroyed the brazen serpent of Moses: several other Old Testament characters bore this name.

hieromania (hī'ĕr-o-mā-'nĭ-â), *n.* religious insanity.

highbrow (hī'brou), *n.* one who has a high forehead; hence, a learned or intellectual person, but generally applied to one who assumes an attitude of intellectual superiority.

high-hat *n.* [Slang], one who considers himself superior to others; a conceited, silly fellow fond of display: *v.t.* to look down upon with contempt; to despise: to scorn or ignore.

Highland Mary (hī'lănd mā'ri), Mary Morrison, the sweetheart of Bobbie Burns, "a winsome wee Scotch lassie, whom he courted on the Brig (bridge) o' Doon."

hill-billy (hĭl-bĭl'ĭ), *n.* mountaineer; especially applied to an inhabitant of the backwood mountainous districts of Kentucky, Tennessee, North Carolina, and Georgia; a rube or inexperienced countryman.

Hindenburg line (hĭn'den-boorgh līn), a line of defense which the Germans placed across northeastern France, in 1916, under General Paul von Hindenburg. Early in 1917 the German troops were swept back to this line, but it was not until September of the following year that the Allied forces were able to break through.

hinsdalite (hĭnz-dâ-līt'), *n.* a mineral related to alunite.

Hippocratic oath (hĭp-ō-krat'ĭk ōth), an oath said to have been imposed by Hippocrates, of Cos, an ancient Greek physician, styled "the father of medicine," upon his disciples, and which was taken by all young men of the time about to begin medical practice; while not administered in modern times, it is still regarded as a basis for medical ethics and all true physicians respect and accept its precepts.

hislopite (hĭs-lō-pīt'), *n.* a grass-green variety of calcite.

Hitlerism (hĭt′lẽr-iz′m), *n.* the extreme nationalistic theories, doctrine, and propaganda of the National Socialist Party in Germany under the leadership of Adolph Hitler since 1930; German fascism.

Hitlerite (-īt), *n.* a follower of Adolph Hitler; one who endorses his policy.

Hivites (hī-vī′tēz), *n.pl.* an ancient race of the land of Canaan, conquered by the Hebrews.

Hodgkin's disease (hŏj′kinz dĭ-zēz′), a disease characterized by progressive anæmia, and enlargement of the lymphatic glands: after Dr. Thomas Hodgkin (1798-1866), an English physician, who described it.

Hohenzollern (hō′ĕn-tsŏl-ẽrn), *n.* name of a princely family of Germany, dating back to the 11th century, from which descended the royal line of Prussia and the last of the German Emperors, down to the former Kaiser, William II., who abdicated in 1918, and took refuge in Holland.

holocaine (hŏl-ō-kā′in), *n.* one of the coal-tar derivatives, a crystalline white substance, used as a local anæsthetic.

holotonia (hŏl-o-tō′ni-å), *n.* a muscular spasm of the body.

Holy Alliance (ă-lī-ăns), an alliance of all the sovereigns of Europe, except the king of England and the Pope, agreed upon in 1815, ostensibly for the purpose of conserving peace in Europe, but really to suppress a tendency to constitutional government, then becoming manifest: the alliance terminated with the French Revolution in 1830.

Holy Rollers (rōl′ẽrz), [Colloq.], members of a religious sect, an off-branch of Methodism, who, when under religious fervor at their meetings, display great emotion, as rolling over the floor and over one another, and often, in their excitement, divesting themselves of clothing.

honorificabilitudinitatibus (ŏn′ẽr-ĭf-ĭ-kȧ-bĭl′ĭ-tū′dĭ-nĭ-tăt′ĭ-bŭs), *n.* [L.] honorableness; state of being honorable.

homitosis (hŏm-i-tō′sis), *n.* a recently coined business word, meaning poor judgment or bad taste in the selection of home furniture and furnishings.

Homo sapiens (hō′mō sā′pĭ-ĕnz), [L.], the one and only human species of the genus Homo, made up of all the various races of mankind, considered as so many varieties of this single species; man as an intelligent, sensible, reasoning being.

Honest Abe (ŏn′ĕst āb), a popular nickname for Abraham Lincoln (1809-1865), sixteenth President of the U. S. (1861-1865).

hooch (hōōch), *n.* [Slang], an alcoholic liquor surreptitiously obtained or manufactured; home brew.

hoosegow (hōōs′gou), *n.* [Slang], a local jail; a prison; a lockup; a guardhouse; penitentiary.

Hoozier (hōō′zhẽr), *n.* a native of, or one living in, the State of Indiana.

Hoosier State, a nickname for the State of Indiana.

Hooverize (hōō′vẽr-īz), *v.i.* to economize in food, or its distribution: after Herbert Hoover, when he was U. S. Food Administrator (1917-'18): now rarely used.

Hopi (hō′pi), *n.pl.* pueblo Indians, noted for snake dances and weird religious rites and customs: have a reservation in Colorado.

hormone (hôr′mōn), *n.* a chemical substance secreted in one organ of the body and carried, through blood circulation, to another organ, which it stimulates and strengthens.

Horus (hō′rŭs), *n.* in Egyptian mythology, the hawk-headed god of day.

Hosea (hŏ-zē′å), *n.* a Hebrew prophet of the 8th century B. C.; a Book of the Old Testament.

Hrasvelg (hras′vĕlg), *n.* in Scandinavian, mythology, the huge eagle that watches by the root of the Tree of the World, to devour the dead: the flap of his wings causes violent storms.

Hudsonia (hŭd-sō′ni-å), *n.* a genus of cistaceous plants of Eastern U. S., of which the heath is typical.

Hudson seal (hud′s′n sēl), the skin or fur of the muskrat dyed to resemble that of the seal in color.

Hull House (hŭl hous), a social settlement founded in Chicago, in 1889, by Jane Addams and Ellen Starr: named after Charles J. Hull, owner of the building on S. Halsted Street, which he gave to the settlement.

Hun (hun), *n.* a term of opprobrium applied by opponents to a German soldier in the World War: Kaiser Wilhelm urged his fighting men to make themselves as dreaded as the Huns under Attila.

Hundred Years' War (hŭn′drĕd yẽrz wôr), a contest between England and France carried on intermittently from 1337 to 1453 to finally decide the claim of the English Kings to the French throne: in the end, England lost all her French possessions, except Calais.

Hyde Park (hīd pärk), a park in London, covering 365 acres, extending in an irregular sweep from Whitehall to Kensington: it is a favorite resort for all classes of citizens, and a "happy hunting ground" for soap-box orators, who are permitted to express very radical views without objection or molestation on the part of the authorities: there is a fashionable equestrian thoroughfare in the park called Rotten Row, and a little lake about a mile in length, known as the Serpentine; also, a park of Sydney, Australia, a favorite recreation place of citizens; the birthplace and estate of F. D. Roosevelt in Duchess County, N.Y.

hydroaeroplane (hī′drō-ā-ẽr-ō-plān), *n.* an æroplane which, in addition to wheels, is equipped with pontoons, enabling it to alight upon, and take off from, water.

hydromonoplane (-mŏn′ō-plān), *n.* a hydroæroplane having but one main supporting plane.

hydrophone (hī′drŏ-fōn), *n.* an instrument by which sounds transmitted through water can be heard.

hydroplane, same as hydroæroplane.

hydrosphere (-sfēr), *n.* the aqueous vapor in the atmosphere surrounding the earth.

hygrology (hī-grŏl′ŏ-ji), *n.* the branch of science that covers the phenomena of humidity.

Hyksos (hĭk′sōs), *n.* the XVth dynasty of six Egyptian kings who ruled about 100 years, supposed to have been Asiatic Semites: often referred to as the *Shepherd kings.*

hyperglycemia (hī-pẽr-glī-sē′mĭ-å), *n.* excess of sugar in the blood.

hyperthroidism (-thī′roid-izm), *n.* a morbid condition, resulting from abnormal functional activity of the thyroid gland.

hyphenate (hī′fĕn-āt), *n.* an American, especially of the U. S., of foreign birth or origin, who designates his nationality by placing a hyphen (-) between the name of his racial country and that in which he lives, as German-American.

Hypnos (hĭp′nŏs), *n.* in Greek mythology, the god of sleep, identified with Somnus, the brother of Death (Mors), and son of Night (Nox).

hyposthenia (-sthē-ni-å), *n.* general weakness of body; lack of strength.

hyposthenuria (hī-pŏs-thĕ-nū′ri-å), *n.* gradual lessening of the quantity of urine secreted.

hyzone (hī′zon), *n.* a variation of hydrogen, unstable and gaseous, obtained from ordinary hydrogen by gaseous ionization: chemically designated H_3 to distinguish it from H_2, ordinary hydrogen.

I

Ice Saints (īs sāntz), Saints Mamertus, Pancratius, and Servetus, whose festival days, according to the R. C. Calendar, occur on May 11, 12 and 13 respectively—days which are popularly reputed to be unseasonably cold throughout Europe.

Idaho (ī′då-hō), *n.* a State of the U. S., the Gem State; from the Indian, meaning "Gem of the Mountain."

Il Duce (dōō′chĕ), the leader; a term especially applied to Benito Mussolini, Premier of Italy.

illinium (ĭ-lĭn′ĭ-ŭm), *n.* a chemical element definitely identified by B. S. Hopkins in 1926, though two Italian chemists, L. Fernandez and L. M. Rolla claim to have identified it two years earlier, and named it *florentium*: its atomic number is 61.

Illinois (ĭl′ĭ-noi,-noiz), *n.* a State of the U. S., the Prairie or Sucker State; from Indian, *Illini*, men, and French *ois*, tribe of men.

imbat (ĭm′băt), *n.* a breeze that blows off the Mediterranean along the northern shore.

Immelmann turn (ĭm′ĕl-man tẽrn), a reverse turn of an airplane in which, after completing half a loop, the machine is driven back in an opposite direction: copied by aviators on both sides in the World War: after Max Immelmann, one of the most spectacular, daring, and skilled of the German fliers, who downed fifteen enemy pilots before his death in 1916.

imshee (im′shē), *interj.* [Australian Slang], begone! get out! depart! vamoose!

incommunicado (ĭn-kŏ-mū′nĭ-kä′dō), *adj.* solitary; alone; without means of communication.

Indiana (ĭn-dĭ-ăn′å), *n.* a State of the U. S., the Hoosier State; name derived from *Indian.*

Indian Territory (tĕr′ĭ-tŏ-rĭ), a former territory of the U. S., incorporated in the State of Oklahoma, when the latter was organized in 1907: in 1829 Congress authorized the use of the territory for all Indians east of the Mississippi River.

Industrial Workers of the World (ĭn-dŭs′trĭ-ăl, wẽrk′ẽrs, wẽrld), in the U. S., a former labor organization favoring international socialism, the abolition of the wage system, and the abolition of employers: usually referred to as the I. W. W.

inferiority complex (in-fē′ri-or′i-ti kom′pleks), a combination of thoughts, ideas, and emotions that causes a person to imagine himself inferior to others, and keeps him from asserting, claiming, or maintaining his individual rights and privileges.

infielder (ĭn-fēld′ẽr), *n.* in baseball, a player in first defensive line of the side not at bat.

infracaninophile (in′frå-kä-nĭn′o-fĭl), *n.* literally, a lover of the under dog; hence, one who pities, helps, or succors the poor, oppressed, downtrodden, or unjustly treated: word coined by Christopher Morley.

ink balls (ingk bôlz), *n.pl.* certain galls made by four-winged flies on various species of oak: so called because they contain a dark fluid, often used as ink by rural folk: in some places they are called *oak apples.*

Innisfail (ĭn′ĭs-fāl), *n.* a poetic name for Ireland.

innocuous desuetude (ĭ-nŏk′ū-ŭs dĕs′we-tūd), a phrase used by President Grover Cleveland in a message to Congress, March 1, 1886, meaning abeyance or harmless disuse. In referring to the Tenure-of-Office Act, passed over President Johnson's veto in 1867, which took from the President the power to remove members of his cabinet without permission of the Senate, President Cleveland stated: "After an existence of nearly twenty years of almost *innocuous desuetude* these laws are brought forth."

inside job (in′sīde job), a position, the work of which is carried on indoors; [Colloq.] a criminal deed, as a theft or burglary, ascribed to a person employed by the victim, or to one in whom confidence is placed and who is considered above suspicion.

insufflator (ĭn′sū-flā-tẽr), *n.* an instrument for blowing something, as powder, gas, vapor, or water, into a cavity, opening, or organ of the body; an injector used for forcing air into a furnace.

insulin (ĭn′sū-lĭn), *n.* an extract from the smaller glands of the pancreas,—known as the islands of Langerhans,—widely prescribed in the treatment of diabetes; it acts as a ferment, and while not a positive cure for the disease, it counteracts the sugar and does much to restore a proper metabolism: it was first isolated in 1922 by Dr. F. G. Banting, of the University of Toronto, but it was not isolated in crystallized form until four years later, by Dr. John J. Abel of Johns Hopkins University.

intelligentsia (in-tel′i-jĕnt′sĭ-å), *n.pl.* collectively, the intellectual or learned classes, as opposed to the common proletariat or unlearned.

interferometer (ĭn-tẽr-fẽr-ŏm′ĕ-tẽr), an instrument for measuring length or displacement by the interference of two beams of light.

internal combustion engine (ĭn-ter′năl kŏn-bŭs′chun ĕn′jĭn), a mechanical contrivance that converts heat into motion by the combustion of whatever kind of fuel is used—gaseous or liquid—within the engine, instead of combustion under a boiler outside the engine.

International Peace Conference (ĭn-tẽr-năsh′ŭn-ăl pēs kon′fẽr-ens), an international conference held at the Hague, May 18 to July 29, 1899, made up of delegates from the principal countries, who principally discussed world peace and the limitation of military and naval armaments.

intracollegiate (ĭn-trå-kŏ-lē′jĭ-āt), *adj.* referring or pertaining to what is done or carried on within one college or university: opposite of *intercollegiate.*

intramine (ĭn-trå-mĭn′), *n.* a sulphur compound often used in the treatment of syphilis.

introvert, *v.t. & n.* see main vocabulary.

introvert (ĭn′trŏ-vẽrt), *n.* in psychology, a person having a habit of almost constant introspection; one who gives much study to his own thoughts, emotions, urgings, and motives.

invar (in-vär′), *n* an alloy of nickel and steel, not appreciably affected by temperature change: it is used as material for measuring instruments that give minute accuracy.

invertase (ĭn-vẽr′tās), *n.* an enzyme that effects the inversion of cane sugar, changing it into invert sugar or glucose: this substance is found in many plants, also in the intestines of animals.

ionization (ī-ŏn-ĭ-zā′shŭn), *n.* the act or process of ionizing; state of being ionized.

ionize (ī′ŏn-īz), *v.t.* to convert, or separate, into ions; to dissociate: when a vapor, or gas, or current, or the like is subjected to some radioactive substance that renders it a conductor of electricity, it is said to be *ionized.*

ionone (ī′ŏ-nōn), *n.* an artificial oil of very strong odor, much used in the preparation of violet perfumes.

Iowa (ī′ŏ-wå), *n.* a State of the U. S., the Hawkeye State; from the Algonquin word, *ajawa*, meaning "across" or "beyond."

irisation (ī-rĭ-sā′shŭn), *n.* the act or process of making iridescent; iridescence.

Irish elk (ī′rish elk), a huge elk or deer, long extinct, remains of which are found under the peat bogs of Ireland: it stood over six feet in height, and had palmated antlers with a spread of from twelve to fifteen feet.

Iron Chancellor (chăn′sĕl-ẽr), Prince Eduard Leopold von Bismarck-Schönhausen (1815-

1898), commonly called Bismarck, German statesman: in allusion to his iron will and determination.

Iron City, Pittsburgh, Pa.: in allusion to its iron manufactures.

iron horse (hôrs), a locomotive engine.

Isaac (ī'zăk), *n.* a Hebrew patriarch, the son of Abraham and Sarah, husband of Rebekah, and father of Jacob and Esau: See *Gen.* xv.-xxxv.

ischesis (ĭs-kē'sĭs), *n.* suppression of a discharge.

ischiagra (ĭs-kĭ-ăg'rȧ), *n.* gout in the hip.

ischidrosis (ĭs-kĭ-dro'sĭs), *n.* suppression of sweat or perspiration.

ischochymia (ĭs-kō-kī'mĭ-ȧ), *n.* retention and stagnation of food in the stomach.

Ishmael (ĭsh'mā-ĕl), *n.* the son of Abraham and Hagar, ancestor of the Ishmaelites, a wild and wayward man, with "his hand against every man, and every man's hand against him"; hence, a social outcast; a quarrelsome person; one who antagonizes others.

Ishtar (ĭsh'tär), in Babylonian mythology, the Earth Mother; the goddess of the reproductive powers of nature: to the Assyrians, the goddess of war, represented as clothed in fire, with bow and arrow in her hands.

Island of Saints and Scholars (ī'lănd, săntz, skŏl'ẽrz), Ireland after the advent of St. Patrick: on account of the zeal with which the Irish embraced Christianity, of the many devoted to the religious life, of the monasteries, schools, and halls of learning that were established, and of the eminent scholars they produced, many of whom went to other countries to teach and preach.

island universe (ū'nĭ-vẽrs), a group of stars outside the galaxy.

isograph (ī'sō-grȧf), *n.* a drawing instrument which serves as a protractor and square: it consists of two short straight edge pieces of metal, joined at top by a circular plate marked with angular degrees.

Israel (ĭz'rā-ĕl), *n.* Jacob, after he wrestled with the angel.—*Gen.* xxxii-28; the descendants of Jacob; the children of Israel; the Jews or Hebrews; the Jewish world.

J

Jack Ketch (jak ketch), a public hangman: from an individual so named who acted as such under James II of England.

Jack Johnson (jăk jŏn's'n), [Slang], in the World War, a gun or shell of very large size: in allusion to the colored prize-fighter.

Jack Tar (tär), a sailor: sailors formerly wore hats made of tarred cloth: Charles Dickens was the first to use this term.

Jael (jā'ĕl), *n.* in Biblical literature, the wife of Heber the Kenite, she who killed Sisera in her tent with a nail. See *Judges* iv: 17-22.

jalouse (jȧ-lōōz'), *v.i.* in Scotland, to suspect; to surmise; to be suspicious of.

Jameson raid (jām's'n rād), an unauthorized raid on the Transvaal in December, 1895, led by Sir Leander Starr Jameson, English official in S. Africa. Jameson was captured, recalled to England, and jailed for a few months; he returned to S. Africa, where he succeeded Cecil Rhodes as Progressive leader; from 1900 to 1908 he was prime minister of Cape Colony; he died in 1917.

jack (jăk), *n.* [Slang], money; funds; spondulix.

jambosa (jăm-bō'sȧ), *n.* the rose apple.

jambosine (-bō'sēn), *n.* a crystalline alkaloid, $C_{10}H_{15}O_3N$, obtained from the root of jambosa.

jami (jä'mĭ), *n.* a mosque centrally located.

jampan (jăm'păn), *n.* in India, a sedan, consisting of a bamboo frame covered with silk, and carried on two poles.

jandia (jăn'dĭ-ȧ), *n.* a catfish found in the rivers of Brazil.

Jane (jān), *n.* [Slang], a woman, or girl: used derisively.

Japhetic nations (jā-fĕt'ĭk nā'shŭnz), a popular division of the White Race, including the Teutonic, Celtic, Slavic, Italic and Iranian.

Jason (jā's'n), *n.* in Greek mythology, the nephew of a king of Iolcus, sent in quest of the Golden Fleece, kept by the king of Colchis, who set him the task of harnessing to a plow two brazen-hoofed, fire-breathing bulls, of sowing dragons' teeth, and of destroying the armed men who would spring up from the teeth, which task Jason accomplished and secured the Fleece; hence, a person who accomplishes what is considered impossible.

jaunting-car (jänt'ing-kär), *n.* a two-wheeled, open vehicle, peculiar to, and until recently common in, Ireland, having a seat on each side above the wheels, in which the passengers sit sidewise, back to back: now fast disappearing, being superseded by the motor-car.

javel water (jȧ-vel' wô'tẽr), a bleaching preparation, composed of potassium carbonate, chlorine, and water: used sometimes in photography.

jawbreaker ('brēk-ẽr), *n.* [Slang], a long word: a pedantic word; a word hard to pronounce, or obscure of meaning.

jawfish (-fĭsh), *n.* a marine fish, having but one dorsal fin, found in tropical seas.

jawsmith (-smĭth), *n.* [Slang], a loud-voiced demagogue; a professional talker.

Jayhawker State, a nickname for the State of Kansas.

jaywalker ('wôk-ẽr), *n.* one who crosses a street or avenue diagonally, instead of at right angles; one who forgets, ignores, or defies traffic regulations, and crosses a street elsewhere than at intersections.

jazz (jăz), *n.* a form of musical expression which had its inception in the U. S. in the beginning of the present century; at first, it was played in rag-time, a cadence in which certain notes were accented: as it developed, many innovations were made in the instrumentation—banjos, saxophones, clarinets, cymbals, drums, and other instruments were introduced, the whole making a syncopated music hilarious and often boisterous.

jazz band (bănd), a band of musicians who play ragtime in a very lively and boisterous way.

jazz boes (bōz), [Slang], American colored troops in the World War.

Jefferson Bible (jef'ẽr-s'n bī'b'l), a compilation made by Thomas Jefferson, consisting of passages from the four gospels, cut out and pasted in a book according to a scheme of his own.

Jeffersonianism (jef-ẽr-sō'nĭ-ăn-izm), *n.* the simplicity and absence of pomp or display which characterized the administration (1801-1809), of President Jefferson; the principles of Thomas Jefferson as diplomat and statesman.

Jehol (yĕ-hōl'), *n.* a town and district of Manchukuo, taken by the Japanese early in 1933, an act emphatically condemned by the World Powers and which led to Japan's withdrawal from the League of Nations.

Jehoshaphat (jĕ-hŏsh'ȧ-fat), *n.* the fourth king of Judah after the revolt of the ten tribes: he made peace with the kings of Israel, and in his reign the people were prosperous and happy.

Jekyll Act (ăkt), an Act (1763) of the British Parliament, restricting the sale of spirituous or intoxicating liquors.

jenny-jo (jen'ĭ-jō), *n.* [Slang], in Ireland, a contemptuous term for an effeminate boy, or one who fails to take part in boyish sports.

Jephthah (jĕf'thȧ), *n.* in Biblical literature, a judge of Israel who sacrificed his only daughter to make good a vow. See *Judges* xi: 30-40.

Jeremiah (jĕr-ē-mī'ȧ), *n.* a great prophet and judge of Judæa who flourished about the 6th century B. C., whose prophecies, teachings, preachings, and denunciations are recorded in the "Book of the Prophet Jeremiah" and "The Lamentations of Jeremiah:" on account of the latter he is called *the weeping prophet.*

jerked beef (jẽrk'd bēf), beef cut into long strips and dried in the wind and sun.

jerks (jẽrkz), *n.pl.* chorea or involuntary twitchings, due to nervous excitement: used with *the.*

jerry (jĕr'ĭ), *n.* [Slang], a round, stiff, felt hat.

Jersey cattle (jẽr'sĭ kat''l), a valuable breed of cattle, well known for large flow of milk and fine quality of butter produced: they are rather small, have short horns, and are generally yellowish brown in color: so called because they originated on the island of Jersey, in the English channel: now, they are widely distributed in both Europe and America.

Jersey lightning (līt'nĭng), [Slang], applejack; an inferior, but strong kind of intoxicating liquor; bad whiskey; rotgut.

Jersey Lily (lĭ'ĭ), Mrs. Hugo de Bathe (1852-1929), better known as Lillie Langtry, an English actress, born on the island of Jersey, famous for her beauty, talent, and social graces: she visited the U. S. many times professionally.

jessur (jĕs'ŭr), *n.* a large viperine snake of southeastern Asia, beautifully marked, and extremely venomous.

Jew lizard (lĭz'ȧrd), an agamoid lizard of Australia, having a jular pouch which, when inflated, suggests a beard, hence, the name.

jiggered (jĭg'ẽrd), *p.a.* a euphemistic swearword, as in 'I'll be *jiggered.*'

jiharo (jĭ-här'ō), *n.* a warlike tribe of Indians of South America.

Jim Crow car, a street car, or railroad coach, set apart for the exclusive use of colored persons.

jipijapa (hē-pē-hä'pä), *n.* a South American plant the leaves of which are extensively used in the manufacture of the best Panama hats; a Panama hat made from these leaves: after a town of this name in Eucador.

jitters (jĭt'ẽrz), *n.* a dizzy or half-sick feeling experienced by some persons when ascending in elevators, or at the top, or on the roof, of high buildings; a nervous state caused by fear, or dread, or the anticipation of evil or misfortune.

jivatma (jē-vät'mȧ), *n.* in theosophy, the mind, soul, or spirit; the intellectual part of the ego.

Joab (jō'ăb), *n.* the nephew of King David, and commander-in-chief of his armies: he was slain at the altar by order of Solomon for taking part in the rebellion of Adonijah. See I. *Kings* ii:28-34.

Joan (jōn), *n.* a mythical female pope who, according to one of various legends, was of English descent, went to Rome, donned male attire, studied for the priesthood, was ordained, rose to be a cardinal, was elected pope in 855 with the title of John VIII, and ruled three years. In 1647, a French Calvinist, David Blondel, pronounced the story a fraud; however, it was not until 1863 that it was finally disposed of and metaphorically buried, by Johann Josef Ignaz Döllinger, a German Old Catholic theologian. In recent years several have tried to resurrect it, but with no success.

Joan of Arc, the heroine of France, historically known as the Maid of Orleans. Believing she heard heavenly voices, she became convinced God was calling her to liberate France from the English. She donned a suit of white armor, mounted a black charger, and led an army of 6,000 men to the siege of Orleans; after 14 days fighting, the English were forced to retreat, and Charles II was crowned king. In the last of her campaigns, Joan was taken by the Burgundians, who turned her over to the English. She was imprisoned at Ronen, condemned as a heretic, and, finally, burned at the stake May 30, 1431, in her 19th year. The Church canonized her 1920 during the popedom of Benedict XV.

job-lot, a miscellaneous, low-priced assortment of goods, usually sold in the lump.

jodhpurs (jod'pōōrz), *n.* close-fitting riding breeches: after Jodhpur, a native state of the province of Rajputana, in northwestern India.

John the Baptist (băp'tĭst), in Biblical literature, the son of Zacharias and Elizabeth, cousin of the Virgin Mary, and forerunner of Jesus Christ; he preached repentance, predicting the Kingdom of God was at hand, and baptized many in the Jordan, among them Jesus; he censured Herod Antipas for espousing Herodias, was thrown into prison, and finally beheaded at the request of Salome, the dancing daughter of Herodias. See *Matt.* xiv.

joint liability (joint lī-ȧ-bil'ĭ-tĭ), the state of being legally responsible with co-partners for contracts, losses, expenses, debts, etc.

joint ownership (ōn'ẽr-ship), ownership of property in common with two or more persons.

Joseph (jō'zef), *n.* in the Old Testament, a Hebrew patriarch, the favorite son of Jacob who gave him "a coat of many colors," and whom his brothers sold into slavery in Egypt —*Gen.* xxx to l.; in the New Testament, the husband of Mary the Mother of Christ, a lowly carpenter of Nazareth. See *Matt.* i:19.

Joshua (jŏsh'ū-ȧ), *n.* in Biblical literature, the son of Nun; he succeeded Moses as leader of the Israelites, whom he conducted into the land of Canaan; a Book of the Old Testament.

josser (jŏs'ẽr), *n.* [Slang], a foolish fellow; a simpleton.

jour gras (zhōōr grä'), [Fr.], a fast day on which the Church permits flesh-meat to be eaten: literally, a fat day.

jovite (jō'vīt), *n.* a high explosive, made up of nitro compounds and sodium nitrate.

joy-stick (-stĭk), *n.* the lever that operates the elevating planes of an aeroplane.

Jubaea (jōō-bē'ȧ), *n.* a genus of palms, native to Chili, having pinnate leaves, and producing one-seeded fruit: the coquita palm is typical.

Judge Lynch (linch), the personification of lynch law which, in southern U. S., is the act of punishing a person accused of, or guilty of, crime, without due process of established or constitutional law: the term is said to be derived from a traditional Virginian, named Lynch, who took the law into his own hands.

Jukes (jōōks), *n.pl.* fictitious name for the descendants of a family that early settled in N. Y. State, nearly all of whom have been morons, degenerates and criminals. The record begins with the marriage of two sons of Max, a Dutch backswoodsman, to two sisters, known as the *Jukes sisters.* One of these women, Margaret, has been styled "the mother of criminals"; some 1200 of the descendants of these two women were investigated, and of these, 150 were criminals of one kind or another, 310 were supported at public expense, and most of the remainder were diseased, licentious, or morally depraved; in 75 years, the Jukes family, in all, cost the State almost $1,500,000. The Jukes are often contrasted with the Edwards family, the descendants of the Rev. Jonathan Edwards (1703-1758), all of whom have been good and useful citizens, many of them rising to high eminence in Church and State.

Julian the Apostate (jōōl'yăn, ȧ-pŏs'tāt), Roman Emperor, nephew of Constantine the Great. Brought up a Christian, he apostatized to paganism, and began to persecute all Christians under his sway,—he tried to bribe some to become pagans; he was indulgent to Jews, and attempted to rebuild the Temple at

Jerusalem, so as to falsify the prophecy of Christ, but his plan failed; he was killed (363 A. D.), in an expedition against the Persians.

jumbuk (jum'buk), *n.* in Australia, a sheep: so called by the aborigines and bushmen.

June beetle (jo͞on bē't'l), a large brown beetle of northern U. S.: so called because it begins to fly about June 1.

jungftak (jŭngf' tăk), *n.* a fabled Persian bird, the male of which had only one wing, on the right side, and the female only one wing, on the left side; instead of the missing wings, the male had a hook of bone, and the female an eyelet of bone, and it was by uniting hook and eye that they were enabled to fly,—each, when alone, had to remain on the ground.

junior college (jo͞on'yẽr kol'ej), a college in which but a two-years' course in regular college work is given.

junior high school (hī sko͞ol), a school in which the course of instruction covers the 7th and 8th grades of grammar school, with the first year of regular high school.

justifiable homicide (jŭs-tĭ-fī'ȧ-b'l hŏm'ĭ-sīd), the killing of a person when the act is absolutely necessary to prevent murder, or the commission of some other serious crime; the killing of a criminal by an officer of the law to prevent the former's escape, or to protect the latter from death or violence.

juvenile delinquency (jo͞o'vĕ-nĭl dĕ-lĭng'kwĕn-sĭ), the commission by children, under sixteen years old, of acts that would be punishable as crimes, if perpetrated by persons over that age, in other words, by adults. In most of the States, boys and girls under 16, are classed as delinquents, who are deemed incorrigible, or who associate with depraved or vicious persons older than themselves, or who frequent resorts of unsavory reputation.

juzail (jū-zāl') *n.* a long-barreled, heavy Afghan gun.

K

kabaragoya (kä-bä-rä-gō'yä), *n.* a large aquatic lizard of the Malay archipelago: esteemed as a food by the natives.

kabaite (kăb'ȧ-īt), *n.* hydrocarbon found in meteorites.

Kadarite (kăd'ȧ-rīt), *n.* one of a sect of Mohammedans who assert the power of free will.

kadikane (kä-dĕ-kä'nĕ), *n.* broom corn millet.

kadischi (kä-dĭsh'ĭ), *n.* a mixed breed of Arabian horses.

kahuna (kä-ho͞o'nä), *n.* in the Hawaiian Islands, a shaman or medicine man.

kaik (kä'ĭk), *n.* in New Zealand, a village or community made up of Maoris exclusively.

kainozoölogy (kī-nō-zō-ŏl'ō-ji), *n.* the zoölogy of present-day, or existing animals.

kaiserdom (kī'zẽr-dŭm), *n.* the dominion, jurisdiction, or office of a kaiser.

Kaiserin (-ĭn), *n.* the wife of a Kaiser; an Empress.

kaiserism (-izm), *n.* any arbitrary rule or domination, such as that ascribed to the former Emperor of Germany, William II.

kajugaru (kä-yo͞o-gä'ro͞o), *n.* a tree of the Malayan archipelago, valued for its hard wood.

kakawahie (kä'kä-wä-hē'ā), *n.* a bird of a brilliant scarlet plumage, found on the Island of Molokai, one of the Hawaiian group.

kakidrosis (kăk-ĭ-drō'sĭs), *n.* a heavy secretion of sweat, having a very strong disagreeable odor: usual from fat persons who take little or no exercise.

kakogenesis (kăk-ō-jĕn-'ĕ-sĭs), *n.* a defective or abnormal formation, as a monstrosity; also, incapacity of animals of the same genus, but different species, to produce a hybrid.

kala-azar (kä'lä-zär'), *n.* a virulent type of malaria, prevalent in Assam and other parts of India, in which the skin assumes a dark hue, for which reason, it is also called the *black sickness*: it is very infectious.

kalinite (kăl'ĭ-nīt), *n.* common alum, as found in the natural state.

kaliege, see *kaleege* main vocabulary.

kamarezite (kă-mä'rĕ-zīt), *n.* a hydrated basic copper sulphate.

kangaroo closure (kang-ä-ro͞o' klō'zhŭr), [Slang, Eng.], a parliamentary plan, adopted by a chairman or speaker to shorten, or end, a debate or discussion, by limiting consideration of the subject to only a few of its leading features.

kangaroo court (kōrt), a petty local court, presided over by a mayor and justices of the peace, whose fees are contingent on the fines paid by defendants found guilty of trivial transgressions of the law.

kangarooer (-ro͞o'ẽr), *n.* in Australia, one of a party mounted on horseback who hunt kangaroos for sport.

Kang Teh (tā), official title of Henry Pu-yi, former Manchu boy-emperor of China, since he was called to head the government of the State of *Manchukuo*, formed 1932-33 with Japanese aid.

Kansas (kăn'zȧs), *n.* a State of the U. S., the Sunflower State; from an Indian term, meaning "Smoky Water."

kapa (kä'pä), *n.* tapa cloth, made from the bark of the paper mulberry, as worn by native Hawaiians and Polynesians.

kappa (kăp'ȧ), *n.* the tenth letter of the Greek alphabet, corresponding to English *k*.

karakul (kä-rȧ-ko͞ol'), *n.* a fine grade of astrakhan.

karao (kȧ-rä'ō), *n.* in India, the marriage of a widow to a brother of her deceased husband.

Karoo system (kȧ-ro͞o' sis'tĕm), a large series of sandstones and shales in South Africa, which includes the Permian and Triassic of that country.

karri (kă'rĭ), *n.* a giant gum tree of Western Australia that yields a hard, red wood, much used for paving blocks: this tree should not be confounded with the kauri tree which is a giant pine of New Zealand, and also grows in several parts of Australia.

karsivan (kär'si-vän), *n.* in England, the name given to the blood specific which, in America, is called salvarsan; "606."

kashima (kăsh'ĭ-mȧ), *n.* an igloo or house which the Eskimos use as a common assembly place or meeting room; also called *kashga*.

katabasis (kȧ-tăb'ȧ-sis), *n.pl.* -ses (-sēz). [Gr.], literally, a going down; the return march of the Greek auxiliaries of the Anabasis; hence, a return from an expedition; a retreat.

katabatic (kăt-ȧ-băt'ik), *adj.* in meteorology, pertaining to a downward motion of the air, due to surface cooling.

katamorphism (-mŏr'fiz'm), *n.* the breaking down of rocks by chemical or mechanical process: the opposite of *anamorphism*.

katharsis (kȧ'thär'sis), *n.* same as catharsis; a purgation; in philosophy, a word, which has caused much discussion and comment, as it is hard to determine the meaning, though it is directly based on the Greek verb *kathairein*, to cleanse, and consequently, the natural inference is, that it signifies a cleansing or purification. Aristotle used it in his definition of tragedy; he seems to have held, that 'tragedy purifies the spectator by showing him how his feelings and convictions will result when carried out.' In regard to the effects of tragedy on the spectator, he writes: "Through pity and fear working a *purification* of these emotions."

Kathleen Mavourneen (mȧ-vŭr-nyēn'), literally, Catherine, my darling,—the title of a once famous Irish song, still rendered in country districts of Ireland.

katuka (kȧ-to͞o'kȧ), *n.* a venomous viperine snake of India and Ceylon.

kaus (kous), *n.* a southeast wind that blows off the Persian Gulf.

K-boat (-bōt), *n.* a British submarine.

keena (kē'nȧ), *n.* a tree of India that yields a hard, light-wood, much used for spars; the poon tree.

keener (kēn'ẽr), *n.* in Ireland, a professional mourner at a wake or funeral, who simulates sorrow by weeping and wailing.

keffel (kĕf''l), *n.* in Northern Ireland, and Scotland, an old, done-out work-horse.

Kehama (kĕ-hä'mȧ), *n.* in Southey's "Curse of Kehama," an Indian rajah who, after a long tyranny on earth, was sent to Pandalon (Hell) where, in order to obtain domination, he drank the cup of immortality, but instead of the immortality of *life* he drank the immortality of *death* and was compelled to become one of the four props that support the throne of Yamen (Pluto): his curse, instead of withering, benefited those who incurred it.

kelene (kĕ-lēn'), *n.* ethyl chloride.

kelep (kĕl'ĕp), *n.* a stinging ant of Central America; as a destroyer of the boll weevil it has been introduced into the cotton fields of southern U. S.

Kelvin scale (kĕl'vĭn skāl), the absolute scale of temperature: after William Thomson, first Baron Kelvin (1824-1907), professor of physics, Glasgow University.

kenotron (kĕn'ō-trŏn), *n.* a vacuum discharge tube, having an incandescent filament as cathode, with a tungsten anode.

Kensington (kĕn'zĭng-tŭn), *n.* a metropolitan borough on the west side of London, noted for its fine residences and social advantages.

Kensington Gardens (gär'd'nz), a public park in London, covering about 375 acres, world-famous for its scenic beauty; it has many attractions, among them the Sunken Garden, the Broad Walk, and the Albert Memorial: it lies between Westminster Palace and Hyde Park: adjacent is South Kensington, the location of the Victoria and Albert Museum, the Natural History Museum, the Indian Museum, the Imperial Institute, and the Royal College of Science and Art.

Kentia (kĕn'ti-ȧ), *n.* a small genus of Australian palms, with pinnate leaves; [k-], any of several well-known small house palms, some of which are referred to this genus.

Kentucky (kĕn-tŭk'ĭ), *n.* a State of the U. S., the Blue Grass State; from an Indian term, signifying "At the Head of the River."

Ker (kẽr), *n.* in Greek legend, a ghost; an avenging spirit; man's fate personified as a spirit.

keratalgia (kĕr-ȧ-tăl'ji-ȧ), *n.* pain in the cornea.

keratectasia (-tĕk-tā'zhĭ-ȧ), *n.* protrusion of the cornea.

keratectomy (-tĕk'tō-mĭ), *n.* excision of the whole, or part, of the cornea.

keratolysis (-tŏl'ĭ-sis), *n.* a peeling or scaling off of the horny layer of the skin.

keratosis (-tō'sis), *n.* a condition in which the skin becomes covered with horny excrescences.

keratotomy (-tot'ō-mi), *n.* incision of the cornea.

Keraunia (kĕ-rō'nĭ-ȧ), *n.* in Greek mythology, an earth Goddess, mother of Dionysus by Zeus, who asked the latter to permit her to see him in his majesty; her request was granted and his thunders and lightnings destroyed her: in Greek, the word, literally, means thunder-stricken.

kerion (kē'ri-ŏn), *n.* a disease of the scalp caused by parasites.

kerril (kĕr'ĭl), *n.* a water snake found along the shores of southern Asia.

kerrite (kĕ-rīt'), *n.* a variety of mica, of a yellowish-green color.

Kerry, a small, black cow, one of a breed of Irish cattle highly prized for the richness of their milk and for the excellent butter it produces: from the County Kerry, Ireland, famous for these cattle, and where they thrive on the scant pasture of its poor soil, and almost barren hills.

ketonuria (kĕt-ō-nū'ri-ȧ), *n.* the presence of ketone bodies in the urine.

kettle of fish (ket''l), muddle; confusion; miscarriage; disappointment; the expression is a corruption of *kiddle of fish*, a kiddle being a basket set in the opening of a weir for catching fish, and often the fish escape, causing confusion and disappointment.

Kew (kū), *n.* a suburb of London, on the Thames, some 7 miles up the river from Hyde Park corner.

Kew Gardens (gär'd'nz), formerly, the name of the now Royal Botanical Gardens, at Kew, containing the largest and finest collection of plants in the world: adjacent to the Gardens is Richmond Park, in which is the Kew Observatory.

Khalifat (kä'lĭ-făt), *n.* formerly, the spiritual headship of Islam, as represented by, or embodied in, the Sultan of Turkey, at Istanbul, formerly Constantinople.

khediviate (kĕ-dē'vĭ-āt), *n.* the government, jurisdiction, power, or position of a khedive.

Khmer (k'mĕr), *n.* one of a tall native race of Cambodia, supposed by some to have Dravidian affinities, by others, as a Mongoloid race, mixed with Malay, or Hindu, blood.

kick, *n.* see main vocabulary.

kick (kĭk), *n.* [Slang] something quick in action or effect, somewhat suggestive of a kick; immediate effect of strong liquor; a side-partner; a pal; aclose friend; a pants-pocket; any pocket in which one carries money or valuables.

kiddies (kĭd'ĭz), *n.pl.* [Slang], children: plural of *kid*.

kike (kīk), *n.* [Slang] opprobrious name for a Jew; a Yid.

kiley (kī'lĭ), *n.* in Western Australia, the native name for a boomerang.

Kilkenny cats (kil-ken'i kats), according to legend, two cats of County Kilkenny, Ireland, that fought so desperately to a finish, nothing but their tails were left; hence applied to persons who fight, quarrel, or contend until both sides are irretrievably ruined.

Kilkenny quarrel (kwor'el), a quarrel, dispute, or disagreement long continued, in which both parties finally lose all worth having.

killadar (kĭl'ȧ-där), *n.* in India, the governor or commandant of a fortress.

kilocycle (kĭl'ō-sī-k'l), a measurement of frequency in electricity and radio, denoting 1,000 cycles per second, a cycle being the interval between two impulses or waves in sequence: the rapidity of these impulses or waves in succession is what is termed frequency.

kiltie (kĭl'tĭ), *n.* a Scottish Highland soldier: the distinctive uniforms of Scottish soldiers in the British service are still kilts, with pendant sporrans.

kinema (kĭn'ĕ-mȧ), *n.* cinema: so spelt in England and Ireland.

King Charles Spaniel (chärlz span'yel), one of a breed of English toy dogs, kept as a household pet; also known as black-and-tan on account of its coloring.

king cobra (kō'brä), a very large and extremely venomous snake of southeastern Asia, allied to the true cobra of India: many reach a length of 15 feet.

king of swat (swŏt), [Slang], a title conferred on George Herman ("Babe") Ruth, professional baseball player: also, called the *home run king*.

kiosk, *n.* see main vocabulary.
kiosk (kĭ-ŏsk′), *n.* a structure covering the entrance to a subway or underground railroad; a light, open-air arrangement, erected as for a news stand, band stand, fruit stand, or the like.
kippeen (kĭ-pēn), *n.* in Ireland, a light, but tough, walking-stick; an ash-plant.
kitchen police (kich′ĕn pŏ-lēs′), in the army, men detailed to help the cook: they scrub, clean, carry, wait on table, etc.
kite, *n.* see main vocabulary.
kite (kīt), *n.* in aviation, a heavier than air machine, depending for propulsion on a towline pull sustained by wind force.
Kiwanian (kĭ-wä′nĭ-ăn), *n.* a member of Kiwanis Club.
Kiwanis Club (-wä′nis klŭb), one of many such clubs in the U. S. and Canada, the first of which was organized in Detroit, in 1915: the Clubs, are mostly composed of business men whose principles are square dealing, and living up to the precept inculcated by the Golden Rule, not only in business affairs but also in private, social and civic relationship.
kiyi (kī′yī), *n.* [Colloq.], the howl or yelp of a dog: *v.i.* to howl or yelp, as a dog.
kleinite (klī′nīt), *n.* natural mercury-aluminum chloride.
Klieg light (klēg līt), a very strong electric light: mostly used in the taking of moving pictures.
Knights of Columbus (nīts, ko-lum′bus), a fraternal and benevolent body of Catholic men, organized by the Rev. J. C. McGinley at New Haven, Conn., 1882, the object of which is to promote Catholic interests and foster good feeling between all creeds and classes.
kosher (kō′shĕr), *adj.* [Heb.] clean; denoting a shop or store where food, considered clean by Jews, is sold or obtained: *n.* food ceremonially clean according to Jewish ritual, especially the meat of animals slaughtered in conformity with Jewish laws and traditions.
Kulturkampf (kōōl-tōōr′kämpf), *n.* the struggle between the R. C. Church and the former German government, over the latter's efforts to control schools, educational establishments and the appointments of churchmen in the interests of centralization. The struggle began in 1873 when the socalled *May Laws* were passed, aiming at the regulation of the clergy: these laws were practically nullified from 1880 to 1887.
kyphosis (kī-fō-sis), *n.* angular curvature of the spine: the deformity of the humpbacked.
kyphotic (-fŏt′ik), *adj.* pertaining to humpback, or those so afflicted.

L

lachrymator (lăk′ri-mā′tĕr), *n.* a tear-producing substance: anything that causes tears.
lactase (lăk′tās), *n.* an enzyme, found in some yeasts, that changes lactose into glucose in an animal body.
Lady Bountiful (boun′ti-fōōl), any lady in a community who is good, generous, and charitable, especially to the poor and sick: after a country gentlewoman in Farquhar's comedy, "The Beaux' Stratagem."
Lady of Babylon (băb′ĭ-lŏn), the R. C. Church: opprobriously so called in reference to an interpretation of the 'scarlet woman' (*Rev.* xvii), as given by some Protestants.
lady of pleasure (plĕzh′ŭr), a courtesan; mistress; prostitute.
Laetare Medal (lē-tā′rē mĕd′al), a medal conferred once a year on some distinguished Roman Catholic by the University of Notre Dame, South Bend, Indiana.
Lais (lā′ĭs), *n.* the most famous, or rather, most infamous hetæra of ancient Greece, said to have been the most beautiful woman of her age; she lived in Corinth: the filthy Diogenes the Cynic was one of her favorites, but she ignored Demosthenes the Orator.
laitance (lā-tangs′), *n.* [Fr.], a jelly-like fluid that exudes from cement under water.
Lake of the Cat, name given to Lake Erie by the first white men who discovered it.
Lake of the Clouds (kloudz), a lake in New Hampshire about 6,000 feet above sea level.
Lake State (lāk stāt), popular name for State of Michigan, which borders on Lakes Huron, Erie, Michigan, and Superior.
Lakshmi (lăks′mĭ), *n.* in Hindu mythology, the wife of Vishnu, and goddess of good luck.
Lammas floods (flŭdz), torrential rain-storms which usually occur in the British Isles around August 1.
lame ducks (lām dŭks), in the U. S. Congress, members defeated for reëlection, who hold office until the term expires.
landing chassis (shă′sē), the under formations of an aeroplane or aircraft, considered as a whole, consisting of wheels, struts, skids, and wires.
landing ground, a place prepared, or suitable, for the landing of an aëroplane or aircraft.
land lies (līz), a phrase generally used with the interrogative adverb *how*, signifying state, conditions, circumstances, expectations, as all depends upon *how the land lies*, that is, all depends upon the circumstances or conditions, etc.
Land o' Cakes (kāks), Scotland: because oatmeal cakes are the favorite bread.
Land of Beulah (bū′lȧ), a land of rest and quiet: symbolical of peace of mind: see Bunyan's "Pilgrim's Progress."
Land of Flowers (flou′ĕrz), Florida: named by Ponce de Leon, 1512.
Land of Promise (prŏm′is), Canaan, to the Israelites; figuratively, Heaven, to be reached by crossing the Jordan of death; any expected land or haven of contentment and peace.
Land of the Rose (rōz), England, of which the rose is the national emblem.
Land of the Shamrock (shăm′rŏk), Ireland, of which the shamrock is the emblem.
Land of the Thistle (this″l), Scotland, of which the thistle is the emblem.
landplane (-plān), *n.* an aircraft designed to ascend from, and light on, solid earth; an ordinary aëroplane.
Land's End, the most westerly point in England, rising from granite cliffs in Cornwall, about 75 feet high.
Langley plane (lăng′li), an American bombing plane.
Latvian (lat′vi-ăn), *adj.* pertaining to Latvia, an independent republic, formerly included in the Baltic provinces of the then Russian Empire.
laubanite (lô′băn-īt), *n.* a hydrous silicate of calcium and aluminum, snow-white in color.
lavaliere (lăv-ȧ-lēr′), *n.* a chain worn around the neck as an ornament, with a pendant or drop attached.
lavrovite (lăv′rŏ-vīt), *n.* pyroxene of a greenish color, due to the presence in it of vanadium.
League of Nations (lēg, nā′shŭnz), an association of nations, organized in 1920, in accordance with a covenant of the Peace Conference at Paris, the object being prevention of war by limitation of armament, and arbitration.
learned blacksmith (lĕrnd blak′smith), Elihu Burritt (1810-1879), distinguished American linguist, who began his career as a blacksmith in Connecticut.
leery (lēr′i), *adj.* [Slang], vulgar; low; mean; also, cunning; suspicious.
legal tender (lē′gal ten′dĕr), all money that must be accepted for goods purchased, and also for the discharge of just debts: treasury notes are legal tender to unlimited amounts, silver coins up to $10, and pennies up to 25c.
legionnaire (lē-jŭn-âr′), *n.* member of a legion: especially in the U. S., a soldier of the American Legion who served in the World War.
Legion of Honor (on′ĕr), a French order of merit instituted by Napoleon Bonaparte in 1802 to honor performers of distinguished service to France, whether military or civil: the emblem is a white enameled 5-ray star, having on one side a symbol of the republic, and two flags on the obverse: it is worn with a red ribbon on the left breast.
Legree (lē-grē′), *n.* in "Uncle Tom's Cabin," a character typifying the cruel, brutal, ruthless slave dealer; hence, one who is tyrannical and cruel; a hard taskmaster.
lei (lā′ĭ), *n.pl. leis.* in the Hawaiian Islands, a garland or wreath of flowers and leaves: natives place *leis* around the necks of incoming visitors and tourists, while welcoming them with cries of "Aloha." Any ornamental headdress worn by native Hawaiians.
Leibnitzianism (līp-nĭt′si-ăn-iz′m), *n*] the philosophy of Gottfried Wilhelm von Leibnitz or Liebniz (1646-1716), German philosopher, scholar, scientist and mathematician who, independent of Newton, discovered the infinitesimal calculus, a stroke of genius which stamped him the foremost mathematician of the age. It is on his philosophy, however, that his fame rests. He was a very deep student of the Aristotelian philosophy, particularly the entelechy of the little Stagirite, which gave him the idea of his own monads. Leibnitz maintained that all beings are monads, or groups of monads, that is, self-active beings or substances, each in its own activity illustrating or reflecting the activity of the entire universe. The monads of Leibnitz are of five different degrees, the highest being those who have attained thought—these are human souls; the next are animals—they have sense perception and locomotion; the third are plants—they are capable of reproduction; the fourth are minerals, which have crystallization, and below these are elements that have chemical affinities. The monads who have attained thought, the human souls, are "members of the City of God."
leiodermatous (lī-o-der′mȧ-tŭs), *adj.* denoting a smooth glossy skin.
leiodermia (lī-ŏ-der′mi-ȧ), *n.* a disease in which the skin becomes glossy, as if polished.
Leningrad (len′in-gräd), *n.* the former capital of the Russian empire on the delta of the River Neva, at the head of the gulf of Finland, founded by Peter the Great, 1703. It was known as St. Petersburg until 1914, when, on account of its German origin, it was changed to Petrograd. After the death of Lenin, in 1924, it was again changed to Leningrad; pop. (1933), 2,810,375.
Leninism (lĕn′in-ĭzm), *n.* Russian Communism as developed from Bolshevism by the teachings and policies of Vladimir Ilich Ulianor, better known as Nikolay Lenin; especially, the dictatorship of the protelariat, as later modified by the New Economic Policy. **Leninist, Leninite.**
leno (lē′nō), *n.* a fabric, in the manufacture of which, some of the warp ends are twisted so as to give an open-work effect.
leprechaun (lĕp-rĕ-chŏn′), *n.* in Irish folklore, a goblin conceived as a wrinkled old man; the fairy shoemaker who, if caught, gives untold wealth to his captor for liberation, but who is seldom, if ever, caught.
leprosarium (lĕp′rŏ-sā′rĭ-ŭm), *n.* an asylum or retreat for lepers.
leptochroa (lep-tŏk′rō-ȧ), *n.* the condition of having a very thin, delicate skin.
leptodermatous (-dĕr′mȧ-tŭs), *adj.* thin-skinned.
leptodermic (′mĭk), *adj.* same as leptodermatous.
leptophonia (-fō′nĭ-ȧ), *n.* weakness of voice.
Lesbianism (lez′bĭ-ăn-izm), unnatural sex relation between one woman and another woman; tribadism: Sapphism; the sin of Sappho.
lesbian love, the same as Lesbianism.
Lesghians (les′gĭ-ănz), *n.pl.* the hardy mountain people of Daghestan on the Eastern slopes of the Caucasian range of mountains in Soviet Russia: they are not of high culture, but they are good weavers.
leuconychia (lū-kŏ-nik′i-ȧ), *n.* white spots under the nails.
leucopenia (-pē′ni-ȧ), *n.* a condition in which there is a reduced number of leucocytes in the blood.
leucoplakia (-plā′ki-ȧ), *n.* a diseased condition characterized by white spots on the tongue.
levanter (le-văn′tĕr), *n.* a strong easterly wind blowing from the Mediterranean.
leveche (le-vā′chā), *n.* a hot, dry, southerly wind blowing from the southeast coast of Spain.
Leviathan of Literature (lē-vī′ȧ-thăn, lĭt′ĕr-ȧ-tūr) Dr. Samuel Johnson (1709-1784), lexicographer.
levoversion (lē-vŏ-ver′shŭn), *n.* the turning of both eyes to the left.
levulosuria (lĕv-ū-lŏ-sū′rĭ-ȧ), *n.* the presence of levulose in the urine.
Libby Prison (lĭb′ĭ prĭz″n), a notorious prison of Civil War days, at Richmond, Va., where, sometimes, over 1,000 Federal prisoners were confined under unsanitary conditions, which resulted in a heavy mortality.
Liberty Bell (lĭb′ĕr-ti bĕl), a bell in Independence Hall, Philadelphia, rung on July 8, 1776 to announce the proclamation of the Declaration of Independence, adopted four days previously. It cracked in 1835, on the anniversary of its first ringing, while being tolled for the funeral of Chief Justice Marshall.
libido (lĭb′ĭ-dō), *n.* strong sexual urge or desire.
Lick Observatory (ŏb-zer′vȧ-tō-ri), a building, devoted to astronomical purposes, containing large telescope and other instruments, on the summit of Mt. Hamilton, 30 miles east of San Jose, California, donated by James Lick (1796-1876) to the University of California, at a cost of more than $700,000 for construction and equipment.
Light Horse Harry, a popular sobriquet for General Henry Lee (1756-1818), a cavalry officer in the American Revolution, famous for his marches through the Carolinas.
Light of the Age, Rabbi Moses ben Maimon (1135-1204), of Cordova, Spain, more generally known as Maimonides, the philosopher.
Light of the World, to Christians, Christ, the Savior; a famous painting by W. Holman Hunt (1827-1910), English artist, representing Christ, thorn-crowned, and with a lantern pending from his left hand.
Limerick (lĭm′ĕr-ĭk), *n.* a nonsense poem, consisting of five anapæstic lines, of which the first, second, and fifth are of three feet, and rime, while the third and fourth lines are of two feet and rime: after Limerick, a county and city, of the Irish Free State.
limnobiology (lĭm-nŏ-bī-ŏl′ŏ-ji), *n.* the branch of biology that treats of the life found in fresh water.
limnobios (-bī′ŏs), *n.* the collective animal and plant life of fresh water.
limnology (lĭm-nŏl′ŏ-ji), *n.* the scientific study of fresh water pools, ponds, lakes, rivers, etc. and whatever is found in these waters.
Lincoln Memorial (ling′kun mē-mō′rĭ-ăl), a building erected in Potomac Park, Washington, D. C., at a cost of $2,594,000, to honor

and commemorate Abraham Lincoln; it was begun on Lincoln's birthday, 1914: it consists of one great, oblong-shaped hall surrounded by a Doric colonnade.

Lincoln's Inn, an incorporated law society, of London, which, with the Inner and Middle Temples, and Gray's Inn, has the sole right to admit and call law students to the English bar.

lipoid (lĭp'oid), *adj.* resembling fat: *n.* a substance resembling the fats proper, as cholesterin.

lipolysis (lĭ-pol'i-sĭs), *n.* decomposition of fat.

lipophrenia (lĭp-ō-frē'nĭ-å), *n.* deficiency of the mental powers.

lipstick (lĭp'stik), *n.* rouge compressed to the form of a short pencil, used by females to heighten the color of the lips.

lipuria (lĭ-pū'rĭ-å), *n.* the presence of fat in the urine.

Little Church around the Corner, the Protestant Episcopal Church of the Transfiguration on East 29th street, near Fifth Avenue, New York City, the Mecca and magnet of religious life among theatrical folk: often called the Actors' Church.

Little Entente (äng'tängt'), the union of Czecho-Slovakia, Rumania, and Jugo-Slavia in 1920.

Little Giant (jī'ant), a popular sobriquet conferred on Stephen A. Douglas (1813-1861), U. S. Senator from Illinois: in allusion to his small body and large intellect.

Little Mac (mĕk), General George B. McClellan (1826-1885), Union Commander in the Civil War: because of his short stature and great popularity.

Little Magician (må-jĭsh'ăn), sobriquet of Martin Van Buren (1782-1862), eighth President of the U. S. (1837-1841), in allusion to his supposed political sagacity.

Little Nell, in "The Old Curiosity Shop" by Dickens, a lovable little girl who, though living amid scense of sordidness, wretchedness, misery, and crime, still preserves the purity and innocence of her character.

Little Red Riding-hood, in a famous nursery tale, a little girl in a red cloak who, when carrying food to her sick grandmother, meets a wolf to whom she talks; the wolf runs ahead, kills the old woman, eats her, and takes her place in bed; when the little girl arrives, she thinks the big bad wolf is her grandmother; he eats her, too, but a hunter chances to pass, who rips open the wolf, and out step Little Red Riding-Hood and her grandmother, well and happy.

Little Rhody (rŏd'i), Rhode Island, the smallest State of the U. S.

livedo (lĭv'e-dō), *n.* a black-and-blue mark or spot.

live load (līv lōd), the weight upon a structure exclusive of its own weight; a load of varying strain.

live oak (ōk), an evergreen oak of southern U. S. with glossy leaves, and yielding a hard, heavy wood.

live wire (wīr), [Slang], a person of keenness and activity; one who keeps abreast of the times and well-posted on current events; an alert business man; a hustler.

lobstick (lŏb'stĭk), *n.* in Canada, a tree denuded of the lower branches, and having the top ones trained to point the way in several directions.

loganberry (lō'găn-bĕr'ĭ), *n.* a hybrid fruit produced from a graft of a blackberry bush and a raspberry bush.

loggy (lŏg'i), *adj.* in aviation, denoting the rocking motion of an airplane.

logion (log'i-on), *n.pl.* LOGIA (-å), a maxim or saying attributed to a religious leader or teacher; in the plural [L-], the sayings supposed to have been uttered by Jesus, including the Agrapha.

London Bridge (brĭj), of several bridges that spanned the Thames, the bridge of song and story, which was a structure of solid stone, about half-a-mile from the Tower, completed in 1209; there were houses on either side—these were removed in 1756, and the bridge itself was pulled down in 1832: this was the bridge of the nursery rhyme, "London Bridge is falling down, falling down."

Londoner (lŭn'dŭn-ēr), *n.* a native, or resident, of London.

Londonese (-ēz'), *adj.* pertaining to London: *n.* the speech of London; cockney.

Lone Star State (lōn stär stāt), appellation of the State of Texas: from the device on its coat-of-arms.

Lonjius (lŏn'ji-ŭs), *n.* the name of the Roman soldier who pierced the side of Christ with a spear, as the latter was about to expire on the Cross on Calvary.

Loo (lōō), *n.* an abbreviation for the Louvre in Paris; abbreviation for Woolloomooloo (wully-mully), formerly a suburb of, but now incorporated in, the city of Sydney, Australia.

loop, *n.* & *v.t.* see main vocabulary.

loop (lōōp), *n.* in aviation, an ǣrial stunt in which an airplane is made to perform a somewhat circular path in the plane of the longitudinal and normal axes.

Lord Chancellor (chăn'sĕl-ēr), the highest legal dignitary of the British government: he is adviser to the King and Parliament, and Keeper of the Great Seal.

Lord Chief Justice (jŭs'tĭs), the second highest law officer of the British government, next to the Lord Chancellor: he is head of the King's Bench Division of the High Court of Justice.

Lord Protector (prō-tek'tēr), title of Oliver Cromwell, as head of the British Commonwealth (1653-1658).

Lord's Prayer (prâr), the prayer taught by Jesus to his disciples, commonly called the "Our Father," English translation of the Latin, *Pater Noster.*

Lord's Supper (sŭp'ēr), the celebration of the Jewish Passover by Jesus and the twelve apostles, on the night before He was crucified: commemorated by Christians on Holy Thursday: the sacrament of Holy Communion or the Eucharist derives from this supper, in fact, the term is used as a synonym for the communion service in many Christian Churches.

Lost Battalion (bă-tăl'yŭn), a detachment of some 550 American troops, under the command of Major Charles W. Whittlesey, most of them belonging to the 308th Infantry of the 77th Division, who were surrounded by Germans in the Argonne forest for four days (Oct. 3-7, 1918), and thus cut off from the remainder of the Division during the battle of the Meuse-Argonne.

Lost Cause (kôz), the cause of the Southern Confederacy in the Civil War; the conflict began at Fort Sumter, Charleston, S. C., on April 12, 1861, and ended with the surrender of General Robert E. Lee at Appomattox, a village in Virginia, on April 26, 1865; hence, any cause or undertaking that is lost or defeated.

lost tribes (trībz), the Jews who seceded from the kingdom of Israel after the death of Solomon, and established a separate kingdom which lasted about 200 years, or until Sargon, King of Assyria swooped down upon them in 722 B. C. and carried them into captivity. What became of them is one of the riddles of history.

loud-speaker (loud-spē'kēr), *n.* in radio, one of various devices for increasing the volume of sound; an amplifying vacuum tube.

Louisiana (lōō-ē-zē-ăn'å), *n.* a State of the U. S., the Creole State; named in honor of Louis XIV of France.

Louisiana purchase (pûr'chas), the territory purchased by the U. S. from France in 1803, at a cost of $15,000,000; it covered a vast sweep of country, extending westward from the Mississippi to the Rockies, and northward from the Gulf of Mexico to Canada: at the time of the deal, Napoleon was First Consul in France, and Thomas Jefferson was president of the U. S.

Lourdes (lōōrd), *n.* a town in southern France, formerly famed for its castle, called "the key to the Pyrenees," but now better known as a resort for pilgrims who come from all parts of the world in April to visit a shrine of the Virgin in the expectation of being cured of physical ills: the shrine is on the spot where, it is claimed, the Blessed Virgin appeared to a peasant girl named Bernadotte.

Louvre (lōō'vēr), *n.* formerly, a royal palace of Paris, now a museum and national storehouse for treasures and rare articles brought from many lands; it contains famous paintings, statues, bronzes, and tapestries, being especially rich in antiques: additions have been made from time to time, so that the building is now, probably, the largest of its kind in the world, 1900 feet long, with a great Corinthian colonnade of the time of Louis XIV.

lowbrow (lō'brou), *n.* a person having a low forehead; [Slang] one of limited education, not interested in books or literature in general.

Loyal Order of Moose (loi'ăl, ôr'dēr, mōōs), a secret fraternal and beneficiary society, founded in 1888, at Louisville, Ky.

louvres (lōō'vērz), *n.pl.* metal, or wood, slots placed in the ventilating opening of a building.

luargol (lū-är'gŏl), *n.* a chemical preparation used in the treatment of syphilis.

luau (lōō-ou'), *n.* in the Hawaiian Islands, a native feast or banquet.

Lumber State (lŭm'bēr stāt), the State of Maine: on account of the large amount of lumber it supplies.

lumber-jack (-jak), *n.* in northwestern U. S., a workman engaged in lumbering; one who helps to float logs.

lumbricus (lŭm'brĭ-kŭs), *n.* [L], the common earthworm.

Lusitania (lū-si-tā'nĭ-å), *n.* name of an ancient region in southwest Europe to which Portugal now corresponds: name of a Cunard liner, torpedoed by a German submarine, off the south coast of Ireland, May 7, 1915. Some 1200 passengers were drowned, 115 of them American citizens, including Alfred G. Vanderbilt, Elbert Hubbard, and Charles Frohman.

Lynch law, see *Judge Lynch* above.

lypemania (lĭp-ĕ-mā'nĭ-å), *n.* profound melancholy; depressive insanity; great mental prostration.

lypothymia (lī-pō-thī'mĭ-å), *n.* same as lypemania.

M

MacAllum and Laughton extract (măk'ŏl'ŭm, lô'tŭn, ĕks'trăkt), an extract derived from the duodenum, the first portion of the small intestine: said to be much more effective than insulin in the treatment of diabetes: originally prepared, in 1932, by Drs. A. B. MacAllum and N. B. Laughton of the physiology department of the University of Western Ontario, London, Canada.

macroæsthesia (măk-rō-ĕs-thē'si-å), a state indicated by a false sensation that objects are much larger than they are.

macrobian (må-krō'bi-ăn), *adj.* long-lived.

macrocephalia (-sĕ-fā'li-å), **macrocephaly** (-sĕf'å-lĭ), *n.* abnormal or excessive size of the head: exemplified in a certain type of idiots.

macrography (må-krŏg'rå-fĭ), *n.* handwriting of very large size; usually indicative of some nervous disorder in the writer.

macromastia (-măs'ti-å), *n.* excessive development of the breasts.

macromelia (-mē'li-å), *n.* abnormal largeness of one or more members of the body.

macron (mā'krŏn), *n.* a short straight line over a vowel, to indicate long sound, as ō in gōld.

macropodia (-pō'dĭ-å), *n.* excessive largeness of the feet.

macropsy (măk'rŏp-si), *n.* vision in which things seem larger than they are: also *macropia.*

macroscelia (-sĕl'ĭ-å), *n.* abnormal growth of the legs.

macrosomia (măk-rō-sō'mi-å), *n.* abnormal largeness of the body.

Mad Anthony (ăn'tō-nĭ), a sobriquet of General Anthony Wayne (1745-1796), distinguished for military skill and dashing qualities as an officer in the War of the Revolution.

magneton (mag'nĕ-tŏn), *n.* the ultimate magnetic particle having polarity.

mahamari (må-hä-mä'rē), *n.* in India, the plague.

mahant (må-hănt'), *n.* in India, the head or superior of a native monastery.

mahar (må-här'), *n.* one of a very low caste, inhabiting Central India.

maharani (må-hä-rä'nē), *n.* in India, queen of a native state.

mahat (må-hăt'), *n.* in theosophy, the principle of universal intelligence.

mah jongg (mä jŏng), a Chinese game, dating back to the time of Confucius: it consists of a set of ivory tiles (136), divided into six suits—the honor suit, the four winds suit, the flowers and seasons suit, and three suits of bamboos, dots, and characters: very popular in U. S. 1920-1924.

maianthemum (mī-an'thĕ-mum), *n.* wild lily-of-the-valley; the Mayflower.

Maid of Orleans (mād, ôr-lā-äng'), Joan of Arc.

Maine (mān), *n.* a State of the U. S., the Pine Tree State; name signifies "The Main" or "Mainland."

Maine, a battleship of the U. S., destroyed in Havana harbor, on the night of February 15, 1898, with a loss of 250 lives: the sinking of this ship precipitated the Spanish-American War.

main stem (mān stĕm), the principal street of a town or city; specifically, (M- S-), Broadway, New York City, from 34th to 59th street.

maitre d'hotel (mā'tr' dō-tĕl'), [Fr.], literally, master of the house; the landlord or keeper of an hotel; a major-domo, butler, house-steward, or chief officer or servant in an hotel or house of entertainment.

major (mā'jēr), *v.i.* to specialize in, or make a chief study of, some particular subject during one's term at a school, college, or university.

Makassar (må-kăs'år), *n.* a district of Celebes; one of the half-civilized people of this district; their language: also, spelt *Macassar.*

Makassar oil, an oil originally obtained from Makassar, probably derived from the sandal-wood tree: it was much used in hair-dressing: now the term is applied to a substitute consisting of cocoanut oil, olive oil, or castor oil, highly perfumed.

makimaki (mä'ki-mä'ki), *n.* a puff fish widely distributed in both the Pacific and Indian oceans, the flesh of which is extremely poisonous.

malabonga (mä-lä-bong'å), *n.* a tree of the Philippines, resembling a laurel: it yields a light, red wood.

mallee bird (măl'ĕ bērd), a peculiar bird of Australia that inhabits the mallee scrubs: it forms the one species of the genus, Leipoa, the mound building megapodes, called mound-birds because they do not hatch their eggs, but scratch warm sand around them, thus forming a heap or mound, hence, the name; the plumage of the leipoa is ocellated, that is, it is covered with dots resembling little eyes, and these are of various colors: it is a plump bird, from two to two-and-a-half feet long, and has a little crest on top of the head.

malocclusion (măl-ŏ-klōō'shŭn), *n.* improper closure of the upper set of teeth upon the lower set.

mammalgia (mă-măl'ji-å), *n.* pain in the breast.

Mammoth Cave (măm'ŏth kāv), a huge cavern in Kentucky, convenient to the town of Glasgow, and about 80 miles southwest of Louisville: it has over 100 miles of passage-ways, avenues, windings, chambers, pits, domes, etc., and is traversed by several underground rivers, in which it, is said, there are blind fish: the main cave is 3 miles long, 50 to 200 feet wide and from 3 to 150 feet high: it attracts many tourists.

mampalon (măn'på-lŏn), *n.* a little web footed animal of the civet family, resembling an otter, found in the jungles of Borneo, Sumatra, and the Malay Peninsula: it is of a reddish-brown color and has a short tail.

Manchester ship canal (man'chĕs-tẽr ship kå-nal'), a canal 35 miles long connecting the city of Manchester, in Lancashire, England, with the Irish Sea: it has a minimum depth of 30 feet and width of 130 feet; cost 16,000,000 pounds ($80,000,000); opened in 1894.

Manchoukuo (măn-jō-kwō'), a state established in Manchuria, a division of Eastern China, in 1932, under Japanese influence: it includes the former provinces of Fengtien, Hielung-kiang, and Khinghan, with Jehol, formerly a province of Central Mongolia.

mancinism (măn'si-nĭzm), *n.* left-handedness.

mandate, *n.* see main vocabulary.

mandate, *n.* a commission granted by the League of Nations to a nation member of that League, for the establishment of a proper and responsible government over colonies lost by Germany as a result of the World War, or over other conquered territory inhabited by people not capable of developing its resources or bringing about satisfactory economic conditions.

manikinism (măn'ĭ-kĭn-ĭz'm), *n.* conduct or behaviour suggestive of what one expects from a manikin: pettiness of action; silly or puerile conduct.

man hunt (hŭnt), a hunt or search for a man or men, especially, for a criminal or criminals, or those accused of, or suspected of crime.

manhunter ('ẽr), *n.* one who leads, or takes part, in a man hunt; a detective; an investigator.

manjak (man'jăk), *n.* natural bitumen found in the Barbados or Lesser Antilles, West Indies.

Mann Act. See *White Slave Act* below.

Mantuan swan (man'tū-ăn swŏn), Vergil, the Roman poet, born at Mantua, Lombardy, Italy, 90 B. C., died 19 B. C.

Man Without a Country (kŭn'tri), a fictitious character named Philip Nolan, as portrayed by Edward Everett Hale in his story of this title.

marcel (mâr-sel'), *v.t.* to wave the hair in tiers: after the French hairdresser, M. Marcel.

marcel wave (wāv), a style of hairdressing in which the hair is first waved, then coiled in rows from the forehead up to a crowning pinnacle.

marchantia (mär-kăn'shi-ā), *n.* the most common and most widely distributed of the liver-worts.

mariposite (mär-i-pŏ-sīt'), *n.* a light-green variety of muscovite.

marquisette (mär'ki-zĕt'), *n.* a sheer cotton fabric, woven from a mercerized thread composed of two strands—it is more or less lustrous; also, a sheer light silk material, used for overdresses.

maru (må-rōō'), *n.* a word used in the names of Japanese vessels to distinguish them from warships and other craft: its application in this respect is obscure, as it is said to be derived from a Chinese character representing anything round. A standard Japanese dictionary defines it—"a circle, sphere, full, complete, all, whole."

Marvelous Boy (mär'vĕl-ŭs), Thomas Chatterton (1752-1770)—so called because of his remarkable literary precocity.

Mary (mā'ri), *n.* the Mother of Jesus, commonly called the Blessed Virgin; the sister of Martha; Mary of Magdala, better known as Mary Magdalen, or the Magdalene, believed to have been "the woman which was a sinner" (*Luke* vii:37*ff*); [Australian Slang], any girl or woman.

Maryland (-lănd), *n.* a State of the U. S., the Old Line State; named in honor of Henrietta Maria, Queen of Charles I. of England.

maschalephidrosis (măs-kăl-ĕf-ĭ-drō'sis), *n.* excessive profusion of sweat in the armpits.

masochism (măz'ŏk-iz'm), *n.* indulgence in excessive passion during which each participant derives pleasure proportionate to the abuse and cruelty inflicted by the other: after Leopold von Sacher, Austrian novelist.

Mason and Dixon's line (mā's'n, dik's'nz līn), a survey line as marking the southern boundary of Pennsylvania, the course of which was mapped by two English astronomers, Charles Mason and Jeremiah Dixon between 1763 and 1767: famous in U. S. history as indicating or defining the boundary between the Free and the Slave States.

Massachusetts (mås-å-chōō'sets), *n.* a State of the U. S., the Bay State; from the Indian, "About the Green Hills."

Massachusetts Bay Colony (kŏl'ŏ-ni), a small band, made up of Puritans, chartered in 1629, for the purpose of planting a colony on Massachusetts Bay. It founded Boston the following year.

Massacre of St. Bartholomew (bär-thŏl'ŏ-mū), a massacre of Huguenots which began in Paris on St. Bartholomew's Day (August 24), 1572. The number of Protestants slaughtered throughout France was estimated at 70,000. The massacre was instituted under Charles IX by Catherine de' Medici and the Guises.

massotherapy (măs'o-ther'å-pi), *n.* the treatment of bodily ailments by massage.

masthelcosis (măs-thĕl-kō'sis), *n.* ulceration of the breast.

mastigosis (măs-ti-gō'sis), *n.* whipping or beating as a treatment for the purpose of stimulation, or as a counter-irritant.

mastochondrosis (-kŏn-drō'sis), *n.* a cartilaginous tumor of the breast.

mastopathy (măs-tŏp'å-thi), *n.* any disease of the breast.

matrilinear (mă-tri-lĭn'ĕ-år), *adj.* tracing descent on the female side; denoting people who thus trace their descent.

matzoon (måt-sōōn'), *n.* an Armenian medicinal drink consisting chiefly of fermented milk: used for digestive complaints.

mavrone (må-vrōn'), *n.* [It.], literally, my grief; a word much used by the Irish peasantry, to express sorrow, regret, loss, etc.

maxixe (măk-sēks'), *n.* Portuguese dance in polka time, somewhat resembling the two-step in action and rhythm.

Medici (mĕd'i-chē), *n.pl.* an illustrious family of Florence, Italy, many members of which rose to great wealth and influence during the 14th, 15th and 16th centuries: they were patrons of art and literature, and entertained royally in their magnificent palace: they gave two Popes to the Church—Leo X and Clement VII, and one of the daughters became Queen of France, the famous Catherine de Medici, wife of Henry II, and mother of Francis II, Charles IX, and Henry III.

medulitis (mĕd-ŭ-lī'tis), *n.* inflammation of the spinal cord or bone marrow; myelitis.

megalgia (mĕg-ăl'ji-å), *n.* severe pain, as in muscular rheumatism.

megalodactylous (mĕg-ă-lŏ-dăk'ti-lŭs), *adj.* having abnormally large fingers.

megalogastria (-găs'tri-å), *n.* enlargement of the stomach.

megalomaniac (-mā'ni-ăk), *n.* one who has delusions of greatness: one who imagines himself as great, learned, or powerful; an egomaniac.

meiosis (mī-ō'sis), *n.* the representation of a thing which causes it to appear less or smaller then it really is.

Melanesian (mĕl-å-nē'shăn), *n.* one of the dominant race of Melanesia, distinguished for dark skins, frizzy hair, and thick beards: ethnologists regard these people as a cross between the Polynesians or Malays and the Negroid Papuan race: their language seems intermediate between that of the true Malayans and that of the Polynesians.

melder (mĕl'dẽr), *n.* in Scotland, the quantity of meal or flour ground in a mill at one time.

melichroous (mĕ-lĭk'rŏ-ŭs), *adj.* of the color of honey.

melitis (mĕ-lī'tĭs), *n.* inflammation of the cheek.

melomania (mĕl-ŏ-mā'nĭ-å), *n.* a morbid desire for music.

melomaniac (-mā'ni-ăk), *n.* one having a mania, or morbid desire for music at all times.

Melospiza (mĕl-ŏ-spī'zå), *n.* the genus that contains the American song sparrows and the swamp sparrows.

melting pot, a name applied to the U. S. as a place of the amalgamation of races and of manners and customs.

Melungeon (mĕ-lŭn'jŭn), *n.* one of a mixed Indian and white people inhabiting the Carolinas and southern Tennessee, said to be descendants of the early white settlers or pioneers and the native Indians whom the former found there.

memento mori (mĕ-men'tō mō'rī), [L.], literally, remember to die; a warning, or reminder, of death; something that causes one to think of death, as a skull, crossbones, death's-head, etc.

mendicant orders (ôr'dẽrz), in the R. C. Church certain orders of priests who live chiefly on alms, being forbidden to have or hold property; they include Franciscans, Dominicans, Augustinians, and Carmelites.

meningoencephalitis (me-ningk'gō-ĕn-sĕf-å-lī'-tis), *n.* inflammation of the brain and its membranes.

meningomyelitis (-mī-ĕ-lī'tis), *n.* inflammation of the spinal cord and its membranes.

meningosis (mĕn-ĭn-gō'sis), *n.* attachment of the bones by membranes.

meninting (mĕ-nĭn'tĭng), *n.* the kingfisher of East India.

meniscitis (mĕn-ĭ-sī'tĭs), *n.* inflammation of the interarticular cartilages of the knee.

meralgia (mĕ-răl'ji-å), *n.* neuralgic pain in the thigh.

meraline (mĕr'å-lin), *n.* a striped woolen fabric which, on account of durability and heating quality, is much used for dresses and cloaks.

Mercator's projection (mẽr-kā'tẽrz prŏ-jĕk'-shŭn), a method of map making in which meridians of longitude and parallels of latitude are represented by straight lines that cross each other at right angles, which has the effect of enlarging the intervals between the degrees of longitude as they approach the poles: the intervals between the parallels are proportionately increased in order to preserve the relation between latitudinal and longitudinal distances: after Gerardus Mercator (1512-1594), Flemish mathematician and geographer.

metabiosis (mĕt-å-bī-ō'sis), *n.* a kind of relationship between two organisms by which one can flourish only after the other has preceded, and prepared the way for it.

metopodynia (mĕt-ŏ-pŏ-dĭn'i-å), *n.* a frontal headache.

metopomancy (-man'si), *n.* devination or fortune telling by the physiognomy.

metroptosis (mē-trŏp-tō'sis), *n.* prolapse of the uterus.

metachysis (mĕ-tăk'i-sis), *n.* transfusion of blood.

Michigan (mĭsh'i-găn), *n.* a State of the U. S., the Wolverine State; from the Indian, signifying "Great Sea."

microbiophobia (mī-krŏ-bī-ŏ-fō'bi-å), *n.* morbid dread of microbes.

micromania (-mā'ni-å), *n.* insane belief that one's body is becoming smaller.

microphthalmia (mī-krŏf-thăl'mi-å), *n.* unnatural smallness of the eyes, as the result of disease or retarded development.

micropia (mī-krō'pi-å), *n.* abnormality of vision in which objects appear smaller than they are.

microtia (mī-krō'shi-å), *n.* congenital abnormal smallness of the ear.

midnight sun (mĭd'nīt), the sun shining at midnight in either the arctic or antarctic summer.

mika operation (mī'ka ŏp-ẽr-ā-shŭn), an operation to prevent impregnation, long practiced by Australian aborigines: this operation undoubtedly is *vasectomy*, commended by advocates of birth control.

mike (mīk), *n.* [Slang], in radio, an abbreviation for microphone; variant of Mick, an abbreviation of Michael.

Mill-boy of the Slashes (slăsh'ĕz), Henry Clay (1777-1852), born near a place known as the "Slashes," in Hanover County, Va., and where there was a mill to which Henry was often sent as a boy.

millionocracy (mĭl-yŭn-ŏk'rå-si), *n.* the rule or government of millionaires.

milo (mī'lō), *n.* a coarse yellow-seeded sorghum, grown in the U. S. as a dry-land crop: popularly called *milo-maize*.

mine layer (lā"r), a vessel equipped for the laying of under-water mines.

Minenwerfer (mē'nen-vĕr-fẽr), *n.* [G.], literally, mine-thrower; a heavy, muzzle-loading, 3-inch German gun, having a range of about 2,000 yards, and of flat trajectory fire: it weighs over 500 pounds, is mounted on wheels, and furnished with oil-filled recoil cylinders: it is dismounted before being fired.

mineralography (mĭn-ẽr-ăl-og'rå-fi), *n.* a description of minerals, especially in regard to their structure.

Ming (mĭng), *n.* a Chinese dynasty, dating from 1368 to 1644, during which there was peace, and the arts encouraged: it was succeeded by the late Manchu dynasty.

Minnesota (mĭn-ĕ-sō'tå), *n.* a State of the U. S., the Gopher State; from the Indian, *Minne Sotah*, signifying "Cloudy Water."

minyan (mēn-yän)', *n.* in Jewish religious service, the number necessary for the conducting of public worship.

miotic (mī-ŏt'ĭk), *adj.* causing the pupils of the eyes to contract.

Mississippi (mĭs-i-sĭp'i), *n.* a State of the U. S., the Bayou State: from the Indian, signifying "Great Long River."

2. A river of the U. S.

Missouri (mĭ-sōō'rĭ), *n.* a State of the U. S., the "Show-Me State": from the Indian, signifying "Muddy."

mitochondria (mĭt-ō-kŏn'drĭ-å), *n.pl.* very minute bodies found in the protoplasm of some cells, believed to be responsible for the transmission of hereditary characteristics.

mizpah (mĭz'pä), *n.* [Heb.], literally, a watchtower; name of several places in ancient Palestine; name was especially applied to heap of stones gathered in Mt. Gilead by Jacob and his brethren as a remembrance of the covenant made with Laban; in modern usage the word signifies a parting salutation, suggested by Laban's prayer—"The Lord watch between me and thee, when we are absent from one another."

mob psychology (mŏb-sī-kŏl'ō-ji), the spirit that seems to arouse persons collectively to act in a disorderly way which they would never think of doing individually.

mochy (mŭh'i), *adj.* misty; muggy; moist: used only in Scotland and Northern Ireland.

model school (mŏd''l skōōl), a graded school in which approved methods of instruction are practiced by student teachers under competent directors: usually connected with a training college for teachers.

modern Athens (mŏd'ẽrn ăth'ĕnz), Edinburgh; also applied to Boston.

modern Babylon (băb'i-lŏn), London.

mogiphonia (mŏj-i-fō'ni-å), *n.* difficulty in speaking, due to strain on the voice.

mogo (mō'gō), *n.* a stone hatchet used by Australian aborgines.

Mohammedan calendar (mŏ-hăm'ĕd-an kăl'ĕn-dẽr), the calendar as used by Mohammedans, reckoning from the year of the hegira, 622 A. D.: it is a lunar calendar, the Mohammedan year consisting of twelve lunar months, without intercalation—(1) Muharram, 30 days; (2) Safar, 29 days; (3) Rabia I. 30 days; (4) Rabia II. 29 days; (5) Jumada I. 30 days; (6) Jumada II. 29 days; (7) Rajab 30 days; (8) Shaban 29 days; (9) Ramadan 30 days; (10) Shawwal, 29 days; (11) Zu'lkadah, 30 days, and (12) Zu'lhijjah, 29 days.

Mohave (mŏ-hä'vä), *n.* an Indian of the Yuma tribe inhabiting Arizona and southern California: these Indians are of good physique, but they are diminishing.

mojarra (mŏ-här'å), *n.* any of many marine food fishes of tropical waters with compressed bodies, resembling bass.

moki (mō'ki), *n.* a spiny-finned food fish of New Zealand waters—the bastard trumpeter; a kind of raft made by the Maoris with dried bubrushes.

moko (mō'kō), *n.* a kind of tatooing admired, and practiced by the higher-class Maoris.

moko-moko, *n.* a small lizard of New Zealand.

molariform (mŏ-lăr'ĭ-fôrm), *adj.* having the shape of a molar tooth.

moli (mō'li), *n.* a liliaceous tree of East Africa, that yields a variety of dragon's blood.

Moll (mŏl), *n.* [Slang], a female who assists or encourages a professional crook or desperado in his lawless deeds; specifically, the mistress of a gunman; a gun-moll.

Moll Cutpurse (kŭt'pûrs), a notorious woman thief and highway robber who carried on her depredations in and around London about the middle of the 17th century. On one occasion she held up, and robbed General Fairfax on Hounslow Heath. She was a handsome woman, of good family—her real name was Mary Frith.

Moll Flanders (flăn'dẽrz), a woman of great beauty, born in the Old Bailey, London. She was twelve years a courtezan, five years a wife, twelve years a thief, and eight years a convict in Virginia: she died a penitent in the reign of Charles II. Daniel Defoe wrote her life and adventures, "The Fortunes of Moll Flanders," which is still a best seller.

monadism (mŏn'ăd-izm), *n.* see *monadology* main vocabulary.

Mona Lisa (mō'nä lē'zä), a famous portrait of Lisa, wife of Francesco del Giocondo, a Florentine gentleman, painted by Leonardo da Vinci. Millions of copies have been distributed throughout the world. The original is in the Louvre, Paris.

money-grubber (-grŭb'ẽr), *n.* a person who concentrates his energies on the acquiring of money.

moniker (mŏn'i-kẽr), *n.* [Slang], a name; usually, in the sense of nickname.

monilithrix (mō-nĭl'i-thriks), *n.* a disease of the hair characterized by the appearance of a series of little nodes on each hair.

monkey business (bĭz'nĕs), [Slang], trickery; fooling; mischievous pranks; deception; action that arouses suspicion.

monkey face (fās), a human face resembling that of a monkey: term is opprobriously applied.

monkey-faced owl (-fāsd oul), the common American barn owl.

monkey meat (mēt), [Soldier Slang], in the World War, a French ration—canned beef from Madagascar.

Mon-Khmer (mōn'k'mẽr'), *adj.* designating a division of the Indo-Chinese language which includes the Khmer spoken in Cambodia, the Khasi spoken in Assam, the Mon of Pegu, and Anamese, all of which are monosyllabic.

monophagy (mŏ-nŏf'å-ji), *n.* eating by one's self; eating but one kind of food.

monophasia (mŏn-ŏ-fā'zhi-å), *n.* a form of aphasia in which only one word can be spoken.

monophthalmus (mŏn-ŏf-thăl'mŭs), *n.* in teratology, a monster marked by the absence of one eye.

Montana (mŏn-tä'nå), *n.* a State of the U. S., the Stub Toe State: from the Spanish, signifying "Mountainous,"; in geology, a major subdivision of the Cretaceous in Northwestern U. S.; [m-], a large tract of country covered with forests; specifically, the wooded region along the eastern slopes of the Andes in Peru.

Montessori method (mŏn-tĕs-sō'rē mĕth'ŭd), a method of child training and instruction, devised by Dr. Marie Montessori, of Rome, Italy, which stresses freedom of action and emphasizes the importance of sense development, as through vision, touch, and the perception of movement.

Monumental City (mŏn-ū-mĕn'tăl), the City of Baltimore, on account of its many fine monuments.

Moose (mōōs), *n.* a member of the Progressive Party organized by the adherents of Theodore Roosevelt in the presidential campaign of 1912; a Bull-Moose; a member of the Loyal Order of Moose, a secret fraternal and beneficiary society, founded in 1888 at Louisville, Ky.; there are many lodges of the Order throughout the Country, and a home and school at Mooseheart, Ill.

Morea (mŏ-rē'å), *n.* the modern name for the large southern peninsula of Greece, the ancient Peloponnesus.

mores (mō'rēz), *n.pl.* [L], customs; habits; manners; customary laws.

Moros (mŏr'ŏz), *n.pl.* a Mohammedan people inhabiting the southwestern section of the Philippine Islands: they indulged in slavery and polygamy until the U. S. authorities put a stop to both. There have been several revolts, each quickly suppressed. The Moros now (1935) number about 160,000.

Mormon State (môr'mŭn stāt), the State of Utah.

moron (mō'ron), *n.* a feeble-minded person; an adult whose mentality is not higher than that of an average child of eight or nine years.

mortician (mŏr-tish'ăn), *n.* an undertaker.

mosaic (mŏ-zā'ik), *n.* a destructive disease that attacks potatoes, tobacco, sugar cane, and other crops: it bleaches the chlorophyll in the leaves irregularly, leaving them spotted or mottled, hence the name.

Mother of Presidents (mŭth'er, prĕz'i-dĕnts), a name frequently applied to Virginia, which has furnished several presidents of the U. S.

Mother of States (stāts), Virginia, so called from having been the first settled of the original Thirteen States, which united in the Declaration of Independence.

Mother's Day, a day appointed for the honoring of motherhood by both public and individual remembrance: it is observed in most States on the second Sunday in May, though exercises in celebration of it are held in the public schools the preceding Friday: a white carnation is usually worn as a symbol of the day.

motograph (mō'tŏ-grăf), *n.* a moving picture.

motography (-tŏg'rå-fi), *n.* the art or process of making motographs.

motor-bus (-bŭs), *n.* an automobile bus.

motorcade (mō'tẽr-kād), *n.* a fleet of moving motor cars in line.

motordrome (mō'tẽr-drōm), *n.* an enclosed area with seats for spectators around a circular track, on which races, tests, and tryouts of automobile vehicles are held.

motorize (mō'tẽr-īz), *v.t.* to substitute motor vehicles, or automobiles for horse-drawn vehicles, especially in regard to the equipment of a public fire department.

Mound City, popular name of St. Louis, on account of the number of mounds on the site it now occupies.

movie (mōō'vi), *n.* [Slang], a moving picture or a moving picture show; *pl.* moving pictures collectively, or moving picture shows as a class.

movieboner (-bōn'ẽr), *n.* [Slang], a slip, mistake defect, incongruity, or the like in the scene represented, as, for instance, in a Civil War scene, when one of the characters is observed reading a newspaper with a 1935 headline.

moviegoer (-gō'ẽr), *n.* [Slang], a regular patron of the movies; one who frequently goes to the movies.

multiplane (mŭl'ti-plān), *n.* an airplane having three or more main supporting surfaces, one immediately above the other.

Muscle or Mussel Shoals (mus''l shōlz), the name of the rapids in the Tennessee River, Tennessee. The spelling is still open to question, some favoring *Muscle*, others, *Mussel*, though both words are etymologically the same.

Mut (mōōt), *n.* in Egyptian mythology, the lion-headed consort of Amon-Ra, the sun, and mother of Chunsu, the moon.

mutt (mŭt), *n.* [Slang], a stupid fellow; a person of no account; a worthless character; a mongrel or nondescript dog; a cur.

mysophobia (mī-sŏ-fō'bi-å), *n.* morbid dread of dirt.

N

Nabal (nā'băl), *n.* in Biblical literature, a wealthy but parsimonious and evil-minded owner of many sheep and goats who refused to pay tribute to David for protecting his herds, and who escaped punishment because of the appeal his wife, Abigail, made to David, whom she afterwards married—See *I Sam.* xxv; any churlish, evil-minded, niggardly man; a miser.

Nana (nä'nä), *n.* in Babylonian mythology, a goddess of Ur, identified with the planet Venus and, afterwards, with the goddess Ishtar; a Parisian courtezan, heroine of the well known novel of this title by Émile Zola (1840-1902).

nancy (năn'si), *n.* an NC type of seaplane; in rural England, a fancy name for the narcissus; in Tasmania, a small plant of the lily family.

napoo (nå-pōō'), *adj.* [Soldier Slang], all gone; no more; finished; dead.

naprapath (năp'rå-påth), *n.* one who believes in, or who practices, naprapathy.

naprapathy (nå-prăp'å-thĭ), *n.* a therapeutic system of healing without medicines, by manipulating and massaging, based on the theory that strained muscles and ligaments are the cause of the illness.

narcism (när'siz'm), *n.* a mental state or condition in which one falls in love with his own person; self-admiration; self-love.

narcist (när'sist), *n.* a lover of his own body.

nark (närk), *n.* [Australian Slang], a churlish fellow; a disagreeable person; a spoil-sport: *v.t.* to foil; to annoy; to spoil sport.

Nasua (nă'shū-å), *n.* the genus made up of the coatis; [n-], a coati.

Natick (nā'tik), *n.* one of the "praying Indians" brought together by the Rev. John Eliot in 1651 and by whom Natick, Mass., was founded.

Natick Cobbler (kob'lẽr), Henry Wilson, Vice President of the U. S. (1873-1875), who was a shoemaker of the town of Natick, Mass.

national anthem (năsh'ŭn-ăl ăn'thĕm), the most popular patriotic song of a nation. *The Star Spangled Banner* is generally regarded as the national anthem of the U. S., though it has not been officially designated as such. Many favor *My Country 'Tis of Thee* as the national hymn.

National Army, in the U. S., that part of the army which consists of drafted men, in distinction from the men of the Regular Army and those who constitute the National Guard.

national monument (mŏn'ū-mĕnt), any place of natural attraction, as a mountain, or a cañon, or of historic interest, as a battlefield, taken over and reserved by the government as public property.

national park (pärk), a plot, tract, or section of land reserved as public property under act of Congress.

nation of shopkeepers (nā'shŭn shŏp-kēp'ẽrz), England: used contemptuously. The phrase is erroneously attributed to Napoleon, and to Samuel Adams, the American patriot. It was originated by Adam Smith (1723-1790), Scottish political economist; in his "Wealth of Nations," published in 1776; he writes,—"To found a great Empire for the sole purpose of raising up a nation of shopkeepers, may at first sight appear a project fit only for a nation of shopkeepers."

natricine (năt'ri-sīn), *n.* a snake of the genus Natrix; the grass snake of Europe: *adj.* pertaining to a snake or snakes of the genus Natrix.

Natrix (nā'triks), *n.* a genus of Colubrine snakes, which includes water snakes, garter snakes, and other similar forms: the European grass snake is typical.

natural realism (năt'ū-răl rē'ăl-izm), in philosophy, the doctrine that perception gives direct and incontestable evidence of the independent existence of both mind and matter: often called *commonsense philosophy*: its chief protagonists were the philosophers of the Scottish school.

natural theology (thē-ŏl'ō-ji), the study of God through nature, independent of revelation.

naturopathist (nā-tūr-op'å-thist), *n.* one who practices, or believes in, naturopathy.

naturopathy (nā-tūr-ŏp'å-thi), *n.* the helping of nature to overcome disease by the use of home remedies; the drugless treatment of ills; the 'back-to-nature' cure.

naval observatory (nā′val ŏb-zer′vȧ-tō-rĭ), a government institution at Washington, D. C., a division of the Bureau of Navigation of the Navy Department, the function of which is to make general astronomical observations, to purchase instruments for the navy and keep them in repair, to announce twice daily by radio and telegraph the correct standard time for the use of navigators, and to compile the "Nautical Almanac" or "American Ephemeris."

Nazi (nä′tsi), *n.* the National Socialist Party of Germany, or a member thereof. See *Hitlerism.*

N C an abbreviation of *Navy-Curtiss*, used to designate a certain type of seaplane designed, built and equipped under the joint supervision of the U. S. Navy and the Curtiss Engineering Corporation.

N C boat (bōt), a Navy-Curtiss seaplane.

near seal (nēr sēl), any of several skins or furs prepared to imitate true seal; specifically, the fur of the European rabbit or coney, treated and dyed in such a way as to give it a close resemblance to genuine sealskin.

neat's-foot (nēts′fŏŏt), *n.* the foot of an ox or cow.

neat's-foot oil, a pale, yellow, odorless oil, obtained from the feet and leg bones of cattle: much used for softening leather.

neat's tongue (tŭng), ox tongue.

Nebiim (nĕb-ē-ēm′), *n.pl.* the books of the Hebrew Bible, generally called the *Prophets*: they are placed between the Torah and the Hagiographa.

Nebo (nē′bō), *n.* the mountain from which Moses viewed Canaan, the Promised Land, and on which he died alone. This mountain is the Jebel Neba, 2700 ft. high, near the northern end of the Dead Sea.

Nebraska (nĕ-brăs′kȧ), *n.* a State of the U. S., the Black-water State; from the Indian, signifying "Water Valley."

Nebuchadnezzar (nĕb-ū-kăd-nĕz′ăr), *n.* a corruption of Nebuchadrezzar, King of Babylon from 604 to 561 B. C.: he restored Babylon, built the hanging gardens, and made it the most wonderful City of the ancient world: he invaded Jerusalem several times and finally destroyed it 586 B. C.: he also conquered Egypt.

needle beer (nē′d'l bēr), weak beer strengthened by a shot of alcohol: very common in the U. S. during the Prohibition period.

Nehemiah (nē-hē-mī′ȧ), *n.* a famous Jewish statesmen and leader who was governor of Judæa, 445-433 B. C., in the reign of Artaxerxes I.; a Book of the Old Testament, forming the concluding portion of Chronicles-Ezra-Nehemiah.

neoarsphenamine (nē-ō-ärs-phĕn′ȧ-mēn′), *n.* see *neosalvarsan* main vocabulary.

neobotany (nē-ō-bŏt′ȧ-ni), *n.* the science of living plants.

Neo-Catholic (-kăth′ō-lik), *adj.* pertaining to a party in the Church of England with leanings towards the Roman Communion: *n.* one of a party in the Church of England in sympathy with the Roman, rather than the Anglican Communion.

neon (nē′on), *n.* a recently discovered gaseous element, found in the atmosphere in very minute proportion, about $^1/_{2000}$ by volume; it has a specific gravity of 0.69 and anatomic weight of 20.2.

neophobia (nē-o-fō′bi-ȧ), *n.* morbid fear or dread of anything new.

nephroptosis (nĕf-rŏp-tō′sis), *n.* sinking of a kidney; a floating kidney.

nephrorrhagia (nĕf-rō-rā′ji-ȧ), *n.* hemorrhage from the kidneys.

Ne Temere (nē tĕm′ĕr-ē), in the R. C. Church, a papal decree which declares invalid any marriage of a Roman Catholic not contracted before a priest, or bishop, of that Church in good standing.

neurodermitis (nū-rō-dēr-mī′tis), a nervous affection of the skin characterized by itching.

neurodynia (-din′i-ȧ), *n.* pain in a nerve.

neutrodyne (nū′trō-dīn), *n* in radio, a receiver in which the circuit is different from other tuners, being designed for rapid frequency amplification, with the neutralization of capacity coupling.

Nevada (nĕ-vä′dȧ), *n.* a State of the U. S., the Silver State; from the Spanish, signifying "Snowy."

Never-Never Land (nĕv′ĕr), the remote part of western Queensland, Australia, a weird, desolate tract of country, mostly covered by scrub and sand.

New Albion (ăl′bi-ŏn), a territory in America granted by Charles I in 1634 to Sir Edmund Plowden and others as a county palatine: it comprised what is now included in Long Island, New Jersey, Pennsylvania, Maryland and Delaware; an extensive territory on the Pacific coast now included in the States of Oregon and Washington.

New Amsterdam (ăm′stĕr-dăm), early name of New York City, when occupied by the Dutch.

newchum (nū-chum), *n.* in Australia, a recent arrival; a tenderfoot.

New Deal (dēl), a collective term for the various policies adopted and put into practice by the U. S. government, under President Franklin D. Roosevelt, to end depression and bring about recovery.

New England (ing′gland), the name under which are grouped Maine, New Hampshire, Vermont, Massachusetts, Rhode Island and Connecticut.

Newgate (nū′găt), *n.* London's famous old prison, many times rebuilt and, finally, razed in 1902: so called because it stood near the western gate (new gate) in the wall of the old city of London where Watling street or road passes through.

New Hampshire (hămp′shĭr), a State of the U. S., the Granite State: named after the County of Hampshire, England.

New Jersey (jer′zi), a State of the U. S., the Sharp Backs State: so named by its first proprietor, Sir George Carteret, in honor of the defense of the Isle of Jersey.

New Jerusalem (jē-roo′sȧ-lem), the heavenly or celestial city; abode of the blessed in the after life.

New Mexico (mĕk′sĭ-kō), a State of the U. S., the Sunshine State: from Mexitl, the Aztec god of War.

New Netherlands (nĕth′ĕr-lăndz), original Dutch name for the province that is now New York State.

New Sweden (swē′dĕn), the territory between Virginia and New York, claimed by Sweden in the seventeenth century.

New Testament (tĕs′tȧ-mĕnt), see under *Testament* main vocabulary.

New Thought (thôt), an eclectic form of philosophy which takes an optimistic view of life; belief in mental healing, that man has the power within himself to regulate his life as regards health and success by the mental attitude he assumes.

New York (yôrk), a State of the U. S., the Empire State: named after the Duke of York, afterward Charles II.

nidology (nī-dŏl′ō-ji), *n.* the branch of ornithology that treats of nests and their construction.

Nietzscheism (nē′che-izm), *n.* the doctrine of Frederick W. Nietzsche (1844-1900), German philosopher, based on the theory that man can perfect himself through forcible self-assertion. Nietzsche's philosophy is a kind of egoism: he was the apostle of the Overman, the advocate of what Geo. Bernard Shaw, later, styled the Superman. Nietzsche died insane.

night-blooming cereus (sē′rē-ŭs), a well-known cactus of tropical America, with large fragrant white flowers which open at night: abounds in the Hawaiian Islands.

Nimrod (nĭm′rŏd), *n.* a very successful hunter; a keen sportsman: from Nimrod, son of Cush,—see *Gen.* x:8.

niphablepsia (nif′ȧ-blep′si-ȧ), *n.* snow blindness.

Nira (nī′rȧ), *n.* an abbreviation for National Industrial Recovery Act of 1933, intended to restore industry and promote general welfare.

Nobel prize (nō-bĕl′ prīz), an annual prize, value about $40,000, given by the Nobel Foundation to a person who has achieved distinction in any of various fields, as literature, science, art, peace promotion, etc.: after Alfred Bernard Nobel (1833-1896), Swedish chemist, inventor of dynamite, who left a large sum to keep up the prizes.

no man's land, in time of war, the space between hostile trenches.

Nordic race (nor′dik rās), a race of tall, blond people who once inhabited Scandinavia, Scotland, and northern England, including the ancient Goths.

Nordic theory (thē′o-ri), a theory held by many that the people of Nordic descent are biologically superior to all other races, as well as to other branches of the Caucasian race.

Norfolk jacket (nor′fŏk jak′et), a singlebreasted, loosefitting, belted jacket or coat, with a box-pleat on both front and back.

North Carolina (kăr-ō-lī′nȧ), a State of the U. S., the Tar State: named in honor of Charles I. of England.

North Dakota (dȧ-kō′tȧ), *n.* a State of the U.S., the Flickertail State: from the Indian word, *Dahkotah*, meaning "Leagued."

North River (rĭv′ĕr), the Hudson on the west side of New York City, to distinguish it from the Delaware or South River.

Northwest Territory (nôrth-west′ tĕr′i-tō-ri), the former non-slavery region, north of the Ohio River, between Pennsylvania and the Mississippi, now divided into five States.

Notre Dame (nō′tr′ dăm), [Fr.], Our Lady; the famous cathedral of Paris. built in the 13th century.

novocaine (nō-vō-kān′), *n.* a synthetic alkaloid, used as a local anæsthetic: less toxic then cocaine.

Nutmeg State, a nickname for the State of Connecticut: so nicknamed from a jocular accusation, in the early days, that some of the people sold wooden nutmegs for genuine ones.

nyctophobia (nĭk-to-fō′bi-ȧ), *n.* morbid dread of the night time; fear of darkness.

nycturia (nĭk-tū′ri-ȧ), *n.* nocturnal bed-wetting.

O

objectivism (ŏb-jĕk′tiv-izm), *n.* the philosophical doctrine that emphasizes the objective, while ignoring the subjective, that is, which gives undue prominence to the realities as manifested by the physical senses, and neglects the mental processes; the practice of objective art in literature by treating subjects apart from the personality of the writer; the theory that moral good is an objective.

ocean greyhound (ō′shăn grā′hound), a very fast ocean steamship.

ochone (awh′-ŏn′), *interj.* [Ir.], an exclamation of grief or lamentation, loss or disappointment.

October bird (ŏk-tō′bĕr bērd), the bobolink.

odontonecrosis (ŏ-dŏn-tō-nĕk-rō′sis), *n.* necrosis of the teeth.

odontonosology (-nō-sŏl′ō-ji), *n.* the branch of medical science which treats of diseases of the teeth.

odontorthosis (ŏ-dŏn-tŏr-thō′sis), *n.* the process of straightening irregular teeth.

odontotripsis (-trip′sis), *n.* the wearing away of a tooth or teeth.

odontotrypy (-tŏt′ri-pi), *n.* the operation of drilling into a tooth.

œciomania (ē-si-ō-mā′ni-ȧ), *n.* a mental derangement characterized by bullying, browbeating, scolding and obstreperous conduct in the home.

œcophobia (ē-kŏ-fō′bi-ȧ), *n.* morbid dislike of home.

œnophobist (ĕ-nŏf′ō-bĭst), *n.* one who hates wine or any strong drink.

Ohio (ŏ-hī′ō), *n.* a State of the U. S., the Buckeye State: from the Indian, signifying "Beautiful."

okeh (ō′kā), *interj.* it is so; all right: abbreviated O. K.

Oklahoma (ō-klȧ-hō′mȧ), *n.* a State of the U. S., the Sooner State: from the Indian, signifying "Home of the Red Man."

Old Boy (boi), [Slang], the Devil.

Old Catholic (kăth′ō-lik), a member of a religious body organized in 1870 by a party in the R. C. Church who refused to accept the doctrine of papal infallibility.

old country (kŭn′tri), Ireland: so called by Irish emigrants in the U. S.

Old English (ĭng′glĭsh), the English language of the period between 450 A. D. and 1150 A. D.; Anglo-Saxon.

Old French (frĕnch), the French language from the 9th to the 16th century.

Old Guard (gärd), the imperial guard organized by Napoleon I. in 1804; the remnant of soldiers who fought for the Union cause in the Civil War—the G. A. R.; the conservative or "stand-pat" element in the Republican party.

Old Hickory (hik′o-ri), Andrew Jackson (1767-1845), 7th president of the U. S. (1829-1837): so called by his soldiers.

Old Ironsides (ī′ẽrn-sīdz), the U. S. frigate "Constitution," launched at Boston, September 20, 1797; she was active in the war with Tripoli, and gained much fame in the War of 1812. Dr. Oliver Wendell Holmes celebrated her in a poem with this title.

old man, [Slang] a familiar term for father; a husband; captain of a ship; head of a business concern; a large male kangaroo.

Old Man Eloquent (el′o-kwent), a title applied to John Quincy Adams (1767-1848), sixth President of the U. S. (1825-1829).

Old Masters (măst′ẽrz), the celebrated artist-painters of the 16th and 17th centuries.

Old Nick, [Slang] the Devil.

Old North State, a popular designation of the State of North Carolina.

Old Rough-and-Ready (rŭf, rĕd′ĭ), Gen. Zachary Taylor (1784-1850), afterwards President of the U. S. This nickname was given to him by his soldiers during the Mexican War.

Old Style (stīl), the former mode of reckoning time according to the Julian year of 365¼ days.

oligodactylia (ŏl-ĭ-gō-dăk-til′i-ȧ), congenital state of having less fingers than normal; also, extreme slenderness of the fingers.

oligodontous (-dŏn′tŭs), *adj.* having few teeth.

oligomenorrhea (-mĕn-ō-rē′ȧ), *n.* scantiness of menstruation; deficiency of monthly flow.

oligotrichia (-trĭk′i-ȧ), *n.* congenital sparseness or scarcity of hair; deficiency in hair growth.

Olympiad (ō-lim′pi-ăd), *n*, the quadrennial celebration of the modern Olympic games.

Olympic games, see main vocabulary.

Olympic games (gāms), a modern revival of the ancient contests held on Mt. Olympus: they occur every four years and are held in various capitals, chosen for facility of athletic accommodations in the way of large arenas and other conveniences: all the events are international, open to all competitors, and consist of marathon races, high- and broad-jumping, pole-vaulting, discus-throwing, wrestling, etc.: the first competition was held at Athens, 1896.

omalgia (ō-măl'ji-ȧ), *n.* pain in the shoulder-joint.

O. M. I., abbreviation of Order of Mary Immaculate, a congregation of R. C. priests, popularly called Oblates; they are engaged in teaching and missionary work, especially in Canada.

omitis (ō-mī'tis), *n.* inflammation of the shoulder.

omniarch (ŏm'ni-ärk), *n.* a ruler of all.

omnilingual (-lĭng'gwăl), *adj.* speaking all languages.

omniloquent (-nĭl'ō-kwĕnt), *adj.* speaking on all topics.

omnilucent (-lū'sĕnt), *adj.* giving or shedding light in every direction.

omninescience (-nes'shi-ĕnz), *n.* ignorance of everything.

omninescient (-nĕs'shi-ĕnt), *adj.* ignorant of everything.

oncosis (ŏng-kō'sis), *n.* a condition characterized by the development of tumors.

one-step (wŭn-stĕp), *n.* a quick lively round dance in two-four time, demonstrating a variety of steps, including the coupee, the grapevine, the whirl, and the dip.

onomatomania (ŏn-ō-măt-ō-mā'ni-ȧ), *n.* mental distress over inability to remember a word or name; constant concentration of the mind on some particular word.

ontologism (-tŏl'ō-jizm), *n.* the doctrine that the knowledge of God is intuitive, and that all other knowledge springs from it.

oodle (ōō'd'l), *n.* [Slang], a large amount; a heap; abundance.

oomancy (ō'ō-măn-si), *n.* divination or foretelling by a study of eggs.

Opata (ō'pä-tä), *n.* an Indian of an important Piman tribe, inhabiting Chihuahua and Sonora in Mexico. Most of the Opatas are engaged in farming, and all of them are Christians.

opisthotonos (ŏp-is-thŏt'ō-nŏs), *n.* a tetanic spasm that bends the body backward until the back of the head almost touches the heels.

Opium War (ō'pi-ŭm), a war between England and China (1840-1842), due to the latter's attempt to stop the importation of opium.

opotherapy (ŏp-ō-ther'ȧ-pi), *n.* treatment of disease with animal extracts, chiefly of the glands of internal secretion, as the thyroid, adrenals, and pituitary body; organotherapy.

opsonin (ŏp'sō-nin), *n.* a substance in the blood that renders pathogenic bacteria more susceptible to the action of the phagocytes.

optophone (ŏp'tō-fōn), *n.* an instrument which, by combining a selenium cell and telephone apparatus, converts light energy into sound energy, enabling a blind person to locate and estimate varying degrees of light through the ear, and thus to read ordinary printed matter.

optotechnics (ŏp-tō-tĕk'niks), *n.* the technology of lenses, optometers, and other optical instruments and apparatus.

oralogy (ō-răl'ō-ji), *n.* the science that treats of the mouth, especially in regard to the teeth, their preservation and prevention of decay, based on the orderly processes of the cellular activity which maintains a margin of biologic safety of all parts of the body.

Orcus (ôr'kŭs), *n.* the god of the underworld; the underworld; Hades.

Oreamnos (ō-rē-ăm'nŏs), *n.* the genus consisting of the mountain goat.

Oregon (ŏr'ē-gŏn), *n.* a State of the U. S., the Beaver or Sunset State: from the Algonquin word, *Wau-re-gan*, meaning "Beautiful Water."

Orpington (ôr'pĭng-tŭn), *n.* one of a valuable breed of deep-breasted domestic fowl, with single combs and unfeathered legs: originally bred at Orpington, Kent, England.

osteophyma (ŏs-tē-ō-fī'mȧ), *n.* a bony outgrowth or tumor.

osteopsathyrosis (ŏs-tē-ŏp-săth-i-rō'sis), *n.* abnormal brittleness of the bones.

osteorrhaphy (ŏs-tē-ŏr'ȧ-fi), *n.* the operation of suturing or wiring bones.

otogenous (ō-toj'ē-nŭs), *adj.* originating within the ear.

otorrhagia (ō-tō-rā'ji-ȧ), *n.* hemorrhage from the ear.

ototomy (ō-tŏt'ō-mi), *n.* dissection of the ear.

ovariectomy (ō-vā-ri-ĕk'tō-mi), *n.* the operation of removing an ovary.

overhead, *adj.* see main vocabulary.

overhead, *n.* expenses incurred in conducting a business, which, cannot be charged to any particular department of the business, or to any of the products handled, as rent, lighting, heating, etc.

over there, to Americans, the battlefields of Europe during the World War.

over the top, in war time, jumping out of trenches or dugouts to charge the enemy.

oxan (ŏk'săn), *n.* a colorless gas of which there are two kinds: it is formed by the contact of nitrogen oxides and hot charcoal.

oxozone (ŏk'sō-zōn), *n.* an allotropic variety of oxygen believed by some chemists to exist in ozone in solution.

oxozonide (-zōn'īd), *n.* an organic oxidation product, obtained from unsaturated hydrocarbons: similar to oxozone.

oxyacetylene blowpipe (ŏk-si-ȧ-sĕt'i-lēn blō'pīp), a specially constructed blowpipe in which the oxyacetylene flame produced is much hotter than the oxyhydrogen flame: used in the welding of steel.

Oyster State (ois'tẽr), a name frequently applied to Maryland, on account of its oyster industries.

ozonate (ō'zō-nāt), *n.* one of a series of orange salts produced by the action of ozonified oxygen on an alkali.

ozostomia (ō-zŏs-tō'mi-ȧ), *n.* bad breath; foul odor from the mouth.

P

pacifism (păs'i-fizm), *n.* the advocacy of peace as opposed to militarism; protestation against war and all that pertains to it; an attitude or stand that favors the settlement of international disputes by arbitration.

paddy fields (păd'i fēldz), in China and East India, the rice fields when the crop is at an early stage of its growth, requiring almost constant irrigation.

pahmi (pä'mi), *n.* the European marmot; the fur of this animal.

painted desert (pān'tĕd dĕz'ẽrt), the wide tract of country consisting of plateaus and low mesas, lying east of the valley of the Little Colorado in Central Arizona; it is interspersed with rocks of various colors, hence the name.

Palmetto State (păl-met'ō stāt), a nickname given to South Carolina, in allusion to the representation of a palmetto tree on its coat-of-arms.

Panama Canal (păn-ȧ-mä' kȧ-năl'), a canal connecting the Atlantic with the Pacific ocean, cut through the Isthmus of Panama, the connecting link of N. and S. America. It was constructed by the U. S. at a cost of $525,815,000 to completion in 1921. It is about 50 miles in length from deep water to deep water, the width of the bottom channel is from 300 to 1000 feet, and the locks average 1000 feet long and 110 feet wide. The transit or passage of the canal takes from 12 to 15 hours.

Pan-American Union (-ȧ-mĕr'ĭ-kȧn ūn'yŭn), formerly International Bureau of American Republics, an association for fostering friendly relations between the twenty-one republics of the American continent.

pancake (păn'kāk), *v.i.* in aviation, the making of a descent by steering an airplane higher than for ordinary landing, then coming down at a very wide angle, almost without bank, on a steeply inclined path.

pancreatitis (păng-krē-ȧ-tī'tis), *n.* inflammation of the pancreas.

pancreatomy (-ăt'ō-mi), *n.* incision into the pancreas.

pancreatorrhagia (-ō-rā'ji-ȧ), *n.* hemorrhage from the pancreas.

pandaram (păn-dä'răm), *n.* a low-caste Hindu priest of southern India; also, a mendicant of the Sudra, practicing severe asceticism.

Pan-Germanism (-jẽr'man-izm), *n.* prior to the World War, the imperialistic doctrine or belief that Germany was destined to dominate the world.

Panhandle State (pan'han-d'l), a nickname for West Virginia, on account of its long narrow projection between the State of Pennsylvania and the Ohio River.

panophthalmia (păn-ŏf-thăl'mi-ȧ), *n.* severe inflammation of the eye, involving the whole structure of the eyeball.

panophthalmitis (-thăl-mī'tĭs), *n.* same as panophthalmia.

panosteitis (-ŏs-tē-ī'tis), *n.* inflammation of bone structure.

panotitis (-ō-tī'tis), *n.* inflammation of all parts of the ear.

panpneumatism (-nū'mȧ-tiz'm), *n.* the philosophical doctrine that noumenal reality, the world, is both unconscious thought and unconscious will: put forward by E. von Hartmann in an attempt to reconcile the pantheism of Schopenhauer and the panlogism of Hegel.

pantalgia (păn-tăl'ji-ȧ), *n.* pain affecting every part of the body.

pantograph, *n.* see main vocabulary.

pantograph (păn'tō-grăf), *n.* a frame structure on roof of a trolley car from which a connecting metal rod arises to take current from an overhead wire.

papal infallibility (pā'păl ĭn-făl-ĭ-bĭl'ĭ-ti), the R. C. dogma, that the Pope cannot err, when, in his official capacity, or ex cathedra (from the chair), he proclaims a doctrine of faith or morals.

Papal States, dominions in the center of Italy formerly subject to the Holy See. Prior to the wars for Italian independence they comprised about 17,500 square miles, but after 1870 only the Vatican and Lateran palaces remained. In 1929 through treaty with the Italian government the Pope was given sovereignty over the State of Vatican City, comprising about 110 acres in the heart of Rome.

papillon (pȧ-pē'yon), *n.* a tiny European dog, kept as a household pet, like a poodle; closely resembles the Mexican chihuahua; color, usually brown.

parasitotropic (păr-ȧ-sī-tō-trŏp'ik), *adj.* denoting a substance in the blood that absorbs parasites: *n.* a parasitotropic substance.

parasol, *n.* see main vocabulary.

parasol (păr-ȧ-sŏl'), *n.* a monoplane having parasol wings, that is, wings raised above the head of the pilot, so as to permit of downward vision.

parochial schools (pȧ-rō'ki-ăl skōōlz), parish schools conducted under the auspices of the R. C. Church, and supported by voluntary contributions of the parishioners: nearly all are in charge of monks and nuns.

parsec (pär'sĕk), *n.* a unit of measure for interstellar space, equal to a distance of 3.2 light years, or 100,000 times the diameter of the earth's orbit.

Parseval (pär'sē-văl), *n.* a nonrigid, dirigible balloon consisting of a single gas bag from which a small car is suspended: designed by A. von Parseval, German engineer.

passing the buck (pås'ing, bŭk), shifting responsibility from self to another: from a small object or marker called a "buck" used in playing poker, which is put in the pot, and passed from player to player, according to the rules of the game.

pastorium (pås-tō'ri-ŭm), *n.* in southern U. S., the parsonage of a Baptist minister.

pastrame (pås-trä'mē), *n.* a table delicatessen consisting of cooked meat highly spiced.

pathomania (păth-ō-mā'ni-ȧ), *n.* moral insanity.

pathophobia (-fō'bi-ȧ), *n.* morbid dread of disease; hypochondria.

pathophorous (pȧ-thŏf'ō-rŭs), *adj.* producing disease; conveying disease.

patrilineal (păt-ri-lin'ē-ăl), *adj.* denoting or relating to descent through the male line or paternal ancestors: contrasted with *matrilineal.*

patrioteer (pā-tri-ot-ẽr'), *n.* one who boasts of his patriotism, or tries to make capital of it.

patroclinous (păt-rō-klī'nus), *adj.* denoting or designating that which is inherited from a father in the way of temperament, disposition, traits, and general character.

patrogenesis (-jĕn'ē-sis), *n.* a kind of reproduction in which the chromatin for the embryo is wholly supplied from the sperm or pollen cell: the offspring in such reproduction manifests the characteristics of the male parent.

Peace Conference (pēs kŏn'fẽr-ens), a conference in the interests of peace, especially, either of the International Peace Conferences held at The Hague. See *International Peace Conference.*

Peace Day (dā), May 18, the anniversary of the opening of the first Hague Peace Conference, May 18,1899.

peace dollar (dol'ẽr), a silver dollar of the U. S. struck 1918 to commemorate the Treaty of Peace.

peg, [Colloq.] in England, a small drink of alcoholic liquor.

Pekinese (pē-kĭn-ēz'), *n.* one of a Chinese breed of small dogs, very intelligent and affectionate; they have long hair, short legs, drooping ears, and pug noses.

penguin, *n.* see main vocabulary.

penguin (pĕng'gwin), *n.* a small-winged airplane used in training schools for aviators, but not adapted for flight; one of the Women's Royal Air Force of England, organized in 1918: so called because these women did not fly.

Pennsylvania (pĕn-sĭl-vā'nĭ-ȧ), *n.* a State of the U. S., the Keystone State: from Penn (William, an English quaker, who founded it) and *sylvania*, forest or wooded country.

pentathlon (pĕn-tăth'lŏn), *n.* in the modern Olympic games, a composite contest in which the events are throwing the discus, throwing the javelin, 200- and 1500-meter runs, and a running broad jump.

pep, [Slang] vim; vigor; dash; spirit.

perfidious Albion (pẽr-fĭd'ĭ-ŭs ăl'bi-ŏn), a name applied to England by Napoleon Bonaparte.

Persian lamb (per'zhan lăm), the young of sheep of Central Asia, from which is obtained the karakul and astrakhan of furriery; the finest grade of karakul, or astrakhan.

Petticoat Lane (pĕt'ĭ-kōt lān), a notorious street of Whitechapel, London, formerly known as Hog Lane, and now Middlesex Street.

Pfeiffer bacillus (p'fīf'ẽr bȧ-sĭl'ŭs, *n.* the bacillus or germ that causes influenza: discovered by Richard Pfeiffer, German bacteriologist in 1892.

phallic worship (făl'ik wûr'ship), a form of religion, practiced by most ancient peoples, in which the genital organs, or representations of them, were worshipped.

phaneromania (făn-ẽr-ō-mā'niȧ), *n.* a morbid habit as of biting the finger-nails, plucking at some abnormal growth or defect on hands or face, etc.

pharmacomania (fär-må-kŏ-mā'ni-å), *n.* insane fondness for taking, or administering, drugs.

phony (fō'ni), *adj.* denoting something not genuine; crooked; dishonest; faked.

photolysis (fō-tŏl'i-sis), *n.* chemical decomposition through the action of light.

photostat (fō'tō-stăt), *n.* a device for making photographic copies of printed matter, manuscripts, records, maps, drawings, illustrations, etc. on specially prepared paper with the image not reversed, as in a negative.

phrenalgia (frĕ-năl'ji-å), *n.* melancholia.

phrenoplegia (-plē'ji-å), *n.* sudden loss or failure of the mental powers.

phytotoxin (fī-tō-tŏk'sin), *n.* a poisonous protein found in plants.

piaba (pē-ä'bå), *n.* a small edible fish found in Brazilian rivers.

piarrhæmia (pī-å-rē'mi-å), *n.* the presence of fat in the blood.

picturedrome (pik'tŭr-drōm), *n.* a theatre in which moving pictures are shown.

picturize (pik'tŭr-īz), *v.t.* to make a picture of; to represent by means of moving pictures.

Pilate (pī'lăt), cognomen of the Roman governor, Pontius Pilate, who was procurator of Judea at the time of Christ's crucifixion: he was banished to Gaul, where, it is said, he committed suicide.

Pilate's wife (wīf), Procla, venerated in the Greek Church as a saint, her feast day occurring on October 27.

pilosis (pī-lō'sis), *n.* abnormal growth of hair.

Piltdown man (pilt'doun), one of a primitive race of humans: from Piltdown, Sussex, England, where parts of a skull were found in 1911.

pimiento (pē-myĕn'tō), *n.* the Spanish sweet pepper, the fruit of which is used in stuffing pickles, olives, etc., and for salads: often confounded with *pimento.*

pinch-hitter; (pinch-hit'ĕr), *n.* [Cant] in baseball, a player who is called to bat in place of another, in case of emergency.

Pine-tree State, the State of Maine: on account of its pine forests.

pinochle, *n.* see *Penuchle* main vocabulary.

pistology (pis-tŏl'ō-ji), *n.* the part of theology that treats of faith.

pituitrin (pĭ-tū'i-trin), *n.* an extract from the pituitary body.

pixol (pĭk'sōl), *n.* a composition of potash, green soap, and wood tar, used as an antiseptic in skin affections.

plasmocyte (plas'mŏ-sīt), *n.* a white blood corpuscle.

player piano (plā'ĕr pĭ-ăn'ō), a piano having an inside mechanism, controlled by a perforated strip of paper—the perforations corresponding to notes—which moves the keys without the manipulation of hands; a self-playing piano.

pleiobar (plī'ō-bär), *n.* an area of high barometric pressure.

pliotron (plī'ŏ-trŏn), *n.* an electric detector and amplifier for fluctuating currents, consisting of a discharge tube in which is mounted a grid of wires between the incandescent cathode and the anode: trade name.

Plough Monday (plou mŭn'dā), the Monday after Epiphany, on which the ploughing season begins in rural England: until recently it was celebrated with much merrymaking.

plumcot (plŭm'kŏt), *n.* a fruit produced by crossing a plum with an apricot.

pneumonoultramicroscopicsilicovolcanokoniosis (ŭl'trå-mi''krŏ-skŏp'ĭk-sĭl'ĭ-kŏ-vŏl-kā'nō-kō''-nĭ-ō'sĭs), a special form of silicosis or lung affection, caused by ultramicroscopic particles of siliceous volcanic dust, breathed into the lungs.

Pocahontas (pō-kå-hŏn'tăs), *n.* an Indian maiden (1595-1617), daughter of Powhatan, chief of Virginia: she rescued Captain John Smith when her father was about to kill him: she was baptized with the name of Rebecca and married John Rolfe, an Englishman, thus preserving peace between her father's tribe and the colonists.

podiatrist (pŏ-dī'å-trĭst), *n.* one skilled in the care and treatment of the feet; a foot doctor.

podiatry (-dī'å-tri), *n.* the study of disorders and affections of the feet; treatment of disordered feet.

Poet's Corner (pō'ĕtz kôr'nĕr), a corner in Westminster Abbey, in the south transept, where there are memorials to many of England's famous poets, and one to an American poet, H. W. Longfellow.

pogo (pō'gō), *n.* a slender but strong pole or stick with foot-treads on each side near the bottom and immediately above a strong spring which enables boys and girls to hop along in sport.

poilu (pwå-lü'), *n.* [Fr.] literally, hairy; popular and international name for a French private-soldier: probably, from the unkempt appearance of many, without hair-cut or shave, during the World War.

police dog, a German wolf-dog, trained to assist police in tracking criminals.

poliomyelitis (pŏl-i-ō-mī-ĕ-lī'tĭs), *n.* an acute inflammation of the gray matter of the spinal cord which, in some cases, extends to the brain; infantile paralysis.

poltergeist (pŏl'tĕr-gīst), *n.* [G.] literally, a noisy ghost; a ghost said to indulge in table-tipping, rapping, knocking, bumping, breaking delft, and tossing furniture around.

pomato (pŏ-mā'tō), *n.* a succulent vegetable resembling a tomato, produced by grafting tomato scions on potato plants.

Popocrat (pŏp'ŏ-krăt), *n.* a term applied by opponents to a Democrat who favored or supported the Populists or People's party in the campaigns of 1896 and 1900.

poppy day (pŏp'i), the day on which artificial poppies made by disabled veterans are sold to the public: usually, Decoration Day.

poppycock (-kŏk), *n.* [Colloq.] empty or foolish talk; bosh; buncombe; nonsense.

pork, *n.* see main vocabulary.

pork (pōrk), *n.* money, position, or favors obtained from the Federal government, not as reward for services rendered, but as a result of political influence and patronage.

pork barrel (băr'ĕl), formerly, a fund of money appropriated from the Federal treasury ostensibly for public improvements, as the erection of buildings, the deepening of harbors, etc., but really for local patronage and as a sop to obstreperous politicians.

Porkopolis (pōrk-ŏp'ŏ-lis), *n.* Cincinnati, at a time when that city was noted as a hog-slaughtering center; later, Chicago, on account of its large pork-packing industries.

poste restante (pōst rĕs-tängt'), [Fr.] literally, remaining post; to be left at post office until called for—used in addressing letters; a department of the post office having charge of letters waiting to be called for.

post-impressionism (-ĭm-prĕsh'ŭn-iz'm), *n.* the practice of a group of French artists, including cubists and futurists, who, in painting, sculpture, music, etc., put into their work what they term self-expression, that is, they treat their subjects in their own way, according to their own ideas, regardless of professional ethics or traditions. See *expressionism.*

potamophilous (pŏt-å-mŏf'ĭ-lŭs), *adj.* loving rivers.

Prairie State (prā're stāt), the State of Illinois: on account of its wide-spreading prairies.

preschool (prē-skōōl), *n.* a kindergarten or nursing school where children of preschool age, sometimes in age groups, are entered for observation, and social, and educational training: *adj.* pertaining to or designating the period in a child's life from infancy to the age of five years.

presentationism (prĕz-ĕn-tā'shŭn-izm), *n.* the philosophic doctrine that reality is immediately manifested in perception; the theory that the psychical life is altogether made up of cognitive elements.

preventorium (pre-ven-tō'ri-um), *n.* a sanitarium; especially an institution devoted to the prophylactic treatment of persons showing tendency towards consumption or tuberculosis of the lungs.

progestion (prŏ-jĕs'chŭn), *n.* a hormone recently discovered.

psychoanalysis (sī-ko-å-nal'ĭ-sis), *n.* diagnosis of mental and nervous afflictions by analyzing the emotions and investigating the history of the patient: based on the theory of Sigmund Freud, Viennese psychologist, that in many forms of neurosis and mental disorders, certain factors persist unconsciously, while rejected consciously.

psychotic (sī-kot'ik), *adj.* of or pertaining to psychosis; insane.

psychroesthesia (sī-krŏ-ĕs-thē'si-å), *n.* a perverted feeling or sensation in which part of the body, while warm, feels cold.

psychrophobia (-fō'bi-å), *n.* a morbid fear or dread of anything cold.

Ptah (p'tä), *n.* an ancient god of Egypt, regarded as "the father of both gods and men": a magnificent temple was erected in his honor at Memphis.

pulmonitis (pŭl-mŏ-nī'tis), *n.* pneumonia.

pyophylactic (pī-ō-fi-lăk'tik), *adj.* counteracting, or guarding against, pus.

Pyramid of Cheops (pĭr'å-mĭd, kē'ops), the largest of the three great pyramids at Gizeh, Egypt, 482 feet high, and having a base covering an area of 13 acres: built for King Cheops, probably, about 3720 B. C.

pyrex (pī'reks), *n.* trade name for glassware that has been subjected to a chemical process which causes it to withstand a high degree of heat; the articles, chiefly cooking utensils, made of this ware.

Q

Q-boat (-bōt), *n.* a boat classified in the British navy under the letter, Q, hence, a mystery boat.

quadricinium (kwŏd-ri-sĭn'ĭ-ŭm), *n.* a musical composition in four voice parts.

quadriparous (-rĭp'å-rŭs), *adj.* bringing forth four children at a birth.

quadrisect ('r-sekt), *v.t.* to divide into four equal parts.

quadruplane (kwod'rōō-plān), *n.* an airplane having four supporting surfaces, one above another.

Quadruple Alliance (kwŏd'rōō-p'l ă-lī-ăns), in the World War, the alliance between Germany, Austria-Hungary, Turkey, and Bulgaria; also, the alliance, at the same time, between Gt. Britain, France, Russia, and Italy.

quæstuary (kwĕs'tū-ā-ri), *adj.* denoting or designating a person in business solely for profit.

Quai d'Orsay (kā' dŏr-sā'), a part of the left bank of the Seine in the center of Paris, opposite the Place de la Concorde. Because the Foreign Office, the Chamber of Deputies, and other government buildings front on this Quai, it is taken as a synonym for the French government, just as Downing Street, in London, is used to designate the British goverment.

Quaker City (kwāk'ĕr sĭt'i), Philadelphia, on account of its being first settled by Quakers.

Quaker meeting (mēt'ing), a gathering of Quakers; a meeting of Quakers for worship: as these meetings are usually characterized by intervals of complete silence, it follows that any silent assemblage of people is termed a *Quaker* or *Quakers' meeting.*

Quaker poet (pō'et), John Greenleaf Whittier (1809-1865), who was a member of the Society of Friends.

qualtagh (kwăl'tah'), *n.* in the Isle of Man, the first individual a person sees or meets of a morning when setting out from home, and whom he regards as an omen of good, or bad, luck for that day.

quantum, *n.* see main vocabulary.

quantum (kwŏn'tŭm), *n.* the elemental unit of energy, according to the quantum theory: designated by the symbol E.

quantum theory (thē'ŏ-ri), in physics, a theory that the radiation emitted from any body is not a continuous process, but that each radiator sends off units of energy in equal amounts, called *quanta,* the value of these depending upon a universal constant and the frequency of the radial vibrations; in finance, a theory that any change in the amount of available money will result in a corresponding change in the prices of things.

Quartier Latin (kwŏr'tyer lăt'in), a student section of Paris, south of the Seine, containing the College de France, the Luxembourg, Pantheon, Sorbonne, etc.: it is the synonym for a careless, free, Bohemian life, and of late years is said to be a nursery for the fostering and development of socialistic and communistic ideas.

Quapaw (kwä'păw), *n.* one of a tribe of Indians of the Sioux family, formerly dwelling in the lower reaches of the Mississippi, now living on the Indian reservation in Oklahoma: only a few hundred are left.

Quasimodo, *n.* see main vocabulary.

Quasimodo (kwăs'i-mō'dō), *n.* the ugly and strong foundling hunchback in Victor Hugo's romance, "Notre Dame de Paris," who lives in the tower of the cathedral of Notre Dame, Paris.

queen bee (kwēn bē), the fully developed female of the honeybee.

Queen City (kwen sit'i), a popular name for Cincinnati, when it was the commercial metropolis of the West.

Queen City of the Lakes (kwēn, lākz), Buffalo: on account of its location and commercial importance.

Queen City of the South, Adelaide, South Australia: built of white stone and surrounded by green hills.

Queen of Heaven (hĕv''n), a title given to the Virgin Mary by Roman Catholics.

Queen of Sheba (shē'bå), the woman ruler who became famous through her visit to King Solomon, with a great retinue, bearing costly gifts,—see *I Kings* x. It is supposed by some that *Sheba* is a variation of *Saba,* on ancient country, adjacent to the Red Sea, in southwestern Arabia, now known as Yemen. Other authorities say, that the woman who visited Solomon was Queen Balkis of the Sabeans, a people allied to the Arabs and Jews, and who had colonies in Africa where they intermarried with Ethiopians. Abyssinian tradition states that the *Queen of Sheba* was ruler of ancient Ethiopia, and that the present monarch of Abyssinia is a descendant of the first Menelik (Melech), who was a son of the Queen by King Solomon.

Queen of Song (sŏng), Madame Otto Goldschmidt (1820-1887), better known as Jenny Lind, Swedish operatic soprano, popularly styled "The Swedish Nightingale."

Queen of the Adriatic (ăd-ri-ăt′ik), the city of Venice, Italy: on account of its location, and its control of commerce to the East.
Queen of the Antilles (ăn-tĭl′ēz), Cuba, island republic of the West Indies, capital, Havana.
Queen of the Lakes (lākz), Windermere, the largest lake in England, 11 miles long and one mile wide, between the Counties of Lancashire and Westmoreland.
Queen of the Mississippi Valley (mĭs-ĭ-sĭp′ĭ val′ĭ), St. Louis, Missouri.
queen olive (ŏl′iv), a large oblong olive, having a very small stone or pit: grown in the neighborhood of Seville, Spain.
Queensberry Rules (rōōlz), the rules that govern modern prize-ring fighting and pugilistic exhibitions: after John Sholto Douglas (1844-1930), Marquis of Queensberry who formulated the Rules.
questionnaire (kwes-chŭn-âr′), *n.* a series of questions submitted to a number of persons in order to obtain information on a given subject by comparing the answers.
Quetzalcoatl (kĕt-säl-kō-ä′t′l), *n.* a nature god of the various races in Mexico before the Spanish conquest: represented in various ways,—deity of storms, god of rains, of fertile fields, of industry, etc. Tradition says he was a king who imparted culture to the early Aztecs, and that his own brother, Tezcatlipoca, drove him out to seek a refuge in the land to the southeast.
Quichua (kē′chwä), *n.* one of a South American Indian family of several tribes, all of the same linquistic stock, who once occupied the ancient Peruvian Empire under the Incas.
quinquesect (kwin′kwē-sĕkt), *v.t.* to cut or divide into five equal parts or segments.
quod erat demonstrandum (kwŏd ē′răt dĕm-ŏn-străn′dŭm), [L.], which was to be demonstrated.

R

raash (rȧ-ăsh′), *n.* the electric catfish.
race suicide (rās sū′i-sīd), the gradual lessening, until final passing, of a race through failure of the people to keep the birth rate, at least, equivalent to the death rate.
Rachel (rā′chel), *n.* in Biblical literature, the younger daughter of Laban, wife of Jacob, and mother of Joseph and Benjamin — See *Gen.* xxix.
rachioparalysis (rā-kĭ-ō-pȧ-răl′i-sis), *n.* paralysis of the spine.
rachiotomy (rā-ki-ŏt′ō-mi), **rachitomy** (rȧ-kĭt′-o-mi), *n.* incision into the spinal column.
racialism (rā′shal-izm), *n.* racial qualities, characteristics, tendencies, likes, dislikes, etc.
racket, *n.* see main vocabulary.
racket (rak′et), *n.* a term used in a number of loose ways, some apparently contradictory; it may signify (1) an honest means, or manner, of making a livelihood; (2) an unlawful occupation or profession; extortion of money from victims by threat or violence; (3) conversion of lawful organizations, as labor unions, into bodies of force for the purpose of extortion; (4) in general, the activities of gangsters and members of the underworld against the powers of law, order, and organized society for the protection of lives and property.
racketeer (rak-e-tēr′), *n.* one who preys upon organized society for a living; a member of the underworld who plans, or takes part in, criminal acts; a gangster; desperado; bootlegger.
radicivorous (rā-dĭ-sĭv′ō-rŭs), *adj.* feeding on roots.
radiculitis (rȧ-dĭk-ū-lī′tis), *n.* inflammation of a spinal nerve root.
radio (rā′dĭ-ō), *n.* in North America, the name given to the transmission of messages through space, without wires, by means of electric waves, or more specifically, by means of wireless telephony, wireless telegraphy, and photography; also, the instruments or apparatus used for sending out and receiving the messages, particularly, the receiving apparatus or set: in England called *wireless*: *adj.* of, pertaining to, using, or operated by radiant energy, specifically, that of electric waves.
radiodynamic (-dī-năm′ik), *adj.* pertaining to, or designating, any of the wonderful things due to the radiant energy of electric waves.
radio-frequency (frē-kwĕn′si), *n.* the frequency of electric waves in radiotelegraphy, which has been estimated from 100,000 to 1,100,000 cycles per second.
radiologist (rā-di-ŏl′ō-jist), *n.* one skilled in radiology.
radiology (rā-di-ŏl′ō-ji), *n.* the art or practice of using X-rays to determine the cause of disease for the purpose of removing or remedying the cause.
radiophare (rā′dĭ-ō-fār), *n.* a radio telegraphic station, used only for the purpose of determining the location or whereabouts of ships.
radiophone, *n.* see main vocabulary.
radiotelephony (-tĕl′ĕ-fō-ni), *n.* see *radiophony* main vocabulary.
radiotron (rā′dĭ-ō-trŏn), *n.* trade name for a vacuum tube used in radio or wireless.
Raffles (răf′ĕls), *n.* a fictional character, represented as a gentleman burglar in a series of well-known stories by the late Ernest William Hornung (1866-1921), English novelist.
rail-bird, see *fence-sitter*.
rail splitter (rāl split′ĕr), one who splits rails; especially, [R-S-] a term applied to Abraham Lincoln.
rain-rot, *n.* a skin disease, resembling scab, that attacks sheep when exposed to rain for several days.
raisin tree (rā′z′n trē), the common red currant bush.
Rama (rä′mȧ), *n.* in Hindu mythology, one of the incarnations of Vishnu.
Ramachandra (-chăn′drȧ), *n.* the seventh and most famous incarnation of Vishnu.
ramarama (rä′mȧ-rä′mȧ), *n.* a New Zealand myrtle.
rats (răts), *interj.* [Slang], an exclamation expressing incredulity, disbelief, annoyance, disgust, or the like.
rattled (răt′l′d), *adj.* [Slang], excited; mentally confused.
rattlers (rat′lērz), *n.pl.* [Tramps' Slang] empty freight cars in movement over a railroad.
rayon (rā′on), *n.* a generic term applied to chemically produced textile filaments, and the fabrics derived from them: the filaments constitute the yarn which is made by any one of four chemical processes: the cloth is woven or knit into various kinds of garments.
razz (răz), *v.t.* to taunt; rile; poke fun at; delude; deceive; annoy.
real McCoy (rēl mā-koi′), [Slang] the genuine article; something that proves its own genuineness or reality: said to be derived from "Kid McCoy" (Norman Selby), prize-fighter who once knocked out a bully who doubted his personality.
realtor (rē-ăl′tŏr), *n.* a real estate operator, member of a local organization of brokers in good standing with the National Association of Real Estate Boards.
receptionism (rē-sĕp′shŭn-iz′m), *n.* the religious belief that in the Sacrament of Holy Communion the bread and wine remain substantively the same, but that with them the communicant receives the body and blood of Christ.
rectorite (rĕk′tŏ-rīt), *n.* hydrated aluminum silicate.
Red Army (är′mi), in Russia, the army of radical socialists, otherwise the Bolsheviki or Communists who, since 1918, have controlled the government of the U.S.S.R.; any similar revolutionary armed forces.
reddingtontite (rĕd′ing-tŏn-tīt), *n.* in mineralogy, hydrous chromium sulphate.
red-light district (-līt′ dĭs′trĭkt), a section of a town or city in which there are many disorderly resorts, or houses of ill-fame: so called because, formerly, it was customary to display a red lantern light above the doors of such houses.
Red Star, an international organization having for its objective the humane treatment of animals: it had its inception in Switzerland.
red tape (tāp), official formality; adhering strictly to rules and regulations.
red triangle (trī′ăng-g′l), the symbol of the Y. M. C. A.
register, *v.t.* see main vocabulary.
register (rĕj′is-tēr), *v.t.* in the part of an actor or actress, in the taking of moving pictures, to display feelings or emotions, or assume facial expressions, or form body postures appropriate to the scene being enacted, as to appear sad or joyous, cry or laugh, or raise or lower eyes, arms, etc.
Reich (rīh′, rīk), *n.* the modern federated republic of Germany since 1919, now (1935) under the chancellorship of Adolph Hitler, leader of the National Socialist Party (Nazi) which gained complete political control of the country in the 1933 elections; formerly, the German Empire from 1871 to 1919.
Reichsfuehrer (rīks′fū-rĕr), *n.* [G.], leader or head of the Reich; specifically, Adolph Hitler, leader of the National Socialist Party of Germany—the Nazi.
relativity (rel′ȧ-tiv′ĭ-ti), *n.* the quality of being relative; specifically, a theory of *relativity* put forward by Albert Einstein, German physicist, based on a belief that our knowledge of velocity must, of a necessity, be relative; it claims that the velocity of light is independent of the relative velocity of its source, and of the observer, and that such velocity can never be attained by any material body; it also assumes that the mass of a body depends upon its velocity.
Rembrandt (rĕm′brănt), one of the paintings by the celebrated Dutch master, Rembrandt van Rijn (1606-1669), characterized by strongly contrasted light and shade.
Republican elephant (rē-pŭb′li-kăn ĕl′ē-fănt), a picture, figure, or representation of an elephant as a symbol of the National Republican Party—the G. O. P.: originated by Thomas Nast (1840-1902), illustrator and caricaturist, in a cartoon in *Harper's Weekly*, Nov. 7, 1874.
requiescat in pace (rĕk-wi-ĕs′kăt in pā′si), [L.], may he (or she) rest in peace: abbreviated to R. I. P., frequently inscribed on headstones, tombstones, and cemetery vaults.
reserve bank (rē-zerv′ băngk), any of the twelve banks instituted under the Federal Reserve Act of 1913 to serve member banks of the system in its own particular district, as a bank of reserve and rediscount.
resinol (res′ĭ-nol), *n.* trade name for a healing ointment.
resinosis (rĕz-i-nō′sis), *n.* an overflow of resin from pine trees.
restaurate (rĕs′tō-rāt), *v.t.* to eat in a restaurant.
rest treatment, see *rest cure* main vocabulary.
retrogressionist (rĕ-trō-grĕs′shŭn-ist), *n.* one who retrogrades or goes back; a person disposed to retrogression.
Reuter's News Agency (roi′tērz nūz ā′jĕn-si), an agency for gathering and transmitting news of current interest: established 1849 by Baron Paul J. von Reuter (1821-1899), a German who became a British subject and lived in London.
revisionist (rē-vizh′ŭn-ist), *n.* one in favor of revision; a reviser, especially, one of those who prepared the Revised Version of the Bible.
revue (rē-vū′), *n.* [Fr.], a burlesque comedy in which well-known or lately performed plays are burlesqued or imitated.
rex begonia (rĕks bē-gō′ni-ȧ), a begonia with very large and beautifully variegated leaves, cultivated as a foliage plant.
rezzle (rez″l), *n.* in rural England, a weasel.
rhabdomyoma (răb-dō-mi-ō′mȧ), *n.* a tumor of striated muscle fibers.
rhachialgia (rā-kĭ-ăl′ji-ȧ), *n.* Pott's disease.
rhachianesthesia (răk-ĭ-ăn-ĕs-thē′si-ȧ), *n.* spinal anesthesia.
rhachiocentesis (-sĕn-tē′sis), *n.* puncture of the spine.
rhapsodomancy (rap′sŏ-dō-măn-si), *n.* divination by means of verses.
Rheims cathedral (rēmz kȧ-thē′drăl), a famous cathedral, built in the Gothic style of architecture in the 13th century at Rheims, a city in the Department of the Marne, France; it was much damaged in the World War, but has been repaired.
rhenium (rē′ni-ŭm), a chemical element discovered in very minute traces in manganese salts by Tacke and Noddack in 1925: atomic number 75, symbol Re.
rheumatalgia (rōō-mȧ-tăl′ji-ȧ), *n.* rheumatic pain.
rheumatic fever (-mat′ik fēv′ĕr), a disease in which the joints swell and become painful, and there is much constitutional disturbance: in many cases, there is inflammation of the pericardium and valves of the heart: believed caused by a micro-organism known as streptodiplococcus; considered infectious.
Rhiannon's birds (rī-ăn′-yŭnz bērdz), birds belonging to *Rhiannon*, the wife of a Welsh prince, named Pwyll: they sang so charmingly that they entranced the old Welsh bards for considerable periods of time,—one of them, a white bird sang so enchantingly, that it kept the monk Felix spell-bound for one hundred years listening to it. See Longfellow's "Golden Legend".
rhinalgia (rī-nal′ji-ȧ), *n.* pain in the nose.
rhinopharyngitis (rī-nō-făr-ĭn-jī′tis), *n.* an inflammation of the mucous membranes of nose and pharynx.
rhinorrhagia (rī-nō-rā′ji-ȧ), *n.* nosebleed.
rhinorrhea (-rē′ȧ), *n.* a mucous running or discharge from the nose.
rhodamine (rō′dȧ-mĭn), *n.* a rose-colored dye obtained by condensing an amino derivative of phenol with phthalic anhydride.
Rhode Island (rōd ī′lănd), the smallest State of the U. S., Little Rhody, the Plantation State: named after the Island of Rhodes, in the Mediterranean Sea, off the south-west coast of Asia Minor.
Rhodes grass (rōdz grȧs), a South African grass, cultivated as a forage crop in dry districts: after C. J. Rhodes.
Rhodes scholar (skŏl′ĕr), one who is taking, or has taken, the course in a Rhodes scholarship.
Rhodes scholarship (-shĭp), one of a number of scholarships, of an annual value of $1500, at Oxford University, England, under the will of Cecil J. Rhodes (1853-1902), English administrator in South Africa: these scholarships are tenable for three consecutive year and are open to 90 students from the British dominions, and 96 from the U. S.: 15, open to German students, were rescinded in 1916.
Rhodope (rō′dŏ-pā), **Rhodopsis** (rō-dŏp′sis), *n.* a celebrated Greek courtezan of about 600 B. C. who had been a slave in Egypt and was bought at very great cost by Charaxus, brother of the famous lyric poetess, Sappho, who became so enraged at the extravagance, she attacked the purchase in vitriolic verse. Rhodope eventually became the wife of

Psammeticus, king of Egypt and, it is said, built the third pyramid.

rhumba (rŭm′bȧ), *n.* a form of dance, recently introduced in the U. S.

rice Christians (krĭs′chănz), in Protestant missionary fields, especially in China, converts from heathenism who join the church solely for material assistance or gain: analogous to "soupers" during the famine time (1846-1848) in Ireland.

rice table (tā′b′l), in Java, the noonday meal, with rice as the principal dish, to which are added cooked meat, chicken, fish, eggs, pickles, and curries.

Richebourg (resh-bōōr′), *n.* Burgundy red wine of rare delicacy and bouquet.

riddlings (rĭd′lingz), *n.pl.* the coarse material left in a riddle after the firm grain has been sifted through; hence, siftings or leavings of any kind.

ridge myrtle (rij mẽr′t′l), an Australian tree of the myrtle family.

ridgepiece, ridgeplate, see *ridgepole* main vocabulary.

Riggs' disease (rĭgs dĭ-zēz′), pyorrhea alveolaris, a form of pyorrhea: after J. M. Riggs, American dentist.

right wing, European cant for the conservative element in a political group, party, or legislature.

rigid, *adj.* see main vocabulary.

rigid (rij′ĭd), *adj.* in aviation, said of an airship that carries its gas containers inside a rigid framework, as of metal, in which are also the cabins, gondolas, and motors.

rigsmaal (rĭgz′mäl), *n.* the official language of Norway; the Dano-Norwegian "language of the realm."

rima (rē′mä), *n.* in the Philippine Islands, the breadfruit.

rimulose (rĭm′ū-lōs), *adj.* having many small chinks: showing numerous minute fissures.

ring-dropper (-drŏp′ẽr), *n.* [Slang], a sharper who offers to sell a ring, dropped by himself, but which he pretends to have found, the ring being of little or no value.

ringer, *n.* see main vocabulary.

ringer (rĭng′ẽr), *n.* in Australia, the head-man in a shearing shed, the one who shears the most sheep in a day.

ringhals (rĭng′hȧls), *n.* the spitting snake.

riparian (rī-pā′ri-ăn rītz), the legal rights, in regard to a waterway, of one who owns land bordering upon same.

ritz, *n.* [Slang], swank; pretension; presumption: putting on the *ritz* equivalent to putting on dog, that is, pretending, or trying to play a role for which one is not qualified or adapted.

ritzy (rĭt′zi), *adj.* [Slang], extravagant; flashy; pretentious; presumptuous.

roaring days (rōr′ing dāz), the exciting, roistering, and rowdy time, chiefly in and around Ballarat, immediately after gold was first discovered in Australia, in 1851.

roaring forties (fôr′tiz), the stormy areas of ocean, north and south, between the fortieth and fiftieth parallels of latitude.

robot (rō′bŏt), *n.* a mechanical contrivance, somewhat in the form of a man, and operated by electricity, which performs some functions, hitherto deemed beyond anything save human intelligence and activity to carry out; it walks, talks, operates, and controls machinery, but of course the human brain is behind it, not only in its construction, but in the person who manipulates it.

Rockefeller Center (rŏk′ĕ-fĕl-ẽr sen′t′r), a set or series of buildings in N. Y. City, not yet (1935) completed, designed for both amusement and commercial purposes: it is the largest business enterprise ever privately undertaken. Six buildings have been constructed and are occupied: when the group is completed there will be twelve in all, taking up three city blocks, from 48th to 51st street, between 5th and 6th Avenues. Radio City comprises four units—the International Music Hall, the RKO Theater, the RCA Building, and the RKO Building. The whole is under the presidency of John D. Rockefeller, Jr.

Rockefeller Foundation (foun-dā′shŭn), a philanthropic trust, established in 1913, by John D. Rockefeller, Sr. with an endowment of $165,281,624. Its chief departmental bureaus or agencies are (1) the International Health Board, which coöperates with governments throughout the world in safeguarding public health; (2) the China Medical Board which maintains Peiping Union Medical College, and promotes medical education in other Chinese Colleges: (3) the Division of Medical Education, the function of which is the study of present day needs in medical science, and coöperation with Medical Colleges by helping them to extend their work, and (4) the Division of Studies, created in 1924, which concerns itself with investigations of work the Foundation may undertake in the future.

Rockefeller Institute for Medical Research (ĭn′stĭ-tūt, mĕd′i-kăl rē-serch′), an institution incorporated in 1901 by John D. Rockefeller, Sr. having for its objective the promotion and encouragement of medical research, with a special view to the treatment and prevention of disease. It has many laboratories and departments, including those of pathology, physiological and pathological chemistry, bacteriology, physiology, pharmacology and therapeutics.

Rocky Mountain goat (rŏk′i moun′tin gōt), an animal resembling a goat, inhabiting the upper ranges of the Rockies: it has long white hair, underneath which is a thick coat of wool: the horns are black and curve backward.

Roentgenogram (rŏnt-jĕn′ō-grăm), *n.* a picture made with the X-ray: after William Konrad Roentgen (1845-1923), German physicist.

Roentgenologist (-ol′ō-jist), *n.* a specialist in the use of X-rays.

Roentgen rays (rāz), **X-rays,**—see under *ray* main vocabulary.

roller, *n.* see main vocabulary.

roller (rōl′ẽr), *n.* a Harz Mountains canary having a trilling kind of song.

rolling kitchen (kĭch′ĕn), a large metal vessel on wheels, with an under compartment for fire: from it are served hot soup and other warm foods to soldiers on the march.

rollmop (rōl′mŏp), *n.* a salt herring, cleaned and stuffed with onion, pepper, and cucumber sliced, then rolled up and sewed or skewered.

rorty (rôr′ti), *adj.* [Australian Slang], boisterous; hilarious; rowdy; drunken.

Rosalie (rŏz′ȧ-li), *n.* [Soldier Slang], a bayonet.

Rotarian (rō-tā′ri-ăn), *n.* a member of a Rotary Club.

Rotary Club (klub), one of an association of clubs in the U. S., the object of which is to improve civic service.

rotisserie (rō-tēs′-rē′), *n.* [Fr.], a grill or restaurant in which patrons can have food prepared under their direct supervision, and then served.

rotograph (rō′tō-grȧf), *n.* a photograph produced by a process in which a sensitized strip of paper automatically rolls over the negative, making a series of prints.

rotogravure (-grȧ-vūr′), *n.* a process in photogravure for printing illustrations and text by means of etched cylindrical plates attached to the rollers of a rotary machine; an illustration thus produced.

roughneck (rŭf′nĕk), *n.* [Slang], a disorderly fellow; a rowdy; a tough; a blackguard.

Royal Air Force (roi′ăl ār fōrs), a British organization for air defense, formed in 1918 by combining the Royal Flying Corps with the Royal Naval Air Service: under the jurisdiction of the Department of the British Government known as the *Air Ministry*.

Royal Flying Corps (roi′ăl flī′ing kōr), in England, an organization formed in 1912 under the jurisdiction of the War Office, but later amalgamated with the Royal Naval Air Force: abbreviated R. F. C.

rucksack (rŭk′săk), *n.* a canvas knapsack carried on the back with the straps passing over the shoulders.

rumenitis (rōō-mĕn-ī′tis), *n.* inflammation of the rumen.

rumgumption (rŭm-gŭm′shŭn), *n.* in rural England and in Scotland, shrewdness: sharpness; cleverness.

rum jar (jär), [Soldier Slang], the shell of a Minenwerfer.

Ruritania (rōō-ri-tā′ni-ȧ), *n.* an imaginary kingdom in the novel, "The Prisoner of Zenda" by Anthony Hope Hawkins.

Ruritanian (-tā′ni-ăn), *adj.* pertaining to, or characteristic of, Ruritania.

Russell Sage Foundation (rŭs′l sāj foun-dā′shŭn), an institution founded by Mrs. Russell Sage, April 1907, in memory of her husband, with an endowment of $12,000,000 for improving social conditions throughout the U. S.

Russian apple (rŭsh′ăn ap″l), the red astrachan apple, originating in Russia.

Russian bath (bȧth), a vapor bath in which the body is exposed to steam for a considerable time, then washed and shampooed.

Russian thistle (this″l), a prickly European plant which flourishes in Russia: in middle and western U.S., under the name of *tumbleweed*, it is very troublesome to farmers.

Russian wolfhound (wōōlf′hound), the borzoi,—see *wolfhound* main vocabulary.

S

sable-fish (sā′b′l-fĭsh), *n.* a spiny-finned foodfish found in the temperate waters of the North Pacific Ocean.

sabulite (săb′ū-līt), *n.* a high stable explosive about three times more powerful than dynamite.

Sacajawea (săk′ȧ-jȧ-wē′ȧ), *n.* bird woman, an Indian squaw, who joined the Lewis and Clark Expedition when the explorers reached Mandan, a section now included in North Dakota, whence she guided them through the Northwest, carrying her papoose on her back.

sacred geese (sā′kred gēs), geese kept by the ancient Romans in the temple of Juno on the Capitoline Hill. When the Gauls stealthily climbed up the rocks to attack, neither the sentinels nor the watchdogs heard them, but the geese did, and sounded the alarm by cackling: the defenders rushed out, repulsed the invaders, and thus saved the capitol.

sacred number (nŭm′bẽr), seven, which is frequently used in the Bible as a mystical and symbolical number; also, it was so used among the principal nations of antiquity,—Babylonia, Assyria, Persia, India, Egypt, Greece and Rome.

safety island (sāf′ti ī′lănd), one of the small, elevated, and usually concreted, areas in the center of a street or roadway, where there is much vehicular traffic, to afford safety to pedestrians in crossing in case they cannot reach the sidewalk in time to escape accident, from motor cars, wagons, and the like.

Sage of Monticello (sāj, mon-ti-sel′o), sobriquet of Thomas Jefferson: so called from his home in Virginia.

Ste Anne de Beaupre (ăn, bō′prā), a village in Montmorency County, Quebec, Canada, on the St. Lawrence river, famous for its ancient parish church to which large numbers come annually in July to venerate relics of Ste Anne, mother of the Virgin Mary, in the hope of being cured of physical ills.

St. Brendan (brĕn′d′n), an Irish saint of the 6th century who, it is said, was the first white man to reach the North American continent.

St. Crispin (krĭs′pĭn), the tutelary or patron saint of shoemakers, whose feast day is observed on October 25. Crispin, or Crispianos was one of two brothers, born at Rome, who journeyed to Soissons, France, in 303 A. D. to preach the gospel: as they wanted to be independent of any one, both worked as shoemakers. By order of the French governor both were beheaded.

St. James' Palace (jāmz′ păl′ȧs), the residence of the British sovereigns in London, from the time of William III to the accession of Queen Victoria, in 1837, when Buckingham Palace became the royal home: the British court still retains the official designation of the *Court of St. James.*

St. Patrick's Purgatory (păt′riks pûr′gȧ-tō-ri, a small islet in a little mountain lake called Lough Derg, in the County Donegal, Ireland, to which many devout Roman Catholics make pilgrimage to do penance for their sins: they fast and pray almost constantly for several days, meditate on the Stations of the Cross, going around the rocks on bare knees, and, finally, go to confession and communion in the little chapel on the islet.

St. Paul's (pôlz), the great Anglican cathedral in London, the most famous church of its denomination in the world; standing on the summit of Ludgate Hill, it is the most conspicuous building of the city. It dates back to early Saxon times, though the original vast structure was destroyed by the great fire of 1666. The present edifice was built on the same site by the famous architect, Christopher Wren, at a cost of almost $4,000,000; it was begun in 1765 and completed in 1810; to the top of the great dome the height is 405 feet. It contains the tombs of many distinguished men, including those of Nelson, Wellington, and Sir John Moore.

St. Swithin's Day (swĭth′ĭnz), July 15, observed in honor of Swithin (793-862 A. D.), bishop of Winchester, England, who, though not canonized by the Church, is traditionally styled *St. Swithin*: legend says that if rain fall on his day, it will rain in the same locality for forty succeeding days.

Sakdalista (săk-dȧ-lēs′tȧ), *n.* a political party in the Philippines, aiming at the complete independence of the Islands: they revolted against U. S. sway in 1935, but were soon crushed.

salpingectomy (săl-pin-jek′tō-mi), *n.* the operation of cutting out a Fallopian tube.

salpingitis (-jī′tis), *n.* inflammation of the Fallopian tubes.

samantics (sȧ-măn′tiks), *n.* the science of word meanings, or of determining how many meanings a word can or may have.

Sammy (săm′i), *n.* [Slang], in the World War, the British name for an American soldier.

Samnite (săm′nīt), *n.* one of an ancient people who inhabited southern Italy and were allied to the Sabines.

sancy diamond (săn′si dī′ȧ-mŭnd), a large diamond, formerly in the possession of the late imperial family of Russia: was 53 carats when cut.

Sandalphon (săn-dăl′fŏn), *n.* according to Jewish doctrine or belief, a flaming angel who accepts the prayers of men and weaves them into crowns, which he presents to Jehovah.

sandy blight (săn′di blīt), [Australian Slang] ophthalmia.

Santa Casa (sänt′ȧ kä′sä), [Sp.] literally, Holy House; according to tradition, the house in which the Virgin Mary, Mother of Christ, lived at Nazareth, and which was miraculously transferred to Loretto, in Italy, in the 13th century.

Sapphira (să-fī'râ). *n.* in Biblical literature, the wife of Ananias, who tried, with her husband to deceive Peter and who fell dead at the apostle's feet, as did Ananias. See *Acts* v.

Satyagraha (sat'yâ-gră-hâ), *n.* a doctrine preached and practiced by M. K. Gandhi, Hindu reformer, in which great stress is put upon the efficacy of passive resistance and noncoöperation in opposing abuses.

satyromaniac (săt-i-rō-mā'nĭ-ăk), *n.* one affected with satyriasis.

scarlet letter (skär'let lĕt''r), in Puritan times in New England, a scarlet A, sewn or pinned, ou the garment of a woman who had sinned.

scenario, *n.* see main vocabulary.

scenario (sĕ-nā'ri-o), *n.* in moving pictures, the full description of a photoplay, unfolding the plot scene by scene, bringing out every detail in connection therewith, giving the cast of characters, and whatever other matters are essential for the understanding and performance of the story.

Schick test (shĭk), the injection of a diluted diptheria toxin, which causes the skin of a person susceptible to diptheria to become hard and red surrounding the point of injection: after Dr. *Schick* of Vienna.

schipperke (schĭp'ĕr-kē), *n.* one of a breed of small, tailless, usually black dogs, which originated in Holland: they somewhat resemble the Pomeranians, but the hair is much shorter: so called from the Dutch *schipper*, a boatman, because they were used as watchdogs on boats.

schizophrenia (skĭz-o-frē'nĭ-â), *n.* dementia praecox.

Schrecklichkeit (shrĕk'lih'-kīt), *n.* [G.], horrible atrociousness; frightfulness: a word often used during the World War.

scooter, *n.* see main vocabulary.

scooter (skōōt'ĕr), *n.* a kind of push-board used by boys, consisting of a stout narrow piece of wood about a yard long to which are attached two strong wheels, one at either end; to the wheel that is used in front is attached a handle, with bar, by which the manipulator impels the vehicle along; in Western U. S., a plough with one handle, used for marking or laying out furrows.

Scotch-Irish, *n.pl.* descendants of the Lowland Scotch Presbyterians whom James I sent over to colonize Ulster, the northern province of Ireland, early in the 17th century; they intermarried with the Ulster natives, and more than a million of their progeny came to the U. S. during the 18th century. At the outbreak of the Revolution one-sixth of the population of all the colonies were Scotch-Irish.

Scotland Yard (skŏt'lănd yärd), the Metropolitan Police of London, especially, the detective or criminal investigation department, popularly known as the C. I. D., whose headquarters, until 1890, was in Scotland Yard, a short street off Whitehall: at present, headquarters, called New Scotland Yard, is located on the Thames embankment.

Scourge of God (skûrj), Attila, king of the Huns (434-453); he extended his dominions over Germany and Gaul and all his conquests were marked with extreme cruelty and ferocity.

scoutcraft (skout'krăft), *n.* the work, practice, craft, or skill of scouts.

scout cruiser (krōōz'ĕr), a high-speed vessel having an armament heavier than that of a light cruiser.

scram (skram), *v.i.* [Slang] get out; depart; go away: used imperatively.

scrimshank (skrĭm'shăngk), *v.i.* [Slang], to dodge or evade; to shirk duty.

scrimshanker (-ĕr), *n.* [Slang] one who shirks or dodges duty.

scrounge (skrounj), *v.i.* [Slang], to fawn; sponge; pilfer; steal on the sly.

scrounger('ĕr), *n.* [Slang] a low, petty fellow; a loafer; one who pilfers on the sly.

sealine (sēl-ēn'), *n.* rabbit skin so treated and prepared as to resemble near seal.

seaplane (sē'plăn), *n.* an airplane so constructed that it can ascend from, and descend upon, water.

secretarial (sĕk-rē-tā'rĭ-ăl), *n.* secretaries considered collectively as a body; the force of employes under a chief secretary; the place or office where a secretary does his work, or where he stores his records.

Secretary of State (sĕk'rē-tă-ri), in the U. S., the executive head of the Dept. of State, having charge of all foreign relations—the highest cabinet officer: in England there are five Secretaries of State in the Cabinet, *viz*, for Home Affairs, for Foreign Affairs, for India, for the Colonies, and for War.

Secretary of State for Air, in England, a minister, not in the Cabinet, who has control of all the air units in the service: office was created in 1921.

self-service (ser'vis), *adj.* designating a type of café or restaurant in which patrons select their own foods, and wait upon themselves, paying a cashier when leaving.

semipro (sĕm-i-prō'), *n.* [Cant.] abbreviation of semiprofessional, one who engages in sport for pay, but does not follow it as a profession or calling.

serology (sē-rŏl'ō-ji), *n.* the branch of medical science that treats of serums, their preparation, use, reaction, etc.

Seroot fly (sē-rōōt'), a bloodsucking fly with a long proboscis, very troublesome to man and animals in Northern Africa.

Seven Champions of Christendom (chăm-pi-ŭnz, krĭs''n-dŭm), St. George for England, St. Patrick for Ireland, St. Andrew for Scotland, St. David for Wales, St. Denys for France, St. James for Spain, and St. Anthony for Italy.

Seven-hilled City (sĕv''n-hĭld sit'i), ancient Rome, built on seven hills.

Seven Seas, all oceans, namely, the North and South Atlantic, the North and South Pacific, the Indian, and the Arctic and Antarctic oceans.

Shan Van Vocht (shân vân vō), [Ir.], poor old woman or, in order, old woman poor, a mystical or symbolical name for Ireland, often used by the poets and romancers.

Shavian (shā'vi-ăn), *adj.* relating to George Bernard Shaw (Irish litterateur in London), or his works.

shellac (she-lak'), *v.t.* [Slang] to beat soundly; thresh; give a drubbing to.

shiner (shī'nĕr), *n.* [Slang] a black eye.

shinty (shĭn'ti), *n.* a game resembling hockey.

shirty (shĕrty), *adj.* [Slang] chesty; vainglorious; proud; aggressive; forward; bold.

shock-absorber (-ab-sôrb'ĕr), *n.* a hydraulic or pneumatic cushion device used in automobiles to lessen the shock from bumps on rutted or uneven roads: any of several springs attached to an airplane to help effect a smooth landing.

shock troops (trōōpz), well-trained troops of high morale, chosen for offensive work.

shoful (shō'fōōl), *n.* [Eng. Slang] counterfeit money; also, a hansom cab.

shoneen (shō-nyēn'), *n.* [Ir.] a would-be gentleman who puts on airs, and imagines himself superior to those of his surroundings: a swell-head; megalomaniac.

short ballot (băl'ŭt), a system that reduces the number of elective offices in public elections, so that only a few offices are filled by election at one time.

sialism (sī'â-lĭzm), *n.* increased flow of saliva.

sidekick (sīd'kĭk), *n.* [Slang] a comrade; pal; fellow-worker; buddy.

side car, a small car of one seat attached to the side of a motorcycle for the accommodation of a single passenger, who sits abreast of the cyclist.

Siegfried (sēg'frēd), *n.* the hero of several German tales and legends, notably of the Nibelungenlied. He accomplishes wonderful deeds, marries the beautiful Kriemhild, and is treacherously slain by the fierce Hagen. Wagner makes him the chief character in two of his operas.

silundum (si-lŭn'dŭm), *n.* a refractory substance, exceedingly hard, which is formed in the electric furnace: it is used for articles that require great resistory power, as electric resistors.

silver wedding, see under *wedding* main vocabulary.

sin offering (of'ĕr-ing), anything offered as a sacrifice for sin; something offered as an atonement or an expiation of sin, especially, any of the sacrifices offered by the early Jews, which were of two kinds, *bloody* and *bloodless.*

Sinophile (sĭn'ō-fīl), *n.* one, not Chinese, who upholds and defends Chinese policies and customs.

Sinophilism (sī-nŏf'ĭ-lĭzm), *n.* praise or admiration of, or friendship for, the Chinese, their institutions, laws, policies, manners, customs, etc.

Sinophilist (-list), *n.* one, not a Chinese, who displays friendship for the Chinese people.

sin-shifter (-shĭf'tĕr), *n.* [Australian Slang], in the World War, a name applied to an army chaplain by the Anzacs.

sippio (sĭp'ĭ-ō), *n.* a game resembling bagatelle, played with eight balls, cue, and cue ball.

sitosterol (sī-tŏs'tĕr-ōl), *n.* an oily alcohol of a white color, extracted from maize, wheat, and cocoa beans: also, called *sitosterin.*

skirt (skĕrt), *n.* [Vulgar Slang], a woman or girl: used derisively.

skite (skīt), *v.i.* [Australian Slang], to boast; brag; talk wildly, especially of oneself.

skiter ('ĕr), *n.* [Australian Slang] a braggart; a boaster, especially one who boasts of his deeds or actions.

skoal (skōl), *interj.* [Nor.], hail! health! used in giving a Norseland toast.

Skoda gun (skō'dâ), a rapid-firing automatic gun acting on the recoil principle: a fly-wheel set in motion by the recoil returns the recoiling parts to firing position: after Emil von Skoda (1839-1900), proprietor of the Skoda Steel and Munitions Works, formerly in Austria-Hungary, now in Czecho-Slovakia.

skookum (skōō'kŭm), *adj.* [Chinook Indian], first-rate; exceedingly good; superlatively fine: used colloquially in Western U. S.

sláinte (shlaun'te), *interj.* [Ir.] health! hail! here's to you—introducing an Irish toast.

slapstick (slăp'stik), *n.* a device consisting of two pieces of flatboard held by a string, used by cheap somedians to make a noise resembling a heavy blow.

slapstick comedy (kŏm'ĕ-di), low-class comedy in which something suggestive of a slapstick is used to evoke laughter.

slats (slăts), *n.pl.* [Vulgar Slang] the ribs.

sleeping sickness, see *encephalitis lethargica* above.

slick (slik), *adj.* [Slang] smart; plausible; adroit; cunning; also, pleasant; effective.

slushy (slŭsh'i), *n.* a toiler in a scullery; a drudge; a ship's cook; a cook's assistant at an Australian shearing shed.

Smithsonian Institution (smĭth-sō'nĭ-ăn in-sti-tū'shŭn), a national institution of learning established in Washington, D. C. in 1846, under Act of Congress, through an endowment of $120,000 bequeathed for the purpose by James Smithson (1765-1829), an English physicist. It administers the National Museum, National Gallery of Art, Bureau of American Ethnology, International Exchange Service, and the National Zoölogical Park: supported by Congressional appropriations.

smoke-bomb (smōk-bŭm), *n.* a shell which emits a thick white smoke when exploded: used to hide the approach of advancing troops; also, a bomb, emitting a black or white smoke, dropped from an airplane for the purpose of signaling.

smoke-screen (-skrēn), *n.* a curtain of heavy smoke dropped by a ship to conceal her own location or that of a fleet: it is usually produced by the incomplete combustion of coal, but sometimes by specially prepared chemicals.

smooge (smōōj), *v.t.* [Australian Slang] to flatter or fawn; to bill and coo.

smooger ('ĕr), *n.* [Australian Slang] a flatterer; a sycophant; a courtier.

snake juice (snāk jōōs), [Slang] strong liquor.

sniperscope (snīp'ĕr-skōp), *n.* a device, on the principle of the periscope, attached to a rifle near the rear sight, and pointing downward, so that a soldier in a trench can take aim without exposing himself.

snitch (snĭch), *v.i.* [Slang] to inform; betray: reveal: *v.t.* to pilfer; pinch; snatch; steal: *n.* an informer; a betrayer.

snowbird, *n.* see main vocabulary.

snowbird (snō'bĕrd), *n.* [Slang], one who sniffs cocaine powder, which resembles snow in color; a drug fiend.

soft soap (soft sōp), [Slang] fulsome flattery; hypocritical praise; insincere profession of friendship.

soggarth (sŏg'ărt), *n.* [Ir.] a priest.

Sokol (sō'kol), *n.* one of many gynastic societies in Czecho-Slovakia and the U. S., which aim at strength and grace of body, courage, and keenness of mind,—characteristics attributed to the falcon, which the word signifies in Bohemian: a member of a Sokol society or gymnasium.

soldier's heart (sōl'jĕrz härt), the heart in a disordered state, generally characterized by palpitation, pain in the chest, and a feeling of lassitude or fatigue.

southpaw (south'paw), *n.* [Cant] in baseball, a left-handed pitcher: *adj.* denoting or pertaining to such pitcher.

sovietize (sō-vyet'īz), *v.t.* to convert to the principles of sovietism; to change a government by a soviet; to communize.

Solomon (sŏl'ō-mŭn) ,*n.* son of David, and third king of Israel, born about 1030 B. C. During his reign he made the nation a great political power, and adorned Jerusalem by erecting the most gorgeous temple of worship the world has known; reputed to have been the author of *Proverbs, Canticles, Ecclesiastes* and the *Wisdom of Solomon*; renowned for his judicial decisions: hence, any wise man, but especially a wise judge, is termed a Solomon.

Solon (sō'lŏn), *n.* a legislator: a wise man: a sage: after *Solon*, one of the Seven Wise Men of Greece.

sooner (sōōn'ĕr), *n.* one who settles on government land before the legal time for settlement, in order that he can claim, as first-settler, priority over others when the land is legally open to settlement; hence, one who tries to get an unfair advantage; one who acts prematurely for his own advantage.

Sooner State, the State of Oklahoma, because many rushed to what is now that state, before March 23, 1889, the day appointed by President Harrison, in a proclamation, as the one on which a large tract of land would be open for settlement.

soused (sousd), *adj.* [Slang] intoxicated to stupefaction; beastly drunk

South Carolina (kăr-ō-lī'nâ), a State of the U. S., the Palmetto State: named in honor of Charles I of England.

South Dakota (dȧ-kō'tȧ), a State of the U. S., the Coyote State: after the Sioux Indian word *Dahkotah*, meaning "An Alliance of Friends."

South Sea, the Pacific Ocean; so called by Vasco Nuñez de Balboa, in 1513.

sovietism (sō-vyĕt'izm), the principles and practices of the soviets, especially, the form of government carried on by soviets, or approved by them; Bolshevism; communism.

sovietist ('ist), *n.* a member of a soviet body or society; one who believes in sovietism: one who approves the principles of soviet government.

span, *n.* in aëronautics, the spread of an airplane, that is, the maximum distance across or laterally from tip to tip of the machine.

Spanish Main (span'ish mān), in the days of the buccaneers, a name applied to the southern waters of the Caribbean Sea.

Spartacism (spär'tȧ-sizm), *n.* the principles, practices, doctrines and teachings of the Spartacists, members of an extreme radical party organized in Germany after the fall of the Hohenzollerns.

Spartacist (-sist), *n.* a member of the former Spartacus party in Germany; an extreme socialist: a radical.

Spartacus party (spär'tȧ-kŭs pär'ti), *n.* the former Bolshevist party of Germany, a group organized in 1918 along extreme socialistic lines by Karl Liebknecht, who adopted the term in allusion to Spartacus, a Thracian, who at the head of an army of slaves devastated a large part of Italy during 73-71 B. C.

speedster (spēd'stẽr), *n.* a two-seat, high-speed automobile with low body.

sphingomyelin (sfĭng-gō-mī'ĕ-lĭn), *n.* a crystalline compound, containing phosphoric acid radicals, extracted from the white matter of the brain.

spondylotherapeutics (spŏn-di-lō-thĕr-ȧ-pū'tiks), *n.* the massage treatment; the treatment of disease by physical methods, especially, in the region of the spine.

spoonerism (spōōn'ẽr-izm), *n.* the transposition of letter sounds, especially of the sounds of the initial letters of two or more words, as *sh*ower *fl*ow for *fl*ower *sh*ow: after Rev. W. A. Spooner, an English clergyman.

spridhogue (sprĭd'ōg), *n.* [Ir.] a worthless fellow; also a little fellow, one of low stature; a puny, dwarfish creature.

squattocracy (skwŏt-ŏk'rȧ-si), *n.* [Australian Slang] the wealthy and influential squatters as a class; squatters considered collectively or as a whole.

squaw bush (skwô bŏŏsh), the cranberry tree.

sruti (shrŏŏ'ti), *n.* in India, the literature that is regarded as revelation of deity, as the Veda.

staphylitis (stăf-ĭ-lī'tis), *n.* inflammation of the uvula.

Stalinism (stâl'in-izm), *n.* the political theories, doctrine, and practices of Josef Stalin (real name, Josef Dzugashvili), Russian political leader; Russian communism.

static (stat'ik), *n.* in radio, an atmospheric disturbance, caused by electrical discharges, as lightning flashes, which interfere with reception.

Stations of the Cross (stā'shŭnz, krŏs), a series of fourteen pictures or images representing the successive stages of Christ's passion: these are usually placed around the walls of R. C. Churches; sometimes they are placed, as in France, on roads leading to shrines or churches: the devotion called "making the stations" consists in reciting a special prayer before each and meditating upon the particular suffering the picture or image illustrates. In many Anglican churches, also, the Stations are displayed and prayers recited before them.

steam roller (stēm rōl'ẽr), a heavy roller, driven by steam, used for crushing broken stone, gravel, grout, etc. into a consolidated state to form a roadway; hence, any crushing power, force, or influence exerted to down or overcome opposition.

sterilize, *v.t.* see main vocabulary.

sterilize (ster'ĭ-līz), *v.t.* to deprive of virility; to render, by operation, a male or female, incapable of reproduction; to make a region barren of military power by preventing erection of forts or camps, and the assembling of troops.

sterol (ster'ōl), *n.* an abbreviation of cholesterol, one of the solid higher alcohols.

stethemia (stĕ-thē'mi-ȧ), *n.* congestion of the lungs.

stir (stẽr), *n.* [Slang] prison; jail; hoosegow.

stomatitis (stō-mȧ-tī'tis), *n.* inflammation of the mouth.

stooge (stōōj), *n.* [Slang] a toady who follows a performer of stage, screen, or radio and is paid for trying to bring attention to the act of his employer by applauding, shouting, clapping, and in other ways; one who assists an actor on the stage by giving prepared answers to questions or uttering prepared responses, while sitting in a box in orchestra or gallery; an understudy.

stoush *v.t.* [Australian Slang] to beat; punch; pummel; strike violently.

Stradivarius (străd-ĭ-vā'ri-us), a violin made by Antonio Stradivari (1644-1737), of Cremona, Italy: all of his instruments were famed for beauty of design and sweetness and richness of tone: now very scarce and valuable.

stratosphere (strā'tō-sfēr), *n.* the upper region of the atmosphere, about seven miles, less or more, above the earth, the distance varying according to latitude, season, and weather, in which there is but little change in temperature and, consequently, little or no convection, and where clouds never form.

streamline (strēm'līn), *n.* a make or construction, especially of motor-propelled vehicles, as locomotives, automobiles, airplanes, etc., the outlines of which are so designed as to increase air resistance as much as possible; the course taken by a small part of a fluid relative to a solid body to which such fluid is flowing; a curve, the tangent of which at any point shows the direction of the velocity vector at the same tangential point: *adj.* pertaining to a streamline; designating a body, surface, outline, construction, etc., shaped in such a form as to permit the undisturbed flow of a fluid coming towards it, particularly, when the resistance to such flow will be as low as possible; denoting a body, as of a locomotive, automobile, airplane, or the like which gives the least possible resistance to the air: *v.t.* to construct with a streamline form; design a form that presents little resistance to air.

streamline flow (flō), a flow that does not change direction: a flow the direction of which at any point remains the same.

stuffed shirt (stŭf'd shẽrt), [Slang] a vain, pompous, but worthless individual who does little or no good to any one.

submachine gun (sŭb-mȧ-shēn'), a double-firing light weapon which is operated on the automatic principle and can be used either as pistol or gun: by means of a pistol grip it can be fired as the former, and a detachable buttstock enables one to fire it from the shoulder, as a gun; the firing rate is about 500 shots a minute, and the range about 600 yards. It is fed from a drum containing from 50 to 100 cartridges.

Sucker State (sŭk'ẽr stāt), the State of Illinois, whose inhabitants are called "Suckers" because, it is said, early travelers over its prairies sucked their drinking water through a reed from holes made by freshwater crawfish.

superheterodyne (sū-pẽr-hĕt'ẽr-ō-dīn), *adj.* in radio or wireless, designating a type or form of beat reception for extremely high frequencies, by means of which beats of a frequency above audible are produced but lower than that of the received signals: these beats or oscillations, after being rectified, are amplified so as to reproduce in the telephone receivers the sounds of the music, speech, or whatever is being transmitted.

superman (sū'pẽr-măn), *n.* the Overman of Nietzsche, German philosopher; a hypothetical being supposed to have gained power and ascendancy over others through dominant force of character; one considered superior to others in mental and moral qualities and attributes, especially, one who excels in intellectual attainments: word first introduced by G. B. Shaw.

Supreme Council, the executive body of the Peace Conference at Paris, 1919, afterwards the executive body of the Allied and Associated Powers.

Swadeshi (swȧ-dā'shē), *n.* in India, one of the phases of the agitation for Swaraj, aiming at the production and use of home goods, instead of foreign importations.

swank (swengk), *n.* [Eng. Dial.] swagger; pomposity; brag; pretension; braggadocio.

swan song (swŏn sŏng), the last work of a poet or composer, produced immediately before his death: from the tradition that the swan sings melodiously when it is about to die.

Swaraj (swȧ-räj'), *n.* in India, home rule; self-government; independence.

swastika, *n.* see *fylfot* main vocabulary.

sword of Damocles (sōrd, dam'o-klēz), an impending evil; an ever-constant fear; dread of immediate danger: from the sword which Dionysius I. of Syracuse, suspended by a single hair over the head of Damocles, court flatterer, to rebuke him for constantly babbling of the happiness of kings.

synchilia (sin-kī'li-ȧ), *n.* adhesion of one lip to the other.

synovitis (sĭn-ō-vī'tis), *n.* inflammation of a synovial membrane.

syphiloma (sĭf-ĭ-lō'mȧ), *n.* a syphilitic tumor.

syphilophobia (-lō-fō'bi-ȧ), *n.* morbid dread of becoming infected with syphilis.

syringomyelia (sĭ-rĭng-gō-mi-ē'li-ȧ), *n.* a chronic disease of the spine due to cavities in the spinal cord: it is characterized by muscular atrophy of the upper extremities, loss of feeling, and various vasomotor irregularities.

syringomyelitis (-mī-ē-lī'tis), *n.* inflammation of the spinal cord accompanying syringomyelia.

szopelka (sō-pĕl'kȧ), *n.* a musical instrument; a kind of oboe, with brass mouthpiece, popular among Russian peasants around the Black Sea.

T

tabloid, *n.* see main vocabulary.

tabloid (tab'loid), *n.* a small-sized condensed newspaper.

tag day, a day on which funds are publicly solicited from passers-by for some charitable or worthy purpose, each contributor receiving a tag.

taiga, tayga (tī'gȧ, tā'gȧ), *n.* a vast, cold, swampy section of Siberia, covered by forests of stunted pines, lying immediately beyond the tundra or treeless plain of that northern region.

tailors of Tooley street (tāl'ẽrz, tōō'le), applied to any petty or obscure group who imagine themselves of vast importance, or who think they represent the people: from a few poor tailors who met in a house in Tooley street, London, in 1820, and drew up a petition to the House of Commons for redress of popular grievances, beginning "We, the people of England . . ."

tail spin, in aviation, an aerial maneuver in which an airplane descends in a spiral of small radius, with the longitudinal axis of the plane inclined downward at a steep angle.

talkies (tôk'iz), *n.pl.* [Colloq.] movies or moving pictures accompanied by sounds produced synchronously with the actions of the scene represented, and in which the characters talk correspondently to the parts they play.

tamarao (tȧ-mȧ-rä'o), *n.* a small wild buffalo of the Philippines.

Tamworth (tăm'wŭrth), *n.* one of a breed of English pigs that are very large, many weighing from 300 to 500 lbs. and over: they yield excellent bacon: usual color reddish-brown with black patches: after Tamworth in Staffordshire, where first raised.

tandan (tăn'dăn), *n.* a freshwater catfish of Australian rivers: so called by the natives.

Tang (täng), *n.* a Chinese dynasty that flourished from the beginning of the 7th century to the beginning of the 10th century, marked by great progress, especially the invention of printing and the advancement of literature.

taphephobia (tăf-ĕ-fō'bi-ȧ), *n.* an insane fear of being buried alive.

Tara (tä'rȧ), *n.* a famous hill in County Meath, Irish Free State where, in olden days, kings and princes, nobles, courtiers, and bards met to discuss public affairs; in recent times, the scene of many great political gatherings.

Tar State, a nickname for the State of North Carolina, on account of its tar products.

tart (tärt), *n.* [Slang] a sweetheart; a young girl.

tashlik (täsh-lēk'), a propitiatory rite of orthodox Jews, performed on the afternoon of Rosh Hashana, in which they assemble on the bank of a river or stream and pray, while shaking part of their garments over the water, believing that their sins are thus washed away.

taxi (tak'si), *v.i.* to ride in a taxicab.

Taxidea (tăk-sĭd'ĕ-ȧ), *n.* the genus made up of the American badger.

tea wagon (wag'"n), a small table on wheels, used in serving tea and light refreshments.

tear bomb (tēr bŏm), a bomb or shell containing chemicals which, when exploded, temporarily blinds with tears the eyes of those within range.

tear gas, the gas exploded from a tear bomb.

Teddy bear, a stuffed toy for children resembling a bear in miniature.

tefillah (tĕf-ĭ-lä'), *n.* [Heb.] a phylactery.

teju (tĕ-yōō'), *n.* a large South American lizard, about three feet long, of a blackish color, interspersed with yellow spots: eaten by the natives as a delicacy.

telautomatics (tĕl-aw-tō-măt'iks), *n.* control of boats, torpedoes, etc., at a distance, by radio-telegraphic waves.

telemechanics (-mȧ-kăn'iks), *n.* the science of operating apparatus or mechanism at a distance.

telergy (tĕl'ẽr-jĭ), *n.* the influence one brain is supposed to have over that of another at a distance through hypothetical mental force.

telesis (tĕl'e-sĭs), *n.* progress clearly planned and accomplished by consciously directed effort.

televise (tĕl'ĕ-vīz), *v.t.* to transmit representations of places, persons, or objects by radio.

television (tĕl'e-vizh-un), *n.* vision at a distance, specifically, views of places, or of objects and persons, still or in motion, transmitted and reproduced by a recently invented device, in connection with radio, which turns light rays into electrical waves, and re-converts these electrical waves into visible light rays, which form pictures, thus enabling one, through a receiving station, to see, as in the 'movies', representations of the scenes and persons at the transmitting station.

Temple Bar (tĕm′p′l bär), a famous gateway that formerly stood before the Temple in London, at the junction of Fleet Street and the Strand: removed in 1878.
Tennessee (tĕn-ĕ-sī′), *n.* a State of the U. S., the Volunteer State: from the Indian, signifying "River of Big Bend."
tenontagra (tĕn-ŏn-tăg′rȧ), *n.* a disease of the tendons of the nature of gout.
tenontodynia (tĕn-ŏn-tō-dĭn′ĭ-ȧ), *n.* pain in a tendon.
teraglin (tĕr′ȧ-glĭn), *n.* native name of a silvery-scaled fish, abundant along the coast of New South Wales.
terranean (tĕ-rā′nē-ăn), *adj.* belonging to the earth; living in the earth.
terrazzo (tĕr-răt′sō), *n.* [It.] a flooring composed of cement in which fragments of colored stone are set irregularly.
territorialism, *n.* see main vocabulary.
Territorialism (tĕr-ĭ-tō′rĭ-ăl-iz′m), *n.* a theory or doctrine entertained by many Jews, looking forward to the settlement of their race in some country where they would be autonomous or self-governing, or, at least, be given all political rights and privileges.
Terror of the World (tĕr′ĕr, wẽrld), Attila (406-453), King of the Huns; also termed the *Scourge of God.*
Teufel-hund, *n.* [G.] see Devil Dog above.
Texas (tĕk′sȧs), *n.* a State of the U. S., the Lone Star State: from the Indian word, *Tachies,* meaning "Friends."
thana (tä′nä), *n.* in India, a police station: a unit of local administration.
thanadar (-där′), *n.* in India, the chief officer of a police station.
theic (thē′ik), *n.* a lover of tea; one who drinks large quantities of the beverage, or who drinks it often; a tea drunkard.
thevetin (thĕv′ē-tĭn), *n.* a poisonous glucoside extracted from the seeds of certain apocynaceous plants: there are many such plants and trees, all tropical, and all belong to the dogbane family: recently, from the nuts of one of them, the oleander, a crystalline drug, has been extracted which, it is claimed, is more effective then digitalis in the treatment of cardiac affections.
Thian Shan stag (tē-än′ shän), a very large deer of the Thian Shan range in Western China, allied to the American wapiti.
Thian Shan sheep, a sheep of the Thian Shan mountains, allied to the bighorn but having much longer horns.
thigmotropism (thĭg-mŏt′rō-pizm), *n.* response to contact stimuli.
thioform (thī′ō-fôrm), *n.* a yellowish powder used as an antiseptic, and as a substitute for iodoform.
thiol (thī′ōl), *n.* a brown liquid used in the treatment of skin diseases: it is obtained by heating paraffin oil and sulphur.
third degree (thẽrd dē-grē′), in Freemasonry, the degree of Master Mason, conferred with elaborate ceremonies; hence, a severe hackling or examination of a prisoner or suspect in order to extort a confession of guilt.
thoracodynia (thō-rȧ-kō-dĭn′ĭ-ȧ), *n.* pain in the chest.
thorn bird (bẽrd), a small bird of South America, so called because it builds a very large nest of thorns in a bush or tree.
thorn devil (thôrn dev′′l), an exceedingly spiny agamoid lizard of South Australia.
thrasher (thrăsh′ẽr), a very large shark of the Atlantic coasts, having a huge, long tail with which it threshes the water to attract the fish it devours.
three balls (thrē bôlz), three gilt balls used as a sign for a pawnbroker's shop: from the coat of arms of Lombardy, the first pawnbrokers in London being Lombards.
three-card monte (-kärd mŏn′tē), three cards thrown quickly on a table by a gambler who challenges his victim to pick out the one that has been previously shown.
Three Musketeers (mŭs-kĕt-ērz′), three close friends in the romance of this name (Fr. *Les Trois Mousquetaires*) by Alexander Dumas, *pere,* who stick together and adopt as their motto "one for all, and all for one."
Three Wise Men, the "wise men from the East" who followed the star of the new-born Christ to Bethlehem where, at the crib, they offered gold, frankincense, and myrrh: legend, not the Bible, gives their names as Gaspar, Melchior, and Balthasar.
thymopathy (thī-mŏ′pȧ-thĭ), *n.* a mental disorder; a disease of the thymus gland.
Tib's eve (tĭbz ēv), never; a time that never comes: there is no saint of this name.
ticker tape (tĭk′ẽr tāp), a continuous ribbon or narrow band of paper, issuing from a ticker machine, operated by a telegraphic device, on which are printed daily quotations from the stock exchange.
tickled (tik′′ld), *adj.* marked with small specks on a plain ground; [Slang] pleased: satisfied.
tickled to death, [Slang] exceedingly well pleased; highly satisfied; happy over some occurrence or event.
Tiger, the, a nickname given to Georges E. B. Clemenceau (1841-1929), who was premier of France, 1917-1920.
tightwad (tīt′wȧd), *n.* [Slang] one who keeps a tight hold of his 'wad'; a person who hates to part with money; one who grudgingly or reluctantly pays his just debts or dues: a miser.
tilpah (tĭl′pä), *n.* in Southwestern U. S., a parti-colored rug used between the saddle and the saddle blanket.
timber rattlesnake (tĭm′bẽr răt′′l-snāk), the banded rattlesnake.
time clock (tīm klŏk), a clock having a mechanical arrangement which when punched records the time of arrival and departure of employees.
tinitus (tĭ-nī′tus), *n.* a singing, or ringing, sound in the ears.
tinker's dam (tingk′ẽrz), something worthless, or of no account: formerly, a tinker, in soldering, made a little dam of clay to retain melted solder, which dam was worthless after the job was finished.
Tippecanoe (tĭp-ĕ-kȧ-nōō′), *n.* a sobriquet of General William Henry Harrison (1773-1841), ninth president of the U. S. (1841), from his victory over the Indians near the Tippecanoe River.
Titanic (tī-tan′ik), name of an English steamship, struck by an iceberg on the night of April 14, 1912, on her maiden voyage from Liverpool to New York, and sunk with a loss of 1,513 out of a total of 2,213.
Toby (tō′bi), *n.* Punch's dog in a Punch-and-Judy show, wearing a frill, and bells to scare the Devil away.
tohunga (tō-hōō′ngä), *n.* among the Maoris of New Zealand, a wise man; a priest.
tommyrot (tŏm′ĭ-rŏt), *n.* [Slang] foolishness; nonsense; false statement.
tonguetacked (tŭng′tăk-it), *adj.* defective in utterance; impeded or hesitating in speech.
tongue tree (trē), the tongue of a wagon or other vehicle.
topesthesia (tŏp-ĕs-thē′si-ȧ), *n.* determination of a place or locality by the sense of touch.
tophaceous (tŏ-fā′shŭs), *adj.* sandy; gritty; stony; rough.
tophyperidrosis (tŏf-ĭ-pĕr-ĭ-drō′sis), *n.* excessive secretion or exudation of sweat, localized in a part.
topknotcher (-nŏch′ẽr), *n.* [Slang] a superior person; one who excels in some particular activity.
totalitarian (tō-tăl-ĭ-tăr-ĭ-ăn), *adj.* pertaining to, or designating, a closely centralized government under control of a particular political group or organization which does not recognize, nor permit representation to, any other political party: *n.* one who supports, or favors, totalitarian government.
totalitarianism (-ĭzm), *n.* the principles and practices of those in control of totalitarian government; the support or advocacy of totalitarian government.
tower wagon (tou′ẽr wăg′′n), a wagon having a movable platform which can be raised to enable workmen to repair overhead trolley wires.
toxiferous (tŏk-sif′ẽr-ŭs), *adj.* producing, containing, or bearing poison.
trachle (trä′h′l), *v.t.* [Scot.] to drudge; drag wearily along; toil listlessly: *n.* drudgery; wearisome toil; prolonged exertion; a long, exhausting walk.
tranka (trăng′kȧ), *n.* a silver coin of Tibet, worth about 12 cents in U. S. currency.
traumatropism (trô-măt′rō-piz′m), *n.* the sensitiveness of certain plants to wounds, especially wounds of the roots.
Treacle Bible (trē′k′l bī′b′l), Beck's Bible of 1549 in which the word balm is rendered treacle; also known as the Bishops' Bible. In *Jer.* viii:22, the line reads:—"Is there no *tryacle* (treacle) in Gilead?"
treacle miner (mīn′ẽr), [Slang] one of the squattocracy of Australia; a squatter who has become pompous and proud of his wealth.
tresis (trē′sis), *n.* perforation.
tribadism (trib′ȧ-dizm), *n.* sensual desire of one woman for another; lewdness; Sapphism; Lesbianism.
tricolette (trĭk-ō-lĕt′), *n.* a kind of dress goods, usually made of cotton but sometimes of fiber silk.
Trilbies (trĭl′bēz), *n.pl.* [Slang] feet, or shoes, especially large feet, or large shoes: in allusion to the heroine of George du Maurier's novel, "Trilby."
triskelion (trĭs-kĕl′ĭ-ŏn), *n.* a figure representing three parts or branches radiating from a common center, and adopted as a badge or symbol, as three legs, bent at the knees, which is the symbol of the Isle of Man.
tristimania (trĭs-tĭ-mā′nĭ-ȧ), *n.* melancholia.
tritural (trit′ū-rȧl), *adj.* adapted for grinding, as the teeth of certain animals.
trollop (trŏl′up), *v.i.* [Scot.] to walk or work in a slovenly manner: *n.* a slovenly woman: a slattern: a wanton woman.
tromomania (trŏm-ō-mā′nĭ-ȧ), *n.* delirium tremens.
troposphere (trŏp′ō-sfēr), *n.* the portion of the atmosphere below the stratosphere, in which clouds form and temperature decreases with altitude.
trotol, TNT. see *trinitrotoluol* main vocabulary.
tryout (trī′out), *n.* a test by which fitness or capacity is determined.
tsamba (säm′bȧ), *n.* barley scorched and ground: constitutes the principal cereal food of the inhabitants of Tibet and Mongolia.
tuberculophobia (tū-ber-kū-lō-fō′bĭ-ȧ), *n.* a morbid dread of tuberculosis.
Tuileries (twē′lẽr-iz), *n.* a royal palace in Paris, connected with the Louvre, the scene of stirring revolutionary activities: it was burned by the Commune, in 1871.
tune in, in radio, to adjust the frequency of a receiving set or apparatus to correspond to that of the sending station, so as to hear a desired program.
turkey-trot (tûr′ki-trot), a modern one-step, syncopated or ragtime dance, characterized by eccentric sensational motions and positions.
tussol (tŭs′ōl), *n.* a salt of antipyrine, used as a remedy in whooping cough.
twilight sleep (twī′līt slēp), a partial narcosis induced by scopolamine, or a morphine derivative, for the purpose of rendering the pains of childbirth less painful.
typhemia (tī-fē′mĭ-ȧ), *n.* typhus fever.
typomania (tī-pō-mā′nĭ-ȧ), *n.* a mania for writing for public reading: nonce word.
typtology (tĭp-tŏl′ō-ji), *n.* the study or lore of spirit rappings.
tyriasis (tĭ-rī′ȧ-sis), *n.* elephantiasis; also, alopecia.

U

udasi (ōō-dä′sē), *n.pl.* in India, members of the Sikh sect who go around begging; Sikh mendicants.
ukulele (ōō′kōō-lā′lā), *n.* a kind of guitar, with four strings, originally played by the Kanakas or natives of the Hawaiian Islands, and now in frequent use in U. S.
Ulad (ū′lăd), *n.* the ancient name of Ulster, the northern province of Ireland, now Northern Ireland.
ulæmorrhagia (ū-lē-mō-rā′ji-ȧ), *n.* hemorrhage from the gums.
ullagone (ŭl-ȧ-gŏn′), *n.* [Ir.] a wail of sorrow; a cry of grief; a dirge or lament.
ullalulla (ŭl′ȧ-lŭl′ȧ), *n.* [Ir.] a dirge for the dead.
Ulster King-of-Arms (ŭl′stẽr), the chief heraldic officer of Ireland, a member of the Heralds' College, ranking next to Garter King-of-Arms.
ultimate stress (ŭl′tĭ-māt), stress at which material will fail or break.
ultramicroscopic (ŭl′trȧ-mi-krŏ-skŏp′ik), *adj.* too small or minute to be seen through the lens of a microscope.
ultra valorem (ŭl′trȧ vȧ-lō′rĕm), [L.] beyond the value.
ultra-violet rays (ul′trȧ-vī′o-let rāz), *n.* the very short rays beyond the violet of the visible spectrum, and which have strong actinic and bactericidal power: used in the treatment of superficial skin diseases.
Ulva, *n.* see main vocabulary.
Ulva (ōōl′vä), *n.* one of a tribe of Indians inhabiting Nicaragua, and constituting a linguistic stock.
umbra tree (ŭm′brȧ), a South American tree with large dark leaves, which give it a gloomy appearance: the juice of the berries is used for coloring wine.
underground railway (un′dẽr-ground rāl′wā), a railway or railroad beneath a tunnel or running under the streets of a city; formerly, an understanding or coöperation among those opposed to slavery for the purpose of permitting, and even assisting, fugitive slaves to escape from their bondage in the South to freedom elsewhere, especially in Canada.
underslung (ŭn′dẽr-slŭng), *adj.* designating the body of an automobile suspended from the springs in a way that causes the axles to be above the frame of the chassis.
unigenesis (ū-nĭ-jĕn′ĕ-sis), *n.* asexual reproduction.
union shop (ūn′yŭn shŏp), a shop in which the rules and regulations of a trade-union are strictly observed.
union station (stā′shŭn), a railroad station used jointly by two or more railroad companies.
Universal Prayer (ū-nĭ-ver′sȧl prer), the Lord's Prayer, beginning "Our Father etc."
unknown soldier (ŭn′nōn sōl′jẽr), an unidentified soldier whose body has been selected to represent all those of a nation who were killed in the World War. His grave, which is specially honored, is a symbol of the graves of all the fallen soldiers.
uranophane (ū-răn′ō-fān), *n.* hydrous silicate of uranium and calcium.
uranalysis (ū-rȧ-năl′ĭ-sis), *n.* the chemical analysis of urine; urinalysis.
uraniferous (ū-rȧ-nĭf′ẽr-ŭs), *adj.* containing or yielding uranium.

uratæmia (ū-rȧ-tē′mĭ-ȧ), *n.* accumulation of urates in the blood.
uratosis (-tō′sis), *n.* a deposit of urates in the tissues.
ureterectomy (ŭ-rē′tĕr-ĕk′tŏ-mĭ), *n.* excision of a ureter.
ureterolith (-ŏ-lith), *n.* stone or concretion in the ureter.
ureteropyosis (-pī-ō′sis), *n.* inflammation of the ureter, with a purulent exudation.
ureterostenoma (ŭ-rē′tĕr-ŏ-stē-nō′mȧ), *n.* stricture of the ureter.
ureterotomy (-ŏt′ŏ-mĭ), *n.* the act or operation of cutting into the ureter.
urethralgia (ŭ-rĕ-thrăl′ji-ȧ), *n.* pain in the urethra.
urethrism (ŭ-rē′thriz′m), *n.* a condition in which the liver is irritable.
urodynia (ū-rŏ-dĭn′i-ȧ), *n.* painful urination.
urœdemia (ŭ-rŏ-dē′mĭ-ȧ), *n.* a swelling due to the extravasation of blood into the tissues.
uropoiesis (ŭ-rŏ-poi-ē′sis), *n.* secretion of urine.
ushabti (ōō-shăb′ti), *n.* in ancient Egypt, a small mummy-like figure deposited in a tomb with the real mummy, bearing inscriptions about the latter.
Utah (ū′tä), *n.* a State of the U. S., the Mormon State, named after the Ute tribe of Indians.
uteritis (ū-tĕr-ī′tis), *n.* inflammation of the womb.
uteromania (-ŏ-mā′ni-ȧ), *n.* nymphomania.

V

Valley Forge (val′i fōrj), name of place where Gen. George Washington and his army camped during the winter, 1777-1778; Washington's encampment: now a State park in Chester county, Pennsylvania.
vamp, *v.* & *n.* see main vocabulary.
vamp (vămp), *v.t.* [Slang] to allure; entice; beguile; seduce by look, posture, or action: said of an adventuress: *n.* one who vamps: a designing female; an adventuress.
varicosis (vă-ri-kō′sis), *n.* the formation of varices or varicose veins; varicosity.
varicotomy (-kŏt′ŏ-mi), *n.* excision of a varicose vein.
varicula (vă-rĭk′ū-lȧ), *n.* a swelling or varicosity of the veins of the conjunctiva.
varus (vā′rŭs), *n.* a deformity in which one of the feet is turned inward: *adj.* denoting a deformed foot; bent inwards: knock-kneed.
vasectomy (văs-ĕk′tŏ-mi), the operation of cutting into the vas deferens or seminal duct; —a modern way of rendering sterile, as it prevents impregnation.
Vazimba (vȧ-zĭm′bȧ), *n.* one of a Negroid people inhabiting Madagascar.
velamen (vĕ-lā′mĕn), *n.* a membrane; a velum.
veldt sore (vĕlt sōr), a sore which frequently breaks out, usually on the feet, of those who often walk on the veldt in South Africa: supposed due to a special microörganism.
venetian (vĕ-nē′shăn), *n.* a fabric of twilled cotton, mostly used for lining garments.
verano (vĕr-ăn′ŏ), *n.* the dry season in tropical America.
verbomania (ver-bŏ-mā′ni-ȧ), *n.* an inordinate desire for acquiring words, especially new ones; a mania for talking; word-madness.
verbomaniac (-ăk), *n.* one who devotes much time to the study of words, and to the acquirement of new words; one addicted to much talk; one who indulges in almost incessant and foolish chatter.
verminiferous (ver-mĭ-nĭf′ĕr-ŭs), *adj.* breeding, or bearing, vermin.
Vermont (vĕr-mŏnt′), *n.* a State of the U. S., the Green Mountain State: from the French *vert*, green, and *mont*, mountain.
verrucosity (vĕr-ŏŏ-kos′i-ti), *n.* the state or condition of being covered with warts.
verrucoseness (-kōs′nĕs), *n.* same as verrucosity.
versipel (ver′sĭ-pĕl), *n.* a creature that is supposed to change from one form to another, as the werewolf.
Very's lights (ver′iz litz), a system of signaling by means of balls of green and red fired from a pistol in an arrangement representing numbers, which have a code significance: from Samuel W. *Very* who invented the system in 1877.
Victorian (vik-tō′ri-an), *n.* one who lived in England, particularly in London, during the reign of Queen Victoria: *adj.* referring to Queen Victoria, especially, her reign.
Victory Medal (vĭk′tŏ-ri mĕd′ăl), a bronze medal cast in 1920 by order of the U. S. government for distribution among the soldiers, sailors and others who had been in service in the World War: the medal on the obverse shows Liberty, and the reverse, the shield of the U. S., with names of Allied Nations.
vioform (vī′ŏ-fôrm), *n.* an odorless derivative of quinoline, used as a substitute for iodoform.
viosterol, see *ergosterol* above.
Virginia (vĕr-jĭn′i-ȧ), *n.* a State of the U. S., the Old Dominion State; named in honor of Queen Elizabeth of England—the "Virgin Queen."
Virgin Queen (vĕr′jin kwēn), a title applied by some to Elizabeth, Queen of England (1533-1603), daughter of Henry VIII and Anne Boleyn.
vitamin (vī′tȧ-min, vit′a-min), *n.* any one of a group of constituents, some of which are in nearly all natural foods, more or less, even a small quantity of some particular one being necessary to the proper maintenance of bodily health and vigor. There are several vitamins, but the exact chemical properties or principles of some have not as yet been determined. All of the known vitamins, except the D vitamin or factor, come, originally, from plant sources, and are present in the oils, organs, and milk of animals only as they come originally from plant sources, and from vitamin rich or vitamin low foods. The lack of essential vitamins in foods causes what is called "deficiency disease," which simply is the effect of malnutrition. In the absence of these vitamins, neither proteins, nor fats, nor carbohydrates, nor salts, are properly utilized—some of these are largely wasted, while others are harmful to the organism. The principal known vitamins are A, B, C, and D. Vitamin A is contained in the oils of vegetables and fruits, and in the adipose tissue and fatty parts of the livers and kidneys of animals, but butter and cream are the staple and larger sources of this vitamin; cod liver oil is also rich in it. Yeast is the richest known source of Vitamin B which, also, is found in green leaves, vegetables, eggs, and milk; the absence of this vitamin causes loss of appetite and cessation of growth. Vitamin C is in goodly quantity in fresh vegetables and fresh fruits, in fresh milk, too, and in some animal products; a deficiency in this vitamin is directly associated with bad teeth; it has an important part in bone development. Vitamin D largely comes from animal source, but to some extent it is also found in cod liver oil; away from vitamins A, B, and C, its use should be restricted, as it is likely to do harm; this vitamin is an outstanding factor in the preventing of rickets.
vitreograph (vit′rē-ŏ-grȧf), *n.* a photographic printing on glass.
volplane (vŏl′plān), *v.i.* to descend in an aeroplane from a high altitude without motor power; to come down at a wider angle than that of a glide.
Volstead Act (vŏl′sted ăkt), an act of Congress to enforce the Eighteenth or Prohibition Amendment to the Constitution of the U. S., passed into law October 28, 1919, and effective the following January 19. The Eighteenth Amendment was repealed, 1933.
vulturine eagle (vŭl′tū-in ē′g′l), a South African eagle having a black plumage except the lower part of the back, which is white.

W

Waac (wak), *n.* a member of the Women's Auxiliary Army Corps of England, organized in 1917 to help in the World War by serving as nurses, secretaries, stenographers, attendants, ambulance drivers, etc.: the word is an acrostic from the title.
Walpurgis Night (väl-pōōr′gis nīt), in Germany, May Eve, the festival of an English female saint, said to have converted the Saxons to Christianity: the superstitious believe that the spirits of the dead walk abroad on this night: corresponds to Hallowe'en, the Eve of All Saints, in Ireland, October 31.
wangle (wang′g′l), *v.t.* [Slang] to cheat; swindle; obtain by unfair methods; to act unscrupulously.
war baby (wôr bā′bi), an illegitimate child born while the father is serving as a soldier in war.
war bride (brīd), a girl or woman who marries a soldier while the latter is actively engaged in war service.
war is hell, a famous epigram attributed to Gen. William Tecumseh Sherman (1820-1891) after the fall of Vicksburg (1863), while he was leading his troops across the Pearl River, at Jackson, Mississippi, in pursuit of Gen. Joseph E. Johnston and his forces.
warrant officer (wŏr′ănt ŏf′is-ĕr), in the U. S. navy, a minor or subordinate official appointed (warranted) by the President, whose duty is manifested by his title, such as gunner, machinist, carpenter, etc.
Washington (wŏsh′ing-tŭn), *n.* a State of the U. S., the Chinook State: named in honor of the first President.
Washington Monument (mŏn′ū-mĕnt), a marble obelisk, the highest (555 ft.), of its kind in the world, on the left bank of the Potomac, in Washington, D. C., erected as a national memorial of George Washington: it was begun during the President Polk administration in 1848, and finished in 1884; total cost $1,500,000.
washout, *n.* see main vocabulary.
washout (wŏsh′out), *n.* a failure; an empty, useless, or ineffectual thing: in aëronautics, decrease in the angle of attack; in gunnery, a miss in shooting at a target.
Wasserman test (väs′ĕr-män), a complicated test for syphilis in which serum from the patient is involved: after August von Wasserman (1866-1933), German bacteriologist.
Watchdog of the Treasury (wŏch′dŏg, trĕzh′ŭ-ri), a nickname applied to the member of Congress who makes the greatest efforts to prevent excessive appropriations. It was first applied, in 1867, to Elihu B. Washburne, of Illinois, who served in Congress from 1853 to 1869.
watchful waiting (wŏch′fŭl wāt′ing), refraining from interfering with another, but keeping close watch on his actions and attitude: from President Wilson's first annual message (Dec. 2, 1913) in reference to his policy regarding the then disturbances in Mexico.
watered stock (wô′tĕrd stŏk), capital stock increased without increase of assets.
water wagon (wăg″n), [Slang] a synonym for abstention from intoxicating liquors, on the *water wagon* signifying "off the booze."
Waterloo (wô-tĕr-lōō′), *n.* a village in the province of Brabant, Belgium, about ten miles south of Brussels, pop. (1932) 5,053, scene of the battle, June 15, 1815, in which the French army under Napoleon was defeated by the allied forces under Blücher and Wellington; hence, a decisive defeat; a disastrous reverse.
Watling Street (wŏt′ling strēt), a great Roman road of England; beginning at Dover it ran through Canterbury to London, thence in a northwesterly direction to Chester, Holyhead, and Anglesea, in Wales.
Wazir (wȧ-zēr′), *n.* one of a hardy mountainous people of the northwest frontier Province of India, closely resembling the Afghans in physique.
Wea (wā′ä), *n.* one of a remnant of a tribe of Indians, originally a division of the Miamis, now dwelling in northern Oklahoma.
weasel words (wē′z′l wĕrdz), words that contradict each other; words so applied that one *sucks* the meaning, as it were, from the other, so that the latter is deprived of its original interpretation or force: after the weasel's habit of sucking eggs until only the light and useless shells remain: the term was used by Theodore Roosevelt in a speech at St. Louis, May 31, 1916, criticizing President Wilson, but Mr. Roosevelt was not the originator.
weeping philosopher (fĭ-lŏs′ŏ-fĕr), Heraclitus of Ephesus, from his gloomy view of life and his habit of bewailing the failings and foibles of others: contrasted with Democritus, of Abdera, who laughed at the failings and foibles of others.
Weird Sisters (wērd sis′tĕrz), in Scandinavian mythology, the three sisters who had control over Fate, one named Urth (the Past), the second, Verthandi (the Present), and the third Skuld (the Future).
weirrasthrue (wĕr′ăs-thrōō), *interj.* [Ir.] an expression of grief, signifying my sorrow.
Westminster Abbey (west′min-stĕr ab′i), the Collegiate Church of St. Peter, in London, built by Edward the Confessor (1049-1065): burial place of English sovereigns, statesmen, heroes, and poets, painters, and others of distinction.
Westinghouse brake (wĕs′tĭng-hous brāk), a railroad airbrake controlled by compressed air from a pump on the engine of a locomotive: it acts automatically when a coupling is disconnected.
West Virginia (vĕr-jin′i-ȧ), a State of the U. S., the Panhandle State, or the Little Mountain State, formed from western and northwestern parts of Virginia.
wet-my-foot, in Ireland, the quail, on account of its peculiar cry from the meadows in the summer evenings.
whiffenpoof (whif′ĕn-pōōf), *n.* a piece of board or log, studded with protruding nails, which boy scouts use in their forest work to blaze or mark trails on the trunks of trees.
whippet, *n.* see main vocabulary.
whippet (whĭp′ĭt), *n.* a small armored tank which the Allies used in the World War: equipped with two engines, it was very mobile and speedy, and required only two men to operate it.
Whitechapel (hwīt-chăp′ĕl), *n.* a district in the northeast section of London, mostly made up of narrow, irregular streets, notorious as the scene of a series of murders, chiefly of unfortunate women, in 1888 and 1889, by a supposed degenerate who signed his name as Jack the Ripper.
whiskey insurrection (hwĭs′ki in-sŭ-rĕk′shŭn), an outbreak in western Pennsylvania in 1794, on account of the excise tax on whiskey imposed under a law of 1791: it spread to Virginia but was suppressed by an armed force under Gen. Henry Lee, governor of Virginia.
white clergy (kler′ji), formerly in Russia, the parish priests in contradistinction to the *black* clergy or monks.
white coal (kōl), [Fr. *houille blanche*] falling, flowing, or rushing water, capable of being used for power purposes: term originated in France; also, a compound of carbon, hydrogen,

oxygen and sulphur, found in the form of minute reddish-brown scales in certain shales of Tasmania.

white-haired boy (-hār″d), [Colloq.] a favorite; a pet; a popular person; one who performs a conspicuous or meritorious act, or deed of bravery.

Whitehall (-hôl), *n.* formerly a royal palace in London, originally called York House, of which only a royal chapel now remains, which was built for James I.

White King, Charles I. of England: he wore a white robe of State instead of a purple one, and on the day of his funeral, snow covered his pall.

White Lady (lā′di), a ghost seen in different castles and palaces formerly belonging to the royal family of Germany, whose appearance was supposed to forebode the death of a member; often termed the *White Lady of Berlin.*

White Lady of Ireland (ir′lănd), the banshee.

white man's burden (bur′d′n), the supposed responsibility of the white race for the moral and physical welfare of the other races of mankind; title of a poem by Rudyard Kipling.

white man's grave (grāv), Sierra Leonê, a British protectorate in Africa, area 31,109 sq. m., pop. (1930) 1,313.

White League (lēg), a term applied to the Ku-Klux Klan; a military society organized in Louisiana immediately after the Civil War, having for its objective the maintenance of white supremacy.

whites (hwītz), *n.pl.* leucorrhea.

White Slave Act, an act of Congress, passed June 25, 1910, to regulate interstate and foreign commerce by prohibiting the transportation therein of women and girls for immoral purposes: also, called the *Mann Act,* after Congressman James R. Mann, of Illinois, who introduced the bill.

whoopee (hwōōp′ē), *n.* [Slang] hilarious rejoicings; merry pranks; antics; fun; in general, a gay time: *interj.* an exclamation of joy, delight, gladness, or the like.

Wicked Bible (wĭk′ĕd bĭb′l), a Bible, published in 1631, in which the word, *not,* is omitted from the seventh commandment, causing it to read—"Thou shalt commit adultery."

Widow of Windsor (wid′o, win′sor), a sobriquet of Queen Victoria after the demise of Albert, the Prince Consort.

wild potato (pŏ-tā′tō), a low twining vine of the morning-glory family, having a very large, more or less bulbous root, cordate leaves, and large purplish flowers, with dark corollas; another kind of twining vine with an enormous tuberous root, in some cases, three feet long, which is confined to the American tropics: it is regarded by some as the original of the sweet potato.

wild tobacco (tŏ-băk′ō), a species of tobacco, formerly cultivated by the Indians, but now growing wild in Eastern U. S. and Canada.

wilgar (wil-gär′), *n.* a corruption of *wilga,* so pronounced by the natives, an Australian scrub bush resembling the willow, and having numerous and strong scented leaves and flowers: see *wilga* main vocabulary.

Wilhelmstrasse (vĭl′hĕlm-shträs″ē), *n.* [G.] literally, William's street; a street in the center of Berlin, beginning on the south side of the Unter den Linden and ending at the Belle Alliance Platz: as there are many government buildings and offices on this street, including the Foreign Office, it was figuratively used for the German Foreign Office in the time of the monarchy.

wind cave (wĭnd kāv), a large cave, covering about 11,000 acres, in South Dakota: it is a cañon running into an extensive cave containing miles of galleries and chambers of peculiar formation.

wind shield (shēld), a shield or plate of glass in front of an automobile or motor car to protect the face of the driver or chauffeur from the force of the wind and from wind-driven particles; a similar device in an airplane to break or resist the force of the wind upon the aviator.

Windsor Castle (käs′l), one of the residences of the royal family of Great Britain, located in Berkshire.

windy city (wĭn′dĭ sĭt′ĭ), Chicago: from the breezes blowing through and over it off Lake Michigan.

winter bird (win′tẽr bẽrd), the woodcock.

Wisconsin (wĭs-kŏn′sĭn), a State of the U. S., the Badger State; from the Indian, signifying "Wild rushing Channel."

wise guy (wīz gī), [Slang] a cunning fellow; a sharper; a shrewd, calculating person; one not easily deceived.

wisest man, Socrates (469-399 B. C.), the Athenian philosopher: so pronounced by the Oracle at Delphi.

Witch of Endor (wĭch, en-dŏr), the woman with a familiar spirit whom King Saul consulted at En-dor, and for whom she summoned the spirit of Samuel. See I *Sam.* xxviii.

witches' Sabbath (săb′ăth), in medieval times, a blasphemous revelry at midnight in which witches and evil spirits were supposed to participate; a profane orgy at midnight in which holy things were desecrated and the ceremonies of the Church travestied and mocked: it is said that such orgies are still practiced, at which the so-called Black Mass is celebrated.

Wizard of the North (wĭz′ărd), a title applied to Sir Walter Scott (1771-1832), on account of the conjuring power of his fertile imagination.

wobbles (wŏb′l′z), *n.pl.* the blind staggers; in Australia, a disease of horses and cattle, said to be due to their eating the hard, peltate or shield-shaped leaves of certain plants.

Wolof (wō′lŏf), *n.* one of an intensely black Negro tribe of the western Sudan.

Wolverine State (wol-vẽr-ĭn′), the State of Michigan: named for the animal, the Wolverine.

woman of pleasure (wōōm′ăn, plĕzh′ūr), a woman who indulges in sensuality; a profligate.

Woman's Christian Temperance Union (′ănz krĭs′chăn tĕm′pẽr-ăns ūn′yŭn), an organization of women founded in 1874 in the U. S. for the purpose of promoting the cause of temperance by example, education, social activity, evangelistic work and by endeavoring to get legislation favorable to their undertaking.

woman suffrage (sŭf′rāj), the right to vote, possessed or exercised by females.

wooden horse (hôrs), an enormous wooden figure of a horse, which the Trojans dragged into Troy as a palladium, but the Greeks concealed themselves in it, and at night dashed out, slew the Trojan guards, opened the gates, and set fire to the city.

wooden Indian (wŏŏd″n in′dĭ-ăn), a representation of an Indian, carved from wood and painted, formerly placed before tobacco shops and cigar stores as a trade sign or symbol.

wop (wŏp), *n.* [Slang] derisive nickname for an Italian; a Dago; any unskilled laborer of Latin origin or extraction.

World Court (wẽrld kōrt), the permanent court of international justice at The Hague, the chief office of which is to settle disputes between conflicting states and thus prevent war.

World Series (sē′rēz), a series of baseball games played during the autumn of each year, in which the champion teams of the two major leagues of the U. S. contend to decide the professional championship of the game in America.

World War (wẽrld wŏr), the great international conflict begun on July 28, 1914, and which involved on the one side the Central Powers (Germany and Austria-Hungary), and their allies (Turkey and Bulgaria), and on the other side, the twenty-three Allied and Associated Powers, including the U. S.: the signing of an armistice by Germany, November 11, 1918, brought about the cessation of hostilities, and practically ended the war.

Wraf (răf), *n.* one of the Women's Royal Air Force which was organized in England, in 1917, to assist in the war: the word is an acrostic.

wrangle-tangle (răng′g′l-tăng′g′l), *adj.* confused; mixed; snarled; knotted.

Wren (rĕn), *n.* a member of the Women's Royal Naval Service, organized in England, in 1917, as an auxiliary to the regular navy.

wrist watch (rĭst wŏch), a small watch set in a bracelet, or attached to a strap around the wrist, for the purpose of determining the time easily and quickly.

writing on the wall (rīt′ĭng, wôl), something that presages evil or misfortune; an omen of disaster; a warning: the reference is to Belshazzar's feast. See *Dan.* v.

wungee (wŭn′jē), *n.* in East India, a muskmelon.

Würzburg (wŭrz′bŭrg), *n.* one of the best known of Rhine wines; also, a favorite brew of lager beer: after Wurzburg, on the Stein, Germany, famous for its vineyards.

Wyoming (wī-ō′mĭng), *n.* a State of the U. S., the Equality State; from the Indian, *Maughwanwame,* signifying "Broad Valley."

X

Xanthippe (zăn-thĭp′ē), *n.* the scolding, nagging, quarrelsome, sharp-tempered wife of Socrates (469-399 B. C.), the Greek philosopher; hence, a scolding or nagging woman; a troublesome wife; a vixen; a termagant.

xanthochroism (zăn-thŏk′ro-ĭzm), *n.* an obnormal coloration of the feathers of certain birds, as some parrots, in which yellow replaces the natural color.

xanthoconite (zăn-thŏ-kō′nīt), *n.* silver-arsenic-sulphide.

xanthosderite (-sĭd′ẽr-īt), *n.* hydrated oxide of iron.

X chromosome (krō′mŏ-sōm), a particular chromsome found in certain eggs, and in the sperm cells of a few animals: the presence of only one in the fertilized egg causes a female to be produced, of two, a male.

Xenocrates (zĕ-nŏk′ră-tēz), *n.* the Greek philosopher (396-314 B. C.), whom the famous courtezan Lais tried to vamp, but in vain, and to whom she referred as a stone, not a man.

Xenocratic (-krăt′ĭk), *adj.* pertaining to the doctrine of Xenocrates, which was a combination of Pythagoreanism and Platonism.

xenoderm (zĕm′o-derm), *n.* a wart snake.

xenolith (zĕn′ŏ-lĭth), *n.* a concretion or substance enclosed in an organ; an enclave.

xerophyte (zē′rŏ-fīt), *n.* a plant growing in a dry region; a plant that can live without water for a considerable time.

Xmas, *n.* abbreviation for Christmas: the Greek for Christ is *Cristo,* and in the Greek alphabet the *ch* sound is represented by X.

xyloglyphy (zī-lŏg′lĭ-fĭ), *n.* fancy wood carving: the carving of wood in artistic designs.

xylology (zī-lŏl′ŏ-jĭ), *n.* a study of the structure of wood; a treatise on the fibrous structure of wood.

xylotomy (-lŏt′ŏ-mĭ), *n.* the art or practice of preparing sections of wood, cross, longitudinal, and tangential, by means of an instrument called a microtome, for microscopic examination.

Xyrichthys (zī-rĭk′thĭs), *n.* a genus which includes the razor fishes.

Y

Y, short for Y.M.C.A., Young Men's Christian Association; also, used attributively, as a "Y", campaign.

Yakker (yăk′ẽr), *n.* [Australian Slang] hard toil; drudgery.

Yale lock (yāl lok), a cylinder lock invented by Linus Yale (1797-1868), of Herkimer County, New York; a modified form of this original lock.

Yankee dime (yăng′kĕ dīm), [Slang] in Southern U. S., a kiss.

Yankeeism (-iz′m), *n.* a Yankee idiom, manner, custom, habit, or the like.

Yankeeland (-lănd), *n.* [Colloq.] formerly New England, later the whole U. S.

yankie (yangk′ĭ), *adj.* [Scot.] clever; cunning; sharp.

yellow peril (yĕl′ō per′ĭl), the danger of an invasion by the yellow race, Japanese or Chinese, of countries occupied by the white race, which some are inclined to believe is real, not fancied.

Yellow Race (yel′o rās), the Mongolian race of mankind.

Yellow River, the Hwang-Ho, a river of China flowing into the Yellow or Chinese Sea, popularly called *China's Sorrow* and the *Scourge of China,* owing to its devastating floods which destroy lives and crops.

Yellowstone Park (-stōn pärk), a famous reservation, partly located in Wyoming, Montana, and Idaho, containing boiling springs, geysers, petrified forests, a mountain lake, river scenery, the Grand Canyon, and other natural phenomena: it covers an area of 2,142,720 acres.

yerba mate (yẽr′bä mä′tē), the yerba herb, infused as tea, commonly called Paraguay tea.

Y-gun, *n.* an antisubmarine gun, having two barrels in the form of the letter Y.; used to fire a depth charge simultaneously on each side of the vessel.

yield point (yēld point), the point from which material quickly stretches without increase in stress.

Yoruba (yō′rŏŏ-bä), *n.* a Negro of a large linguistic family inhabiting the African Slave Coast, north of the lower Niger.

Yosemite National Park (yŏ-sĕm′ĭ-tē năsh′ŭn-ăl pärk), a park in California, with an area of 967,680 acres, comprising the world-famous Yosemite Valley, 10 miles long, high waterfalls, lofty cliffs, and groves of huge trees in the Sierras.

Yoshiwara (yō-shē-wä′rå), a section or quarter of the city of Tokyo, Japan, set apart for prostitutes; hence, a name applied to a red-light district in any large city or town.

Yuki (yōōk′ĭ), *n.* an Indian of a small group of tribes in northern California, now nearly extinct.

Yuruk (yŏŏ-rōōk′), *n.* one of the wandering Turks of the mountainous parts of western Asia Minor.

Yuzen process (yoo′zen pros′es), a Japanese secret method of dyeing painted fabrics, as silk, velvet, etc., keeping true to the outlines of design; after *Yuzen,* the inventor.

Y. W. C. T. U., abbreviation for Young Women's Christian Temperance Union, an organization for promoting the welfare of young women: originated in 1855 in England, in a home for young women, established by Lady Kinnaird.

Z

Zabernism (tsä′bẽrn-iz′m), *n.* the act of committing a cowardly deed; approval of a cowardly or treacherous act: from Zabern, a town of Alsace, where, on Dec. 1, 1913, a German lieutenant struck a helpless lame cobbler, and was commended for the deed by the then Crown Prince.

zapatera (sä-pä-tā'rä), *n.* a spoiled or rejected olive.

zarp (zärp), *n.* a policeman of the former South African Republic: from the initial letters of that state, South being *Zuid*, in Dutch.

Zarathustra (zär-å-thōō'strä), *n.* original name of Zoroaster.

Zarathustrian ('strĭ-ăn), *n.* a disciple or follower of Zoroaster.

Zarathustrianism (-iz'm), *n.* the doctrines or teachings of Zoroaster.

zemeism (zĕm'ĕ-iz'm), *n.* worship of totemistic ancestors.

zemzem (zĕm'zĕm), *n.* a fountain at Mecca which Mohammedans believe was the very spring God made to slake the thirst of Ishmael when he and his mother Hagar were driven into the wilderness by Abraham.

Zenelophon (zē-nĕl'ŏ-fŏn), *n.* the beggar maid who married King Cophetua of Africa: Shakespeare's *Loves Labor Lost*, act iv.

Zenobia (zĕ-nō'bi-å), *n.* Queen of Palmyra, who claimed the title of "Queen of the East."

zigaboo (zig'å-bōō), *n.* [Slang] a contemptuous name for a negro.

zinc sulphide (zingk sŭl'fīd), sulphide of zinc (ZnS), a white amorphous precipitate resulting from an zinc solution with an alkaline sulphide.

zipper (zip'ẽr), *n.* a metallic contrivance for quickly fastening and opening garments, as coats, vests, jumpers, blouses, also shoes, leggings, pocket-books, handbags, etc., consisting of a running catch fitting into serrated metallic edgings attached to the articles; at will, the running catch immediately separates, or brings together, the edges, thus opening or fastening the article.

zircite (zerk'īt), *n.* zirconium oxide: as it is very refractory to the action of heat, it is much used for lining furnaces.

zinsang (zin'sang), *n.* a carnivorous animal of East India, allied to the civet.

zoöphysiology (zō-ŏ-fiz-ĭ-ŏl'ŏ-jĭ), *n.* the physiology of animals, as distinguished from that of human beings.

A DICTIONARY

OF THE

ENGLISH LANGUAGE

A (ā). The first letter of the alphabet in most of the known languages of the earth; in the Ethiopic, however, it is the thirteenth, and in the Runic the tenth. It is the first letter because it represents the first vocal sound naturally formed by the human organs; being the sound uttered with a mere opening of the mouth without constraint, and without any effort to alter the natural position or configuration of the lips. Hence this letter is found in many words first uttered by infants; which words are the names of the objects with which infants are first concerned, as the breast and the parents. Hence in Hebrew *am* is mother, and *ab* is father. In Chaldee and Syriac, father is *abba*; in Arabic, *aba*; in Ethiopic, *abi*; in Malayan and Bengalese, *bappa*; in Welsh, *tad*, whence we retain *dad*; in Old Greek and in Gothic, *atta*; in Irish, *aithair*; in Cantabrian, *aita*; in Lapponic, *atki*; in Abyssinian, *abba*; in Amharic, *aba*; in Shilhic and Melindane, African dialects, *baba*; and *papa* is found in many languages. Hence the Latin *mamma*, the breast, which is, in popular use, the name of mother; in Swedish, *amma* is a nurse. This list might be greatly extended; but these examples prove *A* to be the first natural vocal sound, and entitled to the first place in alphabets. The Hebrew name of this letter, *aleph*, signifies an ox or a leader.

a (ȧ *or* ā), *indef. art.* An abbreviation of Anglo-Saxon *an* or *ane*, one, used before words beginning with an articulation; as, *a* table, instead of *an* table or *one* table. [See *An*.]

a-, *prefix.* A combining form in many English words, as in *a*sleep, *a*wake, *a*foot, *a*ground, *a*going. In some cases, this is a contraction of the Teutonic *ge-*, as in *a*sleep, *a*ware, from the Anglo-Saxon *geslapan*, to sleep, *gewarian*, to beware; the Dutch *gewaar*. Sometimes it is a corruption of the Anglo-Saxon *on*; as, again, from *ongean*; awake, from *onwacian*, to watch or wake. Before participles, it may be a contraction of the Celtic *ag*, the sign of the participle of the present tense; as, *ag-radh*, saying; *a*saying, *a*going. Or this may be a contraction of *on*, or, what is equally probable, it may have proceeded from a mere accidental sound produced by negligent utterance. In some words, *a-* may be a contraction of *at*, *of*, *in*, *to*, or *an*.

In some words of Greek origin *a-* is privative, giving to them a negative sense, as in *agastric*, from *a* and *gaster*, stomach. In some words derived from the Greek and Latin, *a* is used as a prefix and as a suffix; as, *a*spire, *a*mend, *a*byss, com*a*, Afric*a*, etc.

A, a, *as a symbol.* In Hebrew, Syriac, Chaldee, Samaritan, and Arabic, *A* denotes *one* or unity. In the Julian calendar, *A* is the first of the seven dominical letters.

Among logicians, *A*, as an abbreviation, stands for a universal affirmative proposition. *A* asserts; E denies. Thus in *barbara*, *A*, thrice repeated, denotes so many of the propositions to be universal.

The Romans used *A* to signify a negative or dissent in giving their votes; *A.* standing for *antiquo*, I oppose or object to the proposed law. Opposed to this letter were U. R., *uti rogas*, be it as you desire—the words used to express assent to a proposition. These letters were marked on wooden ballots, and each voter had an affirmative and a negative put into his hands, one of which, at pleasure, he gave as his vote. In criminal trials, *A.* stood for *absolvo*, I acquit; C. for *condemno*, I condemn; and N. L. for *non liquet*, it is not evident; and the judges voted by ballots thus marked. In inscriptions, *A.* stands for *Augustus*; or for *ager*, *aiunt*, *aurum*, *argentum*, etc.

A. is used for *anno*, as in A. D., for *anno Domini*, the year of our Lord, and A. M., for *anno mundi*, the year of the world; and also for *ante*, as in A. M., for *ante meridiem*, before noon; and for *artium*, as in A. M., for *artium magister*, master of arts.

In algebra, *a* and other first letters of the alphabet usually represent known quantities—the last letters being used to represent unknown quantities.

In music, *A* is the nominal of the sixth note in the natural diatonic scale—called by Guido *la*. It is also the name of one of the two natural modes; and is the open note of the second string of the violin, by which the other strings are tuned and regulated.

In pharmacy, *ā* or *āā*, abbreviations of the Greek *ana*, signifies *of each separately*, or, that the things mentioned should be taken in quantities of the same weight or measure.

In chemistry, *aaa.* stand for *amalgama*, or *amalgamation*.

In commerce, *A* stands for *accepted*, as in case of a bill of exchange. Merchants also number their books by the letters A, B, C, instead of figures. Public officers number their exhibits in the same manner; as, the document *A*, or B.

In Scripture, *alpha* and *omega*, the first and last letters of the Greek alphabet, are used for the *beginning* and *end*—representative of Christ.

A 1 (ā-wun). In shipping-lists, a mark used to denote a ship of the highest class, the *A* referring to the quality of the ship, and the *1* to that of the equipment; hence, colloquially, first-rate.

ä-ä′, *n.* [Hawaiian.] A bed of lava that has become solidified with a rough surface.

äal, äl, *n.* [Hind. *āl*, a plant.] A plant of the genus *Morinda*, commonly called Indian mulberry.

äam, *n.* [D.] A measure of liquids among the Dutch, varying in different cities from thirty-seven to forty-one English wine-gallons.

äard′värk, *n.* [D., earth-pig.] The name given in South Africa to a kind of ant-eater, *Orycteropus capensis*.

äard′wolf (-wụlf), *n.* [D., earth-wolf.] A digitigrade, carnivorous quadruped, *Proteles lalandi*, of South Africa, akin at once to the hyenas, the foxes, and the civets.

Aa-ron′iç, Aa-ron′iç-ăl, *a.* Pertaining to Aaron, the Jewish high priest, or to the priesthood of which he was the head.

Âar′ŏn's-beard, *n.* The flowered St.-John's-wort, *Hypericum calycinum*.

Âar′ŏn's-rod, *n.* 1. A rod with a serpent twined round it, used in architecture as an ornament.

2. Any plant of the goldenrod kind.

ab-, *pre.* A combining form used with words of Latin origin, as in *ab*duct; it is the Latin preposition *ab*, the Greek *apo*, and the English *of*; written in ancient Latin, *af*. It denotes *from*, *separation*, or *departure*.

ab, *n.* The Hebrew name of father. [See *Abba*.]

Ab, *n.* The eleventh month of the Jewish civil year, and the fifth of the ecclesiastical year, answering to a part of July and a part of August. In the Syriac calendar, the name of the last summer month.

ab′ȧ-çȧ, *n.* The native Filipino name for the manila hemp plant, and its fiber.

Brig laid aback.

ȧ-bac′i-nāte, *v.t.* [It. *ad*, to, and *bacino*, basin.] To destroy the sight of by placing a red-hot copper basin close to the eyes. [Rare.]

ȧ-bac-i-nā′tion, *n.* The act of destroying eyesight by placing a red-hot copper basin close to the eyes; a form of medieval torture.

ab-ȧ-cis′çus, *n.* In ancient architecture, the square compartment of a mosaic pavement.

ab′ȧ-cist, *n.* [L. *abacus*, a counting-board.] One who casts accounts; a calculator.

ȧ-back′, *adv.* [AS. *on bæc*, at, on, or toward the back.] Toward the back; on the back part; backward. In seamen's language, it signifies the situation of the sails when pressed back against the mast by the wind.

Laid aback; having the sails purposely placed aback to give the ship sternway.

Taken aback; having the sails carried back suddenly by the wind.

ab′ȧ-çot, *n.* The cap of state, formerly used by English kings, wrought into the figure of two crowns.

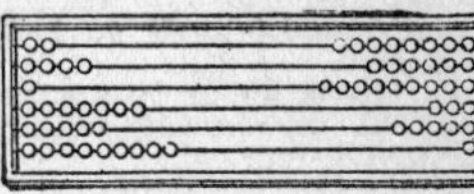

Abacot, from Great Seal of Henry VII.

ab-ac′ti-năl, *a.* [L. *ab*, from, and E. *actinal*.] Pertaining to or situated at the opposite extremity from the mouth; said of a radiate animal.

ab-aç′tion, *n.* A stealing of cattle by the herd.

ab-aç′tŏr, *n.* [L. *abigere*, to drive from.] In law, one who feloniously drives away or steals a herd or numbers of cattle at once, in distinction from one who steals a head or two.

ab-aç′ū-lus, *n.* Same as *Abaciscus*.

ab′ȧ-çus, *n.* [L. *abacus*, anything flat, as a sideboard, a bench, a slate, a table or board for games; Gr. *abax*, a counting-board.]

Abacus for Calculations.

1. Among the Romans, a cupboard or buffet.

2. An instrument to facilitate operations in arithmetic. On this are drawn lines; a counter on the lowest line is one; on the next, ten; on the third, a hundred, etc. On the spaces, counters denote half the number of the line above. Other schemes are called by the same name, as the calculating frame still employed by the Chinese, which consists of wires stretched in a framework, with counters sliding on the wires.

3. In architecture, a table constituting the upper member or crowning division of a column and its capital. It is square in the Tuscan, Doric, and Ionic orders, but its sides are

Ionic Capital. A. The Abacus.

Doric Capital. A. The Abacus.

arched inward in the Corinthian and Composite. The name is also given to a concave molding on the capital of the Tuscan pedestal, and to the plinth above the boltel in the Tuscan and Doric orders.

4. A game among the Romans; so called from its being played on a board, somewhat in the manner of chess.

Abacus harmonicus; the structure and disposition of the keys of a musical instrument.

Abacus major; a trough used for washing ore in mines.

Ȧ-bad′dŏn, *n.* [Heb., from *abad*, to perish.]

1. The destroyer, or angel of the bottomless pit. Rev. ix. 11.

2. The bottomless pit.

ȧ-bȧft′, *adv.* and *prep.* [AS. *be*, by, and *æftan*, behind.] A sea term, signifying in or at the hinder part of a ship or the parts which lie

fāte, fär, fȧst, fạll, fināl, cãre, at;—mēte, prey, hẽr, met;—pīne, marïne, bïrd, pin;—nōte, möve, fọr, atŏm, not;—mọ̈on, book;
ūse, bụll, brüte, tũrn, up;—crȳ, myth;—çat, maçhine, church, ḡhord;—ġem, añger, (Fr.) boṅ, miṣer;—this, thin;—azure.—See Key.

toward the stern; opposed to *afore.* Relatively, it denotes *further aft,* or toward the stern; as, *abaft* the mainmast.

Abaft the beam; in that arc of the horizon which is between a line drawn at right angles with the keel, and the point to which the stern is directed.

à-bāi'sănce, *n.* See *Obeisance.*

à-bāi'sēr, *n.* Ivory-black or animal charcoal.

ab-āl'ien-āte (-yen-), *v.t.*; abalienated, *pt., pp.*; abalienating, *ppr.* 1. To transfer the title of; a civil law term.

2. To alienate or estrange, in the general sense.

3. In medicine, to effect mental aberration.

ab-āl'ien-ā-ted, *a.* 1. In medicine, so corrupted, diseased, or injured as to require amputation; applied to a part or member of the body; alienated; deranged.

2. Transferred, as a title to property; estranged.

ab-āl-ien-ā'tion, *n.* 1. Mental derangement.

2. Bodily disease or corruption.

3. The act of abalienating; transfer of title.

4. Estrangement.

ab-à-lō'nē, *n.* [Sp. origin.] A name used on the Pacific coast of the United States to designate the univalve shellfish commonly called ear-shells.

ab-à-mū'rus, *n.* [L.] A buttress.

à-ban'dŏn, *v.t.*; abandoned (-dund), *pt., pp.*; abandoning, *ppr.* [Fr. *abandonner*; *a-* to, and *bandon,* decree, authority, ban; that is, to place under a ban or authority of another.]

1. To forsake entirely; as, to *abandon* a hopeless enterprise.

2. To renounce and forsake; to leave with a view never to return; to desert as lost or desperate; as, to *abandon* a cause or party.

3. To give up or resign without control, as when a person yields himself, without restraint, to a propensity; as, to *abandon* oneself to intemperance.

4. To resign; to yield, relinquish, or give over entirely; as, to *abandon* a throne.

5. In commerce, to relinquish to insurers (all claim to a ship or goods insured), as a preliminary toward recovering for a total loss.

Syn.—Desert, forsake, leave, quit, forego, give up, take leave of, evacuate.

à-ban'dŏn, *n.* 1. One who totally forsakes or deserts. [Obs.]

2. A relinquishment. [Obs.]

à-bàn-doṅ', *n.* [Fr.] Unrestrained impulsiveness; frankness or enthusiasm of manner.

à-ban'dŏned (-dund), *a.* 1. Wholly forsaken or deserted.

2. Given up, as to a vice; hence, extremely wicked, or sinning without restraint; irreclaimably wicked.

Syn.—Corrupt, depraved, forsaken, profligate, reprobate.

à-ban-dŏn-ee', *n.* In law, one to whom anything is abandoned.

à-ban'dŏn-ēr, *n.* One who abandons.

à-ban'dŏn-ing, *n.* A forsaking; total desertion.

à-ban'dŏn-ment, *n.* 1. A total desertion; the state of being forsaken.

2. In commerce, the relinquishment to underwriters of all property saved from loss by shipwreck, capture, or other peril stated in a policy. This *abandonment* must be made before the insured can demand indemnification for a total loss.

à-ban'dum, *n.* In old law, anything forfeited or confiscated.

ab-an-ni'tion (-nish'un), *n.* [LL.] A banishment for one or two years for manslaughter. [Rare.]

à-bap-tis'tŏn, *n.* The perforating part of the old trephine, an instrument used in trepanning. [Obs.]

ab"ăr-tic"ū-lā'tion, *n.* In anatomy, that species of articulation or structure of joints which admits of manifest motion; called also *diarthrosis* and *dearticulation.*

à-bāse', *v.t.*; abased (-bāst'), *pt., pp.*; abasing, *ppr.* [Fr. *abaisser,* from LL. *abassare,* to lower.]

1. Literally, to lower or depress; to throw or cast down; as, to *abase* the eye. [Rare.]

2. To cast down; to reduce low; to depress; to humble; to degrade; applied to the passions, rank, office, and condition in life.

Syn.—Debase, degrade, depress, disgrace, humble, humiliate, lower.

à-bāsed' (-bāst'), *a.* 1. Reduced to a low state; humbled; depressed.

2. In heraldry, a term used of the wings of eagles, when the tops are turned downward toward the point of the shield; or when the wings are shut, the natural way of bearing them being spread, with the top pointing to the chief of the angle.

à-bāse'ment, *n.* The act of humbling or bringing low; also, a state of depression, degradation, or humiliation.

à-bash', *v.t.*; abashed (-basht'), *pt.,pp.*; abashing, *ppr.* [OFr. *esbahir,* to astonish.] To disconcert; to discomfit; to cast down the countenance; to make ashamed; to confuse or confound, as by exciting suddenly a consciousness of guilt, error, or unworthiness.

Syn.—Disconcert, confuse, shame.

à-bash'ed-ly, *adv.* In a confused manner.

à-bash'ment, *n.* Confusion from shame.

à-bas'si, à-bas'sis, ab-bas'si, *n.* [Per. from Shah *Abas* II.]

1. A silver coin formerly current in Persia, worth about twenty-nine cents.

2. A silver coin current in some parts of Russia, equal to twenty copecks, worth about fifteen cents.

à-bāt'à-ble, *a.* That may or can be abated; as, an *abatable* writ or nuisance.

à-bāte', *v.t.*; abated, *pt., pp.*; abating, *ppr.* [Fr. *abattre,* to beat down.]

1. To beat down; to pull down; to destroy in any manner; as, to *abate* a nuisance.

2. To lessen; to diminish; to moderate; as, to *abate* zeal; to *abate* pride; to *abate* a demand.

3. To lessen; to mitigate; as, to *abate* pain, sorrow, or misery.

4. To overthrow; to cause to fail; to frustrate by judicial sentence; as, to *abate* a writ.

5. To deject; to depress; as, to *abate* the soul. [Obs.]

6. To deduct from; to lower; as, to *abate* a price.

7. To cause to fail; to annul. By the English law, a legacy to a charity is *abated* by a deficiency of assets.

8. To remit; as, to *abate* a tax.

à-bāte', *v.i.* 1. To decrease, or become less in strength or violence; as, pain *abates*; a storm *abates.*

2. To fail; to be defeated, or come to naught; as, a writ *abates.*

3. In law, to enter into a freehold after the death of the last possessor, and before the heir or devisee takes possession; with *in* or *into.* —Blackstone.

4. In horsemanship, to perform well a downward motion. A horse is said to *abate,* or take down his curvets, when, working upon curvets, he puts both his hind legs to the ground at once, and observes the same exactness in all his motions.

Syn.—Decrease, diminish, lessen, lower, reduce, subside, decline, intermit.

à-bä'te, *n.*; *pl.* **à-bä'ti.** [It.] A title given in Italy to ecclesiastics not otherwise designated. Compare *abbé.* Also written *abbate.*

à-bāt'ed, *a.* Lessened; decreased; destroyed; mitigated; defeated; remitted; overthrown; depressed.

à-bāte'ment, *n.* 1. The act of abating; the state of being abated.

2. A reduction, removing, or pulling down, as of a nuisance. —Blackstone.

3. Diminution, decrease, or mitigation, as of grief or pain.

4. Deduction; the sum withdrawn, as from an account.

5. Overthrow, failure, or defeat, as of a writ. —Blackstone.

6. In law, the entry of a stranger into a freehold after the death of the last possessor, before the heir or devisee. —Blackstone.

7. In heraldry, a mark of dishonor in a coat of arms, by which its dignity is debased for some stain on the character of the wearer.

à-bāt'ēr, *n.* A person or thing that abates.

ab'à-tis, ab'āt-tis, *n.* [Fr. *abatis.*] In fortification, piles of trees, or branches of trees sharpened and laid with their points outward, in front of ramparts, to prevent assailants from mounting the walls; an old form of barricade.

à-bat-jour' (à-bä-zhör'), *n.* [Fr. *abattre,* to throw down, and *jour,* daylight.] A skylight; any device that admits or deflects light from above.

à-bāt'ŏr, *n.* A person who enters into a freehold on the death of the last possessor, before the heir or devisee; also, one who abates anything, as a nuisance. —Blackstone.

a-bat-toir' (à-bàt-twär'), *n.* [Fr.] A building for the slaughtering of cattle.

ab'à-tūre, *n.* The track left in grass or herbage by any animal of the chase.

a-bat-voix' (à-bä-vwä'), *n.* [Fr. *abattre,* to throw down, and *voix,* the voice.] A canopy or sounding-board over a pulpit or rostrum.

abb, *n.* [AS. *ab, āweb,* woof.] Among weavers, yarn for the warp. Hence, *abb*-wool is wool for the *abb.*

ab'bà, *n.* [Syr., a father.] In the Syriac, Coptic, and Ethiopic churches, a title given to the bishops, the bishops bestowing the title, by way of distinction, on the bishop of Alexandria. Hence the title Baba, or Papa, Pope or Great Father, which the bishop of Alexandria bore, before the bishop of Rome.

ab'bà-cy, *n.* [From *abba.*] The dignity, rights, and privileges of an abbot.

ab-bä'te, *n.* Same as *Abate,* n.

ab-bā'tiăl (-shăl), *a.* Belonging to an abbey.

ab-bat'iç-ăl, *a.* Abbatial. [Obs.]

ab-bé' (à-bā'), *n.* [Fr., from *abba.*] In a monastic sense, an abbot; the superior of an abbey; but more generally, a title given to Roman Catholic clergy without any determinate rank or office.

ab'bess, *n.* A female superior or governess of a nunnery, or convent of nuns, having the authority over the nuns which the abbots have over the monks. [See *Abbey.*]

ab'bey, *n.*; *pl.* **ab'beyṣ.** [Fr. *abbaye,* abbey.]

1. A monastery or society of persons of either sex, secluded from the world and devoted to religion. The males are called monks, and governed by an abbot; the females are called nuns, and governed by an abbess.

2. A church connected with a monastery.

Syn.—Cloister, convent, monastery, nunnery, priory.

ab'bey-lub"bēr, *n.* A name formerly given to idle monks or abbey pensioners.

ab'bŏt, *n.* [AS. *abbod,* L. *abbas,* from Syr. *abba,* father.]

1. The superior or governor of an abbey or monastery.

2. A title sometimes borne by bishops whose sees were formerly abbeys.

Abbot, or *Lord, of Misrule*; one formerly chosen to direct the sports and revels of a family during Christmas holidays.

ab'bŏt-ship, *n.* The state of an abbot.

ab-boz'zō (-bot'sō) *n.* [It., a sketch.] A rough sketch or outline of anything, as of a picture or a poem; a preliminary draft.

ab-brē'vi-āte, *v.t.*; abbreviated, *pt., pp.*; abbreviating, *ppr.* [L. *abbreviare*; *ad,* to, and *breviare,* from *brevis,* short.]

1. To shorten, to make shorter by contracting the parts. [Rare.]

2. To shorten; to abridge by the omission or defalcation of a part; to reduce to a smaller compass; as, to *abbreviate* a writing or a word.

3. In mathematics, to reduce to lower terms.

Syn.—Abridge, curtail, condense, compress, epitomize, reduce, shorten, contract, boil down.

ab-brē'vi-ā-ted, *a.* Shortened; reduced to lower terms, abridged. In botany, an *abbreviated* perianth is shorter than the tube of the corolla.

ab-brē-vi-ā'tion, *n.* 1. The act of shortening or contracting.

2. A letter or a few letters used for a word or phrase; as, *Gen.* for Genesis; *U. S. A.* for United States of America.

3. The reduction of fractions to lower terms.

4. In music, one dash, or more, through the stem of a note, dividing it respectively into quavers, semiquavers, or demisemiquavers.

Written. Played.

5. A summary; an abridgment; a contracted or abbreviated form.

Syn.—Contraction, abridgment, curtailment.

ab-brē'vi-ā-tŏr, *n.* 1. One who abridges or reduces to a smaller compass.

2. One of a number of secretaries in the chancery of Rome, whose duty is to draw up the pope's briefs, and reduce petitions, when granted, to a due form for bulls.

ab-brē'vi-à-tō-ry, *a.* Shortening; contracting.

ab-brē'vi-à-tūre, *n.* A letter or character for shortening; an abridgment; a compend. [Obs.]

ab-brŏch'ment, *n.* The act of monopolizing goods or forestalling a market. It was formerly a criminal offense in England. [Obs.]

A B C. The first three letters of the alphabet, used for the whole alphabet; also used to denote the rudiments or first principles of anything; as, the *A B C* of farming.

A-B-C book; a little book or primer for teaching the elements of reading.

A B C Powers; Argentina, Brazil and Chile, which countries entered into a mutual five-year peace treaty May 25, 1915.

ab-çà-ree, *n.* See *Abkari.*

àb'dàl, *n.* In Persia and other Asiatic countries, a Mohammedan devotee or fanatic.

ab-dà-lā'vī, ab-dē-lā'vī, *n.* The Egyptian muskmelon.

Ab-dē'ri-ăn, *a.* [Gr. *Abdera,* a Thracian town, birthplace of Democritus, the Laughing Philosopher.] Given to foolish or immoderate laughter.

Ab'dē-rīte, *n.* An inhabitant of Abdera, a maritime town in Thrace, the home of Democritus, the Laughing Philosopher, who is called *the Abderite.*

ab'dest, *n.* [Per. *abdast*; *ab,* water, and *dast,* hand.] Purification by washing; a Mohammedan rite.

ab-dev'en-ham, *n.* An astrological term applied to the ruler of the twelfth house of the heavens.

ab'di-çà-ble, *a.* Able to be abdicated.

ab'di-çănt, *a.* Abdicating; renouncing.

ab'di-çāte, *v.t.*; abdicated, *pt., pp.*; abdicating, *ppr.* [L. *abdicare*; *ab* and *dicare,* to proclaim.]

1. In a general sense, to relinquish, renounce, or abandon.

2. To abandon (an office or trust) without a formal resignation to those who conferred it,

or without their consent: also, to abandon a throne without a formal surrender of the crown. —Blackstone.

3. To relinquish an office before the expiration of the term of service.

4. To reject; to renounce; to abandon, as a right.

5. In the civil law, to disclaim and expel from the family, as a father his child; to disinherit during the life of the father.

Syn.—Resign, renounce, abandon, give up, vacate, quit, relinquish.

ab′di-ċāte, *v.i.* To renounce; to abandon; to cast off; to relinquish, as a right, power, or trust.

> Though a king may *abdicate* for his own person, he cannot *abdicate* for the monarchy. —Burke.

ab′di-ċā-ted, *a.* Renounced; relinquished without a formal resignation; abandoned.

ab-di-ċā′tion, *n.* 1. The act of abdicating; the abandoning of an office or trust, without a formal surrender, or before the usual or stated time of expiration.

2. A casting off; rejection; disinheritance.

ab′di-ċā-tive (*or* ab-dig′ȧ-tive), *a.* Causing or implying abdication.

ab′di-ċā-tŏr, *n.* A person who abdicates.

ab′di-tive, *a.* [L. *abdere*, to hide.] Having the power or quality of hiding. [Rare.]

ab′di-tō-ry, *n.* A place for secreting or preserving goods.

ab-dō′men (*or* ab′dō-men), *n.* [L.]

1. The belly, or that part of the body which lies between the thorax and the bottom of the pelvis. It is lined with a membrane called peritoneum, and contains the stomach, liver, spleen, pancreas, kidneys, bladder, and intestines. It is separated from the breast internally by the diaphragm, and externally by the extremities of the ribs.

2. In insects, that part of the body posterior to the corselet. In some species, it is covered with wings and a case. It is divided into segments, or rings, on the sides of which are small spiracles by which the insect respires.

ab-dom′i-năl, *a.* 1. Pertaining to the belly; as, the *abdominal* regions.

2. Having ventral fins under the abdomen; applied to fishes.

Abdominal ring; an oblong tendinous ring in each groin, through which passes the spermatic cord in men, and the round ligaments of the uterus in women; called also *inguinal ring*.

ab-dom′i-năl, *n.* [L. *abdominalis*; pl., *abdominales*.] In ichthyology a member of a class of fishes whose ventral fins are placed behind the pectoral, and which belong to the division of bony fish. The class contains, among other fishes, the salmon, pike, mullet, flying-fish, herring, and carp.

Ab-dom-i-nā′lēṣ, *n. pl.* A class of fishes, the abdominals.

Ab-dom-i-nā′li-ȧ, *n. pl.* A group of *Crustacea* having appendages to the abdomen.

ab-dom-i-nā′li-ăn, *a.* Pertaining to the *Abdominalia*.

ab-dom-i-nos′cō-py, *n.* [L. *abdomen* and Gr. *skopein*, to look at.] Inspection of the abdomen in order to detect disease.

Abdominal Regions.

1. Epigastric. 2. Umbilical. 3. Hypogastric. 4. 4. Hypochondriac. 5. 5. Lumbar. 6. 6. Inguinal.

ab-dom″i-nō-thō-rac′iç, *a.* Pertaining to the abdomen and the thorax.

ab-dom′i-nous, *a.* Relating to the abdomen; having a large belly.

ab-dūce′, *v.t.*; abduced (-dūst′), *pt., pp.*; abducing, *ppr.* [L. *abducere*, to lead away.] To draw from; to withdraw, or draw to a different part; formerly used in anatomy.

ab-dū′cens, *n.*; *pl.* **ab-dū-cen′tēṣ.** One of the abducent nerves.

ab-dū′cent, *a.* Drawing from; pulling back; used of those muscles which pull back certain parts of the body, in separating, opening, or bending them. The *abducent* muscles, called *abductors*, are opposed to the *adducent* muscles or *adductors*.

Abducent nerves; the sixth pair of cranial nerves.

ab-duçt′, *v.t.*; abducted, *pt., pp.*; abducting, *ppr.* To take away stealthily and by force.

ab-duç′tion, *n.* 1. In a general sense, the act of drawing apart, or carrying away.

2. In surgery, a species of fracture, in which the broken parts recede from each other.

3. In logic, a kind of argumentation, called by the Greeks *apagoge*, in which the major is evident, but the minor is so obscure as to require further proof; as in this syllogism, "All whom God absolves are free from sin; God absolves all who are in Christ; therefore all who are in Christ are free from sin."

4. In law, the taking and carrying away of a child, a wife, etc., either by fraud, persuasion, or open violence. —Blackstone.

ab-duç′tŏr, *n.* 1. In anatomy, a muscle which serves to withdraw, or pull back, a certain part of the body; as, the *abductor oculi*, which pulls the eye outward.

2. A person guilty of abduction.

ȧ-bēam′, *adv.* On the beam; a nautical term signifying at right angles to the keel of the ship.

ȧ-bēar′, *v.t.* [AS. *aberan*.] To bear; to endure. [Obs.]

ȧ-bēar′ănce, *n.* Behavior. [Obs.]

ȧ-bēar′ing, *n.* Demeanor. [Obs.]

ā″bē-cē-dā′ri-ăn, *n.* [Formed from the first four letters of the alphabet.] One who teaches the letters of the alphabet; also, a learner of the letters; hence, a novice.

ā-bē-cē′dā-ry, ā″bē-cē-dā′ri-ăn, *a.* Pertaining to or formed by the letters of the alphabet.

ȧ-bed′, *adv.* On or in bed.

ȧ-begge′, *v.t.* An old form of *aby*. [See *Aby*.]

ȧ-bēle′, ā′bel-tree, *n.* A name of the white poplar. [See *Poplar*.]

Ā-bel′i-ăn, *a.* Relating to or named after the Norwegian mathematician Abel (1802-1829); as, *Abelian* equations; *Abelian* integrals.

Ā-bel′ian (-yăn), **Ā-bel-ō′ni-ăn, Ā′bel-ite,** *n.* In church history, one of a temporary sect in Africa, mentioned only by Augustine, who states that the members married, but lived in continence, after the manner, as they pretended, of Abel, and attempted to maintain the sect by adopting the children of others.

Ā-bel-mos′ċhus, *n.* Former name of a genus of plants to which the okra and abelmosk belong.

ā′bel-mosk, *n.* A popular name of a species of *Hibiscus*, or Syrian mallow. The plant rises on a herbaceous stalk to a height of three or four feet, sending out two or three side branches. The seeds have a musky odor (whence its name from the Greek *moschos*), for which reason the Arabians mix them with coffee.

ab″ēr-dē-vīne′, *n.* The European siskin, *Carduelis spinus*, a small green and yellow finch.

ab-ērr′, *v.i.* To deviate. [Obs.]

ab-ēr′răn-cy, ab-ēr′rănce, *n.* [L. *aberrans*, from *ab* and *errare*, to wander.] A wandering or deviating from the right way; rarely used in a literal sense. In a figurative sense, a deviation from truth, an error, mistake; and in morals, a fault, a deviation from rectitude.

ab-ēr′rănt, *a.* Wandering; straying from the right way.

ab′ēr-rāte, *v.i.* To wander.

ab-ēr-rā′tion, *n.* 1. The act of wandering from the right way; deviation from truth or moral rectitude; deviation from a straight line.

2. In astronomy, a slight apparent motion or displacement of the fixed stars, occasioned by the progressive motion of light and the earth's motion in its orbit.

3. In optics, a deviation in the rays of light, when inflected by a lens or mirror, by which they are prevented from meeting in the same point. It is occasioned by the figure of the glass or mirror, or by the unequal refrangibility of the rays of light.

4. Partial alienation of mind; mental wandering.

Crown of aberration; a luminous circle surrounding the disk of the sun, depending on the aberration of its rays, by which its apparent diameter is enlarged.

Syn.—Insanity, delusion, divergence, mania, alienation, illusion, deviation.

ab-ēr-rā′tion-ăl, *a.* Marked by aberration.

ab-ē-run′ċāte, *v.t.* [L. *aberuncare*, to weed out.] To pull up by the roots; to extirpate utterly. [Obs.]

ab-ē-run′ċā-tŏr, *n.* 1. A weeding-machine.

2. Same as *Averruncator*.

ȧ-bet′, *v.t.*; abetted, *pt., pp.*; abetting, *ppr.* [OFr. *abeter*, to incite, to deceive.]

1. To encourage by aid or countenance; now used chiefly in a bad sense; as, to *abet* an evil-doer.

2. In law, to encourage, counsel, incite, or assist in a criminal act.

Syn.—To aid, encourage, countenance, incite, instigate, assist, connive at.

ȧ-bet′, *n.* The act of aiding or encouraging in a crime. [Obs.]

ȧ-bet′ment, *n.* The act of abetting.

ȧ-bet′tăl, *n.* Same as *Abetment*.

ȧ-bet′tēr, ȧ-bet′tŏr, *n.* One who abets, or incites, aids, or encourages another to commit a crime. The legal form of the word is *abettor*.

Syn.—Accessory, accomplice, ally, assistant.

ab-ē-vaç-ū-ā′tion, *n.* In medicine, a partial evacuation.

ȧ-bey′ănce, *n.* [OFr. *abeance*, expectation; Fr. *bayer*, to gape, stare at.]

1. In law, a state of expectation or contemplation. The fee simple or inheritance of lands and tenements is in *abeyance* when there is no person in being in whom it can vest, so that it is in a state of expectancy or waiting until a proper person shall appear. Thus, if land is leased to A for life, remainder to the heirs of B, the remainder is in *abeyance* till the death of B —Blackstone.

2. Popularly, a state of suspension, or temporary extinction.

ȧ-bey′ăn-cy, *n.* Abeyance.

ȧ-bey′ănt, *a.* In a state of suspense.

ab′grē-gāte, *v.t.* To separate from a herd. [Obs.]

ab′hăl, *n.* An East Indian berry; the juniper.

ab-hom′i-nȧ-ble, *a.* An obsolete spelling of *abominable*.

ab-hom′i-năl, *a.* Not human. [Obs.]

ab-hor′, *v.t.*; abhorred, *pt., pp.*; abhorring, *ppr.* [L. *ab*, from, and *horrere*, to shrink.]

1. To hate extremely, or with contempt; to loathe, detest, or abominate.

2. To despise or neglect.

3. To cast off or reject. [Obs.]

4. To be opposed or averse to.

ab-horred′, *a.* Hated extremely; detested.

ab-hor′rence, *n.* Extreme hatred; detestation; great aversion.

Syn.—Antipathy, aversion hatred, dislike.

ab-hor′ren-cy, *n.* Abhorrence. [Obs.]

ab-hor′rent, *a.* 1. Hating, detesting, struck with abhorrence.

2. Contrary; odious; inconsistent with; expressive of extreme opposition, as, slander is *abhorrent* to all ideas of justice In this sense it should always be followed by *to*.

3. Exciting horror; as, *abhorrent* scenes.

Syn.—Loathsome, odious, hateful, detestable, abominable, revolting, repugnant.

ab-hor′rent-ly, *adv.* With abhorrence.

ab-hor′rēr, *n.* One who abhors.

ab-hor′ri-ble, *a.* Detestable. [Rare.]

ab-hor′ring, *n.* 1. Loathing; the feeling of abhorrence.

2 An object of abhorrence; as, an *abhorring* to all flesh. [Obs.]

Ā′bib, *n.* [Heb. *abib*, an ear of corn.] The first month of the Jewish ecclesiastical year, called also *Nisan*. It begins at the spring equinox, and answers to the latter part of March and beginning of April. Its name is derived from the full growth of wheat in Egypt, which took place anciently, as it does now, at that season.

ȧ-bīd′ănce, *n.* Continuance; abode; stay. [Rare.]

ȧ-bīde, *v.i.*; abode, *pt., pp.*; abiding, *ppr.* [AS. *abidan*, to abide.]

1. To rest, or dwell.

2. To tarry or stay for a short time.

3 To continue permanently, or in the same state; to be firm and immovable.

4. To remain; to continue.

Syn.—Inhabit, dwell, live, lodge, rest, sojourn, stay, tarry, wait.

ȧ-bīde′, *v.t.* 1. To wait for; to be prepared for; to await; as, bonds and afflictions *abide* me. (*For* is here understood.)

2. To endure or sustain.

> To *abide* the indignation of the Lord. —Joel ii. 11.

3. To bear or endure; to bear patiently; as, I cannot *abide* his impertinence.

In general, *abide by* signifies to adhere to, maintain, defend, or stand to; as, to *abide by* a bargain, a promise, or a friend; or to suffer the consequences of; as, to *abide by* the event.

ȧ-bīd′ēr, *n.* One who dwells or abides.

ȧ-bīd′ing, *a.* Without change in existence or place.

Syn.—Continuing, lasting, permanent, durable, steadfast, changeless, remaining, dwelling, awaiting.

ȧ-bīd′ing-ly, *adv.* In a manner to continue; permanently.

Ā′bi-ēṣ, *n.* [L.] A genus of trees, the conifers, including some of the best known fir-trees.

ab′i-ē-tēne, *n.* [From L. *abies*, a fir-tree.] A hydrocarbon obtained by distilling the resinous exudation of the nut-pine of California.

ab-i-et′iç, *a.* Relating to the products of the fir-tree; pertaining to the genus *Abies*.

ab′i-ē-tin, ab′i-ē-tine, *n.* A neutral resin, extracted from the turpentine of some species of *Abies*.

ab″i-ē-tin′iç, *a.* Relating to abietin.

ab′i-ē-tite, *n.* A kind of manna obtained from the silver fir, *Abies pectinata*, of Europe.

ab′i-găil, *n.* [Originally a Hebrew proper name.] A waiting-maid; from the name bestowed upon a lady's-maid in a popular play by Beaumont and Fletcher.

ȧ-big′ē-ăt, *n.* [L *abigeatus*, cattle-stealing.] The crime of cattle-stealing.

ȧ-bil′i-ment, *n.* An obsolete form of *habiliment*.

ȧ-bil′i-ty, *n.* [Fr. *habileté*; L. *habilitas*, ableness, fitness.]

1. Physical power, whether bodily or mental, natural or acquired; force of understanding; skill in arts or science. *Ability* is active power, or power to perform, as opposed to *capacity*, or power to receive In the plural, *abilities* is

much used in a like sense; and also for faculties of the mind, and acquired qualifications.

2. Riches, wealth, substance, which are the means, or which furnish the power, of doing certain acts. [Rare.]

3. The state or quality of being able.

4. Moral power, depending on the will—a metaphysical and theological sense.

5. Civil or legal power; the power or right to do certain things; as, *ability* to inherit.

Syn.—Capacity, skill, talent, aptitude.

ȧ-bīme′, ȧ-byme′ (-bēm′), *n.* [Obs.] See *Abyss.*

ab-in-tes′tāte, *a.* [L. *ab* and *intestatus*, dying without a will, from *in* and *testari*, to bear witness.] In the civil law, inheriting from one dying without a will.

ab″i-ō-gen′e-sis, *n.* [Gr. *a* priv.; *bios*, life; *genesis*, generation.] Generation of living from nonliving matter; spontaneous generation.

ab″i-ō-ġē-net′iç, *a.* Of or pertaining to abiogenesis.

ab″i-ō-ġē-net′iç-ăl-ly, *adv.* By spontaneous generation.

ab-i-oġ′e-nist, *n.* One who holds the doctrine of abiogenesis.

ab-i-oġ′e-nous, *a.* Produced by abiogenesis.

ab-i-oġ′e-ny, *n.* Same as *Abiogenesis.*

ab″i-ō-loġ′iç-ăl, *a.* Relating to the study of lifeless matter; not biological.

ab-i-ol′ō-ġy, *n.* The science of non-animate things; in contra-distinction to biology.

ab′i-on, *n.* Inanimate things in the aggregate as contrasted with animate beings.

ab-ir′ri-tănt, *n.* A drug that allays irritation.

ab-ir′ri-tāte, *v.t.* To deaden sensibility in; to debilitate.

ab-ir-ri-tā′tion, *n.* Debility; low vitality.

ab-ir′ri-tā-tive, *a.* Characterized by debility.

ab-ject′, *v. t.* To throw away; to cast down. [Obs.]

ab′ject, *a.* [L. *abjectus*; *abjicere*, to throw away, from *ab* and *jacere*, to throw.]

1. Sunk to a low condition; applied to persons or things.

2. Worthless; mean; despicable; low in estimation; without hope or regard.

Syn.—Low, degraded, contemptible, pitiful.

ab′ject, *n.* A person in the lowest condition, and despicable. [Obs.]

ab-jeçt′ed-ness, *n.* A very low or despicable condition. [Obs.]

ab-jeç′tion, *n.* A state of being cast away; hence, a low state; meanness of spirit; baseness.

ab′jeçt-ly, *adv.* In a contemptible manner; meanly; servilely.

ab′jeçt-ness, *n.* Meanness; servility.

ab-judġe′, *v.t.* To reject or remove by law. [Rare.]

ab-jū′di-çāte, *v.t.* To abjudge. [Rare.]

ab-jū-di-çā′tion, *n.* Rejection or deprivation by judgment.

ab′jū-gāte, *v.t.* [L. *abjugatus.*] To unyoke. [Obs.]

ab-junç′tive, *a.* Isolated. [Rare.]

ab-jū-rā′tion, *n.* 1. The act of abjuring; a renunciation upon oath; as, an *abjuration* of the realm, by which a person swore to leave the country, and never to return. Formerly, in England, felons, taking refuge in a church, and confessing their guilt, might save their lives by abjuring the realm.

2. A formal rejection or denial; a solemn renunciation; as, an *abjuration* of heresy.

Oath of abjuration; an oath whereby an alien, seeking naturalization, renounces allegiance to all foreign sovereignties; also formerly, in England, an oath asserting the right of the present royal family to the crown, and disclaiming such right in the descendants of the house of Stuart.

ab-jū′rȧ-tō-ry, *a.* Containing abjuration.

ab-jūre′, *v. t.*; abjured, *pt.*, *pp.*; abjuring, *ppr.* [L. *abjurare*, to deny upon oath.]

1. To renounce upon oath; to abandon; as, to *abjure* allegiance to a prince.

2. To renounce or reject with solemnity; to reject; as, to *abjure* errors; to *abjure* reason.

3. To recant or retract.

Syn.—Abnegate, recant, renounce, retract, deny, recall, revoke, forswear.

ab-jūre′, *v.i.* To take an oath of abjuration.

ab-jūre′ment, *n.* Renunciation. [Rare.]

ab-jūr′ẽr, *n.* One who abjures.

ab-kä′ri, *n.* [Hind. *abkar*, a distiller.] In India, the manufacture and traffic in intoxicating liquors; also, the government tax paid by distillers and dealers. Also written *abcaree*, *abkary*, etc.

ab-laç′tāte, *v.t.* [L. *ablactare*; *ab* and *lac*, milk.] To wean from the breast. [Rare.]

ab-laç-tā′tion, *n.* 1. The weaning of a child from the breast.

2. The old name of a method of grafting, in which the scion is not separated from the parent stock till it is firmly united to that in which it is inserted; now called grafting by approach or inarching. [See *Graft.*]

ab-lā′quē-āte, *v.t.* To lay bare, as the roots of a tree or vine. [Obs.]

ab-lā-quē-ā′tion, *n.* [L. *ablaqueare.*] A laying bare the roots of trees or vines to expose them to the air and water.

ab-las-tem′iç, *a.* [Gr. *a* priv., and *blastēma*, sprout.] Nongerminal.

ȧ-blas′tous, *a.* [Gr. *ablastos*, barren.] Having no bud or germ.

ab-lā′tion, *n.* [L. *ablatus*, pp. of *auferre*, to carry away.]

1. A carrying away.

2. In medicine, the taking from the body whatever is hurtful; evacuations in general.

3. In chemistry, the removal of whatever is finished or no longer necessary.

4. In geology, the melting of a glacier, the detrition of rocks, etc.

ab-lȧ-ti′tious (-tish′us), *a.* Lessening.

ab′lȧ-tive, *n.* [L. *ablativus*, from *ablatus*, pp. of *auferre*, to carry away.] In grammar, the case of a noun, in Latin and other languages, which chiefly signifies a taking away, removal, separation.

Ablative absolute; in Latin grammar, a construction corresponding to the *nominative absolute* in English, in which a noun or pronoun, combined with a participle expressed or understood, or some other qualifying word, forms an adverbial clause which, if omitted, leaves a perfect or complete sentence.

ab′lȧ-tive, *a.* 1. Taking away or tending to remove. [Rare.]

2. In grammar, noting removal; as, the *ablative* case.

ab′laut, *n.* [G. *ab*, off, and *laut*, sound.] Vowel gradation, such as takes place in the verb, *sing, sang, sung.*

ȧ-blāze′, *adv.* On fire, in a blaze.

ā′ble, *a.*; *comp.* abler; *superl.* ablest. [OE. *abil*, *habil*; OFr. *able*, Fr. *habile*, from L. *habilis* suitable, fit, from *habere*, to have, hold.]

1. Having physical power sufficient; having competent power or strength, bodily or mental; as, a man *able* to perform military service; a child is not *able* to reason on abstract subjects.

2. Having strong or unusual powers of mind, or intellectual qualifications; as, an *able* minister.

3. Having large or competent property, or simply having property or means; as, he is *able* to support a wife.

4. Having competent strength or fortitude; as, he is *able* to sustain great pain.

5. Having competent, legal power or qualifications; as, *able* to take by inheritance.

Syn.—Capable, efficient, skillful, clever, strong, powerful, effective.

ā′ble, *v.t.* To enable. [Obs.]

-a′ble, *suffix.* [L. *-abilis.*] A combining form very common as a termination of adjectives, especially those based on verbs, and signifying capable of, worthy of, etc.; as, toler*able*, obtain*able*, laud*able*.

ā′ble-bod″ied (-id), *a.* Having a sound, strong body, or a body of competent strength for service. In marine language, it denotes skill in seamanship.

ā″ble-bod′ied-ness, *n.* Physical soundness; robustness.

ab′lē-gāte, *v.t.* [L. *ablegare*, to send away.] to send abroad. [Rare.]

ab′lē-gāte, *n.* In the Roman Catholic church, a papal envoy of high rank, intrusted with important diplomatic missions; also, the envoy who bears to a newly-created cardinal his insignia of office.

ab-lē-gā′tion, *n.* The act of sending abroad.

ā′ble-mind′ed, *a.* Having mental power.

ā″ble-mind′ed-ness, *n.* Intellectual ability.

ab′len, ab′let, *n.* [Fr. *ablette*, from L. *albus*, white, hence the name *bleak.*] A small fresh-water fish, the bleak.

ā′ble-ness, *n.* Ability of body or mind; force; vigor. [Obs.]

ab-lep′si-ȧ, ab′lep-sy, *n.* [Gr. *ablepsia*, blindness.] Want of sight; blindness.

ab′li-gāte, *v.t.* [L. *abligare.*] To keep from by tying up. [Obs.]

ab-lig-ū-ri′tion (-rish′un), *n.* [L. *abliguritio*, feasting.] Extravagance in the preparation and serving of food. [Obs.]

ā′bliņş, *adv.* See *Aiblins.*

ȧ-blōōm′, *adv.* In bloom.

ab-lūde′, *v. i.* [L. *ab* and *ludere*, to play.] To be unlike; to differ. [Rare.]

ab′lū-ent, *n.* [L. *abluere*, to wash away.] Washing clean; cleansing by water or liquids.

ab′lū-ent, *a.* In medicine, that which purifies the blood; also, that which removes filth or viscid matter from the skin, ulcers, etc.

ȧ-blush′, *adv.* and *a.* Rosy; blushing.

ab-lū′tion, *n.* 1. In a general sense, the act of washing; a cleansing or purification by water.

2. Appropriately, the washing of the body as a preparation for religious duties, enjoined by Moses, and still practised in many countries.

3. In chemistry, the purification of bodies by the affusion of a proper liquid, as water to dissolve salts.

4. In medicine, the washing of the body externally, as by baths, or internally, by diluting fluids.

5. The water used in cleansing. [Rare.]

6. In the Roman Catholic church, a small quantity of wine and water, which is used to wash the chalice and the priest's fingers after the communion, and which then, as containing portions of the consecrated elements, is drunk by the priest.

ab-lū′tion-ā-ry, *a.* Pertaining to ablution.

ab-lū′vi-ŏn, *n.* That which is washed off. [Rare.]

ā′bly, *adv.* In an able manner; with great ability.

-a′bly, *suffix.* A combining form for adverbs; as, accept*ably*.

ab′nē-gāte, *v.t.*; abnegated, *pt.*, *pp.*, abnegating, *ppr.* To deny; to renounce.

Syn.—Abjure, disown, disclaim, surrender.

ab-nē-gā′tion, *n.* [L. *ab*, from, and *negare*, to deny.] A denial; a renunciation; self-denial.

Syn.—Denial, renunciation, abjuration.

ab′nē-gā-tŏr, *n.* One who denies, renounces, or opposes anything.

ab-nẽrv′ăl, *a.* [L. *ab*, from, and *nervus*, nerve.] Proceeding from or away from a nerve or nerval source; applied to electrical currents traversing a muscular fiber.

ab′net, *n.* The girdle of a Jewish priest.

ab-neū′răl, *a.* Situated in or pertaining to the region opposite to the neural axis.

ab′nō-dāte, *v.t.* [L. *abnodare*; *ab*, from, and *nodare*, to cut.] To cut knots from (trees). [Obs.]

ab-nō-dā′tion, *n.* The act of cutting away the knots of trees. [Obs.]

ab-nọr′măl, *a.* [L. *abnormis*; *ab*, from, and *norma*, rule.] Not conformed to rule; irregular; deformed; varying from an established type or standard; contrary to system; anomalous; as, an *abnormal* appetite or thirst; an animal of *abnormal* shape.

Syn.—Eccentric, strange, unusual, unnatural, irregular, anomalous.

ab-nọr-mal′i-ty, *n.* 1. The state of being abnormal.

2. That which is abnormal.

ab-nọr′măl-ly, *adv.* In an abnormal manner; as, a plant or animal developed *abnormally*.

ab-nọr′mi-ty, *n.*; *pl.* **ab-nọr′mi-tieş.** [L. *abnormis*, irregular.] Irregularity; deformity; monstrosity.

ab-nọr′mous, *a.* Abnormal.

ȧ-bōard′, *adv.* 1. Within a ship, vessel, or boat; on board; as, he came *aboard* at midnight; also, within or upon a railroad train, or street-car.

2. By the side of; as, to lie close *aboard.*

Aboard main tack; an order to draw a corner of the mainsail down to the chesstree.

All aboard; an imperative phrase, notifying passengers to get upon a train or other vehicle; an announcement of the intention of starting.

To fall aboard; to strike a ship's side.

To get aboard; to get foul of, as a ship.

To go aboard; to enter a ship; to embark.

ȧ-bōard′, *prep.* On board of; as, *aboard* a ship; *aboard* a car.

ȧ-bō′brȧ, *n.* A South American gourd.

ȧ-bōd′ănce, *n.* An omen. [Obs.]

ȧ-bōde′, *v.*, past tense of *abide.*

ȧ-bōde′, *n.* [See *Abide.*]

1. Stay; continuance in a place; residence for a longer or shorter time.

2. A place of continuance; a dwelling; a habitation.

To make abode; to dwell or reside.

Syn.—Dwelling, domicile, residence, house, home, sojourn, stay.

ȧ-bōde′, *v.t.* [Obs.] See *Bode.*

ȧ-bōde′, *v.i.* To be an omen. [Obs.]

ȧ-bōd′ing, *n.* Presentiment. [Obs.]

ä-bō-gä′dō, *n.* [Sp.] A lawyer or advocate.

ȧ-bol′ish, *v.t.*; abolished (-isht), *pt.*, *pp.*; abolishing, *ppr.* [Fr. *abolir*; L. *abolere*; from *ab* and *olere*, to grow.]

1. To make void; to annul; to abrogate; applied chiefly and appropriately to established laws, contracts, customs, and institutions; as, to *abolish* laws; to *abolish* slavery.

2. To destroy, or put an end to; as, to *abolish* idols.

Syn.—Abrogate, nullify, annul, repeal, revoke, cancel, destroy, do away with, annihilate.

ȧ-bol′ish-ȧ-ble, *a.* That may be annulled, abrogated, or destroyed, as a law, rite, custom, etc.

ȧ-bol′ish-ẽr, *n.* One who abolishes.

ȧ-bol′ish-ment, *n.* The act of annulling; abrogation; destruction.

ab-ō-li′tion (-lish′un), *n.* 1. The act of abolishing, or the state of being abolished; an annulling; abrogation; utter destruction; as, the *abolition* of laws, decrees, ordinances, rites, customs, debts, etc.

2. Specifically, in modern times, the putting an end to slavery; emancipation.

ab-ō-li′tion-işm, *n.* The principles of an abolitionist; belief in the abolition of slavery.

ab-ō-li′tion-ist, *n.* A person who favors abolition; specifically, one who favored the abolition of slavery.

ab-ō-li′tion-ize, *v.t.*; abolitionized, *pt.*, *pp.*; abolitionizing, *ppr.* To teach abolitionism; to imbue with belief in abolitionism.

a-bol′lȧ, *n.* [L.] A garment, worn by the Greeks and Romans.

Romans wearing the Abolla.

ab-ō-mā′sum, ab-ō-mā′sus, *n.* [L. *ab*, from, and *omasum*, a third stomach.] The fourth stomach of a ruminant animal, lying next to the omasum, or third stomach.

ȧ-bom′i-nȧ-ble, *a.* [See *Abominate.*]

1. Very hateful; detestable; loathsome; odious to the mind; offensive to the senses.

2. Excessive; extreme; as, his pride is *abominable.* [Colloq.]

Syn. — Execrable, detestable, hateful, abhorrent, foul, horrible, loathsome, odious, nauseous.

ȧ-bom′i-nȧ-ble-ness, *n.* The quality or state of being odious; hatefulness.

ȧ-bom′i-nȧ-bly, *adv.* 1. Very odiously; detestably; sinfully.

2. In colloquial language, extremely, excessively; as, *abominably* conceited.

ȧ-bom′i-nāte, *v.t.*; abominated, *pt.*, *pp.*; abominating, *ppr.* [L. *ab*, from, and *ominari*, to regard as an omen.] To hate extremely; to abhor; to detest.

Syn.—Abhor, detest, execrate, hate, loathe.

ȧ-bom-i-nā′tion, *n.* 1. Extreme hatred; detestation.

2. The object of detestation; a common signification in Scripture.

> The way of the wicked is an *abomination* unto the Lord. —Prov. xv. 9.

3. Hence, defilement; pollution; any object of extreme hatred.

ȧ-bom-i-nā′tŏr, *n.* One who abominates.

ȧ-boon′, *prep.* and *adv.* [Scot.] Above.

ab-ō′răl, *a.* [L. *ab*, from, and *os* (*oris*), mouth.] Away from the mouth.

ȧ-bōrd′, *n.* [Fr.] Literally, arrival, but formerly used for first appearance, manner of accosting, or address. [Obs.]

ȧ-bōrd′, *v.t.* To approach; to accost. [Rare.]

ab-ō-rig′i-năl, *a.* [L. *ab*, from, and *origo*, origin.] First; original; *aboriginal* people are the first inhabitants of a country.

Syn.—Native, primeval, original.

ab-ō-rig′i-năl, *n.* An original inhabitant. The first inhabitants of a country are called *aboriginals*, as the Celts in Europe and Indians in America.

ab-ō-rig-i-nal′i-ty, *n.* The state of being aboriginal.

ab-ō-rig′i-năl-ly, *adv.* In an aboriginal manner; originally.

ab-ō-rig′i-nēs, *n.pl.*; *sing.* **ab-ō-rig′i-nē.** 1. The first inhabitants of a country.

2. The flora and fauna native to a region.

ȧ-bŏrse′ment, *n.* Abortion. [Obs.]

ȧ-bŏr′sive, *a.* [Obs.] See *Abortive.*

ȧ-bŏrt′, *v.i.*; aborted, *pt.*, *pp.*; aborting, *ppr.* [L. *ab*, from, and *oriri*, to rise.]

1. To miscarry; to give birth prematurely.

2. To remain undeveloped, as the organs of an animal or plant.

ȧ-bŏrt′, *n.* An abortion. [Obs.]

ȧ-bŏr′ti-cide, *n.* [L. *abortus*, and *cidium*, from *caedere*, to kill.] The crime of abortion; the act of destroying a fetus; feticide.

ȧ-bŏr-ti-fā′cient (-shent), *a.* [L. *abortio*, miscarriage, and *facere*, to make.] Tending to produce abortion.

ȧ-bŏr-ti-fā′cient, *n.* That which is used to produce abortion.

ȧ-bŏr′tion, *n.* [L. *abortio*, a miscarriage.]

1. The act of miscarrying, or producing young before the natural time, or before the fetus is perfectly formed.

2. The fetus brought forth before it is perfectly formed; hence, anything misshapen or imperfectly developed; a monstrosity.

3. In a figurative sense, any fruit or produce that does not come to maturity, or anything which fails in its progress, before it is matured or perfect, as a design or project.

4. The criminal offense of causing or procuring miscarriage. [Colloq.]

5. In biology, the incomplete or arrested development of an organ.

ȧ-bŏr′tion-ăl, *a.* Relating to abortion; unsuccessful.

ȧ-bŏr′tion-ist, *n.* One who causes or seeks to cause abortion.

ȧ-bŏr′tive, *a.* 1. Brought forth in an immature state; failing, or coming to naught, before it is complete.

2. Failing in its effect; miscarrying; producing nothing; as, an *abortive* scheme.

3. Productive of nothing; chaotic; as, the *abortive* gulf. [Rare.]

4. Pertaining to abortion, as, *abortive* vellum, made of the skin of an *abortive* calf.

5. In medicine, producing abortion; as, *abortive* drugs.

6. In biology, incompletely developed; barren; non-productive; imperfect or stunted, as an organ.

ȧ-bŏr′tive, *n.* 1. That which is brought forth or born prematurely. [Obs.]

2. A drug used to cause abortion; an abortifacient.

ȧ-bŏr′tive-ly, *adv.* Immaturely; in an untimely manner.

ȧ-bŏr′tive-ness, *n.* The state of being abortive; want of success.

ȧ-bŏrt′ment, *n.* An untimely birth. [Obs.]

ȧ-bou′li-ȧ, *n.* Same as *Abulia.*

ȧ-bound′, *v.i.*; abounded, *pt.*, *pp.*; abounding, *ppr.* [L. *abundare*, to overflow.]

1. To have or possess in great quantity; to be copiously supplied; followed by *with* or *in*; as, to *abound with* provisions; to *abound in* good things.

2. To be in great plenty; to be very prevalent; as, vice *abounds*; game *abounds.*

Syn.—Flourish, luxuriate, teem, overflow, swarm.

ȧ-bound′ing, *n.* Increase; abundance.

ȧ-bout′, *prep.* [AS. *abutan*, *onbutan*, *embutan*, about, around.]

1. Around; on the exterior part or surface; as, a girdle *about* the waist.

2. Near to in place, with the sense of circularity; close to; as, enemies *about* him on every hand.

3. Near to in time, number, quantity, degree, etc.; as, *about* 12 o'clock; *about* three weeks; *about* 500 men; *about* a bushel; *about* the best; *about* my height. This is practically the adverbial sense.

4. Near to in action, or near to the performance of some act; as, Paul was *about* to open his mouth.

5. Near to the person; appended to the clothes; as, everything *about* him is in order.

6. Concerned in; engaged in; as, what is he *about?*

7. Around, referring to compass or circumference; as, two yards *about* the stem.

8. Here and there; in different parts and directions; as, the gossip *about* the village; a man *about* town.

9. In relation to; having regard to; as they will talk *about* you; much ado *about* nothing.

ȧ-bout′, *adv.* 1. Near to in quality, degree, etc.; as, *about* as high, or as cold. [See *About*, prep.]

2. Here and there; around; in one place and another; as, wandering *about.*

3. Around, or by the longest way, opposed to *across*, or by the shortest way; as, a mile *about*, and half a mile *across.*

4. In an opposite direction; as, to face or turn *about.*

5. In readiness; as, *about* to sail; *about* to begin.

About ship, ready about; orders to sailors to prepare for tacking.

To bring about; to bring to the end; to effect or accomplish a purpose.

To come about; to happen; to change or turn; to come to the desired point. In a like sense, seamen say *go about*, when a ship changes her course to go on the other tack.

To go about; to enter upon; also, to prepare; to seek the means.

ȧ-bout′-sledge, *n.* A blacksmith's largest sledgehammer.

ȧ-bŏve′, *prep.* [AS. *abufan*; *a*, on, and *bufan*, *beufan*; *be*, by, and *ufan*, above.]

1. Literally, higher in place; as, *above* the earth.

2. Figuratively, superior in any respect; as, *above* reproach; the colonel is *above* the captain in rank.

3. More in number or quantity; as, the weight is *above* a ton; *above* five hundred members. This is practically the adverbial sense.

4. More in degree; in a greater degree; as, happiness is to be preferred *above* riches.

5. Beyond; in a state to be unattainable; as, things *above* comprehension.

6. Too proud for; as, this man is *above* his business.

7. Too elevated in mind or rank; having too much dignity for; as, this man is *above* mean actions.

ȧ-bŏve′, *adv.* 1. Overhead; in a higher place; as, the stars *above*; the powers *above.*

2. Before; in a former place; as, what was said *above.*

3. Higher in authority; as, an appeal to the court *above.*

4. More than; as, *above* a score. [See *Above*, prep.]

Above ground; alive; not buried.

ȧ-bŏve′, *a.* Preceding; foregoing; as, the *above* citation; also used substantively, by ellipsis; as, since writing the *above.*

ȧ-bŏve′bōard, *a.* and *adv.* Above the board or table; in open sight; without trick, concealment, or deception.

ȧ-bŏve′-cīt″ed, *a.* Cited before, in the preceding part of a book or writing.

ȧ-bŏve′deck, *a.* and *adv.* On deck; aboveboard.

ȧ-bŏve′-men″tioned, *a.* Mentioned before.

ȧ-bŏve′-said (-sed), *a.* Mentioned or recited before.

ȧ-box′, *adv.* and *a.* In the position of a vessel's head-yards when the head-sails are laid aback.

Ab″rȧ-çȧ-dab′rȧ, *n.* The name of a deity worshiped by the Syrians. Sammonicus wrote the letters of this name in the form of an inverted triangle on pieces of paper, which he recommended as an antidote against certain diseases. Hence, any cabalistic word or formula used to deceive the credulous; unmeaning language; jargon.

ab-rā′dănt, *n.* A substance used for polishing or grinding, as emery.

ab-rāde′, *v.t.*; abraded, *pt.*, *pp.*; abrading, *ppr.* [L. *abradere*; *ab*, away, and *radere*, to scrape.] To rub or wear off; to waste by friction.

Syn.—Scrape off, wear away, wear off, waste away, erase.

Ā-brȧ-ham′iç, Ā″brȧ-ham-it′iç, *a.* Pertaining to Abraham, the patriarch; as, the *Abrahamic* covenant.

Ā′brȧ-ham-man, Ā′brăm-man, *n.* One of a class of impostors, in England, who wandered about the country, pretending lunacy.

To sham Abraham; to feign sickness.

ȧ-brāid′, *v.t.* To arouse. [Obs.]

Ȧ-bran′çhi-ȧ, *n.pl.* [Gr. *a* priv., and *branchia*, gills.] A term applied to an order of *Annelida*, because the species composing it have no external organs of respiration; including worms and leeches.

ȧ-bran′çhi-ăn, *a.* Abranchiate.

ȧ-bran′çhi-ăn, ȧ-bran′çhi-āte, *n.* One of the *Abranchia.*

ȧ-bran′çhi-āte, *a.* Pertaining to the *Abranchia*; having no gills.

ȧ-bran′çhi-ous, *a.* Abranchiate. [Rare.]

Ab′rȧ-sax, *n.* See *Abraxas.*

ab-rāșe′, *v.t.*; abrased, *pt.*, *pp.*; abrasing, *ppr.* To wear away; to smooth; to abrade.

ab-rā′șion, *n.* 1. The act of wearing or rubbing off.

2. Substance worn off by attrition or rubbed off.

3. The result of rubbing; a wound of the skin caused by rubbing.

ab-rā′sive, *a.* Tending to cause abrasion.

ȧ′braum, *n.* [G. *ab*, off, and *raumen*, to take.] A red ocher used to color mahogany.

Abraum salts; a combination of salts found at Stassfurt, Prussia, used largely in the manufacture of potassic salts.

Ab-rax′ăs, Ab′rȧ-sax, *n.* [The Greek letters *a*, *b*, *r*, *a*, *x*, *a*, *s*, as numerals express 365.]

1. A word denoting a power which presides over 365 others, the number of days in a year, and used as a mystical term to express the supreme God, under whom the Basilidians supposed 365 dependent deities. It was the principle of the Gnostic hierarchy, whence sprang their multitude of eons.

2. In antiquities, a gem or stone with the word *abraxas* engraved on it.

ȧ-breast′ (-brest′), *adv.* 1. Side by side, with the breasts in a line; as, the two men rode *abreast.*

2. Opposite; against; on a line with; as, the ship was *abreast* of Montauk Point.

In nautical language, ships are *abreast* when their heads are equally advanced; and they are *abreast* of objects when the objects are on a line with the beam.

3. Figuratively, on a level with; up to; in line with; as, to keep *abreast* of the times.

ab-rē-nounce′, *v.t.* [L. *ab*, from, and *renuntiare*, to renounce.] To renounce. [Obs.]

ab-rep′tion, *n.* [L. *ab*, from, and *rapere*, to snatch.] A carrying away; or state of being seized and carried away. [Obs.]

ȧ-breu-voir′ (ȧ-brū-vwär′), *n.* [Fr. *abreuvoir*, a watering-place, from *abreuver*, to water.] Among masons, the joint between stones, to be filled with mortar.

ā′bri-çock, *n.* An obsolete form of *apricot.*

ȧ-bridge′, *v.t.*; abridged, *pt.*, *pp.*; abridging, *ppr.* [Fr. *abréger*, from L. *abbreviare*; *ad*, to, and *brevis*, short.]

1. To make shorter; to epitomize; to contract by using fewer words, yet retaining the sense in substance; used of writings; as, Justin *abridged* the history of Trogus Pompeius.

2. To lessen; to shorten in duration; to diminish; as, to *abridge* labor; to *abridge* power or rights.

3. To deprive; to cut off; followed by *of*; as, to *abridge* one *of* his rights or enjoyment.

4. In algebra, to reduce a compound quantity or equation to its more simple expression.

Syn.—To abbreviate, contract, shorten, cut down, prune.

ȧ-bridġ′ẽr, *n.* One who abridges; one who makes a compend.

ȧ-bridġ′ment, *n.* 1. An epitome; a compend or summary of a book.

2. Diminution; contraction; reduction; as, an *abridgment* of expenses.

3. Deprivation; a debarring or restraint; as, an *abridgment* of pleasures.

Syn.—Abstract, abbreviation, compend, compendium, contraction, digest, epitome, summary, synopsis.

ā′brin, *n.* [Gr. *habros*, graceful.] A vegetable poison obtained from the seed of the wild licorice.

ȧ-brōach′, *adv.* Broached; letting out or yielding liquor, or in position for letting out; as, a cask is *abroach*. Figuratively used by Shakspere for setting loose, or in a state of being diffused; as, set mischief *abroach*; but this sense is unusual.

ȧ-brọad′, *adv.* 1. In a general sense, at large; widely; not confined to narrow limits; in the open air.

2. Beyond or out of the walls of a house; as, to walk *abroad*.

3. Beyond the limits of a camp or fortified place.

4. Beyond the bounds of a country; in foreign countries; as, to go *abroad* for an education.

5. Extensively; before the public at large; as, to tell the news *abroad*.

6. Widely; with expansion; as, a tree spreads its branches *abroad*.

ab′rō-gȧ-ble, *a.* That may be abrogated.

ab′rō-gāte, *v.t.*; abrogated, *pt.*, *pp.*; abrogating, *ppr.* [L. *abrogare*, to repeal; *ab*, from, and *rogare*, to ask or propose.] To repeal; to annul by an authoritative act; to abolish by the authority of the maker or his successor; applied to the repeal of laws, decrees, ordinances, the abolition of established customs, etc.

Syn.—Abolish, nullify, rescind, annul, repeal.

ab-rō-gā′tion, *n.* The act of abrogating; repeal by authority of the legislative power.

ab′rō-gā-tive, *a.* Causing repeal; tending to abrogate.

ab′rō-gā-tŏr, *n.* One who abrogates.

Ȧ-brō′ni-ȧ, *n.* [Gr. *habros*, delicate.] A genus of North American trailing plants, bearing heads of fragrant verbena-like flowers.

ȧ-brọọd′, *adv.* In the function of brooding. [Obs.]

ȧ-brook′, *v.t.* To brook; to endure. [Obs. See *Brook*.]

ab-rot′ȧ-noid, *n.* [Gr. *abrotonon*, aromatic plant, and *eidos*, form.] A species of coral belonging to the genus *Madrepora*. It is one of the reef-corals of the East Indies.

ab-rot′ȧ-num, *n.* [Gr. *abrotonon*.] A species of evergreen plants arranged under the genus *Artemisia*; called also *southernwood*.

ab-rupt′, *a.* [L. *abruptus*, from *abrumpere*, to break off.]

1. Literally, broken off, or broken short.

2. Steep; craggy; applied to rocks, precipices, and the like.

3. Figuratively, sudden; without notice to prepare the mind for the event; as, an *abrupt* entrance or address.

4. Unconnected; having sudden transitions from one subject to another; as, an *abrupt* style.

5. In botany, terminating suddenly; ending as if broken or cut off; an *abrupt-pinnate* leaf is one which has neither leaflet nor tendril at the end.

1. Abrupt Root.
2. Abrupt Leaf.
3. Abrupt-pinnate.

Syn.—Rugged, rough, sudden, unexpected, blunt, bluff, unceremonious.

ab-rupt′, *n.* A chasm; an abrupt place. [Poet.]

> Over the vast *abrupt*. —Milton.

ab-rupt′ed, *a.* Torn off; torn asunder.

ab-rup′tion, *n.* A sudden breaking off; a violent separation of bodies.

ab-rupt′ly, *adv.* Suddenly; without giving notice, or without the usual forms; as, the minister left France *abruptly*.

ab-rupt′ness, *n.* 1. A state of being broken; craggedness; steepness.

2. Figuratively, suddenness; unceremonious haste or vehemence.

Ā′brus, *n.* [Gr. *habros*, graceful.] A genus of papilionaceous plants, including the Jamaica wild licorice.

ab′scess, *n.* [L. *abscessus*, from *ab* and *cedere*, to go from.] A cavity containing pus, or a collection of purulent matter, in some part of the body, formed by suppuration, consequent on inflammation.

ab-sces′sion, *n.* Departure. [Obs.]

ab-scind′, *v.t.*; abscinded, *pt.*, *pp.*; abscinding, *ppr.* [L. *ab*, off, and *scindere*, to cut.] To cut off. [Rare.]

ab-scis′sȧ, ab′sciss, *n.* [L. *abscissus*, from *ab* and *scindere*, to cut.] In conics, a part of the diameter or transverse axis of a conic section, intercepted between the vertex or some other fixed point and a semiordinate.

Generally, any part of the diameter or axis of a curve, comprised between any fixed point where all the *abscissas* begin, and another line, called the ordinate. In the diagram, AD is the ordinate; CD the *abscissa*.

ab-sciṣ′ṣion (-sizh′un), *n.* [L. *abscissio*, from *ab*, and *scindere*, to cut off.]

1. A cutting off, or a being cut off. In surgery, the separation of any corrupted or useless part of the body, by a sharp instrument; applied to the soft parts, as amputation is to the bones and flesh of a limb.

2. In rhetoric, a figure of speech used when, having begun to say a thing, a speaker stops abruptly, as supposing the matter sufficiently understood; thus, "He is a man of so much honor and candor, and such generosity—but I need say no more."

ab-sco̤nd′, *v.i.*; absconded, *pt.*, *pp.*; absconding, *ppr.* [L. *abscondere*; *abs*, from or away, and *condere*, to hide.]

1. To retire from public view, or from the place in which one resides or is ordinarily to be found; to withdraw, or absent oneself in a private manner; to conceal oneself; appropriately used of persons who secrete themselves to avoid a legal process.

2. To hide, withdraw, or be concealed.

> The marmot *absconds* in winter. —Ray.

ab-sco̤nd′ence, *n.* Concealment.

ab-sco̤nd′ẽr, *n.* One who withdraws from public notice, or conceals himself from public view.

ab′sence, *n.* [L. *absentia*, being away.]

1. A state of being at a distance in place, or not present in company. It is used to denote any distance indefinitely, either in the same town, or country, or in a foreign country, and primarily supposes a prior presence; as, speak well of one in his *absence*.

2. Want; destitution; implying no previous presence.

> In the *absence* of conventional law. —Kent.

3. In law, non-appearance; a not being in court to answer.

4. Heedlessness; inattention to things present; as, *absence* of mind.

ab′sent, *a.* 1. Not present; not in company; at such a distance as to prevent communication; as, a gentleman is *absent* on his travels.

2. Heedless; inattentive to persons present, or to subjects of conversation in company; as an *absent* man is uncivil to the company.

3. Lacking; non-existent.

Syn.—Abstracted, dreamy, inattentive, listless.

ab-sent′, *v.t.*; absented, *pt.*, *pp.*; absenting, *ppr.* [L. *absens* (*-entis*), ppr. of *absum*, *abesse*; *ab*, away, and *esse*, to be.] To depart to such a distance as to prevent intercourse; to retire or withdraw; to forbear to appear in presence; used with the reciprocal pronoun; as, let a man *absent himself* from the company.

ab-sen-tā′nē-ous, *a.* Pertaining to absence. [Obs.]

ab-sen-tā′tion, *n.* The act of remaining away or absenting oneself.

ab-sen-tee′, *n.* 1. One who withdraws or absents himself from his country, office, post, etc.; one who removes to a distant place or to another country.

2. A landowner or capitalist who derives his revenue from one country and resides in and expends it in another.

ab-sen-tee′iṣm, *n.* Absence from duty or station; applied specifically to the act of residing in a country different from that from which one's resources are derived.

ab-sent′ẽr, *n.* One who absents himself.

ab′sent-ly, *adv.* In an absent manner.

ab-sent′ment, *n.* The state of being absent. [Rare.]

ab″sent-mīnd′ed, *a.* Characterized by inattention to present needs or surroundings; preoccupied; abstracted.

ab″sent-mind-ed-ly, *adv.* In an absent-minded or preoccupied manner.

ab″sent-mind-ed-ness, *n.* The state of being preoccupied or abstracted.

ab′sent-ness, *n.* Absent-mindedness.

ab′sey-book, *n.* An alphabet-book. [Obs.]

ab-sid′i-ōle, *n.* Same as *Apsidiole*.

ab′sinth, ab′sinthe, *n.* [L. *absinthium*.]

1. Wormwood.

2. An aromatic liqueur of an opaline-green color, flavored with wormwood and other plants containing absinthin.

ab-sin′thāte, *n.* A chemical compound containing absinthic acid.

ab-sin′thi-ăl, *a.* Bitter; pertaining to wormwood.

ab-sin′thi-ăn, *a.* Of the nature of wormwood.

ab-sin′thi-āte, *v.t.*; absinthiated, *pt.*, *pp.*; absinthiating, *ppr.* To compound or impregnate with absinth.

ab-sin′thi-ā-ted, *a.* Impregnated with or containing absinth.

ab-sin′thiç, *a.* Pertaining to absinth; as, *absinthic* acid.

ab-sin′thin, *n.* The crystalline bitter principle inherent in absinthium.

ab′sin-thiṣm, *n.* Absinth poisoning.

ab-sin′thi-um, *n.* [L.] The common wormwood, *Artemisia absinthium*, a bitter plant, used as a tonic.

ab′sis, *n.* Same as *Apsis*.

ab-sist′, *v.i.* [L. *ab*, from, and *sistere*, to stand.] To stand apart; to desist. [Obs.]

ab-sist′ence, *n.* A standing apart. [Obs.]

ab′sō-lūte, *a.* [L. *absolutus*, from *ab* and *solvere*, to loose.]

1. Literally, in a general sense, free or independent of anything extraneous.

2. Complete in itself; positive; as, an *absolute* declaration.

3. Unconditional; as, an *absolute* promise.

4. Existing independent of any other cause; as, God is *absolute*.

5. Unlimited by extraneous power or control; as, an *absolute* government or monarch.

6. Not relative; as, *absolute* space.

7. In chemistry, pure, unmixed; as, *absolute* alcohol.

8. In grammar, independent; as, the *absolute* case; applied to a word or member of a sentence not immediately dependent on the other parts of the sentence in government.

Absolute curvature; see *Curvature*.

Absolute equation; in astronomy, the sum of the optic and eccentric equations.

Absolute numbers; in algebra, such as have no letters annexed; as, $2a+36=48$. The two latter numbers are *absolute* or pure.

Absolute space; in physics, space considered without relation to any object.

Absolute temperature; the temperature measured from absolute zero, and useful in dealing with gases.

Absolute unit of current; a current possessing a degree of strength, and which when transmitted through a wire curved in the shape of an arc of a circle of one centimeter radius, will act on a one-unit power magnetic pole, stationed at the center of the arc, with a force equal to one degree.

Absolute velocity; the velocity of a body with reference to a body not in motion.

Absolute zero; in thermodynamics, the lowest possible temperature. It corresponds with $-273.7°$ centigrade ($-460.66°$ Fahr.). It has no existence in fact, but is deduced from theoretical considerations based on the expansion of gases.

Syn.—Arbitrary, positive, imperious, despotic, peremptory, tyrannous, tyrannical, autocratic, supreme.

Ab′sō-lūte, *n.* 1. The independent, unrestricted, and perfect Being; God; generally with *the*; as, the power of *the Absolute*.

2. [a—] That which is perfect or unrestricted; a condition of perfection.

ab′sō-lūte-ly, *adv.* 1. Completely; wholly; as, a thing is *absolutely* unintelligible.

2. Without dependence or relation; in a state unconnected.

> *Absolutely* we cannot discommend, we cannot *absolutely* approve, either willingness to live, or forwardness to die. —Hooker.

3. Without restriction or limitation; as, God reigns *absolutely*.

4. Without condition; as, God does not forgive *absolutely*, but upon condition of faith and repentance.

5. Positively; peremptorily; as, command me *absolutely* not to go.

Syn.—Completely, unrestrictedly, unconditionally.

ab′sō-lūte-ness, *n.* 1. Independence; completeness in itself.

2. Despotic authority, or that which is subject to no extraneous restriction or control.

ab-sō-lū′tion, *n.* 1. The act of absolving or freeing from the consequences of sin or crime.

2. In the civil law, an acquittal, or sentence of a judge declaring an accused person innocent.

3. In the Roman Catholic church, a remission of sins, pronounced by a priest in favor of a penitent.

4. The act of absolving from excommunica-

tion or freeing a person from its penalties on his reconciliation to the church.

5. In some Protestant churches, a declaration of remission of sins on the ground of repentance.

Absolution day; in the Roman Catholic church, the Tuesday before Easter.

ab′sō-lū-tism, *n.* 1. The state of being absolute; or the principles of absolute government.

2. The doctrine of predestination.

ab′sō-lū-tist, *n.* One who is in favor of absolutism.

ab′sō-lū-tist, ab″sō-lū-tis′tiç, *a.* Of the nature of absolutism.

ab-sol′ū-tō-ry, *a.* Giving absolution; absolving; as, an *absolutory* sentence.

ab-solv′ȧ-ble, *a.* Capable of being absolved.

ab-solv′ȧ-tō-ry, *a.* Conferring absolution, pardon, or release; having power to absolve.

ab-solve′, *v.t.*; absolved, *pt.*, *pp.*; absolving, *ppr.* [L. *ab*, from, and *solvere*, to loose.]

1. To set free or release from some obligation, debt, or responsibility; or from that which subjects a person to a burden or penalty; as, to *absolve* a person from a promise; to *absolve* an offender, which amounts to an acquittal and remission of his punishment.

2. To forgive for sin or free from a penalty.

3. To finish or accomplish. [Obs.]

Syn.—Acquit, clear, exculpate, exonerate, forgive, pardon, remit.

ab-solv′ent, *a.* Having the power or quality to absolve.

ab-solv′ent, *n.* One who absolves, or possesses the power to absolve. [Rare.]

ab-solv′ēr, *n.* One who absolves; one who pronounces sin to be remitted.

ab′sō-nănt, *a.* [L. *ab*, from, and *sonans*, ppr. of *sonare*, to sound.] Wide from the purpose; contrary to reason.

ab′sō-nous, *a.* [L. *absonus*; *ab*, from, and *sonus*, sound.] Contrary to reason; discordant; unmusical. [Obs.]

ab-sorb′, *v.t.*; absorbed, *pt.*, *pp.*; absorbing, *ppr.* [L. *absorbere*; *ab*, from, and *sorbere*, to drink in.]

1. To drink in; to suck up; to imbibe like a sponge, or the lacteals of the body.

2. To drink in, swallow up, or overwhelm with water; as, his body was *absorbed* by the whirlpool.

3. To waste wholly or sink in expenses; to exhaust; as, to *absorb* an estate in luxury.

4. To engross or engage wholly; as, *absorbed* in study or the pursuit of wealth.

5. To receive or take up by chemical or molecular action; as, to *absorb* gases.

6. To receive or gather in by political action; as, a great nation may *absorb* smaller states.

Syn.—Consume, engulf, imbibe, drink in, suck up, engross.

ab-sorb-ȧ-bil′i-ty, *n.* The state or quality of being absorbable.

ab-sorb′ȧ-ble, *a.* That may be imbibed or swallowed.

ab-sorb′ed-ly, *adv.* In an absorbed manner.

ab-sorb′en-cy, *n.* Absorptiveness.

ab-sorb′ent, *a.* Imbibing; swallowing.

Absorbent ground; in painting a prepared ground, possessing the power of absorbing the oil of the colors used and thus hastening drying.

ab-sorb′ent, *n.* 1. In anatomy, a vessel which imbibes, as the lacteals and lymphatics.

2. In medicine, a substance used to absorb acidity in the stomach, as magnesia, chalk, etc.

3. Any substance which absorbs.

ab-sorb′ẽr, *n.* A person who or a thing which absorbs.

Shock absorber; any device which lessens a jar, as in an automobile, for reducing the jar resulting from rough roads, or in an aeroplane when alighting.

ab-sorb′ing, *a.* Imbibing; engrossing; occupying very fully.

ab-sorb′ing-ly, *adv.* In an absorbing manner.

ab-sor-bi′tion (-bish′un), *n.* Absorption. [Obs.]

ab-sorp-ti-om′e-tēr (-ti- *as* -shi-), *n.* [L. *absorptio*, absorption, and Gr. *metron*, a measure.] An instrument invented by Bunsen for measuring the extent to which particular gases may be absorbed by certain liquids.

ab-sorp′tion, *n.* 1. The act or process of imbibing or swallowing; either by water, which overwhelms, or by substances which drink in and retain liquids; as, the *absorption* of a body in a whirlpool, or of water by the earth, or of the humors of the body by dry powders.

2. Entire occupation or engrossment of mind; as, *absorption* in business.

3. In physiology, one of the vital organic functions, which conveys to the circulating system the materials of nutrition, by means of the lacteals, and the effete particles of the body by means of the lymphatics.

4. In chemistry, the conversion of a gaseous fluid into a liquid or solid, by union with another substance.

ab-sorp′tive, *a.* Having power to imbibe.

ab-sorp′tive-ness, *n.* The power of absorption.

ab-sorp-tiv′i-ty, *n.* Absorbency.

ab-squăt′ū-lāte, *v.i.* To leave suddenly; to decamp. [Slang

abs′quē-hoc. [L. Without this or that; in law, words used in traversing what has been alleged and is repeated.

ab-stāin′, *v.i.*; abstained, *pt.*, *pp.*; abstaining, *ppr.* [L. *abstinere*, to keep from; *abs* and *tenere*, to hold.] In a general sense, to forbear, or refrain from, voluntarily; but used chiefly to denote a restraint upon the passions or appetites; to refrain from indulgence; as, to *abstain* from the use of intoxicating liquors as beverages; to *abstain* from luxuries.

Syn.—Forbear, cease, refrain, give up, withhold, relinquish.

ab-stāin′, *v.t.* To prevent. [Rare.]

Abstain men from marrying. —Milton.

ab-stāin′ẽr, *n.* One who abstains, particularly from intoxicants.

ab-stē′mi-ous, *a.* [L. *abstemius*, abstaining from intoxicating liquor; *abs*, from, and *temetum*, strong drink.]

1. Sparing in diet; refraining from a free use of food and strong drinks.

2. Sparing in the enjoyment of animal pleasures of any kind.

3. Sparingly used, or used with temperance; marked by abstinence; as, an *abstemious* diet.

4. Inspiring abstinence. [Rare.]

The virtue of the *abstemious* well. —Dryden.

Syn.—Sober, temperate, abstinent.

ab-stē′mi-ous-ly, *adv.* Temperately; with a sparing use of meat or drink.

ab-stē′mi-ous-ness, *n.* The quality of being temperate or sparing in the use of food and strong drinks. This word expresses a greater degree of abstinence than *temperance*.

ab-sten′tion, *n.* The act of abstaining.

ab-sten′tious, *a.* Characterized by abstinence.

ab-stērge′, *v.t.*; absterged, *pt.*, *pp.*; absterging, *ppr.* [L. *abstergere*; *abs*, away, and *tergere*, to wipe.] To wipe or make clean by wiping; to cleanse by lotions or similar applications; to purge. [Rare.]

ab-stēr′gent, *a.* Wiping; cleansing.

ab-stēr′gent, *n.* Anything which removes foulness, as lotions or soap.

ab-stērse′, *v.t.* To clean. [Obs.]

ab-stēr′sion, *n.* [From L. *abstergere*, *abstersus*.] The act of wiping clean; or a cleansing by lotions or similar applications.

ab-stēr′sive, *a.* Cleansing; having the quality of removing foulness. [See *Detersive*.]

ab-stēr′sive, *n.* That which cleanses.

ab-stēr′sive-ness, *n.* The quality of being abstersive.

ab′sti-nence, *n.* [L. *abstinentia* abstinence from anything.]

1. In general, the act or practice of voluntarily refraining from, or forbearing any action.

2. The refraining from an indulgence of appetite, or from customary gratifications of animal propensities; it denotes a total forbearance, as in fasting, or a forbearance of the usual quantity; as, *abstinence* from meat; *abstinence* from whisky.

Total abstinence; the specific name for the act and practice of refraining from the use of intoxicating liquors as beverages.

ab′sti-nen-cy, *n.* Abstinence. [Rare.]

ab′sti-nent, *a.* Refraining from indulgence, especially in the use of food and drink.

ab′sti-nent-ly, *adv.* With abstinence.

Ab′sti-nents, *n.pl.* A sect which appeared in France and Spain in the third century, opposing marriage and the eating of flesh, and placing the Holy Spirit in the class of created beings.

ab-stort′ed, *a.* [L. *abs*, from, and *tortus*, twisted.] Forced away. [Obs.]

ab-stract′, *v.t.*; abstracted, *pt.*, *pp*; abstracting, *ppr.* [L. *abstractus*, dragged away, pp. of *abstrahere*, to draw from or separate.]

1. To draw from, or to separate; as, to *abstract* an action from its evil effects.

2. To separate (ideas) by the operation of the mind; to consider one part of a complex object by itself.

3. To select or separate (the substance of a book or writing); to epitomize or reduce to a summary.

4. To take secretly for one's own use from the property of another; to purloin; as, to *abstract* goods from a parcel.

5. In chemistry, to separate, as the more volatile parts of a substance by repeated distillation, or at least by distillation; to extract.

6. To draw away the attention of; as, he was *abstracted* by thoughts of the morrow.

ab′stract, *a.* [L. *abstractus*, pp. of *abstrahere*; *abs*, from, and *trahere*, to draw.]

1. Separate; distinct from something else; treated by itself; as, *abstract* mathematics.

2. Separate; existing in the mind only; general; not concrete; as, an *abstract* subject; an *abstract* question; hence, difficult, abstruse.

3. Having the senses unemployed, insensible to outward objects; abstracted.

Abstract as in a trance. —Milton.

4. Lacking a concrete object; refined; pure. [Rare.]

Abstract idea; in metaphysics, an idea separated from a complex object, or from other ideas which naturally accompany it; as the solidity of marble contemplated apart from its color or figure.

Abstract or *pure mathematics*; that which treats of magnitude or quantity, without restriction to any species of particular magnitude, as arithmetic and geometry; distinguished from *mixed* mathematics, which treats of simple properties and the relations of quantity, as applied to sensible objects, as hydrostatics, navigation, optics, etc.

Abstract nouns or *terms*; those which express abstract ideas, as beauty, whiteness, roundness, without regarding any subject in which they exist; or the names of orders, genera, or species of things, in which there is a combination of similar qualities.

Abstract numbers; numbers used without application to things, as six, eight, ten; but when applied to anything, as six feet, ten men, they become concrete.

ab′stract, *n.* 1. A summary, or epitome, containing the substance, a general view, or the principal heads of a treatise or writing.

2. In grammar, a noun used as a general term; an abstract noun; as virtue, goodness, paternity.

3. In pharmacy, a solid preparation in which two parts of the drug are represented by one part of the *abstract*, which is compounded with milk-sugar. *Abstracts* are double the strength of the fluid extracts.

4. Any generality.

In the abstract; in a state of separation; as a subject considered *in the abstract*, i.e., without reference to particular persons or things.

Abstract of title; a summary of the successive title-deeds of real estate.

Syn.—Abridgment, summary, digest, synopsis, compendium, epitome.

ab-stract′ed, *a.* Separated; purloined; refined; exalted; abstruse; absent in mind.

Syn.—Absent, preoccupied, absorbed.

ab-stract′ed-ly, *adv.* In a separate state, or in contemplation only.

ab-stract′ed-ness, *n.* The state of being abstracted.

ab-stract′ēr, *n.* 1. One who makes an abstract or summary.

2. Specifically, one engaged in the business of making abstracts of title.

ab-strac′tion, *n.* [L. *abstractio*, from *abs*, away, and *trahere*, to draw.]

1. The act of separating, or state of being separated.

2. The operation of the mind when occupied by abstract ideas; as when we contemplate some particular part or property of a complex object as separate from the rest. Thus, when the mind considers the branch of a tree by itself, or the color of the leaves as separate from their size or figure, the act is called *abstraction*. So, also, when it considers whiteness, softness, virtue, existence, as separate from any particular objects. *Abstraction* is the groundwork of classification, by which things are arranged in orders, genera, and species. We separate in idea the qualities of certain objects which are of the same kind, from others which are different in each, and arrange the objects having the same properties in a class, or collected body.

3. A separation from worldly objects; a recluse life; as, a hermit's *abstraction*.

4. Absence of mind; inattention to present objects; as, a fit of *abstraction*.

5. The taking for one's own use part of the property of another.

6. In distillation, the separation of the volatile parts, which rise, come over, and are condensed in a receiver, from those which are fixed. It is chiefly used when a fluid is repeatedly poured upon any substance in a retort, and distilled off, to change its state or the nature of its composition.

7. In logic, the power which the understanding has of separating the combinations which are presented to it.

8. Something abstract; an abstract idea; an impracticable notion.

ab-strac′tion-ăl, *a.* Pertaining to abstraction.

ab-strac′tion-ist, *n.* A person who has lofty ideals.

ab-strac-ti′tious (-tish′us), *a.* Obtained by distillation. [Obs.]

ab-strac′tive, *a.* Having the power or quality of abstracting.

ab-strac′tive-ly, *adv.* Separately.

ab-strac′tive-ness, *n.* The quality of being abstractive.

ab′stract-ly, *adv.* Separately; absolutely; in

a state or manner unconnected with anything else; as, matter *abstractly* considered.

ab'stract-ness, *n.* A separate state; a state of being in contemplation only, or not connected with any object.

ab-strict'ed, *a.* Cut off by abstriction.

ab-stric'tion, *n.* [L. *abstringere*; *abs*, from, and *strictio*, from *stringere*, to bind.] In botany, a cutting off of cells, as in some algæ and fungi, in which a decided constriction of the cell-walls occurs at the place of division.

ab-stringe', *v.t.* [L. *abs*, from, and *stringere*, to bind.] To unbind. [Obs.]

ab-strude', *v.t.* To thrust away. [Obs.]

ab-struse', *a.* [L. *abstrusus*, pp. of *abstrudere*, to thrust away, to conceal; *abs*, away, and *trudere*, to thrust.] Hid; concealed; hence, remote from apprehension; difficult to be comprehended or understood; opposed to what is *obvious*; not used of material objects; as, metaphysics is an *abstruse* science.

Syn.—Complex, mysterious, obscure.

ab-struse'ly, *adv.* In a concealed manner; obscurely; in a manner not to be easily understood.

ab-struse'ness, *n.* Obscurity of meaning; the state or quality of being difficult to be understood.

ab-strū'sion, *n.* The act of thrusting away; that which is put aside. [Rare.]

ab-strū'si-ty, *n.* Abstruseness; that which is abstruse.

ab-sūme', *v.t.* [L. *absumere*; *ab*, away, and *sumere*, to take.] To bring to an end by a gradual waste; to consume. [Obs.]

ab-sump'tion, *n.* The act of consumption.

ab-sūrd', *a.* [L. *absurdus*, from *ab* and *surdus*, deaf, insensible.] Opposed to manifest truth; inconsistent with reason, or the plain dictates of common sense; logically contradictory. An *absurd* man acts contrary to the clear dictates of reason or sound judgment. An *absurd* proposition contradicts obvious truth. An *absurd* practice or opinion is repugnant to the reason or common apprehension of men.

Syn.—Foolish, irrational, ridiculous, preposterous, silly, unreasonable, nonsensical.

ab-sūrd'i-ty, *n.* 1. The quality of being inconsistent with obvious truth, reason, or sound judgment; want of judgment, applied to men; want of propriety, applied to things.

2. That which is absurd; in this sense it has a plural; as, the *absurdities* of men.

ab-sūrd'ly, *adv.* In a manner inconsistent with reason, or obvious propriety.

ab-sūrd'ness, *n.* Same as *Absurdity*.

ab-tēr'mi-năl, *a.* [L. *ab*, from, and *terminalis*, end.] In electricity, proceeding inward from the end; applied to currents traversing a muscle, etc.

ab'thāin, ab'thāne, *n.* [Gael.] A Scotch abbacy in the tenth century.

ȧ-bū'li-ȧ, ȧ-bou'li-ȧ, *n.* [Gr. *aboulia*; *a* priv., and *boulē*, advice.] Loss of will-power.

ȧ-bū'nȧ, *n.* [Eth. and Ar., our father.] The established head of the Christian church in Abyssinia.

ȧ-bun'dănce, *n.* [Fr. *abondance*; L. *abundare*; *ab*, and *unda*, wave.]

1. Great plenty; an overflowing quantity; ample sufficiency; strictly applicable to quantity only, but sometimes used of number; as, an *abundance* of laborers.

2. Abundant wealth or means; as, to give of one's *abundance*.

3. Fullness; overflowing; as, the *abundance* of the heart.

Syn. — Plenteousness, exuberance, plenty, plentifulness, plenitude, riches, affluence, copiousness, wealth.

ȧ-bun'dănt, *a.* [L. *abundans* (*-antis*), from *abundare*, to overflow.]

1. Plentiful; in great quantity; fully sufficient; as, an *abundant* supply.

2. Abounding; having in great quantity; overflowing with.

Abundant number; in arithmetic, a number the sum of whose aliquot parts exceeds the number itself. Thus, 1, 2, 3, 4, 6, the aliquot parts of 12, make the sum of 16. This is opposed to a *deficient* number, as 14, whose aliquot parts are 1, 2, 7, the sum of which is 10; and to a *perfect* number, which is equal to the sum of its aliquot parts, as 6, whose aliquot parts are 1, 2, 3.

Syn.—Ample, copious, exuberant, luxuriant, plentiful, plenteous.

ȧ-bun'dănt-ly, *adv.* Fully; amply; plentifully; in a sufficient degree.

ȧ-būrst', *a.* Bursting.

ȧ-būr'tŏn, *adv.* and *a.* A nautical term applied to casks placed athwartships.

ȧ-būs'ȧ-ble, *a.* Capable of being abused.

ȧ-būs'ăge, *n.* Abuse. [Obs.]

ȧ-būse', *v.t.*; abused, *pt.*, *pp.*; abusing, *ppr.* [Fr. *abuser*; It. *abusare*; L. *abutor*, *abusus*; *ab*, and *uti*, to use.]

1. To use ill; to maltreat; to misuse; to use with bad motives or to wrong purposes; as, to *abuse* rights or privileges.

2. To violate; to defile.

3. To deceive; to impose on. [Obs.]

> Nor be with all these tempting words *abused*. —Pope.

4. To treat rudely, or with contumelious language; to revile.

5. To pervert the meaning of; to misapply; as, to *abuse* words.

Syn.—Misuse, insult, revile, traduce.

ȧ-būse', *n.* 1. Ill use; improper treatment or employment; application to a wrong purpose; as, an *abuse* of our natural powers; an *abuse* of civil rights, or of religious privileges; *abuse* of advantages, etc.

> Liberty may be endangered by the *abuses* of liberty, as well as by the *abuses* of power. —Madison.

2. A corrupt practice or custom; as, the *abuses* of government.

3. Rude speech; rudely contemptuous language addressed to a person; contumely; reviling words.

4. Violation; defilement.

5. Perversion of meaning; improper use or application; as, an *abuse* of words.

ȧ-būse'fụl, *a.* Using or practising abuse; abusive.

ȧ-būs'ēr, *n.* One who abuses.

ȧ-bū'sion, *n.* Abuse; evil or corrupt usage; reproach; deception. [Obs.]

ȧ-bū'sive, *a.* 1. Practising abuse; offering harsh words, or ill treatment; as, an *abusive* author; an *abusive* fellow.

2. Containing abuse, or constituting the instrument of abuse; rude; reproachful; as, *abusive* words.

Syn.—Insolent, insulting, offensive, opprobrious, reproachful, rude, scurrilous, saucy.

ȧ-bū'sive-ly, *adv.* In an abusive manner; rudely; reproachfully.

ȧ-bū'sive-ness, *n.* Ill usage; the quality of being abusive; rudeness of language, or violence to the person.

ȧ-but', *v.i.*; abutted, *pt.*, *pp.*; abutting, *ppr.* [Fr. *aboutir*; *a*, to, and *bout*, *but*, end.] To border upon; to be contiguous to; to meet; strictly, to adjoin to at the end; used with *on* or *upon*; sometimes *against*; as, his land *abuts upon* mine; the building *abuts on* the highway; the bridge *abuts against* the solid rock.

A-bū'tȧ, *n.* A genus of climbing plants of the moonseed family.

A-bū'ti-lon, *n.* [Ar. *aubutilun.*] A genus of plants belonging to the family *Malvaceæ*, or mallowworts.

ȧ-but'ment, *n.* 1. The head or end; that which unites one end of a thing to another; chiefly used to denote the solid pier or mound of earth, stone, or timber, which is erected on the bank of a river to support the end of a bridge and connect it with the land.

2. That which abuts or borders on another, as a building or piece of land.

3. The state of abutting.

ȧ-but'tăl, *n.* The butting or boundary of land at the end; a headland.

ȧ-but'tēr, *n.* A person who or a thing which abuts; said of a building or land, or its owner.

ȧ-but'ting, *a.* Touching at the end; contiguous; as, *abutting* property; resting on or against; as, *abutting* rocks.

Syn.—Adjacent, neighboring, next.

ȧ-buzz', *a.* Buzzing. [Colloq.]

ȧ-bȳ', ȧ-bȳe', *v.t.* and *v.i.* [AS. *a*, out, and *bycgan*, to buy.] To endure; to pay dearly; to remain. [Obs.]

ȧ-bysm', *n.* [Fr. *abisme*; L. *abyssus*, from Gr. *abyssos*; *a* priv., and *byssos*, depth.] A gulf; a chasm.

ȧ-bys'măl, *a.* Pertaining to an abyss.

ȧ-bys'măl-ly, *adv.* Profoundly; to the lowest depths; as, sunk *abysmally* in crime.

ȧ-byss', *n.* [Gr. *abyssos*, bottomless; *a* priv., and *byssos*, bottom.]

1. A bottomless gulf; also a deep mass of waters, once supposed to have encompassed the earth in the beginning; as, the face of the *abyss*, in the Septuagint.

2. That which is immeasurable; that in which anything is lost.

> Thy throne is darkness, in the *abyss* of night. —Milton.

3. The bottomless pit; hell; Erebus.

4. An immensity of time, space, depth, or scope, usually with the idea of intellectual or moral depravity; as, an *abyss* of ignorance; an *abyss* of crime.

5. In heraldry, the center of an escutcheon; as, he bears azure, a fleur-de-lis, in *abyss*.

Syn.—Chasm, cleft, crevasse, gorge, gulf, pit.

ȧ-byss'ăl, *a.* 1. Pertaining to an abyss.

2. Pertaining to the ocean's greatest depths; as, the *abyssal* fauna and flora.

Ab-ys-sin'i-ăn, *a.* and *n.* [Ar. *Habashon*, Abyssinians, Ethiopians, from *habasha*, to collect, or congregate; L. *Abassini.*]

I. *a.* Belonging to Abyssinia.

II. *n.* A native of Abyssinia.

Ab-ys-sin'i-ăns, *n.pl.* A sect of Christians in Abyssinia, which admits but one nature in Jesus Christ and rejects the council of Chalcedon. It is governed by a bishop, or metropolitan, called the abuna.

aç, *n.* [AS. *ac*, *ake*, *oke*, oak.] A prefix used in place-names; as, *Ac*ton, *oak*town, etc.

aç-, *prefix.* A euphonious change for *ad-*, used before *c* and *q*, as in *ac*cuse, *ac*quire.

-aç, *suffix.* [L. *acus*, Gr. *akos.*] Characteristic of, pertaining to, having; as mani*ac*, demoni*ac*. It is preceded by *i* and may be followed by *al*.

A-çā'ciȧ (-shȧ *or* -shi-ȧ), *n.*; *pl.* **A-çā'ciȧs** (-shȧz); L. *pl.* **A-çā'ciæ** (-shi-ē). [L. *acacia*, a thorn, from Gr. *akakia*, a point.]

Acacia Arabica.

1. A genus of plants, natural order *Leguminosæ*, suborder *Mimoseæ*, for the most part natives of Arabia, Barbary, and the East Indies. As objects of ornament the *acacias* are usually of striking beauty. Some of the species produce catechu, as *Acacia Catechu*, and some exude gum arabic, as *Acacia Verek*, *Acacia Arabica*, *Acacia vera* (Egyptian thorn), *Acacia Adansoni*; the bark of others yields a large quantity of tannin, as *Acacia decurrens* and *Acacia mollissima*. Several species afford timber of good quality.

2. [a—] In medicine, the inspissated juice of several species of *Acacia*, known popularly as gum arabic.

3. [a—] Among antiquaries, a name given to an object resembling a roll or bag, seen on medals, in the hands of several emperors and consuls. Some take it to represent a handkerchief rolled up, with which signals were given at the games; but its exact import has not been determined.

A-çā'ciăns, *n.pl.* In church history, certain sects, so denominated from their leaders, Acacius, bishop of Cæsarea, and Acacius, patriarch of Constantinople.

aç'ȧ-cin, aç'ȧ-cine, *n.* Gum arabic.

aç-ȧ-dēme', *n.* [L. *academia.*]

1. An academy; a society of persons. [Obs.]

2. [A—] The academy or school of Plato.

aç-ȧ-dē'mi-ăl, *a.* Academic.

aç-ȧ-dē'mi-ăn, *n.* A member of an academy; a student in a university or college.

aç-ȧ-dem'iç, aç-ȧ-dem'iç-ăl, *a.* 1. Belonging to an academy, or to a college or university; as, *academic* studies.

2. [A—] Pertaining to the school or philosophy of Plato; as, the *Academic* sect.

Aç-ȧ-dem'iç, *n.* 1. One who belonged to the school or adhered to the philosophy of Socrates and Plato. The latter is considered as the founder of the Academic philosophy in Greece. He taught that matter is eternal and infinite, but without form, refractory, and tending to disorder; and that there is an intelligent cause, the author of spiritual being and of the material world.

2. [a—] A student in a college or university.

aç-ȧ-dem'iç-ăl-ly, *adv.* In an academical manner.

aç-ȧ-dem'iç-ăls, *n.pl.* The cap and gown or other costume worn at colleges.

aç″ȧ-dē-mi'cian (-mish'un), *n.* [Fr. *académicien.*] A member of an academy, or society for promoting arts and sciences; particularly, a member of the French Academy.

Aç-ȧ-dem'i-çism, *n.* 1. An Academic law.

2. [a—] A custom peculiar to an academy.

A-çad'e-mism, *n.* The doctrine of the Academic philosophy.

ȧ-çad'e-mist, *n.* 1. A member of an academy for promoting arts and sciences.

2. [A—] An Academic philosopher.

ȧ-çad'e-my, *n.* [L. *academia*; Gr. *akadēmeia*. Originally a garden, grove, or villa, near Athens, where Plato and his followers held their philosophical conferences.]

1. [A—] The school of Plato.

2. A school or seminary of learning, holding a rank between a university, or college, and a common school; also, a school for teaching a particular art, or particular sciences; as, a military *academy*.

3. A building in which the students or members of an academy meet; a place of education.

4. A society of men united for the promotion of arts and sciences in general, or of some particular art or science.

5. Specifically, an institution for the cultivation and promotion of the fine arts, partaking of the character both of an association of artists for mutual improvement and of a school of instruction.

Academy figure; in art, a drawing usually

made with black and white chalk, on tinted paper, after the living model.

Syn.—College, institute, school, seminary, university.

ȧ-çā′di-ăl-īte, *n.* [*Acadia*, Nova Scotia, and *lite* from Gr. *lithos*, stone.] A kind of mineral; chabazite.

Ȧ-çā′di-ăn, *n.* and *a.* I. *n.* An inhabitant of Acadia or Nova Scotia.

II. *a.* Pertaining to Acadia.

aç′ȧ-jöu, *n.* [Fr.] 1. A name given to the cashew-tree.

2. A gum exuding from the cashew-tree.

aç′ȧ-jöu, *n.* [Fr.] Mahogany.

Aç-ȧ-lē′phæ, *n. pl.* [Gr. *akalēphē*, a nettle.] A large class of marine, radiate animals or zoöphytes; so called from the property, possessed by most of the species, of irritating and inflaming the skin when touched; including the medusa, sea-nettle, jelly-fish, etc. The most typical of the *Acalephæ*, the *Medusidæ*, are gelatinous, free-swimming animals, consisting of an umbrella-shaped disk, containing canals which radiate from the center whence hangs the digestive cavity.

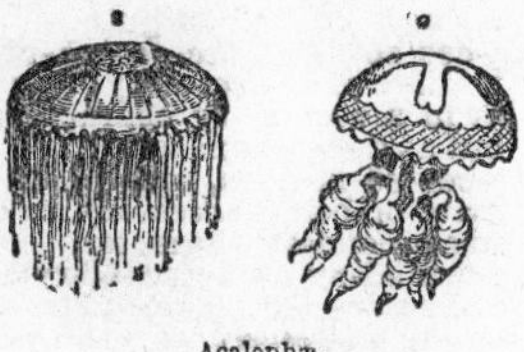
Acalephæ.
1. *Medusa pellucens.*
2. *Rhizostoma cuvieri.*

aç-ȧ-lē′phăn, *a.* Pertaining to the *Acalephæ*.

aç-ȧ-lē′phăn, *n.* One of the *Acalephæ*.

aç-ȧ-lē′phoid, *a.* Resembling an acalephan.

ȧ-çal′y-çine, aç-ȧ-lyç′i-nous, *a.* [Gr. *a* priv., and *kalyx*, calyx.] Without a calyx or flower-cup.

aç-ȧ-lyç′ū-lāte, *a.* Without a calycle.

Ȧ-çal′y-phȧ, *n.* [Gr. *akalēphē*, nettle.] A genus of herbaceous plants, family *Euphorbia*, some of which are cultivated while others grow as weeds, as *Acalypha Virginica*, the three-seeded mercury.

aç-ȧ-nā′ceous, *a.* [Gr. *akanos*, from *akē*, point, a prickly shrub.] Armed with prickles.

ȧ-çan′thȧ, *n.* [Gr. *akantha*, from *akē*, a spine or thorn.] In botany, a prickle; in zoölogy, a spine or prickly fin; the spinous process of the vertebræ.

Aç-an-thā′cē-æ, *n.pl.* A family of plants of which the acanthus is a type.

aç-an-thā′ceous, *a.* Armed with prickles, as a plant; also, pertaining to the *Acanthaceæ*.

ȧ-çan′thine, *a.* Pertaining to the plant acanthus. The *acanthine* garments of the ancients were made of the down of thistles, or embroidered in imitation of the acanthus.

ȧ-çan′thīte, *n.* Sulphid of silver.

ȧ-çan-thō-cär′pous, *a.* [Gr. *akantha*, thorn, and *karpos*, fruit.] Thorny, as fruit.

Ȧ-çan-thō-ceph′ȧ-lȧ, *n.pl.* [Gr. *akantha*, thorn, and *kephalē*, head.] An order of intestinal worms having a thorny head.

ȧ-çan-thō-ceph′ȧ-lous, *a.* [Gr. *akantha*, thorn, and *kephalē*, head.] Pertaining to the *Acanthocephala*.

aç-an-thog′lȧ-dous, *a.* [Gr. *akantha*, thorn, and *klados*, branch.] Thorny.

ȧ-çan′thoid, *a.* Formed like or resembling a spine.

aç-an-thoph′ō-rous, *a.* [Gr. *akantha*, thorn, and *pherein*, to bear.] Bearing spines.

ȧ-çan′thō-pod, *n.* [Gr. *akantha*, a spine, and *pous*, foot.] A term applied to clavicorn coleopterous insects, including those species with spiny legs.

ȧ-çan-thō-pō′di-ous, aç-an-thop′ō-dous, *a.* [Gr. *akantha*, thorn, and *pous*, foot.] In zoölogy, having spine-bearing feet.

Aç-an-thop′tēr-i, *n. pl.* [Gr. *akantha*, thorn, and *pteron*, wing.] A group of fishes with spiny fins.

aç-an-thop′tēr-ous, *a.* Pertaining to the *Acanthopteri*.

Aç-an″thop-tēr-yġ′i-ī, *n.pl.* [Gr. *akantha*, a thorn, and *pterygion*, the fin of a fish, from *pteryx*, a wing.] One of the two primary divisions of the osseous fishes established by Cuvier, and including by far the greatest number of ordinary fishes. They are characterized by having one or more of the first rays of the fins in the form of unjointed spines. In some species the first dorsal fin is represented by a few unconnected spines. The first rays of the anal fins consist of simple spines, and each ventral fin has usually one. The swim-bladder is in all a shut sac. They include the perch, mackerel, gudgeon, bass, flying-fish, mullet, braize, tunny, etc. Many fishes belonging to this division are used as food.

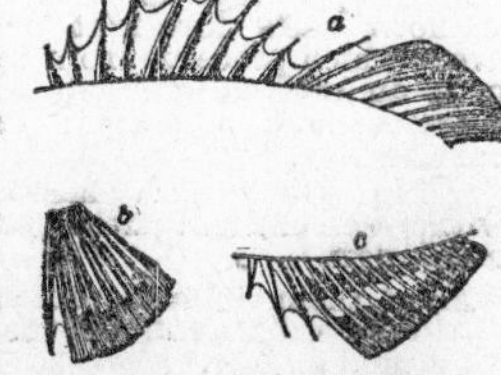
a, b, c, Spines of the dorsal, anal, and ventral fins of *Acanthopterygii*.

aç-an″thop-tēr-yġ′i-ous, *a.* In zoölogy, having the characteristics of the *Acanthopterygii* or spine-finned fishes; belonging to the *Acanthopterygii*.

Ȧ-çan′thus, *n.* [Gr. *akanthos*, L. *acanthus*, from *akantha*, a prickle or thorn.]

1. A genus of prickly plants, natural order *Acanthaceæ*, the bear's-breech or brankursine.

2. [a—] In architecture, an ornament resembling the foliage or leaves of the acanthus, used in the capitals of the Corinthian and Composite orders.

Acanthus.

3. [a—] Any plant of the genus *Acanthus*.

ȧ çap-pel′lȧ. [It., from L. *ad*, to, according to, and *capella*, chapel.] In the style of church or chapel music; especially in the old style, without accompaniment.

ȧ-çap′sū-lăr, *a.* [Gr. *a* priv., and *kampsa*, or L. *capsula*, a box or chest.] Without a capsule.

ȧ-çär′di-aç, *a.* [Gr. *a* priv., and *kardia*, heart.] Without a heart.

aç-ȧ-rī′ȧ-sis, *n.* The itch; a parasitic skin disease.

Ȧ-çar′i-dȧ, *n.pl.* [Gr. *akarēs*, too short to be cut, small, tiny; *a* priv., and *keirein*, to cut.] A division of *Arachnida*, including the mites, ticks, and water-mites. Of the true mites, the domestic or cheese-mite and the itch-mite are examples. The garden-mites and spider-mites live upon plants; the wood-mites and harvest-ticks are found amongst moss and herbage, or creeping on trees and stones; while the true ticks (*Ixodidæ*) attach themselves parasitically to the bodies of various mammals, as sheep, oxen, dogs, etc. The water-mites (*Hydrachnidæ*) are parasitic for at least a portion of their existence upon water-beetles and other aquatic insects. The mouth in all is formed for suction. Also called *Acarina*.

1 2 3
Acarida.
1. Itch-mite (*Sarcoptes scabiei*).
2. Cheese-mite (*Acarus domesticus*).
3. Harvest-tick (*Leptus autumnalis*).

ȧ-çar′i-dăn, *a.* Of or pertaining to the *Acarida*.

ȧ-çar′i-dăn, *n.* One of the *Acarida*.

Aç-ȧ-rī′nȧ, *n.pl.* Same as *Acarida*.

aç′ȧ-rine, *a.* [Gr. *akari*, a mite.] Caused by mites.

aç′ȧ-roid, *a.* Having the appearance of a mite.

ȧ-çär-pel′ous, *a.* [Gr. *a* priv., and L. *carpellum*, from Gr. *karpos*, fruit.] Without carpels.

ȧ-çär′pous, *a.* Not fruitful.

Aç′ȧ-rus, *n.* 1. The typical genus of the *Acarida*; it includes the mites and ticks.

2. [a—] A mite; a tick.

ȧ-çat-ȧ-leç′tiç, *n.* [Gr. *akatalēktos*, incessant, from *a* priv., and *katalēgein*, to stop.] A verse which has the complete number of syllables without defect or superfluity.

ȧ-çat′ȧ-lep-sy, ȧ-çat-ȧ-lep′si-ȧ, *n.* [Gr. *a* priv., and *katalambanein*, to comprehend.]

1. Impossibility of complete discovery or comprehension; incomprehensibility.

2. In medicine, uncertainty in the diagnosis or prognosis of disease.

ȧ-çat-ȧ-lep′tiç, *a.* [Gr. *akatalēptos*; *a* priv., and *kata*, down, and *lambanein*, to seize.] Incomprehensible.

ȧ-çā′tēr, *n.* [Obs.] See *Caterer*.

ȧ-çātes′, *n.* [Obs.] See *Cates*.

aç-ȧ-thär′si-ȧ (*or* -shȧ), *n.* [Gr. *akatharsia*, impurity, from *a* priv., and *kathartos*, pure.]

1. In medicine, impurity of the blood and humors.

2. In surgery, the filth or sordes proceeding from a wound.

ȧ-çau′dăl, *a.* [L. *a*, without, and *cauda*, tail.] Without a tail.

ȧ-çau′dāte, *a.* Same as *Acaudal*.

aç-au-les′cent, ȧ-çau′line, *a.* Same as *Acaulous*.

ȧ-çau′lous, *a.* [Gr. *a* priv., and *kaulos*, a stalk.] In botany, without the stem called caulis.

Aç-çā′di-ăn, *n.* An inhabitant of Accad in ancient Babylon.

aç-çēde′, *v.i.*; acceded, *pt.*, *pp.*; acceding, *ppr.* [L. *accedere*; *ad*, to, and *cedere*, to yield.]

1. To agree or assent, as to a proposition, or to terms proposed by another.

2. To become a party, by agreeing to the terms of a treaty, convention, or other form of contract.

3. To attain, as to an office or rank; to enter into possession; as, Edward VII. *acceded* to the British throne in 1901.

Syn.—Acquiesce, agree, consent, assent, comply, succeed, attain, enter upon.

aç-çēd′ence, *n.* The act of acceding.

aç-çēd′ēr, *n.* One who accedes.

aç-çel-ēr-an′dō (*or* ät-chā-le-rän′dō), *adv.* [It.] With an acceleration of the time in a tune; gradually quicker.

aç-çel′ēr-āte, *v.t.*; accelerated, *pt.*, *pp.*; accelerating, *ppr.* [L. *accelerare*; *ad*, to, and *celerare*, to hasten.]

1. To cause to move faster; to hasten; to quicken (motion); to add to the velocity of a moving body.

2. To add to (natural or ordinary progression); as, to *accelerate* the growth of a plant, or the progress of knowledge.

3. To bring nearer in time; to shorten (the time) between the present time and a future event; as, to *accelerate* the ruin of a government; to *accelerate* a crisis.

Accelerated motion; in mechanics and physics, that which continually receives accessions of velocity.

Accelerating force; the force which causes accelerated motion, as gravity.

Accelerating gun; an accelerator.

Syn.—Hasten, expedite, further, quicken, forward, advance.

aç-çel-ēr-ā′tion, *n.* The act of increasing velocity or progress; the state of being quickened in motion or action; as, a falling body moves toward the earth with an *acceleration* of velocity. It is the opposite of *retardation*.

Acceleration of the moon; the increase of the moon's mean motion around the earth; the moon moving with more velocity now than in ancient times.

Diurnal acceleration of the fixed stars; the time by which they anticipate the apparent mean diurnal revolution of the sun, which is nearly three minutes, fifty-six seconds of mean time.

Acceleration of the planets; the increasing velocity of their motion in proceeding from the apogee to the perigee of their orbits.

Acceleration of the tides; priming of the tides which occurs in the first and third quarters of the moon.

aç-çel′ēr-ȧ-tive, *a.* Adding to velocity; quickening progression.

aç-çel′ēr-ā-tŏr, *n.* [L. *ad*, to, and *celerare*, to hasten.]

1. One who or that which accelerates; anything that quickens action.

2. A cannon with several powder-chambers whose charges are exploded consecutively in order to accelerate the speed of the projectile.

3. In anatomy, a muscle which contracts to expel or accelerate the passage of the urine.

4. In photography, any substance which shortens the time required for exposure.

aç-çel′ēr-ȧ-tō-ry, *a.* Accelerating; quickening motion.

aç-çel′ēr-ō-graph, *n.* [L. *accelerare*, to hasten, and Gr. *graphos*, a writer.] An accelerometer.

aç-çel-ēr-om′e-tēr, *n.* [L. *accelerare*, to hasten, and Gr. *metron*, measure.] An appliance for ascertaining the propulsive power of gunpowder.

aç-çend′, *v.t.* [L. *accendere*; *ad*, to, and *candare*, to kindle.] To kindle; to set on fire. [Obs.]

aç-çend-i-bil′i-ty, *n.* Capacity of being kindled or of becoming inflamed.

aç-çend′i-ble, *a.* Capable of being inflamed or kindled.

aç-çen′sion, *n.* The act of kindling or setting on fire, or the state of being kindled; inflammation.

aç-çen′sŏr, *n.* One who sets on fire or kindles; specifically, in the Roman Catholic church, a minister or servant whose business it is to light and trim the candles and tapers.

aç′cent, *n.* [L. *accentus*, from *ad*, to, and *canere*, to sing.]

1. Originally, the modulation of the voice in reading or speaking, as practised by the ancient Greeks, which rendered the rehearsal musical.

2. A particular stress or force of voice upon certain syllables of words, which distinguishes them from the others. When the full *accent* falls on a vowel, that vowel has its long sound, as in *vō′cal*; but when it falls on an articulation or consonant, the preceding vowel is short, as in *hab′it*. *Accent* alone regulates English verse. It must not be confounded with *emphasis*, the latter being used in reference to some one word or part of a sentence to which a speaker wishes to draw attention, by giving it a more marked pronunciation. There are two kinds of *accent* in many English words, the primary and the secondary; thus, in uttering the word *aspiration*, the *first* and *third* syllables are distinguished—the *third* by a full sound, which constitutes the primary *accent*; the *first*, by a degree of force in the voice which is less than that of the primary *accent*, but evidently

greater than that which falls on the second and fourth syllables.

3. A mark or character used in writing to direct the stress of the voice in pronunciation. Our ancestors borrowed from the Greek language three of these characters, the acute (ʹ), the grave (\`), and the circumflex (˜, or ˆ) In the Greek, the first shows when the voice is to be raised; the second, when it is to be depressed; and the third, when the vowel is to be uttered with an undulating sound.

4. A modulation of the voice expressive of passion or sentiments; as, the tender *accents* of love.

5. Manner of speaking; as, a man of plain *accent*.

6. [*pl.*] Poetically, words, language, or expressions in general.

Winds! on your wings to heaven her *accents* bear. —Dryden.

7. In music, either the stress laid on the accented parts of the bar, called *grammatical accent*; or the emphasis dictated by feeling, and giving the music its peculiar expression, called *oratorical accent*.

8. A peculiar tone or inflection of voice; as, a French *accent*.

9. In mathematics, a mark used to distinguish magnitudes of the same or similar kind, expressed by the same letter, but differing in value; as, a', a''.

10. A mark at the right hand of a number used to express a minute of a degree; two such *accents* express a second, etc.; thus, 26° 43′ 58″ west longitude; similar *accents* are used to denote feet and inches.

Syn.—Cadence, intonation, emphasis, stress, tone.

aç-cent′, *v.t.*; accented, *pt.*, *pp.*; accenting, *ppr.*

1. To give accent to; to utter (a syllable) with a particular stress or modulation of the voice; to emphasize.

2. In poetry, to utter or pronounce in general. [Rare.]

3. To note (accents) by marks in writing.

aç′cent-less, *a.* Devoid of accent.

aç-cen′tŏr, *n.* [L. *ad*, to, and *canere*, to sing.]

1. In music, one who sings the leading part. [Obs.]

2. [A—] A genus of insessorial birds, so named from their sweetness of note. It includes the English hedge-sparrow.

aç-cen′tū-ȧ-ble, *a.* Capable of being accented.

aç-cen′tū-ăl, *a.* Pertaining to accent; rhythmical.

aç-cen-tū-al′i-ty, *n.* The quality of being accentual; the quality of possessing rhythm.

aç-cen′tū-ăl-ly, *adv.* With due observance of accent; rhythmically.

aç-cen′tū-āte, *v.t.*; accentuated, *pt.*, *pp.*; accentuating, *ppr.* [L. *accentuatus*, pp. of *accentuare*; *ad*, to, and *canere*, to sing.]

1. To mark or pronounce with an accent or with accents.

2. To emphasize.

aç-cen-tū-ā′tion, *n.* The act of placing accents in writing, or of pronouncing them in speaking.

aç-cept′, *v.t.*; accepted, *pt.*, *pp.*; accepting, *ppr.* [L. *acceptare*, from *accipere*; *ad*, to, and *capere*, to take.]

1. To take or receive (what is offered) with a consenting mind; to receive with approbation or favor; as, he made an offer which was *accepted*.

2. To regard with partiality; to value or esteem.

It is not good to *accept* the person of the wicked. —Prov. xviii. 5.

3. To consent or agree to; to receive as terms of a contract; as, to *accept* a treaty; often followed by *of*; as, *accept of* the terms.

4. To understand; to have a particular idea of; to receive in a particular sense; as, how is this phrase to be *accepted?*

5. In commerce, to agree or promise to pay; as, to *accept* a bill of exchange. [See *Acceptance.*]

6. To receive as sufficient; as, to *accept* an apology.

Syn.—Receive, take, admit.

aç-cept-ȧ-bil′i-ty, *n.* Acceptableness.

aç-cept′ȧ-ble, *a.* [L. *acceptabilitas*, from *ad*, to, and *capere*, to take.]

1. That may be received with pleasure; pleasing to a receiver; gratifying; as, an *acceptable* present.

2. Agreeable or pleasing in person; as, a man makes himself *acceptable* by his services or civilities.

Syn.—Agreeable, grateful, pleasing, welcome.

aç-cept′ȧ-ble-ness, *n.* The quality of being agreeable to a receiver, or to a person with whom one has intercourse; acceptability.

aç-cept′ȧ-bly, *adv.* In a manner to please, or give satisfaction.

aç-cept′ănce, *n.* 1. A receiving with approbation or satisfaction; favorable reception; as, work done to *acceptance*; the *acceptance* of gifts.

2. The receiving of a bill of exchange or order, in such a manner as to bind the acceptor to make payment. This must be by express words; and, to charge the drawer with costs, in case of non-payment, the *acceptance* must be in writing, under, across, or on the back of the bill. —Blackstone.

3. An agreeing to terms or proposals in commerce, by which a bargain is concluded and the parties bound.

4. An agreeing to the act or contract of another, by some act which binds the person in law; as, a landlord's taking rent agreed upon in a lease made by his predecessor is an *acceptance* of the terms of the lease.

5. In mercantile language, a bill of exchange accepted; as, a merchant receives another's *acceptance* in payment.

aç-cept′ăn-cy, *n.* The act of acceptance.

aç-cept′ănt, *a.* and *n.* I. *a.* Accepting.

II. *n.* One who accepts.

aç-cep-tā′tion, *n.* 1. Kind reception; a receiving with favor or approbation.

2. A state of being acceptable; favorable regard.

Some things are of great dignity and *acceptation* with God. —Hooker.

3. The meaning or sense in which a word or expression is understood, or generally received; as, a term is to be used according to its usual *acceptation*.

aç-cept′ed, *a.* 1. Kindly received; as, an *accepted* favor.

2. Received with a pledge to pay; as, an *accepted* bill of exchange.

3. Acceptable; as, now is the *accepted* time.

4. Understood; generally received; as, the *accepted* meaning of a word.

aç-cept′ẽr, *n.* [L. *acceptor*, one who receives; from *accipere*; *ad*, to, and *capere*, to take.] A person who accepts; the person who receives a bill of exchange so as to bind himself to pay it. [See *Acceptor.*]

aç-cep′ti-lāte, *v.t.* To remit (a debt) by acquittance without receiving the money.

aç-cep-ti-lā′tion, *n.* [L. *acceptilatio*, from *accipere*, to receive or take, and *latio*, from *latus*, pp. of *ferre*, to bear.] Remission of a debt by an acquittance from the creditor without receiving the money.

aç-cep′tion, *n.* Acceptation. [Obs.]

aç-cept′ive, *a.* Acceptable.

aç-cept′ŏr, *n.* Same as *Accepter*, but more used in commerce and law.

aç-cess′ (*or* aç′cess), *n.* [L. *accessus*, approach.]

1. A coming to; near approach; admittance; admission; as, to gain *access* to a prince.

2. Approach, or the way by which a thing may be approached; as, the *access* is by a neck of land.

3. Means of approach; liberty to approach; implying previous obstacles.

4. Admission to sexual intercourse.

5. Addition; increase by something added; as, an *access* of territory; but in this sense *accession* is more generally used.

6. The return of a fit or paroxysm of disease, or fever.

7. In the Roman Catholic church, the approach of the celebrant to the altar.

8. In the Anglican and Protestant Episcopal churches, the prayer before consecration of the eucharistic elements; the prayer of humble *access*.

Syn.—Admission, approach, entrance, admittance, increase, reception.

aç-ces′sā-ri-ly, *adv.* See *Accessorily.*

aç-ces′sā-ri-ness, *n.* See *Accessoriness.*

aç-ces′sā-ry, *a.* and *n.* See *Accessory.*

aç-cess-i-bil′i-ty, *n.* The quality of being approachable, or of admitting access.

aç-cess′i-ble, *a.* 1. That may be approached or reached; approachable; applied to things; as, an *accessible* town or mountain.

2. Easy of approach; affable; used of persons.

Syn.—Attainable, complaisant, civil, courteous, familiar, sociable, friendly.

aç-cess′i-bly, *adv.* So as to be accessible.

aç-ces′sion, *n.* [L. *accessio*, an approach, from *accedere*; *ad*, to, and *cedere*, to move.]

1. A coming to and joining; as, a king's *accession* to a confederacy.

2. Increase by something added; that which is added; augmentation; as, an *accession* of wealth or territory.

3. In law, a mode of acquiring property, by which the owner of a corporeal substance, which receives an addition by growth, or by labor, has a right to the thing added or the improvement; provided the thing is not changed into a different species. Thus the owner of a cow becomes the owner of her calf. —Blackstone.

4. The act of arriving at a throne, an office, or dignity; as, the *accession* of a new president; the *accession* of the house of Hanover.

5. The invasion of a fit of a periodical disease; as, an *accession* of fever; a paroxysm; as an *accession* of folly.

Syn.—Addition, augmentation, coming to, growth, increase.

aç-ces′sion-ăl, *a.* Additional. [Rare.]

aç-ces′sit, *n.* [L., 3d pers. sing., perf. ind. of *accedere*, to come near, and meaning "he came near."]

1. A certificate or prize awarded to a student second in merit. [Eng.]

2. In the election of a pope, the opportunity given to cardinals to revise their votes.

aç-ces′sive, *a.* Additional.

aç-ces-sō′ri-ăl, *a.* [L. *accessorius*, from *accessus*, pp. of *accedere*; *ad*, to, and *cedere*, to yield.] Pertaining to an accessory; as, *accessorial* agency; *accessorial* guilt.

aç-ces′sō-ri-ly, aç-ces′sā-ri-ly, *adv.* In the manner of an accessory; by subordinate means, or in a secondary character; not as principal, but as a subordinate agent.

aç-ces′sō-ri-ness, aç-ces′sā-ri-ness, *n.* The state of being accessory, or of being or acting in a secondary character.

aç-ces′sō-ry (*or* aç′ces-sō-ry), **aç-ces′sā-ry**, *a.* [L. *accessorius*, from *accessus*, pp. of *accedere*; *ad*, to, and *cedere*, to yield.—The second, or old pronunciation, while not now generally in favor, has a respectable usage among cultured people. Dr. Webster explained that the natural accent of this word is on the second syllable, although he gave the accent on the first because of the derivatives, which require a secondary accent on the third.]

1. Acceding; contributing; aiding in producing some effect, or acting in subordination to the principal agent. Usually in a bad sense; as, he was *accessory* to the felony.

2. Aiding in certain acts or effects in a secondary manner; as, *accessory* sounds in music.

Accessory fruit; fruit formed with a part of the floral envelope attached to the pericarp as additional substance; the mulberry and checkerberry are examples.

Accessory nerves; in anatomy, the eleventh pair of cranial nerves; the spinal accessory nerves.

Accessory valves; in zoölogy, small additional valves, as those placed near the umbones of the genus *Pholas* among the *Mollusca*.

aç-ces′sō-ry, *n.*; *pl.* **aç-ces′sō-rieş**. 1. In law, one who is guilty of a felony, not by committing the offense in person or as principal, but by advising or commanding another to commit the cri e, or by concealing the offender. There may be *accessories* in all felonies, but not in treason. An *accessory before* the fact is one who counsels or commands another to commit a felony, and is not present when the act is executed; an *accessory after* the fact, one who receives and conceals the offender. Also written *accessary*.

2. That which belongs to something else, as its principal; an accompaniment or adjunct; as, the *accessories* of a banquet.

3. Among artists, any part of a historical or other painting which is merely ornamental and not essential, as a vase, armor, etc.

Syn.—Abettor, accomplice, ally, confederate, assistant, associate, coadjutor, companion, helper, henchman, partner, auxiliary, participator.

ac-ciaç-ça-tū′ra (ät-chäk-kä-tö′rä), *n.* [It.] In music, a grace note, one semitone below the note to which it is prefixed.

aç′ci-dence, *n.* [Misspelled plural of *accident*. L. *accidentia*, from *accidere*, to happen.]

1. A book containing the rudiments of grammar.

2. The part of grammar treating of the accidents, or inflection of words.

3. The rudiments of any language, art, science, etc.

aç′ci-dence, *n.* [L. *accidens*, ppr. of *accidere*; *ad*, to, and *cadere*, to fall.] A happening by accident; a chance.

aç′ci-dent, *n.* [L. *accidens*, falling, from *ad*, to, and *cadere*, to fall.]

1. A happening; an event that takes place without one's foresight or expectation; an event which proceeds from an unknown cause, or is an unusual effect of a known cause, and therefore not expected; chance; casualty; contingency.

2. That which takes place or begins to exist without an efficient intelligent cause and without design.

All of them, in his opinion, owe their being to fate, *accident*, or the blind action of stupid matter. —Dwight.

3. In logic, a property, or quality of a thing, which is not essential to it, as whiteness in paper; also applied to all qualities in opposition to substance, as sweetness and softness, and to things not essential to a body, as clothes.

4. In grammar, something belonging to a word, but not essential to it, as gender, number, and case.

5. In heraldry, a point or mark, not essential to a coat of arms.

Syn.—Casualty, contingency, misadventure, mischance, misfortune, mishap, disaster.

aç-ci-den'tăl, *a.* 1. Happening by chance, or, rather, unexpectedly; casual; fortuitous; taking place not according to the usual course of things; opposed to that which is constant, regular, or intended; as, an *accidental* visit.

2. Non-essential; not necessarily belonging to; as, songs are *accidental* to a play.

Accidental colors; in optics, the imaginary complementary colors seen after fixing the eye for a short time on a bright-colored object, and then turning it suddenly to a white or light-colored surface. If the object is blue, the accidental color is yellow; if red, green.

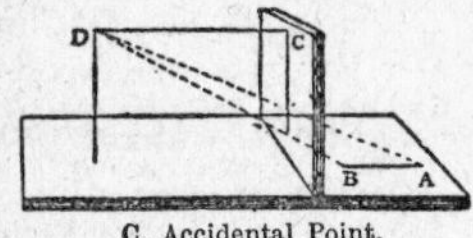

C, Accidental Point.

Accidental point; in perspective, that point (C) where a line (DC) drawn from the eye (D) parallel to a given right line (BA) meets the perspective plane.

Syn.—Casual, chance, contingent, fortuitous, incidental.

aç-ci-den'tăl, *n.* 1. Anything happening, occurring, or appearing accidentally, or as if accidentally; a casualty; a property not essential. [Rare.]

2. In music, a sharp, flat, or natural which does not occur in the clef, and which implies some change of key or modulation different from that in which the piece began.

3. In painting, one of those fortuitous or chance effects, occurring from luminous rays falling on certain objects, by which they are brought into stronger light than they otherwise would be, and their shadows are consequently of greater intensity.

aç-ci-den'tăl-işm, *n.* Accidental character.

aç"ci-den-tal'i-ty, *n.* The quality of being accidental.

aç-ci-den'tăl-ly, *adv.* By chance; casually; fortuitously; not essentially.

aç-ci-den'tăl-ness, *n.* The quality of being casual.

aç'ci-den-ted, *a.* Varied and uneven in surface; applied to land.

Aç-ci-pen'sẽr, *n.* See *Acipenser.*

aç-cip'i-ent, *n.* [L. *accipiens,* ppr. of *accipere; ad,* to, and *capere,* to take.] A receiver. [Rare.]

aç-cip'i-tẽr, *n.* [L., a bird of prey, from *accipere; ad,* to, and *capere,* to take or seize.]

1. In ornithology, one of the order of rapacious birds, *Accipitres* or *Raptores.*

2. A surgical name for a nose-bandage, from its resemblance to a hawk's claw.

aç-cip'i-trăl, *a.* Accipitrine.

Aç-cip'i-trēş, *n.pl.* The name given by Linnæus and Cuvier to the rapacious birds, now usually called *Raptores.*

Aç-cip-i-tri'næ, *n.pl.* A sub-family of *Raptores* including the hawks, family *Falconidæ,* having the wings shorter than the tail and the bill short and hooked from the base. They pounce on their prey when flying.

aç-cip'i-trine, *a.* 1. Seizing; rapacious; as, the *accipitrine* order of birds.

2. Pertaining to the *Accipitres.*

aç-cis'mus, *n.* [Gr. *akkismos,* coyness.] In rhetoric, a feigned refusal.

aç-cite', *v.t.* [L. *accitus,* pp. of *accire; ad,* to, and *cire,* to go, and contains causative force of *cieri,* cause to go.] To call; to cite; to summon. [Rare.]

aç-çlāim', *v.t.*; acclaimed, *pt., pp.*; acclaiming, *ppr.* [L. *acclamare; ad,* to, and *clamare,* to cry out.]

1. To applaud. [Rare.]

2. To salute or declare by acclamation; as, to *acclaim* the president on his inauguration.

3. To cry aloud or shout; as, he *acclaimed* his grief.

aç-çlāim', *v.i.* To applaud loudly; as, the people *acclaimed* with one voice.

aç-çlāim', *n.* A shout of joy; acclamation.

aç-çlāim'ẽr, *n.* One who acclaims.

aç-çlȧ-mā'tion, *n.* [L. *acclamatio,* a shouting, from *ad,* and *clamare,* to cry out.]

1. A shout of applause uttered by a multitude; a token of public approbation. Anciently, *acclamation* was a form of words, uttered with vehemence, somewhat resembling a song, sometimes accompanied with applause given by the hands. In modern times, *acclamation* is expressed by hurrahs, by clapping of hands, and often by repeating words expressive of joy and good wishes.

2. In archæology, a representation, in sculpture or on medals, of people expressing joy. *Acclamation medals* are those on which laudatory acclamations are recorded.

3. Spontaneous and unanimous action by a multitude or meeting in favor of a person or proposition; as, he was nominated, and the platform was adopted, by *acclamation.*

Syn.—Applause, plaudit, acclaim, approval, cheer, exultation, shouting.

aç-çlam'ȧ-tō-ry, *a.* Expressing joy or applause by shouts, or clapping of hands.

aç-çli'mȧ-tȧ-ble, *a.* Capable of being acclimated.

aç-çli-mȧ-tā'tion, *n.* Same as *Acclimatization.*

aç-çli'māte, *v.t.*; acclimated, *pt., pp.*; acclimating, *ppr.* [Fr. *acclimater,* from L. *ad,* to, and *climat,* climate; Gr. *klima(t),* a belt or zone of the earth, from *klinein,* to slope or lean.] To habituate to a climate not native, so as not to be peculiarly liable to attack by its endemic diseases.

aç-çli'māte-ment, *n.* Acclimation. [Rare.]

aç-çli-mā'tion, *n.* 1. The process of becoming habituated to a foreign climate.

2. The state of being habituated or inured to a climate.

aç-çli'mȧ-tī-zȧ-ble, *a.* Acclimatable.

aç-çli"mȧ-ti-zā'tion, *n.* Acclimation.

aç-çli'mȧ-tīze, *v.t.*; acclimatized, *pt., pp.*; acclimatizing, *ppr.* To inure to a climate different from that which is natural; applied to persons, animals, or plants.

aç-çli'mȧ-tīzed, *a.* Inured to a strange climate.

aç-çli'mȧ-tūre, *n.* The act of acclimating, or state of being acclimated. [Rare.]

aç'çli-nāte, *a.* [L. *acclinatus,* pp. of *acclinare; ad,* to, and *clinare,* to lean.] Bending upward.

aç-çliv'i-ty, *n.* [L. *acclivitas,* a slope, from *ad,* to, and the root *kli,* to lean.] A slope or inclination of the earth, as the side of a hill, considered as *ascending,* in opposition to *declivity,* or a side *descending;* rising ground; ascent; in fortification, the talus of a rampart.

aç-çli'vous, aç-çliv'i-tous, *a.* Rising, as a slope of a hill.

aç-çloy', *v.t.*; accloyed, *pt., pp.*; accloying, *ppr.* [Fr. *encloyer,* to drive in a nail, from L. *in,* and *clavus,* nail.] To fill; to stuff; to fill to satiety. [Obs.]

aç-çōast', *v.t.* and *v.i.* To fly near the earth. [Rare.]

aç-çoil', *v.i.*; accoiled, *pt., pp.*; accoiling, *ppr.* [OFr. *acoillir,* from L. *ad,* to, and *colligere,* to collect.]

1. To encircle; to gather around. [Obs.]

2. In nautical language, to coil up.

aç-çō-lāde', *n.* [Fr. *accolade,* from L. *ad,* to, and *collum,* neck.]

1. A ceremony used in conferring knighthood, anciently consisting in putting the hand on the knight's neck, afterwards in giving a blow with the naked fist, and still later with the flat of a sword, which last is the form in which the ceremony is now observed.

2. In music, a brace connecting several staves.

3. In architecture, a form of decoration for windows and doors.

aç'çō-lā-ted, *a.* Bearing two or more profile heads, one overlapping another; as, an *accolated* coin.

aç'çō-lent, *a.* [L. *accolo,* dwell by, from L. *ad,* and *colo,* dwell.] Dwelling in the same vicinity.

aç'çō-lent, *n.* One who dwells near by; a borderer.

aç-çom-bi-nā'tion, *n.* Combination. [Rare.]

aç-çom'mō-dȧ-ble, *a.* [Fr. *accommodable.*] That may be fitted, made suitable, or made to agree. [Rare.]

aç-çom'mō-dȧ-ble-ness, *n.* The capability of accommodating. [Rare.]

aç-çom'mō-dāte, *v.t.*; accommodated, *pt., pp.*; accommodating, *ppr.* [L. *accommodatus,* pp.; from *ad,* to, and *commodare,* to fit; *con,* and *modus,* a measure.]

1. To fit, adapt, or make suitable; as, to *accommodate* ourselves to circumstances; to *accommodate* the choice of subjects to the occasion.

2. To supply with or furnish; followed by *with*; as, to *accommodate* a man *with* apartments.

3. To supply with conveniences; as, to *accommodate* a friend.

4. To reconcile (things which are at variance); to adjust; as, to *accommodate* differences.

5. To show the fitness or agreement of; to apply; as, to *accommodate* prophecy to events.

6. To lend money to, or give commercial credit to.

Syn.—Adapt, adjust, fit, suit, serve, oblige.

aç-çom'mō-dāte, *v.i.* To be in or come to adjustment, as the eye in order to see distinctly at a certain distance; to be in or come to conformity with; to agree. [Rare.]

aç-çom'mō-dāte, *a.* Suitable; fit; adapted; as, means *accommodate* to the end. [Rare.]

aç-çom'mō-dāte-ly, *adv.* Suitably; fitly. [Rare.]

aç-çom'mō-dāte-ness, *n.* Fitness. [Rare.]

aç-çom'mō-dā-ting, *a.* Adapting oneself to; obliging; yielding to the desires of others; disposed to comply, and to oblige another; as, an *accommodating* man.

aç-çom-mō-dā'tion, *n.* 1. Fitness; adaptation; followed by *to.*

2. Adjustment of differences; reconciliation; as of parties in dispute.

3. The provision of conveniences.

4. [*pl.*] Conveniences; things furnished for use; chiefly applied to board, lodging, etc.; as, the *accommodations* at a hotel.

5. In mercantile language, a loan of money, or an extension of credit.

6. In theology, the application of a passage to something not originally intended by it, on the ground of resemblance or analogy.

> Many of those quotations were probably intended as nothing more than *accommodations.* —Paley.

7. Automatic adjustment or the power of conforming, as that of the eye to see at different distances.

Accommodation bill; in England, a bill or note given instead of a loan of money.

Accommodation ladder; in nautical language, a ladder hung over the side of a ship at the gangway, as for the accommodation of ladies or landsmen.

Accommodation Ladder.

Accommodation note; a note drawn and offered for discount, for the purpose of borrowing its amount, in distinction from a note which the owner has received in payment for goods; the term is also used of a note lent merely to accommodate the borrower.

aç-çom'mō-dā-tive, *a.* Furnishing accommodation.

aç-çom'mō-dā-tive-ness, *n.* The state or quality of being accommodative.

aç-çom'mō-dā-tŏr, *n.* One who accommodates or adjusts.

aç-çŏm'pȧ-nȧ-ble, *a.* Sociable. [Obs.]

aç-çŏm'pȧ-ni-ẽr, *a.* A person who accompanies.

aç-çŏm'pȧ-ni-ment, *n.* [Fr. *accompagnement;* L. *ad,* to, with, and *compania,* associate; from *con,* together, and *panis,* bread.]

1. That which attends as a circumstance, or which is added by way of ornament to the principal thing, or for the sake of symmetry.

2. In music, the subordinate part, or parts, accompanying the voice or a principal instrument; also, the harmony of a figured bass.

3. In painting, an object accessory to the principal object, and serving for its ornament or illustration.

aç-çŏm'pȧ-nist, *n.* The performer in music who takes the accompanying part.

aç-çŏm'pȧ-ny, *v.t.*; accompanied, *pt., pp.*; accompanying, *ppr.* 1. To go with or attend as a companion or associate on a journey, walk, etc.; as, a man *accompanies* his friend to church, or on a tour.

2. To be with, as connected; to attend; as, pain *accompanies* disease.

3. In music, to act as an accompanist for.

Syn.—Attend, escort.

aç-çŏm'pȧ-ny, *v.i.* 1. To attend; to be an associate; as, to *accompany* with others. [Obs.]

2. To cohabit. [Obs.]

3. In music, to perform the accompanying part in a composition.

aç-çom'plē-tive, *a.* Tending to accomplish. [Rare.]

aç-çom'plice, *n.* [L. *ad,* to, and *complex,* from *con,* together, and *plectere,* to twist, also *plicare,* to fold.] An associate in a crime; a partner or partaker in guilt. It was formerly used in a good sense for *coöperator,* but this sense is wholly obsolete. It is followed by *with* or *of* before a person; as, A was an *accomplice with* B in the murder of C. Dryden uses it with *to* before a thing, but *in* is generally used.

Syn.—Accessory, abettor, ally.

aç-çom'plice-ship, *n.* The state of being an accomplice. [Rare.]

aç-çom-plic'i-ty, *n.* Complicity. [Rare.]

aç-çom'plish, *v.t.*; accomplished, *pt., pp.*; accomplishing, *ppr.* [Fr. *accomplir,* to finish, from L. *ad,* and *complere,* to complete, to fill up.]

1. To complete; to finish entirely; as, to *accomplish* a ride of fifty miles.

2. To execute; as, to *accomplish* a vow.

3. To gain; to obtain or effect by successful exertions; as, to *accomplish* a purpose.

4. To fulfil or bring to pass; as, to *accomplish* a prophecy.

5. To furnish with qualities which serve to render the mind or body complete, as with valuable endowments and elegant manners.

6. To arm and equip. [Obs.]

Syn.—Achieve, complete, effect, do, execute, finish, fulfil, perform, realize, bring about, carry out, consummate.

aç-çom'plish-ȧ-ble, *a.* Capable of being accomplished.

aç-çom'plished, *a.* 1. Finished; completed; fulfilled; executed; effected.

2. Well endowed with good qualities and manners; complete in acquirements; having a finished education; applied usually to acquired

qualifications, without including moral excellence; as, an *accomplished* musician.

Syn.—Skilled, proficient, polished, refined, cultured, educated.

aç-çom′plish-ẽr, *n.* One who accomplishes.

aç-çom′plish-ment, *n.* 1. Completion; fulfilment; entire performance; as, the *accomplishment* of a prophecy.

2. The act of carrying into effect, or obtaining an object designed; attainment; as, the *accomplishment* of our desires or ends.

3. Acquirement; that which constitutes excellence of mind, or elegance of manners, acquired by education; as, full of *accomplishments*.

aç-çompt′ (-count′), *n.* [Obs.] See *Account*.

aç-çompt′ănt, *n.* [Obs.] See *Accountant*.

aç-çord′, *n.* 1. Agreement; harmony of minds; consent or concurrence of opinions or wills.

> They all continued with one *accord* in prayer. —Acts i. 14.

2. Concert; harmony of sounds; the union of different sounds, which is agreeable to the ear; agreement in pitch and tone; as, the *accord* of notes.

3. Agreement; just correspondence of things; as, the *accord* of light and shade in painting.

4. Will; voluntary or spontaneous motion; used of the will of persons, or the natural motion of other bodies, and preceded by *own*.

> Being more forward of his own *accord*. —2 Cor. viii. 17.

5. In law, an agreement between parties in controversy, by which satisfaction for an injury is stipulated, and which, when executed, bars a suit. —Blackstone.

6. The settlement of a dispute; agreement.

aç-çord′, *v.t.*; accorded, *pt.*, *pp.*; according, *ppr.* [OE. *acord*; Fr. *accorder*; from L. *ad*, to, and *cor*, *cordis*, heart.]

1. To make to agree or correspond; to adjust.

> Her hands *accorded* the lute's music to the voice. —Sidney.

2. To bring to an agreement; to settle, adjust, or compose; as, to *accord* suits or controversies.

3. To grant; to give; to concede; as, to *accord* due praise.

aç-çord′, *v.i.* 1. To agree; to be in correspondence; as, his dress *accords* with his duties.

2. To agree in pitch and tone.

aç-çord′ȧ-ble, *a.* Capable of accordance.

aç-çord′ănce, *n.* Agreement with a person; conformity with a thing.

Syn.—Agreement, concord, harmony.

aç-çord′ăn-çy, *n.* Accordance.

aç-çord′ănt, *a.* Corresponding; consonant; agreeable.

aç-çord′ănt-ly, *adv.* In accordance or agreement.

aç-çord′ẽr, *n.* One who accords. [Rare.]

aç-çord′ing, *a.* 1. Agreeing; harmonizing; as, *according* music.

2. Suitable; agreeable; in accordance; used with *to*; as, *according to* Hoyle.

aç-çord′ing, *adv.* Accordingly; in accordance; agreeably; used with *to* or *as*; as, *according to* him, every man has his price.

According as; agreeably, conformably, or proportionately as.

aç-çord′ing-ly, *adv.* Agreeably; suitably; in a manner conformable to; consequently; as, to be rewarded *accordingly*.

Syn. — Therefore, wherefore, conformably, consequently, then.

aç-çor′di-ŏn, *n.* A small keyed wind-instrument, whose tones are generated by the play of wind upon metallic reeds. It is constructed on the same principle as the concertina.

aç-çor′di-ŏn-ist, *n.* An accordion-player.

aç-çor′di-ŏn-plāit, *n.* See *Plait*.

aç-çor′pō-rāte, *v.t.* [Obs.] See *Incorporate*.

aç-çost′, *v.t.*; accosted, *pt.*,*pp.*; accosting, *ppr.* [Fr *accoster*; L. *accostare*, to bring side by side; *ad*, to, and *costa*, rib, side.]

1. To approach; to draw near; to front, or face. [Obs.]

2. To speak first to; to address; as, he *accosted* the lady.

aç-çost′, *v.i.* To adjoin. [Obs.]

aç-çost′ȧ-ble, *a.* Easy of access; familiar.

aç-çost′ed, *a.* In heraldry, side by side; a term used when charges are placed on each side of another charge; as, a pale *accosted* by six mullets; also applied to two beasts walking or running side by side.

aç-çouçhe′ment, *n.* [Fr.] Delivery in childbed.

aç-çou-çheur′, *n.* [Fr.] A medical practitioner who attends women in childbirth; a man-midwife.

aç-çou-çheuse′, *n.* [Fr.] A midwife.

aç-çount′, *n.* [OE. *acounten*; Fr. *aconter*; L. *ad*, to, and *computare*, to reckon.

1. A sum stated on paper; a registry of a debit or credit, of debts and credits, or charges; an entry in a book or on paper of things bought or sold, of payments, services, etc., including the names of the parties to the transaction, date, and price or value of the thing. An *account* may be either a single entry, or charge, or a statement of a number of particular debts and credits, in a book or on a separate paper.

2. A computation of debts and credits, or a general statement of particular sums; as, the *account* stands thus; let them exhibit his *account*.

3. A computation or mode of reckoning; applied to other things than money or trade; as, the Julian *account* of time.

4. [*pl.*] The books containing entries of financial transactions; generally used in connection with a particular set of books; as, his *accounts* are neatly kept.

5. Narrative; relation; statement of facts; recital of particular transactions and events, verbal or written; as, an *account* of the revolution in France.

6. An assignment of reasons; explanation by a recital of particular transactions, given by a person in an employment, or to a superior, sometimes implying responsibility; an answering for conduct; a report; as, the congressman came home to give an *account* of his stewardship.

7. Reason or consideration, as a motive; as, on all *accounts*; on every *account*.

8. Value; importance; estimation; that is, such a state of persons or things as renders them worthy of more or less estimation; as, men of *account*.

9. A general statement in explanation of some event or phenomenon; as, no satisfactory *account* of the matter has yet been given.

10. Profit; advantage; that is, a result or production worthy of estimation; as, to find our *account* in a pursuit; to turn to *account*.

11. Regard; behalf; sake; as, I have incurred this trouble on your *account*.

To open an account; to commence pecuniary transactions with a banker or merchant; to enter an account for the first time in a ledger or other book.

Account current, running account, open account; one continuing without formal balancing or settlement, so far approximating balance as to be satisfactory to the parties concerned; the statement of items of such an account.

Account rendered; a bill or account previously rendered or presented.

Account sales; a statement of daily transactions between two firms or individuals on a board of trade, or similar institution; also, a separate account rendered to a merchant by his broker, showing goods sold, prices obtained, and the net result after deduction of all necessary expenses; also, a similar account rendered by a merchant to the consigner of goods, showing the net proceeds of each consignment, after deduction of freight, commission, etc.

Account stated, or *stated account*; an account presented by the creditor and accepted as correct by the debtor.

Bank account; the balance on deposit, or the business transactions of an individual or firm with a bank.

Private accounts; individual accounts.

Public accounts; those of public institutions or offices of government.

Settled account; one which has been discharged.

Statement of account; usually contracted to *statement*; the periodical statement which a business firm sends to every debtor.

Writ of account; in law, a writ which the plaintiff brings, demanding that the defendant should render his just account, or show good cause to the contrary; called also an *action of account*.

Payment on account; partial payment of a debt.

To balance accounts; to settle accounts between two parties or firms formally by exchanging accounts and settling such difference as may appear.

To make account; to have a previous opinion or expectation. [Obs.]

To close an account; to settle an account with the object of discontinuing further credit or business with a firm.

Syn.—Record, report, sum, balance, statement, recital, narrative, relation, explanation, rehearsal

aç-çount′, *v.t.*; accounted, *pt.*, *pp.*; accounting, *ppr.* 1. To deem, judge, consider, think, or hold in opinion; as, he is *accounted* a learned judge.

2. To reckon, or compute; as, the motion of the sun whereby years are *accounted*; also, to assign as a debt; as, a project is *accounted* to his service. [Obs.]

3. To give an account of; to account for; to explain; as, a way of *accounting* the solidity of ice. [Obs.]

aç-çount′, *v.i.* 1. To render an account or relation of particulars; as, an officer must *account* with or to the treasurer for money received.

2. To give reasons; to assign the causes; to explain; with *for*; as, idleness *accounts for* poverty.

3. To render reasons; to answer for in a responsible character; as, we must *account* for all the talents intrusted to us.

aç-çount-ȧ-bil′i-ty, *n.* 1. The state of being liable to answer for one's conduct; liability to give account, and to receive reward or punishment for actions.

> The awful idea of *accountability*. —R. Hall.

2. Liability to the payment of money or of damages; responsibility for a trust.

3. Accountableness.

aç-çount′ȧ-ble, *a.* 1. Liable to be called to account; answerable to a superior; as, every man is *accountable* to God for his conduct.

2. Subject to pay, or make good, in case of loss; as, a sheriff is *accountable* as bailiff and receiver of goods.

3. That may be accounted for. [Rare.]

Syn. — Amenable, responsible, answerable, liable.

aç-çount′ȧ-ble-ness, *n.* Liability to answer or to give account; the state of being answerable, or liable to the payment of money or damages.

aç-çount′ȧ-bly, *adv.* In an accountable manner.

aç-çount′ăn-çy, *n.* The position or business of an accountant.

aç-çount′ănt, *n.* [Fr. *acomptant*, ppr. of *acompter*; L. *ad*, to, and *computare*, to reckon.] One skilled in mercantile accounts; more generally, a person who keeps accounts for private business concerns or in public offices.

Expert accountant; one who, as an independent business, examines or balances books or accounts, either public or private.

aç-çount′ănt-gen′ẽr-ăl, *n.* The principal or responsible accountant in a public office or in a mercantile or banking house or company, as in the Bank of England, etc.

aç-çount′ănt-ship, *n.* The office or employment of an accountant.

aç-çount′-book, *n.* A book in which accounts are kept.

aç-çount′ing, *n.* The act of reckoning or adjusting accounts.

aç-çou′ple (-kup′pl), *v.t.* [Fr. *accoupler*, to join; L. *accopulare*; *ad*, to, and *copulare*, to join.] To couple; to join or link together. [Rare.]

aç-çou′ple-ment (-kup′pl-), *n.* A coupling; a connecting in pairs; junction. [Rare.]

aç-çou′tẽr, aç-çou′tre (ak-ko͞o′tẽr), *v.t.*; accoutered, *pt.*, *pp.*; accoutering, *ppr.* [Fr. *accoutrer*, to dress; L. *ad*, to, and *custos*, keeper.] In a general sense, to dress; to equip; but appropriately, to array in a military dress; to put on, or to furnish with, a military dress and arms; to equip the body for military service.

Syn.—Arm, equip, fit out, furnish, prepare, provide, supply.

aç-çou′tẽr-ments, aç-çou′tre-ments (-ko͞o′-tẽr-), *n.pl.* 1. Dress; equipage; furniture for the body; appropriately, military dress and arms; equipage for military service.

2. The regulation equipment which a soldier carries in addition to his weapons.

ac-coy′, *v.t.* [OFr. *acoyer*, to appease; L. *ad*, to, and *quietus*, pp. of *quiescere*, to rest.] To render quiet or diffident; to soothe; to caress. [Obs.]

aç-çred′it, *v.t.*; accredited, *pt.*, *pp.*; accrediting, *ppr.* [Fr. *accréditer*, to give authority or reputation; L. *ad*, to, and *creditum*, a belief, from *credere*, to lend, to believe.]

1. To repose confidence in; to trust; to esteem or have a high opinion of; as, their most considerable and *accredited* ministers.

2. To confer credit or authority on; to stamp with authority.

3. To send with credentials, as an envoy; as, the minister *accredited* by France.

4. To believe; to put credit in; as, they *accredited* stories of witchcraft.

To accredit with; to lay to one's charge; to give credit for; as, statesmen are often *accredited with* sentiments they do not hold.

aç-çred-i-tā′tion, *n.* The act of accrediting, or state of being accredited.

aç-çred′it-ed, *a.* Allowed; received with reputation; authorized in a public character; as, our *accredited* representatives abroad.

aç″çrē-men-ti′tial (-tish′ăl), *a.* Relating to accrementition.

aç″çrē-men-ti′tion, *n.* [L. *accrementum*, from *ad*, to, and *crescere*, to grow.] The production of a new type by budding; gemmation.

aç-çresce′, *v.i.* To accrue. [Rare.]

aç-çres′cence, *n.* Growth; accretion.

aç-çres′cent, *a.* 1. Increasing; growing.

2. In botany, continuing to grow after flowering.

aç-çres-çi-men′tō, *n.* [It., from L. *accrescere,* to increase.] The addition to a note of half its length in time; indicated by placing after it a small dot.

aç-çrēte′, *v.i.* To grow together; to be added.

aç-çrēte′, *v.t.* To cause to adhere; to add.

aç-çrēte′, *a.* Increased; added to; formed by accretion; in botany, grown together.

aç-çrē′tion, *n.* [L. *accretio,* increase, from *ad,* to, and *crescere,* to grow.]

1. A growing to; an increase by natural growth.

2. An increase by an accession of parts externally; as, a mineral vein is augmented by *accretion.*

3. In civil law, an increase to property by fortuitous circumstances, without cost to the owner; as, an increase of land by flood or alluvial deposit, or change in the course of a stream; increase of inheritance by death, surrender, or failure on the part of a colegatee.

4. In medicine, the union by gradual growth of organs or parts naturally separate, as the fingers.

aç-çrē′tive, *a.* Increasing by growth; growing; adding to by growth; as, the *accretive* motion of plants.

aç-çrim′i-nāte, *v.t.* [L. *ad,* to, and *criminari,* to accuse.] To accuse of a crime. [Obs.]

aç-çrim-i-nā′tion, *n.* Accusation. [Obs.]

aç-çrōach′, *v.i.* [Fr. *accrocher,* to fix on a hook; from *croc, crochet,* a hook, from the same elements as *crook.*]

1. To hook, or draw to, as with a hook. [Obs.]

2. To encroach; to draw away from another. Hence, in old laws, to assume the exercise of royal prerogatives. —Blackstone.

aç-çrōach′ment, *n.* Encroachment; especially in the sense of usurpation, or attempt to exercise royal power. [Obs.]

aç-çrū′ăl, *n.* Act or process of accruing; accretion.

aç-çrūe′, *v.i.*; accrued, *pt., pp.*; accruing, *ppr.* [Fr. *accroitre, accru,* to increase; L. *accrescere; ad,* to, and *crescere,* to grow.] Literally, to grow to; hence, to arise, proceed, or come; to be added, as increase, profit, or damage; as, a profit *accrues* to government from the coinage of copper; a loss *accrues* from the coinage of gold and silver.

aç-çrūe′, *n.* Something that accedes to or follows the property of another. [Obs.]

aç-çrū′ẽr, *n.* A legal term signifying accretion; as, title by *accruer.*

aç-çrū′ment, *n.* Addition; increase; the act of accruing.

aç-çū-bā′tion, *n.* [L. *accubatio,* a reclining, from *ad,* to, and *cubare,* to lie down.] A lying or reclining on a couch, as the ancients at their meals, with the head resting on a pillow or on the elbow. Two or three men lay on one couch, the feet of one extended behind the back of another.

aç-çul-tū-rā′tion, *n.* [Prefix *ac-,* and *culture.*] The impartation of culture by one race to another through proximity.

aç-çumb′, *v.i.* To recline, as at table. [Obs.]

aç-çum′ben-çy, *n.* State of being accumbent or reclining.

aç-çum′bent, *a.* [L. *accumbens,* ppr. of *accumbere,* from *ad,* to, and *cubare,* to recline.]

1. Leaning or reclining, as the ancients at their meals.

2. In botany, lying against anything; said of leaves, organs, etc.; as, an *accumbent* ovule.

Accumbent Ovule. (*Thlaspi arvense.*)

aç-çum′bent, *n.* One who reclines at table.

aç-çū′mū-lāte, *v.t.*; accumulated, *pt., pp.*; accumulating, *ppr.* [L. *accumulatus,* pp. of *accumulare; ad,* to, and *cumulare,* to heap.]

1. To heap up; to pile; to amass; as, to *accumulate* earth and stones.

2. To collect or bring together; as, to *accumulate* causes of misery; to accumulate wealth.

Syn.—Amass, collect, gather, heap up, hoard.

aç-çū′mū-lāte, *v.i.* To grow to a great size, number, or quantity; to increase greatly; as, public evils *accumulate.*

aç-çū′mū-lāte, *a.* Collected into a mass or quantity.

aç-çū-mū-lā′tion, *n.* 1. The act of accumulating; the state of being accumulated; an amassing; a collecting together; as, an *accumulation* of earth, or of evils.

2. In law, the concurrence of several titles to the same thing, or of several circumstances to the same proof.

3. That which is accumulated; as, a great accumulation of sand at the mouth of a river.

Accumulation of degrees; in universities, the taking of several degrees together, or at smaller intervals than usual, or than are allowed by the rules.

Accumulation of power; a term applied to that amount of force or capacity for motion which exists in some machines at the end of intervals of time, during which the velocity of the moving body has been constantly accelerated.

aç-çū′mū-lā-tive, *a.* Given to accumulating; heaping up; accumulating.

aç-çū′mū-lā-tive-ly, *adv.* In an accumulative manner; in heaps.

aç-çū′mū-lā-tive-ness, *n.* The quality of being accumulative.

aç-çū′mū-lā-tŏr, *n.* One who or that which accumulates, gathers, or amasses. Specifically, an apparatus for storing power or energy, as a secondary or storage battery; a kind of battery by which electric energy is stored and rendered portable till required for use.

aç′çū-rȧ-çy, *n.* [L. *accuratio,* from *accurare,* to take care of; *ad,* to, and *curare,* to take care; *cura,* care.] Exactness; exact conformity to truth, or to a rule or model; freedom from mistake; nicety; correctness; precision which results from care, as, the *accuracy* of ideas or opinions is conformity to truth; the value of testimony depends on its *accuracy;* copies of legal instruments should be taken with *accuracy.*

aç′çū-rāte, *a.* [L. *accuratus,* pp. of *accurare,* to take care.]

1. In exact conformity to truth, or to a standard or rule, or to a model; free from failure, error, or defect; as, an *accurate* account; *accurate* measure; an *accurate* expression.

2. Determinate; precisely fixed, as, one body may not have a very *accurate* influence on another. [Obs.]

Syn.—Exact, correct, just, nice, precise.

aç′çū-rāte-ly, *adv.* Exactly; in an accurate manner; with precision; without error or defect; as, a writing *accurately* copied.

aç′çū-rāte-ness, *n.* Accuracy; exactness; nicety; precision.

aç-çũrse′, *v.t.*; accursed *or* accurst, *pt., pp.*; accursing, *ppr.* [A wrong spelling, in imitation of *ad-* and *curse,* AS. *a* and *cursian; acursien.*] To doom to destruction; to imprecate misery or evil upon; to excommunicate from the faithful, or the church. [Rare. See *Curse.*]

aç-çũrsed′ (*or* ak-kũrs′ed), **aç-çũrst′,** *a.* 1. Worthy of curses; detestable; execrable; cursed; as, deeds *accursed.*

2. Doomed to evil of any kind; lying under a curse; ruined; blasted.

Thro' you my life will be *accurst.*
—Tennyson.

aç-çũrs′ed-ly, *adv.* Execrably; detestably; in an accursed manner.

aç-çũrs′ed-ness, *n.* The state or quality of being accursed.

aç-çūş′ȧ-ble, *a.* [L. *accusabilis,* from *accusare,* to call to account.] That may be accused; chargeable with a crime; blamable; liable to censure; followed by *of;* as, *accusable of* being heterodox.

aç-çūş′ăl, *n.* Accusation.

aç-çūş′ănt, *n.* One who accuses. [Obs.]

aç-çū-şā′tion, *n.* 1. The act of charging with a crime or offense; the act of accusing of any wrong or injustice.

2. The charge of an offense or crime; the declaration containing the charge; that which is charged.

They set up over his head his *accusation.*
—Matt. xxvii. 37.

Syn.—Charge, impeachment, arraignment, indictment, crimination.

aç-çū-şȧ-ti′văl, *a.* Relating to the accusative case.

aç-çū′şȧ-tive, *n.* The case of nouns on which the action of a verb terminates or falls; called in English grammar the objective case; in Latin and Greek, the fourth case.

aç-çū′şȧ-tive, *a.* 1 The term applied to the fourth case in Latin and Greek grammar, corresponding to the objective case in English.

2. Charging with offense or crime. [Obs.]

aç-çū′şȧ-tive-ly, *adv.* 1. In an accusative manner.

2. In relation to the accusative case in grammar.

aç-çū-şȧ-tō′ri-ăl, *a.* Accusatory.

aç-çū-şȧ-tō′ri-ăl-ly, *adv.* By way of accusation.

aç-çū′şȧ-tō-ry, *a.* Accusing; containing an accusation; as, an *accusatory* libel.

aç-çūşe′, *v.t.* [Fr. *accuser;* L. *accusare,* to call to account, from *ad,* to, and *causa,* a reason, case, or suit at law.]

1. To charge with, or declare to have committed a crime, either by plaint, or complaint, information, indictment, or impeachment; to charge with an offense against the laws, judicially or by a public process; as, to *accuse* one of a high crime or misdemeanor.

2. To charge with a fault; to blame.

It is followed by *of* before the subject of accusation; as, to *accuse* one *of* greed.

Syn.—Charge, indict, arraign, impeach, blame.

aç-çūşed′, *n.* One charged with a crime; as, the *accused* was seen to enter the house. It has the same form in the plural; as, the *accused* are charged with conspiring.

aç-çūşe′ment, *n.* An accusation. [Obs.]

aç-çūş′ẽr, *n.* One who accuses or blames; an officer who prefers an accusation against another for some offense, in the name of the government, before a tribunal that has cognizance of the offense.

aç-çūş′ing-ly, *adv.* In an accusing manner.

aç-çus′tŏm, *v.t.*; accustomed *pt., pp.*; accustoming, *ppr.* [Fr. *accoutumer,* from *ad* and *coutume, coustume,* custom; L. *consuetumen,* habit, from root in *consuescere; con* and *suere,* to make one's own, from *suus,* one's own.] To make familiar by use, to form (a habit) by practice; to habituate or inure; as, to *accustom* oneself to a spare diet.

aç-çus′tŏm, *v.i.* 1. To be wont, or habituated to do anything. [Rare.]

2. To cohabit. [Obs.]

aç-çus′tŏm, *n.* Custom. [Obs.]

aç-çus′tŏm-ȧ-ble, *a.* Of long custom; habitual; customary. [Rare.]

aç-çus′tŏm-ȧ-bly, *adv.* According to custom or habit. [Rare.]

aç-çus′tŏm-ănce, *n.* Custom; habitual use or practice. [Obs.]

aç-çus′tŏm-ā-ri-ly, *adv.* [Rare.] See *Customarily*

aç-çus′tŏm-ā-ry, *a.* [Rare.] See *Customary.*

aç-çus′tŏmed, *a.* Customary; habitual; usual; often practised; as, in their *accustomed* manner.

aç-çus′tŏmed-ness, *n.* Familiarity. [Rare.]

-ace, *suffix.* [Fr *ace;* It. *accio, accia.*] A noun-suffix, occurring in such words as popul*ace,* pinn*ace,* and having a depreciatory force.

āce, *n.* [L. *as,* a unit or pound.]

1. A unit; a single point on a card or die; or the card or die so marked.

2. A very small quantity; a particle; an atom; a trifle; as, a creditor will not abate an *ace* of his demands.

3. A single point in scoring, in various games, as tennis.

4. Any "Great War" aviator who brought down five or more enemy aeroplanes inside his own lines.

-ā′ce-a (-ā′she-ȧ), *suffix.* [LL. neut. pl. of *aceus.*] A combining form for names of classes or orders of animals; as, Crust*acea,* Cet*acea;* properly agreeing with *animalia* (animals) understood.

-ā′cē-æ (-ā′cē-ē), *suffix.* [L. f. pl. of *aceus.*] A combining form for names of orders or families of plants; as, Lili*aceæ,* Ros*aceæ;* and properly agreeing with L. *plantæ* (plants) understood.

-acean, *suffix.* Anglicized form of *-acea,* from L. *aceus,* and same as *-aceous.*

ȧ-cē′di-ȧ, *n.* [Gr. *akēdia,* from *akēdos; a* priv., and *kēdos,* care.] Melancholia; sloth; ennui; listlessness; a mental condition marked by apathy.

Ā-cel′dȧ-mȧ, *n.* [L. *Aceldama,* from Gr. *Akeldama,* for Syr. *ōkēl damō.*] A field said to have lain south of Jerusalem, the same as the potter's field, purchased with the bribe which Judas took for betraying his master, and therefore called the field of blood. It was appropriated to the interment of strangers. Figuratively, any place stained by slaughter.

ac-ē-naph′thēne, *n.* A crystalline hydrocarbon, $C_{12}H_{10}$, obtained from coal-tar by distillation.

ȧ-cen′triç, *a.* [Gr. *a* priv., and *kentron,* a center.] Not centric; without a center.

-ā′ceous (-ā′shus), *suffix.* [L. *-aceus,* of the nature of.] Of the nature of; belonging to; characterized by; like; as, in crust*aceous,* farin*aceous.*

Ȧ-ceph′ȧ-lȧ, *n.pl.* [Gr. *a* priv., and *kephalē,* head.] A class of molluscous animals, comprehending those which have no apparent head, as the oyster and mussel; the *Lamellibranchiata.*

ȧ-ceph′ȧ-lăn, *n.* An individual of the *Acephala.*

Ȧ-ceph′ȧ-lī, *n.pl.* [LL. nom. pl. of *acephalus,* from Gr. *a* priv., and *kephalē,* head.]

1. An Egyptian sect of the fifth century, who renounced communion with the patriarch of Alexandria.

2. Clergy and monks unattached, not living under episcopal jurisdiction, and bishops exempt from patriarchal jurisdiction.

3. A council of the Roman communion summoned without the authority of the pope.

4. A class of levelers in the reign of Henry I. of England, who would acknowledge no head or superior.

5. A fabulous nation in Africa—the Blemmyes—reported by ancient writers to have no heads.

ȧ-ceph′ȧ-list, *n.* One who acknowledges no head or superior; one of the *Acephali.*

ȧ-ceph′ȧ-lō-cyst, *n.* [Gr. *akephalos,* headless, and *kystis,* bladder.] A larval tapeworm embedded in the tissues.

ȧ-ceph″ȧ-lō-cys′tiç, *a.* Pertaining to or of the nature of an acephalocyst.

ȧ-ceph′ȧ-lous, *a.* [Gr. *a* priv., and *kephalē,* head.]

1. Without a head; headless; a term applied specifically, in early history, to several sects of levelers called *Acephali*, and to independent bishops, etc.

2. In botany, a term applied to ovaries, the style of which springs from their base instead of their apex.

3. In anatomy, lacking a head; applied to a fetus.

4. In prosody, defective or lacking something at the beginning; applied to a verse or line of poetry.

5. Wanting something essential; as, a false or *acephalous* structure of sentence.

6. Having no chief or leader.

ȧ-ceph′ȧ-lus, *n.* [Gr. *a* priv., and *kephalē*, head.]

1. In prosody, a verse defective at the beginning.

2. In anatomy, a fetus without a head; a headless monstrosity.

āce′-point, *n.* The single point on a card or die; also, the side of a die that has but one point.

ȧ-ce̤′quï-ä (ä-sā′kē-ä), *n.* [Sp.] An irrigating ditch.

Ā′cēr, *n.* [L., a maple-tree, so called from its sharp leaves. From root *ak*, sharp, appearing in *acid, acetic*, etc.] The generic name of the maple-tree. *Acer saccharinum* is the sugar-maple.

Ac′e-rȧ, *n.* [Gr. *a* priv., and *keras*, horn.] A genus of shell-bearing gasteropods, belonging to the family *Bullidæ*, and of which *Acera bullata* is a common form.

Ac-e-rā′cē-æ, *n. pl.* [L. *acer*, maple, and suffix *-aceæ*.] A natural order of plants, including the maples and box-elders, and belonging to the thalamifloral division of dicotyledonous plants. There are about fifty species, belonging to three genera; they are all trees or shrubs, and inhabit the temperate parts of Europe and Asia, the north of India, and North America. They yield a sweet mucilaginous sap, from which sugar is often made. The bark is astringent, and yields yellow and reddish dyes.

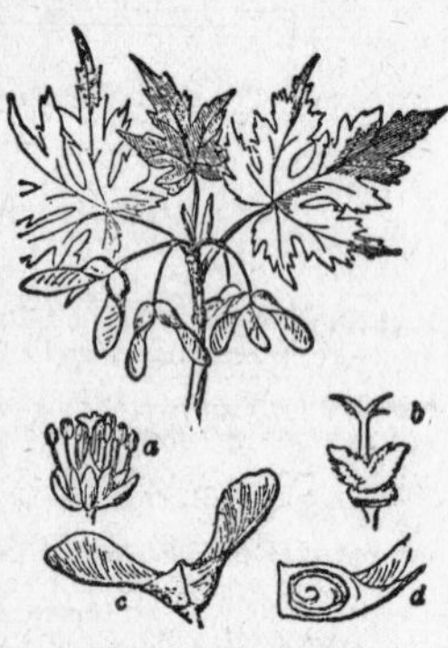

Aceraceæ—Common Maple (*Acer campestre*).

a, Flower. *b*, Pistil (ovary, style, and stigma). *c*, Double-winged fruit or samara. *d*, Section of fruit (single carpel with inclosed seed).

ac-e-rā′ceous, *a.* Of or pertaining to the *Aceraceæ*.

ac′e-răn, *n.* [Gr. *a* priv., and *keras*, horn.] An individual of the genus *Acera*.

ac′ēr-āte, *n.* [L. *acer*, maple.] A salt of aceric acid.

ac′ēr-āte, *a.* Needle-shaped.

Ac-e-rā′tēs, *n.* A genus of plants to which the green milkweed belongs.

ȧ-cērb′, *a.* [Fr. *acerbe*, L. *acerbus*, bitter, sour, from *acer*, sharp.] Sour, bitter, and harsh to the taste; sour, with astringency or roughness; a quality of unripe fruits.

ȧ-cērb′āte, *v.t.*; acerbated, *pt., pp.*; acerbating, *ppr.* 1. To make sour, bitter, or harsh to the taste. [Rare.]

2. To embitter; to exasperate.

ȧ-cērb′ic, *a.* Sour; harsh; severe.

ȧ-cērb′i-ty, *n.* 1. A sourness with bitterness and astringency.

2. Harshness, bitterness, or severity; applied to persons or things; as, *acerbity* of temper; *acerbity* of pain.

ȧ-cer′ic, *a.* [L. *acer*, a maple-tree.] Pertaining to the maple; obtained from the maple; as, *aceric* acid.

Ac-e-rin′ē-æ, *n. pl.* Same as *Aceraceæ*.

ac′ēr-ōse, ac′ēr-ous, *a.* [L. *acerosus*, chaffy, from *acus*, genit. *aceris*, needle.]

1. In botany, chaffy; resembling chaff.

2. Linear and permanent in form like a needle, as the leaves of pine, juniper, etc.

ȧ-cēr′rȧ, *n.* [L.] In Roman antiquity, a vessel in which incense was burned; a censer.

Acerose Leaves—Juniper.

ȧ-cēr′vȧl, *a.* [L. *acervalis*, from *acervus*, heap.] Pertaining to a heap. [Obs.]

ȧ-cēr′vāte, *v.t.* [L. *acervatus*, pp. of *acervare*, to heap up, from *acervus*, heap.] To heap up. [Obs.]

ȧ-cēr′vāte, *a.* In natural history, heaped, or growing in heaps, or in closely compacted clusters.

ac-ēr-vā′tion, *n.* The act or process of heaping up.

ȧ-cēr′vȧ-tive, *a.* Tending to grow in heaps.

ȧ-cēr′vū-line (*or* -lin), *a.* Shaped like little heaps.

ȧ-ces′cence, *n.* Acescency.

ȧ-ces′cen-cy, *n.* [L. *acescens*, ppr. of *acescere*, to become sour.] The state of turning sour by spontaneous decomposition, and hence a moderate sourness; a tendency to turn sour.

ȧ-ces′cent, *a.* Turning sour; readily becoming tart or acid by spontaneous decomposition. Hence, slightly sour; acidulous; subacid.

ȧ-ces′cent, *n.* Any substance which is slightly acid, or likely to become sour.

acet-. Combining form of *acetic, acetyl*, before vowels. [See *Aceto-*.]

ac-e-tab′ū-lăr, *a.* Cup-shaped.

Ac-e-tab-ū-lif′ēr-ȧ, *n.pl.* [L. *acetabulum*, a cup, and *ferre*, to bear.] The order of cephalopods which contains the cuttlefishes, squids, etc., having rows of little cups or suckers on their arms or tentacles; the *Dibranchiata*.

ac-e-tab-ū-lif′ēr-ous, *a.* Having cup-shaped suckers like the cuttlefish.

ac-e-tab′ū-li-fo̤rm, *a.* Acetabular.

ac-e-tab′ū-lum, *n.* [L. *acetabulum*, a vinegar-cup, from *acetum*, vinegar.]

1. Among the Romans, a vinegar cruet or like vessel; also, a measure of about one-eighth of a pint.

2. In anatomy, the cavity of a bone for receiving the protuberant end of another bone, and therefore forming the articulation called enarthrosis; especially, the cavity of the os innominatum, which receives the head of the thigh-bone.

3. A cotyledon in the placenta of ruminating animals.

4. In entomology, the socket on the trunk, in which the leg is inserted.

5. A sucker of the cuttlefish and others of the *Dibranchiata*.

6. In botany, the acetabular fructification of many lichens.

7. In music, a very ancient kind of kettle-drum.

ȧ-cē′tăl, *n.* [*Acet-, -ic*, and *al*(cohol).] A colorless liquid obtained by the imperfect oxidation of alcohol under the influence of platinum-black.

ac-et-al′dē-hȳde, *n.* Acetic aldehyde.

ac-et-am′id, ac-et-am′īde, *n.* [*Acet-, -ate*, and *amid.*] A white crystalline solid obtained by the distillation of ammonium acetate.

ac-et-an′i-lid, ac-et-an′i-līde, *n.* [Eng. *acetyl*, and *anilid.*] A white pungent powder, formed by the action of acetyl chlorid or acetic anhydrid on aniline; also called *antifebrin*.

ac-e-tā′ri-ous, *a.* Used in salads; as, *acetarious* plants.

ac′e-tȧ-ry, *n.* An acid pulpy substance in certain fruits, as the pear, inclosed in a small gritty mass toward the base of the fruit.

ac′e-tāte, *n.* [L. *acetum*, vinegar, from *acere*, to be sour.] A salt formed by the union of acetic acid with any salifiable base.

ac′e-tā-ted, *a.* Combined with acetic acid.

ȧ-cē′tic (*or* ȧ-set′), *a.* [L. *acetum*, vinegar.] Relating to vinegar; having the properties of vinegar; sour.

Acetic acid; an acid, $C_2H_4O_2$, prepared by the dry distillation of wood, by the oxidation of alcohol, by decomposing an acetate, etc., and existing in vinegar in a dilute and impure form.

Acetic ethers; compounds consisting of acetates of alcohol radicals. Common *acetic ether* is a colorless, apple-flavored, volatile fluid, and is a flavoring constituent in many wines. It is made artificially by distilling a mixture of alcohol, oil of vitriol, and acetate of potash.

ȧ-cet″i-fi-cā′tion, *n.* The act of making or becoming acetous or sour; the operation of making vinegar.

ȧ-cet′i-fi-ēr, *n.* A device used to facilitate the process of acetification.

ȧ-cet′i-fȳ, *v.t.*; acetified, *pt., pp.*; acetifying, *ppr.* To convert into acid or vinegar.

ȧ-cet′i-fȳ, *v.i.* [L. *acetum*, vinegar, and E. *-fy*.] To turn acid.

ac-e-tim′e-tēr, ac-e-tom′e-tēr, *n.* [L. *acetum*, vinegar, and Gr. *metron*, measure.] An instrument for ascertaining the strength of vinegar.

ac-e-tim′e-try, *n.* The act or method of ascertaining the strength of vinegar or the proportion of acetic acid contained in it.

ac′e-tin, *n.* A mixture of acetic acid and glycerin.

ac′e-tīze, *v.i.* To acetify.

ac′e-tō-, acet-. [L. *acetum*, vinegar.] A combining form used in chemistry to indicate compounds derived from acetic acid, acetyl, etc.; as, *aceto*-gelatin; *aceto*-bromide.

ac″e-tō-næ′mi-ȧ, *n.* [E. *acetone*, and Gr. *aima*, blood.] In pathology, a morbid condition due to the presence of acetone in the blood.

ac′e-tōne, *n.* 1. A limpid mobile liquid, C_3H_6O, with an agreeable odor and a strong peppermint-like taste, produced by the destructive distillation of acetates. It occurs in small quantities in the blood.

2. The general name for a class of compounds which may be regarded as built up of an acid and an alcoholic radical.

ac-e-ton′ic, *a.* Pertaining to acetone.

ac″e-tō-phe′nōne, *n.* A chemical compound derived from acetic and benzoic acids.

ac′e-tōse, *a.* Acetous.

ac-e-tos′i-ty, *n.* Sourness.

ȧ-cē′tous (*or* ac′e-tous), *a.* 1. Sour; acid; as *acetous* spirit.

2. Causing acetification; as, *acetous* fermentation.

Acetous acid; a term formerly applied to impure and dilute acetic acid, under the notion that it was composed of carbon and hydrogen in the same proportions as in acetic acid, but with less oxygen. No such acid exists. [Obs.]

Acetous fermentation; the process by which alcoholic liquids, as beer or wine, yield acetic acid by oxidation.

ȧ-cē′tum, *n.* [L. *acere*, to be sour.] Vinegar.

ac′e-tyl, *n.* [L. *acetum*, vinegar, and *hyle*, substance.] The hypothetical radical of acetic acid.

ȧ-cet′y-lēne, *n.* A colorless gas prepared by the decomposition of water with calcium carbide; also formed by the imperfect combustion of illuminating gas and other hydro-carbons. It has a characteristic, unpleasant odor, and burns with a luminous smoky flame. As an illuminant it is made to give a brilliant light and is widely used.

A-chæ′ăn, *a.* See *Achean*.

Ach-æ-men′i-ăn, *n.* A Persian of the period of Achæmenes; also, the language of his dynasty.

ȧ-chæ′tous, *a.* [Gr. *a* priv., and *chaitē*, hair.] Without hairs, as some caterpillars, plants, etc.

ȧ-chär′, *n.* [Per.] An Anglo-Indian name for a pickle or relish.

ach′āte, *n.* Agate. [Obs.]

ȧ-chāte′, *n.* [Fr. *achat*, purchase, from *acheter*; LL. *accaptare*; *ad*, to, and *captare*, to take.]

1. Purchase; bargaining. [Obs.]

2. [*pl.*] Same as *Cates*.

Ach-ȧ-ti′nȧ, *n.* A genus of land-snails, popularly called agate-snails. Some of them have shells which are among the largest of land shells. They feed on trees and shrubs in warm climates.

ȧ-chä-tōur′, *n.* [Fr.] A caterer. [Obs.]

āche (āk), *v.i.*; ached, *pt., pp.*; aching, *ppr.* [AS. *ace, ece*, ache, from *acan*, to ache.]

1. To suffer pain; to have or be in pain, or in continued pain; as, the head *aches*.

2. To suffer grief, or extreme grief; to be distressed; as, the heart *aches*.

āche (āk), *n.* Pain, or continued pain, in opposition to sudden twinges, or spasmodic pain; as, the *aches* and pains of old age.

A-chē′ăn, A-chæ′ăn, *a.* Pertaining to Achaia in Greece, and to a celebrated league or confederacy established there. This state lay on the Gulf of Corinth, within Peloponnesus. Also written *Achaian*.

ȧ-chei′lȧ-ry, *a.* See *Achilary*.

ȧ-chei′lous, *a.* See *Achilous*.

ȧ-chēne′, *n.* An achenium.

ȧ-chē′ni-ăl, *a.* Pertaining to an achenium.

ȧ-chē′ni-um, *n.* [Gr. *achanēs*, from *a* priv., and *chainein*, to gape.] In botany, a small dry carpel, having a single seed, which neither adheres to the pericarp nor opens when ripe. It is exemplified in the buttercup.

Achenium—Lettuce and Ranunculus.

Ach′e-ron, *n.* A fabled river of hell; hence, the lower regions.

Ach-e-ron′tic, *a.* Dark and forbidding; like the lower regions.

ȧ-chiev′ȧ-ble, *a.* That may be performed.

ȧ-chiev′ănce, *n.* Performance. [Obs.]

ȧ-chiēve′, *v.t.*; achieved, *pt., pp.*; achieving, *ppr.* [Fr. *achever, achiever*, to finish, from L. *ad*, to, and Fr. *chief*, from L. *caput*, head, end.]

1. To perform or execute; to accomplish; to finish, or carry on to a final close. It is appropriate to the completion of bodily activity; as, he *achieved* his laborious task.

2. To gain or obtain, as the result of exertion, to bring about by effort; as, to *achieve* a fortune.

Syn.—Accomplish, consummate, realize, attain, effect, execute, finish, fulfil, gain, perform, win.

ȧ-chiēve′ment, *n.* [Fr. *achevement*, from *achever*, to end.]

1. The performance of an action; the act of achieving; an obtaining by exertion.

2. A great or heroic deed; a feat; something accomplished by valor, or boldness.

3. An escutcheon or ensigns armorial, granted for the performance of a great or honorable action. Especially applied to the escutcheon of a person deceased, it being displayed at the obsequies and over the tomb; a hatchment.

Funeral Achievement or Hatchment impaled and showing that a widow survives.

à-chiēv′ẽr, *n.* One who achieves or accomplishes.

à-chī′là-ry, à-cheī′là-ry, *a.* [Gr. *a*, priv., and *cheilos*, lip.] Without a lip or labellum; applied to flowers, etc.

Ach-il-lē′à, *n.* A genus of composite plants, including the milfoil or yarrow.

Ach-il-lē′ăn, *a.* Unconquerable, like Achilles.

à-chī′lous, à-cheī′lous, *a.* In anatomy and botany, possessed of no lips or of only rudimentary ones.

āch′ing, *n.* Pain; continued pain or distress.

āch′ing, *a.* Painful.

āch′ing-ly, *adv.* In a manner to give continued pain.

à-chī-ō′te, *n.* [Sp. *achiote*, from Indian *achiotl*.] Same as *Arnotto*.

ach′i-rīte, *n.* An old name for dioptase, after its discoverer, Achir Mahmed.

à-chī′rous, *a.* Without hands.

à-chlam′y-dāte, *a.* [Gr. *a* priv., and *chlamys*, cloak.] Having no mantle; a term applied to certain gasteropods.

Ach-là-myd′ē-æ, *n. pl.* A group of plants in which both the calyx and corolla are wanting, as the willows, oaks, and birches.

ach-là-myd′ē-ous, *a.* [Gr. *a* priv., and *chlamys*, a garment.] In botany, naked; having no floral envelope.

à-chō′li-à, *n.* [Gr. *a* priv., and *cholia*, bile.] Lack of bile.

à-chol′ic, *a.* Deficient in bile.

ach′ō-lous, *a.* Acholic.

ach′ŏr (*or* ā′chŏr), *n.* [Gr. *achōr*, dandruff.] Scald-head, a disease of infants, the face, and often the neck and breast, becoming incrusted with thin yellowish or greenish scabs. It arises in minute whitish pustules which discharge a viscid fluid, which dries into a scab, and is believed to be due to the growth of a fungus.

à-chor′dăl, *a.* [Gr. *a* priv., and *chordē*, a chord.] Having no notochord.

Ach-or-dā′tà, *n. pl.* A general name for the animals which have no notochord.

à-chō′ri-ŏn, *n.* [LL. *achor*, from Gr. *achōr*, scurf.] The parasitic fungus which causes the disease achor.

Ach-rō-an′thēs, *n.* [Gr. *achroos*, colorless, and *anthos*, flower.] A genus of orchids; also called *Microstylis* or *adder's-mouth*.

ach′rō-īte, *n.* [Gr *achroos*, from *a* priv., and *chroa*, color.] A colorless variety of tourmalin.

ach-rō-mat′ic, *a.* [Gr. *a* priv., and *chrōma*, *chrōmatos*, color.] Destitute of color; applied to lenses, etc.

Achromatic lens; a compound lens so made and adjusted as to transmit light without decomposing it into its primary colors.

Achromatic telescope or *microscope*; a telescope or microscope having an achromatic object-glass, by means of which the chromatic aberration is corrected.

ach-rō-mà-tic′i-ty, *n.* The state of being achromatic.

à-chrō′mà-tin, *n.* Organic tissue not easily colored or stained.

à-chrō′mà-tism, *n.* 1. The destruction of the prismatic colors, which accompany the image of an object seen through a prism or lens.

2. The state of being achromatic; as, the *achromatism* of a lens.

à-chrō″mà-ti-zā′tion, *n.* The process of achromatizing.

à-chrō′mà-tīze, *v.t.*; achromatized, *pt.*, *pp.*; achromatizing, *ppr.* [Gr. *a* priv., and *chrōma*, color.] To decolorize; to deprive of color.

à-chrō-mà-top′sy, à-chrō-mà-top′si-à, *n.* [Gr. *a* priv., and *chrōma*, color, and *opsis*, sight.] Color-blindness.

à-chrō-mà-tō′sis, *n.* A disease characterized by absence of coloring matter, as albinism.

à-chrō′mà-tous, à-chrō′mous, *a.* Lacking color; colorless.

ach-rō-moph′i-lous, *a.* [Gr. *a* priv., and *chrōma*, color, and *philos*, fond.] Not easily colored by dyes or pigments.

à-chron′ic, *a.* See *Acronych.*

ach-rō-ō-dex′trine, *n.* [Gr. *achroos*, colorless, and Eng. *dextrine*.] Dextrine not colorable by iodine.

à-chrō′ous, *a.* Achromatic.

à-chȳ′lous, *a.* [Gr. *a* priv., and *chylos*, juice.] Devoid of chyle.

à-chȳ′mous, *a.* Devoid of chyme.

à-cic′ū-là, *n.*; *pl.* **à-cic′ū-læ.** [L. *acicula*, a small needle.] A name given by naturalists to a spine or prickle of an animal or plant.

à-cic′ū-lăr, *a.* [L. *acicula*, a small needle.] Slender and pointed; resembling a needle, as certain leaves and crystals.

à-cic′ū-lăr-ly, *adv.* In the manner of needles, or prickles.

à-cic′ū-lāte, à-cic′ū-lā-ted, *a.* [L. *acicula*, a needle.] In the form of a needle.

à-cic′ū-li-fọrm, *a.* Having the form of needles.

à-cic′ū-līte, *n.* [L. *acicula*, needle, and Gr. *lithos*, stone.] Acicular ore of bismuth; also called *needle-ore* and *aikinite*.

à-cic′ū-lum, *n.*; *pl.* **à-cic′ū-là.** A strong bristle.

ac′id, *a.* [L. *acidus*, sour, from root *ak*, sharp.] Sour, sharp, or biting to the taste; having the taste of vinegar; as, *acid* fruits or liquors.

ac′id, *n.* 1. In popular language, a sour substance.

2. In chemistry, a compound of an electronegative element with one or more atoms of hydrogen which can be replaced by electropositive or basic atoms. The majority of *acids* contain oxygen, and are known as *oxyacids*; those not containing oxygen are termed *hydrogen acids*. *Acids* usually have the following properties: (a) a sour taste; (b) solubility in water; (c) the power of changing most organic blue and violet colors into red, and of restoring original colors altered by an alkali; (d) the power of uniting in definite proportions with the metals, called bases, forming salts, the metal replacing the hydrogen of the acid; (e) the power of decomposing most carbonates, causing effervescence; (f) the power of exchanging the whole or part of their hydrogen for an alkaline metal presented to them in the form of a hydrate, this last being the only essential property of *acids*. *Acids* vary in their terminations according to the quantity of oxygen or other electro-negative constituent. Those having the maximum of oxygen end in *-ic*; those of a lower degree in *-ous*. *Acids* that end in *-ic*, as sulphuric *acid*, form salts terminating in *-ate*; those ending in *-ous* form salts terminating in *-ite*.

à-cid′ic, *a.* 1. Acid.

2. In geology, containing a high percentage of silica; opposed to *basic*.

ac-id-if′ẽr-ous, *a.* [L. *acidus*, sour, and *ferre*, to bear.] Containing acids, or an acid.

Acidiferous minerals; minerals which consist of an earth combined with an acid, as carbonate of lime, aluminite, etc.

à-cid′i-fī-à-ble, *a.* Capable of being converted into an acid, by union with an acidifying principle.

ac-id-if′ic, *a.* Producing an acid or acidity.

à-cid″i-fi-cā′tion, *n.* The act or process of changing into an acid.

à-cid′i-fī-ẽr, *n.* 1. One who or that which acidifies.

2. In chemistry, that which has the property of changing a substance into an acid, as oxygen, chlorin, etc.

à-cid′i-fȳ, *v.t.*; acidified, *pt.*, *pp.*; acidifying, *ppr.* [*Acid*, and L. *facere*, to make.]

1. To make acid; but appropriately, to convert into an acid, chemically so called, by combination with any substance.

2. Figuratively, to sour or embitter.

ac-id-im′e-tẽr, *n.* [L. *acidus*, sour, acid, and Gr. *metron*, measure.] An instrument for ascertaining the strength of acids.

ac-id-im′e-try, *n.* The measurement of the strength of acids; especially, the process of estimating the amount of acid in any liquid by finding how much of a standard alkaline solution is required exactly to neutralize a measured quantity of the given solution.

à-cid′i-ty, *n.* [Fr. *acidité*, from L. *aciditas*, sourness.] The quality of being sour; sourness; tartness; sharpness to the taste.

ac′id-ly, *adv.* In an acid manner.

ac′id-ness, *n.* The quality of being sour; acidity.

à-cid′ū-læ, *n.pl.* [L.] An old name for medicinal springs impregnated with carbonic acid.

à-cid′ū-lāte, *v.t.*; acidulated, *pt.*, *pp.*; acidulating, *ppr.* [L. *acidulus*, slightly sour, and *-ate*.] To tinge with an acid; to make acid in moderate degree.

à-cid′ū-lent, *a.* Having an acid quality; tart; peevish.

à-cid′ū-lous, *a.* [L. *acidulus*, slightly sour.] Slightly sour; subacid; as oranges, gooseberries, etc.

Acidulous mineral waters; such as contain carbonic acid.

ac′i-ẽr-āge, *n.* [Fr. from *acier*, steel.] The process of coating another metal with a layer of iron or steel, by electricity; stereotypes are sometimes steel-faced in this way.

ac′i-fọrm, *a.* [L. *acus*, a needle, and *forma*, form.] Shaped like a needle.

à-cil′i-āte, *a.* Without cilia.

ac-i-nā′ceous, *a.* [L. *acinus*, grapestone, and *-aceous*.] Full of kernels.

à-cin′à-cēs, *n.* [L., from Gr. *akinakēs*, a short sword.] A short straight dagger worn on the right side by the Scythians, Medes, and Persians.

Figure wearing the Acinaces.

à-cin′à-ci-fọrm, *a.* [L. *acinaces*, a simitar; Gr. *akinakēs*, and *-form*.] In botany, formed like or resembling a simitar; as, an *acinaciform* leaf, that is, one which has one edge convex and sharp and the other straight and thick.

ac-i-nē′si-à, *n.* Same as *Akinesia*.

Ac-i-nē′tæ, *n.pl.* [L., from Gr. *a* priv., and *kinētos*, movable.] An order of the *Infusoria* which are non-locomotive and suctorial.

ac-i-net′i-fọrm, *a.* Having the form of *Acinetæ*.

Ac″i-nē-ti′nà, *n.pl.* A group of infusorians equivalent to the *Acinetæ*.

ac″i-nē-ti′năn, *a.* Pertaining to the *Acinetina*.

ac″i-nē-ti′năn, *n.* One of the *Acinetina*.

à-cin′i-fọrm, *a.* [L. *acinus*, a grapestone, and *-form*.] Having the form of grapes, or being in clusters like grapes; in anatomy, applied to glands.

ac′i-nōse, ac′i-nous, *a.* Consisting of minute granular concretions.

ac′i-nus, *n.*; *pl.* **ac′i-nī.** [L. *acinus*, grapestone.]

1. In botany, one of the small grains which compose the fruit of the blackberry, and other similar plants.

2. In anatomy, the ultimate secernent follicles of glands, or the granulations composing the structure of some conglomerate glands, as the liver.

-ā′cious. [L. *-ax*, *-aci*; It. *-ace*, and OFr. *-ous*.] A suffix; full of, characterized by; added to verb stems to form adjectives; as, (*capax*) capacious, holding much; (*audax*) audacious, full of boldness.

Ac-i-pen′sẽr, *n.* [L., from Gr. *akkipēsios*, a sturgeon.] A genus of cartilaginous ganoid fishes, distinguished by the bony scales or plates arranged at intervals along the body in five longitudinal rows. The gills are free as in osseous fishes, the snout long and conical, and the mouth retractile, toothless, and projecting from the under surface of the head. The genus includes the sturgeon, sterlet, huso, etc.

Acipenser—Head of Sturgeon.

ac′i-ūr-gy, *n.* [Gr. *akis*, a point, and *ourgia*, from *o-ergia*, from *ergein*, to work.] Surgery. [Obs.]

ac-knōw′, *v.t.* To avow; to acknowledge. [Obs.]

ac-knowl′edge (ak-nol′ej), *v.t.*; acknowledged, *pt.*, *pp.*; acknowledging, *ppr.* [OE. *ac* (*a*), *knowlechen*, *knoulechen*, acknowledge, from *knouleche*, *cnawleche*, know, *knowlage*, *knowen*, to know, and Ice. *leikr*, *leiki*, Sw. *lek*, a suffix used to form abstract nouns, as AS. *lac*, in *wedlac*, and meaning game, play.]

1. To own, avow, or admit to be true, by a declaration of assent; as, to *acknowledge* the being of a God.

2. To own or notice with particular regard.

In all thy ways *acknowledge* him.
—Prov. iii. 6.

3. To own or confess, as implying a consciousness of guilt.

4. To own with assent; to admit or receive with approbation.

5. To own with gratitude; to own as a benefit; as, to *acknowledge* a favor, or the receipt of a gift.

6. To own or admit to belong to oneself; as, to *acknowledge* a son.

7. To receive with respect.

8. To own or avow receiving; as, please to *acknowledge* this letter.

9. To show recognition of by an act, as by a bow, nod, smile, lifting the hat, etc., as a mark of friendship or respect; to salute; as, she met him in the street, but barely *acknowledged* him.

10. To own, avow, or assent to (an act) in a legal form, to give it validity; as, to *acknowledge* a deed.

Syn.—Allow, avow, confess, concede, admit, grant, own, recognize, accept, indorse, certify, profess.

aç-knowl′edġed-ly, *adv.* Avowedly.

aç-knowl′edġ-ẽr, *n.* One who acknowledges.

aç-knowl′edġ-ment, *n.* 1. The act of owning; confession; as, the *acknowledgment* of a fault.

2. The act of recognizing with approbation, or in the true character; as, the *acknowledgment* of a God, or of a public minister.

3. Concession; admission of the truth; as of a fact, position, or principle.

4. The owning of a benefit received, accompanied with gratitude; with the idea of an expression of thanks. Hence, it is used also for something given or done in return for a favor.

5. A declaration or avowal of one's own act, to give it legal validity; as, the *acknowledgment* of a deed before a proper officer.

Acknowledgment money; in some parts of England, a sum paid by tenants, on the death of their landlords, as an acknowledgment of their new lords.

Syn.—Admission, avowal, concession, recognition, confession.

ȧ-elas′tiç, *a.* [Gr. *aklastos*, unbroken, from *a* priv., and *klastos*, from *klaein*, to break.] Unable to refract light.

aç′lē, *n.* A tree of the bean family, native to India, Burma, and the Philippine Islands. Its trunk rises upward of seventy feet, bare of branches. The timber is one of the hardest known woods, close-grained, heavier than water, and its heartwood is unassailable by insects. Largely used for gun-carriages, etc. It is also called *ironwood* and *pyengadu*.

ȧ-elin′iç, *a.* [Gr. *a* priv., and *klinein*, to bend.] Not dipping or bending; as, the *aclinic* line, or magnetic equator, where the needle ceases to dip.

aç′lis, aç′lide, *n.*; *pl.* **aç′li-dēs.** [L. *aclis*, a javelin.] A short club studded with sharp points and attached to a cord which enabled the thrower to draw it back after having launched it against an enemy; a very ancient weapon.

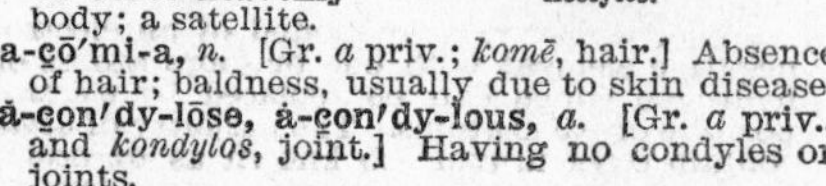

Aclis.—From Chesnel.

aç′mē, *n.* [Gr. *akmē*, a point.]

1. The top or highest point; the height or crisis of anything.

2. The maturity or perfection of an animal.

3. In medicine, the crisis of a disease, or its utmost violence.

4. Mature age; people of mature age collectively. [Rare.]

Syn.—Apex, height, culmination, climax, zenith.

aç′mite, *n.* [Gr. *akmē*, a point.] A mineral of the augite family, occurring in long, pointed crystals, of a dark brownish color, and a bright and somewhat resinous luster.

aç′nē, *n.* [A corruption of Gr. *acmē*, point.] A skin disease, characterized by pustules, which, after suppurating, become hard tubercles.

aç-nō′dăl, *a.* Pertaining to acnodes.

aç′nōde, *n.* [L. *acus*, needle; *nodus*, a node.] In mathematics, a point outside but belonging to a curve.

ȧ-cock′, *adv.* In a cocked or turned-up manner.

ȧ-cock′bill, *adv.* [Prefix *a-*, on, and *cock*, and *bill*, point, edge.] A nautical term, used of the anchor when hanging at the cathead, and of the yards when tipped at an angle with the deck.

Bark, with Yards Acockbill.

A-cœ′lȧ (ȧ-sē′lȧ), *n. pl.* [L. *acœlus*, from Gr. *akoilos*; *a* priv., and *koilos*, hollow.] A group of worms belonging to the *Turbellaria*, having no digestive tract.

ȧ-cœ′lō-māte, *a.* Without a body-cavity.

ȧ-cœ-lom′ȧ-tous, *a.* Same as *Acœlomate*.

ȧ-cœ′lō-mous, *a.* Acœlomate.

ȧ-cœ′lous, *a.* Without an alimentary canal.

A-cœm′ē-ti, A-cœm′ō-tæ (-sem-), *n.pl.* [Gr. *akoimetoi*, the sleepless ones, from *a* priv., and *koimasthai*, to fall asleep.] An order of Eastern monks and nuns of the fifth century who kept up prayer and praise both day and night by sleeping in relays. In the sixth century the monks embraced Nestorianism and their order became extinct, but the nuns maintained their organization until the sixteenth century.

ȧ-cōld′, *a.* Cold; very cold; as, Tom's *acold*. [Obs.]

aç-ō-log′iç, *a.* Relating to acology.

ȧ-col′ō-ġy, *n.* [Gr. *akos*, remedy, and *logos*, discourse.] The doctrine of remedies, or the materia medica.

ȧ-col′ō-thist, ȧ-col′y-thist, *n.* An acolyte. [Obs.]

aç-ō-lyç′tine, *n.* An alkaloid obtained from aconite.

aç′ō-lȳte, aç′ō-lyth, *n.* [Gr. *akolouthos*, a follower.]

1. One who waits on a person; an attendant.

2. In the Roman Catholic church, the highest of the inferior orders of clergy, whose office it is to follow and serve the superior orders in the ministry of the altar, light the candles, prepare the elements of the sacrament, etc.

Acolytes.

3. In astronomy, an attendant or accompanying star or other heavenly body; a satellite.

ȧ-cō′mi-ȧ, *n.* [Gr. *a* priv.; *komē*, hair.] Absence of hair; baldness, usually due to skin disease.

ȧ-con′dy-lōse, ȧ-con′dy-lous, *a.* [Gr. *a* priv., and *kondylos*, joint.] Having no condyles or joints.

aç-ō-nī′tăl, *a.* Having the quality of aconite.

aç′ō-nīte, *n.* [L. *aconitum*; Gr. *akoniton*, a poisonous plant, probably from *akōn*, a dart, it having been used to poison darts.]

1. The herb called wolf's-bane, or monk's-hood, a poisonous plant.

2. Any plant of the genus *Aconitum*.

aç-ō-ni′ti-ȧ (-nish′i-ȧ), *n.* Aconitin.

aç-ō-nit′iç, *a.* Pertaining to aconite.

ȧ-con′i-tin, ȧ-con′i-tine, *n.* A poisonous, narcotic vegetable principle or alkaloid, extracted from several species of aconite.

Aç-ō-nī′tum, *n.* [L.] A genus of poisonous plants, natural order *Ranunculaceæ*. The species are hardy and many of them of great beauty.

ȧ-con′ti-ȧ (-shi-ȧ), *n.pl.* [L., from Gr. *akontion*.] The defensive organs of the sea-anemone.

A-con′ti-as, *n.* [Gr. *akontias*, a dart, from *akōn*, a dart, *akontion*, dim.]

1. A genus of timid lacertian reptiles, which have rudiments only of the hind limbs, allied to the slowworm of Great Britain. They occur in almost all regions, particularly the warm and dry. *Acontias meleagris* is sometimes called *dart-snake*, from its manner of darting on its prey. This snake-like animal is about three feet in length, of a light gray color, with black spots resembling eyes; the belly perfectly white. It is a native of Africa and the Mediterranean isles.

2. In botany, a genus of Brazilian plants, with spots on their stems like those of the reptiles so called.

ȧ-cop′, *adv.* [Prefix *a-*, on, and *cop*, top.] At the top. [Obs.]

ȧ-cop′iç, *a.* [Gr. *a* priv., and *kopos*, a striking, weariness, from *koptein*, to strike.] In medicine, fitted to relieve weariness; restorative.

ā′corn (*or* ā′kẽrn), *n.* [ME. *akorn*, *eykorn*, *akecorn*, *okecorn*, *akern*; AS. *æcern*, acorn, an adj. form of *æcer*, field; Ice. *akarn*, from *akr*, a field; properly, any fruit of the field.]

1. The seed or fruit of the oak; an oval nut which grows in a rough permanent cup.

2. In nautical language, a small ornamental piece of wood, of a conical shape, fixed on the point of a spindle above the vane, on the masthead, to keep the vane from being blown off.

3. See *Acorn-shell*.

Acorn of Coasting Craft.

ā′corn-cup, *n.* The capsule which holds the acorn.

ā′corned, *a.* Bearing acorns, as the oak.

ā′corn-shell, *n.* 1. The shell of the acorn.

2. One of the cirripeds of the genus *Balanus*, allied to the barnacles, called by this name from a supposed resemblance of some of the species to acorns.

Aç′ō-rus, *n.* [L., from Gr. *akoros*, sweet-flag.] A genus of plants of the natural order *Araceæ*. The aromatic calamus of the druggists, *Acorus calamus*, or sweet-flag, is widely prevalent in northern temperate regions.

ȧ-coş′mişm, *n.* [Gr. *a* priv., and *kosmos*, world, and *-ism*.] A belief which denies the existence of an external world.

ȧ-coş′mist, *n.* One who professes acosmism.

ȧ-cot-y-lē′dŏn, *n.* [Gr. *a* priv., and *kotylēdōn*, cavity, cup.] In botany, a plant in which the seed-lobes, or cotyledons, are not present, or are very indistinct. The *acotyledons* form a grand division of the vegetable kingdom including the ferns, lichens, etc., and correspond to the *Cryptogamia* of Linnæus.

ȧ-cot-y-led′ŏn-ous, *a.* Having either no seed-lobes, or such as are indistinct.

Acotyledons.

1. Spores of lichens, germinating; 2. Spores of horsetails (*Equisetaceæ*), germinating; 3. Spores of mosses, germinating.

ȧ-cöu′chy, *n.* [Fr. *acouchi*, *agouchi*, from the native name in Guiana.] A rodent of the genus *Dasyprocta*, found in the West Indies and South America; the olive agouti, or Surinam rat; it is related to the guinea-pig.

ȧ-cöu′me-tẽr (*or* -kow′), *n.* [Gr. *akouein*, to hear, and *metron*, measure.] An instrument for determining the acuteness of the hearing.

ȧ-cöu′me-try, *n.* The measurement of hearing.

aç-öu-sim′e-tẽr (*or* -kow-), *n.* Same as *Acoumeter*.

ȧ-cöus′tiç (*or* -kows′), *a.* [Gr. *akoustos*, heard, from *akouein*, to hear.] Pertaining to the ears, to the sense of hearing, or to the doctrine of sounds.

Acoustic duct; in anatomy, the *meatus auditorius*, or external passage of the ear.

Acoustic vessels; in ancient theaters, brazen tubes or vessels, shaped like a bell, used to propel the voice of the actors, so as to render them audible to a great distance.

ȧ-cöus′tiç, *n.* Any remedy or remedial agent designed to assist in hearing.

ȧ-cöus′tiç-ăl, *a.* Of or pertaining to acoustics.

ȧ-cöus′tiç-ăl-ly, *adv.* In relation to sound or hearing.

ȧ-cöus-ti′cian (-tish′un), *n.* One skilled in acoustics.

ȧ-cöus′ti-cŏn, *n.* [L. *acousticus*, Gr. *akoustikos*, relating to hearing, from *akouein*, to hear.] An adjustable apparatus for transmitting sounds to deaf persons, consisting of an ear piece, a transmitter and a small electric battery, connected by a small silk-covered wire, all of which may be so arranged on the person that no part except the ear piece need be visible. It is capable of nearly 3,000 different adjustments in applying it to various individual needs. The penetrating quality of the sound-wave affects the inner ear direct. Sounds are transmitted inversely, a whisper seeming louder than a shout, and a shout becoming a whisper. Ordinary conversational tones are heard with ease by the deafest person, if the auditory nerve is not paralyzed.

ȧ-cöus′tiçs (*or* -kows′), *n.* The science of sound, teaching the cause, nature, and phenomena of the vibrations of elastic bodies which affect the organ of hearing. The manner in which sound is produced, its transmission through air and other media (sometimes called *diacoustics*), the doctrine of reflected sound or echoes (sometimes called *catacoustics*), the properties and effects of different sounds, including musical sounds or notes, the structure and action of the organ of hearing, are all treated of under *acoustics*.

ȧ-cöus-tom′e-tẽr (*or* -kows), *n.* An apparatus for testing the acoustic properties of a room.

aç-quāint′, *v.t.*; acquainted, *pt.*, *pp.*; acquainting, *ppr.* [ME. *acquentin*, Fr. *acointer*, from L. *adcognitare*, to make known, from *ad*, and *cognitus*, pp. of *accognoscere*, to know thoroughly; *con* and *noscere*, to know.]

1. To make familiar; usually followed by *with*.

> A man of sorrows and *acquainted with* grief.
> —Isa. liii. 3.

2. To inform; to communicate notice to; as, a friend in the country *acquaints* me *with* his success.

Syn.—Apprise, enlighten, inform, make aware, tell.

aç-quāint′ȧ-ble, *a.* Affable; easily approached. [Obs.]

aç-quāint′ănce, *n.* 1. A state of being acquainted, or of having more or less intimate knowledge; used with reference both to persons and things.

2. A person known to one, especially a person with whom one is not on terms of great intimacy; as, he is not a friend, only an *acquaintance*.

3. The whole body of those with whom one is acquainted; as, my *acquaintance* is large.

Syn.—Familiarity, fellowship, intimacy. —*Intimacy* is the result of close connection, and hence is the stronger word; *familiarity* springs from frequent intercourse.

aç-quāint′ănce-ship, *n.* The state of being acquainted.

aç-quāint′ănt, *n.* An acquaintance. [Rare.]

aç-quāint′ed-ness, *n.* Extent of acquaintance. [Rare.]

aç-quest′, *n.* [OFr. *acquest*, L. *acquæsitum*,

anything acquired, from *acquisitum*, pp. of *acquirere*, to acquire.]

1. Acquisition; the thing gained. [Obs.]

2. Conquest; a place acquired by force. [Obs.]

3. In English law, property not descended by inheritance, but acquired by purchase or donation.

aç-qui-esce′ (-wi-es′), *v.i.*; acquiesced, *pt.*, *pp.*; acquiescing, *ppr.* [Fr. *acquiescer*, to yield to, from L. *acquiescere*; *ad*, to, and *quiescere*, to rest.]

1. To rest satisfied, or apparently satisfied, or to rest without opposition and discontent; usually implying previous opposition, uneasiness, or dislike, but ultimate compliance, or submission; as, to *acquiesce* in the dispensations of Providence.

2. To assent to, upon conviction; as, to *acquiesce* in an opinion; that is, to rest satisfied of its correctness or propriety.

Acquiesced in; in a passive sense, complied with; submitted to, without opposition; as, a measure has been *acquiesced in*.

Syn.—Accede, agree, consent, submit, yield, comply, concur, conform.

aç-qui-es′cence, *n.* A quiet assent; a silent submission, or submission with apparent consent, distinguished from avowed consent on the one hand, and on the other from opposition or open discontent; as, an *acquiescence* in the decisions of a board of arbitration.

aç-qui-es′cen-cy, *n.* Acquiescence.

aç-qui-es′cent, *a.* Resting satisfied; easy; submitting; disposed to submit.

aç-qui-es′cent-ly, *adv.* In an acquiescent manner.

aç-quī′et, *v.t.* To ease. [Obs.]

aç-quīr-à-bil′i-ty, *n.* Capability of being acquired or possessed.

aç-quīr′à-ble, *a.* That may be acquired.

aç-quīre′, *v.t.*; acquired, *pt.*, *pp.*; acquiring, *ppr.* [L. *acquirere*; *ad*, to, and *quærere*, to seek.] To gain, by any means, as a thing which is in a degree permanent, or which becomes vested or inherent in the possessor; as, to *acquire* a title, estate, learning, habits, skill, dominion, etc.; as, plants *acquire* a green color from the solar rays.

Syn.—Attain, compass, earn, gain, get, obtain, procure, realize, win.—A mere temporary possession is not expressed by *acquire*, as by *gain*, *obtain*, *procure*; thus, we *obtain* or *procure* a book on loan, but do not *acquire* ownership or permanent possession.

aç-quīre′ment, *n.* The act of acquiring, or that which is acquired; attainment. It is used in opposition to natural gifts; as, eloquence and skill in music and painting are *acquirements*.

aç-quīr′ẽr, *n.* A person who acquires.

aç-quīr′ing, *n.* Acquirement.

aç-qui-ṣi′tion (-zish′un), *n.* [L. *acquisitio*, the act of acquiring, from *acquirere*, to seek for.]

1. The act of acquiring; as, a man takes pleasure in the *acquisition* of property, as well as in the possession.

2. The thing acquired, or gained; as, learning is an *acquisition*.

aç-quiṣ′i-tive, *a.* 1. Acquired, as distinguished from native. [Obs.]

2. Naturally inclined to obtain or possess property, or knowledge; as, a man of *acquisitive* disposition.

aç-quiṣ′i-tive-ly, *adv.* In an acquisitive manner.

aç-quiṣ′i-tive-ness, *n.* Desire of possession; propensity to acquire.

aç-quiṣ′i-tŏr, *n.* A person who acquires. [Rare.]

aç-quit′, *v.t.*; acquitted, *pt.*, *pp.*; acquitting, *ppr.* [Fr. *acquitter*, to free, from L. *acquitare*, to settle a claim, from *ad*, to, and *quietare*, to quiet.] To set free; to release or discharge from an obligation, accusation, guilt, censure, suspicion, or whatever lies upon a person as a charge or duty; as, the jury *acquitted* the prisoner; we *acquit* a man of evil intentions. It is followed by *of* before the object; to *acquit from* is obsolete. In a reciprocal sense, as, the soldier *acquitted* himself well in battle, the word has a like meaning, implying the discharge of a duty or obligation. Hence its use in expressing excellence in performance; as, the orator *acquitted* himself well.

Syn.—Absolve, discharge, justify, clear, release, pardon, exonerate, forgive, set free.

aç-quit′ment, *n.* The act of acquitting, or state of being acquitted. [Rare.]

aç-quit′tăl, *n.* A judicial setting free, or deliverance from the charge of an offense, as by verdict of a jury, or sentence of a court; as, the *acquittal* of a principal operates as an *acquittal* of the accessories.

aç-quit′tănce, *n.* 1. A discharge or release from a debt; the state of being so discharged or released.

2. The writing which is evidence of a discharge; a receipt in full, which bars a further demand.

aç-quit′tẽr, *n.* A person who acquits.

à-çrā′ni-à, *n.* [Gr. *a* priv., and *kranion*, skull.] 1. A malformation characterized by total or partial absence of the bones and integuments of the cranium.

2. [A— *pl.*] The lowest group of vertebrates; also called *Acephala*.

à-çrā′ni-ăl, *a.* Skull-less.

A-çras′pē-dà, *n.pl.* [Gr. *a* priv., and *kraspedon*, border.] A group of jellyfishes; the *Discophora*.

aç′rà-sy, à-çrā′si-à, *n.* [L. *acrasia*, from Gr. *a* priv., and *krasia*, power, temperance.] Excess; irregularity; intemperance. [Rare.]

à-çrāze′, à-çrāṣe′, *v.t.* To make crazy; to infatuate. [Obs. See *Craze*.]

ā′çre, (-kẽr), *n.* [ME. *aker*, AS. *æcer*, L. *ager*, Gr. *agros*, all meaning field, and from Sans. root *ajra*.]

1. Originally an open, plowed, or sowed field.

2. A superficial measure of land, containing 160 square rods or perches, or 4840 square yards. This is the statute *acre* in the United States and Great Britain. The Irish *acre* is 7840 square yards. The *acre* of Scotland contains 6150⅖ square yards.

God's acre; a burial-ground; a churchyard; God's field.

ā′çre-à-ble, *a.* According to the acre; measured or estimated in acres or by the acre.

ā′çre-āġe, *n.* Extent of a piece of land in acres; acres taken collectively; as, the *acreage* of New York state.

ā′çred (-kẽrd), *a.* Possessing acres or landed property; used chiefly in composition; as, wide-*acred* landlords.

ā′çre-fight, *n.* A sort of duel in the open field, formerly fought by English and Scotch combatants on their frontiers.

ā′çre-foot, *n.* A unit of water-volume, equal to that of a prism having an acre in extent of base, and one foot high, or 43,560 cubic feet; a term used in hydraulics.

aç′rid, *a.* [L. *acer* (f. *acris*), sharp.]

1. Sharp; pungent; bitter; sharp or biting to the taste; acrimonious; as, *acrid* salts.

2. Severe; virulent; violent; stinging; as, an *acrid* temper.

Acrid poisons; those poisons which irritate, corrode, or burn the parts to which they are applied, producing intense burning sensation, and acute pain in the alimentary canal when taken internally. They include concentrated acids and alkalis, compounds of mercury, arsenic, copper, etc.

à-çrid′i-ăn, *n.* One of the *Acrididæ*.

A-çrid′i-dæ, *n.pl.* [Gr. *akridion*, dim. of *akris*, locust.] A family of orthopterous insects, including the grasshoppers; all the species of this family can leap.

aç′rid-in, aç′rid-ine, *n.* An acrid crystalline substance found in coal-tar.

à-çrid′i-ty, *n.* The state or quality of being bitter, sharp, or acrimonious; acridness.

aç′rid-ly, *adv.* Bitterly; sharply.

aç′rid-ness, *n.* The state or quality of being acrid.

aç-ri-mō′ni-ous, *a.* [L. *acrimoniosus*, from *acrimonia*, sharpness.]

1. Sharp; bitter; corrosive; abounding with acrimony. [Rare.]

2. Figuratively, severe, sarcastic; applied to language or temper.

aç-ri-mō′ni-ous-ly, *adv.* With sharpness or bitterness.

aç-ri-mō′ni-ous-ness, *n.* The state or quality of being acrimonious.

aç′ri-mō-ny, *n.* [L. *acrimonia*, sharpness.]

1. Sharpness; a quality of bodies which corrodes, dissolves, or destroys others; harshness or bitterness of taste; pungency. [Rare.]

2. Figuratively, sharpness or severity of temper; bitterness of expression proceeding from anger, ill nature, or petulance.

Syn.—Harshness, asperity, smartness, bitterness, tartness.

aç′ri-sy, à-çris′i-à, *n.* [Gr. *akrisia*, from *a* priv., and *kritos*, discernible, from *krinein*, to judge, to separate.]

1. A state or condition of which no right judgment can be formed; matter in dispute; inability to judge.

2. In medicine, defective or unfavorable crisis in disease, making prognosis doubtful.

Aç′ri-tà, *n. pl.* [Neut. pl. of Gr. *akritos*, undecided, from *a* priv., and *krinein*, to judge.] A term applied to that division of radiate animals in which there is no distinct discernible nervous system, and no separate alimentary canal, as the sponges, polyps, etc.

aç′ri-tăn, *a.* Pertaining to the *Acrita*.

aç′ri-tăn, *n.* One of the *Acrita*.

aç′rīte, *a.* Acritan.

à-çrit′iç-ăl, *a.* In medicine, without crisis or indications of crisis.

aç″ri-tō-chrō′mà-cy, *n.* [Gr. *akritos*; *a* priv., and *kritos*, distinguishable, and *chrōma*, color.] Achromatopsy or color-blindness.

aç′ri-tūde, *n.* An acrid quality; bitterness to the taste; biting heat. [Rare.]

aç′ri-ty, *n.* Sharpness; eagerness. [Obs.]

aç′rō-. A combining form from Gr. *akros*, summit, extreme, topmost. F. form *akra*, neut. *akron*; from root *akē*, point. Sometimes *acro*, from L. *acer*, sharp, is confused with it.

aç′rō-à-mat′iç, aç″rō-à-mat′iç-ăl, *a.* See *Acroatic*.

aç-rō-at′iç, *a.* [L. *acroaticus*, Gr. *akroatikos*, connected with hearing, from *akroasthai*, to hear.] Abstruse; pertaining to deep learning, and opposed to *exoteric*. Aristotle's lectures were of two kinds, *acroatic*, *acroamatic*, or *esoteric*, which were delivered privately to a class of select disciples, who had been previously instructed in the elements of learning; and *exoteric*, which were delivered in public. The former respected being, God, and nature; the principal subjects of the latter were logic, rhetoric, and policy. The abstruse lectures were called *acroatics*.

aç′rō-bat, *n.* [Fr. *acrobate*, Gr. *akrobatos*, to walk on tiptoe, to go aloft; from Gr. *akros*, high, tip, and *bainein*, to go.] A gymnast; a tumbler; one who practises daring and difficult feats of agility and strength on the tight rope, trapeze, horizontal bar, and other apparatus, or on the ground.

Aç-rob′à-tēs, *n.* [L.] A genus of marsupial animals found in Australia, including the opossum or flying mouse, so called from its size and appearance. [See *Phalanger*.]

Opossum Mouse (*Acrobates pygmæus*).

aç-rō-bat′iç, *a.* Pertaining to an acrobat.

aç-rō-bat′iç-ăl-ly, *adv.* In an acrobatic manner.

aç′rō-bat-ism, *n.* The art of acrobats.

aç′rō-blast, *n.* See *Mesenchyma*.

Aç-rō-cär′pi, *n.pl.* [*Acro-*, and Gr. *karpos*, fruit.] A division of the mosses, containing the species in which the capsule terminates the growth of a primary axis.

aç-rō-cär′pous, *a.* A term applied to mosses whose flower terminates the growth of a primary axis.

aç″rō-cē-phal′iç, *a.* Characterized by a pyramidal skull.

aç-rō-ceph′à-ly, *n.* [*Acro-*, and Gr. *kephalē*, head.] In ethnology, a pyramidal or lofty form of skull.

Aç″rō-cē-rau′ni-ăn, *a.* [*Acro-*, and Gr. *keraunos*, thunderbolt.] An epithet applied to certain mountains which project into the Adriatic, and are often struck by lightning.

aç-rō-dac′tyl-um, *n.* [*Acro-*, and Gr. *daktylos*, finger.] The upper surface of each digit of a bird.

aç′rō-dont, *n.* and *a.* [*Acro-*, and Gr. *odous* (*odontos*), tooth.]

I. *n.* A lizard characterized by having the bases of the teeth attached to the edge of the jaw without sockets.

II. *a.* Resembling an acrodont or its teeth.

aç′rō-drōme, *a.* [*Acro-*, and Gr. *dromos*, course.] A botanical term signifying terminating in a point.

aç-rō-dyn′i-à, *n.* An epidemic disease marked by disturbances of the alimentary canal and the nervous system.

aç′rō-ġen, *n.* [*Acro-*, and Gr. *genēs*, from *gignesthai*, to bear.] A cryptogamic plant which increases in growth chiefly at its summit.

aç-rō-ġen′iç, *a.* Acrogenous.

à-çroġ′e-nous, *a.* Increasing by growth at the apex, as the tree-ferns; pertaining to the acrogens.

aç-roġ′rà-phy, *n.* [*Acro-*, and Gr. *graphia*, from *graphein*, to write.] The art of producing designs in relief on metal or stone by etching, for the purpose of printing from them along with type, and thus superseding wood-engraving.

aç-rō′lē-in, *n.* [L. *acer*, *acris*, sharp, and *olere*, to smell, and *-in*.] A colorless liquid obtained by the distillation of glycerin; its odor is intensely irritating.

aç′rō-lith, *n.* [Gr. *akros*, summit, and *lithos*, stone.] In Grecian sculpture, a statue whose head and extremities only were of stone, the body and limbs being of wood covered with fabric or thin metal.

à-çrol′i-thăn, *a.* Pertaining to an acrolith; formed like an acrolith; as, an *acrolithan* statue.

aç-rō-lith′iç, *a.* Acrolithan.

aç′rō-logue (-log), *n.* A symbolic letter or picture employed in acrology.

à-çrol′ō-ġy, *n.* [*Acro-*, and Gr. *logia*, from *legein*, to say.] The science of denoting names by means of initials, pictorial representations, etc.

aç-rō-meg′à-ly, *n.* [Gr. *akros*, extremity, and *megas* (*megalē*), large.] A disease which enlarges and prolongs the bones of the extremities; also, hypertrophy of the facial bones.

à-çrom′e-tẽr, *n.* [L. *acer*, sharp, and Gr. *metron*, measure.] An instrument for ascertaining the density of oil.

ȧ-çrō'mi-ăl, *a.* In anatomy, relating to the acromion.

ȧ-çrō'mi-on, *n.* [Gr. *akromion*, from *akromia*, the point of the shoulder.] In anatomy, that part of the spine of the scapula which receives the extreme part of the clavicle.

aç"rō-mon"ō-gram-mat'iç, *a.* In poetry, having each line or verse begin with the letter with which the preceding line or verse ends.

aç"rō-när-çot'iç, *n.* A drug that is both narcotic and acrid.

ȧ-çron'yçh, ȧ-çron'yçh-ăl, *a.* [*Acro-*, and Gr. *nyx*, night.] In astronomy, culminating at midnight; said of a star which rises as the sun sets, and sets as the sun rises, and is, therefore, directly opposite the sun; opposed to *cosmical*. Spelled also, though improperly, *acronic*, *acronical*.

ȧ-çron'yçh-ăl-ly, *adv.* In an acronychal manner.

aç-rō-nyç'tous, *a.* Acronychal.

ȧ-çrook', *adv.* In a crooked manner. [Rare.]

ȧ-çrop'e-tăl, *a.* In botany, developing in a basifugal manner.

aç-rō-phō'bi-ȧ, *n.* [Gr. *akros*, high, and *phobos*, fear.] Morbid fear of being on any height, as at the top of a building.

aç-roph'ō-ny, *n.* [*Acro-*, and Gr. *phōnē*, sound.] The science of using picture symbols to represent the initial sound of the name of an object.

aç-rō-pō'di-um, *n.* [*Acro-*, and Gr. *pous* (*podos*), foot.] In zoölogy, the whole of the upper surface of the foot.

ȧ-çrop'ō-lis, *n* [Gr. *akropolis*, *akros*, high, and *polis*, city.] A citadel; specifically [A—] the citadel in Athens.

aç-rō-pol'i-tăn, *a.* Pertaining to an acropolis.

aç-rō-sär'çum, *n.* [L., from Gr. *akros*, extreme, and *sarx* (*sarkos*), flesh.] A berry resulting from an ovary with an adnate calyx, as the cranberry.

aç'rō-sōme, *n.* [*Acro-*, and Gr. *sōma*, body.] The apical body at the anterior end of a spermatozoön.

aç'rō-spire, *n.* [Gr. *akros*, extreme, and *speira*, spire, coil.] The sprout at the ends of seeds when they begin to germinate; the plumule, so called from its spiral form; the first sprout of malting grain.

aç'rō-spire, *v.i.* To grow the first leaf; to sprout.

aç'rō-spōre, *n.* [*Acro-*, and Gr. *spora*, seed.] In some fungi, a naked spore borne at the end of the mother-cell.

aç'rō-spōr-ous, *a.* Bearing acrospores.

ȧ-çross', *prep.* 1. From side to side; opposed to *along*, which is in the direction of the length; athwart; quite over; as, a bridge is laid *across* a river.

2. Intersecting; passing over at any angle; as, a line passing *across* another.

3. On the other side of; as, *across* the ocean.

4. Opposite; as, the window *across* from mine.

ȧ-çross', *adv.* Crosswise; transversely from one side to the other; as, his arms were folded *across*; beyond or at the other side of; as, the house stands *across*

ȧ-çros'tiç, *n.* [Gr. *akrostichos*, from *akros*, extreme, and *stichos*, order, line, verse.]

1. A composition, usually in verse, in which certain letters of the lines, taken in order, form a name, title, motto, etc., which is the subject of the composition.

2. A Hebrew poem of which the initial letters of the lines, or stanzas, were made to run over the letters of the alphabet in their order. Twelve of the psalms are of this character, of which Psalm cxix. is the best example.

ȧ-çros'tiç, ȧ-çros'tiç-ăl, *a.* Relating to or containing an acrostic; as, *acrostic* verses.

ȧ-çros'tiç-ăl-ly, *adv.* In the manner of an acrostic.

aç-rō-tär'si-um, *n.* [L., from Gr. *akros*, highest, and *tarsos*, tarsus.] The instep, or upper surface of the tarsus.

aç"rō-te-leu'tiç, *n.* [Gr. *akros*, extreme, and *teleutē*, end, and *-ic*.] Among ecclesiastical writers, an appellation given to anything added to the end of a psalm or hymn, as a doxology.

aç-rō-tē'ri-ăl, *a.* Pertaining to an acroterium; as, *acroterial* ornaments.

aç-rō-tē'ri-um, *n.*; *pl.* **aç-rō-tē'ri-ȧ.** [L., from Gr *akrōtērion*, pl. *akrōtēria*.] In architecture, a term applied to one of the pedestals, usually without a base, anciently placed at the two extremes or in the middle of pediments or frontispieces, serving to support statues, etc It is also applied to figures placed as ornaments on the tops of churches and other buildings.

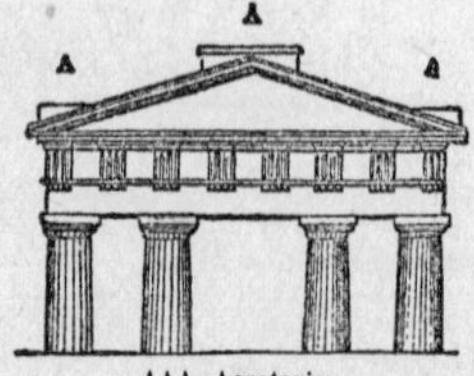

AAA, Acroteria.

aç-rō-thym'i-ŏn, *n.* [Gr. *akros*, extreme, and *thymos*, thyme.] A species of wart, with a narrow base and broad top, having the color of thyme; also called *thymus*.

ȧ-çrot'iç, *a.* [Gr. *akrotēs*, an extremity.] Relating to or affecting external surfaces.

aç'rō-tişm, *n.* [Gr. *a* priv., and *krotos*, sound of beating.] Weakness of the pulse.

ȧ-çrot'ō-mous, *a.* [*Acro-*, and Gr. *temnein*, to cut.] In mineralogy, having a cleavage parallel with the top.

aç'ryl, *n.* In chemistry, a hypothetical radical of acrolein.

ȧ-çryl'iç, *a.* Relating to or containing acryl; as, *acrylic* acid.

açt, *v.i.*; acted, *pt.*, *pp.*; acting, *ppr.* [OE. *act*; Fr. *acte*; L. *actum*, a thing done, neut. of pp. of *agere*, to do; Gr. *agein*, to do, drive, lead; Ice. *aka*, drive, from Sans. root *ajr*, drive.]

1. To exert power; as, the stomach *acts* upon food; to have effect; to fulfil functions.

2. To be in action or motion; to move.

3. To behave, demean, or conduct, as in morals, private duties, or public offices; as, we know not why a minister has *acted* so.

To act up to; to equal in action; to fulfil, or perform a correspondent action; as, he has *acted up to* his engagement or his advantages.

açt, *v.t.* 1. To perform; to represent (a character) on the stage; to simulate or play (a rôle); hence, to feign or counterfeit; as, to *act* the villain.

2. To transact; to do or perform. [Obs.]

3. To put in motion; to actuate; to regulate movements. [Obs.]

Syn.—Personate, simulate, perform, feign, work, make, move, execute, effect, do.

açt, *n.* 1. The exertion of power; the effect, of which power exerted is the cause; as, the *act* of giving or receiving. In this sense it denotes an operation of the mind as well as of the body. Thus, to discern is an *act* of the understanding; to judge is an *act* of the will.

2. That which is done; a deed, exploit, or achievement, whether good or ill; as, all the *acts* of a man's career.

3. Action; performance; production of effects; as, an *act* of charity.

4. A state of reality or real existence, as opposed to a possibility. [Obs.]

5. In general, action completed; but preceded by *in* it denotes incomplete action; as, he was taken *in the act*. *In act* is used also to signify incipient action, or a state of preparation to exert power; as, *in act* to strike.

6. A part or division of a play to be performed without interruption, after which the action is suspended to give respite to the performers.

7. The result of public deliberation, or the decision of a legislative body, council, court of justice, or magistrate; a law, judgment, resolve, award, determination; as, an *act* of congress or of parliament. The term is also transferred to the book, record, or writing containing the laws and determinations.

8. Any instrument in writing to verify facts; as, this is my *act* and deed.

Acts; the title of a book in the New Testament, containing a history of the acts of the apostles.

Act of faith; see *Auto da fé*.

Act of God; in law, an inevitable, accidental, or extraordinary episode in the course of events, which cannot be foreseen to guard against, as the consequences arising from storms, lightning, etc.

Act of grace; a general public pardon or amnesty to a number of offenders, as at the accession of a sovereign, etc.

Adamson Act; an act passed by Congress in 1916 providing for an eight-hour day for employees of carriers engaged in interstate commerce which went into effect Jan. 1, 1917.

Syn.—Action, accomplishment, performance, achievement, transaction, proceeding, exertion, exercise, doing, effect, feat, work, deed.

aç'tȧ, *n. pl.* [L., pl. of *actum*, neut. of *actus*, pp. of *agere*, to do.] Acts; the proceedings of ecclesiastical or judicial bodies, or the minutes thereof.

Acta Sanctorum; collections of accounts of the lives of saints and martyrs of the Roman and Greek churches.

açt'ȧ-ble, *a.* Capable of being acted.

Aç'ti-ăn, *a.* Relating to Actium, a town and promontory of Epirus; as, *Actian* games, which were instituted by Augustus to celebrate his naval victory over Antony, near that town, Sept. 2, B. C. 31. They were celebrated every five years.

aç-tin-. See *Actino-*.

aç'ti-năl, *a.* [Gr. *aktis* (*aktinos*), a ray, and *-al*.] Relating to the side where the mouth is situated; applied to radiate animals.

aç'tine, *n.* A ray, as those in the spicule of a sponge.

aç-ti-nen'çhy-mȧ, *n.* [L., from *actin-* and Gr. *enchyma*, a pouring together; *en*, in, and *chein*, to pour.] The radiated cellular tissue of some medullas; stellate cellular tissue.

açt'ing, *n.* Action; the act of performing a part of a play; the art of an actor.

Aç-tin'i-ȧ, *n.* [L., from Gr. *aktis* (*aktinos*), a ray.] A genus of radiate zoöphytes, having a circle of tentacles or rays around the mouth; including the animal-flowers or sea-anemones.

aç-tin'i-ăn, *a.* Pertaining to the *Actinia*.

aç-tin'iç, *a.* Pertaining to actinism; specifically, pertaining to the chemical rays of the sun.

Actinic focus; the focus at which the actinic rays are brought together by a lens.

aç'ti-nid, *n.* One of the *Actinia*.

aç-tin'i-fôrm, *a.* [Gr. *aktis*, a ray, and *-form*.] Having a radiated form, like one of the *Actinia*.

aç-tin'i-ō-çhrōme, *n.* [*Actino-*, and Gr. *chrōma*, color.] A red pigment obtained from certain radiate zoöphytes.

aç'tin-işm, *n.* [Gr. *aktis*, *aktinos*, a ray.]

1. The radiation of heat or light; or that branch of natural philosophy which treats of the radiation of heat or light.

2. The property of the chemical part of the sun's rays which, as seen in photography, produces chemical combinations and decompositions. A ray, when decomposed by refraction through a prism, is found to possess three properties, viz., the luminous, the heating, and the chemical or actinic, the two latter acting at opposite ends of the spectrum. The actinic property or force, or *actinism*, begins among the violet rays, and extends a long way beyond the visible spectrum.

aç-tin'i-um, *n.* A substance said to be obtainable from zinc and to turn dark on exposure to sunlight.

aç'ti-nō-, aç'ti-ni-, aç'tin-. [Gr. *aktis*, *aktinos*, a ray.] A combining form denoting usually, in zoölogy, the possession of tentacles, or a radiated structure; in physics and chemistry, the presence of actinic rays.

aç"ti-nō-çhem'is-try, *n.* The chemistry of the action of light-rays.

aç"ti-nō-çri'nite, aç"ti-nō-çri'noid, *n.* A fossil species of radiate crinoid.

aç-tin'ō-grȧph, *n.* [*Actino-*, and Gr. *graphein*, to write.] An instrument for computing the chemical effect of solar rays.

aç'tin-oid, *a.* Radiated, as one of the *Actinia*.

aç-tin'ō-lite, *n.* [*Actino-*, and Gr. *lithos*, a stone.] The bright green variety of hornblende, occurring usually in glassy prismatic crystals.

aç"tin-ō-lit'iç, *a.* Like or containing actinolite.

aç-tin'ō-logue (-log), *n.* Any part in a radiate animal that has a homologous relation to another in a different segment of the animal.

aç-ti-nol'ō-ġy, *n.* [*Actino-*, and Gr. *logos*, from *legein*, to say.] 1. The science which treats of the action of actinic rays.

2. The homologous relation of similar segments in a radiate animal.

aç-tin'ō-mēre, *n.* [*Actino-*, and Gr. *meros*, part.] One of the segments of a radiate animal.

aç-ti-nom'e-tẽr, *n.* [*Actino-*, and Gr. *metron*, measure.] An instrument for measuring the intensity of the sun's actinic rays. Several of these instruments have been invented, based upon the production of certain chemical reactions by means of the chemical rays.

aç"ti-nō-met'riç, *a.* Of or belonging to the actinometer, or the measurement of the chemical-action of the sun's rays.

aç-ti-nom'e-try, *n.* The measurement of the intensity of actinic rays.

aç"ti-nō-mȳ'çēs, *n.* [*actino-*, and Gr. *mykēs*, a mushroom.] A bacterium which causes lumpy jaw, or actinomycosis, in cattle.

aç"ti-nō-mȳ-çō'sis, *n.* [*Actino-*, and Gr. *mykēs*, a mushroom, excrescence, and *-osis*.] An infectious disease of cattle which may affect human beings. It is caused by the bacterium called actinomyces, and is characterized by tumors on the jaw, usually, but sometimes on the tongue, or in the lungs; commonly called lumpy jaw.

aç"ti-nō-mȳ-çot'iç, *a.* Pertaining to actinomycosis.

aç-tin'ō-phōre, *n.* [Gr. *aktinophoros*, ray-bearing.] One of the bones that support the finrays of a fish.

aç-ti-noph'ō-rous, *a.* Having radiating spines.

aç"tin-ō-sō'mȧ, *n.* [*Actino-*, and Gr. *sōma*, body.] The body of an actinozoan, whether simple or compound.

aç'tin-ost, *n.* [*Actin-*, and Gr. *osteon*, bone] One of the bones at the base of the pectoral fin of a fish.

aç-tin'ō-stōme, *n.* [*Actino-*, and Gr. *stoma*, mouth.] The mouth of a cœlenterate.

aç-ti-nō-ther'ȧ-py, *n.* Same as *radiotherapy*.

aç-ti-not'rō-çhȧ, *n.* [*Actino-*, and Gr. *brochē*, wheel.] The larva of certain marine worms of the genus *Phoronis*.

Aç"ti-nō-zō'ȧ, *n.pl.* [*Actino-*, and Gr. *zoon*

animal.] A group of *Cœlentera*, including the *Anthozoa*; the sea-anemones, corals, etc.

aç″ti-nō-zō′ăl, *a.* Pertaining to the *Actinozoa.*

aç″ti-nō-zō′ăn, aç″ti-nō-zō′on, *n.* One of the *Actinozoa.*

aç-tin′ū-lȧ, *n.* [L., dim. of Gr. *aktis, aktinos,* ray.] A larval condition of certain hydroids; the embryo after the formation of the mouth circlet of tentacles.

aç′tion, *n.* [ME. *accion*; OFr. *action*; L. *actio(n),* from *agere,* to do, drive.]

1. Literally, a driving; hence, the state of acting or moving; exertion of power or force, as when one body acts on another; or, the effect of power exerted on one body by another; motion produced. Hence, *action* is opposed to *rest. Action,* when produced by one body on another, is mechanical; when produced by the will of a living being, spontaneous or voluntary.

2. An act or thing done; a deed.

3. In mechanics, agency; operation; driving impulse; effort of one body upon another; as, the *action* of wind upon a ship's sails; also, the effect of such action.

4. [*pl.*] In ethics, the external signs or expression of the sentiments of a moral agent; conduct; behavior; demeanor.

5. In poetry and the drama, a series of events on which the interest of the piece depends; as, a play full of *action.*

6. In oratory, gesture or gesticulation; the external deportment of the speaker.

7. In physiology, the motions or functions of the body, vital, animal, and natural; as, the *action* of the heart and lungs; the *action* of the stomach in the digestive process.

8. In law, literally, an urging for right; a suit or process, by which a demand is made of a right; a claim made before a tribunal. *Actions* are civil or penal; *civil,* when instituted solely in behalf of private persons to recover debts or damages; *penal,* when instituted to recover a penalty, imposed by way of punishment. The word is also used for a *right of action*; as, the law gives an *action* for every claim. —Blackstone.

9. In painting and sculpture, the attitude or position of the several parts of the body, by which they seem to be actuated by passions or emotions; as, the arm extended, to represent the act of giving or receiving.

10. A battle; a fight; an engagement between enemies in war, whether on land or water, or by a large or small number of combatants.

11. The mechanism of a piano, organ, or other compound instrument of like kind.

12. The stride of a horse or its movements generally; as, a horse of spirited *action.*

13. The mechanism of a gun, by which a breech is opened.

Chose in action; in law, a right to a thing, in opposition to the possession. A bond or note is a *chose in action* [Fr. *chose,* a thing], and gives the owner a right to prosecute his claim to the money, as he has an absolute property in a *right,* as well as in a *thing,* in possession.

Quantity of action; in physics, the product of the mass of a body by the space it runs through and its velocity.

Syn.—Act, deed, case, accomplishment, behavior, feat, performance, exploit, achievement, exercise, proceeding, transaction.—In many cases, *action* and *act* are synonymous; but some distinction between them is observable. *Action* seems to have more relation to the power that acts, and its operation and process of acting; and *act,* more relation to the effect or operation complete. *Action* is also more generally used for ordinary transactions; and *act* for such as are remarkable, or dignified; as, all our *actions* should be regulated by prudence; a citizen is distinguished by *acts* of heroism or humanity.

aç′tion-ȧ-ble, *a.* Furnishing ground for an action at law; as, to call a man a thief is *actionable.*

aç′tion-ȧ-bly, *adv.* In a manner that subjects to legal process.

aç′tion-less, *a.* Without action.

aç′ti-vāte, *v.t.* To make active. [Obs.]

aç′tive, *a.* [ME. *actif*; OFr. *actif*; L. *activus,* from *agere,* to act.]

1. Having the power or quality of acting; containing the principle of action, independent of any visible external force; as, attraction is an *active* power; communicating action or motion; opposed to *passive*; as, the *active* powers of the mind.

2. Having the power of quick motion, or the disposition to move with speed; nimble; lively; brisk; agile; as, an *active* animal.

3. Busy; constantly engaged in action; pursuing business with vigor and assiduity; diligent; energetic; as, an *active* life; an *active* officer.

4. Requiring action or exertion; practical; producing real effects; opposed to *theoretical, ideal,* or *speculative*; as, the *active* duties of life.

5. In grammar, expressing action; as, an *active* verb. *Active* verbs are subdivided into two classes, namely, *active intransitive* and *active transitive*; the former implying action confined to the actor; as, I *walk, run, think*; the latter action passing from the actor to an object; as, I *chase* the hare; I *teach* the boy.

6. In commerce, lively; brisk; as, an *active* demand for wheat; freights are *active.*

7. In medicine, effective and quick; as, an *active* remedy; also, developing rapidly; as, an *active* disease.

Active bonds; those having fixed interest payable from date of issue, distinguishing them from passive bonds, which bear no interest, but entitle the holder to a future benefit.

Active capital; money, or property that may readily be converted into money, and used in commerce or other employment for profit.

Active commerce; the commerce in which a nation carries its own productions and foreign commodities in its own ships, or which is prosecuted by its own citizens.

Active list; the military or naval officers of a country's forces, liable to be called into active service.

Active service; actual military activity in the face of an enemy.

Syn.—Agile, alert, assiduous, brisk, busy, lively, nimble, quick, spirited, vigorous, sprightly, prompt, energetic, operative, industrious.

aç′tive-ly, *adv.* In an active manner; by action; nimbly; briskly. In grammar, in an active signification; as, a word is used *actively.*

aç′tive-ness, *n.* The quality of being active; activity.

aç-tiv′i-ty, *n.* The quality of being active; the active faculty; exertion of energy; briskness of movement; nimbleness; agility; animation; as, *activity* of a market; human *activities.*

Sphere of activity; the whole space in which the virtue, power, or influence of any object is exerted.

Syn.—Briskness, liveliness, animation.

act′less, *a.* Without action or spirit. [Rare.]

äç′tō, *n.* [Sp., literally, an act.] In Spanish-American law, a lawsuit; a proceeding in court.

aç′tŏn, *n.* [OFr. *aketon, hoqueton,* a quilted jacket; Sp. *alcoton,* cotton.] A stuffed vest or tunic formerly worn under a coat of mail.

aç′tŏr, *n.* [L. *actor,* a doer, an advocate.]

1. One who acts or performs; an active agent.

2. One who represents a character, or acts a part in a play; a professional player.

3. In law, an advocate or proctor in civil courts or causes; also, a plaintiff.

aç′tress, *n.* A woman who acts; specifically, a woman who acts a part in a play.

aç′tū-ăl (*or* ak′chū-ăl), *a.* [ME. *actuel,* active; L. *actualis,* from *actus,* pp. of *agere,* to do.]

1. Real or effectual, or existing truly and absolutely; as, *actual* heat, opposed to virtual or potential heat.

2. Existing in act; real; in opposition to *speculative,* or existing in theory only; as, an *actual* crime; *actual* receipts.

3. Existing at the present time; as, the *actual* condition of the country.

Actual cautery; burning by a red-hot iron, etc.; opposed to *potential cautery,* or a caustic application.

Actual sin; that which is committed by a person himself; opposed to *original sin,* or the corruption of nature supposed to be communicated from Adam.

Syn.—Certain, genuine, positive, real, true, authentic, veritable, unquestioned.

aç′tū-ăl, *n.* In finance, something actually in hand or received, as distinguished from estimated assets or receipts. [Colloq.]

aç′tū-ăl-ist, *n.* A realist; one who believes in actualities.

aç-tū-al′i-ty, *n.* Reality, as opposed to *ideality.*

aç″tū-ăl-i-zā′tion, *n.* A making real or actual.

aç′tū-ăl-ize, *v.t.*; actualized, *pt., pp.*; actualizing, *ppr.* To make actual.

aç′tū-ăl-ly, *adv.* 1. In fact; really; in truth.

2. With outward and active manifestation.

aç′tū-ăl-ness, *n.* The quality of being actual.

aç-tū-ā′ri-ăl, *a.* Relating to an actuary or the business of an actuary.

aç′tū-ā-ry, *n.* [L. *actuarius,* clerk, from *actus,* pp. of *agere,* to do.]

1. A registrar or clerk; a term of the civil law, and used originally in courts of civil law jurisdiction; specifically, in England, an officer appointed to keep savings-banks' accounts.

2. An official statistician and computer of an insurance company; one who calculates insurance risks and premiums.

aç′tū-āte, *a.* Put in action. [Obs.]

aç′tū-āte, *v.t.*; actuated, *pt., pp.*; actuating, *ppr.* [L. *actuatus,* pp. of *actuare,* from *actus,* act.]

1. To put into action; to move or incite to action; as, men are *actuated* by motives, or passions.

2. To carry out; to execute. [Obs.]

Syn.—Act upon, impel, induce, instigate, move, prompt.

aç-tū-ā′tion, *n.* The state of being put in action; effectual operation.

aç′tū-ā-tŏr, *n.* A person who actuates.

aç′tū-ōse, *a.* Full of action. [Obs.]

aç-tū-os′i-ty, *n.* 1. In metaphysics, a state of activity which is complete in itself without leading to any result which must be regarded as its completion; as, to think.

2. The power to act; energy. [Obs.]

aç′tūre, *n.* Action. [Obs.]

aç-tū′ri-ence, *n.* A desire to act. [Rare.]

aç′tus, *n.* In law, a public highway. [Rare.]

aç′ū-āte, *v.t.* [L. *acuatus,* pp. of *acuare,* from *acuere,* to sharpen.] To sharpen; to make pungent, or corrosive. [Rare.]

aç′ū-āte, *a.* Sharpened.

aç-ū-ā′tion, *n.* The act of sharpening.

aç-ū-i′tion (-ish′un), *n.* [L. *acuere,* to sharpen.] The sharpening of medicines, as by the addition of acid, to increase their effect. [Obs.]

ȧ-çū′i-ty, *n.* Sharpness.

ȧ-çū′lē-āte, *a.* [L. *aculeatus,* from *aculeus,* a sting.]

1. In botany, having prickles, or sharp points; pointed; used chiefly to denote prickles fixed in bark, in distinction from thorns, which grow from the wood.

2. In zoölogy, having a sting, or prickles.

ȧ-çū′lē-ā-ted, *a.* Aculeate.

ȧ-çū′lē-i-fŏrm, *a.* [L. *aculeus,* prickle, and *-form.*] Resembling a prickle.

ȧ-çū′lē-ō-lāte, *a.* Having small prickles.

ȧ-çū′lē-ous, *a.* Aculeate. [Obs.]

ȧ-çū′lē-us, *n.*; *pl.* **ȧ-çū′lē-ī.** [L., dim. of *acus,* needle.]

1. A prickle, or rigid point, growing from the epidermis of a plant; distinguished from a thorn, which grows from the wood.

2. The sting of hymenopterous insects, like the bee and the wasp.

ȧ-çū′men, *n.* [L. *acumen,* a point, a sting.]

1. Quickness of perception; penetration of mind; the faculty of nice discrimination; sharpness; sagacity.

2. In botany, a sharp point.

ȧ-çū′mi-nāte, *a.* Having a long, projecting, and highly tapering point. In botany, applied to leaves; when the narrowing takes place at the base it is so expressed; as, *accuminate* at the base; when used without any limitation it always refers to the apex of the leaf.

Acuminate Leaf.

ȧ-çū′mi-nāte, *v.t.*; acuminated, *pt., pp.*; acuminating, *ppr.* [L. *acuminatus,* pp. of *acuminare,* to sharpen.] To make sharp.

ȧ-çū′mi-nāte, *v.i.* To come to, or end in, a sharp point.

ȧ-çū-mi-nā′tion, *n.* A sharpening; termination in a sharp point.

ȧ-çū′mi-nōse, *a.* Acuminate.

ȧ-çū′mi-nous, *a.* Keen; possessing acumen; also, acuminate.

aç-ū-min′ū-lāte, *a.* Somewhat acuminate.

aç-ū-pres′sūre, *n.* [L. *acus,* a needle, and *pressura,* pressure.] A method of stopping hemorrhages during surgical operations, by means of a needle or wire.

aç″ū-pung″tū-rā′tion, *n.* Same as *Acupuncture.*

aç-ū-pung′tūre, *n.* [L. *acus,* needle, and *punctura,* a pricking.] A surgical operation, performed by pricking the part affected with a needle, as in headaches and lethargies.

aç-ū-pung′tūre, *v.t.* To prick with a needle; to perform the operation of acupuncture on.

ȧ-çus′tum-ançe, *n.* [Obs.] See *Accustomance.*

ȧ-çūt′an″gū-lăr, *a.* Acute-angled.

ȧ-çūte′, *a.* [L. *acutus,* pp. of *acuere,* to sharpen.]

1. Sharp at the end; ending in a sharp point; opposed to *blunt* or *obtuse*; as, an *acute* angle.

2. Figuratively, applied to mental powers, penetrating; having nice discernment; perceiving or using minute distinctions; opposed to *dull* or *stupid*; as, an *acute* reasoner.

3. Applied to the senses, having nice or quick sensibility; susceptible of slight impressions; having power to feel or perceive small objects; as, a man of *acute* eyesight, hearing, or feeling.

4. In medicine, sharp; severe; coming speedily to a crisis; said of disease; the opposite of *chronic.*

5. In oratory, sharp, shrill and high, as the accents of pain and excitement.

6. In music, sharp or high in tone or pitch; said of sound; opposed to *grave.*

7. In botany, ending in an acute angle, as a leaf or perianth.

Acute angle; in geometry, one which is less than a right angle, or which subtends less than ninety degrees.

Syn.—Keen, penetrating, shrewd, sagacious, piercing, pointed, sharp.

ȧ-çūte′, *v.t.* To give a sharp sound to. [Rare.]

ȧ-çūte′=an″gled, *a.* Having acute angles.

Acute-angled triangle; a triangle whose three angles are each less than a right angle.

ȧ-cūte′ly, *adv.* Sharply; keenly; with nice discrimination.

ac″ū-tē-naç′ū-lum, *n.*; *pl.* **ac″ū-tē-naç′ū-lȧ.** [L. *acus*, needle, and *tenaculum*, holder.] An instrument for facilitating the use of a needle in surgical operations.

ȧ-çūte′ness, *n.* 1. Sharpness; the quality of being acute.

2. Figuratively, the faculty of nice discernment or perception; applied to the senses, or the understanding. By an *acuteness* of feeling, we perceive small objects or slight impressions; by an *acuteness* of intellect, we discern nice distinctions.

3. Sharpness, or elevation of sound, in rhetoric or music.

4. In medicine, violence of a disease, which brings it speedily to a crisis.

Syn.—Sharpness, sagacity, penetration, keenness, shrewdness.

ȧ-çū′ti-, ȧ-çū′to-. Combining forms, from L. *acutus*, sharp.

ȧ-çū-ti-fō′li-āte, *a.* [*Acuti-*, and L. *folium*, leaf.] Having sharp-pointed leaves.

ȧ-çū-ti-lō′bāte, *a.* [*Acuti-*, and L. *lobus*, lobe.] In botany, having acute lobes; said of certain leaves.

-ȧcy, *suffix.* [L. *-acia.*] A combining form used in nouns denoting state, office, etc.; as, democ*racy*, cur*acy*.

ȧ-cyç′lic (*or* -sīk′), *a.* Without cycles, or whorls.

ac-y-rol′ō-gy, *n.* [L. *acyrologia*, from Gr. *akyrologia*; *a* priv., and *kyros*, authority, and *logos*, word.] Faulty diction.

ad-, *prefix.* [L. *ad*, to, unto, toward.] A combining form used in a great number of words of Latin origin, and in many others assimilated to the first letter of the word to which it is prefixed; thus, in *ac*claim, *af*firm, *al*ligation, *ap*prove, *ar*rive, *at*trition, etc., the *ac-*, *af-*, *al-*, *ap-*, *ar-*, *at-*, etc., are all modified forms of *ad-*. In *ascend*, *ascribe*, the *d* has been lost altogether.

Ad hominem; to the man; in logic, applied to an argument adapted to touch the prejudices of the person addressed.

Ad infinitum; to infinity; without limit.

Ad libitum; at pleasure; to any extent desired.

Ad valorem; according to the value; in commerce and finance, a term used to denote duties or charges laid upon goods, at a certain rate per cent upon their value, as stated in their invoices; in opposition to a specific sum upon a given quantity or number.

-ad, *suffix.* [Gr. *-as, -ad.*] A combining form signifying of or pertaining to, and found in words of Greek origin, as Il*iad*, dry*ad*, mon*ad*, etc.

-ad, *suffix.* [L. *ad*, to.] A combining form signifying toward; used especially in anatomical terms; as, dors*ad*, toward the back.

ad-açt′, *v.t.* To compel; to drive. [Obs.]

ȧ-daç′tyl, *n.* [Gr. *a* priv., and *daktylos*, a digit.] In zoölogy, a locomotive extremity without digits.

ȧ-daç′tyl-ism, *n.* The state of being without fingers or toes.

ȧ-daç′tyl-ous, *a.* Without fingers or toes; having no claws.

ad′āge, *n.* [Fr. *adage*; L. *adagium*, *adagio*, from *ad*, and *aio*, I say; Gr. *ēmi*, say; Sans. root *ah*, say.] A proverb; an old saying which has obtained credit by long use; a wise observation handed down from antiquity.

Syn.—Maxim, proverb, saw, saying, dictum, motto, aphorism, apothegm, byword, axiom.

ȧ-dā′gi-ăl, *a.* Proverbial.

ā-dä-giet′tō (-jet′), *a.* and *adv.* [It.] Not quite so slow as adagio.

ȧ-dä′giō (-jō), *n.* [It. *ad*, to, at, and *agio*, leisure.] In music, a slow movement; a piece of music to be performed in adagio; as, an *adagio* of Haydn.

ā-dä′giō, *a.* and *adv.* Slow, slowly; leisurely, and with grace. When repeated, *adagio, adagio*, it directs the movement to be very slow.

Ad′ăm, *n.* In Hebrew, Chaldee, Syriac, Ethiopic, Arabic, *man*; primarily, the name of the human species, mankind; appropriately, the first man, the progenitor of the human race. The word signifies form, shape, or suitable form; hence, species. It is used symbolically to mean original sin.

Adam's ale; water. [Colloq.]

Adam's apple; the thyroid cartilage, the prominent part of the throat, particularly in males; so called from the superstition that it was caused by the forbidden apple sticking in Adam's throat; also, a variety of the lime, *Citrus limetta*.

Adam's needle; the popular name of the *Yucca filamentosa*, or bear-grass.

ad′ȧ-mant, *n.* [OE. *adamaunt*; L. *adamas, adamantis*, the hardest metal, from Gr. *adamas, adamantos*; *a* priv., and *daman*, to subdue.] A stone imagined by some to be of impenetrable hardness; a name formerly given to the diamond and other substances of extreme hardness. The name has also been given to the lodestone. In modern mineralogy it has no technical signification, but it has a general figurative use, meaning indefinitely something very hard.

ad″ȧ-man-tē′ăn, *a.* Hard as adamant.

ad-ȧ-man′tine, *a.* 1. Made of adamant; having the qualities of adamant; that cannot be broken, dissolved, or penetrated; as, *adamantine* bonds, or chains.

2. Resembling the diamond in hardness or sparkling luster.

Adamantine spar; a variety of corundum, with gray, brown, or greenish shades.

ad-ȧ-man′toid, *n.* A hexoctahedron; a crystal bounded by forty-eight equal triangles.

ad-am-bū-lā′çrăl, *a.* [L. *ad*, to, and *ambulacrum*, a walk.] Next to the ambulacra.

A-dam′iç, A-dam′iç-ăl, *a.* Pertaining to Adam.

Adamic earth; a term applied to common red clay, through a mistaken idea that *Adam* means *red earth*.

Ad′ăm-īte, *n.* 1. A descendant of Adam; one of mankind.

2. [a—] A hydrous arsenate of zinc, named after Adam, a French mineralogist; called also *adamine*.

Ad′ăm-ītes, *n.pl.* In church history, a sect of visionaries, who pretended to establish a state of innocence, and, like Adam, went naked. They abhorred marriage, holding it to be the effect of sin.

Ad-ăm-it′iç, *a.* Pertaining to the Adamites.

ȧ-dănce′, *adv.* In a dancing manner.

ȧ-dan′gle, *adv.* In a dangling manner.

Ad-an-sō′ni-ȧ, *n.* [From M. *Adanson*, a French botanist who traveled in Senegal.] A genus of large low trees, of which *Adansonia digitata* is the African calabash-tree, or baobab-tree of Senegal. *Adansonia Gregorii*, the only other species, is the cream-of-tartar tree of North Australia.

ȧ-dapt′, *v.t.*; adapted, *pt.*, *pp.*; adapting, *ppr.* [L. *ad*, to, and *aptare*, to fit.]

1. To make suitable; to fit, or suit; as, to *adapt* an instrument to its uses; we have provisions *adapted* to our wants. It is applied to things material or immaterial.

2. Specifically, to remodel, work up, and render fit for representation on the stage, as a novel, or a play from a foreign language.

Syn.—Accommodate, adjust, suit, arrange, fit, conform.

ȧ-dapt-ȧ-bil′i-ty, *n.* The quality of being capable of adaptation.

ȧ-dapt′ȧ-ble, *a.* Capable of being adapted.

ȧ-dapt′ȧ-ble-ness, *n.* Suitableness; adaptability.

ad-ap-tā′tion, *n.* 1. The act of making suitable, or the state of being suitable, or fit; fitness.

2. That which is adapted; specifically, a play translated or constructed from a foreign language or a novel, and rendered suitable for representation; as, this comedy is a free *adaptation* from a French author.

ȧ-dapt′ȧ-tive, *a.* Adaptive.

ȧ-dapt′ed-ness, *n.* State of being adapted; suitableness.

ȧ-dapt′ẽr, *n.* 1. One who or that which adapts; specifically, one who translates, remodels, or works up, rendering fit to be represented on the stage, as a play from a foreign tongue or from a novel.

2. In chemistry, same as *Adopter*.

ȧ-dap′tion, *n.* Adaptation; the act of fitting. [Rare.]

ȧ-dapt′ive, *a.* Tending to adapt; suitable; pertaining to adaptation.

ȧ-dapt′ive-ly, *adv.* In an adaptive manner.

ȧ-dapt′ive-ness, *n.* The state or quality of being adaptive; suitableness.

ȧ-dapt′ly, *adv.* In a suitable or convenient manner. [Rare.]

ȧ-dapt′ness, *n.* The state of being fitted. [Obs.]

Ā′dăr, *n.* [Heb. *adār.*] A Hebrew month, answering to the latter part of February and the beginning of March, the twelfth of the sacred and sixth of the civil year.

ȧ-där′çē, *n.* [L. *adarce*, Gr. *adarkē*, salt found in marshes.] A saltish concretion on reeds and grass in marshy ground; especially noted in ancient Galatia. It is soft and porous, and was formerly used to cleanse the skin from various blemishes.

ad′ȧ-ti, ad′ȧ-tis, *n.* A muslin or kind of fine cotton cloth made in India.

ȧ-däunt′, *v.t.* To subdue. [Obs.]

ȧ-dąw′, *v.t.* To daunt; to subject. [Obs.]

ȧ-dąw′, *v.i.* To awake. [Obs.]

ȧ-dāyş′, *adv.* On or in days; used now only in the word now*adays*.

ad çap-tan′dum. [L. *ad*, to, and gerund of *captare*, to take.] For the purpose of catching; often applied as an adjective to specious attempts to catch popular favor or applause; as, *ad captandum* oratory.

Ad captandum vulgus; to please and catch the crowd.

add, *v.t.*; added, *pt.*, *pp.*; adding, *ppr.* [L. *addere*, from *ad*, to, and *dare*, to give.]

1. To set or put together, join, or unite, as one thing or sum to another, in an aggregate; as, *add* three to four; *add* this to your store.

2. To unite in idea or consideration; to subjoin; as, let me *add* this.

To add to; in Scripture, to give or bestow upon.—Gen. xxx. 24.

Syn.—Annex, adjoin, adduce.

add, *v.i.* 1. To be or serve as an addition; to be added; to augment; with *to*; as, the consciousness of folly often *adds to* one's regret.

2. To perform the arithmetical operation of addition; as, he *adds* very rapidly.

Syn.—Augment, increase, cast up, total, sum up.

add′ȧ-ble, *a.* See *Addible.*

ad′dax, *n.* A species of African antelope, *Hippotragus nasomaculatus*, and one of the largest of the genus, being of the size of a large ass, which it greatly resembles in shape. The horns of the male are about four feet long, twisted, and particularly magnificent.

Head of Addax (*Hippotragus nasomaculatus*).

ad-deem′, *v.t.* To award; to sentence. [Obs.]

ad-den′dum, *n.*; *pl.* **ad-den′dȧ.** [L. gerund of *addere*, to add, place.] Something to be added; an addition; an appendix.

Addendum circle; in mechanics, the circle which might be described around the outer ends of gear-teeth on a wheel, the length of the teeth being the *addendum*.

ad′dẽr, *n.* [ME. *adder, addre*, from *nadder, neddre*, confused with *a nadder*, an adder; AS. *nædre*; G *natter*; Ice. *nathra*, a snake.]

1. A venomous serpent of several species, belonging to the viper family The common European *adder*, *Pelias berus* or *Vipera communis*, attains a length of from two to three feet, and is the only venomous snake found in Great Britain. Its bite is rarely fatal to man.

2. Any one of several harmless American snakes, as the puffing *adder*, the milk *adder*, the spreading *adder*, etc.

3. A European fish; the sea-*adder*, or fifteen-spined stickleback.

add′ẽr, *n.* One who or that which adds; an adding machine.

ad′dẽr-bōlt, *n.* An English name for the dragon-fly

ad′dẽr-flȳ, *n.* The dragon-fly or *Libellula*; sometimes called *adder-bolt*.

ad′dẽr-pīke, *n.* The lesser weever, *Trachinus vipera*; also called *sting-fish*, *etter-pike*, etc.

ad′dẽr's-mēat, *n.* A name sometimes given to the English wake-robin or cuckoo-pint; also, the chickweed.

ad′dẽr's-mouth, *n.* A delicate North American orchid, *Microstylis ophioglossoides*.

ad′dẽr's-spēar, *n.* Same as *Adder's-tongue.*

ad′dẽr's-tongue (-tung), *n.* 1. A variety of fern, genus *Ophioglossum*, whose seeds are produced on a spike, supposed to resemble a serpent's tongue.

2. The dog's-tooth violet.

ad′dẽr-wŏrt, ad′dẽr's-wŏrt, *n.* Snakeweed, *Polygonum bistorta*, so named from its supposed virtue in curing the bite of serpents; called also *bistort*.

add-i-bil′i-ty, add-ȧ-bil′i-ty, *n.* The condition of being addible; the capability of being added.

add′i-ble, add′ȧ-ble, *a.* That may be added.

ad′dice, *n.* [Obs.] See *Adz.*

ad-diçt′, *v.t.*; addicted, *pt.*, *pp*; addicting, *ppr.* [L. *addictus*, pp. of *addere*, to devote, to deliver over.] To apply habitually; to devote or give up entirely; to habituate; to attach closely; generally with a reflexive pronoun, and sometimes in a good sense, but, as now used, generally in a bad sense; as, to *addict* oneself to intemperance, to gambling, or the like; and most frequently in the past participle; as, she was *addicted* to gossip.

To addict oneself to a person, formerly, to attach or devote oneself to a person; a sense borrowed from the Romans, who used the word (*addico*) for assigning debtors in servitude to their creditors.

Yours entirely *addicted*, madam.—B. Jonson.

ad-diçt′, *a.* Addicted. [Rare.]

If he be *addict* to vice,
Quickly him they will entice. —Shak.

ad-diçt′ed, *a.* Devoted by customary practice.

Syn.—Devoted, accustomed, prone, attached, habituated, disposed, inclined, abandoned, wedded.

ad-diçt′ed-ness, *n.* The quality or state of being addicted.

ad-diç′tion, *n.* 1. The act of devoting or giving up to in practice; the state of being devoted.

2. Among the Romans, a making over of goods to another by sale or legal sentence; also, an assignment of debtors in service to their creditors.

ad-dit′ȧ-ment, *n.* [L. *additamentum*, an increase.] An addition, or rather the thing added. [Rare.]

ad-di′tion (-dish′un), *n.* [L. *additio*, from *addere*; *ad*, to, and *dare*, to give.]

1. The act of adding; opposed to *subtraction*, or *diminution*; as, a sum is increased by *addition*.

2. Anything added, whether material or immaterial; an accession.

3. In arithmetic, the uniting of two or more numbers in one sum; also the rule or branch of arithmetic which treats of adding numbers.

4. In law, a title annexed to a man's name, to show his rank, occupation, or place of residence; as, Adam Brown, *Esq.*; John Jones, *electrician*; George Johnson *of Chicago*.

5. In music, a dot at the right side of a note, to lengthen its sound one-half.

6. In heraldry, something added to a coat of arms, as a mark of honor; opposed to *abatement*; as bordure, quarter, canton, gyron, pile, etc.

7. In popular language, an advantage, ornament, or improvement; anything added by way of improvement.

Syn.—Increase, accession, augmentation, annexation, superaddition, additament, increment, appendage, adjunct.

ad-di′tion-ăl, *a.* Supplemental; added; increased or increasing in any manner.

ad-di′tion-ăl-ly, *adv.* By way of addition.

ad-di′tion-ā-ry, *a.* Additional. [Rare.]

ad-di-ti′tious (-tish′us), *a.* Additive. [Rare.]

ad′di-tive, *a.* That may be added, or that is to be added; opposed to *subtractive*.

ad′di-tō-ry, *a.* Adding, or capable of adding; making an addition. [Rare.]

ad′dle (ad′l), *a.* [ME. *adel*; AS. *adela*, mud, filth.] Having lost the power of development; in a morbid state; putrid; applied to eggs. Hence, barren; producing nothing; muddled.

His brains grow *addle*. —Dryden.

ad′dle, *v.t.*; addled, *pt.*, *pp.*; addling, *ppr.* To make addle; to make corrupt or rotten.

ad′dle, *n.* 1. Mire; liquid manure. [Obs.]

2. Dregs; the dry lees of wine.

ad′dle-brained, *a.* Stupid; useless as to mentality; muddled.

ad′dled (ad′ld), *a.* Rotten, corrupt, putrid, or barren; as, an *addled* egg.

ad′dle-pāte, *n.* A stupid, muddled fellow. [Colloq.]

ad′dle-pā″ted, *a.* Addle-brained.

ad′dle-pā″ted-ness, *n.* Stupidity; denseness; obtuseness; silliness.

ad-dōom′, *v.t.* To adjudge. [Obs.]

ad-dorsed′, *a.* Same as *Adorsed*.

ad-dress′, *v.t.*; addressed, *pt.*, *pp.*; addressing, *ppr.* [ME. *addressen*; OFr. *adresser*, *addrescer*; from L. *ad*, to, and *directio*, from *dirigere*, to lay straight, to direct.]

1. To prepare; to make suitable dispositions for; to enter upon; as, he now *addressed* himself to the business.

2. To aim or direct (words); to pronounce, as a discourse.

3. To aim or direct; to throw or hurl. [Obs.]

4. To accost personally; to direct words to; to talk to; as, he *addressed* the judges; he *addressed* himself to the speaker.

5. To direct in writing, as a letter; or to direct and transmit; as, he *addressed* a letter to the governor

6. To present an address to, as a letter of thanks or congratulation, a petition, or a testimony of respect; as, the legislature *addressed* the president.

7. To court or approach as a lover.

8. In commerce, to consign or intrust to the care of another, as agent or factor; as, the ship was *addressed* to a merchant in Baltimore.

9. In golf, to assume position to strike (the ball).

Syn.—Approach, salute, hail, accost, apostrophize, greet, court, woo.

ad-dress′, *n.* 1. A speaking to; verbal application; a formal manner of speech; a discourse; as, the president made a short *address*.

2. A written or formal application; a message of respect, congratulation, thanks, petition, etc.; as, an *address* of thanks; an *address* to constituents.

3. Manner of speaking to another; as, a man of pleasing *address*.

4. Courtship; more generally in the plural, *addresses*; as, he makes or pays his *addresses* to a lady.

5. Skill; dexterity; skilful management; as, the envoy conducted the negotiation with *address*.

6. Direction of a letter, parcel, etc., including the name, title, and place of residence of the person for whom it is intended. Hence, these particulars are called a person's *address*.

Syn.—Direction, superscription, discourse, speech, harangue, oration, lecture, sermon, tact, skill, ability, ingenuity, adroitness.

ad-dress-ee′, *n.* One to whom anything is addressed, as a letter.

ad-dress′ẽr, *n.* One who addresses or petitions.

ad-dress′ing-mȧ-chïne″, *n.* A mechanical device for addressing envelopes and newspaper wrappers.

ad-dres′sion, *n.* The act of laying out one's route or course. [Obs.]

ad-dres′sō-gräph, *n.* A trade name for a machine which addresses letters, etc., printing each address separately from an embossed plate.

ad-dūce′, *v.t.*; adduced, *pt.*, *pp.*; adducing, *ppr.* [L. *adducere*, to lead or bring to; *ad*, to, and *ducere*, to lead.] To bring forward, present, or offer; to cite, name, or introduce; as, to *adduce* an authority or an argument.

Syn.—Advance, allege, assign, cite, quote, bring forward, urge, name, mention.

ad-dū′cent, *a.* Bringing forward, or together; applied to those muscles of the body which pull one part toward another. [See *Adductor*.]

ad-dū′cẽr, *n.* One who adduces.

ad-dū′ci-ble, *a.* Capable of being adduced.

ad-duct′, *v.t.* [L. *adductus*, pp. of *adducere*, to lead to.]

1. To draw toward something.

2. To draw on; to allure. [Obs.]

ad-duc′tion, *n.* 1. The act of bringing forward, as authority or evidence.

2. In anatomy, the action of the adducent muscles.

ad-duc′tive, *a.* Adducing; bringing forward.

ad-duc′tŏr, *n.* [L. *adducere*, to lead to.]

1. A muscle which draws one part of the body toward another; as, the *adductor* of the eye, which turns the eye toward the nose; the *adductor* of the thumb, which draws the thumb toward the fingers.

2. In zoölogy, one of the muscles which bring together the valves of the shell of the bivalve mollusks.

ad-dulce′, *v.t.* [Fr. *adoulcir*; L. *adulcir*, from *ad*, to, and *dulcis*, sweet.] To sweeten. [Obs.]

ȧ-deem′, *v.t.* A legal term signifying to revoke, as a legacy, substituting a gift.

ä-de-län-tä-dil′lō (-dēl′yō), *n.* [Sp.] A Spanish red wine, made of the earliest ripe grapes.

ä″de-län-tä′dō, *n.* [Sp.] Formerly, a Spanish title for a governor of a province; a lieutenant-governor; a commander.

ad-e-las′tẽr, *n.* [Gr. *adēlos*, not manifest, and *aster*, star.] In botany, a name proposed for those garden plants which have come into cultivation without their flowers being known, and have not therefore been referred to their genera.

ad′el-ing, *n.* See *Atheling*.

ȧd″ē-lō-cō-don′iç, *a.* [Gr. *a* priv., *dēlos*, manifest, and *kōdon*, bell.] Describing a gonophore having no umbrella developed.

ad″ē-lō-mor′phous, *a.* [Gr. *adēlos*, not manifest, and *morphē*, form.] Not easily seen; said of certain glandular cells.

ȧ-del′ō-pod, *n.* [Gr. *a* priv., *delos*, apparent, and *pous*, foot.] An animal whose feet are not apparent.

ȧ-del′phi-ȧ, *n.* [Gr. *adelphos*, brother.] A botanical term applied to a bunch or bundle of stamens; used of those plants in which the stamens, instead of growing singly, combine by the filaments into one or more parcels, or brotherhoods.

ȧ-del′phous, *a.* In botany, forming an adelphia or adelphias; uniting by the filaments into one or more parcels; said of stamens.

ȧ-dempt′, *a.* [L. *ademptus*, pp. of *adimere*, to take away.] Taken away. [Obs.]

ȧ-demp′tion, *n.* [L. *ademptio*, from *adimere*, to take away.] In civil law, the revocation of a grant, donation, or the like.

aden-, aden-i-, aden-o-, *prefix.* [Gr. *adēn*, gland.] A combining form, signifying connected with or affecting a gland.

ad-ē-nal′ġi-ȧ, ad-ē-nal′ġy, *n.* [*Aden-*, and Gr. *algos*, pain.] Pain in a gland.

ȧ-dē′ni-ȧ, *n.* Enlargement of the glands.

ȧ-den′i-fōrm, *a.* [*Adeni-*, and *-form*.] Shaped like a gland.

ad′ē-nine, *n.* A substance, $C_5H_5N_5$, obtained from glands.

ad-ē-ni′tis, *n.* Inflammation of the lymphatic glands.

ad″ē-nō-graph′iç, *a.* Pertaining to adenography

ad-ē-nog′rȧ-phy, *n.* [*Adeno-*, and Gr. *graphein*, to describe.] That part of descriptive anatomy which treats of the glands.

ad′ē-noid, ad-ē-noid′ăl, *a.* [*Aden-*, and Gr. *eidōs*, form.] In the form of a gland; glandiform.

ad″ē-nō-log′iç-ăl, *a.* Pertaining to the doctrine of the glands.

ad-ē-nol′ō-ġy, *n.* [*Adeno-*, and Gr. *logos*, discourse.] In anatomy, the doctrine of the glands, their nature, and their uses.

ad-ē-nō′mȧ, *n.* A glandular tumor.

ȧ-den′ō-phōre, *n.* The stalk of a nectar gland.

ad-ē-noph′ō-rous, *a.* [*Adeno-*, and Gr. *phoros*, from *pherein*, to bear.] In botany, gland-producing.

ad-ē-noph′yl-lous, *a.* [*Adeno-*, and Gr. *phyllon* leaf] Bearing glands upon the leaves.

ad′ē-nōse, ad′ē-nous, *a.* Pertaining to or resembling a gland.

ad″ē-nō-tom′iç, *a.* Relating to adenotomy.

ad-ē-not′ō-my, *n.* [*Adeno-*, and Gr. *tomē*, from *temnein*, to cut.] In anatomy and surgery, a cutting or incision of a gland.

ȧ-deph′ȧ-gous, *a.* [Gr. *adēphagos*, gluttonous.] Gluttonous; applied to certain voracious beetles.

ad′eps, *n.* [L.] Fat; animal oil; the contents of the cells of the adipose tissue.

ȧ-dept′, *n.* [L. *adeptus*, pp. of *adipisci*, to arrive at, from *ad*, to, and *apisci*, to pursue.] One fully skilled or well versed in any art; a proficient; a master. The term is borrowed from the alchemists, who applied it to one who pretended to have found the philosopher's stone or the panacea.

ȧ-dept′, *a.* Well skilled; completely versed or acquainted with.

Syn.—Expert, dexterous, skilful, versed in.

ȧ-dep′tion, *n.* [L. *adeptio*.] An obtaining; acquirement. [Obs.]

ȧ-dept′ist, *n.* An adept. [Obs.]

ȧ-dept′ness, *n.* Skill; the quality of being adept.

ad′ē-quȧ-cy, *n.* The state or quality of being equal to, proportionate, or sufficient; a sufficiency for a particular purpose; as, the *adequacy* of supply to demand.

ad′ē-quāte, *a.* [Formerly, *adæquate*, from L. *adæquatus*, pp. of *ad*, and *æquare*, to make equal.] Equal; proportionate; correspondent to; fully sufficient; as, we have no *adequate* ideas of infinite power.

ad′ē-quāte-ly, *adv.* In an adequate manner; in exact proportion; with just correspondence, representation, or proportion; in a degree equal to the object.

ad′ē-quāte-ness, *n.* The state of being adequate; justness of proportion or representation; sufficiency.

ad-ē-quā′tion, *n.* Adequateness; the making or being adequate; also, the resulting equivalence or equivalent. [Obs.]

ȧ-des′my, *n.* [Gr. *a* priv., and *desmos*, fetter. In botany, the separation of an organ usually entire, or of parts usually united.

Ad-es″sē-nā′ri-ăns, *n.pl.* [L. *adesse*, to be present.] In church history, a sect which held the real presence of Christ's body in the eucharist, but not by transubstantiation.

ad-fect′ed, *a.* In algebra, compounded; consisting of different powers of the unknown quantity. [See *Affected*.]

ad-fil′i-ā-ted, *a.* [Obs.] See *Affiliate*.

ad-fil-i-ā′tion, *n.* [Obs.] See *Affiliation*.

ad-flux′ion (-fluk′shun), *n.* See *Affluxion*.

ad-hā′mănt, *a.* [L. *adhamare*, to catch; from *ad*, to, and *hamus*, hook.] Holding tightly, as by hooks.

ad-hēre′, *v.i.*; adhered, *pt.*, *pp.*; adhering, *ppr.* [L. *adhærere*; *ad*, to, and *hærere*, to stick.]

1. To stick fast, as glutinous substances; to become joined by natural growth; as, the lungs sometimes *adhere* to the pleura; a stamp *adheres* to an envelope.

2. To be joined, or held in contact; to cleave.

3. Figuratively, to hold to, be attached, or remain fixed, either by personal union or conformity of faith, principle, or opinion; as, men *adhere* to a party, a leader, a church, or a creed.

4. To be consistent; to hold together as the parts of a system.

Syn.—Attach, cling, stick, cleave, fasten, unite, join.

ad-hēr′ence, *n.* 1. The quality or state of sticking or adhering; the state of being adherent.

2. Figuratively, a being fixed in attachment; fidelity; steady attachment; as, an *adherence* to a party or opinions.

ad-hēr′en-cy, *n.* Adherence. [Rare.]

ad-hēr′ent, *a.* 1. Sticking; uniting, as glue or wax.

2. In botany, attached; used of parts that are nominally separate; as, an *adherent* ovary, an ovary attached or united by its whole surface to the tube of the calyx.

3. In logic and metaphysics, accidentally connected with; not belonging to the nature of a thing; not inherent in; as, if a cloth is wet, its wetness is a quality *adherent* to, not inherent in, it.

ad-hēr′ent, *n.* A person who adheres; one who follows a leader, party, or profession; a follower, or partisan; a believer in a particular faith or church.

Syn.—Follower, partisan, supporter, friend, aid, ally, companion, backer.

ad-hēr′ent-ly, *adv.* In an adherent manner.

ad-hēr′ẽr, *n.* One who adheres; an adherent.

ad-hē′ṣion, *n.* [Fr. *adhesion*; L. *adhæsio*, from *ad*, to, and *hærere*, to stick.]

1. The act or state of sticking, or being

united and attached to; as, the *adhesion* of glue, or of parts united by growth, cement, and the like. *Adhesion* is generally used in a literal, *adherence* in a metaphorical, sense.

2. Adherence; union; steady attachment; firmness in opinion; as, *adhesion* to vice; *adhesion* to party or principles.

3. In physics, the force by which bodies of different kinds adhere when united, as distinguished from *cohesion*, which unites the particles of homogeneous bodies; molecular attraction.

4. In medicine, the reunion of divided parts by adhesive inflammation.

5. In botany, the union of parts or organs nominally separate.

6. Agreement to adhere in loyal union; assent; concurrence.

ad-hē′sive, *a.* Sticky; tenacious, as glutinous substances; apt or tending to adhere.

Adhesive inflammation; in medicine, that kind of inflammation which causes union by adhesion, or union by first intention, without suppuration.

Adhesive plaster; sticking plaster; used especially for uniting the lips of wounds, and made of litharge, resin, etc.

Adhesive slate; a variety of slaty clay, adhering strongly to the tongue, and rapidly absorbing water.

ad-hē′sive-ly, *adv.* In an adhesive manner.

ad-hē′sive-ness, *n.* 1. The quality of sticking or adhering; stickiness; tenacity.

2. In phrenology, an organ, or supposed organ, whose function it is to promote attachment to objects, animate or inanimate, lasting friendships, social intercourse, etc.

ad-hib′it, *v.t.* [L. *adhibere*; *ad*, to, and *habere*, to have.] To use or apply; to affix or fasten, as a label. [Rare.]

ad-hi-bi′tion (-bish′un), *n.* Application; use.

ad-hort′, *v.t.* To advise; to exhort. [Obs.]

ad-hor-tā′tion, *n.* [L. *adhortatio*, advice.] Advice. [Obs.]

ad-hor′tā-tō-ry, *a.* [L. *adhortari*, to advise.] Advisory; containing counsel or warning. [Obs.]

ad″i-ȧ-bat′ic, *a.* [Gr. *adiabatos*, not able to go through, from *a* priv., *dia*, through, and *bainein*, to go.] In thermodynamics, the term applied to a line which exhibits the variations of pressure and volume of a fluid when it expands without either receiving or giving out heat.

ad″i-ȧ-bat′ic-ăl-ly, *adv.* In an adiabatic manner.

ad″i-ac-tin′ic, *a.* [Gr. *a* priv., *dia*, through, and *aktis*, a ray.] Impervious to the actinic rays of light.

Ad-i-an′tum, *n.* A large genus of ferns, including the common maidenhair ferns.

ad″i-aph″ō-rē′sis, *n.* Lack of perspiration.

ad-i-aph′ō-rism, *n.* Indifference to religion.

Ad-i-aph′ō-rist, *n.* [Gr. *adiaphoros*, from *a* priv., *dia*, through, and *pherein*, to bear.] A moderate or indifferent person; specifically, a name given in the sixteenth century to certain followers of Melanchthon, who held some opinions and ceremonies to be indifferent which Luther condemned as sinful or heretical.

ad″i-aph″ō-ris′tic, *a.* Pertaining to adiaphorism.

Ad-i-aph′ō-rīte, *n.* Same as *Adiaphorist*.

ad-i-aph′ō-ron, *n.* An indifferent moral or religious principle.

ad-i-aph′ō-rous, *a.* 1. Indifferent; neutral.

2. A term applied to medicines which will do neither harm nor good.

ad″i-ȧ-thĕr′măn-cy, *n.* [Gr. *a* priv., *dia*, through, and *thermē*, heat.] Imperviousness to radiant heat.

ad″i-ȧ-thĕr′mic, *a.* Impervious to radiant heat.

ad″i-ȧ-thet′ic, *a.* [Gr. *a* priv., *diathesis*, from *diatithenai*, to place separately.] Not chargeable or due to diathesis, or constitutional predisposition.

A-dic′ē-ȧ, *n.* A genus of plants, of the nettle family, but without nettles; also called *Pilea.*

ȧ-dieū′, *interj.* [OE. *adew*; OFr. *à Dieu*; L. *ad*, to, and *Deum*, acc. of *Deus*, God.] Farewell; an expression of kind wishes at the parting of friends.

ȧ-dieū′, *n.*; *pl.* **ȧ-dieūs′** *or* **ȧ-dieūx′** (-dūz′). A farewell, or commendation to the care of God; as, an everlasting *adieu*.

Syn.—Good-by, farewell, valediction, valedictory.

ȧ-dīght′ (-dīt′), *v.t.* To put in order; to dress; to equip. [Obs.]

ä-di-ōs′, *interj.* [Sp.] Adieu; farewell; good-by; used in southwestern United States.

ad-i-pes′cent, *a.* [L. *adeps* (*adip*), fat, and *-escent*.] Growing fatty.

ȧ-dip′ic, *a.* [L. *adeps*, fat.] Pertaining to or derived from fat; as, *adipic* acid.

ad-i-poc′ĕr-āte, *v.t.* To convert into adipocere.

ad″i-poc″ĕr-ā′tion, *n.* The act or process of being changed into adipocere.

ad′i-pō-cēre″, *n.* [Fr. *adipocire*; L. *adeps* (*adip*), and *cera*, wax.] A soft, unctuous, or waxy substance of a light brown color, into which the muscular fibers of dead animal bodies are converted by long immersion in water or spirit, or by burial in moist places. It is speedily produced when the body is immersed in running water.

Adipocere mineral; a fatty substance found in certain iron ores and peat-mosses.

ad″i-pō-cēr′i-form, *a.* Resembling adipocere.

ad-i-poc′ĕr-ous, *a.* Pertaining to or of the nature of adipocere.

ad-i-poḡ′e-nous, *a.* [L. *adeps*, *adipis*, fat, and *genous*, producing.] Capable of producing fat.

ad″i-pō-lyt′ic, *a.* [L. *adeps*, fat, and Gr. *lytikos*, able to loose, from *lyein*, to loose.] Effecting the digestion of fats.

ad-i-pō′mȧ, *n.* A fatty tumor; lipoma.

ad-i-pom′ȧ-tous, *a.* Composed mostly of fatty tissue, as a tumor.

ad′i-pōse, *a.* [L. *adiposus*, fatty, from *adeps*, fat.] Fatty; consisting of, partaking of the character of, or resembling, fat.

Adipose arteries; the branches of the diaphragmatic, capsular, and renal arteries which nourish the fat around the kidneys.

Adipose fin; in zoölogy, a soft fatty dorsal fin.

Adipose substance; animal fat.

Adipose tissue; an aggregation of minute cells (*adipose cells* or *vesicles*), which draw fat or oily matter from the blood, dispersed in the interstices of common areolar tissue, or forming distinct masses. *Adipose tissue* underlies the skin, surrounds the large vessels and nerves, invests the kidneys, etc. It sometimes accumulates in large quantities, and forms swellings, which are called in pathology adipose tumors.

ad′i-pōse, *n.* Fat in general; specifically, the fat on the kidneys.

ad′i-pōse-ness, *n.* The state of being adipose.

ad-i-pos′i-ty, *n.* Adiposeness.

ad′i-pous, *a.* Fat; of the nature of fat; adipose.

ȧ-dip′si-ȧ, ad′ip-sy, *n.* [Gr. *a* priv., and *dipsa*, thirst.] A total absence of thirst.

ȧ-dip′sous, *a.* Thirst-quenching, as certain fruits.

ad′it, *n.* [L. *aditus*, pp. of *adire*, to approach; *ad*, and *ire*, to go.] An entrance or passage; specifically, in mining, the more or less horizontal opening giving access to the shaft of a mine, or by which water and ores can be carried away. The word is sometimes used for air-shaft, but not with strict propriety. In the specific sense called also the *drift* or *tunnel*.

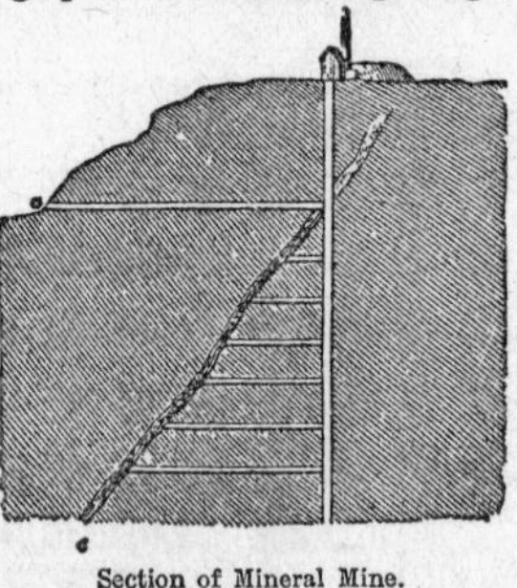

Section of Mineral Mine. *a*, Adit. *c*, Vein.

ad-jā′cence, *n.* The state of being adjacent; adjacency.

ad-jā′cen-cy, *n.* The state of lying close or contiguous; a bordering upon or lying next to; as, the *adjacency* of lands or buildings.

ad-jā′cent, *a.* [L. *adjacens*, ppr. of *adjacere*, to lie near.] Lying near, close, or contiguous; bordering upon; as, a field *adjacent* to the highway.

Syn.—Adjoining, approximating, contiguous, nigh, bordering, close to, near to, abutting.

ad-jā′cent, *n.* That which is next to or contiguous. [Rare.]

ad-jā′cent-ly, *adv.* So as to be adjacent.

ad-ject′, *v.t.* [L. *adjectus*, pp. of *adjicere*, to throw to; *ad*, to, and *jacere*, to throw.] To add or put, as one thing to another. [Rare.]

ad-jec′tion, *n.* The act of adding, or thing added. [Rare.]

ad-jec-ti′tious (-tish′us), *a.* Added. [Rare.]

ad-jec-ti′văl (*or* ad′jec-tiv-ăl), *a.* Pertaining to an adjective.

ad-jec-ti′văl-ly, *adv.* By way of or as an adjective.

ad′jec-tive, *n.* [L. *adjectivus*, a grammatical term, from *adjectus*, pp. of *adjicere*, to add to.] In grammar, a word used with a noun, or a word or phrase used as a noun, to express a quality of the thing named, or something attributed to it, or to limit or define it, or to specify or describe a thing, as distinct from something else. It is called also an *attributive* or *attribute*. Thus, in the phrase, a *wise* ruler, *wise* is the *adjective*, or attribute, expressing a particular quality of *ruler*.

ad′jec-tive, *a.* 1. Pertaining to an adjective; as, the *adjective* use of a noun.

2. Adjunctive; additional. [Rare.]

Adjective color; a color which requires to be fixed by some mordant or base to render it permanent.

ad′jec-tive, *v.t.* To make an adjective of (a word). [Rare.]

ad′jec-tive-ly, *adv.* In the manner of an adjective; as, a word is used *adjectively*.

ad-join′, *v.t.*; adjoined, *pt.*, *pp.*; adjoining, *ppr.* [ME. *ajoinen*; Fr. *ajoindre*; L. *adjungere*; *ad*, to, and *jungere*, to join.] To join or add; to put in addition; to unite; to annex or append.

ad-join′, *v.i.* To lie or be next to, or in contact; to be contiguous; as, a farm *adjoining* to the highway. This is the common use of the word, *to* being usually omitted; as, *adjoining* the highway; my house *adjoins* the church.

ad-join′ănt, *a.* Contiguous to. [Obs.]

ad-join′ing, *a.* Joining to; adjacent; contiguous.

ad-joint′, *n.* One joined with another in company or an enterprise. [Rare.]

ad-journ′ (-jŭrn′), *v.t.*; adjourned, *pt.*, *pp.*; adjourning, *ppr.* [ME. *ajournen*; Fr. *ajourner*; L. *adjurnare*, to fix a day, from *a* (L. *ad*) and *diurnus*, belonging to a day.] Literally, to put off, or defer to another day; but generally used to denote a formal intermission of business, a putting off to any future meeting of the same body; as, the court *adjourned* the consideration of the question.

Syn.—Suspend, defer, postpone, put off.

ad-journ′, *v.i.* To suspend business for a time, as from one day to another, or for a longer period; usually public business, as of legislatures and courts, for repose or refreshment.

ad-journ′ăl, *n.* Same as *Adjournment*. [Rare.]

ad-journ′ment, *n.* 1. The act of adjourning, as in legislatures.

2. The putting off till another day or time specified, or without day; as, the *adjournment* of a debate.

3. The time or interval during which a public body defers business; but a suspension of business, between the forming of a house and an *adjournment*, is called a recess.

In Great Britain, the close of a session of parliament is called a prorogation; and the close of a parliament is a dissolution. But in Great Britain, as in the United States, *adjournment* is used for an intermission of business for any indefinite time; as, an *adjournment* of parliament for six weeks.

ad-judge′, *v.t.*; adjudged, *pt.*, *pp.*; adjudging, *ppr.* [ME. *adjugen*; Fr. *adjuger*; L. *adjudicare*; *ad*, to, and *judicare*, to judge, decide.]

1. To decide, or determine, in the case of a controverted question; to decree by a judicial opinion; used appropriately of courts of law and equity; as, a criminal was *adjudged* to suffer death; he was *adjudged* the victor.

2. To pass sentence on; to sentence or condemn; as, rebel spirits *adjudged* to hell.

3. To deem; to judge; as, he *adjudged* him unworthy of his friendship.

Syn.—Decree, award, assign, decide, determine, settle, adjudicate.

ad-judg′ĕr, *n.* One who adjudges.

ad-judg′ment, *n.* The act of judging; sentence.

ad-jū′di-cāte, *v.t.*; adjudicated, *pt.*, *pp.*; adjudicating, *ppr.* [L. *adjudicatus*, pp. of *adjudicare*; *ad*, to, and *judicare*, to judge.] To adjudge; to try and determine, as a court.

ad-jū′di-cāte, *v.i.* To try and determine upon judicially; as, the court *adjudicated* upon the case.

ad-jū-di-cā′tion, *n.* 1. The act of adjudicating; the act or process of trying and determining judicially; as, a ship was taken and sent into port for *adjudication*.

2. A judicial sentence; judgment or decision of a court.

3. Specifically, in law, the act of a court declaring a person bankrupt.

4. In Scots law, an action by which a creditor attaches the estate of his debtor, in payment or security of his debt.

ad-jū′di-cā-tive, *a.* Adjudicating.

ad-jū′di-cā-tŏr, *n.* A person who adjudicates.

ad-jū′di-cā-tūre″, *n.* An adjudication.

ad′jū-gāte, *v.t.* To yoke to. [Obs.]

ad′junct, *n.* [L. *adjunctus*, pp. of *adjungere*; *ad*, to, and *jungere*, to join.]

1. Something added to another, but not essentially a part of it; as, water absorbed by a sponge is its *adjunct*.

2. In metaphysics, a quality of the body or the mind, whether natural or acquired; as color, in the body; thinking, in the mind.

3. In grammar, words added to illustrate or amplify the force of other words; as, the history *of the American Revolution*; the words in italics are the *adjuncts* of *history*.

4. An associate or assistant in work or duty to be done.

5. In music, a relative scale or key; an attendant key.

Syn.—Appurtenance, attribute, addition, complement, help.

ad′junct, *a.* Added to or united with; joined

in office or in action of any kind; as, an *adjunct* professor.

ad-junc′tion, *n.* The act of joining; the thing joined.

ad-junc′tive, *a.* Joining; having the quality of joining.

ad-junc′tive, *n.* That which is joined.

ad-junc′tive-ly, *adv.* In an adjunctive manner.

ad-junct′ly, *adv.* In connection with; consequently.

ad-jū-rā′tion, *n.* 1. The act of adjuring; a solemn charging on oath, or under the penalty of a curse.

2. The form of oath.

ad-jū′rȧ-tō-ry, *a.* Containing an adjuration.

ad-jūre′, *v.t.*; adjured, *pt., pp.*; adjuring, *ppr.* [ME. *adjuren*; L. *adjurare*; *ad*, to, and *jurare*, to swear.]

1. To charge, bind, or command on oath, or under the penalty of a curse; as, Joshua *adjured* the children of Israel.

2. To charge earnestly and solemnly; to charge, urge, or summon impressively; as, the mayor *adjured* the people to keep the peace.

I *adjure* thee by the living God.—Matt. xxvi.

ad-jūr′ēr, *n.* One who adjures; one who exacts an oath.

ad-just′, *v.t.*; adjusted, *pt., pp.*; adjusting, *ppr.* [Fr. *adjuster*, to join fitly or dispose in an orderly manner; L. *adjuxtare*, to put side by side; *ad*, and *juxta*, near. Confused with L. *adjustus*.]

1. To make exact; to fit; to make correspondent, or conformable; generally with *to* before the remoter object; as, to *adjust* a garment *to* the body, or things *to* a standard.

2. To put in order; to regulate or reduce to system.

3. To make accurate; to settle or bring to a satisfactory state, so that parties are agreed in the result; as, to *adjust* accounts; specifically, in insurance losses, to settle or agree upon the amount of loss and the indemnity to be paid.

Syn.—Accommodate, adapt, settle, conform, regulate, classify, arrange, fit, suit.

ad-just′ȧ-ble, *a.* That may or can be adjusted.

ad-just′ēr, *n.* One who or that which adjusts; specifically, one whose business it is to adjust differences, grievances, or claims; most frequently, one who adjusts insurance claims.

ad-just′ive, *a.* Tending to regulate.

ad-just′ment, *n.* 1. The act of adjusting; regulation; a reducing to just form or order; a making fit or conformable; settlement.

2. The arrangement of the different parts of an instrument into their proper places; as, the microscope is out of *adjustment*.

3. In insurance, the settling of the amount of indemnity which the party insured is entitled to receive under the policy after all proper allowances and deductions have been made, and, in marine insurance, fixing the proportion of that indemnity which each underwriter is liable to bear.

Syn.—Arrangement, regulation, settlement, adaptation, disposal, disposition.

ad′jū-tāge, *n.* Same as *Ajutage*.

ad′jū-tăn-cy, *n.* The office or rank of an adjutant; skilful arrangement; assistance.

ad′jū-tănt, *n.* [L. *adjutans*, ppr. of *adjutare*, freq. of *adjuvare*, to help, assist.]

1. In military affairs, an officer whose duty is to assist the commanding officer of a regiment or garrison by receiving and communicating orders. The *adjutant* has to make known the orders of his chief, to receive reports intended for him, to see that proper discipline is kept up, and to regulate the rotation of duty among the different portions of the body of troops with which he is connected.

2. A helper; an assistant; an aid. [Rare.]

A fine violin must be the best *adjutant* to a fine voice. —W. Mason.

3. The adjutant-bird.

ad′jū-tănt-bird, *n.* [So called on account of its stiff figure in walking.] A very large grallatorial bird, *Ciconia argala*, allied to the storks; a native of the warmer parts of India. It is one of the most voracious carnivorous birds known, and in India, from its devouring all sorts of carrion and noxious animals, is protected by law. Called also the *gigantic crane*.

Adjutant-bird (*Ciconia argala*).

ad′jū-tănt-crāne, *n.* The adjutant-bird.

ad′jū-tănt-gen′ēr-ăl, *n.* In military affairs, a staff officer, the chief aid to a commanding general in the execution of the duties of his office. He superintends the details of all the dispositions ordered by the commander-in-chief, communicates general orders, and receives and registers the reports of the state of each separate command as to numbers, discipline, equipments, etc. In the United States army he is at the head of the most important bureau of the war department. Each state also has its *adjutant-general*, who superintends the details of management of the state militia.

ad-jū′tŏr, *n.* [L., from *adjuvare*, to assist.] A helper. [Rare.]

ad-jū′tō-ry, *a.* Aiding. [Obs.]

ad-jū′trix, *n.* [L., f. of *adjutor*.] A female assistant. [Rare.]

ad′jū-vănt, *a.* [L., ppr. of *adjuvare*, to assist.] Helping; assisting.

ad′jū-vănt, *n.* An assistant; in medicine, a substance added to a prescription, to aid the operation of the principal ingredient.

ad-lē-gā′tion, *n.* [L. *adlegatio*, from *adlegare*; *ad*, to, in addition to, and *legare*, to send on an embassy.] In the law of the old German empire, a right claimed by the states of joining their own ministers with those of the emperor, in public treaties and negotiations relating to the common interests of the empire.

ad-lō-cū′tion, *n.* See *Allocution*.

ad-mär′gin-āte, *v.t.* [L. *ad*, to, and *margo*, margin, and *-ate*.] To make marginal notes on. [Rare.]

ad-max′il-lā-ry, *a.* Connected with the jawbone. [See *Maxilla*.]

ad-meas′ūre (ad-mezh′ūr), *v.t.* [ME. *amesuren*; OFr. *admesurer*; L. *admensurare*, from *ad*, to, and *metiri*, to measure.]

1. To measure or ascertain dimensions, size, or capacity; to measure.

2. In law, formerly, to apportion; to assign to each claimant his right; as, to *admeasure* dower or common of pasture. —Blackstone.

ad-meas′ūre-ment, *n.* 1. The measuring of dimensions by a rule, as of a ship, cask, and the like; measurement; mensuration.

2. The measure of a thing, or dimensions ascertained.

3. In law, formerly, the adjustment of proportion, or ascertainment of shares, as of dower or pasture held in common. This was done by writ of *admeasurement*, directed to the sheriff. —Blackstone.

ad-meas′ūr-ēr, *n.* One who admeasures.

ad-men-sū-rā′tion, *n.* [Rare.] See *Mensuration*.

ad-min′i-cle, *n.* [L. *adminiculum*, support; originally, a support for the hand; *ad*, to, and *manus*, hand, with dim. ending *-culum*.]

1. Help; support; an auxiliary.

2. In law, corroborative or explanatory proof. In Scots law, any writing helpful in establishing the existence or terms of a lost deed.

3. In medicine, anything that helps the action of a remedy.

ad-mi-nic′ū-lăr, *a.* Supplying help; helpful.

ad-mi-nic′ū-lā-ry, *a.* Adminicular.

ad-mi-nic′ū-lāte, *v.t.* In Scots law, to reproduce a lost legal document by written evidence.

ad-min′is-tēr, *v.t.*; administered, *pt., pp.*; administering, *ppr.* [OE. *aministren*; Fr. *administrer*; L. *administrare*; *ad*, to, and *ministrare*, to serve.]

1. To have charge of as chief agent in managing public affairs, under laws or a constitution, as a president, king, or other supreme officer. It is used of absolute monarchs, but is more strictly applicable to constitutional officers. A president or king *administers* the laws when he executes them, or carries them into effect. A judge *administers* the laws when he applies them to particular cases or persons. In short, to *administer* is to direct the execution or application of laws.

2. To dispense; as, to *administer* justice, or the sacraments.

3. To afford; to give or furnish; as, to *administer* relief, that is, to act as the agent; to *administer* medicine, that is, to direct and cause it to be taken.

4. To give, as an oath.

5. In law, (a) to manage (an estate) of one who has died intestate, or without a competent executor; (b) to manage (an estate) of a deceased person as an executor.

Syn.—Manage, conduct, minister, furnish, afford, supply, dispense, distribute, direct, discharge, control, execute, superintend.

ad-min′is-tēr, *v.i.* 1. To contribute; to bring aid or supplies; to add something; as, a shade *administers* to our comfort.

2. To perform the office of administrator; as, A *administers* upon the estate of B.

ad-min-is-tē′ri-ăl, *a.* Pertaining to administration, or to the executive part of government.

ad-min′is-trȧ-ble, *a.* Capable of being administered.

ad-min′is-trănt, *n.* and *a.* I. *n.* A person who administers.

II. *a.* Managing; governing; executive.

ad-min′is-trāte, *v.t.* [L. *administratus*, pp. of *administrare*; *ad*, to, and *ministrare*, to serve.] To administer; to supply. [Rare.]

ad-min-is-trā′tion, *n.* 1. The act of administering; direction; management; government of public affairs; the conducting of any office or employment.

2. The executive part of government, consisting in the exercise of the constitutional and legal powers, the general superintendence of national affairs, and the enforcement of laws.

3. The persons collectively who are intrusted with the execution of laws, and the superintendence of public affairs, as the president and cabinet; or the council alone, as in Great Britain.

4. Dispensation; distribution; exhibition; as, the *administration* of justice, of the sacrament, or of grace.

5. The management of the estate of an intestate person, under a commission from the proper authority. This management consists in collecting debts, paying debts and legacies, and distributing the property among the heirs. Also, the management of a deceased person's estate by an executor under a will.

6. The power, office, or commission of an administrator.

7. The term or period during which an administrative official holds office; as, the war with Spain occurred during President McKinley's *administration*.

8. The act of prescribing medically.

9. The act of tendering, as an oath.

Administration with the will annexed; administration granted in cases where a testator makes a will without naming executors, or where the executors named in the will are incapable of acting or refuse to act.

Letters of administration; the commission from a court of probate, or other proper authority, under which an administrator proceeds.

ad-min′is-trā-tive, *a.* Pertaining to administration; executive; as, *administrative* ability.

ad-min′is-trā-tive-ly, *adv.* In an administrative manner.

ad-min′is-trā″tŏr, *n.* 1. One who, by virtue of a commission from a surrogate, court of probate, or other proper authority, has charge of the goods and estate of one dying without a will.

2. One who administers, or who executes, directs, manages, distributes, or dispenses laws and rites, either in civil, political, judicial, or ecclesiastical affairs.

ad-min′is-trā-tŏr-ship, *n.* The office of an administrator.

ad-min′is-trā-trix, *n.* A woman who administers the estate of an intestate; also, a woman who administers government.

ad″mi-rȧ-bil′i-ty, *n.* Admirableness. [Rare.]

ad′mi-rȧ-ble, *a.* [L. *admirabilis*, from *admirari*; *ad*, to, at, and *mirari*, to wonder.]

1. Worthy of admiration; having qualities to excite wonder, with approbation, esteem, reverence, or affection most excellent; used of persons or things; as, an *admirable* work of art; an *admirable* teacher.

What a piece of work is a man! How noble in reason! How infinite in faculty! In form and moving, how express and *admirable*! —Shak.

2. Causing wonder; strange; amazing. [Obs.]

Syn.—Wonderful, excellent, astonishing, surprising, pleasing, worthy, choice.

ad′mi-rȧ-bly, *adv.* In an admirable manner.

ad′mi-răl, *n.* [ME. *admiral*, *admiralle*; OFr. *admiral*; L. *admiralis*, properly *amiralis*. (The *ad* is a wrong spelling, due to associating the word with *admirabilis*.) From Ar. *amir*, *emir*, a ruler, commander.]

1. A naval commander-in-chief; the commander of a navy or of a fleet; the highest naval rank. In the United States navy the rank, vacant since 1891, was revived in 1898 by the appointment of Admiral Dewey. The rank of *vice-admiral*, existing in the British navy, became extinct in the United States navy in 1890. The next rank is that of *rear-admiral*, and is usually held by an officer in command of a fleet or of a navy-yard, etc. He ranks next above the captains.

2. The commander of any single fleet, or, in general, any flag-officer.

3. The ship which carries the admiral; also the most considerable ship of a fleet of merchantmen, of yachts, or of fishing-vessels.

4. A name given to two species of butterflies: *Vanessa atalanta*, or red admiral, and *Limenitis camilla*, or white admiral.

Lord high admiral; in Great Britain, an officer who (when this rare dignity is conferred) is at the head of the naval administration. There have been few high admirals since 1632, when the office was first put in commission.

ad′mi-răl-ship, *n.* The office of an admiral; the superior seamanship or naval skill of an admiral.

ad'mi-răl-ty, *n.* 1. The office, functions, or jurisdiction of an admiral.

2. The branch of jurisprudence which takes cognizance of maritime causes; as, a suit in *admiralty*; an *admiralty* court.

3. [A—] In Great Britain, the board of commissioners appointed for the administration of naval affairs; the lords of the *Admiralty*; they are five in number, including a civil lord.

Admiralty court, or *court of admiralty*; a court for the trial of causes arising on the high seas, as suits for damage by collision, and the like. In the United States, there is no admiralty court distinct from others; but the federal district courts, established in the several states by congress, are invested with admiralty powers.

ad-mi-rā'tion, *n.* [L. *admiratio*, from *admirari*, to admire.]

1. Wonder mingled with pleasing emotions, as approbation, esteem, love, or veneration; a compound emotion excited by something novel, rare, great, or excellent; applied to persons and their works; it often includes a degree of surprise; as, we view the solar system with *admiration*.

2. Wonder with disapprobation. [Rare.]

Your boldness I with *admiration* see. —Dryden.

3. That which is admired; as, the picture is the *admiration* of all beholders.

Note of admiration; the exclamation point (!).

Syn.—Amazement, surprise, astonishment, wonder, approval, adoration, reverence, worship.

ad-mi'rā-tive, *a.* Pertaining to admiration. [Rare.]

ad-mire', *v.t.*; admired, *pt.*, *pp.*; admiring, *ppr.* [L. *admirari*; *ad*, at, and *mirari*, to wonder; Fr. *admirer*; It. *ammirare*.]

1. To regard with wonder or delighted surprise, mingled with approbation, esteem, reverence, or affection; to feel admiration for; to look on or contemplate with pleasure; as, to *admire* virtue; to *admire* a landscape or a statue; to *admire* a woman.

2. To approve or esteem, in an ironical sense; a frequent modern usage; as, one is forced to *admire* the stupidity of the ass.

3. To wonder at; to regard with wonder. [Obs.]

Syn.—Approve, commend, applaud, esteem, adore, respect, revere, love, praise.

ad-mire', *v.i.* 1. To be surprised; to marvel; to wonder; often followed with *at*; as, he *admired at* his own contrivance. [Rare.]

2. To feel trivial or superficial pleasure; as, I should *admire* to go with you; a rural colloquial use of the word.

ad-mired', *a.* 1. Regarded with admiration; as, a greatly *admired* novel.

2. Wonderful. [Obs.]

ad-mir'ēr, *n.* One who admires; one who esteems or loves greatly.

ad-mir'ing-ly, *adv.* With admiration; in the manner of an admirer.

ad-mis-si-bil'i-ty, *n.* The quality of being admissible.

ad-mis'si-ble, *a.* That may be admitted, allowed, or conceded; as, the testimony is *admissible*.

ad-mis'si-ble-ness, *n.* Admissibility.

ad-mis'si-bly, *adv.* So as to be admitted; in an admissible manner.

ad-mis'sion, *n.* [ME. *admyssion*; L. *admissio(n)*, from *admissus*, pp. of *admittere*, to admit.]

1. The act or practice of admitting; as, the *admission* of aliens into our country; also, the state of being admitted.

2. Admittance; power or permission to enter; entrance; access; power to approach; as, our laws give to foreigners easy *admission* to the rights of citizens; the free *admission* of air.

3. Allowance; grant of an argument or position not fully proved.

4. Confession; acknowledgment; concession; as, an *admission* of guilt.

5. A fee or price charged for entrance; as, the *admission* is fifty cents.

6. In law, an essential fact or matter, the necessity of proving which is removed by the opposite party admitting it. *Admissions* are either upon the record or by agreement between the parties to a suit.

Syn. — Access, admittance, approach, entrance, confession, acknowledgment.

ad-mis'sive, *a.* Admitting; implying admission.

ad-mis'sō-ry, *a.* Pertaining to admission.

ad-mit', *v.t.*; admitted, *pt.*, *pp.*; admitting, *ppr.* [ME. *admitten*; L. *admittere*; *ad*, to, and *mittere*, to send.]

1. To suffer to enter; to grant entrance, whether into a place or an office, or into the mind or consideration; as, to *admit* a student into college, or an attorney to the bar; to *admit* a serious thought into the mind.

2. To give right of entrance; as, a ticket *admits* one to a theater.

3. To allow; to receive as true; to concede; to acknowledge; as, the argument or fact is *admitted*.

4. To permit, grant, or allow, or to be capable of; as, the words do not *admit* of such a construction. In this sense, *of* may be used after the verb, or omitted.

Syn.—Acknowledge, allow, assent, grant, concede, own.

ad-mit'tá-ble, *a.* That may be admitted or allowed.

ad-mit'tănce, *n.* 1. The act of admitting.

2. Permission to enter; the power or right of entrance; hence, actual entrance; as, he gained *admittance* into the church.

3. Concession; admission; allowance; as, the *admittance* of an argument. [Obs.]

4. The state of being personally acceptable. [Obs.]

Sir John, you are a gentleman of excellent breeding, of great *admittance*. —Shak.

ad-mit-tā'tŭr, *n.* [L., let him be admitted.] A certificate of admission in some colleges.

ad-mit'ted, *a.* Allowed; granted; conceded.

ad-mit'ted-ly, *adv.* With acknowledgment or concession.

ad-mit'tēr, *n.* One who admits.

ad-mix', *v.t.* To mingle with something else. [Rare. See *Mix*.]

ad-mix'tion (-chun), *n.* [L. *admixtio*, from *admiscere*; *ad*, to, and *miscere*, to mix.] A mingling of bodies; a union by mixing different substances together. [Rare.]

ad-mix'tūre, *n.* 1. The close intermingling of different substances.

2. The act of mingling or mixing.

3. That which is mingled or formed by mingling; a compound of substances mixed together.

ad-mon'ish, *v.t.*; admonished, *pt.*, *pp.*; admonishing, *ppr.* [ME. *admonyshen*; OFr. *admonester*, advise; ML. *admonitare*, freq. of *admonere*; *ad*, to, and *monere*, to warn, advise.]

1. To warn or notify of a fault; to reprove with mildness.

2. To counsel against wrong practices; to caution or advise.

3. To instruct or direct; to guide; to inform or acquaint with; as, *admonished* by his ear.

4. In ecclesiastical affairs, to reprove (a member of the church) for a fault, either publicly or privately; the first step of church discipline. It is followed by *of* or *against*; as, to *admonish of* a fault committed, or *against* committing a fault. It has a like use in colleges.

Syn.—Caution, rebuke, counsel, censure, advise, reprove, forewarn, warn.

ad-mon'ish-ēr, *n.* One who reproves or counsels.

ad-mon'ish-ment, *n.* Admonition. [Rare.]

ad-mō-ni'tion (-nish'un), *n.* [OE. *amonicioun*; Fr. *admonition*; L. *admonitio*, from *admonere*, to warn, advise.]

1. Gentle reproof; warning against a fault; instruction in duties; caution; direction.

2. In church discipline, public or private reproof.

Syn.—Warning, caution, rebuke, reproof, advice, counsel, censure.

ad-mō-ni'tion-ēr, *n.* A dispenser of admonitions. [Rare.]

ad-mon'i-tive, *a.* Containing admonition.

ad-mon'i-tive-ly, *adv.* By admonition.

ad-mon'i-tŏr, *n.* [L.] An admonisher; a monitor.

ad-mon-i-tō'ri-ăl, *a.* Admonitory. [Rare.]

ad-mon'i-tō-ri-ly, *adv.* In an admonitory manner.

ad-mon'i-tō-ry, *a.* Containing admonition; admonishing.

ad-mon'i-trix, *n.*; *pl.* **ad-mon-i-tri'cēs.** [L.] A female admonitor.

ad-mor-ti-zā'tion, *n.* The reducing of lands or tenements to mortmain. [See *Mortmain*.]

ad-mōve', *v.t.* [L. *admovere*; *ad*, to, and *movere*, to move.] To move to; to bring one thing to another. [Obs.]

ad-nas'cent, *a.* [L. *adnascen(t)s*, ppr. of *adnasci*; *ad*, to, and *nasci*, to be born, to grow.] Growing to or on something else.

ad'nāte, *a.* [L. *adnatus*, pp. of *adnasci*, to be born, to grow to.]

1. In botany, pressing close to another part, or attached to it. Thus *adnate* anthers are such as are united to their filaments throughout their whole length, as in the ranunculus. *Adnate* stipules are such as grow to the petiole or leaf-stalk, as in the rose.

1. Adnate Anther. 2. Adnate Stipule.

2. In anatomy, growing attached by cartilage.

ad-na'tion, *n.* The growing together of floral organs.

ad-nērv'ăl, *a.* [L. *ad*, to, and *nervus*, nerve.] Moving toward the nerve; applied to an electrical current passing along an animal fiber.

ad-nom'i-năl, *a.* Relating to an adnoun.

ad-nom'i-năl-ly, *adv.* In the manner of an adnoun; adjectively.

ad'noun, *n.* [*Ad-* and *noun*.] In grammar, an adjective, or attribute. [Rare.]

ad-nū'bi-lā-ted, *a.* [L. *adnubilatus*, pp. of *adnubilare*; *ad*, to, and *nubilare*, to cloud.] Clouded; obscure. [Rare.]

à-dō', *n.* [OE. *ado*, *at do*, to do.] Bustle; trouble; labor; difficulty; as, to make a great *ado* about nothing; to persuade one with much *ado*.

à-dō'be, *n.* [Sp. *adobe*, dried brick.]

1. The sun-dried brick used in Mexico, Arizona, California, and elsewhere, for building houses; also, the clay used in making the bricks.

2. In quicksilver mining, a brick composed of the finer ores mixed with clay for convenience in handling.

à-dō'be, *a.* Built of sun-dried bricks; as, an *adobe* house.

ad-ō-les'cence, *n.* [Fr. *adolescence*; L. *adolescentia*, from *adolescen(t)s*, ppr. of *adolescere*, to grow; *ad*, to, and incept. form of *olere*, to grow, from *alere*, to nourish.] The state of growing, applied to the young of the human race; youth, or the period of life between childhood and maturity.

ad-ō-les'cen-cy, *n.* Youthfulness.

ad-ō-les'cent, *a.* [L. *adolescen(t)s*, ppr. of *adolescere*; *ad*, to, and *olescere*, to grow.] Growing; advancing from childhood to manhood.

ad-ō-les'cent, *n.* A youth.

ā-don', *n.* An apparatus enlarging the image in a fixed-focus camera without necessitating a change of focus. When used alone it is a powerful telephotographic lens.

Ad-ō-nā'ī, *n.* [Heb., my lords.] A Hebrew word for God.

Ad-ō-nē'ăn, *a.* Pertaining to Adonis.

A-dō'ni-á, *n pl.* [L., from Gr. neut. pl. of adj. *Adōnios*, pertaining to *Adōnis*.] Festivals celebrated anciently in honor of Adonis, by females, who spent two days in alternate lamentation and feasting.

A-don'iç, *n.* A verse, consisting of a dactyl and a spondee, as those used in bewailing the death of Adonis.

A-don'iç, *a.* Pertaining to Adonis.

A-dō'nis, *n.* 1. In mythology, the handsome favorite of Venus, who is fabled to have changed him at his death into the flower which bears his name.

2. One of preëminent, manly beauty; also, a fop; a dandy; as, he is quite an *Adonis*.

3. A genus of plants belonging to the natural order *Ranunculaceæ*. In the pheasant's-eye, *Adonis autumnalis*, the petals are bright scarlet, and are considered as emblematical of the blood of Adonis, from which the plant is fabled to have sprung.

A-dō'nist, *n.* [Hebrew, Chaldee, and Syriac, *Adōn*, Lord, a scriptural title of the Supreme Being.] One who maintains that the Hebrew points ordinarily annexed to the consonants of the word *Jehovah* are not the natural points belonging to that word, and that they do not express the true pronunciation of it; but that they are vowel-points belonging to the words *Adonai* and *Elohim*, applied to the ineffable name *Jehovah*, which the Jews were forbidden to utter and the true pronunciation of which was lost; they were, therefore, always to pronounce the word *Adonai*, instead of Jehovah.

ad'ō-nize, *v.t.* To beautify; used of males.

à-dōor', à-dōors', *adv.* At the door. [Obs.]

à-dopt', *v.t.*; adopted, *pt.*, *pp.*; adopting, *ppr.* [L. *adoptare*; *ad*, to, and *optare*, to desire, choose.]

1. To take a child of other parents as one's own in affection and law.

2. To choose or receive an adult person into intimate relationship, as a friend, heir, or citizen.

3. To take or receive as one's own that which is not so naturally; as, to *adopt* the opinions of another; to *adopt* resolutions; or to receive that which is new, as a late invention; to *adopt* a foreign country as one's own.

4. To select and take; as, to *adopt* a style.

Syn.—Affiliate, embrace, espouse, choose, select, elect, assume, appropriate, arrogate.

à-dopt'á-ble, *a.* Capable of being adopted; suitable for adoption, or selection.

à-dopt'ed, *a.* Taken as one's own; received as son and heir; selected for use; as, an *adopted* child; an *adopted* style.

à-dopt'ed-ly, *adv.* In the manner of something adopted.

à-dopt'ēr, *n.* 1. One who adopts.

2. In chemistry, a large, round receiver, with two necks, diametrically opposite to each other, one of which admits the neck of a retort, and the other is joined to another receiver. It is used in distillations, to give more space to elastic vapors, or to increase the length of the neck of a retort. Also called *adapter*.

à-dop'tion, *n.* [L. *adoptio*, from *adoptare*, to adopt.]

1. The act of adopting or the state of being adopted; the taking and treating of the child of another as one's own; the taking into fellowship or intimate relationship; as, the *adoption* of a person into a society.

2. The receiving as one's own what is new or not natural; acceptance.

ȧ-dop'tion-ist, *n.* One who maintains that Christ was the son of God by adoption only.

ȧ-dop'tious, *a.* Adoptive. [Obs.]

ȧ-dopt'ive, *a.* [L. *adoptivus*, from *adoptare*, to adopt.] That adopts; as, an *adoptive* father; or that is adopted; as, an *adoptive* son.

ȧ-dopt'ive, *n.* A person or thing adopted.

ȧ-dopt'ive-ly, *adv.* By adoption.

ȧ-dōr-ȧ-bil'i-ty, *n.* Adorableness.

ȧ-dōr'ȧ-ble, *a.* [Fr. *adorable*; L. *adorabilis*, from *adorare*, to adore.]

1. Worthy of being adored; worthy of divine honors.

2. Worthy of the utmost love or respect.

ȧ-dōr'ȧ-ble-ness, *n.* The quality of being adorable, or worthy of adoration.

ȧ-dōr'ȧ-bly, *adv.* In a manner worthy of adoration.

ad-ō'răl, *a.* [L. *ad*, to, and *oral*, from *os*, *oris*, mouth.] Situated near the mouth.

ad-ō-rā'tion, *n.* [Fr. *adoration*, L. *adoratio*, from *adorare*, to worship.]

1. The act of paying honors to a divine being; the worship paid to God; the act of addressing as a god. *Adoration* consists in external homage, accompanied by the highest reverence. It is used for the act of praying, or preferring requests or thanksgiving to the Supreme Being.

2. Homage paid to one in high esteem; profound reverence.

3. A mode by which the cardinals in conclave sometimes elect the pope. In *adoration*, unlike scrutiny, the cardinals elect a pope by acclamation.

4. In art, a pictorial representation of the *adoration* of the infant Jesus by the magi and the shepherds.

ȧ-dōre', *v.t.*; adored, *pt.*, *pp.*; adoring, *ppr.* [ME. *adouren*; OFr. *adoren*, from L. *adorare*, to worship; *ad*, to, and *orare*, to speak, from *os*, *oris*, mouth.]

1. To worship with profound reverence; to address with exalted thoughts, by prayer and thanksgiving; to pay divine honors to; to honor as a god, or as divine.

2. To love in the highest degree, as a man a woman; to regard with the utmost esteem, affection, and respect.

ȧ-dōre'ment, *n.* Adoration. [Obs.]

ȧ-dōr'ēr, *n.* One who worships, or honors as divine; in popular language, an admiring lover.

ȧ-dōr'ing-ly, *adv.* With adoration.

ȧ-dorn', *v.t.*; adorned, *pt.*, *pp.*; adorning, *ppr.* [OE. *adornen*; Fr. *adorner*, from L. *adornare*; *ad*, to, and *ornare*, to deck out.]

1. To deck or decorate; to make beautiful; to add to the beauty of, by dress; to deck with external ornaments; as, a bride *adorns* herself for the altar.

2. To set off to advantage; to add ornaments to; to embellish by anything external or adventitious; as, to *adorn* a speech by appropriate action, sentiments with elegance of language, or a gallery with pictures.

3. To display the beauty or excellence of; as, to *adorn* the doctrine of God.

Syn.—Deck, decorate, embellish, ornament, bedeck, garnish, beautify, grace, exalt, honor.

ad-or-nā'tion, *n.* Adornment. [Obs.]

ȧ-dorn'ēr, *n.* One who adorns.

ȧ-dorn'ing, *n.* Ornament; decoration.

ȧ-dorn'ing-ly, *adv.* By way of adorning.

ȧ-dorn'ment, *n.* An adorning; ornament.

ȧ-dorsed', **ȧ-dossed'** (-dost'), *a.* [Fr. *adossée*, pp. of *adorser*, to set back to back; *à*, to, and *dos*, back; L. *dorsum*.] In heraldry, applied to two figures or bearings placed back to back.

ad-os-cū-lā'tion, *n.* [L. *adosculatio*, from *adosculari*, to kiss.]

1. In botany, the impregnation of plants by the falling of the pollen on the pistil; also, the insertion of one part of a plant into another.

2. In physiology, impregnation by external contact merely, as in most fishes.

ȧ-dossed', *a.* See *Adorsed.*

ȧ-down', *adv.* From a higher to a lower situation; downward. [Rare.]

ȧ-down', *prep.* Down; on the ground; at the bottom. [Rare.]

A-dox'ȧ, *n.* [Gr. *adoxos*; *a* priv., and *doxa*, glory.] A genus of plants, natural order *Caprifoliaceæ*. The moschatel is the only species.

ad-press', *v.t.* Same as *Appress.*

ad-rā'di-ăl, *a.* [L. *ad*, to, *radius*, ray, and *-al*.] Located near a ray; a term applied to certain processes in some hydrozoans.

ad-rā'di-ăl-ly, *adv.* In an adradial manner.

ad'rȧ-gant, *n.* [Fr., a corruption of *traganthe*.] Formerly, gum tragacanth.

ȧ-dread' (-dred'), *a.* Affected by dread. [Obs.]

ad-rec'tăl, *a.* [L. *ad*, to, *rectum*, and *-al*.] Situated near the rectum.

ad-rē'năl, *n.* [L. *ad*, to, *ren*, kidney, and *-al*.] In anatomy, a small capsular body above the kidney; also called the *atrabiliary capsule.*

ad-rē'năl, *a.* Situated above the kidney.

Ā'dri-ăn, *a.* Relating to the Adriatic.

Ā'dri-ăn-ist, **Ā'dri-ăn-īte**, *n.* In church history, one of a sect who denied the immaculate conception of Jesus Christ; so called after Adrian Hamstedius, an Anabaptist of the sixteenth century.

Ā-dri-at'ic, *a.* [L. *Adriatus*, *Hadriaticus*, from *Adria*, *Hadria*, a town of the Venetians.] Pertaining to or situated on the Gulf of Venice, or *Adriatic* Sea; as *Adriatic* ports.

ȧ-drift', *a.* or *adv.* 1. Literally, driven; floating at random; impelled or moving without direction; at the mercy of winds and currents; as an adjective it always follows its noun; as, the boat is *adrift.*

2. Figuratively, swayed by any chance impulse; also, all abroad; at sea; at a loss; as, their minds are all *adrift.*

ȧ-drip', *a.* and *adv.* Dripping.

ad'rō-gāte, *v.t.* To adopt by adrogation.

ad-rō-gā'tion, *n.* [L. *adrogatio*, from *ad*, to, and *rogare*, to ask.] A species of adoption in ancient Rome, by which a person capable of choosing for himself was admitted into the relation of a son; so called from the questions put to the parties.

ȧ-droit', *a.* [Fr. *adroit*, from L. *directus*, pp. of *dirigere*, to set in a straight line.] Dexterous; skilful; active in the use of the hand, and, figuratively, in the exercise of the mental faculties; ingenious; ready in invention or execution; as, an *adroit* mechanic; an *adroit* statesman.

Syn.—Expert, artful, clever, skilful, dexterous, proficient.

ȧ-droit'ly, *adv.* With dexterity; in a ready, skilful manner.

ȧ-droit'ness, *n.* Dexterity; readiness in the use of the limbs, or of the mental faculties.

ȧ-drȳ', *a.* Thirsty; in want of drink.

ad-sci-ti'tious (-tish'us), *a.* [L. *adscitus*, pp. of *adsciscere*, to take knowingly; *ad*, to, and *sciscere*, to approve, from *scire*, to know.] Added; taken as supplemental; additional; not requisite.

ad-sci-ti'tious-ly, *adv.* In an adscititious manner.

ad'script, *n.* [L. *adscriptus*, pp. of *adscribere*, to enroll.] One who is held to service as attached to some object or place, as when a slave is made an *adscript* of the soil.

ad-scrip'tion, *n.* Attachment to an estate or to a feudal lord.

ad-scrip-ti'tious (-tish'us), *a.* Adscriptive.

ad-scrip'tive, *a.* Attached to and transferable with an estate.

ad-sig"ni-fi-cā'tion, *n.* A modification of meaning by means of a prefix or suffix.

ad-sig'ni-fȳ, *v.t.* [L. *adsignificare*, from *ad*, to, and *significare*, to point out.] To add meaning to (a word) by a prefix or suffix.

ad-sorp'tion, *n.* [L. *ad*, to, and *sorbere*, to suck in.] The condensation of gases on solids.

ad-stip'ū-lāte, *v.i.* [L. *adstipulari*; *ad*, to, and *stipulari*, to stipulate.] To stipulate, as a second or accessory party to an agreement.

ad-stip'ū-lā-tōr, *n.* One who stipulates, as a second or accessory party to a contract.

ad-strict', *v.i.* See *Astrict.*

ad-stric'tion, *n.* See *Astriction.*

ad-stric'tō-ry, *a.* See *Astrictory.*

ad-strin'gent, *a.* See *Astringent.*

ad-tēr'mi-năl, *a.* [L. *ad*, to, and *terminalis*, from *terminus*, end.] A term descriptive of electrical currents passing toward the extremities of a muscle.

ad-ū-lā'ri-ȧ, *n.* [From *Adula*, a mountain in the Swiss Alps.] A very pure, limpid, translucent variety of the common feldspar, called by lapidaries *moonstone*, on account of the play of light exhibited by the arrangement of its crystalline structure.

ad'ū-lāte, *v.t.*; adulated, *pt.*, *pp.*; adulating, *ppr.* [L. *adulatus*, pp. of *adulari*, to flatter.] To flatter servilely.

ad-ū-lā'tion, *n.* Servile flattery; praise in excess, or beyond what is merited; high compliment.

Syn.—Flattery, compliment, sycophancy, blandishment, obsequiousness.

ad'ū-lā-tōr, *n.* A flatterer; one who offers praise servilely.

ad'ū-lā-tō-ry, *a.* Flattering fulsomely; containing excessive praise or compliments; servilely praising; as, an *adulatory* address.

ad'ū-lā-tress, *n.* A female adulator.

A-dul'lăm-īte, *n.* 1. A dweller in the village of Adullam. —Gen. xxxviii. 12.

2. In English politics, one of a party of Liberals who seceded from their own leaders in 1866, and were likened to the political outlaws who took refuge with David in the cave of Adullam. —1 Sam. xxii. 1, 2.

ȧ-dult', *a.* [L. *adultus*, pp. of *adolescere*; *ad*, to, and *olescere*, from *alere*, to nourish.]

1. Having arrived at mature years, or to the full size and strength; as, an *adult* person or plant.

2. Pertaining to adults; suitable for adults; as, *adult* age; an *adult* school.

ȧ-dult', *n.* A person grown to full size and strength, or to the years of manhood or womanhood. It is also applied to full-grown plants and animals.

ȧ-dul'tēr, *v.i.* To commit adultery; to adulterate. [Obs.]

ȧ-dul'tēr-ănt, *n.* The person or thing that adulterates.

ȧ-dul'tēr-āte, *v.t.*; adulterated, *pt.*, *pp.*; adulterating, *ppr.* [L. *adulteratus*, pp. of *adulterare*, from *adulter*, an adulterer; *ad*, to, and *alter*, another.]

1. To corrupt, debase, or make impure by an admixture of baser materials; as, to *adulterate* liquors; to *adulterate* drugs.

2. To give a hybrid character to; as, to *adulterate* plants and flowers. [Rare.]

Syn.—Alloy, debase, defile, corrupt, vitiate, contaminate.

ȧ-dul'tēr-āte, *a.* Tainted with adultery; debased by foreign mixture.

ȧ-dul'tēr-āte-ly, *adv.* In an adulterate manner.

ȧ-dul'tēr-āte-ness, *n.* The quality or state of being debased or corrupted.

ȧ-dul-tēr-ā'tion, *n.* 1. The act of adulterating, or the state of being adulterated, corrupted, or debased by foreign mixture; the use of ingredients in the production of any professedly genuine article, which are cheaper and of a worse quality, or which are not considered so desirable by the consumer as other or genuine ingredients for which they are substituted. The *adulteration* of many articles, especially of food, is punishable by law.

2. An adulterated product.

ȧ-dul'tēr-ēr, *n.* 1. A man guilty of adultery; a married man who has sexual intercourse with any woman except his wife.

2. In Scripture, an apostate from the true faith; a very wicked person.

ȧ-dul'tēr-ess, *n.* A married woman guilty of adultery.

ȧ-dul'tēr-ine, *a.* Proceeding from adulterous intercourse; spurious.

ȧ-dul'tēr-ine, *n.* In law, a child issuing from an adulterous connection. [Rare.]

ȧ-dul'tēr-ize, *v.i.* To commit adultery. [Rare.]

ȧ-dul'tēr-ous, *a.* 1. Guilty of adultery; pertaining to adultery.

2. In Scripture, idolatrous; very wicked.

3. Spurious; corrupt; adulterated. [Rare.]

4. Born of adultery.

ȧ-dul'tēr-ous-ly, *adv.* In an adulterous manner.

ȧ-dul'tēr-y, *n.* [L. *adulterium*, from *adulter*, an adulterer.]

1. Violation of the marriage bed; sexual unfaithfulness, which introduces or may introduce into a family a spurious offspring. *Adultery* is a common ground of divorce. The common law governs this matter generally in the United States, with some variations in the different states. It is a civil injury for which damages may be recovered from the corespondent by either wife or husband. In Great Britain, *adultery* on the part of the husband is punishable by ecclesiastical censure only; but a claim for civil injury arises against the corespondent when the wife is in the wrong.

2. In Scripture, all manner of lewdness or unchastity, as forbidden by the seventh commandment; also, idolatry or apostasy.

3. In old laws, the fine and penalty imposed for the offense of adultery.

4. In ecclesiastical affairs, the intrusion of a person into a bishopric, during the life of the bishop.

ȧ-dult'ness, *n.* The state of being adult.

ad-um'brănt, *a.* Giving a faint shadow, or slight resemblance.

ad-um'brāte, *v.t.* [L. *adumbratus*, pp. of *adumbrari*, to shade; *ad*, and *umbra*, shade.] To give a faint shadow, or slight likeness; to exhibit a faint resemblance, like a shadow.

ad-um-brā'tion, *n.* 1. The act of making a shadow or faint resemblance.

2. A faint sketch; an imperfect representation of a thing.

3. In heraldry, the shadow only of a figure, outlined, and painted of a color darker than the field.

ad-um'brȧ-tive, *a.* Faintly reproducing; lightly sketched.

ad-ū-nā'tion, *n.* [L. *adunatio*, from ppr. of *adunare*, to make one; *ad*, to, and *unare*, from *unus*, one.] The state of being united; union. [Obs.]

ȧ-dunc', *a.* Aduncous.

ȧ-dun'cāte, **ȧ-dun'cā-ted**, *a.* [L. *aduncatus*, pp. of *aduncare*, to hook; *ad*, to, and *uncare*, to hook, from *uncus*, a hook.] Hook-shaped.

ȧ-dun'ci-ty, *n.* [L. *aduncitas*, hookedness; *ad*, to, and *uncus*, a hook.] Hookedness; a bending in form of a hook.

ȧ-dun'cous, *a.* [L. *aduncus*, hooked.] Hooked; bent or made in the form of a hook.

ȧ-dūre', *v.t.* [L. *adurere*; *ad*, to, and *urere*, to burn.] To burn up. [Obs.]

ȧ-dust′, *a.* [L. *adustus*, burnt, pp. of *adurere*, to burn.]

1. Burnt; scorched; become dry by heat; hot and fiery.

2. Sunburnt; sallow.

3. In medicine, heated; applied to the condition of the blood and other bodily fluids; hence, ardent; impetuous. [Obs.]

ȧ-dust′ed, *a.* Become hot and dry; burnt; scorched. [Obs.]

ȧ-dus′tion, *n.* The act of burning, scorching, or heating to dryness; a state of being thus heated or dried. [Obs.]

ad-vȧnce′, *v.t.*; advanced, *pt., pp.*; advancing, *ppr.* [ME. *advaunce, avauncen, avancen*; OFr. *avancer*, to forward, promote, from L. *abantiare, ab* and *ante*, before; Fr. *avant*. The *a* was made *ad* on the supposition that it came from L. *ad*.]

1. To bring forward; to move further in front.

2. To promote; to raise to a higher rank; as, to *advance* one from the bar to the bench.

3. To improve or make better; to benefit; to promote the good of; as, to *advance* one's true interests.

4. To forward; to accelerate; as, to *advance* the growth of plants.

5. To offer or propose; to bring to view or notice; as, to *advance* an opinion or an argument.

6. In commerce, to supply beforehand; to furnish on credit, or before goods are delivered, or work done; or to furnish as a part of a stock or fund; as, to *advance* money on loan or contract, or toward a purchase or enterprise.

7. To furnish for others; to supply or pay for others, in expectation of reimbursement.

8. To raise; to enhance; as, to *advance* the price of goods.

Syn.—Forward, promote, further, raise, elevate, exalt, improve, heighten, accelerate, allege, adduce, assign.

ad-vȧnce′, *v.i.* 1. To move or go forward; to proceed; as, the troops *advanced*.

2. To improve, or make progress; to grow better, greater, wiser, or older; as, to *advance* in knowledge, in stature, in wisdom, or in years.

3. To rise in rank, office, or consequence; to be preferred or promoted; as, to *advance* from captain to colonel.

Syn.—Proceed, progress, rise, increase.

ad-vȧnce′, *a.* Being before, in time or place; used for *advanced*; as, *advance* money; an *advance* agent.

ad-vȧnce′, *n.* 1. Movement forward, or toward the front; the act of advancing.

2. The front; the position before anything.

3. The first approach, or overture, toward opening negotiations or personal relations; often in the plural; as, *advances* with a view to matrimony.

4. The military order to move forward; as, to sound the *advance*.

5. Gradual progression; improvement; as, an *advance* in religion or knowledge.

6. Advancement; promotion; preferment; as, an *advance* in rank or office.

7. In trade, additional price; profit; as, an *advance* on the prime cost of goods.

8. A giving beforehand; a furnishing of something, on contract, before an equivalent is received, as money or goods toward a capital or stock, or on loan; or the money or goods thus furnished; as, A made large *advances* to B.

9. A furnishing of money or goods for others, in expectation of reimbursement; or the property so furnished.

> I shall, with great pleasure, make the necessary *advances*. —Jay.

In advance; in front; before; also, beforehand; before an equivalent is received; as, to send an agent *in advance*; to be paid *in advance*.

ad-vȧnced′, *a.* Moved forward; promoted; improved; furnished beforehand; situated in front, or before the rest; also, old, having reached the decline of life; as, *advanced* in years; an *advanced* age; *advanced* ideas, etc.

ad-vȧnce′-guȧrd, *n.* 1. The vanguard; the first line or division of an army in order of battle, in front of the main body; opposed to *rear-guard*.

2. A small party in advance of the main-guard.

ad-vȧnce′ment, *n.* 1. The act of moving forward or proceeding.

2. The state of being advanced; preferment; promotion in rank or excellence; the act of promoting.

3. Settlement on a wife, or jointure. [Obs.]

4. Provision made by a parent for a child by gift of property, during the parent's life to which the child would be entitled as heir, after his parent's death.

5. The payment of money in advance; money paid in advance.

Syn.—Improvement, progress, progression, proficiency, promotion, exaltation, elevation, preferment, enhancement.

ad-vȧn′cẽr, *n.* 1. One who advances; a promoter.

2. The second start or branch of the horns on the head of a stag or similar animal.

ad-vȧn′cive, *a.* Tending to advance or promote. [Rare.]

ad-vȧn′tȧge, *n.* [ME. *avantage, avauntage*; Fr. *avantage*, an advantage, benefit.]

1. Any state, condition, or circumstance specially favorable to success, prosperity, interest, or reputation; as, the enemy had the *advantage* of elevated ground.

2. Benefit; gain; profit.

3. Means to an end; opportunity; convenience for obtaining benefit; as, students enjoy great *advantages* for improvement.

4. Favorable state or circumstances; as, jewels set to *advantage*.

5. Superiority, or prevalence over; with *of* or *over*; as, to get the *advantage of* an enemy.

6. Superiority, or that which gives it; as, the *advantage* of a good constitution; superiority of personal knowledge; as, when we say to a stranger, you have the *advantage* of me.

To take advantage of; to use or make useful, in a good sense; also, to abuse the confidence of; to overreach.

Syn.—Benefit, good, profit, gain, avail, emolument, interest, help, utility, vantage.

ad-vȧn′tȧge, *v.t.*; advantaged, *pt., pp.*, advantaging, *ppr.* To benefit; to yield profit or gain to; to promote; to advance the interest of.

ad-vȧn′tȧge-ȧ-ble, *a.* Profitable; convenient; gainful. [Rare.]

ad-vȧn′tȧge-ground, *n.* Vantage-ground. [Rare.]

ad-văn-tā′ġeous, *a.* Being of advantage; furnishing convenience, or opportunity to gain benefit; gainful; profitable; useful; beneficial; as, an *advantageous* position of the troops; trade is *advantageous* to a nation.

ad-văn-tā′ġeous-ly, *adv.* In an advantageous manner; profitably; usefully; conveniently.

ad-văn-tā′ġeous-ness, *n.* The quality or state of being advantageous; profitableness; usefulness; convenience.

ad-vēne′, *v.i.* [L. *advenire*, to come to.] To accede, or come; to be added, or become a part, though not essential. [Rare.]

ad-vēn′ient, *a.* Advening; coming from outward causes. [Obs.]

ad′vent, *n.* [L. *adventus*, pp. of *advenire*; *ad*, to, and *venire*, to come.]

1. A coming; approach; visitation.

2. [A—] Specifically, the coming of Christ; in the church calendar, the period including four Sundays before Christmas, beginning on St. Andrew's day, November 30, or the Sunday nearest to it, either before or after.

Ad′vent-ist, *n.* One of a sect believing in the second personal coming of Christ.

ad-ven-ti′ti-ȧ (-tish′i-ȧ), *n.* [L., f. sing. of *adventitius*, coming from abroad, extraneous; with *membrana* understood; from *ad*, to, and *venire*, to come.] In anatomy, any membranous covering not properly belonging to an organ.

ad-ven-ti′tious, *a.* [L. *adventitius*, extraneous.]

1. Added extrinsically; accidental; not essentially inherent; casual; foreign; as, *adventitious* aids to oratory.

2. In botany, applied to anything produced in an abnormal position, as leaf-buds on the surface of a stem, or roots from aerial stems or branches, as in the banian-tree.

3. In zoölogy, occurring as a straggler, or away from its natural position or habitat.

ad-ven-ti′tious-ly, *adv.* Accidentally; in an adventitious or extrinsic manner.

ad-ven-ti′tious-ness, *n.* The state of being adventitious.

ad-ven′tive, *a.* 1. Accidental; adventitious. [Rare.]

2. In botany, applied to plants not commonly indigenous appearing spontaneously in a country.

ad-ven′tive, *n.* A thing or person that comes from without. [Rare.]

Ad-ven′tū-ăl, *a.* Relating to the season of Advent.

ad-ven′tūre, *n.* [OE. *aventure*; Fr. *aventure*; L. *adventura*, from *advenire*; *ad*, to, and *venire*, to come.]

1. Hazard; risk; chance.

2. An enterprise of hazard; a bold undertaking, in which hazards are to be encountered, and the issue is staked upon unforeseen events.

3. A remarkable occurrence in one's personal history; a striking event; as, the *adventures* of one's life.

4. A consignment of goods to be sold at the owner's risk; a speculative business enterprise.

Syn.—Event, incident, occurrence, undertaking, enterprise.

ad-ven′tūre, *v.t.*; adventured, *pt., pp.*; adventuring, *ppr.* 1. To risk, or hazard; to jeopardize; to venture. [See *Venture*.]

2. To venture on; to attempt.

ad-ven′tūre, *v.i.* To dare; to try the chance; as, to *adventure* on the tempestuous sea of liberty.

ad-ven′tūre-fụl, *a.* Given to adventure; full of enterprise. [Rare.]

ad-ven′tūr-ẽr, *n.* 1. One who hazards, or puts something at risk; as, merchant *adventurers*.

2. One who seeks occasions of chance, or attempts bold, novel, or extraordinary enterprises.

3. A speculator; specifically, in English mining, a shareholder in working a mine.

4. One who gains or strives to gain social standing unduly, or by questionable means.

ad-ven′tūre-sŏme, *a.* Bold; daring; incurring hazard. [See *Venturesome*.]

ad-ven′tūre-sŏme-ness, *n.* The quality of being bold and venturesome.

ad-ven′tūr-ess, *n.* A female adventurer; a woman who seeks to gain position by fraudulent means, or engages in enterprises of a questionable character.

ad-ven′tūr-ous, *a.* [ME. *aventurous*; Fr. *aventureux*, from *aventurer*, to venture.]

1. Inclined or willing to incur hazard; bold to encounter danger; daring; courageous; enterprising; applied to persons.

2. Full of hazard; attended with risk, exposing to danger; requiring courage; applied to things; as, an *adventurous* undertaking.

Syn.—Rash, audacious, brave, enterprising, venturesome, bold, hazardous, reckless, foolhardy.

ad-ven′tūr-ous-ly, *adv.* Boldly; daringly; in a manner to incur hazard.

ad-ven′tūr-ous-ness, *n.* The act or quality of being adventurous.

ad′vẽrb, *n.* [L. *adverbium*; *ad*, to, and *verbum*, word.] In grammar, a word used to modify the sense of a verb, participle, adjective, or other adverb, and usually placed near it; as, he writes *well*; paper *extremely* white.

ad-vẽr′bi-ăl, *a.* Pertaining to an adverb.

ad-vẽr-bi-al′i-ty, *n.* The quality of being adverbial.

ad-vẽr′bi-ăl-ize, *v.t.* To use as an adverb; to give the quality of an adverb to.

ad-vẽr′bi-ăl-ly, *adv.* In the manner of an adverb.

ad-vẽr-sā′ri-ȧ, *n. pl.* [L. *adversaria*, neut. pl. of *adversarius*, opposing, turned toward.]

1. A commonplace book.

2. In literature, a miscellaneous collection of notes, remarks, or selections; used as a title of books or papers of such character.

ad-vẽr-sā′ri-ous, *a.* Antagonistic; inimical. [Obs.]

ad′vẽr-sā-ry, *n.* [OE. *adversie*; OFr. *adversier*, from L. *adversarius*, turned toward, opponent.]

1. An enemy or foe; one who has enmity at heart. In Scripture, Satan is called *the adversary* by way of eminence.

2. An opponent or antagonist, as in a suit at law, or in single combat; an opposing litigant.

Syn.—Opponent, antagonist, enemy, foe.—Unfriendly feelings mark the *enemy*; habitual hostility the *adversary*; active hostility the *foe*. *Opponents* are those who are pitted against each other; *antagonists* those who struggle in the contest with all their might.

ad′vẽr-sā-ry, *a.* 1. Opposed; opposite to; adverse.

2. In law, having an opposing party; in distinction from an application, in law or equity, to which no opposition is made; as, an *adversary* suit.

ad-vẽrs′ȧ-tive, *a.* [L. *adversativus*, from *adversatus*, pp. of *adversari*, to be opposed to.] Noting some difference, contrariety, or opposition; as, John is an honest man, but a fanatic. Here *but* is called an *adversative* conjunction.

ad-vẽrs′ȧ-tive, *n.* A word denoting contrariety or opposition.

ad-vẽrs′ȧ-tive-ly, *adv.* In an adversative manner or sense.

ad′vẽrse, *a.* [ME. *adverse*; Fr. *adverse*; L. *adversus*, pp. of *advertere*; *ad*, to, and *vertere*, to turn.]

1. Opposite; opposing; acting in a contrary direction; conflicting; counteracting; opposed to; hostile; as, *adverse* winds; an *adverse* party; *adverse* criticism.

2. Figuratively, opposing desire; contrary to the wishes, or to supposed good; hence, unfortunate; calamitous; pernicious; unprosperous; as, *adverse* fate or circumstances.

3. In botany, turned toward the stem; applied to leaves.

Adverse possession; in law, occupancy of realty without molestation, which may at length ripen into an unimpeachable title.

Syn.—Opposite, opposing, contrary, inimical, hostile, unfortunate, calamitous, unprosperous.

ad-vẽrse′, *v.t.* To oppose. [Obs.]

ad′vẽrse-ly, *adv.* In an adverse manner; oppositely; unfortunately; unprosperously; in a manner contrary to desire or success.

ad′vẽrse-ness, *n.* Opposition; adversity; unprosperousness.

ad-vẽrs-i-fō′li-āte, ad-vẽrs-i-fō′li-ous, *a.* [L. *adversus*, opposite, and *folium*, a leaf.] In botany, having the leaves opposite to each other on the stem.

ad-vẽr′si-ty, *n.* [ME. *adversite*; L. *adversitas*, from *adversus*, pp. of *advertere*, to oppose.] An event, or series of events, which opposes success or desire; misfortune; calamity; affliction; distress; state of unhappiness.

Sweet are the uses of *adversity*. —Shak.

Syn.—Disaster, misfortune, calamity, bad luck, misery, distress.

ad-vẽrt′, *v.i.*; adverted, *pt.*, *pp.*; adverting, *ppr.* [L. *advertere*; *ad*, to, and *vertere*, to turn.] To turn the mind or attention to; to regard, observe, or notice; to refer or allude; with *to*; as, he *adverted to* what was said, or *to* a circumstance that occurred.

ad-vẽrt′ence, ad-vẽrt′en-cy, *n.* [OFr. *advertence*; L. *advertentia*, from *advertens*, ppr. of *advertere*, to turn to.] A direction of the mind to; attention; notice; regard; consideration; heedfulness.

ad-vẽrt′ent, *a.* Attentive; heedful.

ad-vẽrt′ent-ly, *adv.* In an advertent manner.

ad′vẽr-tīse (*or* ad-ver-tīz′), *v.t.*; advertised, *pt.*, *pp.*; advertising, *ppr.* [ME. *advertisen*; OFr. *advertiss*, from *advertir*, to inform, certify.]

1. To take note of; to observe. [Obs.]

2. To inform; to give notice, advice, or intelligence to, whether of a past or present event, or of something yet to come.

I will *advertise* thee what this people will do to thy people. —Num. xxiv. 14.

3. To publish a notice of; to give conspicuous notice or information of to the public, through newspapers, signs, circulars, posters, periodical publications, etc.; as, to *advertise* goods for sale, entertainments to occur, etc.

Syn.—Announce, declare, proclaim, promulgate, publish, make known, apprise, inform.

ad′vẽr-tīse, *v.i.* To exploit anything before the public; to announce publicly one's desires or purposes; as, to *advertise* for help.

ad-vẽr′tīse-ment (*or* -tīz′ment), *n.* 1. Information; admonition; notice given. [Obs.]

2. A written or printed notice intended to make something known to the public; especially a printed and paid notice in a newspaper or other public print.

ad′vẽr-tīs-ẽr (*or* -tīz′-), *n.* One who or that which advertises; the word is frequently adopted as an appropriate title for newspapers.

ad′vẽr-tīs-ing (*or* -tīz′-), *a.* 1. Furnishing or fond of using advertisements; as, *advertising* merchants.

2. Monitory, or active in giving intelligence. [Obs.]

ad′vẽr-tīs-ing (*or* -tīz′-), *n.* 1. The art or practice of obtaining commercial or personal publicity through the press or other mediums.

2. The business or profession of writing and otherwise preparing advertising matter, or of securing contracts for the publication of advertisements.

Advertising is now a recognized profession. —Collier.

ad-vīce′, *n.* [ME. *advyse*, *avys*; OFr. *avis*; L. *advisum*, a view, opinion, from *advisus*, pp. of *advidere*; *ad*, to, and *videre*, to see.]

1. Counsel; an opinion recommended or offered, as worthy to be followed.

We may give *advice*, but we cannot give conduct. —Franklin.

2. Prudence; deliberate consideration. [Obs.]

3. Information as to the state of an affair or affairs; notice; intelligence; as, we have late *advices* from China; usually in the plural.

4. In commerce, a notification by one person to another, usually by mail, as of a draft drawn or other business transacted in which both are interested.

To take advice; to consult with others; specifically, to consult one who has a special knowledge of a subject; to take the opinion of a professional or skilful man, as a physician, lawyer, and the like.

Syn.—Counsel, instruction, information, notice, deliberation, admonition, recommendation, exhortation, intelligence

ad-vīce′-bōat, *n.* A despatch-boat.

ad-vīs-ȧ-bil′i-ty, *n.* The quality of being advisable; expediency.

ad-vīs′ȧ-ble, *a.* 1. Proper to be advised; prudent; expedient; proper to be done or practised; as, it is not *advisable* to proceed at this time.

2. Open to advice. [Rare.]

Syn.—Prudent, expedient, proper.

ad-vīs′ȧ-ble-ness, *n.* The quality of being advisable or expedient.

ad-vīs′ȧ-bly, *adv.* With advice.

ad-vīṣe′, *v.t.*; advised, *pt.*, *pp.*; advising, *ppr.* [OE. *avisen*; L. *advisare*; *ad*, to, and *visare*, from *videre*, to see.]

1. To give counsel to; to offer an opinion, as worthy or expedient to be followed; as, I *advise* you to be cautious of speculation.

2. To give information to; to communicate notice to; to make acquainted with; followed by *of* before the thing communicated; as, the merchants were *advised of* the risk.

Syn.—Counsel, admonish, inform, apprise, acquaint.

ad-vīṣe′, *v.i.* 1. To deliberate, weigh well, or consider. [Obs.]

2. To consult with others; to join others in deliberating; followed by *with*; as, I shall *advise with* my friends.

ad-vīṣ′ed-ly, *adv.* With deliberation or advice; heedfully; purposely; by design; as, an enterprise *advisedly* undertaken.

ad-vīṣ′ed-ness, *n.* Deliberate consideration; prudent procedure.

ad-vīṣe′ment, *n.* 1. Counsel; information. [Obs.]

2. Consultation; deliberation; as, to take a case under *advisement*.

ad-vīṣ′ẽr, *n.* One who gives advice or admonition; as, a legal *adviser*.

ad-vīṣ′ing, *n.* Advice; counsel.

ad-vī′ṣō, *n.* [*Ad*, for *a*, Sp. *aviso*, advice.]

1. Advice; suggestion. [Obs.]

2. An aviso, or advice-boat.

ad-vī′ṣō-ry, *a.* 1. Having power to advise; as, an *advisory* board.

2. Containing advice; as, their opinion is merely *advisory*.

ad′vō-cȧ-cy, *n.* 1. The act of pleading for or supporting; vindication; defense; intercession.

2. Judicial pleading; lawsuit. [Obs.]

ad′vō-cāte, *n.* [OE. *avocat*; L. *advocatus*, one called to another.]

1. One who pleads the cause of another in a court of law; a counsel or counselor; as, he is a learned lawyer and an able *advocate*.

2. One who defends, vindicates, or espouses a cause by argument; one who is friendly to; an upholder; a defender; as, an *advocate* of peace, or of the oppressed.

Judge advocate; in courts martial, a person who manages the prosecution.

ad′vō-cāte, *v.t.*; advocated, *pt.*, *pp.*; advocating, *ppr.* 1. To plead in favor of; to defend by argument before a tribunal or the public; to support or vindicate; as, to *advocate* total abstinence.

2. In Scotland, formerly, to appeal from a lower to a higher court.

Syn.—Plead for, favor, support, maintain.

ad′vō-cāte, *v.i.* To plead; to act as an advocate. [Obs.]

ad′vō-cāte-ship, *n.* The office or duty of an advocate.

ad′vō-cā-tess, *n.* A female advocate. [Rare.]

ad-vō-cā′tion, *n.* A pleading for; plea; apology; advocacy. [Obs.]

Bill of advocate; in Scotland, formerly, a written application to a superior court, to call an action before it from an inferior court. This form of process was abolished in 1868, a simple appeal being substituted.

ad-vō-lū′tion. *n.* [L. *advolvere*; *ad*, to, and *volvere*, to roll.] A rolling toward something; evolution philosophically considered with regard to its ultimate trend.

ad-vou′trẽr, *n.* [ME. *advouter*, OFr. *avouter*, *avoltre*, L. *adulter*, adulterer.] An adulterer. [Obs.]

ad-vou′tress, *n.* An adulteress. [Obs.]

ad-vou′try, ad-vow′try, *n.* Adultery. [Obs.]

ad-vow-ee′, *n.* One who has the right of advowson.

ad-vow′ṣon, *n.* [ME. *advowson*, *avowiesoun*; OFr. *avoeson*; L. *advocatio*, a summoning, a calling to, from *ad*, to, and *vocare*, to call.] In English law, a right of presentation to a vacant benefice; or, in other words, a right of nominating a person as rector or vicar of a vacant parish. The name is derived from *advocatio*, because the right was first obtained by such as were founders, benefactors, or strenuous defenders, *advocates*, of the church. The *advowsons* of more than half the benefices of the Church of England are held by private persons.

ad-voy′ẽr, *n.* See *Avoyer*.

ad-wạrd′, *n.* Same as *Award*. [Obs.]

ad-y-nā′mi-ȧ, *n.* [L., from Gr. *adynamia*, want of strength, from *a* priv., and *dynamis*, power.] In medicine, weakness; want of strength occasioned by disease; a deficiency of vital power.

ad-y-nam′iç, *a.* [Gr. *adynamia*, without power, and *-ic*.]

1. Weak; destitute of strength.

2. In physics, characterized by the absence of force.

ȧ-dyn′ȧ-my, *n.* Same as *Adynamia*.

ad′y-tum, *n.* [L., from Gr. *adyton*, neut. of *adytos*, not to be entered, from *a* priv., and *dyein*, to enter.] In ancient temples, a secret place whence oracles were given.

adz, adze, *n.* [ME. *adis*, *adse*, AS. *adesa*, an adze, ax.] An iron instrument with an arching blade, across the line of the handle, and ground from a base on its inside to the outer edge; used for chipping a horizontal surface of timber.

Adz.

æ (*e or ē*). A diphthong in the Latin language; used also by the Anglo-Saxon writers. It answers to the Greek *ai*. The Anglo-Saxon *æ* has been changed into *e* or *ea*. In derivatives from the learned languages, it is mostly superseded by *e*, and many words formerly spelled with the initial diphthong *æ* will now be found defined under the letter E.

Æ-cid″i-ō-my-cē′tēṣ, *n.pl.* [L. *æcidium*, dim. of Gr. *aikia*, injury, and *mykētes*, pl. of *mykēs*, a fungus.] A group of minute parasitic fungi, including many rusts and mildews infesting cultivated plants.

æ-cid′i-ō-spōre, *n.* [L. *æcidium*, dim. of Gr. *aikia*, injury, and *spora*, seed.] A spore formed by a process of abstriction in certain parasitic fungi.

æ-cid′i-ō-stāġe, *n.* The stage in the growth of certain fungi at which occurs the formation of æcidiospores.

Æ-cid′i-um, *n.* [L., dim. of Gr. *aikia*, injury.] A genus of parasitic fungi, or a stage in the development of the fungi commonly called rusts, which infest plants.

æ′dīle, ē′dīle, *n.* [L. *ædilis*, from *ædes*, building, temple.] In ancient Rome, an officer or magistrate who had the care of the public buildings (*ædes*), streets, highways, public spectacles, etc.

æ′dīle-ship, ē′dīle-ship, *n.* The office of an ædile.

æ-gȧ-grop′i-lȧ, æ-gag′rō-pīle, *n.* [L., from Gr. *aigagros*, a wild goat, and L. *pila*, ball, from *pilus*, hair.] A concrete mass of hair, etc., found in the stomach of some ruminants, as the goat.

Æ-ġē′ăn, *a.* [L. *Ægeum*; Gr. *Aigaion*.] Of or pertaining to the arm of the Mediterranean Sea east of Greece, or the Archipelago.

Æ-ġē′ri-ȧ, Ē-ġē′ri-ȧ, *n.pl.* [L., after *Ægeria*, a prophetic nymph of Roman legend.] In entomology, a typical genus of *Lepidoptera*, consisting of bright-colored moths with transparent wings.

Æ-ġē′ri-ăn, Ē-ġē′ri-ăn, *a.* Of or pertaining to the *Ægeria*, commonly called clearwings.

æ-ġi-çrā′ni-ȧ, *n.pl.* [L., from Gr. *aix*, *aigos*, goat, and *kranion*, skull.] In classical architecture, the heads of rams or goats sculptured in ornamentation.

æ′ġi-lops, ē′ġi-lops, *n.* [L., from Gr. *aigilōps*; *aix*, *aigos*, goat, and *ōps*, eye.]

1. In medicine, goat-eye; an abscess in the inner canthus of the eye.

2. [Æ—] In botany, a genus of grasses growing wild in southern Europe.

æ′ġir-īte, æ′ġir-īne, *n.* [Ice. *Ægir*, the god of the sea, and *-ite*, *-ine*.] Same as *Acmite*.

æ′ġis, *n.* [L., from Gr. *aigis*, a goatskin, from *aix*, *aigos*, a goat; also, a storm, hurricane, probably from *aissein*, to glance, dart.]

1. A shield, or defensive armor; originally applied to the shield given by Jupiter to Minerva. In later times, part of the armor of Pallas Athena, appearing as a kind of breastplate covered with metal scales, and made terrible by the head of the Gorgon Medusa, being also fringed with serpents.

Pallas Wearing the Ægis.—From an antique statue.

2. Figuratively, any power or influence which protects or shields; as, under the *ægis* of American citizenship.

Æ-ġi-thog′nȧ-thæ, *n.pl.* [L., from Gr. *aigithos*, a bird, and *gnathos*, a jaw.] A large group or suborder of birds of the order *Carinatæ*.

æ-ġi-thog′nȧ-thiṣm, *n.* The state or quality of being ægithognathous; that form of the bony palate of birds consisting in the union of the vomer with the alinasal walls and turbinals, characteristic of the large group *Ægithognathæ*, including the passerine and gallinaceous birds.

æ-ġi-thog′nȧ-thous (-thus), *a.* In ornithology, having the structure of the palate disposed as in the sparrow and other passerine birds; applied also to the swifts and woodpeckers.

Æ′glē, *n.* [L., from Gr. *aiglē*, splendor.] In botany, a small genus of trees of the family *Rutaceæ*, found in tropical Asia and Africa, and resembling the citrus or orange-tree. *Ægle Marmelos* produces the golden orange of India.

æ-gō-phon′iç, *a.* Relating to or having the character of ægophony.

æ-goph′ō-ny, *n.* [Gr. *aix* (*aigos*), a goat, and

phōnē, voice.] The sound of the voice of a person affected with pleurisy, when heard through the stethoscope; so called because it is tremulous and broken, so as to suggest the bleatings of a goat.

Æ-nē'id, *n.* [L. *Æneis, Æneidos.*] The epic poem by Virgil, of which Æneas is the hero.

ā-ē'nē-ous, *a.* [L. *aëneus*, of bronze.] Colored like or having the appearance of bronze; a term used in zoölogy.

æ-nig'mȧ-tīte, *n.* [L. *ænigma*, enigma.] An amphibolic mineral which crystallizes in the triclinic system.

Æ-ō'li-ăn, Ē-ō'li-ăn, *a.* [L. *Æolius*; Gr. *Aiolios.*]

1. Pertaining to Æolus, the god of the winds.

2. Of or pertaining to Æolia, or Æolis, in Asia Minor; as, the *Æolian* dialect.

3. [æ—] Produced by atmospheric action; blown by the wind; æolic; as, an *æolian* deposit.

Æolian harp; a simple stringed instrument that is made to sound by the currents of air. It is usually placed in a window, and consists of a box of thin wood in which are stretched numerous strings of equal length and tuned in unison. Also called *Æolian lyre.*

Æ-ol'iç, Ē-ol'iç, *a.* 1. Same as *Æolian.*

2. [æ—] In physical geography, pertaining to or caused by the action of the wind upon the earth's surface.

æ-ō-li'nȧ, *n.* [L. *Æolus*; Gr. *Aiolos*, god of the winds.] A small free-reed musical instrument, the forerunner of the accordion.

æ-ol'i-pīle, æ-ol'i-pȳle, ē-ol'i-pīle, *n.* [L. *æolipilæ*; *Æolus*, god of the winds, and *pila*, a ball.] A hollow ball of metal with a pipe or slender neck, used in hydraulic experiments.

Æ'ō-lis, Ē'ō-lis, *n.* [L., from Gr. *Aiolis*, from *aiolos*, quick-moving.] A genus of slug-like mollusks with gill-like papillæ in clusters along the back.

æ"ō-lō-trop'iç, *a.* [Gr. *aiolos*, changeful, and *tropē*, from *trepein*, to turn.] In physics, exhibiting changeful qualities; non-isotropic; used with reference to the action upon bodies of light, heat, etc.

æ-ō-lot'rō-py, *n.* In physics, the quality of being æolotropic.

Æ'ō-lus, *n.* [L., from Gr. *Aiolos.*] In Greek and Roman mythology, the god of the winds.

æ'ŏn, *n.* See *Eon.*

æ-ō'ni-ăn, *a.* See *Eonian.*

æ-py-ọr'nis, ē-py-ọr'nis, *n.* [Gr. *aipus*, high, and *ornis*, bird.] A gigantic ostrich-like bird found in a fossil state in Madagascar.

ā-ēr-, ā-ēr-i-, ā-ēr-ō-. [Gr. *aēr*, air.] Combining forms, denoting situation, motion, growth in, or relation to, air or gas.

æ-rā'ri-ăn, *a.* and *n.* [L. *ærarius*, from *æs, æris*, pertaining to ore, money.]

I. *a.* Pertaining to the Roman public treasury; fiscal.

II. *n* A Roman citizen of the lowest class of freemen, who paid only a poll-tax and had not the suffrage.

ā'ēr-āte, *v.t.*; aerated, *pt., pp.*; aerating, *ppr.* [Gr. *aēr*, air, and *-ate.*]

1. To combine with air; to combine with carbonic acid, formerly called fixed air; to combine, charge, or impregnate with gas.

2. In physiology, to change the circulating fluids of (animals) by the agency of the air.

3. In agriculture, to expose (soils) to the action of the air by plowing, harrowing, etc.

ā-ēr-ā'tion, *n.* 1. The act or operation of combining with air, carbonic acid, or oxygen.

2 In physiology, the change in the circulating fluids of animals effected by the agency of the air, as the arterialization of the blood by respiration in the higher animals, and the corresponding change in the lower animals.

3. In agriculture, the exposure of soil to the free action of the air, by plowing, etc.

ā'ēr-ā-tŏr, *n.* 1. An apparatus for forcing gas into combination with fluids, as in making soda-water, or charging mineral waters.

2. An apparatus for blowing a stream of air or gas upon wheat, etc., to destroy fungi or injurious insects; a fumigator.

ā-ēr-en'ċhy-mȧ, *n.* [Gr. *aēr*, air, and *enchyma*, an infusion.] In botany, a form of cellular tissue found in the stems of some marsh and aquatic plants; it resembles the tissue of cork.

ā-ē'ri-ăl, *a.* [*Aeri-*, and *-al.*]

1. Belonging to the air, or atmosphere.

2. Consisting of air; partaking of the nature of air; as, *aerial* particles.

3. Growing, existing, or happening in the air.

4. Inhabiting or frequenting the air.

5. Placed in the air; high; lofty; elevated.

6. Possessed of a light and graceful beauty; as, *aerial* melodies.

7. Ethereal; visionary; as, *aerial* fancies.

Aerial sickness; the illness caused by the rolling of an aircraft or by the rapid change of altitude. It combines the symptoms of seasickness and mountain sickness.

Aerial tints; in painting, tints or modifications of color by which the expression of distance is attained.

ā-ē'ri-ăl, *n.* In radiotelegraphy, the wire or wires insulated from and suspended at a certain height above the ground used to radiate energy as electric-magnetic waves produced by a transmitter.

ā-ē'ri-ăl-ly, *adv.* In an aerial manner; from or like the air.

A-ē'ri-ăns, *n.pl.* In church history, a branch of Arians, so called from Aerius, who maintained that there is no difference between bishops and priests.

ae'rie (ē'rē *or* ā'ẽr-y), *n.* See *Aery.*

ā-ẽr-if'ẽr-ous, *a.* [*Aeri-*, and *-ferous*, from L. *ferre*, to bear.] Conveying or containing air; air-bearing; as the larynx and bronchial tubes, and the trachea of insects.

ā"ẽr-i-fi-cā'tion, *n.* 1. The act of combining air with; the state of being filled with air.

2. The act of becoming air, or of changing into an aeriform state, as substances which are converted from a liquid or solid form into gas or an elastic vapor.

ā'ẽr-i-fọrm, *a.* Having the form or nature of air, or of an elastic fluid.

ā'ẽr-i-fȳ, *v.t.*; aerified, *pt., pp.*; aerifying, *ppr.* To infuse air into; to fill with air, or to combine air with; to change into an aeriform state.

ā'ẽr-ōbe, *n.* One of the aerobia.

ā-ẽr-ō'bi-ȧ, *n. pl.* [*Aero-*, and Gr. *bios*, life.] Bacteria that live in contact with the air and absorb oxygen from it.

ā-ẽr-ō'biç, *a.* Of the nature of aerobia.

ā-ẽr-ō'biç-ăl-ly, *adv.* In the manner of the aerobia.

ā'ẽr-ō-bieṣ (-biz), *n.pl.* [Fr.] The term originally applied by Pasteur to the aerobia.

ā"ẽr-ō-bi-ō'sis, *n.* Life in and by means of air, or an atmosphere containing oxygen.

ā"ẽr-ō-bi-ot'iç, *a.* Relating to aerobiosis.

ā"ẽr-ō-boat', *n.* [*Aero-*, and *boat.*] A flying boat.

Ā"ẽr-ō-bran'ċhi-ȧ, *n. pl.* [*Aero-*, and Gr. *branchia*, gills.] A subclass of *Arachnida*, including the scorpions and spiders.

ā"ẽr-ō-bran'ċhi-āte, *a.* Pertaining to the *Aerobranchia.*

ā"ẽr-ō-bus', *n.* [*Aero-*, and *bus.*] An aeroplane of sufficient size to carry several passengers.

ā'ẽr-ō-cũrve, *n.* An aeroplane having a curved sustaining surface.

ā'ẽr-ō-cyst, *n.* [*Aero-*, and Gr. *kystis*, bladder.] An air-cell or air-bladder of an algal.

ā'ẽr-ō-drōme, *n.* [*Aero-* and Gr. *dromos*, course.]

1. A building or shed for housing aircraft; a hangar.

2. A field or ground used for flying purposes, particularly one with hangars and other facilities.

3. A flying-machine.

ā"ẽr-ō-dȳ-nam'iç, *a.* Relating to the force of air in motion.

ā-ẽr-ō-dȳ-nam'ics, *n.* [*Aero-*, and Gr. *dynamis*, power.] The science relating to the effects produced by air in motion; this is, therefore, the term to be applied to the science of aviation.

ā'ẽr-ō-foil, *n.* An aeroplane whose sustaining surfaces are not strictly planes.

ā-ẽr-og'nō-sy, *n.* [*Aero-*, and Gr. *gnōsis*, knowledge.] The science which treats of the properties of air and the part it performs in the operations of nature.

ā'ẽr-ō-gram, *n.* [*Aero-*, and Gr. *gramma*, a writing.] A message sent by wireless telegraphy.

ā'ẽr-ō-grȧph, *n.* [*Aero-*, and Gr. *graphos*, a description, or writing.] An apparatus, or a process, for conducting wireless telegraphy.

ā-ẽr-og'rȧ-phẽr, *n.* One versed in the science of aerography; an aerologist.

ā"ẽr-ō-graph'iç, *a.* Of or pertaining to aerography.

ā"ẽr-ō-graph'iç-ăl-ly, *adv.* In an aerographic manner.

ā-ẽr-og'rȧ-phy, *n.* [*Aero-*, and Gr. *graphein*, to describe.]

1. A description of the air or atmosphere. [See *Aerology.*]

2. A name given to wireless telegraphy.

ā'ẽr-ō-gun", *n.* A gun designed to battle aircraft.

ā"ẽr-ō-hȳ"drō-dȳ-nam'iç, *a.* [*Aero-*, Gr. *hydor*, water, and *dynamis*, power.] Acting by the force of air in water; as, an *aerohydrodynamic* wheel.

ā'ẽr-ō-līte, *n.* [*Aero-*, and Gr. *lithos*, a stone.] A stone which has fallen from atmospheric regions; a meteoric stone; a meteorite.

ā"ẽr-ō-li-thol'ō-ġy, *n.* [*Aero-*, Gr. *lithos*, stone, and *logos*, word, description.] The science of aerolites.

ā"ẽr-ō-lit'iç, *a.* Of or pertaining to aerolites.

ā"ẽr-ō-loġ'iç, ā"ẽr-ō-loġ'iç-ăl, *a.* Pertaining to aerology.

ā-ẽr-ol'ō-ġist, *n.* One versed in aerology.

ā-ẽr-ol'ō-ġy, *n.* [*Aero-*, and Gr. *logos*, description.] A description of the air; that branch of physics which treats of the air, its constituent parts, properties, and phenomena.

ā'ẽr-ō-man"cy, *n.* [*Aero-*, and Gr. *manteia*, divination.] Divination by means of the air and winds; hence, sometimes used to denote the practice of forecasting changes in the weather.

ā"ẽr-ō-mē-ċhan'iç, *n.* [*Aero-*, and *mechanic.*] An expert in aeronautics.

ā"ẽr-ō-mē-ċhan'iċs, *n.* The science of aerial navigation.

ā-ẽr-om'e-tẽr, *n.* [*Aero-*, and Gr. *metron*, measure.] An instrument for weighing air, or for ascertaining the density of air and gases.

ā"ẽr-ō-met'riç, *a.* Pertaining to aerometry.

ā-ẽr-om'e-try, *n.* The science of measuring the weight or density of air and gases, including the doctrine of their pressure, elasticity, rarefaction, and condensation.

ā'ẽr-ō-naut, *n.* [*Aero-*, and Gr. *nautēs*, a sailor.] One who sails or floats in the air; an aerial navigator; applied to persons who ascend in balloons or air-ships.

ā"ẽr-ō-naut'iç, ā"ẽr-ō-naut'iç-ăl, *a.* Sailing or floating in the air; pertaining to aerial sailing.

ā"ẽr-ō-naut'iċs, *n.* The doctrine, science, or art of sailing in the air, by means of a balloon or air-ship.

ā'ẽr-ō-naut"ism, *n.* The practice of ascending and floating in the atmosphere in balloons or air-ships.

ā"ẽr-ō-phō'bi-ȧ, ā-ẽr-oph'ō-by, *n.* [*Aero-*, and Gr. *phobos*, fear.] In medicine, a morbid dread of a current of air, often accompanying hydrophobia, hysteria, and other nervous affections.

ā'ẽr-ō-phōne, *n.* [*Aero-*, and Gr. *phōnē*, voice.]

1. An apparatus for intensifying soundwaves, as those from spoken words, and thus making the sounds audible at a greater distance, without diminishing their distinctness.

2. An appliance for the relief of the deaf.

ā'ẽr-ō-phȳte (-fīt), *n.* [*Aero-*, and Gr. *phyton*, a plant.] A plant that lives exclusively in air, absorbing all its food from air alone, as some orchids; an epiphyte.

ā'ẽr-ō-plāne, *n.* [*Aero-*, and Gr. *planos*, a wanderer.]

1. A light framework, usually covered with balloon-cloth, used as a supporting surface in flying-machines.

2. A flying-machine that is supported in the air by aeroplanes instead of rarefied air or gas.

ā'ẽr-ō-sçep"sy, ā"ẽr-ō-sçep'sis, *n.* [*Aero-*, and Gr. *skepsasthai*, to explore.] The faculty of perception by the medium of the air, supposed to reside in the antennæ of insects; aeroscopy.

ā'ẽr-ō-sçōpe, *n.* [*Aero-*, and Gr. *skopein*, to look out.] In biology, an apparatus for gathering germs, bacteria, etc., from the atmosphere.

ā-ẽr-os'çō-py, *n.* [*Aero-*, and Gr. *skopia*, from *skopein*, to look out.]

1. The investigation or observation of the atmosphere.

2. Aeroscepsy.

æ-rōse', *a.* Resembling copper or brass.

ā"ẽr-ō-sid'ẽr-īte, *n.* [*Aero-*, and Gr. *siderites*, of iron.] A meteorite consisting chiefly of iron.

ā"ẽr-ō-sid'ẽr-ō-līte, *n.* [*Aero-*, and Gr. *sidēros*, iron, and *lithos*, stone.] A meteorite containing both iron and stone.

ā'ẽr-ō-sphēre, *n.* [*Aero-*, and *sphere*, from Gr. *sphaira*, a ball.] The air surrounding the earth; the atmosphere.

ā'ẽr-ō-stat, *n.* [*Aero-*, and Gr. *statos*, sustaining.]

1. A machine or vessel sustaining weights in the air; a name given to air-balloons.

2. An aeronaut. [Rare.]

ā"ẽr-ō-stat'iç, ā"ẽr-ō-stat'iç-ăl, *a.* Suspending in air; pertaining to the art of aerial navigation.

ā"ẽr-ō-stat'iċs, *n.* The science that treats of the equilibrium of elastic fluids or of bodies sustained in them; hence, the science of aerial navigation.

ā"ẽr-os-tā'tion, *n.* 1. Aerial navigation; the science of raising, suspending, and guiding machines in the air, or of ascending in balloons.

2. The science of weighing air. [Obs.]

ā"ẽr-ō-trop'iç, *a.* [*Aero-*, and Gr. *tropē*, from *trepein*, to turn.] In botany, turning away from the natural course, as roots by the action of gases.

ā-ẽr-ot'rō-pism, *n.* The deviation of roots from their natural direction of growth, by the action of gases.

æ-rū'ġi-nous (ē-), *a.* [L. *æruginosus*, adj. from *ærugo*, rust of copper, from *æs*, copper.] Pertaining to or resembling copper-rust.

æ-rū'gō (ē-), *n.* [L., from *æs*, brass, copper.] The rust of brass or copper; verdigris.

ā'ẽr-y, *a.* Ethereal; airy; spiritual; also, high; lofty. [Rare.]

aer'y, aer'ie (*also pronounced* ē'rē, ā'ẽr-y), *n.* [W. *eryr*, Corn. *er*, an eagle.]

1. The nest of a bird of prey, as of an eagle.

2. A brood of such birds.

3. Any small, high-perched human habitation.

Formerly written *eyrie, eyry, eirie.*

ā'ẽr-y-light (-līt), *a.* Light as air; used for *airy light.*

æs'ċhy-nīte (es'), *n.* [Gr. *aeschynē*, shame.] A rare mineral found in the Ural Mountains; an ore containing titanium, zirconium, cerium, etc.

Æs-chy-nom′e-nē, *n.* [L., a sensitive plant, from Gr. *aischynomenē*, f. ppr. of *aischynein*, to disfigure.] In botany, a genus of plants of the bean family, *Leguminosæ*, mostly found in South America. Some of the species, as *Æschynomene hispida*, bear sensitive leaves.

æs-chy-nom′e-nous, *a.* Sensitive, as the leaves of some varieties of *Æschynomene*.

Æs-cū-lā′pi-ăn, Es-cū-lā′pi-ăn, *a.* Relating to Æsculapius or the art of healing.

Æs-cū-lā′pi-us, *n.* [L., from Gr. *Asklēpios*.] In mythology, the god of medicine, the son of Apollo by the nymph Coronis. His worship prevailed over all Greece. In the Homeric poems, *Æsculapius* is not a divinity but simply "the blameless physician." The most characteristic emblem of *Æsculapius* is the serpent. The name is often used as a general term for doctor, usually in a humorous sense.

æs′cū-lin, *n.* See *Esculin.*

Æ′sir (ā′sir *or* ē′sir), *n.pl.* [Ice. pl. of *as*, a god.] In Norse mythology, the heathen gods of Scandinavia.

Æ-sō′pi-ăn, Ē-sō′pi-ăn, *a.* Pertaining to Æsop, the famous Greek fabulist, or in his style.

Æ-sop′ic, Ē-sop′ic, *a.* Same as *Æsopian.*

æs′thā-cyte, *n.* [Gr. *aisthanesthai*, to feel, and *kytos*, cell.] One of the sensitive cells of a sponge.

æs″thē-mȧ-tol′ō-ġy, es″thē-mȧ-tol′ō-ġy, *n.* [Gr. *aisthēma, aisthēmatos*, sensation, and *logos*, description.] The branch of physiology treating of the senses and their organs.

æs-thē′si-ȧ, es-thē′si-ȧ, *n.* [Gr. *aisthēsis*, sensation, from *aisthanesthai*, to perceive.] In physiology, perception; feeling; sensibility.

æs-thē′si-ō-ġen, es-thē′si-ō-ġen, *n.* [Gr. *aisthēsis*, feeling, and *genēs*, producing.] A substance supposed to produce an effect upon the nervous system when touched.

æs-thē-si-ol′ō-ġy, es-thē-si-ol′ō-ġy, *n.* The branch of physiology which treats of the sensations.

æs-thē″si-ō-mā′ni-ȧ, *n.* [Gr. *aisthēsis*, feeling, and *mania*, madness.] Insanity accompanied by moral depravity or eccentricity.

æs-thē-si-om′e-tēr, es-thē-si-om′e-tēr, *n.* [Gr. *aisthēsis*, feeling, and *metron*, measure.] In medicine, an instrument for testing the tactile sensibility of the human body in health and disease, by ascertaining, through the application of the points of the instrument to the skin, the shortest distance at which two points can be perceived as distinctly separate.

æs-thē′sis, es-thē′sis, *n.* Æsthesia.

æs-thē-sod′ic, *a.* [Gr. *aisthēsis*, feeling, and *hodos*, a way.] Conveying sensory impulses or impressions; sensitive; applied to the nerves.

æs′thēte, es′thēte, *n.* [Gr. *aisthētēs*, one who perceives.] One who has great regard for æsthetics.

æs-thet′ic, æs-thet′ic-ăl, es-thet′ic, es-thet′ic-ăl, *a.* Of or pertaining to æsthetics; as, *æsthetic* persons, studies, etc.

æs-thet′ic-ăl-ly, es-thet′ic-ăl-ly, *adv.* According to the principles of æsthetics; with reference to the sense of the beautiful.

æs-thē-ti′ciăn, es-thē-ti′ciăn (-tish′un), *n.* One versed in æsthetics; an authority in matters of taste.

æs-thet′i-cism, es-thet′i-cism, *n.* 1. The doctrine or principles of æsthetics.

2. Attachment to æsthetics; a proneness to indulge and cultivate the sense of the beautiful.

æs-thet′ics, es-thet′ics, *n.* [Gr. *aisthētikos*, perceptive by feeling.] The science of deducing from nature and taste the rules and principles of art; the theory of the fine arts; the science or that branch of philosophy which deals with the beautiful; the doctrines of taste.

æs″thō-phys-i-ol′ō-ġy, *n.* [Gr. *aisthanesthai*, to perceive, and *physiologia*; *physis*, nature, and *logos*, discourse.] The physiology of sensation; that part of physiology which treats of the organs of sense and the parts of the body which exercise subsidiary functions.

æs-tif′ēr-ous, *a.* See *Estiferous.*

æs′ti-văl, *a.* [L. *æstivalis*, from *æstas*, summer.] See *Estival.*

æs′ti-vāte, *v.i.* [L. *æstivare, æstivatum*, to spend the summer.] See *Estivate.*

æs-ti-vā′tion, *n.* See *Estivation.*

æs′tū-ā-ry, *n.* See *Estuary.*

æs′tū-āte, es′tū-āte, *v.i.* [L. *æstuatus*, pp. of *æstuare*, to burn, boil up.] To be agitated; to rage; to boil. [Obs.]

æs-tū-ā′tion, es-tū-ā′tion, *n.* Agitation, as of a fluid in boiling; hence, mental agitation or excitement. [Obs.]

æs′tūre, es′tūre, *n.* Violent commotion. [Obs.]

Æ-thā′li-um, *n.*; *pl.* **Æ-thā′li-ȧ.** [L., from Gr. *aithalos*, smoke, soot.] A genus of slime-molds, *Myxomycetes*, often found in greenhouses where spent tan is used for heating purposes, and hence sometimes called *flowers of tan.*

ā-ē-thē-og′ȧ-mous, *a.* [Gr. *aēthēs*; *a* priv., *ēthos*, custom, and *gamos*, marriage.] A term applied to cryptogamic plants, founded on the opinion that their mode of propagation is not hidden, but only unusual.

æ′thēr, *n.* See *Ether.*

æ′thi-ops, *n.* A name formerly given by pharmacists to certain mineral preparations, which were black or very dark in color.

Æthiops martial; black oxid of iron; iron in the form of a very fine powder.

Æthiops mineral; a combination of mercury and sulphur, of a black color; black sulphid of mercury.

æth′ō-ġen (*or* æ′thō-ġen), *n.* [Gr. *aithos*, fire, and *genēs*, producing.] In chemistry, boric nitride; it burns with a greenish phosphorescence.

æ′thri-ō-scōpe, *n.* [Gr. *aithrios*, clear, and *scopein*, to observe.] An instrument, including a differential thermometer, for measuring minute changes in the heat radiated from the sky.

Æ-thū′sȧ, *n.* [Gr. *aithousa*, f. ppr. of *aithein*, to burn.] A genus of poisonous plants of the parsley family, *Umbelliferæ*.

æ″ti-ō-loġ′ic-ăl, ē″ti-ō-loġ′ic-ăl, *a.* Pertaining to ætiology.

æ″ti-ō-loġ′ic-ăl-ly, ē″ti-ō-loġ′ic-ăl-ly, *adv.* With regard to the cause, or the discovery of a cause.

æ-ti-ol′ō-ġy, ē-ti-ol′ō-ġy, *n.* [Gr. *aitia*, cause, and *logos*, description.] The science of the causes of disease; an account of the causes of anything, particularly of disease.

ā-ē-tī′tēs, *n.* [L., from Gr. *aetitēs*, from *aetos*, eagle.] Eaglestone; a variety of bog-iron.

ȧ-fär′, *adv.* At a distance in place; to or from a distance; used absolutely or with *from* preceding, or *off* following; as, he was seen *from afar*; I saw him *afar off*.

ȧ-fēard′, *a.* [AS. *afæred*, pp. of *afæran*, to frighten, from *a* and *fær*, terror.] Afraid. [Obs.]

Ā′fēr, *n.* [L.] The southwest wind.

aff, *adv.* and *prep.* [Scot.] Off.

af-fȧ-bil′i-ty, *n.* The quality of being affable; readiness to converse; civility and courteousness in receiving others, and in conversation; winning sociability.

Syn.—Civility, courtesy, politeness, suavity, urbanity, benignity.

af′fȧ-ble, *a.* [Fr. *affable*; L. *affabilis*, easy to be spoken to; from *ad*, to, and *fari*, to speak.]

1. Easy of conversation; admitting others to free conversation without reserve; courteous; complaisant; of easy manners; as, an *affable* gentleman.

2. Kindly of aspect; winning; inviting to friendliness and intercourse; benign; gracious; opposed to *forbidding*.

Syn.—Courteous, civil, complaisant, accessible, mild, benign, condescending, gracious, urbane, polite.

af′fȧ-ble-ness, *n.* Affability.

af′fȧ-bly, *adv.* In an affable manner; courteously; invitingly.

af-fab-ū-lā′tion, *n.* The moral of a fable. [Obs.]

af-fāir′, *n.* [ME. *afere*; OFr. *afaire*; Fr. *affaire*, from *à faire*, to do; L. *ad*, to, and *facere*, to do.]

1. Business of any kind; that which is done, or is to be done.

2. [*pl.*] Transactions in general; as, human *affairs*; political or ecclesiastical *affairs*; public *affairs*; a man of *affairs*.

3. [*pl.*] Matters; state; condition of business or concerns; as, his business *affairs* are tangled.

4. A personal concern, entanglement, or adventure; as, an *affair* of honor, or duel; a small engagement of forces; as, his little *affair* with the Indians.

5. [*pl.*] Ordinary and general happenings and experiences.

> Services to those around in the small *affairs* of life. —Herbert Spencer.

6. A thing or contrivance indefinitely expressed; as, the machine is a useless *affair*; her hat is a marvelous *affair*.

Syn.—Business, concern, matter, subject, transaction, topic, occurrence.

af-fam′ish, *v.t.* To starve. [Obs. See *Famish.*]

af-fam′ish-ment, *n.* A starving. [Obs.]

af-fat′ū-āte, *v.t.* [Obs.] See *Infatuate.*

af-fēar′, *v.t.* To frighten. [Obs.]

af-fect′, *v.t.*; affected, *pt.*, *pp.*; affecting, *ppr.* [ME. *affecten*; OFr. *affecter*; L. *affectare*, to strive after.]

1. To act upon; to produce an effect or change upon; as, cold *affects* the body; loss *affects* our interests.

2. To act upon, or touch, as the passions; as, *affected* by grief.

3. To aim at; aspire to; to desire, or entertain pretension to; as, to *affect* imperial sway.

4. To tend to by natural affinity or disposition; as, the drops of a fluid *affect* a spherical form; the deer *affects* the forest glades.

5. To love, or regard with fondness. [Obs.]

> Think not that wars we love and strife *affect*. —Fairfax.

6. To be pleased with or take a fancy to. [Obs.]

> Study what you most *affect*. —Shak.

7. To imitate as a model; as, he *affects* the airs of his superiors.

8. To make a pretentious display of; as, he *affects* a style of dress that is ridiculous.

9. To attempt to imitate, in a manner not natural; to assume the appearance of (what is not natural or real); as, to *affect* to be grave; *affected* friendship.

> Spenser, in *affecting* the ancients, writ no language. —B. Jonson.

Syn.—Assume, arrogate, like, pretend, feign, presume, put on, influence, move, interest, act on, concern, melt, soften, subdue, overcome.

af-fec-tā′tion, *n.* [L. *affectatio(n)*, from *adfectare*, to strive after, imitate.] An attempt to assume or exhibit what is not natural or real; false pretense; artificial appearance, or show; as, an *affectation* of wit, or of virtue.

af-fect′ed, *a.* 1. Inclined or disposed; followed by *to* or *toward*; as, well *affected to* or *toward* the government.

2. Given to false show; assuming, or pretending to possess what is not natural or real; as, an *affected* young woman.

3. Assumed artificially; not natural; as, *affected* airs.

4. In algebra, a term applied to an equation into which two or more powers of the unknown quantity enter; adfected.

af-fect′ed-ly, *adv.* In an affected manner; hypocritically; with more show than reality; formally; studiously; unnaturally; as, to walk *affectedly*; *affectedly* civil.

af-fect′ed-ness, *n.* The quality of being affected; affectation.

af-fect′ēr, af-fect′ŏr, *n.* A person who practises affectation; one who affects.

af-fect-i-bil′i-ty, *n.* The state of being affectible. [Rare.]

af-fect′i-ble, *a.* That may be affected. [Rare.]

af-fect′ing, *a.* 1. Exciting or touching the emotions; tending to move the affections; pathetic; as, an *affecting* address.

> The most *affecting* music is generally the most simple. —Mitford.

2. Full of affectation. [Obs.]

Syn.—Moving, pathetic, touching, tender, impressive, exciting.

af-fect′ing-ly, *adv.* In an affecting manner; in a manner to excite emotions.

af-fec′tion, *n.* [Fr. *affection*; L. *affectio*, from *afficere*, to affect.]

1. The state of being affected.

2. A bent of mind toward a particular object, holding a middle place between disposition and passion.

3. In a more particular sense, a settled good-will, love, or zealous attachment; as, the *affection* of a parent for his child. It was formerly followed by *to*, but is now generally followed by *for* or *toward*. The word is also often used in this sense in the plural; as, he won her *affections*.

4. Desire; inclination; propensity, good or evil; as, virtuous or vile *affections*.

5. In a general sense, an attribute, quality, or property, which is inseparable from its object; as, love, fear, and hope are *affections* of the mind; form, weight, and dimensions are *affections* of bodies.

6. In ethics, one of those principles of action in man which have persons for their immediate object, as esteem, gratitude, friendship, which are *benevolent affections*; hatred, envy, jealousy, revenge, which are *malevolent affections*.

7. A disease, or any morbid state; as, a gouty *affection*; hysteric *affection*.

8. In painting, a lively representation of passion. [Rare.]

Syn.—Fondness, attachment, kindness, love, liking, tenderness.

af-fec′tion-ăl, *a.* Implying affection.

af-fec′tion-āte, *a.* 1. Having great love, or affection; fond; as, an *affectionate* brother.

2. Warm in feeling; zealous. [Obs.]

> Man, in his love to God, and desire to please him, can never be too *affectionate*.—Sprat.

3. Proceeding from affection; indicating love; benevolent; tender; as, the *affectionate* care of a parent; an *affectionate* disposition.

4. Strongly inclined; used with *to*. [Rare.]

Syn.—Tender, attached, loving, devoted, warm, fond, earnest, kind, ardent.

af-fec′tion-āte-ly, *adv.* With affection; fondly; tenderly; kindly.

af-fec′tion-āte-ness, *n.* Fondness; good-will; affection.

af-fec′tioned, *a.* Disposed; having an affection of heart. [Obs.]

> Kindly *affectioned* one to another.—Rom. xii.

af-fec′tive, *a.* That affects or excites emotion; suited to affect. [Rare.]

af-fec′tive-ly, *adv.* In an affective or impressive manner.

af-fec′tū-ous, *a.* Full of passion. [Obs.]

af-feer′, *v.t.* [ME. *affeer*; OFr. *affeurer*; L. *afforare*, to fix a price; from, *ad*, to, and *forum*, market.]

1. In old English law, to assess or reduce (an arbitrary penalty or amercement) to a precise sum.

2. To confirm. [Obs.]

af-feer′ment, *n.* The act of affeering, or assessing an amercement, according to the circumstances of the case.

af-feer′ŏr, af-feer′ēr, *n* A person sworn to assess a penalty, or reduce an arbitrary fine to a reasonable amount.

af′fēr-ent, *a.* [L. *afferens*, ppr. of *afferre*; *ad*, to, and *ferre*, to bear.] In physiology, bringing to; conducting to; as, *afferent* nerves.

af-fet-tū-ō′sō, *a.* [It.] Tender; affecting; in music, giving a direction to render notes softly and affectingly.

af-fī′ănce, *n.* [ME. *affiance*, *afiance*; OFr. *afiance*, from *afier*, to trust in.]

1. The marriage contract or promise; faith pledged.

2. Strong trust, reliance, or faith.

The Christian looks to God with implicit *affiance*. —Atterbury.

af-fī′ănce, *v.t.*; affianced, *pt.*, *pp.*; affiancing, *ppr.* 1. To betroth; to pledge one's faith or fidelity in marriage, or to promise marriage.

2. To give assurance. [Obs.]

af-fī′ănced (-ănst), *n.* One betrothed; a future husband or wife.

I with my *affianced*. —Tennyson.

af-fī′ăn-cēr, *n.* One who makes a contract of marriage between parties.

af-fī′ănt, *n.* [OFr. *affiant*, ppr. of *affier*, to pledge one's faith.] In law, one who makes affidavit.

af-fīche′, *n.* [Fr. *afficher*, to fasten to.] A paper of any kind or bill pasted or affixed to a wall to be seen or read; a poster.

af-fi-dā′vit, *n.* [L., he has made oath. Perf. tense of *affidare*.] A declaration upon oath; a declaration in writing, signed by the party, and sworn to before an authorized magistrate or notary.

af-file′, *v.t.* [Fr. *affiler*; L. *ad*, to, and *fil*, thread, a polish.] To polish. [Obs.]

af-fil′i-ȧ-ble, *a.* Capable of being affiliated.

af-fil′i-āte, *v.t.*; affiliated, *pt.*, *pp.*; affiliating, *ppr.* [Fr. *affilier*, from L. *adfiliare*, to adopt as a son; *ad*, to, and *filius*, son.]

1. To adopt; to receive into a family as a son.

2. To receive into a society as a member, and initiate into its mysteries, objects, plans, etc.

3. To trace origin to; used with *upon*.

4. To determine the paternity of (an illegitimate child); with *on* or *upon*; as, a woman *affiliates* a child *upon* a man.

Syn.—Adopt, admit, initiate, receive.

af-fil′i-āte, *v.i.* To unite or associate oneself; as, to *affiliate* with a political party.

af-fil-i-ā′tion, *n.* 1. Adoption; association in the same family or society.

2. In law, the assignment of a child, as a bastard, to its father.

3. The assignment of anything to its origin; connection by way of descent.

af-fī′năl, *a.* [OFr. *affin*, *afin*, a kinsman or ally; L. *affinis*, from *ad*, to, and *finis*, border, end.] Related by affinity.

af-fine′, *v.t.* To refine. [Obs.]

af-fined′, *a.* Joined in affinity. [Obs.]

af-fin′i-tā-tive, *a.* Of the nature of affinity.

af-fin′i-tā-tive-ly, *adv.* By means of affinity.

af-fin′i-tive, *a.* Closely connected.

af-fin′i-ty, *n.* [L. *affinitas*, from *affinis*, adjacent, related by marriage; *ad*, to, and *finis*, end.]

1. The relation contracted by marriage between a husband and his wife's kindred, and between a wife and her husband's kindred; in contradistinction from consanguinity, or relation by blood.

Solomon made *affinity* with Pharaoh. —1 Kings iii. 1.

2. Applied to things generally, agreement; relation; conformity; resemblance; connection; as, the *affinity* of sounds, of colors, or of languages.

3. In chemistry, that force by which bodies of dissimilar nature unite in certain definite proportions to form a compound, different in its nature from any of its constituents; called *chemical* or *elective affinity*.

4. In biology, a resemblance in general plan or structure, or in the essential structural parts, existing between two organisms or groups of organisms.

5. A psychical attraction supposed to exist between individuals of opposite sex; also, either of the individuals so attracted; as, there is an *affinity* between us; she is my *affinity*.

6. Intercourse; acquaintance. [Obs.]

Syn.—Alliance, kindred, relationship.

af-fīrm′, *v.t.*; affirmed, *pt.*, *pp.*; affirming, *ppr.* [ME. *affermen*; OFr. *affirmer*; L. *affirmare*, to present as fixed; *ad*, to, and *firmare*, to make firm.]

1. To assert positively; to tell with confidence; to aver; to declare the existence of; to maintain as true; opposed to *deny*.

Affirming each his own philosophy. —Tennyson.

2. To declare in the affirmative, or sense of *yes*, as opposed to the negative; as, the convention *affirmed* the resolution.

3. To establish, confirm, or ratify, as an act already accomplished by oneself, or by another person or body; as, the supreme court *affirmed* the judgment.

Syn.—Aver, protest, assert, asseverate, assure, protest, avouch, confirm, establish, ratify, declare, pronounce.—We *affirm* a thing with confidence; we *assert* it against all denial we *aver* its truth with solemnity; we *protest* it, as what ought not to be called in question.

af-fīrm′, *v.i.* 1. To make a positive statement, as of fact.

2. To declare formally and solemnly before a court without taking the usual oath; to make a legal affirmation.

af-fīrm′ȧ-ble, *a.* Capable of being asserted or declared; followed by *of*; as, charity in judgment is *affirmable of* every just man.

af-fīrm′ȧ-bly, *adv.* In a way capable of affirmation.

af-fīrm′ănce, *n.* 1. Confirmation; ratification; as, the *affirmance* of a judgment; a statute in *affirmance* of common law.

2. Declaration; affirmation. [Rare.]

They swear it till *affirmance* breeds a doubt. —Cowper.

af-fīrm′ănt, *n.* One who affirms; one who makes a legal affirmation

af-fīr-mā′tion, *n.* [L. *affirmatio*, from *affirmare*, to affirm.]

1. The act of affirming or asserting as true; opposed to *negation* or *denial*.

2. That which is asserted; position declared as true; averment.

3. Confirmation; ratification; an establishment of what has been before done or decreed.

4. A solemn declaration made under the penalties of perjury, by persons who conscientiously decline taking an oath; such *affirmation* being in law equivalent to an oath.

af-fīrm′ȧ-tive, *a.* [Fr. *affirmatif*; L. *affirmativus*, from *affirmare*, to affirm.]

1. Affirming or asserting; declaratory of what exists; opposed to *negative*; as, an *affirmative* proposition.

2. Confirmative; ratifying; as, an act *affirmative* of common law.

3. In algebra, positive; a term applied to quantities which have the sign + (plus), denoting addition, and opposed to *negative*, or such as have the sign — (minus), denoting subtraction.

4. Positive; dogmatic. [Obs.]

af-fīrm′ȧ-tive, *n.* 1 That side of a debated question which affirms or maintains; opposed to the *negative*; as, there were seventy votes in the *affirmative* and thirty-five in the negative.

2. A short expression of assent, as the word *yes*.

3. A statement in which anything is affirmed; an affirmative proposition; an affirmation.

The *affirmatives* are indemonstrable. —Stillingfleet.

af-fīrm′ȧ-tive-ly, *adv.* In an affirmative manner; positively; on the affirmative side of a question; opposed to *negatively*.

af-fīrm′ȧ-tō-ry, *a.* Affirmative; assertive.

af-fīrm′ēr, *n.* One who affirms.

af-fix′, *v.t.*; affixed, *pt.*, *pp.*; affixing, *ppr.* [L. *affixare*, freq. of *affigere*, to fasten.]

1. To join to; to subjoin; to annex; to add; as, to *affix* a syllable to a word; to *affix* a seal to an instrument.

2. To attach, unite, or connect with; as, names *affixed* to ideas, or ideas *affixed* to things.

3. To fix or fasten in any physical manner. In this sense, *fix* is more generally used.

Syn.—Attach, add, annex, subjoin, connect, adjoin, append, fasten, fix.

af′fix, *n.* 1. Anything applied or put on, in the sense of a smaller or lesser to a greater; an addition; an attachment; that which is joined.

2. A letter or syllable added to a word or root; a prefix or suffix.

3. In decorative art, any small ornament added or attached, as the dragons on Japanese bronzes.

af-fix′ion (-fik′shun), *n.* The act of affixing, or the state of being affixed. [Rare.]

af-fix′tūre, *n.* That which is affixed. [Rare.]

af-flā′tion, *n.* [L. *afflatus*, pp. of *afflare*, to blow, or breathe upon; *ad*, to, and *flare*, to blow.] A blowing or breathing on.

af-flā′tus, *n.* 1. A breath or blast of wind.

2. Inspiration; communication of divine knowledge, or the power of prophecy; often called the *divine afflatus*; inspiration or impulse of a poetic, oratorical, or religious nature.

af-flict′, *v.t.*; afflicted, *pt.*, *pp.*; afflicting, *ppr.* [L. *afflictare*, to trouble, agitate, freq. of *affligere*, to strike down.]

1. To give (the body or mind) pain which is continued or of some permanence; to trouble, grieve, or distress; as, one is *afflicted* with the gout, or with melancholy, or with losses and misfortunes.

2. To humiliate; to persecute. [Obs.]

Syn.—Torment, distress, trouble, grieve, harass, pain, disquiet.

af-flict′ed-ness, *n.* The state of being afflicted; affliction. [Obs.]

af-flict′ēr, *n.* One who afflicts, or causes pain of body or of mind.

af-flict′ing, *a.* Grievous; distressing; as, an *afflicting* event.

af-flict′ing-ly, *adv.* In an afflicting manner.

af-flic′tion, *n.* [Fr. *affliction*; L. *afflictio(n)*, from *affligere*, to strike down.]

1. The state of being afflicted; a state of pain, distress, or grief; as, some virtues are seen only in *affliction*.

2. The cause of continued pain of body or mind; as sickness, losses, calamity, adversity, persecution.

Many are the *afflictions* of the righteous. —Ps. xxxiv. 19.

Syn.—Trouble, distress, sorrow, adversity, misfortune, grief, regret, sadness, tribulation, trial.—*Affliction* is the strongest of these terms, being a state of prolonged suffering; *adversity* and *misfortune* are general states; *distress* is particular, being the case of one under the *stress* or *pressure* of severe pain, bodily or mental; *trouble* and *sorrow* are less strong.

af-flic′tion-less, *a.* Having no affliction.

af-flic′tive, *a.* Giving pain; causing continued or repeated pain or grief; painful; distressing.

af-flic′tive-ly, *adv.* In a manner to give pain or grief.

af′flū-ence, *n.* [Fr. *affluence*; L. *affluentia*, abundance, from *affluere*, to flow to; *ad*, to, and *fluere*, to flow.]

1. Literally, a flowing to, or concourse; influx; as, an *affluence* of new settlers.

2. Figuratively, abundance; as, *affluence* of language; specifically, abundance of riches; wealth; as, a man of *affluence*.

Many new men rose rapidly to *affluence*. —Macaulay.

Syn.—Abundance, wealth, opulence, plenty, exuberance, prosperity, riches.

af′flū-en-cy, *n.* Affluence. [Rare.]

af′flū-ent, *a.* 1. Flowing to.

2. Wealthy; abounding in goods or riches; abundant.

Syn.—Rich, opulent, fluent.

af′flū-ent, *n.* [L. *affluens*, ppr. of *affluere*, to flow to.] A tributary stream.

af′flū-ent-ly, *adv.* In abundance; abundantly.

af′flū-ent-ness, *n.* The state of being affluent.

af′flux, *n.* [L. *affluxum*, pp. of *affluere*, to flow to; *ad*, to, and *fluere*, to flow.] The act of flowing to; a flowing to, or that which flows to; as, an *afflux* of blood to the head.

af-flux′ion (-fluk′shun), *n.* Afflux.

af-fōrce′, *v.t.* [OFr. *afforcier*; L. *affortiare*, from *ad*, to, and *fortis*, strong.] To reinforce; to support.

af-fōrce′ment, *n.* 1. A fortress; a fortification for defense. [Obs.]

2. A reinforcement, especially of a deliberative body. [Obs.]

af-fōrd′, *v.t.*; afforded, *pt.*, *pp.*; affording, *ppr.* [ME *aforthen*; AS. *gefarthien*, further, advance; *ge-* and *farthian*, further.]

1. To yield or produce, as fruit, profit, issues, or result. Thus, the earth *affords* grain; trade *affords* profit.

2. To yield, grant, or confer; as, a good life *affords* consolation in old age.

3. To be able to grant or sell with profit or without loss; as, A *affords* wine at a less price than B.

4. To be able to expend without suffering; as, a man can *afford* a sum yearly in charity; or to be able to bear expenses, or the price of the thing purchased; as, one man can *afford* to buy a farm, which another cannot.

5. To be able without loss or with profit; used with *can, could, might*, in the last two senses.

The merchant can *afford* to trade for smaller profits. —Hamilton.

Syn.—Spare, supply, give, impart, furnish, bestow.

af-fōrd′ȧ-ble, *a.* That may be afforded.

af-for′est, *v.t.* [L. *afforestare*, to convert into a forest; *ad*, to, and *foresta*, forest.] To convert (ground) into forest, as was done by the first Norman kings in England, for the purpose of affording themselves the pleasures of the chase.

af-for-es-tā'tion, *n.* The act of turning ground into forest or woodland. —Blackstone.

af-fọrm'ȧ-tive, *n.* A formative added to the stem; an affix; as *-ly* in king*ly*, *-ous* in virtu*ous*.

af-fran'chīse (*or* -chiz), *v.t.*; affranchised, *pt.*, *pp.*; affranchising, *ppr.* [Fr. *affranchir*, to make free; *a* for L. *ad*, to, and *franc*, free.] To free from any controlling power; to liberate; to make free.

af-fran'chīse-ment, *n.* The act of making free, or liberating from dependence or servitude. [Rare.]

af-frap', *v.t.* or *v.i.* [It. *affrappare*; L. *ad*, to, and Fr. *frapper*, to strike.] To strike. [Obs.]

af-frāy', *v.t.* To frighten; to startle. [Obs.]

af-frāy', *n.* [ME. *affray*, terror, brawl; OFr. *esfrai*; Fr. *affray*, from *affrayer*, to disquiet.]

1. In law, a public fight between two or more persons, to the terror of others. A private fight is not an *affray* in the legal sense.

2. As popularly used, any fight, quarrel, or brawl; tumult; disturbance.

Syn.—Quarrel, brawl, scuffle, encounter, fight, contest, tumult, disturbance.

af-frāy'ẽr, *n.* One who engages in affrays.

af-freight' (-frāt'), *v.t.*; affreighted, *pt.*, *pp.*; affreighting, *ppr.* [Fr. *affreter*; *a* and *freter*, freight, charter.] To hire for the transportation of goods or freight, as a vessel.

af-freight'ẽr, *n.* The person who hires or charters a ship to convey goods.

af-freight'ment, *n.* The act of hiring a ship for the transportation of goods.

af-fright' (-frīt'), *n.* 1. Sudden or great fear; terror.

2. The cause of terror; a frightful object.

The gods upbraid our suff'rings,
By sending these *affrights*. —B. Jonson.

af-fright', *v.t.*; affrighted, *pt.*, *pp.*; affrighting, *ppr.* [ME. *afrighten*; AS. *afyrhtan*, to terrify.] To impress with sudden fear; to frighten; to terrify or alarm. It expresses a stronger impression than *fear* or *apprehension*, and perhaps less than *terror*.

Syn.—Alarm, appal, dismay, shock, terrify.

af-fright'ed-ly, *adv.* With fright.

af-fright'en, *v.t.* [Obs.] See *Frighten*.

af-fright'ẽr, *n.* One who frightens. [Rare.]

af-fright'fụl, *a.* Terrifying; terrible; that may excite great fear; dreadful. [Obs.]

af-fright'fụl-ly, *adv.* Frightfully. [Obs.]

af-fright'ment, *n.* Fright; terror; the state of being frightened. [Rare.]

af-frŏnt', *v.t.*; affronted, *pt.*, *pp.*; affronting, *ppr.* [Fr. *affronter*, to encounter face to face; L. *affrontare*; *ad*, to, and *frons*, front, forehead.]

1. Literally, to meet or encounter face to face, in a good or bad sense. [Obs.]

The seditious *affronted* the king's forces. —Milton.

2. To offer abuse to the face; to insult, dare, or brave openly; to offer abuse or insult in any manner, by words or actions; to offend by insolence; as, to *affront* one by giving him the lie.

af-frŏnt', *n.* 1. Opposition to the face; open defiance; encounter. [Obs.]

2. Rude treatment; abuse; an insult; anything reproachful or contemptuous, that excites or justifies resentment, as foul language, or personal abuse; incivility.

3. Shame; disgrace; anything producing a feeling of shame or disgrace.

Syn.—Insult, abuse, offense, annoyance, indignity, wrong, outrage.

af-frŏn-té' (-tā'), *a.* [Fr.] In heraldry, front to front; an epithet applied to animals that face each other on an escutcheon; also, facing the spectator, as the lion in the crest of Scotland.

af-frŏnt'ed-ly, *adv.* In a manner to affront; provokingly. [Obs.]

af-frŏnt'ẽr, *n.* One who affronts.

af-frŏnt'ing-ly, *adv.* In an affronting manner.

af-frŏnt'ive, *a.* Giving offense; tending to offend; abusive.

af-frŏnt'ive-ness, *n.* The quality that gives offense. [Rare.]

af-fūṣe', *v.t.* [L. *affusus*, pp. of *affundere*, to pour to; *ad*, to, and *fundere*, to pour.] To pour upon; to sprinkle, as with a liquid. [Rare.]

af-fū'ṣion, *n.* 1. The act of pouring upon, or sprinkling with a liquid, as water upon a child in baptism.

2. In medicine, the act of pouring water, etc., on the whole or part of the body, as a remedy in disease.

af-fȳ', *v.t.* To betroth; to bind or join. [Obs.]

af-fȳ', *v.i.* To trust or confide. [Obs.]

Af'ghăn (-găn), *n.* 1. A native of Afghanistan.

2. [a—] A kind of woolen blanket or carriage-robe.

Af'ghăn, *a.* Pertaining to Afghanistan.

ȧ-fiēld', *adv.* To the field; in the field; abroad; at large.

ȧ-fīre', *adv.* and *a.* On fire.

ȧ-flāme', *adv.* and *a.* Flaming; ablaze.

ȧ-flat', *adv.* and *a.* On a level with the ground. [Obs.]

ȧ-flaunt', *adv.* and *a.* Showy; flaunting; in a flaunting manner.

ȧ-flick'ẽr, *adv.* and *a.* Flickering; wavering.

ȧ-flōat', *adv.* and *a.* 1. Borne on the water; floating; swimming; as, the ship is *afloat*.

2. On board ship; at sea; as, much wheat is *afloat*.

3. Figuratively, moving; in circulation; passing from place to place; as, a rumor is *afloat*.

4. Unfixed; moving without guide or control; as, our affairs are all *afloat*.

5. Flooded; awash; as, the deck is *afloat*.

ȧ-flōw', *adv.* and *a.* Flowing; in a flowing state.

ȧ-flush', *adv.* and *a.* 1. Flushed or blushing.

2. On the same level.

ȧ-flut'tẽr, *adv.* and *a.* In an agitated manner; agitated.

ȧ-fōam', *adv.* and *a.* In a foaming state; foaming; as, the water is all *afoam*.

ȧ-foot', *adv.* and *a.* 1. On foot; traveling or moving on the feet.

2. In action astir; about.

3. In a state of preparation; as, a design is *afoot*.

ȧ-fōre', *adv.* [ME. *aforn*; AS. *onforan*; *on*, on, and *foran*, at the front.]

1. In front of; before. [Rare.]

2. In the fore part of a vessel.

3. In time foregone and past.

4. Before in position.

ȧ-fōre', *prep.* 1. Before; as, *afore* God; *afore* the mast; none is *afore* or after another.

Afore the mast; applied to a common sailor whose berth is in the forecastle.

ȧ-fōre', *conj.* Rather than; before; as, *afore* I'll endure tyranny I'll die.

Afore is still retained in common speech, in the Scriptures, and certain compounds, but its use in pure literature is rare.

ȧ-fōre'cit-ed, *a.* Previously quoted.

ȧ-fōre'gō-ing, *a.* Going before; referring to something previous.

ȧ-fōre'hand, *adv.* and *a.* I. *adv.* In time previous; by previous provision.

II. *a.* Prepared; previously provided; as, to be *aforehand* in business; well supplied with means of living, by one's own efforts; popularly changed into *forehanded*; as, a *forehanded* farmer.

ȧ-fōre'men-tioned, *a.* Mentioned before in the same writing or discourse.

ȧ-fōre'nāmed, *a.* Named before.

ȧ-fōre'said (-sed), *a.* Said or recited before, or in a preceding part.

ȧ-fōre'thought (-that), *a.* Premeditated; prepense; as, malice *aforethought*, which is required to constitute murder.

ȧ-fōre'thought, *n.* Previous deliberation; forethought.

ȧ-fōre'time, *adv.* In time past; in a former time.

ā fọr-ti-ō'rī (-shi-). [L.] With stronger reasons.

ȧ-foul', *adv.* or *a.* Entangled; in a state of collision; not free.

To run afoul of; to collide with so as to cause entanglement or injury.

ȧ-frāid', *a.* [ME. *afraied*, pp. of *afraien*, to frighten.] Fearful; filled with alarm; timid; stricken with fear; apprehensive of disaster; dreading. It is followed by *of* before the object of fear.

I am afraid; a colloquial phrase used to break the harshness of the statement which follows; as, *I am afraid* he lies.

Syn.—Alarmed, apprehensive, cautious, timid, fearful, timorous, cowardly, frightened.

af'reet, *n.* Same as *Afrit*.

ȧ-fresh', *adv.* Anew; again; recently; after intermission.

Af'riç, *a.* and *n.* Same as *African*.

Af'ri-căn, *a.* and *n.* [L. *Afer*, an African.]

I. *a.* Pertaining to Africa.

II. *n.* A native of Africa.

Af'ri-can''dẽr, *n.* One born in South Africa, of white parents; also spelled *Afrikander*.

Af'ri-căn-ism, *n.* A word, idiom, custom, or other characteristic of natives of Africa.

Af'ri-căn-ize, *v.t.* To place under African or negro domination; to give an African character to.

af'rit, af'rite, af'reet, *n.* [Ar. *frit*, a demon.] In Mohammedan mythology, a powerful kind of demon.

Af'rō-. A combining form, signifying pertaining to Africa; from Africa.

Af'rō-A-mer'i-căn, *n.* A person of the African race or of African descent, residing in America.

ȧ-frŏnt', *adv.* In front.

ȧ-frŏnt', *prep.* In front of.

ȧft, *a.* or *adv.* [AS. *æftan*, behind, in the rear.] In nautical use, at or toward the stern or pertaining to the stern of a ship; abaft; astern.

ȧft'ẽr, *a.* [ME. *after*; AS. *æfter*, after; Ice. *aptr*; Gr. *apōterō*, further off.]

1. A marine term, signifying more aft, or toward the stern of the ship; as, *after*-sails; *after*-hatchway.

2. Subsequent; later in time; as, in *after* life.

After-hands shall sow the seed. —Whittier.

ȧft'ẽr, *prep.* 1. Behind in place; as, men placed in line one *after* another.

2. Later in time; as, *after* supper. This word often precedes a sentence, as a governing preposition.

After I am risen again, I will go before you into Galilee. —Matt. xxvi. 32.

3. In pursuit of; moving behind; following; in search of; as, the police are *after* him.

4. In imitation of; as, to make a thing *after* a model; a portrait *after* Vandyke.

5. According to; as, consider a thing *after* its intrinsic value.

6. According to the direction and influence of.

To live *after* the flesh. —Rom. viii. 12.

7. In honor of; for the sake of; as, to name a boy *after* his father.

8. Below in order of rank or excellence; as, Milton comes *after* Shakspere.

9. In consequence of; as, *after* this experience, I will take greater precautions.

10. In opposition to; as, *after* all warnings, he persisted.

11. Concerning; about; as, to inquire *after* one who is absent.

ȧft'ẽr, *adv.* Subsequently; later in time; also, behind; in the rear; as, he comes *after*. This is really an elliptical use of the preposition, the object being understood.

ȧft'ẽr-ac''cep-tā'tion, *n.* A sense not at first admitted.

ȧft'ẽr-ac-çount'', *n.* A subsequent reckoning.

ȧft'ẽr-act, *n.* A subsequent act.

ȧft'ẽr-ā''ġeṣ, *n.pl.* Later ages; succeeding times. *After-age*, in the singular, is not improper.

ȧft'ẽr-birth, *n.* The placenta in which the fetus is involved, and which comes away after delivery.

ȧft'ẽr-brāin, *n.* The medulla oblongata; the part of the brain behind the hindbrain.

ȧft'ẽr-çast, *n.* A play after the game is ended; hence, any attempt made too late.

ȧft'ẽr-çlap, *n.* An unexpected subsequent event; something disagreeable happening after an affair is supposed to be at an end.

ȧft'ẽr-çost, *n.* Later cost; expense after the execution of the main design.

ȧft'ẽr-çourse, *n.* Future conduct; also, a following course at a meal.

ȧft'ẽr-çrop, *n.* The second crop in the same year.

ȧft'ẽr-damp, *n.* Choke-damp arising from an explosion of fire-damp.

ȧft'ẽr-dāyṣ, *n.pl.* Future days.

ȧft'ẽr-ēat''āġe, *n.* A second growth; aftermath; the stalks or stubble remaining after harvesting.

ȧft'ẽr-eye (-ī), *v.t.* To keep (one) in view; to look after. [Rare]

ȧft'ẽr-gāme, *n.* A subsequent scheme, or expedient.

ȧft'ẽr-glōw, *n.* A reflected light in the western sky after sunset.

ȧft'ẽr-grȧss, *n.* A second crop of grass.

ȧft'ẽr-grōwth, *n.* Second growth; figuratively, development.

ȧft'ẽr-guärd, *n.* The seamen stationed on the poop or after-part of the ship, to attend the after-sails.

ȧft'ẽr-hōpe, *n.* Future hope.

ȧft'ẽr-im''āġe, *n.* The impression retained by the eye after withdrawing it from a steadfast look at a brilliant object.

ȧft'ẽr-ingṣ, *n.pl.* The last milk drawn in milking; strippings.

ȧft'ẽr-life, *n.* 1. Future life, or the life after this.

2. A later period of life; subsequent life.

ȧft'ẽr-mȧth, *n.* A second crop of grass in the same season; hence, figuratively, any supplementary result; as, the *aftermath* of a crime.

ȧft'ẽr-mōst, *a. superl.* Hindmost; nearest the stern; opposed to *foremost*.

ȧft-ẽr-nŏŏn', *n.* The part of the day which follows noon, between noon and evening.

ȧft-ẽr-nŏŏn'-lā'dieṣ, *n.pl.* A plant of the genus *Mirabilis*. [See *Four-o'clock*.]

ȧft'ẽr-nōte, *n.* In music, a second or unaccented note.

ȧft'ẽr-pāinṣ, *n.pl.* The pains which succeed childbirth.

ȧft'ẽr-pärt, *n.* The latter part; in nautical language, the part of a ship toward the stern.

ȧft'ẽr-piēce, *n.* A piece performed after a play; a farce or other short dramatic entertainment.

ȧft'ẽr-rāke, *n.* In nautical language, a part of the hull jutting out at the stern.

ȧft'ẽr-sāilṣ, *n.pl.* The sails on the mizzenmast and on the stays between the main- and mizzenmasts.

ȧft'ẽr-shȧft, *n.* A supplementary feather

springing from the stem of the main feather; the shaft of such a feather; the hypoptilum, or the hyporachis.

ȧft'ẽr-swarm, *n.* A swarm of bees which leaves the hive after the first.

ȧft'ẽr-tāste, *n.* The taste left in the mouth after eating or drinking.

ȧft'ẽr-thought (-that), *n.* Reflection after an act or experience; a useful later thought; a thought or expedient occurring too late to be available.

ȧft'ẽr-times, *n.pl.* Succeeding times. It may be used in the singular.

ȧft'ẽr-wȧrd, ȧft'ẽr-wȧrds, *adv.* In later or subsequent time.

ȧft'ẽr-wīse, *a.* Wise afterward or too late.

ȧft'ẽr-wit, *n.* Subsequent wit; wisdom that comes too late.

ȧft'ẽr-wit"ted, *a.* Slow-witted.

ȧft'mōst, *a.* In seamen's language, nearest to the stern.

ȧft'wȧrd, *a.* Approaching the stern.

ā-gä', ā-ghä' (-gä'), *n.* [Turk. *agha*, commander.] In the Turkish dominions, a commander or chief officer. The title is given to various chief officers, whether civil or military. It is also given by courtesy to any distinguished individual.

ȧ-gä'dȧ, *n.* Same as *Haggadah*.

ȧ-gad'iç, *a.* Same as *Haggadic*.

ȧ-gain' (ȧ-gen'), *adv.* [ME. *agen*; AS. *ongegn, ongean*; *on*, for *an*, on, and *gean*, like G. *gegen*, against.]

1. Back; referring to movement toward a former position, place, or person; as, bring us word *again*.

2. Back; in return, as a reply, etc.; as, to give back *again*.

3. A second time; once more; as, I will not *again* curse the ground.—Gen. viii. 21.

4. Moreover; further; in addition; as, *again*, let me add; *again*, it is further to be considered.

5. Once more; once repeated; used of number and quantity, in the phrases *as large, as much*, or *as many, again*.

6. Anew; another time; as, if a man die, shall he live *again?*—Job xiv. 14.

Again and again; often; repeatedly.

Now and again; now and then; occasionally.

Again as a compound with verbs or verbal derivatives was used somewhat in Anglo-Saxon and frequently in Old English. As a preposition in the sense of opposed to, *against* now displaces it entirely, although in the form of *agen* or *agin*, it still remains in illiterate use.

ȧ-gain', ȧ-gains', *prep.* Against; toward, in order to meet. [Obs.]

ȧ-gain'bu̇y (-bī), *v.t.* To redeem. [Obs.]

ȧ-gain'sāy, *v.t.* To gainsay. [Obs.]

ȧ-gainst' (-genst'), *prep.* [ME. *againest, again*, from AS. *ongegn*, and *es*, a genit. ending, and *t*, intensive.] The elementary sense of this word is *opposition*, variously modified according to its application to different objects.

1. In enmity or disapprobation of.

His hand will be *against* every man.
—Gen. xvi. 12.

2. In contrariety, contradiction, or repugnance to; as, a decree *against* law, reason, or public opinion.

3. In competition with, as between different sides or parties; as, there are twenty votes in the affirmative *against* ten in the negative.

4. In an opposite direction to; as, to ride *against* the wind.

5. Opposite in place; abreast; as, a ship is *against* the mouth of a river. In this sense it is often preceded by *over*.

6. In opposition, noting adversity, injury, or contrariety to wishes; as, this change of measures is *against* us.

7. Bearing upon; as, one leans *against* a wall.

8. In provision for; in preparation for; as, have things ready *against* our return.

ȧ-gain'stand, *v.t.* To withstand. [Obs.]

ȧ-gain'wȧrd, *adv.* Back again. [Obs.]

ag-ȧ-lac'ti-ȧ, *n.* [Gr. *agalaktia*, from *a* priv., and *gala, galaktos*, milk.] Failure of milk secretion after childbirth.

ag-ȧ-lac'tous, *a.* Characterized by agalactia.

ä'gal-ä'gal, *n.* Same as *Agar-agar*.

ag'ȧ-lax-y, *n.* Same as *Agalactia*.

ȧ-gal'lō-chum, ag'al-loch, *n.* [L., from Gr. *agallochon*, the fragrant aloe.] A very soft, resinous wood, of a highly aromatic smell, brought from the East Indies, and burnt as a perfume. It is the Scriptural aloes-wood, but has no connection with the common aloe. It yields uggur oil. Also called *agal-wood*.

ag-al-mat'ō-lite, *n.* [Gr. *agalma, agalmatos*, image, and *lithos*, stone.] A soft stone, carved into images in China, and hence called figure-stone. It has the appearance of soapstone, but contains alumina instead of magnesia. Also called *steatite* and *pagodite*.

ag'al-wood, *n.* Same as *Agallochum*.

Ag'ȧ-mȧ, *n.* A genus of small saurian reptiles.

ag'ȧ-mȧ, *n.* [Guiana name.] A species of the genus *Agama*.

ag'ȧ-mī, *n.* [Fr., from the Guiana name.] A grallatorial bird of Central America, commonly called the golden-breasted trumpeter, from its cry.

Agami (*Psophia crepitans*).

ȧ-gam'iç, *a.* [Gr. *agamos*; *a* priv., and *gamos*, married.] Produced without sexual union; asexual.

ȧ-gam'iç-ăl-ly, *adv.* In an agamic manner.

ag'ȧ-mist, *n.* [Gr. *agamos*; *a* priv., and *gamos*, married.] An unmarried person, or one who is opposed to marriage.

ag"ȧ-mō-gen'e-sis, *n.* [Gr. *agamos*; *a* priv., and *gamos*, married, and *genesis*, reproduction.] In biology, reproduction without the congress of distinct sexes.

ag"ȧ-mō-gē-net'iç, *a.* Produced asexually.

ag"ȧ-mō-gē-net'iç-ăl-ly, *adv.* By or with asexual generation.

ag'ȧ-moid, *n.* and *a.* I. *n.* An agama.

II. *a.* Pertaining to or having the characteristics of lizards of the genus *Agama*.

ȧ-gam'ō-spōre, *n.* [Gr. *agamos*; *a* priv., and *gamos*, married, and *spora*, seed.] A spore produced asexually.

ag'ȧ-mous, *a.* [Gr. *a* priv., and *gamos*, marriage.]

1. In botany, having no visible organs of fructification. A term applied to cryptogamic plants, because they have no distinct sexual organs, or to those inferior groups of cryptogamic plants in which there is nothing analogous to such organs, as the fungi, lichens, and confervæ.

2. In biology, asexual.

ȧ-gañ-gli-on'iç, *a.* Having no ganglion cells.

ag-ȧ-pan'thus, *n.* [Gr. *agapē*, love, and *anthos*, flower.] Any cultivated plant of the order *Liliaceæ*.

ȧ-gāpe' (*or* -gāp), *adv.* or *a.* Gaping, as with wonder, expectation, or eager attention; having the mouth wide open.

ag'ȧ-pē, *n.*; *pl.* **ag'ȧ-pæ**. [Gr. *agapē*, love.] Among the primitive Christians, a love feast or feast of charity, held before or after the communion, when contributions were made for the poor. This feast was held at first without scandal, but afterward being abused, it was condemned at the council of Carthage, A. D. 397.

Ag-ȧ-pem'ō-nē, *n.* [Gr. *agapē*, love, and *monē*, abode.] The abode of love; an association of men and women living promiscuously on a common fund; specifically, the association formed by Rev. H. J. Prince in 1846 at Charlynch, England.

ä'gär-ä'gär, *n.* The native Ceylonese name for Ceylon moss, a seaweed—the *Gracilaria lichenoides*—much used in the East for soups and jellies. It is employed by scientists in bacterial culture, and in China as a glue; sometimes called *Bengal isinglass*.

ag'ȧ-riç (*or* ȧ-gar'iç), *n.* A fungus of the genus *Agaricus*.

ȧ-gar'i-cin, *n.* An extract of the white agaric, *Polyporus officinalis*.

ȧ-gar'i-çoid, *a.* Of the nature of an agaric; mushroom-like.

A-gar'i-cus, *n.* [L. *agaricum*, from Gr. *agarikon*.] In botany, a genus of fungi, containing numerous species, including many of the most common mushrooms, some of which are valued as articles of food, while others are poisonous.

Agaricus disseminatus.

In pharmacy, the term was applied to two species of fungi, belonging to the Linnæan genus *Boletus*; that of the larch, *Boletus laricis*, called also *male agaric*; and that of the oak, *Boletus igniarius*, called also *female agaric* and *touchwood*, from its readiness to take fire. The former was used as a cathartic; the latter as a styptic, and also for tinder and in dyeing.

Agaric mineral; a light, chalky deposit of carbonate of lime, rubbing to a powder between the fingers; formed in caverns or fissures of limestone. In composition it is identical with chalk.

ȧ-gȧsp', *adv.* and *a.* In a gasping manner; out of breath.

ȧ-gȧst', *a.* Old form of *aghast*.

A-gas'tri-ȧ, *n.pl.* [Gr. *a* priv., and *gastēr*, stomach.] Formerly, a low class of animals, supposed to be destitute of intestines.

ȧ-gas'triç, *a.* Without a stomach or digestive canal, as the tapeworm.

ȧ-gāte', *adv.* On the way; going. [Obs.]

ag'āte, *n.* [Fr. *agate*; L. *achates*; Gr. *achatēs*, an agate.]

1. A semipellucid, uncrystallized variety of quartz, presenting various tints in the same specimen. Its colors are delicately arranged in stripes or bands, or are blended in clouds; when they are in angular shapes, like the outline of a fortification, it is called *fortification agate*; when in mossy threads, *moss-agate*. The Scotch pebble is a fortification *agate*. *Ribbon-agate, zone-agate, star-agate*, etc., obtain their names from their characteristic appearance. Striking varieties are produced in Oldenburg, Germany, by the aid of artificial coloring. *Agates* are the least valuable of the precious stones. They are found chiefly in trap-rocks and serpentine, often as geodes.

2. An instrument used by gold-wire drawers, so called from the agate in the middle of it.

3. In printing, type of a size between pearl and nonpareil. In England it is called *ruby*.

This line is printed in agate.

4. In bookbinding, a burnisher.

5. A boy's marble made of *agate*, or of some material in imitation of *agate*.

6. A belittling epithet, found in Shakspere, derived from the little figures carved on *agate* seals; as, manned with an *agate*.

ag'āte-shell, *n.* A shell of the genus *Achatina*.

Ag'ȧ-this, *n.* [Gr. *agathis*, a ball of thread.] A genus of Australasian trees commonly called *Dammara*, including the wax-pine.

ag'ȧ-thişm, *n.* [Gr. *agathos*, good, and *-ism*.] The doctrine that all things tend toward ultimate good.

ag-ȧ-tif'ẽr-ous, *a.* Composed of or producing agates.

ag'ȧ-tine, *a.* Pertaining to agate.

ag'ȧ-tize, *v.t.* To change to or make to resemble agate.

ag'ȧ-tized, *a.* Having the colored lines and figures of agate.

Agatized wood; a kind of agate, resulting from the petrifaction of wood, and still showing something of its texture.

ag'ȧ-ty, *a.* Of the nature of agate.

A-gā'vē, *n.* [Gr. *agauos*, noble.] A genus of plants; the best-known species is the American aloe, or century-plant, native to Mexico, where it is largely cultivated under the name of *maguey*. It attains maturity in from ten to fifty or sixty years. The magnificent scape of flowers which at this time it throws up from the center to a height of forty feet, marks its death. The plant has many uses. From its sap the native intoxicant *pulque* is made. An extract from its leaves serves as soap, and the withered flower-stem is cut up for razor-strops. Thread, rope, and even paper, are made from the fiber of its leaves.

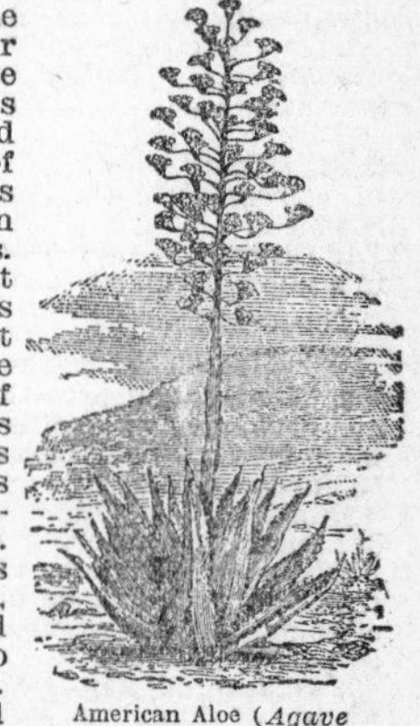
American Aloe (*Agave Americana*).

ȧ-gāzed', *a.* Struck with amazement; aghast; used only by a few old writers. [Obs.]

āge, *n.* [OFr. *aage*; Fr. *âge*; L. *ætа(t)s*; Gr. *aiōn*, a period of existence.]

1. The whole duration of a being, whether animal, vegetable, or other kind; as, the usual *age* of a man is seventy years.

2. That part of the duration of a being which is between its beginning and any given time; as, what is the present *age* of a man, or of the earth?

3. The latter part of life, or long-continued duration; oldness; as, the eyes of Israel were dim for *age*.

4. A certain period of human life, marked by a difference of state, as infancy, youth, manhood, and old age; the *age* of youth; the *age* of manhood.

5. The period when a person of either sex becomes his own master in the legal sense; as, in the United States, both males and females are of *age* at twenty-one years.

6. The period of life at which a person may be held legally responsible for certain acts, or capable of exercising certain powers; as, the *age* of discretion; the *age* of consent, in females.

7. A particular period of time, as distinguished from others; as, the golden *age*; the *age* of iron; the *age* of heroes or of chivalry.

8. The people who live at a particular period hence, a generation, and a succession of generations; as, *ages* yet unborn.

9. In geology, a great period of earth-existence, marked by certain classes of rocks and animal or vegetable forms; as, the Carboniferous *age*; the Silurian *age*.

10. A century, as in the phrases, dark *ages*, middle *ages*.

11. In the game of poker, the position of the player first to the left of the dealer, his being the oldest hand; he leads in betting or has the right to pass till the last.

Syn.—Century, date, epoch, era, generation, period, time.

āge, *v.i.*; aged (ājd), *pt., pp.*; aging, *ppr.* To grow old; to show signs of age; as, he became fleshy as he *aged*.

āge, *v.t.* To produce the effect of age upon; to cause to grow or appear old.

ā′ged, *a.* 1. Old; having lived long; having lived almost the usual time allotted to that species of being; applied to animals or plants; as, an *aged* man, or an *aged* oak.

2. [ājd.] Having a certain age; having lived; as, a man *aged* forty years.

3. Pertaining to old age; as, *aged* wrinkles.

Syn.—Elderly, old, senile.

ā′ged, *n.* Old persons, collectively.

ā′ged-ly, *adv.* Like an aged person.

ā′ged-ness, *n.* The state of being aged; oldness.

āge′less, *a.* Without limit of existence; absence of old age.

ȧ-gen′, *adv.* and *prep.* [Obs.] See *Again*.

ā′gen-cy, *n.* [L. *agentia*, from *agen(t)s*, ppr. of *agere*, to act.]

1. The quality of moving, or of exerting power; the state of being in action; action; operation; instrumentality; as, the *agency* of Providence in the natural world.

2. The office of an agent, or factor; business of an agent intrusted with the concerns of another; as, the principal pays the expenses of the *agency*.

3. The headquarters of an agent; as, an insurance *agency*.

ā′gend, *n.* [Obs.] See *Agendum*.

ȧ-gen′dum, *n.*; *pl.* **ȧ-gen′dȧ.** [L., neut. of the gerundive of *agere*, to act.]

1. Something to be done; usually in the plural.

2. [*pl.*] A memorandum-book; the service or office of a church; a ritual or liturgy; items of business to be brought before a meeting, etc.

aġ-e-nes′iç, *a.* Imperfectly developed.

ȧ-gen′e-sis, *n.* [Gr. *a* priv., and *genesis*, birth.] Any imperfect development of an organ, or variation in construction.

aġ-en-nē′siç, *a.* Impotent; sterile; unproductive.

aġ-en-nē′sis, *n.* [Gr. *a* priv., and *gennesis*, generation.] Sterility; unproductiveness.

ā′gent, *a.* Acting; opposed to *patient*, or sustaining action; as, the body *agent*. [Rare.]

ā′gent, *n.* [L. *agens*, *agentis*, ppr of *agere*, to act; Gr. *agein*, to drive; Ice. *aka*; Sans. *aj*, drive.]

1. An actor; one who exerts power, or has the power to act; as, a moral *agent*.

2. An active power or cause; that which has the power to produce an effect; as, heat is a powerful *agent*.

3. A substitute, deputy, or factor; one intrusted with the business of another; one who acts for another, as his representative.

Syn.—Deputy, substitute, actor, factor.

ā-ġen′tiăl (-shăl), *a.* Pertaining to an agent or agency.

ā′gent-ship, *n.* The office of an agent; agency. [Obs.]

A-ġĕr′ȧ-tum, *n.* [L., from Gr. *ageraton*, a plant; *a* priv., and *geras*, age.] A genus of American plants. *Ageratum Mexicanum* is cultivated as a border plant.

ȧ-geū′si-ȧ, *n.* Same as *Ageustia*.

ȧ-geūs′ti-ȧ, *n.* [L., from Gr. *ageustia*, a fasting, from *ageustos*; *a* priv., and *geustos*, tasting.] In medicine, loss of the sense of taste, from nervous disease.

aġ-ġen-ẽr-ā′tion, *n.* [L., from *aggenerare*, to beget in addition.] The state of growing to another. [Obs.]

aġ′ġẽr, *n.* [L.] A fortress, or mound. [Obs.]

aġ′ġẽr-āte, *v.t.* [L. *aggeratus*, pp. of *aggerare*, to heap up.] To heap. [Obs.]

aġ-ġẽr-ā′tion, *n.* A heaping; accumulation; as, *aggerations* of sand [Rare.]

aġ-ġẽr-ōse′, *a.* In heaps, or formed in heaps.

aġ-ġest′, *v.t.* To heap up. [Obs.]

ag-glom′ẽr-āte, *v.t.*; agglomerated, *pt., pp.*; agglomerating, *ppr.* [L. *agglomeratus*, pp. of *agglomerare*; *ad*, to, and *glomerare*, to form into a ball.] To wind, or collect into a ball; to gather into a mass.

ag-glom′ẽr-āte, *v.i.* To gather, grow, or collect into a ball or mass.

ag-glom′ẽr-āte, ag-glom′ẽr-ā-ted, *a.* Wound or collected into a ball.

ag-glom′ẽr-āte, *n.* 1. A mass or ball.

2. A mass of volcanic fragments compacted by heat.

ag-glom-ẽr-ā′tion, *n.* The act of winding into a ball; the state of being gathered into a mass; an agglomerated mass or cluster.

ag-glom′ẽr-ā-tive, *a.* Having a tendency to agglomerate.

ag-glū′ti-nănt, *n.* [L. *agglutinans*, ppr. of *agglutinare*, to glue to.] Any viscous substance which unites other substances, by causing an adhesion; any application which tends to unite parts which have too little adhesion.

ag-glū′ti-nănt, *a.* Uniting, as glue; tending to cause adhesion.

ag-glū′ti-nāte, *v.t.*; agglutinated, *pt., pp.*; agglutinating, *ppr.* [L. *agglutinatus*, pp. of *agglutinare*, to cement to, *ad*, to, and *glutinare*, from *gluten*, glue.] To unite, or cause to adhere, as with glue or other viscous substance; to unite by causing an adhesion of substances.

ag-glū′ti-nāte, *a.* 1. Cemented together, as with glue.

2. Formed by combining root-words without materially changing their form or meaning; as, *agglutinate* languages. Turkish is an *agglutinate* tongue.

ag-glū-ti-nā′tion, *n.* 1. The act of uniting by glue or other tenacious substance; the state of being thus united.

2. In philology, a combination of root-words, in which their form and meaning remain practically unchanged.

ag-glū′ti-nā-tive, *a.* 1. That tends to unite, or has power to cause adhesion.

2. Formed or distinguished by agglutination, as a language.

ag-grāce′, *v.t.* To favor [Obs.]

ag-grāce′, *n.* Kindness; favor. [Obs.]

ag-grȧ-dā′tion, *n.* The act of aggrading; specifically, in physiography, the deposition of detritus by running water, as in the channel of a river, tending to form a regular grade, or, in a plain, the building up of the low places to a regular grade; opposed to *degradation*

ag-grāde′, *v. t.* [L. *aggradi*; *ad*, to, and *gradi*, to step, from *gradus*, step.] In geology, to grade up; the opposite of *degrade*, or wear away.

ag′gran-di-zȧ-ble, *a.* That may be aggrandized.

ag-gran-di-zā′tion, *n.* The act of aggrandizing. [Obs.]

ag′gran-dīze, *v.t.*; aggrandized (-dīzd), *pt., pp.*; aggrandizing, *ppr.* [Fr. *agrandir*, to augment, from L. *ad*, to, and *grandire*, to increase, from *grandis*, great.]

1. To make great or greater in power, rank, or honor; to exalt; as, to *aggrandize* a family.

2. To enlarge; applied to immaterial things; as, to *aggrandize* our conceptions.

Syn.—Exalt, promote, advance.

ag′gran-dīze, *v.i.* To enlarge or become great. [Obs.]

ag-gran′dīze-ment (*or* ag′gran-dīze-ment), *n.* The act of aggrandizing; the state of being exalted in power, rank, or honor; exaltation; enlargement.

ag′gran-dīz-ẽr, *n.* One who aggrandizes or exalts in power, rank, or honor.

ag-grāte′, *v.t.* [It. *aggratare*; from L. *ad*, to, and *gratus*, pleasing.] To please. [Obs.]

ag′grȧ-vāte, *v.t.*; aggravated, *pt., pp.*; aggravating, *ppr.* [L. *aggravatus*, pp. of *aggravare*; *ad*, to, and *gravis*, heavy.]

1. To make heavy; not now used in this literal sense.

2. To make worse, more severe, or less tolerable; as, to *aggravate* the evils of life.

3. To make more enormous, or less excusable; as, to *aggravate* a crime

4. To exaggerate; to give coloring in description; to give an exaggerated representation; as, to *aggravate* a charge against an offender.

5. To irritate; provoke; tease. [Colloq.]

Syn.—Intensify, irritate, enhance, increase, magnify.

ag′grȧ-vā-ting, *a.* 1. Increasing in severity, enormity, or degree, as evils, misfortunes, pain, punishment, crimes, guilt; exaggerating.

2. Provoking; exasperating; vexing. [Colloq.]

ag′grȧ-vā-ting-ly, *adv.* In an aggravating manner.

ag-grȧ-vā′tion, *n.* [Fr. *aggravation*; L. *aggravatio*, a making heavy.]

1. The act of making worse; used of evils, natural or moral; the act of increasing severity or heinousness; addition to that which is evil or improper; as, an *aggravation* of pain or grief.

2. Exaggerated representation, or heightened description of anything wrong, improper, or unnatural; as, an *aggravation* of features in a caricature.

3. Irritation; provocation; the act of irritating or provoking. [Colloq.]

ag′grȧ-vā-tive, *a.* and *n.* I. *a.* Tending toward aggravation.

II. *n.* Anything causing aggravation.

ag′grē-gāte, *v.t.*; aggregated, *pt., pp.*; aggregating, *ppr.* [L. *aggregatus*, pp. of *aggregare*, to lead to a flock, add to; *ad*, to, and *gregare*, to herd; *grex*, *gregis*, a herd.]

1. To bring together; to collect into a sum, mass, or body.

2. To unite to, as a person to a society.

3. To make the sum total of; to amount to.

Syn.—Accumulate, collect, pile, heap up.

ag′grē-gāte, *a.* 1. Formed by a collection of particulars into a whole mass or sum, united; combined; total; as, the *aggregate* amount of charges.

2. In anatomy, zoölogy, and botany, specifically used in the sense of clustered or associated together, as the lymph-follicles of the conjunctiva, called the clusters of Bruch, or *aggregate glands*; *aggregate* animals, composed of a number of individuals, like various polyps; *aggregate* fruit, which is formed when a cluster of distinct carpels belonging to a flower are assembled upon the common receptacle, as in the blackberry.

3. In mechanics, resulting from a combination or summing up of forces, etc.

Aggregate combination; the combined movement of parts which causes another part to move with a compound motion; as the combination of a cam, cam-roller, and arm of a machine causes another part to move with an oscillatory movement.

Aggregate path; the path through which a part of a machine travels, resulting from the aggregate combination of the parts moving it; as the path through which a part of a machine travels when moved by cam, cam-roller, and arm.

Aggregate velocity; the resultant velocity produced by a combination of two or more forces, or parts of a machine, moving at different speed; as, a gear twelve inches in circumference, in mesh with a gear six inches in circumference, will cause the latter to move with double the velocity of the former, producing an *aggregate velocity* in the shaft of the latter of double the velocity of the former.

ag′grē-gāte, *n.* 1. A mass, assemblage, or collection of particulars; as, a house is an *aggregate* of stones, brick, timber, etc.

2. Any hard material added to a cement to make concrete.

3. The total of a military force, including officers and men.

4. A mass formed by the union of homogeneous particles; an agglomerate of different minerals which are separable by mechanical means.

5. The total sum, quantity, or number of anything.

ag′grē-gāte-ly, *adv.* Collectively; taken in a sum or mass.

ag-grē-gā′tion, *n.* [Fr. *aggregation*.]

1. The act of aggregating; the state of being collected into a sum or mass; a collection of particulars; an aggregate.

2. In logic, the combination of terms into a term true of anything of which any of its parts are true; the union of species to form a genus.

3. The affiliation of a member with an association or body. [Rare.]

ag′grē-gā-tive, *a.* Taken together; collective.

ag′grē-gā-tŏr, *n.* One who collects into a whole or mass.

ag-greġe′, *v.t.* To aggravate. [Obs.]

ag-gress′, *v.i.*; aggressed, *pt., pp.*, aggressing, *ppr.* [L. *aggressus*, pp. of *aggredi*, to attack, to go to; *ad*, to, and *gradi*, to step, from *gradus*, step.] To make a first attack; to commit the first act of hostility or offense; to begin a quarrel or controversy; to assault first, or invade.

ag-gress′, *v.t.* To attack; to set upon. [Rare.]

ag-gress′, *n.* Aggression. [Obs.]

ag-gres′sion, *n.* [L. *aggressio*, from *aggredi*, to attack.] The first attack, or act of hostility; the first act of injury, or first act leading to a war or controversy.

ag-gres′sive, *a.* Tending to aggress; making the first attack.

ag-gres′sive-ly, *adv.* In an aggressive manner.

ag-gres′sive-ness, *n.* The quality of being aggressive, or quarrelsome.

ag-gres′sŏr, *n.* The person who first attacks; he who first commences hostility or a quarrel; an assaulter; an invader.

Syn.—Assaulter, invader.—An *aggressor* is one who begins a quarrel or encroachment; an *assaulter* is one who makes a violent onset; an *invader* is one who enters by force into the possessions of another.

ag-griēv′ănce, *n.* Oppression; hardship; injury. *Grievance* is more generally used.

ag-griēve′, *v.t.*; aggrieved (-grēvd′), *pt., pp.*; aggrieving, *ppr.* [ME. *agreven*; OFr. *agrever*, *aggraver*, to aggravate; L. *aggravare*, to make heavy; *ad*, to, and *gravis*, heavy.]

1. To give pain or sorrow; to afflict.

2. To bear hard upon; to oppress or injure in one's rights; to vex or harass by civil or political injustice.

ag-griēve′, *v.i.* [Obs.] See *Grieve*.

ag-grōup′, *v.t.*; aggrouped (-grōpt′), *pt., pp.*; aggrouping, *ppr.* [Fr *agrouper*; It. *aggruppare*; a, L. *ad*, to, and *gruppo*, a knot, heap, group.] To bring together; to group; to collect in a crowd or into a whole, either in statuary, painting, or description.

ag-gröup'ment, *n.* Arrangement in one or more groups; subdivision; grouping.

ag'gry, ag'gri, *n.* A kind of colored glass bead, supposed to be of ancient Egyptian origin, found among the natives of Africa.

ȧ-ghȧst' (ȧ-gȧst'), *a.* [ME. *agast*, full form, *agasted*, pp. of *agasten*, to terrify; *a*, AS. *ā*, and *gasten*, AS. *gæstan*, to terrify.] Struck with amazement; stupefied with sudden fright or horror.

ȧ-ghȧst', *v.t.* To terrify. [Obs.]

ag'i-ble, *a.* [L. *agibilis*, from *agere*, to do.] Possible; practicable. [Obs.]

ag'ile, *a.* [Fr. *agile*; L. *agilis*, from *agere*, to move, to act.] Nimble; having the faculty of quick motion in the limbs; apt or ready to move; brisk; active.

> And bending forward struck his *agile* heels.
> —Shak.

Syn.—Active, nimble, quick, spry, alert.

ag'ile-ly, *adv.* In a nimble manner.

ag'ile-ness, *n.* Nimbleness; activity; the faculty of moving the limbs quickly; agility.

ȧ-gil'i-ty, *n.* [Fr. *agilité*; L. *agilitas*, *agilis*, from *agere*, to move, to do.] The power of moving the limbs quickly; nimbleness; briskness; activity; quickness of motion.

ȧ-gil'lō-chum, *n.* See *Agallochum*.

ā'ging, āge'ing, *n.* Act or process of giving age or the appearance of age to, as wines.

ag'i-ō (*or* ā'gi-ō), *n.* [It. *aggio*, exchange, premium.]

1. In commerce, the difference in value between metallic and paper money, or between one sort of metallic money and another. The term is used principally on the continent of Europe.

2. Premium; sum given above the nominal value, as, the *agio* of exchange.

3. The rate of exchange between the currencies of different nations.

4. Premium on appreciated, or discount on depreciated, currency.

5. Allowance for the wear and tear on metallic currency, in Amsterdam, Hamburg, etc.

ag'i-ō-tāge (*or* ā'gi-ō-tāge), *n.* [Fr. *agiotage*, from *agioter*, to job in stocks; from *agio*, premium.] A European commercial term denoting stock-jobbing; the exchange business.

ȧ-gist', *v.t.* [OFr. *agister*; *a*, L. *ad*, to, and *gister*, to assign a lodging; L. *gistum*, from *jacitum*, pp. of *jacere*, to lie.]

1. To assess for a specific public purpose.

2. To feed or pasture (the cattle of others) for a price; originally applied to feeding or grazing cattle in the king's forest.

ag'is-tā-tŏr, *n.* Same as *Agistor*.

ȧ-gist'ment, *n.* 1. Formerly, the taking and feeding of other men's cattle in the king's forest, or on one's own land; also, the price paid for such feeding.

2. Any burden, charge, or tax laid against land

3. An embankment or dyke against the encroachment of water.

ȧ-gist'ŏr, ȧ-gist'ẽr, *n.* 1. One who for hire takes cattle to feed or pasture.

2. Formerly, an officer of the king's forest who had the care of cattle agisted, and collected the money for the same; hence called *gist-taker*, which in England was corrupted into *guest-taker*.

ag'i-tȧ-ble, *a.* That may be agitated, shaken, or discussed. [Rare.]

ag'i-tāte, *v.t.*; agitated, *pt., pp.*; agitating, *ppr.* [L. *agitatus*, pp. of *agitare*, to put in motion; from *agere*, to move.]

1. To stir violently; to move back and forth with a quick motion; to shake or move briskly; as, to *agitate* water in a vessel.

2. To move or force into violent irregular action; as, the wind *agitates* the sea.

3. To disturb, or excite into tumult; as, to *agitate* the mind or passions.

4. To discuss; to debate; to controvert; as, to *agitate* a question.

5. To consider on all sides; to revolve in the mind, or view in all its aspects; to contrive by mental deliberation; as, politicians *agitate* desperate designs.

6. To move or actuate. [Obs.]

Syn.—Disturb, rouse, ruffle, discompose, deliberate upon, debate, canvass, excite.

ag'i-tāte, *v.i.* To seek to stir up the public mind on any subject; as, to *agitate* in every state of the Union.

ag'i-tā-ted-ly, *adv.* In an agitated manner.

ag-i-tā'tion, *n.* 1. The act of shaking; the state of being moved with violence, or with irregular action; commotion; as, the sea after a storm is in *agitation*.

2. Disturbance of tranquillity; perturbation; excitement of passion with physical disturbance.

3. Discussion; examination of a subject in controversy.

4. Deliberation, with a view to contrivance or plan to be adopted; as, a scheme is in *agitation*.

5. Public excitement over any matter; as, the free-silver *agitation*; the *agitation* for municipal ownership.

Syn.—Disturbance, emotion, tremor, trepidation, debate, discussion.

ag-i-tā'tion-ăl, *a.* Relating to agitation.

ag'i-tā-tive, *a.* Having a tendency to agitate.

ag'i-tā-tŏr, *n.* 1. One who agitates; especially, one who makes a livelihood by stirring up excitement or commotion; also, an insurgent; one who excites sedition or revolt.

2. In antiquity, a charioteer.

3. In Cromwell's time, one of certain officers appointed by the army to manage its concerns.

4. A utensil for shaking or mixing.

ag'lēaf, *n.* The common mullein.

ȧ-glēam', *a.* and *adv.* Gleaming.

ȧ-glee', ȧ-gley', *adv.* [Scot.] Off the right line; wrong.

ag'let, āig'let, *n.* [OFr. *aguillette*; Fr. *aiguillette*, a point, dim. of *aiguille*; L. *acucula*, dim. of *acus*, needle.]

1. In olden times, an ornamental image at the ends of laces, tabs, points, braid, or cord, used in dress.

2. A metal point on a ribbon to facilitate insertion into an eyelet-hole; any metal ornament at the ends of ribbons or laces.

3. A staylace, round and white, used in the drapery trade in England.

4. In botany, a pendant at the ends of the stamens of flowers, as in the rose and tulip; a pendent anther; a loose catkin.

ag'let-bā"by, *n.* A small image serving as an aglet.

ag'let-hōle, *n.* An eyehole.

ȧ-glim'mẽr, *a.* and *adv.* Glimmering.

ȧ-glit'tẽr, *adv.* and *a.* In a glitter; sparkling.

ȧ-glob'ū-lism, *n.* [Gr. *a* priv., and L. *globulus*, dim. of *globus*, a ball.] In pathology, a diminution of the proportion of red corpuscles in the blood.

A-glos'sȧ, *n.pl.* [Gr. *a* priv., and *glōssa*, tongue.] A suborder of batrachians that are without a tongue.

ȧ-glos'săl, ȧ-glos'sāte, *a.* [Gr. *aglōssos*, without tongue.] Tongueless; as, *aglossal* toads.

ȧ-glos'sāte, *n.* An aglossal batrachian.

ȧ-glōw', *adv.* and *a.* In a glow; glowing; as, the horizon all *aglow*.

ag-lū-ti'tion (-tish'un), *n.* [Gr. *a* priv., and L. *glutitio*, from *glutire*, to swallow.] Inability to swallow.

ȧ-glyph'ō-dont, *a.* [Gr. *aglyphos*, uncarved; *a* priv., and *glyphein*, to carve, and *odous*, *odont*, tooth.] Having no grooved teeth for venom; applied to snakes.

ag'mi-năl, *a.* [L. *agminalis*; *agmen*, *agminis*, a train.] Pertaining to an army or troop. [Rare.]

ag'mi-nāte, ag'mi-nā-ted, *a.* [L. *agmen*, *agminis*, a train, crowd.] Clustered together; as, *agminate* glands.

ag'nāil, *n.* [ME. *agnayle*, *angnail*; AS. *angnægle*, a corn, wart.]

1. A whitlow; an inflammation round the nail.

2. A hangnail; a piece of half-severed skin beside or at the base of a nail.

ag'nāmed, *a.* [*Ag*, L. *ad*, to, and *name*.] Designated by an epithet added to the surname.

ag'nāte, *a.* 1. Related or akin by the father's side.

2. Allied; from a common source; as, *agnate* words.

ag'nāte, *n.* [L. *agnatus*, pp. of *agnasci*, to be born in addition to; *ad*, to, and *nasci*, to be born.] Any male relation by the father's side.

ag'nȧ-thous, ag-nath'ic, *a.* [Gr. *a* priv., and *gnathos*, jaw.] Without jaws.

ag-nā'ti, *n. pl.* [L. pl., from *agnatus*, pp. of *agnasci*, to be born to.] Relations by the father's side.

ag-nat'ic, *a.* Pertaining to descent by the male line of ancestors.

ag-nā'tion, *n.* 1. Relation by the father's side only, or descent in the male line, distinct from *cognation*, which includes descent in the male and female lines.

2. Relationship or kinship in a general sense. [Rare.]

ag'nel, *n.* [OFr. *agnel*, a lamb; L. *agnellus*, dim. of *agnus*, a lamb.] An ancient French gold coin, value twelve sols, six deniers. It was called also *mouton d'or* and *agnel d'or*.

ag'ni, *n.*, pl. of *agnus*.

ag-ni'tion (-nish'un), *n.* [L. *agnitio*, from *agnoscere*, to acknowledge.] Acknowledgment. [Obs.]

ag-nize', *v.t.* To acknowledge. [Obs.]

Ag-nō-ē'tæ, *n.pl.* [L., from Gr. *agnoētai*, ignorant, from *agnoein*, to be ignorant.]

1. A sect of the fourth century who denied the omniscience of God; also called *Theophronians*, after their leader.

2. A sect of the sixth century who denied the omniscience of Christ; called also *Themistians*, after their leader.

ag-noi-ol'ō-gy, *n.* [Gr. *agnoia*, ignorance, and *logia*, from *legein*, to say.] The metaphysical theory of true ignorance; the doctrine which seeks to determine those things of which we are necessarily ignorant.

ag-nō'men, *n.* [L. *ad*, to, and *nomen*, name.]

1. An additional fourth name, given by the Romans on account of some exploit or event; as *Africanus* added to *Publius Cornelius Scipio*.

2. A name added in praise or dispraise.

ag-nom'i-nāte, *v.t.* To name. [Rare.]

ag-nom-i-nā'tion, *n.* [L. *agnominatio*, from *ad*, to, and *nomen*, name.]

1. A name or title added to another, as expressive of some act, achievement, etc.; a surname.

2. Similarity of sound in two or more words, usually made apparent by alliteration.

ag-nos'tic, *n.* [Gr. *a* priv., and *gnōstikos*, knowing, from *gignōskein*, to know.] One who holds the doctrine of agnosticism; one who accepts the general doctrine of nescience. The name was suggested by Huxley in 1869.

ag-nos'tic, *a.* Relating to an agnostic or to agnosticism.

ag-nos'tic-ăl-ly, *adv.* In the manner of an agnostic.

ag-nos'ti-cism, ag-nos'tics, *n.* 1. The doctrines of the agnostics.

2. Belief in agnostic doctrines.

3. In theology, the doctrine that God is unknown and unknowable; because God has not revealed himself to man; because finite mind cannot comprehend God; because Absolute God cannot come into intimacy nor make himself known to finite mind.

4. In philosophy, the doctrine that First Cause and the essential nature of things are unknowable to man; that it is impossible to know the existence of the human soul and Ultimate Cause, or to prove or disprove it.

> By *agnosticism*, I understand a theory of things which abstains from either affirming or denying the existence of God; all it undertakes to affirm is, that, upon existing evidence, the being of God is unknown.
> —G. J. Romanes.

ag'nus, *n.*; *pl.* **ag'nus-es** or **ag'nī**. [L., a lamb.] An image of a lamb as emblematic of Christ; Agnus Dei.

ag'nus cas'tus. [L.] A species of *Vitex*, so called from Gr. *agnos*, chaste, from its imagined virtue of preserving chastity. The Athenian ladies reposed on the leaves of this plant at the feast of Ceres. The Latin *castus*, chaste, now added to the name, forms a duplication of the sense.

Ag'nus Dē'ī. [L., Lamb of God.]

1. One of the titles of Christ.

2. In the Roman Catholic church, a medallion of wax, or other object, stamped with the figure of a lamb, supporting the banner of the cross. It is worn as an entreaty to be preserved from diseases and all other calamities. Also, a part of the mass, in which the prayer beginning with these words is repeated by the priest.

Agnus Dei that belonged to Charlemagne. — From Aix-la-Chapelle Cathedral.

3. A prayer beginning with these words.

Ag'nus Scyth'i-cus (sith'). [L., Scythian lamb.] A name applied to the roots of a species of fern, *Dicksonia Barometz*, covered with brown, woolly scales, and in shape resembling a lamb; found in Russia and Tartary.

Agnus Scythicus (*Dicksonia Barometz*).

ȧ-gō', *adv.* and *a.* [OE. *ago*, *agon*, pp. of *agon*, to go; AS. *āgān*, to pass away; *ā* and *gān*, to go.] Past; gone; as, a year *ago*.

ȧ-gog', *adv.* and *a.* [Earlier form, *on gog*; Fr. *en gogue*, mirth, glee.] In a state of desire; highly excited by eagerness after an object.

> The gaudy gossip, when she's set *agog*.
> —Dryden.

ȧ-gō'ing, *adv.* In motion; as, to set a mill *agoing*.

ȧ-gom'phi-ous, *a.* [Gr. *a* priv., and *gomphios*, molar.] Having no teeth.

ag′ŏn, *n.*; *pl.* **ȧ-gō′nēṣ.** [Gr.] The contest for a prize at public games.

ag′ō-năl, *a.* Same as *Agonic.*

ȧ-gŏne′, *a.* and *adv.* Ago; past; since. [Rare.]

ā′gōne, *n.* An agonic line.

ȧ-gon′iç, *a.* [Gr. *agōnos*, without angles; *a* priv., and *gōnia*, angle.] Not forming an angle.

Agonic line; an irregular line on the earth's surface connecting those points where the magnetic needle points to the true north, or where the magnetic and geographical meridians coincide. There are two principal *agonic lines*; one, called the *American agone*, is in the western hemisphere, and the other, or *Asiatic*, is in the eastern hemisphere. Although they extend from south to north, they do not coincide with the meridians, but intersect them under different angles.

ag′ō-niṣm, *n.* [Gr. *agōnismos*, from *agonizesthai*, to contend for a prize.] Contention for a prize. [Obs.]

ag′ō-nist, *n.* [Gr. *agōnistēs*, contestant.] One who contended for a prize in the public games. Milton has used *agonistes* in this sense, and so called his tragedy, from the similitude of Samson's exertions in slaying the Philistines to prize-fighting. In church history, the disciples of Donatus are called *Agonists.*

ag-ō-nist′iç, ag-ō-nist′iç-ăl, *a.* Pertaining to prize-fighting, contests of strength, or athletic combats.

ag-ō-nist′iç-ăl-ly, *adv.* In an agonistic manner. [Rare.]

ag-ō-nist′içs, *n.* The science of athletic contests, or contending in public games.

ag′ō-nize, *v.i.*; agonized, *pt., pp.*; agonizing, *ppr.* [Fr. *agonizer*; L. *agonizare*, labor, strive; Gr. *agōnizesthai*, to contend for a prize.]

1. To writhe with extreme pain; to suffer violent anguish.

> To smart and *agonize* at every pore.—Pope.

2. To struggle; to contend; to strive.

ag′ō-nize, *v.t.* To distress with extreme pain; to torture.

ag′ō-nīz-ing, *a.* Giving extreme pain.

ag′ō-nīz-ing-ly, *adv.* With extreme anguish.

ag′ō-nō-thēte, *n.* [Gr. *agōnothetēs*; *agōn*, contest, and *tithenai*, to appoint.] An officer who presided over the public games in Greece.

ag″ō-nō-thet′iç, *a.* Pertaining to the president of the Grecian games.

ag′ō-ny, *n.* [ME. *agonie*; L. *agonia*; Gr. *agōnia*, a contest or struggle, from *agōn*, a struggle for a prize.]

1. In strictness, pain so extreme as to cause writhing or contortions of the body, similar to those made in the athletic contests in Greece.

2. Extreme pain of body or mind; anguish; appropriately, the pangs of death, and the sufferings of Christ in the garden of Gethsemane.

3. Violent contest or striving.

4. Any violent emotion; a paroxysm.

Syn.—Anguish, pang, distress, suffering, pain, torture.—*Agony* and *pang* denote a severe paroxysm of pain (*agony* being the greatest); *anguish* is prolonged suffering; the *anguish* of remorse; the *pangs* or *agonies* of dissolution.

ȧ-good′, *adv.* In earnest. [Obs.]

ag′ō-rȧ, *n.* [Gr.] The public square and market-place in an ancient Greek city.

ȧ-gō-stä-de′rō, *n.* [Sp. Am.] A cattle-pasture.

ȧ-gōu-ä′rȧ, *n.* [S. Am. name.] A species of racoon, *Procyon cancrivorus*, commonly called crab-eating racoon.

ȧ-gōu′tȧ, *n.* [Native name.] An insectivorous mammal peculiar to Haiti, of the *Centetes* family, and belonging to the genus *Solenodon*. It was so puzzling to naturalists that it was

Agouta (*Solenodon paradoxus*).

called *Solenodon paradoxus*. Its tail is devoid of hair and covered with scales, its eyes are small, and its nose elongated. It is of the size of a rat.

Agouti (*Dasyprocta agouti*).

ȧ-gōu′ti, ȧ-gōu′ty, *n.* [Fr. *agouti, acouti*; Sp. *aguti*, native Am. *aguti, acuti.*] A quadruped of the order *Rodentia*, genus *Dasyprocta*. It is of the size of a rabbit. The upper part of the body is brownish, with a mixture of red and black; the belly yellowish. Three varieties are peculiar to South America and the West Indies.

ȧ-graffe′ (-graf′), *n.* [Fr. *agrafe, agraffe*, a clasp, hook; also, *agrappe*; *a*, L. *ad*, to, and *grappe*, L. *grappa*; O.H.G. *chrapfo*; G. *krapfe*, a hook.]

1. An ornamental hook or clasp for armor or costume.

2. A device for clasping a piano-string so as to prevent vibration.

3. A builder's cramp-iron.

ȧ-gram′mȧ-tiṣm, *n.* In pathology, a form of aphasia characterized by inability to form connected or grammatical sentences.

ȧ-gram′mȧ-tist, *n.* [Gr. *agrammatos*, illiterate; *a* priv., and *grammata*, letters, from *graphein*, to write.] An illiterate person.

ȧ-graph′i-ȧ, *n.* [Gr. *a* priv., and *graphein*, to write.] A form of aphasia in which there is a loss of the power of expressing ideas by written symbols.

ȧ-graph′iç, *a.* Pertaining to agraphia.

ȧ-grappes′ (-graps′), *n.pl.* Hooks and eyes for fastening armor. [See *Agraffe.*]

ȧ-grā′ri-ăn, *a.* [L. *agrarius*, from *ager*, a field, country.]

1. Relating to lands, particularly public lands. Appropriately, denoting or pertaining to an equal division of lands; as, the *agrarian* laws of Rome, which distributed the conquered and other public lands equally among all the citizens, limiting the quantity which each might enjoy.

2. Pertaining to agrarianism.

3. In botany, wild; growing without cultivation; said of plants growing in the fields.

ȧ-grā′ri-ăn, *n.* One in favor of an equal division of land and other property among the inhabitants of a country.

ȧ-grā′ri-ăn-iṣm, *n.* An equal division of lands or property, or the principle of such a division.

ȧ-grā′ri-ăn-ize, *v.t.*; agrarianized, *pt., pp.*; agrarianizing, *ppr.* 1. To imbue with the principles or ideas of agrarianism.

2. To distribute lands equally among all.

ȧ-grē′, ȧ-gree′, *adv.* [Fr. *agre.*] In good part; kindly. [Obs.]

ȧ-gree′, *v.i.*; agreed, *pt., pp.*; agreeing, *ppr.* [ME. *agreen*; Fr. *agréer*, to receive kindly, from OFr. phrase, *à gré*, favorably; *à*, L. *ad*, to, and *gré*, good will, from L. *gratus*, pleasing.]

1. To be of one mind; to harmonize in opinion; as, in the expediency of the law, all the parties *agree.*

2. To live in concord, or without contention; as, parents and children *agree* well together.

3. To yield assent; to approve or admit; followed by *to*; as, to *agree to* an offer, or *to* an opinion.

4. To settle by stipulation, the parties being *agreed* as to the terms; as, to *agree* on articles of partnership.

5. To come to a compromise of differences; to be reconciled; as, they have *agreed* at last.

6. To come to one opinion or mind; to concur; as, to *agree* on a place of meeting. This sense often implies a resolving to do an act.

7. To be consistent; to harmonize; not to contradict, or be repugnant; as, this story *agrees* with what has been related by others.

8. To resemble; to be similar; as, the picture does not *agree* with the original.

9. To suit; to be accommodated or adapted to; as, the same food does not *agree* with every constitution.

10. In grammar, to correspond in number, case, gender, or person; as, a verb should *agree* with its subject.

Syn.—Accede, acquiesce, accept, coincide, concur, consent, harmonize, correspond, promise, engage, contract.

ȧ-gree′, *v.t.* To admit, or come to one mind concerning; as, to *agree* the fact. Also, to reconcile or make friends; to put an end to variance. Let the parties *agree* the fact, is really elliptical: let them *agree on* the fact. [Obs.]

ȧ-gree-ȧ-bil′i-ty, *n.* 1. Easiness of disposition. [Obs.]

2. Agreeableness of manner or deportment.

ȧ-gree′ȧ-ble, *a.* [ME. *agreable*; OFr. *agreable*, from *agreer* to accept, to please.]

1. Suitable; conformable; correspondent; consistent with; as the practice of virtue is *agreeable* to the law of God and our own nature.

2. In pursuance of; in conformity with; as, *agreeable* to the order of the day, the house took up the report of the committee. It is not correctly followed by *with*, and in this sense is used for *agreeably.*

3. Pleasing, either to the mind or senses; as, *agreeable* manners; fruit *agreeable* to the taste.

4. Willing; ready to agree; as, we found the opposition *agreeable* to our suggestion. [Colloq.]

Syn.—Acceptable, grateful, pleasant, pleasing.

ȧ-gree′ȧ-ble-ness, *n.* 1. Suitableness; conformity; consistency; as, the *agreeableness* of virtue to the laws of God.

2. The quality of pleasing; that quality which gives satisfaction or moderate pleasure to the mind or senses; as, an *agreeableness* of manners; there is an *agreeableness* in the taste of certain fruits. This is the usual sense of the word.

3. Resemblance; likeness; with *to* or *between.* [Obs.]

ȧ-gree′ȧ-bly, *adv.* 1. Pleasingly; in an agreeable manner; in a manner to give pleasure; as, to be *agreeably* entertained with a discourse.

2. Suitably; consistently; conformably.

> Marriages grow less frequent, *agreeably* to the maxim above laid down. —Paley.

3. Alike; in the same manner. [Obs.]

ȧ-greed′, *a.* Mutually determined or decided upon; as, an *agreed* amount.

ȧ-gree′ing-ly, *adv.* In conformity to. [Rare.]

ȧ-gree′ment, *n.* 1. Concord; harmony; conformity; as, to live in *agreement* with one's neighbors.

2. Union of opinions or sentiments; as, a good *agreement* subsists among the members of the council.

3. Resemblance; conformity; similitude.

> Expansion and duration have this further *agreement.* —Locke.

4. Union of minds in regard to a transfer of interest; bargain; compact; contract; stipulation; as, he made an *agreement* for the purchase of a house.

5. The terms in which a contract or bargain is set down in writing; a written compact.

6. In grammar, concord.

Syn.—Accordance, bargain, concurrence, compact, contract, covenant, harmony, stipulation.

ȧ-grē′ēr, *n.* One who agrees.

ȧ-gres′tiăl (-chăl), *a.* 1. Same as *Agrestic.*

2. Growing wild.

ȧ-gres′tiç, ȧ-gres′tiç-ăl, *a.* [L. *agrestis*, rural, from *ager*, field.] Rural; rustic; pertaining to fields or the country, in opposition to the city; unpolished.

ȧ-griç-ō-lā′tion, *n.* Cultivation of the soil. [Obs.]

ȧ-griç′ō-list, *n.* A husbandman; an agriculturist. [Obs.]

ag′ri-çul-tŏr, *n.* [L. *ager*, a field, and *cultor*, a cultivator.] One whose occupation is to till the ground; a farmer; a husbandman; one skilled in husbandry. [Rare.]

ag-ri-çul′tūr-ăl, *a.* Pertaining to husbandry, tillage, or the culture of the earth; as, *agricultural* implements; *agricultural* pursuits.

Agricultural ant; a species of ant, the best known of which is the *Pogonomyrmex barbatus* of Texas, which clears large spaces around its nest.

ag-ri-çul′tūr-ăl-ist, *n.* See *Agriculturist.*

ag-ri-çul′tūr-ăl-ly, *adv.* As regards agriculture; for agricultural purposes.

ag′ri-çul-tūre, *n.* [L. *ager*, a field, and *cultura*, cultivation.] Farming; tillage; the cultivation of the ground, for the purpose of producing vegetables and fruits for the use of man and beast; or the art of preparing the soil, sowing and planting seeds, dressing the plants, and removing the crops. In this sense, the word includes gardening, or horticulture, and also the raising and feeding of cattle or stock. But in the more common and appropriate sense, the cultivation which is intended to raise grain and other field crops. It is equivalent to *husbandry* and is the most general occupation of man.

ag-ri-çul′tūr-iṣm, *n.* The art or science of agriculture. [Rare.]

ag-ri-çul′tūr-ist, *n.* One skilled in the art of cultivating the ground; a skilful husbandman; a farmer

ȧ-grief′, *adv.* In grief; amiss. [Obs.]

Ag′ri-mō-ny, Ag-ri-mō′ni-ȧ, *n.* [ME. *agrimony*; OFr. *aigremoine*; L. *agrimonia*, for *argemonia*; Gr. *argemōnē*, from *argemon*, a white speck in the eye, for which the plant is said to have been a cure.] A genus of plants of the rose family, having several species. Of these, the *eupatoria*, or common *agrimony*, and the *odorata*, or sweet-scented, were formerly used in medicine.

ȧ-grin′, *adv.* and *a.* [AS. *a*, on, and *grin.*] Grinning; on the grin.

ag″ri-ō-log′iç-ăl, *a.* Pertaining to agriology.

ag-ri-ol′ō-ġist, *n.* One versed in agriology.

ag-ri-ol′ō-ġy, *n.* [Gr. *agrios*, wild, savage, and *logia*, from *logos*, word, description.] The comparative study of the customs of uncivilized tribes or races of men.

ȧ-grīṣe′, *v.i.* [ME. *agrisen*; AS. *agrisan*; *a*, and *grisan*, be terrified.] To shiver. [Obs.]

ȧ-grīṣe′, *v.t.* To terrify; also, to make frightful. [Obs.]

ag′rŏm, *n.* [Native name.] A disease frequent in the East Indies, in which the tongue chaps and cleaves, becomes rough and sometimes covered with white spots.

ag-rō-nom′iç, ag-rō-nom′iç-ăl, *a.* Pertaining

to agronomy, or the management of lands or farms.

ag-rō-nom′ics, *n.pl.* The science of the distribution of land, and its management.

ȧ-gron′ō-mist, *n.* One versed in agronomy; a student of the science of agronomics.

ȧ-gron′ō-my, *n.* [Gr. *agronomos*, an overseer of the public lands; *agros*, field, and *nomos*, from *nemein*, to deal out, manage.] The art of cultivating the ground; the management of land; agriculture.

ȧ-grōpe′, *adv.* In the act of groping.

Ag-rō-stem′mȧ, *n.* [Gr. *agros*, field, and *stemma*, wreath.] A genus of plants of several species, containing the common corn-cockle, wild lychnis or campion, etc.

A-gros′tis, *n.* [Gr. *agrōstis*, grass.] Bent-grass; a genus of many species.

ag-ros-tog′rȧ-phēr, *n.* One who writes about grasses; an agrostologist.

ȧ-gros-tō-graph′iç, ȧ-gros-tō-graph′iç-ăl, *a.* Pertaining to agrostography.

ag-ros-tog′rȧ-phy, *n.* [Gr. *agrōstis*, grass, and *graphia*, from *graphein*, to write.] A description of grasses.

ag-ros-tō-loġ′iç, ag-ros-tō-loġ′iç-ăl, *a.* Pertaining to agrostology.

ag-ros-tol′ō-ġist, *n.* One skilled in agrostology; an authority upon grasses.

ag-ros-tol′ō-ġy, *n.* [Gr. *agrōstis*, grass, and *logos*, discourse.] That part of botany which relates to the grasses.

ȧ-ground′, *adv.* 1. On the ground; a marine term, signifying that the bottom of a ship rests on the ground for want of sufficient depth of water. When the ground is near the shore, the ship is said to be ashore or stranded.

2. Figuratively, stopped; impeded by insuperable obstacles.

ȧ-gröup′ment, *n.* See *Aggroupment.*

ȧ-gryp′ni-ȧ, *n.* [Gr. *agrypnia*, from *agrypnios*, sleepless; *agreuein*, to hunt, and *hypnos*, sleep.] Morbid wakefulness; insomnia.

ȧ-gryp-nō-cō′mȧ, *n.* [Gr. *agrypnos*, sleepless, and *kōma*, coma.] Lethargy, without actual sleep.

ag-ryp-not′iç, *a.* Preventing sleep.

ag-ryp-not′iç, *n.* In medicine, any agency or drug which tends to prevent sleep.

A-gryp′nus, *n.* [Gr. *agrypnos*, sleepless.] A genus of *Coleoptera.* The species are among those destructive beetles whose larvæ are called wire-worms.

ä′guȧ (-gwȧ), *n.* [Native name.] A large, voracious, bellowing toad, the *Bufo marinus*, found in the West Indies and South America.

ä-guȧ-çȧ′te, *n.* [Sp.] A tropical tree bearing a pear-shaped fruit; the avocado.

ä-guȧ-jï′ (-gwȧ-), *n.* [Sp. Am.] The gag, a large food-fish of the Florida reefs; the *Nycteroperca microlepis.*

ä-guär-dï-en′te (ä-gwär-), *n.* [Sp., contraction of *agua ardiente*, burning water; L. *aqua*, water, and *ardens*, burning.]

1. A popular brandy of Spain and Portugal; a brandy made in all Spanish countries from the native red wines.

2. Any common spirituous liquor, especially Mexican pulque. In the southwestern United States, the term is often applied to inferior whisky.

ā′gūe, *n.* [ME. *agu, ague*; OFr. *agu*, f. *ague*; L. *acutus*, f. *acuta*, sharp, violent; L. *febris acuta*, a violent fever.]

1. The cold fit which precedes a fever, or a paroxysm of fever in intermittents. It is accompanied with shivering.

2. Chilliness; a chill, or state of shaking with cold, though in health.

3. A periodical fever; an intermittent, whether quotidian, tertian, or quartan. In this case, the word, which signifies the preceding cold fit, is used for the disease.

ā′gūe, *v.t.* To cause a shivering in; to strike with a cold fit.

ā′gūe-çāke, *n.* An enlargement and hardening of the spleen from the effect of intermittent fevers.

ā′gūed (-gūd), *a.* Chilly; having a fit of ague; shivering with cold or fear.

ā′gūe-drop, *n.* A solution of potassium arsenite used as a remedy for ague.

ā′gūe-fit, *n.* A paroxysm of cold, or shivering; chilliness.

ā′gūe-grȧss, *n.* In botany, the colicroot, *Aletris farinosa*; star-grass. It is of the bloodwort family.

ā′gūe-root, *n.* Same as *Ague-grass.*

ȧ-guēr′ry (-gēr′), *v.t.* [Fr. *aguerrir*, to make war-like; *à*, to, and *guerre*, war.] To inure to the hardships of war; to instruct in the art of war. [Obs.]

ā′gūe-spell, *n.* A charm or spell to cure or prevent ague.

ā′gūe-tree, *n.* A name sometimes applied to sassafras, on account of its febrifuge qualities.

ā′gūe-weed, *n.* Thoroughwort or boneset, *Eupatorium perfoliatum*; also, the stiff gentian, *Gentiana quinqueflora.*

ȧ-guilt′ (-gilt′), *v.t.* To be guilty of; to sin against; to offend; to wrong. [Obs.]

ȧ-guīṣe′ (-gīz′), *v.t.* To dress; to adorn. [Obs.]

ȧ-guīṣe′, *n.* Dress. [Obs.]

ā′gū-ish, *a.* 1. Chilly; somewhat cold or shivering; also, having the qualities of an ague.

2. Productive of ague; as, an *aguish* district.

ā′gū-ish-ly, *adv.* In the manner of ague, or of a person affected by ague.

ā′gū-ish-ness, *n.* Chilliness; the quality of being aguish.

ȧ-gū′jȧ (-hȧ), *n.* [Sp., literally, needle.]

1. The spearfish of the West Indies.

2. A large, voracious garfish, *Tylosurus fodiator*, much dreaded by fishermen of western Mexico.

ȧ-gush′, *adv.* and *a.* In a gushing state.

aġ′y-nȧ-ry, *a.* [Gr. *a* priv., and *gynē*, woman.] A botanical term applied to flowers without female organs.

aġ′y-nous, *a.* Same as *Agynary.*

ȧ-ġȳ′rāte, *a.* [L. *agyratus*, pp. of *agyrare*; Gr. *a* priv., and *gyros*, circle.] In botany, without whorls.

äh, *interj.* [ME. *a*; OFr. *ah*; G. *ach*; L. *ah*; Gr. *a.*] An exclamation, expressive of surprise, pity, complaint, contempt, dislike, joy, exultation, etc., according to the manner of utterance.

ȧ-hä′, *interj.* and *n.* I. *interj.* An exclamation, expressing triumph, contempt, or simple surprise; the senses are distinguished by very different modes of utterance, and different modifications of features.

II. *n.* A sunk fence, not visible without near approach; more commonly called *ha-ha.*

ȧ-han′i-gēr, *n.* A name of the garfish. [Obs.]

ȧ-head′ (ȧ-hed′), *adv.* 1. Further forward than another thing; in front; originally, a sea-term, denoting further forward than another ship, or on the point to which the stem is directed, in opposition to *astern.*

2. Onward; forward; toward the point before the stem or head; as, move *ahead.*

3. Headlong; without restraint; precipitantly; as, children suffered to run *ahead.* [Obs.]

ȧ-hēap′, *adv.* In a heap.

ȧ-height′ (-hīt′), *adv.* Aloft; on high. [Obs.]

ȧ-hem′, *interj.* An exclamation used to attract the attention of someone.

ȧ-hey′, *interj.* Hey.

ȧ-high′ (-hī′), *adv.* On high. [Obs.]

ȧ-hold′, *adv.* Near the wind; as, to lay a ship *ahold.* [Obs.]

ȧ-horse′back, *adv.* On horseback.

ȧ-hoy′, *interj.* A sea-term used in hailing.

Äh′ri-mȧn, *n.* See *Ariman.*

ä′hū, *n.* [Per. *āhū*, deer.] The native name for the Persian gazel.

ä′hū-atle (ä′ō-atl), *n.* [Mex.] The eggs of a fly, used as a food by Indians, in Mexico.

ȧ-hull′, *adv.* With the sails furled, and the helm lashed; applied to ships in a storm.

ȧ-hun′gēred, *a.* Hungry.

ä′i, *n.* [Braz. *aï, haï*, from the animal's cry.] The three-toed sloth.

ai-ai′ä, ai-ai′ai, *n.* [Sp. Am.] 1. The trivial name of a species of *Platalea*, or spoonbill; called also the *roseate spoonbill.*

2. The American jabiru, genus *Mycteoria*, of Paraguay.

āi′bliṇs, ā′bliṇs, *adv.* A Scotch word for perhaps.

Aich′-met″ăl, *n.* A kind of gun-metal.

āid, *v.t.*; aided, *pt., pp.*; aiding, *ppr.* [ME. *aiden*; OFr. *aider*; L. *adjutare*, freq. of *adjuvare*, to help, assist; *ad*, to, and *juvare*, to help.]

1. To help; to assist; to support, either by furnishing strength or means to effect a purpose, or to prevent or remove anything detrimental to another.

2. To forward; to facilitate.

3. In law, to correct (a fault) subsequently in proceedings, so that it may be eliminated from consideration.

Syn.—Abet, assist, help, relieve, support, succor, coöperate.

āid, *n.* 1. Help; succor; support; assistance.

2. The person who aids or yields support; a helper; an auxiliary; also, the thing that aids or yields succor.

3. In English law, a subsidy or emergency tax granted by parliament, and making a part of the king's revenue.

4. In English feudal law, a tax paid by a tenant to his lord; originally, a mere gift, which afterward became a right demandable by the lord. The aids of this kind were chiefly three: (a) to ransom the lord when a prisoner; (b) to make the lord's eldest son a knight; (c) to marry the lord's eldest daughter.

—Blackstone.

5. In law, a remedy of defect in pleadings or procedure.

6. The help of whip, rein, spur, heel, etc., by which a horseman aids the action of his horse.

7. An aide-de-camp, by abbreviation; as, a general's *aid.*

āid′ănce, *n.* Aid; help; assistance. [Rare.]

āid′ănt, *a.* Helping; helpful; supplying aid.

āid′-de-çamp, *n.* See *Aide-de-camp.*

āide′-de-çamp (*Fr. pron.* äd′d′-käṅ), *n.*; *pl.* **āideṣ′-de-çamp.** [Fr. *aide*, aid, *de*, L. *de*, of, and *camp*, L. *campus*, field.] In military affairs, an officer whose duty is to receive and communicate the orders of a general officer; an aid. Sometimes written *aid-de-camp.*

āid′ēr, *n.* One who helps; an assistant.

āid′fụl, *a.* Helpful; giving aid. [Rare.]

āid′ing, *a.* Helping; assisting.

āid′less, *a.* Helpless; without aid; unsupported; undefended.

āid′-mä″jŏr, *n.* A regimental adjutant. [Obs.]

āig′let, *n.* Same as *Aglet.*

āi′gre (-gēr), *a.* [Fr.] Sour; sharp. [Obs. Compare *Eager.*]

āi′gre-mōre (-gēr-), *n.* [Fr. Origin unknown.] Prepared charcoal ready for use in making gunpowder.

āi′gret, āi-grette′, *n.* [Fr., a heron with a tuft of feathers on its head; tufted.]

1. A tuft formed of feathers, diamonds, etc., surmounting a headdress.

2. The small white heron, with tufted head.

3. A crown of feathery seed, as the dandelion or thistle-top. [See *Egret.*]

āi-guï-ēre′ (ā-gē-âr′), *n.* [Fr.] A tall pitcher, with handle and tall spout.

āi-guille′ (-gwēl′), *n.* [Fr., a needle.]

1. A sharp, rocky, mountain peak; especially those Alpine peaks in the neighborhood of Mount Blanc.

2. A slender rock-drill.

āi-guil-lette′ (-gwil-let′), *n.* [Fr., dim. of *aiguille*, needle.]

1. An aglet; a tag or point at the end of a detail of dress.

2. In cookery, a side-dish served on a small ornamental skewer.

āi′gū-let, *n.* [Fr. Usually contracted into *aglet.*] A point or tag, as at the ends of fringes.

āi′kin-īte, *n.* [Named after Dr. A. *Aikin.*] A mineral composed of sulphid of lead, copper, and bismuth; commonly called *needle-ore.*

āik′rąw, *n.* The obsolete name of a species of lichen, or moss.

āil, *v.t.*; ailed (āld), *pt., pp.*; ailing, *ppr.* [ME. *ailen, aylen*; AS. *eglian, eglan*, trouble, pain.] To trouble; to affect with uneasiness, either of body or mind; used to express some uneasiness or affection whose cause is unknown; as, what *ails* the man? I do not know what *ails* him. It is never used to express a specific disease. We never say, pleurisy *ails* him; but something *ails* him.

āil, *v.i.* To be ill or indisposed; to be affected with pain or uneasiness; to be in trouble; as, one day the child began to *ail.*

āil, *n.* Indisposition, or morbid affection.

āi-lan′tiç, *a.* Relating to or derived from the ailantus.

āi-lan′tine, *n.* Silk obtained from the silkworm that feeds on the ailantus. Also used as an adjective.

Āi-lan′tus, Āi-lan′thus, *n.* [L., from *ailanto*, tree of heaven; Malacca name.] A genus of trees, native to the East Indies and cultivated in America and Europe for their leaves, which are fed upon by silkworms.

āi′lēr-on, *n.* [Fr.] A small hinged or separated wing tip or surface of an aeroplane, for maintaining lateral balance.

āi-lette′ (ā-let′), *n.* [Fr. *ailette*, dim. of *aile*, wing; L. *ala*, wing.] A metal shield worn upon the shoulder by knights; the original form of the modern epaulet.

Ailettes.

āil′ment, *n.* Disease; indisposition; morbid affection of the body; but the word is not applied ordinarily to acute diseases.

Āi-lū-roid′ē-ȧ, *n. pl.* [L., from Gr. *ailouros*, cat, and Gr. *eidos*, form.] In zoölogy, a group of carnivorous mammals which includes the cats, civets, and hyenas.

āil′weed, *n.* A parasitic plant that attaches itself to clover.

āim, *v.i.*; aimed, *pt., pp.*; aiming, *ppr.* [ME. *aymen, amen*; OFr. *amer, esmer*; L. *æstimare*, to estimate.]

1. To point with a weapon, as a lance or a gun, with the purpose or assumed purpose of hitting the object pointed at.

2. To direct the intention or purpose; to attempt to reach or accomplish an object or purpose; to tend toward something; to endeavor; as a man *aims* at distinction.

3. To guess or conjecture. [Obs.]

āim, *v.t.* 1. To direct at, simultaneously with the act of impelling, with the intention of hitting; as, to *aim* a blow with a club.

2. To point, direct, or level, as a gun or other weapon, at any object.

3. To direct (something intangible) at, as a sarcastic remark, an innuendo, a look of scorn.

All these senses imply something in the nature of attack.

4. To estimate; to conjecture; to consider. [Obs.]

Syn.—Aspire, endeavor, direct, purpose.

āim, *n.* 1. The pointing or directing of a weapon; the direction of anything to a particular point or object, with a view to strike or affect it; as of a lance, a blow, a discourse, or remark.

2. The point intended to be hit, or object intended to be affected; as, a man missed his *aim*.

3. Figuratively, a purpose; intention; design; scheme; as, men are often disappointed of their *aim*.

4. Conjecture; guess. [Obs.]

āim′ẽr, *n.* One who aims.

āim′less, *a.* Without aim or purpose; having no end or object in view.

āim′less-ly, *adv.* In an aimless or purposeless manner.

āim′less-ness, *n.* The state of being without aim or purpose, or of having no object in view.

āin′hum, *n.* [Negro name.] A disease said to attack negroes only; it causes loss of the toes.

Ai′nō, Ai′nū, *n.* [Native name.] One of a peculiar, hairy race found as uncivilized tribes in northern Japan, and often called the aborigines of the Japanese empire; also, their language, which is unlike Japanese. They are mild, and have Caucasian features.

āin't (ānt). A contraction in very common use for *am not*, *is not*, and *are not*. [Colloq.]

Ai′nū, *n.* See *Aino*.

āir, *n.* [ME. *eier*, *aire*; OFr. *air*, air, breath; L. *aër*; Gr. *aēr*, air, mist, from *aein*, to breathe, blow.]

1. The gaseous fluid which we breathe and which envelops the earth; the atmosphere. *Air* is inodorous, invisible, insipid, colorless, elastic, possessed of gravity, and easily moved, rarefied, and condensed. It is composed of mechanically mixed oxygen and nitrogen in the relative volume of twenty-one to seventy-nine; or twenty-three to seventy-seven by weight. It contains also small percentages of carbon dioxid, aqueous vapor, nitric acid, ozone, and organic matter. A thousand cubic inches of *air* at mean temperature and pressure weigh thirty and one-half grains.

2. Any aeriform or gaseous body; an old chemical term now employed only to express the fumes of shops and foundries.

3. A breeze, zephyr, or gentle wind.

> Let vernal *airs* through trembling osiers play. —Pope.

4. Publicity; public utterance.

> You gave it *air* before me. —Dryden.

5. Intelligence; advice; news. [Obs.]

6. The characteristic look, appearance, manner, or mien of a person; as, the *air* of a youth; a lofty *air*.

7. The general character or appearance of anything; as, the room had an *air* of refinement.

8. [*pl.*] An affected manner; show of pride; haughtiness; as, he puts on *airs*.

9. Anything light or uncertain.

10. The motive or theme of a musical composition; a song; a rhythmical melody.

11. In painting, the effect of air; atmosphere; also, that which expresses action; manner; attitude.

12. In the Greek church, a delicate veil spread over the paten and the chalice together, in addition to the individual veils of those vessels.

Liquid air; see under *Liquid*.

To take the air; to ride or walk outdoors.

In the air; flying hither and thither, without apparent source or authority, as a rumor; in an unsettled or unstable position; in special military usage, expressive of a force in a helpless position, unsupported and incapable of either giving or receiving aid; visionary; uncertain; foundationless.

Syn.—Appearance, bearing, mien, carriage, demeanor, behavior, expression, look, manner, style.

āir, *v.t.*; aired, *pt.*, *pp.*; airing, *ppr.* 1. To expose to the air; to give access to the open air; to ventilate; as, to *air* clothes; to *air* a room.

2. To expose to heat or fire to expel dampness; as, to *air* linen by the fire.

3. To expose to public notice, generally with the suggestion of ostentatiousness; as, to *air* a grievance.

4. To make a vain display of in public or before others; as, she *aired* her charms at the opera.

Ai′rȧ, *n.* [L., from Gr. *aira*, a kind of darnel.] A genus of perennial grasses, including the hair-grass.

āir′-bal-loon″, *n.* See *Balloon*.

āir′-bal-loon″ist, *n.* One who makes or uses air-balloons.

āir′-bath, *n.* 1. An apparatus for applying air to the body.

2. An arrangement for drying substances in air of regulated temperature.

āir′-bed, *n.* A mattress filled with air.

āir′-blad″dẽr, *n.* 1. A vesicle filled with air, as the cells of the lungs.

2. The bladder of a fish, containing air, by which it is enabled to maintain its equilibrium in the water.

āir′-born, *a.* Born of the air.

āir′-bōrne, *a.* Borne in or by the air.

āir′-brāke, *n.* A system of railroad-brakes operated by means of compressed air.

āir′-brāv″ing, *a.* Braving the winds.

āir′-brush, *n.* A brush, in the form of an atomizer, operated by compressed air; used to apply paint or liquid color.

āir′-built (-bilt), *a.* Erected in the air; having no solid foundation; chimerical; as, an *air-built* castle; *air-built* hopes.

āir′-cell, *n.* A cavity or cell containing air. In plants, a certain cavity in the cellular tissue, by the multiplication of which they are rendered buoyant in water; in birds, the same as an air-sac; in insects, a dilatation of the air-vessels; in man, a cavity in the air-tubes of the lungs.

Air-cells in Gulf-weed (*Sargassum vulgare*).

āir′-chām″bẽr, *n.* A chamber filled with air, as in a force-pump or lifeboat.

āir′-cock, *n.* A faucet to regulate the supply of air.

āir′-cŏm-press″ŏr, *n.* An apparatus for compressing air for mechanical purposes.

āir-craft, *n.*: *pl.* aircraft. Any type of machine for flying or sailing through the air.

āir′-cross″ing, *n.* A passage for air in a mine, running over or under another one.

āir′-cush″ion (-un), *n.* 1. A bag inflated with air and used as a cushion or pillow.

2. An air-spring for arresting motion without shock.

āir′-drawn, *a.* Drawn in air; imaginary.

āir′-drill, *n.* A pneumatic drill.

āired, *a.* Ventilated; warmed; thoroughly freed from dampness; as, *aired* sheets.

āir′-en″gine, *n.* An engine operated by compressed air.

āir′ẽr, *n.* 1. One who exposes to the air.

2. A frame on which clothes are aired.

āir′-foun″tain (-tin), *n.* An apparatus for producing a jet of water by the power of compressed air.

āir′-fŭr″nāce, *n.* A furnace which works with a natural draft of air, and has no forced draft.

āir′-gun, *n.* A pneumatic gun, which discharges bullets by means of the elastic force of compressed air.

āir′-hōld″ẽr, *n.* An instrument for holding air, as for the purpose of counteracting the pressure of a decreasing column of mercury.

āir′-hōle, *n.* An opening to admit or discharge air.

āir′i-ly, *adv.* In an airy manner.

āir′i-ness, *n.* 1. Exposure to a free current of air; openness to the air; as, the *airiness* of a country-seat.

2. Gaiety; levity; as, the *airiness* of young persons.

āir′ing, *n.* An exposure to the air, or to a fire, for warming or drying; also, a walk or ride in the open air; a short excursion; the exercise of horses in the open air.

āir′-jack″et, *n.* A jacket having air-tight cells or cavities which can be filled with air, to render persons buoyant in swimming.

āir′less, *a.* Not open to a free current of air; wanting fresh air, or communication with open air.

āir′-lev″el, *n.* A spirit-level.

āir′like, *a.* Resembling air.

āir′-line, *n.* A straight line; a bee-line; shortest distance between two points.

āir′-line, *a.* Direct; straight; as, an *air-line* road.

āir′ling, *n.* A thoughtless, gay person.

āir-lock, *n.* 1. An air-tight compartment in a submarine caisson.

2. In the World War, the space between two damp blankets hung at the openings of dugouts to render them gas proof.

āir-man, *n.* In aviation, one skilled in maneuvering aircraft and in matters pertaining to aviation.

āir-om′e-tẽr, *n.* An instrument for measuring the flow of air; also, an air-holder similar to a gasometer.

āir′-pipe, *n.* 1. A pipe used to draw foul air from a ship's hold, by means of a communication with the furnace and the rarefaction of the air by fire.

2. Any pipe used to conduct air into or out of close places, for ventilation, etc.

āir′-plant, *n.* A name given to certain plants, which will grow for a long time without being rooted in earth or in any other substance. The term is applied to many epiphytic orchids.

āir′-poise, *n.* An instrument to measure the weight of the air.

āir′-pōre, *n.* In botany, a stoma.

āir-port, *n.* 1. On board ship, a porthole or scuttle to admit air.

2. A terminal for aircraft, corr. to sea port for ships.

āir′-pump, *n.* A machine, of varying construction, for exhausting the air from a vessel or inclosed space, for transmitting air, or for compressing air in any inclosed space. In the common forms the air is exhausted by means of a cylinder and piston. The forms of *air-pumps* vary according to the uses they are intended to serve.

āir′-sac, *n.* In birds, a receptacle for air, or one of the vesicles lodged in the fleshy parts, in the hollow bones, and in the abdomen, all communicating with the lungs. These are supposed to render the body specifically lighter, and to supply the place of a muscular diaphragm.

āir′-shăft, *n.* A passage for air into a mine, usually opened in a perpendicular direction, and meeting the adits or horizontal passages, to cause a free circulation of fresh air through the mine.

āir-ship, *n.* A self-propelling dirigible balloon or kite-like machine, generally operated by a motor.

In 1909 Bleriot crossed the English Channel in an air-ship, a feat marking a new era in aviation. Gaudart, French, on Aug. 7, 1909, made an endurance record for an aeroplane, his flight lasting 2 hrs., 27 min., 15 sec. The Wright brothers met the U. S. government specifications on July 30, 1909, their air-ship averaging 42.58 mi. per hr., tests being made at Ft. Myer. On July 23, 1909, Farman made the longest cross country flight recorded, from Chalons to Suippes, Fr., a distance of 40 mi.

āir′-slacked (-slakt), *a.* Slacked or pulverized by exposure to the air; as, *air-slacked* lime.

āir′-spring, *n.* A spring in which the elastic principle of atmospheric air is utilized.

āir′-stōve, *n.* A stove for heating air to be distributed through a house; a furnace.

āir′-thẽr-mom″e-tẽr, *n.* A form of thermometer in which the changes of temperature are measured by the expansion and contraction of atmospheric air.

āir′-thread (-thred), *n.* A name given to the spider's webs, which are often seen floating in the air, and serve to support the spider when in quest of prey.

āir′-tight (-tit), *a.* So tight or compact as to be impermeable to air.

āir′-tight, *n.* 1. A stove with a draft which can be shut off almost entirely.

2. Any sealed can or tin.

āir′-trap, *n.* A contrivance for the escape of foul air from drains, sewers, etc.

āir′-trunk, *n.* A shaft for conducting heated or vitiated air from a room.

āir′-valve, *n.* A valve to regulate the admission of air; especially, a valve to admit air to a steam-boiler.

āir′-ves″sel, *n.* A tube, duct, cell, or chamber for conveying or holding air; as, the *air-vessels* of the human body, of a plant, or of a machine.

āir′wărd, āir′wărds, *adv.* Up into the air; upward.

āir′-wāy, *n.* A passage for air.

āir′y, *a.* 1. Consisting of air; as, an *airy* substance.

2. Relating or belonging to air; high in air; as, an *airy* flight; *airy* region.

3. Open to a free current of air; as, an *airy* situation.

4. Light as air; resembling air; thin; unsubstantial; without solidity; delicate or graceful in appearance or quality; ethereal; immaterial.

5. Without reality; having no solid foundation, vain; trifling; as, an *airy* scheme; *airy* notions.

6. Gay; sprightly; full of vivacity and levity; light of heart; lively; as, an *airy* girl.

Aisle, Salisbury Cathedral.

7. Having affected manners; putting on airs. [Colloq.]

8. In painting, having the appearance or qualities of atmosphere.

ãir′y, *n.* An old form of *aery*, an eagle's nest.

aisle (īl), *n.* [Fr. *aile*, a wing; L. *ala*, wing.]

1. In architecture, a term applied to the side divisions, or wings, of a church or other building, in distinction from the central portion or nave; usually separated from the nave by arches or columns, supporting the roof or walls of a clearstory. [See illus., page 37.]

2. The passage between the rows of pews in a church; a similar passage in any auditorium.

aisled (īld), *a.* Furnished with aisles.

aisle′less, *a.* Without an aisle.

āit, *n.* [ME. *eyt*, *æit*; in comp. *eytlond*; AS. *eget*, *iget*, an island.] An islet, or little isle, in a river or lake; an eyot.

āit, *n.* [Scot.] Oat.

āitch (āch), *n.* The letter *h*, *H*.

āitch′bōne, *n.* [ME. *nache-bone*; OFr. *nache*, the buttock; L. *natica*, from *natis*, buttock.] The rump-bone of a beef.

āi-ti-ol′ō-gy, *n.* See *Ætiology*.

A″i-zō-ā′cē-æ, *n.pl.* [L., probably from Gr. *aei*, always, and *zōos*, alive.] A family of plants, with opposite leaves and apetalous; the carpetweed family, with twenty-two genera and 500 species.

ā″i-zō-ā′ceous, *a.* Belonging or pertaining to the *Aizoaceæ*.

ȧ-jär′, *adv.* and *a.* [ME. *on char*, on the turn; AS. *cerr*, *cyrr*, turn.] Partly open, as a door.

ȧ-jär′, *adv.* and *a.* Out of harmony; as, he is *ajar* with all men.

aj′ȧ-vä, *n.* See *Ajowan*.

ȧ-jog′, *adv.* Moving leisurely along; on the jog.

aj′ōw-ăn, aj′ōu-ăn, *n.* [E. Ind.] The fruit of a species of parsley that grows in Persia, India, and Egypt; used both as a drug and as a condiment.

aj′ū-tāge, *n.* [Fr. *ajoutage*, from *ajouter*, to add to; L. *adjuxtare*: *ad*, to, and *jungere*, to join.] A spout or nozle; a tube or nozle fitted into a vessel and calculated to facilitate the discharge of water or liquid by reducing friction.

ȧ-kä′lȧ, *n.* [Hawaiian.] A shrub of the family *Rosaceæ* growing in the Hawaiian Islands, producing large, red berries, edible and agreeable.

A-kē′bi-ȧ, *n.* [L., from Japan. *akebi*.] A genus of hardy Japanese climbing plants, of which *Akebia quinata* is much cultivated and admired.

ȧ-kee′, *n.* [Native name in Guiana.] The *Cupania sapida*, a small tree growing throughout the West Indies, introduced from Guinea in 1793 by Captain Bligh. It produces a fruit whose spongy aril, or seed-covering, is esteemed as food, resembling custard when cooked.

Akee Fruit.

ȧ-kēne′, *n.* Same as *Achene*.

ȧ-kim′bō, *a.* and *adv.* [Etymology unknown, many attempted explanations having proved unsatisfactory.] In a sharp bend; at an acute angle; said of the arms when the hands rest on the hips and the elbows project outward.

ȧ-kin′, *a.* [*A-*, of, and *kin*.]

1. Related by blood, used of persons; as, the two families are near *akin*.

2. Allied by nature; partaking of the same properties; as, envy and jealousy are near *akin*.

ak-i-nē′si-ȧ, *n.* [Gr. *akinēsia*, *akinēsis*, from *a* priv., and *kinein*, to move.] Paralysis of the motor nerves; loss of the control of movement.

ak-i-nē′sic, ak-i-net′ic, *a.* Pertaining to akinesia.

ȧ-knee′ (-nē′), *adv.* On the knees. [Rare.]

ak-nōw′, *v.t.* [Obs.] See *Acknow*.

al-, *prefix.* In Arabic, an adjective or inseparable prefix, answering to the Italian *il*, and the Spanish *el* and *la*. As a combining form, its use is to render nouns definite, like the English *the*; as, *al*koran, the koran, or the book, by eminence; *al*cove, *al*chemy, *al*embic, *al*manac, etc.

Al-, in English, is sometimes a contraction of the Saxon *æthel*, noble or illustrious.

More generally, *al-*, in composition, is a contraction of *ald* or *alt*, old, and is prefixed to many names, as *Al*burg.

Al-, in the composition of Latin words, is written before *l* for *ad*, for the ease of pronunciation, as in *allevo*, *alludo*, for *ad levo*, *ad ludo*.

-al, *suffix.* [L. *-alis*.] An adjectival suffix denoting belonging to, of, or pertaining to, etc. Also appearing as part of nouns which were originally adjectives, used as substantives, as riv*al*, anim*al*, etc.; and used to form nouns of action from verbs, as, arriv*al*, acquitt*al*, etc.

äl, *n.* [Hind.] An Indian plant, *Morinda citrifolia*, yielding a madder, used in Madras for dyeing. Written also *aal*, *awl*.

ā′lȧ, *n.* [L.] An organ or part resembling a wing.

à la (ä lä). [Fr.] To the, or in the; hence, according to, or in the fashion of; as, *à la carte*, according to the menu card, or bill of fare; *à la française*, in the French fashion; *à la duchesse*, in the style of a duchess.

al-ȧ-ban′dite, al-ȧ-ban′dine, *n.* Manganese sulphid; named after *Alabanda*, an old city of Asia Minor, which produced it.

al′ȧ-bas-tēr, *n.* [L. *alabaster*; Gr. *alabastros*, adj. The mineral was called *alabastrites*, alabaster.]

1. A compact variety of sulphate of lime, or gypsum, of fine texture, and usually white and semipellucid, but sometimes yellow, red, or gray. It is soft and costly and carved into statuettes, vases, mantel ornaments, etc. The finest variety is found near Florence, Italy.

2. A subvariety of carbonate of lime, found in large masses formed by the deposition of calcareous particles in caverns of limestone rocks. These concretions have a foliated, fibrous, or granular structure, and are of a pure white color, or present shades of yellow, red, or brown, in undulating or concentric stripes, or in spots. Also called *stalagmite*, *stalactite*, and *travertine*.

Among antiquaries and artists, the name *alabaster* is given to varieties both of carbonate of lime and gypsum, the *alabaster* vessels of the ancients having been formed of both those substances.

3. Among the ancients, a vessel in which odoriferous liquors or ointments were kept; so called from the stone of which it was made. Also, the name of a measure, containing ten ounces of wine, or nine of oil.

al′ȧ-bas-tēr, *a.* Made of alabaster, or resembling it.

al-ȧ-bas′tri-ăn, al-ȧ-bas′trine, *a.* Pertaining to or like alabaster.

al″ȧ-bas-trī′tēs, *n.* Oriental alabaster; carbonate of lime deposited by hot springs or by percolation through limestone into caves.

al-ȧ-bas′trum, *n.*; *pl.* **al-ȧ-bas′trȧ.** [L.]

1. A flower-bud.

2. A small pear-shaped, wide-lipped vessel used by the ancient Greeks as a receptacle for perfumes and unguents.

ȧ-lack′, *interj.* An exclamation of sorrow.

ȧ-lack′ȧ-dāy, *interj.* An exclamation uttered to express regret or sorrow.

ȧ-lac′ri-fy, *v.t.* To arouse. [Rare.]

ȧ-lac′ri-ous, *a.* Cheerful.

ȧ-lac′ri-ous-ly, *adv.* With alacrity; cheerfully.

ȧ-lac′ri-ous-ness, *n.* Briskness. [Obs.]

ȧ-lac′ri-ty, *n.* [Fr. *alacrité*; L. *alacritas*, briskness, from *alacer*, *alacris*, brisk, lively.]

1. Cheerfulness; gaiety; sprightliness.

2. A readiness or promptitude to act or serve; cheerful willingness; as, he responded with *alacrity* to the demand.

3. Quickness or facility of thought or action.

A-lad′din-ist, *n.* A freethinker among the Mohammedans; so named from *Aladdin* (meaning *height of religion*), a learned priest of the time of Mohammed II.

à-lä-grecque′ (-grek′), **à-lä-grec′,** *n.* [Fr., after the Greek fashion.] A name for one of the varieties of fret ornament used for running friezes and borders, and frequently seen in ancient Roman pavements. Sometimes written *aligreek*.

À-la-grecque.

ȧ-lā′li-ȧ, *n.* [L., from Gr. *alalia*, from *a* priv., and *lalein*, to talk.] A paralysis of the larnyx or muscles of speech; loss of vocal control is the result.

al′ȧ-līte, *n.* [*Ala*, a valley in Piedmont, and *-lite*, Gr. *lithos*, stone.] A bright green variety of pyroxene, in prisms; first obtained in the valley of Ala.

al-ȧ-lon′gȧ, al-i-lon′ghi (-gi), *n.* [L. *ala*, wing, fin, and *longa*, long.] The tunny.

ä-lȧ-me′dȧ, *n.* [Sp.] A public promenade shaded by trees.

ä-lȧ-mī′re, *n.* [Formed from *a*, *la*, *mi*, *re*, names of notes in the musical scale.] The lowest note but one in Guido Aretino's scale of music.

al″ȧ-mō-dal′i-ty, *n.* [Fr. *à la mode* and *-ality*.] Conformity to the fashion.

al′ȧ-mōde, *adv.* [Fr. *à la mode*, after the fashion.] According to the fashion or prevailing mode.

al′ȧ-mōde, *n.* A thin, glossy black silk for hoods, scarfs, etc.

al′ȧ-mort, *a.* [Fr. *à la mort*.] Depressed; melancholy; in a moribund state.

ȧ-lan′, *n.* [OFr. *alant*; L. *alanus*, a hunting-dog.] A wolf-dog. [Obs.]

ȧ-land′, *adv.* At or on land.

al′ȧ-nine, *n.* A compound derived from aldehyde ammonia.

al′ant-cam″phor, *n.* Camphor obtained from elecampane.

ȧ-lan′tin, *n.* An amylaceous or starchy substance extracted from the root of the *Angelica Archangelica*; identical with inulin.

ā′lär, *a.* [L. *alaris*, from *ala*, wing.]

1. Possessing wings; relating to wings; shaped like or resembling wings.

2. In botany, located in the forks of a plant or a stem; axillary.

3. In anatomy, of or pertaining to the armpit.

A-lā′ri-ȧ, *n.* [L. *alarius*, from *ala*, wing.] A genus of seaweeds.

ȧ-lärm′, *n.* [ME. *alarme*; OFr. *alarme*; It. *all' arme*, fright. alarm; from *all' arme*, to arms! *a*, L. *ad*, to; *le*, L. f. pl. of *ille*, the; *arme*, L. *arma*, neut. pl., arms.]

1. Any sound, outcry, or information, intended to give notice of approaching danger; as, to sound an *alarm*.

2. A summons to arms.

3. Sudden surprise with fear or terror; as, the fire of the enemy excited *alarm*.

4. Terror; a sensation excited by an apprehension of danger, from whatever cause; as, we felt *alarm* at the cry of fire.

5. A mechanical contrivance for awaking persons from sleep, or rousing their attention.

6. In fencing, an appeal or challenge.

Syn.—Fright, terror, consternation, apprehension, affright, dread, fear, panic.—*Alarm* is the dread of impending danger; *apprehension*, fear that it may be approaching; *terror* is agitating and excessive fear; *consternation* is terror which overpowers the faculties.

ȧ-lärm′, *v.t.*; alarmed, *pt.*, *pp.*; alarming, *ppr.*

1. To give notice of danger; to rouse to vigilance and exertions for safety.

2. To call to arms for defense.

3. To surprise with apprehension of danger; to disturb with terror; to fill with anxiety by the prospect of evil.

ȧ-lärm′ȧ-ble, *a.* Liable to be alarmed; easily alarmed.

ȧ-lärm′-bell, *n.* A bell that gives notice of danger.

ȧ-lärm′-bird, *n.* See *Turacou*.

ȧ-lärm′-clock, *n.* A clock which can be so set as to ring loudly at a particular hour, to wake one from sleep, or excite attention.

ȧ-lärmed′, *a.* Notified of sudden danger; surprised with fear; roused to vigilance or activity by apprehension of approaching danger; solicitous at the prospect or expectation of evil.

ȧ-lärm′ed-ly, *adv.* In an alarmed manner.

ȧ-lärm′ing, *a.* Exciting apprehension; terrifying; awakening a sense of danger; as, an *alarming* message.

ȧ-lärm′ing-ly, *adv.* With alarm; in a manner to excite apprehension.

ȧ-lärm′ist, *n.* One who excites alarm.

ȧ-lärm′-post, *n.* A place to which troops are to repair in cases of an alarm.

ȧ-lärm′-watch (-wäch), *n.* A watch that can be so set as to strike frequently at a particular hour, to attract attention.

ȧ-lär′um, *n.* A variant of *alarm*, now used only in poetry, and in England as a popular term for alarm-clock.

ā′lȧ-ry, *a.* [L. *alarius*, from *ala*, wing.] Pertaining to wings; wing-like.

ȧ-las′, *interj.* [ME. *alas*, *allas*; OFr. *a las*, *ha las*; Fr. *hélas*; *a*, ah, and *las*, wretched; L. *lassus*, weary.] An exclamation expressive of sorrow, grief, pity, concern, or apprehension of evil; formerly, sometimes followed by *day* or *while*; *alas the day*, like alackaday; or *alas the while*.

ȧ-lāte′, *adv.* Lately. [Obs.]

ā′lāte, ā′lā-ted, *a.* [L. *alatus*, winged, from *ala*, wing.] In natural history, winged; bordered by a membranous or leafy expansion.

al-ȧ-tēr′nus, al′ȧ-tērn, *n.* The popular name of a species of *Rhamnus* or buckthorn.

ȧ-lā′tion, *n.* The state of being winged; the formation of wings, as in insects.

ȧ-launt′, *n.* [Obs.] See *Alan*.

alb, *n.* [OE. *albe*; L. *alba*, f. of *albus*, white.] A tunic or vestment of white linen, reaching to the feet, worn by the Roman Catholic clergy. Also, a white garment worn in the early church, by new converts, from the Saturday before Easter until the first Sunday after Easter, which is called *Alb* Sunday.

Alb.

al′bȧ, *n.* [L. *alba*, f. of *albus*, white.] The white nervetissue of the brain and spinal cord.

al′băn, *n.* [L. *albus*, white.] A crystalline substance obtained from gutta-percha.

Al-bā′ni-ăn, *a.* and *n.* I. *a.* Relating to Albania.

II. *n.* An inhabitant of Albania; the language of Albania.

al-bā′tȧ, *n.* [L. *albatus*, pp. of *albare*, to make white, from *albus*, white.] German silver; a white metal much used in manufactures.

al'bȧ-tross, *n.* [Port. *alcatraz*, a cormorant; Sp. *alcatruz*, a pelican, from Ar. *al*, the, and *qādūs*, bucket; Gr. *kados*, bucket.] An aquatic fowl, belonging to the petrel family. The bill is straight; the upper mandible crooked at the point, and the lower one truncated; the nostrils are oval, open, and but little prominent, and placed on the sides; the wings are pennated, and there are three webbed toes on each foot. The upper part of the body is sometimes white, but usually of a spotted brown, and the belly white. It is the largest sea-bird known and very voracious, preying on fish and small water-fowl. The *albatross* is found in great numbers about the capes of the northern continents, and especially on the northeastern shores of Asia. It is sometimes called the *great gull*.

Wandering Albatross (*Diomedea exulans*).

al'bȧ-tross-cloth, *n.* A kind of thin woolen cloth.

al-bē', al-bee', *conj.* Albeit. [Obs.]

al-bē'dō, *n.* [L. *albus*, white.] In astronomy, the ratio between the light reflected from a surface and the total light falling upon the surface; as, the *albedo* of the moon.

al-bē'it, *conj.* [ME. *al be it*; *al*, all, and *be it*.] Be it so; admit all that; although; notwithstanding

Albeit so mask'd, madam, I love the truth.
—Tennyson.

al'bērt-īte, *n.* [Named from the county, *Albert*, and *-ite*.] A mineral closely resembling asphaltum, found in Albert county, New Brunswick.

al'bēr-type, *n.* 1. A process of printing a picture in ink from a photographic plate; the invention of Joseph Albert, whence its name.

2. A picture produced by this process.

al-bes'cence, *n.* Whitishness.

al-bes'cent, *a.* [L. *albescens*, ppr. of *albescere*, to become white, from *albus*, white.] Becoming white, or whitish; moderately white.

al'bē-spine, *n.* [OFr. *albespine*; L. *alba spinus*, white thorn; *alba*, f. of *albus*, white, and *spina*, thorn.] The European hawthorn. [Obs.]

al'bi-cant, *a.* [L. *albicans*, ppr. of *albicare*, to be white.] Turning white.

al-bi-cā'tion, *n.* The process of turning white.

al'bi-cōre, *n.* [Port. *albacor*; Ar. *al*, the, and *bukr*, a young camel.] One of several marine fishes of the mackerel family; the tunny.

al"bi-fi-cā'tion, *n.* The act of making white. [Obs.]

al-bi-flō'rous, *a.* [L. *albiflorus*; *albus*, white, and *flos*, *floris*, flower.] A botanical term signifying bearing white flowers.

Al-bi-gen'sēs, Al-bi-geois' (-zhwä'), *n.pl.* [L. from Fr. *Albigeois*, inhabitants of *Albi*.] A party of reformers who opposed the Church of Rome, in the twelfth century; so called from Albi, Latin *Albija*, in the south of France, where they resided. Although confounded with, they were not of, the Waldenses, but were a branch of the Cathari. The *Albigenses* defied the authority of the church, discarded sacraments, and looked upon marriage as sinful. They died out, gradually, under the rigors of the Crusades and the Inquisition, till the Reformation, when what remained of them joined the Genevan Protestants and the followers of Zwingli.

Al-bi-gen'sian (-shun), *a.* Pertaining to the Albigenses.

al'bin, *n.* [L. *albus*, white.] A variety of opaque white apophyllite found in Bohemia.

al-bī'ness, *n.* A female albino.

al'bi-nism, *n.* The state of being an albino; leucopathy; albinoism.

al-bi-nis'tic, *a.* Inclined to albinism.

al-bī'nō, *n.*; *pl.* **al-bī'nōs.** [Port. *albino*, from L. *albus*, white.]

1. A person of any race, having, through deficiency of coloring matter, abnormally white skin and hair, accompanied by pink eyes.

2. Any animal having the same abnormal peculiarity.

3. A term applied to plants which are white through abnormal lack of chlorophyl.

4. An appellation originally given by the Portuguese to white negroes found on the coast of Africa. [Obs.]

al-bī'nō-ism, *n.* The state of an albino.

al-bi-not'ic, *a.* Albinistic.

Al'bi-ōn, *n.* An ancient name of England, still used in poetry. It is supposed that this name was given to it on account of its white cliffs.

al'bite, *n.* [L. *albus*, white, and *-ite*.] A species of mineral, of the feldspar group, of a white color; differing from the common feldspar in containing soda instead of potash. It is a constituent of many varieties of granitic rocks.

Al-biz'zi-ȧ (-bit'si-), *n.* [L., from It. *Albizzi*, a noble family in Tuscany.] A genus of plants allied to the *Acacia*.

al'bō-lith, al'bō-lite, *n.* [L. *albus*, white, and Gr. *lithos*, stone.] Artificial stone or cement composed of calcined magnesite and silica. It is used as a fireproofing and for plastic decorations in buildings.

Al'bō-rak, *n.* [Ar. *al-buraq*, from *baraqa*, to shine.] The fabled white mule on which Mohammed is said to have journeyed to heaven.

al'bronze, *n.* An alloy of copper and aluminium.

al-bū-gin'ē-ȧ, *n.* [L., f., as if from *albugineus*, white, with *tunica* understood.] The partial coat of the eye, formed by the expansion of the tendons of its straight muscles, at their insertion into the sclerotica around the cornea. It forms the white of the eye, so called.

al-bū-gin'ē-ous, *a.* Pertaining to or resembling the white of the eye, or of an egg.

Albugineous humor; the aqueous humor of the eye.

al-bū'gō, *n.*; *pl.* **al-bū'gi-nēs.** [L., whiteness, from *albus*, white.] A disease of the eye occasioned by a white opaque spot growing on the cornea and obstructing vision; also called *leucoma*.

al'bum, *n.* [L., neut. of *albus*, white.]

1. Among the Romans, a white tablet, board, or register, on which the names of public officers and records of public transactions were entered.

2. A blank book for the complimentary record of autographs, personal sentiments of friends, or appropriate lines.

3. A book for preserving photographs.

4. A book for the registry of visitors' names.

5. A book for various collections of special or miscellaneous matter, as a scrapbook of poetry, a collection of stamps, etc.

al'bum græ'cum, *n.* [L., Greek white.] A preparation for tanning and dressing leather. It is made from the weather-dried dung of dogs, etc.

al-bū'men, *n.* [L. *albumen*, from *albus*, white.]

1. A substance which forms a constituent part of both the animal and vegetable fluids and solids, and which exists nearly pure in the white of an egg; albumin. The latter form of the word is usually employed by chemists, *albumen* being used for the white of an egg.

Albumen Section of a grain of Wheat.

2. In botany, any form of nutritive matter in seeds of plants, without regard to its chemical composition; the endosperm, or perisperm. In grain, it is farinaceous; in nuts, fatty; in vegetable ivory, bony.

al-bū'men-ize, *v.t.* See *Albuminize*.

al-bū'min, *n.* A chemical substance, existing naturally in the purest form as the white of egg, which is found in animal tissue, blood, and serous fluids, and in plant tissue and juices. Heat, alcohol, and the stronger acids coagulate it; water dissolves it. Nitrogen, hydrogen, carbon, oxygen, and sulphur are its component elements. The dry commercial *albumin* is made from eggs and from blood. It has varied uses in the arts, as a vehicle and fixative for colors or dyes, a mordant for aniline dyes, a varnish or dressing for fabrics, etc.

al-bū'mi-nāte, *n.* A substance formed by the union of albumin with an alkali.

al-bū"mi-nif'ēr-ous, *a.* [*Albumen*, and *-ferous*, from L. *ferre*, to bear.] Producing albumin.

al-bū"mi-nim'e-tēr, *n.* [*Albumen*, and Gr. *metron*, measure.] An instrument for discovering the amount of albumin in a liquid.

al-bū'mi-nin, *n.* The substance of the cells in the tissue that surrounds the white of a bird's egg.

al-bū"mi-nip'ȧ-rous, *a.* [*Albumen*, and L. *parere*, to bring forth.] Yielding albumin.

al-bū'min-ize, *v.t.*; albuminized, *pt.*, *pp.*; albuminizing, *ppr.* To coat, treat with, or convert into albumin

al-bū'mi-noid, *a.* and *n.* I. *a.* Resembling albumin.

II. *n.* A proteid.

al-bū-mi-noid'ăl, *a.* Relating to or having the nature of an albuminoid.

al-bū'mi-nōne, *n.* Peptone.

al-bū'mi-nōse, *n.* See *Peptone*.

al-bū'mi-nous, al-bū'mi-nōse, *a.* Relating to or containing albumin.

al-bū'mi-nous-ness, *n.* The condition of being albuminous.

al-bū"mi-nū'ri-ȧ, *n.* [L. *albumen*, whiteness, and Gr. *ouron*, urine.] A disease characterized by albumin in the urine.

al'bū-mōse, *n.* A compound formed by albuminoids during the process of digestion.

al'burn, *a.* Auburn. [Obs.]

al'bŭrn, *n.* [L. *alburnus*, whitish, from *albus*, white.] The bleak, a small fish, the scales of which are used in the manufacture of artificial pearls

al-bŭr'nous, *a.* Relating to alburnum.

al-bŭr'num, *n.* [L., neut. of *alburnus*, whitish, from *albus*, white.] The white and softer part of wood, between the inner bark and the heartwood or duramen; popularly called the sapwood. This annually acquires firmness, and thus becomes heartwood.

Alburnum. *aa*, Alburnum or sapwood. *bb*, Heartwood. *c*, Pith. *dd*, Bark.

Al'byn, *n.* [*Albion*, a name applied to Great Britain, probably on account of its white cliffs; L. *albus*, white.] Scotland, especially the Highlands; compare *Albion*.

al-çāde', *n.* See *Alcaid*.

al'çȧ-hest, *n.* See *Alkahest*.

Al-çā'iç, *a.* Pertaining to Alcæus, a lyric poet of Mitylene, in Lesbos, who flourished about 600 B. C.; or to other poets of the same name, of whom three are mentioned; one an Athenian tragic poet, and another a Messenian.

Al-çā'içs, *n.pl.* Several kinds of verse, so called from Alcæus. One kind consists of five feet, a spondee or iambic, an iambic, a long syllable, and two dactyls.

al-çāid', *n.* [Sp. *alcaide*, *alcayde*, a governor, from Ar. *al-qāid*; *al*, the, and *qāid*, leader, from *qāda*, to lead.] Among the Moors, Spaniards, and Portuguese, a governor of a castle or fort; also, a jailer.

äl-çäl'de, *n.* [Sp. *alcalde*, from Ar. *al-qādī*, judge, from *qada*, to judge.] In Spain and Spanish countries, a magistrate or judge; a chief magistrate or mayor.

äl-çal-dī'ȧ, *n.* [Sp.] The territory in which an alcalde has jurisdiction; also, the office in which he conducts business.

al-çȧ-lim'e-tēr, *n.* See *Alkalimeter*.

al-çan'nȧ, *n.* [Sp. *alcana*, *alhena*, Ar. *alhinnā*; *al*, the, and *hinnā*.] A plant, a species of *Lawsonia*; and a powder, prepared from its leaves, used by the Turkish women to give a golden color to the nails and hair. Infused in water, it forms a yellow color; with vinegar, it forms a red. In Cairo, it is an article of commerce. From the berries is extracted an oil, used in medicine. Also called *henna*.

al-çap'ton, *n.* See *Alkapton*.

al-çär-rä'zȧ (*Sp.* äl-kä-rä'thä), *n.* [Sp., from Ar. *al-kurrāz*; *al*, the, and *kurrāz*, earthen vessel.] An earthenware vessel for cooling liquids.

al-çä'zär (*Sp.* äl-kä'thär), *n.* [Sp., from Ar. *al qacr*; *al*, the, and *qacr*, a fortified place.] A fort or royal residence.

Al-çē'dō, *n.* [L.; Gr. *Alkyōn*.] A genus of kingfishers whose species are numerous. They usually live about rivers, feeding on fish, which they take by darting into the water with surprising velocity. [See *Halcyon*.]

al-chem'iç, al-chem'iç-ăl, *a.* Relating to alchemy, or produced by it.

al-chem'iç-ăl-ly, *adv.* In the manner of alchemy.

Al-che-mil'lȧ, *n.* [Fr. *alchemille*; Port. *alchemila*, from Ar. *alkmelyeh*, alchemy. So called because it was thought to have alchemical virtues.] A genus of plants of the rose family.

al'che-mist, *n.* One who practises alchemy.

al-che-mis'tiç, al-che-mis'tiç-ăl, *a.* Practising alchemy, or relating to it.

al'che-mis-try, *n.* Alchemy. [Obs.]

al'che-mize, *v.t.*; alchemized (-mīzd'), *pt.*, *pp.*; alchemizing, *ppr.* To change by alchemy.

al'che-my, *n.* [L. *alchimia*; Gr. *archēmia*; Ar. *alkimia*; *al*, the, and *kimia*, Gr. *chēmia*, alchemy; *chēmia*, for *chymeia*, a pouring together; *chymos*, juice, from *cheein*, to pour.]

1. Formerly, the doctrine, study, and practice of the more sublime and difficult parts of chemistry, and chiefly such as related to the transmutation of metals into gold, the finding of a universal remedy for diseases, and an alkahest, or universal solvent, together with other things now dismissed from serious consideration. The art was much practised from the thirteenth to the seventeenth century, and paved the way for modern chemical science.

2. Formerly, a mixed metal used for utensils.

3. Any imaginary power or process of transmuting the common into the precious.

Alç-mā'ni-ăn, *a.* Pertaining to Alcman, a Spartan lyric poet of the seventh century B. C., celebrated for his amorous verses. The *Alcmanian* verse consisted of six anapests or their equivalents, wanting the two last syllables.

al'çō, *n.* [Native name.] A small, hairless, dog-like quadruped, native to Peru and Mexico, and domesticated by the aborigines. The animal was used for food by the earlier Spanish settlers.

al'çō-hol, *n.* [Fr. *alcohol*; Sp. *alcohol*, from Ar. *al*, the, and *kohl*, powder of antimony, used to color the eyebrows; *kahala*, to stain, paint.]

1. Originally, powdered antimony; any impalpable powder. [Obs.]

2. Pure or highly rectified spirit obtained by distillation from the product of the vinous fermentation of sugar and from fruit and vegetable juices. It consists of hydrogen, carbon,

and oxygen, the chemical formula of common or ethyl alcohol being C_2H_5OH. It is highly volatile, inflammable, colorless, and is a powerful stimulant and antiseptic. *Alcohol* is extensively used in the arts and medicine as a general solvent.

3. The intoxicating element of wines and liquors.

4. In a popular sense, any alcoholic intoxicant.

Wood alcohol; methylic or methyl alcohol, derived from the destructive distillation of wood, and a by-product in the manufacture of charcoal; used in making aniline dyes and as a solvent, etc.

al′ço-hol-āte, al′ço-āte, al′ço-hāte, *n.* A compound in which alcohol undergoes the substitution of an atom of metal alkali for one of hydrogen.

al-ço-hol′ȧ-tūre, *n.* [Fr. *alcoolature.*] An alcoholic tincture made from fresh plants.

al-ço-hol′iç, *a.* 1. Pertaining to alcohol, or partaking of its qualities.

2. Containing alcohol; as, an *alcoholic* thermometer.

al-ço-hol′iç, *n.* 1. One addicted to the use of alcoholic intoxicants.

2. [*pl.*] Alcoholic beverages.

al′ço-hol-ism, *n.* A morbid or diseased condition induced in the human system by the excessive or continuous use of alcoholic stimulants. It is acute when arising from an inordinate consumption in a short period, as plain drunkenness; or chronic when the stimulus is maintained for a length of time by small and oft-repeated doses.

al″ço-hol-i-zā′tion, *n.* The act of rectifying spirit till it is wholly dephlegmated; or of saturating the system with alcoholic drinks; or [Obs.] of reducing a substance to an impalpable powder.

al′ço-hol-īze, *v.t.*; alcoholized, *pt., pp.*; alcoholizing, *ppr.* 1. To convert into alcohol.

2. To rectify until wholly dephlegmated.

3. To reduce to an impalpable powder. [Obs.]

4. To saturate with alcohol.

al-ço-hol′me-tēr, al″ço-hol-om′e-tēr, al-ço-hom′e-tēr, al-ço-om′e-tēr, *n.* [*Alcohol*, and Gr. *metron*, measure.] An instrument for determining the strength of spirits, with a scale graduated so as to indicate the percentage of pure alcohol, either by weight or volume.

al″ço-hol-met′riç-ăl, al″ço-hol-ō-met′riç-ăl, al″ço-hō-met′riç, al″ço-ō-met′riç-ăl, *a.* Relating to the alcoholmeter; as, *alcoholmetrical* tables.

al-ço-hol′ō-gy, *n.* The study of diseases caused by using alcoholic beverages.

al″ço-hol-om′e-try, *n.* The act and method of determining the relative proportion of pure alcohol in spirits.

al-ço-met′riç-ăl, *a.* See *Alcoholmetrical.*

al-ço-om′e-tēr, *n.* See *Alcoholmeter.*

Al′çor, *n.* [Ar.] A small star in Ursa Major.

Al′ço-răn, *n.* See *Koran.*

Al-ço-ran′iç, *a.* Pertaining to the Koran.

Al-ço-ran′ist, *n.* One who adheres strictly to the letter of the Koran, rejecting all comments upon it. The Persians are generally *Alcoranists*; the Turks, Arabs, and Tartars admit many traditions.

äl-çor-no′que (-kȧ), *n.* [Sp., cork tree.] The bark of several Brazilian trees, used medicinally.

al′çove (*or* **al-çōve′**), *n* [Fr. *alcôve*; Sp. *alcoba*; Ar. *al-qobbah*; *al*, the, and *qobbah*, arch, vault, dome.]

1. Originally, in Spain, a recess, or part of a room separated by an estrade, partition of columns, or other means, in which may be placed a bed of state, or seats for company.

Alcove.

2. A recess in a room, or a small room attached to a larger one for the reception of a piano, a bed, etc.

3. A small ornamental building, or recess, in a garden.

4. A compartment or recess for books in a library.

5. A niche for a statue, a seat, etc.

6. Any natural recess, as in a grove; a secluded spot.

7. In geology, a deep niche formed by erosion.

al′cy-on, *n.*; *pl.* **al-cy′ō-nēş.** [L., from Gr. *alkyōn*, the kingfisher.] The general name of the kingfishers. [See *Halcyon.*]

Al cy-ō-nā′ce-ȧ, *n. pl.* Group of *Alcyonaria.*

Al″cy-ō-nā′ri-ȧ, *n.pl.* An order of actinozoan corals found only in deep water, and usually attached to a foreign body.

Al-cy′ō-nē, *n.* [L., from Gr. *Alkyonē*, a daughter of King Æolus. She was changed into a kingfisher.] One of the stars in the Pleiades.

al-cy-on′iç, *a.* Pertaining to the group or family of zoöphytes, allied to the sponges, and called the *cork-polyps.*

al′cy-on-ite, *n.* A fossil zoöphyte of or resembling the genus *Alcyonium.*

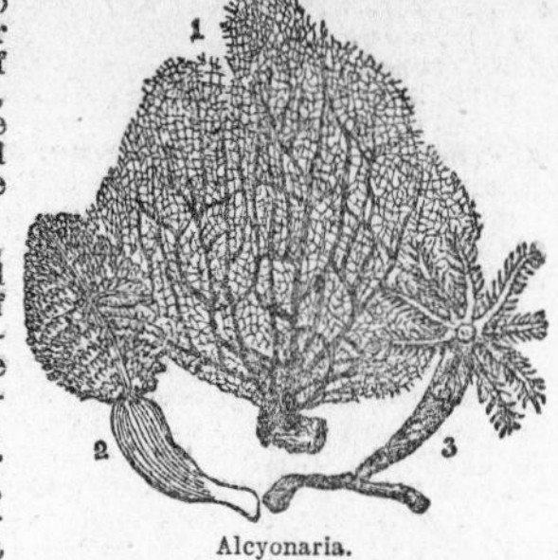

Alcyonaria.
1. Sea-fan (*Gorgonia flabellum*). 2. Sea-pen (*Pennatula phosphorea*). 3. *Cornularia rugosa.*

Al-cy-ō′ni-um, *n.* [L., from Gr. *alkyonion*, a zoöphyte, so called from its resemblance to the nest of the *alkyon.*] A genus of zoöphytes, branching somewhat like a plant, and when alive covered with small polyps, shaped like an expanded pink.

al′cy-ō-noid, *a.* Relating to the *Alcyonaria.*

al′dāy, *adv.* Continually. [Obs.]

Al-deb′ȧ-ran, *n.* [Ar. *al-debarān*; *al*, the, and *debarān*, following, from *dabar*, to follow.] A star of the first magnitude in Taurus, forming the Bull's Eye. It is the bright star in the group of five called the *Hyades.*

al′dē-hȳde, *n.* [Abbrev. of *al*cohol, and L. *dehyd*rogenatus; L. *de*, from, without, and *hydrogen.*] A colorless, pungent, volatile liquid produced by the oxidation of ethyl alcohol.

al-dē-hȳ′diç, *a.* Pertaining to aldehyde.

al′dēr, *n.* [ME. *alder, aldir, aller*; AS. *alr, alor*; Ice. *ölr, elrir*; Norw. *older*; L. *alnus*, from Fr. *aune*, alder.] A tree usually growing in moist land and belonging to the genus *Alnus.* The name is applied also to some species of other genera which resemble true alders.

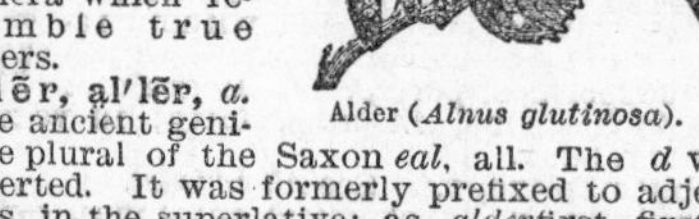

Alder (*Alnus glutinosa*).

al′dēr, al′lēr, *a.* The ancient genitive plural of the Saxon *eal*, all. The *d* was inserted. It was formerly prefixed to adjectives in the superlative; as, *alder*first, first of all; *alder*best, best of all. [Obs.]

al′dēr-măn, *n.*; *pl.* **al′dēr-men.** [AS. *ealdorman*; *ealdor*, prince, chief, and *man.*]

1. Among the Anglo-Saxons, a senior or superior. The title was applied to princes, dukes, earls, senators, and presiding magistrates; also to archbishops and bishops, implying superior wisdom or authority. Thus, Ethelstan, duke of the East-Anglians, was called *alderman* of all England; and there were *aldermen* of cities, counties, and castles, who had jurisdiction within their respective districts.

2. Generally, in the United States, a member of a municipal council elected by the people for a term of one or more years; a city councilor; a councilman. In cities having a dual council, the members of the upper chamber are usually called *aldermen*, while those of the lower body are styled councilors, councilmen, etc. In many cities the *aldermen* have certain magisterial powers, as that of performing the marriage ceremony, etc.

3. In England, a municipal councilor and magistrate, generally elected for a term of years, but in the city of London holding the office for life, the lord mayor being chosen each year from among the *aldermen* who have not yet held the office.

al′dēr-măn-cy, *n.* The position of alderman.

al-dēr-man′iç, *a.* Characteristic of, or relating to, an alderman.

al-dēr-man′i-ty, *n.* Aldermen regarded collectively; the whole body of aldermen.

al′dēr-măn-like, *a.* Like an alderman.

al′dēr-măn-ly, *a.* Pertaining to or like an alderman.

al′dēr-măn-ry, *n.* A district having an alderman; a ward.

al′dēr-măn-ship, *n.* An alderman's office.

al′dērn, *a.* Made of alder. [Obs.]

Al′dēr-ney, *n.* One of the breed of cattle originally raised on the island of Alderney, in the English Channel. *Alderneys* are of a tawny color, much resembling Jerseys.

Al′dine (*or* **al′din**), *a.* A distinguishing term applied to those editions, chiefly of the classics, which proceeded from the press of Aldus Manutius, of Venice, for the most part in the sixteenth century. The term was later applied to certain elegant editions of English works, and has also been used of some American editions.

āle, *n.* [ME. *ale*; AS. *ealu.*]

1. An intoxicating beverage made from an infusion of malt by top-fermentation. It differs from beer in having a smaller proportion of hops, and hence being sweeter, and of a lighter color. It is of different sorts, chiefly *pale* and *brown*; the first made from malt slightly dried; the second, from malt more considerably dried or roasted. *Ale* was the common drink of the ancient inhabitants of Europe. It is usually made with barley, but sometimes with other grains.

2. A merry meeting in English country places, so called from the liquor drunk. [Rare.]

On ember eves and holy *ales.* —Shak.

Medicated ales; those which are prepared for medicinal purposes, by an infusion of herbs during fermentation.

ȧ-lēak′, *a.* and *adv.* Leaking; in a leaking state.

ā′lē-ȧ-tō-ry, *a.* [L. *aleatorius*, pertaining to gaming; from *aleator*, a gamester; *alea*, a game with dice.] In law, depending upon a contingency; applied to contracts, etc.; the literal meaning is, depending upon a throw of dice.

āle′bench, *n.* A bench in or before an alehouse.

āle′ber-ry, *n.* A beverage formerly made by boiling ale with spice, sugar, and sops of bread.

āle′-brew″ēr, *n.* One whose occupation is to brew ale.

ȧ-lec′i-thăl, *a.* [Gr. *a* priv., and *lekithos*, yolk.] Pertaining to certain ova from which the food yolk is missing, or in which it occurs uniformly segmented.

āle′çon-nēr, *n.* [*Ale* and *con*, to know or see.] An officer in London, in former times, whose business was to inspect the measures used in public-houses, to prevent frauds in selling liquors; an aletaster.

āle′çost, *n.* [*Ale* and L. *costum*; Gr. *kostos*, an Oriental, aromatic plant.] Costmary, a plant formerly used to give an aromatic flavor to ales.

Al-eç-tor′i-dēş, *n.pl.* [L., from Gr. *alektoris*, pl. *alektorides*, f. of *alektōr*, a cock.] A group of birds delimited in various ways, but ordinarily understood to include the domestic fowls and pheasants.

ȧ-leç-try-om′ȧ-çhy, ȧ-leç-tō-rom′ȧ-çhy, *n.* [Gr. *alektōr*, a cock, and *machē*, a fight.] Cock-fighting.

ȧ-leç′try-ō-man″cy, ȧ-leç′tō-rō-man″cy, *n.* [Gr. *alektōr*, a cock, and *manteia*, divination.] An ancient practice of foretelling events by means of a cock. The letters of the alphabet were traced on the ground, and a grain of corn laid on each; a cock was then permitted to pick up the grains, and the letters under the grains selected, being formed into words, were supposed to foretell the event desired.

ȧ-lee′, *adv.* In seamen's language, on the side opposite to the wind, that is, opposite to the side on which it strikes. The helm of a ship is *alee*, when pressed close to the lee side.

Hard alee, or *luff alee*; an order to put the helm to the lee side.

Helm's alee; that is, *the helm is alee*, a notice given as an order to the seamen to let the head-sails fly in the wind, with a view to bring the ship about.

al′e-găr, *n.* [*Ale*, and *egar*; Fr. *aigre*, sour.] Sour ale; the acid of ale; vinegar made of ale.

al′e-ġēr, *a.* [OFr *alegre*; It. *allegro*; L. *alacer*, brisk, cheerful.] Gay; cheerful; sprightly. [Obs.]

āle′hoof, *n.* [ME. *alehoofe*, a corruption of *haihove*; *hai*, a hedge, and *hoofe*, ivy; AS. *hofe*, ivy.] Ground-ivy; so called by the Anglo-Saxons as being a chief ingredient in making ale.

āle′house, *n.* A house where ale is retailed; a tippling-house.

āle′-knight, *n.* A pot-companion. [Obs.]

al′em, *n.* [Turk. *alem*, a flag, banner.] The Turkish standard.

Al-ē-man′niç, *a.* [L. *Alemannicus*, pertaining to the Alemanni, from Goth. *alamans*, all men.] Relating to the Alemanni, ancient Germans, and to Alemannia, or Alemagne.

Al-ē-man′niç, *n.* The language of the Alemanni.

ȧ-lemb′där, *n.* [Turk. *'alemdār*; *'alem*, flag, and *dār*, from Per. *dār*, a bearer.] In Turkey, an officer who bears the green standard of Mohammed, when the sultan appears in public.

ȧ-lem′biç, *n.* [L. *alambicus*; Ar. *alanbiq*; *al*, the, and *anbiq*, Per. *ambiq*, a still; Gr. *ambix*, a cup of a still.]

Alembic.

1. A chemical vessel formerly used in distillation, and usually made of glass or metal. The bottom part containing the liquor to be distilled, was called the cucurbit; the upper part which received and condensed the steam was called

the head, the beak of which was fitted to the neck of a receiver. The head was more properly the *alembic*. This vessel has been superseded by the worm-still and retort.

2. Figuratively, anything which transforms or works a change; as, the *alembic* of a vivid imagination.

ȧ-lem′broth, *n.* A compound of corrosive sublimate and sal-ammoniac, formerly used by alchemists.

ȧ-length′, *adv.* At full length; along; stretched at full length.

ȧ-lep′i-dōte, *n.* [Gr. *a* priv., and *lepis* (*lepidotis*), scale.] Any fish whose skin is not covered with scales.

ȧ-lep′i-dōte, *a.* Having no scales.

āle′pōle, *n.* A pole set up in front of an alehouse as a sign. [Obs.]

A-lep′pō ē′vil. [Named from *Aleppo*, a province of Syria.] An ulcerous affection of the skin.

ȧ-lērce′, *n.* [Sp. *alerce*, the larch tree; L. *larix*; Gr. *larix*, the larch.] A Chilean timber-tree of the pine family; also, the wood of the sandarac-tree of Morocco.

ȧ-lērt′, *a.* [Fr. *alerte*; It. *all' erta*, on the watch; *all'* for *alla*, for L. *ad* and *illam*, on the, and *erta*, watch, f. of *erto*, raised aloft, pp. of *ergere*, from L. *erigere*, to raise.]

1. Watchful; vigilant; active in vigilance.

2. Brisk; nimble; moving with celerity.

Syn.—Active, brisk, lively, vigilant, watchful, wide-awake, prompt, ready.

ȧ-lērt′, *n.* An attitude of vigilance; used principally in the phrase *on the alert*; as, the watch stood *on the alert*.

ȧ-lērte, *n.* [Fr.] A warning against attack, as a military bugle-call.

ȧ-lērt′ly, *adv.* In an alert manner; promptly; agilely.

ȧ-lērt′ness, *n.* Briskness; nimbleness; sprightliness; levity.

-a′lēs. [L., pl. of *-alis*.] A suffix used in plant classification.

āle′-sil″vēr, *n.* A duty paid to the lord mayor of London by the sellers of ale within the city.

āle′stāke, *n.* A stake-sign for an alehouse. [Obs.]

āle′tāst-ēr, *n.* An officer, in former times in England, appointed and sworn to inspect ale, beer, and bread, and examine the quality and quantity within a district.

ȧ-lē-thi-ol′ō-gy, *n.* [Gr. *alētheia*, truth, and *logos*, discourse.] The science of truth and error; a department of logic.

ȧ-leth′ō-sçōpe, *n.* [Gr. *alēthēs*, true, and *skopein*, to view.] An instrument for viewing pictures, producing a stereoscopic effect.

Al′e-tris, *n.* [L., from Gr. *aletris*, a grinder of corn, from *aletreuein*; *alein*, to grind.] A genus of plants of the bloodwort family.

ȧ-lette′ (ȧ-let′), *n.* [Dim. of L. *ala*, a wing.] A small wing of a building; a pilaster or buttress; the face of the pier of an arch, extending from the edge of the opening; but more particularly, that portion between the edge of the opening and the pillar or pilaster used to decorate the arch.

a, Arch. *bb*, Pillars. *cc*, Alettes.

Al-eū-ri′tēs, *n.* [L., from Gr. *aleuritēs*, pertaining to *aleuron*, meal, from *alein*, to grind.] A genus of euphorbiaceous plants, including the candleberry-tree.

ȧ-leū′rō-man-cy, *n.* [Gr. *aleuromanteion*, divination by meal; *aleuron*, meal, and *manteia*, divination.] A kind of divination by flour or meal, used by the ancients.

al-eū-rom′e-tēr, *n.* [Gr. *aleuron*, meal, and *metron*, measure.] An instrument for testing the quality of gluten in flour.

ȧ-leū′rō-nat, *n.* Nutriment made of aleurone.

ȧ-leū′rōne, *n.* An albuminoid substance found in small granules in ripening seeds; also called *protein granules*.

al-eū-ron′iç, *a.* Pertaining to or resembling aleurone.

A-leū′tian, A-leū′tic, *a.* Designating or pertaining to certain islands in the Pacific Ocean, forming part of the territory of Alaska. The word is formed from *aleut*, an Indian term for a bald rock.

al′e-vin, *n.* [Fr. *alevin*; OFr. *alever*; L. *adlevare*, to raise.] A young fish of any kind but especially of the salmon and herring families.

ȧ-lew′, *n.* [Obs.] Same as *Halloo*.

āle′-wăshed, *a.* Steeped or soaked in ale.

āle′wife, *n.*; *pl.* **-wives.** A fish, *Clupea vernalis*, of the herring family, the name being given probably on account of its appearance.

Big-bellied *alewives*. —Clarke.

āle′wife, *n.* A woman who keeps an alehouse.

al-ex-an′dēr̤ṣ (-eg-zan′), *n.* [ME. *alisandre*; OFr. *alisaundre*; AS. *alexandrie*, from L. *Alexandria*.]

1. The *Smyrnium Olusatrum*, a plant of the parsley family, formerly much cultivated in Europe for salads.

2. In this country, the *Thaspium aureum*, or meadow-parsnip.

Al-ex-an′dri-ăn, Al-ex-an′drine, *a.* 1. Pertaining to one of the cities of the name of Alexandria, but usually the old Egyptian Alexandria, which was founded by Alexander the Great, 332 B. C. It was highly celebrated for its learning, literature, and magnificence; its library, said to have contained 700,000 volumes, was the largest collection of books in antiquity.

2. Pertaining to Alexander the Great.

Al-ex-an′dri-ăn, *n.* A citizen of Alexandria; a professor of sciences in the ancient school of Alexandria.

Al-ex-an′drine, *a.* See *Alexandrian*.

Al-ex-an′drine, *n.* A verse of twelve syllables, or of twelve and thirteen alternately, receiving its name from its use in early French romantic poetry on the life of Alexander.

al-ex-an′drite, *n.* [Named from *Alexander*, Czar of Russia.] A variety of chrysoberyl, emerald-green by direct, columbine-red by transmitted, light.

ȧ-lex′i-ȧ, *n.* [L., from Gr. *a* priv., and *lexis*, speech, from *legein*, to speak.] A disease of the visual nerve-centers causing word-blindness.

ȧ-lex′in, *n.* [Gr. *alexein*, to ward off.] A proteid found in the blood, hostile to pathogenic bacteria.

ȧ-lex-i-phär′maç, ȧ-lex-i-phär′miç, *a.* [L., from Gr. *alexipharmakon*; *alexein*, to ward off, and *pharmakon*, poison.] Expelling or resisting poison; antidotal; also, sudorific; having the quality of expelling poison or infection by sweat.

ȧ-lex-i-phär′maç, ȧ-lex-i-phär′miç, *n.* A medicine that is intended to obviate the effects of poison; an antidote to poison or infection. In the latter sense, applied to remedies in malignant fevers.

ȧ-lex-i-phär′maç-ăl, ȧ-lex-i-phär′miç-ăl, *a.* See *Alexipharmac*.

ȧ-lex″i-py-ret′iç, *a.* and *n.* [Gr. *alexein*, to ward off, and *pyretos*, fever; from *pyr*, fire.]

I. *a.* Curative in fevers.

II. *n.* A medicine efficacious in fevers; a febrifuge.

ȧ-lex-i-ter′iç, ȧ-lex-i-ter′iç-ăl, *a.* [Gr. *alexitērios*, able to keep off, from *alexitēr*, one who defends, from *alexein*, to ward off.] Resisting poison; obviating the effects of venom.

ȧ-lex-i-ter′iç, *n.* A medicine to resist the effects of poison, or the bite of venomous animals; nearly synonymous with *alexipharmac*.

āle′yärd, *n.* An elongated form of drinking-glass and measure for ale, formerly used. There were also half-yards and quarter-yards, for pints and half-pints respectively. A "tricky" aleyard was also used, in which the narrow end opened into a small globe, so contrived that, in the process of draining, the ale came out with a spurt on the drinker's face.

1. Aleyard.
2. Tricky Aleyard.

al′fȧ, *n.* The name of a North African plant of the genus *Stipa*; also, its fiber, used in the manufacture of paper.

al′fȧ-grass, *n.* Alfa.

al-fal′fȧ, *n.* [Sp. *alfalfez*, from Ar. *al-faç*, *façah*, the best fodder.] The common name of lucerne, a valuable forage-grass. [See *Lucerne*.]

al′fe-nid, al′fe-nide, *n.* An alloy of silver and nickel with a thick silver electroplating.

al-fē′reṣ, *n.* [Sp. *alferez*, ensign, from Ar. *al-fāris*; *al*, the, and *fāris*, a knight, horseman.] A standard-bearer. [Obs.]

al′fet, *n.* [L. *alfetum*; AS. *alfaet*, a pot to boil in.] An early English ordeal to determine the innocence or guilt of an accused person, who was required to plunge his arm into a pot of boiling water; also, the pot of boiling water used for this purpose.

al″fi-le-ril′lȧ, al-fil″ȧ-rī′ȧ, *n.* [Sp. Am.] The naturalized European plant, *Erodium cicutarium*, a valuable forage-grass of California, called *pin-grass* and *pin-clover*.

ȧl-fi-ō′nȧ, ȧl-fi-ō′ne, *n.* [Sp. Am.] The largest of the edible surf-fish on the coast of California; the *Rhacochilus toxotes*.

al-fres′çō, *adv.* and *a.* [It.; *al*, for *a il*, in the, and *fresco*, fresh, cool.] Out of doors.

al′gȧ, *n.*; *pl.* **al′gæ.** [L., seaweed.] A seaweed; one of the *Algæ*.

Al′gæ (*or* -ge), *n.pl.* [L.] A division of submerged or subaqueous plants, including the seaweeds (*Fucus*) and the lavers (*Ulva*) growing in salt water, and the fresh-water confervæ. Irish moss, dulse, and laver are nutritious edible *Algæ*. The ashes of the *Algæ*, formerly used in various arts, are now employed in making iodine.

Algæ.
1. *Dictyota dichotoma*: *a*, Spore. *b*, Vertical view of a sorus. *c*, Vertical section of a sorus.
2. *Plocamium coccineum*: *f*, Tetraspore. *g*, Stichidium. *h*, Branchlet with a tubercle.

al′găl, *a.* Pertaining to, or characteristic of, the *Algæ*.

Algal fungus; a fungus of the group *Phycomycetes*.

al′gȧ-rot, al′gȧ-roth, *n.* [Fr. *algaroth*, from *Algarotti*, a Venetian scholar.] An emetic powder, antimony oxychlorid, precipitated by compounding the trichlorid and trioxid of antimony.

al-gär-rō′bȧ, al-gȧ-rō′bȧ, *n.* [Sp., from Ar. *al-kharrubah*; *al*, the, and *kharrubah*, the carob.] A name given to a tree growing in the Mediterranean region, which bears an edible bean, known as St. John's bread; also applied to the mesquit and its fruit, and the West Indian locust.

al″gär-rō-bil′lȧ, al″gȧ-rō-vil′lȧ, *n.* The seeds and husks of certain leguminous South American shrubs; used in tanning and dyeing.

al′gāte, al′gātes, *adv.* [ME. *al*, all, and *gate*, gate; AS. *algeats*, a gate, a way.] By all means; on any terms. [Obs.]

al′gȧ-zel, *n.* [Ar. *al*, the, and *ghazāl*, gazelle.] The gazel.

al′ge-brȧ, *n.* [Fr. *algèbre*; Russ. *algebra*; Ar. *al-jabr*, *al-jebr*, the reunion of broken parts, as the reduction of fractions to whole numbers; *jabara*, to reunite, bind together.]

1. The science of quantity in general, or universal arithmetic. *Algebra* is a general method of computation, in which signs and symbols, which are commonly the letters of the alphabet, are made to represent numbers and quantities. It takes an unknown quantity sought, as if granted; and, by means of one or more quantities given, proceeds till the quantity supposed is discovered, by some other known quantity to which it is equal.

This science was of Oriental discovery; but whether among the Arabians or Indians is uncertain.

2. A treatise on this division of mathematics.

al-ġe-brā′iç, al-ġe-brā′iç-ăl, *a.* Pertaining to algebra; containing an operation of algebra, or deduced from such operation.

Algebraic curve; a figure whose intercepted diameters bear always the same proportion to their respective ordinates.

al-ġe-brā′iç-ăl-ly, *adv.* By algebraic process.

al′ġe-brā-ist, *n.* One who is versed in the science of algebra.

al′ġe-brā-ize, *v.t.*; algebraized, *pt.*, *pp.*; algebraizing, *ppr.* To perform by algebra, or to reduce to algebraic form.

al-ġē-fā′cient (-shient), *a.* [L. *algere*, be cold, and *faciens*, ppr. of *facere*, to make.] Cooling.

Al-ġē′ri-ăn, Al-ġe-rine′, *a.* Relating to Algiers.

Al-ġē′ri-ăn, Al-ġe-rine′, *n.* An inhabitant or native of Algiers.

al-ġē′si-ȧ (*or* -zi-ȧ), *n.* [Gr. *algesis*, sense of pain, from *algein*, to suffer.] Pain.

al-ġet′iç, *a.* Causing pain.

-al′ġi-ȧ, -al′ġy, *suffix.* A combining form used to denote pain.

al′ġid, *a.* [L. *algidus*, cold, from *algere*, to be cold.] Cold.

Algid cholera; Asiatic cholera.

al-ġid′i-ty, al′ġid-ness, *n.* Chilliness; coldness.

al-ġif′iç, *a.* Producing cold.

al-god′ō-nite, *n.* [From *Algodones*, in Chile.] A copper arsenide found in Chile.

al′goid, *a.* Resembling one of the *Algæ*.

Al′gol, *n.* [Ar. *al-ghūl*, destruction, from *ghala*, to destroy.] A fixed star in Medusa's head, in the constellation Perseus, remarkable for its periodic variation in brightness.

al-gō-loġ′iç-ăl, *a.* Pertaining to algology; of the nature of seaweeds or algæ.

al-gol′ō-ġist, *n.* A specialist in, or a student of, algology.

al-gol′ō-ġy, *n.* [L. *alga*, seaweed, and Gr. *logos*, description.] The study of seaweeds.

al-gom′e-tēr, *n.* [Gr. *algos*, pain, and *metron*, measure.] An instrument for testing sensibility to pain.

al-gom′e-try, *n.* The science of pain-sensibility.

Al-gon′ki-ăn, Al-gon′qui-ăn, *a.* 1. Relating to the Algonkins.

2. In geology, characterizing the period between the Archæan and the Cambrian.

Al-gon′kin, Al-gon′quin, *n.* A member of the Algonkin tribe of Indians.

al′gor, *n.* [L., from *algere*, to be cold.] Cold; especially when abnormal, as in certain diseases.

al′gō-rism, al′gō-rithm, *n.* [OFr. *algorisme*; L. *algorismus*, the Arabic system of numbers; from Ar. *al-Khowārazmī*, a native of Khwarazm (Khiva), an Arabic mathematician of the ninth century.] An Arabic term signifying numerical computation, or the operations of arithmetic. Also, the common rules of computation in any branch of analysis; as, the *algorithm* of the differential calculus.

al′gous, *a.* [L. *alga*, seaweed.] Pertaining to seaweed; abounding with, or like, seaweed.

al-guä-zil′ (-gwä-), *n.* [Sp., from Ar. *al-wazīr*; *al*, the, and *wazīr*, officer.] An inferior officer of justice in Spain; a constable.

al′gum, *n.* Probably a pine, or similar tree, which grew on Mount Lebanon in Bible times, and was used in the construction of Solomon's temple. It has been supposed to be identical with *almug*, but the latter was a wood brought from Ophir.

> Send me also cedar trees, fir trees, and *algum* trees, out of Lebanon. —2 Chron. ii. 8.

Al-ham′brȧ, *n.* A fortress and palace erected by the Moors in Granada during the thirteenth and early fourteenth centuries. It is the finest existing example of Moorish architecture.

Al-ham-brā′iç, Al-ham-bresque′ (-bresk′), *a.* After the pattern of the decoration of the Alhambra.

al-hen′nȧ, *n.* See *Henna*.

ā′li-ăs, *adv.* [L.] Otherwise; in another place; at another time; used in legal phraseology to connect false names, or names assumed with questionable motives for concealment; as, Smith *alias* Jones, *alias* Robinson.

ā′li-ăs, *n.* [L., from *alius*, other.]

1. A name assumed for the purpose of questionable concealment.

2. A second writ or execution issued when the first has failed of effect.

al′i-bī, *adv.* [L., locative case of *alius*, other.] Elsewhere, or in another place.

al′i-bi, *n.* 1. In law, a plea showing that the person charged with offense was in another place at the time it was committed.

2. The fact of being elsewhere at the time of an offense charged.

al-i-bil′i-ty, *n.* The state of being alible.

al′i-ble, *a.* [L. *alibilis*, from *alere*, to nourish.] Nutritive; possessing nourishment.

al′i-cănt, *n.* A kind of wine, deriving its name from Alicant, in Spain, near which town it was first made.

al′i-dāde, *n.* [L. *alidada*, from Ar. *al-'idādah*, a revolving radius; *al*, the, and *'adad*, the upper arm.] A name for the index of a graduated instrument (such as a quadrant), carrying sights or a telescope, and showing the degrees cut off on the arc of the instrument.

āl′ien (-yen), *a.* [OFr. *alien*; L. *alienus*, from *alius*, another.]

1. Foreign; not belonging to the same country, land, or government.

2. Belonging to one who is not a citizen.

3. Estranged; foreign; not allied; adverse to; as, principles *alien* from our religion.

Alien enemy; the subject of a government at war with the state in which he has residence.

Syn.—Foreign, distant, unsympathetic, remote, irrelevant.

āl′ien (-yen), *n.* 1. A foreigner; one born in, or belonging to, another country; one who is not a denizen, or entitled to the privileges of a citizen.

2. In Scripture, one who is a stranger to the church of Christ, or to the covenant of grace.

> *Aliens* from Israel. —Eph. ii. 12.

3. A stranger. [Obs.]

In France, a child born of residents who are not citizens is an *alien*. In the United States and Great Britain, children born of resident *aliens* are looked upon as natural-born citizens, if they remain in these countries; and foreign-born children of citizens are generally considered natural-born citizens.

āl′ien, *v.t.*; aliened (-yend), *pt.*, *pp.*; aliening, *ppr.* 1. To convey, sell, or make over (any property) to another; to alienate.

2. To alienate; to deflect; to estrange, as the affections.

āl″ien-ȧ-bil′i-ty, *n.* The capacity of being alienated or transferred.

> The *alienability* of the domain. —Burke.

āl′ien-ȧ-ble, *a.* Possessing the right to be sold, transferred, or conveyed; as real estate.

āl′ien-āge, *n.* The state of being an alien.

> Why restore estates forfeitable on account of *alienage*? —Story.

āl′ien-āte (-yen-), *v.t.*; alienated, *pt.*, *pp.*; alienating, *ppr.* [L. *alienatus*, pp. of *alienare*, from *alius*, another.]

1. To transfer (title, property, or right) to another; as, to *alienate* lands, or sovereignty.

2. To estrange; to withdraw; as the affections; to make indifferent or averse, where love or friendship before subsisted; with *from*; as, to *alienate* the heart or affections; to *alienate* a man *from* the friends of his youth.

Syn.—Estrange, transfer, wean, disaffect.

āl′ien-āte, *a.* Estranged; withdrawn; strange; with *from*.

> O *alienate from* God, O spirit accurst! —Milton.

āl′ien-āte, *n.* A stranger; an alien. [Obs.]

āl-ien-ā′tion, *n.* [Fr. *aliénation*; L. *alienatio*, from *alienare*; *alius*, another.]

1. In law, a transfer of title, or a legal conveyance of property to another.

2. The state of being alienated.

3. A withdrawing or estrangement, as of the heart or affections.

4. Delirium; derangement of mental faculties; insanity.

āl′ien-ā-tŏr, *n.* One who or that which alienates.

āl-iēne′ (-yēn′), *v.t.*; aliened, *pt.*, *pp.*; aliening, *ppr.* 1. To transfer (title or property) to another; to sell.

> Nor could he *aliene* the estate even with the consent of the lord. —Blackstone.

2. To estrange; to make averse or indifferent; to turn the affections of; to alienate. [Rare.]

> The prince was *aliened* from all thoughts of the marriage. —Clarendon.

āl-ien-ee′, *n.* One to whom the title of property is transferred.

āl′ien-iṣm, *n.* 1. The state of being an alien.

2. The science of mental alienation.

āl′ien-ist, *n.* A specialist in mental diseases.

āl-ien-or′, *n.* A person who transfers property.

al-i-eth′moid, al″i-eth-moid′ăl, *a.* [L. *ala*, wing, and *ethmoid*.] Relating to expansions of the ethmoid region.

ȧ-life′, *adv.* On my life. [Obs.]

ȧ-lif′ẽr-ous, *a.* [L. *ala*, wing, and *ferre*, to bear.] Having wings. [Rare.]

al′i-fŏrm, *a.* [L. *ala*, wing, and *forma*, shape.] Resembling a wing in shape; applied to bone or muscle processes.

ȧ-lig′ẽr-ous, *a.* [L. *ala*, wing, and *gerere*, to carry.] Having wings. [Rare.]

ȧ-light′ (-līt′), *v.i.*; alighted, *pt.*, *pp.*; alighting, *ppr.* [ME. *alighten*; AS. *alīhtan*; *a*, out, off, and *līhtan*, to dismount, to render light.]

1. To get down or descend, as from horseback or from a carriage.

2. To descend and settle; as, a flying bird *alights* on a tree.

3. To fall or descend and lodge; as, snow *alights* on a roof.

4. To hit (upon) accidentally or unexpectedly.

Alighting gear; the under mechanism of an aeroplane, designed to cushion its descent and stop it as it reaches the ground.

ȧ-light′, *a.* Lighted; lighted up; as, the candles are *alight*.

ȧ-lign′, *v.t.* and *v.i.*; aligned, *pt.*, *pp.*; aligning, *ppr.* Same as *Aline*.

ȧ-lign′ment, *n.* Same as *Alinement*.

ȧ-like′, *a.* [ME. *alike*; AS. *onlic* and *gelic*, similar, correspondent.] Having resemblance or similitude; similar.

ȧ-like′, *adv.* Equally; in the same manner, form, or degree; in common; as, we are all *alike* concerned in religion.

ȧ-like′-mind″ed, *a.* Having the same mind; like-minded. [Obs.]

ä′lim, *n.* [Ar. *'ālim*, learned, from *'alama*, to know.] A Mohammedan religious teacher.

al′i-mȧ, *n.* [L., from Gr. *halimos*, of the sea.] The larval stage of a stomatopod.

al′i-ment, *n.* [L. *alimentum*, from *alere*, to nourish.]

1. That which nourishes; food; nutriment; anything which feeds or adds to a substance, animal or vegetable, in natural growth.

2. In Scotland, an allowance for support, as that of a pensioner.

al′i-ment, *v.t.*; alimented, *pt.*, *pp.*; alimenting, *ppr.* 1. To nourish; to support.

2. In Scotland, to provide means of support for.

al-i-men′tăl, *a.* Supplying food; nourishing; furnishing the materials for natural growth; as, chyle is *alimental*; *alimental* sap.

al-i-men′tăl-ly, *adv.* So as to serve for nourishment or food.

al-i-men′tȧ-ri-ness, *n.* The quality of supplying nutriment. [Rare.]

al-i-men′tȧ-ry, *a.* Pertaining to aliment or food; having the quality of nourishing; as, *alimentary* particles.

Alimentary canal; the duct extending from the mouth to the anus, which receives the food, conveying and digesting it, assimilating part and excreting the remainder.

al″i-men-tā′tion, *n.* [Fr. *alimentation*; L. *alimentatio*, from *alimentare*, to provide.]

1. The act or power of affording nutriment; assimilation.

2. The state of being nourished.

al-i-men′tive-ness, *n.* 1. In phrenology, the alimentary faculty.

2. The desire for food and drink.

al-i-mō′ni-ous, *a.* Nourishing; affording food. [Rare.]

al′i-mō-ny, *n.* [L. *alimonia*, food, support, from *alere*, to nourish.]

1. Means of living; aliment.

2. An allowance made for the support of the wife in case of divorce or legal separation from the husband. It is granted at the discretion of the court, and when awarded must be paid out of the husband's estate or income.

Alimony pendente lite; the maintenance awarded the wife out of the husband's income or estate while divorce proceedings are pending.

Permanent alimony; that adjudged to the wife after divorce or legal separation obtained by her.

al-i-nā′ṣăl, *a.* [L. *ala*, wing, and *nasus*, nose.] Characterizing the expansions of the nasal region.

ȧ-line′, ȧ-lign′, *v.t.* and *v.i.*; alined, *pt.*, *pp.*; alining, *ppr.* [L. *ad*, to, and *lineare*, to reduce to a line, from *linea*, line. *Align* is from Fr. *aligner*.]

I. *v.t.* To adjust to a line; to lay out or regulate by a line; to form or bring into line.

II. *v.i.* To form in line; to take one's assigned place in line.

ȧ-lin′ē-āte, *v.t.* To aline. [Rare.]

ȧ-lin-ē-ā′tion, *n.* The act of bringing objects in line with each other; a method of locating remote or obscure objects by an imaginary line extending between two distinct objects; as the familiar method of searching out the North Star by means of the pointers of the Great Dipper.

ȧ-line′ment, ȧ-lign′ment, *n.* 1. The act of adjusting to a line; the state of being so adjusted; the formation or arrangement in a line; the line of adjustment.

2. In engineering, the ground-plan of any work, as distinguished from its profile-plan.

ȧ-lin′ẽr, *n.* A person who alines.

Al′i-oth, *n.* [Ar. *alyāt*, the tail of a fat sheep.] A star in the tail of the Great Bear, much used in finding the latitude.

al′i-ped, *a.* [L. *ala*, wing, and *pes*, *pedis*, foot.] Wing-footed; having wings formed by a membrane connecting the toes.

al′i-ped, *n.* An animal whose toes are connected by a membrane, which has the functions of a wing; as the bat.

Aliped.

al-i-phat′iç, *a.* [Gr. *aleiphar*, *aleiphatos*, fat.] Fatty.

al′i-quănt, *a.* [L. *aliquantus*, some, moderate, from *alius*, other, and *quantus*, how great.] Dividing a number with a remainder; as, 5 is an *aliquant* part of 16.

al′i-quot, *a.* [L. *aliquot*, some, several, from *alius*, other, and *quot*, how many.] Dividing a number without a remainder; as, 5 is an *aliquot* part of 15.

al-i-sep′tăl, *a.* [L. *ala*, wing, and *sæptum*, *septum*, septum.] Pertaining to the aliseptal.

al-i-sep′tăl, *n.* The cartilage which forms lateral expansions of the septum in the nasal cavity in the skulls of embryonic birds.

āl′ish, *a.* Like ale; having the qualities of ale.

Al-is-mā′cē-æ, *n.pl.* [L., from Gr. *alisma*, plantain, and *-aceæ*.] A botanical order consisting of monocotyledonous aquatic or marsh plants, the leaves of which are elliptical with long stalks, and the flowers white in color, regular in structure, and either monœcious or diœcious. The typical genus is *Alisma*.

al-is-mā′ceous, *a.* Pertaining or belonging to the order *Alismaceæ*.

al-i-sphē′noid, al″i-sphē-noid′ăl (-sfē-), *a.* [L. *ala*, wing, and *sphenoid*.] Pertaining to the alisphenoid bones.

al-i-sphē′noid, *n.* In anatomy, either of the two bones which form the large wing-like plates on the sides of the sphenoid bone.

ȧ-lis′son, *n.* See *Alyssum*.

al′i-trunk, *n.* [L. *ala*, a wing, and *trunk*.] The segment of the body of an insect to which the wings are attached.

al-i-tūr′giç-ăl, *a.* Without liturgy; an ecclesiastical term applied to those days on which the liturgy or eucharistic service is not performed.

ā-li-un′dē, *adv.* [L. *alius*, other, and *unde*, whence.] In law, from another source; as, evidence *aliunde*, that is, evidence to support or contradict a written instrument from sources outside of itself.

ȧ-live′, *a.* [ME. *alive*, *alyfe*, *on live*; AS. *on life*, *on*, in, and *life*, dat. case of *lif*, life.]

1. Having life, in opposition to *dead*; living; being in a state in which the organs perform their functions, and the fluids move, whether in animals or vegetables; as, the man or plant is *alive*.

2. In a state of action; unextinguished; undestroyed; unexpired; in force or operation; as, to keep the interest *alive*.

3. Cheerful; sprightly; lively; full of alacrity; as, the company were all *alive*.

4. Susceptible; easily impressed; having lively feelings, as when the mind is solicitous about some event; as, one is *alive* to whatever is interesting to a friend.

5. Exhibiting motion or moving bodies in great numbers; as, the city was all *alive*, when the general entered.

6. In a scriptural sense, regenerated; born again.

7. Of all living persons; as, the proudest man *alive*.

8. Often used as an intensive; as, woman *alive*; sakes *alive*. [Colloq.]

9. In printing, see *Live*.

ȧ-liz′ȧ-rāte, *n.* A salt of alizarin obtained by the action of an alkali.

ȧ-li-zä′ri, *n.* [Probably from Ar.] An Oriental name for madder.

ȧ-li-zä′riç, *a.* Pertaining to or containing alizari.

ȧ-liz′ȧ-rin, ȧ-liz′ȧ-rine, *n.* [From *alizari*, the Levantine name of madder.] A peculiar yellowish-red coloring matter, formerly obtained exclusively from madder, but now also made from anthracene. It is acid and unites with bases. It is used extensively in dyeing fabrics—silk, wool, or cotton.

al′kȧ-hest, *n.* A term supposed to have been invented by Paracelsus to designate an imaginary universal solvent, capable of dissolving all bodies.

al-kȧ-hes′tiç, *a.* Pertaining to the alkahest.

al-kal-am′ide, al-kal-am′id, *n.* [*Alkali* and *amide*.] In chemistry, a compound in which part of the hydrogen in ammonia has been replaced by acid, and another part by basic, radicals. Written also *alkalimide*.

al-kȧ-les′cence, al-kȧ-les′cen-cy, *n.* [*Alkali* and *-escence*.] A tendency to become alkaline; or a tendency to the properties of an alkali; or the state of a substance in which alkaline properties begin to be developed, or to be predominant.

al-kȧ-les′cent, *a.* Tending to the properties of an alkali; slightly alkaline.

al′kȧ-li (*or* -lī), *n.*; *pl.* **al′kȧ-lis** *or* **al′kȧ-lies**. [ME. *alkaly*; OFr. *alcali*; Ar. *al-qaliy*; *al*, the, and *qaliy*, ashes of the plant saltwort; *qalay*, to roast in a pan.]

1. In chemistry, any one of various classes of bodies having the following properties in common: (a) solubility in water; (b) the power of neutralizing acids, and forming salts with them; (c) the property of corroding animal and vegetable substances; (d) the property of altering the tint of many coloring matters—thus, they turn red litmus, blue; turmeric, brown. The alkalis are hydrates, or water in which half the hydrogen is replaced by a metal or compound radical. In its restricted and common sense the term is applied to four substances only: hydrate of potassium (potash), hydrate of sodium (soda), hydrate of lithium (lithia), and hydrate of ammonium (an aqueous solution of ammonia). In a more general sense, *alkali* is applied to the hydrates of the so-called alkaline earths and to a large number of organic substances, both natural and artificial, commonly called vegetable alkalis, or alkaloids. Potash, soda, and lithia are known as the *fixed* alkalis, in distinction from ammonia, called the *volatile* alkali.

2. The *Salsola kali*, or saltwort, formerly called glasswort, from its use in manufacturing glass.

3. Soda-ash.

al′kȧ-li-fī″ȧ-ble, *a.* That may be alkalified, or converted into an alkali.

al′kȧ-li-flat, *n.* A barren, arid plain, the soil of which contains large quantities of alkali, usually the bed of some ancient, but long evaporated, lake.

al′kȧ-li-fȳ, *v.t.*; alkalified, *pt.*, *pp.*; alkalifying, *ppr.* To form or to convert into an alkali.

al′kȧ-li-fȳ, *v.i.* To become an alkali.

al-kȧ-lig′e-nous, *a.* [*Alkali*, and *-genous*; Gr. *genēs*, producing.] Producing or generating alkali.

al′kȧ-li-land, *n.* An arid region, particularly in western United States, where the soil is strongly impregnated with alkalis which are destructive to vegetation. They appear on the surface in the form of a powder or crust.

al-kȧ-lim′e-tẽr, *n.* [*Alkali*, and Gr. *metron*, measure.] An instrument for ascertaining the strength of alkalis, or the quantity of alkali in any solution or mixture.

al″kȧ-li-met′riç, al″kȧ-li-met′riç-ăl, *a.* Pertaining to alkalimetry.

al-kȧ-lim′e-try, *n.* The process of ascertaining the strength of alkalis, or the amount of alkali present in any alkaline mixture.

al′kȧ-lin (*or* -lin), *a.* Pertaining to an alkali; having the properties of, obtained from, or containing, alkali.

Alkaline earths; baryta, lime, magnesia, and strontia.

Alkaline metals; cæsium, lithium, potassium, rubidium, and sodium, and the hypothetical element ammonium.

al-kȧ-lin′i-ty, *n.* The quality which constitutes an alkali.

al-kā′li-ous, *a.* Having the properties of alkali. [Obs.]

al′kȧ-li-zāte, *a.* Alkaline; impregnated with alkali. [Obs.]

al′kȧ-li-zāte, *v.t.* To render alkaline. [Rare.]

al′kȧ-li-zā′tion, *n.* The act of rendering alkaline by impregnating with an alkali; the process of converting into alkali.

al′kȧ-lize, *v.t.*; alkalized, *pt.*, *pp.*; alkalizing, *ppr.* To make alkaline; to communicate the properties of an alkali to; to convert into alkali.

al′kȧ-loid, *n.* One of a class of nitrogenized compounds found in living plants, and containing their active principles, usually in combination with organic acids; frequently termed the *organic bases* of plants. Although formed originally within the plant, it has been found possible to prepare numerous *alkaloids* by synthesis. Most natural *alkaloids* contain carbon, hydrogen, nitrogen, and oxygen, but the greater number of artificial ones lack oxygen. The only property common to all *alkaloids* is that of combining with acids to form salts, and some exhibit an alkaline reaction with colors. Many have a high value as toxic medicines, such as morphine, strychnine, quinine, etc.

al′kȧ-loid, *a.* Of, pertaining to, or resembling, an alkali; containing an alkali or alkaloid.

al-kȧ-loid′ăl, *a.* Pertaining to or resembling an alkaloid.

al′kȧ-net, *n.* [Sp. *alcaneta*, *orcaneta*, dim. of *alcana*, henna.]

1. A deep-red dye, made from the roots of *Alkanna tinctoria*, and other plants, as the *Anchusa officinalis*, of England, and *Lithospermum canescens*, commonly called puccoon, of America.

2. Any of the various plants from which the dye is obtained.

Al-kan′nȧ, *n.* [L.; Sp. *alcana*.] A genus of perennial herbs of the family *Boraginaceæ*, found in Oriental and Mediterranean countries, including the dye-yielding *Alkanna tinctoria*.

al-kap′ton, *n.* A crystalline body, $C_4H_6(OH)_2$, found in the urine and in the cerebrospinal fluid, formed by the decomposition of the proteids.

al-kär′gen, *n.* [*Alkar*sin and oxy*gen*.] Cacodylic acid.

al-kär′sin, al-kär′sine, *n.* [*Al*cohol, *ar*senic, and *-in*.] A liquid containing cacodyl together with its oxidation products; it is poisonous and spontaneously inflammable, and has an extremely offensive odor. Called also *Cadet's fuming liquid*.

al-kä′zär, *n.* See *Alcazar*.

al-kē-ken′gi, *n.* [Fr. *alkékenge*, from Ar. *al-kākanj*, a kind of resin found in the mountains near Herat.] *Physalis alkekengi*, a plant of the nightshade family, found in southern parts of Europe; the winter-cherry. The scarlet fruit inclosed in the enlarged red calyx makes the plant very ornamental in the beginning of winter. The fruit is edible.

al-ken′nȧ, al-hen′nȧ, *n.* Same as *Henna*.

al-kẽr′mēs, *n.* [Fr. *alkermes*; Ar. *al-qirmiz*; *al*, the, and Sans. *krimija*, worm-begotten, from *krimi*, worm.] The name of a once celebrated compound cordial, to which a fine red color was given by kermes. Its ingredients are said to have been cider, rose-water, sugar, and various fragrant flavoring matters.

Al′kō-rän (*or* al-kō-rän′), *n.* See *Koran*.

Al-kō-ran′iç, *a.* Same as *Alcoranic*.

al′kyl, *n.* An alcohol radical; methyl, ethyl, etc.

ąll, *a.* [AS. *all*, *al*; D. *al*, *alle*; W. *oll*; Arm. *oll*; Gr. *holos*; O.H.G. *alanc*, entire, complete.]

1. Every one of; the whole number of persons (or particulars) of, taken individually or together; used often with a collective noun; as, *all* sections should be indicated; *all* the Republicans favor the plan; *all* the company was uneasy.

2. The whole quantity of, with reference to extent, duration, amount, quality, or degree; used especially with nouns which have no plural forms; as, *all* China, *all* the year, *all* strength. Among the various modifiers of the same noun, *all* precedes the definite article and any pronoun.

3. The greater portion or number of; as, *all* the cattle in Egypt died.

4. Any; any whatsoever; as, beyond *all* doubt; free from *all* care.

5. Every; used mostly with *kind*, *manner*, and *sort*; as, *all manner* of evil; *all kind* of experiences.

6. The greatest possible; as, he made *all* speed.

7. Alone; nothing but; only; as, he was *all* nerves.

For all the world; exactly; precisely; as, she looks *for all the world* like her mother.

ąll, *adv.* 1. Wholly; completely; entirely; in the highest degree; very; as, it is *all* ready; *all* bedewed; he is *all* for amusement; *all* too dear.

2. Formerly used with various significations now obsolete: (a) equivalent to the conjunction *although*, and, used together with *as*, to *when*, *as*, *as if*; (b) with the adverbial sense of *only*, *exclusively*; and (c) as an intensive or an expression of emphasis meaning *even*, *just*, *at the exact moment or place*. This last meaning is retained, especially in ballad poetry, with its force often weakened to that of a mere expletive; as, *all* in the month of May.

All as an adjective and an adverb is used extensively in compounds, usually with a hyphen. In a few instances it has become a part of the word, as in *also*, *always*.

All along; all the time; throughout.

All but; very nearly; almost.

All in the wind; with sails so nearly parallel to the course of the wind that they flutter; applied to a vessel standing too close to the wind.

All one; a matter of indifference; just the same.

All over; everywhere; as, he searched *all over*; in every respect, exactly; as, that was his father *all over*; entirely past, ended; as, the storm, or the bitter feeling, is *all over*.

All the better, worse, etc.; so much the better, worse, etc.

All the same; notwithstanding; nevertheless; indifferently.

ąll, *conj.* Albeit; although. [Obs.]

ąll, *n.* (often approaching a pronominal use.)

1. The whole; the total; the actual aggregate of particulars or persons, or those involved in any particular consideration; everything or every one; often used with *of*; as, *all* that I aspired to be; *all* the parts assembled into an effective whole; *all* that thou seest is thine.

2. The whole, in a relative sense; one's entire property or interest; as, he was fighting for his *all*.

After all; even after everything is considered; nevertheless.

All in all; everything desired, everything together; as, thou shalt be *all in all*; also, adverbially, everything considered, altogether; as, taking things *all in all*.

At all; in any degree, to any extent, for any reason, under any circumstances; a phrase much used in negative and interrogative clauses; as, he has no time *at all* for recreation; would such a measure be considered *at all*?

For all; for all time, finally; as, let me say once *for all*.

äl′lä, *prep.* [It., dat. f. of the def. article, *la*; Fr. *à la*.] After the manner of; in the style of; as, *alla francese*, in the French style.

Alla breve; with one breve to a measure.

Alla cappella; same as *A cappella*.

al′lȧ-gite, *n.* [Gr. *allagē*, change, from *allassein*, to change, and *-ite*.] An impure, brownish variety of manganese spar.

Al′läh, *n.* The Arabic name of the Supreme Being.

ąll-ȧ-mort′, *a.* See *Alamort*.

al′lăn-ite, *n.* [Named after Thomas *Allan*, the discoverer.] An ore of the metals cerium and lanthanum, pitch-black or brownish in color.

al-lan-tō′iç, *a.* Pertaining to, or contained in, the allantois.

Allantoic acid; an acid found in the liquor of the allantois of the fetal calf. This was formerly called amniotic acid.

al-lan′toid, al-lan-toid′ăl, *a.* [L. *allantoides*, from Gr. *allantoeidēs*, sausage-shaped.] In anatomy, relating to the allantois.

Al-lan-toid′ē-ȧ, *n.pl.* In zoölogy, a division of vertebrates, including those reptiles, birds, and mammals which, when in embryo, have an allantoid enveloping membrane.

al-lan′tō-in, *n.* A crystalline compound, $C_4H_6N_4O_3$, obtained from the allantoic fluid of the cow, and from other sources.

al-lan′tō-is, al-lan′toid, *n.* [Gr. *allas*, *allantos*, a sausage, and *eidos*, form.] A thin membrane situated between the chorion and amnion in quadrupeds, and forming one of the membranes which invest the fetus in those animals. It is also developed as an appendage of the embryos of some birds and reptiles.

al-lan-tū′riç, *a.* Of, related to, or derived from allantoin and uric acid.

al-las-sō-ton′iç, *a.* [Gr. *allassein*, to change, and *tonos*, tension.] A term applied to the movements, taking place under stimulation, of vegetable organs.

al′lȧ-trāte, *v.i.* [L. *allatratus*, pp. of *allatrare*, to bark.] To bark. [Obs.]

al-lāy′, *v.t.*; allayed, *pt.*, *pp.*; allaying, *ppr.* [OE. *alaien*; AS. *ālecgan*; *ā*, out, and *lecgan*, to lay.]

1. To make quiet; to pacify or appease; as, to *allay* the tumult of the passions; to *allay* civil commotions.

2. To abate, mitigate, subdue, or destroy; as, to *allay* grief or pain.

> Females, who soften and *allay* the bitterness of adversity. —Rawle.

3. To alloy. [Obs.]

Syn.—Check, repress, assuage, appease, abate, subdue, destroy, compose, soothe, calm, quiet, alleviate.

al-lāy′, *v.i.* To abate; to assuage; to subside.

al-lāy′, *n.* 1. An alloy. [Obs.]

2. That which allays, or abates. [Obs.]

al-lāy′ēr, *n.* One who or that which allays.

al-lāy′ment, *n.* The act of quieting, or a state of tranquillity; a state of rest after disturbance; that which allays; abatement; as, the *allayment* of grief. [Obs.]

al′lē-çret, *n.* [OFr. *alecret*, *halecret*.] A kind of armor worn by the Swiss in the sixteenth century.

Allecret Armor, A. D. 1540.

al-leçt′, *v.t.* To entice. [Obs.]

al-lec-tā′tion, *n.* Enticement; allurement. [Obs.]

al-ledge′, *v.t.* [Obs.] See *Allege*.

al-lē-gā′tion, *n.* 1. Affirmation; positive assertion or declaration.

2. That which is affirmed or asserted; that which is offered as a plea, excuse, or justification.

3. In ecclesiastical courts, a formal complaint, or declaration of charges.

4. In law, the first plea of the plaintiff in a case testamentary; in criminal or civil proceedings, the statement which a party undertakes to prove.

al-lēġe′ (-lej′), *v.t.*; alleged (-lejd′), *pt.*, *pp.*; alleging, *ppr.* [OE. *alegen*, to bring forward as evidence; OFr. *esligier*, from L. *ex*, out, and *litigare*, to dispute at law.]

1. To declare; to affirm; to assert; to pronounce with positiveness; as, to *allege* a fact.

2. To produce, as an argument, plea, or excuse; to cite or quote; as, to *allege* the authority of a judge.

Syn.—Bring forward, adduce, advance, assign, produce, cite, quote, declare, affirm, assert.

al-leġe′, *v.i.* To mitigate; to lighten, as a burden. [Obs.]

al-leġe′ȧ-ble, *a.* That may be alleged or affirmed.

al-lēġe′ănce, *n.* Allegation. [Obs.]

al-leġe′ment, *n.* Allegation. [Obs.]

al-leġ′ēr, *n.* One who affirms or declares.

al-lē′ġiănce (*or* -ji-ăns), *n.* [ME. *alegeaunce*; *a*- and *legeaunce*, from OFr. *ligance*; L. *ligantia*, from *ligare*, to bind.]

1. The tie or obligation of a citizen or subject to his government or ruler; the duty of fidelity to a king, government, or state. Every native citizen owes *allegiance* to the government under which he is born. This is called natural or implied *allegiance*, which arises from the connection of a person with the society in which he is born, and his duty to be a faithful citizen, independent of any express promise.

2. Loyalty and devotion in general; as to a church, a political party, a principle, a leader.

Express allegiance; that obligation which proceeds from an express promise, or oath of fidelity. The paramount *allegiance* of a citizen of the United States has been decided to be due the general government before that due his own state.

Syn.—Devotion, fealty, loyalty, obedience.

al-lē′ġiănt, *a.* Loyal.

al-lē-gor′iç, al-lē-gor′iç-ăl, *a.* In the manner of allegory; figurative; describing by resemblances.

al-lē-gor′iç-ăl-ly, *adv.* In a figurative manner; by way of allegory.

al-lē-gor′iç-ăl-ness, *n.* The quality of being allegorical.

al′lē-gō-rist, *n.* One who allegorizes, or uses allegory, as Bunyan or Spenser.

al″lē-gor-i-zā′tion, *n.* The act of construing allegorically; the act of turning into allegory.

al′lē-gō-rize, *v.t.*; allegorized (-rīzd), *pt.*, *pp.*; allegorizing, *ppr.* 1. To form in allegory; to turn into allegory; as, to *allegorize* the history of a people.

2. To understand in an allegorical sense; as, when a passage in a writer may be understood literally or figuratively, he who gives it a figurative sense is said to *allegorize* it.

al′lē-gō-rize, *v.i.* To use allegory; as, a man may *allegorize* to please his fancy.

al′lē-gō-rī″zēr, *n.* One who allegorizes, or turns matter into allegory.

al′lē-gō-ry, *n.*; *pl.* **al′lē-gō-rieṣ**. [L. *allegoria*; Gr. *allēgoria*, description of one thing under the image of another; from *allos*, other, and *agoreuein*, to speak in the assembly; *agora*, a place of assembly.]

1. A figurative sentence or discourse, in which the principal subject is described by another subject resembling it in its properties and circumstances. The principal subject is thus kept out of view, and we are left to collect the intentions of the writer or speaker by the resemblance of the secondary to the primary subject.

2. In painting and sculpture, a symbolical representation.

3. Any emblem or symbolic suggestion.

Syn.—Fable, fiction, metaphor, illustration, parable, simile.

al-le-gresse′, *n.* [Fr. *allégresse*, from L. *alacer*, sprightly.] Joy.

al-le-gret′tō, *a.* [It., dim. of *allegro*.] In music, a term applied to a movement or time quicker than andante, but not so quick as allegro.

al-le-gret′tō, *n.* In music, a movement or passage in allegretto time.

al-le′grō, *a.* [It., from L. *alacer*, brisk, sprightly, cheerful.] In music, a term denoting a brisk movement, the quickest except presto.

al-le′grō, *n.* In music, a movement or passage in allegro time.

al-lē-lū′iȧ, al-lē-lū′iȧh, *interj.* Same as *Halleluiah*.

al-lē-lū′iȧ, al-lē-lū′iȧh, *n.* [L. *alleluia*; Heb. *hal-lēlū-yāh*, praise ye Jehovah.] Same as *Halleluiah*.

al-le-mȧnde′, *n.* 1. An old-style German waltz in $\frac{3}{4}$ time.

2. A sprightly German national dance in $\frac{2}{4}$ time.

3. A movement after the prelude in a musical suite, often omitted. It is an accelerated andante, consisting of two repeated strains in $\frac{4}{4}$ time.

4. A dance-figure.

al-lē-man′niç, *n.* and *a.* See *Alemannic*.

al-len′ăr-ly, *adv.* Only; a Scotch legal term.

ąl′lēr, *a.* [Obs.] Same as *Alder*.

al-lē′ri-on, *n.* [Etymology doubtful; Fr. *alérion*; L. *alarius*, from *ala*, wing.] In heraldry, an eagle or eaglet, displayed without beak and legs, with wings outspread and tips pointing downward; denoting imperialists vanquished and disarmed.

al-lē′vi-āte, *v.t.*; alleviated, *pt.*, *pp.*; alleviating, *ppr.* [L. *alleviatus*, pp. of *alleviare*, from *allevare*; *ad*, to, and *levis*, light.]

1. To lessen or lighten the weight of. [Obs.]

2. To remove in part; to lessen, mitigate, or make easier to be endured; as, to *alleviate* sorrow, pain, care, punishment, a burden, etc.; opposed to *aggravate*.

3. To make less by representation; to lessen the magnitude or criminality of; to extenuate; applied to moral conduct; as, to *alleviate* an offense. [Rare.]

Syn.—Lessen, diminish, mitigate, assuage, allay, ameliorate, moderate, soften.—These words are all figurative. *Alleviate* supposes a load, as of care, which is lightened; *mitigate*, something fierce, which is made mild, as suffering; *assuage*, something violent which is quieted, as sorrow; *allay*, something excited, but now brought down, as grief; *lessen* and *diminish* refer to amount or degree.

al-lē-vi-ā′tion, *n.* 1. The act of lightening, allaying, or extenuating; a lessening, or mitigation.

2. That which lessens, mitigates, or makes more tolerable; as, the sympathy of a friend is an *alleviation* of grief.

al-lē′vi-ā-tive, *a.* and *n.* I. *a.* Tending to lessen or mitigate.

II. *n.* Anything which alleviates or makes more bearable.

al-lē′vi-ā-tōr, *n.* A person who alleviates.

al-lē′vi-ȧ-tō-ry, *a.* Alleviative.

al′ley, *n.*; *pl.* **al′leyṣ**. [OE. *aly*, *ally*; OFr. *alée*, *allée*, a going, passage, from *aler*, *aller*, to go.]

1. A narrow foot-passage between buildings.

2. A narrow and rather obscure passageway, narrower than a street, for people or vehicles, in cities and towns; a minor thoroughfare through the center of city blocks or squares.

3. A garden path or walk, between flower-beds, shrubs, etc.

4. A passage between seats, counters, desks, shelving, or cases, orderly arrangement being inferred.

5. A long, narrow, inclosed space, with smooth floor, for the game of bowls; a place containing bowling-alleys.

6. The space between rows of composing-stands in a printing-office.

al′ley, *n.*; *pl.* **al′leyṣ**. [Said to be contracted from *alabaster*, from which it was formerly made.] A choice taw or large marble; a boy's plaything; also written *ally*.

al′leyed (-lid), *a.* Having an alley or alleys, or forming an alley.

al′ley-way, *n.* A passageway; an alley.

Ąll-Fools′ dāy. The first day of April.

ąll-fourṣ′, *n.* A game at cards, played by two or four persons; so called from the four chances of which it consists, viz.: high, low, jack, and the game.

ąll-fourṣ′, *n.* The four extremities of a beast, or the arms and legs of a person.

On all-fours; being sustained by, or traveling on, the four extremities; on an equal or like footing.

ąll-hāil′, *interj.* [*All* and AS. *hæl*, health.] All health; a phrase of salutation, expressing a wish of all health or safety to the person addressed.

ąll-hāil′, *v.t.* To salute; to greet. [Poet.]

Ąll-hal′lond, *n.* Allhallows. [Obs.]

Ąll-hal′lōwṣ, Ąll-hal′lōw, *n.* All-Saints' day, the first of November; a feast dedicated to all the saints in general.

Allhallow eve; Halloween.

Ąll-hal′lōw-mas, *n.* The feast of All-Saints.

Ąll-hal′lōwn, *a.* Of or pertaining to the season of Allhallows. [Obs.]

Ąll-hal′lōw-tīde, *n.* [AS. *tid*, time.] The time near All-Saints, or November 1.

ąll′hēal, *n.* The popular name of several plants; as cat's valerian.

al-lī′ȧ-ble, *a.* Capable of entering into an alliance.

al-li-ā′ceous (-shus), *a.* [L. *allium*, garlic, and *-aceous*.] Pertaining to the plants of the genus *Allium*, including garlic; having the properties of garlic. [See *Allium*.]

al-lī′ănce, *n.* [OFr. *alliance*; L. *alligantia*, from *alligare*; *ad*, to, and *ligare*, to bind.]

1. The relation or union between families, contracted by marriage.

2. The union between nations, contracted by compact, treaty, or league.

3. The treaty, league, or compact, which is the instrument of confederacy between states or provinces; sometimes the act of confederating.

4. Any union or connection of interests between persons, families, states, or corporations; as, an *alliance* between church and state.

5. The persons or parties allied; as, men or states may secure any *alliances* in their power.

6. A subdivision of the vegetable kingdom; a series.

Syn.—Connection, affinity, union, confederacy, league, coalition.

al-lī′ănce, *v.t.* To ally. [Obs.]

al-lī′ănt, *n.* An ally. [Obs.]

al′lice, al′lis, *n.* [L. *alosa*; Fr. *alose*.] An English name for the shad, *Clupea vulgaris*.

al-li′cien-cy (-lish′en-), *n.* Hypnotic power; attraction; magnetism. [Obs.]

al-li′cient, *n.* and *a.* [L. *alliciens*, ppr. of *allicere*, to draw gently to, to entice.]

I. *n.* That which attracts. [Rare.]

II. *a.* Having power to attract.

al-lied′, *a.* Connected by marriage, treaty, or similitude; united; joined.

al′li-gāte, *v.t.*; alligated, *pt.*, *pp.*; alligating, *ppr.* [L. *alligatus*, pp. of *alligare*, to bind to; *ad*, to, and *ligare*, to bind.] To tie together; to unite by some tie.

al-li-gā′tion, *n.* 1. The act of tying together; the state of being tied. [Rare.]

2. A rule of arithmetic for finding the price or value of compounds of ingredients of different values and varying proportions.

Alligation alternate; the process which ascertains what proportions of given price will produce a compound of given cost.

Alligation medial; the process of finding the cost of a mixture, the prices and proportions of the ingredients being given.

Alligator (*Alligator lucius*).

al′li-gā-tōr, *n.* [Sp. *el lagarto*, lizard; L. *lacerta*, *lacertus*, lizard.]

1. Any one of a genus of saurian reptiles of the family *Crocodilidæ*; the American crocodile; the cayman. This animal has a long naked body, four feet, armed with claws, and a serrated tail. The mouth is very large, and

furnished with sharp teeth; the skin is brown, tough, and, on the sides, covered with tubercles. The largest of these animals grow to the length of seventeen or eighteen feet. They live in and about the rivers in warm climates, eat fish, and sometimes catch and eat small animals. In winter, they burrow in the earth, which they enter under water, and work upward, lying torpid till spring. The *alligator* differs from the true crocodile in important respects.

2. In mechanics, any machine, tool, or apparatus with powerful jaws.

al'li-gā-tŏr-ap"ple, *n.* A West Indian fruit eaten by alligators but not by man.

al'li-gā-tŏr-fish, *n.* The *Podothecus acipenserinus*, a marine fish, found along the northwestern coast of North America.

al'li-gā-tŏr-gär, *n.* A very large garpike found in the rivers of the South.

al'li-gā-tŏr-peār (-pār), *n.* See *Avocado.*

al'li-gā-tŏr-tũr"tle, *n.* 1. The common snapping-turtle, *Chelydra serpentina.*

2. A fresh-water turtle of southern United States, the *Macrochelys lacertina.* It commonly attains a weight of fifty or sixty pounds, often more, and is esteemed for food.

al'li-gā-tŏr-wood, *n.* A kind of West Indian timber.

al'li-gā-tŏr-wrench, *n.* A kind of wrench with toothed, V-shaped jaws.

al-lign'ment, *n.* See *Alinement.*

al-lin'ē-āte, *v.t.* See *Alineate.*

al-lin-ē-ā'tion, *n.* See *Alineation.*

al-li'sion, *n.* [L. *allisio*, from *allidere*, to strike against; *ad*, to, and *lædere*, to strike.] A striking against; as, the *allision* of the sea against the shore.

al-lit'ẽr-ăl, *a.* Alliterative; characterized by alliteration.

al-lit'ẽr-āte, *v.t.*; alliterated, *pt.*, *pp.*; alliterating, *ppr.* To place (letters or words) so as to produce alliteration.

al-lit'ẽr-āte, *v.i.* [L. *alliteratus*, pp. of *alliterare*; *ad*, to, and *litera, littera*, letter.] To construct alliteratively.

al-lit-ẽr-ā'tion, *n.* [Fr. *allitération*, from L. *alliterare*; *ad*, to, and *littera*, letter.] The repetition of the same letter at the beginning of two or more words immediately succeeding each other, or at short intervals; as the repetition of *f* and *g* in the following line:

Fields ever fresh, and groves ever green.

al-lit'ẽr-ā-tive, *a.* Pertaining to or consisting of alliteration.

al-lit'ẽr-ā-tive-ly, *adv.* In an alliterative manner.

al-lit'ẽr-ā-tive-ness, *n.* The state or quality of being alliterative.

al-lit'ẽr-ā-tŏr, *n.* One who uses alliteration.

Al'li-um, *n.* [L., the garlic.] A genus of bulbous plants of about three hundred species. It includes the garlic, onion, and leek.

all'mouth, *n.* A fish commonly known as the angler, *Lophius piscatorius.*

all'ness, *n.* Entirety; totality. [Rare.]

all'night, *n.* Food, fuel, or light sufficient to last through the night. [Obs.]

al'lo-, *prefix.* [Gr. *allos*, other.] A combining form bearing the signification of other, another.

al'lō-cāte, *v.t.*; allocated, *pt.*, *pp.*; allocating, *ppr.* [L. *allocatus*, pp. of *allocare*; *ad*, to, and *locare*, to place; *locus*, a place.]

1. To parcel out; to assign.

2. To localize. [Rare.]

al-lō-cā'tion, *n.* 1. Allotment, apportionment, assignment, or the act thereof; as, the *allocation* of shares in a stock company.

2. Arrangement; disposition; the act of putting in place.

3. In England, an allowance made upon accounts in the exchequer.

al-lō-cā'tũr, *n.* [L., it is allowed, from *allocare*, to allow.] The indorsement of a judge on a writ or legal document to designate it as approved or allowed.

al-lō-chi'ri-ȧ, *n.* [*Allo-*, and Gr. *cheir*, hand.] In pathology, a confusion of the two sides of the body in the localization of sensation.

al-lō-chrō'ic, *a.* [Gr. *allochroos*, of another color.] Variable or changeable in color.

al-loch'rō-īte, *n.* [Gr. *allochroos*, of another color, and *-ite.*] The common garnet. [See *Garnet.*]

al-loch'rō-ous, *a.* [Gr. *allochroos*, changed in color.] Of a variety of colors; said of minerals.

al-lō-cryp'tic, *a.* [*Allo-*, and Gr. *kryptos*, hidden.] Hiding from view by the use of extraneous objects of similar color to itself; imitating the color of plants or trees by changing colors, for the purpose of concealment, as the chameleon.

al-lō-cū'tion, *n.* [L. *allocutio*, from *alloqui*, to speak to; *ad*, to, and *loqui*, to speak.]

1. The act or manner of speaking to, or of addressing in words.

2. An address; a formal address, as of a general to his troops, or of the pope to the clergy.

al'lod, *n.* See *Allodium.*

al-lō'di-ăl, *n.* Any property held as a freehold.

al-lō'di-ăl, *a.* Pertaining to allodium; free of rent or service; held independent of a lord paramount; opposed to *feudal.*

al-lō'di-ăl-ism, *n.* The allodial system.

al-lō'di-ăl-ist, *n.* One who holds land allodially.

al-lō'di-ăl-ly, *adv.* In allodial tenure.

al-lō'di-ā-ry, *n.* Same as *Allodialist.*

al-lod"i-fi-cā'tion, *n.* The conversion of title from feudal tenure to a freehold.

al-lō'di-um, *n.* [L. *allodium, alodium*, from O.H.G. *allōd*; *all*, all, and *ōt*, property.] Freehold estate; land which is the absolute property of the owner; real estate held in absolute independence, without being subject to any rent, service, or acknowledgment to a superior. It is thus opposed to *feud.*

al-log'ȧ-mous, *a.* Relating to allogamy, or cross-fertilization.

al-log'ȧ-my, *n.* [*Allo-*, and Gr. *gamos*, marriage.] Cross-fertilization of flowers.

al-lō-ġē'nē-ous, *a.* [*Allo-*, and Gr. *genos*, kind.] Varying in nature or kind. [Rare.]

al'lō-graph, *n.* [*Allo-*, and Gr. *graphein*, to write.] A signature made by proxy. In law, an instrument written by a person who is not a party to its execution.

al-lom'ẽr-ism, *n.* [*Allo-*, and Gr. *meros*, part, and *-ism.*] In chemistry, a change in the chemical constituents or their proportions while the crystalline form remains unvaried.

al-lom'ẽr-ous, *a.* Characterized by allomerism.

al'lō-morph, *n.* [*Allo-*, and Gr. *morphē*, figure, form.]

1. Any substance having more than one crystalline form.

2. A pseudomorph formed with partial change in its chemical composition.

al-lō-mor'phic, *a.* Pertaining to allomorphism.

al-lō-mor'phism, *n.* The state of being or becoming an allomorph.

al-lŏnġe', *n.* [Fr. *allonger*, to lengthen, to thrust.]

1. A pass with a sword; a thrust made by stepping forward and sharply extending the arm; now contracted into *lunge.* [Obs.]

2. A long rein. [Obs.]

3. In commerce, the name applied to a slip or rider attached to a bill of exchange to receive indorsements when the reverse of the bill is filled.

al-lŏnġe', *v.i.* [Fr. *allonger*, to lengthen; *a*, L. *ad*, to, and *longare*, from *longus*, long.] To make an allonge; to lunge. [Obs.]

al'lō-nym, *n.* [*Allo-*, and Gr. *onyma*, name.]

1. A pseudonym; especially, the name of another assumed by an author; a false name.

2. The work published under such a name.

al-lon'y-mous, *a.* Published under a false name.

al-loo', *v.t.* or *v.i.* To incite dogs by a call. [Obs. See *Halloo.*]

al'lō-path, al-lop'ȧ-thist, *n.* One who practises allopathy.

al-lō-path'ic, *a.* Pertaining to or in accordance with allopathy.

al-lō-path'ic-ăl-ly, *adv.* In a manner conformable to allopathy.

al-lop'ȧ-thy, *n.* [*Allo-*, and Gr. *pathos*, from *paschein*, to suffer.] That method of medical practice which seeks to cure disease by the production of a condition of the system either different from, opposite to, or incompatible with, the condition essential to the disease to be cured; the ordinary mode of medical practice, as distinguished from *homeopathy.*

al'lō-phāne, *n.* [Gr. *allophanēs*, appearing otherwise; *allos*, other, and *phanēs*, from *phaneisthai*, to appear.] A hydrosilicate of aluminium, occurring in amorphous, botryoidal, or reniform masses.

al-lō-phan'ic, *a.* Pertaining to anything which changes its appearance, or color.

al-lō-phyl'i-ăn, al-lō-phyl'ic, *a.* [L. *allophylus*, from Gr. *allophylos*; *allos*, other, and *phylē*, tribe.] A term applied to those languages of Europe and Asia which are non-Aryan and non-Semitic; Turanian.

al'lō-quy, *n.* A speaking to another. [Obs.]

al-lot', *v.t.*; allotted, *pt.*, *pp.*; allotting, *ppr.* [OFr. *alloter*; *a*, to, and *loter, lotir*, to assign by lot; AS. *hlot*; O.H.G. *hlōz*, lot, share.]

1. To divide or distribute by lot.

2. To distribute or parcel out in parts or portions, or to distribute (a share) to each individual concerned.

3. To grant, as a portion; to give, assign, or appoint in general; as, to be content with what fate *allots.*

Syn.—Distribute, assign, apportion, appoint, destine.

al'lō-thē-ism, *n.* [*Allo-*, Gr. *theos*, god, and *-ism.*] The worship of other gods.

al-loth'i-ġēne, al-loth-i-ġen'ic, *a.* [Gr. *allothi*, elsewhere, and *-gene*, Gr. *genēs*, produced.] Produced elsewhere; said in geology of fragments of rocks found elsewhere than in their place of origin.

al-loth"i-ġē-net'ic, al-lō-thoġ'e-nous, *a.* Same as *Allothigene.*

al-lot'ment, *n.* 1. The act of allotting.

2. That which is allotted; a share, part, or portion granted or distributed; that which is assigned by lot, or by the act of God.

3. A part, portion, or place appropriated; as, an *allotment* of ground for a garden.

al-lō-tri-oph'ȧ-ġy, *n.* [Gr. *allotrios*, another's, and *phagia*, from *phagein*, to eat.] In pathology, a depraved appetite.

al-lō-troph'ic, *a.* [*Allo-*, and Gr. *trophos*, nourishing.] Modified in such a way as to be innutritious.

al-lō-trop'ic, al-lō-trop'ic-ăl, *a.* Relating to or characterized by allotropy.

al-lō-trop'ic-ăl-ly, *adv.* In an allotropical manner.

al"lō-trō-pic'i-ty, *n.* Power of becoming allotropic.

al-lot'rō-pism, *n.* Allotropy.

al-lot'rō-pize, *v.t.* To render allotropic.

al-lot'rō-py, *n.* [Gr. *allotropos*, of or in another manner; *allos*, other, and *tropos*, way, manner.] The capability or characteristic exhibited by some elements, of existing in more than one form, and with different physical and chemical properties. Carbon is a good example, as it crystallizes perfectly in the diamond, imperfectly in graphite, and is amorphous, yet quite distinct, in anthracite and charcoal.

al-lot'tȧ-ble, *a.* Capable of being allotted, or distributed.

al-lot'ted, *a.* Distributed by lot; granted; assigned.

al-lot-tee', *n.* The person to whom an allotment is made; one who receives a share.

al-lot'tẽr, *n.* One who allots.

al-lot'tẽr-y, *n.* Allotment. [Obs.]

al-low', *v.t.*; allowed, *pt.*, *pp.*; allowing, *ppr.* [OE. *alouen*; OFr. *alouer*; Fr. *allouer*; L. *allocare*, to admit as approved, to place; *ad*, to, and *locare*, to place.]

1. To grant, give, or yield; as, to *allow* a servant his liberty; to *allow* a pension.

2. To admit; as, to *allow* the truth of a proposition; to *allow* a claim.

3. To approve, justify, or sanction.

Ye *allow* the deeds of your fathers.
—Luke xi. 48.

4. To afford, or grant, as a compensation; as, to *allow* a dollar a day for wages.

5. To abate or deduct; as, to *allow* a sum for tare or leakage.

6. To permit; to grant license to; as, to *allow* a son to be absent.

Syn.—Permit, suffer, tolerate.—*Allow* and *permit* are often used synonymously; but *permit* rather implies a formal sanction; *allow*, that we merely do not hinder; *suffer* is still more passive than *permit*, and may imply that we do not prevent something, though we feel it to be disagreeable, or know it to be wrong; *tolerate* is always used in the sense of permitting or bearing something unpleasant.

al-low', *v.i.* [OE. *alouen*; OFr. *alouer*; L. *allaudare*, to praise much; *ad*, to, and *laudare*, to praise.] To admit; to acknowledge; to concede.

al-low'ȧ-ble, *a.* Permissible; lawful; admitted as true and proper; not forbidden; not unlawful or improper; as, a certain degree of freedom is *allowable* among friends.

al-low'ȧ-ble-ness, *n.* The quality of being allowable.

al-low'ȧ-bly, *adv.* In an allowable manner.

al-low'ănce, *n.* 1. The act of allowing or admitting.

2. Permission; license; approbation; sanction; usually slight approbation.

3. Admission; assent to a fact or state of things; a granting.

4. Freedom from restraint; indulgence.

5. That which is allowed; a portion appointed; a stated quantity, as of food or drink; hence, a limited quantity of meat and drink, when provisions fall short.

6. Abatement; deduction; as, to make an *allowance* for the inexperience of youth.

7. Established character; reputation; as, a pilot of approved *allowance.* [Obs.]

8. In commerce, a customary deduction from the gross weight of goods, different in different countries, such as tare and tret.

9. A sum of money granted or allowed at stated intervals; as, his *allowance* is $500 a year.

Syn.—Concession, grant, permission, pay, stipend, consent, authority.

al-low'ănce, *v.t.*; allowanced (-ănst), *pt.*, *pp.*; allowancing, *ppr.* [ME. *alouance*; OFr. *alouance*, from *allouer*, to grant, permit.] To put upon allowance; to restrain or limit to a certain quantity of provisions or drink; as, distress compelled the captain of the ship to *allowance* his crew.

al-low'ed-ly, *adv.* Admittedly; by acknowledgment.

al-low'ẽr, *n.* One who allows, permits, grants, or authorizes.

al-lox'ăn, *n.* [*Allantoin*, *oxalic*, and *-an.*] A crystalline compound, $C_4H_2N_2O_4$, obtained by the action of strong nitric acid on uric acid.

al-lox′ȧ-nāte, *n.* A salt of alloxanic acid.

al-lox-an′iç, *a.* Pertaining to alloxan.

al-lox-an′tin, *n.* A crystalline substance obtained by the action of reducing agents on alloxan.

al-loy′, *n.* 1. In coinage, a baser metal mixed with a finer.

2. In chemistry, the mixture, generally by fusion, of different metals; any metallic compound except that of mercury with another metal, which is called an amalgam.

3. Figuratively, that which detracts from the value of anything; as, no happiness is without *alloy*.

al-loy′, *v.t.*; alloyed (-loid), *pt., pp.*; alloying, *ppr.* [Fr. *aloyer*; OFr. *allier, allayer*; L. *alligare*; *ad*, to, and *ligare*, to bind.]

1. To reduce the purity of (a metal) by mixing with it a portion of one less valuable; as, to *alloy* gold with silver, or silver with copper.

2. To mix (metals) so as to form an alloy.

3. To reduce or abate by mixture; as, to *alloy* pleasure with misfortunes.

al-loy′, *v.i.* To unite to form a metallic compound.

al-loy′āġe, *n.* The act of alloying metals, or the mixture so made.

al-lō-zō′oid, *n.* A zoöid differing from the parent organism.

all′-pos-sessed′ (-zest′), *a.* Wild; raging; as if possessed by evil spirits.

All′-Sāints, *n.* Allhallows or Hallowmas, a feast day celebrated on the first day of November; All-Saints' day.

all′seed, *n.* A name applied to several plants; as the goosefoot, *Chenopodium polyspermum*, found in waste places.

All′-Sōuls, *n.* The second day of November, a festival in the Roman Catholic church, when prayers are publicly offered up for the release of souls from purgatory; All-Souls' day.

all′spīce, *n.* The fruit of *Eugenia pimenta*, a tree of the West Indies; a spice of a mildly pungent taste, and agreeably aromatic. Its odor and flavor are supposed to combine those of cinnamon, cloves, and nutmeg, hence the name. Also called *Jamaica pepper* and *pimento*.

all′thing, *n.* Everything. [Obs.]

al-lūde′, *v.i.*; alluded, *pt., pp.*; alluding, *ppr.* [L. *alludere*, to joke, jest, refer to; *ad*, to, and *ludere*, to play.] To refer to something not directly mentioned; to have reference; to hint by remote suggestions; as, that story *alludes* to a recent transaction.

Syn.—Hint, refer, suggest, intimate, glance at, advert to.

al-lūde′, *v.t.* To make an allusion to; to refer to indirectly. [Obs.]

al-lū-mette′ (-met′), *n.* [Fr.] A slip of paper or splinter of wood for lighting lamps; literally, a match.

al-lū′mi-nŏr, *n.* An illuminator; an illustrator. [Obs.]

al-lūr′ănce, *n.* Enticement. [Obs.]

al-lūre′, *v.t.*; allured, *pt., pp.*; alluring, *ppr.* [OFr. *alurer, aleurer*, to attract, allure; *a*, to, and *lurer*, to lure; Fr. *leurre*, a decoy.] To attempt to draw to; to tempt by the offer of some good, real or apparent; to invite by something flattering or acceptable; as, rewards *allure* men to brave danger.

Syn.—Entice, decoy, seduce, attract, tempt, lead astray.—We are *allured* to evil by some promised good; we are *enticed* into it through our passions; we are *seduced* when drawn aside from the path of rectitude.

al-lūre′, *n.* Allurement. [Obs.]

al-lūre′, *n.* [Fr.] Bearing; mien; air.

al-lūre′ment, *n.* That which allures; any real or apparent good held forth, or operating, as a motive to action; temptation; enticement; as, the *allurements* of pleasure, or of honor.

al-lūr′ēr, *n.* One who or that which allures.

al-lūr′ing, *a.* Inviting; having the quality of attracting or tempting.

al-lūr′ing-ly, *adv.* In an alluring manner; enticingly.

al-lūr′ing-ness, *n.* The quality of alluring or tempting.

al-lū′şion, *n.* [Fr. *allusion*; L. *allusio(n)*, a playing or sporting with; from ppr. of *alludere*, to play or sport with.]

1. A reference to something supposed to be known, but not explicitly mentioned; a hint; a suggestion.

2. In rhetoric, a reference to some striking incident in history, or passage in some writer, by way of illustration.

al-lū′sive, *a.* Having reference to something not fully expressed.

al-lū′sive-ly, *adv.* By way of allusion; by implication, remote suggestion, or insinuation.

al-lū′sive-ness, *n.* The quality of being allusive.

al-lū′sō-ry, *a.* Allusive. [Rare.]

al-lū′vi-ȧ, *n.*; Latin plural of *alluvium*.

al-lū′vi-ăl, *a.* Pertaining to or having the character of alluvium; deposited or thrown up by the action of waves or currents of water; as, *alluvial* deposits; *alluvial* soil.

al-lū′vi-ŏn, *n.* [Fr. *alluvion*; L. *alluvio*, an overflowing, from *alluere*; *ad*, to, and *luere*, to wash.]

1. A gradual washing or carrying of earth or other substances to a shore or bank; the earth thus added.

2. In law, the gradual increase of earth on a shore or bank of a river, by the force of water, as by a current or by waves.

3. In physical geography, a tract of alluvial formation; particularly applied to the bottom-lands and deltas of rivers.

al-lū′vi-ous, *a.* [Obs.] Same as *Alluvial*.

al-lū′vi-um, *n.*; *pl.* **al-lū′vi-umş** or **al-lū′vi-ȧ.** [L. *alluvium*, from *alluere*, to wash upon.] Earth, sand, gravel, and other transported matter, which has been washed away, and thrown down by rivers, floods, or other causes, upon land not permanently submerged beneath the waters of lakes or seas.

all′where, all′whereş (-whârz), *adv.* Everywhere. [Rare.]

all′wŏrk, *n.* Common manual work of all kinds, especially domestic, or work about a house; as, a maid of *allwork*; a man of *allwork*.

al-lȳ′, *v.t.*; allied, *pt., pp.*; allying, *ppr.* [OE. *alien*; OFr. *alier*; Fr. *allier*; from L. *alligare*; *ad*, to, and *ligare*, to bind.]

1. To unite, or form a relation, as between families by marriage, or between princes and states by treaty, league, or confederacy.

2. To form a relation between by similitude, resemblance, or friendship. This word is more generally used in the passive form; as, families are *allied* by blood; or reciprocally; as, princes *ally themselves* to powerful states.

al-lȳ′, *n.*; *pl.* **al-līeş′.** 1. A prince or state united to another by treaty or league; a confederate.

2. One related to another by marriage or other tie; but seldom applied to individuals, except to princes in their public capacity.

3. A helper; an auxiliary; as, science may be the *ally* of religion.

4. Any organism akin to another by structure, etc.

The Allies; originally the nations comprising the Triple Entente, but later all the nations which fought against the Central Powers in the World War.

Syn.—Accessory, confederate, accomplice, associate, companion.

al′ly, *n.* A taw or marble. [See *Alley*.]

al′lyl, *n.* [L. *allium*, garlic, and *-yl*.] The unsaturated radical C_3H_5, forming on liberation diallyl, C_6H_{10}, a pungent, ethereal liquid.

al′ly-lēne, *n.* A gaseous hydrocarbon, C_3H_4, standing in the same relation to allyl, C_3H_5, as ethylene, C_2H_4, to ethyl, C_2H_5.

al′mȧ, al′mȧh, *n.* [Ar. *'almah*, learned, knowing, from *'alama*, to know.] An Egyptian singing and dancing girl of the better class, whose business it is to entertain and amuse the rich, sing dirges at funerals, etc.

al-mȧ-can′tăr, *n.* See *Almucantar*.

al-mȧ-dī′ȧ, al′mȧ-die (-di), *n.* [Ar. *alma 'dīyah*; *al*, the, *ma 'dīyah*, ferryboat.] A bark canoe used by the Africans; also, a river-boat used at Calicut, in India, and shaped like a shuttle.

Al′mȧ-ġest, *n.* [ME. *almagest*; L. *almageste*; Ar. *almajisti*; *al*, the, and Gr. *megistē*, greatest, superl. of *megas*, great.] A collection of problems in astronomy and geometry drawn up by Ptolemy.

al-mȧ′grȧ, *n.* [Sp. *almagra*; Ar. *al-maghrah*, red ocher.] A fine deep-red ocher, with an admixture of purple, used in India for staining the person. Sometimes used as a paint, and for polishing silver and glass, under the name of *Indian red*.

Al′māin, *n.* 1. A German; also used adjectively. [Obs.]

2. [a—] A kind of dance, or dance-music in slow time. [Obs. See *Allemande*.]

Al′māin-riv″et, *n.* A kind of light, flexible armor invented in Germany about 1450, and used in England in the sixteenth and seventeenth centuries. It consisted of overlapping plates sliding on rivets.

al′mȧ mā′tēr (*or* mä′tēr). [L., fostering mother.] A college or university where one is educated.

al′mȧ-naç, *n.* [Sp. *almanac*; L. *almanac*, probably from Ar. *almanakh*; *al*, the, and *manakh*, a calendar.] A book or table, containing a calendar of days, weeks, and months, with the times of the rising and setting of the sun and moon, changes of the moon, eclipses, hours of full tide, stated festivals of churches, stated terms of courts, observations on the weather, etc., for the year.

Nautical almanac; an official annual publication of great service to mariners, astronomers, and others, giving in advance the positions of the heavenly bodies, predictions of astronomical phenomena, and many other calculations of value to navigators.

al′măn-dine, *n.* [LL. *alamandina*, a corruption of *alabandina*.] The common garnet, a reddish iron-alumina stone found crystallized as a rhombic dodecahedron. Precious *garnet* is this stone when deep red and transparent. Written also *almandite*.

al′me, al′meh, *n.* Same as *Alma*.

äl-men-drōn′, *n.* [Sp., from *almendra*, almond.] The tree yielding the Brazil nut of commerce, *Bertholletia excelsa*.

al′mēr-y, *n.* [Obs.] See *Ambry*.

älm′esse (äm′es), *n.* [Obs.] See *Alms*.

ąl-mīght′fụl, ąl-mīght′i-fụl, *a.* All-powerful. [Obs.]

ąl-mīght′i-ly, *adv.* With almighty power.

ąl-mīght′i-ness, *n.* Omnipotence; infinite or boundless power.

ąl-mīght′y, *a.* [ME. *almighty*; AS. *ealmihtig*; *eal*, all, and *mihtig*, mighty.]

1. Possessing all power; omnipotent.

2. A slang term for great; terrible; enormous; astonishing; as, an *almighty* mistake.

Almighty dollar; a phrase forcibly expressive of the power of money, first used by Washington Irving in 1837.

Ąl-mīght′y, *n.* The omnipotent God.

älm′nēr (äm′), *n.* An almoner. [Obs.]

älm′ŏnd (*or* al′mŏnd), *n.* [OE. *almande*; L. *amygdala*; Gr. *amygdalē*, an almond.]

1. The *Prunus* or *Amygdalus communis*, a tree of the rose family, or its popular edible nut, which is the kernel or stone of the fruit; the bitter, sweet, and Jordan *almonds* being varieties. The leaves and flowers of the *almond*-tree resemble those of the peach.

Almond (*Amygdalus communis*)

2. By comparison, anything having a close resemblance to an almond-nut; applied specifically to a tonsil and various ornaments.

äl′mŏnd-fūr″năce, *n.* [*Almond* is probably a corruption of *Almain*, German.] A kind of furnace used in the refining process, to separate the metal from cinders and other foreign matter.

al′mŏn-dine, *n.* See *Almandine*.

älm′ŏnd-oil, *n.* A bland, fixed oil, obtained from almonds by pressure.

älm′ŏnd-pēach, *n.* A hybrid between the almond and the peach, cultivated in France.

älm′ŏnd-wil″lōw, *n.* The *Salix amygdalina*, the leaves of which are light green on both sides.

al′mŏn-ēr, *n.* [OFr. *aumoniere, almosniere*; L. *eleemosyna*, alms.]

1. A functionary or agent who distributes alms or charity, as for a monastery, a noble's establishment, etc.

2. Any one who dispenses charity, benefits, or blessings.

al′mŏn-ēr-ship, *n.* The office and duties of an almoner.

al′mŏn-ry, *n.*; *pl.* **al′mŏn-rieş.** The place where an almoner resides, or where alms are distributed.

al′mōse, *n.* Alms. [Obs.]

ąl′mōst, *adv.* [AS. *ēalmaēst*.] Nearly; well-nigh; for the great part.

Almost never; scarcely ever.

Almost nothing; scarcely anything at all.

älm′ry, *n.* Almonry. [Obs.]

älmş (ämz), *n., sing.* and *pl.* [ME. *alms, ælmesse*; AS. *ælmesse*; L. *eleemosyna*, alms; Gr. *eleēmosynē*, pity, compassion; *eleēmōn*, pitiful; *eleos*, pity.] Anything given gratuitously to relieve the poor, as money, food, or clothing; charity.

Tenure by free alms; frankalmoin.

älmş′deed, *n.* An act of charity; a charitable gift.

älmş′fōlk (ämz′fōk), *n.pl.* Persons supported by alms. [Obs.]

älmş′giv″ēr, *n.* One who gives to the poor

älmş′giv″ing, *n.* The bestowment of charity.

älmş′house, *n.* A house appropriated for the use of the poor who are supported by the public; a poorhouse.

älmş′măn, *n.*; *pl.* **älmş′men.** 1. A man who lives by alms.

2. One who gives alms. [Rare.]

al-mū-çan′tăr, *n.* [Sp. *almicantarat*; Ar. *almuqantarāt*; *al*, the, and *muqantarāt*, pl. of *muqantarah*, a sundial.] A term applied to circles of the sphere parallel to the horizon, conceived to pass through every degree of the meridian.

al-mū-çan′tăr-staff, *n.* An instrument having an arc of fifteen degrees, formerly used to take observations of the sun, about the time of its rising or setting, to find the amplitude and the variation of the compass.

al′mūce, au′mūce, *n.* [Sp. *almuce*; L. *almussa, almucia*.] A furred hood worn by the clergy in the thirteenth, fourteenth, and fifteenth centuries, when officiating in churches during inclement weather; also written *amice*.

al-mūde′, *n.* [Port. *almude*; Ar. *al-mudd*, a dry measure.] A variable measure for liquids and grain in Spain and Portugal, ranging for liquids from three and one-half to five and one-half English gallons; for grain, from three and one-half to eleven pints.

al′mug, *n.* [Heb.] In Scripture, a tree or wood about which the learned are not agreed. The latest probable conjecture is that the word denotes the sandalwood of the East. [See *Algum*.]

Priest wearing Almuce.—From a sepulchral brass.

al′nāġe, ąul′nāġe, *n.* [OFr. *aulnage*; Fr. *aunage*, *aulner*, to measure by the ell; *alne*, *aune*, ell.] A measuring by the ell of cloth for duty.

al′nā-ġẽr, ąul′nā-ġẽr, *n.* A measurer by the ell; formerly, in England, a sworn officer, whose duty was to inspect and measure woolen cloth for duty.

Al′nus, *n.* [L. *alnus*, alder.] A genus of cupuliferous trees, commonly called alders.

al′od, ȧ-lō′di-ăl, ȧ-lō′di-um. Same as *Allod*, etc.

Al′ō-ē, *n.* [L. *aloe*; Gr. *aloē*, the aloe.] A genus of plants of the lily family, of many species; all natives of warm climates, and most of them of the southern part of Africa.

al′ōe, *n.* Any plant of the genus *Aloë*, as *Aloë Socotrina*, one of the species used in medicine.

al′ōeṣ, *n. sing.* or *pl.* In medicine, a purgative obtained from the inspissated juice of aloe-leaves.

al′ōeṣ-wood, *n.* See *Agallochum*.

al-ō-et′iç, *a.* 1. Pertaining to the aloe or aloes; having the qualities of aloes.

2. Consisting chiefly of aloes; having aloes as a principal ingredient; as, an *aloetic* preparation.

Aloë Socotrina.

al-ō-et′iç, *n.* A medicine, the chief ingredient of which is aloes.

ȧ-lọft′, *adv.* 1. On high; in the air; high above the ground; as, the eagle soars *aloft*.

2. In nautical language, in the top; at the masthead, or on the higher yards or rigging.

3. On the upper part, as of a building.

ȧ-lọft′, *prep.* On top of; on the upper surface of. [Rare.]

A-lō′ġi-ăn, *n.* [L. *Alogiani*, *Alogii*; Gr. *Alogos*; *a* priv., and *logos*, word.] In church history, a member of a sect of the second and third centuries, that denied Jesus Christ to be the *Logos*, and consequently rejected the Gospel of St. John.

al″ō-gō-trō′phi-ȧ, al-ō-got′rō-phy, *n.* [Gr. *alogos*; *a* priv., and *logos*, reason, and *trophē*, nourishment, from *trephein*, to nourish.] A disproportionate nutrition and growth of the parts of the body, especially of the bones.

al′ō-ġy, *n.* [Gr. *a* priv., and *logos*, reason.] Irrational behavior; unreasonableness. [Obs.]

al′ō-in, *n.* The active principle of aloes.

al′ō-man-cy, *n.* Same as *Halomancy*.

ȧ-lōne′, *a.* and *adv.* [*All* and *one*.]

1. Single; solitary; separate from others or from the mass; without the presence or aid of another; by oneself; as, he toiled *alone* and in the dark.

2. Only; exclusively; sole; with no person or thing else; as, he *alone* has the power of pardon.

3. Unequaled in attributes or position; peerless; as, among modern chemists, he stands *alone*.

To let alone; to leave unaltered or undisturbed; to refrain from interfering.

ȧ-lōne′ly, *a.* and *adv.* Only; merely; singly. [Obs.]

ȧ-lōne′ness, *n.* The condition of being alone.

ȧ-lọng′, *adv.* [ME. *along*, *anlong*; AS. *andlang*, along; *and*, over against, and *lang*, long.]

1. By the length; lengthwise; in a line with the length; by the side; frequently used with *by*; as, a forbidding fence was built *along by* the river.

2. Onward, in time or space; in a forward line, or with a progressive motion; as, let us walk *along*; the years creep *along* unnoticed.

3. In connection or company; often used with *with*; as, he took his dog *along*; he carried the odor of sanctity *along with* him.

To get along; to progress; to fare.

ȧ-lọng′, *prep.* 1. By the length of; in the line or direction of; as, the ship sailed *along* the coast.

2. Throughout the length of; by the side of; in the line of; in the course of; as, the wagons moved slowly *along* the highway.

ȧ-lọng′, *adv.* On account; because; followed by *of*; as, all *along of* this change; sometimes shortened to *long*; as, this is all *long* of you. [Colloq. or Dial.]

ȧ-lọng′shōre, *adv.* Lengthwise by the shore, on land or water.

ȧ-lọng′shōre-măn, *n.* See *Longshoreman*.

ȧ-lọng′sīde, *adv.* By the side; along the side; side by side; as, their vessel lay *alongside* of the pier.

ȧ-lọngst′, *adv.* and *prep.* Along; by the length. [Obs.]

ȧ-lọọf′, *n.* In zoölogy, same as *alewife*.

ȧ-lọọf′, *adv.* [ME. *aloofe*; *a*, on, and *loof*, from D. *loef*, *luff*, to windward.]

1. At a short distance; apart; aside; by oneself; as, to stand *aloof*.

2. In a figurative sense, without sympathy; with no inclination to associate; coldly; askance; unfavorably.

ȧ-lọọf′, *prep.* Separate or clear from; as, *aloof* the crowd. [Rare.]

ȧ-lọọf′ness, *n.* The state or quality of keeping aloof.

al-ō-pē′ci-ȧ (-shi-ȧ), **ȧ-lop′e-cy**, *n.* [L. *alopecia*; Gr. *alōpekia*, from *alōpēx*, a fox.] A disease of the skin in which there is a falling off of the hair, and sometimes of the nails; baldness.

ȧ-lop′e-cist, *n.* One who gives treatment for the prevention or cure of alopecia or baldness.

al-ō-pē′coid, *a.* [Gr. *alōpēx*, fox, and *eidos*, like.] Foxlike; vulpine.

Al″ō-pē-cū′rus, *n.* [L., from Gr. *alōpēx*, fox, and *oura*, tail.] A genus of grasses, commonly called foxtail-grass. The meadow-foxtail, *Alopecurus pratensis*, furnishes valuable fodder; but some other species are troublesome as weeds.

ȧ-lọr′ciç, al-ọr-cin′iç, *a.* Pertaining to or obtained from aloes.

ȧ-lōse′, *n.* [Fr., from L. *alosa*.] A shad, especially the European shad.

ȧ-lōse′, *v.t.* [OFr. *aloser*.] To praise. [Obs.]

al-ōu-ate′ (-at′), *n.* [Fr., from native name.] A general name for any South American howling-monkey. [See *Howler*.]

ȧ-loud′, *adv.* 1. Loudly; with a loud voice, or great noise.

2. Audibly; out loud; as, to speak or read *aloud*.

ȧ-lōw′, *adv.* In a low place, or a lower part; opposed to *aloft*.

ȧ-low′, *adv.* On fire. [Scot.]

alp, *n.*; *pl.* **alps.** [L. *alpes*, high mountains; Gael. *alp*; Ir. *ailp*, a high mountain; O.H.G. *Alpen*, the Alps.]

1. A high mountain.

2. Figuratively, something difficult of attainment or hard to surmount; an obstacle.

3. In Switzerland, a mountain pasture.

alp, *n.* The common European bullfinch.

al-pag′ȧ, *n.* [Sp. *alpaca*, *alpaco*, from Ar. *al*, the, and *paco*, the Peruvian name of the animal.]

1. A ruminant, native to the mountains of Chile and Peru, allied to the llama; the *Auchenia pacos*. It is somewhat like a sheep, and can be domesticated. Its wool, called also *alpaca*, is very valuable, being long, fine, and dark in color.

Alpaca (*Auchenia pacos*).

2. Any fabric woven from *alpaca*-wool, or made in part of it; especially, a thin cloth made of cotton and wool, with a hard, shiny surface.

3. Any garment made of *alpaca*-cloth.

al′pen, *a.* Same as *Alpine*. [Rare.]

al′pen-horn, *n.* [G. *Alpen*, genit. pl. of *Alp*, of the Alps, and *horn*.] A very long, powerful horn, nearly straight, but curving slightly and widening toward its extremity; used on the Alps by cowherds, and formerly by the Swiss to convey signals, and as a musical instrument.

Alpenhorn.

al′pen-stock, *n.* An iron-pointed staff used as an aid in mountain-climbing.

al-pes′trine, *a.* [L. *alpestris*, pertaining to mountains, from *alp*, a mountain.]

1. Pertaining to high mountains, as the Alps. [Rare.]

2. Growing on mountain heights, but below the tree-limit.

al′phȧ, *n.* [L., from Gr. *alpha*, from Heb. *āleph*, an ox or leader.]

1. The first letter in the Greek alphabet, corresponding to A; and used to denote first, beginning, or chief; as, Plato, the *alpha* of the wits.

I am *Alpha* and Omega. —Rev. i. 8.

2. In cataloguing stars, the symbol of the brightest in the constellation; as, α Lyræ, α Tauri, etc.

al′phȧ-bet, *n.* [L. *alphabetum*, from Gr. *alpha* and *bēta*, the first two letters of the Greek alphabet.]

1. The letters of a language arranged in the customary order; the series of letters which form the elements of a written language.

2. The simplest elements of anything; rudiments; first principles; fundamentals; as, the *alphabet* of science.

3. Any series of signs representing letters or syllables; as, the telegraph *alphabet*; the deaf-and-dumb *alphabet*.

al′phȧ-bet, *v.t.* To arrange in the order of an alphabet; to designate by the letters of the alphabet. [Rare.]

al″phȧ-bet-ā′ri-ăn, *n.* A learner while in the A, B, C.

al-phȧ-bet′iç, al-phȧ-bet′iç-ăl, *a.* 1. Of or pertaining to an alphabet; expressed by an alphabet; as, *alphabetic* languages.

2. In the order of the letters of the alphabet; having its parts or its matter arranged according to the letters of the alphabet; as, an *alphabetical* classification.

al-phȧ-bet′iç-ăl-ly, *adv.* In an alphabetical manner; in the customary order of the letters; by means of an alphabet.

al-phȧ-bet′içs, *n.* The science of the origin, growth, and use of alphabetic letters or symbols to represent language.

al′phȧ-bet-iṣm, *n.* The representation of spoken sounds by alphabetic characters.

al′phȧ-bet-īze, *v.t.*; alphabetized (-īzd), *pt.*, *pp.*; alphabetizing, *ppr.* 1. To arrange in the order of the letters of the alphabet.

2. To express by or furnish with an alphabet.

al-phen′iç, *n.* [Fr. *alfénic*, *alphénic*; Sp. *alfeñique*; Ar. *al-fānīd*; *al*, the, and *fānīd*, from Per. *fānīd*, *pānīd*, sugar.] White barley-sugar, sometimes prescribed for affections of the respiratory tract.

al-phit′ō-man-cy, *n.* [Gr. *alphiton*, barley, and *mantis*, a diviner, soothsayer; *manteia*, divination.] Divination by barley-meal.

al-phō′sis, *n.* [Gr. *alphos*, white, and *-osis*.] The state of being, or process of becoming, an albino.

al′phus, *n.* [L., from Gr. *alphos*, white.] A disease of the skin characterized by the appearance and development of smooth white patches; a non-contagious form of leprosy found frequently among the Arabs.

al′pi-ġēne, *a.* [L. *alpes*, alps, and *-gene*, from *genus*, produced.] Produced or growing in Alpine regions.

Al′pine (*or* -pīn), *a.* [L. *alpinus*, from *Alpes*, the Alps.]

1. Pertaining to the Alps.

2. [a—] Resembling the Alps; very high; elevated; towering.

3. [a—] Growing on mountain heights above the tree-limit; as, *alpine* plants.

al′pin-ist, *n.* One who climbs the Alps or other high mountains.

al′pist, al′pi-ȧ, *n.* The seed of various kinds of canary-grass or foxtail-grass, used for feeding birds.

al′qui-fōu (-ki-), *n.* [Fr. *alquifoux*; Sp. *alquifol*; Ar. *al-koh'l*, a fine powder.] A sort of lead ore (galena), found in Cornwall, England; used by potters to give a green glaze to their wares; called also *potter's ore*.

ąl-read′y (-red′), *adv.* Before a certain time, past, present, or future; previously; beforehand; by the time specified; even now; as, it had been *already* discovered; the results are *already* apparent.

ąls, *adv.* Also. [Obs.]

ąls, *conj.* As. [Obs.]

Al-sā′tiăn (-shăn), *n.* 1. A native of Alsatia, or Alsace, a German territory between the Rhine and the Vosges Mountains.

2. A frequenter of Alsatia, formerly a resort of criminals in London.

Al-sā′tiăn, *a.* Pertaining to Alsace or Alsatia.

al′sike (al′sik), *n.* [From *Alsike* in Sweden.] A forage-plant, *Trifolium hybridum*, commonly called Swedish clover.

Al-sī′nē, *n.* [L., from Gr. *alsinē*, a kind of plant.] A large genus of herbs of the pink or chickweed family, *Caryophyllaceæ*.

al'sō, *adv.* and *conj.* [ME. *al so, al swo, al swa,* from AS. *eal swā*; *eal,* all, and *swa,* so.]

1. Likewise; in like manner.

2. As something additional tending the same way or in the same direction; besides; as well; further; too; as, he is *also* an orator.

3. Even as; so; as; used as a conjunction. [Obs.]

Al-soph'i-lȧ, *n.* [Gr. *alsos,* a grove, and *philos,* loving.] A genus of tropical ferns, most of which are arborescent.

Al-stō'ni-ȧ, *n.* [From Dr. *Alston,* a botanist of Edinburgh.] A genus of trees of the dogbane family. *Alstonia* bark is used as an antiperiodic and tonic.

al'stŏn-ite, *n.* Same as *Bromlite.*

alt, al'tō, *a.* [It., from L. *altus,* high.] In music, a term applied to high notes in the scale. In sculpture, *alto-rilievo,* high relief, a form of relief in which the figures project half or more, without being entirely detached from the ground.

äl'tȧ, *a.* [It.] In music, high; usually denoting an octave higher; feminine of *alto.*

Al-tā'ic, Al-tā'iăn, *a.* Pertaining to the Altai, a vast ridge of mountains in north central Asia.

Al-tāir', *n.* [Corrupted Ar.] The chief star in the constellation Aquila.

al-tā'ite, *n.* A mineral, telluride of lead, found first in the Altai Mountains, in central Asia.

al'tăr, *n.* [ME. *alter*; L. *altare,* an altar, a high place, from *altus,* high.]

1. A mount; a table or elevated place, on which sacrifices were anciently offered to some deity. *Altars* were originally made of turf, afterward of stone, wood, or horn; some were round, others square, others triangular. They differed also in height, but all faced the east. The principal *altars* of the Jews were the *altars* of incense, of burnt offering, and of showbread; all of shittim-wood, and covered with gold or brass.

Ancient Heathen Altars.

2. In Christian churches, the communion table; and, figuratively, a church; a place of worship.

Gothic Altar.—Church of St. Waudru, Mons.

3. In ship-building, one of the steps or ledges, the flights of which form the sides of a dry-dock.

al'tăr-āge, *n.* 1. The revenue accruing from offerings made at the altar.

2. Offerings made upon an altar or to a church.

al'tăr-cloth, *n.* A cloth to lay upon an altar in churches.

al'tăr-cush"iŏn (-un), *n.* A cushion laid upon the altar in some churches to support the service-book.

al'tăr-fire, *n.* Sacrificial fire on an altar; hence, figuratively, religious fervor, or religious service.

al'tăr-ist, *n.* In old law, an appellation given to the priest to whom the altarage belonged; also, a chaplain.

al'tăr-piece, *n.* 1. A painting, mosaic, or piece of sculpture placed over the altar in a church; a reredos.

2. The entire decoration of an altar taken collectively.

al'tăr-rail, *n.* A low railing in front of the altar or communion table.

al'tăr-screen, *n.* A wall or partition built behind an altar.

al'tăr-stōne, *n.* The stone constituting the surface of an altar; also, loosely, the chancel or sanctuary.

al'tăr-tā"ble, *n.* A table, generally of wood, and supported on four legs, on which, in the Church of England, the communion elements are placed; the communion table. At first this table was placed by the Reformers in the situation occupied by the old stone altars, namely, attached to an eastern wall. This position gave umbrage to the Puritans, and Cromwell caused it to be removed to the middle of the chancel, and to be surrounded with seats for the communicants. At the Restoration it was almost universally replaced in its ancient position. When used it is covered with a white linen cloth.

Wooden Altar-table, time of James I.

al'tăr-thāne, *n.* Same as *Altarist.*

al'tăr-tōmb, *n.* A raised monument surmounting a tomb, having a general resemblance to an altar; *altar-tombs* are often surmounted by a recumbent effigy.

Altar-tomb.—Tomb of the Black Prince, Canterbury Cathedral.

al'tăr-wise, *adv.* In the usual position of an altar, at the east end of the church, with the front facing the west.

alt-az'i-muth, *n.* An astronomical instrument having two graduated circles, one vertical and one horizontal, for simultaneously measuring altitude and azimuth.

al'tēr, *v.t.*; altered, *pt., pp.*; altering, *ppr.* [L. *alterare,* to make other, from *alter,* other.]

1. To change in some particular or degree, without entire change; as, snow *altered* the landscape; age had *altered* the singer's voice.

2. To change entirely or materially; as, to *alter* an opinion.

3. To castrate.

Syn.—Change, modify, metamorphose, transform, vary.

al'tēr, *v.i.* To become, in some respects, different; to vary; as, the weather *alters* almost daily; the world *alters* as we grow older.

al"tēr-ȧ-bil'i-ty, *n.* The quality of being alterable.

al'tēr-ȧ-ble, *a.* That may be altered.

al'tēr-ȧ-ble-ness, *n.* The quality of admitting alteration; variableness.

al'tēr-ȧ-bly, *adv.* In a manner that may be altered, or varied.

al'tēr-ănt, *a.* [L. *alteran(t)s,* ppr. of *alterare,* to make other.] Altering; gradually changing.

al'tēr-ănt, *n.* 1. That which causes change or modification.

2. An alterative medicine.

al-tēr-ā'tion, *n.* [L. *alteratio.*] The act of making different; the state of being altered; as, a cold substance suffers an *alteration* when it becomes hot.

al'tēr-ȧ-tive, *a.* Causing alteration; specifically, in medicine, having the power to gradually restore the normal functions of the body.

al'tēr-ȧ-tive, *n.* A medicine which gradually induces bodily change, and restores healthy functions without sensible evacuations.

al'tēr-cāte, *v.i.*; altercated, *pt., pp.*; altercating, *ppr.* [L. *altercatus,* pp. of *altercari,* to dispute; from *alter,* other.] To contend in words; to dispute with zeal, heat, or anger; to wrangle.

al-tēr-cā'tion, *n.* Warm contention in words; dispute carried on with heat or anger; controversy; wrangle.

al'tēr-cā-tive, *a.* Wrangling; disputing; scolding. [Rare.]

al-ter'i-ty, *n.* The state or quality of being different; oppositeness. [Rare.]

al'tērn, *a.* [L. *alternus,* from *alter,* other.]

1. Acting by turns; succeeding one another; alternate. [Obs.]

2. In crystallography, exhibiting, on two parts, an upper and a lower part, faces which alternate among themselves, but which, when the two parts are compared, correspond with each other.

Altern base; in trigonometry, a term used in distinction from the true base. Thus, in oblique triangles the true base is the sum of the sides, and then the difference of the sides is the *altern base*; or the true base is the difference of the sides, and the sum of the sides is the *altern base.*

al-tēr'nȧ-cy, *n.* Performance or action by turns. [Rare.]

al-tēr'nănt, *a.* [L. *alternans,* ppr. of *alternare,* to alternate.] In geology, having alternate layers.

Al-tēr-nan'the-rȧ, *n.* [L. *alternus,* alternate, and *anthera,* anther.] A genus of dwarf tufted plants having opposite leaves and small tribracteate flowers arranged in heads. Some of the species have richly colored foliage.

al-tēr-nāt' (-nä'), *n.* [Fr.] Rotation in precedence, as among diplomats of equal rank, in signing treaties and in international conventions.

al-tēr'nāte, *a.* [L. *alternatus,* pp. of *alternare,* to do by turns.]

1. Being by turns; following each the other in succession of time or place; hence, reciprocal.

And bid *alternate* passions fall and rise. —Pope.

Alternate Leaves.

2. Intervening regularly between the members of two similar series; as the odd and even numbers in a numerical list, or every second, or every other, rank in a military company.

3. In botany, placed at nearly regular distance from each other around an axis, and not opposite.

Alternate alligation; see *Alligation.*

Alternate angles; in geometry, the internal angles made by two lines with a third, on opposite sides of it. If the two lines are parallel, the alternate angles are equal. Thus, if the parallels *ab, cd,* be cut by the line *eh,* the angles *bfg* and *cgf* are alternate angles, as are also the angles *afg* and *fgd.*

Alternate Angles.

Alternate quarters; in heraldry, the first and fourth, and the second and third; they are usually of the same nature.

al-tēr'nāte, *n.* 1. That which happens by turns with something else; vicissitude. [Rare.]

2. A regularly appointed substitute for a delegate or appointee; as, he attended the national convention as an *alternate.*

3. In mathematics, a proportion, the derivative of another; obtained by interchange of the means.

4. An alternative. [Obs.]

al'tēr-nāte, *v.t.*; alternated, *pt., pp.*; alternating, *ppr.* To perform by turns, or in succession; to cause to succeed by turns; to change (one thing for another) reciprocally; as, congress *alternated* a high tariff with a low one.

al'tēr-nāte, *v.i.* 1. To follow one another in time, place, or condition, reciprocally; often followed by *with*; as, the flood and ebb tides *alternate with* each other.

2. In electricity, to change rapidly from positive electricity to negative, and the reverse; as in a current.

al-tēr'nāte-ly, *adv.* In an alternate manner: (a) in reciprocal succession; by turns; in the same way as night follows day and day follows night; (b) with the omission or intervention of one between each pair; as, read the lines *alternately.*

al-tēr'nāte-ness, *n.* The quality of being alternate, or of following in succession.

al-tēr-nā'tion, *n.* [L. *alternatio,* ppr. of *alternare,* to do by turns.]

1. The reciprocal succession of things, in time or place; the act of following and being followed in succession; as, the *alternation* of day and night, cold and heat, summer and winter.

2. In mathematics, same as *permutation.*

3. In church ritual, the response of the congregation speaking alternately with the minister.

al-tēr'nā-tive, *a.* [Fr. *alternatif.*]

1. Offering a choice of two things.

2. Designating alternation; as the word *either,* having an *alternative* (conjunctive) use.

al-tēr'nā-tive, *n.* 1. That which may be chosen or omitted as one of two things, so that if one is taken, the other must be left. Thus, when *two* things offer a choice of *one* only, the two things are called *alternatives*. When one thing only is offered it is said there is no *alternative*.

2. By extension, a choice of a number; as, one of numerous *alternatives*.

The fourth and last of these *alternatives*. —Gladstone.

al-tẽr′nā-tive-ly, *adv.* In the manner of alternatives.

al-tẽr′nā-tive-ness, *n.* The quality or state of being alternative.

al-tẽr′ni-ty, *n.* Alternation. [Rare.]

Al-thæ′ȧ, *n.* [L., from Gr. *althaia*, wild mallow.]

1. A genus of the mallow family, including the common garden hollyhock, *Althæa rosea*, and the common marshmallow, *Althæa officinalis*.

2. [a—] The flowering shrub *Hibiscus Syriacus*; called also *rose of Sharon* and *shrubby althæa*.

al′thē-in, *n.* See *Asparagine*.

Al′thing (-ting), *n.* [Ice. *allr*, all, and *thing*, office, court.] The parliament of Iceland.

Al′thing-măn, *n.* A member of the Icelandic parliament.

alt′hŏrn, *n.* A musical instrument used extensively in military bands. It is of the saxhorn class.

ạl-thōugh′ (-thō′), *conj.* [*All* and *though*.] Grant all this; be it so; allow all; suppose that; admit all that; notwithstanding.

Syn.—Though.—These words approach very nearly in meaning. *Although* is perhaps the stronger and more pronounced, bringing the adversative proposition into greater prominence. It is, therefore, generally preferred to commence a sentence.

Although all shall be offended, yet will not I. —Mark xiv. 29.

The sound of love makes your soft heart afraid,
And guard itself, *though* but a child invade. —Waller.

al-til′ō-quence (-kwens), *n.* [L. *altus*, high, and *loqui*, *loquens*, speaking.] Lofty speech; pompous language. [Rare.]

al-til′ō-quent, *a.* High-sounding. [Rare.]

al-tim′e-tẽr, *n.* [L. *altus*, high, and *metrum*; Gr. *metron*, measure.] An instrument for taking altitudes by mathematical principles, as a quadrant, sextant, or theodolite.

al-tim′e-try, *n.* The art of ascertaining altitudes by means of an altimeter, without actual mensuration.

ăl-tin′cȧr, *n.* See *Tincal*.

al′ti-scōpe, *n.* [L. *altus*, high, and Gr. *skopein*, to look at.] An instrument consisting of mirrors and lenses arranged in a telescopic tube, so designed as to permit a view around an obstacle to direct vision.

al-tis′ō-nănt, al-tis′ō-nous, *a.* [L. *altus*, high, and *sonans*, ppr. of *sonare*, to sound.] High-sounding; lofty or pompous, as language.

äl-tis′si-mō, *n.* [It., superl. of *alto*, high.] In music, the sounds that lie in the octave above the pitch of sounds in alt.

al′ti-tūde, *n.* [L. *altitudo*, from *altus*, high.]

1. Space extended upward; height; the elevation of an object above its foundation, the ground, or a given level; or the elevation of one object above another; as, the *altitude* of a mountain or column; the *altitude* of a cloud, or of a bird above a tree.

2. In astronomy, the elevation of a point, or star, or other object above the horizon, measured by the arc of a vertical intercepted between such point and the horizon. It is either *apparent* or *true*. *Apparent altitude* is that which appears by observations made at any place on the surface of the earth; *true altitude*, that which results by correcting the apparent for refraction, parallax, and dip of the horizon.

3. In geometry, the perpendicular distance between the base of a figure (or its base produced), and a point in the figure most remote therefrom.

4. Highest point or degree.

Partly proud; even to the *altitude* of his virtue. —Shak.

5. Elevation of spirit, especially from liquor; haughty air; in this sense generally used in the plural.

The man of law began to get into his *altitudes*. —Scott.

Meridian altitude; an arc of the meridian between the horizon and any star or point on the meridian.

al-ti-tū′di-năl, *a.* Of, relating, or pertaining to altitude.

al″ti-tū-di-nā′ri-ăn, *a.* Aspiring to great heights.

al-tiv′ō-lănt, *a.* [L. *altus*, high, and *volans*, flying.] Flying high.

al′tō (*or* äl′tō), *n.*; *pl.* **al′tōṣ.** [It., from L. *altus*, high.]

1. In music, the lowest part taken by a female voice; contralto.

2. Formerly, the highest part taken by a male voice; the counter-tenor.

3. One having a voice adapted for singing *alto*.

al′tō, *a.* High; a common element in terms in music and art, derived from the Italian; as, *alto*-rilievo.

al′tō-clef, *n.* The counter-tenor clef, or the C clef, placed on the third line of the staff.

ạl-tō-geth′ẽr, *adv.* [*All* and *together*.] Wholly; entirely; completely; without exception.

Every man at his best estate is *altogether* vanity. —Ps. xxxix. 5.

ạl-tō-geth′ẽr, *n.* 1. A pose of the whole figure in the nude, as distinguished from a pose exhibiting part of the figure.

2. The entire effect; the whole taken together.

al-tom′e-tẽr, *n.* [L. *altus*, high, and *metrum*, Gr. *metron*, measure.] An altimeter.

al″tō-rē-liē′vō, *n.* The anglicized form of the Italian *alto-rilievo*.

äl″tō-ri-lie′vō (äl″tō-ri-lyā′vō), *n.* [It. *alto*, high, and *rilievo*, relief.]

Alto-rilievo, Battle of Centaurs and Lapithæ.

1. In sculpture, carving or modeling which stands out boldly from the background, approximating the natural form; the form of relief that stands out farthest from the background.

2. Any work done in high relief.

al′tri-căl, *a.* Of, relating, or pertaining to the *Altrices*. Also spelled *altricial*.

Al-tri′cēṣ, *n.pl.* [L., pl. of *altrix*, nurse.] A division of birds characterized by young which remain in the nest for a comparatively long time; in opposition to *Præcoces*.

al′trụ-iṣm, *n.* [Fr. *altruisme*, from It. *altrui*, of or to others, from L. *alter*, another.] A term first employed by the Positivists, or followers of the French philosopher Comte, to signify devotion to others or to humanity; the opposite of *selfishness*.

al′trụ-ist, *n.* An exponent of altruism.

al-trụ-is′tic, *a.* Of or exhibiting altruism.

al-trụ-is′tic-ăl-ly, *adv.* In an altruistic manner; unselfishly.

al′ū-del, *n.* [Sp. *aludel*, from Ar. *al-uthāl*, for *ithāl*, pl. of *athla*, utensil.] One of a series of bottomless vessels, generally of earthenware, which fit into each other, making a continuous tube used in sublimation of ores.

al′ū-lȧ, *n.*; *pl.* **al′ū-læ.** [Dim. of L. *ala*, a wing.]

1. The bastard wing of a bird.

2. A membrane-like flap having a basilar attachment, on the wings of certain insects; also, a like structure similarly placed on certain beetles.

al′ū-lăr, *a.* In zoölogy, pertaining to the alula.

al′ū-let, *n.* See *Alula*, 2.

al′um, *n.* [L. *alumen*, alum.] A compound, as $AlK(SO_4)_2 12 H_2O$, the potassium or aluminium of which may be replaced by various elements, in which case it retains its principal characteristics, and crystallizes in regular octahedrons. Potassium and ammonium *alums* are important members of this class, being used as mordants in dyeing and in the preparation of skins, etc.

al′um, *v.t.* To expose to the action of alum. [Rare.]

ȧ-lū′men, *n.* [L.] The pharmaceutic term for alum.

ȧ-lū′mi-nȧ, *n.* [L., from *alumen*, alum.] An earth having the chemical formula Al_2O_3; aluminium oxid. It is the most abundant of the earths, being widely diffused over the globe in the shape of clay, loam, and other similar substances. In the crystalline forms of corundum, the ruby, etc., it is, next to the diamond, the hardest substance known. It is of value in the arts, being used in dyeing.

ȧ-lū′mi-nāte, *v.t.*; aluminated, *pt.*, *pp.*; aluminating, *ppr.* [L. *alumen*, alum; *-ate*.] To impregnate with alum; to wash with alum-water.

ȧ-lū′mi-nāte, *n.* A compound formed by replacing the hydrogen in the trihydrate of aluminium by a metal.

al-ū-min′ic, *a.* Of, pertaining to, or containing, aluminium.

ȧ-lū″mi-nif′ẽr-ous, *a.* [L. *alumen*, alum, and *-ferous*, from *ferre*, to bear.] Containing alum.

ȧ-lū′mi-ni-fọrm, *a.* Having the form of alumina.

ȧ-lū′mi-nite, *n.* Subsulphate of alumina, a whitish mineral occurring in small roundish or reniform masses.

al-ū-min′i-um, *n.* [L. *alumen*, alum.] A bluish white metal, chemical symbol Al, the base of alumina. It is remarkable for lightness and resistance to oxidation. It forms one-twelfth of the crust of the earth in its various compounds. The most important of its mineral compounds is with the feldspars, whose decomposition forms clay. It is a most valuable metal because of its great strength, lightness, non-tarnishing and non-poisonous qualities, but the high cost of extracting it from its compounds limits its use chiefly to alloys. By electrolytic methods it is now produced at the cost of copper. The specific gravity of aluminium is remarkably low, being one-third that of iron; it is malleable, ductile, and hard as zinc, sonorous, and a good conductor

This word was first proposed by Sir Humphry Davy, who discovered the metal, in the form of *alumium* and later *aluminum*. *Aluminum* has an extensive popular use, but the usage of scientists and scholars appears to be in favor of *aluminium*.

Aluminium bronze; an alloy of aluminium and copper, of a pale gold color, used for journal-bearings, cheap jewelry, etc., and in yacht-building.

Aluminium silver; an alloy with silver, which, while having the brilliant color of the latter, will not tarnish by gas.

ȧ-lū′mi-nīze, *v.t.*; aluminized, *pt.*, *pp.*; aluminizing, *ppr.* To treat or impregnate with alum; to aluminate.

ȧ-lū′mi-nous, *a.* Pertaining to or containing alum.

ȧ-lū′mi-num, *n.* Same as *Aluminium*.

al′um-ish, *a.* Having the nature of alum; somewhat resembling alum.

ȧ-lum′nȧ, *n.*; *pl.* **ȧ-lum′næ.** [L.] A female graduate of an educational institution.

ȧ-lum′nus, *n.*; *pl.* **ȧ-lum′nī.** [L., from *alere*, to nourish.] Formerly, a pupil; now a graduate of an educational institution.

al′um-rọọt, *n.* A name given to the astringent root of several plants, as *Heuchera Americana*.

al′um-sçhist, al′um-shāle, *n.* A fissile rock of varying colors, often glossy, composed chiefly of silica and alumina and the source of the greater part of the alum of commerce.

al′um-stōne, *n.* The silicious subsulphate of alumina and potash; a mineral of a grayish or yellowish white color, found at Tolfa in Italy, in secondary rocks.

al′ū-nīte, *n.* Same as *Alum-stone*.

ȧ-lū′nō-gen, *n.* [Fr. *alun*, alum, and *-gen*, Gr. *-genēs*, producing.] The native hydrous aluminium sulphate common in clays.

al′ūre, *n.* [ME. *alure*; OFr. *aler*, *aleor*, gallery, passage.] An alley, passageway, or pavement. [Obs.]

ȧ-lū′tȧ, *n.* [L.] A pliable, alum-dressed leather.

al-ū-tā′ceous, *a.* Leather-like in qualities or color.

al-ū-tā′tion, *n.* The tanning or dressing of leather. [Obs.]

al′vē-ā-ry, *n.*; *pl.* **al′vē-ā-rieṣ.** [L. *alvearium*, a beehive, bulging vessel; *alveus*, a hollow vessel.]

1. A beehive; hence, anything like a beehive.

2. The hollow of the external ear, where the wax is contained.

al′vē-ā-ted, *a.* Formed like a conical beehive.

al′vē-ō-lăr, al-vē′ō-lā-ry (*or* al′vē-), *a.* [L. *alveolus*, a small hollow or cavity, diminutive of *alveus*, a hollow vessel.] Containing sockets, hollow cells, or pits; pertaining to sockets, specifically the sockets of the teeth; as, the *alveolar* artery.

Alveolar processes; the processes of the maxillary bones containing the sockets of the teeth.

al-vē′ō-lāte (*or* al′vē-), *a.* Deeply pitted, so as to resemble a honeycomb.

al′vē-ōle, *n.* Same as *Alveolus*.

al-vō′ō-li-fọrm (*or* al-vē-ō′), *a.* Having the form of an alveolus.

al-vē′ō-lō-. [L. *alveolus*, a socket.] A combining form denoting connection with, or relation to, an alveolus or alveolar process.

al-vē″ō-lō-den′tăl, *a.* [*Alveolo-*, and L. *dens*, *dentis*, tooth.] Relating to the tooth-sockets.

al-vē″ō-lō-lā′bi-ăl, *a.* [*Alveolo-*, and L. *labia*, lip.] Relating to the lips and alveoli.

al-vē″ō-lō-lin′guăl (-gwăl), *a.* [*Alveolo-*, and L. *lingua*, tongue.] Relating to the alveolar processes and the tongue.

al-vē′ō-lus, *n.*; *pl.* **al-vē′ō-lī.** [L., dim. of *alveus*.] A small cell, cavity, or depression in a surface; applied particularly in biology, as to a cavity in a shell, an air-cell in the lungs, or a tooth-socket.

al′vē-us, *n.*; *pl.* **al′vē-ī.** [L.]

1. The channel or bed of a river.

2. In anatomy, a tube or canal through which some fluid flows, as the thoracic duct.

al′vine, *a.* [Fr. *alvin*, from L. *alvus*, the belly.] Pertaining to the belly or intestines; as, *alvine* discharges.

al′wāy, *adv.* [ME. *alway*, *alle wey*; AS. *ealne weg*; *ealne*, acc. of *eal*, all, and *weg*, acc. of *weg*, way; all the way.] The original form of *always*, now having a poetic use only.

al′wāys, *adv.* [ME. *alwayes*, the genit. sing. with an adverbial *s* added.]

1. Perpetually; throughout all time; as, God is *always* the same.

2. Continually; without variation; as, to do *always* the things that please.

3. Regularly at periodical times; as, he shall eat *always* at my table.

4. At all convenient times; regularly as opportunity offers; invariably; as, Cornelius prayed to God *always*; he *always* treated his friends the same.

Syn.—Ever, constantly, continually, permanently, perpetually.

Ȧ-lys′sŏn, *n.* [Obs.] See *Alyssum*.

Ȧ-lys′sum, *n.* [L., from Gr. *alysson*, neut. of *alyssos*, a cure for canine madness; *a* priv., and *lyssa*, madness.]

1. An extensive genus of cruciferous plants, including the well-known sweet *alyssum*, *Alyssum maritimum*, cultivated for its white, fragrant blossoms.

2. [a—] Any plant of this genus; as, sweet *alyssum*.

am, *v.* [AS. *am*, *eom*.] The first pers. sing. of the verb *to be*, in the indicative mode, present tense.

I *am* that I *am*. —Ex. iii. 14.

ā′mȧ, *n.* [L. *ama*, *hama*; Gr. *hamē*, a water-bucket.] In the early Christian church, a vessel for mixing and storing wine for the purposes of the eucharistic service. The wine was poured from the *ama* into smaller vessels when it was required for the service. Now called *cruet*.

Amas which belonged to the Abbey of St. Denis.

ā′mȧ, *n.* A wine measure, as a cask, a pipe, etc. [Obs.]

am-ȧ-bil′i-ty, *n.* [Fr. *amabilité*; L. *amabilitas*, lovableness.] Lovableness.

am-ȧ-crat′iç, *a.* [Gr. *hama*, together, and *kratos*, power.] Same as *Amasthenic*.

am″ȧ-dȧ-vat′, *n.* [E. Ind.] A pugnacious singing cage-bird of India; also called *strawberry-finch*, and *red waxbill*.

am′ȧ-dōu, *n.* [Fr.] Black match; German tinder; pyrotechnical sponge; punk. A tinder made from various fungi growing on old trees, and treated with saltpeter. It has been used in surgery as a styptic.

ȧ-māin′, *adv.* With force, strength, or violence; violently; furiously; suddenly; at once.

ȧ-mal′gam, *n.* [Fr. *amalgame*, a corruption of L. *malagma*, from Gr. *malagma*, a poultice, an emollient, from *malassein*, to soften.]

1. A compound of mercury or quicksilver with another metal; any metallic alloy of which mercury forms an essential constituent part.

2. A native compound of mercury and silver found in fine crystals in mines in which veins of copper and silver cross each other.

3. A mixture or compound of different things.

ȧ-mal′gam, *v.t.* and *v.i.* To amalgamate. [Rare.]

ȧ-mal′gȧ-mȧ, *n.* Same as *Amalgam*.

ȧ-mal′gȧ-māte, *v.t.*; amalgamated, *pt.*, *pp.*; amalgamating, *ppr.* 1. To make an amalgam of, as one metal with another; to coat or plate with mercury.

> To *amalgamate* a zinc plate, a drop of mercury is placed on it and spread with a brush. —Ganot.

2. To mix (different things) to make a compound; to blend; to unite.

ȧ-mal′gȧ-māte, *v.i.* To unite as an amalgam; to blend; to coalesce; to combine; as, languages *amalgamate* in time.

ȧ-mal′gȧ-māte, ȧ-mal′gȧ-mā-ted, *a.* Compounded with quicksilver; blended; coalesced; united.

ȧ-mal-gȧ-mā′tion, *n.* 1. The act or operation of compounding mercury with another metal; applied particularly to the process of separating gold and silver from their ores by means of mercury.

2. The mixing, blending, or union of separate elements or things.

3. The union or combination of two or more companies into one concern.

ȧ-mal′gȧ-mā-tive, *a.* Tending to amalgamate.

ȧ-mal′gȧ-mā-tŏr, *n.* One who or that which amalgamates; especially, an apparatus used in mining for extracting precious metals from pulverized ore by means of amalgamation.

ȧ-mal′gȧ-mīze, *v.t.* [Rare.] Same as *Amalgamate*.

ȧ-mȧnd′, *n.* [Fr. *amende*, fine, penalty.] In Scots law, a fine or penalty; also, a sum of money deposited in court by a defendant as security against evasive delay.

am′ȧn-din, *n.* [Fr. *amande*, almond.]

1. The legumin of sweet almonds.

2. A kind of paste or cold-cream for chapped hands, or any compound containing almond extract.

ȧ-man′dō-lȧ, *n.* [It. and Per. *amandola*, an almond.] A green marble having the appearance of honeycomb, and containing white spots; of 100 parts, 76 are mild calcareous earth, 20 schist, and 2 iron. The cellular appearance proceeds from the schist.

Am-ȧ-ni′tȧ, *n.* [L.] A subgenus of *Agaricus*, containing the poisonous mushrooms.

ȧ-man′i-tin, ȧ-man′i-tine, *n.* [Gr. *amanitai*, pl., a sort of fungi.] An organic base, the supposed poisonous principle of certain mushrooms, as *Agaricus muscarius*, *Agaricus bulbosa*, etc.

ȧ-man-ū-en′sis, *n.*; *pl.* **ȧ-man-ū-en′sēs**. [L. *amanuensis*; *a*, *ab*, from, and *manu*, abl. of *manus*, hand; *-ensis* equals *servus*, servant.] One whose employment is to write what another dictates, or to copy what another has written.

ȧ-mar′ȧ-cus, *n.* [L.] Marjoram.

am′ȧ-rănt, *n.* Amaranth. [Obs.]

Am″ȧ-ran-tā′cē-æ, Am″ȧ-ran-thā′cē-æ, *n.pl.* A natural order of plants, the amaranths.

am″ȧ-ran-tā′ceous, am″ȧ-ran-thā′ceous, *a.* Pertaining to the order *Amarantaceæ*.

am-ȧ-ran′tad, am-ȧ-ran′thad, *n.* Any plant of the amaranth family.

am′ȧ-ranth, *n.* [L. *amarantus*; Gr. *amarantos*, unfading; *a* priv., and *marainein*, to fade.]

1. A plant of the genus *Amarantus*, or in a wider sense, one of the *Amarantaceæ*.

2. In poetry, an imaginary flower that never fades.

3. A color inclining to purple.

Am″ȧ-ran-thā′cē-æ, *n. pl.* See *Amarantaceæ*.

am-ȧ-ran′thine, *a.* 1. Pertaining to amaranth.

2. Never-fading, like the amaranth of the poets; imperishable.

3. Purplish in color.

Am-ȧ-ran′tus, Am-ȧ-ran′thus, *n.* [L.] A genus of tropical annual plants of many species, much cultivated for their flowers; as, *Amarantus caudatus*, love-lies-bleeding.

ä-mär-gō′sō, *n.* [Sp., bitter.] The bark of the goatbush, *Castela erecta*, a shrub of southern Texas and northern Mexico. It is very bitter, and is much used medicinally by the Mexicans.

am′ȧ-rin, am′ȧ-rine, *n.* [L. *amarus*, bitter.] A poisonous, acrid, crystalline substance obtained from the oil of bitter almonds.

ȧ-mar′i-tūde, *n.* [L. *amaritudo*, from *amarus*, bitter.] Bitterness. [Rare.]

Am″ȧ-ryl″li-dā′cē-æ, *n. pl.* [L. *Amaryllis* (*id*), and *-aceæ*.] In botany, an order of plants, the amaryllis family, closely allied to the *Liliaceæ*, and embracing several hundred species, including the snowdrop, narcissus, daffodil, etc.

am″ȧ-ryl″li-dā′ceous, am″ȧ-ryl-lid′ē-ous, *a.* Pertaining to the order *Amaryllidaceæ*.

Am-ȧ-ryl′lis, *n.* [Gr., a female name in Virgil and Theocritus.]

1. A large genus of plants, the type genus of *Amaryllidaceæ*.

2. [a—] Any plant of this genus.

ȧ-măss′, *v.t.*; amassed, *pt.*, *pp.*; amassing, *ppr.* [Fr. *amasser*; L. *amassare*; *ad*, to, and *massa*, heap, mass.]

1. To collect into a heap; to gather a great quantity of; to accumulate; as, to *amass* a treasure.

2. To collect in great numbers; to add (many things) together; as, to *amass* words or phrases.

Syn.—Accumulate, aggregate, heap together, hoard, lay up.

ȧ-măss′, *n.* An assemblage; a heap; an accumulation. [Obs.]

ȧ-măss′ȧ-ble, *a.* Capable of being amassed.

ȧ-măss′ẽr, *n.* One who amasses.

ȧ-mas-sette′ (-set′), *n.* [Fr.] A spatula or painter's knife.

ȧ-măss′ment, *n.* A heap collected; a large quantity or number brought together; an accumulation.

am-as-then′iç, *a.* [Gr. *hama*, together, and *sthenos*, strength.] In optics, uniting the actinic or chemical rays of light into one focus.

ȧ-mas′ti-ȧ, *n.* [L., from Gr. *amastos*; *a* priv., and *mastos*, breast.] In anatomy, absence of the mammæ, or nipples.

ȧ-māte′, *v.t.* [OFr. *amatir*, to subdue.] To terrify; to dishearten. [Rare.]

ȧ-māte′, *v.t.* To be a mate to; to accompany. [Obs.]

am′ȧ-teūr (am′ȧ-tūr *or* -tūr′), *n.* [Fr., from L. *amator*, a lover, from *amare*, to love.]

1. A person attached to a particular pursuit, study, or science, as to music or painting; one who has a taste for the arts, especially the fine arts; specifically, one who cultivates any study or art, from taste or attachment, without pursuing it professionally.

2. In modern athletic sports, an athlete who has never used any athletic art professionally or as a means of livelihood; one who has not taken part in contests open to professionals. The term is variously and more specifically defined by different athletic associations.

am-ȧ-teūr′ish, *a.* Characteristic of an amateur.

am-ȧ-teūr′ish-ly, *adv.* In an amateurish manner; crudely; unskilfully.

am-ȧ-teūr′ish-ness, *n.* The quality of being amateurish.

am-ȧ-teūr-ism, *n.* State of being an amateur.

am′ȧ-teūr-ship, *n.* The character, position, or procedure of an amateur.

am-ȧ-tī′tō, *n.* [It. *amatita*, lead or chalk for pencils; L. *hæmatites*, hematite.] A red pigment derived from hematite.

am′ȧ-tive, *a.* [L. *amatus*, pp. of *amare*, to love.] Amorous.

am′ȧ-tive-ness, *n.* In phrenology, a faculty which is supposed to influence sexual desire; propensity to love.

am-ȧ-tō′ri-ăl, *a.* [L. *amatorius*, from *amare*, to love.]

1. Relating to love; as, *amatorial* verses; produced by sexual intercourse; as, *amatorial* progeny.

2. In anatomy, a term applied to the oblique muscles of the eye, from their use in ogling.

am-ȧ-tō′ri-ăl-ly, *adv.* In an amatorial manner; by way of love.

ä-mä-tō′ri-ō, *n.* [It.] A love-gift; specifically, a gift bearing the portrait of a lady and a complimentary inscription.

am-ȧ-tō′ri-ous, *a.* Pertaining to love. [Obs.]

am′ȧ-tō-ry, *a.* Pertaining to, expressing, or causing love; amatorial; as, *amatory* potions.

am-au-rō′sis, *n.* [Gr. *amaurosis*, from *amauros*, dark, dim.] A loss or decay of sight from a palsy of the optic nerve, without any visible defect in the eye, except an immovable pupil; formerly called *gutta serena*, the "drop serene" of Milton.

am-au-rot′iç, *a.* Pertaining to or having the characteristics of amaurosis.

ȧ-mau′site, *n.* Felsite or petrosilex.

ȧ-māze′, *v.t.*; amazed, *pt.*, *pp.*; amazing, *ppr.* [ME. *amasen*; *a* and *masen*, to confuse, perplex.]

1. To confound with fear, sudden surprise, or wonder; to astound, perplex, or astonish; to awe; as, he *amazes* people by his boldness.

2. To puzzle; to daze; to bring into a maze. [Obs.]

Syn.—Astonish, astound, bewilder, dumbfound, surprise, perplex, confound.

ȧ-māze′, *v.i.* To be astounded or bewildered; as, my soul *amazes* at God's goodness. [Obs.]

ȧ-māze′, *n.* Astonishment; confusion; perplexity, arising from fear, surprise, or wonder.

ȧ-māz′ed-ly, *adv.* With amazement; in a manner to confound.

ȧ-māz′ed-ness, *n.* The state of being confounded with fear, surprise, or wonder; astonishment; great wonder.

ȧ-māze′fụl, *a.* Full of amazement; tending to cause amazement. [Obs.]

ȧ-māze′ment, *n.* 1. Astonishment; confusion or perplexity, from a sudden impression of fear, surprise, or wonder, sometimes accompanied by fear or terror; sometimes merely extreme wonder or admiration at some great, sudden, or unexpected event, at an unusual sight, or at the narration of extraordinary events.

2. Frenzy; madness; infatuation. [Obs.]

Syn.—Wonder, admiration, astonishment, surprise, confusion, perturbation, awe, bewilderment.

Am-ȧ-zil′i-ȧ, *n.* [L., from *amazili*, a word of probable South American origin.] A genus of humming-birds, native to Mexico and Central and South America. Their coloring is mostly green and chestnut.

ȧ-māz′ing, *a.* Very wonderful; exciting astonishment or perplexity.

Syn.—Wonderful, marvelous, astonishing, surprising, incredible.

ȧ-māz′ing-ly, *adv.* In an astonishing degree; in a manner to excite astonishment, or to perplex, confound, or terrify.

Am′ȧ-zŏn, *n.* [L., from Gr. *Amazōn*; *a* priv., and *mazos*, breast. A doubtful derivation, which arises from the mythical Greek legend that the Amazons cut off the right breast that it might not incommode them in the use of the bow and javelin.]

1. One of a race of female warriors, described in Greek mythology, who founded an empire on the river Thermodon, in Asia Minor, on the coast of the Euxine. They are said to have excluded men from their society, and by their warlike character and skill to have conquered

surrounding nations. The *Amazons* were a favorite subject with the ancient Greek writers.

2. A female warrior of Dahomey in Africa.

3. [a—] A large, masculine, truculent woman; a virago; any female warrior.

am′á-zŏn, *n.* 1. A South American parrot of the genus *Chrysotis.*

2. One of various humming-birds, named from the River Amazon.

Amazons.
1. From Hope's Costumes of the Ancients.
2. From Museo Borbonico.

Am′á-zŏn-ánt, *n.* An interesting species of ant, the *Formica rufescens*, found in Europe and North America. They rob the nests of other ants, capturing neuters in the pupa or larval state, and making slaves of them.

am-á-zō′ni-ăn, *a.* 1. Pertaining to or resembling an Amazon; bold; of masculine manners; warlike; applied to females.

2. [A—] Belonging to the River Amazon in South America, or to the country lying on that river.

am′á-zŏn-īte, *n.* Amazon-stone.

Am′á-zŏn-stōne, *n.* A beautiful bright green species of microlite, used as a gem, occurring on the banks of the Amazon River, also in Colorado, and in Siberia.

amb-, am′bi-, *prefix.* [L.] A combining form signifying around, about. Equivalent to Greek *amphi.*

am′bāġe, *n.* [*Amb-*, and L. *agere*, to drive.]

1. Circumlocution; circuit of words to express ideas which may be expressed in fewer words; equivocation.

2. A winding or turning. Generally used in the plural, *ambages*, to denote secret or devious ways.

am-baġ′i-nous, *a.* Indirect; roundabout; ambagious. [Rare.]

am-bā′ġious (-jus), *a.* [L. *ambagiosus.*] Characterized by circuitous methods; devious; ambiguous. [Rare.]

am-baġ′i-tō-ry, *a.* Circumlocutory. [Rare.]

am′bá-ri, *n.* [Hind.] A covered seat on the back of an elephant or camel; a howdah.

am-băr-vā′li-á, *n. pl.* [*Ambi-*, and L. *arvum*, a field.] An ancient Roman festival in which sacrifices were offered to Ceres as an invocation for fertile fields. The sacrificial animals were first led about the fields.

am′bá-ry, *n.* [Native name.] An East Indian fiber plant, *Hibiscus cannabinus*; brown Indian hemp.

am′bash, *n.* [Probably native name.] In botany, a leguminous African shrub, *Herminiera Elaphroxylon*, esteemed on account of its light white wood; called also the *pith-tree of the Nile.*

am′băs-sāde, em′băs-sāde, *n.* The mission or functions of an ambassador; an embassy. [Obs.]

am-bas′sá-dŏr, em-bas′sá-dŏr, *n.* [Fr. *ambassadeur*; L. *ambasciator.*] The highest diplomatic representative that one sovereign power or state sends officially to another. An *ambassador* represents his sovereign personally, as well as the state. Otherwise, the difference between *ambassadors* and diplomatic agents of the second class—envoys, and ministers resident and plenipotentiary—is one of dignity, privilege, and etiquette. An *ambassador* ranks next to royal blood, and may ask audience at any time of the chief of the state to which he is accredited; he and his household are exempt from local jurisdiction, and from imposts and duties; he enjoys immunity of person, and freedom of religious worship. Until 1893, the United States accredited abroad no higher diplomatic agents than envoys extraordinary and ministers plenipotentiary. At that time Congress made provision for raising to the ambassadorial rank ministers to foreign powers sending *ambassadors* to the United States.

am-bas-sá-dō′ri-ăl, *a.* Pertaining or belonging to an ambassador or embassy.

am-bas′sá-dŏr-ship, *n.* The office, dignity, or functions of an ambassador.

am-bas′sá-dress, *n.* A female ambassador; or the wife of an ambassador.

am′băs-sāġe, *n.* [Rare.] Same as *Embassage.*

am′băs-sy, *n.* [Rare.] Same as *Embassy.*

am′bē, am′bi, *n.* [Gr. *ambē*, ridge.]

1. An obsolete surgical instrument for reducing dislocated shoulders; so called from the jutting of its extremity.

2. A projection or ridge on a bone. [Obs.]

am′bẽr, *n.* [Fr. *ambre*; from Ar. *'anbar*, ambergris.]

1. A hard, semipellucid substance, tasteless and without smell, except when pounded or heated, when it emits a fragrant odor. It is found in alluvial soils, or on the seashore, in many places; on the shores of the Baltic, in Europe, most abundantly. It is a fossil pine resin. Though usually pale yellow or reddish-brown, and translucent, it is sometimes clouded and quite opaque, and sometimes bluish, greenish, or violet. It is highly electrical, is the basis of amber varnish, and is used for cigarette-holders, mouthpieces for pipes, fancy pipes, beads, etc. In mineralogy, called *succinite.*

2. A pale yellow color, like that of amber.

3. Liquidambar, a balsam.

4. Ambergris; the original meaning. [Obs.]

Black amber; jet.

White amber; spermaceti.

am′bẽr, *a.* Consisting of, made of, or resembling amber; as, *amber* bracelets; the *amber* sky.

am′bẽr, *v.t.*; ambered, *pt., pp.*; ambering, *ppr.*

1. To scent or flavor with ambergris.

2. To incase or preserve in amber; as, an *ambered* fly.

3. To give an amber or yellowish color to.

am′bẽr-fish, *n.* One of several brilliantly colored fishes, genus *Seriola*, found in tropical waters. Some are valued as food.

am′bẽr-grēase, *n.* Ambergris.

am′bẽr-gris, *n.* [Fr. *ambre gris*; *ambre*, amber, and *gris*, from O.H.G. *gris*, gray.] A solid, opaque, ash-colored, inflammable substance, variegated like marble, remarkably light, rugged on its surface, and when heated having a fragrant odor. It does not effervesce with acids; it melts easily into a kind of yellow resin, and is soluble, but not readily, in alcohol. It is a morbid secretion in the intestines of the spermaceti-whale, a species of *Physeter.* It is usually found floating on the surface of the ocean, in regions frequented by whales; sometimes in masses of from 60 to 225 lbs. weight. It is highly valued as a material in perfumery.

am′bẽr-jack, *n.* An amber-fish, *Seriola lalandi.*

am′bẽr-seed, *n.* Musk-seed; a seed somewhat resembling millet. It is of a bitterish taste, and found in Egypt and the West Indies.

am′bẽr-tree, *n.* The English name of a species of *Anthospermum*, a shrub with evergreen leaves, which, when bruised, emit a fragrant odor.

āmbeş′-āce, āmbeş′-ās (āmz-), *n.* [L. *ambo*, both, and *as*, ace.] The double ace, the lowest count in dice; hence, ill-luck. [Rare.]

am′bi-, *prefix.* See *Amb-.*

am′bi, *n.* See *Ambe.*

am-bi-dex′tẽr, *n.* [*Ambi-*, and L. *dexter*, the right hand.]

1. A person who uses both hands with equal facility.

2. A double-dealer; one equally ready to act on either side in party disputes.

3. In law, a juror who takes money from both parties for giving his verdict.

am-bi-dex′tẽr, *a.* Ambidextrous.

am″bi-dex-ter′i-ty, *n.* The faculty of using both hands with equal facility; double-dealing; the taking of money from both parties for a verdict.

am-bi-dex′trăl, *a.* Pertaining equally to the right and left.

am-bi-dex′trous, *a.* Having the faculty of using both hands with equal ease; practising or siding with both parties.

am-bi-dex′trous-ly, *adv.* In an ambidextrous manner; with both hands.

am-bi-dex′trous-ness, *n.* Ambidexterity.

am′bi-ent, *a.* [L. *ambiens*, ppr. of *ambire*, to go round.] Surrounding; encompassing on all sides; investing; applied to fluids or diffusible substances; as, the *ambient* air.

am′bi-ent, *n.* That which encompasses on all sides.

am-biġ′e-năl, *a.* [*Ambi-*, and L. *genus*, born.] Of two kinds; used only in the Newtonian phrase, *ambigenal hyperbola.*

Ambigenal hyperbola; one of the triple hyperbolas of the third order, having one of its infinite legs falling within an angle formed by the asymptotes, and the other without.

am-biġ′e-nous, *a.* Of two kinds; specifically, in botany, sharing in two natures; said of certain perianths having the inner members petaloid and the outer calycine.

am′bi-gū, *n.* [Fr. *ambigu*, doubtful.] An entertainment or feast, consisting of a medley of dishes served at once.

am-bi-gū′i-ty, *n.* [L. *ambiguitas*, from *ambiguus*, doubtful.] Doubtfulness or uncertainty of signification; double meaning; as, words should be used which admit of no *ambiguity.*

am-biġ′ū-ous, *a.* [L. *ambiguus*, from *ambigere*, to wander; *ambi*, about, around, and *agere*, to drive.] Having two or more meanings; doubtful; being of uncertain signification; susceptible of different interpretations; hence, obscure. It is applied to words and expressions; not to a dubious state of mind, though it may be to a person using words of doubtful signification; as, the ancient oracles were *ambiguous.*

Syn.—Doubtful, indefinite, dubious, equivocal, uncertain, involved.

am-biġ′ū-ous-ly, *adv.* In an ambiguous manner; with doubtful meaning.

am-biġ′ū-ous-ness, *n.* The quality of being ambiguous; uncertainty of meaning; ambiguity; hence, obscurity.

am-bi-lē′vous, *a.* [*Ambi-*, and L. *lævus*, left.] Awkward, as though both hands were the left; opposed to *ambidextrous.* [Rare.]

am-bil′ō-quy, *n.* The use of doubtful or ambiguous expressions. [Obs.]

am-bip′á-rous, *a.* [*Ambi-*, and L. *parere*, to bear.] In botany, having the beginnings of both flowers and leaves, as a bud.

am′bit, *n.* [L. *ambitus*, a circuit, from *ambire*, to go about.] An encompassing line; scope.

am-bi′tion (-bish′un), *n.* [L. *ambitio*, from *ambire*, to go about; from the practice of Roman candidates for office, who went about the city to solicit votes.]

1. An eager and sometimes inordinate desire after some object, as preferment, honor, pre-eminence, superiority, power, fame, or whatever confers distinction; desire to distinguish oneself in some way.

2. The object of ambitious desire or endeavor.

3. Desire to work; spirit. [Colloq.]

am-bi′tion, *v.t.* Ambitiously to seek after. [Rare.]

am-bi′tion-ist, *n.* One actuated excessively by ambition. [Obs.]

am-bi′tion-less, *a.* Devoid of ambition.

am-bi′tious, *a.* 1. Greatly desirous of power, honor, office, superiority, or excellence; aspiring; overeager for fame; also, in colloquial use, spirited; energetic.

2. Showy; adapted to command notice or praise; as, *ambitious* ornaments.

3. Showing or having characteristics of ambition.

am-bi′tious-ly, *adv.* In an ambitious manner; with an eager desire after preferment or superiority.

am-bi′tious-ness, *n.* The quality of being ambitious, or pretentious; ambition.

am′bi-tus, *n. sing.* and *pl.* [L.] 1. The circumference or exterior edge or border of a thing.

2. In Roman history, a canvassing for votes.

am′ble, *v.i.*; ambled (-bld), *pt., pp.*; ambling, *ppr.* [Fr. *ambler*, from L. *ambulare*, to walk.]

1. To move with the peculiar gait called *amble.*

2. To ride or walk in a careless, lounging fashion; as, he *ambled* through the park.

am′ble, *n.* 1. A gait natural to the elephant, and at times to the horse, ass, and mule. Instantaneous photography shows the movement of the feet in the *amble* to be, right hind, right fore, left hind, left fore, and repeating in the same order.

2. A loose, easy, swinging or lounging gait.

am′blẽr, *n.* One who ambles; an ambling horse.

am′bling-ly, *adv.* With an ambling movement.

am-blō′sis, *n.* [L., from Gr. *amblōsis*, abortion.] Abortion; miscarriage.

am-blot′iç, *a.* and *n.* I. *a.* Causing, or tending to cause, abortion.

II. *n.* A drug designed to produce abortion.

am-bly-ā′phi-á, *n.* [L., from Gr. *amblys*, dull, and *haphē*, touch, from *haptein*, *haptesthai*, to touch.] In pathology, dullness or insensibility of touch; physical apathy.

am′bly-gon, *n.* [Gr. *amblys*, dull, obtuse, and *gōnia*, an angle.] An obtuse-angled triangle; a triangle with one angle of more than ninety degrees.

am-blyġ′ō-năl, *a.* Containing an obtuse angle. [Obs.]

am-blyġ′ō-nīte, *n.* [Gr. *amblygōnios*, having an obtuse angle, and *-ite.*] A mineral of Saxony, Norway, and parts of the United States, pale green in color, sometimes columnar, and containing phosphoric acid, alumina, and lithium.

am″bly-ō-çăr′pous, *a.* [Gr. *amblys*, dull, and *karpos*, fruit.] In botany, having abortive seeds; applied to fruit.

am-bly-ō′pi-á, am′bly-ō-py, *n.* [L., from Gr. *amblys*, dull, and *ōps*, eye.] Dullness or obscurity of sight, without any apparent defect of the organs; the first stage of amaurosis.

am-bly-op′iç, *a.* Relating to amblyopia.

Am″bly-ō-pī′næ, *n. pl.* [*Amblyopus*, and *-inæ.*] A subfamily of fishes, exemplified by the genus *Amblyopus*, having the two dorsal fins united.

am-bly-op′sid, *n.* A fish of the family *Amblyopsidæ.*

Am-bly-op′si-dæ, Am-bly-op′i-dæ, *n. pl.* A family of haplomous fishes, including the blindfish of the Mammoth and other caves of North America.

am-bly-op′sis, *n.* [L., from Gr. *amblys*, dull, dim, and *opsis*, countenance, sight.]
1. The typical genus of *Amblyopsidæ*.
2. A crustacean genus.

am-bly-op′soid, *a.* and *n.* I. *a.* Characteristic of the *Amblyopsidæ*.
II. *n.* An amblyopsid.

Am-bly-ō′pus, *n.* [Gr. *amblyōpos*, dim-sighted.]
1. A genus of fishes, family *Gobiidæ*.
2. A genus of orthopterous insects.

am′bly-ō-py, *n.* See *Amblyopia*.

Am-blyp′ō-dȧ, *n. pl.* [L., from Gr. *amblys*, blunt, and *pous*, *podos*, foot.] A group of extinct mammals whose fossil remains are found in the Eocene beds of North America.

Am-bly-rhyn′chus, *n.* [L., from Gr. *amblys*, dull, and *rhynchos*, snout.] A genus of blunt-snouted lizards of the family *Iguanidæ*, found in the Galapagos Islands.

Am-blys′tō-mȧ, *n.* [L., from Gr. *amblys*, dull, and *stoma*, mouth.] A genus of tailed batrachians, the type of the family *Amblystomidæ*. Sometimes erroneously written *Ambystoma*.

am-blys′tō-mid, am′bly-stōme, *n.* One of the amphibian *Amblystomidæ*.

Am-bly-stom′i-dæ, *n.pl.* A family of amphibians of which *Amblystoma* is the typical genus. They are salamanders without prolonged palatines.

am′bō, am′bon, *n.*; *pl.* **am′bōs** *or* **am-bō′nēs.** [L., from Gr. *ambōn*, a stage, platform.]
1. An oblong, elevated pulpit, in the early Christian churches, but disused after the fourteenth century.
2. In anatomy, a circumferential fibrocartilage, as the glenoid fossa of the scapula.

Ambo, Church of San Lorenzo, Rome.

am-bō-dex′tēr, *a.* and *n.* Same as *Ambidexter*.

am-bol′iç, *a.* [Gr. *ambolikos*, from *anabolikos*, *anabolē*, that which is thrown up.] Having the power of producing abortion.

Am-boy-nēse′ (*or* -nēz′), *n.* A native or natives of Amboyna, the most important of the Moluccas or Spice Islands.

ȧm-brē-ä′dȧ, *n.* [Port.] A kind of factitious amber, made in Europe for the African trade.

am′brē-āte, *n.* A salt of ambreic acid.

am-brē′iç, *a.* Pertaining to or obtained from ambrein; as, *ambreic* acid.

am-brē′id, *n.* See *Ambroid*.

am′brē-in, *n.* A peculiar fatty, crystalline substance, the chief constituent of ambergris.

am-brette′, *n.* [Fr., dim. of *ambre*, amber.]
1. Same as *Amber-seed*.
2. A kind of pear with the odor of ambergris.

am′brīte, *n.* [Eng. *amber*, and *-ite*.] A fossil resin, occurring in parts of New Zealand in large masses.

am′broid, am-brē′id, *n.* [*Amber* and *-oid*.] An amber substance composed of amber chips pressed into a mass; made principally in Germany.

am-brol′ō-ġy, *n.* [L. *ambra*, and Gr. *logia*, from *legein*, to speak.] The natural history of amber.

am′brōṣe, *n.* 1. Ambrosia.
2. An early English name of the Jerusalem oak; also, the wood-germander.

am-brō′ṣiȧ (*or* -zhi-ȧ), *n.* [Gr. *ambrosia*, f. of *ambrosios*, immortal, from *abrotos*; *a* priv., and *brotos*, *mortos*, mortal; Sans. *amrita*, immortal.]
1. In mythology, the food of the gods, supposed to confer immortality; also, perfumed ointment.
2. Figuratively, anything very pleasing to taste or smell.
3. [A—] In botany, a genus of the aster family, with lobed leaves, as the ragweed.

am-brō′ṣi-aç (*or* -zhi-ak), **am-brō′ṣiăn** (-zhăn), *a.* Having the qualities of ambrosia.

am-brō′ṣiăl (-zhăl *or* -zhi-ăl), *a.* 1. Pertaining to or having the nature of ambrosia; fragrant; delicious.

> We have only to live right on and breathe the *ambrosial* air. —Thoreau.

2. Befitting the gods; heavenly; divinely beautiful; as, *ambrosial* curls.

am-brō′ṣiăl-ly, *adv.* Deliciously; delightfully.

Am-brō′ṣiăn, *a.* 1. Pertaining to St. Ambrose.
2. [a—] Same as *Ambrosiac*.

Ambrosian chant; a mode of singing or chanting introduced by St. Ambrose. It was more monotonous than the Gregorian, which succeeded it.

Ambrosian ritual; a formula of worship instituted in the church of Milan by St. Ambrose.

am′brō-ṣin, *n.* [L. *Ambrosinus nummus*.] In the middle ages, a coin struck by the dukes of Milan, on which St. Ambrose was represented on horseback.

am′brō-tȳpe, *n.* [Gr. *ambrotos*, immortal, and *typos*, type.] An old style of photograph, produced by reversing a negative and backing it with some dark material that shows through as a background, against which the portions of silver preparation remaining on the negative stand out as light.

am′bry, *n.* [OE. *ambry*, *amrie*; Hind. *almārī*; L. *armarium*, a chest for tools, arms.]
1. A storage-place, chest, cupboard, pantry, or the like.
2. An almonry; an improper use of the word.
3. A niche or closet in or near the altar of early churches for the deposit of the sacred vessels used in the service; in modern churches, a locker or chest for the same purpose.

Ambry.

ambṣ′-āce (āmz′ās), *n.* Same as *Ambes-ace*.

am-bū-lā′çrȧ, *n.*, pl. of *ambulacrum*.

am-bū-lā′çrăl, *a.* Of or pertaining to an ambulacrum or to ambulacra.

am-bū-lā′çri-fọrm, *a.* Shaped like an ambulacrum.

am-bū-lā′çrum, *n.*; *pl.* **am-bū-lā′çrȧ.** [L., a walk, avenue, from *ambulare*, to walk.] In zoölogy, an external section or division extending from the apex to the base of an echinoderm, as the sea-urchin, and containing a series of perforations through which the tube-feet or tentacles are protruded and withdrawn.

am′bū-lănce, *n.* [Fr. *ambulance*, *hôpital ambulant*; from L. *ambulare*, to walk, move.]
1. A movable hospital; a hospital establishment designed to accompany an army in the field.
2. A wagon specially adapted to carry the sick or wounded; used on the battlefield, by hospitals, etc.

am′bū-lănt, *a.* [L. *ambulans*, ppr. of *ambulare*, to walk.] Walking; moving from place to place.

am′bū-lāte, *v.i.* [L. *ambulatus*, pp. of *ambulare*, to walk.] To walk; to move to and fro. [Rare.]

am-bū-lā′tion, *n.* A moving about; the act of walking.

am′bū-lā-tive, *a.* Walking. [Rare.]

am′bū-lā-tŏr, *n.* 1. A walker; one who moves about.
2. A kind of longicorn beetle.
3. The odometer.

am′bū-lā-tō-ry, am″bū-lā-tō′ri-ăl, *a.* 1. Pertaining to walking or a person who walks; able to walk or move about; adapted to walking.
2. Moving from one place to another; not stationary; as, *ambulatory* jurisdiction.
3. In ornithology, (a) formed for walking; applied to the feet of birds with three toes before and one behind; opposed to *scansorial*; also, (b) moving one foot after the other; applied to birds or to their gait; opposed to *saltatory*.
4. In medicine, shifting from one part to another; also applied to that form of typhus which allows the patient to be about.
5. In law, not fixed; able to be altered, as a will during the life of the testator.

am′bū-lā-tō-ry, *n.* A place designed for walking; a corridor or arcade; generally, a sheltered walk connected with a convent.

am′būr-y, *n.* Same as *Anbury*.

am-bus-çāde′, *n.* [Fr. *ambuscade*; Port. and It. *ambuscado*, *emboscata*; L. *imboscata*, an ambush, f. of pp. of *imboscare*, to set in ambush.]
1. A hiding or lying in wait in order to make an unexpected attack; used generally with reference to a body of soldiers or other fighting men.
2. A place where men lie concealed, with a view to attack an enemy; an ambush.
3. A body of men lying in ambush.

am-bus-çāde′, *v.t.* and *v.i.*; ambuscaded, *pt.*, *pp.*; ambuscading, *ppr.* I. *v.t.* To lie in wait for; to attack from a concealed position.
II. *v.i.* To lie in concealment for the purpose of attacking.

am-bus-çā′dō, *n.* and *v.* [Obs.] See *Ambuscade*.

am′bụsh, *n.* [ME. *embusshen*; OFr. *enbuscher*; L. *imboscare*, to set in ambush; *in*, in, and *boscus*, wood, bush.]
1. A hiding or lying concealed, for the purpose of attacking; a lying in wait; a snare; a trap.
2. The person or body of persons posted in a concealed place. [Obs.]
3. A place of concealment from which an unexpected attack may be made; an ambuscade.

am′bụsh, *v.t.*; ambushed, *pt.*, *pp.*; ambushing, *ppr.* To lie in wait for; to assail unexpectedly; also, to post in ambush.

am′bụsh, *v.i.* To lie in wait, for the purpose of attacking by surprise. [Rare.]

am′bụsh-ēr, *n.* One who waylays; one who hides in ambush.

am′bụsh-ment, *n.* An ambush; also, the act of laying an ambush.

am-bus′tion (-chun), *n.* [L. *ambustio*, from *amburere*, to burn or scorch; *amb-*, about, and *urere*, to burn.] A burn or scald. [Obs.]

Am-bys′tō-mȧ, *n.* See *Amblystoma*.

ȧ-mē′bȧ, am-ē-bē′ăn, ȧ-mē′boid. See *Amœba*, etc.

ȧ-meer′, ȧ-mïr′, *n.* [Ar. *amīr*, ruler.] A ruler or governor in Mohammedan countries; an Oriental title of dignity; an emir; especially applied to the ruler of Afghanistan.

ȧ-meer′ship, ȧ-mïr′ship, *n.* The station or dignity of an ameer.

am′el, *n.* and *v.* [Obs.] See *Enamel*.

am′el-çorn, *n.* [Gr. *amelkorn*; O.H.G. *amar*, amelcorn; L. *amylum*, starch; Gr. *amylon*.] A wild or degenerate wheat, from which starch is made in Switzerland; also called *French rice*.

ȧ-mēl′iō-rȧ-ble (-yō-), *a.* Capable of betterment.

ȧ-mēl′iō-rāte, *v.t.*; ameliorated, *pt.*, *pp.*; ameliorating, *ppr.* [L. *amelioratus*, pp. of *ameliorare*, to make better; *ad*, to, and *meliorare*, from *melior*, better.] To make better; to improve; to meliorate.

ȧ-mēl′iō-rāte, *v.i.* To grow better or less severe.

ȧ-mēl-iō-rā′tion, *n.* A making or becoming better; improvement.

ȧ-mēl′iō-rā-tive, *a.* Tending to produce improvement.

ȧ-mēl′iō-rā-tŏr, *n.* One who or that which ameliorates.

ā-men′ (*in singing and in ritualistic service*, ä-men′), *n.* [L. *amen*; Gr. *amēn*; Heb. *āmēn*, truly, certainly.]
1. A term used in Scripture to denote Christ.

> These things saith the *Amen*, the faithful and true witness. —Rev. iii. 14.

2. An expression of formal assent, concurrence, or conviction.
3. The conclusion, in word or act; the end.

ā-men′, *adv.* and *interj.* 1. So be it; used as an expression of hearty assent or formal confession of faith; also, as the formal conclusion of prayers, etc.
2. Truly; verily.

ā-men′, *v.t.* To assent to or concur in; to sanction; to say *amen* to; to conclude.

ȧ-mē-nȧ-bil′i-ty, *n.* The state of being amenable; liability to answer.

ȧ-mē′nȧ-ble, *a.* [Fr. *a*, L. *ad*, to, and *mener*, L. *minare*, to drive.]
1. In old law, easy to be led; governable, as a woman by her husband. [Obs.]
2. Under authority; liable to be called to account; answerable; responsible.
3. Tractable; yielding submission; recognizing authority or control.

Syn.—Accountable, answerable, responsible, liable.

ȧ-mē′nȧ-ble-ness, *n.* Amenability.

ȧ-mē′nȧ-bly, *adv.* In an amenable manner.

am′ē-nāġe, *v.t.* To manage. [Obs.]

am′ē-nănce, *n.* Conduct; behavior. [Obs.]

ȧ-mend′, *v.t.*; amended, *pt.*, *pp.*; amending, *ppr.* [Fr. *amender*; L. *amendare*, free from fault; *e*, *ex*, from, without, and *mendum*, fault, blemish.]
1. To make better by some change; to correct errors in; to supply deficiencies in, or to free from whatever is faulty or wrong; as, to *amend* one's ways.
2. To alter (a motion, law, etc.) by formal action of an authorized body.

Syn.—Correct, reform, rectify, better, improve, mend.—To *amend* is literally to take away blots, and hence to remove faults; to *reform* is to form over again for the better; to *correct* is to make straight or right; to *rectify* is to set right. We *rectify* abuses, mistakes, etc.; *correct* errors; and *reform* or *amend* our lives.

ȧ-mend′, *v.i.* To become better; to improve by correcting something previously wrong.

ȧ-mend′ȧ-ble, *a.* Capable of correction; as, an *amendable* fault.

ȧ-mend′ȧ-ble-ness, *n.* Capability of correction; the state or quality of being amendable.

ȧ-mend′ȧ-tō-ry, *a.* Intended to amend; corrective.

ȧ-mende′ (*Fr. pron.* ȧ-mond′), *n.* [Fr., a fine, penalty.] A fine or other pecuniary punishment; also, any recantation or making of amends.

Amende honorable; formerly, in French law, a humiliating punishment imposed for treason, parricide, and sacrilege. The guilty person was led into court with a halter around his neck; and with feet bare and a lighted torch in his hand was compelled publicly to confess his guilt and to beg for pardon from God, from the legal authorities, and from the injured persons. The phrase has come to mean at present an open recantation or apology, with reparation to the injured person.

ȧ-mend′ẽr, *n.* A person who amends.

ȧ-mend′fụl, *a.* Full of improvement. [Obs.]

ȧ-mend′ment, *n.* 1. An alteration or change for the better; correction of a fault or faults; reformation of life, by quitting vices.

2. In legislative or deliberative proceedings, any formal alteration in a bill, motion, or law.

3. In law, the correction of an error in a writ or process.

Syn.—Correction, improvement, reformation, amelioration, betterment.

ȧ-mend′ment-mŏn″gẽr, *n.* One constantly occupied in bringing forward amendments, as to the constitution of the United States; the Anti-Federalists were formerly given this name.

ȧ-mends′, *n.pl.* [Fr. *amendes*, pl. of *amende.*] Compensation for an injury; recompense; satisfaction; equivalent; as, the happiness of a future life will more than make *amends* for the miseries of this.

Syn.—Reparation, restitution, restoration, compensation.

ȧ-men′i-ty, *n.* [Fr. *aménité*; L. *amœnitas*, from *amœnus*, pleasant, delightful.] Pleasantness; gentility; civility; agreeableness of situation, temper, or disposition; in the plural, the pleasant features of anything.

ȧ-men-ō-mā′ni-ȧ, ȧ-mœn-ō-mā′ni-ȧ, *n.* [L. *amœnus*, pleasant, and Gr. *mania*, madness.] Insanity in the form of pleasing delusions.

ȧ-men-or-rhē′ȧ, ȧ-men-or-rhœ′ȧ, *n.* [Gr. *a* priv., *mēn*, month, and *rhein*, to flow.] Suppression of the menses.

ȧ-men-or-rhē′ăl, ȧ-men-or-rhœ′ăl, *a.* Pertaining to amenorrhea.

am′ent, ȧ-men′tum, *n.* [L. *amentum*, a thong, or strap.] In botany, a species of inflorescence, consisting of many scales, massed about a stalk or slender axis, which is the common receptacle; a catkin; as in the birch, oak, and chestnut.

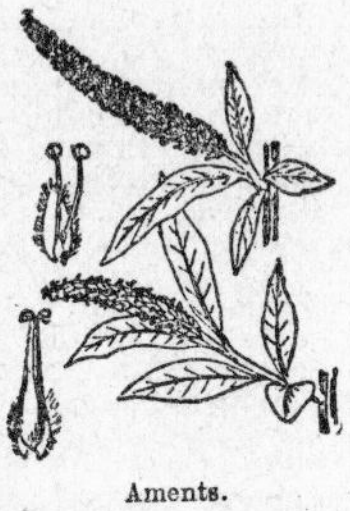

Aments.
Willow (*Salix fragilis*), male and female, with separate flowers.

ȧ-men′tȧ, *n.*; pl. of *amentum.*

Am-en-tā′cē-æ, *n. pl.* [LL., from *amentum*, strap.] In botany, a group of plants which bear flowers in aments; now separated into other orders, among which are the *Salicaceæ*, *Cupuliferæ*, etc.

am-en-tā′ceous, *a.* 1. Growing in an ament; resembling an ament; as, the chestnut has an *amentaceous* inflorescence.

2. Furnished with aments; having flowers arranged in aments; as, *amentaceous* plants.

ȧ-men′tăl, *a.* Relating to aments; having aments.

ȧ-men′tăl, *n.* A plant bearing aments.

ȧ-men′ti-ȧ (-shi-), *n.* [L., want of reason; *a*, away, from, and *mens, mentis*, mind.] Mental imbecility; lack of intelligence. Formerly sometimes written *amenty.*

am-en-tif′ẽr-ous, *a.* [L. *amentum*, a strap, and *ferre*, to bear.] Bearing aments or catkins.

ȧ-men′ti-fọrm, *a.* Resembling an ament in shape.

ȧ-men′tum, *n.*; *pl.* **ȧ-men′tȧ.** See *Ament.*

ȧ-men′ty, *n.* See *Amentia.*

am′ē-nụse, *v.t.* To diminish. [Obs.]

ȧ-mērce′, *v.t.*; amerced, *pt., pp.*; amercing, *ppr.* [ME. *amercen, amercien*; OFr. *amercier*, from *a merci*, at the mercy of, liable to punishment.]

1. To fine, mulct, or inflict an arbitrary penalty upon.

2. To impose a legal pecuniary punishment upon, the amount being left to the discretion of the court.

ȧ-mērce′ȧ-ble, *a.* Subject to amercement; justifying amercement.

ȧ-mērce′ment, *n.* A pecuniary assessment inflicted on an offender at the discretion of the court. It differs from a fine, in that the latter is, or was originally, a fixed and certain sum prescribed by statute for an offense; while an *amercement* is arbitrary.

Amercement royal; in English law, a penalty imposed on an officer for a misdemeanor in his office.

ȧ-mēr′cẽr, *n.* One who sets a fine at discretion upon an offender.

ȧ-mēr′ci-ȧ-ment (*or* -shȧ-), *n.* Same as *Amercement.*

A-mer′i-căn, *a.* 1. Pertaining to America, the western hemisphere, or either of the continents composing it. The name is derived from *Americus Vespuiius*, the Latinized form of Amerigo Vespucci, in whose honor it was named.

2. Relating to the United States: a specific use based on the preëminent activity and power of the United States in the western hemisphere.

American ivy; a favorite ornamental climbing vine of this country, *Ampelopsis quinquefolia*; called also the *American woodbine* and *Virginia creeper.*

American party; a political organization in existence from 1853 to 1856, whose object was to exclude foreign-born citizens from participating in government; called also the *Know-nothing* party, the members, after the first secret organization of the party, declaring they knew nothing about it.

American plan; a system of hotel charges, common in the United States, consisting of a fixed rate per day for food, lodging, and all ordinary services and conveniences; contrasted with the *European plan* of separate charges for each item.

American Protective Association; a secret society formed in Iowa, in 1887, for the purpose of keeping Roman Catholics out of public office, professedly to protect American institutions. Colloquially abbreviated to A. P. A.

American system; the original name for the protective tariff system of the United States.

Native American party; a short-lived political party, organized about 1843, whose object was somewhat similar to that of the American party.

A-mer′i-căn, *n.* 1. An aboriginal, or one of the various copper-colored natives found on the American continent by the Europeans; the original application of the name.

2. An American-born descendant of European settlers.

3. A native-born or naturalized citizen of the United States.

> The name *American* must always exalt the pride of patriotism. —Washington.

A-mer′i-căn-ism, *n.* 1. The doctrine of United States citizenship; patriotic attachment to the United States, its interests and institutions.

2. Any custom, trait, or idea peculiar to the United States or its people.

3. A word, phrase, or idiom original with the people of the United States, or any peculiar use of English by them.

4. The condition of being a citizen of the United States.

A-mer′i-căn-ist, *n.* A student of things American, more particularly in their relation to the aborigines.

A-mer″i-căn-i-zā′tion, *n.* The state of becoming American, or the process of making American.

A-mer′i-căn-īze, *v.t.* and *v.i.*; Americanized, *pt., pp.*; Americanizing, *ppr.* To impress with the American spirit and aspirations; to cause to become American or be like Americans; to stamp with the character of the American life.

A-mer″i-cō-mā′ni-ȧ, *n.* A craze for things American. [Rare.]

am-e-ris′tiç, *a.* [Gr. *a* priv., and *meristos*, divided, from *merizein*, to divide; *meros*, part.] In zoölogy, unsegmented, and in botany, wanting certain parts.

āmes′-āce (āmz′ās), *n.* See *Ambes-ace.*

am′ess, *n.* Same as *Amice.*

Am-ē-tab′ō-lȧ, Am″ē-tab-ō′li-ȧ, *n.pl.* [L., from Gr. *ametabolos*, unchangeable.] A subclass of insects, consisting of those which do not pass through regular metamorphosis.

ȧ-met-ȧ-bō′li-ăn, *a.* and *n.* I. *a.* Pertaining to the *Ametabola.*

II. *n.* One of the *Ametabola.*

ȧ-met-ȧ-bol′iç, *a.* Not subject to metamorphosis.

am-ē-tab′ō-lous, *a.* Ametabolic.

ȧ-meth′ō-dist, *n.* One lacking method; a quack. [Obs.]

am′ē-thyst, *n.* [L. *amethystus*; Gr. *amethystos*, resisting wine, the Greeks believing the stone and plant of that name to be preventives of intoxication; *a* priv., and *methystos*, drunken, from *methyein*, to be drunk; *methy*, strong drink.]

1. A variety of quartz, of a bluish-violet color or of different degrees of intensity. It is ranked among precious stones and is wrought into various articles of jewelry.

2. In heraldry, a purple color. It is the same in a nobleman's escutcheon as purpure in a gentleman's, and mercury in that of a sovereign prince.

3. A stone in the breastplate of the Jewish high priest.

Oriental amethyst; the violet-blue variety of transparent crystallized corundum.

am-ē-thys′tine, *a.* [Gr. *amethystinos*, pertaining to amethyst.]

1. Pertaining to or resembling amethyst, as distinguished from the Tyrian and hyacinthine purple.

2. Composed of amethyst; as, an *amethystine* cup.

am-ē-trom′e-tẽr, *n.* [Gr. *ametros*, irregular, and *metron*, measure.] An instrument used in ascertaining the qualities of refraction in the eye, and for determining and examining conditions of ametropia.

am-ē-trō′pi-ȧ, *n.* [L., from Gr. *ametros*, irregular, and *ops*, eye.] An abnormal condition of the refracting powers of the eye, producing poor sight.

am-e-trop′iç, *a.* Pertaining to or produced by ametropia.

am′gärn, *n.* [W., ferrule.] A stone implement probably used as the ferrule of a spear-shaft by the ancient inhabitants of Europe.

Am-har′iç, *a.* and *n.* I. *a.* Pertaining to Amhara, in Abyssinia, its people or their language.

II. *n.* The language in use at present by the upper classes in Abyssinia.

Am-hẽrs′ti-ȧ, *n.* [LL., named after the Countess of *Amherst.*] A genus of Burmese plants, with but a single species (*Amherstia nobilis*), bearing large vermilion flowers spotted with yellow. It is regarded as sacred to Buddha. The bloom is a large, pendulous raceme of extraordinary beauty.

Am′i-ȧ, *n.* [L., from Gr. *amia*, a kind of tunny.] A genus of fishes found in North American waters, and including the bowfin, *Amia calva*, or dogfish, etc.

ā″mi-ȧ-bil′i-ty, *n.* Amiableness; excellence of disposition.

ā′mi-ȧ-ble, *a.* [Fr. *aimable*, from L. *amicabilis*, friendly; *amicare*, to make friendly, from *amicus*, a friend.]

1. Friendly; amicable; kindly.

2. Tending to excite love or delight; lovely; pleasing. [Obs.]

> How *amiable* are thy tabernacles, O Lord. —Ps. lxxxiv. 1.

3. Possessing sweetness of temper, kind-heartedness, etc.; having an excellent disposition; lovable; as, an *amiable* girl; an *amiable* disposition.

4. Exhibiting love, or a show of love. [Obs.]

Syn.—Charming, lovable, kind, loving, obliging.

ā′mi-ȧ-ble-ness, *n.* The quality of deserving love; loveliness.

ā′mi-ȧ-bly, *adv.* In an amiable manner; sweetly; graciously; lovably.

am′i-anth, *n.* Same as *Amianthus.*

am-i-an′thi-fọrm, *a.* Having the form or likeness of amianthus; as, *amianthiform* arseniate of copper.

am-i-an′thoid, *n.* A variety of asbestos, composed of long capillary filaments, flexible, but coarser than the ordinary forms; the color is olive-green, or greenish-white.

am-i-an′thoid, *a.* Resembling asbestos in form.

am-i-an′thus, *n.* [L. *amiantus*, from Gr. *amiantos*; *a* priv., and *miainein*, to stain.] Earth-flax, or mountain-flax; a mineral substance belonging to the grade of hornblende known as asbestos. It is quite like flax in appearance, and in color is of a greenish white or gray; sometimes of a yellowish or silvery white, olive, mountain-green, pale flesh-red, or ocher. It has been wrought into cloth and paper, and is in familiar use in gas-grates and lamp-wicks and for fireproof coverings. Also *Amiantus.*

am′iç, *a.* Derived from ammonia; related to ammonia.

Amic acid; a nitrogenized acid of the nature of an amide.

am″i-cȧ-bil′i-ty, *n.* The quality of being kind; friendliness; conciliation.

am′i-cȧ-ble, *a.* [L. *amicabilis*, from *amicus*, a friend, from *amare*, to love.] Friendly; peaceable; characterized by good will; harmonious in social or mutual transactions; usually applied to the dispositions of men who have business with each other, or to their intercourse and transactions; as, nations or men have come to an *amicable* adjustment of their differences.

Amicable action; in law, an action entered in court by the amicable arrangement of both parties, for the purpose of getting judgment upon a point of law connected with it.

Amicable numbers; in mathematics, any two numbers, either of which is equal to the sum of all the aliquot parts of the other.

Syn.—Friendly, peaceable, fraternal.—*Amicable* always supposes two parties, as an *amicable* arrangement. We cannot say of a single individual that he was *amicable*, though we can say he was *friendly*. *Amicable* rather implies a negative sentiment, and *friendly* a positive feeling of regard, the absence of indifference.

am′i-cȧ-ble-ness, *n.* The quality of being peaceable, friendly, or disposed to peace; friendliness; amicability.

am′i-cȧ-bly, *adv.* In a friendly manner; with harmony or good will; as, the dispute was *amicably* adjusted.

am′ice, *n.* See *Almuce.*

am′ice, am′içt, *n.* [Fr. *amict*, from L. *amictus*, a cloak.] A square linen cloth worn as a collar by Roman Catholic priests, and also attached to a hood to symbolize the helmet of salvation. A similar piece of linen is worn by some priests of the Anglican church. It is usually embroidered with a cross, and worn with the upper edge fastened round the neck under the alb.

ȧ-mid′, *prep.* [ME. *amid, on midde, on midden*; AS. *on middan*; *on*, in, and *middan*, dat. of *midde*, middle. *Amid* is used chiefly in poetry, *amidst* being preferred in general use.]

1. In the midst or middle of; amidst.

2. Among; mingled with; as, *amid* the crowd.

3. Surrounded, encompassed, or enveloped by; as, *amid* the waves. [See *Amidst.*]

1. Amice round the neck. 2. Amice worn as a hood.

am′id-, am′i-dō-. [From *amide.*] Combining forms indicating that a chemical compound has had one atom of hydrogen replaced by amidogen; as, *amido*-benzene.

am′ide, am′ine, *n.* In chemistry, names given to a series of salts produced by the substitution of elements or radicals for the hydrogen atoms of ammonia; often used as terminations of the names of such salts. When these hydrogen atoms are replaced by acid radicals, the salts are called *amides*, as $NH_2C_2H_3O$ (acetamide); while if the replacing radicals are basic, the salts are termed *amines*, as NH_2K (potassamine) and $NH_2C_2H_5$ (ethylamine).

am′i-din, am′i-dine, *n.* [Fr. *amidine*, from *amidon*; L. *amylum*; Gr. *amylon*, neut. of *amylos*, not ground at the mill, the finest meal; *a* priv., and *mylos*, mill.] The soluble part of starch, yellow or white when hydrous.

am′i-dō-. See *Amid-*.

am″i-dō-ac′id, *n.* An acid in which the amido-group is substituted for a part of the non-acid hydrogen.

ȧ-mid′ō-gen, *n.* [*Amido-*, and Gr. *-genēs*, producing.] A supposed radical composed of two equivalents of hydrogen and one of nitrogen; so far it has not been obtained in a separate state, but may be traced in the compounds called amides and amines. Also called the *amido-group.*

am′i-dōl, *n.* A white crystalline substance obtained from phenol by replacing two atoms of hydrogen with two amido-groups, and used as a developer for bromide plates in photography.

am′i-dō-plast, am″i-dō-plas′tid, *n.* Same as *Leucoplast.*

ȧ-mid′ships, *adv.* In nautical language, in the middle part of a ship; midway between stem and stern; also, on the fore-and-aft line, or mid way as to breadth.

ȧ-midst′, *prep.* [AS. *on-middan*, in the middle; OE. *amidde, amiddes* (*es* being an adverbial genitive termination), and *t*, a later addition, as in *against.*] In the middle of; in the midst of; among; mingled with; surrounded by; amid; as, *amidst* the trees; *amidst* the enemy; *amidst* the clouds.

am′ine (*or* -in), *n.* See *Amide.*

am′i-oid, *a.* and *n.* I. *a.* Pertaining to or resembling the *Amioidei.*

II. *n.* One of the *Amioidei.*

Am-i-oi′dē-i, *n. pl.* [L., from Gr. *amia*, a kind of tunny, and *-oid.*] A family of ganoid fishes typified by the genus *Amia.*

ȧ-mir′, *n.* Same as *Ameer.*

ȧ-mir′ship, *n.* Same as *Ameership.*

Am′ish, *a.* Pertaining to, or designating, a sect of Mennonites, founded by Jacob Amman in the seventeenth century.

ȧ-miss′, *a.* and *adv.* I. *a.* Wrong; faulty; out of order; improper; used in the predicate; as, it may not be *amiss* to ask advice.

II. *adv.* In a faulty manner; contrary to propriety, truth, law, or morality; as, to ask *amiss.*

To take amiss; to be displeased or offended because of.

ȧ-miss′, *n.* A fault or mistake. [Obs.]

ȧ-mis-si-bil′i-ty, *n.* The quality of being amissible; liability to be lost. [Rare.]

ȧ-mis′si-ble, *a.* [LL. *amissibilis.*] Apt to be lost. [Rare.]

ȧ-mis′sion, *n.* [L. *amissio*, a losing.] Loss; privation. [Obs.]

ȧ-mit′, *v.t.* [L. *amittere*, to lose.] To lose. [Obs.]

am-i-tō′sis, *n.* Same as *Karyostenosis.*

am-i-tot′ic, *a.* Pertaining to amitosis; karyostenotic.

am′i-ty, *n.* [Fr. *amitié*, from a supposed L. *amicitas, amicus*, friendly; from *amare*, to love.] Friendship, in a general sense, between individuals, societies, or nations; harmony; good understanding; as, our nation is in *amity* with all the world; a treaty of *amity* and commerce.

Syn.—Friendship, attachment, esteem, good will, comity, harmony, peace.

am′mȧ, *n.* [L. *amma*; Gr. *amma*, mother in a convent; Syr. *ama*, mother, nurse; Anglo-Ind. *amah.*] An abbess or spiritual mother.

am′mȧ, *n.* [Gr. *hamma*, band, from *haptein*, to fasten, bind.] A girdle or truss used for ruptures.

am′măn, *n.* [G. *amtmann*; AS. *ambaht*, or *embeht*, office, duty, charge, and *man.*] In some of the German cantons of Switzerland, the chief executive, who also has judicial cognizance of civil causes.

Am′măn-ite, *n.* A member of a sect of Swiss Mennonites, who followed Jacob Amman, in the seventeenth century; one of the upland Mennonites.

am′me-lin, am′me-line, *n.* A white crystalline chemical compound, $C_3H_5N_5O$.

am′me-tẽr, *n.* An ampere-meter.

Am′mi, *n.* [L.] A genus of umbelliferous plants found around the Mediterranean; sometimes called *bishop's-weed.*

am′mi-răl, *n.* An admiral. [Obs.]

am′mīte, ham′mīte, *n.* [Gr. *ammitēs*, sandstone, from *ammos*, sand.] An old name for roestone or oölite.

am′mō-chryse (-kris), *n.* [Gr. *ammos*, sand, and *chrysos*, gold.] A yellow, soft stone, found in Germany, consisting of glossy yellow particles. When rubbed or ground fine, it was formerly used to strew over writing, as a blotter

am′mō-dȳte, *n.* A sand-eel; also, a European viper, commonly called the *sand-natter.*

Am-mō-dȳ′tēs, *n.* [Gr. *ammos*, sand, and *dytēs*, a diver, from *dyein*, to dive.] A genus of fishes (sand-eels) of the family *Ammodytidæ*, about a foot in length, with a compressed head, a long, slender body, and scales hardly perceptible. Two species are recognized by naturalists.

Am′mŏn, Am′ŏn, *n.* [L. *Ammon*; Gr. *Ammōn*; Heb. *'Āmōn*; Egypt. *Amūn, Amen*, He who is hidden.]

1. The sun-god of the Egyptians, who was considered by the Greeks to correspond to their god Zeus and the Roman Jupiter. The Greek and Roman conception of the Egyptian deity included a ram's horns, or ears, confounding the true Amen-Ra, always represented in human form, with the god of life, a lesser, ram-headed divinity of the Libyan oasis.

2. [a—] The argal, or *Ovis ammon*, more modernly named *Caprovis argali.* [See *Argal.*]

Ammon, from a bronze in British Museum.

am-mō′ni-ȧ, *n.* [Gr. *Ammoniakos*, pertaining to Ammon; L. *sal ammoniacum*, the salt from which it is manufactured. The name came from the district in Libya where *ammonia* was first produced by burning camels' dung at the temple of Jupiter Ammon.] An alkali, gaseous or aeriform in its uncombined state, and composed of three equivalents of hydrogen and one of nitrogen; called also *volatile alkali, aqua ammonia*, and *spirits of hartshorn.*

am-mō′ni-ac, am-mō-nī′ȧ-căl, *a.* Pertaining to ammonia, or possessing its properties.

Ammoniacal engine; an engine whose motive power is derived from the vapor of ammonia.

Sal ammoniac; chlorid of ammonium.

am-mō′ni-ac, *n.* The concrete juice of an umbelliferous tree, *Dorema ammoniacum*, brought from Persia in large masses, composed of tears, internally white, and externally yellow. It has a fetid smell, and a nauseous, sweet taste, followed by a bitter one. It is inflammable, soluble in water and spirit of wine, and is used in medicine as a deobstruent and resolvent; called also *gum ammoniac.*

Am-mō′ni-ăn, *a.* 1. Relating to Ammonius, surnamed Saccas, who flourished at the end of the second century, and was one of the founders of the eclectic system of philosophy.

2. Relating to Ammonius of Alexandria, a Christian philosopher of the third or fourth century, who divided the gospels into the *Ammonian* sections.

Am-mō′ni-ăn, *a.* Of or pertaining to the Egyptian deity Ammon, or to his temple and worship.

am-mō′ni-āte, *n.* Any organic substance used as a source of ammonia in the manufacture of fertilizers.

am-mō′ni-ā-ted, *a.* In chemistry, combined, saturated, or impregnated to any degree with ammonia.

am-mō′nic (*or* -mon′ic), *a.* Of or pertaining to ammonium or ammonia.

am-mō′ni-ō-. A combining form, denoting the presence of ammonium in a chemical compound.

am′mŏn-ite, *n.* [L. *cornu Ammonis*, horn of Ammon, from *Jupiter Ammon*, whose statues were represented with ram's horns.] The serpentstone, or *cornu Ammonis*, a fossil shell, curved into a spiral, like a ram's horn; of various sizes, from the smallest grains to three feet in diameter. This fossil is found in strata of limestone and clay, and in argillaceous iron-ore. It is smooth or ridged; the ridges being straight, crooked, or undulated.

am″mŏn-i-tif′ẽr-ous, *a.* [*Ammonite*, and *-ferous*, from L. *ferre*, to bear.] Containing the remains of ammonites.

Am-mon″i-toid′ē-ȧ, *n.pl.* A family of extinct mollusks of the class *Cephalopoda* (cuttlefishes).

am-mō′ni-um, *n.* A compound radical, consisting of four equivalents of hydrogen and one of nitrogen, and having the chemical relations of a basic element.

am-mō-ni′ū-ret, *n.* Same as *Ammoniate.*

Am-moph′i-lȧ, *n.* [L., f. of *ammophilus*; Gr. *ammos*, sand, and *philos*, loving.]

1. A genus of hymenopterous insects, popularly called sand-wasps.

2. A genus of grasses peculiar to the sandy coasts of North America and northern Europe.

am-moph′i-lous, *a.* Sand-loving; applied to the *Ammophila.*

am-mū-ni′tion (-nish′un), *n.* [Fr. *amunition*, from L. *munitio*, from *munire*, to fortify; the *a* is probably due to mistaking *l'amunition* for *la munition.*]

1. Military stores, or provisions for attack or defense. In modern usage, the signification is confined to the articles which are used in the discharge of firearms and ordnance of all kinds, as cartridges for rifles, carbines, shotguns, or pistols, and powder, balls, bombs, projectiles, shells, etc., for cannon and machine guns.

2. Any stock or supply of missiles, or resources that may be used for attack and repulse, considered either literally or figuratively; as, boys use snow for *ammunition*; the congressman has plenty of *ammunition* for his speech.

Ammunition bread, shoes, etc.; such as are supplied by government contractors for use by troops. [Eng.]

Ammunition shoes; safety-shoes for wear in a magazine of explosives.

Fixed ammunition; explosives and projectiles combined for use, as in bombs, cartridges, etc.

am-mū-ni′tion, *v.t.*; ammunitioned, *pt., pp.*; ammunitioning, *ppr.* To provide or equip with ammunition.

am-nē′si-ȧ (*or* -zi-ȧ), *n.* [L., from Gr. *a* priv., and *mnasthai*, to remember.] Loss of memory for certain kinds of words; a variety of aphasia.

am-nē′sic, *a.* Characterized by amnesia.

am-nes′tic, *a.* Producing amnesia.

am′nes-ty, *n.* [L. *amnestia*, from Gr. *amnēstia*, forgetfulness, *amnestos*, forgotten; *a* priv., and *mnasthai*, to remember.] An act of oblivion; a general pardon of the offenses of citizens or subjects against a government, or the proclamation of such pardon.

Syn. — Absolution, exoneration, pardon, acquittal, oblivion.

am′nes-ty, *v.t.*; amnestied, *pt., pp.*; amnestying, *ppr.* To grant pardon or amnesty to.

am′nic, *a.* Same as *Amniotic.*

am-nic′ō-list, *n.* [L. *amnis*, a river, and *colere*, to inhabit.] One who lives near a river. [Obs.]

am-nig′e-nous, *a.* [L. *amnigenus*, born in a river.] Born of or in a river. [Obs.]

am′ni-ŏn, *n.* [Gr. *amnion*, the membrane around the fetus, dim. of *amnus*, lamb.] The innermost membrane surrounding the fetus in mammals, birds, and reptiles.

False amnion; in anatomy, the outer layer of the amnion, which, in a state of maturity, disappears or unites with the chorion.

Am-ni-ō′tȧ, *n.pl.* The group of vertebrates having an amnion.

am-ni-ot′ic, *a.* Pertaining to the amnion; contained in the amnion; as, the *amniotic* fluid.

Amniotic acid; same as *Allantoin.*

ȧ-mœ′bȧ, *n.*; *pl.* **ȧ-mœ′bȧs** or **ȧ-mœ′bæ.** [LL., from Gr. *amoibē*, change, from *ameibein*, to change.]

1. A microörganism of the simplest structure, being a mere mass of protoplasm which absorbs its food at every point of its body by means of processes which are also locomotive, being protruded and withdrawn at will, so that it constantly changes its shape. Written also *ameba.*

2. [A—] A genus of microscopic *Protozoa*, of which *Amœba diffluens* is the type.

Amœba, or Fresh-water Proteus, showing some of the shapes which it assumes, and the vacuoles in its sarcodic substance.

am-œ-bæ′um, *n.* [L., neut. of *amœbæus*, from Gr. *amoibaios*, alternate; *amoibē*, change.] A poem in which persons are represented as speaking alternately, as the third and seventh eclogues of Virgil.

Am-œ-bē′ȧ, *n. pl.* In zoölogy, the division of the protozoans which includes the amœbas and similar organisms.

am-œ-bē′ăn, *a.* Of or pertaining to the *Amœbea*; written also *amebean.*

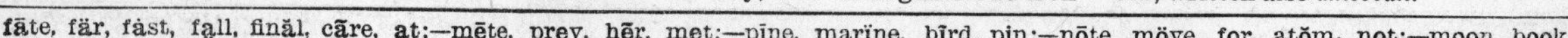

am-œ-bē′ăn, *a.* Alternately answering or responding. [See *Amœbæum.*]

ȧ-mœ′bi-ăn, *n.* A protozoan of the genus *Amœba.*

ȧ-mœ′bi-fọrm, ȧ-mœ′boid, *a.* Relating to or characteristic of an amœba; written also *amebiform, ameboid.*

Amœboid movements; the alternate prolongation and retraction of an amœba or other simple mass of protoplasm, as a colorless blood corpuscle.

ȧ-mœ′bō-cȳte, *n.* See *Leucocyte.*

ȧ-mœ′bous, *a.* Resembling an amœba in structure.

ȧ-mœ′bū-lȧ, *n.* A diminutive amœba.

ȧ-mœn-ō-mā′ni-ȧ, *n.* See *Amenomania.*

ä-mō′le, *n.* [Mex.] A name applied in Mexico and Spanish America to the cleansing roots of several plants; also, the century-plant, *Agave Americana*, or any other plant having cleansing and soap-like roots.

am-ō-li′tion (-lish′un), *n.* Removal. [Obs.]

A-mō′mum, *n.* [L., from Gr. *amōmon*, an Eastern plant.] A genus of aromatic plants of the ginger family, natives of warm climates, and remarkable for their pungency. It includes species yielding cardamoms and grains of paradise.

Am′ŏn, *n.* Same as *Ammon.*

ȧ-mon′este, *v.t.* To admonish. [Obs.]

ȧ-mŏng′, ȧ-mŏngst′, *prep.* [ME. *among, amang;* AS. *amang, onmang, gemang,* contr. for *ongemang; on,* in, and *gemang,* crowd, company.]

1. In a general or primitive sense, mixed or mingled with; surrounded by; as, tares *among* wheat.

2. Conjoined or associated with, or making part of the number of.

Blessed art thou *among* women.—Luke i. 28.

3. According to the customs of; in the time or country of; as, *among* the Romans; *amongst* civilized people.

4. In the power of, or by the action of, all jointly, or one or other of the number; as, I know you have the purse *among* you.

Syn.—Amid, amidst, between, betwixt.

ȧ-mon-til-lä′dō (-yä′dō), *n.* [Sp.] A dry sherry, light in color and of aromatic bouquet.

am-ō-rä′dō, *n.* [Sp. *enamorado;* L. *inamorare; in,* in, and *amare,* to love.] A lover. [Rare.]

Am-ō-rē′ănṣ, *n.pl.* A sect of Gemaric doctors or commentators on the Jerusalem Talmud. The *Amoreans* succeeded the Mishnic doctors, and were followed by the Sebureans.

am′ō-ret, am-ō-rette′, *n.* [OFr. *amorette, amourette;* It. *amoretta,* a little love, dim. of *amor.*]

1. A trifling love affair; a slight amour.
2. A lover; a person enamoured.
3. A love-knot.
4. A love-song or love-sonnet.

äm-ō-rī′nō, *n.; pl.* **äm-ō-rī′nī.** [It., dim. of *amore,* love, cupid.] A young cupid, such as is used in decorative art.

am′ō-rist, *n.* A lover; a gallant; an inamorato. [Rare.]

ȧ-mọrn′ings, *adv.* On or in the mornings. [Obs.]

am-ō-rō′sȧ, *n.* [It.] An amorous or wanton woman.

am-ō-ros′i-ty, *n.* The quality of being amorous; amorousness. [Rare.]

am-ō-rō′sō, *n.* [It.] A lover; a man enamoured.

am-ō-rō′sō, *adv.* [It.] In music, in a soft and amatory manner.

am′ō-rous, *a.* [ME. *amorous;* OFr. *amorous;* L. *amorosus,* full of love; *amor,* love.]

1. Inclined to love; having a propensity to love, or to sexual enjoyment; loving; fond.
2. In love; enamoured.
3. Pertaining to love; produced by love; indicating love; as, *amorous* delight; *amorous* airs.

Syn.—Loving, fond, affectionate.—These words are used to indicate the degree or excess of a tender sentiment. Those who have not a well-regulated affection for each other will be *loving* by fits and starts; children and animals who have no control over their appetites will be apt to be *fond* to those who indulge them. An *amorous* temper should be regulated; a *fond* temper should be checked. When taken generally, *loving* and *fond* may be used in an indifferent sense.

am′ō-rous-ly, *adv.* In an amorous manner; fondly; lovingly.

am′ō-rous-ness, *n.* The quality of being inclined to love, or to sexual pleasure; fondness; lovingness.

A-mọr′phȧ, *n.* [L., f. of *amorphus,* without form, irregular, from Gr. *amorphos.*] A genus of leguminous plants; bastard indigo.

ȧ-mọr′phiç, *a.* Same as *Amorphous.*

ȧ-mọr′phiṣm, *n.* 1. That state or property of matter in which it is without regular or definite shape; the state of being non-crystalline even in minute particles; opposed to *crystallization.*

2. Complete anarchy.

ȧ-mọr′phous, ȧ-mọr′phiç, *a.* [Gr. *amorphos,* from *amorphē; a* priv., and *morphē,* form.]

1. Having no determinate form; of irregular shape.
2. Having no regular structure; non-crystalline.
3. Formless; characterless; clumsy.

ȧ-mọr′phous-ly, *adv.* In an amorphous manner.

ȧ-mọr′phous-ness, *n.* The quality of being amorphous or without regular shape.

A-mọr-phō-zō′ȧ, *n. pl.* [L., from Gr. *amorphos,* without form, and *zōon,* animal.] A name for the *Protozoa.*

ȧ-mọr-phō-zō′iç, *a.* Relating to the *Amorphozoa.*

ȧ-mọr′phy, *n.* Irregularity of form; deviation from a determinate shape. [Rare.]

ȧ-mọrt′, *a.* [From Fr. *à la mort,* to the death, after the manner of death.] In the state of the dead; dejected; spiritless.

ȧ-mọr′tiṣe, ȧ-mọr-ti-ṣā′tion, ȧ-mọr′tiṣ-ȧ-ble, ȧ-mọr′tiṣe-ment. Same as *Amortize, etc.*

ȧ-mọr′tiz-ȧ-ble, *a.* [Fr. *amortissable.*] Capable of being settled or cleared off, as a debt.

ȧ-mọr-ti-zā′tion, ȧ-mọr′tize-ment, *n.* 1. The act or right of alienating lands or tenements to a corporation in mortmain.

2. The extinction of debt, especially by a sinking fund.

ȧ-mọr′tize, *v.t.;* amortized, *pt., pp.;* amortizing, *ppr.* [Sp. *amortizare;* LL. *admortizare;* OFr. *amortir,* to extinguish, to deaden; L. *ad,* to, and *mors,* death.]

1. In English law, to alienate in mortmain, that is, to sell to a corporation.
2. To kill; to destroy. [Obs.]
3. To apply to a debt for the purpose of extinction, as by a sinking-fund.

ȧ-mọr′tize-ment, *n.* 1. Same as *Amortization.*

2. In architecture, the crown or finial at the top of any member or part, whether in itself an ornament or not.

ȧ-mọr′we, *adv.* [ME.] In the morning, or on the following morning. [Obs.]

ȧ-mō′tion, *n.* [L. *amotio,* from *amovere; a, ab,* from, and *movere,* to move.]

1. Removal; especially, the ousting of a corporate officer.

2. In law, deprivation of possession. —Blackstone.

ȧ-mō′tus, *a.* [L., withdrawn, pp. of *amovere.*] Drawn up from its proper place; said of an animal's toe that is so short that it does not touch the ground.

ȧ-mount′, *v.i.;* amounted, *pt., pp.;* amounting, *ppr.* [ME. *amounten,* mount up to; OFr. *amounter,* from *amont, a mont;* L. *ad montem,* to a mountain, *ad,* to, and *montem,* acc. sing. of *mons,* mountain.]

1. To rise or reach, by an accumulation of particulars or items, to an aggregate whole; to compose in the whole; as, the interest on the several sums *amounts* to fifty dollars.

2. To rise, reach, or extend to, in effect or substance; to result in, by consequence, when all things are considered; as, the testimony of these witnesses *amounts* to very little.

3. To ascend; to go up. [Obs.]

ȧ-mount′, *v.t.* To imply; to amount to. [Obs.]

ȧ-mount′, *n.* 1. The sum total of two or more particular sums or quantities; as, the *amount* of 7 and 9 is 16.

2. The effect, substance, or result; the sum; the import; as, the *amount* of the testimony is this.

ȧ-mọur′, *n.* [Fr., from L. *amor,* love.] An unlawful connection in love; a love intrigue; an affair of gallantry.

ȧ-mọu-rette′, *n.* Same as *Amoret.*

ȧ-mōv-ȧ-bil′i-ty, *n.* Liability to removal from office. [Rare.]

ȧ-mōv′ȧ-ble, *a.* Removable.

ȧ-mōv′ăl, *n.* Total removal. [Obs.]

ȧ-mōve′, *v.t.* [L. *amovere; a, ab,* from, and *movere,* to move.]

1. To remove. [Obs.]
2. In law, to remove from a post or station.

ȧ-mōve′, *v.t.* To set in motion; to excite; to arouse from sleep. [Obs.]

äm-pä′rō, *n.* [Sp. and Port., defense, protection.] A preliminary certificate of title to land.

Am″pe-li-dā′cē-æ, *n.pl.* [LL., from Gr. *ampelis,* dim. of *ampelos,* vine.] In botany, a small order of polypetalous plants; the vine family; called also *Vitaceæ.*

am″pe-li-dā′ceous, *a.* Of, relating, or pertaining to the *Ampelidaceæ.*

am′pe-līte, *n.* [L. *ampelitis;* Gr. *ampelites,* from *ampelos,* vine.] An earth abounding in pyrites, used by the ancients to kill insects, etc., on vines; later, a kind of schist.

Am-pe-lop′sis, *n.* [Gr. *ampelos,* vine, and *opsis,* appearance.]

1. A genus of plants, natural order *Vitaceæ,* scarcely distinguishable from *Vitis,* except that the flowers have a ring round the base of the ovary. *Ampelopsis hederacea* is the Virginia creeper, a well-known climbing shrub.

2. [a—] A plant of this genus.

am-per′āġe, *n.* The strength of an electric current in amperes.

am-pēre′, *n.* [Named after André Marie *Ampère,* French electrician.] The standard unit of electric-current strength. It is the amount of current that would be produced by an electromotive force of one volt acting through a resistance of one ohm. The *ampere* was officially defined as the standard of measurement by the International Electrical Congress of 1893, and by United States statute of 1894.

am-pēre′=bal″ănce, *n.* A form of amperemeter.

am-pēre′=foot, *n.* An ampere running through one foot of the length of a conductor; a unit of electrical measurement.

am-pēre′=hour (-our), *n.* The quantity of electricity transferred by a current of one ampere in one hour.

am-pēre′=mē″tẽr, *n.* An instrument for measuring the strength of an electric current in amperes.

am-pēre′=tūrn, *n.* A unit of magnetomotive force equal to the force resulting from the effect of one ampere passing around a single turn of wire.

am-pe-rom′e-tẽr, *n.* An ampere-meter.

am′pẽr-sand, *n.* [A corruption of *and per se and; per se,* Latin, by itself. The last *and* is equivalent to the character &c or &, made by combining the letters of Latin *et,* and.] A term applied to the character &, and.

am-phi-, *prefix.* [Gr. *amphi,* on both sides.] A combining form meaning on both sides; round about; on all sides. [See *ambi-.*]

am″phi-är-thrō′di-ăl, *a.* Of or pertaining to amphiarthrosis.

am″phi-är-thrō′sis, *n.* [*Amphi-,* and Gr. *arthrōsis,* a jointing, from *arthron,* a joint.] In anatomy, a form of articulation in which the bones are connected by cartilaginous substance permitting slight motion, as the articulation of the vertebræ.

Am′phi-as-tẽr, *n.* [*Amphi-,* and Gr. *astēr,* a star.]

1. A genus of starfishes, including *Amphiaster insignis,* a beautiful species found in California waters.

2. [a—] In embryology, a stage of development in a maturing ovum in which the figure appears radiated at either end, like two stars conjoined.

Am-phib′i-ȧ, *n.pl.* [*Amphi-,* and Gr. *bios,* life.]

1. In zoölogy, a class of vertebrate animals whose young have gills and which are equally at home in the water and on land. They include (a) the frogs or *Anura;* (b) the tailed *Amphibia* (*Urodela*), as the salamanders and the sirens (*Sirenoidea*); and (c) the serpent *Amphibia* (*Ophiomorpha*), which have small scales and are limbless.

2. [a—] Amphibious animals in general.

am-phib′i-ăl, *a.* Amphibian. [Rare.]

am-phib′i-ăn, *a.* and *n.* I. *a.* Of or pertaining to the *Amphibia;* as, *amphibian* reptiles.

II. *n.* One of the *Amphibia.*

am-phib′i-ō-līte, *n.* [*Amphi-,* and Gr. *bios,* life, and *lithos,* stone.] A fossil of the *Amphibia.*

am-phib″i-ō-loġ′iç-ăl, *a.* Pertaining to amphibiology.

am-phib-i-ol′ō-ġy, *n.* [*Amphi-,* and Gr. *bios,* life, and *logos,* discourse.] A treatise on amphibious animals, or the history and description of such animals; the department of science which treats of them.

Am″phi-bi-ot′i-çȧ, *n.pl.* [*Amphi-,* and Gr. *bios,* life, and the term. *-ōtikos.*] An entomological division of insects embracing those with aquatic larvæ.

am-phib′i-ous, *a.* 1. Having the power of living in two elements, air and water, as frogs, crocodiles, beavers, and the like.

2. Of a mixed nature; partaking of two natures; as, an *amphibious* breed.

3. Suited to both land and water.

The Greeks were of an *amphibious* character. —Hare.

am-phib′i-ous-ly, *adv.* In an amphibious manner.

am-phib′i-ous-ness, *n.* The quality of being able to live in two elements, or of partaking of two natures.

am-phib′i-um, *n.; pl.* **am-phib′i-ȧ** or **am-phib′i-umṣ.** An amphibian.

am-phi-blas′tiç, *a.* [*Amphi-,* and Gr. *blastikos,* tending to sprout.] In embryology, segmenting unequally.

am-phi-blas′tū-lȧ, *n.* A blastula having its origin in an ovum in which the larger part of the yolk-material lies toward one pole.

am′phi-bōle, *n.* [Gr. *amphibolos,* doubtful, from *amphiballein; amphi,* around, and *ballein,* to throw.] A kind of mineral constituent of granitic rocks, including tremolite, asbestos, actinolite, and hornblende, of many colors and of varied composition, occurring in both massive and crystalline form, composed mainly of silica, magnesium, and calcium, often with aluminium and iron added. [See *Hornblende.*]

am-phi-bol′iç, *a.* Pertaining to amphibole; resembling amphibole, or partaking of its nature.

Amphibolic rocks; such as contain amphibole or hornblende as a leading constituent.

am-phib′ō-lite, *n.* Trap, or greenstone; a rock with a base of amphibole or hornblende.

am″phib-ō-loġ′iç-ăl, *a.* Doubtful; of doubtful meaning.

am″phib-ō-loġ′iç-ăl-ly, *adv.* With a doubtful meaning.

am-phi-bol′ō-ġy, *n.* [Gr. *amphibolos*, doubtful, and *logia*, from *legein*, to speak.]

1. The use of language of doubtful meaning arising from the construction; ambiguity.

2. In logic, a sentence, etc., capable of double meaning, owing to doubtful syntax or figure; as, "the Duke yet lives that Henry shall depose."

am-phib′ō-loid, *n.* and *a.* I. *n.* A rock composed of amphibole and feldspar, in which the amphibole predominates; a variety of greenstone.

II. *a.* Pertaining to or containing amphibole.

am-phib′ō-lous, *a.* [Gr. *amphibolos*, doubtful.] Doubtful in meaning; ambiguous; equivocal; applied, in logic, to a sentence susceptible of two meanings. [Rare.]

am-phib′ō-ly, *n.* 1. In logic, uncertain meaning of a proposition, owing to faulty syntax or ambiguous figure.

2. Employment of ambiguous language; quibbling.

am′phi-braçh, am-phib′rȧ-çhys, *n.* [Gr. *amphybrachys*; *amphi*, on both sides; and *brachys*, short.] In poetry, a foot of three syllables, a short, a long, and a short (⏑—⏑); as, ăc-cēntĕd.

Ăm-phib-rā- | *chys* hastes with | ă state-ly | stride. —Coleridge.

am-phi-cär′pous, am-phi-cär′piç, *a.* [*Amphi-*, and Gr. *karpos*, fruit.] Bearing two kinds of fruit, differing either in shape or in the time of maturing.

am-phi-çhī′răl, am-phi-cheī′răl, *a.* [*Amphi-*, and Gr. *cheir*, hand.] Literally, both-handed, or capable of being transferred from one hand, or side, to the other without changing form; undistinguishable as to the right and left sides.

am-phi-chrō′iç, *a.* [*Amphi-*, and Gr. *chroa*, color.] In chemical tests of color, having the power to bring out two different colors in the same substance, as red and blue in litmus paper.

am-phi-cœ′li-ăn, am-phi-cœ′lous, *a.* [Gr. *amphikoilos*, hollowed all round; *amphi-*, and *koilos*, hollow.] Hollowed out at both ends; doubly concave; said of the vertebræ of fishes.

am′phi-çōme, *n.* [Gr. *amphikomos*, with hair all around; *amphi-*, and *komē*, hair.] A kind of figured stone, of a round shape, but rugged, with eminences; used by the ancients in divination. [Obs.]

am″phi-çrē-at′i-nin, *n.* A leucomaine derived from muscle.

Am-phiç′ty-on, *n.* [Gr. *Amphictyones*, probably from *amphiktiones*; *amphi*, around, and *ktiones*, dwellers.] In Grecian history, a member of the Amphictyonic council.

Am-phiç-ty-on′iç, *a.* Pertaining to the august council of the Amphictyons.

Amphictyonic council; in ancient Grecian history, an assembly composed of delegates from all the confederated states, who met alternately at Thermopylæ and Delphi to discuss measures of interest to the states.

Am-phiç′ty-ō-ny, *n.* In Grecian history, a league of states; especially the confederation represented by the Amphictyonic council.

am′phid, *n.* A term applied to salts formed by combining an acid with a base, in contradistinction to *haloid* compounds. [Rare.]

am′phi-disk, *n.* [*Amphi-*, and Gr. *discos*, a round plate.] A spicule, peculiar to fresh-water sponges, with a finely-notched disk-like wheel at each end.

am-phi-drō′mi-ȧ, *n.pl.* [Gr. *amphidromia*, running around, from *amphidromos*, a running around.] A christening ceremony in Greece, in which the child was carried around the hearth before being named.

am-phi-drom′iç-ăl, *a.* Pertaining to the amphidromia.

am-phi-dū′rȧ, *n.* [A corruption of Gr. *amphithyra*, pl. of *amphithyron*; *amphi-*, and *thyron*, door.] In the Greek church, a veil or curtain opening to dwarf folding doors, and separating the chancel from the rest of the church. When the priest has passed the folding doors the curtain is drawn across, so that while officiating at the altar he is hidden from the congregation.

am-phig′ȧ-mous, *a.* [*Amphi-*, and Gr. *gamos*, marriage.] A term formerly applied to the cryptograms, or lowest class of plants.

am-phi-ġē′ăn, *a.* [*Amphi-*, and Gr. *gē*, *gaia*, earth.] Covering the earth; embracing every zone.

am′phi-ġen, *n.* [*Amphi-*, and Gr. *genēs*, producing.]

1. In chemistry, any element that may combine to form acids and basic compounds, as sulphur or oxygen.

2. In botany, any cryptogamous plant that grows by cellular accretion alone, as the lichens.

Amphidura, in Greek Church.

am′phi-ġēne, *n.* Same as *Leucite.*

am-phi-ġen′e-sis, *n.* [*Amphi-*, and Gr. *genesis*, generation.] Genesis through sexual coöperation.

am-phiġ′e-nous, *a.* In botany, growing and spreading in every lateral direction, as lichens.

am-phi-gon′iç, *a.* Relating to amphigony. [Rare.]

am-phig′ō-nous, *a.* Transmitting to progeny the characteristics of both parents. [Rare.]

am-phig′ō-ny, *n.* Sexual generation; propagation by the sexes.

am-phi-gor′iç, *a.* Relating to an amphigory; meaningless.

am′phi-gō-ry, *n.* [Fr. *amphigouri*, perhaps from Gr. *amphi*, about, and *gyros*, circle.] A nonsensical poem; a succession of words apparently coherent, but which really mean nothing.

am-phil′ō-ġism, am-phil′ō-ġy, *n.* [Gr. *amphilogia*, doubt; *amphi*, on both sides, and *logia*, from *legein*, to speak.] An ambiguous mode of speech; equivocation; amphibology.

am-phim′ȧ-cēr, *n.* [Gr. *amphimakros*, long on both sides; *amphi-*, and *makros*, long.] In ancient poetry, a foot of three syllables, the middle one short and the others long, as in *cāstĭtās.*

am-phi-mix′is, *n.* [LL., from Gr. *amphimixis*; *amphi-*, and *mixis*, mingling.] In biology, interchange of germ-plasm, as in the sexual connection of some of the *Infusoria.*

Am-phi-neū′rȧ, *n.pl.* [L., from Gr. *amphineuron*; *amphi*, around, and *neuron*, nerve.] One of the kingdom of vermes, members of which are distinguished by the symmetrical arrangement of the nerves along the sides of the body.

Am-phi-ox′us, *n.* [*Amphi-*, and Gr. *oxys*, sharp.] A genus of small lance-shaped translucent fish-like animals without bones, representing in structure a very low type of *Vertebrata*. *Amphioxus lanceolatus*, the lancelet, is the type.

am-phi-plat′y-ăn, *a.* [*Amphi-*, and Gr. *platys*, flat, broad.] Having both ends flat; said of vertebræ.

am′phip-neūst, *n.* [*Amphi-*, and Gr. *pnein*, to breathe.] One of a division of amphibians which have both air-breathing and water-breathing organs at the same time; as the siren.

am′phi-pod, *n.* and *a.* [*Amphi-*, and Gr. *pous*, *podos*, foot.]

I. *n.* An amphipodous animal.

II. *a.* Relating to the *Amphipoda.*

Am-phip′ō-dȧ, *n. pl.* An order of sessile-eyed crustaceans, having usually seven pairs of legs, with feet directed partly forward and partly backward. The sand-hopper and shore-jumper are examples.

Amphipod.
1. Shore-jumper (*Orchestia littoralis*). 2. Portion of Orchestia to show the respiratory organs *aaa*.

am-phip′ō-dăn, *a.* Same as *Amphipod.*

am-phip′ō-dous, *a.* Relating to the *Amphipoda*; amphipod; amphipodan.

am-phip′rō-stȳle, *n.* [Gr. *amphiprostylos*, having a double prostyle; *amphi-*, and *prostylos*, prostyle.] A double prostyle, or an edifice with columns in front and behind, but not on the sides.

Am-phi-rhī′nȧ, *n. pl.* [*Amphi-*, and Gr. *rhis*, *rhinos*, nose.] A division of fishes or fish-like animals having two nasal openings; opposed to *Monorhina.*

Am-phis-bæ′nȧ, *n.* [Gr. *amphisbaina*; *amphis*, *amphi*, at both ends, and *baina*, from *bainein*, to go.]

1. [a—] In mythology, a serpent having a head at each end and capable of moving either way.

2. A genus of snake-like lizards with similar ends, and hence seeming to have a head at each end; they possess the ability to move either way.

am-phis-bæ′noid, *a.* Resembling the lizards of the genus *Amphisbæna.*

am-phis′ci-ī (-fish′i-ī), **am-phis′ciăns** (-fish′ănz), *n. pl.* [L., from Gr. *amphiscios*, pl. *amphiscioi*, throwing a shadow both ways; *amphi*, and *skia*, shadow.] A term applied to the inhabitants of the tropics, because their shadows at noon in one part of the year are cast to the north, and in the other to the south, according as the sun is north or south of their zenith.

Am-phis′i-lē, *n.* A genus of acanthopterygious fishes in which the back is plated and the dorsal fin is placed quite at the extremity of the body, and produced into a long and strong spine.

Part of *Amphisile strigata.*

am-phis′tō-moid, am-phis′tō-mous, *a.* [*Amphi-*, and Gr. *stoma*, mouth, and *-oid.*] Pertaining to entozoa of the genus *Amphistomum.*

Am-phis′tō-mum, *n.* A genus of parasitic worms having a minute cup-shaped mouth or sucker at each end of the body, by which they adhere to the intestines of the animals in which they are parasitic.

am-phi-stȳ′liç, *a.* [*Amphi-*, and Gr. *stylos*, pillar.] A term applied to the skulls of certain sharks which have supports for both the upper and lower mandibular arches.

am-phi-thē′ȧ-tēr, am-phi-thē′ȧ-tre (-tēr), *n.* [Gr. *amphitheatron*, from *amphi*, about, and *theatron*, theater, from *theasthai*, to see or look.]

1. An ancient edifice, oval or circular, having a central arena encompassed with rows of seats, rising higher as they receded from the arena, on which people sat to view the combats of gladiators and wild beasts, and other sports.

Amphitheater at Verona.

The *amphitheater* at Rome, known as the Colosseum, the greatest architectural monument left by the Romans, seated about 90,000 people.

2. In gardening, a disposition of shrubs, trees, or turf in amphitheatrical form.

3. In a general sense, any arena or place where public contests are held.

am-phi-thē′ȧ-trăl, *a.* Same as *Amphitheatrical.*

am″phi-thē-at′riç, *a.* Same as *Amphitheatrical.*

am″phi-thē-at′riç-ăl, *a.* Relating to an amphitheater; as, an *amphitheatrical* structure; an *amphitheatrical* contest.

am″phi-thē-at′riç-ăl-ly, *adv.* In an amphitheatrical form or manner.

am-phit′ō-ky, *n.* [Gr. *amphitokia*; *amphi*, on both sides, and *tokia*, from *tiktein*, to produce.] Parthenogenetic propagation of sexual forms.

am-phit′rō-çhȧ, *n. pl.* [LL., from *amphi-*, and Gr. *trochos*, wheel.] A form of annelid larvæ having both a dorsal and a ventral ring of extra cilia.

am-phit′rō-păl, am-phit′rō-pous, *a.* [*Amphi-*, and Gr. *tropos*, from *trepein*, to turn.] In botany, applied to an ovule curved upon itself so that the ends are brought near to each other with the hilum in the middle.

Amphitropal Ovule.

Am-phi-ū′mȧ, *n.* [A corruption of Gr. *amphipneuma*; *amphi*, on both sides, and *pneuma*, breath.] A genus of amphibians, of which the Congo-snake is the type, having the form of a serpent but with permanent gill openings and four poorly developed limbs. They are found in southern United States.

am-phō-pep′tōne, *n.* [Gr. *amphō*, both, and *peptone.*] A compound of hemipeptone and antipeptone, produced by gastric digestion.

am-phoph′i-lous, *a.* [Gr. *amphō*, both, and *philein*, to love.] Capable of being stained by either acid or basic dyes.

am′phō-rȧ, *n.*; *pl.* **am′phō-ræ.** [L., from Gr. *amphoreus*, a jar with handles.] Among the Greeks and Romans, a two-handled vessel, used for holding wine, oil, etc. [See illus., p. 57.]

am′phō-răl, *a.* Pertaining to or resembling an amphora.

am-phor′iç, *a.* Having a hollow sound, as if produced by blowing across the mouth of a belly-shaped bottle; as, *amphoric* breathing.

am-phō-ter'iç, *a.* [Gr. *amphoteros*, both.] Partaking of the nature of both an acid and an alkali; neutral.

am'ple, *a.*; *comp.*, ampler; *superl.*, amplest. [Fr. *ample*; L. *amplus*, prob. from *am*, *ambi*, around, and *plus*, *plenus*, full.]

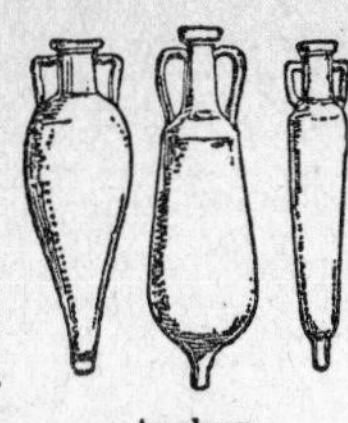
Amphoræ.

1. Large; wide; spacious; extended; great in bulk, size, or capacity; as, an *ample* house.

2. Liberal; unrestrained; without parsimony; fully sufficient; as, *ample* provision for the table; *ample* justice.

3. Diffusive; not brief or contracted; as, an *ample* narrative.

Syn.—Spacious, capacious, extensive, abundant, sufficient, plenteous, copious, plentiful.—When we mean by *ample* large in extent, we say *spacious* or *extensive*; large in size, *capacious*; large in quantity, *abundant* or *plenteous*. *Ample* is opposed to *scanty*, *spacious* to *narrow*, *capacious* to *small*. What is *ample* suffices and satisfies; it imposes no constraint.

am-pleç'tănt, *a.* [L. *amplectans*, ppr. of *amplecti*, to embrace.] Twining about; clasping hold of; as, an *amplectant* creeper.

am'ple-ness, *n.* Largeness; spaciousness; sufficiency; abundance.

am-plex-i-çau'dāte, *a.* [L. *amplexus*, pp. of *amplecti*, to embrace, and *cauda*, tail.] A term applied to certain bats in which the tail is united to the hind legs by a web.

am-plex'i-çaul, *a.* [L. *amplexus*, pp. of *amplecti*, to embrace, and *caulis*, stem.] In botany, nearly surrounding or embracing the stem, as the base of a leaf.

Amplexicaul Leaves (*Inula Helenium*).

am-plex-i-fō'li-āte, *a.* [L. *amplexus*, pp. of *amplecti*, to embrace, and *folium*, leaf.] Having stem-embracing leaves.

am'pli-āte, *a.* Having an enlarged outer edge, as the wings of some insects.

am'pli-āte, *v.t.* [L. *ampliatus*, pp. of *ampliare*, to enlarge.] To enlarge; to make greater; to extend. [Rare.]

am-pli-ā'tion, *n.* 1. Enlargement; amplification; diffuseness. [Rare.]

2. In old law, a delaying to pass sentence; a postponement of a decision, to obtain further evidence or hear additional argument.

am'pli-ā-tive, *a.* Enlarging; in logic, adding to the primary idea or attributes of a subject; synthetic.

am'pli-fi-çāte (*or* am-plif'i-çāte), *v.t.* To enlarge; to amplify. [Obs.]

am"pli-fi-çā'tion, *n.* [L. *amplificatio*, from *amplificare*, to make large.]

1. Enlargement; extension; the act of amplifying.

2. In rhetoric, diffusive description; exaggerated representation; copious argument, intended to present the subject in every view; a dilating upon all the particulars of a subject; a description given in more words than are necessary, or an illustration by various examples and proofs.

3. The additional matter which amplifies.

am'pli-fi-çā-tive (*or* am-plif'i-çā-tive), *a.* Serving or tending to amplify; ampliative.

am'pli-fi-ça-tō-ry (*or* am-plif'i-çā-tō-ry), *a.* Having a tendency to amplify.

am'pli-fi-ēr, *n.* 1. One who amplifies or enlarges; one who treats a subject diffusively.

2. A device in a radio receiving set which magnifies the waves or sounds.

am'pli-fȳ, *v.t.*; amplified, *pt.*, *pp.*; amplifying, *ppr.* [Fr. *amplifier*; L. *amplificare*, from *amplus*, large, and *facere*, to make.]

1. To enlarge; to augment; to increase or extend, in a general sense; applied chiefly to immaterial things.

2. In rhetoric, to enlarge in discussion or by representation; to treat copiously, so as to present the subject in every view, and in the strongest light.

3. To enlarge by addition; to improve or extend, as to *amplify* the sense of an author by a paraphrase.

am'pli-fȳ, *v.i.* 1. To speak largely or copiously; to be diffuse in argument or description; to dilate; often followed by *on* or *upon*; as, to *amplify on* the several topics of discourse.

2. To exaggerate; to enlarge by representation or description.

am'pli-tūde, *n.* [L. *amplitudo*, from *amplus*, large.]

1. Largeness; extent; applied to bodies; as, the *amplitude* of the earth.

2. Largeness; extent of capacity or intellectual powers; as, *amplitude* of mind.

3. Extent of means or power; abundance; sufficiency.

4. In astronomy, an arc of the horizon intercepted between the true east or west point and the center of the sun or a star at its rising or setting.

5. In gunnery, the horizontal line which measures the range of a projectile.

6. In mathematics, an angle upon which the value of one of the forms of elliptic functions is based.

Magnetic amplitude; the arc of the horizon between the sun or a star, at its rising or setting, and the east or west point of the horizon, by the compass. The difference between this and the true amplitude is the variation of the compass. [See 4, above.]

am'ply, *adv.* Largely; liberally; fully; sufficiently; copiously; in a diffusive manner.

am'pul, *n.* Same as *Ampulla*.

am-pul'là, *n.*; *pl.* **am-pul'læ**. [L.] 1. A narrow-necked globular vessel used among the Romans in anointing the body after bathing.

2. A vessel to contain the oil used in church ceremonials, particularly in the consecration of sovereigns.

3. A vessel for the wine of the eucharist.

4. In biology, any membranous sac shaped like a bottle, as the expanded part of the semiround canals of the ear.

5. A small membranous float attached to the leaves of some aquatic plants.

Pure gold Ampulla and Spoon used at Coronation of English Sovereigns.

am-pul-lā'ceous, *a.* Like an ampulla, bottle, or inflated bladder; swelling.

Ampullaceous sac; one of the ciliated chambers of sponges.

am'pul-lăr, **am'pul-lā-ry**, *a.* Like an ampulla.

am'pul-lāte, **am'pul-lā-ted**, *a.* Provided with an ampulla; bellied or bottle-shaped.

am-pul'li-fọrm, *a.* Shaped like an ampulla; flask-shaped.

am'pū-tāte, *v.t.*; amputated, *pt.*, *pp.*; amputating, *ppr.* [L. *amputatus*, pp. of *amputare*; *amb-*, about, and *putare*, to prune.]

1. To prune; to cut off, as branches of trees or vines.

2. To cut off, as a limb or other part of an animal body; a term used in surgery.

am-pū-tā'tion, *n.* [L. *amputatio*.] The act of amputating; especially, the surgical operation of cutting off a limb or other part of the body.

Spontaneous amputation; a cutting off by disease which unnaturally constricts the part; occurring in the disease known as ainhum, the toes being amputated by constriction.

am'pū-tā-tŏr, *n.* One who performs amputation.

am'pyx, *n.*; *pl.* **am'pyx-eṣ** or **am'py-çēṣ**. [Gr.]

1. Among the Greeks, a band or plate of metal, often enriched with precious stones, worn round the head by ladies of rank, and often having an ornament over the forehead.

2. The headband of a horse.

am-ri'tȧ, *n.* [Sans. *amrita*; *a* priv., and *mrita*, dead, from the root *mar*, to die.] In Hindu mythology, immortality; also, the nectar which produced it.

am'ṣel, *n.* Same as *Amzel*.

ȧmt, *n.*; *pl.* **ȧmt'ēr** or **ȧmts**. [Dan. and Norw. *amt*, a district.] A territorial administrative division of the Scandinavian countries, Norway being divided into eighteen administrative *amter*.

ȧ-muck', *adv.* [Malay *amoq*, engaging furiously in battle.] In the manner of a frenzied Malay. The word is used only in the phrase *to run amuck*.

To run amuck; to attack all persons within reach indiscriminately, while frenzied by insanity, liquor, or drugs, as the Malays do at times when under the influence of the native intoxicant.

am'ū-let, *n.* [Fr. *amulette*; Sp. *amuleto*; L. *amuletum*, a charm.] A charm; a preservative; something worn as a remedy or protection against evils or mischief. *Amulets* were common in earlier days. They consisted of stones, metals, or plants; sometimes of words, characters, or sentences, arranged in a particular order. They are still worn in many parts of the world.

Amulets, from Vatican (1) and private collection (2).

am-ū-let'iç, *a.* Pertaining to an amulet.

ȧ-mŭr'cous, *a.* Foul; full of dregs or lees. [Rare.]

ȧ-mūṣ'ȧ-ble, *a.* Able to be amused.

ȧ-mūṣe', *v.t.*; amused, *pt.*, *pp.*; amusing, *ppr.* [Fr. *amuser*; *a*, L. *ad*, to, and OFr. *muser*, to gaze at, stare fixedly.]

1. To entertain; to occupy or detain the attention of with agreeable objects; to divert; to please with comedy.

2. To delude; to engage the attention of by hope or expectation; as, to *amuse* one by flattering promises. [Rare.]

3. To occupy the attention of; to distract; to bewilder. [Obs.]

Syn.—Divert, entertain, beguile, enliven.—We *amuse* or *entertain* by engaging the attention on some occupation; we *divert* by drawing the attention from any object. Whatever *amuses* serves to lull the faculties and banish reflection; whatever *diverts* causes mirth and provokes laughter; it will be active, lively, and tumultuous; whatever *entertains* acts on the senses, and awakens the understanding.

ȧ-mūṣe', *v.i.* To muse; to ponder; to meditate. [Obs.]

ȧ-mūṣe'ment, *n.* 1. That which amuses, detains, or engages the mind; an entertainment or pastime; as a play, any sport, dancing, or music.

2. The act of amusing; diversion; recreation; the state of being amused.

Syn.—Diversion, pastime, recreation, sport, fun, merriment.

ȧ-mūṣ'ēr, *n.* One who amuses, or affords an agreeable entertainment to the mind.

am-ū-ṣette', *n.* [Fr., dim. of *amuse*, a toy, from *amuser*, to amuse.] A French term for a small field-gun.

ȧ-mū'si-ȧ, *n.* [L., from Gr. *amousos*; *a* priv. and *mousos*, song, music.] A condition characterized by inability to recognize musical sounds, or to play or sing them.

ȧ-mūṣ'ing, *a.* Entertaining; diverting; exciting mirth; pleasing.

ȧ-mūṣ'ing-ly, *adv.* In an amusing manner.

ȧ-mū'ṣive (*or* -siv), *a.* Having the power to amuse or entertain. [Rare.]

ȧ-mū'ṣive-ly, *adv.* In a manner to give amusement.

ȧ-mū'ṣive-ness, *n.* The quality of being amusing.

ȧ-my' (ȧ-mē'), *n.* [Fr. *ami*; L. *amicus*, friend.] Friend. [Obs.]

ȧ-myç'tiç, *a.* [Gr. *amyktikos*, lacerating, from *amyssein*, to tear.] Abrasive; irritating.

ȧ-mȳ-ē-lin'iç, *a.* Devoid of a medullary sheath; applied to nerve-fibers.

ȧ-mȳ'e-lous, *a.* [L., from Gr. *amyelos*; *a* priv., and *myelos*, marrow.] Without a spinal cord; applied to a fetus.

ȧ-myg'dȧ-lȧ, *n.*; *pl.* **ȧ-myg'dȧ-læ**. [L., from Gr. *amygdalē*, almond.] In anatomy, any almond-shaped organ or part, as a tonsil.

ȧ-myg-dȧ-lā'ceous, *a.* Derived from or allied to the almond.

ȧ-myg'dȧ-lāte, *a.* Made from almonds, or like almonds.

ȧ-myg'dȧ-lāte, *n.* 1. An emulsion made of almonds; milk of almonds. [Obs.]

2. A salt of amygdalic acid.

am-yg-dal'iç, *a.* Pertaining to or obtained from almonds; as, *amygdalic* acid, an acid obtained from bitter almonds.

ȧ-myg-dȧ-lif'ēr-ous, *a.* [L. *amygdala*, almond, and *-ferous*, L. *ferre*, to bear.] Bearing almonds; also yielding almond-shaped bodies or kernels.

ȧ-myg'dȧ-lin, **ȧ-myg'dȧ-line**, *n.* A crystalline substance existing in bitter almonds, the leaves of the common laurel, and many other plants.

ȧ-myg'dȧ-line, *a.* 1. Pertaining to or resembling almonds.

2. Relating to an almond-shaped part in anatomy, as a tonsil, or a lateral lobe of the brain.

ȧ-myg'dȧ-lō-. A combining form used in anatomy to express relation to an amygdala.

ȧ-myg'dȧ-loid, *n.* [Gr. *amygdalē*, almond, and *eidos*, form.] A variety of basaltic rock containing small cavities, occupied, wholly or in part, by nodules or geodes of different minerals, particularly agates, quartz, calcareous spar, and the zeolites. When the imbedded minerals are detached, it is porous, like lava.

ȧ-myg'dȧ-loid, **ȧ-myg-dȧ-loid'ăl**, *a.* 1. Pertaining to or consisting of amygdaloid.

2. Almond-shaped.

A-myg'dȧ-lus, *n.* A genus of rosaceous trees and shrubs, natives of Asia, especially known by the stone of the drupaceous fruit which incloses the kernel or seed being coarsely furrowed, and by the young leaves being folded in halves. *Amygdalus communis* is the almond-tree, *Amygdalus Persica* the peach and nectarine.

ȧ-myg'dūle, *n.* A nodule occurring in amygdaloid.

am'yl, **am'yle**, *n.* [L. *amylum*; Gr. *amylon*, starch, and *-yl*, Gr. *hylē*, matter.] A hypothetical radical (C_5H_{11}), said to exist in many compounds, as amylic alcohol, etc. This substance cannot exist in the free state, the molecules at the moment of its liberation combining to form the substance decane ($C_{10}H_{22}$).

Amyl acetate; a compound composed of acetic acid and amylic alcohol.

Amyl alcohol; an oily, colorless liquid, the chief principle of fusel-oil.

Amyl nitrate; an amber-colored fluid, smelling and tasting like essence of pears, used as a resuscitator in cases of drowning and prolonged fainting. It is generally inhaled by the nostrils, and it accelerates the action of the heart more than any known agent.

am-y-lā′ceous, *a.* Pertaining to starch, or the farinaceous part of grain; starchy; resembling starch.

am-yl-am′ine (*or* -ēn), *n.* An organic base produced by treating amyl cyanate with caustic potash. There are three *amylamines* known, which are regarded as ammonia in which one, two, and three hydrogen-atoms are respectively replaced by one, two, and three molecules of the radical amyl.

am′y-lāte, *n.* A compound made of starch and a base.

am′y-lēne, *n.* A hydrocarbon (C_5H_{10}) obtained by the dehydration of amylic alcohol by means of zinc chlorid, etc. It is a light, limpid, colorless liquid with a faint odor. At ordinary temperatures it speedily evaporates. It possesses anæsthetic properties, and has been tried as a substitute for chloroform, but unsuccessfully, as it has been proved to be extremely dangerous.

ȧ-myl′iç, *a.* Pertaining to amyl; derived from the radical amyl; as, *amylic* ether.

Amylic acid; a volatile acid obtained from starch.

Amylic alcohol; hydroxid of amyl; amyl alcohol.

Amylic fermentation; the process of fermentation in starch or sugar, which produces amylic alcohol.

am′y-lin, am′y-line, *n.* [L. *amylum*; Gr. *amylon*, neut. of *amylos*, unground; *a* priv., and *mylē*, mill.] The insoluble portion of starch which constitutes the covering of the sphericles; starch cellulose.

am′y-lō-. A combining form, from L. *amylum*, Gr. *amylon*, starch.

am″y-lō-bac′tēr, *n.* [*Amylo-*, and Gr. *bacterion*, a staff.] A bacillus present in putrefied vegetable tissue.

am″y-lō-dex′trin, *n.* [*Amylo-*, and *dextrin.*] A product obtained in changing starch into sugar.

ȧ-myl′ō-ġen, *n.* [*Amylo-*, and *-gen*, Gr. *genēs*, born.] Soluble starch.

am″y-lō-ġen′e-sis, *n.* The formation of starch.

am″y-lō-ġen′iç, *a.* Pertaining to amylogen.

am′y-loid, am-y-loid′ăl, *a.* [*Amylo-*, and *-oid*, Gr. *eidos*, form.] Resembling or being of the nature of amyl; starch-like.

Amyloid degeneration; in pathology, a change of structure by which the tissue or organ affected presents chemical characteristics of *amyloid* compounds or sometimes of albuminoid substances; called also *lardaceous* or *waxy degeneration.*

am′y-loid, *n.* 1. A semigelatinous substance, analogous to starch, met with in some seeds, which becomes yellow in water after having been colored blue by iodine.

2. The albuminoid substance deposited or developed in morbid animal tissues in *amyloid* degeneration.

3. A food of non-nitrogenous or starch-like nature; a gummy substance.

am-y-lol′y-sis, *n.* [*Amylo-*, and Gr. *lysis*, from *lyein*, to loose.] The process of converting starch into sugar.

am″y-lō-lyt′iç, *a.* Relating to amylolysis.

am-y-lom′e-tēr, *n.* [*Amylo-*, and Gr. *metron*, measure.] A device for ascertaining the quantity of starch in farinaceous substances.

am′y-lō-plast, *n.* [*Amylo-*, and Gr. *plastos*, verbal adj. of *plassein*, to form.] A starch-forming granule found within the protoplasm of vegetable cells; a leucoplast.

am″y-lō-plas′tid, am″y-lō-plas′tide, *n.* Same as *Amyloplast.*

am-y-lop′sin, *n.* [*Amylo-*, and Gr. *opsis*, appearance.] A ferment found in pancreatic juice and capable of converting starch into sugar.

am′y-lōse, *n.* One of the three groups into which the carbohydrates are divided, the others being glucose and saccharose.

am′y-lum, *n.* [Gr. *amylon.*] Starch.

Amylum body; an amyloplast.

Amylum center; a small portion of protoplasm about which starch is formed; a pyrenoid.

am″y-ō-sthē′ni-ȧ, *n.* [L., from Gr. *a* priv., *mys, myos*, muscle, and *sthenos*, strength.] Lack of muscular strength; imperfection or deficiency of muscular contraction.

am″y-ō-sthen′iç, *n.* A medicinal compound that diminishes muscular action.

am″y-ō-troph′iç, *a.* Pertaining to amyotrophy.

am-y-ot′rō-phy, *n.* [L., from Gr. *a* priv., and *mys, myos*, muscle, and *trophia*, from *trephein*, to nourish.] Atrophy of the muscles.

am′y-ous, *a.* [Gr. *amyos*; *a* priv., and *mys, myos*, muscle.] Lacking or deficient in muscle.

Am-y-rald′iṣm, *n.* In church history, the doctrine of universal grace, as taught by Amyraldus, or Amyrault, of France, in the seventeenth century.

Am-y-rald′ist, *n.* A believer in the doctrine of Amyraldism.

am′y-rin, *n.* A crystalline resin found in various gums, as Mexican gum elemi, etc.

Am′y-ris, *n.* A genus of tropical trees belonging to the myrrh family and yielding resinous products.

am′yss, *n.* Same as *Almuce.*

ȧ-myzt′li (-mist′), *n.* [Native name.] A large otary or eared seal found on the Pacific coast of North America.

am′zel, am′ṣel, *n.* [Dan. and G. *amsel.*] The blackbird of Europe; also, the ring-ouzel, *Turdus torquatus*, of Europe.

an, *indef. art.* and *a.* [AS. *ān*, pl. *ane*, an; declined as an adj; G. *ein*; Fr. *on, un, une*; L. *unus*, one.] One; noting an individual, either definitely, known, certain, specified, or understood; or indefinitely, not certain, known, or specified. Definitely; as, "Paul was *an* eminent apostle." Indefinitely; as, "Bring me *an* orange." Before a consonant the letter *n* is dropped; as, *a* man; although formerly retained; as, *an* man, *an* king. The letter *a* represents *an* definitely or indefinitely Definitely; as, "I will be to you *a* God." Ex. vi. Indefinitely; as, "The province of *a* judge is to decide controversies." Although *an*, *a*, and *one* are the same word, and always have the same sense, yet by custom, *an* and *a* are used exclusively as a definite adjective, and *one* is used in numbering. *An* and *a* are never used except with a noun, but like other adjectives, *one* is sometimes used without its noun, and as a substitute for it; as, "*one* is at a loss to assign a reason for such conduct." *An* is used before nouns of the singular number only, and before a vowel and silent *h*; as, *an hour.* It is also used by some writers (especially in England) before *h* when the accent of the word falls on any syllable except the first, as in *historian*, and *historiographer.* In such expressions as once *an* hour, twenty cents *an* ounce, etc., *an* has the meaning of each, every.

an, *conj.* An obsolete form used by old English authors to signify *if*; as, "*An* it please your honor." So in Greek *an* or *ean*, Latin *an*, if or whether; Irish *an.*

an-, a-, *prefix.* *An* is the fuller form of *a*, called *alpha privative*; *an* is used before vowels, and *a* before consonants, with a negative force, as in *an*omalous, *a*theist.

ā′nȧ, *adv.* [Gr. *ana*, with a distributive force.] In medical prescriptions, a term denoting an equal quantity of the several ingredients. It is often contracted to *āā* or *ā*, when the mark over the *a* indicates the omission of *n*; as, wine and honey, *ana, āā*, or *ā oz. ii*, that is, of wine and honey each two ounces.

ana-, *prefix.* [L. *ana-*; Gr. *ana-*, from Gr. prep. *ana*, up, upon, throughout.] Denoting up, upon, back, again, anew, throughout.

-a′nȧ, *suffix.* [Neut. pl. of L. *-anus*, a suffix used to form adjectives from proper names; as, *Cicero*, Ciceroni*anus*; the *i* being added for euphony.] In modern use it forms collective plurals; as, Johnson*iana*, Scaliger*ana*, the sayings, anecdotes, literary gossip, etc., of or pertaining to Johnson or Scaliger. It is also used as a substantive; as, the *ana* of the continent.

ā′nȧ, *n. pl.* Interesting or curious sketches, scraps, notes, etc., relating to a place, a personage, or notable subject; as, all the *ana* of Europe.

ȧ-nab′ȧ-mous, *a.* [Gr. *ana*, up, and *bainein*, to go.] Having ability to climb; applied by exaggeration to the climbing-fish of India, *Anabas scandens.*

an-ȧ-ban′tid, *n.* A fish belonging to the family *Anabantidæ.*

An-ȧ-ban′ti-dæ, An-ȧ-bat′i-dæ, *n. pl.* A family of fresh-water fishes, of which the genus *Anabas* is the type.

an-ȧ-ban′toid, *a.* and *n.* I. *a.* Of, or pertaining to, the *Anabantidæ.*

II. *n.* An anabantid.

An-ȧ-bap′tiṣm, *n.* [Gr. *anabaptismos.*] The doctrine of the Anabaptists.

An-ȧ-bap′tist, *n.* [LL. *anabaptista*, from Gr. *anabaptizein*; *ana*, again, and *baptizein*, to baptize.]

1. One who holds the doctrine of the baptism of adults alone, or of the invalidity of infant baptism, maintaining that those who have been baptized in infancy ought to be baptized again. With these sentiments is generally united the belief that baptism should always be by immersion.

2. In church history, one of a radical German sect whose zeal agitated Germany and the Netherlands during the Reformation.

an″ȧ-bap-tis′tiç, an″ȧ-bap-tis′tiç-ăl, *a.* Relating to the Anabaptists, or to their doctrines.

an″ȧ-bap-tis′tiç-ăl-ly, *adv.* In conformity with anabaptistic doctrine or practice.

An-ȧ-bap′tist-ry, *n.* Anabaptism.

an″ȧ-bap-tīze′, *v.t.* To rebaptize. [Obs.]

An′ȧ-bas, *n.* [LL., from Gr. *anabas*, second aor. p. of *anabainein*, to go up; *ana*, up, and *bainein*, to go.] A genus of fishes resembling the perches in form, but having their respiratory organs so constructed as to enable them to sustain life for a long time out of water. *Anabas scandens* is the climbing-fish of India.

Climbing Perch (*Anabas scandens*).

ȧ-nab′ȧ-sis, *n.*; *pl.* **ȧ-nab′ȧ-sēṣ.** [Gr. *anabasis*, from *anabainein*, to go up; *ana*, up, and *bainein*, to go.]

1. [A—] The name of a work in which Xenophon gives an account of the expedition of the younger Cyrus into central Asia, 401 B. C.

2. Any military expedition; as, the *anabasis* of Napoleon; the *anabasis* of Sherman.

3. The course of a disease from beginning to climax. [Obs.]

an-ȧ-basse′, *n.* [Fr.] A coarse blanketing manufactured in Holland and France, chiefly for the African trade.

an-ab′ȧ-tȧ, *n.* [LL.] A hooded cape, usually longer than the closed cape, and often worn in ecclesiastical processions.

An-ab′ȧ-tēṣ, *n.* [LL., from Gr. *anabatēs*, one who mounts, from *anabainein*, to mount, go up.] A genus of birds founded by Temminck, in 1820, upon the South American bird, *Anabates ruficaudus.*

an-ȧ-bat′iç, *a.* [Gr. *anabatikos.*] Relating to an anabasis; as, an *anabatic* rash. [Obs.]

An-ȧ-bat′i-dæ, *n. pl.* See *Anabantidæ.*

an″ȧ-bi-ō′sis, *n.* [LL., from Gr. *anabioein*, to come to life again.] Resuscitation. [Rare.]

an″ȧ-bi-ot′iç, *a.* Restoring animation; reviving.

An″ȧ-blē-pī′nȧ, *n. pl.* A division of carnivorous fishes, including the genus *Anableps*, and several other genera.

An′ȧ-bleps, *n.* [LL., from Gr. *anablepein*, to look up; *ana*, up, and *blepein*, to look.] A genus of malacopterygian fishes, remarkable for the structure of their eyes. These project and have two pupils, and each eye appears as if double, so that the fish apparently has four eyes; but there is only one crystalline humor, one vitreous humor, and one retina. The *Anableps tetraophthalmus* inhabits the rivers of Guiana.

Anableps tetraophthalmus.

an-ab′ō-lē, *n.* [Gr. *anabolē*, a throwing up, from *anaballein*; *ana*, up, and *ballein*, to throw.] In medicine, a throwing up, an ejection, as in vomiting.

an-ȧ-bol′iç, *a.* Constructively metabolic.

an-ab′ō-liṣm, *n.* [Gr. *anabolē*, a rising up, and *-ism.*] Constructive metabolism; assimilation.

an′ȧ-branch, *n.* A branch of a river which flows back into the main stream.

an-ȧ-brō′sis, *n.* [LL., from Gr. *anabrōsis*, an eating up, from *ana*, up, and *bibroskein*, to eat.] An ulceration of soft tissues; a wasting away of the body.

an-ȧ-brot′iç, *a.* Corrosive.

An-ab′rus, *n.* [LL., from Gr. *an* priv., and *abros*, pretty, graceful.] A genus of orthopterous insects belonging to the family *Locustidæ.*

ä″nä-çä-huï′te (-hwē′), *n.* [Mex.] A boraginaceous shrub, *Cordia Boissieri*, of Mexico, the wood of which was formerly reputed to be a remedy for consumption and to have been the source of Aztec papyrus.

an″ȧ-çȧ-lyp′sis, *n.*; *pl.* **an″ȧ-çȧ-lyp′sēs.** [L., from Gr. *anakalypsis*, an uncovering.] Revelation; an unveiling.

an-ȧ-çamp′tiç, *a.* [Gr. *anakamptein*, to bend back.] Reflecting or reflected; a word formerly applied to that part of optics which treats of reflection; *catoptric* is now used.

Anacamptic sounds; among the Greeks, sounds produced by reflection, as in echoes; or such as proceeded downward from acute to grave.

an-ȧ-çamp′tiç-ăl-ly, *adv.* By reflection; as, echoes are sounds produced *anacamptically.*

an-ȧ-çamp′tiçs, *n.* 1. The doctrine of reflected light. [See *Catoptrics.*]

2. The doctrine of reflected sounds.

an′ȧ-çanth, *n.* One of the *Anacanthini.*

An-ȧ-çan′thī, *n.pl.* Same as *Anacanthini.*

An-ȧ-çan′thi-nī, *n.pl.* [LL., from Gr. *an* priv., and *akanthinos*, thorny, from *akantha*, thorn.] A group of fishes of the order *Teleostia*, characterized by the absence of spines in the rays of the fins.

an-ȧ-çan′thous, *a.* Having no spines; said of certain fishes; also, pertaining to the *Anacanthini.*

an′ȧ-çärd, *n.* [Fr. *anacarde*; L. *anacardium*, from Gr. *ana*, according to, resembling, and *kardia*, heart.]

1. The cashew-nut.

2. Any plant of the genus *Anacardiaceæ.*

An″ă-ça̤r″di-ā′çē-æ, *n.pl.* A large and widely distributed order of polypetalous trees or shrubs, natives of tropical America, Africa, and India. There are 450 species, among which the most widely known are the poisonous sumac, the cashew, the pistachio, the mango, and the varnish-tree.

an″ă-ça̤r″di-ā′ceous, *a.* Belonging to, or resembling, the *Anacardiaceæ.*

an-ȧ-ça̤r′diç, *a.* Pertaining to the cashew-nut, or its shell.

Anacardic acid; a strong, burning acid obtained from the cashew-nut. It is crystalline and white.

An-ȧ-ça̤r′di-um, *n* A genus of shrubs of the American tropics, including the cashew.

an″ȧ-çȧ-thär′sis, *n.* [LL., from Gr. *anakatharsis,* a clearing away; *ana,* up, away, and *kathairein,* to cleanse.] Purgation upward; also, a cough accompanied by expectoration.

an″ȧ-çȧ-thär′tiç, *a.* [LL., from Gr. *anakathartikos,* from *anakathairein,* to cleanse upward, vomit.] Cleansing by exciting discharges from the mouth and nostrils.

an″ȧ-çȧ-thär′tiç, *n.* A medicine which excites discharges through the mouth or nose, as expectorants, emetics, sternutatories, and masticatories.

an-ȧ-ceph″ȧ-læ-ō′sis, *n.* [L., from Gr. *anakephalaiosis,* from *anakephalaioein,* to sum up, bring under heads; *ana,* up, and *kephalē,* head.] In rhetoric, a recapitulation of the heads of a discourse. [Rare.]

An-ach′ȧ-ris, *n.* [LL., from Gr. *ana,* up, and *charis,* grace.] A genus of plants of the frogbit family, *Hydrocharidaceæ,* natives of North America; water-thyme or water-weeds.

an-ach′ō-ret, *n.* See *Anchoret.*

an-ach-ō-ret′iç-ăl, *a.* [Obs.] See *Anchoretic.*

an-ach′ō-rişm, *n.* [Gr. *ana,* up, against, and *chōros,* place.]

1. Opinion, or sentiment, foreign to the spirit of reasonable citizenship.

2. Something unsuited to the locality or country.

3. Error regarding place. [Rare.]

an-ȧ-çhron′iç, an-ȧ-çhron′iç-ăl, *a.* Containing an anachronism; anachronous.

an-ach′rō-nişm, *n.* [Gr. *anachronismos,* from *anachronizein,* to refer to a wrong time; *ana,* against, and *chronos,* time.] An error in computing time; any error which implies the misplacing of persons or events in time, as where Shakspere makes Hector quote Aristotle, who lived several hundred years after the assumed date of Hector.

an-ach′rō-nist, *n.* One who commits an anachronism.

an-ach-rō-nis′tiç, *a.* Erroneous in date; characterized by or involving anachronism.

an-ach′rō-nize, *v.t.* To commit an anachronism. [Rare.]

an-ach′rō-nous, *a.* Anachronistic.

an-ach′ō-nous-ly, *adv.* Erroneously as to time or date.

an-ȧ-çlas′tiç, *a.* [Gr. *anaklastos,* reflected, from *anaklān; ana,* back, and *klān,* to bend.] Refracting light; also, springing or bending back with sound.

Anaclastic glass; a sonorous phial with a thin, flexible, convex bottom. When the air is partially exhausted from the vessel, the bottom emits a sharp sound, which is repeated when the pressure becomes normal.

an-ȧ-çlas′tiçs, *n.* That part of optics which treats of the refraction of light; commonly called *dioptrics.*

an-ȧ-çli′năl, *a.* [Gr. *ana,* back, and *klinein,* to bend.] Sloping contrary to the dip; as, an *anaclinal* valley.

an″ȧ-cœ-nō′sis, *n.* [L., from Gr. *anakoinōsis,* from *anakoinoun,* to make common.] A figure of rhetoric by which a speaker asks an opinion of the point in debate by appeal to either his opponents or the audience.

an″ȧ-çō-lū′thi-ȧ, *n.* [Gr. *anakolouthia,* inconsequence.] In grammar, lack of sequence or coherence; abrupt change from one construction, leaving it incomplete, to another; used legitimately in rhetoric with strong emotional effect.

an″ȧ-çō-lū′thiç, *a.* Wanting in sequence; pertaining to anacoluthia.

an″ȧ-çō-lū′thiç-ăl-ly, *adv.* In a manner lacking sequence.

an″ȧ-çō-lū′thon, *n.; pl.* **an″ȧ-çō-lū′thȧ.** [Gr. *anakolouthos,* wanting sequence, not following; *an* priv., and *akolouthos,* following.] Want of grammatical sequence in a sentence; anacoluthia.

an-ȧ-çon′dȧ, *n.* [Probably of Ceylonese origin.] The popular name of two of the largest species of the serpent tribe; (a) a Ceylonese species, *Python tigris,* and (b) *Eunectes murinus,* a native of tropical America allied to the boa constrictor.

Ȧ-naç-rē-on′tiç, *a.* and *n.* I. *a.* Pertaining to Anacreon, a Greek poet, whose odes and epigrams are celebrated for their delicate, easy, and graceful air, and for their exact imitation of nature. They were devoted to the praise of love and wine. Hence, *Anacreontic* sometimes signifies amatory, convivial.

II. *n.* [a—] A poem composed in the manner of Anacreon.

an-ȧ-çrot′iç, *a.* Pertaining to or displaying anacrotism.

ȧ-naç′rō-tişm, *n.* [Gr. *ana,* up, again, and *krotos,* a beating, clapping.] A secondary wave in the ascending curve of the tracing made by any wave-recording instrument, as a seismograph.

an-ȧ-çrū′sis, *n.* [Gr. *anakrousis,* from *anakrouein,* to strike back; *ana,* up, back, and *krouein,* to strike.] An unemphasized syllable introducing a verse properly beginning with an accented syllable.

an-ȧ-çrus′tiç, *a.* Pertaining to an anacrusis.

an-ȧ-çū′sis, *n.* [Gr. *anakousis,* from *an* priv., and *akouein,* to hear.] In pathology, deafness resulting from nervous lesion.

an′ȧ-dem, *n.* [L. *anadema;* Gr. *anadēma,* from *ana,* up, and *dein,* to find.] A garland or fillet; a chaplet or crown of flowers.

an″ȧ-di-plō′sis, *n.* [L., from Gr. *anadiplōsis,* from *anadiploun,* to double; *ana,* up, again, and *diploos,* double.] Grammatical duplication; the repetition of the last or any important word or words in a line or clause of a sentence, in the beginning of the next; as. "He retained his virtues amidst all his misfortunes —misfortunes which no prudence could foresee or prevent."

an′ȧ-drom, *n.* [Gr. *anadromos,* a running; *ana,* up, and *dromos,* from *dramein,* to run.] A marine fish that ascends rivers to spawn.

ȧ-nad′rō-mous, *a.* A term in biology for ascending; going up; applied to sea-fish spawning in rivers, or to ferns branched secondarily above the pinnæ.

ȧ-næ′mi-ȧ, *n.* See *Anemia.*

ȧ-næ′miç, *a.* See *Anemic.*

an-æ-ret′iç, an-ē-ret′iç, *n.* and *a.* [Gr. *anairetikos,* taking away, destructive, from *anairetēs,* a destroyer.]

I. *n.* In medicine, anything that destroys or tends to destroy animal tissue.

II. *a.* Destructive of animal tissue.

an-ā′e-rōbe, *n.* One of the anaerobia.

an-ā-e-rō′bi-ȧ, *n.pl.* [LL., from Gr. *an* priv., *aēr, aeros,* air, and *bios,* life.] Microscopic organisms having the power of living without free oxygen.

an-ā-e-rō′bi-ăn, *a.* Pertaining to, or of the nature of, the anaerobia.

an-ā-e-rob′iç, *a.* Of the nature of the anaerobia.

an-ā′e-rō-bieş (-biz), *n.pl.* Same as *Anaerobia.*

an-ā″e-rō-bi-ot′iç, an-ā-e-rō′bi-ous, *a.* Capable of living in the absence of air or free oxygen; applied to microörganisms.

an-ā′e-rō-phȳte, *n.* [Gr. *an* priv., *aēr, aeros,* air, and *phyton,* a plant.] In botany, a plant which does not require a direct supply of air.

an-æs-thē′si-ȧ, an-es-thē′si-ȧ, *n.* [Gr. *anaisthēsia,* from *an* priv., and *aisthēsis,* feeling, from *aisthanein,* to feel, perceive.] A condition of total or partial insensibility, especially to touch, produced commonly by anæsthetics, though sometimes due to disease.

an-æs-thē′sis, *n.* Same as *Anæsthesia.*

an-æs-thet′iç, an-es-thet′iç, *a.* Pertaining to, characterized by, or producing, anæsthesia.

an-æs-thet′iç, an-es-thet′iç, *n.* A substance producing anæsthesia, as chloroform, etc.

an-æs″thē-ti-zā′tion, an-es″thē-ti-zā′tion, *n.* The act or process of producing anæsthesia; the state of the nervous system when under the influence of anæsthetics.

an-æs′thē-tize, an-es′thē-tize, *v.t.;* anæsthetized, *pt., pp.;* anæsthetizing, *ppr.* To cause anæsthetization in.

An-ȧ-gal′lis, *n.* [LL., from Gr. *ana,* again, and *agallein,* to adorn.] A genus of plants belonging to the order *Primulaceæ,* the pimpernels.

an′ȧ-glyph, *n.* [Gr. *anaglyphon,* embossed work, from *ana,* up, and *glyphein,* to cut out, engrave.] An ornament in relief chased or embossed in precious metal or stone, as a cameo.

an-ȧ-glyph′iç, an-ȧ-glyph′iç-ăl, *a.* Of or relating to the art of anaglyphy.

ȧ-nag′ly-phy, *n.* 1. The art of sculpturing in low relief.

2. The work thus executed.

an-ȧ-glyp′tiç, *a.* [L. *anaglypticus;* Gr. *anaglyptikos,* from *ana,* up, and *glyptos,* wrought in relief.] Wrought in low relief.

an-ȧ-glyp′tiç, *n.* Anything wrought in low relief.

an-ȧ-glyp′tiçs, *n.* The art of anaglyphy.

an-ȧ-glyp′tō-gräph, *n.* 1. A device for producing drawings or etchings on a plane surface, having the appearance of relief-work.

2. An engraving made by this machine.

an-ȧ-glyp-tō-gräph′iç, *a.* Pertaining to anaglyptography.

an″ȧ-glyp-tog′rȧ-phy, *n.* The art or process of producing anaglyptographic drawings or etchings.

an-ag-nor′i-sis, an-ag-nō′sis, *n.* [Gr. *anagnōrisis,* from *ana* and *gnōrizein,* to recognize.] Recognition; the unraveling or dénouement of a dramatic plot. [Rare.]

an-ȧ-gō′ġē, *n.* [Gr. *anagōgē,* a leading up; *ana,* up, and *agein,* to lead, drive.]

1. A heavenly or elevated state of the mind.

2. Spiritual meaning or application, especially of the Scriptures.

3. In medicine, vomiting.

an″ȧ-gō-ġet′iç-ăl, *a.* Mysterious; spiritual.

an-ȧ-goġ′iç, an-ȧ-goġ′iç-ăl, *a.* Mysterious; elevated; spiritual; allusive.

an-ȧ-goġ′iç-ăl-ly, *adv.* Mysteriously; with religious exaltation.

an-ȧ-goġ′içs, *n.* The study of hidden or mystical allusions, particularly of the Scriptures.

an′ȧ-gō-ġy, *n.* Same as *Anagoge.*

an′ȧ-gram, *n.* [Fr. *anagramme;* LL. *anagramma,* from Gr. *ana,* back, and *gramma,* from *graphein,* to write.] In its proper sense, the letters of one or several words read backward, and then forming a new word; thus, *evil* is an *anagram* of *live.* In a wider and more usual sense, a transposition of the letters of a word or sentence, to form a new word or sentence; thus, *Galenus* is an *anagram* of *angelus.*

an′ȧ-gram, *v.t.* Same as *Anagrammatize.* [Rare.]

an″ȧ-gram-mat′iç, an″ȧ-gram-mat′iç-ăl, *a.* Making an anagram; relating to an anagram.

an″ȧ-gram-mat′iç-ăl-ly, *adv.* In the manner of an anagram.

an-ȧ-gram′mȧ-tişm, *n.* The act or practice of making anagrams.

an-ȧ-gram′mȧ-tist, *n.* A maker of anagrams.

an-ȧ-gram′mȧ-tize, *v.t.* and *v.i.;* anagrammatized, *pt., pp.;* anagrammatizing, *ppr.* I. *v.t.* To transpose, as the letters of an anagram are transposed.

II. *v.i.* To make an anagram or anagrams.

an′ȧ-gräph, *n.* An inventory; a commentary. [Obs.]

ȧ-nä′guȧ (-gwȧ), **ȧ-nä′quȧ** (-kwȧ), *n.* [Sp. Am.] A Texan name for *Ehretia elliptica,* a small tree of the borage family, with hard, close-grained wood.

An′ȧ-kim, Ā′naks, *n.pl.* [Heb.] The sons of Anak, giants of Scripture.

ā′năl, *a.* [LL. *analis,* pertaining to the anus.] Pertaining to the anus; situated near the anus.

ā′năl, *n.* An anal fin.

ȧ-nal′cīte, ȧ-nal′cim, ȧ-nal′cime, *n.* [Gr. *analkis,* without strength.] A white or flesh-red mineral, of the zeolite family, occurring in twenty-four-sided (trapezoidal) crystals, and in cubes. It is common in amygdaloid and lavas. By friction, it acquires a weak electricity; hence its name.

an′ȧ-leçt, *n.; pl.* **an-ȧ-leç′tȧ** or **an′ȧ-leçts.** [Gr. *analecta,* from *analegein,* to collect; *ana,* and *legein,* to gather.] A literary fragment; an extract.

an-ȧ-leç′tiç, *a.* Collecting or selecting; made up of selections; as, an *analectic* magazine.

an-ȧ-lem′mȧ, *n.* [L. *analemma,* a sundial which showed the latitude and meridian of a place; Gr. *analēmma,* a sundial, support, from *analambanein,* to take up.]

1. In geometry, a projection of the sphere on the plane of the meridian, orthographically made by straight lines, circles, and ellipses, the eye being supposed at an infinite distance, and in the east or west point of the horizon.

2. An instrument of wood or brass, on which such projection is drawn, with a horizon or cursor fitted to it; formerly used by astronomers.

3. A scale drawn across the torrid zone on a terrestrial globe, by which the declination of the sun may be ascertained for every day of the year.

4. In surgery, support for a fractured limb [Obs.]

an-ȧ-lep′sis, an-ȧ-lep′si-ȧ, *n.* [Gr. *analēpsis,* restoration.]

1. The nutrition of an emaciated body; recovery of strength.

2. Epilepsy caused by gastric derangement.

an′ȧ-lep-sy, *n.* Same as *Analepsis.*

an-ȧ-lep′tiç, *a.* Restorative; invigorating.

an-ȧ-lep′tiç, *n.* A medicine which gives strength; a restorative.

an-al-ġē′si-ȧ, *n.* [LL., from Gr. *analgēsia; an* priv., and *algēsia,* from *algēsis,* pain.] The incapacity to feel pain.

an-al-ġet′iç, an-al-ġē′siç, *n.* A medicine that allays pain.

an-al-ġet′iç, *a.* Allaying pain.

an″al-lag-mat′iç, *a.* [Gr. *an* priv., and *allagma,* a change, from *allassein,* to change.] In mathematics, remaining unchanged by inversion.

Anallagmatic curves and *surfaces;* quartic curves and surfaces having nodes on the absolute; such curves are sometimes called bicircular quartics.

an″al-lan-tō′iç, *a.* In anatomy or zoölogy, without an allantois.

An″al-lan-toid′ē-ȧ, *n.pl.* In zoölogy, the division

of vertebrates having no allantois, including amphibians, fishes, and lower forms.

ȧ-nal'ō-găl, *a.* Analogous. [Obs.]

an-ȧ-log'iç-ăl, an-ȧ-log'iç, *a.* [L. *analogicus*; Gr. *analogikos*, proportionate, analogous.] Having analogy; founded on analogy.

an-ȧ-log'iç-ăl-ly, *adv.* In an analogical manner; deducibly from some agreement or relation.

an-ȧ-log'iç-ăl-ness, *n.* The quality of being analogical; fitness to be applied as the illustration of some analogy.

ȧ-nal'ō-ġism, *n.* [Gr *analogismos*, consideration; reasoning; from *analogizesthai*, to calculate, reckon, consider.]

1. An argument from cause to effect.

2. Investigation of things by the analogy they bear to each other.

ȧ-nal'ō-ġist, *n.* One who adheres to analogy.

ȧ-nal'ō-ġize, *v.t.*; analogized, *pt., pp.*, analogizing, *ppr.* To demonstrate by analogy.

ȧ-nal'ō-ġize, *v.i.* To use analogy; to be analogous.

ȧ-nal'ō-gon, *n.* [Gr.] Analogue.

ȧ-nal'ō-gous, *a.* [L. *analogus*; Gr. *analogos*, according to a due ratio, or proportion.] Having analogy; bearing some resemblance or proportion; followed by *to*; as, there is something in the exercise of the mind *analogous to* that of the body.

Analogous pole; in electricity, that pole of a pyroelectric crystal or other body which becomes positively electrified when subjected to heat.

ȧ-nal'ō-gous-ly, *adv.* In an analogous manner.

ȧ-nal'ō-gous-ness, *n.* The quality of being analogous.

an'ȧ-logue, *n.* [Fr. *analogue*, from L. *analogus*, from Gr. *analogos*, analogous.]

1. In the broadest sense, a thing similar to another thing; that which corresponds with something else in construction, function, qualities, etc.

2. In philology, a word corresponding to one in another language.

3. An animal or plant having a representative or counterpart in another group, species, etc., corresponding in some essential part or function. The essential element of an *analogue* is a similarity in some respect between two things dissimilar as a whole.

ȧ-nal'ō-ġy, *n.* [Gr. *analogia*, proportion, equality of ratios; from *analogos*, analogous.]

1. An agreement or likeness between things in some circumstances or effects, when the things are otherwise entirely different; as, learning *enlightens* the mind, because it is to the mind what *light* is to the eye, enabling it to discover things before hidden; a plant has some *analogy to* or *with* an animal.

2. In grammar, conformity of words to the genius, structure, or general rules of a language.

3. In biology, a likeness in function; physiological resemblance; as, the *analogy* between the legs of a crab and those of a quadruped.

4. In mathematics, an equation between ratios; as, Napier's *analogies*.

5. In logic, resemblance of any kind in one or more respects on which an argument falling short of induction may be based.

Syn.—Resemblance, agreement, likeness, similarity, similitude, conformity, relation.

an-al'phȧ-bet, an-al'phȧ-bēte, *n.* One not knowing the alphabet; an ignorant person.

an-al-phȧ-bet'iç, *a.* Having no knowledge of the alphabet; illiterate.

an'ȧ-lyse, *v.t.* See *Analyze.*

ȧ-nal'y-sis, *n.*; *pl.* **ȧ-nal'y-sēs.** [Gr. *analysis*, dissolving, a resolution of a whole into parts; *ana*, up, back, and *lysis*, a loosing, from *lyein*, to loose.]

1. Separation into constituent parts or elements; a resolving.

2. A consideration of anything in its separate parts, as the words which compose a sentence or the various propositions which enter into an argument; opposed to *synthesis*.

3. In mathematics, the resolving of problems by reducing them to equations. The *analysis* of finite quantities is algebra; the *analysis* of infinites is the method of fluxions, or the calculus.

4. In chemistry, the process of decomposing a compound substance with a view to determine either what elements it contains (*qualitative analysis*), or how much of each element is present (*quantitative analysis*).

5. In logic, the tracing of things to their source; the resolving of knowledge into its original principles.

6. The regressive method of philosophical and scientific investigation; induction.

7. A syllabus, or table of the principal heads of a continued discourse, disposed in their natural order.

8. A brief, methodical illustration of the principles of a science. In this sense it is nearly synonymous with *synopsis*.

Syn.—Abridgment, digest, dissection.

an'ȧ-lyst, *n.* One who analyzes, or is versed in analysis.

an-ȧ-lyt'iç, an-ȧ-lyt'iç-ăl, *a.* [Gr. *analytikos*, analytic, from *analytos*, dissoluble, from *analyein*, to loosen, dissolve.] Pertaining to analysis; resolving into first principles; separating into parts or original principles; resolving a compound body or subject; as, *analytic* chemistry, an *analytical* investigation. It is opposed to *synthetic*.

Analytic language; a language in which modifications of the meanings of words are not expressed by inflections, but rather by particles, auxiliaries, etc.

an-ȧ-lyt'iç-ăl-ly, *adv.* In the manner of analysis; by way of separating a body into its constituent parts, or a subject into its principles.

an-ȧ-lyt'iċs, *n.* The science of analysis.

an'ȧ-ly̆-zȧ-ble, *a.* Capable of being analyzed.

an'ȧ-ly̆-zȧ-ble-ness, *n.* The state of being analyzable.

an-ȧ-ly-zā'tion, *n.* Analysis.

an'ȧ-lȳze, *v.t.*; analyzed, *pt., pp.*; analyzing, *ppr.* To resolve into constituent elements; to separate (a compound subject) into its parts or propositions, for the purpose of an examination of each separately; as, to *analyze* a fossil substance; to *analyze* an action to ascertain its morality. Sometimes written *analyse*.

an'ȧ-lȳ-zēr, *n.* 1. One who analyzes; that which analyzes or has the power to analyze.

2. In optics, that part of a polariscope which exhibits the properties of polarized light.

An-ȧ-mēse', *a.* and *n.* I. *a.* Relating to Anam, in southeastern Asia.

II. *n.* An inhabitant of Anam; the language of Anam, akin to Chinese.

An-ȧ-mir'tȧ, *n.* [LL., probably from native name.] A genus of climbing shrubs, native to the East Indies; *Anamirta cocculus* yields cocculus indicus, and is the sole species.

an-am-nē'sis, *n.* [Gr. *anamnēsis*, a calling to mind, from *anamimnēskein*; *ana*, again, and *mimnēskein*, to call to mind.]

1. A figure in rhetoric which calls to remembrance something omitted.

2. In medicine, the history of a case previous to the physician's diagnosis.

an-am-nes'tiç, *a.* and *n.* I. *a.* Aiding the memory.

II. *n.* The art of recollection or reminiscence; mnemonics. [Rare.]

an-am-ni-ot'iç, *a.* [Gr. *an* priv., and *amnion*, amnion, and *-ic*.] In anatomy, having no amnion, as fishes and amphibians.

an-ȧ-mor'phism, *n.* 1. A distorted image of any object.

2. In biology, a gradual change from one type to another, generally from lower to higher.

an-ȧ-mor'phō-sċōpe, *n.* [Gr. *anamorphōsis*; *ana*, again, *morphē*, form, and *skopos*, a watcher, from *skopein*, to see.] A vertical cylindrical mirror, which destroys anamorphosis and gives a correct representation of the object mirrored.

an-ȧ-mor'phō-sis (*or* -mor-phō'-), *n.* [Gr. *anamorphōsis*, a forming anew, from *ana*, again, and *morphoun*, to form.]

1. In perspective, a deformed or distorted portrait or figure which, in one point of view, is confused or unintelligible, and in another is an exact and regular representation; or which is confused to the naked eye, but, reflected from a plain or curved mirror, appears regular and in right proportion.

2. In biology, a gradual change of form to a higher type.

Anamorphosis.

an-ȧ-mor'phō-sy, *n.* Same as *Anamorphosis*.

ȧ-nan', *interj.* Eh? what? what is it? [Obs.]

ȧ-nä'nas, *n.* [Sp., from native American name.]

1. The pineapple.

2. A wild kind of pineapple, *Bromelia Pinguin*, of the West Indies.

An-an-chy̆'tēs, *n.* [Etym. uncertain.] A genus or subdivision of fossil sea-urchins belonging to the tribe *Spatangidæ*, called in the south of England shepherds' crowns and fairy loaves, and especially characteristic of the Upper Chalk. They have a raised helmet-like form, simple ambulacra, transverse mouth, and oblong outlet.

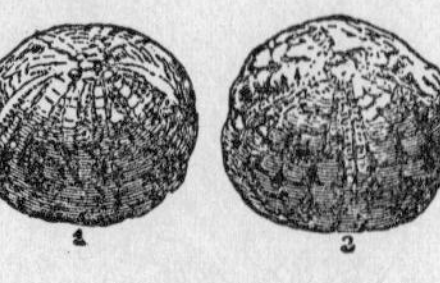

Ananchytes.
1. *A. ovatus*. 2. *A. tuberculatus.*

an-an'drous, *a.* [Gr. *an* priv., and *anēr*, *andros*, man.] Without stamens; said of female flowers.

an-an'gū-lăr, *a.* Without angles. [Rare.]

an-an'thēr-ous, *a.* Without anthers.

an-an'thēr-um, *n.* A staminodium.

an-an'thous, *a.* [Gr. *ananthēs*; *an* priv., and *anthos*, flower.] Flowerless.

an'ȧ-pæst, *n.*; **an-ȧ-pæs'tiç,** *a.* See *Anapest, Anapestic.*

an"ȧ-pei-rat'iç, *a.* [Gr. *anapeirasthai*, to try again.] Caused by the too frequent or continuous use of the same muscles; applied to affections like writer's or telegrapher's cramp.

an'ȧ-pest, an'ȧ-pæst, *n.* [L. *anapæstus*; Gr. *anapaistos*, an anapest; from *ana*, back, and *paiein*, to strike.]

1. In poetry, a foot consisting of three syllables, the first two short, the last long; as, the word *in-tēr-vēne'*.

2. A verse composed of or characterized by such feet. Example:

Can a bo | som so gen | tle remain
Unmoved | when her Cor | ydon sighs?
—Shenstone.

an-ȧ-pes'tiç, an-ȧ-pæs'tiç, *n.* The anapestic measure.

an-ȧ-pes'tiç, an-ȧ-pes'tiç-ăl, *a.* Pertaining to an anapest; consisting of anapestic feet.

ȧ-naph'ō-rȧ, *n.*; *pl.* **ȧ-naph'ō-ræ.** [Gr. *anaphora*, from *anapherein*, to carry up or back.]

1. A figure in rhetoric in which the same word or words are repeated at the beginning of succeeding verses or clauses; as, "*Where* is the wise? *Where* is the scribe? *Where* is the disputer of this world?"

2. The most solemn part of the eucharistic service.

3. In astronomy, the oblique ascension of a star.

an-aph-rō-dis'i-ȧ, *n.* [Gr. *anaphrodisia*, from *anaphroditos*; *an* priv., and *Aphroditē*, Venus.] Lack of sexual desire; impotence.

an-aph-rō-dis'i-ac, ant"aph-rō-dis'i-ac, *a* and *n.* I. *a.* Tending to cool or quench sexual desire.

II. *n.* A drug or treatment tending to produce anaphrodisia.

an-aph-rō-dit'iç, *a.* [Gr. *anaphroditos*, without love.] In biology, produced without sexual coöperation.

an'ȧ-plast, *n.* In botany, a leucoplast.

an-ȧ-plas'tiç, *a.* Pertaining to or used in anaplasty; as, an *anaplastic* operation.

an-ȧ-plas'tiç, *n.* A medicine that increases the plastic force.

an'ȧ-plas-ty, *n.* [Gr. *anaplastos*, verbal adj. of *anaplassein*; *ana*, again, and *plassein*, to mold.] Plastic surgery; the restoration of injured or deformed parts by the use of healthy tissue from other parts.

an"ȧ-plē-rō'sis, *n.* [LL., from Gr. *anaplērōsis*, from *anaplēroun*, to fill up.] A filling up of tissue to replace lost substance, as in the healing of wounds.

an"ȧ-plē-rot'iç, *a.* and *n.* I. *a.* Filling up; promoting anaplerosis.

II. *n.* A medicine which produces anaplerosis.

ȧ-nap'nō-grȧph, *n.* [Gr. *anapnoē*, respiration, and *graphein*, to write.] An automatic apparatus that measures and registers the lung capacity, that is, the greatest volume of air the lungs can expel after the deepest inspiration.

an-ap-nō'iç, *a.* Pertaining to respiration.

an-ap-nom'e-tēr, *n.* A spirometer.

an-ap-ō-diç'tiç, an-ap-ō-deiç'tiç, *a.* [Gr. *anapodeiktos*; *an* priv., and *apodeiktos*, demonstrable.] Not demonstrable.

an-ȧ-poph'y-sis, *n.*; *pl.* **an-ȧ-poph'y-sēs.** [Gr. *ana*, back, *apophysis*, offshoot.] An auxiliary process found on some lumbar vertebræ, as in the hare and most rodents.

an-ap-tot'iç, *a* [Gr. *ana*, again, and *aptotikos*, indeclinable.] Losing or having lost the use of inflections; applied to languages undergoing phonetic decay.

an-ap'ty-chus, *n.*; *pl.* **an-ap'ti-chi.** [Gr. *anaptychos*; *ana*, back, and *ptyssein*, to fold.] A shelly, heart-shaped plate found in some fossil cephalopods.

ȧ-nä'quȧ, *n.* See *Anagua.*

an'ärch, *n.* [Gr. *anarchos*, without head or chief.] An anarchist; an advocate and promoter of revolt.

ȧ-när'chăl, *a.* Anarchic. [Rare.]

ȧ-när'chiç, ȧ-när'chiç-ăl, *a.* Pertaining to anarchy or anarchism; tending toward anarchy; in a condition of lawless confusion; as, *anarchic* ideas; *anarchical* turbulence.

an'ärch-ism, *n.* 1. The theory that formal government of any kind is unnecessary and wrong in principle; the doctrine and practice of anarchists.

2. Anarchy; confusion; lawlessness.

an'ärch-ist, *n.* 1. An advocate of anarchism as a social and political theory.

2. One who advocates the use of violence to overthrow government and established social

institutions; one who excites revolt, or promotes disorder in a state.

an-ärçh-is'tiç, *a.* Pertaining to anarchism; favoring or promoting anarchy.

an'ärçh-ize, *v.t.*; anarchized, *pt.*, *pp.*; anarchizing, *ppr.* To put in a state of anarchy.

an'ärçh-y, *n.* [Gr. *anarchia*, lack of ruler or government, from *anarchos*, without chief or ruler; *an* priv., and *archos*, ruler.]

1. A social theory, advocated especially by Pierre Joseph Proudhon (1809-1865), that holds formal government to be unnecessary for the maintenance of order and therefore unjustifiable, regarding individual liberty as the only just rule of society.

2. Want of government; a state of society in which there is no law or supreme power; general confusion; lawless disorder; a disorganized state of affairs; chaos; as, a state of *anarchy* prevails.

Syn.—Lawlessness, disorder, tumult, rebellion, riot, insubordination.

An-är'rhi-çhas, *n.* [Gr. *anarrhichāsthai*, to clamber up.] A genus of ravenous fishes, including the sea-wolf or wolf-fish, *Anarrhichas lupus*, found in the northern seas.

An-är-throp'ō-dȧ, *n. pl.* [LL., from Gr. *an* priv., *arthron*, joint, and *pous*, *podos*, foot.] A division of the *Articulata*, having no jointed legs.

an-är-throp'ō-dous, *a.* Relating to or resembling the *Anarthropoda*.

an-är'throus, *a.* [Gr. *anarthros*, without joints, without the article; *an* priv., and *arthron*, joint, article.]

1. In grammar, without the article; applied to a few Greek nouns in certain rare uses.

2. In zoölogy, having neither wings nor legs, as worms, leeches, etc.

A'nas, *n.* [L. *anas*, a duck.] A genus of swimming birds comprising an indefinite number of species of fresh-water ducks.

an-ȧ-sär'çȧ, *n.* [L., from Gr. *ana*, up, and *sarka*, acc. of *sarx*, flesh.] An accumulation of serous fluid in the cellular tissue; cellular dropsy.

an-ȧ-sär'çous, *a.* Pertaining to or characteristic of anasarca; dropsical.

an-ȧ-seis'miç, *a.* [Gr. *anaseisma*, a shaking up and down, from *ana*, up, and *seiein*, to shake.] Heaving; applied to an earthquake.

an-ȧ-stal'tiç, *a.* [Gr. *anastaltikos*, fitted for checking, from *anastellein*, to check, send back.] In medicine, astringent; styptic. [Obs.]

an'ȧ-stāte, *n.* [Gr. *ana*, up, and *histanai*, to cause to stand.] In biology, a substance formed in the anabolic processes; opposite of *catastate*.

an-ȧ-stat'iç, *a.* Raised; embossed; in relief; also, having raised characters.

Anastatic engraving; a process of transferring an ink design to a metal plate, the uninked portions of which are then etched away by the action of acid, leaving the letters or design raised from the surface.

Anastatic printing; the process of printing from anastatic plates.

An-ȧ-stat'i-çȧ, *n.* A genus of cruciferous plants, native to the Orient, of which the resurrection plant, or rose of Jericho, is the only species. It is remarkable for the property the dried plant possesses of absorbing water when placed in it and appearing to live.

Rose of Jericho (*Anastatica hierochuntina*).
1. The plant. 2. The root dried. 3. The root expanded after being put in water.

an-as"tig-mat', *n.* A combination of lenses used in photography to overcome distortion of the image and to obtain a flat field; an anastigmatic lens.

an-as"tig-mat'iç, *a.* Not astigmatic; corrected for astigmatism, as a lens.

ȧ-nas'tō-mōse, *v.i.*; anastomosed, *pt.*, *pp.*; anastomosing, *ppr.* [Gr. *ana*, throughout, and *stoma*, mouth.] To communicate with each other; to have common canals; to connect by anastomosis.

ȧ-nas-to-mō'sis, *n.*; *pl.* **a-nas-tō-mō'sēs.** [LL., from Gr. *anastomōsis*, opening, from *ana*, again, and *stoma*, mouth.] The intercommunication or inosculation of vessels; the opening of one vessel into another; applied in anatomy to the connection between vessels containing fluids, as blood and lymph; and in botany to the cross-veining of leaves.

ȧ-nas-tō-mot'iç, *a.* Pertaining to anastomosis.

ȧ-nas'trō-phē, *n.* [Gr. *anastrophē*, a turning or inversion, from *anastrephein*; *ana*, back, and *strephein*, to turn.] In rhetoric and grammar, an inversion of the natural order of words; as, *back he came*, for *he came back*.

an'ȧ-tāse, *n.* [Gr. *anatasis*, extension, from *ana*, back, and *teinein*, to stretch.] Octahedrite.

ȧ-nath'ē-mȧ, *n.*; *pl.* **ȧ-nath'ē-mȧṣ** or **ȧ-nath-ē-mȧ'tȧ.** [L., from Gr. *anathema*, anything devoted to evil, a curse; *anathēma*, a votive offering set up in a temple, from *anatithenai*, to set up.]

1. A ban or curse pronounced against an offender; a malediction or imprecation; especially, the solemn ban of excommunication pronounced in the Roman Catholic church against great offenders.

2. A person or thing considered as accursed or forbidden.

Abjuratory anathema; in church history, an anathema pronounced by a proselyte against the faith or church he was leaving for another.

Anathema maranatha; an expression the significance of which is taken to be an intensified form of *anathema*.

Syn.—Curse, ban, denunciation, imprecation.

ȧ-nath-ē-mat'iç, ȧ-nath-ē-mat'iç-ăl, *a.* Pertaining to or resembling an anathema.

ȧ-nath-ē-mat'iç-ăl-ly, *adv.* In the manner of an anathema.

ȧ-nath'ē-mȧ-tiṣm, *n.* The uttering of anathemas; denunciation. [Rare.]

ȧ-nath"ē-mȧ-ti-zā'tion, *n.* The act of anathematizing.

ȧ-nath'ē-mȧ-tīze, *v.t.*; anathematized, *pt.*, *pp.*; anathematizing, *ppr.* [LL. *anathematizare*; Gr. *anathematizein*, to make accursed, from *anathema*, a curse.] To curse; to make a formal denunciation of; to pronounce anathemas against.

ȧ-nath'ē-mȧ-tī-zēr, *n.* One who pronounces an anathema.

ȧ-nat'i-fȧ, *n.*; *pl.* **ȧ-nat'i-fæ.** [LL., a contraction of *anatifera*, f. of *anatiferus*, from *anas*, *anatos*, duck, and *ferre*, to bear.] A stalked cirriped of the genus *Lepas*, commonly called goose-barnacle.

ȧ-nat'i-fēr, *n.* Same as *Anatifa*.

an-ȧ-tif'ēr-ous, *a.* [L. *anas*, *anatos*, a duck, and *ferre*, to bear.] Producing geese; applied to anatifæ, or goose-barnacles, and to the trees on which they were thought to grow, from a former belief that they fell into the water and became geese.

an'ȧ-tine, *a.* Pertaining to or resembling a duck; duck-like.

ȧ-nat'ō-ciṣm, *n.* [L. *anatocismus*, from Gr. *anatokismos*, from *ana*, again, and *tokizein*, to lend at interest; *tokos* interest.] Interest upon interest; the taking of compound interest; or the contract by which such interest is secured. [Rare.]

an'ȧ-toid, *a.* In zoölogy, belonging to or resembling the ducks and geese.

an-ȧ-tom'iç, an-ȧ-tom'iç-ăl, *a.* [Gr. *anatomikos*, from *anatomē*, *anatomia*, anatomy.] Pertaining to anatomy or dissection; produced by or according to the principles of anatomy, or natural structure of the body.

an-ȧ-tom'iç-ăl-ly, *adv.* In an anatomical manner; by means of dissection; according to anatomy.

ȧ-nat'ō-miṣm, *n.* 1. The theory that the phenomena of life in organized bodies are the result of anatomical structure.

2. The application of the principles of anatomical structure and the display of anatomical details, as in sculpture, painting, etc.

ȧ-nat'ō-mist, *n.* One who is proficient in the science of anatomy or expert in dissection.

ȧ-nat"ō-mi-zā'tion, *n.* The act of dissection; structural analysis.

ȧ-nat'ō-mīze, *v.t.*; anatomized, *pt.*, *pp.*; anatomizing, *ppr.* 1. To dissect; to cut apart for the purpose of examining the structure and relationship of the constituent parts.

2. To analyze; to examine in detail.

ȧ-nat'ō-mī-zēr, *n.* One who anatomizes; a dissector; an anatomist.

ȧ-nat'ō-my, *n.* [Fr. *anatomie*; L. *anatomia*; Gr. *anatomia*, *anatomē*, a cutting up, from *anatemnein*; *ana*, up, and *temnein*, to cut.]

1. The dissection of organized bodies for the examination of their structure and economy.

2. The science of the structure of animals and plants.

3. Anatomical structure; the arrangement of parts in an organism.

4. A pamphlet or treatise on anatomy.

5. A critical analysis, physical or mental, of an animate or inanimate thing.

6. A subject for dissection; a result of dissection; variously applied, as to a corpse, a skeleton, an anatomical model, and, figuratively, to an emaciated person or a shadowy and immaterial thing.

Comparative anatomy; comparison of higher and lower types, variations, and modifications of organism, in different classes and groups of animals.

Syn.—Dissection, division, analysis, dismemberment.

ȧ-nat'ō-piṣm, *n.* [Gr. *ana*, back, and *topos*, place, and *-ism*.] Faulty arrangement; in art, inharmonious grouping.

an-ȧ-trep'tiç, *a.* [Gr. *anatreptikos*, from *anatrepein*; *ana*, up, and *trepein*, to turn.] Refuting; defeating; applied to the dialogues of Plato which represent a defeat in the gymnastic exercises.

an'ȧ-tron, *n.* [Sp., from Ar. *an-natrūn*, from *al*, the, and *natrūn*, natron.]

1. Soda; a native form of sodium carbonate. [Obs.]

2. A scum which forms upon the molten mixture from which glass is made; glass-gall; sandiver.

3. An efflorescence of saltpeter as it appears on the walls of vaults.

ȧ-nat'rō-pous, ȧ-nat'rō-păl, *a.* [L. *anatropus*, from Gr. *ana*, up, and *trepein*, to turn.] In botany, inverted; applied to an ovule which has been so reversed that the apex of the nucleus, and consequently the foramen, corresponds with the base of the ovule.

Anatropal Ovule.

ȧ-nat'tō, *n.* Same as *Arnotto*.

an-ax'i-ăl, *a.* Without a distinct axis; of irregular form.

An-ax-ō'ni-ȧ, *n.pl.* [LL., from Gr. *an* priv., and *axōn*, axle.] Organisms lacking a distinct axis, and having consequently an irregular form.

an'bŭr-y, am'bŭr-y, *n.* [AS. *ampre*, *ompre*, a crooked, swelling vein, perhaps from *ange*, painful, and *berie*, berry.]

1. A tumor, wart, or swelling, full of blood and soft to the touch, appearing on horses and cattle.

2. A sort of woody gall, produced by insects on the roots of certain vegetable plants, as the turnip; also called *clubroot*.

-ance, -an'cy, *suffix.* [Fr. *-ance*; L. *-antia*, *-entia*.] Used in forming nouns from adjectives in *-ant*, and denoting action, quality, or state; as abund*ance*, defi*ance*, forbear*ance*.

an'ces-tŏr, *n.* [OFr. *ancestre*; L. *antecessor*, one who goes before, from *antecedere*; *ante*, before, and *cedere*, to go.]

1. One from whom a person descends, either by the father or the mother, at any distance of time; a forefather; as, an *ancestor* of mine was one of the Pilgrim fathers.

2. In biology, a progenitor; a hypothetical form or an early type from which an organism is developed.

3. In law, a predecessor in line of inheritance; a person from whom an estate has descended.

Syn.—Progenitor, forefather, forebear.

an-ces-tō'ri-ăl, *a.* Ancestral.

an-ces-tō'ri-ăl-ly, *adv.* As far as one's ancestors are concerned.

an-ces'trăl, *a.* Relating or belonging to ancestors; claimed or descending from ancestors; as, an *ancestral* estate.

an'ces-tress, *n.* A female ancestor.

an'ces-try, *n.* A series of ancestors, or progenitors; lineage, or those who compose the line of natural descent; hence, birth or honorable descent; as, he is proud of his *ancestry*.

an̄'çhi-lops, *n.* [Gr. *anchilops*; *anchi*, near, and *ops*, eye.] An abscess in the inner angle of the eye; an incipient lachrymal fistula; the goat-eye.

an̄'çhŏr, *v.t.*; anchored, *pt.*, *pp.*; anchoring, *ppr.* 1. To place at anchor; to hold at rest by lowering an anchor; as, to *anchor* a ship.

2. To fix or fasten; to fix in a stable condition.

an̄'çhŏr, *v.i.* 1. To cast anchor; to come to anchor; as, our ship *anchored* off the Isle of Wight.

2. To stop; to fix or rest.

an̄'çhŏr, *n.* An anchoret. [Obs.]

an̄'çhŏr, *n.* [AS. *ancor*; Dan. *ancer*; O.H.G. *anchar*; L. *ancora*; Gr. *ankyra*, an anchor, hook.]

1. An iron implement of varying size and shape, attached to a ship by a rope or chain cable and which, when thrown overboard, fastens itself in the earth, mud, etc., at the bottom and holds the ship in the position required.

The *anchor* in common use is formed with a strong shank, *a*, at one extremity of which is the crown, *c*, from which branch out two arms, *bb*, terminating in broad palms or flukes, *dd*, the sharp extremity of which is the peak or bill; at the other end of the shank is the stock, *ee*, a transverse piece, behind which is a shackle or ring, to which the cable can be attached. Other types of *anchor* are sometimes used, effective forms being those known as Martin's and Trotman's *anchors*.

Common Anchor.

Anchors of various sizes are carried by every vessel. They are named according to their relative importance and varying uses. The principal one, and that on which most dependence is placed, is the *sheet-anchor*. Then come the *best bower*, the *small bower*, the *spare anchor*, the *stream-anchor*, and *kedge anchors* which are the smallest.

2. Any instrument, device, or contrivance for a purpose akin to that of a ship's *anchor*—to hold an object in place; as, the *anchor* (timbers) of a dam; the *anchor* of a cable supporting a bridge, etc.

Martin's Anchor.

3. In architecture, (a) a metal band holding walls or other parts of a building together; a clamp or brace, often with ornamental visible ends; (b) carved work, resembling anchors, in moldings, cornices, etc.

4. In zoölogy, a spicule of certain sponges, in shape like an anchor; also, an ancora, or one of the anchor-shaped calcareous hooks serving certain holothurians, particularly the *Synaptæ*, as means of locomotion.

5. In a figurative sense, that which gives stability or security; that on which we place dependence for safety.

Which hope we have as an *anchor* of the soul, both sure and steadfast. —Heb. vi. 19.

6. In heraldry, an emblem of hope.

At anchor; said of a ship when she rides by her anchor or is anchored. Hence, *to lie* or *ride at anchor*.

To cast anchor; to let go an anchor, to keep a ship at rest.

To weigh anchor; to heave or raise the anchor out of the ground.

Trotman's Anchor.

Anchor acockbill; said of any anchor when it is suspended perpendicularly from the cathead, ready to be let go.

Anchor apeak; the position of the anchor when the cable is drawn in so tight as to bring the ship directly over the anchor.

Anchor atrip, or *aweigh*; the position of the anchor when it is just drawn out of the ground.

The anchor comes home; a phrase used of an anchor when it is dislodged from its bed, so as to drag as the vessel drifts.

Foul anchor; (a) said of an anchor when hooked or entangled with another anchor, or with a wreck or cable, or when the slack of its own cable becomes entangled with it; (b) a design showing an anchor with chain or hawser twisted around it, used on the flag of the secretary of the navy in the United States, and in England by the Admiralty as a crest.

To back an anchor; to lay down a small anchor ahead of that by which the ship rides, with the cable fastened to the crown of the latter to prevent its coming home.

To cat the anchor; to hoist the anchor to the cathead and make it fast there.

an'chŏr-ȧ-ble, *a.* Fit for anchorage.

an'chŏr-āge, *n.* 1. Anchor-ground; a place where a ship can anchor.

The water was so deep that no *anchorage* could be found. —Darwin.

2. An anchor and all its necessary tackle. [Rare.]

3. A harbor-toll.

4. The condition of being at anchor.

5 Something which holds like an anchor; as, the *anchorages* of a bridge.

6. That which is steadfast; that upon which one may rely.

an'chŏr-āge, *n.* The dwelling-place of an anchoret.

an'chŏr-āte, *a.* Shaped like an anchor.

an'chŏr-bolt, *n.* A bolt to hold down or secure a machine.

an'chŏr-chock, *n.* A block on which an anchor rests when stowed.

an'chŏr-drag, *n.* An anchor attached to a floating beam, restraining the swing of a vessel in a bad sea.

an'chŏred, *a.* 1. Lying or riding at anchor; fixed in safety.

2. In heraldry, the term applied to a cross with ends like the flukes of an anchor.

Anchored.

An-chō-rel'lȧ, *n.* [LL., dim. of L. *ancora*, spelled *anchora*, anchor.] A genus of entomostracans parasitic upon fishes.

An-chō-rel'li-dæ, **An-chō-rel'lȧ-dæ**, *n.pl.* The family of entomostracans of which the *Anchorella* are typical; fish-lice.

an'chō-ress, *n.* A female anchoret.

an'chō-ret, **an'chō-rite**, *n.* [OFr. *anachorete*; L. *anachoreta*; Gr. *anachōrētēs*, one retired, from *anachōrein*; *ana*, back, and *chōrein*, to retire.] A hermit; a recluse; one who retires to a solitary place, to devote himself to religious duties; also, a monk who retires to a cave or cell, to live in solitude.

an-chō-ret'iç, **an-chō-ret'iç-ăl**, *a.* Pertaining to a hermit, or his mode of life; written also *anachoretical*.

an'chō-ret-ish, *a.* Hermit-like.

an'chō-ret-işm, *n.* The mode of life of an anchoret; the condition of an anchoret.

an'chŏr-gāte, *n.* A lock-gate whose upper bearing has a heavy anchor-like collar embedded in masonry, to support the gate when it swings.

an'chŏr-ground, *n.* Ground for anchoring.

an'chŏr-hōld, *n.* The hold of an anchor upon the ground; security.

an'chŏr-hoy, *n.* A lighter for conveying anchors and chains in a harbor, etc.

an'chō-rite, *n.* See *Anchoret.*

an'chō-ri-tess, *n.* [Rare.] See *Anchoress*.

an'chŏr-less, *a.* Having no anchor; hence, drifting; unstable.

an'chŏr-lift, *n.* A device for raising from the bottom a heavy pointed timber or pile that has served as an anchor.

an'chŏr-light, *n.* The light required to be shown by a vessel at anchor in a harbor at night.

an'chŏr-lin"ing, *n.* Sheathing used to protect the sides of a vessel when weighing anchor.

an'chŏr-plāte, *n.* A metal bearing-plate that anchors the end of a cable in a suspension bridge.

an'chŏr-ring, *n.* 1. The ring to which a cable is fastened.

2. In geometry, the surface generated by the revolution of a plane curve round an axis external to the revolving plane.

an'chŏr-rock"et, *n.* A rocket with a fluked anchor-head, for carrying a line to a wreck; used in the life-saving service.

an'chŏr-shot, *n.* A shot furnished with anchor-like flukes; propelled from a mortar to carry a life-saving line to wrecks.

an'chŏr-trip"pēr, *n.* A device for casting off an anchor.

an'chŏr-wätch, *n.* The night-watch while a vessel is anchored; also called *harbor-watch*.

an'chŏr-well, *n.* A protecting recess for an anchor; used on monitors, etc., to guard the anchor from the enemy's fire.

an-chō'vy, *n.* [Port. and Sp. *anchova*; Basque, *anchova*, *anchua*, anchovy, related to *antzua*, dry, dried fish.] A small fish about three inches in length, of the genus *Clupea* or *Engraulis*. It is found and caught in vast numbers in the Mediterranean, and pickled for exportation. It is used as a sauce or seasoning.

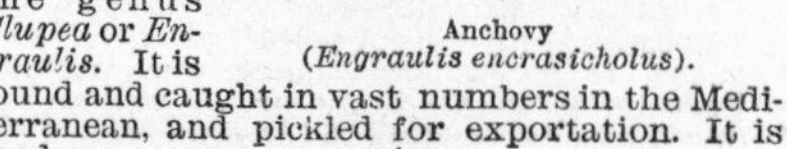

Anchovy (*Engraulis encrasicholus*).

an-chō'vy-peăr (-pãr), *n.* A fruit of the West Indies, produced by the tree *Grias cauliflora*. It resembles the mango in taste, and, like it, is sometimes pickled when green.

An-chū'sȧ, *n.* [LL., from Gr. *anchousa*, the plant alkanet.] A genus of plants belonging to the natural order *Boraginaceæ*, with downy, spear-shaped leaves and clusters of small purple or reddish flowers. Alkanet is a well-known species.

an'chū-sin, *n.* In chemistry, the principle of the red coloring matter, alkanet.

an'chy-lōse, *v.t.* and *v.i.* See *Ankylose*.

an'chy-lōsed, *a.* See *Ankylosed*.

an-chy-lō'sis, *n.* See *Ankylosis*.

an-chy-los'tōme, *n.* [Gr. *ankylos*, crooked, and *stoma*, mouth.] A parasitic worm, *Dochmius duodenalis*, which pierces the intestines of man, sucks the blood, and causes what is known as Egyptian chlorosis.

an"chy-los"tō-mī'ȧ-sis, *n.* [Gr. *ankylos*, crooked, and *stoma*, mouth.] An anemic condition caused by anchylostomes.

an-chy-lot'iç, *a.* See *Ankylotic*.

ān'cient (-shent), *a.* [ME. *auncient*; OFr. *ancien*; L. *antianus*, *ancianus*, former, old, from *ante*, before.]

1. Old; existing in times long ago; as, *ancient* authors, *ancient* days. In general, *ancient* is opposed to *modern*. When we speak of a thing that existed formerly, which has ceased to exist, we commonly use *ancient*; as, *ancient* republics, *ancient* heroes.

The voice I hear this passing night, was heard
In *ancient* days by emperor and clown. —Keats.

2. Of great age; having been of long duration; as, an *ancient* forest; an *ancient* city.

3. Known from long ago; as, the *ancient* continent, opposed to the *new* continent.

4. In law, of more than twenty or thirty years' continuous existence; used specifically in cases of defective proof; as, an *ancient* boundary.

5. In heraldry formerly worn, now out of date or obsolete; opposed to *modern*.

Ancient demesne; in English law, tenure of manors belonging to the crown in the times of Edward the Confessor or William the Conqueror. These were entered in Doomsday Book. —Blackstone.

Syn.—Primitive, pristine, antiquated, obsolete, antique, old, old-fashioned, immemorial.—A thing is *ancient* when it is old; it is *antiquated*, *antique*, and *obsolete*, when it is gone out of use or fashion.

ān'cient, *n.* [Early E. *antient*, *antesign*; corruption of Fr. *ensign*.]

1. A flag or streamer on a ship of war, or the colors of a regiment. [Obs.]

2. An ensign; the bearer of a flag. [Obs.]

'Tis one Iago, *ancient* to the general. —Shak.

ān'cient-ly, *adv.* 1. In old times; in times long since past; as, Rome was *anciently* more populous than at present.

2. In an old or ancient manner. [Rare.]

ān'cient-ness, *n.* The state of being ancient; antiquity; existence from old times.

Their melancholy grandeur, and the awe
Their *ancientness* and solitude beget. —R. H. Stoddard.

ān'cient-ry, *n.* 1. Dignity of birth; the honor of ancient lineage.

2. Antiquity; that which is aged.

By gain thereof it could not fail to find
Much proof of *ancientry*. —Jean Ingelow.

3. Old age, or aged persons collectively. [Rare.]

ān'cients, *n.pl.* 1. Those who lived in former ages; opposed to the *moderns*.

2. In Scripture, very old men; also, governors, rulers, political and ecclesiastical.

The Lord will enter into judgment with the *ancients* of his people. —Isa. iii. 14.

3. In England, senior members of the Inns of Court; there are benchers, *ancients*, barristers, and students under the bar.

4. [*sing.*] A senior or predecessor. [Obs.]

Ancient of Days; an appellation of the Deity, signifying eternal existence.

Come and reign over us, *Ancient* of Days. —C. Wesley.

Council of Ancients; in French history, the higher branch of the legislative body, under the constitution of 1795.

ān'cient-y, *n.* 1. Age; antiquity. [Obs.]

2. In some old English statutes and writings, eldership or seniority. [Obs.]

an-ci'lē, *n.* [L.] In Roman antiquity, the sacred shield of Mars, said to have fallen from heaven in the reign of Numa, or one made in imitation of it.

an'cil-lā-ry, *a.* [L. *ancillaris*, from *ancilla*, a maidservant.]

1. Pertaining to a maidservant, or female service. —Blackstone.

2. Subservient or subordinate to; as, a court *ancillary* to another jurisdiction.

Ancillary administration; in law, a subordinate administration of such assets of a deceased person as are found in a state other than that in which he resided.

Ancillary letters; letters issued to give authority for ancillary administration.

an-cille' (-sil'), *n.* A maid; a maidservant. [Obs.]

an-cip'i-tăl, *a.* [L. *anceps*, *ancipitis*, two-headed, double, doubtful; *an*, *amb*, on both sides, and *caput*, head.]

1. Doubtful, or double; double-faced; double-formed.

2. In botany, two-edged; compressed, and forming two opposite angles, as a stem; having two prominent, longitudinal angles, with a convex disk, as a leaf.

an-cip'i-tous, *a.* Ancipital.

an-cis'troid, *a.* [Gr. *ankistron*, hook, and *eidos*, form.] Shaped like a hook.

an'cle, *n.* See *Ankle*.

an'cōme, *n.* A small ulcerous swelling, coming suddenly. [Obs.]

an'con, *n.*; *pl.* **an-cō'nēs**. [L. *ancon*; Gr. *ankōn*, the elbow; *ankos*, a bend.] The olecranon, or elbow; the larger posterior process at the upper end of the ulna.

Ancon sheep; the name of a breed of sheep, once celebrated but now extinct, which originated in Massachusetts in 1791; called also the *otter* breed.

an'con, **an'cōne**, *n.* [L. *ancon*; Gr. *ankōn*, a bend.]

1. In architecture, the bracket supporting a cornice, as in doorways, etc.

2. The corner of a crossbeam, or wall, etc. [Obs.]

an̄′çō-năl, an̄-çō′nē-ăl, *a.* Pertaining to the ancon.

an̄-çō′nē-us, *n.*; *pl.* **an̄-çō′nē-ī.** [L. *ancon*, elbow.] A muscle used in extending the fore-arm.

an̄′çō-noid, *a.* Elbow-shaped; anconal.

an̄′çō-ny, *n.* [Probably from Gr. *ankōn*, elbow, on account of its shape.] In iron-works, a piece of half-wrought iron, in the shape of a bar in the middle, but rude and unwrought at the ends.

an̄′çō-rȧ, *n.*; *pl.* **an̄′çō-ræ.** In zoölogy, same as *Anchor.*

-an′cy, *suffix.* See *-ance.*

an-cȳ′roid, *a* [Gr. *ankyra*, anchor, and *eidos*, shape.] Resembling the fluke of an anchor.

and, *conj.* [ME. *and, ant, an*; AS. *and, ond*; Dan. *en, ende*; G *und*; O.H.G. *ant*, and; Ice. *enda*, and if, in case that, and yet, *an*, and, *and, if*, AS. *ant*, are forms of the same word and are akin to L. *ante*, Gr. *anti*, Sans. *anti*, over against.] A conjunctive, connective, or conjoining word. It signifies that a word, phrase, clause, or sentence is to be added to what precedes. In Scripture especially it often opens a narrative, where the connection with anything going before is not obvious; thus, "*And* the Lord spake unto Moses." Num. i. 1; Ex. xxiv. 1. It is also sometimes used as a particle introducing interrogative and other clauses, expressive of surprise, or surprise conjoined with incredulity, joy, indignation; as, *And* shall I see him again? *And* you dare thus address me! It is also found used by a Latinism for *both*; as, thrones *and* civil and divine. In old popular songs it is sometimes a mere redundant expletive; as, When that I was *and* a tiny little boy. It is frequently used in an emphatic manner; as, there are men *and* men, that is, there are two different kinds of men. *And* is also used colloquially with the verbs *go, try, come*, as a substitute for *to* in the infinitive; as, try *and* be there, that is, try *to* be there.

And so forth; and the rest; and such things; *et cetera* (etc.).

an-dab′ȧ-tism, *n.* Blind struggling; uncertainty. [Obs.]

an-dȧ-lū′site, *n.* A mineral, occurring usually in thick lamellar forms, of a grayish or pale reddish tint, and sometimes in rhombic prisms, composed chiefly of silica and alumina. Its name is derived from Andalusia, in Spain, where it was first discovered.

än-dän′te (*or* an-dan′tē), *a.* and *n.* [It., ppr. of *andare*, to walk.]

I. *a.* In music, having a moderately slow movement; faster than larghetto and slower than allegretto.

II *n.* A musical passage or composition in *andante* time.

än-dän-tī′nō, *a.* and *n.* [It., dim. of *andante.*]

I. *a.* In music, having a movement a little faster than andante.

II. *n.* Any composition or passage in *andantino* time.

an′dȧ-raç, *n.* Same as *Sandarac.*

An-dē′ăn, *a.* Pertaining to the Andes, the great chain of mountains extending through South America.

an′dēs-ine, *n.* A triclinic feldspar containing both lime and soda. It was first discovered in the Andes.

an′dēs-ite, *n.* [From the *Andes* mountains, in which it occurs.] A volcanic rock, the ground-mass of which is usually composed of feldspar microliths, scattered through which are abundant crystals of plagioclase feldspar.

An′dine, *a.* Pertaining to the Andes; Andean.

An-dī′rȧ, *n.* [LL., from the native name.] A genus of tropical American trees, including the *Andira inermis* of the West Indies, a showy flowering tree, yielding building timber and a medicinal bark; called also the *cabbage-tree.*

and′ī-ron (-ūrn), *n.* [ME. *andyron, aundiren, andyre*; the ending was associated with ME. *iron, yron, yre*, iron. The word was confused with AS. *brand-isen*, a brandiron.] An iron support for sticks of wood in an open fireplace.

an′drȧ-dite, *n.* [Named after the Portuguese mineralogist *d'Andrada.*] A variety of garnet containing calcium and iron.

an-drȧ-nat′ō-my, *n.* [Gr. *anēr, andros*, a man, and *anatomē*, dissection.] The dissection of a human body, especially of a male.

an′drē-ō-lite, *n.* [Named from *Andreas*, in the Hartz Mountains, and *-lite*, Gr. *lithos*, stone.] An old name of the mineral harmotome, or cross-stone.

an′drō-, andr-. [Gr. *anēr, andros*, man.] A combining form, denoting man, male, and in botany the male organs or stamens of the flowers.

an-drō-ceph′ȧ-lous, *a.* [*Andro-*, and Gr. *kephalē*, a head.] Having a human head and an animal's body, as the sphinx of Egypt.

an-drō-clin′i-um, *n.* Same as *Clinandrium.*

an-drō-çō′ni-ȧ, *n.pl.* [*Andro-*, and Gr. *konia*, dust.] Minute scales on certain parts of the wings of some male butterflies.

an″drō-di-œ′cious, *a.* [*Andro-*, and *diœcious*; LL., from Gr. *dis*, twice, and *oikos*, house.] In botany, having hermaphrodite flowers on one plant and male on another plant of the same species, but none with female flowers only.

an-drō-dȳ′nȧ-mous (*or* -dyn′ȧ-mus), *a.* [*Andro*, and Gr. *dynamis*, power.] In botany, having stamens of unusual development.

an-drœ′ci-um (-shi-um), *n.* [*Andr-*, and Gr. *oikos*, house.] In botany, the stamens of a flower, taken as a whole.

an″drō-gō-nid′i-um, *n.*; *pl.* **an″drō-gō-nid′i-ȧ.** Same as *Androspore.*

an-droġ′y-năl, *a.* See *Androgynous.*

an-droġ′y-năl-ly, *adv.* With the organs of both sexes. [Rare.]

an′drō-ġyne, *n.* [*Andro-*, and Gr. *gynē*, woman.] A hermaphrodite; in botany, an androgynous plant.

an-droġ′y-nism, *n.* 1. Same as *Androgyny.*

2. In botany, the condition of diœcious plants when they become monœcious.

an-droġ′y-nous, *a.* [*Andro-*, and Gr. *gynē*, woman.]

1. Having the characteristics of both sexes; hermaphroditical.

2. In botany, bearing staminate and pistillate flowers on the same parent stem.

an-droġ′y-ny, *n.* Hermaphroditism; the state of being androgynous.

an′droid, *a.* Resembling a man; in human form.

an′droid, an-droi′dēs, *n.* A machine or automaton in human form, which, by means of springs, performs natural motions of a living man.

an-drō-lep′si-ȧ, an′drō-lep-sy, *n.* [*Andro-*, and Gr. *lēpsis*, from *lambanein*, to seize.] In international law, the seizure by one nation of a citizen or citizens of another nation to enforce some claim or right; derived from Athenian law.

an-drol′ō-ġy, *n.* [*Andro-*, and Gr. *logia*, from *legein*, to speak.]

1. The science of man, especially of the male sex.

2. The science of the diseases of the male genito-urinary organs.

an-drō-mā′ni-ȧ, *n.* [*Andro-*, and Gr. *mania*, madness.] Nymphomania.

An-drom′e-dȧ, *n.* [L., from Gr *Andromedē*, daughter of Cepheus, king of Ethiopia.]

1. A northern constellation.

2. A genus of plants, family *Ericaceæ*, found in northern latitudes and bearing white or rose-colored flowers in masses.

an′drō-mēde, an′drō-med, *n.* One of a stream of meteors which appear to radiate from the constellation Andromeda.

an″drō-mō-nœ′cious, *a.* [*Andro-*, and Gr. *monos*, single, alone, and *oikos*, house.] In botany, having male and hermaphrodite flowers on the same plant, but without female flowers.

an-drō-mor′phous, *a.* [*Andro-*, and Gr. *morphē*, form.] Formed like a man; of masculine appearance; as, an *andromorphous* woman.

an′dron, *n.* [Gr. *andrōn*, from *anēr, andros*, man.] In Grecian and Roman architecture, the apartment appropriated for the males. This was in the lower part of the house, while the *gynæceum*, or apartment for females, was in the upper part.

an-drō-pet′ăl-ous, *a.* [*Andro-*, and Gr. *petalon*, a leaf or petal.] In botany, a term applied to double flowers, produced by the conversion of the stamens into petals, as in the garden ranunculus.

an-droph′ȧ-ġī, *n.pl.* [*Andro-*, and Gr. *phagein*, to eat.] Man-eaters; cannibals. [Rare.]

an-droph′ȧ-gous, *a.* Man-eating. [Rare.]

an-droph′ȧ-gus, *n.* A man-eater; a cannibal; singular of *androphagi.* [Rare.]

an-drō-phō′bi-ȧ, *n.* [*Andro-*, and Gr. *phobos*, fear.] Abnormal fear of, or repugnance to, the male sex.

an″drō-phō-nō-mā′ni-ȧ, *n.* [Gr. *androphonos*, man-killing, and *mania*, madness.] A mania for killing persons; homicidal insanity.

an′drō-phōre, *n.* [*Andro-*, and Gr. *phoros*, from *pherein*, to bear.]

1. In botany, a stamineal column formed by the union of the filaments, as in a monadelphous plant.

2. In zoölogy, a part in some pelagic *Hydrozoa* which bears male gonophores.

an-droph′ō-rous, *a.* In zoölogy, of the nature of an androphore.

an′drō-phyll, *n.* [*Andro-*, and Gr. *phyllon*, leaf.] In botany, a stamen.

An-drō-pō′gon, *n.* [*Andro-*, and Gr. *pōgōn*, a beard.] A large genus of widely distributed grasses, including the varieties of sorghum, and the well-known broom-sedge.

an′drō-sphin̄x, *n.* [*Andro-*, and Gr. *sphinx*, a sphinx.] In Egyptian sculpture, a man-sphinx; a sphinx with a man's head, as distinguished from one with the head of an animal.

an′drō-spōre, *n.* [*Andro-*, and Gr. *sporē*, seed.] In botany, a spore of some algæ, from which proceed a large number of small bodies having male functions.

an-drot′ō-mous, *a.* In botany, having the stamens divided.

an-drot′ō-my, *n.* [*Andro-*, and Gr. *tomē*, a cutting, from *temnein*, to cut.] A cutting of human bodies; dissection of the human body, as distinguished from *zoötomy.* [Rare.]

-an′drous. [Gr. *anēr andros*, a man, a male.] An adjective termination used in botany to indicate the presence of stamens; as, mon*androus*, di*androus.*

āne, *n.* and *a.* One. [Scot. and Eng. dialect.]

-āne, *suffix* [L. *-ānus.*]

1. Generally, the same as *-an.*

2. In chemistry, it denotes a hydrocarbon of the paraffin series; as, meth*ane*, eth*ane*, etc.

ȧ-nēal′, *v.t.* [ME. *anele*; AS. *an*, on, and *elian*, from *ele*, oil.] To anoint; specifically, to give extreme unction to. [Obs.]

ȧ-nēar′, *prep.* and *adv.* Near. [Rare.]

ȧ-nēar′, *v.t.* and *v.i.* To approach. [Rare.]

ȧ-nēath′, *prep.* and *adv.* Beneath. [Scot.]

an′eç-dō-tȧ, *n.* A plural form of *anecdote.*

an′eç-dō-tāge, *n.* 1. Anecdotes and anecdotal matter as a whole. [Rare.]

2. The latter part of life, when one is supposed to be garrulous and fond of telling anecdotes; a play on the word *dotage.* [Colloq.]

an′eç-dō-tăl, *a.* Pertaining to or containing anecdotes.

an′eç-dōte, *n.* [Fr. *anecdote*; L. *anecdota*, from Gr. *anekdota*, neut. pl. of *anekdotos*, unpublished; *an* priv., and *ekdotos*, from *ekdidonai*; *ek*, out, and *didonai*, to give.] A short story or narrative, being the relation of a particular or detached incident or fact of an interesting nature; a biographical incident; a single passage of private life. Details of the private life of public men and of the inside or secret history of courts and governments are frequently collected for publication under the title of *anecdotes* or *anecdota*

Syn.—Story, incident, tale, narrative, legend, myth, narration.—An *anecdote* is the relation of an interesting or amusing incident, generally of a private nature, and is always reported as true. A *story* may be true or fictitious, and generally has reference to a series of incidents so arranged and related as to be entertaining.

an-eç-dot′iç, an-eç-dot′iç-ăl, *a.* Pertaining to, containing, or given to telling, anecdotes.

an′eç-dō-tist, *n.* A person who relates or collects anecdotes.

an′ē-lāce, *n.* See *Anlace.*

ȧ-nēle′, *v.t.* Same as *Aneal.*

an-ē-leç′triç, *a.* and *n.* I. *a.* Not electrifiable by friction.

II *n.* A substance that friction cannot electrify.

an-ē-leç′trōde, *n.* The positive voltaic pole of an electric battery.

an″ē-leç-trot′ō-nus, *n.* [Gr. *an* priv., *ēlectron*, amber, and *tonos*, strain.] The state of lessened irritability of a nerve or muscle near the anode by the passage of an electric current through it.

an-el′y-trous, *a.* In entomology, without elytra.

ȧ-nē′mi-ȧ, ȧ-næ′mi-ȧ, *n.* [L., from Gr. *anaimia*; *an* priv., and *aima*, blood.] A deficiency of blood in the system or of the red corpuscles in the blood.

ȧ-nē′miç, ȧ-næ′miç, *a.* Pertaining to or affected with anemia.

anemo-. A combining form, from Gr. *anemos*, wind.

ȧ-nem′ō-gram, *n.* [*Anemo-*, and Gr. *gramma*, a writing.] The record of an anemograph.

ȧ-nem′ō-grȧph, *n.* [*Anemo-*, and Gr. *graphein*, to write.] An instrument that measures and records the velocity and direction of the wind.

ȧ-nem-ō-graph′iç, *a.* Of or pertaining to anemography; ascertained by the anemograph.

an-ē-mog′rȧ-phy, *n.* [*Anemo-*, and Gr. *graphē*, a writing.]

1. A description of the winds.

2. The automatic registration of the wind's force and direction.

an-ē-mol′ō-ġy, *n.* [*Anemo-*, and Gr. *logos*, a discourse.] The branch of science which deals with the winds and their phenomena.

an-ē-mom′e-tẽr, *n.* [*Anemo-*, and Gr. *metron*, measure.] An instrument or machine for measuring the force and velocity of the wind. In the simplest form, four hemispherical hollow cups *a a* are extended upon strong metal arms, with their concave surfaces facing the same way, upon a vertical axis *b*, which has at its lower extremity an endless screw *d*. The axis is strengthened and supported at *c*. The endless screw is placed in gear with a train of wheel-work; and

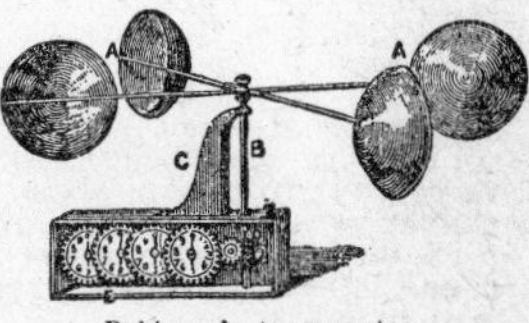

Robinson's Anemometer.

the indication is given by a hand which moves round a dial, or, in some instruments, by several hands moving round different dials, like those of a gas-meter.

an″ē-mō-met′riç, an″ē-mō-met′riç-ăl, *a.* Relating to anemometry.

an″ē-mō-met′rō-grȧph, *n.* An anemograph.

an-ē-mom′e-try, *n.* The process of ascertaining the velocity, force, and direction of the wind, as by an anemometer.

A-nem′ō-nē, *n.* [Gr. *anemōnē*, windflower, from *anemos*, wind.]

1. A genus of plants, natural order *Ranunculaceæ*, having numerous species. Those with double flowers form striking ornaments under garden cultivation.

Vine-leaved Anemone (*Anemone vitifolia*).

2. [a—] A plant of the genus *Anemone*, the wood-*anemone* being the best known. Written also *anemony*.

3. [a—] A sea-*anemone*. [See *Actinia*.]

an-ē-mon′iç, *a.* Of, pertaining to, or derived from an anemone, or from anemonin; as, *anemonic* acid.

ȧ-nem′ō-nin, *n.* An acrid, crystallizable substance, obtained from some species of anemone. It burns like camphor.

ȧ-nem′ō-ny, *n.* See *Anemone*.

ȧ-nem′ō-phile, *n.* [*Anemo-*, and Gr. *philos*, loving.] A plant which depends upon the wind for the distribution of its seeds.

an-ē-moph′i-lous, *a.* Literally, loving the wind; specifically, in botany, denominative of flowers whose pollen is conveyed from the anther to the stigma by the agency of the wind.

ȧ-nem′ō-sçōpe, *n.* [*Anemo-*, and Gr. *skopein*, to view.] A device which shows the course or direction of the wind; often consisting of an exterior weathercock exposed to the wind and connected with a dial or index inside.

an-en-cē-phal′iç, an-en-ceph′ȧ-lous, *a.* [L., from Gr. *an* priv., and *enkephalos*, brain.] In zoölogy, without a brain.

ȧ-nenst′, *prep.* and *adv.* See *Anent*.

ȧ-nent′, ȧ-nenst′, *prep.* [ME. *anent*, *anente*, *onefent*; AS *on-efen*; *on*, on, and *efen*, even, on a level with.]

1. With regard to; as to; about; concerning.

2. Toward; before; over against. [Obs.]

ȧ-nent′, ȧ-nenst′, *adv.* On the other side; in an opposite situation.

an-en′tēr-ous, *a.* [Gr. *an* priv., and *enteron*, intestine.] In zoölogy, without a stomach or alimentary canal.

an-e-pig′rȧ-phous, *a.* [Gr. *anepigraphos*, from *an* priv., and *epi*, on, and *graphein*, to write.] Without an inscription; said of coins.

an-ē-ret′iç, *a.* See *Anæretic*.

an′ē-roid, *a.* [Gr. *a* priv., *nēros*, wet, liquid, and *eidos*, form.] Without liquid; hence applied to a kind of barometer which consists of a metallic box from which the air has been exhausted, the pressure of the atmosphere being shown by the movements of its elastic top, which are registered by an index.

Aneroid Barometer.

an′ē-roid, *n.* An aneroid barometer.

ānes, *adv.* Once. [North Eng. and Scot.]

an-es-thē′si-ȧ, *n.*; **an-es-thet′iç,** *a.* and *n.*; **an-es″thē-ti-zā′tion,** *n.*; **an-es′thē-tize,** *v.* Same as *Anæsthesia*, *Anæsthetic*, *Anæsthetization*, *Anæsthetize*.

an′et *n.* [Fr. *aneth*; L. *anethum*; Gr. *anēthon*, *anisson*, the anise.] The dill or dill-seed. [Obs.]

an′ē-thōl, *n.* [L. *anethum*, anise, and *-ol*.] A compound contained in the oils of anise and fennel.

ȧ-net′iç, *a.* [L. *aneticus*; Gr. *anetikos*, relaxing; from *ana*, back, and *ienai*, to send.] Soothing.

ȧ-neū′ri-ȧ, *n.* [LL., from Gr. *a* priv., and *neuron*, nerve.] Lack of nervous power.

ȧ-neū′riç, *a.* Lacking nervous power; characterized by aneuria.

an′eū-rişm, an′eū-ryşm, *n.* [LL., from Gr. *aneurysma*, from *aneurynein*, to widen.] A soft, pulsating tumor, arising from the unnatural dilation or rupture of the coats of an artery.

an-eū-riş′măl, an-eū-ryş′măl, *a.* Pertaining to an aneurism.

ȧ-new′, *adv.* Over again; another time; in a new form; as to arm *anew*; to create *anew*.

an-frac′tū-ōse, *a.* See *Anfractuous*.

an-frac-tū-os′i-ty, *n.* 1. A state of being full of windings and turnings.

2. In anatomy, a sinuous depression or channel like those between the convolutions of the brain.

an-frac′tū-ous, an-frac′tū-ōse, *a.* [L. *anfractus*, pp. of *anfringere*; *an*, *ambi*, around, and *frangere*, to break.] Winding; full of windings and turnings.

an-frac′tū-ous-ness, *n.* A state of being anfractuous.

an-frac′tūre, *n.* A mazy winding. [Obs.]

añ-gā′ri-ȧ, *n.* In law, an act made compulsory by a government or feudal lord. [Obs.]

añ-gā-ri-ā′tion, *n.* [L. *angaria*; Gr. *angareia*, post-service, from *angaros*, a courier.] Compulsory service; exertion. [Obs.]

an-ġei-ol′ō-ġy (-ji-), **an-ġei-ot′ō-my** (-ji-), *n.* See *Angiology*, *Angiotomy*.

ān′ġel, *a.* Resembling angels; angelic; as, *angel* whiteness; *angel* face.

ān′ġel, *n.* [L. *angelus*; Gr. *angelos*, a messenger.]

1. Literally, a messenger; one employed to communicate news or information from one person to another at a distance. [Rare.]

2. A spirit, or a spiritual being, employed by God, according to the Scriptures, to communicate his will to man; a ministering spirit.

3. In a bad sense, an evil spirit; as, the devil and his *angels*.

4. A minister of the gospel, or pastor; as, the *angel* of the church at Ephesus.

5. An attendant spirit or demon.

6. In the language of affection, a very beautiful or lovable person; one of angelic qualities.

7. An English gold coin current in the fifteenth, sixteenth, and seventeenth centuries, and varying in value from 6s. 8d. to 10s.; so called from bearing on its obverse a figure of the archangel Michael piercing a dragon.

Angel of Queen Elizabeth.

8. A species of fish. [See *Angel-fish*.]

Destroying angel; (a) the angel of death; (b) in Mormon church history, a Danite. [See *Danite*.]

ān′ġel-āġe, *n.* The existence or state of angels.

ān′ġel-bed, *n.* An open bed without posts. [Obs.]

ān′ġel-et, *n.* 1. A small gold coin formerly current in England, of half the value of an angel.

2. A little angel. [Rare.]

ān′ġel-fish, *n.* A species of shark, of the genus *Squatina*. It is from six to eight feet long, and takes its name from its pectoral fins, which are very large and extend horizontally, like wings when spread.

ān′ġel-fọọd, *n.* A kind of cake.

ān′ġel-hood, *n.* The state of being angelic.

an-ġel′iç, an-ġel′iç-ăl, *a.* [L. *angelicus*.] Resembling angels; belonging to angels, or partaking of their nature; suiting the nature and dignity of angels.

Angelic hymn; an ancient hymn of the Christian church, beginning with the song of the angels on the Nativity. Luke ii. 14.

Angel fish (*Squatina angelus*).

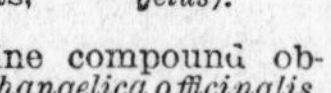

an-ġel′iç, *a.* In chemistry, of or derived from angelica; as, *angelic* ether.

Angelic acid; a crystalline compound obtained from the roots of *Archangelica officinalis*, etc.

An-ġel′i-cȧ, *n.* [LL., from *angelicus*, angelic.]

1. A genus of umbelliferous plants, found in the northern temperate regions and in New Zealand.

2. [a—] Any plant of this genus, including *Archangelica officinalis* or *Angelica Archangelica*, the leaf-stalks of which are used in confectionery, and the roots and seeds in medicine.

3. [a—] The blanched and candied stems of the plant *angelica*.

4. [a—] A sweet, white California wine.

Angelica tree; a thorny shrub, *Aralia spinosa*, the berries of which are used in medicine.

an-ġel′iç-ăl-ly, *adv.* Like an angel.

an-ġel′iç-ăl-ness, *n.* The quality of being angelic; excellence more than human.

an-ġel′i-cō, *n.* A large plant of the parsley family found in North America.

an-ġel′i-fȳ, *v.t.* To angelize. [Obs.]

an′ġe-lin, *n.* The common name of several tropical timber-trees of the genus *Andira*.

ān′ġel-ize, *v.t.*; angelized, *pt.*, *pp.*; angelizing, *ppr.* To make angelic.

ān-ġel-ol′ȧ-try, *n.* [Gr. *angelos*, angel, and *latreia*, worship.] Angel-worship.

ān-ġel-ol′ō-ġy, *n.* A discourse or treatise on angels; theories regarding the angelic host.

ān-gel-oph′ȧ-ny, *n.* [Gr. *angelos*, angel, and *phania*, from *phainesthai*, to appear.] The manifestation of an angel or angels to man by actual appearance.

an′ġe-lot, *n.* [Fr. *angelot*; LL. *angelotus*, dim. of *angelus*, angel.]

1. Formerly, an instrument of music, somewhat resembling a lute.

2. A French coin of gold, first struck in the fourteenth century, and so called because stamped with the figure of an angel; also, an English coin, struck at Paris while the city was in the possession of the English under Henry VI.; so called from bearing the figure of an angel supporting the escutcheons of England and France.

3. A small, rich cheese, made in Normandy, and stamped similarly to the French coin. [Obs.]

ān′ġel-shot, *n.* [Fr. *ange*, an angel, a chain-shot; so named from its appearance in the air.] A chain-shot, formed of hollow segments, which are fastened by chains to a central disk, and spread wing-like when fired.

an′ġe-lus, *n.* 1. A prayer to the Virgin, commemorating the annunciation by the angel Gabriel, offered in Roman Catholic countries at the sound of a bell. It is named from its first word.

2. The bell, rung at morning, noon, and night, as a signal for the *angelus* to be said.

ān′ġel-wa̤″tẽr, *n.* A perfume formerly prepared from rose-water, musk, etc. [Obs.]

an′ġe-ly-wood, *n.* See *Angili-wood*.

añ′gẽr, *n.* [ME. *anger*, *angre*, affliction, anger; Ice. *angr*; Dan. *anger*, regret; G. *angst*, anguish, fear; L. *angor*, anguish, a strangling, from *angere*, to strangle; Gr. *anchein*, to strangle.]

1. A violent passion of the mind excited by a real or supposed injury; often accompanied by a desire to take vengeance, or to obtain satisfaction from the offending party; resentment; wrath; ire.

2. The pain or smart of a sore or swelling; the original sense of the word. [Obs.]

3. Inflammation.

4. An individual paroxysm of wrath or an expression of deep displeasure. [Obs.]

Syn.—Indignation, resentment, wrath, fury, rage, ire.—*Anger* is a stronger term than *resentment*, but not so strong as *indignation*, which is awakened by what is flagitious in character or conduct; nor as *wrath*, *fury*, *rage*, in which *anger* is wrought up to a still higher point in the order of these words. *Anger* is a sudden sentiment of displeasure; *resentment* is a continued *anger*; *wrath* is a heightened sentiment of *anger*, which is poetically expressed by the word *ire*.

añ′gẽr, *v.t.*; angered, *pt.*, *pp.*; angering, *ppr.*

1. To excite anger in; to provoke; to rouse resentment in.

2. To make painful; to cause to smart; to inflame; as, to *anger* an ulcer. [Rare.]

Syn.—Enrage, exasperate, inflame, irritate, provoke.

añ′gẽr-ly, *adv.* [Obs.] See *Angrily*.

An′ġe-vin, An′ġe-vine, *a.* 1. Of or pertaining to Anjou, an old French province, or to the family that formerly reigned over it.

2. Of or pertaining to the Plantagenet family, which was descended from Geoffrey of Anjou.

3. In architecture, pertaining to or resembling the style of architecture followed in Anjou in the middle ages.

An′ġe-vin, An′ġe-vine, *n.* A native or inhabitant of Anjou; specifically, a member of its ancient royal family.

an-ġi-eç′tȧ-sis, *n.* [Gr. *angeion*, a vessel, and *ektasis*, extension.] In medicine, enlargement of the blood-vessels, as in varicose veins.

an-ġi-eñ′chy-mȧ, *n.* [L., from Gr. *angeion*, vessel, and *enchyma*, infusion.] The tissue of plants, which is supplied with vessels and ducts for the circulation of the sap.

an′ġi-li-wood, an′ġe-ly-wood, *n.* [Tamil, *angili*.] The wood of an evergreen tree of India, *Artocarpus hirsuta*.

an′ġi-nȧ (*or* an-ġi′nȧ), *n.* [LL., from *angere*, to choke.] In medicine, a term applied to all inflammatory affections of the throat or fauces, from the accompanying choking or difficulty of breathing; including quinsy, malignant sore throat, croup, mumps, etc.

Angina pectoris; a painful, periodic, nervous affection of the chest; neuralgia of the heart.

an′ġi-nous, an′ġi-nōse, *a.* Relating to angina, or angina pectoris.

an′ġi-ō-. A combining form from Gr. *angeion*, a case, vessel, capsule, and used in compounds relating to seed, or blood-vessels, or to something contained in or covered by a vessel.

an′ġi-ō-blast, *n.* [*Angio-*, and Gr. *blastos*, a sprout or shoot.] The embryonic cell of a blood-vessel or corpuscle.

an″ġi-ō-blas′tiç, *a.* Relating to or resembling an angioblast.

an″ġi-ō-çär′pous, *a.* [*Angio-*, and Gr. *karpos*,

fruit.] Having the fruit inclosed in an envelope, as in the case of a chestnut within its husk; also applied to certain lichens and fungi which have their seeds or spores covered.

an-ġi-og′rȧ-phy, *n.* [*Angio-*, and Gr. *graphē*, description.]
1. A description of the vascular system of the human body.
2. A treatise on standards of weight and measure, the instruments, and the utensils, used by various nations. [Rare.]

an-ġi-ol′ō-ġy, *n.* [*Angio-*, and Gr. *logia*, from *legein*, to speak.] That section of anatomy which treats of the vessels of the human body, as the arteries, veins, lymphatics, etc.

an-ġi-ō′mȧ, *n.* [*Angio-*, and *-oma.*] A tumor formed of blood-vessels in a state of distention.

an″ġi-ō-mon-ō-spẽr′mous, *a.* [*Angio-*, and Gr. *monos*, alone, and *sperma*, seed.] Producing one seed only in a seed-pod.

an″ġi-ō-neū-rō′sis, *n.* [*Angio-*, and Gr. *neuron*, nerve, and *-osis.*] A neurosis of the blood-vessels; a disturbance of the vasomotor system, either of the nature of a spasm or of paralysis.

an″ġi-ō-neū-rot′iç, *a.* Pertaining to or afflicted with angioneurosis.

an′ġi-ō-sçōpe, *n.* [*Angio-*, and Gr. *skopein*, to view.] In anatomy and botany, an instrument for examining capillary vessels.

an′ġi-ō-spẽrm, *n.* [*Angio-*, and Gr. *sperma*, seed.] In botany, an exogenous plant or tree bearing its seeds in a closed seed-vessel, as the apple, the oak, etc.

an″ġi-ō-spẽr′mous, an″ġi-ō-spẽr′mȧ-tous, *a.* Having seeds inclosed in a pod or other pericarp; opposed to *gymnospermous*, or naked-seeded.

ăn-ġi-os′pō-rous, *a.* [*Angio-*, and Gr. *spora*, seed.] Having the spores inclosed in a cell or shell, as certain fungi.

An″ġi-ō-stō′mȧ-tȧ, *n. pl.* [*Angio-*, and Gr. *stomata*, pl. of *stoma*, mouth.]
1. A suborder of serpents, characterized by cloven mouths that do not dilate.
2. A family of gasteropods, having shells with contracted apertures.

an″ġi-ō-stom′ȧ-tous, *a.* Pertaining to or resembling the *Angiostomata.*

an-ġi-os′tō-mous, *a.* In zoölogy, having a narrow mouth.

an-ġi-ot′ō-my. *n.* [*Angio-*, and Gr. *tomē*, a cutting, from *temnein*, to cut.]
1. Formerly, in medicine, the opening of a vessel, whether a vein or an artery, as in bleeding. It included both arteriotomy and phlebotomy.
2. In anatomy, the dissection of the vessels which operate in the circulation of the fluids of the body.

aṅ′gle, *v.i.*; angled, *pt., pp.*; angling, ppr. [ME. *angle*; AS. *angel*, *angul*, a hook, fishhook; Ice. *angi*, a sting, spine, probably the same root as Gr. *ongkos*, a hook, barb.]
1. To fish with an angle or with line and hook.
2. To fish; to try to gain by some bait or insinuation; as, men *angle* for fish; to scheme; as, to *angle* for the hearts of people; to *angle* for compliments.

aṅ′gle, *v.t.* 1. To fish in with hook or line; as, to *angle* a river. [Rare.]
2. To allure; to entice; as, he *angled* their hearts. [Obs.]

aṅ′gle, *n.* [Fr. *angle*; Sp. *angulo*, from L. *angulus*, a corner, angle; Gr. *angkylos*, bent, crooked.]
1. The point where two lines meet, or the meeting of two lines in a point; also, the space inclosed; a corner; a nook.
2. In geometry, (a) the figure formed by two straight lines meeting in a point; (b) the space comprised between them; (c) the extent of their divergence; as, an *angle* of forty-five degrees. The point where the lines meet is the vertex of the *angle*, and the lines themselves are its sides or legs. Strictly, an angle is measured by the amount of rotation required to make either side coincide with the other; that is, rotation of so many degrees. Straight lines which converge but do not meet are said to lie at a certain *angle* to each other.
3. Any well-defined projection, sharp point, or corner; as, the *angles* of a crystal, or of a brickbat.
4. A hook; an instrument to take fish, consisting of a rod, a line, and a hook, or a line and hook.
5 One who may be easily enticed; a gull. [Obs.]
6. In astrology, either of the first, fourth, seventh, or tenth houses, situated at the cardinal points and being those of life, relations, marriage, and dignities. [Obs.]
7. In heraldry, a bend or curve in the band or ribbon of an armorial charge.
Angle of incidence; see under *Incidence.*
Angle of refraction; see under *Refraction.*
Acute angle; one that is less than a right angle, or less than ninety degrees.
Adjacent or *contiguous angles*; two angles having one side common as well as a common vertex.
Alternate angles; see under *Alternate.*
Complementary angles; two angles whose sum is ninety degrees.
Curvilineal angle; an angle formed by two curved lines.
External or *exterior angles*; angles formed outside of a rectilineal figure by continuing or extending its sides.
Facial angle; see under *Facial.*
Internal or *interior angles*; angles which are within any right-lined figure.
Mixtilineal angle; an angle, one side of which is a right line and the other a curved line.
Oblique angles; either acute or obtuse angles, as distinguished from right angles.
Obtuse angle; an angle greater than a right angle, or more than ninety degrees.
Optic angle; see under *Optic.*
Outward angles; same as *External angles.*
Rectilineal or *right-lined angle*; an angle formed by two right lines.
Right angle; an angle formed by a right line falling on another perpendicularly, or an angle of ninety degrees, measured by an arc which is one quarter of a circle.
Solid angle; an angle formed by the meeting of three or more plane angles at one point and not lying in the same plane.
Spherical angle; an angle made by the meeting of two arcs of great circles, cutting one another on the surface of a globe or sphere.
Supplementary angles; two angles whose sum is 180 degrees.
Visual angle; same as *Optic angle.*

aṅ′gle=bär, *n.* 1. In carpentry, a vertical bar at the angle made by the meeting of two faces of a bay window.
2. In machinery, same as *angle-iron.*

aṅ′gle=bēad, *n.* In architecture, a piece of wood fixed vertically upon the exterior or salient angles of apartments to preserve them, and also to serve as a guide by which to float the plaster; called also *staff-bead.*

aṅ′gle=brāce, *n.* 1. A piece of timber fixed at each extremity to one of the two pieces forming the adjacent sides of a system of framing and subtending the angle formed by their junction. When it joins opposite corners of a rectangular frame, it is called a *diagonal brace.*
2. An instrument consisting of a rectangular crank-frame like the carpenter's brace, used for boring holes in angular positions.

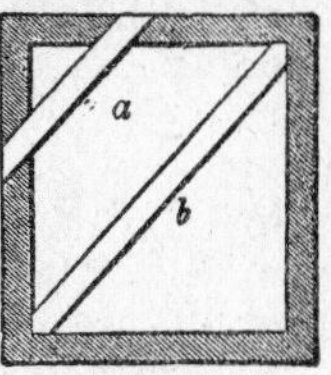

a, Angle-brace.
b, Diagonal brace.

aṅ′gled (-gld), *a.* 1. Having angles; composed of angles; used principally in compounds; as, a many-*angled* figure.
2. In heraldry, said of a line, usually straight, which is broken short, as at an angle.
3. Driven into an angle or nook. [Obs.]

aṅ′gle=ī″ron (-ŭrn), *n.* A piece of iron rolled into the shape of the letter L or V, used for forming the joints of iron plates in girders, boilers, etc., to which it is riveted.

A. Angle-iron.

aṅ′gle=lēaf, *n.* An architectural detail, often leaf-shaped, employed as a device for strengthening and decorating an angle.

an′gle=mē″tẽr, *n.* [*Angle*, and Gr. *metron*, measure.] An instrument for measuring angles; a clinometer.

aṅ′glẽr, *n.* 1. One who angles; a fisherman.
2. A fish, *Lophius piscatorius*, of Europe and America, having peculiar filaments projecting from its head, with which it is said to entice the fish on which it feeds.

Aṅ′gleṣ (-glz), *n.pl.* [L. *Angli.*] An ancient tribe from northern Europe that settled in Great Britain and gave it the name Angle-land (England), outnumbering the Saxons, Jutes, etc., and founding the kingdoms of East Anglia, Mercia, and Northumbria. Their occupation of the island began in the fifth century.

aṅ′gle-sīte, *n.* [From *Anglesea*, Wales, where it was first found, and *-ite.*] Native sulphate of lead. It occurs in white or yellowish prismatic crystals, semitransparent, with a glassy or adamantine luster, and is found associated with other ores of lead.

aṅ′gle=staff, *n.* An angular wooden strip used in building to preserve projecting corners and serve as a guide for floating the plaster.

aṅ′gle-wīṣe, *adv.* Angularly.

aṅ′gle-wŏrm, *n.* An earthworm; so called because often used by fishermen for bait.

Aṅ′gli-ăn, *a.* and *n.* I. *a.* Of or pertaining to the Angles, or their land.
II. *n.* One of the Angles.

Aṅ′gliç, *a.* Anglian. [Rare.]

Aṅ′gli-çăn, *a.* [L. *Anglicanus*, from *Anglicus*, pertaining to the Angles, or to England.]
1. English; pertaining to England or the English nation; as, an *Anglican* characteristic.
2. Of or pertaining to the Church of England, or the churches in accord with it as to doctrines and government; especially to the High-church party in such churches.
Anglican Church; a term which strictly embraces only the Church of England and the Protestant Episcopal churches in Ireland, Scotland, and the British colonies, but is sometimes made to include also the Episcopal churches of the United States.

Aṅ′gli-çăn, *n.* A member of the Church of England or any of the churches in accord with it; especially, a High-churchman.

Aṅ′gli-çăn-iṣm, *n.* 1. Belief in the principles and ritual of the established Church of England.
2. The principles and forms of the Church of England; often, in a restricted sense, the doctrines of the High-church party, or advanced ritualists.
3. Partiality to England and things that are English.

Aṅ′gli-cē, *adv.* [L.] In English; in the English manner.

Aṅ-glic′i-fȳ, *v.t.* To Anglicize. [Rare.]

Aṅ′gli-ciṣm, *n.* 1. An English idiom; a form of language or method peculiar to the English; a Briticism.
2. The quality of being English.

Aṅ-glic′i-ty, *n.* The quality of being English.

Aṅ″gli-ci-zā′tion, *n.* The act of Anglicizing or of becoming English in tone or character.

Aṅ′gli-cīze, *v.t.*; Anglicized, *pt., pp.*; Anglicizing, *ppr.* To make English; to give English characteristics to; to convert into English. Also written without a capital.

Aṅ′gli-fȳ, *v.t.* To Anglicize.

aṅ′gling, *n.* The act or art of one who angles or fishes with rod and line.

Aṅ′glō=. A combining form from Latin *Anglus*, English, and signifying *English*, *English and*, or *English joined with*; as, *Anglo*-Indian troops *Anglo*-American friendship, *Anglo*-German alliance, etc.

Aṅ″glō=A-mer′i-çăn, *a.* 1. Pertaining to Englishmen who live in America or the descendants of Englishmen in America.
2. Of or pertaining to England and America, or to their people jointly.

Aṅ″glō=A-mer′i-çăn, *n.* A citizen of America, especially of the United States, who is English by birth or extraction.

Aṅ″glō=Çath′ō-liç, *a.* 1. Of or pertaining to the churches which adopted the principles of the English Reformation; especially to the Church of England.
2. Of or pertaining to the High-church party of the Church of England, which favors doctrines and forms closely approaching those of the Roman Catholic church.

Aṅ″glō=Çath′ō-liç, *n.* A member of the Church of England; especially of the High-church party.

Aṅ″glō=Çȧ-thol′i-ciṣm, *n.* 1. The principles or doctrines of the Anglican church as embodied in the Book of Common Prayer and the Thirty-nine Articles.
2. The doctrines or ritualistic forms of the High-church party of the Anglican church.

Aṅ″glō=In′di-ăn, *n.* and *a.* I. *n.* A resident of India who is English by birth or extraction.
II. *a.* Relating to the English in India or to the Anglo-Indians; partaking of both the English and Indian nature or habits; as, an *Anglo-Indian* trait.

Aṅ″glō=Ī′rish, *a.* 1. Pertaining to England and Ireland; as, *Anglo-Irish* relations.
2. Of English and Irish parentage.

Aṅ′glō-măn, *n.*; *pl.* **Aṅ′glō-men.** 1. An Anglomaniac.
2. A strong partisan of British customs and interests; a term used by Thomas Jefferson.

Aṅ-glō-mā′ni-ȧ, *n.* [*Anglo-*, and Gr. *mania*, madness.] A love for English customs; especially by one of another nationality.

Aṅ-glō-mā′ni-aç, *n.* A person imbued with Anglomania.

Aṅ′glō-phōbe, *n.* [*Anglo-*, and Gr. *phobos*, from *phobein*, to fear.] One who manifests a constant and unreasonable dislike for and dread of the English people and their customs.

Aṅ-glō-phō′bi-ȧ, *n.* The abnormal mental attitude or condition of an Anglophobe.

Aṅ″glō=Sax′ŏn, *a.* Pertaining to the Saxons who settled in England, or to their language, customs, etc.; pertaining to the English race.

Aṅ″glō=Sax′ŏn, *n.* 1. One of the nation formed by the union of the Angles, Saxons, and other early Teutonic settlers in Britain, or one of their descendants: a native of England or Lowland Scotland, or one descended from natives of those countries; one belonging to the English race.
2. The earliest form of the English language, the language taken to England by the Teutonic invaders in the fifth century.

Aṅ″glō=Sax′ŏn-dŏm, *n.* The entire area throughout which the language, laws, and usages of the Anglo-Saxon race predominate.

Añ″glō-Sax′ŏn-işm, *n.* An Anglo-Saxon word or custom; also, the inherent quality of an Anglo-Saxon.

añ-gō′lȧ, *n.* An incorrect form of *angora*, a fabric woven from the hair of the Angora goat.

añ-gō′lȧ-pēa, *n.* A species of *Cajanus*; called also *pigeon-pea*.

añ′gŏr, *n.* [L.] 1. Anguish; intense bodily pain. [Obs.]

2. In medicine, extreme anxiety, producing constriction in the epigastric region, and often palpitation and oppression.

añ-gō′rȧ, *n.* [From *Angora*, a city in Asia Minor.] A fine fabric made from the wool of the Angora goat.

Angora cat; one of the finest varieties of the domestic cat, distinguished by its size and beautiful silky hair.

Angora goat; a kind of domestic goat, native to the district about Angora, and having long silky hair, which is used in the manufacture of fabrics; called by the Arabs *chamal goat, chamal* signifying silky or fine.

añ-goş-tū′rȧ-bärk, *n.* [From *Angostura*, a town in Venezuela.] The bark of the *Galipea cusparia*, a plant of the rue family growing in the mountains of Venezuela. It was formerly used in medicine as a tonic, and is now used in the preparation of bitters.

añ-gos-tūr′in, *n.* The essential medicinal element in angostura-bark.

añ′gri-ly, *adv.* In an angry manner; with indications of resentment.

añ′gri-ness, *n.* 1. The state of being angry.

2. Inflammation of a sore or swelling.

añ′gry, *a.*; *comp.* angrier; *superl.* angriest. 1. Roused to resentment; provoked; energetically indignant.

> God is *angry* with the wicked every day. —Ps. vii. 11.

2. Manifesting anger; marked by anger; caused by anger; as, an *angry* countenance; *angry* words.

3. In medicine, inflamed; red and sore; said of swellings, wounds, etc.

4. Raging; furious; tumultuous; as, *angry* waves.

Syn.—Enraged, irate, wroth, incensed, choleric, ireful, inflamed, hot, irascible, passionate, resentful, irritated, indignant, provoked, raging.

añ′guid (-gwid), *n.* One of the *Anguidæ*.

Añ′gui-dæ (-gwi-), *n.pl.* [L. *anguis*, a serpent, snake, and *-idæ*.] A family of double-tongued serpentiform lizards, including the blindworms or slowworms.

añ′gui-fọrm, *a.* [L. *anguis*, snake, and *forma*, shape.] In the form of a snake or serpent.

añ-guil′li-fọrm (-gwil′), *a.* [L. *anguilla*, an eel, and *forma*, shape.] In the form of an eel; resembling an eel.

añ-guil′lous, *a.* Anguilliform.

Añ-gui′næ, *n.pl.* Same as *Anguidæ*.

añ′guine (-gwin), *a.* Pertaining to or resembling a snake.

añ-guin′ē-ăl, *a.* Anguineous.

añ-guin′ē-ous, *a.* [L. *anguineus*, from *anguis*, a serpent.] Pertaining to or resembling a snake.

añ′gui-ped, añ′gui-pēde, *a.* and *n.* [L. *anguis*, snake, and *pes, pedis*, a foot.]

I. *a.* Having serpent-shaped legs and feet.

> A winged *anguipede* giant. —A. S. Murray.

II. *n.* A mythological being having feet and legs resembling serpents.

Añ′guis (-gwis), *n.* [L. *anguis*, serpent.] A genus of reptiles typical of the *Anguidæ*, the best known species being *Anguis fragilis*, the common blindworm.

añ′guish (-gwish), *n.* [ME. *anguisse*; OFr. *anguisse*; It. *angoscia*, anguish, from L. *angustia*, narrowness, straitness; from *angere*, to press tight, to choke.]

1. Extreme pain, either of body or of mind.

> And they hearkened not unto Moses, for *anguish* of spirit, and for cruel bondage. —Ex. vi. 9.

2. Any keen affection of the emotions or feelings; as, an *anguish* of delight.

Syn.—Agony, pang, torture, torment, grief, sorrow, distress.

añ′guish, *v.t.*; anguished, *pt., pp.*; anguishing, *ppr.* To distress with extreme pain or grief.

añ′gū-lăr, *a.* 1. Having an angle, angles, or corners; pointed; as, an *angular* figure.

2. Forming an angle; as, an *angular* point.

3. Measured by an angle; as, *angular* distance; *angular* velocity.

4. Physically, lean and awkward; socially, testy and unsympathetic.

Angular advance; in machinery, the advance of an eccentric from the point where it is perpendicular to the line of its motion to the point it occupies when the crank-shaft has reached its dead-center.

Angular aperture of lenses; the angular width of a pencil of light whose point is in the object and which is transmitted to the eye by the lenses of a microscope; as, a microscope of 60° aperture.

Angular artery; any artery passing around, over, or under an angular bone or process, as under the angle of the jaw.

Angular belting; in machinery, a belt constructed to run over a grooved pulley in such a way as to give it greater tractive capacity.

Angular chain-belt; a chain-belt constructed to bear hard against the grooved sides of a V-shaped pulley.

Angular distance; see under *Distance*.

Angular intervals; in astronomy, those arcs of the equator which are intercepted between circles of declination passing through the objects observed.

Angular motion; the motion of a body, swinging or moving in an arc, as a pendulum or a planet.

Angular perspective; in drawing, that kind of perspective in which neither of the sides of the principal object is parallel to the plane of the picture; and therefore in the representation the horizontal lines of both converge to vanishing points; called also *oblique perspective*.

Angular velocity; in physics, the rate at which a body revolves round a fixed axis; that is, the rate at which a line continually drawn from the one body to the other shifts its position in space.

añ′gū-lăr, *n.* The name applied to a bone occurring in the lower classes of vertebrates, situated at the base of the lower jaw.

añ-gū-lar′i-ty, *n.* The quality of being angular.

añ′gū-lăr-ly, *adv.* With angles or corners; in the direction of the angles.

añ′gū-lăr-ness, *n.* The quality of being angular.

añ′gū-lāte, añ′gū-lā-ted, *a.* Formed with angles or corners; as, *angulate* stems, leaves, petioles, etc.

añ′gū-lāte, *v.t.*; angulated, *pt., pp.*; angulating, *ppr.* [L. *angulatus*, pp. of *angulare*, to make angled; from *angulus*, an angle.] To put into angular shape.

añ-gū-lā′tion, *n.* The act or process of making angles; formation by angles; the state of being angulated.

añ-gū-lif′ẽr-ous, *a.* [L. *angulus*, an angle, and *ferre*, to bear.] In conchology, having a whorl, especially the last one, angular in shape.

añ′gū-li-nẽrved, *a.* Applied to the veins of a leaf branching angularly; pinnately veined, as many leaves of exogens.

añ″gū-lō-den′tāte, *a.* [L. *angulus*, angle, and *dentatus*, from *dens, dentis*, a tooth.] In botany, angularly toothed; said of the margin of a leaf.

añ-gū-lom′e-tẽr, *n.* [L. *angulus*, angle, and *metrum*; Gr. *metron*, measure.] Any instrument constructed for and used in the measurement of external angles.

añ′gū-lōse, *a.* [Rare.] Same as *Angulous*.

añ-gū-los′i-ty, *n.* The state or quality of having angles; angularity. [Rare.]

añ′gū-lous, *a.* Angular; having corners; hooked.

añ′gū-lus, *n.*; *pl.* **añ′gū-lī.** [L.] In anatomy, an angle of any kind, as of the jawbone or of a rib.

an-gust′, *a.* [L. *angustus*, narrow.] Narrow; strait. [Obs.]

añ-gus′tāte, *a.* Narrow; diminishing rapidly in breadth.

añ-gus-tā′tion, *n.* [L. *angustus*, narrow.] The act of making narrow; a straitening, or being made narrow.

añ-gus′ti-çlāve, *n.* [L. *angustus*, narrow, and *clavus*, a nail, a stripe.] A mark of distinction worn by a Roman of the order of equestrians, consisting of two narrow purple stripes attached to the shoulders of his tunic and extending downward in front and behind.

añ-gus-ti-fō′li-āte, añ-gus-ti-fō′li-ous, *a.* [L. *angustus*, narrow, and *folium*, leaf.] In botany, narrow-leaved; that is, having leaves very much less in width than in length.

añ-gus-ti-ros′trāte, *a.* [L. *angustus*, narrow, and *rostratus*, beaked, from *rostrum*, a beak.] In ornithology, having a narrow beak.

añ-gus-tū′rȧ-bärk, *n.* Same as *Angostura-bark*.

añ-gwăn-tī′bō, *n.* [Native name.] A small animal (*Arctocebes calabarensis*) of western Africa, which bears a strong resemblance to the lemur, but has only a rudimentary tail.

an-här-mon′iç, *a.* [Fr. *anharmonique*, from Gr. *anharmonikos*; *an* priv., and *harmonikos*, harmonic.] In mathematics, not harmonic; as, an *anharmonic* ratio.

Anharmonic ratio; a kind of ratio introduced into mathematics by the German mathematician Möbius and employed in defining the metrical properties of variables.

an-hē-lā′tion, *n.* [L. *anhelatio*, from *anhelare*, to breathe with difficulty, to pant; *an*, *ambi*, around, and *helare*, to breathe.]

1. Shortness of breath; a panting; difficult respiration.

2. Breathless anxiety, or panting desire.

> These *anhelations* of divine souls after the adorable object of their love.—Glanville.

an-hēle′, *v.i.* To be eager. [Obs.]

an′hē-lōse, an-hē′lous, *a.* Out of breath; panting; breathing with difficulty. [Rare.]

an-hi-drot′iç, *n.* [Gr. *anhidrōs*; *an* priv., and *hidrōs*, perspiration.] A drug that arrests perspiration.

an-hi-drot′iç, *a.* Deficient in perspiration; tending to check perspiration.

an′hi-mȧ, *n.* [Braz.] A Brazilian aquatic fowl, larger than a swan, and somewhat like a crane; the *Palamedea cornuta*, or horned screamer.

an-hiñ′gȧ, *n.* [S. Am. name.] The snakebird, *Plotus anhinga*, an aquatic bird of the South.

an-his′tous, *a.* [Gr. *an* priv., and *histos*, web, tissue.] Without a decided structure; said of membranes, etc.

an-huñ′gẽred, *a.* Hungry. [Rare.]

an-hȳ′drid, an-hȳ′dride, *n.* [Gr. *an* priv., and *hydōr*, water.] An oxid that becomes an acid by the addition of water.

an-hȳ′drīte, *n.* Anhydrous gypsum, differing from gypsum in not containing water. It occurs in rectangular crystals, nearly colorless, or of pale shades of blue or red; also fibrous, radiated, and granular. A silicious variety is called vulpinite.

an-hȳ′drous, *a.* [Gr. *anydros*, dry; *an* priv., and *hydōr*, water.] Destitute of water; as, *anhydrous* salts or acids.

ä′nī, ä′nō, *n.* [Braz.] A tropical American cuckoo.

an′i-çut, *n.* See *Annicut*.

an-id″i-ō-mat′iç-ăl, *a.* Not idiomatical. [Obs.]

an′i-ent, an-i-en′tise, *v.t.* [OFr. *anienter*; Fr. *anéantir*, to destroy.] To frustrate; to make void; to annihilate. [Obs.]

ȧ-nigh′ (-nī′), *prep.* and *adv.* Nigh. [Rare.]

ȧ-night′ (-nīt′), *adv.* In the nighttime. *Anights* is used of frequent and customary acts.

> You must come in earlier *anights*. —Shak.

an′il, *n.* [Port. *anil*; Ar. *an-nīl*; *an, al*, the, and *nīl*, from Sans. *nīlī*, indigo, from *nīla*, dark-blue.] A shrub from whose leaves and stalks indigo is made; a species of *Indigofera*, or indigo-plant.

an′ile, *a.* [L. *anilis*, from *anus*, an old woman.] Old-womanish.

an′ile-ness, *n.* Anility. [Rare.]

an-il′iç, *a.* Relating to or obtained from anil. [Rare.]

an′i-lide (*or* -lĭd), *n.* Phenylamide; any one of those amide compounds in which phenyl has to a great degree replaced the hydrogen.

an′i-line (*or* -lēn), *n.* A substance formerly made from indigo, but now from nitrobenzene. It is a base from which many dyes are produced.

an′i-line, *a.* Resembling or containing aniline.

ȧ-nil′i-ty, *n.* [L. *anilitas*, from *anilis*, from *anus*, an old woman.] The state of being an old woman; the old age of a woman; dotage.

an′i-mȧ-ble, *a.* [L. *animare*, to animate.] Susceptible of animation.

an″i-mad-vẽr′săl, *n.* That which has the power of perceiving and judging. [Obs.]

an″i-mad-vẽr′sion, *n.* [L. *animadversio*, from *animadvertere*, to turn the mind to, criticize, censure.]

1. Remarks by way of censure or criticism; reproof; blame.

2. The act or faculty of observing or noticing. [Obs.]

3. A kind of ecclesiastical punishment. [Rare.]

Syn.—Blame, censure, chiding, comment, criticism, reproof.

an″i-mad-vẽr′sive, *a.* Having the power of perceiving.

an″i-mad-vẽr′sive-ness, *n.* The power of animadverting.

an″i-mad-vẽrt′, *v.i.*; animadverted, *pt., pp.*; animadverting, *ppr.* [L. *animadvertere*, to observe, consider, censure, punish; *animum*, acc. of *animus*, mind, *ad*, to, and *vertere*, to turn.]

1. To take cognizance; to perceive: to notice.

2. To consider or remark by way of criticism or censure.

3. To inflict punishment; followed by *upon*. [Rare.]

an″i-mad-vẽrt′ẽr, *n.* One who animadverts or utters censure.

an′i-măl, *n.* [L. *animal*, from *anima*, air, breath, soul; Gael. *anam*, breath; W. *envil*, *en*, a being, soul, spirit, and *mil*, a beast; Arm. *aneval*; Sans. *ana, animi*.]

1. An organized, sentient, living being. *Animals* are essentially distinguished from plants by the property of sensation, the power of voluntary motion, the active and intelligent ability of nourishing themselves, by the predominance of nitrogen in their composition, and by their incapacity to originate protein or nitrogenous compounds, plants possessing this power.

2. A brute beast, or any animal lower than man.

3. A stupid or gross person; used as an expression of contempt.

4. A domestic quadruped; as, he rides a fine *animal*.

an′i-măl, *a.* [L. *animalis*, living, animate, from *anima*, breath, air, soul.]

1. Belonging or relating to animals; as, *animal* habits.

2. Relating to the purely physical functions and sensations of men and animals, as opposed in man to mentality, spirituality, etc.; as, *animal* appetites; *animal* pleasures.

3. Of, pertaining to, or consisting of, the flesh of animals; as, *animal* food.

Animal economy; the system of animal functions.

Animal electricity; the electricity generated in some animal bodies, as in certain eels.

Animal kingdom; the entire class of living beings; one of the three great divisions of nature, embracing all animals. It comprises several subkingdoms, and under these are classes, orders, families, genera, and species differently arranged by writers and naturalists. Linnæus, in his famous system promulgated in 1766, divided animals into the following six primary divisions or classes: 1. Mammalia; 2. Aves; 3. Amphibia; 4. Pisces; 5. Insecta; 6. Vermes. Cuvier in 1817, and Owen in 1860, proposed different divisions, and in 1869 Huxley devised an arrangement of the *animal kingdom* into eight primary groups, as follows: Vertebrata, Mollusca, Molluscoida, Cœlenterata, Annulosa, Annuloida, Infusoria, and Protozoa.

Animal magnetism; the term by which Mesmer (1733-1815), the proponent and exemplifier of the phenomenon, designated mesmerism, now called hypnotism under its more scientific development.

Animal spirits; vivacity; liveliness; natural buoyancy of spirits.

an-i-mal′çū-lăr, an-i-mal′çū-line, *a.* Pertaining to an animalcule or animalcules.

an-i-mal′çūle, *n.* [L. *animalculum*, dim. of *animal*, animal.] A minute animal, especially one that is indiscernible without the aid of a magnifying glass.

an-i-mal′çū-lişm, *n.* 1. A theory in biology that animalcules are the cause of life and decay.

2. Spermatism.

an-i-mal′çū-list, *n.* One versed in the knowledge of animalcules; one believing in the theory of animalculism.

an-i-mal′çū-lum, *n.*; *pl.* **an-i-mal′çū-lȧ.** Same as *Animalcule*.

an′i-măl-flow″ẽr, *n.* A name sometimes given to the sea-anemones or other animal productions having some resemblance to flowers.

An-i-mā′li-ȧ, *n.pl.* [L., pl. of *animal*.] The animal kingdom; animals as a division of nature.

an′i-măl-ish, *a.* Like an animal; brutish. [Rare.]

an′i-măl-işm, *n.* 1. The state of a mere animal; the state of being actuated by sensual appetites only, and not by intellectual or moral qualities; sensuality.

2. In physiology, a theory which holds that the embryo is entirely formed from the spermatic communication of the male.

an′i-măl-ist, *n.* 1. An animalculist.

2. A sensualist.

3. An artist whose chief work is the study and representation of animals.

an″i-măl-is′tiç, *a.* Pertaining to animalism.

an-i-mal′i-ty, *n.* Animal life or nature.

An″i-mȧ-liv′ō-rȧ, *n.pl.* [L., neut. pl. of *animalivorus*, from *animal*, animal, and *vorare*, to devour.] In zoölogy, a suborder of carnivorous and insectivorous bats.

an″i-mȧ-liv′ō-rous, *a.* Feeding on animals; carnivorous; pertaining to the *Animalivora*.

an-i-mal-i-zā′tion, *n.* 1. The act of giving animal life, or endowing with the properties of an animal.

2. Conversion into animal matter, by the processes of assimilation.

3. The process of being animalized or degraded in life or habits.

an′i-măl-īze, *v.t.*; animalized, *pt.*, *pp.*; animalizing, *ppr.* 1. To give animal life to; to endow with the properties of animals.

2. To convert into animal matter by assimilation.

3. To sensualize; to render brutish; as, to *animalize* a man.

an′i-măl-ly, *adv.* Physically; in an animal manner

an′i-măl-ness, *n.* Animality. [Rare.]

an′i-mănt, *a.* and *n.* I. *a.* Having life and reason; quickening. [Obs.]

II. *n.* An animate creature. [Obs.]

an′i-mȧ-ry, *a.* Pertaining to the soul. [Obs.]

an-i-mas′tiç, *a.* Spiritual; psychic.

an-i-mas′tiç, *n.* The doctrine of the soul; psychology. [Obs.]

an′i-māte, *v.t.*; animated, *pt.*, *pp.*; animating, *ppr.* [L. *animatus*, pp. of *animare*, to make alive, fill with breath.]

1. To give life to; to quicken; to make alive; as, the soul *animates* the body.

2. To give powers to, or to heighten the powers or effect of; as, to *animate* a lyre.

3. To give spirit or vigor to; to infuse courage, joy, or other enlivening passion into; to stimulate or incite; as, to *animate* dispirited troops.

Syn.—Inspire, quicken, exhilarate, revive, inspirit.

an′i-māte, *a.* Alive; possessing animal life.

an′i-mā-ted, *a.* Endowed with animal life; as, *animated* beings; lively; vigorous; full of spirit; indicating animation; as, an *animated* discourse.

an′i-mā-ted-ly, *adv.* With life; briskly.

an′i-mā-tẽr, *n.* One who or that which animates

an′i-mā-ting, *a.* Giving life; infusing spirit; enlivening; causing animation.

an′i-mā-ting-ly, *adv.* So as to animate or excite feeling.

an-i-mā′tion, *n.* [L. *animatio*, from *animare*, to make alive.]

1. The act of infusing life; the state of being animated.

2. The state of being lively, brisk, or full of spirit and vigor; as, he recited the story with great *animation*.

3. In the fine arts, the character of a figure or group designed with such energy and vigor as to suggest the idea of life and motion.

Suspended animation; temporary loss of vital force; suspension of the vital functions, as in persons half drowned.

Syn.—Life, vivacity, spirit, buoyancy, gaiety, liveliness.—A person with *animation* takes an interest in everything; a *vivacious* man catches at everything that is pleasant and interesting; a *spirited* man enters into plans, makes great exertions, and disregards difficulties.

an′i-mā-tive, *a.* Capable of giving life or spirit; inspiriting.

an′i-mā-tŏr, *n.* One who or that which infuses life or spirit.

an′i-mē (*or* -mā), *n.* [Fr., Sp., Port.] A resin exuding from the stem of a large American tree, *Hymenæa Courbaril*. It dissolves in rectified spirit of wine, and is used as a varnish.

an′i-mé (-mā), *a.* [Fr., animated.] In heraldry, a term denoting that the eyes of a rapacious animal are borne of a different tincture from the animal itself.

an-i-met′tȧ, *n.* [It.] Among ecclesiastical writers, the cloth which covers the cup of the eucharist.

an′i-min, an′i-mine, *n.* A chemical compound derived from bone-oil.

an′i-mişm, *n.* [L. *anima*, soul, and *-ism*.] The doctrine that the phenomena of the animal economy are produced by the agency of the soul, as taught by Stahl; also, the doctrine that the living phenomena of organized bodies are produced by an actuating or vital principle, distinct from the substance of those bodies; hence, belief in a spiritual world as apart from a material world.

an′i-mist, *n.* One who maintains the doctrine of animism.

an-i-mis′tiç, *a.* Of or pertaining to animism.

an′i-mōse, an′i-mous, *a.* Full of spirit; hot; vehement; resolute. [Obs.]

an-i-mōse′ness, *n.* Spirit; vehemence of temper. [Obs.]

an-i-mos′i-ty, *n.* [Fr. *animosité*; It. *animosita*; from L. *animositas*, courage, spirit, from *animus*, courage, life.]

1. Violent hatred; active enmity.

2. Courage; spiritedness. [Obs.]

Syn.—Enmity, hostility, malice, rancor, antipathy, antagonism.—*Animosity* differs from *enmity* in that it is accompanied by passion, and is generally avowed and active; while *enmity* may be secret and inactive, though more deep-seated and inveterate. It is a less criminal passion than *malice*. One who harbors *animosity* seeks to gain a cause or destroy an enemy or rival from hatred or private interest; a person actuated by *malice* seeks to do injury to another merely for the sake of giving pain.

an′i-mus, *n.* [L. *animus*, mind.] Animating temper, or motive; prejudice; unfriendly spirit.

an′i-on, *n.* [Gr. *aniōn*, ppr. of *anienai*; *ana*, up, and *ienai*, to go.] That product of electrolysis appearing at the anode, opposed to *cation*. [See *Anode*.]

an′is-. A combining form used in chemistry to denote derivation from anise or anisic acid.

an-i-san′drous, *a.* Same as *Anisostemonous*.

an′ise, *n.* [Sp. *anis*; L. *anisum*; Gr. *anison*; Ar. *anīsūn*, anise.]

1. An annual plant, *Pimpinella anisum*. It grows naturally in Egypt, and is cultivated in Spain and Malta, whence the seeds or fruit are imported.

2. The fruit or seeds of the anise-plant; aniseed.

an′i-seed, *n.* The ovate, ribbed, aromatic seed of the anise; also, the cordial prepared from it, also called *anisette*.

an-i-sette′, *n.* [Fr.] A cordial prepared from, or flavored with, and sometimes called, aniseed.

ȧ-nis′iç, *a.* Pertaining to anise.

an′i-sō-. [Gr. *anisos*, unequal; *an* priv., and *isos*, equal.] A combining form signifying unequal, dissimilar; as, *aniso*meric, *aniso*dont.

an″i-sō-cẽr′çăl, *a.* [*Aniso-*, and Gr. *kerkos*, tail.] Having the terminal fin unequally lobed.

an″i-sō-çō′ri-ȧ, *n.* [*Aniso-*, and Gr. *korē*, pupil of the eye.] Inequality of the diameters of the pupils of the eye.

an″i-sō-daç′tyl, an″i-sō-daç′tyle, *n.* [*Aniso-*, and Gr. *daktylos*, finger.]

1. One of an order of birds, *Anisodactyli*, whose toes are of unequal length.

2. One of the *Anisodactyla*.

an″i-sō-daç′tyl, an″i-sō-daç′tyle, *a.* Same as *Anisodactylic*.

An″i-sō-daç′ty-lȧ, An″i-sō-daç′tyls, *n. pl.* A division of pachydermatous quadrupeds, like the elephant, rhinoceros, etc., having several hoofs forming a single series, about the bottom of the foot.

An″i-sō-daç′ty-lī, *n. pl.* A group of birds, variously divided by naturalists, of the order *Picariæ*.

an″i-sō-daç′tyl-iç, an″i-sō-daç′ty-lous, *a.* 1. Pertaining to the *Anisodactyla*.

2. Pertaining to the *Anisodactyli*.

an′i-sō-dont, *a.* and *n.* [*Aniso-*, and Gr. *odous*, *odontos*, tooth.]

I. *a.* Having teeth unequal in size and spacing.

II. *n.* Any snake having such teeth.

an-i-sog′nȧ-thous, *a.* [*Aniso-*, and Gr. *gnathos*, jaw.] Having the molar teeth unlike in form or size in the upper and lower jaws.

an-i-sog′y-nous, *a.* [*Aniso-*, and Gr. *gynē*, woman.] Having carpels less or (usually) greater in number than sepals.

an-i-sō′iç, *a.* Same as *Anisic*.

an′i-sōl, *n.* Methyl-phenyl ether, an ethereal liquid derived from phenol.

an″i-sō-mer′iç, *a.* [*Aniso-*, and Gr. *meros*, part.] Not consisting of symmetrical or corresponding parts; unsymmetrical; not isomeric.

an-i-som′ẽr-ous, *a.* Characterized by an unequal number of floral organs.

an″i-sō-met′riç, *a.* [*Aniso-*, and Gr. *metron*, measure.] Not isometric.

an″i-s‾-mē-trō′pi-ȧ, *n.* [*Aniso-*, and Gr. *metron*, measure, and *ōps*, eye.] A difference in the refractory power of the two eyes.

an″i-sō-mē-trop′iç, *a.* Unequally refractive; pertaining to anisometropia.

an″i-sō-pet′ăl-ous, *a.* [*Aniso-*, and Gr. *petalon*, leaf.] With petals unequal.

an-i-soph′yl-lous (*or* -sō-phyl′lous), *a.* [*Aniso-*, and Gr. *phyllon*, leaf.] With leaves unequal.

An″i-sō-pleū′rȧ, *n.pl.* [*Aniso-*, and Gr. *pleura*, side.] A division of gasteropods having unequal sides.

an″i-sō-pleū′răl, an″i-sō-pleū′rous, *a.* Having unequal sides; asymmetrical; pertaining to the *Anisopleura*.

An-i-sop′ō-dȧ, *n.pl.* [*Aniso-*, and Gr. *pous*, *podos*, foot.] A division of *Crustacea*, having an unequal number of legs anteriorly and posteriorly.

an-i-sop′ō-dous, *a.* Pertaining to the *Anisopoda*.

an-i-sop′tẽr-ous, *a.* [*Aniso-*, and Gr. *pteron*, wing.] Having wings unequal, as certain flowers.

an′i-sō-spōre, *n.* [*Aniso-*, and Gr. *sporos*, seed.] One of two classes of spores, particularly of colonial radiolarians, supposed to unite or couple; opposite of *isospore*.

an″i-sō-stem′ō-nous, *a.* [*Aniso-*, and Gr. *stēmōn*, a thread.] Having stamens not equal to the petals or the sepals in number.

an″i-sō-sthen′iç, *a.* [*Aniso-*, and Gr. *sthenos*, strength.] Of unequal muscular power.

an″i-sō-trop′iç, an-i-sot′rō-păl, an′i-sō-trōpe, an-i-sot′rō-pous, *a.* [*Aniso-*, and Gr. *tropos*, a turning, from *trepein*, to turn.] Not exhibiting the same physical properties in all directions; not isotropic.

an-i-sot′rō-py, *n.* The state of being anisotropic.

aṅ′kẽr, *n.* [D.] A measure of wine and spirits (particularly the latter), formerly used in England, and containing ten wine gallons. It is still used in Russia and Denmark.

aṅ′kẽr-ite, *n.* [Named after Prof. *Anker* of Austria, and *-ite*.] A mineral consisting of the carbonates of lime, magnesium, and iron, used for smelting and as a flux.

aṅkh (aṅk), *n.* [Egypt., life, soul.] A sacred Egyptian emblem symbolic of life; a cross with a ring at the top.

aṅ′kle, aṅ′çle, *n.* [ME. *ankle*, *ancle*, *anclowe*; AS. *ancleow*; Dan. *enkel*; O.H.G. *encha*, *einka*, leg, ankle; L. *angulus*; Gr. *angkylos*, bent, angle; Sans. *anga*, limb.] The joint which connects the foot with the leg; also, that part of the leg about the ankle-joint.

an′kle-bōne, *n.* The bone of the ankle; the astragalus.

an̄′kled (-kld), *a.* Possessing ankles; used in composition.

an̄′klet, *n.* 1. A little ankle. [Rare.]

2. Anything surrounding or inclosing the ankle, as an ornament, support, clasp, or fetter.

an̄′kus, *n.* [Hind. *ankus*, from Sans. *ankuça*.] An elephant-goad.

an̄′ky-lōse, an̄′chy-lōse, *v.t.* and *v.i.*; ankylosed, *pt.*, *pp.*; ankylosing, *ppr.* To consolidate bones; to stiffen joints, or to become united and stiffened.

an̄′ky-lōsed, an̄′chy-lōsed, *a.* United; stiffened; as the movable bones of joints, by disease; affected with or consolidated by ankylosis.

an̄-ky-lō′sis, an̄-chy-lō′sis, *n.* [Gr. *ankylōsis*, a stiffening of the joints, from *angkyloein*, to crook, stiffen; *angkylos*, crooked, bent.] Union of the bones forming an articulation; stiffness and immovability of a joint.

an̄″ky-los″tō-mi′ȧ-sis, *n.* [Gr. *ankylos*, crooked, and *stoma*, mouth.] Anemia produced by an intestinal parasite, *Ankylostoma duodenale*; also called *dochmiasis*.

an̄-ky-lot′ic, an̄-chy-lot′ic, *a.* Pertaining to ankylosis.

an-ky′roid, *a.* Ancyroid.

an′lāce, an′ē-lāce, *n.* [ME. *anlas*, *anlace*; W. *anglas*, a sword.] A broad knife or dagger, from eighteen inches to two feet long, worn at the girdle. It appears to have been used from an early period.

1. Anlace (time of Edward IV).
2. Anlace (time of Henry VII).

ȧn′lā-ge, *n.* [G.] The first stage of growth of an organ in an embryo.

an′laut, *n.* [G. *an*, on, the beginning, and *laut*, a sound.] The initial sound of a word.

ann, *n.* Same as *Annat*.

an′nȧ, *n.* [Hind. *ānā*.] An East Indian coin, the sixteenth part of a rupee, or about three cents.

an′nāl, *n.* In the Roman Catholic church, a mass said for any person daily for a year, or a mass said on a particular day every year.

an′nāl, *n.* A single event, recorded or registered. [See *Annals*.]

an′nāl-ist, *n.* A writer of annals.

an-nāl-is′tic, *a.* Pertaining to annals or an annalist.

an′nāl-ize, *v.t.* To record; to write annals of. [Rare.]

an′nāls, *n.pl.* [L. *annalis*, pl. *annales*, from *annus*, year.]

1. A kind of history arranged in order of time, or a relation of events in chronological order, year by year. *Annals* differ from history in merely relating events, without observations on the motives, causes, and consequences.

2. Books containing *annals*; as, the *Annals* of Tacitus.

Syn.—History, chronicles, records, registers.

an′nat, an′nāte, *n.* [L. *annus*, a year.] In Scots law, the right of the executor of a deceased clergyman to a half-year's net revenue of his benefice.

an′nāte, *n.* See *Annat*.

an′nats, an′nātes, *n.pl.* [L. *annus*, a year.] In England, a certain sum, as a year's income, formerly given by an ecclesiastic to the church on succeeding to a benefice.

an-nat′tō, *n.* Same as *Arnotto*.

an-nēal′, *v.t.*; annealed, *pt.*, *pp.*; annealing, *ppr.* [ME. *anelen*, *onelen*; AS. *anǣlan*, *onǣlan*, to burn; *an*, *on*, on, and *ǣlan*, to burn, set on fire; *al*, *æl*, fire.]

1. To heat, as glass or iron vessels, in an oven or furnace, and then cool slowly, for the purpose of rendering less brittle; to temper by a gradually diminishing heat. Metals made hard and brittle by hammering, by this process recover their malleability.

2. To heat, as glass or tiles, in order to fix colors; to bake.

And like a picture shone in glass *annealed*.
—Dryden.

an-nēal′ēr, *n.* One who or that which anneals.

an-nēal′ing, *n.* The process or art of heating gradually and cooling gradually, as applied to glass, metals, etc., to reduce brittleness and increase ductility and strength; also, the process of fixing colors or enamel, as in glass, earthenware, etc., by heating and cooling.

an-nēal′ing-ärch, *n.* An oven for annealing glassware; also called a *leer*.

an-nēal′ing-box, *n.* A box in which articles are inclosed while in the annealing-oven.

an-nēal′ing-col″ŏr, *n.* The color assumed by steel in annealing.

an-nēal′ing-ōv″en, *n.* An annealing-arch.

an-nēal′ing-pot, *n.* A closed pot in which articles to be annealed are placed to prevent them from being oxidized.

an-nect′, *v.t.* [L. *annectere*; *ad*, to, and *nectere*, to bind.] To connect; to attach; to join. [Obs.]

an-nec′tent, *a.* Connecting; annexing.

an′nē-lid, an′nē-lide, *a.* and *n.* I. *a.* Pertaining to the *Annelida*.

II. *n.* An animal belonging to the class *Annelida*.

an-nel′i-dăn, *a.* and *n.* Same as *Annelid*.

An-nel′i-dȧ, An-nel′i-dēs, *n.pl.* [LL., from *annellus*, *anellus*, dim. of *anulus*, a ring.] A division of the *Articulata*, without jointed legs but with segmented body; it includes the earthworms, similar marine and fresh-water worms, and leeches.

an-nel′i-dous, *a.* Pertaining to or resembling an annelid.

An-nel-lā′tȧ, *n.pl.* Same as *Annelida*.

an′nē-loid, *a.* and *n.* I. *a.* Annelidous.

II. *n.* An animal like an annelid.

an-nex′, *v.t.*; annexed, *pt.*, *pp.*; annexing, *ppr.* [Fr. *annexer*, from L. *annexus*, pp. of *annectere*; *ad*, to, and *nectere*, to tie, bind.]

1. To unite at the end; as, to *annex* a codicil to a will; to subjoin; to affix.

2. To unite, as a smaller thing to a greater; as, to *annex* a province to a kingdom.

3. To unite to something preceding, as the main object; to connect with, as a condition or consequence; as, to *annex* a penalty to a prohibition, or punishment to crime.

Syn.—Add, attach, fasten, affix, subjoin, append, connect, unite.

an-nex′, *v.i.* To join; to be united.

an-nex′ (*or* an′nex), *n.* Something annexed; as, an *annex* to a building; an appendix; an addition; a supplementary part to a writing, a structure, or a service.

an-nex-ā′tion, *n.* The act of annexing, or uniting at the end; conjunction; addition; the act of connecting; union; as, the *annexation* of Alaska or the Philippine Islands.

an-nex-ā′tion-ăl, *a.* Pertaining to annexation.

an-nex-ā′tion-ist, *n.* One who favors annexation.

an-nex′ion (-nek′shun), *n.* The act of annexing; annexation; addition. [Rare.]

an-nex′ion-ist, *n.* [Rare.] Same as *Annexationist*.

an-nex′ment, *n.* The act of annexing; the thing annexed. [Rare.]

an′ni-cut, an′i-cut, *n.* An East Indian term for an irrigation dam.

an-nī′hi-lȧ-ble, *a.* Capable of being annihilated.

an-nī′hi-lāte, *v.t.*; annihilated, *pt.*, *pp.*; annihilating, *ppr.* [L. *annihilatus*, pp. of *annihilare*, to reduce to nothing; *ad*, to, and *nihilare*, from *nihil*, nothing.]

1. To reduce to nothing; to destroy absolutely; as, no human power can *annihilate* matter.

2. To destroy the identity, form, or distinctive properties of, so that the specific thing no longer exists; as, to *annihilate* a forest by cutting and carrying away the trees, though the timber may still exist; to *annihilate* a house by demolishing the structure.

3. To annul or destroy the force of; to abolish; as, to *annihilate* an argument; to *annihilate* law.

Syn.—Abolish, destroy, extinguish, extirpate, nullify.

an-nī′hi-lāte, *a.* Annihilated. [Obs.]

an-nī-hi-lā′tion, *n.* 1. The act of reducing to nothing, or non-existence; or the act of destroying the form or combination of parts under which a thing exists, so that the name can no longer be applied to it; as, the *annihilation* of a corporation.

2. The state of being reduced to nothing.

an-nī-hi-lā′tion-ism, *n.* The belief that the wicked shall be destroyed; a theological doctrine involving the punishment of the wicked by annihilation.

an-nī-hi-lā′tion-ist, *n.* One who believes in annihilationism.

an-nī′hi-lā-tive, *a.* Destructive.

an-nī′hi-lā-tŏr, *n.* One who or that which annihilates.

an-nī′hi-lā-tō-ry, *a.* Annihilative.

an-ni-vēr′sȧ-ri-ly, *adv.* Annually. [Rare.]

an-ni-vēr′sȧ-ry, *a.* [L. *anniversarius*; *annus*, year, and *vertere*, to turn; pp. *versum*.] Returning every year, at a stated time; annual; yearly; as, an *anniversary* feast.

Anniversary days; in the Roman Catholic church, the days on which an office is yearly performed for the souls of the deceased, or on which the martyrdom of the saints is yearly celebrated.

Anniversary week; the week in the year when annual meetings of religious and benevolent societies are held, as in Boston and New York.

an-ni-vēr′sȧ-ry, *n.* 1. A stated day returning with the revolution of the year. The term is usually applied to a day on which some remarkable event is annually celebrated or commemorated; as, the *anniversary* of the Declaration of Independence.

2. In the Roman Catholic church, an observance on the recurring date of a person's death.

3. The act of celebration, as of a birth, marriage, death, or notable event.

an′ni-vērse, *a.* Anniversary. [Obs.]

an′nō-dā-ted, *a.* [L. *annodatus*, pp. of *annodare*, to knot; *ad*, to, and *nodare*, from *nodus*, a knot.] In heraldry, shaped or curved in a form resembling that of the letter S, as the serpents in the caduceus of Mercury.

Annodated.

an′nō Dom′i-nī. [L. *anno*, abl. of *annus*, year, and *Domini*, genit. of *Dominus*, Lord, master.] In the year of our Lord, noting the time from the Saviour's incarnation; as, *anno Domini*, or *A. D.*, 1904.

an-nom′i-nāte, *v.t.* To name. [Rare.]

an-nom-i-nā′tion, *n.* [L. *annominatio*; *ad*, to, and *nominatio*, from *nomen*, name.]

1. A pun; the use of words nearly alike in sound but of different meanings; paronomasia.

2. Alliteration, or the use of two or more words successively beginning with the same letter. [Obs.]

an′nō mun′dī. [L.; abbreviated to A. M.] In the year of the world; used in chronological reckoning, with the creation as the starting-point; as, *A. M.* 5908.

an-nō′nȧ, *n.* [L. *annona*, from *annus*, a year.]

1. A year's crop production or increase; hence, provisions for a year's subsistence.

2. In the Roman empire, a contribution or tax, payable in corn, imposed on some of the more fertile provinces for provisioning the army.

an′nō-tāte, *v.t.*; annotated, *pt.*, *pp.*; annotating, *ppr.* To make expository or critical notes on; to comment upon; as, to *annotate* the works of Shakspere.

an′nō-tāte, *v.i.* [L. *annotatus*, pp. of *annotare*, to put a note to, write down; *ad*, to, and *notare*, to note, mark; *nota*, a mark, sign.] To comment; to make notes; to make remarks on a writing; as, to *annotate* on the margin of a book.

an-nō-tā′tion, *n.* [L. *annotatio*, from *ad*, to, and *notatio*, a marking, from *notare*, to mark.]

1. A remark, note, or commentary on some passage of a book, intended to illustrate or elucidate its meaning; generally used in the plural; as, *annotations* on the Scriptures.

2. The act of annotating.

3. In civil law, a judicial or decisive remark or note settling a legal point of doubtful significance.

4. The first symptoms of an intermittent fever, or attack of a paroxysm.

Syn.—Comment, commentary, remark, criticism, elucidation.

an-nō-tā′tion-ist, *n.* An annotator. [Rare.]

an′nō-tā-tive, *a.* Of the nature of or characterized by annotations.

an′nō-tā-tŏr, *n.* A writer of annotations, or one who annotates; a commentator; a scholiast.

an-nō′tā-tō-ry, *a.* Containing or marked by annotations. [Rare.]

an′nō-tine, *n.* [L. *annotinus*, a year old.] In zoölogy, a bird one year old, or that has molted once.

an-not′i-nous, *a.* [L. *annotinus*, a year old, from *annus*, year.] In botany, one year old, as branches.

an-not′tō, *n.* Same as *Arnotto*.

an-nounce′, *v.t.*; announced, *pt.*, *pp.*; announcing, *ppr.* [Fr. *annoncer*; It. *annunziare*; L. *annunciare*, *annuntiare*, make known, proclaim; *ad*, to, and *nuntiare*, to report; *nuntius*, a messenger.]

1. To publish; to proclaim; to give notice or first notice of; to make known; as, to *announce* a sale; to *announce* a meeting.

2. To pronounce; to declare by judicial sentence.

Syn.—Proclaim, publish, make known, advertise, declare, promulgate.—To *publish* is to make publicly known; to *announce* is to make known for the first time; to *proclaim* is to give the widest publicity; to *advertise* is to make known through the public prints.

an-nounce′ment, *n.* The act of giving notice; proclamation; publication; that which is announced; as, he made a startling *announcement*.

an-noun′cēr, *n.* One who announces, or first gives notice; a proclaimer.

an-noy′, *v.t.*; annoyed, *pt.*, *pp.*; annoying, *ppr.* [OE. *anoyen*, *anoien*; OFr. *anoier*, *ennuyer*, to annoy, weary; It. *inodio*, from L. *in odio*, in hatred.] To incommode; to irritate; to injure or disturb by continued or repeated acts; to tease, vex, or molest; as, the mosquitoes *annoyed* us: your mistakes *annoy* me: the enemy *annoyed* the garrison by a midnight bombardment.

Syn.—Disturb, worry, plague, harass, tantalize, discommode, molest, vex, pester.

an-noy′, *n.* Injury; molestation; annoyance. [Rare.]

an-noy'ănce, *n.* That which annoys or injures; the act of annoying; the state of being annoyed; as, he showed his *annoyance.*

an-noy'ẽr, *n.* One who annoys.

an-noy'ful, *a.* Giving trouble; incommoding; molesting. [Obs.]

an-noy'ing, *a.* Incommoding; hurting; molesting; as, an *annoying* noise.

an-noy'ing-ly, *adv.* In an annoying manner.

an-noy'ing-ness, *n.* Vexatiousness; the quality of being annoying.

an-noy'ous, *a.* Troublesome. [Obs.]

an'nū-ăl, *a.* [ME. *annual*; OFr. *annuel*; L. *annualis*, yearly, from *annus*, a year.]

1. Yearly; returning every year; coming yearly; as, an *annual* feast.

2. Lasting or continuing only one year or season; requiring to be renewed every year; as, an *annual* plant.

3. Performed in a year; as, the *annual* motion of the earth.

Annual assay; a test of coins which the director of the United States mint makes every year to assure the standard of fineness.

an'nū-ăl, *n.* 1. Any compilation or literary work published yearly.

2. A plant, or other organism, that lives but one year, or for a single season.

3. In the Roman Catholic church, a yearly mass for the dead, or for a special purpose.

an'nū-ăl-ist, *n.* One who edits, writes for, or publishes, an annual. [Rare.]

an'nū-ăl-ly, *adv.* Yearly; returning every year; year by year.

an'nū-ā-ry, *a.* and *n.* I. *a.* Annual. [Obs.]

II. *n.* A year-book.

an'nū-el-ẽr, *n.* A priest who says anniversary masses for persons deceased. [Obs.]

an'nū-ent, *a.* [L. *annuens*, ppr. of *annuere*, to nod at; *ad*, to, and *nuere*, from Gr. *neuein*, to nod.] Nodding; specifically applied to the muscles that bend the head.

an-nū'i-tănt, *n.* One who receives, or is entitled to receive, an annuity.

an-nū'i-ty, *n.* [Fr. *annuité*; L. *annuitas*, from *annus*, year.] A sum of money, payable yearly, to continue for a given number of years, for life, or forever; an annual sum granted to another and charged on the person of the grantor; an annual allowance.

an-nul', *v.t.*; annulled, *pt.*, *pp.*; annulling, *ppr.* [Fr. *annuler*, from L. *annullare*, to bring to nothing; *ad*, to, and *nullus*, none, *nullum*, nothing.]

1. To make void; to nullify; to abrogate; to abolish; used appropriately of laws, decrees, edicts, decisions of courts, or other established rules, permanent usages, and the like, which are made void by competent authority.

2. To reduce to nothing; to obliterate. [Rare.]

Syn.—Abolish, repeal, cancel, quash, nullify, revoke, abrogate, reverse, rescind, destroy, set aside, obliterate.

an'nū-lăr, *a.* [L. *annularis*, pertaining to a ring, from *annulus*, *anulus*, a ring.]

1. Having the form of a ring; pertaining to a ring; ringed, or ring-shaped; as, *annular* ducts.

2. Marked with rings or bands.

Annular crystal; the form of crystal when a hexahedral prism has six, or an octahedral prism eight, marginal faces, disposed in a ring about each base; or when these prisms are truncated on all their terminal edges.

Annular eclipse; an eclipse of the sun, in which the moon conceals the whole of the sun's disk except a bright ring around the border.

Annular finger; the fourth digit of each hand; the ring-finger.

An-nū-lā'ri-ȧ, *n.pl.* In botany, a genus of fossil plants supposed to represent branches of *Calamitea*; so called from the annuli or ring-like parts formed by the whorled leaves when sheathing.

an-nū-lar'i-ty, *n.* The quality or state of being annular.

an'nū-lăr-ly, *adv.* In an annular fashion or manner; after the form of a ring.

an'nū-lā-ry, *a.* Having the form of a ring.

An-nū-lā'tȧ, *n.pl.* [L., neut. pl. of *annulatus*, furnished with a ring, from *annulus*, a ring.] In zoölogy, a class of animals including the marine and fresh-water worms, earthworms, leeches, etc.; the *Annelida.*

an'nū-lāte, *n.* One of the *Annulata.*

an'nū-lāte, an'nū-lā-ted, *a.* [L. *annulatus*, furnished with a ring.]

1. Furnished with rings, or circles like rings; having belts; surrounded by rings.

2. Pertaining to the *Annulata.*

an-nū-lā'tion, *n.* A circular or ring-like formation; a ring or belt.

an'nū-let, *n.* [Dim. of L. *annulus*, a ring.]

1. A small ring.

2. In architecture, a small fillet or band several times repeated, in the Doric capital, under the quarter-round; also, a narrow, flat molding, which is common to many parts of columns, as in the bases or capitals; called also a *fillet*, *listel*, *cincture*, *tænia*, etc.

3. In heraldry, a little circle borne as a charge in coats of arms; formerly reputed a mark of nobility and jurisdiction. It denotes strength and eternity, by its circular form.

4. In decorative art, a stripe around a vase or other ornamental vessel.

an-nul'lȧ-ble, *a.* Capable of being annulled, repealed, or abrogated.

an-nul'lẽr, *n.* One who annuls. [Rare.]

an'nū-li, *n.*, pl. of *annulus.*

an-nul'ment, *n.* The act of annulling; invalidation.

an'nū-loid, *n.* One of the *Annuloida.*

an'nū-loid, *a.* 1. Ring-like.

2. Pertaining to or resembling the *Annuloida.*

An-nū-loid'ȧ, An-nū-loi'dē-ȧ, *n.pl.* [LL., from L. *annulus*, a ring, and Gr. *eidos*, form.] In zoölogy, a subkingdom classified by Huxley, including the *Echinodermata* and *Scolecida*; called also *Echinozoa.* [Rare.]

An-nū-lō'sȧ, *n.pl.* [LL., from L. *annulosus*, from *annulus*, a ring.] In modern zoölogical classifications, a division (subkingdom) of animals regarded by some as synonymous with the *Arthropoda* or *Articulata*; according to other systematists, including both the *Articulata* and *Annulata* or worms; so called from their ringed appearance.

an-nū-lō'săn, *n.* One of the *Annulosa.*

an'nū-lōse, *a.* 1. Furnished with rings; composed of rings.

2. Of or pertaining to the *Annulosa.*

an'nū-lus, *n.*; *pl.* **an'nū-li.** [L., a ring.]

1. A ring-like figure; a ring.

2. In geometry, the ring-like area between the circumferences of two concentric circles.

3. In botany, the elastic ring which surrounds the sporecase in ferns; also, the slender membrane surrounding the stems of certain agarics (mushrooms) after the spreading of the cap.

aa, Annulus of a Fungus (*Agaricus rubescens*).

4. In zoölogy, a ring-shaped marking.

5. In astronomy, the visible edge of the sun in an annular eclipse.

an-nū'mẽr-āte, *v.t.* [L. *annumeratus*, pp. of *annumerare*, to add to, to reckon with; *ad*, to, and *numerare*, to count.] To add to a former number; to unite to something before mentioned. [Obs.]

an-nū-mẽr-ā'tion, *n.* Addition to a former number. [Obs.]

an-nun'ci-ȧ-ble (-shi-ȧ-bl), *a.* That may be announced. [Rare.]

an-nun'ci-āte (-shi-), *v.t.*; annunciated, *pt.*, *pp.*; annunciating, *ppr.* [L. *annunciatus*, *annuntiatus*, pp. of *annuntiare*, to proclaim.] To bring tidings to; to announce.

an-nun'ci-āte (-shi-), *a.* Announced; foretold. [Obs.]

an-nun-ci-ā'tion (-shi-), *n.* 1. The act of announcing; promulgation; proclamation; announcement; as, the *annunciation* of a decree.

2. In church history, specifically, the announcement of the incarnation of Christ, made to the Virgin Mary by the angel Gabriel.

3. [A—] The festival celebrated in some churches (on March 25) in commemoration of the angel's announcement to Mary.

4. Among the Jews, a part of the ceremony of the Passover.

an-nun'ci-ȧ-tive (-shi-), *a.* Making an announcement; pertaining to annunciation. [Rare.]

an-nun'ci-ā-tŏr (-shi-), *n.* 1. One who announces.

2. Formerly, an officer of the Greek or Eastern church, whose duty was to announce holy days and festivals.

3. A device, operated by electricity, etc., for showing the whereabouts of persons desiring service; used in hotels, steamboats, elevators, etc.

an-nun'ci-ȧ-tō-ry (-shi-), *a.* Relating to announcement. [Rare.]

ā'nō-. [Gr. *anō*, upward, from *ana*, up.] A combining form signifying upward.

An'ō-ȧ, *n.* [Native name.] A subgenus of ruminating animals. The typical species is a small forest-ox, *Anoa depressicornis*, found on the island of Celebes.

an-ō-căr'pous, *a.* [*Ano-*, and Gr. *karpos*, fruit.] In botany, having the sori or fruit-dots on the upper side of the frond, as ferns.

an'ōde, *n.* [Gr. *anodos*, a way up; *ana*, up, and *hodos*, way.] The positive pole of an electric battery, or preferably, the path by which the current passes out and enters the electrolyte on its way to the other pole; opposed to *cathode.*

ȧ-nod'iç, *a.* 1. Relating to an anode.

2. Proceeding in an upward direction.

3. In medicine, astringent; styptic.

An-ō-don'tȧ, *n.* [LL., from Gr. *an* priv., and *odous*, *odontos*, tooth.] A genus of fresh-water mollusks without hinge-teeth.

an'ō-dyne, *n.* [Gr. *anōdynos*, without pain; *an* priv., and *odynē*, pain.] Any medicine which allays pain, as an opiate or narcotic.

an'ō-dyne, *a.* Assuaging pain.

ȧ-nod'y-nous, *a.* Having the qualities of an anodyne.

ȧ-noil', *v.t.* To anoint with oil. [Obs.]

ȧ-noint', *v.t.*; anointed, *pt.*, *pp.*; anointing, *ppr.* [ME. *anoynten*, *enoynten*; OFr. *enoindre*; L. *inungere*, to anoint; *in*, on, and *ungere*, to smear.]

1. To pour oil upon; to smear or rub over with oil or unctuous substances.

2. To consecrate by the use of oil, a sacred rite of great antiquity. Monarchs, prelates, and priests were *anointed* as part of their consecration ceremonies, and the custom still survives, as in the coronation of British monarchs. King Edward VII. and his queen, Alexandra, were both *anointed* at their coronation in 1902.

Anoint Hazael to be king over Syria.
—1 Kings xix. 15.

A-noint'ed, *n.* 1. The Messiah, or Son of God, consecrated to the great office of Redeemer; called the *Lord's Anointed.*

2. [a—] A consecrated person.

ȧ-noint'ẽr, *n.* One who anoints.

ȧ-noint'ing, *n.* The act of smearing with oil; a consecrating.

ȧ-noint'ment, *n.* The act of anointing, or state of being anointed.

A-nō'lis, *n.* [LL. from *anoli*, *anoalli*, the native name in the Antilles.] A genus of American lizards of the family *Iguanidæ*; called also *chameleons.*

an'om-, *prefix.* See *Anomo-.*

ȧ-nom'ăl, *n.* An anomaly. [Rare.]

ȧ-nom''ȧ-li-flō'rous, *a.* [L. *anomalus*, irregular; *flos*, *floris*, flower.] In botany, producing anomalous flowers.

ȧ-nom'ȧ-li-ped, ȧ-nom'ȧ-li-pēde, *a.* and *n.* [LL. *anomalus*, irregular, and *pes*, *pedis*, foot.]

I. *a.* Having abnormal feet; syndactylic.

II. *n.* In ornithology, a syndactyl; a bird whose toes are firmly united together for some distance, as the kingfisher.

ȧ-nom'ȧ-lişm, *n.* An anomaly; a deviation or departure from rule.

ȧ-nom'ȧ-list, *n.* In philology, one who claims the right to create language arbitrarily; opposed to *analogist.*

ȧ-nom-ȧ-lis'tiç, ȧ-nom-ȧ-lis'tiç-ăl, *a.* 1. Irregular; departing from common or established rules.

2. In astronomy, pertaining to the anomaly or angular distance of a planet from its perihelion.

Anomalistic revolution; the period in which a planet or satellite passes from any one point in its elliptic orbit to the same point again, completing a cycle of its changes of anomaly.

Anomalistic year; in astronomy, the time in which the earth passes through its orbit, which is 24 minutes 45 seconds longer than the tropical year on account of the precession of the equinoxes.

ȧ-nom-ȧ-lis'tiç-ăl-ly, *adv.* In an anomalistic manner.

ȧ-nom''ȧ-lō-gon'ȧ-tous, *a.* [LL. *anomalogonatus*, from Gr. *anōmalos*, irregular, and *gony*, knee.] Having abnormal knees, through lack of the ambiens muscle; applied to some birds.

ȧ-nom'ȧ-lous, *a.* [Gr. *anōmalos*, irregular, uneven; *an* priv., and *homalos*, from *homos*, the same, common.] Irregular; deviating from a general rule, method, or analogy; applied, in grammar, to words which deviate from the common rules in inflection; and in astronomy, to the seemingly irregular motions of the planets; but applied also generally to whatever is irregular; as, an *anomalous* character; *anomalous* pronunciation.

ȧ-nom'ȧ-lous-ly, *adv.* Irregularly; in a manner different from common rule, method, or analogy.

ȧ-nom'ȧ-lous-ness, *n.* The condition of being anomalous.

ȧ-nom'ȧ-ly, *n.*; *pl.* **ȧ-nom'ȧ-lies.** [Fr. *anomalie*; L. *anomalia*; Gr. *anōmalia*, inequality.]

1. Irregularity; deviation from the common rule; the state of being anomalous; thus *oxen*, the plural of *ox*, is an *anomaly* in grammar, as the regular plural would be *oxes.*

2. In astronomy, the angular distance of a planet from its perihelion, as seen from the sun; called *true anomaly* when the angle is measured to the real position of the planet, and *mean anomaly* when measured to its mean position.

3. In music, a slight deviation from a perfect interval in tuning instruments with fixed notes or keyboards.

4. In natural history, a deviation from the essential characteristics of any given type, as a bird that cannot fly.

Syn.—Irregularity, abnormality, exception, informality, peculiarity, eccentricity.

A-nō'mi-ȧ, *n.* [LL., from Gr. *anomoios*, unlike; *an* priv., and *homoios*, like, similar.] In conchology, a genus of bivalve mollusks having unequal valves, the lower being perforated for adhesion to oysters and other shells.

an'ō-mite, *n.* 1. A fossil of the genus *Anomites.*

2. In mineralogy, a variety of the mica called biotite.

an'ō-mō-, an'om-, *prefix.* [Gr. *anomos,* irregular; *a* priv., and *nomos,* law.] A combining form signifying unusual or abnormal.

an"ō-mō-cär'pous, *a.* [*Anomo-,* and Gr. *karpos,* fruit.] In botany, producing abnormal fruit.

an'ō-mō-dont, *a.* and *n.* I. *a.* Relating to the *Anomodontia.*

II. *n.* One of the *Anomodontia.*

An"ō-mō-don'ti-ȧ, *n.pl.* [*Anomo-,* and Gr. *odous, odontos,* tooth.] A name given by Owen to an order of extinct reptiles of the Trias, either without teeth or having the premaxillaries sheathed with a horny plate like the turtles, or only one pair of canine tusks in the upper jaw, and divided by him into three families in accordance with these distinctions. Called by Huxley *Dicynodontia.*

An-ō-mœ'ăn, *n.* [LL., from Gr. *anomoios,* dissimilar; *an* priv., and *homoios,* similar.] In church history, one of a sect of extreme Arians of the fourth century, as distinguished from the Semi-Arians. They held the Son to be unlike the Father in his essential nature. [See *Eunomian.*]

an-ō-moph'yl-lous, *a.* [*Anomo-,* and Gr. *phyllon,* leaf.] In botany, having leaves arranged without regularity.

An-ō-mū'rȧ, An-ō-möü'rȧ, *n.pl.* [*Anomo-,* and Gr. *oura,* tail.] A suborder of crustaceans, having the tail unfitted for swimming, as the hermit-crab; the section is intermediate between the crabs and the lobsters.

an-ō-mū'răl, *a.* Of or pertaining to the *Anomura.*

an-ō-mū'răn, *a.* and *n.* I. *a.* Same as *Anomural.*

II. *n.* One of the *Anomura.*

an-ō-mū'rous, an-ō-möü'rous, *a.* Having an irregular abdomen or tail; anomural.

an'ō-my, *n.* A violation of law. [Rare.]

ȧ-non', *adv.* [ME. *anon, anoon, onon, onoon;* AS. *on ān,* acc., in one, together, straightway.]

1. In a little while; soon; with little delay; as, I will be there *anon.*

2. At another time; again.

Ever and anon; now and then; time after time.

A-nō'nȧ, *n.* [LL., from *menona,* the Malay name.] A genus of plants, the type of the natural order *Anonaceæ. Anona squamosa* (sweet-sop) grows in the West Indian islands, and yields an edible fruit having a thick, sweet, luscious pulp. *Anona muricata* (sour-sop) is cultivated in the West and East Indies; it produces a large pear-shaped fruit, of a greenish color, containing an agreeable, slightly acid pulp. *Anona reticulata* is the custard-apple.

Anona or Sour-sop (*Anona muricata*).

An-ō-nā'cē-æ, *n.pl.* In botany, a natural order of polypetalous plants, embracing several hundred species, including the custard-apple, sweet-sop, sour-sop, etc.

an-ō-nā'ceous, *a.* Of or relating to the *Anonaceæ.*

an'ō-nym, an'ō-nyme, *n.* 1. One whose name is unknown; an anonymous person or writer.

2. A pen-name; a pseudonym.

3. A book bearing no author's name. [Rare.]

4. In zoölogy, an appellation; a name having no basis of scientific authority. [Rare.]

an-ō-nym'i-ty, *n.* 1. The quality or state of being anonymous.

2. That which is anonymous. [Rare.]

ȧ-non'y-mous, *a.* [Fr. *anonyme;* L. *anonymus;* Gr. *anōnymos,* nameless.]

1. Nameless; without the real name of the author; as, an *anonymous* pamphlet.

2. Of unknown name; as, an *anonymous* author.

3. Lacking a name, as an animal not assigned to any species. [Rare.]

Syn.—Nameless, unattested, authorless, unidentified, unauthenticated.

ȧ-non'y-mous-ly, *adv.* Without a name; in an anonymous manner.

ȧ-non'y-mous-ness, *n.* The state of being anonymous.

A-noph'e-lēs, (lēz) *n.* A genus of mosquitoes of the family *Culicidæ,* characterized by the long, slender palpi which nearly equal the beak in length. The No. Am. species is the malarial mosquito.

An-ō-phy'tȧ, *n.pl.* [LL., from Gr. *anō,* upward, and *phyton,* plant, from *phyein,* to grow.] A section of cryptogamic plants comprising the mosses and liverworts.

an'ō-phyte, *n.* One of the *Anophyta.*

An'ō-plȧ, *n.pl.* [LL., from Gr. *anoplos,* unarmed; *an* priv., and *hoplon,* shield, *hopla,* arms.] A division of nemertean worms with unarmed proboscis.

an-op'lō-thēre, *n.* An individual of the genus *Anoplotherium.*

An-ō-plō-thē'ri-um, *n.* [LL., from Gr. *an* priv., *hoplon,* weapon, and *thērion,* a beast.] A genus of extinct quadrupeds of the order *Pachydermata,* whose bones were first found in the gypsum quarries near Paris; characterized by the shortness and feebleness of their canine teeth, whence the name.

An-ō-plū'rȧ, *n.pl.* [LL., from Gr. *an* priv., *hoplon,* weapon, and *oura,* tail.] An aberrant order of insects, sometimes termed *Parasitica* or *Epizoa,* and including the lice proper, as those parasitic on man, and bird-lice.

an'op-sy, ȧ-nop'si-ȧ, *n.* [LL., from Gr. *an* priv., *opsis,* sight.] Deficient sight; blindness.

an-ō-rec'tic, *a.* Pertaining to, affected with, or causing, anorexia.

an-ō-rec'tous, *a.* Without appetite.

an-ō-rex'i-ȧ, an-ō-rex'y, *n.* [Gr. *anorexia,* want of appetite; *an* priv., and *orexia,* from *oregein,* to desire.] Want of appetite.

ȧ-nor'măl, *a.* Not according to rule; abnormal. [Obs.]

ȧ-norn', *v.t.* To adorn. [Obs.]

ȧ-nor'thic, *a.* [Gr. *an* priv., and *orthos,* straight.] In crystallology, irregular; triclinic.

ȧ-nor'thite, *n.* [Gr. *an* priv., *orthos,* straight, and *-ite.*] A species of mineral of the feldspar family, occurring in small glassy crystals.

ȧ-nor'thō-clāse, *n.* [Gr. *an* priv., *orthos,* straight, and *klān,* to break.] A sodium potassium feldspar, that is triclinic in crystallization.

an-or-thŏp'si-ȧ, *n.* [Gr. *an* priv., *orthos,* straight, and *ōps,* eye.] Obliquity of vision; squinting.

ȧ-nor'thō-scōpe, *n.* [Gr. *an* priv., *orthos,* straight, *skopein,* to view.] An instrument or toy for producing a particular kind of optical illusion by means of two disks rotating rapidly in opposite directions, the hinder disk having certain distorted figures painted upon it, which appear in normal shape when viewed through slits in the other disk.

an-os-mat'ic, *a.* Without the sense of smell.

ȧ-nos'mi-ȧ, *n.* [LL., from Gr. *an* priv., and *osmē,* smell.] Absence of the sense of smell.

an-ŏth'ẽr, *a,* and *pron.* [ME. *an other, an,* one, the, and *other.*]

1. Not the same; different; as, we have *one* form of government, England *another.*

2. One more, in addition to a former number, indefinitely; as, grant one request, they will ask *another* favor, *another,* and *another.*

3. Any other; any different person, indefinitely; as, let *another* praise thee, and not thy own mouth. This word is often thus used as a pronoun, becoming a substitute for the name of a person or thing. *Another* is also used in opposition to *one,* and frequently with *one* in a reciprocal sense; as love *one another;* bear *one another's* burdens; that is, love each other, or let one love another, etc.

an-ŏth'ẽr-gāines, *a.* Of another kind. [Obs.]

an-ŏth'ẽr-gātes, *a.* Of another sort. [Obs.]

an-ŏth'ẽr-guess (ges), *a.* [Corrupted from *another-gates.*] Of another sort. [Rare.]

ȧ-not'tȧ, *n.* Same as *Arnotto.*

An-öü'rȧ, *n.* See *Anura.*

an-öü'rous, *a.* See *Anurous.*

an'sȧ, *n.; pl.* **an'sæ.** [L. *ansa,* a handle.]

1. In archæology, a vase-handle.

2. [*pl.*] In astronomy, the projections or arms of the ring on each side of the planet Saturn.

an'sā-ted, *a.* [L. *ansatus,* from *ansa,* a handle.] Having a handle or handles, or something in the form of handles.

An'sẽr, *n.* [L., a goose.]

1. A genus of birds, family *Anseridæ.* The ordinary name of the goose, whether tame or wild.

2. In astronomy, a small star visible in the constellation known as the Fox and Goose.

an'sẽr-ā-ted, *a.* [L. *anser,* a goose, and *-ated.*] In heraldry, a term applied to a cross with its extremities shaped like the heads of lions, eagles, geese, reptiles, etc.

Anserated.

An'sẽr-ēs, *n.pl.* [L., geese.] In Linnæus's system, the third order of birds, whose characteristics are a smooth bill, broadest at the point, covered with a smooth skin, and furnished with teeth. The toes are webbed or palmated. It includes all the web-footed water-fowl, as geese, ducks, gulls, petrels, etc.

An-ser'i-dæ, *n.pl.* A family of web-footed birds, containing the geese proper (genus *Anser*), distinguished by having the bill not longer than the head, and thicker at the base than it is broad; they have longer and stronger legs than ducks, and shorter wings. [See *Goose.*]

An"ser-i-for'mēs, *n. pl.* [L. *anser,* a goose, and *forma,* form.] A class of birds approximately equivalent to the *Anseres.*

an'sẽr-ine, *a.* [L. *anserinus,* from *anser,* a goose.]

1. Resembling the skin of a goose; uneven, like the human skin after a chill; as, an *anserine* skin.

2. Pertaining to the *Anseres.*

an'sẽr-ous, *a.* Resembling a goose; stupid, as a goose seems; silly.

an'swẽr (-sẽr), *v.t.;* answered, *pt., pp.;* answering, *ppr.* [ME. *answeren, andsweren;* AS. *andswarian;* Ice. *andsvara;* Sw. *ansvara, and-,* against, in reply, and *svara,* from *swaran,* to swear, affirm.]

1. To speak in return to, as a call or question, or a speech, declaration, or argument of another person; to respond to; as, to *answer* a fool according to his folly; to *answer* a proper question.

This word may be applied to a great variety of objects, expressing the idea of a *return;* as, to *answer* the notes or sounds of birds and animals; an echo *answers* a voice, etc.

2. To speak in one's defense; to defend; to refute; as, to *answer* a charge of murder.

3. To write in reply to; to reply to (another writing) by way of explanation, refutation, or justification; as, to *answer* a letter; to *answer* an editorial.

4. To comply with, fulfil, pay, or satisfy; as, he *answered* my order; to *answer* a debt.

5. To act in return or opposition to; as, the enemy *answered* our fire with a twelve-inch shell.

6. To be equivalent to; to be adequate to, or sufficient to accomplish.

7. To bear a due proportion to; to be equal or adequate to; to suit; as, our success does not *answer* our expectation.

8. To be opposite to; to face; as, fire *answers* fire.

9. To respond to, or attend upon; as, an attentive maid instantly *answers* the bell; or to respond to by signifying one's presence; as, to *answer* a roll-call; or by granting a petition; as, God *answers* prayer.

10. To solve, as a proposition or problem in mathematics; to give a correct solution of; as, to *answer* a riddle.

an'swẽr, *v.i.* 1. To reply; to speak or write by way of return; to respond; as, there is none to *answer;* he *answered* quickly.

2. To be accountable, liable, or responsible; followed by *to* before the person to whom, and *for* before the thing for which, one is liable; as, the man must *answer to* his employer *for* the money intrusted to his care; we must *answer to* the law *for* our offenses.

3. To vindicate, or give a justificatory account of; to atone or take punishment for; followed by *for;* as, a man cannot *answer for* his friend.

4. To correspond with; to suit; followed by *to.*

> As in water face *answereth to* face, so the heart of man *to* man. —Prov. xxvii. 19.

5. To return, as sound reverberated; to echo; as, the noise seems to fly away and *answer* at a great distance.

6. To succeed; to effect the object intended; to have a good effect; as, gypsum *answers* as a manure on a dry soil.

7. In law, to make a defense to a civil suit by a written statement filed in the court; to defend oneself against a criminal charge.

8. To take the place of; as, a piece of sail *answered* for clothes.

an'swẽr, *n.* 1. A reply; that which is said in return to a call, a question, an argument, an allegation, or address.

2. An account rendered to justice; a reply to a charge.

> He will call you to so hot an *answer* for it. —Shak.

3. In law, a counterstatement of facts, in a course of pleadings; a refutation of what the other party has alleged; the formal reply of one side in a lawsuit to the allegations of the other.

4. A writing, letter, pamphlet, or book, in reply to another.

5. A reverberated sound; an echo.

6. A return; that which is sent in consequence of some petition; as, a blessing sent in *answer* to a prayer.

7. A solution, as of a puzzle, rebus, etc.; the result of a mathematical calculation; as, the *answer* to an equation.

8. An act done in response or return for another; retaliation; as, his *answer* was an immediate assault.

9. In music, the reply of one instrument to another in orchestration, or of one phrase to another.

10. In fencing, a return thrust.

Syn.—Reply, rejoinder, retort, response, replication, solution.—An *answer* is given to a question; a *reply* is made to an assertion; a *rejoinder* is made to a *reply*; a *response* is made in accordance with the words of another.

an′swẽr-ȧ-ble (-bl), *a.* 1. Capable of being answered, or satisfied by reply; as, an *answerable* argument.

2. Obliged to give an account, or liable to be called to account; amenable; responsible; as, an agent is *answerable* to his principal.

3 Obliged or liable to pay, indemnify, or make good; as, to be *answerable* for a debt or for damages.

4. Correspondent; agreeing with; in conformity with; as, the features portrayed in a picture are *answerable* to the original.

5. Suitable; suited; proportionate; commensurate; as, an achievement *answerable* to the preparation for it.

6. Equal; equivalent to. [Rare.]

Syn.—Amenable, accountable, responsible, liable.

an′swẽr-ȧ-ble-ness, *n.* The quality of being answerable, liable, responsible, or correspondent.

an′swẽr-ȧ-bly, *adv.* In an answerable manner.

an′swẽr-ẽr, *n.* One who answers.

an-swẽr-less, *a* Having no answer, or unanswerable.

an't. A contraction of *an it*, that is, *if it*. [Obs. See *An*.]

ăn't. Same as *Ain't*.

ant-, *prefix* Contraction of *anti-*, which see.

-ant, *suffix.* [Fr. *-ant*; L. *-antem* or *-entem*, the ppr. ending.] A combining form most frequently denoting *the act of doing*, or *one who does* what is suggested by the stem of the word with which it is combined; and forming nouns of adjectival origin; as, milit*ant*, merch*ant*, radi*ant*.

ȧnt, *n.* [ME. *amte, amete*; AS. *æmete, æmette*; O H.G. *ameize*; G. *ameise*, ant.] One of a genus of insects (*Formica*) of the order *Hymenoptera*, having a characteristic scale between the breast and belly, with a joint so deep that the insect appears as if almost cut in two; an emmet; a pismire.

Ants, like bees, keep together in companies, and maintain a sort of republic. Some raise hillocks of earth, in which they live, propagate and nurture their young, and store their provisions, the nests containing an intricate system of passages and chambers. Others, in rainy climates, build nests on trees. As among bees, there are neuter or working *ants* as well as males and females, the so-called neuter *ants* being without wings and female without the faculty of being fertilized. They do most of the work of the community, and care for the young. Many of the species are distinguished by names derived from their habits, as *agricultural ants, amazon ants, carpenter ants, honey ants, mason ants*, and *soldier ants*.

an′tȧ, *n*; *pl* **an′tæ** or **an′tēs.** [L., from *ante*, before.] In architecture, a pilaster, especially a pilaster on each side of a door or standing opposite a pillar; in Greek and Roman architecture, the pilaster used to terminate the side walls of temples prolonged beyond the face of the end wall. A portico having its columns standing between *antæ* is said to be *in antis* Written also *ante*.

A A

Portico *in Antis*. *AA*, Antæ.

ant-ac′id, *n* In medicine, a substance counteracting or neutralizing acidity.

ant-ac′id, *a.* Neutralizing acidity.

ant-ac′rid, *a* Having power to correct acridity.

An-tæ′ăn, *a.* Relating to or like Antæus, a giant killed by Hercules.

an-tag′ō-niṣm, *n.* 1. The act of antagonizing or opposing; the characteristic quality or temper of persons opposed.

2. The state of being antagonized; mutual resistance, as between persons, forces, or things acting in opposition to each other; contrariety or disagreement, as between conflicting principles

an-tag′ō-nist, *n.* [Gr *antagōnistēs*, an opponent; from *antagōnizesthai*, to struggle against.]

1. One who struggles for mastery with another; an opponent in a contest of any kind.

2. In anatomy, a muscle which acts oppositely to another; as, a flexor is the *antagonist* of an extensor.

3. In medicine, a counteractive; an antidote.

Syn.—Adversary, opponent, competitor, enemy, rival, foe.

an-tag′ō-nist, *a.* Counteracting; opposing; combating; antagonistic; as, an *antagonist* muscle.

an-tag-ō-nis′tiç, an-tag-ō-nis′tiç-ăl, *a.* Opposing in combat; contending against.

an-tag-ō-nis′tiç-ăl-ly, *adv.* With antagonism; in opposition; adversely.

an-tag′ō-nīze, *v.t.*; antagonized, *pt., pp.*; antagonizing, *ppr.* 1. To contend against; to oppose; to counteract or neutralize.

2. To arouse antagonism in; to render antagonistic; as, this subterfuge *antagonized* his associates.

an-tag′ō-nīze, *v.i.* To be in opposition; to act antagonistically.

an-tag′ō-ny, *n.* Contest; opposition. [Obs.]

ant-al′ġiç, *a.* [Gr. *anti*, against, and *algos*, pain.] Having the tendency to allay pain.

ant-al′ġiç, *n.* A drug having the power of allaying pain; an anodyne.

ant-al′kȧ-li, ant-al′kȧ-line (*or* -līn), *n.* In medicine, a substance which neutralizes an alkali, or counteracts an alkaline tendency in the system.

ant-al′kȧ-line (*or* -līn), *a.* Having the property of neutralizing alkalis.

ant-am-bū-lā′çrăl, *a.* In zoölogy, distant from or opposite to the region of the ambulacra.

ant″an-ȧ-çlā′sis, *n.* [Gr. *antanaklasis*, a bending back against; *anti*, against, and *anaklān*, to bend back.]

1. In rhetoric, a figure which consists in repeating the same word in a different sense; as, while we *live*, let us *live*; learn some *craft* when young, that when old you may live without *craft*.

2. In grammar, a repetition of words, resuming a sentence after a long parenthesis; as, shall that heart (which not only feels them, but which has all motions of life placed in them), *shall that heart*, etc.

ant″an-ȧ-gō′ġē, *n.* [Gr. *anti*, against, and *anagogē*, a taking up.] In rhetoric, a figure which consists in replying to an adversary with recrimination; as, when the accusation of one party is unanswerable, the accused person charges him with the same or another crime.

ant″aph-rō-dis′i-aç, *a.* and *n.* Same as *Anaphrodisiac*.

ant″aph-rō-dit′iç, *a.* Antivenereal.

ant″aph-rō-dit′iç, *n.* [*Anti-*, and *aphroditē*, Venus.] A medicine to cure venereal disease.

ant″ap-ō-pleç′tiç, *a.* and *n.* I. *a.* Serving to prevent or to cure apoplexy.

II. *n.* A medicine for the prevention or cure of apoplexy.

ant-är′çhiṣm, *n.* [*Anti-*, and Gr. *archē*, government.] Opposition to all government, or to all restraint of individuals by law. [Rare. See *Anarchism*.]

ant-är′çhist, *n.* One who opposes all social government, or all control of individuals by law. [Rare.]

ant-är-çhis′tiç, ant-är-çhis′tiç-ăl, *a.* Opposed to all human government. [Rare.]

ant-ärç′tiç, *a.* [*Anti-*, and Gr. *arktos*, the Bear, a northern constellation.] Opposite to the northern or arctic pole; relating to the southern pole or to the region near it; as, the *antarctic* circle, the *Antarctic* Ocean, etc.

Antarctic circle; an imaginary circle around the earth, distant from the antarctic pole 23° 28′.

An-tā′rēs, *n.* [Gr. *Antarēs*; *anti*, against, resembling, and *Arēs*, Mars, so called from its resemblance to Mars in color.] The Arabic name of a star of the first magnitude in the constellation of Scorpio; called also the *Scorpion's Heart*.

ant-är-thrit′iç, an″ti-är-thrit′iç, *a.* [*Anti-*, against, and Gr. *arthritis*, gout.] Having power to relieve or cure gout.

ant-är-thrit′iç, an″ti-är-thrit′iç, *n.* A remedy which cures or alleviates the gout.

ant-asth-mat′iç (-as-mat′ik), **an″ti-asth-mat′iç,** *a.* [*Anti-*, and Gr. *asthma*, asthma.] Having power to relieve or cure asthma.

ant-asth-mat′iç, an″ti-asth-mat′iç, *n.* A remedy for the asthma.

Ant-bear (*Myrmecophaga jubata*).

ȧnt′=beãr (-bãr), *n.* 1. A name sometimes given to any of the larger species of ant-eaters, but generally restricted to *Myrmecophaga jubata*, a native of the warmer parts of South America. Its body is covered with long hair, and the tail is long and bushy. The snout or muzzle is extended and toothless, and the tongue extensile and glutinous. Called also *tamanoir* and *great ant-eater*.

2. The aardvark, *Orycteropus capensis*, of South Africa.

ȧnt′=bīrd, *n.* One of several species of birds common in South America, which feed on ants.

ȧnt′=çat″tle, *n.pl.* A name given to various aphids kept by ants for the sake of a kind of honey-dew secreted by them, which forms a source of food for the ants.

ȧnt′=çow, *n.* Any individual of the group of insects known as ant-cattle.

an′tē-, *prefix.* [L. *ante*, before; Gr. *anti*; Sans. *anti*; Goth. *and-*.] A combining form signifying before in time, order, or position.

an′tē, *n.* In the game of poker, a stake put up by a player before cards are dealt to him.

an′tē, *v.t.* and *v.i.*; anteed, *pt., pp.*; anteing, *ppr.* In the game of poker, to put up a stake or ante; often followed by *up*.

an′tē, *n.* Same as *Anta*.

an′tē=act, *n.* A preceding act.

an′tē-ăl, *a.* Being before or in front. [Rare.]

ȧnt′=ēat″ẽr, *n.* Any one of various animals that live on ants, as the ant-bear, the aardvark, etc.

an′tē=bel′lum, *a.* [L.] Before the war; as, *ante-bellum* days.

an-tē-braçh′i-ăl, *a.* Pertaining to the forearm.

an-tē-braçh′i-um, *n.* [*Ante-*, and L. *brachium*, arm.] The forearm.

an″tē-çē-dā′nē-ous, *a.* Antecedent; preceding in time.

an-tē-çēde′, *v.t.* and *v.i.*; anteceded, *pt., pp.*; anteceding, *ppr.* [*Ante-*, and L. *cedere*, to go.] To go before in place, order, or time.

an-tē-çēd′ence, *n.* 1. The act or state of going before in time; precedence.

2. In astronomy, an apparent motion of a planet toward the west, or contrary to the order of the signs.

an-tē-çēd′en-cy, *n.* The condition or quality of being anterior or prior; priority; precedency.

an-tē-çēd′ent, *a.* [L. *antecedens*, ppr. of *antecedere*, to go before.]

1. Going before in time; prior; anterior; preceding; as, an event *antecedent* to the deluge.

2. Presumptive; previous to examination or observation; as, an *antecedent* improbability.

Syn.—Prior, preceding, foregoing, previous, anterior, former.—*Antecedent* is specific, referring to something consequent; *foregoing, preceding*, and *previous*, are more general, being opposed to *subsequent*; *prior*, like priority, implies a preference if there is competition.

an-tē-çēd′ent, *n.* 1. A person or thing that goes before, with reference to time, place, position, etc.

2. In grammar, the noun or substantive to which a pronoun refers; in the sentence, Solomon was the prince who built the temple, *prince* is the *antecedent*.

3. In mathematics, the first term of a ratio, or that which is compared with the other.

4. In logic, the first of two propositions in an enthymeme, or argument of two propositions; as, *every man is mortal*; therefore every king is mortal; the first proposition being the *antecedent*, the second the *consequent*. Also, the first and conditional part of a hypothetical proposition; as, if the sun is fixed, the earth must move.

5. [*pl.*] The events that have gone before in one's life; facts and circumstances constituting one's previous history; as, his *antecedents* are against him.

an-tē-çēd′ent-ly, *adv.* Previously; at a time preceding.

an-tē-çes′sŏr, *n.* [L. *antecessor*, a foregoer, teacher, from *antecedere*, to go before.]

1. One who goes before; a predecessor or a principal. [Rare.]

2. In Roman antiquity, a soldier who went ahead of troops to arrange for quarters and supplies, select camp-grounds, etc.; also, a title given to those who excelled in any science, especially to professors of civil law.

3. In law, one who possessed land before the present possessor; an ancestor or predecessor. [Obs.]

an′tē-chām″bẽr, *n.* An outer room; a chamber leading to a principal apartment and used as a waiting-room.

an′tē-chap″el, *n.* The part of a chapel through which is the passage to the choir.

an′tē-çhoir (-kwīr), *n.* In a church, a space between the choir and the nave, usually partly inclosed.

an-tē′ciănṣ, an-tœ′ciănṣ, *n.pl.* [LL. *antœci*, from Gr. pl. *antoikoi*; *anti*, opposite, and *oikein*, to live.] Persons living in corresponding latitudes north and south of the equator, and in the same longitude.

an″tē-çom-mūn′ion (-yun), *n.* In the Anglican church, a portion of the liturgy preceding the communion service

an-tē-çūr′sŏr, *n.* [L., a forerunner, from *ante*, before, and *currere*, to run.] One who runs before; a forerunner. [Obs.]

an′tē-dāte, *n.* 1. Prior date; a date antecedent to the actual one.

2. Anticipation. [Obs.]

an′tē-dāte, *v.t.*; antedated, *pt., pp.*; antedating, *ppr.* [*Ante-*, and L. *datum*, from *dare*, to give.]

1. To precede; to be antecedent to; to belong to an earlier time than; as, folklore *antedates* history.

2. To anticipate; to take before the true time.

And *antedate* the bliss above. —Pope.

3. To date too early; to give a date earlier than the actual one; as, to *antedate* a deed or note.

an″tē-di-lū′vi-ăn, an″tē-di-lū′vi-ăl, *a.* [*Ante-*, and L. *diluvium*, a flood.]

1. Before the flood, or deluge, in Noah's time; relating to things or times antecedent to the deluge.

2. Apparently antedating the flood; of great age; antiquated; ancient; primitive; as, *antediluvian* methods; *antediluvian* machinery.

an″tē-di-lū′vi-ăn, *n.* One who lived before the deluge.

An′tē-don, *n.* [LL., from Gr. *Anthēdōn*, a nymph.]

1. A genus of crinoids, the type of the family *Antedonidæ*.

2. [a—] Any comatula belonging to the genus *Antedon*.

An-tē-don′i-dæ, *n.pl.* A jointed family of the *Crinoidea* class with five branching arms.

an′tē-fact, *n.* [*Ante-*, and L. *factum*, a thing done.] Something done before another. [Obs.]

an′tē-fix, *n.*; *pl.* **an-tē-fix′ēs** or **an-tē-fix′á.**

Antefixes.

[L. *antefixum*; *ante*, before, and *fixus*, pp. of *figere*, to fasten.] An ornamental tile placed on the cornices and eaves of ancient buildings.

an-tē-flect′ed, *a.* Same as *Anteflexed.*

an′tē-flexed, *a.* [L. *ante*, before, and *flexus*, pp. of *flectere*, to bend.] Bent or inclined forward; showing anteflexion; applied particularly to the uterus.

an-tē-flex′ion (-flek′shun), *n.* The forward displacement or curvature of an organ, especially of the uterus.

ant′=eggs, *n.pl.* Little white cocoons found in the hillocks of ants, usually supposed to be their eggs, but in reality the larvæ in their first and second states, particularly the latter. They are vermicules, wrapped in a film composed of a silky substance spun by themselves, like the cocoons of silkworms.

an-tē′li-os, *n.* [Gr. *anti*, opposite, and *hēlios*, sun.] A name applied to the position of a heavenly body when in front of the sun.

an′tē-lōpe, *n.* [LL. *antilope*; Gr. *antholops*, deer.] In zoölogy, the name of one of a group of ruminant quadrupeds, intermediate between the deer and goat, of which there are a large number of species. Their horns are solid and permanent, straight or curved, sometimes annulated, sometimes surrounded by a spiral, occasionally smooth. They resemble deer in elegance of form and in agility. The only American species is the pronghorn of the Rockies. *Antilocapra americana.*

An-tē-lop′i-dæ, An-ti-lop′i-dæ, *n.pl.* The antelopes regarded as a family.

an′tē-lō-pine, an-tē-lō′pi-ăn, *a.* Pertaining to the antelope.

an-tē-lū′căn, *a.* [L. *antelucanus*; *ante*, before, and *lux*, light.] Being before light; a word applied, in times of the Roman persecution, to Christian assemblies held in the morning before daylight.

an′tē lū′cem. [L. *ante*, before, and *lux*, light.] Before dawn or daylight.

an″tē-mē-rid′i-ăn, *a.* [L. *antemeridianus*; *ante*, before, and *meridianus*, pertaining to midday.] Being before noon; pertaining to the forenoon, or to the time between midnight and the following noon.

ant-ē-met′iç, *a.* [Gr. *anti*, against, and *emein*, to vomit.] Restraining or allaying vomiting.

ant-ē-met′iç, *n.* A medicine which checks vomiting.

an′tē=mor′tem, *a.* [L.] Occurring before death; as, an *ante-mortem* examination.

Ante-mortem statement; a statement made under the pressure of impending death, and often received in evidence.

an′tē=Mō-ṣā′iç, *a.* Being before the time of Moses.

an-tē-mun′dāne, *a.* [L. *antemundanus*, from *ante*, before, and *mundus*, world.] Being before the creation of the world.

an-tē-mū′răl, *n.* [L. *antemurale*; *ante*, before, and *murus*, wall.] In old castles, a barbican or outwork, consisting of a strong high wall, with turrets in front of the gate, for defending the entrance.

an-tē-nā′tăl, *a.* [L. *ante*, before, and *natalis*, pertaining to birth.] Happening before birth.

an-tē-nā′tī, *n.pl.* [L. *ante*, before, and *nati*, pl. of *natus*, pp. of *nasci*, to be born.] Persons born before a certain event. Used particularly in connection with the claiming of political rights, as Americans born before the Declaration of Independence.

an′tē-nāve, *n.* That part of the nave which is farthest from the choir.

an′tē=Nī′cēne, *a.* [*Ante-*, and *Nicene*, from *Nice*.] Anterior to the first council of Nice, A. D. 325.

an-ten′næ, *n.pl.*; *singular*, **an-ten′ná.** [L., from Gr. *anateinein*; *ana*, up, and *teinein*, to stretch.] In zoölogy, certain movable, articulated organs of sensation, attached to the heads of insects, and of *Crustacea*; two in the former, and usually four in the latter. They are used as organs of touch, and in some species the cavity of the ear is situated near the basal joint. In insects, they are popularly called horns, and also feelers, but this latter term is more properly applied to the palpi.

Antennæ.

1. 1. Filiform Antennæ of Cucujo Firefly of Brazil (*Pyrophorus luminosus*); 2. Denticulate Antenna; 3. Bipinnate; 4. Lamellicorn; 5. Clavate; 6. Geniculate; 7. Antenna and Antennule of Crustacean.

2. The aerial of a receiving radio which intercepts the waves and brings the energy down to the receiving set.

an-ten′năl, *a.* Belonging to the antennæ.

An-ten-nā′ri-á, *n.* A genus of plants belonging to the composite family. They are commonly known as everlasting.

an-ten-nif′ēr-ous, *a.* [L. *antenna*, and *-ferous* from *ferre*, to bear.] Bearing antennæ.

an-ten′ni-fọrm, *a.* Shaped like antennæ.

an-ten′nūle (-yūl), *n.* A small antenna; one of the shorter pair of antennæ of a crustacean.

an′tē-num-bēr, *n.* A number that precedes another. [Rare.]

an-tē-nup′tiăl (-shăl), *a.* Being before marriage; as, an *antenuptial* agreement.

an-tē-ọr′bit-ăl, *a.* [L. *ante*, before, and *orbitus*, orbit.] In anatomy, anterior to the orbit.

an-tē-pag′ment, an″tē-pag-men′tum, *n.* [L. *ante*, before, and *pagmentum*, from *pangere*, to fasten.] An ornamental molding placed on a jamb, post, etc., of a window or doorway.

an-tē-pas′çhăl, *a.* Pertaining to the time before Easter.

an′tē-pȧst, *n.* [*Ante-*, and L. *pastus*, food.] A foretaste; something taken before the proper time. [Rare.]

an-tē-pen′di-um, *n.*; *pl.* **an-tē-pen′di-á.** [LL., from L. *ante*, before, and *pendere*, to hang.] An altar-cloth; the hangings in front of an altar.

an″tē-pē-nult′, an″tē-pē-nult′i-mȧ, *n.* [L. *ante*, before, *pæne*, almost, and *ultimus*, last.] The last syllable of a word except two; as, *syl* in *syllable*.

an″tē-pē-nult′i-māte, *a.* Pertaining to the antepenult.

an″tē-pē-nult′i-māte, *n.* The antepenult.

ant-eph-i-al′tiç, an″ti-eph-i-al′tiç, *a.* [Gr. *anti*, against, and *ephialtēs*, nightmare.] Curing nightmare.

ant-eph-i-al′tiç, an″ti-eph-i-al′tiç, *n.* A cure for nightmare.

ant-ep-i-lep′tiç, an″ti-ep-i-lep′tiç, *a.* [Gr. *anti*, against, and *epilēptikos*, epileptic.] Resisting or curing epilepsy.

ant-ep-i-lep′tic, an″ti-ep-i-lep′tiç, *n.* A remedy for epilepsy.

an′tē-pōrt, *n.* [*Ante-*, and L. *porta*, gate.] An outside door.

an-tē-pōr′ti-çō, *n.* An outer porch or colonnade.

an″tē-pō-ṣi′tion (-zish′un), *n.* [*Ante-*, and L. *positio*, from *ponere*, to place.]

1. In grammar, the placing of a word before another, which, by ordinary rules, ought to follow it.

2. In botany, a change in the arrangement of parts which usually alternate in the circle of flowers.

an-tē-pran′di-ăl, *a.* [*Ante-*, and L. *prandium*, luncheon.] Occurring before dinner; being before breakfast or luncheon.

an″tē-prē-dic′á-ment, *n.* [*Ante-*, and L. *prædicamentum*, that which is predicted, a category.] A term applied in logic to certain previous matters requisite to a clear understanding of the predicaments and categories, as definitions of common terms.

an-tē-pros′tāte, *n.* The gland in front of the prostate gland.

an-tē′ri-ŏr, *a.* [L., from *ante*, before.]

1. Before in time; prior; antecedent; preceding in time.

2. Before or in front, in place; as, the *anterior* lobes of the brain.

3. In botany, opposite or distant from the axis; as, the *anterior* side of a flower.

4. In anatomy, situated in front.

Syn.—Previous, former, preceding.—*Anterior* is opposed to and implies *posterior*; the others are opposed to *subsequent*.

an-tē″ri-or′i-ty, *n.* The state of being anterior, preceding, or in front; a state of being before in time or situation.

an-tē′ri-ŏr-ly, *adv.* In an anterior manner; previously.

an′tē-rō-. A combining form used to express *anterior*, *front*; as, *antero*lateral, *antero*posterior.

an″tē-rō-lat′ēr-ăl, *a.* [*Antero-*, and L. *lateralis*, from *latus*, side.] At the front side; anterior.

an′tē-rọọm, *n.* A room, usually small, before or in front of another; a waiting-room used as a temporary reception room.

an″tē-rō-pā-rī′e-tăl, *a.* [*Antero-*, and L. *parietalis*, from *paries*, a wall.] In anatomy, pertaining to the parietal plates of the cranium.

an″tē-rō-pos-tē′ri-ŏr, *a.* Reaching from the front to the back; relating to the direction from front to back.

an′tēṣ, an′tæ, *n.*, plurals of *anta*.

an″tē-stat′ūre, *n.* In fortification, a small retrenchment or work formed of palisades, or sacks of earth.

an′tē-stŏm″ăçh, *n.* A cavity which leads into the stomach, as in birds.

an-tē-tem′ple, *n.* The nave in an ancient church. [Obs.]

an′tē-tȳpe, *n.* A prototype.

an-tē-vēr′sion, *n.* [L. *anteversion*, from *ante*, before, and *vertere*, to turn.] A forward displacement of an organ, as the uterus.

an-tē-vērt′, *v.t.* [*Ante-*, and L. *vertere*, to turn.]

1. To prevent. [Obs.]

2. In medicine, to dislodge by anteversion.

an-thē′lá, *n.*; *pl.* **an-thē′læ.** [Gr. *anthēlē*, from *anthein*, to bloom.] In botany, a form of cymose inflorescence, in which the lateral branches extend beyond the axis.

ant-hel′i-cine, *a.* Pertaining to the antihelix.

ant-hē′li-ŏn, *n.*; *pl.* **ant-hē′li-á.** [L., from Gr. *anti*, against, and *hēlios*, sun.] A luminous ring, or rings, seen by an observer, especially in alpine and polar regions, around the shadow of his head, projected on a cloud or fog bank, or on grass covered with dew, 50 or 60 yards distant, and opposite the sun when rising or setting. It is due to the diffraction of light.

ant′hē-lix, *n.* Same as *Antihelix.*

an-thel-min′thiç, *a.* and *n.* Same as *Anthelmintic.*

an-thel-min′tiç, *a.* and *n.* [Gr. *anti*, against, and *helmins*, a worm.]

I. *a.* Destructive or expurgative of intestinal worms.

II. *n.* A remedy for worms in the intestines; a vermifuge.

an′them, *n.* [ME. *antem*, *antefne*; AS. *antefen*; L. *antiphona*, an anthem, from Gr. *antiphōnon*; *anti*, in return, and *phōnē*, voice.]

1. Formerly, a hymn sung in alternate parts; in modern usage, a sacred tune or piece of music set to words, taken from the Psalms or other parts of the Scriptures, and usually sung in parts; first introduced into the English church service in Elizabeth's reign.

2. A song of praise or reverence.

an′them, *v.t.* To praise with song; usually used poetically.

an-thē′mi-á, *n.pl.* In botany, any flower-cluster. [Rare.]

an-thē′mi-ŏn, *n.* [Gr. *anthemion*, a flower or flower-ornament.] Specifically, the honeysuckle or spreading design in classic Greek ornamentation; any common pattern of flower-and-leaf ornament.

Anthemion, from Pediment of Temple, Phigalia.

Anthemion molding; an ornamental molding characteristic of Greek decoration.

An′thē-mis, *n.* [L., from Gr *anthemis*, a flower, or herb resembling the camomile, from *anthos*, a flower.] In botany, a genus of herbaceous plants belonging to the aster family (*Compositæ*); the camomile.

ănt″hem-or-rhaġ′iç (-raj′), *a.* Same as *Antihemorrhagic.*

an′thẽr, *n.* [L. *anthera,* a flowery plant, from Gr. *antheros,* flowery, from *anthein,* to bloom; *anthos,* a flower.] In botany, the summit or top of the stamen, elevated by means of the filament or thread. It contains the pollen, or fertilizing dust, which, when mature, is emitted for the impregnation of the ovary.

bb, Anthers.

an′thẽr-ăl, *a.* Pertaining to anthers.

an′thẽr-dust, *n.* The dust or pollen of an anther.

an-thẽr-id′i-ăl, *a.* Pertaining to the antheridia.

an-thẽr-id′i-um, *n.*; *pl.* **an-thẽr-id′i-ȧ.** [LL., from *anthera,* anther, and Gr. dim. *-idion.*] A term used in describing the male organs of mosses, which are relatively the same as the anthers of flowering plants.

an-thẽr-if′ẽr-ous, *a.* [L. *anthera,* anther, and *-ferous,* from *ferre,* to bear.] Producing anthers, as plants; supporting anthers, as filaments.

an-thėr′i-fọrm, *a.* Anther-shaped.

an-thẽr-oġ′e-nous, *a.* [L. *anthera,* and Gr. *genēs,* producing.] Engendered from anthers.

an′thẽr-oid, *a.* [L. *anthera,* anther, and Gr. *eidos,* form.] Presenting the appearance of an anther.

an″thẽr-ō-zō′id, an″thẽr-ō-zō′oid, *n.* [Gr. *antheros,* flowering, *zōon,* animal, and *-oid.*] One of the minute bodies in the antheridia of cryptogamic plants by which the female organs are fertilized.

an-thē′sis, *n.* [Gr. *anthēsis,* bloom, from *anthein,* to bloom.] The time, state, or process of full unfoldment or expansion in a flower.

ȧnt′-hill, *n.* A little mound, as of earth, sand, or leaves, thrown up by ants for, or in the process of constructing, their dwelling or nest.

An-thī′næ, *n.pl.* [LL., from Gr. *anthos,* masc., a small bird, and *-inæ.*] A subfamily of singing, passerine birds, including the titlarks or pipits. There are about fifty species found in various parts of the world.

an′thō-, *prefix.* [Gr. *anthos,* flower.] A combining form used to express some relation to a flower or flowers.

an-thō′bi-ăn, *n.* [*Antho-,* and Gr. *bios,* life.] A beetle that lives on flowers.

An-thō-brañ′chi-ȧ, *n.pl.* [*Antho-,* and Gr. *branchia,* gills.] A suborder of gasteropods, including the family *Dorididæ* and allied forms; also called *Pygobranchia.*

an′thō-çärp, *n.* [*Antho-,* and Gr. *karpos,* fruit.] In botany, a fruit characterized by thick or fleshy floral envelopes which are united with or matted together about the ovary, though not usually belonging to it. The checkerberry, strawberry, mulberry, and pineapple belong to this class of fruits.

an-thō-çär′piç, *a.* Anthocarpous.

an-thō-çär′pous, *a.* Having thick or fleshy floral envelopes, as certain fruits.

an-thō-clin′i-um, *n.* Same as *Clinanthium.*

an-thō-çȳ′ȧ-nin, an-thō-çȳ′ȧ-nine, *n.* The coloring matter in blue flowers.

an-thō′di-um, *n.*; *pl.* **an-thō′di-ȧ.** [L., from Gr. *anthos,* flower, and *eidos,* form.] In botany, the inflorescence of a compound flower, as the aster; also, the common calyx of a compound flower.

an-thō-ġen′e-sis, *n.* [*Antho-,* and Gr. *genesis,* production.] A mode of reproduction occurring in certain plant-lice, the sexual individuals, male and female, arising from pupæ furnished by an intervening form; a form of production in the alternation of generations.

an″thō-ġē-net′iç, *a.* Pertaining to anthogenesis.

an-thoġ′rȧ-phy, *n.* [*Antho-,* and Gr. *graphein,* to write.] The division of botany that describes and treats of flowers.

an′thoid, *a.* Flower-like.

an-thō-kȳ′ăn, *n.* [*Antho-,* and Gr. *kyanos,* blue.] Same as *Anthocyanin.*

an-thō-leū′cin, an-thō-leū′cine, *n.* [*Antho-,* and Gr. *leukos,* white.] The coloring matter in white flowers.

an′thō-līte, *n.* [*Antho-,* and *-lite,* Gr. *lithos,* stone.] A fossil plant; an impression, as on the shales of the coal measures, resembling a flower.

an-thō-loġ′iç-ăl, *a.* Pertaining to anthology.

an-thol′ō-ġist, *n.* One who compiles an anthology.

an-thol′ō-ġy, *n.* [Gr. *anthologia,* a flower-gathering, from *anthologos*; *anthos,* flower, and *legein,* to gather.]

1. A discourse on flowers. [Rare.]

2. A collection of flowers; a garland. [Rare.]

3. A collection of beautiful passages from authors; a collection of poems or epigrams; particularly applied to a collection of ancient Greek epigrams.

4. In the Greek church, a collection of devotions, or book of offices.

an-thol′y-sis, *n.* [*Antho-,* and Gr. *lysis,* from *lyein,* to loose.] In botany, a retrograde transformation of the organs of a flower, as of stamens into petals.

an-thō-mā′ni-ȧ, *n.* [*Antho-,* and Gr. *mania,* madness.] A mania or extravagant affection for flowers.

an-thoph′ȧ-gous, *a.* [*Antho-,* and Gr. *phagein,* to eat.] Flower-eating; applied to certain insects.

An-thoph′i-lȧ, *n.pl.* [*Antho-,* and Gr. *philos,* loving.] A division of hymenopterous insects, including the bees.

an-thoph′i-lous, *a.* Having a fondness for flowers; especially said of insects, as bees, that live among and feed upon flowers.

an′thō-phōre, *n.* [*Antho-,* and Gr. *phoros,* from *pherein,* to bear.] In botany, the name given to the lengthened internode below the receptacle in *Caryophyllaceæ,* which bears the petals and stamens at its summit.

an-thoph′ō-rous, *a.* Flower-bearing.

an-thoph′yl-līte, *n.* [*Antho-,* and Gr. *phyllon,* leaf.] A brownish-gray mineral of the hornblende group, occurring in brittle fibers, or fibrous or bladed masses, and consisting chiefly of silica, magnesia, and oxid of iron.

an″thō-phyl-lit′iç, *a.* Pertaining to anthophyllite or containing it.

An-thoph′y-tȧ, *n.pl.* Same as *Spermophyta.*

an′thō-riṣm, *n.* [Gr. *anthorismos*; *anti,* against, and *horizein,* to define.] In rhetoric, a description or definition contrary to that which is given by the adverse party. [Rare.]

an′thō-tax-y, *n.* [*Antho-,* and Gr. *taxis,* order.] The arrangement of flowers in the several kinds of inflorescence; the science of such arrangement.

-an′thous, *suffix.* [Gr. *anthos,* flower.] A terminal form used principally in botany; as, gymn*anthous,* mon*anthous.*

An-thō-zō′ȧ, *n.pl.* [LL., from Gr. *anthos,* flower, and *zōon,* animal.] Flower-animals; a class of zoöphytes which includes the corals and sea-anemones; the polyps.

an-thō-zō′ăn, *a.* Relating to the *Anthozoa.*

an-thō-zō′ăn, *n.* One of the *Anthozoa.*

an-thō-zō′iç, *a.* Pertaining to the *Anthozoa.*

an-thō-zō′oid, *n.* An individual zoöid or polyp in a compound colony. In a piece of coral each of the animals that build the coral mass is an *anthozoöid.*

an′thrȧ-cēne, an′thrȧ-cin, *n.* A hydrocarbon obtained in the last stages of coal-tar distillation, and used as a base in the manufacture of alizarin.

an-thrac′iç, *a.* Pertaining to or affected with anthrax; as, *anthracic* blood.

an-thrȧ-cif′ẽr-ous, *a.* Containing anthracite.

an′thrȧ-cin, *n.* Same as *Anthracene.*

an′thrȧ-cīte, *n.* [Gr. *anthrakitēs,* resembling coal, from *anthrax,* a burning coal.] A hard, compact variety of mineral coal, of high luster, differing from bituminous coal in containing little or no bitumen, in consequence of which it burns almost without flame. The purer specimens consist wholly of carbon. It is popularly called *hard coal.*

an-thrȧ-cit′iç, *a.* Pertaining to anthracite.

an-thraç′nōse, an-thraç-nō′sis, *n.* [Gr. *anthrax, anthrakos,* carbuncle, and *nosos,* disease.] A destructive disease, caused by fungi, which attacks the grape, bean, cotton, melon, and other plants.

an′thrȧ-çō-, an′thraç-. A combining form from Gr. *anthrax,* and signifying coal, a precious stone, or an ulcer.

an′thrȧ-çoid, *a.* [*Anthraco-,* and *-oid,* Gr. *eidos,* resembling.]

1. Resembling anthrax; partaking of the nature of a malignant disease.

2. Resembling the carbuncle, a precious stone of deep red color.

an-thraç′ō-līte, *n.* Anthracite.

an′thrȧ-çō-man″cy, *n.* [*Anthraco-,* and Gr. *manteia,* divination.] Divination by observing certain peculiarities of burning coal.

an-thrȧ-çom′e-tẽr, *n.* [*Anthraco-,* and Gr. *metron,* measure.] An instrument for ascertaining the amount of carbonic acid in a gaseous mixture.

an″thrȧ-çō-met′riç, *a.* Relating to an anthracometer.

an-thraç′ō-nīte, *n.* [Gr. *anthrakōn,* a pile of coals, from *anthrax,* coal.] A variety of marble of a coal-black luster, occurring at Kilkenny, Ireland. It gives off a fetid odor when heated or rubbed; also called *stinkstone.*

an-thrȧ-çō′sis, *n.* [*Anthrac-,* and *-osis.*] A disease of the lungs caused by inhaling coal-dust, and common among coal-workers. Called also *black lung, collier's lung,* and *miner's phthisis.*

An″thrȧ-çō-thē′ri-um, *n.* [*Anthraco-,* and Gr. *thērion,* beast.] A genus of extinct pachydermatous quadrupeds, first found in Italy in Tertiary lignite or brown coal, whence its name.

an-thrȧ-pūr′pū-rin, *n.* An orange-colored dye produced during the conversion of anthracene into alizarin.

an″thrȧ-quī-nōne′, *n.* A crystalline compound of yellow color produced by the oxidation of anthracene. It is valued as the source of artificial alizarin.

an′thrax, *n.*; *pl.* **an′thrȧ-çēṣ.** [Gr., a burning coal.]

1. A carbuncle; a malignant ulcer.

2. A gem of the ancients, probably identical with the carbuncle.

3. A microscopic bacterial organism, *Bacillus anthracis,* found in the blood of persons affected with splenic fever.

4. An infectious disease of cattle and sheep, which may be transmitted to man by inoculation; splenic fever.

An-thrē′nus, *n.* [LL., from Gr. *anthrēnē,* a hornet.] A genus of small beetles, the larvæ of which are destructive to woolens, furs, etc.

an-throp′iç, an-throp′iç-ăl, *a.* [Gr. *anthrōpikos,* from *anthrōpos,* man.] Of or pertaining to man; manlike; human. [Rare.]

An-throp′i-dæ, *n.pl.* [LL., from Gr. *anthrōpos,* man.] The group that includes man only, and therefore stands at the head of *Mammalia.*

an′thrō-pō-. A combining form from Gr. *anthrōpos,* man, and signifying of, pertaining to, or like man; human; as, *anthropology.*

an″thrō-pō-cen′triç, *a.* [*Anthropo-,* and Gr. *kentron,* center.] Regarding man as the central fact or final aim of all creation; applied to scientific or philosophical theories of the universe.

an″thrō-pō-ġen′iç, *a.* Relating to anthropogeny.

an-thrō-poġ′e-ny, *n.* [*Anthropo-,* and Gr. *genos,* birth.] The science of the origin and development of man; a branch of anthropology.

an-throp′ō-glot, *n.* [*Anthropo-,* and Gr. *glōtta,* tongue.] An animal having a tongue like that of a man, as the parrot.

an-thrō-poġ′rȧ-phy, *n.* [*Anthropo-,* and Gr. *graphia,* from *graphein,* to write.] A description of man or the human race; especially, that branch of anthropology which treats of the geographic distribution, variations, and peculiarities of the human race; in contradistinction to *ethnography,* which treats historically of races and nations.

an′thrō-poid, *a.* and *n.* [*Anthropo-,* and Gr. *eidos,* resembling.]

I. *a.* Resembling a human being; applied especially to the most highly developed apes, as the gorilla, orang, gibbon, and chimpanzee.

II. *n.* An anthropoid ape.

an-thrō-poid′ăl, *a.* Resembling man; anthropoid.

An-thrō-poid′ē-ȧ, *n.pl.* [LL., from Gr. *anthrōpos,* man, and *eidos,* resembling.] The suborder of primate mammals which comprises man, apes, and monkeys.

an-thrō-pol′ȧ-try, *n.* [*Anthropo-,* and Gr. *latreia,* worship.] Man-worship; the bestowing of divine honors upon a human being.

an-throp′ō-līte, *n.* [*Anthropo-,* and *-lite,* Gr. *lithos,* stone.] A petrifaction of the human body, skeleton, or any bodily part, as by the action of calcareous waters; also, any stony deposit or concretion in the body.

an″thrō-pō-loġ′iç-ăl, an″thrō-pō-loġ′iç, *a.* Pertaining to anthropology, or the natural history of man; relating to man in any aspect; as, *anthropological* facts.

an″thrō-pō-loġ′iç-ăl-ly, *adv.* From an anthropological point of view.

an-thrō-pol′ō-ġist, *n.* One who studies, describes, or is versed in, the natural history of man; a specialist in the science of anthropology.

an-thrō-pol′ō-ġy, *n.* [*Anthropo-,* and Gr. *logia,* from *legein,* to speak.]

1. A discourse upon human nature. [Rare.]

2. That manner of expression by which the inspired writers attribute human parts and passions to God. [Rare.]

3. The science of man and mankind, including the study of man's place in nature, that is, of the measure of his agreement with and divergence from other animals; of his physical structure and psychological nature, together with the extent to which these act and react on each other; of the various tribes of men, determining how these may have been produced or modified by external conditions, and consequently taking account also of the advance or retrogression of the human race.

Anthropology is much more extensive in its scope than ethnology, which concerns itself only with the division of mankind into races, their origin, distribution, relations, and peculiarities. It puts under contribution all sciences which have man for their object, as archæology, comparative anatomy, physiology, psychology, climatology, etc. By some, *anthropology* has been divided as follows: (a) *zoölogical anthropology,* which investigates man's relations to the brute creation; (b) *descriptive anthropology* or *ethnology,* describing the divisions and groups of mankind; (c) *general anthropology,* or, as it has been called, the biology of the human race. This last is *anthropology* proper.

an′thrō-pō-man″cy, *n.* [*Anthropo-*, and Gr. *manteia*, divination.] Divination by inspecting the entrails of a human being.

an″thrō-pō-met′riç, an″thrō-pō-met′riç-ăl, *a.* Relating to anthropometry.

an-thrō-pom′e-try, *n.* [*Anthropo-*, and Gr. *metria*, from *metron*, measure.] The measurement of the human body.

An″thrō-pō-mor′phȧ, *n.pl.* [*Anthropo-*, and Gr. *morphē*, form.] A group of anthropoid apes.

an″thrō-pō-mor′phiç, *a.* 1. Relating to or characterized by anthropomorphism.

2. Resembling man.

an″thrō-pō-mor′phiç-ăl-ly, *adv.* In an anthropomorphic manner.

an″thrō-pō-mor′phişm, *n.* [*Anthropo-*, and Gr. *morphē*, form.]

1. The representation or conception of Deity under a human form, or with human attributes and affections.

2. The doctrine which attributes to animals mental faculties of the same nature as those of man.

an″thrō-pō-mor′phist, *n.* One who ascribes human attributes to Deity.

an″thrō-pō-mor′phīte, *n.* One who believes the Supreme Being possesses a human form and is swayed by human passions; specifically, one of an ancient sect holding such views.

an″thrō-pō-mor′phi-tişm, *n.* The doctrines of anthropomorphites.

an″thrō-pō-mor′phīze, *v.t.* and *v.i.*; anthropomorphized, *pt.*, *pp.*; anthropomorphizing, *ppr.* To invest (a god) with human form; to indulge in anthropomorphism.

an″thrō-pō-mor-phol′ō-gy, *n.* [*Anthropo-*, and Gr. *morphē*, form, and *logia*, from *legein*, to speak.] The use of anthropomorphic terms.

an″thrō-pō-mor′phō-sis, *n.* Transformation into human form.

an″thrō-pō-mor′phous, *a.* [*Anthropo-*, and Gr. *morphos*, from *morphē*, form.] Belonging to that which has the form of man; having the figure of or resemblance to a man.

an″thrō-pō-path′iç, an″thrō-pō-path′iç-ăl, *a.* Subject to human passions; said of a deity.

an″thrō-pō-path′iç-ăl-ly, *adv.* In an anthropopathic manner.

an-thrō-pop′ȧ-thişm, *n.* [*Anthropo-*, and Gr. *pathos*, feeling, affection.]

1. The affections or passions of man. [Obs.]

2. The ascription of human passions to the Supreme Being.

an-thrō-pop′ȧ-thy, *n.* Anthropopathism.

an-thrō-poph′ȧ-gī, *n.pl.* [*Anthropo-*, and Gr. *phagein*, to eat.] Man-eaters; cannibals.

an″thrō-pō-phag′iç, an″thrō-pō-phag′iç-ăl, *a.* Pertaining to cannibalism.

an″thrō-pō-phag′iç-ăl-ly, *adv.* In the manner of a cannibal.

an″thrō-poph-ȧ-gin′i-ăn, *n.* A cannibal.

an-thrō-poph′ȧ-gist, an-thrō-poph′ȧ-gīte, *n.* A cannibal.

an-thrō-poph′ȧ-gous, *a.* Feeding on human flesh.

an-thrō-poph′ȧ-gus, *n.* A cannibal; singular of *anthropophagi*. [Rare.]

an-thrō-poph′ȧ-gy, *n.* Cannibalism; the act or practice of eating human flesh.

an″thrō-pō-phō′bi-ȧ, *n.* [*Anthropo-*, and Gr. *phobia*, from *phobein*, to fear.] A morbid shrinking from human beings; aversion to society.

an-thrō-poph′ū-işm, *n.* [*Anthropo-*, and Gr. *phyē*, nature.] The investment of spiritual beings with human attributes. [Rare.]

an-thrō-poph′y-sīte, *n.* One who ascribes human attributes to God.

an-thrō-pos′çō-py, *n.* [*Anthropo-*, and Gr. *skopia*, from *skopein*, to view.] Character-reading from the features. [Rare.]

an-thrō-pos′ō-phy, *n.* [*Anthropo-*, and Gr. *sophia*, wisdom.] Knowledge of the nature of man.

an″thrō-pō-tom′iç-ăl, *a.* Relating to anthropotomy.

an-thrō-pot′ō-mist, *n.* One who is skilled in human anatomy.

an-thrō-pot′ō-my, *n.* [*Anthropo-*, and Gr. *tomē*, a cutting, from *temnein*, to cut.] The anatomy or dissection of the human body.

an″thrō-pō-zō′iç, *a.* [*Anthropo-*, and Gr. *zōon*, life.] Pertaining to the time during which man has existed; quaternary.

An-thū′ri-um, *n.* [L., from Gr. *anthos*, flower, and *oura*, tail.] An important genus of tropical American flowering plants, epiphytically attached to trees, and belonging to the family *Araceæ*, of which the well-known genus *Arum* is typical. They are largely cultivated in greenhouses for their effective beauty.

ant-hyp-not′iç, *a.* and *n.* See *Antihypnotic.*

ant″hyp-ō-chon′dri-aç, *a.* and *n.* See *Antihypochondriac.*

ant-hys-ter′iç, *a.* and *n.* See *Antihysteric.*

an′ti-, *prefix.* A combining form, from Gr. *anti*, against, Sans. *anti*, over against, and signifying against, contrary to, opposed to, in place of, etc.; as *anti*pathy, *anti*christ. It is shortened to *ant-* before vowels; as, *ant*acid, *ant*arctic, and before an aspirate it becomes *anth-*. In words of English formation, *anti-* is frequently retained before a vowel or aspirate.

an′ti, *n.* One who opposes; used colloquially in many parts of the United States with local signification; often in connection with the liquor traffic, and meaning one opposing prohibition or opposed to license, as the case may be.

An″ti-ab-ō-li′tion-ist (-lish′un-), *n.* One who opposes abolition; specifically, one who opposed the abolition of slavery; a term used in the United States before and during the Civil War.

an′ti-æ, *n.pl.* [LL. *antiæ*, the forelock, from *ante*, before.] The extensions of the feathers on each side of the bill, seen on some birds.

anti-aircraft, *a.* Used for defence against aeroplanes, balloons, etc.; as a gun, a shell, a battery. Esp. a semi-automatic gun firing at great heights and at great angles.

an″ti-al-bū′māte, *n.* The product of albumin and dilute hydrochloric acid.

an″ti-al-bū′mid, *n.* A product of the digestion of albumin by pancreatic and gastric juices.

an″ti-al-bū′mōse, *n.* A product of the digestive action of pancreatic juice on albumin. [See *Albumose.*]

an″ti-Ȧ-mer′i-căn, *a.* Opposed to America, or to the true interests or government of the United States.

an″ti-aph-rō-diş′i-aç, *a.* and *n.* Same as *Anaphrodisiac.*

an″ti-ap-ō-pleç′tiç, *a.* and *n.* Same as *Antapoplectic.*

an′ti-ăr, *n.* [Javanese *antjar.*] A poison extracted from the upas-tree, *Antiaris toxicaria*; also, the tree itself.

an′ti-ȧ-rin, *n.* The poisonous principle of antiar.

An-ti-ā′ris, *n.* [LL., from *antiar.*] A genus of plants of the nettle family, including the upas-tree. They are mostly found in the East Indies.

an″ti-ăr-thrit′iç, *a.* and *n.* See *Antarthritic.*

an″ti-asth-mat′iç (-as-mat′ik), *a.* and *n.* See *Antasthmatic.*

an″ti-at-tri′tion (-trish′un), *n.* A lubricating substance applied to machinery to lessen friction; often consisting of plumbago with oil or grease.

an″ti-baç-çhī′us, *n.*; *pl.* **an″ti-baç-çhī′ī.** [L., from Gr. *antibakcheios*; *anti*, against, and *bakcheios*, a bacchius.] In poetry, a foot of three syllables, the first two long, and the last short; as, *āmbīrĕ*; opposed to the *bacchius*, in which the first syllable is short and the last two long.

an″ti-baç-tē′ri-ăl, *a.* Preventing or noxious to bacterial growth.

an-ti-bil′ious (-yus), *a.* Counteractive of bilious complaints.

an″ti-bī-ot′iç, *a.* [*Anti-*, and Gr. *biotikos*, from *bios*, life.] Denying the presence of life; specifically, denying the existence of life at great ocean-depths.

an″ti-bī-ot′iç, *n.* One holding an antibiotic theory.

an-ti-braçh′i-ăl, *a.* See *Antebrachial.*

an-ti-braçh′i-um, *n.* See *Antebrachium.*

an-ti-brō′miç, *n.* [*Anti-*, and Gr. *brōmos*, a smell.] A deodorizer.

An-ti-bŭrgh′ẽr, *n.* A member of a Scottish sect which arose in 1747, in opposition to the so-called burgess oath.

an′tiç, *a.* [Fr. *antique*; Pr. *antic*, ancient, old; It. *antico*, from L. *antiquus*, former, old; *ante*, before.]

1. Odd; fantastic; ludicrous; as, *antic* tricks.

2. Antique. [Obs.]

an′tiç, *n.* 1. A buffoon or merry-andrew; one who practises odd gesticulations; a clown.

2. An odd appearance; a fantastic figure.

3. A piece of buffoonery; a comical trick; a prank; a caper.

4. In architecture, a grotesque representation or figure. [Obs.]

an′tiç, *v.i.* To perform or practise antics.

an′tiç, *v.t.* To make grotesque or antic. [Obs.]

an-ti′căl, *a.* Same as *Anticous.*

an-ti-căr′di-um, *n.* [L., from Gr. *antikardion*; *anti*, over against, and *kardia*, heart.] The pit of the stomach; the upper part of the abdomen.

an″ti-çȧ-tărrh′ăl, *a.* [*Anti-*, and Gr. *katarrhoos*, a catarrh.] Beneficial against catarrh.

an″ti-çȧ-tărrh′ăl, *n.* A remedy for catarrh.

an-ti-çath′ōde, *n.* A platinum deflection-plate supported inside an X-ray tube to receive the cathodic bombardment.

an″ti-çau-sot′iç, an″ti-çau-sod′iç, *a.* and *n.* [*Anti-*, and Gr. *kausos*, fever, from *kaiein*, to burn.]

I. *a.* Efficacious against inflammatory fever.

II. *n.* A remedy for inflammatory fever.

an-ti-çaus′tiç, *a.* 1. Neutralizing the action characteristic of caustics.

2. In mathematics, designating a caustic curve produced by refraction.

an-ti-çaus′tiç, *n.* 1. A remedy for neutralizing caustic action.

2. A caustic curve produced by refraction.

an′ti-chām″bẽr, *n.* [Obs.] See *Antechamber.*

an′ti-çhlor, *n.* A substance employed to remove free chlorin from fabrics, etc., that have been bleached. Sodium hyposulphite is usually the substance used.

an-ti-çhrē′sis, *n.*; *pl.* **an-ti-çhrē′sēş.** [Gr. *antichrēsis*, from *anti*, in return, and *chrēsthai*, to use.] In civil law, a mortgage contract in which the borrower gives possession and use of property, the revenues therefrom being applied on account of the principal and interest of the debt.

an′ti-çhrīst, *n.* [L. *antichristus*; Gr. *antichristos*; *anti*, against, and *Christos*, Christ.] An adversary of Christ or Christianity; especially, that great adversary who, as some suppose, will precede the second coming of Christ. [Often spelled with a capital.]

an-ti-çhris′tiăn (-chăn), *a.* Pertaining to antichrist; opposing the Christian religion.

an-ti-çhris′tiăn, *n.* A follower of antichrist; one opposed to the Christian religion.

an-ti-çhris′tiăn-işm, *n.* Antichristianity.

an″ti-çhris-ti-an′i-ty, *n.* Opposition to Christianity.

an-ti-çhris′tiăn-ly, *adv.* In an antichristian manner.

an-ti-çhron′iç-ăl, *a.* [*Anti-*, and Gr. *chronos*, time.] Deviating from the proper order of time; erroneously dated.

an-ti-çhron′iç-ăl-ly, *adv.* In an antichronical manner.

an-tiçh′rō-nişm, *n.* Deviation from the true order of time. [Rare.]

an-tiçh′thon, *n.*; *pl.* **an-tiçh′thō-nēş.** [Gr. *antichthōn*; *anti*, against, opposite, and *chthōn*, the earth.]

1. An imaginary planet similar to the earth, but on the opposite side of the sun; the counter-earth of Pythagoras.

2. [*pl.*] The inhabitants of such a planet.

an-tiç′i-pănt, *a.* 1. Anticipating; applied to periodic diseases, having intermitting attacks, each occurring at an earlier period than the one preceding.

2. Expectant; used with *of*; as, *anticipant of* death.

an-tiç′i-pāte, *v.t.*; anticipated, *pt.*, *pp.*; anticipating, *ppr.* [L. *anticipatus*, pp. of *anticipare*, to anticipate, take beforehand; *ante*, before, and *capere*, to take.]

1. To take or act before another, so as to forestall him; to take first possession of.

2. To take up before the proper time; as, the advocate has *anticipated* that part of his argument.

3. To foretaste or foresee; to have a previous view or impression of; to consider beforehand; as, to *anticipate* the pleasures of an entertainment.

4. To prevent by acting beforehand; to preclude.

5. To foresee, as a wish, etc., and do in advance (what is desired); as, he *anticipated* our orders.

Syn.—Foresee, expect, preoccupy, forestall, foretaste, prejudge.—*Expect* is stronger than *anticipate*. We may *anticipate* difficulties when we do not really *expect* them.

an-tiç-i-pā′tion, *n.* 1. The act of anticipating; the act of taking up, placing, or considering something before the proper time in natural order.

2. Foretaste; previous view or impression of what is to happen afterward; as, the *anticipation* of the joys of heaven.

3. Previous notion; preconceived opinion, produced in the mind before the truth is known; slight previous impression.

4. In medicine, the occurrence in the human body of any phenomenon, morbid or natural, before the usual time.

5. In music, the introduction into a chord of one or more of the component notes of the chord which follows, producing a passing discord.

Syn.—Expectation, preconception, foresight, forethought, foretaste, prelibation, antepast, forecast, provision.

an-tiç′i-pā-tive, *a.* Containing anticipation; tending to anticipate.

an-tiç′i-pā-tive-ly, *adv.* In an anticipative manner.

an-tiç′i-pā-tŏr, *n.* One who anticipates.

an-tiç′i-pā-tō-ry, *a.* Before the time.

an-ti-çiv′iç, *a.* Hostile to citizenship.

an-ti-çiv′işm, *n.* Hostility to a state of citizenship, or to republicanism. [Rare.]

an-ti-çlas′tiç, *a.* [Gr. *antiklān*; *anti*, back, and *klān*, to bend.] Curved oppositely in different directions; applied to a surface having concave and convex curvatures transversely opposite, as that of a saddle.

an-ti-çlī′max, *n.* [*Anti-*, and Gr. *klimax*, a ladder, climax.] A sentence in which the ideas first increase in force, and then terminate in something less important and striking; opposed to *climax*. For example—

Next comes Dalhousie, the great god of war, Lieutenant-colonel to the Earl of Mar.
—Waller.

an-ti-çli′năl, *a.* [*Anti-*, and Gr. *klinein*, to incline.] Inclining in opposite directions.

Anticlinal line, or *anticlinal axis*; in geology,

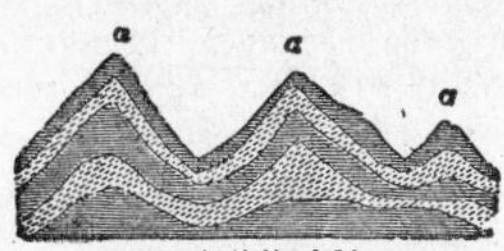

aaa, Anticlinal Line.

the ridge of a wave-like curve, the strata dipping from it on either side as from the ridge of a house; opposed to *synclinal*.

Anticlinal vertebra; in man, the tenth thoracic vertebra.

an-ti-çli′năl, *n.* In geology, an anticlinal line or axis.

an′ti-çline, *n.* Same as *Anticlinal*.

an″ti-çli-nō′ri-um, *n.*; *pl.* **an″ti-çli-nō′ri-ȧ.** [LL., from Gr. *anti*, against, *klinein*, to lean, and *oros*, mountain.] An elevation of the earth's crust caused by an upward flexure.

an′tiç-ly, *adv.* In an antic manner.

an′tiç=mȧsk, *n.* See *Antimask*.

an′tiç-ness, *n.* The state of being antic.

an″ti-çon-sti-tū′tion-ăl, *a.* Opposed to or against the constitution.

an″ti-çon-tā′ġious (-jus), *a.* Opposing or destroying contagion.

an″ti-çon-vul′sive, *a.* In medicine, efficacious against convulsions.

an′ti-çor, *n.* [*Anti-*, and L. *cor*, the heart.] An inflammation in a horse's breast, opposite the heart; a sort of quinsy.

an-ti′çous (-çus), *a.* [L. *anticus*, in front, from *ante*, before.] In botany, turned inward toward the axis; introrse.

an′ti-çȳ-çlōne, *n.* The name for a condition of atmospheric pressure, in which there is a current from the central (high) area, outward.

an″ti-çȳ-çlon′iç, *a.* Of the nature of an anticyclone.

an″ti-çȳ-çlon′iç-ăl-ly, *adv.* In a manner opposite to that of a cyclone.

an″ti-dem-ō-çrat′iç, *a.* 1. Opposing democracy; contrary to government by the people.

2. In the United States, opposed or contrary to the principles of the Democratic party.

An″ti-diç-ō-mā′ri-ăn-īte, *n.* [*Antidikos*, opponent; *anti*, against, *dikē*, right, and *Mariaim*, Mary.] One of a sect of Arabian Christians, late in the fourth century, who denied the perpetual virginity of Mary, maintaining that she had children by Joseph after the birth of Jesus. Also called *Antidicomarian* and *Antimarian*.

an-ti-dō′ron, *n.* See *Eulogia*.

an′ti-dō-tăl, an′ti-dō-tȧ-ry, *a.* Preventive of the ill effects of poisons, or of anything noxious or mischievous.

an′ti-dō-tăl-ly, *adv.* In an antidotal manner.

an′ti-dō-tȧ-ry, *n.* 1. A pharmacopœia, or a treatise on antidotes.

2. An antidote.

an′ti-dōte, *n.* [Gr. *antidotos*, an antidote; *anti*, against, and *dotos*, given, from *didonai*, to give.]

1. A medicine to counteract the effects of poison, or of anything noxious taken into the system.

2. Anything tending to prevent mischievous effects, or to counteract the evil which something else might produce; as, an *antidote* for poverty.

Syn.—Remedy, counteraction, preventive.

an′ti-dōte, *v.t.*; antidoted, *pt.*, *pp.*; antidoting, *ppr.* 1. To counteract the effects of, as a poison.

2. To provide an antidote for, as a disease or condition.

an-ti-dot′iç-ăl, *a.* Serving as an antidote.

an-ti-dot′iç-ăl-ly, *adv.* By way of antidote.

an-tid′rō-măl, an-tid′rō-mous, *a.* [LL. *antidromus*, from Gr. *antidromein*; *anti*, against, and *dromein*, to run.] Of, relating, or pertaining to antidromy.

an-tid′rō-my, *n.* In botany, direction-change of ascending spirals connecting leaf-attachments.

an″ti-dys-en-ter′iç, *a.* Remedial for dysentery, or bloody flux.

an″ti-dys-en-ter′iç, *n.* A remedy for dysentery.

an″ti-ē-met′iç, *a.* and *n.* See *Antemetic*.

an″ti-eph-i-al′tiç, *a.* and *n.* See *Antephialtic*.

an″ti-ep-i-lep′tiç, *a.* and *n.* See *Antepileptic*.

an-ti-fē′brile, *a.* and *n.* See *Febrifuge*.

an-ti-feb′rine, *a.* and *n.* Same as *Antipyretic*.

an-ti-fed′ẽr-ăl, *a.* Opposing federalism.

An-ti-fed′ẽr-ăl-iṣm, *n.* 1. Opposition to the ratification of the constitution of the United States, in the early days of the government.

2. [a—] Opposition to federalism.

An-ti-fed′ẽr-ăl-ist, *n.* One who, at the formation of the constitution of the United States, opposed its adoption and ratification.

an-ti-friç′tion, *a.* Lessening friction.

an-ti-friç′tion, *n.* A lubricant.

an″ti-gȧ-laç′tiç, *n.* [*Anti-*, and Gr. *gala*, *galaktos*, milk.] A medicine which tends to diminish the secretion of milk.

an-ti=Gal′li-căn, *n.* and *a.* I. *n.* One who is opposed to France or anything French.

II. *a.* Hostile to what is French.

an′ti-grȧph, *n.* [Gr. *antigraphon*, a copy; *anti*, corresponding to, and *graphon*, from *graphein*, to write.] A copy.

an-ti-gug′glẽr, *n.* A tube permitting the entrance of air into a narrow-mouthed bottle or carboy, thus preventing splashing of the contents when turned out.

an-ti-hē′lix, *n.* [*Anti-*, and Gr. *helix*, from *helissein*, to turn round.] The semicircular prominence of the external ear, situated before and within the helix.

an″ti-hem-or-rhaġ′iç, *n.* and *a.* I. *n.* A remedy for hemorrhage.

II. *a.* Remedial for hemorrhage.

an″ti-hȳ-drō-phō̆b′iç, *n.* and *a.* I. *n.* A medicine for hydrophobia.

II. *a.* Curative of hydrophobia.

an″ti-hȳ-drop′iç, *n.* and *a.* I. *n.* A medicine to counteract dropsy.

II. *a.* Efficacious against dropsy.

an″ti-hyp-not′iç, ant-hyp-not′iç, *n.* and *a.* [*Anti-*, and Gr. *hypnotikos*, from *hypnos*, sleep.]

I. *n.* A medicine that prevents or tends to prevent sleep.

II. *a.* Tending to prevent sleep or lethargy.

an″ti-hyp-ō-ċhon′dri-aç, *a.* Counteracting or tending to cure hypochondriac affections and depression of spirits.

an″ti-hys-ter′iç, *n.* and *a.* I. *n.* A medicine for hysteria.

II. *a.* Remedial for hysteria.

an″ti-iç-ter′iç, *n.* and *a.* [*Anti-*, and Gr. *ikterikos*, from *ikteros*, the jaundice.]

I. *n.* A medical remedy for jaundice.

II. *a.* Remedial for jaundice.

an″ti=im-pē′ri-ăl-ist, *n.* One opposed to the policy of imperialism; specifically, in United States politics, one opposed to an extension of territory and the consequent colonial policy.

an″ti-lē-gom′e-nȧ, *n. pl.* [Gr. *antilegomena*, things spoken against, from *antilegein*; *anti*, against, and *legein*, to speak.] Those books of the New Testament which were not at first received as canonical. They were the Epistle to the Hebrews, James and Jude, Second Peter, Second and Third John, and Revelation. Opposed to *homologoumena*.

an″ti-lī-brā′tion, *n.* Equipoise. [Rare.]

an-ti-lith′iç, *n.* and *a.* [*Anti-*, and Gr. *lithos*, stone.]

I. *n.* A medicine that tends to prevent or destroy urinary calculi.

II. *a.* Having the properties of an antilithic.

an-ti-log′ȧ-rithm, *n.* 1. The complement of the logarithm of any sine, tangent, or secant, to that of ninety degrees. [Rare.]

2. The number corresponding to any logarithm; as, 100 is the antilogarithm of 2.

an″ti-log-ȧ-rith′miç, *a.* Pertaining to antilogarithms.

an-til′ō-gous, *a.* Of a character the reverse of analogous; specifically, in electricity, designating that pole of a crystal or like body which exhibits negative electricity when heated.

an-til′ō-ġy, *n.*; *pl.* **an-til′ō-ġies.** [Gr. *antilogia*, from *antilogos*, contradictory; *anti*, against, and *logos*, from *legein*, to speak.] A contradiction between any words or passages in an author.

an-ti-loi′miç, *n.* [*Anti-*, and Gr. *loinos*, plague.] A remedy for the plague.

an-til′ō-pine, *a.* Pertaining to an antelope.

an-til′ō-quist, *n.* A contradicter. [Obs.]

an-til′ō-quy, *n.* [*Anti-*, and L. *loqui*, to speak.] Contradiction. [Obs.]

an-ti-lys′siç, *a.* [*Anti-*, and Gr. *lyssa*, rage, madness.] Antihydrophobic.

an″ti-mȧ-ças′săr, *n.* [*Anti-*, and *macassar*, an oil.] A kind of tidy, as for a chair, formerly used to protect it from the oil of the hair.

an″ti-mȧ-ġis′triç-ăl, *a.* Opposed to the office of magistrates. [Obs.]

an″ti-mȧ-lā′ri-ăl, *a.* Efficacious against malaria.

An-ti-mā′ri-ăn, *n.* Same as *Antidicomarianite*.

an′ti-mȧsk, *n.* A ludicrous secondary mask; also spelled *antimasque*. [Obs.]

an-ti-mā′sŏn, *n.* One opposed to freemasonry.

an″ti-mȧ-son′iç, *a.* Opposing freemasonry.

an-ti-mā′sŏn-ry, *n.* Opposition to freemasonry.

an-ti-men′si-um, *n.*; *pl.* **an-ti-men′si-ȧ.** [LL., from Gr. *anti*, in place of, and L. *mensa*, a table.] In the Greek church, an altar-cloth used in celebrating the eucharist in churches having no altar.

an″ti-me-phit′iç, *a.* and *n.* [*Anti-*, and L. *mephitis*, a poisonous gas.]

I. *a.* Efficacious against poisonous gases.

II. *n.* A remedy for poisonous gases.

an′ti-mēre, *n.* [*Anti-*, and Gr. *meros*, part.] In biology, one of two bilaterally symmetrical sides.

an-ti-mer′iç, *a.* Relating to an antimere.

an″ti-me-tab′ō-lē, *n.* [L., from Gr. *antimetabolē*; *anti*, against, and *meta*, beyond, and *ballein*, to throw.] A form of speech characterized by an inverted repetition of words or ideas; as, a wit amongst fools, and a fool amongst wits.

an″ti-me-tath′e-sis, *n.* [L., from Gr. *antimetathesis*; *anti*, against, and *metathesis*, transposition.] In rhetoric, counter-transposition; a figure of speech by which the position of the two leading words in one clause are changed by inversion in a succeeding one. For example—

A poem is a speaking picture; a picture a mute poem.
—Crabbe.

an-tim′e-tẽr, *n.* [*Anti-*, and Gr. *metron*, measure.] A modification of Hadley's quadrant, for measuring angles under 10°. [Obs.]

an″ti-mō-när′ċhiç, an″ti-mō-när′ċhiç-ăl, *a.* Opposed to monarchy.

an-ti-mon′ärċh-ist, *n.* An opposer of monarchy.

an-ti-mō′nāte, *n.* See *Antimoniate*.

an-ti-mō′ni-ăl, *a.* Relating to or containing antimony.

Antimonial powder; an emetic compound, composed of oxid of antimony and phosphate of calcium in the proportion of one and two.

an-ti-mō′ni-ăl, *n.* An antimonial compound.

an-ti-mō′ni-āte, *n.* A salt of antimonic acid; an antimonate.

an-ti-mō′ni-ā-ted, *a.* In combination with antimony mixed or prepared with antimony.

an-ti-mon′iç, *a.* Relating to or produced from antimony; particularly applied to compounds with this element in its highest valence.

an-ti-mō′ni-ous, *a.* Containing antimony, with a valency next below the highest.

an′ti-mō-nite, *n.* 1. A compound of antimonious acid and a base or a radical acting as a base.

2. Stibnite.

an-ti-mō′ni-ū-ret″ed, *a.* Combined with antimony.

an′ti-mō-ny, *n.* [Fr. *antimoine*; L. *antimonium*, antimony.] One of the elements, symbol Sb (Latin *stibium*); sp.gr. 6.7; at.wt. 120. A brittle metal of a bluish-white or silver-white color occurring in two forms, crystalline and amorphous, sometimes found native or alloyed with other metals. Owing to the fact that it expands at the moment of solidifying it is of use in type-founding and in casts, as a constituent of an alloy. It is also used in medicine and in fireworks.

an″ti-nē-phrit′iç, *n.* and *a.* [*Anti-*, and Gr. *nephritis*, from *nephros*, kidney.]

I. *n.* A medicine that tends to cure diseases of the kidneys.

II. *a.* Remedial for diseases of the kidneys.

an-tin′i-ăl, *a.* Of, relating, or pertaining to the antinion.

an-tin′i-on, *n.* [Gr. *anti*, opposite, and *inion*, the back of the head.] The part of the skull between the eyebrows.

an′ti-nōde, *n.* [*Anti-*, and L. *nodus*, a knot.] In physics, the middle point of a loop. [See *Loop*, n., 5.]

an-ti-nō′mi-ăn, *a.* and *n.* I. *a.* Pertaining to the antinomians or to antinomianism.

II. *n.* One who believes in antinomianism.

an-ti-nō′mi-ăn-iṣm, *n.* The belief of a sect originating with John Agricola about 1538 holding the view that the church was subservient only to the gospel, and that faith is the essential of salvation.

an-tin′ō-my, *n.* [L. *antinomia*, a contradiction between laws, from Gr. *antinomia*; *anti*, against, and *nomia*, from *nomos*, law.]

1. Antagonism between laws; contradiction in the same law; a rule, principle, or law opposed to another.

2. The unavoidable contradiction to pure reasoning which human limitations introduce, as formulated by Kant; paradoxical conclusion.

An-ti-ō′ċhi-ăn, *a.* Pertaining to the eclectic school of philosophy of Antiochus, who flourished just previous to the Christian era, and who deduced his system from the doctrines of Plato, Aristotle, and the Stoics.

Antiochian epoch; a name given to various epochs of time, particularly to one dating from 48 B. C.

An-ti-ō′ċhi-ăn, *n.* 1. A resident of Antioch.

2. A follower of, or a believer in, the school of religious philosophy, founded at Antioch, Syria, in the fourth century, which propounded a course of scriptural interpretation midway between the literal and allegorical.

an″ti-ō-pel′mous, *a.* [Gr. *antios*, opposite, and *pelma*, sole.] Having one of the tendons of the foot trisected and a part running to the first, second, and fourth toes; a term applied to the foot of a bird, or the bird itself.

an″ti-ŏr-gas′tiç, *a.* [*Anti-*, and Gr. *orgaein*, to swell.] Having a tendency to repress sexual excitement.

an-ti-pā′pal, *a.* Opposed to the pope or papacy.

an-ti-par′al-lel, *a.* Running in a contrary direction.

an-ti-par′al-lels, *n.pl.* In geometry, lines which make equal angles with two other lines, but in a contrary order; thus, supposing *ab* and *ac* any two lines, and *fc* and *fe* two others, cutting them so as to make the angle *abc* equal to the angle *aed*, and the angle *acb* equal to the angle *ade*; then *fc* and *fe* are *antiparallels* with respect to *ab* and *ac*; also these latter are *antiparallels* with respect to the two former.

an″ti-par-ȧ-lyt′ic, an″ti-par-ȧ-lyt′ic-ăl, *a.* Remedial for paralysis.

an-ti-par-ȧ-lyt′ic, *n.* A remedy for paralysis.

An′ti-pasch, *n.* The first Sunday after Easter.

An″ti-pȧ-thā′ri-ȧ, *n.pl.* [LL., from Gr. *antipathēs*, of opposite feelings or properties.] An order of corals having a noncalcareous, hollow, external sclerobase, and colonial in habit.

an″ti-pȧ-thā′ri-ăn, *a.* and *n.* I. *a.* Of or pertaining to the *Antipatharia*.

II. *n.* One of the *Antipatharia*.

an″ti-pȧ-thet′ic, an″ti-pȧ-thet′ic-ăl, *a.* Inherently averse; contrary; having or showing aversion to.

an-tip′ȧ-thist, *n.* An antagonist; one naturally averse. [Rare.]

an-tip′ȧ-thize, *v.i.* To feel or show aversion. [Rare.]

an-tip′ȧ-thous, *a.* Adverse; having a natural contrariety. [Obs.]

an-tip′ȧ-thy, *n.* [Gr. *antipatheia*; *anti*, against, and *patheia*, from *pathein*, to suffer, feel.]

1. Inherent aversion or antagonism of feeling; repugnancy; revulsion; as, *antipathy* to snakes; *antipathy* to an offensive person.

2. Incompatibility, in a physical or chemical sense. [Obs.]

3. Any object of repugnancy or idiosyncratic aversion.

Antipathy is regularly followed by *to*, sometimes by *for*, etc., and is opposed to *sympathy*.

Syn.—Abhorrence, aversion, contrariety, detestation, dislike, hatred, opposition, repugnance.

an-ti-pep′tōne, *n.* One of the two varieties of peptone; peptone unchanged by tripsin.

an″ti-pē-ri-od′ic, *n.* A remedy possessing the property of preventing the return of periodic diseases, as intermittents.

an″ti-per-i-stal′sis, *n.* [Gr. *anti*, against, and *peristaltikos*, clasping and compressing.] A reversion of the normal downward peristaltic motion of the intestinal system.

an″ti-per-i-stal′tic, *a.* Checking peristalsis; characteristic of antiperistalsis.

an″ti-pe-ris′tȧ-sis, *n.* [Gr. *antiperistasis*; *anti*, against, and *peristasis*, a standing around, from *peristanai*, to stand around; *peri*, around, and *histanai*, to stand.] Opposition, resulting in the intensification or consequent strength of the thing opposed.

an″ti-per-i-stat′ic, *a.* Pertaining to antiperistasis.

an-ti-pet′ăl-ous, *a.* [*Anti-*, and Gr. *petalon*, a leaf.] Placed opposite or in front of a petal.

an-ti-phär′mic, *a.* Counteractive of poison; antidotal.

an″ti-phlō-gis′tiăn (-chăn), *n.* An opposer of the theory of phlogiston.

an″ti-phlō-gis′tic, *a.* 1. Counteracting a phlogistic condition.

2. Opposed to the doctrine of phlogiston; as, the *antiphlogistic* system.

an″ti-phlō-gis′tic, *n.* Any medicine or diet which tends to reduce inflammation or fever.

an′ti-phon, an′ti-phōne, *n.* [LL. *antiphona*, from Gr. *antiphōna*; *anti*, in return, and *phōnē*, voice, a sound.]

1. The chant or alternate singing in choirs of cathedrals; antiphony.

2. An echo or response. [Rare.]

an-tiph′ō-năl, *a.* Pertaining to antiphony or alternate singing.

an-tiph′ō-năl-ly, *adv.* In an antiphonal manner.

an-tiph′ō-nā-ry, *n.* A book of antiphons or anthems; specifically, a service-book containing whatever is sung by the choir. Also written *antiphonal*, *antiphonar*.

an-ti-phon′ic, an-ti-phon′ic-ăl, *a.* Antiphonal.

an-tiph′ō-ny, *n.* 1. The response of one choir to another, when an anthem or psalm is sung alternately by two choirs; alternate singing.

2. The words given out at the beginning of a psalm, to which both the choirs are to accommodate their singing.

3. A musical composition of several verses extracted from different psalms.

an-tiph′rȧ-sis, *n.*; *pl.* **an-tiph′rȧ-sēs.** [L., from Gr. *antiphrasis*, from *antiphrazein*, to express by antithesis or negation; *anti*, against, and *phrazein*, to speak.] The use of words in a sense opposite to their proper meaning; as when a court of justice is called a court of vengeance.

an-ti-phras′tic, an-ti-phras′tic-ăl, *a.* Pertaining to antiphrasis.

an-ti-phras′tic-ăl-ly, *adv.* In the manner of antiphrasis.

an-ti-phthis′ic (-tiz′), *a.* and *n.* I. *a.* Remedial for consumption.

II. *n.* A remedy for consumption.

an-ti-phys′ic-ăl, *a.* [*Anti-*, and Gr. *physis*, nature.] Contrary to physics or to nature.

an-ti-phys′ic-ăl, *a.* [*Anti-*, and Gr. *physa*, breath, wind.] Carminative.

an-ti-plas′tic, *a.* 1. Reducing plasticity.

2. In medicine, unfavorable to the healing process.

an″ti-pō-dag′ric, *a.* and *n.* I. *a.* Remedial for gout.

II. *n.* A remedy for gout.

an-tip′ō-dăl, *a.* 1. Of or relating to the antipodes.

2. Opposed diametrically or directly.

an′ti-pōde, *n.* A person living at the opposite side of the globe; an exact opposite.

an-tip′ō-dēs, *n.*, *sing.* and *pl.* [Gr. *antipodes*, opposite feet; *anti*, against, opposite, and *pous*, pl. *podes*, feet.]

1. People who live at the opposite side of the earth.

2. Regions on the opposite side of the globe.

3. Any person or persons, thing or things, opposite in quality or attribute; contraries; as, he is my *antipodes*.

an′ti-pōle, *n.* The pole opposite; a thing at the extreme of difference.

an′ti-pōpe, *n.* In the great schism, a usurping pope or one not canonically elected.

an-tip-sor′ic, *a.* and *n.* [Gr. *anti*, against, and *psora*, the itch.]

I. *a.* Efficacious in curing the itch.

II. *n.* A remedy for the itch.

an-tip-tō′sis, *n.* [Gr. *antiptōsis*; *anti*, against, instead of, and *ptōsis*, a falling, case, from *piptein*, to fall.] In grammar, the putting of one case for another.

an″ti-pū-trē-fac′tive, *a.* Checking or preventing putrefaction; antiseptic.

an″ti-pū-tres′cent, *a.* Antiputrefactive.

an-ti-py′ic, *a.* and *n.* [*Anti-*, and Gr. *pyon*, pus.]

I. *a.* Unfavorable to pus formation.

II. *n.* A remedy for pus formation.

an″ti-py̆-rē′sis, *n.* [LL., from Gr. *anti-*, against, and *pyressein*, to be feverish; from *pyr*, fire.] Absence of fever; treatment of fever by antipyretics.

an″ti-py̆-ret′ic, *a.* and *n.* I. *a.* Cooling; allaying fever.

II. *n.* Any agent allaying fever, as cold.

an-ti-py̆′rin, an-ti-py̆′rine, *n.* An antipyretic medicine derived from the benzene group, C_6H_6. It is a white crystalline substance, dissolving readily in water.

an″ti-py̆-rot′ic, *a.* and *n.* I. *a.* Remedial for burns or catarrh of the stomach.

II. *n.* A medicine for burns or pyrosis.

an-ti-quā′ri-ăn, *a.* 1. Pertaining to antiquaries.

2. A term applied to a drawing paper 52½ by 30½ inches.

an-ti-quā′ri-ăn, *n.* An antiquary.

an-ti-quā′ri-ăn-ism, *n.* The science of antiquities.

an-ti-quā′ri-ăn-īze, *v.i.* To pursue antiquarian researches. [Rare.]

an′ti-quā-ry, *n.*; *pl.* **an′ti-quā-ries.** [L. *antiquarius.*] One who makes a study of the history of ancient things, as statues, coins, medals, paintings, inscriptions, books, and manuscripts, or searches for them, and explains their origin and purport; a scholar versed in antiquities.

an′ti-quāte, *v.t.*; antiquated, *pt., pp.*; antiquating, *ppr.* [L. *antiquitatus*, pp. of *antiquare*, to restore a thing to its former condition, to make old; *antiquus*, ancient, old.] To make old or obsolete; to make old in such a degree as to put out of use; to make void or abrogate, as laws or customs.

> Christianity might introduce new laws and *antiquate* or abrogate old ones. —Hale.

an′ti-quā-ted, *a.* Grown old; obsolete; out of use; having lost its binding force, by nonobservance; as, an *antiquated* law.

Syn.—Old, ancient, antique, old-fashioned, obsolete.

an′ti-quā-ted-ness, *n.* The state of being obsolete.

an′ti-quāte-ness, *n.* Antiquatedness. [Obs.]

an-ti-quā′tion, *n.* The state of being antiquated.

an-tique′ (-tēk′), *a.* [Fr. *antique*, ancient, old, from L. *antiquus*, former, old, from *ante*, before.]

1. Old; ancient; of genuine antiquity; in this sense it usually refers to the flourishing ages of Greece and Rome; as, an *antique* statue.

2. Old, as respects the present age, or a modern period of time; of old fashion; as, an *antique* robe.

3. In imitation of ancient fashions; as, *antique* customs.

4. Old; wild; fantastic; more generally written *antic*.

Syn.—Old, ancient, antiquated, old-fashioned, obsolete, archaic, obsolescent.

an-tique′, *n.* 1. Anything very old; specifically, a term applied to the remains of ancient art, as statues, paintings, vases, cameos, and the like, and more especially to the works of Grecian and Roman antiquity.

2. In printing, a term applied to a style of type in which each stroke of the face has an equal thickness.

an-tique′ly, *adv.* In an antique manner.

an-tique′ness, *n.* The quality of being antique; an appearance of ancient origin and workmanship.

an′ti-quist (-kwist), *n.* One who collects antiques; an antiquarian. [Rare.]

an-tiq-ui-tā′ri-ăn, *n.* One holding to or admiring antique customs.

an-tiq′ui-ty, *n.* [Fr. *antiquité*, from L. *antiquitas*, from *antiquus*, former, old.]

1. The quality of being ancient; ancientness; great age; as, a family of great *antiquity*.

2. Ancient times; former ages; times long since past; as, Cicero was the most eloquent orator of *antiquity*.

3. The ancients; the people of ancient times; as, the fact is admitted by all *antiquity*.

4. Old age. [Obs.]

5. An old person. [Obs.]

6. The remains of ancient times; ancient institutions or customs; in this sense usually or always plural; as, Greek or Egyptian *antiquities*.

an″ti-rā-chit′ic, *a.* Remedial for rachitis or rickets.

an-ti-rent′ēr, *n.* One opposed to the payment of rent; specifically, [A—] one of the Antirent party, an organization which (1839-1848) resisted the payment of rent on certain manorial estates in New York.

an-ti-rent′ism, *n.* The policy or principles of the Antirent party.

an″ti-rheū-mat′ic (-rū-), *a.* Efficacious in cases of rheumatism.

An-tir-rhī′num, *n.* [LL., from Gr. *antirrhinon*; *anti*, corresponding to, like, and *rhis*, *rhinos*, nose.] A genus of plants belonging to the figwort or *Scrophulariaceæ* family; the snapdragons.

an″ti-sab-bȧ-tā′ri-ăn, *n.* One of a sect which opposes the observance of the Christian Sabbath, maintaining that the Jewish Sabbath was one of ceremonial, not of moral obligation, and was consequently abolished by Christ.

an″ti-sac-ēr-dō′tăl, *a.* Adverse to priests or their office.

an-tis′ciăns, an-tis′ci-ī (-tish′), *n.pl.* [L. *antiscii*, from Gr. *antiskioi*, pl. of *antiskios*, with opposite shadows; *anti*, opposite, and *skios*, from *skia*, shadow.] In geography, the inhabitants of the earth, living on the same meridian on opposite sides of the equator, whose shadows at noon are cast in contrary directions.

an″ti-scō-let′ic, an-ti-scol′ic, *a.* [*Anti-*, and Gr. *skolex*, a worm.] Anthelmintic.

an″ti-scor-bū′tic, an″ti-scor-bū′tic-ăl, *a.* Counteracting the scurvy.

an″ti-scor-bū′tic, *n.* A remedy for the scurvy.

an-ti-scrip′tūr-ăl, *a.* Not accordant with the Scriptures.

an″ti-Sem′īte, *n.* One who is antagonistic to the Jews, or who favors their persecution, especially by political methods.

an″ti-Sem-it′ic, *a.* Pertaining to or of the nature of anti-Semitism.

an″ti-Sem′i-tism, *n.* Political or social persecution of the Jews.

an-ti-sep′ăl-ous, *a.* Standing opposite to sepals, as the stamens of some flowers.

an-ti-sep′sis, *n.* [L., from Gr. *antisēpsis*; *anti*, against, and *sēpsis*, putrefaction.] The exclusion of bacteria from wounds, etc., by the use of antiseptics or other means; antiseptic surgery.

an-ti-sep′tic, an-ti-sep′tic-ăl, *a.* Opposed to or counteracting a putrescent tendency in the system.

Antiseptic surgery; surgery practised with proper precautions to render the wound aseptic.

an-ti-sep′tic, *n.* A substance which resists or corrects putrefaction, or counteracts a putrescent tendency in the system, as certain acids and saline substances.

an-ti-sep′tic-ăl-ly, *adv.* In an antiseptic manner, or by the aid of antiseptics.

an-ti-slāv′ēr-y, *n.* and *a.* I. *n.* Opposition to slavery.

II. *a.* Opposed to slavery; as, *antislavery* literature.

an-ti-sō′ciăl, *a.* 1. Averse to society; tending to interrupt or destroy social intercourse or its enjoyment.

2. Hostile to the existence of society, or the principles on which it is founded; as, *antisocial* agitators.

an-ti-sō′ciăl-ist, *a.* Antagonistic to or tending to undermine the theories and practices of socialism.

an-ti-sō′lăr, *a.* Opposite to or occurring in the heavens at a point 180° from the sun; used especially as an astronomical term.

an-tis′pȧ-sis, *n.* [Gr. *antispasis*, from *antispān*, to draw in the opposite direction; *anti*, opposite, and *spān*, to draw.] In medicine, the turning or diverting of a disease from one part of the body to another; counter-irritation.

an″ti-spaș-mod′iç, *a.* Of a nature to prevent or relieve spasms; resisting convulsions, as anodynes.

an″ti-spaș-mod′iç, *n.* A remedy for spasms or convulsions.

an′ti-spast, an-ti-spas′tus, *n.* [Gr. *antispastos*, from *antispān*, to draw in the contrary direction; *anti*, opposite, and *spān*, to draw.] In prosody, a tetrasyllabic foot, in which the first and last syllables are short, and the middle syllables long.

an-ti-spas′tiç, *a.* 1. Causing a revulsion of fluids or humors; of the nature of antispasis. [Obs.]

2. Counteracting spasms; antispasmodic.

an-ti-spas′tiç, *a.* In prosody, pertaining to, of the nature of, or embodying an antispast.

an-ti-spas′tiç, *n.* 1. In medicine, an agent supposed to act by causing a revulsion of the humors; anything causing antispasis. [Obs.]

2. A remedy which counteracts spasms; an antispasmodic.

an-ti-spas′tus, *n.* See *Antispast.*

an″ti-splē-net′iç (*or* an-ti-splen′e-tiç), *a.* and *n.* I. *a.* Counteracting or relieving diseases of the spleen.

II. *n.* A medicine for disorders of the spleen.

an-tis′tȧ-sis, *n.* [Gr. *antistasis*, a counter-plea, opposition, from *anti*, against, and *stēnai*, to stand.] In oratory, the defense of an action on the ground that if it had been omitted, something worse would have happened.

an-tis′tēș, *n.*; *pl.* **an-tis′ti-tēș.** [L.] A prelate or chief priest. [Rare.]

an″ti-strep-tō-coç′çus, *n.*; *pl.* **an″ti-strep-tō-coç′çi.** [L., from Gr. *anti*, against, *streptos*, twisted, and *kokkos*, a berry, seed.] A serum remedy for scarlet fever, obtained by repeated injections of scarlet fever bacteria (*streptococcus*) into a horse or other animal until immunized against the disease. The serum of the animal thus immunized is an *antistreptococcus*.

an-tis′trō-phē, *n.* [Gr. *antistrophē*, from *antistrephein*, to turn about; *anti*, against, opposite, and *strephein*, to turn.]

1. In rhetoric, the reversal of terms mutually depending on each other; reciprocal conversion; as, the master of the servant, the servant of the master.

2. The construing of an adversary's plea or argument to his disadvantage.

3. That part of a Greek choral ode, which was sung while turning from the left to the right, in opposition to the *strophe*, which was sung while turning from the right to the left.

an-ti-stroph′iç, *a.* Belonging to the antistrophe.

an-ti-stroph′iç-ăl-ly, *adv.* In an antistrophic style.

an-tis′trō-phon, *n.* [Neut. of Gr. *antistrophos*, turned against.] In rhetoric, the turning of an opponent's argument upon himself.

an″ti-strū-mat′iç, an-ti-strū′mous, *a.* [*Anti-*, and L. *struma*, a scrofulous swelling.] Remedial for scrofulous disorders.

an″ti-strū-mat′iç, *n.* An agent for curing or preventing scrofula.

an″ti-syph-i-lit′iç, *a.* and *n.* I. *a.* Remedial in cases of syphilis; antivenereal.

II. *n.* A medicine given in cases of syphilis.

An-ti-taç′tēș, *n.*; *pl.* **An-ti-taç′tæ.** [Gr. *antitactēs*, a heretic, from *antitassein*, to oppose; *anti*, against, and *tassein*, to arrange, draw up.] One of the sect which Clement of Alexandria named Gnostics; they considered that the decalogue originated from the Demiurge, or so-called second Maker, and wilfully despised and defied it.

an-ti-thā′li-ăn, *a.* [*Anti-*, and L. *Thalia*, muse of comedy.] Antagonistic to merriment and merry-making. [Rare.]

an′ti-thē-ișm, *n.* Opposition to belief in a God.

an′ti-thē-ist, *n.* One who opposes the belief in a God.

an″ti-thē-is′tiç, *a.* Pertaining to the doctrine of antitheism; opposing the belief of a God.

an-tith′ē-sis, *n.*; *pl.* **an-tith′ē-sēș.** [Gr. *antithesis*, from *antitithenai*; *anti*, against, and *tithenai*, to place, set.]

1. In rhetoric, an opposition or contrast of words, phrases, or sentiments; as, the prodigal robs his heir, the miser robs himself; excess of ceremony shows want of breeding.

2. The second of two balanced clauses; opposed to *thesis*.

3. The opposite; extreme contrast.

4. Opposition of opinions; controversy.

an′ti-thet, *n.* [Gr. *antitheton*, an antithesis, neut. of *antithetos*, opposed.] A statement which partakes of the nature of antithesis. [Rare.]

an-ti-thet′iç-ăl, an-ti-thet′iç, *a.* Pertaining to antithesis; containing or abounding with antithesis.

an-ti-thet′iç-ăl-ly, *adv.* By antithesis.

an-ti-tox′iç, *a.* Protecting against poison; antidotal.

an-ti-tox′in, an-ti-tox′ine, *n.* Virus used to neutralize the action of toxin; specifically, serum used hypodermically as a preventive of, or cure for, diphtheria.

an′ti-trāde, *n.* A wind moving above the trade-winds and in an opposite direction.

an-ti-traġ′i-çus, *n.*; *pl.* **an-ti-trăġ′i-çī.** A muscle on the antitragus.

an-tit′rā-gus, *n.*; *pl.* **an-tit′rā-ġī.** [LL., from Gr. *antitragos*; *anti*, opposite, and *tragos*, a part of the ear.] That process of the external ear behind the opening and opposite the tragus.

an″ti-trin-i-tā′ri-ăn, *a.* and *n.* I. *a.* Antagonistic to the doctrine of the Trinity.

II. *n.* A disbeliever or opponent of the doctrine of the Trinity, or the triune Godhead.

an″ti-trin-i-tā′ri-ăn-ișm, *n.* The opposition existing against, and the denial of the doctrine of, the Trinity.

an″ti-trō-çhan′tẽr, *n.* In anatomy, a smooth surface on the ilium against which the great trochanter plays and forms a joint, as in birds.

an″ti-trō-çhan-ter′iç, *n.* Pertaining to the antitrochanter.

an-tit′rō-păl, *a.* See *Antitropous.*

an′ti-trōpe, *n.* [Fr. *antitrope*, from Gr. *anti*, against, and *tropos*, from *trepein*, to turn.] In anatomy, a part of an organism reversely repeated, so as to form a pair; as, the right and left ears are *antitropes* to each other.

an-ti-trop′iç, an-ti-trop′iç-ăl, *a.* 1. In anatomy, symmetrically related in position, as the two arms.

2. In botany, same as *sinistrorse*.

an-tit′rō-pous, an-tit′rō-păl, *a.* [L. *antitropus*; Gr. *antitropos*; *anti*, against, and *tropos*, from *trepein*, to turn.] In botany, denoting that the radicle, in a seed, is at the extremity most remote from the hilum, or that the embryo is inverted with respect to the seed.

an-tit′rō-py, *n.* Reversed repetition of a part or organ.

an′ti-trust, *a.* Antagonistic to or not in sympathy with trusts or corporations formed for the purpose of controlling trade, industries, etc., by overcoming competition, lessening the cost of production, and fixing prices.

an-ti-tȳ′păl, *a.* Pertaining to an antitype.

an′ti-tȳpe, *n.* [Gr. *antitypos*; *anti*, against, corresponding to, and *typos*, form, figure.]

1. That of which the type is the prefiguration; something formed according to a model, or pattern, and bearing strong features of resemblance to it; especially, in theology, something in the New Testament which was symbolized by a type in the Old Testament, as Christ is the *antitype* of the serpent raised up in the wilderness by Moses.

2. In anatomy, an antitrope.

an-ti-typ′iç-ăl, an-ti-typ′iç, *a.* 1. Pertaining to an antitype; explaining the type.

2. In anatomy, same as *antitropic.*

an-ti-typ′iç-ăl-ly, *adv.* By means of an antitype.

an-tit′y-pous, *a.* Characterized by antitypy. [Obs.]

an-tit′y-py, *n.* [Gr. *antitypia*, from *antitypos*; *anti*, against, and *typos*, from *typtein*, to strike.] The property of matter known as impenetrability.

an″ti-vaç-ci-nā′tion, *n.* Opposition to vaccination.

an″ti-vaç-ci-nā′tion-ist, an-ti-vaç′cin-ist, *n.* One who is opposed to vaccination.

an″ti-vā-ri′ō-lous, *a.* Preventing or supposed to prevent smallpox contagion.

an-ti-vē′nin, *n.* [*Anti-*, and L. *venenum*, poison.] The serum of animals vaccinated against a virulent venom, such as that of the cobra. It is antitoxic to the poisons of all kinds of serpents, and even scorpions.

an″ti-vē-nē′rē-ăl, *a.* Resisting venereal poison.

an″ti-viv-i-seç′tion, *n.* Antagonism to vivisection.

an″ti-viv-i-seç′tion-ist, *n.* One antagonistic to vivisection.

an-ti-zym′iç, an″ti-zȳ-mot′iç, *a.* Preventing or checking fermentation or putrefaction; antiseptic.

an″ti-zȳ-mot′iç, *n.* That which prevents fermentation or putrefaction; an antiseptic.

ant′lẽr, *n.* [ME. *anntelere*; OFr. *antoiller*, from an assumed L. *antocularis*; *ante*, before, and *oculus*, eye.] The entire deciduous, bony outgrowth of a cervine animal, as of the stag. The first year a stag has only frontal protuberances or *bossets*; the second year, a simple *snag* or *stem*; the third, a longer stem garnished with a branch or *brow-antler*; in the fourth, the *bes-*, *bez-*, or *bay-antler*; in the fifth, the *antler-royal* is added; in the sixth, the *crown* or *surroyal* diverges on the top of the horn, forming the cup, which consists of two or three snags or prongs curving upward. To these in future years others are added, the total number of branches often amounting to ten in a stag seven or eight years old.

ant′lẽred (-lẽrd), *a.* 1. Furnished with or bearing antlers.

2. Ornamented with antlers.

ant′lẽr-mọth, *n.* A European moth, *Charæas graminis*, the larvæ of which are ruinous to grass and meadows.

Antlers.
a, Brow-antler; *b*, Bez-antler; *c*, Antler-royal; *d*, Sur-royal or Crown-antler.

ant′li-ȧ, *n.*; *pl.* **ant′li-æ.** [L., a pump, from Gr. *antlia*, the hold of a ship, bilge-water.] The haustellum of a lepidopter.

ant′-li″ŏn, *n.* An insect resembling the dragon-fly and belonging to the order *Neuroptera*, the larvæ of which build a trap in the earth to catch ants and other small insects.

an-tœ′ci-ănș, an-tœ′ci, *n.pl.* Same as *Antecians.*

ăn-tō-ni′nō, *n.* The mackerel-scad.

an-tō-nō-mā′și-ȧ (-zhi-ȧ), *n.* [L., from Gr. *antonomasia*, from *antonomazein*, to call by another name; *anti*, instead of, and *onomazein*, to name; *onoma*, name.] The use of the name of some office, dignity, profession, science, or trade, instead of the proper name of a person; as when *his honor* is used for a judge, or when, instead of Aristotle, we say, *the philosopher*; also, conversely, the use of a proper name instead of an appellative, as when an eminent orator is called *a Demosthenes.*

an-tō-nō-mas′tiç, an-tō-nō-mas′tiç-ăl, *a.* Of or pertaining to the figure antonomasia.

an-tō-nō-mas′tiç-ăl-ly, *adv.* By the use of the figure antonomasia.

an-ton′ō-mȧ-sy, *n.* Same as *Antonomasia.*

an′tō-nym, *n.* [Gr. *antonymia*, a word used instead of another; *anti*, opposite, and *onoma*, *onyma*, name.] A word meaning the opposite of some other word; as, unhappy is the *antonym* of happy, agreeable of disagreeable, good of bad.

ant-ọr′bit-ăl, *a.* and *n.* Same as *Anteorbital.*

ant-ọr-gas′tiç, *a.* Same as *Antiorgastic.*

ant-ō′zōne, *n.* A name given to hydrogen dioxid, which, when combined with ozone, produces oxygen.

an′trȧ, *n.*, pl. of *antrum.*

an′trăl, *a.* Of or pertaining to an antrum.

an′tre (-tẽr), *n.* [Fr. *antre*; L. *antrum*; Gr. *antron*, a cave.] A cavern. [Obs.]

an-trorse′, *a.* [L. *ante*, before, and *versus*, turned, from *vertere*, to turn.] In biology, leaning forward, or forward and upward.

an-trō-vẽrt′, *v.i.* [L. *ante*, before, and *vertere*, to turn.] To incline or bend forward. [Rare.]

an′trum, *n.*; *pl.* **an′trȧ.** [L., a cave.] A cavity; specifically, an anatomical hollow; a sinus.

an-trus′tion (-chun), *n.* [Fr.] A follower of the Frankish princes of the seventh century similar to the Anglo-Saxon thanes.

ănt′-thrush, *n.* The common name of the birds of the genus *Pitta*, allied to the *Turdidæ* or thrush family. The name is also given to the ant-bird.

A-nū′bis, *n.* [L., from Gr. *Anoubis*, Egypt. *Anepu.*] A god of the Egyptians who was supposed to have the care of the entombed and to perform the part of a conductor of departed spirits; represented as having a human body with a head like that of a jackal.

Anubis, from an Egyptian Painting.

A-nū′rȧ, *n.pl.* [LL., from Gr. *an* priv., and *oura*, tail.] An order of batrachians which lose the tail when they reach maturity, as the toad and frog. Written also *anoura.*

an-ū-rē′sis, *n.* Same as *Anuria.*

an-ū-ret′iç, *a.* Pertaining to anuresis.

ȧ-nū′ri-ȧ, *n.* [LL., from Gr. *an* priv., and *ouron*, urine.] Inability to excrete urine.

ȧ-nū′riç, *a.* Relating to anuria.

ȧ-nū′rous, *a.* Tailless; relating to the *Anura.* Written also *anourous.*

an′ū-ry, *n.* Same as *Anuria.*

ā′nus, *n.* [L. *anus*, a ring.] The opening of the body from which excrement is expelled.

an′vil, *n.* [OE. *anvelt*, *andvell*, *anvylte*; AS.

anfilt, onfilte, an anvil; *an,* on, and *fealdan,* to fold.]

1. An iron block with a smooth face of steel, on which smiths hammer and shape their work.

Anvil.

2. Figuratively, anything on which blows are laid; anything that in any way resembles an anvil; as one of the small bones in the ear.

To be on the anvil; to be in a state of discussion or preparation, as when a scheme or measure is forming, but not matured.

an'vil, *v.t.* To use an anvil in forming or forging. [Rare.]

aṅx-ī'e-tūde, *n.* Anxiety. [Rare.]

aṅx-ī'e-ty (ang-zī'), *n.* [Fr. *anxieté;* L. *anxietas,* from *anxius,* anxious.]

1. Concern or solicitude respecting some event, future or uncertain, which disturbs the mind, and keeps it in a state of painful uneasiness.

2. A condition of eagerness; as, *anxiety* to please one's instructor.

3. In medicine, a state of restlessness and agitation of the mind, accompanied by a distressing sense of pressure in the vicinity of the abdomen.

Syn.—Solicitude, care, foreboding, uneasiness, perplexity, disquietude, disquiet, watchfulness, restlessness.

aṅx'ious (angk'shus), *a.* [L. *anxius,* anxious, troubled, from *angere,* to trouble, choke.]

1. Greatly concerned respecting something unknown; being in suspense; applied to persons; as, to be *anxious* for the issue of a battle.

2. Full of solicitude; disquieting; as, *anxious* thoughts; or, *anxious* to commit no serious error.

Syn.—Solicitous, careful, uneasy, concerned, restless, watchful, disturbed, unquiet, uneasy, worried.

aṅx'ious-ly, *adv.* In an anxious manner.

aṅx'ious-ness, *n.* The condition of being anxious.

an'y (en'y), *a.* and *pron.* [AS. *anig, ænig;* D. *eenig;* G. *einig.*]

1. One, indefinitely; one of three or more (which one not specified).

2. Some; an indefinite number or quantity; for, though the word is formed from *one,* it may signify several; as, are there *any* witnesses present?

At any rate, in any case; whatever the state or the case may be; no matter what else may be true or may happen.

an'y, *adv.* [ME. *any, eny, anie;* AS. *ænig;* O.H.G. *einag;* from *ān,* one.] To an indefinite extent; somewhat; in any degree; as, *any* farther; *any* better; *any* more.

an'y-bod"y, *pron.* 1. Of all, any person that may be specified.

2. A person of some note; as, is he *anybody?* opposed to *nobody.* [Colloq.]

an'y-how, *adv.* 1. Under any circumstances; in whatever way considered; without regard to consequences; whatever else may be.

2. Carelessly; as, he performs his work *anyhow.*

an'y-thing, *pron.* 1. An indiscriminate thing of whatsoever character or importance, or unimportance. Written as one word when the stress is on *any,* but as two words when the stress is on *thing.*

2. A word used to express comparison unspecified and unlimited; as, the turkey spreads his tail as proudly as *anything.* [Colloq.]

Anything but; not in the least; as, the entertainment was *anything but* pleasing.

Anything like; by a great deal, as, the property did not sell for *anything like* its value.

an'y-thing, *adv.* In any degree. [Obs.]

an'y-thing-ā'ri-ăn, *n.* One careless as to creed or belief or indifferent in his views.

an'y-wāy, an'y-wāyṣ, *adv.* In any manner or under any circumstances whatever; in spite of anything; as, he will go *anyway.*

an'y-where (-hwâr), *adv.* In, to, from, or at any place.

an'y-whith-ẽr, *adv.* Toward no specified place; in no specified direction.

an'y-wiṣe, *adv.* In any way or wise; to any extent; by any means.

An'zaç, *n.* [From the initials of Australian and New Zealand Army Corps.] A member of this corps. [Colloq.]

An'zaç, *a.* Belonging or pertaining to the Australian and New Zealand Army Corps.

Ā-ō'ni-ăn, *a.* [L. *Aonius,* from *Aonia,* a part of Bœotia, in Greece.] Pertaining to the Muses or to Aonia in Bœotia, the supposed abode of the Muses.

Aonian fount; the fount of Aganippe at the foot of Mount Helicon not far from Thebes; it was sacred to the Muses.

ā'ō-rist, *n.* [Gr. *aoristos,* indefinite, from *a* priv., and *orizein,* to define; *oros,* a boundary, limit.] The name of certain tenses in the grammar of the Greek language, which express an action as completed in past time, but leave it, in other respects, wholly indeterminate.

ā-ō-ris'tiç, *a.* Indefinite; pertaining to an aorist, or indefinite tense.

ā-or'tȧ, *n.* [L., from Gr. *aortē,* aorta, from *aeirein,* to raise, heave.] The great artery, or trunk of the arterial system, proceeding from the left ventricle of the heart, and giving origin to all the arteries, except the pulmonary. It rises as the ascending *aorta,* then makes a great curve and gives branches to the head and upper extremities; then it proceeds as the descending *aorta,* giving branches to the trunk, and finally divides into the two iliacs, which supply the pelvis and lower extremities.

ā-or'tăl, *a.* Aortic.

ā-or'tiç, *a.* Pertaining to the aorta, or great artery.

ā-or-tī'tis, *n.* Aortic inflammation.

ā-os'miç, *a.* [Gr. *aosmos,* odorless; *a* priv., and *osmē,* odor.] Without odor.

ä'ōu-dad, *n.* [Moorish name.] The *Ammotragus tragelaphus,* or bearded argali, an ovine quadruped, allied to the sheep, most closely to the mouflon, from which, however, it may be easily distinguished by the heavy mane commencing at the throat and falling as far as the knees. It is a native of North Africa.

Aoudad (*Ammotragus tragelaphus*).

ȧ-pāce', *adv.* With a quick pace; fast; speedily; hastily; implying motion or progression; as, birds fly *apace;* weeds grow *apace.*

A-pä'chē, *n.* 1. One of a warlike tribe of North American Indians, formerly very numerous in New Mexico and Arizona; also their language.

2. A member of a criminal gang infesting the streets of the city of Paris.

ȧ-pä'chē-plūme, *n.* A shrub, *Fallucia paradoxa,* found in New Mexico.

ap-ȧ-gō'gē, *n.* [L., from Gr. *apagogē,* a leading away; *apo,* away, and *agein,* to lead, drive.]

1. In logic, the form of proving a proposition by showing that anything else is absurd; indirect demonstration.

2. In mathematics, a passage from one proposition to another, when the first, having been demonstrated, is employed in proving others.

ap-ȧ-gog'iç, ap-ȧ-gog'iç-ăl, *a.* Of or pertaining to apagoge.

ȧ-paid', *a.* [Obs.] Same as *Paid.*

Ap-ȧ-lā'chi-ăn, *a.* Same as *Appalachian.*

ap'ăn-āġe, *n.* See *Appanage.*

ȧ-pan'thrō-py, *n.* [Gr. *apanthrōpia,* from *apanthrōpos,* unsocial; *apo,* away, and *anthrōpos,* man.] An aversion to the company of men; a love of solitude.

ap'ăr, ap'ȧ-rȧ, *n.* Same as *Mataco.*

ȧ-pä-re'jō (-hō), *n.* [Sp.] A Mexican pack-saddle in use in western United States, made of two pads of leather stuffed with soft material.

ap-ȧ-rith'mē-sis, *n.* [Gr. *aparithmēsis,* from *aparithmein,* to count off, *apo,* off, and *arithmein,* to count.] In rhetoric, enumeration of details.

ȧ-pärt', *adv.* [ME. *apart,* OFr. *a part;* It. *a parte,* from L. *ad partem; ad,* to, at, and *partem,* acc. of *pars,* part, side.]

1. Separately; at a distance; in a state of separation as to place.

> Jesus departed thence into a desert place apart. —Matt. xiv. 13.

2. In a state of distinction or exclusion as to purpose, use, or character.

3. Distinctly; separately; as, consider the two propositions *apart.*

4. Aside; in exclusion of; as, *apart* from all regard to his morals, he is not qualified, in other respects, for the office he holds.

5. Into parts, or pieces; asunder; as, to take a watch *apart.*

To tell apart; to distinguish one from another.

Syn.—Separately, aside, secretly, privately, aloof.

ȧ-pärt'ment, *n.* [Fr. *appartement;* It. *appartamento,* an apartment, from L. *ad,* to, and *partire,* to separate; from *pars,* a part.]

1. A room in a building; a division in a house, separated from others by partitions; a place separated by inclosure.

2. A suite or number of rooms; a flat.

3. A compartment. [Obs.]

Syn.—Flat.—*Apartment* and *flat* are commonly used interchangeably, though strictly an *apartment* is a suite of rooms none of which are used for cooking; a *flat,* a number of rooms used for housekeeping purposes.

ȧ-pärt'ness, *n.* The state of being or holding oneself apart; isolation.

ap-as'tron, *n.* [L., from Gr. *apo,* from, and *astron,* a star.] In astronomy, the point in the orbit of a double star where the primary and its satellite are separated farthest.

ap-ȧ-tet'iç, *a.* [Gr. *apatetikos,* from *apatē,* deceit.] In animal coloration, denoting a form or color which resembles some other animal or thing, for the purpose of concealment, applied, for example, to the zebra.

ap-ȧ-thet'iç, ap-ȧ-thet'iç-ăl, *a.* Devoid of feeling; free from passion; insensible; indifferent.

ap-ȧ-thet'iç-ăl-ly, *adv.* In an apathetic manner.

ap'ȧ-thist, *n.* One destitute of feeling.

ap-ȧ-this'tiç-ăl, *a.* Apathetic. [Rare.]

ap'ȧ-thy, *n.* [L. *apathia;* Gr. *apatheia; a* priv., and *pathos,* from *pathein,* to feel; *paschein,* to suffer.] Want of feeling, privation of passion, or insensibility to pain; applied either to the body or the mind. As applied to the mind, it is stoicism, a calmness of mind incapable of being ruffled by pleasure, pain, or passion. In the first ages of the church, the Christians adopted the term to express a contempt of earthly concerns.

> The helpless *apathy* of Asiatics.—Macaulay.

Syn.—Impassiveness, indifference, insensibility, lethargy, stoicism, unconcern.

ap'ȧ-tīte, *n.* [Gr. *apatē,* deceit, and *-ite.*] Native phosphate of lime. It occurs usually in six-sided prisms, of a greenish color, resembling beryl.

ȧ-pau-mée' (-pō-mā'), *n.* Same as *Appaumée.*

āpe, *n.* [ME. *ape;* AS. *apa;* Ice. *api,* ape, Gr. *kēpos;* Sans. *kapi,* ape.]

1. An animal of the order *Quadrumana,* an inhabitant of the tropical Old World, resembling man in structure. The arms are very long, the dentition the same as in man, the body nearly erect, and tailless.

2. One who imitates servilely, in allusion to the manners of the ape; a silly fellow.

Long-armed Ape (*Hylobates camboja*).

āpe, *v.t.;* aped (āpt), *pt., pp.;* aping, *ppr.* To imitate servilely; to mimic as an ape imitates human actions.

> Thus while I *ape* the measure wild,
> Of tales that charmed me yet a child.
> —Scott.

Syn.—Mimic, imitate, simulate, personate, represent.

ȧ-peak', *adv.* 1. On the point; in a posture to pierce.

2. Among seamen, in a vertical line. The anchor is *apeak,* when the cable is drawn so as to bring the ship directly over it.

ȧ-peek', *adv.* Same as *Apeak.*

āpe'hood, *n.* The condition of being an ape.

ȧ-pel'lous, *a.* [*A* priv., and L. *pellis,* skin.] Without skin.

Ap'en-nīne, *a.* [L. *Apenninus,* from Celt. *pen, ben;* Ir. *benn,* a peak, mountain.] Pertaining to the Apennines, a chain of mountains which extend in a southeasterly direction through Italy.

ȧ-pep'si-ȧ, ȧ-pep'sy, *n.* [L., from Gr. *apepsia,* from *apeptos,* undigested; *a* priv., and *peptos,* from *peptein,* to cook, digest.] Indigestion.

āp'ẽr, *n.* One who apes.

ȧ-per-çu' (ȧ-pâr-sụ'), *n.* [Fr. *aperçu,* pp. of *apercevoir,* to perceive, discover.] A quick examination or view; a brief, comprehensive glance.

ȧ-pē're-ȧ, *n.* [L.] The restless cavy, *Cavia aperea.*

ȧ-pē'ri-ent, *a.* and *n.* [L. *aperiens,* ppr. of *aperire,* to open, uncover; *ab,* from, and *parire,* to produce.]

I. *a.* Opening; laxative.

II. *n.* A remedy that promotes excretion; a laxative.

ȧ-pē-ri-od'iç, *a.* Not occurring periodically.

ȧ-per-i-spẽr'miç, *a.* Same as *Exalbuminous.*

ȧ-per'i-tive, *a.* Opening; aperient.

ȧ-pẽrt', *a.* [OFr. *apert,* from L. *apertus,* pp. of *aperire,* to open.] Open; evident; undisguised. [Obs.]

ȧ-pẽrt', *adv.* Undisguisedly. [Obs.]

ȧ-pẽr'tion, *n.* The act of opening; a gap, aperture, or passage. [Rare.]

ȧ-pẽrt'ly, *adv.* Apert. [Obs.]

ȧ-pẽrt'ness, *n.* Openness. [Rare.]

ap-ẽr-tom'e-tẽr, *n.* [*Aperture,* and Gr. *metron,* measure.] A measuring instrument used to determine the angular aperture of an object-glass.

ap′ẽr-tūre, *n.* [L. *apertura*, an opening; from *apertus*, pp. of *aperire*, to open; *ab*, from, and *perire*, to produce.]

1. An opening; a gap, cleft, or chasm; a passage perforated; a hole through any solid substance.

2. The act of opening. [Obs.]

3. In geometry, the space between two right lines forming an angle.

4. In optics, the clear space which receives the light of an object, as in a microscope.

Angular aperture; see under *Angular*.

Syn.—Opening, hole, orifice, perforation, passage, gap, cleft.

āp′ẽr-y, *n.* 1. The practice of aping.

2. A place where apes are kept. [Rare.]

A-pet′ȧ-læ, *n.pl.* [L., from Gr. *a* priv., and *petalon*, a leaf.] A subclass of exogenous plants, the flowers of which have no petals.

ȧ-pet′ăl-ous, *a.* In botany, having flowers without petals; having no corolla; pertaining to the *Apetalæ*.

ȧ-pet′ăl-ous-ness, *n.* A state of being without petals.

ā′pex, *n.*; *pl.* **ā′pex-eṣ** or **ā′pi-cēṣ.** [L. *apex*, a point.]

1. The tip, point, or summit of anything.

2. In botany, the end farthest from the point of attachment, or base of an organ.

3. In geometry, the angular point of a cone or conic section; the angular point of a triangle opposite the base.

4. In mining, the summit of a stratum or slope.

Apex of the earth's motion; the orbital point which the earth is nearing.

Apex of the sun's way; that point in space which is being approached by the sun and solar system.

Syn.—Summit, vertex, acme, top.

ȧ-phær′e-sis, *n.* See *Apheresis*.

ȧ-phā′ki-ȧ, *n.* [Gr. *a* priv., and *phakos*, lentil-seed, lens.] Absence of the crystalline lens of the eye.

ȧ-phā′ki-ăl, *a.* Relating to aphakia; as, *aphakial* eyes.

Aph-ȧ-nip′te-rȧ, *n.pl.* [L., from Gr. *aphanēs*, unseen; *a* priv., and *phainesthai*, to appear, and *pteron*, wing.] An order of apterous, haustellate insects, having indistinct rudimentary wings. It is composed of the different species of fleas.

aph-ȧ-nip′tẽr-ous, *a.* Pertaining to or resembling the *Aphaniptera*.

aph′ȧ-nīte, *n.* [Gr. *aphanēs*, invisible; *a* priv., and *phainesthai*, to appear, and *-ite*.] A very compact, dark-colored rock, consisting chiefly of hornblende, its texture being visible only under the microscope.

aph-ȧ-nit′iç, *a.* Relating to or like aphanite; being of microscopic structure.

aph-ȧ-noz′y-gous, *a.* [Gr. *aphanēs*, indistinct, and *zygon*, for *zygōnia*, a cheek-bone.] Having the cheek-bones invisible when the cranium is seen from above.

Aph-ȧ-ryn′ġē-ȧ, *n.pl.* [L., from Gr. *a* priv., and *pharynx*, throat.] An order of planarioid worms having no pharynx.

aph-ȧ-ryn′ġē-ăl, *a.* Having no pharynx.

ȧ-phā′ṣi-ȧ, *n.* [L., from Gr. *aphasia*, from *aphatos*, unuttered; *a* priv., and *phatos*, from *phanai*, to speak.] A cerebral disease in which one or more of the powers of speech, sight, motion, or hearing are impaired or lost.

Motor or *ataxic aphasia*; loss of control of the muscles used in speech.

Sensory aphasia; a loss of memory for words.

ȧ-phā′siç, *a.* Of, relating, or pertaining to aphasia.

aph′ȧ-sy, *n.* Aphasia. [Obs.]

ȧ-phē′li-ŏn or **ȧ-phēl′ion** (-yun), *n.*; *pl.* **ȧ-phē′li-ȧ** (-li-ȧ or -yȧ). [Gr. *apo*, from, and *hēlios*, the sun.] That point of a planet's orbit which is most distant from the sun; opposed to *perihelion*.

ȧ-phē″li-ō-trop′iç, *a.* [Gr. *apo*, from, *hēlios*, sun, and *tropikos*, from *trepein*, to turn.] In botany, avoiding the light.

ȧ-phē-li-ot′rō-piṣm, *n.* The tendency of some plants to avoid the light.

ȧ-phē′mi-ȧ, *n.* [L., from Gr. *a* priv., and *phēmē*, voice, from *phanai*, to speak.] Motor aphasia.

ȧ-pher′e-sis (-fer-), *n.* [L. *aphæresis*; Gr. *aphairesis*, from *aphairein*, to take away; *apo*, away, and *hairein*, to take.]

1. In grammar, omission of a letter or syllable from the beginning of a word, as *'tis* for *it is*.

2. Amputation of a part, or the removal of noxious substance from the body. [Obs.]

aph′e-sis, *n.* [Gr. *aphesis*, a letting go; *apo*, from, and *hienai*, to send.] A form of apheresis in which the syllable lost is short and unaccented, as in *down* for *adown*.

aph′e-tȧ, *n.* [L., from Gr. *aphetēs*, one who lets go, from *aphetos*, let go; *aphienai*, to let go; *apo*, away, and *hienai*, to send.] In astrology, the ruling planet; the planet that rules one's life.

ȧ-phet′iç, ȧ-phet′iç-ăl, *a.* Of, relating, or pertaining to an apheta.

aph′e-tiṣm, *n.* A word formed by aphesis.

aph′e-tīze, *v.t.*; aphetized (-tīzd), *pt.*, *pp.*; aphetizing, *ppr.* To form (a word) by aphesis.

aph′id (*or* ā′phid), *n.* An insect of the genus *Aphis*.

aph′i-dēṣ, *n.*, pl. of *aphis*.

ȧ-phid′i-ăn, *a.* and *n.* I. *a.* Relating to the genus *Aphis*.

II. *n.* An insect of the genus *Aphis*; an aphid.

aph-i-diph′ȧ-gous, *a.* [L., from *Aphis*, and Gr. *phagein*, to eat.] Subsisting on insects of the genus *Aphis*.

aph-i-div′ō-rous, *a.* Aphidiphagous. [Obs.]

aph-i-lan′thrō-py, *n.* [Gr. *aphilanthropos*, not loving man; *a* priv., *philein*, to love, and *anthrōpos*, man.]

1. Want of philanthropy.

2. In medicine, aversion to society.

Ā′phis, *n.* [L., from Gr. *apheideis*, pl. of *apheidēs*, unsparing.]

1. A genus of insects belonging to the order *Hemiptera*. They are furnished with an inflected beak, and with antennæ longer than the thorax. In the same species, some individuals have four erect wings, and others are entirely without wings. The feet are of the ambulatory kind, and the belly usually ends in two horns, from which is ejected the substance called honeydew. The species are very numerous.

2. [a—; *pl.* aph′i-dēṣ.] Any insect of this genus.

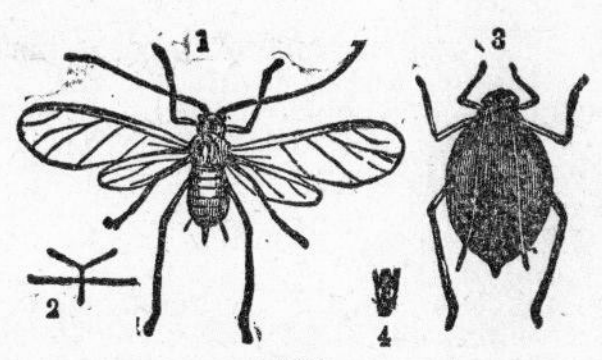

Aphides.

Wheat plant-louse (*Aphis granaria*).—1. 2. Male, enlarged and natural size; 3. 4. Wingless Female, enlarged and natural size.

ā′phis-fly, *n.* [L., *aphides*, unsparing.] Any fly of the genus *Syrphus*, or a related genus, the larvæ of which devour aphids.

ā′phis-lī″ŏn, *n.* Any larva, as that of the lacewing or ladybird, preying upon aphids.

aph-lō-ġis′tiç, *a.* [Gr. *a* priv., and *phlogistos*, inflammable, from *phlogizein*, to burn, to set on fire.] Flameless; as, an *aphlogistic* lamp, in which a coil of wire is kept in a state of continued ignition by alcohol, without flame.

ȧ-phō′ni-ȧ, *n.* [LL., from Gr. *a* priv., and *phōnē*, sound, tone, voice, from Gr. *phanai*, to speak.] A loss of voice; dumbness; hoarseness.

ȧ-phon′iç, *a.* and *n.* I. *a.* Affected with aphonia; without voice.

II. *n.* One who suffers from aphonia.

aph′ō-nous, *a.* Having the voice lacking.

aph′ō-ny, *n.* Aphonia. [Obs.]

aph′ō-riṣm, *n.* [Fr. *aphorisme*, from Gr. *aphorismos*, a definition, a short, pithy sentence; from *aphorizein*, to divide, mark off; *apo*, from, and *horizein*, to bound; *horos*, a boundary.] A maxim; a precept or principle expressed in a few words; a detached sentence containing some important truth.

Syn.—Axiom, maxim, adage.—An *axiom* is a self-evident proposition of high importance; a *maxim* expresses some great practical truth; an *adage* is a saying which has gained credit by long use.

aph-ō-riṣ′mẽr, *n.* One who uses aphorisms in speaking or writing. [Rare.]

aph-ō-riṣ′miç, aph″ō-riṣ-mat′iç, *a.* Relating to aphorisms; containing an aphorism.

aph′ō-rist, *n.* A writer of aphorisms.

aph-ō-ris′tiç, aph-ō-ris′tiç-ăl, *a.* In the form of an aphorism; in the form of short unconnected sentences; as, an *aphoristic* style.

aph-ō-ris′tiç-ăl-ly, *adv.* In the form or manner of aphorisms.

aph′ō-rīze, *v.i.*; aphorized, *pt.*, *pp.*; aphorizing, *ppr.* To make aphorisms.

aph′rīte, *n.* [Gr. *aphros*, foam, froth, and *-ite*.] A variety of calcite approaching argentite when hard, and chalk when soft.

aph-rō-diṣ′i-ȧ, *n.* [Gr. *aphrodisios*, pertaining to Aphrodite.]

1. Violent sexual desire; erotomania.

2. Sexual commerce; coition.

aph-rō-diṣ′i-aç, aph″rō-di-ṣī′ȧ-căl, *a.* Exciting venereal desire; increasing the appetite for sexual connection.

aph-rō-diṣ′i-aç, *n.* Food or medicine believed to be capable of exciting sexual desire.

aph-rō-diṣ′i-ăn, *a.* Relating to Aphrodite; hence, given to sexual gratification.

Aph-rō-dī′tē, *n.* [Gr. *Aphroditē*, the goddess of love; so named because she was said to have sprung from the foam of the sea; *aphros*, foam, and *ditē*.]

1. In mythology, the Greek name of the goddess of love, called by the Romans Venus, supposed to have originated from the foam of the sea.

2. [a—] In zoölogy, a marine annelid, the sea-mouse.

3. [a—] A beautifully colored butterfly of the United States, *Argynnis aphrodite*.

aph-rō-dit′iç, *a.* Venereal. [Rare.]

aph′thȧ, *n.*; *pl.* **aph′thæ.** [Gr. *aphthai*, pl. of *aphtha*, eruption, ulceration, from *aptein*, to set on fire, inflame.]

1. A small ulcer that occurs upon the lips, gums, and palate.

2. An eruptive disease, commonly called thrush.

Aph-thär″tō-dō-cē′tæ, *n.pl.* [Gr. *aphthartos*, incorruptible, and *dokein*, to think.] Religionists of the sixth century who believed that the body of Christ was ever incorruptible, his death not being a literal reality.

aph-thit′ȧ-līte, *n.* [Gr. *aphthitos*, unchangeable, indestructible; *a* priv., and *phthitos*, destructible, from *phthinein*, to destroy, and *alis*, salt, and *lithos*, a stone.] A compound salt, consisting chiefly of the sulphates of potash and soda, and common salt; found in the lava at Vesuvius.

aph′thoid, *a.* Like, resembling, or pertaining to aphtha or thrush.

aph′thong, *n.* [Gr. *aphthongos*, voiceless, without sound, from *a* priv., and *phthongos*, voice.] A letter, or combination of letters, which, in the customary pronunciation of a word, has no sound; as *p* in *pneumonia*.

aph-thon′găl, *a.* Pertaining to an aphthong.

aph′thous, *a.* Aphthoid.

A-phyl′lon, *n.* [Gr. *aphyllos*, leafless, from *a* priv., and *phyllon*, a leaf.] A genus of leafless plants of North America; the naked broom-rape.

aph′yl-lōse, *a.* Same as *Aphyllous*.

aph′yl-lous, *a.* [Gr. *a* priv., and *phyllon*, leaf.] In botany, leafless, as the cactus.

ā-pi-ā′ceous, *a.* [L. *apium*, parsley, celery.] Pertaining to the *Umbelliferæ* or parsley family.

ā′pi-ăn, *a.* [L. *apianus*, belonging to bees, from *apis*, bee.] Relating to bees.

ā-pi-ā′ri-ăn, *a.* Pertaining to bees; apian.

ā′pi-ā-rist, *n.* One who keeps an apiary.

ā′pi-ā-ry, *n.* [L. *apiarium*, beehive.] Any place where bees are kept; specifically, a number of colonies of bees tended for their honey.

ap′iç-ăl, *a.* [L. *apex*, the tip or top of a thing, the point, summit.] Relating to an apex.

ap′i-cēṣ, *n.*, pl. of *apex*.

A-pi′ciăn (-pish′ăn), *a.* [L. *Apicianus*, from *Apicius*, a celebrated Roman gormand.] Relating to Apicius; pertaining to cookery or delicate viands; epicurean.

ȧ-piç′ū-lăr, *a.* Having or pertaining to an apiculus.

ȧ-piç′ū-lāte, ȧ-piç′ū-lā-ted, *a.* [LL., *apiculatus*, *apiculus*, dim. of L. *apex*, point.] In botany, terminated by an apiculus, as a leaf.

ap′i-çul-tūre, *n.* [L. *apis*, bee, *cultura*, cultivating, culture.] Bee-culture.

ȧ-piç′ū-lus, *n.*; *pl.* **ȧ-piç′ū-lī.** In botany a small point formed by the projection of the midrib beyond the leaf.

ȧ-piēce′, *adv.* [OE. *apeece*, *a piece*; ME. *a pece*.] To each; noting the share of each; as, an orange *apiece*.

ȧ-piē′ceṣ, *adv.* In pieces. [Obs.]

ȧ-pīk′ed, *a.* Trimmed. [Obs.]

ā′pi-ŏl, *n.* [L. *apinum*, parsley, and *-ol*.] A crystalline principle obtained by distillation from parsley-seeds.

ā-pi-ol′ō-ġist, *n.* [L. *apis*, bee; Gr. *empis*, a gnat, and *logos*, description.] A student or master of apiology.

ā-pi-ol′ō-ġy, *n.* The branch of science that treats of bees.

Ā′pis, *n.* [L. *apis*, bee.] A Linnæan genus of insects of the order *Hymenoptera*; the bees. [See *Honeybee*.]

Ā′pis, *n.* [L. *Apis*; Gr. *Apis*; Egypt. *Hapi*, lit. the hidden.] A bull to which divine honors were paid by the ancient Egyptians, who regarded him as a symbol of Osiris.

āp′ish, *a.* Apelike; hence, imitative; silly.

āp′ish-ly, *adv.* In an apish manner.

āp′ish-ness, *n.* The quality of being apish.

ȧ-pit′pat, *adv.* Same as *Pitapat*.

Ā′pi-um, *n.* [L. *apium*, celery, parsley.] A genus of umbelliferous plants, among which is the common celery, *Apium graveolens*.

ā-piv′ō-rous, *a.* [L. *apis*, bee, and *vorare*, to devour.] Making prey of bees; subsisting upon bees.

ap-lȧ-cen′tăl, *a.* Having no placenta; unplacental.

Ap-lȧ-çoph′ō-rȧ, *n.pl.* [Gr. *a* priv., *plax*, a tablet, or plate, and *pherein*, to bear or carry.] In conchology, a division of *Amphineura* in which the body is shell-less.

ap-lȧ-nat′iç, *a.* [Gr. *aplanētos*, not wandering; *a* priv., and *planētos*, wandering, from *planasthai*, to wander.] In optics, having the quality of correcting spherical and chromatic aberration; as, an *aplanatic* lens or telescope.

Aplanatic focus; in a lens, the point at which divergent rays of light pass through the lens without spherical or chromatic aberration.

ȧ-plan′ȧ-tiṣm, *n.* The state of being aplanatic.

ȧ-plā′ṣi-ȧ, *n.* [Gr. *a* priv., and *plasis*, formation, from *plassein*, to form.] Incomplete or defective development; agenesis; as of an organ or tissue.

ȧ-plas′tiç, *a.* [Gr. *aplastos*, not capable of being molded.] 1. Not plastic or easily molded.

2. Characterized by or pertaining to aplasia.

ap′līte, *n.* [Gr. *haplos*, late form of *haploos*, single, simple.] A fine-grained granite, of which quartz and feldspar are the principal constituents.

ȧ-plomb′ (ȧ-plom̃′), *n.* [Fr. *à plomb*, lit. perpendicularity, self-possession, assurance.] Self-possession; self-confidence.

ȧ-plot′ō-my, *n.* [Gr. *haplotomia*, from *haplotomein*, to cut by a simple incision.] In surgery, a simple cutting or incision.

ȧ-plus′tre (-tẽr), *n.* [L. *aplustre*, the curved stern of a ship with its ornaments.] In Roman antiquity, an ornament made of wooden planks, rising from the stern of a ship, corresponding to the Greek *aphlaston*, by the side of which a pole was erected with a flag or ribbons attached, to indicate the course of the wind.

Aplustre, from the British Museum.

A-plys′i-ȧ, *n.* [LL. *aplysiæ*; Gr. *aplysiai*, pl. of *aplysia*, filthiness, from *aplytos*, unwashed.] A genus of gasteropodous mollusks. Some of the species have the power of discharging a fluid of a deep-purple color, by which, when in danger, they can discolor the water for a considerable distance around. The *Aplysia depilans*, or depilatory sea-hare, is found in the European seas, adhering to rocks, and it was long supposed that the acrid humor which it throws out was capable of removing hair.

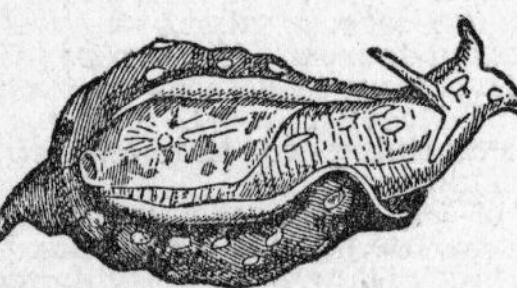

Depilatory Sea-hare (*Aplysia depilans*).

ap-neū-mat′iç, *a.* Without air; as, an *apneumatic* lung.

Ap-neū′mō-nȧ, *n.pl.* [Gr. *a* priv., and *pneumōn*, lung, from *pnein*, to breathe.] An order of holothurians, destitute of a system of respiration.

ap-neūs′tiç, *a.* [Gr. *apneustos*, without breath; *a* priv., and *pnein*, to breathe.] In zoölogy, without stigmata.

ap-nœ′ȧ, *n.* [Gr. *apnoos*, without wind, breathless; *a* priv., and *pnein*, to blow, breathe.] Partial or complete suspension of respiration, as in case of swoon.

ap′ō-, *prefix.* [Gr.] A combining form signifying off, from, away from, separation, in respect of time, place, or origin.

ȧ-poç′ȧ-lypse, *n.* [ME. *apocalipse*; L. *apocalypsis*; Gr. *apokalypsis*, an uncovering, revelation, from *apokalyptein*, uncover, reveal; *apo*, from, and *kalyptein*, to cover or conceal.]

1. Revelation; discovery; disclosure.

2. [A—] A book of the New Testament, written by St. John, in Patmos, near the close of the first century; the book of Revelation.

3. Certain Jewish religious writings which appeared between the years 250 B.C. and 150 A.D.

ȧ-poç-ȧ-lyp′tiç, ȧ-poç-ȧ-lyp′tiç-ăl, *a.* 1. Containing or pertaining to revelation; disclosing.

2. Pertaining to the Apocalypse.

Apocalyptic number; the number 666, spoken of in Rev. xiii. 18.

ȧ-poç-ȧ-lyp′tiç, ȧ-poç-ȧ-lyp′tist, *n.* One making an apocalyptical communication.

ȧ-poç-ȧ-lyp′tiç-ăl-ly, *adv.* In an apocalyptical manner.

ap-ō-cär′pous, *a.* [*Apo-*, and Gr. *karpos*, fruit.] In botany, a term denoting that the carpels of a compound pistil are either entirely or partially distinct.

Apocarpous Fruit of Aconite.

ap″ō-çȧ-tas′tȧ-sis, *n.* [Gr. *apokatastasis*, return, restoration, from *apokathistanai*, to restore, return; *apo*, from, *kata*, down, and *histēmi*, to stand.]

1. In astronomy, the period of a planet's orbital revolution.

2. In theology, the final restoration.

ap″ō-chrō-mat′iç, *a.* [*Apo-*, and Gr. *chrōma*, color.] In optics, without aberration.

ȧ-poç′ō-pāte, *v.t.*; apocopated, *pt.*, *pp.*; apocopating, *ppr.* [Gr. *apokopē*, a cutting off, from *apokoptein*, to cut off.] To cut off or drop, as the last letter or syllable of a word.

ȧ-poç′ō-pāte, ȧ-poç′ō-pā-ted, *a.* Shortened by the omission of the last letter or syllable.

ȧ-poç-ō-pā′tion, *n.* Abbreviation by apocope.

ȧ-poç′ō-pē, *n.* [Gr. *apokopē*, a cutting off, from *apokoptein*, to cut off.]

1. The cutting off or omission of the last letter or syllable of a word; as the Latin *di* for *dii*.

2. In surgery, removal of substance by cutting off or out.

ap-ō-çris′i-ā-ry, ap″ō-çris-i-ā′ri-us, *n.* [Gr. *apokrisis*, an answer, from *apokrinesthai*, to answer.] An ecclesiastical term for one delegated by another; specifically, a legate of the pope at Constantinople.

ap-ō-çrus′tiç, *a.* and *n.* [Gr. *apokroustikos*, able to drive off; *apo*, off, and *kronein*, to beat.]

I. *a.* In medicine, astringent; repellent.

II. *n.* An astringent medicine.

Ȧ-poç′ry-phȧ, *n.*, *sing.* and *pl.* [Gr. *apokryphos*, hidden, concealed, obscure, from *apokryptein*, to hide away; *apo*, away, and *kryptein*, to hide, conceal.]

1. Those books whose authenticity, as inspired writings, is not admitted, and which are therefore not considered a part of the sacred canon of the Scripture by the Protestant churches generally. The books of the *Apocrypha* are as follows: 1 and 2 Esdras, Tobit, Judith, Esther x. 4-xvi, Wisdom, Ecclesiasticus, Baruch, Song of the Three Holy Children, History of Susanna, Bel and the Dragon, Prayer of Manasses, and 1 and 2 Maccabees.

2. [a—] Anything, as a writing, of doubtful authenticity. [Obs.]

3. [a—] Things hidden, secret, or set apart.

Ȧ-poç′ry-phăl, *a.* 1. Of, relating to, or found in the Apocrypha.

2. [a—] Having no authority ecclesiastically; hence, fictitious; false; doubtful.

ȧ-poç′ry-phăl-ist, *n.* A student or advocate of, or believer in, the Apocrypha. [Rare.]

ȧ-poç′ry-phăl-ly, *adv.* In an apocryphal or false manner.

ȧ-poç′ry-phăl-ness, *n.* The state of being apocryphal or false.

Ȧ-poc-y-nā′cē-æ, *n.pl.* A natural order of dicotyledonous plants, having for its type the genus *Apocynum* or dogbane. There are upward of 1,000 species of this genus, having widely varying characteristics, but nearly all yield a milky juice, as caoutchouc, while fruits, dyes, or drugs are the products of others.

ȧ-poc-y-nā′ceous, ap-ō-cyn′ē-ous, *a.* Resembling the dogbane, *Apocynum*.

ȧ-poc′y-nin, *n.* The precipitate from a tincture of Canadian hemp-root.

Ȧ-poc′y-num, *n.* [L. *apocynon*, dogbane; Gr. *apokynon*, a plant; *apo*, from, away, and *kyōn*, *kynos*, a dog.] Dogbane, a genus of perennial herbs with small, pale, cymose flowers, and possessing a fibrous bark.

ap′od, ap′ō-dăl, *a.* Literally, having no feet; specifically, in zoölogy, destitute of ventral fins; relating or belonging to the *Apoda*.

ap′od, ap′ōde, *n.*; *pl.* **ap′odṣ** or **ap′ōdeṣ.** An animal that has no feet; one of the *Apoda*.

Ap′ō-dȧ, *n.pl.* [Gr. *apous*, footless; *a* priv., and *pous*, foot.]

1. A term given to certain teleostean fishes, from the fact of their being destitute of ventral fins (which correspond to the legs and feet of man), as the eel, sand-eel, swordfish, etc.

2. The former name of an order of amphibian or batrachian reptiles, without apparent limbs, and of a serpent-like form. Now called *Ophiomorpha*.

Sand-eel (*Ammodytes tobianus*), one of the *Apoda*.

3. An order of cirripeds, destitute of locomotive organs.

ap′ō-dăl, ap′ō-dăn, *a.* See *Apod*.

ap′ō-dăn, *n.* One of the *Apoda*.

ap-ō-deiç′tiç, *a.* Same as *Apodictic*.

ap-ō-deix′is, *n.* Same as *Apodixis*.

ȧ-pod′e-măl, *a.* Having an apodeme.

ap′ō-dēme, *n.* [*Apo-*, and Gr. *demas*, body.] A name given to the plates of chitin which pass inward from the integuments, and divide as well as support the internal organs in crustaceans.

Ap′ō-dēṣ, *n.pl.* See *Apoda*, 1.

ap-ō-diç′tiç, ap-ō-diç′tiç-ăl, *a.* [Gr. *apodeiktikos*, demonstrative, from *apodeiknynai*, to point out, demonstrate.] Demonstrative; evident beyond contradiction; clearly proving. Spelled also *apodeictic*, *apodictical*.

ap-ō-diç′tiç-ăl-ly, ap-ō-deiç′tiç-ăl-ly, *adv.* Uncontradictorily self-evident.

ap-ō-dix′is, *n.* [L. *apodixis*, absolute demonstration.] Clear demonstration.

ȧ-pod′ō-sis, *n.* [Gr. *apodosis*, a giving back; *apo*, back, and *didonai*, to give.] The latter part of a conditional sentence, which results from, or is dependent on, the protasis or condition. Thus in the sentence, if it rain, I shall not go, the former clause is the *protasis*, the latter the *apodosis*. By some grammarians the term is not restricted to conditional sentences, but is extended to others similarly constructed; thus in a simile the *apodosis* is the application or latter part.

ap′ō-dous, *a.* Apodal.

ȧ-pod-y-tē′ri-um, *n.* [Gr. *apodytērion*, an undressing room, from *apodynai*, to strip, undress; *apo*, off, and *dynai*, to put.] An apartment in Greek and Roman baths or in the palestra, where the bathers or those engaged in gymnastic exercises dressed and undressed.

ap-ō-gā′iç, *a.* Relating to the apogee.

ap-ō-gam′iç, *a.* Relating to apogamy.

ȧ-pog′ȧ-my, *n.* [*Apo-*, and Gr. *gamos*, marriage.] The reproduction or perpetuation of a plant without the usual sexual organs, but by prothallic spores or buds, as in the ferns.

ap-ō-ġē′ăn, ap-ō-ġē′ăl, *a.* Relating to the apogee; as, *apogean* tides.

ap′ō-ġee, *n.* [Fr. *apogée*; Gr. *apogaion*; *apo*, from, and *gē*, earth.]

1. In astronomy, that point in the orbit of any heavenly body at its greatest distance from the earth; especially applied to the moon. The ancients regarded the earth as the center of the system, and therefore assigned to the sun, with the planets, an orbit and an *apogee*; but modern astronomy, considering the sun as the center, uses the terms, *perihelion* and *aphelion*. The sun's *apogee*, therefore, is the earth's *aphelion*.

2. Figuratively, the culmination of anything.

ap″ō-ġē-ō-trop′iç, *a.* [Gr. *apogaios*, from the earth, and *tropikos*, a turning, from *trepein*, to turn.] Characterized by apogeotropism, as the inclination of a plant-leaf.

ap″ō-ġē-ot′rō-piṣm, *n.* A term applied by Darwin to the propensity of the organs of a plant above the earth to bend away from it.

ap′ō-grȧph, *n.* [Gr. *apographē*, a copy; *apo*, from, and *graphein*, to write.] A transcript made from an original; a copy.

ap-ō-hȳ′ăl, *a.* Designating a cartilaginous portion of the hyoid bone.

ȧ-poiṣe′, *adv.* In a balanced position.

ȧ-pō′lăr, *a.* [Gr. *a* priv., and *polos*, a pivot or axis.] Not having a pole; applied specifically to processless nerve-cells.

ap-ō-laus′tiç, *a.* [Gr. *apolaustikos*, of or for enjoyment, from *apolauein*, to enjoy.]

1. Pertaining to enjoyment or pleasure.

2. Self-indulgent.

A-pol-li-nā′ri-ăn, *a.* [L. *Apollinaris*, from Gr. *Apollōn*.] Designating, in honor of, or pertaining to Apollo, as the *Apollinarian* games.

A-pol-li-nā′ri-ăn, *n.* One of a sect deriving their name from *Apollinaris*, bishop of Laodicea in the fourth century, who denied the proper humanity of Christ, maintaining that his body was endowed with a sensitive, not a rational soul, and that the divine nature supplied the place of intellectual principle in man.

A-pol-li-nā′ri-ăn-iṣm, *n.* The doctrine of the Apollinarians.

A-pol-li-nā′ris wa̤′tẽr. A German alkaline mineral water, having a high percentage of carbonic acid in solution, used in medicine and as a beverage.

A-pol′lō, *n.* [Gr. *Apollōn*, from *apollynai*, to destroy; *apo*, from, and *ollynai*, to destroy.] A deity among the Greeks and Romans, worshiped under the name of Phœbus, the sun, as the god of light and heat. He was the presiding deity of archery, prophecy, medicine, and music, and protector of the Muses, and always represented as the highest type of masculine beauty and grace.

Apollo Belvedere; a celebrated statue of Apollo in the Belvedere gallery of the Vatican palace at Rome, esteemed one of the noblest representations of the human frame, and one of the finest pieces of sculpture extant.

Ap-ol-lō′ni-ăn, Ap-ol-lon′iç, *a.* Apollinarian.

Ȧ-pol′ly-ŏn (*or* -pol′yun), *n.* [Gr. *apollyon*, destroying, ppr. of *apollynai*, to destroy.] The destroyer; a name used, Revelation ix. 11, for the angel of the bottomless pit, answering to the Hebrew *Abaddon*.

ȧ-pol′ō-ġẽr, *n.* [*Apo-*, and Gr. *logos*, description.] A writer or narrator of apologues. [Obs.]

ȧ-pol-ō-ġet′iç, ȧ-pol-ō-ġet′iç-ăl, *a.* [Gr. *apologētikos*, fit for a defense, from *apologeisthai*, to speak in defense; *apo*, from, and *legein*, to speak.] Defending by words or arguments; excusing; said or written in defense, or by way of apology; as, an *apologetic* essay.

ȧ-pol-ō-ġet′iç-ăl-ly, *adv.* By way of excuse.

ȧ-pol-ō-ġet′iços, *n.* That branch of theology by which Christians are scientifically enabled to justify and defend the peculiarities of their faith, and to answer its opponents.

ap-o-lō′ġi-ȧ, *n.* An apology or argument in defense of what may appear to others to be wrong.

ȧ-pol′ō-ġist, *n.* One who makes an apology; one who speaks or writes in defense of another, especially a defender of the Christian religion.

ȧ-pol′ō-ġize, *v.i.*; apologized, *pt.*, *pp.*; apologizing, *ppr.* 1. To make an apology.

2. To write or speak in favor of, or to make excuse for something; followed by *for*; as, to *apologize for* his rudeness.

Syn.—Defend, justify, exculpate, excuse, plead.

ȧ-pol′ō-ġīze, *v.t.* To defend. [Obs.]

ȧ-pol′ō-ġīz-ẽr, *n.* One who makes an apology or defends.

ap′ō-logue (-log), *n.* [Gr. *apologos*, a long speech, a fable.] A moral fable; a story or relation of events to convey truths. A parable is drawn from human life; an *apologue* is founded on supposed actions of brutes or things. Æsop's fables are good examples of *apologues.*

ȧ-pol′ō-ġy, *n.* [Gr. *apologia*, a defense, from *apologeisthai*, to speak in defense.]

1. Something said or written in defense or justification of what appears to others wrong or unjustifiable, or of what may be liable to disapprobation; defense; justification; vindication.

2. A formal admission, acknowledgment, or confession of a wrong or offensive course of action, with overtures of reparation and conciliation.

3. A makeshift; generally implying haste and carelessness; as, an *apology* for a building.

Syn.—Excuse, evasion, plea, pretense, pretext, subterfuge.—We make an *apology* for something rude, unbecoming, etc.; we offer an *excuse* for some failure or neglect of duty.

ȧ-pol′ō-ġy, *v.i.* To make an apology. [Obs.]

ap″ō-mē-çom′e-tẽr, *n.* An instrument for measuring heights.

ap″ō-mē-çom′e-try, *n.* [*Apo-*, and Gr. *mēkos*, distance, and *metron*, measure.] The art of measuring the height of distant objects. [Rare.]

ap-ō-mor′phine, ap-ō-mor′phi-ȧ, *n.* [*Apo-*, and Gr. *Morpheus*, the son of sleep, god of dreams.] An artificial alkaloid; morphine with one molecule of water abstracted; used as an emetic.

ap″ō-neū-rō′sis, *n.*; *pl.* **ap″ō-neū-rō′sēs.** [Gr. *aponeurōsis*, the end of a muscle where it becomes tendon; *apo*, from, and *neuron*, a nerve.] A white, shining, and very resisting membrane, composed of interlacing fibers, being the expansion of a tendon, serving to attach or to inclose and bind down muscles.

ap″ō-neū-rot′iç, *a.* Relating to an aponeurosis.

ap″ō-neū-rot′ō-my, *n.* Aponeurotic dissection.

ap-ō-pemp′tiç, *a.* and *n.* [Gr. *apopemptikos*, valedictory, from *apopempein*, to send off, dismiss; *apo*, from, and *pempein*, to send.]

I. *a.* Valedictory; parting; used especially of a song or hymn among the ancients, sung or addressed to a stranger, on his departure.

II. *n.* A valedictory hymn.

ap-ō-pet′ăl-ous, *a.* [*Apo-*, and Gr. *petalon*, a leaf.] In botany, polypetalous.

ȧ-poph′ȧ-sis, *n.* [Gr. *apophasis*, a denial, from *apophanai*, to deny.] In rhetoric, a pretended denial or omission of what one plainly insinuates or really gives; as, "I will not mention the other argument," proceeding to give it.

ap″ō-phleg-mat′iç, *a.* [Gr. *apophlegmatikos*, from *apophlegmatizein*, to discharge phlegm; *apo*, from, and *phlegma*, phlegm.] Having the quality of exciting discharges of phlegm or mucus.

ap″ō-phleg-mat′iç, *n.* A medicine which excites discharges of phlegm or mucus.

ap-ō-phleg′mȧ-tiṣm, *n.* 1. The action of an apophlegmatic.

2. An apophlegmatic. [Obs.]

ap′ŏph-thegm (ap′ō-them), *n.* See *Apothegm.*

ap″ŏph-theg-mat′iç, ap″ŏph-theg-mat′iç-ăl (ap-ō-), *a.* Same as *Apothegmatic.*

ȧ-poph′y-ġē, *n.* [Gr. *apophygē*, escape from; *apo*, from, and *pheugein*, to flee.] In architecture, the part of a column where it springs out of its base, usually molded into a concave sweep or cavetto. It is sometimes called the scape or spring of the column.

ȧ-poph′yl-līte, *n.* [Gr. *apophillizein*, to strip of its leaves; *apo*, from, and *phyllon*, leaf.] A zeolitic mineral, occurring in pearly, laminated masses, or crystallized in prisms, with a cleavage surface having a pearly luster. Sometimes called *ichthyophthalmite*, or *fish-eye stone.*

ȧ-poph′yl-lous, *a.* [*Apo*, away, and Gr. *phyllon*, a leaf.] In botany, having free leaves; applied to a perianth.

ȧ-poph′y-sis, *n.*; *pl.* **ȧ-poph′y-sēṣ.** [Gr. *apophysis*, an offshoot, from *apophyesthai*, to grow off from.]

1. A process, prominent part, outgrowth, or swelling, as of a bone or other organ.

2. In botany, a swelling under the base of the theca or spore-case of certain mosses.

3. In geology, a lateral insert or offshoot in igneous intrusive rock-formations.

ap-ō-pleç′tiç, ap-ō-pleç′tiç-ăl, *a.* [Gr. *apoplēktikos*, from *apoplēktos*, disabled by a stroke, stricken.] Pertaining to or symptomatic of apoplexy; as, an *apoplectic* fit; or predisposed to apoplexy; as, an *apoplectic* habit of body.

ap-ō-pleç′tiç, *n.* One affected, or liable to affection with apoplexy.

ap-ō-pleç′ti-form, ap-ō-pleç′toid, *a.* Resembling apoplexy.

ap′ō-plex, *n.* Apoplexy. [Obs.]

ap′ō-plexed, *a.* Affected with apoplexy. [Obs.]

ap′ō-plex-y, *n.* [Fr. *apoplexie*; L. *apoplexia*; Gr. *apoplēxia*, from *apoplēssein*, to strike down; *apo*, from, and *plēssein*, to strike.] Loss of sense and voluntary motion, from suspension of the functions of the brain; usually as a result of hemorrhage causing pressure on the brain-tissue; often called *cerebral apoplexy.* Sometimes used of a hemorrhage in some other organ; as, *apoplexy* of the liver.

ap-ō-ret′iç, ap-ō-ret′iç-ăl, *a.* Doubting. [Obs.]

ȧ-pō′ri-ȧ, *n.* [Gr. *aporia*, doubt; *apo*, from, and *horos*, boundary.]

1. In rhetoric, an affectation of doubting or being at a loss where to begin, or what to say, on account of the variety of matter.

2. In medicine, febrile anxiety; uneasiness.

Ap-ō-rō′sȧ, *n.pl.* [Gr. *aporos*, without passage.] A group of corals having the corallum solid, and not perforated with minute apertures.

ap′ō-rōse, *a.* Not porous.

ȧ-pōrt′, *adv.* On or toward the left or larboard side.

ap″ō-sē-mat′iç, *a.* [Gr. *aposēmainein*, to announce by signs; *apo*, from, and *sēma*, sign.] In animal coloration, furnished with warning colors or some special means of defense or hiding, as the sea-anemone.

ap-ō-sep′ȧ-lous, *a.* [*Apo-*, and Fr. *sépale*; L. *sepalum*, from Gr. *petalon*, a leaf.] Same as *Polysepalous.*

ap″ō-si-ō-pē′sis, *n.* [Gr. *aposiōpēsis*, a becoming silent, from *aposiōpān*, to be silent; *apo*, from, and *siōpān*, to be silent.] Reticency or suppression; as when a speaker suddenly breaks off his discourse, before it is ended and passes over something in such a way as to call attention to it.

ap-ō-sit′iç, *a.* [Gr. *apositia*; *apo*, from, and *sitos*, food.] Taking away or diminishing the appetite.

ȧ-pos′pō-ry, *n.* A feature of certain cryptogamous plants having the prothallus generated directly from the sporangium instead of by spores.

ȧ-pos′tȧ-sis, *n.* [Gr. *apostasis*, a standing away from; *apo*, from, and *histanai*, to stand.] In botany, a resultant of extreme internodal growth, which separates whorls or other parts of a plant.

ȧ-pos′tȧ-sy, *n.* [ME. *apostasie*; Fr. *apostasie*, Gr. *apostasia*, from *apostasis*, defection, revolt; from *aphistasthai*, to stand away from.] An abandonment or falling away from real or imagined allegiance; as, *apostasy* from one's religion, creed, or politics.

ȧ-pos′tāte, *n.* [Gr. *apostatēs*, a runaway, deserter, from *aphistasthai*, to stand away from.] One guilty of apostasy; specifically, in the Roman Catholic church, one who, without a dispensation, forsakes a religious order of which he has made profession.

Syn.—Convert, proselyte, pervert.

ȧ-pos′tāte, *a.* False; traitorous.

ȧ-pos′tāte, *v.i.* To apostatize. [Obs.]

ap-ō-stat′iç, ap-ō-stat′iç-ăl, *a.* Apostate.

ȧ-pos′tȧ-tīze, *v.i.*; apostatized, *pt.*, *pp.*; apostatizing, *ppr.* To abandon one's belief or church; to forsake principles or faith which one has professed.

ap′os-tem, *n.* [Gr. *apostēma*, interval.] An abscess; a swelling filled with purulent matter; also spelled *aposteme, apostume, impostume.*

ȧ-pos′tē-māte, *v.i.* To form into an abscess; to swell and fill with pus. [Rare.]

ȧ-pos-tē-mā′tion, *n.* The formation of an apostem; the process of gathering into an abscess.

ap-os-tem′ȧ-tous, *a.* Pertaining to an abscess; partaking of the nature of an apostem.

ā pos-tē-ri-ō′ri. [L. *a*, or *ab*, from, and *posteriori*, abl. of *posterior*, comp. of *posterius*, subsequent, following.]

1. In logic, reasoning backward from effects, consequences, or facts, to causes; in opposition to *a priori.* [See *Induction.*]

2. In philosophy, relating to observed knowledge, either empirical or inductive.

ȧ-pos′til, ȧ-pos′tille, *n.* [Fr. *apostille*; L. *ad*, to, in, *post illa*; *post*, after; *illa*, neut. pl. of pron. *ille*, that.] A marginal note or reference.

ȧ-pos′tle (-pos′l), *n.* [AS. *apostol*; ME. *apostle*, *apostel*; L. *apostolus*; Gr. *apostolos*, a messenger; from *apostellein*, to send away; *apo*, from, and *stellein*, to send.]

1. A person deputed to execute some important business; specifically, a disciple of Christ commissioned to preach the gospel. Twelve persons were selected by Christ for this purpose.

2. The person first preaching Christianity in any part of the world; hence, one especially zealous in promoting any cause, doctrine, or movement; as, an *apostle* of reason.

3. In law, a brief statement of a case sent by a court whence an appeal has been taken to a superior court; a sense which belonged to the Latin *apostolus* among the Roman jurists.

4. In the Greek church, a book containing the epistles of St. Paul, printed in the order in which they are to be read in churches throughout the year.

5. In certain churches, as the Mormon, a high official.

Apostles' creed; a confession of faith supposed to have been drawn up by the apostles. This creed as it now stands in the liturgy of the English church is to be found in the works of St. Ambrose, bishop of Milan, in the fourth century.

Apostle spoon; a spoon of silver gilt, with a handle terminating in the figure of an apostle, one or more of which at one time formed the usual present of sponsors to the infant at christenings.

ȧ-pos′tle-ship, *n.* The office or dignity of an apostle.

ȧ-pos′tō-lāte, *n.* A mission; the dignity or office of an apostle. Ancient writers use it for the office of a bishop; but it is now restricted to the dignity of the pope, whose see is called the *apostolic see.*

ap-os-tol′iç, ap-os-tol′iç-ăl, *a.* 1. Pertaining or relating to the apostles; as, the *apostolic* age.

2. According to the doctrines of the apostles; delivered or taught by the apostles; as, *apostolic* faith or practice.

3. Relating to the pope; as, the *apostolic* see.

Apostolic Brothers; a sect of the thirteenth century led by Segarelli, a monk of northern Italy, in opposition to the pope.

Apostolic Constitutions and *Canons*; a collection of regulations attributed to the apostles, but generally supposed to be spurious. They appeared in the fourth century, are divided into eight books, and consist of rules and precepts relating to the duty of Christians, and particularly to the ceremonies and discipline of the church.

Apostolic fathers; the Christian writers who during any part of their lives were contemporary with the apostles. There are five—Clement, Barnabas, Hermas, Ignatius, Polycarp.

Apostolic king; a title granted by the pope to the kings of Hungary, first conferred on St. Stephen, the founder of the royal line of Hungary, on account of what he accomplished in the spread of Christianity.

Apostolic see; the see of the popes or bishops of Rome; so called because the popes profess themselves the successors of Peter.

Apostolic succession; the unbroken line of apostles having direct authority to preach, holding such authority by regular ordination as well as by right of succession.

ap-os-tol′iç, *n.* The pope; or, formerly, any bishop.

ap-os-tol′iç-ăl-ly, *adv.* In the manner of the apostles.

ap-os-tol′iç-ăl-ness, *n.* Same as *Apostolicity.*

ap-os-tol′i-ciṣm, ȧ-pos-tō-lic′i-ty, *n.* The condition of being apostolic.

ȧ-pos′trō-phē, *n.* [Gr. *apostrophē*, a turning away, from *apostrephein*, to turn away from; *apo*, from, and *strephein*, to turn.]

1. In rhetoric, a diversion of speech; strictly, a changing the course of a speech, and making a short address to a person different from those to whom the speech is generally directed, or even to an inanimate object; often, any abrupt interjectional speech.

> . . . produces at the right moment in parliamentary harangue a pocket crucifix, with the *apostrophe*, "Will ye crucify him afresh?" —Carlyle.

2. In grammar, (a) the contraction of a word by the omission of a letter or letters, a figure or figures, denoted by a sign like a comma, placed at the top instead of at the foot of the character, as *call'd* for *called*; class of *'03*; (b) the sign used to mark the omission; (c) a sign of the possessive singular or plural; as, a girl's dress, girls' dresses; denoting the omission of the letter *e*, formerly added in forming the possessive.

The *apostrophe* is used to mark the plural of letters, figures, or other characters; as, mind your p's and q's; several 2's; numerous ¶'s; also, singly or doubly, to close a quotation.

ap-os-troph′iç, *a.* Pertaining to an apostrophe; noting the contraction of a word.

ȧ-pos′trō-phīze, *v.t.*; apostrophized (-fīzd), *pt.*, *pp.*; apostrophizing, *ppr* To address by an apostrophe, as in a speech; to mark with an apostrophe.

ȧ-pos′trō-phīze, *v.i.* To make use of the rhetorical apostrophe.

ap′os-tūme, *n.* [Obs.] See *Apostem.*

Ap-ō-taç′tīte, *n.* [Gr. *apotaktos*, set apart, from *apotassein*, to set apart, or assign specially.] One of a sect of ancient Christians, who, in imitation of the first believers, renounced all their effects and possessions.

ȧ-pot′e-leṣm, *n.* [Gr. *apotelesma*, result, effect,

the result of certain positions of the stars on human destiny; from *apotelein*, to complete, accomplish; *apo*, from, and *telein*, to end.] Fulfilment; calculation of nativity in astrology. [Obs.]

ap″ō-tel-es-mat′ic, *a.* 1. Relating to astrology; teaching by the science of the stars. [Obs.]

2. Pertaining to a fulfilment.

ȧ-poth′ē-ca-ry, *n.*; *pl.* **ȧ-poth′ē-ca-ries.** [ME. *apothecarie*; L. *apotheca*, a repository, from Gr. *apothēkē*, a place where a thing is stored up; *apo*, away, and *tithenai*, to put.] One who prepares and sells drugs and medicines; a druggist or pharmacist.

In England and Ireland the term is now specifically applied to an inferior sort of practitioners, who are licensed to practise medicine and at the same time deal in drugs. In Scotland the *apothecary*, as such, is only a dispenser of drugs.

Apothecaries' weight; the weight employed in dispensing drugs, differing only in its subdivisions from troy weight.

ap-ō-thē′ci-um (-shi-um), *n.*; *pl.* **ap-ō-thē′ci-ȧ** (-shi-ȧ). [Gr. *apothēkē*, a storehouse.] In botany, the receptacle of lichens, consisting of the spore-cases or asci, and of the paraphyses or barren threads.

ap′ō-thegm (-them), *n.* [Fr. *apophthegme*; Gr. *apophthegma*, a terse, pointed saying; from *apophtheggesthai*, to speak out plainly; *apo*, from, and *phtheggesthai*, to cry out, utter.] A saying; a short, instructive remark; also spelled *apophthegm*.

ap″ō-theg-mat′ic, **ap″ō-theg-mat′ic-ăl**, *a.* Sententious; pertaining to or containing apothegms.

ap-ō-theg′mȧ-tist, *n.* A collector or maker of apothegms.

ap-ō-theg′mȧ-tīze, *v.i.* To utter apothegms, or short, instructive sentences. [Rare.]

ap′ō-them, *n.* [Fr. *apotheme*, from Gr. *apotithenai*, to set off, put aside.]

1. In geometry, a perpendicular dropped from the center of a regular polygon upon one of its sides.

2. In pharmacy, a brown deposit which forms in vegetable extracts exposed to the air.

ap-ō-thē′ō-sis, *n.*; *pl.* **ap-ō-thē′ō-sēs.** [Gr. *apotheōsis*, a deification, from *apotheoein*, *apotheoun*, to deify; *apo*, from, and *theos*, god.]

1. Deification; the act of placing a person among the deities or gods. This honor was often bestowed on illustrious men in Rome, and followed by the erection of temples, and the institution of sacrifices to the new deity.

2. By extension, an honoring or glorification of any kind; as, the *apotheosis* of a career.

ap-ō-thē′ō-size, *v.t.*; apotheosized, *pt.*, *pp.*; apotheosizing, *ppr.* To consecrate, or exalt to the place of a god; to deify.

ȧ-poth′e-sis, *n.* [Gr. *apothesis*, a laying up or putting away, from *apotithenai*, to put back or away.]

1. In surgery, the reduction of a dislocated bone.

2. A place in primitive churches furnished with shelves for books, vestments, etc.

ȧ-pot′ō-mē, *n.* [Gr. *apotemnein*, to cut off.]

1. In mathematics, the difference between two incommensurable quantities.

2. In music, a major semitone.

ap′ō-zem, *n.* [Gr. *apozema*, a decoction, from *apozein*, to boil off, throw off by fermenting; *apo*, from, and *zein*, to boil.] A decoction. [Obs.]

ap-ō-zem′ic-ăl, *a.* Like a decoction. [Obs.]

ap-pāir′, *v.t.* and *v.i.* [ME. *apairen*, *apayren*, *empair*.] To impair. [Obs.]

ap-pạl′, **ap-pạll′**, *v.t.*; appalled, *pt.*, *pp.*; appalling, *ppr.* [ME. *appallen*, *apallen*; Fr. *pâle*; L. *ad*, to, and *pallidus*, pale, from *pallere*, to grow pale.]

1. To depress or discourage with fear; to impress with fear, in such a manner that the mind shrinks, or loses its firmness; as, the sight *appalled* the stoutest heart.

2. To reduce, allay, or destroy; as, to *appal* thirst. [Obs.]

3. To cause to turn pale. [Obs.]

Syn.—Affright, alarm, terrify, daunt, cow, shock, dishearten, horrify, dismay, astound.

ap-pạl′, **ap-pạll′**, *v.i.* 1. To grow faint; to be dismayed. [Obs.]

2. To become stale or weak. [Obs.]

ap-pạl′, **ap-pạll′**, *n.* Fright; dismay. [Poet.]

Ap-pȧ-lā′chi-ăn, *a.* Of, relating, or pertaining to, (a) the system of mountains extending along the eastern coast of the United States; (b) the Alleghanies.

ap-pạll′ing, *a.* Fitted to appal or dismay.

ap-pạll′ing-ly, *adv.* In a manner to appal.

ap-pạl′ment, **ap-pạll′ment**, *n.* Depression caused by fear; discouragement. [Obs.]

ap′pȧ-nāge, **ap′ăn-āge**, *n.* [Fr. *apanage*, an estate assigned to a younger son for his maintenance; an appendix, dependence, appurtenance, from L. *ad*, to, *panis*, bread.]

1. The portion of land assigned by a sovereign prince for the subsistence of his younger sons; an allowance from the public treasury to a prince.

2. A general or customary adjunct; any belonging by right; a natural endowment.

3. A territory which is dependent.

ap-pan′ȧ-gist, *n.* An owner or possessor of an appanage, especially a prince holding or receiving an appanage.

ap-pȧ-rā′tus, *n.*; *pl.* **ap-pȧ-rā′tus** (*or rarely* ap-pȧ-rā′tus-es). [L. *apparere*, to prepare; *ad*, to, and *parare*, to prepare.]

1. Things provided as means to some end, as the tools of an artisan, the furniture of a house; more especially, a complete set of instruments or materials used in any scientific, artistic, or professional work; machinery; mechanism.

2. In physiology, the system of organs which coöperate to perform some one special function; as, the *apparatus* of hearing or of digestion.

ap-par′el, *n.* [ME. *aparel*, *apparail*; Fr. *appareil*, preparation; L. *apparere*, to prepare.]

1. Clothing; vesture; garments; dress.

2. External appearance; guise; as, science parading in the *apparel* of mystery.

3. The furniture of a ship, as sails, rigging, anchors, etc.

4. A piece of embroidery done in silk and gold, sometimes enriched with pearls and precious stones, worn from the thirteenth to the fourteenth century, attached to the alb and other ecclesiastical vestments.

Syn.—Clothes, robes, vesture, vestment, raiment, garniture, habiliments, habit, dress, clothing.

Apparels.

ap-par′el, *v.t.*; appareled (-eld), *or* apparelled, *pt.*, *pp.*; appareling *or* apparelling, *ppr.* 1. To prepare clothing for. [Obs.]

2. To dress; cover with garments; adorn.

> They which are gorgeously *apparelled* . . . are in kings' courts. —Luke vii. 25.

3. To furnish with outward equipment or covering; as, ships *appareled* for sea.

ap-pâr′ence, **ap-pâr′en-cy**, *n.* 1. State of being apparent. [Obs.]

2. Appearance; outward semblance. [Obs.]

3. The state of getting ready, or preparing. [Obs.]

4. The condition of being heir apparent. [Rare.]

ap-pâr′ent, *a.* [L. *apparens*, *-entis*, ppr. of *apparere*, to become visible, to appear.]

1. Visible; able to be seen; in sight; as, the coast was *apparent* but once.

2. Plain to the perception; visible; manifest; obvious; clear; evident; as, the mechanical ingenuity of the American is *apparent* on every side.

3. Seeming; appearing to the inward or outward vision; distinguished from *actual* and *real*; as, this *apparent* victory soon demonstrated its own weakness.

Apparent horizon; the visible horizon distinguished from the rational horizon.

Apparent time; see under *Time*.

Heir apparent; an heir having indisputable rights; one who, if he lives, will by course of law succeed his ancestor.

Syn.—Evident, obvious, clear, plain, manifest, visible.—What is *apparent* is easily and quickly understood by the senses or the mind; what is *evident* is made clear by the exercise of the mental faculties, as judgment or reason.

ap-pâr′ent, *n.* An heir apparent. [Rare.]

ap-pâr′ent-ly, *adv.* 1. Plainly; openly; clearly.

2. To all appearances; seemingly; in semblance.

ap-pâr′ent-ness, *n.* Plainness to the eye or the mind; visibleness; obviousness. [Rare.]

ap-pȧ-ri′tion (-rish′un), *n.* [Fr. *apparition*; L. *apparitio*, in sense of attendance, service, from *apparere*, to attend, to appear.]

1. Appearance; visibility; or, the act of appearing, particularly in some unusual or wonderful form.

2. The thing appearing; a visible object; more especially, a strange or extraordinary vision; a ghost; a specter; a visible spirit.

3. In astronomy, the first appearance of a star or other luminary, after having been obscured; opposed to *occultation*.

ap-pȧ-ri′tion-ăl, *a.* Relating to apparitions.

ap-par′i-tŏr, *n.* [L. *apparere*, to prepare or make ready.]

1. Among the Romans, any officer who attended magistrates and judges to execute their orders.

2. In England, a messenger or officer who serves the process of a spiritual court; also, a beadle, in a university, who carries the mace.

ap-pau-mée′, **a-pau-mée′** (-pō-mā′), *a.* [Fr. *appaumé*, from L. *ad*, to, and *palma*, palm.] In heraldry, with fingers and thumb extended; open; applied to a hand.

Hand Appaumée.

ap-pāy′, *v.t.* To satisfy. [Obs. See *Pay*.]

ap-pēach′, *v.t.* To accuse; to censure or reproach. [Obs. See *Impeach*.]

ap-pēach′ēr, *n.* One who accuses. [Obs.]

ap-pēach′ment, *n.* Impeachment; accusation. [Obs.]

ap-pēal′, *v.i.*; appealed (-pēld), *pt.*, *pp.*; appealing, *ppr.* [ME. *appelen*, *apelen*; Fr. *appeler*; L. *appellare*, to call upon, address; *ad*, to, and *pellere*, to drive.]

1. In law, to apply for taking up a cause to a superior judge or court, for revision or reversal.

2. To refer (to some person, authority, or power) for decision, justification, proof, or defense; to have recourse; to resort; to call upon; as, they *appealed* to the head of the department; let us *appeal* to reason.

3. To supplicate or solicit earnestly; to make entreaty; as, they *appealed* for public help.

4. To arouse sympathy or peculiar interest; as, music *appeals* to nearly every one.

ap-pēal′, *v.t.* 1. In law, to call or remove from an inferior to a superior judge or court for rehearing.

2. To accuse; to charge with crime. [Obs.]

3. To challenge. [Rare.]

ap-pēal′, *n.* 1. In law, the removal of a cause or suit from an inferior to a superior tribunal for review; also, the right of such action.

2. In old law, (a) an accusation of crime brought by an accomplice; (b) a vindictive process instituted by a private person for some heinous crime by which he has been injured, when the accused has already been acquitted or pardoned.

3. A summons to answer to a charge; a challenge. [Rare.]

4. A call upon or reference to some authority or power for decision, proof, or assistance; a recourse or resort; as, an *appeal* to the house; an *appeal* to force.

5. A call for help, sympathy, encouragement, etc.; a prayer for mercy; as, an *appeal* for contributions.

ap-pēal′ȧ-ble, *a.* 1. Able to be appealed or removed to a higher tribunal for decision; as, the cause is *appealable*.

2. Liable to be accused or called to answer by appeal; applied to persons; as, a criminal is *appealable* for manslaughter. [Obs.]

ap-pēal′ănt, *n.* One who appeals; an appellant. [Obs.]

ap-pēal′ēr, *n.* One who appeals; an appellor.

ap-pēal′ing, *a.* Making or carrying an appeal; beseeching.

ap-pēal′ing-ly, *adv.* In an appealing or imploring manner.

ap-pēal′ing-ness, *n.* The quality of containing or making an appeal.

ap-pēar′, *v.i.*; appeared (-pērd′), *pt.*, *pp.*; appearing, *ppr.* [L. *apparere*, to appear; *ad*, to, and *parere*, to come forth, be visible.]

1. To come or be in sight; to be in view; to be visible.

> And God said . . . Let the dry land *appear*. —Gen. i. 9.

2. To become visible to the apprehension of the mind; to be obvious; to be known, as a subject of observation or comprehension; to become manifest; to be clear or made clear by evidence.

> It doth not yet *appear* what we shall be. —1 John iii. 2.

3. To come into the light of publicity; to become generally noticed or known; to come before the public; as, a great statesman has *appeared*; this magazine *appears* monthly.

4. To come into the presence of, as parties or advocates before a court, or as persons to be tried; as, the defendant, being called, did not *appear*, either in person or by attorney.

5. To seem; to look; to have the appearance of being; as, the facts *appear* favorable; the man *appears* to be a mile off.

ap-pēar′, *n.* Appearance. [Obs.]

ap-pēar′ănce, *n.* 1. The act of coming in sight; the act of becoming visible to the eye; as, his sudden *appearance* surprised me.

2. The thing seen; an extraordinary spectacle; a phenomenon; as, an *appearance* in the sky.

3. External semblance; outward aspect; hence, outward sign, indication, or evidence; as, the *appearance* of the place was altogether pleasing; the writing had every *appearance* of genuineness; to all *appearances*, the case is hopeless; often used in the plural to signify outward circumstances collectively or the general aspect of external facts; as, *appearances* were against them.

4. Presence; mien; aspect, as presented by the person, dress, or manners; as, the man had a commanding *appearance*.

5. A coming into notice; an appearing before the public; as, the *appearance* of an actor, of a new book, etc.

6. Probability; likelihood. [Obs.]

7. In law, a being present in court; a coming into court as party to an action; an appearing, in person or by attorney, of anybody against whom action is taken, for the purpose of defense.

To put in an appearance; to appear.

To save appearances; to maintain a good showing.

Syn.—Air, aspect, look, manner, mien, semblance.

ap-pēar′ẽr, *n.* One who or that which appears. [Rare.]

ap-pēar′ing-ly, *adv.* Seemingly. [Obs.]

ap-pēaṣ′ȧ-ble, *a.* Able to be appeased, quieted, or conciliated.

ap-pēaṣ′ȧ-ble-ness, *n.* The quality of being appeasable.

ap-pēaṣe′, *v.t.*; appeased (-pēzd′), *pt., pp.*; appeasing, *ppr.* [ME. *apesen, apeisen*; Fr. *apaiser*; L. *ad*, to, and *pax*, peace, from *pacisci*, to pacify.]

1. To make quiet; to calm; to still; as, to *appease* the tumult of the ocean, or of the passions; also, to reduce to peace; to pacify; to soothe; to conciliate; as, to *appease* wrath.

2. To allay or assuage, as grief or suffering; to satisfy or relieve the acuteness of, as hunger, thirst, etc.

Syn.—Calm, pacify, quiet, still, allay, assuage, compose, conciliate, propitiate, reconcile, soothe, tranquilize.—To *appease* is to allay agitation which demands satisfaction; to *calm* is to bring into a tranquil state. *Appease* respects matters of force or violence, *calm* those of inquietude and distress. *Pacify* corresponds to *appease*, and *quiet* to *calm*; in sense they are the same, but in application they differ; *appease* and *calm* are used only in reference to objects of importance; *pacify* and *quiet* to those of a more familiar nature. *Still* is a loftier expression, serving for restraining or putting to silence that which is noisy and boisterous.

ap-pēaṣe′ment, *n.* The act of appeasing; the state of being in peace.

ap-pēaṣ′ẽr, *n.* One who appeases or pacifies.

ap-pēa′sive, *a.* Having the power to appease; mitigating; quieting.

ap-pel′, *n.* [Fr. *appel.*] In fencing, a feint, usually accompanied by a tap of the foot.

ap-pel′lȧ-ble, *a.* Same as *Appealable.*

ap-pel′lăn-cy, *n.* Appeal; capability of appeal.

ap-pel′lănt, *n.* 1. One who makes an appeal.

2. In law, one who appeals, or removes a cause from a lower to a higher tribunal.

3. One who prosecutes another for a crime. [Obs.]

4. One who challenges or summons another to single combat. [Obs.]

5. In church history, one of a division of the clergy in France in the early eighteenth century, who rejected the bull Unigenitus, and appealed to a general council.

ap-pel′lănt, *a.* [Fr. *appelant*, from *appeler*, to call; L. *appellans*, ppr. of *appellare*, to call upon.] Pertaining to an appeal. In law, the *party appellant* is the party who appeals, as opposed to the *respondent*, or *appellee*.

ap-pel′lāte, *n.* A person appealed, or prosecuted for a crime. [Obs. See *Appellee.*]

ap-pel′lāte, *a.* Pertaining to appeals; having cognizance of appeals; as, *appellate* jurisdiction.

Appellate court; a court having the power to pass upon appeals.

Appellate judges; judges of appellate courts.

Party appellate; in law, the party appealed against.

ap-pel-lā′tion, *n.* [L. *appellatio*, an addressing, accosting, from *appellare*, to call upon.]

1. A name; the word by which a person, thing, or class is called and known; a title; as, to give a man his proper *appellation*.

2. The act of appealing; an appeal. [Obs.]

3. The act of naming or calling by a title.

Syn.—Name, title, cognomen, style, denomination, appellative, epithet.

ap-pel′lȧ-tive, *a.* 1. Pertaining to a common name; noting the common name of a species; naming; denominative.

2. In grammar, denoting a class; said of *common*, as opposed to *proper*, nouns.

ap-pel′lȧ-tive, *n.* 1. A common name, in distinction from a proper name. A common name, or *appellative*, stands for a whole class, genus, or species of beings, or for universal ideas. Thus, man is the name of the whole human race, and bird of all winged animals. Tree is the name of all plants of a particular class; plant and vegetable are names of things that grow out of the earth. A proper name, on the other hand, stands for a single thing; as, Chicago, Washington, Lake Michigan.

2. A descriptive name or title; an appellation.

Many a fair flower is burdened with preposterous *appellatives*. —Tupper.

ap-pel′lȧ-tive-ly, *adv.* According to the manner of nouns appellative; in a manner to express whole classes or species; as, Hercules is sometimes used *appellatively*; that is, as a common name to signify a strong man.

ap-pel′lȧ-tive-ness, *n.* The quality of being appellative.

ap-pel′lȧ-tō-ry, *a.* Containing an appeal; as, an *appellatory* libel.

ap-pel-lee′, *n.* 1. The defendant, or respondent, in an appeal; opposed to *appellant.*

2. The person appealed against, or prosecuted for a crime; opposed to *appellor.*

ap-pel′lŏr (*or* ap-pel-lọr′), *n.* 1. In old English law, the person who instituted an appeal, or prosecuted another for a crime.—Blackstone.

2. A criminal who confesses a felony and accuses his accomplices.

This word is rarely or never used for the plaintiff in appeal from a lower court, who is called the *appellant.*

ap′pen-āġe, *n.* Same as *Appanage.*

ap-pend′, *v.t.*; appended, *pt., pp.*; appending, *ppr.* [Fr. *appendre*, to hang up; ME. *appenden*; L. *appendere*, to weigh, consider; *ad*, to, and *pendere*, to hang.]

1. To hang or attach, as by a string, so that the thing is suspended; as, a seal *appended* to a record.

2. To add or annex as an accessory to the principal thing; as, a glossary is *appended* to this dialect story.

Syn.—Affix, supplement, subjoin, attach, add.

ap-pend′āġe, *n.* 1. Something added to a principal or greater thing, though not neccessary to it, as a portico to a house.

Modesty is the *appendage* of sobriety. —Jer. Taylor.

2. In biology, any part or organ which is subordinate or supplementary; an external organ, or limb, as an antenna, a tail, a leaf, a hair, etc.

Syn.—Appendix, accessory, supplement, concomitant, addition.

ap-pend′āġed, *a.* Furnished with an appendage.

ap-pend′ănce, *n.* 1. Something annexed. [Obs.]

2. The condition of being annexed.

ap-pend′ănt, *a.* 1. Hanging; annexed; adjunct; accompanying; attached; as, a seal *appendant* to a paper.

2. In law, appended by prescription, or by long-continued usage; a term applied to a right or privilege belonging by inheritance to a superior inheritance. A common of fishing may be *appendant* to a freehold, or a pew in the parish church *appendant* to a manor. —Blackstone.

Common appendant; in English law, a right belonging to the owners or occupiers of land to pasture commonable beasts, as horses, cows, etc., upon the waste land of the lord of the manor, or upon the lands of other persons within the same manor.

Advowson appendant; a right of patronage or presentation, as the appointment to a rectorate or vicarage, annexed to the possession of a manor.

ap-pend′ănt, *n.* 1. That which belongs to another thing, as incidental or subordinate to it; an appendage.

2. In law, an inherited right annexed by prescription to a more important inheritance; as, a right of common, a right of fishing in certain waters, etc.

ap-pen-deç′tō-my, ap-pend-i-ceç′tō-my, *n.* [L. *appendix*, an appendage, and Gr. *ektemnein*, to cut.] In surgery, the removal, by excision, of the vermiform appendix.

ap-pend′ence, ap-pend′en-cy, *n.* 1. The state of being appendant. [Rare.]

2. Something appended. [Obs.]

ap-pend′i-căl, *a.* Pertaining to or of the nature of an appendix.

ap-pend′i-cāte, *v.t.* To append; to add. [Obs.]

ap-pend-i-cā′tion, *n.* An appendage or adjunct. [Obs.]

ap-pend-i-ceç′tō-my, *n.* See *Appendectomy.*

ap-pen′di-çēṣ, *n.*, pl. of *appendix.*

ap-pend-i-cī′tis, *n.* In pathology, inflammation of the vermiform appendix of the cæcum, a peculiar little blind process extending from the end of the cæcum and varying in man from 3 to 6 inches in length. The disease often causes death, sometimes within a very short time.

ap-pend′i-cle, *n.* A small appendage.

ap-pen-diç′ū-lȧ, *n.*; *pl.* **ap-pen-diç′ū-læ.** An appendicle; specifically, in botany, a branching, hair like process, at the apex of the conceptacle or sporocarp in certain fungi.

ap-pen-diç′ū-lăr, *a.* Appendiculate. [Rare.]

Ap-pen-diç-ū-lā′ri-ȧ, *n.* [LL. *appendicularius*, from L. *appendicula.*] A genus of minute ascidians, or tunicates, with a tail-like appendage which gives them a resemblance to tadpoles.

ap-pen-diç-ū-lā′ri-ăn, *n.* One of the *Appendicularia.*

ap-pen-diç-ū-lā′ri-oid, *a.* Pertaining to the genus *Appendicularia.*

Ap-pen-diç-ū-lā′tȧ, *n.pl.* In zoölogy, an order of annelids, including the marine worms or *Polychæta.*

ap-pen-diç′ū-lāte, *a.* 1. In botany, having an appendage, as a leaf with lobes attached to the petiole, a calyx with expansions, or a corolla with a nectary.

2. Of or pertaining to the *Appendiculata.*

Appendiculate leaf; a small appended leaf.

ap-pen′dix, *n.*; *pl.* **ap-pen′dix-eṣ** or **ap-pen′di-çēṣ.** [L. *appendix*, an appendage, from *appendere*, to hang to, or from; *ad*, to, and *pendere*, to hang.]

1. Something appended or added.

Normandy became an *appendix* to England. —Hale.

2. An adjunct, concomitant, or appendage.

3. An addition appended to a literary work or book relating, but not essential, to the main body of the work.

4. In anatomy, an appendage, or prolongation; a projecting process; the vermiform appendix.

Vermiform appendix; a slender blind process at the end of the cæcum in man and some other mammals. [See *Appendicitis.*]

Syn.—Addition, supplement, addendum.

ap-pen-dix′ious (-dik′shus), *a.* Pertaining to or resembling an appendix. [Rare.]

ap-pense′, *a.* [L. *appensus*, pp. of *appendere*, to hang to.] Hanging from above; pendulous, as an ovule. [Rare.]

ap-pen′sion, *n.* The act of appending. [Obs.]

ap-pen′tis, ap-pen′tice, *n.* [ME. *appentice*; OFr. *apentis*; Fr. *appentis*, a shed; L. *appendere*, to hang to.] An architectural name for a lean-to roof or a kind of open shed supported on columns or brackets let into a wall, or otherwise, with the view of affording protection from the weather to a door, window, flight of steps, etc., over which it projects. Corrupted in English into *penthouse.*

Appentis, Cathedral of Meaux (fifteenth century).

ap-pẽr-cēive′, *v.t.* [ME. *aperceiven*; OFr. *apercevir*; Fr. *apercevoir*, to perceive; Sp. *apercibir*; L. *ad*, to, and *percipere*, to perceive.] To comprehend. [Rare.]

ap-pẽr-cep′tion, *n.* [Fr. *aperception*, perception, from *apercevoir*, to perceive; from L. *ad*, to, and *percipere*, to perceive.]

1. Perception that reflects upon itself; consciousness by the mind of its own perception; self-reflective perception applied to metaphysical or anthropological ends.

Apperception is the essential mental act in the three great stages of mental generalization, perception, conception, and judgment. —Baldwin.

2. The adjustment or coalescence of parts of new ideas with what is already in the mind, or with old ideas, by modification.

ap-pẽr-cep′tive, *a.* Pertaining to apperception; as, the *apperceptive* function.

ap-per′il, *n.* Peril; danger. [Obs.]

ap-pẽr-tāin′, *v.i.*; appertained, *pt., pp.*; appertaining, *ppr.* [ME. *apperteinen, aperteinen, apertinen*; OFr. *apartenir*; Fr. *appartenir*, to appertain, belong to; L. *ad*, to, and *pertinere*, to belong to.] To belong, whether by right, nature, or appointment; to pertain; to relate; as, give to whom it *appertains.*

ap-pẽr-tāin′ingṣ, *n.pl.* The things which belong to one; appurtenances. [Rare.]

ap-pẽr-tāin′ment, *n.* That which belongs to a person; appurtenance. [Obs.]

ap-pẽr′tē-nence, ap-pẽr′ti-nănce, ap-pẽr′ti-nence, *n.* Same as *Appurtenance.*

ap-pẽr′ti-nent, *a.* Belonging; appertaining. [Obs. See *Appurtenant.*]

ap-pẽr′ti-nent, *n.* That which belongs to some thing else. [Obs. See *Appurtenance.*]

ap-pēte′, *v.t.* To crave for; to desire. [Obs.]

ap′pē-tence, ap′pē-ten-cy, *n.*; *pl.* **ap′pē-ten-cieṣ.** [Fr. *appétence, appétit*; L. *appetentia*, a longing after, appetite, from *appetere*, to strive after.]

1. In a general sense, desire; especially desire for that which gratifies the senses; sensual appetite; as, *appetence* for liquor.

2. The disposition of organized bodies to select and imbibe such portions of matter as serve to support and nourish them.

These lacteals have mouths, and by animal selection or *appetency* they absorb such part of the fluid as is agreeable to their palate. —Erasmus Darwin.

3. An inclination or propensity in animals to perform certain actions, as in the young to suck, and in aquatic birds to enter into water and to swim.

4. Natural attraction, or the tendency in inanimate bodies to move toward each other and unite.

5. The principle that a change of desires or needs produces in an organism a corresponding modification in its structure.

ap′pē-tent, *a.* [L. *appetens*, ppr. of *appetere*, to strive for.] Desiring; very desirous. [Rare.]

ap″pē-ti-bil′i-ty, *n.* The quality of being desirable.

ap′pē-ti-ble, *a.* [LL. *appetibilis*, from *appeto*.] Desirable; that may be the object of desire.

ap′pē-tite, *n.* [ME. *appetit, apetite*; Fr. *appétit*, appetite; L. *appetitus*, a passionate longing or desire, from *appetere*, to seek for.]

1. The natural desire for pleasure; desire for gratification, either of the body or of the mind; as, the *appetite* for glory or riches; the *appetites* of hunger, thirst, etc. Hunger and thirst are natural *appetites*; the *appetites* for olives, tobacco, snuff, etc., are artificial or cultivated. *Appetite* should be followed by *for*; as, an *appetite for* pleasure.

2. A desire for food or drink; as, dining with a good *appetite*.

3. Strong desire; longing; as, a vulgar *appetite* for the sensational.

4. The thing desired. [Obs.]

Power being the natural *appetite* of princes. —Swift.

5. Appetency. [Obs.]

To be given to appetite; to be voracious or gluttonous.

Syn.—Passion, desire, propensity, proclivity, inclination, propension, appetency, want, craving, disposition, tendency, proneness.

ap-pē-ti′tion (-tish′un), *n.* Desire; craving; a longing for.

ap′pē-ti-tive, *a.* 1. Desiring gratification; as, *appetitive* power or faculty.

2. Producing appetite; appetizing.

ap′pē-tize, *v.t.*; appetized, *pt., pp.*; appetizing, *ppr.* To give zest to the hunger of; as, to *appetize* one for his food.

ap′pē-ti-zēr, *n.* That which appetizes; anything that gives relish, especially for food.

ap′pē-ti-zing, *a.* Whetting the appetite.

ap′pē-ti-zing-ly, *adv.* In an appetizing manner.

Ap′pi-ăn, *a.* Pertaining to Appius or to any member of the Appii, a Roman family.

Appian Way, or *Via Appia*; a celebrated road from Rome south through Capua to Brundusium (Brindisi), commenced by the censor Appius Claudius B. C. 312. It is above 330 miles in length, 14 to 18 feet in breadth.

ap′plȧ-nāte, *a.* [*Ad-*, and L. *planus*, flat.] In botany, expanded or flattened out.

ap-plaud′, *v.t.*; applauded, *pt., pp.*; applauding, *ppr.* [Fr. *applaudir*; L. *applaudere*, to strike the hands together; *ad*, to, and *plaudere*, to strike.]

1. To praise or show approval of by clapping the hands, acclamation, shouting, or other significant sign.

2. To praise by words, actions, or other means; to express approbation of; to commend.

I do *applaud* his courage. —Shak.

Syn.—Approve, cheer, commend, extol, encore, laud, praise.

ap-plaud′, *v.i.* To give expression to praise or approval by clapping the hands, stamping the feet, shouting, or other demonstration; as, the audience *applauded*.

ap-plaud′ēr, *n.* One who applauds.

ap-plaus′ȧ-ble, *a.* Worthy of applause. [Obs.]

ap-plause′, *n.* [Fr. *applaudissement*, applause; L. *applausus*, pp. of *applaudere*, to applaud.]

1. The act of applauding; approbation and praise; acclamation; approbation publicly expressed.

2. Demonstration of approval by hand-clapping, cheering, waving handkerchiefs, etc.

Syn.—Commendation, approbation, acclamation, encomium, approval, plaudit, praise.

ap-plau′sive, *a.* Expressive of applause; containing applause.

ap-plau′sive-ly, *adv.* In a manner expressing applause.

ap′ple (-pl), *n.* [OE. *appl, appil*; ME. *apple, aple*; AS. *æppl, æpl*; Arm. *aval*. This word primarily signifies fruit in general, especially of a round form.]

1. The edible pome or fruit of the apple-tree, *Pyrus Malus*, which is cultivated in almost all the temperate regions of the earth. It is usually spheroidal in form, the ends being considerably depressed. The name is also applied to the fruit of many related trees bearing fruit of a similar shape, as the American crab-*apple*, *Pyrus coronaria*. The European crab-*apple* is thought to be the original species. Many varieties of *apple* are raised in this country for the manufacture of cider, and for eating raw or cooking. These are called by distinctive names, some of general and others of local significance. Such terms as *russet*, *pippin*, etc., are applied to many varieties; while names such as American Beauty, Canada Baldwin, Northern Spy, Fall Pippin, Golden Russet, Virginia Greening, etc., are specific.

2. Any tree on which the apple grows, especially *Pyrus Malus*.

3. Any growth resembling the apple; as, the love-*apple*, the oak-*apple*, etc.

Apple brandy; a liquor distilled from apple cider; apple-jack.

Apple of Cain; the strawberry-tree, *Arbutus Unedo*; also, its fruit.

Apple of discord; anything which produces dissension among people. The expression is founded on the classical myth that Eris, the goddess of discord, flung among the immortals a golden apple inscribed, "For the fairest." It produced great jealousy among the goddesses, and three—Juno, Minerva, and Venus—contended for it, the last named being the winner. The result of the competition so enraged Juno, that she did not cease her machinations against the Trojans till Troy had been destroyed.

Apple of love, or *love-apple*; an old name for the tomato, *Lycopersicum esculentum*.

Apple of Peru; a Peruvian herb, *Nicandra physaloides*.

Apple of Sodom, or *Dead Sea apple*; a plant growing near the Dead Sea, thus described by Josephus. ". . . Which fruits have a color as if they were fit to be eaten; but if you pluck them with your hands they dissolve into smoke and ashes." Hence, anything of promising appearance which disappoints or deceives.

Apple of the eye; the pupil of the eye; figuratively, something precious.

Apple-pie bed; a bed made up, as a practical joke, with a sheet so doubled that it prevents one from stretching at full length.

Apple-pie order; perfect order. [Colloq.]

Apple sauce; a sauce made of stewed apples.

Bitter apple; see *Colocynth*.

ap′ple, *v.i.* To form like an apple; to yield apples; to grow like an apple. [Rare.]

ap′ple-blight (-blīt), *n.* A species of aphis.

ap′ple-bōr″ēr, *n.* A beetle whose larvæ bore into the apple and other trees.

ap′ple-but″tēr, *n.* A preserve or sauce made of apples stewed in cider, and seasoned with spices.

ap′ple-cärt, *n.* A cart or barrow from which apples are sold or peddled.

To upset one's apple-cart; figuratively, to upset one's plans or business; to overthrow an adversary or competitor.

ap′ple-cōr″ēr, *n.* A device for cutting out the cores of apples.

ap′ple-fāced, *a.* Having a full rosy face like an apple.

ap′ple-flȳ, *n.* Any fly whose larvæ bore into apples.

ap′ple-grȧft, *n.* A scion of the apple-tree ingrafted.

ap′ple-green, *n.* A color resembling the light-green hue of some apples.

ap′ple-head″ed (-hed″ed), *a.* A term applied to dogs whose heads are round on top rather than flat.

ap′ple-jack, *n.* Apple brandy.

ap′ple-john (-jon), *n.* A kind of apple which keeps for a long time, but becomes shriveled and dry; called also *John-apple*.

ap′ple-midġe (-mij), *n.* An insect whose larvæ bore into apples.

ap′ple-mọth, *n.* A lepidopterous insect, the larvæ of which infest apples.

ap′ple-shell, *n.* An apple-snail.

ap′ple-snāil, *n.* A shell of the genus *Ampullaria*.

ap′ple-squire (-skwīr), *n.* A courtezan's page; a pimp. [Obs.]

ap′ple-tree, *n.* Any tree that yields apples, especially *Pyrus Malus*.

ap′ple-wine, *n.* Cider made from apples.

ap′ple-wŏrm, *n.* The larva of a moth, *Carpocapsa pomonella*, which infests apples.

ap-pli′ȧ-ble, *a.* Capable of being applied; applicable. [Obs.]

ap-pli′ănce, *n.* 1. The act of applying; application; as, the *appliance* of a theory.

2. Pliability; compliance; subservience. [Obs.]

3. Something applied to a particular use; a tool; an apparatus or instrument; as, a mechanical *appliance*; the *appliances* of a trade.

Syn.—Arrangement, contrivance, apparatus, device, machine, instrument, tool.

ap″pli-cȧ-bil′i-ty, *n.* The quality of being applicable or fit to be applied.

ap′pli-cȧ-ble, *a.* [Fr. *applicable*; L. *applicare*, to join or fasten to.] Capable of being applied; fit to be applied; bearing relation; relevant; as, this observation is *applicable* to the case.

Syn.—Available, convenient, useful, pertinent, suitable, appropriate, adaptable.

ap′pli-cȧ-ble-ness, *n.* Fitness to be applied; the quality of being applicable.

ap′pli-cȧ-bly, *adv.* In an applicable manner.

ap′pli-căn-cy, *n.* The state of being applicable. [Rare.]

ap′pli-cănt, *n.* [L. *applicans*, ppr. of *applicare*, to join or attach to.] One who applies or makes application; a petitioner; as, an *applicant* for charity; an *applicant* for divorce.

ap′pli-cāte, *a.* Applied or put to practical use; as, *applicate* sciences. [Rare.]

Applicate number; in mathematics, a number applied in a concrete case.

Applicate ordinate; a straight line applied at right angles to the axis of any conic section, and bounded by the curve.

ap′pli-cāte, *n.* A straight line drawn across a curve, so as to be bisected by the diameter; an ordinate.

ap′pli-cāte, *v.i.* To apply. [Obs.]

ap-pli-cā′tion, *n.* [Fr. *application*; L. *applicatio*, a binding on, or joining to, from *applicatus*, pp. of *applicare*, to join or fasten to.]

1. The act of applying or laying on; as, the *application* of emollients to a diseased limb.

2. The thing applied; as, the pain was abated by the *application*.

3. The act of making request or soliciting; as, he made *application* to a court of chancery; an *application* for employment.

4. The act of applying as a means; the employment of means; as, children may be governed by a suitable *application* of rewards and punishments.

5. Applicability; relevancy; as, a rule of universal *application*.

6. A formal request or solicitation, or the writing embodying such request; as, his *application* was well written.

7. The act of fixing the mind; intensity of thought; close study; as, to injure the health by *application* to study.

Had his *application* been equal to his talents his progress might have been greater. —J. Jay.

8. The act of referring something to a particular case; as, I make the remark and leave you to make the *application*.

9. In sermons, that part of the discourse in which the principles before laid down are applied to practical purposes.

10. The act of applying the principles of one science to another; as, the *application* of algebra to geometry.

11. A device in which the principles of a science are applied to secure a practical result; as, the trolley-car is an *application* of electrodynamics.

12. In astrology, the approach of a planet to a particular aspect.

Syn.—Solicitation, supplication, requisition, petition, request, demand, suit.

ap′pli-cā-tive, *a.* Applicable.

ap′pli-cā-tive-ly, *adv.* In an applicative manner.

ap′pli-cȧ-tō-ri-ly, *adv.* In an applicatory manner.

ap′pli-cȧ-tō-ry, *a.* Suitable for application; applicative.

ap′pli-cȧ-tō-ry, *n.* That which applies. [Rare.]

ap-pli′ed-ly, *adv.* By application. [Rare.]

ap-pli′ēr, *n.* One who or that which applies.

ap-pli′ment, *n.* Application. [Obs.]

ap-pli-qué′ (-kā′), *a.* [Fr.] Decorated with a design cut out of other material and transferred; as, *appliqué* work.

ap-plot′, *v.t.*; applotted, *pt., pp.*; applotting, *ppr.* To allot; to divide into plots. [Obs.]

ap-plot′ment, *n.* Allotment. [Obs.]

ap-plȳ′, *v.t.*; applied, *pt., pp.*; applying, *ppr.* [ME. *applyen, applien*; OFr. *aplier*; Fr. *appliquer*; L. *applicare*, to attach to, apply.]

1. To lay on; to put (one thing) to another; as, to *apply* the hand to the breast; to *apply* liniment to a part of the body.

2. To employ for a particular purpose; as, to *apply* a sum of money to the payment of a debt.

3. To refer as relative; as, to *apply* the testimony to the case; to *apply* an epithet.

4. To fix wholly; to engage and employ with attention; sometimes reflexive; as, to *apply* oneself to study.

5. To address or direct. [Obs.]

6. To keep busy. [Obs. See *Ply*.]

7. To visit. [Obs.]

Syn.—Dedicate, engage, employ, devote, allot, use, direct.

ap-plȳ′, *v.i.* 1. To suit; to agree; to have analogy; as, this argument *applies* well to the case.

2. To make request; to solicit; as, to *apply* to the president for an office.

3. To devote or direct one's attention closely. [Rare.]

ȧp-pŏg-giä′tō (ȧp-pō-jä′tō), *a.* [It., supported.] In music, a direction signifying that the notes are to glide and melt into each other without break; sustained.

ȧp-poġ-ġiȧ-tū′rȧ (äp-poj-ä-tū′rä), *n.* [It., from *appogiare*, to prop, lean.] In music, an ornamental and embellishing note, usually written in a smaller character than the regular notes of the piece, interposed between two of the latter, and sharing the time of the following note; used for transition or expression. Also called *grace-note*.

ap-point′, *v.t.*; appointed, *pt.*, *pp.*; appointing, *ppr.* [ME. *appointen*, *apointen*; OFr. *apointer*; Fr. *appointer*; L. *ad*, to, and *punctum*, a point, from *pungere*, to prick.]

1. To fix; to settle; to establish; to constitute, ordain, or fix by decree or decision; as, to *appoint* a holiday.

> When he *appointed* the foundations of the earth. —Prov. viii. 29.

2. To allot or assign; to designate by authority; as, to *appoint* a committee; to *appoint* a guardian; to *appoint* a time for the meeting.

3. To ordain, command, or order.

> Thy servants are ready to do whatsoever my lord the king shall *appoint*.—2 Sam. xv. 15.

4. To equip; to furnish; to provide; as, his person and house are well *appointed*.

5. To point out by way of censure, or correction; to blame. [Obs.]

> *Appoint* not heavenly disposition.—Milton.

6. In law, (a) to designate, or nominate, as an executor, administrator, or guardian; (b) to allot or divide, by virtue of a clause contained in a conveyance, conferring a power on some person to do so. [See *Appointor*.]

Syn.—Allot, constitute, depute, fix, ordain, designate, name, order, prescribe, nominate.

ap-point′, *v.i.* To ordain; to decree.

> The Lord had *appointed* to defeat the good counsel of Ahithophel. —2 Sam. xvii. 14.

ap-point′ȧ-ble, *a.* Capable of being appointed; as, officers are *appointable* by the executive.

ap-point-ee′, *n.* 1. A person appointed.

2. In law, one receiving appointment from a legally constituted appointor.

ap-point′ẽr, *n.* One who appoints.

ap-point′ive, *a.* Filled by or subject to appointment. [Rare.]

ap-point′ment, *n.* 1. The act of appointing or the state of being appointed; designation to office; also, the office to which one may be appointed; as, he erred by the *appointment* of unsuitable men; he received his *appointment* yesterday.

2. Stipulation; assignation; engagement; as, they made an *appointment* to meet at six o'clock.

3. Decree; established order or constitution; direction; order; command; as, it is our duty to submit to the divine *appointments*.

4. Equipment; outfit; commonly in the plural; as, the *appointments* of a hotel; the *appointments* of an ocean steamer.

5. An allowance to a person; a salary or pension, as to a public officer; properly used only in the plural. [Obs.]

6. In law, the act performed by an appointor in transferring to a person any specific property; also, the deed or conveyance containing the disposition of such property.

Syn.—Establishment, station, order, designation, equipment, position, command.

ap-point′ŏr, *n.* In law, one empowered to allot or divide an estate by virtue of a clause contained in a conveyance previously drawn up; as where a parent has the life interest in a fund with a power to appoint the fund to his children after death.

ap-pōr′tẽr, *n.* [L. *apportare*, bring to; *ad*, to, and *portare*, to bring.] A bringer-in; a procurer. [Obs.]

ap-pōr′tion, *v.t.*; apportioned, *pt.*, *pp.*; apportioning, *ppr.* [*Ad-*, and L. *portio*, portion.] To divide and assign in proportion; to distribute among, as persons, etc., a just part to each; as, to *apportion* undivided rights; to *apportion* time among various employments.

Syn. — Distribute, deal out, divide, share, allot, dispense, dispose.

ap-pōr′tion-āte-ness, *n.* Just proportion. [Obs.]

ap-pōr′tion-ẽr, *n.* One who apportions.

ap-pōr′tion-ment, *n.* 1. The act of allotting; a just division into shares; a true distribution of property of any kind.

2. The allotment or distribution of representatives in Congress, and in the state legislatures. In the former case, a new *apportionment* is made by Congress every ten years, after the census.

3. An allotment of direct taxes proportionate to the population; a power possessed by Congress under the constitution but rarely exercised.

ap-pōṣ′ȧ-ble, *a.* Capable of being closed together, as the fingers and thumb, or able to be arranged in juxtaposition.

ap-pōṣe′, *v.t.* [Fr. *apposer*; L. *apponere*, to put or lay at; *ad*, to, and *ponere*, to put.]

1. To put questions to; to examine. [Obs. See *Pose*.]

2. To apply; to place before or opposite to.

3. To arrange side by side.

ap-pōṣed′, *a.* Arranged in apposition; fitting into one another.

ap-pōṣ′ẽr, *n.* An examiner. In the English Court of Exchequer there was, prior to 1833, an officer called the *apposer*, who audited the accounts of the sheriff.

ap′pō-ṣite, *a.* [L. *appositus*, pp. of *apponere*, to put or lay at or near; *ad*, to, and *ponere*, to place.] Suitable; fit; adapted; pertinent; apt; followed by *to*; as, his remarks were *apposite to* the subject before us.

ap′pō-ṣite-ly, *adv.* In a suitable manner.

ap′pō-ṣite-ness, *n.* Fitness; propriety; suitability.

ap-pō-ṣi′tion (-zish′un), *n.* [Fr. *apposition*; L. *appositus*, pp. of *apponere*, to place against or to.]

1. The act of adding to; addition; accretion.

2. In grammar, the connection between two nouns or pronouns in the same case but without any word between them; as, he supported Blaine, the statesman, but disapproved Blaine, the man; in such an instance the second noun explains the first.

3. The placing of things side by side; also, the state of being side by side.

4. In surgery, (a) the development of tissue by propinquity; (b) the act of bringing together separated parts, or restoration in that manner.

5. In rhetoric, the method of adding a word or set of words to emphasize a meaning, or show examples of other words.

Growth by apposition; (a) in physiology, a form of growth by transformation of nutritive matter from the blood into tissue on the surface of an organ; (b) in botany, growth in thickness by formation of laminæ, as of cellulose in cell-walls and of starch in starch-grains.

ap-pō-ṣi′tion-ăl, *a.* Relating to apposition.

ap-poṣ′i-tive, *n.* A noun, pronoun, or clause in apposition. [See *Apposition*.]

ap-poṣ′i-tive, *a.* Apposite; applicable.

ap-poṣ′i-tive-ly, *adv.* In an appositive manner.

ap-prāiṣ′ȧ-ble, *a.* Capable of appraisal.

ap-prāiṣ′ăl, *n.* An official valuation; an appraisement.

ap-prāiṣe′, *v.t.*; appraised (-prāzd′), *pt.*, *pp.*; appraising, *ppr.* [ME. *apraysen*; OFr. *apreiser*, *apretier*, *aprisier*; LL. *appretiare*, to value, esteem.]

1. To set a value on; to estimate the worth of, particularly by persons appointed for the purpose; to value officially.

2. To make an estimate of; to judge.

3. To praise; to speak well of. [Rare.]

ap-prāiṣe′ment, *n.* 1. The act of setting the value; the business of an appraiser.

2. A valuation.

ap-prāiṣ′ẽr, *n.* One who values; particularly, a person appointed and sworn to make a thorough and correct valuation of property of any kind. [See *Apprizer*.]

ap-prē-ċā′tion, *n.* [L. *apprecari*, to worship, pray to; *ad*, to, and *precari*, to pray.] Earnest prayer. [Obs.]

ap′prē-ċā-tō-ry, *a.* Intercessory. [Obs.]

ap-prē′ci-ȧ-ble (-shi-ȧ-bl), *a.* That may be justly estimated; capable of being duly estimated; perceptible; as, an *appreciable* amount.

ap-prē′ci-ȧ-bly, *adv.* In an appreciable manner.

ap-prē′ci-ănt (-shi-), *a.* Capable of appreciating. [Rare.]

ap-prē′ci-āte (-shi-), *v.t.*; appreciated, *pt.*, *pp*; appreciating, *ppr.* [Fr. *apprécier*; L. *appretiare*, to value or estimate, from *ad*, to, and *pretium*, price.]

1. To value; to be conscious of the significance, desirability, or worth of; to estimate justly; as, we seldom sufficiently *appreciate* the advantages we enjoy.

2. To increase the price set on; contrary of *depreciate*.

3. To be alive to; to note distinctions in; as, to *appreciate* differences of color.

Syn. — Esteem, estimate, value, regard, reckon, prize.—We *estimate* things when we learn by calculation their real amount; we *appreciate* when we prize them according to their true value or worth; we *esteem* when we regard them with moral approbation.

ap-prē′ci-āte, *v.i.* To rise in value; as, public securities *appreciated* when the debt was funded.

ap-prē′ci-ā-ting-ly, *adv.* With appreciation.

ap-prē-ci-ā′tion, *n.* 1. A setting a value; accurate estimate; recognition of good points; also, a keen perception of differences, or true understanding of changes.

2. A rising in value; increase of worth of value.

ap-prē′ci-ȧ-tive, *a.* Having or exhibiting appreciation.

ap-prē′ci-ȧ-tive-ly, *adv.* In an appreciative manner.

ap-prē′ci-ȧ-tive-ness, *n.* The quality of being appreciative.

ap-prē′ci-ā-tŏr, *n.* One who appreciates.

ap-prē′ci-ȧ-tō″ri-ly, *adv.* Appreciatively.

ap-prē′ci-ȧ-tō-ry, *a.* Appreciative; as, *appreciatory* words.

ap-prē-hend′, *v.t.*; apprehended, *pt.*, *pp.*; apprehending, *ppr.* [Fr. *apprehender*; L. *apprehendere*, to take hold of; *ad*, to, and *prehendere*, to take hold.]

1. To take or seize; to take hold of. In this literal sense, applied chiefly to arresting persons by legal process, or with a view to trial; as, to *apprehend* a thief.

2. To take with the understanding; to perceive with the mind; to understand. Usually, to understand only partially; to imagine; to have an opinion concerning; as, how much can we *apprehend* of truth?

3. To fear; to anticipate evil of; as, we *apprehend* calamities.

4. To note; to learn by observation; to discover by experience.

> Each man avails him of what worth he *apprehends* in you. —Browning.

5. To have perception of by the senses; to have a clear impression of; as, if a man sees two distinct persons, he *apprehends* them as different persons.

Syn.—Understand, comprehend, anticipate, conceive, arrest, dread, take.

ap-prē-hend′, *v.i.* 1. To think, believe, or suppose.

2. To be apprehensive; to expect calamity; to fear.

3. To gain an impression; to perceive; as, he *apprehends* very thoroughly.

ap-prē-hend′ẽr, *n.* One who perceives an idea; one who arrests.

ap-prē-hend′ing-ly, *adv.* With apprehension or perception; understandingly.

ap-prē-hen-si-bil′i-ty, *n.* The state or quality of being apprehensible. [Rare.]

ap-prē-hen′si-ble, *a.* Capable of being apprehended or conceived.

ap-prē-hen′si-bly, *adv.* In an understanding manner.

ap-prē-hen′sion, *n.* 1. The act of taking or arresting; as, the felon, after his *apprehension*, escaped.

2. Suspicion; fear; dread; the thought of future evil, accompanied with uneasiness of mind; apprehensiveness.

3. The act of taking in mentally, as cognition or conception; as, the special charm of Stevenson's works is that, to our *apprehension*, the characters always seem real people.

4. The faculty by which new ideas are conceived; as, a man of dull *apprehension*.

5. Opinion; the result of a mental impression; as, in our *apprehension*, the facts prove the issue.

Syn.—Arrest, disquietude, alarm, suspicion, comprehension, estimation.

ap-prē-hen′sive, *a.* 1. Quick to understand; apt; as, an *apprehensive* scholar.

2. Fearful; in expectation of evil; as, we were *apprehensive* of fatal consequences.

3. Suspicious; inclined to believe; as, I am *apprehensive* that he does not understand me.

4. Cognizant; aware; conscious. [Rare.]

5. Sensible; having perception. [Rare.]

ap-prē-hen′sive-ly, *adv.* In an apprehensive manner.

ap-prē-hen′sive-ness, *n.* The quality of being apprehensive; readiness to understand; fearfulness.

> In ninety-nine cases out of a hundred the *apprehensiveness* of women is gratuitous. —Hawthorne.

ap-pren′tice, *n.* [ME. *apprentice*, *aprentis*; OFr. *apprentis*; Fr. *apprenti*, from *apprendre*, to learn; L. *apprehendere*, to seize, take hold of.]

1. One who serves, for a certain time, with a view to learn an art, trade, profession, or occupation, in which his master undertakes to instruct him. In England, apprentices are regularly bound by indentures. The name is applied specifically to a boy on a merchantship who is made part of a ship's company with a view to his training as a future officer of the mercantile marine.

2. In old English law, a barrister, considered a learner of law till of sixteen years' standing. [Obs.] —Blackstone.

3. One not proficient in a subject; a beginner in a trade, occupation, or profession; as, a literary *apprentice*.

Parish or *town apprentice*; in England, a pauper child bound out as an apprentice by the parish or town authorities.

ap-pren'tice, *v.t.*; apprenticed, *pt.*, *pp.*; apprenticing, *ppr.* To bind to, or put under the care of a master, for the purpose of instruction in the knowledge of a trade or business.

ap-pren'tice-ship, *n.* 1. The term for which an apprentice serves.

2. The service, state, or condition of an apprentice; preliminary practice or training.

ap-pressed', ap-prest', *a.* [L. *appressus*, pp. of *apprimere*, to press to; *ad*, to, and *premere*, to press.] In botany, pressed close; lying near the stem.

ap-prīse', *v.t.*; apprised, *pt.*, *pp.*; apprising, *ppr.* [Fr. *appris*, pp. of *apprendre*, to teach or inform, from L. *apprendere*, to lay hold of.] To inform, verbally or in writing.

Syn.—Notify, inform, acquaint.

ap-prīse', *n.* Notice. [Obs.]

ap-prīz'ăl, *n.* Appraisal.

ap-prīze', *v.t.*; apprized, *pt.*, *pp.*; apprizing, *ppr.* Same as *Appraise.*

ap-prīze'ment, *n.* Same as *Appraisement.*

ap-prīz'ẽr, *n.* 1. Same as *Appraiser.*

2. In Scots law, a creditor for the benefit of whom an appraisal is made.

ap-prōach', *v.i.*; approached, *pt.*, *pp.*; approaching, *ppr.* [ME. *aprochen*; OFr. *aprochier*; LL. *appropiare*, from L. *ad*, to, and *propius*, comp. of *prope*, near.]

1. To come or go near, in place; to draw near; to advance nearer; as, to *approach* the city; to draw near in point of time; as, the dinner-hour *approaches.*

2. To draw near, in a figurative sense; to advance near to a point aimed at, in science, literature, government, morals, etc.; to approximate; as, he *approaches* to the character of the ablest statesman.

ap-prōach', *v.t.* 1. To come near to in character or quality; as, Pope *approaches* Virgil in smoothness of versification.

2. To draw nearer to, in place or time; as, to *approach* home.

3. To bring near; to advance; as, the colonel *approached* his troops to the town. [Obs.]

4. To make military approaches to, including the necessary works and fortifications; as, the Prussians *approached* Paris with due care.

5. To draw near the person of; to have access to; as, I *approached* the king with ease.

6. To get the private ear of; to draw near in secrecy; as, the ambassador *approached* the minister privately.

ap-prōach', *n.* 1. The act of drawing near; a coming or advancing near; as, he was apprised of the enemy's *approach*; the *approach* of the holidays.

2. Access; as, the *approach* to kings.

3. The path or avenue which leads from the public road or highway to a house or dwelling; a means of access.

4. A term used in golf; when the player drives his ball to the putting-green his stroke is known as the *approach.*

5. A term used in horticulture. [See *Approaching.*]

6. [*pl.*] In fortification, the works thrown up by besiegers to protect them in their advances toward a fortress or fortified town.

Syn.—Admittance, admission, access, advance, way.

ap-prōach-ȧ-bil'i-ty, *n.* Approachableness.

ap-prōach'ȧ-ble, *a.* Able to be approached; easy of access; friendly; informal.

ap-prōach'ȧ-ble-ness, *n.* The state of being approachable; accessibility.

ap-prōach'ẽr, *n.* One who approaches.

ap-prōach'ing, *n.* In horticulture, the act of ingrafting a sprig or shoot of one tree into another, without cutting it from the parent stock; called also *inarching*, or *grafting by approach.*

ap-prōach'less, *a.* Unapproachable; without an approach.

ap-prōach'ment, *n.* The act of coming near. [Obs.]

ap'prō-bāte, *a.* Approved. [Obs.]

ap'prō-bāte, *v.t.*; approbated, *pt.*, *pp.*; approbating, *ppr.* 1. To express approbation of; to manifest a liking, or degree of satisfaction for; to approve officially; as, to *approbate* one's choice.

2. To license, as a preacher or an innkeeper.

3. In Scots law, to approve as valid.

To approbate and reprobate; in Scots law, to accept and reject; as when one tries to profit by part of a deed while rejecting the rest.

ap-prō-bā'tion, *n.* [L. *approbatio*, an approving, assenting to, from *approbare*, to approve.]

1. The act of approving; that state or disposition of the mind in which one assents to the propriety of a thing with some degree of pleasure or satisfaction; approval: commendation; as, the *approbation* of one's own conscience; he was rewarded by royal *approbation.*

2. A novitiate or probation. [Obs.]

3. Attestation; proof. [Obs.]

4. In the Roman Catholic church, the official approval by a bishop of a priest in his character of confessor.

Syn.—Approval, assent, concurrence, commendation, praise, permission, liking, consent.

ap'prō-bā-tive, *a.* Approving; implying approbation.

ap'prō-bā-tive-ness, *n.* 1. In phrenology, love of approbation.

2. The quality of being approbative.

ap'prō-bā-tŏr, *n.* One who approves. [Rare.]

ap'prō-bā-tō-ry, *a.* Containing approbation, expressing approval or sanction.

ap-prompt', *v.t.* To prompt; to stimulate. [Obs.]

ap-proof', *n.* 1. Approval.

2. Proof; the act of testing. [Obs.]

ap-prō-pin'quāte, *v.i.* [L. *appropinquare*, to approach, draw near.] To draw near. [Obs.]

ap″prō-pin-quā'tion, *n.* A drawing nigh. [Rare.]

ap-prō-pin'qui-ty, *n.* Propinquity; nearness. [Rare.]

ap-prō'pre (-pẽr), *v.t.* To appropriate. [Obs.]

ap-prō'pri-ȧ-ble, *a.* Capable of being appropriated, set apart, sequestered, or assigned exclusively to a particular use.

ap-prō'pri-ȧ-ment, *n.* A characteristic peculiar to oneself. [Obs.]

ap-prō'pri-āte, *v.t.*; appropriated, *pt.*, *pp.*; appropriating, *ppr.* [ME. *apropren*; OFr. *aproprier*; Fr. *approprier*; LL. *appropriare*, to appropriate; L. *ad*, to, and *proprius*, one's own.]

1. To set apart for, or assign to, a particular use, in exclusion of all other uses; as, a spot of ground is *appropriated* for a garden; money is *appropriated* by Congress for public buildings. The latter illustrates the common use of the word in the United States, namely, the setting apart of a sum of money for a particular object.

2. To take to oneself in exclusion of others; to claim or use as by an exclusive right; as, let no man *appropriate* the use of a common benefit.

3. To make peculiar; to render suitable; as, to *appropriate* names to ideas. [Rare.]

4. In English ecclesiastical law, to sever (an ecclesiastical benefice) and annex it to a spiritual corporation, for its perpetual use. —Blackstone.

Syn.—Arrogate, assume, seize, usurp.

ap-prō'pri-āte, *a.* Belonging peculiarly; peculiar; set apart for a particular use or person; fit or proper; suitable; as, *appropriate* duties; *appropriate* language; *appropriate* manners.

Syn.—Particular, becoming, congruous, suitable, adapted, peculiar, proper, meet, fit, apt.

ap-prō'pri-āte, *n.* A peculiar characteristic; proper function; property. [Obs.]

ap-prō'pri-āte-ly, *adv.* In an appropriate or proper manner; suitably; fitly.

ap-prō'pri-āte-ness, *n.* Peculiar fitness; the quality of being appropriate, or peculiarly suitable.

ap-prō-pri-ā'tion, *n.* [LL. *appropriatio*, from L. *ad*, to, and *proprius*, one's own.]

1. The act of sequestering, setting apart, or assigning to a particular use or person, or of taking as one's own, to the exclusion of all others; application to a special use or purpose; as of a piece of ground for a park; of a right to oneself; of words to ideas; of a sum of money to a particular purpose or object.

2. In English law, (a) the severing or sequestering of a benefice to the perpetual use of a spiritual corporation; (b) the application of money belonging to a debtor or bankrupt's estate to the payment of a particular debt, when more than one debt is due the same creditor.

3. A sum of money, or any other thing, officially set apart for a given purpose; as, an *appropriation* for street-paving; an *appropriation* for schools.

ap-prō'pri-ā-tive, *a.* Appropriating; pertaining to appropriation; as, an *appropriative* act of Congress.

ap-prō'pri-ā-tive-ness, *n.* The state or quality of being appropriative, or of making appropriations.

ap-prō'pri-ā-tŏr, *n.* 1. One who appropriates.

2. In law, one who is possessed of an appropriated benefice. —Blackstone.

ap-prŏv'ȧ-ble, *a.* Meriting approbation.

ap-prŏv'ȧ-ble-ness, *n.* The quality of being approvable.

ap-prŏv'ăl, *n.* Approbation; sanction.

ap-prŏv'ănce, *n.* Approval. [Obs.]

ap-prŏve', *v.t.*; approved, *pt.*, *pp.*; approving, *ppr.* [ME. *aproven*; OFr. *aprover*; Fr. *approuver*; L. *approbare*, to approve, to assent to as good; *ad*, to, and *probare*, to try, test; from *probus*, good.]

1. To like; to be pleased with; to admit the propriety of; to commend; as, we *approve* the measures of the administration. This word, when it signifies to be pleased, is sometimes followed by *of*, in which use it is intransitive; as, I *approve of* the measure.

2. To prove; to show to be real or true; to justify; to make good. [Obs.]

> Wouldst thou *approve* thy constancy? *Approve*
> First thy obedience. —Milton.

3. To make or show to be worthy of approbation; as, to *approve* oneself to God by righteousness.

4. To demonstrate; to show by proof; to prove practically.

> He had *approved* himself a great warrior. —Macaulay.

5. To improve. [Obs.] —Blackstone.

6. To sanction officially; to ratify; as, to *approve* the decision of a court-martial.

Syn.—Commend, sanction, encourage, authorize, support, promote, praise, admire, ratify.

ap-prŏve', *v.t.* [OFr. *aproer*, to profit.] In English law, to convert to one's own profit; used particularly of waste land appropriated by the lord of the manor for improvement.

ap-prŏv'ed-ly, *adv.* In a manner to gain approval.

ap-prŏve'ment, *n.* 1. Approbation; liking. [Obs.]

2. The act of turning state's evidence. In old English law, when a prisoner confessed a crime before pleading, and appealed or accused his accomplices of the same crime, to obtain his pardon, this confession and accusation were called *approvement* and the person an approver. —Blackstone.

The term is no longer in use; the act represented by *approvement* being now called, in England, turning king's (or queen's) evidence, and in the United States, turning state's evidence.

ap-prŏve'ment, *n.* In old English law, improvement of waste or common lands by inclosing and converting them to the uses of husbandry, for the benefit of the lord of the manor. —Blackstone.

ap-prŏv'ẽr, *n.* 1. One who approves; formerly, one who made proof or trial.

2. In old English law, one who confessed a crime and accused another. [Obs. See *Approvement.*]

3. In old law-writers, a bailiff or steward of a manor.

ap-prŏv'ing, *a.* Yielding, implying, or expressing approbation; as, an *approving* conscience.

ap-prŏv'ing-ly, *adv.* In an approving manner.

ap-prox'i-māte, *a.* 1. Near in time, position, or character.

2. Approaching; closely resembling; proximate.

Approximate quantities; in mathematics, those which are nearly, but not absolutely, equal.

ap-prox'i-māte, *v.t.*; approximated, *pt.*, *pp.*; approximating, *ppr.* [LL. *approximatus*, pp. of *approximare*, to come near; L. *ad*, to, and *proximus*, superl. of *prope*, near.]

1. To carry or advance near; to cause to approach.

> To *approximate* the inequality of riches to the level of nature. —Burke.

2. To come near to; to approach.

> The telescope *approximates* perfection. —J. Morse.

ap-prox'i-māte, *v.i.* To come near; to approach; as, they do not *approximate* in style.

Syn.—Approach, resemble, border, near.

ap-prox'i-māte-ly, *adv.* Nearly; also, by approximation.

ap-prox'i-mā-ting, *a.* Close; resembling; near; approaching.

ap-prox-i-mā'tion, *n.* 1. Approach; a drawing, moving, or advancing near; the act of approximating.

2. The result of approximating; an approach to correctness in estimating, calculating, or conjecturing; a coming near to a given quantity or quality.

3. In mathematics, a continual approach or coming nearer and nearer to a definite result in the process of finding values; also, a result or value that is approximately correct.

ap-prox'i-mā-tive, *a.* Approaching; nearing a correct result; as, *approximative* estimates.

ap-prox'i-mā-tive-ly, *adv.* In an approximative manner.

ap-prox'i-mā-tive-ness, *n.* Closeness to correct results; approximation; the quality or state of being approximative.

ap-prox'i-mā-tŏr, *n.* One who or that which approximates.

ap-puĭ' (-pwē'), *n.* [Fr. *appui*, a support or prop, from *appuyer*, to prop up.]

1. In horsemanship, the reciprocal feeling of support between the mouth of the horse and the hand of the rider or driver.

2. A prop; a support. [Obs.]

Point d'appui; the point of support; a good position for defense; a rallying point; a phrase used in military strategy.

ap-pulse′, *n.* [L. *appulsus*, pp. of *appellere*, to drive forward; *ad*, to, and *pellere*, to strike.]

1. The act of striking against; as, in all consonants there is an *appulse* of the organs.

2. An active or energetic approach; a driving or running upon; impulse, as of a ship.

3. In astronomy, the approach of any planet to a conjunction with the sun or a star.

ap-pul′sion, *n.* The act of striking against by a moving body.

ap-pul′sive, *a.* Striking against; driving toward; as, the *appulsive* influence of the planets.

ap-pul′sive-ly, *adv.* By appulsion.

ap-pŭr′te-năn̄ce, *n.* [ME. *appertenaunce*; OFr. *apertenance*; from L. *ad*, to, and *pertinere*, to reach, extend.] That which belongs to something else; an adjunct; an appendage; as, small buildings are the *appurtenances* of a mansion. In law, such buildings, rights, and improvements as belong to a house or to land are called the *appurtenances*, as outbuildings, gardens, pasturage, etc., to a house, and a right of way or other easement to land. But land can never properly pass as an *appurtenance* to land. In admiralty law, in the United States, the *appurtenances* of a ship include, besides her sails, spars, tackle, etc., all other articles provided for a voyage, though not essential to navigation.

ap-pŭr′te-nănt, *a.* Belonging to or annexed; pertaining to of right; as, a right of way *appurtenant* to land or buildings. —Blackstone.

Common appurtenant; in old English law, that which is annexed to land, and can be claimed only by prescription or immemorial usage, on a legal presumption of a special grant.

ap-pŭr′te-nănt, *n.* An appurtenance.

ȧ-prax′i-ȧ, *n.* [Gr. *apraxia*, inaction, from *a* priv., and *praktos*, from *prassein*, to do, practise.] In pathology, loss of power to recognize objects or their uses, often accompanied by inability to communicate ideas.

ap′ri-ċāte, *v.i.* and *v.t.* [L. *apricari.*] To bask in the sun; to expose to sunlight. [Obs.]

ap-ri-ċā′tion, *n.* The act of basking in the sun; the heat of the sun in winter. [Obs.]

ā′pri-cot, *n.* [OE. *apricock*; Fr. *abricot*; from Sp. *albaricoque*; L. *præcoqua*, from *præ*, beforehand, and *coquere*, to cook.] The fruit of the *Prunus Armeniaca*, natural order *Rosaceae*, growing wild in parts of India, allied to the plum, and of an oval shape and delicious taste. It is cultivated throughout the temperate zone.

Ā′pril, *n.* [Fr. *April*; L. *Aprilis*; from *aperire*, to open.]

1. The fourth month of the English calendar year.

2. Figuratively, used in reference to the sprouting of vegetation in that month or to its changeable weather; hence, the early or hopeful period, as of life; also, a period of emotional inconstancy.

> The *April's* in her eyes; it is love's spring.
> —Shak.

April fool; one who is sportively imposed upon by others on the first of April.

April-fool's day; the first day of April.

ā pri-ō′ri. [*A*, and L. *prior*, comp. of *prius*, first.]

1. Pertaining to or characterized by reasoning which deduces consequences from definitions formed, or principles assumed, or which infers effects from causes previously known; deductive; the reverse of *a posteriori.*

2. Presumptive; without, or before, examination.

3. In philosophy, prior to, and furnishing the basis of, experience; innate, or based upon innate ideas.

ā-pri-ō′riṣm, *n.* An *a priori* principle or method of reasoning.

ā-pri-or′i-ty, *n.* The quality of antecedency in thought.

A-proç′tȧ, *n.pl.* [L., from Gr. *a* priv., and *prōktos*, anus.] One of the divisions of the *Turbellaria*, including those species which are without an anal opening.

ȧ-proç′tous, *a.* Devoid of an anal opening.

ā′pron (ā′pŭrn *or* ā′prun), *n.* [Early Eng. *a napron*, *an apron*; ME. *napron*; OFr. *naperon*, from *nape*, a cloth; L. *mappa*, a cloth.]

1. An article of dress worn by women and men on the front part of the body to keep the clothes clean, to protect them from injury, or as a covering or ornament. It is made of cloth, leather, or fine fabrics, and is usually tied at the waist with strings.

> They sewed fig-leaves together and made themselves *aprons*. —Gen. iii 7.

2. In gunnery, a cap or lid covering the vent of a gun.

3. In shipbuilding, a piece of curved timber just above the foremost end of the keel.

4. A platform or flooring of plank at the entrance of a dock, against which the dock-gates are shut.

5. A piece of leather or other material to be spread before a person riding in a vehicle, to protect him from rain, snow, or dust.

6. A part of the dress of an Anglican bishop, or of the regalia of Freemasons, etc.

7. A platform placed before a dam or sluiceway to cause the water to fall less precipitously.

8. The wedge holding the cutting tool of a plane.

9. In plumbing, a strip of lead to guide the water from a wall into a gutter.

Apron. 2. Lower Apron.

10. The abdomen of the short-tailed decapod crustaceans, as the crab.

11. Any device to protect the banks of rivers, etc., from the action of running water.

12. A piece of boarding, leather, etc., used to conduct loose moving material past an opening, as grain in a separator; also called a *traveling apron.*

ā′proned (ā′pŭrnd *or* ā′prund), *a.* Wearing an apron.

ā′pron-fụl, *n.*; *pl.* **ā′pron-fụlṣ**. The entire contents of an apron.

ā′pron-less, *a.* Not furnished with an apron.

ā′pron=man, *n.* A man who wears an apron; a laboring man; a mechanic. [Obs.]

ā′pron=piēce, *n.* A horizontal piece of timber in the landing of a staircase against which the slanting pieces bearing the steps are supported.

ā′pron=string, *n.* The tie-string of an apron.

To be tied to a woman's apron-strings; to be completely under a woman's control, usually as a son or a husband; to render servile obedience to a woman's wishes.

ap-rō-pōs′ (-pō′), *adv.* [Fr. *à propos*, to the purpose; *à* (L. *ad*), to, and *propos*, from L. *propositum*, purpose, from *proponere*; *pro*, before, and *ponere*, to place.]

1. Opportunely; seasonably; pertinently.

2. By the way; to the purpose; a word used to introduce an incidental observation, suited to the occasion, though not strictly belonging to the narration; usually with *of*; as, *apropos of* your argument, I will tell a story.

ap-rō-pōs′, *a.* Opportune; seasonable; as, an *apropos* remark.

ap-rō-sex′i-ȧ, *n.* [L., from Gr. *aprosexia*, lack of attention.] A condition characterized by lack of the power of mental concentration.

ap-rō-sō′pi-ȧ, *n.* [Gr. *aprosōpos*, without a face; *a* priv., and *prosōpon*, a face.] The condition of being nearly devoid of a face; lacking development of face.

ap-rō-ter′ō-dont, *a.* [Gr. *a* priv., *proteros*, in front, and *odous*, *odontos*, tooth.] Without front teeth, as some serpents.

apse, ap′sis, ab′sis, *n.*; *pl.* **ap′sēṣ, ab′sēṣ.**

1. In architecture, (a) a portion of any building forming a termination or projection semicircular or polygonal in plan, and having a dome or vaulted roof; especially, the vaulted semicircular or polygonal recess at the east end of the choir or chancel of a church, in which the altar is placed; (b) an arched roof, as of a room or of an oven.

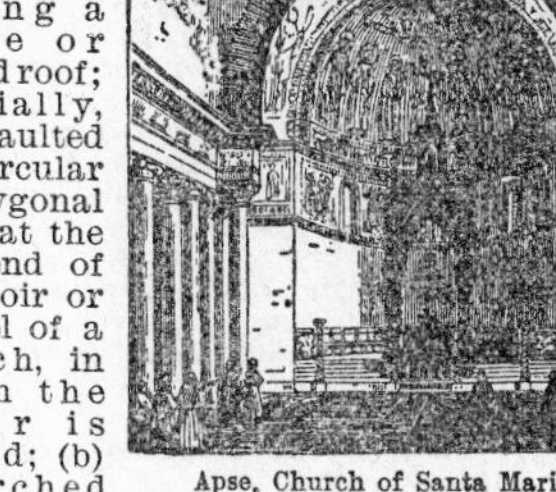

Apse, Church of Santa Maria-in-Trastevere, Rome.

2. A cabinet for preserving mementos of saints.

3. In ancient churches, the bishop's seat or throne.

ap′si-dăl, *a.* 1. Relating to an architectural apse.

2. Pertaining to the apsides of planetary bodies.

ap-sid′i-ōle, ab-sid′i-ōle, *n.* In architecture, a diminutive apse; an apse of an apse.

ap′sis, *n.*; *pl.* **ap′si-dēṣ.** [L. *apsis*, pl. *apsides*, from Gr. *hapsis*, an arch, bow, vault, a tying, fastening, from *haptein*, to fasten.]

1. In astronomy, one of those points in the orbit of a primary planet at its greatest and least distances from the sun; corresponding to the aphelion and the perihelion; one of those points in the orbit of a secondary planet at its greatest and least distances from its primary; corresponding, in relation to the moon, to the apogee and perigee. The more distant is the *higher* and the other the *lower apsis*. The line connecting these is called the *line of the apsides.*

2. In mathematics, a point in a curve with polar coördinates, where the radius vector is either minimum or maximum.

3. In architecture, same as *apse*; the plural form in this case is *apses.*

apt, *a.* [Fr. *apte*; L. *aptus*, pp. of *apere*, to fasten, join, from Gr. *haptein*, to fasten.]

1. Fit; suitable; appropriate; as, he used very *apt* metaphors.

2. Having a usual tendency; usually liable; used of things; as, wheat on moist land is *apt* to blast or be winter-killed.

3. Inclined; disposed customarily; used of persons; as, men are too *apt* to slander others.

4. Quick of perception; quick to learn; ready; prompt; as, an *apt* scholar; an *apt* wit.

5. Qualified; expert.

> All the men of might, strong and *apt* for war
> —2 Kings xxiv. 16.

Syn.—Appropriate, suitable, qualified, inclined, disposed, dexterous, fitted, applicable.—One who is *disposed* or *inclined* to anything is *apt* to do it. He who is *apt* at any employment is *qualified* or *dexterous*. An *apt* quotation is one which is *appropriate*, *suitable*, or *fitted* to the case.

apt, *v.t.* To fit; to suit or adapt. [Obs.]

apt′ȧ-ble, *a.* That may be adapted. [Obs.]

ap′tāte, *v.t.* To make fit. [Obs.]

Ap′te-rȧ, *n.pl.* [L., from Gr. *aptera*, animals without wings.] A suborder of *Insecta*, embracing the wingless insects.

ap′tēr-ăl, *a.* 1. In zoölogy, destitute of wings.

2. In architecture, without lateral columns; applied to buildings which have no series of columns along their sides but are either prostyle or amphiprostyle; opposed to *peripteral.*

ap′tēr-ăn, *n.* One of the suborder *Aptera.*

ap-tē′ri-um, *n.*; *pl.* **ap-tē′ri-ȧ.** [L., from Gr. *apteros*, wingless, without feathers; *a* priv., and *pteron*, wing.] A space on the skin of a bird where there are no feathers.

ap′tēr-oid, *a.* Having some resemblance to a wingless bird; having very small or rudimentary wings.

ap′tēr-ous, *a.* 1. In zoölogy, destitute of wings; applied to insects of the suborder *Aptera.*

2. In botany, destitute of membranous expansions; opposed to *alate.*

Ap-ter′y-ġēṣ, *n.pl.* [L., from Gr. *apterygos*, wingless; *a* priv., and *pteryx*, from *pteron*, a wing.] A suborder of ratite birds, including the family *Apterygidæ.*

Ap-te-ryġ′i-dæ, *n.pl.* A family of ratite birds made up of the one genus *Apteryx.*

Ap′te-ryx, *n.* [Gr. *a* priv., and *pteryx*, wing.]

1. A genus of birds, typical of the family *Apterygidæ.*

2. [a—] One of the birds belonging to this genus, a native of New Zealand, having only short rudiments of wings, and no vestige of a tail.

Apteryx (*Apteryx mantelli*).

apt′i-tūde, *n.* [Fr. *aptitude*; L. *aptitudo*, from *aptus*, fit, apt, pp. of *apere*, to fit, join; Gr. *haptein*, to fasten; Sans. *āpta*, from *ap*, to reach, attain.]

1. A natural or acquired disposition for a particular purpose, or tendency toward particular action or effect; as, oil has an *aptitude* to burn; men acquire an *aptitude* for particular vices.

2. Fitness; suitableness.

3. Aptness; readiness in learning; docility.

apt-i-tū′di-năl, *a.* Having aptitude. [Obs.]

apt′ly, *adv.* In an apt or suitable manner; with proper correspondence of parts; fitly; properly; justly; pertinently; readily.

apt′ness, *n.* 1. Fitness; suitableness; as, the *aptness* of things to their end.

2. Disposition of the mind; propensity; as, the *aptness* of men to follow example.

3. Quickness of apprehension; readiness in learning; docility; as, an *aptness* to learn is more observable in some children than in others.

4. Tendency, in things; as, the *aptness* of iron to rust.

Syn.—Fitness, tendency, adaptability, suitableness, propensity, docility, teachableness, aptitude.

ap-tō″sō-ċhrō′mȧ-tiṣm, *n.* [Gr. *aptōs*, not falling off, from *a* priv., and *piptein*, to fall, and *chrōmatismos*, coloring, from *chrōma*, color.] Change of color without change of feathers, as in some species of birds.

ap′tōte, *n.* [L. *aptotum*, pl. *aptota*, from Gr. *aptōton*, neut. of *aptōtos*, not fallen, undeclined; *a* priv., and *ptōtos*, from *piptein*, to fall.] In grammar, a noun which has no variation of termination or distinction of cases; an indeclinable noun.

ap-tot′iç, *a.* Containing or characterized by aptotes; without inflection; as, an *aptotic* language.

ap-tȳ′ȧ-lişm, *n.* [Gr. *a* priv., and *ptyalismos*, from *ptyalizein*, to spit much, from *ptyein*, to spit.] Inability, total or partial, to secrete saliva.

ap′ty-chus, *n.*; *pl.* **ap′ty-chī**. [L., from Gr. *a* priv., and *ptychos*, a fold, from *ptyssein*, to fold.] A fossil body regarded as the operculum of an ammonite.

A′pus, *n.* [L., from Gr. *apous*; *a* priv., and *pous*, foot.] A genus of phyllopod crustaceans of the subclass *Entomostraca*.

ap-y-ret′iç, *a.* [Gr. *apyretos*, without fever; *a* priv., and *pyretos*, from *pyr*, fire.] Having no fever; applied to periods during the progress of an intermittent fever.

ap-y-rex′i-ȧ, ap′y-rex-y, *n.* [Gr. *apyrexia*; *a* priv., and *pyressein*, to be feverish; from *pyr*, fire.] The temporary cessation of fever.

ap-y-rex′i-ăl, *a.* Pertaining to apyrexia.

ȧ-pȳ′rō-tȳpe, *n.* [Gr. *apyros*, without fire; *a* priv., and *pyr*, fire, and *typos*, a blow, impress, from *typein*, to strike.] Printing-type made with dies from cold metal, instead of by casting in molds.

ȧ-pȳ′rous (*or* ap′y-rous), *a.* [Gr. *apyros*, without fire; *a* priv.,and *pyr*, fire.] Incombustible, or able to sustain a strong heat without alteration of form or properties. *Apyrous* substances differ from those simply refractory. *Refractory* substances cannot be fused by heat, but may be altered.

ā′quȧ (-kwȧ), *n.* [L.] Water; a term much used in pharmacy and the old chemistry in various significations, determined by the word or words annexed.

Aqua ammonia; liquid ammonia.

Aqua fortis; the old name for nitric acid.

Aqua marina; same as *Aquamarine*.

Aqua pura; pure or distilled water.

Aqua regia; the old name for nitro-muriatic acid.

Aqua Tofana; a poison containing arsenic prepared by an Italian woman named Tofana in the seventeenth century. By its means she is said to have killed some six hundred persons.

Aqua vitæ; literally, water of life; a name given to all distilled alcoholic beverages.

ā″quæ-mȧ-nā′lē, ā″quȧ-mȧ-ni′lē, *n.* [L. *aquæmanalis*, a washbowl; *aqua*, water, and *manus*, hand.]

1. The basin in which, according to an ancient church ceremony, the priest washed his hands before celebrating mass.

2. A name applied to vessels of the ewer kind, formerly used in private houses, and frequently made into grotesque forms representing a real or fabulous animal, or the like.

Aquæmanale.

ā″quȧ-mȧ-rïne′, *n.* [L. *aqua marina*, sea-water.]

1. A variety of beryl; so called on account of its color.

2. A sea-green color; a pigment.

ȧ-quȧ-plāne, *n.* [L. *aqua*, water, and *planus*, plane.] An apparatus towed by a motor-boat, on which one may glide over the water.

ā-quȧ-punç′tūre, *n.* [L. *aqua*, water, and *punctura*, from *pungere*, to prick.] In medicine, counter-irritation by the projection of a fine jet of water against the skin, for the alleviation of pain.

aq-uȧ-relle′ (ak-wȧ-rel′), *n.* [Fr., from It. *acquerella*, water-color, from *acqua*, water; L. *aqua*, water.] The process of making pictures by means of thin water-colors; also, a picture made by this process; as, a scene in *aquarelle*.

aq-uȧ-rel′list, *n.* One who makes pictures in aquarelle.

ȧ-quā′ri-ăn, ȧ-quā′ri-ăl, *a.* Relating to an aquarium, or to aquariums.

A-quā′ri-ăn, *n.* One of a sect of early Christians who substituted water for wine in the celebration of the Lord's Supper.

ȧ-quā′ri-um, *n.*; *pl.* **ȧ-quā′ri-umş** or **ȧ-quā′ri-ȧ**. [L., neut. of *aquarius*, pertaining to water, from *aqua*, water.] An artificial pond, tank, glass globe, etc., for the care and exhibition of living specimens of aquatic plants and animals; also, a building containing *aquariums*.

A-quā′ri-us, *n.* [L., the water-carrier, from *aqua*, water.]

1. In astronomy, the Water-bearer; the eleventh sign of the zodiac.

2. A zodiacal constellation south of Pegasus.

ȧ-quar′tẽr, *adv.* In navigation, in a course 45° abaft the beam; on the quarter.

ȧ-quat′iç, *a.* [L. *aquaticus*, from *aqua*, water.]

1. Of or pertaining to water.

2. Growing, living, or feeding in, or swimming on, water; as, *aquatic* fowl.

ȧ-quat′iç, *n.* A plant that grows, or an animal that lives, in water.

ȧ-quat′iç-ăl, *a.* Aquatic.

ȧ-quat′içs, *n.pl.* The exercises and sports practised in or upon water, as swimming, rowing, yachting, etc.

aq′uȧ-tile, *a.* Inhabiting water; aquatic. [Rare.]

ā′quȧ-tint, ā-quȧ-tin′tȧ, *n.* [Fr. *aquatinte*; It. *acqua tinta*, dyed in water; *acqua*, from L. *aqua*, water, and *tinta*, from L. *tintus*, pp. of *tingere*, to dye, tinge.]

1. A method of engraving or etching by means of aqua fortis, by which an effect is produced resembling a drawing in water-colors or India ink.

2. An engraving in the *aquatint* method.

ā′quȧ-tint, *a.* Pertaining to the process of etching known as *aquatint*.

ā′quȧ-tint, *v.i.* To etch in *aquatint*.

aq′uē-duçt, *n.* [OFr. *aqueduct*; L. *aquæductus*, a conveyance of water; *aquæ*, genit. of *aqua*, water, and *ductus*, a channel,leading, from *ducere*, to lead.]

Aqueduct at Segovia, Spain.

1. A conductor, conduit,canal,or other channel, open or inclosed, for conveying water, especially one for conveying the water-supply of cities.

2. An ancient structure raised on one or more series of arches and sustaining one or more channels for water, built on a slightly descending plane.

3. A structure somewhat similar to the ancient *aqueducts*, for conveying a water-channel or conduit over a river or hollow; called also an *aqueduct-bridge*; as High Bridge, the old Croton *aqueduct* over the Harlem River in New York.

4. In anatomy, a term applied to certain canals occurring in different parts of the body.

ā-quē′i-ty, *n.* Wateriness; moistness. [Obs.]

ā″quē-ō-ig′nē-ous, *a.* [L. *aqua*, water, and *igneus*, from *ignis*, fire.] In geology, pertaining to or characterized by the joint effect of water and heat; as, *aqueo-igneous* rocks.

ā′quē-ous, *a.* [L. *aquosus*, watery, from *aqua*, water.]

1. Watery; partaking of the nature of water, or abounding with it.

2. Made by means of water; as, an *aqueous* solution.

3. Formed by settlings; sedimentary; as, *aqueous* rocks.

Aqueous extract; an extract obtained by soaking or boiling a vegetable substance in water.

Aqueous humor; in anatomy, one of the humors of the eye; a transparent, limpid fluid, occupying the space, divided into two chambers by the iris, between the crystalline lens and the cornea.

Aqueous lava; a kind of muddy lava formed during or after the eruption of a volcano by the commingling of volcanic ashes with water formed by the condensation of cooling volcanic vapors.

Aqueous rocks; rocks composed of matter deposited by water and laid in strata, as distinguished from igneous rocks.

Aqueous tint; in painting, a very light, almost colorless, tint.

ā′quē-ous-ness, *n.* The quality of being watery; wateriness.

ā-qui-çul′tūr-ăl, *a.* Pertaining to aquiculture.

ā′qui-çul-tūre, *n.* [Fr. *aquiculture*, from L. *aqua*, water, and *cultura*, from *colere*, to cultivate.] The cultivation of any animal organism native in fresh or salt water.

ā-quif′ẽr-ous, *a.* [L. *aqua*, water, and *ferre*, to bear.] Conducting or containing water or watery fluid; as, the *aquiferous* system of the sponges.

A″qui-fō″li-ā′cē-æ, *n.pl.* [L. *aquifolium*, the holly, from *acus*, needle, and *folium*, leaf.] In botany, an old name for the holly family.

ā″qui-fō″li-ā′ceous, *a.* Of or pertaining to the *Aquifoliaceæ*.

ā′qui-fọrm, *a.* [L. *aqua*, water, and *forma*, form.] In the form of water; like water.

Aq′ui-lȧ, *n.* [L., eagle.]

1. In ornithology, a genus of raptorial birds containing the true eagles.

2. In astronomy, a northern constellation in the Milky Way, containing about eighty stars that range from first to sixth magnitude.

3. [a—] A reading-desk or lectern shaped like an eagle.

Aq-ui-lā′ri-ȧ, *n.* [L. *aquila*, eagle.] A typical genus of evergreen trees belonging to the family *Thymelæaceæ*, found in eastern parts of Asia and the Malay group, and having tough bark, alternate leaves, and pear-shaped fruit in a valved capsule.

aq′ui-lā-ted, *a.* In heraldry, ornamented with eagles' heads; as, a cross *aquilated*.

Aq-ui-lē′gi-ȧ, *n.* [L. *aquila*, eagle.] In botany, a genus of perennial plants of the crowfoot family (*Ranunculaceæ*), found in the north temperate zone, and characterized by showy flowers with five-spurred petals; called also *columbines*.

Aq-ui-lī′næ, *n.pl.* In ornithology, a conventional subfamily of falconoid birds; the eagles.

aq′ui-line (*or* -lin), *a.* [L. *aquilinus*, from *aquila*, eagle.]

1. Belonging to the eagle.

2. Curving; hooked; prominent, like the beak of an eagle; as, an *aquiline* nose.

Aq′ui-lon, *n.* [Fr. *aquilon*; L. *aquilo*, the north wind.] The north wind personified. [Rare.]

ȧ-quip′ȧ-rous, *a.* [L. *aqua*, water, and *parere*, to yield.] In anatomy, secreting a watery substance, as certain glands.

Aq-ui-tā′ni-ăn, *a.* Pertaining to Aquitania, afterward called Gascony, one of the great divisions of Gaul, which, according to Cæsar, lay between the Garonne River, the Pyrenees, and the ocean.

ȧ-quiv′ẽr, *a.* Agitated; tremulous; quivering.

ȧ-quiv′ẽr, *adv.* In an agitated manner; quiveringly.

ā″quō-çap-sū-li′tis, *n.* [L. *aqua*, water, *capsula*, box, and *-itis*.] In medicine, watery inflammation of the chamber-linings of the eye.

ā-quom′e-tẽr, *n.* [L. *aqua*, water, and *metrum*, Gr. *metron*, a measure.] A device in the form of a pump acting both by steam and vacuum, for lifting and forcing water.

ā′quōse, *a.* Watery. [Rare.]

ā-quos′i-ty, *n.* The state of being watery; moistness.

aq′uū-lȧ (ak′wū-lȧ), *n.* [L., a little stream; dim. of *aqua*, water.]

1. In anatomy, a small quantity of watery matter.

2. The aqueous humor of the eye.

3. The crystalline lens of the eye.

är, *conj.* Ere; before. [Obs.]

-ar, *suffix.* [ME. *-er*; OFr. *-er*, *-ier*, *-air*; Fr. *-aire*; L. *-aris*; in nouns, *-are*; used for *-alis*, when *l* precedes.]

1. A combining form signifying pertaining to or like, as in singul*ar*, regul*ar*, schol*ar*.

2. A variation of *-ary* or *-er*, as in vic*ar*, which in old English was vik*er* or vic*ary*.

3. A variant form of *-er*, as in begg*ar*, begg*er*, li*ar*, li*er*.

A′rȧ, *n.* [L.] In astronomy, the constellation of the Altar, which may be seen south of the Scorpion.

A′rȧ, *n.* [Native Braz. name.] In ornithology, a genus of South American birds, including the macaw; the type genus of the *Arinæ*.

Ar′ăb, *n.* [L. *Arabs*; Gr. *Araps*; Ar. *'Arab*; Heb. *arabah*, a desert.]

1. A native of Arabia, or a member of the Arabic division of the Semitic race.

2. [a—] A neglected outcast of the streets, particularly a homeless boy or girl; called also *street arab*.

Ar′ăb, *a.* Of or pertaining to the Arabs or Arabia; as, an *Arab* steed.

ȧ-rä′bȧ, *n.* [Bulg. *araba*; Hind. and Pers. *arāba*; Turk. and Ar. *'arabah*, a cart.] An Indian or Turkish cart drawn by oxen or cows, and used for traveling; sometimes richly ornamented but without springs; called also *aroba*.

Cinque-cento Arabesque, from tomb in Church of S. Pietro-in-Vinculo, Rome.

ar′ȧ-bä, *n.* See *Araguato*.

ar-ȧ-bä′tȧ, *n.* Same as *Araguato*.

ar-ȧ-besque′ (-besk′), *a.* [Fr. *arabesque*; It. *arabesco*; Port. *arabesco*, from *Arabo*, an Arab.]

1. Arabian.

2. Relating to or exhibiting the ornamentations described as *arabesques*.

ar-ȧ-besque′, *n.* In decorative art, a term applied to paintings, inlaid work, and carvings in low relief containing fanciful groupings of plant and animal forms, and often human figures, fantastically intertwined with lines and geometrical patterns. This kind of ornamentation is found in Greek, Roman, and Renaissance art. The *arabesques* of the Moors, who are prohibited by their religion from representing animal forms, consist essentially of complicated ornamental designs based on the suggestion of plant-growth, combined with extremely complex geometrical forms.

ar-ȧ-besqued′ (-beskt′), *a.* Ornamented in arabesque fashion.

ar-ȧ-besque′ly, *adv.* In the manner of arabesque ornamentation.

Ȧ-rā′bi-ăn, *a.* Pertaining to Arabia; belonging to Arabia.

Arabian architecture; a term generally applied to the examples of Mohammedan, Moorish, or Saracenic architecture found in Egypt and Syria.

Ȧ-rā′bi-ăn, *n.* 1. A native of Arabia; an Arab.

2. In church history, one of the Arabici.

Ar′ȧ-biç, *a.* Belonging to Arabia, or the language of its inhabitants.

Arabic numerals; the nine digits and the cipher (0), the numeral characters used in our arithmetic. They were introduced into Europe from Arabia during the twelfth century, being taken from the work of Al-Khowarazmi. The system as now known originated in India; but the source of the separate characters and their history remain a mystery.

Gum arabic; see under *Gum.*

Ar′ȧ-biç, *n.* The language of the Arabians. It is a Semitic language, like the Hebrew, and is the language of the Koran.

Ȧ-rab′iç-ăl, *a.* Arabic.

Ȧ-rab′iç-ăl-ly, *adv.* In an Arabic or Arabian manner.

Ȧ-rab′i-cī, *n.pl.* In church history, a Christian sect of the third century whose members asserted that the body and soul are equally affected by death and resurrection. The sect existed in Perea, beyond the Jordan, often regarded as part of Arabia.

ar-ȧ-bil′i-ty, *n.* The state of being arable.

ar′ȧ-bin, *n.* In chemistry, a white, soluble substance, the principal constituent of gum arabic.

ar′ȧ-bin-ōse, *n.* In chemistry, a sugar prepared by the action of sulphuric acid on arabin. It crystallizes and is non-fermentable.

ar″ȧ-bin-ō′siç, *a.* Pertaining to arabinose.

Ar′ȧ-bis, *n.* [L., from Gr. *Arabis*, Arabian, from *Arabia*, Arabia.] In botany, a genus of plants of the cruciferous order, found in the north temperate regions of both hemispheres, and having clusters of purple or white flowers; called also *rock-cress.*

Ar′ȧ-biṣm, *n.* An Arabic idiom or peculiarity of language.

Ar′ȧ-bist, *n.* One versed in the Arabic language or literature.

ar′ȧ-ble, *a.* and *n.* [Fr. *arable*; L. *arabilis*, from *arare*, to plow.]

I. *a.* Fit for plowing or tillage; cultivable; as, *arable* land.

II. *n.* Land suitable for tillage.

Ar′ȧ-by, *n.* Arabia; poetically, a land of sweet delightsomeness. [Rare.]

Ar″ȧ-çȧ-nēṣe′, Ar″ȧ-kȧ-nēṣe′, *n., sing.* and *pl.* 1. A native or an inhabitant, or natives or inhabitants, of Aracan or Arakan, a province of British Burma.

2. [*sing.*] The language spoken by the Aracanese.

Ar″ȧ-çȧ-nēṣe′, *a.* Pertaining to Aracan, or Arakan, or to its inhabitants.

ä-rä-çä′rï, *n.* [Port. *aracari*, from the native name.] A name of the birds belonging to the genus *Pteroglossus*, included in the *Ramphastidæ* or toucan family, but differing from the typical toucans by a smaller bill and smaller size; native to the warm parts of South America.

ȧ-rāce′, *v.t.* [ME. *aracen*; OFr. *aracier, arachier*, from L. *exradicare, eradicare*, to root out; *ex*, out, and *radicare*, from *radix, radicis*, root.] To tear up by the roots. [Obs.]

Ȧ-rā′cē-æ, *n.pl.* [L., from *arum*; Gr. *aron*, the wake-robin, and *-aceæ.*] A natural order of monocotyledonous plants, having the genus *Arum* as the type. The species are herbaceous, with leaves sheathing at the base; the flowers are unisexual and without a perianth, on a spadix protected, when young, by a spathe; the anthers are nearly sessile, and the fruit succulent. Most of the species have tuberous roots abounding in starch, which forms a wholesome food after the acrid juice has been washed out.

Araceæ.
Wake-robin or Cuckoo-pint (*Arum maculatum*). *a*, Spadix; *bb*, Stamens or male-flowers; *cc*, Ovaries or female flowers; *d*, Spathe or sheath; *e*, Cormus.

ȧ-rā′ceus, *a.* Pertaining to the natural order of plants *Araceae.*

Ar′ȧ-çhis, *n.* [L., from Gr. *arakis*, name of a plant.] A genus of leguminous food-plants much cultivated in warm climates; remarkable for the fact that when the flower falls, the stalk supporting the ovaries lengthens, and bending downward, pushes the fruit into the ground, where it begins to enlarge and ripen. The best-known species is *Arachis hypogæa*, the common peanut.

ar-aċh-naç′tis, *n.* [L., from Gr. *arachnē*, spider, and *aktis*, ray.] A name given to the free-swimming young of certain sea-anemones.

ar-aċh-nē′ăn, *a.* [Gr. *arachnē*, a spider.] Web-like; filmy; gossamery.

ȧ-raċh′nid, *n.* An arachnidan.

Ȧ-raċh′ni-dȧ, *n.pl.* [L., from Gr. *arachnē*, spider.] A class of arthropods without wings or antennæ, including spiders, mites, and scorpions.

ȧ-raċh′ni-dăn, *a.* Pertaining to the *Arachnida.*

ȧ-raċh′ni-dăn, *n.* One of the *Arachnida.*

ar-aċh-nid′i-ȧ, *n.*, pl. of *arachnidium.*

ar-aċh-nid′i-ăl, *a.* Relating to the *Arachnida.*

ar-aċh-nid′i-um, *n.*, *pl.* **ar-aċh-nid′i-ȧ.** The gland of a spider having for its function the secretion of a sticky, semifluid substance spun into the web.

ar-aċh-nī′tis, *n.* Inflammation of the arachnoid membrane.

ȧ-raċh′noid, *a.* 1. Like a cobweb; filmy; gossamery.

2. In botany, consisting of soft fibers or hairs, so as to appear like a cobweb.

3. Relating to the *Arachnida.*

4. In anatomy, of or pertaining to the arachnoid membrane.

Arachnoid membrane; a very thin and delicate semitransparent membrane, spread over the brain and the spinal cord between the *dura mater* and *pia mater.*

ȧ-raċh′noid, *n.* 1. In zoölogy, one of the class *Arachnida.*

2. In anatomy, the arachnoid membrane.

ar-aċh-noid′ăl, *a.* Arachnoid.

Ar-aċh-noid′ē-ȧ, *n.pl.* The *Arachnida.* [Obs.]

ȧ-raċh-nō-loġ′iç-ăl, *a.* Relating to arachnology.

ar-aċh-nol′ō-ġist, *n.* One versed in arachnology.

ar-aċh-nol′ō-ġy, *n.* [Gr. *arachnē*, spider, and *logia*, from *legein*, to speak.] The science of spiders and other *Arachnida.*

ar-aċh-noph′ȧ-gous, *a.* [Gr. *arachnē*, spider, and *phagein*, to eat.] In zoölogy, preying upon arachnids.

ā-ræ-om′e-tēr, *n.* See *Areometer.*

ā-ræ′ō-stȳle, *a.* and *n.* Same as *Areostyle.*

ā-ræ-ō-sys′tȳle, *a.* and *n.* Same as *Areosystyle.*

Ar″ȧ-gō-nēṣe′, *n.* and *a.* I. *n., sing.* and *pl.* A native or inhabitant, or the natives or inhabitants of Aragon, in Spain.

II. *a.* Relating to Aragon or its people.

ȧ-rag′ō-nīte, *n.* [From *Aragon*, in Spain, and *-ite.*] A dimorphous form of carbonate of lime, occurring in orthorhombic crystals.

är-ä-guä′tō (-gwä′tō), *n.* [S. Am.] A species of monkey found in South America; the ursine howler, *Mycetes ursinus.* Also called *araba*, etc.

ȧ-rāiṣe′, *v.t.* To raise. [Obs.]

ar′ak, *n.* Same as *Arrack.*

Ȧ-rā′li-ȧ, *n.* [Origin unknown.] A genus of plants, the type of the order *Araliaceæ*, eight species of which are found in North America.

Ȧ-rā-li-ā′cē-æ, *n.pl.* An order of plants, indigenous to warm climates, akin to the *Umbelliferæ*, but of a more shrubby character. The ginseng and the English ivy are two well-known genera of this order.

ȧ-rā-li-ā′ceous, *a.* Belonging or pertaining to the order *Araliaceæ.*

Ar-ȧ-mæ′ăn, *a.* and *n.* See *Aramean.*

Ar-ȧ-mā′iç, *a.* [Gr. *Aramaia*, f. of *Aramaios*, from Heb. *'Arām*, a name given to Syria, and Mesopotamia.] A term applied to the people, country, language, and literature of Syria and Mesopotamia; specifically to that branch of Semitic tongues to which the Syriac and Chaldee belonged.

Ar-ȧ-mā′iç, *n.* 1. The northern branch of the family of Semitic languages, most of which are now dead, including the languages of the cuneiform inscriptions of the Babylonians and Assyrians.

2. The language of Palestine after the captivity, in which tongue Christ and his disciples spoke.

Ar-ȧ-mā′iṣm, *n.* An idiom of the Aramaic language; also written *Arameanism, Aramism.*

Ar-ȧ-mē′ăn, Ar-ȧ-mæ′ăn, *a.* Pertaining to the ancient countries, Aram and Aramæa, to their people, the Syrians and Chaldeans, or to their language.

Ar-ȧ-mē′ăn, Ar-ȧ-mæ′ăn, *n.* A native or inhabitant of Aram or Aramæa; also, the Aramaic language.

Ar-ȧ-mē′ăn-iṣm, *n.* See *Aramaism.*

Ar′ȧ-mism, *n.* See *Aramaism.*

Ar-ȧ-nē′i-dȧ, *n.pl.* [L. *aranea*, spider.] An order of *Arachnida*, including the spiders. They have the abdomen unsegmented and connected with the thorax by a narrow peduncle. They breathe by means of pulmonary sacs and two stigmata connected with tracheæ, and have from four to six spinnerets for making the silken threads from which their webs are spun.

Ar-ȧ-nē′i-dæ, *n.pl.* The spider family, a tribe of the pulmonary order of arachnidans and containing the true spinning spiders.

ar-ȧ-nē′i-dăn, *a.* and *n.* I. *a.* Relating to the *Araneida*, especially to the spiders.

II. *n.* One of the *Araneida.*

Ar-ȧ-nē-i-dē′ȧ, *n.pl.* Same as *Araneida.*

ar-ȧ-nē′i-fọrm, *a.* [L. *aranea*, spider, and *forma*, form.] Having the shape of a spider.

Ȧ-rā-nē-ī′nȧ, *n.pl.* Same as *Araneida.*

Ar-ȧ-nē-oid′e-ȧ, *n.pl.* Same as *Araneida.*

ȧ-rā′nē-ōse, *a.* [L. *araneosus*, full of or like spider's web, from *aranea*, spider.] Resembling the web of a spider; arachnoid.

ȧ-rā′nē-ous, *a.* Like the web of a spider; as, the *araneous* membrane of the eye.

ȧ-ran′gō, *n.*; *pl.* **ȧ-ran′gōeṣ** (-gōz). [Native name.] A rough bead made of carnelian, imported from Bombay and used extensively by slave-traders in the days of the African slave-trade.

ȧ-rä-pai′mȧ, *n.* [Native name.] The largest known fresh-water food-fish; found in South America. It frequently measures fifteen feet in length, and sometimes weighs more than 400 pounds.

Ar-ȧ-pun′gȧ, *n.* [S. Am. native name.] A genus of South American dentirostral insessorial birds, the chatterers, including the curious white bell-bird or campanero, *Arapunga alba*, remarkable for its clear, far-sounding, bell-like notes, and for the strange tubular horn-like structure which grows on its forehead. When this structure is empty of air it is pendulous, but rises to the height of three inches when the bird is excited. As the horn has a communication with the palate, it has probably something to do with the peculiar sound of the bird's voice.

Head of Arapunga or Bell-bird (*Arapunga alba*).

ȧ-rä′rȧ, *n.* The native name for the black macaw or palm cockatoo of Australia.

ar-ȧ-rō′bȧ, *n.* Same as *Goa powder.*

ȧ-rā′tion, *n.* Tillage. [Rare.]

ar′ȧ-tō-ry, *a.* [L. *aratorius*, from *arator*, a plower, from *arare*, to plow.] Pertaining to tillage.

Ar-au-cā′ri-ȧ, *n.* [L., from the *Araucanos*, a tribe of Indians in the southern parts of Chile.] A genus of *Coniferæ*, found in South America and Australasia, being large evergreen trees with verticillate spreading branches, and bearing large cones, each scale having a single large seed.

ar-au-cā′ri-ăn, *a.* and *n.* I. *a.* Pertaining to the *Araucaria.*

II. *n.* Any tree of the genus *Araucaria.*

är′bȧ-list, är′bȧ-lest, *n.* [ME. *arbaleste*; Port. *arbalesta*, from L. *arcuballista*; *arcus*, bow, and *ballista*, an engine for hurling projectiles; from Gr. *ballein*, to throw.] A crossbow very common in Europe during the middle ages, consisting of a steel bow set in a shaft of wood, furnished with a string and a trigger, and bent by a crank-windlass.

är′bȧ-list-ēr, är′bȧ-lest-ēr, *n.* [ME. *arbalester*; OFr. *arbalestier*; L. *arcubalistarius*, one who uses an arcubalist.] A crossbowman. [Obs.]

är′bi-tēr, *n.* [L. *arbiter*, a witness, judge, from *ar-*, *ad*, to, and *bitere*, *betere*, to come or go.]

1. In civil law, a person appointed, or chosen, to decide a controversy; an arbitrator.

2. One who has the power of judging; one whose power of deciding and governing is not limited.

Syn.—Adjudicator, arbitrator, umpire, referee, judge.

är′bi-tēr, *v.t.* To act as arbiter for; to judge. [Obs.]

är′bi-trȧ-ble, *a.* 1. Arbitrary; depending on the will. [Obs.]

2. Subject to arbitration.

är′bi-trāġe, *n.* [Fr. *arbitrage*, from *arbitrer*; L. *arbitrari*, to give a decision, from *arbiter*, a witness, judge.]

1. Arbitration. [Rare.]

2. A strictly stock-exchange business, consisting of the calculation of relative values of securities, stocks, and shares at different places at the same time, with the view of speculative profit, through differences in payments, favorable or unfavorable circumstances, etc.

är′bi-trăl, *a.* Relating to an arbitrator or arbitration. [Rare.]

är-bit′rȧ-ment, *n.* 1. Determination; the final decision of an arbitrator; also, the power to make an absolute and final decision; as, the *arbitrament* of war.

2. The award of arbitrators.

är′bi-trā-ri-ly, *adv.* In an arbitrary manner.

är′bi-trā-ri-ness, *n.* The quality of being arbitrary; despotic caprice.

är-bi-trā′ri-ous, *a.* Arbitrary; despotic. [Obs.]

är-bi-trā′ri-ous-ly, *adv.* Arbitrarily. [Obs.]

är′bi-trā-ry, *a.* [L. *arbitrarius*, from *arbiter*, a witness, judge.]

1. Not governed by principle; depending on volition; capricious; tyrannical; despotic.

> *Arbitrary* power is most easily established on the ruins of liberty abused to licentiousness.
> —Washington.

2. In law, left to the discretion or judgment; not fixed; not determined by statute; as, *arbitrary* fines.

Arbitrary constant, or *function*; in mathematics, a function given an assigned value in order to solve a special problem.

Arbitrary quantity; in mathematics, a quantity whose assigned value varies by choice and exigency.

Syn.—Tyrannical, imperious, unlimited, capricious, absolute, positive, despotic, peremptory, tyrannous.

är′bi-trāte, *v.t.*; arbitrated, *pt.*, *pp.*; arbitrating, *ppr.* [L. *arbitratus*, pp. of *arbitrari*, to see, give a decision, from *arbiter*, a witness, judge.]

1. To hear and decide, as arbitrators; as, to *arbitrate* a dispute.

2. To decide or determine by arbitration; to surrender to arbitration.

Syn.—Settle, adjust, compose, decide, determine, accommodate, adjudicate.

är′bi-trāte, *v.i.* 1. To decide; to determine.

2. To act as arbitrator.

är-bi-trā′tion, *n.* The hearing and determination of a cause between parties in controversy, by a person or persons chosen by the parties.

A board of *arbitration* usually consists of an odd number of persons chosen equally by the opposing sides, excepting the *umpire* or odd man, who is the choice of the arbitrators before chosen. An award in writing, signed by a majority of the board, is usually binding.

Arbitration bond; a bond which is generally entered into by parties wishing to submit their differences to arbitration. It binds them to acquiesce in the award given. —Blackstone.

Arbitration court; a permanent court, for the arbitration of international disputes, which was provided for by an international arbitration treaty adopted by the accredited representatives of all the great maritime powers, at a "Universal Peace Conference" held at The Hague in 1899. The treaty was subsequently ratified by all the governments whose representatives participated in the conference.

Arbitration of exchange; the fixing of the ratio of exchange of the moneys of two countries; also, the changing of money of one country to that of another.

Arbitration treaty; a treaty for the adjustment of differences between nations. The United States has been a party to more arbitration treaties than any other nation, having within the last hundred years settled by this means more than forty international disputes.

är′bi-trā-tŏr, *n.* [L. *arbitrator*, from *arbitrari*, to see, give judgment, from *arbiter*, a witness, judge.]

1. A person who is chosen by agreement of parties in a controversy, to settle the dispute; or, one of two or more persons so chosen.

2. An arbiter; one who has absolute power to decide any matter.

Syn.—Arbiter, judge, umpire.

är′bi-trā-trix, *n.* A woman who arbitrates; also, a woman who has entire control, as in the settlement of an estate.

är′bi-tress, *n.* A female arbiter.

är′blȧst, *n.* Same as *Arbalist.*

är′bŏr, är′bŏur, *n.* [ME. *erber*, *herber*; OFr. *erbier*, *herbier*; from L. *herbarium*, a place covered with grass or herbage, from *herba*, grass, a herb.] A frame of latticework, covered with vines, or other plants, for shade; a bower.

är′bŏr, *n.* [L., a tree, a beam.]

1. In botany, a tree, as distinguished from a shrub.

2. In mechanics, the principal spindle or axis which communicates motion to the rest of the machinery; called also the *shaft*, or *mandrel.*

Arbor day; a day appointed by law, in many states of the United States, for the planting of trees by the pupils of the public schools and others, to foster interest in the preservation of forests; in Canada, the first Friday in May.

är′bō-rā-ry, *a.* [L. *arborarius*, from *arbor*, a tree.] Belonging to a tree or trees.

är′bō-rā-tŏr, *n.* One who plants or who prunes trees. [Obs.]

är-bō′rē-ăl, *a.* 1. Pertaining to or of the nature of trees.

2. Living in or found among trees; pertaining to life in woods or among trees; as, *arboreal* animals; *arboreal* pursuits.

är′bōred, *a.* Furnished with an arbor, or bower; as, an *arbored* garden.

är-bō′rē-ous, *a.* [L. *arboreus*, from *arbor*, a tree.]

1. Belonging to, or growing on, a tree; resembling a tree; as, *arboreous* moss.

2. Forming a trunk and having the habits or constitution of a tree, as distinguished from a shrub.

är-bō-res′cence, *n.* [L. *arborescens*, ppr. of *arborescere*, to become a tree, from *arbor*, a tree.] The state of having the figure of a tree; resemblance to a tree in minerals, or crystallizations.

är-bō-res′cent, *a.* 1. Resembling a tree; having the figure of a tree; dendritic.

2. Becoming woody in stalk.

är′bō-ret, *n.* [It. *arboreto*, from L. *arbor*, a tree.] A small tree or shrub; a place planted or overgrown with trees. [Obs.]

är-bō-rē′tum, *n.*; *pl.* **är-bō-rē′tȧ.** [L., a place grown with trees, from *arbor*, a tree.] A place in a park or nursery where rare trees and shrubs are propagated; a botanical or tree-garden cultivated for scientific purposes.

är-bor′iç-ăl, *a.* Relating to trees. [Obs.]

är-bor′i-cōle, *a.* [Fr. *arboricole*, from L. *arbor*, a tree, and *colere*, to dwell, inhabit.] Inhabiting trees, as birds of various kinds.

är-bō-riç′ō-line, *a.* Growing upon trees, as certain parasitic plants, lichens, etc.

är″bor-i-çul′tūr-ăl, *a.* Relating to arboriculture.

är″bor-i-çul′tūre, *n.* [Fr. *arboriculture*, from L. *arbor*, tree, and *cultura*, culture.] The art of cultivating trees and shrubs, chiefly for timber or ornamental purposes.

är″bor-i-çul′tūr-ist, *n.* One who cultivates trees.

är-bor′i-fọrm, *a.* Having the form of a tree.

är′bŏr-ist, *n.* One who makes trees his study, or who is versed in the knowledge of trees.

är″bor-i-zā′tion, *n.* The appearance or figure of a tree or plant, as in minerals or fossils.

är′bŏr-ized, *a.* Resembling a tree.

är′bŏr-ous, *a.* Consisting of trees. [Obs.]

är′bŏr-vine, *n.* A species of bindweed, a climber native to the West Indies.

är″bŏr-vī′tæ, *n.* [L., tree of life.]

1. An evergreen tree, extensively planted for ornament and for hedges, the species common to America being the *Thuja occidentalis.*

2. In anatomy, a dendriform arrangement which appears in the medullary substance of the brain when the cerebellum is cut vertically.

är′bus-cle (-bus-sl), *n.* [L. *arbusculus*, a little tree, dim. of *arbor*, tree.] A dwarf tree, or one in size between a shrub and a tree.

är-bus′çū-lăr, *a.* Resembling a shrub; having the shape of a small tree.

är-bus′çūle, *n.* In zoölogy, a tuft of small, vibratory swimming organs, or hairlike processes; a gill with fine branches.

är-bus′tive, *a.* [L. *arbustivus*, from *arbustum*, a place where trees are planted.] Containing copses of trees or shrubs; covered with shrubs.

är′būte, *n.* The strawberry-tree.

är-bū′tus, *n.* [L. *arbutus*, the wild strawberry-tree.]

1. Any plant of the genus *Arbutus.*

2. [A—] A genus of evergreen plants belonging to the natural order *Ericaceæ.* It has panicles of large, pale greenish-white flowers and red fruit, which, with the evergreen leaves, are especially beautiful in the months of October and November.

Trailing arbutus; a creeping or trailing plant, *Epigæa repens*, with rose-colored blossoms, found chiefly in New England in the spring; the mayflower, or ground-laurel.

ärç, *n.* [Fr. *arc*, from L. *arcus*, a bow, arch.]

1. In geometry, any part of a curve; a segment of a circle.

2. In architecture, an arch, used in French phrases. [Rare.]

3. In astronomy, a segment of the apparent circle of a heavenly body.

Arc lamp; a lamp in which the light is produced by a voltaic arc.

Arc light; light produced by the voltaic arc; an arc lamp.

Voltaic arc; a luminous arc between two carbon electrodes barely separated, the pencils of carbon forming terminals in the circuit. [See *Electric lamp*, under *Electric.*]

ärç, *v.i.* In electricity, to discharge in voltaic arc form.

är′çȧ, *n.*; *pl.* **är′cæ.** [L., a box or coffin.]

1. In the early church, (a) a chest for receiving pecuniary offerings; (b) a box or casket in which the eucharist was carried; (c) a reliquary.

2. [A—] A genus of lamellibranch mollusks, typical of the family *Arcidæ*; the ark-shells.

är-çāde′, *n.* [Fr. *arcade*; It. *arcata*, an arcade, from L. *arcata*, from *arcus*, a bow, arch.] 1. A series of arches on pillars; used as the screen and roof support of an ambulatory or walk, but in the architecture of the middle ages ornamentally applied to a wall.

2. An arched opening in a wall. [Rare.]

3. A vault. [Rare.]

4. A lane or passage in a town or building, containing shops or stores, and usually covered with glass.

är-çād′ed, *a.* Furnished with an arcade.

Är-çā′di-ȧ, *n.* [L. *Arcadia*; Gr. *Arkadia.*]

1. A picturesque district of Greece, in the Peloponnesus, whose people were noted for simplicity and contentment.

2. Figuratively, any place where rural simplicity and happiness prevail.

Är-çā′di-ăn, Är-çā′diç, *a.* 1. Pertaining to Arcadia.

2. Poetically pastoral; characterized by simplicity and contentment.

Är-çā′di-ăn, *n.* A native of Arcadia.

Är′çȧ-dy, *n.* A poetic form of *Arcadia.*

är-çāne′, *a.* Hidden; secret. [Rare.]

är-çā′num, *n.*; *pl.* **är-çā′nȧ.** [L. *arcanum*, neut. of *arcanus*, shut in, hidden; from *arcere*, to shut up; *arca*, a chest.]

1. Profound knowledge, beyond the perception of ordinary men; mystery; a secret.

2. The great secret of nature which the alchemists sought.

3. A secret and wonderful medicine.

ärç″-bōu-tänt′ (-täṅ′), *n.* [Fr.] In architecture, an arch-formed buttress; a flying buttress.

ärch, *n.* [Fr. *arche*; L. *arcus*, a bow, an arc.]

1. An archway; any place covered by an arch; as, the *arch* of an arcade; the *arch* of a bridge.

2. Any curvature in the form of an arch; as, the *arch* of the eyebrow; the *arch* of a horse's neck.

> Whereon a sapphire throne, inlaid with pure Amber, and colors of the showery *arch.*
> —Milton.

3. In mining, a piece of ground left unworked near a shaft.

4. In geometry, any part of the circumference of a circle or other curve; an arc.

5. In architecture, a structure composed of separate inelastic bodies, having the shape of truncated wedges arranged on a curved line, so as to retain their position by mutual pressure. Arches are usually constructed of stones or of brick. The separate stones which compose the arch are called voussoirs or archstones; the extreme or lowest voussoirs are termed springers, and the uppermost or central one is called the keystone. The under or concave side of the voussoirs is called the intrados, and the upper or convex side the extrados of the arch. When the curves of the intrados and extrados are concentric or parallel, the arch is said to be extradosed. The supports which afford resting and resisting points to the arch are called piers and abutments. The upper part of the pier or abutment where the arch rests—technically, where it springs from—is the impost. The span of an arch is, in circular arches, the length of its chord; for the span is generally the width between the points of its opposite imposts whence it springs. The rise of an arch is the height of the highest point of its intrados above the line of the impost; this point is sometimes called the under side of the crown, the highest point of the extrados being the crown. Arches are designated in two ways; first, in a general manner, according to their properties, their uses, their position in a building, or their exclusive employment in a

Extradosed Arch.

a, Abutments. *i*, Impost. *v*, Voussoirs or Archstones. *s*, Springers. *In*, Intrados. *p*, Piers. *k*, Keystone. *Ex*, Extrados.

Ogee. Equilateral.

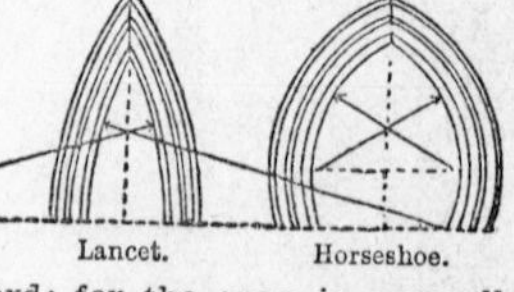

Lancet. Horseshoe.

Segmental. Semicircular.

particular style of architecture. Thus, there are arches of equilibration, equipollent arches, arches of discharge, skew and reversed arches, Roman, pointed, and Saracenic arches. Second, they are named specifically according to the curve the intrados assumes, when that curve is the section of any of the geometrical solids; as, segmental, semicircular, cycloidal, elliptical, parabolical, hyperbolical, or catenarian arches; or from the resemblance of the whole contour of the curve to some familiar object, as lancet arch and horseshoe arch; or from the method used in describing the curve, as equilateral, three-centered, four-centered, ogee, and the like. When any arch has one of its imposts higher than the other it is said to be rampant.

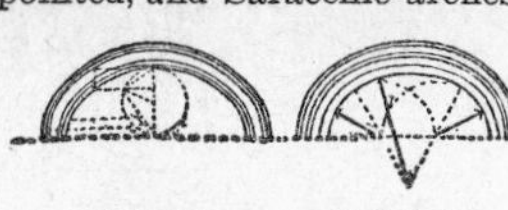
Cycloidal. Elliptical.

6. A fire-chamber, as in a brick-kiln and certain kinds of furnaces and ovens; also, the door of an ash-pit.

Triumphal arch; in Roman antiquity, a simple arch festooned and otherwise decorated, under which a victorious general and army passed in triumph.

ärch, *v.t.*; arched, *pt.*, *pp.*; arching, *ppr.* To cover with an arch; to form with a curve; as, to *arch* a gate.

ärch, *v.i.* To make an arch or arches; to curve.

ärch, *a.* 1. Cunning; sly; shrewd; waggish; mischievous; mirthful; roguish; as, an *arch* look.

2. Chief; of the first class; principal; as, an *arch* deed.

ärch, *n.* A chief. [Rare.]

ärch-, *prefix.* [L. *archi-*, *arch-*; Gr. *archi-*, *arch-*, from *archos*, a ruler, *archein*, to rule.] A combining form signifying chief; as, *arch*duke, *arch*bishop.

-ärch, *suffix.* [Gr. *archos*, ruler, from *archein*, to rule.] A combining form signifying a ruler, as in hept*arch*.

Är-chæ'ăn, *a.* [Gr. *archaios*, ancient, from *archē*, beginning.] Of or pertaining to the first or oldest strata, preceding the Cambrian.

Är-chæ'ăn, *n.* A series of crystalline schists and rocks beneath the most ancient fossiliferous strata. The name was first proposed by James Dwight Dana, the American geologist, and has been generally adopted for this ancient formation and its period. The *Archæan* includes the Azoic and Eozoic ages. Geologists differ as to whether the latter includes the earliest forms of life or not, many believing the entire *Archæan* age to be destitute of all fossil remains of life.

är-chæ-ō-. [Gr. *archaios*, ancient, from *archē*, the beginning, from *archein*, to be first.] A combining form signifying ancient, as in *archæ*ology, *archæ*ozoic.

är-chæ-og'ră-phy, *n.* [*Archæo-*, and Gr. *graphia*, from *graphein*, to write.] A treatise or writing on antiquity or antiques.

är″chæ-ō-lith'ic, *a.* [*Archæo-*, and Gr. *lithikos*, from *lithos*, stone.] Of, relating to, or designating, the earliest Stone age.

är″chæ-ō-lō'gi-ăn, *n.* See *Archæologist.*

är″chæ-ō-log'ic, är″chæ-ō-log'ic-ăl, *a.* Pertaining to archæology.

är″chæ-ō-log'ic-ăl-ly, *adv.* In an archæological manner.

är-chæ-ol'ō-gist, *n.* One versed in antiquity, or ancient learning.

är-chæ-ol'ō-gy, *n.* [*Archæo-*, and Gr. *logia*, from *legein*, to speak.] The study of antiquity; particularly the scientific investigation, study, and classification of the history, use, and meaning of prehistoric antiquities and remains of every kind; in a popular sense, the bringing together of any facts that throw light on the remote past of a country.

är-chæ-op'te-ryx, *n.* [*Archæo-*, and Gr. *pteryx*, wing.] One of a family of reptile-like birds of the Jurassic period.

är-chæ-os'tō-mȧ, *n.* [*Archæo-*, and Gr. *stoma*, mouth.] A primitive or elementary blastopore.

Är″chæ-ō-stō'mȧ-tȧ, *n.pl.* [*Archæo-*, and Gr. *stoma*, pl. *stomata*, mouth.] In zoölogy, a group of gastrular animals retaining an elementary mouth during life.

är″chæ-ō-stō'mȧ-tous (*or* -stom'ȧ-tous), *a.* Of, relating to, or characteristic of, the *Archæostomata.*

är'chæ-ō-stōme, *n.* Same as *Archæostoma.*

är″chæ-ō-zō'ic, *a.* [*Archæo-*, and Gr. *zōon*, animal.] Resembling, pertaining to, or containing, the early or primitive forms of life.

är-chā'ic, *a.* [Gr. *archaikos*, from *archaios*, old, ancient.] A term applied particularly to language, meaning passing out, or nearly out of use; becoming obsolete.

Syn.—Ancient, antiquated, obsolescent, obsolete.—*Ancient* denotes merely age; *antiquated*, both aged and passing out of style; *obsolescent* or *archaic*, a passing out of use; *obsolete*, having passed out of use.

är-chā'ic-ăl, *a.* Archaic. [Rare.]

är-chā'ic-ăl-ly, *adv.* In an archaic manner.

är'chā-ism, *n.* [Fr. *archaïsme*, from Gr. *archaismos*, from *archaios*, ancient; *archē*, the beginning.]

1. A word, expression, or idiom passing out of use or becoming obsolete.

2. Grammatical or rhetorical obsolescence.

är'chā-ist, *n.* 1. An archæologist.

2. One who uses archaic expressions.

är-chā-is'tic, *a.* Of the nature of or pertaining to archaism; affecting what is antiquated.

är'chā-ize, *v.i.*; archaized (-īzd), *pt.*, *pp.*; archaizing, *ppr.* To give an ancient character or effect; to imitate an old or archaic style.

ärch″an'gel, *n.* [L. *archangelus*; Gr. *archangelos*, chief angel, from *archos*, chief, first, and *angelos*, messenger, angel.]

1. An angel of the highest order; an angel occupying the eighth rank in the celestial hierarchy.

2. A name applied to several labiate plants of different genera, and to *Angelica archangelica.*

ärch″bish'ŏp, *n.* [ME. *archbisshop*, *archebiscop*; AS. *arcebiscop*; from L. *archiepiscopus*, from Gr. *archiepiskopos*, an archbishop; *archi*, chief, and *episkopos*, a bishop, overseer.] A chief bishop; a church dignitary of the first class; a metropolitan bishop who superintends the conduct of the suffragan bishops in his province, and also exercises episcopal authority in his own diocese.

ärch″bish'ŏp-ric, *n.* [ME. *archebischopriche*; AS. *arcebiscoprice*; *arcebiscop*, archbishop, and *rice*, jurisdiction.] The jurisdiction, trust, or office of an archbishop.

ärch'-brick, *n.* A brick shaped like a keystone, used in arches; also, a glazed brick, as in the roof of a kiln.

ärch″but'lēr, *n.* The chief butler; an officer of the old German empire.

ärch″chăm'bēr-lain (-lin), *n.* The chief chamberlain; an officer of the old German empire whose office was similar to that of the great chamberlain of England.

ärch″chăn'cel-lŏr, *n.* A chief chancellor; an officer in the old German empire who presided over the secretaries of the court.

ärch″chem'ic, *a.* Of supreme chemical power. [Rare.]

ärch″dēa'cŏn, *n.* [AS. *arcediacon*, *archidiacon*; L. *archidiaconus*; Gr. *archidiakonos*; *archos*, chief, and *diakonos*, servant, minister.] In England, an ecclesiastical dignitary, next in rank below a bishop, who has jurisdiction either over a part or over the whole of the diocese.

The term is now variously used in the Anglican and Roman Catholic churches to designate an administrator of the affairs of a diocese, having jurisdiction delegated from the bishop. The word has been in use as the title of an ecclesiastical dignitary since the fourth century.

ärch″dēa'cŏn-ry, *n.* The office, jurisdiction, or residence of an archdeacon.

ärch″dēa'cŏn-ship, *n.* The office of an archdeacon.

ärch″dī'ō-cēse, *n.* The diocese of an archbishop.

ärch″dū'căl, *a.* Pertaining to an archduke.

ärch″duch'ess, *n.* The wife of an archduke; a princess of the reigning family of Austria.

ärch″duch'y, *n.* The territory of an archduke or archduchess.

ärch″dūke', *n.* A prince belonging to the reigning family of Austria; formerly, either (a) one of various European sovereigns, or (b) the emperor of Austria.

ärch″dūke'dŏm, *n.* An archduchy.

är″chē-bī-ō'sis, *n.* [*Arche-*, and Gr. *biōsis*, from *bios*, life.] Spontaneous generation; abiogenesis.

ärched (ärcht), *a.* Made with an arch or curve; covered with an arch; in the form of an arch.

är-chē-gō'ni-um, *n.*; *pl.* **är-chē-gō'ni-ȧ.** [L., from Gr. *archegonos*, first of a race: *archē-*, first, and *gonos*, race.] The flasklike female organ of reproduction analogous to the pistil in the higher cryptogamous plants.

är-cheg'ō-ny, *n.* Abiogenesis; archebiosis.

är-chel'ō-gy, *n.* [Gr. *archē*, the beginning, and *logia*, from *legein*, to speak.] The science of first principles.

Är-chen-ceph'ȧ-lȧ, *n.pl.* [*Archi-*, and Gr. *enkephalos*, the brain; *en*, in, and *kephalē*, head.] In zoölogy, a subfamily having a single genus, man.

ärch″en'e-my, *n.* A principal enemy; Satan.

ärch-en-ter'ic, *a.* Pertaining to an archenteron.

ärch-en'tēr-on, *n.* [*Arch-*, and Gr. *enteron*, intestine.] In biology, the primitive form of the digestive tract of an embryo.

ärch″ē-ō-log'ic-ăl, *a.* See *Archæological.*

ärch-ē-ol'ō-gy, *n.* See *Archæology.*

ärch-ē-os'tō-mȧ, är'chē-ō-stōme, *n.* Same as *Archæostoma.*

ärch″ē-ō-zō'ic, *a.* See *Archæozoic.*

ärch'ēr, *n.* [Fr. *archer*, *archier*; L. *arcarius*, a bowman, from *arcus*, a bow.]

1. One who uses a bow; one who is skilled in the use of the bow and arrow; a bowman.

2. The archer-fish.

ärch'ēr-ess, *n.* A female archer.

ärch'ēr-fish, *n.* A name given to the *Toxotes jaculator*, a scaly-finned, acanthopterygian fish, about six inches long, inhabiting the sea around Java; it has the faculty of shooting drops of water to the distance of three or four feet, with sure aim, at insects, thereby causing them to fall into the water, when it seizes and devours them. The soft, and even the spiny, portions of their dorsal fins are so covered with scales as to be scarcely distinguishable from the rest of their body.

Archer-fish (*Toxotes jaculator*).

ärch'ēr-ship, *n.* An archer's art or skill.

ärch'ēr-y, *n.* 1. The use of the bow and arrow; the practice, art, or skill of archers; the act of shooting with a bow and arrow.

2. A number of archers; a company of bowmen.

ärch'es, *n.*; pl. of *arch.*

Court of Arches; an English ecclesiastical court, the chief and most ancient consistory court, belonging to the archbishopric of Canterbury, for the debating of spiritual causes; so called from the church in London, known as *St. Mary le Bow* (*de arcubus*), where it was formerly held. The jurisdiction of this court extends over the province of Canterbury.

är'chē-spōre, *n.* The cell or cell-group inclosing and productive of the mother-cells of pollen or spores.

är'chē-ty̆-păl, *a.* Original; constituting a model or pattern; pertaining to an archetype.

Archetypal world; the world existing only in the mind of God, antedating the created world.

är'chē-ty̆-păl-ly, *adv.* Originally.

är'chē-tȳpe, *n.* [Fr. *archétype*; L. *archetypum*; Gr. *archetypon*, from *archetypos*, stamped first; *archi-*, and *typos*, from *typtein*, to strike.]

1. The original pattern or model of a work; or the model from which a thing is made.

2. In coinage, the standard weight or coin by which others are adjusted.

3. In biology, the theoretical basic design from which any group of organisms may be said to have sprung.

är-chē-typ'ic-ăl, *a.* Archetypal.

är-chē'us, *n.* [L., from Gr. *archaios*, ancient, old, from *archē*, beginning.] In alchemy, the internal efficient cause of all things; the *anima mundi* or plastic power of the old philosophers. [Obs.]

är'chi-, *prefix.* [L. *archi-*; Gr. *archi-*, from *archos*, chief, *archein*, to be first, to rule.] A combining form signifying chief, first, or, in biology, primitive.

är″chi-am″phi-as'tēr, *n.* [*Archi-*, and Gr. *amphi*, about, and *astēr*, a star.] In biology, the initial amphiaster produced in an ovum at the time of polar cell expulsion.

Är″chi-an-nel'i-dȧ, *n.pl.* [*Archi-*, and *Annelida.*] A primary group of *Annelida* characterized by archaic arrangement of parts.

är'chi-ā-tēr, *n.* [*Archi-*, and Gr. *iatros*, physician.] Chief physician; a term applied on the continent of Europe, to the first or body physician of princes, and to the first physician of some cities; in Russia, the first imperial physician.

är'chi-blast, *n.* [*Archi-*, and Gr. *blastos*, germ.] In biology, the body that contains the germ and ultimately becomes the embryo.

är-chi-blas'tic, *a.* Pertaining to the archiblast.

är-chi-blas'tū-lȧ, *n.* [*Archi-*, and *blastula*, dim. of Gr. *blastos*, sprout.] A hollow, globular blastula.

är'chi-cärp, *n.* [*Archi-*, and Gr. *karpos*, fruit.] In botany, the female organ of reproduction in some of the lower cryptograms; the ascogonium.

är″chi-dī-ac'ō-năl, *a.* Pertaining to an archdeacon; as, an *archidiaconal* visitation.

Arch'ie, *n.* An anti-aircraft gun. Derived from the catchwords "Archibald, certainly not;" popular with the British Expeditionary Force and applied to the ineffective work of the anti-air craft guns during early years of the World War.

är″chi-ē-pis'cō-pȧ-cy, *n.* 1. The office of an archbishop.

2. An episcopacy the head of which is an archbishop.

är″chi-ē-pis'cō-păl, *a.* Of or pertaining to an archbishop; as, Chicago is an *archiepiscopal* see.

är″chi-ē-pis-cō-pal'i-ty, *n.* Archiepiscopacy.

är″chi-ē-pis'cō-pāte, *n.* [*Archi-*, and L. *episcopatus*, from *episcopus*; Gr. *episkopos*, a bishop, overseer.] An archbishopric; the office of an archbishop.

är-chi'e-rey, *n.* [*Archi-*, and Gr. *hiereus*, a

priest, from *hieros*, holy.] The higher order of the clergy of the Greek church, including the metropolitans, archbishops, and bishops.

är-chi-gas′trū-lȧ, *n.* [*Archi-*, and L. *gastrula*, dim. of Gr. *gaster*, stomach.] In biology, a bell-gastrula of an archiblastic ovum.

är′chil, *n.* [ME. *orchell*; OFr. *orchell*; It. *orcella*; Sp. *orchillo*.]

1. A purple-red or violet dye made from the lichen *archil*.

2. A lichen, especially the *Roccella tinctoria*, which grows on rocks in the Canary and Cape Verde Isles, and yields rich dyestuffs and litmus. Also spelled *orchal*, *orchil*.

Roccella tinctoria, from which Archil is obtained.

Är-chi-lō′chi-ăn, *a.* Pertaining to the Greek poet Archilochus, who was noted for the severity of his satire; or designating one of the metrical combinations which he first used. There are three dactylic *Archilochian* distichs and one iambic *Archilochian* distich.

ärch′i-lūte, *n.* See *Archlute.*

är′chi-māġe, är-chi-mā′gus, *n.* [L., from Gr. *archimagos*, chief of the magi; *archi-*, chief, and *magos*, one of the magi.]

1. The high priest of the Persian magi, or worshipers of fire.

2. A great magician or wizard.

är-chi-man′drite, *n.* [L. *archimandrita*; Gr. *archimandritēs*; *archi-*, chief, and *mandra*, an inclosure, monastery.] In the Greek church, a chief of a monastery, corresponding to abbot in the Latin church; or a superintendent of several monasteries, corresponding to a superior abbot, or father provincial, in the Latin church.

Greek Archimandrite, from an original sketch.

Är″chi-mē-dē′ăn, *a.* Pertaining to Archimedes, a celebrated Greek philosopher, or constructed on the principle of his famous screw; as, an *Archimedean* propeller.

Archimedean screw, or *Archimedes's screw*; an instrument or device for raising water or loose material, as salt, cement, etc., from a lower to a higher level. It is said to have been invented by Archimedes, and consists of a spiral conduit wound around an inclined axis. The lower end being dropped into the liquid or material to be raised, the screw is revolved and the substance rises to the upper level.

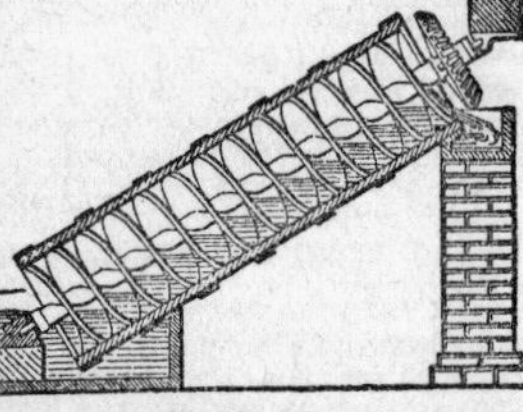
Archimedean Screw.

är-chi-neph′ric, *a.* Relating to the archinephron.

är-chi-neph′ron, *n.* [*Archi-*, and Gr. *nephron*, kidney.] In embryology, the primitive kidney.

ärch′ing, *a* Curving like an arch.

ärch′ing, *n.* 1. The arched portion of a structure; any arched work.

2. An arch-like form; as, the *arching* of her eyebrows.

3. In nautical language, a hogging, or drooping at the ends; opposed to *sagging*.

är″chi-pē-laġ′ic, *a.* Relating to or resembling an archipelago.

är-chi-pel′ȧ-gō, *n.*; *pl.* är-chi-pel′ȧ-gōeṣ or är-chi-pel′ȧ-gōṣ. [It. *arcipelago*, from Gr. *archi-*, chief, and *pelagos*, sea.]

1. Any large body of water studded with islands; also, the islands themselves; a group of islands.

2. [A—] The Grecian *Archipelago*, or Ægean Sea, abounding with islands and lying between Greece and Asia Minor.

är″chip-te-ryġ′i-um, *n.*; *pl.* är″chip-te-ryġ′i-ȧ. [L., from Gr. *archi-*, first, and *pterygion*, a wing, fin.] The primitive type of limb of the *Vertebrata*; the primitive form of fin.

är′chi-stōme, *n.* [*Archi-*, and Gr. *stoma*, mouth.] In embryology, the primitive mouth of bilateral animals.

är′chi-tect, *n.* [L. *architectus*, from Gr. *architektōn*; *archi-*, chief, and *tektōn*, a worker.]

1. One skilled in the art of building; one who understands architecture, or makes it his occupation to form plans and designs of buildings, and to superintend the artificers employed.

2. A contriver; a former, designer, or maker; one who builds up something; as, men are the *architects* of their own fortunes.

är-chi-tec′tive, *a.* Used in building; proper for building.

är″chi-tec-ton′ic, är″chi-tec-ton′ic-ăl, *a.* 1. Pertaining to an architect or architecture; having skill in designing or construction.

2. In logic, pertaining to the scientific arrangement or systematization of knowledge.

är″chi-tec-ton′ic, *n.* 1. Architectonics.

2. In logic, the art of systematizing knowledge.

är″chi-tec-ton′ics, *n.* The science of architecture.

är′chi-tec-tŏr, *n.* An architect. [Obs.]

är′chi-tec-tress, *n.* A female architect.

är-chi-tec′tūr-ăl, *a.* Pertaining to the art of building; relating to the rules of architecture.

är-chi-tec′tūr-ăl-ly, *adv.* In an architectural manner; from an architect's point of view.

är′chi-tec-tūre, *n.* [Fr. *architecture*; L. *architectura*, from *architectus*; Gr. *architektōn*, a chief worker, master-builder; *archi-*, chief, and *tektōn*, worker.]

1. The art or science of building; particularly the art of constructing houses, bridges, churches, and other buildings for the purposes of civil life, often called *civil architecture.*

2. Construction; structure; workmanship; as, the *architecture* of that house is defective.

3. A system or style of building, having certain characteristics of structure, decoration, etc.; as, Gothic *architecture*; ecclesiastical *architecture.*

4. Architectural productions collectively; as, ancient *architecture.*

Military architecture; the art of fortification.

Naval architecture; the art of building warships.

Marine architecture; shipbuilding of all kinds.

Är-chi-teū′this, *n.* [*Archi-*, and Gr. *teuthis*, a kind of squid.] The giant squids, a genus of cephalopods of immense size.

är′chi-trāve, *n.* [Fr. *architrave*; It. *architrave*, from L. *archi-*, and *trabs*, a beam.]

1. In architecture, the lower division of an entablature, or that part which rests immediately on the column; a chief beam.

2. The ornament or molding at sides of and above a door, window, or other square opening.

är′chi-trāved, *a.* Having an architrave.

är′chi-văl, *a.* Pertaining to archives or records; contained in records.

är′chive, *n.* [L. *archivum*, *archium*; Gr. *archeion*, a government-house; *ta archeia*, archives; *archē*, beginning, government.]

1. A record or document preserved in evidence of facts; almost always used in the plural and signifying documents or records relating to the rights, privileges, claims, treaties, constitutions, etc., of a family, corporation, community, city, state, or nation.

2. [*pl.*] The chamber or building where such documents are kept.

Syn.—Annal, chronicle, record, register.

är′chi-vist, *n.* The keeper of archives or records.

är′chi-vōlt, *n.* [Fr. *archivolte*; It. *archivolto*; *archi-*, chief, and *volto*, an arch, vault.] In architecture, the mass of molding usually on the face and soffits of a medieval arch; also, the grouped ornaments on the face of a classical arch.

är-chi-zō′ic, *a.* [*Archi-*, and Gr. *zōon*, animal.] Pertaining to the earliest forms of life.

ärch′lūte, ärch′i-lūte, *n.* [Fr. *archiluth*; It. *arciliuto*.] Formerly, a large lute, or theorbo.

ärch′ly, *adv.* In an arch manner.

ärch-mär′shăl, *n.* The grand marshal of the old German empire; an office of the elector of Saxony.

ärch′ness, *n.* Sly humor without malice; the quality of being arch.

är′chon, *n.* [Gr. *archōn*, a ruler, from *archein*, to be first, to rule.] In ancient Athens, one of nine chief magistrates, chosen from the most illustrious families to superintend civil and religious matters.

är′chon-ship, *n.* The office of an archon.

är′chon-tāte, *n.* The term of office of an archon.

Är-chon′tic, *n.* One of a fourth century sect who held that the world was not created by God, but by heavenly rulers called archons.

Är′chonts, *n.pl.* [Gr. *archōn*, ruler, from *archein*, to be first, to rule.] In zoölogy, the group of mammals which includes only man.

är′chō-plaṣm, *n.* [Gr. *archē*, beginning, and *plasma*, from *plassein*, to form, mold.] In biology, an element in cell protoplasm which has a formative function.

är-chō-plaṣ′mic, *a.* Containing or relating to archoplasm.

ärch-prel′āte, *n.* A chief prelate.

ärch-pres′by-tēr, *n.* [L. *archipresbyter*; Gr. *archipresbyteros*; *archi-*, chief, and *presbyteros*, elder, comp., from *presbys*, an old man.] A chief presbyter or priest.

ärch-pres′by-ter-y, *n.* The absolute dominion of presbytery, or the chief presbytery.

ärch-priēst′, *n.* A chief priest.

ärch-prī′māte, *n.* The chief primate; an archbishop over other bishops.

ärch′stōne, *n.* The wedge-shaped stone that binds an arch; the keystone.

ärch-trāi′tŏr, *n.* A principal traitor.

ärch-treaṣ′ūr-ēr (-trezh′), *n.* The great treasurer of the old German empire; also, any head treasurer.

ärch′wāy, *n.* A passage under an arch.

ärch′wife, *n.* A married woman of masculine physique or mind. [Obs.]

ärch′wīse, *adv.* In the form of an arch.

ärch′y, *a.* Having arches; as, *archy* eyebrows.

är′ci-fôrm, *a.* [L. *arcus*, a bow, and *forma*, form.] Shaped like a bow; curved.

är′cō-gráph, *n.* [L. *arcus*, bow, and Gr. *graphein*, to write.] An instrument for drawing a circular arc without using a central point.

är-cōse′, *n.* See *Arkose.*

Ärc-tā′li-ȧ, *n.* [L., from *arctic*, and Gr. *hals*, sea.] The zoölogical zone embracing the northern seas southward as far as floating ice descends.

ärc-tā′tion, *n.* [Fr. *arctation*, from L. *arctus*, shut in, narrow, pp. of *arcere*, to shut in.] Contraction of a natural opening, as of the anus.

ärc′ti-ăn, *a.* and *n.* I. *a.* Of, relating, or pertaining to the *Arctiidæ*, a family of moths having very hairy caterpillars.

II. *n.* A moth of this family.

ärc′tic, *a.* [Fr. *arctique*; L. *arcticus*; Gr. *arktikos*, from *arktos*, bear.]

1. Pertaining to the northern constellations known as Little Bear and Great Bear.

2. Pertaining to the north, particularly to the region within the arctic circle; hence, cold, frigid.

Arctic circle; a lesser circle parallel to the equator, 23° 28′ from the north pole, marking the southern limit of the north frigid zone.

ärc′tic, *n.* 1. The arctic circle.

2. A fleece-lined waterproof overshoe or rubber.

Ärc-tī′i-dæ, *n.pl.* [L., from Gr. *arktos*, bear.] A family of moths belonging to the *Heterocera*. Their larvæ are thickly covered with hair, whence they have obtained the name of woolly-bears.

Ärc-tis′cȧ, *n.pl.* [L., from Gr. *arktos*, a bear.] An order of *Arachnida* including the water-bears.

Ärc′ti-um, *n.* [L., from Gr. *arktos*, a bear.] A genus of plants of the natural order *Compositæ*, of which several species are weeds. The genus includes *Arctium lappa*, the common burdock.

Ärc-tō-gæ′ȧ, *n.* [L., from Gr. *arktos*, north, and *gaia*, land.] A faunal zone comprising the land area of the northern regions.

Ärc-tō-ġē′ăl, *a.* Of, relating, or pertaining to the zone Arctogæa.

ärc′toid, ärc-toi′dē-ăn, *a.* and *n.* I. *a.* Pertaining to the *Arctoidea*; resembling the bears.

II. *n.* One of the *Arctoidea.*

Ärc-toi′dē-ȧ, *n.pl.* [L., from Gr. *arktos*, bear, and *eidos*, form.] A subfamily of the *Carnivora*, comprehending the bears, racoons, weasels, etc.

ärc-toi-dē-ăn, *a.* and *n.* See *Arctoid.*

Ärc-tō-staph′y-los, *n.* [L., from Gr. *arktos*, a bear, and *staphylē*, a bunch of grapes.] A genus of ericaceous plants nearly related to *Arbutus*, and including the bearberry and the manzanitas.

Ärc-tū′rus, *n.* [L., from Gr. *Arktouros*; *arktos*, bear, and *ouros*, a guard.] A fixed star of the first magnitude in the constellation Boötes. It is one of the stars observed to have a proper motion.

ärc′ū-ăl, *a.* Relating to an arc.

ärc′ū-āte, ärc′ū-ā-ted, *a.* [L. *arcuatus*, pp. of *arcuare*, to arch, bend like a bow, from *arcus*, a bow.] Bent or curved in the form of a bow.

ärc′ū-āte-ly, *adv.* In an arcuate manner.

ärc-ū-ā′tion, *n.* 1. The act of bending; the state of being bent.

2. A method of raising trees by layers, by bending branches to the ground and covering the small shoots with earth.

ärc′ū-bȧ-list, *n.* [L. *arcuballista*; *arcus*, a bow, and *ballista*, an engine for hurling missiles.] A crossbow; an arbalist.

ärc-ū-bal′ist-ēr, *n.* A crossbowman.

ärc′ū-bus, *n.* [Obs.] See *Harquebus.*

är′cus, *n.* [L.] In anatomy, a bow or arch.

Arcus senilis; a ring of fatty degeneration marginal to the cornea; seen in old persons. [L., the bow of old age.]

-ard, -art. [Fr. *-ard*, from G. *-hart*, from *hart*, hard.] A suffix forming personal nouns from adjectives, and denoting that one has to a high degree the quality expressed by the adjective, as in drunk*ard*, cow*ard*.

är-das-sēne′, *n.* [Fr., from *ardasse*, a fine silk thread, from Per. *ardan*, raw silk.] A very fine sort of Persian silk, used in costly French fabrics.

är′deb, *n.* [Ar. *irdab.*] An Egyptian weight and measure equivalent to 226 lbs., or to about 40½ gallons.

är′den-cy, *n.* 1. Warmth of passion or affection; ardor; eagerness; as, the *ardency* of love or zeal.

2. Heat. [Rare.]

är′dent, *a.* [L. *ardens*, ppr. of *ardere*, to burn.]

1. Hot; burning; causing a sensation of great heat; as, *ardent* spirits; an *ardent* fever.

2. Having the appearance or quality of fire; fierce; as, *ardent* eyes.

3. Warm, as applied to the passions and affections; passionate; affectionate; zealous; as, *ardent* love or vows; *ardent* zeal.

Syn.—Burning, eager, fervent, fiery, hot, intense, passionate, vehement, zealous.

är′dent-ly, *adv.* In an ardent manner.

är′dent-ness, *n.* Ardency. [Rare.]

är′dish, *n.* [E. Ind.] An East Indian style of mural decoration, made by arranging pieces of colored glass in a background of plaster.

Är-dis′i-ȧ, *n.* [L., from Gr. *ardis*, the point of an arrow.] A genus of shrub-like trees of the family *Myrsinaceæ*, ornamental plants native to the East and West Indies, cultivated for their evergreen leaves, showy flowers, and strikingly-colored berries.

är′dŏr, är′dŏur, *n.* [OFr. *ardor*, *ardour*; L. *ardor*, a burning fire, flame, from *ardere*, to burn.]

1. Heat, in a literal sense; as, the *ardor* of the sun's rays.

2. Warmth, or heat, applied to the passions and affections; eagerness; as, he pursues study with *ardor*; they fought with *ardor*.

3. A bright spirit; brilliancy.

Thousand celestial *ardours*, where he stood. —Milton.

4. In medicine, a feeling of heat or burning.

Syn.—Devotion, earnestness, excitement, fervor, intensity, passion, rapture, zeal.

är′dū-ous, *a.* [L. *arduus*, high, steep.]

1. Steep, and therefore difficult of ascent; hard to climb.

And pointed out those *arduous* paths they trod. —Pope.

2. Attended with great labor, like the ascending of acclivities; difficult; as, an *arduous* employment, task, or enterprise.

Syn.—Difficult, hard.—*Arduous*, requiring extraordinary effort, energy, and perseverance to overcome, and mostly applied to a protracted undertaking; *hard*, requiring less endurance and energy, and more within the reach of common powers than *arduous*, but tasking the energies more than *difficult*; *difficult*, not easy, laborious, but attainable or to be accomplished by fair effort or application. *Hard* sometimes applies to passive suffering, as a *hard* lot; *arduous* and *difficult* do not.

är′dū-ous-ly, *adv.* In an arduous manner.

är′dū-ous-ness, *n.* The quality of being arduous; difficulty of execution.

är′dū-rous, *a.* Possessed of ardor. [Rare.]

äre, *v.* [AS. *aron*; Ice. *erum*; L. *sumus*; Gr. *esmen*; Sans. *smas*, from the root *as*; *are* is a Scand. form, the *s* being changed to *r*.] The present tense plural of the verb *to be*, *art* being the second person singular.

äre (*or* är), *n.* [Fr., from L. *area*, a level piece of ground.] The unit of French square measure, containing 100 square meters, or 1076.44 square feet.

ā′rē-ȧ, *n.* [L. *area*, a level piece of ground.]

1. Any plane surface within boundaries; as the floor of a room, of a church, or other building, or a piece of inclosed ground; the space or site on which a building stands, or, by extension, any range of surface, particularly of the earth's surface; as, the *area* of heavy rainfall.

2. A yard attached to a house or a space sunk below the general surface of the ground before windows in the basement story of a building.

3. In geometry, the superficial contents of any figure; the surface included within any given lines; as, the *area* of a square or a triangle.

4. In biology, any spot upon a surface differing from the normal.

5. Figuratively, range of action or view; extent; as, the expanding *area* of culture.

ȧ-rēad′, ȧ-reed′, *v.t.* [AS. *arædan*, to determine, read, counsel.]

1. To read; as, a book or riddle; hence, to divine. [Obs.]

2. To counsel; to warn; to make known. [Obs.]

ā′rē-ăl, *a.* Pertaining to an area.

ȧ-rēar′, *v.t.* and *v.i.* To raise; to exalt; to arouse. [Obs.]

ȧ-rēar′, *adv.* To the rear. [See *Arrear.*]

A-rē′çȧ, *n.* [Port.] 1. A genus of palm-trees, including the betel-nut tree.

2. [a—] Any plant of this genus.

ȧ-reed′, *v.t.* See *Aread.*

ȧ-reek′, *adv.* and *a.* In a reeking condition.

ar-ē-fac′tion, *n.* [Fr. *arefaction*, from L. *arefacere*, to make dry; *arere*, to be dry, and *facere*, to make.] The act of drying.

ar′ē-fȳ, *v.t.* To dry or make dry. [Rare.]

ȧ-rē′nȧ, *n.*; *pl.* **ȧ-rē′nȧṣ** or **ȧ-rē′næ.** [L. *arena*, *harena*, sand, a sandy place, arena.]

1. In Roman antiquity, the area in the central part of an amphitheater, in which the gladiators fought and other shows were exhibited; so called because it was covered with sand.

2. Figuratively, any place of public contest or exertion; as, the *arena* of debate; the *arena* of life.

3. In pathology, sand or gravel in the kidneys.

ar-ē-nā′ceous, *a.* Made up of sand; sandy.

Ar-ē-nā′ri-ȧ, *n.* [L. *arenarius*, sandy.] In botany, the sandworts, a genus of plants belonging to the *Caryophyllaceæ*, or pink family.

ar-ē-nā′ri-ous, *a.* [L. *arenarius*, sandy, from *arena*, sand.] Sandy; as, *arenarious* soil.

ar-ē-nā′tion, *n.* In medicine, a bath of hot sand.

ar-en-dā′tŏr, *n.* [Russ. *arendatoru*; L. *arrendator*, *arendator*, a farmer of revenue, from *arrendare*, *arrentare*, to pay rent; from *ad*, to, and *renda*, rent.] In Livonia and other provinces of Russia, a farmer of rents or other incomes.

ȧ-reng′, ȧ-reṅ′gȧ, *n.* [E. Ind.] A sago-palm, *Arenga saccharifera.* [See *Gomuti.*]

ar-ē-niç′ō-līte, *n.* [L. *arena*, sand, and *colere*, to inhabit.] A name formerly given to certain holes in rocks, believed to have been caused by marine annelids; scientists claim they were caused by the sea.

ar-ē-niç′ō-lous, *a.* Burrowing in the sand.

ȧ-ren-i-lit′iç, *a.* [L. *arena*, sand, and Gr. *lithos*, a stone.] Pertaining to or composed of sandstone; as, *arenilitic* mountains.

ar′ē-nōse, *a.* Sandy.

ȧ-ren′ū-lous, *a.* Full of fine sand. [Obs.]

ȧ-rē′ō-lȧ, *n.*; *pl.* **ȧ-rē′ō-læ.** [L. *areola*, a small open place, dim. of *area.*]

1. In physical science, any small area.

2. In anatomy, (a) the circle surrounding the nipple, varying from pink to brown; (b) the circle surrounding the pustule in vaccination; (c) one of the cells in areolar tissue.

3. In entomology, one of the small areas, or veinlets, into which the wings of insects are divided by the nervures.

4. In botany, the minute meshes on the surface of a plant.

ȧ-rē′ō-lăr, *a.* Pertaining to an areola.

ȧ-rē′ō-lāte, ȧ-rē′ō-lā-ted, *a.* Divided into small spaces or areolations, as the wings of insects, and the leaves of plants.

ā″rē-ō-lā′tion, *n.* 1. Any small space, bounded by some part differing in color or structure, as the spaces bounded by the nervures of the wings of insects, or those by the veins of leaves.

2. The quality of being areolate; the division into or space containing areolæ.

ā′rē-ōle, *n.* Same as *Areola.*

ȧ-rē′ō-let, *n.* [Dim. of L. *areola*, a small place.] A small areola.

ā-rē-om′e-tēr, *n.* [Fr. *aréomètre*, from Gr. *araios*, thin, rare, and *metron*, measure.] An instrument for measuring the specific gravity of liquids; also spelled *aræometer.*

ā″rē-ō-met′riç, ā″rē-ō-met′riç-ăl, *a.* Pertaining to an areometer.

ā-rē-om′e-try, *n.* [Gr. *araios*, thin, rare, and *metria*, from *metron*, measure.] The process or act of measuring the specific gravity of fluids.

Ar-ē-op′ȧ-ġist, Ar-ē-op′ȧ-ġīte, *n.* A member of the Areopagus.

ar-ē-op-ȧ-ġit′iç, *a.* Pertaining to the Areopagus.

Ar-ē-op′ȧ-gus, *n.* [L., from Gr. *Areiopagos*; *Areios*, *pagos*; *Areios*, pertaining to *Arēs*, Mars, and *pagos*, hill.]

1. A supreme tribunal at Athens, famous for the justice and impartiality of its decisions. It was originally held on the hill of the same name.

2. Any final court or tribunal.

ȧ-rē′ō-stȳle, ȧ-ræ′ō-stȳle, *a.* [L. *aræostylos*; Gr. *araiostylos*, with columns far apart; *araios*, not dense, thin, and *stylos*, pillar.] Pertaining to the style of intercolumnation having the intermediate spaces upward of three columnar diameters in extent.

ȧ-rē-ō-sys′tȳle, ȧ-ræ-ō-sys′tȳle, *a.* Pertaining to the style of arrangement attendant on coupled columns.

ā-rē-ot′iç, *a.* [Gr. *araiōtikos*, from *araioun*, to rarefy; *araios*, rare, thin, not dense.] Attenuating; making thin, as liquids; rarefying.

A′rēṣ, *n.* The god of war in Greek mythology, corresponding to Mars in Roman mythology.

ȧ-rest′, *n.* 1. A rest for a spear. [Obs.]

2. Arrest. [Obs.]

ȧ-ret′, ȧ-rette′, *v.t.* [ME. *aretten*; OFr. *areter*, *aretter*; *a* (L. *ad*, to) and *reter*, from L. *reputare*, to count, reckon again.] To assign; to impute. [Obs.]

ar-ē-tā′içṣ, *n.* Same as *Aretology.*

ȧ-rēte′, *n.* [Fr., from OFr. *areste*; L. *arista*, an ear of corn, a spine.] A bold mountainous crest or sharp ridge.

Ar-ē-thū′ṣȧ, *n.* [L. *Arethusa*; Gr. *Arethousa*, one of Diana's nymphs, transformed into a fountain.] A genus of orchids of which one species, *Arethusa bulbosa*, is a native of North America; the only other species known is found in Japan.

ar-ē-tol′ō-ġy, *n.* [Fr. *aretologie*; Gr. *aretalogia*; *aretē*, virtue, and *logia*, from *legein*, to speak.] That part of ethics which treats particularly of virtue.

ȧ-rew′, *adv.* An obsolete form of *arow.*

är′gal, *n.* See *Argol.*

är′gal, *adv.* A corruption of Latin *ergo*, therefore.

är′gal, *n.* Same as *Argali.*

är′gȧ-lȧ, *n.* The Indian name of the adjutant-bird, *Ciconia argala.*

är′gȧ-li, *n.* [Mongolian.] A species of wild sheep, *Caprovis argali* or *Ovis ammon*, found on the mountains of Siberia, central Asia, and Kamchatka. It is nearly as large as an ox. The horns are nearly four feet in length, and at their base are about nineteen inches in circumference.

Argali (*Caprovis argali*).

Är′gand, *a.* Of, relating, or pertaining to a lighting-system using *Argand* lamps.

Argand lamp; an improved lamp, invented by Argand, of Geneva, in 1782, in which, by means of a hollow wick and a glass chimney, a strong and clear light is produced by placing the flame between two currents of air.

är′gan-tree, *n.* [Ar. *argān*, *arjān.*] A low-branched evergreen tree, *Argania Sideroxylon*, of Morocco, yielding a compact wood and fruit resembling the olive.

Är′gas, *n.* [L., from Gr. *argos*, *aergos*; *a* priv. and *ergos*, working.] A genus of eyeless mites or ticks.

Är-ġē′ăn, *a.* Pertaining to the ship or the constellation Argo.

är′gel, *n.* A Syrian name for *Solenostemma Argel*, an asclepiadaceous plant, the leaves of which are used in Egypt for adulterating senna.

Är-ge-mō′nē, *n.* [L. *argemone*; Gr. *argemōnē*, from *argema*, a small white speck in the eye, from *argos*, white.] A genus of plants belonging to the family *Papaveraceæ*. The *Argemone Mexicana*, believed to have come from Mexico, is now common in other warm countries.

är′ġent, *n.* [Fr. *argent*; L. *argentum*, silver; Gr. *argyros*, silver.]

1. The white color in coats of arms, intended to represent silver, or figuratively, purity, innocence, beauty, or gentleness.

2. Silver, or silver money; hence, whiteness, or anything white. [Obs.]

är′ġent, *a.* Silvery; of a pale white, or bright like silver.

Ask of yonder *argent* fields above. —Pope.

är-ġen′tăl, *a.* Pertaining to silver; consisting of silver; combined with silver.

är′ġen-tan, *n.* [L. *argentum*, silver.] An alloy of nickel with copper and zinc; German silver.

är′ġen-tāte, *a.* Silvery white; said of certain leaves.

är-ġen-tā′tion, *n.* An overlaying with silver. [Rare.]

är-ġen′tiç, *a.* Pertaining to, containing, or derived from silver; applied to compounds of silver in its lower valence.

är-ġen-tif′ēr-ous, *a.* [L. *argentum*, silver, and *ferre*, to produce.] Producing silver; as, *argentiferous* ore.

Är-ġen-tī′nȧ, *n.* [L. *argentum*, silver.] A genus of malacopterygious fishes, belonging to the salmon family, so named from their silvery scales.

är′ġen-tīne, *a.* [Fr. *argentin*, from L. *argentum*, silver.]

1. Of, relating, or pertaining to silver.

2. [A—] Pertaining to the South American republic, Argentina.

är′ġen-tīne, *n.* 1. In mineralogy, a silicious variety of carbonate of lime, having a silvery-white luster, and a lamellar structure.

2. A name common to the species of the genus *Argentina.*

3. White metal, silver-plated.

4. A gold coin of Argentina worth about $4.82.

5. [A—] An inhabitant of Argentina.

är′ġen-tīte, *n.* [L. *argentum*, silver, and *-ite.*] Sulphid of silver, Ag_2S.

är-ġen′tous, *a.* Containing silver in its higher valence.

är′ġent-ry, *n.* Silver plate. [Rare.]

är′gil, *n.* [Fr. *argile*; L. *argilla*, white clay; Gr. *argilla*, *argillos*, argil, from *argos*, white.] Clay, or potter's earth; in a technical sense, pure clay, or alumina.

är-ġil-lā′ceous, *a.* [L. *argillaceus*, from *argilla*, white clay.] Partaking of the nature of clay; consisting of argil.

Argillaceous sandstone; in geology, sandstone which contains a large percentage of clay.

Argillaceous schist or *slate*; argillite.

är-ġil-lif′ẽr-ous, *a.* [L. *argilla*, clay, and *ferre*, to bear.] Producing clay; applied to such earths as abound in argil.

är′ġil-lite, *n.* [L. *argilla*, white clay, and *-ite*.] Argillaceous schist or slate; clay-slate. Its usual color is bluish gray.

är-ġil-lit′iç, *a.* Pertaining to argillite.

är-ġil″lō-ar-ē-nā′ceous, *a.* [L. *argilla*, white clay, and *arena*, sand.] Consisting of clay and sand, as a soil.

är-ġil″lō-çal-çā′rē-ous, *a.* Consisting of clay and calcareous earth.

är-ġil″lō-fer-rū′ġi-nous, *a.* Containing or consisting of iron and clay.

är-ġil′lous, *a.* [ME. *argillous*; OFr. *argillos*; L. *argillosus*, from *argilla*, white clay.] Consisting of clay; clayey.

är′ġi-nin, *n.* [L. *argentum*, silver, and *-in*.] An alkaline germicidal agent composed of silver and casein.

Är′ġive, *a.* Pertaining to Argos, the capital of ancient Argolis in Greece, or to the whole of Greece; Greek.

Är′ġive, *n.* An inhabitant of ancient Argos; in the plural, a poetical designation for Greeks generally.

Är′gō, *n.* [Gr. *Argō*, from *argos*, swift, bright, glancing.]

1. In mythology, the ship which carried Jason and his fifty-four companions to Colchis, in quest of the golden fleece.

2. In astronomy, the southern constellation of the Ship, containing 9 clusters, 3 nebulæ, 13 double and 540 single stars, of which about 64 are visible.

Är-gō′ăn, *a.* Pertaining to the ship Argo.

är′gol, är′gal, *n.* Unrefined or crude cream of tartar, a substance deposited on the sides of wine-casks.

Är-gol′iç, *a.* Pertaining to Argolis, a territory or district of Peloponnesus, between Arcadia and the Ægean Sea; as, the *Argolic* gulf.

är′gon, *n.* [Gr. *argon*, from *aergos*, inactive; *a* priv., and *ergon*, work.] A constituent of the air discovered in 1894, thought to be a triatomic form of nitrogen.

Är′gō-naut, *n.* [L. *Argonauta*; Gr. *Argonautēs*; *Argō*, Jason's ship, and *nautēs*, a sailor, from *naus*, ship.]

1. One who sailed to Colchis with Jason, in the Argo, in quest of the golden fleece.

2. One going to California to seek gold, after its discovery in 1849.

3. [a—] One of the molluscoid animals belonging to the genus *Argonauta*.

Är-gō-nau′tȧ, *n.* [L., an Argonaut.] A genus of the class *Cephalopoda*. The shell consists of one spiral involuted valve. The species *argo*, with a subdentated carina, is the famous nautilus, which was thought to extend two of its arms, spreading a membrane for a sail. It really propels itself by means of a jet of water, as do other cephalopods. The animal is quite like an octopus in appearance, having eight arms.

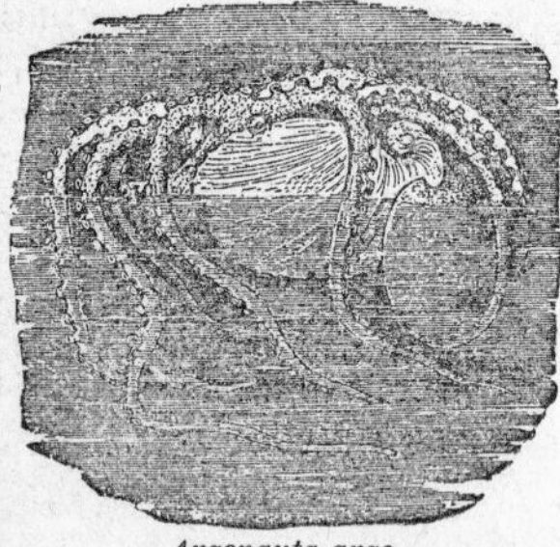

Argonauta argo.

Är-gō-nau′tiç, *a.* Pertaining to the Argonauts.

är′gō-sy, *n.*; *pl.* **är′gō-sieṣ.** [ME. *argosie*, *ragosie*, *rhaguse*, *ragusye*; It. *Ragusea*, a vessel of Ragusa.] A large merchantman; a carack.

är-got′ (*or* är′gō), *n.* [Fr.] A term applied to the language in use among thieves and bad characters, intended to conceal from the uninitiated the real import of what is said; hence, any slang.

är′gū-ȧ-ble, *a.* That may be argued; admitting argument.

är′gūe, *v.i.*; argued, *pt.*, *pp.*; arguing, *ppr.* [ME. *arguen*; OFr. *arguer*; L. *arguere*, to make clear, to prove; from same root as Gr. *argos*, white, clear.]

1. To invent and offer reasons in support of, or against, a proposition, opinion, or measure.

2. To dispute; to reason; followed by *with*; as, he *argued with* his friend.

är′gūe, *v.t.* 1. To debate or discuss; to treat by reasoning; as, the counsel *argued* the cause.

2. To prove or evince; to manifest by inference or deduction; to imply; as, the order visible in the universe *argues* a divine cause.

3. To persuade by reasons; as, to *argue* a man into a different opinion.

4. To accuse or charge with. [Obs.]

Syn.—Discuss, debate, dispute, prove, evince. —To *discuss*, *debate*, or *dispute* is the act of parties interchanging arguments between themselves. To *prove* is the strongest term, implying decisive evidence; to *evince* is next in strength, implying evidence sufficient to remove doubt; *argue* is the weakest.

är′gū-ẽr, *n.* One who argues; a disputer.

är′gū-fȳ, *v.t.* and *v.i.* To argue persistently; to wrangle; also, to signify. [Colloq.]

Är′gū-lus, *n.* [L., dim. of Gr. *argos*; contr. for *aergos*; *a* priv., and *ergon*, work.] A genus of entomostracans. The *Argulus foliaceus* is a common parasite upon fresh-water fishes.

är′gū-ment, *v.i.* To argue. [Obs.]

är′gū-ment, *n.* [Fr. *argument*; L. *argumentum*, evidence, proof, from *arguere*, to make clear, prove.]

1. A reason offered for or against a proposition, opinion, or measure; a reason offered in proof, to induce belief, or convince the mind; as, the only *argument* used was force.

2. A debate or discussion; a series of reasoning; as, an *argument* was had before the court, in which *argument* all the reasons were urged.

3. The subject of a discourse or writing; in a more restricted meaning, an outline of the plot or a summary of any literary production; as, the *argument* of a play.

> The abstract or *argument* of the piece is shortly as follows. —Jeffrey.

4. Something to make one take action; matter for controversy. [Obs.]

5. In astronomy, the quantity on which another quantity in a table depends; as, the altitude is the *argument* of the refraction.

6. In logic, the mean or middle term of a syllogism.

7. In mathematics, an independent variable the functional values of which are tabulated.

Syn.—Controversy, reasoning, discussion, dispute, topic.

är-gū-men′tȧ-ble, *a.* Capable of being argued.

är-gū-men′tăl, *a.* Belonging to or consisting of argument.

är″gū-men-tā′tion, *n.* [Fr. *argumentation*; L. *argumentatio*, from *argumentari*, to adduce, as proof.]

1. Reasoning; the act of forming reasons, making inductions, drawing conclusions, and applying them to the case in discussion; the operation of inferring propositions, not known or admitted as true, from facts or principles known, admitted, or proved to be true.

2. Argument; debate.

är-gū-men′tȧ-tive, *a.* 1. Abounding in argument; consisting of argument; containing a process of reasoning; as, an *argumentative* discourse.

2. Addicted to argument; as, an *argumentative* writer.

3. Tending to proof; indicating reasons; as, illustrations *argumentative* of a proposition.

är-gū-men′tȧ-tive-ly, *adv.* In an argumentative manner.

är-gū-men′tȧ-tive-ness, *n.* The state of being argumentative.

är′gū-men-tīze, *v.i.* To engage in discussion; to produce argument. [Obs.]

Är′gus, *n.* [L., from Gr. *Argos*; *argos*, bright.]

1. A fabulous being of antiquity, said to have had a hundred eyes, who was placed by Juno to guard Io.

2. [a—] One noted for watchfulness.

3. A genus of birds, the only species of which is the *Argus giganteus*, family *Phasianidæ*, a large, beautiful, and very singular species of pheasant, found native in the southeast of Asia, more especially in Sumatra. The males measure from five to six feet from the tip of the beak to the extremity of the tail. The general body-plumage is brown. When divested of its plumage, the bird is not much larger than a barnyard fowl.

Argus Pheasant (*Argus giganteus*).

är′gus-eyed (-īd), *a.* Keenly watchful.

är′gus-shell, *n.* A species of seashell, *Cypræa argus*, distinguished by its many beautiful eye-like spots.

är-gū-tā′tion, *n.* Frivolous argument; cavil. [Obs.]

är-gūte′, *a.* [L. *argutus*, clear, sharp, pp. of *arguere*, to make clear.] Sharp of taste; shrill; acute; keen; cunning. [Obs.]

är-gūte′ly, *adv.* Cunningly; wittily.

är-gūte′ness, *n.* Wittiness; keenness.

är-ġy-ran′thē-mous, är-ġy-ran′thous, *a.* [Gr. *argyros*, silver, and *anthos*, flower.] Having silver-colored inflorescence.

är-ġyr′i-ȧ, *n.* Argyrism.

är′ġyr-iṣm, *n.* [Gr. *argyrismos*, a money-getting, from *argyrizesthai*, to get money, from *argyros*, silver, money.] Skin-discoloration; an effect produced by the continued internal use of silver compounds.

är-ġyr′ō-dite, *n.* [L., from Gr. *argyrōdēs*, like silver; *argyros*, silver, and *eidos*, form.] A mineral compound, Ag_6GeS_5, of a grayish steel color.

ȧ-rhi′zăl, *a.* Same as *Arrhizal*.

ā′ri-ȧ, *n.* [It., from L. *aer*, air.] In music, an air of unusual length and importance, constituting a prominent part of an opera and sung as a solo.

-arian. [L. *-arius*, -ary, and *-anus*, -an.] A suffix used in forming adjectives and nouns from adjectives, denoting age, sect, social belief, occupation, etc.; as, antiqu*arian*, nonagen*arian*, Unitar*ian*.

Är′iăn, Ar′i-ăn, *a.* and *n.* See *Aryan*.

Ā′ri-ăn, *a.* and *n.* I. *a.* Related to Arius or his doctrines.

II. *n.* A believer in or an advocate of the doctrines of Arius.

Ā′ri-ăn-iṣm, *n.* The doctrines of the Arians; specifically, the doctrine promulgated by Arius, an Alexandrian of the fourth century, in substance denying the divinity of Christ.

Ā′ri-ăn-īze, *v.i.* To believe in the doctrine of Arianism.

Ā′ri-ăn-īze, *v.t.* To convert to the doctrines of Arius.

ar′i-cin, ar′i-cine, *n.* [From *Arica*, the principal seaport in northern Chile.] An alkaloid, a constituent of Arica bark and of *Cinchona cuprea*.

ar′id, *a.* [L. *aridus*, dry, from *arere*, to be dry.]

1. Dry; exhausted of moisture; parched with heat; having little rainfall; as, an *arid* waste.

2. Without profit; dry; tedious; as, an *arid* speech.

ȧ-rid′i-ty, *n.* Dryness; the state or quality of being arid.

ar′id-ness, *n.* Aridity.

Ā′ri-el, *n.* [L. *ariel*; Gr. *ariēl*; Heb. *ariēl*, Lion of God; a name applied to Jerusalem in the Old Testament.]

1. A name given by Sir John Herschel to the inner satellite of Uranus.

2. [a—] An Australian phalanger.

ā′ri-el, *n.* [Ar. *aryil*, *ayyil*, a stag.] A kind of gazel, *Gazella dama*, common to Arabia.

ā′ri-el, *a.* Light and airy on the wing; applied to certain birds.

Ā′ri-ēṣ, *n.* [L. *aries*, a ram.]

1. In astronomy, (a) the Ram, a northern constellation of 156 stars, of which 50 are visible; (b) the first sign of the zodiac.

2. [a—] A battering-ram of the Romans.

ar′i-e-tāte, *v.i.* [L. *arietatus*, pp. of *arietare*, to butt like a ram, from *aries*, a ram.] To butt, as a ram. [Obs.]

ar″i-e-tā′tion, *n.* 1. The act of butting. [Obs.]

2. The act of striking or conflicting. [Rare.]

ȧ-ri-et′tȧ, ar-i-ette′, *n.* [It., dim. of *aria*, from L. *aer*, air.] A short song; an air, or little air.

ȧ-right′ (ȧ-rīt′), *adv.* [*A-* and *right*, AS. *gericht*.] Rightly; in a right form; without mistake.

Syn.—Appropriately, suitably, properly, justly.

ar′il, *n.* [Fr. *arill*; Sp. *arilla*; L. *arilli*, dried grapes, from *aridus*, dry.] The exterior coat or covering of a seed, fixed to it at the base only, investing it wholly or partially, and falling off spontaneously, as the mace of a nutmeg.

ar′il-lāte, ar′il-lā-ted, *a.* Furnished with an aril.

ȧ-ril′lus, *n.* Same as *Aril*.

Är′i-măn, Äh′ri-măn, *n.* [Per.] The evil genius or demon according to the dualistic doctrine of Zoroaster. *Ariman* is the personification of malignity, the original source of all moral and physical evil, the chief of the devils and malignant spirits, the king of darkness and of death, and the eternal foe of Ormazd and his kingdom of light and life.

ar″i-ō-lā′tion, *n.* Same as *Hariolation*.

ar′i-ōse, *a.* [It. *arioso*, from *aria*; L. *aer*, air.] Characterized by melody, as distinguished from harmony.

ȧ-ri-ō′sō, *adv.* and *a.* [It., from *aria*; L. *aer*, air.] Combining the style of an aria and a recitative.

Ar-i-sæ′mȧ, *n.* [L. *aris*; Gr. *aron*, arum, and *haima*, blood.] A genus of low perennial plants of the *Arum* family, including the Indian turnip, or Jack-in-the-pulpit, *Arisæma triphyllum*.

ȧ-rīṣe′, *v.i*; arose, *pt.*; arising, *ppr.*; arisen, *pp.* [ME. *arisen*; AS. *arīsan*; *ā*, out, and *rīsan*, to rise.]

1. To ascend; mount up; as, vapors *arise* from humid places.

2. To get out of bed; to leave a restful posture.

The king *arose* early and went to the den.
—Dan. vi. 19.

3. To begin; to spring up; to originate.

The persecution that *arose* about Stephen.
—Acts xi. 19.

4. To begin to act; to exert power; to move from a state of inaction.

Let God *arise*; let his enemies be scattered.
—Ps. lxviii. 1.

Syn.—Rise, spring, flow, mount, scale, issue, emanate.

ȧ-rīṣe′, *n.* Rising. [Obs.]

ȧ-rist′, *v.* Ariseth. [Obs.]

ȧ-ris′tȧ, *n.* [L.] 1. In botany, the awn.

2. In zoölogy, any awn-like appendage.

ar′is-tärch, *n.* [From *Aristarchus*, a critic distinguished among the ancients for severity.] A severe critic.

ar-is-tär′chi-ăn, *a.* Severely critical.

ar′is-tär-chy, *n.* Severe criticism. [Obs.]

ar′is-tär-chy, *n.* [Gr. *aristarchia*, from *aristarchos*, best ruling; *aristos*, best, and *archos*, from *archein*, to rule.] A body of good men in power, or government by excellent men.

ȧ-ris′tāte, *a.* 1. Awned; having a pointed, beardlike process, as the glumes of wheat.

2. In zoölogy, having a slender, sharp tip.

ar-is-toc′rȧ-cy, *n.* [Fr. *aristocracie*; Gr. *aristokratia*, the rule of the best-born, or nobles; *aristos*, best, and *kratia*, from *kratein*, to be strong, to rule.]

1. Government exercised by the best class in a community. [Obs.]

2. A titled class or nobility of a country.

3. Those who rise above the rest of the community in any important respect, as in wealth, knowledge, character, etc.

4. The quality of being an aristocrat; as, his *aristocracy* was in keeping with his education.

ar-is′tō-crat (*or* ar′is-), *n.* A member of the aristocracy; one believing in aristocracy.

ar″is-tō-crat′ic, ar″is-tō-crat′ic-ăl, *a.* Related in any way to aristocracy; having the qualities and inclinations of an aristocrat.

ar″is-tō-crat′ic-ăl-ly, *adv.* In an aristocratic manner.

ar″is-tō-crat′ic-ăl-ness, *n.* The condition or quality of being aristocratic.

ar′is-tō-crat″ism, *n.* Aristocratic principles or rank; the state of being an aristocrat.

Ar″is-tō-lō′chi-ȧ, *n.* [From Gr. *aristolocheia*, a herb, promoting childbirth; *aristos*, best, and *locheia*, childbirth.] The typical genus of the natural order *Aristolochiaceæ*. They are herbs and woody climbers, tropical, and have flowers of dull color, and curiously formed to entrap insects, which appear to be necessary to fertilization, though just how is not known. Some species have been popularly considered remedial for snake-bites, and as vermifuges. *Aristolochia Serpentaria*, the Virginia snakeroot, is a tonic and diaphoretic. *Aristolochia Sipho*, Dutchman's-pipe, or pipe-vine, native to the Alleghany mountains, is cultivated for ornamental purposes.

Ar″is-tō-lō-chi-ā′cē-æ, *n.pl.* An order of tropical climbers and twiners, with dull, heavy-scented, often offensive, flowers; the birthwort family.

ar″is-tō-lō-chi-ā′ceous, *a.* Relating to the *Aristolochiaceæ*.

ar-is-tol′ō-gy, *n.* [Gr. *ariston*, breakfast, and *logia*, from *legein*, to speak.] The science of dining. [Rare and humorous.]

Ar″is-tō-phan′ic, *a.* Pertaining to the classic Greek poet, Aristophanes, and to his comedies.

Ar″is-tō-tē′li-ăn, *a.* and *n.* I. *a.* Pertaining to the classic Greek philosopher, Aristotle, or to his philosophy.

II. *n.* A disciple of Aristotle.

Ar″is-tō-tē′li-ăn-iṣm, *n.* The philosophical system of Aristotle, the ancient Greek philosopher of the fourth century B.C. Aristotle was a disciple of Plato and founded the sect of Peripatetics or Peripatetic School; his system is called the Aristotelian philosophy. He maintained the deductive method in opposition to the inductive, and experimentalism as opposed to intuitionalism. In his cosmology, a thing exists only in potentiality; form is its actuality; matter, which makes it to be, is identical in an unformed state with the potentiality of a germ.

Ar″is-tō-tel′ic, *a.* Pertaining to Aristotle or to his philosophy.

ȧ-ris′tō-tȳpe, *n.* [Gr. *aristos*, best, and *typos*, an impression, mark of a blow; from *typtein*, to strike.] A photographic picture on any printing-out paper specially prepared with collodion or gelatin, the name *aristo paper*—strictly the trade name of one variety—being generally applied to all kinds of such paper.

ȧ-ris′tū-lāte, *a.* [L., dim. of *arista*, awn, or beard of grain.] In botany, with a small awn.

ar′ith-man-cy, *n.* [Gr. *arithmos*, number, and *manteia*, divination.] Same as *Arithmomancy*.

ȧ-rith′me-tic, *n.* [L. *arithmetica*; Gr. *arithmētikē*, from *arithmein*, to reckon, count; *arithmos*, number.]

1. The science of numbers, or the art of computation, the fundamental operations of which are performed by addition, subtraction, multiplication, and division.

2. A treatise on the science of numbers or their use in computation.

Arithmetic of sines or *series*; trigonometry.

Political arithmetic; statistics relating to the condition of a country

Universal arithmetic; algebra.

ar-ith-met′ic-ăl, ar-ith-met′ic, *a.* Pertaining to arithmetic; according to the rules or methods of arithmetic.

ar-ith-met′ic-ăl-ly, *adv.* According to the rules, principles, or methods of arithmetic.

ȧ-rith-me-ti′ciăn (-tish′un), *n.* One skilled in arithmetic, or versed in the science of numbers.

ȧ-rith′mō-man-cy, *n.* Divination, or the foretelling of future events by the use or observation of numbers; also written *arithmancy*.

ar-ith-mom′e-tēr, *n.* [From Gr. *arithmos*, a number, and *metron*, a measure.] A machine for performing the fundamental operations of arithmetic.

ärk, *n.* [ME. *ark*, *arche*; AS. *earc*, arc; L. *arca*, a chest, box, from *arcere*, to shut up, inclose; Gr. *arkein*, to keep off.]

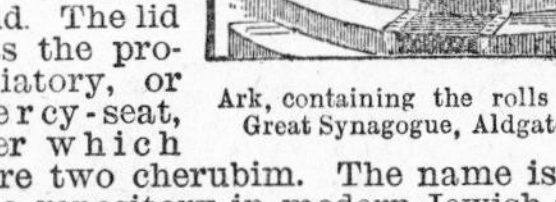

Ark, containing the rolls of the Law.—Great Synagogue, Aldgate, London.

1. A small, close vessel, chest, or coffer, which was the repository of the tables of the covenant among the Jews. It was about three feet nine inches long, and two feet six inches wide, and was made of acacia wood overlaid with gold. The lid was the propitiatory, or mercy-seat, over which were two cherubim. The name is also given to a repository in modern Jewish synagogues for the books used in the service.

2. The large, floating vessel in which Noah and his family were preserved during the deluge.

3. A refuge; that which shelters or protects.

4. In western United States, a river flatboat, used for transporting produce and other freight; on the eastern coast, a house-scow used for the transaction of fish and oyster business; also in the eastern states, a bin for grain.

ärk′ite, *a.* Belonging to the ark. [Rare.]

är-kōse′, är-cōse′, *n.* [Fr.] A fragmental sandstone composed largely of granite crystals with feldspar present.

ärk′-shell, *n.* A bivalve of the genus *Arca*.

ärleṣ (ärlz), *n.pl.* [Scot. *arles*; Gael. *iarlas*, earnest-money; Fr. *arrhes*; L. *arrha*, earnest-money.] Earnest-money, given in confirmation of a bargain, contract, or agreement. The practice is now discontinued except in the case of hiring servants in Scotland or the north of England.

ärleṣ′-pen″ny, *n.* Same as *Arles*.

ärm, *n.* [AS. *arm*, *earm*; L. *armus*, shoulder; Gr. *harmos*, a joining, joint.]

1. In anatomy, one of the two upper limbs; especially that portion extending from the shoulder to the elbow.

2. In zoölogy, the corresponding limb of vertebrate animals; also, in general, any part extending from the body like an arm, as the ray of a starfish.

3. Anything formed on the type of or resembling an arm; any slender part projecting from the main body, trunk, base, axis, or fulcrum; applied widely in machinery.

4. Any branch or division; any separate part; as, the cavalry forms a distinct *arm* of the service; an *arm* of the gulf runs back into the forest.

5. Nautically, the end of the yard of a sailing vessel; also, one of the ends of the bar of an anchor.

6. A weapon of any kind. [See *Arms*.]

7. Figuratively, strength or support; as, the secular *arm*.

Arm in arm; with arms intertwined, or with the hand of one person in the arm of another.

Arm of a force; in a couple, the rod or bar which connects the force with the axis of rotation; as, the weight-arm of a balance is the *arm of the force* exerted by the weight.

At arm's length; at a distance, literally or figuratively; beyond familiarity; as, to keep a person *at arm's length*; also, at a disadvantage; with inconvenience; as, to work *at arm's length*.

ärm, *v.t.*; armed (ärmd), *pt.*, *pp.*; arming, *ppr.* [ME. *armen*; OFr. *armer*; It. *armare*; L. *armare*, to arm, from *arma*, pl., arms.]

1. To equip with any means of offense or defense; to prepare for war.

2. To equip or provide with anything advantageous or tending toward greater strength or efficiency, in a material or immaterial way; as, he had *armed* himself with proper passports; to *arm* the younger generation with an adequate education.

3. To raise in the arms; to grasp by the arm; to supply with arms. [Obs.]

To arm a magnet; to provide a magnet with a keeper or armature.

Syn.—Fortify, equip, furnish, attire, array, supply.

ärm, *v.i.* To take arms; to prepare for attack or defense; as, the nations *arm* for war.

är-mȧ′dȧ, *n.* [Sp. *armada*; It. *armata*, an armed force; L. *armata*, f. of *armatus*, pp. of *armare*, to arm; *arma*, arms.] A fleet of armed ships; a squadron; specifically, the Spanish fleet, consisting of 130 ships, intended to act against England, in the reign of Queen Elizabeth, A.D. 1588.

är-mȧ-dil′lō, *n.*; *pl.* **är-mȧ-dil′loṣ**. [Sp. dim. of *armada*, from L. *armatus*, armed, pp. of *armare*, to arm.]

Yellow-footed Armadillo (*Dasypus encoubert*).

1. A name given to different species of edentate quadrupeds, belonging to the genus *Dasypus*; peculiar to America. These animals are covered with a hard, bony shell, divided, over the back, into movable belts, which are connected by a membrane which allows them to roll up like a ball when attacked, and present their armor on all sides to an assailant. In size, they vary, the largest being more than three feet in length, without the tail. They subsist chiefly on fruits, roots, and insects, and their flesh is esteemed good food.

2. [A—] A genus of isopod crustaceans, including the pill-bugs, that roll themselves up like the armadillos.

är-mȧ′dō, *n.* [Obs.] See *Armada*.

är′mȧ-ment, *n.* [L. *armamentum*, pl. *armamenta*, implements, tackle of a ship, from *armare*, to arm; *arma*, arms.]

1. A land or naval force, or a combination of both, in fighting order; as, the entire *armament* of Japan.

2. The offensive equipment of a ship of war or a fortification, including guns, rifles, etc.; as, the enemy's *armament* was heavier than ours.

3. Any means of offensive or defensive operations, by an individual or a nation.

är″mȧ-men-tā′ri-um, *n.* [L.] Same as *Armamentary*.

är-mȧ-men′tȧ-ry, *n.* [L. *armamentarium*, an arsenal, from *armamenta*, arms, equipment.] An armory; a magazine or arsenal. [Rare.]

är′mȧ-tūre, *n.* [Fr. *armature*; L. *armatura*, arms, equipment, from *armatus*, pp. of *armare*, to arm; *arma*, arms.]

1. Defensive armor or offensive weapons; equipment for battle. [Rare.]

2. The natural defenses of animals and vegetables, as prickles, spines, and horns.

3. In architecture, any means of bracing or stiffening a weak part, as supports for slender columns, etc.

4. A system of natural organs; a physiological apparatus; as, the gastric *armature*.

5. In magnetism, a piece of iron connecting the two poles of a horseshoe magnet, in order to maintain the magnetic power undiminished.

6. In a dynamo-electric machine, the part generating useful currents, consisting of a series of coils of insulated wire, grouped on a central core, and moved through the magnetic field.

ärm′chāir, *n.* A chair with supports on the sides for the elbows or arms.

ärmed, *a.* 1. Equipped with weapons or any means of offense or defense; fortified.

2. Having means of strength or efficiency; made powerful or firm; used in mental and moral as well as physical senses.

3. In biology, having defensive parts or weapons, as horns, claws, prickles, thorns, etc.

4. In magnetism, fitted with an armature, as a magnet or dynamo.

5. In heraldry, furnished with beaks, talons, horns, etc., of a different color from the rest of the body.

Armed at all points; completely covered with armor; armed cap-à-pie.

Armed neutrality; see under *Neutrality*.

Armed at all points.

Är-mē′ni-ăn, *n.* [Fr. *Arménien*; L. *Armenius*; Gr. *Armenios*, from *Armenia*.]

1. A native or inhabitant of Armenia.

2. The language of Armenia.

3. A member of the Armenian church.

Är-mē′ni-ăn, *a.* Pertaining to Armenia.

Armenian bole; a bright red clay found in Armenia.

Armenian church; the church founded in the fourth century by Gregory, called the Illuminator. It is separate from the Greek church, though resembling it in some doctrines and practices.

Armenian stone; a soft, blue stone, consisting of calcareous earth or gypsum, with the oxid of copper; used in the preparation of certain blue pigments; also, a popular name for lapis lazuli.

ärm′et, *n.* [Fr. *armet*, *armette*, dim. of *armes*, armor.] A steel helmet used from the fourteenth to the sixteenth centuries.

Armet-grand. Armet-petit.

ärm′fụl, *n.* As much as the arm (or arms), can hold; anything so held.

ärm′gäunt, *a.* Slender, as the arm; having thin limbs. [Obs.]

ärm′=greāt, *a.* [ME. *arm-gret*, arm-great.] As thick as a man's arm. [Obs.]

ärm′hōle, *n.* 1. The cavity under the shoulder; the armpit.

2. A hole for the arm in a garment.

är-mif′ẽr-ous, *a.* [L. *arma*, arms, and *ferre*, to bear.] Bearing arms. [Rare.]

är′mi-gẽr, *n.* [L. *armiger*, an armor-bearer; *arma*, arms, and *gerere*, to carry, bear.] An esquire; a knight's armor-bearer and companion; hence, later, one just below a knight in degree of rank; a person having the right of armorial ensigns. [See *Esquire*.]

är-mig′ẽr-ous, *a.* 1. Bearing arms. [Rare.]

2. Having the right to use armorial bearings.

är′mil, *n.* [L. *armilla*, an armlet, bracelet, from *armus*, arm.]

1. An armillary sphere, or a ring in such a sphere.

2. A bracelet. [Obs.]

är-mi-lạu′sȧ, *n.* [L., probably from *armus*, the shoulder, and *clausus*, shut in, pp. of *claudere*, to shut in.] A name of a medieval garment, worn in Europe, which probably differed in shape at different times. It has been described as a body garment, the prototype of the surcoat. One form of it, in the fourteenth century, was a kind of short cloak with a hood.

Armilausa, from an illumination of 14th century.

är-mil′lȧ, *n.*; *pl.* är-mil′læ. [L., armlet.]

1. An armlet; a circular or spiral ornament worn round the upper arm; also, a bracelet or ornament for the wrist.

2. In machinery, an iron ring, hoop, or brace, in which the gudgeons of a wheel move.

3. In anatomy, a circular ligament of the wrist binding the tendons of the whole hand.

4. In zoölogy, a ring of hair or feathers around the lower part of the tibia.

är′mil-lā-ry, *a.* [L. *armilla*, an armlet, armring, from *armus*, shoulder.] Resembling a bracelet, or rings; consisting of rings or circles.

Armillary sphere; an ancient astronomical instrument used before the invention of the telescope, consisting of an artificial sphere, composed of a number of circles of the same sphere. This artificial sphere revolved upon its axis within a horizon divided into degrees, and movable every way upon a brass supporter.

Armillary sphere.

ärm′ing, *n.* 1. The act of taking up, or furnishing with, arms; also, that which arms.

The *arming* was now universal.—Macaulay.

2. Nautically, (a) tallow attached to a sounding-lead to bring up specimens from the sea-bottom; (b) [*pl.*], waist-cloths, hung about a ship's upper works.

ärm′ing=press, *n.* In bookbinding, a kind of press used in impressing designs, as of gold-leaf, on a cover.

Är-min′i-ăn, *a.* Pertaining to Arminius or his followers, or designating his principles and doctrines.

Är-min′i-ăn, *n.* One of a sect or party of Christians, so called from Arminius, or Harmansen, of Holland, who flourished at the close of the sixteenth century and beginning of the seventeenth.

The *Arminian* doctrines are: (1) conditional election and reprobation, in opposition to absolute predestination; (2) universal redemption, or that the atonement was made by Christ for all mankind, though none but believers can be partakers of the benefit; (3) that man, in order to exercise true faith, must be regenerated and renewed by the operation of the Holy Spirit, which is the gift of God; but that this grace is not irresistible, and may be lost; so that men may lapse from a state of grace, and die in their sins.

Är-min′i-ăn-ism, *n.* The doctrines or tenets of the Arminians.

är-mip′ō-tence, *n.* [L. *armipotentia*, power in arms; *arma*, arms, and *potens*, ppr. of *posse*, to be able.] Power in arms. [Rare.]

är-mip′ō-tent, *a.* Powerful in arms; mighty in battle. [Rare.]

är-mis′ō-nănt, är-mis′ō-nous, *a.* [L. *arma*, arms, and *sonans*, ppr. of *sonare*, to sound.] Sounding or rustling in arms. [Obs.]

är′mis-tice, *n.* [Fr. *armistice*, from L. *arma*, arms, and *stare*, to stand still.] A cessation of arms, for a short time, by convention; a truce; a temporary suspension of hostilities by agreement of the parties.

ärm′less, *a.* 1. Without an arm or branch.

2. Having no arms or weapons.

ärm′let, *n.* 1. A small arm; as, an *armlet* of the sea.

2. A piece of armor for the arm.

3. An ornamental ring for the upper arm; a bracelet.

Persian. Armlets. Egyptian.

är-mō′ni-aç, *a.* Ammoniac. [Obs.]

är′mŏr, är′mour, *n.* [ME. *armour*, *armure*; OFr. *armure*; It. *armatura*; L. *armatura*, armor, from *armare*, to arm; *arma*, arms.]

1. Defensive arms; any covering worn to protect the body in battle; a coat or suit of mail; formerly called *harness*; often named from the material, as *plate armor*, *ring armor*, *chain armor*, etc. A complete *armor* formerly consisted of a casque or helmet, a gorget, cuirass, gauntlets, tassets, brassarts, cuishes, and covers for the legs, to which the spurs were fastened. In the illustration are shown the various parts of a complete suit of *plate armor* of the fifteenth century; A, bascinet; B, jeweled orle round the bascinet; C, gorget, or gorgiere of plate; D, pauldrons; E, breastplate-cuirass; F, rerebraces; G, coudes or elbow-plates; H, gauntlets; I, vambrace; J, skirt of tassets; K, military belt or cingulum, richly jeweled; L, tuilles or tuillettes; M, cuishes; N, genouillières or knee-pieces; O, jambes; P, spur-straps; Q, sollerets; R, misericorde or dagger; S, sword, suspended by a transverse belt.

Armor, from the effigy of Sir Richard Peyton.

2. The metallic protection given to warships or forts, usually consisting of supercarbonized steel plates of varying thickness, to enable them to withstand the fire of heavy artillery.

3. Figuratively, any protection or safeguard.

Put on the whole *armour* of God.—Eph. vi. 11.

4. Any protective covering, as the shells of some animals, the husk of grain, etc.

Submarine armor; a diving suit.

är′mŏr, *v.t.*; armored, *pt.*, *pp.*; armoring, *ppr.* To cover with armor or armor-plate.

är′mŏr=beār″ẽr, *n.* One who carried the armor of another; a squire; an armiger.

är′mŏred (-mẽrd), *a.* Equipped, furnished, or clad with armor; as, an *armored* train, ship, or knight.

är′mŏr-ẽr, *n.* [ME. *armurer*, *armerer*; OFr. *armurier*, from *armure*, armor.]

1. A maker of armor or arms; a manufacturer of instruments of war.

2. Formerly, a body-servant who cared for a knight's armor and arms and arrayed him in them.

3. The custodian of arms, either on board a man-of-war or in the army; one who cleans and repairs arms.

är-mō′ri-ăl, *a.* Belonging to armor, or to the arms or escutcheon of a family.

Armorial bearings; in a coat of arms, the devices displayed.

Är-mor′iç, Är-mor′i-căn, *a.* [L. *armoricus*; Celtic *ar*, upon, and *mor*, the sea.] Of or pertaining to ancient Armorica, in the northwestern part of France, now Bretagne, or Brittany, where a branch of the Celtic is spoken.

Är-mor′iç, *n.* The language of the Armoricans; one of the Celtic dialects which have remained to the present time.

Är-mor′i-căn, *n.* A native of Armorica, or Brittany.

är′mŏr-ist, *n.* [Fr. *armoriste*, from *armoiries*, a coat of arms, arms.] One well-versed in heraldry or skilled in the blazoning of arms.

är′mŏr=plāte, *n.* Plates of iron or steel for covering the sides of a ship or fort.

är′mŏr=plāt″ed, *a.* Covered with armor-plate; steel-clad.

är′mŏr-y, *n.* [Fr. *armoire*; OFr. *armaire*, *armarie*, from L. *armarium*, a place for keeping arms.]

1. A place where arms and instruments of war are deposited for safe-keeping.

2. Armor; defensive and offensive arms.

3. Ensigns armorial.

4. The knowledge of coat-armor; that branch of heraldry which treats of coat-armor.

5. A place or building in which arms are manufactured.

6. A place where arms are kept and soldiers are drilled; as, the First Regiment *armory*; often, in this sense, a building containing apartments for social as well as military use, as company rooms, halls, etc.

är′mŏur, *n.* and *v.t.* See *Armor*.

är-mō-zeen′, är-mō-zīne′, *n.* [Fr. *armoisin*; OFr. *armesin*; L. *ermesinus*, taffeta.] A heavy silk, generally black, formerly used in making robes for the clergy.

ärm′pit, *n.* The hollow place or cavity under the shoulder; the axilla.

ärmṣ, *n.pl.* [ME. *armes*; Fr. *arme*, pl. *armes*, from L. *arma*, arms, equipment.]

1. Weapons of offense, or armor for defense and protection of the body.

2. Military science; the occupation of war; deeds done in war; the profession of a soldier; as, a comrade in *arms*; an assault at *arms*.

Arms and the man I sing. —Dryden.

3. In heraldry, the ensigns armorial of a family, consisting of figures and colors borne in shields, banners, etc., as marks of dignity and distinction, and descending from father to son.

4. In law, anything which a man takes in his hand in anger, with which to strike or assault another.

5. In botany, the various defensive parts or armor of plants, as prickles, thorns, forks, and stings, which seem intended to protect the plants from injury by animals.

6. Any device adopted, as by a state or city, to be its official emblem; as, the *arms* of the city of New York; the *arms* of Illinois.

7. In falconry, the legs of a hawk from the thigh to the foot.

A stand of arms; a rifle, bayonet, cartridge-box and belt; or the rifle and bayonet alone.

Arms of precision; modern firearms.

Repeating arms; arms that can be fired several times without reloading.

Rifled arms; firearms that are cut with a spiral groove, or rifled.

Small arms; firearms that can be carried, as rifles, carbines, pistols, etc.

To be in arms; to be in a state of hostility, or preparation for war.

To arms; a summoning to war or battle.

To take arms; to arm for attack or defense.

Bred to arms; educated to the profession of a soldier.

Under arms; having arms ready for use, as troops ready for parade or battle.

är′mūre, *n.* 1. Armor. [Obs.]

2. A kind of ribbed woolen cloth.

3. In weaving, the manner of preparing a loom for different weaves. The four principal *armures* are called taffeta, serge, twill, and sateen.

är′my, *n.* [ME. *armye, armeye*; OFr. *armee*; It. *armata*; L. *armata*, f. of *armatus*, pp. of *armare*, to arm; *arma*, arms.]

1. A collection or body of men armed for war, and usually organized in companies, battalions, regiments, brigades, and divisions, under proper officers. In general, an *army*, in modern times, consists of infantry, cavalry and artillery; although the union of all is not essential to its organization.

2. The military forces of a nation as distinguished from its navy; the land forces; as, to join the *army*; an *army* officer.

3. A great number; a vast multitude; as, an *army* of locusts or caterpillars.

4. A body of persons organized for some particular object; as, the Salvation *Army*.

Standing or *regular army*; an army of regular soldiers always ready for duty, in distinction from the reserves, as militia or volunteers.

Syn.—Multitude, phalanx, soldiery, legion, soldiers, troops, host.

är′my-ȧnt, *n.* A foraging ant, of the genus *Eciton*.

är′my-cōrps (-kōr), *n.* The largest unit of an army under one command, including every branch of the service, and often acting as an independent army.

är′my-list, *n.* An official register of an army.

är′my-wŏrm, *n.* The larva of *Leucania unipuncta*; so called because vast numbers move like a destroying army, completely devouring all vegetation in their path; also, any related species with similar habits.

är′nȧ, är′nee, *n.* [Hind. *arnā*.] One of the numerous Indian varieties of the buffalo, *Bos bubalus*, remarkable as being the largest animal of the ox kind known.

är′nee, *n.* See *Arna*.

Är′ni-çȧ, *n.* [Probably from *Ptarmica*; Gr. *ptarmikos*, causing to sneeze.]

1. A genus of plants belonging to the order *Compositæ*.

2. [a—] Any plant of this genus, especially the perennial *Arnica montana*, or mountain arnica, common in the mountainous parts of Germany, Sweden, Lapland, and Switzerland. It is used in medicine as a narcotic and stimulant.

3. [a—] Tincture of arnica, applied externally as a remedy for sores, wounds, bruises, and ailments of a similar kind.

är′ni-cin, är′ni-cine, *n.* In chemistry, a bitter resin that contains the active principle of arnica.

Är′nōld-ist, *n.* A disciple of Arnold of Brescia, who, in the twelfth century, was executed for insurrection against Roman Catholic authority.

är′not, *n.* [Obs.] See *Earthnut*.

är-not′tō, *n.* [Native S. Am. name, origin unknown.]

1. The *Bixa Orellana*, a small tree, natural order *Flacourtiaceæ*, a native of tropical America. It is common in Jamaica and other parts of the West Indies, and has been introduced into tropical regions of the Old World.

Arnotto (*Bixa Orellana*).

2. The dye or coloring-matter obtained from the seeds of this plant. The seeds are covered with a reddish or reddish-yellow, waxy pulp, which is dissolved in water, dried to the consistency of putty, and made up in rolls or cakes or folded in leaves. It is employed as a dye for silken stuffs, as an auxiliary in giving a deeper shade to the simple yellows and as a coloring for butter, cheese, and chocolate. Called also *anotta, annatto, anatto, arnatto*, etc.

är′nut, *n.* See *Earthnut*.

ä-rō-ei′rȧ (-ā′rȧ), *n.* [Native Brazilian name.] Any one of several South American shrubs of the cashew family, from which a medicinal resin is extracted.

ar′oid, ȧ-roid′ē-ous, *a.* Resembling or belonging to the *Arum* family.

ar′oid, *n.* [L. *arum*; Gr. *aron*, wake-robin, and *eidos*, shape, form.] A member of the *Arum* family.

A-roi′dē-æ, *n.pl.* [L., from Gr. *aron*, the wake-robin, and *eidos*, form.] See *Araceæ*.

ȧ-roint′, ȧ-roynt′, *interj.* [Provincial English of Cheshire, *rynt, runt*; AS. *gerȳman*, make room.] A word used apparently as a standard formula for exorcising witches; as, *aroint*, thou witch! [Rare.]

ȧ-roint′, *v.t.* To exorcise; to frighten away. [Rare.]

ȧ-rol′lȧ, *n.* [Fr. *arolle*.] The stone-pine of the Old World, *Pinus Cembra*.

ȧ-rō′mȧ, *n.* [ME. *aromat*; OFr. *aromat*; L. *aroma*; Gr. *arōma*, a sweet spice, a sweet smell.]

1. The fragrance of plants, or other substances, which is perceived by an agreeable smell; spicy perfume.

2. Figuratively, a characteristic charm or flavor; as, the *aroma* of culture.

Syn.—Fragrance, perfume, savor.

ar-ō-mat′iç, ar-ō-mat′iç-ăl, *a.* Fragrant; spicy; strong-scented; odoriferous; having an agreeable odor.

Aromatic compounds; in chemistry, those which are mostly obtained from aromatic oils and resins, differing in many respects from the fatty bodies. The lowest of the series is benzene, C_6H_6.

Aromatic vinegar; see under *Vinegar*.

ar-ō-mat′iç, *n.* A plant, drug, or medicine, characterized by a fragrant smell, and usually by a warm, pungent taste, as ginger.

ar-ō-mat-i-zā′tion, *n.* The act of impregnating or scenting with aroma, or rendering aromatic.

ȧ-rō′mȧ-tize, *v.t.*; aromatized, *pt., pp.*; aromatizing, *ppr.* To impregnate with aroma; to infuse with an aromatic odor; to give a spicy scent or taste; to perfume.

ȧ-rō′mȧ-ti-zēr, *n.* That which communicates an aromatic quality; one who aromatizes.

ȧ-rō′mȧ-tous, *a.* [Obs.] See *Aromatic*.

ar′oph, *n.* [A contraction of *aroma philosophorum*.] In old chemistry, various pharmaceutical preparations. [Obs.]

ȧ-rōşe′, *v.*, past tense of *arise*.

ȧ-round′, *prep.* 1. About; on all sides; encircling; encompassing.

2 From place to place; at random in. [Colloq.]

ȧ-round′, *adv.* 1. In a circle; on every side.

2. At random; without any fixed direction; as, to travel *around* from town to town.

3. In the vicinity; about; near by; as, he visited *around*. [Colloq.]

ȧ-rous′ăl, *n.* The act of arousing.

ȧ-rouşe′, *v.t.*; aroused, *pt., pp.*; arousing, *ppr.* [*A-* and ME. *rowsen, rouzen*.] To excite into action (that which is at rest); to stir, or put in motion or exertion (that which is languid); as, to *arouse* one from sleep; to *arouse* the dormant faculties.

Syn.—Stimulate, provoke, animate, awaken, excite.

ȧ-rōw′, *adv.* In a row; successively.

är-peġ′giō, här-peġ′giō (-pej′ō), *n.* [It. *arpeggiare*, to play on a harp.]

1. In music, the sounding of the notes of a chord in rapid succession, as in harp-playing.

2. A chord played *à arpeggio*.

är′pent, *n.* [Fr. *arpent*; LL. *arapennes*; L. *arepennis*; a word of Celtic origin.] An old and varying measure of land in France, the *arpent* of Paris containing about five-sixths of an acre; retained in Louisiana, and Quebec, Canada.

är-pen-tā′tŏr, *n.* A land surveyor. [Rare.]

är′pine, *n.* [Obs.] See *Arpent*.

är′quā-ted, *a.* [L. *arcuare*, to bend like a bow, from *arcus*, bow.] Arcuate; curved. [Rare.]

är′quē-bus, är′quē-buse, *n.* See *Harquebus*.

är″quē-bus-āde′, *n.* See *Harquebusade*.

är″quē-bus-iēr′, *n.* See *Harquebusier*.

är′qui-fōux (är′ki-fọọ), *n.* [Fr. *alquifoux*.] Same as *Alquifou*.

är-rȧ-çȧ′chȧ, *n.* [Sp.] A Mexican plant, belonging to the genus *Arracacia*.

Är-rȧ-çā′ci-ȧ (-shi-ȧ), *n.* [Sp., from a native name.] A genus of umbelliferous plants growing in Mexico and South America.

ar′răch, *n.* See *Orach*.

ar′rack, *n.* [Fr. *arac*; Ar. *araq*, sweat, spirit, juice.]

1. An Oriental name for all spirituous liquors.

2. An Oriental beverage, varying in different countries, being distilled from rice, molasses, or the sap of the cocoa-palm.

ar-rāign′ (-rān′), *v.t.*; arraigned (-rānd), *pt., pp.*; arraigning, *ppr.* [ME. *araynen, arenen*; OFr. *aranier*; L. *ad*, to, and *ratio*, reason.]

1. In law, to call or set (a prisoner) at the bar of a court, to answer to the matter charged against him in an indictment or complaint.

2. To accuse; to charge with faults; to call before the bar of reason, or taste; to call in question, for faults, before any tribunal.

> They will not *arraign* you for want of knowledge. —Dryden.

Syn.—Accuse, attack, censure, impeach, inculpate.

ar-rāign′, *v.t.* In old English law, to appeal to; to demand.

ar-rāign′, *n.* Arraignment; as, clerk of the *arraigns*.

ar-rāign′ēr, *n.* One who arraigns.

ar-rāign′ment, *n.* [Norm. *arresnement, arraynement*.]

1. The act of arraigning; the act of calling a person or prisoner before a court to answer to a complaint or indictment and to plead guilty or not guilty.

2. A calling in question for faults; accusation.

ar-rāi′ment, *n.* [Obs.] See *Raiment*.

ar-rānġe′, *v.t.*; arranged (-rānjd), *pt., pp.*; arranging, *ppr.* [ME. *arayngen, arengen*; OFr. *arangier*; Fr. *arranger*, from *ad* and *ranger*, to set in order.]

1. To put in proper order; to dispose (the parts of a whole) in the manner intended, or best suited for the purpose; as, to *arrange* troops for battle.

2. To adjust; to settle; to put in order; to prepare; as, to *arrange* details.

3. To adapt (a musical composition).

Syn.—Class, dispose, place, range, group, adjust.

ar-rānġe′ment, *n.* 1. The act of putting in proper order; the state of being put in order; disposition in suitable form.

2. That which is disposed in order; system of parts disposed in due order.

3. Preparatory measure; previous disposition; as, we have made *arrangement* for receiving company.

4. Final settlement; adjustment by agreement; as, the parties have made an *arrangement* between themselves concerning their disputes,

5. Classification of facts relating to a subject or of objects, in regular, systematic order; as, the Linnæan *arrangement* of plants.

6. The adaptation of a musical composition; also, a composition so adapted.

Syn.—Classification, adjustment, agreement, disposition, grouping, disposal, order.

ar-rān′ġēr, *n.* One who or that which puts in order.

ar′rănt, *a.* [A variant spelling of *errant*, wandering, from L. *errare*, to wander.]

1. Notorious, in an ill sense; infamous; mere; vile; as, an *arrant* rogue or coward.

2. Earnest; genuine: thorough. [Obs.]

Syn.—Consummate, notorious, flagrant, vile, utter.

ar′rănt-ly, *adv.* Notoriously, in an ill sense; infamously; impudently; shamefully.

ar′răs, *n.* [So called from *Arras*, from L. *Atrebates*, a people of Belgic Gaul.] Tapestry; hangings woven with figures.

ar′răs, *n.* [Sp.] In Spanish law, a marriage pledge or settlement.

ar′răs, *n.* A kind of powder probably made of the root of the orris. [Obs.]

ar′răs, *v.t.* To hang or furnish with arras.

ar-răs-ēne′, *n.* A silk or woolen cord or thread, used for embroidery.

är-răs′tră, *n.* See *Arrastre*.

är-răs′tre, *n.* [Sp. *arrastrar*, to drag along the ground; L. *ad*, to, and *radere*, to scrape.] In gold-mining, a rude machine formerly used for ore-crushing.

ar′răs-wişe, *adv.* See *Arriswise*.

ar-rąught′ (-rąt′), *a.* [Imperf. of *areach*.] Seized by violence.

ar-rāy′, *n.* [ME. *arayen*; OFr. *areyer, arraier*; L. *ad*, to, and *res*, thing.]

1. Regular order or arrangement; disposition in regular lines; specifically, disposition of a body of men for attack or defense; as, troops in battle *array*.

2. An orderly collection or assemblage; especially, a body of men in an imposing order; a body of men in order of battle or prepared for battle; hence, military force; soldiery; troops.

> A gallant *array* of nobles and cavaliers. —Prescott.

3. Dress; garments disposed in order upon the person; raiment or apparel.

> Emily ere day
> Arose, and dress'd herself in rich *array*. —Dryden.

4. Situation; circumstances; position. [Obs.]

> Thou stondest yet (quod sche) in swiche *array*. —Chaucer.

5. In law, (a) the number of persons summoned to serve upon a jury; (b) the act of impaneling a jury; (c) the jury impaneled.

> Challenge to the *array*, when exception is taken to the whole number impannelled. —Fonblanque.

6. Formerly in England, the muster of a county for military purposes; the men so mustered; as, a commission of *array*.

ar-rāy′, *v.t.*; arrayed (-rād), *pt., pp.*; arraying, *ppr.* 1. To place or dispose in order, as troops for battle.

2. To deck or dress; to adorn with dress; applied especially to dress of a splendid kind.

Pharaoh *arrayed* him (Joseph) in vestures of fine linen. —Gen. xli. 42.

3. To set (a jury) in order for the trial of a cause; that is, to call (them) man by man. —Blackstone.

4. To envelop.

In gelid caves with horrid glooms *arrayed.* —Trumbull.

To array a panel; to call, in order, men that are impaneled as a jury.

Syn.—Arrange, marshal, dispose, rank, place, deck, adorn, dress.

ar-rāy′ẽr, *n.* 1. One who arrays.

2. In English history, an officer who had care of soldiers' armor, and who saw them duly accoutered; later, a commissioner of array, who was charged with putting the soldiers of a county in condition for service.

ar-rēar′, *adv.* Behind; in the rear or toward the hinder part.

ar-rēar′, *n.* [Fr. *arriere*, the back part, stern; ME. *arere*; L. *ad*, to, and *retro*, back, backward.] That which is behind in payment, or remains unpaid, though due. It is generally used in the plural; as, the *arrears* of rent, wages, or taxes; and it implies a part of the money already paid.

In arrear or *in arrears*; behindhand, as in payment; in debt; owing a balance due or past due.

ar-rēar′āġe, *n.* Arrears; any sum of money remaining unpaid, after previous payment of a part. One may be in arrear for the whole amount of a debt; but arrears and *arrearage* imply that a part has been paid.

ar-reçt′, ar-reçt′ed, *a.* [L. *arrectus*, pp. of *arrigere*, to set upright.]

1. Erect; raised; upright.

2. Attentive, as a person listening. [Obs.]

ar-reçt′, *v.t.* 1. To erect; to direct. [Obs.]

2. To accuse; to impute. [Obs.]

ar-reçt′ȧ-ry, *n.* An upright post; a vertical beam. [Obs.]

ar-re-not′ō-kous, *a.* [Gr. *arrenotokos*, bearing males, from *arrēn*, male, and *tiktein*, to bring forth.] See *Arrhenotokous.*

ar-ren-tā′tion, *n.* [OFr. *arrenter*; L. *ad*, to, and *redditus*, pp. of *reddere*, to return, give back.] In old English law, the act of licensing the owner of land in a forest to inclose it with a small ditch and low hedge, in consideration of a yearly rent.

ar-rep′tion, *n.* [L. *arripere*, to snatch away.] A removing; the act of taking away. [Obs.]

ar-rep-ti′tious (-tish′us), *a.* Snatched away; hence, carried away by dementia, or possessed; frantic; mad. [Obs.]

ar-rep-ti′tious, *a.* [L. *arrepere*, to creep toward, to steal softly.] Creeping or having crept in privily. [Obs.]

ar-rest′, *v.t.*; arrested, *pt., pp.*; arresting, *ppr.* [ME *arresten, aresten*; OFr. *arester*; Fr. *arrêter*; L. *ad*, to, and *restare*, to stay back, remain.]

1. To obstruct; to stop; to check or hinder the motion of; as, to *arrest* the current of a river; to *arrest* the senses; to *arrest* the course of justice.

2. To take, seize, or apprehend by virtue of a warrant from authority; as, to *arrest* one for debt, or for a crime.

3. To attract, seize on, and fix; as, to *arrest* the eyes, or attention.

4. To rest or fix; as, to *arrest* our thoughts upon divine mercy. [Obs.]

Syn.—Apprehend, withhold, capture, restrain, detain, seize, take, hold, stop.

ar-rest′, *v.i.* To tarry; to stop; to rest. [Obs.]

ar-rest′, *n.* 1. The act of arresting or state of being arrested; a stop, hindrance, or restraint; any stay, seizure, check, or interruption, as of movement, growth, or development.

2. The taking or apprehending of a person by virtue of a warrant from authority; apprehension; legal custody, or restraint; also, a warrant or decree. An *arrest* is made by seizing or touching the body.

3. Any seizure, or taking by power, physical or moral.

4. In farriery, a mangy humor between the ham and pastern of the hind leg of a horse; also called *rat-tails.*

Arrest of judgment; in law, the staying or stopping of a judgment after verdict, for causes legally assigned. The motion for this purpose is called a motion in *arrest of judgment.* —Blackstone.

ar-res-tā′tion, *n.* Arrest. [Rare.]

ar-res-tee′, *n.* In Scots law, the person in whose hands an arrester seizes or attaches property.

ar-rest′ẽr, ar-rest′ŏr, *n.* 1. One who or that which arrests.

2. In Scots law, the person at whose suit an arrestment is made.

ar-rest′ive, *a.* Having a tendency to arrest.

ar-rest′ment, *n.* 1. The act of arresting or stopping: obstruction; stoppage.

2. In Scots law, (a) a process by which a creditor may attach money or movable property which a third party holds for behoof of his debtor; (b) the arrest or detention of a criminal till he gives bail to stand trial, or the securing of a debtor until he pays the debt or gives security for its payment.

ar-rest′ŏr, *n.* Same as *Arrester.*

ar-ret′ (*or* -rā′), *n.* [Fr. *arrêt*; OFr. *arest*, to detain, to fix, to determine.]

1. The decision of a court, tribunal, or council; a decree published; the edict of a sovereign prince; a French term, applied particularly to the judgments and decisions of courts and tribunals in France.

2. An arrest; a seizure by legal authority.

ar-ret′, *v.t.* To assign; to allot. [Obs.]

ar′rhȧ (-rȧ), *n.*; *pl.* **ar′rhæ.** [L. *arrha*, or *arra*; Gr. *arrabon*, earnest-money.] Anciently, earnest-money on betrothment. In Scots law, earnest; used in evidence of a completed bargain. Same as *Arles.*

ar-rhȧ-phos′tiç, *a.* [Gr. *arrhaphos*, seamless; *a* priv., and *rhaphē*, a seam.] Seamless. [Rare.]

ar-rhe-not′ō-kous, *a.* Producing males only, as the females of certain bees and sawflies, by means of ova which have the power of developing without the intervention of the male element; also written *arrenotokous.*

ar-rhi′zous, ar-rhī′zăl, *a.* [Gr. *arrhizos*, without roots; *a* priv., and *rhiza*, a root.] Having no true roots, as certain parasitical plants.

ar-rhyth′mi-ȧ, *n.* [Gr. *arrhythmos*, without rhythm; *a* priv., and *rhythmos*, rhythm.] Irregularity, or lack of rhythm, as of the pulse.

ar-rhyth′miç, ar-rhyth′mous, *a.* Lacking in rhythm; irregular.

ar-rhyth′my, *a.* Destitute of rhythm or meter. [Rare.]

ar′riāġe (-rāj), *n.* [Scot. contr. of *average.*] In Scots law, an indefinite service performed by horses, formerly demandable from tenants, but now abolished; used chiefly in the phrase *arriage and carriage.*

ar-ride′, *v.t.* [L. *arridere*, to laugh at; *ad*, to, *ridere*, to laugh.] To laugh at; to please well. [Obs.]

ar-riēre′ (-rēr′), *n.* [Fr. *arrière*, from OFr. *ariere*, rear.]

1. The last body of an army; now called *rear.*

2. The reserve force of the French National Guard.

ar-riēre′-ban, *n.* [Fr. *arrière-ban*; LL. *aribannum, herebannum*, from O.H.G. *heriban*, the summoning of an army to the field.] An edict of the ancient kings of France and Germany commanding all their noblesse and vassals to assemble with their vassals prepared for war or forfeit their estates; formerly written *arrierban.*

ar-riēre′-fee, ar-riēre′-fiēf, *n.* A fee or fief dependent on a superior fee, or a fee held of a feudatory.

ar-riēre′-vas″săl, *n.* The vassal of a vassal.

ar-riere″-vōus-sūre′ (ar-rār″-vö-sür′), *n.* A rear vault; an arch placed within the opening of a window or door, and of a different form, to increase the size of the aperture internally, or for other purposes.

Arriere-voussure.

ar′ris, *n.* [Fr. *areste, arête*; OFr. *areste*; L. *arista*, the awn or beard of an ear of grain.] In architecture, the edge formed by two surfaces meeting each other, whether plane or curved; applied particularly to the edges in moldings, and to the raised edges which separate the flutings in a Doric column.

ar′ris-fil″let, *n.* A triangular wooden molding, used to raise the slates or shingles of a roof against a chimney or a wall, to throw off the rain more effectually; also called *tilting-fillet.*

ar′ris-gut″tẽr, *n.* A wooden eaves-gutter having the form of the letter V.

ar′ris-wīse, ar′răs-wīse, *adv.* 1. Diagonally arranged, a mode of laying tiles or slates.

2. In heraldry, a term employed when anything of a square form is placed with one corner in front, showing the top and two of the sides.

Arriswise.

ar-rīv′ăl, *n.* [ME. *aryvaile, arrivaile.*]

1. The act of arriving; a coming to or reaching a place from a distance, whether by water, as in its original sense, or by land.

2. The attainment or reaching of any object or state by effort or action, or by natural process; as, *arrival* at a just decision.

3. The person or thing arriving; as, news brought by the last *arrival.*

The next *arrivals* here will gladlier build their nests. —Warner.

ar-rīv′ănce, *n.* 1. People coming.

2. Arrival; a reaching in progress. [Obs.]

ar-rīve′, *v.i.*; arrived, *pt., pp.*; arriving, *ppr.* [Fr. *arriver*; ME. *ariven, aryven*; OFr. *ariver, arriver*; L. *ad*, to, and *ripa*, bank.]

1. Literally, to come to the shore, or bank. Hence, to come to or reach in progress by water, or by traveling on land, followed by *at*, also by *in* and *from*; as, we *arrived at* Havre de Grace; he *arrived in* Boston; many *arrived from* Europe.

2. To reach a point, conclusion or result by progressive motion; to gain an end or compass an object by effort, practice, study, inquiry, reasoning, or experiment; as, to *arrive* at an unusual degree of excellence or wickedness; to *arrive* at a conclusion.

3. To be at hand; to come to pass; as, the time has *arrived.*

4. To happen or occur. [Obs.]

Happy! to whom this glorious death *arrives.* —Waller.

Syn.—Achieve, get to, reach, attain, enter, come, land.

ar-rīve′, *v.t.* To reach; to come to; also, to bring to shore. [Obs.]

ar-rīv′ẽr, *n.* One who or that which arrives.

ăr-rō′bä, *n.* [Sp. and Port. *arroba*; Ar. *arrob*; *al*, and *rob.*] A Spanish and Portuguese weight; also, an old Spanish wine and oil measure of varying capacity.

ar′rō-gănce, *n.* [ME. *arrogance, arrogaunce*; OFr. *arrogance*; L. *arrogantia*, arrogance; *arrogare*, to claim.] The act or quality of taking much upon oneself; that species of pride which consists in exorbitant claims of rank, dignity, estimation, or power, or which exalts the worth or importance of the person to an undue degree; pride with contempt for others; conceitedness; presumption.

Supple knees
Feed *arrogance*, and are the proud man's fees. —Shak.

Syn.—Assumption, pride, haughtiness, presumption, self-conceit, vanity.

ar′rō-găn-cy, *n.* Arrogance.

ar′rō-gănt, *a.* 1. Assuming; making, or having the disposition to make, exorbitant claims of rank or estimation; giving oneself an undue degree of importance; haughty; conceited; applied to persons; as, an *arrogant* churchman.

2. Containing arrogance; marked with arrogance; proceeding from undue claims or self-importance; applied to things; as, *arrogant* pretensions, or behavior.

Syn.—Overbearing, domineering, presumptuous, imperious, insolent, stately, haughty, lordly, proud, rude.

ar′rō-gănt-ly, *adv.* In an arrogant manner; with undue pride, or self-importance.

ar′rō-gănt-ness, *n.* Arrogance. [Rare.]

ar′rō-gāte, *v.t.*; arrogated, *pt., pp.*; arrogating, *ppr.* [L. *arrogare*, to claim; *ad*, to, or for, and *rogare*, to ask.] To claim or demand unduly or presumptuously; to claim from vanity or false pretensions; to lay claim to in an overbearing manner; as, to *arrogate* power or dignity to oneself.

Who, not content
With fair equality, fraternal state,
Will *arrogate* dominion undeserved
Over his brethren. —Milton.

Syn.—Appropriate, assume, affect, seize.

ar-rō-gā′tion, *n.* 1. The act of arrogating, or making exorbitant claims; the act of taking more than one is justly entitled to.

2. In civil law, the act of adopting into a family an adult; anciently done among the Romans by popular vote, later by imperial rescript. Also called *adrogation.*

ar′rō-gā-tive, *a.* Assuming or making undue claims and pretensions. [Rare.]

ar-roṅ-disse′ment (-dis′moṅ), *n.* [Fr., from *arrondir*, to make round.] Literally, a circuit, or district. In France, an administrative district forming a subdivision of a department.

ar-rōṣe′, *v.t.* [Fr. *arroser*, to sprinkle; LL. *adrorare*, to bedew; L. *ad*, to, and *rorare*, to distil.] To wet; to drench. [Obs.]

ar-rō′ṣion, *n.* [L. *arrosus*, pp. of *arrodere*, to gnaw at.] A gnawing. [Obs.]

ar′rōw, *n.* [ME. *arow*; AS. *arwa, arewe*, arrow; L. *arquus, arcus*, a bow.] A missile weapon of offense, straight, slender, pointed, and often barbed, to be shot with a bow.

ar′rōw-grȧss, *n.* A popular name of different grasslike plants, species of the genus *Triglochin.* Two well-known species are the marsh arrow-grass, *Triglochin palustre*, and the seaside arrow-grass, *Triglochin maritimum.* They have small greenish flowers.

ar′rōw-head (-hed), *n.* 1. The head of an arrow.

2. The popular name of different aquatic plants, species of the genus *Sagittaria*; so called from the resemblance of their leaves to the head of an arrow.

ar′rōw-head″ed, *a.* Shaped like the head of an arrow.

Arrow-headed characters; certain characters found inscribed on the ruins of Persepolis, the bricks of Babylon, and monuments in some other places of the East; formed by a combination of triangular, or wedge-like figures, hence called also *cuneiform characters*.

Arrow-headed Characters.

ar′rōw-rọọt, *n.* 1. A popular name applied to the different species of the genus *Maranta*. The Indians are said to have employed the roots of *Maranta Galanga* to counteract the poison of arrows, whence the name.

2. A nutritive starch obtained from the rhizomes or rootstocks of *Maranta arundinacea*, or arrowroot plant; it is an easily digested food much used in medicine.

Arrowroot Plant. (*Maranta arundinacea*). *a. a.* Rhizomes.

ar′rōw-snāke, *n.* A snake-like lizard of the genus *Acontias*; also called the *dart-snake*.

ar′rōw-stōne, *n.* A name sometimes given to a belemnite.

ar′rōw-wood, *n.* A name given to various shrubs and small trees of the genera *Viburnum* and *Cornus*.

ar′rōw-wŏrm (-wẽrm), *n.* One of the *Sagitta*, a genus of transparent arrow-shaped marine worms.

ar′rōw-y, *a.* 1. Consisting of arrows.

2. Resembling an arrow in form, appearance, or manner of motion; slender; sharp; darting; piercing.

ar-roy′ō, *n.* [Sp.] 1. A natural bed for flowing water.

2. A rivulet or its dry bed.

3. In geology, a deep channel worn in the earth by running water.

ärse, *n.* [ME. *ars*; AS. *ears, ærs*; Gr. *orros*, or *orsos*, the rump.] The buttocks, or hind part of an animal. [Low.]

är′se-năl, *n.* [ME. *arcenal, arsinal, archinale*; Sp., Port., Fr., Arm. *arsenal*, a magazine or repository of stores; in It. and Sp., a dock or dockyard; probably from L. *arx navalis*, a naval citadel or repository.] A repository or magazine of arms and military stores, whether for land or naval service; also, a public establishment where naval or military arms and equipments are manufactured as well as stored.

är-se-nī′ă-sis, *n.* Arsenious poisoning.

är-sē′ni-āte, är′se-nāte, *n.* A salt formed by arsenic acid combined with any base.

är′se-niç, *n.* [ME. *arsenik, arsnek*; OFr. *arsenic*; L. *arsenicum*; Gr. *arsenikon*, from *arsenikos*, strong, masculine.] A substance of a steel-gray color and brilliant luster, and quite brittle. It forms alloys with most of the metals and is occasionally found native. Combined with sulphur, it forms orpiment and realgar, which are the yellow and red sulphids of *arsenic*. Orpiment is the true *arsenicum* of the ancients. *Arsenic* is actively poisonous, as are also its compounds, but when judiciously employed it is a safe and useful medicine, especially in skin diseases. The commercial substance known as *arsenic* is arsenious oxid or *white arsenic*.

är-sen′iç, är-sen′iç-ăl, *a.* Belonging to arsenic; consisting of or containing arsenic.

är-sen′i-çāte, *v.t.*; arsenicated, *pt.*, *pp.*; arsenicating, *ppr.* To combine with arsenic.

är-sen′i-çişm, *n.* Arseniasis.

är′sen-ide (*or* -īd), *n.* A compound of arsenic and a metallic base.

är-sen-if′ẽr-ous, *a.* Composed partly of arsenic.

är-sē′ni-ous, *a.* Pertaining to, consisting of, or containing, arsenic; as, *arsenious* powder.

är′sen-īte, *n.* A salt formed by uniting arsenious acid with a base.

är-se-nī′ū-ret, *n.* A combination of arsenic with a metallic or other base.

är-se-nī′ū-ret-ed, *a.* Combined with arsenic so as to form an arseniuret.

är-sen′ō-blast, *n.* [Gr. *arsēn*, male, and *blastos*, bud.] In embryology, one of the male elements into which a sexual cell separates.

är″sen-ō-pȳr′īte, *n.* [Gr. *arsen*, male, and *pyritēs*, a flint, from *pyr*, fire.] Mispickel; a white mineral containing arsenic, sulphur, and iron.

ärse′smärt, *n.* Smartweed.

är′shin, är′shīne, *n.* [Russ. *arshinŭ*; Bulg., Serv. *arshin*; Turk., Pers. *arshin*; of Tartar origin.] A Turkish and Persian measure of length; formerly a Russian measure.

är′sine, *n.* Arseniureted hydrogen.

är′sis, *n.* [Gr. *arsis*, a raising, from *airein*, to lift up.] 1. In prosody, that point in a measure where the ictus is put, or which is marked by a greater stress or force.

2. That elevation of voice now called metrical accentuation; opposed to *thesis*, or depression of the voice.

Arsis and thesis; in music, the strong position and weak position of the bar, indicated by the down-beat and up-beat in marking time.

är′sŏn, *n.* [OFr. *arson, arsoun*; from L. *arsus*, pp. of *ardere*, to burn.] In law, the malicious burning of a dwelling-house or outhouse of another man, which by the common law is felony; the intentional burning of a building, a ship, etc., the offense being aggravated if human life is endangered. The definition of the crime varies in the statutes of different countries and states.

ärt, *v.*; the second person, singular number, indicative mood, present tense, of the verb *to be*; as, where *art* thou?

ärt, *n.* [ME. *art, arte*; OFr. *art*; L. *ars* (*artis*), root *ar*, to join; Gr. *artunein*, to arrange.]

1. The disposition or modification of things by human skill, to answer the purpose intended. In this sense *art* stands opposed to *nature*.

2. A system of rules, serving to facilitate the performance of certain actions; opposed to *science*, or to speculative principles; as, the *art* of building or engraving. *Arts* are divided into the useful or *mechanical arts*, that is, those in which the hands and body are more concerned than the mind, as in making clothes and utensils; the *fine arts*, or such as give scope to genius, as music, painting, sculpture, etc.; and the *liberal, polite*, or *elegant arts*, in which category may be classed all the branches of academic learning, as well as fine art. Formerly the circle of the sciences was confined to the seven *liberal arts*—grammar, rhetoric, logic, arithmetic, music, geometry, and astronomy. In this sense, the term *arts* is still employed when we speak of the *arts* classes in the universities, a *master of arts*, etc.

3. Business or employment; as, the various *arts* of life.

4. Skill, dexterity, or the power of performing certain actions, acquired by experience, study, or observation; as, a man has the *art* of managing his business to advantage.

5. Cunning; artifice; as, animals practise *art* when opposed to their superiors in strength.

6. One of the *fine arts*, more especially one of the imitative members of the group, and in particular, painting or sculpture; as, he has adopted *art* as his profession.

7. The special skill required by those who practise one of the fine arts; artistic faculty; skill in counterfeiting nature or natural expression.

8. Black *art*; necromancy.

Art and part; in Scots law, a term denoting the charge of contriving a criminal design as well as of participating in the perpetration of the criminal act.

Syn.—Aptitude, readiness, skill, dexterity, adroitness, contrivance, profession, business, trade, calling, cunning, artifice, deceit, duplicity.

är′te-făct, *n.* Same as *Artifact*.

Är-tē′mi-ȧ, *n.* [Gr. *Artemis*, a goddess usually identified with the Roman Diana.] A genus of entomostracans belonging to the order *Branchiopoda*. The *Artemia salina*, or brine-shrimp, inhabits water so salt that most other marine animals die in it.

Är′tē-mis, *n.* [L. and Gr. *Artemis*.]

1. In mythology, a celebrated Grecian goddess, worshiped in Arcadia and elsewhere. She corresponded to the Roman Diana.

2. A genus of bivalves.

3. A genus of coleopterous insects.

Är-tē-mi′şi-ȧ, *n.* [Gr. *Artemisia*.] A genus of plants of numerous species, including the plants called mugwort, southernwood, and wormwood. *Artemisia absinthium* is the common wormwood.

är-tē′ri-ăç, *a.* and *n.* [Gr. *artēriakos*, pertaining to the windpipe, from *artēria*, windpipe.]

I. *a.* Relating to the windpipe.

II. *n.* A remedy for diseases of the windpipe.

är-tē′ri-ăl, *a.* 1. Pertaining to an artery or the arteries; as, *arterial* action.

2. Like an artery; composed of a principal channel and a system of branches; as, an *arterial* river.

Arterial blood; blood that has been arterialized by passing through the lungs. It differs from venous blood particularly in its lighter florid red color and its greater warmth and coagulability—changes produced by the process of respiration.

är-tē″ri-ăl-i-zā′tion, *n.* The process of changing venous into arterial blood by the absorption of oxygen in the lungs.

är-tē′ri-ăl-īze, *v.t.*; arterialized, *pt.*, *pp.*; arterializing, *ppr.* To communicate, as to venous blood, the qualities of arterial blood; to make arterial.

är′tẽr-in, *n.* A term for the arterial blood pigment as contained in the red corpuscles.

är-tē′ri-ō-. [Gr. *artēria*, artery.] A combining form used in anatomy, etc., to express relation to an artery.

är-tē-ri-og′rȧ-phy, *n.* [Gr. *artēria*, artery, and *graphein*, to write, describe.] A description of the arterial system.

är-tē′ri-ōle, *n.* Any one of the small arteries.

är-tē-ri-ol′ō-ġy, *n.* [Gr. *artēria*, artery, and *logos*, discourse.] A treatise or discourse on the arteries.

är-tē″ri-ō-sçlē-rō′sis, *n.* The thickening and hardening of the walls of the arteries.

är-tē-ri-ot′ō-my, *n.* [Gr. *artēriotomia*, the cutting of an artery; *artēria*, artery, and *temnein*, to cut.]

1. The opening of an artery by a lancet, or other instrument, for the purpose of letting blood.

2. That part of the science of anatomy which treats of the dissection of the arteries.

är-tē-rī′tis, *n.* Inflammation occurring in the arteries.

är′tẽr-y, *n.* [ME. *arterie*; OFr. *artere*; L. *arteria*, the windpipe, an artery; Gr. *artēria*, from *aeirein*, to lift up, to heave.]

1. A name formerly given to the trachea or windpipe.

2. One of a system of vessels or tubes which convey the blood from the heart to all parts of the body. There are two principal *arteries*; the *aorta*, which rises from the left ventricle, and ramifies through the whole body; and the *pulmonary artery*, which conveys the blood from the right ventricle to the lungs, to undergo arterialization.

3. Figuratively, any large channel, or part of a ramified system of communication; as, the *arteries* of commerce.

Är-tē′şiăn, *a.* [Fr. *artésien*, properly, pertaining to *Artois* in France.]

1. Of or belonging to Artois in France.

2. [a—] A term descriptive of a particular kind of well, believed to have been first used in Artois.

Artesian well; a perpendicular boring into the ground through which water rises to the surface of the soil, producing a constant flow or stream. The term is often applied in the United States to deep borings for oil.

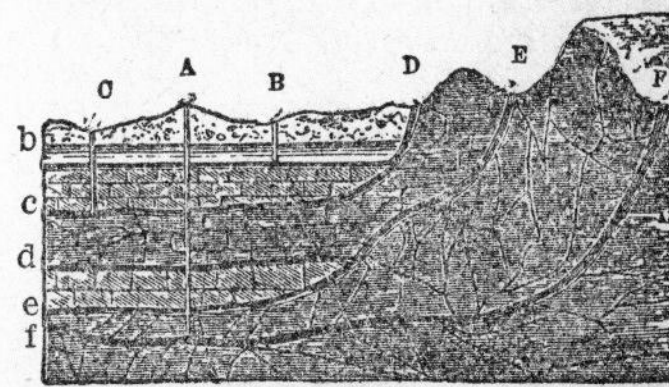

Artesian Well.

Diagram showing pervious strata in a basin-shaped curve. *A, B, C*, three wells communicating at *b, c, d, e, f*, with underground pervious strata containing water which descends by gravitation from the higher levels *D, E, F*.

ärt′fụl, *a.* 1. Performed with art or skill. [Obs.]

2. Artificial, as opposed to *natural*. [Obs.]

3. Cunning; practising art, or stratagem; crafty; as, an *artful* boy.

4. Proceeding from art or craft; as, an *artful* scheme.

Syn.—Dexterous, designing, cunning, shrewd, crafty, subtle, wily, sly, adroit, deceitful.

ärt′fụl-ly, *adv.* In an artful manner.

ärt′fụl-ness, *n.* Art; craft; cunning; address.

är′then, *a.* Earthen. [Obs.]

ärthr-, *prefix.* See *Arthro-*.

är′thrăl, *a.* [Gr. *arthron*, a joint.] Of or pertaining to a joint.

är-thral′ġi-ȧ, *n.* A sharp pain, as of neuralgia, in a joint.

är-threç′tō-my, *n.* In surgery, the excision of a joint.

är-thrit′iç, är-thrit′iç-ăl, *a.* 1. Pertaining to arthritis; affecting the joints.

2. Pertaining to the gout; gouty.

är-thrī′tis, *n.* [Gr. *arthritis*, from *arthron*, a joint.] In a general sense, any inflammation of the joints; but more particularly, the gout.

är′thri-tişm, *n.* A gouty tendency.

är′thrō-, ärthr-. [L. *artus*; Gr. *arthron*, a joint.] A combining form used to express relation to or connection with a joint.

är-thrō-brañ′chi-ȧ, *n.*; *pl.* **är-thrō-brañ′chi-æ.** [*Arthro-*, and Gr. *branchia*, gills.] A distinct gill of a crustacean.

är′thrō-dẽrm, *n.* [*Arthro-*, and Gr. *derma*, skin.] The horny envelope or shell of an articulate, as the shell of a crab.

är-thrō′di-ȧ, *n.* [Gr., from *arthron*, joint, and *eidos*, form.] In anatomy, a species of articulation, in which the head of one bone is received into the shallow socket of another; as that of the humerus into the glenoid cavity of the scapula.

är-thrō′di-ăl, är-throd′iç, *a.* Relating to arthrodia.

är-thrō-dyn′i-ȧ, *n.* [*Arthro-*, and Gr. *odynē*, pain.] Pain in the joints; chronic rheumatism.

är-thrō-dyn′iç, *a.* Pertaining to arthrodynia.

Är-thrō-gas′trȧ, *n.pl.* [*Arthro-*, and Gr. *gastēr*, the belly.] In Huxley's classification, an order of *Arachnida* (spiders), in which the abdomen is distinctly divided into somites, or segments, each with an upper and lower pair of appendages. It includes the scorpions.

är-throg′rȧ-phy, *n.* [*Arthro-*, and Gr. *graphē*, description.] A scientific delineation or description of the joints.

är-throl′ō-ġy, *n.* [*Arthro-*, and Gr. *logos*, description.] That part of anatomical science which treats of the joints.

är′thrō-mēre, *n.* [*Arthro-*, and Gr. *meros*, a part.] One of the segments or rings of an articulate.

är′thron, *n.*; *pl.* **är′thrȧ.** A joint.

är-throp′ȧ-thy, *n.* [*Arthro-*, and Gr. *pathos*, suffering.] A disease of the joints.

är-thrō-pleū′rȧ, *n.* [*Arthro-*, and Gr. *pleura*, side.] The side or limb-bearing part of one of the segments of an arthropod.

är′thrō-pod, *n.* One of the *Arthropoda.*

Är-throp′ō-dȧ, *n.pl.* [*Arthro-*, and Gr. *pous*, genitive *podos*, a foot.] One of the two primary divisions (*Anarthropoda* being the other) into which modern naturalists have divided the subkingdom *Articulata*, characterized by a body composed of a series of segments arranged about a longitudinal axis, each segment occasionally and some always being provided with articulated appendages.

är-throp′ō-dăl, *a.* Of or pertaining to the *Arthropoda.*

Är-thrō-pom′ȧ-tȧ, *n.pl.* One of the two orders of the *Brachiopoda.*

är-throp′tẽr-ous, *a.* [*Arthro-*, and Gr. *pteron*, a wing.] Having the fin-rays articulated, as those of many fishes.

är-thrō′sis, *n.* [Gr. *arthrōsis*, a joining, from *arthroun*, to join.] In anatomy, an articulation; a joint.

är′thrō-spōre, *n.* [*Arthro-*, and Gr. *sporos*, seed, from *speirein*, to sow.] A spore belonging to a series united like a string of beads and formed by fission.

är-thrō-spōr′ous, är-thrō-spōr′iç, *a.* Forming spores by fission; as, *arthrosporous* bacteria.

Är-thros′trȧ-çȧ, *n.pl.* [*Arthro-*, and Gr. *ostrakon*, a shell.] A division of *Crustacea*, having the thorax and abdomen segmented.

Är-thrō-zō′ȧ, *n.pl.* [*Arthro-*, and Gr. *zōon*, an animal, from *zēn*, to live.] A group of invertebrates; one of the divisions of the *Metazoa.*

är-thrō-zō′iç, *a.* Of or pertaining to the *Arthrozoa.*

Är-thū′ri-ăn, *a.* Relating to King Arthur or the knights of the Round Table.

är′ti-ad, *n.* and *a.* [Gr. *artios*, even.]

I. *n.* In chemistry, an atom whose valence is denoted by an even number.

II. *a.* Even; of the nature of an artiad.

är′ti-chōke, *n.* [Fr. *artichaut*; It. *articiocco*; Ar. *alkharshuf.*] The *Cynara Scolymus*, a plant somewhat resembling a thistle, with a dilated, imbricated, and prickly calyx. The head is large, rough, and scaly, on an upright stalk. It is composed of numerous oval scales, inclosing the florets, sitting on a broad receptacle, which, with the fleshy base of the scales, is the eatable part of the plant.

Jerusalem artichoke; a species of sunflower (*Helianthus tuberosus*), whose roots are used like potatoes. The term *Jerusalem* is here a corruption of the Italian *girasole*, sunflower.

är′ti-çle, *n.* [ME. *article*; OFr. *article*; L. *articulus*, dim. of *artus*, a joint; Gr. *arthron*, from Indo-Eur. root, *ar*, fit, join.]

1. A single clause in a contract, account, system of regulations, treaty, or other writing; a particular separate charge or item in an account; a term, condition, or stipulation in a contract. In general, a distinct part of a writing, instrument, or discourse, consisting of two or more particulars; as, *articles* of agreement; an account consisting of many *articles.*

2. A point of faith; a doctrinal point or proposition in theology; as, The Thirty-nine *Articles.*

3. A complete and independent, or partially independent, portion of a literary publication, especially of a newspaper, magazine, review, or other periodical; as, an *article* on child labor; a series of *articles* on immigration.

4. A distinct part.

Upon each *article* of human duty. —Paley.

5. A particular commodity, or substance; as, an *article* of merchandise; salt is a necessary *article.* In common usage, this word is applied to almost every separate substance or material.

The *articles* which compose the blood. —Darwin.

6. A point of time. [Obs.]

7. In grammar, an adjective used before nouns, to limit or define their application. In the English language, *a*, or *an*, is the indefinite article and *the* the definite article.

In the article of death [L. *in articulo mortis*]; literally, in the moment of death; in the last struggle or agony.

Articles of impeachment; a formal document in a case of impeachment, similar in function to an indictment filed in a criminal court.

Articles of war; the code or regulations for the government of the army and navy.

Lords of articles; in Scottish history, a committee of the parliament, whose business was to prepare and digest all matters that were to be laid before it, including the preparation of all bills for laws; called also *lords articulars.*

The Thirty-nine Articles; a statement of the particular points of doctrine, thirty-nine in number, maintained by the English Church, first promulgated by a convocation held in London in 1562-63; it was founded on and superseded an older code issued in the reign of Edward VI.

är′ti-çle, *v.t.*; articled (-kld), *pt.*, *pp.*; articling, *ppr.* 1. To draw up in distinct particulars; as, to *article* the errors or follies of man.

2. To accuse or charge by an exhibition of articles; as, he shall be *articled* against in the High Court of Admiralty.

3. To bind by articles of covenant or stipulation; as, to *article* an apprentice to a mechanic.

är′ti-çle, *v.i.* To agree by articles; to stipulate. [Rare.]

är-tiç′ū-lăr, *a.* [L. *articularis*, adj., from *articulus*, joint.] Belonging to the joints; as, the gout is an *articular* disease.

är-tiç′ū-lăr, är-tiç′ū-lā-ry, *n.* A bone in the lower jaw of some birds, reptiles, and fishes.

är-tiç′ū-lăr-ly, *adv.* In such a manner as to sound every letter.

Är-tiç-ū-lā′tȧ, *n.pl.* [L. neut. pl. nom. of *articulatus*, pp. of *articulare*, to join.]

1. The third great section of the animal kingdom, according to the arrangement of Cuvier. It includes all the invertebrates with the external skeleton forming a series of rings articulated together and enveloping the body, distinct respiratory organs, and an internal ganglionated nervous system along the middle line of the body. They are divided into five classes, viz.: *Crustacea, Arachnida, Insecta, Myriapoda*, and *Annelida.* The first four classes are now commonly placed together under the name of *Arthropoda.*

2. A term applied to a section of the *Brachiopoda* having shells united by a hinge.

är-tiç′ū-lāte, *n.* One of the *Articulata.*

är-tiç′ū-lāte, *a.* [L. *articulatus*, jointed, pp. of *articulare*, to join.]

1. Formed by the distinct and intelligent movement of the organs of speech; uttered by suitably modifying the position of the vocal organs; as, an *articulate* sound; *articulate* speech.

2. Clear; distinct; as, *articulate* pronunciation.

3. Expressed in articles, or in separate particulars. [Obs.]

4. In natural history, jointed; formed with joints; as, an *articulate* animal.

är-tiç′ū-lāte, *v.i.*; articulated, *pt.*, *pp.*; articulating, *ppr.* 1. To utter articulate sounds; to utter distinct syllables or words; as, to *articulate* distinctly.

2. To connect by articulation.

3. To treat, stipulate, or make terms. [Obs.]

är-tiç′ū-lāte, *v.t.* 1. To form into elementary sounds; to form into distinct syllables, or words; as, to *articulate* letters or language.

2. To draw up or write in separate particulars. [Obs.]

3. To joint; to unite by a joint or joints; as, to *articulate* a skeleton.

4. To utter with distinctness.

Syn.—Pronounce, enunciate, syllabify, joint, form, utter.

är-tiç′ū-lā-ted, *a.* 1. Uttered distinctly in syllables or words.

2. Jointed; having joints, as a plant or animal.

är-tiç′ū-lāte-ly, *adv.* 1. With distinct utterance of syllables or words.

2. Article by article; in detail.

3. In the manner of a joint.

är-tiç′ū-lāte-ness, *n.* The quality of being articulate.

är-tiç-ū-lā′tion, *n.* 1. In anatomy, the joining or juncture of the bones. This is of three kinds; (a) diarthrosis, or a movable connection, including enarthrosis, or the ball and socket joint; arthrodia, which is the same, but more superficial; ginglymus, or hinge-like joint; and trochoid, or the wheel and axle; (b) synarthrosis, immovable connection, as by suture, or junction by serrated margins; harmony, or union by straight margins; and gomphosis, like a nail driven in a board, as the teeth in their sockets; (c) symphysis, or union by means of another substance; as synchondrosis, union by a cartilage; syssarcosis, union by muscular fibers; synneurosis, union by tendons; syndesmosis, union by ligaments; and synostosis, union by a bony substance.

2. In botany, a term applied to the connection of the parts of a plant by joints, as in pods; also, to the nodes or joints, as in cane and maize; and to the parts intercepted between the joints.

3. The forming of words; the distinct utterance of syllables and words by the human voice; the act of articulating; as, he spoke with perfect *articulation.*

4. An articulate sound, especially that of a consonant.

5. An anatomical joint.

6. The act of jointing or putting together; as, the *articulation* of a skeleton.

är-tiç′ū-lā-tive, *a.* Relating or pertaining to articulation.

är-tiç′ū-lā-tŏr, *n.* 1. A person who articulates; specifically one who puts together the bones of skeletons.

2. A thing which articulates; specifically an apparatus for the cure of stammering; also, a telephone attachment that produces even vibrations and insures perfect sounds.

är-tiç′ū-lā-tō-ry, *a.* Pertaining to articulation.

är-tiç′ū-lus, *n.*; *pl.* **är-tiç′ū-lī.** [L., dim. of *artus*, a joint.] A joint of the appendage, or stem, of a crinoid.

är′ti-fact, är′tē-fact, *n.* [L. *art* (*artis*), art, and *factus*, pp. of *facere*, to make.]

1. Something produced, or modified, artificially.

2. In archæology, a simple form of aboriginal art.

3. A modification of the appearance, or structure, of protoplasm, caused by some exterior or chemical agent, as death or a reagent. [Rare.]

är′ti-fact, *a.* Artificial; unnatural. [Rare.]

är′ti-fice, *n.* [L. *artificium*, a trade or profession, from *ars*, art, and *facere*, to make.]

1. Artful contrivance; an artful or ingenious device, in a good or bad sense. In a bad sense, it corresponds with trick, or fraud.

2. Art; trade; skill acquired by science or practice. [Obs.]

Syn.—Cheat, deception, deceit, finesse, imposition, ruse, stratagem, trick.—A *trick* is crude, low, malicious; an *artifice*, fine, or as the word implies, artful.

är-tif′i-cẽr, *n.* [L. *artifex*, an artist, one skilled in a profession, from *ars*, art, and *facere*, to make.]

1. An artist; a mechanic or manufacturer; one whose occupation requires skill or knowledge of a particular kind, as a silversmith or saddler.

2. One who makes or contrives; an inventor; as, an *artificer* of fraud or lies.

3. A cunning or artful fellow. [Obs.]

4. In military life, a carpenter, blacksmith, or other mechanic, attached to the service; or a skilled worker in a military laboratory.

är-ti-fi′ciăl (-fish′ăl), *a.* [Fr. *artificiel*; L. *artificialis*, from *artificium*, a trade or profession.]

1. Made or contrived by art, or by human skill and labor, in opposition to *natural*; as, *artificial* heat or light; an *artificial* magnet.

2. Feigned; fictitious; not genuine or natural; as, *artificial* tears.

3. Contrived with skill or art; artistic. [Obs.]

4. Cultivated; not indigenous; not being of spontaneous growth; as, *artificial* grasses.

5. Full of affectation; not natural; as, *artificial* manners.

Artificial arguments; in rhetoric, arguments invented by the speaker, in distinction from laws, authorities, and the like, which are called inartificial arguments or proofs.

Artificial light, light other than that produced by the sun, moon or stars.

Artificial lines; on a sector or scale, lines so contrived as to represent the logarithmic sines and tangents, which, by the help of the line of numbers, solve, with tolerable exactness, questions in trigonometry, navigation, etc.

Artificial numbers; logarithms.

Syn.—Manufactured, constructed, simulated, pretended, assumed, false.

är-ti-fi-ci-al′i-ty, *n.* The quality of being artificial; appearance of art.

är-ti-fi′ciăl-ize, *v.t.*; artificialized, *pt.*, *pp.*; artificializing, *ppr.* To render artificial.

är-ti-fi′ciăl-ly, *adv.* In an artificial manner.

är-ti-fi′ciăl-ness, *n.* The quality of being artificial.

är-ti-fi′cious, *a.* [L. *artificiosus*, accomplished in an art.] Same as *Artificial.* [Obs.]

ärt′i-līze, *v.t.* To make to resemble art, or to render artificial; as, to *artilize* nature, or to render the artificial aspects of nature. [Obs.]

är-til′lēr-ist, *n.* A person skilled in gunnery.
är-til′lēr-y, *n.* [ME. *artylerye*; OFr. *artillerie*; LL. *artillaria*; from L. *ars*, gen. *artis*, art, skill.]

1. In a general sense, offensive weapons of war, whether large or small. Hence, it was formerly used for bows and arrows.

And Jonathan gave his *artillery* unto his lad. —1 Sam. xx. 40.

2. Cannon; great guns; ordnance; also ordnance and its necessary equipment both in men and material (thus including carriages, horses, ammunition, etc.); or simply the men and officers that manage the guns in land battles and sieges.

3. The science which treats of the use and management of great guns.

Field artillery; artillery designed to be taken with an army to the field of battle.

Flying artillery; artillery, the gunners of which are trained to rapid evolutions, so as to change position with facility.

Park of artillery; a body or force of artillery, with the carriages, horses, and stores of all kinds necessary for its effective use; also, the scene of its operations or encampment.

Siege artillery; heavy artillery designed to be employed in destroying fortifications.

Train of artillery; a certain number of pieces of cannon mounted on carriages, with all their equipment ready for the march.

är-til′lēr-y-măn, *n.* A soldier of the artillery.
är-til′lēr-y-plant, *n.* A South American plant of the nettle family, which discharges its pollen in an explosive manner.
är″ti-ō-daç′tyl, *n.* One of the *Artiodactyla.*
Är″ti-ō-daç′ty-là, *n.pl.* [Gr. *artios*, even, and *daktylos*, a toe.] An order of the *Ungulata* or hoofed mammals, comprising all those in which the number of the toes is even (two or four), including the ruminants, and also a number of nonruminating animals, as the hippopotamus and the pig. This division includes all the hoofed animals used for human food, and domesticated from time immemorial.
är″ti-ō-daç′ty-lous, *a.* Having toes even in number.
är′ti-şăn, är′ti-zăn (*or* är-ti-zan′), *n.* [Fr. *artisan*; L. *artitus*, skilled in arts; pp. of *artire.*]

1. One trained to manual dexterity in any art, mystery, or trade.

2. A handicraftsman; a skilled mechanic; an artificer.

ärt′ist, *n.* [Fr. *artiste*; from L. *ars*, art.]

1. In a general sense, one who is skilled in the practice of some art.

2. In present usage, one who professes and practises one of the liberal arts, in which science and taste preside over the manual execution. It is thus that the *artist* is distinguished from the *artisan*, who follows mechanically the rules of his handicraft or art. The term is particularly applied to painters, sculptors, engravers, and architects.

3. Specifically, a painter.

är-tiste′, *n.* [Fr.] A term of very extensive application to denote one who is peculiarly dexterous and tasteful in almost any art, as an opera-dancer, a hairdresser, or a cook. This term should not be confounded with the English word *artist.*
är-tis′tiç, är-tis′tiç-ăl, *a.* Pertaining to an artist; made in the manner of an artist; conformable to art; regular.
är-tis′tiç-ăl-ly, *adv.* In an artistic manner.
ärt′ist-ry, *n.* 1. Artistic finish or touch; artistic effect.

2. Works of art, as a whole.

ärt′ize, *v.t.* and *v.i.* To form or live by art; to render artificial. [Obs.]
ärt′less, *a.* 1. Unskilful; wanting art, knowledge, or skill.

2. Free from guile, art, craft, or stratagem; simple; sincere; unaffected; undesigning; as, an *artless* mind.

3. Contrived without skill or art; as, an *artless* tale.

Syn.—Candid, fair, frank, honest, ingenuous, open, plain.

ärt′less-ly, *adv.* In an artless manner; unaffectedly.
ärt′less-ness, *n.* The quality of being void of art or guile; simplicity; sincerity; unaffectedness.
ärt′ly, *adv.* Artificially; by human skill or contrivance. [Obs.]
är-tō-çär′pad, *n.* One of the *Artocarpeæ.*
Är-tō-çär′pē-æ, *n.pl.* [Gr. *artos*, bread, and *karpos*, fruit.] A natural order of plants, the breadfruit order.
är-tō-çär′pous, är-tō-çär′pē-ous, *a.* Relating to breadfruit or the breadfruit tree.
Är-tō-çär′pus, *n.* The breadfruit, a genus of plants, natural order *Artocarpeæ.*
är′tō-tȳpe, *n.* An improved form of albertype, or a photograph produced by the exposure of a sensitized gelatin plate.
Är-tō-tȳ′rite, *n.* [Gr. *artos*, bread, and *tyros*, cheese.] One of a sect of heretics, in the primitive church, who celebrated the eucharist with bread and cheese, alleging that the first oblations of men were not only of the fruit of the earth, but of their flocks. They admitted females to the priesthood and episcopacy.
ärts′măn, *n.* A learned man. [Obs.]
Ā′rum, *n.* [L. *arum*; Gr. *aron*, the wake-robin.] A genus of plants, natural order *Araceæ. Arum maculatum* is the common wake-robin. It has acrid properties, but its cormus yields a starch, which is known by the name of arrowroot.

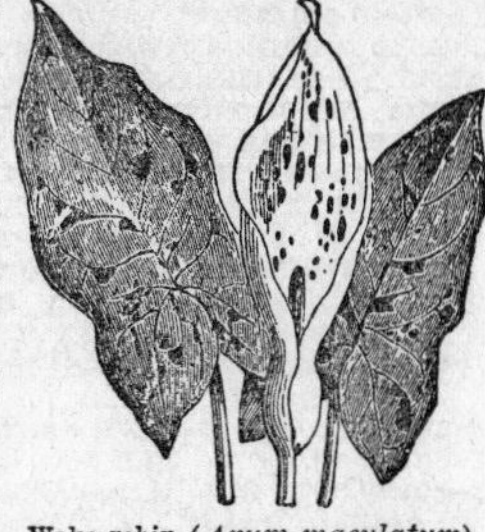
Wake-robin (*Arum maculatum*).

Ar-un-dē′li-ăn (-yăn), *a.* Pertaining to the earl of Arundel; as, *Arundelian* marbles.

Arundelian marbles; a collection of ancient stones, containing a chronological detail of the principal events of Greece, from about 1582 B.C. to 264 B.C. The engraving was done in Paros, and the chronology is called the Parian Chronicle. These stones are called *Arundelian*, from the earl of Arundel, who employed William Petty to procure relics of antiquity in the East, in 1624, and were later presented to the University of Oxford. They are also called *Oxford marbles.*

ar-un-dif′ēr-ous, *a.* [L. *arundo*, reed, and *ferre*, to bear.] Bearing canes or reeds.
à-run-di-nā′ceous, *a.* [L. *arundinaceus*, like a reed.] Pertaining to a reed; resembling the reed or cane.
À-run-di-nā′ri-à, *n.* [L. *arundo.*] A genus of tall, reed-like grasses, native to both Asia and America, and embracing the cane of the southern United States.
ar-un-din′ē-ous, *a.* Abounding with reeds.
À-run′dō, *n.* [L., a reed.] A genus of grasses, with reedy stems and large leaves, embracing some half-dozen species, which are found in the warmer sections of America and the Old World.
à-rū′rà, à-röu′rà, *n.* [Gr.] An ancient Grecian and Egyptian measure of surface.
à-rus′pex, à-rus′pice, *n.*; *pl.* **à-rus′pi-cēs.** [L. *aruspex* or *haruspex*, a soothsayer or diviner.] See *Haruspex.*
à-rus′pi-cy, *n.* See *Haruspicy.*
är′văl, *a.* [L. *arvalis*, relating to cultivated land; from *arvum*, a field, neut. of *arvus*, that has been plowed, but not sown, from *arare*, to plow.] Pertaining to plowed ground.

Arval Brethren; a body of priests in ancient Rome, who offered sacrifices to the rural goddess Dia Dea.

är′văl, är′vel, *n.* [ME. *arvell*; AS. *erfe*; W. *arwyl*, funeral, from *ar*, over, and *wylo*, to weep.] A funeral feast. [Prov. Eng.]
Ar-viç′ō-là, *n.* The typical genus of the subfamily *Arvicolinæ.*
Är-viç-ō-lī′næ, *n.pl.* [From L. *arvum*, plowed land, field, and *colere*, to inhabit.] One of several subfamilies of rodents, which includes the field-mice of America, the water-rats of Europe, etc.
är-viç′ō-line, är-viç′ō-lous, *a.* Living in the fields; relating to the *Arvicolinæ.*
är-viç′ō-line, *n.* One of the *Arvicolinæ*; a field-mouse.
-ary. [L. *-arius, -aria, -arium.*] A suffix occurring (a) in nouns and denoting persons, things, or places; as, antiqu*ary*, diction*ary*, libr*ary*; (b) in adjectives, as prim*ary*, auxili*ary*.
Är′yăn, Är′iăn (*or* ar′yăn), *n.* [L. *Arianus*; Gr. *Areia*; Sans. *Ārya*, origin uncertain, perhaps from *ārya*, noble.]

1. One of the Asiatic or Eastern divisions of the Indo-European family, inhabiting Persia and India, between the Bay of Bengal and Mesopotamia.

2. In a more modern sense, a member of the European section of the human family called Indo-European, which embraces as its eastern section the Persians and Hindus.

3. One of that primitive people of Central Asia whose emigrants formed the stock of the Hindus, Persians, Greeks, Latins, Teutons, Celts, Slavonians, etc., or the races of the Indo-European family. Both the blonde and brunette divisions of Europe are included. The languages of these peoples show unmistakably their origin in a common tongue.

The whole framework of grammar had become settled before the separation of the *Aryan* or Japhetic family. —Max Müller.

4. The original language of the Aryans.

Är′yăn, Är′iăn, *a.* Pertaining to the Aryans or their language; Indo-European, Japhetic, or Indo-Germanic.
Är′yăn-ize (*or* Ar′y-ăn-ize), *v.t.* To make Aryan in character.
à-ryt′ē-noid, *a.* and *n.* [Gr. *arytainoeides*, cup-shaped; *arytēr*, a cup, and *eidos*, form.]

I. *a.* Ladle-shaped or cup-shaped.

II. *n.* One of the two arytenoid cartilages.

Arytenoid cartilages; two pyramidal bodies articulated by their bases with the oval articular substances which exist on the upper margin of the cricoid cartilage in the human larynx; they assist to regulate the action of the vocal cords.

Arytenoid muscle; a muscle which passes from one of the arytenoid cartilages to the other.

aṣ, *adv.* and *conj.* [ME. *as, ase*; AS. *alswā, ealswā.*]

In most of its uses, *as* is a conjunctive adverb, its use as a pure adverb being confined to the beginning of sentences, particularly such as contain the correlative *so* or *as.* At times it almost becomes a preposition, as in the sentence, he appeared *as* Romeo; and it is practically a relative pronoun when introducing an attributive clause after *such* or *same*; as, he did not expect *such* a result *as* that.

1. Literally, like; even; similar to. "Ye shall be *as* gods, knowing good and evil." "*As* far *as* we can see"; that is, like far, equally far. Hence, it may be explained by *in like manner*; as, do *as* you are commanded.

2. In the character or idea of, with a view to qualities, attributes, or circumstances. "New York *as* a financial center"; "to appear on the stage *as* Hamlet."

3. While; during; at the same time. "He trembled *as* he spoke."

4. Since; because. "The jury acquitted him, *as* the evidence was insufficient."

5. Though; however. "Careful *as* it was, the committee failed in some respects."

6. For instance; for example; thus.

7. Formerly, equivalent to the relative *that* after *so.* [Obs.]

The relations are so uncertain *as* they require a great deal of examination. —Bacon.

8. Formerly, and in vulgar speech to this day, used in other positions as a relative, equivalent to *who* or *that*, without a preceding *such*; as, the man *as* goes to market.

That gentleness *as* I was wont to have. —Shak.

9. Formerly, used for *as if.* [Obs.]

He lies, *as* he his bliss did know. —Waller.

In most of its uses, *as* is resolvable into *like, equal, even*, or *equally, in like manner.* In some phrases it is equivalent to the relative *that.* "Appoint to office such men *as* deserve public confidence." This phrase, however, may be elliptical for "such men *as* those who deserve public confidence."

As, in a subsequent part of a sentence, answers to *such*; give us *such* things *as* you please; and in a preceding part of a sentence, has *so* to answer to it; *as* with the people, *so* with the priest.

As far as; to the distance or degree of.

As for, or *as to*; in or with regard or respect to.

As good as; equal with, or the same as.

As it were; a phrase used to soften or excuse some expression that might be regarded as in any way unsuitable.

As well as; equally with; just as much.

As yet; up to the present time; up to this moment.

ās, *n.* An ace. [Obs.]
as, *n.*; *pl.* **as′sēṣ.** [L.] 1. A Roman weight of twelve ounces, answering to the libra or pound.

2. A Roman coin, originally of a pound weight, but reduced, after the first Punic war, to two ounces, and subsequently to half an ounce; the most common form had the two-faced head of Janus on one side and the prow of a ship on the other.

As (half size).

As, *n.* In Norse mythology, one of the Æsir gods.
as′à, as′sä, *n.* [Per. *aza*, mastic.] An ancient name of a gum. The word is used now mostly in composition, as in *asafetida.*
as-à-dul′cis, *n.* [*Asa*, gum, and L. *dulcis*, sweet.] A much-used drug of former times, and called also *laser*, probably obtained from an umbelliferous plant of Europe and Africa. It was at one time thought to be the same as benzoin.
as-à-fet′i-dà, as-à-fœt′i-dà, *n.* [*Asa*, gum, and L. *fetida, fœtida*, f. of *fetidus* or *fœtidus*, pp. of *fœtere*, to have a disagreeable smell, stink.] A fetid inspissated sap, from Persia and the East Indies. It is the concrete juice of a large umbelliferous plant, the *Ferula*, or

Narthex, Asafœtida, and is much used in medicine as an antispasmodic and a stimulant. Written also *Assafœtida*.

as'ăk, *n.* See *Asok*.

As'ȧ-phēṣ, *n.* [Gr. *asaphēs*, obscure, not clear; *a* priv., and *saphēs*, clear.] A genus of ichneumon-flies; also, a genus of coleopterous beetles.

ȧs-ā'phi-ȧ, *n.* [Gr. *asaphēs*, not clear; *a* priv., and *saphēs*, distinct.] A condition characterized by a thick utterance, as when a person is tongue-tied.

As'ȧ-phus, *n.* [Gr. *asaphēs*, obscure; *a* priv., and *saphēs*, clear.] A genus of trilobites, characteristic of the lower Paleozoic rocks; so called from their true nature having been long obscure.

as"ȧ-rȧ-baç'çȧ, *n.* [L. *asarum*, from Gr. *asaron*, and L. *bacca*, berry.] The English name of the *Asarum Europæum*. The leaves are emetic, cathartic, and diuretic.

as'ȧ-rin, as'ȧ-rōne, *n.* Camphor of asarum; a crystallized substance obtained from the *Asarum Europæum*.

As'ȧ-rum, *n.* [L. *asarum*; Gr. *asaron*; from *a* priv., and *seira*, a cord, string, or band.] A genus of plants belonging to the order *Aristolochiaceæ*, or birthworts. It contains the species *Asarum Europæum*.

as-bes'tiç, as-bes'tous, *a.* [See *Asbestos*.] Having the qualities of, or resembling, asbestos.

as-bes'ti-fọrm, *a.* Having the structure of asbestos.

as-bes'tine, *a.* Pertaining to asbestos, or partaking of its nature and qualities; incombustible.

as-bes'tin-īte, *n.* Actinolite.

Calciferous asbestinite; a variety of steatite.

as-bes'tŏs, as-bes'tus, *n.* [Fr *asbeste*; ME. *asbeston*; L. *asbestos*; Gr. *asbestos*, inextinguishable; *a* priv., and *sbennunai*, to extinguish.] A fibrous variety of several members of the hornblende family, as augite, actinolite, and tremolite, composed of separable filaments with a silky luster. It is incombustible, and, being capable of being wrought into cloth and other flexible shapes, is valuable for a variety of purposes. It is used as fireproofing material for buildings, safes, etc.; for lampwicks and gas-logs in grates; for firemen's clothing and glassworkers' gloves; for roofing and flooring material, and for packing steam-joints and pistons. It is mined in many parts of the United States and in Canada. Its powder is soft to the touch; its colors are some shade of white, gray, or green, passing into brown, red, or black. A fine variety is called *amianthus*.

Ligniform asbestos; a variety of a brown color, of a slaty or splintery fracture, and, if broken across, presenting an irregular filamentous structure, like wood.

as-bes'tous, *a.* Asbestic.

aṣ'bō-lin, *n.* [Gr. *asbolos*, *asbole*.] A yellow, oil-like matter, acrid and bitter, obtained from soot.

as'căn, *a.* Relating to or derived from an ascus.

as-çar'i-cīde, *n.* [*Ascaris*, and L. *caedere*, kill.] A vermifuge, used especially to expel ascarids.

as'çȧ-rid, *n.* One of the *Ascaridæ*.

As-çar'i-dæ, *n.* A family of worms including several genera of pinworms, roundworms, and other intestinal parasites.

As'çȧ-ris, *n.* [Gr.] In zoölogy, a genus of intestinal worms.

as-cend', *v.i.*; ascended, *pt.*, *pp.*; ascending, *ppr.* [L. *ascendere*, from *scandere*, to mount or climb; W. *esgyn*, to rise.]

1. To move upward; to mount; to go up; to rise, whether in air or water, or upon a material object.

2. To rise, in a figurative sense; to proceed from an inferior to a superior degree, from mean to noble objects, from particulars to generals, etc., and from modern to ancient times.

3. In a corresponding sense, to proceed in a line toward ancestors; as, to *ascend* to our first progenitors.

4. To rise, as a star; to proceed or come above the horizon.

5. In music, to rise in vocal utterance; to pass from any note to one more acute.

Syn.—Surmount, mount, go up, climb, scale, tower, rise, soar.

as-cend', *v.t.* [ME. *ascenden*; L. *ascendere*; *ad*, to, and *scandere*, to climb.] To go or move upward upon; as, to *ascend* a hill or ladder; to climb; as, to *ascend* a tree.

as-cend'ȧ-ble, as-cend'i-ble, *a.* That may be ascended.

as-cend'ănce, as-cend'ence, *n.* Same as *Ascendancy*.

as-cend'ăn-cy, as-cend'en-cy, *n.* Power; governing or controlling influence; the state of being in the ascendant.

> Custom has an *ascendency* over the understanding. —Watts.

Syn.—Superiority, authority, domination, mastery, sway.

as-cend'ănt, as-cend'ent, *n.* 1. Superiority, or commanding influence; as, one man has the *ascendant* over another.

2. An ancestor, or one who precedes in genealogy or degrees of kindred; opposed to *descendant*.

3. Height; elevation; as, sciences in their highest *ascendant*.

4. In astrology, the sign of the zodiac which rises above the horizon at the time of one's birth; supposed to have influence on a person's life and fortune.

To be in the ascendant; to have commanding power or influence.

Lord of the ascendant; one who has possession of ruling power or influence.

as-cend'ănt, as-cend'ent, *a.* 1. Superior; predominant; surpassing.

2. In astrology, above the horizon.

3. Moving up; soaring.

as-cend'en-cy, *n.* See *Ascendancy*.

as-cend'i-ble, *a.* Same as *Ascendable*.

as-cend'ing, *a.* Rising; moving upward; as, an *ascending* star.

Ascending latitude; the latitude of a planet when moving toward the north pole.

Ascending node; that point of a planet's orbit wherein it passes the ecliptic to proceed northward. It is also called the *northern node*.

Ascending vessels; in anatomy, those vessels which carry the blood upward or toward the superior parts of the body.

Ascending embryo; in botany, an embryo the apex of which is pointed toward the apex of the fruit.

Ascending ovule; an ovule which grows from a little above the base of the ovary.

as-cend'ing-ly, *adv.* In an ascending manner.

as-cen'sion, *n.* 1. The act of ascending; a rising. Specifically, *the Ascension*, the visible elevation of Christ to heaven.

2. The thing rising or ascending. [Obs.]

Right ascension; in astronomy, the arc of the equator intercepted between the first point of Aries and that point of the equator that comes to the meridian with the sun or star.

Oblique ascension; the arc of the equator intercepted between the first point of Aries and that point of the equator that comes to the horizon with a star. [Rare.]

Ascension day; a festival of some Christian churches, held ten days, or on the Thursday but one, before Whitsuntide, in commemoration of Christ's ascension into heaven, after his resurrection; called also *Holy Thursday*.

as-cen'sion-ăl, *a.* Relating to ascension; ascending or rising up.

Ascensional difference; in astronomy, the difference between the right and oblique ascension of the same point on the surface of the sphere. [Rare.]

as-cen'sive, *a.* 1. Rising; tending to rise, or causing to rise.

2. In grammar, intensive; increasing the force; augmentative.

as-cent', *n.* [L. *ascensus*, from *ascendere*, to ascend.]

1. The act of rising; motion upward, whether in air, water, or other fluid, or on elevated objects; rise; a mounting upward; as, the *ascent* of vapors from the earth.

2. The way by which one ascends; the means of ascending.

3. An eminence, hill, or high place.

4. The degree of elevation of an object, or the angle it makes with a horizontal line; as, a road has an *ascent* of five degrees.

5. Acclivity; the rise of a hill; as, a steep *ascent*.

6. The act of proceeding from an inferior to a superior degree, from particulars to generals, etc.

as-cẽr-tāin', *v.t.*; ascertained, *pt.*, *pp.*; ascertaining, *ppr.* [OFr. *acertainer*; L. *ad*, to, and *certus*, fixed.]

1. To make certain; to define or reduce to precision, by removing obscurity or ambiguity; to determine.

> The divine law *ascertains* the truth. —Hooker.

2. To make certain, by trial, examination, or experiment, so as to know what was before unknown; as, to *ascertain* the weight of a commodity, or the purity of a metal.

3. To make certain or confident, followed by an objective and *of*; as, to *ascertain us of* the goodness of our work. [Obs.]

4. To fix; to establish with certainty; to render invariable, and not subject to will. [Rare.]

> The mildness and precision of their laws *ascertained* the rule and measure of taxation. —Gibbon.

Syn.—Find out, discover, determine, detect, discern, learn.

as-cẽr-tāin'ȧ-ble, *a.* Capable of being ascertained.

as-cẽr-tāin'ȧ-ble-ness, *n.* The quality or state of being ascertainable.

as-cẽr-tāin'ȧ-bly, *adv.* In an ascertainable manner or condition.

as-cẽr-tāin'ẽr, *n.* One who ascertains or makes certain.

as-cẽr-tāin'ment, *n.* The act of ascertaining; a reducing to certainty; certainty; fixed rule.

as-ces'săn-cy, *n.* See *Acescency*.

as-ces'sănt, *a.* See *Acescent*.

as-cet'iç, *a.* [Gr. *askētikos*, exercised, from *askein*, to exercise.] Retired from the world; rigid; severe; austere; unduly rigid in devotions and mortifications.

as-cet'iç, *n.* 1. In the early church, one who retired from the customary business of life, and devoted himself to the duties of piety and devotion; a hermit; a recluse.

2. One who practises undue rigor and self-denial in religious things.

as-cet'i-ciṣm, *n.* The state or practice of ascetics.

as'çham, *n.* [Named after Roger *Ascham*.] A receptacle for archery implements.

as'cī, *n.*, pl. of *ascus*.

as'ciăn (ash'yăn), *n.*; *pl.* **as-ciăns, or as'ci-ī** (ash'i-ī). [L. *ascius*, shadowless; Gr. *askios*; *a* priv., and *skia*, a shadow.] A person who on certain occasions casts no shadow at noon. The inhabitants of the torrid zone alone attain this peculiarity, having the sun exactly above their heads twice a year at noon.

As-cid'i-ȧ, *n.pl.* [Gr. *askidion*, a little bottle, from *askos*, a leathern bag, a bottle.] A name given to the *Tunicata*, or sea-squirts, molluscous animals of a low grade; ascidians. They are found at low-water mark on the seabeach, and are dredged from deep water attached to stones, shells, and fixed objects. An ascidian presents externally the appearance of a wine-jar or double-necked bottle. A large proportion of the tough outer case or test is composed largely of cellulose. A single nervous mass of ganglion represents the nervous system, this mass being placed between the two apertures of the body. Male and female reproductive organs exist in each specimen. Ascidians may be single or simple, social, or compound. In social ascidians, the peduncles of a number of individuals are united into a common tubular stem, with a partial, common circulation of blood.

Ascidians.

1. Perophora; *a*, mouth; *b*, vent; *c*, intestinal canal; *d*, stomach; *e*, common tubular stem. 2. *Ascidia echinata*. 3. *Ascidia virginea*. 4. *Cynthia quadrangularis*. 5. *Botryllus violaceus*.

as-cid'i-ȧ, *n.*, pl. of *ascidium*.

as-cid'i-ăn, *a.* and *n.* I. *a.* Of or belonging to the *Ascidia*.

II. *n.* One of the *Ascidia*; a sea-squirt.

as-cid-i-ā'ri-um, *n.*; *pl.* **as-cid-i-ā'ri-ȧ**. [L.] A compound ascidian.

as-ci-diç'ō-lous, *a.* In zoölogy, parasitic in or on ascidians.

as-cid'i-fọrm, *a.* Resembling an ascidian in shape; bottle-shaped.

as-cid'i-oid, *a.* Pertaining to, or of the nature of, an ascidian.

As-cid-i-oi'dȧ, *n.pl.* Same as *Ascidia*.

as-cid"i-ō-zō'oid, *n.* [*Ascidium*, and Gr. *zōon*, a living being, from *zēn*, to live.] One of the component members of an ascidiarium.

as-cid'i-um, *n.*; *pl.* **as-cid'i-ȧ**. In botany, a hollow tube or pitcher-like appendage found in some plants, and formed by a modified leaf. It is often closed by a lid, as in the true pitcher-plant.

as-cig'ẽr-ous, as-cif'ẽr-ous, *a.* [LL. *ascus*, a bag, and L. *gerere*, to bear, or *ferre*, to bear.] In botany, bearing asci, as lichens and ascomycetous fungi.

as'ci-ī (ash'i-ī), *n.*, pl. of *ascian*.

As-ci'tănṣ, *n.pl.* [Gr. *askos*, a bag or bottle of skin.] A sect or branch of Montanists, who appeared in the second century, and introduced bacchanals into their assemblies.

as-cī'tēṣ, *n.* [Gr. *askos*, a bladder.] Dropsy of the abdomen.

as-cit'iç, as-cit'iç-ăl, *a.* Pertaining to ascites; dropsical; hydropical.

as-ci-ti'tious (-tish'us), *a.* [LL. *ascititius*; L. *ascitus*, pp. of *asciscere*, to approve or adopt.] Additional; added; supplemental; not inherent or original; same as *adscititious*.

> Homer has been reckoned an *ascititious* name. —Pope.

as-çlē'pi-ad, *n.* In ancient prosody, a form of

verse first used by the Greek poet, Asclepiades.

as-clē′pi-ad, *n.* A plant of the natural order *Asclepiadaceæ.*

As-clē′pi-ad, *n.* One of an order of Greek physicians and priests who claimed to be descendants of Asklepios (Æsculapius), the god of healing.

As-clē″pi-ȧ-dā′cē-æ, *n.pl.* [From *Asclepias*, the typical genus.] A natural order of monopetalous dicotyledonous plants (the milkweed family), known by the grains of pollen adhering together in a waxlike mass within the cell of the anther, and by the fruit consisting of two spreading follicles. Over a thousand species are known, chiefly in the tropics.

as-clē″pi-ȧ-dā′ceous, *a.* Of, pertaining to, or resembling plants of the milkweed family.

as-clē-pi-ad′ic, *a.* Of or pertaining to the asclepiad, a kind of verse.

As-clē′pi-as, *n.* [Gr. *Asklēpios*, son of *Apollo* and *Coronis*, tutelary god of medicine.] A genus of plants, the type and the largest genus of the natural order *Asclepiadaceæ.* Most of the species are North American herbs, having opposite, alternate, or verticillate leaves. Many of them possess powerful medicinal qualities.

as′cō-. [Gr. *askos*, a bag or wine-skin.] A combining form used especially in zoölogical words in relation to an *ascidian*, and in botanical, in relation to an *ascus.*

as′cō-cärp, *n.* [*Asco-*, and Gr. *karpos*, fruit.] In botany, the fruit of ascomycetous fungi.

As-cō-coc′cus, *n.* [*Asco-*, and Gr. *kokkos*, kernel.] A genus of bacteria occurring in peculiarly formed masses in putrid infusions of meat, etc.

as-cog′e-nous, *a.* [*Asco-*, and Gr. *genos*, kind, species.] Producing asci.

as-cō-gō′ni-um, *n.*; *pl.* **as-cō-gō′ni-ȧ.** [*Asco-*, and Gr. *gonos*, the produce of anything.] The female organ in some of the lower cryptogams, which produces asci.

as″cō-mȳ-cē′tăl, *a.* Relating to the *Ascomycetes.*

As″cō-mȳ-cē′tēs, *n.pl.* [*Asco-*, and Gr. *mykēs*, a mushroom.] A large group of fungi, whose spores or sporidia are contained within asci.

as″cō-mȳ-cē′tous, *a.* Of or pertaining to the *Ascomycetes.*

as′con, *n.* One of the *Ascones.*

As-cō′nēs, *n.pl.* [Gr. *askos*, a bag.] A group of the lowest chalk-sponges, with thin ventricular walls.

as′cō-phōre, *n.* [*Asco-*, and Gr. *pherein*, to bear.] A seed-bearer from which asci are produced.

as-coph′ō-rous, *a.* In botany, of, pertaining to, or like an ascophore.

as′cō-spōre, *n.* [*Asco-*, and Gr. *spora*, seed.] In botany, a cluster of spores borne within an ascus.

as-crīb′ȧ-ble, *a.* Capable of being ascribed or attributed.

as-crībe′, *v.t.*; ascribed, *pt.*, *pp.*; ascribing, *ppr.* [ME. *ascriven*; OFr. *ascrire*; L. *ascribere*; *ad*, to, and *scribere*, to write.]

1. To attribute, impute, or set down to, as to a cause; to refer an effect to its cause; as, losses are often to be *ascribed* to imprudence.

2. To attribute, as a quality or an appurtenance; to consider or allege to belong to; as, to *ascribe* perfection to God.

Syn.—Attribute, impute, assign, allege, charge.

as′cript, *a.* Enrolled; appointed. [Obs.]

as-crip′tion, *n.* [L. *ascriptus*, pp. of *ascribere*, to ascribe.]

1. The act of ascribing, imputing, or affirming to belong.

2. A sentiment ascribing glory and praise to God, repeated by a clergyman, immediately after his sermon.

as-crip-ti′tious (-tish′us), *a.* 1. Ascribed.

2. Attached; said of serfs or villains under the feudal system, who were annexed to the freehold and transferable with it; also written *adscriptitious.*

as′cū-lȧ, *n.* [Dim. of LL. *ascus*, sponge.] The stage of a larval sponge in which its cilia have disappeared and it has become fixed.

as′cus, *n.*; *pl.* **as′cī** (as′ī). [Gr. *askos*, a leather bottle or bag.] In botany, a bag; a term applied to the little membranous bags or thecæ in which the reproductive particles or spores of lichens, some fungi, and some other cryptogams are produced.

as′cy-phous (as′i-fus), *a.* [Gr. *ascyphos*, without a cup; *a* priv., and *scyphos*, a cup.] In botany, without scyphi.

ȧ-sēa′, *adv.* At sea; in the direction of or toward the sea.

ȧ-sē′i-ty, *n.* [Fr. *aséité*; from L. *a*, *ab*, from, and abl. of reflexive pron. *se*, oneself, of oneself.] In metaphysics, the state or condition of having an independent existence.

ȧ-sē′mi-ȧ, *n.* [Gr. *asēmos*, without sign; *a* priv., and *sēma*, sign.] Loss of ability to express or understand thought or ideas by means of signs or symbols, written, uttered, or gesticulated.

ȧ-sep′sis, *n.* [Gr. *a* priv., and *sēpsis*, putrefaction.] The condition of being free from putrefaction; absence of toxic or pathogenic bacteria.

ȧ-sep′tȧ, *n.pl.* [Gr. *aseptos*; *a* priv., and *septein*, to putrefy.] Substances which, except under extraordinary circumstances, do not putrefy.

ȧ-sep′tic, *a.* Not liable to putrefy; free from septic matter or toxic bacteria.

Aseptic operation; the asepticizing of a wound by the introduction into it of antiseptic solutions.

ȧ-sep′tic, *n.* Any aseptic substance.

ȧ-sep′ti-cişm, *n.* The doctrine or principles of antiseptic surgery, or treatment by aseptic methods.

ȧ-sep-tic′i-ty, *n.* The quality of being aseptic.

ȧ-sep′ti-cīze, *v.t.*; asepticized, *pt.*, *pp.*; asepticizing, *ppr.* To cause to become aseptic.

ȧ-sex′ū-ăl, *a.* Having no distinct sex; also, produced without sexual agency.

ȧ-sex′ū-ăl-ly, *adv.* In an asexual manner.

ash, *n.* [ME. *asch*, *ashe*, *assh*; AS. *asce*, *æsc.*]

1. The popular name of different species of timber trees of the genus *Fraxinus*, natural order *Oleaceæ*; as, the white *ash*, *Fraxinus Americanus.*

2. The wood of the ash-tree.

3. Any one of several trees resembling the ash.

ash, *a.* Pertaining to or like the ash; made of ash; ashen.

Ash keys or *ashen keys*; the keys or fruit of the ash-tree; in heraldry, a somewhat conventional figure, as represented in the adjoining cut.

Ash Keys.

ash, *v.t.*; ashed, *pt.*, *pp.*; ashing, *ppr.* To strew or sprinkle with ashes; as, to *ash* the hair.

ash, *n.* [ME. *ash*, *ashe*, *asche*; pl. *ashes*, *asches*, *askes*; AS. *asce*, *æsce*; pl. *ascan*, *æscan.*] The incombustible residue of a body that is burned; as, the *ash* of a cigar; when used in the singular generally denoting a particular kind of ash; also, frequently used in composition; as, *ash*-bin, pot-*ash*, etc. [See *Ashes.*]

ȧ-shāme′, *v.t.* To shame. [Rare.]

ȧ-shāmed′, *a.* [ME. *aschamen*; AS. *ascamian*, *gescamian.*]

1. Affected by shame; abashed or confused by guilt, or a conviction of some criminal action or indecorous conduct, or by the exposure of some gross error or misconduct, which tends to impair honor or reputation; followed by *of* or a dependent phrase, introduced by *that.*

> Israel shall be *ashamed of* his own counsel.
> —Hosea x. 6.

2. Hesitating to perform an action, because of the shame or mortification connected with it; reluctant; followed by an infinitive; as, I am *ashamed* to tell you.

Syn.—Abashed, confused, mortified, confounded, humiliated.

ȧ-shām′ed-ly, *adv.* Bashfully; with shame. [Rare.]

A-shan′tĭ, A-shan′tee, *n.* and *a.* [Native name.]

I. *n.* An inhabitant or native of Ashanti, in western Africa.

II. *a.* Relating to Ashanti.

ash′=bin, *n.* A receptacle for ashes and other refuse.

ash′=col″ŏred, *a.* Of a color between brown and gray.

ash′en, *a.* Pertaining to the ash-tree; made of the wood of the ash; as, an *ashen* stick.

ash′en, *a.* Resembling or consisting of ashes; pale; as, *ashen* lips.

ash′en, *n.*, pl. of *ash.* [Obs.]

A-shē′räh, *n.*; *pl.* **A-shē′rim.** [Heb.]

1. Sacred wood; sometimes a tree or stump of a tree, found beside Canaanitish altars.

2. A Semitic goddess; also, a name applied generally to her symbolic representations.

ash′ẽr-y, *n.* 1. A place where ashes are deposited.

2. A place where potash is made.

ash′eş, *n.pl.*; *sing.* **ash.** 1. The incombustible residue of combustible substances remaining after combustion, as of wood or coal.

2. As a commercial term, the residue of vegetable substances, from which are extracted the alkaline matters called potash, pearlash, kelp, barilla, etc.

3. The remains of the human body when burned. Hence, figuratively, a dead body or corpse.

4. In Scripture, figuratively, vileness, meanness, frailty, or humiliation.

> I, which am but dust and *ashes.*
> —Gen. xviii. 27.

Volcanic ashes; the loose, earthy matter ejected by volcanoes during eruption.

In sackcloth and ashes; in great grief or humiliation; an ancient phrase borrowed from the Oriental customs of grieving.

ash′=fire, *n.* A low fire used in chemical operations.

ash′=fûr″nāce, *n.* An oven in which the materials used in glassmaking are fritted.

ȧ-shine′, *a.* Shining.

ash′lẽr, ash′lăr, *n.* [ME. *asheler*, *ascheler*; OFr. *aiseler*, from L. *assula*, a chip; dim. of *assis*, plank.]

1. In architecture, a facing made of squared stones; or a facing made of thin slabs, used to cover walls of brick or rubble.

2. A common or free stone as brought from the quarry.

3. In carpentry, an upright from a garret floor to a rafter.

ash′lẽr-ing, ash′lăr-ing, *n.* 1. The short upright pieces between the floor-beams and rafters in garrets, for the attachment of lath.

2. Masonry of ashler.

ȧ-shōre′, *adv.* 1. On shore; on the land adjacent to water; to the shore; as, bring the goods *ashore*; the ship was driven *ashore.*

2. On land, opposed to *aboard*; as, the captain of the ship remained *ashore.*

ash′=ŏv″en, *n.* Same as *Ash-furnace.*

Ash′tō-reth, *n.* [Heb.] The moon-goddess Astarte, worshiped by the ancient Syrians and Phenicians.

Ash Wednes′dāy (wenz′dā). The first day of Lent; so called from an old Roman Catholic custom of sprinkling the heads of penitents with ashes on that day.

ash′weed, *n.* [From Fr. *ache*, celery; so named because its leaves resemble those of celery.] See *Goutweed.*

ash′y, *a.* Belonging to, consisting of, or resembling ashes; ash-colored; pale; as, a quantity of *ashy* matter.

A′siăn (-shăn), *a.* and *n.* I. *a.* Pertaining to Asia; Asiatic.

II. *n.* An Asiatic.

ā′si-ärch (-shi-ärk), *n.* [Gr. *Asia*, and *archōn*, ruler, from *archein*, to rule.] A chief or pontiff of proconsular Asia, who had the superintendence of the public games.

A-si-at′ic (-shi-at′ik), *a.* and *n.* I. *a.* Pertaining to Asia.

II. *n.* A native of Asia.

A-si-at′i-cişm, *n.* Something characteristic or imitative of Asia or Asiatics.

ȧ-sīde′, *adv.* 1. On or to one side; to or at a short distance off; apart; away from some normal direction; as, to turn or stand *aside*; to draw a curtain *aside.*

> He took him *aside* from the multitude.
> —Mark vii. 33.

2. Out of one's thoughts, consideration, or regard; away; off; as, to lay *aside* one's animosity; to put one's cares *aside.*

3. So as not to be heard by some one present; in a secret or private manner. [See *Aside*, *n.*]

To set aside; in law, to reverse, as a decision; to nullify or render inoperative, as a judgment or injunction.

ȧ-sīde′, *n.* Something spoken and not heard, or supposed not to be heard by some one present; especially, a speech or other remark uttered by an actor on the stage, and supposed not to be heard by the other characters on the stage, or heard only by those for whom it is intended.

ȧ-sid′ẽr-īte, *n.* [Gr. *a* priv., and *sideros*, iron.] A meteorite in which there is no iron.

Ȧ-sil′i-dæ, *n.pl.* A family of insects belonging to the order *Diptera*, and the tribe *Brachycera*; the hornet-flies.

As′i-lus, *n.* [L. *asilus*, a gadfly, a horsefly.] A genus of flies typical of the *Asilidæ.*

Ȧ-sim′i-nȧ, *n.* A genus of shrubby trees common to temperate North America of which the papaw, *Asimina triloba*, is a species.

As-i-nā′ri-i, *n.pl.* [L. *asinarius*, ass-like, from *asinus*, ass.] Ass-worshipers; a defamatory term first applied to the Jews by the Romans; later to the early Christians by the Romans and Jews.

as-i-nē′gō, as-si-nē′gō, *n.* [Sp. *asnico*, dim. of *asno*, ass; L. *asinus.*] A foolish fellow. [Obs.]

as′i-nīne, *a.* [L. *asininus*, ass-like, from *asinus*, ass.] Belonging to the ass; having ass-like qualities; stubborn; stupid.

as-i-nin′i-ty, *n.* The state of being asinine.

A-sī-phō-nā′tȧ, *n.pl.* [Gr. *a* priv., and *siphōn*, a siphon.] An order of lamellibranchiate bivalve mollusks, destitute of a siphon; including the oysters, the mussels, and in general those mollusks most useful to man.

ȧ-sī′phon-āte, *a.* Of or pertaining to the *Asiphonata.*

ȧ-si′ti-ȧ (-sish′i-ȧ), *n.* [Gr. *asitia*, want of appetite; *a* priv., and *sitos*, food.] Loss of appetite; loathing of food; also, want of food.

ask, *v.t.*; asked, *pt.*, *pp.*; asking, *ppr.* [ME. *ashen*, *esken*; AS. *ascian*, *acsian*, to ask; originally from Sans. root, *ish*, to seek.]

1. To request; to seek to obtain by words; to petition; sometimes with *of*, in the sense of *from*, before the person to whom the request is made.

> *Ask* counsel of God. —Judges xviii. 5.

2. To require as necessary or useful; to exact; as, the nation *asks* little of its representatives.

3. To interrogate, or inquire; to put a question to, with a view to an answer.

He is of age, *ask* him. —John ix. 21.

4. To claim, require, or demand, as the price or value of a commodity; to set (a price); as, what price do you *ask?*

5. To invite; as, to *ask* guests to a wedding or entertainment; *ask* my friend to step into the house.

6. To inquire concerning; to seek to be informed about; as, to *ask* the way to the courthouse.

To ask in church; to publish banns of marriage.

Syn.—Demand, entreat, inquire, request, solicit, crave, beg, petition, question, interrogate, invite, require, beseech.

ȧsk, *v.i.* 1. To request or petition; used with or without *for*; as, *ask for* bread.

Ask, and it shall be given you.—Matt. vii. 7.

2. To inquire, or seek by request; to make inquiry; sometimes followed by *after*; as, to *ask after* one's health.

ȧsk, *n.* The asker or water-newt. [Prov. Eng.]

ȧ-skȧnce′, ȧ-skȧnt′, *adv.* [Origin uncertain.] Sideways; obliquely; out of one corner of the eye; hence, distrustfully; with suspicion; as, they regarded us *askance*.

ȧ-skȧnce′, *v.t.* To turn away. [Rare.]

ȧsk′ẽr, *n.* One who asks; a petitioner; an inquirer.

ȧsk′ẽr, *n.* [ME. *aske*; AS. *āthexe*, a lizard or newt.] The water-newt. [Prov. Eng.]

ȧ-skew′, *adv.* [ME. *askue, ascue.*] With a wry look; aside; askance; sometimes indicating scorn, contempt, or envy.

ȧsk′ing, *n.* 1. The act of requesting, petitioning, or interrogating; also the thing requested.

2. The publishing or proclamation of marriage banns.

ȧ-slāke′, *v.t.* [ME. *aslaken*; AS. *āslacian*, to slacken.] To remit; to slacken; to diminish. [Obs.]

ȧ-slănt′, *a.* and *adv.* On one side; obliquely; not perpendicularly or at a right angle.

The shaft drove through his neck *aslant*. —Dryden.

ȧ-slănt′, *prep.* In a slanting direction; across, through, or over; as, a ray of light *aslant* the room.

ȧ-sleep′, *a.* and *adv.* 1. Sleeping; in a state of sleep; at rest; as, the boy was fast *asleep*.

2. To a state of sleep; as, to fall *asleep*.

3. Figuratively, dead; in a state of death.

Concerning them which are *asleep*, sorrow not. —1 Thess. iv. 13.

4. Numbed, accompanied with a tingling sensation; as, my foot is *asleep*.

ȧ-slōpe′, *a.* and *adv.* In a leaning, slanting, or inclined position.

ȧ-slug′, *adv.* In a sluggish manner. [Obs.]

ȧ-smeăr′, *a.* and *adv.* Smeared.

As-mō-nē′ăn, *a.* and *n.* I. *a.* Pertaining to Asmoneus, the father of Simon, and chief of a family that reigned over the Jews 126 years; Maccabean.

II. *n.* One of the family of Asmoneus, the ancestor of the Maccabees.

ȧ-sōak′, *a.* or *adv.* Soaking.

as′ŏk, ȧ-sō′kȧ, as′ăk, *n.* [Native name.] A sacred East Indian tree, *Saraca Asoka*.

ȧ-sō′mȧ-tous, *a.* [Gr. *asōmatos*, without body; *a* priv., and *sōma*, body.] Without a material body; incorporeal.

as′ō-nănt, *a.* Soundless. [Rare.]

ȧsp, ȧsp′iç, *n.* [L. *aspis*; Gr. *aspis*, an asp.]

1. A species of Egyptian viper, *Naja haje*, having a distensive neck like the cobra. This small, greenish-brown snake, native near the Nile, has been celebrated for ages on account of the quick and easy death resulting from its bite. Its figure is often found carved on the portals of the temples of the ancient Egyptians.

Asp, from ancient Egyptian monument.

2. A species of viper found all over the continent of Europe, the *Vipera aspis*.

ȧsp, *n.* Same as *Aspen*.

As-pal′ȧ-thus, *n.* [Gr. *aspalathos*, a sweet-scented shrub.]

1. The African broom, a large genus of African plants of the bean family, with small heath-like leaves and generally yellow flowers.

2. [a—] A thorny shrub of uncertain species, mentioned in ancient writings.

as-pȧ-rag′iç, *a.* Same as *Aspartic*.

as-par′ȧ-ġin, as-par′ȧ-ġine, *n.* An alkaloid found in the seeds of many plants, in asparagus, beets, and other vegetables. It is rhombically crystalline and soluble in hot water.

as-pȧ-raġ′i-nous, *a.* Relating or allied to asparagus; with esculent shoots like asparagus.

As-par′ȧ-gus, *n.* [OFr. *esparage*; L. *asparagus*; Gr. *asparagos*, asparagus.]

1. A large genus of perennial plants, of the natural order *Liliaceæ*.

2. [a—] The vernal shoots or tips of *Asparagus officinalis*, forming a well-known esculent. The former name, *sparrowgrass*, is now obsolete or vulgar.

3. [a—] Any plant of this genus.

as-par′ȧ-gus=bee″tle, *n.* A leaf-beetle, as *Crioceris asparagi*, feeding on asparagus plants.

as-par′ȧ-gus=stone, *n.* A crystalline form of apatite.

as-pär′tiç, *a.* Of, relating to, or obtained from asparagin.

as′peçt, *n.* [ME. *aspect*; L. *aspectus*, from *aspicere*, to look at.]

1. Look; view; appearance to the eye or the mind; as, to present an object or a subject in its true *aspect*, or under a double *aspect*; public affairs have a favorable *aspect*.

2. Countenance; look, or particular appearance of the face; as, a mild or severe *aspect*.

3. Look; glance; the act of seeing. [Rare.]

4. Position or situation with regard to seeing, or that position which enables one to look in a particular direction; or, in a more general sense, position in relation to the points of the compass; as, a house has a southern *aspect*, that is, a position which faces or looks to the south.

5. In astrology, the situation of one planet with respect to another, or the angle formed by the rays of light proceeding from two planets, and meeting at the eye. This situation of a planet determines, astrologically, its influence for good or evil.

6. In heraldry, the position of an animal with reference to the spectator; as, in full *aspect*.

Syn.—Appearance, countenance, complexion, deportment, bearing, feature, phase, look, view, light mien, air.

as′peçt, *v.t.* To behold. [Obs.]

as-peçt′ȧ-ble, *a.* [L. *aspectabilis*, visible.] That may be seen; visible. [Rare.]

as-peçt′ănt, *a.* [L. *aspectans*, ppr. of *aspectare*, to look at repeatedly.] In heraldry and art, facing each other.

as-peçt′ed, *a.* Having an aspect. [Rare.]

as-peç′tion, *n.* The act of viewing. [Obs.]

as-peç′tŏr, *n.* A beholder. [Obs.]

asp′en, asp, *n.* [ME. *asp, aspe*; AS. *aespe, aspe*, aspen.] A species of poplar, *Populus tremula*, proverbial for the trembling of its leaves, which move with the slightest impulse of the air.

asp′en, *a.* Pertaining to the aspen, or resembling it; made of aspen wood.

as′pẽr, *a.* Rough; rugged. [Rare.]

All base notes have an *asper* sound.—Bacon.

as′pẽr, *n.* [L. *asper*, rough.] In Greek grammar, the accent (ʽ) importing that the letter over which it is placed should be aspirated, or pronounced as if the letter *h* preceded it.

as′pẽr, *n.* [LL. *asprum*; Gr. *aspron*, neut. of *aspros*, white.] A Turkish monetary unit, formerly a coin, equivalent to about one cent and one-fifth.

as′pẽr-āte, *v.t.*; asperated, *pt., pp.*; asperating, *ppr.* [L. *asperatus*, pp. of *asperare*, to make rough.] To make rough or uneven.

as′pẽr-āte, *a.* In botany, rough; uneven.

as-pẽr-ā′tion, *n.* A making rough.

as-pẽr′ġēs, *n.* [L. *aspergere*, to sprinkle; *asperges*, you will sprinkle.] In the Roman Catholic church, a short service introductory to the mass, during which the congregation is sprinkled with holy water by the officiating priest.

as′pẽr-ġill, as-pẽr-ġil′lum, *n.* See *Aspergillus*, 1.

as-pẽr-ġil′li-fŏrm, *a.* Resembling an aspergillus.

as-pẽr′ġil′lus, *n.*; *pl.* **as-pẽr-ġil′lī.** [L. from *aspergere*, to sprinkle, and dim. *-illus*.]

1. A device used in the Roman Catholic church for sprinkling holy water on the congregation; said to have been originally made of hyssop.

Aspergillus.

2. [A—] A genus of hyphomycetous fungi, some species of which form mold on various substances, especially in a state of decay.

as″pẽr-i-fō′li-āte, as″pẽr-i-fō′li-ous, *a.* [L. *asper*, rough, and *folium*, a leaf.] Having rough leaves; a term applied to the natural order of plants named by Linnæus *Asperifoliæ*, now called *Boraginaceæ*.

as-per′i-ty, *n.* [ME. *asprete*; OFr. *asprete*; L. *asperitas*, roughness, from *asper*, rough.]

1. Roughness of surface; unevenness; opposed to *smoothness*.

2. Roughness of sound; that quality which grates upon the ear; harshness of pronunciation.

3. Roughness to the taste; sourness.

4. Roughness or ruggedness of temper; moroseness; sourness; crabbedness.

5. Difficulty; disagreeableness; as, the pleasures and *asperities* of life.

Syn.—Roughness, harshness, sharpness, moroseness, acrimony, acerbity, severity.

ȧ-spẽr′mȧ-tism, *n.* Defective secretion of semen or lack of formation of spermatozoa.

ȧ-spẽr′mȧ-tous, ȧ-spẽr′mous, *a.* [Gr. *aspermos*, seedless; *a* priv., and *sperma*, seed.] In botany, destitute of seeds.

ȧ-spẽr′mi-ȧ, *n.* A condition characterized by defective secretion of semen.

ȧ-spẽr′mous, *a.* Same as *Aspermatous*.

as′pẽr-ous, *a.* [L. *asper*, rough.] Rough; uneven. [Obs.]

as-pẽrse′, *v.t.*; aspersed, *pt., pp.*; aspersing, *ppr.* [L. *aspersus*, pp. of *aspergere*, to scatter.]

1. To bespatter, as with foul reports or false and injurious charges; to tarnish in point of reputation or good name; to slander or calumniate; as, to *asperse* a poet or his writings; to *asperse* a man's motives.

2. To cast upon or over; to besprinkle.

Syn.—Calumniate, scandalize, backbite, slander, traduce, malign, defame, vilify.

as-pẽrsed′, *a.* 1. In heraldry, strewed or powdered.

2. Slandered; vilified; bespattered, as with dust or water.

as-pẽrs′ẽr, *n.* One who asperses or slanders another.

as-pẽr′sion, *n.* 1. A sprinkling, as of water or dust, in a literal sense.

2. The spreading of calumnious reports or charges which tarnish reputation, like the bespattering of a body with foul water; calumny; censure.

as-pẽrs′ive, *a.* Slanderous.

as-pẽrs′ive-ly, *adv.* In an aspersive manner.

as-pẽr-sō′ri-um, as-per-soir′ (-swär′), *n.*; *pl.* **as-pẽr-sō′ri-ȧ.** [L., from *aspersus*, pp. of *aspergere*, to sprinkle.]

1. The stoup or vessel for holy water in Roman Catholic churches, usually of stone and fixed permanently close to the entrance. Sometimes, however, the *aspersorium* is portable, of metal, ivory, etc., and often highly ornamented with bas-reliefs.

Portable Aspersorium.

2. A name sometimes applied to the aspergillus or brush with which the priest sprinkles the people.

as-pẽr′sō-ry, *a.* Tending to asperse; defamatory.

as-pẽr′ū-lous, *a.* In botany, slightly rough to the touch.

as′phalt (*or* as-falt′), **as-phal′tum, as-phalte′**, *n.* [Gr. *asphaltos*, asphalt, a word of foreign origin.]

1. The most common variety of bitumen; mineral pitch; a compact, glossy, brittle, black or brown mineral which breaks with a polished fracture, melts easily with a strong, pitchy odor when heated, and when pure burns without leaving any ashes. It is found in the earth in many parts of Europe, Asia, and America, and in a soft state on the surface of the Dead Sea, which Josephus called *Lacus Asphaltites*. It is of organic origin, the *asphalt* of the great Pitch Lake of Trinidad being derived from bituminous shales, containing vegetable remains in the process of transformation.

2. A composition of natural bitumen or refined asphalt, sand, and carbonate of lime used for street pavements, roofing, etc.; asphaltic cement.

3. An artificial product secured in making coal-gas; it is the residue of the tarry matter left in the retorts.

as′phalt, *v.t.*; asphalted, *pt., pp.*; asphalting, *ppr.* To spread over with asphalt.

as-phal′tiç, *a.* Pertaining to asphalt, or containing it; bituminous.

as-phal′tīte, *a.* Asphaltic.

as′phō-del, *n.* [L. *asphodelus*; Gr. *asphodelos*, a plant like the lily.]

1. The common name of different species of the genus *Asphodelus*; cultivated for the beauty of their flowers.

2. A name popularly and poetically applied to plants of other genera, especially to the daffodil or narcissus.

Branched Asphodel (*Asphodelus ramosus*).

As-phod′el-us, *n.* [L.] A genus of hardy perennial plants, of the lily family.

as-phyç′tiç, *a.* Relating to asphyxia.

as-phyx′i-ȧ, as-phyx′y, *n.* [Gr. *asphyxia*, a stopping of the pulse; *a* priv., and *sphyzein*, to beat violently.] Originally, want of pulse, or cessation of the motion of the heart and arteries; as now used, apparent death, or suspended animation, particularly from suffocation or drowning, or the inhalation of irrespirable gases; the suspension of vital phenomena resulting when the lungs are deprived of oxygen.

as-phyx′i-ăl, *a.* Pertaining to asphyxia.

as-phyx′i-ănt, *n.* An agent capable of producing asphyxia.

as-phyx′i-ănt, *a.* Producing asphyxia.

as-phyx′i-āte, *v.t.*; asphyxiated, *pt.*, *pp.*; asphyxiating, *ppr.* To suffocate; to produce or cause asphyxia; as, they were *asphyxiated* by coal-gas.

as-phyx-i-ā′tion, *n.* The act or process of causing suffocation; the condition of asphyxia.

as-phyx′ied (-id), *a.* In a state of asphyxia; asphyxiated.

as-phyx′y, *n.* Same as *Asphyxia.*

as′piç, *n.* [Fr. *aspic*; L. *aspis*, asp.]

1. The asp.

2. Formerly, a piece of ordnance carrying a twelve-pound shot. [Obs.]

as′piç, *n.* [Fr. *aspic*; OFr. *espic*; L. *spica*, a spike, an ear of corn.] A European species of lavender (*Lavandula spica*), which resembles the common kind (*Lavandula vera*) in the blue color of its flowers, and in the figure and green color of its leaves; also called *male lavender* and *Spica nardi.*

as′piç, *n.* [Fr.] In cookery, a meat jelly.

ȧ-spiç′ū-lāte, ȧ-spiç′ū-lous, *a.* [Gr. *a* priv., and L. *spiculum*, point.] Having no spicules.

As-pid′i-um, *n.* [Gr. *aspidion*, a small round shield, dim. of *aspis*, a round shield.] A genus of ferns including all those which have round sori protected with a roundish covering or indusium; shield-fern.

As″pi-dō-brañ′chi-ȧ, *n.pl.* A group of gasteropods having bipectinate gills and a shield-like shell.

as″pi-dō-brañ′chi-āte, *a.* and *n.* [Gr. *aspis*, shield, and *branchia*, gills.]

I. *a.* Resembling the *Aspidobranchia.*

II. *n.* One of the *Aspidobranchia.*

as-pir′ănt, *a.* Aspiring.

as-pir′ănt, *n.* [L. *aspirans*, ppr. of *aspirare*, to breathe upon, to endeavor to reach.] One who aspires or seeks with eagerness; as, an *aspirant* to public office.

as′pi-rāte, *v.t.*; aspirated, *pt.*, *pp.*; aspirating, *ppr.* [L. *aspiratus*, pp. of *aspirare*, to breathe; Gr. *aspairein*, to struggle for breath.] To pronounce with a breathing or full emission of breath; as, we *aspirate* the words *horse* and *house.*

as′pi-rāte, *v.i.* To give or impart a strong breathing; as, the letter *h aspirates.*

as′pi-rāte, *n.* A letter marked with an asper, or note of breathing; a sound characterized by a full breath; the letter *h* or a similar sound; a mark of aspiration, as the Greek accent.

as′pi-rāte, as′pi-rā-ted, *a.* Uttered with a strong emission of breath.

as-pi-rā′tion, *n.* 1. The pronunciation of a letter with a full emission of breath; the act of aspirating.

2. A breathing in; inspiration, as opposed to exhalation; a breath.

3. The act of aspiring or of ardently desiring; an ardent wish or desire, particularly for what is noble, elevated, or spiritual.

Syn.—Ambition, longing, craving, desire, hope, wish.

as′pi-rā-tŏr, *n.* 1. In medicine, an explorative instrument for the evacuation of the fluid contents of tumors, serous and synovial effusions, collections of blood and pus, etc.

2. An instrument for creating a vacuum, or for passing a current of air through fluids, gases, etc.; much used in the chemical analysis of gases.

as-pir′ȧ-tō-ry, *a.* Pertaining to breathing; suited to the inhaling of air.

as-pire′, *v.i.*; aspired, *pt.*, *pp.*; aspiring, *ppr.* [ME. *aspire*; Fr. *aspirer*; L. *aspirare*, to breathe upon, to aspire to; Gr. *aspairein*, to pant for breath.]

1. To breathe.

2. To desire with eagerness; to pant after an object, great, noble, or spiritual; followed by *to* or *after*; as, to *aspire to* a crown, or *after* immortality.

3. To aim at something elevated; to rise or tower with desire.

4. To rise; to ascend; as, the flames *aspire.*

Syn.—Desire, aim, seek, long, rise, mount, ascend, soar.

as-pire′, *n.* Aspiration. [Obs.]

as-pire′ment, *n.* Aspiration. [Obs.]

as-pir′ĕr, *n.* One who aspires.

as′pi-rin, *n.* A drug compound of acetyl and salicylic acid, valued because it liberates the salicylic acid in the intestines.

as-pir′ing, *a.* Ambitious; animated with an ardent desire of power, importance, or excellence; as, an *aspiring* citizen.

as-pir′ing-ly, *adv.* In an aspiring manner.

as-pir′ing-ness, *n.* The state of being aspiring.

asp′ish, *a.* Resembling an asp.

ȧ-splañ′chniç, *n.* [Gr. *a* priv., and *splanchna*, bowels.] Lacking an alimentary canal.

As-plē′ni-um, *n.* [Gr. *asplēnion*, the spleenwort, a fern; *a*, euphonic, and *splēn*, spleen.] Spleenwort. A large genus of ferns belonging to the order *Polypodiaceæ.* Among the best-known species are the *Asplenium Ruta-muraria*, or wall-rue, and the *Asplenium Trichomanes*, or maidenhair spleenwort.

as-pōr-tā′tion, *n.* [L. *asportatio*, a carrying away; *ab*, from, and *portare*, to carry.]

1. A carrying away. [Rare.]

2. In law, the felonious removal of goods from the place where they were deposited, which is adjudged to be theft, though the goods are not carried from the house or apartment. —Blackstone.

ȧ-sprawl′, *a.* and *adv.* I. *a.* Sprawling.

II. *adv.* In a sprawling condition.

ȧ-squät′, *a.* and *adv.* I. *a.* Squatting.

II. *adv.* In a squatting posture.

ȧ-squint′, *a.* Oblique; squinting.

ȧ-squint′, *adv.* To the corner or angle of the eye; obliquely; toward one side; not in the straight line of vision; as, to look *asquint.*

ȧss, *n.* [ME. *ass*, *asse*; OFr. *asne*; AS. *assa*; L. *asinus*, ass.]

1. A quadruped, *Equus asinus*, of the same genus, but smaller than the average horse. It has long, slouching ears, a short mane, and a tail covered with long hairs at the end. It is usually of an ash color, with a black bar across the shoulders. The tame or domestic *ass* is slow, but very sure-footed, and for this reason very useful on rough, steep hills; called also *donkey*, *jack*, and *burro.*

2. A dull, heavy, stupid fellow; a dolt; a fool.

Asses' bridge; in mathematics, a name given to the fifth proposition of the first book of Euclid.

To make an ass of oneself; to act or talk foolishly.

äss, *n.* [Scot.] Ashes.

as′sä, *n.* See *Asa.*

as′sä-çú, as′sȧ-çöu, *n.* [Braz.] A euphorbiaceous tree (*Hura crepitans*) of South America, the bark and sap of which contain a poisonous acrid principle.

as′sȧ-gai, as′se-gai, *n.* [Fr. *archegaie*, from Ar. *az-zaghāyah*, the spear.]

1. A war weapon of the Kaffirs; a kind of javelin or throwing spear.

2. In botany, a tree of the dogwood family, from which the South African natives make their spears.

ȧs-sä′i, *adv.* [It. *assai*, very much; from L. *ad*, to, and *satis*, enough.] In music, an augmentative often joined to a word indicating the movement of an air or other passage; as, *adagio assai*, very slow; *allegro assai*, very quick.

as-sai′ (as-sī′), *n.* [Native name.]

1. A palm-tree of Brazil, the *Euterpe edulis.*

2. A beverage made from the fruit of this tree.

as-sāil′, *v.t.*; assailed, *pt.*, *pp.*; assailing, *ppr.* [ME. *assailen*; OFr. *asaillir*; L. *assilire*, to spring upon; *ad*, to, and *salire*, to leap.]

1. To leap or fall upon by violence; to assault; to attack suddenly, as when one person falls upon another to beat him.

2. To invade or attack, in a hostile manner, as an army, or nation.

3. To attack with arguments, censure, abuse, criticism, appeals, entreaties, and the like, with a view to injure, bring into disrepute, or overcome mentally or morally.

Syn.—Encounter, assault, fall upon, invade, attack, storm.

as-sāil′ȧ-ble, *a.* That may be assailed, attacked, or invaded.

as-sāil′ănt, *n.* [Fr. *assaillant.*] One who assails, attacks, or assaults.

as-sāil′ănt, *a.* 1. Assaulting; attacking; invading with violence.

2. In heraldry, salient; applied to beasts borne in coat-armor.

as-sāil′ĕr, *n.* One who assails.

as-sāil′ment, *n.* Assault; attack. [Rare.]

as′sȧ-mär, *n.* [L. *assus*, roasted, from *assare*, to roast, and *amarus*, bitter.] In chemistry, a yellow-colored bitter substance formed during the process of roasting meat, bread, starch, sugar, and the like till they are browned.

As-sȧm-ēse′, *a.* and *n. sing.* and *pl.* I. *a.* Of or pertaining to Assam, a province of British India, or to its inhabitants.

II. *n. sing.* and *pl.* A native or natives of Assam.

as-sȧ-pan′, as-sȧ-pan′iç, *n.* [Native Am. Indian name.] One of the species of flying-squirrels (*Pteromys volucella*).

as-särt′, *n.* [OFr. *assarter*, to grub up; LL. *exsartare*; from L. *ex*, out, and *sarrire*, to hoe.]

1. In ancient laws, the offense of grubbing up trees, and thus destroying thickets or coverts of a forest.

2. A tree plucked up by the roots; also, a piece of land cleared. [Obs.]

as-särt′, *v.t.* To grub up (trees). [Obs.]

as-sas′sin, *n.* [Fr. *assassin*, from Ar. *Hashshāshin*, hashish-drinkers; a sect so called because those selected to do murder were maddened with hashish.]

1. One who kills, or attempts to kill, by surprise or secret assault. The circumstance of surprise or secrecy seems essential to the signification of this word, though it is sometimes used to denote one who takes any advantage, in killing or attempting to murder, as by attacking one when unarmed.

2. [A—] One of a tribe or clan in Syria noted for deeds of blood committed under the inspiration of hashish. They originated in Persia about the year 1090.

as-sas′sin, *v.t.* To assassinate. [Obs.]

as-sas′sin-āte, *v.t.*; assassinated, *pt.*, *pp.*; assassinating, *ppr.* 1. To kill, or attempt to kill, by surprise or secret assault; to murder by sudden violence.

2. To waylay; to take by treachery. [Rare.]

Syn.—Kill, murder, massacre, slay.

as-sas′sin-āte, *n.* A murder or murderer. [Obs.]

as-sas-si-nā′tion, *n.* The act of killing or murdering, by surprise or secret assault; murder by violence.

as-sas′si-nā-tŏr, *n.* One who assassinates; an assassin.

as-sas′sin-ous, *a.* Murderous. [Obs.]

as-sā′tion, *n.* [L. *assare*, to roast.] A roasting. [Obs.]

as-sault′, *n.* [ME. *assaut*; OFr. *assaut*, *assalt*, assault, from L. *ad*, to, *saltare*, to leap.]

1. An attack or violent onset, whether by an individual, a company, or an army.

2. An attack by hostile words or measures; as, an *assault* upon the prerogatives of a prince, or upon the constitution of a state; also, an attack by argument or appeal.

3. In law, an unlawful setting upon one's person; an attempt or offer to beat another without touching his person, as by lifting the fist, or a cane, in a threatening manner, or by striking at him, and missing him. If the blow aimed takes effect, it constitutes *assault and battery.* —Blackstone.

Syn.—Attack, onset, onslaught, storm, charge.

as-sault′, *v.t.*; assaulted, *pt.*, *pp.*; assaulting, *ppr.* 1. To attack or fall upon by violence, or with a hostile intention; as, to *assault* a man, a house, or town.

2. To invade or fall on with force; as, the cry of war *assaults* our ears.

3. To attack by words, arguments, or unfriendly measures, with a view to shake, impair, or overthrow; as, to *assault* a character, the laws, or the administration.

Syn.—Encounter, assail, engage, attack, invade, storm, charge.

as-sault′ȧ-ble, *a.* Capable of being assaulted.

as-sault′ĕr, *n.* One who assaults, or violently attacks.

as-saut′, *n.* An old spelling of *assault.*

as-sāy′, *n.* 1. In metallurgy, the determination of the quantity of any particular metal in an ore or other metallic compound alloy; more especially the determination of the quantity of gold or silver in coin or bullion.

2. The substance to be assayed.

3. In law, an examination of weights and measures by the standard.

4. Examination; trial; effort; first entrance upon any business; attempt. [Obs. See *Essay.*]

5. Value; ascertained purity. [Obs.]

Pearls and precious stones of great *assay.*
—Spenser.

as-sāy′, *v.t.*; assayed, *pt.*, *pp.*; assaying, *ppr.* [ME. *assayen*; OFr. *asaier*, *essaier*, to try, from LL. *exagium*, a weighing out, from L. *exigere*, to weigh, try; *ex*, out, and *agere*, to drive.]

1. To determine (the amount of a particular metal) in an ore, alloy, or other metallic compound.

2. Figuratively, to apply to, as to the touchstone; to try. [Obs.]

as-sāy′, *v.i.* To attempt, try, or endeavor. [Obs. See *Essay.*]

as-sāy′ȧ-ble, *a.* Capable of being assayed.

as-sāy′=bal″ănce, *n.* A balance used in the process of assaying.

as-sāy′ĕr, *n.* One who assays.

as-sāy′=fŭr″nāce, *n.* A furnace used in the process of assaying.

as-sāy′ing, *n.* The determination of the amount of any particular metal in a metallic compound.

as-sāy′=mås″tĕr, *n.* A chief assayer.

asse, *n.* In zoölogy, a small African fox, *Vulpes caama*, yielding a valuable fur.

ass′=ēar, *n.* An old name for the common comfrey, *Symphytum officinale.*

as″sē-cū-rā′tion, *n.* Assurance; a making sure. [Obs.]

as-sē-cūre′, *v.t.* [L. *ad*, to, and *securus*, secure.] To make sure. [Obs.]

as-sē-cū'tion, *n.* [L. *assequi*, to follow after.] An obtaining or acquiring. [Obs.]

as'se-gai, *n.* See *Assagai.*

as-sem'blāge, *n.* 1. A collection of individuals or of particular things; the state of being assembled; as, an *assemblage* of men of note

2. The act of assembling.

3. The act of fitting together, as parts of a machine.

Syn.—Collection, concourse, convention.

as-sem'blănce, *n.* 1. Representation; likeness. [Obs.]

2. An assembling. [Obs.]

as-sem'ble, *v.t.*; assembled, *pt., pp.*; assembling, *ppr.* [ME. *assemblen*; OFr. *assembler, asembler*, to assemble, from L. *ad*, to, and *simul*, together.]

1. To collect (a number of individuals or particulars) into one place or body; to bring or call together; to convene; to congregate; as, to *assemble* an army-corps.

2. To put together the parts of; as, to *assemble* a bicycle.

Syn.—Collect, convene, convoke, gather, muster.

as-sem'ble, *v.i.* To meet or come together; to convene, as a number of individuals; as, congress *assembles* every winter.

as-sem'ble, *v.t.* To compare. [Obs.]

as-sem'blẽr, *n.* One who assembles.

as-sem'bling, *n.* 1. A collection or meeting together.

2. In manufacture, the bringing or fitting together of the different parts of an article or machine, as a bicycle, gun, or sewing-machine.

as-sem'bly, *n.* [ME. *assemble, assemblaye*; OFr. *assemblee*, an assembly.]

1. A company or collection of individuals, in the same place, usually for the same purpose; an assemblage.

2. In a civil or political sense, a meeting convened by authority, for the transaction of public business; as, the *assemblies* of the Roman people; the *assembly* of the states-general, and the national *assembly* in France.

3. In some of the United States, the legislature, or the lower branch of it, whether in session or not; sometimes called the *general assembly.*

4. A collection of persons for amusement; as, a dancing *assembly.*

5. In the Presbyterian church, a convocation, convention, or council of ministers and ruling elders, delegated from each presbytery; as, the General *Assembly* of Scotland, or of the United States.

6. In military tactics, the drumbeat or bugle-call summoning a body of troops to form ranks.

Unlawful assembly; in law, a gathering of three or more persons whose actions cause a reasonable doubt of their peaceful intent.

Westminster Assembly; a convocation summoned in 1643 by the Long Parliament to determine the constitution of a church for England and Scotland. The chief fruits of its labors were the Directory of Public Worship, the Confession of Faith, and the Larger and Shorter Catechisms.

Syn.—Assemblage, congregation, convocation, collection, audience, concourse.

as-sem'bly-măn, *n.* A member of an assembly, especially of a legislative assembly.

as-sem'bly-room, *n.* A room in which persons assemble, especially for amusement.

as-sent', *n.* 1. The act of the mind in admitting or agreeing to the truth of a proposition.

> Faith is the *assent* to any proposition, on the credit of the proposer. —Locke.

2. Consent; concurrence; agreement to a proposal respecting some right or interest; acquiescence; as, the bill before the house has the *assent* of a great majority of the members.

3. Agreement; accord; approval; as, to read an author's works with *assent* and admiration.

Royal assent; formal royal sanction to a legislative act.

Syn.—Acquiescence, approbation, concurrence, consent, agreement, compliance.—The distinction between *assent* and *consent* seems to be this: *assent* is the agreement to an abstract proposition. We *assent* to a statement, but we do not *consent* to it. *Consent* is an agreement to some proposal or measure which affects the rights or interests of the consenter. *Assent* is an act of the understanding; *consent* is an act of the will.

as-sent', *v.i.*; assented, *pt., pp.*; assenting, *ppr.* [ME. *assenten*; OFr. *assenter*; L. *assentari, assentire*, to approve, consent; *ad*, to, and *sentire*, to feel.] To admit as true; to agree; to yield, or concede; to express an agreement of the mind to what is alleged or proposed; to answer in the affirmative.

> The Jews also *assented.* —Acts xxiv. 9.

as-sen-tā'tion, *n.* [L. *assentatio*, from *assentari*, to comply.] Compliance with the opinion of another, from flattery or dissimulation.

as'sen-tā"tŏr, *n.* A flatterer. [Rare.]

as-sent'ă-tō-ri-ly, *adv.* With adulation. [Obs.]

as-sent'ă-tō-ry, *a.* Flattering. [Obs.]

as-sent'ẽr, *n.* See *Assentor.*

as-sen'tient (-shient), *a.* Agreeing; assenting.

as-sent'ing, *a.* Agreeing to, or admitting as true; yielding to.

as-sent'ing-ly, *adv.* In a manner to express assent; by agreement.

as-sent'ive, *a.* Complying. [Rare.]

as-sent'ment, *n.* Assent; agreement. [Obs.]

as-sent'ŏr, *n.* A person who assents; in Great Britain, one of eight voters legally required to indorse the nomination of a parliamentary candidate.

as-sẽrt', *v.t.*; asserted, *pt., pp.*; asserting, *ppr.* [L. *assertus*, pp. of *asserere*, to join to; *ad*, to, and *serere*, to join, bind.]

1. To affirm positively; to declare with assurance; to aver.

2. To maintain or defend by words or measures; to vindicate a claim or title to; as, to *assert* our rights and liberties.

Syn.—Asseverate, maintain, declare, affirm, allege, protest, aver, state.

as-sẽrt'ẽr, *n.* One who affirms positively; one who maintains or vindicates a claim; an affirmer, supporter, or vindicator.

as-sẽr'tion, *n.* 1. The act of asserting; the maintaining of a claim.

2. Positive declaration or averment; affirmation; position advanced.

as-sẽr'tion-ăl, *a.* Containing an assertion.

as-sẽrt'ive, *a.* Positive; affirming confidentially; peremptory; dogmatic.

as-sẽrt'ive-ly, *adv.* Affirmatively.

as-sẽrt'ive-ness, *n.* The state or quality of being assertive.

as-sẽrt'ŏr, *n.* See *Asserter.*

as-sẽr-tō'ri-ăl, *a.* Asserting anything to exist; asserting a thing as a fact; relating to an assertion.

as-sẽrt'ō-ry, *a.* Affirming; maintaining.

as-sẽrve', *v.t.* To assist; to serve. [Obs.]

ȧs-sẽr'vile, *v.t.* To make servile. [Obs.]

as-sess', *v.t.*; assessed, *pt., pp.*; assessing, *ppr.* [ME. *assesse*; OFr. *assesser*, from L. *assessare*, to impose a tax, set a rate, from *assidere*; *ad*, to, and *sedere*, to sit.]

1. To set or fix a certain sum against, as a tax, fine, or forced contribution; as, to *assess* each citizen in due proportion.

2. To value; to fix the value of (property) for the purpose of being taxed; as by the law of the United States. Also, to value or fix the profits of business, for the purpose of taxation.

3. To set, fix, or ascertain; as, it is the province of a jury to *assess* damages.

as-sess'ȧ-ble, *a.* That may be assessed.

as-sess'ȧ-bly, *adv.* By assessment.

as-ses'sion, *n.* A sitting down beside a person; a session. [Rare.]

as-sess'ment, *n.* 1. A valuation of property or profits of business, for the purpose of taxation. An *assessment* is a valuation made by authorized persons according to their discretion, as opposed to a sum certain or determined by law. It is a valuation of the property of those who are to pay the tax, for the purpose of fixing the proportion which each man shall pay; on which valuation the law imposes a specific sum upon a given amount. —Blackstone.

2. A tax or specific sum charged on persons or property.

3. In the United States, (a) payment asked on a stock subscription, usually at stated intervals; (b) a levy for political purposes, called a *political assessment.*

4. The act of assessing; the act, by a jury, of determining the amount of damages.

as-sess'ŏr, *n.* [L., an assistant judge, from *assidere*; *ad*, to, by, and *sedere*, to sit.]

1. One appointed to assess the person or property.

2. An inferior officer of justice, who assists the judge.

3. In England, a person chosen to assist the mayor and aldermen of corporations, in matters concerning elections.

4. One who sits by another, as next in dignity; an official associate.

as-ses-sō'ri-ăl, *a.* Pertaining to assessors, or a court of assessors.

as-sess'ŏr-ship, *n.* The office of an assessor.

as'set, *n.* A separate item included in collective *assets*; as, his mining stock proved to be a good *asset*; an item of value; as, his name was his only available *asset.* [See *Assets.*]

as'sets, *n.pl.* [OFr. *assez, asset*; L. *ad satis*; *ad*, to, and *satis*, enough, sufficient.]

1. The goods or estate of a deceased person, subject by law to the payment of his debts and legacies; so called because sufficient to render the executor or administrator liable to the creditors and legatees, so far as such goods or estate may extend. *Assets* are real or personal; *real assets* are lands which descend to the heir, subject to the fulfilment of the obligations of the ancestor; *personal assets* are the money or goods of the deceased, or debts due to him, which come into the hands of the executor or administrator, or which he is bound to collect and convert into money. —Blackstone.

2. The effects of an insolvent debtor.

3. The entire property of all sorts belonging to a merchant or to a trading association.

as-sev'ẽr, *v.t.* An obsolete form of *asseverate.*

as-sev'ẽr-āte, *v.t.*; asseverated, *pt., pp.*; asseverating, *ppr.* [L. *asseveratus*, pp. of *asseverare*, to assert strongly; *ad*, to, and *severus*, earnest, severe.] To affirm or aver positively, or with solemnity.

Syn.—Affirm, aver, avow, avouch, declare, assert.

as-sev-ẽr-ā'tion, *n.* Positive affirmation or assertion; a solemn declaration unaccompanied by an official oath.

as-sev'ẽr-ā-tive, as-sev'ẽr-ā-tō-ry, *a.* Positively affirming.

ass'-head (-hed), *n.* A blockhead.

as-sib'i-lāte, *v.t.*; assibilated, *pt., pp.*; assibilating, *ppr.* [L. *assibilatus*, pp. of *assibilare*, to whisper at, or to; *ad*, to, and *sibilare*, to whisper.] To speak in a hissing manner; to alter (a mute letter) into a sibilant, as in changing the *t* in *position* into *sh.*

as-sib-i-lā'tion, *n.* The change of a nonsibilant letter to a sibilant.

As-si-dē'ăn, Chas-i-dē'ăn, *n.* One of a sect of Jews who resorted to Mattathias, the father of the Maccabees, to oppose the Hellenistic Jews. From these sprang the Pharisees and Essenes.

as'si-dent, *a.* [L. *assidens*, ppr. of *assidere*, to sit by; *ad*, to, and *sedere*, to sit.] In pathology, concomitant. *Assident* signs, in medicine, are such as usually attend a disease, but not always; distinguished from *pathognomonic* signs, which are inseparable from it.

as-sid'ū-āte, *a.* Continuous; assiduous. [Obs.]

as-si-dū'i-ty, *n.* 1. Diligent application to any enterprise.

2. Attention; attentiveness to persons. *Assiduities*, in the plural, are studied and persevering attentions.

as-sid'ū-ous, *a.* [L. *assiduus*, from *assidere*, to sit by; *ad*, to, and *sedere*, to sit.]

1. Constant in application; as, a person *assiduous* in his occupation.

2. Attentive; careful; regular in attendance; as, an *assiduous* physician or nurse.

3. Performed with constant diligence or attention; as, *assiduous* labor.

Syn.—Industrious, unremitting, sedulous, persevering, zealous, attentive.

as-sid'ū-ous-ly, *adv.* Diligently; attentively; with earnestness and care; with regular attendance.

as-sid'ū-ous-ness, *n.* Constant or diligent application.

as-siēge', *v.t.* To besiege. [Obs.]

as-siēge', *n.* A siege. [Obs.]

as-si-en'tist, *n.* One in any way connected with an assiento.

as-si-en'tō, *n.* [Sp. *assiento, asiento*, a seat, contract, agreement; *a*, L. *ad*, to, and *sentar*, from L. *sedens*, ppr. of *sedere*, to sit.] A contract between the king of Spain and other countries, or between Spain and a company of merchants, for furnishing slaves to the Spanish dominions in America in return for special privileges.

as-sign' (-sīn'), *v.t.*; assigned (-sīnd'), *pt., pp.*; assigning, *ppr.* [ME. *assignen*; OFr. *assigner*; L. *assignare*, to mark out, allot; *ad*, to, and *signare*, to mark.]

1. To allot; to appoint or grant by distribution or apportionment.

2. To designate or appoint for a particular purpose.

3. To fix, specify, or designate; as, to *assign* a day for a judicial hearing.

4. In law, to transfer or make over to another, as an estate; in bankruptcy, to transfer (property) to, and vest in certain persons, called assignees, for the benefit of creditors.

5. To allege or show in particular; as, to *assign* a reason for one's conduct.

Syn.—Apportion, appoint, transfer, grant, adduce, convey, give.

as-sign', *v.i.* To transfer one's property in trust for the benefit of creditors.

as-sign', *n.* 1. A person to whom property or an interest is transferred; as, a deed to a man and his heirs and *assigns.*

2. An asset; a belonging. [Obs.]

as-sign-ȧ-bil'i-ty, *n.* The quality of being assignable.

as-sīgn'ȧ-ble, *a.* 1. That may be allotted, appointed, or assigned.

2. That may be transferred by writing; as, an *assignable* note or bill.

3. That may be specified, shown with precision, or designated; as, an *assignable* quantity.

as'sig-nat (*or* a-sē-nyä'), *n.* [Fr., from L. *assignatus*, pp. of *assignare*, to assign, allot.]

1. In French law, the assignment of an annuity (*rente*) on an estate, by which the annuity is based on the security of the latter.

2. A form of currency, issued by the revolutionary government of France, based on the security of lands appropriated by the state.

as-sig-nā′tion, *n.* 1. A special appointment for meeting; used chiefly of illicit love affairs.
2. A making over by transfer of title. [See *Assignment.*]
3. The act of apportioning or assigning.
House of assignation; a house where meetings for immoral sexual purposes take place.
as-sign-ee′ (-si-nē′), *n.* 1. A person to whom property or rights at law have been transferred for the benefit of others or himself, and who administers or conducts such affairs for another in trust; as, an *assignee* in bankruptcy, or the *assignee* of an insolvent debtor. An *assignee* may be created by law, specially appointed, or named in a deed.
2. [*pl.*] In English insolvency proceedings, those who administer the property of a debtor.
as-sign′ẽr, *n.* [Rare.] See *Assignor*
as-sign′ment, *n.* 1. An allotting, or an appointment to a particular person or use.
2. In law, a transfer of title or interest by writing, as of a lease, bond, note, or bill of exchange.
3. The writing by which an interest is transferred.
4. The appointment or designation of causes or actions in court, for trial on particular days.
5. The conveyance of the whole interest which a man has in an estate, usually for life, or a term of years. It differs from a *lease*, which is the conveyance for a shorter term than the lessor has in the estate.
Assignment in bankruptcy; the transfer of the property of a bankrupt to certain persons called assignees, in whom it is vested for the benefit of creditors.
Assignment of dower; the apportionment of the widow's share in an estate, particularly by determining the legal bounds of her real estate.
Assignment system; the system which formerly prevailed in Australia of assigning convicts as servants.
as-sign-ọr′, *n.* One who assigns or allots; a person who assigns or transfers a property interest; as, the *assignor* of a bill of exchange.
as-sim″i-lȧ-bil′i-ty, *n.* The state of being assimilable. [Rare.]
as-sim′i-lȧ-ble, *a.* That may be assimilated.
as-sim′i-lāte, *v.t.*; assimilated, *pt.*, *pp.*; assimilating, *ppr.* [L. *assimilatus*, pp. of *assimilare*, to make like; *ad*, to, and *similis*, like.]
1. To bring to a likeness; to cause to resemble.
2. To convert into a like substance; as, food is *assimilated* by conversion into animal substance.
as-sim′i-lāte, *v.i.* 1. To become similar. [Rare.]
2. To perform the act of converting food to the substance of the body; as, birds *assimilate* less than beasts.
3. To be converted into the substance of the body; as, meat *assimilates* more readily than vegetables.
as-sim-i-lā′tion, *n.* 1. The act of bringing to a resemblance; or a state of resemblance.
2. The act or process by which bodies convert other bodies into their own nature and substance; as, flame *assimilates* oil.
3. In physiology, the conversion of nutriment into the fluid or solid substance of the body.
4. In old pathology, the supposed conversion of the fluids of the body to the nature of any diseased matter.
The term *assimilation* has been limited by some to the final process by which the blood is converted into actual substance.
as-sim′i-lā-tive, *a.* Having power of converting to a likeness, or to a like substance; possessing the faculty of assimilation; as, an *assimilative* mind.
as-sim′i-lā-tō-ry, *a.* Tending to assimilate.
as-sim′ū-lāte, *v.t.* To feign. [Obs. See *Simulate.*]
as-sim-ū-lā′tion, *n.* A counterfeiting. [Obs. See *Simulation.*]
as-si-nē′gō, *n.* See *Asinego.*
ȧss′ish, *a.* Stupid; asinine.
as-sist′, *v.t.*; assisted, *pt.*, *pp.*; assisting, *ppr.* [L. *assistere*, to stand by or near; *ad*, to, and *sistere*, to stand.] To help; to aid; to succor; to give support to in some undertaking or effort, or in time of distress.
Syn.—Coöperate, befriend, relieve, succor, support, second, help, aid.
as-sist′, *v.i.* 1. To lend aid.
2. In euchre, to aid one's partner by ordering up as trumps the card which said partner has turned.
3. To be present; to attend; as, to *assist* at a public meeting. [Gallicism.]
as-sist′ănce, *n.* Help; aid; furtherance; succor; a contribution of support in bodily strength or other means.
Writ of assistance; a writ issued to the successful suitor in chancery giving him possession of the property; in the colonial times in America, a judicial writ authorizing officers engaged in searching premises for contraband goods to call upon others to assist them.
as-sist′ănt, *a.* Helping; lending aid or support; auxiliary.
as-sist′ănt, *n.* 1. One who aids, or who contributes his strength or other means to further the designs or welfare of another; an auxiliary; a means of help.
2. An attendant.
3. Formerly, in some of the New England colonies, a member of the upper house of the legislature, or of the governor's council.
Syn.—Confederate, associate, coadjutor, aid, helper, ally, auxiliary, partner.
as-sist′ănt-ly, *adv.* In a manner to give aid. [Rare.]
as-sist′ẽr, *n.* One who lends aid; a helper. [See *Assistor.*]
as-sist′fụl, *a.* Helpful.
as-sist′ive, *a.* Helping.
as-sist′less, *a.* Without aid or help. [Rare.]
as-sist′ŏr, *n.* An assister; this spelling is the usual legal one.
as-sith′ment, *n.* See *Assythment.*
as-size′, *n.* [ME. *assize*; OFr. *assise*, *asise*, a sitting, session of a court, judgment, tax, impost, from L. *assidere*; *ad*, to, and *sedere*, to sit.]
1. Originally, an assembly of knights and other substantial men, with a bailiff or justice, in a certain place and at a certain time, for public business. The general council, or Witenagemote, of England, was called the *General Assize.* —Blackstone.
2. In England, the *courts of assize*, popularly called the *assizes*, are the sessions held, by at least one of the judges of the superior courts, in each of the counties, under commissions of assize for civil cases, and of oyer and terminer, and jail-delivery, for criminal cases. The commission of assize originally directed the judges to take *assizes*, or the verdicts of a particular jury called the *assize.*
3. A jury. In England the word was formerly used in this sense in the terms *grand assize* and *petty assize*, but is now obsolete. In Scotland at present, the *assize* exists for the trial of criminal cases.
4. A name formerly given to certain writs, summoning juries, etc.
5. A particular species of rents, established and not subject to be varied. [Obs.]
6. The time or place of holding the court of assize; generally in the plural, *assizes.*
7. In a more general sense, any tribunal or court of justice.
8. A statute, or ordinance, generally; as, the *assizes* of the realm; the *assizes of the forest*, rules and regulations for the management of the royal forests; *assize of arms*, a statute of Henry II. for arming the kingdom; *assizes of Jerusalem*, a code of feudal laws formed by the crusaders for their kingdom of Jerusalem.
9. A statute of regulation; an ordinance regulating the weight, measure, and price of articles sold in market; and hence the word came to signify the weight, measure, or price itself; as, the *assize* of bread. —Blackstone.
10. An ordinance fixing the standard of weights and measures; and, therefore, the standard weights and measures themselves; as, the custody of the *assize.* —Blackstone.
11. Measure; dimension. [Obs.]

> An hundred cubits high by just *assize.*
> —Spenser.

Maiden assize; a session of an English criminal court in which no defendant appears for trial.
as-size′, *v.t.* 1. To fix the weight, measure, or price of, by an ordinance or regulation of authority. [Obs.]
2. To fix the rate of; to assess. [Obs.]
as-siz′ẽr, *n.* 1. An officer who has the care or inspection of weights and measures.
2. In Scotland, a juror.
as-siz′ŏr, *n.* See *Assizer.*
as-sō-bẽr′, *v.t.* To make or keep sober. [Obs.]
as-sō-ciȧ-bil′i-ty (-shȧ-), *n.* The quality of being capable of association; the quality of suffering some change by sympathy, or of being affected by bodily conditions.
as-sō′ciȧ-ble, *a.* 1. That may be joined or associated.
2. Sociable; companionable. [Obs.]
3. In a medical sense, liable to be affected by sympathy, or to receive from other parts correspondent feelings and affections.

> The stomach, the most *associable* of all the organs of the animal body. —Med. Rep.

as-sō′ciȧ-ble-ness, *n.* Associability.
as-sō′ci-āte (-shi-āte), *v.t.*; associated, *pt.*, *pp.*; associating, *ppr.* [L. *associatus*, pp. of *associare*, to join to, unite with; *ad*, to, and *sociare*, to join, or unite with.]
1. To join in company, as a friend, companion, partner, or confederate; as, to *associate* others with us in business, or in an enterprise.
2. To unite in the same mass; as, particles of matter *associated* with other substances.
Syn.—Incorporate, combine, couple, unite, link, join.
as-sō′ci-āte, *v.i.* 1. To unite in company; to keep company, implying intimacy; as, congenial minds are disposed to *associate.*
2. To unite in action, or to be affected by the action of a different part of the body.
as-sō′ci-āte, *a.* 1. Joined in interest or purpose; confederate.
2. Joined in employment or office; as, an *associate* judge.
3. In medicine, connected by habit or sympathy; as, *associate* motions, such as occur sympathetically in consequence of preceding motions.
as-sō′ci-āte, *n.* 1. A companion; one frequently in company with another, implying intimacy or equality; a mate; a fellow.
2. A partner in interest, as in business; or a confederate in a league.
3. A companion in a criminal transaction; an accomplice.
4. A member of a public body not enjoying full fellowship with its privileges; as, an *associate* of the Royal Academy.
Syn.—Companion, comrade, mate, friend, fellow, coadjutor, partner, accomplice.
as-sō′ci-ā-ted, *a.* United in company or in interest; joined; accompanying.
as-sō′ci-āte-ship, *n.* The state or office of an associate.
as-sō-ci-ā′tion, *n.* 1. The act of associating; union; connection of persons.
2. Union of persons in a company; a society formed for transacting or carrying on some business for mutual advantage; a partnership.
3. Union of things; apposition, as of particles of matter.
4. Union or connection of ideas.
5. An exertion or change of some extreme part of the sensorium observed in the muscles or organs of sense, in consequence of some antecedent or attendant fibrous contractions.
6. A term first used among Congregationalists for a society of the clergy, consisting of a number of pastors of neighboring churches, united for promoting the interests of religion and the harmony of the churches; a coöperative organization formed for the advancement of a common cause.
Association of ideas; in psychology, the conditions under which one idea is able to recall another to consciousness. These conditions may be classified under two general heads, the *law of contiguity*, and the *law of association.* The first states the fact that actions, sensations, emotions, and ideas, which have occurred together, or in close succession, tend to suggest each other when any one of them is afterward presented to the mind. The second indicates that the present actions, sensations, emotions, or ideas tend to recall their like from among previous experiences. On their physical side the principles of association correspond with the physiological facts of reëxcitation of the same nervous centers.
Syn.—Denomination, community, connection, fellowship, fraternity, alliance, sodality, union, society, club.
as-sō-ci-ā′tion-ăl, *a.* 1. Pertaining to an association of any kind.
2. Pertaining to the philosophical doctrine known as associationism, or to the social doctrine of Fourierism (communism).
as-sō-ci-ā′tion-ịsm, *n.* 1. The doctrine based upon the theory that the development of the soul is reached through the association of ideas and especially through the medium of the senses; opposed to *idealism.*
2. The doctrine of association as applied to peoples, or communities; communism.
as-sō-ci-ā′tion-ist, *n.* One who holds the doctrine of associationism in any of its forms, philosophical or social.
as-sō′ci-ā-tive, *a.* Having the quality of associating, or of being affected by sympathy.
as-sō′ci-ā-tŏr, *n.* A confederate; an associate.
as-soil′, *v.t.* [ME. *assoilen*; OFr. *assoiler*; L. *absolvere*; *ab*, from, and *solvere*, to loosen, untie.] To solve; to release; to absolve. [Obs.]
as-soil′, *v.t.* To soil; to stain. [Obs.]
as-soil′ment, *n.* The act of assoiling; absolution. [Obs.]
as-soil′ment, *n.* Defilement.
as-soil′yiē, as-soil′ziē, *v.t.* In Scots law, to absolve.
as′sō-nănce, *n.* [Fr. *assonance*, from L. *assonans*, ppr. of *assonare*, to sound, to respond to.]
1. Resemblance of sounds. In rhetoric and poetry, a concurrence of words or lines, terminated by sounds approximating to, but not concurring in, a rime.
2. Resemblance of things not completely corresponding; as, *assonance* of facts. [Rare.]
as′sō-nănt, as-sō-nan′tăl, *a.* Having a resemblance of sounds. In Spanish poetry, *assonant rimes* are those in which a resemblance of sounds serves instead of a natural rime; as, *ligera, tierra.* Such rimes require only the same vowel in the last or last two syllables, without any concurrence of consonants, as is found in regular rime.

as'sō-nāte, *v.i.*; assonated, *pt.*, *pp.*; assonating, *ppr.* To accord in sound.

as-sort', *v.t.*; assorted, *pt.*, *pp.*; assorting, *ppr.* [ME. *assorte*; Fr. *assortir*; *a*, L. *ad*, to, and *sortir*, from L. *sortiri*, to cast lots, select; *sors*, a lot, condition.]

1. To distribute in classes, as similar things, or things which are suited to a like purpose; sometimes applied to persons as well as things.

2. To furnish with all sorts.

as-sort', *v.i.* To agree; to be in accordance with; to suit.

as-sort'ed, *a.* 1. Furnished with an assortment, or with a variety; as, a well-*assorted* store.

2. Fitted or adapted to.

They appear no way *assorted* to those with whom they must associate. —Burke.

Syn.—Classified, separated, selected, chosen, arranged.

as-sort'ment, *n.* 1. The act of distributing into sorts, kinds, or classes, or of selecting and suiting things.

2. A mass or quantity distributed into kinds, or sorts; or a number of things assorted.

3. A number of things of the same kind, varied in size, color, quality, price, or form, to suit the market, the wants of people, or for various purposes; as, an *assortment* of thread, of silks, or of calicoes; an *assortment* of paintings.

4. A variety of sorts or kinds adapted to various wants, demands, or purposes; as, an *assortment* of goods.

Syn.—Collection, selection, miscellany, variety, class, stock, lot.

as-sot', *v.t.* [Fr. *assoter*; *a*, L. *ad*, to, and *sot*, foolish.] To infatuate; to besot. [Obs.]

ȧss's-foot, *n.* A medicinal herb, more commonly known as coltsfoot.

as-suāge' (-swāj'), *v.t.*; assuaged, *pt.*, *pp.*; assuaging, *ppr.* [ME. *asuagen*; OFr. *asouager*, *asuager*, from L. *ad*, to, and *suavis*, sweet.] To soften, in a figurative sense; to allay, mitigate, ease, or lessen, as pain or grief; to appease or pacify, as passion or tumult. In strictness, it signifies rather to moderate than to quiet, tranquilize, or reduce to perfect peace or ease.

Syn.—Abate, alleviate, diminish, soothe, pacify, compose, appease, calm, tranquilize.

as-suāge', *v.i.* To abate or subside. [Obs.]

The waters *assuaged.* —Gen. viii. 1.

as-suāge'ment, *n.* Mitigation; abatement; also, an alleviative.

as-suā'ġẽr, *n.* One who allays or pacifies; that which mitigates or abates.

as-suā'sive, *a.* Softening; mitigating; tranquilizing. [Rare.]

as-sub'jū-gāte, *v.t.* To bring into subjection. [Obs.]

as-suē-fac'tion (as-swē-), *n.* [L. *assuefacere*, to accustom to; *assuetus*, pp. of *assuescere*, to accustom, and *facere*, to make.] The act of accustoming. [Obs.]

as'suē-tūde, *n.* [L. *assuetudo*, from *assuetus*, pp. of *assuescere*, to accustom.] Custom; habitual use; habit. [Obs.]

as-sūm'ȧ-ble, *a.* Capable of being assumed.

as-sūm'ȧ-bly, *adv.* In an assumable manner; by assumption.

as-sūme', *v.t.*; assumed, *pt.*, *pp.*; assuming, *ppr.* [L. *assumere*, to take up, claim; *ad*, to, and *sumere*, to take, from *sub*, under, and *emere*, to take, buy.]

1. To take, or take upon oneself. It differs from *receive*, in not implying an offer to give.

The god *assumed* his native form again. —Pope.

2. To take (what is not just); to take with arrogant claims; to arrogate; to seize unjustly; as, to *assume* haughty airs; to *assume* unwarrantable powers.

3. To take for granted, or without proof; to suppose as a fact; as, to *assume* a principle in reasoning.

4. To appropriate, or take to oneself; as, to *assume* the debts of another.

5. To take (what is fictitious); to pretend to possess; to take in appearance; as, to *assume* the garb of humility.

6. To receive or adopt; as, *assumed* into that honorable company.

Syn.—Appropriate, arrogate, affect, pretend, usurp, claim, feign.

as-sūme', *v.i.* 1. To be arrogant; to claim more than is due.

2. In law, to take upon oneself an obligation; to undertake or promise; as, A *assumed* upon himself, and promised to pay.

as-sūmed', *a.* 1. Supposed; taken for granted.

2. Pretended; fictitious; as, an *assumed* character.

as-sūm'ed-ly, *adv.* By or according to assumption.

as-sūm'ent, *n.* An addition. [Obs.]

as-sūm'ẽr, *n.* One who assumes; an arrogant person.

as-sūm'ing, *a.* Taking or disposed to take upon oneself more than is just; haughty; arrogant.

as-sūm'ing, *n.* Presumption.

as-sump'sit, *n.* [L., he undertook, perf. tense of *assumere*, to assume.]

1. In law, a promise or undertaking, founded on a consideration. This promise may be verbal or written. An *assumpsit* is express or implied; express, when made in words or writing; implied, when, in consequence of some benefit or consideration accruing to one person from the acts of another, the law presumes that person has promised to make compensation. In this case, the law, upon a principle of justice, implies or raises a promise, on which an action may be brought to recover the compensation. Thus, if A contracts with B to build a house for him, by implication and intendment of law, A promises to pay B for the same, without any express words to that effect.

2. An action founded on a promise. When this action is brought on a debt, it is called *indebitatus assumpsit*, which is an action on the case to recover damages for the nonpayment of a debt. —Blackstone.

as-sumpt', *v.t.* To take up; to raise. [Obs.]

as-sumpt', *n.* That which is assumed. [Obs.]

as-sump'tion, *n.* [ME. *assumpcioun*, *assumptioun*; L. *assumptio*, from *assumere*, to take up.]

1. The act of taking to oneself; adoption.

2. The act of taking for granted, or supposing a thing without proof; supposition.

This gives no sanction to the unwarrantable *assumption* that the soul sleeps from the period of death to the resurrection of the body. —Thodey.

3. The thing supposed; a postulate, or proposition assumed. In logic, the minor or second proposition in a categorical syllogism.

4. The taking up of a person into heaven. Hence, in the Roman Catholic and Greek churches, a festival in honor of the miraculous ascent of the Virgin Mary into heaven.

Syn.—Supposition, postulate, appropriation, undertaking, arrogance, assurance.

as-sump'tive, *a.* That is or may be assumed.

Assumptive arms; in heraldry, formerly, such arms as a person had a right, with the approbation of his sovereign, and of the heralds, to assume, in consequence of an exploit; armorial bearings not inherited.

as-sump'tive-ly, *adv.* By way of assumption.

as-sūr'ănce (-shūr'), *n.* [ME. *assuraunce*; OFr. *asseurance*, from L. *assecurantia*, from *assecurare*, to assure.]

1. The act of assuring, or of making a declaration in terms that furnish ground for confidence; as, I trusted to his *assurances*; or the act of furnishing any ground for full confidence.

2. Firm persuasion; full confidence or trust; freedom from doubt; certain expectation; the utmost certainty.

3. Firmness of mind; undoubting steadiness; intrepidity.

Brave men meet danger with *assurance.* —Knolles.

4. Excess of boldness; impudence; as, his *assurance* is intolerable.

5. Freedom from excessive modesty, timidity, or bashfulness; laudable confidence; self-reliance.

Conversation with the world will give them knowledge and *assurance.* —Locke.

6. Insurance; a contract for the payment of a sum on occasion of a certain event, as loss or death. The word *assurance* has been used, in England, in relation to life contingencies, and *insurance* in relation to other contingencies. [See *Insurance.*]

7. Any written or other legal evidence of the conveyance of property. In England, such evidences are called the *common assurances* of the kingdom. —Blackstone.

Syn.—Confidence, conviction, impudence, promise, certainty, effrontery, presumption.

as-sūre', *v.t.*; assured, *pt.*, *pp.*; assuring, *ppr.* [ME. *assuren*, from L. *assecurare*, to assure; *ad*, to, and *securus*; *se*, without, and *cura*, care.]

1. To make certain; to give confidence by a promise, declaration, or other evidence; as, he *assured* me of his sincerity.

2. To confirm; to make certain or secure.

3. To embolden; to make confident.

4. To affiance; to betroth. [Obs.]

5. To insure; to covenant to indemnify for loss. [See *Insure.*]

as-sūred', *a.* Certain; indubitable; not doubting; bold to excess.

as-sūred', *n.* One who has his life or property insured.

as-sūr'ed-ly, *adv.* Certainly; indubitably.

as-sūr'ed-ness, *n.* The state of being assured; certainty; full confidence.

as-sūr'ẽr, *n.* 1. One who assures; one who insures against loss; an insurer or underwriter.

2. A person who takes out an insurance policy.

as-sūr'ġen-cy, *n.* The tendency to rise.

as-sūr'ġent, *a.* [L. *assurgens*, ppr. of *assurgere*, to rise up.]

1. Rising.

2. In botany, rising upward in a curve from a declining base.

3. In heraldry, applied to a bearing rising from the ocean, as the sun.

as-sūr'ing-ly, *adv.* In a way to create assurance.

as-swāġe', *v.t.* and *v.i.* See *Assuage.*

As-syr'i-ăn, *a.* Pertaining to Assyria.

As-syr'i-ăn, *n.* A native of Assyria; the language of Assyria.

As-syr"i-ō-loġ'iç-ăl, *a.* Relating to Assyriology.

As-syr-i-ol'ō-ġist, *n.* One who makes the history of Assyria his special study.

As-syr-i-ol'ō-ġy, *n.* [Gr. *Assyria*, and *logia*, from *legein*, to speak.] The science of Assyrian antiquities; the archæology of Assyria.

as-syth'ment, *n.* [Scot., from *assyth*; OFr. *asset*, from L. *ad satis facere*; *ad*, to, *satis*, enough, and *facere*, to make.] In Scots law, an indemnification due to the heirs of a person murdered, from the person guilty of the crime. Where the penalty of the law is suffered by the criminal no claim for indemnity is allowed.

as-tā'ciăn, *n.* An animal belonging to the genus *Astacus*, or the family *Astacidæ*.

As-tac'i-dæ, *n.pl.* A family of crustaceans belonging to the order *Decapoda* and the suborder *Macrura*.

as'tȧ-cīte, *n.* [L., from Gr. *astakos*, and *-ite*.] Any fossil crustacean resembling a lobster or crawfish.

As-tȧ-çoi'dē-ȧ, *n.pl.* A group or series of crustaceans that embraces the crawfish and the lobster.

as-taç'ō-līte, *n.* [Gr. *astakos*, a lobster, and *lithos*, stone.] Same as *Astacite*.

As'tȧ-cus, *n.* [L., from Gr. *astakos*, a lobster, crawfish.] A genus of decapod, long-tailed crustaceans, the typical one of the family *Astacidæ*. It embraces the *Astacus marinus*, or lobster, and the *Astacus fluviatilis*, or crawfish. Curious specimens of this genus of crawfish, without eyes, abound in the Mammoth Cave, Kentucky.

ȧ-stär'bōard, *adv.* On the starboard side, as a rudder.

ȧ-stärt', ȧ-stẽrt', *v.i.* To start from, to escape; to flee, to get free. [Obs.]

That oft out of her bed she did *astart*,
As one with vew of ghastly feends affright. —Spenser.

ȧ-stärt', *v.t.* To cause to start; to startle; to terrify; to affright; to release; to avoid. [Obs.]

As-tär'tē, *n.* [Gr. *Astartē*.]

1. A Phenician goddess corresponding to the *Ashtoreth* of Scripture. [See *Ashtoreth.*]

With these in troop
Came Astoreth, whom the Phœnicians call'd
Astarte, queen of heaven, with crescent horns. —Milton.

2. In zoölogy, a genus of bivalve mollusks.

3. [a—] Any species of this genus.

4. The moon.

as-tā'si-ȧ, *n.* [L., from Gr. *astasia*, unsteadiness, from *astatos*; *a* priv., and *statos*, from *histanai*, to stand.] A condition characterized by inability to maintain an erect position.

ȧ-stāte', *n.* Estate. [Obs.]

ȧ-stat'iç, *a.* [Gr. *astatos*, unstable, uncertain; *a* priv., and *statos*, from *histanai*, to stand.] Not influenced by the earth's magnetism; without polarity.

Astatic needle; a needle movable about an axis in the plane of the magnetic meridian, and parallel to the inclination. When so situated, the terrestrial magnetic couple acting in the direction of the axis cannot impart to the needle any determinate direction, and therefore it is *astatic*.

Astatic system; a combination of two needles of equal force joined parallel to each other, with the poles in contrary directions.

ȧ-stat'iç-ăl-ly, *adv.* In an astatic manner.

ȧ-stat'i-çism, *n.* The state or condition of being astatic.

as'tȧ-tize, *v.t.*; astatized, *pt.*, *pp.*; astatizing, *ppr.* To make astatic.

ȧ-stāy', *adv.* A term used in regard to an anchor which, on being hauled up, takes such a position that the cable or chain from which it depends forms an acute angle with the surface of the water, appearing to be in line with the ship's *stays*.

ȧ-stē-ȧ-tō'sis, *n.* [L., from Gr. *a* priv., and *stear*, *steatos*, fat, tallow.] Faulty secretion by the sebaceous glands.

as'tē-işm, *n.* [Gr. *asteismos*, from *asteizesthai*, to be witty, talk cleverly, from *asteios*, witty, clever, from *asty*, city.] In rhetoric, genteel irony; a polite and ingenious manner of deriding another.

as'tel, *n.* [ME. *astelle*; OFr. *astelle*; L. *astula*, dim. of *assis*, a board.] An arch or ceiling in a mine.

-as′tẽr, *suffix.* [L. *-aster*, a dim. suffix.] A combining form denoting diminutiveness, slight resemblance, inferiority, or worthlessness, as in medic*aster*, a quack; poet*aster*, a dabbler in poetry.

as′tẽr-, as′tẽr-i-, as′tẽr-ō-. Combining forms from Gr. *astēr*, a star.

As′tẽr, *n.* [Gr. *astēr*, star.]

1. A genus of plants with compound flowers, many of which are cultivated for their beauty, particularly the China aster.

2. [a—] A plant of the genus *Aster*.

3. [a—] A term used in biology to express starlike structures in mitotic cell division.

As-tẽr-ā′cē-æ, *n.pl.* [L., from Gr. *astēr*, star, and *-aceæ*.] An order of plants of which the genus *Aster* is the type.

as-tē′ri-ȧ, *n.* [L., from Gr. *astēr*, a star.] A variety of sapphire, not perfectly transparent, but showing a starlike opalescence in the direction of the axis of the crystal if cut round.

As-tē′ri-as, *n.* [L., from Gr. *asterias*, starred, a fish, from *astēr*, star.] A genus of common starfishes of the family *Asteriidæ*.

as-tē′ri-ā-ted, *a.* [Gr. *asterios*, radiated.] Radiated; presenting diverging rays, like a star; as, *asteriated* sapphire.

as′tẽr-id, *n.* A starfish; one of the *Asterias*.

As-tẽr-id′ē-ȧ, *n.pl.* An order of *Echinodermata* which includes the true starfishes; called also *Asteroidea*.

As-tē-rī′i-dæ, *n.pl.* [L., from Gr. *asterias*, radiated, starred, and *-idæ*.] A family of radiated animals belonging to the class *Echinodermata*, order *Stellerida*. It contains the so-called starfishes.

as-tē′ri-on, *n.* The point on the skull where the sutures formed by the union of the occipital, temporal, and parietal bones intersect one another.

As-tẽr-is′çus, *n.* [L., from Gr. *asteriskos*, a little star.]

1. A genus of starfishes.

2. [a—] A small bone found in the inner ear of certain fishes.

as′tẽr-isk, *n.* [Gr. *asteriskos*, a little star, from *astēr*, a star.]

1. The figure of a star, thus, *, used in printing and writing as a reference to a passage or a note in the margin, or to fill the space where words are omitted.

2. In the Greek church, an appliance in the form of a star or cross, with the ends bent to serve as supports, placed during the liturgy over the paten so as to keep the cover of the latter from touching the sacred bread.

Asterisk.

as′tẽr-iṣm, *n.* [Gr. *asterismos*, a marking with stars, from *asterizein*, to mark with stars; *astēr*, a star.]

1. Formerly, a constellation; as now used, a small cluster of stars.

2. In printing, (a) an asterisk, or mark of reference,—a rare use; (b) three asterisks placed thus, ⁂, calling attention to a special passage.

3. The property possessed by cleft sapphires, mica, and other stones, of exhibiting a starlike reflection.

ȧ-stẽrn′, *adv.* 1. In or at the hinder part of a ship; or toward the hinder part, or backward; as, to go *astern*.

2. Behind a ship, at any indefinite distance.

To back astern; to move with the stern foremost.

To be astern of the reckoning; to fail to make the distance required by the schedule, or reckoning.

To drop astern; to fall behind.

To go astern; to go backward.

ȧ-stẽr′năl, *a.* [Gr. *a* priv., and *sternon*, breastbone.] Not joined to or proceeding from the sternum, or breastbone, as the floating ribs.

as′tẽr-oid, *n.* [*Aster-*, and Gr. *eidos*, form.] A name given by Herschel to the small planets, or planetoids, between the orbits of Mars and Jupiter, of which about three hundred have been discovered.

as′tẽr-oid, *a.* Starlike; specifically, in zoölogy, belonging to the *Alcyonaria*, or *asteroid* polyps; in botany, resembling the aster.

as-tẽr-oid′ăl, *a.* 1. Resembling a star.

2. Pertaining to the asteroids.

3. Pertaining to the starfishes.

As-tẽr-oid′ē-ȧ, *n.pl.* A term sometimes used as the equivalent of *Asteridea*, sometimes as including, along with that order, the *Ophiuroidea*, or starfishes with discoid bodies; the *Alcyonaria*.

As-te-rol′ē-pis, *n.* [*Aster-*, and Gr. *lepis*, a scale.] A genus of gigantic ganoid fishes, now found only in fossil state in the Old Red Sandstone. These fishes sometimes attained the length of eighteen or twenty feet. The engraving shows one of their most characteristic bones, the hyoid plate, with its central strengthening ridge. The stellate markings from which the genus derives its name seem to have been restricted to the dermal plates of the head.

1. Hyoid plate of *Asterolepis*, 1-9th natural size.
2. Internal ridge of hyoid plate, 1-4th natural size.

as″tẽr-ō-phyl′-lite, *n.* One of the genus *Asterophyllites*.

As″tẽr-ō-phyl-lī′tēṣ, *n.* [*Aster-*, and Gr. *phyllon*, a leaf.] Star-leaf, a genus of fossil plants (horse-tail family), so called from the stellated disposition of the leaves round the branches. They abound in the coal-measures, and are believed to be the foliage of the *Calamites*.

ȧ-stẽrt′, *v.i.* See *Astart*.

as′tẽr-wŏrt, *n.* Any composite plant of the aster family.

as-the-nī′ȧ, as′the-ny, *n.* [L., from Gr. *astheneia*, weakness, from *asthenēs*, weak.] A debilitated condition of body; want of bodily vigor.

as-then′iç, *a.* [Gr. *a* priv., and *sthenos*, strength.] Weak; characterized by debility.

as-the-nol′ō-ġy, *n.* [Gr. *asthenēs*, without strength, and *logia*, from *legein*, to speak.] The science which treats of debility and of the diseases connected with it.

as-the-nō′pi-ȧ, *n.* [L., from Gr. *asthenēs*, weak, and *ōps*, *opis*, eye.] An affection of the eye arising from an impaired condition of one or more of the muscles controlling its movements.

as-the-nop′iç, *a.* Relating to asthenopia.

as′the-ny, *n.* Same as *Asthenia*.

asth′mȧ (az′mȧ, ast′mȧ, *or* as′mȧ), *n.* [L. *asthma*; Gr. *asthma*, a panting, asthma, from *azein*, to breathe hard; Sans. root *vā*, blow.] A chronic disorder of the respiratory processes, accompanied by paroxysms of the bronchi, a shortness of breath, a wheezing sound, a feeling of tightness and compression of the lungs, and labored coughing to remove tenacious mucus from the air-passages.

Asthma herb; *Euphorbia pilulifera*, a weed used as a remedy for asthma.

Asthma weed; *Lobelia inflata*, a plant containing properties which are supposed to give it value as a remedy for asthma.

Hay asthma; same as *Hay-fever*.

asth-mat′ic, *n.* A person who suffers from asthma.

asth-mat′iç, asth-mat′iç-ăl, *a.* Pertaining to or affected by asthma.

asth-mat′iç-ăl-ly, *adv.* In an asthmatic manner.

as-tig-mat′iç, *a.* Pertaining to or characterized by astigmatism.

ȧ-stig′mȧ-tiṣm, *n.* [Gr. *a* priv., and *stigma*, *stigmatos*, a mark, spot.] In optics, any want of symmetry in the focusing of a lens; in pathology, a defect of vision arising from the faulty focusing of the light by the crystalline lens upon the retina; the variation of refraction in different meridians.

as-tip′ū-lāte, *v.i.* To agree. [Obs.]

as-tip-ū-lā′tion, *n.* Agreement; concurrence. [Obs.]

ȧ-stir′, *adv.* and *a.* On the stir; on the move; stirring; active; as, the people are *astir*.

A-stō′mȧ-tȧ, *n.pl.* [L., from Gr. *a* priv., and *stoma*, *stomatos*, mouth.] One of the two groups into which the *Protozoa* are divided with regard to the presence or absence of a mouth, of which organ the *Astomata* are destitute. The group comprises two classes, *Gregarinida* and *Rhizopoda*. [See *Protozoa*.]

ȧ-stom′ȧ-tous, *a.* Not possessing a mouth; astomous; specifically, belonging or pertaining to the *Astomata*.

as′tō-mous, *a.* Without a mouth; astomatous; specifically applied in botany to a division of mosses the capsules of which have no aperture.

as-ton′, as-tōne′, *v.t.* To astound. [Obs.]

as-ton′ied, *a.* Astounded. [Obs.]

as-ton′ied-ness, *n.* The state of being astonished. [Obs.]

as-ton′ish, *v.t.*; astonished, *pt.*, *pp.*; astonishing, *ppr.* [ME. *astonien*, *astunian*; OFr. *estoner*, *estuner*, *estonner*, from L. *attonare*, to thunder at, astonish, stun; *ad*, to, at, and *tonare*, to thunder.] To stun, or strike dumb with sudden fear, terror, surprise, or wonder; to amaze; to confound with some sudden passion; to surprise exceedingly.

as-ton′ish-ȧ-ble, *a.* Astonishing. [Rare.]

as-ton′ished, *a.* Amazed; confounded with fear, surprise, or admiration.

Syn.—Appalled, dismayed, astounded, overwhelmed, surprised, amazed, dumfounded, thunderstruck.

as-ton′ished-ly, *adv.* In an astonished manner [Rare.]

as-ton′ish-ing, *a.* Calculated to astonish; amazing; wonderful; as, with *astonishing* celerity.

as-ton′ish-ing-ly, *adv.* In an astonishing manner.

as-ton′ish-ing-ness, *n.* The quality of exciting astonishment.

as-ton′ish-ment, *n.* 1. A state of benumbing surprise, often creating confusion so overwhelming as to prevent rational action.

2. A cause or matter of astonishment.

Thou shalt become an *astonishment*, a proverb, and a byword among all nations.
—Deut. xxviii. 37.

as-ton′y, *v.t.* 1. To astonish; to terrify; to confound. [Obs.]

2. To stun, as with a blow. [Obs. See *Astonish*.]

ȧ-stoop′, *adv.* In a stooping posture.

as-tound′, *a.* Astounded. [Obs.]

as-tound′, *v.t.*; astounded, *pt.*, *pp.*; astounding, *ppr.* [ME. *astouned*, *astoned*, pp. of *astounen*, *astonen*, to astonish.] To astonish; to strike dumb with amazement.

as-tound′ed, *a.* Astonished to dumbness.

Syn.—Astonished, stunned, stupefied, confounded, dazed.

as-tound′ing, *a.* Adapted to astonish; astonishing.

as-tound′ing-ly, *adv.* In an amazing manner.

as-tound′ment, *n.* Amazement.

as′trȧ-chan, *n.* Same as *Astrakhan*.

ȧ-strad′dle, *adv.* With one leg on either side; astride; as, to sit *astraddle*.

As-træ′ȧ, As-trē′ȧ, *n.* [L., from Gr. *Astraia*, goddess of justice, f. of *astraios*, starry, from *astron*, a star.]

1. The goddess of justice. A name sometimes given to the sign *Virgo*, the virgin. The poets feign that Justice quitted heaven, in the golden age, to reside on earth; but becoming weary of the iniquities of men, she returned to heaven, and commenced a constellation of stars.

2. A small planet, discovered in December, 1845, revolving round the sun in 1511 days, and belonging to the group sometimes called asteroids.

3. A genus of coral zoöphytes, the typical one of the family *Astræidæ*.

as-træ′ăn, as-trē′ăn, *a.* Pertaining to the genus *Astræa*.

as-træ′ăn, *n.* A coral of the family *Astræidæ*; a star coral; an astrean.

As-træ′i-dæ, *n.pl.* A family of radiated animals belonging to the class *Actinozoa* and the order *Sclerodermata*. It is specially to this family that the formation of coral reefs is to be attributed. Among others it contains the genera *Astræa* and *Meandrina*.

as′trȧ-gal, *n.* [L. *astragalus*, from Gr. *astragalos*, a turning joint, vertebra, an architectural molding.]

1. In architecture, a little round molding which surrounds the top or bottom of a column, in the form of a ring, representing a ring or band of iron to prevent the splitting of the column. It is often cut into beads or berries, and is used in ornamental entablatures to separate the several faces of the architrave.

2. In gunnery, a round molding on a cannon near the mouth.

3. In anatomy, the astragalus.

4. [*pl.*] Dice, the Greeks using huckle-bones for that purpose.

as-trag′ȧ-lăr, *a.* Relating to the astragalus.

as-trag′ȧ-lō-. A combining form from Gr. *astragalos*, and used in anatomy to indicate connection with or relation to the *astragalus*; as, *astragalo*navicular.

as-trag′ȧ-loid, *a.* [*Astragalo-*, and Gr. *eidos*, form.] Like the astragalus in shape.

as-trag′ȧ-lō-man″cy, *n.* [Gr. *astragalos*, in the pl., dice, and *manteia*, divination.] Pretended divination performed by throwing down huckle-bones (called astragals) or dice with marks corresponding to letters of the alphabet, and observing what words they formed. It was practised in the temple of Hercules, in Achaia. [See *Astragal*, 4.]

as-trag′ȧ-lus, *n.*; *pl.* **as-trag′ȧ-lī.** [L., from Gr. *astragalos*, a vertebra, ankle-bone, a die, an architectural molding.]

1. In anatomy, the huckle, ankle, or sling bone; the upper bone of that part of the foot called the tarsus, supporting the tibia; the astragal.

2. [A—] A genus of papilionaceous plants, of the natural order *Fabaceæ*, containing numerous species, including milk-vetch and licorice-vetch. Gum tragacanth is obtained from different species, particularly the *Astragalus verus*.

3. In architecture, same as *Astragal*.

as′trȧ-khan, *n.* A name given to curled, woolly skins obtained from sheep found in the Russian province of Astrakhan, and in Persia and

Syria; also, a fabric with a pile in imitation of this fur.

as′trȧ-khan, *a.* Made of or resembling astrakhan.

as′trăl, *a.* [L. *astralis*, from *astrum*, a star.]

1. Belonging to the stars; starry.

2. In biology, showing an aster; of or pertaining to an aster.

3. In theosophy, a term applied to the fluid that is believed to permeate space.

Astral body; a phrase used by modern theosophical occultists to designate an ethereal or spiritual body, the spirit, or double, inhabiting the material body in life and surviving as the astral or thought body, after death.

Astral lamp; an Argand lamp in which the oil is contained in a vessel in the form of a flattened ring, obliquely inclined outward and downward, and surmounted by a flattened hemispherical ground glass; the whole being designed to throw a strong and uninterrupted light on the table below.

ȧ-strand′, *adv.* On the strand; aground; as, a boat washed *astrand.*

ȧ-strāy′, *adv.* [ME. *astray, astraei*; OFr. *estraié, estrayé*, from *estraier*, to stray; Pr. *estraguar*, from L. *extravagare*; *extra*, out, and *vagare*, to wander.] Out of the right way or proper place, both in a literal and figurative sense.

As-trē′ȧ, *n.* See *Astræa.*

as-trē′ăn, *a.* See *Astræan.*

as-trict′, *v.t.* [L. *astrictus*, pp. of *astringere*, to draw close; *ad*, to, and *stringere*, draw.]

1. To bind fast; to confine. [Rare. See *Astringe.*]

2. To constrict; to contract.

as-trict′, *a.* Compendious; contracted. [Obs.]

as-tric′tion, *n.* 1. The act of binding fast, or confining.

2. A contraction of parts by applications; the stopping of fluxes or hemorrhages.

3. Constipation.

4. In Scotland, an obligation to have corn raised on certain land ground at a specified mill, paying a toll called multure; also called *thirlage.*

as-tric′tive, *a.* Binding; constricting; astringent.

as-tric′tive-ly, *adv.* In an astrictive manner.

as-tric′tō-ry, *a.* Astringent; binding; tending to bind. [Rare.]

ȧ-stride′, *adv.* With a leg on each side; as, to ride horseback *astride.*

as-trif′ẽr-ous, *a.* [L. *astrifer*, from *astrum*, a star, and *ferre*, to bear.] Bearing or containing stars. [Rare.]

as-tringe′, *v.t.*; astringed, *pt., pp.*; astringing, *ppr.* [L. *astringere*, to draw close, contract; *ad*, to, and *stringere*, to bind, strain.]

1. To bind fast; to constrict; to contract; to cause (parts) to draw together.

2. To bind by obligation.

as-trin′gen-cy, *n.*; *pl.* **as-trin′gen-cies**. The state or quality of being astringent; that quality in medicines by which soft or relaxed parts of the body are contracted; as, the *astringency* of acids or bitters; hence, also, harshness or austerity in disposition; as, the *astringencies* of character or human nature.

as-trin′gent, *a.* [L. *astringens*, ppr. of *astringere*, to contract, draw close; *ad*, to, and *stringere*, to draw, bind.]

1. Binding; contracting; strengthening, or drawing together, as the soft organic tissues.

2. Austere, harsh, or stern in character.

as-trin′gent, *n.* A medicine which contracts the organic textures and canals of the body, condensing the soft solids, and thereby checking or diminishing excessive discharges. The chief *astringents* are the mineral acids, alum, lime-water, chalk, salts of copper, zinc, iron, lead, silver; and among vegetables catechu, kino, oak-bark, and galls. Vegetable *astringents* owe their efficacy to the presence of tannin.

as-trin′gent-ly, *adv.* In an astringent manner.

as-trin′gẽr, *n.* See *Austringer.*

as′trite, *n.* [L. *astroites*, a precious stone; Gr. *astron*, a star.] A radiated or starlike fossil, as one of the detached articulations of fossil encrinites; star-stone; also, a precious stone valued by the ancients, probably the sapphire. Written also *astroite* and *astrion.* [Obs.]

as′trō-. A combining form from Gr. *astron*, a star, and used in zoölogy and botany to denote resemblance to a star.

as′trō-fel, as′trō-phel, *n.* [L. *astrum*, star, and *fel*, gall, bitter.] A bitter herb; supposed to be identical with the aster, or starwort.

as-trog′e-ny, *n.* [*Astro-*, and Gr. *gennaein*, to produce.] The theory or doctrine of the creation or evolution of the heavenly bodies.

as-trog′nō-sy, *n.* [*Astro-*, and Gr. *gnōsis*, knowledge.] Knowledge of the stars, especially the fixed stars, in respect to their names, magnitudes, situations, and the like.

as-trō-gon′ic, *a.* Relating to the genesis or evolution of the stars.

as-trog′ō-ny, *n.* Same as *Astrogeny.*

as-trog′rȧ-phy, *n.* [*Astro-*, and Gr. *graphia*, from *graphein*, to describe.] A description of, or the art of describing, mapping, or delineating the stars.

as′trō-ite, *n.* Same as *Astrite.*

as′trō-lābe, *n.* [Fr. *astrolabe*; LL. *astrolabium*; Gr. *astrolabon*, an astrolabe, from *astron*, star, and *lambanein, labein*, to take.]

1. An instrument formerly used for taking the altitude of the sun or stars, now superseded by the quadrant and sextant.

2. A stereographic projection of the sphere, on the plane of a great circle, usually either upon the plane of the equator, the eye being supposed to be in the pole of the world, or upon the plane of the meridian, the eye being in the point of intersection of the equinoctial and the horizon.

Sir Francis Drake's Astrolabe. —Royal Naval College, England.

3. Among the ancients, the same as the modern armillary sphere.

as-trol′ȧ-tẽr, *n.* One who worships or adores the stars.

as-trol′ȧ-try, *n.* [Fr. *astrolatrie*, from Gr. *astron*, star, and *latreia*, worship.] The worship or adoration of the stars.

as″trō-li-thol′ō-gy, *n.* [*Astro-*, and Gr. *lithos*, stone, and *logia*, from *legein*, to speak.] The science of aerolites or meteoric stones.

as-trol′ō-gẽr, as-trō-lō′gi-ăn, *n.* [ME. *astrologer*; L. *astrologus*; Gr. *astrologos*, an astronomer, astrologer; *astron*, star, and *logos*, from *legein*, to speak.]

1. One who professes to interpret or determine the supposed influence of the stars on events, qualities, or the destinies of men; one who practises astrology, or foretells events by the situations and aspects of the stars. *Astrologian* is little used.

2. An astronomer. [Obs.]

as-trō-log′ic, as-trō-log′ic-ăl, *a.* Pertaining to astrology; professing or practising astrology.

as-trō-log′ic-ăl-ly, *adv.* By means of or in accordance with astrology.

as-trol′ō-gize, *v.t.*; astrologized, *pt., pp.*; astrologizing, *ppr.* To interpret by means of astrology; to apply astrology to.

as-trol′ō-gize, *v.i.* To study or practise astrology.

as-trol′ō-gy, *n.* [ME. *astrology*; L. *astrologia*; Gr. *astrologia*, astronomy, astrology; *astron*, star, and *logia*, from *legein*, to speak.] Literally, the science or doctrine of the stars, and formerly often used as equivalent to *astronomy*, but now restricted in meaning to the pseudoscience which pretends to enable men to judge of the effects and influences of the heavenly bodies on mundane affairs and human character, and to foretell events by their situations and conjunctions.

The belief in *astrology* was almost universal in the middle of the seventeenth century. It was in such great repute during the middle ages that men ignorantly supposed the heavenly bodies to have a ruling influence over the physical and moral world; thus, one's temperament was ascribed to the planet under which he was born, as saturnine from Saturn, jovial from Jupiter, mercurial from Mercury, etc.; and the virtues of herbs, gems, and medicines were supposed to be due to their ruling planets. *Astrology* became the parent of modern astronomy, as alchemy did of chemistry.

Judicial astrology; that branch of astrology which pretended to foretell events connected with the life of men or nations.

Natural astrology; that branch of astrology which professed to predict natural effects, as changes of the weather, winds, and storms.

as′trō-man-cy, *n.* [*Astro-*, and Gr. *manteia*, divination.] Stellar prophecy; astrology.

as-trō-man′tic, *a.* Of or pertaining to astromancy.

as″trō-mē″tē-ọr-ō-log′ic-ăl, *a.* Of or pertaining to astrometeorology.

as″trō-mē″tē-ọr-ol′ō-gist, *n.* One who studies or practises astrometeorology.

as″trō-mē″tē-ọr-ol′ō-gy, *n.* [*Astro-*, and Gr. *meteōrologia*, meteorology; *meteōron*, meteor, and *logia*, from *legein*, to speak.] The so-called art of foretelling the weather and its changes from the appearance of the moon and stars; a branch of natural astrology; or, a scientific investigation of the influence of the heavenly bodies upon atmospheric conditions.

as-trom′e-tẽr, *n.* [*Astro-*, and Gr. *metron*, measure.] An instrument, invented by Sir John Herschel, for measuring the relation, brightness, and apparent magnitude of the fixed stars.

as-trom′e-try, *n.* A branch of astronomy relating to measurements among the stars. The apparent magnitudes and positions of the heavenly bodies are determined by the measurement of angles and time.

as-tron′ō-mẽr, *n.* [ME. *astronomer*; L. *astronomia*; Gr. *astronomia*, from *astronomos*, an astronomer; *astron*, star, and *nemein*, to distribute, arrange.]

1. One who is versed in astronomy; one who has a knowledge of the laws of the heavenly bodies, or the principles by which their motions are regulated, with their various phenomena.

2. An astrologer. [Obs.]

as-trō-nō′mi-ăn, *n.* An astrologer. [Obs.]

as-trō-nom′ic-ăl, as-trō-nom′ic, *a.* Pertaining to astronomy; in harmony with the principles of astronomy.

Astronomical clock; a clock regulated to keep sidereal, not mean time.

Astronomical signs; the signs of the zodiac.

Astronomical year; also called the *solar* and *tropical year*; the period of time covered by the passage of the earth around the sun, or by the changes of the seasons, i. e., 365 days, 5 hours, and 48 minutes.

as-trō-nom′ic-ăl-ly, *adv.* In an astronomical manner; by the principles of astronomy.

as-tron′ō-mize, *v.i.* To study or discourse upon astronomy. [Rare.]

They *astronomized* in caves.—Sir T. Browne.

as-tron′ō-my, *n.* [Gr. *astronomia*, from *astronomos*, an astronomer; *astron*, star, and *nomos*, from *nemein*, to arrange, distribute.]

1. The science which treats of the celestial bodies—fixed stars, planets, satellites, and comets—their nature, distribution, magnitudes, motions, distances, periods of revolution, eclipses, etc. That part of the science which gives a description of the motions, figures, periods of revolution, and other phenomena of the heavenly bodies, is called *descriptive astronomy*; that part which teaches how to observe the motions, figures, periodical revolutions, distances, etc., of the heavenly bodies, and how to use the necessary instruments, is called *practical astronomy*; and that part which explains the causes of their motions, and demonstrates the laws by which those causes operate, is termed *physical astronomy.*

2. Astrology. [Obs.]

3. A text-book or treatise on the heavenly bodies.

as′trō-phel, *n.* See *Astrofel.*

as″trō-phō-tog′rȧ-phy, *n.* [*Astro-*, and Gr. *phōs, phōtos*, light, and *graphia*, from *graphein*, to write, describe.] The art or practice of photography as applied to the delineation of the sun, moon, and stars, and their phenomena, and to other astronomical ends.

as″trō-phō-tom′e-tẽr, *n.* [*Astro-*, and Gr. *phōs, phōtos*, light, and *metron*, measure.] An instrument fitted to a telescope and used to determine the brightness of stars, the standard of comparison being an artificial light.

as″trō-phō″tō-met′ric-ăl, *a.* Of or pertaining to an astrophotometer or to astrophotometry.

as″trō-phō-tom′e-try, *n.* The science of determining the brightness of the heavenly bodies.

as-trō-phyṣ′ic-ăl, *a.* Pertaining to physical astronomy.

as′trō-phyṣ-ics, *n.* [*Astro-*, and Gr. *physikos*, natural, *physis*, nature.] That branch of astronomy which deals with the physical characteristics of the heavenly bodies.

As-troph′y-ton, *n.* [*Astro-*, and Gr. *phyton*, plant.] A genus of starfishes, including the basket-urchin or sea-basket.

as′trō-scōpe, *n.* [*Astro-*, and Gr. *skopein*, to view.] An old astronomical instrument, composed of two cones, on whose surface the constellations were delineated; an old form of celestial globe.

as-tros′cō-py, *n.* Observation of the stars by means of the astroscope.

as″trō-thē-ol′ō-gy, *n.* [*Astro-*, and Gr. *theologia*, theology.] The treatment of natural religion, or theology, from the standpoint of astronomy.

ȧ-struc′tive, *a.* [L. *astructus*, pp. of *astruere*, to build in addition, add; *ad*, to, and *struere*, to heap up.] Constructive; opposed to *destructive.* [Obs.]

ȧ-strut′, *a.* Strutting; pompous. [Obs.]

ȧ-strut′, *adv.* In a swelling or strutting manner, as in walking.

as-tū′cious, as-tū′tious, *a.* [Fr. *astucieux*, astute.] Crafty; subtle; astute; wise in the ways of the world. [Rare.]

as-tū′cious-ly, *adv.* Astutely. [Rare.]

as-tū′ci-ty, *n.* Astuteness. [Rare.]

ȧ-stun′, *v.t.* To stun. [Obs.]

As′tūr, *n.* [L. *astur, astor*, a goshawk.] A genus of rapacious birds including the goshawk, *Astur palumbarius.*

As-tū′ri-ăn, *a.* Pertaining to Asturias, a province of northern Spain, or to the Asturians.

As-tū′ri-ăn, *n.* A native or inhabitant of Asturias.

as-tūte′, *a.* [L. *astutus*, from *astus*, craft, cunning.] Of a shrewd and penetrating mind; cunning; sagacious.

That *astute* little lady of Curzon street. —Thackeray.

Syn.—Penetrating, sagacious, discerning, critical, shrewd, subtle, keen.

as-tūte′ly, *adv.* In an astute manner; shrewdly; sharply; cunningly.

as-tūte′ness, *n.* The quality of being astute or cunning; shrewdness.

as-tū′tious, *a.* Same as *Astucious*.

ȧ-stȳ′lăr, *a.* [Gr. *a* priv., and *stylos*, a column.] In architecture, having no columns or pilasters.

ȧ-styl′len, *n.* In mining, a small ward or stoppage in an adit, or nearly horizontal tunnel or drift, to prevent the free passage of water, made by damming up. [Eng.]

ȧ-sun′dẽr, *adv.* [ME. *a sundir, on sunder*; AS. *on sundran*; *on*, on, and *sunder*, apart.]

1. In a sundered or divided state; into or in a different place or direction; apart; separately; as, wide *asunder* as right and wrong. [See *Sunder*.]

2. Into or in parts, as by an explosion.

ȧ-sụ′rȧ, *n.* [Sans. *asura*, spiritual, a spirit.] In Hindu mythology, an antagonist of the gods; especially one of a race of Titans or demons; a son of Asu.

as′wail, *n.* The native name of the sloth-bear, *Ursus labiatus*, of the mountains of India. It is an uncouth, unwieldy animal, with very long black hair, and inoffensive when not attacked. It never devours vertebrate animals except when pressed by hunger, its usual diet consisting of roots, bee-nests, grubs, snails, ants, etc. Its flesh is esteemed as food.

Aswail (*Ursus labiatus*).

ȧ-swēve′, *v.t.* To stupefy. [Obs.]

ȧ-swing′, *adv.* In a state of swinging.

ȧ-swọọn′, *adv.* In a swoon.

ȧ-swọọned′, *adv.* Aswoon.

ȧ-sȳ′lum, *n.* [L. *asylum*; Gr. *asylon*, an asylum, neut. of *asylos*; *a* priv., and *sylē*, right of seizure.]

1. A sanctuary or inviolable place of protection, where criminals and debtors, in ancient times, sheltered themselves from capture and punishment, and from which they could not be forcibly taken without sacrilege. Temples and altars were anciently *asylums*, as were tombs, statues of the gods, and monuments.

2. Any place of retreat and security.

3. An institution for the protection or relief of unfortunate, afflicted, destitute, or defective persons; as, an *asylum* for the poor, for the insane, for orphans, or for the aged.

Right of asylum; in ancient times, the right recognized for Greek and other heathen sanctuaries, and for sacred meeting places of the early Christians, of protecting those who fled to them to escape molestation or capture. Modernly, the right of one state to receive, shelter, and protect those accused of offenses in another.

Syn.—Refuge, retreat, sanctuary, shelter, covert, retirement.

ȧ-sym′me-trăl, ȧ-sym′me-trous, *a.* [Obs.] Same as *Asymmetric*.

as-ym-met′riç, as-ym-met′riç-ăl, *a.* 1. Wanting symmetry; without proper proportion of parts.

2. In crystallography, relating to the triclinic system, crystals belonging to this classification having three unequal axes or being without a plane of symmetry.

ȧ-sym′me-try, *n.* [Gr. *asymmetria*, disproportion; *a* priv., and *symmetros*; *syn*, with, and *metron*, measure.]

1. The want of proportion between the parts of a thing; lack of symmetry.

2. In mathematics, incommensurability, as when there is no common measure between two quantities. [Obs.]

as′ymp-tōte (as′im-tōt), *n.* [Gr. *a* priv., and *sympiptein*, to fall together; *syn*, with, together, and *ptōtos*, from *piptein*, to fall.] A line which continually approaches nearer to some curve, but, though infinitely extended, would never meet it. This may be conceived as a tangent to a curve at an infinite distance.

as-ymp-tot′iç-ăl, as-ymp-tot′iç, *a.* Belonging to an asymptote.

Asymptotical lines or *curves*; such as continually approach when extended, but never meet.

as-ymp-tot′iç-ăl-ly, *adv.* In an asymptotic manner.

ȧ-syn′ăr-tēte, ȧ-syn″ăr-tet′iç, *a.* [Gr. *asynartētos*, disconnected; *a* priv., *syn*, with, and *artein*, to join, fasten.] Literally, disconnected; not fitted or adjusted.

Asynartete sentence; one in which the members are not united by connective particles; as, I came, I saw, I conquered.

Asynartete verse; in prosody, a verse consisting of two members, having different rhythms; as when the first consists of iambuses and the second of trochees, or the first of dactyls and the second of iambuses.

ȧ-syn′çhrō-niṣm, *n.* Lack of correspondence in time.

ȧ-syn′çhrō-nous, *a.* [Gr. *a* priv., and *syn*, with, and *chronos*, time.] Without coincidence in time; not simultaneous.

as-yn-det′iç, *a.* Of or pertaining to asyndeton; not connected by conjunctions.

as-yn-det′iç-ăl-ly, *adv.* In an asyndetic manner.

ȧ-syn′de-ton, *n.* [Gr. *asyndeton*, asyndeton, neut. of *asyndetos*; *a* priv., and *syndetos*, from *syndein*, to bind together.] In rhetoric, a figure which omits the connective; as, *veni, vidi, vici*; I came, I saw, I conquered. It stands opposed to *polysyndeton*, which is a multiplication of connectives.

as-y-nẽr′gi-ȧ, ȧ-syn′ẽr-ġy, *n.* [Gr. *a* priv., and *synergein*, to work together.] In medicine, want of coördination of muscles normally acting in unison.

ȧ-sys′tō-lē, ȧ-sys′tō-liṣm, *n.* [Gr. *a* priv., and *systole*, contracting, from *syn*, with, and *stellein*, to set, arrange.] In medicine, imperfect contraction of the ventricles of the heart.

at, *prep.* [ME. *at*; AS. *æt*; Ice. *at*; L. *ad*; Sans. *ādhi*, unto, on.]

In general, *at* denotes the relations (1) of *coincidence* or *contiguity* in time or place, actual or approximate; presence or nearness; (2) of *direction toward*; in both senses it is used both literally and figuratively.

1. Denoting presence or nearness: (a) In time; as, *at* the ninth hour; *at* first; *at* last; *at* length; *at* once; *at* the same time. (b) In space; as, *at* home; *at* church; *at* sea; *at* hand. (c) In occupation or condition; as, *at* work; *at* hunting; *at* arms; *at* prayer; *at* peace; *at* war. (d) In degree or condition; as, *at* best; *at* the worst; *at* least; *at* all; *at* his last shift; *at* his utmost need. (e) In effect, as coincident with the cause; as, *at* the word; *at* the sight. (f) In relation, as existing between two objects; as, all shall be *at* your command; he deserves well *at* your hands; *at* my cost. (g) In value; as, *at* a shilling a head.

2. Denoting direction towards, literally or figuratively; as, fire *at* the target; look *at* him; up, guards, and *at* 'em; what would he be *at*; she set her cap *at* him.

At last; a phrase implying difficulties overcome, or impediments causing unforeseen delay; as, I brought him to hear reason *at last*; we reached the top *at last*; or disappointment by having had to wait longer for an object than we expected; as, you have come *at last*.

At length; a phrase implying long continuance of effort, either mental or physical, for a definite end, or long-continued hope, expectation, suspense, or suffering; as, *at length* my toils are rewarded; *at length* my wishes are realized; *at length* my sufferings have come to an end.

At large; an adverbial phrase meaning (a) generally; as a whole; as, the country *at large* must be consulted; (b) at liberty; unconfined; as, the culprit is *at large*; (c) not subject to usual limitations; as, a delegate *at large*, that is, one representing the people, the state, etc., *at large*, and not a particular district.

at′ȧ-bal, *n.* [Sp. *atabal*, from Ar. *at-tabl*; *al*, the, and *tabl*, drum.] A kettledrum; a kind of tabor used by the Moors.

ȧ-taç′ȧ-mīte, *n.* A native muriate of copper, originally found in the desert of Atacama, between Chile and Peru.

ȧ-taç′tiç, *a.* [Gr. *ataktos*, without order; *a* priv., and *taktos*, from *tassein*, to order, arrange.]

1. Without order or arrangement; irregular.

2. In grammar, not syntactic.

3. In medicine, ataxic; incoördinate.

at-ȧft′ẽr, *prep.* After. [Obs.]

at′ȧ-ghan, *n.* Same as *Yataghan*.

ȧ-tāke′, *v.t.* To overtake. [Obs.]

at′ȧ-man, *n.* [Russ. *ataman*; Pol. *ataman*, a chief, headman.] The hetman, or chief military commander of the Cossacks.

at-ȧ-mas′çō, *n.* [Am. Ind.] A plant, *Zephyranthes Atamasco*, of the amaryllis family, found in southern United States; also called *atamasco lily*.

at-ȧ-rax′i-ȧ, at′ȧ-rax-y, *n.* [Gr. *ataraxia*, calmness, from *a* priv., and *taraktos*, from *tarassein*, to disturb.] Calmness of mind; a term used by the Stoics and Skeptics to denote a freedom from the emotions which proceed from vanity and self-conceit.

ȧ-tąunt′, ȧ-tąunt′ō, *adv.* [ME. *ataunt*; OFr. *ataunt, altant*; *al*, L. *alius*, other, and *tant*, L. *tantus*, so much.] In nautical parlance, fully rigged; set on end; set right; commonly applied to the masts of a ship.

All ataunt, or *all atаunto*; a sailor's phrase denoting that a vessel is fully rigged, with all her upper masts and yards aloft; hence, all right; all in good order, or in readiness.

ȧ-tav′iç, *a.* Pertaining to atavism.

at′ȧ-viṣm, *n.* [Fr. *atavisme*, from L. *atavus*, the father of a great-grandfather, from *avus*, a grandfather.]

1. The resemblance of offspring to a remote ancestor or to a distant member in the collateral line; the return to the original type, or the restoration of characters acquired by crossing or otherwise at a remote period.

2. In medicine, the recurrence of any peculiarity or disease of an ancestor in remote generations.

at-ȧ-vis′tiç, *a.* Same as *Atavic*.

ȧ-tax′i-ȧ, ȧ-tax′y, *n.* [Gr. *ataxia*, disorder, from *ataktos*; *a* priv., and *taktos*, from *tassein*, to order, arrange.]

1. Want of order; disturbance; irregularity.

2. In medicine, irregularity in disease, or in the functions; irregularity in the crises and paroxysms of fever; a condition characterized by inability to coördinate muscular movements, as in *locomotor ataxia*.

ȧ-tax′iç, *a.* In medicine, irregular; characterized by great irregularity.

Ataxic fever; a term applied to malignant typhus fever.

at-ȧ-zīr′, *n.* [Sp., from Ar. *altasīr*, influence.] In astrology, the influence of a star upon other stars, or upon man. [Obs.]

āte, *v.*, past tense of *eat*.

-āte, *suffix.* [L. *-atus*, the pp. ending of verbs belonging to the first conjugation.]

1. As a termination in adjectives it is equivalent to the participle or participial adjective ending *-ed*; as anim*ate*, adjective, the same as anim*ated*, possessed of breath, life, or spirit; determin*ate*, determined.

2. As a termination in verbs it signifies to make, to act, or to do that which is indicated by the adjective or substantive from which the verb is made; as, propiti*ate*, to make propitious; domin*ate*, to act as a dominus, or lord over; radi*ate*, to make or emit radii or rays.

3. As a termination in ordinary nouns, it denotes an agent, an office, or dignity; as, tribun*ate*, the office or dignity of a tribune. In chemistry, it is used in naming salts. The *-ic* of the acid is changed into *-ate*, and the word thus formed is connected by *of* with the name of the substance combined with the acid. Thus, from acet*ic* acid come acet*ates*; as, acet*ate* of lead.

ȧ-teçh′niç, *a.* and *n.* [Gr. *atechnos*, without art; *a* priv., and *technē*, art.]

I. *a.* Having neither technical nor artistic knowledge.

II. *n.* One who lacks technical or artistic knowledge.

at′el-. See *Atelo-*.

at′e-lēne, *a.* [Gr. *atelēs*, imperfect.] In mineralogy, imperfect; wanting regular forms in the genus.

At′e-lēṣ, *n.* [L., from Gr. *atelēs*, incomplete; *a* priv., and *telos*, end, completion.] A genus of American monkeys having attenuated bodies, long slender limbs, and a prehensile tail; so called because the thumbs are but rudimentary; the spider-monkeys.

ȧ-te-lier′ (ȧ-te-lyā′), *n.* [Fr.] A studio.

A-tel′lăn, *a.* and *n.* I. *a.* Relating to the dramas at Atella, in ancient Italy.

II. *n.* One of the plays given at Atella; later, applied to any dramatic representation which was satirical or licentious. [Obs.]

at′e-lō-. [Gr. *atelēs*, imperfect.] A combining form denoting incomplete or undeveloped structure; as, *atelo*cardia.

at″e-lō-cär′di-ȧ, *n.* [*Atelo-*, and Gr. *kardia*, heart.] An imperfect or undeveloped state of the heart.

at″e-lō-çhī′li-ȧ, *n.* [*Atelo-*, and Gr. *cheilos*, lip.] Imperfect development of a lip; also written *atelocheilia*.

at″e-lō-glos′si-ȧ, *n.* [*Atelo-*, and Gr. *glōssa*, tongue.] Congenital defect in the tongue.

at″e-log-nā′thi-ȧ, *n.* [*Atelo-*, and Gr. *gnathos*, jaw.] Imperfect development of a jaw, especially of the lower jaw.

at″e-lō-stō′mi-ȧ, *n.* [*Atelo-*, and Gr. *stoma*, mouth.] Incomplete development of the mouth.

ȧ-thal′ȧ-mous, *a.* [Gr. *a* priv., and *thalamos*, bed.] In botany, lacking thalami; applied to certain lichens.

ȧ-thal′line, *a.* [Gr. *a* priv., and *thalos*, a shoot, branch.] Without a thallus.

ath′ȧ-mąnt, *n.* Adamant. [Obs.]

ath-ȧ-nā′ṣi-ȧ (-zhi-ȧ), **ȧ-than′ȧ-sy,** *n.* [Gr. *athanasia*, from *a* priv., and *thanatos*, death.] Immortality.

Ath-ȧ-nā′ṣiăn (-zhăn), *a.* Pertaining to Athanasius, bishop of Alexandria in the fourth century.

Athanasian creed; a creed, confession, or exposition of faith, supposed formerly to have been drawn up by Athanasius, though this opinion is now generally rejected and the composition often ascribed to Hilary, bishop of Arles, about 430 A.D. It is an explicit avowal of the doctrines of the Trinity, as opposed to Arianism, and of the incarnation.

Ath-ȧ-nā′ṣiăn, *n.* A follower of Athanasius, or a believer in the Athanasian creed.

ath′ȧ-nor, *n.* [ME. *athanor*; Sp. *atanor*, from Ar. *at-tannūr*; *al*, the, and *tannūr*, from Heb. *tannūr*, an oven; *nūr*, fire.] A digesting furnace, formerly used in alchemy, and so constructed as to maintain a uniform and durable heat.

Ath-ē-çā′tȧ, *n.* [L., from Gr. *a* priv., and *thēkē*, a box, chest.] A division of the *Hydroidea* in which the zoöids are not sheathed.

ath′ē-çāte, *a.* Resembling the *Athecata.*

ā′thē-iṣm, *n.* [Fr. *athéisme*, from Gr. *atheos*, without a god; *a* priv., and *theos*, god.] The disbelief of the existence of a God, or supreme intelligent Being.

> A little philosophy inclineth men's minds to *atheism*, but depth in philosophy bringeth men's minds to religion. —Bacon.

ā′thē-ist, *n.* One who disbelieves in the existence of a God, or supreme intelligent Being.

> By night an *atheist* half believes a God. —Young.

ā′thē-ist, *a.* Atheistical; disbelieving or denying the being of a supreme God.

ā-thē-is′tiç, ā-thē-is′tiç-ăl, *a.* 1. Pertaining to atheism.

2. Disbelieving the existence of a God; impious; applied to persons; as, an *atheistic* writer.

3. Implying or containing atheism; applied to things; as, *atheistic* doctrines or opinions.

ā-thē-is′tiç-ăl-ly, *adv.* In an atheistic manner.

ā-thē-is′tiç-ăl-ness, *n.* The quality of being atheistical.

ā′thē-īze, *v.i.* To discourse as an atheist. [Rare.]

ā′thē-īze, *v.t.* To render atheistic. [Rare.]

ā′thē-ī-zẽr, *n.* One who atheizes. [Rare.]

ath′el-ing, ad′el-ing, *n.* [ME. *atheling*; AS. *ætheling*; O.H.G. *adaling*, from *athele*, noble.] In Anglo-Saxon times, a prince; one of the royal family; a nobleman.

Ath-e-næ′um, Ath-e-nē′um, *n.* [L., from Gr. *Athēnaion*, a temple of Athene.]

1. In ancient Athens, a place where poets, philosophers, and rhetoricians declaimed, and repeated their compositions; a temple dedicated to Athene, the patroness of literature, art, and industry.

2. An academy founded at Rome by Hadrian for the promotion of literary and scientific studies, and imitated in the provinces.

3. In modern times, an institution for the encouragement of literature and art, where a library, periodicals, etc., are kept for the use of the members; or an association for the study of art, science, and literature.

A-thē′ni-ăn, *a.* Pertaining to Athens, the metropolis of Attica, in Greece.

A-thē′ni-ăn, *n.* A native or inhabitant of Athens.

ā″thē-ō-lō′ġi-ăn, *n.* One who is opposed to a theologian. [Obs.]

ā″thē-ō-loġ′iç-ăl, *a.* Not theological.

ā-thē-ol′ō-ġy, *n.* Opposition to theology; atheism.

ā′thē-ous, *a.* 1. Atheistic; impious. [Rare.]

> The hypocrite or *atheous* priest. —Milton.

2. Not taking God into account; neither accepting nor denying God. [Rare.]

Ath-e-rī′nȧ, *n.* [L., from Gr. *atherinē*, a kind of smelt.] A genus of abdominal fishes, characterized by a rather flat upper jaw, six rays in the gill-membrane, and a silvery side belt or line. It includes the sand-smelts.

ath′ẽr-ine, *n.* A name common to the species of the genus *Atherina.*

ȧ-thẽr′măn-cy, *n.* [Gr. *athermantos*, not heated; *a* priv., and *thermainein*, to heat, from *thermē*, heat.] The state or condition of being impervious to radiant heat; the power existing in some substances of retaining all the heat which they receive.

ȧ-thẽr′mȧ-nous, ȧ-thẽr′mous, *a.* Pertaining or relating to athermancy; opposed to *diathermanous.*

ath′ẽr-oid, *a.* [Gr. *atheros*, an ear of grain.] Formed like an ear of grain.

ath-e-rō′mȧ, *n.* [L., from Gr. *athērōma*, from *atharē*, porridge.]

1. A species of wen or encysted tumor, containing cheesy matter.

2. The fatty degeneration of the walls of the arteries in arteriosclerosis, or the whole process of arteriosclerosis.

ath″e-rō-mā′ṣi-ȧ (-zhi-ȧ), *n.* An atheromatous condition.

ath-e-rom′ȧ-tous, *a.* Characterized by or affected with atheroma.

Ath″e-rō-spẽr′mȧ, *n.* [Gr. *athēr*, *atheros*, the beard, or spike, of an ear of corn, and *sperma*, a seed.] A genus of plants, of Australia and Tasmania, containing but one species, the plume-nutmeg, *Atherosperma moschatum.*

ath′e-tīze, *v.t.*; athetized, *pt.*, *pp.*; athetizing, *ppr.* [Gr. *athetein*, to set aside; *a* priv., and *thetos*, from *tithenai*, to set.] To reject; to set aside.

ath′e-toid, *a.* Relating to or characteristic of athetosis.

ath-e-tō′sis, *n.* [L., from Gr. *athetos*, without place; *a* priv., and *thetos*, from *tithenai*, to place.] In medicine, a condition characterized by involuntary twitchings and tremors of the hands and feet; a form of St. Vitus's dance.

ȧ-think′, *v.t.* To repent. [Obs.]

ȧ-thirst′, *a.* 1. Thirsty; wanting drink.

2. Having a keen appetite or desire; as, *athirst* for knowledge.

ath′lēte, *n.* [L. *athleta*; Gr. *athlētēs*, a contestant in the games; from *athlein*, to contest for a prize; *athlos*, a contest; *athlon*, a prize.]

1. Among the ancients, one who contended for a prize in the public games.

2. One trained to engage or strive for victory in exercises and contests requiring physical strength, endurance, or agility.

3. Figuratively, one fitted or trained for mental contests; as, *athletes* of debate.

ath-let′iç, *a.* 1. Pertaining to an athlete or to wrestling, boxing, running, and other exercises; as, *athletic* sports.

2. Strong; lusty; robust; vigorous; fitted for vigorous exertions; as, an *athletic* young man.

Syn.—Strong, muscular, vigorous, able, robust, sinewy, lusty, mighty, stalwart.

ath-let′iç-ăl-ly, *adv.* In an athletic manner.

ath-let′i-ciṣm, *n.* The act or practice of taking part in athletics.

ath-let′içs, *n.* The art of physical training; athletic games or exercises, as boxing, running, etc.

ath′lē-tiṣm, *n.* The condition or characteristics of an athlete; muscularity.

ȧ-threp′si-ȧ, *n.* [L., from Gr. *a* priv., and *threpsis*, nourishment, from *trephein*, to nourish.] Want of nourishment; extreme weakness or debility, especially among children, resulting from lack of food and neglect of hygiene.

ȧ-thwạrt′, *prep.* 1. Across; from side to side; transverse to; as, *athwart* the path.

2. In marine language, across the line of a ship's course; as, a fleet standing *athwart* our course.

Athwart hawse; the situation of a ship when it lies across the stem of another, whether in contact or at a small distance.

Athwart the forefoot; a phrase applied to the flight of a cannon-ball, fired by one ship across another ship's course, ahead, as a signal for her to be brought to.

ȧ-thwạrt′, *adv.* Across; transversely; hence, in a manner to perplex; crossly; wrongly; wrongfully.

ȧ-thwạrt′ships, *adv.* Athwart or across the ship from side to side, or in that direction.

ȧ-thy′mi-ȧ, *n.* [Gr. *athymia*, faint-heartedness; *a* priv., and *thymos*, soul, courage.] In medicine, (a) despondency; (b) loss of consciousness; (c) insanity.

-at′iç, *suffix.* [A compound L. suffix composed of a pp. stem in *-at* and *-icus*; Gr. *-atikos*, in which *ikos* is added to a noun stem in *-at.*] A combining form used in adjectives of Greek and Latin origin and signifying of, of the kind of.

ȧ-tilt′, *adv.* 1. In the manner of a tilter; in the position or with the action of a man making a thrust; as, to stand or run *atilt.*

2. In the manner of a cask tilted, or with one end raised.

at′i-my, *n.* [Gr. *atimia*, from *a* priv., and *timē*, honor.] In ancient Greece, public disgrace; exclusion from office or magistracy, by some disqualifying act or decree.

-ā′tion, *suffix.* [Fr. *-ation*, from L. *atio(n)*; a suffix added to verbs of the first conjugation.] A combining form used in forming nouns of action often equivalent to abstract nouns in *-ing*, and explaining the state resulting from the action. These nouns are usually formed from verbs in *-ate* or verbs without a suffix, as fix, fix*ation*, quote, quot*ation.*

-ā′tious. A compound adjective suffix consisting of *-atio(n)* and *-ous*, and used to form adjectives from nouns in *-ation*, as disput*atious.*

ȧ-tip′tōe, *adv.* 1. On tiptoe.

2. Figuratively, in a state of high expectation or eagerness.

At-lan′tȧ, *n.* [L., from Gr. *Atlas*, *Atlantos.*] A genus of pelagic gasteropodous mollusks typical of the family *Atlantidæ.*

at-lan′tăl, *a.* In anatomy, relating to the atlas.

At-lan-tē′ăn, *a.* 1. Pertaining to Atlas; resembling Atlas.

2. Pertaining to the island Atlantis, which the ancients allege was sunk and overwhelmed by the sea, or to Bacon's ideal commonwealth of that name.

at-lan′tēṣ, *n.pl.* [Gr. *Atlantes*, pl. of *Atlas.*] In architecture, figures or half figures of men used in the place of columns or pilasters to support an entablature; called by the Romans *telamones.* Female figures so employed are called *caryatides.*

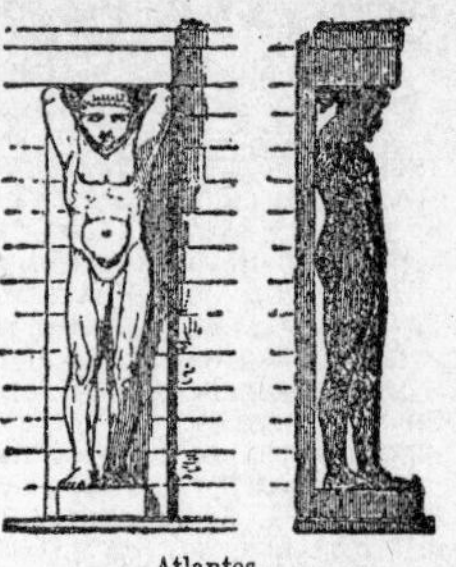
Atlantes.

At-lan′tiç, *a.* [L. *Atlanticus*, from Gr. *Atlas*, *Atlantos*, a mountain in west Africa whose shores the Atlantic Ocean washes; so named because fabled to be the pillar of heaven.]

1. Pertaining to or descended from Atlas.

2. Pertaining to that division of the ocean which lies between Europe and Africa on the east and America on the west; as, the *Atlantic* cable; *Atlantic* gales.

3. Pertaining to the island Atlantis. [See *Atlantean*, 2.]

At-lan′ti-dæ, *n.pl.* [L., from Gr. *Atlas*, *Atlantos*, Mt. Atlas.]

1. One of the three great divisions into which some ethnologists divide the human family, the other two being *Mongolidæ* and *Japetidæ.* It comprises all the tribes of Africa, as well as those of Syria and Arabia.

2. In zoölogy, a family of gasteropodous mollusks of the order *Nucleobranchiata*, with a small shell resembling that of the nautilus, and at one time supposed to be the living representatives of the fossil ammonites.

At-lan′ti-dēṣ, *n.pl.* A name given to the Pleiades or seven stars, which were fabled to be the daughters of Atlas, who were translated to heaven.

at-lan′tō-. A combining form of *atlas*, *atlantos*, meaning of or pertaining to the atlas of the vertebral column.

At-lan-tō-sau′ri-dæ, *n.pl.* A family of dinosaurian reptiles, of which the genus *Atlantosaurus* is the type.

At-lan-tō-sau′rus, *n.* [*Atlanto-*, and Gr. *sauros*, a reptile.] A genus of gigantic dinosaurian reptiles, remains of which have been found in the Jurassic strata of Colorado.

at′lăs, *n.* [Gr. *Atlas*, one of the Titans, who attempted to storm heaven, and was therefore condemned to bear the vault of heaven, or, according to some legends, the earth, on his shoulders.]

1. [A—] Figuratively, one who bears a great burden.

2. A collection of maps in a volume; supposed to be so called from a picture of Atlas supporting the globe, prefixed to some collections.

3. A book in which subjects are exhibited in tabular form or arrangement; as, a historical or ethnographical *atlas.*

4. A large, square folio, resembling a volume of maps; called also *atlas-folio.*

5. The first vertebra of the neck, articulating immediately with the occipital bone, and thus sustaining the head, whence the name.

6. A size of drawing paper, 26 by 33 or 34 inches.

7. A collection or volume of plates or engravings explanatory of some subject.

8. The atlas-beetle, *Chalcosoma atlas.*

Atlas powder; a compound of nitroglycerin used in blasting.

at′lăs, *n.* [Ar., smooth, bare, satin.] A fine fabric of silk and satin, manufactured in the East Indies.

at″lăs-fōl′iō, *n.* A large square folio size of books.

at′lee, *n.* [Native name.] The East Indian tamarisk salt-tree, *Tamarix orientalis.*

at′lō-, at-loid′ō-. A combining form used in anatomy, signifying pertaining or referring to the atlas.

at′loid, *a.* [*Atlo-*, and Gr. *eidos*, form.] In anatomy, pertaining to the atlas.

at-mi-dom′e-tẽr, *n.* [Gr. *atmis*, *atmidos*, vapor, and *metron*, a measure.] An instrument used in measuring the evaporation from water, ice, or snow.

at-mi-dom′e-try, *n.* The science of ascertaining and measuring evaporation in the atmosphere.

at′mō, *n.* [Contraction of *atmosphere.*] A standard barometric pressure of the atmosphere, consisting of 760 millimeters in the latitude of Paris, at sea-level, and 0° centigrade.

at-mō-loġ′iç, at-mō-loġ′iç-ăl, *a.* Pertaining to atmology.

at-mol′ō-gist, *n.* One skilled in atmology; a student of atmology.

at-mol′ō-gy, *n.* [Gr. *atmos*, vapor, and *logia*, from *legein*, to speak.] That branch of science which treats of the laws and phenomena of aqueous vapor.

at-mol′y-sis, *n.* [Gr. *atmos*, vapor, and *lysis*, a loosing, from *lyein*, to loose.] A method of separating the constituent elements of a compound gas, as atmospheric air, by causing it to pass through a vessel of porous material, such as graphite.

at″mol-y-zā′tion, *n.* The separation of compound gases by atmolysis.

at′mō-lyze, *v.t.*; atmolyzed, *pt., pp.*; atmolyzing, *ppr.* To separate by atmolysis.

at′mō-ly-zēr, *n.* One who or that which produces atmolysis; specifically, an instrument for separating compound gases.

at-mom′e-tēr, *n.* [Gr. *atmos*, vapor, and *metron*, a measure.] An instrument used in measuring the quantity of evaporation from a humid surface in a given time; an evaporometer.

at′mŏs-phēre, *n.* [Gr. *atmos*, vapor, and *sphaira*, a sphere.]

1. The whole mass of aeriform fluid surrounding the earth; also, the gaseous envelope surrounding any other planet; in general, any gaseous medium; as, the *atmosphere* of a house.

2. A hypothetical medium surrounding electrical bodies, through which their electrical influence extends.

3. Figuratively, pervading influence; environment; as, a moral *atmosphere*.

4. An established unit of atmospheric pressure. In the United States and England the unit of pressure is the pressure of a column of mercury 30 inches high, at a temperature of 32° Fahrenheit, at the level of the sea at London. The weight of the atmosphere per square inch (about 14.7 pounds) is frequently regarded as the conventional unit for ordinary purposes.

at-mŏs-pher′ic, at-mŏs-pher′ic-ăl, *a.* 1. Pertaining to, characteristic of, or existing in the atmosphere; as, *atmospheric* air or vapors; *atmospheric* currents.

2. Dependent on the atmosphere. [Rare.]

> I am an *atmospheric* creature. —Pope.

3. Produced or acted upon by the atmosphere; as, an *atmospheric* effect.

Atmospheric churn; a churn of various forms, in which atmospheric air is driven into the milk in order to agitate it, and also to obtain the specific effect of the air upon the milk in aggregation of the oleaginous globules.

Atmospheric engine; a steam-engine in which the steam is admitted only to the under side of the piston and for the up stroke, the steam being then condensed, and a vacuum thereby created under the piston, which in consequence descends by the pressure of the atmosphere acting on its upper surface.

Atmospheric line; in a steam-pressure diagram, a line drawn by the pencil when the steam is shut off from the piston of the indicator, and it is acted on by the pressure of the atmosphere alone. The height of the steam-line above this shows the pressure of the steam, and the depth of the vacuum-line below shows the degree of condensation which is then taking place in the engine.

Atmospheric pressure; the weight of the atmosphere per square inch of surface; the pressure of 14.7 pounds per square inch exerted in all directions, at the sea level, by the atmosphere.

Atmospheric railway; a railway so constructed that the motive power is derived from the pressure of the atmosphere; a pneumatic railway.

Atmospheric spring; a spring formed by compressed air; an air-spring.

at-mŏs-pher′ic-ăl-ly, *adv.* With regard to the atmosphere.

at-mŏs-pher′ics, *n.* Natural electrical discharges in the ether which travel through the same medium as radio waves. They therefore are readily picked up by radio receivers, often proving troublesome as it is difficult to tune out the disturbances because they do not have a definite wave length.

at-mŏs-phē-rol′ō-gy, *n.* [Gr. *atmos*, vapor, *sphaira*, sphere, and *logia*, from *legein*, to speak.] The science which treats of the atmosphere.

at-mos′tē-ăl, *a.* Relating to or of the nature of an atmosteon.

at-mos′tē-on, *n.*; *pl.* **at-mos′tē-ȧ**. [Gr. *atmos*, air, and *osteon*, bone.] In ornithology, an air-bone; an ossified membranous tube that conveys air into the interior of a bone.

at′ō-kous, *a.* [Gr. *atokos*, barren; *a* priv., and *tokos*, offspring.]

1. In zoölogy, producing only asexual offspring, as the eggs of certain species of the *Annelida*.

2. Asexual; applied to certain worms.

ȧ-toll′, *n.* [Malay *adal*, closing, uniting.] A name given to coral islands consisting of a strip or ring of coral surrounding a central lagoon, very common in the Indian and Pacific Oceans.

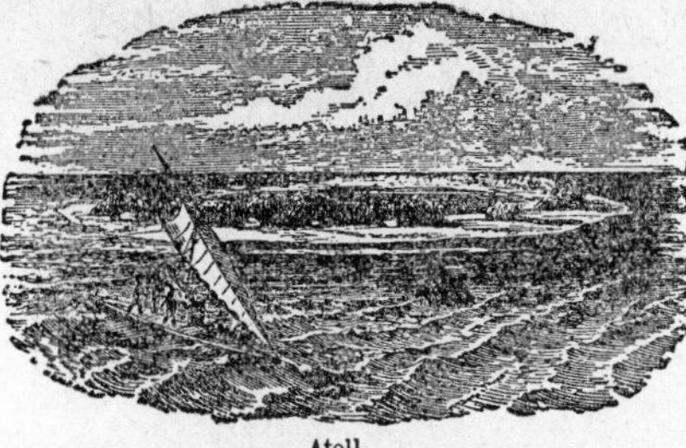

Atoll.

at′ŏm, *n.* [Fr. *atome*; L. *atomus*; Gr. *atomos*, an atom, indivisible; *a* priv., and *tomos*, from *temnein*, to cut.]

1. In physics, a particle of matter so minute as to admit of no division; also, a particle of matter, without regard to whether it is divisible or indivisible; a molecule. *Atoms* are conceived to be the first principles or component parts of all bodies.

2. In chemistry, a supposed ultimate particle or component part of a body; the smallest particle supposed to result from the division of a body, without decomposition.

3. Anything extremely small; as, he has not an *atom* of sense.

at′ŏm, *v.t.* To change to atoms. [Obs.]

at″ō-mē-chan′ics, *n.* Atom mechanics; the science which treats of motions and forces of atoms.

ȧ-tom′ic, ȧ-tom′ic-ăl, *a.* Pertaining to atoms; consisting of atoms; extremely minute.

Atomic philosophy, or *doctrine of atoms*; a theory said to have been first broached by Leucippus, but much cultivated and improved by Epicurus, teaching that atoms are endued with gravity and motion, by which all things were formed, without the aid of a supreme intelligent Being.

Atomic theory; the doctrine of definite proportions, in chemistry, teaching that all chemical combinations take place between the supposed ultimate particles or *atoms* of bodies, and that these unite, either one atom with one atom, or by sums of atoms which are integral multiples of unity. This theory was first presented by Dalton.

Atomic weight; the weight of a supposed ultimate particle or atom of a body, compared with an atom of hydrogen as a unit.

ȧ-tom′ic-ăl-ly, *adv.* In accord with the theory or nature of atoms.

at-ō-mi′ciăn (-mish′un), *n.* One who believes in the atomic theory. [Rare.]

ȧ-tom′i-cism, *n.* Atomism. [Obs.]

at-ō-mic′i-ty, *n.* 1. Valence.

2. The number of atoms in the group forming a molecule.

at′ŏm-ism, *n.* The doctrine of atoms.

at′ŏm-ist, *n.* One who holds to the atomic philosophy.

at-ŏm-is′tic, *a.* Relating to atomism. [Rare.]

at″ŏm-i-zā′tion, *n.* The state of being atomized, or the process of atomizing; specifically, in medicine, the reduction of liquids into spray.

at′ŏm-ize, *v.t.*; atomized, *pt., pp.*; atomizing, *ppr.* To reduce to atoms.

at′ŏm-i-zēr, *n.* One who or that which atomizes.

at-ŏm-ol′ō-gy, *n.* The doctrine of atoms.

at′ŏm-y, *n.* An atom; a pygmy.

at′ŏm-y, *n.* [*Anatomy*, separated into *an atomy*.] A very lean person; a skeleton.

ȧ-tōn′ȧ-ble, *a.* Capable of being atoned for.

at-one′ (-wun′), *adv.* At one; together; at once. [Obs.]

ȧ-tōne′, *v.i.*; atoned, *pt., pp.*; atoning, *ppr.* [ME. *attone*, *atoon*, *aton*, *at one*, at one, agreed.]

1. To agree; to be in accordance. [Obs.]

> He and Aufidius can no more *atone*,
> Than violentest contrariety. —Shak.

2. To stand as an equivalent; to make reparation, amends, or satisfaction for an offense or a crime, by which reconciliation is procured between the offended and offending parties. Usually followed by *for*.

ȧ-tōne′, *v.t.* 1. To expiate; to answer or make satisfaction for.

> Or each *atone* his guilty love with life. —Pope.

2. To reduce to concord; to reconcile; to appease. [Obs.]

3. To unite. [Obs.]

ȧ-tōne′ment, *n.* 1. Agreement; concord; reconciliation after enmity or controversy.

> He seeks to make *atonement*
> Between the Duke of Glo'ster and your brothers. —Shak.

2. Expiation; satisfaction or reparation made by giving an equivalent for an injury, or by doing or suffering that which is received in satisfaction for an offense or injury; with *for*.

> Great as Sawyer's offenses were, he had made great *atonement* for them. —Macaulay.

3. In theology, the expiation of sin made by the obedience and personal sufferings of Christ; more specifically, the crucifixion.

Day of atonement; a Jewish fast-day; the tenth of Tizri, on which the faults of the year were expiated by sacrifice and fasting.

ȧ-tōn′ēr, *n.* One who makes atonement.

at-ōnes′, *adv.* At once. [Obs.]

ȧ-ton′ic, *a.* [Gr. *atonos*, not stretched; *a* priv., and *tonos*, from *teinein*, to stretch.] 1. In medicine, characterized by atony, or want of tone or vital energy; as, an *atonic* disease.

2. In grammar or philology, (a) unaccented; (b) produced by the breath alone; surd.

ȧ-ton′ic, *n.* 1. In medicine, a drug capable of allaying organic excitement or irritation.

2. In grammar or philology, (a) a word that has no accent; (b) an elementary sound produced by the breath; a surd consonant; a breathing.

at′ō-ny, *n.* [Fr. *atonie*; L. *atonia*; Gr. *atonia*, languor; *a* priv., and *teinein*, to stretch.] In medicine, lack of power, especially muscular power.

ȧ-top′, *adv.* On or at the top.

-ator. [L. *-ator*, in which *-tor*, an agency suffix is added to stems in *-a* of the first conjugation.] A suffix signifying the doer, agent, actor, as in cre*ator*, liber*ator*, educ*ator*.

-atory. [L. *-atorius*, a compound suffix in which *-ius* is added to nouns in *-ator*.] A suffix signifying of or pertaining to, of the nature of, produced by, as in accus*atory*, exclam*atory*, declam*atory*.

at″rȧ-bi-lā′ri-ăn, at″rȧ-bi-lā′ri-ous, *a.* [L. *atrabilarius*, from *atra bilis*, black bile.] Affected with melancholy, which the ancients attributed to the black bile; replete with black bile.

at″rȧ-bi-lā′ri-ăn, *n.* A melancholy person.

at″rȧ-bi-lā′ri-ous-ness, *n.* The state of being melancholy, or atrabilious.

at-rȧ-bil′iăr (-yăr), *a.* Melancholy.

at-rȧ-bil′iȧ-ry (-yȧ-ry), *a.* In medicine, (a) of, relating, or pertaining to black bile; (b) pertaining to or designating certain renal organs; as, the *atrabiliary* capsules or blood-vessels.

at-rȧ-bil′ious (-yus), *a.* 1. Melancholic or hypochondriacal; from the supposed preponderance of black bile.

2. Atrabiliary.

at-rac-ten′chy-mȧ, *n.* [L., from Gr. *atraktos*, a spindle, and *enchyma*, infusion.] Vegetable tissue consisting of spindle-shaped cells.

at″rȧ-men-tā′ceous, *a.* Black as ink. [Obs.]

at-rȧ-men′tăl, at-rȧ-men′tous, *a.* [L. *atramentum*, black ink, from *ater*, black.] Inky; black, like ink.

at″rȧ-men-tā′ri-ous, *a.* Like ink; suitable for making ink. Sulphate of iron, or copperas, is called *atramentarious*, as being one of the materials used in making ink.

at-rēde′, *v.t.* To excel in council. [Obs.]

at-ren′, *v.t.* To outrun. [Obs.]

ȧ-trē′si-ȧ, (-shi-ȧ), *n.* [L., from Gr. *atrētos*, not perforated; *a* priv., and *trētos*, from *tetrainein*, to perforate.] Absence or abnormal constriction of any natural passage of the body.

ā′tri-ȧ, *n.*, pl. of *atrium*.

ā′tri-ăl, *a.* Pertaining to an atrium; in zoölogy, of or pertaining to the atrium in the *Tunicata*.

ā′tri-ō-. A combining form used in anatomical and medical terms to denote some relation to an atrium, as in *atrio*ventricular.

ā-tri-op′ō-răl, *a.* Pertaining to the atrial pore.

ā′tri-ō-pōre, *n.* [*Atrio-*, and Gr. *poros*, a passage.] The atrial pore.

ȧ-trip′, *adv.* In nautical language, said of an anchor when the purchase has just made it break ground, or raised it clear. Sails are *atrip* when they are hoisted from the cap, sheeted home, and ready for trimming. Yards are *atrip* when swayed up, ready to have the stops cut for crossing; so an upper mast is said to be *atrip* when the fid is loosed.

At′ri-plex, *n.* [L., from Gr. *atraphaxys*, an orach.] A genus of plants, natural order *Chenopodiaceæ*; orach. They are mealy or scaly herbs or shrubs, with small unisexual flowers, growing on shores and in waste places.

ā′tri-um, *n.*; *pl.* **ā′tri-ȧ**. [L.]

1. In ancient Roman architecture, the entrance-hall, the most important, and usually the most splendid, apartment of a Roman house, generally ornamented with statues and pictures, and forming the reception-room for visitors and clients.

2. A hall or court in front of the entrance of certain great ancient temples, pagan and early Christian.

3. An auricle of the heart; by extension, the entire auricular cavity.

4. In zoölogy, the large chamber or cloaca

into which the intestine opens in the *Tunicata*.

at'rō-chȧ, *n.pl.* [L., from Gr. *a* priv., and *trochos*, a wheel, from *trechein*, to run.] The larva, or embryo, of a chætopod worm, in which the cilia are spread over the body and do not appear in distinct rings.

at'rō-chous, at'rō-chal, *a.* Pertaining to or like atrocha.

ȧ-trō'cious, *a.* [L. *atrox*, fierce, cruel, from *ater*, black.]

1. Extremely heinous, criminal, or cruel; outrageously wicked.

2. Expressing or revealing great atrocity.

The fierce *atrocious* frown of sinewed Mars. —Thomson.

3. Very grievous; violent; as, *atrocious* distempers. [Obs.]

Syn.—Outrageous, flagitious, monstrous, villainous, flagrant, heinous, wicked, cruel.

ȧ-trō'cious-ly, *adv.* In an atrocious manner; with supreme cruelty or guilt.

ȧ-trō'cious-ness, *n.* The state or quality of being atrocious; atrocity.

ȧ-troc'i-ty, *n.* [Fr. *atrocité*; L. *atrocitas*, from *atrox*, *atrocis*, cruel; *ater*, black.]

1. Enormous wickedness; extreme heinousness or cruelty.

2. A specific act of extreme heinousness or cruelty.

The *atrocities* committed in that holy name. —DeQuincey.

At'rō-pȧ, *n.* [L., from Gr. *Atropos*, one of the Fates, who cut the thread of life, unchangeable; from *a* priv., and *trepein*, to turn.] A genus of poisonous narcotic plants, of the natural order *Solanaceæ*. *Atropa belladonna*, or deadly nightshade, has a shining black berry like a cherry, inclosed in the permanent calyx. It has a sweetish taste, but is poisonous. [See *Belladonna*.]

at'rō-pal, *a.* In botany, erect; orthotropous; said of an ovule.

ȧ-troph'ic, *a.* Pertaining to or affected with atrophy.

at'rō-phied (-fid), *a.* Affected with atrophy; wasting or wasted away.

at'rō-phy, *n.* [Fr. *atrophie*; L. *atrophia*; Gr. *atrophia*, a wasting away; *a* priv., and *trephein*, to nourish.] A wasting of the flesh with loss of strength, the result of a morbid condition of the body, especially of the digestive organs; emaciation.

at'rō-phy, *v.t.*; atrophied, *pt.*, *pp.*; atrophying, *ppr.* To cause to be wasted away.

ȧ-trō'pi-ȧ, *n.* Same as *Atropin*.

at'rō-pin, at'rō-pine, *n.* [Gr. *atropos*, inflexible; *a* priv., and *trepein*, to turn.] A crystalline alkaloid, $C_{17}H_{23}NO_3$, obtained from the deadly nightshade, *Atropa belladonna*. It is very poisonous, and produces persistent dilatation of the pupil of the eye.

at'rō-pism, *n.* The morbid condition produced by atropin.

at'rō-pous, *a.* Same as *Atropal*.

ā'trous, *a.* [L. *ater*, black.] Intensely black.

A-try̆'pȧ, *n.* [L., from Gr. *a* priv., and *trypa*, a hole.] An extinct genus of brachiopods, having rigid branchial appendages spirally coiled toward the center of the shell, the shell-substance being fibrous and impunctate.

at'tȧ-bal, *n.* See *Atabal*.

ȧt-tȧc'cȧ. [It., imper. of *attaccare*, to tie, bind.] In music, a direction which denotes that the next movement is to follow immediately, without any pause.

at-tach', *v.t.*; attached (-tacht'), *pt.*, *pp.*; attaching, *ppr.* [Fr. *attacher*, to tie, fasten; *a*, L. *ad*, to, and Breton *tach*, a nail.]

1. To make to adhere; to tie, bind, or fasten; as, to *attach* one thing to another by a string, by glue, etc.

2. Figuratively, to connect; to associate; as, to *attach* great importance to a particular circumstance.

3. To lay hold of; to seize. [Obs.]

Then, homeward, every man *attach* the hand
Of his fair mistress. —Shak.

4. In law, to take by legal authority; to arrest (a person) by writ to answer for a debt; applied to a taking of a person by a civil process, being now never used for the arrest of a criminal, although formerly applied to arrests of all kinds. Thus we find Shakspere using it with *of* before the charge: "*Of* capital treason I *attach* you both." Now applied also to the taking of goods and real estate by an officer, by virtue of a writ or precept, to hold the same to satisfy a judgment to be rendered in a suit.

5. To take, seize, and lay hold on, by moral force, as by affection or interest; to fasten or bind by moral influence; to gain over; to win; as, his kindness *attached* us all to him.

Songs, garlands, flow'rs,
And charming symphonies *attached* the heart
Of Adam. —Milton.

Syn.—Add, affix, append, annex, connect, fasten, fix, stick, tack.

at-tach', *v.i.* To be attached or connected; to be joined or bound up with; to belong; with *to*.

at-tach', *n.* Attachment. [Obs.]

at-tach'ȧ-ble, *a.* Capable of being attached, legally or otherwise; liable to be taken by writ or precept.

at-ta-ché' (ȧ-tȧ-shā'), *n.* [Fr., pp. of *attacher*, to attach.] One attached to another, as attendant or a part of his suite; specifically, one attached to an embassy or legation to a foreign government.

at-tach'ment, *n.* 1. The act of attaching or binding; the condition of being held fast or connected; close adherence or affection; fidelity; regard; any passion or affection that binds a person; as, an *attachment* to a friend, or to a party.

2. That by which one thing is attached to another; as, to cut the *attachments* of a muscle; also, the place at which a fastening or joining is made; as, the *attachment* was too low for convenience.

3. Some adjunct attached to an instrument, machine, or other object; as, the Æolian *attachment* to the pianoforte.

4. In law, (a) the taking of a person, goods, or estate, by a writ or precept in a civil action, to secure a debt or demand; (b) the writ directing such action. *Attachments* also issue against persons failing to appear upon summons, and those guilty of contempt of court.

Foreign attachment; the taking of the money or goods of a debtor in the hands of a third person, considered in law as the agent, attorney, factor, or trustee of the debtor; as when the debtor is not within the jurisdiction of the court, or has absconded.

Syn.—Adherence, fondness, affection, inclination, bond, tie, adjunct, appendage.

at-tack', *v.t.*; attacked (-takt'), *pt.*, *pp.*; attacking, *ppr.* [Fr. *attaquer*, to attack; another form of *attacher*, to fasten, join; *a*, L. *ad*, to, and Breton *tach*, a nail.]

1. To assault; to fall upon with force; to assail, as with force and arms.

2. To fall upon with unfriendly words or writing; to begin a controversy with; to attempt to overthrow or bring into disrepute, by satire, calumny, or criticism; as, to *attack* a man or his opinions in the newspapers.

3. To begin to perform; to undertake; to enter upon; as, to *attack* a piece of work.

4. To begin to destroy or affect injuriously; to seize; to cause to decompose or dissolve; as, he was *attacked* by malaria; restlessness *attacked* the community; sulphuric acid *attacks* zinc vigorously.

Syn.—Encounter, assail, assault, charge, invade, fall upon.

at-tack', *v.i.* To make an onset or beginning; as, to *attack* methodically.

at-tack', *n.* 1. The act of attacking; an onset; first invasion; a falling on with force or violence, or with calumny, satire, or criticism.

2. The offensive part in a contest; as, his *attack* was better than his defense.

3. In military matters, the body of men making an assault; as, the *attack* was composed of cavalry alone.

4. The beginning of any action or undertaking; the start; as the entering upon a piece of work.

5. Sickness or an affection of any kind.

6. Destructive action, as by a chemical agent.

Syn.—Assault, invasion, onset, inroad, charge.

at-tack'ȧ-ble, *a.* Open to attack; assailable.

at-tack'ẽr, *n.* One who assaults or invades.

at'tȧ-gen, at'tȧ-gas, *n.* [L. *attagena*, from Gr. *attagēn*, *attagas*, a bird.] Names variously applied by former naturalists, now designating several European birds, as the common partridge.

at'tȧ-ghan, *n.* See *Yataghan*.

at-tāin', *v.i.*; attained (-tānd'), *pt.*, *pp.*; attaining, *ppr.* [ME. *attainen*, *atteinen*; OFr. *ataindre*; L. *attingere*, to touch upon, attain; *ad*, to, and *tangere*, to touch.]

1. To reach; to come or arrive by motion, bodily exertion, or efforts toward a place or object.

If by any means they might *attain* to Phenice. —Acts xxvii. 12.

2. To reach; to come or arrive by an effort of mind.

Such knowledge is too wonderful for me; it is high; I cannot *attain* to it. —Ps. cxxxix. 6.

This verb is usually followed by *to* or *unto*.

at-tāin', *v.t.* 1. To gain; to compass; to achieve or accomplish, that is, to reach by efforts.

Is he wise who hopes to *attain* the end without the means? —Tillotson.

2. To reach or come to (a place or object) by progression or motion.

But ere such tidings shall his ears *attain*. —Hoole's Tasso.

3. To reach in excellence or degree; to equal.

4. To ascertain; to get possession of. [Obs.]

5. To overtake. [Obs.]

Syn.—Accomplish, acquire, compass, procure, achieve, reach, gain, get, earn, win.

at-tāin', *n.* Attainment; acquirement. [Obs.]

at-tāin-ȧ-bil'i-ty, *n.* Attainableness.

at-tāin'ȧ-ble, *a.* Capable of being attained.

at-tāin'ȧ-ble-ness, *n.* The quality of being attainable.

at-tāin'dẽr, *n.* [ME. *attayndere*; OFr. *ataindre*, *ateindre*, to accuse, convict, from L. *attingere*; *ad*, to, and *tangere*, to touch, attain.]

1. The act of attainting or state of being attainted; the legal consequences of judgment of death or outlawry pronounced in respect of treason or felony; as, a bill of *attainder*; to remove an *attainder*. By English common law, the consequences to the person attainted were forfeiture of lands, tenements, and hereditaments; corruption of blood, by which he could no longer inherit, or transmit an inheritance; and loss of reputation, and of civil rights generally. By modern English legislation the consequences of *attainder* are limited to the life of the person attainted. By the Constitution, no bill of *attainder* can be passed in the United States.

2. A bringing under some disgrace, stain, or imputation; a state of being in dishonor.

at-tāin'ment, *n.* 1. The act of attaining; the act of arriving at or reaching; hence, the act of obtaining by efforts; as, the *attainment* of excellence.

2. That which is attained to, or obtained by exertion; acquisition; applied especially in the plural to acquirements in an intellectual or moral way; as, a man of great *attainments*.

at-tāint', *v.t.*; attainted, *pt.*, *pp.*; attainting, *ppr.* [ME. *atāynten*, *atteinten*, to convict; OFr. *ateint*, pp. of *ateindre*, from L. *attingere*; *ad*, to, and *tangere*, to touch, fasten.]

1. To affect with attainder; to find guilty of a crime, as of felony or treason, involving forfeiture of civil privileges.

2. To convict; to taint the credit of, as jurors found guilty of giving a false verdict. [Obs.]

3. To disgrace; to cloud with infamy; to stain.

4. To taint or corrupt; to render unsound or unhealthy; to infect with some noxious quality.

5. To make a charge of crime or misconduct against; to accuse. [Rare.]

6. To reach; to touch. [Obs.]

at-tāint', *n.* 1. A stain, spot, or taint; especially some mark of personal dishonor or social corruption.

2. Anything injurious; that which impairs. [Obs.]

3. In farriery, a blow or wound on the legs or feet of a horse, from overreaching.

4. The conviction of a jury for the rendering of a false verdict; also, a writ issued after such conviction, reversing the original verdict.

at-tāint'ment, *n.* The state of being attainted, or the act of attainting; conviction; attainder.

at-tāin'tūre, *n.* A staining or rendering infamous; reproach; imputation; also, attainder.

at'tăl, *n.* See *Attle*.

At-tā'lē-ȧ, *n.* [L., from Gr. *Attalos*, a king of Pergamum.] A genus of palms belonging to the cocoanut family, found in tropical America. One species, *Attalea funifera*, yields a valuable fiber, the piassava.

at-tāme', *v.t.* 1. To begin. [Obs.]

2. To make an incision into. [Obs.]

at-tam'i-nāte, *v.t.* To contaminate. [Obs.]

at'tap, *n.* The Malay name for the nipa-palm.

at'tăr, *n.* [Pers. *'atar*, fragrance, from Ar. *'atara*, to smell sweet.] A highly fragrant essential oil obtained from flowers, especially from the petals of roses; also called *ottar*, or *otto*, *of roses*.

at-tȧsk', *v.t.* [Obs.] See *Task*.

at-tāste', *v.t.* [Obs.] See *Taste*.

at'tē. At the; an obsolete contraction.

at-tem'pẽr, *v.t.*; attempered, *pt.*, *pp.*; attempering, *ppr.* [ME. *attempren*; OFr. *atemprer*; L. *attemperare*, to fit, adjust; *ad*, to, and *temperare*, to control, moderate.]

1. To reduce, modify, or moderate by mixture; as, to *attemper* heat by a cooling mixture, or liquors by diluting with water.

2. To soften, mollify, or moderate; as, to *attemper* rigid justice with clemency.

3. To mix in just proportion; to regulate; as, a mind well *attempered* with kindness and justice.

4. To accommodate; to fit or make suitable.

Acts *attempered* to the lyre. —Pope.

In all senses, *temper* is now the commoner word.

at-tem'pẽr-ȧ-ment, *n.* A regulating or mixing in proper proportion.

at-tem'pẽr-ănce, *n.* Temperance. [Obs.]

at-tem′pẽr-āte, *a.* Tempered; proportioned; suited.

> Hope must be proportioned and *attemperate* to the promise. —Hammond.

at-tem′pẽr-āte, *v.t.* To attemper. [Obs.]

at-tem-pẽr-ā′tion, *n.* 1. The act of attempering, adjusting, or accommodating. [Obs.]

2. The act of regulating the temperature of the wort in brewing and distilling.

at-tem′pẽr-ly, *adv.* In a temperate manner. [Obs.]

at-tem′pẽr-ment, *n.* Attemperament.

at-tempt′, *v.t.*; attempted, *pt.*, *pp.*; attempting, *ppr.* [OFr. *atempter, attenter*; It. *attentare*; L. *attemptare, attentare*, to try, solicit; *ad*, to, and *temptare, tentare*, to try, attack.]

1. To make an effort to effect; to try; to endeavor to perform; to undertake; as, to *attempt* to sing; to *attempt* a bold flight.

2. To attack; to make an effort upon; as, to *attempt* the enemy's camp.

3. To make a trial or experiment of; to venture upon; as, to *attempt* the wilderness.

4. To make an assault upon the feelings or passions of; to try to win or seduce.

> He will never *attempt* us again. —Shak.

Syn.—Try, endeavor, essay, undertake, strive.

at-tempt′, *v.i.* To make an attack; to make an attempt. [Obs.]

at-tempt′, *n.* 1. An essay, trial, or endeavor; an effort to gain a point; particularly applied to an unsuccessful endeavor.

> The *attempt*, and not the deed, confounds us. —Shak.

2. An attack or assault; an endeavor to gain a point by force or violence; as, an *attempt* upon one's life.

3. In law, an act having for its ultimate object the accomplishment of something criminal.

Syn.—Effort, endeavor, essay, trial, enterprise, undertaking.

at-tempt′ȧ-ble, *a.* Able to be attempted, tried, or attacked; liable to an attempt, or attack.

at-tempt′ẽr, *n.* One who attempts or attacks.

at-tempt′ive, *a.* Inclined to make attempts; willing to venture. [Obs.]

at-tend′, *v.t.*; attended, *pt.*, *pp.*; attending, *ppr.* [OFr. *atendre*, to wait, expect; It. *attendere*; L. *attendere*, to stretch toward, give heed to; *ad*, to, and *tendere*, to stretch.]

1. To go with, or accompany, as a companion or servant; to be present with, for some duty, implying charge or oversight; to serve professionally; to wait on; to watch over or care for; as, a physician *attends* the sick; a large retinue *attended* the prince.

2. To be associated with; to accompany; to be consequent to, from connection of cause; as, fever *attends* a cold; a measure *attended* with ill effects.

3. To be present at, from some connection in affairs; as, lawyers or spectators *attend* a court.

4. To await; to remain, abide, or be in store for; as, happiness or misery *attends* us after death.

5. To regard; to fix the mind upon; to give attention to. [Obs.]

6. To wait for; to expect. [Obs.]

Syn.—Accompany, escort, serve, wait upon.

at-tend′, *v.i.* 1. To exercise attention; to pay regard or heed, often to pay such regard as combines with it compliance; mostly followed by *to*; as, my son, *attend to* my words.

> *Attend to* the voice of my supplications. —Ps. lxxxvi. 6.

2. To be present, in pursuance of duty; to act as an attendant; used by itself or followed by *on* or *upon*; as, who *attends* here? to *attend upon* a committee.

3. To wait on in worship; to serve.

> That ye may *attend upon* the Lord without distraction. —1 Cor. vii. 35.

4. To stay; to wait; to delay. [Obs.]

> For this perfection she must yet *attend*,
> Till to her Maker she espoused be.—Davies.

Syn.—Heed, listen, give regard to, observe.

at-tend′ănce, *n.* [ME. *attendaunce*; OFr. *atendance*; L. *attendantia*, from *attendens*(*-entis*), ppr. of *attendere*, to stretch toward, give heed; *ad*, to, and *tendere*, to stretch.]

1. The act of waiting on or serving; service; ministry; as, to receive *attendance*.

2. A being present on business of any kind; presence; as, the *attendance* of witnesses in court.

3. The persons attending; a train; a retinue.

4. Attention; regard; careful application of mind. [Obs.]

5. Expectation. [Obs.]

at-tend′ăn-cy, *n.* Attendance; a train or retinue. [Obs.]

at-tend′ănt, *a.* [Fr. *attendant*, ppr. of *attendre*, to wait, from L. *attendere*, to give heed; *ad*, to, and *tendere*, to stretch.]

1. Accompanying; being present, or in the train.

> Other suns with their *attendant* moons. —Milton.

2. Accompanying, connected with, or immediately following; consequential; as, intemperance with all its *attendant* evils.

3. In law, depending on, or owing duty or service to.

Attendant keys; in music, the keys or scales on the fifth above, and fifth below (or fourth above) any keynote or tonic, considered in relation to the key or scale on that tonic.

at-tend′ănt, *n.* 1. One who attends or accompanies in any character whatever, as a friend, companion, or servant; one who belongs to a train or retinue.

2. One who is present; as, an *attendant* at or upon a meeting.

3. In law, one who owes duty or service to, or depends on another.

4. That which accompanies or is consequent to.

> A love of fame, the *attendant* of noble spirits. —Pope.

at-tend′ẽr, *n.* One who attends; a companion; an associate. [Rare.]

at-tend′ment, *n.* An accompanying circumstance. [Obs.]

at-tent′, *a.* Attentive. [Obs.]

at-tent′, *n.* Attention; as, due *attent*. [Obs.]

at-ten′tāte, at-ten′tat, *n.* [Fr. *attentat*; L. *attentatum*, a crime, from *attentare*, to attempt; *ad*, to, and *tentare*, to try, attack.]

1. An assault. [Obs.]

2. In law, (a) a proceeding in a court of judicature, pending suit, and after an inhibition is decreed; (b) a thing done after an extra judicial appeal.

at-ten′tion, *n.* 1. The act of attending or heeding; the due application of the mind to any object presented for contemplation; mental concentration.

> They say, the tongues of dying men
> Enforce *attention* like deep harmony.—Shak.

2. An act of civility, courtesy, or gallantry; said especially of a lover; as, he paid her very marked *attention*.

3. The word of command given to soldiers to prepare them for the performance of any exercise or evolution; also, the attitude taken at such command.

Syn. — Application, heed, consideration, study, watchfulness.

at-ten′tive, *a.* 1. Heedful; intent; observant; regarding with care. It is applied to the senses of hearing and seeing, as, an *attentive* ear or eye; to the application of the mind, as in contemplation; or to the application of the mind, together with the senses above-mentioned, as when a person is *attentive* to the words, and to the manner and matter of a speaker, at the same time.

2. Characterized by thoughtful regard or attention; courteous; polite.

Syn.—Careful, thoughtful, heedful, mindful, intent, observant, watchful.

at-ten′tive-ly, *adv.* Heedfully; carefully; with fixed attention.

at-ten′tive-ness, *n.* The state of being attentive; heedfulness; attention.

at-tent′ly, *adv.* Attentively. [Obs.]

at-ten′ū-ănt, *a.* [Fr. *atténuant*; L. *attenuans*, ppr. of *attenuare*, to make thin.] Making thin, as fluids; diluting; rendering less dense and viscid.

at-ten′ū-ănt, *n.* A medicine that thins the fluids; a diluent.

at-ten′ū-āte, *v.t.*; attenuated, *pt.*, *pp.*; attenuating, *ppr.* [L. *attenuatus*, pp. of *attenuare*, to make thin; *ad*, to, and *tenuare*, from *tenuis*, thin.]

1. To make thin or less consistent; to render less viscid.

2. To comminute; to break or wear solid substances into finer or very minute parts; as, to *attenuate* rocks.

3. To make slender; to reduce in thickness.

at-ten′ū-āte, *v.i.* To become thin, slender, or fine; to diminish; to lessen.

at-ten′ū-āte, at-ten′ū-ā-ted, *a.* 1. Made thin or less viscid; comminuted; made slender.

2. In botany, growing slender toward an extremity.

at-ten-ū-ā′tion, *n.* [L. *attenuatio*, from *attenuare*, to make thin.]

1. The act of making thin, as fluids or gases.

2. The act of making fine, by comminution or attrition; pulverization, as of rocks.

3. The act or process of making slender, thin, or lean.

4. The act or process of lessening in intensity or virulence, as of medicine or of virus.

5. In brewing, the change which takes place in the saccharine worts during fermentation by the sugar being converted into alcohol and carbonic acid.

at′tẽr, *n.* [AS. *ættor*, poison.] Poison; venom; pus. [Obs.]

at′tẽr-āte, *v.t.* Same as *Atterrate*.

at-tẽr-ā′tion, *n.* Same as *Atterration*.

at′tẽr-çop, *n.* [ME. *attercop*; AS. *attercoppe*; *ator*, poison, and *cop*, head, lungs.]

1. A spider. [Obs.]

2. A testy, ill-natured person. [Prov. Eng.]

at-tẽr′mi-năl, *a.* Same as *Adterminal*.

at′tẽr-rāte, at′tẽr-āte, *v.t.*; atterrated, *pt.*, *pp.*; atterrating, *ppr.* [L. *atterratus*, pp. of *atterrare*, to carry earth to another place; *ad*, to, and *terra*, earth.]

1. To wear away. [Obs.]

2. To form with alluvial earth. [Obs.]

at-tẽr-rā′tion, at-tẽr-ā′tion, *n.* The operation of forming land by deposition. [Obs.]

at-test′, *v.t.*; attested, *pt.*, *pp.*; attesting, *ppr.* [Fr. *attester*, from L. *attestari*, to bear witness to; *ad*, to, and *testis*, a witness.]

1. To bear witness to; to certify; to affirm to be true or genuine; to make a solemn declaration, in words or writing, for the support of; as, to *attest* the truth of a writing; to *attest* a copy of record.

2. To bear witness to, or support the truth of a fact, by other evidence than words; as, the ruins of Palmyra *attest* its ancient magnificence.

3. To call to witness; to invoke. [Obs.]

> Streams which heaven's imperial state
> *Attests* in oaths, and fears to violate. —Dryden.

at-test′, *n.* Witness; testimony; attestation. [Rare.]

at-tes-tā′tion, *n.* Testimony; witness; a solemn or official declaration, verbal or written, in support of a fact; evidence.

at-test′ȧ-tive, *a.* Serving to attest or corroborate.

at-test′ẽr, at-test′ŏr, *n.* One who attests.

at-test′ive, *a.* Giving attestation; attesting.

At′tiç, *a.* [L. *Atticus*; Gr. *Attikos*.] Pertaining to Attica, in Greece, or to its principal city, Athens; marked by such qualities as were characteristic of the Athenians.

Attic base; a peculiar base used by the ancient architects in the Ionic and Corinthian orders, and by Palladio and some others in the Doric, and revived during the Renaissance.

Attic dialect; the dialect of the ancient Greek language used by the Athenians; the purest Greek.

Attic faith; inviolable faith.

Attic order; an order of small square pillars placed by Athenian architects at the uppermost parts of a building.

Attic style; a style pure, classical, and elegant.

Attic wit, Attic salt; a poignant, delicate wit, peculiar to the Athenians.

at′tiç, *n.* [Fr. *attique*; It. *attico*, an attic; from L. *Atticus*, Attic.]

1. A low story erected over a principal one, generally decorated with pilasters and a cornice, but having neither capital nor base.

A, Attic.

2. A story in the upper part of a house, immediately beneath the roof; a garret.

3. [A—] An Athenian; an Athenian author.

At′tiç-ăl, *a.* Pertaining to Athens; pure, classical.

At′ti-çişm, *n.* [Gr. *Attikismos*, a siding with Athens, Attic style, from *Attikos*, Attic.]

1. The peculiar style and idiom of the Greek language, used by the Athenians; refined and elegant Greek; concise and elegant expression.

2. A particular attachment to or taking the part of the Athenians; specifically applied to the act of siding with the Athenians during the Peloponnesian war.

At′ti-çize, *v.t.*; Atticized, *pt.*, *pp.*; Atticizing, *ppr.* To conform or make conformable to the language or idiom of Attica; thus, the adjective ending *-os*, when *Atticized*, becomes *-ōs*.

At′ti-çize, *v.i.* 1. To use Atticisms, or the idiom of the Athenians.

2. To side with the Athenians, or to subserve the interests of Athens.

at-tig′ū-ous, *a.* [L. *attiguus*, from *attingere*, to touch.] Near; adjoining; contiguous. [Obs.]

at-tig′ū-ous-ness, *n.* The state of being attiguous. [Obs.]

at-tinge′, *v.t.* [L. *attingere*, to touch.] To touch lightly. [Obs.]

at-tire′, *v.t.*; attired, *pt.*, *pp.*; attiring, *ppr.* [ME. *atiren*; OFr. *atirer*, put in order, arrange, from *a tire*, in a row, in order; *a*, L. *ad*, to, and *tire*, order, row, dress.] To dress; to array; to adorn; particularly, to adorn with elegant or splendid garments.

With the linen mitre shall he be *attired.* —Lev. xvi. 4.

at-tīre′, *n.* 1. Dress; clothes; habit; especially, rich ornamental dress.

Can a bride forget her *attire?* —Jer. ii. 32.

2. In heraldry, a term applied to the horns of stags and similar animals in blazoning arms.

3. In botany, a name formerly applied to the stamens.

at-tīred′, *a.* In heraldry, provided with antlers or headgear.

at-tīre′ment, *n.* Attire.

at-tīr′ẽr, *n.* One who adorns with attire.

at′ti-tūde, *n.* [Fr. *attitude*; It. *attitudine*, attitude, aptness; L. *aptitudo*, from *aptus*, fitted, from *apere*, to fasten, join.]

1. The posture or position of a person, or the manner in which the parts of his body are disposed, particularly in relation to some purpose or emotion; as, a threatening *attitude*; an *attitude* of entreaty.

2. Figuratively, position resulting from feeling, mood, or condition; as, a nation's *attitude*; one's mental *attitude*.

3. In painting and sculpture, the posture in which a figure is placed, expressing the action and sentiments of the person represented.

To strike an attitude; to pose for effect.

Syn.—Situation, standing, position, posture, pose.

at-ti-tū′di-năl, *a.* Pertaining to attitude.

at-ti-tū-di-nā′ri-ăn, *n.* One who gives particular attention to attitudes.

at-ti-tū-di-nā′ri-ăn-ism, *n.* The practice of using studied or affected attitudes.

at-ti-tū′di-nize, *v.i.*; attitudinized, *pt.*, *pp.*; attitudinizing, *ppr.* To practise or assume attitudes.

They had the air of figurantes, *attitudinizing* for effect. —De Quincey.

at-ti-tū′di-nī-zẽr, *n.* One who poses.

at′tle, **at′tăl**, *n.* [Corn., refuse, waste.] In mining, refuse containing no ore worth extraction.

at-tol′lent, *a.* [L. *attollens*, ppr. of *attollere*; *ad*, to, and *tollere*, to lift.] Lifting up; raising; as, an *attollent* muscle.

at-tol′lent, *n.* A muscle which raises some part; a levator or elevator. [Rare.]

at-tŏnce′, *adv.* At once; at the same time. [Obs.]

at-tŏrn′, *v.t.*; attorned, *pt.*, *pp.*; attorning, *ppr.* [OFr. *attorner*; L. *attornare*, to commit business to another; *ad*, to, and *tornare*, to turn.]

1. In law, to turn over; to assign to another; to transfer.

2. In feudal law, to turn or transfer, as homage or service, to a new possessor, and accept tenancy under him.

at-tŏr′ney, *n.* [ME. *atturny*; OFr. *attorne*, *atorne*; L. *attornatus*, pp. of *attornare*, to commit business to another.] One who is legally appointed by another to transact any business for him. An *attorney* is either public or private. A *private attorney* is a person appointed by another, by a letter or power of attorney, to transact any business for him out of court. A *public attorney*, or attorney at law, is an officer of a court of law, legally qualified to prosecute and defend actions in such court, on the retainer of clients or order of the court. An *attorney* is commonly known as a lawyer. He may have general powers to transact business for another; or his powers may be special, or limited to a particular act or acts. In Great Britain, *attorneys* are not admitted to plead at the bar, or to be advocates or counsel, in the higher courts; this privilege being confined to barristers or counsel.

A power, letter, or *warrant of attorney*; a written authority from one person empowering another to transact business for him.

at-tŏr′ney, *v.t.* To perform by proxy; to employ as a proxy. [Obs.]

at-tŏr′ney-gen″ẽr-ăl, *n.* [*Pl.* attorney-generals or attorneys-general.] 1. The highest officer of the law of a state or nation.

2. In England, the public prosecutor on behalf of the crown, having general powers to act in all legal proceedings in which the crown is a party, particularly to prosecute in criminal matters affecting the state.

3. In the United States, (a) a member of the cabinet whose duties are those connected with the portfolio of justice; the trying of such Supreme Court cases as affect the government, and the legal advising of the President and members of his cabinet; (b) an elective officer of each state, having duties analogous to those of the United States *attorney-general*.

at-tŏr′ney-ism, *n.* Shrewdness or unscrupulousness commonly ascribed to attorneys.

at-tŏr′ney-ship, *n.* The office or duties of an attorney; agency for another.

at-tŏrn′ment, *n.* [OFr. *attornment*, from *attorner*; L. *attornare*, to commit business to another.] The act of a feudatory, vassal, or tenant, by which he consents, upon the alienation of an estate, to receive a new lord or superior, and transfers to him his homage and service. —Blackstone.

at-traçt′, *v.t.*; attracted, *pt.*, *pp.*; attracting, *ppr.* [L. *attractus*, pp. of *attrahere*, to draw to; *ad*, to, and *trahere*, to draw.]

1. To draw to or toward; to exert the power of attraction on; to cause or tend to cause to move toward and cohere to or unite with; as, all physical bodies mutually *attract* each other.

2. To draw by influence of a moral kind; to invite or allure; to engage; as, to *attract* admirers; to *attract* attention.

Syn.—Draw, allure, invite, entice.

at-traçt′, *n.* Attraction. [Obs.]

at-traçt-ȧ-bil′i-ty, *n.* The quality of being attractable or of being subject to the law of attraction.

at-traçt′ȧ-ble, *a.* That may be attracted; subject to attraction.

at-traçt′ȧ-ble-ness, *n.* The state or quality of being susceptible to attraction.

at-traçt′ẽr, *n.* One who attracts; that which attracts.

at-traçt′ile, *a.* Having attractive power.

at-traçt′ing-ly, *adv.* In an attracting manner.

at-traç′tion, *n.* [L. *attractio*, from *attrahere*, to draw to; *ad*, to, and *trahere*, to draw.]

1. In physics, the tendency, force, or forces through which all particles of matter, as well as all individual masses of matter, are attracted or drawn towards each other; the inherent tendency in bodies to approach each other, to unite, and to resist separation.

2. The act of attracting; the effect of the principle of attraction.

3. The power or act of alluring, drawing to, inviting, or engaging; as, the *attraction* of beauty or eloquence.

4. Anything exerting an attractive force or influence; as, the *attraction* of pleasure.

Adhesive attraction; see *Adhesion.*

Attraction of gravitation; see *Gravitation.*

Capillary attraction; a form of cohesion between a solid and a liquid meeting it, by which the latter rises; also, the phenomena so produced. [See *Capillary.*]

Chemical attraction or *affinity*; the force which is exerted between molecules not of the same kind, as when two molecules of hydrogen unite with one molecule of oxygen to form water.

Cohesive attraction; the force uniting adjacent molecules of the same nature; cohesion.

Magnetic, diamagnetic, and *electrical attraction*; similar attractive polar forces dependent upon certain conditions of matter.

Syn.—Allurement, charm, fascination, inclination, tendency.

at-traç′tion-sphēre, *n.* A minute globule adjacent to the nucleus of the greater number of cells, supposed to be directly related to the phenomena of cell-division.

at-traçt′ive, *a.* [Fr. *attractif.*]

1. Having the power or quality of attracting; drawing to; as, the *attractive* force of bodies.

2. Drawing to by moral influence; alluring; inviting; engaging; as, the *attractive* graces.

at-traçt′ive, *n.* An attraction.

at-traçt′ive-ly, *adv.* In an attractive manner.

at-traçt′ive-ness, *n.* The quality of being attractive or engaging.

at-traç-tiv′i-ty, *n.* The measure of the attractive power of an object.

at-traçt′ŏr, *n.* A person or thing that attracts.

at′trā-hent, *a.* [L. *attrahens*, ppr. of *attrahere*, to draw to; *ad*, to, and *trahere*, to draw.] Drawing to; attracting.

at′trā-hent, *n.* 1. That which draws to or attracts, as a magnet.

2. In medicine, an application that attracts fluids to the part where it is applied, as a blister or a rubefacient.

at-trap′, *v.t.* To clothe; to dress; to adorn with trappings. [Obs.]

at-trap′, *v.t.* [Fr. *attraper*, to trap, insnare; *a*, L. *ad*, to, and *trappe*, trap.] To catch in a trap. [Obs.]

at-treç-tā′tion, *n.* [L. *attrectatio*, from *ad* and *tractare*, to handle.] Frequent handling. [Obs.]

at-trib′ū-tȧ-ble, *a.* Capable of attribution.

at-trib′ūte, *v.t.*; attributed, *pt.*, *pp.*; attributing, *ppr.* [L. *attributus*, pp. of *attribuere*, to assign; *ad*, to, and *tribuere*, assign, give.] To ascribe; to impute; to consider as belonging or as due; to assign.

Faulty men use oftentimes
To *attribute* their folly unto fate. —Spenser.

Syn.—Ascribe, impute, assign, refer, charge.

at′tri-būte, *n.* [L. *attributum*, attribute, predicate, from *attribuere*, to assign, ascribe.]

1. Any property, quality, or characteristic that can be ascribed to a person or thing; as, strength and bravery are two of his *attributes.*

But mercy is above this sceptered sway; . . .
It is an *attribute* to God himself. —Shak.

2. In grammar, the word that expresses what is affirmed concerning another, as an adjective; an attributive.

3. A term descriptive of an attribute or quality, or of a combination of such. [Rare.]

4. In the fine arts, a symbol of office or character added to any figure; thus, the eagle is the *attribute* of Jupiter, a club of Hercules, the bow and arrow of Love.

The ladder is a striking *attribute* for the patriarch Jacob, and the harp for King David. —Fairholt.

5. Reputation; honor. [Obs.]

Much *attribute* he hath; and much the reason
Why we ascribe it to him. —Shak.

Syn.—Property, quality, characteristic, attainment.

at-tri-bū′tion, *n.* 1. The act of attributing.

2. That which is ascribed; attribute; function.

3. Commendation; praise. [Obs.]

at-trib′ū-tive, *a.* Pertaining to or expressing an attribute, as, an *attributive* word.

at-trib′ū-tive, *n.* In grammar, a modifying word expressing an attribute; also, a phrase used adjectively or adverbially.

at-trib′ū-tive-ly, *adv.* In an attributive manner.

at-trīte′, *a.* [L. *attritus*, pp. of *atterere*, to wear, rub away; *ad*, to, and *terere*, to rub.]

1. Worn by rubbing or friction.

2. In theology, repentant only from fear of punishment.

at-tri′tion (-trish′un), *n.* [Fr. *attrition*; L. *attritio*, a rubbing; from *attritus*, pp. of *atterere*, to rub, wear away.]

1. Abrasion; the act of wearing by friction, or by rubbing substances together; as, the *attrition* of rocks.

2. The state of being worn.

3. In theology, grief for sin, arising only from fear of punishment; the lowest degree of repentance.

at-trī′tus, *n.* Finely ground or powdered matter resulting from attrition.

at′try, *a.* Venomous. [Obs.]

at-tūne′, *v.t.*; attuned, *pt.*, *pp.*; attuning, *ppr.*

1. To tune, or put in tune; to adjust one sound to another; to make accordant; as, to *attune* the voice to a harp.

2. To make musical. [Obs.]

Vernal airs *attune* the trembling leaves. —Milton.

3. Figuratively, to arrange fitly; to make accordant; as, to *attune* the thoughts.

ȧ-twāin′, *adv.* In twain; asunder. [Obs.]

ȧ-tween′, *adv.* and *prep.* Between. [Obs.]

ȧ-twīrl′, *a.* and *adv.* Twirling; in a twirl.

ȧ-twist′, *a.* and *adv.* Awry; twisted. [Rare.]

ȧ-twīte′, *v.t.* To reproach; to twit. [Obs.]

ȧ-twixt′, *adv.* Betwixt. [Obs.]

ȧ-twō′ (-tö′), *adv.* In two. [Obs.]

ȧ-typ′iç, **ȧ-typ′iç-ăl**, *a.* [Gr. *atypos*; *a* priv., and *typos*, type.] Having no type; devoid of typical character; irregular; in medicine, said of certain intermittent fevers.

au-bāde′ (ō-bäd′), *n.* [Fr., from *aube*, dawn.] Open-air music performed in the morning, distinguished from *serenade.*

au-bāin′ (ō-băn′), *n.* [Fr., from L. *albanus*, an alien; *alibi*, elsewhere, and *-anus.*] An alien liable to *droit d'aubaine.*

au-bāine′ (ō-bān′), *n.* In French law, the disposition of the goods of a deceased alien.

Droit d'aubaine; the king's right—not in force since 1819—to the personal property of an alien dying in France.

ąube, *n.* An alb. [Obs.]

ąu-bẽrge′ (*or* ō-bärzh′), *n.* [Fr.] An inn.

ąu′bẽr-gine (*or* ō-bär-zhēn′), *n.* [Fr.] The egg-plant or its fruit.

ąu′bũrn, *a.* [ME. *auburne*; OFr. *auborne*, *alborne*; L. *alburnus*, from *albus*, white.] Originally, whitish or flaxen-colored; now, reddish brown; generally applied to hair.

ąu-chē′ni-um, *n.* [L., from Gr. *auchēn*, neck.] In ornithology, the scruff of the neck, below the nape. [Rare.]

ąuç′tā-ry, *n.* Augmentation. [Obs.]

ąuç′tion, *n.* [L. *auctio*, an increasing, a public sale, from *augere*, to increase.]

1. A public sale of property to the highest bidder, usually by a person licensed and authorized for the purpose.

2. The property sold or offered for sale at auction. [Obs.]

Dutch auction; an auction in which a certain price is set, and lowered by the auctioneer until a bid is received, the first bidder becoming the buyer.

Auction pitch; a card game in which the players bid for the privilege of pitching trump; also called *smear.*

ąuç′tion, *v.t.* To sell by or at auction.

ąuç′tion-ā-ry, *a.* Pertaining to an auction or public sale. [Rare.]

ąuç-tion-eer′, *n.* One whose business it is to cry sales at auction; one licensed to sell property at public sale.

auc-tion-eer′, *v.t.*; auctioneered, *pt.*, *pp.*; auctioneering, *ppr.* To sell at auction.

Au′cū-bȧ, *n.* [L., from Japan. *aoki*, green, and *ba*, leaf.] A genus of plants of the dogwood family, natural order *Cornaceæ*, consisting of six species from eastern Asia. They are branching shrubs, with smooth opposite leaves and small unisexual flowers. *Aucuba Japonica* has been long in cultivation, and is prized for its mass of glossy leathery-green leaves mottled with yellow, and its coral-red berries.

au-cū-pā′tion, *n.* [L. *aucupatio*, from *aucupari*, to go bird-catching; *auceps*, *aucupis*, a bird-catcher, from *avis*, a bird, and *capere*, to take.] The art or practice of taking birds; fowling; bird-catching. [Obs.]

au-dā′cious, *a.* [Fr. *audacieux*; L. *audacia*, from *audax*, bold, from *audere*, to be bold, to dare.]

1. Very bold or daring; impudent; contemning the restraints of law, religion, or decorum; bold in wickedness; applied to persons; as, an *audacious* wretch.

2. Committed with, or proceeding from, daring effrontery, or contempt of law; as, an *audacious* crime.

3. Bold; fearless.

Syn.—Impudent, insolent, shameless, unabashed, daring, bold.

au-dā′cious-ly, *adv.* In an impudent manner; with excess of boldness.

au-dā′cious-ness, *n.* The quality of being audacious; impudence; audacity.

au-dac′i-ty, *n.* [L. *audax*, bold, from *audere*, to be bold, dare.]

1. Boldness; daring spirit; venturesomeness; resolution; confidence; used indifferently either in a good or bad sense.

> The freedom and *audacity* necessary in the commerce of men. —Tatler.

2. Audaciousness; presumptuous impudence; effrontery; in a bad sense, and often implying a contempt of law or moral restraint; as, arrogant *audacity*.

Syn.—Boldness, effrontery, impudence, hardihood.

Au′di-ăn, *n.* A follower of Audius, a Syrian of the fourth century, who held that God had a body in the image of which that of man was created.

Au′di-ăn-ism, *n.* Anthropomorphism; or the doctrine of Audius. [See *Audian*.]

au-di-bil′i-ty, *n.* Audibleness.

au′di-ble, *a.* [L. *audibilis*, from *audire*, to hear.] That may be heard; perceivable by the ear; loud enough to be heard; as, an *audible* voice or whisper.

au′di-ble, *n.* Anything that may be heard. [Rare.]

au′di-ble-ness, *n.* The quality of being audible.

au′di-bly, *adv.* In an audible manner; in a manner so as to be heard.

au′di-ence, *n.* [ME. *audience*; OFr. *audience*; L. *audientia*, a hearing, listening, from *audiens*, ppr. of *audire*, to hear.]

1. The act of hearing, or attending to sounds.

> His bold discourse had *audience*. —Milton.

2. Admittance to a hearing; reception to an interview, especially with a sovereign or the head of a government, for conference or the transaction of business; as, the senator had an *audience* of the president.

3. An auditory; an assembly of hearers.

Court of audience; an English ecclesiastical court formerly held before an archbishop or the dean of the arches, as his representative; also written *audience-court*.

In general audience; in public.

To give audience; to grant an interview.

au′di-ence-chām″bẽr, *n.* An apartment for an audience or formal meeting.

au′di-ence-cōurt, *n.* See *Court of audience*, under *Audience*.

au′di-ent, *a.* [L. *audiens*, ppr. of *audire*, to hear.] Listening; attentive; hearing.

au′di-ent, *n.* A hearer. [Obs.]

au′dile, *n.* One who is especially acute of hearing.

au-di-om′e-tẽr, *n.* [L. *audire*, to hear, and *metrum*, Gr. *metron*, measure.] An instrument for determining the acuteness of hearing.

au′di-phōne, *n.* See *Dentiphone*.

au′dit, *n.* [L. *auditus*, a hearing, from *audire*, to hear.]

1. An examination of an account or of accounts, with the hearing of the parties concerned, by proper officers, or persons appointed for that purpose, who compare the charges with the vouchers, examine witnesses, and report the result.

2. The result of such an examination, or an account as adjusted by auditors; a final account.

3. The act of having audience. [Obs.]

au′dit, *v.t.*; audited, *pt.*, *pp.*; auditing, *ppr.* To make an audit of; to examine.

au′dit, *v.i.* To check an account; to act as an auditor.

au′dit-āle, *n.* A kind of ale specially brewed at some English colleges, and originally broached for the first time on audit-day, which was made an occasion of festivity.

au′dit-house, *n.* An appendage to a cathedral, in which the business belonging to it is transacted. [Eng.]

au-di′tion (-dish′un), *n.* A hearing; the sense of hearing.

au′di-tive, *a.* Having the power of hearing.

au′di-tŏr, *n.* [L. *auditor*, a hearer, from *audire*, to hear.]

1. A hearer; one who listens, as to a lecture, concert, etc.

2. A person appointed and authorized to examine an account or accounts; specifically, a national, state, or county officer whose duty it is to audit the accounts of the nation, state, or county.

3. Ecclesiastically, a judicial hearer, as in an audience-court.

au-di-tō′ri-ăl, *a.* Auditory; also, relating to an auditor.

au-di-tō′ri-um, *n.* [L. *auditorium*, neut. of *auditorius*, of or for hearing.]

1. In an opera-house, public hall, and the like, the space allotted to the hearers.

2. An apartment in monasteries for the reception of strangers.

3. A building used for public purposes, usually large, and distinguished from a theater by being chiefly used for public meetings, etc.

au′di-tŏr-ship, *n.* The office of auditor.

au′di-tō-ry, *a.* [L. *auditorius*, from *auditor*, a hearer; *audire*, to hear.] Relating to hearing or to the sense or organs of hearing; as, the *auditory* nerve.

Auditory passage; the passage of entrance into the ear, which conveys the sound to the auditory nerve.

Auditory nerve; the eighth cranial nerve, supplying the internal ear; formerly, the portio mollis of the seventh pair of cranial nerves.

au′di-tō-ry, *n.* 1. An assembly of hearers, as in a church.

2. An auditorium; specifically, in ancient churches, the nave where the hearers stood to be instructed.

> When Agrippa and Bernice entered into the *auditory*. —Acts xxv. 23, Wyclif's Trans.

3. A bench on which a judge sits to hear causes. [Obs.]

au′di-tress, *n.* A female hearer.

au-dit′ū-ăl, *a.* Auditory. [Rare.]

auf, *n.* A fool; a simpleton. [See *Oaf*.]

au fait (ō fā). [Fr., lit. to the fact; *au*, to the, and *fait*, from L. *factum*, fact.] Skilled; accomplished; equal to the mastery of anything.

Au-gē′ăn, *a.* 1. In Grecian mythology, of or relating to Augeas, one of the Argonauts, and afterward king of Elis.

2. Resembling the stables of Augeas; hence, extremely filthy; foul; corrupt.

Augean stables; the stables of Augeas, containing 3,000 oxen and uncleaned for thirty years, but cleaned by Hercules in a day by diverting the river Alpheus through them.

au′gẽr, *n.* [ME. *nauger*, *naugor*, *navegor*; AS. *nafegār*; *nafa*, *nafu*, the nave of a wheel, and *gār*, a spear, bore.]

Augers.

1. An instrument used for boring holes in wood, or other soft substances. It is used by carpenters, shipwrights, joiners, wheelwrights, and cabinetmakers. It consists of a wooden handle and an iron shank, with a steel bit terminating it at the bottom.

2. A large, three-piece boring-tool, consisting of a handle, extensible rod, and cutting-piece, used for boring in the earth.

au′gẽr-bit, *n.* An auger fitted for using with a brace.

au-get′ (*or* ō-zhā′), *n.* [Fr., dim. of *auge*, a trough, from L. *alveus*, hollow, a trough; *alvus*, belly.] A tube filled with powder and extending from the chamber of a mine to the extremity of the gallery; used in exploding mines.

aught (at), *n.* [ME. *aught*; AS. *awiht*; *a*, *an*, one, and *wiht*, a creature, thing.]

1. Anything, indefinitely.

> But go, my son, and see if *aught* be wanting. —Addison.

2. Any part, the smallest; a jot or tittle.

aught (at), **aucht** (at), *n.* [ME. *aught*, *auhte*, *ahte*; AS. *æht*, from *agan*, to own.] Property, possession. [Scot.]

aught, *adv.* At all; in any manner.

au′gīte, *n.* See *Pyroxene*.

au-git′ic, *a.* Of, relating to, or containing augite.

au-gi-toph′y-ric (-tof′), *a.* [Gr. *augitēs*, from *augē*, brightness, and *porphyritic*.] Containing porphyritic crystals of augite.

aug-ment′, *v.t.*; augmented, *pt.*, *pp.*; augmenting, *ppr.* [Fr. *augmenter*; L. *augmentare*, from *augmentum*, increase; *augere*, to increase.]

1. To increase; to enlarge in size or extent; to swell; to make bigger; as, to *augment* an army by reinforcement; impatience *augments* an evil.

2. In grammar, to add an augment to; as, the Greek language *augments* certain tenses of the indicative.

aug-ment′, *v.i.* To increase; to grow larger; as, a stream *augments* by rain.

aug′ment, *n.* 1. Increase; enlargement by addition; state of increase.

2. In grammar, a syllable prefixed to a word; or an increase of the quantity of the initial vowel.

3. In medicine, the increase of a disease, or the period intervening between its attack and height.

aug-ment′ȧ-ble, *a.* That may be increased; capable of augmentation.

aug-men-tā′tion, *n.* 1. The act of increasing, or making larger, by addition, expansion, or dilatation.

2. The state of being increased or enlarged.

3. The thing added by which some other thing is enlarged.

4. In music, a doubling the value of the notes of the subject of a fugue or canon.

5. In heraldry, an additional charge to a coat-armor, often as a mark of honor, and generally borne on the escutcheon or a canton.

6. In medicine, the period of a fever between its commencement and its height.

7. In botany, a greater number than normal, as of petals or sepals; multiplication.

Syn.—Accession, expansion, enlargement, extension, increase, addition.

aug-ment′ȧ-tive, *n.* A derivative expressing more force than the original word; as, *drunkard*, one who is drunk habitually.

aug-ment′ȧ-tive, *a.* Having the quality or power of augmenting.

aug-ment′ȧ-tive-ly, *adv.* In an augmentative manner.

aug-ment′ẽr, *n.* One who or that which augments.

au′grim, *n.* [Obs.] See *Algorism*.

au′grim-stōnes, *n.pl.* Stones or counters formerly used to aid in arithmetical calculation.

au′gūr, *n.* [L. *augur*, perhaps from *avis*, a bird, and *gar*; Sans. *gar*, to call.]

1. Among the Romans, an officer whose duty was to foretell future events by the singing, chattering, flight, and feeding of birds, or by other signs or omens, derived from celestial phenomena, appearances of quadrupeds, or certain accidents. There was a college or community of *augurs*, originally three in number, and afterward nine, four patricians and five plebeians. They bore each a staff or wand, and were held in great respect.

Cæsar as an Augur.—From a Roman bas-relief.

2. One who pretends to foretell future events by omens.

> We all know that *augur* cannot look at *augur* without laughing. —Buckminster.

au′gūr, *v.i.*; augured (-gūrd) *pt.*, *pp.*; auguring, *ppr.* To guess; to conjecture by signs or omens; to prognosticate.

au′gūr, *v.t.* To predict or foretell; as, to *augur* ill success.

Syn.—Predict, forebode, betoken, portend, presage.

au′gū-răl, *a.* [L. *auguralis*, from *augur*, an augur.] Pertaining to augurs or to augury; as, *augural* consultations.

au′gū-rāte, *v.i.* [L. *auguratus*, pp. of *augurare*, to augur.] To judge by augury; to predict. [Obs.]

au′gū-rāte, *n.* An augurship.

au-gū-rā′tion, *n.* The practice of augury.

au′gūr-ẽr, *n.* An augur. [Obs.]

au-gū′ri-ăl, *a.* Relating to augurs, or to augury.

au′gū-rist, *n.* An augur.

au′gūr-ize, *v.t.* To augur. [Obs.]

au′gū-rous, *a.* Predicting; foretelling; foreboding. [Obs.]

au′gūr-ship, *n.* The office, or period of office, of an augur.

au′gū-ry, *n.*; *pl.* **au′gū-ries**. [L. *augurium*, divination, from *augur*, an augur.]

1. The art or practice of foretelling events by signs or omens.

> She knew by *augury* divine. —Swift.

2. That which forebodes; that from which a prediction is drawn; a prognostication.

Sad *auguries* of winter thence she drew.
—Dryden.

au-gust′, *a.* Grand; magnificent; majestic; impressing awe; inspiring reverence; as, *august* in visage.

Au′gust, *n.* [ME. *August, Augst*; L. *Augustus*; named from Emperor Augustus; name originally from *augere*, to increase.] The eighth month of the year, containing thirty-one days. The old Roman name was *Sextilis*, the sixth month from March, the month in which the primitive Romans, as well as Jews, began the year. The name was changed to *August* in honor of the emperor Octavius Augustus, on account of his victories and his entering on his first consulate in that month.

Au-gus′tăn, *a.* 1. Pertaining to Augustus Cæsar; as, the *Augustan* age.

2. Pertaining to the town Augusta Vindelicorum, now Augsburg; as, the *Augustan* Confession.

Augustan age; the most brilliant period in Roman literature; hence, in any national literature, the supposed period of its highest state of purity and refinement. So the reign of Louis XIV. has been called the *Augustan age* of French literature, and that of Queen Anne the *Augustan age* of English literature.

Augustan Confession; the confession drawn up at Augsburg, by Luther and Melanchthon, in 1530, and containing the principles of the Protestants and their reasons for separating from the Roman Catholic church.

Au-gus′tin, Au-gus′tine, Au-gus-tin′i-ăn, *n.* One of an order of monks, called after St. Augustine, and also called *Austin* friars.

Au-gus-tin′i-ăn, *a.* Pertaining to St. Augustine or the doctrines he originated.

Augustinian canons; an order of monks formerly numerous and popular in England and Ireland.

Augustinian hermits; an order of austere mendicant friars originally hermits, who were congregated into a body in 1265.

Augustinian nuns; an order of nuns who wait on the sick. The Hotel Dieu of Paris is served by them.

Augustinian rules; a set of rules governing religious orders, based on the letters of St. Augustine.

Au-gus-tin′i-ăn, *n.* [L. *Augustinus*, pertaining to Augustus.] One of those divines, who, from St. Augustine, maintain that grace is effectual from its nature, absolutely and morally, not relatively and gradually.

Au-gus-tin′i-ăn-ism, Au-gus′tin-ism, *n.* The doctrines of St. Augustine; the practices of the Augustinians.

au-gust′ly, *adv.* In an august manner.

au-gust′ness, *n.* Dignity of mien; grandeur; magnificence.

auk, *n.* [Prov. Eng. *alk*, from Ice. *alka.*] A popular name applied to different species of aquatic birds of the genus *Alca* and order *Anseres*; as, the great *auk* or northern penguin; the little *auk* or black and white diver; the Labrador *auk* or puffin, and the razorbill, *Alca torda*.

Razorbill (*Alca torda*).

auk′let, *n.* One of several species of small auks, among them the sea-dove or little auk, *Mergulus alle*.

auk′wărd, *a.* Awkward. [Obs.]

au′lȧ, *n.* [L. *aula*; Gr. *aulē*, a hall or court.] The anterior portion of the third ventricle of the cerebrum.

au-lā′ri-ăn, *a.* and *n.* [LL. *aularis*, pertaining to a hall.]

I. *a.* Pertaining to a hall.

II. *n.* At Oxford university, a member of a hall.

auld, *a.* Old. [Prov. Eng. and Scot.]

Take thine *auld* cloak about thee. —Shak.

Auld lang syne; a Scotch phrase employed to express days or times long since past, especially happy times.

Auld Reekie; literally, Old Smoky; a name applied by Scotchmen to the city of Edinburgh.

au-let′iç, *a.* [Gr. *aulētēs*, a flute-player, from *aulein*, to play a flute.] Pertaining to pipes or instruments of the flute kind. [Rare.]

au′liç, *a.* [L. *aulicus*; Gr. *aulikos*, pertaining to a court; from *aulē*, court.]

1. Pertaining to a royal court.

2. In anatomy, relating to the aula.

Aulic Council; a supreme court of the old German empire. It ceased at the death of each emperor, and was renewed by his successor. It became extinct when the German empire was dissolved in 1806. The title is now applied in Germany in a general sense to the chief council of any department, political, administrative, judicial, or military.

au′liç, *n.* The ceremony formerly observed in conferring the degree of doctor of divinity at the University of Paris; so called because it took place in the great hall (L. *aula*) of the archbishopric.

auln (an), *n.* See *Aune*.

aul′nāge, *n.* See *Alnage*.

aul′nā-gēr, *n.* See *Alnager*.

au′lō-phȳte (-fīt), *n.* [Gr. *aulos*, pipe, and *phyton*, plant.] A nonparasitic plant living inside another, as some of the algæ.

Au-los′tō-mȧ, *n.* [Gr. *aulos*, pipe, and *stoma*, mouth.] A genus of fishes, family *Aulostomidæ*, so called from having the mouth lengthened into the form of a pipe.

Head of *Aulostoma maculatum*.

Au-lō-stom′i-dæ, *n.pl.* A family of fishes, with elongated body and pipe-shaped snout.

aum, *n.* Same as *Aam*.

aum, *n.* Same as *Om*.

au-māil′, *v.t.* [OE. for *enamel*.] To figure or variegate. [Obs.]

aum′bry, *n.* Same as *Ambry*.

au′mē-ry, *n.* Same as *Ambry*.

au′mil, au′mil-dăr, *n.* [Anglo-Ind.] In India, a revenue collector.

aun′cel, *n.* [ME. *auncel, aunselle*; It. *lancelle*, a balance; L. *lanx*, genit. *lancis*, a plate.] A kind of inaccurate balance anciently used in England for weighing.

aun′cet-ry, *n.* Ancestry. [Obs.]

aune (ōn), *n.* [Fr. *aune*; OFr. *alne*, ell, from L. *ulna*; Gr. *ōlenē*, the elbow.] An old French cloth measure, of different lengths in different parts of the country. The meter as a standard of measure has now taken its place.

ȧunt (ȧnt), *n.* [ME. *aunte*; OFr. *ante, aunte*; L. *amita*, aunt.]

1. The sister of one's father or mother; correlative to nephew or niece.

2. The wife of one's uncle.

3. An elderly woman.

4. An old gossip; also, a lewd woman. [Obs.]

Aunt Sally; a game which consists of throwing sticks or balls at a clay pipe stuck in the mouth of a wooden figure of a woman's head; also, the figure itself.

aun′tēr, *n.* [ME.] Adventure. [Obs.]

aun′tēr, aun′tre, *v.t.* To venture. [Obs.]

aun′trous, *a.* Venturesome. [Obs.]

ȧunt′y, ȧunt′ie (ȧnt′i), *n.* A familiar form of *aunt*; specifically, an elderly negress. [Colloq.]

au′rȧ, *n.* [L. *aura*; Gr. *aura*, air, from *aēnai*, to breathe, blow.]

1. Literally, a breeze, or gentle current of air; but technically used to denote any subtle, invisible fluid supposed to flow from a body; an effluvium, emanation, or exhalation, as the aroma of flowers, the odor of the blood; a supposed fertilizing emanation from the pollen of flowers, etc.

2. A peculiar sensation resembling that produced by a current of air.

Electric aura; a term applied to a supposed electric fluid emanating from an electrified body, and forming a sort of atmosphere around it; called also *electric atmosphere*.

Epileptic aura; a sensation as of a current of air, rising from some part of the body to the head, preceding an attack of epilepsy.

Hysteric aura; a similar sensation preceding an attack of hysteria.

au′răl, *a.* Pertaining to the air or to an aura.

au′răl, *a.* [L. *auris*, the ear.] Relating to the ear; as, the *aural* orifice; *aural* surgery.

au′răm-ine (*or* au-ram′ine), *n.* [L. *aurum*, gold, and *amine*, from L. *ammoniacum*, ammonia.] A yellow dye obtained from coal-tar.

Au-ran-ti-ā′cē-æ, *n.pl.* [LL. *aurantium*, an orange, from L. *aurum*, gold.] The orange tribe, formerly a natural order of plants, now classified as a tribe of the natural order *Rutaceæ*.

au-ran-ti-ā′ceous, *a.* Pertaining to or like the *Aurantiaceæ*.

au′rāte, *n.* [L. *auratus*, pp. of *aurare*, to overlay with gold.]

1. A combination of auric acid with a base; as, *aurate* of potash.

2. A kind of pear.

au′rā-ted, *a.* 1. Resembling gold; gold-colored; gilded.

2. In chemistry, combined with gold.

au′rā-ted, *a.* [L. *auris*, the ear.] Eared; having ears like the scallop-shell.

au′rē-āte, *a.* [LL. *aureatus*, from L. *aureus*, golden, from *aurum*, gold.] Golden; gilded.

au-rē′li-ȧ, *n.* [It., from L. *aureolus*, golden, dim. of *aureus*, golden.]

1. In zoölogy, the nymph, chrysalis, or pupa of a lepidopterous insect. [See *Chrysalis*.]

2. [A—] A genus of *Acalephæ*, or medusiform *Hydrozoa*, which passes through several changes of form in its development.

3. A term sometimes applied to the adult state of any medusa.

au-rē′li-ăn, *a.* Like or pertaining to the aurelia; as, the *aurelian* form of an insect.

au-rē′li-ăn, *n.* An entomologist who devotes himself particularly to the study of lepidopterous insects; a lepidopterist.

au-rē′ō-lȧ, au′rē-ōle, *n.* [L. *aureolus*, dim. of *aureus*, golden, from *aurum*, gold.]

1. In painting, an illumination surrounding a holy person, as Christ, a saint, a martyr, and the like, and intended to represent a luminous cloud or haze supposed to emanate from the person. *Aureola, glory*, and *nimbus* are in popular usage frequently confounded, though technically they have quite distinct uses. [See *Glory* and *Nimbus*.]

Aureola.

2. Anything resembling an *aureola*; specifically, (a) in astronomy, the ring of light seen round the moon in total eclipses of the sun; (b) in meteorology, a kind of halo surrounding a shadow cast upon a cloud or fog-bank or dew-covered grass; often observed by aeronauts on the upper surface of clouds.

3. In Roman Catholic theology, a reward given after death to those who have been spiritually victorious on earth.

4. In anatomy, an areola.

au-rē′ō-lin, *n.* [L. *aureolus*.] Cobalt yellow.

au re-voir′ (ō rē-vwär′). [Fr., from L. *revidere*, to see again; *re*, again, and *videre*, to see.] Until we meet again, good-by.

au′riç, *a.* [L. *aurum*, gold.] Pertaining to gold.

Auric oxid; a saturated combination of gold and oxygen (Au_2O_3).

au-ri-ĉhal′cē-ous, *a.* Brass-colored.

au-ri-ĉhal′cite, *n.* [L. *aurichalcum*; Gr. *oreichalkon*, from *oros*, mountain, and *chalkos*, brass or copper.] A mineral occurring in transparent verdigris-green, needle-shaped crystals, which when reduced yields a gold-colored alloy of copper and zinc.

au-ri-ĉhal′cum, *n.* See *Orichalch*.

au′ri-çle, *n.* [L. *auricula*; dim. of *auris*, ear.]

1. The external ear, or that part which is prominent from the head.

2. One of two cavities in the mammalian heart, placed above the two cavities called ventricles, and resembling in shape the external ear. It receives the blood from the veins, and communicates it to the ventricles. [See *Heart*.]

3. An instrument applied to the ears to assist in hearing; a kind of ear-trumpet.

4. One of the internal processes curving over the ambulacra near the mouth, as in sea-urchins; also called *auricula*.

au′ri-çled (-kld), *a.* 1. Having ears or auricles; having appendages resembling ears.

2. In botany, applied to leaves when they are furnished with a pair of leaflets, generally distinct, but sometimes joined to them.

au-riç′ō-mous, *a.* [L. *auricomus*, from *aurum*, gold, and *coma*, hair; Gr. *komē*, hair.] Golden-haired.

au-riç′ū-lȧ, *n.* [L., the external ear, dim. of *auris*, an ear.]

1. In botany, a garden-flower derived from the yellow *Primula Auricula*, found native in the Swiss Alps, and sometimes called *bear's-ear* from the shape of its leaves.

2. [A—] In zoölogy, a genus of phytophagous or plant-eating gasteropodous mollusks, whose organs of respiration are formed for breathing air.

3. In echinology, same as *auricle*.

Auricula (*Primula Auricula*).

au-riç′ū-lăr, *a.* 1. Pertaining to the ear or to the sense of hearing; as, the *auricular* nerves.

2. Confided to one's ear; especially, privately confided to the ear of a priest; as, *auricular* confession.

3. Perceived by the ear; known or obtained by the sense of hearing; as, *auricular* evidence.

You shall by an *auricular* assurance have your satisfaction. —Shak.

4. Communicated or known by report.

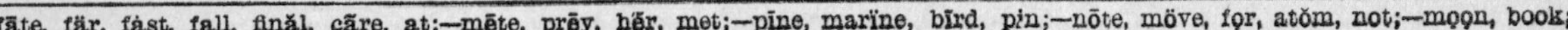

Auricular traditions and feigned testimonies. —Bacon.

5. Pertaining to the auricles of the heart.

Auricular feathers; the circle of feathers surrounding the opening of the ear in birds.

Auricular finger; the little finger, so called from its being most easily introduced into the ear.

Auricular tube; a speaking-tube, either portable, for the use of deaf persons, or carried between different parts of a building for the conveyance of messages.

au-ric-ū-lā′ri-ȧ, *n.* In zoölogy, a term applied to an early stage in the development of certain holothurians.

au-ric′ū-lăr-ly, *adv.* In an auricular manner; specifically, in a secret manner; by way of whisper; by words addressed to the ear.

au-ric′ū-lărs, *n.pl.* In ornithology, a term applied to the auricular feathers.

au-ric′ū-lāte, au-ric′ū-lā-ted, *a.* 1. Shaped like the ear.

2. Having ears or some kind of expansions resembling ears; eared; in botany, said of a leaf with a pair of small blunt projections or ears at the base.

au-ric′ū-lō-. [L. *auricula.*] A combining form used in medical and anatomical terms, meaning of or pertaining to an auricle.

au-rif′ĕr-ous, *a.* [L. *aurifer*, gold-producing; from *aurum*, gold, and *ferre*, to bring forth.] Yielding or producing gold; containing gold; as, *auriferous* quartz; *auriferous* strata.

au-rif′ic, *a.* [L. *aurum*, gold, and *facere*, to make.] Yielding gold; also, having the power of changing into gold.

au-ri-flam′mȧ, au′ri-flamme, *n.* [L. *aurum*, gold, and *flamma*, flame.] See *Oriflamme.*

au′ri-form, *a.* [L. *auris*, the ear, and *forma*, form.] Shaped like the human ear; as, an *auriform* shell.

Au-ri′gȧ, *n.* [L. *auriga*, a charioteer.]

1. In astronomy, the Wagoner, a constellation in the northern hemisphere, consisting of sixty-eight stars, including Capella of the first magnitude.

2. [a—] In medicine, the fourth lobe of the liver; also, a bandage for the sides.

au-ri′găl, *a.* Pertaining to a chariot or carriage. [Rare.]

au-ri-gā′tion, *n.* [L. *aurigatio*, the act of chariot-driving.] The act or practice of driving horses harnessed to carriages. [Rare.]

au-rig′rȧ-phy, *n.* [L. *aurum*, gold, and *graphium*, style, from Gr. *graphein*, to write.] The art or practice of writing in golden characters.

au′ri-lāve, *n.* [L. *auris*, the ear, and *lavare*, to wash.] An ear-brush, or ear-sponge.

au′rin, au′rine, *n.* [L. *aurum*, gold.] An aromatic compound obtained from coal-tar, used as a dye under the name of corallin or rosalic acid.

au-ri-phryġ′i-āte (-frij′), *a.* [L. *aurum*, gold, and *phrygius*, embroidered with Phrygian needlework; by metonymy, embroidered.] Ornamented with embroidery in gold. [Rare.]

> Nor wore he mitre here, precious or *auriphrygiate.* —Southey.

au-ri-pig′ment, *n.* Same as *Orpiment.*

au′ri-scalp, *n.* [L. *auris*, ear, and *scalpare*, to scrape.] An instrument to clean the ears; used also in surgical operations on the ear.

au′ri-scōpe, *n.* [L. *auris*, ear, and Gr. *skopein*, to view.] An instrument for ascertaining the condition of the ear and the Eustachian tube.

au-ris′cō-py, *n.* The act or practice of using the auriscope.

au′rist, *n.* One who is expert in and treats disorders of the ear.

au′ri-ted, *a.* [L. *auritus*, furnished with ears, from *auris*, ear.] In botany and zoölogy, eared; having any part resembling an ear; auriculate.

au-riv′ō-rous, *a.* [L. *aurum*, gold, and *vorare*, to devour.] Subsisting on gold. [Rare.]

au-rō-ceph′ȧ-lous (-sef′), *a.* [L. *aurum*, gold, and Gr. *kephalē*, the head.] In zoölogy, characterized by a head of golden color.

au-rō-chlō′rid, au-rō-chlō′ride (*or* -rīd), *n.* [L. *aurum*, gold, and Gr. *chlōros*, green.] A chemical compound in which gold chlorid and a chlorid of another metal combine to form a double chlorid.

Aurochs (*Bison bonasus*).

au′rochs, *n.* [G. *auerochs*, from O.H.G. *urohso*; L. *urus*; Gr. *ouros*, wild ox.] The *Bison bonasus*, a species of wild bull or bison, now almost extinct, once roaming over the plains and through the forests of northern Europe, and resembling the buffalo of the American plains, but having a less shaggy head and neck, a lighter thorax, a heavier pelvic development, and a longer and larger tail. The few remaining animals of this species are kept under the protection of the Russian government in the forests of Lithuania.

au-rō-cy′ȧ-nide (*or* -nīd), *n.* [L. *aurum*, gold, and Gr. *kyanos*, a dark blue substance used in the heroic age to adorn works in metal.] A double cyanid in which gold and some other metal are combined.

au-rō′rȧ, *n.* [L. *aurora*, dawn.]

1. The rising light of the morning; the dawn of day.

2. [A—] The goddess of the morning, or twilight, deified by fancy. The poets represented her as rising out of the ocean, in a chariot, with rosy fingers dropping gentle dew

Aurora Borealis.

3. The polar lights; the *aurora borealis* or the *aurora australis*; in this sense the word has the plural form *auroræ.*

Aurora borealis; northern lights; a phenomenal species of illumination in the northern part of the heavens, supposedly due to electromagnetic influences in the rare upper atmosphere. It occurs at various times, by night or day, and is usually characterized by the appearance of ribbon-like streams of light radiating from the region of the north magnetic pole, and extending toward the zenith. These phenomena constantly shift their positions and assume a variety of colors. They often exhibit a tremulous motion, presenting a spectacle of rare beauty, and suggesting the name of *merry dancers*, given to them by the people of the Shetland Isles.

Aurora australis; a corresponding phenomenon in the southern hemisphere, the streams of light ascending in the same manner from near the southern horizon.

Aurora glory; same as *Corona.*

au-rō′răl, *a.* Belonging to the aurora, or to the northern lights; resembling the dawn; roseate.

au′rous, *a.* Pertaining to gold; in chemistry, containing gold in its lower valence.

au′rum, *n.* [L.] Gold.

Aurum fulminans; fulminating gold; a precipitate obtained from a solution of gold in nitromuriatic acid. This precipitate is of a brownish yellow, or orange color, and when exposed to a moderate heat, or when struck, detonates with considerable noise. It is a compound of auric acid and the oxid of ammonium.

Aurum mosaicum; mosaic gold; a sparkling gold-colored substance, containing about equal quantities of copper and zinc, and used as a pigment.

aus-cult′, *v.i.* and *v.t.* To auscultate.

aus′cul-tāte, *v.i.* and *v.t.*; auscultated, *pt., pp.*; auscultating, *ppr.* [L. *auscultare*, to listen.] In medicine, to investigate by listening; to practise auscultation.

aus-cul-tā′tion, *n.* [L. *auscultatio*, a listening, from *auscultare*, to listen.]

1. The act of listening, or hearkening to. [Obs.]

2. In medicine, a method of distinguishing diseases, particularly in the thorax, by listening to the sounds in the part. It is called *immediate* when the ear is directly applied to the part, and *mediate* if practised by the aid of the stethoscope.

aus′cul-tā-tŏr, *n.* An expert in auscultation.

aus-cul′tȧ-tō-ry, *a.* Pertaining to or determined by auscultation.

aus′laut, *n.* [G. *aus*, denoting completion, from, and *laut*, loud.] The sound of the final syllable of a word.

Au-sō′ni-ăn, *a.* [L. *Ausonia*, a name given to middle and lower Italy.] Of or relating to Italy or to the inhabitants of Italy. [Poet.]

aus′pi-cāte, *v.t.*; auspicated, *pt., pp.*; auspicating, *ppr.* [L. *auspicari*, to take the auspices.]

1. To give a favorable turn to, in commencing; a sense derived from the practice of the Romans of taking the *auspicium*, or inspection of birds, before they undertook any enterprise.

2. To foreshow. [Obs.]

aus′pi-cāte, *a.* Giving promise of a favorable issue; auspicious. [Obs.]

aus′pice, *n.* [L. *auspicium*, an omen, from *auspicari*, to take the auspices.]

1. An augury from birds; an omen or sign in general; as, to take the *auspices*; an *auspice* of a good fortune.

2. Protection; favor shown; influence.

> Great father Mars, and greater Jove,
> By whose high *auspice* Rome hath stood
> So long. —B. Jonson.

3. The good fortune that follows a person; favorable influence arising from the presence of some person; now always in the plural; as, under his *auspices* the war was soon brought to a successful termination; an entertainment under the *auspices* of a church.

aus-pi′ciăl (-pish′ăl), *a.* Relating to auspices. [Rare.]

aus-pi′cious (-pish′us), *a.* [L. *auspicium*, auspice, from *auspicari*, to take the auspices.]

1. Having omens of success, or favorable appearances; as, an *auspicious* beginning.

2. Prosperous; fortunate; applied to persons; as, *auspicious* chief.

3. Favorable; kind; propitious; applied to persons or things; as, an *auspicious* mistress; *auspicious* gales.

Syn.—Favorable, propitious, promising, encouraging, advantageous, lucky.

aus-pi′cious-ly, *adv.* In an auspicious manner.

aus-pi′cious-ness, *n.* A state of fair promise; prosperity.

aus′tĕr, *n.* [L.] The south wind.

aus-tēre′, *a.* [ME. *austere*; OFr. *austere*; L. *austerus*, harsh; Gr. *austēros*, dry, harsh.]

1. Severe; harsh; rigid; stern; applied to persons and things; as, an *austere* master; an *austere* look.

2. Sour with astringency; harsh; rough to the taste; applied to things; as, *austere* fruit or wine.

3. Simple; plain; without adornment or embellishment.

4. In the fine arts, a term applied to a rigid rendering of what the artist conceives to be unadorned truthfulness; severely and scrupulously truthful.

aus-tēre′ly, *adv.* In an austere manner.

aus-tēre′ness, *n.* 1. Severity in manners; harshness; austerity.

2. Pungency or bitterness as to taste.

aus-ter′i-ty, *n.* 1. Severity of manners or life; rigor; strictness; harsh discipline; particularly applied to the mortifications of a monastic life, which are called *austerities.*

2. Sourness; harshness as to taste. [Obs.]

3. The absence of adornment or embellishment; severe plainness.

Aus′tin, *a.* Same as *Augustinian.*

aus′trăl, *a.* [L. *australis*, southern, from *auster*, the south wind, or south.] Southern; lying or being in the south; as, *austral* land; *austral* ocean.

Austral signs; the last six signs of the zodiac, or those south of the equator.

Aus-trăl-ā′siăn (-shăn), *a.* and *n.* I. *a.* Pertaining to Australasia; as, *Australasian* region.

II. *n.* A native of Australasia.

Aus-trā′liăn, *a.* and *n.* I. *a.* Relating to Australia.

II. *n.* A native or inhabitant of Australia.

Australian ballot; a system of voting originating in Australia and intended to maintain the utmost secrecy. An official ballot-paper prepared by a legally constituted board of election-officers is furnished to voters when they appear at the proper place for voting. It contains the names of all candidates that may be voted for, arranged in such a way that a voter may readily express his choice by marking his ballot, which he does alone in a secluded stall or booth, thus securing secrecy and freedom from restraint.

aus′trăl-īze, *v.i.* To tend toward the south or south pole, as a magnet. [Obs.]

Aus′tri-ăn, *a.* and *n.* [LL. *Austria*; G. *Oesterreich*; O.H.G. *Ostarrihhi*; from O.H.G. *ostar*, eastern, and *rihhi*, kingdom.]

I. *a.* Of or relating to Austria.

II. *n.* A native or inhabitant of Austria.

aus′trine, *a.* [L. *austrinus*, southern, from *auster*, south.] Southern; southerly. [Obs.]

aus′trin-ġĕr, as′trin-ġĕr, *n.* [OFr. *ostruchier*; L. *austurgo*, from *austur*, a goshawk.] A falconer who kept or trained a goshawk. [Obs.]

Aus″trō-Hun-gā′ri-ăn, *a.* Relating to Austro-Hungary.

aus′trō-man-cy, *n.* [L. *auster*, the south wind, and Gr. *manteia*, divination.] Soothsaying, or prediction of future events, from observations of the winds.

au′tăr-chy, *n.* [Gr. *autarchia*, absolute power; *autos*, self, and *archein*, to rule.] Unlimited sovereignty; autocracy.

au′tăr-chy, *n.* The state or quality of being self-sufficient. [Obs.]

au-tĕr-foits′ (ō-tr-fwä), *adv.* [Fr. *autrefois*, at another time.] A law term introduced into the plea of former trial as a bar to a second prosecution for the same offense.

Auterfoits acquit; the plea of a former acquittal.

Auterfoits attaint; the plea of former attaint. *Auterfoits convict*; the plea of former conviction.

au-then′tic, *a.* [ME. *autentike*; OFr. *autentique*; LL. *autenticus*; Gr. *authentikos*, warranted, authentic, from *autos*, self, and *entea*, instruments, tools.]

1. Having a genuine original or authority, in opposition to that which is false, fictitious, or counterfeit; being what it purports to be; genuine; true; applied to things; as, an *authentic* paper or register.

2. Of approved authority; as, an *authentic* writer.

3. In law, vested with all due formalities, and legally attested.

4. In music, having an immediate relation to the keynote or tonic; in distinction from *plagal*, having a corresponding relation to the fifth or dominant, in the octave below the keynote.

Syn.—Genuine, true, certain, faithful, credible, reliable, official, authorized.—A distinction is made between *authentic* and *genuine*, the former being opposed to *false*, and the latter to *spurious*; as, an *authentic* history; a *genuine* manuscript.

au-then′tic, *n.* An original production; not a copy; as, *authentics* and transcripts. [Obs.]

au-then′tic-ăl, *a.* Authentic.

au-then′tic-ăl-ly, *adv.* In an authentic manner; with the requisite or genuine authority.

au-then′tic-ăl-ness, *n.* The quality of being authentic; authenticity. [Rare.]

au-then′ti-cāte, *v.t.*; authenticated, *pt.*, *pp.*; authenticating, *ppr.* 1. To render authentic; to give authority to, by the proof, attestation, or formalities, required by law, or sufficient to entitle to credit.

> The king serves only as a notary to *authenticate* the choice of judges. —Burke.

2. To determine as genuine; to prove the authenticity of; as, to *authenticate* a portrait.

au-then-ti-cā′tion, *n.* The act of authenticating; the giving of authority by the necessary formalities; confirmation.

au-then-tic′i-ty, *n.* 1. The quality of being authentic, or of having established authority for truth and correctness.

2. Genuineness; the quality of being authentic.

au-then′tic-ly, *adv.* Authentically.

au-then′tic-ness, *n.* Authenticity. [Rare.]

Au-then′tics, *n.* In civil law, a Latin translation from the Greek of the novels or new constitutions of Justinian, made by an anonymous author; so called, because the novels were translated entire, to distinguish it from the epitome made by Julian.

au-thi-gen′ic, **au″thi-ġē-net′ic**, **au-thig′e-nous**, *a.* [Gr. *authi*, on the spot, and *gignesthai*, to be born.] In geology, born or produced where found, as rock-crystals.

au′thŏr, *n.* [ME. *autour*; OFr. *autor*; L. *auctor*, author, from *augere*, to cause to grow, increase.]

1. One who produces, creates, or brings into being; as, God is the *author* of the universe.

2. The beginner, former, or first mover of anything; hence, the efficient cause of a thing; appropriately applied to one who composes or writes a book, or whose occupation is to compose and write books.

3. An editor. [Obs.]

4. One who furnishes information, or is responsible for a statement; as, the *author* of a report.

au′thŏr, *v.t.* To occasion; to effect. [Obs.]

au′thŏr-ess, *n.* A female author.

au-thō′ri-ăl, *a.* Pertaining to an author. [Rare.]

au′thŏr-ism, *n.* Authorship. [Rare.]

au-thor′i-tā-tive, *a.* 1. Having due authority; sanctioned by authority; entitled to obedience or credence.

2. Having an air of authority; positive; peremptory; as, an *authoritative* manner.

au-thor′i-tā-tive-ly, *adv.* In an authoritative manner.

au-thor′i-tā-tive-ness, *n.* The quality of being authoritative.

au-thor′i-ty, *n.* [ME. *autorite*, *auctorite*; OFr. *autoritet*; L. *auctoritas*, authority, from *auctor*, author.]

1. Legal power, or a right to command or to act; as, the *authority* of the president or a governor; the *authority* of parents over children.

> By what *authority* doest thou these things? —Matt. xxi. 23.

2. The power derived from opinion, respect, or esteem; influence of character or office; credit; as, a magistrate of great *authority* in the city; the *authority* of age or example.

3. Testimony; witness; or the person who testifies; as, the Gospels or the evangelists are our *authorities* for the miracles of Christ.

4. Weight of testimony; credibility; as, a historian of no *authority*.

5. A person or thing that may be appealed to for support of an opinion or act.

6. Warrant; justification.

7. In law, a precedent or decision of a court; an official declaration; an eminent opinion or saying; anything calculated to influence the opinions of others, as the decision of a higher court.

8. The author of an authoritative statement, or one commanding the respect of others; or a book containing the writings of such an author.

9. [*pl.*] The officers of government; the persons or the body exercising power or command; as, the local *authorities* of the states.

Syn.—Ascendancy, dominion, rule, influence, force, power, command, sway, control.

au′thŏr-i-ză-ble, *a.* Capable of being authorized.

au-thŏr-i-zā′tion, *n.* The act of giving authority, or legal power; establishment by authority.

au′thŏr-ize, *v.t.*; authorized, *pt.*, *pp.*; authorizing, *ppr.* 1. To give authority, warrant, or legal power to; to give a right to act; to empower; as, to *authorize* commissioners to settle the boundary of the state.

2. To make legal; as, to *authorize* a marriage.

3. To establish by authority, as by usage, or public opinion; as, idioms *authorized* by usage.

4. To give authority, credit, or reputation to; to sanction; as, to *authorize* a report, or opinion.

5. To justify; to support as right; as, suppress desires which reason does not *authorize*.

au′thŏr-ized, *a.* Warranted by right; supported or established by authority; derived from legal or proper authority; having power or authority.

Authorized Version; the version of the Bible into English, made by forty-seven learned divines at the suggestion of James I. It was first published in 1611. It was appointed to be read in churches, and till quite recently its title-page contained the words "printed by authority." It has held its place thus long more by its own great merits than by the support of law. The Revised Version succeeded it, without superseding it, in 1885.

au′thŏr-ī-zēr, *n.* One who authorizes.

au′thŏr-less, *a.* Without an author; unacknowledged; anonymous.

au′thŏr-ly, *a.* Authorial. [Rare.]

au′thŏr-ship, *n.* 1. The quality or state of being an author.

2. Origin; source; as, the *authorship* of a book, a deed, or a condition.

au′thō-tȳpe, *n.* [Gr. *autos*, self, and *typos*, a stamp or imprint.] A type or block bearing the facsimile of an autograph.

au′tō-, *prefix.* [Gr. *autos*, self.]

1. A combining form implying some idea of self, oneself, itself, one's own, its own, etc.; hence, often meaning natural, independent, alone, etc. Sometimes *auto-* is used subjectively, as *auto*graph, that which one himself writes; and sometimes objectively, as *auto*biography, a writing about the life of oneself.

2. An abbreviation of *automobile*, self-moving, used as a combining form in names given to vehicles to convey the idea of self-propulsion; as, *auto*car, *auto*truck, etc.

au′tō, *n.* An automobile. [Colloq.]

au′tō, *n.* [Sp.] 1. A miracle-play.

2. In Spanish law, an order; a decree.

3. The proceedings of a lawsuit; in this sense, used in the plural.

au″tō-bi-og′rȧ-phēr, *n.* [*Auto-*, and Gr. *bios*, life, and *graphein*, to write.] A person who writes his or her own life or memoirs.

au″tō-bi-ō-graph′ic, **au″tō-bi-ō-graph′ic-ăl**, *a.* Pertaining to, resembling, or containing autobiography.

au″tō-bi-ō-graph′ic-ăl-ly, *adv.* In the manner of autobiography.

au″tō-bi-og′rȧ-phist, *n.* An autobiographer.

au″tō-bi-og′rȧ-phy, *n.* [*Auto-*, and Gr. *bios*, life, and *graphein*, to write.] A biography or narrative of one's life, written by oneself.

au′tō-bōat, *n.* Same as *Motor-boat.*

au′tō-cär, *n.* 1. A self-propelling vehicle, used chiefly for passenger traffic in cities.

2. A military conveyance propelled by a motor, and carrying machine guns.

au-tō-cär′pous, **au-tō-cär′pi-ăn**, *a.* [*Auto-* (meaning nothing but), and Gr. *karpos*, fruit.] In botany, a term applied to fruits consisting of the pericarp, without any organ, such as the calyx, outwardly adhering.

au-tō-ceph′ȧ-lous, **au-tō-ceph′ȧ-lic** (-sef′-), *a.* [*Auto-*, and Gr. *kephalē*, head.] In church history, having a head of its own; ecclesiastically independent.

au-tō-chrōn′ō-grȧph, *n.* [*Auto-*, and Gr. *chronos*, time, and *graphein*, to write.] An instrument for the recording or printing of time instantaneously and automatically.

au-toch′thon, *n.*; *pl.* **au-toch′thō-nēs**. [Gr. *autochthōn*, sprung from the land itself; *autos*, self, and *chthōn*, the earth, the ground.] One of the aborigines of a country; a man, animal, or plant indigenous to the country or the soil.

au-toch′thō-năl, **au-toch-thon′ic**, **au-toch′thō-nous**, *a.* Aboriginal; primitive; native; indigenous.

au-toch′thō-nism, **au-toch′thō-ny**, *n.* The state of being autochthonal.

au′tō-clāve, *n.* [Fr., from *auto-*, and L. *clavis*, key, from *claudere*, to shut.] A form of French stewpan with a lid kept steam-tight by the force of the steam rising from the contents of the vessel.

au-toc′rȧ-cy, *n.* [Fr. *autocratie*; Gr. *autokrateia*, absolute power, from *autos*, self, and *kratein*, to rule.]

1. Independent or absolute power; supreme, uncontrolled, unlimited authority or right of governing, in a single person.

2. Absolute power of determining one's own actions; independent or self-derived power; self-rule.

3. Right of self-government in a state; autonomy.

4. In medicine, the tendency and power of the vital principle to preserve life and organic soundness; in this sense, written also *autocrasy*.

au′tō-crat, *n.* [Gr. *autokratēs*, an absolute ruler.]

1. An absolute prince or sovereign; a ruler or monarch who holds and exercises the powers of government by inherent right, not subject to restriction; a title assumed by the emperors of Russia.

2. One who is invested with or assumes absolute independent power or unlimited authority in any relation.

au-tō-crat′ic, **au-tō-crat′ic-ăl**, *a.* Pertaining to autocracy; absolute; holding independent and unlimited powers of government.

au-tō-crat′ic-ăl-ly, *adv.* In a haughty, despotic, or autocratic manner.

au-toc′rȧ-tŏr, *n.* An autocrat. [Obs.]

au″tō-crȧ-tor′ic-ăl, *a.* Pertaining to an autocrator. [Obs.]

au-toc′rȧ-trix, *n.*; *pl.* **au-toc-rȧ-trī′cēs**. A female sovereign, who is independent and absolute; a title given to the reigning empresses of Russia.

au′tō-crat-ship, *n.* The office of an autocrat.

au′tō dä fe, *n.*; *pl.* **au′tōs dä fe**. [Port. *auto de fe*: *auto*, from L. *actum*, act; *de*, from L. *de*, from, and *fe*; from L. *fides*, faith; L. *actum de fide*.]

1. A solemnity held by the Spanish Inquisition, for the punishment of heretics and the absolution of the innocent accused.

2. A sentence given by the Inquisition, and read to a criminal, or heretic, on the scaffold, just before he was executed.

3. A session of the Inquisition.

au′tō de fe, *n.* Same as *Auto da fe.*

au″tō-di-ag-nō′sis, *n.* Self-diagnosis.

au′tō-di-dact″, *n.* [Gr. *autodidaktos*, self-taught; *autos*, self, and *didaskein*, to teach.] A person who is self-taught.

au″tō-di-ġes′tion (-chun), *n.* [*Auto-*, and L. *digestio*, digestion, distribution.] In pathology, the absorption or digestion of the walls of the stomach, as the result of an abnormal condition of the gastric juice; self-digestion.

au″tō-dȳ-nam′ic, *a.* [*Auto-*, and Gr. *dynamis*, power.] Operating by its own power or force.

au-tœ′cious, **au-toi′cous**, *a.* [*Auto-*, and Gr. *oikos*, a dwelling.]

1. In botany, having both male and female inflorescence on the same plant.

2. Passing through all stages of growth on a single host, as some parasitic fungi.

au-tō-fec-un-dā′tion, *n.* [*Auto-*, and L. *fecundare*, to make fruitful.] In biology, the act of self-impregnation.

au-tog′ȧ-mous, *a.* In botany, fertilized by its own pollen.

au-tog′ȧ-my, *n.* [*Auto-*, and Gr. *gamos*, marriage.] In botany, self-fertilization.

au-tō-ġē′nē-ăl, *a.* Self-begotten. [See *Autogenous.*]

au-tō-ġē′nē-ous, *a.* Same as *Autogenous.*

au-tō-ġen′e-sis, *n.* Self-production; spontaneous generation.

au-tō-ġē-net′ic, *a.* [*Auto-*, and Gr. *genesis*, production.] Produced independently; pertaining to autogenesis.

au″tō-ġē-net′ic-ăl-ly, *adv.* In an autogenetic manner; independently; spontaneously.

au-toġ′e-nous, *a.* [Gr. *autogenēs*, self-produced; from *autos*, self, and *genesis*, origin, or birth.]

1. Self-engendered; self-produced; arising spontaneously.

2. In anatomy, proceeding from distinct and separate centers of ossification, as in the knitting together of fractured bones.

Autogenous soldering; a method of uniting metals by fusion of the parts to be joined, instead of by the employment of other materials.

au-toġ′e-nous-ly, *adv.* In an autogenous manner; autogenetically.

au-toġ′e-ny, *n.* Autogenesis.

au′tō-gram, *n.* An autographic telegram. [See *Autographic telegraph*, under *Autographic.*]

au′tō-grȧph, *n.* [Fr. *autographe*; from Gr.

autos, self, and *graphein*, to write.] Anything written with one's own hand, as a letter or a signature; an original manuscript, as distinguished from a copy.

au'tō-gräph, *a.* Written by one's own hand; as, the *autograph* letters of a king.

au-tō-graph'ic, au-tō-graph'ic-ăl, *a.* Written by one's own hand; pertaining to an autograph; pertaining to or used in autography.

Autographic ink; ink used for executing writings or drawings on prepared paper, and of such a character that it is possible afterward to transfer them to stone.

Autographic paper; the prepared paper used for the original copy in autography.

Autographic press; the printing-press used in reproducing autographs.

Autographic telegraph; an instrument for transmitting autographic messages or portraits executed in insulating ink upon prepared paper; also called *telautograph*.

au-tog'rȧ-phy, *n.* 1. A person's own handwriting; an autograph; a personal or original manuscript.

2. In lithography, a process for transferring a writing or drawing from paper to stone.

3. The study and deciphering of autographs; a branch of the science of diplomatics.

au'tō-härp, *n.* [*Auto-*, and OE. *harpe*; AS. *hearpe*, harp.] A musical instrument resembling the zither.

au"tō-hyp-not'ic, *a.* Self-hypnotizing.

au"tō-hyp-not'ic, *n.* One who induces hypnotism in himself.

au-tō-hyp'nō-tism, *n.* [*Auto-*, and Gr. *hypnos*, sleep.] Mental stupor induced by dwelling intensely upon some all-absorbing thought.

au-toi'cous, *a.* Same as *Autœcious*.

au"tō-in-fec'tion, *n.* Same as *Autointoxication*.

au"tō-in-oc-ū-lā'tion, *n.* [*Auto-*, and L. *inoculare*, to inoculate.] In medicine, the inoculation of a healthy part of a body with virus from a diseased part.

au"tō-in-tox-i-cā'tion, *n.* [*Auto-*, and LL. *intoxicare*, to drug or poison, from L. *toxicum*, a poison in which arrows were dipped.] The state of being infected by poisonous substances in the body, as virus from a malignant sore.

au"tō-ki-net'ic, au"tō-ki-net'ic-ăl, *a.* Moving automatically; as, an *autokinetic* fire-alarm system.

au-tol'ȧ-try, *n.* [*Auto-*, and Gr. *latreia*, worship.] The worship of self.

au-tol'ō-ġy, *n.* [*Auto-*, and Gr. *logos*, description.] The study of self.

au-tō-mat', *n.* [Gr. *automatos*, self-acting.]

1. An apparatus for serving foods mechanically in response to a coin or token dropped in a slot.

2. A restaurant or café where such an apparatus is used.

3. A camera shutter operated by a pneumatic bulb.

au-tom'ȧ-tȧ, *n.*, pl. of *automaton*.

au'tō-māte, *n.* [Fr.; Gr. *automatos*, self-acting.] An automatic telephone, or telephonic system including an automatic mechanical device for making connections at the central switchboard at the will of the person calling.

au'tō-math, *n.* [*Auto-*, and Gr. *manthanein*, to learn.] A self-taught person. [Rare.]

au-tō-mat'ic, au-tō-mat'ic-ăl, *a.* [Gr. *automatos*, self-moving; *autos*, self, and *matenein*, to strive to do.]

1. Belonging to an automaton; having the power of moving itself; applied particularly to self-acting machinery, or such as has within itself the power of regulating entirely its own movements, although the moving force is derived from without.

2. Conducted or carried on by self-acting machinery; as, *automatic* operations.

3. Mechanical; done without conscious effort.

4. In physiology, not voluntary; not depending on the will; instinctive; applied to animal actions.

Automatic arts; such economic arts or manufactures as are carried on by self-acting machinery.

au-tō-mat'ic-ăl-ly, *adv.* In an automatic manner; involuntarily; mechanically.

au-tom'ȧ-tism, *n.* 1. The state of being automatic; the power of involuntary action.

2. In metaphysics, a theory that animals lack consciousness, that their actions are governed only by physical laws, and that they are automata.

3. In medicine, the involuntary action caused by certain diseases, as epilepsy.

au-tom'ȧ-ton, *n.*; *pl.* **au-tom'ȧ-tȧ** or **au-tom'ȧ-tons**. [Gr. *automatos*, acting of one's own will, self-moving.]

1. Any object or being possessing the power of automatic action; especially a mechanical device or toy, so constructed as to imitate the form and motions of men or animals.

2. A person whose actions are mechanical or of such a routine nature as to seem to be done without thought or will being expended on them.

au-tom'ȧ-tous, *a.* Having in itself the power of motion; automatic. [Obs.]

au-tō-mō'bile, *a.* Self-moving; as, an *automobile* carriage, an *automobile* bicycle.

au"tō-mō-bïle' (*or* ą-tō-mō'bil), *n.* [*Auto-*, and L. *mobilis*, movable.] A self-moving vehicle, especially a carriage driven by steam, gasoline, electric, or other power, by means of a motor borne on the vehicle.

Automobile.

au-tō-mō'bil-ism, *n.* The act or practice of using an automobile.

au-tō-mō'bil-ist, *n.* One who uses an automobile.

au-tom'ō-līte, *n.* [Gr. *automolos*, a deserter.] A name sometimes given to gahnite.

au-tō-mor'phic, *a.* [*Auto-*, and Gr. *morphē*, form.]

1. Made similar in form to oneself, or drawn after the pattern of oneself.

2. Idiomorphic; occurring in separate crystals.

au-tō-mor'phism, *n.* The attribution of one's own traits to another.

au"tō-mō'tive, *a.* [*Auto-*, and L. *motivus*, moving.]

1. Self-propelling.

2. Having to do with any machine that is self-propelling; as a motorboat, aeroplane, etc.

au-tō-mō'tŏr, *n.* [*Auto-*, and L. *motus*, motion, from *movere*, to move.] Any automobile vehicle.

au-tō-nom'ȧ-sy, *n.* See *Autonomasia*.

au-tō-nom'ic, *a.* Relating to autonomy; having the power of self-government.

au-ton'ō-mist, *n.* An advocate of autonomy.

au-ton'ō-mous, *a.* 1. Independent in government; having the right of self-government.

2. In biology, applied to a separate organism, not one dependent on any other.

au-ton'ō-my, *n.* [Gr. *autonomia*, independence, from *autos*, self, and *nemein*, to hold sway.]

1. The power or right of self-government, whether in a community which elects its own magistrates and makes its own laws, or in an individual who lives according to his own will.

2. In the philosophy of Kant, the right of reason to dominate in matters of ethics; the right of the individual to govern himself according to his own reason.

3. In biology, an autonomous organism.

au'tō-nym, *n.* [*Auto-*, and Gr. *onoma*, name.]

1. One's real name; opposed to *pseudonym*.

2. A production bearing the originator's real name.

3. A homonym. [Rare.]

au-tō-path'ic, *a.* [Gr. *autopatheia*, one's own feelings or experience; *autos*, self, and *pathos*, feeling.] In pathology, caused by or influenced by the peculiar structure and physical tendencies of the individual.

Au-toph'ȧ-ġi, *n.pl.* [*Auto-*, and Gr. *phagein*, to eat.] A division of birds that can run about and feed themselves as soon as hatched.

au-toph'ȧ-gous, *a.* 1. Pertaining to or resembling the *Autophagi*.

2. In medicine, of the nature of autophagy.

au-toph'ȧ-ġy, *n.* [*Auto-*, and Gr. *phagein*, to eat.] The act of the body drawing its nourishment from its own tissues, as in fasting; self-consumption.

au-toph'ō-by, *n.* [*Auto-*, and Gr. *phobos*, fear.] A shrinking from reference to oneself; a morbid dread of being egotistical. [Rare.]

au'tō-phōn, *n.* [*Auto-*, and Gr. *phōnein*, to make a sound.] A musical instrument, the sounds of which are determined by perforations, corresponding to notes, in a band or ribbon of material which unreels within the instrument.

au-toph'ō-ny, *n.* [*Auto-*, and Gr. *phōnē*, sound.]

1. A form of auscultation in which the examiner speaks close to the patient's chest and notes the modification of his own voice as affected by the conditions of the patient's chest.

2. A form of deafness in which the patient's voice seems very loud to himself.

au"tō-phyl-log'e-ny, *n.* [*Auto-*, and Gr. *phyllon*, leaf, and *genea*, offspring.] In botany, the abnormal duplication of a leaf.

au'tō-pis-ty, *n.* [*Auto-*, and Gr. *pistos*, worthy of credence.] Internal worthiness of belief. [Rare.]

au'tō-plast, *n.* [*Auto-*, and Gr. *plastos*, formed, from *plassein*, to form.]

1. A cell in the yolk of an ovum, formed spontaneously and not developed in the usual way from protoplasm.

2. Same as *Chloroplastid*.

au-tō-plas'tic, *a.* Relating to autoplasty.

au'tō-plas-ty, *n.* In surgery, the operation of building up an extensive wound with the living tissue of some other part of the same body.

au-top'si-ȧ, *n.* Same as *Autopsy*. [Rare.]

au-top'sic, au-top'sic-ăl, *a.* Same as *Autoptic*. [Rare.]

au'top-sy, *n.* [Gr. *autopsia*, a seeing with one's own eyes; *autos*, self, and *opsis*, a sight, appearance.]

1. Personal inspection; ocular view.

2. In medicine, post-mortem examination; inspection of the body after death to discover the cause and seat of the disease, or wound, of which the person died.

3. Figuratively, a critical examination of anything, as a scientific theory, a poem, etc.

au-top'tic, au-top'tic-ăl, *a.* Relating to or based on autopsy or personal observation; as, *autoptic* evidence.

au-top'tic-ăl-ly, *adv.* By means of ocular view or one's own observation.

au-tō-sche-di-as'tic, au-tō-sche-di-as'tic-ăl, *a.* [Gr. *autoschediazein*, to do a thing offhand; *autos*, self, and *schediazein*, to do a thing suddenly.] Impromptu; offhand; slight; hasty; not fully considered.

au'tō-scōpe, *n.* [*Auto-*, and Gr. *skopein*, to look at, examine.] An instrument whereby one is enabled to examine his own eye.

au-tos'cō-py, *n.* The examination of oneself, particularly of the eyes or throat, by instruments designed for the purpose.

au'tos dä fe, *n.*, pl. of *auto da fe*.

au"tō-si-tā'ri-us, *n.*; *pl.* **au"tō-si-tā'ri-ī**. Either individual body of a double monster, in which two equally developed bodies are joined, as by the umbilicus.

au'tō-site, *n.* [*Auto-*, and Gr. *sitos*, food.] Any living organism supporting a parasite; especially, that autositarius which supplies nourishment to the other, which is called the *parasite*.

au-tō-sit'ic, *a.* Pertaining to or having the characteristics of an autosite.

au-tō-styl'ic, *a.* [*Auto-*, and Gr. *stylos*, column.] In anatomy, lacking a regular suspensorium; having the jaws attached directly to the cranium.

au"tō-sug-ges'tion (-chun), *n.* [*Auto-*, and L. *suggestio*, a suggestion, from *suggerere*, to put under.] In hypnotism, suggestion arising within one's own mind, as distinguished from suggestion initiated by another; also called *traumatic suggestion*.

au-tō-tem'nous, *a.* [*Auto-*, and Gr. *temnein*, to cut.] In biology, capable of self-division, as tissue-cells, etc.

au'tō-thē-ism, *n.* [*Auto-*, and Gr. *theos*, God.]

1. The doctrine of the self-existence of Deity; used particularly with reference to Christ, or the second person of the Trinity. [Rare.]

2. Self-worship; excessive vanity.

au'tō-thē-ist, *n.* 1. A believer in autotheism.

2. A worshiper of self.

au-tot'ō-mic, *a.* Self-intersecting.

au"tō-tox-ē'mi-ȧ, *n.* Toxemia caused by generation or retention of poisons within the system. [See *Autointoxication*.]

au-tō-tox'ic, *a.* Pertaining to or producing autotoxemia.

au"tō-tox-i-cā'tion, *n.* Autointoxication.

au"tō-trans-form'ẽr, *n.* [*Auto-*, and L. *transformare*, to change in shape.] In electrical engineering, a transformer sometimes used when a small additional electro-motive force is temporarily required, as in the case of the starting of a motor. It consists of a coil of wire wound on an iron core, and connected across the mains. To some point in it, at a greater or less distance from one end, according to the voltage required, a branch wire is attached and a current drawn off between this branch and one end. In this way, a much greater current can be drawn off than is actually supplied by the mains, as the piece between the branch and the end in use acts as the secondary of a transformer.

au'tō-tȳpe, *n.* [*Auto-*, and Gr. *typos*, a stamp.]

1. A photographic process of reproducing works of art in one color or different shades of one color by printing from a gelatin plate.

2. A picture produced by this process.

3. A facsimile.

au"tō-tȳ-pog'rȧ-phy, *n.* [*Auto-*, and Gr. *typos*, an impression, stamp, and *graphein*, to write.] A process of printing in which relief drawings in gelatin are transferred to a soft metal plate, from which copies may be printed.

au-tot'y-py, *n.* The art of reproducing by the autotype process.

au-tre-fois' (ō-tr-fwä'), *adv.* [Fr.] Same as *Auterfoits*.

au'tumn, *n.* [ME. *autumpne*; OFr. *autompne*; L. *autumnus*, autumn, from root *av*, to satisfy oneself.]

1. The third season of the year, or that between summer and winter, often called *fall* in the United States. Astronomically, it dates in

the northern temperate zone from the autumnal equinox, September 22, when the sun enters Libra, to the winter solstice, December 21, when the sun enters Capricorn. Popularly, however, *autumn* in the United States comprises the months of September, October, and November. In the southern hemisphere, *autumn* corresponds to spring in the northern.

2. The period of ripeness; maturity; the beginning of old age and decay; as, life's *autumn*.

au-tum′năl, *a.* Belonging or peculiar to autumn; as, an *autumnal* tint: produced or gathered in autumn; as, *autumnal* fruits: flowering in autumn; as, an *autumnal* plant: belonging to a period corresponding to autumn in the year; hence, past the middle stage of life; as, an *autumnal* matron.

Autumnal equinox; the time when the sun crosses the equator, as it proceeds southward, or when it passes the autumnal point.

Autumnal point; the point of the equator intersected by the ecliptic, as the sun proceeds southward; the first point of Libra.

Autumnal signs; the signs Libra, Scorpio, and Sagittarius, through which the sun passes between the autumnal equinox and winter solstice.

au-tum′năl, *n.* A plant that blossoms in autumn.

au′tumn-bells, *n.* The European plant *Gentiana Pneumonanthe*, whose bell-shaped flowers appear in autumn.

au′tun-ite, *n.* [From *Autun*, a city in France.] An orthorhombic mineral, of a citron or sulphur-yellow color. It is a native hydrous phosphate of uranium and calcium.

aux-ă-nom′e-tēr, *n.* [Gr. *auxein*, to increase, and *metron*, measure.] An instrument for measuring and recording the growth of plants.

aux-ē′sis, *n.* [Gr. *auxēsis*, increase.]

1. In rhetoric, a figure by which anything is magnified too much; the use of a more unusual and high-sounding word for the ordinary and proper word; hyperbole; exaggeration.

2. In mathematics, the ratio in which an element in one figure must be increased to conform to the corresponding element in a conformable figure.

3. Increase in magnitude or extent.

aux-et′ic, *a.* Relating to auxesis; amplifying; increasing.

aux-il′iăr (agz-), *n.* An auxiliary. [Rare.]

aux-il′iăr, *a.* Auxiliary. [Rare.]

aux-il′iăr-ly, *adv.* By means of aid or help.

aux-il′iă-ry, *a.* [L. *auxiliaris*, helpful, from *auxilium*, aid, from *augere*, to increase; Gr. *auxanein*, to grow.] Helping; aiding; assisting; subsidiary; conferring aid or support by joint exertion, influence, or use; as, *auxiliary* troops.

Auxiliary notes; in music, notes representing tones subsidiary to harmony but inserted for variety.

Auxiliary quantity; in mathematics, a quantity employed to elucidate an equation or trigonometrical problem.

Auxiliary scales; in music, the six keys or scales, consisting of any key major, with its relative minor, and the attendant keys of each.

Auxiliary verb; a verb used in the conjugation of other verbs. [See *Auxiliary*, n. 3.]

aux-il′iă-ry, *n.* 1. A helper; an assistant; a member of a band of *auxiliaries*; a confederate in some action, enterprise, or undertaking.

2. [*pl.*] Troops secured from a foreign country to assist a nation at war.

3. In grammar, a verb which is used in the formation of the voices, modes, and tenses of other verbs; as, *have, be, may, can, do, must, shall*, and *will*, in English.

4. In mathematics, an auxiliary quantity. [See *Auxiliary*, a.]

aux-il′iă-tō-ry, *n.* and *a.* I. *n.* Help; aid. [Obs.]

II. *a.* Helping; aiding. [Obs.]

aux-ol′ō-gy (aks-), *n.* [Gr. *auxanein*, to increase, and *logos*, description.] Embryology.

aux-om′e-tēr, *n.* [Gr. *auxanein*, to increase, and *metron*, a measure.] An instrument for measuring the magnifying powers of an optical apparatus.

aux-ō-ton′ic, *a.* [Gr. *auxanein*, to grow, and *tenos*, a strain, tension.] In botany, determined or induced by growth; applied to movements of the organs in plants.

ä-va′, *adv.* Of all; at all. [Scot.]

ä′vä, *n.* The native name of a South Sea Island fermented drink, made from the roots of a shrub by the same name; also called *kava*, or *kawa*.

av′ă-dă-vat′, *n.* An East Indian bird of the finch variety. [See *Amadavat*.]

ȧ-vāil′, *v.t.*; availed, *pt., pp.*; availing, *ppr.* [ME. *availen*; OFr. *avaler*; from L. *ad*, to, or for, and *valere*, to be strong.]

1. To profit; to turn to advantage; followed by the pronouns *myself, thyself, himself, herself, itself, ourselves, yourselves, themselves*, with *of* before the thing used; as, let him *avail himself of* his license.

2. To assist or profit; to aid in effecting a design, or bringing it to a successful issue; as, what will skill *avail* us against numbers?

ȧ-vāil′, *v.i.* To be of use or advantage; to answer the purpose; to have strength, force, or efficacy sufficient to accomplish the object; as, the plea in bar must *avail*, that is, be sufficient to defeat the suit; medicines will not *avail* to check the disease; suppositions, without proof, will not *avail*.

ȧ-vāil′, *n.* 1. Profit; advantage tending to promote success; benefit; as, labor, without economy, is of little *avail*; I doubt whether it will be of much *avail*.

2. Profits or proceeds; as, the *avails* of a year's trade. [Rare.]

Syn.—Benefit, profit, service, use, utility.

ȧ-vāil′, *v.t.* and *v.i.* [Obs.] See *Avale*.

ȧ-vāil-ȧ-bil′i-ty, *n.* Availableness; the state or quality of being available.

ȧ-vāil′ȧ-ble, *a.* 1. Capable of being used; attainable; possessing availability; usable; profitable; advantageous; having efficacy; as, a measure is more or less *available*; *available* resources.

2. Having sufficient power, force, or efficacy for the object; valid; as, an *available* plea. [Obs.]

ȧ-vāil′ȧ-ble-ness, *n.* 1. The quality of being available; power or efficacy in promoting an end in view.

2. Competent power; legal force; validity; as, the *availableness* of a title. [Obs.]

ȧ-vāil′ȧ-bly, *adv.* In an available manner.

ȧ-vāil′ment, *n.* Profit; efficacy; successful issue. [Rare.]

ā′văl, *a.* [L. *avus*, grandfather.] Relating to a grandparent.

ȧ-văl′, *n.* [Fr. *à val*, at the bottom.] In Canada, a legal term signifying an indorsement or surety.

av′ȧ-lanche, *n.* [Fr., from *avaler*, to descend.]

1. A snowslide; a mass or body of snow or ice sliding down a mountain.

2. A similar falling mass of earth or rock; a landslide.

3. Figuratively, anything sudden or violent befalling a person; as, an *avalanche* of misfortune.

ȧ-vāle′, *v.t.* [ME. *avalen*; OFr. *avaler*, to let down; from L. *ad vallem*, to the valley.]

1. To let down; to lower; to cause to descend; as, to *avale* a sail. [Obs.]

2. To depress; to make abject; as, to *avale* the sovereignty. [Obs.]

ȧ-vāle′, *v.i.* To fall, as rain, or the tide; to descend; to dismount. [Obs.]

ȧ-vănt′, *n.* The van of an army. [Obs.]

ȧ-vănt′-cōu″ri-ēr, *n.* [Fr. *avant*, before, and *courir*, to run, from L. *currere*, to run.] A person despatched before another person or company, to give notice of his or their approach.

ȧ-vănt′-guärd, *n.* The van or advanced body of an army. [See *Vanguard*.]

av′ȧ-rice, *n.* [ME. *avarice*; OFr. *avarice*; L. *avaritia*, avarice, from *avarus*, greedy, from *avere*, to wish, desire.] An inordinate desire of gaining and possessing wealth; covetousness; greediness or insatiable desire of gain; cupidity; also, in a figurative sense, an excessive desire for some benefit or advantage.

> *Avarice* sheds a blasting influence over the finest affections and sweetest comforts of mankind. —Buckminster.

Syn.—Covetousness, greediness, cupidity, eagerness.

av-ȧ-ri′cious (-rish′us), *a.* Covetous; greedy of gain; immoderately desirous of accumulating property; characterized by avarice.

Syn.—Covetous, parsimonious, penurious, miserly, niggardly.—The *covetous* eagerly desire wealth, even at the expense of others; the *avaricious* hoard it; the *penurious, parsimonious*, and *miserly* save it by disgraceful self-denial; and the *niggardly*, by meanness in their dealings with others.

av-ȧ-ri′cious-ly, *adv.* Covetously; with inordinate desire of gaining wealth.

av-ȧ-ri′cious-ness, *n.* The quality of being avaricious; insatiable or inordinate passion for property.

av′ȧ-rous, *a.* Greedy of gain. [Obs.]

ȧ-văst′, *interj.* [Corrupted from D. *hou′vast, houd vast*, hold fast.] In seamen's language, an order to cease, stop, or stay in any operation.

Avast heaving; a nautical cry to arrest the capstan when nippers are jammed, or any other impediment occurs in heaving the cable.

av-ȧ-tär′, av-ȧ-tä′rȧ, *n.* [Sans. *avatāra*, from *ava*, down, and root *tri*, to go, or pass beyond.]

1. A descent, or the act of descending from heaven; particularly applied to the incarnations of the Hindu deities, or their appearance in some manifest shape upon earth.

2. An incarnate form.

ȧ-vaunce′, *v.t.* and *v.i.* To advance. [Obs.]

ȧ-vaunt′, *interj.* [ME. *avaunt*; OFr. *avant*, forward; LL. *abante*, from L. *ab*, from, and *ante*, before.] Begone; depart; a word of contempt or abhorrence, equivalent to the phrase "Get thee gone."

ȧ-vaunt′, *v.t.* and *v.i.* To advance; also, to boast. [Obs.]

ȧ-vaunt′, *n.* A boast. [Obs.]

ȧ-vaunt′ēr, ȧ-vaunt′ōur, *n.* A boaster. [Obs.]

Ā′vē (*or* ä′vē), *n.* [L., imper. of *avere*, to be well.]

1. A salutation and prayer to the Virgin Mary; a Hail Mary.

2. [a—] A salutation; a welcoming hail; a farewell.

av′el, *n.* [ME. *aile, eile*; AS. *egl*, the beard of grain.] The beard or awn of barley, oats, and some other grains.

av′el-ēr, av′el-lēr, *n.* A machine for avelling grain; a hummeler.

av′ell, *v.t.* To pull or tear away.

ȧ-vel′lāne, ȧ-vel′lan, *a.* [OFr. *avelane*, the filbert-nut; name derived from L. *Avellana*, or *Abellana*, a town in Campania.] In heraldry, a term applied to a cross whose quarters resemble filbert-nuts (the fruit of *Corylus Avellana*), as in the accompanying figure. Crosses of this form when placed on the mondes of kings or emperors are ensigns of sovereignty.

Avellane Cross.

Ā′vē Mä-rī′ä, Ā′vē Mā′ry. [From the first words of the Roman Catholic prayer to the Virgin Mary; L. *ave, Maria*, hail, Mary.]

1. A form of devotion in the Roman Catholic church, chaplets and rosaries being divided into a certain number of *Ave Marys* and paternosters.

2. A particular time, in Roman Catholic countries, as in Italy, about half an hour after sunset, and also at early dawn, when the bells ring and the people repeat the *Ave Maria* or Hail Mary.

Ȧ-vē′nȧ, *n.* [L., oats.] A genus of plants belonging to the order *Gramineæ*. The most important species is the cultivated oat, *Avena sativa*.

av-ē-nā′ceous, *a.* [L. *avenaceus*, from *avena*, oats.] Belonging to or partaking of the nature of oats.

av′ē-nāge, *n.* [OFr. *avenage*, from L. *avena*, oats.] In old English law, a certain quantity of oats paid by a tenant to a landlord in lieu of rent or other duty.

av′ē-nēr, av′ē-nor, *n.* [Fr.] In English feudal law, an officer attached to the king's stables, whose duty was to provide oats. [Obs.]

ȧ-venge′, *v.t.*; avenged, *pt., pp.*; avenging, *ppr.* [ME. *avengen*; OFr. *avengier*, to avenge; *a-*, and *vengier*, to avenge; from L. *ad*, to, and *vindicare*, to punish.] To take satisfaction for (a wrong) by punishing the injuring party; to vindicate by inflicting pain or evil on the wrongdoer; to deal punishment on account of. *Avenge* and *revenge*, radically, are synonymous, but modern usage makes a valuable distinction in the use of these words, restricting *avenge* to the taking of just punishment, and *revenge* to the infliction of pain or evil maliciously.

ȧ-venge′, *v.i.* To obtain satisfaction; to take vengeance.

ȧ-venge′, *n.* Vengeance. [Obs.]

ȧ-venge′ănce, *n.* [Obs.] See *Vengeance*.

ȧ-venge′fụl, *a.* Vengeful. [Obs.]

ȧ-venge′ment, *n.* Vengeance; punishment; the act of taking satisfaction for an injury by inflicting pain or evil on the offender; satisfaction taken; revenge.

ȧ-ven′gēr, *n.* One who avenges or vindicates; a vindicator; a revenger.

ȧ-ven′gēr-ess, *n.* A female avenger. [Obs.]

ȧ-vē′nin, *n.* [L. *avena*, oats.] A proteid substance found in oats.

av′ē-nor, *n.* See *Avener*.

ȧ-vē′nous, ȧ-vē′ni-ous, *a.* [Gr. *a* priv., and L. *vena*, vein.] In botany, lacking veins or nerves.

av′ens, *n.* [ME. *avans*; OFr. *avence*.] The popular name of plants belonging to the genus *Geum*. Common avens, or herb-bennet, is *Geum urbanum*, and water-*avens* is *Geum rivale*.

av′en-tāil, av′en-tāile, *n.* [ME. *aventayle*; OFr. *esventail*, lit. air-hole, from L. *ex*, out of, and *ventus*, wind.] The movable part of the front of a helmet.

Av′en-tine (*or* -tīn), *a.* and *n.* I. *a.* Pertaining to *Mons Aventinus*, one of the seven hills on which Rome stood.

II. *n.* A post of safety. [Obs.]

ȧ-ven′tre (-tēr), *v.t.* To hurl, as a spear. [Obs.]

ȧ-ven′tūre, *n.* [Fr. *aventure*, from L. *advenire*, to come to.] In old law, a mischance causing a person's death without felony; as by drowning, or falling from a house. [See *Adventure*.]

ȧ-ven′tū-rin, ȧ-ven′tū-rine, *n.* [Fr. *aventure*, adventure.]

1. A variety of translucent quartz, spangled throughout with scales of yellow mica; the gold-stone of New Mexico and Arizona; also, a form of glittering feldspar; sunstone.

2. An ornamental glass, brown with gold

specks, now made in Venice by a process first discovered in Spain. Also written *avanturin(e)*.

av′e-nūe, *n.* [Fr. *avenue*, avenue, from *avenir*, to happen, to come, from L. *advenire*, to come tc.]

1. A passage; a way or opening for entrance into a place; any opening or passage by which a thing is or may be introduced.

2. An alley or walk planted on each side with trees, and leading to a house, gate, wood, etc.; any wide walk or driveway bordered by trees.

3. A wide street.

4. Figuratively, means of access or attainment; as, the *avenues* to public office.

ȧ-vẽr′, *v.t.*; averred, *pt.*, *pp.*; averring, *ppr.* [ME. *averren*; OFr. *averrer*, to confirm; from L. *ad*, to, and *verus*, true.]

1. To affirm with confidence; to declare in a positive or peremptory manner, as in confidence of asserting the truth.

2. In law, to offer to verify; to verify.

Syn.—Affirm, declare, assert, asseverate, allege, avow, depose.

ā′vẽr, *n.* [OFr., from L. *habere*, to have.] In England, a horse or ox when used as a beast of burden. [Obs.]

av′ẽr-āġe, *n.* [Fr. *avaris*, decay of wares or merchandise; OFr. *average*; LL. *averagium*, property, probably from L. *habere*, to have.]

1. In feudal law, a duty or service which a tenant was bound to render to his lord, by his horses, carts, etc., such as the carrying of grain.

2. In commerce, a contribution to a general loss. When, for the safety of a ship in distress, any destruction of property is incurred, either by cutting away the masts, throwing goods overboard, or other means, all persons who have goods on board, or property in the ship, contribute to the loss according to their *average*, that is, according to the proportionate value of the goods of each on board.

3. A mean proportion, medial sum or quantity, made out of unequal sums or quantities. Thus, if A loses five dollars, B nine, and C sixteen, the sum is thirty, and the *average* ten. This is the present popular sense of the word.

4. A small duty payable by the shippers of goods to the master of a ship, over and above the freight, for his care of the goods. Hence, the expression in bills of lading, "paying so much freight, with primage and *average* accustomed."

5. A mean estimate in several different instances, as to number, size, amount, degree, quality, etc.; the ordinary run; a medium.

> On an *average* the male and female births are tolerably equal. —Buckle.

6. In games and sports, the mean proportional, or ordinary record of a player; as, a batting *average* in baseball.

General average; a term employed in marine insurance. Where maritime property is in peril and a sacrifice of a part is made for and causes the safety of the rest, that which is saved contributes to make up the loss of that which is sacrificed, the proportional contribution being called *general average*.

Particular average; a term signifying that the damage to maritime property is borne by the individual owners of the articles damaged, or by their insurers.

Upon or *on an average*; usually; estimated from a number of instances; taking the mean deduced from a great number of examples.

av′ẽr-āġe, *a.* 1. Medial; containing a mean proportion; resulting from estimation or calculation of sizes, numbers, amounts, etc.; as, an *average* price.

2. Based on an average; as, an *average* division of expense.

av′ẽr-āġe, *v.t.*; averaged, *pt.*, *pp.*; averaging, *ppr.* 1. To find the mean of (unequal sums or quantities); to reduce to a medium; to divide among a number, according to a given proportion; as, to *average* a loss.

2. To result in, as a mean term; to form or to exist in, as a mean sum or quantity; as, to *average* $50 per week; these spars *average* ten feet in length.

To average out; a commercial term meaning to increase the amount of an investment when a market temporarily declines, so that, upon a subsequent rise in value, the total investment will yield a profit sooner.

av′ẽr-āġe, *v.i.* To come to an average; to amount to on an average; as, the results *average* well.

av′ẽr-āġe-ly, *adv.* In an average manner; on the average.

ȧ-vẽr′ment, *n.* [ME. *averren*; OFr. *averrer*, to confirm; from L. *ad*, to, and *verus*, true, and *-ment*.]

1. Affirmation; positive assertion; the act of averring.

2. Verification; establishment by evidence.

3. In law, formerly, an offer of either party to justify or prove what he alleged. In any stage of pleadings, when either party advanced new matter, he averred it to be true, by using this form of words, "and this he is ready to verify." This was called an *averment*. It is now termed a *verification*. —Blackstone.

A-vẽr′năl, A-vẽr′ni-ăn, *a.* [L. *Avernus*, from Gr. *aornos*, without birds; *a* priv., and *ornos*, bird.] Pertaining to *Avernus*, a lake of Campania, in Italy, represented by classical poets as the entrance to hell. From its waters mephitic vapors arose which are said to have killed the birds that attempted to fly over it.

av′ẽr-pen″ny, *n.* In old English law, money paid by a tenant instead of the service of average. [See *Average*, n. 1.]

A-ver′rō-iṣm, A-ver′rhō-iṣm, *n.* The doctrines of the Averroists.

A-ver′rō-ist, A-ver′rhō-ist, *n.* One of a sect of Peripatetic philosophers who appeared in Italy before the restoration of learning; so denominated from *Averroes* or *Averrhoes*, a celebrated Arabian author.

av-ẽr-run′ċāte, *v.t.* [L. *averruncare*, to avert, or turn away; *a*, or *ab*, from, and *verruncare*, to turn about.]

1. To root up; to scrape or tear away by the roots. [Obs.]

2. To prune.

3. To avert; to turn aside; to ward off. [Obs.]

Two forms of Averruncator.

av″ẽr-run-ċā′tion, *n.* 1. The act of tearing up or raking away the roots.

2. The act of pruning, or cutting off superfluous branches.

3. The act of turning aside or averting. [Obs.]

av″ẽr-run-ċā′tŏr, *n.* In arboriculture, an instrument for pruning trees, consisting of two blades fixed on the end of a rod, and so constructed as to operate like a pair of shears.

ȧ-vẽr′sănt, *a.* [L. *aversans*, turning away, ppr. of *aversari*, to turn away.] In heraldry, said of a right hand when it is turned to show the back; also called *dorsed*.

Aversant.

av-ẽr-sā′tion, *n.* A turning from with disgust or dislike; aversion; hatred; disinclination. [Obs.]

ȧ-vẽrse′, *a.* [L. *aversus*, pp. of *avertere*, to turn away.]

1. Literally, turned from, in manifestation of dislike, or turned backward, in a reverse direction.

2. Disliking; unwilling; having a repugnance of mind; unfavorable; indisposed; malign.

> And Pallas, now *averse*, refused her aid. —Dryden.

3. In botany, turned away from the axis.

This word and its derivatives are now regularly followed by *to*, and not by *from*.

Syn.—Adverse, backward, loath, reluctant, repugnant, unwilling, disinclined, hostile, indisposed, opposed.—*Averse* implies habitual dislike or unwillingness, though not of a very strong character, and is nearly synonymous with *disinclined*; as, *averse* to study, to active pursuits. *Reluctant*, literally, struggling back from, implies some degree of struggle, either with others who are inciting us on, or between our own inclination and some compelling motive, as sense of duty, whether it operate as an impelling or restraining influence.

ȧ-vẽrse′, *v.t.* and *v.i.* To avert. [Obs.]

ȧ-vẽrse′ly, *adv.* 1. With repugnance; unwillingly.

2. Backward; behind; as, an arm stretched *aversely*. [Rare.]

ȧ-vẽrse′ness, *n.* Opposition of mind; dislike; unwillingness; backwardness.

ȧ-vẽr′sion, *n.* [L. *aversus*, pp. of *avertere*, to turn away; *a*, or *ab*, from, and *vertere*, to turn.]

1. Opposition or repugnance of mind; dislike; disinclination; reluctance; hatred; followed by *to* before the object; although sometimes it admits of *for*.

> A freeholder is bred with an *aversion* to subjection. —Addison.

2. Opposition or contrariety of nature; applied to inanimate substances. [Obs.]

> Magnesia, notwithstanding this *aversion* to solution, forms a kind of paste with water. —Fourcroy.

3. The cause or object of dislike.

Syn.—Antipathy, disgust, reluctance, repugnance, abhorrence, contrariety, detestation, dislike, hatred, opposition.—*Aversion* is not so strong as *reluctance*; nor *reluctance* as *repugnance*. *Disgust* is a repugnance of feeling or taste; *antipathy* is properly a constitutional disgust, though sometimes an acquired one.

ȧ-vẽrt′, *v.t.*; averted, *pt.*, *pp.*; averting, *ppr.* [L. *avertere*, to turn away; *a*, or *ab*, from, and *vertere*, to turn.]

1. To turn from; to turn off or away; as, to *avert* the eyes from an object.

2. To keep off, divert, or prevent; as, to *avert* an approaching calamity.

3. To dislike; to oppose. [Obs.]

ȧ-vẽrt′, *v.i.* To turn away. [Obs.]

ȧ-vẽrt′ed, *a.* Turned from or away; unfavorable; unpropitious.

ȧ-vẽrt′ẽr, *n.* A person or thing that averts.

ȧ-vẽrt′i-ble, *a.* Capable of being averted or prevented.

ȧ-vẽr′ti-ment, *n.* Advertisement. [Obs.]

A′vēṣ, *n.pl.* [L., pl. of *avis*, bird.] The class of vertebrates including the birds: they breathe by lungs; have warm, red blood and a double circulation; are produced from eggs; covered with feathers; have a prominent naked toothless bill; and four limbs, the two anterior being organized for flight, and called wings.

A-ves′tȧ, *n.* The sacred writings of Zoroaster. [See *Zend-Avesta*.]

A-vest′ăn, *a.* and *n.* I. *a.* Of or pertaining to the Avesta.

II. *n.* The language in which the Avesta is written. [See *Zend*.]

ä″vï-ä-dōr′, *n.* [Sp. Am.] A person who supplies funds and materials for working a mine.

ā′vi-ăn, *a.* Of or pertaining to birds.

ā′vi-ā-ry, *n.* [L. *aviarium*, an aviary, from *avis*, a bird.] A building or inclosure for the breeding, rearing and keeping of birds.

ā″vi-ā′tion, *n.* That part of aerial navigation dealing with dynamically-raised or "heavier-than-air" machines.

ā″vi-ā-tor, *n.* [L. *avis*, bird.] One who practices aviation.

ȧ-vic′ū-lȧ, *n.* [L., dim. of *avis*, bird.]

1. A small bird; a fledgeling.

2. [A—] A genus of bivalve mollusks, including the wing-shells.

ȧ-vic′ū-lăr, *a.* Of or pertaining to birds.

ȧ-vic-ū-lā′ri-um, *n.*; *pl.* **ȧ-vic-ū-lā′ri-ȧ.** A prehensile process found in the cells of many of the *Polyzoa*, resembling a bird's bill in shape.

ā′vi-cul-tūre, *n.* [L. *avis*, bird, and *cultura*, culture.] The raising and care of birds.

av′id, *a.* [L. *avidus*, covetous.] Eager; greedy.

ȧ-vid′i-ous, *a.* Avid.

ȧ-vid′i-ous-ly, *adv.* Eagerly; with greediness.

ȧ-vid′i-ty, *n.* [Fr. *avidite*; L. *aviditas*, greed, from *avere*, to desire.]

1. Greediness; strong appetite; applied to the senses.

2. Eagerness; intenseness of desire; applied to the mind.

3. In chemistry, the degree of affinity.

Syn.—Greediness, eagerness, gluttony, cupidity, graspingness.

ȧ-vie′, *adv.* In an emulous manner. [Obs.]

ā-vi-fau′nȧ, *n.* [L. *avis*, bird, and *faunus*, faun, from *favere*, to favor.] A collective name for the birds of a district.

av-i-gä′tō, *n.* Same as *Avocado*.

A-vi-gnon′-ber″ry (ȧ-vēn-yaṅ′), *n.* The fruit of *Rhamnus infectorius*, so called from the city *Avignon*, in France. It is used by dyers and painters for staining yellow; also called *French berry* and *yellow berry*.

ȧ-vile′, *v.t.* [ME. *avilen*; OFr. *aviler*, to debase, from L. *ad*, to, and *vilis*, base.] To depreciate; to debase. [Obs.]

ȧ′vis′, *n.* [Fr.] Advice. [Obs.]

ȧ-viṣe′, *v.t.* and *v.i.* [Fr. *aviser*, to advise.] To consider; to counsel. [Obs.]

ȧ-vīsed′, *a.* Complexioned; as, black-*avised*. [Scot.]

ȧ-viṣe′ful, *a.* Circumspect. [Obs.]

ȧ-viṣe′ly, *adv.* Advisedly. [Obs.]

ȧ-viṣe′ment, *n.* Advisement; deliberation. [Obs.]

ȧ-vi′ṣion, *n.* Vision. [Obs.]

ȧ-vi′ṣō, *n.* [Sp.] 1. Advice; information; intelligence. [Obs.]

2. An advice-boat; a despatch-boat.

av-i-zan′dum, *n.* [Fr. *aviser*, to advise; L. *avisandum*, gerund of *avisare*, to advise; a term used in Law Latin.] In Scots law, private consideration. A judge *makes avizandum* with a cause when he removes it from court and takes it into his private consideration.

av-ō-ċä′dō, av-ō-ċä′tō, av-i-gä′tō, *n.* [Corrupted from Mex. *ahuacatl*.] The alligator-pear, *Persea gratissima*, a native of the West Indies. The fruit, when fully ripe, is considered a delicacy.

av′ō-ċat (-kȧ), *n.* [Fr., from L. *avocatus*, pp. of *avocare*, to call away.] An advocate.

av′ō-ċāte, *v.t.* [L. *avocare*, from *a*, from, and *vocare*, to call.] To call off or away. [Obs.]

av-ō-ċā′tion, *n.* [L. *avocatio*, a calling off; from *avocare*, to call away.]

1. The act of calling aside, or diverting from some employment; as, an *avocation* from sin or from business. [Obs.]

2. The business which calls aside. The word is generally used for the smaller affairs of life,

or occasional calls which summon a person to leave his ordinary or principal business.

3. A person's regular business or occupation; vocation; employment. [This use of the word, though improper, is common.]

The ancient *avocation* of picking pockets.
—Sydney Smith.

The wandering *avocation* of a shepherd.
—Buckle.

This use of *avocation* for vocation, however common, has seldom had the sanction of good writers. On the other hand the plural, *avocations*, was long ago used, sometimes to denote *pursuits, duties*, and such is, I think, almost exclusively, its modern import.—Fitzedward Hall.

4. [*pl.*] Daily pursuits; duties; vocation.

5. The removal of a case or process from an inferior to a superior court, or from one tribunal to another.

Syn.—Employment, occupation, business, vocation, calling.

ȧ-vō′çȧ-tive, *a.* [Obs.] See *Avocatory*.

av-ō-çȧ′tō, *n.* Same as *Avocado*.

ȧ-voc′ȧ-tō-ry, *a.* Calling away or aside.

Letters avocatory; letters from a ruler recalling subjects from another country or directing them to discontinue certain proscribed acts.

av′ō-cet, *n.* Same as *Avoset*.

ȧ-void′, *v.t.*; avoided, *pt., pp.*; avoiding, *ppr.* [ME. *avoiden*, to avoid; OFr. *esvuidier, esveudier*, to empty out, from L. *ex*, out, and *viduare*, to deprive of.]

1. To shun; to keep at a distance from; to keep clear of; to escape; to abstain from; that is, literally, to go from; as, to *avoid* the company of gamesters; to *avoid* expense.

2. To emit or throw out; to make empty; to quit; to evacuate; to shun by leaving. [Obs.]

3. To make void; to annul or vacate; as, to *avoid* a deed or grant.

4. In pleading, to defeat or evade (the allegation of the other party) by setting up some new matter. Thus, in a replication, the plaintiff may deny the defendant's plea, or confess it, and *avoid* it by stating new matter.
—Blackstone.

Syn.—Shun, elude, eschew, avert, escape, evade, keep away from, keep clear of.—*Avoid* is negative; it is simply to keep away from. *Shun* is positive; it is to *turn* from. Prudence may induce us to *avoid*; fear or dislike leads us to *shun*. We *avoid* bad habits; we ought to *shun* vice.

ȧ-void′, *v.i.* 1. To retire; to withdraw. [Obs.]

David *avoided* out of his presence.
—1 Sam. xviii. 11.

2. To become void, vacant, or empty, as a benefice. [Obs.]

ȧ-void′ȧ-ble, *a.* 1. That may be avoided, left at a distance, shunned, or escaped.

2. That may be vacated; liable to be annulled.

ȧ-void′ănce, *n.* 1. The act of avoiding or shunning.

2. The act of becoming vacant, or the state of being vacant. It is appropriately used for the state of a benefice becoming void by the death, deprivation, or resignation of the incumbent.

3. The act of annulling.

4. A retiring from or leaving a place. [Obs.]

5. An emptying out; an outlet. [Obs.]

ȧ-void′ẽr, *n.* 1. One who avoids, shuns, or escapes.

2. One who or that which empties or carries things away.

ȧ-void′less, *a.* That cannot be avoided; inevitable.

av″oir-dū-poiṣ′ (-ẽr-dū-), *n.* [ME. *aver de poiz*; OFr. *aver de peis*; *aver*, goods, from L. *habere*, to have; *de*, from, L. *de*, from; *peis*, from L. *pensum*, weight.]

1. A system of weight commonly used in the United States and England for commodities of all kinds except precious metals, precious stones, and drugs. The pound, the unit weight, contains 16 ounces instead of 12 ounces, as in troy weight; 2,000 pounds constitute the common or "short" ton, while the "long" ton contains 2,240 pounds. The pound *avoirdupois* contains 7,000 troy grains, and is equivalent to $1\frac{51}{144}$ pound troy.

2. Commodities sold by weight. [Obs.]

3. Weight; heaviness; as, *avoirdupois* counts in football. [Colloq.]

ȧ-vōke′, *v.t.* [L. *avocare*, to call away.] To call back or away. [Obs.]

av′ō-lāte, *v.i.* [L. *avolare*, to fly away.] To fly off; to escape; to evaporate. [Obs.]

av-ō-lā′tion, *n.* The act of flying away; flight; escape; exhalation; evaporation. [Obs.]

av′ō-set, av′ō-cet, *n.* [Fr. *avocette*; Sp. *avoceta*.]

1. Any one of various species of aquatic birds, of the genus *Recurvirostra*. The bill of these birds is long, slender, flexible, and bent upward toward the tip. They have very long legs, and palmated feet. *Recurvirostra americana* is the American species; *Recurvirostra avosetta*, the European. Written also *avocette*.

2. A humming-bird of the genus *Avocetta*, with a slender up-curved bill.

Avoset (*Recurvirostra avosetta*).

ȧ-vouch′, *v.t.*; avouched, *pt., pp.*; avouching, *ppr.* [ME. *avouchen*; OFr. *avochier*, to affirm positively; from L. *advocare*, to summon.]

1. To affirm openly; to declare or assert with positiveness; to avow; also, to acknowledge openly; as, to *avouch* one's guilt; to *avouch* the Lord to be thy God.

2. To maintain, vindicate, or justify; to make good; to answer for; to establish; to substantiate; to guarantee.

3. To appeal to; to cite as authority. [Obs.]

ȧ-vouch′, *v.i.* To give assurance or guarantee; as, to *avouch* for another's character or reputation.

ȧ-vouch′, *n.* Evidence; testimony; declaration. [Rare.]

ȧ-vouch′ȧ-ble, *a.* Capable of being avouched or maintained.

ȧ-vouch′ẽr, *n.* One who avouches.

ȧ-vouch′ment, *n.* Declaration; the act of avouching. [Obs.]

ȧ-vöu-é′ (-ā′), *n.* [Fr., from OFr. *avoue*, pp. of *avouer*, to avow, from L. *advocare*, to call upon or summon.]

1. In France, formerly, a protector of a church or religious community, corresponding to the English *advowee*.

2. A French lawyer, the term in this connection corresponding to the English *attorney at law*.

ȧ-vou′trẽr, *n.* [Obs.] Same as *Advoutrer*.

ȧ-vou′trie, *n.* [Obs.] Same as *Advoutry*.

ȧ-vow′, *v.t.*; avowed, *pt., pp.*; avowing, *ppr.* [ME. *avowen*; OFr. *avouer*, to avow, or confess; from L. *advocare*, to call upon.]

1. To declare openly, with a view to justify, maintain, or defend; or simply to own, acknowledge, or confess frankly; as, a man *avows* his principles or his crimes.

2. In law, to acknowledge and justify, in one's own right, as when the distrainer of goods defends in an action of replevin, and *avows* the taking in his own right, but insists that such taking was legal. —Blackstone.

Syn.—Acknowledge, profess, declare, confess, admit, aver, own.

ȧ-vow′, *n.* A vow or determination. [Rare.]

ȧ-vow′, *n.* An avowal; acknowledgment. [Obs.]

ȧ-vow′, *v.t.* and *v.i.* To devote; to promise; to bind. [Obs.]

ȧ-vow′ȧ-ble, *a.* Capable of being avowed, or openly acknowledged with confidence.

ȧ-vow′ăl, *n.* An open declaration; frank acknowledgment.

ȧ-vow′ănce, *n.* 1. Avowal.

2. Defense or vindication. [Obs.]

ȧ-vow′ănt, *n.* In law, the defendant in replevin, who avows the distress of the goods, and justifies the taking. —Cowell.

ȧ-vowed′, *a.* Openly declared; owned; frankly acknowledged.

ȧ-vow′ed-ly, *adv.* In an open manner; with frank acknowledgment.

ȧ-vow-ee′, *n.* One who has a right to present to a benefice; the patron; an advowee. [Obs.]

ȧ-vow′ẽr, *n.* One who avows, owns, or asserts.

ȧ-vow′ry, *n.* 1. In law, the act of the distrainer of goods, who, in an action *avowed* and justified the taking by maintaining that he took them in his own right; thus distinguished from *cognizance*, which was the defense of one who maintained that he took them in the right of another as his bailiff or servant.

2. Justification. [Obs.]

Therefore away with these *avowries*; let God alone be our *avowry*. —Latimer.

ȧ-vow′try, *n.* Same as *Advoutry*.

ȧ-voy′ẽr, *n.* [Fr. *avoyer*.] Formerly, the chief magistrate of an imperial city or canton of French Switzerland. [Obs.]

ȧ-vulse′, *v.t.* [L. *avulsus*, pp. of *avellere*, to pluck off.] To pull off; to pluck. [Rare.]

ȧ-vul′sion, *n.* [L. *avulsio*, from *avello*; *a*, from, and *vello*, to pull.]

1. A pulling or tearing from or asunder; a rending or forcible separation.

2. That part which is torn away.

3. In law, a sudden removal of soil from the land of one and its deposit upon or addition to the land of another by the violent action of water, or a sudden change in the course of a stream.

ȧ-vun′çū-lăr, *a.* [L. *avunculus*, uncle.] Of, pertaining to, or like an uncle.

ȧ-wä′, *adv.* [Scot.] Away.

ȧ-wāit′, *v.t.*; awaited, *pt., pp.*; awaiting, *ppr.* [ME. *awaiten*; OFr. *awaiter*, to wait for; *a*, to, and *waiter*; later *guaitier*, Fr. *guetter*, to watch.]

1. To lie in wait for. [Obs.]

2. To wait for; to look for, or expect.

Betwixt these rocky pillars Gabriel sat,
Chief of the angelic guards, *awaiting* night.
—Milton.

3. To be in store for; to attend; to be ready for; as, a glorious reward *awaits* the good.

4. To wait upon; to serve. [Obs.]

ȧ-wāit′, *v.i.* 1. To watch. [Obs.]

2. To remain in waiting; to wait.

ȧ-wāit′, *n.* Ambush; a state of waiting. [Obs.]

ȧ-wāke′, *v.t.*; awoke *or* awaked, *pt.*; awaking, *ppr.*; awaked, *pp.* [ME. *awecchen*; AS. *aweccan*, to awaken.]

1. To rouse from sleep; to cause to cease from sleep.

I go, that I may *awake* him out of sleep.
—John xi. 11.

2. To excite or rouse from a state resembling sleep, as from death, stupor, or inaction; to put into action, or new life; as, to *awake* the dead; to *awake* the dormant faculties.

Syn.—Arouse, excite, provoke, stimulate, incite, animate.

ȧ-wāke′, *v.i.* [ME. *awaken*, awake; AS. *āwacian*, to be awake.]

1. To cease to sleep; to come from a state of natural sleep.

Jacob *awaked* out of his sleep.
—Gen. xxviii. 16.

2. To bestir, revive, or rouse from a state of inaction; to be invigorated with new life; as, the mind *awakes* from its stupidity; he *awoke* to life's higher significance.

3. Figuratively, to rouse from spiritual sleep; as, to *awake* to righteousness.

ȧ-wāke′, *a.* Not sleeping; in a state of vigilance or action.

ȧ-wāk′en, *v.t.* and *v.i.*; awakened, *pt., pp.*; awakening, *ppr.* 1. To rouse from inactivity of any kind; to stir into life and energy.

2. To become awake; to awake.

ȧ-wāk′en-ẽr, *n.* One who or that which awakens.

ȧ-wāk′en-ing, *n.* The act of rousing from sleep or inactivity; specifically, a revival of religion, or more general attention to religion than usual.

ȧ-wāk′en-ing-ly, *adv.* In a manner to awaken.

ȧ-wāk′en-ment, *n.* An awakening; a revival. [Rare.]

ȧ-wạnt′ing, *a.* Wanting; lacking. [Scot. and Prov. Eng.]

ȧ-wạrd′, *v.t.*; awarded, *pt., pp.*; awarding, *ppr.* [ME. *awarden*; OFr. *eswarder*, to award; *es*, out, and *warder*, to guard, from O.H.G. *warten*, to guard.]

1. To adjudge; to give by sentence or judicial determination; to assign as the result of careful consideration, as to competitors in any contest; specifically, used to express the act of arbitrators, etc., in pronouncing upon the rights of parties; as, the arbitrators *awarded* damages to A. B.

2. To grant; to allot; to bestow.

The child had many more luxuries and indulgences than had been *awarded* to his father.
—Thackeray.

ȧ-wạrd′, *v.i.* To judge; to determine; to make an award.

ȧ-wạrd′, *n.* 1. A judgment, sentence, or final decision; as, the *award* of Providence; the *award* of posterity.

2. Specifically, the decision of arbitrators, a jury, etc., in a case submitted.

3. The paper containing the decision of arbitrators, etc.; as, a sealed *award*.

ȧ-wạrd′ẽr, *n.* One who awards, or assigns by sentence or judicial determination; a judge.

ȧ-wāre′, *a.* [ME. *aware, iwar*; AS. *gewær*, aware, from *wær*, cautious.]

1. Watchful; vigilant; guarded.

2. Apprised; cognizant; expecting an event from information, or probability; as, the general was *aware* of the enemy's designs.

Syn.—Cognizant, conscious, apprised, informed, sensible, acquainted.

ȧ-warn′, *v.t.* To warn. [Obs.]

ȧ-wash′, *a.* and *adv.* 1. Level with the surface of the water, as a rock just above the waves, or an anchor when hove up to the surface of the water.

2. Wet by the waves; as, the decks are *awash*.

3. Washed about by the water.

ȧ-wāy′, *adv.* [ME. *away, awey*; AS. *aweg, on weg*, on way.]

1. Literally, on the way; along; as, come *away*.

2. Absent; at a distance; distant; as, the master is *away* from home; the river is two miles *away*.

3. From here or there; from proximity; off; as, to go *away*; to clear *away* rubbish.

4. Separate; detached; out of one's keeping, attention, or interest; as, that is *away* from the discussion; to give *away* a secret; to put *away* a temptation; to lay *away* one's clothes.

5. In another direction; off; aside; as, to turn *away*.

6. Out of existence; to another condition or state; to an end; as, to pass *away*; to fade *away*.

7. On; without intermission; steadily; continuously; as, sing *away*. From this sense, it comes to have a merely intensive force; as, fire *away*. [Colloq.]

8. Used without a verb with an idea of separation or moving; as, whither *away* so fast? It often has an imperative force equivalent to *begone*; as, *away*, slight man!

Away back; at a great distance back, in time or space.

Away with; take away; as, *away with* him; also, endure or bear; as, I cannot *away with* it.

Far away; at a great distance.

Far and away; greatly; by far.

Right away; at once; instantly.

To do away with; to discard or destroy.

To make away with; to kill or destroy; also, to carry off or to use wastefully.

ȧ-wāy′=gō″ing, *a.* and *n.* I. *a.* Departing; leaving.

II. *n.* A departure.

Away-going crops; in law, crops sown during the last year of a tenancy, but not ripe until after the expiration of it. The right which an outgoing tenant has to take an *away-going crop* is sometimes given to him by the express terms of the contract, but where this is not the case he is generally entitled to do so by the custom of the district.

ȧ-wāy′wȧrd, *adv.* Away. [Obs.]

awe (a), *n.* [ME. *aw, awe*, from Ice. *agi*, awe, fear; same root as in Gr. *achos*, fear.]

1. Fear mingled with admiration or reverence; reverential fear; a feeling produced by a sense of the dreadful and the sublime.

Stand in *awe*, and sin not. —Ps. iv. 4.

2. Fear; dread, as of something evil. [Rare.]

To stand in awe of; to reverence deeply; to have great fear, dread, or respect for.

Syn.—Dread, veneration, reverence.—*Dread* is strong personal fear; *reverence* is high respect slightly mingled with fear; in *awe*, the fear predominates. *Veneration* is the highest reverence we can pay to human beings.

awe, *v.t.*; awed, *pt.*, *pp.*; awing, *ppr.* To strike with fear and reverence; to influence by fear, terror, or respect; as, his majesty *awed* them into silence.

ȧ-wēa′ry, *a.* Same as *Weary*.

ȧ-weath′ẽr (-weth′), *adv.* A nautical term, signifying on the weather side, or toward the wind; as, the helm is *aweather*; opposed to *alee*.

ȧ-weigh′ (-wā′), *adv.* Among seamen, atrip; said of an anchor. The anchor is *aweigh* when it is just drawn out of the ground and hangs perpendicular.

awe′=in-spir″ing, *a.* Impressing with awe.

awe′less, aw′less, *a.* [ME. *awles*; AS. *egeleas*, aweless; *ege*, awe, and *-leas*, less.] Lacking awe or reverence; also, lacking the ability to inspire awe or reverence.

awe′less-ness, *n.* The quality or condition of being aweless.

awe′sōme, aw′sōme, *a.* Awe-inspiring; indicating awe. [OE. or Scot.]

awe′sōme-ness, *n.* The quality of causing awe.

awe′=strick″en, *a.* Impressed with awe.

awe′=strike, *v.t.* To impress or strike with awe. [Rare.]

awe′=struck, *a.* Impressed or struck with awe; awe-stricken.

aw′fụl, *a.* [ME. *awful, agheful*; AS. *egeful*, awful.]

1. Inspiring with awe; filling with profound reverence; impressive; as, the *awful* majesty of Jehovah.

2. Filling with terror and dread; frightful; dreadful; as, the *awful* approach of death.

3. Struck with awe; evidencing awe.

A weak and *awful* reverence for antiquity. —Watts.

4. Obedient; under due awe of authority or dignity; lawful; reverential. [Obs.]

5. Frightful; ugly; detestable; as, an *awful* bonnet; also excessive; great; remarkable; as, an *awful* lie. [Colloq.]

Syn.—Dreadful, fearful, solemn, direful, impressive, appalling.

aw′fụl-ly, *adv.* 1. In a manner to fill with awe; in a reverential manner.

2. Very; exceedingly; as, *awfully* bad taste. [Colloq.]

aw′fụl-ness, *n.* 1. The quality of striking with awe, or with reverence; solemnity; as, the *awfulness* of this sacred place.

2. The state of being struck with awe. [Obs.]

A help to prayer, producing in us reverence and *awfulness*. —Taylor.

ȧ-whāpe′ (-hwāp′), *v.t.* [ME. *awhaped.*] To strike with amazement; to confound. [Obs.]

ȧ-while′ (-hwīl′), *adv.* For a space of time; for some time; for a short time; also properly written as two words.

ȧ-wing′, *a.* or *adv.* On the wing; in flight.

awk, *n.* An auk.

awk, *a.* [ME. *awke, auke*, from Ice. *öfigr, öfugr*, contrary; root *af*, off, away.]

1. Contrary; backward; hence, perverse, wrong, erroneous. [Obs.]

2. Not dexterous; unhandy; awkward; ungainly.

3. Left; left-handed. [Obs.]

awk, awk′ly, *adv.* 1. Awkwardly. [Obs.]

2. Perversely; in the wrong way. [Obs.]

awk′wȧrd, *a.* [ME. *awkwarde*, from *awk-*, off, and *-ward*, AS. *-weard*; same root as L. *vertere*, to turn.]

1. Wanting dexterity in the use of the hands or of instruments; unskilful; not dexterous; bungling.

2. Inelegant; ungainly; ungraceful in manners; clumsy.

3. Troublesome to handle or to manage; embarrassing; as, an *awkward* situation.

4. Unfavorable; untoward; adverse; unfortunate. [Obs.]

Awkward squad; a squad of raw recruits.

Syn.—Clumsy, uncouth, unhandy, bungling, ungainly, unskilful, rough.

awk′wȧrd-ly, *adv.* Clumsily; in a rude or bungling manner; inelegantly; badly; uneasily.

awk′wȧrd-ness, *n.* Clumsiness; ungracefulness in manners; want of dexterity in the use of the hands or instruments; unsuitableness; embarrassment.

awl, *n.* [ME. *aul, awel*; AS. *æl, awel*, an awl.] A tool for piercing small holes in leather, wood, and other soft materials. It is made in various shapes for special uses.

aw′less, *a.* Same as *Aweless*.

aw′less-ness, *n.* Same as *Awelessness*.

awl′=shāped (-shāpt), *a.* 1. Having the shape of an awl.

2. In botany, subulate; tapering to a point.

awl′wŏrt, *n.* The popular name of *Subularia aquatica*; so called from its awl-shaped leaves, which grow in clusters round the root. It is a native of the British Isles.

awm, aum, *n.* Same as *Aam*.

awn, *n.* [ME. *awne, agun*, from Ice. *ögn*, chaff.] The beard of grain or grass; a slender, sharp process issuing from the chaff or glume in grain and grasses.

awned, *a.* 1. In botany, furnished with an awn, as a glume.

2. Covered with an awning.

awn′ing, *n.* [Fr. *auvent*, a penthouse; Per. *āwan*, anything suspended; origin uncertain.]

1. A cover, similar to a roof, to shelter from the sun's rays, the rain, and the wind; usually made of canvas or similar material. Originally employed as a shelter to a vessel's deck, or a boat, but now used for various other purposes, as in front of store and other windows.

2. That part of the poop-deck which is continued forward beyond the bulkhead of the cabin.

awn′inged, *a.* Equipped with an awning.

awn′less, *a.* Without awn or beard.

awn′y, *a.* Having awns.

ȧ-wōke′, *v.*, past tense of *awake*.

ȧ-wŏrk′, *adv.* [ME. *awerke.*] At work; in or into a state of labor or action.

ȧ-wŏrk′ing, *adv.* At work; in or into a state of working or action. [Obs.]

ȧ-wrēak′, ȧ-wrēke′ (-rēk′), *v.t.* [ME. *awreken*; AS. *awrecan*, to take vengeance on.] To avenge; to take vengeance on. [Obs.]

ȧ-wrŏng′ (-rŏng′), *adv.* In a wrong manner.

ȧ-wrȳ′ (-rī′), *a.* or *adv.* [ME. *awry, awrye, on wry*, turned or twisted.]

1. Turned or twisted toward one side; not in a straight or true direction or position; asquint; with oblique vision; as, to glance *awry*; the lady's cap is *awry*.

2. In a figurative sense, turned aside from the line of truth, or right reason; perverse or perversely.

aw′sōme, *a.* See *Awesome*.

ax, axe, *v.t.* To ask. [Obs. or Vulgar.]

ax, axe, *n.*; *pl.* **ax′eṣ.** [ME. *ax, axe*; AS. *æx, eax*, ax; L. *ascia*; Gr. *axinē*, an ax, mattock.] A tool for hewing, chopping, etc., consisting of a head of iron or steel with a cutting-edge, and a handle or helve. The shape and size vary with the specific use to which the *ax* is to be put, as in the broad*ax*, the stonecutter's *ax*, the fireman's *ax*, the old battle-*ax*, etc.

ax′ăl, *a.* See *Axial*.

axe, *n.* See *Ax*.

axed (axt), *a.* In stonemasonry, having a surface dressed smooth with a stone-ax.

axe′măn, *n.* See *Axman*.

ax′ēṣ, *n.*, pl. of *axis*; also of *ax*.

ax′fitch, *n.* [Old Dutch *akes*, ax, and *vitsche*, fitch.] A leguminous plant having the pods ax-shaped.

ax′=fọrm, *a.* In botany, same as *Ax-shaped*.

ax′i-ăl, *a.* 1. Of or pertaining to an axis; moving about an axis; constituting an axis.

2. In anatomy, pertaining to the axis of the entire body or of any part or organ; as, the *axial* skeleton; an *axial* bone.

Axial filament; the central filament of the flagellum of a spermatozoan. It extends through the middle piece and terminates anteriorly in the end-knob.

ax′i-ăl-ly, *adv.* In reference to an axis; in a direction corresponding to that of an axis.

ax′i-fọrm, *a.* [L. *axis* and *forma.*] In the form of an axis.

ax′il, *n.* [L. *axilla*, shoulder-joint, from *ala*, wing.] In botany, the angle between an axis and the upper side of any organ growing from it, as between a branch and the stem of a leaf. Buds usually appear in the *axils* of leaves.

aa, Axils.

ax′ile, *a.* [L. *axis*, an axle.] Belonging to, occupying, or lying in the direction of an axis.

ax-il′lȧ, *n.*; *pl.* **ax-il′læ.** [L. *axilla*, the armpit.]

1. The hollow underneath the shoulder; the armpit.

2. In botany, an axil.

ax-il′lănt, *a.* In botany, inclosing an axil; forming an axil.

ax′il-lăr, ax′il-lā-ry, *n.* In ornithology, one of the feathers on the under side of the wing near its juncture with the body; usually in the plural.

ax′il-lā-ry, ax′il-lăr, *a.* 1. In anatomy, pertaining to the axilla or armpit.

2. In botany, pertaining to or proceeding from an axil.

ax′in, *n.* [Sp. *axina.*] A secretion of the Mexican cochineal; used in the preparation of certain medicines and varnishes.

ax′i-nite, *n.* [Gr. *axinē*, an ax.] A dark-brown mineral, occurring in sharply edged crystals, somewhat resembling an ax. It consists chiefly of silica, alumina, lime, and oxid of iron.

ax-in′ō-man-cy (*or* ax′in-ō-man″cy), *n.* [Gr. *axinē*, an ax, and *manteia*, divination.] An ancient kind of divination for the detection of crime by means of an ax. Thus, an ax might be poised on a bar, and the names of the persons suspected repeated; if the ax moved at the name of any one he was pronounced guilty.

ax′i-ō-lite, *n.* [L. *axis*; Gr. *axōn*, an axle, and *lithos*, stone.] A collection of crystal fibers, grouped about an axis; found in certain rocks.

ax″i-ō-lit′iç, *a.* Pertaining to or resembling axiolite.

ax′i-ŏm, *n.* [Gr. *axiōma*, authority, an authoritative sentence, from *axioun*, to think worthy.]

1. A self-evident truth, or a proposition whose truth is so evident at first sight that no process of reasoning or demonstration can make it plainer; as, the whole is greater than a part.

2. An established principle in some art or science; a principle received without new proof.

Syn.—Maxim, aphorism, adage.—*Axioms* are the foundations of science; *maxims* are guiding principles in our practical concerns. An *aphorism* is a detached sentence expressing a weighty sentiment; an *adage* is a saying of long-established authority.

ax″i-ō-mat′iç, ax″i-ō-mat′iç-ăl, *a.* Pertaining to an axiom; of obvious truth; self-evident; also, replete with or based on axioms.

ax″i-ō-mat′iç-ăl-ly, *adv.* By the use of or in accordance with axioms.

ax′i-ō-pis-ty, *n.* [Gr. *axiopistos*, trustworthy; *axios*, worthy, and *pistos*, trusty.] The quality which renders a thing worthy of belief; worthiness of credit. [Obs.]

ax′is, *n.*; *pl.* **ax′ēṣ.** [L. *axis*; Gr. *axōn*, axis, axle.]

1. The straight line, real or imaginary, passing through a body, on which it revolves, or may be imagined to revolve; as, the *axis* of the earth; also, any central line of symmetry.

2. In mechanics, the support for any rotating body; a shaft, axle, or spindle.

3. In geometry, the imaginary line passing through the center of a figure or solid; the central line with reference to which a figure is symmetrical; any fixed line with reference to which positions of points are determined or distances measured.

4. In anatomy, (a) the central portion of the body, i.e., the vertebral column, or of an organ; (b) the second cervical vertebra, which has a tooth-like process passing upward through the central foramen of the first vertebra or atlas, thus serving as a pivot on which the latter turns; hence, also, the tooth-like process itself.

5. In botany, the central line or column; that part around which subsidiary parts are disposed. Thus, the stem and root are known as

the *ascending* and *descending axes* respectively.

6. In crystallography, an imaginary line assumed through a crystal, with reference to its different faces and angles.

7. In physical geography and geology, the principal mountain region; the crest-line; the main line of direction of ranges, valleys, etc. The axis running along a crest is an *anticlinal axis*; the axis running along a valley is a *synclinal axis*.

8. In art and architecture, one of the main central lines of design.

9. Figuratively, a turning-point or condition; that upon which a matter depends; a pivot.

Axes of coördinates; two intersecting straight lines with reference to which the relative positions of points are determined.

Axis of a curve; a right line dividing a curve into two symmetrical parts, so that the part on one side exactly corresponds to that on the other, as in a parabola, ellipse, or hyperbola.

Axis of a lens; a straight line drawn through the optical center of the lens, and perpendicular to both its surfaces.

Axis of an Ionic capital; a line passing perpendicularly through the middle of the eye of the volute.

Axis of horizon; a right line assumed at the point of observation, perpendicular to the horizon.

Axis of oscillation; a right line parallel to the horizon, passing through the center about which a pendulum vibrates.

Axis of refraction; a straight line drawn perpendicular to the surface of the refracting medium, through the point of incidence of the refracted ray. Some crystals have two *axes of refraction*.

Axis of symmetry of a body; a line on both or all sides of which the parts of a body or magnitude are symmetrically disposed.

Conjugate or *minor axis*; in conic sections, the diameter perpendicular to the transverse axis.

Neutral axis (*of a beam, etc.*); in mechanics, the line or plane along which neither tension nor compression is operative.

Optic axis; the line passing through the center of the pupil of the eye and of the crystalline lens, perpendicularly to the surface. The ray of light passing along this line is the only one which is not refracted.

Optic axis of a crystal; a line of direction through a crystal in which a ray of light is not refracted.

Spiral axis; in architecture, the axis of a twisted column or shaft drawn spirally so that the circumvolutions may be traced externally.

Transverse or *major axis*; in conic sections, the diameter which passes through the foci.

Visual axis; the line of any of the several rays of light which enter the eye; distinguished from the *optic axis*.

ax'is, *n.* In zoölogy, the spotted deer of India (*Cervus axis*); also called *hog-deer* and *chittra*.

ax'is-cyl"in-dẽr, *n.* The core of white tissue in the center of a nerve-fiber, constituting its essential part.

ax'le (ax'l), *n.* [ME. *axel*, *exel*, shoulder; AS. *æx*, *eax*, axle; L. *axilla*, the armpit.]

1. A shaft on or with which a wheel revolves.

2. An axletree; a crossbar serving to connect wheels on opposite sides of a vehicle, etc.

3. An axis, as of the earth or sun. [Rare.]

ax'le-box, *n.* A box inclosing that part of an axle or shaft that rotates in a bearing; also, the metal lining of a wheel-hub.

ax'led (ax'ld), *a.* Equipped with an axle or with axles.

ax'le-guärd (-gärd), *n.* That portion of a railroad truck by means of which the axle-box is permitted to move vertically, through the action of the springs.

ax'le-hook, *n.* A hook on an axle to which the doubletree is attached.

ax'le-pin, *n.* A pin inserted through the end of an axletree to keep the wheel in place; a linchpin.

ax'le-tree, *n.* A bar of iron or wood, fitted for insertion in the hubs of wheels, and on which the wheels turn; an axle.

ax'măn, **axe'măn**, *n.*; *pl.* **ax'men**. 1. One who uses an ax.

2. In civil engineering, one who cuts away obstructions and sets stakes for the rodman.

3. Formerly, one who carried a battle-ax.

Ax'min-stẽr, *n.* A kind of carpet having a thick pile; so called from *Axminster*, England.

ax'oid, **ax-oid'e-ăn**, *a.* [L. *axis*, axle.] In anatomy, pertaining to the axis.

ax'ō-lotl, *n.* [Mex.] An amphibian of the genus *Amblystoma*, found in the lakes of Mexico.

ax-om'e-tẽr, *n.* [L. *axis*; Gr. *axōn*, an axle, and *metron*, a measure.] In spectacle-making, an instrument for adjusting the axes of lenses.

ax'on, *n.*; *pl.* **ax-ō'nēs**. [Gr. *axōn*, axis.] The axis of the body or skeleton of a vertebrate.

Ax-ō'ni-ȧ, *n.pl.* [Gr. *axōn*, axle.] Organisms, animal or vegetable, which have definite axes; opposed to *Anaxonia*.

ax-ot'ō-mous, *a.* [Gr. *axōn*, axis, and *tomos*, cut; from *temnein*, to cut.] In mineralogy, having a cleavage with a single face, perpendicular to the axis.

ax'-shāped, *a.* In botany, having a resemblance to the head of an ax or hatchet; dolabriform.

ax'stōne, *n.* A light green or greenish-gray mineral, remarkable for its toughness; a variety of jade or nephrite. It is used by the natives of the South Sea Islands for making axes or hatchets.

ax'tree, *n.* An axletree. [OE. and Scot.]

ax'unġe, *n.* [Fr., from L. *axis*, axle, and *ungere*, to grease.] Animal fat; especially, in pharmacy, hog's lard or goose-grease. [Rare.]

aȳ (ī), *interj.* Ah; alas; as, *ay me!*

aȳ (ī), *adv.* Same as *Aye*.

āy (ā), *adv.* Same as *Aye*.

ä'yȧh, *n.* [Anglo-Ind., from Hindu *āya*, from Port. *aia*, nurse, governess.] The ordinary appellation given by Anglo-Indians to a lady's-maid or nursemaid of one of the native races of India.

aȳe, **aȳ** (ī), *adv.* [ME. *ay*; Ice. *ei*, ever.] Yes; yea; a word expressing assent, or an affirmative answer to a question. It is used also to enforce the sense of what is asserted, equivalent to even so, truly, certainly. In deliberative bodies, it is used to express an assenting vote.

aȳe (ī), *n.* One who votes in the affirmative; an affirmative vote; as, the *ayes* have it; the *ayes* and *noes*.

āye, **āy** (ā), *adv.* [ME. *ay*, *aye*, *ai*, ever, from Ice. *ei*, *ey*, ever, from AS. *awa*, *awi*, ever.] Always; ever; continually; for an indefinite time; used principally in poetry.

For aye; forever.

aȳe'-aȳe (ī'ī), *n.* [The native name, from its peculiar cry.] A singular nocturnal quadruped, about the size of a hare, found in Madagascar, the *Chiromys madagascariensis*, in its habits resembling the sloth, and remarkable for the hand-like structure of its hind feet.

ȧ-yen', **ȧ-yein'** (-yen'), **ȧ-yeins'** (-yens'), *adv.* and *prep.* Again. [Obs.]

ȧ-yen'wărd, *adv.* Backward. [Obs.]

āy'green, **āye'green** (ā'), *n.* The houseleek, *Sempervivum tectorum*; so called because of its hardiness.

āyle, *n.* [ME. *aiel*; Fr. *aieul*; OFr. *aiel*, grandfather, from L. *avus*, grandfather.] In law, a grandfather. [Obs.]

Writ of ayle; a writ in lieu of an assize of *mort d'ancestor*, when the abatement happens on the death of the demandant's grandfather. —Blackstone.

ȧ-yont', **ȧ-yond'**, *prep.* and *adv.* Beyond; past; farther. [Prov. Eng. and Scot.]

ā'y-rie, **ā'y-ry**, *n.* Same as *Aery*.

Āyr'shire (âr'), *a.* and *n.* I. *a.* Relating to *Ayrshire*, Scotland, and applied to a famous breed of cattle originating there; as, an *Ayrshire* bull.

II. *n.* One of the Ayrshire breed of cattle.

ä-yun"tä-mi-en'tō, *n.* [Sp. and Sp. Am.] The officers of a municipality; a town council; as, the *ayuntamiento* of San Francisco in 1849.

A-zā'lē-ȧ, *n.* [Gr. *azaleos*, dry, the allusion being to the dry, arid habitation of the plant.]

1. A genus of plants, natural order *Ericaceæ*, remarkable for the beauty and fragrance of its flowers, and distinguished from the rhododendrons chiefly by its deciduous leaves and its flowers, which have ten stamens instead of five. The species are principally native to North America and Asia.

Azalea (*Azalea Indica*).

2. [a—] A plant of the genus *Azalea*.

Alpine azalea; a small procumbent evergreen shrub, *Loiseleuria procumbens*, growing in mountainous districts of the eastern states and Canada and in the Scottish Highlands.

az'ȧ-rōle, *n.* [Fr. *azerole*.] The *Cratægus azarolus*, or Neapolitan medlar; a fruit-bearing shrub allied to the whitethorn.

ȧ-zed'ȧ-rach, *n.* [Fr. *azédarac*, from Per. *azaddirakht*, noble tree.]

1. A beautiful oriental tree (*Melia Azedarach*), extensively cultivated in southern United States.

2. The bark from the root of the *azedarach*, used in medicine.

az-ē-lā'iç, *a.* [Gr. *a* priv., and *zōē*, life, and *elaion*, oil.] Of, pertaining to, or containing a substance derived from the action of nitric acid on an oil; as, *azelaic* acid.

az'i-muth, *n.* [ME. *azymuth*; OFr. *azimut*, from Ar. *as-sumut*; *as*, from *al*, the, and *sumut*, pl. of *samt*, way or path.] In astronomy, angular distance measured on a horizon circle either eastward or westward from either the north or the south point in the horizon; the complement of *amplitude*.

Azimuth circle; any great circle which passes through the zenith and the nadir, and cuts the horizon at right angles.

Azimuth of a star; the angular distance, either east or west, of that star from the meridian of the observer.

Magnetic azimuth; angular distance of any heavenly body, east or west, from the magnetic meridian. This is found by observing the object with an *azimuth* compass.

Azimuth Compass.

Azimuth compass; an instrument resembling the ordinary mariner's compass, so fitted as to ascertain the magnetic azimuth of a heavenly body, whose variation from the true azimuth shows the variation of the needle.

az'i-muth-ăl (*or* -mū-thăl), *a.* Pertaining to the azimuth.

Azimuthal error; any error arising out of a deviation from the vertical plane passing through the north and south points of the heavens; as, the *azimuthal error* of a transit-instrument.

az'i-muth-ăl-ly (*or* az'i-mū-thăl-ly), *adv.* In the manner or direction of the azimuth.

az'i-muth-di"ăl, *n.* A dial whose style or gnomon is at right angles to the plane of the horizon. The shadow marks the sun's azimuth.

az'ō-. [Gr. *azōos*, lifeless; *a* priv., and *zōē*, life.] A combining form (derived from *azote*), used in chemistry to denote nitrogen compounds, especially those in which two atoms of nitrogen unite two hydrocarbon radicals.

az-ō-ben'zēne, *n.* [*Azo-*, and Fr. *benjoin*, benzene.] A chemical compound obtained from nitrobenzene by the action of reducing agents.

az"ō-ben-zō'iç, *a.* Pertaining to azobenzene.

ä-zō'gue (ä-thō'gā), *n.* A Spanish-American name for quicksilver.

ȧ-zō'iç, *a.* [Gr. *azōos*, lifeless; from *a* priv., and *zōē*, life.] Destitute of organic life; formed previous to the existence of animal life; applied to rocks in which no fossils have been found.

Azoic age; in geology, the age preceding the beginning of animal life.

A-zō'iç, *n.* The Azoic age.

az-ō-lē'iç, *a.* In chemistry, designating an acid formed by the action of nitric acid on oleic.

A-zol'lȧ, *n.* [Gr. *azein*, to dry, and *ollynai*, to kill.] A genus of cryptogamous plants of the *Salvinia* family.

ȧ-zon'iç, *a.* [Gr. *a* priv., and *zonē*, region.] Not restricted to any particular zone or region; not local.

A-zō'ri-ăn, *a.* and *n.* [Sp. *Azores*, the Azores, from *azor*, a hawk.]

I. *a.* Of or pertaining to the Azores.

II. *n.* An inhabitant of the Azores.

az'ōte (*or* ȧ-zōte'), *n.* [Gr. *a* priv., and *zōē*, life.] An early name for nitrogen; so called by Lavoisier from its inability to sustain life. [Rare.]

az'oth, *n.* [Ar. *az-zaug*, mercury.] A name given by alchemists to mercury, they assuming it to be the first principle of all metals; the universal specific of Paracelsus.

ȧ-zot'iç, *a.* Pertaining to azote; formed or consisting of azote in its higher valence; nitric. [Rare.]

az'ō-tīte, *n.* [Gr. *a* priv., and *zōein*, to live.] A salt of nitrous acid; a nitrite. [Rare.]

az'ō-tīze, *v.t.*; azotized, *pt.*, *pp.*; azotizing, *ppr.* To impregnate with nitrogen or azote; to nitrogenize.

az-ō-tom'e-tẽr, *n.* [*Azo-*, and Gr. *metron*, a measure.] An instrument for ascertaining the proportion of nitrogen in a substance; a nitrometer.

ȧ-zō'tous, *a.* [Obs.] Same as *Nitrous*.

az-ō-tū'ri-ȧ, *n.* [*Azo-*, and L. *urina*, urine.] A pathological condition characterized by an excess of nitrogenous matter in the urine.

Az'rā-el, *n.* [Heb. *Azraël*, help of God.] A Mohammedan name for the angel of death.

Az'teç, *a.* and *n.* [A native name.]

I. *a.* Of or pertaining to the Aztecs, the ruling race in Mexico at the time of the Spanish invasion under Cortes in 1519.

II. *n.* A member of the Aztec race.

ä-zu-le'jō (ä-thū-lā'hō), *n.* [Sp.] A kind of richly decorated tile.

ä-zum'bre (ä-thōm'brā), *n.* [Sp.] A Spanish

liquid measure varying in capacity from two to three quarts.

az'ūre (*or* ā'zūre), *a.* [ME. *azure*; OFr. *azur*; LL. *azura*; Ar. *lazward*; Per. *lazhward*, azure; the initial *l* lost through confusion with the definite article, Fr. *l'*, *le*, etc.]

1. Sky-blue; resembling the color of the clear blue sky.

2. Figuratively, cloudless; spotless, like the clear sky; as, an *azure* reputation.

az'ūre (*or* ā'zūre), *n.* 1. The fine blue color of the sky.

Her eyes a bashful *azure*. —Tennyson.

2. A name common to several sky-colored or blue pigments, of which there are two well-known varieties: (a) that made of lapis lazuli, called *ultramarine*, a color of great value to the artist; (b) that made by fusing glass with oxid of cobalt reduced to powder; in large masses called *smalt*.

3. The sky, or azure vault of heaven.

4. The lapis lazuli. [Obs.]

5. In heraldry, blue; in uncolored engraving represented by parallel horizontal lines.

az'ūre, *v.t.* To color blue.

ȧ-zū'rē-ous, *a.* In zoölogy, of a blue color.

az'ūre-stōne, *n.* A name applied to lazulite or azurite.

az'ū-rine, *a.* Azure. [Obs.]

az'ū-rine, *n.* 1. The blue roach, common in Europe.

2. The blue wren of Australia.

az'ū-rīte, *n.* In mineralogy, lazulite; also, blue malachite.

az'ūrn (*or* ā'zūrn), *a.* Of a blue color. [Obs.]

az-y-gom'ȧ-tous, *a.* [Gr. *a* priv., and *zygoun*, to yoke.] Lacking zygomatic arches.

az'y-gos, *n.* In anatomy, an azygous part.

ȧ-zy'gō-spōre, *n.* [Gr. *a* priv., and *zygon*, a yoke, and *sporos*, a sowing.] In botany, a parthenogenetic spore corresponding to a zygospore.

az'y-gous, *a.* [Gr. *azygos*, unmatched; *a* priv., and *zygoun*, to yoke.] In anatomy, a term applied to certain parts or organs which have no fellows, or are not found in pairs, as certain muscles, veins, bones, etc.

az'ym, az'yme, *n.* [Gr. *azymos*, unleavened; *a* priv., and *zymē*, leaven.] Unleavened bread.

ȧ-zym'ic, *a.* Pertaining to unleavened bread.

Az'y-mīte, *n.* In church history, one of a sect of Christians who administered the eucharist with unleavened bread; also, a term of reproach applied by the Greeks in the eleventh century to the Latins for consecrating the host with unleavened bread.

az'y-mous, *a.* [Gr. *azymos*, unleavened; *a* priv., and *zymē*, leaven.] Unleavened; unfermented.

B

B (bē). The second letter and the first consonant in the English alphabet, as it is also in the other languages of the Aryan family spoken in Europe. The characters in use in these several tongues having come through the Greek from some old language, probably the Phenician, belonging to the Semitic, or Syro-Arabian family, it was to be expected that the letter corresponding to *B* would occupy the same place in the Semitic as in the Aryan alphabets. Investigation shows this to be the case, at least, to a considerable extent. A sound and character corresponding to the English *b* and the Greek *beta*, is the second letter and the first consonant in Phenician, Hebrew, Samaritan, Aramaic, Arabic, and Coptic. In some of the Aryan languages of Asia, we find that *b* is given as the twenty-sixth of thirty-eight letters; and in Sanskrit, Mahratta, etc., *bŭ* or *bă* is generally placed twenty-third in the list of consonants. In the Semitic, *beth*, the name given to the second letter of the Hebrew alphabet, is really Aramean. Like the corresponding word in Hebrew, *baith*, it signifies a house, to which it has some faint resemblance. The form *B* is Latin, from the Greek *Beta* β; the smaller or lower case *b* came by gradual modification.

B is a flat mute, the sound being produced by compressing the lips, and adding the long vowel *ē* to render it audible. It is called a labial, from the Latin *labia*, lips; its other associates in the same category being *p*, *f*, and *v*, with which it is often interchanged in the cognate languages. Thus to *bake* is in Old German *pachan*, and in Slavic *peshtshi*. The English *life* is the German *leben*; and while *life* is the noun, *live* is the verb. So the Latin *balæna* is from the Greek *phallaina*, *phalaina* with *ph* pronounced as *f*, while from one or other comes the English *whale*. The English *have* is from the Latin *habeo*. So also the Sanskrit *vyagra*, a tiger, becomes the Mahratta *vagh* (pronounced *wagh*), and is transformed into the Hindi *bagh*. Other letters than the labials can be interchanged with *b*; thus the Greek *molubdos* and the Latin *plumbum*, lead, unlike as they appear, are akin, *m* being exchanged for *p*; and the old form of the Latin *bellum*, war, was *duellum*, whence the English words *bellicose* and *duel*.

B, b, *as a symbol*. In Greek, Hebrew, Arabic, and occasionally in English numeration, *B* is used for 2.

In music, *B* is the nominal of the seventh note of the diatonic scale. It answers to the Italian and French *si*.

In Biblical criticism of the codices, *B* is the Codex Vaticanus.

In abstract reasoning or arguments, *B* is used to designate persons or things; as, if *B* ships the goods promptly; volume *B*, etc.

In a series of any kind, *B* is used to designate the second; as, Company *B*.

In abbreviations, *B.* stands for *Bachelor* (Latin *Baccalaureus*), in degrees, as in *B.A.*, Bachelor of Arts; *B.D.*, Bachelor of Divinity; *B.L.*, Bachelor of Laws. It also indicates *before*, as in *B.C.*, before Christ; or *born*, as *b.* 1564.

In nautical records, *b* represents *blue sky*.

bä, *v.t.* [OFr. *baer*, to open the mouth.] To kiss. [Obs.]

bäa, *n.* The cry or bleating of a sheep.

bäa, *v.i.* To cry or bleat as sheep.

bäa'ing, *n.* The bleating of sheep.

Bā'ăl, *n.*; *pl.* **Bā'ăl-im.** [Gr. *Baal*, from Heb. *Ba'al*, lord, or owner.]

1. The supreme male divinity of the Syro-Phenicians; the sun-god, the lord or master, representing productive power. The name is used in Scripture in combinations designating different ideas of a lord, or different functions of a divine character; as, *Baal-berith* is the lord of the covenant; *Baal-phegor*, the lord of the dead; *Baal-zebub*, literally the god of flies, meaning the god of the Philistines.

2. [*pl.*] The idols or divinities called *Baal*, taken as a whole.

Bā'ăl-işm, *n.* The worship of Baal; idolatry.

Bā'ăl-ist, Bā'ăl-īte, *n.* One who worships Baal; an idolater.

bä'bä, *n.* A diminutive term of endearment; a young child; a childish form of *papa*.

bä'bä, *n.* [Fr.] A kind of fruit-cake.

bab'bitt, *v.t.*; babbitted, *pt.*, *pp.*; babbitting, *ppr.* To apply Babbitt metal to.

Bab'bitt, *n.* An antifriction metal composed of antimony, tin, and copper; named after the inventor, Isaac *Babbitt*; called also *Babbitt metal*.

bab'ble, *v.i.*; babbled (-bld), *pt.*, *pp.*; babbling, *ppr.* [ME. *babelen*; Fr. *babiller*, to babble; origin probably a repetition of *ba*.]

1. To utter words imperfectly or indistinctly, as children.

2. To talk idly or irrationally; to talk thoughtlessly.

3. To talk much; to prate; to chatter; to tell secrets.

4. To utter sounds frequently, incessantly, or indistinctly; as, a *babbling* echo; a *babbling* stream.

Syn.—Chatter, chat, prattle, prate, gabble, twaddle.

bab'ble, *v.t.* 1. To prate; to utter.

2. To tell a secret or secrets; to blat.

bab'ble, *n.* 1. Idle or senseless talk; as, gossipy *babble*.

2. Murmur; as, the *babble* of the stream.

bab'ble-ment, *n.* [Obs.] See *Babble*.

bab'blẽr, *n.* 1. One who or that which babbles; specifically, a hunting-dog that yelps or bays noisily after having struck the scent.

2. In zoölogy, a bird of the family *Timaliinæ*, a subfamily of thrushes of the East Indies.

bab'ble-ry (-bl-), *n.* Babble. [Obs.]

bābe, *n.* [ME. *babe*; earlier form *baban*, babe, probably so called from saying *ba-ba*.]

1. An infant; a young child of either sex.

2. A child's doll.

bābe'hood, *n.* Babyhood. [Rare.]

Bā'bel, *n.* [Heb. *Bābel*, Babylon, confusion.] A place or circumstances in which confusion of sounds is the predominating characteristic; from the tower of *Babel*.

Syn.—Hubbub, confusion, clamor, jargon, din, discord, clang.

bāb'ẽr-y, *n.* Finery to please a child; any trifling toy for children. [Obs.]

ba'bi-ăn, bā'bi-ŏn, *n.* A baboon. [Obs.]

bab'il-lärd, *n.* [Fr. *babiller*, to chatter.] The lesser whitethroat or chatterer, *Sylvia curruca*, of Europe.

bab'ing-tŏn-īte, *n.* [Named after Wm. *Babington*, of England.] A vitreous, greenish-black mineral placed by Dana under his amphibole group, the pyroxene subgroup, and the section of it with triclinic crystallization.

Bab'ing-tŏn's-cũrse, *n.* An aquatic plant, *Elodea Canadensis*, troublesome to navigation and fisheries. It was falsely supposed to have been introduced into England by Charles *Babington*.

bā'bi-ŏn, *n.* [Obs.] See *Babian*.

bab-i-rŭs'sȧ, bab-i-rōus'sȧ, *n.* [Name from Malay *babi*, hog, and *rusa*, deer.] A species of wild hog, *Babirussa alfurus*; sometimes called *horned hog* or *hog-deer*, from the fact that its upper tusks, which are of great length and curved form, grow upwards like the horns of a ruminant. It is a native of the Indian Archipelago.

Babirussa (*Babirussa alfurus*).

bāb'ish, *a.* Like a babe; childish. [Obs.]

bāb'ish-ly, *adv.* Childishly. [Obs.]

bāb'ish-ness, *n.* Childishness. [Obs.]

Bäb'işm, *n.* [Per. *bab*, a gate; so called because the founder claimed that no one could know God except through him.] The pantheistic doctrine and principles of a religious sect founded in Persia in 1843.

Bäb'ist, *n.* One who believes in Babism.

bab'lȧh, *n.* [Hind.] A pod of several species of *Acacia*, which comes from the East, and from Senegal under the name of *neb-neb*. It contains gallic acid and tannin and is used in dyeing to produce shades of drab.

bä'bo͞o, *n.* See *Babu*.

bȧ-bo͞ol', *n.* See *Babul*.

bab-o͞on', *n.* [ME. *babewyne*; OFr. *babuin*, baboon. Origin of name unknown.] The dog-faced ape, a term applied to Old World *Quadrumana* of the genera *Cynocephalus* and *Mandrilla*. They have elongated abrupt muzzles like a dog, strong tusks or canine teeth, usually short tails, cheek-pouches, small, deep eyes with huge eyebrows, and naked callosities on the buttocks. They constitute the link uniting the monkeys with the lower animals, and include the chacma, drill, common baboon, and mandrill.

Mandrill or Rib-nosed Baboon (*Cynocephalus maimon*).

bab-o͞on'ẽr-y, *n.* 1. An assemblage of baboons.

2. Baboonish behavior or condition.

bab-o͞on'ish, *a.* Resembling a baboon.

bȧ-bo͞osh', bȧ-bouche' (-bo͞osh'), *n.* [Fr. *babouche*; Ar. *babush*; Per. *paposh*, a slipper, from *pa*, foot, and *posh*, covering.] A heelless slipper, consisting of a vamp and sole, worn in Eastern countries.

bä-bü′, *n.* A Hindu title of respect nearly equivalent in application to English *Mr.*

bā-bŭl′, *n.* Same as *Bablah.*

bā′by, *n.*; *pl.* **bā′bieṣ.** [Dim. of *babe.*]

1. An infant or young child of either sex; a babe.

2. A small image in form of an infant for girls to play with; a doll.

3. The image of oneself reflected in another's eyes. [Obs.]

bā′by, *a.* Babyish; infantine; pertaining to an infant.

> Moulded thy *baby* thought. —Tennyson.

bā′by, *v.t.*; babied (-bid), *pt.*, *pp.*; babying, *ppr.* To treat like a young child.

bā′by-färm, *n.* A place where infants are cared for and reared for pay.

bā′by-färm″ẽr, *n.* One who practises baby-farming.

bā′by-färm″ing, *n.* A system by which newly-born, generally illegitimate, infants are received from their parents, to be secretly cared for.

bā′by-hood, *n.* The state of being a baby; infancy.

bā′by-house, *n.* A place for children's dolls and babies.

bā′by-ish, *a.* Like a baby; very childish.

bā′by-ish-ly, *adv.* In a babyish manner.

bā′by-ish-ness, *n.* The quality of being like a baby; extreme childishness.

bā′by-iṣm, *n.* 1. The state of being a baby; babyhood.

2. A childish mode of speech.

bā′by-jump″ẽr, *n.* An apparatus for the amusement of children, consisting of a safety seat suspended from the ceiling by a strong elastic band, by means of which the child may jump up and down without falling.

Bab-y-lō′ni-ăn, Bab-y-lō′nish, *a.* [Gr. *Babylōnia*; Heb. *Bābel.*]

1. Pertaining to Babylon, the great and luxurious capital of the ancient kingdom of Babylonia, or to the kingdom.

2. Resembling or having the characteristics of ancient Babylon, the Babylon of Revelation (Rev. xiv. 8), or any great center of luxury and vice; as, *Babylonian* splendors; *Babylonish* orgies.

3. Like the confusion of tongues at Babel; mixed; confused.

Bab-y-lō′ni-ăn, *n.* 1. An inhabitant of Babylonia; a Chaldean.

2. An astrologer; so called because the Chaldeans were remarkable for the study of astrology.

Bab-y-lon′iç, Bab-y-lon′iç-ăl, *a.* 1. Pertaining to Babylon, or made there; as, *Babylonic* garments, carpets, or hangings.

2. Tumultuous; disorderly. [Obs.]

Bab-y-lō′nish, *a.* Same as *Babylonian.*

bā′by-pin, *n.* A safety-pin.

bab-y-rŭs′sȧ, bab-y-rous′sȧ, *n.* Same as *Babirussa.*

bā′by-ship, *n.* The state of being an infant; babyhood.

baç, *n.* See first *Back*, n.

bȧ-çä′bȧ, *n.* [S. Am. name.] A Brazilian palm, *Œnocarpus distichus*, or *bacaba*, from the fruit of which the natives make a refreshing beverage or a thin oil.

bȧ-çȧ-lä′ō, *n.* [Cuban.] A West Indian fish, called the *scamp.*

baç′çȧ, *n.* [L. *baca*, or *bacca*, berry.] In botany, a berry; more precisely, a fruit, with many cells and seeds, indehiscent, in which, when ripe, the seeds lose their attachment and scatter throughout the flesh, as the gooseberry.

baç-çȧ-lau′rē-āte, *n.* [LL. *baccalaureatus*, from LL. *baccalaureus*, a bachelor, in the sense of one who has attained the first degree in a university; from *bacca*, a berry, and *laurus*, a laurel, referring to the custom of the bachelors wearing garlands of bayberries.] The degree of Bachelor of Arts; a baccalaureate sermon; a farewell discourse to a graduating class.

baç-çȧ-lau′rē-āte, *a.* Pertaining to a Bachelor of Arts; as, a *baccalaureate* sermon; *baccalaureate* pranks.

Baç-çȧ-när′ist, *n.* One of an order founded in Italy in the latter part of the eighteenth century by *Baccanari*, having as its object the restoration of the Jesuits.

baç-çȧ-rä′, baç-çȧ-rät′ (-rä′), *n.* [Fr., origin unknown.] A game of cards introduced from France into England and America. It is played by any number of players, or rather betters, and a banker.

baç-çȧ′rē, *interj.* See *Backare.*

baç′çāte, *a.* [L. *bacca*, berry.] 1. In botany, succulent, or having a pulpy texture like a berry.

2. Having or bearing berries; berried.

baç′çȧ-ted, *a.* [L. *baccatus*, garnished with berries or pearls, from *bacca*, a berry.]

1. Having many berries.

2. Set or adorned with pearls. [Obs.]

baç′chȧ-năl, *a.* [L. *bacchanal*, a place devoted to *Bacchus*, the god of wine.]

1. Reveling in intemperate drinking; riotous; noisy.

2. Relating to Bacchus or the bacchanalia.

baç′chȧ-năl, *n.* 1. A votary of Bacchus; one who indulges in drunken revels; one who is noisy and riotous when intoxicated; a drunkard.

> Each bold *bacchanal.* —Byron.

2. Any orgy of drunkenness and debauchery; specifically in the plural, the bacchanalia.

3. A dance or song after the bacchanalian style.

> Then Genius danced a *bacchanal.*—Cowper.

baç-chȧ-nā′li-ȧ, *n.pl.* [L.] In classical antiquity, feasts in honor of Bacchus, the god of wine, which were celebrated in spring and autumn, with games and shows; hence, drunken feasts; debauchery.

baç-chȧ-nā′li-ăn, *n.* and *a.* Same as *Bacchanal.*

baç-chȧ-nā′li-ăn-iṣm, *n.* The practice of bacchanalian rites; drunken revelry; riotous festivity.

baç-chȧ-nā′li-ăn-ly, *adv.* In a bacchanalian manner.

baç′chănt, *n.*; *pl.* **baç′chănts** or **baç-chan′tēṣ.** [L. *bacchans*, ppr. of *bacchari*, to celebrate the feast of Bacchus.]

1. A priest, priestess, or devotee of Bacchus.

2. A bacchanal; one given to intemperate reveling.

> They appear in a state of intoxication and are the *bacchants* in a delirium. —Rees.

3. Formerly, in Germany, a wandering student.

baç′chănt, *a.* Bacchanalian; wine-loving; reveling; carousing.

baç′chănte (*or* baç-çant′), *n.*; *pl.* **baç-chan′tēṣ.** A priestess of Bacchus, or one who joined in the celebration of the feasts of Bacchus; one in a state of bacchanal frenzy; hence, a woman addicted to intemperance or bacchanalian revelry.

Bacchante, from a marble in British Museum.

baç-chan′tiç, *n.* Same as *Bacchanal.*

baç′chȧ-ric, *n.* Same as *Bacharach.*

Baç′chȧ-ris, *n.* [The name of a shrub dedicated to Bacchus.] A large genus of plants, natural order *Compositæ.* They are shrubs or herbs, the genus containing more than two hundred species, all natives of America. Sudorific and tonic virtues are ascribed to some of the species.

baç′chiç, baç′chiç-ăl, *a.* 1. Relating to Bacchus, the god of wine; as, a *bacchic* feast or song; *bacchic* mysteries.

> The *bacchic* orgia were celebrated on the tops of hills and desolate wild places.—Stukeley.

2. Jovial; drunken; mad with intoxication.

baç-chī′us, *n.*; *pl.* **baç-chī′ī.** [Gr. *Bakcheios*, a metrical foot.] In ancient prosody, a foot composed of a short syllable and two long ones, as in *ăvārī.*

Baç′chus, *n.* [L.; Gr. *Bakchos.*] In Greek and Latin mythology, another name of Dionysos, the god of wine, son of Zeus (Jupiter) and Semele. He is said first to have taught the cultivation of the grape, and the preparation of wine and other intoxicating liquors.

Bacchus, from an antique statue.

baç-cif′ẽr-ous, *a.* [L. *baccifer*, berry-bearing.] Bearing or producing berries.

baç′ci-form, *a.* [L. *bacca*, berry, and *forma*, shape.] Of the shape of a berry.

baç-civ′ō-rous, *a.* [L. *bacca*, berry, and *vorare*, to devour.] Subsisting on berries; as, *baccivorous* birds.

bāce, *n.*, *a.*, and *v.* [Obs.] Same as *Base.*

Bach′ȧ-rach, *n.* A kind of Rhine wine made at *Bacharach*, a small town in Rhenish Prussia. Formerly written *Backarack*, *Backrag*, etc.

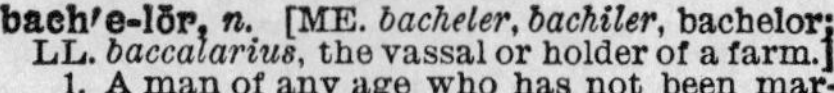

bach′e-lŏr, *n.* [ME. *bacheler*, *bachiler*, bachelor; LL. *baccalarius*, the vassal or holder of a farm.]

1. A man of any age who has not been married.

2. A person who has taken the baccalaureate or first degree in the liberal arts and sciences, or in divinity, law, etc., at a college or university.

3. A knight of the lowest order, or novice in arms, who fought under another's banner; styled a *knight bachelor.*

4. In the livery companies of London, a person not yet admitted to the livery.

5. A fresh-water fish, resembling the bass, found in the waters of the Mississippi valley; the crappie.

6. A woman who has not been married. [Obs.]

bach′e-lŏr-dŏm, *n.* 1. The state or condition of bachelorhood.

2. Bachelors collectively.

bach′e-lŏr-hood, *n.* The state of being a bachelor.

bach′e-lŏr-iṣm, *n.* The state of a bachelor; a bachelor's mannerism.

bach′e-lŏr′ṣ-but″tŏnṣ, *n.pl.* The popular name of several plants, as the double-flowered variety of *Lychnis diurna*, the red campion; *Centaurea nigra*, knapweed; especially of the double-flowered varieties of *Ranunculus aconitifolius*, white *bachelor's-buttons*, and *Ranunculus acris*, yellow *bachelor's-buttons.*

bach′e-lŏr-ship, *n.* Bachelorism.

bach′el-ry, *n.* The whole company of young candidates for knighthood. [Obs.]

baç′il-lär (*or* bȧ-cil′lär), *a.* Pertaining to or resembling a bacillus or bacilli.

Bac-il-lā′ri-ȧ, *n.* A genus of microscopic *Algæ*, belonging to the class *Diatomaceæ.*

baç′il-lā-ry, *a.* Like or containing bacilli; also, rod-like.

bȧ-cil′li-cīde, *n.* [L. *bacilli*, and *cædere*, to kill.] A substance intended to kill bacilli or disease-germs.

bȧ-cil′li-form, *a.* Having the form of a bacillus.

bȧ-cil′lus, *n.*; *pl.* **bȧ-cil′lī.** [L. *bacillum*, a small staff; dim. of *baculus*, a stick, from Gr. *baktron*, a staff.]

1. A minute rod-like body; especially, a microscopic vegetable organism like a minute rod, found in diseased tissues of the body, and the cause of putrefaction in many organic substances. The term is applied to all elongated forms of bacteria, except such as are spiral and have a gyratory motion.

2. [B—] A genus of the *Bacteriaceæ.*

back, *n.* [Fr. *bac*, trough, ferryboat.]

1. A vat used by brewers, dyers, and others, for mixing, holding water, etc.

2. A ferryboat, hauled by rope or chain, especially one adapted to carry vehicles.

3. A wooden trough, or scuttle for fuel. [Scot.]

> Narrowly escaping breaking my shins on a turf *back.* —Scott.

back, *n.* [Sw. and D. *balk*, a beam, a partition, a joist, a rafter, a bar.] In carpentry, one of the principal rafters of a roof.

back, *n.* [ME. *bak*, *bac*; AS. *baec*, back.]

1. The posterior part of the trunk extending from the inferior and posterior region of the neck as far as the loins; the region of the spine; the hinder part of the body in man and the upper in other animals.

2. A part behind or furthest from the face or front, like the back in man; as, the *back* of a house; the *back* of a book (the part which is behind when the book is opened for use); the *back* of the leg.

> Trees set upon the *backs* of chimneys do ripen fruits sooner. —Bacon.

3. A part behind, or in the furthest distance, with reference to the spectator, speaker, scene of action, or the like; as, the *back* of an island; the *back* of a wood; the *back* of a village.

4. A part which comes behind in the ordinary movements of a thing, or when it is used; as, the *back* of the hand; the *back* of a knife, saw, etc.

5. A part forming the upper, and especially the outer and upper portion of a thing, like the *back* of one of the lower animals; as, the *back* of a handrail; the *back* of a rafter; in mining, the *back* of a lode (the upper part of it); the *back* of a level (the ground above a level separating it from the next level above or the surface of the ground).

> (The mountains) their broad, bare *backs* upheave. —Milton.

6. A part which supports the ribs; as, the *back* of a ship—the keel and keelson.

7. By synecdoche, the whole body; as, he has no clothes to his *back.*

8. [*pl.*] A term given by leather merchants to the thickest and best-tanned hides.

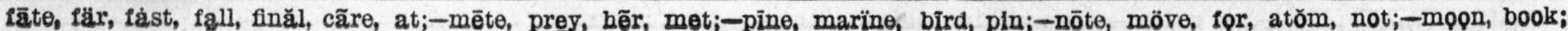

9. The address of a letter, formerly written on the back of the letter itself.

10. A reserve or secondary resource; now supplanted by *backing*.

11. In football, a player behind the rush-line, or his position; as, quarter-*back*; half-*back*.

Behind the back; treacherously; secretly.

On one's back; helpless; sick.

To bow the back; to submit to oppression.

To cast behind the back; to forget and forgive; or to treat with contempt.

To plow the back; to oppress and persecute.

To put or *set one's back up against*; to show antipathy or aversion toward; to resist; a metaphor probably taken from the practice of cats. [Colloq.]

To turn the back on; to desert, or to leave the care or cognizance of.

To turn the back to; to dismiss contemptuously.

back, *a.* 1. Lying or being behind; opposite to the front; remote in place or condition; as, a *back* district; the *back* seat.

2. Acting or moving in reverse direction; as, *back* action; *back* course.

3. Delayed, as in payment, labor, or time; in arrear; overdue; as, *back* dues; *back* work; previous in time; as, *back* numbers of a magazine.

Back charges; after charges of any kind.

To take the back track; to go back the same way as one came. [Colloq.]

back, *adv.* [Formed from *aback*, by apheresis; from ME. *abak*; AS. *on bæc*, backward.]

1. At the rear; behind; as, the sun passed *back* of the cloud.

2. Rearward; to the rear; as, the men fell *back*.

3. Rearward to a previously occupied point, whether of state, condition, or place; as, *back* to the old home; he gave *back* the gift; *back* to his old duties; *back* to civilization.

4. Rearward in return by a previous course; as, he found his way *back*.

5. Restrictively or preventively as to progress; as, the blockade held him *back*.

6. Toward times or things past; as, to look *back* on former ages.

7. In return or as a reward; as, how shall I pay you *back*?

8. In reserve; as, to keep *back* the truth.

To go back on; to forsake.

back, *v.t.*; backed, *pt.*, *pp.*; backing, *ppr.* 1. To mount; to get upon the back of; to sit (a horse); sometimes, to place or carry upon the back; as, to *back* a horse; to *back* a load.

2. To support; to second or strengthen by encouragement or financial aid; as, the court was *backed* by justice and public sentiment; he *backed* his agent without limit.

3. To put backward; to cause to recede; as, to *back* oxen.

4. To adjoin behind; to lie back of; as, the orchard *backs* the garden.

5. To strengthen or support at the back; to furnish with a back; as, to *back* a book.

6. To indorse or sign on the back, as a document, note, etc.; to write on the back of, as a letter.

7. To gamble on; as, to *back* a horse or a pugilist.

To back the field; in horse-racing, to bet that some one of all the other horses in a race will beat a specified horse.

To back an anchor; in seamanship, to lay down a small anchor ahead of a large one, the cable of the small one being fastened to the crown of the large one, to prevent its coming home.

To back astern; in rowing, to manage the oars in a direction contrary to the usual method, so as to move a boat stern foremost.

To back the oars; to row backward.

To back a rope; to put on a preventer so as to reduce the strain upon the rope.

To back water; to reverse the power so as to force the boat or ship backward.

To back the sails; to put them in such a position that the wind acts upon their forward surfaces, thus arresting or reversing the motion of the ship.

To back an engine; to reverse the action of the engine.

To back up; to lend support to, or substantiate.

back, *v.i.* 1. To move or go backward; as, the horse refuses to *back*.

2. To move in the reverse direction; opposite to *haul*; said of the wind.

To back and fill; to navigate a vessel in a river or channel when the wind is against the tide and there is no room to tack, by so managing the sails that the wind strikes them alternately in front and behind, so as to make the vessel shoot from side to side of the channel while being carried forward by the tide. Figuratively, to vacillate in opinion; to be irresolute.

To back down; to retreat from a position or attitude; to give in.

To back out; to retreat from a difficulty or engagement.

back′ăche (-āk), *n.* An ache or a pain in the back.

back′ăche-brāke, *n.* A fern supposed to possess medicinal qualities, the *Asplenium Filix-fœmina*, or lady-fern.

back′ăche-root, *n.* A variety of button-snake-root, belonging to the aster family.

back′ȧ-rack, *n.* See *Bacharach*.

baç-kā′rē, baç-çā′rē, *interj.* [A humorously-formed pseudo-Latin word, being merely the Eng. *back* with a Latin termination, apparently that of the infinitive of the first conjugation.] Stand back! Go back! A cant word of Shakspere's time.

> *Baccare!* you are marvelous forward.—Shak.

back′band, *n.* The strap worn over the back of a horse to support the thills of a carriage.

back′bīte, *v.t.* and *v.i.*; backbit, *pt.*, *pp.*; backbiting, *ppr.* [ME. *bakbiten*, *bacbiten*.] To censure, slander, reproach, or speak evil of the absent.

back′bīt″ẽr, *n.* One who backbites.

back′bīt″ing, *n.* The act of a backbiter; secret calumny.

back′bīt″ing-ly, *adv.* With secret slander.

back′bōard, *n.* [AS. *bæcbord*.]

1. A board for the support or rest of the back.

2. A board across the stern of a boat for the passengers to lean against.

3. A board attached to the rim of a water-wheel to prevent the water running off the floats or paddles into the interior of the wheel.

4. A thin sheet of wood, veneering, or pasteboard, to sustain and protect the back of a picture or a mirror in a frame.

5. A board worn on the back to contribute to erectness.

back′bond, *n.* In Scots law, a deed attaching a qualification or condition to the terms of a conveyance, or other instrument.

back′bōne, *n.* [ME. *bakbone*, *bakbon*, *bacbon*, backbone.]

1. The bone of the back; the spine; the vertebral column.

2. Something resembling a backbone in appearance, position, or office; as, the Apennines are the *backbone* of Italy.

3. Figuratively, firmness; stability of purpose; decision of character; resolution; moral principle; as, he has no *backbone* in him.

To the backbone; to the utmost extent of one's power or nature; out and out; thoroughly; entirely.

back-bōned′, *a.* Having a backbone.

back′-box, *n.* In printing, one of the boxes on the top of the upper case, usually appropriated to small capitals.

back′çar″ry, *n.* In old English forest law, the crime of having game on the back, as deer unlawfully killed.

back′-căst, *n.* 1. A cast or throw back.

2. A backward stroke, or a stroke driving one back; hence, figuratively, any discouragement or cause of relapse or failure. [Scot.]

back′-cen″tẽr, *n.* The point on the back or dead spindle of a lathe which supports that end of the work.

back′-chāin, *n.* A chain which passes over the cart-saddle of a horse to support the shafts.

back-dōor′, *n.* and *a.* I. *n.* A door at the rear of a house; an obscure entrance or passage.

II. *a.* Acting from behind and in secret; as, *backdoor* politics.

back′down, *n.* A yielding or surrender. [Colloq.]

backed (bakt), *a.* 1. Having a back or backing; used chiefly in composition; as, broad-*backed*, hump*backed*.

2. Mounted; placed on the back.

back′ẽr, *n.* One who or that which backs; specifically, (a) a supporter of, or better for a party in a contest; (b) in architecture, a narrow slate laid on the back of a broad square-headed one, where the slates begin to diminish in width.

back′fạll, *n.* In wrestling, a throw in which one contestant strikes upon his back.

back′-fill″ing, *n.* Any substance, as mortar, small stone, etc., used in filling a space between two walls or parts of a wall.

back-fire, *v.i.*; back-fired, *pt.*, *pp.*; back-firing, *ppr.*

1. To set fire in advance of a forest or prairie fire, thus giving protection by a burnt area.

2. In engineering, to have an explosion within the cylinder in the return stroke, as in a gas-engine.

3. To light from the inner rather than the outer jet, as in a Bunsen burner.

back-fire, *n.* 1. A fire purposely started in front of an advancing forest or prairie fire which is being fought.

2. An untimely explosion in an engine cylinder which tends to drive the piston in the wrong direction.

back′friend (-frend), *n.* 1. An enemy in secret. [Obs.]

2. One who stands behind one as a friend. [Rare.]

back′fur″rōw, *v.t.* and *v.i.*; backfurrowed, *pt.*, *pp.*; backfurrowing, *ppr.* To plow (land) so as to leave a ridge between two furrows.

back″gam′mŏn, *v.t.* To win at backgammon.

back″gam′mŏn, *n.* [ME. *bak*; AS. *bæc*, back, and AS. *gamen*, sport, game.] A game played by two persons, upon a board, with box and dice. The board is in two parts, on which are twenty-four black and white spaces, called points. Each player has fifteen men, of different colors for the purpose of distinction. The advance of the men is determined by the throw of the dice.

back″gam′mŏn-bōard, *n.* A board divided into two rows of triangular points at each end, upon which to play the game of backgammon. Usually the board is hinged in the middle, folding together flat, or like two trays, according to the build.

back′-ġēar, *n.* An arrangement of toothed wheels by which the power of a driving-belt is proportionately increased.

back′ground, *n.* 1. Ground in the rear or behind, as opposed to the front.

2. The part of a picture represented as farthest from the spectator; that which is represented as behind a figure or group of figures.

3. Figuratively, a situation little seen or noticed; a position in which one tries to avoid notice.

back′hand, *n.* and *a.* I. *n.* Handwriting in which the letters slope backward, or from left to right downward.

II. *a.* Sloping backward; oblique.

back′hand″ed, *a.* 1. With the hand turned backward; as, a *backhanded* blow.

2. Having an ambiguous or double meaning; as, a *backhanded* reply.

3. Having an oblique inclination; as, a *back-handed* type-face.

back′hand″ed-ly, *adv.* With the hand directed backward; as, to strike *backhandedly*.

back′hand″ed-ness, *n.* The state of being backhanded or unfair.

back′hand″ẽr, *n.* A backhanded blow.

back′house, *n.* A rear building; a privy.

back′ing, *n.* 1. The act expressed by the verb *to back* in its various senses.

2. Support, physical or moral, from some agency behind, or, figuratively, at the back of a principal; as, he would have gone on with it, but he could get no *backing* from anybody.

3. The address of a letter.

4. In technology, something put at or attached to the back of something else by way of support or finish, or the act of putting it there; as, (a) a layer or layers of timber, generally teak, on which the iron plates of armor-clad ships are bolted; (b) in bookbinding, the preparing of the back of a book with glue, etc., before putting on the cover; (c) in weaving, the web of coarser or stronger material at the back of such piled fabrics as velvet, plush, Brussels carpet, etc.

back′ing-up, *n.* A term used in cricket and other games for the act of supporting a fielder lest he fail to hold or misses the ball.

back′joint, *n.* In masonry, a rebate such as that made on the inner side of a chimneypiece to receive a slip.

back′lash, *n.* The backward surge of a pair or of a train of toothed wheels acting under a variable driving pressure; the loose play of such a part. It equals the clearance allowance between the flanks of the teeth in gear.

back′less, *a.* Having no back.

back′-link, *n.* In engines, one of the links in a parallel motion which connect the air-pump rod to the beam.

back′log, *n.* A log of wood against which a fire is made on a hearth or in a fireplace.

back′-look, *n.* A review of time past.

> After a serious *back-look* of all these forty-eight years. —Walker.

back′-pāint″ing, *n.* A term sometimes applied to the painting of mezzotint prints pasted on glass to produce the effect of painted glass.

back′piēce, *n.* The piece or plate, in a suit of armor, covering the back.

back′plāte, *n.* Same as *Backpiece*.

back′-pres″sūre (-presh″ŭr), *n.* The resistance of the atmosphere or waste steam to the action of the piston of a steam-engine on its return stroke.

back′rack, back′rag, *n.* Same as *Bacharach*.

back′-rest, *n.* A lathe traversing rest used for the support of long shafts or other pieces of work being turned.

back′-rōpe, *n.* In nautical language, the rope or wire stay running from the end of the dolphin-striker to the ship's bows.

back′sạw, *n.* A saw having a web stiffened by a metallic back of greater substance, such as a tenon-saw.

back′set, *n.* 1. One who or that which checks; a relapse.

2. An eddy or backwater.

back′set, *v.t.* To give a second plowing in the fall to (sod-ground broken in the spring). [Western U. S.]

back′set″tlẽr, *n.* One who lives in a district remote from a settled part of the country.

back′sheesh, bak′shĭsh, *n.* [Hind. *bakhshīsh*; Per. *bakhshish*, a present, from *bakhshidan*, to give.] The customary gratuity exacted in the countries of the East; a tip.

back′side, *n.* 1. The back side; rear part. [Obs.]

2. The buttocks. [Vulgar.]

back′sight (-sit), *n.* 1. The first reading from a leveling-staff taken from any position of the instrument. All other readings are called *foresights.*

2. The rear sight of a gun.

back′-slang, *n.* A species of slang in which the words are pronounced or written backward, or as nearly so as the skill of the speaker or writer or the nature of the word will permit; thus, penny becomes *ynnep*, woman *namow*, and so on.

back-slide′, *v.i.*; backslid, *pt.*, *pp.*; backsliding, *ppr.* To fall off; to apostatize; to turn gradually from a faith, principle, or profession, as from the practice of Christianity.

back-slid′ẽr, *n.* One who backslides.

back-slid′ing, *n.* Apostasy; a falling away from a faith.

back′-speed, *n.* A back-gear.

back′stȧff, *n.* [So called from its being used with the observer's back toward the sun.] An instrument formerly used for taking the sun's altitude at sea.

back′stāir, back′stāirṣ, *a.* Indirect; secret; intriguing; as if finding admittance by way of the backstairs.

back′stāirṣ, *n.pl.* Stairs in the back part of a house; private stairs; figuratively, a private or indirect way.

back′stāy, *n.* 1. A long rope or stay extending from the masthead to the side of a ship, slanting a little aft, to assist the shrouds in supporting the mast; usually in the plural.

2. In printing, a strap used to check the carriage of a press.

3. In mining, a fork placed at the back of a car to act as a brake in case of accident. [Eng.]

4. A spring used to maintain the contact of the cutting-edges of shears.

5. In a lathe, a doctor or back-rest.

back′-step, *n.* Rearward movement, as of a body of troops, while maintaining the same front.

back′stẽr, *n.* A baker. [Obs.]

back′stitch (-stich), *v.t.* and *v.i.*; backstitched (-sticht), *pt.*, *pp.*; backstitching, *ppr.* To sew with stitches overlapping each other.

back′stitch, *n.* A stitch lapping over a former one.

back′-strapped (-strapt), *a.* Compelled to sail to leeward by head winds or adverse currents.

back′stress, *n.* A woman baker. [Obs.]

back′swōrd (-sōrd), *n.* 1. A sword with one sharp edge.

2. In England, a stick with a basket handle used in fencing; also, the game of singlestick.

back′wãrd, back′wãrdṣ, *adv.* 1. With the back in advance or to the front; reversely; as, to ride *backward*; the servant withdrew *backward*.

2. Toward the back; as, to throw the arms *backward*; to move *backward* and forward.

3. On the back, or with the back downward; as, to fall *backward*.

4. Toward past times or events; as, to look *backward* on the history of man.

5. By way of reflection; reflexively; as, the mind turns *backward* on itself.

6. Inertly lapsing from better to worse; as, public affairs go *backward*.

7. Reversely; toward the beginning; contrary to the natural order; as, to read *backward*.

8. In an opposite direction; as, to drive the enemy *backward*.

back′wãrd, *a.* [ME. *bakward*, *bacward*, from *aback*; AS. *on bæc*, back, and *-weard*, toward.]

1. Retiring; bashful; unwilling; averse; reluctant; hesitating.

> For wiser brutes are *backward* to be slaves. —Pope.

2. Slow; sluggish; dilatory.

> The mind is *backward* to undergo the fatigue of weighing every argument. —Watts.

3. Dull; not quick of apprehension; unprogressive; as, a *backward* youth; a *backward* people.

4. Late; behind in time; coming after something else, or after the usual time; as, *backward* fruits; the season is *backward*.

5. Retrogressive; reversed; directed toward the rear; as, a *backward* look; a *backward* course; *backward* steps.

6. Already past. [Rare.]

Syn.—Averse, bashful, dull, retiring, reluctant.

back′wãrd, *n.* The things or state behind or past. [Obs.]

back′wãrd, *v.t.* To delay. [Obs.]

back-wãr-dā′tion, *n.* In English stock transactions, a mutual arrangement whereby the seller delays delivery by payment of a premium to the buyer; also, the premium itself.

back′wãrd-ly, *adv.* Unwillingly; reluctantly; aversely; perversely. [Obs.]

back′wãrd-ness, *n.* 1. Unwillingness; reluctance; dilatoriness, or dullness in action.

2. A state of being behind in progress; slowness; tardiness; as, the *backwardness* of the spring.

back′wäsh, *v.t.* To cleanse from oil, as wool after being combed.

back′wäsh, *n.* The wash of a wave or backwater from a boat.

back′wa″tẽr, *n.* 1. Water thrown back by the turning of a water-wheel or some similar movement.

2. Water held or forced back, as in a mill-race, or in a tributary of a stream, in consequence of some obstruction, as a dam or the swelling of the river below.

3. A water-reserve obtained at high tide and to be discharged at low tide for clearing off deposits in channel beds and tideways.

4. A creek or arm of the sea near to and parallel to the coast, and communicating with the sea by barred entrances.

back′woodṣ, *n.pl.* Woody districts in thinly-settled regions of the United States and Canada, remote from populous centers; any wild region of country with vegetation.

back-woodṣ′măn, *n.*; *pl.* **back-woodṣ′men.** An inhabitant of the backwoods; a pioneer.

back′wŏrm, *n.* A minute worm-like parasite causing a disease in hawks. [See *Filanders*.]

bā′çŏn, *n.* [ME. *bacon*; OFr. *bacon*; O.H.G. *bahho*, *bacho*, a side of bacon.] Hog's flesh, especially the back and sides, salted or pickled and dried, usually in smoke.

To save one's bacon; to preserve oneself or one's property from harm. [Colloq.]

bā′çŏn-bee″tle, *n.* A beetle, *Dermestes lardarius*, which attacks bacon and provisions of similar kind.

Bā-çō′ni-ăn, *a.* Pertaining to Lord Bacon, or his system of philosophy. This system is founded upon induction, and is also known as the *Inductive Philosophy*. [See *Induction*.]

Bā-çō′ni-ăn, *n.* 1. A believer in the philosophy of Bacon.

2. One holding to the theory that Bacon was the author of Shakspere's plays.

Bā′çŏn-iṣm, *n.* The essence or the philosophy of Bacon's writings; the philosophy or scientific method propounded by Bacon in his Novum Organum, a revolt against antiquated authority and an advocacy of induction from facts as the basis for scientific investigation.

baç-tē′ri-ȧ, *n.*, pl. of *bacterium*.

baç-tē′ri-ăl, *a.* Pertaining to or caused by bacteria.

baç-tē′ri-çī″dăl, *a.* Destructive to bacteria.

baç-tē′ri-cide, *n.* [L. *bacterium*, bacterium, and *cædere*, to kill.] A germicide.

baç-tē′ri-ō-. A combining form, derived from *bacterium*.

baç-tē′ri-oid, *a.* Of, relating, or pertaining to bacteria.

baç-tē″ri-ō-loġ′iç-ăl, *a.* Pertaining to bacteriology.

baç-tē-ri-ol′ō-ġist, *n.* One skilled in bacteriology.

baç-tē-ri-ol′ō-ġy, *n.* [*Bacterio-*, and Gr. *logos*, a description.] That branch of biology that treats of bacteria.

baç-tē″ri-ō-sçop′iç, *a.* Pertaining to bacterioscopy.

baç-tē-ri-os′çō-pist, *n.* A person skilled in bacterioscopy.

baç-tē-ri-os′çō-py, *n.* [*Bacterio-*, and Gr. *skopein*, to see.] The microscopic study of bacteria.

baç-tē′ri-um, *n.*; *pl.* **baç-tē′ri-ȧ.** [LL. *bacterium*, pl. *bacteria*, bacteria, from Gr. *baktērion*, a little stick, dim. of *baktron*, a staff.]

1. A microscopic organism of various shapes—spherical, elliptical, cylindrical, filamentoid, etc.,—constituting the most elemental forms of vegetable life. They are very widely diffused in nature, and multiply with marvelous rapidity. Certain species, the *Saccharomycetes* or budding fungi, are active agents in alcoholic fermentation, while others, the *Schizomycetes* or fission fungi, appear to be the cause of certain infectious diseases. Their nourishment consists of albuminous substances, which they convert into complex chemical compounds, many of which are highly poisonous. These poisons are called toxins, and a very minute quantity is sufficient to produce destructive changes in the blood and tissue of man and animals. The study of the chemistry of *bacteria* has shown that many of them do not grow upon living matter, but will flourish upon decomposing and putrefying substances. *Bacteria* existing in the soil convert inert matter into available plant-food, changing organic nitrogenous substances into soluble nitrates. *Bacteria* are classified by Cohn, according to their form, into four groups: *spherobacteria*, characterized by spherical cells, separate or joined in groups; *microbacteria*, having rod-shaped cylindrical cells joined end to end; *desmobacteria*, those in the form of short, slender filaments; and *spirobacteria*, in the form of fine spiral threads.

2. [B—] A genus of microscopic fungi, consisting of cylindrical or elliptical cells, capable of spontaneous movement. *Bacterium termo* is the best known species; it is found in all infusions of animal or vegetable matter.

baç′tē-roid, baç-tē-roid′ăl, *a.* Resembling bacteria.

Baç′tri-ăn, *a.* and *n.* I. *a.* Relating to Bactria, in Asia.

II. *n.* A native or inhabitant of Bactria.

Bactrian camel; the two-humped camel.

baç′ūle, *n.* [Fr. *bascule*.] A bascule.

baç′ū-line, *a.* Relating to the rod, or punishment with the rod.

Baç-ū-lī′tēṣ, *n.pl.* [L. *baculum*; Gr. *baktron*, a staff, and *lithos*, a stone.] A genus of polythalamous or many-chambered cephalopods belonging to the family *Ammonitidæ*. The species are only known in a fossil state, having become extinct at the close of the Cretaceous period.

Portion of *Baculites faujasii*.

baç-ū-lom′e-try, *n.* [L. *baculum*, a staff, and Gr. *metron*, measure.] The act of measuring distance or altitude by a staff or staves.

bad, *a.*; *comp.* worse; *superl.* worst. [ME. *bad*, *badde*, bad, worthless.] The opposite of *good*; wanting good qualities, physical or moral: a word of the widest application, being applied in the most general way to whatever falls below an assumed type or standard or the average of objects of its class, to whatever is injurious or offensive, or intended to be so; and both to what is *bad* (as, a *bad* heart, *bad* health) and what makes *bad* (as, *bad* influence, *bad* example).

Syn.—Wicked, evil, ill, vile, wrong, corrupt, vicious, abandoned, base, unsound, abominable.

bad, *n.* 1. Collectively, those who are bad; those things which are bad; as, in conflict with the *bad*.

2. A condition of badness; as, gone to the *bad*.

bad, *v.*, old form of *bade*.

bad′dẽr, *a.*, old comp. of *bad*, now superseded by *worse*.

bad′dẽr-locks, *n.* [Perhaps for *Balder's locks*, from *Balder*, the hero of Scandinavian mythology; the termination may be the *-lock* in char*lock*, hem*lock*; AS. *leac*, a plant, a leek.] A common name for the *Alaria esculenta*, a seaweed found on the shores of the north of Europe. It is sometimes eaten by the people of Scotland, Ireland, Denmark, etc. Called also *henware* and *murlins*.

bad′dest, *a.*, old superl. of *bad*.

bad′dish, *a.* Somewhat bad; indifferently bad.

bade, *v.*, past tense of *bid*.

badġe (baj), *n.* [ME. *badge*, *bagge*; LL. *bagea*, *bagia*, a badge; origin unknown.]

1. A mark, sign, or token worn on the person, by which one's relation to a particular occupation, society, or superior is distinguished; an honorable decoration; a mark of rank or of service.

2. The mark or token of anything; as, the *badge* of bitterness.

3. An ornament or carving formerly placed on ships near the stern, decorated with figures and containing a window or a resemblance of one.

Syn.—Mark, sign, insignia, token, emblem.

badġe, *v.t.* To mark or distinguish with a badge.

badġe′less, *a.* Having no badge.

badġ′ẽr, *n.* In England, a licensed porter, carrier, or hawker required to wear a badge.

badġ′ẽr, *n.* [For *bladger*, from LL. *bladarius*, a corn-dealer, from *bladum*, corn; origin unknown.] In old law, a person who was licensed to buy grain in one place and sell it in another.

badġ′ẽr, *n.* [OE. *bageard*, from *badge*, and *-ard*, so called from the white mark on its forehead.] A plantigrade quadruped of the genus *Meles* or some allied genus, of a clumsy build, with short, thick legs, and long claws on the forefeet. It inhabits the northern parts of Europe, Asia, and North America. *Taxidea americana* is the American *badger*.

European Badger (*Meles vulgaris*).

badġ′ẽr, *v.t.*; badgered, *pt.*, *pp.*; badgering, *ppr.*

1. To follow up or pursue with great eagerness, as the badger is hunted; to pester or worry.

2. To beat down in price; to cheapen; to bargain. [Colloq.]

badg′ẽr=dog, *n.* The dachshund.

badg′ẽr-ẽr, *n.* 1. A person who badgers.

2. A dog trained for badger-baiting.

badg′ẽr-ing, *n.* 1. The act of pestering or worrying.

2. The practice of buying any kind of provisions in one place and selling them elsewhere at a profit; formerly an offense in England.

badg′ẽr=legged, *a.* Having a leg or legs shorter on one side than on the other, as the badger was erroneously supposed to have.

bad-i-ä′gä (*or* bad-yä′gä), *n.* [Russ. *badyaga*, or *bodyaga*, the river-sponge.] A small sponge of the genus *Spongilla*, common in the north of Europe, the powder of which is used to take away the livid marks of bruises.

bā′di-ăn, bā′di-āne, *n.* [Fr. *badiane*; L. *badius*, bay-colored, from the color of the capsules.] The Chinese anise-tree, *Illicium anisatum*, or its fruit. It abounds in a volatile oil, giving it an aromatic flavor and odor. On this account it is much used in China and India as a condiment, and is imported into France for flavoring.

bȧ-di′ġeōn (-jun), *n.* [Fr.] 1. A mixture of plaster and freestone, ground together and sifted, and used by sculptors to fill the small holes and repair the defects of the stones of which they make their statues.

2. A mixture of sawdust and glue, or of whiting and glue, used by joiners to fill up defects in their work.

3. A preparation for coloring houses, consisting of powdered stone, sawdust, slacked lime, alum, etc.

bȧ-di-näge′ (-näzh′, *or* bad′i-nāge), *n.* [Fr. *badiner*, to jest or make merry; Pr. *badar*, to gape, from LL. *badare*, to gape, to trifle.] Light or playful discourse; banter.

> He seems most to have indulged himself only in an elegant *badinage*.—Warburton.

bȧ-di′ne-rīe, *n.* [Fr., from *badiner*, to jest.] Light or playful discourse; nonsense; badinage. [Rare.]

> The fund of sensible discourse is limited; that of *badinerie* is infinite. —Shenstone.

bȧd-i-neūr′, *n.* [Fr.] One who indulges in badinage; a banterer; a trifler. [Obs.]

bad′ly, *adv.* [ME. *badly*, *baddeliche*.] In a bad manner; not well; unskilfully; grievously; unfortunately; imperfectly. Colloquially, it is used, in connection with *want* or *need*, etc., for *very much*; as, help is *badly* needed.

bad′mash, *n.* Same as *Budmash*.

bad′min-tŏn, *n.* [From *Badminton*, an English country-seat.]

1. An outdoor game, similar to lawn-tennis, but played with shuttlecocks, the net being narrow and suspended at some height above the ground.

2. Claret-cup and soda, flavored with cucumber. [Eng.]

bad′ness, *n.* The state of being bad, vicious, evil, or depraved; want of good qualities, physical or moral.

bä′el, *n.* The Indian name of the Bengal quince-tree, *Ægle Marmelos*; written also *bel*, *bhel*.

bæ′nō-mēre, *n.* [Gr. *bainein*, to walk, and *meros*, a part.] A segment of the thorax of an arthropod.

bæ′nō-pod, *n.* [Gr. *bainein*, to walk, and *pous*, *podos*, foot.] A thoracic leg of an arthropodal animal.

bæ′nō-sōme, *n.* [Gr. *bainein*, to walk, and *sōma*, body.] The thorax of an arthropodal animal.

bæ′ty-lus, *n.*; *pl.* **bæ′ty-li.** [Gr. *baitylos*, a sacred stone.] In classical antiquity, a sacred meteoric stone, or any stone shaped so as to serve as a symbol of divinity.

baff, *n.* and *a.* [Scot.] I. *n.* A blow; a heavy thump.

II. *a.* In provincial English, valueless.

Baff week; in English mining, the week in which no pay is received when the system of biweekly payments is practised.

baff, *v.i.*; baffed (baft), *pt.*, *pp.*; baffing, *ppr.* In golf, to strike the ground with the club-head in playing, and so send the ball in air.

baf′fe-tȧ, *n.* Same as *Baft*.

baf′fle (baf′l), *v.t.*; baffled, *pt.*, *pp.*; baffling, *ppr.* [ME. *baffelen*, *baffulen*, to baffle; OFr. *beffler*, *beffer*, to baffle, mock; of Germanic origin.]

1. To mock or elude by artifice; to elude by shifts and turns; hence, to defeat, or confound; as, to *baffle* the enemy.

2. To frustrate; to thwart; to defeat.

> They make a shift to break the precept, and at the same time to *baffle* the curse. —South.

3. To force submission to disgraceful public punishment, as a recreant or perjured knight. [Obs.]

Syn.—Defeat, disconcert, confound. — *Baffle* expresses less than *defeat*; *disconcert* less than *confound*; one is *baffled* in argument who is, for the time, discomposed and silenced; one is *defeated* if his opponent has altogether the advantage of him; one is *disconcerted* who loses his presence of mind or has his feelings in any way discomposed; one is *confounded* when the powers of thought and consciousness become torpid or vanish.

baf′fle, *v.i.* 1. To practise deceit. [Obs.]

2. To struggle ineffectually; as, to *baffle* with the wind.

3. In mining, to render fire-damp nonexplosive by the admission of air.

baf′fle, *n.* 1. A defeat by artifice, shifts, and turns. [Obs.]

2. A baffle-plate.

baf′fle-ment, *n.* The act of baffling or state of being baffled.

baf′fle=plāte, *n.* A metal plate in a fire-box to divert the flame and hot gases against the best heating surfaces.

baf′flẽr, *n.* One who or that which baffles.

baf′fling, *a.* Eluding by shifts and turns, or by stratagem; defeating; confounding.

Baffling wind; among seamen, one that frequently shifts from one point to another.

baf′fling-ly, *adv.* In a baffling manner.

baf′fling-ness, *n.* The quality of baffling.

baft, baf′tȧ, *n.* [Per.] A fine cotton fabric, originally made in India. The name is now applied to similar fabrics of British manufacture.

baft, *adv.* Same as *Abaft*.

bag, *n.* [ME. *bagge*; Ice. *baggi*, a bag, from *belgr*, skin, bellows.]

1. A sack; a pouch, usually of cloth, paper, or leather, used to hold, preserve, or convey anything; as, a *bag* of money; a *bag* of grain.

2. A sac, in animal bodies, containing some fluid or other substance; the udder of a female mammal.

3. Formerly, a sort of silken pouch in which the back hair of the wig was worn. [Obs.]

4. In commerce, a certain quantity of a commodity, such as it is customary to carry to market in a sack; as, a *bag* of coffee or hops; a *bag* of oats.

5. The quantity of game killed in one day or during a hunting expedition; as, our trip to the woods resulted in a good *bag*.

6. In fisheries, the bulging part of a seine full of fish.

7. In mining, a hole or cavity filled with water or gas.

8. [*pl.*] Garments, especially when they fit badly; more specifically, a man's trousers; as, a pair of flannel *bags*. [Colloq.]

9. In baseball, any one of the bases; so called because they are frequently marked by square *bags* of sand; as, he reached third *bag*, for third *base*; hold the *bag*.

Bag and baggage; all of one's belongings.

Bag of bones; an epithet applied to a very thin person.

To give one the bag; to leave or to dismiss without warning. [Colloq.]

bag, *v.t.*; bagged, *pt.*, *pp.*; bagging, *ppr.* 1. To put into a bag; as, to *bag* oats.

2. To load with bags.

3. To entrap; to capture; to snare; to kill; as, to *bag* game.

4. To steal; also, to play truant. [Slang.]

bag, *v.i.* 1. To swell like a full bag, as sails when filled with wind, or the worn knees of a man's trousers.

2. To swell with haughty pride. [Obs.]

bag′ȧ-rȧ, *n.* [Port. *bagre*, a fish.] A sciænoid fish, *Menticirrus undulatus*, of the Pacific coast.

bȧ-gasse′, *n.* [Fr. *bagasse*, or *bagace*, from Sp. *bagazo*, the refuse of sugar-cane.] The refuse of sugar-cane, sugar-beets, grapes, olives, etc., after the juice has been expressed; when dried, used as fuel.

bag-ȧ-telle′, *n.* [Fr.; Sp. *bagatela*, bagatelle; It. *bagatella*, a trifle.]

1. A trifle; a thing of no importance.

2. A game played on a board having numbered cups, arches, or holes, into which balls are to be struck with a rod held in the hand of the player.

bag′gāge, *n.* [ME. *baggage*, *bagage*; OFr. *bagage*, *baggage*, baggage, from *baguer*, to tie up.]

1. The tents, clothing, provisions, utensils, and other necessaries of a military force.

2. The trunks, valises, satchels, bags, or cases, containing clothing and other conveniences, which a traveler carries with him on a journey; called by the English *luggage*.

3. Rubbish; a worthless thing; an incumbrance. [Obs.]

bag′gāge, *n.* [Fr. *bagasse*; Sp. *bagasa* (Obs.), a strumpet.]

1. A playful, saucy young woman; a flirt.

2. A loose woman; a strumpet.

bag′gāge=cär, *n.* The car of a railroad-train used for carrying the baggage of passengers.

bag′gāge-man, *n.* A man who handles the baggage of passengers on a railroad or steamship line.

bag′gāge=mas″tẽr, *n.* An officer of a railroad or steamship company whose duty it is to care for baggage intrusted to the company.

bag′gȧ-gōr, *n.* One who carries baggage; especially, one who assists in carrying the baggage of an army. [Obs.]

bag′gȧ-lȧ, bag′lō, *n.* [Ar. *baggala*, a female mule.] A two-masted Arab boat used for trading in the Indian Ocean, generally from two hundred to two hundred and fifty tons burden, exceedingly weatherly, and remarkable for the elevation of the stern, which is highly ornamented.

Baggala.

bag′gi-ly, *adv.* In the manner of a bag; loosely.

bag′ging, *n.* 1. Any coarse fabric cut of which bags are made, or with which bales are covered.

2. The act of putting into bags.

3. The act of swelling, or becoming baggy.

4. Filtration through canvas bags.

5. A method of reaping peas, beans, wheat, etc., by chopping with a reaping-hook. [Eng.]

bag′git, *n.* [Scot.] An adult female salmon that has lately spawned.

bag′gy, *a.* Having the appearance of a bag; bulging out like a bag; puffy; as, *baggy* trousers.

bag′lō, *n.* See *Baggala*.

bag′măn, *n.*; *pl.* **bag′men.** In England, a name formerly given to commercial travelers from their traveling on horseback, carrying their samples or wares in saddlebags; now used only as a term of moderate contempt.

bag′net, *n.* A net in the form of a bag for catching fish.

bagn′iō (ban′yō), *n.* [It. *bagno*, from L. *balneum*, a bath.]

1. A bath; a house for bathing. [Obs.]

2. A brothel; a house of ill fame.

3. In Turkey, a prison. In France, one of the prisons (*bagnes*) used instead of the galleys.

Bag-nō′li-ăn, *n.* [From *Bagnoles*, in Languedoc, where the heresy had its rise.] One of a sect of French heretics of the eighth century, who rejected the whole of the Old and part of the New Testament.

bag′nut, *n.* A plant of the soapberry family with a pod like a bag; also called *bladdernut*.

bag′ō-net, *n.* An obsolete form of *bayonet*.

bag′pīpe, *n.* A musical wind-instrument of very great antiquity, having been used among the Hebrews and Greeks, and being a favorite instrument throughout Europe in the fifteenth century. It still continues in use among the country people of Poland, Italy, and the south of France, and more especially in Scotland and Ireland. The *bagpipe* consists of a leathern bag, which receives the air from the mouth, or from bellows, and of pipes, into which the air is pressed from the bag by the performer's elbow. One pipe (called the chanter) plays the melody, others (called drones) sound respectively the keynote (an octave lower) and the fifth of the scale, the sound being produced by means of reeds. The chanter has eight holes, which the performer stops and opens at pleasure. There are several species of *bagpipes*, as the soft and melodious Irish *bagpipe*, the more martial Highland *bagpipe*, and the Italian *bagpipe*.

Old English Bagpipe.

bag′pīpe, *v.t.* To cause to resemble a bagpipe.

To bagpipe the mizzen; in nautical language, to lay it aback by carrying the sheet to the mizzen shrouds.

bag′pīp″ẽr, *n.* One who plays the bagpipe; usually called a *piper*.

bag′=pụd″ding, *n.* A pudding cooked in a bag.

bag′=pump, *n.* A kind of pump in which there is an elastic bag distended at intervals by rings, fastened at one end to the bottom of the piston-chamber, and at the other to the valve-disk.

bag′re, *n.* [Sp. and Port.] A catfish of the genus *Bagrus*.

bag′reef, *n.* A British nautical term to indicate the lowest reef of a fore-and-aft sail.

bag′rōom, *n.* In a ship, a room wherein are stored the clothing-bags of the crew.

Bag′rus, *n.* [L., from Sp. and Port. *bagre*, a fish.] A genus of fishes of the order *Siluroidei*.

bȧ-guet′, bȧ-guette′ (-get′), *n.* [Fr. *baguette*, a rod, wand; It. *baccheta*, dim. of *bacchio*, from L. *baculum*, a rod, stick.]

1. In architecture, a little round molding like the astragal, called, when plain, a bead, when enriched with foliage, a chaplet.

2. In zoölogy, a germinal process found after the union or conjugation of the divided nucleoli of certain *Infusoria*.

bag′wig, *n.* An eighteenth-century wig for the back hair, shaped like a bag.

bag′wŏrm, *n.* A larva inclosed in a protecting case or bag, as *Platœceticus gloveri*, or *Thyridopteryx ephemeræformis*; called also the *basketworm*.

bäh, *interj.* An exclamation expressive of contempt or disgust.

bȧ-ha′dųr, bȧ-hau′dųr, *n.* [Hind. *bāhadur*, brave, hero.] A native title of respect given to European officials in India.

bȧ-här′, *n.* [Ar. *bahār*.] An East Indian measure of weight, varying, according to the locality and the substances weighed, from 223 to 625 pounds.

bȧ-hī′ä (-ē′), *n.* A Spanish word meaning bay.

bȧ-hụt′, *n.* [Fr.] 1. A richly carved or ornamented chest or cabinet of a medieval type.

2. An extra wall built above the cornice proper in convex form and on which the roof is supported.

baī′där, *n.* [Native name.] A canoe used in the Aleutian and Kurile islands. It has a covering of hides, and usually is about twenty feet long.

bāigne (bān), *v.t.* [Fr. *baigner*, to bathe.] To soak or drench. [Obs.]

bāi-gnoire′ (-nwär′), *n.* [Fr.] A lower box in a theater.

baī′kăl-īte, *n.* [From *Baikal*, a lake in northern Asia.] A greenish variety of augite, occurring in grouped or radiated needle-like prisms.

bāil, *v.t.*; bailed (bāld), *pt., pp.*; bailing, *ppr.* [OFr. *bailler*, to keep in custody, to deliver, from L. *bajulare*, to bear a burden, from *bajulus*, a bearer, carrier.]

1. To set free, deliver, or liberate from arrest and imprisonment, upon security given that the person *bailed* shall appear and answer in court.

The magistrate *bails* a man, when he liberates him from arrest or imprisonment, upon bond given with sureties. The surety *bails* a person when he procures his release from arrest, by giving bond for his appearance.—Blackstone.

2. To deliver (goods in trust) upon a contract, expressed or implied, that the trust shall be faithfully executed on the part of the bailee, or person intrusted; as, to *bail* cloth to a tailor to be made into a garment, or to *bail* goods to a carrier. —Blackstone.

3. To release from imprisonment. [Obs.]

4. To secure or protect. [Obs.]

bāil, *n.* [OFr. *bail*, power, control, jurisdiction, from *bailler*, to control, keep in custody.]

1. The person or persons who procure the release of a prisoner from custody, by becoming surety for his appearance in court.

2. The security given for the release of a prisoner from custody; as, the man is out upon *bail*. *Bail* must be given by men of real property, sufficient to pay their bond or recognizance.

Excessive *bail* ought not to be required.
—Blackstone.

Bail court; an auxiliary British court particularly concerned with the arrangement of bailbonds.

Common bail; imaginary bondsmen offered as surety for the appearance of defendant; as, John Doe and Richard Roe. [Obs.]

Out on bail; under bonds for trial, but at large.

Special bail; bail secured by real responsible bondsmen.

Straw bail; worthless or irresponsible bail, a term arising from a former custom, adopted by the professional bailors who frequented courts of law, of wearing straw in their shoes as a sign of their occupation.

To admit to bail; to release upon security given by bondsmen.

To find bail; to procure persons to act as bondsmen.

To go bail; (a) to act as bail or surety; (b) to vouch for (a thing), as, I'll go *bail* for that.

To hold to bail; to oblige to find bail.

To perfect or *justify bail*; to prove by the oath of the proposed bondsman that he is worth the sum for which he is surety, beyond his debts.

To stand bail; to act as bail or surety.

bāil, *v.t.* and *v.i.* [Fr. *baille*, a bucket, pail, from L. *bacula*, dim. of *bacca*, a vessel.]

I. *v.t.* To dip water out of (a boat); usually with *out*; as, he started to *bail out* the canoe.

II. *v.i.* To clear water from a boat by dipping; as, he began to *bail* vigorously.

bāil, *v.t.* [OFr. *baillier*, to shut in, bar, from *baille*, a bar, crossbar.]

1. To confine.

2. To furnish with a bail or handle.

To bail up; to detain for the purpose of robbery. [Australia.]

bāil, *n.* [ME. *bayle, baile*; OFr. *bail, baille*, barrier, palisade; L. *baculum*, stick, rod, staff.]

1. An advance wall or palisade-defense outside the solid defenses of a town; written also *bayle*. [Obs.]

2. A specific forest limit.

3. A post; a bar; specifically applied to the little sticks, about four inches long, laid on the tops of cricket-wickets or stumps.

4. A jail or justice's court; a bailey. [Eng.]

5. A division, as a bar, between the stalls of a stable.

bāil, *n.* [ME. *bayle*; Dan. *beugel*, a hoop, ring, handle; G. *biegel, bügel*, a bow, ring.]

1. A hoop made of any material.

2. A hoop-handle on a bucket or kettle.

3. An iron yoke by which to lift heavy objects, as guns, or to suspend a life-car from the hawser, or the support of a wagon-cover or boat-awning.

4. A supporting arch for a millstone.

bāil′ȧ-ble, *a.* 1. Able to be released under bailbonds.

2. Admitting of bail; as, a *bailable* offense.

bāil′=bond, *n.* A bond or obligation given by a prisoner and his surety, to insure the prisoner's appearance in court, at the return of the writ. Also, special bail in court to abide the judgment.

bāil-ee′, *n.* The person to whom goods are committed in trust, and who has a temporary possession and a qualified property in them, for the purposes of the trust. —Blackstone.

bāil′ẽr, *n.* One who bails or frees from water; anything used to bail out water, especially a small, shallow vessel with a handle made for the purpose.

bāil′ẽr, *n.* See *Bailor*.

bāi′ley, *n.* [ME. *baily, bailie*; OFr. *bail, baille*, a palisade, from *baillier*, to inclose.] The outside wall of a fortress or castle; also, the space inclosed by the outer wall; later applied to any court of a defensive post.

Old Bailey; the seat of the central criminal court of London; the building was formerly within the confines of the ancient bailey, between Lud Gate and New Gate, which gave rise to the appellation.

bāil′ie, *n.* A municipal officer in Scotland, corresponding to an alderman in England.

bāil′iff, *n.* [ME. *bailif, baillif*; OFr. *bailif*, from L. *bajulus*, a guardian, administrator.]

1. A sheriff's deputy who serves warrants, writs, and other court papers; an officer of a court when in session into whose care prisoners are committed during trial and who preserves order.

2. A custodian of property or a business, under judicial authority.

3. In England, an officer appointed by the sheriff. *Bailiffs* are either special, and appointed to arrest persons; or *bailiffs* of hundreds, who collect fines, summon juries, attend the assizes, and execute writs and processes; *bailiffs* of forests and of manors, who direct the husbandry, collect rents, etc.; and *water-bailiffs* who protect rivers from fish-poachers and illegal fishing. The sheriff, in England, is the king's *bailiff*.

bāil′i-wick, *n.* [ME. *bailie*, a bailiff, and *wick*; AS. *wic*, a village.] The precincts in which a bailiff has jurisdiction; the limits of a bailiff's authority, as a hundred, a liberty, or a forest, over which a bailiff is appointed.

bāil′ment, *n.* [OFr. *baillement*, from *bailler*, to deliver, bail.] A delivery of goods, in trust, upon a contract, expressed or implied, that the trust shall be faithfully executed.—Blackstone.

bāil′ŏr, *n.* One who delivers goods to another in trust for some particular purpose.

bāil′piēce, *n.* A judicial certificate containing a recognizance of bail. —Blackstone.

bāin, *n.* [Fr.] A bath. [Obs.]

bain=mȧ-rie′ (baṅ-mȧ-rē′), *n.* [Fr., from L. *balneum Mariæ*, bath of Mary.] A large pan or bath of water, in which food contained in another vessel may be cooked without burning; used also in pharmaceutical and chemical compounding.

Baī′răm, *n.* The name of two Mohammedan festivals, of which one is held at the close of the fast Ramadan and the other seventy days after.

bāirn, *n.* [ME. *barn*; AS. *bearn*, a child, from *beran*, to bear.] A child. [Scot. and Prov. Eng.]

bāiṣe′māin, *n.* [Fr.] The act of kissing the hands; in the plural, respects or compliments. [Obs.]

bāit, *n.* [ME. *baiten, beiten*; Ice. *beita*, food; *beit*, pasture.]

1. Any substance, such as a grub, a grasshopper, or a piece of meat, used to catch fish, or other animals, by alluring them to swallow a hook, or to be caught in snares, or in an inclosure or net.

2. A portion of food and drink, or a hasty luncheon taken on a journey; a small grazing of green grass.

3. An allurement; enticement; temptation.

bāit, *v.t.*; baited, *pt., pp.*; baiting, *ppr.* 1. To put meat on (a hook), or in (an inclosure), or among (snares), to allure fish, fowls, and other animals into human power.

2. To give a portion of food and drink, as a beast upon the road; as, to *bait* horses.

bāit, *v.t.* 1. To provoke and harass by dogs; to harass by the help of others; as, to *bait* a bull or a boar.

2. To attack with violence; to harass in the manner of small animals.

bāit, *v.i.* 1. To take a portion of food and drink for refreshment on a journey; as, we stopped to *bait*.

2. To act in a manner calculated to torment.

bāit, *v.i.* [Fr. *battre de l' aile*, to flap or flutter; *battre*, to beat.] To clap the wings; to flutter as if to fly; or to hover as a hawk when she stoops to her prey.

bāit′ẽr, *n.* A person who baits; a tormenter.

bāit′ing, *n.* 1. The act of baiting; refreshment at an inn, particularly food for a horse.

2. The act of teasing or tormenting bears, bulls, and other animals.

bāize, *n.* [OFr. *baie*, pl. *baies*, baize.] A coarse woolen stuff, with a long nap, sometimes frizzed on one side, without wale, and woven with two treadles, like flannel.

bȧ-joc′cō (bȧ-yok′ō), *n.* An obsolete papal copper coin, of the value of a cent and a half.

bāke, *v.t.*; baked, *pt., pp.*; baking, *ppr.* [ME. *baken*; AS. *bacan*, to bake.]

1. To heat, dry, and harden by continued heat, as in an oven or furnace, under coals of fire, on hot stones or metal, etc.; to prepare for food in a close place, heated; as, to *bake* bread.

2. To dry and harden by heat, either in an oven, kiln, or furnace, or by the solar rays; to vitrify; as, to *bake* bricks; to *bake* the ground.

bāke, *v.i.* 1. To do the work of baking; as, she brews, washes, and *bakes*.

2. To be baked; to dry and harden in heat; as, the bread *bakes*; the ground *bakes* in a hot sun.

bāke, *n.* The process of baking, or the results of it; usually with a specifying adjective; as, a clam*bake*.

bāked (bākt), *a.* Dried and hardened by heat; dressed in heat; as, *baked* meat.

bāked′=ap′ple, *n.* The cloudberry, especially its dried fruit.

bāke′house, *n.* A house or building for baking.

bāke′meat, bāked′=meat, *n.* Meat which is baked, especially in the form of a pie. [Obs.]

bāk′en, *v.*, past participle of *bake*. [Obs.]

bāk′ẽr, *n.* [ME. *baker*; AS. *bæcere*, from *bacan*, to bake.]

1. One whose occupation is to bake bread, biscuit, pastry, or any kind of flour food.

2. A small oven in which baking is performed.

Baker's dozen; thirteen; a generous measure.

Baker's foot; an ill-shaped foot.

Baker's itch; a skin disease of the hands, peculiar to bakers.

Baker's knee or *leg*; legs that crook inward at the knees; commonly termed *knock-knee*.

bāk′ẽr-y, *n.* 1. The trade of a baker. [Rare.]

2. A bakeshop; a place devoted to the business of baking and selling such goods as bread, biscuit, rolls, pies, cakes, cookies, and crackers.

bāk′ing, *n.* 1. A drying or hardening by heat.

2. The quantity baked at once; as, a *baking* of bread.

Baking powder; a powder used in baking as a substitute for yeast. It usually consists of tartaric acid, bicarbonate of soda, and rice or potato flour. These ingredients are powdered and dried separately, and then thoroughly mixed together. The flour is added to keep the powder dry, and prevent it from absorbing moisture from the atmosphere.

bāk′ing-ly, *adv.* In a baking manner.

bak′shĭsh, *n.* See *Backsheesh*.

bal′ȧ-chong, *n.* [Malay.] A condiment made of fishes and shrimps pounded up with salt and spices, and dried; it is much used on rice and other food eaten by the inhabitants of Farther India and Malaysia.

Balæniceps rex.

Bȧ-læ′ni-ceps, *n.* [L. *balæna*, a whale, and *-ceps*, from *caput*, head.] A genus of birds embracing the *Balæniceps rex*, or whale-headed stork, a gigantic wading bird about three and one-half feet in height, with a large beak. It has been found in the upper part of the White Nile.

Bȧ-læ′ni-dæ, *n.pl.* [L. *balæna*, a whale, and *-idæ*.] A family of whales especially productive of long narrow baleen, including always the bowhead, or Greenland right whale.

bȧ-læ′noid, *a.* Pertaining to the *Balænoidea*.

bȧ-læ′noid, *n.* A right whale which yields baleen, or whalebone; the whalebone-whale.

Bal-æ-noi′dē-ȧ, *n.pl.* [L. *balæna*, whale, and Gr. *eidos*, form.] One of the three divisions of *Cetacea*, including the right and fin-whales.

bal′ȧ-hoọ, *n.* [Native name in West Indies.] A marine fish; the halfbeak.

bal′ănce, *n.* [ME. *balance*; OFr. *balance*, from L. *bilanx*, *bilancis*; *bis*, twice, and *lanx*, a dish, scale.]

1. An instrument for ascertaining the weight of bodies.

In its original and simplest form it consists of a beam or lever suspended exactly in the middle on a pivot as its center of gravity, with a scale or basin of precisely equal weight hung to each extremity. The annexed illustration represents the common *balance*. AB is the beam, which rests in a horizontal position, and is capable of turning on the center of motion C. D and E are the scales, which are suspended from the points A and B, the extremities of the beam, called the centers of suspension. Midway between the centers of suspension, and directly above the center of motion, there rises from the upper surface of the beam a perpendicular slender stem called the tongue, which, when the beam is horizontal, points to the top of the handle F, by which the whole is suspended. In a properly constructed *balance* the beam should rest in a horizontal position when the scales are either empty or loaded with equal weights; a very small addition of weight put into either scale should cause the beam to deviate from the horizontal position; and the arms of the beam should be inflexible, exactly similar, equal in weight and length.

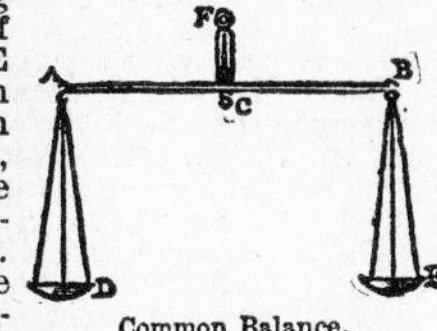

Common Balance.

2. Figuratively, the act of mentally comparing or estimating two things, one against the other.

> Upon a fair *balance* of the advantages on either side. —Atterbury.

3. The weight or sum necessary to make two unequal weights or sums equal; that which is necessary to bring them to a balance or equipoise; the excess by which one thing is greater than another; surplus, real or figurative; as, I have still a *balance* at my banker's. In accounts, the difference of two sums; as, upon an adjustment of accounts, a *balance* was found against A in favor of B.

4. An equality of weight, power, advantage, and the like; equipoise or just proportion, as of emotions and the like; as, *balance* of force; to lose one's *balance*.

5. That which renders power or authority equal; a counterpoise; as, the *balance* between the executive, legislative, and judicial bodies of the United States government is carefully maintained.

6. The part of a clock or watch which regulates the beats, formerly a pin oscillating on its center, and thus resembling the beam of a *balance*; now a wheel.

7. In astronomy, a sign in the zodiac, called Libra, which the sun enters at the equinox in September.

Alloy balance; a balance for weighing metals which are to be combined in decimal proportions.

Assay balance; one used in experimental or testing operations for weighing minute bodies. Such balances, besides being made with extraordinary care, are always placed under glass cases to protect them from currents of air.

Balance of power; such a relation between ruling political parties that a minority party or faction by its vote may turn the scale either way, or block action.

In international politics, a certain equality of power among a number of different states; or, more specifically, such an equality among the most powerful of a number of states, along with a disposition to maintain their relative power. When a few of the leading powers or a number of separate and sovereign states counterpoise each other the *balance of power* is maintained, and the safety of the smaller states secured. The international policy by which this has been effected in Europe has been for the majority to oppose every new arrangement which threatens either materially to augment the strength of one of the great powers or to diminish that of another.

Balance of trade; a phrase used to denote the relation in respect of amount or value which subsists between the exportation of domestic productions from a country and the importation of foreign, or the difference between the amount or value of the commodities exported and imported. The *balance of trade* is against or in favor of a country.

Bent-lever balance; a weighing-scale in which the scale-pan is attached to the short arm of a bent lever, the long arm indicating the weight in the pan by traversing a graduated arc.

Electric balance; same as *Balance-electrometer*.

False balance; a balance constructed for fraudulent purposes, having the arms of unequal lengths but of equal weights. When the scales are empty the beam rests in a horizontal position, and the balance appears to be just; but when a weight is put into the scale suspended from the short arm a less weight of goods put into the other scale will be sufficient to cause the beam to settle in a horizontal position and produce an apparent equilibrium. The readiest way of detecting such a balance is to make the weight and the article weighed to change places, for then the scale suspended from the longer arm will immediately preponderate.

Hydrostatic balance; a balance for weighing substances in water.

Torsion balance; an appliance for measuring electricity and magnetism.

To pay a balance; to pay the difference and make the two accounts equal.

To strike a balance; a term in bookkeeping which indicates the final writing-up of the accounts, so that the debits and credits balance; figuratively, to finally adjust matters in an equitable way.

bal′ănce, *v.t.*; balanced (-ănst), *pt.*, *pp.*; balancing, *ppr.* 1. To adjust, as weights in the scales of a balance so as to bring them to an equipoise; to weigh in a pair of scales or balance.

2. To poise on a point or small base; to keep in equilibrium; as, to *balance* oneself on a tightrope; the juggler *balanced* a plate on his nose.

3. To weigh (reasons); to compare, by estimating the relative force, importance, or value of different things; as, to *balance* good and evil.

4. To regulate (different powers), so as to keep them in a state of just proportion; as, to *balance* Europe, or the powers of Europe.

5. To counterpoise; to make of equal weight or force; to neutralize; as, one species of attraction *balances* another.

6. To settle and adjust, as an account; to find the difference of (two accounts), and to pay the balance, or difference, and make them equal.

7. In bookkeeping, to adjust or correct, as a system of accounts so that the sum of the debits equals the sum of the credits; as, to *balance* a set of books.

8. In seamanship, to reef (a fore-and-aft sail) by taking it in at the peak.

9. In dancing, to move toward, and then away from (one another); as, to *balance* partners.

10. To offset.

Syn.—Adjust, counterpoise, equalize, neutralize, poise, weigh.

bal′ănce, *v.i.* 1. To have equal weight on each side; to be on a poise; to preserve the equipoise of the body.

2. To hesitate; to fluctuate between motives which appear of equal force.

3. In dancing, to move toward a person or couple opposite, and then back.

bal′ănce-ȧ-ble, *a.* Capable of being balanced.

bal′ănce-bēam, *n.* A beam constituting part of the machinery for lowering a drawbridge, and which, moving upward, caused it to descend.

bal′ănce-ē-lec-trom′e-tēr, *n.* An instrument constructed on the principle of the common balance and weights, used to estimate the mutual attraction of oppositely electrified surfaces. A glass pillar is fixed in a stand A, to which the beam of a delicate balance B′B is suspended at the point D. A scale-pan *d* is suspended from one arm, and lightly rests upon the support E, likewise insulated and fixed upon the stand A. From the other arm is suspended a light gilt cone *c*, the base of which is opposed to the base of another inverted cone *b*, which may be fixed at any distance from it by sliding upon the insulated pillar *d′*. The metallic balance *c* may be connected with the interior of a Leyden jar or battery, and the cone *b* with the exterior, and the attractive power of any charge at any variable distance between the cones may be estimated by weights placed in the scale-pan.

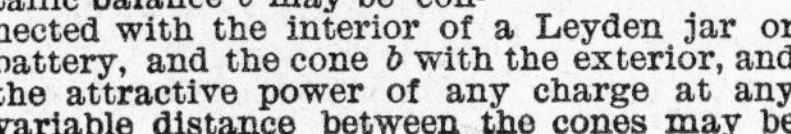
Balance-electrometer.

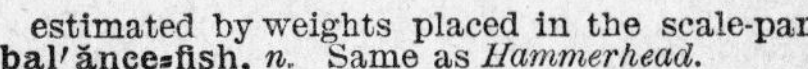

bal′ănce-fish, *n.* Same as *Hammerhead*.

bal′ănce-knife (-nīf), *n.* A table- or carving-knife, which, when laid on the table, rests wholly on the handle, without the blade touching the cloth; so called because the weight of the handle counterbalances that of the blade.

bal′ăn-cēr, *n.* 1. One who weighs, or uses a balance.

2. In entomology, a member of the dipterous insects used in balancing the body; a rudimentary wing; a poiser.

3. One skilled in balancing or preserving the equipoise of his body.

4. In aeroplanes, an organ—usually a plane—for maintaining lateral equilibrium.

bal′ănce-reef, *n.* A reef-band that crosses a fore-and-aft sail diagonally.

bal′ănce-rud″dēr, *n.* A rudder supported on a projection from the keel so that part of it is forward of its vertical axis of motion; also called *equipoise-rudder*.

bal′ănce-sheet, *n.* In bookkeeping, a sheet or tabular statement showing the balances of all the open accounts of a business, the sum of the debits balancing the sum of the credits, if the books have been correctly kept; a statement of the assets and liabilities of an individual, firm, or corporation.

bal′ănce-step, *n.* In military tactics, one of the steps of the squad drill taught in laying down the principles of marching.

bal′ănce-thēr-mom′e-tēr, *n.* A thermometer mounted as a balance, the variations of temperature causing changes in the inclination of the tube containing the mercury; used, with the aid of electric and other devices, in the automatic regulation of artificial heat, and to give an alarm in case of fire.

bal′ănce-valve, *n.* A valve in which steam is admitted to both sides so as to render it more readily operated, by relieving its pressure on the seat.

bal′ănce-wheel, *n.* That part of a watch or chronometer which regulates the action of the power, and determines the regularity and time of beat or strike; a fly-wheel in machinery.

bal′ăn-cing, *n.* The art or act of maintaining balance or equipoise, either of one's own body or of an object.

ba-lan′drȧ, *n.* [Sp., from Dan. *bijlander*; *bij*, by, and *land*, land.] A coasting-vessel used on the South American coasts.

bal-an′drȧ-nȧ, *n.* [OFr. *balandran*.] A wide cloak or mantle, used as a surtout in the twelfth and thirteenth centuries; called also *supertotus*.

bal-an-i-, bal-an-ō-. Combining forms from Gr. *balanos*, an acorn, a gland.

bal′ȧ-nid, *n.* A cirriped of the family *Balanidæ*; the acorn-barnacle.

Bal-an′i-dæ, *n.pl.* [L., from Gr. *balanos*, acorn.] A family of cirripeds, of which the genus *Balanus* is the type. The animals of this family are frequently called *acorn-shells*. [See *Balanus*.]

bal-ȧ-nif′ēr-ous, *a.* [*Balani-*, and L. *ferre*, to bear.] Acorn-bearing.

bal′ȧ-nīte, *n.* A cirriped fossil; similar to a balanid; also, a precious stone.

Bal-ȧ-nī′tēs, *n.* [L., from Gr. *balanites*, acorn-shaped; *balanos*, an acorn.]

1. A genus of plants, natural order *Simarubaceæ*, containing two species, which are small spiny trees, found in desert places in Asia and Africa. The oval fruits are purgative; they contain a very hard nut, used in India for fireworks.

2. Another name for *Balanus*, a genus of cirripeds.

bal-ȧ-nī′tis, *n.* [L., from Gr. *balanos*, a gland, an acorn.] A kind of gonorrhea.

Bal″ȧ-nō-glos′si-dæ, *n.pl.* [*Balano-*, and Gr. *glōssa*, tongue.] A family of *Enteropneusta*, having a system of gill-like structures at the side of the alimentary canal.

Bal″ȧ-nō-glos′sus, *n.* [*Balano-*, and Gr. *glōssa*, tongue.] A remarkable genus of soft-bodied marine worms, having gill-like openings along the alimentary canal, allying them to the vertebrates; the type of the *Balanoglossidæ*.

bal′ȧ-noid, *a.* [Gr. *balanos*, acorn, and *eidos*, like.] Like an acorn; applied, in zoölogy, to certain barnacles with acorn-shaped shells.

Bal″ȧ-nō-phō-rā′cē-æ, *n.pl.* [*Balano-*, and Gr. *phoros*, from *pherein*, to bear.] A curious order of parasitic, leafless, flowering plants. There are about thirty known species grouped into ten genera. They are generally of a bright yellow or red color. Their small flowers, in most cases unisexual, are aggregated into dense masses. The fruit is one-celled, with a single seed.

bal″ȧ-nō-phō-rā′ceous, *a.* Related to the family *Balanophoraceæ*.

Bal′ȧ-nus, *n.* [L., from Gr. *balanos*, a gland or acorn.] A genus of sessile cirripeds, family *Balanidæ*, of a great variety of forms. Colonies are found on rocks left dry at low water, on

ships, on timber, on lobsters and other crustaceans, and on the shells of conchifers and other mollusks. They differ from the barnacles (genus *Lepas*) in having a symmetrical shell and in being destitute of a flexible stalk. They pass through a larval stage of existence, at which period they are not fixed, but move about by means of swimming-feet, and possess large stalked eyes, both feet and eyes disappearing when they attach themselves to their final place of repose. Often called *acorn-shells*.

Group of *Balanus tintinnabulum*.

bä-lä′ō, *n.* Same as *Balahoo*.

bal′ăs, bȧ-lass′, *n.* [ME. *balas*; OFr. *balais*; Port. *balache*; from Ar. *balakhsh*, a ruby.] A ruby named from a country of Central Asia (called *Balasian* by Marco Polo). It is a variety of the spinel ruby, of a pale rose-red color, sometimes inclining to orange. Its crystals are usually octahedrons, composed of two four-sided pyramids, applied base to base. Called also *balas ruby*.

bal′ȧ-tȧ, *n.* [Sp., from native name.]

1. A sapotaceous tree (*Mimusops globosa*) of tropical America, from the inspissated juice of which a gum somewhat similar to gutta-percha is made; the bastard bully-tree.

2. The dried juice or gum of the *balata*, used in the insulation of wires and the manufacture of chewing-gum.

bȧ-lạus′tȧ, *n.* [L. *balaustium*; Gr. *balaustion*, the flower of the wild pomegranate.] Any fruit (of which the pomegranate is a type) whose ovary is many-seeded and pulpy and whose tough skin is surmounted by the adnate or united calyx.

bȧ-lạus′tine, *n.* The root-bark and fruit-rind of the wild pomegranate-tree; the tree itself.

Balaustine flowers; the dried flowers of the pomegranate, used in medicine as an astringent.

Bȧ-lạus′ti-on, *n.* [Gr. *balaustion*, the flower of the wild pomegranate.] A genus of plants, order *Myrtaceæ*, containing one known species, *Balaustion pulcherrimum*, a shrub inhabiting southwestern Australia, and considered one of the most beautiful of plants, with numerous flowers resembling in shape and color those of the dwarf pomegranate.

bȧ-lȧ-yeụse′, *n.* [Fr., f. of *balayeur*, sweeper, from *balayer*, to sweep.] A ruffle placed on the inside of the bottom of a woman's dress to protect it.

Bal-brig′găn, *n.* [From *Balbriggan*, Ireland.] A fine cotton fabric made at Balbriggan, Ireland, and used in manufacturing hosiery and underwear.

bal-bū′ti-āte (-shi-), *v.i.* [L. *balbutire*, from *balbus*, stammering.] To stammer in speaking. [Obs.]

bal-bū′ti-ēṣ (-shi-), *n.* Stammering; also, a vicious and incomplete pronunciation, in which almost all the consonants are replaced by *b* and *l*.

bal′çon, bal′çone, *n.* A balcony or gallery. [Obs.]

bal′çō-net, *n.* [Fr., dim. of *balcon*, balcony.] A low ornamental railing to a door or window, projecting but slightly beyond the threshold or sill.

bal′çō-nied (-nid), *a.* Fitted with balconies.

The house was double-*balconied*. —North.

bal′çō-ny, *n.* [Fr. *balcon*; It. *balcone*, from *balcon*, a beam, scaffold.]

1. A stage or platform projecting from the wall of a building, supported by columns, pillars, or consoles, and encompassed by a balustrade, railing, or parapet. *Balconies* are common before windows.

Balcony.

2. The projecting gallery in the interior of a building, as of a theater.

3. A stern gallery in a ship of war: (a) in a modern vessel, for the accommodation of the flag-officer; (b) in the old-style craft, an open structure for general purposes.

bạld, *a.* [ME. *balde, belde, ballede*, pp. of *ball*, to reduce to roundness like a ball, as when the hair is removed.]

1. Destitute of hair, especially on the top and back of the head.

2. Destitute of the natural covering at the summit; as, a *bald* oak; a *bald* mountain.

3. Figuratively, without attempt to conceal; naked; bold; as, *bald* blasphemy, egotism, sophistry.

4. Unadorned; inelegant; as, a *bald* literary style.

5. In biology, without the usual appendage or mark; as, *bald* wheat; *bald* eagle.

Bald eagle; see under *Eagle*.

bạld, *n.* A bare mountain top, especially among the southern Appalachians of the United States.

Bạld-, -bạld. [AS. *bald*, bold.] A common prefix and suffix to many proper names; as, *Bald*win, bold in battle; Ethel*bald*, bold noble, or nobly bold.

bal′dȧ-çhin, bal-dȧ-çhī′nō, bal′dȧ-quin (-kin), *n.* [It. *baldacchino*; Sp. *baldaquino*, a rich silk cloth or canopy carried over the host; from *Baldacco*, the Italian form of *Bagdad*, where the cloth was manufactured.] A canopy or covering of various kinds, as (a) a canopy borne over the host or sacramental elements; (b) a covering of silk or stuff supported on four poles and upheld over the pope on ceremonial occasions; (c) a covering on four columns of marble or stone, or a canopy hanging from the roof over the high altar in some churches; (d) a canopy over a bed to which curtains are attached; (e) a canopy or covering above the seats of kings, imperial personages, and bishops and other ecclesiastical dignitaries. [See *Baudekin*.]

Baldachin, Church of St. Ambrose, Milan.

bạld′-buz″zărd, bal′bū-särd, *n.* A name sometimes given to the osprey or fishhawk (*Pandion haliaëtus*).

bạld′-çoot, *n.* See *Baldicoot*.

Bạl′dẽr, *n.* [Ice. *Baldr*, from *baldor*, bold, a prince.] In Scandinavian mythology, the son of Odin and Freya, the young and beautiful god of light and peace. Written also *Baldur*.

bạl′dẽr-dash, *n.* [Dan. *balder*, noise, and *dask*, a dash, a slap.]

1. Senseless prate; a jargon of words; ribaldry; noisy nonsense; as, his speech was nothing but *balderdash*.

2. A worthless mixture of frothy liquors. [Obs.]

To drink such *balderdash* or bonnyclabber. —B. Jonson.

Syn.—Gasconade, flummery, rodomontade, bombast, fustian, froth, verbosity, wordiness.

bạl′dẽr-dash, *v.t.* To mix or adulterate. [Rare.]

bạld′-fāced, *a.* White-faced, or with white on the face; said of animals; as, a *bald-faced* horse.

bạld′head (-hed), *n.* 1. A head destitute of hair.

2. A man bald on the head.

3. A kind of pigeon, so called from its white head; also, the widgeon, or fresh-water duck, the top of whose head is white.

bạld′head″ed, *a.* Having little or no hair on the head, especially on the top of the head.

bạl′di-çoot, *n.* 1. The common European coot, *Fulica atra*; also called *bald-coot*.

2. A term applied to a monk, from his shaven head.

bạld′ly, *adv.* Nakedly; meanly; inelegantly; openly.

bạld′mon″ey, *n.* [ME. *baldmony*, from *baldemoin*, a name given the gentian.] A name for the mew, or *Meum athamanticum*, a European umbelliferous plant; called also *spicknel*.

bạld′ness, *n.* 1. The state or quality of being bald; want of hair or natural covering on the head or top; lack of hair.

2. Deficiency of appropriate ornament, as in writing; meanness or inelegance; want of ornament; as, *baldness* of style.

Baldness of allusion and barbarity of versification. —T. Warton.

bạld′pāte, *n.* 1. A pate or head without hair.

2. A person with a bald head.

Come hither, goodman *baldpate*. —Shak.

3. A widgeon, *Anas americana*.

bạld′pāte, bạld′pāt″ed, *a.* Destitute of hair; shorn of hair.

bạld′rib, *n.* 1. A rib, as of pork, from which the fat has been removed.

2. A very lean person. [Obs.]

bạl′driç, bạl′drick, bạu′drick, *n.* [ME. *baudrik*; OFr. *baudrei, baldrei*; G. *balderich*, a girdle; O.H.G. *balz*, a belt.]

1. A belt or ornament resembling a belt.

2. A belt worn round the waist, as the Roman *cingulum* or military belt. [Rare.]

3. A jeweled ornament worn round the neck by both ladies and gentlemen in the sixteenth century.

4. A broad belt, worn pendent from the right or left shoulder, diagonally across the body, to the waist or below it, either simply as an ornament or to suspend a sword, dagger, or horn. Some were magnificently decorated and garnished with bells and precious stones. The *baldric* was worn in feudal times, partly as a military and partly as a heraldic symbol, and its style served to indicate the rank of the wearer.

A radiant *baldric* o'er his shoulder tied. —Pope's *Iliad*.

bạl′driç-wīṣe, *adv.* After the manner of a baldric; over one shoulder and hanging diagonally across the body.

Bạl′dūr, *n.* Same as *Balder*.

Bạld′win, *n.* A large winter apple of a reddish color and a tartish flavor, raised in the United States.

bāle, *n.* [ME. *bale*; OFr. *bale, balle*; L. *bala, balla*, a package, ball.] A bundle or package of goods in a cloth cover, and corded for carriage or transportation; specifically, a large package of compressed material; as, a *bale* of hay, or cotton.

bāle, *v.t.*; baled (bāld), *pt., pp.*; baling, *ppr.* To make into a compressed package.

bāle, *v.t.* To free from water. [See *Bail*.]

bāle, *n.* [ME. *bale, balw*; AS. *balw*, evil, calamity.]

1. Mischief; danger; calamity. [Rare.]

2. Sorrow; misery. [Rare.]

Bal-e-ar′iç, *a.* [L. *Balearicus*; Gr. *Balearikos*, from *Baliareis*, the name of a group of islands.] Pertaining to the isles of Majorca, Minorca, Iviça, etc., in the Mediterranean Sea, known as the *Balearic* Isles.

Balearic crane; the crowned crane. [See *Crane*.]

bȧ-leen′, *n.* [ME. *balene*; OFr. *balene*; L. *balæna*, a whale.] The narrow, elastic plates extending in a fringe from the upper jaw of certain whales, *Balænoidea*, for use in straining and retaining their food; the whalebone of commerce.

bāle′fīre, *n.* [ME. *balefyre*; AS. *bælfȳr*; *bæl*, bale, and *fȳr*, fire.] A signal-fire; an alarm-fire.

bāle′fụl, *a.* [ME. *baleful, baluful*; AS. *bealu-full*; *bealu*, bale, and *-full*, full.]

1. Mischievous; destructive; pernicious; calamitous; deadly; as, *baleful* enemies; *baleful* war.

2. Sorrowful; woeful; sad. [Rare.]

bāle′fụl-ly, *adv.* In a baleful manner; sorrowfully.

bāle′fụl-ness, *n.* The state or quality of being baleful; destructiveness.

bal′i-sä-ür, *n.* [Hind. *bālusūr*, a sandhog.] An East Indian mammal, *Arctonyx collaris*, allied to the badger; found only in the hill country of Hindustan.

bal′is-tẽr, *n.* [ME. *balester*, from L. *ballista*, a crossbow.] A crossbow, or a crossbowman. [Obs.]

Bȧ-lis′tēṣ, *n.* The typical genus of the family of fishes known as *Balistidæ*; called also the *trigger-fish* because the large first ray of the dorsal fin cannot be pressed down until the second ray is depressed, when the first shuts down like the hammer of a gun.

Bȧ-lis′ti-dæ, *n.pl.* [L., from *balista*, a military engine.] A family of hard-scaled, bright-colored fishes of the order *Plectognathi*, frequenting coral beds for their food. They have no ventral fins or spines.

bal′is-toid, *a.* Of, relating, or pertaining to the trigger-fishes, genus *Balistes*.

bal-is-trā′ri-ȧ, *n.* [L., from *balistra*, a form of *ballista*, a crossbow.] A cross-shaped loophole in a fortress for the discharge of arrows; also, a storeroom for crossbows.

bȧ-līze′, *n.* [Fr. *balise*, a beacon.] A seamark; a pole raised on a bank.

bạlk (bạk), *n.* [ME. *balk*; AS. *balca*, a ridge; G. *balke*, a beam, a bar.]

1. Anything acting as a hindrance or interference; a temporary or complete check; a delay or thwarting; a stop; failure; as, a *balk* in negotiations.

2. Anything left untouched, as a ridge between furrows in plowing.

3. In athletic sports, a deceptive motion, as of a pitcher in baseball, retaining the ball when seeming to pitch it.

4. In billiards, the space bounded by the

cushions and balk-line; also, the space back of a line passing through the spot.

5. A beam or piece of timber of considerable length and thickness; as, (a) a crossbeam or tiebeam in a roof; (b) any squared timber or square log; (c) a connecting beam for the supports of a trestle- or bateau-bridge.

bạlk, *v.t.*; balked (bạkt), *pt.*, *pp.*; balking, *ppr.*
1. To leave untouched in plowing.
2. To leave untouched generally; to omit; to pass over; to neglect; to shun.
3. To disappoint; to frustrate.
4. To heap up so as to form a balk or ridge. [Rare.]

Syn.—Estop, bar, thwart, frustrate, foil, stop, prevent, hinder, neutralize, nullify, mar, counteract, disappoint, defeat, baffle.

bạlk, *v.i.* 1. To turn aside or stop in one's course; as, the horse *balked*; he *balked* in his speech.
2. To deal at cross-purposes; to talk beside one's meaning. [Obs.]

bạlk, *v.i.* [ME. *balken*, *belken*; AS. *bælcian*; Dan. *balken*, to brawl, brag.] To indicate by calls or signs from shore, to fishermen at sea, the direction of schools of herring.

bạlk'ēr, *n.* One who or that which balks.

bạlk'ēr, *n.* One who warns fishermen by balking.

bạlk'ing-ly, *adv.* In a manner to balk or frustrate.

bạlk'ish, *a.* Uneven; furrowy; ridged. [Rare.]

bạlk'=line, *n.* In billiards, one of four lines drawn parallel to and usually fourteen or eighteen inches from each side and end of the table for restricting the play; also, the line at the end of the table marking the position of the cue-balls at the opening of the game.

bạlk'y, *a.* Obstinate; inclined to balk; as, a *balky* horse.

bạll, *n.* [ME. *ball*, *bal*; M.H.G. *bal*, *balle*, a ball.]
1. A round body; a spherical substance, whether natural or artificial; or, a body nearly round; as, a *ball* for play; a *ball* of thread; a *ball* of snow.
2. Any part of a thing, especially of the human body, that is rounded or protuberant; as, the *ball* of the eye; the *ball* of the thumb; the *ball* of a dumb-bell; the *ball* of a pendulum, that is, the weight at the bottom.
3. The globe or earth, from its figure. [Rare.]
4. In farriery, a form of medicine, corresponding to the term *bolus* in pharmacy.
5. The projectile of a firearm; a bullet; such projectiles having formerly been always spherical. In this sense the word is also used collectively; as, to supply a regiment with powder and *ball*.
6. In printing, a cushion-like dauber, attached to a handle, for inking the type; now obsolete, rollers being used.
7. In pyrotechnics, a composition of combustible ingredients, which serve to burn, smoke, or give light.
8. In athletics, a general name for games in which a ball is used, particularly baseball.
9. In baseball, (a) the mode of delivery of a pitcher; as, a high *ball*; specifically, a delivery by the pitcher to the batsman, not passing over the plate and between the knee and shoulder limits, when the umpire is said to call *a ball* upon the pitcher; opposed to *a strike*; (b) any strike or throw; as, a foul *ball*; a wild *ball*.

Ball and socket joint; a joint formed by a ball or rounded end of anything working within a socket, so as to admit of motion in all directions. This kind of joint is much employed in the construction of gasaliers, and, anatomically, has an example in the hip-joint.

Ball of the eye; the globe moving in the orbit as distinguished from the remaining parts; formerly, the *pupil*.

Three balls, or *three golden balls*; the customary sign of a pawnbroker, from the coat of arms of the Medici family, the members of which were money-lenders.

bạll, *n.* [G. *ball*; Fr. *bal*, a dance, from *baler*, to dance; L. *ballare*; Gr. *ballizein*, to dance, jump about; *ballein*, to throw.] A social assembly of persons of both sexes for the purpose of dancing.

bạll, *v.i.*; balled (bạld), *pt.*, *pp.*; balling, *ppr.* To form into balls, as snow on horses' hoofs, or on the feet; as, the horse's feet *ball*.

bạll, *v.t.* To make into a ball, as of snow; or in winding cotton or heating a metal for rolling.

bal'lăd, *n.* [Fr. *ballade*, a dancing-song, from L. *ballare*, to dance.]
1. A short narrative poem, especially such as is adapted for singing; a poem partaking of the nature both of the epic and the lyric.
2. In music, a short, simple, repeated air having a subordinate accompaniment.

bal'lăd, *v.i.* To make or sing ballads. [Obs.]

bal'lăd, *v.t.* To make the subject of a ballad. [Obs.]

bal-lāde', *n.* [Fr.] An early style of poetry having seven- or eight-line stanzas, generally followed by a refrain and closed by an envoy.

bal'lăd-ēr, *n.* A writer of ballads.

bal'lăd-ism, *n.* The quality in a literary or musical composition which fixes its character as a ballad.

bal'lăd-ist, *n.* The author or singer of a ballad.

bal'lăd=mŏn"gēr, *n.* A dealer in ballads.

bal'lăd-ry, *n.* Compositions of the ballad kind; the style of ballads.

bal'lā-hōu, **bal'lā-hoo**, *n.* [Native name.] A fast-sailing two-masted vessel, rigged with high fore-and-aft sails, much used in the West Indies.

bal'lăn=wrasse, *n.* [Gael. and Ir. *ballach*, spotted, and *wrasse*.] A fish, of little flesh value (*Labrus maculatus*), found on the British coast; called also *ballan*.

bal'la-rag, **bal'ly-rag**, *v.t.* To bully; to threaten. [Obs. See *Bullyrag*.]

bal'lăst, *n.* [G. *ballast*; D. *barlast*; *bar*, bare, waste, and *last*, a load.]
1. Any weighty, compact substance, as stone, sand, or iron, placed in the hold of a ship or car of a balloon to keep it steady; as, the *ballast* was replaced by cargo.
2. Any material, as gravel, cinders, or crushed stone placed on the roadbed of a railway to render the track firm and lasting; also, similar material used as a basis for concrete.
3. That which gives firmness to the mind or steadiness to the character.

In ballast; said of a ship which sails without a commercial cargo, carrying only ballast.

bal'lăst, *v.t.*; ballasted, *pt.*, *pp.*; ballasting, *ppr.* To provide with ballast; as, to *ballast* a ship.

bal'lăst-āge, *n.* A toll paid for the privilege of taking up ballast in a port or harbor.

bal'lăst=fin, *n.* An extension of the keel of a sailing vessel, acting as ballast.

bal'lăst-ing, *n.* Ballast; that which is used for ballast.

bal'lăst=line, *n.* A ship's water-line when in ballast.

bal'lăst=plant, *n.* A plant, the seeds of which have been introduced to a country by being carried in ballast.

bal'lăst-tank, *n.* A tank in a ship's hold, into or out of which water for ballast can be pumped.

bal'lā-try, *n.* [Obs.] Same as *Balladry*.

bạll'=bear"ing, *n.* In mechanics, a bearing made of small steel balls turning in a socket round the shaft, thus reducing friction.

bạll'=cock, *n.* A kind of self-acting stopcock opened and shut by means of a hollow sphere or ball of metal attached to the end of a lever connected with the cock. Such cocks are often

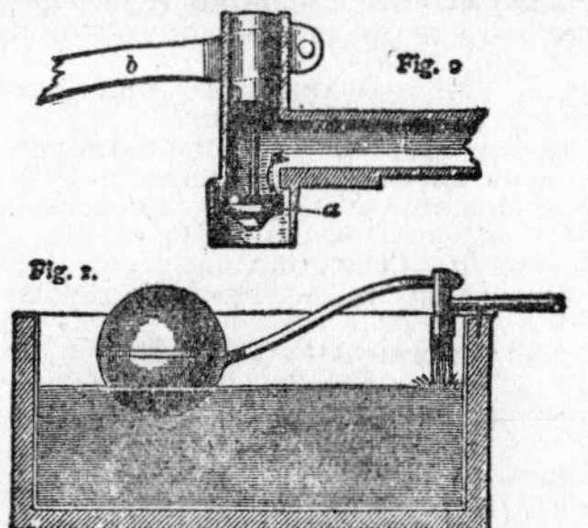

Fig. 1. Cistern with Ball-cock attached.
Fig. 2. Internal structure of Cock.
a, valve shown open so as to admit water; *b*, arm of the lever, which, being raised, shuts the valve.

employed to regulate the supply of water to cisterns. The ball floats by its buoyancy, and rises and sinks with the water, thus shutting it off or letting it on.

bal'let (ba'lā), *n.* [Fr. *ballet*; dim. of *bal*, a dance.]
1. A picturesque dance, more or less intricate, generally on an elaborate scale as to steps, costumes, and light-effects, performed as a dramatic or operatic interlude by a corps of dancers, usually by women in tights.
2. A dance in which a story is told in pantomime.
3. Collectively, the entire number of dancers so performing.

bal'let, *n.* [Fr. *ballette*, dim. of *bal*, *balle*, a ball.] In heraldry, a bearing representing small balls, or *ballets*, and denominated, according to their color, bezants, plates, hurts, etc.

bạll'fish, *n.* The diodon, or globefish.

bạll'=flow"ēr, *n.* An ornament resembling a ball placed in a circular flower, the three petals of which form a cup round it. This ornament is usually found inserted in a hollow molding, and is generally characteristic of the decorative style of the fourteenth century.

Ball-flower.

bạll'=gud"geŏn, *n.* A spherical journal which permits a freer motion of the shaft than mere rotation.

bal'liărds, *n.* Billiards. [Obs.]

bal-lis'mus, *n.* [L., from Gr. *ballismos*, from *ballizein*, to dance, jump about.] St. Vitus's dance.

bal-lis'tā, *n.*; *pl.* **bal-lis'tæ**. [L. *ballista*, from Gr. *ballein*, to throw.] A machine or engine, shaped like a crossbow and used by the ancients, in war, for throwing darts, stones, and other missiles.

bal'lis-tēr, *n.* A crossbow. [Obs.]

bal-lis'tic, *a.* Pertaining to the ballista or its use.

Ballistic curve; the path actually traveled by a projectile, as distinguished from its theoretical or parabolic path.

Ballistic pendulum; a heavy suspended mass against which a shot is fired and the deflection of the mass noted. From the laws of impact and those of the pendulum the velocity of the projectile may be calculated.

bal-lis'tics, *n.* 1. The science or art of throwing missiles by the use of an engine.
2. The modern science of projectiles.

bal'li-um, *n.* Same as *Bailey*.

bal"lon-et', **bal-loon'et**, *n.* A small balloon in a larger balloon for controlling the ascent or descent, and for maintaining pressure on the outer envelope to prevent its collapse.

bal-loon', *n.* [Fr. *ballon*, a balloon, football.]
1. A bag or hollow vessel filled with hydrogen gas or heated air, or any other gas lighter than common air, the contained gas causing it to rise and float in the atmosphere; also, the entire mechanism used in such an ascension.
2. In chemistry, a round vessel with a short neck to receive whatever is distilled; a glass receiver of a spherical form.
3. In architecture, a ball or globe on the top of a pillar.
4. In pyrotechnics, a ball of pasteboard or kind of bomb stuffed with combustibles, which, bursting like a bomb, exhibits sparks of fire like stars.
5. In weaving, a cylindrical reel on which sized woolen yarn for warp is wound in order to be dried by rapid revolution in a heated chamber.
6. In a drawing, the line inclosing words supposed to be spoken by a figure or character.
7. A large ball of leather inflated; the game played with it, a kind of football. [Obs.]

Captive balloon; a balloon permanently fixed or supplied with an anchor, used in military operations.

Dirigible balloon; a balloon which can be steered. [See *Air-ship*.]

Kite balloon; a captive balloon which is so constructed that it may be held against the wind, somewhat like a kite; esp. an elongated, cylindrical balloon of this kind having hemispherical ends and at the rear an air bag which fills automatically, serving to hold the balloon nearly stationary. (Called also *sausage balloon kite sausage* or *sausage*.)

bal-loon', *v.t.*; ballooned, *pt.*, *pp.*; ballooning, *ppr.* To cause to be carried up; to carry up in a balloon. [Rare.]

bal-loon', *v.i.* 1. To go up; to voyage in a balloon.
2. To puff up; to swell; as, the sails *balloon* to the wind.

bal-looned', *a.* Inflated like a balloon.

bal-loon'ēr, *n.* An aeronaut.

bal-loon'et, *n.* Same as *ballonet*.

bal-loon'=fish, *n.* A curious tropical malacopterygian or soft-spined fish of the order *Plectognathi*; the *Tetraodon lineatus* or striped spinebelly. Like the diodonts, it has the power of distending itself by swallowing air and making it pass into cavities beneath the skin, and of causing its spines to become erect.

bal-loon'ing, *n.* 1. The art or practice of managing balloons.
2. Inflation of values; also, extravagant praise, especially of a political candidate. [Slang.]

Ballooning spider; a spider that floats through the air on its web.

bal-loon'ist, *n.* One who ascends in a balloon.

bal-loon'=jib, *n.* A triangular sail used by yachts in light winds, set between the foretop-mast-head and the end of the jib-boom.

bal-loon'=kite, *n.* A combination of balloon and kite used for meteorological observations and formerly for military scouting.

bal-loon'ry, *n.* The art or practice of ascending in a balloon.

bal-loon'=vine, *n.* A tropical climbing plant belonging to the soapberry family (*Sapindaceæ*).

bal'lŏt, *n.* [It. *ballotta*; Fr. *ballotte*, a little ball.]
1. A ball used in voting. *Ballots* are usually of two colors, white and black, the former being used for an affirmative and the latter for a negative.
2. A printed or written vote; sometimes called a *ticket*.

3. The act of voting by balls or tickets, or by means of a voting-machine.

4. The entire number of votes cast at an election.

Australian ballot; see *Australian*.

bal′lŏt, *v.i.*; balloted, *pt.*, *pp.*; balloting, *ppr.* To vote by ballot.

bal′lŏt, *v.t.* To vote for or against by ballot; to choose or elect by ballot. [Obs.]

None of the competitors arriving at a sufficient number of balls, they fell to *ballot* some others. —Sir H. Wotton.

bal′lō-tāde, bal′lŏt-tāde (*or* -täd′), *n.* [Fr. *ballattade*, from *ballotter*, to toss; *ballotte*, a little ball, from *bal*, a ball.] A fancy leap of a horse made so that he exposes only the shoes of his hind feet while his fore feet are elevated, without jerking out.

bal-lō-tā′tion, *n.* A voting by ballot. [Obs.]

bal′lŏt-box, *n.* A box for receiving ballots.

bal′lŏt-ēr, *n.* One who ballots or votes by ballot.

bal′lō-tin, *n.* The carrier of the ballot-box; the taker of the votes by ballot. [Obs.]

bal′lŏt-ing, *n.* The act of voting by ballot.

bal-lotte′ment, *n.* [Fr., from *ballotter*, to toss.] A manual test to determine pregnancy.

bal′lōw, *n.* A cudgel. [Obs.]

bạll′rọọm, *n.* An apartment in which balls and dances are given.

bal′ly-rag, *v.t.* See *Ballarag*.

bälm (bäm), *n.* [ME. *baume*; OFr. *basme*; L. *balsamum*, from Gr. *balsamon*, balsam.]

1. The sap or juice of trees or shrubs remarkably odoriferous or aromatic.

2. Any fragrant or valuable ointment.

3. Anything which heals, soothes, or mitigates pain.

4. In botany, the name of several plants, particularly of the herb *Melissa officinalis*. They are aromatic, and used as corroborants.

Balm of Gilead; an Oriental evergreen tree, the *Balsamodendron Gileadense* of Decandolle. Its leaves yield, when bruised, a strong aromatic scent; and from this plant is obtained the *balm of Gilead* of the shops, or *balsam of Mecca*, or *of Syria*, as it is also called. It has a yellowish or greenish color, a warm, bitterish, aromatic taste, and a fragrant smell.

bälm, *v.t.* 1. To anoint with balm, or with anything medicinal.

2. To soothe; to mitigate; to assuage. [Obs.]

bälm′-ap″ple, *n.* Same as *Balsam-apple*.

bälm′i-fȳ, *v.t.* To render balmy. [Obs.]

bälm′i-ly, *adv.* In a balmy manner.

bal′mō-ny, *n.* A name sometimes given to the *Chelone glabra* or turtlehead.

Bal-mor′ăl, *n.* [After the English royal residence at Deeside, Aberdeenshire.]

1. A heavy, serviceable, striped, woolen cloth.

2. A heavy, laced shoe.

3. A striped woolen petticoat worn under the dress, which is looped up in places to show it.

4. A cap worn in Scotland.

Bal-mor′ăl, *a.* Relating to the special kind of cloth, garments, or shoes originating at Balmoral; usually capitalized.

bälm′y, *a.* 1. Having the qualities of balm; aromatic; fragrant.

2. Producing balm; as, the *balmy* tree.

3. Soothing; soft; mild; assuaging; mitigating.

bal′nē-ăl, *a.* [L. *balneum*, a bath.] Pertaining to a bath or bathing-place.

bal′nē-ā-ry, *n.* A bathing-room.

bal-nē-ā′tion, *n.* The act of bathing. [Rare.]

bal′nē-ā-tō-ry, *a.* [L. *balneatorius*, from *balneator*, a bath-keeper; *balneum*, a bath.] Belonging to a bath or a bath attendant. [Obs.]

bal′nē-ō-. [L. *balneum*, a bath.] A combining form designating relation to baths or bathing.

bal-nē-og′rā-phy, *n.* [*Balneo-*, and Gr. *graphia*, from *graphein*, to write.] A description of baths, especially from the medical standpoint.

bal-nē-ol′ō-ġy, *n.* [*Balneo-*, and Gr. *logia*, from *legein*, to write.] The science of curing by means of baths, especially in mineral springs.

bal″nē-ō-ther′ā-py, *n.* [*Balneo-*, and Gr. *therapeuein*, to heal.] The treatment of diseases by means of baths or water-cure.

bȧ-lō′nē-ȧ, *n.* [Gr. *balania*, the holm-oak; *balanos*, an acorn.] A name for an oak, *Quercus Ægilops*, native to Greece and the Levant. It is a large handsome tree, the wood of which is valuable in cabinetwork. The cups of the acorns are used in tanning; called also *valonia*.

Fisherman with his Balsa.

bạl′sȧ, bạl′zȧ, *n.* [Sp. and Port. from Peruvian *balza*, the native name of light porous wood used in Peru for rafts.]

1. A raft used on the coasts and rivers of South America for fishing, or landing goods and passengers through a heavy sea. It is formed generally of two inflated seal-skins, connected by a sort of platform on which the fisherman, passengers, or goods are placed.

2. A sailing canoe of Ceylon.

3. A tree (*Ochroma Lagopus*) flourishing on the coasts of tropical America; the corkwood.

bạl′săm, *n.* [AS. *balsam*; L. *balsamum*, from Gr. *balsamon*, *balsamos*, a balsam-tree.]

1. An oily, aromatic, resinous substance, flowing spontaneously or by incision from certain trees and shrubs. A great variety of substances pass under this denomination. The *balsams* are either liquid or solid; of the former are the balm of Gilead and the *balsams* of copaiba, Peru, and Tolu; of the latter, benzoin, dragon's-blood, and storax. The substances known as *balsams* are properly compounds of resin and essential volatile oils, fragrant and aromatic.

2. A preparation for preservative purposes, as embalming.

3. Any aromatic, fragrant, and healing ointment.

4. Figuratively, anything that heals, soothes, mitigates suffering, or ministers to the mind.

5. In botany, (a) a tree that exudes aromatic resin, especially one of the genus *Abies*; as, *Abies balsamea*, the balsam-fir, from which Canada *balsam* is produced; (b) an ornamental flowering plant, annual, as *Impatiens balsamina*, garden-balsam, lady's-slipper, touch-me-not.

Balsam of copaiba; see *Copaiba*.

Balsam of Mecca; see *Balm of Gilead* under *Balm*.

Balsam of Peru; a product of a Peruvian tree, grown in Central America (*Myroxylon Pereiræ*), used as an expectorant and also in perfumery.

Balsam of Saturn; an ointment compounded of acetate of lead dissolved in turpentine and mixed with camphor.

Balsam of Tolu; the product of *Myroxylon Toluiferum*, the tolu tree of Colombia and Venezuela. It is of a yellowish somber-red color, semisolid, turning brittle by age. It is very fragrant, allied to balsam of Peru, and likewise used as a stomach cure and expectorant.

Canada balsam; the liquid resin of *Abies balsamea*, used to preserve the objects mounted on microscopic slides.

bạl′săm, *v.t.*; balsamed, *pt.*, *pp.*; balsaming, *ppr.* To treat with balsam.

bạl′săm-ap″ple, *n.* An East Indian plant, annual; a small gherkin-shaped gourd, yellowish red in color, of the genus *Momordica*.

Wild balsam-apple; a climbing vine, *Echinocystis lobata*, of the gourd family.

bạl-săm-ā′tion, *n.* 1. The act of rendering balsamic.

2. The art or act of embalming. [Obs.]

bạl′săm-fīr, *n.* See *Balsam*, n. 5.

bạl-sam′iç, bạl-sam′iç-ăl, *a.* Having the qualities of balsam; stimulating; unctuous; soft; mitigating; mild.

bạl-sam′iç, *n.* A warm, stimulating, demulcent medicine, of a smooth and oily consistence.

bạl-sam′iç-ăl-ly, *adv.* In a balsamic manner.

bạl-săm-if′ēr-ous, *a.* [L. *balsamum*, balsam, and *ferre*, to bear.] Producing balsam.

Bạl″săm-i-nā′cē-æ, *n.pl.* [L. *balsamina*, the balsam plant, and *-aceæ*.] A small group of plants formerly separated from the *Geraniaceæ* because of their irregular flowers, but again restored to that order, as the discovery of additional species of *Impatiens*, the only genus in the group, shows these differences not to be of sufficient importance to establish an order.

bạl″săm-i-nā′ceous, *a.* Relating to the *Balsaminaceæ*.

bạl′sam-ine, *n.* The common name of the *Impatiens balsamina*, garden balsam.

Bạl″săm-ō-den′drŏn, *n.* [Gr. *balsamon*, balsam, and *dendron*, a tree.] A genus of trees remarkable for their powerful balsamic juice. They have compound leaves, small green flowers and, in season, small oval nuts.

bạl′săm-ous, *a.* Balsamic; abounding in balsam.

bạl′săm-sweat″ing (-swet″), *a.* Yielding balsam.

bạl′tēr, *v.t.* 1. To tangle. [Obs.]

2. To walk on clumsily.

bạl′tēr, *v.i.* 1. To become tangled.

2. To dance. [Obs.]

Bạl′tiç, *a.* Pertaining to the Baltic Sea, which separates Norway and Sweden from Denmark, Germany, and Russia; situated on the Baltic Sea.

Bȧ-lū′chī, *n.* 1. A native or inhabitant of Baluchistan.

2. The language of the Baluchis.

bal′us-tēr, *n.* [Fr. *balustre*; It. *balaustra*, a pillar, from *balausto*; L. *balaustium*; Gr. *balaustion*, the flower of the wild pomegranate.] A small column or pilaster of various forms and dimensions, often adorned with moldings, used for balustrades.

bal′us-tēred, *a.* Having balusters.

bal′us-trāde, *n.* [Fr. *balustrade*; It. *balaustrata*, from *balaustro*, a baluster.] A row of balusters, joined by a rail, serving as a fence or inclosure, for altars, balconies, staircases, terraces, tops of buildings, etc.

Balustrade.

bam′ȧ-lip, *n.* A word in logic, expressing a mood of the fourth figure; this word is artificially and mnemonically composed, that is, six of the seven letters, or b, a, m, a, i, and p, are significant, representing the initial letters of special definitions in logic. [See *Mood*.]

bäm-bī′nō, *n.*; *pl.* **bäm-bī′nī.** [It., a child, dim. of *bambo*, childish.] In the fine arts, the figure of Christ represented as an infant in swaddling clothes, often surrounded by a halo and watched over by angels, and forming the altarpiece in several churches. The *Santissimo Bambino* in the church of Ara Cœli at Rome, a richly decorated figure carved in wood, is claimed to have a miraculous virtue in curing diseases. *Bambini* of a similar though inferior description, are set up for the adoration of the faithful in many places in Catholic countries.

The Bambino, Church of Ara Cœli, Rome.

bam-boç′cī-āde, *n.* [It. *bambocciata*, a grotesque painting, from *bamboccio*, a little child, simpleton, a nickname given to Pieter Van Laer, the painter.] In painting, a term applied to lively or amusing scenes from common life, as rustic games, tavern scenes, and penny weddings.

bam-bọọ′, *n.* [Malay *bambu*.]

1. A plant of the reed kind, growing in the East Indies, and in some other warm climates, sometimes to a height of more than a hundred feet; originally placed by Linnæus in the genus *Arundo*, but afterward ranked by him in a distinct genus, *Bambusa*. The best-known species is *Bambusa Arundinacea*. From the main root, which is long, thick, and jointed, spring several round, jointed stalks. At a distance of ten or twelve feet from the ground, these, in turn, send out shoots from their joints. The offshoots are united at their base, spinose at the joints, with one or two sharp, rigid spines, and furnished with oblong, oval leaves, eight or nine inches long, on short footstalks. The flowers are arranged in pyramidal form, growing from the joints, three in a group. The mature stalk, which often attains a diameter of half a foot, is so durable as to be used for house frames, furniture, ship masts, palanquin poles, and water-pipes. The smaller stalks are used for fishing-poles, canes, and reed musical instruments.

1. Bamboo (*Bamboo Arundinacea*), showing its mode of growth.
2. Flowers, leaves, and stem on a larger scale.

2. The wood or fiber of the *bamboo*.

3. In pottery, an unglazed Wedgwood ware of the color of *bamboo* or straw.

4. An Eastern measure of length, about eleven feet; also, the name of an Eastern measure of capacity.

Bamboo books; ancient Chinese writings

inscribed on bamboo slips, discovered about A.D. 279.

bam-bōō′, *v.t.* To flog or beat with a bamboo. [See *Bastinado.*]

bam-bōō′-rat, *n.* A mole-like rodent of India, found chiefly in its bamboo jungles.

bam-bōō′zle, *v.t.*; bamboozled, *pt.*, *pp.*; bamboozling, *ppr.* [A slang word.] To confound; to deceive; to play low tricks upon. [Colloq.]

bam-bōō′zlēr, *n.* A cheat; one who plays low tricks; a swindler.

Bam-bū′sȧ, *n.* [L., from Malay *bambu*, bamboo] A genus of gigantic tropical grasses containing nearly seventy species, embracing the two which furnish the commercial bamboo, i.e., *Bambusa vulgaris* and *Bambusa Arundinacea.* [See *Bamboo.*]

ban, *n.* [ME. *ban*; AS. *bann*, an edict, decree; Ice. *bann*; Dan. *band*; G. *bann*, a proclamation; L. *fari*, to speak; Gr. *phanai*, to say; Sans. *bhan*, to speak.]

1. A public proclamation or edict; a public order or notice, mandatory or prohibitory, on the body summoned.

The *ban* was sometimes convoked.—Hallam.

2. In the plural, the word *bans*, or (commonly) *banns*, denotes notice of a marriage proposed, or of a matrimonial contract, proclaimed in a church, or other place prescribed by law, that any person may object, if he knows of any kindred between the parties, of any precontract, or other just cause why the marriage should not take place.

3. An edict of interdiction, prohibition, or proscription. In the former German Empire, to put a prince under the *ban of the empire*, was to divest him of his dignities, and to interdict all intercourse and all offices of humanity with the offender. Sometimes cities or districts were put under the *ban of the empire*, that is, deprived of their rights and privileges.

4. Interdiction; prohibition.

5. Curse; excommunication; anathema.

6. A pecuniary mulct or penalty laid upon a delinquent for offending against a *ban.*

7. A mulct paid to the bishop by one guilty of sacrilege and other crimes.

8. In military affairs, a proclamation by beat of drum, or sound of trumpet, requiring a strict observance of discipline, either for declaring a new officer, or for punishing an offender; in France and Germany, the forces summoned to duty by the government or sovereign.

ban, *n.* [From *banana*, from the stalk-fiber of which it is made.] In commerce, a smooth, fine muslin, imported from the East Indies.

ban, *v.t.*; banned, *pt.*,*pp.*; banning, *ppr.* 1. To curse; to execrate.

2. To interdict; to prohibit.

ban, *v.i.* To curse. [Obs.]

ban, *n.* [Per. *bān*, master, lord.] Formerly, a title belonging to the chief of the eastern marches of Hungary; now, the governor of Slavonia and Croatia. The territory over which he rules is called a banat. He is appointed by the emperor of Austria, acting as king of Hungary.

ban′ăl, *a.* [Fr. *banal*; L. *bannalis*, from *bannum*, a proclamation, decree.] Commonplace; trivial.

ban′ăl, *a.* Pertaining to a ban or a banat.

bȧ-nal′i-ty, *n.* [Fr. *banalité*, from *banal*; L. *bannum*, a decree, proclamation.]

1. The state of being banal; anything trite or trivial; a commonplace.

2. A compliment uttered to every one alike, and therefore devoid of special significance.

3. In French law, the authority by which a landed proprietor forced his tenants to use his agricultural machinery; also, the district over which such authority extended.

bȧ-nä′nȧ (*or* bȧ-nan′ȧ), *n.* [Sp.] A large, perennial plant or tree, *Musa sapientum*, akin to the plantain; also its fruit. It grows in the tropics to a height of fifteen or twenty feet, has a soft stalk, and leaves six feet long and a foot broad. The fruit is usually five or six inches long, and the pulp is soft and of a luscious taste. *Bananas* grow in large bunches, weighing as much as eighty pounds. They constitute not only a staple article of food to the natives, but are largely exported.

Banana (*Musa sapientum*).

bȧ-nä′nȧ-bird, *n.* A pretty bird (*Icterus leucopteryx*) perching in the fruit-trees around the houses in the West Indies and the warmer parts of America. It is very fond of the ripe fruit of the banana; hence its name.

bȧ-nä′nȧ-quit, *n.* A bird of the genus *Certhiola*, commonly known as *honey-creeper* and found in tropical America.

Banana-bird (*Icterus leucopteryx*).

ban′at, ban′āte, *n.* [Fr. and G. *banat*; Per. *bān*, a master, lord.]

1. The territory or jurisdiction of a ban.

2. The office of a ban. [See *Ban.*]

banc, bañk, *n.* [Fr. *banc*; L. *bancus*, a bench.] A bench; a seat of justice; a court.

In banc or *in banco*; in full session; as, sitting *in banc*, all the judges of a court being present, or, before a full bench.

bañ′cȧ, *n.* [Sp., from native name.] A boat resembling a canoe used by the natives in the Philippine islands.

bañ′căl, *n.* [Fr., bowlegged.] A curved saber in use in France from 1792-1810.

bȧñ′căl, *n.*; *pl.* **bȧñ-că′les.** [Sp., from *banca*, a bench.] A cover for a bench or seat, made of ornamented carpet, leather, or similar material.

bañ′cō, *n.* [It.] 1. A bank, particularly, the bank of Venice.

2. In commerce, a term employed to designate the money in which the banks of some countries keep or kept their accounts, as distinguished from the current depreciated money of the place.

band, *n.* [ME. *band*; Ice., G., Sw., Dan., *band*; Sans. *bandha*, a binding; *bandh*, to bind.]

1. A fillet; a cord; a tie; a chain; anything by which a thing is bound, tied, or fastened, or by which a number of things are bound together.

2. In architecture, (a) any flat, low strip or molding, broad, but not deep, called also fascia, face, or plinth; more specifically, the round molding, or series of moldings, which encircles the middle of the shaft in the early English style; (b) the tablet or stringcourse round a tower or other part of a building.

3. Figuratively, any fetter or chain; any means of restraint; that which draws or confines.

4. Means of union or connection between persons; as, Hymen's *band.*

5. Anything bound round or encircling another; as, a hat*band.*

6. [*pl.*] A pair of linen strips hanging in front from the neck; as, the *bands* worn by clergymen.

7. A company of persons united in any common design; a body of men united under one flag or ensign; a troop; a body of armed men.

8. A slip of canvas sewn across a sail to strengthen it.

9. A company of persons organized for the purpose of playing upon portable musical instruments; as, a string *band.*

10. A narrow strip of cloth sewn upon a garment to strengthen and complete it, or as a means of fastening it together; as, a neck*band*, wrist*band*, etc.

11. In zoölogy, a stripe around, or partly around, the body of an animal.

12. In mechanics, a driving-belt.

13. A bond; an agreement; security. [Obs.]

Thy oath and *band.* —Shak.

14. A metal ring shrunk on to the axle, hub, or circumference of a wheel; a tire.

15. In botany, the space between the ribs or lines of umbelliferous fruits.

16. A kind of ruff or collar worn in the sixteenth and seventeenth centuries.

17. In mining, a layer of rock containing seams of coal; sometimes the coal itself.

band, *v.t.*; banded, *pt.*, *pp.*; banding, *ppr.* 1. To bind together; to tie with a band.

2. To unite in a troop, company, or confederacy; as, *banded* against the throne.

3. To mark with a band or stripe, as a flag.

band, *v.i.* To unite; to associate; to confederate for some common purpose; to conspire.

band, *v.t.* To beat to and fro; to bandy; to drive away. [Obs.]

band, *v.*, past tense of *bind.* [Obs.]

band′āge, *n.* [Fr., from *bande*, a band, strip.]

1. A fillet, roll, or strip, used in dressing and binding up wounds, restraining hemorrhages, and joining fractured and dislocated bones.

2. Something resembling a *bandage*; that which is bound over something; a ligature.

band′āge, *v.t.*; bandaged, *pt.*, *pp.*; bandaging, *ppr.* To bind or cover with a bandage or similar appliance; as, to *bandage* a wound.

ban-dä′lȧ, *n.* [Native name.] Cloth or cordage (especially white rope) woven in Manila, from the outer fiber of the abaca.

ban-dan′ȧ, ban-dan′nȧ, *n.* [Hind. *bāndhnū*, a mode of dyeing.]

1. A species of silk or cotton handkerchief originally made by the Hindus, having a uniformly dyed ground, usually of red or blue, with white figures of a circular or lozenge form.

2. A style of calico-printing, in which white or bright spots are produced on a red or dark ground.

band′box, *n.* A light paper box for bands, caps, hats, bonnets, muffs, or other light articles.

ban′deau (-dō), *n.*; *pl.* **ban′deaux** (-dōz). [Fr., a fillet, diadem.] A narrow band or fillet around a cap or other headdress; a narrow band or bandage worn as a headdress.

band′ed, *a.* Being encircled by a band, either as a means of fastening, or striped in form or color; as, the *banded* serpent; the *banded* sheaves of grain.

Banded architrave, column, pier, shaft, etc.; any of these architectural forms whose outline is broken by bands or projections running across it at right angles.

Banded mail; a style of medieval armor in which the rings were arranged in bands around the body.

band′e-let, *n.* A small band. [See *Bandlet.*]

band′ẽr, *n.* One banded or associated with others. [Rare.]

ban-de-rïl′lä (ban-dā-rēl′yä), *n.* [Sp.] A small dart having a barbed head and bearing a banderole, which is directed at the bull by a banderillero during a bullfight.

ban″de-rïl-le′rō (-lyā′rō), *n.* One who directs a banderilla at a bull during a bullfight.

band′e-rōle, band′rōl, *n.* [Fr. *banderole*; It. *banderuola*, dim. of *bandiera*, a banner.]

1. A small banner or flag; a streamer. Written also *bannerol.*

2. In heraldry, a streamer attached to the head of a bishop's staff or crozier and folding over it.

3. In art, a painted or sculptured band, frequently bearing an inscription.

Banderole.

4. In bullfighting, the small flag forming part of the banderilla.

band′-fish, *n.* A small fish, the *Cepola rubescens*; also called the *ribbon-fish.*

ban′di-cōōt, *n.* [Corruption of native *pandikokku*, pig-rat.]

1. A name given to *Mus giganteus*, a very large rat of India and Ceylon. It is as large as a rabbit, and very destructive to growing crops.

2. An Australasian marsupial of the genus *Perameles*, resembling the *bandicoot* of India.

band′ing-plāne, *n.* A plane for making grooves for the reception of bands and strings.

band′ing-ring, *n.* In hatmaking, a ring which keeps the hat in place upon the block, slipped around it at a place corresponding to the hatband.

ban′dit, *n.*; *pl.* **ban′dits** or **ban-dit′ti.** [It. *bandito*, from *bandire*; L. *bandire*, to banish, outlaw.] An outlaw; a brigand; also, in a general sense, a robber; a highwayman; a lawless or desperate fellow.

ban′dle (-dl), *n.* [Ir. *bannlamh*; *bann*, a measure, and *lamh*, the arm, hand.] An Irish measure two feet in length.

ban′dle-lin″en, *n.* A coarse Irish linen made by hand and about a bandle in width.

band′let, band′e-let, *n.* [Fr. *bandelette*, dim. of *bandel*, a band.] Any little band or flat molding, as that which crowns the Doric architrave.

band′mȧs″tẽr, *n.* The leader or conductor of a band of music.

ban′dog, *n.* A large, fierce kind of dog; a mastiff; usually kept chained, hence the name *band*-dog or *bandog.*

ban-dō-leer′, *n.* [Fr. *bandoulière*; It. *bandoliera*, from *banda*, band.] A large leather belt, thrown over the right shoulder, and hanging under the left arm, and containing receptacles for cartridges; formerly worn by musketeers for sustaining their firearms. The term was also applied to small leather cases, of which every musketeer wore twelve, each containing a charge of powder. Also spelled *bandolier, bandilier.*

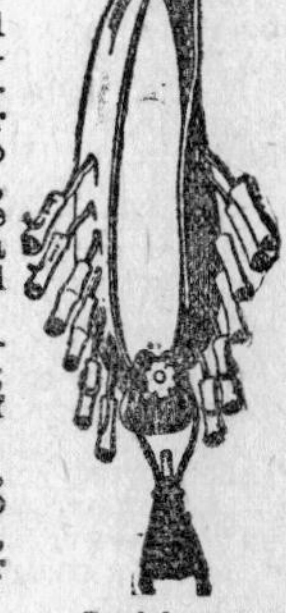

Bandoleer.

ban′dō-line, *n.* A gummy pomatum used for the hair; usually a preparation of quince seeds.

ban′dō-line, *v.t.*; bandolined, *pt.*, *pp.*; bandolining, *ppr.* To use bandoline upon, as the hair, for the purpose of glossing or keeping in shape.

ban′dŏn, *n.* Disposal; license. [Obs.]

ban′dōre, *n.* [Sp. *bandurria*; L. *pandura*; Gr. *pandoura*, a musical instrument.] A musical stringed instrument resembling a guitar; a pandore.

band'-pul"ley, *n.* A flat-faced wheel or pulley fixed on a shaft, driven by a band and employed in the transmission of power.

band'-saw, *n.* 1. A saw in the form of a narrow, endless steel band, carried between two wheels.

2. The entire mechanism, including the band-like saw.

band'-stand, *n.* A stand or platform for the use of a band of musicians.

band'-string, *n.* A string or lace in early times attached to a neckband.

band'wag"on, *n.* A vehicle intended for the use of a band of musicians.

To get into the bandwagon; to go with the crowd; to side with a successful candidate or cause. [Colloq.]

band'-wheel, *n.* A wheel with a face nearly flat or grooved to retain the band that drives it, as in the lathe; a band-pulley.

ban'dy, *n.* [Anglo-Ind.] A cart or conveyance, generally drawn by bullocks.

ban'dy, *n.* [Fr. *bander*, to bend.]

1. A club bent at the lower part for striking a ball at play; a hockey-stick.

2. The play with such a club; shinney; hockey.

ban'dy, *v.t.*; bandied (-did), *pt., pp.*; bandying, *ppr.* [Fr. *bander*, to bandy at tennis, from *bande*, a band, side, party.]

1. To beat to and fro, as a ball when playing at bandy.

2. To exchange; to give and receive reciprocally; as, to *bandy* words.

3. To agitate; toss about, as from man to man.

ban'dy, *v.i.* 1. To drive the ball, as in a return stroke at tennis.

2. To form into a band or union. [Obs.]

3. To emulate, either in a friendly or hostile spirit.

ban'dy, *a.* Crooked; bent; especially bent or crooked outward; said of legs, as *bandy*-legged.

bāne, *v.t.* To poison; to ruin. [Obs.]

bāne, *n.* [ME. *bane*; AS. *bana*, a slayer, murderer; O.H.G. *bano*, murder; Gr. *phonē*, murder.]

1. Poison of a deadly quality; hence, any fatal cause of mischief, injury, or destruction; as, vice is the *bane* of society.

2. A disease in sheep, more commonly termed the *rot*.

3. Death; destruction. [Obs.]

bāne'ber"ry, *n.* A common name of the genus of herbs *Actæa*, belonging to the crowfoot family, whose berries are poisonous.

bāne'ful, *a.* Poisonous; pernicious; destructive; deadly.

bāne'ful-ly, *adv.* In a baneful manner; dangerously.

bāne'ful-ness, *n.* The state or quality of being baneful or pernicious.

bāne'wŏrt, *n.* A poisonous plant, of the crowfoot family, especially the deadly nightshade and the lesser spearwort, the latter being particularly baneful to sheep.

bang, *v.t.*; banged (bangd), *pt., pp.*; banging, *ppr.* [G. *bangen*, to strike, beat; Ice. *banga*, to hammer.]

1. To beat, as with a club or cudgel; to thump.

2. To handle roughly; to treat with violence; as, to *bang* a drum.

bang, *v.i.* To make a great noise, as by striking a series of blows; to slam.

bang, *v.t.* To cut straight across, as a horse's tail, or hair over the human forehead; to dock.

bang, *n.* 1. A hard blow, as with a club; a resounding thump.

2. An explosive noise; as, the *bang* of a door; the *bang* of a gun.

bang, *n.* The front hair cut squarely across the forehead; a curl of the front hair or a false front brought down low upon the forehead.

bang, *n.* [Per. *bang*; Sans. *bhangā*, hemp.] See *Bhang*.

ban'gle (-gl), *v.t.*; bangled (-gld), *pt., pp.*; bangling, *ppr.* To waste gradually; to squander in bits. [Obs.]

ban'gle, *v.i.* To hang loosely; to flutter.

ban'gle, *n.* [Hind. *bangrī*, glass bracelet.]

1. A form of bracelet; a circlet of gold, silver, glass, or other material, worn by the women of eastern countries; also, an ornament worn on the ankle in India and Africa.

Bangles, from East India Museum.

2. Among sailors, a hoop around a spar.

ban'gle-ear, *n.* An ear that hangs loosely, like that of a spaniel or bloodhound.

bang'ling, *n.* Trivial disputation; wrangling.

ban'iăn, ban'yăn, *n.* [Hind. *banya*, from Sans. *vanij*, a merchant; the banian-tree was originally called the merchants' tree.]

1. An Indian tree of the fig genus, the *Ficus Indica*, natural order *Moraceæ*, remarkable for its vast rooting branches. It has ovate leaves, and produces figs about the size of a cherry. The horizontal branches send down shoots which take root when they reach the ground and enlarge into trunks, which in their turn send out branches; the tree in this manner covering a prodigious extent of ground, and enduring for many ages. On the banks of the Nerbudda is a celebrated banian-tree with 350 stems, each equal to a large tree, and 3,000 smaller ones, which has been known to shelter 7,000 men. Some of these trees are 500 yards in circumference and 100 feet in height. A species of birdlime and abundance of gum-lac are obtained from its juice, and the bark is used by the Hindus as a tonic.

Banian-tree (*Ficus Indica*).

2. A Hindu trader or merchant, one of a class or caste wearing a peculiar dress and abstaining from the use of animal meat.

3. An Anglo-Indian name for a kind of loose cotton shirt, and also for a loose house-dress resembling the native costume.

Banian day; in nautical language, the day on which no meat is served out. The term seems to be derived from the Hindu banians, who, believing in metempsychosis, eat no flesh and do not even kill beasts of prey. In the British navy, *banian day* formerly occurred once a week; the term is now applied to days on which ship-fare is meager.

ban'iăn-tree, *n.* The banian, *Ficus Indica*.

ban'ish, *v.t.*; banished, *pt., pp.*; banishing, *ppr.* [ME. *banishen*; OFr. *banir, bannir*; L. *bandire*, to proclaim, banish; *bannum*, a ban.]

1. To condemn to leave one's country, by authority of the sovereign or government, either temporarily or for life.

2. To drive away; to forcibly dismiss; as, to *banish* sorrow.

3. To drive out, as from a familiar place; as, St. Patrick *banished* the snakes from Ireland.

Syn.—Exile, expel.—A man is *banished* when forced to depart; *exiled* when sent from his own into a foreign country; *expelled* when forcibly ejected, usually with disgrace.

ban'ish-ẽr, *n.* One who compels another to quit his country; one who banishes.

ban'ish-ment, *n.* 1. The action of a monarch or a government, compelling a citizen to leave his country.

2. The state of being banished.

3. The act of driving away or dispelling; as, the *banishment* of care.

ban'is-tẽr, *n.* A small upright or pillar supporting a railing; a baluster.

ban'jō, *n.* [Corrupted by negro usage from *bandore*.] A musical instrument usually with five strings, resembling the tambourine as to body and the guitar as to head and neck; it is played with the hand and fingers.

ban'jō, *n.* A metallic frame in which the propeller of a steamship is sometimes hung when not in use; also called *banjo-frame*.

ban'jō-ist, *n.* A player of the banjo.

bank, *n.* [ME. *bank*; Ice. *bakki*, a bank of a river, ridge; Dan. *bakke*, a hill.]

1. A mound or pile of earth raised above the surrounding ground, either as a defense or for any other purpose.

2. Any steep acclivity rising from a river, lake, etc.; the side of a ravine, or the steep side of a hillock.

3. A bench, or a bench of rowers, in a galley; a seat running across a boat; a thwart.

4. The ground bordering a watercourse, whether steep or flat; as, the river overflowed its *banks*.

5. An elevation, or rising ground, in the sea, even though many fathoms below the surface; as, the *banks* of Newfoundland. Flats, shoals, shelves, or shallows are in reality forms of *banks*, but they may rise to the surface of the water or near to it.

6. In law, the bench on which judges sit. [See *Banc*.]

7. In mining: (a) the ground at the top of a shaft; (b) the face of the coal at which a miner is working; (c) a deposit of ore or coal so situated that it can be worked by excavations above the water-level.

8. A table or sloping-shelved rack used by printers; the dump.

9. The track of the moving carriage of a printing-press.

10. In billiards, the cushion; as, along the *bank*.

11. A row of keys in an organ or similar instrument.

12. Any objects placed in order, one above the other, or material in a pile; as, a *bank* of boxes.

13. Any formation similar to a bank; as, a *bank* of clouds.

14. An oyster-bed in a river or the sea.

15. Any hill or acclivity; a grade; as, up the *bank*, for *uphill*. [Local, Eng.]

bank, *n.* [ME. *banke*; Fr. *banque*; It. *banca*, a bench, money-changer's bench. bank.]

1. An institution which trades in money; an establishment for the deposit, custody, and issue of money, as also for making loans and discounts, and facilitating the transmission of remittances from one place to another.

2. A company or association carrying on such a business.

3. The building or office in which the transactions of a banker or banking company are conducted.

4. The funds of a gambling establishment; the visible or ostensible capital of a gambler; as, to break the *bank*; a faro-*bank*.

5. A joint stock or capital. [Obs.]

Bank discount; an amount deducted by a bank from the face value of a note, and equal to the interest for the period from the date of deduction to that of maturity.

Bank of deposit; a bank whose operations are limited to receiving the money of its customers, and circulating it in loans, etc.

Bank of England; the great national bank closely connected with the government of England, custodian of the public funds and manager of the public debt.

Bank of issue; a bank duly authorized by law to issue its own bank-notes, which circulate as currency.

Bank of the United States; one of two institutions that formerly acted as fiscal agents of the United States government.

National bank; in the United States, a bank chartered by federal law and under the supervision of the controller of the currency, which issues circulating notes secured by United States bonds deposited with the government.

Private bank; a bank of discount carrying on practically the same business as a state bank, and sometimes owned and operated by one person, though usually several persons are associated for the purpose.

State bank; a bank which receives, lends, and transmits money and buys, sells, and collects bills of exchange, under the authority of state law and under state supervision.

To break the bank; in gambling, to win all of the amount which has been designated as the limit which the bank is willing to lose in a single day.

bank, *v.t.*; banked, *pt., pp.*; banking, *ppr.* 1. To raise a mound or bank; around; to inclose or fortify with a bank; as, to *bank* a house.

2. To pass by the banks of. [Obs.]

As I have *banked* their towns. —Shak.

3. To heap up or make a pile of; as, to *bank* earth or sand.

4. To bring to the shore, or bank; as, to *bank* logs.

5. In aeronautics, to tilt the aircraft sidewise as is done in rounding a curve.

To bank a fire; to cover up and shut in a fire so that it may burn low, or keep.

bank, *v.t.* and *v.i.* To deposit in a bank.

bank, *v.i.* 1. To engage in banking; to keep a bank.

2. To wager, or to form a bank, as in gambling.

3. In general terms, and colloquially, to feel secure as to the honesty or reliability of a thing, event, or person; as, I will *bank* on him.

bank'a-ble, *a.* Receivable at a bank, as bills or coin; or discountable, as notes.

bank'-bill, *n.* 1. In the United States, the same as *bank-note*.

2. In England, a bill drawn on a bank or a private individual. It is payable at sight, or at a certain specified time after its date, but is no part of the legal currency.

bank'-book, *n.* A book in which the debit and credit items of a depositor's account are entered by the officers of a bank, this book remaining in possession of the depositor as a voucher.

bank'-cred"it, *n.* A specified sum up to which one will be allowed to draw money from a bank upon the deposit of security.

bank'ẽr, *n.* 1. One who keeps a bank or is engaged in the business of banking; one who receives money on deposit and makes loans, negotiates bills of exchange, etc.

2. One who keeps the bank, or handles the money, in a gambling-house or private game of chance; the dealer.

3. The backer of any individual or enterprise; one who furnishes funds.

4. A vessel engaged in the cod-fishery on the banks of Newfoundland.

5. A money-changer. [Obs.]

6. A sculptor's modeling-table, provided with a circular revolving platform.

7. A bench used by masons or bricklayers in cutting or squaring stone or brick; a banket.

8. One who makes banks or mounds.

9. In provincial English, one who digs ditches or drains; a ditcher.

10. A cushion or covering for a seat; an altar-hanging.

bank'ẽr-ess, *n.* A woman banker, or the wife of a banker.

bank'et, *n.* [AS. *benc*, bench, and E. dim. *-et*.] The workbench of a mason or bricklayer, used for trimming and squaring.

bank'-hol'i-day, *n.* A holiday upon which banks are legally closed. [See *Holiday*.]

bank'ing, *n.* The business of a bank or employment of a banker; the business of establishing a common fund for lending money, discounting notes, issuing bills, receiving deposits, collecting the money on notes deposited, negotiating bills of exchange, etc.

bank'ing, *n.* 1. The act of raising a mound or bank, or of inclosing with a bank.

2. A general term applied to cod-fishing on the banks of Newfoundland.

bank'ing, *a.* Relating to a bank or banker; as, *banking* operations.

bank'ing-house, *n.* Any establishment engaged in a banking business.

bank'-man, *n.* In printing, a compositor who attends to the proving of galleys on the bank.

bank'-mär"tin, *n.* Same as *Bank-swallow*.

bank'-nōte, *n.* 1. A note issued by a bank legally empowered to send it forth; commonly called a bank-bill. It promises to pay to the bearer a certain specific sum of money conspicuously printed upon its face. *Bank-notes* or bills are issued by the national banks in this country in denominations from $1 to $1,000. The Bank of England issues *bank-notes* of £5 (about $25) and upward.

2. A promissory note in which a bank is named as the place of payment.

bank'-pōst, *n.* Letter-paper of large size, varying in weight from five and a half to ten pounds per ream.

bank'rupt, *n.* [Fr. *banqueroute*, a bankrupt, from It. *banca rotta*, lit. broken-benched; *banca*, bench, and *rotta*, f. of *rotto*, broken; from the fact that the bench or table which a merchant or banker formerly used was broken on his bankruptcy.]

1. In a popular sense, one who fails in business, or becomes unable to pay his debts; an insolvent individual.

2. In old English law, a trader who defrauded or sought to defraud his creditors by secreting himself or his property. In England, prior to the Bankruptcy Act of 1861, only insolvent traders were termed *bankrupts*, all others unable to pay their debts being styled insolvents; but since the passage of that act, insolvent traders and non-traders alike are called *bankrupts*.

3. In law, a person who has been declared by legal authority unable to pay his debts and adjudged to be discharged from his indebtedness under the provisions of the bankruptcy laws, either on showing that he has no assets to meet his liabilities or on surrender of his property for distribution among his creditors under a decree of court. In the United States, the bankruptcy laws of 1841 and 1867 applied the term *bankrupt* to other insolvents besides those engaged in trade. As the Federal Constitution confers on Congress authority to establish a uniform law concerning bankruptcies, the statutes in the various states relating to this subject are generally called insolvent laws.

4. In a legal sense, any person unable to pay his just debts when they become due and payment of the same is demanded of him.

bank'rupt, *a.* 1. In the condition of having been legally declared insolvent; as, a *bankrupt* firm.

2. Out of funds; depleted of means; having no money to meet liabilities; as, a *bankrupt* treasury.

3. Lacking something desirable to possess; as, *bankrupt* in health, in gratitude, etc.

4. Pertaining to bankruptcy.

5. Hopelessly discredited, as in resources or character.

Bankrupt law, bankruptcy law; a law formed with the view of protecting a person who cannot pay his debts from unduly harsh proceedings by his creditors, and those creditors from any fraudulent conduct on the part of their debtor. Bankrupt laws have the double object of enforcing a complete discovery and equitable distribution of the property and effects of an insolvent, and of conferring on the bankrupt the advantage of security of person, and a relief from all future annoyance, harassment, or claims on the part of his creditors.

bank'rupt, *v.t.*; bankrupted, *pt.*, *pp.*; bankrupting, *ppr.* To break (one) in trade or commerce; to make insolvent; to exhaust the resources of; to impoverish.

bank'rupt-cy, *n.*; *pl.* **bank'rupt-cies**. 1. The state of being bankrupt or insolvent; inability to pay just or legal debts.

2. The act of becoming a bankrupt; the act of rendering oneself a bankrupt; failure in trade or commerce.

3. In law, the condition of being judicially declared bankrupt.

4. The legal act or process of applying for relief from debts under the bankruptcy law; as, to go into *bankruptcy*.

5. Serious or complete loss, as of faith, belief, reputation, etc.

bank'-shot, *n.* In billiards, a shot which rebounds from the cushion or bank.

Bank'si-à, *n.* [From Sir Joseph *Banks*, a distinguished naturalist, and companion of Captain Cook.] A genus of apetalous evergreen shrubs, natives of Australia and Tasmania. Many of the species are cultivated in conservatories, where they are much esteemed for their handsome foliage and singular heads of flowers, a single head often containing six hundred flowers.

bank'side, *n.* The side of a bank; applied to a brook or river.

bank'-stock, *n.* A share or shares in the capital-stock of a bank.

bank'-swäl"lōw, *n.* A name for the sand-martin, *Clivicola riparia*, which makes its nest by burrowing in banks; also called *bank-martin*.

ban'li-eue (ban'li-ū), *n.* [Fr., from *ban*, a command, and *lieue*, league.] The territory without the walls, but within the legal limits, of a town or city.

ban'nẽr, *n.* [ME. *baner*; Fr. *bannière*; from LL. *banderia*, a banner; from O.H.G. *bant*, a band, a strip of cloth.]

1. A flag; a military ensign or standard; an official emblem; as, the star-spangled *banner*; an army with *banners*.

2. A streamer, formerly borne at the end of a lance or spear, as the standard of a military chief, to mark a rallying-point.

3. In botany, the upper petal of a papilionaceous corol; the vexillum.

4. Any moral or religious ensign; as, the *banner* of the Cross.

5. One of the eight divisions of the Chinese imperial or Manchu army, each having its distinctive flag, the army being known as the eight banners and its soldiers as bannermen. Four of the flags are of solid colors, red, white, yellow, and blue, the others having variegated borders.

6. A large square or piece of heavy silk or other material inscribed with the emblem, name, etc., of a society, union, or other organization, borne at the end of a staff or staves, often attached to a crosspiece, and displayed in parades, processions, or public assemblies.

7. A form of sign or advertisement for outdoor display, usually consisting of a large square or rectangular piece of cloth, netting, etc., duly inscribed and suspended in public view, as across a street, in front of a building, or along the sides of a railroad car or other vehicle.

8. In heraldry, a little flag or banneret of various forms, used as the emblem of a knight.

To carry the banner; to have no place to sleep, or no place of abode; as, he *carried the banner* all night. [Slang.]

ban'nẽr-cry, *n.* A rallying-cry; as, the *banner-cry* of freedom.

ban'nẽred, *a.* Equipped with or carrying banners; as, a *bannered* host.

ban'nẽr-et, *n.* [OE. *baneret*; Fr. *banneret*.]

1. A small banner; called also a *banderole*.

2. Formerly, an independent knight or feudal lord; a knight *banneret*; one of a middle grade of knights between barons and simple knights, in the middle ages, having his own battle-flag.

3. A title or dignity earned by heroic deeds upon the battlefield; hence, an order of knighthood; also, the person elevated to this order. The dignity of knight *banneret* was conferred in the field by removing the points of the pennant on the lance or spear of the person knighted, thus changing the emblem to the square form of a *banneret* or little banner.

4. Formerly, a magisterial officer of the second rank in some Swiss cantons; also, a civil officer in certain Italian republics.

ban'nẽr-fish, *n.* A large salt-water fish of the swordfish family, having a large, erect dorsal fin like a banner; also called *sailfish* and *spikefish*.

ban'nẽr-man, *n.*; *pl.* **ban'nẽr-men**. 1. A standard-bearer. [Obs.]

2. One who is a member of a banner in the Chinese army; a Manchu. [See *Banner*, 5.]

ban'nẽr-ōl, *n.* Same as *Banderole*.

ban'nẽr-plant, *n.* A plant of the genus *Anthurium*, having bright scarlet spathes or modified leaves of banner-like appearance.

ban'nẽr-stōne, *n.* In archæology, a stone ornament resembling a two-edged ax with an eye for a handle or staff, supposed to have been a symbol of authority among aboriginal tribes in North America, many having been found in various parts of the United States.

ban-ni'tion (-nish'un), *n.* The act of expulsion. [Obs.]

ban'nŏck, *n.* [ME. *bannok*; from AS. *bannuc*; from Gael. *bannach*, a cake.] A cake made of coarse meal, usually oatmeal, pease-meal, or barley-meal, common in Scotland and northern England. It is baked on an iron or stone griddle.

ban'nŏck-flūke, *n.* The turbot. [Scot.]

banns, *n.pl.* [ME. *bannen*, from AS. *bannan*, to summon.] Proclamation or notice of a proposed marriage, especially in a church by a priest or minister, such notice being given that anyone may object who is aware that there is just impediment to the union of the parties concerned. [See *Ban*, n.]

The publication of *banns* is not essential to a valid civil marriage in the United States, England, or Scotland, though it occurs, as a matter of form, in several churches, as the Anglican or Protestant Episcopal. In the Roman Catholic church it is regarded as highly reprehensible to omit such public notice of a marriage, though the omission does not invalidate a marriage ceremony. *Banns* are proclaimed three times, usually on three successive Sundays or festival days, and, in the Latin church, during the celebration of the mass.

To forbid the banns; to make public or formal objection to a proposed marriage, an opportunity for such objection being offered during the proclamation of the banns.

ban'quet, *n.* [Fr. *banquet*, a feast, from dim. of *banc*, a table.]

1. A feast; a sumptuous entertainment; literally, of food and drink; figuratively, of anything delightful.

2. A formal or ceremonious feast in honor of some particular person or occasion, and usually followed by speeches, music, etc.; as, a *banquet* in honor of the president; the St. Patrick's day *banquet*.

3. Dessert; sweets to be eaten after meat. [Obs.]

Syn.—Feast, festivity, treat, entertainment, festival, carousal, carouse, regalement, cheer.

ban'quet, *v.t.* and *v.i.*; banqueted, *pt.*, *pp.*; banqueting, *ppr.* I. *v.t.* To treat with a feast, or sumptuous entertainment.

II. *v.i.* To feast; to regale oneself with good eating and drinking; to attend a banquet.

ban'quet-ẽr, *n.* 1. A feaster; one who banquets.

2. One who gives banquets or sumptuous entertainments.

ban'quet-hall, *n.* A hall, either public or private, provided for the giving of banquets.

ban-quette' (-ket'), *n.* [Fr., dim. of *banc*, a bench.]

1. In fortification, an elevated earthen footbank, running along the inside of a parapet, on which soldiers stand to fire upon the enemy; also, an outer earthwork.

2. A bench-seat for passengers on the top of public vehicles, as of stagecoaches and diligences.

3. The footway of a bridge, when raised above the carriageway; a sidewalk; used in this sense in southern United States.

4. In architecture, a small window-seat; a narrow shelf.

ban'shee, ben'shïe, *n.* [Gael. *ban-sìth*; Ir. *beansidhe*; from *ban*, woman, and *sìth*, fairy; lit. woman of the fairies.] In Gaelic folklore, a supernatural being, commonly supposed by the superstitious among the Irish and Scotch peasantry to take the shape of an old woman and to foretell death by mournful singing or wailing outside a dwelling. The *banshee* superstition is peculiarly Celtic. Written also *banshie* and *benshi*.

ban'stic-kle, *n.* [ME. *banstickle*, lit. prickle bone, from AS. *bān*, bone, and *sticels*, prickle.] The three-spined stickleback, a small fish of the genus *Gasterosteus*. [Prov. Eng.]

ban'tam, *n.* 1. One of numerous breeds of the common domestic fowl characterized by diminutive size, the varieties including the Japanese, African, game, Pekin, Polish, and Sebright *bantams*. Probably named from Bantam, Java.

2. A person of small size or weight; especially, a boxer of very light weight; a *bantam-weight*.

3. A small person who struts like a *bantam*, or puts on consequential airs.

ban'tam-weight (-wāt), *n.* A boxer capable of entering the ring weighing not more than 105 pounds; the lightest class of boxers recognized by athletic associations.

ban'tăm-wŏrk, *n.* A gaudy carved and painted work, produced in the East Indies in imitation of Japan-work.

ban'teng, *n.* A species of small wild ox, *Bos banteng* or *Banteng sondaicus*, native to the Malayan archipelago.

ban'tēr, *v.t.*; bantered (-tērd), *pt., pp.*; bantering, *ppr.* [Prob. corrupted from Fr. *badiner*, to joke.]

1. To play upon with words and in good humor; to rally; to joke or jest with; to chaff; to tease.

2. To ridicule; to joke or jest about. [Rare.]

3. To trick; to impose upon; to befool.

4. To provoke to a trial or contest; to challenge. [Colloq. Southern and Western U. S.]

Syn.—Deride, jest, ridicule, rally, mock, chaff, make a butt of, make game of.

ban'tēr, *n.* 1. A joking or jesting; good-humored raillery; pleasantry.

2. A challenge to a match or contest. [Colloq. Southern and Western U. S.]

Syn.—Badinage, chaff, mockery, derision, ridicule, irony, jeering, raillery.

ban'tēr-ēr, *n.* One who banters or jests; one who teases.

ban'tēr-ing, *n.* The act of joking, teasing, or jesting.

ban'tēr-ing-ly, *adv.* In a bantering manner.

ban'ting-ism, *n.* The banting cure or banting system; a course of diet for reducing corpulence, adopted and recommended in 1864 by William *Banting*, of London. The method recommended was the use of lean meat principally, and abstinence from liquids and fat-producing foods, especially those containing a large percentage of farinaceous, saccharine, or oily matter.

bant'ling, *n.* [Corruption from *bandling*, one wrapped in swaddling-clothes; from *band*; or from G. *bäntling*, a bastard.]

1. A young child; an infant.

2. A foundling; a bastard. [Obs.]

3. Figuratively, an immature product, as of an author or artist; used in a contemptuous or depreciatory sense.

Ban'tū, *n., sing.* and *pl.* [Native name, meaning, literally, people.]

1. A name sometimes applied to an extensive South African family of languages, excluding only the Hottentot and Bushman dialects. One peculiarity of this family, especially of the Kaffir branch, is the use of clucks or clicks in speaking. It is essentially different from the pure negro tongues.

2. One of the *Bantu* race; or, collectively, the *Bantu* people.

Ban'tū, *a.* Pertaining to the Bantu.

banx'ring, *n.* The native name of a small insectivorous mammal resembling the squirrel, found in the East Indies; *Tupaia javanica.*

ban'yăn, *n.* See *Banian.*

ban-zai', *interj.* [Jap., lit., ten thousand years.] A Japanese shout of honor or joy; hurrah.

bā'ō-bab, *n.* The African name of the *Adansonia digitata.* The trunk is sometimes thirty feet in diameter, but not more than seventy

Baobab without foliage, but showing the fruit.

feet high. It bears white flowers and has been naturalized in India. A Madagascar variety of *baobab* bears red flowers.

Baph'ō-met, *n.* [Fr., derived from Mahomet, or Mohammed.] An idol or spiritual symbol which the medieval Knights Templars were supposed to use in their secret ceremonies.

Bap-ti'si-ȧ (-tizh'-ȧ), *n.* [Gr. *baptein*, to dye.] A genus of leguminous plants, ornamental as border-flowers; some of the species which are found mainly in the eastern parts of North America, are used in dyeing; called also *wild indigo.*

bap'tism, *n.* [OFr. *baptesme*, from LL. *baptisma*, from Gr. *baptismos*, that which is dipped; from *baptizein*, to dip.]

1. The application of water to a person, as a sacrament or religious ceremony, by which he is initiated into the visible church of Christ. This is usually performed by sprinkling, pouring, or immersion, the manner of performing the act varying with the tenets of various churches.

2. A religious ceremony consisting of an ablution symbolizing purification or dedication, as in the case of the christening of bells.

3. A christening; as, the child's *baptism* occurs next Sunday.

Baptism of blood; (a) in Christian church history, martyrdom before baptism, regarded as an effective substitute for the baptismal rite; (b) the first actual experience of the horrors of war, as by a regiment of soldiers, a state, nation, or people, as, the Rough Riders received their *baptism of blood* at Las Guasimas.

Baptism of fire; (a) in theology, the baptism of the Spirit, as distinguished from the rite of baptism; variously interpreted among theologians; (b) in early church history, martyrdom; (c) the first experience of a soldier or regiment, etc., under fire.

bap-tis'măl, *a.* Relating to baptism; taken or used at baptism; as, a *baptismal* vow.

Baptismal name; the Christian name bestowed at baptism; as, his *baptismal name* is Henry.

bap-tis'măl-ly, *adv.* By means of baptism; in a baptismal manner.

Bap'tist, *n.* 1. One who holds that baptism ought to be administered only to believers upon formal profession of faith in Christ and that the ceremony should be performed by immersion alone.

2. A member of one of the branches of the Baptist church or denomination.

3. One who administers baptism; specifically, John the *Baptist.* [Obs.]

Freewill Baptist; one of a sect of Baptists who are Arminians and believe in open communion.

German Baptist; see *Dunkard.*

Hard-shell Baptist; same as *Primitive Baptist.*

Primitive Baptist; one of a sect of Baptists who are rigid Calvinists, opposed to foreign missionary work and to special education for their ministers; popularly styled *Hard-shell Baptist.*

Seventh-day Baptist; one of a sect of Baptists who observe Saturday as the Sabbath.

Bap'tist, *a.* Of or pertaining to the religious denominations that believe in the baptism by immersion of confessed believers; as, a *Baptist* church; a *Baptist* preacher.

bap'tis-tēr-y, bap'tis-try, *n.*; *pl.* **bap'tis-tēr-ies** (-iz), or **-tries** (-triz). [L. *baptisterium*, a place for bathing, from Gr. *baptizein*, to dip.]

1. A place where the rite of baptism is administered.

2. A building or a portion of a building in which is administered the rite of baptism. In the early Christian church the *baptistery* was distinct from the basilica or church, but was situated near its west end, and was generally circular or octagonal in form, and dome-roofed. About the end of the sixth century the *baptistery* began to be absorbed into the church, the font being placed within and not far from the western door. As a separate building it was often of considerable size and highly decorated, that of Florence being 108 feet in diameter externally and its wall-spaces and dome richly ornamented.

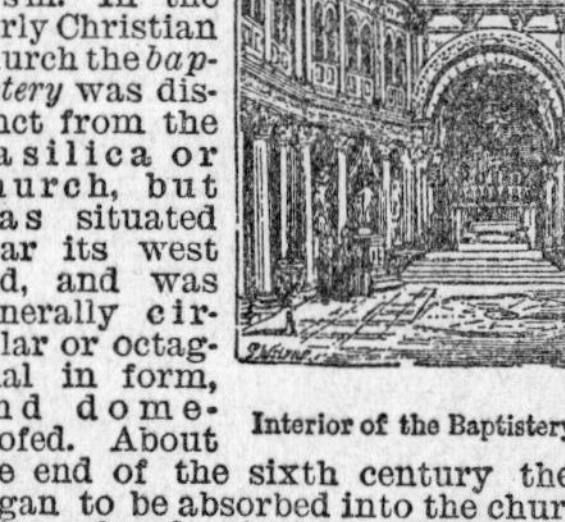

Interior of the Baptistery at Florence.

3. Part of a church furnished with a font and used only for baptisms.

4. In Baptist churches, the reservoir used for baptism by immersion, usually concealed beneath removable flooring of the pulpit or auditorium.

bap-tis'tic, *a.* [Gr. *baptistikos.*] Relating to baptism or the doctrines of the Baptist church.

bap-tis'tic-ăl, *a.* Baptistic. [Rare.]

bap-tis'tic-ăl-ly, *adv.* In a baptistic manner.

bap'tis-try, *n.* See *Baptistery.*

bap-tiz'ȧ-ble, *a.* Capable of being, or fit to be baptized. [Rare.]

bap-ti-zā'tion, *n.* The act of baptizing; the state of being baptized. [Obs.]

bap-tize', *v.t.*; baptized (-tizd), *pt., pp.*; baptizing, *ppr.* [Gr. *baptizein*, to dip under water.]

1. To administer the sacrament of baptism to.

2. To christen; to name; to give a name to; as, to *baptize* a child Thomas.

3. To consecrate to special purposes; as, to *baptize* a ship.

4. To receive into a new state; to sanctify; as, *baptized* with the Spirit.

bap-tize', *v.i.* To observe or to administer the sacrament of baptism; as, an elder is authorized to *baptize* and marry.

bap-tized', *a.* Having received baptism; christened.

bap-tize'ment, *n.* Baptism; the act of baptizing. [Rare.]

bap-tiz'ēr, *n.* One who christens, or administers baptism.

bȧ-quet' (-kā'), *n.* [Fr.] A small tub.

bär, *n.* [ME. *barr, barre*, from OFr. *barre*, from LL. *barra*, a bar.]

1. A piece of wood, iron, or other solid substance, long in proportion to its diameter, used for various purposes, but especially for a hindrance or obstruction; as, the *bars* of a fence; the *bar* of a door.

2. [*pl.*] In athletics, various forms of gymnastic apparatus in the shape of *bars*; as, *parallel bars* and *horizontal bars.*

3. Any obstacle which obstructs, hinders, or defends; an obstruction; a fortification.

> Must I new *bars* to my own joy create?
> —Dryden.

4. A bar-like piece or quantity of a substance, of indefinite size or weight; as, a *bar* of chocolate.

5. The railing that incloses the place which counsel occupy in courts of justice. Hence the phrase *at the bar of the court* signifies in open court. Hence, also, licensed lawyers are called *bar*risters; and the legal profession is called the *bar.*

6. Figuratively, any tribunal; as, the *bar* of public opinion; the *bar* of God, or the final judgment.

7. The room in a hotel, saloon, etc., where liquors, etc., are served to customers; also, the counter over which the articles are served.

8. A bank of sand, gravel, or earth, forming a shoal at the mouth of a river or harbor, obstructing entrance, or rendering it difficult; as, crossing the *bar.*

9. A rock or other obstruction in the sea.

10. Anything laid across another, as *bars* in heraldry, stripes in color, and the like.

Bar.

11. [*pl.*] The part of the jaw of a horse between the tusks and grinders, which bears no teeth, and to which the bit is applied.

12. In music, a line drawn perpendicularly across the lines of the staff and dividing it into spaces called measures. A *double bar* is placed at the end of a strain.

Bar. Bar. D'ble-bar.

Weak accent. Strong accent. Weak accent. Strong accent.

13. In law, a peremptory exception sufficient to destroy the plaintiff's action; a plea in *bar*; an *ordinary bar* constitutes a sufficient answer and destroys the plaintiff's declaration.
—Blackstone.

14. An ingot, lump, or wedge of gold or silver from the mines, run in a mold, and unwrought. A *bar* of iron is wrought and hammered from a pig or block.

15. In architecture, a strip of wood dividing and supporting the glass of a window; as, a sash-*bar.*

16. A barrier across a city gateway; as, old *Temple Bar* in London.

17. A place in the United States Senate, the House of Representatives, the state legislatures, and deliberative bodies, usually near the speaker or presiding officer, where persons, not members, stand when they are permitted to address those assemblies, or are called before them for any reason. In both houses of the British parliament an inclosed space near the main entrance which bars the way to all but members and officials. In the House of Commons, the *bar* is an actual obstruction, in the form of a sliding rod, drawn out to hinder further progress when any person is summoned to the *bar* of the House.

Bar sinister; in heraldry, a mark of illegitimacy. [See *Baton.*]

Case at bar; the case before the court; the case in course of hearing.

Flinders bar; an iron bar placed near a mariner's compass to reduce any deviation caused by local influence.

Trial at bar; in English law, a trial before the full bench of a superior court.

bär, *n.* [Fr.] The maigre; a European fish whose flesh is white and bloodless.

bär, *v.t.*; barred (bärd), *pt., pp.*; barring, *ppr.* [ME. *barren*, from OFr. *barrer*, to fasten with a bar.]

1. To fasten with a bar; as, to *bar* a door or gate.

2. To hinder; to obstruct; to prevent; as, to *bar* the entrance of evil.

3. To prevent; to exclude; to hinder; to

make impracticable; as, the distance between us *bars* our intercourse.

4. To prohibit; to restrain or exclude by express or implied prohibition; as, the statute *bars* my right; the law *bars* the carrying of concealed weapons.

5. To obstruct, prevent, or hinder by any intervening obstacle; as, the right is *barred* by time; a release *bars* the plaintiff's recovery.

6. To except; to exclude by exception; as, I *bar* none.

7. To cross with stripes of a different color.

8. In mechanics, to operate by using a bar as a lever.

To bar a vein; in veterinary surgery, to operate upon a horse by disengaging a vein, tying it above and below, and then striking between the two ligatures; usually undertaken as a means of scattering malignant humors.

bar′ad, *n.* [Gr. *barys*, weighty, and Eng. *farad*.] An electrical unit of pressure; the pressure of one dyne per square centimeter.

băr-æs-thē-si-om′e-tēr, *n.* See *Baresthesiometer.*

bar-ȧ-lip′ton, *n.* [Composed of symbolical letters, especially the vowels. *A* is equivalent to a universal affirmative, *I* is equivalent to a particular affirmative, and *ton* is a termination given for euphony.] In logic, the first indirect mood of the first figure of syllogisms. A syllogism in *baralipton* is one in which the first two propositions are universal affirmatives, and the third a particular affirmative; the middle term being the subject of the first and the attribute of the second. One example generally given of the *baralipton* is the following:

BA. Every evil ought to be feared.
RA. Every violent passion is an evil.
LIP. Therefore something that ought to be feared is a violent passion.

The *baralipton* is an imperfect kind of syllogism.

bar-ȧ-mun′dȧ, *n.* Same as *Barramunda.*

bar′ȧ-thrum, *n.*; *pl.* **bar′ȧ-thrȧ.** [Gr. *barathron*, a gulf.]

1. A pit; an abyss.

2. A rocky pit outside the walls of Athens, into which criminals, dead or alive, were cast.

3. The fathomless pit; hades.

4. In figurative use, a relentless devourer; a glutton; an extortioner.

bärb, bärbe, *n.* [OFr. *barbe*; L. *barba*, beard.]

1. Beard, or that which resembles it, or grows in place of it; as, the *barb* of a fish.

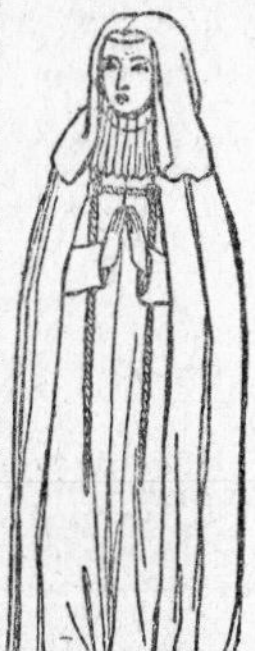

2. A sharp point turning backward, as in a fishhook or arrow, making withdrawal difficult.

3. In botany, a bristle or hair that has a double hook at its end.

4. A lateral branch of the shaft of a feather, one of the processes of the vane.

5. [*pl.*] Projections of the mucous membrane under the tongues of horses and cattle, usually pathological; called also *paps*. In this sense, written also *barbels* and *barbles*.

6. A roughness or imperfection occurring in the process of metal-working; a bur.

7. In heraldry, one of the five green leaves that appear around the outer edge of a full-blown rose and extend beyond the petals.

Nun wearing a Barb.

8. A scarf or muffler worn by women, particularly nuns or women in mourning. [Obs.]

9. A kind of bit for a horse. [Obs.]

bärb, *v.t.*; barbed, *pt.*, *pp.*; barbing, *ppr.* 1. To shave; to dress, as the head. [Obs.]

2. To furnish with barbs, as an arrow, fishhook, spear, or other implement.

3. To put armor on, as a horse.

bärb, *n.* [Fr. *barbe*, a Barbary horse, from *Barbarie*; Ar. *Barbar*, the Berbers.]

1. A horse of Barbary, *barb* being a contraction of Barbary.

2. A common name of the Barbary pigeon, a bird of a black or dun color.

3. A kingfish of the eastern coasts of the United States.

bärb, *n.* Armor for a horse; same as *Bard.*

bär′bȧ-ça̤n, *n.* See *Barbican.*

bär′bȧ-ça̤n-āġe, *n.* See *Barbicanage.*

bär′bȧ-çūe, *n.* and *v.t.* See *Barbecue.*

Bär-bā′di-ăn, *a.* and *n.* [Port. *barbadas*, the bearded, from L. *barbatus*, bearded.]

I. *a.* Relating to Barbados.

II. *n.* An inhabitant of Barbados.

Bär-bā′dōṣ, Bär-bā′dōeṣ, *n.* A West Indian island of the Lesser Antilles. Its name is applied to such fruits as the *Barbados cherry* and the *Barbados gooseberry*. The oily seeds of the *Barbados nut* are especially purgative.

Bär-bā′dōṣ-prīde, *n.* 1. A name given to a low, spiny shrub, *Poinciana pulcherrima*, with an odor like savin. In Barbados it is used for fences, and hence is called *flower-fence.*

2. An East Indian tree, bearing yellow blossoms and now cultivated for ornamental purposes in the West Indies.

bär′bȧ-rȧ, *n.* A mnemonic word in logic, being the first word in the mnemonic verses intended to represent the various forms of syllogism. It indicates a syllogism, the three propositions of which are universal affirmatives.

Bär-bȧ-resque′ (-resk′), *a.* 1. Relating to Barbary.

2. [b—] Characteristic of barbarians.

bär-bā′ri-ăn, *n.* [L. *barbarus*; Gr. *barbaros*, foreign; so called by the Greeks because the talk of a foreigner sounded like *bar-bar*.]

1. A man in his rude state; an uncivilized person; strictly defined, one in the intermediate condition between savagery and civilization.

2. A cruel, savage, brutal man; one destitute of pity or humanity.

3. A foreigner. The Greeks and Romans denominated most foreign nations *barbarians*, but employed the word in a less reproachful sense than is conveyed by modern usage.

bär-bā′ri-ăn, *a.* 1. Relating to an uncivilized state of society.

2. Cruel; inhuman.

bär-bar′iç, *a.* [L. *barbaricus*, from Gr. *barbarikos*, barbaric, foreign.]

1. Foreign; imported from foreign nations.

2. Exhibiting the characteristics of a barbarian, as in taste and dress; unrefined; barbarous.

bär′bȧ-riṣm, *n.* 1. Any offense against purity of style or language; any form of speech contrary to the pure idioms of a particular language.

2. Ignorance of arts; want of learning.

3. Rudeness of manners; barbarity; a savage state of society.

bär-bar′i-ty, *n.* 1. The manners of a barbarian; savageness; cruelty; ferocity; inhumanity.

2. An act of cruelty.

3. Barbarism; impurity of speech. [Rare.]

bär′bȧ-rize, *v.t.*; barbarized, *pt.*, *pp.*; barbarizing, *ppr.* To make barbarous.

bär′bȧ-rize, *v.i.* 1. To fall into a barbarous state.

2. To employ unrefined modes of expression.

bär′bȧ-rized, *a.* Made barbarous.

bär′bȧ-riz-ing, *a.* Making barbarous.

bär′bȧ-rous, *a.* 1. Uncivilized; savage; ignorant; inhabited by barbarians.

2. Cruel; ferocious; inhuman; as, *barbarous* usage.

bär′bȧ-rous-ly, *adv.* 1. In the manner of a barbarian; ignorantly; contrary to the rules of speech.

2. In a savage, cruel, ferocious, or inhuman manner.

bär′bȧ-rous-ness, *n.* 1. Rudeness or incivility of manners.

2. Impurity of language.

3. Cruelty; inhumanity; barbarity.

Bär′bȧ-ry, *n.* 1. The countries, exclusive of Egypt, lying along the Mediterranean coast of Africa.

2. [b—] A Barbary horse; a barb.

Barbary ape; a tailless ape, intelligent and easily trained, found in northern Africa and Gibraltar, and the only monkey living in a natural state in Europe.

bär′bȧ-stel, *n.* [Fr. *barbastelle*; L. *barba*, beard.] A species of bat with hairy or bearded cheeks.

bär′bāte, bär′bā-ted, *a.* [L. *barbatus*, bearded, from *barba*, beard.] In botany, bearded; having long, weak hairs. In zoölogy, fringed with hair; having hair or feathers.

bär′bē-çūe, bär′bȧ-çūe, *n.* [Sp. *barbacoa*, from Haitian *barbacoa*, a framework of sticks.]

1. A framework of wood to hold fish or meat over a fire to be smoked or dried.

2. A framework of iron for supporting large pieces of meat or entire animals over a fire to be roasted.

3. The entire animal—usually an ox or a hog—that is roasted.

4. A popular social gathering, usually in the open air, at which the roasting of and feasting upon whole animals are features; also, a political gathering similarly conducted.

5. A smooth floor, or other space, exposed to the sun for the drying of coffee-beans.

bär′bē-çūe, bär′bȧ-çūe, *v.t.*; barbecued (-kūd), *pt.*, *pp.*; barbecuing, *ppr.* 1. To cure by drying or smoking on a framework.

2. To roast whole, as an animal, after it has been properly prepared.

bärbed, *a.* 1. Bearded; jagged with hooks or points.

2. In heraldry, (a) having barbs or green leaves; as, a rose *barbed*; (b) having wattles, as a cock; (c) having ends with arrowhead barbs.

3. Furnished with armor; applied to a horse; as, a *barbed* steed.

4. Shaved or trimmed. [Obs.]

Barbed shot; a shot to be fired from a mortar to a wreck, carrying a life-line and provided with barbs to hold it wherever it strikes.

Barbed wire; wire for fences, having twisted into the strands at regular intervals sharp barbs or points of metal.

bär-bei′rō (-bā′rō), *n.* [Port., meaning barber.] Same as *Barbero.*

bär′bel, *n.* [Fr. *barbeau*, from OFr. *barbel*, a barbel-fish, from L. *barba*, beard.]

1. A fish of the genus *Barbus*, especially the *Barbus vulgaris*, having four beard-like appendages on the upper jaw.

2. A slender appendage on the mouths or nostrils of certain fishes.

3. An inflamed swelling in the mouths of cattle and horses, usually under the tongue. Also written *barble* and *barb.*

bär′bel-lāte, *a.* Having bristles or short stiff barbed hairs, as some kinds of plants.

bär-bel′lū-lāte, *a.* Having barbules or very small barbs or hairs.

bär′bēr, *n.* [ME. *barbour*, *barbor*, from OFr. *barbeor*, from L. *barba*, a beard.] A person whose occupation is that of shaving, trimming, or dressing the hair. Formerly, a *barber's* practice included primitive surgery. In this sense formerly called *barber-chirurgeon* or *barber-surgeon.*

Barber's basin; a rimmed basin for lather, formerly fitted to the neck and used while shaving.

Barber's itch; an eruption upon the scalp or face, medically known as *sycosis.*

Barber's pole; a sign used by barbers, striped spirally with alternate colors, usually red, white, and blue or black, denoting the barber's old-time practice of surgery, by symbolizing a ribbon bandage for a bleeding arm.

bär′bēr, *v.t.*; barbered, *pt.*, *pp.*; barbering, *ppr.* To shave the beard of, or dress the hair of.

bär′bēred (-bērd), *a.* Having had the head and face dressed by a barber.

bär′bēr-ess, *n.* A female barber.

bär′bēr-fish, *n.* A berycoid, spiny-finned fish found in the Mediterranean; the surgeon-fish, equipped with spines near the tail that pierce like a lance.

bär′bēr-mŏn″gēr, *n.* A man who frequents the barber's shop, or prides himself on being dressed by a barber; a fop. [Obs.]

bär′ber-ry, bēr′ber-ry, *n.* [ME. *barbere*, from OFr. *berbere*; LL. *berberis*, the barberry.] A plant of the genus *Berberis*; specifically, *Berberis vulgaris*, a shrubby plant with yellow flowers that have a rank odor; native in Europe and naturalized in the United States; it bears acidulous red berries, and furnishes bark for the manufacture of yellow dyes.

bär′ber-y, *n.* 1. A barber's shop. [Obs.]

2. Formerly, the process and practice of shaving and surgery combined. [Rare.]

bär′bet, bär′bett, *n.* [Fr., from L. *barba*, a beard.]

1. A small beard. [Obs.]

2. A part of a helmet used about the sixteenth century. [Obs.]

bär′bet, *n.* [Fr., from L. *barbatus*, bearded.]

1. A dog, so called from its long curly hair; a poodle.

2. A species of larva that feeds on aphides.

African Barbet (*Pogonias hirsutus*).

3. In ornithology, a bird resembling the cuckoo, the type of the family *Bucconidæ*, and found in both hemispheres. Their conical beaks are bearded with stiff bristles, hence the name.

bär-bette′ (-bet′), *n.* [Fr., from L. *barbatus*, bearded.] A platform or elevation of earth from which cannon may be fired over a parapet.

Barbette battery; a battery placed on a barbette.

Barbette carriage; a carriage to raise a gun for firing over a parapet.

Barbette gun; a gun placed on a barbette.

Barbette ship; a vessel on which the guns are mounted to fire over the bulwarks.

Barbette turret; a revolving, armored turret on a barbette.

En or *in barbette*; mounted on a barbette; applied to guns.

bärb′-feath″ērṣ (-feth-), *n.pl.* [*Barb*, from L. *barba*, beard.] The feathers under the beak of a hawk.

bär′bi-ça̤n, bär′bȧ-ça̤n, *n.* [ME. *barbican*, from OFr. *barbicane*, a barbican; a word of Arabic or

Portuguese origin, introduced into Europe by the crusaders; perhaps from Ar. *babh-khānah*, a gate-house, or house on a wall.]

1. A fortification or outer defense to a city or castle, consisting of an elevation of earth about three feet high, along the foot of the rampart.

Barbican, Walmgate Bar, York.

2. A fort at the end of a bridge, or at the outlet of a city; any advanced work or outwork.

3. An opening in a fortress-wall through which guns were fired upon an enemy.

bär′bi-căn, *n.* [L. *barba*, beard.] A climbing barbet of Africa, genus *Pogonias*.

bär′bi-căn-āge, bär′bȧ-căn-āge, *n.* Money expended to maintain a barbican. [Obs.]

bär′bi-cel, *n.* [L. *barba*, beard.] One of the minute processes on the barbule of a feather.

bär′biērs, *n.* [Cingalese *beri*, weakness.] A paralytic disease common in India, closely resembling, and considered by some identical with, *beriberi*.

bär-big′ēr-ous, *a.* [L. *barba*, beard, and *gerere*, to carry.] Having hair, as a petal; bearded, as a man.

bär′bi-ŏn, *n.* [L. *barba*, beard.] A barbet found in Africa, genus *Barbatula*.

bär′bi-ton, bär′bi-tos, *n.*; *pl.* **bär′bi-tȧ.** [Gr. *barbiton*, a lyre.] A musical instrument of ancient Greece resembling a lyre.

bär′ble, *n.* See *Barbel*.

bär′bō-tine, *n.* [Fr. *barbotine*, wormwood, from *barboter*, to dabble.]

1. A thin potter's clay used for relief decoration.

2. One of the various species of wormseed.

3. A substance produced in the East Indies, consisting largely of wax, gum, and bitter ingredients.

bär′bre (-bēr), *a.* Barbarous. [Obs.]

bär′bū, bär-bū′dō, *n.* Same as second *Barbet*, 3.

Bär′bū-lȧ, *n.* [L.] 1. A large genus of the true mosses.

2. A genus of bivalve mollusks.

bär′būle, *n.* [L. *barbula*, a little beard.]

1. A very small barb or beard.

2. One of the finely divided, hair-like processes that bind together the barbs of a feather.

3. The part of a medieval helmet which covered the cheeks and chin.

Bär′bus, *n.* [L. *barba*, beard.] A large genus of cyprinoid fishes, of which the barbel is a common species; characterized by four soft barbels, or fleshy tentacles, around the nose and mouth.

bärb′=wire, *n.* Barbed wire.

bär′cȧ-rōle, bär′cȧ-rōlle (-rōl), *n.* [It. *barcarolo*, boatman.]

1. An Italian boatman.

2. The typical boat-song of a Venetian gondolier.

Bär′clāy-īte, *n.* A member of a sect of dissenting Scotch Protestants of the eighteenth century; so called from the founder of the sect, John Barclay; a Berean.

bär′cŏn, bär′cō-ne, *n.* [It. *barcone*, a bark.] A Mediterranean freight-boat.

bär′=cut″tēr, *n.* A machine for cutting bars of metal into lengths.

bärd, *n.* [Gael. and Ir. *bard*; of Celtic origin.]

1. A poet.

2. Among the ancient Celts, a poet who sang or recited verses composed in honor of the achievements of warriors and kings, and accompanied such recital with the music of the lyre.

3. Formerly, a minstrel or wandering musician of Scotland.

4. In Wales, a member of a hereditary order of poets holding competitive meetings or festivals.

Horse-armor of Maximilian I. of Germany.

a, Chamfron; *b*, Manefaire; *c*, Poitrel, or breastplate; *d*, Croupiere or buttock-piece.

bärd, bärde, *n.* [Fr. *barde*, horse-armor.]

1. A piece of horse-armor in medieval times. It generally consisted of leather studded with metal points.

2. [*pl.*] The ornamental trappings of a horse in medieval tournaments.

3. [*pl.*] In late medieval times, plate-armor worn by a man.

bärd, *n.* A slice of bacon used to cover game or meat while cooking.

bärd, *v.t.*; barded, *pt., pp.*; barding, *ppr.* 1. To equip (a man or horse) with defensive armor.

2. To harness (a horse) with rich caparison.

bärd, *v.t.* To cover (meat) with slices of bacon for cooking.

Bär-des′ȧ-nist, *n.* One of that branch of Gnostics of the second century who were followers of Bardesanes of Edessa, in Mesopotamia. They held to two original self-existent beings, one good, the other evil; that human souls had no material bodies before the fall; that Christ had only the semblance of a body, and did not die on the cross, nor rise from the dead; and that redemption consists in being divested of our gross, material bodies, and being clothed in ethereal or spiritual bodies.

bärd′iç, *a.* Pertaining to bards, or having the characteristics of bardism.

bärd′ish, *a.* Having the characteristics of a bard or of bardism.

bärd′işm, *n.* The science of bards; the poetry, learning, and maxims of bards.

bärd′ling, *n.* An immature or minor bard.

bärd′ship, *n.* The condition of being a bard; the office or rank of a bard.

bāre, *a.* [ME. *bare*, *bar*; AS. *bær*, without covering.]

1. Naked; without covering, as a body unclothed, an animal when deprived of its natural covering, or the ground when barren; as, a *bare* plain.

2. With the head uncovered, from respect.

3. Without embellishment or refinement; simple; unadorned; as, *bare* facts.

4. Laid open to view; detected; no longer concealed.

5. Poor; destitute; indigent; empty; unfurnished; as, *bare* rooms.

6. Mere; alone; unaccompanied by more than is absolutely necessary; as, *bare* expenses; *bare* majority.

7. Threadbare; much worn.

Under bare poles; in nautical language, having no sail set.

Syn.—Destitute, naked, nude, uncovered, stripped, unadorned, undressed, unclothed.

bāre, *v.t.*; bared, *pt., pp.*; baring, *ppr.* [ME. *baren*, from AS. *barian*, to make bare.] To strip of the covering; to make naked; as, to *bare* the breast.

bāre, *v.*, past tense of *bear*. [Obs.]

bāre′back, *adv.* Without a saddle; as, to ride *bareback*.

bāre′backed, *a.* With the back uncovered; having no saddle.

bāre′bone, *n.* A very lean person. [Rare.]

bāre′bōned, *a.* Lean, so that the bones show their forms.

bāre′fāced, *a.* 1. With the face uncovered; not masked.

2. Undisguised; unreserved; without concealment; hence, shameless; impudent; audacious; as, a *barefaced* falsehood.

bāre′fāced-ly, *adv.* Without disguise or reserve; openly; impudently.

bāre′fāced-ness, *n.* Effrontery; assurance; audaciousness.

bāre′foot, *a.* and *adv.* With the feet bare; as, to dance *barefoot*.

bāre′foot″ed, *a.* Having the feet bare.

bȧ-rēge′ (-räzh′), *n.* [Fr. *barège*, from *Barèges*, a town famous as a watering-place in the Pyrenees.] A gauzy dress-goods woven from worsted and silk or cotton.

bāre′hand″ed, *a.* With hands bare; empty-handed; hence, without means or resources.

bāre′head″ed, *a.* Having the head uncovered, either from respect or other cause.

bāre′head″ed-ness, *n.* The state of being bareheaded.

bāre′legged, *a.* Having the legs bare.

bāre′ly, *adv.* Nakedly; poorly; indigently; without decoration; hardly; scarcely; merely; only; without anything to spare; as, *barely* furnished with the necessities of life.

bāre′necked, *a.* Having the neck uncovered.

bāre′ness, *n.* The state of being bare; nakedness; leanness; poverty; indigence.

bāre′ribbed (-ribd), *a.* Excessively lean.

bāre′särk, *n.* [Ice. *berserkr*, without a shirt; *bera*, bare, and *serkr*, shirt.] A mythological Norse warrior who went into battle without armor; called also a *berserker*.

bāre′särk, *adv.* Without armor.

bar-es-thē-si-om′e-tēr, *n.* [Gr. *baros*, weight, *aisthēsis*, perception, and *metron*, a measure.] A device for determining muscular sensibility.

bar″es-thē″si-ō-met′riç, *a.* Relating to a baresthesiometer.

bar′et, *n.* See *Barret*.

bär′fish, *n.* Same as *Calico bass*.

bär′fụl, *a.* Full of obstructions. [Obs.]

bär′gain (bär′gen), *n.* [ME. *bargain*, *bargayne*; OFr. *bargaine*, a bargain.]

1. An agreement between parties concerning the sale of property; or a contract by which one party binds himself to transfer the right to some property for a consideration, and the other party binds himself to receive the property and pay the consideration.

2. Anything which is bought; specifically, a gainful transaction; as, this was a *bargain*.

3. A mutual agreement between two or more persons; a pledge; a stipulation.

Bargain and sale; in law, a species of conveyance, by which the bargainer contracts to convey the lands to the bargainee, and becomes by such contract a trustee for and seized to the use of the bargainee. The statute then completes the purchase; that is, the bargain vests the use, and the statute vests the possession. —Blackstone.

Into the bargain; in addition to what is stipulated; furthermore.

To strike a bargain; to ratify an agreement, originally by striking or shaking hands.

Syn.—Agreement, contract, stipulation, purchase, pledge, compact.

bär′gain, *v.i.*; bargained, *pt., pp.*; bargaining, *ppr.* [ME. *bargainen*, from OFr. *bargaigner*, to traffic.] To make a contract or conclusive agreement for the transfer of property; often with *for* before the thing purchased; as, to *bargain for* a house.

bär′gain, *v.t.* To sell; to transfer for a consideration.

To bargain away; to part with a thing, usually in the sense of a losing transaction.

bär′gain=coun″tēr, *n.* A counter on which are goods for sale at special or reduced prices.

bär′gain=dāy, *n.* A day on which certain goods are sold by a business house at special or reduced prices.

bär-gain-ee′, *n.* The party to a contract who stands as the recipient of the property.

bär′gain-ēr, *n.* One who makes a bargain.

bär′gain-ēr, bär′gain-ŏr, *n.* In law, the party to a contract who stipulates to sell and convey property to another.

bärge, *n.* [OFr. *barge*; LL. *barca*, a bark; L. *baris*, an Egyptian rowboat; Gr. *baris*, a skiff, raft.]

1. A flat-bottomed vessel of burden, for loading and unloading ships; a lighter; also a carrier of goods or a freight-boat used on inland waters.

2. A pleasure-boat; a medieval vessel or boat of state, handsomely furnished with apartments, canopies, and cushions, gorgeously decorated and equipped with rowers; as, a Venetian *state barge*.

State Barge.

3. A large rowboat used by naval officers of high rank.

4. A vessel with double decks, for passengers or freight, intended to be towed by a steamboat.

5. A large boat-shaped vehicle used as an omnibus. [U. S.]

bärge′bōard, *n.* A term applied to inclined projecting boards placed at the gable of a building, and hiding the horizontal timbers of the roof.

bärge′çoup″le (-kup″l), *n.* One of a pair of projecting rafters placed behind the bargecourse and which support the overhanging roof of a gable.

Bargeboard of 15th century.

bärge′çourse, *n.* In architecture, (a) a part of the tiling which projects beyond the principal rafters, in buildings where there is a gable; (b) a course of bricks, laid on end, capping a gable-wall.

bär-gee′, *n.* One who manages a barge; a bargeman.

bärge′măn, *n.*; *pl.* **bärge′men.** A man who manages a barge, or is one of the crew on a barge.

bärge′mas″tēr, *n.* The proprietor or master of

a barge, especially of one conveying goods for hire.

bär′gẽr, *n.* The manager of a barge.

bär′=gown, *n.* The gown of a lawyer.

bär′guest, bär′ghest (-gest), *n.* [Origin uncertain, possibly G. *berggeist*, mountain demon.] A goblin or spirit, generally in the shape of a dog, supposed to mean death or bad fortune to the person to whom it appeared.

bā′ri-ȧ, *n.* [Gr. *barytēs*, weight, from *barys*, heavy.] Same as *Baryta*.

bar′iç, *a.* Pertaining to barium.

bar′iç, *a.* [Gr. *barys*, weighty.] Relating to weight, particularly to the pressure of the air.

bȧ-ril′lȧ, *n.* [Fr. *barille*, from Sp. *barrilla*, impure soda.]

1. A plant cultivated in Spain for its ashes, from which the best commercial carbonate of soda is obtained. The plant is cut and laid in heaps and burned, the salts running into a hole in the ground, where they form a vitrified lump.

2. The alkali procured from this plant and other varieties of the genus *Salsola*, or saltworts, being, more specifically, an impure carbonate of soda, used in making glass and soap, and in bleaching linen.

bar′il-let, *n.* [Fr., dim. of *baril*.] A little barrel, or cylinder; especially that of a clock or watch, or the funnel of a suction-pump.

bā′rite, *n.* [Gr. *barytēs*, weight.] A native form of barium sulphate of high specific gravity, occurring usually in colorless tabular crystals. It is found, however, in granular and massive forms, and of yellow, red, blue, and brown color. It is known also as *heavy-spar* and *barytes*.

bar′i-tōne, *a.* and *n.* See *Barytone*.

bā′ri-um, *n.* [Gr. *barys*, weighty.] A chemical element occurring mainly as the sulphate, barite, and the carbonate, witherite. It is prepared by electrolysis from the chlorid, being a powder which oxidizes rapidly in the air. Its melting temperature is high, and its atomic weight 137. *Barium* is susceptible of two degrees of oxygenation: the first, or protoxid of barium, is called baryta.

bärk, *n.* [ME. *barke*; AS. *barc*, bark or rind.]

1. The outermost covering of a tree, corresponding to the skin of an animal. This is composed of the cuticle or epidermis, the outer bark or cortex, and the inner bark or liber. The rough, broken matter on bark is sometimes called ross in the northeastern part of the United States.

2. Any specific bark; as, Peruvian *bark*.

bärk, *v.t.*; barked, *pt.*, *pp.*; barking, *ppr.* 1. To peel; to strip off bark.

2. To rub off the outer surface or covering of, as the skin.

3. To cover or inclose with bark.

4. To color or tan by means of bark.

5. To kill or make insensible (such game as birds or squirrels) by the concussive force of an object striking the bark of a tree.

bärk, bärque (bärk), *n.* [ME. *barke*; Fr. *barque*; OFr. *barge*, a small boat.] A small ship; specifically, a ship which carries three masts, but which has no mizzentopsail. The English mariners in the coal trade apply this name to a broad-sterned ship without a figurehead.

Bark.

bärk, *v.i.* [ME. *barken*, *berken*; AS. *beorcan*, to bark.]

1. To make the typical noise of dogs.

2. To clamor; to pursue with unreasonable reproach. It is followed by *at*.

To *bark at* sleeping fame. —Spenser.

bärk, *n.* The short, explosive noise made by a dog; also, the similar cry of any other animal.

bärk′ăn-tīne, bärk′en-tīne, *n.* A vessel having three masts, the forward one square-rigged, the other two schooner-rigged; spelled also *barquantine*.

bärk′=bed, *n.* A hotbed having a foundation of tan-bark.

bärk′bee″tle (-tl), *n.* A beetle of the *Scolytidæ* family, that injures trees by boring under the bark.

bärk′bound, *a.* Having the bark too firm or close, as trees. This disease is cured by slitting the bark.

bär′keep″ẽr, *n.* One who sells liquor over a bar; a bartender.

bärk′en, *a.* Made from bark. [Rare.]

bärk′en-tine, *n.* See *Barkantine*.

bärk′ẽr, *n.* 1. One who or that which barks; one who clamors or cries out.

2. In zoölogy, the spotted redshank.

3. A person who stands at a shop-door to invite passing people to enter, or who calls out excursions at docks, etc.; a tout. [Colloq.]

4. A gun on the lower deck of a ship.

5. A pistol. [Slang.]

bärk′ẽr, *n.* One who strips bark from trees.

Bärk′ẽr's mill. A machine, moved by the centrifugal force of water, invented more than a century ago by Dr. *Barker*; one of the simplest water-mills constructed. It has a vertical axis C D, moving on a pivot at D, and carrying the upper millstone *m*, after passing through an opening in the fixed millstone *n*. Round this axis is a tube T T, communicating with a horizontal tube A B, with two apertures in opposite directions A and B. When water from the mill-course M N is introduced into the tube T T, it flows out of the apertures A and B, and by pressure the arm A B (and the whole machine) is put in motion. The bridge-tree *a b* is raised or lowered by turning the nut *c* at the end of the lever *c b*. The grain is passed into the hopper H, and thence to the grindstones. In a modified form *Barker's mill* is also known as the *Scotch turbine*.

Barker's Mill.

bärk′ẽr-y, *n.* A tanhouse.

bärk′ing=i″rons (-ī″ŭrnz), *n.pl.* Instruments used in taking off the bark of trees.

bärk′less, *a.* Without bark.

bärk′louse, *n.* A coccid insect which frequents the bark of vines and trees.

bärk′=pit, *n.* A pit filled with bark and water, in which hides are steeped in tanning.

bärk′=stōve, *n.* A glazed structure for keeping tropical plants, having a bed of tanner's bark, or other fermentable matter, which produces a moist heat.

bärk′y, *a.* Like bark; consisting of bark; containing bark.

bär′ley, *n.* [ME. *barly*, from AS. *bærlic*, barley.] A species of grain, of the genus *Hordeum*, used especially for making malt, from which are prepared liquors of extensive use, as beer, ale, and porter. As a domestic grain it is among the most ancient of species, is remarkably hardy, and is cultivated over a greater range of territory than any other. Medicinally, it possesses decided emollient and expectorant qualities.

bär′ley=bīrd, *n.* 1. A European finch; called also the *siskin*.

2. The nightingale.

bär′ley-brāke, bär′ley-break, *n.* A rural play; a trial of swiftness, or tag, usually played around stacks of barley or in other grain fields.

bär′ley=bree, bär′ley=broo, *n.* A strong liquor made from barley; ale or whisky. [Scot.]

bär′ley=broth, *n.* A contemptuous word for malt liquors.

bär′ley-corn, *n.* A grain of barley, the average length of which was considered one-third of an inch; an old linear measure.

John Barleycorn; a humorous personification of liquor.

bär′ley=sug″ăr (-shug″ẽr), *n.* Sugar boiled till it is brittle (formerly with a decoction of barley), and candied.

bär′ley=wa̤″tẽr, *n.* A decoction of barley, which is soothing and nourishing and much used in medicine.

bär′ley=wine, *n.* The ancient name for malt liquors.

bär′=loom, *n.* A loom for weaving ribbons.

bärm, *n.* [ME. *barme*, *berme*, from AS. *beorma*, yeast.] Foam rising upon beer, or other malt liquors, when fermenting, and used as leaven in bread to make it rise, causing it to be softer, lighter, and more delicate. It may be used in liquors to make them ferment or work. *Barm* is also called *brewers' yeast*.

bärm, *n.* [AS. *bearm*.] The bosom or lap. [Obs.]

bär′=mag″net, *n.* A magnet in the form of a bar.

bär′maid, *n.* A girl or woman who tends bar.

bär′mas″tẽr, *n.* [Perhaps from G. *bergmeister*, a surveyor of mines; *berg*, a hill, a mine, and *meister*, a master or overseer.]

1. Formerly, in mining, a surveyor or local judge who looked after the interests of the owner and the rights of the miners.

2. A magistrate of the barmote. [Eng.]

bärm′brack, *n.* [Ir. *bairin*, cake, and *breac*, speckled.] A currant-bun. [Ir. and Prov. Eng.]

bärm′cloth, *n.* An apron. [Obs.]

Bär′mē-ci-dăl, Bär′ma-ci-dăl, *a.* Like Barmecide or Barmecide's entertainment; illusive; unreal.

Bär′mē-cide, Bär′mȧ-cide, *n.* and *a.* I. *n.* A person who offers a pretended pleasure or spurious gift; a reference to the imaginary food given by *Barmecide*, in the "Arabian Nights Tales."

II. *a.* Barmecidal; unreal.

bär′mōte, *n.* [G *berg*, a hill, and AS. *mote*, meeting.] In Derbyshire, England, a court established to adjudicate among the miners.

bärm′y, *a.* Containing barm or yeast.

bärn, *n.* [ME. *barn*, *bern*; AS. *bern*, contracted from *berern*; *bere*, barley, and *ern*, a place for storing.] A building for storing farm-produce, stabling live-stock, etc.

bärn, *v.t.* To lay up in a barn. [Obs.]

bärn, *n.* A child. [Obs. See *Bairn*.]

Bär′nȧ-bite, *n.* A member of an old Roman Catholic order named after St. Barnabas, and which still exists.

bär′nȧ-cle, *n.* [ME. *barnakylle*, dim. of *bernak*, a goose.]

1. A species of wild goose, *Anser bernicla*, found in northern European waters. The head and neck are black, the back brown or black, flecked with white. Formerly a strange notion prevailed that these birds grew out of the barnacles attached to wood in the sea, hence the name. In this use, written also *bernacle* and *bernicle*.

2. The name applied to several species of the *Cirripedia*, particularly the sessile and stalked species (*Lepas anatifera*). They are found adhering to submerged bottoms of vessels or to rocks.

Barnacle (*Lepas anatifera*).

3. Any person or thing that resembles a barnacle in clinging persistently, as to some office or support; a hanger-on.

bär′nȧ-cle=eat″ẽr, *n.* A fish of the *Alutera* genus; the New England filefish.

bär′nȧ-cleş (-klz), *n.pl.* [OFr. *bernac*, a kind of bit.]

1. An instrument consisting of two branches joined at one end with a hinge, to put upon a horse's nose, to confine him, while shoeing, bleeding, or dressing.

2. Spectacles. [Colloq.]

bär′nȧ-cle=scāle, *n.* A barnacle-shaped louse infesting the bark of orange and quince trees.

Bärn′bŭrn″ẽr, *n.* A member of a section of the Democratic party in New York State, that in 1846 opposed the extension of slavery to the territories. The name was bestowed by its opponents, the Hunkers, who likened the party to the man who burned down his barn to clear it of rats.

bärn′dook, *n.* Rifle. [English soldiers' slang.]

bärn′=owl, *n.* An owl which frequents buildings, especially barns, in search of mice; zoölogically known as *Strix flammea*.

bärn′storm″ẽr, *n.* A traveling actor who gives performances in barns or any available building; an actor who plays in country districts; an inferior actor.

bärn′storm″ing, *n.* The giving of theatrical performances in barns or similar buildings; the practice of playing in country districts.

bärn′=swal″lōw, *n.* A swallow which frequents barns, attaching its mud nest to the rafters; especially the American variety (*Hirundo horreorum*).

bärn′yärd, *n.* The yard or space adjacent to a barn.

bȧ-rō′cō, bȧ-rō′kō, *n.* In logic, a combination of letters collectively destitute of meaning, but which, taken separately, imply that the first proposition (A) is a universal affirmative, the second and third (O) particular negatives, and the middle term the predicate in the first two propositions. *Baroco* is the fourth mode of the second figure of syllogisms. Written also *baroque*. Example:

All scholars of the first rank have, as one essential characteristic, intense love of knowledge.
But the mass of mankind does not possess this.
Therefore the mass of mankind cannot reach the first rank of scholarship. [See *Bamalip*.]

bar′ō-gram, *n.* The tracings of a barograph.

bar′ō-grȧph, *n.* [Gr. *baros*, weight, and *graphein*, to write.] In meteorology, an instrument for recording, by automatic tracings, variation in the pressure of the atmosphere. In aviation, an instrument used for recording altitudes attained during an ascent.

bȧ-rō′kō, *n.* See *Baroco*.

bar′ō-līte, *n.* [Gr. *baros*, weight, and *lithos*, a stone.] In mineralogy, a form of barium carbonate. [See *Witherite*.]

bȧ-rol′ō-gy, *n.* [Gr. *baros*, weight, and *logos*, description.] The science of the weight of bodies or of gravity.

bar″ō-mȧ-crom′e-tẽr, *n.* [Gr. *baros*, weight, *macros*, long, and *metron*, measure.] An instrument invented by Prof. Stein for determining the weight and length of infants at birth.

bȧ-rom′e-tẽr, *n.* [Gr. *baros*, weight, and *metron*, measure.]

1. An instrument for measuring the weight

or pressure of the atmosphere; consisting of a glass tube, about thirty-three inches long, hermetically sealed at one end, filled with quicksilver, well defecated and freed from air, and inverted in a basin of quicksilver. A column of quicksilver is then supported in the tube of equal weight with the incumbent atmosphere. This instrument was invented by Torricelli, of Florence, in 1643. Its uses are to indicate changes of weather, and to determine altitudes, by the falling and rising of the mercury. For this purpose, the tube is fixed to a graduated scale, so that the smallest variation in the column is visible.

Marine Barometer. Common Upright Barometer.

2. Figuratively, anything employed to ascertain the prevailing sentiment, especially its changes; as, the newspaper is the *barometer* of public opinion.

Aneroid barometer; see under *Aneroid*, a.

Marine barometer; a barometer whose tube is contracted at the neck to avoid oscillations of the mercury. It is hung in gimbals so as to remain upright regardless of the vessel's motion.

Mountain barometer; a mercurial barometer, with tripod attachment, used for measuring altitudes.

bȧ-rom′e-tẽr-flow″ẽr, *n.* An artificial flower, tinted with chlorid of cobalt, which shows blue when dry and pink when wet.

bȧ-rom′e-tẽr-gāuge, *n.* A gauge attached to a steam-chamber for indicating the degree of vacuum therein.

bar-ō-met′riç, bar-ō-met′riç-ăl, *a.* Pertaining to the barometer; made by a barometer; as, *barometrical* records.

Barometric gradient; the variation of atmospheric pressure; a diagram of such variation.

bar-ō-met′riç-ăl-ly, *adv.* By means of a barometer; in accordance with barometric observations.

bar-ō-met′rō-grȧph, *n.* [Gr. *baros*, weight, *metron*, measure, and *graphein*, to write.] A self-recording barometer. Same as *Barograph*.

bȧ-rom′e-try, *n.* The science of ascertaining atmospheric pressure through the use of the barometer.

bar′ō-metz (-mets), *n.* [An incorrect transliteration of Russ. *baranetsŭ*, club-moss.] In botany, the Scythian lamb; a singular vegetable production, consisting of the prostrate hairy stem of the fern *Dicksonia Barometz*, which, from its shaggy nature and position, has the appearance of a recumbent lamb.

bar′ŏn, *n.* [ME. *baron*, *barun*, a baron; OFr. *baron*, *barun*; O.H.G. *baro*, a man.]

1. In Great Britain, a title or degree of nobility; one who holds the rank of nobility next below that of a viscount, and above that of a knight or baronet. Originally, the *barons* were the proprietors of land held by honorable service. Hence, in ancient records, the word *barons* comprehends all the nobility. All such, in England, had, in early times, a right to sit in parliament. As a *baron* was the proprietor of a manor, and each manor had its *court-baron*, the *barons* claimed, and to this day, enjoy, the right of judging in the last resort, a right pertaining to the house of lords, or peers, as the representatives of the ancient *barons*, landholders, or manor-holders.

Coronet of a Baron.

Anciently, *barons* were greater, or such as held their lands of the king *in capite*; or lesser, such as held their lands of the greater *barons* by military service *in capite*.

The title of *baron* is no longer attached to the possession of a manor, but given by the king's letters patent, or writ of summons to parliament; that is, the dignity is personal, not territorial.

The radical word *vir*, *fir*, a man, is Celtic, as well as Teutonic; but the word *baron* was not known in the British Isles till introduced from the continent under the Norman princes.

2. *Baron* is a title of certain officers; as, *barons of the exchequer*, who were formerly the four judges who tried cases between the king and his subjects relating to the revenue. *Barons of the Cinque Ports* were, before the Reform Act, members of the House of Commons, elected by the seven Cinque Ports, two for each port. These ports were Dover, Sandwich, Romney, Hastings, Hythe, Winchelsea, and Rye. —Blackstone.

3. In old law, a husband; as, *baron and feme*, husband and wife. —Cowell.

4. In cookery, a *baron of beef* consists of two sirloins not cut entirely apart.

5. A capitalist, especially one who attempts to monopolize a necessity of life; as, a *coal baron*. [Colloq.]

bar′ŏn-āġe, *n.* [ME. *baronage*, from OFr. *barnage*, baronage.]

1. The whole body of barons or peers.

2. The dignity of a baron.

3. The land which gives title to a baron. [Obs.]

bar′ŏn-çōurt, *n.* Same as *Court-baron*.

bar′ŏn-ess, *n.* A baron's wife or widow; or a woman who holds the baronial title in her own right.

bar′ŏn-et, *n.* [Fr., dim. of *baron*.] A dignity or degree of honor, next below a baron, and above a knight. It is inheritable and has precedency of all degrees of knighthood except that of the Garter. The order was founded by James I. in 1611, and is given by patent. In the official title *baronet* is usually abbreviated; as, Sir Thomas Jones, *Bart.*

bar′ŏn-et-āġe, *n.* 1. The collective body of baronets.

2. The state or rank of a baronet.

bar′ŏn-et-cy, *n.* The rank or title of a baronet.

bȧ-rō′ni-ăl, *a.* Pertaining to a baron, his estate or class.

bar′ŏn-y, *n.* [ME. *baronie*, from OFr. *baronie*, barony.]

1. The lordship, honor, or domain of a baron, whether spiritual or temporal.

2. In Ireland, a territorial division, corresponding nearly to the English hundred, and supposed to have been originally the district of a native chief.

3. Any extensive freehold estate in Scotland, which may be held by a commoner.

bȧ-rōque′ (-rōk′), *a.* [Fr. *baroque*, odd, irregular, from Port. *barroco*, rough, uneven.]

1. In architecture, odd; grotesque; bizarre.

2. Having unusual formation; distorted; as, a *baroque* pearl.

bȧ-rōque′, *n.* In the fine arts, especially architecture, any form or ornamentation of a grotesque character that prevailed in the early part of the eighteenth century.

bar′ō-sçōpe, *n.* [Gr. *baros*, weight, and *skopein*, to view.] A weatherglass to show the approximate weight of the atmosphere; superseded by the *barometer*.

bar-ō-sçop′iç, bar-ō-sçop′iç-ăl, *a.* Pertaining to the baroscope.

bar-ō-sel′e-nīte, *n.* [Gr. *baros*, weight, and *selēnē*, the moon.] In mineralogy, native barium sulphate. [See *Barite*.]

Ba-ros′mȧ, *n.* See *Buchu*.

bȧ-rouçhe′, *n.* [G. *barutsche*; It. *baroccio*, from LL. *birota*, a two-wheeled vehicle, from L. *bis*, two, and *rota*, a wheel.] A four-wheeled carriage, having a falling top, with a driver's seat on the outside and two inside seats facing each other.

bȧ-rōu-ċhet′ (-shā′), *n.* A variety of small barouche.

bȧ-rox′y-ton, *n.* [Gr. *barys*, heavy, and *oxytonos*, sharp sounding.] A wind-instrument sometimes used in military bands.

bär′pōst, *n.* One of the side posts of a field-gate.

bär′quăn-tīne (-kăn-), **bär′quen-tīne** (-ken-), *n.* Same as *Barkantine*.

bärque (bärk), *n.* See *Bark*.

bärr, *v.i.* [Fr. *barrir*, from L. *barrire*, to cry like an elephant, from *barrus*, an elephant.] To imitate the cry of an elephant.

bär′rȧ, *n.* A measure for cloth, equivalent to about one-and-a-quarter yards, used in Portugal and some parts of Spain.

bär′rȧ-ble, *a.* In law, capable of being barred.

bar′rȧ-çan, *n.* [Fr. *barracan*; Turk. *barrakan*; Ar. *barrakān*, a sort of black gown; from Per. *barak*, a stuff made of camel's hair.] A thick, strong stuff, something like camlet; used in the Levant for cloaks, surtouts, and other outer garments.

bar′răck, *n.* [Fr. *baraque*, from It. *barraca*, a tent or soldier's hut.]

1. A building for soldiers, especially in garrison; used in the plural, *barracks*.

2. A detachable roof, on posts, to cover hay, etc. [Colloq.]

bar′răck, *v.t.* To furnish with barracks; to put (soldiers) in barracks.

bar′răck, *v.i.* To occupy barracks.

bar′rȧ-çlāde, *n.* [D. *baare*, bare, and *kleed*, cloth.] A woolen blanket manufactured at home, undressed or without nap; invented by the Dutch of New Amsterdam (New York).

bar′rȧ-çoon, *n.* [Sp. *barracon*, a stronghold, from *barraca*, a barrack.] An African barrack, pen, or inclosure for slaves, sometimes fortified; a slave-mart.

bar-rȧ-çū′dȧ, bar-rȧ-çōu′tȧ, *n.* [Native name.]

1. In ichthyology, a large sea-fish, of the pike kind, attaining ten feet in length, found in the West Indian and Mediterranean seas.

2. An edible Australian fresh-water fish, *Thyrsites atun*.

bar′rad, *n.* A conical cap worn by the Irish previous to the seventeenth century.

bär′rāġe, *n.* [Fr. *barrage*, a dam, from *barrer*, to stop.] 1. In engineering, especially for irrigating purposes, an artificial bar or dam placed in a watercourse to increase the depth of water.

2. A wall of shell fire which is thrown against an advancing enemy with such regularity that the troops are unable to pierce it. Used to prevent an enemy's advance or retreat, and also to protect troops as they advance for an attack.

Rolling barrage; A barrage which affords a zone of safety between it and the stationary barrage.

bar-rȧ-mun′dȧ, *n.* [Native name.] In ichthyology, (a) an Australian fresh-water fish of the genus *Ceratodus*; (b) an Australian river-fish having large scales.

bar-ran′çȧ, bar-ran′çō, *n.* [Sp.] A ravine caused by rain, or a watercourse.

bar′răs, *n.* [Fr. *barre*, a bar; on account of its resemblance to a bar.] The resin which exudes from wounds made in the bark of *Pinus Pinaster*; called also *galipot*.

bar′rȧ-tŏr, *n.* [ME. *barator*, from OFr. *barateor*, a trader, from *barater*, to barter, cheat.]

1. In law, one guilty of barratry.

2. In maritime law, any employee of a ship who commits fraud in the management of the ship, or in relation to his duties, by which the owner or insurers are injured.

bar′rȧ-trous, *a.* Tainted with barratry.

bar′rȧ-trous-ly, *adv.* In a barratrous manner.

bar′rȧ-try, *n.* [ME. *barratrie*; OFr. *baraterie*, barratry, from *barater*, to barter, cheat.]

1. In law, the practice of exciting and encouraging lawsuits and quarrels.

2. In maritime law, any species of cheating or fraud, by a shipmaster, by which the owners or insurers are injured, as by sinking or deserting, wilful deviation, or embezzling the cargo.

3. In Scots law, the acceptance by a judge of a bribe designed to influence his decision.

bärred (bärd), *a.* Fastened with a bar; hindered; restrained; excluded; forbidden; striped; checkered.

Barred owl; a large American species, *Syrnium nebulosum*, having broad brown stripes or bars across the breast.

bar′rel, *n.* [ME. *barel*, *barayl*; OFr. *bareil*; LL. *barillus*, *barile*, a barrel.]

1. A round vessel or cask, of more length than breadth, and bulging in the middle, made of staves and heading, and bound with hoops.

2. The quantity which a *barrel* contains by custom or state enactment; as, the wine *barrel* of the United States, thirty-one gallons, and the beer *barrel*, thirty-one and one-half; the imperial beer *barrel* of Great Britain, thirty-six gallons; a *barrel* of flour (U. S.), 196 pounds.

3. Anything hollow and long; as, the *barrel* of a gun; a tube.

4. A cylinder; as, the *barrel* of a watch, within which the spring is coiled, and round which is wound the chain.

5. In ornithology, the hollow or quill part of a feather.

Barrel of the ear; the cavity of the ear; the tympanum.

Barrel organ; an organ whose music is produced by a revolving cylinder, usually turned by a crank.

bar′rel, *v.t.*; barreled (-reld), *pt.*, *pp.*; barreling, *ppr.* To put in a barrel; to pack in a barrel.

bar′rel-bel″lied (-lid), *a.* Having a large belly.

bar′rel-bulk, *n.* A measure for estimating the freight capacity of a ship, being five cubic feet in space, holding one-eighth of a ton weight.

bar′reled, *a.* 1. Put or packed in a barrel.

2. Having a barrel or tube.

bar′rel-fish, *n.* The rudder-fish, barred with broad bands like the hoops of a barrel.

bar′rel-sçrew (-skrū), *n.* In mechanics, same as *Bed-screw*.

bar′rel-set″tẽr, *n.* In gun-making, a cylindrical mandrel for testing and truing gun-barrels.

bar′ren, *a.* [ME. *barein*, *barain*; OFr. *baraigne*, barren.]

1. Not producing young or offspring; sterile.

2. Not producing plants; unfruitful; not fertile; unproductive; as, *barren* fields.

3. Unproductive; not inventive; dull; as, a *barren* mind.

4. Empty; fruitless; unprofitable; as, a *barren* enterprise.

Barren flower; in botany, a flower without stamens and pistils, or having only stamens.

Barren Grounds; in geography, a vast region in British America, north of the forest line.

Barren stamens; in botany, stamens that yield no pollen.

bar′ren, *n.* [ME. *barein*; OFr. *brahain*, barren.]

1. In the western states, a tract of slightly elevated land, partly prairie and partly covered by small trees; not necessarily barren as the name imports.

2. Any unproductive tract of land.

bar′ren-ly, *adv.* Unfruitfully.

bar′ren-ness, *n.* 1. The quality of not producing its kind; want of the power of conception.

2. Unfruitfulness; sterility; infertility; the quality of not producing at all, or only in small quantities; as, the *barrenness* of soil.

3. Want of invention; want of the power of producing anything new; applied to the mind.

4. Want of matter; scantiness; as, the *barrenness* of a cause.

5. Defect of emotion, sensibility, or fervency; as, the *barrenness* of devotion.

bar′ren-spir″it-ed, *a.* Of a poor spirit.

bar′ren-wŏrt, *n.* A low, herbaceous plant, *Epimedium alpinum*, with a creeping root, having many stalks, each of which has three flowers.

bar′ret, *n.* [Fr. *barrette*; LL. *barretum*, a cap.]

1. A cap formerly worn by soldiers; called also *barret-cap*.

2. The flat cap worn by priests of the Roman Catholic church. [See *Biretta*.]

bär-rette′, *n.* [Fr. *barrette*, dim. of *barre*, a bar.] The cross-guard or bar of a fencing foil.

bärr′fụl, *n.* Same as *Barful*.

bar-ri-çāde′, *n.* [Fr. *barricade*; Sp. *barricada*, a barricade; literally, made of barrels, from *barrica*, a barrel.]

1. A fortification, made in haste of anything that will obstruct the progress of an enemy, or serve for defense or security; usually formed in streets; as, to make a *barricade* of carts and barrels.

2. Any bar or obstruction; that which defends.

bar-ri-çāde′, *v.t.*; barricaded, *pt.*, *pp.*; barricading, *ppr.* 1. To stop up a passage; to obstruct.

2. To fortify with any hasty or slight work that hinders the approach of an enemy.

bar-ri-çād′ēr, *n.* One who builds barricades.

bar-ri-çā′dō, *n.* and *v.* Same as *Barricade*.

bar-ri′çō, *n.* [Sp. *barrica*, a cask.] A small cask.

bar′ri-ēr, *n.* [ME. *barrere*; OFr. *barriere*, a barrier; LL. *barra*, a bar.]

1. In fortification, a kind of fence to obstruct an enemy's advance.

2. A wall for defense.

3. A fortress or fortified town on the frontier of a country.

4. Any obstruction; anything which confines, or which hinders approach or attack; as, constitutional *barriers*.

5. A bar to mark the limits of a place; any limit or boundary; a line of separation.

Barrier reef; a coral reef which parallels a coast.

Syn.—Bar, barricade, bulwark, hindrance, obstacle, obstruction, prohibition, rampart, restraint, restriction.

bar′ri-ēr-gāte, *n.* A strong heavy barrier to a stockade or palisade.

bar-ri-gŭ′dō, *n.* [Sp., big-bellied.] The Brazilian name for several monkeys of the genus *Lagothrix*. They are the largest of South American monkeys, and have a long prehensile tail.

bär′ring, *ppr.* used as *prep.* Excepting; excluding; as, *barring* accidents, I shall be there.

bar′ris-tēr, *n.* [Early Eng. *barrester*, *barester*, from *barre*, a bar.] A counselor or advocate learned in the law, qualified and admitted to plead at the bar and to undertake the defense of clients; called in full, a *barrister at law*. [Eng.]

bar-ris-tē′ri-ăl, *a.* Pertaining to a barrister.

bär′room, *n.* A room in which liquors are retailed over a bar.

bar′rōw, *n.* [ME. *barrow*, *barow*, *barowe*, a barrow, from AS. *beran*, to bear, carry.]

1. A frame or box having handles or shafts, and with or without a wheel, used in transporting small, heavy loads; a handbarrow or wheelbarrow.

2. A wicker case in salt-works, where the salt is put to drain.

bar′rōw, *n.* [ME. *barow*, *barowe*; AS. *bearg*, *bearh*, a castrated boar.] A castrated hog.

bar′rōw, *n.* [ME. *berw*; AS. *beorg*, a grove.]

1. A hillock or mound of earth, intended as a repository of the dead. Such *barrows* are

Bowl Barrow.

found in England, in the north of the European continent, and in the United States. They sometimes were formed of stones, and, in Scotland and the north of England, are called

Long Barrow.

cairns. They are distinguished, according to their peculiarities of form and construction, as long, bowl, bell, cone, and broad *barrows*, etc.

Twin Barrow.

2. In mining, a heap of accumulated rubbish or attle.

bar′rōw, *n.* A flannel swaddling-cloth. [Prov. Eng.]

bar′rōw-çōat, *n.* An infant's first underdress.

Bar′rōw-ist, *n.* A disciple of Henry Barrowe, executed in 1593, one of the founders of Congregationalism in England.

bar′rŭ-let, *n.* [Dim. of OFr. *barre*, a bar.] In heraldry, a stripe one-fourth the width of a bar.

bar′rŭ-ly, *a.* In heraldry, traversed by barrulets; said of the field.

Barry of six.

bär′ry, *a.* [Fr. *barré*, pp. of *barrer*, to bar, hinder.] In heraldry, divided into bars; said of the field.

bärse, *n.* [ME. *barse*; AS. *bærs*, *bears*, perch.] An English name for the common perch.

bärs′-gem″el, *n.pl.* In heraldry, parallel barrulets placed in couples.

bär′-shēar, *n.* A machine for cutting metallic bars.

bär′-shōe, *n.* A kind of horseshoe having a bar across the hinder part—the open part—of the heel, to protect the tender frog of the foot from injury.

Bars-gemel.

bär′-shot, *n.* Two cannon-balls, or half-balls, joined together by an iron bar, and formerly used in sea-fights to cut the masts or rigging of an adversary's vessel.

Bar-shot.

bär′-sight (-sīt), *n.* A rifle-sight, consisting of a bar placed across a ring.

bär′tend″ēr, *n.* One who serves liquors across a bar.

bär′tēr, *v.i.*; bartered, *pt.*, *pp.*; bartering, *ppr.* [ME. *bartren*; OFr. *bareter*, to barter, trick, cheat.] To traffic or trade by exchanging one commodity for another, in distinction from a sale and purchase, in which money is paid for the commodities transferred.

bär′tēr, *v.t.* To exchange (one thing for another) in commerce; sometimes followed by *away*; as, to *barter away* goods or honor.

bär′tēr, *n.* The act or practice of trading by exchanging commodities; exchange.

Syn.—Exchange, dealing, traffic, trade, truck.

bär′tēr-ēr, *n.* One who trades by exchange of commodities.

bär′tēr-y, *n.* Exchange of commodities in trade. [Obs.]

bärth, *n.* A place of shelter for cattle. [Eng.]

Bär-thol′ō-mew, *n.* One of the Apostles; the name is now used in composition.

Bartholomew fair; a fair at West Smithfield, England, held annually at Bartholomew-tide from 1133 to 1855 A.D.

Bär-thol′ō-mew-tīde, *n.* The time of the festival of St. Bartholomew, August 24.

bär′ti-zăn, *n.* [A corrupted Scot. spelling of *bratticing*.] A small overhanging turret, which projects from the angles of a tower, or from the parapet and other parts of a building.

Bartizan, Micklegate Bar, York.—*aa*, Balistraria.

Bärt′lett, *n.* A species of English pear, named after Enoch *Bartlett*, of Dorchester, Mass., who introduced it into the United States.

bär′tŏn, *n.* [AS. *bere-tun*, a courtyard; *bere*, barley, and *tūn*, inclosure.] The demesne lands of a manor; the manor itself; and sometimes the outhouses. [Eng.]

bär′trăm, *n.* Same as *Bertram*.

bȧ-rụ′, *n.* [Malay.] A woolly substance contained in the leafstock bases of the East Indian sago-palm, used for filling cushions, calking wooden vessels, etc.

bär′wāy, *n.* A passage into a field or yard, closed by bars which are easily taken down.

bär′-weir, *n.* A device to stay fish from returning seaward.

bär′wīse, *adv.* In heraldry, horizontally across the field.

bär′wood, *n.* A strong flexible red dyewood from Africa, useful in the arts. It is produced by a leguminous plant, *Baphia nitida*.

bar-y-. A combining form from Gr. *barys*, heavy, difficult.

bar-y-cen′triç, *a.* [*Bary-*, and Gr. *kentron*, center.] Pertaining to the center of gravity.

bar-y-phō′ni-ȧ, bȧ-ryph′ō-ny, *n.* [*Bary-*, and Gr. *phōnē*, voice.] Difficulty of speech.

bȧ-rȳ′tȧ, *n.* [Gr. *barytēs*, weight, from *barys*, heavy.] Oxid of barium, the heaviest of the earths, the specific gravity being 4.7. It is generally found in combination with sulphuric and carbonic acids, forming sulphate and carbonate of *baryta*, the former of which is called *heavy-spar*.

bȧ-rȳ′tēş, *n.* [Gr. *barytēs*, weight.]

1. Native sulphate of baryta, generally called heavy-spar.

2. Baryta.

bȧ-ryt′iç, *a.* Pertaining to baryta; formed of baryta or containing it.

bȧ-rȳ-tō-çal′cite, *n.* [LL. *baryta*, barium, from Gr. *barytēs*, weight, and L. *calx*, *calcis*, lime.] A compound of carbonate of lime and carbonate of baryta, of a dark or light gray color, occurring massive or crystallized.

bar′y-tōne, bar′i-tōne, *n.* [It. *baritono*; Gr. *barytonos*, deep-toned; *barys*, deep, and *tonos*, tone.]

1. In music, a male voice not reaching so low as bass nor so high as tenor.

2. A singer who possesses a barytone voice.

3. In Greek grammar, a word which has no accent marked on the last syllable, the grave accent being understood.

4. A musical instrument of deep tone.

bar′y-tōne, bar′i-tōne, *a.* 1. Ranging between tenor and bass; as, a *barytone* voice.

2. Suited to a barytone; as, a *barytone* solo.

bȧ-rȳ′tum, *n.* [Gr. *barytēs*, weight.] A metal, the basis of baryta. [Rare. See *Barium*.]

bā′săl, *a.* Pertaining to the base; constituting the base.

Basal plane; in crystallology, a plane parallel to the horizontal axis.

bȧ-sā′lē, *n.*; *pl.* **bȧ-sā′li-ȧ.** [L. *basis*, base.] A cartilage at the base of the fins of certain fishes.

bā′săl-nērved, *a.* In botany, having the nerves springing from the base; said of leaves.

bȧ-sạlt′, *n.* [L. *basaltes*, dark, hard marble.] A fine-grained, heavy, crystalline, igneous rock, consisting of Labrador feldspar, augite, magnetic iron, and sometimes a little olivin. It is amorphous, columnar, tabular, or globular. It is usually of a greenish-black color but sometimes dull brown or black. Fingal's Cave, in the island of Staffa, and the Giant's Causeway, Ireland, furnish remarkable instances of basaltic columns.

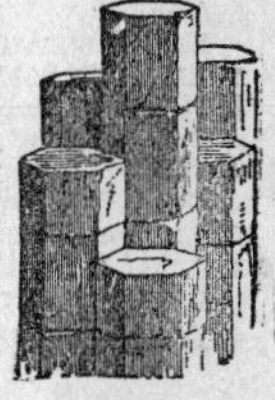

Basalt.

bȧ-sạlt′iç, *a.* Pertaining to basalt; formed of or containing basalt.

bȧ-sạlt′i-fọrm, *a.* In the form of basalt; columnar.

bȧ-sạlt′ine, *n.* A variety of common hornblende, found in basalt and lavas. [Obs.]

bȧ-sạlt′oid, *a.* Formed like basalt; basaltiform.

baş′ăn, *n.* A sheepskin. [See *Basil*.]

baş′ȧ-nīte, *n.* [Gr. *basanos*, the touchstone.] Lydian stone, or black jasper; a variety of silicious or flinty slate. Its color is a grayish or bluish black, often interspersed with veins of quartz. It is employed to test the purity of gold.

bäs-bleu′ (bä-blū′), *n.* [Fr., blue stocking; *bas*, stocking, *bleu*, blue.] A literary lady; a bluestocking.

bas′ci-net, *n.* Same as *Basinet*.

bas′çūle, *n.* [Fr., a seesaw.] A mechanical device based on the principle of a seesaw, one end rising as the other falls; more properly, a balanced lever.

Bascule bridge; a balanced drawbridge, so counterbalanced that it may be raised in whole or in halves to a vertical position when not in use, or, when it crosses a stream, to let vessels pass.

bāse, *a.*; *comp.* baser; *superl.* basest. [ME. *base*, *bass*; OFr. *bas*, base, low; L. *basis*, a base or pedestal.]

1. Low in place. [Obs.]

2. Mean; vile; worthless; that is, low in value or estimation; used of things.

3. Of low station; of mean account; without rank, dignity, or estimation among men; used of persons.

4. Of mean spirit; disingenuous; illiberal; low; without dignity of sentiment; as, a *base* and abject multitude.

5. Of little comparative value; applied to metals, in distinction from the *precious* metals, as gold and silver.

6. Deep; grave; applied to sound; as, the *base* sounds of a viol.

7. Of illegitimate birth; born out of wedlock.

8. In law, not held by honorable tenure. A *base* estate, in England, is an estate held by services not honorable, but by villienage. Such a tenure is called *base*, or low, and the tenant, a *base* tenant.

Syn.—Mean, vile, low, dishonorable, worthless, ignoble, lowminded, shameful, inferior.—*Base* is a stronger term than *vile*, and *vile* than *mean*. The first two denote what is wicked as well as low, the last what is disgraceful or dishonorable.

bāse, *n.* [ME. *base*, *bas*, *baas*; OFr. *base*; L. *basis*, a base or pedestal; Gr. *basis*, a pedestal, step; from *bainein*, to go, to walk.]

1. The bottom of anything, considered as its support, or the part of a thing on which it stands or rests; as, the *base* of a column, the pedestal of a statue, the foundation of a house, etc.

2. In architecture, that part of a column which is between the top of the pedestal and the bottom of the shaft or the part between the bottom of the column and the plinth. Usually it consists of circles. The pedestal also has its *base*.

3. In fortification, the exterior side of the polygon, or an imaginary line drawn from the flanked angle of a bastion to the angle opposite to it.

4. In gunnery, the smallest kind of ordnance. [Obs.]

5. The part of any ornament which hangs down, as housings.

6. The broad part of anything, as the bottom of a cone.

7. The place from which a start is made; the bottom of the field; the starting-post.

8. The lowest or gravest part in music; now commonly written *bass*.

9. An old game; called also *prisoner's base* or *prison-bars*.

10. In war, a tract of country protected by fortifications, or by natural advantages, from which the operations of an army proceed.

11. In geometry, the lowest side of the perimeter of a figure, on which it is supposed to stand.

12. In chemistry, the positive or nonacid component of a salt.

13. In pharmacy, the principal ingredient of a compound.

14. In baseball, any one of the four corners of the square, or diamond, which forms the infield.

15. In botany, the part of fruit where it is united with the peduncle; the extremity of a leaf next the stem, opposed to the *apex*.

Base broom; in botany, the woodwaxen, *Genista tinctoria*.

Base bullion; crude lead, containing silver, antimony, etc.

bāse, *v.t.*; based (bāst), *pt.*, *pp.*; basing, *ppr.*

1. To found; to lay the base or foundation of.

> To *base* and build the commonwealth of man. —Columbiad.

2. To debase; to reduce the value of, by the admixture of meaner metals. [Obs.]

bāse'ball, *n.* The national game of the United States, and played to some extent in Canada, England, the West Indies, Australia, and the island possessions of the United States. It is founded on the old English game of rounders, early known in the United States as *town-ball*. It reached its present state of development and popularity in the latter half of the nineteenth century. The game is played with ball and bat on an open field, marked with a *diamond* ninety feet square, known as the *infield*. The indefinite extension of lines on adjacent sides of this square mark off the *outfield* from *foul ground*. Nine men constitute a team. The ball used in the game is also called a *baseball*.

bāse'bōard, *n.* A board around the walls of a room, meeting the floor and furnishing protection to the plastering.

bāse'born, *a.* 1. Born out of wedlock.

2. Born of low parentage.

3. Vile; mean.

bāse'-bürn"ēr, *n.* A stove or furnace with a fire-box and grate at the bottom and supplied with fuel through a tube projected from above.

bāse'-çourse, *n.* The first or lowest layer, as of stone in a wall.

bāse'-çourt, *n.* 1. The back yard, opposed to the chief court in front of a house.

2. In law, an inferior court.

bāse'-heärt"ed, *a.* Vile in heart.

bāse'-hit, *n.* In baseball, a hit which allows a batsman to reach the first base safely, without any error of the opponents.

bas'e-lärd, *n.* See *Baslard*.

bāse'less, *a.* Without a base; having no foundation or support.

> The *baseless* fabric of this vision. —Shak.

bāse'-lev"el, *n.* In geology, the lowest level to which erosion can be carried on.

bāse'-līne, *n.* 1. An established line from which to measure and to which all other lines are secondary; the principal line, as in engineering.

2. Any line establishing a limit on a playground or table; as, the *base-line* of a tennis-court or baseball diamond.

Bā-sel'lȧ, *n.* [Native name in Malabar.] In botany, a typical genus of East Indian herbs, some species being used in China as spinach plants.

bāse'ly, *adv.* 1. In a base manner; meanly; dishonorably.

2. Illegitimately; in bastardy.

bāse'ment, *n.* [Fr. *soubassement*, base.] In architecture, the lowest story of a building, whether above or below the ground.

Basement membrane; in anatomy, a delicate membrane found beneath the epidermis or epithelium on all the free surfaces of the body, both external and internal; also called the *primary membrane*.

bāse'-mīnd"ed, *a.* Of a low spirit or mind; mean.

bāse'-mīnd"ed-ly, *adv.* With a base mind.

bāse'-mīnd"ed-ness, *n.* Meanness of spirit.

bāse'-mōld"ing, *n.* In architecture, a projecting molding at the base of any architectural feature, as a wall or column.

Base-moldings.

bāse'ness, *n.* 1. Meanness; vileness; worthlessness.

2. The quality of being base; applied to metals, coin, etc.

3. Bastardy; illegitimacy of birth.

bas'ē-net, *n.* A helmet. [See *Basinet*.]

bāse'-plāte, *n.* Same as *Home-plate*.

bā'sēs, *n.*, pl. of *basis*.

bāse'-sōuled, *a.* Vile in soul.

bāse'-spir"it-ed, *a.* Low in courage; mean; cowardly.

bash, *v.t.*; bashed, *pt.*, *pp.*; bashing, *ppr.* [ME. *basshen*, *baschen*, for *abashen*, abash.]

1. To make ashamed. [Obs.]

2. To strike heavily; to beat; to crush. [Prov. Eng. and Scot.]

> *Bash* her open with a rock. —Kipling.

bash, *v.i.* To be ashamed; to be confounded with shame. [Obs.]

bash, *n.* A heavy crushing blow. [Prov. Eng. and Scot.]

bȧ-shaw', *n.* [Turk. *bāshā*, head, ruler; Per. *pādshāh*, a governor, king.]

1. Same as *Pasha*.

2. A large catfish of the Mississippi; the mudcat (*Leptops olivaris*).

bash'fụl, *a.* [OE. *baschen*, *baissen*, to bash, abash.]

1. Having a downcast look; hence, very modest.

2. Modest to excess; sheepish; diffident; shy.

Syn.—Modest, diffident, reserved, shy, timid, unassuming, unobtrusive.

bash'fụl-ly, *adv.* Very modestly; in a bashful manner.

bash'fụl-ness, *n.* Excessive or extreme modesty; a quality of mind often visible in external appearance, as in blushing, a downcast look, confusion, etc.

bash'i-bȧ-zöuk', *n.* [Turk. *bashi-bozuq*, one in no special dress; *bashi*, headdress, and *bozuq*, disorderly, unkempt.] An irregular soldier of the Turkish army.

bash'less, *a.* Shameless; unblushing. [Obs.]

bash'lyk, bash'lik, *n.* [Russ. *bashluik*.] A cloth hood, covering the ears, worn in Russia as a protection against cold.

bas'hyle, *n.* Same as *Basyl*.

bā'si-. [From L. *basis*; Gr. *basis*, base.] A combining form, used in biology to denote some intimate relation to the base; as, *basi*cranial, at the base of the cranium.

bā'sic, *a.* [L. *basis*, base.]

1. In chemistry, having more than one equivalent of the base for each equivalent of acid.

2. Relating to a base; performing the office of a base in a salt.

3. In mineralogy, having a low percentage of silica; said of crystalline rocks.

Basic slag; a part of the refuse in the manufacture of steel, useful as a fertilizer because of the phosphate it contains.

bā-sic'ēr-ite, *n.* [*Basi-*, and Gr. *keras*, horn.] In zoölogy, the part of the long feeler of a crustacean next to the coxocerite, or first joint.

bā-sic'i-ty, *n.* In chemistry, the quality that characterizes a base; the combining power of an acid compared with its replaceable hydrogen.

bā"si-dig-i-tā'lē, *n.*; *pl.* **bā"si-dig-i-tā'li-ȧ**. [*Basi-*, and L. *digitus*, finger.] A cartilage or bone at the base of a finger or a toe.

bā-sid"i-ō-ġē-net'iç, *a.* [Gr. *basis*, base, and *genesis*, origin.] In botany, originating from basidia.

Bā-sid"i-ō-mȳ-cē'tēs, *n.pl.* [Gr. *basis*, base, and *mykes*, a mushroom.] A large subdivision of fungi named from and characterized by spore-bearing basidia, including the common mushrooms and toadstools.

bā-sid"i-ō-mȳ-cē'tous, *a.* Pertaining to the *Basidiomycetes*.

bā-sid'i-ō-phōre, *n.* [Gr. *basis*, base, and *phoros*, something brought, from *pherein*, to bear.] A part of a fungus which holds or bears basidia.

bā-sid'i-ō-spōre, *n.* [Gr. *basis*, base, and *spora*, seed.] A spore originating in a basidium.

bā-sid"i-ō-spōr'ous, *a.* Relating to or having the characteristics of spores borne on basidia.

bā-sid'i-um, *n.*; *pl.* **bā-sid'i-ȧ**. [L., from Gr. *basis*, a base.] In botany, a cell, somewhat pear-shaped, on which are borne the spores in such fungi as mushrooms, toadstools, etc.

bā'si-fī-ēr, *n.* [*Basi-*, and L. *fieri*, to be made.] That which converts into a salifiable base.

bā-sif'ū-găl, *a.* [*Basi-*, and L. *fugere*, to flee.] In botany, tending away from the base; as, a *basifugal* growth.

bā'si-fȳ, *v.t.*; basified, *pt.*, *pp.*; basifying, *ppr.* To convert into a salifiable base.

bā-sig'nȧ-thite, *n.* The second joint in one of the mouth-appendages of an arthropod.

bā-si-ġyn'i-um, *n.* [*Basi-*, and Gr. *gynē*, a female.] The pedicel on which the ovary of certain flowers is situated.

bā-si-hȳ'ăl, *a.* and *n.* [*Basi-*, and the Gr. letter upsilon, Υ; from its arch-shaped appearance.]

I. *a.* Relating to the components of the hyoid arch.

II. *n.* The body or middle part of the hyoid bone.

bā-si-hȳ'oid, *a.* and *n.* I. *a.* Pertaining to the basihyal.

II. *n.* Same as *Basihyal*.

bas'il, *n.* See *Bezel*.

bas'il, *v.t.*; basiled, *pt.*, *pp.*; basiling, *ppr.* See *Bezel*.

bas'il, *n.* [ME. *basile*; OFr. *basile*, the basil plant; name from Gr. *basilikos*, royal; *basileus*, king.] A name common to different species of plants of the mint family, all natives of warm climates. They are fragrant and aromatic. The sweet *basil*, *Ocymum basilicum*, is used in cookery.

Holy basil; a kind of tropical basil of the Old World (*Ocymum sanctum*), held sacred to Vishnu in India.

Wild basil; an aromatic herb, *Calamintha clinopodium*.

bas'il, *n.* The skin of a sheep, tanned; written also *basan*.

bas'i-lăr, bas'i-lā-ry, *a.* 1. Relating to the base; situated at the base.

2. In anatomy, applied to the sphenoid bone, and the cuneiform process of the occipital bone, situated at the base of the cranium, and to an artery of the brain, resting on the cuneiform process of the occipital bone; also, to the os sacrum, at the base of the spine.

3. Figuratively, debased; corrupted; applied to motives and inclinations; as, *basilar* instincts. [Rare.]

Bȧ-sil'i-ăn, *a.* and *n.* I. *a.* Pertaining to the order of St. Basil, who founded it in Cappadocia.

II. *n.* A member of a society under the *Basilian* rule; a *Basilian* monk.

Basilian rule; a rule established by Basilius, a father of the church in the fourth century, requiring physical labor in all monasteries. It is still in force throughout the Greek church, and in some parts of the Roman.

bȧ-sil'iç, *n.* Same as *Basilica*.

bȧ-sil'iç, bȧ-sil'iç-ăl, *a.* 1. In the manner of or pertaining to a basilica.

2. Pertaining to the middle vein of the right arm and the interior branch of the axillary vein, from their being supposed by the ancients to have specially important functions in the animal economy.

bȧ-sil'i-çȧ, *n.* [Gr. *basilikē*, f. of *basilikos*, royal (supply *stoa*), portico. *Basilikē* alone came to mean a basilica or court.]

1. Anciently, a public hall or court of judicature, where princes and magistrates sat to administer justice. The same ground-plan was generally followed in the early Christian churches, which, therefore, long retained the name of *basilica*, and it is still applied to some of the churches in Rome by way of distinction, and sometimes to other churches built in imitation of the Roman *basilicas*.

2. In the middle ages, a large structure

erected over the tomb of a person of distinction.

3. A large piece of ordnance. [Obs. See *Basilisk.*]

Basilica of San Apollinare, Ravenna.

Bȧ-sil'i-çȧ, *n.pl.* An abridgment, in Greek, of the Justinian code, made in the ninth century, under Basil I.

bȧ-sil'i-căn, *a.* Pertaining to or like a basilica.

bȧ-sil'i-cok, *n.* [Obs.] Same as *Basilisk.*

bȧ-sil'i-con, *n.* [Gr. *basilikos*, royal.] A name formerly given to several ancient medical compounds; now restricted to an ointment consisting largely of pitch, resin, wax, and some fat, as olive-oil or lard.

Bas-i-lid'i-ăn, *a.* and *n.* I. *a.* Pertaining to Basilides, an Alexandrian Gnostic of the second century, or to the doctrines taught by him.

II. *n.* One of the followers of Basilides.

bas'i-lisk, *n.* [ME. *basilisk*, from Gr. *basiliskos*, dim. of *basileus*, king.]

1. A fabulous serpent, sometimes called a cockatrice. The ancients alleged that its hissing would drive away all other serpents, and that its breath, and even its look, was fatal.

2. One of a genus of lizards (*Basiliscus*) characterized by their ability to distend the skin on the head to form a bag-like protrusion, and by an erectile crest or ridge along the back.

3. Formerly, a large piece of ordnance, so called from its supposed resemblance to the mythical serpent of the same name, or from its size.

bas'il-thȳme (-tīm), *n.* A name by which two fragrant species of *Calamintha* are known, *Calamintha Nepeta* of North America and *Calamintha Acinos* of Europe.

bas'il-weed, *n.* A variety of basil that grows wild in woods and thickets; also called *wild basil*, *field-basil*, and *stone-basil.*

bā'sin (bā'sn), *n.* [ME. *basin*, *bacin*; OFr. *bacin*; LL. *bachinus*, a bowl; from L. *baca*, a berry; by metonymy, a thing shaped like a berry, hence, bowl.]

1. A vessel or dish of some size, usually circular, rather broad and shallow, used to hold liquids and for various other purposes; a pan.

A silver *basin* full of rose-water. —Shak.

2. The contents of a *basin*; the quantity it will contain.

3. Any reservoir for water, natural or artificial, as a pond, bay, or dock for ships.

4. In glass-grinding, a concave piece of metal with which convex glasses are formed.

5. Among hatters, a large shell or case, usually of iron, on which hats are molded into shape.

6. Any hollow vessel, as the scale of a balance; applied to various forms used in the arts and manufactures.

7. In physical geography, a circular or oval valley, or depression of the surface, the lowest part of which is generally occupied by a lake, or traversed by a river; also, the region drained by a river and its tributaries.

8. In geology, any dipping or disposition of strata toward a common axis or center, due to upheaval and subsidence; sometimes used almost synonymously with *formation*, to express the deposits lying in a certain cavity or depression in older rocks; applied especially to the coal formations, called *coal-basins* or *coal-fields.*

Basinets.
1. Unvizored Basinet, used by infantry.
2. Vizored Basinet, Tower of London.
3. Coroneted Basinet with Camail, Westminster Abbey.

9. In anatomy, a round cavity between the anterior ventricles of the brain; the third ventricle of the brain.

bā'sined (bā'snd), *a.* Situated or confined in a basin.

bas'i-net, bas'net, *n.* [ME. *basinet*; OFr. *bacinet*, dim. of *bacin*, a basin; a helmet basin-shaped.] A small steel cap or helmet, constructed with or without a vizor, in its simplest form somewhat resembling a basin. Spelled also *bascinet*, *basenet*, *bassinet.*

bā″si-oc-cip'i-tăl, *a.* and *n.* [*Basi-*, and L. *occiput*, pl. *occipita*, the occipital bone, from *ob*, against, and *caput*, head.]

I. *a.* Pertaining to the base, or basilar process, of the occipital bone.

II. *n.* The bone, separate in infants, forming in adults the lower part of the occipital.

bā'si-on, *n.* [L. *basis*, a base.] The middle point of that part of the basioccipital bone which forms the anterior border of the great foramen of the human skull.

bā-sip'e-tăl, *a.* [L. *basis*, a base, and *petere*, to seek.] In botany, developing from the top downward, as in compound leaves, or from the center outward, as in certain inflorescence; the reverse of *acropetal.*

bā-sip'ō-dīte, *n.* [*Basi-*, and Gr. *pous*, genit. *podos*, foot.] The joint connecting the limb of a crustacean with its body.

bā-sip-te-ryḡ'i-ăl, *a.* Pertaining to the basipterygium; lying near the base of a fin.

bā-sip-te-ryḡ'i-um, *n.* [*Basi-*, and Gr. *pteryx*, *pterygos*, wing, fin.] In some fishes, one of the main basal cartilages of an embryonic fin, which later forms the metapterygium.

bā-sip-ter'y-goid, *a.* and *n.* [*Basi-*, and Gr. *pterygion*, dim. of *pteryx*, a wing, or fin.]

I. *a.* Pertaining to the base of the sphenoid bone, or the pterygoid process.

II. *n.* The base of the pterygoid bone or the pterygoid process of the sphenoid bone.

bā'sis, *n.*; *pl.* **bā'sēṣ.** [L. *basis*; Gr. *basis*, a base or pedestal, from *bainein*, to go.]

1. The foundation of anything; that on which a thing stands or lies; the bottom or foot of a thing; with reference to material things, *base* is now the commoner word.

2. The groundwork or first principle; that which supports; foundation; as, the charge is without *basis.*

The *basis* of public credit is good faith. —Hamilton.

3. The chief ingredient or component; as, oil constitutes the *basis* of the preparation.

4. In prosody, an introductory foot, usually a trochee, preceding a logaœdic verse; also, the portion of a metrical foot receiving the stress.

5. In chemistry, same as *base.*

6. In architecture, a pedestal or base. [Obs.]

Syn.—Foundation, ground, support, footing, base.

bā-sis'ō-lūte, *a.* [*Basi-*, and L. *solutus*, free.] In botany, extended at the base below the point of origin; applied to some leaves.

bā-si-sphē'noid, bā″si-sphē-noid'ăl (-sfē-), *a.* Pertaining to or situated near the basisphenoid bone.

bā-si-sphē'noid, *n.* [*Basi-*, and Gr. *sphēn*, a wedge, and *eidos*, form.] The posterior part or main body of the sphenoid bone, as distinct from its processes.

bȧsk, *v.i.*; basked, *pt.*, *pp.*; basking, *ppr.* [ME. *basken*, to bask; from Scand. *badhask*, bathe oneself; *badha*, to bathe, and *sk* for *sik*, reflexive pron., oneself.] To lie in warmth; to be exposed to genial heat; to be at ease and thriving under benign influences; as, to *bask* in the blaze of day; to *bask* in the sunshine of royal favor. The word includes the idea of some continuance of exposure.

bȧsk, *v.t.* To warm by continued exposure to heat; to warm with genial heat.

bȧs'ket, *n.* [ME. *basket*; W. *basged*, a basket; of Celtic origin.]

1. A domestic vessel, made of twigs, rushes, thin strips of wood, or other flexible things, interwoven. The forms and sizes of *baskets* are very various, as well as the uses to which they are applied; as, corn-*baskets*, clothes-*baskets*, fruit-*baskets*, and work*baskets.*

2. The contents of a *basket*; as much as a *basket* will contain; as, a *basket* of grapes.

3. In old English stagecoaches, the two outside seats facing one another behind.

4. In architecture, the central portion of the Corinthian capital.

5. In military defenses, a gabion.

6. A basket-hilt.

7. In hat-making, a wickerwork or wire screen of an oval shape for receiving the filaments of hair deposited on it, in the operation of bowing.

bȧs'ket, *v.t.*; basketed, *pt.*, *pp.*; basketing, *ppr.* To put in a basket.

bȧs'ket-bąll, *n.* A game between two opposing parties of players, the object of the play being to toss a large inflated ball into an iron basket or goal at each of the two opposite ends of the room or field; commonly played indoors.

bȧs'ket-fish, *n.* A species of sea-star, or starfish, of the genus *Astrophyton.* It has five rays issuing from an angular body, and dividing into innumerable branches.

bȧs'ket-fụl, *n.*; *pl.* **bȧs'ket-fụlṣ.** The amount a basket will hold.

bȧs'ket-hilt, *n.* A hilt, as of a sword, with a covering wrought like basketwork, to protect the hand.

bȧs'ket-hoop, *n.* A shrub, *Croton lucidus*, native to the West Indies, the bark of which has medicinal properties.

bȧs'ket-pälm (-päm), *n.* The talipot, a palm-tree native to Ceylon and India.

bȧs'ket-ry, *n.* The making of baskets; basketware.

bȧs'ket-wood, *n.* A climbing shrub, *Serjania polyphylla*, having pliable stems used in the making of baskets; found in the West Indies.

bȧs'ket-wŏrk, *n.* Anything made of woven twigs, osiers, or other material, to resemble a basket; wickerwork.

bȧs'ket-wŏrm, *n.* One of various lepidopterous insects which weave a basket or bag of silk, together with bits of leaves and twigs, for protection during the pupal stage; a bag-worm.

bȧsk'ing-shärk, *n.* A species of shark, the *Cetorhinus maximus.* It grows from ten to forty feet in length, is viviparous, and frequents the northern seas; so called from its habit of lying on the surface of the water basking in the sun. It yields a large quantity of oil.

bas'lärd, bas'e-lärd, *n.* [ME. *baselard*; OFr. *basalart*, from *base*, a short knife or saber.] An ornamental dagger worn hanging at the girdle, in front of the person; generally worn in the fifteenth century by those who had pretensions to gentility.

Figure wearing a Baslard.

bas'net, *n.* Same as *Basinet.*

Bā-som-mȧ-toph'ō-rȧ, *n.pl.* [Gr. *basis*, base, *omma*, eye, and *pherein*, to bear.] A group or division of gasteropods of the order *Pulmonifera*, in which the eyes are situated at the base of the tentacles, as in the pond-snail.

bā'sŏn, *n.* A basin. [Obs.]

bā-sō-phil'iç, bā-soph'i-lous, *a.* [Gr. *basis*, base, and *philos*, friendly.] Combining readily with bases; stainable by means of basic dyes.

Bȧsque (bȧsk), *a.* [Fr.] Pertaining to the people or language of Biscay.

Bȧsque, *n.* [Fr.] 1. An individual of a race of people occupying a district of the Pyrenees contiguous to the Bay of Biscay and lying in both France and Spain.

2. The language of the Basques. No connection between it and any other language has as yet been found; it is supposed to represent the tongue of the ancient Iberians, the primitive inhabitants of Spain.

3. [b—] A woman's waist or jacket, usually tight-fitting, and made with or without a short skirt attached; so named because of its resemblance to the costume of the *Basque* women.

bȧs-quine' (-kēn'), **bȧs-quï'nä** (-kē'nyä), *n.* An elaborate outer petticoat worn by Basque women on great occasions. It is also worn in the Spanish provinces adjacent to the Basque district.

Bȧsqu'ish (bȧsk'ish), *a.* Pertaining to the people or language of Biscay. [Obs.]

bȧs-rē-liēf' (bä-rē-leef'), **bȧss-rē-liēf',** *n.* [Fr. *bas-relief*; It. *basso-rilievo*; *basso*, low, and *rilievare*, to raise up.] Low relief; a mode of sculpturing with figures nearly flat; sculpture in which the figures stand out but little from the background.

Bas-relief, from the Elgin Marbles.

In *alto-rilievo*, high relief, the figures project boldly and strongly; in *demi-relief*, half relief, they are given a medium prominence; while in *bas-relief*, low relief, the projection is less than half of the real proportion. Called also *basso-rilievo.*

bȧss, *n.*, *sing.* and *pl.* [ME. *base*, *bace*, bass, a corruption of ME. *barse*, bass; AS. *bærs.*]

1. One of many species of valuable food-fishes of the perch family, especially abundant in the coast and inland waters of the United States. The varieties include the striped bass, *Roccus*

lineatus; the black bass, *Micropterus salmoides*; the sea-bass, *Centropristis atrarius*; the white or silver bass, *Roccus chrysops*; the rock-bass or redeye, and the calico bass.

2. A European food-fish, *Labrax lupus*, called also *sea-dace*, and from its voracity *sea-wolf*.

bȧss, *n.* [A corruption of ME. *bast*; AS. *bæst*, the strong inner bark of various trees.]

1. The American linden or lime-tree; called also *basswood*.

2. The inner fibrous bark of the lime-tree; bast; used in making rope or coarse mats.

3. A coarse mat, originally one made of bast; a hassock.

bāss, *n.* In mining, a dark-colored shale containing considerable carbon.

bāss, *n.* [ME. *base*, *bace*, *bas*; OFr. masc. *bas*, f. *basse*, low, from L. *basis*, a base, a pedestal.]

1. A deep sound; especially in music, a bass tone; the deepest or lowest part in the harmony of a musical composition.

2. A man's voice of the deepest vocal register; also, a singer having such a voice.

3. Any musical instrument adapted to or used in the playing of a bass part.

4. The bass singers or instruments collectively.

bāss, *a.* Deep and grave in tone; also, adapted to or used in the bass.

Bass string; the string of a musical instrument which produces the lowest note.

bāss, *v.t.* To sound in a deep tone. [Rare.]

Bas-sā'li-ȧ, *n.* [LL. *bassus*, low, from L. *basis*, base, from Gr. *basis*, a base, and *halia*, an assembly.] The faunal realm of the deep sea.

Bas-sā'li-ăn, *a.* Pertaining to or found in Bassalia.

bas'set, *n.* [Fr. *bassette*, from It. *bassetta*, basset, f. adj., dim. of *basso*, low.] A game at cards, resembling the modern faro, popular in Europe during the seventeenth and eighteenth centuries.

bas'set, *n.* [Fr., from *bas*, small, low.] A very old breed of dog, used for fox-hunting, and allied to the dachshund; also called *basset-hound*.

bas'set, *n.* [OFr. *basset*, dim. of *bas*, low.] In geology and mining, the outcrop of strata.

bas'set, *v.i.*; basseted, *pt.*, *pp.*; basseting, *ppr.* Among coal-miners, to incline upward. Thus, a vein of coal *bassets*, when it takes a direction toward the surface of the earth.

bas'set, *a.* Inclined upward; as, the *basset* edge of strata.

bas'set-hǫrn, *n.* A musical instrument, blown with a reed, and resembling a clarinet, but of much greater compass, embracing nearly four octaves.

bas'set-ing, *n.* The upward direction of a vein or a stratum.

bas-set'tō, *n.* [It. *bassetto*, somewhat low, dim. of *basso*, low.] A tenor or small bass-viol.

Bas'si-ȧ, *n.* [Named after Ferd. *Bassi*, an Italian botanist of the eighteenth century.] A genus of valuable sapotaceous trees, native to Africa, India, and the Malay peninsula, embracing the gutta-percha and mahwa.

bas'si-net, *n.* [OFr. *bacinet*, dim. of *bacin*, a basin.]

1. A wicker basket with a covering or hood over one end, in which young children are placed, as in a cradle; also, a child's carriage with a wicker top or hood.

2. A kind of helmet. [See *Basinet*.]

bȧs'sō, *n.* [It., from L. *bassus*, low.]

1. In music, the Italian word for bass.

2. One who sings bass.

bȧs'sō-buf'fō, *n.* A bass singer of comic opera.

bȧs'sŏck, *n.* A thick mat; a hassock.

bȧs'sō-cǫn-ti'nū-ō, *n.* Figured bass; thorough-bass.

bas-sǫǫn', *n.* [Fr. *basson*; It. *bassone*, a bassoon; *basso*, low.] A musical wind-instrument, blown with a reed, and furnished with holes, which are stopped as in other large flutes. Its compass comprehends three octaves. It serves for the bass in a concert of oboes, clarinets, etc.

Bassoon.

bas-sǫǫn'ist, *n.* A performer on the bassoon.

bȧs'sō-os-ti-nä'tō, *n.* [It. *basso*, bass, *ostinato*, obstinate; lit. obstinate bass.] Fundamental bass; ground bass; obstinate bass.

bȧs'sō-prō-fon'dō, *n.* [It. *basso*, low, bass, and *profondo*, deep; L. *profundus*, deep.] The deepest-toned bass voice or bass singer.

bȧs'sō-ri-lie'vō (-rē-lyā'vō), *n.* See *Bas-relief*.

bas'sō-rin, *n.* A constituent part of a species of gum from Bassora, a vilayet of Mesopotamia, as also of gum tragacanth, and some gum-resins.

bȧss-rē-liēf', *n.* See *Bas-relief*.

bȧss'wood, *n.* The bass (*Tilia*) or its wood.

bast, *n.* [ME. *bast*, from AS. *bæst*.]

1. The inner bark of the lime-tree, and hence matting or cordage made of the bark of the linden or lime-tree.

2. A thick mat or hassock.

bäs'tȧ, *interj.* [Imper. of It. *bastare*, to stop.] Enough! stop!

bäs'tȧ, *n.* [Sp. *basto*, the ace of clubs.] The queen of spades, the third trump in the Spanish game of solo.

Bas'tä-ard, *n.* One of the Griquas, or half-breeds of South Africa, descended from Dutch fathers and native mothers.

bas'tȧrd, *n.* [ME. *bastard*; OFr. *bastard*, *bastart*, from *bast*, a pack-saddle; equivalent to *fils de bast*, lit. son of a pack-saddle.]

1. A natural child; a child begotten and born out of lawful wedlock; an illegitimate child. By the civil and canon laws, and by the statutes of many of the United States, a *bastard* becomes a legitimate child by the marriage of the parents at any future time. But by the laws of some of the states of the United States, as by those of England, a child, to be legitimate, must at least be born after the lawful marriage.

2. Anything of inferior quality; a mongrel.

3. Specifically, a refuse brown sugar obtained from thin syrups.

4. A large mold for draining sugar.

5. A large, valuable food-fish of Australasia; also called *trumpeter* or *bastard trumpeter*.

bas'tȧrd, *a.* 1. Begotten and born out of lawful matrimony; illegitimate.

2. Spurious; not genuine; false; supposititious; adulterate; as, a *bastard* hope; *bastard* honors.

3. Of unusual size; not conforming to standard measure; as, a *bastard* bolt.

Bastard bar; in heraldry, the baton or bar of bastardy.

Bastard file; a file neither coarse nor medium, but between the grades.

Bastard title; not the true, full, or legitimate title of a book, but a short title on a preceding page.

Bastard type; type whose face is too large or too small for its body.

Bastard wing; in ornithology, a term applied to from three to five quill-like feathers placed on a small joint rising from the middle part of the wing, and corresponding to the thumb in some mammals.

bas'tȧrd, *v.t.*; bastarded, *pt.*, *pp.*; bastarding, *ppr.* To make or show to be a bastard.

bas'tȧrd-ișm, *n.* The state of a bastard.

bas'tȧrd-ize, *v.t.*; bastardized, *pt.*, *pp.*; bastardizing, *ppr.* 1. To make or prove to be a bastard; to convict of being a bastard; to declare, legally, illegitimate.

> The law is so indulgent as not to *bastardize* the child, if born, though not begotten, in lawful wedlock. —Blackstone.

2. To beget illegitimately. [Rare.]

bas'tȧrd-ly, *adv.* In the manner of a bastard; spuriously. [Obs.]

bas'tȧr-dy, *n.* 1. The state of being a bastard, or begotten and born out of lawful wedlock; illegitimacy.

2. The offense of begetting an illegitimate child.

3. A legal proceeding to determine the paternity of a bastard child and compel its father to support it.

bāste, *v.t.*; basted, *pt.*, *pp.*; basting, *ppr.* [Sw. *basa*, to beat with a stick.]

1. To beat with a stick.

2. To drip butter or fat upon, as meat in roasting; to moisten with fat or other liquid.

bāste, *v.t.* [ME. *basten*, from OFr. *bastir*, from O.H.G. *bestan*, to sew, from *bast*; AS. *bæst*, bast, the fibers of which were used for sewing.] To sew with long stitches; to sew slightly.

bas-tīde', *n.* A small fort or a fortified house or tower; a bastile. [Obs.]

bas-tīle', **bas-tille'**, *n.* [ME. *bastile*; Fr. *bastille*; OFr. *bastir*, to build.]

1. A tower or elevated work used for the defense or in the siege of a fortified place. [Obs.]

2. [B—] An old castle in Paris, built in the fourteenth century and long used as a state prison; demolished by the populace July 14, 1789, the anniversary of that date being now observed as a national holiday.

3. A prison.

bas-ti-nāde', *n.* and *v.t.* Same as *Bastinado*.

bas-ti-nā'dō, *n.*; *pl.* **bas-ti-nā'dōeș**. [Fr. *bastonnade*.] A sound beating with a stick or cudgel; the blows given with a stick; particularly, a Turkish and Chinese punishment, consisting of beating an offender on the soles of his feet.

bas-ti-nā'dō, *v.t.* To beat with a stick or cudgel.

bas'tion (-chun), *n.* [Fr. *bastion*; OFr. *bastir*, to build.] In fortification, a huge mass of earth, faced with sods, brick, or stones, standing out from the angles of a fortified work to protect the wall; formerly called a bulwark. It usually consists of two flanks, and two faces. Each flank commands and defends the adjacent curtain, or that portion of the wall extending from one *bastion* to another. The two faces form an acute angle called the salient angle, and command the outworks and ground before the fortification. The distance between the two flanks is the gorge, or entrance into the *bastion*. The use of the *bastion* is to bring every point at the foot of the rampart as much as possible under the guns of the place.

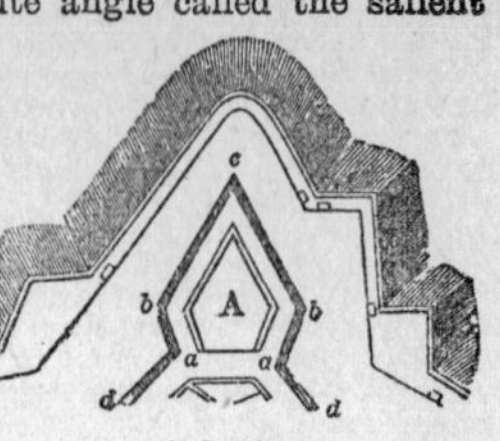

A. Bastion.
a, curtain angle; *b*, shoulder angle; *c*, salient angle; *ab*, flank; *bc*, face; *aa*, gorge; *ad*, part of curtain.

bas'tioned (-chund), *a.* Provided with a bastion or bastions.

bast'nä-site, *n.* A fluocarbonate of the cerium metals, named from *Bastnas*, Sweden, and also occurring in Colorado.

bas'tō, *n.* [Sp.] The ace of clubs in the games of quadrille and omber.

bas'tŏn, *n.* [ME. *baston*; OFr. *baston*, a stick.]

1. A staff; sometimes written *batoon*. [Obs.]

2. Formerly, a royal court officer who bore a painted staff. [Obs.]

3. In heraldry, a staff borne sinister, as a badge of bastardy.

4. In architecture, a round molding at the base of a column; called also *torus*.

Baston.

Bȧ-sū'tōș, *n.pl.* A warlike South African people, divided into many tribes; also called *Bechuanas* and *Sutos*.

bas'yl, **bas'yle**, *n.* [Gr. *basis*, base, and *hylē*, substance, matter.] In chemistry, a term employed to denote any elementary ingredient of a compound, or a constituent which performs the functions of an element; a nonacid or basic element; the electropositive constituent of a salt.

bas'y-lous, *a.* Pertaining to a basyl; basic.

bat, *n.* [OE. *batte*, *botte*; AS. *batt*.]

1. A heavy stick or club; a piece of wood or a wooden instrument with one end thicker or broader than the other, used in the games of baseball, cricket, etc.

2. A term applied by miners to shale or bituminous shale.

3. A sheet of loose cotton prepared for filling quilts or comfortables, or for padding garments; batting.

4. A piece of a brick with one whole end; hence, any part of a brick; a brickbat.

5. A blow; as, a *bat* in the face. [Slang.]

6. A wooden tool used in dressing and flattening sheet lead.

7. In hat-making, a felted mass of fur or wool; also spelled *batt*.

At the bat; in the position of the batsman.

To go on a bat; to go on a protracted spree or debauch. [Slang.]

bat, *v.t.*; batted, *pt.*, *pp.*; batting, *ppr.* 1. To strike or hit with a bat or pole.

2. To wink or flutter; as, to *bat* the eyes; the bird *bats* its wings.

bat, *v.i.* To manage a bat, or use one.

bat, *n.* [Corruption of *back*; ME. *bakke*, from Dan. in compounds *aften-bakke*, evening-bat, from Ice. *blaka*, to flutter, flap.] One of the *Chiroptera*, an order of flying mammalia, divided into several distinct genera. The fore feet have the toes connected by membranes, expanded into elongated wings, by means of which the animals fly. The species are numerous. [See *Chiroptera*.]

Greater Horseshoe Bat (*Rhinolophus ferrumequinum*).

bāt'ȧ-ble, *a.* Disputable. [Obs.]

bat'āiled, *a.* Having embrasures like a battlement. [Obs.]

bä-tä'rȧ, *n.* [S. Am.] A species of bush-shrike.

bȧ-tär-deau' (-dō'), *n.* [Fr. *battre*, to repel, and *eau*, water.] A coffer-dam; a defensive wall built across a ditch, and having a sluice-gate.

bȧ-tä'tȧ, *n.* The aboriginal American name of the sweet potato.

Bȧ-tā'vi-ăn, *a.* [L. *Batavi*, the people who inhabited the isle by that name.] Pertaining to ancient Batavia, an island in Holland, between the Rhine and the Waal; hence, pertaining to the Netherlands or the Dutch; also, pertaining to Batavia, chief city of Java, a Dutch possession.

Bă-tā′vi-ăn, *n.* A native of Batavia, or of the Netherlands. [Rare.]

bat′-bōlt, *n.* A bolt barbed or jagged at its butt or tang to give it a firmer hold.

batch (bach), *n.* [ME. *bacche, batche,* from AS. *bacan,* to bake.]

1. The quantity of bread baked at one time; a baking of bread.

2. Any quantity of a thing made at once, or so united as to have like qualities; as, a *batch* of new colonels; a *batch* of bills.

bāte, *n.* Strife; contention; debate. [Obs.]

bāte, *v.t.*; bated, *pt., pp.*; bating, *ppr.* [ME. *baten*; OFr. *batre,* to beat; L. *batuere,* to beat, strike.]

1. To lessen by retrenching, deducting, or reducing; to beat down; to lessen; to abate; as, to *bate* the laborer's wages.

2. To deduct in abatement; as, to *bate* the price.

bāte, *v.i.* To grow or become less; to remit or retrench a part; with *of.*

Abate thy speed, and I will *bate of* mine. —Dryden.

bāte, *v.t.* To attack; to bait. [Obs.]

bāte, *v.i.* To flutter, as a sparrow-hawk. [Obs.]

bāte, *n.* An alkaline solution of chemicals or manure, used in the preparation of hides and skins.

bāte, *v.t.* To soak or steep in bate, as hides in the process of making leather.

bȧ-teau′ (bȧ-tō′), *n.*; *pl.* **bȧ-teaux′** (-tōz′). [Fr. *bateau*; OFr. *batel,* boat.]

1. A long light boat, wider in the middle than at the ends.

2. A bridge-pontoon.

bāte′-breed″ing, *a.* Breeding strife. [Obs.]

bāt′ed, *a.* Restrained; checked; lowered; used especially in the phrase, with *bated* breath.

bāte′fụl, *a.* Contentious; given to strife; exciting contention.

bāte′less, *a.* Not to be abated. [Obs.]

bāte′ment, *n.* Abatement; deduction; diminution.

bāte′ment-light, *n.* A window, or part of a window, with lower edge cut to fit a staircase; an arch, etc.

bat′fish, *n.* 1. A fish of the genus *Malthe,* especially *Malthe vespertilio* of the southern Atlantic coast.

2. The flying robin or gurnard, *Cephalacanthus volitans* of the Atlantic.

3. The sting-ray of the Pacific coast.

bat′fowl″ēr, *n.* One who practises batfowling.

bat′fowl″ing, *n.* A mode of catching birds at night, by holding a torch or other light, and beating the bush or perch where they roost. The birds, flying to the light, are caught with nets or otherwise.

bat′fụl, *a.* Rich; fertile; said of land. [Obs.]

bȧth, *n.*; *pl.* **bȧths.** [AS. *bæth,* a bath.]

1. A place for bathing; a convenient receptacle of water for persons to plunge into or wash their bodies in; as, a porcelain *bath*; swimming-*bath.*

2. A building or apartment for the use of bathers, and containing receptacles for hot or cold water.

3. The act of immersing or showering and washing the body or part of the body in hot or cold water for the sake of cleanliness, health, and comfort; also, the act of exposing the body, as a medical or hygienic measure, to steam, vapor, hot air, etc.; as, to take a hot *bath,* a medicated *bath.*

4. Figuratively, exposure of the body to action of the sun, the wind, etc.; as, I sat beside my cottage door taking a sun-*bath.*

5. Any arrangement, preparation, or solution for the immersion of an object; as, the silver-*bath* used in photography.

6. In chemistry, any medium through which heat may be applied to a body, as hot sand, steam, ashes, oil, etc.; also, the apparatus with which heat is applied.

7. Water or other liquid prepared for bathing; as, your *bath* is ready.

Dry bath; a bath of hot sand or other heated material applied to the body.

Electric bath; a bath in which a current of electricity is passed through the water.

Russian bath; a bath taken in an apartment filled with steam or vapor in which the body perspires freely.

Sitz bath; a bath in which only the parts of the body about the hips are immersed.

Turkish bath; a kind of bath taken in several stages, the body being first exposed to the action of hot air in an apartment specially constructed for the purpose. This induces profuse perspiration, and then, in a cooler atmosphere, the body is thoroughly rubbed and shampooed, the bath being usually concluded with a plunge into a tank or pool of tepid water, followed by a period of gradual cooling in an apartment of suitable temperature.

Order of the Bath; an order of British knighthood conferred upon persons who distinguish themselves in civil and military life. It is supposed to have been originally instituted in 1399, and received its name from the fact that candidates for initiation were placed in a bath to denote their purification from all evil before joining the order. There are three classes in the order: knights companions, knights commanders, and knights grand cross; the members being entitled to use after their names the initials C. B., K. C. B., and G. C. B. respectively. The badge (fig. 1) is a golden cross of eight points, with the lion of England between the four principal angles, and having in the center the rose, thistle, and shamrock. Stars are also worn by the two first classes. That of the knights grand cross (fig. 2) is of silver, with eight points of rays wavy, on which is a gold cross bearing three crowns.

bȧth, *n.* [Heb.] A measure of the ancient Hebrews, containing the tenth of a homer, if used for liquids; and less if for a dry measure.

Bȧth, *n.* A city in the county of Somerset, England, famous for its hot springs and medicinal baths. It has given its name to numerous objects, as *Bath* chair, *Bath* stone, *Bath* brick, etc.

Bath brick; a fine calcareous earth, molded in the shape of a brick, used for cleaning polished metal, etc.; originally found near Bath.

Bath chair; a kind of wheel-chair for invalids; first used at Bath.

Bath metal; a variety of brass which is an alloy of zinc and copper, consisting of four and one-half ounces of the former to one pound of the latter.

Bath note; a kind of folio writing-paper measuring, when opened, eight and one-half by fourteen inches.

Bath stone; a creamy limestone found near Bath, very easily quarried and used in England for building since the twelfth century.

bāthe, *v.t.*; bathed, *pt., pp.*; bathing, *ppr.* [ME. *bathien*; AS. *bathian,* to bathe.]

1. To wash by immersion, as in a bath.

2. To wash or moisten, for the purpose of making soft and supple, or for cleansing, as a wound.

3. To moisten or suffuse with a liquid.

Her bosom *bathed* in blood. —Dryden.

4. To apply water or other liquid to, for healing or soothing; as, to *bathe* the hands with oil.

5. To lave; to wash; as, waters *bathing* the foot of a mountain.

6. To suffuse or envelop, as with a liquid; as, the moonlight *bathed* the plain.

bāthe, *v.i.* To be or lie in a bath; to be in water, or in other liquid, or to be immersed in a fluid, as in a bath; as, to *bathe* in fiery floods.

bāthe, *n.* The immersion of the body in water; a swim; as, to take one's usual *bathe.*

bāth′ēr, *n.* One who bathes.

bath′ēr, *v.i.* To bathe or rub in dust, as some birds do.

bȧ-thet′iç, *a.* Of, pertaining to, or of the nature of bathos.

bȧth′-house, *n.* A house or building set apart for bathing purposes.

bath′iç, *a.* [Gr. *bathys,* deep.] Deep; pertaining to the depths of the sea.

bāth′ing, *n.* The act of taking a bath, or washing oneself or another; used especially in compounds; as, a *bathing*-suit, etc.

bath′mișm, *n.* [Gr. *bathmos,* a step or stair, from *bainein,* to go, to step.] The power of growth as one of the vital forces; growth-force.

bath′mō-dont, *a.* [Gr. *bathmos,* step, and *odous,* tooth.] Having the upper molars ranged obliquely.

bath′ō-lith, bath′ō-līte, *n.* Same as *Bathylith.*

bȧ-thom′e-tēr, *n.* [Gr. *bathos,* depth, and *metron,* a measure.] An instrument for taking depths or soundings, consisting of a peculiarly constructed spring-balance, instead of a sounding-line.

bat′hörse, *n.* A horse formerly allowed a batman, in the British army, for conveying the utensils in his charge; a horse employed to carry an officer's baggage; a packhorse.

bā′thos, *n.* [Gr. *bathos,* depth.] A ludicrous descent from the elevated to the commonplace, in writing or speech; an anticlimax.

bȧth′-tub, *n.* A receptacle for water for bathing purposes.

bath′y-. A combining form from Greek *bathys,* deep, and signifying deep, or of the deep.

bȧ-thyb′i-ăn, *a.* Of or pertaining to bathybius.

bȧ-thyb′iç, *a.* Pertaining to, native to, or living in the deep waters.

bȧ-thyb′i-us, *n.* [*Bathy-,* and Gr. *bios,* life.] A gelatinous substance of chemical origin, found in deep-sea mud; once supposed by Huxley to be living protoplasm.

bath-y-çol′pi-ăn, *a.* [*Bathy-,* and Gr. *kolpos,* bosom.] Deep-bosomed.

bath′y-lith, bath′y-līte, *n.* [*Bathy-,* and Gr. *lithos,* a stone.] A mass of compact igneous rock which has forced itself in a dome-like form from a lower position to an overlying stratum.

bath-y-lith′iç, bath-y-lit′iç, *a.* Pertaining to a bathylith.

bȧ-thym′e-tēr, *n.* Same as *Bathometer.*

bath-y-met′riç, bath-y-met′riç-ăl, *a.* Pertaining to bathymetry.

bȧ-thym′e-try, *n.* [*Bathy-,* and Gr. *metron,* a measure.] The science of measuring depths; the art of deep-sea sounding.

Bȧ-tid′ē-æ, *n.pl.* A natural order instituted by Martius for the *Batis maritima,* a succulent shrub growing in salt marshes in the West Indies, sometimes used in West India pickles.

bä tïk′ (Malay, bātik). A process for coloring fabrics, originating among Dutch East-Indian natives, and now used in Europe for velvet, velour, etc., in which the design is covered with melted wax and the uncovered portions dyed, the wax then being dissolved in boiling water.

bāt′ing, *prep.* Abating; taking away; deducting; excepting.

Bā′tis, *n.* [Gr. *batis,* the prickly roach, a kind of plant.] A monotypic genus of saline plants containing a single species. [See *Batideæ.*]

bȧ-tïste′, *n.* [Fr. *batiste*; OFr. *baptiste,* so called from its alleged first maker, *Baptiste.*] A kind of cambric, lawn, or fine linen; also applied to cotton cloth of fine texture, and sometimes to a thin, fine woolen cloth.

bat′lēr, bat′let, *n.* A small bat, or square piece of wood with a handle, for beating clothes in washing them.

bat′man, *n.* [Turk.] A weight used in Smyrna and other places in the East, varying according to the locality.

bat′măn, *n.*; *pl.* **bat′men.** [Fr. *bât,* a pack-saddle.] A person formerly allowed to each company of the British army, on foreign service, who had charge of the cooking utensils; now, a military servant.

Bȧ-toi′dē-i, *n.pl.* [Gr. *batos,* a kind of ray, and *eidos,* form.] A suborder of the division *Selachii,* which includes flatfishes such as rays and skates.

bat′ŏn (*or* bȧ-ton′ *or Fr.* bä-tọṅ′), *n.* [Fr.]

1. A staff or truncheon.

2. A field-marshal's staff; a badge of the highest military honor.

3. The badge or truncheon of inferior officers of justice; as, the *baton* of a constable.

4. The staff used by the conductor of an orchestra, band, or choir, to direct the musicians or singers and mark the time.

5. In heraldry, an ordinary, borne sinister, as a mark of bastardy; called also *bastard bar.*

bat′-print″ing, *n.* The process of printing on glazed ware with a gelatinous pad upon which the pattern has been stamped.

Bȧ-trā′çhi-ȧ, *n.pl.* [Gr. *batrachos,* a frog.] An order of reptiles having naked bodies, and two or four feet; including frogs, toads, salamanders, etc.

bȧ-trā′çhi-ăn, *a.* Pertaining to animals of the order *Batrachia.*

bȧ-trā′çhi-ăn, *n.* An animal of the order *Batrachia.*

bat′rȧ-çhīte, *n.* [Gr. *batrachos,* a frog.] A fossil or stone in color resembling a frog.

bat′rȧ-çhoid, *a.* [Gr. *batrachos,* a frog, and *eidos,* form.] Having the form of a frog.

Bat″rȧ-çhō-my̆-om′ȧ-çhy, *n.* [Gr. *batrachos,* frog; *mys,* mouse; and *machē,* battle.] An ancient Greek parody on the Iliad, of uncertain authorship and describing a battle between the frogs and mice.

bat-rȧ-çhoph′ȧ-gous, *a.* [Gr. *batrachos,* frog, and *phagein,* to eat.] Feeding on frogs.

bats′măn, *n.*; *pl.* **bats′men.** The player who wields the bat, or strikes or bats the ball, in baseball, cricket, and similar games.

bat′tä, *n.* [Anglo-Ind., from Hind. *batta, bhata,* allowance for maintenance.]

1. Rate or difference of exchange; the discount on coins which are not in circulation. [India.]

2. Extra allowance, as to English troops serving in India.

bat′tȧ-ble, *a.* Capable of cultivation. [Obs.]

bat′tāil-ănt, *n.* A combatant. [Obs.]

bat′tāil-ous, *a.* Warlike; having the form or appearance of an army arrayed for battle; marshaled, as for an attack. [Obs.]

bat-tāl′iȧ (-yȧ), *n.* [It. *battaglia,* battle.]

1. Order of battle; troops arrayed in their proper brigades, regiments, battalions, etc., as for action. [Obs.]

2. The main body of an army in array, distinguished from the wings. [Obs.]

bat-tal′ion (-yun), *n.* [Fr. *bataillon*; It. *battaglione,* battalion.]

1. An army in battle array or a division of an army in order of battle. [Obs.]

2. A body of troops, consisting of two or more companies paraded together or serving together.

3. In the United States army, a body made up of four companies of infantry; three *battalions* constitute a regiment.

bat'tel (bat'tl), *n.* Battle. [Obs.]

bat'tel, *v.i.* [College slang; of uncertain origin.]

1. To grow fat. [Obs.]

2. To stand indebted on the college books at Oxford for provisions and drink from the buttery.

bat'tel, *v.t.* To render fertile; to batten. [Obs.]

bat'tel, *a.* Fertile; fruitful. [Obs.]

bat'tel-ēr, bat'tlēr, *n.* At Oxford university, one who battels.

batte'ment, *n.* [Fr. *battre*, to beat.] A beating; striking; impulse. [Obs.]

bat'ten (bat'tn), *v.t.*; battened, *pt.*, *pp.*; battening, *ppr.* [Ice. *batna*, to improve.]

1. To fatten; to make fat; to make plump by plenteous feeding.

2. To fill with nourishment or enrich, as land.

bat'ten, *v.i.* To grow or become fat; to live in luxury, or to grow fat in ease and luxury.

bat'ten, *n.* [Fr. *bâton*, a stick.]

1. A long piece of sawed wood; a scantling. The *battens* of commerce are seven inches broad and two and one-half inches thick; split into two boards, each one and one-fourth inches thick, they are used for flooring; and split into three, for putting on roofs, wainscot, and as uprights for lathing.

2. A nautical term for one of several thin pieces of oak or fir, nailed to the masthead, and to the midship post of the yard.

3. In weaving, the swinging bar which drives the weft firmly into the warp.

Batten door; a door of boards held in position by cleats of battens.

bat'ten, *v.t.* To furnish or fasten with battens.

To batten down; to fasten down with battens, as the hatches of a ship during a storm.

bat'ten-ing, *n.* 1. A number of battens.

2. The operation of fixing battens to a wall for nailing laths upon.

bat'tēr, *v.t.*; battered, *pt.*, *pp.*; battering, *ppr.* [ME. *bateren*, from OFr. *batre*, from LL. *battere*, from L. *batuere*, to beat.]

1. To beat with successive blows; to beat repeatedly with violence, so as to bruise, shake, or demolish; as, to *batter* a wall.

2. To wear or impair, as by beating or by use; as, a *battered* jade.

3. In welding, to beat in order to widen, as a piece of metal.

bat'tēr, *n.* 1. In cookery, a mixture of two or more ingredients, as flour, eggs, salt, etc., beaten together into a semi-liquid consistence.

2. In printing, a defect in a form of type or a plate, caused by bruising.

3. A Scotch term for paste.

bat'tēr, *n.* A backward and upward slope in the face of a wall.

Batter rule; an instrument for determining the slope of a wall.

bat'tēr, *v.i.* In architecture, to slope gently backward.

bat'tēr, *n.* One who bats; a batsman.

bat'tēr-ēr, *n.* One who batters or beats.

bat'tēr-ing-ram, *n.* 1. In ancient times, a military engine used to beat down the walls of besieged places. It was generally a large beam, with a head of iron somewhat resembling the head of a ram, whence its name.

Battering-ram.

2. A blacksmith's hammer, swinging horizontally, used for heavy work.

bat'tēr-ing-trāin, *n.* A train of artillery for siege purposes.

bat'tēr-y, *n.* [Fr. *batterie*, battery, from *battre*, to beat; L. *batuere*, to beat.]

1. The act of battering; attack or assault, with the view of beating down. [Obs.]

2. In law, the beating or forcible touching of another's person in anger.

3. The instrument or agency employed in battering or attacking; as, a *battery* of guns; a *battery* of abuse.

4. In military affairs, (a) a body of artillery for field operations consisting generally of from four to eight guns, with its complement of wagons, artillerymen, etc.; (b) the armament, or part of the armament of a warship.

5. The personnel or complement of officers and men attached to a *battery* of artillery.

6. In fortification, a parapet thrown up to cover the gunners and others employed about them from the enemy's shot, with the guns employed.

7. In baseball, the pitcher and catcher.

8. In manufacturing or the arts, any series of similar parts arranged for a certain purpose or process; as, a *battery* of ore-crushers; a *battery* of prisms, condensers, or boilers.

9. In hat-making, a vat for boiling material in dilute sulphuric acid.

10. Metal objects or utensils collectively; as, a *battery* of dishes.

11. A hunting-boat showing little above the water.

12. In mining, (a) a working platform; (b) a brace.

13. In electricity, (a) a plurality of generators of electric energy so connected as to act as a single source of difference of potential and of current; specifically, a number of galvanic cells or couples, the electrodes of which are so interconnected as to act on the external circuit as one cell, whose electromotive force will vary according to the method of connecting the cells. In the general sense, a *battery* may have as its units galvanic cells, secondary or storage cells, dynamos, thermoelectric couples, or even Leyden jars. In the last case, the *battery* can produce only a joint discharge and is then a source of only momentary electric currents; also, (b) a single galvanic cell or element: a common, but incorrect, use of the word.

Barbette battery; see under *Barbette*.

Bunsen battery; an electrical battery in which the carbon of gas coke is used with zinc, instead of copper or platinum; also called *carbon battery*.

In battery; placed in position and ready for firing; said of a gun.

Masked battery; a concealed battery.

Out of battery or *from battery*; withdrawn from action, as for loading.

Storage or *secondary battery*; in electricity, any combination of storage cells; an accumulator.

bat'tēr-y-gun, *n.* A repeating gun; a machine gun.

bat'ting, *n.* 1. The management of a bat at play; the act of a batter.

2. Cotton in sheets, prepared for use in making quilts or bed-covers.

bat'tle (-tl), *n.* [ME. *batel*, *batelle*, from OFr. *bataille*, battle, from LL. *battere*; L. *batuere*, to beat, to fight.]

1. The act of fighting or struggling; an encounter; an engagement, either between large bodies of men or between individuals; figuratively, anything in the nature of a struggle or contest; as, the *battle* of life.

2. A division of an army or the main body itself. [Obs.]

Battle royal; a battle with fists or cudgels, in which more than two are engaged; a melée. The term is also applied to a fight of gamecocks, in which more than two are engaged.

Drawn battle; one in which neither party gains the victory.

Pitched battle; one in which the parties were previously drawn up in regular and threatening formation.

To give battle; to attack the enemy.

To join battle; to counter-attack; to meet in battle.

Wager of battle; see under *Wager*, n.

Syn.—Fight, combat, engagement, conflict.—*Battle* embraces all the movements and maneuvers in face of the enemy, as well as the actual contact of the soldiery, and implies premeditation. It is the appropriate word for great engagements; as, the *battle* of Manila Bay. *Fight* has reference to actual conflict; a man may take part in a *battle*, and have no share in the *fighting*. A *battle* may be made up of many subordinate *fights*; as, the *battle* of Gettysburg and the *fight* for Little Round Top. *Combat* is a word of greater dignity than *fight*, but agrees with it in denoting close encounter. *Engagement* supposes distinctly organized bodies engaged in contact with the enemy. *Conflict*, literally a clashing together, implies fierce physical encounter.

bat'tle, *v.i.*; battled, *pt.*, *pp.*; battling, *ppr.* [ME. *batailen*, *batailen*; OFr. *batailler*, to join battle; from L. *batuere*, to strike.] To join in battle; to contend in fight.

bat'tle, *v.t.* To attack in battle; to cover with armed force.

bat'tle-ax, bat'tle-axe, *n.* A kind of broadax used in ancient times as a weapon of war.

bat'tled (-t'ld), *a.* 1. Furnished or strengthened with battlements.

2. In heraldry, a term employed when the chief, chevron, fesse, etc., is borne in the form of the battlements of a castle.

bat'tle-dōre, bat'tle-door, *n.* [OE. *batyldoure*, a beetle or wooden bat used in washing clothes.]

1. An instrument of play, with a handle and a flat board or palm, used to strike a ball or shuttlecock; a racket; also, the game so played.

2. A child's hornbook; so called from its shape. [Obs.]

bat'tle-ment, *n.* [ME. *batelment*; OFr. *bastiller*, to fortify.] A notched or indented parapet, formed by a series of rising parts called cops or merlons, separated by openings called crenelles or embrasures. *Battlements* were originally military, but were afterward used freely in ecclesiastical and civil buildings by way of ornament, both on parapets and on cornices, tabernacle-work, transoms of windows, etc.

Battlemented Parapet.
aa, Merlons. *bb*, Embrasures.

bat'tle-ment-ed, *a.* Having battlements.

bat'tle-plane″, *n.* An aeroplane which carries machine-guns, etc., for fighting purposes.

bat'tle-range, *n.* The effective firing distance for small arms.

bat'tle-ship, *n.* A warship of the first class, carrying the heaviest armor and guns; corresponding to the former *line-of-battle ship*.

bat-tol'ō-gist, *n.* One who uses battology. [Rare.]

bat-tol'ō-gize, *v.t.* To use battology.

bat-tol'ō-gy, *n.* [Gr. *battologein*, to stammer, from *battos*, a stammerer, and *legein*, to speak.] A needless repetition of words in speaking or writing.

bat'tŏn, *n.* A baton or a batten. [Obs.]

bat'tūe, *n.* [Fr., pp. f. of *battre*, to beat.]

1. A hunt conducted by driving game from cover to a place within reach of waiting sportsmen.

2. Any kind of reckless or wanton slaughter of the weak or unresisting.

bat-tūre', *n.* [Fr., from *battre*, to beat.] An elevated portion of a river- or sea-bottom, at times not submerged.

bat-tū'tā, *n.* [It., from *battere*, to beat.] In music, the measuring of time by beating; a measure; a bar.

bat'ty, *a.* Pertaining to or like a bat.

bat'ūle, *n.* A springboard used by acrobats in leaping and vaulting.

batz, *n.*; *pl.* **bat'zen.** [G., a coin having the image of a bear, from *bätz*, a bear.] A small copper coin with a mixture of silver, formerly current in some parts of Germany and Switzerland, and worth about four cents.

bau-bee', *n.* See *Bawbee*.

bau'ble, *n.* [ME. *bable*; OFr. *babel*, *baubel*, a toy.]

1. A short stick with a fool's head, frequently ornamented with asses' ears, fantastically carved on it, anciently carried by the fools attached to courts and great houses. It frequently had at the other end a flapper with which they pretended to belabor people.

> The kynges foole
> Sate by the fire upon a stoole,
> As he that with his *bauble* plaide.
> —Gower.

Fool's Bauble.

2. A trifling piece of finery; that which is gay or showy without real value; a gewgaw; a trifle.

bau'bling, *a.* [Obs.] See *Bawbling*.

baugh, *a.* [Scot. and Prov. Eng.] Poor; weak; without strength; distasteful; also spelled *baugh*.

bau'dē-kin, *n.* [ME. *baudkin*; OFr. *baudekin*; It. *baldacchino*.] A rich kind of cloth for garments used by the nobility of the middle ages, and composed of silk interwoven with threads of gold. Spelled also *baudkin*, *bawdekin*, *bawdkyn*, and *baldakin*.

bau'drick, *n.* A belt. [See *Baldric*.]

Bau-hin'i-ȧ, *n.* [From Jean and Caspar *Bauhin*, noted Swiss botanists.] A genus of leguminous tropical plants, usually twining and conspicuous.

baulk, *n.* and *v.* Same as *Balk*.

baun'scheidt-ism, *n.* [Named after Karl *Baunscheidt*, who introduced it.] A method of treating rheumatism by counter-irritation, by pricking the affected part with needles dipped in an irritant.

bau'sŏn, *n.* An old name for the badger, sometimes applied to a fat or ponderous person; also written *bawsin*, *bawson*.

baux'ite (bōks'-), **beaux'ite** (bōks'-), *n.* [Fr., from *Baux* or *Beaux*, near Arles.] A clay containing about one-third of its weight of alumina, with silica, iron, and water.

Bā-vā'ri-ăn, *a.* and *n.* I. *a.* Of or pertaining to Bavaria.

II. *n.* A native or inhabitant of Bavaria.

bav'ȧ-roy, *n.* [Fr. *bavarois*, Bavarian.] A kind of cloak or surtout. [Obs.]

bā'vi-ăn, *n.* [OE. *babewin*, baboon.] A baboon.

bav'in, *n.* A piece of waste wood or stick; a fagot. [Prov. Eng.]

bav'in, *n.* Limestone containing impurities. [Prov. Eng.]

baw-bee', *n.* A halfpenny. In the plural, money; cash. [Scot. and Prov. Eng.]

baw'ble, *n.* Same as *Bauble*.

bawb'ling, *a.* Trifling; contemptible. [Obs.]

baw'cock, *n.* A fine fellow. [Obs.]

bawd, *n.* [ME. *baude*, a lewd person; OFr. *baud*, from O.H.G. *bald*, bold.] A procurer or procuress; a person who keeps a house of prostitution, and conducts criminal intrigues; a lewd person.

bawd, *v.i.* 1. To procure; to provide women for lewd purposes.

2. To befoul or dirty. [Obs.]

bawd′i-ly, *adv.* Obscenely; lewdly.

bawd′i-ness, *n.* Obscenity; lewdness.

bawd′rick, *n.* A belt.

bawd′ry, *n.* 1. The acts or practice of a procurer or bawd.

2. Obscenity; filthy, unchaste language.

3. Illicit intercourse; fornication.

bawd′y, *a.* Obscene; filthy; unchaste; applied to language.

bawd′y-house, *n.* A house of ill fame.

baw′hŏrse, *n.* Same as *Bathorse.*

bawl, *v.i.*; bawled, *pt.*, *pp.*; bawling, *ppr.* [ME. *baul*; Ice. *baula*, to low, as a cow.]

1. To cry out with a loud, full sound; to hoot; to cry with vehemence, as in calling, or in pain or exultation.

2. To cry aloud, as a child from pain or vexation.

Syn.—Shout, vociferate, halloo, roar, bellow.

bawl, *v.t.* To proclaim by outcry, as a common crier.

bawl, *n.* A loud, prolonged cry; an outcry.

bawl′ẽr, *n.* One who bawls.

bawn, *n.* An inclosure with mud or stone walls for keeping cattle; a fortification. [Obs.]

baw′rel, *n.* A kind of hawk. [Obs.]

baw′sin, baw′sŏn, *n.* [Obs.] See *Bauson.*

bax′tẽr, *n.* [ME. *baxter*, *bakestre*; AS. *bæcestre*, a baker.] A baker; formerly a female baker.

Bax-tē′ri-ăn, *a.* Pertaining to Baxter, a celebrated English divine; as, the *Baxterian* scheme.

bāy, *a.* [Fr. *bai*; L. *badius*, bay.] Red, or reddish, inclining to a chestnut color; applied to the color of horses.

bāy, *n.* [Fr. *baie*; LL. *baia*, bay.]

1. An arm of the sea, extending into the land, not of any definite form, but smaller than a gulf, and larger than a creek. The name, however, is not used with much precision, and is often applied to large tracts of water around which the land forms a curve, as Hudson's *Bay.* Nor is the name restricted to tracts of water with a narrow entrance, but it is used for any recess or inlet between capes or headlands, as the *Bay* of Biscay.

2. A pond-head, or a pond formed by a dam for the purpose of driving mill-wheels.

3. A place for storing hay or grain in a barn.

4. Any large division in a structure or building, as the space between two piers of a bridge; the space for a window between mullions, or the space between beams in a ceiling.

5. An anchorage or roadstead for ships; a harbor.

bāy, *n.* [OFr. *baie*, *baye*, a berry; L. *baca*, a berry.]

1. The laurel-tree, *Laurus nobilis.*

2. An honorary garland or crown, bestowed as a prize for victory or excellence, anciently made or consisting of branches of the laurel; in this sense, chiefly used in the plural.

> Beneath his reign shall Eusden wear the *bays.*
> —Pope.

bāy, *n.* A bay horse.

bāy, *v.i.*; bayed, *pt.*, *pp.*; baying, *ppr* [ME. *bayen*; OFr. *bayer*, to bark.] To bark, as a dog at his game; especially, to bark with a deep sound.

bāy, *v.t.* 1. To bark at; to follow with barking.

2. To drive to a stand; to bring to bay; as, to *bay* the wolf.

3. To express by barking.

> 'Tis sweet to hear the watchdog's honest bark
> *Bay* deep-mouthed welcome as we draw near home. —Byron.

bāy, *n.* [ME. *bay*, *abay*; OFr. *abai*; Fr. *aboi*, a barking.]

1. A long, deep cry or bark.

2. The turning of a hunted animal when it makes its last stand against its foe; as, the stag stood at *bay.*

3. The state of being kept at a standstill, or of being warded off, by an enemy.

bāy, *v.t.* To bathe. [Obs.]

bāy, *v.t.* To dam up or back, as water.

bä′yä, *n.* [Native name.] The East Indian weaver-bird, *Ploceus phi′ippinus*, a passerine remarkable for its curious nest, which resembles a bottle.

bā-yȧ-dēre′, *n.* [Fr. *bayadère*; Port. *bailadeira*, a dancer.] A female dancer in British India, resembling a nautch-girl.

bȧ-yä′mo, *n.* [Cuban.] A storm peculiar to the vicinity of Bayamo on the south coast of Cuba, consisting of violent gusts of wind, accompanied by thunder, lightning, and rain.

bāy′-ant″lẽr, *n.* The second prong of a stag's horn.

bāy′ärd, *n.* [OFr. *bayard*, *baiard*, a bay horse.]

1. A bay horse; a horse of any color. [Obs.]

2. An unmannerly beholder. [Obs.]

bāy′ärd-ly, *a.* Blind; stupid. [Obs.]

bāy′ber″ry, *n.* The fruit of the bay-tree or *Laurus nobilis*; also applied to the fruit of *Myrica cerifera* (wax-myrtle), and to the plant itself.

bāy′ber-ry-tal″lōw, *n.* A waxy substance obtained from the bayberry, or wax-myrtle; called also *myrtle-wax.*

bāy′bōlt, *n.* A bolt having a sharp-pointed shank.

bāyed (bād), *a.* Having bays, as a building.

bāy′-gall, *n.* In the southern states, a kind of watercourse overspread with soft earth and fibrous matter, the whole mass being strongly impregnated with acid.

bāy′-ice, *n.* See under *Ice.*

bāy′-lēaf, *n.* The leaf of the laurel.

bāy′măn, *n.*; *pl.* **bāy′men.** Aboard a man-of-war, a nurse in the sick-bay; specifically, a hospital apprentice.

bāy′ō-net, *n.* [Fr. *bayonnette*; so called because the first bayonets were made at *Bayonne.*]

1. A short, pointed weapon of iron, or a broad dagger, made with an iron handle and ring, which go over the muzzle of a rifle.

1. Common bayonet.
2. Sword-bayonet.

2. In machinery, a term applied to pins which play in and out of holes made to receive them, and which thus serve to engage or disengage parts of the machinery.

bāy′ō-net, *v.t.*; bayoneted, *pt.*, *pp.*; bayoneting, *ppr.* 1. To stab with a bayonet.

2. To compel or drive by the bayonet.

bāy′ō-net-clutch (-kluch), *n.* In machinery, a form of clutch armed usually with two prongs, *a a*, which, in gear, act on the ends or lugs of a friction-strap *b*, fitted on a side-boss of the wheel to be driven, and which is loose on the same shaft. The clutch is attached to the shaft by a feather-key, and when drawn back or out of gear with the strap the wheel remains at rest, and the clutch continues to revolve with the shaft. When it is required to set the machinery again in motion, the clutch is thrown forward by the fork *c*, and its prongs, engaging with the strap, gradually put the wheel in motion.

Bayonet-clutch.

bāy′ou (bȳ′ö), *n.* [Corruption of Fr. *boyau*, a gut, a long, narrow passage.] In Louisiana, the outlet of a lake; a channel for water. Also, one of the outlets from the Mississippi, in the delta of that river, to the Gulf of Mexico. The term is also applied to other lateral outlets from the river, apparently constituting its former channel.

bāy′-rum′, *n.* A liquid obtained by distilling the leaves of the bay-tree, and in very common use as a cosmetic and lotion.

bāys, bāyze, *n.* See *Baize.*

bāy′-salt, *n.* A general term for coarse-grained salt, but properly applied to salt obtained by spontaneous or natural evaporation of seawater in large shallow tanks or *bays.*

bāy′-tree, *n.* The bay, a species of laurel; the *Laurus nobilis.*

bāy′-win′dōw, *n.* A window built in an angular form from the ground up and projecting from the wall, in stores or dwellings, forming a bay or recess in the room back of it. The name is often popularly given to *bow-* and *oriel-windows.*

Interior of a Bay-window.

bāy′-wood, *n.* A kind of mahogany, particularly that from Campêche Bay and Honduras.

bāy′-yärn, *n.* Woolen yarn for weaving baize.

bȧ-zäar′, bȧ-zär′, *n.* [Per. *bazar*, a market.]

1. In the East, an exchange, market-place, or place where goods are exposed to sale.

2. A spacious hall, or suite of rooms, fitted up with counters or stands for the sale of goods.

3. A fair, lasting usually for a few days, at which all manner of articles are sold for the benefit of some hospital, church, or the like.

bdel′lium (del′yum), *n.* [L., from Gr. *bdellion.*] A gummy, resinous juice, brought from the East Indies, Arabia, etc., in pieces of different sizes and figures, externally of a dark reddish-brown, internally clear, and not unlike glue. It is used as a perfume and a medicine, being a weak deobstruent. Indian *bdellium* (the kind above referred to) is a product of *Balsamodendron Roxburghii*, a native of the East Indies and Madagascar. This is the *bdellium* of Scripture, and is also called *false myrrh.* African *bdellium* is a product of the *Balsamodendron Africanum.*

bdel′loid (del-), *a.* and *n.* [Gr. *bdella*, a leech, and *eidos*, form.]

I. *a.* Pertaining to leeches.

II. *n.* Any leech.

Bdel-loi′dē-ȧ (del-), *n.pl.* The order of *Annulata* to which belong the leeches.

bdel-lom′e-tẽr (del-), *n.* [Gr. *bdella*, a leech, from *bdellein*, to suck, and *metron*, measure.] An instrument used to take the place of a leech, consisting of a cupping-glass, a scarificator, and an exhausting syringe.

Bdel-lō-mor′phȧ (del-), *n.* [L., from Gr. *bdella*, leech, and *morphē*, form.] An order of *Nemertina*, of which the sucking worms found in clams are good examples.

bē, *v.i.*; been, *pp.*; being, *ppr.* [AS. *beon*, to be, *beom*, I am; O.H.G. *bim*; G. *bin.* The verb *be* is defective, its missing parts being supplied by *am*, *art*, *is*, *are*, *was*, *wast*, and *were.*]

1. To exist; to be fixed; to have a real state or existence, for a longer or shorter time.

> To *be*, contents his natural desire. —Pope.

2. To be made to be; to become.

> And they twain shall *be* one flesh.
> —Matt. xix. 5.

3. To remain; as, let the garment *be* as it was made.

4. To be present in a place; as, where *was* I at the time? When will you *be* at my house?

5. To have a particular manner of being or happening; as, how *is* this affair? How *was* it? What *were* the circumstances?

This verb is used as an auxiliary in forming the tenses of other verbs, and particularly in giving to them the passive form; as, he has *been* disturbed. It forms, with the infinitive, a particular future tense, which often expresses duty, necessity, or purpose; as, government *is to be* supported; we *are to pay* our just debts.

Let be; to omit, or leave untouched; to let alone.

> *Let be*, said he, my prey. —Dryden.

Syn.—Become.—To *be* simply denotes existence; to *become* marks a transition from one state to another; as, it *is* cold, and is *becoming* colder.

bē-, *prefix.* [AS. *bi-*, *be-*; G. *be-*; Goth. *bi-*; from AS. prep. *be*, *bi*, by, about.] A combining form signifying by, about, on, near. Its uses are: (a) with its original prepositional force; (b) joined with verbs it intensifies the meaning of the verb, or renders an intransitive verb transitive, or makes the action of the verb particular or definite; (c) it is joined to substantives and adjectives to form verbs; (d) with nouns, adjectives, or adverbs it forms conjunctions, adverbs, or prepositions; (e) with privative force.

bēach, *v.t.*; beached, *pt.*, *pp.*; beaching, *ppr.* To run or haul onto the beach; as, to *beach* a boat.

bēach, *n.* [Perhaps from Ice. *bakki*, a bank, shore, with *k* softened to *ch*, as in *kirk*, church.] The shore of the sea, or of a lake, which is washed by the tide and waves; the strand. It may sometimes be used in reference to the shore of large rivers.

Syn.—Shore, coast, strand, seacoast, seaboard, seashore.

bēach′-cōmb″ẽr (-kōm″ẽr), *n.* 1. A long wave that curls up to a beach.

2. A seaman of lazy and vicious character, who loafs about wharves and beaches in seaports; the word is particularly applied to the vagabond white men found in the islands of the Pacific.

bēached, *a.* Exposed to the waves; washed by the tide and waves; also, driven on a beach; stranded; as, the ship is *beached.*

bēach′-flēa, *n.* In zoölogy, a small crustacean infesting seashores and hopping like a flea; called also *sand-flea*, *sand-hopper*, and *shore-jumper.*

bēach′y, *a.* Having a beach or beaches.

bēa′cŏn, *n.* [AS. *beácen*, *bēcen*, *bēcn*, a signal.]

1. A signal erected on an eminence, consisting of a pitch-barrel, or some combustible matter, to be fired at night, or to cause a smoke by day, as to announce the approach of an enemy.

2. A signal erected on rocks or shoals, to warn of danger. Hence, a lighthouse is sometimes called a *beacon*. In general, a *beacon* is any light or mark intended for direction and security against danger.

3. Figuratively, that which gives notice of danger.

bēa′çŏn, *v.t.*; beaconed (bē′knd), *pt., pp.*; beaconing, *ppr.* To furnish with a beacon; to light up.

bēa′çŏn-āġe, *n.* Money paid for the maintenance of a beacon.

bēa′çŏn-less, *a.* Having no beacon.

bēad, *n.* [ME. *bede*, a prayer; AS. *bedu*, from *biddan*, to pray.]

1. A little perforated ball, often strung on a thread, and worn about the neck, for ornament. A string of *beads* is called a necklace. *Beads* are made of gold, pearl, amber, steel, garnet, coral, diamond, crystal, paste, glass, etc. Roman Catholics use strings of *beads* in rehearsing their prayers. Hence the phrase, *to tell beads*, or *to be at one's beads*, is to be at prayer.

2. Any small globular body; hence, the glass globules used in traffic with savages and sold in strings, are called *beads*; also, a bubble on wine or spirits; froth or foam; also, a drop of perspiration.

3. A small piece of metal on a gun-barrel to take sight by.

4. In architecture and joinery, a small round molding sometimes cut into short embossments, like pearls in a necklace; an astragal. The *bead* is of frequent occurrence in architecture, particularly in the classical styles, and is

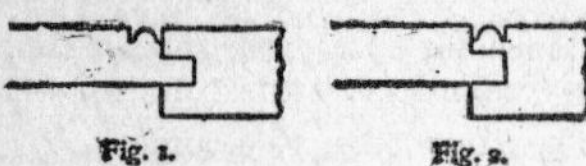

Fig. 1. Fig. 2.

used in picture-frames and other objects carved in wood. Among joiners *beads* are variously modified, as (a) *bead and butt*, framed work, where the panel is flush with the framing, and has a *bead* run on two edges in the direction of the grain only, while the ends are left plain (fig. 1); (b) *bead and flush*, framed work in which a *bead* is run on the edge of the framing (fig. 2); (c) *bead and quirk*, a *bead* formed or stuck, as it is called, on the edge of a piece of stuff flush with its surface (fig. 3); (d) *bead and double quirk*, or *return bead*, a *bead* stuck on a piece of stuff, and quirked or relieved on both surfaces (fig. 4); (e) *bead butt and square work*, when the panel has *beads* on two of its edges on one side only, and the other side is plain; (f) *bead flush and square*, when the framing is beaded on one side only.

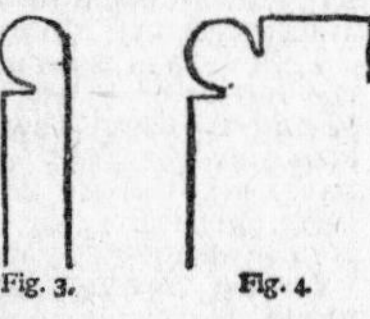

Fig. 3. Fig. 4.

Bidding of beads; a charge given by a priest to his parishioners, to repeat certain prayers upon their beads, for certain objects.

To draw a bead on; to take aim at.

To put a bead on; to pour liquor in such manner that the top is covered with bead-like bubbles.

bēad, *v.t.* and *v.i.*; beaded, *pt., pp.*; beading, *ppr.*

I. *v.t.* To ornament with beads.

II. *v.i.* To form beads, as champagne.

bēad′house, bēde′house, *n.* In England, a refuge for sick and poor, where inmates are expected to pray daily for their benefactors.

bēad′ing, *n.* Molding in imitation of beadwork.

bēa′dle, *n.* [ME. *bedel, bidel, budel*; confused with AS. *bydel*, a messenger, from *beodan*, to bid; OFr. *bedel*.]

1. A messenger or crier of a court; a servitor; one who cites persons to appear and answer; called also an *apparitor* or *summoner*.

2. An officer in a university whose chief business is to walk with a mace in public processions; a bedel.

3. A parish officer whose business is to punish petty offenders; a church officer with various subordinate duties, as waiting on the clergyman, keeping order in church, attending meetings of vestry or session, etc. [Eng.]

bēa′dle-dŏm, *n.* Beadles as a class, and their characteristics; petty and officious stupidity.

bēa′dle-ry, *n.* The jurisdiction of a beadle.

bēa′dle-ship, *n.* The office of a beadle.

bēad′=prọọf, *a.* A term applied to spirituous liquors when, after being shaken, a crown of bubbles will stand, for some time after, on the surface.

bēad′=rōll, *n.* In the Roman Catholic church, a list or catalogue of persons for the repose of whose souls a certain number of prayers is to be said or counted off on the beads of a chaplet or rosary; a roll of prayers or hymns; hence, any list or catalogue.

The *bead-roll* of her vicious tricks. —Prior.

bēadṣ′măn, *n.*; *pl.* **bēadṣ′men.** A man employed in praying for another; a resident of an almshouse in England; a licensed beggar in Scotland.

bēad′snāke, *n.* A small venomous snake of North America, marked with yellow, black, and red bands.

bēadṣ′wom″ăn (-woom″ăn), *n.*; *pl.* **bēadṣ′wom″en** (-wim″en). A praying woman; a woman who resides in an almshouse.

bēad′=tree, *n.* The *Melia Azedarach*, a native tree of the East Indies, growing about twenty feet high. Its nuts are used in Spain and Portugal for the beads of rosaries.

bēad′wŏrk, *n.* Ornamental work with beads.

bēad′y, *a.* 1. Resembling beads; as, *beady* eyes.

2. Decorated with beads, or an imitation thereof.

3. Characterized by beads; as, *beady* wine.

bēa′gle, *n.* [OE. *begele*, small dog.]

1. A small hound, or hunting-dog, used in hunting hares and small game.

2. Figuratively, a detective; in Scotland, a bumbailiff.

bēa′gling, *n.* The sport of hunting with beagles.

bēak, *n.* [ME. *beeke, beke, bek*; OFr. *bec*; L. *beccus*, a beak.]

1. The bill or nib of a bird, consisting of a horny substance, either straight or curving, and usually ending in a point; the form varies much, according to the food and habits of the bird.

2. The prolongation of the mouth or mandibles of some fishes, reptiles, and insects, in form analogous to the *beak* of a bird.

3. A pointed piece of wood, fortified with metal, resembling a *beak*, fastened to the prow of ancient galleys, and intended to pierce the vessels of an enemy.

4. In modern shipbuilding, that portion of a ship, forward of the forecastle, which is made fast to the stem and supported by the main knee.

5. In farriery, a little shoe at the toe about an inch long, turned up and fastened in upon the fore part of the hoof; a toe-clip.

6. Anything ending in a point, like a *beak*.

7. In botany, a process, like the *beak* of a bird, terminating the fruit and other parts in certain plants.

8. In architecture, a slight, continuous projection ending in a narrow fillet; that portion of a drip which casts off the water.

9. The lip or spout of a vessel, like a pitcher, through which the contents are poured.

10. A magistrate, judge, or policeman. [Eng. slang.]

11. The horn of an anvil.

bēak, *v.t.* Among cockfighters, to take hold of with the beak.

bēaked (bēkt), *a.* 1. Having a beak; ending in a point, like a beak.

2. In biology, rostrate; furnished with a process like a beak.

bēak′ẽr, *n.* [ME. *biker*; Ice. *bikarr*, a cup, from L. *bicarium*, a wine-cup; Gr. *bikos*, a wine-jar.]

1. A large drinking-cup with a wide mouth, supported on a standard.

2. An open-mouthed, thin glass vessel having a lip or spout for pouring; used by chemists and druggists.

bēak′head (-hed), *n.* 1. In architecture, an ornament resembling the head and beak of a bird, or sometimes, as used over a Romanesque doorway, a grotesque human head terminating in a beak.

2. In marine architecture, a platform in the forepart of a ship.

bēak′i″ron (-ī″ŭrn), *n.* A bickern; an iron tool, ending in a point, used by blacksmiths; the horn of an anvil.

bēal, *n.* [ME. *beele, bele, bile, bule*, a boil.] A pimple; a small inflammatory tumor; a pustule. [Rare.]

bēal, *v.i.*; bealed, *pt., pp.*; bealing, *ppr.* To gather matter; to swell and come to a head, as a pimple. [Prov. Eng. and Scot.]

bēal, bēl, *n.* [Scot., from Gael. *bealach*, a mountain-pass.] The mouth of a narrow pass or valley between hills. [Scot.]

bē′=ạll, *n.* The whole; everything; all that will ever be.

bēam, *n.* [AS. *beam*, a tree, beam, ray of light; O.H.G. *baum*; Goth. *bagms*; Gr. *phyma*, a growth; Sans. root *bhū*, to grow.]

1. Any one of the largest or principal pieces of timber in a building, that lie across the walls, and serve to support the principal rafters.

2. Any large piece of timber, long in proportion to its thickness, and finished for use.

3. The part of a balance from the ends of which the scales are suspended.

4. The greatest width of a vessel.

5. The main stem bearing the antlers or branches on a stag's head.

6. The pole of a carriage.

7. A wooden cylinder forming that portion of a weaver's loom on which the warp is wound before weaving; also, the cylinder on which the cloth is wound during the process of weaving.

8. The straight part or shank of an anchor.

9. Any one of the main cross timbers or pieces of iron or steel which span the sides of a ship horizontally and support the decks.

10. The main piece of a plow, to which are affixed the handles and colter; a plow-beam.

11. The oscillating lever of a steam-engine, reciprocating upon a center and forming the medium of communication between the piston-rod and the crank-shaft; called also *working-beam* or *walking-beam*.

12. A ray or aggregation of parallel rays of light, the middle ray being the axis.

13. Figuratively, anything analogous to a ray of light; as, a *beam* of hope; *beams* of majesty.

On the beam; in a line with the beams, or at right angles with the keel of the ship.

On her beam-ends; a nautical phrase meaning that the vessel is inclined so far on one side that her beams almost stand on end.

bēam, *v.t.*; beamed, *pt., pp.*; beaming, *ppr.* To send forth; to emit; followed ordinarily by *forth*; as, to *beam forth* light.

bēam, *v.i.* To emit rays of light, or beams; to shine.

He *beamed*, the daystar of the rising age. —Trumbull.

bēam′bĩrd, *n.* A small European bird, *Muscicapa grisola*, so called because it often builds its nest on the projecting end of a beam or rafter in a building; also called *spotted flycatcher*.

bēam′=çal″i-pẽr, *n.* Same as *Caliper-square*.

bēam′=çŏm″pȧss, *n.* An instrument consisting of a beam having sliding sockets that carry steel or pencil points; used for describing large circles and laying off distances.

Beam-compass.

bēamed, *a.* Completely antlered; said of a stag.

bēam′=en″ġine, *n.* A steam-engine having a working-beam to transmit power.

bēam′=feath″ẽr (-feth″ẽr), *n.* One of the long feathers in the wing of a hawk.

bēam′=fill″ing, *n.* The filling in of mason work between beams or joists, its height being equal to the depth of the timbers filled in.

bēam′fụl, *a.* Having many rays of light; radiant.

bēam′i-ly, *adv.* In a radiant manner.

bēam′i-ness, *n.* The state of being radiant.

bēam′ing, *a.* Emitting rays of light or beams.

bēam′ing, *n.* 1. Radiation; the emission or darting of light in rays, materially or mentally.

Such were the *beamings* of an original and gifted mind. —T. Dawes.

2. The use of a beam, as in weaving.

bēam′ing-ly, *adv.* Radiantly.

bēam′less, *a.* Emitting no rays of light.

bēam′let, *n.* A thin shaft of light.

bēam′=tree, *n.* A tree of the pear kind, *Pyrus Aria*, the wood of which is hard, compact, and tough, and used in making axletrees, naves of wheels, and cogs of machinery; called also *whitebeam-tree*.

bēam′y, *a.* 1. Emitting rays of light; radiant; shining.

2. Resembling a beam in size and weight; massy.

3. Having horns, or antlers.

bēan, *n.* [ME. *bene*; AS. *beán*, bean.]

1. The edible seed of any one of various leguminous plants or herbs, the most important of which belong to the genera *Phaseolus*, *Faba*, and *Dolichos*; also, the plant itself. *Beans* are very highly esteemed as an article of vegetable food and are important both in agriculture and in commerce.

2. In popular phraseology, any vegetable seed or fruit resembling the true *beans*; as, a *coffee-bean*.

Calabar bean; the poisonous seed of an African leguminous plant, formerly used as a native test for crime and witchcraft.

Florida bean; (a) the seed of a West Indian plant often cast up by the sea on the shores of Florida; (b) the sea-bean, fruit of the tropical American shrub, *Entada scandens*.

Ignatius bean, or *St. Ignatius' bean*; the seed of *Strychnos Ignatii*, from which strychnine is obtained.

Tonquin bean, or *Tonka bean*; the seed of a leguminous tree, *Dipteryx odorata*; it is esteemed for its fragrance.

bēan′=ā″phis, *n.* A parasite of the bean plant; called also *bean-dolphin*.

bēan′=çā″pẽr, *n.* Any plant whose buds are used as capers, especially a Levantine species, *Zygophyllum Fabago*.

bēan′=çod, *n.* 1. A small fishing-vessel or pilot-boat, used in the rivers of Portugal.

2. A bean-pod.

bēan'-fēast, *n.* A rustic dinner given by an employer to his workmen. [Eng.]

bēan'-fly̆, *n.* A fly found on bean flowers.

bēan'-goose, *n.* A small wild goose, *Anser segetum*, of northern Europe, which migrates to England and other temperate regions in the fall and returns to the north in summer; so called from the likeness of the nail of the bill to a horse-bean.

bēan'-shoot"ēr, *n.* A device for shooting beans; a pea-shooter.

bēan'-shot, *n.* Small copper shot formed by pouring molten metal through a sieve into water.

bēan'-tree, *n.* Any one of various trees or shrubs, as the catalpa or Indian bean.

bēan'-trē"foil, *n.* The laburnum.

bēan'-wee"vil, *n.* A small weevil whose larva is injurious to beans.

bēar, bēre, *n.* [ME. *bere*; AS. *bere*, barley.] A kind of barley, cultivated in Scotland and the north of England; the common four-rowed barley, *Hordeum vulgare*; also the six-rowed barley, *Hordeum hexastichon*. [Local.]

bēar, *v.t.*; bore (formerly, bare), *pt.*; bearing, *ppr.*; borne, born, *pp.* [ME. *beren*; AS. *beran*; O.H.G. *beran*; Ice. *bera*; Goth. *bairan*, to bear; L. *ferre*; Gr. *pherein*; Sans. *bhar*, to bear, carry.]

1. To support; to sustain; to keep afloat; to carry or convey by support; literally or figuratively, to endure by sustaining; to support the character of; to carry by proxy; as, to *bear* a weight or burden; they *bear* him upon the shoulder; the eagle *beareth* them on her wings; a man may *bear* stronger diet, or *bear* punishment.

2. To wear as a mark of authority or distinction; as, to *bear* a sword, a badge, a name; to *bear* a coat of arms.

3. Figuratively, to support in the mind and voluntarily to carry, as the trouble or the animus or consequence; as, to *bear* love for a friend or hate for an enemy; to *bear* neglect.

4. To bring forth, reproduce, or give birth to; to yield; as, to *bear* children; the tree *bears* fruit; to *bear* interest.

5. To admit or be capable of; to suffer or sustain without violence, injury, or change; as, to give words the most favorable interpretation they will *bear*.

6. To possess and use, as power; to exercise; as, to *bear* sway.

7. To carry on, or maintain; to have; as, to *bear* a part in conversation.

8. To show or exhibit; to relate; as, to *bear* testimony or witness.

> *Bear* welcome in your eye. —Shak.

9. To sustain the effect of or be answerable for; as, to *bear* the blame.

10. To sustain; to supply the means of paying; as, to *bear* the expense.

11. To be the object of; as, let me *bear* your love. [Rare.]

12. To behave; to act in any character; with the reciprocal pronoun; as, he hath *borne* himself penitently.

13. To endure the effects of; to give satisfaction for.

> He shall *bear* their iniquities. —Is. liii. 11.

14. To gain or win. [Obs.]

> Some think to *bear* it by speaking a great word. —Bacon.

15. To conduct; to take; as, *bear* the prisoner away. [Obs.]

16. To possess, as a property, attribute, or characteristic; to have in or on; to contain; as, to *bear* signs or traces; to *bear* an inscription; the contents which the letter *bears*.

To bear one another's burdens; to be charitable to one another; to aid one another.

To bear off; to remove; also, to gain or win, as a prize.

To bear down; to crush; to overwhelm, as an enemy.

To bear on; to press against; also, to carry forward, to press, incite, or animate; as, confidence shall *bear* him *on*.

To bear out; to support; to confirm; as, his statement *bears* me *out*.

To bear through; to maintain or support to the end; as, religion will *bear* us *through* the evils of life.

To bear up; to support; to keep from falling; as, religious hope *bears up* the mind.

To bear a body; in painting, said of a color when it is capable of being ground so fine, and mixed so entirely with the oil, as to seem only a very thick oil of the same color.

To bear date; to have the mark of time when written or executed; as, a letter or bond *bears date* January 1, 1904.

To bear a price; to have a certain price. In common mercantile language, it often signifies or implies to bear a good or high price.

To bear in hand; to amuse with false pretenses; to deceive. [Obs.]

To bear a hand; in seamanship, to make haste; to be quick.

To bear in mind; to remember.

To bear one company; to guide, protect, furnish companionship to, and share the vicissitudes of; as, his faithful dog always *bore* him *company*.

Bear, signifying *to bring forth*, has the past participle, when used passively, spelled *born*, but when used after the verb *to have*, it is spelled *borne*. Thus, a child was *born*; but, she has *borne* a child. In all the other senses, both participles are spelled *borne*; as, I have *borne* the expenses; the expenses must be *borne*.

bēar, *v.i.* 1. To suffer, as with pain, or the carrying of a heavy burden.

> But man is born to *bear*. —Pope.

2. To endure; to be patient; as, my burden is greater than I can *bear*.

3. To produce fruit; to be fruitful, in opposition to *barren*.

> This age to blossom, and the next to *bear*. —Dryden.

4. To press; with *on* or *upon*; as, to *bear* hard *upon* an opponent.

5. To take effect; to succeed; to have an influence; as, to bring matters to *bear*.

6. To be situated, as to the point of compass, with respect to something else; as, the land *bore* southeast by east from the ship.

7. To relate or refer (to); with *on* or *upon*; as, his argument *bears upon* the subject with force.

8. To convey intelligence or meaning; to have a definite effect or intent; to mean.

> Her sentence *bore* that she should stand a certain time upon the platform. —Hawthorne.

9. To be capable of sustaining weight; as, the ice will *bear*.

10. To have a certain direction or tendency; as, bringing the guns to *bear*.

To bear away; in nautical language, to keep a ship away from the wind; to change her course and make her run before the wind.

To bear back; to retire in retreat.

To bear in; to tend toward, as a ship approaching the land; opposed to *bear off*.

To bear off; to remove to a greater distance.

To bear up; to tend or move toward; as, to *bear up* to one another; also, to be supported; to have fortitude; to be firm; as, to *bear up* under afflictions.

To bear with; to endure what is disagreeable; to be indulgent; to forbear to resent, oppose, or punish.

Syn.—Suffer, endure, support, maintain, uphold, sustain, undergo, tolerate, carry, convey, waft, produce, yield.—To *bear* is the general term taken in the proper sense without any qualification; the other terms denote different modes of *bearing*. To *bear* is applied either to ordinary or extraordinary evils, and is either a temporary or a permanent act of the resolution; to *endure* is applied only to great evils requiring strong and lasting resolution. To *bear* and *endure* signify to receive becomingly the weight of what befalls ourselves; to *support* signifies to bear either our own or another's evils.

bēar, *n.* A bier. [Obs.]

bēar, *n.* [ME. *bere*; AS. *bera*; Ice. *bera*; G. *bär*, a bear.]

1. A plantigrade carnivorous mammal of the genus *Ursus*, family *Ursidæ*. There are many species, of which the grizzly *bear* and polar *bear* are the most formidable. *Bears*, while belonging to the *Carnivora*, live, to a large extent, on insects, fruits, roots, etc. They have stout, heavy bodies, usually thickly covered with fur. The brown or black *bear* of Europe and Asia is the *Ursus arctos*. It is a native of almost all the northern parts of Europe and Asia. The American black *bear*, *Ursus americanus*, of which the brown or cinnamon *bear* is a variant, has black shining hair, and is rarely above five feet in length. The grizzly *bear* (*Ursus ferox* or *horribilis*) is a ferocious animal, and has a bulky and unwieldy form, but is nevertheless capable of great rapidity of motion. The polar or white *bear*, *Ursus maritimus*, is an animal possessed of great strength and fierceness. It lives in the polar regions, chiefly on the ice, feeds on fish, seals, etc., and usually is seven to eight feet in length. The only South American species of *bear* is the *Ursus ornatus*, or spectacled *bear*, so called because of a peculiar marking about the eye suggesting spectacles. The Syrian *bear*, *Ursus syriacus*, and the sloth *bear*, *Ursus*, or *Melursus*, *labiatus*, the latter a native of India and Ceylon, are among the notable species. *Ursus torquatus* and *Ursus japonicus* are the black *bears* of the Himalayas and Japan respectively.

Brown Bear (*Ursus arctos*).

Polar Bear (*Ursus maritimus*).

2. In zoölogy, any one of several animals allied to the true *bears* by resemblance in form or habits, as the ant-*bear*, the woolly *bear*, the sea-*bear*, the water-*bear*, and the sand-*bear*.

3. [B—] In astronomy, the name of two constellations in the northern hemisphere, called the *Great* and *Little Bear*, or Ursa Major and Ursa Minor. In the tail of the *Little Bear* is the polestar.

4. In nautical parlance, a scouring-block used in cleaning decks.

5. In metal-working, a portable punching-machine for iron plates.

6. In metallurgy, a rough, conglomerate mass found in blast-furnaces after long use.

7. Figuratively, an ill-mannered, morose person; a person of coarse, rough habits or speech.

8. In stock-exchange or board-of-trade parlance, a trader who does all he can to bring down the price of grain, produce, or stocks (as a bear pulls down with its paws), in order that he may buy cheap; opposed to a *bull*, who tries to raise the price (as a bull tosses with his horns) that he may sell dear.

Bear's grease; a perfumed unguent made from the fat of the bear, formerly extensively used in hair-dressing; hence, any unctuous substance or compound used on the hair. [Eng.]

bēar, *v.t.*; beared (bārd), *pt.*, *pp.*; bearing, *ppr.* In the language of the stock exchange or grain market, to strive to depress the price of, for speculative purposes; as, to *bear* a railroad stock; to *bear* oats.

bēar'á-ble, *a.* Capable of being borne; tolerable; endurable.

bēar'á-bly, *adv.* In a bearable manner.

bēar'-bāit"ing, *n.* The act of harassing, tormenting, badgering, or worrying a bear, as by setting on dogs, for the entertainment of spectators.

bēar'bāne, *n.* A poisonous plant, of the aconite family.

bēar'ber"ry, *n.* A medicinal plant, *Arctostaphylos uva-ursi*, of the heath family, yielding red berries for which bears have a partiality.

bēar'bīne, *n.* In botany, the bindweed, *Convolvulus arvensis*.

bēar'-cat"ēr-pil-lăr, *n.* A larval tiger-moth, especially of the genus *Euprepia*; a woolly bear.

bēar'-cloth, *n.* Same as *Bearing-cloth*.

bēard, *n.* [ME. *berde*; AS. *beard*; O.H.G. *bart*; Dan. *baard*; L. *barba*, beard.]

1. The hair that grows on the chin, lips, and adjacent parts of the face, chiefly of male adults; hence a mark of virility.

2. The awn or sharp prickles on the ears of some kinds of grain; also, parallel hairs, or a tuft of stiff hairs terminating the leaves of plants.

3. A barb or sharp process of an arrow, or other instrument, bent backward from the point to prevent its being easily drawn out.

4. The part of a horse's lower jaw which bears the curb of a bridle, underneath the lower mandible and above the chin.

5. The rays of a comet, emitted toward that part of the heaven to which its proper motion seems to direct it.

6. The byssus of certain kinds of mollusks, consisting of fine threads or hairs, by which they fasten themselves to rocks, etc. The term is also applied to the gills or respiratory organs of the oyster and other bivalves.

7. In insects, two small, oblong, fleshy bodies, placed just above the trunk, as in gnats, moths, and butterflies.

8. The long hairs around the face or chin of some animals, as the goat, the cat, etc.

9. In printing, the outside, beard-like shading of some kinds of ornamental type, formerly much used.

bēard, *v.t.*; bearded, *pt.*, *pp.*; bearding, *ppr.*

1. To take by the beard; to seize, pluck, or pull the beard of, in contempt or anger.

2. To oppose to the face; to set at defiance.

> I have been *bearded* by boys. —More.

bēard'ed, *a.* 1. Having a beard, as a man.

> *Bearded* like the pard. —Shak.

2. In botany, having sharp prickes or stiff hairs, as ears or heads of grain.

3. Barbed or jagged, as an arrow.

bēard′-grȧss, *n.* A name common to different species of coarse grass of the genus *Andropogon.*

bēard′ie (-i), *n.* [Dim. of *beard.*] A Scotch name for the loach, *Nemachilus barbatus.*

bēard′less, *a.* 1. Without a beard; young; not having arrived at manhood.

2. In botany, destitute of parallel hairs, or tufts of hairs; having no awn.

bēard′less-ness, *n.* The state or quality of being beardless.

bēard′-mȯss, *n.* A grayish moss, *Usnea barbata*, growing on trees.

bēard′tŏngue (-tung), *n.* A plant of the genus *Pentstemon*, so called from its tongue-shaped bearded stamen.

bēar′ẽr, *n.* 1. In a general sense, one who or that which bears, sustains, or carries.

2. One who carries packages, letters, or intelligence; as, a *bearer* of good news; a *bearer* of despatches.

3. One who carries a body to the grave, at a funeral; a pallbearer.

4. One who wears or carries anything officially, or as a duty; a sword-bearer; an armor-bearer.

5. A tree or plant that yields its fruit; as, a good *bearer.*

6. In architecture, a post or brick wall between the ends of a piece of timber, to support it; often, any support.

7. In heraldry, a figure in an achievement, placed by the side of a shield, and seeming to support it; generally the figure of a beast. The figure of a human being, used for a like purpose, is called a *tenant.*

8. In India, a house-servant similar to a valet, or one of the carriers of a palanquin.

9. In commercial language, any person having, holding, or presenting a note, check, draft, etc.; as, pay to *bearer.*

10. In printing, (a) a type-high metal support for the sides of matter that is to be cast into a plate, to prevent the spreading of or damage to the type on the edges; (b) a piece of wood or metal locked into a platen press, or built onto the bed of a cylinder press, to sustain the impression.

bēar′-gär″den, *n.* 1. Any place where bears are kept for exhibition or sport.

2. Figuratively, a scene of disorderly conduct, or riot; as, the meeting of the city council degenerated into a *bear-garden.*

bēar′hẽrd, *n.* A bear's keeper; an attendant on bears.

bēar′hound, *n.* A dog of the hound variety, used in hunting bears.

bēar′ing, *n.* 1. The manner in which a person bears or conducts himself; gesture; mien; behavior.

I know him by his *bearing.* —Shak.

2. The situation of an object, with respect to another object, by which it is supposed to have a connection with it or influence upon it, or to be influenced by it; relation.

But of this frame, the *bearings* and the ties. —Pope.

3. In architecture, the portion of a piece of timber which rests upon, or is inserted into a wall; also, the wall that supports it.

4. In navigation, the situation of a distant object with regard to a ship's position, as on the bow, on the lee quarter, etc.; the direction or point of the compass in which an object is seen.

5. [*pl.*] In heraldry, the charges on a shield.

A carriage covered with armorial *bearings.* —Thackeray.

6. The act, capacity, or season of producing or giving birth; as, the *bearing* of a child.

7. In machinery, any part that rests on, bears up, or supports another, as a block on which a journal rotates.

8. Endurance; patience under affliction; as, my trials are past *bearing.*

9. Meaning; significance; tendency; connection; application; as, your remarks have no *bearing* upon the subject.

10. [*pl.*] In shipbuilding, (a) the widest part of a ship below the gunwale; (b) a ship's water-line when she is perfectly trimmed.

To lose one's bearings; to become lost or bewildered as to direction.

To take bearings; to ascertain one's position, or the direction, by the compass, in which an object lies; hence, figuratively, to discover how matters stand; to ascertain the conditions.

Syn.—Deportment, demeanor, carriage, behavior, conduct, manner, mien.

bēar′ing-clŏth, *n.* The cloth in which a child is wrapped when carried to church to be baptized.

bēar′ing-rein, *n.* A checkrein.

bēar′ish, *a.* Partaking of the qualities of a bear; resembling a bear in temper or manners.

bēar′ish-ness, *n.* The manner of a bear; rude behavior.

bēar′-lēad″ẽr, *n.* 1. One who leads a bear, or travels with a bear, as for exhibition purposes.

2. Hence, humorously, a tutor; especially, one who conducts a young man on educational travels.

bēar′lïke, *a.* Resembling a bear in appearance or behavior.

bēarn, *n.* A bairn. [Obs.]

bēar′ș′-breech, *n.* 1. A name common to different species of plants of the genus *Acanthus.*

2. The cow-parsnip, *Heracleum Sphondylium*, common in England.

bēar′ș′-ēar, *n.* A popular name of the *Primula auricula*, so called from the form of its leaf.

bēar′ș′-foot, *n.* A species of hellebore widely used in medicine.

bēar′skin, *n.* 1. The skin or fur of a bear.

2. A rough, shaggy cloth for overcoats.

3. A large headdress, made of bear's fur, especially one worn by a drum-major or by the soldiers of certain regiments of the British army.

bēar′ș′-pąw, *n.* An ornamental East Indian bivalve shell.

bēar′wąrd, *n.* A keeper of bears; a bearherd. [Rare.]

bēar′wŏrt, *n.* A European herb, spicknel or mew, *Meum athamanticum.*

bēast, *n.* [ME. *beeste, beste*; OFr. *beste*; L. *bestia*, a beast.]

1. Any four-footed animal, which may be used for labor, food, or sport; distinguished from birds, insects, fishes, and man, and applied especially to large animals; as, *beasts* of burden; *beasts* of the chase; *beasts* of the forest.

2. Any irrational animal, as opposed to *man*; as in the phrase, *man and beast.*

3. Figuratively, a brutal man; a person rude, coarse, filthy, or acting in a manner unworthy of a rational creature.

4. A game at cards similar to loo; also, a forfeit at this game. [Obs.]

Beast royal; the lion. [Obs.]

bēast′hood, *n.* The state of being, or the nature of, a beast.

bēast′ingș, *n.pl.* See *Biestings.*

bēast′ish, *a.* Like a beast; brutal.

bēast′li-head (-hed), *n.* Beastliness. [Obs.]

bēast′lïke, *a.* Like a beast; brutal.

bēast′li-ness, *n.* The state of being beastly; brutality; coarseness; vulgarity; filthiness.

bēast′ly, *a.* 1. Like a beast; brutal; coarse; filthy; contrary to the nature and dignity of man.

2. Having the form and nature of a beast.

3. Nasty; unpleasant; as, *beastly* weather. [Slang.]

Syn.—Brutish, base, bestial, carnal, coarse, sensual, swinish, vile, irrational, degrading.

bēat, *v.t.*; beat, *pt.*; beating, *ppr.*; beaten, beat, *pp.* [ME. *beten*; AS. *beátan*, to beat.]

1. To strike repeatedly; to lay on repeated blows with a stick, with the hand or fist, or with any instrument, and for any cause, just or unjust.

2. To strike, as a drum; to play on, as an instrument of music.

3. To break, bruise, comminute, or pulverize by beating or pounding, as pepper or spices.

4. To extend by beating, as gold or other malleable substance; to hammer into any form; to forge; often followed by *out*; as, to *beat out* gold.

5. To strike, as bushes; to shake by beating, or to make a noise in, to rouse game; as, to *beat* the woods.

6. To break, mix, or agitate by quick strokes; as, to *beat* an egg.

7. To strike or dash against, as water or wind.

8. To tread, as a path.

9. To cheat; to swindle; to defraud; to trick; often followed by *out*; as, he *beat* me *out* of the money. [Colloq.]

10. To overcome in a battle, contest, or strife; to vanquish or conquer; as, he always *beats* her at tennis.

11. To harass; to exercise severely; to perplex; as, to *beat* the brains about logic.

12. To flutter or flap; as, to *beat* the wings.

13. In military life, to signal or give notice of, by beat of drum; as, to *beat* an alarm, the reveille, the tattoo, etc.

14. To puzzle; to perplex; to pass (one's) understanding; as, his actions *beat* me. [Colloq.]

To beat back; to compel to retire or return.

To beat down; to lower the price by importunity or argument; to depress or crush; as, to *beat down* opposition. [Colloq.]

To beat into; to teach or instil by repetition of instruction.

To beat off; to repel or drive back.

To beat out; to extend by hammering.

To beat time; to measure or regulate time in music by the motion of the hand or foot.

To beat up; to attack suddenly; to alarm or disturb; as, to *beat up* an enemy's quarters.

Syn.—Hit, strike, belabor, drub, maul, pummel, thump, bang, thwack, defeat, vanquish, conquer, overcome.

bēat, *v.i.* 1. To move with pulsation; to throb; as, the pulse *beats*; the heart *beats.*

2. To dash with force, as a storm, flood, passion, etc.; as, the tempest *beats* against the house.

3. To knock at a door.

4. To fluctuate; to be in agitation.

5. To give forth sounds on being tapped or struck; as, the drums are *beating.*

6. In seamanship, to make headway against the wind by tacking.

7. In military language, to give a signal by the tap of a drum.

8. To win a victory; to be the victor in a contest.

To beat about; to search for; to try to find; nautically, to tack; hence, figuratively, to follow an aimless course in any enterprise.

To beat about the bush; to approach a subject in a circumlocutory way.

To beat to quarters; to summon the crew of a man-of-war, by beat of drum, to their stations for battle.

bēat, *n.* 1. A stroke; a striking; a blow, whether with the hand or with a weapon.

2. A recurring stroke; a pulsation; as, the *beat* of the pulse.

3. The rise or fall of the hand or foot, in regulating the divisions of time in music; also, the divisions of the measure so marked.

4. A transient grace-note in music, struck immediately before the note it is intended to ornament.

Written. Played.

Beat.

5. In acoustics and music, the pulsation produced by the interference of sound-waves, on the vibration of two tones not quite in unison.

6. A round or course which is frequently gone over; as, a policeman's *beat.*

7. A place of habitual or frequent resort.

8. A cheat or swindler who is tricky in small matters; one who does not pay his debts; a sponge; often intensified by *dead*; as, a *dead beat.* [Colloq.]

9. The act of one who beats a person or thing; especially, in newspaper slang, the act of obtaining and publishing a piece of news by a newspaper before its competitors; also, the news itself; as, the story was a *beat.*

10. In hunting, a diligent search for game, as by striking bushes to drive it forth.

11. In fencing, a quick blow on the adversary's foil.

Beat of a watch or *clock*; the sound or tick made by the action of the escapement.

bēat, *n.* The heavy, matted growth of vegetation from moorland or fallow land, which is burned off to enrich the land for plowing. [Prov. Eng.]

bēat, *v.t.* To remove the sod or surface vegetation from. [Prov. Eng.]

bēat, *n.* Flax or hemp bound in small bundles ready for macerating; written also *beet* and *bait.* [Prov. Eng.]

bēat, *a.* Weary; tired; worn out. [Colloq.]

bēat′en, *a.* 1. Conquered; vanquished.

2. Made smooth by treading; worn by use; hence, figuratively, trite; ordinary; not original; as, his essay was along *beaten* lines.

3. Shaped or formed by beating or hammering; as, *beaten* brass.

4. Exhausted; tired out.

bēat′ẽr, *n.* 1. One who beats, or strikes; one whose occupation is to hammer metals.

2. An instrument for beating, pounding, or comminuting substances.

3. In hunting, one who ranges over a tract, striking bushes, etc., to beat up game.

bēat′ẽr-up, *n.* One who beats for game.

bēath, *v.t.* To bathe. [Obs.]

bē-ȧ-tif′iç, bē-ȧ-tif′iç-ăl, *a.* [L. *beatificus*, from *beatus*, happy, and *facere*, to make.] Having the power to bless or make happy, or the power to complete blissful enjoyment; as, a *beatific* vision.

bē-ȧ-tif′iç-ăl-ly, *adv.* In a beatific manner.

bē-ȧ-tif′i-çāte, *v.t.* To beatify. [Obs.]

bē-at″i-fi-çā′tion, *n.* The act of beatifying, or the state of being beatified; especially, in the Roman Catholic church, the act or process of declaring a person beatified or blessed after death.

bē-at′i-fȳ, *v.t.*; beatified, *pt., pp.*; beatifying, *ppr.* 1. To make happy; to bless with the completion of celestial enjoyment.

2. In the Roman Catholic church, to declare by a decree or public act (a deceased person) to be one of "the blessed," to have been received into heaven, and, though not canonized, to be worthy a degree of homage.

3. To ascribe extraordinary virtue or excellence to; to regard as saintly or exalted.

bēat′ing, *n.* 1. The act of striking blows; punishment by blows.

2. The act of conquering or the state of being conquered.

3. In nautical language, the act of sailing against the wind, by tacking.

4. A pulsation or throbbing; as, the *beating* of the heart.

5. In music, the regular pulsative swelling of sound produced in an organ by pipes when not in unison and their vibrations not coincident. This phenomenon occurs in stringed as well as wind instruments, when sounding together, nearly but not exactly in perfect tune.

bē-at′i-tūde, *n.* [Fr. *béatitude*; L. *beatitudo*, from *beatus*, happy, blessed.]

1. Blessedness; felicity of the highest kind; consummate bliss; used of the joys of heaven.

2. Any one of the declarations of blessedness made by Christ to particular virtues, in the Sermon on the Mount.

3. In the Roman Catholic church, same as *beatification.*

beau (bō), *n.*; *pl.* **beaux** (bōz). [Fr. *beau, bel, f. belle*, from L. *bellus*, pretty, fair.]

1. A man of dress; a fine, gay man; one whose great care is to deck his person; a dandy; a fop.

2. A man who devotes himself to a lady; an escort; a lover. [Colloq.]

Syn.—Gallant, spark, sweetheart, lover, suitor.

beau′fet (bō′), *n.* A wrong spelling of *buffet.*

beau′fin (bō′), *n.* A biffin.

beau′=i-dē′ăl (bō′), *n.* [Fr.] A conception or image of consummate beauty, formed in the mind, free from all the deformities, defects, and blemishes seen in actuality; a standard of excellence; a model.

beau′ish (bō′), *a.* Like a beau; foppish.

beau′pere (bō′pār), *n.* [Fr.] 1. A companion or friend. [Obs.]

2. A father, especially a priest; literally, good father.

beau′pot (bō′), *n.* A vase of large size to contain flowers.

beau-se-ănt′ (bō-sā-äṅ′), *n.* [Fr. *beaucéant*, a flag, black-and-white-spotted.] The Knights Templars' standard, half black and half white.

beau′ship (bō′), *n.* The state or quality of being a beau.

beaū′tē-ous (bū′), *a.* Very fair; very handsome.

beaū′tē-ous-ly (bū′), *adv.* In a beauteous manner.

beaū′tē-ous-ness (bū′), *n.* The state or quality of being beauteous; beauty.

beaū′tied, *a.* Full of beauty; used in poetry.

beaū′ti-fied, *a.* Adorned; made beautiful.

beaū′ti-fī-ẽr (bū′), *n.* One who or that which makes beautiful.

beaū′ti-ful (bū′), *a.* 1. Elegant in form; fair; full of beauty.

2. Having the qualities which constitute beauty; as, a *beautiful* sound.

> A circle is more *beautiful* than a square; a square is more *beautiful* than a parallelogram. —Kames.

Syn.—Fine, handsome, pretty, elegant, fair, lovely.—The *beautiful* is determined by fixed rules; it admits of no excess or defect; it comprehends regularity, proportion, and a due distribution of color, and every particular which can engage the attention; the *fine* must be coupled with a certain grandeur of aspect; it is incompatible with that which is small; the *handsome* is a general assemblage of what is agreeable; it is marked by no particular characteristic, but the absence of all deformity; *prettiness* is always coupled with simplicity and delicacy.

beaū′ti-ful-ly (bū′), *adv.* In a beautiful manner.

beaū′ti-ful-ness (bū′), *n.* Elegance of form; beauty.

beaū′ti-fȳ (bū′), *v.t.*; beautified (-fīd), *pt.*, *pp.*; beautifying, *ppr.* To make or render beautiful; to adorn; to deck; to grace; to add beauty to; to embellish.

Syn.—Adorn, decorate, embellish, deck, ornament.

beaū′ti-fȳ (bū′), *v.i.* To become beautiful; to advance in beauty.

beaū′ti-less (bū′), *a.* Destitute of beauty.

beaū′ty (bū′), *n.* [ME. *bewty, beute*; OFr. *biaute, bealtet, beltet*; L. *bellitas*, beauty, from *bellus*, fair, pretty.]

1 An assemblage of perfections through which an object is rendered pleasing to the eye; those qualities in the aggregate that give pleasure to the æsthetic sense.

Beauty is intrinsic when it is observed objectively or externally, as the *beauty* of a lake, the *beauty* of a landscape; it is relative when the perception requires the aid of understanding and conscious application of knowledge and reason, as the *beauty* of a machine, the *beauty* of the solar system.

2. A particular grace, feature, or ornament; any particular thing which is beautiful and pleasing; as, the *beauties* of nature.

3. A particular excellence, or a part which surpasses in excellence that with which it is united; as, the *beauties* of an author.

4. A beautiful person, especially a beautiful woman; collectively, beautiful women.

5. In the arts, symmetry of parts or form; color; harmony; justness of composition.

6. Fashion. [Obs.]

Syn.—Loveliness, grace, fairness, seemliness, picturesqueness, exquisiteness, adornment, embellishment.

beaū′ty=spot (bū′), *n.* A patch; a foil; a spot placed on the face to heighten beauty.

beaux (bōz), *n.*, pl. of *beau.*

beaux′ite (bŏx′), *n.* See *Bauxite.*

bēa′ver *n.* [ME. *baviere*; OFr. *baviere*, the beaver of a helmet, a bib, from *bave*, foam, saliva.] The movable face-shield of a helmet, so constructed that it could be raised and lowered at will, as for drinking, hence its name.

Helmets, time of Henry VII.
1. Beaver raised; 2. Beaver closed.

bēa′vẽr, *n.* [ME. *bever*; AS. *beofer*; D. *bæver.*]

1. An amphibious quadruped, of the genus *Castor*. It has short ears, a blunt nose, small fore feet, large hind feet, with a flat, ovate tail. It furnishes castor, or castoreum, taken from its preputial glands and used both as a medicine and a perfume. Its fur, which is mostly of a chestnut-brown, is the material formerly used for the best hats, now superseded by silk.

Beaver (*Castor fiber*).

2. The fur of the *beaver*, or a hat, glove, or wrap made of the fur.

bēa′vẽr=eat″ẽr, *n.* The wolverene.

bēa′vẽred (-vẽrd), *a.* Covered with or wearing a beaver.

bēa′vẽr=poi″sŏn, *n.* The water-hemlock.

bēa′vẽr=rat *n.* 1. The common name applied to the members of the genus *Hydromys*, a Tasmanian genus containing certain rodent quadrupeds, inhabiting the banks both of salt and fresh waters.

2. The muskrat.

bēa′vẽr=rọọt, *n.* The yellow pond-lily.

bēa′vẽr-teen, *n.* A species of fustian cloth.

bēa′vẽr=tree, *n.* The sweet-bay, *Magnolia glauca.*

bē-bee′riç, bē-bē′riç, *a.* Pertaining to an acid extracted from the bebeeru.

bē-bee′rin, bē-bī′rine (*or* -rīn), *n.* A tonic used as a substitute for quinine; the bark of the bebeeru.

bē-bee′rū, *n.* [Native name.] A South American tropical tree, *Nectandria Rodiæi*, the wood of which is called greenheart, the bark yielding an acid, bebeeric, and an alkaloid, bebeerin.

bē-bleed′, *v.t.* To make bloody. [Obs.]

bē-blood′, bē-blood′y (-blud′), *v.t.* To make bloody. [Obs.]

bē-blot′, *v.t.* To blot; to stain. [Obs.]

bē-blub′bẽr, *v.t.*; beblubbered *pt.*, *pp.*; beblubbering, *ppr.* To disfigure by weeping.

be′bung, *n.* [G., a trembling, from *beben*, to tremble.] A sustained note having a pulsating or trembling effect.

be′çall, *v.t.* To call; to summon; to challenge. [Obs.]

bē-çälm′ (-käm′), *v.t.*; becalmed, *pt.*, *pp.*; becalming, *ppr.* 1. To still; to make quiet; to appease; to stop or repress motion in; used of the elements and of the passions; as, to *becalm* the ocean, or the mind.

2. To keep from motion by intercepting the current of wind; as, highlands *becalm* a ship.

bē-çāme′, *v.*, past tense of *become.*

beç′ărd, *n.* [Fr. *bec*, a beak.] One of a number of South American birds having hooked bills, particularly those of the genus *Tityra.*

bē-çauṣe′, *conj.* [ME. *because, bi cause, by cause*; *by*, by, and *cause*, cause.] By cause; on this account; for the cause which is explained in the next proposition. Thus, I fled, *because* I was afraid, is to be thus resolved: I fled, *by the cause, for the cause*, which is mentioned in the next affirmation, viz., I was afraid. Hence, *cause* being a noun, *because* may be regularly followed by *of.*

> The spirit is life, *because of* righteousness. —Rom. viii. 10.

Syn.—For, as, since, inasmuch as.

beç-çă-bun′gă, *n.* [L., from G. *beckebunga*, brooklime; *becke*, a brook, and *bung*, a bulb.] The common name of the plant *Veronica Beccabunga*, brooklime.

beç-çă-fī′çō, *n.* [It., from *beccare*, to peck, and *fico*, L. *ficus*, a fig.] A passerine bird (*Sylvia hortensis*), family *Sylviadæ*, resembling a nightingale, which feeds on fruits; known also as the *greater pettychaps* and *garden-warbler.*

beçh′ă-mel, *n.* [Fr., from *Béchamel*, steward to Louis XIV.] A kind of fine, white broth, or sauce, thickened with cream.

bē-chànce′, *v.t.* and *v.i.* To befall; to happen to.

bē-chànce′, *adv.* Accidentally; by chance.

bē-chärm′, *v.t.*; becharmed (-chärmd′), *pt.*, *pp.*; becharming, *ppr.* To charm; to captivate.

bêçhe (bāsh), *n.* [Fr., a spade.] A clutching device to grasp and remove an obstruction in a well-hole.

bêçhe=dē=mer′ (bāsh-), *n.* [Fr., spade of the sea.] The trepang, *Holothuria edulis.*

bē′çhiç, *a.* and *n.* [L. *bechicus*; Gr. *bēchikos*, from *bēx*, cough, *bēssein*, to cough.]

I. *a.* Relieving cough.

II. *n.* A remedy for cough.

Bech-ū-ä′năṣ, *n.pl.* A South African tribe of the Bantu family; the Basutos.

beck, *n.* [ME. *bek, bec*; Fr. *bec*, a beak.] A pendent tippet of the headdress, turned like a beak over the forehead, worn in the time of Henry VI.

Beck.

beck, *n.* [ME. *bek*; AS. *becc*; Ice. *bekkr*, a brook.] A small brook; used as an affix in the names of towns which are situated near streams; as, Wal*beck.*

beck, *n.* [ME. *becken, bekken, becknen*, to beckon.] A nod of the head; a significant motion of the hand, especially as a sign of command.

beck, *v.i.*; becked (bekt), *pt.*, *pp.*; becking, *ppr.* To nod, or make a sign with the head or hand.

beck, *v.t.* To call by a nod; to intimate a command to; to notify by a motion of the head or hand.

beck, *n.* A tank or vat.

beck′ẽr, *n.* [Eng. Dial.] A fish of the genus *Pagrus*, otherwise called braize or king of the seabreams.

beck′et, *n.* A device used on ships to confine loose ropes, tackles, or spars, as a large hook, a rope with an eye at one end, or a wooden cleat; a grommet.

beck′ŏn, *v.i.*; beckoned (-ŏnd), *pt.*, *pp.*; beckoning, *ppr.* [ME. *beknen, becnen*; AS. *bēcnian*, from *beācen*, a sign, beacon.] To make a sign to another, by nodding, winking, or a motion of the hand or finger, etc., intended as a hint or intimation.

beck′ŏn, *v.t.* To make a significant sign to.

beck′ŏn, *n.* A sign made without words.

bē-çlap′, *v.t.* To grab; to seize. [Obs.]

bē-çlip′, *v.t.* [AS. *beclyppan*, to embrace.] To embrace. [Obs.]

bē-çloud′, *v.t.*; beclouded, *pt.*, *pp.*; beclouding, *ppr.* To cloud; to obscure; to dim.

bē-çōme′, *v.i.*; became, *pt.*; becoming, *ppr.*; become, *pp.* [ME. *becumen*; AS. *becuman*, to come, happen; *be*, by, about, and *cuman*, to come.]

1. To pass from one state to another; to enter into some state or condition, by a change from another state or condition, or by assuming or receiving new properties or qualities, additional matter, or a new character; as, a scion *becomes* a tree.

2. To come into being; to begin to come about.

To become of; usually with *what* preceding; to be the fate of; to be the end of; to be the final or subsequent condition of; as, *what* will *become of* our commerce?

bē-çōme′, *v.t.* In general, to suit or to be suitable to; to be congruous with; to befit; to accord with, in character or circumstances; to be worthy of, or proper to; to grace; to adorn; applied to persons or things.

> If I *become* not a cart as well as another man, a plague on my bringing up! —Shak.

This use of the word, however, is less frequent, the verb usually expressing the suitableness of *things* to persons or to other things; as, the dress *becomes* its wearer.

> Nothing in his life *became* him like the leaving it. —Shak.

bē-çōm′ed, *a.* Becoming. [Obs.]

bē-çōm′ing, *a.* Fit; suitable; congruous; befitting; proper; graceful; belonging to the character, or adapted to the circumstances; as, he speaks with *becoming* boldness; a dress is very *becoming.*

bē-çōm′ing, *n.* 1. Anything suitable or appropriate.

2. In philosophy, the state of incompleteness between not being and being.

3. Something used to ornament. [Obs.]

bē-çōm′ing-ly, *adv.* In a becoming or proper manner.

bē-çōm′ing-ness, *n.* Fitness; congruity; propriety; decency; the quality of being appropriate or becoming.

Beç-que′rel rays. See under *Ray.*

bē-crip′ple, *v.t.* To make lame; to cripple. [Rare.]

be-cuī′bȧ (-kwē′-), *n.* [Native name.] A tree growing in Brazil which produces a nut yielding a balsam of efficacy in treating rheumatism. It is the *Myriscati Bicuhyba.*

be-cū′nȧ, *n.* [LL.] A ferocious fish of the Mediterranean, *Sphyræna vulgaris*, resembling the pike. From its scales and air-bladder is obtained a substance useful in the manufacture of artificial pearls.

bē-cūrl′, *v.t.* To curl. [Obs.]

bed, *n.* [AS. *bed*; D. *bed*, bed; G. *bett*, or *beet*, a bed, plat of ground.]

1. A place or an article of furniture to sleep and take rest on; a couch; in modern times, and among civilized men, a sack, tick, or mattress filled with feathers or wool; but a *bed* may be made of straw or any other materials. The word *bed* includes often the bedstead.

2. Lodging; a convenient place for sleep.

3. Marriage; matrimonial connection.

> George, the eldest son of his second *bed*.
> —Clarendon.

4. A plat of ground in a garden, usually a little raised above the adjoining level.

5. The channel of a river, or that part in which the water usually flows.

6. Any hollow place; especially, in the arts, a hollow place in which anything rests; as, the *bed* of a mortar.

7. A layer; a stratum; an extended mass of anything, whether upon the earth or within it; as, a *bed* of coal or iron.

8. In mechanics, the foundation or support for a piece of machinery; as, the *bed* of a lathe.

9. In a printing-press, (a) the base; (b) the part against which the form rests.

10. In building, (a) either of the horizontal surfaces of a building stone in position; (b) the under surface of a brick, shingle, slate, or tile in position; (c) the mortar between courses in which a brick or stone is to be laid; (d) a single horizontal course of brick or stone in a wall.

11. In railway construction, the roadbed.

To be brought to bed; to be delivered of a child.

To make a bed; to put a bed in order after it has been used.

To make one's own bed; to bring about one's own condition.

bed, *v.t.*; bedded, *pt., pp.*; bedding, *ppr.* 1. To place in a bed. [Obs.]

2. To go to bed with. [Rare.]

3. To make partaker of a bed.

4. To furnish with a bed or bedding.

5. To plant and inclose or cover; to set or lay and inclose; as, to *bed* the roots of a plant in soft mold.

6. To lay in any hollow place, surrounded or inclosed; as, to *bed* a stone.

7. To lay in a place of rest or security, covered, surrounded, or inclosed; as, a fish *bedded* in sand.

8. To lay in a stratum; to stratify; to lay in order, or flat; as, *bedded* clay; *bedded* hairs.

9. In masonry, to trim up (a stone or boulder), preparatory to laying.

bed, *v.i.* To cohabit; to use the same bed.

> If he be married and *bed* with his wife.
> —Wiseman.

bē-dab′ble, *v.t.*; bedabbled (-bld), *pt., pp.*; bedabbling, *ppr.* To wet; to sprinkle.

bē-daff′, *v.t.* To make a fool of. [Obs.]

bē-dag′gle, *v.t.*; bedaggled (-gld), *pt., pp.*; bedaggling, *ppr.* To soil, as clothes.

bē-dash′, *v.t.* To wet, as by throwing water.

bē-daub′, *v.t.*; bedaubed, *pt., pp.*; bedaubing, *ppr.* To daub over; to besmear with viscous, slimy matter; to soil with anything thick and dirty.

bē-daz′zle, *v.t.*; bedazzled (-zld), *pt., pp.*; bedazzling, *ppr.* To blind by too strong a light; to dazzle or make dim by luster.

bed′bug, *n.* The *Cimex lectularius*, a wingless insect having a disgusting smell, and infesting beds.

bed′chāir (-chãr), *n.* An adjustable chair for invalids unable to leave their bed.

bed′chām″bēr, *n.* An apartment or chamber intended or appropriated for a bed, or for sleeping purposes.

Lords of the bedchamber; officers of the royal household of England, under the groom of the stole. They are twelve in number, and wait a week each in turn.

Ladies of the bedchamber; ladies whose duties are analogous to those of the lords, in case of a queen regnant.

bed′clothes, *n.pl.* Blankets, sheets, coverlets, etc., for beds.

bed′cord, *n.* A cord or rope fastened to a bedstead so as to support the mattress or bed.

bed′ded, *a.* Laid in a bed; inclosed as in a bed; stratified.

bed′dēr, be-det′tēr, *n.* The nether stone of an oil-mill.

bed′ding, *n.* 1. A bed and its furniture; a bed; the materials of a bed, whether for man or beast.

2. The act of putting to bed; as, the *bedding* of a newly married couple.

3. In geology, the stratification or position of beds and layers.

4. In building, a foundation or bottom layer of some kind.

bēde, *v.t.* To tender; sometimes, to pray. [Obs.]

bēde, *n.* [Eng.] A miner's pickax.

bē-deck′, *v.t.* To deck; to adorn; to grace.

bed′ē-gär, bed′ē-guär (-gär), *n.* [Fr. *bédegar*; Per. *bādāwar*, a white thorn, literally, windbrought, from *bād*, wind, and *āwar*, pp. of *āwardan*, to bring.] A hairy or spongy substance or gall on rosebushes, produced by the puncture of certain insects, and once supposed to have valuable medical properties.

aa, Bedegar on the Rose.

bēde′house, *n.* See *Beadhouse.*

bē′del, bē′dell (bē′dl), *n.* Same as *Beadle.*

bē′del-ry (-dl-), *n.* The extent of a beadle's office. [Obs.]

bed′en, *n.* [Ar. *baden.*] An ibex; probably the wild goat of biblical times.

bēdes′măn, *n.* [Obs.] See *Beadsman.*

bēdes′wom″ăn (-woom″-), *n.* [Obs.] See *Beadswoman.*

bē-dev′il, *v.t.*; bedeviled (-ld), *pt., pp.*; bedeviling, *ppr.* To throw into utter disorder and confusion, as if by the agency of evil spirits; also, to ruin.

bē-dev′il-ment, *n.* Vexatious confusion or bewilderment. [Colloq.]

bē-dew′, *v.t.*; bedewed (-dewd), *pt., pp.*; bedewing, *ppr.* [ME. *bedewen*; G. *bethauen.*] To moisten, as with dew; to moisten in a gentle manner with any liquid; as, tears *bedew* her face.

bē-dew′ēr, *n.* One who or that which bedews.

bē-dew′y, *a.* Moist with dew. [Rare.]

bed′fel″lōw, *n.* One who lies with another in the same bed.

bed′fēre, bed′phēre, *n.* A companion in bed. [Obs.]

bed′gown, *n.* A sleeping robe.

bē-dight′ (-dīt′), *v.t.*; bedight *or* bedighted, *pt., pp.*; bedighting, *ppr.* To adorn; to dress; to set off with ornament. [Rare.]

bē-dim′, *v.t.*; bedimmed (-dimd), *pt., pp.*; bedimming, *ppr.* To make dim; to obscure or darken.

bē-diz′en (*or* -dīz′n), *v.t.*; bedizened, *pt., pp.*; bedizening, *ppr.* To adorn; to deck; especially, to adorn in a loud manner or with vulgarity.

> Remnants . . . with which he had *bedizened* his tatters.
> —Scott.

bē-diz′en-ment, *n.* That which bedizens; the state of being bedizened.

bed′kēy, *n.* A bedwrench.

bed′lăm, *n.* [ME. *bedlem, bedleem, bethlem*, from *Bethlehem*, a religious house in London, converted into a hospital.]

1. A madhouse; a place appropriated for lunatics.

2. A madman; a lunatic; one who lives in bedlam. [Obs.]

3. Figuratively, any scene of wild uproar and madness.

> A division of possessions would make the country a *bedlam* for one short season and a charnel-house ever after. —Brougham.

bed′lăm, *a.* Belonging to a madhouse; fit for a madhouse.

bed′lăm-ism, *n.* A bordering on insanity; madness and disorder.

bed′lăm-īte, *n.* An inhabitant of a madhouse; a madman.

bed′māk″ēr, *n.* One who puts a bed in order, usually involving care of the bedroom, as in English universities and hotels; one who manufactures beds.

bed′=mōld″ing, bed′=mōuld″ing, *n.* In architecture, the moldings of a cornice which are placed below the corona, consisting of an ogee, a list, a large boltel, and another list under the corona.

bē-dōte′, *v.t.* To make to dote. [Obs.]

Bed′ōu-in, *n.* [Fr. *Bédouin*; Ar. *bedāwi*, dwellers in the desert.]

1. One of a tribe of nomadic Arabs, who live in tents and are scattered over Arabia, and Egypt, and other parts of Africa.

2. A nomad; also, a street vagabond.

Bed′ōu-in, *a.* Of, relating, or pertaining to the Bedouins; nomadic.

bed′pan, *n.* A necessary vessel used by one who is bedridden; formerly, a pan for warming beds.

bed′phēre, *n.* See *Bedfere.*

bed′plāte, bed′pīece, *n.* A stayed and stiffened base or support for a piece of machinery.

bed′pōst, *n.* Formerly, one of two posts placed at the side of a bed to keep on the clothes; now, a corner-post supporting the canopy.

bed′quilt, *n.* A quilted spread or cover for a bed.

bē-drab′ble, *v.t.*; bedrabbled (-bld), *pt., pp.*; bedrabbling, *ppr.* To soil with slush, mud, or rain.

bē-drag′gle, *v.t.*; bedraggled (-gld), *pt., pp.*; bedraggling, *ppr.* To soil by splashing, as skirts; to wet in rain, as a flag.

bē-drench′, *v.t.*; bedrenched (-drencht′), *pt., pp.*; bedrenching, *ppr.* To drench; to soak; to saturate with moisture.

bed′rid, bed′rid″den, *a.* [ME. *bedred*; AS. *bedreda*, bedridden, from *bed*, bed, and *rida, ridda*, a rider.] Confined to the bed by age or infirmity.

bed′rīght, bed′rīte, *n.* The privilege of the marriage bed. [Obs.]

bē-driz′zle, *v.t.* To rain upon.

bed′rock, *n.* The solid foundation rock lying under the surface.

bed′room, *n.* 1. A room or apartment intended for or containing a bed; a lodging-room.

2. Room in a bed. [Obs.]

bē-drop′, *v.t.* [ME. *bedroppen.*] To sprinkle, as with drops.

bē-drug′, *v.t.* To drug to excess.

bed′screw, *n.* 1. A bedwrench.

2. A jackscrew used in shipyards.

bed′sīde, *n.* The side of a bed.

bed′sīte, *n.* The place where a bed is to stand.

bed′sōre, *n.* A sore place on the body, caused by lying in bed for a long time.

bed′spread (-spred), *n.* An outer covering for bedclothes, generally of attractive or fancy appearance.

bed′stăff, *n.*; *pl.* **bed′stāves.** A stick formerly used about a bed, sometimes as a means of keeping on the clothes; commonly referred to by old writers as a defensive weapon.

bed′stead, *n.* [ME. *bedstede*, from AS. *bed*, bed, and *stede*, place.] A frame for supporting a bed.

bed′steps, *n.pl.* Steps used to mount a bed.

bed′stock, *n.* Part of the frame of a bed, generally considered the front or back.

bed′straw, *n.* [ME. *beddestrawe.*]

1. Straw put into a bed to make it soft.

2. The popular name of the different species of *Galium.*

Our Lady's bedstraw; a yellow flower, *Galium verum.*

White bedstraw; a wild summer flower, *Galium Mollugo.*

bed′swērv″ēr, *n.* An adulterer or adulteress.

bed′tick, *n.* A case of strong linen or cotton cloth, used for inclosing the feathers or other materials of a bed.

bed′tīme, *n.* The time to go to rest; the usual hour of going to bed.

bē-duck′, *v.t.* To duck; to put under water; to immerse.

bē-dung′, *v.t.* To cover with dung.

bē-dust′, *v.t.* To sprinkle, soil, or cover with dust.

bed′wărd, *adv.* Toward bed.

bē-dwarf′, *v.t.*; bedwarfed, *pt., pp.*; bedwarfing, *ppr.* To make little; to stunt or hinder the growth of; to dwarf.

bed′wrench (-rench), *n.* A wrench formerly used for setting up and taking down beds.

bē-dȳe′, *v.t.* To dye; to stain.

bee, *n.* [ME. *bee*, pl. *been*; from AS. *beo*, or *bi*, pl. *beón.*]

1. An insect of the genus *Apis*; specifically, the common hive-*bee*, which has been cultivated from the earliest periods for its wax and honey. It lives in swarms containing three classes of *bees*: the females or queen *bees*, of which there is only one in each swarm; the males or drones, and the neuters or working *bees*. The queen *bee* propagates the species, the drones serve to impregnate the queen, after which they are destroyed by the neuters, who are the laborers of the hive, collecting the honey from flowers, and conveying it to the hive. The pollen of flowers, also collected by the neuters and called *beebread*, is the food of the larvæ or young. The wax is formed from the honey by a digestive process. The females and neuters have a barbed sting.

2. Any insect related to the common hive-*bee*; as, the mason-*bee*, the bumble-*bee*, etc.

3. A gathering of neighbors or friends, who work together to help out some individual or family; as, a husking-*bee*, a raising-*bee*, a quilting-*bee*. Also, a gathering for friendly competition; as, a spelling-*bee*.

To have a bee in one's bonnet; to be a crank on some subject, especially in regard to one's ambition.

To have a bee in the head; to be full of fancies; to be restless or uneasy.

Bee larkspur; a plant, *Delphinium elatum.*

bee′=bälm (-bäm), *n.* An aromatic plant, *Melissa officinalis*, having an odor like that of a lemon, and used in medicine or as a flavor.

bee′=bee″tle, *n.* A parasitic beetle, *Trichodes apiarius*, which invades beehives.

bee′=bīrd, *n.* A bee-eating bird, as the kingbird or the spotted flycatcher.

bee′=blocks, *n.pl.* Nautically, the pieces of hardwood bolted against the bowsprit of a ship, through which the foretopmast stays are reeved.

bee′bread (-bred), *n.* A brown, bitter substance, made of the pollen of flowers, collected by bees as food for their young.

beech, *n.* [ME. *beche*; AS. *bēce*, beech.] A tree, arranged by Linnæus under the genus *Fagus*, which grows to a large size, with branches forming a beautiful head, with thick foliage. The bark is smooth and was formerly used for writing upon.

Copper beech; the European beech, *Fagus sylvatica*.

beech′=cōal, *n.* Charcoal from beech-wood.

beech′=drops, *n.* A parasitic plant, *Epiphegus Virginiana*, growing upon the roots of the beech.

beech′en, *a.* Consisting of the wood or bark of the beech; belonging to the beech; as, a *beechen* vessel.

beech′=mȧst, *n.* The nuts of the beech.

beech′nut, *n.* One of the nuts or fruits of the beech.

beech′=oil, *n.* The oil of beech-mast or beechnuts.

beech′y, *a.* Of or pertaining to beeches.

bee′=ēat″ẽr, *n.* A bird that feeds on bees. A name common to the different species of birds of the genus *Merops*, of which the *Merops apiaster* of Europe is remarkable for the brilliancy of its plumage.

beef, *n.* [ME. *beef*, *befe*; OFr. *boef*, *buef*, beef; L. *bos*, genit. *bovis*; Gr. *bous*, an ox.]

1. An animal of the bovine genus, whether ox, bull, or cow, in the full-grown state. In this, which is the original sense, the word has a plural, *beeves*, but sometimes formerly *beefs*.

> A herd of *beeves*, fair oxen, and fair kine. —Milton.

> Flesh of muttons, *beefs*, or goats. —Shak.

2. The flesh of an ox, bull, or cow, when killed; in this sense the word has no plural.

3. Colloquially, weight; massive strength; as, a pugilist all *beef*.

beef′ēat″ẽr, *n.* 1. One who eats beef; one who looks well-fed or beefy.

2. A popular appellation for the yeomen of the guard, in England, who attend the sovereign at state banquets and on other ceremonial occasions; and also for the warders of the Tower of London, who wear a quaint medieval uniform.

3. The *Buphaga africana*, an African bird that feeds on the larvæ encysted under the hides of cattle.

4. A bluebottle or flesh-fly.

Beefeater.

bee′=flow″ẽr, *n.* See *Bee-orchis*.

bee′=flȳ, *n.* A fly whose larvæ are parasitic upon bees.

beef′steāk, *n.* A steak or slice of beef, particularly when broiled or for broiling.

beef′=wit″ted, *a.* Dull in intellect; stupid; heavy-headed.

beef′wood, *n.* The timber of some species of Australian trees belonging to the genus *Casuarina*, of a reddish color, hard, and close-grained, with dark and whitish streaks, and used chiefly in fine ornamental work.

beef′y, *a.* Of a heavy build; thickset; often applied to persons.

bee′=gär″den, *n.* A garden or inclosure to set beehives in.

bee′=glūe, *n.* A soft, adhesive matter with which bees cement the combs to the hives, and close up the cells; called also *propolis*.

bee′=hawk, *n.* The honey-buzzard.

bee′hive, *n.* A hive or habitation for a colony of bees; formerly a dome-shaped structure of straw, having a small rectangular door for ingress and egress; now a box or case of various materials and shapes.

Beehive houses; ancient houses, or remains of houses, found in Scotland and Ireland, and so called from their shape, which is that of the old-style beehive.

bee′house, *n.* An apiary.

beeld, *n.* Same as *Bield*.

bee′=line, *n.* The shortest distance between two points or localities.

Bē-el′zē-bub, *n.* [ME. *Belsebub*; L. *Beelzebub*; Gr. *Beelzeboub*; Heb. *Baalzebub*; literally meaning the god of insects; *baal*, lord, and *zebub*, a fly, insect.] A god of the Philistines, who had a famous temple at Ekron. He was worshiped as the destroyer of flies.

Bē-el′zē-bul, *n.* A name given by the Jews to the prince of demons, being an opprobrious change of the term *Beelzebub*.

beem, *n.* [AS. *bēme*.] A trumpet. [Obs.]

bee′=mär″tin, *n.* The kingbird, *Tyrannus carolinensis*.

bee′mȧs″tẽr, *n.* One who keeps bees.

bee′=mọth, *n.* A moth, *Galleria cereana*, having larvæ destructive in beehives.

been (bin *or* bēn), *v.*, past participle of *be*.

been (bēn), *n.* [Hind. *bīn*, a lute or guitar.] A fretted stringed instrument of music of the guitar kind, having nineteen frets; long used in India.

bē′ent, *a.* Having the form of changeless being; a forced translation of the German *seiend*. [Rare.]

bee′=ȯr″chis, *n.* A European orchid, *Ophrys apifera*, having flowers formed somewhat like a bee; called also *bee-flower*.

bee′=plant, *n.* Any plant from which bees obtain honey.

beer, *n.* [ME. *bere*; OE. *beor*; AS. *beór*, beer.]

1. A fermented liquor made from any farinaceous grain, but generally from barley, which is first malted and ground, and its fermentable substance then extracted by hot water. This extract or infusion is boiled in caldrons, and hops or some other substance of an agreeable bitterness added. The liquor is then suffered to ferment in vats. *Beer* is of different degrees of strength, and is denominated lager, ale, porter, brown stout, etc., according to its strength, or other peculiar qualities.

2. A name also given to fermented liquors made of the roots and other parts of various plants, as spruce *beer*, ginger *beer*, root *beer*, etc.

Bitter beer; ale or beer containing a large percentage of hops.

Black beer; any beer of a very dark or black color, especially that made from malt roasted black.

Green beer; beer that has been recently fermented.

Near beer; malt liquor containing so little alcohol it will not intoxicate though used to excess.

Small beer; (a) weak beer; (b) figuratively, matters of little or no importance.

> To suckle fools, and chronicle *small beer*. —Shak.

Weiss beer; a variety of German beer, brewed from wheat and very light in color, whence the name; now made and commonly used in this country.

beer′e-gär, *n.* Vinegar made from beer; sour beer. [Obs.]

beer′=en″gine, *n.* A hydraulic apparatus for raising beer from a cellar to the faucets from which it is retailed.

beer′=gär″den, *n.* Any inclosed outdoor place where beer is sold, usually a yard adjoining a saloon.

beer′house, *n.* A house where malt liquors are sold; an alehouse; a storehouse for beer.

beer′i-ness, *n.* Beery condition.

beer′=mŏn″ey, *n.* An allowance to servants, etc., in lieu of beer.

beer′=pụll, *n.* A beer-pump or its handle.

beer′y, *a.* Of, pertaining to, or resembling beer; in a maudlin condition.

beest′ings, *n. sing.* and *pl.* See *Biestings*.

bees′wax, *n.* The wax collected by bees, and of which their cells are constructed.

bees′wing, *n.* 1. A gauzy film in port wines, indicative of age, much esteemed by connoisseurs.

2. Any wine so crusted over.

beet, *n.* [ME. *bete*; AS. *bēte*; from L. *beta*, beet.]

1. A plant of the genus *Beta*, which produces an edible root. The species cultivated in gardens are the *cicla* and *vulgaris*, or white and red *beet*. There are many varieties; some with long taper roots, and others with flat roots, like turnips.

2. The root of plants of this genus, different species and varieties of which are used for the table, for feeding stock, or for making sugar. Immense quantities of the sugar-*beet* are now raised annually for use in sugar factories.

beete, bēte, *v.t.* [AS. *bētan*, to mend.] Obsolete forms of *beat*.

bee′tle (-tl), *n.* [AS. *bītl*, or *bytl*, a mallet.]

1. A heavy wooden mallet, used to drive wedges, consolidate earth, etc.

2. A machine for producing figured fabrics by pressure from corrugated or indented rollers.

bee′tle, *v.t.*; beetled (-tld), *pt.*, *pp.*; beetling, *ppr.* 1. To use a beetle on; to beat with a heavy wooden mallet, as linen or cotton cloth, as a substitute for mangling.

2. To produce figures on (cloth) by passing it through a beetle.

bee′tle, *n.* [ME. *bitle*, *bityl*; from AS. *bitela*, *bitel*, beetle; from *bitan*, to bite.] Any insect belonging to the order *Coleoptera*. Sometimes the term is used in a more restricted sense, as equivalent to *Scarabæidæ*, a tribe of this order

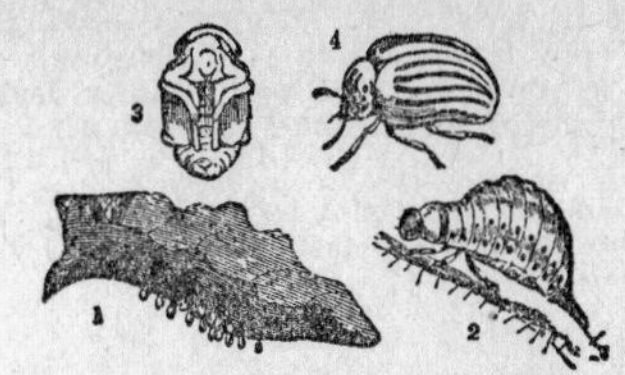

Colorado Beetle (*Doryphora decemlineata*).
1. Part of leaf with eggs of the insect. 2. Caterpillar. 3. Pupa. 4. Perfect insect. (All natural size.)

embracing more than 3,000 species, characterized by clavated antennæ, fissile longitudinally, legs frequently dentated, and wings which have hard cases or sheaths called elytra. *Beetles* vary in size from that of a pin's head to the bulk of a man's fist, the largest being the elephant-*beetle* of South America, four inches long. The black-*beetles* of kitchens and cellars are cockroaches, and belong to the order *Orthoptera*.

Colorado beetle or *potato-bug*; a coleopterous insect, *Doryphora decemlineata*, somewhat larger than a pea, nearly oval, convex, of a yellowish color, marked with black spots, and on the elytra, under which the wings are folded, with ten black longitudinal stripes. This insect works havoc among the potato crops.

bee′tle, *v.i.* To jut; to be prominent; to hang or extend out; as, a cliff that *beetles* over its base.

bee′tle-brow, *n.* A prominent or overhanging brow.

bee′tle=browed, *a.* Having prominent brows; sometimes, ill-humored; gloomy.

bee′tle=head (-hed), *n.* A stupid fellow.

bee′tle=head″ed, *a.* Having a head like a beetle; dull; stupid.

bee′tle-stock, *n.* A beetle-handle.

bee′tling, *a.* Jutting out; prominent; standing out from the main body; as, *beetling* brows.

beet′=rad″ish, beet′rāve, *n.* [Fr. *bette-rave*; *bette*, beet, and *rave*, radish; from L. *beta*, beet, and *rapa*, a turnip.] The common beet.

beet′=sụg″ăr (-shụg″ăr), *n.* Sugar made from beet-roots.

beeve, *n.* An animal of the bovine genus, as a cow, bull, or ox. In the singular rare, and a corruption due to the influence of *beeves*, the plural of *beef*.

> They would knock down the first *beeve* they met with. —Irving.

beeves, *n.*, pl. of *beef*.

bee′=wolf (-wụlf), *n.* A bee-beetle in the larval stage.

bē-fạll′, *v.t.*; befell, *pt.*; befalling, *ppr.*; befallen, *pp.* [ME. *befallen*, fall, happen; AS. *befeallan*, to fall.] To happen to; to occur to; as, the worst that can *befall* one.

bē-fạll′, *v.i.* To happen; to come to pass.

> I have revealed this discord which *befell*. —Milton.

bē-fit′, *v.t.*; befitted, *pt.*, *pp.*; befitting, *ppr.* To suit; to be suitable to; to become.

> That name best *befits* thee. —Milton.

bē-fit′ting, *a.* Appropriate; suitable; consistent.

bē-fit′ting-ly, *adv.* Becomingly; in a suitable or befitting manner.

bē-flat′tẽr, *v.t.* To flatter effusively.

bē-flow′ẽr, *v.t.* To scatter with flowers.

bē-fōam′, *v.t.* To cover with foam. [Rare.]

bē-fog′, *v.t.*; befogged, *pt.*, *pp.*; befogging, *ppr.* To involve in fog; hence, figuratively, to confuse.

bē-fọọl′, *v.t.*; befooled, *pt.*, *pp.*; befooling, *ppr.*

1. To fool; to infatuate; to delude or lead into error.

> Men *befool* themselves. —South.

2. To cause to act foolishly; as, liquor *befooled* him. [Rare.]

bē-fōre′, *prep.* [ME. *beforen*, *biforen*, from AS. *beforan*, *biforan*, from *be*, by, and *foran*, adv., before.]

1. In front of; at the fore part of; in advance of in space; as, *before* the house; *before* the fire.

2. In presence of; in sight of.

> Abraham bowed down himself *before* the people of the land. —Gen. xxiii. 12.

3. Under the cognizance, jurisdiction, or consideration of.

> The cause of both parties shall come *before* the judges. —Ex. xxii. 9.

4. Preceding in time; as, I will return *before* six o'clock. Like *after*, this word often precedes a clause, as a governing preposition, and thus has the function of a conjunction.

Before this treatise can become of use two points are necessary. —Swift.

5. In preference to; prior to; having precedence of in rank, dignity, or the like.

We think poverty to be infinitely desirable *before* the torments of covetousness. —Taylor.

Before the mast; in or into the condition of a common sailor, the portion of a ship behind the mainmast being reserved for the officers.

Before the wind; nautically, in the direction of the wind by its impulse.

bē-fōre′, *adv.* 1. Further onward in place; in front; in the fore part.

Reaching forth unto those things which are *before*. —Phil. iii. 13.

The battle was *before* and behind. —2 Chron. xiii. 14.

2. In time preceding; previously; formerly; already.

You tell me what I knew *before*. —Dryden.

Before is used in composition, retaining its meaning; as, *before*-mentioned.

bē-fōre′hand, *adv.* 1. In a state of anticipation or preoccupation; often followed by *with*; as, you are *beforehand with* me.

2. Antecedently; by way of preparation or preliminary; betimes; as, I got ready *beforehand*.

3. At first; before anything is done. [Obs.]

bē-fōre′hand, *a.* In good pecuniary circumstances.

bē-fōre′time, *adv.* Formerly; of old time.

bē-fọr′tūne, *v.t.* To happen to; to betide.

bē-foul′, *v.t.*; befouled, *pt.*, *pp.*; befouling, *ppr.* [ME. *befoulen*; from AS. *befylan*, to befoul.]

1. To make foul; to soil.

2. To fall foul of; to entangle with; to run against.

bē-friend′ (-frend′), *v.t.*; befriended, *pt.*, *pp.*; befriending, *ppr.* To favor; to act as a friend to; to countenance, aid, or benefit.

bē-friend′ment, *n.* The act of befriending. [Rare.]

bē-frill′, *v.t.* To adorn with a frill or frills.

bē-fringe′, *v.t.* To furnish with a fringe; to adorn as with a fringe.

bē-fud′dle (-dl), *v.t.*; befuddled, *pt.*, *pp.*; befuddling, *ppr.* To mystify; to confuse; to muddle, as with drink.

beg (*or* bā), *n.* [Turk.] In Turkey, a governor; more particularly, the lord of a sanjak or banner; a bey.

beg, *v.t.*; begged, *pt.*, *pp.*; begging, *ppr.* [ME. *beggen*; AS. *bedecian*.]

1. To ask earnestly; to beseech; to entreat or supplicate with humility.

2. To ask or supplicate in charity; as, to *beg* bread.

3. To take for granted; to assume without proof; as, to *beg* the question in debate.

4. To ask respectfully or deferentially; as, to *beg* pardon; to *beg* leave, etc.

To beg a person for a fool; to be appointed his guardian. [Obs.]

To go a-begging; to be valueless or not wanted by reason of being plentiful.

Syn.—Beseech, solicit, entreat, supplicate, implore, crave, ask, pray, petition.—To *beg* denotes a state of want; to *beseech, entreat*, and *solicit*, a state of urgent necessity; *supplicate* and *implore* a state of abject distress; *crave*, the lowest state of physical want. One *begs* with importunity; *beseeches* with earnestness; *entreats* by the force of reasoning and strong representation; *solicits* by virtue of one's interest; *supplicates* by a humble address; *implores* by every mark of dejection and humiliation. *Begging* is the act of the poor when they need assistance; *beseeching* and *entreating* are resorted to by friends and equals when they want to influence or persuade, but *beseeching* is more urgent, *entreating* more argumentative; *solicitations* are employed to obtain favors which have more respect to the circumstances than the rank of the solicitor; *supplicating* and *imploring* are resorted to by sufferers for the relief of their misery, and are addressed to those who have the power of averting or increasing the calamity; *craving* is the consequence of longing; it marks an earnestness of *supplication*.

beg, *v.i.* 1. To ask alms or charity; to practise begging; to live by asking alms.

2. In card games, as seven-up, to ask for a point or new trump.

bē′gȧ, *n.* See *Bigha*.

bē-gan′, *v.*, past tense of *begin*.

bē-gat′, *v.*, past tense of *beget*. [Obs.]

bē-gem′, *v.t.*; begemmed (-jemd), *pt.*, *pp.*; begemming, *ppr.* To decorate with jewels or gems.

bē-get′, *v.t.*; begot *or* begat, *pt.*; begetting, *ppr.*; begot *or* begotten, *pp.* [ME. *begeten*, to obtain; AS. *begitan*, to acquire; *bi*, be-, and *gitan*, to get.]

1. To procreate, as a father or sire; to generate; as, to *beget* a son.

2. To produce, as an effect; to cause to exist; to generate; as, luxuries *beget* vice.

bē-get′tēr, *n.* One who begets or procreates; a father.

beg′gȧ-ble, *a.* Capable of being begged.

beg′gär, *n.* [ME. *beggar*, *beggere*, from *beggen*, to beg.]

1. One who lives by asking alms, or makes it his business to beg for charity.

2. One who assumes in argument what he does not prove.

beg′gär, *v.t.*; beggared (-gärd), *pt.*, *pp.*; beggaring, *ppr.* 1. To reduce to beggary; to impoverish; as, to *beggar* one's family.

2. Figuratively, to exhaust the capacity of; as, to *beggar* description.

beg′gär-hood, *n.* The state of being a beggar; the whole tribe of beggars.

beg′gär-ism, *n.* The state of beggary. [Rare.]

beg′gär-li-ness, *n.* The state of being beggarly; meanness.

beg′gär-ly, *a.* Mean; poor; in the condition of a beggar; extremely indigent; contemptible; used of both persons and things.

Syn.—Miserable, stinted, wretched, niggardly, scant, illiberal.

beg′gär-ly, *adv.* Meanly; indigently; despicably.

beg′gär's-līce, *n.* 1. The bidentate seeds of certain weeds, as *Bidens frondosa*; beggar's-ticks; sticktights.

2. In England, the vulgar name of *Galium Aparine* or goose-grass.

beg′gär's-ticks, *n.* Beggar's-lice.

beg′gär-y, *n.* [ME. *beggerie*; from *beggere*, a beggar.]

1. A state of extreme indigence.

2. The state of being a mendicant or beggar.

3. A beggarly as ect or appearance. [Rare.]

Syn.—Indigence, poverty, want.

beg′gär-y, *a.* 1. Beggarly; mean. [Rare.]

2. Run to weeds; weedy. [Prov. Eng.]

Bē-ghärd′ (-gärd′), *n.* [OFr. *begard*; LL. *Beghardus*, from Lambert le *Begue*, the Stammerer, founder of the Beguins.]

1. A term applied formerly to some of the Franciscans and other mendicant orders of monks.

2. One of a class of persons distinguished for the fervor and frequency of their prayers; they flourished in Flanders in the thirteenth century; called in France *Beguins*.

Sometimes written without the capital.

bē-gild′, *v.t.*; begilded *or* begilt, *pt.*, *pp.*; begilding, *ppr.* To gild.

bē-gilt′, *a.* Gilded.

bē-gin′, *v.i.*; began, begun, *pt.*; beginning, *ppr.*; begun, *pp.* [ME. *beginnen*, from AS. *beginnan*, *onginnan*, to begin.]

1. To have an original or first existence; to take rise; to commence.

2. To do the first act; to enter upon something new; to take the first step.

bē-gin′, *v.t.* 1. To start; to enter on; to commence.

2. To trace from anything, as the first ground; to lay the foundation of.

Syn.—Commence, enter upon, originate, inaugurate, institute, start, set on foot.

bē-gin′, *n.* Beginning. [Obs.]

bē-gin′nēr, *n.* One who begins; also, an elementary student; a novice.

bē-gin′ning, *n.* 1. The first cause; origin; source.

2. That which is first; the first state; commencement; entrance into being.

3. The rudiments, first ground, or materials.

Syn.—Commencement, start, initiation, preface, inauguration, inception, opening, outset.

bē-gird′, *v.t.*; begirt *or* begirded, *pt.*, *pp.*; begirding, *ppr.* [ME. *begirden*, from AS. *begyrdan*, to gird.]

1. To bind with a band or girdle.

2. To surround, as with a girdle; to encompass.

bē-gir′dle, *v.t.*; begirdled (-gir̄dld), *pt.*, *pp.*; begirdling, *ppr.* To encompass as with a girdle.

bē-girt′, *v.t.* To begird.

beg′lēr-beg, *n.* [Turk.] The governor of a province in the Turkish empire, next in dignity to the grand vizier.

bē-gnaw′ (-naw′), *v.t.* [AS. *begnagan*.] To bite or gnaw; to eat away; to corrode.

bē-god′, *v.t.* To deify. [Obs.]

bē-gone′, *interj.* Go away; depart; be gone.

Bē-gō′ni-ȧ, *n.* [Named after Michel *Begon*, a French botanist.] A genus of herbaceous plants, natives of the tropical regions of America. They are called elephant's-ear from the form of their leaves.

Bē-gō-ni-ā′cē-æ, *n.pl.* A natural order of exogens, the members of which occur mostly in the tropical parts of both the Old and New World, particularly in Asia and America.

bē-gō-ni-ā′ceous, *a.* Belonging to the order *Begoniaceæ*.

bē-gōre′, *v.t.* To bespatter with gore.

bē-got′, *v.*, past tense of *beget*.

bē-grāve′, *v.t.* To place in a grave; also, to engrave. [Obs.]

bē-grēase′, *v.t.* To soil or daub with grease, or other oily matter.

be-grīme′, *v.t.*; begrimed, *pt.*, *pp.*; begriming, *ppr.* To dirty, grinding the dirt in.

bē-grīm′ēr, *n.* One who or that which dirties.

bē-grudġe′ (-gruj′), *v.t.*; begrudged, *pt.*, *pp.*; begrudging, *ppr.* To grudge; to envy the possession of.

bē-guīle′ (-gīl′), *v.t.*; beguiled (-gīld′), *pt.*, *pp.*; beguiling, *ppr.* 1. To delude; to deceive; to impose on by artifice or craft.

2. To relieve weariness in, by amusement; to pass pleasingly; to charm, or divert; as, to *beguile* the time with gossip.

3. To elude by craft. [Obs.]

Syn.—Deceive, delude, mislead, divert, entertain.

bē-guīle′ment, *n.* The act of beguiling; the state of being beguiled.

bē-guīl′ēr, *n.* One who or that which beguiles or deceives.

bē-guīl′ing-ly, *adv.* In a manner to beguile.

Bē-guin′ (bā-gaṅ′), *n.* [Fr.] See *Beghard*.

bē-guï-näġe′ (bā-gï-näzh′), *n.* [Fr.] A convent or community of Beguines.

Bē-guīne′ (bā-gēn′), *n.* [OFr. *beguine*; LL. *beguina*, from Lambert le *Begue*, the Stammerer, who founded the order.] One of an order founded in the twelfth century in the Netherlands, composed of women who united for devotion and charity, and lived together without monastic vows.

Beguine.

bē′gum (*or* bā′gum), *n.* [Anglo-Ind. word, from Hind. *begam*, a lady, from Turk. *bigim*, a princess.] In the East Indies, a princess or lady of high rank.

bē-gun′, *v.*, past tense and past participle of *begin*.

bē-hälf′ (-häf′), *n.* [ME. *behalve*, in the phrase *on behalve*, on my side; AS. *on healve*, *on healfe*; *on*, on, and *healve*, dat. of *healf*, half.] Favor; advantage; convenience; profit; support; defense; vindication; as, in *behalf* of the prisoner. *Behalf* is always preceded by the prepositions *in*, *on*, or *upon*.

bē-hap′pen, *v.i.* To happen to. [Obs.]

bē-hāve′, *v.i.*; behaved, *pt.*, *pp.*; behaving, *ppr.* To act; to conduct; applied to manners, conduct, or actions; as, to *behave* badly or well; the ship *behaved* admirably.

bē-hāve′, *v.t.* [ME. *behaven*; AS. *behabban*, to hold, restrain; *be*, about, and *habban*, to have.]

1. To restrain; to govern; to subdue. [Obs.]

2. To conduct; to carry; used in a reflexive manner; as, to *behave* oneself.

Syn.—Conduct, carry, deport, comport, manage, act.

bē-hāv′iōr (-yur), *n.* Manner of behaving, whether good or bad; conduct; manners; carriage of oneself, with respect to propriety or morals; deportment. It expresses external appearance or action; sometimes in a particular character; more generally in the common duties of life; as, our success often depends on our *behavior*. The word is used also of inanimate objects; as, the *behavior* of a ship; the *behavior* of a magnetic needle.

To be upon one's behavior; to be in a state of trial, in which something important depends on propriety of conduct. The modern phrase is, *to be*, or *to be put, upon one's good behavior*.

During good behavior; as long as integrity and fidelity mark official conduct.

Syn.—Conduct, deportment, demeanor, bearing, carriage, manner.—*Behavior* is the manner of our behaving ourselves toward others; *conduct* is the manner of our conducting ourselves, and involves the general tenor of our actions. The former, like *deportment*, is shaped chiefly by circumstances; the latter is a development of the individual.

bē-head′ (-hed′), *v.t.*; beheaded, *pt.*, *pp.*; beheading, *ppr.* To cut off the head of; to sever the head from the body of, with a cutting instrument; appropriately used of the execution of men for crimes.

bē-head′ăl, *n.* The act of beheading.

bē-held′, *v.*, past tense and past participle of *behold*.

bē′hē-mọth, *n.* [Heb. *b'hemoth*, huge beast, supposedly from Egyptian *p-ehe-mau*, water-ox.] An animal described in Job xl. 15-24. Authorities are divided in opinion as to the animal intended, some supposing it to be an ox, others an elephant, hippopotamus, crocodile, mastodon, etc., while many regard it simply as a type or representation of the largest land animals generally.

bē′hen, ben, *n.* [Per. and Ar. *bahman, behmen,* the name of a flower.] A plant, the bladder-campion, *Silene inflata.* The white *behen* of the shops is the root of *Serratula Behen,* a native of the Levant; red *behen* is the root of *Statice Limonium* or sea-lavender.

bē-hest′, *n.* [ME. *behest, bihest,* from AS. *behæse,* a command.]

1. Anything willed; command; precept; mandate.

2. A pledge or solemn vow.

bē-hest′, *v.t.* To swear; to vow. [Obs.]

bē-hēte′, *v.t.* [Obs.] Same as *Behight.*

bē-hight′ (-hīt′), *v.t.* [AS. *behatan,* to promise.] To promise; to intrust; to call or name; to command; to adjudge; to address; to inform; to mean; to reckon. [Obs.]

bē-hight′, *n.* A promise or vow. [Obs.]

bē-hind′, *prep.* [ME. *behinde, behinden,* from AS. *behindan,* behind; *be,* by, and *hindan,* adv., behind.]

1. On the side opposite the front or nearest part, or opposite to that which fronts; on the other side of; as, *behind* a bed; *behind* a hill; *behind* a house, tree, or rock.

2. At the back of another; in the rear of; as, to walk or ride *behind* some one.

3. Remaining; left after departure; as, a man leaves *behind* him his estate

4. At a point less advanced in progress or improvement; as, one student is *behind* another in mathematics; hence, inferior in dignity and excellence.

For I suppose I was not a whit *behind* the very chiefest apostles. —2 Cor. xi. 5.

Behind the back; in Scripture, out of notice or regard; disregarded.

Behind the times; out of date; old-fashioned.

Behind time; late; not up to the proper or appointed time.

bē-hind′, *adv.* 1. Out of sight; not produced or exhibited to view; remaining; as, we know not what evidence is *behind.*

2. Backward; on the back part; in the rear; as, to look *behind;* to walk *behind.*

3. Past, in the progress of time.

Forgetting those things which are *behind.* —Philip. iii. 13.

4. Future, or remaining to be endured.

And fill up that which is *behind* of the afflictions of Christ in my flesh. —Col. i. 24.

5. Remaining after departure of; as, he departed and left us *behind.*

bē-hind′, *n.* The buttocks. [Vulgar.]

bē-hind′hand, *adv.* and *a.* 1. In a state of arrears; in a state in which expenditure has exceeded income, or means are not adequate to supply wants; as, *behindhand* with payments.

2. In a backward state; not equally advanced with some other person or thing; as, *behindhand* in studies.

3. Too late; behind the time set; as, government expeditions are generally *behindhand.*

bē-hith′ēr, *prep.* On this side of. [Obs.]

bē-hōld′, *v.t.;* beheld, *pt., pp.;* beholding, *ppr.* [ME. *beholden, biholden;* AS. *behealdan,* to hold, keep; *be,* be-, intensive force, and *healdan,* to hold, keep.] To fix the eyes upon; to see with attention; to observe; to look at; to see.

Behold the Lamb of God, which taketh away the sin of the world. —John i. 29.

When he *beheld* the serpent of brass, he lived. —Num. xxi. 9.

Syn.—See, regard, view, discern, observe, descry, eye, survey.

bē-hōld′, *v.i.* To look; to direct the eyes to an object; to direct or fix the mind.

And I *beheld,* and, lo, in the midst of the throne, a Lamb. —Rev. v. 6.

Behold, I stand at the door, and knock. —Rev. iii. 20.

bē-hōld′en, *a.* [Past participle of *behold.*] Obliged; bound in gratitude; indebted.

Little are we *beholden* to your love. —Shak.

bē-hōld′ēr, *n.* One who beholds; a spectator; one who looks upon or sees.

bē-hōld′ing, *a.* Beholden. [Obs.]

bē-hōld′ing, *n.* The act of looking or seeing; also, that which is seen.

bē-hōld′ing-ness, *n.* The state of being obliged. [Obs.]

bē-hoof′, *n.* [ME. *behof,* advantage; AS. *behoflic,* advantageous, from *behofiane,* to need, be necessary.] That which is advantageous; advantage; profit; benefit; interest; behalf.

No mean recompense it brings to your *behoof.* —Milton.

bē-hoov′á-ble, *a.* Needful; profitable. [Obs.]

bē-hoove′, *v.t.;* behooved, *pt., pp.;* behooving, *ppr.* [ME. *behoven, behofen;* AS. *behōfian,* to need.] To be necessary for; to be fit for; to be meet for, with respect to necessity, duty, or convenience; used impersonally. Written also *behove.*

And thus it *behoved* Christ to suffer. —Luke xxiv. 46.

bē-hoove′, *v.i.* To be essential, fit, or needful.

bē-hoove′, *n.* [Obs.] Same as *Behoof.*

bē-hoove′fụl, *a.* Needful; useful; profitable; advantageous. [Obs.]

bē-hoove′fụl-ly, *adv.* Usefully; profitably. [Obs.]

bē-hoove′fụl-ness, *n.* Advantageousness. [Obs.]

bē-hōve′, *v.t.* and *v.i.* Same as *Behoove.*

bē-hōve′ly, *a.* and *adv.* Profitable or profitably. [Obs.]

bē-howl′, *v.t.* To howl at. [Obs.]

beige (bāzh), *n.* [Fr.] Same as *Debeige.*

beild (bēld), *n.* See *Bield.*

bē′ing, *v.,* present participle of *be.* Existing in a certain state.

This participle in modern usage is often followed by a past participle when used with *is, are, was,* and *were,* and so denotes progression; as, is *being* made; was *being* constructed; are *being* built; were *being* prepared.

bē′ing, *n.* 1. Existence; the state of existing; any form of existence endowed with life, whether animal or vegetable.

2. Mortal existence. [Obs.]

3. Existence in the widest sense; anything or everything that is; also, anything or everything that exists in actuality, has existed, or may exist, or may be conceived.

4. God; usually with a qualifying term; as, the *Supreme Being.*

5. A human individual; often used contemptuously; as, he is a peculiar *being.*

6. A home; an abode. [Prov. Eng.]

bē′ing, *adv.* Since; such being the case; inasmuch as; as, *being* you are here. [Rare, colloq.]

bē-jāde′, *v.t.* To tire. [Obs.]

bē′jăn, bē′jănt, *n.* [Scot., from Fr. *béjaune;* from OFr. *becjaune,* a novice; literally, a yellow beak.] A Scotch term for a freshman at certain of the universities. [Rare.]

bē-jāpe′, *v.t.* To laugh at; to deceive. [Obs.]

bē-jaun′dice, *v.t.* To spread or infect with the disease known as jaundice.

bē-jew′el, *v.t.;* bejeweled *or* bejewelled, *pt., pp.;* bejeweling *or* bejewelling, *ppr.* To adorn with gems or jewels.

be-jụ′ço (bā-hū′kō), *n.* [Sp.] A name given to various species of lianes in tropical America.

bē-jum′ble, *v.t.* To mix up; to disorder.

bē′kăh, *n.* [Heb.] One-half a shekel.

bē-knāve′ (-nāv′), *v.t.* To call knave. [Obs.]

bē-know′ (-nō′), *v.t.* To acknowledge. [Obs.]

Bel, *n.* The Chaldaic form of the Hebrew *Baal;* the supreme male divinity of the Babylonians.

bel, *n.* [Hind., from Sans. *bilva,* the name of a thorn-tree.] The *Ægle marmelos,* a tree thriving in India and producing an orange-like fruit, which has a medicinal use. From its rind a perfume and yellow dye are obtained. Called also *Bengal quince, wood apple, golden apple.*

bē-lā′bŏr, *v.t.;* belabored, *pt., pp.;* belaboring, *ppr.* 1. To ply diligently.

2. To beat soundly; to thump.

Ajax *belabours* there a harmless ox. —Dryden.

Syn.—Toil, work, cudgel, flog, pommel, thrash, beat.

bel=aç-çoil′, bel=aç-çoyle′, *n.* [Fr. *bel,* beautiful, *accueil,* reception.] A kind salutation and reception. [Obs.]

bē-lāce′, *v.t.* 1 To fasten, as with a lace or cord. [Obs.]

2. To adorn with lace. [Obs.]

3. To beat; to whip. [Obs.]

bē-lam′, *v.t.* To beat; to thrash. [Colloq.]

bel′á-mōur, *n.* [Fr. *bel,* fair, *amour,* love.]

1. A gallant; a lover. [Obs.]

2. An old name for a flower now unknown. [Obs.]

bel′á-my, *n.* [Fr. *bel,* good, *ami,* friend.] A good friend; an intimate. [Obs.]

bē-lāte′, *v.t.;* belated, *pt., pp.;* belating, *ppr.* To retard or make too late.

bē-lāt′ed, *a.* Benighted; abroad late at night; too late; as, a *belated* traveler.

bē-lāt′ed-ness, *n.* The state of being belated.

bē-laud′, *v.t.* To laud; to praise highly.

bē-lāy′, *v.t.;* belayed *or* belaid, *pt., pp.;* belaying, *ppr.* 1. To block up, or obstruct. [Obs.]

2. To await in ambush; to lie in wait for.

3. To adorn, surround, or cover. [Obs.]

4. In seamanship, to fasten, or make fast, by winding a rope round a cleat or belaying-pin. It is chiefly applied to the running rigging.

bē-lāy′ing=pin, *n.* A strong pin in the side of a vessel, or by the mast, round which ropes are wound when they are fastened or belayed.

belch, *v.t.;* belched, *pt., pp.;* belching, *ppr.* [ME. *belkan;* AS. *bealcan,* to belch, to swell or heave.]

1. To throw up or eject from the stomach with violence.

2. To eject violently from within; to emit; as, a volcano *belches* flames and lava; to *belch* forth curses.

belch, *v.i.* 1. To eject wind from the stomach.

2. To issue out noisily and forcibly.

belch, *n.* 1. The act of belching or throwing out from the stomach; eructation.

2. A vulgar name for malt liquor; bad beer. [Obs.]

belch′ēr, *n.* One who or that which belches.

bel′dăm, bel′dāme, *n.* [Fr. *bel;* L. *bellus,* grand, and Fr. *dame,* lady.]

1. An old woman; a hag.

2. A grandmother. [Obs.]

3. Fair lady; the primary sense. [Obs.]

bē-lēa′guēr, *v.t.;* beleaguered, *pt., pp.;* beleaguering, *ppr.* [D. *belegeren,* to besiege.] To besiege; to block up; to surround with an army, so as to preclude escape.

bē-lēa′guēr-ēr, *n.* One who besieges.

bē-lēave′, *v.t.* To leave. [Obs.]

bē-leç′tūre, *v.t.* To weary with lectures; to lecture too frequently.

bē-lee′, *v.t.* To place on the lee, or in a position unfavorable to the wind.

bē-lem′nīte, *n.* [Gr. *belemnon,* a dart, or arrow; from *ballein,* to throw.] An arrowhead, or finger-stone; popularly called *thunderstone.* A generic name for the organic remains of extinct fossil bodies, having straight, tapering shells. They belonged to animals of the class *Cephalopoda,* and are found in Jurassic and Cretaceous formations.

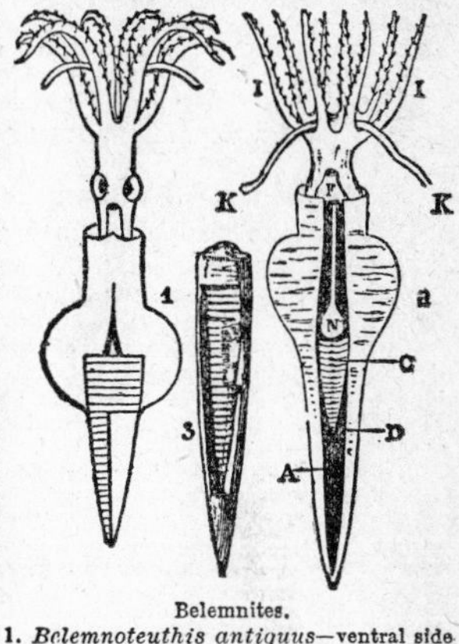

Belemnites.

1. *Belemnoteuthis antiquus*—ventral side
2. *Belemnites Owenii* (restored). A, Guard; C, Phragmacone; D, Muscular tissue of mantle; F, Infundibulum; I, Uncinated arms; K, Tentacula; N, Ink-bag.
3. Belemnite.—British Museum.

bel-em-nit′-iç, *a.* Of the nature of a belemnite.

Bē-lem-nit′i-dæ, *n.pl.* A family of belemnites; the thunderstones.

bē-lep′ēr, *v.t.* To infect with leprosy. [Obs.]

bel=es-prit′ (-prē′), *n.; pl.* **beaux=es-prits′** (bōz-es-prē′). [Fr. *bel,* fine, *esprit,* spirit, genius.] A wit; a fine genius.

bel′fry, *n.* [ME. *belfray,* a watch-tower; OFr. *belfroi;* LL. *berefredus,* a watch-tower; from G. *bercvrit, bercfrit,* literally a protecting shelter; *berc,* from *bergen,* to protect, and *frit,* for *vride,* an inclosed place.]

1. In the middle ages, a tower erected by besiegers to overlook the place besieged.

2. That part of a church, or other building, in which a bell is hung, and, more particularly, the timberwork which supports the bell.

3. A bell-tower.

4. In nautical parlance, the framing on which a ship's bell is suspended.

bel-gärd′, *n.* [It. *bel guardo,* a lovely look.] A soft look or glance. [Obs.]

Bel′ġi-ăn, *a.* and *n.* I. *a.* Pertaining to Belgium or its people.

II. *n.* A native or inhabitant of Belgium.

Bel′ġiç, *a.* [L. *Belgicus,* from *Belgæ,* the Belgians.]

1. Pertaining to the Belgæ, who, in Cæsar's time, possessed the country between the Rhine, the Seine, and the ocean.

How unlike their *Belgic* sires of old. —Goldsmith.

2. Pertaining to Belgium or to its language, customs, or productions.

Bel-grā′vi-ăn, *a.* Pertaining to that part of London in the neighborhood of Belgrave Square, a fashionable quarter of the city; hence, of a fashionable and aristocratic character; especially aristocratic.

Bē′li-ăl, *n.* [Heb. *b'līya'al,* wickedness.] The personification of wickedness; the name of an evil spirit; one of Milton's fallen angels.

Son of Belial; a very wicked and depraved person.

The sons of Eli were *sons of Belial.* —I Sam. ii. 12.

bē-lī′bel, *v.t.* To libel or traduce.

bē-lie′, *v.t.;* belied, *pt., pp.;* belying, *ppr.* [ME. *belyen,* from AS. *beleógan,* to give the lie to; *be,* be-, and *leógan,* to lie.]

1. To give the lie to; to prove to be false; to stamp with falsehood; as, the heart *belies* the

tongue; used of appearances which are false and hypocritical.

2. To counterfeit; to mimic. [Obs.]

With dust, with horses' hoofs, that beat the ground,
And martial brass, *belie* the thunder's sound.
—Dryden.

3. To tell lies concerning; to calumniate by false reports.

Thou dost *belie* him, Percy. —Shak.

4. To fill with lies.

Slander doth *belie* all corners of the world.
—Shak.

bē-liēf′, *n.* [ME. *beleve, beleafe*; AS. *geleāfa*, belief, from *gelēfan*, to believe.]

1. A persuasion of the truth, or an assent of mind to the truth, on the ground of evidence, distinct from personal knowledge.

2. In theology, faith, or a firm persuasion of the truths of religion.

No man can attain [to] *belief* by the bare contemplation of heaven and earth.
—Hooker.

3. Religion; the body of tenets held by the professors of a faith.

In the heat of persecution, to which Christian *belief* was subject upon its first promulgation. —Hooker.

4. The thing believed; the object of believing.

Superstitious prophecies are the *belief* of fools. —Bacon.

Ultimate belief; belief the ground for which cannot be shown; intuitive conviction.

Syn.—Conviction, faith, opinion, credence, creed, trust, persuasion, confidence.

bē-liēf′fụl, *a.* Possessing belief or faith.

bē-liēv′ȧ-ble, *a.* Capable of being believed; credible.

bē-liēv-ȧ-bil′i-ty, *n.* The condition of being believable.

bē-liēv′ȧ-ble-ness, *n.* Credibility.

bē-liēve′, *v.t.*; believed, *pt., pp.*; believing, *ppr.*

1. To credit upon authority or testimony; to be persuaded of the truth of, upon declaration, or upon evidence furnished. When we *believe* another, we put confidence in his veracity.

2. To expect or hope for with confidence; to trust.

I had fainted, unless I had *believed* to see the goodness of the Lord in the land of the living. —Ps. xxvii. 13.

bē-liēve′, *v.i.* 1. To have a persuasion of anything.

2. In theology, to assent to anything; to yield the will and affections, accompanied with humble reliance on Christ for salvation.

3. To think or suppose; as, I *believe* well of you.

To believe in; to trust; to have the utmost confidence in the existence of; to trust implicitly in the ability of.

To believe on; to trust; to place full confidence in; to rest faith upon.

bē-liēv′ẽr, *n.* 1. One who believes; one who gives credit to evidence other than that of personal knowledge.

2. In theology, one who gives credit to the truth of the Scriptures, as a revelation from God. In a more restricted sense, a professor of Christianity.

bē-liēv′ing-ly, *adv.* In a believing manner.

bē-light′ (bē-līt′), *v.t.* To light or illuminate. [Obs.]

bē-līke′, *adv.* Probably; likely; perhaps. [Obs.]

bē-līke′ly, *adv.* Probably. [Obs.]

bē-līme′, *v.t.* To besmear with lime.

bē-lit′tle, *v.t.*; belittled, *pt., pp.*; belittling, *ppr.* To disparage; to lower in character.

bē-līve′, *adv.* Speedily; quickly. [Obs.]

belk, *v.t.* To vomit. [Obs.]

bell, *n.* [ME. *bel, belle*; AS. *belle*, a bell.]

1. A hollow, resounding, metallic instrument of ancient and multifarious use as a signal. It may be cup-shaped, with a wide mouth; saucer-shaped, as a gong, or spherical, as a sleigh*bell*. A *bell* produces sound by being struck with a hammer of some kind, either outside or in; in some, a clapper or tongue is the hammer; in the spherical *bell*, a metal ball. Arranged in series and attuned to the musical scale, *bells* are sometimes used as instruments of music, especially in the form called chimes.

2. Anything in the form of a *bell*, as the cup or calyx of a flower.

To bear the bell; to be the first or leader, in allusion to the bellwether of a flock.

To curse by bell, book, and candle; in the Roman Catholic church, a solemn form of excommunication, the office of execration being read, bells rung, and candles extinguished, to inspire the greater dread.

To shake the bells; to give an alarm.

Liberty Bell; the famous old Philadelphia statehouse bell which was rung when the Continental Congress promulgated the Declaration of Independence. It is a symbol of American liberty. It was cast in 1753, and bears the inscription, "Proclaim liberty throughout all the land, to all the inhabitants thereof."

bell, *v.t.*; belled, *pt., pp.*; belling, *ppr.* 1. To attach a bell or bells to; to furnish or equip with a bell or bells.

2. To make into the form of a bell; as, to *bell* the mouth of a horn.

To bell the cat; a phrase derived from the fable of the mice resolving to put a bell on the cat, to guard them against his attack; hence, to disable or handicap an enemy or a rival.

bell, *v.i.* [ME. *belle*, from AS. *bellan*, to roar.] To call with a peculiar sound, as that of the deer in the rutting season.

The wild buck *bells* from ferny brake. —Scott.

bell, *v.i.* To grow in the form of bells, as the bell-shaped corollas of certain flowers.

bell, *n.* [D. *bel*, a bubble.] A bubble formed by gas in a liquid; as, an air-*bell* in a photographic plate.

bel-lȧ-don′nȧ, *n.* [It. *bella donna*, beautiful lady; from L. *bella*, f. of *bellus*, beautiful, and *domina*, lady.] A European plant of the nightshade family (*Atropa belladonna*). It is a perennial herb, poisonous in all its parts, containing the alkaloid atropin. The plant received its name from the use of its products by ladies as cosmetics. The extracts of root and leaf are largely used medicinally, being anodyne and anti-spasmodic, and in optical surgery to dilate the pupil and temporarily atrophize the muscles. Also called *deadly nightshade*.

bel-lȧ-don′nȧ-lil′y, *n.* An ornamental plant, with large rose-tinted bell-flowers, striated with red; a native of South Africa. The analogy of the color of its blossoms to flesh tint gave it the name; known botanically as *Amaryllis belladonna*.

Belladonna-lily (*Amaryllis belladonna*).

bel-lȧ-don′nin, *n.* A poison found in belladonna.

bell′-an-i-mal″cūle, *n.* [L. *bellus*, fine, and *animal*, a living being.] One of the popular names of the species of the genus *Vorticella*.

bel-lȧ-som′brȧ, *n.* [Sp., beautiful shade.] A South American tree of the pokeweed family (*Phytolacca dioica*). It has large dark leaves and is esteemed for its shade.

bell′-beãr″ẽr, *n.* A leaf-hopper of Brazil (*Bocydium tintinnabuliferum*), distinguished for bearing upon its thorax four appendages in the shape of bells.

bell′-bird, *n.* One of several species of birds named from the bell-like character of their songs, including *Chasmorhynchus niveus* of South America and *Manorhina melanophrys* of Australia.

bell′boy, *n.* A boy who answers calls made by a bell; especially, a hotel employee who answers bells.

bell′-crank, *n.* A lever whose two arms meet the fulcrum at right angles or nearly so. It is used for changing the direction of motion in the wires of bell-pulls and in fixtures for carrying packages, etc., in stores.

Bell-crank.

belle (bel), *n.* [Fr., f. of *beau*, beautiful; OFr. *bel*; L. *bellus*, beautiful, fine.] A handsome or charming woman who is a social favorite and attraction; a reigning beauty in society; a young woman who is a general favorite by virtue of social and personal attractiveness.

belled (beld), *a.* Furnished with bells.

bel-leek′, *n.* A kind of porcelain ware originally produced at Belleek, Ireland; it is very delicate, highly-glazed, and sometimes iridescent.

Bel-ler′ō-phon, *n.* [Gr. *Bellerophōn*, the slayer of the monster Chimæra.] A genus of fossil shells, of the Paleozoic age.

belles-let′tres (bel-let′tr), *n.pl.* [Fr., fine letters; sing. *bel*, pl. *belles*, fine, and sing. *lettre*, letter, pl. *lettres*, literature.] Polite literature; a word of very vague signification. It includes poetry and oratory; but authors are not agreed as to what particular branches of learning the term should include.

bel-let′rist, belle-let′trist, *n.* One devoted to belles-lettres.

bel-let-ris′tic, bel-let-ris′tic-ăl, *a.* Characteristic of belles-lettres.

bell′-fāced, *a.* Having a convex striking surface, as a hammer.

bell′flow″ẽr, *n.* 1. A name common to different species of plants of the genus *Campanula*; so named from the shape of the flower, which resembles a bell.

2. A large winter apple.

bell′-gā″ble, *n.* A gable-shaped structure for hanging a bell.

bell′i-bōne, *n.* [Fr. *belle et bonne*, beautiful and good.] A woman excelling both in beauty and goodness. [Obs.]

bel′lic, bel′lic-ăl, *a.* [Fr. *bellique*; L. *bellicus*, warlike; *bellum*, war.] Concerning war; characteristic of war.

bel′li-cōse, *a.* [L. *bellicosus*, fond of war, warlike; from *bellicus*, pertaining to war; *bellum*, war.] Tending to strife; disposed to quarrel or fight.

Bell-gable.

bel′li-cōse-ly, *adv.* In a quarrelsome manner.

bel′li-cous, *a.* Bellicose. [Obs.]

bel′lied, *a.* 1. Swelled or prominent like the belly; used chiefly in composition; as, a big-*bellied* bottle.

2. In botany, ventricose; swelling out in the middle, as a monopetalous corolla.

bel-lig′ẽr-āte, *v.i.* To make war. [Rare.]

bel-lig′ẽr-en-cy, bel-lig′ẽr-ence, *n.* The state of being belligerent or on the verge of warfare.

bel-lig′ẽr-ent, *n.* [Fr. *belligérant*, waging war, from L. *belligerans*, ppr. of *belligerare*, to wage war.]

1. A nation, power, or state, at war.

2. An individual of a body of men engaged in warfare; a warrior.

bel-lig′ẽr-ent, *a.* 1. Hostile; addicted to war; bellicose; warlike in attitude or intention; threatening war.

2. Pertaining to warfare between nations, tribes, states, or powers; engaged in warfare; pertaining to belligerents, or those at war with one another.

bel-lig′ẽr-ent-ly, *adv.* In a hostile or warlike manner; bellicosely.

bel-lig′ẽr-ous, *a.* Same as *Belligerent*.

bell′ing, *n.* [AS. *bellan*, to bellow.] The noise of deer in rutting time; the baying of hounds in a fox-chase.

bel-lip′ō-tent, *a.* [L. *bellipotens*, powerful in war, from *bellum*, war, and *potens*, powerful.] Powerful or mighty in war. [Rare.]

Bel′lis, *n.* [L., from *bellus*, beautiful.] The daisy, a small genus of annual or perennial flowering plants found in great profusion in North America and Europe.

bell′măn, *n.* A man who rings a bell, especially to give notice of anything in the streets; a town-crier.

bell′-met″ăl, *n.* A mixture of copper and tin, in the proportion of from three to five parts of copper to one of tin, and usually a small portion of brass or zinc; used for making bells.

Bell-metal ore; a sulphid containing about twenty-six per cent of tin, with copper, iron, and zinc; of a steel-gray color; chiefly obtained in Cornwall, England. Also called *stannite*.

bell′-mouthed, *a.* With a bell-like opening at the mouth, as a cornet.

bel′lŏn, *n.* [Origin unknown.] Lead or painter's colic.

Bel-lō′nȧ, *n.* [L.] The goddess of war.

bel′lōw, *v.i.*; bellowed, *pt., pp.*; bellowing, *ppr.* [ME. *belwen*; AS. *bylgean*, to bellow.]

1. To make a hollow, loud noise, as a bull; to make a loud outcry; to roar.

2. To vociferate or clamor.

3. To roar, as the sea in a tempest, or as the wind when violent; to make a loud, hollow, continued sound.

bel′lōw, *v.t.* To shout; to call with a loud voice; followed by *out*; as, he *bellows out* his commands.

bel′lōw, *n.* A loud outcry; a roar.

bel′lōw-ẽr, *n.* One who bellows.

bel′lōw-ing, *n.* A loud, hollow sound or roar, like that of a bull.

bel′lōws, *n. sing.* and *pl.* [ME. *belowes, belwes*; AS. *bælg, bælig*, a bellows.] An instrument, utensil, or machine used primarily for blowing fire. It is so formed that by being expanded, it inhales air by an orifice which is opened and closed with a valve, and by contraction expels a stream of air through a tube upon the fire. It is also used in various forms for ventilating mines, for filling pipes of an organ with wind, etc.

Bellows to mend; a slang phrase, meaning out of breath.

bel′lōws-cam″e-rȧ, *n.* A photographic camera that can be drawn out like a bellows.

bel′lōws-fish, *n.* The trumpet-fish, *Centriscus scolopax*, which has a long tubular snout, like the pipe of a pair of bellows; called also *snipe-fish*.

bell′-pep″pẽr, *n.* The common garden red pepper.

bell′-pụll, *n.* A cord to ring a bell with; the

handle by which to pull a wire to ring a bell.

bell′=punch, *n.* An instrument used to cancel tickets on railroad trains, street-cars, etc. It rings a small bell when a perforation is made.

Bellows-fish (*Centriscus scolopax*).

bell′=ring″ẽr, *n.* 1. One whose business is to ring a church bell or chimes, or hand-bells.

2. An automatic apparatus for ringing a bell on a locomotive.

3. A mechanism, operated by means of hand-levers, for ringing chimes.

bell′=roof, *n.* A roof having the contour of a bell.

bells, *n.pl.* In nautical parlance, strokes of a bell marking the time on shipboard, and used in the same sense as *o'clock*; as, eight *bells* in the afternoon watch, or 4 o'clock.

Bell-roof.

bell′=shāped, *a.* 1. Having the form of a bell.

2. In botany, campanulate; swelling out, without a tube at the base, as a monopetalous corolla.

bel′lū-ine, *a.* [L. *belluinus*, beast-like; from *bellua*, a beast.] Beastly; pertaining to or like a beast; brutal. [Rare.]

bell′weth″ẽr, *n.* A wether or sheep which leads the flock, with a bell on his neck; hence, any leader.

bell′wŏrt, *n.* A name common to different species of plants of the genus *Uvularia*.

bel′ly, *n.* [ME. *bely*, *beli*, the belly, stomach; AS. *belg*, *baelg*, *bielg*, a bag.]

1. That part of the human body, in front, which extends downward from the breast to the thighs, and contains the bowels or intestines; the abdomen; the abdominal cavity.

2. The part of an animal corresponding to the human *belly*.

3. The womb. [Obs.]

4. The part of anything which resembles the human *belly* in protuberance or cavity, as of a harp, a sail, or a bottle; the innermost part.

5. In architecture, the concave part of a timber, the convex part being the *back*.

bel′ly, *v.t.*; bellied, *pt.*, *pp.*; bellying, *ppr.* To fill; to swell out.

bel′ly, *v.i.* To swell and become protuberant, like the belly; to bulge.

bel′ly=āche (-āk), *n.* Pain in the bowels; colic. [Colloq.]

bel′ly=band, *n.* 1. A band that encompasses the belly of a horse and fastens the saddle; a girth.

2. A cloth band worn about the belly.

3. In seamanship, a strengthening band of canvas on a sail.

bel′ly=bōard, *n.* The sounding-board of a musical instrument.

bel′ly=bound, *a.* Constipated.

bel′ly=chēat, *n.* An apron. [Obs.]

bel′ly=cheer, *n.* Good cheer. [Obs.]

bel′ly=fret″ting, *n.* 1. The chafing of a horse's belly with a girth.

2. A violent pain in a horse's belly, caused by worms.

bel′ly-fụl, *n.* 1. As much as fills the belly; sufficient to satisfy all desire.

2. Figuratively, enough or more than enough; as, he had a *bellyful* of war.

bel′ly=god, *n.* One who takes great pleasure in eating; a gluttonous person.

bel′ly=pinched, *a.* Starved; pinched with hunger.

bel′ly=rōll, *n.* A barrel-shaped roller, to roll plowed land between ridges, or in hollows.

bel′ly=slāve, *n.* A slave to the appetite.

bel′ly=wŏrm (-wẽrm), *n.* A worm that breeds in the belly or stomach.

bē-lock′, *v.t.* [AS. *belucan*, to lock.] To lock, or fasten as with a lock. [Obs.]

bel′ō-man-cy, *n.* [Gr. *belos*, an arrow, and *manteia*, divination.] A kind of divination practised by the ancient Scythians and Arabians. A number of arrows, being marked, were put into a bag or quiver, and drawn out at random, and the marks or words on the arrow drawn betokened what was to happen.

bel′ō-nē, *n.* [Gr. *belonē*, a needle.] A name given to the garfish, or sea-needle.

bē-lọng′, *v.i.*; belonged, *pt.*, *pp.*; belonging, *ppr.* [ME. *belongen*, to be the property of, from *be-*, and AS. *langian*, to long for.]

1. To be the property (of); used in this and other senses with *to*; as, a field *belongs to* Richard Roe.

2. To be the concern or proper business (of); to appertain; to be in relation (to); to be appendant (to).

He went into a desert place *belonging* to Bethsaida. —Luke ix. 10.

3. To be the quality or attribute (of).

To the Lord our God *belong* mercies and forgiveness. —Dan. ix. 9.

4. To be suitable (for).

Strong meat *belongeth* to them of full age. —Heb. v. 14.

5. To be a native; to have original or legal residence; in common language, to have a settled residence; to be domiciliated.

bē-lọng′, *v.t.* To be merited by. [Obs.]

bē-lọng′ing, *n.* That which belongs to a person or thing; in the plural, one's effects, such as clothes, household goods, etc.; humorously, a member of one's household or family; as, these are my *belongings*.

bel′ō-nīte, *n.* [Gr. *belonē*, a needle, anything having a sharp point.] A small crystalline formation sometimes found in glassy volcanic rocks.

Bel-ọọ′chē, *n.* See *Baluchi*.

bē-lọrd′, *v.t.* 1. To treat in a manner characteristic of a lord.

2. To address as "my lord."

Bel-os′tō-mȧ, *n.* [Gr. *belos*, a dart, and *stoma*, mouth.] The typical genus of the bug family *Belostomidæ*. The largest species, *Belostoma grandis*, reaches four inches in length, and is found in South America. It is powerful enough to prey upon fish and other animals of considerable size, and is called also the *great water-bug*.

bē-lōve′, *v.t.* To love. [Obs.]

bē-lŏved′, *n.* One greatly loved.

bē-lŏv′ed, *a.* Loved; greatly loved; dear to the heart.

bē-lōw′, *prep.* [ME. *bilooghe*, from *bi*, be, and *logh*, low.]

1. Under in place; beneath; not so high; as, *below* the moon; *below* the knee.

2. Inferior in rank, excellence, or dignity.

3. Unworthy of; unbefitting.

bē-lōw′, *adv.* 1. Lower in place, with respect to any object; beneath; underneath.

2. On the earth, as opposed to heaven.

3. In hell, or the regions of the dead; as, the realms *below*.

4. In a court of inferior jurisdiction; as, at the trial *below*.

Syn.—Beneath, under, underneath.—*Below* is opposed to on high; *beneath* is opposed to above. A person who is *below* us at table is not *beneath* us. *Below* has not properly the sense of unbecoming or unworthy of, but *beneath* has. We say, *beneath* (not *below*) the character of a gentleman, *beneath* contempt, etc.

bē-lowt′, *v.t.* To treat with contempt. [Obs.]

bel′sīre, *n.* A grandsire or any ancestor. [Obs.]

bel′swag″gẽr, *n.* A lewd man; a bully. [Obs.]

belt, *n.* [ME. *belt*, from AS. *belt*, from L. *balteus*, a belt.]

1. A girdle, band, or cincture, of any material, used to encircle the waist, or body; as, a lady's *belt*; a sword-*belt*.

2. Anything having resemblance to a *belt*; a stripe; a strip; as, a *belt* of woods; a *belt* of hills.

3. An extended region characterized by some peculiarity or natural phenomenon; as, the cotton *belt*; a *belt* of calms; a heat *belt*; the wheat *belt*, etc.

4. [B—] A narrow passage of water; a strait; specifically, the Great and Lesser *Belt* in the Baltic Sea, between the islands of Zealand and Fünen, and between Fünen and Jutland.

5. A band of various widths and materials used to transmit power from pulley to pulley.

6. In astronomy, the zones of Jupiter and Saturn.

7. In architecture, a course of stone marking a band across the wall of a building.

8. In heraldry, a knightly badge.

9. A blow; as, a *belt* with a club. [Slang.]

Sam Browne belt; an army officer's leather belt, having a strap over the right shoulder.

belt, *v.t.*; belted, *pt.*, *pp.*; belting, *ppr.* 1. To gird or encircle with or as with a belt; to supply with a belt; to mark with a belt; as, *belted* with children; to *belt* a pulley; to *belt* a pole by painting.

2. To strike a sharp blow. [Slang.]

Bel′tāne, *n.* [Scot., from Gael. *Bealltainn*.]

1. An ancient Scottish festival, formerly celebrated on May 1, Old Style. It marked the beginning of summer.

2. A similar Irish festival anciently celebrated on June 21.

belt′ed, *a.* 1. Wearing a belt; as, a *belted* hunter.

2. Marked or adorned by a belt or girdle; as, a *belted* zebra.

3. Worn at or hanging from the belt; as, a lady's *belted* ornaments.

Belted cattle; a breed of black-and-white cattle originally from Holland, the white being in the form of a wide belt about the body.

Bel′tein, Bel′tin, *n.* See *Beltane*.

belt′ing, *n.* Belts, collectively; also, the material used in making belts for machinery.

belt′=lā″cing, *n.* Strong, pliable leather used in uniting machine-belts.

bē-lū′gȧ, *n.* [Russ. *bieluga*, whitefish.]

1. A large cetacean, *Delphinapterus leucas*, of the northern seas, twelve feet and upwards in length; called also *white whale* or *whitefish*.

2. A Russian name for the white sturgeon, *Acipenser huso*.

bē-lūte′, *v.t.* [L. *lutum*, mud.] To cover or bespatter with mud. [Rare.]

bel-ve-dēre′, *n.* [It. *belvedere*, a beautiful view; *bel*, beautiful, and *vedere*, a view; from L. *bellus*, fine, and *videre*, to see.]

1. In Italian architecture, the uppermost story of a building, open to the air, at least on one side, and frequently on all, for the purpose of giving a view of the country, and to admit the evening breeze. It is sometimes a sort of lantern or kiosk erected on the roof.

AA, Belvedere of the Vatican, Rome.

2. In France, a summerhouse on an eminence in a park or garden.

bel′zē-buth, *n.* [From *Beelzebub*.] A spider-monkey of Brazil, *Ateles belzebuth*.

bē′mȧ, *n.*; *pl.* **bē′mȧ-tȧ.** [Gr. *bēma*, a step.]

1. In the early Christian church, a chancel. [Obs.]

2. In ancient Greece, a stage or platform, on which speakers stood when addressing an assembly.

bē-man′gle, *v.t.* To mangle; to tear asunder. [Rare.]

bē-mȧsk′, *v.t.* To mask; to conceal.

bē-mȧs′tẽr, *v.t.* To master with thoroughness.

bē′mȧ-tȧ, *n.*, pl. of *bema*.

bē-maul′, *v.t.* To beat severely; to bruise.

bē-māze′, *v.t.* To bewilder. [Rare.]

bē-mēan′, *v.t.*; bemeaned, *pt.*, *pp.*; bemeaning, *ppr.* To render mean; to degrade.

bē-meet′, *v.t.* To meet. [Obs.]

bē-mēte′, *v.t.* To measure. [Obs.]

bē-min′gle, *v.t.* To mingle; to mix. [Rare.]

bē-mīre′, *v.t.* To drag or encumber in the mire; to soil by passing through mud or dirt.

bē-mist′, *v.t.* To cover or envelop in mist. [Obs.]

bē-mōan′, *v.t.*; bemoaned, *pt.*, *pp.*; bemoaning, *ppr.* [ME. *bemenen*; AS. *bemænan*; *be*, be-, with intensive force, and *mænan*, to moan.] To lament; to bewail; to express sorrow for; to sympathize with.

Syn.—Deplore, grieve, lament, mourn, regret, sorrow.

bē-mōan′ẽr, *n.* One who laments.

bē-mock′, *v.t.*; bemocked, *pt.*, *pp.*; bemocking, *ppr.* To treat with mockery; to ridicule.

bē-moil′, *v.t.* [Fr. *mouiller*, to wet.] To bedraggle; to soil or encumber with dirt. [Obs.]

bē′mol, *n.* [Fr.] In music, B flat, a semitone below B natural.

bē-mon′stẽr, *v.t.* To make monstrous. [Obs.]

bē-mourn′, *v.t.* To mourn over. [Rare.]

bē-mud′dle, *v.t.*; bemuddled, *pt.*, *pp.*; bemuddling, *ppr.* To muddle; to stupefy or confuse.

bē-muf′fle, *v.t.* To cover; to wrap up; to muffle. [Rare.]

bē-mūse′, *v.t.* To daze, as with liquor. [Rare.]

ben, ben′=nut, *n.* [Ar. *bān*, the name of the ben-nut tree.] The seed of a tree of the genus *Moringa*. [See *Moringa*.]

ben, *adv.* and *prep.* [Scot.] Toward the inner apartment of a house.

Wi' kindly welcome Jenny brings him *ben*. —Burns.

ben, *n.* [Scot.] The inner apartment of a house.

ben, *v.* An obsolete form of the plural indicative present of *be*.

bench, *n.* [ME. *benk*, *bynk*; AS. *benc*, bench.]

1. A long seat, usually of board or plank, of greater length than a stool.

2. The seat where judges sit in court; the seat of justice.

3. The persons who sit as judges; the court; judges collectively; as, the *bench* and the bar.

4. A long work-table for mechanics.

5. A row of exhibition-stalls in a public exhibit, as at a dog-show.

6. Any natural conformation resembling a bench; as a projection of rock formed by erosion or by mining, or an elevated table of land adjacent to a river or lake.

Bench of bishops; a collective name for the bishops having seats in the English House of Lords.

bench, *v.t.* 1. To furnish with benches.

2. To seat on a bench.

bench, *v.i.* To sit on a seat of justice. [Obs.]

bench′ẽr, *n.* 1. In English law, one of the senior members of an inn of court, who have the government of the society.

2. An alderman of a corporation. [Eng.]

3. A judge. [Rare.]

4. An idler; one who frequents the benches of a tavern. [Obs.]

bench′-märk, *n.* In surveying, a permanent mark placed at intervals along a survey-line noting differences of level.

bench′-plāne, *n.* Any hand-plane used for working a flat surface on wood, as a jack-plane.

bench′-shōw, *n.* A dog-show.

bench′-tā″ble, *n.* In architecture, a projection, as of masonry, from an interior wall, of such height as to furnish a seat.

bench′-wär″rănt, *n.* A process issued by a court against a person guilty of some contempt, or indicted for some crime.

bend, *v.t.*; bent *or* bended, *pt.*, *pp.*; bending, *ppr.* [ME. *benden*, from AS. *bendan*, to bend. *Bend* and *bind* are radically the same word.]

1. To strain, or to crook by straining; as, to *bend* a bow.

2. To crook; to make crooked; to curve; to inflect; as, to *bend* the arm.

3. To direct to a certain point; to incline; to turn; as, to *bend* our steps to a particular place.

4. To exert; to apply closely; to exercise laboriously; as, to *bend* the mind to study.

5. To subdue; to cause to yield; to make submissive; as, to *bend* a man to our will.

6. In seamanship, to fasten, as one rope to another or to an anchor, as a sail to its yard or stay, or as a cable to the ring of an anchor.

To bend the brow; to knit the brow; to scowl; to frown.

bend, *v.i.* 1 To be crooked; to crook, or be curving.

2. To incline; to lean or turn; as, a road *bends* to the west.

3. To jut over; to overhang.

4. To bow or be submissive.

Syn.—Curve, deviate, incline, tend, swerve, diverge, mold, persuade, influence, bias, dispose, direct, lower, lean, deflect, bow, condescend, yield, stoop, submit.

bend, *n.* 1. A curve; a crook; a turn; flexure; deflection; as, a *bend* in a stream.

2. In marine language, a knot by which one part of a rope is fastened to another, or to a post, spar, or anchor.

3. In a ship, one of the strongest planks or streaks in its sides, more generally called a *wale*.

4. In the leather trade, a butt or rounded crop cut in two.

5. In mining, indurated clay or any indurated argillaceous substance.

bend, *n.* 1. A band. [Obs.]

2. In heraldry, one of the nine honorable ordinaries, containing a third part of the field when charged and a fifth when plain. It is made by two lines drawn across from the dexter chief to the sinister base point.

Bend sinister; an ordinary similar to a bend but crossing in the opposite direction diagonally, from the sinister chief to the dexter base.

Bend.

bend′ȧ-ble, *a.* Capable of being bent or curved.

bend′ẽr, *n.* 1. One who bends; that which bends.

2. A slang term for an extended spree

bend′let, *n.* [Early modern Eng. *bendelet*.] In heraldry, a narrow bend which occupies a sixth part of a shield.

Bend between two Bendlets.

bends, *n.* A disease incident to caisson work, caused by sudden change in atmospheric pressure affecting the heart.

bend′wīṣe, bend′wāyṣ, *adv.* In heraldry, diagonally; in the direction of a bend.

ben′dy, *a.* [Fr. *bandé*, from OFr. *bende*, a band or fillet.] In heraldry, divided into four, six, or more parts, diagonally, and varying in metal and color; said of the field.

ben′dy-tree, *n.* A naturalized West Indian tree, *Thespesia populnea*; called also *portia* and *umbrella-tree*. It is a native of Eastern Asia, and Polynesia. It produces portia-seeds, from which an oil is made, and a dye is made from the flowers.

A sword bendwise.

bē′nē, *n.* [AS. *ben*.] A prayer; a boon. [Obs.]

ben′e, *n.* Same as *Benne*.

bene, ben, *n.* [Native name.] The *Sus papuensis*, a wild hog of New Guinea.

bē-nēaped′ (-nēpt′), *a.* See *Neaped*.

bē-nēath′, *prep.* [ME. *benethe*, *binethe*; AS. *beneothan*, beneath; *be-*, intensive be-, and *neothan*, below.]

1. Under; lower in place, with something directly over or on; underneath; as, to place a cushion *beneath* one.

2. Under, in a figurative sense, as bearing heavy impositions, taxes, or oppressive government.

3. Lower in rank, dignity, or excellence; as, *beneath* the average.

bē-nēath′, *adv.* 1. In a lower place; underneath.

2. Below; a comparative term; as, in earth *beneath*.

Ben-ē-dic′i-tē, *n.* [L., imp. pl. of *benedicere*, to speak well of one, praise.] A chant or hymn, beginning in Latin with this word, and in English with, "O all ye works of the Lord, bless ye the Lord"; being an expansion of Psalm cxlviii.

ben-ē-dic′i-tē, *interj.* An exclamation meaning, Bless you!

ben′ē-dict, ben′ē-dick, *n.* [From *Benedick*, one of the characters in Shakspere's play, "Much Ado About Nothing."] A man newly married; applied especially to one who has previously scoffed at marriage.

ben′ē-dict, *a.* [L. *benedictus*, pp. of *benedicere*, to speak well of.] Having mild and salubrious qualities. [Obs.]

Ben-ē-dic′tine, *a.* Pertaining to the order or monks of St. Benedict.

Ben-ē-dic′tine, *n.* 1. A member of the most famous and widely spread of all the orders of monks, founded at Monte Casino, about halfway between Rome and Naples, about the year 530, by St. Benedict, whose rule the members profess to follow. Called also Black Friars—though incorrectly—from the color of their habit. The order was introduced into the United States in 1846.

2. [b—] A liqueur formerly made by a branch of this order at Fécamp, Normandy, but in modern times by a secular company.

Benedictine or Black Friar.

Ben-ē-dic′tin-iṣm, *n.* The practices and organization of the Benedictines.

ben-ē-dic′tion, *n.* [LL. *benedictio*, from L. *benedicere*, to speak well of.]

1. The act of blessing; a blessing pronounced in favor of any person or thing; a solemn invocation of happiness. Specifically, the short prayer which closes public worship.

2. The advantage conferred by blessing.

3. The form of instituting an abbot, answering to the consecration of a bishop.

4. The ceremony performed by a priest in the office of matrimony, which is called the *nuptial benediction*.

5. In the Roman Catholic church, a solemn ecclesiastical ceremony by which the ceremonial appurtenances, as bells, candles, etc., are rendered sacred or venerable and dedicated to God.

Syn.—Blessing, commendation, approval, benison.

ben-ē-dic′tion-ăl, *n.* In the Roman Catholic church, a book containing benedictions or blessings.

ben-ē-dic′tion-ā-ry, *n.* A series of blessings in collective form.

ben-ē-dic′tive, *a.* Tending to bless; giving a blessing.

ben-ē-dic′tō-ry, *a.* Expressive of good wishes.

Ben-ē-dic′tus, *n.* [L. *benedicere*, to speak well of; later, to bless.] A canticle beginning, "Blessed be the Lord God of Israel" (Luke i. 68); the song of Zacharias at the birth of John the Baptist.

ben′ē-dight (-dīt), *a.* Blessed. [Rare.]

ben-ē-fac′tion, *n.* [LL. *benefactio*, a kindness, from L. *benefacere*, to do well; *bene*, well, and *facere*, to do.]

1. The act of conferring a benefit; a deed promoted by charity or generosity.

2. A benefit conferred, especially a charitable donation.

Syn.—Alms, bequest, boon, bounty, charity, donation, gift, grant, gratuity, present.

ben-ē-fac′tŏr, *n.* [LL. *benefactor*, from L. *benefacere*, to do well, or to do a kindness.] One who confers a benefit, especially one who makes charitable contributions either to public institutions or in cases of private need.

Syn.—Friend, supporter, contributor, upholder, wellwisher, favorer, welldoer, patron, protector, guardian.

ben-ē-fac′tress, *n.* A woman who confers a benefaction.

bē-nef′ic, *a.* 1. Beneficent, favorable, or kindly.

2. In astrology, of favorable planetary influence.

ben′ē-fice, *n.* [OFr. *benefice*; L. *beneficium*, a favor; *bene*, well, and *facere*, to do.]

1. Literally, a benefit, advantage, or kindness.

2. An ecclesiastical living, as in the Church of England; a church endowed with a revenue, for the maintenance of divine service; the revenue itself. All English church preferments are called *benefices*, except bishoprics, which are called dignities. But, ordinarily, the term dignity is applied to bishoprics, deaneries, archdeaconries, and prebendaries, and *benefice* to parsonages, vicarages, and donatives.

3. A feudal fee or interest in a landed estate, granted for life only, or a term of years, and subject to the will of the donor.

ben′ē-ficed, *a.* Possessed of a benefice or church preferment.

ben′ē-fice-less, *a.* Having no benefice.

bē-nef′i-cence, *n.* [L. *beneficentia*, active kindness, from *benefacere*, to do a kindness.] The practice of doing good; active goodness, kindness, or charity.

Syn.— Benevolence, munificence.—*Benevolence* is literally well-willing, *beneficence* is literally well-doing. The former may exist without the latter, but *beneficence* always supposes *benevolence*. *Munificence* is *beneficence* on a large scale.

bē-nef′i-cent, *a.* Bringing about or doing acts of kindness and charity. It differs from *benign* as the act from the disposition.

bē-nef-i-cen′tiăl (-shăl), *a.* Pertaining to beneficence.

bē-nef′i-cent-ly, *adv.* In a beneficent manner.

ben-ē-fi′ciăl (-fish′ăl), *a.* [LL. *beneficialis*, beneficial, from *beneficium*, a benefit.]

1. Advantageous; conferring benefits; useful; profitable; helpful; contributing to a valuable end; followed by *to*; as, industry is *beneficial to* the body, as well as *to* the property.

2. Receiving or entitled to have or receive advantage, use, or benefit; as, the *beneficial* owner of an estate.

Syn.—Profitable, salutary, advantageous, wholesome, salubrious, useful, good, helpful.

ben-ē-fi′ciăl-ly, *adv.* Advantageously; profitably; helpfully.

ben-ē-fi′ciăl-ness, *n.* The quality of being useful or helpful; wholesomeness.

ben-ē-fi′ci-ā-ry, *a.* [L. *beneficiarius*, one receiving a favor.]

1. Holding some office or valuable possession, in subordination to another; having a dependent and secondary possession.

2. Pertaining to benevolence; of the nature of charity or a gratuity.

Beneficiary interest; an advantage, or benefit, in a contract, as distinct from a strictly legal right.

ben-ē-fi′ci-ā-ry, *n.* [L. *beneficiarii*, pl. of *beneficiarius*, a name given to soldiers who had received some honor or special exemption from duty.]

1. One who holds a benefice. A *beneficiary* is not the proprietor of the revenues of his church, but he has the administration of them without being accountable to any person.

2. In the middle ages, a feudatory or vassal.

3. One who receives anything as a gift, or is maintained by charity; especially one who receives the funds necessary for his education from a church, society, or trust estate.

ben-ē-fi′ci-āte (-fish′i-āt), *v.t.* 1. To work or improve, as a mine.

2. To reduce (ores).

ben-ē-fi-ci-ā′tion (-fish-i-ā′shun), *n.* Improvement, as of a mine.

ben-ē-fi′cien-cy, *n.* Kindness or favor bestowed. [Obs.]

ben-ē-fi′cient, *a.* Doing good. [Obs.]

ben′ē-fit, *n.* [ME. *benefet*, *bienfet*, from OFr. *bienfait*, a kindness; from L. *benefacere*, to do a kindness.]

1. An act of kindness; a favor conferred.

> Bless the Lord, O my soul, and forget not all his *benefits*. —Ps. ciii. 2.

2. Advantage; profit; a word of extensive use, and expressing whatever contributes to promote prosperity and personal happiness, or adds value to property.

> Men have no right to what is not for their *benefit*. —Burke.

3. A performance at a theater, the proceeds of which are given in aid of some individual actor or actress. The term is also applied to any public performance for the advantage of some indigent, deserving person, or of some public institution or charity.

4. In law, benefit of clergy. [See under *Clergy*.]

Benefit society; a coöperative association in which the members, by the regular payment of small sums, become entitled to pecuniary aid in case of sickness, old age, or injury. Fraternal

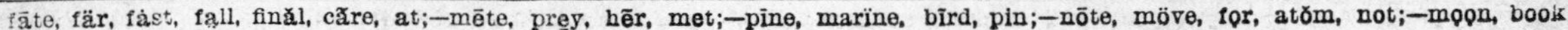

insurance and burial expenses are provided in some instances. Commonly called *friendly society* in Great Britain. Similar organizations existed among the ancient Greeks.

Syn.—Boon, behoof, service, utility, avail, use, good, advantage, profit, favor, blessing.

ben′ē-fit, *v.t.*; benefited, *pt.*, *pp.*; benefiting, *ppr.* To do good to; to advantage; to advance in health or prosperity; applied either to persons or things; as, exercise *benefits* health; trade *benefits* a nation.

ben′ē-fit, *v.i.* To gain advantage; to make improvements; as, he has *benefited* by good advice.

ben′ē-fit-ẽr, *n.* One who bestows a benefit; also, one upon whom a benefit is bestowed.

bē-nēme′, *v.t.* [AS. *benæman.*] To deprive (of); to take away (from). [Obs.]

bē-net′, *v.t.* To catch in a net; to ensnare. [Obs.]

bē-nev′ō-lence, *n.* [ME. *benivolence*; OFr. *benivolence*; L. *benevolentia*, good feeling; *bene*, well, and *volens*, ppr. of *velle*, to wish.]

1. The disposition to do good; good will; kindness; charitableness; the love of mankind, accompanied with a desire to promote its happiness.

2. An act of kindness; good done; charity given.

3. A kind of tax, falsely represented as a gratuity, which some kings of England have arbitrarily exacted.

Syn.—Kindness, benignity, tenderness, almsgiving, beneficence, bounty, charity, generosity, good will, humanity, kindheartedness, kindliness, liberality, munificence, philanthropy, sympathy.—*Kindness* and *tenderness* lean to the side of natural feeling; *benevolence* is considerate kindness, and often overrules mere impulse; *benignity* is condescending kindness; as, the *benignity* of God.

bē-nev′ō-lent, *a.* Having a disposition to do good; possessing love to mankind and a desire to promote its prosperity and happiness; kind; charitable.

Thou good old man, *benevolent* as wise. —Pope.

Syn. — Beneficent, munificent. — Originally, *benevolent* meant well-wishing, and *beneficent* well-doing, but now they differ in their outward exercise chiefly in degree, a *beneficent* act being on a larger scale than a *benevolent* one, while a *munificent* act is greater and more imposing than either.

bē-nev′ō-lent-ly, *adv.* In a kind manner; with good will.

bē-nev′ō-lous, *a.* Kind; benevolent. [Obs.]

ben-gal′, *n.* [From *Bengal*, a province of India.]

1. A fabric of silk and hair for women's apparel.

2. Striped muslin, originally brought from Bengal; sometimes called *Bengal stripes.*

Ben-găl-ēse′ (*or* -ēz′), *n. sing.* and *pl.*, and *a.* I. *n.* The Bengalis collectively, or a native of Bengal.

II. *a.* Pertaining to Bengal, its inhabitants, or their language.

Ben′gal-grass, *n.* A forage-plant, *Setaria Italica*; also called *German millet.*

Ben-gal′ī, Ben-gal′ee (*or* -gäl′), *n.* and *a.* I. *n.* One of the people of Bengal, or his vernacular.

II. *a.* Pertaining to Bengal or its inhabitants, or to its vernacular, which is a mixture of native dialects, Arabic, and Indo-Aryan.

Ben′gal-root, *n.* The root of plants belonging to the ginger family, as *Curcuma Zedoaria* and *Curcuma Zenembel.*

bē-night′ (-nīt′), *v.t.*; benighted, *pt.*, *pp.*; benighting, *ppr.* 1. To involve in darkness; to shroud with the shades of night.

The clouds *benight* the sky. —Garth.

2. To overtake with night, or with darkness; as, the traveler was *benighted.*

3. To involve in moral darkness, or ignorance; to debar from intellectual light; as, absorption in routine *benights* the mind.

bē-night′ed, *a.* Involved in darkness, physical or moral; overtaken by the night.

bē-night′ment, *n.* The condition of being benighted, or shut out from intellectual light.

bē-nign′ (-nīn′), *a.* [ME. *benigne*; OFr. *benigne*; L. *benignus*, good, kind.]

1. Kind; of a kind disposition; gracious; showing favor; kindly; agreeable.

Our Creator, bounteous and *benign.*—Milton.

2. Generous; liberal; as, a *benign* benefactor.

3. Propitious; having a salutary influence; as, the *benign* aspect of the seasons.

4. Wholesome; not pernicious; as, a *benign* medicine.

5. Mild; not malignant; as, a *benign* disease.

bē-nig′năn-cy, *n.* [L. *benignitas*, kindness.] Kindliness; graciousness; amiable quality or manner.

bē-nig′nănt, *a.* Amiable; humane; merciful; benevolent in feeling, character, or aspect.

bē-nig′nănt-ly, *adv.* In a generous, kindly manner.

bē-nig′ni-ty, *n.* [L. *benignitas*, kindness.]

1. Goodness of disposition or heart; kindness of nature; graciousness.

2. Salubrity; wholesome quality; used of climate, etc.

bē-nign′ly (-nīn′ly), *adv.* Favorably; kindly; graciously.

bē-nim′, *v.t.* [AS. *beniman.*] To take away; to rob; to spoil. [Obs.]

ben′i-sŏn, *n.* [ME. *benisoun*; OFr. *beneison*, a blessing, from LL. *benedictio*, a blessing, from L. *benedicere*, to speak well of.] Blessing; benediction.

God's *benison* go with you. —Shak.

bé-ni′tier (bā-nē′tyā), *n.* [Fr., from *bénir*, to bless.] In Roman Catholic churches, a stoop or font for holy water, into which worshipers dip the fingers of the right hand, and bless themselves by making the sign of the cross.

Bénitier.

ben′jȧ-min, *n.* A style of overcoat originally made by an English tailor named Benjamin, and once fashionable; hence, any overcoat. [Slang.]

ben′jȧ-min, *n.* [An earlier form of *benzoin.*] A tree or shrub, *Lindera Benzoin*, a native of America; called also *spicebush.*

ben′jȧ-min-tree, *n.* 1. The *Styrax Benzoin*, from which benzoin is obtained.

2. The East Indian *Ficus Benjamina.*

3. The benjamin or spicebush.

Ben′jȧ-mīte, *n.* A descendant of Benjamin; one of the tribe of Benjamin.

ben′ne, ben′e, *n.* [Malay *bijen.*] In botany, the name of two plants, *Sesamum orientale* and *Sesamum Indicum*, native to Asia; called also *oil-plant.* An oil called *benne-oil* is expressed from the seeds and used universally in India for cooking and anointing, and for soaps, etc.; it is also used in France, England, and the United States in the manufacture of soap and as a substitute for olive-oil.

Benne-plant (*Sesamum orientale*).

ben′net, *n.* [ME. *benet*, from Fr. *benoite*, from LL. *benedictus*, pp. of *benedicere*, to bless. Called the *herba benedicta*, or blessed herb.] The common European avens; the *Geum urbanum.*

ben′sel, *n.* Force or tension; impetus; violence; a harsh rebuke; a pushing blow. [Prov. Eng. and Scot.]

ben′sel, *v.t.* [Ice. *benzl*, a bending, tension, from *benda*, to bend.] To drive; to beat. [Prov. Eng. and Scot.]

bent, *a.* 1. Incurvated; inflected; crooked; as, a *bent* bow; a *bent* knee; a *bent* pin.

2. Inclined; determined; set; used with *on* or *upon*; as, *bent* on war.

bent, *n.* 1. Inclination; disposition; a leaning or bias of mind; propensity; as, the *bent* of the mind or will; the *bent* of a people toward an object.

2. A swerve; a different direction; as, warped souls take an easy *bent.*

If your thoughts should assume so unhappy a *bent.* —Sheridan.

3. Flexion; curvature; state of being bent; as, lowly *bent* of knee; a rod at a *bent.* [Obs.]

4. The limit of force; tension; degree of flexure; a sense, first employed in archery, which is figuratively applied to mental disposition.

Her affections have their full *bent.* —Shak.

5. A section of a frame building; a portion of the framework of a scaffold or building, put together and placed in position, instead of being constructed in position.

6. Declivity or slope. [Rare.]

7. A crook, bend, or curved part. [Obs.]

Syn.—Bias, inclination, prepossession, tendency, propensity, disposition.—*Bent* is applied to the will, affection, and power in general; *bias* mainly to the force of habit or circumstances; *inclination* and *prepossession* to the state of the feelings.

bent, *n.* [ME. *bent*; AS. *beonet*, bent, a rush.]

1. Any stiff wiry grass growing in neglected places; a rush or reed; specifically, *Agrostis vulgaris* and *Agrostis Canina.*

2. A common, heath, or open, neglected pasture. [Obs.]

3. A stalk of coarse withered grass, or of dead grass after bearing seed.

ben′thăl, *a.* [Gr. *benthos*, the depth of the sea.] Pertaining to the greatest depths of the ocean.

Ben-tham′iç, *a.* Relating to Bentham or Benthamism.

Ben′thăm-işm, *n.* A moral doctrine promulgated by Jeremy Bentham (1748-1832), who taught that the love of pleasure and the fear of pain are the sole motives governing human action.

Ben′thăm-īte, *n.* A believer in the doctrine of Benthamism.

ben′thos, *n.* [Gr. *benthos*, depth of the sea.] The bottom or depths of the ocean; also, the fauna and flora found there.

bent′ing-time, *n.* The time when pigeons feed on bents, before peas are ripe.

bent′y, *a.* 1. Having many bents, or stalks of coarse grass.

2. Like bent.

bē-numb′ (-num′), *v.t.*; benumbed, *pt.*, *pp.*; benumbing, *ppr.* [AS. *benumen*, pp. of *beniman*, to deprive; *be-*, and *niman*, to take. The *b* after *m* in numb, thumb, dumb, is an arbitrary addition of comparatively modern writers.] To make stiff and void of feeling; to deprive of sensation; to stupefy; as, fingers *benumbed* by cold; to *benumb* the senses.

bē-numbed′ (-numd′), *a.* Rendered torpid; deprived of sensation; stupefied.

bē-numbed′ness (-numd′), *n.* Destitution of feeling.

bē-numb′ment, *n.* The process of benumbing, or condition of being benumbed.

ben′zal, *n.* In chemistry, a compound organic radical, related to benzoyl and benzyl, and symbolized as C_6H_5CH.

ben-zal′dē-hȳde, *n.* In chemistry, an oily liquid, C_7H_6O; also called *bitter-almond oil.*

ben′zȧ-mide (*or* -mīd), *n.* A substance, consisting of crystals, $C_6H_5CO.NH_2$, obtained by subjecting chlorid of benzoyl to the action of ammonia.

ben′zēne, *n.* An extremely inflammable colorless liquid, C_6H_6, obtained commercially by exhaustive distillation of coal-tar. The aniline colors are derived from it. A low grade is called benzol or benzole.

Benzene ring or *benzene nucleus*; the provisionally accepted type from which the aromatic compounds are derived; it is figured as consisting of six carbon atoms, marking the angles of a six-sided figure, with an atom of hydrogen attendant on each.

ben′zi-dine, *n.* A basic substance used in preparing certain dyes; it is obtained from diphenyl by substitution.

ben′zil, ben′zile, *n.* A compound, $C_{14}H_{10}O_2$, resulting from the oxidization of benzoin.

ben′zin, ben′zine, *n.* A colorless liquid used for cleansing purposes, etc., and obtained from petroleum by fractional distillation. It is a product similar to gasolene. As a single hydrocarbon, it essentially differs from benzene, which is a mixture of hydrocarbons.

ben′zō-āte, *n.* A salt formed by the union of benzoic acid with any salifiable base.

ben-zō′iç, *a.* Relating to or derived from benzoin.

Benzoic acid; a vegetable compound obtained from benzoin, resins, etc. It has a pungent and bitterish taste and somewhat aromatic odor.

ben-zoin′, *n.* [G. *benzoe, benzoin*; Fr. *benjoin*; Ar. *lubān jāwā*, incense of Java.]

1. A concrete resinous juice which flows from incisions in the stem of *Styrax benzoin*, a tree of the East Indies. It yields benzoic acid when submitted to the action of heat. It is solid and brittle, sometimes in yellowish-white tears joined together by a brown substance, and sometimes of a uniform brown substance like resin. It has little taste, but its smell is fragrant and agreeable. It is used in cosmetics and perfumes, and in incense. Also called, by corruption, *benjamin.*

2. In botany, the spicebush.

3. A white crystalline compound derived from benzoic aldehyde.

Flowers of benzoin; benzoic acid.

ben-zoin′ā-ted, *a.* Filled with benzoin.

ben′zōl, ben′zōle, *n.* Adulterated or impure benzene, used for cleansing, etc.

ben′zō-lin, ben′zō-line, *n.* Same as *Benzol.*

ben′zoyl, *n.* The base, C_6H_5CO, of benzoic acid and other compounds.

ben′zō-zōne, *n.* A designation applied to benzoyl acetyl peroxid, the solution of which has been shown to possess marked germicidal properties. —Novy.

ben′zyl, *n.* A compound radical, $C_6H_5CH_2$, existing only in combination.

bē-pāint′ *v.t.* To paint; to cover with paint. [Rare.]

bē-pelt′, *v.t.* To pelt. [Rare.]

bē-pinch′, *v.t.* To mark with pinches.

bē-plas′tẽr, *v.t.* To plaster; to daub; to smear.

bē-plūmed′, *a.* Decorated with feathers.

bē-pom′mel, *v.t.* To beat; to rain blows upon.

bē-pow′dẽr, *v.t.* To powder; to sprinkle or cover with powder

bē-praise′, *v.t.* To praise greatly or extravagantly.

bē-prōse′, *v.t.* To change from verse to prose. [Rare.]

bē-puff′, *v.t.* To puff; to bepraise.

bē-pûr′ple, *v.t.* To tinge or dye with a purple color

bē-quēath′, *v.t.*; bequeathed, *pt.*, *pp.*; bequeathing, *ppr.* [ME. *bequethen*, *bicwethen*; AS. *becwethan*, to declare, give by will; *be-*, and *cwethan*, to say.]

1. To give or leave by will; to devise by testament; as, to *bequeath* an estate or a legacy.

2. To hand down to posterity; as, to *bequeath* a family quarrel.

3. To offer; to give, as services. [Obs.]

Syn.—Devise, give, bestow, confer, consign, grant, impart, yield.—*Bequeath* is the generic term correctly applied to personal property only; *devise* is to bequeath lands or real estate.

bē-quēath′ȧ-ble, *a.* Capable of being bequeathed.

bē-quēath′ăl, *n.* A bequest; the act of bequeathing.

bē-quēath′ẽr, *n.* One who bequeaths.

bē-quēath′ment, *n* The act of bequeathing; a bequest.

bē-quest′, *n.* Something left by will; a legacy.

bē-quēth′en, *v.*, old past participle of *bequeath*.

bē-quōte′, *v.t.* To quote with great frequency.

bē-rāin′, *v.t.* To rain upon. [Obs.]

bē-rāte′, *v.t.*; berated, *pt.*, *pp.*; berating, *ppr.* To chide vehemently; to scold.

bē-rat′tle, *v.t.* To make rattle; to heap abuse upon; to berate. [Obs.]

bē-rāy′, *v.t.* To make foul; to soil. [Obs.]

bẽrbe, *n.* A small African animal, *Genetta pardina*; a kind of genet.

Bẽr′bẽr, *n.* [Ar.] 1. One of a race (Kabyles) akin to the Arabs, formerly occupying all of north Africa, now narrowing down to the Barbary region.

2. The language spoken by the Berbers.

Bẽr″be-ri-dā′cē-æ, *n.pl.* [L., from *berberis*, and *-aceæ*.] The barberry family of plants, bearing fruit in the form of either a berry or a capsule. There are about twenty genera and over one hundred species, including some American varieties, as *Podophyllum*.

bẽr-bẽr-i-dā′ceous, *a.* Belonging to the *Berberidaceæ*.

bẽr′bẽr-ine, *n.* A bitter yellowish substance, obtained as an alkaloid from the root of the barberry, etc.

Bẽr′be-ris, *n* [L.] A widely distributed genus of shrubs, type of the family *Berberidaceæ*. *Berberis vulgaris*, the barberry, is the best-known species.

bẽr′ber-ry, *n.* Same as *Barberry*.

bẽr-ceūse′, *n.* [Fr., a rocker, from *bercer*, to rock, to lull to sleep.] A term applied to a musical composition having a soothing or lulling effect, as a cradle-song.

bẽr′dash, *n.* A cravat formerly worn by men. [Obs.]

bēre, *n.* [AS. *bere*, barley.] In Scottish dialect, barley.

bēre, *v.t.* To pierce. [Obs.]

Bē-rē′ăn, *n.* 1. An inhabitant of the ancient city of Berea, in Asia Minor.

2. A member of a Scottish religious sect, founded toward the end of the eighteenth century by John Barclay, who taught that religion should be derived from the Scriptures alone, according to Acts xvii. 11.

bē-rēave′, *v.t.*; bereaved, bereft, *pt.*, *pp.*; bereaving, *ppr.* [ME. *bereven*; AS. *berēafian*, to rob, bereave; *be-*, and *reāfian*, to rob, plunder.]

1. To deprive; to strip; to make destitute; to deprive by death; with *of* before the person or thing taken away; as, *bereaved of* a father or mother; *bereft of* hope. The first form of the past participle is used only with reference to material objects, and is particularly applied to the loss of relatives or friends by death.

> Me have ye *bereaved* of my children.
> —Gen. xlii. 36.

2. To take away from. [Obs.]

Syn.—Strip, divest, dispossess.

bē-rēaved′, *a.* Deprived; stripped and left destitute; having lost a friend or relative by death; as, a *bereaved* parent.

bē-rēave′ment, *n.* The state of being bereaved; deprivation, particularly by the loss of a friend by death.

Syn.—Destitution, affliction, deprivation, loss.

bē-rēav′ẽr, *n.* One who bereaves or deprives another of something valued.

bē-reft′, *v.*, past tense and past participle of *bereave*. [See *Bereave*.]

Ber-en-gā′ri-ăns, *n.pl.* A sect of the eleventh century which followed Berengarius, archdeacon of Angers, who denied the doctrine of transubstantiation.

ber′et, *n.* [Fr., from L. *berretta*, dim. of *birrus*, a cloak.]

1. A flat cap of woolen or other material, worn by French peasantry.

2. Same as *Biretta*.

bē-ret′tȧ, *n.* Same as *Biretta*.

bẽrg, *n.* [AS. and G. *berg*, a hill.]

1. A hill or eminence.

2. A large mass or floating island of ice; an iceberg.

> Glittering *bergs* of ice. —Tennyson.

bẽr′gȧ-mot, *n.* [From *Bergamo*, a town in Italy.]

1. A variety of pear.

2. A plant of the mint family.

3. A species of citron whose fruit has a fine taste and smell, its essential oil being highly esteemed as a perfume. This oil is extracted from the yellow rind of the fruit. The tree is the *Citrus bergamia*, a distinct species, with a pear-shaped fruit.

4. The essence or perfume produced from the *bergamot* citron.

5. A kind of snuff perfumed with *bergamot*.

6. A coarse tapestry, manufactured out of flock of wool, silk, cotton, hemp, and ox or goat's hair; said to have been invented at Bergamo, in Italy.

bẽr′gan-dẽr, *n.* [ME. *bergander*; *berg*, a burrow, and *gander*, a male goose.] The sheldrake or burrow-duck of England (*Anas tadorna*); a duck that breeds in holes under cliffs.

bẽr′gẽr-et, *n.* [OFr., from *berger*, a shepherd.] A pastoral song. [Obs.]

bẽrgh (bẽrg), *n.* [AS. *beorg*, a hill.] A hill. [Obs.]

bẽrg′măn-īte, *n.* [Named after *Bergman*, mineralogist.] A variety of scapolite, found in Norway.

bẽrg′mȧs″tẽr, *n.* Same as *Barmaster*.

bẽrg′mehl, *n.* [G., from *berg*, a mountain, and *mehl*, meal.] In mineralogy, an earthy substance, of the fineness of flour or meal, consisting of the shells of *Infusoria*; sometimes eaten in times of famine in northern Europe.

bẽrg′mōte, *n.* Same as *Barmote*.

bẽr′gō-mȧsk, *n.* A rustic dance, named after the inhabitants of *Bergamo*, Italy, once proverbial for their awkwardness.

bẽrg′stock, *n.* [G., from *berg*, a mountain, and *stock*, a stick.] A spiked pole used in mountain-climbing: a kind of alpenstock.

bẽr′gylt, *n.* [Norw.] The Norwegian haddock, or rosefish, *Sebastes marinus*.

bē-rhȳme′ (-rīm′), *v.t.* See *Berime*.

ber′i-ber-i, *n.* [Cingalese *beri*, weakness.] A disease characterized by great muscular weakness, inflammation of the nerves, paralysis, and fatal effusion. It occurs among the natives of India and Japan.

ber-i-gor′ȧ, *n.* [Native name.] An Australian falcon, *Hieracidea berigora*, marked with spots of orange or reddish-yellow.

bē-rīme′, **bē-rhȳme′**, *v.t.*; berimed, *pt.*, *pp.*; beriming, *ppr.* To celebrate or extol in rime.

bē-rīme′, *v.i.* To indite verses or compose in rime.

Bẽrke-lē′ăn, *a.* and *n.* I. *a.* Of or pertaining to George Berkeley, bishop of Cloyne (1684-1753), or his system of philosophical idealism.

II. *n.* A follower of Bishop Berkeley, or an adherent of Berkeleianism.

Bẽrke-lē′iăn-ism, **Bẽrke′ley-ism**, *n.* The philosophy of Bishop Berkeley, who held that material things exist only in so far as they are perceived, that the mind is conscious of subjective impressions only, and therefore cannot know external things.

Bẽrke′ley-īte, *n.* See *Berkeleian*.

Bẽrk′shire, *n.* One of a breed of swine, originally from Berkshire, England, characterized by medium size, hair mostly black, short legs and head, and broad, straight back.

bẽr′lin, *n.* 1. A large four-wheeled vehicle with two interior seats and a top or hood that can be raised or lowered, the body being suspended; so called from Berlin, where it was first made in the seventeenth century.

2. Fine dyed worsted used for knitting, embroidery, tapestry, and various other kinds of fancywork; zephyr wool; called also *Berlin wool*.

3. A knitted glove.

4. A dance belonging to the polka class.

Berlin black; black varnish, used in coating ironware, which dries with a dead black surface.

Berlin blue; Prussian blue.

Berlin green; a green dyestuff consisting of a complex cyanide of iron.

Berlin iron; a fusible kind of soft iron, containing phosphorus, largely used in making delicate or ornamental articles, as jewelry and fine smooth castings, which are sometimes stained or lacquered in imitation of bronze.

Berlin shop; a repository for ladies' fancy wares, more especially for Berlin wools, patterns, knitting-needles, etc.

Berlin ware; a kind of pottery marked with a blue stamp, and of such quality as to resist the action of almost all chemical reagents.

Berlin work; embroidery or fancywork made of Berlin or zephyr wool.

bẽrm, **bẽrme**, *n.* [Fr. *berme*; D. *berme*; G. *berme*; Ice. *barmr*, the edge of a river or sea.]

1. A narrow ledge. In fortification, a space of ground, from three to five feet in width, left between the rampart and the moat or foss, designed to receive the earth from the rampart and prevent it from filling the ditch.

2. In engineering, a horizontal ledge or bench at the bottom or part way up a bank or cutting, to catch earth that may roll down the slope, or to strengthen the bank.

3. The bank or side of a canal which is opposite to the towpath.

Bẽr-mū′dȧ-grȧss, *n.* A kind of pasture-grass, *Cynodon Dactylon*, which is widespread in warm countries. Called also *Bermuda devil grass*, *Bahama grass*, and *scutch-grass*.

Bẽr-mū′di-ăn, *n.* and *a.* I. *n.* A native or inhabitant of the Bermuda islands, a group about 600 miles east of Cape Hatteras.

II. *a.* Of or pertaining to the Bermudas or their inhabitants.

bẽr′nȧ-cle, *n.* Same as *Barnacle*.

bẽr′nȧ-fly, *n.* A Brazilian two-winged insect which lays its eggs in wounds of man or beast, where the larvæ work great harm.

Bẽr′när-dine, *n.* and *a.* I. *n.* One of the order of Cistercian monks founded by St. Bernard in the twelfth century.

II. *a.* Of or pertaining to St. Bernard of Clairvaux (1091-1153) or to the Cistercian order founded by him.

Bẽr-nēse′, *a.* Pertaining to the canton or city of Bern, Switzerland, or to its people.

Bẽr-nēse′, *n. sing.* and *pl.* A native or natives of Bern.

bẽr′ni-cle, *n.* See *Barnacle*.

bẽr-nouse′, *n.* Same as *Burnoose*.

bē-rob′, *v.t.* To plunder; to rob. [Obs.]

Ber′ō-ē, *n.* [L., from Gr. *Beroē*, one of the ocean nymphs.]

1. The typical genus of ctenophorans of the family *Beroidæ*.

2. [b—] A small jellyfish or ctenophoran of this genus. These marine invertebrates, which are transparent and gelatinous, are either oval or globular, and float in the ocean, where they are widely diffused. They are phosphoric, and shine at night like lamps suspended in the sea.

ber′ret, *n.* Same as *Beret*.

ber-ret′tȧ, *n.* See *Biretta*.

ber′ried (-rid), *a.* Having or yielding berries; also, consisting of or resembling berries.

ber′ry, *n.*; *pl.* **ber′ries**. [ME. *bery*, *berie*; AS. *berie*; O.H.G. *beri*; Ice. *ber*, berry.]

1. A succulent, indehiscent, pulpy fruit or pericarp, many-celled and many-seeded, as the tomato, grape, and currant, the attachment of the seeds being lost at maturity, and the seeds remaining scattered in the pulp.

1. Fruit of Currant. 2. Section of same.

2. Any of the succulent small fruits having numerous small seeds, as the goose*berry*, black*berry*, straw*berry*, mul*berry*, huckle*berry*, etc.

3. The dry kernel of various grains; also, the coffee-bean.

4. Something resembling a berry, as one of the ova or eggs of a lobster.

In berry; containing spawn.

ber′ry, *v.i.*; berried, *pt.*, *pp.*; berrying, *ppr.* To bear or produce berries; also, to seek for or gather berries.

ber′ry, *n.* [AS. *beorh*, a hill.] A mound or hillock; a corruption of *barrow*.

ber′ry-ing, *n.* The act of seeking for berries.

bẽr′seem, *n.* Egyptian clover. [See *Trifolium*.]

bẽr′sẽrk, **bẽr′sẽrk-ẽr**, *n.* [Ice. *berserkr*; *berr*, bare, and *serkr*, a coat, shirt.]

1. In Norse legends, a warrior who fought with peculiar frenzy, called the "berserker rage."

2. One given to fury and violence.

bẽrs′tle, *n.* A bristle. [Obs.]

bẽrth, *n.* [Probably from the root of *bear*.]

1. The space occupied by a ship riding or ranging at anchor; any situation or place where a vessel lies, or can lie, whether at anchor or at a wharf.

2. An apartment in a vessel in which officers or men mess and sleep; also, a storage-place in a vessel for sailors' chests.

3. A sleeping-place or bunk in a vessel, a railway sleeping-car, or elsewhere.

4. An allotted place, office, appointment, or employment on a vessel; also, office or employment in general; as, a snug *berth* in the civil service.

To give a wide berth to; to keep at a safe distance from; principally in nautical use.

bẽrth, *v.t.*; berthed, *pt.*, *pp.*; berthing, *ppr.* 1. In nautical affairs, to give anchorage-ground to; to give space to lie in, as a ship in a dock, or at a wharf.

2. To allot a berth or berths to; as, to *berth* a ship's company; to *berth* a traveler in a railway sleeping-car.

3. To furnish with employment.

bẽr'thȧ, *n.* [Fr. *berthe*, from *Berthe*, Bertha, a feminine name.] A wide collar or cape, usually of lace, for feminine wear.

bẽrth'āġe, *n.* 1. The place allotted to a vessel at a dock or in a harbor.

2. Fees for a berth at a dock or a place for anchorage.

bẽrth'-deck, *n.* The deck of a vessel on which the *berths* are located; in war-vessels, the deck next below the gun-deck.

bẽr'thi-ẽr-ite (bẽr'ti-), *n.* An ore of antimony, consisting of sulphuret of antimony and protosulphuret of iron. It has a metallic luster, a dark steel-gray color, and occurs massive or in elongated prisms; so called from Pierre *Berthier*, a French mineralogist.

bẽrth'ing, *n.* 1. The exterior planking of the sides of a vessel, above the sheer-strake; the bulwark.

2. The displacement, from rising or working up, of the planks in the side of a vessel.

bẽrth'ing, *n.* 1. The disposal of accommodations for sleeping in a sleeping-car or on a vessel.

2. The act of placing a vessel in a dock or berth.

Bẽr-thol-lē'ti-ȧ (-shi-ȧ), *n.* A genus of South American trees which grow to great size and yield the Brazil-nut; so called from C. L. *Berthollet*, a French chemist. The only species, *Bertholletia excelsa*, composes the genus, which is included in the family *Myrtaceæ*.

Ber-til-lon' sys'tem (bār-tē-yoṅ'). A system of personal identification devised by the French anthropologist, Alphonse *Bertillon*. It records those dimensions of the human body which are least subject to change, confining the principal measurements to the bones, as the skull, ulna, radius, femur, and to proportional measurement from the coccyx to top of cranium, and to the calcaneum or heel-bone, and from point to point of the shoulder; it also notes external physical peculiarities, such as deformities, color, impressions of thumb lines, etc. A distinguishing feature of the system is the classification, by which the anthropometric indices are tabulated to facilitate a prompt identification regardless of change of name or appearance. The system is generally employed by police authorities for the purpose of identifying criminals.

bẽr'trăm, *n.* [Corrupted from L. *pyrethrum*; Gr. *pyrethron*, a spicy plant; *pyr*, fire.] An old name for pellitory, *Pyrethrum Parthenium*, or feverfew, and *Anacyclus Pyrethrum*, or Spanish pellitory, both of which belong to the aster family. Written also *bartram*.

ber'y-ċoid, *a.* [L. *Beryx*, the name of the typical genus, and Gr. *eidos*, form.] Pertaining to the *Berycidæ*, a family of marine fishes.

ber'yl, *n.* [L. *beryllus*; Gr. *bēryllos*, a gem, beryl.] A hard, colorless, yellowish, bluish, or less brilliant green variety of emerald, the prevailing hue being green of various shades, but always pale. The best *beryls* are found in Brazil, in Siberia, and Ceylon, and in Dauria, on the frontiers of China. The stone is also found in many parts of the United States. Some of the finer and transparent varieties of it are called aquamarine and are prized as gems to be set in jewelry.

be-ryl'li-ȧ, *n.* Same as *Glucina*.

ber'yl-line, *a.* Like a beryl as to color; light green, or bluish green.

be-ryl'li-um, *n.* Same as *Glucinum*.

ber'yl-loid, *n.* [*Beryl*, and Gr. *eidos*, form.] A solid, consisting of two twelve-sided pyramids put base to base, as in beryl crystals.

bes'ȧ-bol, *n.* [Ar.] A fragrant balsam resin, formerly called Indian myrrh, and differing from the real myrrh principally in color. It is obtained from the *Commiphora kataf*, a tree growing in Somaliland, eastern Africa. Also written *bissabol*.

bē-saint', *v.t.* To make a saint of. [Obs.]

bē-ṣant', *n.* Same as *Bezant*.

beṣ-ant'lẽr, *n.* Same as *Bez-antler*.

bē-sāyle', **bē-sāiel'**, *n.* [ME. *besayle*; OFr. *besayel*, a great-grandfather; *bes* (L. *bis*), twice, and *ayel*, grandfather.]

1. A great-grandfather. [Obs.]

2. In old English law, a writ of abatement, by which a great-grandchild, illegally excluded from lands of which either of his great-grandfathers died seized, vindicated his claim to it. Written also *besaille*.

bē-sçat'tẽr, *v.t.* To scatter over; also, to strew or cover sparsely, as with flowers.

bē-sçorn', *v.t.* To treat with scorn.

bē-sçratch', *v.t.* To scratch; to tear with the nails.

bē-sçrawl', *v.t.* To scribble over.

bē-sçreen', *v.t.* To cover with a screen; to shelter; to conceal.

bē-sçrib'ble, *v.t.* To scribble over.

bē-sçum'bẽr, **bē-sçum'mẽr**, *v.t.* To befoul with ordure. [Obs.]

bē-see', *v.t.* To see; to mind. [Obs.]

bē-seech', *v.t.*; besought, *pt.*, *pp.*; beseeching, *ppr.* [ME. *besechen*, *bisechen*, *beseken*; *be-*, and *sechen*, to seek.]

1. To entreat; to supplicate; to implore; to ask or pray with urgency; followed by a personal object; as, I, Paul, *beseech you* by the meekness and gentleness of Christ.

2. To beg eagerly for; to solicit; followed by the thing solicited.

> But Eve fell humble, and *besought* his peace. —Milton.

Syn.—Beg, entreat, solicit, supplicate, implore, crave, appeal to, invoke, request, pray.—*Beg* supposes simply a state of want; to *beseech*, *entreat*, and *solicit*, a state of urgent necessity; to *implore* and *supplicate*, a state of overwhelming distress.

bē-seech', *n.* A request; a supplication. [Obs. or Poet.]

bē-seech'ẽr, *n.* One who beseeches.

bē-seech'ing-ly, *adv.* In a beseeching manner.

bē-seech'ing-ness, *n.* Same as *Beseechment*.

bē-seech'ment, *n.* The act of beseeching, supplicating, or earnestly entreating. [Rare.]

bē-seek', *v.t.* To beseech. [Obs.]

bē-seem', *v.t.*; beseemed, *pt.*, *pp.*; beseeming, *ppr.* 1. To become; to be fit for, or worthy of.

2. To seem fit for. [Obs.]

> What form of speech or behaviour *beseemeth* us, in our prayers to God? —Hooker.

bē-seem', *v.i.* 1. To be seemly; to be meet.

2. To seem. [Obs.]

bē-seem'ing, *n.* 1. Appearance. [Obs.]

2. Comeliness.

bē-seem'ing, *a.* Becoming; fit; worthy of. [Rare.]

bē-seem'ing-ly, *adv.* In a beseeming manner.

bē-seem'ing-ness, *n.* The quality of being meet, or suitable.

bē-seem'ly, *a.* Becoming; suitable. [Rare.]

bē-seen', *a.* 1. Seen. [Obs.]

2. Arrayed; equipped. [Rare.]

bē-sen'nȧ, *n.* Same as *Mesenna*.

bē-set', *v.t.*; beset, *pt.*, *pp.*; besetting, *ppr.* [ME. *besetten*, *bisetten*; AS. *besettan*; *be*, about, and *settan*, to set.]

1. To surround; to inclose; to hem in; to besiege; as, we are *beset* with enemies; the city is *beset* with troops.

2. To press on all sides, so as to perplex; to press hard, or to press hard upon; to harass, obstruct, or embarrass.

3. To ornament; to set or stud, as with gems.

4. To employ; to set or place; to become or suit. [Obs.]

Syn.—Surround, inclose, environ, hem in, besiege, encircle, encompass, embarrass, urge, press.

bē-set'ment, *n.* The condition of being beset; also, that by which one is beset, as a sin or failing.

bē-set'tẽr, *n.* One who or that which besets.

bē-set'ting, *a.* Habitually attending; constantly attacking, troubling, or pressing; as, a *besetting* sin.

bē-shine', *v.t.*; beshone, *pt.*, *pp.*; beshining, *ppr.* To shine upon.

bē-show', *n.* [Native name.] The black candlefish, *Anoplopoma fimbria*, of the north Pacific Coast, which grows to a large size and is esteemed as food.

bē-shrew', *v.t.* To curse; to execrate.

bē-shroud', *v.t.* To cover with a shroud; to screen.

bē-shut', *v.t.* To shut up; to shut out. [Obs.]

bē-side', *adv.* 1. Close by; near; at hand; as, the man was close *beside*.

2. Besides. [Rare.]

bē-side', *prep.* [ME. *beside*, *biside*, *byside*; AS. *be sīdan*; *be*, by, and *sīdan*, dat. of *sīde*, side.]

1. At the side of; near; as, he sat *beside* me, or *beside* the stream.

> *Beside* him hung his bow. —Milton.

2. Over and above, distinct from; in addition to. [Now rare in this sense, *besides* having taken its place.]

3. In comparison with; as, my writing is poor *beside* yours.

4. On one side; out of the regular course or order; not according to, but not contrary.

> It is *beside* my present business to enlarge upon this speculation. —Locke.

5. Out of; in a state deviating from.

> Paul, thou art *beside* thyself.—Acts. xxvi. 24.

bē-sīdeṣ', *adv.* and *prep.* Moreover; more than that; over and above; distinct from; not included in the number, or in what has been mentioned.

> *Besides*, the gentleman is full of virtue. —Shak.

bē-siēġe', *v.t.*; besieged, *pt.*, *pp.*; besieging, *ppr.* [ME. *besegen*, *bisegen*; *be-*, and *segen*, to siege; OFr. *siége*, a seat, a siege.]

1. To lay siege to; to beleaguer; as, to *besiege* a fort or city.

2. To beset; to throng round; as, *besieged* with cares.

Syn.—Encompass, surround, hem in, invest, engird, inclose.

bē-siēġe'ment, *n.* The act of besieging or state of being besieged.

bē-siē'ġẽr, *n.* One who lays siege, or is employed in a siege.

bē-siē'ġing, *a.* Surrounding in a hostile manner; laying siege to.

bē-siē'ġing-ly, *adv.* In a besieging manner.

bē-sit', *v.t.* To suit; to become. [Obs.]

bē-slab'bẽr, *v.t.* To beslobber.

bē-slāve', *v.t.* To enslave; to make a slave of. [Obs.]

bē-slav'ẽr, *v.t.*; beslavered, *pt.*, *pp.*; beslavering, *ppr.* To befoul or defile with slaver.

bē-slime', *v.t.* To daub with slime; to soil. [Obs.]

bē-slob'bẽr, *v.t.* To soil or smear with spittle; to bedaub, as with spittle; to slobber over with kisses; figuratively, to bestow fulsome praise.

bē-slub'bẽr, *v.t.* Same as *Beslobber*.

bē-smēar', *v.t.*; besmeared, *pt.*, *pp.*; besmearing, *ppr.* To bedaub; to overspread with any viscous, glutinous matter, or with any soft substance that adheres; to befoul; to soil.

bē-smēar'ẽr, *n.* One who besmears.

bē-smirch', *v.t.*; besmirched, *pt.*, *pp.*; besmirching, *ppr.* To soil; to befoul; to discolor. Hence, to dishonor; to sully.

bē-smōke', *v.t.*; besmoked, *pt.*, *pp.*; besmoking, *ppr.* To foul with smoke; also, to harden or dry in smoke.

bē-smut', *v.t.*; besmutted, *pt.*, *pp.*; besmutting, *ppr.* To blacken with smut; to foul with soot.

bē-snōw', *v.t.*; besnowed, *pt.*, *pp.*; besnowing, *ppr.* 1. To scatter like snow. [Rare.]

2. To whiten with, or as with snow.

bē'ṣŏm, *n.* [ME. *besum*, *besem*, *besma*, a broom, rod; AS. *besema*, a rod, pl., a bundle of twigs.] A broom; a brush of twigs for sweeping. [Rare.]

bē'ṣŏm, *v.t.* To sweep, as with a besom. [Rare.]

bē'ṣŏm-ẽr, *n.* One who uses a besom. [Rare.]

bē-sọrt', *v.t.* To suit; to fit; to become. [Obs.]

bē-sọrt', *n.* Company; attendance; train. [Obs.]

bē-sot', *v.t.*; besotted, *pt.*, *pp.*; besotting, *ppr.* To make sottish; to infatuate; to make drunk.

bē-sot'ted, *a.* Abandoned to infatuation; made a slave to intoxicants or narcotics.

bē-sot'ted-ly, *adv.* In a foolish manner.

bē-sot'ted-ness, *n.* Stupidity; arrant folly; infatuation.

bē-sot'ting-ly, *adv.* In a besotting manner.

bē-sought', *v.*, past tense and past participle of *beseech*.

bē-span'gle, *v.t.*; bespangled, *pt.*, *pp.*; bespangling, *ppr.* To adorn with spangles; to dot or sprinkle with something brilliant; as, the heavens are *bespangled* with stars.

bē-spat'tẽr, *v.t.*; bespattered, *pt.*, *pp.*; bespattering, *ppr.* 1. To soil by spattering; to sprinkle with water, or with dirt and water.

2. To asperse with calumny or reproach.

bē-spawl', *v.t.* To soil or make foul with spittle. [Obs.]

bē-spēak', *v.t.*; bespoke, *pt.*; bespeaking, *ppr.*; bespoken, bespoke, *pp.* 1. To speak for beforehand; to order or engage; as, to *bespeak* a favor.

2. To speak to; to address. [Rare.]

3. To betoken; to indicate by externals; as, his words *bespeak* the fiend.

Syn.—Betoken, foreorder, forestall, prearrange, indicate, evidence.

bē-spēak', *v.i.* To speak out; to exclaim. [Obs.]

bē-spēak', *n.* Among actors, a benefit. [Eng.]

bē-spēak'ẽr, *n.* One who bespeaks.

bē-speç'kle, *v.t.* To mark with speckles or spots.

bē-spew', *v.t.* To soil with spew; to cover with vomit.

bē-spice', *v.t.* To season or flavor with spices.

bē-spirt', *v.t.* [Obs.] See *Bespurt*.

bē-spit', *v.t.* To daub or soil with spittle.

bē-spōke', *v.*, past tense of *bespeak*.

bē-spot', *v.t.*; bespotted, *pt.*, *pp.*; bespotting, *ppr.* To mark with spots; to dapple.

bē-spread' (-spred'), *v.t.*; bespread, *pt.*, *pp.*; bespreading, *ppr.* To spread over; to cover over; as, to *bespread* with flowers.

bē-sprent', *v.* The past participle of the obsolete verb, *bespreng*, to besprinkle or scatter.

bē-sprin'kle, *v.t.*; besprinkled, *pt.*, *pp.*; besprinkling, *ppr.* To sprinkle over; to scatter over; as, to *besprinkle* with dust.

bē-sprin'klẽr, *n.* One who sprinkles over.

bē-sprin'kling, *n.* The act of sprinkling; the state of being besprinkled.

bē-spŭrt', *v.t.* To spurt over or on; to void in a stream. [Obs.]

Bes-sel'ĭăn, *a.* In mathematics, of or pertaining to Bessel, the astronomer, or to Bessel's functions.

Bes′se-mẽr, *a.* and *n.* [Named from Sir Henry *Bessemer*, an English engineer.]

I. *a.* Pertaining to the process of making Bessemer steel.

II. *n.* Any article produced by the Bessemer process.

Bessemer steel; steel produced by the decarburization of molten gray iron by means of air-blasts, which oxidize out and carry off the carbon, silicon, and other impurities, the product being then cast into ingots.

best, *a.*, superl. of *good*. [AS. *best*, contr. from *betest*, *betsta*, *betst*, best. The word has no connection in origin with *good*, of which it is the superlative.]

1. Most good; having good qualities in the highest degree; applied indifferently to physical or moral subjects; as, the *best* man; the *best* road; the *best* cloth; the *best* abilities. Like *most*, and other attributes, it is often used without its noun, when the noun is obvious; as, the *best* of men fail in the performance of duty.

2. Farthest advanced; as, the *best* scholar; this is the literal sense of the word.

3. Most correct, or complete; as, the *best* view of a subject.

4. Largest; most; greatest; as, the *best* part of a day. [Colloq.]

5. Most advantageous; most serviceable for a purpose; as, the *best* way to town.

In commercial usage, the word *best* has various meanings; as, give me your *best* price, meaning the lowest price; get the *best* price you can, meaning the highest, etc. As expressing quality in trade, it does not always signify the highest standard of excellence, such terms as fancy, extra-fancy, etc., being often used for grades higher than *best* goods.

Best man; the groomsman, or friendly supporter and attendant of the bridegroom at a wedding; the principal groomsman, if there be more than one.

Best work; in mining, the richest part of the ore.

best, *n.* Utmost; highest endeavor or state; the most excellent or perfect thing or quality; as, to do one's *best*; he wore his *best* and sang to the *best* of his ability.

At best; in the best manner; in the utmost degree or extent applicable to the case; as, life is *at best* very short.

To get the best of; to best; to defeat; to gain an advantage over, by fair or foul means; as, *to get the best of* a bargain or of an enemy.

To make the best of; to carry to its greatest perfection; to improve to the utmost; as, *to make the best of* a sum of money or a piece of land. Also, to permit the least possible inconvenience; as, *to make the best of* ill fortune or a bad bargain.

best, *adv.*, superl. of *well*. 1. In the highest degree; beyond all other; as, to love one *best*.

2. To the most advantage; with the most ease; as, which instrument can you *best* use?

3. With most profit or success; as, money is *best* employed in manufactures.

4. Most intimately or particularly; most correctly; as, it is *best* known to himself.

best, *v.t.*; bested, *pt.*, *pp.*; besting, *ppr.* To get the better of; to overcome; to defeat. [Colloq.]

bē-stain′, *v.t.* To mark with stains.

bē-stead′ (-sted′), *v.t.*; besteaded, bested, *pt.*, *pp.*; besteading, *ppr.* 1. To aid; to assist.

2. To avail; to benefit; to profit; to serve.

bes′tiăl (bes′chăl), *a.* [L. *bestialis*, from *bestia*, beast.]

1. Belonging to a beast, or to the class of beasts.

2. Having the qualities of a beast; brutal; below the dignity of reason or humanity; carnal; as, a *bestial* appetite.

Syn.—Beastly, depraved, low, vile, sensual, carnal.

bes′tiăl, *n.* 1. In Scots law, the cattle on a farm taken collectively.

2. A work on zoölogy.

bes-tiăl′i-ty (-chăl′), *n.* 1. The quality of beasts; the state or quality of being bestial.

2. Unnatural connection with a beast.

bes′tiăl-īze, *v.t.*; bestialized, *pt.*, *pp.*; bestializing, *ppr.* To make like a beast; to degrade to a bestial condition.

bes′tiăl-ly, *adv.* Brutally; in a bestial manner.

bes′ti-ā-ry, *n.* [L. *bestiarium*, neut. of *bestiarius*, pertaining to wild beasts; *bestia*, a beast.] A name given to old books treating of beasts, often in verse.

bē-stick′, *v.t.*; bestuck, *pt.*, *pp.*; besticking, *ppr.* To stick over, as with sharp points; to mark, by infixing points or spots; to pierce.

bē-still′, *v.t.* To make still; to quiet.

bē-stir′, *v.t.*; bestirred, *pt.*, *pp.*; bestirring, *ppr.* To put into brisk or vigorous action; to move with life and vigor; usually used reflexively; as, *bestir* yourselves.

best′ness, *n.* The state of being best. [Rare.]

bē-storm′, *v.t.* To overtake with a storm.

bē-stōw′, *v.t.*; bestowed, *pt.*, *pp.*; bestowing, *ppr.* [ME. *bestowen*; *be-* and *stowen*, from *stowe*, a place. Literally, to set or place.]

1. To give; to confer; to impart; with the sense of gratuity, and followed by *on* or *upon*.

2. To give in marriage; to dispose of.

3. To apply; to place for the purpose of exertion, or use; as, to *bestow* our whole force upon an object.

4. To lay out, or dispose of; to give in payment for. [Obs.]

5. To lay up in store; to deposit for safe-keeping; to stow; to place.

6. To behave; followed by the reflexive pronoun. [Rare.]

Syn.—Give, grant, confer, present, lodge, arrange, pack.

bē-stōw′ăl, *n.* The act of bestowing; disposal.

bē-stōw′ẽr, *n.* One who bestows; a giver.

bē-stōw′ment, *n.* The act of giving; that which is given.

bē-strad′dle (-dl), *v.t.* To bestride.

bē-straught′ (-strat′), *a.* Distracted; mad. [Obs.]

bē-streak′, *v.t.* To mark with streaks.

bē-strew′, *v.t.*; bestrewed, *pt.*; bestrewed, bestrewn, *pp.*; bestrewing, *ppr.* To scatter over; to besprinkle; to strew. Also written *bestrow*.

bē-stride′, *v.t.*; bestrode, bestrid, *pt.*; bestridden, bestrid, bestrode, *pp.*; bestriding, *ppr.* [ME. *bestriden*; AS. *bestridan*; *be-*, and *stridan*, to stride.]

1. To stride over; to stand or sit with (anything) between the legs, or with the legs extended across; as, to *bestride* a horse.

2. To step over; as, to *bestride* a threshold.

bē-stud′, *v.t.*; bestudded, *pt.*, *pp.*; bestudding, *ppr.* To set with studs; to adorn with bosses; as, to *bestud* with stars.

bē-swike′, *v.t.* [ME. *beswiken*; AS. *beswican*; *be-* and *swican*, to deceive.] To allure. [Obs.]

bet, *n.* [ME. *abet*; OFr. *abet*, from *abeter*, to encourage, excite.] A wager; that which is laid, staked, or pledged in a contest or contingent issue, to be won either by the victorious party himself or by another person in consequence of his victory; the act of betting or making a wager.

bet, *v.i.*; bet, betted, *pt.*, *pp.*; betting, *ppr.* To lay a bet; to lay a wager; to stake or pledge something upon the event of a contest.

bet, *v.t.* To wager; to stake.

bē′tȧ (*or* bā′tȧ), *n.* The second letter in the Greek alphabet (β); used specifically in the sciences to designate the second of a series.

Bē′tȧ, *n.* [L., a beet.] A genus of apetalous plants, natural order *Chenopodiaceæ*, having large succulent roots, and a green calyx in which the hard rugged nut is embedded, valuable for both culinary and agricultural purposes. *Beta vulgaris* is the common beet.

bē′tȧ-in, *n.* [L. *beta*, beet, and *-in*.] A chemical base found in the common beet and mangel-wurzel.

bē-tāke′, *v.t.*; betook, *pt.*; betaking, *ppr.*; betaken, *pp.* [ME. *betaken*; Sw. *betaka*; *be-*, and *taka*, to take, seize.]

1. To take to; to have recourse to; to apply; to resort; used reflexively; as, to *betake* ourselves to arms.

2. To take or seize. [Obs.]

3. To commit; to deliver. [Obs.]

bête, *n.* [Fr., from OFr. *beste*, a beast.] A forfeit.

Bête noire (lit. black beast); a bugbear; something particularly obnoxious to or dreaded by any one.

bēte, *v.t.* To mend; to better. [Obs.]

be-tee′lȧ, *n.* An East Indian muslin, once used largely for veils, neckwear, etc. [Obs.]

bē-teem′, *v.t.* To bring forth; to produce; to shed; to bestow. [Obs.]

bē′tel (bē′tl), *n.* [Fr. *bétel*; Port. *betel*, *betelhe*, *vitele*; Malay, *vettila*, betel.] A species of pepper, *Piper betle*, a creeping or climbing plant, a native of the East Indies, natural order *Piperaceæ*. [See *Betel-nut*.]

Bet′el-guēse (-gēz), *n.* [Fr. *Bételgeuse*, from the Arabic.] A star of the first magnitude in the right shoulder of Orion; written also *Betelgeuse* and *Betelgeux*.

bē′tel-nut, *n.* The nut of the areca palm, *Areca Catechu*, chewed in the East with betel leaves and lime. [See *Betel*.]

Leaf, flowers, and nut of *Areca Catechu*.

beth′el, *n.* [Heb. *bēth-ēl*, house of God.]

1. A worshiping-place; any sacred spot.

2. A house of worship for sailors; sometimes a floating structure.

bē-think′, *v.t.*; bethought, *pt.*, *pp.*; bethinking, *ppr.* To call to mind; to recall or bring to recollection, reflection, or consideration; always used with a reflexive pronoun, with *of* or *that* before the subject of thought.

I have *bethought* me *of* another fault.—Shak.

Syn.—Recollect, remember.

bē-think′, *v.i.* To think; to ponder or deliberate.

Beth′lē-hem, *n.* 1. A hospital for lunatics, so called from the lunatic hospital of St. Mary of Bethlehem, in London, England, which was corrupted into *Bedlam* hospital.

2. In architecture, a small building attached to some Oriental church edifices, in which the communion bread is baked.

Beth′lē-hem-īte, Beth′lem-īte, *n.* 1. An inhabitant of Bethlehem in Judea.

2. [*pl.*] In church history, an order of monks, introduced into England in the year 1257, who dressed like the Dominicans, except that they wore a star with five rays, in memory of the star which appeared over Bethlehem at the nativity of Jesus Christ. There was an order of *Bethlehemites* also in Spanish America.

3. [b—] A bedlamite; a lunatic; a madman. [See *Bedlam*.]

bē-thought′ (-thot′), *v.*, past tense and past participle of *bethink*.

bē-thrall′, *v.t.* To enslave; to reduce to bondage; to bring into subjection. [Rare.]

bē-thumb′ (-thum′), *v.t.*; bethumbed, *pt.*, *pp.*; bethumbing, *ppr.* To handle; to soil by handling; as, his books are well *bethumbed*.

bē-thump′, *v.t.* To beat or thump soundly. [Rare.]

bē-tīde′, *v.t.*; betided, *pt.*, *pp.*; betiding, *ppr.* [ME. *betiden*; *be-*, and AS. *tīdan*, to happen.] To happen to; to befall; to come to; used of good or evil.

What will *betide* the few? —Milton.

bē-tīde′, *v.i.* To come to pass; to happen.

What news else *betideth* here? —Shak.

bē-tīmeṣ′, bē-tīme′, *adv.* 1. Seasonably; in good season or time; before it is late.

2. Soon; in a short time; speedily.

3. Occasionally; at times. [Scot.]

Syn.—Early, soon.

bē-tī′tle (-tl), *v.t.* To supply with a title or titles; to entitle. [Obs.]

bē-tō′ken, *v.t.*; betokened, *pt.*, *pp.*; betokening, *ppr.* [ME. *betokenen*, from AS. *be-*, and *tācn*, *tācen*, a token.]

1. To signify by some visible object; to show by signs.

2. To foreshow by present signs; to indicate (something future) by that which is seen or known; as, a dark cloud often *betokens* a storm.

bē-tǫn′, *n.* [Fr. *béton*, concrete; Pr. *beton*; Sp. *betun*, from L. *bitumen*, bitumen.] In building, concrete made of lime, sand, and hydraulic cement, after the French manner.

bē-tŏngue′ (-tung′), *v.t.* To attack with the tongue; to abuse; to scold.

bet′ō-ny, *n.* [ME. *betony*; OFr. *beteine*; L. *betonica*, a corruption of *vettonica*, called after the Vettones.] The popular name of *Stachys Betonica*, a British plant which grows in woods. It was formerly much employed in medicine, and is sometimes used to dye wool a fine dark yellow color.

bē-took′, *v.*, past tense of *betake*.

bē-torn′, *a.* Torn.

bē-toss′, *v.t.* To toss; to agitate; to disturb; to put in violent motion.

bē-trap′, *v.t.* 1. To entrap; to insnare.

2. To put trappings on; to clothe; to deck.

bē-trāy′, *v.t.*; betrayed, *pt.*, *pp.*; betraying, *ppr.* [ME. *betrayen*, *betrain*; *be-*, and *traien*, betray; OFr. *trair*; L. *tradere*, to hand over, deliver.]

1. To deliver into the hands of an enemy by treachery or fraud, in violation of trust; as, an officer *betrayed* the city.

2. To violate by fraud, or unfaithfulness; as, to *betray* a trust.

3. To break faith with, by disclosing a secret, or that which was intrusted; to expose; followed by the person or the thing; as, my friend *betrayed* me, or *betrayed* the secret.

4. To disclose, or permit to appear, as something intended to be kept secret, or which prudence would conceal; to disclose unintentionally; as, to *betray* one's ignorance.

5. To mislead or expose to inconvenience not foreseen; as, great confidence *betrays* a man into errors.

6. To show; to disclose; to indicate; used of that which is not obvious at first view, or would otherwise be concealed; as, all the names in the country *betray* great antiquity.

7. To fail, or deceive; as, my legs *betray* me.

8. To seduce, by artifice or deceit; to lead astray; to deceive and desert.

Syn.—Deceive, delude, dupe, circumvent, ensnare, dishonor, manifest, indicate, reveal.

bē-trāy′ăl, *n.* The act of betraying; a breach of trust.

bē-trāy′ẽr, *n.* One who betrays; a traitor; a seducer.

bē-trāy'ment, *n* Betrayal. [Rare.]

bē-trim', *v.i.*; betrimmed, *pt. pp.*; betrimming, *ppr.* To deck; to dress, to adorn; to grace; to embellish; to beautify; to decorate.

bē-trọth' (*or* bē-trŏth') *v.t.*; betrothed, *pt., pp.* betrothing, *ppt.* [ME *betrouthen, betreuthen*, to betroth; *be-*, and *treuthe*. AS *treowth*, troth, truth.]

1. To contract to any one, with a view to a future marriage; to promise or pledge to be the future spouse of another; to affiance; used of either sex; as, the father *betroths* his daughter.

2. To contract with for marriage at some future time; to plight one's troth to; to engage oneself to; as, a man *betroths* a lady.

3. To nominate to a bishopric, in order to consecration. [Obs.]

bē-trọth'ăl (*or* -trŏth'ăl), *n.* The act of betrothing, or the state of being betrothed; a promise or engagement between two persons for a future marriage; betrothment; affiance; engagement.

The feast of *betrothal*. —Longfellow.

bē-trọth'mᵉnt (*or* -trŏth'), *n.* Betrothal.

bē-trust', *v t.* To intrust; to commit to another in confidence of fidelity; to trust. [Obs.]

bē-trust'ment, *n.* The act of intrusting; the thing intrusted. [Obs.]

bet'sō, *n.* [It. *pezzo*, a piece, a piece of money.] A small Venetian coin. [Obs.]

bet'tẽr, *a.*, comp. of *good*. [ME. *bettere, betere*; AS. *betera*, better, from a positive not in use, but which appears in the adv. *bet*; D. *beter*; M.H.G. *bezzer*; G. *besser*; Sw. *bättre*; Sans. *bhadra*, excellent.]

1. Having good qualities in a greater degree than another; applied to physical, acquired, or moral qualities; as, a *better* soil, a *better* man, a *better* physician, a *better* house, a *better* air, a *better* harvest.

2. More advantageous, acceptable, safe, useful, or to be preferred for any other reason.

Better is a dinner of herbs where love is, than a stalled ox and hatred therewith.
—Prov. xv. 17.

3. Improved in health; less affected by disease; as, the patient is *better*.

4. Larger in amount, or size; as, he gave me the *better* part of the cake.

5. More nearly perfect or complete; as, *better* acquaintance; to have a *better* understanding; a *better* knowledge of a subject.

All the better; wholly better; better by all the difference.

Better half; a colloquial term for *wife*.

To be better off; to be in better circumstances.

bet'tẽr, *adv.*, comp. of *well*. 1. In a more excellent manner; with more skill and wisdom, virtue, advantage, or success; as, to perform work *better*; to plan a scheme *better*; land *better* cultivated; government *better* administered.

2. More correctly, or fully; as, to understand a subject *better* than another.

3. With more affection; in a higher degree; as, to love one *better* than another.

4. More, in point of distance, time, or value; as, I have walked ten miles and *better*; a colloquial use of the term.

To think better of; to reconsider and change, as an opinion or decision.

bet'tẽr, *v.t.*; bettered, *pt., pp.*; bettering, *ppr.*

1. To improve; to meliorate; to increase the good qualities of; as, manure *betters* land; discipline may *better* the morals.

2. To surpass; to exceed.

The works of nature do always aim at that which cannot be *bettered*. —Hooker

3. To advance; to support; to give advantage to; as, to *better* a party; to *better* a cause. [Obs.]

4. To improve; to increase; to enhance in value; as, to *better* one's position or station in life.

Syn.—Amend, improve, advance, meliorate.

bet'tẽr, *v.i* To become better; to improve.

bet'tẽr, *n.* 1. One of superior rank or standing; one entitled to precedence, generally in the plural; as, he stood in the way of his *betters*.

2. Advantage; victory; used with *of*.

For the better; for advantage or improvement; as, a change *for the better*.

To get or *gain the better of*; to obtain advantage, superiority, or victory over.

To have the better; to have the advantage or superiority; followed by *of* before him or that over which the advantage is enjoyed.

bet'tẽr, bet'tŏr, *n.* A person who bets or lays a wager.

bet'tẽr-ment, *n.* 1. A making better; improvement.

2. In law, an improvement of an estate which renders it better than mere repairs would; generally used in the plural.

bet'tẽr-mōst, *a.* Best; as, the *bettermost* classes. [Rare.]

bet'tẽr-ness, *n.* 1. Superiority. [Rare.]

2. In minting, the excess of fineness of a precious metal above the standard.

bet'tŏng, *n.* [Native name.] The kangaroo-rat, a marsupial of the genus *Bettongia*, about the size of a common hare. It is nocturnal in its habits, and is found in Australia.

bet'tŏr, *n.* See *Better*.

bet'ty, *n.* 1. A small instrument used by thieves in entering houses, etc.; a short bar or wrench; now called a *jimmy*. [Slang.]

2. A man who interferes with or engages in woman's work; from Betty, a short or familiar form of Elizabeth.

3. A pear-shaped Italian flask or bottle for wine or olive-oil, usually covered with maize-leaves, etc.; a Florence flask.

Bet'ū-lȧ, *n.* [L., the birch.] A genus of hardy trees or shrubs, natives of the north temperate and arctic regions; the birches.

Bet-ū-lā'cē-æ, *n.pl.* A natural order of apetalous dicotyledonous plants, of which *Betula* is the typical genus, and containing besides this only the genus *Alnus*, with sixty species belonging to both genera.

bet-ū-lā'ceous, *a.* Relating to the *Betulaceæ*.

bet'ū-lin, bet'ū-line, *n.* A substance discovered in the bark of the common or white birch. It is of a white color, crystallized in the form of long needles, fusible, volatile, and inflammable.

bē-tum'ble (-bl), *v.t.* To tumble; to disarrange. [Rare.]

bē-tū'tŏr, *v.t.*; betutored, *pt., pp.*; betutoring, *ppr.* To tutor; to instruct.

bē-tween', *n.* An interval. [Rare.]

bē-tween', *prep.* [ME. *betwene, bitwenen*; AS. *betweōnum, betwȳnum*; *be*, by, and *tweōnum*, from *twā*, two.]

1. In the intermediate interval, as regards time, space, limit, quantity, etc.; as, *between* trains; *between* buildings; *between* boundaries.

2. From one to another; passing from one to another, noting exchange of actions or intercourse; as, things go well *between* the parties.

3. Belonging to two or more, in common, or partnership; as, twenty proprietors own a tract of land *between* them.

4. Having mutual relation to two or more; as, discord exists *between* the families.

5. Noting difference or discrimination of one from another; as, to distinguish *between* right and wrong.

Between ourselves, between you and me, between themselves; in confidence.

Syn.—Betwixt, among.—*Between* implies two only; *among*, three or more; as, the offices were apportioned *between* the two leading politicians; later, *among* all the political parties. By extension, *between* sometimes expresses a certain relation where more than two are concerned; as, he hesitated *between* a number of precedents.

bē-tween'=decks, *n.* The space between the decks of a ship.

bē-twixt', *prep.* [ME. *betwixt, bytwyxte*; AS. *betwyxt, betwyx*; from *be*, by, and *twā*, two.]

1. Between; in the space that separates two persons or things; as, *betwixt* two oaks.

2. Passing between; from one to another; noting intercourse.

Betwixt and between; a colloquial phrase, signifying in an intermediate position; neither good nor bad; not definitely one thing or another.

beūr-ré' (bũr-rā'), *n.* [Fr., from *beurre*, butter.] A pear, the succulent part of which is luscious and melting; used with a distinguishing word; as, *beurré* d'Anjou.

bev'el, *n.* [Fr. *biveau*, a bevel.]

1. An instrument used by mechanics for drawing angles, consisting of two limbs jointed together, the stock and the blade, movable on a pivot at the joint, and adjustable so as to include any angle between it and the stock; a bevel-square.

Bevel.

2. A slant or inclination of a surface from a right line.

3. In heraldry, a chief broken or opening like a carpenter's *bevel*. It is formed by the long line being cut off in its straightness by another, which makes an acute angle. Written also *bevil, bevile*.

bev'el, *a.* Slant; having the form of a bevel.

bev'el, *v.t.*; beveled, bevelled, *pt., pp.*; beveling, bevelling, *ppr.* To cut to a bevel-angle.

bev'el, *v.i.* To slant or incline off to a bevel-angle, or from a direct line.

bev'el=an"gle, *n.* An angle not a right angle.

bev'eled, bev'elled, *a.* 1. Formed with a bevel-angle.

2. In mineralogy, replaced by two planes inclining equally upon the adjacent planes, as an edge; having its edges replaced by inclining planes, as a cube or other solid.

3. In heraldry, relating to a bevel.

bev'el=gēar, *n.* Wheelwork whose cogs stand beveling, or at an oblique angle to the shaft. The axis of the leader or driver forms an angle with the axis of the follower or the wheel driven. Such wheels are frequently called conical wheels, as they resemble the frustums of fluted cones.

Bevel-gear.

bev'el-ment, *n.* In mineralogy, the replacement of an edge by two similar planes, equally inclined to the including faces or adjacent planes.

bev'el=square, *n.* See *Bevel*, n. 1.

bev'el=wheel, *n.* See *Bevel-gear*.

bē'vẽr, *n.* [ME. *bever*; OFr. *bevre*, from L. *bibere*, to drink.] A collation or small repast between meals. [Obs.]

bē'vẽr, *v.i.* To take a small repast between meals. [Obs.]

bev'ẽr-āġe, *n.* [ME. *beverage*; OFr. *bevrage*, from *bevre*, L. *bibere*, to drink.]

1. Drink; liquor for drinking. It is generally used of a pleasant liquor; as, nectar is called the *beverage* of the gods.

2. Drink-money; a treat. [Prov. Eng.]

bev'ile, *n.* See *Bevel*, n. 3.

bev'iled, bev'illed, *a.* See *Beveled*, 3.

be-vụe', *n.* [Fr. *bévue*; OFr. *besvue*; *bes* (L. *bis*), double, and *vue*, view.] An error; a slip.

bev'y, *n.* [ME. *bevy, bevey*; OFr. *beveye*, from *bevre*, L. *bibere*, to drink.]

1. A flock of birds; especially, a flock of quail or grouse; the term was also applied to a company of roebucks.

2. A company of females.

A lovely *bevy* of fair ladies sat,
Courted of many a jolly paramour.—Spenser.

bē-wāil', *v.t.*; bewailed, *pt., pp.*; bewailing, *ppr.* [ME. *bewailen*; *be-*, and *wailen*, to wail; Ice. *væla*, from *væ*, woe.] To bemoan; to lament; to express deep sorrow for; as, to *bewail* the loss of a child.

Syn.—Lament, bemoan, sorrow, deplore.

bē-wāil', *v.i.* To express grief.

bē-wāil'ȧ-ble, *a.* Lamentable.

bē-wāil'ẽr, *n.* One who laments.

bē-wāil'ing, *n.* Lamentation.

bē-wāil'ing-ly, *adv.* In a mournful manner.

bē-wāil'ment, *n.* The act of bewailing.

bē-wāke', *v.t.* To keep awake; to watch. [Obs.]

bē-wāre', *v.i.* [ME. *be ware*; *be*, AS. *beō*, second pers. imper. of v. *be*, and *ware*; AS. *wær*; O.H.G. *wara*, notice, attention.]

1. To be wary, guarded, or careful; to be watchful; to look out; often with *of*; as, let him *beware*; *beware of* him.

Beware of all, but most *beware of* man.
—Pope.

2. To take heed; to be heedful or attentive; to pay special attention. [Obs.]

Beware of him, and obey his voice.
—Ex. xxiii. 21.

bē-wāre', *v.i.* To avoid; to guard against; to be wary of; as, *beware* the flatterer.

bē-wāsh', *v.t.*; bewashed, *pt., pp.*; bewashing, *ppr.* To soak with water; to drench.

bē-weep', *v.t.*; bewept, *pt., pp.*; beweeping, *ppr.* To weep over; to bedew with tears. [Rare.]

bē-weep', *v.i* To make lamentation. [Rare.]

bē-wet', *v.t.* To wet; to moisten. [Obs.]

bew'et, bew'it, *n.* [ME. *bewette*, dim. of OFr. *beue, bue*, a chain, collar; L. *boja*, a collar.] In falconry, the strap for attaching a bell to the leg of a hawk.

bē-whōre' (-hōr'), *v.t.* To corrupt with regard to chastity; to denounce as unchaste.

bē-wig', *v.t.* To put a wig on.

bē-wil'dẽr, *v.t.*; bewildered, *pt., pp.*; bewildering, *ppr.* [Dan. *forvilde*, to bewilder; G. *verwildern*; AS. *wilde*, wild.] To lead into perplexity or confusion; to lose in pathless places; to confound for want of a plain road; to perplex with mazes; or, in general, to perplex to an extreme degree.

Syn.—Daze, dazzle, confound, mystify, puzzle, embarrass, astonish, perplex, confuse, mislead.

bē-wil'dẽred, *a.* Lost in mazes; perplexed with disorder, confusion, or intricacy.

Lost and *bewildered* in the fruitless search.
—Addison.

Syn.—Confused, amazed, mystified, puzzled, perplexed, embarrassed.

bē-wil'dẽred-ness, *n.* Bewilderment. [Rare.]

bē-wil'dẽr-ing-ly, *adv.* In a bewildering manner.

bē-wil'dẽr-ment, *n.* The state of being bewildered; a chaotic state of the mental forces; confusion; perplexity.

bē-win'tẽr, *v.t.* To make like winter. [Obs.]

bew'it (bū'it), *n.* See *Bewet*, n.

bē-witch' (-wich'), *v.t.*; bewitched (-wicht), *pt.*,

pp.; bewitching, ppr. [ME. bewicchen; be-, and wicchen, a witch; AS. wiṫga, wiṫiga, a witch.]

1. To fascinate; to gain an ascendency over by charms or incantation; an operation which was formerly supposed to injure the person bewitched.

Look, how I am *bewitched*; behold, mine arm Is like a blasted sapling, withered up.—Shak.

2. To charm; to fascinate; to please to such a degree as to take away the power of resistance.

Syn.—Enchant, fascinate, charm, captivate.

bē-witch′ed-ness, *n.* State of being bewitched.

bē-witch′ẽr, *n.* One who bewitches.

bē-witch′ẽr-y, *n.* Fascination; charm; resistless power exerted in a pleasing manner.

bē-witch′fụl, *a.* Alluring; fascinating.

bē-witch′ing, *a.* Having power to bewitch or captivate by the arts of pleasing.

bē-witch′ing-ly, *adv.* In a fascinating manner.

bē-witch′ing-ness, *n.* The quality of bewitching.

bē-witch′ment, *n.* Fascination; power of charming; the act or state of being bewitched.

bē-wŏn′dẽr, *v.t.*; bewondered, *pt.*, *pp.*; bewondering, *ppr.* To cause to wonder; to wonder at.

bē-wrap′ (-rap′), *v.t.* To wrap up.

bē-wrāy′ (-rā′), *v.t.* [AS. *wregan*, to accuse.] To disclose perfidiously; to betray; to show or make visible. [Obs.]

Thy speech *bewrayeth* thee.—Matt. xxvi. 73.

bē-wrāy′ẽr, *n.* A divulger of secrets. [Obs.]

bē-wrāy′ment, *n.* The act of bewraying.

bē-wreck′ (-rek′), *v.t.* To ruin. [Obs.]

bē-wrēke′ (-rēk′), *v.t.* To wreak. [Obs.]

bē-wrọught′ (-rọt′), *a.* Worked; wrought. [Obs.]

bey, *n.* [Turk. *bey*, *beg*; Per. *baig*, a lord.] A governor of a town or particular district of country in the Turkish dominions; also, in some places, a prince; a beg.

bey′liç, *n.* The jurisdiction of a bey.

bē-yond′, *prep.* [ME. *beyonde*, *beyende*; AS. *begeondan*; *be*, by, and *geondan*, from *geond*, across, beyond, over.]

1. On the further side of; as, *beyond* a river or the sea.

2. Past; later than; as, *beyond* the hour of welcome.

3. Above; in a degree to exceed or excel; as, one man is great or good *beyond* another.

4. Out of reach of; further than; as, *beyond* the power of evil.

To go beyond; to exceed in any action or scheme; hence, to deceive or circumvent.

bē-yond′, *adv.* At a distance; yonder; farther off.

bez′ăn, *n.* [E. Ind.] A cotton cloth from Bengal.

bez′ănt (*or* bē-zant′), *n.* [Fr. *bezant*; L. *Besantius*, from *Byzantium*, Gr. *Byzantion*, Byzantium.]

1. An old coin of Byzantium; properly called *solidus*.

2. In heraldry, a circle in or or argent representing this coin, in which the stipends of the higher soldiers of the army in the holy wars are supposed to have been paid.

bez-an-tée′ (-tā′), *n.* [OFr. *besanté*, from *besant*, a gold coin.] An ornamental design, representing a series of bezants, found on Norman moldings.

bez-ant′lẽr, *n.* [OFr. *bes*, from L. *bis*, twice, and *antler*.] The second branch of a deer's horn, next above the brow-antler; also written *besantler*.

bez′el, **bas′il**, *n.* [Fr. *biseau*, sloping edge, from OFr. *bisel*.]

1. The upper part of the collet of a ring, which encompasses and fastens the stone; the rim which fastens the crystal of a watch in the cavity in which it is set.

2. The bevel or beveled edge of any cutting tool.

be-zique′ (bā-zēk′), *n.* [Fr.] 1. A card game, usually played by two persons, with a pack of cards for each player, having the twos to sixes discarded, one thousand points being the game.

2. A combination, the queen of spades and jack of diamonds, counting forty points in the game of *bezique*.

bē′zōar, *n.* [Sp. *bezoar*; Ar. *bāzarh*; Per. *bādzarh*, *pādzahr*; *pād*, expelling, and *zahr*, poison.]

1. A name for certain calculi or concretions found in the stomach or intestines of some animals (especially ruminants), formerly supposed to be efficacious in preventing the fatal effects of poison, and still held in estimation in some countries. Many varieties have been mentioned, but most value was put on the *bezoar* from the East Indies and that from Peru.

2. Any antidotal remedy.

bez-ō-är′diç, *a.* Pertaining to or compounded with bezoar.

bez-ō-är′diç, *n.* A medicine compounded with bezoar.

bē′zōar-goat, *n.* A name given to the gazel, *Antilope dorcas*, from its producing the bezoar.

bez-ō-är′tiç, **bez-ō-är′tiç-ăl**, *a.* Bezoardic. [Obs.]

bē-zō′ni-ăn, *n.* [Fr. *besoin*; It. *bisogno*, need, want.] A beggar; a scoundrel.

bez′zle, *v.t.* To waste in riot. [Obs.]

bez′zle, *v.i.* To carouse; to revel. [Obs.]

Bhag′ă-vad-Gī′tȧ (bag′), *n.* [Sans.] In Sanskrit literature, the philosophical poem relating a discourse between Krishna and his pupil Arjun in the midst of a battle.

bhāng (bäng), *n.* [Hind., from Sans. *bhangā*, hemp.] An Indian variety of the common hemp, the resin of which is highly narcotic and intoxicant, and a popular Oriental stimulant; otherwise called *hashish*. Also employed in medicine, for its anodyne, hypnotic, and antispasmodic qualities; also spelled *bang*, *beng*.

bhär′al, *n.* The blue sheep of Tibet, intermediate in its habits between the sheep and the goat.

bhees′ty, **bhees′tie** (bēs′), *n.* [Anglo-Ind.] An Indian water-carrier for a private family or in military service.

bhun′dẽr (bun′), *n.* [Native name.] A monkey, *Macacus indicus*, considered sacred by many of the Hindus.

bī-, *prefix.* [L. *bis*, *bi-*, twice; the *s* being dropped in composition.] A combining form signifying, (a) two, twice, doubly, twofold; used generally and in composition; as, *bi*angular, *bi*color; (b) in chemistry, having two parts of the substance designated; as, *bi*carbonate; often used interchangeably with *di*.

bī′ă, *n.* A species of cowry-shell formerly used in the East Indies as a medium of exchange.

bī-ac′id, *a.* In chemistry, a term applied to a base capable of combining with an acid in two different proportions.

bī-ȧ-çū′mi-nāte, *a.* In botany, having two diverging points.

bī-an′gū-lăr, *a.* Having two angles or corners.

bī-an′gū-lāte, **bī-an′gū-lā-ted**, **bī-an′gū-lous**, *a.* Same as *Biangular*. [Rare.]

bī-an′nū-ăl, *a.* Occurring or appearing twice a year; semiannual.

bī-an-thẽr-if′ẽr-ous, *a.* Having two anthers.

Bī-ār′mi-ăn, *a.* and *n.* Same as *Permian*.

bī-ār-tiç′ū-lāte, *a.* Consisting of two joints.

bī′ăs, *n.*; *pl.* **bī′ăs-eṣ**. [Fr. *biais*, a slope, slant.]

1. A weight on the side of a ball, in bowling, which causes it to curve in its course.

2. A leaning of the mind; inclination; prepossession; propensity toward an object, not leaving the mind indifferent; as, education gives a *bias* to the mind.

3. That which causes the mind to lean or incline from a state of indifference to a particular object or course. [Rare.]

4. In dressmaking, an oblique line or seam, as a dart in a waist. To cut cloth on the *bias* is to cut it slantingly or diagonally.

Syn.—Tendency, inclination, propensity, disposition, bent, prepossession, prejudice, warp.

bī′ăs, *a.* Loaded or swelled on one side; as, a ball is *bias*; oblique; inclined.

bī′ăs, *adv.* In a bias manner; obliquely; as, a seam sewed *bias*.

bī′ăs, *v.t.*; biased (-ast), *pt.*, *pp.*; biasing, *ppr.* To warp; to prejudice; to prepossess; as, judgment is often *biased* by interest.

bī′ăs-ness, *n.* Inclination to some side.

bī-au-riç′ū-lăr, *a.* Pertaining to the auricular apertures.

bī-au-riç′ū-lāte, *a.* 1. In biology, a term applied to a heart with two auricles, as in most bivalve mollusks, and in all reptiles, birds, and mammals.

2. In botany, having two projections the shape of an ear.

bī-ax′i-ăl, **bī-ax′ăl**, *a.* Having two axes.

bī-ax′i-ăl-ly, *adv.* In a biaxial manner.

bib, *n.* 1. A small piece of linen or other cloth worn by children over the breast.

2. A similar piece of cloth attached to an apron, to cover the breast.

3. A faucet.

4. The whiting-pout, an arctic fish.

bib, **bibbe**, *v.t.* and *v.i.* [ME. *bibben*; L. *bibere*, to drink.] To sip; to tipple; to drink frequently. [Rare.]

bi-bā′cious, *a.* [L. *bibax*, from *bibere*, to drink.] Addicted to drinking; disposed to imbibe.

bi-bac′i-ty, *n.* The habit of drinking much or frequently. [Obs.]

bī-bā′siç, *a.* In chemistry, a term applied to those acids which combine with two equivalents of a base; sometimes also applied to salts, denoting derivation from such an acid.

bibb, *n.* 1. A faucet; a bibcock.

2. A bracket of timber bolted to the hound of a mast for the purpose of supporting the trestletrees.

bib′bẽr, *n.* A tippler; a man given to drinking, chiefly used in composition; as, wine*bibber*.

bib′ble-bab″ble, *n.* Idle talk; prating to no purpose. [Rare.]

bib′cock, *n.* A cock having a turned-down nozzle; a faucet.

bibe′lot (bib′lō), *n.* [Fr.] An artistic and decorative trifle; a shelf-ornament.

bi-bī′rine, *n.* See *Bebeerine*.

bi-bī′rụ, *n.* See *Bebeeru*.

bib′i-tō-ry, *a.* [L. *bibitor*, a drinker, from *bibere*, to drink.] Pertaining to drinking.

Bī′ble (-bl), *n.* [ME. *bible*; OFr. *bible*, from L. *biblia*, neut. pl., from Gr. *biblia*, pl. of *biblion*, a little book; *biblos*, a book.]

1. The book; specifically, the volume believed by Christians to contain revelations of God, as well as the principles of Christian faith, and the rules of practice. It consists of two parts, called the Old and New Testaments.

2. The sacred writings of any religion.

3. [b—] An important book in any art or science.

Bible Christian; a Bryanite, or member of an English Methodist sect started by William Bryan, in 1816, akin to the Wesleyan body.

Douay Bible; a translation into English of St. Jerome's Latin version of the Bible, known as the Vulgate and the authorized version of the Roman Catholic church. The translation, which was made by English scholars living in France, was sanctioned by the Roman Catholic church. The New Testament was published at Rheims, in 1582, and the Old Testament at Douay, in 1609-10. Also called *Rheims Bible*.

King James Bible; the version of the Bible in common use, so called because it was the revision made by a commission of scholars working by authority of parliament, during the reign of James I. (1604-11).

bib′lẽr, *n.* [L. *bibere*, to drink.] A tippler; a great drinker.

bib′li-căl, *a.* Pertaining to or in harmony with the Bible; as, *biblical* criticism.

bib-li-căl′i-ty, *n.* The quality of being biblical; that which is biblical. [Rare.]

bib′li-căl-ly, *adv.* According to the Bible.

Bib′li-cişm, *n.* Biblical learning; biblical literature; adherence to biblical teachings.

Bib′li-cist, *n.* 1. One skilled in the knowledge and interpretation of the Bible; one who adheres to Bible teachings.

2. One who makes the Bible the sole rule of faith.

bib′li-ō-. A combining form from Gr. *biblion*, a book, signifying of or pertaining to books; also, specifically, in reference to the Bible.

bib′li-og-nost, *n.* [*Biblio-*, and Gr. *gnōstēs*, from *gignōskein*, to know.] A well-read lover of books; one learned in bibliography.

bib″li-og-nos′tiç, *a.* Possessing the characteristics of a bibliognost.

bib″li-og′ō-ny, *n.* The production of books.

bib-li-og′rȧ-phẽr, **bib′li-ō-grȧph**, *n.* [Gr. *bibliographos*, a writer of books; *biblion*, a book, and *graphos*, from *graphein*, to write.] One who composes the history of books; a transcriber; one who is well informed in bibliography.

bib″li-ō-graph′iç, **bib″li-ō-graph′iç-ăl**, *a.* Pertaining to the history of books.

bib″li-ō-graph′iç-ăl-ly, *adv.* In the manner of a bibliographer.

bib-li-og′rȧ-phy, *n.* 1. A history of books; an account of manuscripts, different editions, the times when they were printed, and information illustrating the history of literature.

2. A list of an author's writings; or the literature dealing with a certain subject or author; as, the *bibliography* of Omar Khayyam.

bib-li-ol′ȧ-tẽr, **bib-li-ol′ȧ-trist**, *n.* 1. A worshiper of the Bible, and believer in its inspiration.

2. One who loves books to an unwonted extent.

bib-li-ol′ȧ-try, *n.* [*Biblio-*, and Gr. *latreia*, from *latreuein*, to worship.] Worship or homage paid to books, especially to the Bible.

bib′li-ō-līte, *n.* [*Biblio-*, and Gr. *lithos*, stone.] A name formerly applied to certain laminated schistous stones; called also *book-stone*.

bib-li-ō-log′iç-ăl, *a.* Pertaining to bibliology.

bib-li-ol′ō-gist, *n.* One who is well informed or interested in bibliology.

bib-li-ol′ō-gy, *n.* [*Biblio-*, and Gr. *logia*, from *legein*, to speak.]

1. The literature of the Bible or its doctrine.

2. Bibliography; book-lore.

bib′li-ō-man″cy, *n.* [*Biblio-*, and Gr. *manteia*, prophecy.] A kind of divination, by means of the Bible; consisting in selecting passages of Scripture at hazard, and predicting from them future events.

bib′li-ō-māne, *n.* One having a mania for acquiring books.

bib″li-ō-mā′ni-ȧ, *n.* [*Biblio-*, and Gr. *mania*, madness.] Book-madness; a rage for possessing rare and curious books.

bib″li-ō-mā′ni-aç, *n.* One who has a rage for books; sometimes used attributively.

bib″li-ō-mā-nī′aç-ăl, *a.* Pertaining to a passion for books.

bib″li-ō-peg′iç, *a.* Relating to the binding of books. [Rare.]

bib-li-op′e-gist, *n.* One who binds books.

bib″li-op-e-gis′tiç, *a.* Relating to bookbinders or the bookbinding art. [Rare.]

bib-li-op′e-gy, *n.* [*Biblio-*, and Gr. *pēgia*, from

pēgnynai, to fasten, bind.] The bookbinding art. [Rare.]

bib′li-ō-phile (-fil), *n.* [*Biblio-*, and Gr. *philos*, loving.] A book-lover.

bib-li-oph′i-lism, *n.* Love of books.

bib-li-oph′i-list, *n.* A book-lover.

bib″li-ō-phō′bi-ȧ, *n.* [*Biblio-*, and Gr. *phobia*, fear.] A dread of or distaste for books. [Rare.]

bib′li-ō-pōle, *n.* See *Bibliopolist.*

bib″li-ō-pol′iç, bib-li-op′ō-lăr, *a.* Pertaining to bookselling.

bib-li-op′ō-lism, *n.* The business of buying and selling books.

bib-li-op′ō-list, bib′li-ō-pōle, *n.* [L. *bibliopola*; Gr. *bibliopōlēs*; *biblion*, a book, and *polein*, to sell.] A bookseller, especially one who deals in rare or curious books.

bib-li-op-ō-lis′tiç, *a.* Relating to bibliopolism.

bib″li-ō-taph, bib-li-ot′ȧ-phist, *n.* [*Biblio-*, and Gr. *taphos*, from *taphein*, to bury.] One who stows away books, or secretes them. [Rare.]

bib′li-ō-theç, *n.* One who has charge of a collection of books; a librarian; also, a library.

bib″li-ō-thē′çȧ, *n.* [L. *bibliotheca*; Gr. *bibliothēkē*, a library, bookcase; *biblion*, a book, and *thēkē*, from *tithenai*, to place.] A collection of books; a library.

bib″li-ō-thē′çăl, *a.* Belonging to a library.

bib-li-oth′ē-çā-ry, *n.* A librarian.

bib′li-ō-thēke, *n.* A library. [Obs.]

Bib′list, *n.* See *Biblicist.*

bī-brac′tē-āte, *a.* Doubly bracteate.

bib′ū-lous, *a.* [L. *bibulus*, from *bibere*, to drink.]
1. Absorbent; spongy.
2. Fond of or in the habit of tippling.

bib′ū-lous-ly, *adv.* In a bibulous manner.

bī-cal′çȧ-rāte, *a.* Doubly calcarate.

bī-cal′lōse, bī-cal′lous, *a.* In botany, having two protuberant or hardened spots.

bī-cam′ẽr-ăl, *a.* [*Bi-*, and L. *camera*, a vault, chamber.] Consisting of two houses or chambers; applied to a legislative body.

bī-cap′sū-lăr, *a.* [*Bi-*, and L. *capsula*, a little chest, from *capsa*, a chest.] In botany, having two capsules; as, a *bicapsular* pericarp.

bī-cär′bŏn-āte, *n.* A carbonate containing two equivalents of carbonic acid to one of a base; an acid carbonate; sometimes called *supercarbonate.*

bī-cär′bū-ret-ed, bī-cär′bū-ret-ted, *a.* Combined with or containing two atoms of carbon; as, *bicarbureted* hydrogen, C_2H_4.

bī-car′i-nāte, *a.* Having two carinæ.

bī-çau′dăl, bī-çau′dāte, *a.* Having two tails.

bic′ched, *a.* [Origin unknown.] Cursed. [Rare.]
Bicched bones; a term given by old writers to dice.

bice, bīse, *n.* [ME. *bise*, *bys*; OFr. *bis*, *bise*, dusky, dark.] Among painters, a pale blue color, prepared from the native blue carbonate of copper, or from smalt; called also *blue bice.*

bī-cen′te-nā-ry, *a.* and *n.* I. *a.* Consisting of or pertaining to two hundred; usually two hundred years; as, a *bicentenary* celebration.
II. *n.* That which comprehends two hundred; usually two hundred years; the two hundredth anniversary or the celebration of it.

bī-cen-ten′ni-ăl, *a.* and *n.* I. *a.* Consisting of or lasting two hundred years; occurring every two hundred years.
II. *n.* The two hundredth anniversary of an event.

bī-ceph′ȧ-lous, *a.* Having two heads.

bī′ceps, *n.* [L. *biceps*; *bi-*, two, and *caput*, head.]
1. A muscle which has two heads or origins; specifically applied to the *biceps brachii* or *humeri* of the forearm and the *biceps femoris* of the thigh.
2. Figuratively, strength of the muscles, especially of the arm.

bich-ir′, *n.* [Native name.] Any fish of the genus *Polypterus*; specifically, *Polypterus bichir* of the Nile.

bī-chlō′rid, bī-chlō′ride (*or* -rid), *n.* A compound made up of two atoms of chlorine in combination with one or more basic atoms.

bī′chō, *n.* Same as *Chigoe.*

bī-chrō′māte, *n.* A compound in which the hydrogen of chromic acid has been replaced by a base; as, potassium *bichromate* K_2CrO_4; a dichromate.

bī-chrō-mat′iç, *a.* Dichromatic.

bī-chrō′mȧ-tize, *v.t.* To combine or treat chemically with a bichromate.

bī-cip′i-tăl, bī-cip′i-tous, *a.* [L. *biceps*, from *bis*, twice, and *caput*, *capitis*, head.]
1. Having two heads; two-headed. [Rare.]
2. In anatomy, having two origins, as a muscle.
3. In botany, dividing into two parts at the top or bottom.

bick′ẽr, *v.i.*; bickered, *pt.*, *pp.*; bickering, *ppr.* [ME. *bicheren*, *bikkeren*; W. *bicra*, fight.]
1. To skirmish; to fight intermittently; to exchange blows. [Rare.]
2. To quarrel; to contend in words; to wrangle.
3. To move quickly and unsteadily; to be tremulous like flame or water.

bick′ẽr-ẽr, *n.* One who bickers.

bick′ẽr-ing, *n.* 1. A fight or skirmish.
2. Quarreling; wrangling.

bick′ẽr-ment, *n.* Contention. [Obs.]

bick′ẽrn, *n.* [ME. *bickhorn*, *bicorn*; OFr. *bicorne*; L. *bicorna*, a two-handled cup, from *bicornus*, two-horned; *bis*, two, and *cornu*, horn.] An anvil ending in a tapering projection; also, the projection itself.

bī-çol′li-gāte, *a.* [*Bi-*, and L. *colligatus*, pp. of *colligare*; *con*, together, and *ligare*, to bind.] In ornithology, having the anterior toes connected by a web.

bī-çol′ŏred, bī-çol′ŏr, *a.* Of two colors.

bī-çon′çāve, *a.* Having two concave surfaces.

bī-çon′dy-lăr, *a.* [*Bi-*, and L. *condylus*, a joint, knuckle.] Pertaining to the two bony articulated occipital prominences or the articulation of the lower jaw.

bī-çon′iç-ăl, *a.* Similar in form to a double cone.

bī-çon′jū-gāte, *a.* [*Bi-*, and L. *conjugatus*, pp. of *conjugare*; *con*, together, and *jugare*, to join.] In botany, twice-paired.

bī-çon′vex, *a.* Having two convex surfaces.

bī-çor′nous, bī′çorn, bī′çorned, *a.* [L. *bicornis*; *bis*, twice, and *cornu*, horn.] Having two horns; shaped like a crescent; specifically, in botany, having two projections resembling horns.

bī-çor′pō-răl, *a.* Having two bodies.

bī-çor′pō-rāte, *a.* [*Bi-*, and L. *corporatus*, pp. of *corporare*, to shape into a body; from *corpus*, body.] In heraldry, having two bodies.

Bicorporate.

bī-cos′tāte, *a.* In botany, denoting two longitudinal ribs, as of a leaf.

bī-çrē′nāte, *a.* Twice crenated.

bī-çres-cen′tiç, *a.* Formed as a double crescent.

bī-çrū′răl, *a.* Having two legs.

bī-çus′pid, bī-çus′pid-āte, *a.* [L. *bicuspis*; *bis*, twice, and *cuspis*, *cuspidis*, a point.] Having two points; applied to teeth, leaves, etc.
Bicuspid valve; the mitral valve of the heart. [See *Mitral.*]

bī-çus′pid, *n.* A name applied to the two teeth situated between the canines and the molars.

bī-çy′ȧ-nide, *n.* See *Dicyanide.*

bī′cy-çle, *n.* [*Bi-*, and L. *cyclus*; Gr. *kyklos*, a wheel.] A vehicle consisting of two wheels, one before the other, connected by a simple framework of steel tubing bearing a seat or saddle, and propelled by the feet of the rider. The most usual form is that known as the safety-*bicycle*, the two wheels of which are of the same or nearly the same size. Its driving mechanism consists of pedal cranks, communicating with the rear wheel, usually by means of a sprocket and chain, or a shaft and bevel-gear.

Bicycle.

bī′cy-çlẽr, *n.* The rider of a bicycle.

bī-cyç′liç, *a.* Pertaining to bicycles.

bī′cy-çling, *n.* The art or practice of riding a bicycle.

bī′cy-çlist, *n.* A bicycler.

bī-cyç′ū-lăr, *a.* Pertaining to bicycling.

bid, *v.t.*; bade, bad, bid, *pt.*; bidden, bid, *pp.*; bidding, *ppr.* [ME. *bidden*; AS. *biddan*, to ask, pray, invite, and confused with AS. *beódan*, to offer, command, threaten.]
1. To ask; to request; to invite.

> Provide the feast, father, and *bid* the guests. —Shak.

2. To pray; to wish; to say to by way of greeting or benediction; as, to *bid* good-day, farewell, etc.

> Neither *bid* him God speed. —2 John 10.

3. To command; to order or direct; to enjoin; commonly followed by an accusative and infinitive without *to*, though the *to* is sometimes found.

> And Peter answered him and said, Lord, if it be thou, *bid* me come unto thee on the water. —Matt. xiv. 28.

4. To offer; to propose; specifically, (a) to offer (a certain price) at an auction; (b) to offer (to do something specified) for a given sum.

> The king will *bid* you battle presently.—Shak.

5. To proclaim; to make known by a public announcement. [Obs.]
To bid beads; to pray with beads; originally, to pray one's prayers.
To bid defiance to; to defy; to brave.
To bid fair; to open or offer a good prospect; to appear likely.
Syn.—Tell, request, instruct, direct, order, proffer, charge, command, propose, offer.

bid, *n.* An offer of a price; specifically, an offer made at auctions.

bid, *v.i.* 1. To pray. [Obs.]
2. To offer as a bid; to say for what price one will assume a contract or undertake a commission.

bī-daç′tyl, bī-daç′tyle, *a.* Possessing two fingers or toes; didactylous.

bid′āle, *n.* In England, an invitation of friends to drink ale at some poor man's house, and there to contribute in charity; an ancient and local custom.

bī-där′kee, bī-där′kȧ, *n.* [Native name.] A light Aleutian boat made of skins.

bid′dȧ-ble, *a.* Tractable; willing; obedient. [Scot.]

bid′dẽr, *n.* One who bids or offers a price.

bid′dẽr-y-wāre, *n.* See *Bidri.*

bid′ding, *n.* Invitation; command; order; a notifying; the submission of a bid.

bid′ding-prāyer (-prâr), *n.* In Roman Catholic and Anglican churches, the prayer offered before the sermon, in which special persons are petitioned for.

bid′dy, *n.* A name given to a chicken.

Bid′dy, *n.* [Dim. of *Bridget*, Ir. *Brighid*, from *brigh*, strength. A name given in honor of St. Bridget.] A good-natured appellation for an Irish domestic; hence, applied to any female domestic servant. [Colloq.]

bide, *v.i.*; bided *or* bode, *pt.*, *pp.*; biding, *ppr.* [ME. *biden*; AS. *bidan*, to wait, expect.]
1. To dwell; to inhabit.
2. To remain; to continue or to be permanent in a place or state.

bide, *v.t.* 1. To endure; to suffer.
2. To wait for; as, I *bide* my time.
Syn.—Wait, remain, tarry, stay.

Bī′dens, *n.* [L. *bidens*; *bis*, twice, and *dens*, tooth.] A genus of composite plants, known throughout the world; the beggar's-lice or sticktights. They are coarse homely weeds, the achenes of which attach easily to the clothing or to animals by their barbed awns.

bī′dent, *n.* [L. *bidens*, having two prongs; *bis*, twice, and *dens*, *dentis*, a tooth.] A two-pronged weapon or instrument.

bī-den′tăl, *a.* Having two teeth.

bī-den′tăl, *n.*; *pl.* **bī-den-tā′li-ȧ**. A place in ancient Rome that had been struck by lightning, and which was marked by a monument, consecrated, and inclosed by a wall.

bī-den′tāte, *a.* In biology, two-toothed; having two teeth, or two tooth-like processes.

bi-det′, *n.* [Fr.] 1. A small horse, formerly allowed to each trooper or dragoon for carrying his baggage.
2. A vessel used in taking sitz baths.

bī-dig′i-tāte, *a.* Having two fingers, or parts similar to fingers.

bīd′ing, *n.* Residence; habitation.

bid′ri, bid′ry, *n.* [From *Bidar*, a town in India in the Nizam's dominions, once the chief town of the Deccan.] An alloy, primarily composed of copper, lead, and tin, to which zinc is added. Many articles of Indian manufacture are formed from it, being generally inlaid with silver or gold and polished. Also written *bidree*, *biddery*, *beder*, etc.

bid′ū-ous, *a.* [L. *biduus*; *bis*, and *dies*, day.] Lasting two days, as certain flowers.

bield, *n.* A shelter; a place of refuge. Also spelled *beild*, *beeld.* [Scot.]

bield, *v.t.* To shelter. [Scot.]

bī-en′ni-ăl, *a.* [L. *biennialis*, from *biennis*; *bis*, twice, and *annus*, year.]
1. Continuing for two years; happening, or taking place, once in two years; as, a *biennial* election.
2. In botany, continuing for two years, and then perishing, as plants whose root and leaves are formed the first year, and which produce fruit the second.

bī-en′ni-ăl, *n.* 1. Anything that occurs or takes place once in two years.
2. A plant which lives for two years.

bī-en′ni-ăl-ly, *adv.* Once in two years; at the return of two years.

biẽr, *n.* [ME. *beere*, *bere*; AS. *bǣr*, a bier; from *beran*, to bear; L. *feretrum*; Gr. *pheretron*, a litter, bier.]
1. A frame of wood, with handles at each end, for conveying dead human bodies to the grave.
2. In weaving, forty warp-threads, used as a unit of measurement.

biẽr′balk (-bak), *n.* A path through fields, left for funerals. [Obs.]

biest, *n.* Same as *Biestings.*

biest′ings, beest′ings, *n.pl.* [ME. *beestynge*; AS. *bysting*, from *beost*, biest.] The first milk given by a cow after calving.

bī-fā′ciăl, *a.* Having the opposite surfaces alike.

bī-fā′ri-ous, *a.* [L. *bifarius*, twofold; *bis*, twice, and *fari*, to speak.] Divided into two parts; double; twofold; specifically, in biology, pointing two ways, or arranged in two opposite rows, as leaves that grow only on opposite sides of a branch.

bī-fā'ri-ous-ly, *adv.* In a bifarious manner.

bif'ēr-ous, *a.* [L. *biferus*; *bis*, twice, and *ferre*, to bear.] Bearing fruit or flowering twice a year.

bif'fin, *n.* [A corruption of *beefing*; *beef*, and *-ing*, so called from the color of the apple.]

1. A baked apple crushed down into a flat, round cake.

2. An excellent cooking-apple cultivated in England, especially in the county of Norfolk.

bī'fid, *a.* [L. *bifidus*, forked; from *bis*, twice, and *findere*, to cleave, divide.] In botany, two-cleft; opening with a cleft; divided by a linear sinus, with straight margins.

bif'i-dāte, *a.* Cleft; forked; bifid.

bī-fī'lär, *a.* [*Bi-*, and *filar*, from L. *filum*, thread.] Having or requiring the use of two threads, in support or formation.

Bifilar suspension; the suspension of a needle by two fibers; used in electric balances.

bī-fis'tū-lär, *a.* Having two ducts or channels.

bī-flā-bel'lāte, *a.* [*Bi-*, and L. *flabellum*, a fan.] Fan-shaped on both sides.

bī-flā-gel'lāte, *a.* Having two flagella.

bī-flec'nōde, *n.* [*Bi-*, and L. *flectere*, to bend, and *nodus*, node.] In geometry, the crossing point of a curve, simultaneously a point of inflection or change of direction.

bī'flex, *a.* [*Bi-*, and L. *flexus*, pp. of *flectere*, to bend.] Bending in two directions; as, a *biflex* tube.

bī-flō'rāte, bī-flō'rous, *a.* [*Bi-*, and L. *flos*, *floris*, flower.] Bearing two flowers.

bī-fō'cāl, *a.* Having two lenses of different focal power, as certain spectacles.

bī'foil, *n.* [*Bi-*, and ME. *foil*, from L. *folium*, a leaf.] The twayblade, *Listera ovata.*

bī'fōld, *a.* Twofold; double; of two kinds, degrees, etc.

bī-fō'li-āte, *a.* Having two leaves.

bī-fō'li-ō-lāte, *a.* [*Bi-*, and L. *foliatus*, from *folium*, leaf.] Bearing two leaflets.

bif'ō-rāte, *a.* In botany, having two perforations, as the anthers of the rhododendron.

bif'ō-rine, *n.* [L. *biforis*, two-doored; *bis*, twice, and *foris*, a door.] A minute oval sac found in the interior of the green pulpy part of the leaves of some plants; so called because they discharge their contents by an opening at each extremity.

bī'forked (-forkt), *a.* Bifurcate.

bī'form, *a.* [L. *biformis*; *bis*, twice, and *forma*, form.] Having two forms, bodies, or shapes.

bī'formed, *a.* Same as *Biform.*

bī-form'i-ty, *n.* A double form.

bī'forn, *prep.* and *adv.* Before. [Obs.]

bif'ō-rous, *a.* See *Biforate.*

bī-frŏnt'ed, *a.* Having two fronts.

bī-fūr'cāte, bī-fūr'cā-ted, *a.* [L. *bifurcatus*, from *bifurcus*; *bis*, twice, and *furca*, a two-pronged fork.] Forked; divided into two branches.

bī-fūr'cāte, *v.i.* To separate into two branches.

bī-fūr-cā'tion, *n.* A forking, or division into two branches.

bī-fūr'cous, *a.* Forked. [Rare.]

big, *a.*; *comp.* bigger; *superl.* biggest. [ME. *big*, *bigg*, *byg*, strong, powerful.]

1. Bulky; protuberant.

2. Pregnant; followed by *with*; as, *big with* child.

3. Great; large, in a more general sense; applied to any body or object.

4. Distended; full, as with grief or passion.

> Thy heart is *big*; get thee apart and weep. —Shak.

5. Swelled; inflated, as with pride; hence, haughty in air or mien, or indicating haughtiness; proud; as, *big* words; to look *big*.

6. Great in spirit; lofty; brave.

To talk big; to talk boastfully.

Syn.—Large, great, wide, huge, bulky, proud, arrogant, pompous, fat, massive, gross.

big, bigg, *n.* [ME. *byge*; Ice. *bygg*; Dan. *byg*, barley.] A kind of barley.

big, bigg, *v.t.* [ME. *biggen*, *byggen*; Ice. *byggja*, to build, to dwell in.] To construct. [Prov. Scot. and Eng.]

bī'gȧ, *n.* [L.] A chariot drawn by two horses.

big'ăm, *n.* A bigamist. [Obs.]

big'a-mist, *n.* One who has committed bigamy, or has two wives or husbands at once.

big'ȧ-mous, *a.* Involving the crime of bigamy.

big'ȧ-my, *n.* [ME. *bigamie*; OFr. *bigamie*; LL. *bigamus*; *bis*, twice and Gr. *gamos*, marriage.] The statutory crime of having two wives or husbands at once by formal marriage and with actual or presumptive knowledge of the existing married state of either of the parties: sometimes used as synonymous with *polygamy.*

In the canon law, *bigamy* was the marrying of two virgins in succession, or of a second wife after the death of the first, or once marrying a widow. This disqualified a man for orders, and holding ecclesiastical offices. Shakspere uses the word in the latter sense in "Richard III."

big'ȧ-rāde, *n.* [Fr.] The Seville or bitter orange.

big-ȧ-roon', *n.* [Fr. *bigarreau*, from *bigarré*, variegated.] A kind of firm-fleshed, sweet cherry, of which the large white-heart cherry is a type.

big'-bel''lied, *a.* Having a large belly; advanced in pregnancy. [Vulgar.]

bī-gem'i-nāte, *a.* [*Bi-*, and L. *geminatus*, pp. of *geminare*, to double; *geminus*, double.] In botany, a term applied to a decompound leaf having a forked petiole, with leaflets at the end of each division; biconjugate.

bī'gē-nēr, *n.* [L., a hybrid, from *bis*, twice, and *genus*, kind, family.] A cross from species of different genera; a mongrel; a half-breed.

bī-gē-ner'ic, *a.* Of a hybrid nature.

bī-gen'tiăl (-shăl), *a.* [L. *bigens* (*-entis*); *bi-*, *bis*, two, and *gens*, a nation, race.] Embracing two tribes or races of mankind.

big'eye, *n.* A fish of the genus *Priacanthus*, named from its prominent eyes.

big'gēr, *a.*, comp. of *big.*

big'gest, *a.*, superl. of *big.*

big'gin, *n.* [Fr. *béguin*, a cap, from a cap worn by the nuns called *Beguines.*] A child's bonnet; a head-covering varied in form.

big'gin, *n.* A coffeepot containing a metal strainer to hold ground coffee; boiling water is poured through in making coffee. Named after the inventor.

big'ging, big'gin, *n.* A building. [Obs.]

big'gŏn-net, *n.* [Fr. *beguinet*, dim. of *béguin*, a cap.] A cap or hood with ear-flaps.

Biggonet, from Royal MS. British Museum.

big'hȧ, bē'gȧ, *n.* An East Indian measure of land, containing an acre or less.

big'horn, *n.* The long-horned, gregarious goat, *Ovis montana*, of the Rocky Mountains.

bight (bīt), *n.* [ME. *bycht*; AS. *byht*, a bend, a corner, from *būgan*, to bend, to bow.]

1. A bend or small bay between two points of land.

2. The double part of a rope when folded, in distinction from the end; that is, a round bend, or coil anywhere except at the ends; a loop.

3. The inward bend of a horse's chambrel and the bend of the fore knees; also, any angle. [Obs.]

bī-glan'dū-lär, *a.* Having two glands.

big'ly, *adv.* In a bragging, boasting style.

big'ness, *n.* Bulk; size; largeness; dimensions.

Big-nō'ni-ȧ, *n.* [Named for the Abbe *Bignon.*] A large genus of tropical American climbing shrubs of the order *Bignoniaceæ*, the trumpet-flowers.

Big-nō-ni-ā'cē-æ, *n.pl.* A natural order of monopetalous dicotyledonous plants with irregular flowers, a pod-like fruit, winged seeds without albumen, and usually a climbing habit. They are trees or twining or climbing shrubs, inhabiting the hotter parts of Asia, Africa, and America.

big-nō-ni-ā'ceous, *a.* Relating to the *Bignoniaceæ.*

big'ŏt, *n.* [Fr. *bigot*, a bigot or hypocrite; Arm. *bigod.* Supposed to be a corruption of *by God*, and derived from an expression used by Rollo, duke of Normandy, when ordered to kiss the foot of King Charles, "ne se, *bī Gott.*"]

1. A person who is obstinately and unreasonably wedded to a particular church or religious creed, opinion, practice, or ritual; a fanatic.

2. In an extended sense, one who is intolerantly attached to any opinion, or system of belief; as, a *bigot* to a form of government.

big'ŏt, *a.* Bigoted. [Obs.]

big'ŏt-ed, *a.* Having the characteristics of a bigot.

big'ŏt-ed-ly, *adv.* In a bigoted manner.

big'ŏt-ry, *n.* [Fr. *bigoterie*, from *bigot*, a bigot, hypocrite.]

1. Obstinate or blind attachment to a particular creed; unreasonable zeal or warmth in favor of a party, sect, or opinion; excessive prejudice.

2. The beliefs or practices of a bigot.

big'root, *n.* The popular name of a Californian plant of the gourd family which grows with a remarkably large root.

bi-gut'tāte, *a.* [*Bi-*, and L. *guttatus*, from *gutta*, a spot, drop.] In biology, marked with two spots of color resembling drops.

big'wig, *n.* A great man; a person of consequence; one high in authority or rank; as, the *bigwigs* of society. [Slang.]

big'wigged, *a.* Pompous; solemnly authoritative.

bī-hȳ-drog'ū-ret, *n.* A compound of two atoms of hydrogen with one of some element or radical which is nonmetallic or negative.

bī-il'i-ac, *a.* Same as *Bisiliac.*

bī-jou', *n.*; *pl.* **bī-joux'** (bē-zhō'). [Fr.] A jewel; something small and very pretty; especially, an ornament of gold having an elaborate design but without precious stones; a trinket.

bī-jou'terie (-trē), *n.* [Fr., from *bijou*, a jewel.] Jewelry; trinkets.

bī-jou'try, *n.* Same as *Bijouterie.*

bij'ū-gāte, *a.* [*Bi-*, and L. *jugatus*, pp. of *jugare*, to join; *jugum*, a yoke.] Having two pairs of leaflets; used of pinnated leaves.

bij'ū-gous, *a.* Same as *Bijugate.*

bike, *n.* 1. A wild bee's nest; a concealed store of anything. [Scot.]

2. A swarm of bees, ants, etc.; a crowd. [Scot.]

bikh (bik), *n.* [Hind.] Any one of several plants of the aconite group, especially *Aconitum ferox*; also, a medicinal poison obtained from its roots.

bī-lā'bi-āte, *a.* [*Bi-*, and L. *labium*, a lip.] In botany, having two lips or lobes; applied to certain forms of calyx and corolla.

bī-lā-cin'i-āte, *a.* In botany, doubly laciniate or fringed.

bī-lā'lō, *n.* [Native name.] A passenger-boat about sixty-five feet long and ten feet broad, peculiar to the Bay of Manila, combining local characteristics with European forms. Behind the mainmast is a large cabin. It carries an outrigger for use in fresh winds.

Bilalo of Manila.

bī-lam'el-lāte, bī-lam'el-lā-ted, *a.* [*Bi-*, and L. *lamella*, a thin plate.] Doubly lamellate; having two lamellæ; specifically, in botany, composed of two plates, as many stigmas and placentas; or bearing two plates, as in the lip of the flowers of some orchids.

bī-lam'i-när, bī-lam'i-nāte, *a.* [*Bi-*, and L. *lamina*, a plate, scale.] Having two laminæ; consisting of two plates, scales, or layers.

bī'land, *n.* A peninsula; a byland. [Obs.]

bil'ăn-dēr, *n.* [D. *bijlander*, from *bij*, by, and *land*, land.] A small vessel with two masts, distinguished by the form of the mainsail, the gaff or yard of which hangs fore and aft and is inclined at an angle of about forty-five degrees. The *bilander* is used chiefly in the canals of the Low Countries.

Bilander.

bī-lat'ēr-ăl, *a.* [L. *bilateralis*; *bi-*, two, and *latus*, a side.]

1. Two-sided; pertaining to or arranged upon two sides.

2. In biology, of or pertaining to two equal or corresponding sides with reference to a central axis or organ; having symmetrical sides.

Bī-lat-e-rā'li-ȧ, *n.pl.* A collective name for animals that are bilaterally symmetrical.

bī-lat-ēr-ăl'i-ty, *n.* The state or quality of being bilateral.

bī-lat'ēr-ăl-ly, *adv.* In a bilateral manner; with reference to two sides.

bil'ber''ry, *n.* [Probably from Dan. *böllebær*, bilberry.] The name of any one of several shrubs of the genus *Vaccinium*, and of their fruit; especially, the European whortleberry, *Vaccinium Myrtillus*, and two or three common American varieties.

bil'bō, *n.*; *pl.* **bil'bōes** or **bil'bōs**. A rapier; a sword; so named, it is said, from Bilboa, in Spain, where the best were made.

bil'bō, *n.* A long bar or bolt of iron with shackles sliding on it and a lock at the end, formerly used to confine the feet of prisoners or offenders, especially on board ships.

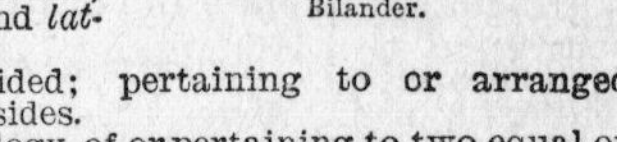

Bilboes, from the Tower of London.

bil-bō-quet' (-ket'), *n.* [Fr.] The toy called cup-and-ball.

bil'cock, *n.* In zoölogy, a popular name for the common European water-rail, *Rallus aquaticus.*

bild'stein, *n.* [G. *bild*, shape, image, and *stein*, stone.] Agalmatolite, figure-stone, or pagodite, the soft unctuous lardstone of China, often cut into grotesque ornaments by the Chinese.

bile, *n.* [Fr. *bile*; L. *bilis*, bile, anger.]

1. A yellow or greenish fluid, slightly alkaline, separated from the blood in the liver, collected in the branches of the hepatic duct, and thence discharged by the common bile duct into the duodenum. It aids in the digestive process, its chief function being to separate the chyle from the chyme.

2. Ill nature; bitterness of feeling; irritability; a meaning derived from the old idea that the *bile* was the humor that produced ill temper.

Bile duct; a canal to convey bile; a term applied, in anatomy, to the duct through which the secretions of the gall-bladder and the liver, after passing through the cystic and hepatic ducts respectively, flow into the duodenum.

bile, *n.* An inflamed tumor; a boil. [Obs.]

bi-leg′tion, *n.* Same as *Bolection.*

bile′stone, *n.* A gallstone, or biliary calculus.

bilġe, *n.* [A variant of *bulge*, a protuberance.]

1. The protuberant part of a cask, which is usually in the middle.

2. That portion of the bottom of a ship, inside or outside, which is most nearly flat; the broadest part of the hull.

3. Bilge-water

bilġe, *v.i.*; bilged, *pt., pp.*; bilging, *ppr.* 1. To suffer a fracture in the bilge; to spring a leak by a fracture in the bilge.

2. To bulge out.

bilġe, *v.t.* 1. To break a hole in the bilge of (a vessel); to fracture the hull of.

2. To cause to swell out or bulge; to make protuberant.

bilġe′=free, *a.* So stowed as to rest entirely on its beds, the bilge being free from pressure or contact; a nautical term applied to a barrel, cask, etc.

bilġe′=pump, *n.* A pump for drawing bilge-water from a ship.

bilġe′=wa″tẽr, *n.* Water which has collected in the bilge of a ship and become foul.

bilġe′wāys, *n.pl.* Planks of timber placed under a vessel's bilge on the building-slip to support her while launching; also termed *launching-ways.*

bil′ġy, *a.* Having the properties (as smell, etc.) of bilge-water.

Bil-hăr′zi-ȧ, *n.* [Named after Theodor *Bilharz.*] A genus of parasitic worms found in the veins of the human body, and especially those of the bladder and mesentery.

bil′iȧ-ry (-yȧ-), *a.* [L. *bilis*, bile.] Pertaining to the bile; conveying the bile; as, a *biliary* duct.

Biliary calculus; a gallstone, or concretion formed in the gall-bladder or its ducts.

Biliary duct; one of the many ducts which combine to form the hepatic duct.

bil-i-ā′tion, *n.* The act or process of secreting and discharging bile.

bil′ic, *a.* Pertaining to or obtained from the bile.

Bilic acid; a compound obtained in the form of white crystals from the oxidation of cholic acid.

bi-lif′ẽr-ous, *a.* [L. *bilis*, bile, and *ferre*, to bear.] Producing bile.

bil-i-fus′cin, *n.* [L. *bilis*, bile, and *fuscus*, dark.] A dark brown pigment present in gallstones and bile.

bi-lim′bi, bi-lim′bing, *n.* The Malayan name of the berries of the *Averrhoa Bilimbi*, which are very acid but edible after cooking, and the juice of which has some medicinal properties.

bil′i-ment, *n.* Part of a woman's attire, particularly an ornament for the head or neck. [Obs.]

bil′in, *n.* [L. *bilis*, bile.] A mixture of the sodium salts forming a constituent of the bile.

bī-lin′ē-ăr, *a.* In mathematics, having reference to or formed of two lines.

bī-lin′ē-āte, *a.* In zoölogy, marked with two parallel lines; striped.

bi-liñ′guăl (-gwăl), **bi-liñ′guăr** (-gwăr), *a.* [*Bi-*, and L. *lingua*, tongue.]

1. Written or expressed in two languages; as, a *bilingual* inscription.

2. Able to speak or use two languages.

bi-liñ′guăl-ism, *n.* The quality of being bilingual; the use of two languages.

bi-liñ′guăl-ly, *adv.* In a bilingual manner; in two languages.

bi-liñ′guăr, *a.* See *Bilingual.*

bi-liñ′guist, *n.* A person able to speak two languages.

bi-liñ′guous (-gwus), *a.* Having two tongues, or speaking two languages.

bil′ious (-yus), *a.* [L. *biliosus*, from *bilis*, bile.]

1. Pertaining to bile; consisting of bile.

2. Having a disordered liver; characterized by or due to an excess of bile; as, a *bilious* fever.

3. Affected with, or characterized by, headache, indigestion, nausea, and related disorders, supposed to be due to an abnormal condition of the liver.

4. Ill-tempered; cross; out of humor; choleric.

bil′ious-ness, *n.* The state or quality of being bilious, in a physical or figurative sense.

bil-i-prā′sin, *n.* [L. *bilis*, bile, and *prasinus*, leek-green.] A pigment of a green color present in human gallstones, icteric urine, and bile.

bil-i-rū′bin, *n.* [From L. *bilis*, bile, and *ruber*, red.] The principal pigment of the bile, orange-red in color; also found in the urine in jaundice.

bī-lit′ẽr-ăl, *a.* and *n.* [*Bi-*, and L. *littera*, a letter.]

I. *a.* Consisting of two letters; as, a *biliteral* root in language.

II. *n.* Something composed of two letters, as a syllable or word.

bī-lit′ẽr-ăl-ism, *n.* The state or quality of being biliteral.

bil-i-vẽr′din, *n.* [L. *bilis*, bile, and *viridis*, green.] A green pigment of the bile produced by oxidation of bilirubin.

bilk, *v.t.*; bilked, *pt., pp.*; bilking, *ppr.* [Origin doubtful; probably a form of *balk.*]

1. To frustrate or disappoint; to deceive or defraud, by nonfulfilment of engagement; as, to *bilk* a creditor.

2. In the game of cribbage, to balk an adversary's crib-score.

3. To steal away from; to elude.

bilk, *n.* 1. A tricky person; a cheat; a swindler.

2. A hoax; a deception; a trick.

3. Meaningless words; nonsense.

4. In cribbage, the spoiling of an adversary's score.

bill, *n.* [ME. *bill*, *bil*; AS. *bil*; G. *bille*, an ax.]

1. A mattock, pickax, or other implement for digging.

2. A variously-shaped tool used for pruning, etc. In general, the head consists of a blade, hook-shaped toward the point, and with a concave cutting edge. When the handle is short, the *bill* is called a hand-*bill*; when long, a hedge-*bill.*

3. The point of the fluke of an anchor.

4. An ancient military weapon consisting of a broad hook-shaped blade with a pike at the end and the back, and fitted to a long handle or staff; used especially by the English infantry of the fourteenth and fifteenth centuries.

Old English Bill. Time of Elizabeth.

bill, *n.* [ME. *bille*, a letter, writing; L. *billa*, *bulla*, a writing, edict.]

1. In law, a declaration in writing, expressing some wrong the complainant has suffered from the defendant, or a fault committed by some person against a law. It contains the fact complained of, the damage sustained, and a petition or process against the defendant for redress. It is used both in civil and criminal cases. In Scots law, every summary application in writing, by way of petition to the court of session, is called a *bill.*

2. An acknowledgment of debt given in writing by one person to another, the sum due and the time of payment, as well as the place and date of signing, being set down; in the United States, more usually known as a note, note of hand, or promissory note.

3. A form or draft of a law, presented to a legislature, but not yet enacted; also, rarely, an enacted law or statute.

4. A paper written or printed, and intended to give public notice of something, especially by being exhibited in some public place; a poster; a placard; as, the *bill* of an auction or of a show.

5. An account of goods sold or delivered, services rendered, or work done, with the price or value annexed to each article; a statement of money due; as, a butcher's *bill.*

6. Any written statement of particulars; as, a *bill* of fare; a *bill* of the play.

7. A note issued by the government or an authorized bank; as, a five-dollar *bill.*

Bill of costs; an itemized statement of the costs of a legal action as charged against the parties to the suit.

Bill of credit; (a) a bill or note for raising money on the mere credit of a state (prohibited by the Constitution of the United States); (b) a written request that the receiver thereof shall credit the bearer as specified, on the security of the writer.

Bill of divorce; in Jewish law, a writing given by the husband to the wife, by which the marriage relation was dissolved.

Bill of entry; a written account of goods entered at the customhouse, whether imported or intended for exportation.

Bill of exchange; an order drawn by one person on another, directing him to pay money to some third specified person, and charge the amount to the drawer. The drawer makes the order; the drawee is directed to make payment; and the payee receives the money.

Bill of fare; a menu; a printed or written list of the articles of food to be served at a meal, or to be obtained at a public eating-house, hotel, or restaurant.

Bill of health; a certificate from the proper authorities as to the state of health of a ship's company, at the time of her leaving port.

Bill of indictment; a formal statement of an accusation of criminal offense presented by a public prosecutor to a grand jury. If the jury sanctions the bill by reason of evidence submitted, it is marked *a true bill.*

Bill of lading; a written receipt for goods accepted for transportation, given by a shipping company to the consignor.

Bill of mortality; an official register of the number and causes of deaths in a place, in a given time.

Bill of parcels; an invoice; a statement giving the different items of purchase, with the value of each.

Bill of particulars; in law, a written statement detailing the various points of a more general pleading.

Bill of rights; a summary of rights and privileges claimed by a people; especially, the declaration presented by the lords and commons of England to the Prince and Princess of Orange in 1688. In the United States, a *bill* or *declaration of rights* is prefixed to most of the constitutions of the several states.

Bill of sale; a writing given by the seller of personal property to the purchaser, answering to a deed of real estate. It is often given to a creditor in security for money borrowed, or obligation otherwise incurred, empowering the receiver to sell the goods if the obligation is not discharged at the appointed time.

Bill of sight; a form of entry at the customhouse by which goods, respecting which the importer is not possessed of full information, may be provisionally landed for examination.

Bill of stores; a license from the customhouse to permit stores required for a voyage to be carried on a merchant vessel without duty.

Bill payable; a promissory note, bill of exchange, or other commercial paper, by which money is to be paid to another.

Bill receivable; a promissory note, bill of exchange, or other commercial paper, by which money is to be received from another.

bill, *v.t.* 1. To invoice; to furnish with a bill; as, to *bill* merchandise.

2. To give notice of by public announcement or advertisement; as, the play is *billed* for next week.

bill, *n.* [ME. *bill*, *bile*; AS. *bile*, a beak.] The beak of a fowl; the beak of other animals, as the turtle, or some similar part, as the rostrum or snout of some fishes.

bill, *v.i.*; billed, *pt., pp.*; billing, *ppr.* To join bills, as doves; to indulge, like doves, in demonstrative caresses.

bill, *n.* A far reverberating noise, as the boom of the bittern; an echoing bellow or roar.

bil′lȧ-bong, *n.* A lagoon; a backwater. [Australia.]

bil′lāge, *n., v.t.,* and *v.i.* Same as *Bilge.*

bil′lărd, *n.* A local English term for the coal-fish.

bill′bee″tle (-tl), *n.* One of a large group of beetles; a weevil; a curculio; also called *bill-bug.*

Bill-bẽr′ġi-ȧ, *n.* [Named after J. G. *Billberg*, a Swedish botanist.] A tropical American genus of air-plants belonging to the *Bromeliaceæ.* The species are cultivated in greenhouses and are crossed into many varieties.

bill′bōard, *n.* 1. A plank or other projection at the bow of a vessel, on which the bill of the anchor rests.

2. A level surface, often part of a wall, on which advertisements are posted; a hoarding.

3. A portable stand for the display of advertising bills.

bill′=book, *n.* A book in which is kept an account of notes, bills, bills of exchange, etc., issued and received.

bill′=brō″kẽr, *n.* One who negotiates bills, promissory notes, etc., at a discount. [Eng.]

bill′bug, *n.* See *Billbeetle.*

billed, *a.* Having a bill.

bil′let, *n.* [Fr. *billet*, dim. of *bille*, a bill.]

1. A small paper or note in writing; a short letter; a note.

2. A ticket directing soldiers to lodgings.

3. The lodging-place of a soldier.

4. A sailor's quarters on board ship.

5. A berth; a situation. [Colloq.]

bil′let, *v.t.*; billeted, *pt., pp.*; billeting, *ppr.* To direct, by a ticket or note, where to lodge. Hence, to quarter, or place in lodgings, as soldiers in private houses.

bil′let, *v.i.* To lodge; as, I *billeted* across the street from my comrade.

bil′let, *n.* [ME. *billette*; OFr. *billette*, dim. of *bille*; L. *billus*, a log.]

1. A small log; a stick of wood.

2. In architecture, an ornament in Norman

work, resembling a billet of wood. [See *Billet-molding.*]

3. A short bar of iron or steel.

4. In harness, etc., a loop receiving the end of a buckled strap.

5. In heraldry, a charge in the form of an oblong figure.

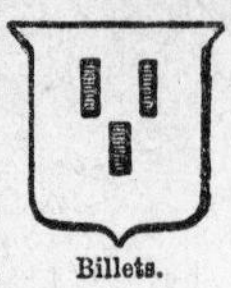

Billets.

bil-let=doux′ (bil-le-dö′), *n.*; *pl.* **bil-lets=doux′** (bil-le-döz′). [Fr. *billet*, a note, and *doux*, L. *dulcis*, sweet.] A love-note or love-letter.

bil′let-head (-hed), *n.* 1. A post at the bow of a whaleboat, around which the harpoon line is paid out.

2. A scroll or ornamental carving taking the place of a figurehead on a ship.

bil′let=mōld-ing, *n.* A molding ornamented with a design of spaced billets, either end to end or upright.

Billet-molding.

bill′fish, *n.* Any one of various fishes having pronounced bills, as species of the garfish, garpike, and saury, and the spearfish.

bill′head (-hed), *n.* A regular printed form on which invoices and accounts are set out.

bill′=hōld″ẽr, *n.* 1. The holder of a bill of acceptance or note.

2. A device for holding bills.

bill′hook, *n.* A thick knife having a hooked point, used to prune shrubs, etc. When it has a short handle it is called a hand-bill; when the handle is long it is generally termed a hedge-bill.

Billhook.

bil′liărd (bil′yărd), *a.* Relating to the game of billiards.

bil′liărds (-yărdz), *n.* [Fr. *billard*, billiards, a billiard-cue, or stick with a curved end, from *bille*, a log, stock of a tree; L. *billus*, a log.] A game played on a table with balls and a cue. The standard size of table used in the United States has a level surface 5x10 feet, composed of solid slate, covered with green cloth of fine glossy finish. This surface is bounded by rubber cushions set in a solid hardwood frame. The balls are ivory, standard size 2⅜ inches in diameter. The cue is heavy at the butt, and diminishes gradually in size to the slender end. The point is furnished with a leather tip. The French game, played with three balls on a pocketless table, is the favorite in the United States. The English game is played upon a larger table, 6x12 feet, furnished with six pockets.

bil′ling, *n.* The act of caressing; fondling.

bil′lings-gāte, *n.* [From a market of this name in London, celebrated for fish and the foul language of its dealers.] Foul language; ribaldry.

bil′liŏn (bil′yun), *n.* [A contr. of L. *bis*, twice, and *million*, a million.] In the United States, a thousand millions (1,000,000,000); in England, a million millions.

bil′liŏn-āire (-yun-ăr), *n.* A perfunctory term for a person rated as having property worth many million dollars; a multimillionaire.

bill′măn, *n.* One who uses a bill or hooked ax; formerly applied to a soldier armed with a bill; as, in rushed the *billmen*.

bil′lon, *n.* [Fr.] An alloy of gold or silver with a baser metal; a silver alloy with a large proportion of copper; used in medals, tokens, etc.

bil′lot, *n.* [Fr., dim. of *bille*, a stick.] Bullion previous to being coined.

bil′lōw, *n.* [Ice. *bylgja*; Sw. *bölja*; Dan. *bölge*, a billow, from AS. *belgan*, to swell, swell up.] A great wave or surge of the sea or other large body of water, occasioned usually by violent wind; figuratively, a wave of anything; as, a *billow* of laughter.

bil′lōw, *v.i.*; billowed, *pt.*, *pp.*; billowing, *ppr.* To swell; to rise and roll in large waves or surges.

bil′lōw-y, *a.* Swelling or swelled into large waves; relating to billows.

bill′pōst″ẽr, *n.* One who puts up advertisements or posters in public places.

bill′stick″ẽr, *n.* A billposter.

bil′ly, *n.* 1. A short club; particularly, a policeman's baton.

2. A slubbing-machine formerly used in wool manufacture.

bil′ly-boy, *n.* A river barge or coasting-vessel with a flat bottom. [Eng.]

Billyboy.

bil′ly-cock, *n.* A stiff, low-crowned felt hat; the English name of the hat known as a *derby* in the United States.

bil′ly=gōat, *n.* A male goat. [Colloq.]

bī-lō′bate, bī′lōbed, *a.* [*Bi-*, and Gr. *lobos*, a lobe.] Separated into two lobes; as, a *bilobate* leaf.

bī-lō-cā′tion, *n.* The ability to be in two places at once; an attribute ascribed to some saints.

bī-lō-cel′lāte, *a.* [*Bi-*, and L. *locellus*, dim. of *locus*, a place.] Having two locelli, or secondary cells, as an ovary or an anther.

bī-loc′ū-lăr, *a.* [*Bi-*, and L. *locularis*, from *locus*, a place.] Divided into two cells, or containing two cells; as, a *bilocular* pericarp.

bī-loph′ō-dont, *a.* [*Bi-*, and Gr. *lophos*, a hill, and *odous*, *odontos*, tooth.] Having two transverse ridges or crests, as the molar teeth of tapirs.

bil′säh, *n.* [E. Ind.] A fine quality of tobacco grown in Central India.

bil′sted, *n.* See *Sweet-gum.*

bil′tong, *n.* Lean meat, as of deer or buffalo, cut into strips and dried in the sun. [South Africa.]

bī-mac′ū-lāte, *a.* [*Bi-*, and L. *maculatus*, from *macula*, a spot.] Having two spots.

Bim′á-ná (*or* **Bī′má-ná**), *n.pl.* [L., neut. pl. of *bimanus*, two-handed.] Two-handed animals; a term applied to the highest order of *Mammalia*, of which man is the type and sole genus.

bim′á-nous, *a.* Having two hands.

bī-man′ū-ăl, *a.* Done with two hands; requiring the use of both hands; as, *bimanual* turning.

bī-mär′gin-āte, *a.* In conchology, a term applied to shells which have a double margin as far as the tip.

bī-mas′tiç, *a.* [*Bi-*, and Gr. *mastos*, a breast.] In anatomy, having two mammæ or teats.

bī-mas′tism, *n.* The state of having two mammæ.

bī-mas′toid, *a.* In anatomy, relating to the two mastoid formations.

bī′mas-ty, *n.* Same as *Bimastism.*

bim-bash′i, *n.* Same as *Binbashi.*

bī-mē′di-ăl, *a.* [*Bi-*, and L. *medialis*, from *medius*, middle.] In geometry, a term applied to a line composed of two mean proportional lines or medials, termed a first *bimedial* line or a second *bimedial* line, according to the nature of the rectangle they form.

bī-mem′brăl, *a.* [L. *bimembris*, from *bi-*, two, and *membrum*, a member.] Having two members (in grammar).

bī-men′săl, *a.* [Obs.] See *Bimonthly.*

bī-mes′tri-ăl, *a.* [L. *bimestris*, from *bi-*, two, and *mensis*, a month.] Lasting two months. [Rare.]

bī-mē-tal′liç, *a.* [*Bi-*, and L. *metallum*, metal.]

1. Pertaining to, or using, a double metallic standard (as gold and silver) for a system of currency or coinage.

2. Formed of two metals; having two parts, and of different metals; as, a *bimetallic* chain.

bī-met′ăl-lism, *n.* The legalized concurrent use of a double metallic standard (as gold and silver) in the coinage or currency of a country, at a fixed ratio of value; also, the doctrine advocating such use, as opposed to monometallism.

bī-met′ăl-list, *n.* A believer in or advocate of bimetallism.

bī-month′ly, *a.* Happening, done, or appearing once in two months; as, *bimonthly* visits.

bī-month′ly, *adv.* Once in two months.

bī-month′ly, *n.* A publication issued once in every two months.

bī-mus′cū-lăr, *a.* Having two attaching muscles and two muscular impressions, as a bivalve mollusk.

bin, *n.* [AS. *binn* or *binne*, a manger or crib.] A wooden compartment, box, or chest, frame or inclosed place, used as a repository for wheat, corn, wine, coal, and other commodities; as, the *bins* of a grain elevator or a coal-yard; the *bins* of a wine-cellar; a corn-*bin*; a *bin* of old Madeira.

bin, *v.t.*; binned, *pt.*, *pp.*; binning, *ppr.* To place in a bin; as, to *bin* corn.

bin, *v.*, old form of *be* and *been.*

bin-, *prefix.* A combining form used for euphony instead of *bi-*.

bī′năl, *a.* Binary. [Rare.]

bin-ăr-sē′ni-āte, *n.* In chemistry, a salt having two parts of arsenic oxid to one of the base.

bī′nā-ry, *a.* [L. *binarius*, from *bini*, two by two, from *bis*, double.] Compounded or consisting of two things or parts.

Binary arithmetic; a system of arithmetic in which two figures only, 0 and 1, are used, in lieu of ten; the cipher multiplying everything by 2, as in common arithmetic by 10. Thus, 1 is one; 10 is two; 11 is three; 100 is four; 101 is five; 110 is six; 111 is seven; 1000 is eight; 1001 is nine; 1010 is ten. It is said this species of arithmetic has been used by the Chinese for 4000 years.

Binary compound; in chemistry, a compound of two elements, or of an element and a compound performing the function of an element, or of two compounds performing the function of elements.

Binary logarithms; an arrangement of logarithms having 2 for its base.

Binary measure; in music, the measure used in common time, in which the time of rising, in beating, is equal to the time of falling.

Binary scale; in arithmetic, a consistent scale of notation with 2 as the ratio.

Binary star; a double star, whose members have a revolution round their common center of gravity.

Binary theory; in chemistry, the suggestion that all chemical compounds are formed of two constituents of contrary and different qualities.

bī′nā-ry, *n.* That which is made up of two figures or parts; a couple.

bī′nāte, *a.* [L. *binatus*, from *bini*, two by two; *bis*, double.] Being double; growing in pairs; as, a *binate* leaf.

bin-au′răl, *a.* [*Bin-*, and L. *auris*, ear.] Of or pertaining to, or used by or with, both ears; as, a *binaural* ear-trumpet.

bin-bash′i, *n.* [Turk. chief of a thousand; *bin*, a thousand, and *bash*, a head.] An officer in the Turkish army having the rank of major.

Binate Leaves.

bind, *v.t.*; bound, *pt.*, *pp.*; binding, *ppr.* [ME. *binden*; AS. *bindan*; O.H.G. *bintan*; M.H.G. *binden*; Goth. *bindan*, to tie, bind; Sans. *bandh*, to tie, bind.]

1. To tie; to secure; to fasten, as with a band or ligature; to confine or restrain, as with bonds.

2. To wrap; to cover, as with a bandage; frequently followed by *up*; as, to *bind up* a wound.

3. To make costive or constipated; as, certain kinds of food *bind* the bowels.

4. To strengthen with stitching; to protect with a band on the edges; as, to *bind* a skirt.

5. To sew together and cover; to cover with anything firm; as, to *bind* the pages of a magazine.

6. To check or restrain by moral force, as a promise, duty, or authority; to hold or attract, as by affection or personal qualities.

To bind to; to contract; as, *to bind* oneself *to* a wife.

To bind over; to oblige by bond to appear at a court.

Bound up in; engrossed in; absorbed in.

Syn.—Tie, fasten, secure, fetter, oblige, restrain, restrict.

bīnd, *v.i.* 1. To contract; to grow hard or stiff; as, clay *binds* by heat.

2. To stick, owing to friction or pressure; as the wheel *binds.*

3. To be obligatory.

4. To tie up anything, as grain in the field.

bīnd, *n.* 1. A stalk of hops, so called from its winding round a pole or tree, or being bound to it; a hop-vine; a bine.

2. Any quantity forming a specific count; as, a *bind* of eels. [Eng.]

3. Among miners, indurated clay, when much mixed with oxid of iron.

4. In music, a ligature or tie for the purpose of grouping notes together.

5. That which binds; a tie.

bīnd′ẽr, *n.* [ME. *byndere*, from AS. *bindere*, binder, from *bindan*, to bind.]

1. A person who binds; one whose occupation is to bind books; also, one who binds sheaves.

2. Anything that binds, as a fillet, cord, rope, or band.

3. A detachable cover, used for magazines, etc.

4. A machine or attachment for binding grain.

bīnd′ẽr-y, *n.* A place where books are bound.

bind′heim-īte, *n.* [After *Bindheim*, a German chemist, who described it.] A shapeless antimoniate of lead, obtained from other ores.

bīnd′ing, *a.* Causing to be bound; obligatory, from a legal or moral standpoint; as, the *binding* force of a moral duty or of a command.

bīnd′ing, *n.* 1. The act or process of fastening, as with a band.

2. Anything that binds; a bandage; the cover of a book, with the sewing and accompanying work.

3. A braid or strip of cloth sewed over an edge for its protection; as, the *binding* of a dress-skirt.

4. In fencing, a method of securing or crossing the adversary's sword with a pressure, accompanied with a spring of the wrist.

5. [*pl.*] The principal timbers used in building and giving stability to a ship.

bīnd′ing=joists, *n.pl.* In architecture, the joists of a floor into which the trimmers of staircases, or wellholes of the stairs and chimney-ways are framed.

bīnd′ing-ly, *adv.* So as to bind.

bīnd′ing-ness, *n.* The state of having force to bind.

bīnd′ing=pōst, *n.* A metallic post connected with electrical apparatus to serve as a convenience in making connections with wires, etc.

bind'weed, *n.* A name common to difference species of the genus *Convolvulus*; as, the white, the blue, the Syrian *bindweed*, etc. The black bryony, or *Tamus communis*, is called *black bindweed*, and a species of smilax is called *rough bindweed*.

bind'with, *n.* In botany, the traveler's-joy, *Clematis Vitalba*.

bine, *n.* [A dialectic form of *bind*.] The winding stem of a climbing plant, as a hop-vine.

bi-nerv'āte, *a.* [*Bi-*, and L. *nerva*, nerve.] Supported by only two nerves, as the wing of an insect; also applied to leaves having two ribs or nerves.

bing, *n.* [ME. *bing*, *binge*, from Ice. *bingr*, a heap.] A heap; specifically, a heap of grain, or, in alum works, a heap of alum thrown together in order to drain.

bin-i'ō-dide, *n.* A salt with two iodine atoms.

bink, *n.* A bench. [Scot.]

bin'nȧ-cle, *n.* [Formerly *bittacle*, from Port *bitacola*, binnacle; L. *habitaculum*, a dwelling-place; *habitare*, to inhabit.] A wooden case or box in which the compass and a light are kept on board ship for use by the steersman.

Binnacle.

bin'nȧ-cle-list, *n.* In the United States navy, a sick-list posted daily in the binnacle.

bin'ny, *n.*; *pl.* **bin'nies.** [Native name.] A species of edible barbel (*Barbus bynni*), found in the Nile.

bin'ō-cle, *n.* [L. *bini*, double, and *oculus*, an eye.] A dioptric telescope, fitted with two tubes joining, so as to enable a person to view an object with both eyes at once; an opera-glass; a field-glass.

bin-oc'ū-lăr, *a.* 1. Having two eyes.

2. Of or pertaining to both eyes at once.

3. Having two apertures or tubes so joined that one may use both eyes at once in viewing a distant object; as, a *binocular* telescope.

bin-oc'ū-lăr, *n.* [L. *bini*, double, and *oculus*, eye.] A glass fitted for the use of both eyes at once, as a telescope, microscope, or opera-glass.

bin-oc'ū-lăr-ly, *adv.* In a binocular manner.

bin-oc'ū-lāte, *a.* Having two eyes.

bi-nōd'ăl, *a.* [*Bi-*, and L. *nodus*, knot.] Having two joints or nodes.

bi-nō'mi-ăl, *n.* [*Bi-*, and L. *nomen*, name.] An algebraic expression of two terms connected by the signs plus (+) or minus (−); as, a+b or 6−4.

bi-nō'mi-ăl, *a.* 1. Pertaining to binomials.

2. In natural history, using two names; applied to the system of denominating animals and plants by generic and specific names.

Binomial theorem; in algebra, the theorem, first demonstrated by Sir Isaac Newton, for raising a binomial to any power, or for extracting any root of it.

bi-nom'i-năl, *a.* Pertaining to two names.

bi-nom'i-nous, *a.* Having two names.

bi-nor'măl, *n.* [*Bi-*, and L. *norma*, a square.] In geometry, a normal perpendicular to the osculating plane.

bi-not'ō-nous, *a.* [L. *bini*, two by two, and *tonus*, a sound, tone.] Consisting of two notes.

bī'nous, *a.* Same as *Binate*.

bin-ox'ȧ-lāte, *n.* [L. *bini*, two by two, and *oxalis*, oxalic acid, from Gr. *oxus*, sharp.] In chemistry, an oxalate having one of its hydrogen atoms replaced by a metal.

bin-ox'id, *n.* Same as *Dioxid*.

bin'tū-rong, *n.* [Native name.] A small carnivorous animal of southern Asia, belonging to the genus *Arctictis*.

bi-nū'clē-ăr, **bi-nū'clē-āte**, *a.* Having two nuclei or central points; as, *binucleate* cells.

bi-nū'clē-ō-lāte, *a.* [*Bi-*, and L. *nucleus*, a nut.] Having two nucleoli; applied to cells.

bī'ō-, *prefix.* [Gr. *bios*, life.] A combining form, indicating relation to or connection with life or living organisms; as, *bio*blast, *bio*graph, etc.

bī'ō-blast, *n.* [*Bio-*, and Gr. *blastos*, a bud.] Same as *Bioplast*.

bi-ō-cel'lāte, *a.* [*Bi-*, and L. *ocellus*, dim. of *oculus*, eye.] In entomology, marked with two eye-like spots, as a wing.

bi-ō-chem'ic, *a.* Pertaining to biochemistry.

bi-ō-chem'ist, *n.* One learned in biochemistry.

bi-ō-chem'is-try, *n.* [*Bio-*, and Fr. *chemique*, chemistry.] The chemistry of living organisms; a science which deals with the vital phenomena dependent upon chemical influences; specifically, with the direct influences and stimuli produced by chemical agents on nerve centers or specific nerves, and the differentiation of such stimuli produced on the same nerve by different chemical elements or compounds. It deals mainly with the effects on cell life as distinguished from the chemical effects on the living macrocosm or complete organism. Thus certain chemical agents directly attract or repel plant germs and lower animals, and certain plants produce and emit certain agents. Recent investigations prove that certain excitations invariably produce reflex functional actions. They show, among other things, that the chemical reaction of food directly causes an appropriate reflex movement of the alimentary organs.

bī'ōd (*or* **bī'od**), *n.* [Gr. *bios*, life.] The od of organic life; a name given by Baron von Reichenbach to the force that he believed connected and explained vital and mesmeric phenomena; the so-called animal magnetism.

bī"ō-dȳ-nam'ic, **bī"ō-dȳ-nam'ic-ăl**, *a.* Relating to biodynamics.

bī"ō-dȳ-nam'ics, *n.* [*Bio-*, and Gr. *dynamis*, strength.] The doctrine of vital energy displayed in organisms; the antithesis of *biostatics*.

bī'ō-gen, *n.* [*Bio-*, and Gr. *genesis*, origin.] Bioplasm.

bī-ō-gen'e-sis, **bī-oğ'e-ny**, *n.* [*Bio-*, and Gr. *genesis*, origin, from *gignesthai*, to become.] The doctrine of the genesis or production of living beings from living beings only; also, the history of the development of life in general; the antithesis of *abiogenesis*.

bī"ō-ğē-net'ic, *a.* Pertaining to biogenesis.

bī-oğ'e-nist, *n.* One who favors the theory of or believes in biogenesis.

bī-og-nō'sis, *n.* [*Bio-*, and Gr. *gnōsis*, inquiry, from *gnōnai*, to know.] The inquiry into or study of life; that branch of science which treats of vital phenomena.

bī'ō-grȧph, *n.* [Gr. *bios*, life, and *graphein*, to write.] A form of instrument for reproducing life-motion as pictures upon a screen. It differs from other instruments of a like nature in employing an extra wide film without perforated edges.

bī-og'rȧ-phẽr, *n.* One who writes an account or history of the life and actions of a particular person; a writer of lives, as Plutarch.

bī-ō-graph'ic, **bī-ō-graph'ic-ăl**, *a.* Pertaining to biography, or the history of the life of a person; containing biography.

bī-ō-graph'ic-ăl-ly, *adv.* In the manner of a biography.

bī-og'rȧ-phy, *n.*; *pl.* **bī-og'rȧ-phies.** [Fr. *biographie*, biography, from Gr. *bios*, life, and *graphein*, to write.]

1. The history of the life and character of an individual.

2. Biographical literature in general.

bī-ō-log'ic, **bī-ō-log'ic-ăl**, *a.* Relating to biology.

bī-ō-log'ic-ăl-ly, *adv.* In relation to biology.

bī-ol'ō-ğist, *n.* One having a thorough knowledge of biology; also, a student of biology.

bī-ol'ō-ğy, *n.* [Fr. *biologie*, biology, from Gr. *bios*, life, and *logos*, description.] The science of life; the branch of science which treats of the phenomena of animals and plants with regard to their morphology, physiology, origin or development, and distribution.

bī-ol'y-sis, *n.* [*Bio-*, and Gr. *ollynai*, to destroy.] The annihilation of life.

bī-ō-lyt'ic, *a.* Pertaining to the destruction of life.

bī"ō-mag-net'ic, *a.* Pertaining to biomagnetism.

bī-ō-mag'net-ism, *n.* Animal magnetism.

bī-om'e-try, *n.* [*Bio-*, and Gr. *metron*, a measure.] Measurement of the probable duration of the life of human beings.

bī'on, *n.* [Gr. *biōn*, living, ppr. of *bioun*, to live.] In biology, the physiological person, characterized by self-reliant function and definiteness; opposed to *morphon*.

bī-on'ō-my, *n.* [*Bio-*, and Gr. *nomos*, law.] The doctrines of the laws of life or animal functions.

bī-oph'ȧ-gous, *a.* [*Bio-*, and Gr. *phagein*, to eat.] Subsisting upon living organisms, as insectivorous plants, of which Venus's flytrap is an example.

bī'ō-phil"ism, *n.* [Gr. *bios*, life, and *philein*, to love.] Literally, the love of all life from highest to lowest forms; giving every creature full credit for every power it possesses.

bī'ō-phil"ist, *n.* One who hopes for the immortality of the sentient universe.

bī'ō-phŏr, **bī'ō-phōre**, *n.* [*Bio-*, and Gr. *phoros*, something brought, from *pherein*, to bear.] In biology, one of the fundamental units of germ-plasm, conveying heredity and vitality.

bī'ō-plasm, *n.* [*Bio-*, and Gr. *plasma*, something molded, as an image, from *plassein*, to mold.] A name suggested for the vital substance constituting the germinal matter in plants and animals.

bī-ō-plas'mic, *a.* Pertaining to or composed of bioplasm.

bī'ō-plast, *n.* [*Bio-*, and Gr. *plassein*, to form.] A bioplasmic cell, as a white blood-corpuscle; a bioblast; any cell containing the essential elements of life.

bī-ō-plas'tic, *a.* Bioplasmic.

bī-or'găn, *n.* [*Bi-*, and L. *organum*, an organ or instrument.] A physiological organ possessing a function; opposed to *idorgan*.

bī'ō-scōpe, *n.* [*Bio-*, and Gr. *skopein*, to view.] A form of instrument for producing moving pictures upon a screen; one of many trade-names for such an apparatus.

bī-ō-stat'ics, *n.* [*Bio-*, and Gr. *statikē* (supply *technē*), statics, the science that treats of bodies at rest.] That branch of biology which deals with structure as related to function.

bī"ō-stȧ-tis'tics, *n.* Statistics relating to life.

bī'ō-tax-y, *n.* [*Bio-*, and Gr. *taxis*, arrangement.] The arrangement or coördination of living forms of matter according to their structural nature; taxonomy.

bī-ot'ic, **bī-ot'ic-ăl**, *a.* Pertaining to biotics.

bī-ot'ics, *n.* [Gr. *biōtikos*, pertaining to life.] That branch of science treating of the functions and phenomena of living organisms.

bī'ō-tīte, *n.* [Named after *Biot*, a French naturalist.] A black or dark-green form of mica, containing iron and magnesia, common in crystalline rocks.

bī'ō-tōme, *n.* [*Bio-*, and Gr. *tomē*, a cutting, section, from *temnein*, to cut.] Any particular metamorphic stage in the life of certain animals, notably the *Entozoa*, that undergo transformation.

bī-ō'vū-lāte, *a.* [*Bi-*, and Fr. *ovule*, an ovule; L. *ovum*, an egg.] Generating two ovules.

bī-pal'māte, *a.* [*Bi-*, and L. *palma*, the palm of the hand.] In botany, having a palmate arrangement on secondary petioles which are palmately arranged on the primary petiole.

bī-par-ȧ-sit'ic, *a.* [*Bi-*, and L. *parasitus*, from Gr. *parasitos*, one who eats off another, a diner-out, from *para*, beside, and *sitos*, food.] In botany, parasitic upon or deriving subsistence from another parasite.

bip'ȧ-rous, *a.* [*Bi-*, and L. *parere*, to bring forth, to bear.] Bringing forth two at a birth.

bī-pärt'i-ble, *a.* [*Bi-*, and L. *partire*, to divide.] Divisible into two parts.

bī-pär'tient (-shent), *a.* and *n.* [*Bi-*, and L. *partire*, to divide.]

I. *a.* Dividing into two parts.

II. *n.* A number which divides another number into two exactly equal parts.

bī-pär'tīle, *a.* Same as *Bipartible*.

bip'är-tīte (*or* **bī-pär'tīte**), *a.* [*Bi-*, and L. *partitus*, divided.]

1. Composed of two distinct parts; having two correspondent parts, as a legal contract or writing, one for each party.

2. In botany, divided into two parts to the base, as a leaf.

bī-pär-ti'tion (-tish'un), *n.* The act of dividing into two parts, or of making two correspondent parts.

bī-pec'ti-nāte, **bī-pec'ti-nā-ted**, *a.* [*Bi-*, and L. *pecten*, a comb.] In botany, having two margins toothed like a comb.

bī'ped, *n.* and *a.* [*Bi-*, and L. *pes* (*pedis*), a foot.]

I. *n.* An animal having two feet, as man.

II. *a.* Two-footed.

bip'e-dăl (*or* **bī'pe-dăl**), *a.* 1. Pertaining to bipeds.

2. Having two feet.

bī-pel'tāte, *a.* [*Bi-*, and L. *pelta*, Gr. *peltē*, a light shield.] Having a defense like a double shield or shell.

bī-pen'nāte, **bī-pen'nā-ted**, *a.* [*Bi-*, and L. *pennæ*, wings.] Having two wings.

bī-pen'ni-form, *a.* In biology, having a median line with parts on both sides symmetrically disposed with reference to it.

bī-pen'nis, *n.* [L. *bipennis*, having two edges, a two-edged ax.] An ax with two blades or heads, one on each side of the handle. It is the weapon usually seen depicted in the hands of the Amazons in ancient works of art.

Bipennis.

bī-pet'ăl-ous, *a.* [*Bi-*, and Gr. *petalon*, a leaf.] In botany, having two petals.

Bī-pin-nā'ri-ȧ, *n.* [*Bi-*, and *pinna*, wing.] In zoölogy, the larvæ of certain echinoderms, as a starfish, developed to the stage of free-swimming; a generic name for such forms.

bī-pin'nāte, **bī-pin'nā-ted**, *a.* [*Bi-*, and L. *pinnatus*, feathered, from *pinna*, a feather.] In botany, having pinnate leaves on each side of the common petiole.

bī-pin-nat'i-fid, *a.* [*Bi-*, and L. *pinnatus*, feathered, and *findere*, to split.] In botany, having both pinnæ and pinnulæ pinnatifid. [See illus., p. 174.]

Bipinnate Leaf.

bī'plane, *n.* An aeroplane with two supporting surfaces. Wright brothers' aeroplanes are typical biplanes.

bī-plic'i-ty, *n.* The state of being biplicate.

bī-pō'lăr, *a.* [*Bi-*, and L. *polus*; Gr. *polos*, the end of an axis.] Having two poles, one at or near each extremity, as in a cell; opposed to *unipolar*, and in contradistinction to *multipolar*; said of ganglionic cells, also of magnetic machinery.

bī-pō-lar′i-ty, *n.* The state of being bipolar.

Bī′pont, Bī-pont′ine, *a.* Relating to certain editions of classic authors, famous as products of the book-printer's art, made at Zweibrücken (Latin *Bipontium*), Bavaria, in the latter part of the eighteenth century.

bī-punc′tāte, *a.* Having two holes or punctures.

bī-punc′tū-ăl, *a.* Having two points.

bī-pū′pil-lāte, *a.* In entomology, having an eye-like spot on the wing, with two dots or pupils within it of a different color, as in some butterflies.

bī-py-ram′i-dăl, *a.* Having two pyramids placed with their bases facing each other, as in the crystal of quartz.

Bipinnatifid Leaf.

bī-quăd-rat′ic, bī-quăd′rāte, *n.* [*Bi-*, and L. *quadratus*, pp. of *quadrare*, to square.] In mathematics, the fourth power of a number or quantity, or its square squared.

bī-quăd-rat′ic, *a.* Pertaining to the fourth power; quartic.

Biquadratic equation; in algebra, an equation of the fourth degree, or one which involves the fourth power of the unknown quantity or quantities.

Biquadratic root of a number; the square root of the square root of that number. Thus the square root of 81 is 9, and the square root of 9 is 3, which is the *biquadratic root* of 81.

bī′quartz, *n.* Two wedge-shaped pieces of quartz placed together, forming a plate, one-half of which will tend to rotate the plane of polarization to the right and the other half to the left, so that by adjustment of the wedges the deviation of the plane of polarization may be overcome. Used with a polariscope.

bī″quā-tēr′ni-ŏn, *n.* [*Bi-*, and L. *quaterni*, four each, by fours.] In mathematics, an imaginary quaternion.

bī-quin′tile, *n.* [*Bi-*, and L. *quintus*, fifth.] An aspect of the planets, when they are distant from each other by twice the fifth part of a great circle, that is, 144 degrees, or twice 72 degrees.

bī-rā′di-ăl, *a.* In biology, having the radii arranged on two sides.

bī-rā′di-ăl-ly, *adv.* In a biradial manner.

bī-rā′di-āte, bī-rā′di-ā-ted, *a.* Having two rays; as, a *biradiate* fin.

bī-rā′mous, *a.* [*Bi-*, and L. *ramus*, a branch.] In biology, having two branches; said of any organ or appendage.

bīrch, *n.* [ME. *birche, birke*; AS. *birce, bierce*, birch.]

1. A name common to different species of trees of the genus *Betula*; as, the white *birch*, the dwarf *birch*, the Canada *birch*, of which there are several varieties, and the black *birch*.

2. The wood of a birch-tree, valuable in furniture-making, etc.

3. A bundle of twigs, or a rod used for chastisement.

4. A very light canoe made of birch-bark.

5. One of several birch-like trees of New Zealand.

Birch of Jamaica; a tree, *Bursera gummifera*, which yields a kind of turpentine; the turpentine-tree.

Birch wine; a beverage made from the juice or sap of the birch.

Oil of birch; see *Birch-oil*.

bīrch, *v.t.*; birched, *pt., pp.*; birching, *ppr.* To beat with a rod of birch; to flog.

bīrch, bīrch′en, *a.* Made of birch; consisting of birch.

bīrch′-cam″phŏr, *n.* Same as *Betulin*.

bīrch′-oil, *n.* 1. An oil obtained from either *Betula alba*, the white birch, or *Betula lenta*, the black birch. The former is used in the manufacture of Russia leather, to which it gives its distinguishing odor, and the latter as a substitute for oil of wintergreen.

2. A whipping; a castigation. [Colloq.]

bīrch′-pärt″ridge (-rij), *n.* The ruffed grouse.

bīrd, *n.* [ME. *bird, berd, byrde*; AS. *brid*, pl. *briddas*, a bird, especially a young bird.]

1. Originally, a chicken; the young of fowls; and hence, a small fowl.

2. In modern use, any feathered animal. Technically, any individual belonging to a class of warm-blooded vertebrate animals (*Aves*), characterized by oviparous generation, a covering of feathers, a beak, the posterior extremities organized as feet, and the anterior extremities as wings, generally formed for flight. *Birds* have a double circulation and are toothless.

3. A game bird, as a partridge or quail. [Eng.]

4. Figuratively, a maiden; a girl. [Obs.]

5. A nestling; an owlet. [Rare.]

Arabian bird; the phenix; the emblem of immortality.

Bird of freedom; the American or bald eagle, which has been taken as an emblem of freedom and installed in the coat of arms of the United States.

Bird of Jove; the eagle.

Bird of Juno; the peacock.

Bird of Minerva, or *bird of night*; the owl.

Bird of paradise; (a) a beautiful bird of the genus *Paradisea*, native in the Orient and in New Guinea. The largest species is over two feet in length. The head and back part of the neck of this species are lemon-colored; the throat of the brightest emerald green, soft like velvet; the breast black; and the wings of a chestnut color. (b) In Australia, the lyre-bird, so named by the first settlers. (c) In astronomy, a small constellation of the southern heavens.

King Bird of Paradise (*Cincinnurus regius*).

Bird of passage; a bird that migrates at the changes of season in spring and autumn; hence, a temporary sojourner; one of a migratory disposition.

Birds of a feather; individuals engaged in a like business; persons having like tastes or characteristics.

Early bird; one who rises early. [Colloq.]

Man-of-war bird; a raptorial sea-bird, *Fregata aquila*, with a strong hooked bill, small webbed feet, and wings and tail fitted for rapid flight.

To hear a bird sing; to receive by some private means intelligence relating to the outcome of some affair.

bīrd, *v.i.* 1. To catch birds, by either shooting or trapping.

2. To seek game or plunder of any kind; to steal by prowling. [Rare.]

bīrd′-bāit″ing, *n.* The catching of birds, especially with nets.

bīrd′bōlt, *n.* An arrow, broad and smooth at the end, for killing birds by concussion, without injuring the plumage.

bīrd′-cāge, *n.* A box or case with wires, small sticks, or wicker, forming open work, for keeping birds in captivity.

bīrd′call, *n.* An instrument for imitating the cry of birds.

bīrd′catch″ēr, *n.* One whose employment is to catch birds; a fowler.

bīrd′catch″ing, *n.* The art or occupation of taking birds or wild fowl.

bīrd′-cher″ry, *n.* A European tree or shrub, *Prunus Padus*, bearing small black fruit, which is eaten only by birds.

bīrd′-dog, *n.* A pointer, setter, or retriever; any dog qualified by breed or training to hunt birds.

bīrd′-duf″fēr, *n.* One who alters the color or form of living or stuffed birds by artificial processes, usually with intent to deceive.

bīrd′ēr, *n.* A birdcatcher.

bīrd′-eyed, *a.* Quick-sighted; catching a glance as one goes.

bīrd′-fan″ci-ēr, *n.* 1. One who is interested in birds; particularly, one who keeps, breeds, or trains birds, more especially cage-birds.

2. One who deals in birds, particularly cage-birds.

bīrd′ie, *n.* A small bird; a pet name for a child or young woman.

bīrd′i-kin, *n.* One of the young of a bird.

bīrd′ing, *n.* The hunting of birds.

bīrd′ing-piēce, *n.* A shotgun or fowling-piece. [Obs.]

bīrd′let, *n.* A small or very young bird.

bīrd′like, *a.* Resembling a bird.

bīrd′lime, *n.* 1. A viscous substance, usually made of the juice of holly-bark or mistletoe berries, extracted by boiling. It is used to catch birds. For this purpose, the twigs of a bush are smeared with it.

2. Figuratively, anything that ensnares or prevents escape.

bīrd′lime, *v.t.* To ensnare and capture by the use of birdlime.

bīrd′ling, *n.* Same as *Birdlet*.

bīrd′-louse, *n.* A parasitic wingless insect infesting birds, and also found on some mammals.

bīrd′măn, *n.* A fowler or birdcatcher.

bīrd′-mīte, *n.* A small parasitic mite, occurring in numerous species and mainly infesting the feathers of birds.

bīrd′-or″găn, *n.* A small organ, used in teaching birds to sing or whistle tunes.

bīrd′-pep″pēr, *n.* A species of *Capsicum* (*Capsicum baccatum*), a shrubby plant, bearing a small red fruit which is one of the most piquant of red peppers.

bīrd′-plant, *n.* A plant flourishing in Mexico, which bears a yellow flower suggestive of a bird.

bīrd′s′-bēak, *n.* A form of molding, a section of which somewhat resembles a bird's beak.

bīrd′seed, *n.* A mixture of seeds used for feeding birds, including the seeds of hemp, millet, canary-grass, and others.

bīrd′s′-eȳe, *n.* 1. The popular name of a genus of plants, called also pheasant's-eye, known in botany by the generic term *Adonis*. There are several species, some of which produce beautiful flowers.

2. A kind of smoking-tobacco containing sections of stalk resembling a bird's eye.

bīrd′s′-eye, *a.* 1. Seen from above, as if by a flying bird; embraced at a glance; hence, general; not minute, or entering into details; as, a *bird's-eye* view of a city; a *bird's-eye* view of a subject or proposition.

2. Having spots looking like a bird's eye.

Bird's-eye maple; a kind of curly-grained maple, the wood of which when dressed and polished presents the appearance of being covered with the images of a bird's eye. It is much in use for fine furniture.

Bird's-eye rot; same as *Anthracnose*.

bīrd′s′-foot, *n.* A plant of the genus *Ornithopus*, whose legume is articulated, cylindrical, and bent in the form of a bow, ending in a point resembling a bird's claw.

Bird's-foot star; a kind of starfish.

Bird's-foot trefoil; a species of *Lotus* with pods resembling claws.

bīrd′s′-mouth, *n.* In architecture, an interior angle or notch cut across a piece of timber, for its reception on the edge of another, as that on a rafter to be laid on a plate.

bīrd′s′-nest, *n.* 1. The nest in which a bird lays eggs and hatches her young.

2. A name popularly given to several plants, as *Neottia nidus-avis*, a British orchid.

3. In cookery, the nest of a small swallow of the Malayan archipelago, much prized in China as an article of food, being mixed with soups. It is of a gelatinous consistence, and formed of a marine plant partly digested by the bird.

4. The wild carrot; so called because its umbels resemble a nest.

5. Same as *Crow's-nest*.

Bird's-nest pudding; an apple pudding in which the apples are cored and the hollows filled with sugar; also, a plain pudding with a fresh fruit dressing.

bīrd′s′-nest″ing, *n.* The act of searching for and taking bird's nests or their eggs.

bīrd′-spēar, *n.* A long arrow used by the Eskimos for shooting birds.

bīrd′-spi″dēr, *n.* A large hairy South American spider that sometimes preys on small birds.

bīrd′s′-tŏngue (-tung), *n.* Same as *Bird-weed*.

bīrd′-tick, *n.* An insect, usually winged, that is parasitic on birds.

bīrd′-weed, *n.* A common weed, the knotgrass, *Polygonum aviculare*.

bīrd′-wit″ted, *a.* Flighty; passing rapidly from one subject to another; not having the faculty of attention.

bī-rec-tan′gū-lăr, *a.* [*Bi-*, and L. *rectus*, right, and *angulus*, angle.] Rectangular in two of its angles; as, a *birectangular* spherical triangle.

bī-rē-frin′gence, *n.* [*Bi-*, and L. *refringere*, to break open.] In optics, the power of double refraction.

bī-rē-frin′gent, *a.* Having the quality of birefringence.

bī′rēme, *n.* [L. *biremis*, a two-oared boat.] An ancient Grecian galley with two banks or tiers of oars.

bi-ret′tȧ, bir-ret′tȧ, *n.* [It. *birretta*; LL. *birrettum*, dim. of *birrus*, a hood or cloak.] A square cap worn by prelates and priests of the Roman Catholic church. The *biretta* of a cardinal is scarlet; those of all other priests are black, a bishop's being lined with green. Also spelled *baretta*, *beretta*, etc.

Biretta.

bīr′gan-dēr, *n.* See *Bergander*.

bī-rhom-boid′ăl (-rom-), *a.* Having a surface composed of twelve rhombic faces, which, being taken six and six and prolonged in idea till they intercept each other, would form two different rhombs.

bï-ri-bï′ri, *n.* Same as *Beriberi*.

bī-rī′mōse, *a.* [*Bi-*, and L. *rimosus*, from *rima*, a chink.] In botany, having two slits or rimæ.

bīrk, *n.* [Prov. Eng.] A birch-tree.

bīrk, *n.* A small European minnow.

bīrk′en, *v.t.* To beat with a birch or rod. [Obs.]

bīrk′en, *a.* Relating to the birch; birchen. [Scot.]

bir'kie, *n.* [Scot.] 1. A pert or lively young fellow.

2. A game of cards.

birl, *v.t.* and *v.i.* [Scot.] To twirl or spin; to make a humming noise by spinning.

birl, *v.t.* and *v.i.* [ME. *birlen*; AS. *byrlian*, *byrelian*, to pour out drink; *byrele*, a cupbearer, from *beran*, to bear.] To ply or furnish with drink; to pour out drink. [Rare.]

bir'law, *n.* See *Byrlaw.*

bi-ros'trāte, bi-ros'trā-ted, *a.* [*Bi-*, and L. *rostrum*, a beak.] Having a double beak, or process resembling two beaks.

birr, *v.i.*; birred, *pt.*, *pp.*; birring, *ppr.* To make a whirring noise, as of wheels in motion; to move with a whirring sound.

birr, *n.* 1. A whirring or buzzing sound.

2. Force or energy; a rushing, as of wind.

3. A rough accent. [See *Bur.*]

bir-ret'tȧ, *n.* See *Biretta.*

bir'rus, *n.*; *pl.* **bir'rī**. [L., a kind of cloak originally of a red color, from Gr. *pyrros*, *pyrsos*, red, flame-colored, from *pyr*, fire.]

1. In Roman antiquity, a cloak or cape with a hood worn hanging down or over the head as a cowl.

2. A coarse species of thick woolen cloth used by the poorer classes in the middle ages, for cloaks and external clothing.

Birrus.

birse, *n.* [Scot.] A bristle or bristles; short hair.

birt, *n.* The brill, or the turbot. [Prov. Eng.]

birth, *n.* [ME. *birth*, *byrthe*, *byrde*; AS. *gebyrde*, from *beran*, to bear; O.H.G. *giburt*; Goth. *gabaurths*; Gael. *breith*; Sans. *bhriti*, birth.]

1. The act or fact of coming into life, or of being born; nativity; generally applied to human beings; as, the *birth* of a son.

2. Lineage; extraction; descent; as, of Grecian *birth*; often used by way of distinction for a descent from noble or honorable parents and ancestors; as, a man of *birth*.

3. The condition to which a person is born; natural state or position; inherited disposition or tendency.

4. That which is born; that which is produced, whether animal or vegetable.

5. The act of bringing forth; as, she had two children at a *birth*.

6. Origin; beginning; as, an empire's *birth*.

Birth stone; a precious stone which is considered to symbolize the influences due to the month of one's birth. Those commonly recognized are: January, garnet; February, amethyst; March, bloodstone; April, diamond; May, emerald; June, pearl; July, ruby; August, sardonyx; September, sapphire; October, opal; November, topaz; December, turquoise.

The new birth; regeneration, or the beginning of a religious life.

Syn.—Parentage, extraction, nativity, family, race, origin, source, rise, lineage, nobility.

birth, *n.* A berth. [Obs.] (is born.)

birth'dāy, *n.* 1. The day on which any person

2. The same day of the same month on and in which a person was born, in any succeeding year; the anniversary of one's nativity.

birth'dāy, *a.* Of or pertaining to the day of one's birth, or its anniversary; as, *birthday* gifts or festivities.

birth'dŏm, *n.* Inheritance by birth; birthright. [Obs.]

birth'ing, *n* See *Berthing.*

birth'less, *a.* Of low extraction. [Rare.]

birth'märk, *n.* Some peculiar mark or blemish found on the body at birth and retained throughout life.

birth'night (-nīt), *n.* The night in which a person is born; also, the anniversary of that night in succeeding years.

birth'plāce, *n.* The town, city, or country, where a person is born. Also, a place of origin or birth, in its more general sense; as, the *birthplace* of freedom.

birth'right (-rīt), *n.* Any right, privilege, or possession into which a person is born, such as an estate descendible by law to an heir, or civil liberty under a free constitution. The word often refers especially to the rights or inheritance of the firstborn.

birth'root, *n.* In botany, a herbaceous plant (*Trillium erectum*) and its astringent rootstock, supposed to possess medicinal properties; birthwort.

birth'-song, *n.* A song sung at the birth of a child

birth'wŏrt, *n.* 1. Any plant of the genus *Aristolochia.*

2. Same as *Birthroot.*

bis, *adv.* [L. *bis*, twice, from *duo*, two.] Twice; a word used to indicate repetition.

bis-, *prefix.* A form of *bi-*, the *s* being added for euphony before *s*, *c*, or a vowel.

bi'sȧ, *n.* 1. An African antelope, *Oryx beisa*; the oryx.

2. A South American monkey, with hairy, non-prehensile tail; the black saki.

bi-sac'cāte, *a.* In botany, having two small sacs, or pouches.

bis-cä'chȧ, *n.* Same as *Viscacha.*

Bis-cāy'ăn, *a.* Of or pertaining to the province of Biscay, Spain.

Bis-cāy'ăn, *n.* A native or inhabitant of the Spanish province of Biscay.

bis'cō-tin, *n.* [Fr.] A confection or biscuit, made of flour, sugar, marmalade, and eggs.

bis'cuit (-kit), *n.* [ME. *bysket*, *biscute*; OFr. *bescoit*, *bescuit*; It. *biscotto*, twice-cooked; L. *bis*, twice, and *coctus*, pp. of *coquere*, to cook.]

1. A kind of unleavened bread, of many varieties, plain, sweet, or fancy, formed into flat thin cakes and baked until crisp; as, ship-*biscuit*. Commonly called *crackers* in the United States, but *biscuits* in England.

2. Bread, raised and shortened or made light with soda or baking powder and baked in tiny loaves, usually with a number in the same pan partially joined together, forming a sheet or batch.

3. Earthenware or porcelain which has undergone the first baking, before it is subjected to the process of glazing.

4. In sculpture, a species of white unglazed porcelain, in which groups and figures are formed in miniature.

Meat biscuit; meat or essence of meat combined with flour and made into biscuit.

bis'cuit-root, *n.* The root of various plants, used as food by the Indians of British Columbia.

bi-scū'tāte, *a.* [*Bi-*, and L. *scutum*, shield.] In botany, resembling two bucklers or shields placed side by side.

bise, *n.* [Fr. *bise*, *bis*, dark brown.] A cold northerly wind prevailing in Switzerland and parts of France, and destructive to vegetation; hence, proverbial for misfortune, or disaster.

bise, *n.* Same as *Bice.*

bi-sect', *v.t.*; bisected, *pt.*, *pp.*; bisecting, *ppr.* [*Bi-*, and L. *sectus*, pp. of *secare*, to cut.] To cut or divide into two parts. In geometry, one line *bisects* another when it crosses it, leaving an equal part of the line on each side of the point where it is crossed.

Biscutate Leaf (*Dionæa muscipula*).

bi-sec'tion, *n.* The act of cutting into two parts; the division of any line or quantity into two equal parts.

bi-sec'tŏr, *n.* 1. One who or that which bisects.

2. In geometry, a straight line which divides an angle or another line into two equal parts

bi-sec'trix, *n.* 1. In crystallography, the line bisecting the angle between the optic axes.

2. In geometry, a bisector.

bi-seg'ment, *n.* One of the parts of a line divided into two equal parts.

bi-sen'nȧ, *n.* See *Mesenna.*

bi-sep'tāte, *a.* [*Bi-*, and L. *sæptum*, a partition.] Having two partitions or septa.

bi-sē'ri-ăl, bi-sē'ri-āte, *a.* Existing in two series.

bi-ser'rāte, *a.* [*Bi-*, and L. *serratus*, from *serra*, a saw.]

1. In botany, doubly serrate, or having the serratures themselves serrate, as in some leaves.

2. In zoölogy, serrate on both sides, as some antennæ.

bi-sē'tōse, bi-sē'tous, *a.* [*Bi-*, and L. *setosus*, from *seta*, a bristle.] Having two bristles.

bi-sette' (-zet'), *n.* [Fr.] A cheap narrow French lace.

bi-sex'ous, *a.* [Obs.] See *Bisexual.*

bi-sex'ū-ăl, *a.* 1. In botany, being of both sexes, as a flower containing both stamens and pistils within the same envelope.

2. In zoölogy, hermaphrodite.

bi-sex'ū-ous, *a.* Bisexual.

bish, *n.* Same as *Bikh.*

bish'ŏp, *n.* [ME. *bishop*; AS. *biscop*, *bisceop*; LL. *episcopus*; Gr. *episkopos*, a bishop, an overseer; *epi*, upon, and *skopos*, from *skopein*, to look.]

1. An overseer; a spiritual superintendent, ruler, or director; applied only once to Christ.

2. In the primitive church, a spiritual overseer; an elder or presbyter; one who had the pastoral care of a church.

3. In the churches maintaining apostolic succession, a prelate superior to the priesthood, consecrated for the spiritual government and direction of a diocese, bishopric, or see; he admits priests to holy orders, and is him self under the rule of an archbishop.

4. In the Methodist Episcopal and some other religious bodies, a church officer higher than a clergyman.

5. One of the pieces in a game of chess, placed next to the royal pieces, and made to resemble a *bishop's* miter.

6. An old mixed drink of port wine, oranges, and sugar, served hot.

7. Formerly, in the United States, a term applied to a woman's bustle.

Bishop sleeve; a wide sleeve sometimes worn by women.

Bishop's length; a canvas measuring fifty-eight by ninety-four inches, used in painting portraits.

bish'ŏp, *v.t.*; bishoped, *pt.*, *pp.*; bishoping, *ppr.* To confirm; to admit solemnly into the church.

bish'ŏp, *v.t.* [From the name of the man who first practised it.] Among horse-dealers, to change the appearance of (a horse), in order to deceive purchasers. [Eng.]

bish'ŏp-bird, *n.* One of the various African weaver-birds.

bish'ŏp-dŏm, *n.* Jurisdiction of a bishop.

bish'ŏp-ly, *adv.* In the manner of a bishop. [Obs.]

bish'ŏp-ly, *a.* Episcopal; bishoplike. [Obs.]

bish'ŏp-rāy, *n.* Same as *Obispo.*

bish'ŏp-ric, *n.* [ME. *bisshoprike*, *bisshopriche*; AS. *bisceoprice*; *bisceop*, a bishop, and *rice*, jurisdiction, kingdom.]

1. A diocese; the district over which the jurisdiction of a bishop extends.

2. The charge of instructing and governing in spiritual concerns; the office of a bishop.

bish'ŏp's-cap, *n.* In botany, any species of the genus *Mitella*; miterwort.

bish'ŏp's-eld"ẽr, *n.* The European goutweed.

bish'ŏp's-mī"tẽr, *n.* 1. A fetid bug injurious to fruit.

2. A miter-shell.

bish'ŏp's-stool, *n.* The see or seat of a bishop.

bish'ŏp's-weed, *n.* A name common to different species of plants of the parsley family; bishop's-elder; goutweed.

bish'ŏp's-wŏrt, *n.* 1. The wood-betony.

2. Fennel-flower.

bis'ie, *v.t.* To employ; to busy. [Obs.]

bis-il'i-ac, *a.* In anatomy, relating to the two crests of the iliac bones; also spelled *bi-iliac.*

bi-sil'i-cāte, *n.* A salt of metasilicic acid, the oxygen of the silica being in the ratio of two to one to the oxygen of the base.

bisk, *n.* [Fr. *bisque.*]

1. Soup or broth, made by boiling several sorts of meat together. [Same as *Bisque.*]

2. A variety of ice-cream in which fine cakes are mixed.

3. In tennis or croquet, odds given to a weaker player.

bis'ket, *n.* A biscuit. [Obs.]

bis'mẽr, bis'măr, *n.* Disgrace; shame; abuse. [Obs.]

bis'mẽr, *n.* 1. A kind of primitive steelyard. [Scot.]

2. In zoölogy, the fifteen-spined stickleback.

bis-mil'lăh, *interj.* [Ar., in the name of God.] An expletive common among the Mohammedans.

bis'mite, *n.* A yellow earthy bismuth trioxid, or bismuth ocher.

bis'muth, *n.* A metal of a yellowish or reddish-white color and a lamellar texture. It is somewhat harder than lead, and scarcely, if at all, malleable, being so brittle as to break easily under the hammer and reducible to powder. Its internal face or fracture exhibits large shining plates, variously disposed. It is often found in a native state, crystallized in rhombs or octahedrons, or in the form of dendrites, or thin laminæ investing the ores of other metals, particularly cobalt. It fuses easily and is useful in the arts and manufactures.

Bismuth ocher; native oxid of bismuth; flowers of bismuth.

bis'muth-ăl, *a.* Consisting of bismuth, or containing it.

bis'muth-ic, *a.* Pertaining to bismuth; containing bismuth in its higher valence; as, *bismuthic* acid.

bis-muth-if'ẽr-ous, *a.* Yielding bismuth.

bis'muth-in, bis'muth-ine, *n.* Same as *Bismuthinite.*

bis-muth'in-ite, *n.* Bismuth trisulphid, found native in orthorhombic crystals isomorphic with stibnite.

bis'muth-ous, *a.* Of, pertaining to, or containing bismuth, in its lower valence.

bis'muth-yl, *n.* The bismuthal radical BiO.

bis'mū-tite, *n.* An uncrystallized brownish or greenish carbonate of bismuth; also written *bismuthite.*

bi'sŏn, *n.* [Fr. *bison*; L. *bison*, a wild ox.] The name of two bovine quadrupeds, (a) *Bos* or *Bonassus bison*, the European *bison* or aurochs; (b) *Bison americanus*, the American *bison*, a wild animal now extinct except in captivity, formerly roaming the plains of central and western United States in herds. The fore parts are massive and shaggy, the hair being rust-colored, and the horns black and curving upward. Commonly, but incorrectly, called *buffalo.*

American Bison.

bi-spi'nōse, *a.* [*Bi-*, and L. *spina*, the spine.] Having two spines.

bi'spōre, *n.* [*Bi-*, and Gr. *sporos*, a sowing.] One of a pair of spores produced by cell-division in certain algæ.

bi-spōr'ous, *a.* Having the qualities of a bispore; two-spored.

bisque (bisk), *n.* In ceramics, same as *biscuit.*

bisque, *n.* [Fr.] In tennis, etc., same as *bisk.*

bisque, *n.* [Fr.] A thick rich soup made from meat or fish, especially crabs and lobsters.

bis-sex'tile, *n.* [L. *bissextilis*, leap-year, from *bissextus* (*bis* and *sextus*), the *sixth* day before the calends of March, or twenty-fourth day of February, which was reckoned *twice* every fourth year, by the intercalation of a day.] Leap-year; every fourth year, in which a day is added to the month of February, on account of the excess of 6 hours which the civil year contains, above 365 days. This excess is 11 minutes, 14 seconds too much; that is, it exceeds by that much the real year, or the period of the annual revolution of the earth. Hence, at the end of every century divisible by 400 it is necessary to retain the bissextile day, and to suppress it at the end of those centuries which are not divisible by 400.

bis-sex'tile, *a.* Pertaining to leap-year.

bis'sŏn, *a.* Purblind. [Obs.]

bis'tēr, bis'tre (-tēr), *n.* [Fr. *bistre*, a dark brown color.] A brown pigment extracted from the soot of wood.

bī-stip'ūled, *a.* Having two stipules.

bis'tort, *n.* [*Bi-*, and L. *tortus*, pp. of *torquere*, to twist.] A plant, *Polygonum Bistorta*; so called because of its twisted root; popularly called *snakeweed.*

bis'tōu-ry, *n.* [Fr. *bistouri*, a bistoury; OFr. *bistorie*, a dagger.] A surgical instrument, the common form of which has a recurving blade; used in minor operations.

bis'tre, *n.* See *Bister.*

bi-sul'çāte, *a.* [*Bi-*, and L. *sulcatus*, pp. of *sulcare*, to furrow.]

1. Two-furrowed.

2. In zoölogy, cloven-footed, or with two hoofed digits.

bī-sul'çous, *a.* Bisulcate. [Obs.]

bī-sul'phāte, *n.* [*Bi-*, and L. *sulfur*, brimstone.] A salt of sulphuric acid in which one-half of the hydrogen of the acid is replaced by a base.

bī-sul'phid (*or* -fid), *n.* A sulphid in which the molecules contain two atoms of sulphur to one of other constituents; a disulphid.

bī-sul'phite, *n.* A salt of sulphurous acid in which one-half of the hydrogen of the acid is replaced by a base.

bī-sul'phū-ret, *n.* A bisulphid. [Obs.]

bit, *n.* [ME. *bite*, a bit, morsel, AS. *bita*, a bit, something bitten off; *bītan*, to bite.]

1. A small piece or morsel of food.

2. A small piece of anything; sometimes used absolutely for a small piece of scenery suitable for a picture.

> Power to grant a patent for stamping round *bits* of copper. —Swift.

> There are several *bits* at Valmontone to delight an artist. —Hare.

The word is often used in certain phrases expressive of extent or degree; thus, a *bit* older means somewhat older; not a *bit*, not a whit, not in any degree; *a bit of* a humorist, somewhat of a humorist.

> Your case is not a *bit* clearer than it was seven years ago. —Arbuthnot.

3. One of several small coins formerly in use in the South and West; now applied colloquially to the sum of twelve and one-half cents, a quarter being two *bits.*

4. The metal part of a bridle which is inserted in the mouth of a horse, and its appendages, to which the reins are fastened.

> We have strict statutes and most biting laws, The needful *bits* and curbs to headstrong steeds. —Shak.

5. The name common to all those exchangeable boring tools for wood applied by means of a brace. The similar tools used for metal are termed *drills* or *drill-bits.* The typical form is the *shellbit* (fig. *a*), which is shaped like a gouge, for shearing the fibers round the circumference of the hole. The *center-bit* (fig. *b*) is another typical form, of which there are many modifications. The *half-round bit* (fig. *c*) is employed for enlarging holes in metal. The *rose-bit* (fig. *d*) is cylindrical, and terminates in a truncated cone, the oblique surface of which is cut into teeth like the rose-countersink, of which it is a modification. It is also used for enlarging holes of considerable depth in metals and hard woods.

Bits.

6. By resemblance, one of several tools or parts of tools; as, (a) the wedge-shaped portion or edge of an ax or like tool; (b) a plane-blade; (c) the blade-like portion of a key, to be inserted in a lock and engage the bolt; the web.

Syn.—Piece, part, fragment, morsel.

bit, *v.t.*; bitted, *pt., pp.*; bitting, *ppr.* To bridle; to put the bit in the mouth of.

bit, *v.*, past tense and past participle of *bite.*

bi-tāke', *v.t.* To betake. [Obs.]

bi-tan'gent, *a.* and *n.* I. *a.* Pertaining to or possessing the qualities of a bitangent.

II. *n.* A straight line that touches a curve at two points.

bī-tär'trāte, *n.* [*Bi-*, and Fr. *tartre*, from LL. *tartarum*, tartar.] A tartrate in which one-half of the replaceable hydrogen of tartaric acid has been replaced; acid tartrate.

bitch (bich), *n.* [ME. *bicche*; AS. *bicce*, bitch.]

1. The female of the canine kind, as of the dog, wolf, and fox.

2. A vulgar epithet applied to a woman, implying obscenity.

bitch'wood, *n.* A tree, *Lonchocarpus latifolius*, found in tropical America; also, its wood.

bīte, *v.t.*; bit, *pt.*; biting, *ppr.*; bitten *or* bit, *pp.* [ME. *biten*; AS. *bītan*, to bite.]

1. To break or crush with the teeth, as in eating; to pierce with the teeth or proboscis, as a serpent or insect; to seize with the teeth, as a dog.

2. To cause a sharp or smarting pain to; to make to smart; to pinch or nip, as with frost; to blast, blight, or injure in various ways; as, pepper *bites* the mouth.

3. To take fast hold of; to grip or catch into or on, so as to act with effect; to get purchase from, as by friction; as, the anchor *bites* the ground; the file *bites* the iron; the wheels *bite* the rails.

4. To cheat; to trick.

5. In etching, to corrode or eat into, by nitric or other acid; as, to *bite* a steel plate; generally with *in*; as, the plate is now *bitten in.*

To bite the tongue; to maintain fixed silence.

To bite the dust or *the ground*; to fall; to be thrown or struck down; to be vanquished or humbled.

To bite the thumb; formerly, a mark of contempt designed to provoke a quarrel.

bīte, *v.i.* 1. To have a habit of biting; to injure by biting or cutting, as if by teeth; as, the dog *bites.*

2. To seize with the teeth or mouth; to take a bait.

3. To take and keep hold; to grip or catch into another object, so as to act on it with effect, obtain purchase or leverage-power from it, and the like; as, the anchor *bites.*

bīte, *n.* [ME. *byte, bite*; AS. *bītan*, to bite.]

1. The seizure of anything by the teeth or with the mouth; specifically, the seizure of a bait; as, the *bite* of a dog; the *bite* of a fish.

2. The wound made by the teeth or other organ connected with the mouth; as, a mosquito *bite.*

3. As much as is taken at once by biting; a mouthful; a bit; as, a *bite* of bread.

4. A cheat; a trick; a fraud.

5. A sharper; one who cheats. [Rare.]

6. In printing, that part of the impression which is improperly printed, owing to the frisket not being sufficiently cut away.

7. The catch or hold that one object or part of an apparatus has on another; as, the *bite* of an anchor on the ground; the *bite* of the wheels of a locomotive on the rails.

bī-tem'pō-răl, *a.* [*Bi-*, and L. *tempora*, the temples.] Pertaining to the two temporal bones.

bīt'ēr, *n.* 1. One who bites; that which bites; a fish apt to take bait.

2. One who cheats or defrauds.

bī-tēr'nāte, *a.* [*Bi-*, and L. *terni*, thrice.] In botany, doubly ternate, as when a petiole has three ternate leaflets.

bī-tēr'nāte-ly, *adv.* In a biternate manner.

bī'thē-ism, *n.* [*Bi-*, and Gr. *theos*, god.] Dualism, or a belief in the existence of two gods.

bi'ti, *n.* A native name for the East Indian rosewood-tree, *Dalbergia latifolia.*

bīt'ing, *a.* Sharp; severe; sarcastic; as, a *biting* affliction; a *biting* jest.

bīt'ing-ly, *adv.* In a sarcastic or caustic manner.

bit'less, *a.* Not having a bit or bridle.

bi'tō, bi'tō-tree, *n.* [Native name.] A small tree, *Balanites Ægyptiaca*, found in dry tropical regions of Asia and Africa; it has valuable wood and bark and an edible fruit.

bit'stock, *n.* The handle or stock by which a boring-bit is held and rotated; a brace.

bitt, *v.t.* To put round the bitts; as, to *bitt* the cable in order to fasten or slacken it. [See *Bitts.*]

bit'tà-çle, *n.* A binnacle. [Obs.]

bit'ten, *v.*, past participle of *bite.*

bit'ten, *a.* In botany, terminating suddenly and irregularly.

bit'tēr, *n.* In nautical language, a turn of the cable which is round the bitts.

bit'tēr, *a.* [ME. *biter*; AS. *biter*, *bitor*, bitter, from *bītan*, to bite.]

1. Sharp or biting to the taste; acrid.

2. Sharp; cruel; severe; as, *bitter* enmity.

3. Sharp; reproachful; sarcastic; as, *bitter* words.

4. Sharp to the feeling; piercing; painful; as, a *bitter* cold day, or *bitter* blast.

5. Painful to the mind; calamitous; poignant; as, a *bitter* fate.

6. Afflicted; distressed; as, to make one's life *bitter.*

7. Hurtful; very sinful.

> It is an evil thing and *bitter.* —Jer. ii. 19.

8. Mournful; distressing; expressive of misery; as, a *bitter* complaint or lamentation.

Bitter apple, cucumber, or *gourd*; same as *Colocynth.*

Bitter cress; a name applied to any plant of the genus *Cardamine.*

Bitter earth; the common name for calcined magnesia.

Bitter principle; a term applied to certain products arising from the action of nitric acid upon animal and vegetable matters, and having an intensely bitter taste.

Bitter salt; Epsom salts; magnesium sulphate.

Bitter vetch; (a) *Ervum Ervilia*, a lentil cultivated for fodder; and (b) all the species of the genus *Orobus*, now frequently included in the genus *Lathyrus.*

To the bitter end; to the last extremity, as in defeat or death.

Syn.—Harsh, sour, sharp, tart, acrimonious, sarcastic, severe, sad, afflictive, intense, stinging, pungent, acrid, cutting.

bit'tēr, *n.* 1. Anything bitter; bitterness; as, the *bitter* and the sweet of life.

2. A bitter concoction. [See *Bitters.*]

bit'tēr, *v.t.* To make bitter. [Rare.]

bit'tēr-blāin, *n.* A name given by the creoles in Guiana to *Vandellia diffusa*, a herb possessing medicinal properties.

bit'tēr-blo͝om, *n.* The North American centaury.

bit'tēr-bump, *n.* The European bittern; the butterbump. [Eng.]

bit'tēr-end, *n.* Nautically, that part of a cable which is abaft the bitts, and therefore within board, when the ship rides at anchor.

bit'tēr-fụl, *a.* Full of bitterness. [Obs.]

bit'tēr-grass, *n.* Colicroot.

bit'tēr-hērb, *n.* The European centaury.

bit'tēr-ing, *n.* A compound of bitter character employed in the adulteration of beer.

bit'tēr-ish, *a.* Bitter in a moderate degree.

bit'tēr-ish-ness, *n.* The quality of being bitter.

bit'tēr-king, *n.* A shrub belonging to the quassia family, found in the East Indies.

bit'tēr-ling, *n.* A fresh-water fish, *Rhodeus amarus*, of Europe.

bit'tēr-ly, *adv.* In a bitter manner.

bit'tērn, *n.* [ME. *bitter*, *bitoure*; OFr. *butor*, the bittern bird.] A bird of the genus *Botaurus*, a native of Europe. It has long legs and neck, and stalks among reeds and sedge, feeding upon fish. It makes a singular noise, called by Dryden *bumping*, and by Goldsmith *booming. Botaurus lentiginosus* is the American species.

European bittern, *Botaurus stellaris.*

bit'tērn, *n.* 1. In salt-works, the brine remaining after the salt is concreted. This, being ladled off, and the salt taken out of the pan, is returned, and, being again boiled, yields more salt. It is used in the preparation of Epsom salt (sulphate of magnesia).

2. A very bitter compound of quassia, used in adulterating beer.

bit′tẽr-ness, *n.* [ME. *bitternesse*, from AS. *biternys*, bitterness.] The state or quality of being bitter; figuratively, extreme enmity; sharpness; severity of temper; biting sarcasm; painful affliction; deep distress of mind.

In the gall of bitterness; in a state of extreme impiety or enmity to God.

Root of bitterness; a dangerous error, or schism, tending to draw persons to apostasy.

Syn.—Acrimony, asperity, harshness, spite, grief, malignity, distress.

bit′tẽr-nut, *n.* The swamp-hickory, *Carya amara*.

bit′tẽr-oak, *n.* The *Quercus Cerris*, a very common European oak-tree.

bit′tẽr-root, *n.* A plant with nutritious roots, flourishing in the mountainous regions of Montana and Idaho. The Bitter Root Mountains and River take their names from it.

bit′tẽrs, *n.pl.* [Pl. of *bitter*.] A liquor in which bitter herbs or roots are steeped; generally a spirituous liquor.

bit′tẽr-spär, *n.* See *Dolomite*.

bit′tẽr-sweet, *a.* Sweet and bitter alternately, especially bitter after sweet; figuratively, pleasant but painful.

bit′tẽr-sweet, *n.* 1. Anything bittersweet in character.

2. The name given to a kind of apple.

3. In botany, (a) *Solanum Dulcamara*, the woody nightshade; (b) *Celastrus scandens*, an American climbing plant.

bit′tẽr-weed, *n.* A variety of ragweed, *Ambrosia artemisiæfolia*, growing in America.

bit′tẽr-wood, *n.* A tree of the West Indies which yields Jamaica quassia; also, the wood of the tree.

bit′tẽr-wŏrt, *n.* The yellow gentian, *Gentiana lutea*, having a remarkably bitter taste.

bit′tŏck, *n.* [Scot.] A little piece of anything; a short distance.

bit′tŏr, **bit′tŏur**, *n.* The bittern. [Obs.]

bitts, *n.pl.* A frame of two strong pieces of timber or iron fixed perpendicularly in the fore part of a ship, on which to fasten the cables. There are sheet-*bitts*, pawl-*bitts*, carrick-*bitts*, etc., used for various purposes aboard ship.

bi-tūme′, *n.* Bitumen. [Rare.]

bi-tūmed′, *a.* Smeared with bitumen. [Rare.]

bi-tū′men, *n.* [L.] 1. A name given by Latin writers to hydrocarbons now known by different names, from naphtha, the most fluid, to petroleum and mineral tar, which are less so, thence to maltha, which is more or less cohesive, and lastly to asphalt and elastic *bitumen* (or elaterite), which are solid.

2. In painting, a mixture of asphaltum with a drying-oil.

bi-tū′mi-nāte, *v.t.*; bituminated, *pt.*, *pp.*; bituminating, *ppr.* To impregnate or coat with bitumen.

bi-tū-mi-nif′ẽr-ous, *a.* [L. *bitumen*, bitumen, and *ferre*, to produce.] Producing bitumen.

bi-tū″mi-ni-zā′tion, *n.* The process of forming bitumen.

bi-tū′mi-nize, *v.t.*; bituminized, *pt.*, *pp.*; bituminizing, *ppr.* To form into, coat, or impregnate with bitumen.

bi-tū′mi-noid, *a.* Bitumen-like.

bi-tū′mi-nous, *a.* Having the qualities of bitumen; compounded with bitumen; containing bitumen.

Bituminous cement or *bituminous mastic*; a cement composed chiefly of asphalt, used for roofing, paving, etc.

Bituminous coal; coal containing from thirty to fifty per cent of volatile matter; commonly called *soft coal*.

Bituminous limestone; limestone of a lamellar structure, susceptible of polish, brown or black in color, and, when rubbed, emitting an unpleasant smell. That of Dalmatia is so charged with bitumen that it may be cut like soap.

Bituminous shale; an argillaceous shale, impregnated with bitumen, usually accompanying coal.

bi′ū-ret, *n.* [*Bi-*, and L. *urina*, urine.] In chemistry, a crystalline, nitrogenous product of urea.

bi′vā-lence (*or* biv′ȧ-lence), *n.* [*Bi-*, and L. *valens*, ppr. of *valere*, to be strong.] A valence twice that of hydrogen.

biv′ȧ-len-cy, *n.* Bivalence.

bi′vā-lent (*or* biv′ȧ-lent), *a.* In chemistry, having double valence; dyad.

bi′valve, *n.* [Fr. *bivalve*, from L. *bis*, two, and *valva*, door.]

1. A molluscous animal, having a shell consisting of two parts or valves, joined together by an elastic ligament at the cardo or hinge, or a shell consisting of two parts, which open and shut. The clam closes its shell by contracting two transverse muscles attached to the shell inside; the oyster has but one such muscle. [See *Mollusca*.]

2. In botany, a separable, two-part seed-case, as in the common pea. [Rare.]

Bivalve Animal of *Mya arenaria*.

a, Anterior adductor muscle; *b*, Posterior adductor muscle; *c*, Heart; *d*, Mantle with its fringe; *e*, Body; *f*, Foot; *g*, Gills or branchiæ; *h*, Mouth; *i*, One of the labial tentacles; *k*, Exhalent siphon; *l*, Branchial siphon.

bi′valve, *a.* Having two shells or valves which open and shut, as the oyster, or two parts or valves which open at maturity, as the seed-vessels of certain plants.

bi′valved, *a.* Same as *Bivalve*.

Bi-val′vi-ȧ, *n.pl.* In zoölogy, a term formerly used for the class *Lamellibranchiata*.

Bivalve Shell of *Cytherea chione*.

A, Right valve; B, Left valve; A, B, Thickness; C, Dorsal margin; D, Ventral margin; E, Anterior side or front margin; F, Posterior side or hinder margin; G, Umbo; H, Hinge and hinge teeth; *o*, Cardinal tooth; *xx*, Lateral teeth; I, Ligament, ligament pit or groove; J, Lunule; K, Anterior muscular impression; L, Posterior muscular impression; M, Pallial impression; N, Abdominal impression; O, Sinus; C, D, Height or breadth; E, F, Length.

bi-val′vous, *a.* Having two valves.

bi-val′vū-lăr, *a.* Bivalvous.

bi-vault′ed, *a.* Having two vaults or arches.

bi-vec′tŏr, *n.* In mathematics, a term made up of two vectors, one of which is taken $\sqrt{-1}$ times.

bi-ven′trăl, *a.* Having two bellies or belly-shaped parts; as, a *biventral* muscle.

biv′i-ăl, *a.* Of or pertaining to the bivium.

biv′i-ous (*or* bi′vi-us), *a.* [L. *bivius*, having two passages, from *bis*, two, and *via*, passage.] Having two ways, or leading two ways.

biv′i-um, *n.* [L. *bivius*, having two passages.] In zoölogy, the two posterior ambulacra of echinoderms, the three anterior ones being known as the *trivium*.

biv′ouac (biv′wak *or* biv′oo-ak), *n.* [Fr. *bivouac*; probably from G. dialect. *beiwacht*, lit. a by-watch; *bei*, by, and *wacht*, a guard.] An encampment of soldiers in the open air without tents, each remaining dressed and with his weapons by him; hence, figuratively, a position or situation demanding extreme watchfulness.

The *bivouac* of life. —Longfellow.

biv′ouac, *v.i.*; bivouacked (-wakt), *pt.*, *pp.*; bivouacking, *ppr.* To watch; to encamp in the open air.

bi-week′ly, *a.* Occurring or appearing at intervals of two weeks; fortnightly.

bi-week′ly, *n.* A periodical issued fortnightly.

bi-week′ly, *adv.* Once every two weeks.

bi-wreye′ (-rā′), *v.t.* To bewray. [Obs.]

Bix′ȧ, *n.* A genus of plants of the Indian plum family, containing a few species of small trees natives of tropical America. The pulp of the fruit of the *Bixa Orellana* affords the arnotto of commerce. [See *Arnotto*.]

Bix-ā′cē-æ, *n.pl.* The Indian plum family, tropical trees and shrubs having simple leaves and showy axillary or terminal flowers.

bix-ā′ceous, *a.* Of or pertaining to the *Bixa* or the *Bixaceæ*.

bix′in, *n.* 1. The orange coloring principle, $C_{16}H_{26}O_2$, of arnotto. It is obtained in small yellowish crystals.

2. A variety of arnotto, having six to ten times the coloring power of common arnotto, from quicker extraction.

Bi-zan′tine, *a.* Same as *Byzantine*.

bi-zärre′, *a.* [Fr.] Odd; fantastic; whimsical; extravagant.

biz-cä′chȧ, *n.* See *Viscacha*.

bi-zet′, *n.* [Fr. *biseau*, a sloping edge.] The upper faceted portion of a brilliant-cut diamond which projects from the setting, having one-third of the full depth of the gem. [See *Brilliant*, n.]

blab, *v.t.*; blabbed, *pt.*, *pp.*; blabbing, *ppr.* [Dan. *blabbre*, babble; an onomatopoetic word.] To utter or tell in a thoughtless manner; to publish (secrets or trifles) without discretion.

blab, *v.i.* To tattle; to tell tales.

blab, *n.* [ME. *blabbe*.] A babbler; a telltale; one who betrays secrets.

blab′bẽr, *n.* [ME. *blaberen*, to stammer; an onomatopoetic word.] A tattler; a telltale.

black, *a.* [ME. *blak*, *blek*, from AS. *blæc*, black.]

1. Of the darkest color; the opposite of *white*. A surface perfectly *black* is absolutely incapable of reflecting light, but the word is often used with less precision to signify very dark in hue, and, as applied to persons, more or less dark in skin or complexion.

Black men are pearls in beauteous ladies' eyes. —Shak.

2. Destitute of light, or nearly so.

In the twilight, in the evening, in the *black* and dark night. —Prov. vii. 9.

3. Figuratively, dismal, gloomy, sullen, forbidding, or the like; destitute of moral light or goodness; mournful; calamitous; evil; wicked; atrocious; thus Shakspere speaks of *black* deeds, thoughts, envy, vengeance, tidings, despair, etc.

Black act; in English history, statute 9 of George I.'s reign, which decreed that to appear armed in any park or warren, etc., or to hunt or steal deer, etc., with the face blacked or disguised, was felony.

Black and blue; having the dark livid color of a bruise in the flesh, which is accompanied with a mixture of blue.

Black angel; a fish of the family *Chætodontidæ*; an angel-fish.

Black antimony; antimonious sulphid, Sb_2S_3, occurring as the mineral stibnite, the principal ore of antimony.

Black art; necromancy; magic; the art of being able to perform wonderful feats by supernatural means, especially means derived from the assistance of the powers of evil.

Black bass; (a) an American game- and food-fish, *Micropterus dolomieu*, found westward as far as Iowa. The name is also given to the large-mouthed or straw bass, *Micropterus salmoides*, having as wide a range. (b) The sea-bass or blackfish.

Black bear; see *Bear*.

Black belt; that territory in the southern part of the U. S. where the negroes predominate.

Black bonnet; the European reed-bunting.

Black book; same as *Black-book*.

Black boy; the Australian grass-tree.

Black bur; yellow avens or the blessed herb, *Geum strictum*.

Black canker; a disease in turnips and other crops produced by a species of caterpillar.

Black cattle; animals of the genus *Bos*, whatever may be their color, raised for slaughter, as distinguished from dairy animals. [Eng.]

Black death; an Oriental plague which, originating in China, spread over Asia and Europe in the fourteenth century.

Black earth; common black dirt or mold.

Black flag; the flag of a pirate.

Black flux; a mixture of carbonate of potash and charcoal, obtained by deflagrating tartar with half its weight of niter.

Black Friar; the English name for a monk of the Dominican order.

Black hand, see *Mafia*.

Black hole; any subterranean or dark prison: commonly used in reference to the Black Hole of Calcutta, an unventilated room about eighteen feet square. Of the one hundred and forty-six prisoners confined there June 20, 1756, only twenty-three came forth alive next morning.

Black horse; a fish, the Missouri sucker, *Cycleptus elongatus*.

Black letter; a term applied to the Old English Gothic or modern text-letter, in which the early English manuscripts were written, and the first English books were printed.

This line is set in black letter.

Black list; a list of persons debarred from employment or credit, or thought unworthy of trust.

Black manganese; the insoluble black substance, manganese dioxid, MnO_2.

Black Maria; a prison-van. [Slang.]

Black Monday; Easter Monday; specifically, April 14, 1360, recorded in history as being so cold that many men of Edward III.'s army investing Paris died from exposure.

Black monks; the Black Friars.

Black oak; the black-barked oak, *Quercus tinctoria*.

Black ocher; a variety of mineral black, combined with iron and alluvial clay; wad.

Black pigment; a very fine, light, carbonaceous substance, or lampblack, prepared chiefly for the manufacture of printers' ink, and obtained by burning common coal-tar.

Black plate; sheet-iron before tinning.

Black pudding; a kind of pudding made of blood, suet, and various other constituents; blood-pudding.

Black quarter; splenic fever; anthrax.

Black rent; anciently, rent paid in produce or copper coin.

Black rod; in England, the usher belonging to the order of the Garter; so called from the black rod which he carries. He is of the king's chamber and usher of parliament.

Black rust; grain-blight, a dark-colored fungus attacking cereals, especially wheat.

Black sheep; a member of a family or society

guilty of loose conduct and unlike the other members.

Black silver; the mineral stephanite.

Black tea; a generic name for various Chinese teas, the principal of which are bohea, congou, pekoe, and souchong.

Black tin; tin ore made ready for smelting, having been finely powdered.

Black turpeth; the di- or sub-oxid of mercury, commonly called the gray, ash, or black oxid.

Black vomit; a copious vomiting of dark-colored matter; a sign of approaching death in yellow fever.

Black walnut; the American walnut, *Juglans nigra.*

black, *n.* [ME. *blak*, *blek*, from AS. *blæc*, black.]

1. The darkest color, or rather the negation of all color; the opposite of *white*; a black dye or pigment or a hue produced by such; as, this cloth has a good *black*.

2. A black part of something, as the black part of the eye; the opening in the iris; in opposition to the *white*.

3. A black dress or mourning; as, to be clothed in *black*; formerly used in the plural; as, to put on *blacks*.

4. A small flake of soot.

A fog that tastes of *blacks* and smells of decomposed frost. —Young.

5. One with the face blacked or disguised; specifically, a deer-stealer. [Obs.]

6. A member of one of the dark-colored races; a negro or other dark-skinned person.

7. A stain or smear.

Defiling her white lawn of chastity with ugly *blacks* of lust. —Rowley.

8. [*pl.*] Ink used in copperplate printing, prepared from the charred husks of the grape and the residue of the wine-press.

Black and white; (a) writing or print; as, a statement in *black and white*; (b) a sketch, drawing, or any picture without color.

Brunswick black; see *Japan black*.

Ivory black; carbonized ivory or bones.

black, *v.t.*; blacked, *pt.*, *pp.*; blacking, *ppr.* To make black; to blacken; to soil.

black′å-mo͝or, *n.* A negro, or black person.

black-and-tan, *n.* A dog having black and yellowish-brown markings; also used attributively.

black′-ash, *n.* Crude carbonate of soda.

black′-å-vised (-vist), *a.* Of dark complexion; swarthy.

black′ball, *n.* 1. A composition used by engravers, shoemakers, etc.; called also *heelball*.

2. An adverse vote rejecting a candidate for membership; the ball or cube used in voting adversely.

black′ball, *v.t.*; blackballed, *pt.*, *pp.*; blackballing, *ppr.* To reject, as in a society, by putting blackballs into a ballot-box; to ostracize.

black′band, *n.* A carbonate of iron, valuable as an iron ore.

black′-bee″tle, *n.* A cockroach.

black′bel″ly, *n.* The blueback or American herring.

black′ber″ry, *n.* One of several species of fruit-bearing plants of the genus *Rubus*; also, the fruit itself, distinguished from the raspberry by retaining the drupelets when ripe. Many varieties are largely cultivated.

black′bird, *n.* 1. A name given to several species of birds of the family *Icteridæ*, common throughout North America. The marsh or red-winged *blackbird* is *Agelæus phœniceus*; the crow-*blackbird*, *Quiscalus purpureus*, etc.

2. In England, the European thrush, *Turdus merula*.

Blackbird (*Turdus merula*).

3. A cant term among slave-traders for a negro or Polynesian.

black′board, *n.* A board or plaster wall painted black, used in schools and lecture-rooms for displaying writing and diagrams.

black′-book, *n.* 1. A record-book for listing violations of rules at some colleges.

2. A book for recording names of those blackballed in a secret order.

3. One of several historical books, as (a) a book of the Exchequer in England, said to have been composed in 1175 by Gervais of Tilbury; (b) a book compiled under Henry VIII., containing a detailed account of the enormities practised in religious houses.

4. A book treating of the black art.

Also written *black book*.

black′-browed, *a.* Having black eyebrows; dismal; threatening; as, a *black-browed* gust.

black′-buck, *n.* An antelope, as either the Indian or sable antelope.

black′cap, *n.* 1. A bird, the chickadee; also, the mock nightingale, *Sylvia atricapilla*, of Europe.

2. In cookery, an apple roasted till black, to be served in a dish of boiled custard.

3. The raspberry shrub; also, its fruit.

black′-cat, *n.* A marten, the fisher.

black′coat, *n.* A common and familiar name for a clergyman, as bluecoat is for a policeman.

black′cock, *n.* The English name for the heath-cock, the male of the black-grouse, *Tetrao tetrix*, a gallinaceous fowl of Europe and Asia. The female and young are called *gray hen* and *poults*, respectively.

Blackcock (*Tetrao tetrix*).

black′-drȧft, *n.* A cathartic composed of senna, magnesia, fennel, etc.

black′-drop, *n.* A liquid preparation of opium in vinegar.

black′en, *v.t.*; blackened, *pt.*, *pp.*; blackening, *ppr.* To make black; to cloud; to soil; to sully; as, vices *blacken* character.

Syn.—Befoul, defame, calumniate, dishonor, asperse, traduce, malign.

black′en, *v.i.* To grow black or dark.

black′en-ẽr, *n.* One who blackens or maligns.

black′-eyed (-īd), *a.* Having black eyes.

Black′feet, *n.pl.* A tribe of North American Indians of the Algonkin stock, formerly widespread and powerful.

black′fel″lōw, *n.* An aboriginal of Australia or Tasmania.

black′fin, *n.* Same as *Bluefin*.

black′fish, *n.* 1. The caaing-whale or a cetacean of an allied genus.

2. A name given to different fishes; as (a) the New England tautog; (b) the common sea-bass or an allied fish; (c) *Centrolophus pompilus*, of Europe; (d) an Alaskan food-fish, *Dallia pectoralis*; (e) in Scotland, a foul or spawning salmon.

black′-flēa, *n.* A coleopterous insect, *Haltica nemorum*, the turnip-flea.

black′-flȳ, *n.* 1. The bean-plant louse, *Aphis fabæ*.

2. A stinging simuliid gnat found in New York and New England.

Black′foot, *n.* One of the Blackfeet, a tribe of North American Indians.

black′-gāme, *n.* The black-grouse.

black′-grȧss, *n.* 1. An American rush, *Juncus Gerardi*.

2. An English grass, *Alopecurus agrestis*.

black′-grouse, *n.* The European grouse, *Tetrao tetrix*.

black′guärd (blag′gärd), *n.* One who uses scurrilous language; a rough; a scamp.

Syn.—Scoundrel, rascal, rapscallion, black-leg, villain.

black′guärd, *a.* Scurrilous; abusive; vicious.

black′guärd, *v.t.* To revile; to abuse scurrilously.

black′guärd-ism, *n.* The conduct of a blackguard.

black′guärd-ly, *a.* and *adv.* I. *a.* Scurrilous; abusive; rascally.

II. *adv.* In the manner of a blackguard.

black′-gum, *n.* The pepperidge *Nyssa multiflora*.

black′head (-hed), *n.* 1. The scaup-duck.

2. A filled pore; comedo.

black′heärt, *n.* A dark-colored, heart-shaped cherry.

black′-heärt″ed, *a.* Having a black or malignant heart.

black′ing, *n.* That which makes black; specifically, a preparation for polishing shoes, stoves, etc.

black′ish, *a.* Somewhat black or dark.

black′-jack, *n.* 1. A large leathern vessel in which beer was generally served in former times, now superseded by vessels of metal, etc.

2. A trade name for caramel used as an adulterant for coffee and other staples.

3. In mining, zinc sulphid. [Prov. Eng.]

4. An oak, *Quercus nigra*.

5. A pirate's flag or ensign.

6. A small bludgeon-like weapon.

Leathern Black-jacks.

black′knot, *n.* A fungoid growth, *Sphæria morbosa*, or the wart-like mass it produces on various fruit-trees.

black′lead (-led), *v.t.* To cover or polish with graphite or plumbago.

black′lead, *n.* 1. Plumbago; graphite.

2. A pencil of graphite.

black′leg, *n.* 1. A professional gambler and cheat; a sharper.

2. A disease of animals; anthrax.

black′-let″tẽr, *a.* 1. Written or printed in black letter; as, a *black-letter* manuscript or book.

2. Studious of black letter or old books; as, a *black-letter* man.

Black-letter days; commonplace or ordinary days, not marked on the calendar by red letters.

black′list, *v.t.* To put upon a black list; to proscribe; to boycott.

black′ly, *adv.* Darkly; atrociously; threateningly.

black′māil, *n.* [Lit. black rent, from ME. *maille*; OFr. *maille*, a coin.]

1. A certain rate of money, corn, cattle, or other things, anciently paid, in the north of England, to certain men, who were allied to robbers, to be by them protected from pillage.

2. Anything, as money, extorted by means of threats of exposure or danger.

3. Black rent, or rent paid in produce or inferior money. [Obs.]

black′māil, *v.t.* To extort by threats.

black′māil″ẽr, *n.* One who blackmails.

black′māil″ing, *n.* and *a.* I. *n.* The act or practice of levying blackmail.

II. *a.* Pertaining to blackmail.

black′mo͝or, *n.* Same as *Blackamoor*.

black′-mouthed, *a.* Using foul or scurrilous language.

black′-neb, *n.* The black-billed or carrion crow.

black′ness, *n.* The quality of being black; black color; darkness; atrociousness or enormity in wickedness.

black′pōll, *n.* The wood-warbler.

black′ro͝ot, *n.* 1. A figwort. [See *Colicroot*.]

2. A plant of the aster family, growing in the Southern pine-barrens.

black′-sạlt″ẽr, *n.* One who prepares black-salts.

black′-sạlts, *n.pl.* The alkaline salts obtained from the lye of wood-ashes by evaporation; crude potash.

black′-scāle, *n.* An insect, *Lecanium oleæ*, causing extensive damage to various trees.

black′smith, *n.* [AS. *blæc*, black, and *smid*, a smith.]

1. A smith who works in iron and makes iron utensils, particularly one who prepares and fits horseshoes.

2. A fish, *Chromis punctipinnis*, having a black back and spotted blue-black fins.

3. The smooth-necked bell-bird of South America.

black′snāke, *n.* 1. An ophidian reptile, the *Coluber constrictor*, common in the United States. It is one of the largest North American serpents, reaching a length of five or six feet, and so agile and swift as to have been named the racer.

Blacksnake (*Coluber constrictor*).

2. A Jamaican snake, *Natrix atra*.

3. A flexible, braided whip used for driving cattle or mule-teams.

black′strap, *n.* 1. A name of a liquor; a cheap concoction of molasses and rum, vinegar, etc.

2. Among sailors, any of the dark red wines of the Mediterranean region.

black′tāil, *n.* 1. A fish, a kind of perch; the ruff or pope.

2. The black-tailed deer, *Cariacus columbianus*, native to California, Washington, and British Columbia; also, the Rocky Mountain mule-deer.

black′thorn, *n.* 1. The sloe or *Prunus communis*.

2. The hedge-hawthorn, *Cratægus tomentosa*, of America.

3. A walking-stick made of the wood of the sloe.

black′-wäd, *n.* An ore of manganese, used as a dryer in paints.

black′wäsh, *n.* 1. A mixture of calomel and limewater; used medicinally.

2. Any preparation to stain black; opposed to *whitewash*.

black′wood, *n.* 1. The West Indian black mangrove, *Avicennia nitida*.

2. The wood of various trees; as (a) a papilionaceous East Indian tree, *Dalbergia latifolia*; (b) *Melharica melanoxylon*, of New South Wales.

black′wõrk, *n.* Unpolished parts of a machine, as those left rough from casting.

blad, *n.* [Scot.] A sharp blow.

blad′dẽr, *n.* [ME. *bladder*, *bleddre*, from AS. *blæddre*, a bladder.]

1. A bag or sac in animals, which serves as the receptacle of some secreted fluid; as, the urinary *bladder*; the gall-*bladder*; in common

language, the urinary *bladder*, either within the animal, or when taken out.

2. Any vesicle or blister, especially if filled with air, or a thin watery liquid.

3. In botany, a distended membranaceous pericarp.

4. Anything having marked distention; something empty or illogical; as, mere *bladders* of argument.

blad'dẽr, *v.t.* 1. To put into a bladder or bladders.

2. To puff up; to fill with wind. [Rare.]

blad'dẽr-hẽrb, *n.* The winter-cherry.

blad'dẽr-kelp, *n.* The bladder-wrack; also, a laminarian North Pacific seaweed bearing an air-bladder six feet in length.

blad'dẽr-nōse, *n.* The hooded arctic seal.

blad'dẽr-nut, *n.* The common name of plants of the genus *Staphylea*, having inflated seed-pods; also called *bladder-tree*.

blad'dẽr-pod, *n.* 1. The English name of a papilionaceous plant, genus *Physolobium*.

2. The common name of a genus of plants, *Vesicaria*, having bladder-like pods.

blad'dẽr-seed, *n.* Any plant of the genus *Physospermum*, having inflated seeds.

blad'dẽr-sen"nȧ, *n.* Any shrub of the genus *Colutea*; specifically, *Colutea arborescens*.

blad'dẽr-tree, *n.* A bladder-nut.

blad'dẽr-wŏrm, *n.* Any encysted worm in its larval stage, as a tapeworm or trichina.

blad'dẽr-wŏrt, *n.* The common name of a genus (*Utricularia*) of slender aquatic plants, the leaves of which are furnished with floating bladders.

blad'dẽr-wrack (-rak), *n.* A seaweed, *Fucus vesiculosus*, having floating vesicles in its fronds.

blad'dẽr-y, *a.* Resembling a bladder; containing bladders.

blāde, *n.* [ME. *blad, blade*, from AS. *blæd*, a leaf.]

1. In botany, (a) the leaf of a plant, particularly of gramineous plants; (b) the broad part of a leaf; the lamina.

2. A thing resembling a blade in shape, etc.; (a) the cutting part of an instrument; as, the *blade* of a knife or sword; (b) the broad part of an oar; (c) the scapula or scapular bone; (d) a commercial name for the four large plates of shell on the sides, and the five large plates in the middle, of the carapace of the turtle, which yield the best tortoise-shell.

3. A dashing or rollicking fellow; a swaggerer; a rakish fellow; strictly, perhaps, one who is sharp and wide-awake.

> He saw a turnkey in a trice
> Fetter a troublesome *blade*. —Coleridge.

4. One of the main rafters of a roof.

blāde, *v.t.*; bladed, *pt., pp.*; blading, *ppr.* To furnish with a blade.

blāde, *v.i.* To come into blade; to produce blades.

blāde'bōne, *n.* The scapula, or upper bone in the shoulder.

blād'ed, *a.* 1. Having a blade or blades; as (a) an instrument; (b) a plant.

2. In mineralogy, composed of long and narrow plates like the blade of a knife.

blāde'fish, *n.* An acanthopterygious fish, *Trichiurus lepturus*; so called from its flatness and resemblance to a sword-blade.

blāde'smith, *n.* A sword-cutler. [Obs.]

blād'y, *a.* Made up of blades. [Rare.]

blæ (blā *or* blē), *a.* [Scot., from ME. *bla, blaa*, blue, from Ice. *blār*, dark blue, livid; AS. *blǣnen*, bluish.] Of a dark blue or bluish-gray color.

blæ'ber"ry, *n.* [Ice. *blāber.*] The Scotch name for the bilberry.

blāgue (blāg), *n.* [Fr. *blaguer*, to humbug.] Arrant jesting; humbug.

blāin, *n.* [ME. *blane, blayn*; AS. *blegen*, a blister, from same root as *blāwan*, to blow.]

1. A pustule; a blister.

2. In farriery, a bladder, growing on the root of the tongue, against the windpipe, which swells so as to stop the breath.

blām'ȧ-ble, *a.* Faulty; culpable; reprehensible; deserving of censure.

blām'ȧ-ble-ness, *n.* Culpableness; fault; the state of being worthy of censure.

blām'ȧ-bly, *adv.* Culpably; in a manner deserving of censure.

blāme, *v.t.*; blamed, *pt., pp.*; blaming, *ppr.* [ME. *blamen*; OFr. *blasmer*, to speak evil of; LL. *blasphemare*; Gr. *blasphēmein*, to speak ill of.]

1. To censure; to express disapprobation of; to find fault with; opposed to *praise* or *commend*, and applicable most properly to persons, but applied also to things.

2. To bring reproach upon; to blemish; to injure. [Obs.]

> She had *blamed* her noble blood. —Spenser.

To blame; blamable; to be blamed; as, inattention is *to blame* for that.

Syn.—Censure, condemn, reprehend, reproach, reprove, upbraid.

blāme, *n.* 1. Censure; reprehension; imputation of a fault; disapprobation; an expression of disapprobation for something deemed to be wrong.

> Let me bear the *blame* forever.—Gen. xliii. 9.

2. Fault; crime; sin; that which is deserving of censure or disapprobation.

> That we should be holy and without *blame* before him in love. —Eph. i. 4.

3. Hurt; injury. [Obs.]

> And glancing down his shield, from *blame* him fairly blest. —Spenser.

blāme'fụl, *a.* Meriting blame; giving blame; reprehensible; faulty; guilty; criminal.

> Thy mother took into her *blameful* bed
> Some stern, untutored churl. —Shak.

blāme'fụl-ly, *adv.* In a blameful manner.

blāme'fụl-ness, *n.* The state of being blameful.

blāme'less, *a.* Without fault; innocent; guiltless; not meriting censure; sometimes followed by *of*.

> We will be *blameless of* this thine oath. —Josh. ii. 17.

Syn.—Faultless, guiltless, innocent, irreproachable, spotless, unblemished.

blāme'less-ly, *adv.* In a blameless manner.

blāme'less-ness, *n.* The state of being blameless.

blām'ẽr, *n.* One who blames or censures.

blāme'wŏr"thi-ness, *n.* The quality of deserving censure.

blāme'wŏr"thy, *a.* Deserving blame; censurable; culpable; reprehensible.

blanç (*Fr. pron.* blaṅ), *n.* [Fr. *blanc*, white.]

1. A base silver coin of the reign of Henry V. of England. It was so called from its color, and to distinguish it from the gold coins which were then coined. Also spelled *blank, blanck.*

2. A small silver coin of France, first coined by Philip of Valois.

3. White paint; a cosmetic.

4. A rich gravy used in serving entrees.

blaṅ'çärd, *n.* [Fr. *blanc*, white.] A kind of linen cloth manufactured in Normandy, so called because the thread is half blanched before it is woven.

blȧnch, *v.t.*; blanched, *pt., pp.*; blanching, *ppr.* [ME. *blaunchen*; OFr. *blanchir*, to whiten.]

1. To whiten; to remove the color of, and make white; to bleach.

2. In gardening, to keep (the leaves of a plant) from the light, as celery, to improve the flavor and texture.

3. Figuratively, to whiten, as a black act or crime; to palliate; to slur; to pass over. [Rare.]

4. In cookery, to soak (as meat or vegetables) in hot water, or to scald by a short, rapid boil, with the view of making firm or white.

5. In the arts, to whiten or make lustrous, as metals, by acids or other means; also, to cover with a thin coating of tin.

blȧnch, *v.t.* To evade; to pass by or avoid, as from fear; to shrink from. [Obs.]

blȧnch, *v.i.* To practise evasion; to fail; to be reserved; to remain blank or silent. [Obs.]

> Books will speak plain, when counsellors *blanch.* —Bacon.

blȧnch, *v.i.* To be or turn white; as, his cheeks *blanched* with fear.

blȧnch, *a.* [OFr. *blanche*, f. of *blanc*, white.] White. [Obs.]

blȧnch, *n.* 1. In mining, a piece of ore found in the hard rock.

2. A cosmetic.

blȧnch'ẽr, *n.* One who or that which blanches or whitens.

blȧnch'-hōld"ing, *n.* [Scot.] In law, a tenure by which the tenant is bound to pay only a nominal or trifling yearly duty to his superior, as an acknowledgment of his right, and only if demanded.

blȧnch-im'e-tẽr, *n.* [*Blanch*, and Gr. *metron*, measure.] An instrument for measuring the bleaching power of chlorid of lime and potash.

blȧnch'ing-liq"uŏr (-lik"ŭr), *n.* A solution of chlorid of lime for bleaching.

blanc-mange' (blȧ-mäṅzh'), *n.* [Fr. *blanc*, white, and *manger*, to eat.] A term applied to various jelly-like preparations of cornstarch, isinglass, calves' feet, seaweed, rice, etc.

blanc-man'ger (blȧ-mäṅ'zhā), *n.* Blancmange. [Obs.]

bland, *a.* [L. *blandus*, mild.]

1. Mild; soft; gentle; balmy.

> Like the bountiful season *bland.*—Tennyson.

2. Affable; suave; kindly; as, *bland* manners.

3. Soothing; said of drugs.

blan-dā'tion, *n.* Gross flattery. [Obs.]

blan-dil'ō-quence, *n.* [L. *blandus*, mild, and *loqui*, to speak.] Fair, mild, flattering speech.

blan-dil'ō-quous (-kwus), *a.* Flattering; smooth of speech.

blan'dise, *v.t.* Same as *Blandish.* [Obs.]

blan'dish, *v.t.*; blandished, *pt., pp.*; blandishing, *ppr.* [ME. *blaundishen*; OFr. *blandir*; L. *blandiri*, to flatter.]

1. To soften; to caress; to cajole; to flatter by kind words or affectionate actions.

2. To render pleasing, alluring, or enticing.

> In former days a country-life
> Was *blandish'd* by perpetual spring. —Cooper.

blan'dish-ẽr, *n.* One who or that which flatters.

blan'dish-ment, *n.* [OFr. *blandissement*, from *blandir*, to flatter; L. *blandiri*, to flatter.] The act of blandishing; soft words; kind speeches; caresses; expressions of kindness; words or actions expressive of affection or kindness, and tending to win the heart; enticement; flattery.

bland'ly, *adv.* In a bland manner.

bland'ness, *n.* The state of being bland.

blaṅk, *a.* 1. White or pale.

> *Blank* as death in marble. —Tennyson.

2. As applied primarily to paper, void of written or printed characters; hence, of any uniform surface; as, a *blank* wall; so also vacant; unoccupied; wanting something necessary to completeness; void; empty; as, a *blank* space; a *blank* ballot; a *blank* cartridge.

> *Blank* and waste it seemed. —Tennyson.

3. Pale from fear or terror; hence, confused; confounded; dispirited; dejected.

> Adam astonished stood, and *blank.*—Milton.

4. Pure; unmingled; entire; complete; as, *blank* stupidity.

5. Unrimed; applied to verse, particularly to the heroic verse of five feet without rime.

Blank bar; in law, a common bar, or a plea in bar, which, in an action of trespass, is put in to oblige the plaintiff to assign the place where the trespass was committed.

Blank cartridge; a cartridge without a bullet.

Blank door, or *blank window*; in architecture, a depressed space in a wall, of the size of a door or window.

Blank line; in printing, a blank space, as wide as a line, on a printed page.

Blank verse; verse without rime.

blaṅk, *n.* [ME. *blank*; OFr. *blanc*, f. *blanche*; O.H.G. *blanch*, white, lustrous.]

1. A piece of paper without writing or printed matter on it; a void space on paper or in any written or printed document; a document remaining incomplete till something essential is filled in.

> The freemen signified their dissent by a *blank.* —Palfrey.

2. A paper, generally of a legal or official nature, with blank or lined spaces for filling in with pen or typewriter; as, a mortgage *blank*; a notary's *blank.*

3. Any void space; a void; a vacancy; as, a *blank* in one's memory.

4. A ticket in a lottery on which no prize is indicated; a lot by which nothing is gained.

> In Fortune's lottery lies
> A heap of *blanks* like this, for one small prize. —Dryden.

5. In archery, the white mark in the center of a target; hence, aim.

> Let me still remain the true *blank* of thine eye. —Shak.

6. A coin, the blanc.

7. A small copper coin formerly current in France.

8. A piece of metal prepared to be formed into something useful, by a further operation, as a piece of metal properly shaped and ready to be made into a file or a screw; specifically, in coining, a plate, or piece of gold or silver, cut and shaped, but not stamped.

9. A blank verse. [Obs.]

blaṅk, *v.t.*; blanked, *pt., pp.*; blanking, *ppr.*

1. To make void; to annul. [Obs.]

2. To deprive of color; to damp the spirits of; to dispirit or confuse; to blanch; as, to *blank* the face of joy. [Obs.]

blaṅ'ket, *n.* [ME. *blanket*; OFr. *blanket*, a blanket; dim. of *blanc*, white.]

1. A cover for a bed, made of coarse wool loosely woven, or of mixed wool and cotton; also, a similar fabric used as a robe or as a cover for a horse, etc.

2. Among printers, woolen cloth, felt, rubber, or other material used to cover the impression-surface, to prevent damage to the type.

3. The layer of blubber stripped from a whale and gradually hoisted aboard a whaleship in sections called *blanket*-pieces.

Blanket act; in legislation, an act to cover or provide for various matters or contingencies.

Blanket ballot; a large ballot-sheet containing the names of the candidates for many offices, to be voted for at the same time.

Blanket mortgage; a mortgage given to secure

various items of indebtedness or to cover numerous items and various forms of property.

Blanket policy; in fire-insurance, a policy written on several risks so as to cover any one of them for the face of the policy in case of loss.

Wet blanket; one who or that which discourages an enterprise or undertaking.

blan'ket, *v.t.*; blanketed, *pt.*, *pp.*; blanketing, *ppr.* 1. To cover with a blanket.

2. To toss in a blanket, either as a punishment or for sport.

3. In seamanship, to take the wind out of the sails of (another vessel), by interposing between her and the wind.

blan'ket-ing, *n.* 1. The punishment or sport of tossing in a blanket.

2. Cloth for blankets.

blan'ket-sheet, *n.* A large folio newspaper.

blank'ly, *adv.* 1 In a blank manner; without expression.

2. Directly; positively; pointblank.

blank'ness, *n.* The state of being blank.

blan-quette' (-ket'), *n.* [Fr., dim. of *blanc*, white.] In cookery, a white fricassee.

blan-quil'lo (-kēl'yō), *n.* [Sp. *blanquillo*, whitish, dim. of *blanco*, white.] A large fish of the genus *Caulolatilus*, one well-known species of which is found off the coast of Florida and in the West Indies, while another is the Pacific whitefish.

blāre, *v i*; blared, *pt.*, *pp.*; blaring, *ppr.* [ME. *bleren*, to cry, weep; an onomatopoetic word.] To roar; to sound loudly.

blāre, *v.t.* To proclaim noisily; to tell abroad as with a trumpet; as, he *blared* the news.

blāre, *n.* A roar; a noise; a blast, as of a trumpet.

blär'ney, *n.* Smooth, deceitful talk; flattery; named from Blarney Castle, near Cork, Ireland, one of the stones of which has long been supposed to give the person who kisses it the gift of smooth speech.

blär'ney, *v t.* blarneyed, *pt.*, *pp.*; blarneying, *ppr.* To influence or wheedle with smooth talk; to bring about by blarney.

blä-ṣé' (-zā'), *a.* [Fr., pp. of *blaser*, to satiate.] Tired or worn out by excess of entertainment or enjoyment; sated with pleasure; surfeited; having the appetite for physical or social pleasures deadened by indulgence.

blas-phēme', *v.t.*; blasphemed, *pt.*, *pp.*; blaspheming, *ppr.* [ME. *blasfemen*; OFr. *blasfemer*; LL. *blasphemare*; Gr. *blasphēmein*, to speak evil of.]

1 To speak of (sacred things) in terms of irreverence; to revile or speak reproachfully of (God, or anything sacred).

2. To speak evil of; to utter abuse or calumny against; to speak reproachfully of, as of persons and things which, although not sacred, are held in high honor by mankind generally.

blas-phēme', *v.i.* To utter blasphemy.

blas-phēm'ēr, *n.* One who blasphemes.

blas'phē-mous, *a.* Containing blasphemy; calumnious.

blas'phē-mous-ly, *adv.* In a blasphemous manner.

blas'phē-my, *n.* 1. An indignity offered to God in words or writing; reproachful, contemptuous, or irreverent words uttered impiously against sacred things; anything which derogates from the prerogatives of God.

In the law of this country, *blasphemy* is an indictable offense defined as wanton and malicious revilement of God and the Christian religion. In English law, according to Blackstone, *blasphemy* is an offense against God and religion, either by impiously denying the Almighty, his existence or providence; or by contumelious reproaches of Jesus Christ; or by profanely scoffing at Holy Scripture, or exposing it to contempt and ridicule.

2. Vilification; malicious detraction; abuse; used figuratively in regard to things held in high esteem; as, *blasphemy* against the theory of equality.

-blast. [Gr. *blastos*, a sprout.] A combining form, or terminal formative, used especially in biological terms to signify growth, formation.

blȧst, *n.* [ME. *blast*, *blest*; AS. *blæst*, a puff of wind.]

1. A gust or violent puff of wind; a sudden gust of wind.

2. The sound made by blowing a wind-instrument; as, he blew a *blast* upon the bugle.

3. Any pernicious or destructive influence upon animals or plants; a blight.

4. A sudden compression of air, attended with a shock, caused by the discharge of cannon.

5 A disease of sheep, in which the stomach and bowels are distended with air.

6. A forcible stream of air from the mouth, from bellows, or the like.

7 A violent explosion of gunpowder, etc., in splitting rocks, or the explosion of inflammable air in a mine.

8. In smelting, the stream of air forced into a furnace to aid combustion.

9. The exhaust steam from an engine, used to create an intense draft through the fire by driving air out of a boiler-chimney.

Hot blast, *cold blast*; terms used to indicate whether the current of air passing through a blast-furnace is heated or not heated on its entrance to the furnace.

In full blast; in full operation, as a blast-furnace at white heat; used figuratively of any business or undertaking; as, the state fair is *in full blast*.

Syn.—Explosion, blight, burst, blaze, frustration, destruction, squall, gale, tempest, hurricane.

blȧst, *v.t.*; blasted, *pt.*, *pp.*; blasting, *ppr.* 1. To cause to wither by some pernicious influence, as too much heat or moisture, or other destructive cause; or to check growth and prevent from coming to maturity and producing fruit; to blight, as trees or plants.

2. To affect with some sudden violence, plague, calamity, or influence, which destroys or causes to fail; to curse.

3. To confound, or strike with force, by a loud blast or din.

4. To split, as rocks, by an explosion of gunpowder, etc.

Syn.—Blight, shrivel, destroy, wither, desolate.

blȧst, *v.i.* 1. To be withered or blighted.

2. To blow, as on a trumpet. [Obs.]

blȧst'ed, *a.* 1. Affected by some cause that checks growth.

2. Split by an explosion, as of gunpowder.

3. Execrable; accursed; used as a mild form of oath.

blas-tē'mȧ, *n.*; *pl.* **blas-tē'mȧ-tȧ.** [Gr. *blastēma*, a bud, from *blastanein*, to bud or sprout.]

1. In botany, the point of growth from which an organ or a part of an organ is produced; an embryonic axis.

2. In anatomy and biology, the protoplasm of the embryo; that from which the generating ovum is developed.

blas-tē'măl, *a.* Pertaining to the blastema.

blas-te-mat'iç, *a.* Pertaining to or proceeding from the blastema.

blȧst'ēr, *n.* One who or that which blasts or destroys.

blȧst'=fūr"nāce, *n.* A furnace for smelting ores, in which the supply of air is furnished by rotary blowers or double-acting pumps. The conical part *c* next above the hearth is termed the *boshes*, and the interior is continued upward, sometimes in a tapered body or cone *d*, sometimes as a perpendicular cylinder, which is surmounted by an opening for the introduction of the materials from an external gallery *f*. The exterior consists of massive masonry of stone or fire-brick, the body part being usually lined with two shells of fire-bricks separated by a thin space, to allow for expansion, and generally filled with sand, ground fire-clay, or the like, to hinder the radiation of heat to the outside. The furnace is said to be *in blast* when in operation and *out of blast* when not being used.

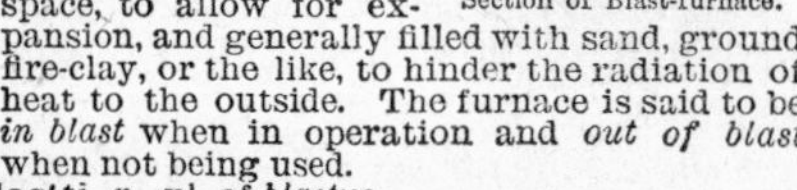

Section of Blast-furnace.

blas'ti, *n.*, pl. of *blastus*.

-blas'tiç. A combining form containing *-blast*, from the Greek *blastos*, a sprout, and *-ic*; used in biological compounds to signify germinal.

blas'tid, *n.* One of the *Blastoidea*.

blas'tide (*or* -tid), *n.* [Gr. *blastos*, sprout, germ.] An ovum after fecundation; the first indication of the nucleus.

blȧst'ing, *n.* 1. A blast; destruction by a pernicious cause.

2. The act of splitting, as by an explosion of gunpowder; the occupation of a blaster.

blȧst'ment, *n.* A blast; a sudden stroke of some destructive cause. [Obs.]

blas'tō-. [Gr. *blastos*, a sprout.] A combining form used in biology to signify connection with or relation to germination, or the early stages of the embryo.

blas-tō-cär'pous, *a.* [*Blasto-*, and Gr. *karpos*, fruit.] In botany, germinating inside the pericarp, as the mangrove.

blas'tō-çhēme, *n.* [*Blasto-*, and Gr. *ochema*, a support, from *ochein*, to carry.] A hydroid medusa which reproduces by means of a special sexual bud.

blas'tō-çhȳle, *n.* [*Blasto-*, and Gr. *chylos*, juice.] The fluid substance that fills the segmentation-cavity.

blas'tō-cœle, *n.* [*Blasto-*, and Gr. *koilos*, hollow.] The segmentation-cavity, or cavity of the blastula.

blas-tō-çol'lȧ, *n.* [*Blasto-*, and Gr. *kolla*, glue.] A balsamic gum that protects the buds of certain plants from the weather.

blas'tō-cyst, *n.* [*Blasto-*, and Gr. *kystis*, bladder.] In an ovum, the nuclear center.

blas'tō-dērm, *n.* [*Blasto-*, and Gr. *derma*, skin.] The germinal membrane; the portion of the ovum from which the organs of the embryo are formed.

blas-tō-dēr'miç, **blas"tō-dēr-mat'iç**, *a.* Relating to the blastoderm.

Blastodermic vesicle; the blastosphere.

blas'tō-disç, *n.* [*Blasto-*, and Gr. *diskos*, a disk.] The germinal disk formed by the division of segments on the germinal side of the ovum.

blas-tō-ġen'e-sis, *n.* [*Blasto-*, and Gr. *genesis*, origin.] The increase of organisms by budding or germination.

blas'toid, *n.* A bud-like fossil; one of the *Blastoidea*; sometimes used attributively.

Blas-toid'ē-ȧ, *n.pl.* [*Blasto-*, and Gr. *eidos*, form, shape.] A division of bud-like fossils found in Paleozoic rocks.

blas'tō-mēre, *n.* [*Blasto-*, and Gr. *meros*, a part.] In embryology, one of the first segments formed by the division of the ovum.

blas-toph'ō-răl, **blas-tō-phor'iç**, *a.* Pertaining to the blastophore.

blas'tō-phōre, *n.* [*Blasto-*, and Gr. *pherein*, to bear.] In a sperm-cell, the neutral part not generating spermatozoa.

blas'tō-pōre, *n.* [*Blasto-*, and Gr. *poros*, a passage.] The duct leading into the primitive enteron.

blas"tor-ly-cē'tē-a, *n.* A rare disease which is manifested by a malignant vegetable growth attaching itself to the intestines.

blas'tō-sphēre, *n.* [*Blasto-*, and Gr. *sphaira*, a sphere.] A blastula.

blas'tō-stȳle, *n.* [*Blasto-*, and Gr. *stylos*, a pillar.] A simple zoöid which produces generative buds.

blȧst'=pipe, *n.* A pipe in a locomotive engine to carry the exhaust steam up the stack so as to create a strong draft.

blas'tū-lȧ, *n.*; *pl.* **blas'tū-læ.** [L., from Gr. *blastos*, a sprout, germ.] In embryology, the stage when the outer cells of the morula develop into the blastoderm, or germinal membrane.

blas'tūle, *n.* Same as *Blastula*.

blas'tus, *n.*; *pl.* **blas'tī.** The plumule, or rudimentary bud, of grasses.

blȧst'y, *a.* 1. Affected by sudden puffs of wind; gusty.

2. Causing blast or blights. [Obs.]

blat, *v.t.*; blatted, *pt.*, *pp.*; blatting, *ppr.* To utter heedlessly; as, he *blatted* the news. [Colloq.]

blat, *v.i.* To speak without thinking; to bleat. [Colloq.]

blā'tăn-cy, *n.* The state of being blatant.

blā'tănt, *a.* 1. Bellowing as a calf.

2. Echoing or vibrating.

3. Loud-mouthed; offensively noisy.

blā'tănt-ly, *adv.* In a noisy manner.

blāte, *a.* [Scot. and Prov. Eng.] 1. Bashful; naturally diffident.

2. Dull or spiritless. [Obs.]

blath'ēr, *v.i.* and *v.t.* To talk nonsensically.

blath'ēr, *n.* Foolish or nonsensical talk in excessive quantity.

blath'ēr-skīte, *n.* 1. Balderdash.

2. A noisy talkative person; a good-for-nothing fellow. [Scot. and Am.]

Blat'tȧ, *n.* [L., a beetle, or cockroach.]

1. A genus of insects, including the cockroach; the type of the family *Blattidæ*.

2. [b—] A cockroach; an insect of the genus *Blatta*.

blat'tȧ, *n.* An interwoven silk of purple and gold used in medieval times.

blat'tēr, *v.i.* [L. *blaterare*, to prate, babble.] To make a senseless noise; to talk volubly; to rattle; to patter; as, the hail *blatters*. [Rare.]

blat'tēr, *n.* A continuous clattering noise; as, the *blatter* of hail.

blat-tēr-ā'tion, *n.* The act of blustering; blattering.

blat'tēr-ēr, *n.* A noisy blustering boaster. [Obs.]

blat'tēr-ing, *n.* Senseless blustering or boasting.

blat-tēr-ọọn', *n.* A blatterer. [Obs.]

blauw'bok, **blau'bok**, *n.* [D., bluebuck.] A small antelope, native of South Africa; the bluebuck.

blā'wort, *n.* [Scot. *bla*, *blae*, blue, and *wort*, a herb.]

1. A flower, commonly called harebell.

2. A plant producing blue bottle-shaped flowers, growing in grainfields

blāy, *n.* A small river fish, the bleak. [Local, Eng.]

blāze, *n.* [ME. *blase*, a flame; AS. *blæse*, *blase*, a flame, torch.]

1. Flame; the stream of light and heat from any substance when burning, proceeding from the combustion of gas.

2. An outburst of any quality or emotion; excitement; ardor; as, a *blaze* of anger.

3. A white spot on the face of a horse or other quadruped.

4. A white spot made on trees by removing the bark with a hatchet.

5. Light; expanded light; light accompanied by heat; as, the *blaze* of day; the *blaze* of the noonday sun.

6. Noise; agitation; tumult.

Syn.—Flame.—A *blaze* and a *flame* are both results of combustion, but the former chiefly implies light and the latter heat.

blāze, *v.i.*; blazed, *pt.*, *pp.*; blazing, *ppr.* 1. To flame; as, the fire *blazes.*

2. To send forth or show a bright and expanded light.

3. To be conspicuous or resplendent; as, his speeches *blaze* with genius.

blāze, *v.t.* [ME. *blasen,* to blow as a trumpet; D. *blazen*; O.H.G. *blāsan*; Ice. *blāsa*; Goth. *blēsan,* from *blāwan,* to blow, breathe.]

1. To make public far and wide.

> To *blaze* those virtues which the good would hide. —Pope.

2. To blazon. [Obs.]

3. To set a white mark on (a tree) by paring off a part of the bark; to indicate by cutting the bark of trees so as to show a succession of white spots; as, to *blaze* a trail.

4. To temper, as steel, by means of oil or tallow, which is burned from the surface.

blāz′ẽr, *n.* 1. One who publishes and spreads reports.

2. One who marks his way by blazing trees.

3. A light outing jacket, usually of bright color, or with definite stripes.

4. Something that is intensely hot, with the implication of intense light; as, the day was a *blazer.*

5. A dish used immediately over a chafing-dish lamp, or coals of a brazier.

blāz′ing, *a.* Emitting flame or light; as, a *blazing* ship.

blāz′ing-stär, *n.* 1. A comet; a star that is accompanied by a coma or train of light.

2. In heraldry, a star having six points and a comet's tail.

3. In botany, any one of various herbaceous plants, known also as colicroot and starwort, some of which are efficacious as antidotes to rattlesnake poison.

blā′zŏn, *v.t.*; blazoned, *pt.*, *pp.*; blazoning, *ppr.* [Fr. *blasonner,* to blazon; It. *blasonare,* from *blason,* a shield, coat of arms; confused with O.H.G. *blāsan,* to blow, to sound a trumpet, proclaim.]

1. To explain in proper terms, as the figures on armorial bearings or heraldic devices.

2. To deck; to embellish; to adorn.

> She *blazons* in dread smiles her hideous form. —Garth.

3. To display; to celebrate by words or writing; to make public far and wide.

> There pride sits *blazoned* on th' unmeaning brow. —Trumbull.

4 To adorn with blazonry; to emblazon.

blā′zŏn, *n.* 1. The art of drawing, describing, or explaining coats of arms.

2. A coat of arms; an armorial shield; heraldic bearings.

3. Publication; show; celebration; pompous display, either by words or by other means.

blā′zŏn, *v.i.* To be conspicuous, shining, or prominent. [Rare.]

blā′zŏn-ẽr, *n.* One who blazons coats of arms; a herald; one who proclaims loudly or extravagantly.

blā′zŏn-ment, *n.* Heraldic description; the act of blazoning.

blā′zŏn-ry, *n.* The art of describing or explaining coats of arms in proper terms; emblazonry.

-ble, *suffix.* [Fr. *-ble*; L *-bilis.*] A combining form used in forming adjectives from verbs and usually preceded by a vowel, as *-able, -ible.*

blēa, *n.* The part of a tree which lies immediately under the bark. [Rare.]

blēa′ber″ry, *n.* Same as *Blaeberry.*

blēach, *v.t.*; bleached, *pt.*, *pp.*; bleaching, *ppr.* [ME. *bleche*; AS. *blæcan*; O.H.G. *bleichen*; Sw. *bleka,* from *blac,* pale, bleak.] To whiten; to make colorless, as by means of chemicals or sunlight

blēach, *v.i.* To grow white in any manner.

blēach′ẽr, *n.* 1. One who whitens, or whose occupation is to whiten cloth.

2. Any utensil or apparatus used for bleaching.

3. [*pl.*] In sporting circles, in the United States, the uncovered seats at exhibition-grounds.

blēach′ẽr-y, *n.* A place for bleaching; as, a wax *bleachery.*

blēach′=fiēld, *n.* A field where cloth or yarn is bleached.

blēach′ing, *n.* The act or art of whitening, especially cloth.

blēach′ing=pow″dẽr, *n.* A powder for bleaching, consisting of chlorid of lime.

blēak, *a.* [ME. *bleke, blake, blak*; AS. *blac, blæc,* pale, wan, from *blican,* to shine.]

1. Pale. [Obs.]

2. Open; desolate; exposed; as, a *bleak* hill.

3. Cold; piercing; as, *bleak* winds.

Syn.—Blank, bare, stormy, nipping.

blēak, *n.* [ME. *bleke*; AS. *blæga,* pale, from the color of its scales.] A small river-fish, five or six inches long, so named from its whiteness. It belongs to the genus *Alburnus,* and is called, also, by contraction, a *blay.* Its scales are used in the manufacture of artificial pearls.

blēak′ish, *a.* Of a bleak cheerless nature.

blēak′ly, *adv.* In a bleak desolate manner.

blēak′ness, *n.* The state or quality of being bleak; openness of situation.

blēak′y, *a.* Bleak; open; unsheltered; cold; chilly. [Obs.]

blēar, *a.* 1. Sore with a watery rheum; applied only to the eye.

2. Producing indistinctness; dim; obscure.

blēar, *v.t.*; bleared, *pt.*, *pp.*; blearing, *ppr.* [ME. *bleren,* to make dim; Dan. *blire,* to blink; G. *blerr,* an ailment of the eyes.] To make sore; to affect with soreness of eyes, or a watery humor; to make dim, or partially obscure (the sight). Figuratively, to render obscure or to hoodwink.

blēar′ed-ness, *n.* The state of being bleared, or dimmed with rheum.

blēar′eȳe, *n.* A chronic disease of the eyelids, causing inflammation of the margins, and attended with gummy secretions.

blēar′=eȳed (-īd), *a.* Having sore eyes; having the eyes dim with rheum; dim-sighted.

blēar′eȳed-ness, *n.* The condition of being blear-eyed.

blēar′y, *a.* Inclined to be blear; somewhat blear.

blēat, *v.i.*; bleated, *pt.*, *pp.*; bleating, *ppr.* [ME. *bleten*; AS. *blætan,* to bleat; L. *balare*; Gr. *blēchē,* a bleating.] To make the noise of a sheep; to cry as a sheep.

blēat, *n.* The cry of a sheep.

blēat′ẽr, *n.* An animal that bleats; a sheep.

blēat′ing, *a.* Crying as a sheep.

blēat′ing, *n.* The cry of a sheep.

bleb, *n.* [Prov. Eng. *bleb, blob,* a blister, bubble.] A little tumor, vesicle, or blister.

> Arsenic abounds with air *blebs.* —Kirwan.

bleb′by, *a.* Full of blebs.

bleck, blek, *v.t.* To pollute; to defile; to blacken. [Obs.]

bled, *v.*, past tense and past participle of *bleed.*

bleed, *v.i.*; bled, *pt.*, *pp.*; bleeding, *ppr.* [ME. *bleden*; AS. *blēdan,* to bleed, from *blōd,* blood.]

1. To lose blood; to run with blood, by whatever means; as, the arm *bleeds.*

2. To die a violent death, or by slaughter.

> The lamb thy riot dooms to *bleed* to-day. —Pope.

3. To issue forth, or drop, as blood from an incision; to lose sap, gum, or juice; as, a tree or vine *bleeds.*

> For me the balm shall *bleed.* —Pope.

4. To lose one's means freely or by extortion; as, to *bleed* for a whim.

The heart bleeds; used to denote extreme pain from sympathy or pity.

bleed, *v.t.* 1. To let blood from; to take blood from by opening a vein.

2. To lose or exude; as, trees *bleed* sap.

3. To extort valuables from; to cheat; to sponge on.

4. To draw liquid from; as, he *bleeds* the barrel.

bleed′ing, *n.* A running or issuing of blood, as from the nose; a hemorrhage; the operation of letting blood, as in old surgery; the drawing of sap from a tree or plant.

bleed′ing=heärt, *n.* 1. A garden-plant, *Dicentra spectabilis,* a native of China.

2. The English wallflower, *Cheiranthus Cheiri.*

bleed′ing=tōoth, *n.* A neritoid shell, having small reddish projections along the border of its mouth, resembling bleeding teeth.

bleit, blāte, *a.* [ME. *blate*; AS. *blāt,* pale, difficult.] Bashful; blunt; dull; used in Scotland and the northern counties of England.

blek, *v.t.* See *Bleck.*

blel′lum, *n.* An idle senseless fellow; a blab. [Scot.]

blem′ish, *v.t.*; blemished, *pt.*, *pp.*; blemishing, *ppr.* [ME. *blemisshen,* to wound, spoil; OFr. *blemir, blesmir,* from *bleme, blesme,* pale, wan.] To mark with deformity; to injure or impair; to mar, either in body or mind; to defame.

blem′ish, *n.* 1. Any mark of deformity; any scar or defect that diminishes beauty, or renders imperfect that which is otherwise well formed.

2. Reproach; disgrace; that which impairs reputation; taint; turpitude; deformity.

Syn.—Stain, spot, speck, flaw, defect, fault, imperfection.—A *stain, spot, speck,* or *flaw,* is a *blemish,* but there are likewise many *blemishes* which are neither *stains, spots, specks,* nor *flaws.* Whatever takes off from the seemliness of appearance is a *blemish.* A *stain* or *spot* sufficiently characterizes itself, as that which is superfluous and out of its place. A *speck* is a small *spot*; and a *flaw* mostly consists of a faulty indenture on a surface. A *blemish* tarnishes; a *stain* spoils; a *spot, speck,* or *flaw* disfigures. A *blemish* is rectified, a *stain* wiped out, a *spot* or *speck* removed.

blem′ish-less, *a.* Without blemish; spotless.

blem′ish-ment, *n.* Disgrace. [Rare.]

blem′mȧ-trōpe, *n.* [Gr. *blemma,* a look, glance, and *trepein,* to turn.] An instrument by which the various positions of the eye are illustrated or exhibited.

blench, *v.i.*; blenched, *pt.*, *pp.*; blenching, *ppr.* [ME. *blenchen,* to evade, shrink back, give way; AS. *blencan,* to deceive.] To shrink; to start from lack of courage; to give way.

blench, *v.t.* To baffle; to foil. [Obs.]

blench, *n.* 1. A start or shrinking back.

2. A side glance. [Obs.]

blench, *v.i.* and *v.t.* To blanch; to become or make pale.

blench′ẽr, *n.* 1. An object or person causing fright; a guard at a deer-hunt stationed to prevent the escape of the game.

2. One who draws back from fear.

blench′=hōld″ing, *n.* See *Blanch-holding.*

blench′ing, *n.* A shrinking back; a giving way.

blend, *v.t.*; blended *or* blent, *pt.*, *pp.*; blending, *ppr.* [ME. *blenden*; AS. *blandan*; Ice. *blanda*; M.H.G. *blanden,* to mix.]

1. To mix together; to combine, so that the separate things mixed cannot be distinguished; hence, to confuse; to confound.

2. To pollute by mixture; to spoil or corrupt. [Obs.]

3. To blind. [Obs.]

blend, *v.i.* To mingle together, or to shade gradually into each other, as colors.

Syn.—Mix, harmonize, unite, combine, fuse, merge, amalgamate, mingle, commingle, coalesce.

blend, *n.* A thorough mixture of two things, as colors, or liquids, so that the various constituents can only with difficulty be distinguished; a shading or merging of one color into another.

blende, *n.* [G. *blende,* from *blenden,* to blind, dazzle.] An ore of zinc, called also mock-lead, false galena, black-jack, and sphalerite. There are several varieties, chiefly zinc sulphids having a nonmetallic luster.

blend′ẽr, *n.* One who mingles or confounds; an object used to blend.

blend′ing, *n.* The act of intermixing or shading, as of colors in painting.

blend′ous, *a.* Pertaining to blende.

blend′=wạ″tẽr, *n.* A cattle-distemper affecting the liver.

bleñk, *v.i.* To look; to blink. [Obs.]

blen′nieṣ, *n.*, pl. of *blenny.*

blen′ni-oid, blen′ni-id, *a.* [L. *blennius,* blenny, and Gr. *eidos,* form.] In zoölogy, pertaining to the blennies.

blen-nog′e-nous, *a.* [Gr. *blennos,* mucus, and *genēs,* producing.] Producing mucus.

blen′noid, *a.* Mucous.

blen-nor-rhē′ȧ, blen-nor-rhœ′ȧ, *n.* [L., from Gr. *blennos,* mucus, and *rhoia,* from *rhein,* to flow.] An inordinate discharge or secretion of mucus, especially from the genitals; gonorrhea.

blen′ny, *n.*; *pl.* **blen′nieṣ.** [L. *blennius*; Gr. *blennos,* a blenny, from *blennos, blenna,* mucus.] A name common to different species of fishes, usually of small size, of the genus *Blennius,* so called from their covering of mucus.

blent, *v.*, past tense and past participle of *blend.*

bleph′ăr-, bleph′ăr-ō-. Combining forms from Gr. *blepharon,* eyelid, and indicating various diseases or conditions of the eyelid; as, *blepharitis, blepharo*spasm.

bleph-ăr-ī′tis, *n.* [Gr. *blepharon,* eyelid, and *-itis.*] In pathology, an ulceration of the eye-lids producing inflammation.

bleph″ăr-op-tō′sis, *n.* [*Blepharo-,* and Gr. *ptōsis,* a fall.] In pathology, a drooping of the upper eyelid.

bleph-ăr-or′rhȧ-phy, *n.* [*Blepharo-,* and Gr. *rhaphē,* a sewing, from *rhaptein,* to sew.] In surgery, the stitching of the eyelids to prevent them from turning back.

bleph′ăr-ō-spaṣm, *n.* [*Blepharo-,* and Gr. *spasmos,* spasm.] A spasmodic twitching of the orbicular muscle, producing continuous winking.

bleph-ăr-ot′ō-my, *n.* [*Blepharo-,* and Gr. *tomē,* a cutting, from *temnein,* to cut.] In optic surgery, an incision into the eyelid to correct some muscular defect.

bles′bok, *n.* [D. *blesbok*; *bles,* blaze, and *bok,* a buck.] A blaze-faced antelope of South Africa, *Alcelaphus albifrons.*

bless, *v.t.*; blessed *or* blest, *pt.*, *pp.*; blessing, *ppr.* [ME. *blessen, blessien*; AS. *blētsian, blēdsian,* to bless, from *blōd,* blood; from the consecration by sprinkling the altar with blood.]

1. To set apart or consecrate to holy purposes; to make and pronounce holy.

And God *blessed* the seventh day, and sanctified it. —Gen. ii. 3.

2. To make happy; to make successful; to make prosperous in temporal concerns; as, we are *blessed* with peace and plenty.
3. To wish happiness to; as, the father *blessed* his son.
4. To consecrate by prayer; to invoke a blessing upon; as, he *blessed* the eucharist.
5. To praise; to magnify; to extol for excellencies.

Bless the Lord, O my soul. —Ps. ciii. 1.

6. To esteem or account happy; used with the reciprocal pronoun.

The nations shall *bless* themselves in him. —Jer. iv. 2.

7. To cross (oneself) as a protection or sanctification.
Bless me; a crude exclamation of astonishment.
God bless the mark; an exclamation of surprise, irony, or scorn, now little used.
Syn.—Felicitate, endow, enrich, gladden, rejoice, cheer, thank.

bless'ed, *a.* 1. Hallowed; sacred; consecrated; holy; beatified.
2. Experiencing or relating to heavenly joys or spiritual felicity.
3. Fraught with happiness; joyful; blissful.
4. Confounded; cursed; worthless; used ironically or intensively; as, that *blessed* rascal; he hasn't a *blessed* cent.
Blessed bread; see *Eulogia.*
Blessed thistle; see under *Thistle.*

bless'ed-ly, *adv.* Happily; in a fortunate manner.

bless'ed-ness, *n.* 1. Happiness; felicity; heavenly joy; the favor of God.
2. Sanctity.
Single blessedness; an unmarried condition.

bless'ẽr, *n.* One who blesses or prospers; one who bestows a blessing.

bless'ing, *n.* [ME. *blessinge, blessunge*; AS. *bletsung*, from *bletsian*, to bless.]
1. Benediction; a prayer from the fullness of the heart for another's welfare; a solemn prophecy of great joy.
2. The granting of divine favor; as, God's *blessing* may be had for the asking.
3. A temporal benefit; as, the *blessings* of nature.
4. Among the Jews, a present; a gift expressive of affection.
5. Worship; praise.

1. Position of hand in blessing in the Latin church; 2 In the Greek church.

blest, *a.* 1. Made happy; blessed.
2. Making happy; cheering.

While these *blest* sounds my ravished ear assail. —Trumbull.

blest, *v.*, past tense and past participle of *bless.*

blet, *n.* [Fr. *blettir*, from *blet, blette*, overripe, soft.] A kind of rot that takes place in overripe fruit.

blet, *v.i.*; bletted, *pt., pp.*; bletting, *ppr.* To decay within, as fruit when overripe.

bleth'ẽr, *v.* and *n.* Same as *Blather.*

blē'tŏn-ism, *n.* The supposed ability to locate subterraneous waters by sensation; so called from Bléton, a Frenchman, who claimed this faculty.

blē'tŏn-ist, *n.* One supposed to possess the power of locating subterraneous waters by sensation.

blet'ting, *n.* [Fr. *blet, blette*, soft, overripe.] A form of incipient fruit-decay, desirable in some species.

blew, *v.*, past tense of *blow.*

blē'wärt, *n.* [Scot.] The germander speedwell.

blew'its, *n.* [Fr. *bluet*, dim. of *bleu*, blue.] An edible mushroom of Europe, of a purplish color.

blēyme, *n.* An inflammation in the foot of a horse, between the sole and the bone. [Obs.]

bleyn'te, *v.*, past tense of *blench.* [Obs.]

blick, *n.* A fish; same as *Bleak.*

blick, *n.* Same as *Fulguration.*

blick'ey, *n.* [G. *blech*, tin.] A local American term for a tin dinner-pail.

blight (blit), *n.* [Origin unknown.]
1. A disease affecting plants variously. Sometimes the plant perishes; sometimes only the leaves and blossoms, which shrivel.
2. Anything nipping, blasting, or destructive.
3. A name given to the aphis, or plant-louse, destructive to fruit-trees.
4. Specifically, two eruptive diseases: (a) in the United States, a kind of rash; (b) in Australia, a disease of the eye in which the eyelids become pustular, inflamed, swollen, and mucous.
5. That which frustrates or impairs one's ambition, brings to naught one's plans, or ruins one's expectations.

blight, *v.t.*; blighted, *pt., pp.*; blighting, *ppr.*
1. To affect with blight; to blast; to prevent the growth of.
2. Figuratively, to frustrate, as hopes or plans; to blast the happiness of.

blight' *v.i.* To injure or blast.

blight'bird, *n.* A bird which clears trees of blight, especially that produced by insects.

blight'ing, *a.* Producing blight.

blight'ing-ly, *adv.* In such a manner as to blight.

blights, *n.pl.* A form of eruptive skin-disease; nettle-rash. [Local, U. S.]

blim'bi, blim'bing, *n.* Same as *Bilimbi.*

blimp, *n.* A small dirigible balloon primarily designed to locate and to observe submarines. [Slang.]

Blight'y, *n.* [Corr. of Hindu *bilāti*, European, hence English.] England. [British soldiers' slang.]

blight'y, *a.* Anything serious enough to furlough a soldier to England; as, a *blighty* wound. [British soldiers' slang.]

blin, *v.t.* and *v.i.* [AS. *blinnan*, to cease.] To stop or cease. [Obs.]

blin, *n.* Cessation. [Obs.]

blind, *a.* [ME. *blind*; AS. *blind*, blind.]
1. Destitute of the sense of seeing, either by natural defect or by deprivation; sightless.
2. Not having the faculty of discernment; destitute of intellectual light; unable to understand or judge; ignorant; as, authors are *blind* to their own defects.
3. Unseen; out of public view; private; dark; obscure; not easy to be found; not easily discernible; as, a *blind* path; a *blind* corner.
4. Heedless; inconsiderate; undeliberating.

This plan is recommended neither to *blind* approbation nor to *blind* reprobation.—Jay.

5. Complicated; winding; difficult to follow or trace; as, the *blind* mazes of the dance.
6. In horticulture, unproductive; as, *blind* buds.
7. Without openings for or impervious to light; as, a *blind* window.
8. Closed at one end; having no outlet; as, the *blind* gut or cæcum; a *blind* alley.
9. Not clear or comprehensive; not legible; as, a *blind* stanza in a poem.
Blind area; a covered space outside the wall of a building to keep it dry.
Blind axle; an axle which turns without communicating motion.
Blind coal; flameless or anthracite coal.
Going it blind; acting without reason or upon impulse; acting recklessly; taking chances.
Syn.—Sightless, unseeing, undiscerning, ignorant, prejudiced, uninformed, unconscious, unaware.

blind, *v.t.*; blinded, *pt., pp.*; blinding, *ppr.* 1. To make blind; to deprive of sight.
2. To darken; to obscure to the eye.
3. To darken mentally; as, to *blind* the mind.
4. To confuse; to dazzle by great brilliancy.
5. In paving, to cover with a layer of fine sand or gravel, that the interstices between paving-blocks, etc., may be filled.
6. In fortification, to cover or conceal with blindages; as, to *blind* a trench.

blind, blinde, *n.* Same as *Blende.*

blind, *n.* 1. Something to obscure vision or obstruct the passage of light; particularly, a shade for a window or a shield for a horse's eye.
2. An artifice to mislead; a deception.
3. In fortification, a blindage or cover for a trench.
4. A halting-place. [Obs.]
5. A place of concealment for hunters.
Venetian blind; an interior window-screen composed of horizontal slats.

blind'āge, *n.* In fortification, a screen or cover for a trench, protecting those in the trench from the enemy's fire; a mantelet.

blind'ball, *n.* In botany, a puffball.

blind'-bee"tle, *n.* Any one of the large bugs that fly blindly at night.

blind'-cat, *n.* A cavern catfish of Pennsylvania whose eyes are almost covered by skin.

blind'ẽr, *n.* 1. A person who or a thing which blinds.
2. A piece of leather on a bridle to screen a horse's eye.

blind'fish, *n.* An eyeless fish found in the waters of caves, especially in the Mammoth Cave of Kentucky.

blind'fōld, *a.* Having the eyes covered; having the mental eye darkened; hence, careless, rash, or unconcerned; as, *blindfold* rage.

blind'fōld, *v.t.*; blindfolded, *pt., pp.*; blindfolding, *ppr.* To cover the eyes of; to hinder from seeing.

blind'ing, *n.* 1. The act of destroying sight.
2. Sand or gravel placed over a road that has been newly paved, for the purpose of filling in crevices.

blind'ing, *a.* Producing blindness; as, *blinding* sleet.

blind'ly, *adv.* Without sight or understanding; without discerning the reason; implicitly; without examination; without judgment or direction; as, to be *blindly* led by another.

blind'man, *n.* 1. In the play of blindman's buff, the one who, blindfolded, seeks to catch some one of his fellows.
2. Same as *Blind-reader.*
Blindman's ball; same as *Blindball.*
Blindman's buff; a game in which a blindfolded person must catch a player and identify him.
Blindman's holiday; the part of the evening between daylight and dark. [Humorous.]

blind'ness, *n.* The state of being without sight; lack of intellectual discernment; ignorance.

blind'-net"tle, *n.* The dead-nettle or hemp-nettle.

blind-pig', *n.* A place where intoxicants are illicitly sold; an unlicensed drinking-place. Especially used in communities having laws or ordinances prohibiting the sale of intoxicating drinks. [Slang.]

blind'-read"ẽr, *n.* A person in a post-office whose duty it is to decipher addresses which are doubtful or blind.

blind'-spot, *n.* The point where the optic nerve enters the retina of the eye. This point is not sensible to light.

blind'stitch, *v.t.* To stitch so that the stitches show on only one side of the material, or do not show at all.

blind'stō"ry, *n.* In medieval architecture, the triforium, which has no windows, in opposition to the *clearstory*, which has apertures admitting light.

blind'-tool"ing, *n.* Impressions made on leather by heated tools; used in bookbinding.

blind'wŏrm, *n.* A small lizard, *Anguis fragilis*, called also *slowworm*. It is about eleven inches long, is covered with scales, has a forked tongue, and is harmless. Its eyes are so small as to be almost indiscernible.

blink, *v.t.*; blinked, *pt., pp.*; blinking, *ppr.* 1. To shut out of sight; to avoid, or purposely evade; as, to *blink* the question before the house.
2. To cheat; to delude. [Scot.]

blink, *v.i.* [ME. *blinken*; Dan. *blinke*; D. *blinken*; Sw. *blinka*, to blink, shine, twinkle; AS. *blican*, to shine.]
1. To wink; to twinkle with the eye.
2. To see with the eyes half shut; to see obscurely.

One eye was *blinking*, and one leg was lame. —Pope.

3. To shine fitfully; to flicker, as a lamp.
4. To become a little stale or sour; used in respect to beer. [Prov. Eng. and Scot.]
Syn.—Wink, ignore, connive, overlook.

blink, *n.* 1. A glimpse or glance.
2. A fitful gleam or flicker; particularly, the gleam reflected from ice in the Arctic regions; also, a spark of fire.
3. [*pl.*] In sporting, boughs broken from trees and thrown where deer are likely to pass, with the view of hindering their running, and of overtaking them the better. [Eng.]

blink'ärd, *n.* 1. A person who blinks or has bad eyes.
2. Figuratively, one who is blind to the truth.
3. That which twinkles, or glances, as a dim star, which appears and disappears.

blink'beer, *n.* Beer kept untapped until it is acidulous.

blink'ẽr, *n.* 1. One who blinks.
2. A shield for horses' eyes; anything which obstructs sight or discernment.
3. [*pl.*] A protection for the eyes from any blinding light; goggles.

blink'-eyed (-īd), *a.* Habitually blinking or winking.

blink'ing, *a.* Winking; twinkling.

blink'ing, *n.* 1. The act of twinkling or winking; as, the *blinking* of an eye.
2. In hunting, the act of a dog in passing by game which it has once located.

blink'ing-chick"weed, *n.* A marsh-herb of the order *Portulacaceæ*; called also *blinks.*

blinks, *n.* Same as *Blinking-chickweed.*

blirt, *n.* A burst of tears; among seamen, a gust of wind and rain.

bliss, *n.* [AS. *blis, blisse*, from *blīds, blīths*, joy, from *blithe*, joyful.] Extreme joy; blessedness; felicity; heavenly joy.
Syn.—Blessedness, joy, ecstasy, rapture.

bliss'ful, *a.* Full of joy and felicity; happy in the highest degree.

bliss'ful-ly, *adv.* In a blissful manner.

bliss'ful-ness, *n.* Exalted happiness; felicity; fullness of joy.

bliss'less, *a.* Destitute of bliss.

blis'sŏm, *v.i.* [Ice. *blæsma*, in heat, as a goat.] To be lustful; to be in heat; said of animals, especially ewes. [Rare.]

blis′sŏm, *a.* In heat, when applied to animals; hence, lascivious.

blis′tẽr, *n.* [ME. *blister*; D. *bluyster*; OFr. *blestre*, a blister, swelling.]

1. An elevation on the surface of the skin, resembling a bladder, caused by a secretion of watery serum beneath the epidermis. It is occasioned by a burn or other hurt, or by a medical application for the purpose.

2. Any similar elevation on the surface of other substances, as plants or metals.

3. Any substance applied to raise a vesicle on the skin.

blis′tẽr, *v.t.*; blistered, *pt.*, *pp.*; blistering, *ppr.* 1. To raise a blister, by any hurt, burn, or violent action upon (the skin); to raise a blister by a medical application or plaster.

2. To raise blisters on iron in a furnace, in the process of converting iron into steel.

3. Figuratively, to painfully injure, as by a blister.

blis′tẽr, *v.i.* To rise in blisters.

blis′tẽr-çop″pẽr, *n.* A kind of copper obtained by calcining the variety known as pimple-metal.

blis′tẽr-fly, blis′tẽr-bee″tle, *n.* The Spanish fly, *Cantharis vesicatoria*, used in raising blisters.

blis′tẽr-plås″tẽr, *n.* A plaster, generally of Spanish flies, designed to raise a blister.

blis′tẽr-y, *a.* Full of blisters.

blite, *n.* [L. *blitum*; Gr. *bliton*, a plant.] A name for various plants with succulent leaves, frequently used as pot-herbs.

blīthe, *a.* [ME. *blithe, blythe*; AS. *blīthe*, joyful.] Gay; joyous; sprightly; mirthful.

Syn.—Light, merry, joyous, happy, bright, buoyant, gladsome, bonny, vivacious, lively, cheerful, blithesome, gay.

blīthe′ful, *a.* Gay; full of gaiety.

blīthe′ly, *adv.* In a gay, joyful manner.

blīthe′ness, *n.* Gaiety; sprightliness; the quality of being blithe.

blīthe′sŏme, *a.* Gay; merry; cheerful.

blīthe′sŏme-ly, *adv.* In a blithesome manner.

blīthe′sŏme-ness, *n.* The quality of being blithesome.

blīve, *adv.* [Contr. of *belive*.] Quickly; at once. [Obs.]

bliz′zärd, *n.* [A word originating on the Atlantic coast of the United States; it came into general use during the winter of 1880-81. Prob. from the same root as *blaze, blow*; AS. *blawan*, to blow.]

1. A gale of cold piercing wind usually accompanied with blinding snow.

2. Figuratively, a rattling volley; a fierce attack.

blōak, *n.* See *Bloke*.

blōat, *v.t.*; bloated, *pt.*, *pp.*; bloating, *ppr.* [ME. *blote*, origin uncertain; doubtless from AS. *blāt*, pale, livid.]

1. To cause to swell or make turgid with water, air, or other means; to puff up, as with dropsical humor.

2. To inflate; to puff up; to make vain.

blōat, *v.i.* To grow turgid; to swell; to dilate.

blōat, *a.* Swelled; turgid. [Obs.]

blōat, *n.* A term used to express contempt, and applied to one who is worthless and dissipated. [Slang.]

blōat′ed-ness, *n.* A turgid state; dilatation from inflation, debility, or any morbid cause.

blōat′ẽr, *n.* [Ice. *blautr*, soaked.]

1. A dried herring.

2. A kind of cisco found in the Great Lakes.

blōat′ing, *n.* A state of being swelled or bloated.

blob, *n.* [Prov. Eng., from Scot. *bleb, bleib, blab*, a bubble.] A drop or lump of something viscid or thick; a bubble; a blister. [See *Bleb*.]

blob′bẽr, *n.* A bubble; commonly pronounced *blubber*. It is a legitimate word, but not in common use.

blob′bẽr-lip, *n.* A thick lip.

blob′bẽr-lipped, *a.* Having thick lips.

blō-çāge′ (-käzh′), *n.* [Fr.] A rough, cheap kind of rubblework in masonry.

block, *n.* [ME. *blok*; Fr. *bloc*, of Germanic origin; M.H.G. *bloch*; L.G. *blok*.]

1. Any mass of matter with an extended surface; as, a *block* of marble, a piece rough from the quarry.

2. A solid body of wood, metal, or stone, with surfaces more or less plane; as, a butcher's *block*; a horse-*block*; A B C *blocks*.

3. A continuous row of buildings; as, a *block* of houses.

4. A city section or square, whether vacant or built upon; the distance between streets.

5. The piece of wood upon which persons expose the neck when beheaded; as, he was brought to the *block*.

6. Any obstruction, or cause of obstruction; a stop; hindrance; obstacle.

7. A pulley, or a system of pulleys, mounted in its frame or shell, with its band or strap. A *block* consists of one or more pulleys or sheaves, with a groove for the rope, fastened in a frame by pins, on which they revolve; a frame inclosing the pulleys; and a band encompassing the frame, attached to some stationary object. *Blocks* for standing rigging, called deadeyes, are shells, without sheaves or pulleys.

8. A blockhead; a stupid fellow. [Obs.]

9. Among cutters in wood, a form of hard wood, on which they cut figures in relief with knives, chisels, etc.

10. The wooden mold on which a hat is formed.

11. In falconry, the perch whereon a bird of prey was kept.

12. In commerce, a number of shares of stock salable in a series or lump.

13. A railroad section operated under the block system.

14. A piece of hard wood used by engravers and printers for the mounting of electrotypes or stereotypes.

15. In cricket, a position of the batter when defending his wicket.

Block system; a system of automatic signals, electric or otherwise, dividing a railroad-track into divisions, called blocks. A train approaching a station or danger-point receives a positive signal if the track is obstructed.

block, *v.t.*; blocked, *pt.*, *pp.*; blocking, *ppr.* [Fr. *bloquer*, to block up, from *bloc*, a block.]

1. To inclose or shut up, so as to hinder egress or passage; to stop up; to obstruct by placing obstacles in the way; often followed by *up*; as, to *block up* a town, or a road.

2. To shape or form by using a block.

3. To support or secure by means of blocks.

4. To stop, as a blow.

5. In athletics, (a) to impede the progress of (an opponent), as in football; (b) to stop (a ball) with the bat, as in cricket.

6. To blot out or deface, as in photography when part of a picture may be removed by erasing it from the plate, or by covering it with some opaque substance when printing.

To block out; to roughly sketch or diagram, omitting details; as, he *blocked out* a plan of action.

block-āde′, *n.* [ME. *blok*, an inclosed space, and *-ade*; from OFr. *bloquer*, to stop.]

1. The closing of one or more ports of a country, by investment with a naval force or troops, to prevent escape and hinder supplies from entering, and to compel a surrender, by hunger and want, without regular attacks. This word is now used mainly when speaking of an investment by naval forces, the word *siege* being preferred when speaking of a land *blockade*.

To constitute a *blockade* the investing power must be able to apply its force to every point of practicable access, so as to render it dangerous to attempt to enter; and there is no *blockade* of that port where its force cannot be brought to bear.

2. A jamming or stoppage of persons or material in transit; as, a *blockade* of freight; a *blockade* of people.

To raise a blockade; to either withdraw or drive away the forces which make a blockade effective.

block-āde′, *v.t.*; blockaded, *pt.*, *pp.*; blockading, *ppr.* To close a port of entry by means of naval investment; to prevent the entry of supplies, succor, etc., by besieging with a land force; to stop up; to block; to obstruct; as, the doorway was *blockaded* with furniture.

Syn.—Beleaguer, shut.

block-ād′ẽr, *n.* 1. A vessel stationed to blockade a port.

2. One employed in blockading.

block′āge, *n.* [From OFr. *bloc*, a barrier, and *-age*.] The act of blocking up or the state resulting therefrom.

block′book, *n.* A book printed from engraved wooden blocks instead of movable type.

block′head (-hed), *n.* A stupid fellow; a dolt; a person deficient in understanding.

Syn.—Dolt, dunderhead, jolterhead, dunce, ninny, numskull, dullard, simpleton, booby, loggerhead, ignoramus.

block′head″ed, *a.* Stupid; dull.

block′head″ism, *n.* Stupidity; that which is characteristic of a blockhead.

block′head″ly, *a.* Stupid.

block′house, *n.* A military edifice or fortress, so called because originally constructed chiefly of timber. In their last war with the Boers the British used octagonal galvanized-iron *blockhouses*.

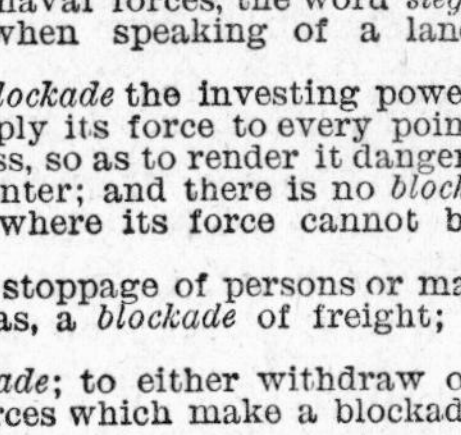

Modern Blockhouse.
a, a, a, a, Loopholes.

block′ing, *n.* 1. The material used to support or prop.

2. The act of obstructing.

3. The act of shaping, stamping, or supporting with blocks.

block′ing-çourse, *n.* The final course of a wall above the cornice.

block′ish, *a.* Stupid; dull; deficient in understanding.

block′ish-ly, *adv.* In a stupid manner.

block′ish-ness, *n.* Stupidity; dullness.

block′like, *a.* Like a block; stupid.

block′print″ing, *n.* 1. The act or process of printing from engraved blocks of wood.

2. A mode of printing paper and cotton with colors from a design cut in relief upon a block.

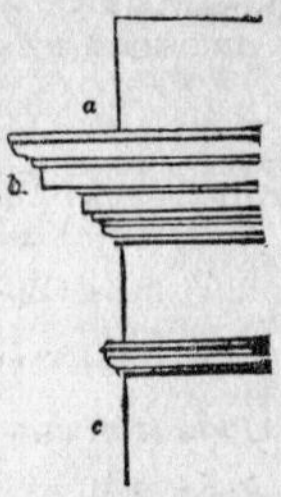

a, Blocking-course; *b*, Cornice; *c*, Front of wall.

block′ship, *n.* An old man-of-war, unfit for use on the open sea, and used as a supply-ship for stores or for the temporary use of seamen; a ship used to block the entrance to a port or harbor; an old hulk.

blö′dite, blœ′dite (blū′), *n.* [Named after the chemist *Blöde*.] A hydrous compound of magnesium, sodium, and sulphur, found chiefly in the salt-mines of upper Austria.

blōke, blōak, *n.* A fellow; a term of disrespect. [Slang.]

blōm′ā-ry, *n.* Same as *Bloomery*.

blond, *a.* [OFr. *blond*, f. *blonde*, light, from LL. *blondus*, yellow.] Possessing a fair or light complexion, light (usually blue) eyes, and hair of a golden or flaxen hue.

blond, *n.* A person of fair complexion, with light hair and blue eyes.

blonde, *a.* and *n.* The feminine of *blond*.

blond′-lāce, *n.* A French lace originally made of unbleached silk, but now sometimes dyed.

blond′-met″ăl, *n.* A clay ironstone used for making tools, and found in Staffordshire, England.

blond′ness, *n.* The condition of being blond.

blon′ket, blonġ′ket, *a.* [OFr. *blanquet*, whitish.] Gray or bluish-gray. [Obs.]

blood (blud), *n.* [ME. *blood, bloud*; AS. *blōd*, blood, from *blōwan*, to flourish, bloom.]

1. The fluid circulating through the arteries and veins of animal bodies, and essential to the preservation of life. This fluid is generally red, except in the case of insects.

2. Kindred; relation by descent; consanguinity; lineage; progeny.

3. Royal or honorable lineage; as, a prince of the *blood*; a gentleman of *blood*.

4. Slaughter, murder, or bloodshed; as, his *blood* shall be avenged.

5. Guilt and punishment.

Your *blood* be upon your own heads.
—Acts xviii. 6.

6. The price of blood; that which is obtained by shedding blood, and seizing goods.

7. Temper of mind; state of the passions. Thus, to commit an act in *cold blood* is to do it deliberately. *Warm blood* denotes a temper inflamed. *Hot blood* denotes the arousing of more violent passions, and *bad blood* the existence of embittered feelings.

8. A man of fire or spirit; a rake.

9. In stock-breeding, pedigree, or superiority of breed. *Half blood* is extraction in which one half of pure blood is in evidence.

10. That which resembles blood; as, the *blood* of grapes.

Blood snow; see *Red snow* under *Snow*.

Flesh and blood; fleshly nature; the carnal part of man, as opposed to the spiritual nature, or divine life; as, to be born of *flesh and blood*.

Whole blood; in law, a kinsman of the *whole blood* is one who descends from the same couple of ancestors; of the *half blood*, one who descends from either of them singly, by a second marriage.

blood, *v.t.*; blooded, *pt.*, *pp.*; blooding, *ppr.* 1. To let blood from; to bleed by opening a vein. [Obs.]

2. To stain with blood. [Obs.]

3. To train or inure to blood, as a hound or a soldier.

4. To heat the blood of; to exasperate. [Obs.]

blood′-ȧ-ven″ġẽr, *n.* One who devotes himself to pursuing and killing the murderer of his relative or friend; one appointed for that purpose. Among primitive peoples, the nearest of kin to the one slain took upon himself this duty.

blood′-bap″tism, *n.* See *Baptism of blood*, under *Baptism*.

blood′-bē-spot″ted, *a.* Spotted with blood.

blood′bird, *n.* A honeysucking bird of Australia, the male bird being of a bright red color.

blood′-blis″tẽr, *n.* A blister full of blood or serum mixed with blood.

blood′-bōlt″ẽred, *a.* Matted or sprinkled with blood. [Obs.]

blood′-çol-ŏred, *a.* Having the color of blood.

blood′-çor″pus-cle, *n.* See *Corpuscle*.

blood′-çups, *n. pl.* In botany, cup-shaped fungi of the genus *Peziza*, of fleshy, waxy, brilliant-red appearance, with naked spores on a

fructifying surface, the gills covered with a delicate membrane.

blood'ed, *a.* 1. Of character or temperament indicated by blood, usually qualified by *cold* or *warm*.

2. Of pure descent or fine breeding; as, *blooded* stock.

blood'flow"ẽr, *n.* Any plant bearing red flowers of the genus *Hæmanthus*, native to the Cape of Good Hope.

blood'guilt"i-ness (-gilt"), *n.* The guilt or crime of shedding blood.

blood'guilt"less, *a.* Not guilty of shedding blood or of murder.

blood'guilt"y, *a.* Guilty of murder.

blood'=hòrse, *n.* A horse of the purest blood or best lineage.

blood'=hot, *a.* As warm as blood at its natural temperature.

blood'hound, *n.* A variety of dog, with long, smooth, and pendulous ears, remarkable for the acuteness of its smell. It is employed to recover game which has escaped wounded from the hunter, by tracing the lost animal by the blood it has lost, by its tracks or contact with any object along its course; whence the name of the dog. It is often employed for the purpose of overtaking and capturing criminals and fugitives from justice.

Bloodhound.

blood'i-ly, *adv.* In a bloody manner; cruelly; with a disposition to shed blood.

blood'i-ness, *n.* The state of being bloody; disposition to shed blood.

blood'=is"lănds (-ī"lăndz), *n pl.* Infinitesimal blood-colored patches or spots dotted over the vascular embryonic tissues, denoting the genesis of corpuscles.

blood'less, *a.* 1. Without or appearing to be without blood; lifeless.

2. Without shedding of blood or slaughter; as, a *bloodless* victory.

3. Without spirit or activity.

blood'less-ly, *adv.* In a bloodless manner.

blood'less-ness, *n.* The state of being without or lacking blood; anemia.

blood'let, *v.t.* To bleed; to let blood. [Rare.]

blood'let"tẽr, *n.* One who lets blood, as in diseases; a phlebotomist. [Rare.]

blood'let"ting, *n.* The act of letting blood, or bleeding by opening a vein.

blood'=mŏn"ey, *n.* 1. Money paid in compensation for murder, to secure immunity from punishment; in accord with an ancient custom by which a murderer could settle with the next of kin to his victim.

2. Money paid as the reward for having committed, or as the inducement to commit, a murder, by those interested in or desiring the death of the victim.

blood'=plāte, blood'=plaque (-plak), *n.* A formative colorless element or disk, found in the blood, smaller than the red and more numerous than the white corpuscles; a hematoblast.

blood'=poi"sŏn-ing, *n.* A dangerous poisoned condition of the blood, caused by disease or wounds, or accidental introduction of harmful foreign matter into the circulation.

blood'pụd"ding, *n.* A pudding made with blood (usually of swine) and other materials.

blood'=rāin, *n.* Rain colored while falling by passing through and collecting coloring matter, particularly red dust, that has been previously drawn up into the atmosphere.

blood'=red, *a.* Red as blood.

blood'rọọt, *n.* A plant so named from the color of its root-sap; a species of *Sanguinaria* (*Sanguinaria Canadensis*); called also *red puccoon, turmeric*, and *redroot*.

blood'shed, *n.* The shedding or spilling of blood; slaughter; waste of life; the crime of shedding blood.

blood'shed"dẽr, *n.* One who sheds blood; a murderer.

blood'shed"ding, *n.* The shedding of blood; the crime of shedding blood.

blood'shot, *a.* Red and inflamed by a turgid state of the blood-vessels, as in diseases of the eye or injuries to it.

blood'shot"ten, *a.* Bloodshot. [Obs.]

blood'=spav"in, *n.* Distension of the parts about the hock-joint of a horse, caused by effusion within the joint.

blood'=stāined, *a.* Stained with blood; hence, figuratively, guilty of murder.

blood'stick, *n.* A piece of wood weighted with lead, used in veterinary surgery to force a lancet into a vein.

blood'stōne, *n.* A green jasper spotted with red, as if with blood.

blood'strōke, *n.* A loss of sensation and motion caused by a hemorrhage or enforced stoppage and gathering of the blood; a form of apoplexy.

blood'suck"ẽr, *n.* 1. Any animal that sucks blood; specifically applied to the leech.

2. A cruel man; a murderer. [Obs.]

3. A hard master, or extortioner.

blood'thĩrst"i-ness, *n.* The desire to shed blood.

blood'thĩrst"y, *a.* Desirous to shed blood; murderous.

blood'=tree, *n.* A small West Indian tree, named from the color of its juice; called *dragon's-blood*.

blood'ulf, *n.* The European species of bullfinch.

blood'=vas"cū-lăr, *a.* Relating to blood-vessels.

blood'=ves"sel, *n.* Any vessel in which blood circulates in an animal body; an artery, a vein, or a capillary.

blood'wīte, *n.* In ancient law, a fine or amercement, paid as a compensation for the shedding of blood; also, a riot in which blood was spilled; sometimes spelled *bloodwit*.

blood'wood (blud'wood), *n.* A name given to several trees, from the color of their wood or sap; especially, the logwood.

blood'wŏrm, *n.* 1. The active red larva of a fly of the dipterous genus *Chironomus*.

2. A parasite living in the blood.

blood'wŏrt, *n.* The bloody dock, a species of *Rumex*; also, a name for the bloodroot.

blood'y, *a.* 1. Stained with blood.

2. Cruel; murderous; given to the shedding of blood; having a cruel, savage disposition; applied to men or animals.

3. Attended with bloodshed; marked by cruelty; applied to things; as, a *bloody* battle.

4. Full of or like blood; as, *bloody* sweat.

5. Excessive; used as an epithet or merely for emphasis. [Vulgar.]

Bloody flux; a form of dysentery in which the discharges from the bowels have a mixture of blood.

Bloody hand; a hand stained with deer's blood, which, under the old English forest laws, was sufficient evidence of trespass; also, a red hand used as the distinctive ensign of the order of baronets.

Bloody man's finger; see *Cuckoopint*.

Bloody sweat; a profuse perspiration tinged with blood; also, a disease called sweating-sickness, formerly common in Europe.

blood'y, *v.t.* To stain with blood.

blood'y, *adv.* Very; as, *bloody* sick; *bloody* drunk. [Vulgar.]

blood'y-bōneṣ, *n.* A terrifying nursery bugbear.

blood'y=eȳed, *a.* Having bloody or cruel eyes.

blood'y=fāced, *a.* Having a bloody face or appearance.

blood'y=fluxed, *a.* Afflicted with the bloody flux.

blood'y=mīnd"ed, *a.* Having a fierce, evil disposition; barbarous; inclined to shed blood.

blood'y=scep"tẽred, *a.* Having a scepter obtained by blood or slaughter.

blood'y=wąr"riŏr (-yẽr), *n.* The wallflower, or bleeding-heart (*Cheiranthus Cheiri*).

blọọm, *n.* [ME. *blome*, a blossom; AS. *blōstma*, a blossom, from *blōwan*, to blow, bloom.]

1. A blossom; the flower of a plant; an expanded bud.

> While opening *blooms* diffuse their sweets around. —Pope.

2. The opening of flowers in general; flowers open, or in a state of blossoming; as, the trees are clothed with *bloom*.

3. The state of youth, resembling that of blossoms; a state of opening manhood; life, beauty, and vigor; a state of health and growth, promising higher perfection; as, the *bloom* of youth.

4. The fine gray dust found upon plums and grapes newly gathered; also, figuratively, anything lending freshness to the appearance; a glow; as, the *bloom* on her cheeks.

5. The appearance of cloudiness sometimes given to a picture by varnish.

6. The yellow powder found on leather after a complete tanning.

7. A name given to some minerals of a bright color, usually produced by a natural decomposition.

8. A trade name for a variety of very choice raisins which are dried in the sun.

blọọm, *v.i.*; bloomed, *pt., pp.*; blooming, *ppr.* 1. To produce or yield blossoms; to flower.

2. To be in a state of healthful, growing youth and vigor; to show the beauty of youth.

blọọm, *v.t.* 1. To put forth, as blossoms. [Obs.]

2. To make blooming. [Rare.]

> Charitable affection *bloomed* them.—Hooker.

blọọm, *n.* [AS. *blōma*, a lump of metal, in a deflected sense from *blōwan*, to blow.]

1. In metallurgy, a rough, heavy, and relatively short bar of wrought iron freed from slag, or of steel made from the puddling balls, usually by shingling, or directly from the ingot, in the case of steel. It is the form in which the metal is handled prior to its being drawn out into bars of commercial sizes between rolls or under the hammer.

2. A billet of iron or steel.

blọọm'ạ-ry, blōm'ạ-ry, *n.* Same as *Bloomery*.

blọọm'ẽr, *n.* [Named after Mrs. *Bloomer*, of New York, who, in 1849-50, attempted to introduce this style of dress for general use.]

1. A costume for women, consisting of a short skirt extending to the knees, loose trousers fastened at the waist and around the ankles, and a large, low hat.

2. A woman attired in this costume.

blọọm'ẽrṣ, *n.pl.* [See *Bloomer*.] The clothes forming the bloomer costume, especially the loose trousers often worn with garments other than the bloomer skirt, as an appropriate costume for athletic exercises and outdoor sports.

blọọm'ẽr-y, *n.* 1. In iron-working, a puddling furnace or forge in which the ore is made directly into wrought iron, taking the form of blooms.

2. A bloom-making machine.

blọọm'ing, *a.* 1. Opening in blossoms; flowering.

2. Thriving in health, beauty, and vigor; showing the freshness and beauties of youth.

3. Thorough-paced; full-fledged; extreme. [Slang.]

Syn.—Flourishing, fair, flowering, blossoming, young, beautiful.

blọọm'ing, *n.* In metallurgy, the process of making blooms.

blọọm'ing, *n.* 1. The clouded appearance, like the bloom of grapes or plums, sometimes assumed by varnish on the surface of a picture.

2. In dyeing, the bright or blooming appearance of goods due to the addition of some substance after the dyeing proper is completed.

blọọm'ing-ly, *adv.* In a flourishing or thriving manner.

blọọm'ing-ness, *n.* A flourishing condition; thriving state.

blọọm'ing=sal"ly, *n.* In botany, the fireweed, *Epilobium angustifolium*.

blọọm'less, *a.* Lacking bloom or flowers.

blọọm'y, *a.* 1. Full of bloom; flowery; flourishing with the vigor of youth; as, a *bloomy* spray; *bloomy* beauties.

2. Covered with bloom, as ripe plums.

blọọth, *n.* The process of blooming or blossoming. [Prov. Eng.]

blōre, *n.* The act of blowing; a blast. [Obs.]

blos'my, *a.* Blossomy. [Obs.]

blos'sŏm, *n.* [ME. *blossome*; AS. *blōstma, blōsthma*, a blossom, flower, from *blowan*, to blow.]

1. The flower of a plant, or the essential organs of reproduction with their appendages; florescence; bloom. The term has been applied by some botanists, and is also applied in common usage, to the corolla. *Blossom* is more commonly used than flower or bloom, when we have reference to the fruit which is to succeed. Thus we use *flowers*, when we speak of plants cultivated for ornament; and *bloom* in a more general sense, as of flowers in general, or in reference to the beauty of flowers.

2. The peculiar color of a horse, when bay or sorrel hairs are mixed freely with white; a kind of peach color.

3. A blooming period of development; as, the *blossom* of youth.

In blossom; in the period of blossoming; applied to plants or trees.

blos'sŏm, *v.i.*; blossomed (-somd), *pt., pp.*; blossoming, *ppr.* 1. To put forth blossoms or flowers; to bloom; to blow; to flower.

2. To flourish and prosper.

> The desert shall rejoice, and *blossom* as the rose. —Isa. xxxv. 1.

blos'sŏm-less, *a.* Destitute of blossom.

blos'sŏm-y, *a.* Having many blossoms.

blot, *v.t.*; blotted, *pt., pp.*; blotting, *ppr.* [ME. *blotten*, to blot, from Ice. *blettr*, a blot, spot.]

1. To spot with ink; to stain or bespatter with ink; as, to *blot* a paper.

2. To obliterate with ink; to cancel or efface; generally with *out*; as, to *blot out* a sentence; to *blot out* a crime.

3. To dry with blotting-paper, as manuscript.

4. To stain with infamy; to tarnish; to disgrace; to disfigure; to impair; to damage.

> *Blot* not thy innocence with guiltless blood. —Rowe.

5. To darken; to eclipse.

> He sung how earth *blots* the moon's gilded wane. —Cowley.

To blot out of the book of life; a scriptural phrase, meaning to reject from the number of those who are to be saved.

To blot out a person or *nation*; to destroy, exterminate, or consume him or it.

To blot out sins; to forgive them.

Syn.—Expunge, erase, efface, cancel, obliterate.—Letters are *blotted out*, so that they cannot be seen again; they are *expunged*, so as to

signify that they cannot stand for anything; they are *erased*, so that the space may be reoccupied with others. *Obliterate* is said of all characters, but without defining the mode in which they are put out. *Efface* is the consequence of some direct action on the thing which is *effaced*; in this manner writing may be *effaced* from a wall by the action of the elements; *cancel* is the act of a person, and always the fruit of design; *obliterate* is the fruit of accident and circumstances in general.

blot, *v.i.* To cause blots, as of ink; to absorb or diffuse, as ink; as, this paper *blots* nicely.

blot, *n.* [ME. *blot*, *blotte*, a blot, probably from Ice. *bletlr*, a stain.]

1. A spot or stain; usually applied to ink on paper.

2. An obliteration of something written or printed.

3. A spot on the reputation; a stain; a disgrace; a reproach; a blemish.

blot, *n.* [Prob. from D. *bloot*, bare, naked, exposed.]

1. In backgammon, (a) an exposure of an unprotected piece; (b) a single man so exposed.

2. An unprotected point; a weak spot; a place inviting attack; a failing.

blotch (bloch), *v.t.*; blotched, *pt.*, *pp.*; blotching, *ppr.* To disfigure with blotches; to put blotches on.

blotch, *n.* 1. A pustule upon the skin; an eruption, usually of a large kind.

2. A blot or spot, as an ink-*blotch*, or a paint-*blotch*; particularly, a spot larger than the ordinary conception of a blot, and of ragged outline; hence, figuratively, a disfiguring stain; as, a moral *blotch*.

3. A disease to which dogs are subject.

blotched, *a.* Covered with blotches.

blotch'y, *a.* Marked with blotches.

blōte, *v.t.* To bloat; to cure; as herrings. [Obs.]

blot'less, *a.* Having no blot.

blot'tēr, *n.* 1. A person or thing which blots; a piece of blotting-paper; a means of removing an excess of liquid ink from the surface of paper by absorption.

2. In bookkeeping, an entry-book for recording current transactions.

blot-tesque' (-tesk'), *a.* and *n.* I. *a.* In painting, characterized by blots or heavy touches; wanting in fine delineation; blotchy.

II. *n.* A blurred or dauby piece of work.

blot'ting, *n.* The making of blots; a staining or obliterating; the act of absorbing ink.

blot'ting-pa"pēr, *n.* A kind of paper made without size, serving to absorb wet ink, and thus prevent blots.

blouse, *n.* [Fr. *blouse*, prob. from OFr. *blaude*, a smock-frock.]

1. A short, loose frock, usually of a cheap blue material, worn by workingmen, particularly in France; also, a short, loose coat, plain and serviceable, such as the coat of the fatigue or service uniforms of soldiers.

2. A short, loose waist, usually belted, worn by women and children.

blōw, *n.* [ME. *blaw*, a blow; origin uncertain.]

1. The act of striking, or the stroke; a sudden and violent impact of the hand, fist, or an instrument, against an object or person.

2. An act of hostility; as, the nation which strikes the first *blow*.

3. A sudden calamity; sudden or severe evil; as, the *blows* of fortune were too hard for him.

At a blow; in a single act; by a sudden event; in one sweep; as, to gain a kingdom *at a blow*.

To come to blows; to engage in combat, whether by individuals, armies, fleets, or nations.

Syn.—Puff, blast, breath, stroke, infliction, wound, disappointment, affliction, knock, shock, calamity, misfortune.

blōw, *v.i.*; blew, *pt.*; blowing, *ppr.*; blown, *pp.* [ME. *blowen*, *blawen*; AS. *blawan*, to blow.]

1. To make a current of air; to move as air; particularly, to move with appreciable force or speed; as, the wind *blows*. Often used impersonally with *it*; as, *it blows* a gale.

2. To pant; to puff; to breathe hard or quick.

> Here is Mistress Page at the door, sweating and *blowing*. —Shak.

3. To give forth sounds or tones on being blown, as a horn or trumpet.

4. To eject a stream of water or other fluid, as a whale or geyser.

5. To be carried about or along by the wind; as, the dust *blows* throughout August in that region.

6. To talk loudly or boastingly. [Colloq.]

To blow great guns; to blow violently; to blow with the force and fury of a heavy gale.

To blow hot and cold; to act inconsistently, particularly in the treatment of a person or attention to a cause; an expression taken from one of Æsop's fables.

To blow in; (a) to squander; (b) to come into a place. [Slang.]

To blow off; to emit a stream of water or steam; to let off pressure, as a boiler.

To blow out; (a) to be torn, disrupted, or ejected by pressure from within, as the gauge-glass or a gasket on a boiler; (b) in electricity, to be melted or burned by the heat of the current, particularly in case of a short circuit.

To blow over; to pass away without effect; to cease or be dissipated; as, the clouds are *blown over*; the scandal will *blow over*.

To blow up; to be violently disrupted by an internal explosion, the wreckage being cast up and around; as, a powder-magazine, a flour-mill, or a gasometer *blows up*.

blōw, *v.t.* 1. To throw or drive a current of air upon; as, to *blow* the fire; also, to fan.

2. To drive by a current of air; to impel; as, the tempest *blew* the ship ashore.

3. To breathe upon, for the purpose of warming; as, to *blow* the fingers on a cold day.

4. To sound (a wind-instrument); as, *blow* the trumpet.

5. To spread by report.

> And through the court his courtesy was *blown*. —Dryden.

6. To deposit eggs on, as flies do on meat.

7. To form by inflating, as glass in the plastic state is formed into a desired shape by the breath, or as soap-bubbles are formed.

8. To put out of breath from fatigue; as, to *blow* a horse.

9. To expel the contents from by forcing air or fluid through; as, to *blow* the nose; to *blow* boiler-tubes.

10. To destroy; to explode; usually followed by *up*, *down*, or *open*. as, the wind *blew* the house *down*; the steam *blew* the boiler *up*.

To blow away; to dissipate; to scatter with wind.

To blow down; (a) to prostrate by wind; (b) to cause fluid under pressure to leave by an orifice at the bottom; as, to *blow down* a boiler.

To blow off, (a) to remove, as by wind; as, to *blow off* fruit from trees; (b) to drive from land; as, to *blow off* a ship; (c) to cause the whole or a part of a fluid under pressure to escape from a receptacle by rising through an opening; as, to *blow off* a boiler; (d) to treat; to pay the expenses of, especially for drink or amusement; in this sense, slang.

To blow one's own trumpet; to resort to fulsome self-praise.

To blow out; (a) to extinguish by a current of air, as a candle; (b) in electricity, to cause to be melted or burned by the current.

To blow out the brains of; to kill by shooting through the head.

To blow through; in condensing engines, to admit live steam into the condenser in order to drive out the air, preliminary to starting the engine.

To blow up; (a) to fill with air; to swell; as, to *blow up* a bladder or a bubble; (b) to inflate; to puff up; as, to *blow* one *up* with flattery; (c) to kindle; as, to *blow up* a contention; (d) to burst, to raise into the air, or to scatter, by the explosion of gunpowder; (e) figuratively, to scatter or bring to naught suddenly; as, to *blow up* a scheme; (f) to remonstrate with; to reprimand; in this sense, slang.

To blow upon; (a) to make stale or worthless; as, to *blow upon* an author's works; (b) to betray; to give information against. [Slang.]

blōw, *n.* 1. The production of or the act of producing a stream or current of air, particularly a strong or violent air-movement; a strong wind; among seamen, a gale of wind; as, the great *blow* of '99.

2. The act of forcing air through any medium, as the mouth or an instrument.

3. The stream of water and air emitted by a whale.

4. A blowhole in a casting.

5. In metallurgy, the time consumed in one blast of the Bessemer process, or the mass of metal acted on at one time.

6. An ovum or egg deposited by a fly on flesh or other substance; also called a *fly-blow*.

7. Inflated speech; boastfulness; brag; as, his speech is all *blow*. [Colloq.]

blōw, *v.i.*; blew, *pt.*; blowing, *ppr.*; blown, *pp.* [AS. *blowan*, to bloom.] To bloom; to flower.

blōw, *v.t.* To cause to bloom or put forth blossoms, as plants. [Rare.]

blōw, *n.* 1. A flower; a blossom; a profusion of blossoms.

2. The condition of blossoming; the period of blooming; hence, a state of high development.

blōw'ball, *n.* The downy head of the dandelion, formed by the pappus, after the blossom has fallen.

blōw'=cock, *n.* A cock for blowing off pressure in a steam-boiler.

blōw'ēr, *n.* 1. One who blows; one who is employed in smelting tin or blowing glass.

2. A plate of iron or tin used to increase the current of air in a chimney.

3. A machine for ventilating a building or shaft, or for cleaning grain; a mechanical fan.

4. A blowing out of gas from a hole in a coal-mine.

5. A name given the whale by seamen.

6. The swellfish, or puffer, *Spheroides maculatus*, found along the Atlantic coast.

7. A loud or boastful talker. [Slang.]

blōw'fish, *n.* Any fish which can blow up or inflate its body.

blōw'fly, *n.* A species of dipterous insect, *Musca carnaria*, very troublesome in summer, from its habit of depositing its eggs on flesh.

blōw'gun, *n.* A tube-shaped weapon, of cane or reed, directing and propelling a missile ejected by a strong puff of breath; used by various savage tribes inhabiting tropical countries; called also *blowpipe*.

blōw'hōle, *n.* 1. A cavity formed at the water-level in a cliff on the seashore, ending in an orifice through which the waters impelled by the waves spout intermittently in high jets.

2. A hole in the ice giving seals and the like access to air.

3. The orifice or nostril through which the whale, dolphin, and similar mammals spout.

4. A hole in a casting made by gas or air.

blōw'ing, *n.* The motion of wind, or act of blowing.

blōw'ing=ad"dēr, *n.* See *Puff-adder*.

blōw'ing=en"gine, blōw'ing=mà-chïne", *n.* A machine for supplying an air-current for any purpose, such as a fan-blower; an engine for ventilation or foundry blast purposes; also, an engine actuating a blower.

blōwn, *v.*, past participle of *blow*.

blōwn, *a.* Opened, as a flower; unfolded; having blossomed; as, a full-*blown* rose.

blōwn, *a.* 1. Driven by wind.

2. Sounded by blowing.

3. Spread by report.

4. Swollen; inflated; in either a literal or a figurative sense.

5. Covered with the eggs and larvæ of flies.

blōw'=off, *n.* and *a.* I. *n.* A blowing off, as of steam; also, the device causing it.

II. *a.* Pertaining to a blow-off; as, a *blow-off* cock.

blōw'=out, *n.* 1. The act or state of blowing out or having blown out, in any of the senses of the word.

2. An entertainment; a festal occasion or celebration, particularly one involving eating and drinking. [Slang.]

blōw'=ō"vēr, *n.* In glass-making, the superfluous material which runs over the top of a mold.

blōw'pīpe, *n.* 1. An instrument by which a blast or current of air is driven through the flame of a lamp or candle, and that flame directed upon a substance, to fuse, vitrify, or heat it intensely. By blowing through this with the mouth, the flame of a Bunsen burner, or similar heat-source, can be directed at will in a flame-pencil of great intensity.

Blowpipe.
a, Ball for catching the moisture of the mouth; *b*, Nozzle.

2. A blowgun.

Blowpipe analysis; a method of rapid qualitative analysis of mineral substances which utilizes the heat of the blowpipe to facilitate the reactions.

blōw'point, *n.* Formerly, a game for children, in which arrows or small pins were blown through a tube at certain numbers. [Obs.]

blowse, *n.* Same as *Blowze*.

blōwth, *n.* Bloom or blossom, or that which is expanded; the state of blossoming; blossoms collectively; blooth. [Obs. or Dial.]

blōw'tūbe, *n.* 1. A blowgun.

2. A metal tube used by boys for discharging light missiles; a pea-shooter.

3. In glass-making, a hollow iron rod, five to six feet long, with which the blower gathers up the semifluid metal from the pot, and by blowing through which he expands the molten material while shaping it on the marver.

blōw'=valve, *n.* The snifting-valve of a condensing engine.

blōw'y, *a.* Windy; breezy; gusty; as, *blowy* weather.

blowze, *n.* [AS. *blyscan*, *bliscan*, to blush, shine.] A ruddy, fat-faced woman; a blowzy woman; a wench. [Obs.]

blowzed, *a.* Blowzy; ruddy; flushed; coarse-complexioned, as from exposure to weather; fat and high-colored.

> Huge women *blowzed* with health and wind and rain. —Tennyson.

blowz'y, *a.* 1. Ruddy-faced; high-colored; fat and flushed; coarse-complexioned.

> A face made *blowzy* by cold and damp. —George Eliot.

2. Unkempt; slatternly; disheveled; as, *blowzy* hair.

blub, *v.t.* To swell; to inflate; to blubber, as with weeping. [Obs.]

blub′bẽr, *n.* [ME. *blubber,* a bubble; formed from the verb.]
1. A bubble.
2. The fat of whales and other large sea animals, from which oil is extracted. The *blubber* lies immediately under the skin and over the muscular flesh.
3. The sea-nettle, or sea-blubber; a jellyfish or medusa.
4. The act of blubbering.

blub′bẽr, *v.i.*; blubbered, *pt., pp.*; blubbering, *ppr.* [ME. *blubren*; G. dial. *blubbern,* to blubber; an onomatopoetic word.] To weep and sob, especially in such a manner as to puff out the cheeks or disfigure the face; used generally in ridicule and contempt.

She wept, she *blubbered,* and she tore her hair. —Swift.

blub′bẽr, *v.t.* 1. To swell (the cheeks) or disfigure (the face) with weeping.
2. To utter in a childish manner; to give vent to sobbingly; usually with *out*; as, he *blubbered out* his confession.

blub′bẽred, *a.* Swollen; marred; turgid; disfigured by or as by weeping; as, a *blubbered* lip.

blub′bẽr-ing, *n.* The act of weeping in a noisy, childish manner.

blub′bẽr-y, *a.* 1. Protuberant; swollen, as lips or cheeks.
2. Resembling blubber; fat; gelatinous; quivering; as, a *blubbery* mass.

blü′chẽr, *n.* A strong leather half-boot or high shoe, named after Field-marshal von Blücher, commander of the Prussian army in the later campaigns against Napoleon Bonaparte.

bludg′eŏn (bluj′ŏn), *n.* [Origin unknown; perhaps from D. *bludsen, blutsen,* to bruise.] A short stick, with one end loaded or thicker and heavier than the other, used as an offensive weapon.

blūe, *n.* [ME. *blew, blewe*; Fr. *bleu*; O.H.G. *blao,* blue; AS. *blǣw,* in deriv. as *blǣwen,* bluish.]
1. One of the seven colors into which the rays of light divide themselves when refracted through a glass prism; the color of the clear sky or deep sea, or a similar color, whether lighter or darker; azure; the natural ultramarine, or a shade or tint resembling it.
2. A dye or pigment of this hue or color. The substances used as blue pigments are of very different natures, and derived from various sources, some being compound bodies, others natural, and still others artificial. They are derived almost entirely from the vegetable and mineral kingdoms. The best *blue* for painters is ultramarine, which is prepared from lapis lazuli, or azure-stone. The principal *blues* used in painting are: *Prussian blue,* which is a compound of cyanogen and iron; *blue bice,* next in quality to Prussian blue; *indigo blue,* from the indigo plant. Besides these there are other shades of blue, as *blue verditer, smalt,* and *cobalt-blue* from *cobalt, lacmus* or *litmus, sky-blue,* etc.
3. The sky; the atmosphere; from its blue tint; as, a bolt from the *blue.*
4. The deep sea.
5. A pedantic literary woman; a contraction of *bluestocking.* [Colloq.]
6. A small blue butterfly.
7. Bluing.
8. A blueprint.
9. A member of a party or any organization of persons which has adopted blue as its distinctive color; as, the buffs and the *blues*; the light *blues* win.
10. [*pl.*] Low spirits; melancholy; usually preceded by the definite article; as, to have a fit of *the blues*; a contraction of *blue devils.*
Cyanine blue; a color between blue-green and blue.
Napoleon blue; a variety of Prussian blue, dyed on silk.
Parma blue; spirit-blue.
Prussian blue; a chemical compound used in dyeing, in ink, etc.; it is obtained by the combination of yellow prussiate of potash with a ferric salt; called also *Berlin blue.*

blūe, *a.*; *comp.* bluer; *superl.* bluest. 1. Having the color of the clear sky, or a color similar to it, whether lighter or darker; as, the *blue* firmament; the deep *blue* sea.
2. Despondent; melancholy; low or depressed in spirits; as, she looked a bit *blue* last night.
3. Tending or suited to cause low spirits; dismal; dreary; lacking cheerfulness; as, a *blue* outlook; a *blue* day. [Colloq.]
4. Austere or puritanic in morals or religion; overstrict; as, a *blue* Covenanter; also, inculcating or prescribing a severe or gloomy code of moral conduct; as, *blue* laws.
5. Genuine; faithful; unwavering; as, his friend was true *blue.*
6. Having a purplish color; livid, as the skin from a bruise, or from extreme cold or fear.
7. Pedantic; learned; said of women, especially those of literary proclivities; an abbreviation of *bluestocking.*
8. Pale, without glare or redness, as a flame; of the color of burning brimstone; hence, figuratively, presaging the presence of imps, ghosts, or devils; as, the air was full of *blue* devils; the air was *blue* with oaths.
9. Indecent; obscene; as, *blue* stories. [Slang.]
Blue asbestos; see *Crocidolite.*
Blue blood; pure, aristocratic descent; from a phrase applied in Spain (*sangre azul*) to the blood of the nobility as distinguished from the blood of the common people.
Blue book; (a) an English parliamentary publication or report, so called from its being issued in blue paper covers; (b) an official register containing the names of the persons in the employ of the United States government.
Blue cod; the buffalo-cod.
Blue crab; the common edible crab found along the Atlantic coast of the United States.
Blue devils; low spirits; melancholy; the imaginary apparitions seen by persons suffering from delirium tremens.
Blue jaundice; see *Jaundice.*
Blue jay; the American jay, *Cyanocitta cristata.* [See *Jay.*]
Blue light; a composition burning with a brilliant blue flame, and used as a night-signal at sea and in pyrotechnic displays.
Blue mantle; one of the pursuivants of the English college of arms; named from the color of his official dress.
Blue mass; a compound of mercury, glycerin, etc., from which blue pills are formed.
Blue mold; the mold or fungus, *Aspergillus glaucus,* which appears on cheese.
Blue Monday; the Monday after a Sunday spent in dissipation, when one is apt to feel blue. [Colloq.]
Blue ointment; in medicine, mercurial ointment.
Blue peter; (a) in the British marine, a blue flag with a white square in the center, used as a signal for sailing, to recall boats, etc.; (b) the call for trumps in the game of whist.
Blue pill; (a) a pill containing mercury, glycerin, honey, etc.; (b) blue mass.
Blue racer; a variety of the common black-snake.
Blue ribbon; (a) a member of the English order of the Garter; so called from the ribbon worn as a badge; (b) a distinction; something worth striving for; a prize, generally a first or principal prize; as, his horse won the *blue ribbon* at the fair; (c) a recognized badge of temperance workers and total abstainers in America and England; also, the designation of a temperance organization; as, she belongs to the *Blue Ribbon* army.
Blue ruin; complete ruin; also, a slang name for gin, from its steel-blue tint.
Blue spar; azure spar. [See *Lazulite.*]
Blue thrush; a European and Asiatic variety of the thrush.
Blue vitriol; sulphate of copper; bluestone.
Blue water; a term applied to the ocean.

blūe, *v.t.*; blued, *pt., pp.*; bluing, *ppr.* To make blue; to dye blue; to cause to become blue by a heating process; as, to *blue* steel.

blūe′back, *n.* 1. A trout found in some of the lakes of Maine.
2. A species of salmon found in the Columbia River and to the northward; also called Fraser *River salmon.*
3. A river herring, *Clupea æstivalis,* closely related to the alewife; the glut-herring.

blūe′-ball, *n.* A name sometimes applied to the nilgau, the dominant color of which is blue.

Blūe′beard, *n.* The name of a character in a French nursery romance of the middle ages, who, when about to absent himself from home, forbade his young wife to enter a certain room in his castle. Her curiosity being thus aroused, she disobeyed the injunction, entered the forbidden chamber, and in it found the heads of several previous wives whom he had murdered. Hence, the word is applied to any cruel or tyrannical husband. It is also used adjectively of forbidden subjects; as, the *bluebeard* chamber of the mind.

blūe′bell, *n.* Any one of several different plants yielding blue bell-shaped flowers. Specifically, (a) in the United States, the grape-hyacinth, *Muscari botryoides,* and the Virginia lungwort; (b) in England, the wild hyacinth, *Scilla nutans*; (c) in Scotland, the well-known beautiful wild plant *Campanula rotundifolia,* or harebell. The term is generally applied to these flowers in the plural, *bluebells.*

blūe′ber″ry, *n.*; *pl.* **blūe′ber″ries.** 1. A berry containing many seeds, produced by any one of several varieties of *Vaccinium,* edible and widely used in the United States. It differs from the American huckleberry, which contains ten nutlets instead of many seeds.
2. The edible berry of an Australian tree, sometimes called the native currant.

blūe′bill, *n.* A duck of the genus *Fuligula,* of which there are two common American species.

blūe′bird, *n.* 1. A small song-bird, *Sialia sialis,* very common in the United States. The upper part of the body is blue, and the throat and breast reddish. It is one of the first spring birds in the East, is allied to the European robin, and makes its nest in the hole of a tree.
2. Any one of a number of other birds; as the slate-colored snowbird, *Junco hyemalis,* and the *fairy bluebird* of the East Indies.

blūe′-black, *a.* Of a very dark blue color, or modified black with a shade of blue.

blūe′-black, *n.* A color or pigment which is nearly black, but has a shade of dark blue.

blūe′bon″net, *n.* 1. A plant, a species of *Centaurea.* [See *Bluebottle.*]
2. The European blue titmouse; the bluecap, *Parus cæruleus.*
3. A broad, flat cap of blue woolen, worn in Scotland; also, one wearing such a cap; a Scotsman; in this sense, commonly two words.

blūe′bot″tle, *n.* 1. A plant, the *Centaurea Cyanus,* which grows among grain, having blue bottle-shaped flowers.
2. A fly with a large blue body.

blūe′breast (-brest), *n.* A small European bird; called also *bluethroat* and *blue-throated warbler.*

blūe′buck, *n.* A South African antelope; the blauwbok.

blūe′bush, *n.* A Mexican shrub, *Ceanothus azureus,* yielding abundant blue flowers and belonging to the buckthorn family.

blūe′but″tons, *n.* In botany, some species of *Scabiosa,* having blue flowers.

blūe′cap, *n.* 1. A one-year-old salmon, with blue spots on its head. [Eng.]
2. The blue titmouse, or tomtit, of Europe.
3. A Scot or Scotsman; so called from wearing a blue bonnet. [Poet.]

blūe′coat, *n.* Any one dressed in a blue uniform, as a United States soldier, a policeman, a sailor, etc.
Bluecoat boy; a pupil of Christ's Hospital school, London; so named from the medieval dress worn by the boys of this institution.

blūe′-curls, *n.* Any one of several herbs of the genus *Trichostema,* belonging to the mint family, and, from its resemblance to pennyroyal, sometimes called bastard pennyroyal.

blūe′-eye, *n.* In zoölogy, the blue-faced honeysucker of New South Wales.

blūe′-eyed (-īd), *a.* Having blue eyes.
Blue-eyed grass; in botany, a delicate grass-like plant common in meadows and bearing tiny flowers of a light blue color.

blūe′fin, *n.* 1. The local name of the lake herring or black-finned whitefish, *Coregonus nigripinnis,* of Lake Michigan.
2. The dollardee.

blūe′fish, *n.* 1. A food-fish, *Pomatomus saltatrix,* common along the Atlantic coast of the United States. It is bluish in color, large, and voracious. Also called *horse mackerel, salt-water tailor,* or *skipjack.*
2. A marine fish of Florida and the West Indies, belonging to the family *Labridæ.*
3. Locally, a name applied to the cunner, sea-bass, and other fishes, found in various parts of the world.

blūe′gown, *n.* One of a class of licensed beggars or paupers in Scotland, called also the king's *beadsmen,* to whom formerly the kings annually distributed certain alms on condition of their praying for the royal welfare. The alms consisted of a blue gown or cloak, a purse containing as many shillings Scots (pennies sterling) as the years of the king's age, and a badge bearing the words "Pass and repass," which protected them from all laws against mendicity.

blūe′-grass, *n.* In botany, a name given to several species of *Poa,* having bluish-green stems and adapted to light, gravelly soils; wire-grass. The *blue-grass* of Kentucky, *Poa pratensis,* spreads rapidly and is valuable for pasture. Texas *blue-grass, Poa arachnifera,* resembles that of Kentucky.
Blue-grass country; the limestone region of Kentucky, in which blue-grass is most plentiful; famous for its production of thoroughbred horses and cattle.

blūe′-gum, *n.* A large, tall gum-tree, *Eucalyptus globulus,* of Australia, valuable for timber and oil, and cultivated in warm, temperate, and tropical countries as a protection against malaria.

blūe′hearts, *n.* An American herb, *Buchnera Americana,* of the figwort genus, having a terminal spike of dark-blue flowers.

blūe′jack″et, *n.* A sailor of the navy; so called from the color of his jacket; a sailor as distinguished from the marines, or soldiers who serve on board vessels of war.

blūe′-john, *n.* A kind of blue fluor-spar, found in the mines of Derbyshire, England, and made into vases and ornamental figures.

blūe′-laws, *n.pl.* Laws or regulations of a puritanical nature; a term first used in the eighteenth century in reference to certain rigorous laws and oppressive regulations supposed to exist in Connecticut.

blūe′ly, *adv.* With a blue color.

blūe′ness, *n.* The quality of being blue; a blue color.

blūe'nōṣe, *n.* A Nova Scotian; so called probably from the deduction that the winter climate in Nova Scotia makes the nose blue. [Colloq.]

blūe'point, *n.* Any oyster much in favor for eating raw because of its small size; originally, an oyster found at Blue Point, Long Island.

blūe'point"ẽr, *n.* A shark, *Lamna glauca*, of the Pacific Ocean.

blūe'pōll, *n.* A kind of salmon-trout, *Salama truita cambricus*, found in the rivers of Ireland, Wales, and northern continental Europe.

blūe'print, *n.* A positive print or photographic copy, in white lines on a blue ground, of a map, plan, or other subject, etc., upon paper sensitized with a solution of potassium ferrocyanide, commonly called *blueprint* or *blue-process paper*.

blūe'-proc"ess, *n.* The process of making blue-prints.

blūe'stärt, *n.* [G. *blausterz*, the blue-tail.] The blue-tailed warbler, *Ianthia cyanura*.

blūe'stock"ing, *n.* 1. A literary lady; applied usually with the imputation of pedantry. The term was first applied to ladies frequenting certain literary meetings in London in Dr. Johnson's time, from a Mr. Stillingfleet whose conversational powers and blue stockings were much in evidence at these meetings.

2. In zoölogy, the American avoset, *Recurvirostra americana*.

blūe'stock"ing-iṣm, *n.* A colloquial term for a taste for the literary, or for pedantry, as evinced by a woman.

blūe'stōne, *n.* 1. Sulphate of copper.

2. Any building-stone of a bluish color; specifically, blue sandstone.

3. A term given by Australian miners to a basaltic lava covering large areas of gold-bearing gravels of the later Tertiary periods in Victoria, etc., and through which they have to sink their mining shafts.

blū'et, *n.* [ME. *blewet, blewit*; Fr. *bluet*, the corn-flower; dim. of *bleu*, blue.] A name common to several blue-flowered plants, as *Houstonia cœrulea*.

blūe'thrōat, *n.* A singing bird, with a tawny breast marked with a sky-blue crescent, inhabiting the northern parts of Europe and Asia.

blūe'wing, *n.* A bird, the blue-winged teal.

blūe'wood, *n.* A compact shrub, *Condalia obovata*, found in southwestern United States and adjacent parts of Mexico.

blūe'y, *n.* A bushman's bundle, or the blue blanket in which it is generally wrapped. [Australia.]

blūe'y, *a.* Somewhat blue; bluish.

bluff, *a.* [Perhaps allied to D. *blaf*, flat, broad; L.G. *blaffen*, to frighten.]

1. Broad and full; specially applied to a full countenance, indicative of frankness and good humor.

> His *bluff* face melted down displeasure.
> —Riddell.

2. Rough and hearty; plain and frank; somewhat boisterous and unconventional.

> *Bluff* Harry broke into the spence,
> And turn'd the cowls adrift. —Tennyson.

3. Blustering; pompous; surly; churlish. [Obs.]

4. Steep and obtuse; rising suddenly and boldly, like a bluff.

Syn.—Bare, open, bold, abrupt, frank, plain-spoken, blunt, surly, rude, blustering, swaggering, brusk, hectoring, coarse, discourteous, rough, bullying.

bluff, *n.* 1. A high bank, almost perpendicular, projecting into the sea or a river; a high bank presenting a steep front.

2. A bold and confident manner assumed for the purpose of deceiving as to real conditions; as, a strong *bluff*; a *bluff* at working. [See *Bluff*, v.t.]

3. The game of poker.

bluff, *v.t.*; bluffed, *pt., pp.*; bluffing, *ppr.* 1. In the game of poker, to deceive by betting a hand for more than it is worth, so as to give a false impression of strength, with the expectation of making subsequent players drop out.

2. Colloquially, to overcome or accomplish by a bold attempt or display designed to cover weakness; as, to *bluff* one's way.

bluff, *v.i.* To act as if making a bluff.

bluff'-bowed, *a.* Having broad and flat bows, as a boat or ship.

bluff'ẽr, *n.* One who bluffs.

bluff'-head"ed (-hed") *a.* In nautical language, having an upright stem.

bluff'ness, *n.* The state or quality of being bluff.

bluff'y, *a.* 1. Having bluffs, or bold projecting points of land.

2. Inclined to bluffness in speech or action.

blū'ing, *n.* 1. The act of making or rendering blue; as, the *bluing* of steel; the *bluing* of clothes in a laundry.

2. Any preparation used to give a bluish tint, as indigo or other blue coloring-matter used in laundry-work.

blū'ish, *a.* Somewhat blue.

blū'ish-ly, *adv.* In a bluish manner.

blū'ish-ness, *n.* A small degree of blue color.

blun'dẽr, *v.i.*; blundered, *pt. pp.*, blundering, *pp.* [ME. *blondren, blunderen*, to blunder; origin uncertain.]

1. To mistake grossly; to err widely or stupidly; as, some one had *blundered*.

2. To move without direction, or steady guidance; to plunge at an object; to move, speak, or write with sudden and blind precipitance; as, to *blunder* upon a reason; to *blunder* round a meaning.

blun'dẽr, *v.t.* 1. To do (something) blunderingly; to botch; as, to *blunder* an example.

2. To cause to blunder. [Obs.]

blun'dẽr, *n.* 1. A mistake through precipitance, or without due exercise of judgment; a gross error.

2. Disturbance. [Obs.]

Syn.—Error, mistake, oversight.—An *error* is a wandering from the right; a *mistake* is the mistaking of one thing for another; a *blunder* is something more gross, a floundering on through carelessness, ignorance, or stupidity. An *error* may be corrected; a *mistake* may be rectified; a *blunder* is always blamed or laughed at.

blun'dẽr-buss, *n.* [*Blunder*, on account of its random action, and D. *bus*, box, gun-barrel; or D. *donderbus*, a thunder-box.]

Blunderbuss.

1. A short gun or firearm, with a large bore, capable of holding a number of balls, and intended to do execution without exact aim.

2. A stupid blundering fellow. [Colloq.]

blun'dẽr-ẽr, *n.* One who is apt to blunder, or to make gross mistakes; a careless person.

blun'dẽr-head (-hed), *n.* A stupid fellow; one who blunders.

blun'dẽr-ing, *a.* Making blunders; as, a *blundering* idiot.

blun'dẽr-ing-ly, *adv.* In a blundering manner.

blunge, *v.t.*; blunged, *pt., pp.*; blunging, *ppr.* [From *plunge*; OFr. *plunger*, to plunge; L. *plumbum*, lead.] In ceramics, to work (clay) with a blunger.

blun'gẽr, *n.* In ceramics, an instrument having a straight, flat, wooden blade, used for mixing clay with water; a plunger.

blun'ging, *n.* The process of mixing clay and water with a blunger.

blunt, *a.*; *comp.* blunter; *superl.* bluntest. [ME. *blunt, blont*, blunt, sluggish; prob. from AS. *blunt*, as found in proper names, *Blunta*, a man's name.]

1. Having a thick edge or point, as an instrument; dull; not sharp.

2. Dull in understanding; slow of discernment.

3. Abrupt in address; plain; unceremonious; wanting the forms of civility; rough in manners or speech; plain, but sincere.

4. Hard to penetrate. [Rare.]

Syn.—Dull, thick, edgeless, obtuse, pointless, coarse, rude, uncivil.

blunt, *v.t.*; blunted, *pt., pp.*; blunting, *ppr.*

1. To dull, as an edge or point, by making thicker.

2. To repress or weaken, as an appetite, desire, or power of the mind; to impair the force of; as, to *blunt* the edge of love; to *blunt* the stings of pain.

blunt, *n.* 1. A kind of needle used for heavy work.

2. A fencing-foil having a blunt point. [Obs.]

3. Money; cash. [Slang.]

blunt'ish, *a.* Somewhat dull or blunt.

blunt'ish-ness, *n.* The state of being blunt.

blunt'ly, *adv.* In a blunt manner; abruptly.

blunt'ness, *n.* The state or quality of being blunt.

blunt'-wit"ted, *a.* Dull; stupid.

blũr, *n.* 1. A confused, ill-defined, or dim figure, outline, or representation; an indistinct appearance.

2. A dark spot; a stain; a blot, whether upon paper or other substance, or upon reputation.

blũr, *v.t.*; blurred, *pt., pp.*; blurring, *ppr.* 1. To obscure by a dark spot, or by any foul matter, without quite effacing.

2. To sully; to stain; to blemish; as, to *blur* reputation.

3. To dim the vision of; to darken; to render vague in outline, or indistinct; as, this illness *blurs* my sight.

blũr'ry, *a.* With many blurs; blurred.

blũrt, *v.t.*; blurted, *pt., pp.*; blurting, *ppr.* [An imitative word.] To throw out, or throw at random, hastily, or unadvisedly, to utter suddenly or inadvertently; commonly with *out*, and applied to words; as, he *blurted out* his confession.

To blurt at; to speak of with disparagement or contempt. [Obs.]

blush, *v.i.*; blushed, *pt., pp.*; blushing, *ppr.* [ME. *bluschen, blyschen*, to glow, glance; AS. *blyscan, bliscan*, to shine.]

1. To redden in the cheeks or over the face, as from a sense of guilt, shame, confusion, or modesty; as, *blush* at your vices; *blush* for your degraded country.

2. To exhibit a red or rosy color; to be red.

> Made the western welkin *blush*. —Shak.

3. To bloom; to blossom.

> Full many a flower is born to *blush* unseen.
> —Gray.

blush, *v.t.* 1. To make red by blushing; as, to *blush* the cheek. [Rare.]

2. To express by blushing. [Rare.]

blush, *n.* 1. A red color suffusing the cheeks only, or the face generally, and excited by confusion, which may spring from shame, guilt, modesty, diffidence, or surprise.

> The rosy *blush* of love. —Trumbull.

2. A red or reddish color; a rosy tint.

At first blush; at first glance; at first sight; prima facie; without further consideration.

To put to the blush; to cause shame, confusion, or embarrassment to one.

Syn.—Bloom, color, aspect, shame, confusion, guiltiness.

blush'ẽr, *n.* One who blushes.

blush'et, *n.* A young, modest girl. [Obs.]

blush'fụl, *a.* Full of blushes.

blush'fụl-ly, *adv.* With many blushes.

blush'ing, *n.* The act of turning red; the appearance of color on the cheeks.

blush'ing-ly, *adv.* In a blushing manner.

blush'less, *a.* Unblushing; past blushing; impudent.

blush'wŏrt, *n.* In botany, a cultivated plant of the gentian family.

blush'y, *a.* Like a blush; having the color of a blush. [Rare.]

blus'tẽr, *v.i.*; blustered, *pt., pp.*; blustering, *ppr.* [An imitative word, from the same root as AS. *blæstan*, to blow.]

1. To threaten noisily without the intention or power to make good the threat.

2. To be loud, noisy, or swaggering; to bully; to puff; to swagger, as a turbulent or boasting person.

3. To roar and be tumultuous, as wind; to be boisterous; to be windy.

blus'tẽr, *v.t.* To utter in a blustering manner; as, to *bluster* out blasphemy.

blus'tẽr, *n.* 1. A blustering threat.

2. Noise; tumult; boasting; boisterousness; turbulence.

3. Roar of a tempest; violent wind; any irregular noise and tumult from wind.

Syn.—Boasting, bragging, bullying, raging, storming, swaggering.

blus'tẽr-ẽr, *n.* One who blusters; that which blusters; specifically, a braggart or bully.

blus'tẽr-ing, *a.* 1. Stormy; windy; as, *blustering* weather.

2. Noisy; tumultuous; swaggering; as, a *blustering* fellow.

blus'tẽr-ing-ly, *adv.* In a blustering manner.

blus'tẽr-ous, blus'trous, *a.* Noisy; tumultuous; boastful.

bō, *interj.* A word used to inspire terror; a customary sound uttered by children to frighten their fellows. Written also *boh* and *boo*.

Not able to say bo! to a goose; very foolish or timid.

Bō'ȧ, *n.* [L. *boa*, also *bova*, a water-serpent, from *bos, bovis*, an ox, cow, perhaps in allusion to the size of the reptile.]

1. A genus of ophidian reptiles, family *Boidæ*, distinguished from allied families by having a prehensile tail, with a single row of scales on its under surface.

2. [b—] Any snake of this genus.

3. [b—] An ornamental neck-wrap of fur, feathers, or other material, worn by women.

Boa constrictor; the name of a large and powerful serpent, sometimes thirty or forty feet long, found in the tropical parts of South America. The name has also been loosely applied to other large serpents, particularly of the genus *Python*, found in Asia and Africa.

Boa constrictor.

Bō-ȧ-nẽr'ġēṣ, *n.pl.* [Gr. *Boanerges*, from Heb. *bnē hargem*, sons of thunder; *bnē*, sons, *ha*, the, and *ra'am*, thunder.]

1. Sons of thunder; an appellation given by Jesus Christ to two of his disciples, James and John.

2. [*sing.*] A vehement and declamatory preacher or speaker.

boar, *n.* [ME *boor, bore*; AS. *bār*, boar.]
1. An uncastrated hog.
2. The undomesticated or wild hog.
3. A military engine used in medieval times.

bōard, *n.* [ME. *bord*; AS. *bord, bred*, a plank, shield, flat surface.]
1. A piece of timber sawed thin, and of considerable length and breadth compared with the thickness, used for building and other purposes; a thin plank.
2. A table at which food is eaten; hence, entertainment; food; diet; specifically, the regular supply of meals necessary for the sustenance of a person; also called *table-board*; as, he works for his *board* and lodging; the price of *board*. Connected with this usage is the application of the word to table-*board* and lodging combined.
3. A table at which a council or court is held; hence, a council convened for business, or any authorized assembly or meeting; as, a *board* of directors; a school-*board*.
4. The deck of a ship; the interior part of a ship or boat; in this sense, primarily, the side of a ship; used in the phrases *on board, aboard*.

Now *board* to *board* the rival vessels row.
—Dryden.

5. The line over which a ship runs between tack and tack. *To make a good board* is to sail in a straight line, when closehauled. *To make short boards* is to tack frequently.
6. A tablet of wood, pasteboard, or other material adapted for a particular work or pursuit; as, a chess*board*, a mortar*board*, a bulletin-*board*, etc.
7. A heavy pasteboard; paper made stiff and thick, to be used for book covers, etc.
8. [*pl.*] The theatrical stage; as, she went on *the boards*.
The American Board; the executive and directory council of the foreign missionary society supported by the Congregational churches of the United States.
Bed and board; food and lodging regularly supplied; as, to work for *bed and board*.
Board of control; (a) a board in control of a corporation or municipality; (b) in England, a board of six privy councilors in whom the government of the East Indies was formerly vested.
Board of directors; the body of directors controlling a corporation.
Board of education; the board directing and supervising the schools of a district or municipality; a school-board.
Board of pardon; a body of commissioners appointed to act on pardons.
Board of trade; (a) in many cities of the United States, an association of the local business men, usually incorporated, for the promotion and defense of all their common interests, as in legislation, transportation, or any other matter affecting industry and commerce; also called *chamber of commerce, merchants' exchange*, etc., the name of such an organization varying in different cities at the will of its founders or members. *Boards of trade* may or may not include a trading feature, or commercial exchange.
(b) Specifically, in the cities of Chicago, Detroit, Duluth, Kansas City, etc., an association incorporated to maintain a commercial exchange; to promote uniformity in the customs and usages of merchants; to inculcate principles of justice and equity in trade; to facilitate the speedy adjustment of business disputes; to acquire and to disseminate valuable commercial and economic information; and, generally, to secure to its members the benefits of coöperation in the furtherance of their legitimate pursuits. The commodities principally dealt in on these *boards of trade* are grain and provisions; on the Chicago *board*, seeds, hay, and straw as well. The business done includes buying and selling for cash or on contract, handling commodities on commission, brokerage, dealing in futures or speculating on future prices, and the shipping of grain, provisions, etc. Most of the business is transacted on the open floor of the board rooms, to which only members or their authorized representatives are admitted, many of the members acting as brokers for non-members desiring to buy, sell, or speculate. The prices of the various commodities are often largely affected by the transactions on the *boards of trade* and in kindred institutions. Similar organizations in New York and Toledo are called *produce exchanges*; in Philadelphia, Boston, Baltimore, Milwaukee, and Minneapolis, *chambers of commerce*, and in St. Louis and Buffalo, *merchants' exchanges*.
(c) The building, rooms, or chamber in which the business of a board of trade is transacted.
(d) In England, a committee of the privy council with wide powers of control over finance, industry, commerce, the patent office, transportation by land or by water, immigration, emigration, and fisheries; it is an important department of the government, and its official head, known as the president of the board of trade, is a member of the cabinet.
Returning board; an official body which canvasses the votes cast and makes the official statement regarding the result of an election.
To go by the board; to be broken off and swept or thrown overboard; said of the mast of a ship; hence, figuratively, to be completely swept away or destroyed.
To sweep the board; to win all the tricks at a game of cards; to win all the prizes in a contest.

bōard, *v.t.*; boarded, *pt.*, *pp.*; boarding, *ppr.*
1. To lay or spread with boards; to cover with boards.
2. To enter (a ship) by force in war, or by courtesy in peace.
3. To furnish with food, or food and lodging, in return for a compensation; as, a man *boards* ten students.
4. To put out to board; as, I *board* my horse at a livery stable.
5. To go on; to enter; as, to *board* a car.
6. To address; to approach; to woo. [Obs.]
To board a tack; to pull down the tack of a course to the deck of a ship.

bōard, *v.i.* To receive table-board or board and lodging at a price; as, he *boards* at a private house.
To board out; to board elsewhere than at home.
To board round; to live in rotation at different houses in the community, as formerly in the case of country school-teachers.

bōard′ȧ-ble, *a.* Capable of being boarded, as a ship.

bōard′-cut″tẽr, *n.* A machine for cutting boards, having a circular saw and moving worktable.

bōard′ẽr, *n.* 1. One who pays for food and lodging in another's house.
2. One who boards a ship in action; one who is selected to board ships; as, *boarders*, away!

bōard′ing, *n.* 1. The act of entering a ship by force or by courtesy.
2. The act of covering with boards; also, the covering itself.
3. The act or practice of obtaining one's food, or food and lodging, in the house of another for a fixed price.

bōard′ing-house, *n.* A private house whose inmates are required to pay for their board.

bōard′ing-net″ting, *n.* A netting formerly triced up above the rail of a ship to keep out the enemy.

bōard′ing-of″fi-cẽr, *n.* A naval or revenue officer who is sent or appointed to board vessels on their arrival from foreign ports.

bōard′ing-pike, *n.* A long pike formerly used by seamen in boarding a ship or repelling boarders.

bōard′ing-school, *n.* A school in which the scholars lodge and are boarded.

bōard′-meas″ūre (-mezh″), *n.* 1. The system of measurement used in ascertaining the number of square feet in boards.
2. A measure or scale used for this purpose.

bōard′-rūle, *n.* A figured scale for finding the number of square feet in a board without calculation.

bōard′-wā″ġeṣ, *n.pl.* Bed and board in return for services rendered; wages hardly sufficient to pay for food and lodging; also, special wages for board and lodging.

boar′fish, *n.* 1. A fish found in the Mediterranean, belonging to the family *Caproidæ*; so named from the shape of its snout.
2. A species of perch found in Australia, and used for food.
3. A New Zealand fish; also called *bastard dory*.

boar′ish, *a.* Swinish; brutal; cruel.

boar′ṣ′-foot, *n.* A herbaceous plant of the crowfoot family; hellebore.

boar′-spēar, *n.* A short spear with a stout shaft, used in hunting boars.

boar′-stag, *n.* A castrated boar.

bōart, *n.* Same as *Bort*.

bōast, *v.i.*; boasted, *pt.*, *pp.*; boasting, *ppr.* [ME. *boosten, bosten*, from *bost*, a boast.]
1. To brag, or vaunt oneself; to make an ostentatious display, in speech, of one's own worth, property, or actions.
2. To glory; to speak with laudable pride and ostentation of meritorious persons or things; usually followed by *of*, sometimes by *in*.

I *boast of* you to them of Macedonia.
—2 Cor. ix. 2.

bōast, *v.t.* 1. To display in ostentatious language; to speak of with pride, vanity, or exultation, with a view to self-commendation.
2. To possess, as something of which one may be proud; as, the town *boasts* not less than five churches.
Syn.—Vaunt, brag, swagger, swell, bluster, vapor, triumph, glory.

bōast, *v.t.* 1. To dress or trim (a stone, etc.) with a broad-faced chisel.
2. In sculpture, to dress or to form roughly; to roughhew to the approximate outline preparatory to elaborating the details.

bōast, *n.* 1. An expression of ostentation, pride, or vanity; a vaunting.

Thou that makest thy *boast* of the law.
—Rom. ii. 23.

2. The cause of boasting; the occasion of pride, vanity, or laudable exultation; as, Shakspere, the *boast* of English literature.

bōast′ănce, *n.* Boasting. [Obs.]

bōast′ẽr, *n.* One who boasts, glories, or vaunts, ostentatiously.
Syn.—Braggadocio, braggart, bully.

bōast′ẽr, *n.* A mason's or stonecutter's broad-faced chisel.

bōast′fụl, *a.* Given to boasting; ostentatious.

bōast′fụl-ly, *adv.* In a boastful manner.

bōast′fụl-ness, *n.* The state of being boastful.

bōast′ing, *n.* Ostentatious display of personal worth or actions; a glorying or vaunting.

bōast′ing-ly, *adv.* In an ostentatious manner; with boasting.

bōast′ive, *a.* Presumptuous. [Rare.]

bōast′less, *a.* Without ostentation.

bōat, *n.* [ME. *boot, bote, bot*; AS. *bāt*, a boat; Sw. *bat*; Ice. *bātr*, a boat.]
1. A small open vessel, or water-craft, usually moved by oars, or rowing. The forms, dimensions, and uses of *boats* are very various, and some of them carry a light sail. The different kinds of *boats* have different names, as long-*boat*, launch, barge, pinnace, jolly-*boat*, cutter, yawl, ferry*boat*, wherry, punt, felucca, etc.
2. A general name for floating craft of all sorts and sizes; as, a mail-*boat*; an Atlantic passenger-*boat*; a fishing-*boat*; a despatch-*boat*; a steam*boat*; a row*boat*.
3. A deep, narrow dish or utensil having a form like a boat; as, a sauce-*boat*.
4. A receptacle for holding incense, used in Catholic churches.
In the same boat; embarked in the same enterprise, or involved in the same predicament.

bōat, *v.i.* To ride in a boat.

bōat, *v.t.*; boated, *pt.*, *pp.*; boating, *ppr.* To transport in a boat; as, to *boat* goods across a lake.

bōat′ȧ-ble, *a.* Navigable by boats, or small river-craft.

bōat′āġe, *n.* The charge for conveying by boat; a carrying by boat.

bōat′bill, *n.* A species of bird, *Cancroma cochlearia*, a native of the tropical parts of South America. It has a bill four inches long, not unlike a boat with the keel uppermost.

bōat′-bug, *n.* Same as *Boat-fly*.

bōat′build″ẽr (-bild″ẽr), *n.* The builder of a boat; a boatwright.

bōat′-flȳ, *n.* A name common to different species of hemipterous insects, which swim on the back, and somewhat resemble small boats.

bōat′fụl, *n.* All that a boat can hold.

bōat′-hook, *n.* An iron hook with a point on the back, fixed to a long pole, with which to pull or push a boat.

bōat′house, *n.* A storehouse for boats.

bōat′ing, *n.* 1. The act or practice of rowing a boat for exercise, amusement, or otherwise.
2. The act or practice of transporting in boats.
3. A Persian mode of punishing capital offenders, by fastening them down on their backs in a boat, which is thereupon covered, and the convict left to perish.

bō-ā′tion, *n.* [L. *boatus*, from *boare*; Gr. *boān*, to cry out.] A reverberation; a roar; loud noise. [Obs.]

bōat′măn, *n.*; *pl.* **bōat′men.** One in charge of or working on a boat.

bōat′măn-ship, *n.* The management of a boat.

bōat′-rōpe, *n.* A rope to fasten a boat; usually called a *painter*.

bōat′-shāped, *a.* Having the shape of a boat; navicular; cymbiform; hollow like a boat.

bōat′-shell, *n.* A marine shell of the genus *Cymba*, so called from its form.

bōats′măn, *n.* A boatman. [Rare.]

bōat′swāin (*pron. by seamen*, bō′sn), *n.* [ME. *botswayne*; boat, and *swain*, a servant.]
1. An officer on board of ships who has charge of the boats, sails, rigging, colors, anchors, cables, and cordage. His office is also to summon the crew to their duty, to relieve the watch, and to assist the first officer in the necessary business of the ship.
2. The tropic-bird; also, the skua or jäger gull.
Boatswain's chair; a swing used by sailors to sit on while at work aloft, or to rescue sailors and passengers from a doomed ship. It is formed of a short board or seat with ropes run through holes at each end.
Boatswain's mate; an assistant to the boatswain.

bōat′-tāil, *n.* A species of blackbird found in the southern part of the United States.

bōat′wom″ăn (-woom″-), *n.*; *pl.* **bōat′wom″en** (-wim″-). A woman who has charge of a boat.

bōat′wright (-rīt), *n.* A boat-carpenter or builder.

bob, *n.* [Principally a colloquial word in origin, and expressing quick, jerky motion; ME. *bob*, *bobbe*, a cluster; Ice. *bobbi*, a cluster; OFr. *bober*, to mock.]

1. A short, jerking action; as, a *bob* of the head.

2. Any little round thing that plays loosely at the end of a string, cord, or chain; a little ornament or pendant that hangs so as to play loosely.

3. The words repeated at the end of a stanza, or the refrain of a song. [Obs.]

4. A blow; a shake or jog; a jeer or flout.

5. The ball of a short pendulum.

6. A mode of ringing bells.

7. A bob-wig, or short curl of hair.

8. A float used in angling to show when a fish bites.

9. A spherical leather tool used for polishing metal, as spoons, etc.

10. The working-beam of a steam-engine.

11. A shilling. [Eng. slang.]

12. A jest or taunt.

bob, *v.t.*; bobbed, *pt.*, *pp.*; bobbing, *ppr.* 1. To move in a short, jerking manner; as, to *bob* one's head; to *bob* a courtesy.

2. To beat; to shake or jog.

3. To cheat; to gain by fraud.

4. To mock or delude.

5. To cut short, as, to *bob* a horse's tail.

bob, *v.i.* 1. To play backward and forward; to play loosely against anything.

2. To angle or fish with a bob.

bō′baç, *n.* [Pol. *bobak.*] The Polish marmot, resembling the American woodchuck.

bō-bance′, *n.* A boasting. [Obs.]

bob′bēr, *n.* That which bobs; one who bobs.

bob′bēr-y, *n.* [Slang, from Hind. *bāp re*, O father.] A disturbance; a noisy quarrel; a squabble.

bob′bēr-y, *a.* Mixed; scrub; as, a *bobbery* lot of horses.

bob′bin, *n.* [Fr. *bobine*, a bobbin.]

1. A small pin or cylindrical piece of wood, bone, or other material, with a head, on which thread is wound for making lace. A similar instrument bored through to receive an iron pivot, and with a border at each end, is used in spinning to wind thread or silk on; a spool.

2. Round tape or narrow braid.

3. A part of some sewing-machines that rotates or slides beneath and works in conjunction with the needle; thread is wound on it and taken up in the operation.

4. An insulated coil of wire for an electromagnet.

5. A piece of wood at the end of a latchstring.

bob-bi-net′, *n.* [A contr. of *bobbin* and *net.*] A kind of machine-made lace which has an open mesh.

bob′bin-wŏrk, *n.* Work woven with bobbins.

bob′bish, *a.* In good spirits. [Eng. slang.]

bob′by, *n.* A policeman; so called from Sir Robert (*Bobby*) Peel, who remodeled the police force of London; also called *peeler*. [Eng. slang.]

bob′çat, *n.* The lynx of America.

bob′=cher″ry, *n.* Among children, a game in which a cherry is hung so as to bob against the mouth, and is to be caught with the teeth.

bob′fly̆, *n.* In angling, an end-fly; a drop-fly.

bob′ō-link, *n.* The popular name of the ricebird or reedbird, *Dolichonyx oryzivorus*, an American song-bird; also called *boblincoln*.

bob′sled, *n.* A sled or sleigh made up of two short sleds or sleighs, the one before the other, and connected by a plank or other coupling.

bob′sleigh (-slā), *n.* A bobsled.

bob′stāy, *n.* A chain or rope employed to retain a vessel's bowsprit down toward the stem or cutwater and counteract the upward strain of the stays. The attachment of the *bobstay* to the stem of the vessel is made by means of iron plates, called *bobstay-plates*.

bob′tāil, *n.* 1. A short tail, or a tail cut short; a short-tailed animal.

2. The rabble; used in contempt, most frequently in the phrase *rag, tag, and bobtail*.

bob′tāil, *a.* Bobtailed; having a bobtail.

bob′tāiled, *a.* Having the hair or tail cut short.

bob′tāil=wig, *n.* Same as *Bob-wig*.

bob′white, *n.* The North American quail; so named from its note or call.

bob′=wig, *n.* A short wig, having the bottom locks curled in small ringlets; also called *bob-tail-wig*.

bō′căl, *n.* [Fr. *bocal*, a bottle with a short, wide neck; L. *bucalis*; Gr. *baukalis*, a vessel in which wine was cooled.]

1. A glass vessel of a cylindrical form, having a short, wide neck and used for preserving solid substances.

2. The mouthpiece of a brass musical instrument, as a horn or trombone.

bō-çăr′dō, *n.* A mood in logic.

boç′ă-sīne, *n.* [Fr. *boccasin*; Turk. *bōhāsi*, a sort of cotton cloth.] A sort of fine linen or buckram.

boç′çȧ, *n.* [L. *bucca*, a cheek.]

1. The round hole of a glass-furnace, for use in taking out the melted glass.

2. The crater of a volcano.

bōce, *n.* A fish found in European waters; also called *bogue*, *boga*, and *box*.

Boçhe, *n.* [Prob. shortened from Fr. *caboche*, head; hence a thick-headed person; a stupid man.] A term applied to the Germans in the Great War. [Slang.]

bock′=beer, buck′=beer, *n.* [From G. *Eimbock-bier*, from *Eimbock* or *Eimbeck*, a town in Prussia, famous for its beer.] A strong beer, usually served in the spring; it is of old brewing, being kept for several months before use.

bock′e-rel, bock′e-let, *n.* A kind of long-winged hawk. [Obs.]

bock′ey, *n.* [D. *bokaal*, *bakje*, a small bowl or vessel.] A cup or bowl made from a gourd.

bock′ing, *n.* A sort of coarse cloth, like baize or drugget, used for covering carpets, generally on stairways; first made in Bocking, England, from which it derives its name.

bock′ing, *n.* [Dan. *bokking.*] A red herring.

bock′land, *n.* See *Bookland*.

bō-därk′, *n.* The Osage orange; also called *bodock*.

bod′dice, *n.* See *Bodice*.

bōde, *v.t.*; boded, *pt.*, *pp.*; boding, *ppr.* [ME. *boden*, *bodien*; AS. *bodian*, to foretell.] To portend; to foreshow; to presage; to indicate (future events) by signs; to be the omen of.

bōde, *v.i.* To foreshow; to presage.

Syn.—To forebode, foreshadow, augur.

bōde, *n.* 1. An omen. [Obs.]

2. A bid; an offer. [Obs.]

bōde, *n.* [ME. *bode*, *bod*, from AS. *bod*, *gebod*, a command, from *beodan*, to command.] A messenger; one who proclaims: a herald.

bōde, *n.* A stop; a halting. [Obs.]

bōde, *v.*, past tense and past participle of *bide*.

bōde, *v.*, past participle of *bid*. [Obs.]

bōde′fụl, *a.* Full of portent; ominous.

bō-dē′gȧ, *n.* [Sp.] A wine-cellar; a place where wine is sold or kept.

bōde′ment, *n.* An omen; a portent; a prognostic; a foreshowing. [Obs.]

bodġe, *n.* A botch; a clumsy patch. [Colloq.]

bodġe, *v.t.* To mend clumsily; to patch; to botch. [Obs.]

bō′di-ăn, *n.* In zoölogy, a large East Indian food-fish, *Diagramma lineatum*.

bod′ice, bod′dice, *n.* [Corruption of *bodies*, pl. of *body*.]

1. Stays; a corset; a sort of under waist, stiffened with whalebone, worn by women.

2. A close-fitting outer waist; the upper portion of a woman's dress.

bod′iced (-ist), *a.* Wearing a bodice.

bod′ied (-id), *a.* Having a body; as, able-*bodied*.

bō-di-ē′rŏn, *n.* [Local name.] The California or Pacific rock-trout

bod′i-less, *a.* 1. Having no body.

2. Having no material form; incorporeal.

bod′i-li-ness, *n.* Corporeality.

bod′i-ly, *a.* 1. Having or containing a body or material form; corporeal; as, *bodily* dimensions.

2. Of or pertaining to the body, in distinction from the mind; as, *bodily* defects; *bodily* pain.

3. Real; actual; as, *bodily* act. [Obs.]

Syn.—Corporeal, corporal, physical.—*Corporal* and *corporeal* both mean relating to the body, but under different aspects of it; *corporal* relating to the body in its outward bearings, *corporeal* to its substance, the latter being opposed to *spiritual* or *immaterial*; *bodily* generally denotes connected with the body or a body, and is frequently opposed to *mental*; hence, *corporal* punishment, *corporeal* existence, *bodily* pain or shape.

bod′i-ly, *adv.* 1. Corporeally; united with a body or matter; in bodily form.

> It is his human nature, in which the Godhead dwells *bodily*. —Watts.

2. In respect to the entire body or mass; entirely; completely; as, to carry away *bodily*.

bōd′ing, *n.* [ME. *bodynge*, *bodunge*, an omen; AS. *bodung*, foretelling, verbal noun from *bodian*, to announce.] Prediction, particularly of evil; a foreshadowing.

bōd′ing, *a.* Predicting evil; fearful.

bōd′ing-ly, *adv.* In a fearful or ominous manner.

bod′kin, *n.* [ME. *bodekyn*, a bodkin; of Celtic origin.]

1. An instrument of steel, bone, ivory, or the like, with a sharp point, for making holes by piercing.

2. An instrument with an eye, for drawing thread, tape, or ribbon through a loop, a hem, etc.

3. A dagger. [Obs.]

4. A style of pin used by women in dressing the hair.

5. In printing, a sharp-pointed tool used for picking up letters in correcting type.

To sit, ride, or *travel bodkin*; to be crowded between two persons on a seat large enough for only two.

bod′kin, *n.* [Obs.] See *Baudekin*.

bō′dle, *n.* [Name said to have come from *Bothwell*, the name of a mint-master.] An old Scottish coin worth about one-sixth of an English penny; hence, a very small coin.

Bod′lēi-ăn, *a.* Pertaining to Sir Thomas Bodley, or to the library founded by him at Oxford, England, in the sixteenth century, and known by this name.

bō-dock′, *n.* Same as *Bodark*.

bod′rāġe, *n.* A raid. [Obs.]

bod′y, *n.*; *pl.* **bod′ieș**. [ME. *body*, *bodi*; AS. *bodig*, body.]

1. The frame or physical part of a man or other animal; the material organism, living or dead, as distinguished from the spirit, soul, or vital principle.

2. The trunk or central part of a human being or animal, in distinction from the head and extremities.

3. In metaphysics, matter, as opposed to spirit.

4. A person; a human being; sometimes alone, more generally with *any*, *some*, or *no*; as, *somebody*; *nobody*; *anybody*.

5. Reality, as opposed to representation.

6. A collective mass; a number of individuals or particulars united; as, the *body* of mankind.

7. The main part; the bulk; as, the *body* of an army; the *body* of a tree.

8. A corporation; a number of men, united by a common tie, by one form of government, or by occupation; as, the legislative *body*; the *body* of the clergy; *body* corporate; *body* politic.

9. In physics, any distinct portion of matter perceived by the senses, or any kind of matter taken generically.

10. In geometry, a solid figure.

11. Any extended solid substance; matter; any substance or mass distinct from others; as, a metallic *body*; a floating *body*; a moving *body*; a light *body*; a heavy *body*.

12. A general collection of things; a code; a system; as, a *body* of laws; a *body* of divinity.

13. Strength; as, wine of a good *body*.

14. Opacity; consistency; as, the *body* of paint.

15. The unrenewed part of man, or sensual affections; a scriptural usage of the word.

16. That portion of a garment which covers the body; as, the *body* of a dress or a coat.

17. In printing, the shank of a type or the width of the shank, by which the size is indicated; as, a nonpareil *body*.

Body corporate; an association of persons incorporated for some specific purpose.

Body politic; the collective body of a nation or state under civil government; the people as a whole.

Body of a church; the nave.

Body of a county; the whole territory embraced within its boundaries.

Body of a law; the operative part.

The bodies seven; in alchemy, the metals supposed to correspond to the planets. [Obs.]

Syn.—Substance, mass, whole, substantiality, collectiveness, assemblage, collection, matter, association, organization, carcass, clay, corpse, dust, form, frame, remains, system.

bod′y, *v.t.*; bodied, *pt.*, *pp.*; bodying, *ppr.* 1. To provide or furnish with a body.

2. To produce in form; to put into outward shape; to represent.

> Imagination *bodies* forth the forms of things unknown. —Shak.

bod′y=bag, *n.* A bag in which to sleep.

bod′y=bōl″stēr, *n.* A crossbeam over the center of the truck and on the under side of a railway-car, supporting the car and transmitting its weight to the truck.

bod′y=brāce, *n.* An inclined timber to brace the panels of a frame.

bod′y=çav″i-ty, *n.* The space between the viscera and the body-wall; the cœloma.

bod′y=çloth, *n.* A horse-blanket.

bod′y=clōtheș, *n.pl.* Clothing or covering for the body, as distinguished from *bed-clothes*, etc.; apparel; also, coverings for a horse or other animal; body-cloths. The plural term *body-clothes* is properly applied to regularly fabricated garments, as of a man or woman, and *body-cloths* to large rugs or cloths, as for covering the bodies of horses.

bod′y=çōat, *n.* A close-fitting dress-coat.

bod′y=çŏl″ŏr, *n.* In painting, a pigment that has substance or thickness in a high degree, as distinguished from tint or wash.

bod′y-guärd, *n.* A guard for the person; a lifeguard; hence, the retinue or personal followers and attendants of a person of note.

bod′y=log, *n.* A log cut from the body of a tree, below the branches.

bod′y=lōop, *n.* An iron connecting the body of a vehicle with the running-gear.

bod′y=louse, *n.* A louse, *Pediculus vestimenti*,

which sometimes infests the human body and clothing; also called *grayback*.
bod'y=plan, *n.* In shipbuilding, an end plan of a ship showing her contour at various points.
bod'y=pōst, *n.* 1. An upright timber which forms part of the frame of a freight-car.
2. In shipbuilding, a post serving to support the propeller-shaft.
bod'y=sẽrv"ănt, *n.* A servant who attends to the personal wants of his employer; a valet.
bod'y=snatch"ẽr, *n.* One who secretly and illegally disinters a dead body; a grave-robber; a resurrectionist.
bod'y=snatch"ing, *n.* The act of robbing a grave, as for the purpose of dissection or the exaction of a ransom.
bod'y=vär"nish, *n.* A thick copal varnish used in carriage-making, etc.
bod'y=wąll, *n.* In anatomy and zoölogy, the envelope or walls of the body.
Boeh-mē'ri-ȧ, *n.* [Named after G. R. *Boehmer*, a German botanist.] A widely distributed genus of shrubs and herbs of the nettle family, some of which furnish valuable fibers, used for making ropes, twine, and thread.
Bœ-ō'tiăn, *a.* 1. Of or pertaining to Bœotia, Greece, noted for the dullness of its inhabitants.
2. Dull; ignorant; stupid.
Bœ-ō'tiăn, *n.* [L. *Bœotia*; Gr. *Boiōtia*, Bœotia.] A native of Bœotia; hence, one who is dull, ignorant, and stupid.
Bōer, *n.* [D. *boer*, a peasant or farmer.] A South African colonist of Dutch descent.
bog, *n.* [Ir. *bogach*, a bog, from Gael. *bog*, soft, moist.]
1. A quagmire covered with grass or other plants.
2. A little elevated spot or clump of earth, in marshes and swamps, covered with roots and grass. This is a common use of the word in New England.
bog, *v.t.*; bogged, *pt.*, *pp.*; bogging, *ppr.* To sink or submerge in mud or mire; as, to *bog* a horse and wagon.
bō'gä, *n.* Same as *Boce*.
bog'=as"phō-del, *n.* A North American plant, *Narthecium Americanum*.
bog'=bēan, *n.* The buck-bean, *Menyanthes trifoliata*, also called the marsh-trefoil, which grows in moist and marshy places and bears beautiful white or reddish flowers and bitter leaves.
bog'ber"ry, *n.* A species of cranberry, *Vaccinium Oxycoccus*, growing in lowlands and marshy places. [Dial., Eng. and Scot.]
bog'=ëarth, *n.* A soil composed for the most part of silicious sand and partially decomposed vegetable matter.
bō'gey, bō'gie, *n.* 1. In golf, a term meaning a fixed number of strokes for each hole, setting the pace for competition.
2. Same as *Bogy*.
Colonel Bogey; in golf, a phantom credited with a certain score for each hole, against which score each player competes.
bog'gle, *v.i.*; boggled, *pt.*, *pp.*; boggling, *ppr.* [Scot. *bogle*, *bogill*, a specter.]
1. To doubt; to hesitate; to stop; to play fast and loose.
2. To dissemble.
3. To perform awkwardly.
bog'gle, *v.t.* To embarrass with difficulties; to make a botch of; a popular or vulgar use of the word.
Syn.—Halt, hesitate, mar, falter, blunder, blotch, spoil, botch, shrink, demur.
bog'glẽr, *n.* A doubter; a timorous man.
bog'glish, *a.* Doubtful; skittish. [Obs.]
bog'gy, *a.* Containing bogs; full of bogs.
bō'gie, *n.* 1. A small truck used to swing logs at right angles to a sawmill carriage.
2. A railway-truck attached by a vertical king-pin.
3. Same as *Bogey*.
bō'gie=en"gine, *n.* An engine having its cylinders and driving-wheels on a pivoted truck.
bō'gle, bog'gle, *n.* [Eng. dial. *boggle*; Scot. *bogle*, a specter.] A bugbear; a specter; a bogy. [See *Bogy*.]
bog'=mọss, *n.* Any aquatic moss-plant or peat-moss of the genus *Sphagnum*.
bog'=nut, *n.* Same as *Bog-bean*.
bog'=ōak, *n.* Bogwood.
Bog'ō-mile, *n.* A member of a Bulgarian sect, of the eleventh and twelfth centuries, who believed that God had two sons, one Jesus and the other Satanaël.
bog'=ōre, *n.* A variety of brown iron ore, or limonite, found in swamps; also, hydrated peroxid of manganese.
bog'=rush, *n.* A rush or sedge (*Cladium mariscoides*) that grows in bogs.
bog'=spav"in, *n.* In horses, an encysted tumor on the inside of the hock, containing gelatinous matter.
bog'suck"ẽr, *n.* The American woodcock.
bog'=trē"foil, *n.* See *Bog-bean*.
bog'trot"tẽr, *n.* One who lives in a boggy country; in allusion to the ability of many of the Irish peasantry, in boggy districts, to elude pursuers by traversing the bogs by leaping from tussock to tussock.
bog'trot"ting, *a.* Dwelling among bogs.
bōgue (bōg), *v.i.* [Sp. *bogar*, to row.] To edge to leeward.
bōgue, *n.* Same as *Boce*.
bō'gus, *a.* [Origin uncertain.] False; sham; counterfeit.
bō'gus, *n.* A mixture of rum and molasses. [Local, U. S.]
bog'wood, *n.* 1. Trunks and large branches of oak found embedded in bogs and preserved by the antiseptic properties of peat, so that the grain of the wood is little affected by the many ages during which it has lain interred. It is of a shining black or ebony color, derived from its impregnation with iron, and is frequently converted into ornamental pieces of furniture and small ornaments, as brooches, earrings, etc.
2. A plant, the *Quercus palustris*.
bog'wŏrt, *n.* The bilberry or whortleberry growing in lowlands.
bō'gy, bō'gey, *n.* 1. A bugbear; a hobgoblin.
2. [B—] The devil; as, *Old Bogy*.

I am *bogey*, and frighten everybody away
—Thackeray.

bō-hēa', *n.* [Chinese *Woo-yē*, hills in Fuhkien, China, where the tea is grown; *w* being sounded like *b*.] A coarse, black, low-priced tea from China.
Bō-hē'mi-ȧ, *n.* 1. A country of central Europe, now part of the Austrian empire.
2. [B— *or* b—] The community or sphere of those known socially as bohemians.
Bō-hē'mi-ăn, *a.* 1. Pertaining to the country of Bohemia or its language.
2. [B— *or* b—] Roving; easy-going; unconventional; especially applied to artists, writers, and musicians.
Bohemian Brethren; a sect formed from the remnants of the Hussites in the fifteenth century; they were the forerunners of the Moravians.
Bō-hē'mi-ăn, *n.* 1. A native of Bohemia.
2. The language of the Bohemians.
3. A gypsy; a vagabond.
4. [b— *or* B—] One who is unconventional in life and habits; especially an artist, writer, or musician who leads a free-and-easy or erratic life.
Bō-hē'mi-ăn-ism, *n.* The life or habits of a bohemian. Written with or without the capital.
bō"hun=ū'pȧs, *n.* See *Upas*.
bō-lär' (bō-yär'), *n.* Same as *Boyar*.
Boi'dæ, *n.pl.* A family of non-venomous ophidian reptiles, of which the type genus is *Boa*.
boil, *v.i.*; boiled, *pt.*, *pp.*; boiling, *ppr.* [ME. *boilen*, *boylen*; OFr. *boillir*; Sp. *bullir*, to boil, move, be active; L. *bullire*, to bubble, boil; *bulla*, a bubble, stud.]
1. To swell, heave, or be agitated by the action of heat; to bubble; to rise in bubbles; as, the water *boils*.
2. In a chemical sense, to pass from a liquid to an aeriform state or vapor, at the boiling point.
3. To simulate the agitation of heat; as, the *boiling* waves which roll and foam.
4. To be hot or fervid; to swell by native heat, vigor, or irritation; as, the *boiling* blood of youth; his blood *boils* with anger.
5. To be in boiling water; to suffer boiling heat in water or other liquid; as, the meat is *boiling*.
6. To bubble; to effervesce, as a mixture of an acid and a carbonate.
To boil away; to evaporate by boiling.
To boil down; to reduce in bulk; to condense.
To boil over; to run over the top of a vessel.
To keep the pot boiling; to provide the means of living.
boil, *v.t.* 1. To dress or cook in boiling water; to seethe; to extract the juice or quality of by boiling.
2. To prepare for some use in boiling liquid; as, to *boil* silk, thread, or cloth. This word is applied to a variety of processes; as, to *boil* salt or sugar, etc. To *boil* a liquid is to subject it to heat till it bubbles, and to *boil* any solid substance is to subject it to heat in a boiling liquid.
boil, *n.* The act of boiling; the state of boiling, or of being at the boiling-point. [Colloq.]
boil, *n.* [ME. *byle*, *bule*; AS. *bȳle*, *bȳl*; G. *beule*; D. *buele*, a boil; Ice. *bola*, a blister, blain.] A circumscribed subcutaneous inflammation, characterized by a pointed pustular tumor, and suppurating with a central core.
boil'ȧ-ry, *n.* Same as *Boilery*.
boiled, *a.* Prepared by boiling; as, *boiled* beef; *boiled* linen.
Boiled oil; linseed oil that has been boiled to give it better drying qualities, and which is in consequence in standard use by house-painters, etc.
boil'ẽr, *n.* 1. Any vessel in which water or other liquids or semiliquids may be raised to ebullition by heat.
2. Specifically, a steam-boiler; a vessel constructed to hold and sustain an internal pressure, in which, by the application of heat, steam is generated and raised to or above the pressure of the atmosphere, for the purpose of utilizing its expansive energy for the production of mechanical work, for supplying heat by conduction of the steam, and for a number of applications in the industrial arts, as for cleaning, bleaching, etc.
The many varieties of *boilers* fall into two main groups: (a) the fire tubular *boilers*, having a number of tubes or flues passing through the water-space and traversed by the heated gases and products of combustion in their passage to the atmosphere; and (b) the water tubular *boilers*, in which the water is contained in tubes or coils, either continuous or connected with one or more larger water-spaces; the heat in this case being applied to the outside of the tubes by the gases playing around them. Tubes or flues are used in *boiler* construction to increase the heating-surface.
3. One who boils.
boil'ẽr=brāce, *n.* A brace used between the shell and the flat end of a boiler.
boil'ẽr=clamp, *n.* A clamp used by riveters to hold boiler-plates in place.
boil'ẽr=fer"rule (-fer"il), *n.* In plumbing, a bushing having a projection to which a lead pipe may be attached.
boil'ẽr=flōat, *n.* An attachment to a steam-boiler that regulates the water-feed or acts as an alarm for low-water.
boil'ẽr=ī"ron (-ūrn), *n.* Rolled iron sheets from which steam-boilers are made; usually from ¼ to ½ inch in thickness.
boil'ẽr=mē"tẽr, *n.* An instrument to measure the water consumed by a steam-boiler.
boil'ẽr=plāte, *n.* 1. Iron plate from which boilers are made.
2. One of the sheets in a boiler.
boil'ẽr=shell, *n.* The outside case of a cylinder boiler.
boil'ẽr=shop, *n.* A shop where boilers are made.
boil'ẽr=smith, *n.* A workman engaged in forging special parts of boilers.
boil'ẽr-y, *n.* 1. A house or apparatus for boiling, as for evaporating salt or refining sugar.
2. In law, the water which arises from a salt-well, belonging to one who does not own the well.
boil'ing, *a.* Bubbling; heaving in bubbles; being agitated; as, *boiling* liquid; swelling with heat, ardor, or passion.
Boiling spring; a spring which gives out hot water and steam, often ejecting it with great force. [See *Geyser*.]
boil'ing, *n.* The act or state of bubbling; agitation by heat; ebullition; the act of cooking by hot water; the act of preparing by hot water, or of evaporating by heat.
boil'ing-ly, *adv.* In a boiling manner; with ebullition.
boil'ing=point, *n.* The degree of heat at which a fluid is converted into vapor with ebullition. This point varies for different liquids, and for the same liquid at different atmospheric pressures, being higher when the pressure of the atmosphere is increased, and lower when it is diminished. When the barometer stands at 30 inches water boils at 212° Fahr., and it is found that the *boiling-point* varies 0.88 of a degree for every half-inch of variation of the barometer.
bois=d'ärc' (bwä-därk'), *n.* [Fr., bow-wood. So called because used for bows by the Indians in the western part of the United States.] The Osage orange.
bois=dūr-ci' (bwä-dūr-sē'), *n.* [Fr., hardened wood.] An artificial wood made by compressing a paste of blood and hardwood sawdust; it takes a high polish.
boist, *n.* [OFr. *boiste*, a box.] A box. [Obs.]
bois'tẽr-ous, *a.* [ME. *boistous*, *buystous*; W. *bwystus*, wild, ferocious.]
1. Loud; roaring; violent; stormy; as, a *boisterous* wind.
2. Turbulent; furious; tumultuous; noisy; as, a *boisterous* man.
3. Large; unwieldy; huge; clumsily violent; as, a *boisterous* club. [Obs.]
4. Violent; as, a *boisterous* heat. [Rare.]
Syn.—Furious, impetuous, noisy, vehement, violent.
bois'tẽr-ous-ly, *adv.* Violently; furiously; with loud noise; tumultuously.
bois'tẽr-ous-ness, *n.* The state or quality of being boisterous; turbulence; disorder; tumultuousness.
bois'tous, *a.* Violent or rude; strong; coarse; noisy. [Obs.]
bois'tous-ly, *adv.* In a boisterous or violent manner. [Obs.]
bois'tous-ness, *n.* Roughness; violence. [Obs.]
bō'kȧ-dam, *n.* See *Cerberus*, 3.
bō'kärk, *n.* A birch-bark basket for maple sugar, used by the Lake Superior Indians.
bōke, *v.t.* and *v.i.* To poke. [Obs.]

bō′lãr, *a.* Having the nature of bole; clayey.

bō′lā-ry, *a.* Pertaining to bole or clay, or partaking of its nature and qualities; bolar.

bō′lăs, *n. sing.* and *pl.* [Sp., pl. of *bola*, a ball; L. *bulla*, a bubble, ball.] A missile employed by the Gauchos of Argentina, Chile, and other parts of South America, to bring down cattle and large game by entangling the legs. It consists of two or three balls of stone or metal separately incased at the ends of braided rawhide cords. A similar device is used by some African tribes and by the Eskimos.

bōld, *a.* [ME. *bold*, *bald*; AS. *beald*, *bald*; O.H.G. *bald*, bold.]

1. Daring; courageous; brave; intrepid; fearless; applied to men or animals; as, *bold* as a lion.

2. Requiring courage in the execution; executed with spirit or boldness; planned with courage and spirit; as, a *bold* enterprise.

3. Confident; not timorous. [Obs.]

4. In a bad sense, rude; forward; impudent.

5. Unconventional; showing great liberty of style or expression; sometimes bordering on the indelicate; as, his descriptions are decidedly *bold*.

6. Standing out to view; striking to the eye; as, *bold* figures in painting, sculpture, and architecture.

7. Steep; abrupt; prominent; as, a *bold* shore, which enters the water almost perpendicularly.

To make bold; to take the liberty; to presume; to venture.

Syn.—Courageous, daring, brave, intrepid, fearless, dauntless, valiant, manful, audacious, stout-hearted, high-spirited, adventurous, confident, strenuous, forward, impudent.—One may be *fearless* where there is no apprehension of danger or no cause for apprehension, but he is *bold* only when he is conscious or apprehensive of danger, and prepared to encounter it. A man may be *fearless* in a state of inaction; he is *bold* only in action, or when in a frame of mind for action; he is *intrepid* who has no fear where the most *fearless* might tremble; he is *undaunted* whose spirit is unabated by that which would make the stoutest heart yield.

bōld, *v.t.* To make daring. [Obs.]

bōld, *v.i.* To be bold; to become bold. [Obs.]

bōld′en, *v.t.* To make bold; to give confidence. [Obs.]

bōld′=fāce, *n.* 1. A person who is impudent, saucy, or bold; a term of reprehension and reproach.

2. In printing, black-faced type; full-face.

bōld′=fāced, *a.* 1. Impudent; saucy.

2. In printing, having a full or black face.

This line is set in bold-faced type.

bōld′ly, *adv.* [ME. *boldly*, *boldliche*; AS. *bealdliche*, from *beald*, bold.] In a bold manner.

bōld′ness, *n.* 1. Courage; bravery; intrepidity; spirit; fearlessness.

2. Prominence; the quality of exceeding the ordinary rules of scrupulous nicety and caution; applied to style, expression, and metaphors in language, and to figures in painting, sculpture, and architecture.

3. Freedom from timidity; liberty.

4. Confidence; confident trust.

5. Freedom from bashfulness; assurance; confident mien.

6. Prominence; steepness; as, the *boldness* of the shore.

7. In a bad sense, rudeness; impudence; sauciness.

Syn.—Intrepidity, assurance, audacity, effrontery, presumption, confidence, daring, bravery.

bōl′dō, *n.* [Native Chilean name.] In botany, a small, aromatic, evergreen tree growing in Chile and bearing edible fruit; the *Boldoa fragrans* or *Peumus Boldus*. The leaves have medicinal value; the bark is used in tanning and the wood in making charcoal.

bōle, *n.* [ME. *bole*; Ice. *bolr*, the trunk of a tree.]

1. The body or stem of a tree.

2. Anything having cylindrical shape, as the trunk of a tree.

3. A small boat suited for a rough sea. [Eng.]

bōle, *n.* An ancient Scotch measure of varying size. [See *Boll*.]

bōle, *n.* [ME. *bole*; OFr. *bol*; L. *bolus*, clay; Gr. *bōlos*, a clod or lump of earth.]

1. In geology, any friable clayey shale or earth used as a pigment, generally yellow or yellowish-red or brownish-black, from the presence of iron oxid.

2. In mineralogy, an amorphous, earthy, hydrous bisilicate of alumina, with iron peroxid in various proportions, and with a little magnesia when soapy or greasy. It is employed in coloring and as an adulterant. There are many varieties, as Armenian *bole*, Bohemian *bole*, and French *bole*. These earths were formerly used as astringent, absorbent, and tonic medicines, and they are still in repute in the Orient.

3. A bolus or dose. [Obs.]

bōle, *n.* 1. An opening in a wall to let in light and air. 2. A small recess in a wall. [Scot.]

bō-lec′tion, *n.* In architecture, a kind of molding which projects beyond the surface of the work which it decorates.

bō-le′rō, *n.* [Sp.] 1. A favorite Spanish dance expressive of the emotion of love; also, the music of the dance.

2. Jacket worn by women, often sleeveless.

bō-let′ic, *a.* Pertaining to or obtained from the *Boletus*, a genus of mushrooms.

Boletic acid; an acid obtained from the juice of *Boletus fomentarius*.

Bō-lē′tus, *n.* [L. *Boletus*; Gr. *bōlitēs*, a species of mushroom; *bōlos*, a lump of earth.] In botany, a genus of mushrooms containing many species, several of which are edible.

bō′ley, **bō′lye**, *n.* Same as *Booly*.

bō′lide (*or* -lid), *n.* A sort of meteor; a brilliant shooting star or exploding fireball.

bol′i-vär, *n.* [Named after Simon *Bolivar*, Bolivian and Venezuelan liberator.] A silver coin, value about 19½ cents, United States coinage; the monetary unit of Venezuela.

Bō-liv′i-ăn, *n.* and *a.* I. *n.* A native or inhabitant of Bolivia.

II. *a.* Pertaining to Bolivia.

bō-li-vi-ä′nō, *n.* The Bolivian dollar, a silver coin worth about 36 cents, United States coinage; the monetary unit of Bolivia.

bōll, *n.* [AS. *bolla*, a bowl.]

1. The pod or capsule of a plant, as of flax or cotton; a globular pericarp.

2. An ancient dry measure used in Scotland and the north of England, varying from two bushels for salt to six bushels for potatoes.

bōll, *v.i.* To form into a pericarp or seed-vessel.

Bol′land-ist, *n.* A Jesuit who edited the *Acta Sanctorum*, succeeding John Bolland, who in 1643 began to edit the material collected by Rosweyd concerning lives of saints.

bol′lard, *n.* 1. In a ship, an upright post used for fastening ropes; a billethead.

2. In docks, one of two large posts set in the ground, securely holding large blocks through which are reeved the transporting hawsers for docking and undocking ships.

bōll′en, *a.* See *Boln*.

bōll′ing, *n.* A tree divested of top and branches; a pollard. [Rare.]

bōll′=rot, *n.* A disease which destroys the boll of the cotton-plant before maturity.

bōll=wee-vil, *n.* A weevil very destructive to cotton bolls in S. Texas and elsewhere, gradually moving N., so far defying scientific extermination.

bōll=wee-vil eat-er, *n.* A species of ant spreading over cotton fields constantly destroying boll-weevil; nature's remedy.

bōll′wŏrm, *n.* In entomology, the larva of the moth *Heliothis armigera*, which ravages the immature bolls of the cotton-plant.

bōln, **bōll′en**, *a.* Puffed out; swelled out, as a sail filled with wind; swollen. [Obs.]

bōln, *v.i.* To swell; to enlarge. [Obs.]

bō′lō, *n.* [Sp.] A large knife used in the Philippine Islands as a weapon or utensil; it is of varied form and size.

bō-lō′gnȧ (bō-lōn′yȧ *or* bō-lō′nȧ), *n.* [From *Bologna*, Italy.] A large sausage made of bacon, veal, pork, etc., chopped fine, and inclosed in a skin.

Bologna stone; radiated sulphate of barium, found in roundish masses, composed of radiating fibers; discovered near Bologna. It is phosphorescent when calcined.

Bologna vial; a wide-mouthed vial or bottle of glass so brittle that it will break into atoms when it is scratched, although a heavy blow will not affect it.

Bō-lō-gnēṣe′ (bō-lōn-yēz′ *or* bō′lō-nēz), *n.* and *a.* I. *n.* A native or inhabitant of Bologna.

II. *a.* Pertaining to Bologna.

Bolognese school; a school of painting established at Bologna by Carracci. Called also *Eclectic school* and *Lombard school*.

Bō-lō′gniăn (bō-lōn′yăn *or* bō-lō′ni-ăn), *n.* and *a.* I. *n.* A Bolognese; a native or inhabitant of Bologna.

II. *a.* Pertaining to Bologna; Bolognese.

Boloism, *n.* The most despicable guise of the doctrine of defeatism. (*q.v.*) Derived from Bolo Pacha, a Frenchman, convicted of treason by a court-martial at Paris, Feb. 14, 1918, and sentenced to death.

bō′lō-măn, *n.* A man armed with a bolo.

bō-lom′e-tẽr, *n.* [Gr. *bole*, a ray, lit. something thrown, from *ballein*, to throw, and *metron*, a measure.] An instrument for measuring minute quantities of radiant heat, and especially used in spectroscopy.

Bol′she-vik (vĕk) *n*; *pl*. **Bol′she-vi″ki** (vē″-kē) [Russ. lit. the larger.] A member of the radical branch of the Social Democratic party in Russian politics, favoring terroristic methods. So called because this was originally the larger group of the party, the Mensheviki being the smaller.

Bol′she-vism (-*vizm*) *n.* The principles of socialism championed by the Bolsheviki.

Bol′she-vist, *n.* and *a.* I. *n.* A believer in Bolshevism.

II. *a.* Pertaining to the Bolsheviki.

bōl′stẽr, *n.* [ME. *bolstre*; AS. *bolster*, a headrest, bolster.]

1. A long cushion, used to support the head of persons lying on a bed; generally laid under the pillows.

2. Anything resembling a bolster in shape or manner of usage.

3. A pad, or quilt, used to relieve pressure, support any part of the body, or make a bandage sit easy upon a wounded part; a compress.

4. The part of a bridge between a truss or girder and the masonry.

5. In architecture, the lateral part of the volute of the Ionic capital; also called *baluster*.

6. In saddlery, a part of a saddle raised upon the bows or hinder part, to hold the rider's thigh.

7. A wooden block on the carriage of a cannon upon which the breech rests when it is moved.

8. In cutlery, the part of such instruments and tools as knives, chisels, etc., which joins the end of the handle; also, a metallic plate on the end of a pocketknife handle.

9. In ships, a cushion or bag, filled with tarred canvas, used to preserve the stays from being worn or chafed by the masts.

10. A piece of timber placed on various parts of a ship to prevent the works or ropes from being abraded.

11. In carbuilding, the principal crossbeam of a truck, or the transverse beam bearing the body of a car; a truck-bolster.

12. The perforated block of a punching-machine.

13. The crossbar, supported by the axle, upon which the body or bed of a vehicle rests.

14. The raised ridge which holds the tuning-pins of a piano.

bōl′stẽr, *v.t.*; bolstered, *pt.*, *pp.*; bolstering, *ppr.* 1. To support with a bolster or pillow.

2. To support; to hold up; to maintain with difficulty or great effort; often followed by *up*; as, he tried to *bolster up* his ridiculous theory.

bōl′stẽr, *v.i.* To lie together, or on the same bolster.

bōl′stẽred, *a.* Swelled out; supported.

bōl′stẽr-ẽr, *n.* A supporter.

bōlt, *n.* [ME. *bolt*, a shaft or arrow; AS. *bolt*, a catapult for throwing bolts.]

1. An arrow; a dart; a quarrel; a pointed shaft, intended to be shot from a crossbow or catapult.

2. A strong cylindrical pin, of iron or other metal, used to hold something in place, often having a head at one end and a screw-thread at the other to receive a nut.

3. A sudden stream of lightning; a thunderbolt; as, a *bolt* from the blue.

4. The quantity of cloth, as of cotton, silk, or canvas, contained in an original roll or package; usually about forty yards.

5. A shackle; a fetter for the legs. [Obs.]

6. That portion of a lock which forms the fastening and is moved back and forth by the key; any movable or sliding catch, bar, or other fastening for a door, window, gate, etc.

7. A bundle, as of osiers or straw.

8. In politics, the withdrawal of one or more delegates from a nominating convention; refusal to support the nominee or platform of one's political party.

9. Precipitate departure or flight; as, a *bolt* from the police; the *bolt* of a horse.

bōlt, *v.t.*; bolted, *pt.*, *pp.*; bolting, *ppr.* [ME. *bolten*, *bulten*, to spring off suddenly, to bolt; AS. *bolt*, a catapult.]

1. To fasten or secure with a bolt.

2. To fasten; to shackle; to restrain.

3. To blurt out; to utter or throw out precipitately.

4. To swallow unmasticated; as, to *bolt* food.

5. To shoot; to drive forth.

6. Among sportsmen, to start or dislodge, as game.

7. In politics, to break from; to refuse to support; as, he *bolted* his party and its candidates.

bōlt, *v.i.* 1. To shoot forth suddenly; to spring out with speed; commonly followed by *out*; as, to *bolt out* of the house.

2. To run away, as a horse.

3. To make a sudden flight or escape; as, he *bolted* to avoid his creditors.

4. In horticulture, to produce seed before the natural time.

5. In politics, to refuse to support the candidate of one's party; to break away from one's political affiliations.

bōlt, *v.t.* [ME. *bulten*; OFr. *bulter*, *buleter*, to bolt, to sift.]

1. To sift or separate, as bran from flour, by passing through a bolter.

2. Figuratively, to examine by sifting; to find the truth of; to purify.

Time and nature will *bolt* out the truth of things. —L'Estrange.

3. To argue privately and for practice, as cases at law by students and attorneys. [Obs.]

To bolt to the bran; to examine and investigate thoroughly.

bolt, *n.* 1. A fine sieve for sifting flour or meal; a bolter.

2. A question debated in a mock court. [Obs.]

bolt, *adv.* In the manner of a bolt; stiffly; unyieldingly.

Bolt upright; in an erect posture; straight up.

bōlt′-au″gẽr, *n.* A large auger used in ship-building to bore holes for bolts.

bōlt′-bōat, *n.* A strong boat that will endure a rough sea.

bōl′tel, bōul′tel, *n.* [ME. *boltel, bowtell*, prob. from *bolt*, with reference to its shaft-like shape.]

1. In architecture, a shaft of a clustered column, or any plain round molding.

2. A rounded border used for strengthening a tray or dish. Written also *boultin*, etc.

bōlt′ẽr, *n.* [ME. *bulter, bulture*, one who bolts, from *bulten*, to bolt.]

1. An instrument or machine for separating bran from flour, or the coarser part of meal from the finer; a milling-sieve.

2. One who sifts flour or meal.

bōlt′ẽr, *n.* One who bolts; specifically, one who bolts his party platform or candidates, or a horse given to running away.

bōlt′ẽr, *n.* A fishing-line. [See *Boulter*.]

bōlt′head (-hed), *n.* 1. A long, straight-necked glass vessel for chemical distillations; called also *matrass* or *receiver*.

2. The head of a bolt.

bōl′ti, *n.* [Ar. *boltuiy*.] An edible fish of the rivers of Egypt and Palestine, belonging to the genus *Chromis*. Written also *bolty, bulti*.

bōlt′ing, *n.* [ME. *bultinge*, verbal noun of *bulten*, to bolt.] The act of fleeing; a darting off or aside.

bōlt′ing, *n.* 1. The act of sifting flour or meal.

2. A private discussion or arguing of cases for practice, as by students in a law school. [Obs.]

bōlt′ing-cloth, *n.* A silk, linen, hair, or wire cloth of which bolters are made for sifting meal.

bōlt′ing-hutch, *n.* A bin or tub in which to keep bolted flour or meal.

bōlt′ing-mill, *n.* A machine or apparatus for sifting meal.

bōl′tŏn-īte, *n.* A granular mineral of a grayish or yellowish color, found in Bolton, Mass.; chiefly composed of silica and magnesia.

bōlt′rōpe, *n.* A rope to which the edges of sails are sewed to strengthen them.

bōlt′sprit, *n.* Same as *Bowsprit*.

bō′lus, *n.* [L. *bolus*; Gr. *bolos*, a throw, a mass, from *ballein*, to throw.]

1. A soft, round mass of anything medicinal to be swallowed at once, as a large pill.

2. Figuratively, an unpalatable doctrine or argument that has to be swallowed or tolerated.

bō′lye, *n.* Same as *Booly*.

bom, *n.* A large South American ringed serpent or boa, the *Epicrates cenchris*; the name is imitative of the sound it emits.

bō′māh-nut, *n.* The fruit of a tropical African plant, *Pycnocoma macrophylla*. It is used in tanning, and its oil in cooking.

Bō-mä′rē-ȧ, *n.* [Named after Valmont de *Bomare*, French naturalist.] A large genus of climbing plants, family *Amaryllis*, having showy flowers; chiefly found in the American tropics.

bomb (bom *or* bum), *n.* [Fr. *bombe*, a bomb, from L. *bombus*, Gr. *bombos*, a deep, hollow sound.]

1. A great noise; a hollow sound. [Obs.]

2. A large shell of cast iron, generally spherical, containing explosive material which is fired by concussion or by a time-fuse.

Bomb.

3. Any receptacle, of any shape or size, containing an explosive; as, a dynamite *bomb*.

4. A mass of lava and scoria, generally spherical in form and varying in size, which has been ejected from a volcano.

Aerial bomb; a steel cylinder filled with high explosives dropped by aircraft.

Incendiary bomb; a shell which throws out a flaming liquid as it explodes, designed to set fire to anything combustible within a wide area.

bomb, *v.t.* To attack with bombs; to bombard; to drop bombs upon, esp. from aircraft.

bomb, *v.i.* To sound. [Obs.]

bom′bāce, *n.* Cotton; padding. [Obs.]

Bom-bā′cē-æ, *n.pl.* [L. *bombyx*, from Gr. *bombyx*, the silkworm.] A family of tropical plants allied to the *Malvaceæ*; the silk-cotton family.

bom-bā′ceous, *a.* Pertaining to the *Bombaceæ*.

bom′bärd, *n.* [ME. *bumbarde, bombarde*, a large leather bottle or jug to hold liquor; OFr. *bombarde*, a cannon; LL. *bombardă*, an engine for throwing stones; L. *bombus*, Gr. *bombos*, a deep, hollow sound.]

1. Formerly, a piece of short, thick ordnance, with a large mouth, sometimes carrying a ball of three hundred pounds' weight. It was called also *basilisk*, and was the earliest type of cannon, at first throwing stones for shot.

2. An attack with bombs; bombardment. [Rare.]

3. A barrel; a drinking-vessel or leather bottle for carrying liquors. [Obs.]

4. [*pl.*] Breeches heavily padded. [Obs.]

bom-bärd′, *v.t.*; bombarded, *pt., pp.*; bombarding, *ppr.* [Fr. *bombarder*, to batter with a cannon.]

1. Formerly, to attack with bombs thrown from bombards. Now, to attack (a fortified place) with artillery; to shell; to fire shot or shells at; as, the fleet *bombarded* the forts. Ships do not, strictly speaking, *bombard* one another, nor does a fort *bombard* a ship; the old sense of throwing bombs into a fortified place being retained in part.

2. Figuratively, to attack with words or speech; as, he *bombarded* me with questions.

3. To assail with missiles of any kind; as, the rioters *bombarded* the police with stones.

bom-bärd′ẽr, *n.* One who bombards; as, at six o'clock the *bombarders* withdrew.

bom-bär-diēr′, *n.* [Fr. *bombardier*, from *bombarde*, a bombard.]

1. A soldier whose business it was to load and fire bombards.

2. An artilleryman placed in charge of mortars; in the British service, specifically, a noncommissioned officer next below a corporal.

Bombardier beetle; one of several varieties of beetle, which, when alarmed, explosively discharge a pungent vapor from their anal glands.

bom′bärd-măn, *n.* One who carried beer or liquor in a bombard. [Obs.]

bom-bärd′ment, *n.* 1. Formerly, an attack with bombs; the act of throwing bombs into a fortified place.

2. An attack with artillery upon a fortified town or fort; as, the *bombardment* of Santiago.

3. Figuratively, an attack by word of mouth; as, a *bombardment* of questions from the audience.

bom-bär′dō, *n.* The bombardon. [Obs.]

bom-bär′dŏn, *n.* [It. *bombardone*, a musical instrument.]

1. Formerly, a musical instrument of the wind kind, much like the bassoon, and used as a bass to the hautboy.

2. A pedal bass reed-stop of the organ.

3. A brass instrument used in orchestras and military bands; the lowest of the saxhorns.

Bombardon.

bom-bȧ-ṣine′, *n.* Same as *Bombazine*.

bom′bast, *n.* [OFr. *bombace*; LL. *bombax*, cotton, *bombasium*, a doublet of cotton, from L. *bombyx*, Gr. *bombyx*, the silkworm, a garment of silk.]

1. Originally, a stuff of soft, loose texture, used to swell garments; also, any kind of stuffing or padding. [Obs.]

2. Figuratively, high-sounding words; an inflated style; fustian; a grandiloquent attempt to elevate something which in reality is unworthy.

Syn.—Rodomontade, braggadocio, gasconade, bluster, inflatedness, pomposity, fustian.

bom′bast, *a.* High-sounding without meaning; inflated; magniloquent.

bom-bast′, *v.t.* To swell; to pad. [Obs.]

bom-bas′tiç, bom-bas′tiç-ăl, *a.* Swelled; high-sounding; bombast.

bom-bas′tiç-ăl-ly, *adv.* In a bombastic manner; grandiloquently.

bom′bast-ry, *n.* Grandiloquent words without much meaning; bombastic language; fustian.

Bom′bax, *n.* [L. *bombyx*; Gr. *bombyx*, the silkworm.] A genus of trees of the mallow family; the silk-cotton trees.

bom-bȧ-zet′, bom-bȧ-zette′, *n.* A thin woolen cloth, either plain or twilled.

bom-bȧ-zïne′, *n.* [Fr. *bombasin*; LL. *bombacinium*, a silk texture; from L. *bombyx*, Gr. *bombyx*, the silkworm.] A twilled fabric of which the warp is silk and the weft worsted; much used for mourning garments.

bomb′-chest, *n.* In military mining, a chest filled with explosives, which is to be buried and exploded near the enemy's works.

bomb′-här-pōōn″, *n.* A harpoon carrying an explosive head; used chiefly in whale-fishing.

bom′biç, *a.* [L. *bombyx*, from Gr. *bombyx*, the silkworm.] Pertaining to or derived from the silkworm; as, *bombic* acid.

Bombic acid; an acid compound found in the silkworm and its chrysalis.

bom′bi-lāte, *v.i.* [L. *bombus*; Gr. *bombos*, any deep, hollow sound.] To buzz, or hum; to boom. [Rare.]

bom-bi-lā′tion, *n.* Sound; report; noise; as, the *bombilation* of guns. [Rare.]

bom′bi-nāte, *v.i.* Same as *Bombilate*.

bom-bi-nā′tion, *n.* [From L. *bombus*; Gr. *bombos*, a deep, hollow sound.] A buzzing or humming.

bomb′-ketch, *n.* A small ship or vessel formerly used for throwing bombs into a fortress from the sea, and strongly built in order to sustain the shocks produced by the discharge of the mortars.

bom′bō-lō, *n.*; *pl.* **bom′bō-lōeṣ.** [It. *bombola*, a bottle.] A spheroidal retort of flint-glass used in the condensation of sublimated camphor. Written also *bumbelo* and *bumbolo*.

bomb′prōōf, *a.* Secured against the force of bombs; able to withstand or resist the impact of bombs or shells.

bomb′prōōf, *n.* A place or structure secure against the bombardment of heavy guns; a place of refuge from a bombardment; as, the British residents were frequently forced to retire to their *bombproofs* during the siege of Ladysmith.

bomb′shell, *n.* A bomb, or hollow globe of iron, to be filled with explosives and thrown from a mortar.

bom′by-çid, *a.* Pertaining to the genus *Bombyx*, or to the silkworm-moth.

bom-byç′i-nous, *a.* [L. *bombycinus*, silken, from *bombyx*, a silkworm.]

1. Silken; made of silk. [Obs.]

2. Having the color of the silkworm; transparent, with a yellow tint.

bom-byl′i-ous, *a.* [Gr. *bombylios*, a bumblebee.] Buzzing, like a bumblebee. [Obs.]

Bom′byx, *n.* [L., from Gr. *bombyx*, the silkworm.] A genus of moths, including the silkworm-moth.

boṅ, *a.* [Fr., from L. *bonus*, good.] Good; valid as security for something.

bō′nä, *n.pl.* [L., neuter pl. of *bonus*, good.] In law, goods or property, movable and immovable.

Bona notabilia; formerly, in English law, goods belonging to one deceased and at the time of his death not situated in the same diocese as that in which he died.

Bona peritura; in law, perishable goods.

Bona vacantia; goods without an apparent owner, as shipwrecks, etc.

bon-aç-çord′, *n.* [Fr. *bon*, good, and *accord*, fellowship, agreement.] Good fellowship; agreement; good will.

bon′āce-tree, *n.* A small West Indian tree, *Daphnopsis tinifolia*, the fibrous inner bark of which (burn-nose bark) is used for making cordage.

bō′nȧ-fī″dē, *a.* [L., ablative of *bona fides*, good faith.] With good faith; without fraud or deception; genuine; as, a *bona-fide* purchase of a *bona-fide* picture.

bō-nāir′, *a.* [ME. *bonair*, from Fr. *debonnaire*, easy-tempered, kind.] Complaisant; yielding; gentle; debonair. [Obs.]

bō-nan′zä, *n.* [Sp. *bonanza*, fair weather at sea, prosperity; Fr. *bonace*, a calm at sea; from L. *bonus*, good.]

1. A rich vein, mine, or body of silver or gold; a rich find in mining or prospecting.

2. Anything which yields a large income; as, his patent proved to be a *bonanza*. [Colloq.]

Bonanza farm; a great modern farm, usually in the western sections of the United States or Canada, whose yields and profits are enormous.

Bonanza mine; a mine of great or unexpected yielding-capacity.

Bō-nȧ-pärt′ē-ăn, *a.* Pertaining to Napoleon Bonaparte or the Bonaparte family.

Bō′nȧ-pärt-iṣm, *n.* 1. The policy of Bonaparte.

2. Loyalty and devotion to the Bonaparte dynasty.

Bō′nȧ-pärt-ist, *n.* One attached to the policy of Bonaparte or to the Bonaparte family.

bō′nȧ-rō″bȧ, *n.* [It.] A gay wanton. [Obs.]

bō-nā′sus, bō-nas′sus, *n.* [L. *bonasus*, Gr. *bonasos*, the wild ox, from *bous*, an ox.] A species of *Bos*, or wild ox; the aurochs.

bon′bon, *n.* [Fr. *bon*, good, emphasized by repetition.] Sugar confectionery; a piece of candy.

boṅ-bon-nière′ (-yãr′), *n.* [Fr.] A bonbon box or dish; a small ornamental bonbon box carried by women.

bonce, *n.* [Origin uncertain.] A game played by boys with large marbles.

Boṅ-chré-tien′ (-krā-tyaṅ′), *n.* [Fr., literally, good Christian.] The original name in England of the Bartlett pear.

bon'ci-lāte, bon'si-lāte, *n.* [A trade term; *bone*, from AS. *bōn*, bone, and *silicate*, from Fr. *silicate*, silicic acid; L. *silex*, a flint.] A composition of mineral substances and ground bone, used for making billiard-balls, etc., after being hardened by pressure.

bond, *n.* [ME. *bond*; AS. *bindan*, to bind.]

1. Anything that binds or fastens, as a cord, a chain, or a rope; a band.

2. A ligament; that which holds things together.

3. Union; connection; a binding.

Let walls be so constructed as to make a good *bond*. —Mortimer.

4. [*pl.*] Chains; fetters; imprisonment; captivity.

This man doeth nothing worthy of death or of *bonds*. —Acts xxvi. 31.

5. Cause of union; a tie which unites; link of connection; as, the *bonds* of affection.

6. An obligation imposing a moral duty, as by a vow or promise, by law, or other means.

7. In law, an obligation or deed by which a person binds himself, his heirs, executors, and administrators, to pay a certain sum on or before a future day appointed. This is a *single bond*. But usually a condition is added, that, if the obligor shall do a certain act, or pay a certain sum of money, etc., on or before a time specified, the obligation shall be void; otherwise it shall remain in full force. If the condition is not performed, the *bond* becomes forfeited, and the obligor and his heirs are liable to the payment of the whole sum. —Blackstone.

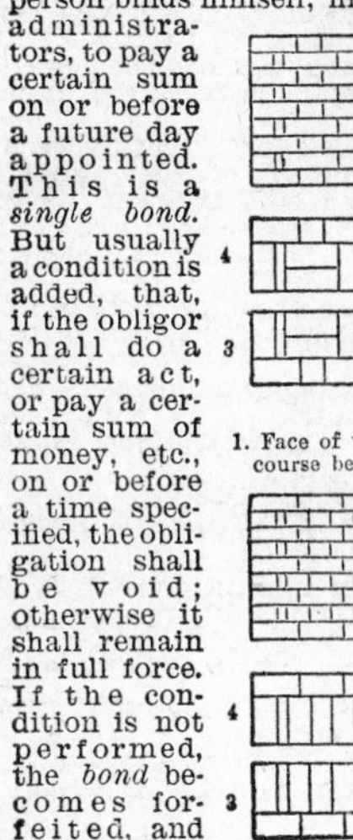

Flemish bond.
1. Face of wall; 2. End of wall; 3. First course bed; 4. Second course bed.

English bond.
1. Face of wall; 2. End of wall; 3. First course bed; 4. Second course bed.

8. In architecture, a peculiar mode of disposing bricks in a wall; as, *English bond*, where one course consists of bricks with their ends toward the face of the wall, called headers, and the next course of bricks with their lengths parallel to the face of the wall, called stretchers; *Flemish bond*, where each course consists of headers and stretchers alternately.

9. A form of the ordinary legal bond issued by a government or corporation, for the purpose of borrowing money; as, a municipal *bond*.

10. The combining power of a hydrogen atom, regarded as a unit of chemical attraction.

11. The condition of goods held in a government or bonded warehouse until the duties are paid; they are then taken out of *bond*.

12. A sum of money, held liable to forfeit, given as a guarantee of good faith or honesty, or to secure one's appearance at a specified time.

13. A confederacy; a league; an association; a bund; as, the Africander *Bond* or league of the Dutch-speaking people of South Africa.

14. A circuit connection of copper, used between the rails in an electric railway-line.

15. [*pl.*] In building, all the timbers employed in constructing the walls of a building.

16. In masonry, a stone holding a wall together, passing through it from side to side, as in walls made of rubble, etc.

17. In carpentry, any timber binding together parts of a frame.

Arbitration bond; a bond given by which one agrees to submit his difference to arbitration and abide by the decision.

Average bond; a bond given to the captain of a ship by the consignees of a cargo, to secure the payment of their share of a general average, their goods having been delivered to them.

Convertible bond; a bond that may be converted into stock at the option of the holder.

Income bond; a bond guaranteeing the payment of certain sums at stipulated times, and pledging the income of a corporation to do so.

Penal bond; a bond by which a sum of money is forfeited in case of failure to do a thing specified.

Straw bond; a fraudulent bond; a bond by which worthless or nonexistent property is pledged as security.

Syn.—Tie, fastening, chain, association, manacle, fetter, compact, obligation, security.

bond, *v.t.*; bonded, *pt.*, *pp.*; bonding, *ppr.* 1. To give bond for, as for duties or customs at a customhouse; to secure payment of, by giving a bond; to mortgage.

2. In building, to make (walls) secure by overlapping the bricks, or by bond-stones.

3. To place in a bonded warehouse; as, the whisky was *bonded*.

bond, *n.* [OE. *bond*, *bonde*, serf.] A serf or slave. [Obs.]

bond, *a.* Held in slavery or serfdom; captive.

Whether we be *bond* or free. —1 Cor. xii. 13.

bond'āge, *n.* [ME. *bondage*; OFr. *bondage*, the condition of being bound; AS. *bonda*, *bunda*, a head of a family, husband.]

1. Slavery or involuntary servitude; captivity; imprisonment; restraint of a person's liberty by compulsion.

2. In ancient English law, villeinage.

3. Obligation; tie of duty.

Brought under the *bondage* of observing oaths. —South.

4. Voluntary or involuntary subjection to any influence; as, the *bondage* of sin; the *bondage* of fashion; the *bondage* of orthodoxy.

Syn.—Servitude, captivity, slavery.

bond'ā-ġēr, *n.* One who works in the field, in payment of rent. [Scot.]

bon'dār, *n.* [Native name.] A small animal, *Paradoxurus bondar*, found in southern Asia; a muskcat; a palm-civet.

bond'-cọọp"ēr, *n.* One who has charge of bonded liquor.

bond'-cred"i-tŏr, *n.* In law, a creditor who has a bond to secure his claim.

bond'-debt (-det), *n.* In law, a debt contracted by forfeiture of a bond; also, a debt secured by a bond or bonds; a bonded debt.

bond'ed, *a.* Secured by bond, as duties; under bond for the faithful performance of a contract.

Bonded debt; a debt secured by a bond or bonds; a bond-debt.

Bonded goods; goods detained in a bonded warehouse, or for which bonds are given at the customhouse to insure the payment of duties.

Bonded warehouse; a place of storage for bonded goods; it is usually in the joint custody of the customs officers and the owner or importer of the goods.

bond'ēr, *n.* 1. One who stores goods under bond.

2. In building, a bondstone.

bond'ēr, *n.* In Norway, one having a small freehold.

bond'hōld"ēr, *n.* One who holds or owns the bonds of a corporation.

bond'māid, *n.* A female slave, or one bound to service without wages, as opposed to a hired servant.

bond'măn, *n.*; *pl.* **bond'men.** 1. A man slave, or one bound to service without wages.

2. In old English law, a villain, or tenant in villeinage.

Syn.—Slave, serf, prisoner, captive, vassal.

bond'-pā"pēr, *n.* Paper of superior quality, used in printing bonds.

bond'-sērv"ānt, *n.* A slave; one in the service of another without pay, or whose person and liberty are restrained.

bond'-sērv"ice, *n.* The condition of a bond-servant; slavery; service without pay.

bonds'măn, *n.*; *pl.* **bonds'men.** 1. Same as *Bondman*. [Obs.]

2. A surety; one who is bound, or who gives security, for another.

bond'stōne, *n.* A stone that binds or holds a wall together, by running through from face to face, thereby strengthening it; used in walls built of rubble, etc.; a binding stone.

bonds'wom"ăn, *n.*; *pl.* **bonds'wom"en.** Same as *Bondwoman*.

bond'-tim"bēr, *n.* A strengthening timber inserted in building a wall, etc.

bon'duc, *n.* [Fr., from Arm. *bondug*, the filbert; Per. *funduq*, the hazel or filbert.] A climbing plant, *Cæsalpinia* or *Guilandina Bonduc*, the nicker-tree or yellow nicker; native in the tropics and bearing a pod containing two hard seeds.

bond'wom"ăn (-woom"-), *n.*; *pl.* **bond'wom"en** (-wim"-). A woman bond-servant.

bōne, *n.* [ME. *boon*, *ban*; AS. *bān*, a bone.]

1. A firm, hard substance, of a dull white color, composing the skeleton or firmer part of the body, in the higher orders of animals. The *bones* of an animal support all the softer parts, as the flesh and vessels. In a fetus they are soft and cartilaginous, but they gradually harden with age. *Bones* are supplied with blood-vessels, nerves, and absorbents. They are covered with a thin, strong membrane, called the *periosteum*, and their cells and cavities are occupied by a fatty substance, called the *medulla* or *marrow*. Earthy matter composes rather more than half, fatty matter one-tenth, and cartilage about one-third of the whole. The earthy matter gives solidity, and consists of phosphate of lime with a small portion of carbonate of lime and phosphate of magnesia.

2. [*pl.*] The skeleton; hence, a corpse; as, lay away my *bones* in peace.

3. Any separate part of a skeleton; as, the collar-*bone*; a *bone* of the wrist; a ham-*bone*.

4. A thin layer of slaty substance found in coal-beds.

5. Stiffening for corsets or dresses, as whalebone or a steel rib.

6. [*pl.*] Clappers of bone or wood, held two together in the hands, which, when struck together, make a rattling noise; also, one who uses them.

7. [*pl.*] Dice. [Colloq.]

Bone in the mouth; a sailor's phrase for the foam dashing up a vessel's bows.

Bone of contention; a subject of dispute.

Bone to pick; a dispute to be settled.

To make no bones; to make no scruple.

To pick a bone with; to quarrel or dispute with.

bōne, *v.t.*; boned, *pt.*, *pp.*; boning, *ppr.* 1. To take out the bones from, as fish.

2. To put whalebone into, as corsets.

3. To steal; to pilfer. [Slang.]

4. To cover with bone for fertilizing.

5. To importune. [Slang.]

bōne, *v.i.* To study diligently. [Slang.]

bōne, *v.t.* [Fr. *bornoyer*, to sight with one eye, from *borgné*, one-eyed.] To look with one eye along (a set of objects) in order to find whether they are level or in line; also written *born*, *bourn*, etc.

bōne'-āce, *n.* A game at cards, in which he who has the highest card turned up to him wins the bone, that is, one-half the stake.

bōne'-ash, *n.* Same as *Bone-earth*.

bōne'-black, *n.* The black carbonaceous substance into which bones are converted by calcination in closed vessels; animal charcoal. It is used as a decolorizing material and as a black pigment.

bōned, *a.* 1. Having bones; used in composition; as, high-*boned*; strong-*boned*.

2. Deprived of bones; as, *boned* turkey.

3. Fertilized with bones.

bōne'dog, *n.* The dogfish.

bōne'-dust, *n.* Ground or pulverized bones, used as manure.

bōne'-earth, *n.* The earthy residuum after the calcination of bone, consisting chiefly of phosphate of lime; used in the arts.

bōne'fish, *n.* See *Ladyfish*.

bōne'-lāce, *n.* A lace made of linen thread; woven with bobbins of bone. [Obs.]

bōne'less, *a.* Without bones; wanting bones.

bōne'set, *n.* A plant, the thoroughwort, *Eupatorium perfoliatum*.

bōne'set"tēr, *n.* One who sets broken bones.

bōne'set"ting, *n.* The practice of setting bones.

bōne'shąw, *n.* Sciatica. [Obs.]

bōne'-spav"in, *n.* A bony excrescence, or hard swelling, on the inside of the hock of a horse's leg.

bō-net'tā, *n.* Same as *Bonito*.

bōne'-whāle (-hwāl), *n.* A right whale.

bon'fire, *n.* [ME. *bonefire*, *bonefyre*, originally a fire of bones.]

1. A fire made in the open air for any purpose, as for amusement, for warmth, or as an expression of public joy or celebration.

2. Anciently, a fire for burning bones; a funeral pyre.

bon'grāce, *n.* [Fr., from *bonne*, f. of *bon*, good, and *grâce*, beauty, charm.] A covering for the forehead; a projecting bonnet or hat. [Obs.]

bon-ho-miē', bon-hom-miē' (bon-o-mē'), *n.* [Fr. *bon*, good, and *homme*, man.] Pleasing manner; cheerful disposition.

bon'i-bell, *n.* [Obs.] See *Bonnibel*.

Bon'i-fāce, *n.* [From *Boniface*, the kind-hearted landlord in Farquhar's comedy, "Beaux' Stratagem."] A hotel proprietor; the keeper of a tavern or inn.

bon'i-fọrm, *a.* [L. *bonus*, good, and *forma*, form.] Of a good form or nature. [Rare.]

bon'i-fȳ, *v.t.* [Fr. *bonifier*, to improve; L. *bonus*, good, and *facere*, to do.] To convert into good. [Rare.]

bōn'i-ness, *n.* The state of being bony.

bōn'ing, *n.* 1. In building, surveying, etc., the act or art of making a level or plane surface by the guidance of the eye; also called *borning*.

2. The treatment of soil with bones as manure.

3. The removing of bones from animal bodies.

bon-i-tā'ri-ăn, *a.* [L. *bonitas*, goodness.] Reasonable; just; honest; bonitary.

bon'i-tā-ry, *a.* Having a beneficiary enjoyment of property without legal title.

bō-nī'tō, *n.*; *pl.* **bō-nī'tōes.** [Sp. *bonito*, dim. of *bueno*, good.]

1. A fish of the tunny kind, *Orcynus pelamys*, growing to the length of three feet, and found on the American coast and in tropical climates.

2. A large, active fish of the genus *Sarda*,

found on both the Atlantic and Pacific coasts of the United States. There are numerous related species which are abundant and important food-fishes.

3. The crabeater or cobia, *Elacate canada*.

4. The madregal, *Seriola fasciata*, of the West Indies.

bon′mōt (-mō), *n.*; *pl.* **bons′mōts** (bon′mō *or* -mōz). [Fr. *bon*, good, and *mot*, a word.] A jest; a witty repartee.

bonne (bon), *n.* [Fr., f. of *bon*, good.] A female caretaker of a young child; a nurse.

bonne′=bouche, *n.* [Fr., from *bonne*, f. of *bon*, good, and *bouche*, mouth.] A delicious morsel or mouthful.

bon′net, *n.* [ME. *bonet*, *bonette*; OFr. *bonet*, *bonnet*, bonnet or cap.]

1. A covering for the head, worn by women or children.

2. In fortification, a small work with two faces, having only a parapet, with two rows of palisades about ten or twelve feet distant. Generally, it is raised above the salient angle of the counterscarp and communicates with the covered way.

3. In nautical language, an addition to a sail, or an additional part laced to the foot of a jib, in small vessels.

4. A seamless woolen cap worn by men. [Scot.]

5. An Indian headdress; as, a Sioux war-*bonnet*.

6. The second stomach of a cud-chewing animal.

7. A decoy; a confederate.

8. Anything used as a bonnet, or resembling one, as the top casting of a valve; a covering over an elevator cage, protecting its occupants from objects falling down the shaft; the wire netting that covers a locomotive smokestack; or the projection over a fireplace to increase the draft, etc.

bon′net, *v.t.*; bonneted, *pt.*, *pp.*; bonneting, *ppr.* 1. To provide with headgear or bonnets.

2. To push the hat down over the eyes of.

bon′net, *v.i.* To uncover the head as a mark of respect. [Obs.]

bon′net-ed, *a.* 1. Wearing a bonnet.

2. In fortification, having a protecting bonnet. [See *Bonnet*, 2.]

bon′net=grass, *n.* White bent-grass, *Agrostis alba*.

bon′net-head (-hed), *n.* A shark, *Reniceps tiburo*, native in the West Indies.

bon′net-less, *a.* Not having a bonnet.

bon′net=lim″pet, *n.* A name given to various species of shells of the family *Calyptræidæ*, which are found adhering to stones and shells.

bon′net=mon″key, *n.* The macaque or munga, *Macacus sinicus*, an East Indian monkey distinguished by the bonnet-like arrangement of the hair on its head.

bon′net=piece, *n.* An old Scottish gold coin on which the head of James V. appears, wearing a bonnet.

bon-net=rouge′ (bon-nā-rözh′), *n.* [Fr.] A red cap worn by French revolutionists as a sign of their patriotism; hence, a red republican or any one with radical ideas of national liberty.

bon′ni-bel, *n.* [Fr. *bonne et belle*, good and beautiful.] A handsome girl. [Obs.]

bon′nie, *a.* Same as *Bonny*.

bon′ni-lasse, *n.* A beautiful girl. [Obs.]

bon′ni-ly, *adv.* Gaily; handsomely.

bon′ni-ness, *n.* Gaiety; handsomeness. [Rare.]

bon′ny, bon′nie, *a.* [Fr. *bon*, *bonne*, good; L. *bonus*, good.]

1. Handsome; beautiful; comely; sweetly attractive; used especially in Scotland and the northern part of England.

> Till *bonny* Susan sped across the plain.—Gay.

2. Gay; merry; frolicsome; cheerful; blithe.

> And be you blithe and *bonny*. —Shak.

Syn.—Fair, pretty, pleasant, lively, cheerful, shapely, buxom.

bon′ny, *n.* [Origin unknown.] Among miners, a round bed of ore; a distinct bed of ore that communicates with no vein.

bon′ny-clab″bēr, *n.* [Ir. *bainne*, milk, and *claba*, thick mud.]

1. Milk that has become thick in the process of souring; clabber; curd.

2. A drink made of beer and buttermilk or sour cream.

bon′spiel, *n.* [Scot.] Formerly, in sports, any match game; now generally restricted to a curling match.

bon′tē-bok, *n.* [D. *bont*, spotted, and *bok*, buck.] A species of antelope, *Alcelaphus pygargus*, of South Africa. It has a blaze on its face, and is closely allied to the blesbok. Written also *buntbok*.

bon′=ton′, *n.* [Fr., good tone, manner.]

1. The style of fashionable people; good breeding; good style.

2. Fashionable society.

bō′nus, *n.* [L. *bonus*, good.]

1. A premium given for a loan, or for a charter or other privilege granted to a company.

2. An extra dividend to the shareholders of a joint-stock company, out of accumulated profits.

3. Extra compensation beyond an amount agreed upon; an extra payment or consideration given as a reward or an inducement, or as a means of avoiding loss, in many contracts and business transactions; an honorarium.

bō′nus, *v.t.*; bonused, *pt.*, *pp.*; bonusing, *ppr.* To promote by giving a bonus to; to add a bonus to. [Rare.]

bon=vi-vant′ (-vē-väṅ′), *n.* [Fr.] A good fellow; a jovial companion; one who lives well.

bōn′y, *a.* 1. Consisting of bones; full of bones; pertaining to bones.

2. Having large or prominent bones; hence, strong; powerful.

3. Thin; gaunt; lean.

bōn′y=fish, *n.* A name given in Connecticut to the menhaden, *Brevoortia tyrannus*.

bōn′y=pike, *n.* The garpike.

bonze (*or* bon′zē), *n.* [Fr., from Port. *bonzo*; Japanese *bozu*, a Buddhist priest.] A name used by Europeans in China and Japan for a Buddhist monk.

boo, booh, *interj.* See *Bo*.

boo′by, *n.* [Sp. *bobo*, a dunce or idiot; OFr. *baube*, a stammerer; L. *balbus*, stammering.]

1. A dunce; a stupid fellow; a lubber.

2. A name given to several birds of the genus *Sula*, the gannet family, as *Sula leucogastra*, the common *booby* of the South Atlantic coast; so called from its apparent stupidity.

3. In cards, the player with the lowest score.

4. The dunce of a class or school.

boo′by, *a.* Having the characteristics of a booby; dull; stupid.

boo′by=hatch (-hach), *n.* A removable covering placed over a hatchway.

boo′by=hut, *n.* A sleigh with a hooded cover. [Local, U. S.]

boo′by=hutch (-huch), *n.* A roughly-built covered carriage used in the east of England.

boo′by-ish, *a.* Like a booby; silly; stupid.

Boodh′, Boodh′ä, *n.* See *Buddha*.

Boodh′ism, *n.* See *Buddhism*.

Boodh′ist, *n.* See *Buddhist*.

boo′dle, *n.* [D. *buidel*; G. *beutel*, a purse; D. *boedel*, possession, property, estate, inheritance, stuff, lumber, etc. The word was used in the seventeenth century, in England, and spelled *buddle*. The meaning, crowd, lot, etc., was produced by association with *caboodle*, a contraction of *kit and boodle*; *kit*, *kith*, a family, and *boodle*, property, possessions.]

1. The whole crowd; the lot; an old term, used in contempt, principally in the phrase *the whole kit and boodle*. [See *Caboodle*.]

2. Money disbursed or received for bribery or corruption in politics or the public service; now popularly applied to any money obtained or paid illegally.

3. Counterfeit money. [Slang.]

boo′dlēr, *n.* One who accepts boodle; one who aids, abets, or participates in corruption involving public funds.

boo-hoo′, *interj.* A word imitating the sound of noisy weeping.

boo-hoo′, *v.i.*; boohooed, *pt.*, *pp.*; boohooing, *ppr.* To cry noisily; to bawl; to blubber.

boo′hoo, *n.* The *Histiophorus americanus*, or sailfish; also called *woohoo*.

book, *n.* [ME. *book*, *boke*, *bok*; AS. *boc*, pl. *bēc*, a writing, record, book, from *boc*, *bece*, a beech (beech-bark probably formed the original writing material of the Teutonic nations); Ice. *bok*, a book, and a beech-tree; D. *boek*, a book, a beech; G. *buch*, a book, *buche*, a beech.]

1. A general name for every literary composition or treatise which is printed; especially, one bound into a volume.

2. Any number of written or printed sheets when bound or sewed together.

3. A volume of blank paper, or of printed blank forms, intended for any species of writing, as for memorandums, accounts, or receipts.

4. A particular part of a literary composition; a division of a subject in the same volume; as, the *books* of the Bible.

5. A volume or collection of sheets in which accounts are kept; a register of debts and credits, receipts and expenditures, etc.; as, to keep a set of *books*.

6. A writing; a written charter; a deed. [Obs.]

> By that time will our *book*, I think, be drawn. —Shak.

7. Specifically, the Bible; commonly written *the Book*.

> Who can give an oath? Where is a *book*? —Shak.

8. Any formal composition of length, whether printed or in manuscript; as, she has written a *book*.

9. In whist, six tricks taken by one side; in some other card games, all the cards forming a set.

10. Figuratively, anything considered as a record or revelation; as, the *book* of nature.

11. The words of a play; the libretto of an opera; as, A wrote the music and B the *book*.

12. In betting, the list of bets made by a bookmaker; an individual's bets upon any sporting event.

13. A package of tobacco leaves, having the stems laid in the same direction.

14. A package of gold-leaf, containing twenty-five leaves placed between covers.

Book of Books; the Bible.

Book of discipline; a book embodying the tenets, and rules for conduct, of the Methodist Episcopal church.

Book of the dead; the priestly and prophetic rules and sacred directions buried in the tombs of the favored Egyptian dead, as an assurance of immortality.

By the book; with authority; with precision; with the conviction of certainty.

Canonical books; collectively, the canon. [See *Canonical*.]

To be in one's good books; to be in favor with.

To be in one's bad or *black books*; to be out of favor with.

To bring to book; to make give an account.

To make a book; in betting, to lay the odds.

Without book; impromptu; spontaneously; by memory; also, without authority.

book, *v.t.*; booked, *pt.*, *pp.*; booking, *ppr.* 1. To enter, write, or register in a book.

2. To engage, as passage, conveyance, or a seat; as, to *book* a seat at the play. [Eng.]

3. To engage to do certain work; as, he has *booked* me for the season. [Theatrical.]

4. To make up in the form of a book, as gold-leaf or tobacco.

5. To select for a certain purpose; as, he was *booked* for the opening address.

book, *v.i.* 1. To engage with any one; to make an engagement to do certain work; as, I *booked* yesterday for the entire season. [Theatrical.]

2. To engage accommodation or contract for transportation, etc. [Eng.]

book′=ac-count″, *n.* An account or register of debt or credit in a book.

book′=ä″gent, *n.* One who solicits orders for books, most frequently for books published in parts or numbers, or sold on the instalment plan.

book′bind″ēr, *n.* One whose occupation is to bind books.

book′bind″ēr-y, *n.* A place for binding books.

book′bind″ing, *n.* The art or practice of binding books.

book′case, *n.* A case with shelves to hold and preserve books.

book′=clamp, *n.* 1. A device to hold books firm in the process of binding.

2. A handle and holder for books, used by schoolchildren.

book′craft, *n.* Literary ability; skill in authorship.

book′=debt (-det), *n.* A debt for goods delivered, and charged by the seller in an account-book.

book′ēr, *n.* One who enters accounts in a book.

book′ēr-y, *n.* 1. A love of books; bookishness.

2. A library or collection of books. [Rare.]

book′=fōld, *n.* See *Book-muslin*.

book′ful, *a.* and *n.* I. *a.* Full of notions gleaned from books; stuffed with book-learning. [Obs.]

II. *n.* As much as would fill a book.

book′hōld″ēr, *n.* 1. One who holds the prompt-book at a theater. [Obs.]

2. A device for supporting a book and holding it open while in use.

book′ing=clērk, *n.* A clerk who sells tickets at a booking-office or who registers passengers, baggage, etc., for conveyance by rail, steamboat, or stage. [Eng.]

book′ing=of″fice, *n.* An office where passage or theater tickets are sold, or where passengers, baggage, etc., are registered for conveyance by transportation lines. [Eng.]

book′ish, *a.* 1. Given to reading; fond of study; more acquainted with books than with men.

2. Having a set style; pedantic; characterized by formality of expression; as, a *bookish* manner of speech.

book′ish-ly, *adv.* In the way of being addicted to books or much reading; pedantically.

book′ish-ness, *n.* Attachment to books; fondness for study.

book′keep″ēr, *n.* One who keeps accounts; the person who has charge of the books and accounts of a business.

book′keep″ing, *n.* The art of recording business transactions in a regular, systematic manner in blank books, or on loose leaves, cards, etc., prepared for the purpose, so as to show their relation to each other, and the state of the business in which they occur; the art of keeping accounts.

There are two systems of *bookkeeping* in common use, known as single entry and double entry. In single entry *bookkeeping*, the record of each transaction is carried either to the debit or the credit side of a single account. In double entry, two entries of every transaction are made and carried to the ledger, one balancing and checking the other.

The books most generally used in keeping accounts are a daybook, cashbook, journal, and ledger. Others are employed to suit individual cases, and the methods used in *bookkeeping* are very numerous and varied.

book′=knowl″edge (-nol″ej), *n.* Knowledge gained by reading books; theoretical learning, as distinct from practical knowledge.

book′land, bock′land, *n.* [AS. *bocland*; *boc*, a charter, writing, and *land*, land.] In old English law, charter land, held by deed under certain rents and free services; free socage land. This species of tenure has given rise to the modern freeholds.

book′=lēarn″ed, *a.* 1. Having knowledge gained from books; learned.

2. Having book-knowledge as opposed to knowledge of life and things from practical experience and observation; bookish.

book′=lēarn″ing, *n.* Knowledge of books and literature; knowledge derived from books without practical experience and observation.

book′less, *a.* Without books; unlearned.

book′let, *n.* A small book.

book′=lōre, *n.* Knowledge acquired from books.

book′=louse, *n.* One of various species of tiny insects that work destruction in books, papers, botanical collections, etc., especially *Atropus pulsatorius*, a wingless insect.

book′=mad″ness, *n.* A rage for possessing books; bibliomania.

book′māk″ēr, *n.* 1. A writer or publisher of books; particularly, a compiler of books.

2. In betting, one who lays the odds on a race or other contingency; one who makes a business of laying odds.

book′māk″ing, *n.* 1. The practice of writing, compiling, or publishing books.

2. The laying of odds in horse-racing, etc.

book′măn, *n.* A student of books; a scholar; a studious or learned man.

book′märk, *n.* 1. Anything placed in a book to mark a place or passage.

2. A label designating the owner of a book; a bookplate.

book′māte, *n.* A schoolfellow or associate in the study of books.

book′mŏn″gēr, *n.* A bookseller.

book′=mọth, *n.* One of various species of moths whose larvæ destroy books.

book′=mus̱″lin, *n.* 1. A kind of muslin used in covering books.

2. A thin white muslin folded like a book in lengths of twenty-four yards; used for ladies' dresses; called also *book-fold*.

book′=nāme, *n.* In zoölogy and botany, a name, other than the technical one, found in scientific works only.

book′=nō″tice, *n.* A review of a book in any publication.

book′=ōath, *n.* An oath taken on the Bible.

I put thee now to thy *book-oath*. —Shak.

book′plāte, *n.* 1. In printing, an electrotype plate, mounted or unmounted, of a book-page, from which impressions are printed.

2. A design, sometimes heraldic, placed in or upon a book, to display the owner's name and identify the book or its library place.

book′=pōst, *n.* An arrangement granting the use of the mails for forwarding books and kindred matter. [Eng.]

book′=scọr″pi-ŏn, *n.* An insect infesting old books, and bearing some resemblance to a scorpion; *Chelifer cancroides* is an example.

book′sell″ēr, *n.* One whose occupation is to sell books.

book′sell″ing, *n.* The employment of selling books.

book′shop, *n.* A bookstore. [Eng.]

book′stạll, *n.* A stand or stall, commonly in the open air, for retailing books.

book′stamp, *n.* A brass or electrotype plate that stamps the cover of a book with title and ornament.

book′stand, *n.* 1. A stand or frame for containing books offered for sale in the streets.

2. A stand or support for books; a portable bookcase.

book′=stōne, *n.* See *Bibliolite*.

book′stōre, *n.* A store where books are kept for sale.

book′wŏrk, *n.* In printing, the specialty of printing books; the process, or any part of the process, of making books, in distinction from printed matter not put in covers, as job or newspaper work.

book′wŏrm, *n.* 1. One of several species of larvæ which bore into books.

2. A student of books; one who absorbs himself in learning and books.

book′y, *a.* Bookish.

book′y, *n.* A colloquial term for a man who makes a book at race-meetings; a bookmaker.

bọọ′ly, bọọ′ley, *n.*; *pl.* **bọọ′lies.** [Ir. *buaile*, a fold, place for milking cows.] Formerly, in Ireland, one who had no settled habitation, but wandered from place to place with his flocks and herds in search of pasture. [Obs.]

bọọm, *n.* [D. *boom*, a tree, a pole.]

1. In ships, a long pole or spar, used to extend the bottoms of particular sails; as, the jib-*boom*, the main-*boom*, etc.

2. A strong iron chain cable, or other obstruction, extended across a river, etc., to prevent an enemy's ships from passing.

3. A pole set up as a mark to direct seamen how to keep the channel in shallow water.

4. A beam which projects from the mast of a derrick, from the outer end of which is suspended the body which is to be lifted.

5. A line of connected floating timbers used to keep sawlogs from floating away.

The booms; in sailing vessels, the space on the spar-deck amidships between the mainmast and foremast and bounded on either side by the gangways; formerly used for stowage of extra spars and booms and boats.

bọọm, *n.* [Imitative word.]

1. A deep hollow sound, as of waves or cannon.

2. A cry like that of the bittern.

bọọm, *v.i.*; boomed, *pt.*, *pp.*; booming, *ppr.* 1. In marine language, to rush with violence, as a ship under a press of sail.

2. To swell; to roll and roar, as waves; to roar and rumble, as heavy guns.

The hoarse waves *booming* to the ocean shore. —Hillhouse.

3. To cry, as the bittern.

bọọm, *v.t.* 1. To push with a boom or pole; as, to *boom* logs downstream.

2. To confine by means of a boom, as logs.

bọọm, *v.t.* and *v.i.* I. *v.t.* To cause to advance rapidly in price or in popular favor.

II. *v.i.* To advance rapidly.

bọọm, *n.* A marked or rapid advance, usually attended with much excitement; applied to stocks, commodities, real estate, political chances of candidates, or to almost anything in which there is public interest or competition; as, the warm weather produced an immediate *boom* in light clothing; the announcement of his action started quite a *boom* in his favor. Sometimes used adjectively; as, *boom* prices; a *boom* town.

A boom town; a town of mushroom-like growth, where there is feverish excitement and activity for a while, usually followed by a collapse when the boom is over. [Colloq.]

bọọm′däs, *n.* [D. *boom*, tree, and *das*, badger.] A small African animal, *Dendrohyrax arboreus*, resembling the rock-rabbit.

bọọm′ēr, *n.* 1. One who or that which booms; one who assists in working up a boom.

2. A North American beaver, *Haplodon rufus*; so named because of its booming noise.

3. In Australia, a name for the male of the giant kangaroo.

bọọm′ēr-ang, *n.* [Australian *bumarin*, *wo-mur-rang*, names of clubs.] A peculiar missile used in hunting and in war by the natives of Australia. It takes the form of a curved stick of hard wood, about two feet long. It describes peculiar curves according to the shape of the instrument and the manner of throwing it, and, taking a backward direction, falls near the place from which it was thrown, or even behind it.

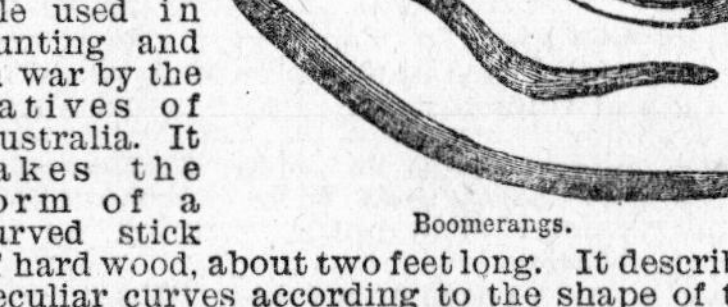
Boomerangs.

2. Figuratively, any speech, act, or thought which recoils upon the originator; as, gossip is a *boomerang*, injuring him who spreads it.

bọọm′ing, *a.* 1. Rushing with violence; roaring, as waves.

2. Advancing in price or in favor quickly and amid excitement; as, a *booming* market; *booming* stocks.

bọọm′ing, *n.* 1. The act of giving out a reverberating, roaring sound; as, the *booming* of surf on the shore.

2. A deep sound, like the cry of the bittern.

bọọm′=ī″ron (-ūrn), *n.* An iron ring on a ship's yard through which the studdingsail-boom passes.

bọọm′kin, *n.* Same as *Bumkin*.

bōō′mō-räh, *n.* [Native name.] A small ruminant allied to the kanchil and the napu, which it somewhat resembles. It belongs to the genus *Tragulus*, and is found in western Africa.

bọọm′slang, *n.* [D. *boom*, a tree, and *slang*, a snake.] A large African tree-snake, *Bucephalus capensis*.

bọọn, *n.* [Fr. *bon*, from L. *bonus*, good; Ice. *bon*, a petition.]

1. A gift; a grant; a benefaction.

2. A prayer or petition. [Obs.]

3. A benefit; a thing to be thankful for; as, the *boon* of good health.

bọọn, *a.* 1. Benign; kind; bountiful. [Obs.]

2. Gay; merry; convivial; as, a *boon* companion.

bọọn, *n.* [Gael. *bunach*, coarse tow, refuse of flax; *bun*, stump, stock.] The refuse or useless vegetable matter from dressed flax.

bọọn′gȧ-ry, *n.* The native name for a small Australian tree-kangaroo, *Dendrolagus lumholtzi*.

bō′ops, *n.* [L., from Gr. *boōpis*, ox-eyed; *bous*, ox, and *ōps*, *opis*, eye.] A fish, *Box boöps*, found mostly in the Mediterranean.

bọọr, *n.* [D. *boer*, a farmer, boor, from *bouwen*, to build, cultivate.] A countryman; a peasant; a rustic; a plowman; hence, one who is rude in manners and illiterate.

bọọr′ish, *a.* Clownish; rustic; awkward in manners; illiterate.

bọọr′ish-ly, *adv.* In a clownish manner.

bọọr′ish-ness, *n.* Clownishness; rusticity; coarseness of manners.

bọọrt, *n.* Same as *Bort*.

bọọs̱e, *n.* A stall or inclosure for an ox, cow, or other animal. [Prov. Eng.]

bọọs̱e, *n.* and *v.i.* See *Booze*.

bọọs̱′ēr, *n.* See *Boozer*.

bọọst, *v.t.*; boosted, *pt.*, *pp.*; boosting, *ppr.* To lift or raise by pushing; to assist in making advancement, or in overcoming difficulties. [Colloq.]

bọọst, *n.* A helping lift; a push upward; hence, commendation; recommendation; as, he gave me a good *boost*. [Colloq.]

bọọst′ēr, *n.* 1. One who boosts; one who speaks or writes in favor of any particular individual or thing. [Colloq.]

2. An appliance for the regulation of electromotive force in an electric circuit; an auxiliary electric dynamo placed in a particular feeder or assemblage of feeders in a distributing system in order to increase the pressure of that particular feeder or assemblage beyond the pressure of the rest of the system.

bọọ′s̱y, *a.* See *Boozy*.

bọọt, *v.t.*; booted, *pt.*, *pp.*; booting, *ppr.* [ME. *boote*, *bote*; AS. *bot*, advantage, reparation; Ice. *bot*; Dan. *bod*; Goth. *bota*; D. *boete*, a making good, reparation.]

1. To profit; to advantage; generally followed by *it*; as, what *boots it?* [Rare.]

2. To enrich; to benefit. [Obs.]

bọọt, *n.* 1. Profit; gain; advantage. [Obs.]

2. Remedy; relief; reparation. [Obs.]

3. That which is given to make an exchange equal, or to supply the deficiency of value in one of the things exchanged.

To boot; in addition to; over and above; besides; in compensation for the difference of value between things bartered; as, I will give my house for yours, with one hundred dollars *to boot*.

bọọt, *n.* [ME. *boote*, *bote*; OFr. *bote*; LL. *botta*, a boot.]

1. A covering for the leg and foot, usually made of leather or rubber.

2. In England, any footwear that reaches above the ankle; used in the same sense as *shoe* in the United States.

3. A woman's outdoor shoe.

4. A kind of rack for the leg, formerly used as an instrument of torture. It was made of boards bound fast to the legs by cords, or was a boot or buskin, made wet and drawn upon the legs, and then dried by a fire, so as to contract and squeeze the legs.

Torture with the Boot.

5. A compartment either in front or at the back of a vehicle, for carrying baggage, parcels, etc.

6. A place at the side of old-fashioned coaches where attendants or passengers might ride.

7. A leather or rubber apron or cover attached to the front of an open vehicle, as a protection from rain or mud.

8. A protective covering for a horse's foot, or a ring worn to prevent interfering.

9. In ornithology, a tarsal envelope occurring in thrushes and warblers.

Boots and saddles; a bugle-call for mounted cavalry drill.

bọọt, *v.t.*; booted, *pt.*, *pp.*; booting, *ppr.* 1. To put boots on, especially for hunting or riding; as, his valet *booted* him.

2. To subject to the torture of the boot. [See *Boot*, n.]

3. To kick with a booted foot. [Slang.]

bọọt, *v.i.* To put on one's boots.

bọọt, *n.* Spoil; plunder; booty. [Obs.]

bọọt′black, *n.* One whose occupation is to black or polish boots; a shoeblack.

bọọt′=clōs̱″ēr, *n.* A workman who sews the

uppers of boots; also applied to a machine used for that purpose.

boot′=crimp, *n.* A machine that crimps boot-uppers by successive operations.

boot′ed, *a.* 1. Wearing boots, especially long-topped riding-boots.

2. In ornithology, having a boot, or tarsal envelope, as thrushes, warblers, etc.

boot-ee′, *n.* [Dim. of *boot.*] A baby's soft shoe or little boot.

Bō-ō′tēs, *n.* [L., from Gr. *boōtēs*, a plowman, from *bous*, an ox.] A northern constellation.

booth, *n.* [ME. *bothe*; Ice. *budh*; Sw. *bod*; G. *bude*, a booth, house; AS. *buan*, to dwell.]

1. A house or shed built of boards, boughs of trees, or other slight materials, for a temporary residence; a shack.

2. A compartment in a fair or market-building, partitioned off for temporary purposes; a market stand.

3. A voting compartment at a polling-place.

boot′hāle, *v.t.* and *v.i.* To go on a foraging expedition; to plunder; to pillage. [Obs.]

boot′=hōșe, *n.pl.* Leggings; spatterdashes.

booth′y, *n.* See *Bothy.*

boot′i-kin, *n.* A small boot.

boot′ing, *n.* Booty; advantage. [Obs.]

boot′ing, *n.* 1. A form of torture. [See *Boot.*]

2. A kicking.

boot′jack, *n.* A device for drawing off boots.

boot′=lȧst, *n.* An implement for shaping boots.

boot′=leg, *n.* Leather cut out for the leg of a boot; the part of a boot above the upper.

boot′less, *a.* Unavailing; unprofitable; useless; without advantage or success.

boot′less-ly, *adv.* Without use or profit.

boot′less-ness, *n.* The state of being unavailing.

boot′lick, *n.* One who cringes or flatters; a toady. [Vulgar.]

boot′māk″ẽr, *n.* A maker of boots.

boot′māk″ing, *n.* The making of boots; the trade of a bootmaker.

boot′=pat″tẽrn, *n.* An apparatus for marking out patterns of various parts of boots.

boots, *n.* A hotel servant who cleans and blacks boots and shoes, and performs small offices or errands for guests. [Eng.]

boot′=stock″ing, *n.* An overstocking to protect the booted foot and leg in cold weather.

boot′top″ping, *n.* 1. The old operation of cleansing a ship's bottom near the surface of the water, by scraping off the grass, slime, shells, etc., and daubing it with a protective mixture of tallow, sulphur, and resin.

2. The act of painting the portion of a ship's copper which is above the water-line.

3. The operation of sheathing a vessel with planking over felt.

boot′tree, *n.* An instrument to stretch and widen the leg of a boot, consisting of two pieces shaped like a leg, between which, when put into the boot, a wedge is driven.

boo′ty, *n.* [ME. *botye*, *buty*; G. *beute*, booty, exchange, barter; Ice. *byte*, give out, distribute, exchange.]

1. Spoil taken from an enemy in war; plunder; pillage.

2. That which is seized by violence and robbery; swag.

To play booty; to play dishonestly, with an intent to lose. [Obs.]

booze, boose, *v.i.*; boozed, *pt.*, *pp.*; boozing, *ppr.* [D. *buizen*; G. *bausen*, to drink.] To drink alcoholic liquor to excess.

booze, boose, *n.* 1. A carouse; a drinking-bout.

2. Liquor; drink.

booz′ẽr, boos′ẽr, *n.* One who makes a practice of drinking alcoholic liquors; a toper.

booz′y, boos′y, *a.* Affected by drink; tipsy; fuddled; stupid or foolish from drink; intoxicated.

bō-peep′, *n.* The act of looking out quickly from behind something and drawing back, as children in play, for the purpose of surprising each other; the game of peek-a-boo.

bō′rȧ, *n.* [It.] In meteorology, a northeast wind, very cold and dry, that blows along the Adriatic coasts.

bōr′ȧ-ble, *a.* Capable of being bored. [Rare.]

bō-rach′iō (-yō), *n.* [Sp. *borracha*, a leather bottle for wine; *borracho*, drunk; *borra*, a lamb.] A leather bottle or wine-skin; figuratively, a winebibber. [Obs.]

bō-rac′iç, *a.* Pertaining to or produced from borax or boron; boric.

Boracic acid; a compound of boron with oxygen and hydrogen; widely used as an antiseptic. It is generally obtained from borax by adding sulphuric or hydrochloric acid.

bō′rȧ-cite, *n.* A mineral composed of boracic acid and magnesia; a native borate of magnesia.

bō′rȧ-çous, *a.* Obtained from borax; relating to or containing borax.

bor′āge (bŭr′), *n.* [ME. *borage*, *burage*; LL. *borrago*, *borago*, from *borra*, the hair of beasts.] A plant of the genus *Borago*; used medicinally for its soothing and perspiratory properties. Written also *burridge*.

bor′āge-wŏrt, *n.* Any plant belonging to the borage family.

Bō-rag-i-nā′cē-æ, *n.pl.* [L., from *borago*, *boraginis*, borage, and *-aceæ*.] A natural order of plants, with cup-shaped blossoms, known as the borage family, chiefly found in the northern temperate regions. All the species have a demulcent, mucilaginous juice and their surfaces covered over with white hairs. Alkanet, comfrey, and the forget-me-not belong to this family.

Common Borage (*Borago officinalis*).

1. Tube of corolla opened up to show the scales (*c c c c*) and lanceolate anthers (*d d d d*); 2. Four-celled, deeply-cleft ovary; 3. Portion of epidermis of the leaf, magnified.

bō-rag-i-nā′ceous, *a.* Pertaining to the *Boraginaceæ*.

bōr-ȧ-gin′ē-ous, *a.* Same as *Boraginaceous*.

Bō-rā′gō, *n.* [LL. *borago*, borage.] The type genus of the order *Boraginaceæ*, natives of the Mediterranean region. It is a small genus, consisting of three species, of which *Borago officinalis* is the most common.

bor′ȧ-mez, *n.* See *Barometz*.

bō-ras′çō, *n.* [Sp. *borrasca*; It. *burasca*, from *bora*, *borea*, the north wind.] A squall of wind sometimes accompanied by thunder and lightning, occurring especially in the Mediterranean.

Bō-ras′sus, *n.* [L., from Gr. *borassos*, the palm-fruit.] A genus of palms having but one species, *palmyra*, found in the tropics of Asia and Africa. [See *Palmyra.*]

bō′rāte, *n.* A salt formed by the combination of boracic acid with a base.

bō′rax, *n.* [LL. *borax*; Ar. *boraq*, *buraq*; Per. *burah*, borax.] Biborate of soda; a salt formed by a combination of boracic acid with soda. It was originally brought from the East Indies, where it was said to be found at the bottom or on the margin of certain lakes, particularly in Thibet. California is now the most important natural source of supply for the United States. It is also made in large quantities from the boric acid found in the hot springs of Tuscany. It is especially valuable, (a) as a reagent in blowpipe analysis; (b) for making colored glazes and enamels for pottery and porcelain; (c) as a flux for cleaning metallic surfaces that are to be brazed or welded; (d) for use in the laundry, in the bath, and in shampooing; and (e) in modified forms in various sanitary, medicinal, and toilet preparations.

bō′rax=bēad, *n.* In chemistry, a glassy drop of molten flux, used in blowpipe analysis as a solvent and color test for certain mineral earths and oxids.

bor′bō-rygm (-rim), *n.* [Gr. *borborygmos*, a rumbling; *borboryzein*, to have a rumbling in the bowels.] The noise produced by wind in the bowels.

bōrd, *n.* 1. A board or a table. [Obs.]

2. In mining, the lateral face of a coal-deposit.

bōrd, *n.* [Obs.] See *Bourd*.

bord, *n.* A striped material made in the Levant and used in the manufacture of garments.

bōrd′āge, *n.* [OFr. *bordage*; *borde*, a hut, cot, and *-age*.] In feudal law, the terms under which a bordar held his dwelling.

bōrd′āge, *n.* [Fr. *bordage*, from *bord*, side of a ship.] The side-planking of a ship.

bōrd′ăr, *n.* [LL. *bordarius*, a cottager, from *borda*, a cottage, hut.] A feudal tenant who gave his services for his cottage or dwelling-house; a cottier; a villain.

Bor-deaux′ (bor-dō′), *a.* and *n.* I. *a.* Pertaining to Bordeaux, a city in southern France.

II. *n.* A wine from Bordeaux.

bor′del, bor-del′lō, *n.* [OFr. *bordel*; It. *bordello*; LL. *bordellum*, a little hut, brothel, dim. of *borda*, a hut, cottage.] A brothel; a bawdy-house; a house devoted to prostitution. [Obs.]

Bor-de-lāis′ (bor-de-lā′), *a.* Pertaining to Bordeaux, or the surrounding district.

bor′del-ẽr, *n.* One who keeps or frequents a brothel. [Obs.]

bor-del′lō, *n.* See *Bordel*.

bor′dẽr, *n.* [ME. *border*, *bordure*; OFr. *bordure*; LL. *bordatura*, border, edging; *bordus*, edge, side.] The outer edge of anything; the extreme part or surrounding line; the confine or exterior limit of a country, or of any region or tract of land; the exterior part or edge of a garment; the rim or brim of a vessel; the exterior part of a garden; the outer edge of an armorial bearing, with a tincture distinct from the field; an overhead piece of scenery in a theater; a limit or boundary; a margin.

bor′dẽr, *a.* Pertaining to that which adjoins, or to outlying districts; as, a *border* ruffian: a desperado of a *border* country or district.

Border states; a name applied to Maryland, Virginia, Delaware, Kentucky, and Missouri, the five slave states which bordered upon the northern free states.

Syn.—Edge, rim, brim, brink, margin, verge.—Of these terms, *border* is the least definite; *edge* the most so; *rim* and *brink* are species of *edge*; *margin* and *verge* are species of *border*. A *border* is a stripe, an *edge* is a line. The *border* lies at a certain distance from the *edge*; the *edge* is the exterior termination of the surface of any substance. Whatever is wide enough to admit of any space round its circumference may have a *border*; whatever comes to a narrow extended surface has an *edge*. A *rim* is the *edge* of any vessel; the *brim* is the exterior edge of a cup; a *brink* is the *edge* of any precipice or deep place; a *margin* is the *border* of a book or a piece of water; a *verge* is the extreme *border* of a place.

bor′dẽr, *v.i.*; bordered, *pt.*, *pp.*; bordering, *ppr.* [ME. *borduren*, *bourduren*, to border, from LL. *bordatura*, from *bordus*, edge, side.]

1. To confine; to touch at the edge, side, or end; to be contiguous or adjacent; with *on* or *upon*; as, Connecticut, on the north, *borders on* or *upon* Massachusetts.

2. To approach; followed by *on* or *upon*.

bor′dẽr, *v.t.* 1. To make a border for; to adorn with a border; as, to *border* a garment or a garden.

2. To reach to; to touch at the edge or end; to adjoin.

3. To confine within bounds; to limit. [Obs.]

bor′dẽred, *a.* Having a border; as, a *bordered* handkerchief.

bor′dẽr-ẽr, *n.* One who dwells on a border or at the extreme part or confines of a country, region, or tract of land; one who dwells near to a place.

bor′dẽr-ing, *a.* Lying adjacent to; forming a border.

bor′dẽr-ing, *n.* Material for a border; specifically, a narrow kind of wall-paper used as a border; also, the act of making a border.

bor′dẽr=land, *n.* Land on the frontiers of adjoining countries; debatable land; frequently used figuratively; as, the *border-land* of science and theology.

bōrd′land, *n.* In old English law, the domain land which a lord kept in his hands for the maintenance of his bord, board, or table; also, land held by a bordar.

bōrd′lōde, bōrd′lōad, *n.* [ME. *bord*, board, and *lode*, a load, way.] The service required of a feudal tenant, as the carrying of timber from the woods to the lord's house; also, the quantity of provisions paid by a bordman for bordland.

bōrd′măn, *n.* A tenant of bordland, who supplied his lord with provisions and rendered menial services.

bord′rāge, bord′rā-ġing, *n.* See *Bodrage*.

bōrd′=sẽrv″ice, *n.* The tenure by which bordland was held.

bor′dūre, *n.* [OFr. *bordure*, border, edge.] In heraldry, a tract or compass of metal, color, or fur, within the escutcheon, and around it.

Bordure.

bōre, *v.t.*; bored, *pt.*, *pp.*; boring, *ppr.* [ME. *boren*, *borien*; AS. *borian*, to bore, from *bor*, an auger.]

1. To perforate or penetrate, and make a round hole in, by turning an auger, gimlet, or other instrument. Hence, to make hollow; to form a round hole in; as, to *bore* a cannon.

2. To eat out or make hollow by gnawing or corroding.

3. To penetrate or break through with difficulty.

4. To tire by annoying repetition; to pester.

5. To delude; to befool. [Obs.]

Syn.—Penetrate, perforate, pierce, weary, fatigue, bother, pester.

bōre, *v.i.* 1. To make a hole or perforation with a boring device, as an auger or gimlet; to penetrate the earth for water, oil, or minerals; to pierce a tree or the ground, as an insect.

2. To be pierced or penetrated by an instrument that cuts as it turns; as, this timber does not *bore* well, or is hard to *bore*.

3. To push forward or advance by persistent action.

4. To thrust out the head or jerk it in the air after the manner of a horse.

bōre, *v.*, past tense of *bear*.

bōre, *n.* [ME. *bore*; AS. *bor*, an auger, gimlet; Ice. *bora*, a hole.]

1. The hole made by boring. Hence, the cavity or hollow of a gun, cannon, pistol, or other firearm, or of any pipe or tube.

2. The diameter of the cavity of a gun-barrel or tube; the caliber.

3. Any instrument for making holes by boring or turning, as an auger or gimlet. [Obs.]

4. A person or thing that wearies by iteration; a dull, garrulous person, or tiresome affair; anything that causes annoyance or weariness of mind.

bōre, *n.* [ME. *bare*, a wave, billow; Ice. *bara*, a billow.] In physical geography, a roaring, high-crested, and destructive wave or flood caused by the rushing of a floodtide up the estuaries of certain rivers, as the Amazon in South America, the Hugli, Ganges, and Indus in India, and Tsientang in China. Similar waves occur, through the meeting of tides, in the Bay of Fundy and the Bristol Channel, though they are neither so high nor so destructive to shipping as those in the great rivers named. In England it is called *eager*.

bō′rē-ăl, *a.* [LL. *borealis*, from *Boreas*, Boreas.] Northern; pertaining to the north, especially the north wind.

Bō′rē-as, *n.* [L., from Gr. *Boreas*, the north wind, the god of the north wind.] The north wind; a cold, northerly wind. Frequently used in personification; as, the blasts of rude *Boreas*.

bōre′cōle, *n.* [D. *boerenkool*, from *boer*, farmer, and *kool*, cabbage.] A variety of cabbage (*Brassica oleracea*) whose leaves are not formed into a compact head, but are loose, and generally curled or wrinkled; called also *kale*.

bōre′dŏm, *n.* 1. The state of being wearied or annoyed by a bore; a condition of ennui.

2. The world of bores; bores, in a collective sense.

bō-ree′, *n.* [Fr. *bourrée*, a rustic dance.] A French dance or movement in common time. Same as *Bourrée*.

bō-reen′, *n.* An Anglo-Irish name for a lane leading from a main road.

bor′ē-gat, *n.* The rock-trout (*Hexagrammus*) of California.

bor′el, *n.* See *Burrel*.

bor′ē-lē, *n.* The smaller of the double-horned rhinoceroses found in South Africa.

bōr′ẽr, *n.* 1. One who bores; also, an instrument to make holes with by turning.

2. In zoölogy, (a) a bivalve mollusk that burrows into wood, as a shipworm; (b) a gasteropod that bores through the shells of oysters, etc.; (c) a beetle, moth, or other insect that bores into trees, usually in the larval state; (d) the hagfish, an eel-like marine fish allied to the lamprey.

bō′riç, *a.* In chemistry, derived from or containing boron.

bō′ride (*or* -rĭd), *n.* Boron in combination with a metallic element.

bōr′ing, *n.* 1. The act of piercing; as, the *boring* of cannon; the *boring* of wells.

2. The hollow made by boring, as a bore-hole.

3. [*pl.*] The shavings or material removed by boring.

bōr′ing-bär, *n.* A bar which rotates in a boring-machine and carries the cutting tools.

bōr′ing-head (-hed), *n.* The head of a diamond drill.

bōr′ing-mȧ-chïne″, *n.* Any mechanism, more complex than a simple drill, used for boring in metal or wood. *Boring-machines* are used in heavy castings, ordnance, structural work, etc.

bōr′ing-spŏnge, *n.* A species of sponge of the genus *Cliona* that bores into the shells of mollusks, and into limestone.

bōr′ing-tool, *n.* A tool which rotates and is used for dressing or finishing holes previously made in metal; a boring-bit.

born, *a.* Of an innate character; having by or from birth; natural; as, a *born* diplomat; a *born* musician.

Born again; regenerated.

In all my born days; during one's lifetime. [Colloq.]

born, bōrne, *v.*, past participle of *bear*.

bor′nē-ōl, *n.* [From *Borneo*.] A superior kind of camphor, somewhat like the common camphor of commerce, from which it can be obtained by chemical process. It is found in the camphor-tree of Borneo and Sumatra (*Dryobalanops camphora*). Also called *Borneo camphor*, *Malay camphor*, and *camphol*.

bor′nīte, *n.* [Named after Dr. Ignatius von *Born*, a metallurgist.] An ore rich in copper and also containing iron and sulphur; called also *purple copper ore* and *horseflesh ore*.

bō-rō-flū′ō-ride (*or* -id), *n.* Same as *Fluoborid*.

bō-rō-glyç′ẽr-ide (*or* -id), *n.* Boric acid and glycerin compounded; an antiseptic.

bō′ron, *n.* [*Borax* and *-on*.] A nonmetallic radical, the base of borax, obtained by applying an intense heat to boric acid in combination with a powerful reagent.

bō-rō-sil′i-çāte, *n.* In chemistry, a compound of silicic and boric acids, found in natural minerals, as in tourmalin.

bŏr′ōugh (bŭr′ō), *n.* [ME. *borwe*, *borgh*, burgh; AS. *burh*, a town, fortified place; from *beorgan*, to protect.]

1. Originally, a fortified city or town; hence, a town or city in general. But in later times, the term *city* was substituted, in England, to denote an episcopal town, in which was the see of a bishop, and *borough* was retained for the rest.

2. In Connecticut, New Jersey, Minnesota, and Pennsylvania, a municipality smaller than a city and incorporated with distinctive privileges.

3. In Scotland, an incorporated municipality; a burgh.

4. Any one of the districts into which Greater New York was divided when the adjacent territory was annexed.

Close or *pocket borough*; a borough with the right of sending to parliament a member, the selection of whom was formerly in the hands of a single person.

Rotten borough; a borough in which there were few voters, yet claiming the right to send a member to parliament; a name applied to such a borough at the time of the passage of the English Reform Bill of 1832.

bŏr′ōugh (bŭr′ō), *n.* [AS. *borhoe*, a surety; *borgian*, to borrow; *borga*, a debtor.] In Saxon times, an association of men mutually pledged to the king for the good behavior of each other. If any offense was committed in their district, they were bound to have the offender forthcoming.

bŏr′ōugh-Eng′lish (-ing′glish), *n.* A customary descent of lands and tenements to the youngest son, instead of the eldest; or, if the owner leaves no son, to the youngest brother.

bŏr′ōugh-head (-hed), *n.* Same as *Headborough*. [Obs.]

bŏr′ōugh-hōld″ẽr, *n.* A headborough; a borsholder.

bŏr′ōugh-mȧs″tẽr, *n.* The mayor, governor, or bailiff of a borough.

bŏr′ōugh-mŏn″gẽr, *n.* One who bought or sold the parliamentary representation of a borough.

bŏr′ōugh-mŏn″gẽr-ing, bŏr′ōugh-mŏn″gẽr-y, *n.* A boroughmonger's practices or dealings.

bōr-rach′iō (-yō), *n.* Same as *Borachio*.

bor′rāge, *n.* Same as *Borage*.

bor-rag-i-nā′ceous, *a.* Same as *Boraginaceous*.

bor′rel, *n.* See *Burrel*.

bor′rel, *a.* Rustic; rude; ignorant. [Obs.]

bor′rōw, *v.t.*; borrowed, *pt.*, *pp.*; borrowing, *ppr.* [ME. *borowen*, *borwen*; AS. *borgian*, to borrow, give a pledge; *borh*, *borg*, a pledge, security.]

1. To take from another by request and consent, with a view to use the thing taken and render an equivalent; as, to *borrow* a book, a sum of money, or a loaf of bread; opposed to *lend*.

2. To take from another, for one's own use, without rendering an equivalent; to copy or select from the writings of another author; to imitate; as, to *borrow* a passage from a printed book; to *borrow* another's manners.

3. In arithmetic, to take (a number) from the next higher order and add it so that a subtraction may be made.

4. To derive; to receive; to take.

To borrow trouble; to be unnecessarily worried or apprehensive.

bor′rōw, *v.i.* 1. To get, take, or receive anything, as a loan.

2. To knock a ball up a hill so that it will roll back toward a hole, as in golf.

3. In nautical language, to come close to land or to the wind.

bor′rōw, *n.* [ME. *borowe*, *borwe*; AS. *borh*, *borg*, a security, pledge, from *beorgan*, to protect, secure.]

1. Any place from which earth is taken for use elsewhere.

2. A surety; a pledge; anything deposited as security. [Obs.]

3. A borrowing; the act of borrowing.

> Yet of your royal presence I'll adventure
> The *borrow* of a week. —Shak.

bor′rōw-ẽr, *n.* 1. One who borrows; opposed to *lender*.

2. One who takes what belongs to another to use as one's own without rendering an equivalent, as in plagiarizing.

bor′rōw-ing-dāyṣ, *n. pl.* The last three days in March, which, according to Scottish folklore, were borrowed from April, because, being always stormy days, they rightfully belonged to March, the stormy month.

bors′hōld″ẽr, *n.* Same as *Headborough*.

bort, *n.* [Origin unknown.] Defective diamonds or fragments of diamonds, fit only for use, when pulverized, in cutting other diamonds.

bō′rụ-ret, *n.* In old chemistry, another name for *boride*.

Bos, *n.* [L.] In zoölogy, the technical name of a genus of quadrupeds. The characteristics are horns hollow within and turned outward in the form of crescents; eight fore teeth in the under jaw, but none in the upper, and no dogteeth. It includes the common ox, the bison, the buffalo, and other species.

bō′ṣȧ, *n.* Same as *Boza*.

bos′çāge, bos′kāge, *n.* [OFr. *boscage*, a grove; LL. *boscus*; from O.H.G. *busc*, a thicket.]

1. Wood; underwood; lands covered with underwood; also, a thicket.

2. In old law, food or sustenance for cattle, yielded by bushes and trees; also, a tax levied on wood brought into a city.

bosçh′bok, bosh′bok, *n.* Same as *Bush-buck*.

bosçh′värk, bosh′värk, *n.* Same as *Bush-hog*.

bosh, *n.* [G. *böschen*, to slope.]

1. One of the sides, forming an obtuse angle at the bottom of a blast-furnace; one of the hollow sides of the foundation of a boiling or puddling furnace, usually made of brick or iron.

2. [*pl.*] The lower part of the sides forming an obtuse angle at the bottom of a blast-furnace.

3. A cooling-trough for ingots and tools, used in forging and smelting.

bosh, *n.* [From Fr. *ébauche*, a rough sketch.] A mere sketch or rough outline. [Obs.]

bosh, *n.* [Turk.] Nonsensical talk; extravagant assertion; as, such talk is *bosh*. [Colloq.]

Bos′jes-man (-yes-), *n.*; *pl.* **Bos′jes-manṣ.** Same as *Bushman*.

bosk, *n.* [ME. *bosc*, *busk*, from O.H.G. *busc*, a bush.] An area covered by a thick growth of shrubbery or small trees. [Rare.]

bos′kāge, *n.* Same as *Boscage*.

bos′ket, *n.* [Fr. *bosquet*, dim. of *bos*, a thicket.] In gardening, a grove.

bosk′i-ness, *n.* The quality of being bosky.

bosk′y, *a.* 1. Woody; covered with thickets.

2. Pertaining to boscage; as, *bosky* gloom.

boṣ′ŏm (booz′), *a.* 1. Of or pertaining to the bosom.

2. Held close; intimate; cherished; dear; as, a *bosom* friend.

3. Secretly cherished; as, a *bosom* sin.

boṣ′ŏm, *n.* [ME. *bosom*; AS. *bosum*, *bosm*; from *bog*, *boh*, the shoulder, arm.]

1. The breast of a human being and the parts adjacent.

2. The folds or covering of clothes about the breast.

> Put now thine hand in thy *bosom*. —Ex. iv. 6.

3. Embrace, as with the arms; inclosure; compass; often implying friendship or affection; as, to live in the *bosom* of a church or a family.

4. The breast, as inclosing the heart, or considered as the seat of the emotions or secret thoughts.

5. Any inclosed place; the interior; as, the *bosom* of the earth or of the deep.

6. Inclination; desire. [Obs.]

7. The smooth, shallow, depressed area around the center of a millstone.

In Abraham's bosom; in paradise; referring to the parable of Dives and Lazarus.

To take to one's bosom; to take to heart; to cherish; to wed.

boṣ′ŏm, *v.t.*; bosomed, *pt.*, *pp.*; bosoming, *ppr.*

1. To inclose in the bosom; to keep with care.

> *Bosom* up my counsel. —Shak.

2. To conceal; to hide from view.

> To happy convents, *bosomed* deep in vines. —Pope.

3. To embrace, as a child.

boṣ′ŏmed, *a.* 1. Having a bosom, or the semblance of a bosom.

2. Held or cherished in the bosom; concealed.

boṣ′ŏm-y, *a.* Having hollows or recesses.

bō′sŏn, *n.* See *Boatswain*.

Bos-pō′ri-ăn, *a.* Pertaining to either the Thracian or the Cimmerian Bosporus.

> The Alans forced the *Bosporian* kings to pay them tribute. —Tooke.

bos′pō-rus, bos′phō-rus, *n.* [L., from Gr. *bosporos*, *boos poros*, ox's ford; *boos*, genit. of *bous*, ox, and *poros*, a ford, from *perān*, to cross.]

1. A narrow sea or a strait between two seas, or between a sea and a lake; so called, it is supposed, as being an ox-passage or strait over which an ox may swim.

2. [B—] Specifically, the strait between the Sea of Marmora and the Black Sea, formerly called the *Thracian Bosporus*; and to the strait of Caffa, or *Cimmerian Bosporus*, which connects the Sea of Azov with the Black Sea.

bos′quet (-ket), *n.* Same as *Bosket*.

boss, *n.* [ME. *bos*, *boce*; OFr. *boce*, the boss of a buckler, a botch; O.H.G. *bozo*, a bundle; *boz*, a blow, from *bozan*, to strike, beat.]

1. A stud or knob; a protuberant ornament, of silver, ivory, or other material, used on bridles, harness, etc.

2. A protuberant part; a prominence; as, the *boss* of a buckler.

3. A projecting ornament at the intersections of the ribs of ceilings and in other situations.

4. A water-conduit swelled out at the middle.

5. A receptacle for mortar, made of wood and hung by means of a hook.

6. A die used for stamping metals into shape.

7. A leather pad used to make the color on pottery uniform.

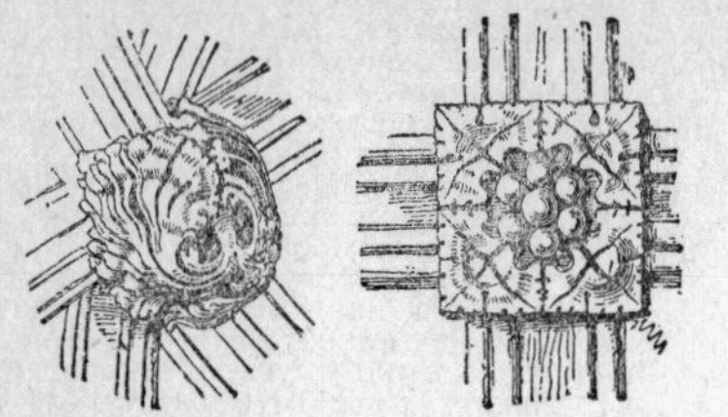

Architectural Bosses.

8. The enlarged part of a shaft or of a hub at the part where a joining is made.

boss, *v.t.*; bossed, *pt.*, *pp.*; bossing, *ppr.* To furnish or adorn with bosses.

bọss, *n.* [D. *baas*, a master.]

1. Among mechanics, the one who directs their work.

2. A political manager who usurps the power of controlling action in his party regardless of the will of the people; an autocratic politician. [Colloq.]

3. Any one who dictates in an arbitrary way to another. [Colloq.]

bọss, *v.i.* To become manager or superintendent; to act the boss. [Colloq.]

bọss, *v.t.* To have control over; to manage or superintend; as, to *boss* the job. [Colloq.]

boss'āġe, *n.* [Fr. *bossage*, from *bosse*, a knob, boss.]

1. In building, an undressed stone projecting beyond the plane of the walls, to be afterward adorned by carving.

2. Rustic finish in a stone wall, the stones being dressed only along the edges of their joinings and at the corners of the building, leaving their rough surfaces projecting beyond the plane of the wall proper.

bossed, *a.* Studded; ornamented with bosses; embossed.

bos'sē-lā-ted, *a.* [Fr. *bosseler*, to ornament with bosses, from *bosse*, a boss, knob.] Studded or covered with bosses or small prominences.

bos'set, *n.* A small bump or boss; specifically, the bump on the head of a young male red deer produced by the underlying rudimentary horn.

bọss'iṣm, *n.* The sway or methods of bosses, particularly political bosses. [Colloq.]

boss'y, *a.* Containing a boss; ornamented with bosses.

His head reclining on his *bossy* shield.—Pope.

bos'sy, *n.* A name for a cow or a calf. [Colloq.]

bos-tan'ji, *n.pl.* [Turk.] The gardeners of the sultan of Turkey; also, his bargemen, guards, and other attendants about the palace.

bọs'tŏn, *n.* A game of cards, played by four persons with two packs of cards, said to have been originated by French army officers in this country during the siege of Boston, in the revolutionary war.

bos'try-ċhite, *n.* [Gr. *bostrychos*, a curl, lock of hair.] A gem bearing some resemblance to a lock of hair.

bos'try-ċhoid, bos-try-ċhoid'ăl, *a.* Having the characteristics of a bostryx.

bos'tryx, *n.* [L., from Gr. *bostrychos*, a curl, lock of hair.] An inflorescence with the flowers in a cyme, or flattish cluster, developed on one side only of the axis, taking a scorpioid form, that is, curved at the end.

Boṣ-wel'li-ȧ, *n.* [Named after Dr. John *Boswell*, of Edinburgh.] A genus of trees belonging to the family *Burseraceæ*, found in eastern Africa and parts of Asia; of importance because various species yield fragrant gums used for making incense or perfumery, such as myrrh and frankincense, also gums and resins of value in the arts, such as gum elemi, an Oriental masticatory.

Boṣ-well'i-ăn, *a.* Pertaining to or characteristic of James Boswell, the biographer of Dr. Johnson.

Boṣ'well-iṣm, *n.* A literary style peculiar to James Boswell, the biographer of Dr. Samuel Johnson, the chief characteristics of which are blind admiration for his hero and most profuse and indiscriminate detail.

bot, bott, *n.* See *Bots.*

bō-tan'iç, bō-tan'iç-ăl, *a.* [LL. *botanicus*; Gr. *botanikos*, from *botanē*, a plant, herb.] Pertaining to botany; relating to plants in general.

Botanic garden; a garden devoted to the culture of plants collected for the purpose of illustrating the science of botany.

Botanic physician; a physician who uses medicines of vegetable origin exclusively.

bō-tan'iç-ăl-ly, *adv.* According to the system of botany.

bot'ȧ-nist, *n.* One skilled in botany; one versed in the knowledge of plants.

bot'ȧ-nize, *v.i.*; botanized, *pt.*, *pp.*; botanizing, *ppr.* 1. To seek for plants, for the purpose of botanical investigation.

2. To investigate plant growth; to examine or classify plants.

bot'ȧ-nize, *v.t.* To examine or survey for specimens of plants or for botanical investigation, as a region or district.

bot'ȧ-ni-zēr, *n.* One who botanizes.

bot-ȧ-nol'ō-ġēr, *n.* A botanist. [Obs.]

bot-ȧ-nol'ō-ġy, *n.* [Gr. *botanē*, a plant, and *logia*, from *legein*, to speak.] The science of botany. [Obs.]

bot'ȧ-nō-man-cy, *n.* [Gr. *botanē*, a plant, and *manteia*, divination.] An ancient method of divination by means of plants.

bot'ȧ-ny, *n.* [Gr. *botanē*, a plant, from *boskein*, to feed, graze.]

1. The science which treats of the structure of plants, the functions of their parts, their places of growth, their classification, and the terms which are employed in their description and denomination.

2. A book expounding the science of *botany*.

Paleontological botany; the department of botany dealing with plants known only from their fossil remains or impressions.

Physiological botany; the department dealing with the organic functions of plants.

Structural botany; the department which deals with the structure and composition of plants.

Systematic botany; the department relating to the nomenclature and classified arrangement of plants.

bō-tär'gō, bō-tär'gȧ, *n.* [Sp.] A relish made of the roes of the mullet or tunny strongly salted after they have become putrid; much used on the Mediterranean coast to induce thirst.

botch (boch), *n.*; *pl.* **botch'eṣ.** 1. A patch, or the part of a garment patched or mended in a clumsy manner.

2. Work which is botched; work done clumsily or unsuitably; a bungle; as, he made a *botch* of the job.

3. One who botches; a bungler.

Syn.—Patch, blunder, jumble, mess, bungle.

botch, *v.t.*; botched, *pt.*, *pp.*; botching, *ppr.* [ME. *bocchen*, to repair; D. *botsen*, *butsen*, to patch, knock together.]

1. To mend or repair awkwardly; to put together unsuitably, or unskilfully; to perform by unsuitable means.

For treason *botched* in rhyme will be thy bane. —Dryden.

2. To spoil or injure by bungling work.

botch, *n.* [ME. *botche*, *bocche*; OFr. *boche*, a botch, swelling.] A swelling on the skin; a large ulcerous affection; a boil. [Obs.]

botch, *v.t.* To mark with botches. [Obs.]

botch'ed-ly, *adv.* In a clumsy or botchy manner.

botch'ēr, *n.* One who botches; a clumsy workman at mending; a mender of old clothes; a bungler.

Let the *botcher* mend him. —Shak.

botch'ēr-ly, *a.* Bungling. [Rare.]

botch'ēr-y, *n.* A botching; awkwardness of performance. [Rare.]

botch'y, *a.* Marked with botches; full of botches.

bōte, *n.* [The old form of *boot*, but retained in law, in compound words.]

1. In old law, compensation; amends; satisfaction; as, man-*bote*, a compensation for a man slain; also, payment of any kind. [Rare.]

2. A privilege or allowance of necessaries; used in composition as equivalent to *estovers*, supplies, necessaries; as, house*bote*, a sufficiency of wood to repair a house, or for fuel, sometimes called fire*bote*; so plow*bote*, cart*bote*, wood for making or repairing instruments of husbandry; hay*bote* or hedge*bote*, wood for hedges or fences, etc. These were privileges enjoyed by tenants under the feudal system. [Rare.] —Blackstone.

bōte'less, *a.* [Obs.] See *Bootless.*

bot'fly, *n.* [Gael. *botus*, a belly-worm; *boiteag*, a maggot.] In zoölogy, a two-winged insect of the family *Œstridæ*. The species common in North America is also called the *gadfly*. A number of species, as the *horse-botfly*, torment domestic animals, and are often the cause of disease in live stock.

bōth, *a.* and *pron.* [ME. *bothe*; Ice. *bathir*, *badhir*; Dan. *baad*, both; Goth. *bai*; AS. *bā*; L. *ambo*; Gr. *ampho*; Sans. *ubhāu*, both.] The one and the other; as, here are two books, take them *both*; the two; the pair or the couple. In such a sentence as '*both* men were there,' it is an adjective; in 'he invited James and John, and *both* went,' it is a pronoun; also in 'the men *both* went,' 'he took them *both*,' it is a pronoun in apposition to *men*, *them*; in the same way it may be explained in '*both* the men,' '*both* of the men.'

bōth, *conj.* As well; equally; not only.

Both, when used conjunctively, often pertains to adjectives or attributes, and in this case generally precedes them in construction; as, he endeavored to render commerce *both* disadvantageous and infamous. This use often obtains in case two or more words or clauses coördinated in use and connected by a common character, purpose, use, or meaning, are joined in the sentence by the conjunction *and*, expressly or by implication, and are sought to be thus collectively attached to the preceding body of the sentence. This construction is sometimes used for emphasis, as to impress upon the mind the unity of the conjoined parts; as, all fled, *both* the disaffected, the lukewarm, the friends, *and* the most avowed partisans.

both'ēr, *v.t.*; bothered, *pt.*, *pp.*; bothering, *ppr.* [Ir. *buaidhirt*, trouble; *buaidhrim*, I vex.] To incommode; to cause trouble to; to tease; to annoy or perplex.

Oh, bother; a mild expletive indicating annoyance.

both'ēr, *v.i.* To be anxious; to worry; to be troubled; to be troublesome.

both'ēr, *n.* Any one or anything that bothers; state of annoyance; worry; trouble.

Syn.—Fuss, worry, excitement, stir, plague, confusion, vexation, flurry, trouble.

both-ēr-ā'tion, *n.* The state of being bothered; the act of bothering; perplexity; worry. [Colloq.]

both'ēr-ēr, *n.* Any one who bothers.

both'ēr-sōme, *a.* Producing or giving bother; perplexing.

bōth'-hands, *n.* A factotum. [Rare.]

both'ie, *n.* Same as *Bothy.*

Both'ni-ăn, Both'niç, *a.* Pertaining to Bothnia, a territory on the Baltic, and also to a gulf of the same name in the same sea, so called from the province which it penetrates.

both-ren'ċhy-mȧ, *n.* [L., from Gr. *bothros*, a trench, and *enchyma*, an infusion; *en*, in, and *cheein*, to pour.] In botany, material of plant structure composed of pitted ducts.

both'ri-um, *n.*; *pl.* **both'ri-ȧ.** [L., from Gr. *bothrion*, dim. of *bothros*, a pit, trench.] A small suctorial organ such as that on the head of the tapeworm.

both'y, both'ie, *n.* A small wooden hut or cottage, particularly a hut for farm servants to live in; a booth.

bō'-tree, *n.* [Cingalese *bo*, a shortened form of Pali *bodhi*, the bo-tree, from *bodhi-taru*; *bodhi*, wisdom, enlightenment, and *taru*, tree.] The pippul-tree at Anuradhapura, Ceylon, under which Buddha is said to have received his enlightenment and revelation; also called the *pagoda-tree*.

Bō-trych'i-um, *n.* [L., from Gr. *botrychos*, curl. So named from the resemblance the spore-cases bear to bunches of grapes.] A genus of cryptogamous plants of the adder's-tongue family, *Ophioglossaceæ*, allied to ferns; also called *grape-ferns*.

bot'ry-ō-ġen, *n.* [Gr. *botrys*, a bunch of grapes, and *-genēs*, producing.] A ferro-ferric sulphate occurring as a crystal containing water of crystallization and having a deep red color. It commonly is found as a bunch or cluster of crystals.

bot'ry-oid, bot-ry-oid'ăl, *a.* [Gr. *botrys*, a bunch of grapes, and *eidos*, form.] Resembling a grape-cluster in form, as the crystallizations of a mineral.

bot'ry-ō-lite, *n.* [Gr. *botrys*, a bunch of grapes, and *lithos*, a stone.] A variety of datolite, occurring in botryoidal forms, and consisting of silica, boracic acid, and lime, being more hydrous than the common varieties.

bot'ry-ōse, *a.* [Gr. *botrys*, a bunch of grapes, and *-ose*.] In botany, (a) resembling a grape-cluster in form; (b) having the buds branching from the axis after the manner of a raceme.

bots, *n.pl.* [Gael. *botus*, belly-worm; *boiteag*, a maggot.] The larvæ of the gadfly when found in the intestines of horses, under the hides of cattle, in the nostrils of sheep, etc. The *bots* with which horses are troubled are caused by the deposition of the larvæ on the tips of the hairs. Being swallowed, the larvæ remain in the stomach several months, are expelled and become pupæ, and later perfect insects.

bott, *n.* 1. In metal-casting, a clay stopper for the hole through which the molten metal runs from a cupola into the pouring ladles.

2. A round cushion, placed on the knees and used in the weaving of lace.

bott'-ham"mēr, *n.* [ME. *botte*, from *batte*, a stick, club, and *hammer*.] A heavy mallet for breaking flax-stalks in order to remove the woody parts from the fiber.

bot-tīne', *n.* [Fr., dim. of *botte*, a boot.]

1. A low boot; a fine shoe for women's wear.

2. A supporting and constraining appliance formed like a boot with adjustable tops and ankle-straps; used for preventing or correcting deformities of the foot and ankle in children.

bot'tle (-tl), *n.* [ME. *botel*; OFr. *botel*, *boutelle*; LL. *buticula*, dim. of *butis*, *butta*, a flask.]

1. A hollow vessel of glass, wood, leather, or

other material, with a narrow **mouth, for holding** and carrying liquids.

Ancient Egyptian Glass Bottles.

Oriental Goatskin Bottles.

2. The contents of a bottle; as much as a bottle contains.

3. Figuratively, intoxicating drink or the use of intoxicants; as, he took to the *bottle*.

bot'tle, *v.t.*; bottled, *pt.*, *pp.*; bottling, *ppr.* 1. To put into bottles and seal; as, to *bottle* wine.

2. To confine or restrain as if placed in a bottle; generally with *up* or *in*; as, the Spanish fleet was *bottled up* in Santiago harbor; to *bottle up* one's anger.

bot'tle=bird, *n.* A bird that builds a nest shaped like a bottle; called also the *weaver-bird*.

bot'tle=brush, *n.* 1. A brush formed of bristles radiating from a wire axis, used for cleaning out bottles.

2. In botany, a number of common plants, having the shape of a *bottle-brush*, as the mare's-tail, the horsetail, etc.

bot'tle=god, *n.* A caper-bearing shrub found in the West Indies; so called from the shape of its pods; the *Capparis cynophallophora*.

bot'tle=cŏm-pan"iŏn (-yun), *n.* A companion in drinking; a boon companion.

bot'tled, *a.* 1. Put into bottles; inclosed in bottles.

2. Having a protuberant belly. [Rare.]

bot'tle=fish, *n.* A deep-sea eel with a body which it can distend, giving it the shape of a bottle. The power of distention enables it to swallow fish much larger than its normal self.

Bottle-fish, inflated. (*Saccopharynx ampullaceus.*)

bot'tle=flow"ẽr, *n.* A plant, the *Centaurea Cyanus*, growing in fields of grain; also called the *bluebottle* from the color and shape of its flowers.

bot'tle=glȧss, *n.* A coarse, green glass, used in the manufacture of bottles.

bot'tle=gōurd, *n.* In botany, the common gourd (*Lagenaria vulgaris*), from the fruit of which cups, dippers, bottles, etc., are made.

bot'tle=grȧss, *n.* Popular name of the *Setaria glauca* or *Setaria viridis*, a meadow-grass; also known as *foxtail-* or *pigeon-grass*.

bot'tle=green, *n.* and *a.* I. *n.* A shade of dark green similar to that of the glass used in ordinary bottles.

II. *a.* Having a dark-green color.

bot'tle-head (-hed), *n.* The bottlenose whale.

bot'tle-hōld"ẽr, *n.* 1. The ring-side attendant of a principal in a prize-fight. The name is given because of the bottle of water he has in readiness to refresh the fighter.

2. A supporter in any contention; a backer. [Colloq.]

3. A stand or rack for a bottle.

bot'tle=imp, *n.* A device used as a toy and as an apparatus in physics, illustrating the specific gravity of bodies; more commonly called the *Cartesian devil*.

bot'tle-nōṣe, *n.* 1. A popular name of several varieties of small whales, especially the *Hyperoödon edentulus* and the *Globicephalus deductor*. It is usually from twenty to thirty feet long, and characterized by a peculiar formation of the snout, whence it derives its name. Also called *bottlehead*.

2. Any one of a number of bottle-nosed varieties of the dolphin, as the *Tursiops tursio*.

3. The puffin, a sea-bird having the beak short and very thick.

4. A bottle-shaped nose; also, a nose discolored or bulbous from drink.

bot'tle=nōṣed, *a.* Having a bottlenose.

bot'tle=ōre, *n.* A name applied to any one of several coarse varieties of North Atlantic seaweed, especially the *Fucus vesiculosus*, or bladder-wrack, and the *Fucus nodosus*.

bot'tlẽr, *n.* One engaged in the bottling of wines, liquors, medicines, etc.

bot'tle-sçrew, *n.* A screw to draw corks out of bottles; a corkscrew.

bot'tle=tit, *n.* In zoölogy, the European titmouse, *Acredula caudata*, which builds a nest shaped like a bottle.

bot'tle=tree, *n.* A tree native to Australia, belonging to the family *Sterculiaceæ*; named from the bottle-like swelling of its trunk, which begins at a very little height above the ground; also called the *barrel-tree*.

bot'tling, *n.* The act, process, or business of putting anything into bottles and corking for preservation and future use.

bot'tling=mȧ-chine", *n.* A machine of various devices which automatically fills and corks bottles.

bot'tŏm, *n.* That on which thread is wound; a ball of thread; the cocoon of a silkworm. [Obs.]

bot'tŏm, *v.t.* To wind, as a ball or skein of thread. [Obs.]

bot'tŏm, *a.* Pertaining to the bottom; situated at the bottom; lowest; fundamental.

bot'tŏm, *v.t.*; bottomed (-tomd), *pt.*, *pp.*; bottoming, *ppr.* 1. To found or build upon; to fix upon as a support; followed by *on*; as, sound reasoning is *bottomed on* just premises.

2. To furnish with a seat or bottom; as, to *bottom* a chair.

3. To get to the root of; to investigate thoroughly, as, to *bottom* a mystery.

4. In mining, to make a channel under for drainage, as in hydraulic gold-mining.

bot'tŏm, *v.i.* 1. To rest upon an ultimate support.

> Find on what foundation a proposition *bottoms*. —Locke.

2. In machinery, to strike against the bottom so as to prevent further movement.

bot'tŏm, *n.* [ME. *bottom*, *botme*; AS. *botm*; D. *bodem*; Ice. *botn*; Sw. *botten*; Dan. *bund*; L. *fundus*; Gr. *pythmēn*, bottom; Sans. *budhna*, depth, ground.]

1. The lowest part of anything; as, the *bottom* of a well, vat, or ship; the *bottom* of a hill.

2. The ground under any body of water; the bed; as, a sandy *bottom*.

3. The foundation or groundwork of anything, material or immaterial, as of an edifice, or a system of reasoning; the base; that which supports any superstructure.

4. The seat of a chair.

5. The lower or hinder extremity of the trunk of an animal; the buttocks.

6. Low ground; a dale; a valley; alluvial land adjoining rivers, etc.

7. The foundation, considered as the cause, spring, or origin; the first moving cause; as, a foreign prince is at the *bottom* of the confederacy.

8. The place farthest away from the head; the least honorable place; as, the *bottom* of the list of eligibles; the *bottom* of the class.

9. The hull of a vessel below the water-line; therefore, a ship or vessel.

10. The lees or dregs; as, the *bottom* of beer.

11. Stamina; endurance; as, an animal of good *bottom*.

12. In a shoe, the sole, shank, and heel, as distinguished from the upper.

13. In painting or in dyeing, the base-color; the color used as a foundation for other colors.

14. In mining, the floor of a seam or vein; also, the channel of a former river in which gold deposits are to be found.

At bottom, at the bottom; in fact or reality; fundamentally; actually.

False bottom; a partition inserted in any receptacle by placing a board or shelf above the true bottom.

To be at the bottom of; to be the real source or cause of; usually restricted to something mischievous or malicious.

To go to the bottom; to become submerged; to sink out of sight; specifically, to sink, as a wreck at sea.

To stand on one's own bottom; to rely on oneself; to be independent.

To touch bottom; to reach the bottom or the utmost depth of anything; to find a place of support.

bot'tŏmed, *a.* Having a bottom of a specified kind; grounded; supported; underlaid; as, a *full-bottomed* ship; a road *bottomed* with gravel.

bot'tŏm=grȧss, *n.* A rich grass, excellent for pasturage, growing on bottom-lands.

bot'tŏm=land, *n.* Land lying low, generally bordering on a river and rich in alluvial soil.

bot'tŏm-less, *a.* 1. Without a bottom; ungrounded; as, a *bottomless* rumor.

2. Fathomless; unknown; visionary; as, a *bottomless* abyss; a *bottomless* speculation.

bot'tŏm-ry, *n.* [ME. *bottomery*, *bodomery*; D. *bodomerij*, bottomry.] In maritime law, the act of borrowing money, and pledging the ship itself as security for the payment of the debt. The contract of *bottomry* is in the nature of a mortgage. If the ship is lost, the lender loses the money; but if the ship arrives safely, he is to receive the money lent, with the interest or premium stipulated, although it may exceed the legal rate of interest. The tackle of the ship, also, is answerable for the debt, as well as the person of the borrower. When a loan is made upon the goods shipped, the borrower is said to take up money at *respondentia*, as he is bound personally to answer the contract. —Blackstone.

bot'tŏn-y, bot'tō-né (-nā), *a.* [OFr. *botonné*, pp. of *botonner*, to ornament with buds or buttons; *boton*, bud, button.] In heraldry, having knobs or buttons at the end.

Cross bottony; a cross bearing three knobs or buds at the end of each arm, in a form somewhat resembling a clover-leaf.

botts, *n.pl.* See *Bots*.

bot'ū-li-fọrm, *a.* [L. *botulus*, sausage, and *forma*, form.] In shape resembling a sausage.

bouche, bouch, *n.* [Fr. *bouche*, mouth, food.]

1. The portion of food formerly allowed servants, or inferior officers, at court or in a feudal lord's household. [Obs.]

2. A notch or hole in a shield, to permit a weapon to be thrust through.

3. The mouth of a firearm.

4. A lining for the vent in breech-loading guns; a bushing.

bouche, bouch, *v.t.*; bouched, *pt.*, *pp.*; bouching, *ppr.* To form or drill a new mouth or vent in, as in a gun which has been spiked.

bou-chée' (-shā'), *n.* [Fr. *bouche*, mouth.] A dainty morsel; in cookery, a small tart.

bou'chẽr-ize, *v.t.*; boucherized, *pt.*, *pp.*; boucherizing, *ppr.* [From *Boucherie*, a French chemist.] To preserve (timber, etc.) by treating with a solution of copper sulphate.

bōud, *n.* An insect that breeds in malt or grain; a weevil. [Obs.]

bou'doir (-dwär), *n.* [Fr., from *bouder*, to pout, sulk.] A lady's private room; an apartment to which only intimates are admitted.

bouf-fănt' (-fäṅ'), **bouf-fănte'**, *a.* [Fr.] Bulging; full; used of a skirt or other drapery.

bouffe, *n.* [Fr., a buffoon.] Comic or light opera; opera *bouffe*.

Bou-gain-vil'lē-ȧ, *n.* A genus of tropical South American plants, climbing shrubs of the family *Nyctaginaceæ*, the flowers of which are nearly inclosed by large colored bracts; named after Louis Antoine de *Bougainville*, a French explorer.

bouge, *v.i.* [Fr.] To swell out; to bulge; also, to spring a leak in the bottom. [Obs.]

bouge, *v.t.* To bilge; to break a hole in. [Obs.]

bouge, *n.* [Obs.] Same as *Bouche*.

bou'get, *n.* [Fr. *bougette*, a little bag.] In heraldry, a leather water-vessel, used as a charge.

Bougets.

bough (bou), *n.* [ME. *bog*, *boh*; AS. *bog*, *boh*, the shoulder, arm; Ice. *bogr*; Sw. *bog*; O.H.G. *buog*; Gr. *pēchys*; Sans. *bahu*, the arm.]

1. The branch of a tree; applied to a branch of considerable size.

2. The hangman's gallows. [Obs.]

bough'pot, bow'pot, beau'pot (bō'), *n.* 1. A bouquet or vase of flowers used as a conventional design in decoration.

2. A vase for flowers, or a large pot for boughs or shrubs.

3. A bouquet.

bought (bout), *n.* 1. A twist; a link; a bend. [Obs.]

2. The part of a sling that contains the stone. [Obs.]

bọught (bọt), *v.*, past tense and past participle of *buy*.

bọught'en, *a.* Obtained by purchase; not homemade. [Colloq. or Poet.]

bought'y (bout'), *a.* Bending. [Obs.]

bou-gie' (-zhē'), *n.* [Fr., a wax candle; Sp. *bugia*, from *Bugia*, in North Africa, whence wax candles were imported.]

1. In surgery, a long, slender instrument, introduced into the urethra, and other canals of the body, to remove obstructions, etc. It was originally made of slips of waxed linen, coiled into a cylindrical or slightly conical form by rolling. *Bougies* are also made of catgut, rubber, and metal.

2. In pharmacy, a thin stick of gelatin or other material impregnated with medicine, to be introduced into the urethra, esophagus, etc., where it is melted by the heat of the body.

3. A wax candle.

bou-illi' (bö-yē'), *n.* [Fr., from *bouillir*, to boil.] Beef or other meat that has been boiled, particularly, that from which soup or bouillon has been made.

bou-illon' (bö-yọṅ'), *n.* [Fr., from *bouillir*, to boil.]

1. Broth; clear soup.

2. In farriery, a growth on a horse's frog; proud flesh.

bouk, *n.* [AS. *buc*, the belly.]

1. Magnitude; volume; bulk. [Scot.]

2. The body; the trunk. [Obs.]

boul, *n.* [Scot.] A kind of semicircular handle, or handle like a loop.

bou-lan′gẽr-ite, *n.* [Named after *Boulanger*, a French mineralogist.] Native sulphid of antimony and lead, occurring in bluish-gray masses.

bōul′dẽr, bōwl′dẽr, *n.* [ME. *bulderston*, a boulder; Sw. *bullersten*; *bullra*, *buldre*, to thunder, roar, and *sten*, a stone.]

1. A water-worn roundish stone of no determinate size, but too large to be regarded as a pebble.

2. In geology, a block lying on the surface of the soil, or embedded in the clays and gravels of the drift formation of the Pleistocene period, generally differing in composition from the rocks in its vicinity, a fact which proves that it has been transported from a distance. *Boulders* lying on the surface are termed *erratic blocks*.

bōul′dẽr-clāy, *n.* The stiff, unlaminated, tenacious clay of the glacial period, usually containing boulders.

bōul′dẽr-head (-hed), *n.* A palisade of piles constructed in front of a breakwater or dike to resist the force of the waves.

bōul′dẽr-ing-stōne, *n.* Hard flint pebbles obtained in gravel-pits, used for dressing the faces of emery-wheels and glazers.

bōul′dẽr-y, *a.* Having many boulders; resembling a boulder.

bōule, bōule′wŏrk, *n.* See *Buhl*, *Buhlwork*.

bou′lē, *n.* The legislative assembly of modern Greece; also, an ancient Greek council or senate.

bou-let′ (*or* -lā′), *n.* [Fr.] In the manège, a horse whose fetlock or pastern-joint bends forward out of its natural position.

bou′le-värd, *n.* [Fr., from G. *bollwerk*, a bulwark.]

1. Originally, a bulwark or rampart of a fortification or fortified town.

2. A public walk or street occupying the site of demolished fortifications, as in many cities and towns of Europe.

3. In the United States, a wide street or avenue, well-paved, usually ornamented with trees and grassplots, and specially intended for walking and driving for pleasure. In many cities the *boulevards* form part of the park system, and only private vehicles, cabs, etc., are permitted to use them, heavy or business traffic being excluded. They form an important feature of modern municipal progress and civic improvement.

bou′le-vär-dier (*Fr. pron.* böl-vär-dyā′), *n.* [Fr.] In Europe, one who frequents the boulevards, particularly those of Paris; a man about town.

bou-le-vẽrse′ment (*Fr. pron.* böl-vers-mäṅ′), *n.* [Fr. *bouelverser*, to overthrow.] Downfall; a complete overthrow; disorder; revolution.

bōult, *n.* A corrupted form of *bolt*.

bōul′tel, *n.* See *Boltel*.

bōul′tẽr, *n.* A long, strong line for deep-sea fishing, having many hooks attached; a trawl; also spelled *bolter*.

bōul′tin, *n.* See *Boltel*.

boun, *a.* [ME. *boun*; Ice. *buinn*, ready, prepared, pp. of *bna*, to till, prepare.] Tending; ready; prepared; a form of *bound*. [Obs.]

boun, *v.t.* To prepare; to get ready.

bounce, *v.i.*; bounced, *pt*, *pp.*; bouncing, *ppr.* [ME. *bounsen*, *bunsen*; D. *bonzen*, to bounce, throw.]

1. To leap or spring; to rush out suddenly.

Out *bounced* the mastiff. —Swift.

2. To spring or leap against anything, so as to rebound; to beat or thump, so as to make a sudden noise.

Another *bounced* as hard as he could knock. —Swift.

3. To boast or bully; to brag; as, he is *bouncing*. [Colloq. Eng.]

bounce, *v.t.* 1. To cause to rebound; as, to *bounce* a ball.

2. To bump; to run against violently.

3. To bully or scold. [Colloq.]

4. To put out unceremoniously, as from a house; to discharge, as from a school, or employment. [Colloq.]

bounce, *n.* 1. A sudden spring or bound; a rebound.

2. A heavy blow, thrust, or thump, with a large, solid body.

The *bounce* burst open the door. —Dryden.

3. A loud sound, as by an explosion. [Obs.]

4. A boast; a threat; a bold lie; as, that was a *bounce*. [Colloq. Eng.]

5. A fish; a species of European dogfish.

6. Dismissal; discharge; as, he received the *bounce*. [Slang.]

bounce, *adv.* Suddenly.

boun′cẽr, *n.* 1. A boaster; a bully; a bold liar; also, an impudent lie. [Colloq.]

2. One who or that which bounces.

3. One who is employed to eject unruly people from a hotel, theater, etc. [Colloq.]

4. One who is strong and stout, or large and healthy-looking; as, the baby is a *bouncer*.

boun′cing, *a.* 1. Stout; strong; buxom; large and heavy; as, a *bouncing* lass.

2. Exaggerated; big; as, a *bouncing* account.

boun′cing-bet, *n.* *Saponaria officinalis*, the soapwort.

boun′cing-ly, *adv.* 1. Boastingly.

2. With a bounce.

bound, *v.*, past tense and past participle of *bind*.

bound, *n.* [ME. *bounde*, *bunne*; OFr. *bunne*, *bonde*; LL. *bodina*, *butina*, a bound, limit.]

1. A limit; any line either imaginary or real which comprehends the whole of any given object or space; a boundary or confine. It is applied to countries, states, cities, towns, tracts of land, and territorial jurisdiction.

2. A limit by which any incursion is restrained; the limit of indulgence or desire; as, the love of money knows no *bounds*.

To beat the bounds; to go around and note the *bounds* of a city or town, *beating* them with willow wands, as is done to this day with ancient ceremonies in many old towns of England.

To keep within bounds; to keep within the limits; to act with regard to propriety.

Syn.—Boundary, limit, confine, extent, border.

bound, *n.* 1. A leap; a jump; a spring.

2. A spring from one foot to the other, as in dancing.

3. A rebound, as of a ball.

4. In artillery practice, when a ball grazes the ground, the distance between any two points of impact.

bound, *v.t.*; bounded, *pt.*, *pp.*; bounding, *ppr.* [ME. *bounden*; AS. *bunden*, pp. of *bindan*, to bind.]

1. To limit; to terminate; to fix the furthest point of extension whether of natural or moral objects, as of land or empire, or of passion, desire, indulgence; to restrain or confine; as, to *bound* our wishes.

2. To mention the boundaries of, as a state; as, to *bound* the state of Ohio.

Syn.—Circumscribe, confine, limit, restrict.

bound, *v.i.* [Fr. *bondir*, to leap, make a noise; LL. *bombitare*, to buzz, hum; L. *bombus*, a humming, buzzing.]

1. To leap; to jump; to spring; to move forward by leaps.

Before his lord the ready spaniel *bounds*. —Pope.

2. To rebound; to recoil, as a ball when thrown against anything.

bound, *v.t.* 1. To make to rebound; to bounce; as, to *bound* a ball against a wall.

2. To cause to leap or bounce. [Rare.]

bound, *a.* 1. Made fast by a band, or by chains or fetters, etc.; confined; restrained.

2. Under legal or moral obligation or compulsion; as, he is *bound* to go.

3. Costive.

4. Inclosed, as a book, in a cover.

5. Sure; destined; certain; as, *bound* to lose. [Colloq.]

6. Determined; as, I am *bound* to go there. [Colloq.]

Often used with a distinguishing prefix in composition; as, weather*bound*, wind*bound*, snow*bound*, hide*bound*, bark*bound*, etc.

Bound bailiff; in England, an officer appointed by a sheriff to execute process; so denominated from the bond given for the faithful discharge of his trust; the name is corrupted into *bumbailiff*.

Bound up in; absorbingly attached or devoted to; inseparable from.

Syn.—Restrained, confined, obliged, destined, compelled, determined, resolved.

bound, *a.* Destined; tending toward; ready; on the way; going, or intending to go; with *to* or *for*; as, the ship is *bound to* New Orleans, or *for* New Orleans; homeward *bound*.

bound′ȧ-ry, *n.*; *pl.* **bound′ȧ-rieṣ** (-riz). [From *bound*, a limit; LL. *bunnarium*, *bonnarium*, a field with limits.] A limit; a bound, real or imaginary. The word is used as synonymous with *bound*, but the original sense is a visible mark designating a limit. *Bound* is the limit itself, or furthest point of extension, and may be an imaginary line; but *boundary* is the thing which marks the limit.

Sensation and reflection are the *boundaries* of our thoughts. —Locke.

Syn.—Limit, border, bound, confine, extent, termination, margin, edge, verge.

bound′en, *a.* [The old pp. of *bind*.]

1. Under legal or moral obligation; obliged; beholden.

I am much *bounden* to your majesty.—Shak.

2. Obligatory; binding; as, our *bounden* duty.

3. Bound by fetters or bonds. [Obs.]

bound′ẽr, *n.* 1. One who or that which bounds; a boundary.

2. An offensive person; a cad. [Eng. Slang.]

bound′ing, *a.* 1. Leaping; springing; rebounding; advancing with leaps; as, a *bounding* deer.

2. Limiting; confining; restraining; as, a *bounding* line.

bound′less, *a.* Unlimited; unconfined; immeasurable; illimitable; as, *boundless* space; *boundless* power; *boundless* love.

Syn.—Illimitable, infinite, unbounded, unlimited, immeasurable, vast.

bound′less-ly, *adv.* Without bound or limit.

bound′less-ness, *n.* The quality of being boundless.

boun′tē-ous, *a.* [ME. *bountevous*; OFr. *bontif*, *bontive*, from *bonte*, goodness, bounty.] Liberal in charity; disposed to give freely; generous; munificent; beneficent; free in bestowing gifts; as, *bounteous* nature.

boun′tē-ous-ly, *adv.* Liberally; generously; largely; freely.

boun′tē-ous-ness, *n.* Liberality in bestowing gifts or favors; munificence; kindness.

boun′ti-fụl, *a.* 1. Free to give; liberal in bestowing gifts and favors; munificent; generous.

God, the *bountiful* author of our being. —Locke.

2. Liberal; abundant; plentiful; as, a *bountiful* harvest.

Syn.—Generous, bounteous, liberal, munificent, plentiful, abundant.

boun′ti-fụl-ly, *adv.* Liberally; largely; in a bountiful manner.

boun′ti-fụl-ness, *n.* The quality of being bountiful.

boun′ti-head (-hed), **boun′ti-hood**, *n.* Goodness; liberality. [Obs.]

boun′ty, *n.*; *pl.* **boun′tieṣ** (-tiz). [ME. *bounte*; OFr. *bonte*; L. *bonitas*, goodness, from *bonus*, good.]

1. Liberality in bestowing gifts and favors; generosity; munificence. The word includes the gift or favor, and the kindness of disposition with which it is bestowed; or a favor bestowed with a benevolent disposition, distinguishing it from a mere gift.

2. A government premium designed to encourage enlistment in the military service, emigration, permanent settlement, the founding of industries, and other acts considered as tending to the public good.

3. Goodness; kindness. [Obs.]

Queen Anne's bounty; a provision made in her reign for augmenting poor clerical livings.

Syn.—Liberality, bounteousness, benevolence, munificence, donation, gift, generosity, charity, benignity.

boun′ty-jump″ẽr, *n.* One who receives a bounty on enlistment and then deserts, as in the United States during the latter part of the Civil War. [Colloq.]

bou-quet′ (-kā′), *n.* [Fr., a plume, a nosegay; OFr. *bosquet*, dim. of *bos*, a wood, thicket.]

1. A nosegay; a bunch of flowers.

2. A perfume; an agreeable aromatic odor emanating from the finer wines.

bou-que-tiēr′, *n.* A device for holding cut flowers, especially one carried in the hand.

bou-que-tin′ (bö-ke-taṅ′), *n.* [Fr.] In zoölogy, an animal of the genus *Ibex*, especially the steinbok of Switzerland.

bour, *n.* A chamber; a bower. [Obs.]

Bour′bŏn, *n.* [From the ancient seigniory of *Bourbon*, France.]

1. A member of the deposed royal family of France, or of any of its branches. The first *Bourbon* to rule France was Henry IV., who succeeded to the throne in 1589. The *Bourbons* have ruled over Spain almost uninterruptedly since 1700.

2. A politician who is behind the times; one opposed to progress; a stubborn conservative. Especially applied before and during the Civil War to certain intensely conservative Democrats. [Political slang.]

Bourbon whisky; see under *Whisky*.

Bour′bŏn-ism, *n.* 1. The policy and principles of the house of Bourbon and the opinions of its adherents.

2. In political slang, obstinate conservatism.

Bour′bŏn-ist, *n.* One who supports the policy and principles of the house of Bourbon.

bourd, *v.i.* To jest. [Obs.]

bourd, *n.* A jest. [Obs.]

bourd′ẽr, *n.* A jester. [Obs.]

bour′dŏn, *n.* [OFr. *bourdon*, a staff; LL. *burdo*, *burdonis*, an ass, mule.] A pilgrim's staff.

bour′dŏn, *n.* [Fr.] 1. In music, (a) the drone of the bagpipe; (b) a bass stop in an organ.

2. Any continuous buzzing or humming sound.

bourg, *n.* [Fr.] A town or borough; a market-town; used especially of a continental town, as distinguished from an English town.

bour-gäde′, *n.* [Fr., from *bourg*, a town, market-town.] An unprotected village or unfortified town in France or Switzerland.

bour-ġeois′ (bũr-jois′), *n.* [So called after a French type-founder *Bourgeois*.] A kind of type, in size between long primer and brevier.

This line is set in bourgeois.

bour-geois′ (bōr-zhwä′), *n.* and *a.* [Fr.] I. *n.* One of the middle class, as a tradesman.

II. *a.* Of or pertaining to the middle class; not aristocratic.

bour-geoi-sie′ (bōr-zhwä-zē′), *n.* [Fr.] The middle class of a country, especially France; used particularly of those depending on trade for a living.

bour′ġeon, *v.i.* See *Burgeon.*

bou′ri, *n.* [Native name.] In zoölogy, a gray mullet (*Mugil capito*) of Europe and Africa.

Bou-rign′ian (-rin′yăn), *a.* In ecclesiastical history, pertaining to Antoinette *Bourignon* (1616-1680), who taught in Great Britain and the Low Countries a religious creed independent of a Bible or church.

Bou-rign′ian, *n.* A member of the Bourignian sect.

Bou-rign′ian-iṣm, *n.* The creed of the Bourignians.

bourn, bourne (*or* bōrn), *n.* [Fr. *borne*; OFr. *bonne, bodne*; LL. *bodina, bonna*, a boundary, limit.] A bound; a limit; a boundary.

The undiscovered country, from whose *bourn*
No traveler returns. —Shak.

bourn, bourne, *n.* [ME. *bourne, burne*; AS. *burne, burna*, a stream.] A brook; a torrent; a rivulet; retained in many names of towns situated on the banks of streams. In Scotland it is still used in the sense of a brook, but written *burn*.

bourn′less, *a.* Without limits.

bour′nŏn-ite, *n.* [Named after Count de *Bournon*, a French mineralogist.] An ore consisting of lead, antimony, copper, and sulphur; occurring in steel-gray crystals, often aggregated into shapes like small cog-wheels.

bour-nous′, *n.* Same as *Burnoose.*

bour-rée′ (-rā′), *n.* [Fr.] An old French dance, similar to the gavotte; written also *boree.*

bourse, *n.* [Fr., a purse, exchange; OFr. *borse*; LL. *bursa*, a purse, bag.] An exchange or place of meeting for business; especially the stock-exchange of Paris.

bouse, *n.* and *v.i.* Same as *Booze.*

bouṣ′ẽr, *n.* Same as *Boozer.*

bou-strō-phē′dŏn, *n.* [Gr. *boustrophēdon*; *bous*, an ox, and *strephein*, to turn.] An ancient Hittite and Grecian mode of writing in alternate lines, one from right to left, and the next from left to right, as fields are plowed.

bou-stroph-ē-don′iç, *a.* Pertaining to the method of writing known as boustrophedon.

bou-stroph′iç, *a.* [Gr. *boustrophos*, ox-guiding.] Boustrophedonic.

bouṣ′y, *a.* Same as *Boozy.*

bout, *n.* [ME. *bout, bowt*; AS. *byht*, a bend, from *bugan*, to bend.]

1. A turn; a single part of an action carried on at successive intervals; essay; attempt.

2. A contest; a match; as, a fencing *bout.*

3. A twist; a bend; a bight. [Obs.]

bou-täde′, *n.* [Fr., from *bouter*, to thrust, butt.] Properly, a start; hence, a whim. [Obs.]

boute′feu, *n.* [Fr.] An incendiary; a firebrand. [Obs.]

Bou-tē-lou′ȧ, *n.* [Named after Claudius *Boutelou*, a Spanish botanist.] An important genus of grasses, abundant in Mexico and southwestern United States, and including the mesquite grasses.

bou-ton-nière′ (-nyãr′), *n.* [Fr., a buttonhole.] A small bouquet worn in a buttonhole.

bouts-ri-més′ (bö-rē-mā′), *n.pl.* [Fr. *bout*, end; *rimé*, pp. of *rimer*, to rime; *rime*, a rime.] Words to be placed at the ends of verses and rimed.

Bou-vär′di-ȧ, *n.* [Named after Dr. Charles *Bouvard*, a French botanist.] A genus of herbs and shrubs with showy flowers, natives of tropical America, and widely cultivated in greenhouses. They belong to the madder family, *Rubiaceæ.*

bō′vāte, *n.* [LL. *bovata*, from L. *bos, bovis*, an ox.] In old English law, an oxgang, or as much land as an ox could plow in a year; an ancient land measure.

bō′vid, *a.* [L. *bos, bovis*, an ox, cow.] Relating to that tribe of ruminant mammals, of which the genus *Bos* is the type.

bō′vi-form, *a.* [L. *bos, bovis*, an ox, and *forma*, form.] Ox-like in form.

bō′vine (*or* -vin), **bō′void**, *a.* [LL. *bovinus*, from L. *bos, bovis*, an ox.]

1. Pertaining to oxen and cows, or the quadrupeds of the genus *Bos.*

2. Sluggish; patient; dull; as, a *bovine* disposition.

bow, *v.t.*; bowed, *pt., pp.*; bowing, *ppr.* [ME. *bowen, buwen, bogen*; AS. *bugan*, to bend, flee; D. *buigen*, O.H.G. *biogan*; Sans. root *bhuj*, to bend.]

1. To cause to bend; as, to *bow* vines.

2. To bend in token of respect, civility, or condescension; as, to *bow* the head.

3. To cause to turn or incline; to exercise great influence upon.

4. To depress; to crush; to subdue.

His heavy hand hath *bowed* you to the grave. —Shak.

5. To express by bowing; as, he *bowed* his thanks.

bow, *v.i.* 1. To bend; to curve; to bend, in token of respect; often with *down*; as, money is the idol to which the world *bows down.*

2. To stoop; to fall upon the knees.

3. To bend the head or body forward as a mark of assent or salutation.

bow, *n.* An inclination of the head, or a bending of the body, in token of respect, civility, or submission.

bow, *n.* [Ice. *bogr*, shoulder, bow of a ship; AS. *bog, boh*, the arm, shoulder.]

1. The stem or prow of a ship.

2. The rounding part of a ship's side forward; often used in the plural; as, under her *bows.*

On the bow; in navigation, situated, at any distance, within 45° of the line ahead of the ship: as, land *on the* weather *bow.*

bōw, *n.* [ME. *bowe, boge*; AS. *boga*, from *bugan*, to bend.]

1. A weapon made of wood, or other elastic material, with a string fastened to each end whereby an arrow is impelled.

2. Anything bent, or in the form of a curve; the rainbow; the doubling of a string in a knot; an ornamental tie, or piece of neckwear, used by men and women; a knot of ribbon worn in the hair, etc.

3. The appliance with which a stringed musical instrument, as a violin, violoncello, etc., is played.

4. A primitive quadrant.

5. An instrument for turning a drill; also, one for turning wood; also, in hat-making, for breaking fur and wool.

6. In architecture, any circular or polygonal projection. A *bow-window* is a window of circular construction; more commonly termed a *bay-window.*

7. [*pl.*] In saddle-making, two pieces of wood, etc., forming the arch in front of a saddle.

8. One of the curved ends of a pair of spectacles, passing over the ear; also called a *riding-bow.*

9. The curved piece of metal forming a guard for the trigger of a firearm; a metal guard about a sword-hilt.

10. An arcograph, or appliance for drawing an arc.

To draw the long bow; to lie; to exaggerate.

To have two strings, or *more than one string, to one's bow*; to have more than one resource.

bōw, *v.t.*; bowed, *pt., pp.*; bowing, *ppr.* 1. In music, to play with the bow; as, to *bow* a difficult passage well.

2. To bend in the form of a bow.

bōw, *v.i.* In music, to play with or handle the bow.

bow′ȧ-ble, *a.* Of a flexible nature or disposition; yielding. [Obs.]

bōw′-ärm, *n.* The arm used in manipulating a bow; (a) in archery, the left arm; (b) in playing the violin and similar instruments, the right arm.

bow′-backed (-bakt), *a.* Having a bent or humped back.

bōw′-beãr″ẽr, *n.* An under officer of the English forests, whose duty was to arrest trespassers.

Bōw′bell, *n.* A figurative appellation for a cockney, or one born within the sound of Bow bells, the bells of St. Mary-le-Bow, a church situated in the heart of London, or cockneydom. *Bow-bells* is therefore another name for cockneydom.

bōw′bent, *a.* Bent like a bow.

bow′-chās″ẽr, *n.* A gun so situated in the bow of a ship that it can be fired at a vessel being chased.

bōw′-cŏm″pȧss, bōw′-cŏm″pȧss-eṣ, *n.* 1. A pair of small compasses having a bow-shaped piece of metal riveted to one of the legs, upon which the other slides.

2. A pair of compasses connected by a bow-shaped spring.

Bowd′lẽr-iṣm, *n.* The practice of omitting passages considered to be indelicate or offensive to refined taste from an author's published works.

Bowd″lẽr-i-zā′tion, *n.* Editorial expurgation.

Bowd′lẽr-ize, *v.t.*; Bowdlerized, *pt., pp.*; Bowdlerizing, *ppr.* [After Dr. Thomas *Bowdler*, who in 1818, published an edition of Shakspere with all indelicate passages omitted.] To expunge indelicate expressions in editing the works of (a writer).

bōw′-drill, *n.* A drill worked by a bow and string.

bōwed (bōd), *a.* Bent like a bow.

bow′el, *n.* [ME. *bowel, boel*; OFr. *boel, buel*; LL. *botellus*, an intestine; L. *botellus*, dim. of *botulus*, a sausage.]

1. An intestine: an entrail; especially, a human entrail; generally used in the plural; as, all his *bowels* gushed out.

2. [*pl.*] In a figurative sense, the interior part of anything; as, the *bowels* of the earth.

3. [*pl.*] The seat of compassion, pity, or kindness, or the attributes themselves; as, *bowels* of compassion; hast thou no *bowels?*

4. [*pl.*] Children; offspring. [Obs.]

bow′el, *v.t.*; boweled, *pt., pp.*; boweling, *ppr.* To take or remove the bowels from; to disembowel; to penetrate the bowels of.

bow′eled, bow′elled, *a.* Possessed of bowels; hollow; as, the *boweled* cavern.

bow′el-less, *a.* Without tenderness or pity.

bōw′en-ite, *n.* [From G. T. *Bowen*, who analyzed it.] A variety of serpentine found in Rhode Island. It is hard and compact in quality, and of a light green color, resembling jade.

bow′ẽr, *n.* 1. An anchor carried near the bows of a ship. There are generally two *bowers*, on the starboard and port sides, called respectively, first and second, great and little, or best and small.

2. One who bows.

3. A muscle used in bending the arm. [Obs.]

bow′ẽr, *n.* [G. *bauer*, a peasant. So called from the figure sometimes designating the knave in a pack of cards.] One of the two best or highest cards in the game of euchre.

Best bower; an extra card sometimes added to the pack in euchre and other games, and taking precedence over all others; the joker.

Left bower: the knave of the same color as the trump but of a different suit; next in value to the right bower.

Right bower; the knave of the trump suit; the highest card in a pack without the joker; used colloquially to describe a trusty friend or valuable assistant.

bow′ẽr, *n.* [ME. *bour*; AS. *bur*, a dwelling, room, chamber, from *buan*, to build; Ice. *bua*, to dwell.]

1. A recess sheltered or covered with foliage; an arbor.

2. A country-seat; a cottage.

3. Poetically, a bedchamber, especially a lady's private apartment.

bow′ẽr, *v.t.*; bowered, *pt., pp.*; bowering, *ppr.* To embower; to inclose.

bow′ẽr, *v.i.* To lodge. [Obs.]

bow′ẽr, *n.* [ME. *bough, bogh*; AS. *bog, boh*, the arm, a branch of a tree.] In falconry, a young hawk before it is fairly on the wing; also written *bowess* and *bowet.*

bow′ẽr-bīrd, *n.* An Australian bird, allied to the crow and starling, so called from its habit of constructing bowers or playhouses of twigs. There are several species, such as the satin *bower-bird* and the spotted *bower-bird.*

Spotted Bower-bird (*Chlamydodera maculata*).

bow′ẽr-y, *n.* [D. *bouwerij*, farm, from *bouer*, a farm.]

1. A farm or plantation; so called by the early Dutch settlers in New York.

2. [B—] A New York street which originally traversed the plantation or *bowery* of Governor Peter Stuyvesant. It is notorious as the location of cheap, vulgar, loud, and tawdry enterprises and amusements.

3. A rustic arrangement for an open-air dance, generally consisting of a dancing platform surrounded by a fence of posts intertwined with branches of trees. The dances given in such a place are called *bowery* dances.

bow′ẽr-y, *a.* 1. Covering; shading, as a bower; also, containing bowers.

A *bowery* maze that shades the purple streams. —Trumbull.

2. [B—] Characteristic of the Bowery, a street in New York City; flashy; loud and vulgar; as, *Bowery* style.

A Bowery boy; a resident in the New York Bowery in the days of its extreme loudness and vulgarity; a loud, flashy, young man.

Bowery dance; (a) a dance conducted in a rustic bowery; (b) a dance of a noisy, vulgar character, like those formerly conducted in the Bowery, New York.

Bowery style; a style of dress, conduct, etc., that is loud and vulgar, or brazen; the style formerly characteristic of the Bowery, New York.

bow'ess, bow'et, *n.* In falconry, same as *bower.* [Obs.]

bōw'fin, *n.* A voracious fresh-water fish, *Amia calva*; the mudfish; called also the *dogfish.*

bowge, *v.i.* To swell out. [Obs. See *Bouge.*]

bowge, *v.t.* To perforate; to cause to leak; as, to *bowge* a ship. [Obs.]

bow'grace, *n.* A frame of timber or junk used to protect the bows or sides of a ship from injury; a kind of ship's fender.

bōw'-hand, *n.* The hand that draws a bow; in archery the left hand, in violin-playing the right. [See *Bow-arm.*]

bōw'head (-hed), *n.* The great Arctic or right whale.

bōw'ie-knife (-nīf), *n.* A long sheath-knife, or dagger, used first by hunters and other frontiersmen in the western and southwestern parts of the United States. It received its name from Col. James *Bowie*, its inventor.

bōw'ing, *n.* 1. The management of the bow judged by the standards of musical technic.

2. In hat-making, the process of preparing hair and fur for felting by means of an instrument called a bow.

bow'ing-ly, *adv.* In a bending manner; with many bows and bends.

bōw'knot (-not), *n.* A knot wherein part of the string, rope, etc., is drawn through in the form of a loop so that it can be easily untied.

bōwl, *n.* [ME. *bolle*; AS. *bolla*, a bowl, round vessel; Ice. *bolli*; O.H.G. *bolla*, a bowl.]

1. A concave vessel usually hemispherical in shape and deeper, as well as larger, than a cup.

2. The hollow part of anything; as, the *bowl* of a spoon; the *bowl* of a pipe.

3. A basin; a fountain.

4. A drinking-vessel for intoxicating liquors; hence, the drink itself; sociable drinking; sometimes termed the *flowing bowl.*

5. The quantity a bowl will hold; a bowlful; as, a *bowl* of soup.

bōwl, *n.* [ME. *bowle*; OFr. *boule*; L. *bulla*, a bubble, stud.]

1. A ball of hard wood used in play on a level surface; a ball used in bowling, often weighted on one side to give it a bias in rolling.

2. [*pl.*] An ancient game, played on the smooth grass of a lawn, with biased or one-sided balls.

3. [*pl.*] The modern game of tenpins, commonly called bowling. [U. S.]

bōwl, *v.t.*; bowled, *pt.*, *pp.*; bowling, *ppr.* 1. To roll, as a ball in the game of bowls; specifically, in cricket to deliver or pitch (the ball) to the batsman.

2. To bear or convey smoothly; to roll as on wheels; as, the horses *bowled* us rapidly along.

3. To strike with anything rolled; hence, to strike down; as, the storm of bullets *bowled* them down.

To bowl out; in cricket, to strike the wicket by bowling, thus retiring the batsman.

To bowl over; in hunters' parlance, to knock over; to kill.

bōwl, *v.i.* 1. To play with bowls, or at bowling.

2. In the game of cricket, to deliver the ball toward the batsman.

3. To move rapidly, smoothly, and like a ball; as, the carriage *bowled* along.

bōwl'dēr, *n.* See *Boulder.*

bōwl'dēr-y, *a.* See *Bouldery.*

bō'leg, *n.* A crooked or bent leg.

bōw'-legged, *a.* Having legs bent like a bow.

bōwl'ēr, *n.* One who plays at bowling, or who delivers the ball in cricket.

bōw'line (*or* -līne), *n.* [ME. *boweline*, *bouline*; D. *boeglijn*; Ice. *boglina*; *bog*, a shoulder, bow of a ship, and *lina*, a line.] A rope fastened near the middle of the leech or perpendicular edge of a ship's square sails, by subordinate parts, called bridles, and used to keep the weather edge of the sail tight forward, when the ship is closehauled.

On a bowline; closehauled; close to the wind.

bōw'line-bri"dle, *n.* A rope by which the bowline is attached to the side of the sail.

bōwl'ing, *n.* The act of rolling bowls, or delivering the ball at cricket; the game of tenpins or bowls.

bōwl'ing-al"ley, *n.* A building or part of a building for the game of bowls or bowling; in England called a *skittle-alley.*

bōwl'ing-green, *n.* A level piece of grass designed for bowling.

bōwls, *n.pl.* An ancient game. [See *Bowl.*]

bōw'măn, *n.*; *pl.* **bōw'men.** An archer.

bow'măn, *n.* The man at the oar which is nearest to the bow of the boat; the bow-oar; also, the man who tends the bow in a boat.

bowne, *v.t.* To make ready. [Obs.]

bōw'-net, *n.* 1. A trap of wickerwork, etc., for catching lobsters and crawfish.

2. A kind of bird-net.

bow'-oar, *n.* The foremost oar used in a boat, except in a whaleboat, where it is the second oar; also, the person who pulls it.

bōw'-pen, *n.* A metallic ruling-pen having the part which holds the ink bowed out toward the middle; also, a bow-compass carrying such a pen.

bōw'-pen"cil, *n.* A bow-compass, on one leg of which there is a pencil.

bow'-piece, *n.* A gun placed at the bow of a ship.

bōw'-pin, *n.* The pin which secures the bows of an ox-yoke.

bow'pot, *n.* See *Boughpot.*

bōw'-saw, *n.* A saw with a narrow blade set in a strong frame resembling a bow.

bowse, *v.i.* 1. To carouse. [See *Booze.*]

2. In seamen's language, to pull hard all together; as, *bowse* away.

bowse, *n.* A drunken revel; carousal; orgie.

bōw'shot, *n.* The distance marked by the flight of an arrow.

bow'sprit (*or* bow'sprit), *n.* [ME. *bowsprit*; D. *boegspriet*; *boeg*, bow of a ship, and *spriet*, a sprit.] A large boom or spar, which projects over the stem of a vessel, to carry sail forward.

Bowsprit.
a, Bowsprit; *b*, Jib-boom; *cc*, Spritsail-yard; *d*, Martingale.

bows'sen, *v.t.* To drench in water; especially, to dip in water supposed to have healing properties for mental disorders. [Obs.]

bōw'string, *n.* 1. The string of a bow.

2. A string used by the Turks in strangling offenders.

Bowstring bridge; a bridge of timber or iron having an arched frame with a strong horizontal tie like a *bowstring.*

Bowstring girder; an arched beam, the two ends of which are connected and strengthened by a horizontal tie or tie-rod.

Bowstring hemp; the tenacious fiber of a hemp which grows in India and Africa, used in making bowstrings.

bōw'string, *v.t.*; bowstringed (-stringd) *or* bowstrung, *pt.*, *pp.*; bowstringing, *ppr.* 1. To throttle by means of a bowstring.

2. To furnish with a bowstring.

bōw'tel, *n.* Same as *Boltel.*

bōw'wood, *n.* The Osage orange of the Mississippi valley, a wood much favored by the Indians in the making of their bows.

bow'wow, *n.* and *a.* I. *n.* The noise made by a dog or a sound like it; a childish term applied to the dog.

II. *a.* Imitative of the sound; as, the *bowwow* philological theory, i. e., that language originated in the imitation of natural sounds; used in ridicule by Max Müller.

bōw'yēr, *n.* [From *bow*, a corruption of *bower*, like *sawyer*, from *saw.*] An archer; one who uses a bow; one who makes bows. [Rare.]

box, *n.* [AS. *box*; L. *buxus*; Gr. *pyxos*, the box-tree.]

1. A tree or shrub, the *Buxus sempervirens*, used for bordering flower-beds. The name is also given to other species of the genus. The African *box* is the *Myrsine Africana.* The wood of the tree varieties is very hard and is extensively used in the manufacture of fine furniture and scientific and musical instruments.

2. Any Australian tree of the various genera *Eucalyptus*, *Murraya*, and *Tristania*; their timber is like boxwood.

box, *n.* [AS. *box*, a box, chest; L. *buxus*, anything made of boxwood; Gr. *pyxos*, the box-tree.]

1. A coffer or chest, either of wood or metal. In general, the word *box* is used for a case of rough boards, more slightly made than a chest, and used for the conveyance of goods. But the name is applied to cases of any size and of any materials; as, a wooden *box*; a tin *box*; a strong-*box.*

2. The quantity that a box contains; as, a *box* of quicksilver. In some cases the quantity called a *box* is fixed by custom; in others, it is uncertain; as, a *box* of tea or sugar.

3. A space with a few seats shut or railed off in a theater or in any public room.

4. The case which contains the mariner's compass.

5. A receptacle for money or other valuables; as, a contribution *box*; a *box* in a safety deposit vault.

6. A cylindrical, hollow iron, in which the axletree of a wheel runs; a journal-*box*; also, a hollow tube in a pump, closed with a valve.

7. A small country-seat, or a huntsman's house.

8. A place for shelter like a box; as, a sentry-*box.*

9. The driver's place on a vehicle.

10. A gift which is contained in a box; as, a Christmas *box.*

11. In baseball, the square allotted to the pitcher.

12. A compartment of a printer's case; as, the comma *box.*

Box beam; in architecture, a hollow beam composed of metal and similar to a box.

Box car; a freight-car with a roof and solid sides.

Box drain; an underground drain boxed up on the sides and top and covered with earth.

Box plait; a form of plaiting consisting of alternate folds in either direction.

Box stall; an inclosure in a stable in which an animal may be kept untied.

In a box, in a tight box; in an embarrassing or difficult situation. [Colloq.]

In the wrong box; in an unnatural position; mistaken. [Colloq.]

box, *v.t.*; boxed (bokst), *pt.*, *pp.*; boxing, *ppr.* 1. To inclose in a box; often followed by *up*; as, to *box up* cloth.

2. To supply with a box, as a wheel.

3. To make an incision into (a tree) to procure the sap; as, to *box* a maple.

4. To turn abruptly; said of a ship.

5. To inclose with boarding or lathing according to a desired form.

To box off; to divide into boxes; in nautical language, to turn the head of a vessel either way by bracing the headyards aback.

To box the compass; to rehearse the thirty-two points of the compass in the proper order; hence, to take every possible attitude on a given subject.

To box up; to inclose in a box; to confine in narrow quarters.

box, *n.* [ME. *box*, a blow, slap; Dan. *bask*, a blow, slap.] A blow on the head with the hand.

box, *v.t.* To strike with the hand or fist, especially on the side of the head.

box, *v.i.* To use the fists; to spar with boxing-gloves.

box'ber"ry, *n.* The checkerberry, or wintergreen.

box'-chrō-nom"e-tēr, *n.* A ship's chronometer suspended in gimbals.

box'-coat, *n.* A thick overcoat used by coachmen; a greatcoat of a peculiar design, square and heavy, especially adapted for travel in inclement weather.

box'-coup"ling (-kup"-), *n.* A metal collar which couples such parts of machinery as shafts.

box'-crab, *n.* A crab of the genus *Calappa*, which, with its pincers folded when resting, resembles a box.

box'el"dēr, *n.* The ash-leaved maple (*Acer negundo*), a native of North America.

box'en, *a.* Made of boxwood or box-trees or pertaining to either. [Rare.]

box'ēr, *n.* One who boxes, spars, or fights, whether with gloves or bare hands; a pugilist.

box'ēr, *n.* One who packs or puts things up in boxes.

Box'ēr, *n.* A member of a powerful secret order in China, antagonistic to foreigners. During the Chinese uprising against foreigners in 1900 the *Boxers* committed many outrages on Europeans, Americans, foreign missionaries, and others, as well as on native Christian converts. Many fell victims to *Boxer* massacres before the foreign powers, under a temporary alliance for the purpose, brought the insurrection to an end in 1901. Why the members of the order are called *Boxers* has never been clearly explained. The organization itself is known by various names, as League of United Patriots and Great Knife (or Sword) Society.

box'fish, *n.* A trunkfish of the genus *Ostracion.*

box'haul, *v.t.*; boxhauled (-hald), *pt.*, *pp.*; boxhauling, *ppr.* In seamanship, to veer or wear (a vessel) short round on her heel when it is not practicable to tack.

box'haul"ing, *n.* A method of changing (a vessel) from one tack to another; so called because the headyards are braced abox or sharp aback, on the wind.

box'-hol"ly, *n.* Butcher's-broom, *Ruscus aculeatus.*

box'ing, *n.* 1. The act of inclosing in a box, or confining in any way; as, *boxing* for storage or shipment.

2. Material suitable for making boxes or used for that purpose.

3. One of the cases on either side of a window-frame into which inside shutters fold back.

4. In shipbuilding, a kind of notched or scarfed diagonal joint used for connecting the stem to the keel.

5. The process of mortising a piece of wood to receive a tenon.

6. The act of giving presents in a box or boxes at Christmas.

7. [*pl.*] Coarse flour from a reel, separated in the process of bolting

box′ing, *n.* The act or practice of fighting with the fists, sparring; pugilism.

box′ing-dāy, *n.* In England, the first week-day after Christmas, a legal holiday; so called from the custom of giving Christmas boxes to letter-carriers, errand-boys, etc., on that day. The night succeeding is called *boxing-night.*

box′ing-glōve, *n.* A glove or mitten with a padded back, used for sparring.

box′ing-match, *n.* A sparring-contest or a prize-fight in which certain rules are prescribed for the combatants.

box′-i″ron (-ūrn), *n.* A hollow smoothing-iron which may be heated from its interior by coals or other means.

box′keep″ẽr, *n.* An attendant in a theater who supervises and regulates admissions to boxes.

box′-kēy, *n.* A socket-key or wrench for turning large nuts.

box′-lob″by, *n.* In a theater, the lobby leading to the boxes.

box′-lock, *n.* A lock made to screw to a surface and not to be mortised in the wood.

box′-met″ăl, *n.* An alloy of copper and tin, or of zinc, lead, and antimony, for making journal-bearings; any metal in the nature of brass or bronze designed to reduce friction to a minimum.

box′-of″fice, *n.* An office for the sale of admission tickets.

box′thorn, *n.* A name given to plants of the genus *Lycium*, particularly *Lycium barbarum.*

box′-tree, *n.* See first *Box.*

box′-tûr″tle, *n.* 1. A land-turtle or -tortoise of the genera *Cistudo* and *Emys*; so named because it is able to shut itself up completely within its shell, as in a box, by means of hinged joints.

2. In a humorous sense, a person of extreme reticence.

box′wood, *n.* 1. The wood of the box (*Buxus sempervirens*), a yellowish, fine, close-grained wood, widely used in engraving, turning, instrument-making, etc.

2. The name given to several species of hardwood trees, more particularly *Cornus florida* of southern United States and *Bignonia Leucoxylon* of the West Indies.

boy, *n.* [ME *boy, boi*; East Friesic, *boi*, a boy, young man; related to D. *boef*, a boy, knave.]

1. A male child, from birth to the age of puberty; but, in general, applied to males under thirteen or fourteen years of age; a lad.

2. A young servant; a page.

3. In some countries, a male servant, slave, or man of inferior race.

4. A familiar name for a comrade or companion. In the plural it is often used colloquially for associates bound together by common ties or tastes, especially in colleges, in the army or navy, or in fraternal or social organizations.

5. One who displays boyish traits or immaturity; as, he is a mere *boy* in judgment.

Boy bishop; in the medieval church, a choirboy sportively elected bishop by his comrades on St. Nicholas' day (December 6), and permitted to serve with some authority over the other boys of the choir until the 28th of the same month. The name is sometimes given to St. Nicholas himself, because of his reputed piety as a boy.

Boy Scout; a member of an organization which aims to develop boys in character through out door activities, camp life, civic service, etc.

Boy's play; a trifling task; childish amusement.

Old boy; Old Nick; the devil. [Slang.]

Yellow boys; gold coins. [Eng. Slang.]

boy, *v.t.* 1. To treat as a boy, or as something belonging to or befitting a boy. [Obs.]

2. To act or represent in the manner of a boy; in allusion to the practice of boys acting women's parts on the stage. [Obs.]

bō-yär′, bō-yärd′ (-yär′), *n.* [Russ. *boyarin′*, pl. *boyare.*] A member of an old Russian aristocratic order or class, next in rank to the ruling princes, which was abolished by Peter the Great; still used in Rumania to designate a privileged person holding a large landed estate or belonging to the conservative party.

boy-au′ (bwä-yō′), *n.*; *pl.* **boy-aux′** (bwä-yōz′). [Fr., a gut.] In fortification, a trench of zigzag form, which protects against an enfilading fire, leading from one parallel of attack to another, or to a magazine or other point; also called a *zigzag.*

boy′cott, *n.* [From Captain *Boycott*, an Irish land-agent who was put under the ban of ostracism by his neighbors during the Land League agitation in Ireland in 1880, the term being first applied by Charles Stewart Parnell in that year.]

1. Originally, a concerted social ostracism or ban openly directed by a community against one of its own members as a mark of disapproval

2. In its later aspect, as defined by the federal commission appointed by President Roosevelt to arbitrate the Pennsylvania coal strike of 1902, a form of coercion by which a combination of many persons seeks to work its will upon a single person, or upon a few persons, by abstaining and compelling others to abstain from social or beneficial business intercourse with such person or persons. The commission distinguished two degrees of *boycott*; first, that directed against the person or persons directly offensive to the instigators; second, that directed against the relatives, associates, or friends of the person or persons offending. The commission declared the secondary *boycott* to be a conspiracy at common law and punishable as such, and also that the primary *boycott* might amount to a conspiracy at law if the element of malicious purpose and concerted action to accomplish it were present. The British Crimes Act of 1887 prohibited the *boycott* under heavy penalties.

boy′cott, *v.t.*; boycotted, *pt., pp.*; boycotting, *ppr.* 1. To combine against by refusing to hold social or business relations with; as, to *boycott* an individual, a firm, or a company; also, to seek to injure by dissuading or preventing others from holding such relations.

2. To place under a ban, as any particular business, products, or commodities.

boy′cott-ẽr, *n.* One who takes part in a boycott.

boy′cott-ing, *n.* The act of embarrassing by means of the boycott.

boy′cott-ism, *n.* The principles and methods peculiar to the boycott.

boy′de-kin, *n.* [Obs.] Same as *Bodkin.*

boy′ẽr, *n.* [Fr. *boyer*, from Fl. *boeyer*, a vessel used for laying buoys; *boey*, a buoy.] A Flemish sloop with a castle at each end.

boy′hood, *n.* The state of being a boy, or the period during which one is a boy.

boy′ish, *a.* Belonging to a boy; childish; trifling; resembling a boy in manners or opinions; puerile.

boy′ish-ly, *adv.* Childishly; in a boyish manner.

boy′ish-ness, *n.* Childishness; the manners or behavior of a boy.

boy′ism, *n.* 1. Childishness; puerility.

2. Boyhood. [Obs.]

boy′ṣ′-lōve, *n.* A name given to the southernwood, *Artemisia abrotanum*; also called *lad's-love.*

bō-yū′nȧ, *n.* 1. A large South American serpent, black and slender, having an intolerable smell.

2. A harmless snake common in Ceylon.

bō′zȧ, *n.* [Ar. *buze*; Per. *buza*; Hind. *buza, boza*; Turk. *boza.*] An Egyptian and Turkish fermented beverage made from an infusion of millet-seed by adding various astringents; also, an intoxicant made from a mixture of darnel-meal, hemp-seed, and water; the name is also given to a beverage made of honey and tamarinds. Written also *bosa, boosa, booza, bozah, bouzah.*

brab, brab′-tree, *n.* [Anglo-Ind.] The palmyra palm, *Borassus flabelliformis.*

Brȧ-bant′ine, *a.* Pertaining to Brabant, an ancient duchy of the Netherlands.

brab′ble, *n.* A broil; a clamorous contest; a wrangle.

brab′ble, *v.i.*; brabbled, *pt., pp.*; brabbling, *ppr.* [D. *brabbelen*, to talk confusedly, to stammer.] To clamor; to contest noisily. [Rare.]

brab′ble-ment, *n.* A noisy dispute; a broil; a brabble. [Rare.]

brab′blẽr, *n.* A clamorous, quarrelsome, noisy fellow; a wrangler. [Rare.]

brac′cāte, *a.* [L. *bracatus*, from *bracæ*, breeches.] In ornithology, furnished with feathers which conceal the feet.

brac′ciō (brät′shō), *n.*; *pl.* **brac′ciȧ** (-shȧ). [It.] An Italian measure of length, varying from half a yard to a yard.

brāce, *n.* [OFr. *brace*, an armful, a fathom; L. *brachia*, pl. of *brachium*, the arm.]

1. In architecture, a diagonal piece of timber with bevel-joints, placed near and across the angles in the frame of a building in order to strengthen it; when used to support a rafter it is called a strut.

2. That which holds anything tightly; a cincture, prop, or bandage.

3. A pair; a couple; as, a *brace* of ducks; used of persons only with a shade of contempt, or in a colloquial style.

4. A thick strap which supports a carriage on wheels.

5. In printing or writing, a sign, usually a vertical doubly curved line or bracket for connecting words, lines, or staves of music.

6. In nautical language, a rope reeved through a block at the end of a yard to square or traverse the yard; also, one of various pieces of iron which are used as supports.

7. Harness; warlike preparation. [Obs.]

8. Tension; tightness.

9. [*pl.*] Suspenders; the straps that sustain trousers, etc.

10. A bitstock; an instrument with a crank motion for holding and rotating bits, to bore or drill holes, drive screws, etc.

11. A defense for the arm, especially in archery; a bracer; a vambrace or piece of armor for the protection of the forearm.

12. A support for any weak part of the body or physical defect.

13. In English mining, a flooring at the mouth of a shaft.

14. A leather slide upon the cords of a drum, used for raising or lowering the tone by tightening or loosening the head.

brāce, *v.t.*; braced (brāst), *pt., pp.*; bracing, *ppr.* [ME. *bracen*; OFr. *bracer*, to brace, embrace; L. *bracchia*, pl. of *bracchium*, an arm.]

1. To draw tight; to tighten; to bind or tie closely; to make tight and firm with or as with bandages.

2. To make tense; to strain up; to increase the tension, tone, or vigor of; to strengthen; as, to *brace* the nerves; to *brace* a drum.

3. In nautical language, to bring (the yards) to either side.

4. To place in a position for bracing; to hold or grasp firmly; as, he *braced* himself against the crowd.

5. To furnish with braces; as, to *brace* a building.

To brace aback; to brace so as to lay the sails aback.

To brace about; to turn the yards round for the contrary tack.

To brace a yard; to trim it, or shift it horizontally, with a brace.

To brace by; to brace the yards in contrary directions on the different masts so as to stop the vessel's progress.

To brace in; to let out the lee braces and haul in the weather braces.

To brace sharp; to cause the yards to have the smallest possible angle with the keel.

To brace to; to check or ease off the lee braces, and round in the weather ones, to assist in tacking.

To brace up; to lay the yards more fore-and-aft to cause the ship to sail closer to the wind.

brāce, *v.i.* To summon one's energies; to restore vigor; followed by *up*; as, he *braced up* when real trouble came. [Colloq.]

brāced (brāst), **brāzed**, *a.* In heraldry, terms applicable to charges when interlaced or linked together

Three Chevrons Braced.

brāce′let, *n.* [Fr. *bracelet*, dim. of OFr. *bracel*, *brachel*, an armlet, defense for the arm.]

1. An ornamental band, ring, or chain for the wrist or arm, now worn mostly by ladies. *Bracelets* were among the very earliest personal ornaments, as is seen from ancient Egyptian and Assyrian sculptures.

Egyptian and Assyrian Bracelets.

> I decked thee also with ornaments, and I put *bracelets* upon thy hands, and a chain on thy neck. —Ezek. xvi. 11.

2. A piece of defensive armor for the arm.

3. A term applied in palmistry to wrist wrinkles.

brā′cẽr, *n.* 1. That which braces, binds, or makes firm; a band or bandage; also, a protection for the arm of a bowman.

2. A medicine which gives tension or tone.

brach, *n.* [OFr. *brache*; O.H.G. *bracho*, a dog that hunts by the scent.] A bitch of the hound kind.

Brach-el′y-trȧ, *n.pl.* [L., from Gr. *brachys*, short, and *elytron*, a covering.] A group of beetles with short sheaths or elytra.

brach-el′y-trous, brach-y-el′y-trous, *a.* Distinguished by short sheaths or elytra.

brach′i-ȧ, *n.*, pl. of *brachium.*

brach′i-ăl, *a.* [L. *bracchialis*, from *bracchium*, the arm.] Pertaining to an arm or its form; as, the *brachial* artery.

Brach-i-ā′tȧ, *n.pl.* [L. *bracchiatus*, from *bracchium*, the arm.] In zoölogy, a branch of the *Crinoidea* furnished with arms.

brach′i-āte, *a.* In botany, furnished with branches in pairs, decussated, all nearly horizontal, and each pair at right angles with the next pair, or widely diverging.

brach′i-ō-. A combining form from L. *bracchium*, Gr. *brachion*, the arm, and used in anatomy and medicine to signify connection with or relation to the arm.

brach″i-ō-gan′oid, *n.* One of the *Brachioganoidei.*

Brach″i-ō-gan-oid′ē-ī, *n.pl.* An order of fishes such as the gar, the sturgeon, and the bichir of the river Nile. Their scales are ganoid, that is, have a bony tissue overlaid by enamel.

Brach″i-ō-lā′ri-ȧ, *n.pl.* [L., from *bracchiolum,* dim. of *bracchium,* an arm.] A peculiar larval stage of certain starfish, wherein they swim by the vibration of ciliated bands; once believed to be a distinct species.

Brach-i-op′ō-dȧ, *n.pl.* [L., from Gr. *brachiōn,* the arm, and *poda,* feet.] A class or order of bivalve molluscous animals characterized by two prehensile fleshy arms or labial processes which they can protrude and withdraw.

One of the *Brachiopoda.*
Terebratula—1. Dorsal valve, with perforated summit of ventral valve; 2. Interior of dorsal valve, showing the shelly loop which supports the arms.

brȧ-chis″tō-cē-phal′ic, brȧ-chis-tō-ceph′ȧ-lous, *a.* [Gr. *brachistos,* superl. of *brachys,* short, and *kephalē,* head.] Having a wide head, indicating the ratio of the breadth of the cranium to the length, according to the cephalic index.

brȧ-chis′tō-chrōne, brȧ-chys′tō-chrōne, *n.* [Gr. *brachistos,* superl. of *brachys,* short, and *chronos,* time.] The curve in which a body moves most swiftly.

brach′i-um, *n.*; *pl.* **brā′chi-ȧ.** [L.] 1. The arm from shoulder to elbow.

2. In biology, a part that is arm-like.

Brach′man, *n.* [Obs.] Same as *Brahman.*

brach′y-. A combining form, from Gr. *brachys,* short.

brach-y-cär′di-ȧ, *n.* [*Brachy-,* and Gr. *kardia,* the heart.] In medicine, slow or retarded heart-action; also called *bradycardia.*

brach″y-cat-ȧ-lec′tic, *a.* and *n.* [L. *brachycatalecticum;* Gr. *brachykatalēkton; brachys,* short, and *katalēgein,* to leave off; *katalektikos,* deficient.]

I. *a.* In prosody, too short by two syllables.

II. *n.* In Greek and Latin prosody, a verse wanting two syllables to complete its length.

brach″y-cē-phal′ic, brach-y-ceph′ȧ-lous, *a.* [*Brachy-,* and Gr. *kephalē,* head.] Short-headed; having a skull very short in proportion to its width.

brach-y-ceph′ȧ-lism, brach-y-ceph′ȧ-ly, *n.* The state or condition of being brachycephalic.

brȧ-chyc′ēr-ous, brȧ-chyc′ēr-ăl, *a.* [*Brachy-,* and Gr. *keras,* a horn.] Possessing short antennæ.

brach-y-dī-ag′ō-nal, *a.* and *n.* I. *a.* Pertaining to the short diagonal or lateral axis.

II. *n.* The shorter diagonal or lateral axis in a rhombic prism.

brach′y-dōme, *n.* [*Brachy-,* and Gr. *dōma,* a house, chamber.] A plane parallel to the brachydiagonal of a prism, as in crystals.

brach′y-dont, *a.* [*Brachy-,* and Gr. *odous, odontos,* a tooth.] Having short-crowned molar teeth, as deer.

Brach-y-el′y-trȧ, *n.pl.* See *Brachelytra.*

brach-y-el′y-trous, *a.* See *Brachelytrous.*

brȧ-chyg′rȧ-phēr, *n.* A shorthand writer.

brȧ-chyg′rȧ-phy, *n.* [*Brachy-,* and Gr. *-graphia,* from *graphein,* to write.] The art or practice of writing in shorthand; stenography.

brȧ-chyl′ō-gy, *n.* [Gr. *brachylogia,* from *brachylogos,* short in speech; *brachys,* short, and *logos,* from *legein,* to speak.] In rhetoric, the expressing of anything in the most concise manner; brevity.

brach-y-pin′ȧ-coid, *n.* In an orthorhombic crystal, a plane parallel to the vertical axis and the brachydiagonal.

brȧ-chyp′ō-dous, *a.* [*Brachy-,* and Gr. *pous, podos,* foot.]

1. In zoölogy, having short feet.

2. In botany, having short stalks.

brach′y-prism, *n.* [*Brachy-,* and Gr. *prisma,* a prism.] A prism lying between the brachypinacoid of an orthorhombic crystal and its unit prism.

Brȧ-chyp′te-rȧ, *n.pl.* [L., from Gr. *brachys,* short, and *pteron,* a wing.] A group of beetles of the order *Coleoptera.*

Brȧ-chyp′te-rī, *n.pl.* A group of short-winged diving-birds, as auks, divers, penguins.

brȧ-chyp′tēr-ous, *a.* [Gr. *brachypteros; brachys,* short, and *pteron,* a wing.] Short-winged.

brach-y-pyr′ȧ-mid, *n.* [*Brachy-,* and Gr. *pyramis,* a pyramid.] An orthorhombic pyramid between the brachydomes and the zone of unit pyramids.

brȧ-chys′tō-chrōne, *n.* See *Brachistochrone.*

brȧ-chyt′y-pous, *a.* [*Brachy-,* and Gr. *typos,* form.] In mineralogy, of a short form.

Brach-y-ū′rȧ, Brach-y-öu′rȧ, *n.pl.* [L., from Gr. *brachys,* short, and *oura,* tail.] A class of decapodous *Crustacea,* as the ordinary crab, with short tail or abdomen folding beneath the cephalothorax.

brach-y-ū′răl, brach-y-ū′rous, *a.* Pertaining to the *Brachyura.*

brach-y-ū′ran, *n.* One of the *Brachyura.*

brā′cing, *n.* 1. The act of bracing, or state of being braced.

2. In engineering, a system of braces.

brā′cing, *a.* Having the quality of giving strength or tone; invigorating.

brack, *n.* [Ice. *brak;* Dan. *bræk,* a break, fissure; AS. *brecan,* to break.] An opening caused by the parting of any solid body; a breach; a broken part; a flaw. [Obs.]

brack, *n.* [D. *brak,* salt.] Brackish water. [Obs.]

brack′en, *n.* A fern.

brack′et, *n.* [OFr. *braguette;* Sp. *bragueta,* a projecting molding, a codpiece, from *bragas;* L. *bracæ,* breeches.]

Ornamental Bracket.

1. In architecture, a projection from the face of a wall to support a statue or other weight, or appearing to do so; in the latter case, often of an ornamental nature.

2. Among workers in timber, an angular wooden stay to support shelves, scaffolds, and the like.

3. A tie for strengthening angles.

4. In machinery, a projection for carrying shafting.

5. The cheek of a mortar-carriage, made of strong plank.

6. In printing, one of the characters used to inclose explanatory or interpolated matter; thus, [ ].

7. A fixture for holding a lamp, etc., attached to the wall or a pillar of a building.

Wall-Bracket.

brack′et, *v.t.*; bracketed, *pt., pp.*; bracketing, *ppr.* To inclose within brackets; to place brackets upon or between.

brack′et-ing, *n.* A number of brackets, taken collectively, especially the wooden ribs or skeleton-pieces used in cornice-work.

brack′et-light (-līt), *n.* A gas or lamp fixture projecting from a wall or pillar of a building.

brack′ish, *a.* Salt, or salt in a moderate degree; applied to any water partially saturated with salt.

brack′ish-ness, *n.* The quality of being brackish; saltness in a small degree.

brack′y, *a.* Brackish.

brac′ō-nid, *n.* An individual of the *Braconidæ.*

Brȧ-con′i-dæ, *n.pl.* [Origin unknown.] A family of ichneumon-flies of which there are many species. Some prey on caterpillars, others on plant-lice.

bract, brac′tē-ȧ, *n.* [L. *bractea,* a thin metal plate.] In botany, an abnormally developed leaf, growing upon the peduncle of a flower. It usually differs from other leaves in shape or color.

brac′tē-ăl, *a.* Resembling a bract in nature and appearance.

brac′tē-āte, bract′ed, *a.* Furnished with bracts.

brac-tē′i-form, *a.* Resembling a bract in form.

brac′tē-ō-lāte, *a.* Furnished with bracteoles.

brac′tē-ōle, *n.* A bract on the individual stalk of a flower, which is a portion of the peduncle; written also *bractlet.*

bract′less, *a.* Destitute of bracts.

bract′let, *n.* Same as *Bracteole.*

brad, *n.* [ME. *brad;* Ice. *broddr,* a spike; Dan. *braad,* a prick, a sting; AS. *brord,* a point, spire of grass.] A small slender flat nail made without a broad head or shoulder over the shank.

brad′=awl, *n.* A chisel-like awl for making holes for brads, etc.

bra-doon′, *n.* Same as *Bridoon.*

brad′y-. A combining form from Gr. *bradys,* slow; delayed; tardy.

brad-y-är′thri-ȧ, *n.* [*Brady-,* and Gr. *arthria,* a joint.] Slow and difficult articulation.

brad-y-cär′di-ȧ, *n.* [*Brady-,* and Gr. *kardia,* heart.] See *Brachycardia.*

brad-y-pep′si-ȧ, brad′y-pep-sy, *n.* [*Brady-,* and Gr. *pepsis,* from *peptein,* to digest.] Slow digestion.

Brad-y-pod′i-dæ, *n.pl.* [L., from Gr. *bradypoda,* neut. pl. of *bradypous,* slow of foot; *bradys,* slow, and *pous, podos,* foot.] A family of edentates, the American sloths.

Brad′y-pus, *n.* The typical genus of the family *Bradypodidæ.*

brāe, *n.* [Scot.] A hillside; a sloping bank or hill.

brag, *v.i.*; bragged, *pt., pp.*; bragging, *ppr.* [ME. *braggen;* OFr. *braguer,* to flaunt, brag; *brague,* pleasure, fun; Ice. *braga,* to creak; *braka,* a noise.] To display one's own actions, merits, or advantages ostentatiously; to tell boastful stories; followed by *of;* as, to *brag of* a good horse, or of a feat.

Syn.—Boast, swagger, vaunt.

brag, *v.t.* To boast of. [Obs.]

brag, *n.* 1. A boast or boasting; ostentatious verbal display of one's deeds, or advantages.

2. Boastfulness, or the person who boasts.

3. That of which one boasts.

4. An old game of cards, similar to poker.

brag, *a.* Lively; boasting; proud. [Obs.]

brag, *adv.* Proudly. [Obs.]

brag-gȧ-dō′ciō (-shō), *n.* [From a bragging character of that name in Spenser's "Faerie Queene"; *brag,* with an Italian ending.]

1. Vain boasting; ostentatious pretension.

2. A puffing, boasting fellow.

brag′gärd-ism, *n.* Boastfulness; vain ostentation.

brag′gärt, *n.* [OFr. *bragard,* from *braguer,* to flaunt, brag; *brague,* amusement, pleasure.] A boaster; a vain fellow.

brag′gärt, *a.* Boastful; vainly ostentatious.

brag′gärt-ly, *adv.* In a vain, ostentatious manner; boastfully.

brag′gēr, *n.* One who brags; a boaster.

brag′get, *n.* [ME. *braket, bragot;* W. *bragawd, bragot, brag,* malt.] A liquor made by fermenting the wort of ale and mead. [Obs.]

brag′ging-ly, *adv.* Boastingly.

brag′less, *a.* Without bragging or ostentation. [Rare.]

brag′ly, *adv.* Finely; in such a way that it may be bragged of. [Obs.]

Bräh′mä, Brähm, *n.* [Hind. *brahm, brahma;* from Sans. *brah′man* (neut.), devotion, divine science, impersonal divinity.] In the old Hindu religion, the absolute, self-existent, eternal essence of the universe, the source of all things, the ultimate of all things; the impersonal, ineffable sacredness, the object of the loftiest philosophic adoration.

Bräh′mä, *n.* [Hind. *Brah′mā,* from Sans. *brahman′* (masc.), worshiper, overseer of sacred things, personal divinity.] In the later Hindu religion, the creator, divine essence, or personified Brahm. *Brahma* was never worshiped by the people and was unknown to the older Hindu religion, but became the object of adoration by the Brahmans, and the first person in the trinity with Vishnu, redeemer, and Siva, destroyer. *Brahma* is represented by a red figure with four heads and four arms.

Brahma, from an Idol in the Indian Museum.

bräh′mä, *n.* [Contr. of *Brahmaputra.*] A well-known variety of domestic chicken of Asiatic origin, divided into two breeds, the light and the dark.

Bräh′man, Bräh′min, *n.* [Hind. *brāhman;* Sans. *brāhmana′,* from *brah′man,* prayer, devotion.] One belonging to the highest or sacerdotal caste among the Hindus. In the beginning the *Brahmans* were individuals or families distinguished for mental or spiritual superiority; but they gradually gathered to themselves powers over public worship, and became a strictly hereditary class, zealously holding in their hands the ministry of holy things. Their persons also became inviolable and objects of worship. In later times, however, the relations of the castes have greatly changed and *Brahmans* are now found in many different walks of life, though retaining much of their former dignity and exclusiveness. Also written *Bramin.*

Bräh′man-ee, Bräh′man-ī, *n.* Any Brahman woman.

Bräh′man-ess, *n.* A Brahmanee.

Bräh-man′ic, Bräh-man′ic-ăl, *a.* Pertaining to the Brahmans.

Bräh′man-ism, Bräh′min-ism, *n.* The religious doctrines of the Brahmans; the cult of Brahma.

Bräh′man-ist, Bräh′min-ist, *n.* A follower of the Brahmans; an adherent to the religion of Brahma.

Bräh′min, *n.* See *Brahman.*

Brāh-min′iç, Brāh-min′iç-ăl, *a.* Same as *Brahmanic.*

Brāh′mō-ișm, *n.* The combined religious tenets of the Brahmo-Somaj.

Brāh′mō-Sō-māj′, *n.* [Hind. *brahma,* Brahma, prayer, and *samaj,* society, assembly.] A modern sect among the Hindus, having reformed and monotheistic views; established by Ram Mohun Roy. Also written *Brahma-Sàmaj.*

brāid, *v.t.*; braided, *pt., pp.*; braiding, *ppr.* [ME. *braiden, breyden*; AS. *bregdan, bredan,* to move to and fro, to weave, braid.]

1. To weave, entwine, or infold by taking three or more strands to form one; to plait.

2. To mingle by rubbing in some fluid or soft substance; as, to *braid* starch.

3. To reproach. [Obs.]

4. To bind or decorate with braid.

brāid, *n.* 1. A string, cord, band, or plait, formed by weaving together different strands of any material.

2. A narrow tape or band of various materials, as cotton, wool, or silk, for binding or for trimming wearing-apparel.

brāid, *v.i.* To start; to awake. [Obs.]

brāid, *a.* [AS. *brǣd, bred,* deceit, from *bregdan,* to move quickly.] Deceitful. [Obs.]

brāid′ing, *n.* 1. Braids, collectively.

2. The act of plaiting or making braids.

brāid′ișm, *n.* The theories of Dr. James Braid, of England, in regard to the phenomena of mesmerism, hypnotism, etc.; also, a method of producing hypnotism similar to that suggested by him.

brāil, *n.* [ME. *brayle*; OFr. *braiel, braiol,* a cincture, from *braie*; L. *bracæ,* breeches.]

1. In falconry, a piece of soft leather to bind up a hawk's wing.

2. In nautical language, one of the ropes passing through pulleys and employed to haul up the foot and leeches of a fore-and-aft sail, preparatory to furling.

3. A staff at the end of a seine upon which to stretch the lines.

brāil, *v.t.* To haul in or to fasten by the brails; used with *up*; as, to *brail up* a sail.

braille (brä′ēl *or* brāl), *n.* A method of printing or writing for the blind, invented by and called after Louis Braille. The characters are represented by points.

brāin, *n.* [ME. *brain, brayne*; AS. *brægan, bregen*; D. *brein*; L.G. *brägen, bregen,* the brain.]

1. The gray and white matter inclosed in the cranium or skull of vertebrates, the most important portion of the nervous system, the seat of consciousness and volition. It consists of two larger portions, the cerebrum and cerebellum; the pons Varolii, which connects the two halves of the cerebellum; and the medulla oblongata, which connects the brain with the spinal cord.

Section of Human Head showing Brain. A, Cerebrum; B, Cerebellum; C, Pons Varolii; D, Spinal Cord.

2. The organ and seat of the intellect or mental power; the mind; hence, the understanding; as, a man of dull *brain*; often used in the plural; as, a man without *brains.*

3. The affections; fancy; imagination. [Rare.]

4. The cephalic or motive ganglion in invertebrates.

Brain coral, brainstone coral; a large reef-building coral, so called because it is so ridged as to bear some resemblance to the surface of the brain.

Brain storm; in pathology, a period when there is an abnormally rapid breaking down of brain cells, resulting in violent derangement of the mind.

To have on the brain; to think of continually; or to be monomaniacal on a particular subject. [Colloq.]

brāin, *v.t.*; brained, *pt., pp.*; braining, *ppr.*

1. To dash out the brains of; to kill by beating out the brains; figuratively, to destroy; to put an end to.

2. To conceive; to understand. [Obs.]

brāin′=box, *n.* The outer covering or skull inclosing the brain; the cranium.

brāined, *a.* Supplied with brains; generally with a descriptive adjective, as, addle-*brained.*

brāin′=fag, *n.* Weariness of the brain.

brāin′=fē′vẽr, *n.* Any acute affection of the brain or its membranes, attended with fever; pathologically known as *phrenitis* or *meningitis,* the latter referring to inflammation of the meninges, or membranes, only.

brāin′ish, *a.* Hot-headed; furious. [Rare.]

brāin′less, *a.* Without understanding; silly; thoughtless; witless.

brāin′less-ness, *n.* The state of being without brains or wit.

brāin′pan, *n.* Same as *Brain-box.*

brāin′sand, *n.* Particles of calcareous matter found either in the pineal gland or the pia mater folds of the brain.

brāin′sick, *a.* Disordered in the understanding; giddy; thoughtless.

brāin′sick-ly, *adv.* Weakly; with a disordered understanding.

brāin′sick-ness, *n.* Disorder of the understanding; giddiness.

brāin′=throb, *n.* The throbbing of the brain from arterial pulsation.

brāin′=wāve, *n.* A psychical undulation supposed to be the means of transferring thought in the process of telepathy.

brāin′y, *a.* Having an active brain.

brāird, *n.* [Scot.] The first shoots or sprouts of grass and grain.

brāit, *n.* Among jewelers, a rough diamond.

brāize, brāiṣe, *n.* 1. In zoölogy, an iridescent marine fish of Europe, *Pagrus vulgaris*; called also *becker.*

2. In Scotland, the roach.

brāize, brāiṣe, *n.* Meat that is braized.

brāize, *n.* Charcoal powder; coal-dust; breeze.

brāize, brāiṣe, *v.t.*; braized, *pt., pp.*; braizing, *ppr.* [Fr. *braiser,* to cook over live coals, from *braise,* live coals, embers; Dan. *brase,* fry.] To stew or broil (meat) in a covered vessel, and then bake.

brāiz′ẽr, *n.* A covered vessel for braizing.

brāke, *v.,* past participle of *break.* [Obs.]

brāke, *n.* [AS. *bracce,* a fern.]

1. A name given to different species of fern, of the genus *Pteris,* particularly to the large fern *Pteris aquilina*; also to different species of fern of other genera.

2. A thicket; a place overgrown with shrubs or canes; as, a cane-*brake.*

brāke, *n.* [ME. *brake*; L.G. *brake,* an instrument for breaking flax.]

1. An instrument or machine to break flax or hemp; that is, to bruise the woody part so that the fiber may easily be separated.

2. The handle or lever by which a pump is worked, as in a hand fire-engine.

3. A baker's kneading-trough.

4. A sharp bit, or snaffle.

5. A device for confining refractory horses while the smith is shoeing them; also, an inclosure for cattle, horses, etc.

6. The fore part of a carriage or engine, which enables it to turn.

7. A large, heavy harrow for breaking clods after plowing; a drag.

8. An ancient engine of war for hurling missiles at the enemy; a ballista.

9. Any mechanical device for retarding or stopping the motion of a vehicle, as a carriage or railroad-car, or the motion of any sliding or rotating body, by the application of pressure or friction. The most common form is that of curved wooden or iron clogs or shoes pressing against the wheels of the vehicle, engine, or other machine to be retarded or stopped.

10. Among engineers, an apparatus designed to ascertain the horse-power of an engine, motor, or driving mechanism, by noting the amount of friction it will overcome; a friction-*brake.*

11. A wagonette, used to break in horses.

12. An instrument of torture used in olden times.

13. A tool used by basket-makers for stripping the bark from willow wands.

14. A large four-wheeled carriage; a kind of wagonette.

Atmospheric brake; a railway-brake operated by compressed air and controlled from the locomotive; called also *air-brake.*

Automatic brake; a brake which sets itself under certain conditions, as when a railroad-car becomes detached from its train.

Continuous brake; a series of car-brakes controllable from a single point, as an atmospheric brake.

Power brake; any brake operated by power, as distinguished from a brake applied by hand.

Vacuum brake; a continuous brake operated by the exhaustion of air from chambers situated under the cars.

To bleed the brakes; to allow air to escape from an air-brake.

brāke′=bär, *n.* The beam on the under side of a carriage or railway-car to which the brake-blocks are attached; called also *brake-beam.*

brāke′=block, *n.* The solid backing of a brake-shoe, or the part which holds the shoe.

brāke′=head (-hed), *n.* The brake-block and shoe combined in one piece or detachable.

brāke′măn, *n.* 1. The man in a train-crew on railroads, whose business is to take care of the brakes and couplings; to signal and flag trains, and generally to oversee the cars under the direction of the conductor.

2. The person in charge of a hoisting-machine in a mine.

brāke′=pow″ẽr, *n.* The frictional resistance developed by a brake.

brāke′=shōe, *n.* The curved part or face of a brake, which presses against a wheel to retard or stop its rotation.

brāke′=sieve (-siv), *n.* In mining, a coarse sieve for sifting ores, worked by a lever.

brāke′=valve, *n.* A valve used in the operation of power-brakes.

brāke′=wheel, *n.* 1. A small hand-wheel used in the operation of a brake.

2. A cam-wheel governing the action of a trip-hammer.

brāk′y, *a.* Full of brakes; abounding with brambles or shrubs; rough; thorny.

Brä′mȧ, *n.* Same as first *Brahma.*

brä′măn-tip, *n.* Same as *Bamalip.*

bram′ble, *n.* See *Brambling.*

bram′ble, *n.* [ME. *brembel*; AS. *bræmbel, bremble,* a bramble.] The raspberry or blackberry bush; a name common to the genus *Rubus,* including these species; any rough, prickly shrub.

bram′ble=bush, *n.* The bramble, or a collection of brambles growing together.

bram′bled (-bld), *a.* Overgrown with brambles.

bram′ble=finch, *n.* The brambling, *Fringilla montifringilla.*

bram′ble=net, *n.* A hallier, or a net with which to catch birds.

bram′bling, *n.* A bird, a species of *Fringilla,* the mountain-finch.

bram′bly, *a.* Full of brambles.

brāme, *n.* Vexation; earnest desire; sharp passion; longing. [Obs.]

Brä′min, *n.* Same as *Brahman.*

Brä′min-ess, Brä′min-ee, *n.* Same as *Brahmanee.*

Brȧ-min′iç, Brȧ-min′iç-ăl, *a.* Same as *Brahmanic.*

Brä′min-ișm, *n.* Same as *Brahmanism.*

bran, *n.* [ME. *bran, bren*; OFr. *bren,* bran, refuse; W. *bran,* bran, husk; Ir. *bran,* chaff.] The outer coat of the seed of wheat, rye, or other farinaceous grain, separated from the flour by bolting.

bran, *n.* A local English name for the common crow.

brañ′çärd, *n.* [Fr.] A horse-litter. [Obs.]

brȧnch, *v.i.*; branched, *pt., pp.*; branching, *ppr.*

1. To shoot or spread in branches; to ramify; as a plant, or as horns.

2. To separate into different parts or subdivisions, as a stream, or a subject of discourse.

To branch off; to grow from the trunk; figuratively, to diverge from the main topic.

To branch out; to speak at length under different heads; to expand the scope of one's enterprises.

brȧnch, *v.t.* 1. To divide, as into branches; to make subordinate divisions in.

2. To adorn with needlework, representing branches, flowers, or twigs.

brȧnch, *n.* [ME. *branche*; OFr. *branche, brance*; Pr. *branca*; LL. *branca,* the claw of a bird or beast.]

1. A shoot of a tree or other plant; a division of the main stem smaller than a limb or bough and larger than a twig.

2. Any arm or part extending from the main body of a thing; as, the *branch* of a candlestick or of an artery; the *branch* of a trunk railroad line; the *branch* of a river; the *branch* of a stag's horn, etc.

3. Any member or part of a body, or system; a section or subdivision; as, charity is a *branch* of Christian duty.

4. Any individual of a family descending in a collateral line; any descendant from a common parent or stock.

5. One of the two pieces of bent iron in a bridle, which bear the bit, the cross chains, and the curb.

6. A warrant or commission given to a pilot.

7. A chandelier. [Obs.]

8. In geometry, a portion of a curve that may extend outward for an unlimited distance.

9. In mining, a vein separating from the main lode.

Syn.—Bifurcation, bough, member, limb, offspring, offshoot, spray, sprig, shoot, scion, ramification, relative, twig.

brȧnch′=chuck, *n.* An attachment to a lathe for holding tools or work, and carrying four branches or jaws.

brȧnched′=work, *n.* The sculptured leaves and branches in monuments and friezes.

brȧnch′ẽr, *n.* 1. One who or that which shoots forth branches.

2. A young hawk when it begins to leave the nest and take to the branches.

brȧnch′ẽr-y, *n.* The ramifications of the vessels dispersed through the pulpy part of fruit.

brañ′chi-, brañ′chi-ō-. Combining forms from Gr. *branchia,* gills.

brañ′chi-ȧ, *n.*; *pl.* **brañ′chi-æ.** [L., from Gr. *branchia,* gills.] A gill; an organ for breathing the air contained in water; as those of crustaceans, mollusks, fishes, and amphibians.

brañ′chi-ăl, *a.* 1. Relating to the branchiæ or gills.

2. Possessed of gills; as, the *branchial* pouch

Branchial aperture; an outlet for water behind the gill of a fish.

Branchial arch; one of the bony arches supporting the gills or branchiæ.

Branchial cleft; an aperture found behind the head in the embryo of a vertebrate, which generally disappears with its development; corresponding to the *branchial aperture* of a fish.

Brañ-chi-ā'tȧ, *n.pl.* [L., from Gr. *branchia*, gills.] A zoölogical name for animals having gills; called also *Branchiogasteropoda*.

brañ'chi-āte, *a.* 1. Provided with branchiæ or gills.

2. Of or pertaining to the *Branchiata*.

brȧnch'i-ness, *n.* Fullness of branches.

brȧnch'ing, *a.* Dividing into branches; shooting out branches.

Brañ'chi-ō-gas-tēr-op'ō-dȧ, *n.pl.* [*Branchio-*, and Gr. *gastēr*, *gastros*, stomach, and *pous*, *podos*, foot.] A division of gasteropodous mollusks, so constructed that they can breathe the air contained in water. They are distinct in sex or hermaphroditic, have the gills exposed or inclosed, and are sessile or free-swimming. The whelks are well-known types.

brañ'chi-ō-pod, *n.* A member of the *Branchiopoda*.

Brañ-chi-op'ō-dȧ, *n.pl.* [*Branchio-*, and Gr. *pous*, *podos*, foot.] A term denoting an order of *Crustaceæ* having the gills or branchiæ situated on the feet; called also *Phyllopoda*.

brañ-chi-os'tē-găl, *a.* and *n.* [*Branchio-*, and Gr. *stegein*, to cover.]

I. *a.* Pertaining to the tissue which covers the branchiæ of fishes.

II. *n.* One of the radiating spines, or rays, which support the branchiostege.

brañ-chi-os'tēge, *n.* The branchiostegal tissue or membrane.

brañ-chi-os'tē-gous, *a.* Same as *Branchiostegal*.

brañ-chi-os'tō-mȧ, *n.* Same as *Amphioxus*.

brañ'chi-rēme, *n.* [*Branchi-*, and L. *remus*, an oar.]

1. An animal that has legs terminating in a bundle of setiform branches having respiratory functions; a branchiopod.

2. Any one of the legs of a branchiopod.

Brañ-chi-ū'rȧ, *n.pl.* [*Branchi-*, and Gr. *oura*, a tail.] A genus of *Entomostraca*, including fish parasites, such as carp-lice, with mouths adapted for sucking, and having four pairs of legs.

brȧnch'-lēaf, *n.* A leaf growing on a branch.

brȧnch'less, *a.* Destitute of branches or shoots; without any valuable product; barren; naked.

brȧnch'let, *n.* A little branch; a twig; the subdivision of a branch.

brȧnch'-pī"lŏt, *n.* A pilot who has a branch or public commission.

brȧnch'y, *a.* Full of branches; having wide-spreading branches.

brand, *n.* [AS. *brand*, *brond*, a burning, sword, from *byrnan*, *beornan*, to burn; Ice. *brandr*, a firebrand, sword; D. *brand*, burning fuel.]

1. A burning stick of wood, or a piece partly burned.

2. A sword; a thunderbolt. [Rare.]

3. Formerly, a mark made upon a criminal, by burning with a hot iron; hence, a stigma.

4. A fungous disease in plants by which their leaves and tender bark are partially destroyed, as if burned; called also *burn*.

5. A device to brand with; a branding-iron.

6. Quality; sort; kind; as, oil of a good *brand*.

7. A mark burned into anything by its owner, as a means of identification, as upon a cask or cattle; a trade-mark.

brand, *v.t.*; branded, *pt.*, *pp.*; branding, *ppr.*

1. To burn or impress a mark upon, with a hot iron; as, to *brand* a steer.

2. To fix a mark or character of infamy upon; to stigmatize as infamous; as, to *brand* a vice.

3. To mark with a stencil, as a box, cask, etc., in order to give a description of the contents, or the name of the manufacturer.

4. To impress indelibly, as with a brand; as, the date is *branded* on my memory.

bran'den-bŭrg, *n.* [Named after *Brandenburg*, a district and town of Prussia.] A sort of trimming for the front of a coat; an ornamental facing worn by military men.

brand'ēr, *n.* 1. One who or that which brands; a branding-iron.

2. A gridiron. [Scot.]

3. In German universities, a student in his second term.

brand'ēr, *v.t.*; brandered, *pt.*, *pp.*; brandering, *ppr.* To broil on a gridiron; to grill. [Scot.]

brand'ēr, *v.i.* To be broiled. [Scot.]

brand'-goose, *n.* Same as *Brent*.

bran'died (-did), *a.* Mingled with brandy; made stronger by the addition of brandy; preserved in brandy; as, *brandied* cherries.

brand'ing-ī"ron (-ŭrn), *n.* See *Brand-iron*.

brand'-ī"ron (-ŭrn), *n.* 1. An iron plate containing the device, trade-mark, or letters desired to be branded on an object.

2. A trivet to set a pot on.

3. The arm of an andiron.

4. A gridiron.

bran'dish, *v.t.*; brandished, *pt.*, *pp.*; brandishing, *ppr.* [ME. *braundishen*, *braundisen*; OFr. *brandir*, to brandish; *brand*, a sword.]

1. To move or wave, as a weapon; to raise and move in various directions; to shake or flourish; often with the meaning of threatening; as, to *brandish* a sword or a cane belligerently.

2. Figuratively, to play with; to flourish; as, to *brandish* syllogisms.

bran'dish, *n.* A motion or flourish, as with a sword, whip, etc.

bran'dle, *v.t.* and *v.i.* To shake; to reel. [Obs.]

brand'ling, bran'lin, *n.* 1. A small red worm, allied to the earthworm; used as fish bait.

2. In ichthyology, a salmon in its parr stage.

brand'-new', bran'-new', *a.* Quite new; glowing like metal fresh from the forge.

bränd'schätz (bränt'shäts), *v.t.* [Gr. *brandschatzen*; *brand*, burning, and *schatzen*, from *schatz*, a tax, contribution.] To levy tribute upon in time of war by threat of the torch. [Rare.]

brand'-spōre, *n.* In botany, one of a series of spores formed by brand fungi.

bran'dy, *n.* [D. *brandewijn*, from *branden*, to burn, and *wijn*, wine.] A spirituous liquor obtained by the distillation of wine, or of the refuse of the wine-press, and containing an average of from 48 to 54 per cent of alcohol. In France, the finest *brandy* is called *cognac*, an inferior sort, distilled from dark red wines, lees, grape-refuse, etc., being called *eau-de-vie*. The name *brandy* is sometimes given to spirit distilled from other liquors, or from cider, peaches, etc. Inferior *brandies* are distilled from grain and malt liquors and given the flavor and color of French *brandy* by artificial means.

Brandy pawnee; in British India, brandy and water.

bran'dy-wine, *n.* Brandy. [Obs.]

brañ'gle, *n.* [Scot., to shake.] A wrangle; a squabble; a noisy contest or dispute. [Rare.]

brañ'gle, *v.i.* To wrangle; to dispute contentiously; to squabble. [Rare.]

brañ'gle-ment, *n.* A quarrel. [Rare.]

brañ'glēr, *n.* One who brangles. [Rare.]

brañk, *n.* Buckwheat. [Prov. Eng.]

brañk, *v.i.* 1. To caper; to prance, like a horse. [Prov. Eng. and Scot.]

2. To toss the head, as a horse.

brañks, *n.pl.* [Gael. *brancas*, a kind of pillory; Ir. *brancas*, a halter; G. *pranger*, a pillory.]

1. A scold's bridle, an instrument for correcting scolding women; formerly used in England and Scotland. It consisted of a headpiece, and a sharp iron which entered the mouth and restrained the tongue.

2. A kind of bridle, having wooden side-pieces, joined to a halter to which a bit or muzzle is attached. [Scot.]

Branks.

3. In medicine, mumps.

brañk'ŭr-sine, *n.* [Fr. *brankursine*; LL. *branca*, a claw, and L. *ursinus*, from *ursus*, a bear.] In botany, bear's-breech, a plant of the genus *Acanthus*.

bran'lin, *n.* See *Brandling*.

bran'ny, *a.* Having the appearance of bran; consisting of bran.

bran'sle, *n.* A brawl; a dance. [Obs.]

brant, *n.* Same as *Brent*.

brant, *a.* Steep. [Prov. Eng.]

bran'tāil, *n.* A small bird with a bright red tail; the redstart of Europe.

brant'-fox, *n.* [For *brand-fox*, so called from its dark color.] In zoölogy, a Swedish fox, *Vulpes alopex*, smaller than the common fox.

bran'ū-lăr, *a.* Pertaining to the brain; cerebral. [Rare.]

Brȧ-sē'ni-ȧ, *n.* [Origin unknown.] A genus of plants having only one species, the water-shield, *Brasenia peltata*.

brȧ-se'rō, *n.* [Sp.] A brasier.

brash, *a.* [Ir. *bras*, *brasach*, hasty, impetuous; G. *barsch*, harsh, impetuous.] Hasty; quick-tempered; impetuous. [Colloq.]

brash, *a.* Brittle; fragile. [Colloq.]

brash, *n.* 1. An eruption or rash; a sudden attack of sickness; as, water-*brash*; teething-*brash*.

2. A sudden shower of rain. [Scot.]

brash, *n.* 1. In geology, a mass of broken pieces of rock consequent on disintegration.

2. A pile of fragments or rubbish.

brash'y, *a.* 1. Broken; crumbling; resembling brash; fragmentary.

2. Showery. [Scot.]

brā'siēr, brā'ziēr (-zhēr), *n.* [Fr. *brasier*, *braisier*, from *braise*, live coals.]

1. An artificer who works in brass.

2. A pan for holding live coals.

brasque (brask), *n.* [Fr.] A paste of coke-dust or charcoal and clay, used in lining crucibles, etc.

brȧss, *n.* [ME. *bras*, *bres*; AS. *bræs*, brass; Ice. *bras*, cement, solder; *brasa*, to harden by fire.]

1. In metallurgy, an alloy of copper and zinc, of a yellow color, usually containing about one-third of its weight of zinc; but the proportions are variable.

2. Impudence; forwardness; rudeness. [Colloq.]

3. In machinery, a journal-bearing made of brass or other hard metal and lined with softer material.

4. Money. [Slang.]

5. [*pl.*] Ornaments, utensils, etc., made of brass.

6. A plate of brass or a slab of stone inlaid with brass, engraved or stamped with a device; especially one intended as a memorial to the dead, generally bearing a coat-of-arms or portrayal.

7. The part of an orchestra or band playing brass instruments.

Brass of Eleanor Bohun (died 1399), in Westminster Abbey.

8. In mining, iron pyrites occurring in small shining particles in coal.

9. In rhetoric, a type of hardness, durability, or obduracy.

brȧss, *a.* Brazen; made of brass; as, a *brass* bedstead.

Brass band; a company of musicians who perform on instruments chiefly of brass; a military band.

brȧs'sāge, *n.* [OFr. *brassage*, *brassaige*, brassage, coinage, mintage.] A sum formerly levied to defray the expense of coinage; seigniorage.

bras'särd, *n.* [Fr., from *bras*, arm.]

1. A badge or emblem, generally worn on the arm, denoting some particular duty, office, or distinction.

2. Same as *Brassart*.

bras'särt, bras'särd, *n.* In late medieval armor, the piece which protected the upper part of the arm, from the elbow to the shoulder; also applied to armor for the entire arm.

brasse, *n.* [G. *brassen*, the bream.]

1. A pale spotted European pike-perch.

2. The European bass.

bras'set, *n.* Same as *Brassart*.

Brassarts.

brȧss'-foil, *n.* Dutch leaf, or Dutch gold; formed by beating out plates of brass to great thinness.

Bras'si-cȧ, *n.* [L., cabbage.] In botany, a genus of plants embracing many important varieties, as the cabbage, *Brassica oleracea*; the cauliflower, turnip, broccoli, kohl-rabi, kale, Brussels sprouts, etc.

bras-si-cā'ceous, *a.* [L. *brassica*, cabbage.] Pertaining to the plants of the cabbage family.

bras-sière', brȧ-syăr', *n.* A tight fitting under-waist worn by women.

brass'i-ness, *n.* 1. The quality of being brassy.

2. Impudence. [Colloq.]

brȧss'y, *a.* 1. Pertaining to brass; containing brass; hard as brass; having the color of brass.

2. Impudent; impudently bold. [Colloq.]

brȧss'y, brȧss'ie, *n.* 1. A brass-soled wooden club used in playing golf.

2. A Scottish name for the bib, a fish of northern waters.

brat, *n.* [ME. *brat*, a coarse cloak; Gael. *brat*, a cloak, mantle, rag.]

1. A child, so called in contempt; progeny; offspring.

2. An apron of coarse fabric; a kind of bib. [Prov. Eng.]

3. A young animal. [Obs.]

brat, *n.* In mining, a thin vein of coal containing pyrites or carbonate of lime.

brät'sche, *n.* [G.] A stringed musical instrument; a viola, or tenor violin.

brat'tach, *n.* [Scot.] A banner or standard.

brat'tice, *n.* [ME. *bretais*, *bretis*, a parapet; OFr. *breteche*, *bretesche*, a wooden tower; O.H.G. *bret*, a board.]

1. In mining, (a) planking used as a roof or wall support; (b) any partition in a level or shaft, especially one designed to control air-currents.

2. An improvised wooden parapet. [Obs.]

brat'tice, *v.t.* To provide with a brattice.

brat'ti-cing, brat'tish-ing, *n.* [ME. *bretasynge*

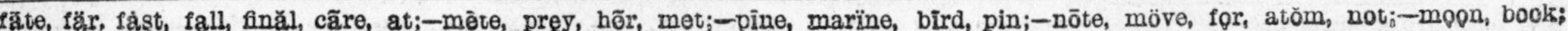

an outwork, from *bretasce*, an outwork, brattice.]

1. A fence of boards in a mine or around dangerous machinery; brattice-work.

2. In architecture, any open or carved work, as on a shrine or parapet.

brat'tle, *v.i.*; brattled, *pt.*, *pp.*; brattling, *ppr.* [Imitative word.]

1. To make a rattling or clattering noise.

2. To run with a clatter; to scamper.

brat'tle, *n.* Any clattering or rattling noise, as of horses' hoofs, thunder, etc.

brau'na, *n.* [Braz.] A leguminous tree, *Melanoxylon Braunia*, found in Brazil; it furnishes a reddish-brown, hard wood, valuable for many uses.

braun'ite, *n.* [Named after Herr *Braun* of Gotha.] In mineralogy, a native oxid of manganese, having a small percentage of silica, and varying from brownish-black to steel-gray in color.

bra-vā'dō, *n.*; *pl.* **bra-vā'dōes**. [Sp.] A boast or brag; an arrogant menace, intended to intimidate; arrogant and threatening conduct.

brāve, *a.* [Fr. *brave*; Sp., Port., It. *bravo*, brave, fine; MD. *brave*, fierce, gallant; Dan. *brav*, brave, worthy.]

1. Courageous; bold; daring; intrepid; fearless of danger; as, a *brave* warrior. It usually unites the sense of courage with generosity and dignity of mind.

2. Gaudy; showy in dress; as, she made a *brave* show at the races.

3. Excellent; admirable. [Rare.]

Syn.—Valiant, gallant, valorous, fearless, undaunted, bold, heroic, intrepid, daring.

brāve, *n.* 1. A bully; a man daring beyond discretion or decency.

Hot *braves* like thee may fight. —Dryden.

2. A boast; a challenge; a defiance. [Obs.]

3. An Indian warrior; a term first applied by the French.

4. A brave man; one who is daring; also, brave people collectively; as, the home of the *brave*.

brāve, *v.t.*; braved, *pt.*, *pp.*; braving, *ppr.* [Fr. *braver*, to brave, defy, from *brave*, brave.]

1. To defy; to challenge; to encounter with courage and fortitude, or without being moved; to set at defiance; to dare.

The rock that *braves* the tempest.—Dryden.

2. To carry a boasting appearance of; as, to *brave* that which they believe not. [Obs.]

3. To make showy; to adorn. [Obs.]

Syn.—Dare, defy, encounter, challenge.

brāve'ly, *adv.* 1. Courageously; gallantly; heroically; splendidly; in a brave manner.

2. Finely; gaudily.

3. Thrivingly; in a prosperous manner.

brāve'ness, *n.* The quality of being brave.

brāv'ēr-y, *n.* [Fr. *braverie*, gallantry, splendor, from *brave*, brave.]

1. Courage; heroism; undaunted spirit; intrepidity; gallantry; fearlessness of danger.

2. Splendor; magnificence; showy appearance; ostentation; fine dress.

The *bravery* of their tinkling ornaments. —Isa. iii. 18.

3. Bravado; boast. [Obs.]

4. A showy person. [Obs.]

Syn.—Courage, intrepidity, heroism, audacity, valor, fearlessness, hardihood, dauntlessness.—*Courage* is that firmness of spirit which meets danger without fear; *bravery* defies or braves it, and shows itself in outward acts; *audacity* is *bravery* running out into rashness.

brāv'ing, *n.* Defiance; challenge or bravado.

brāv'ing-ly, *adv.* In an undaunted or defiant manner.

brä'vō, *n.*; *pl.* **brä'vōes**. [It. and Sp.] A daring villain; a bandit; one who sets law at defiance; a habitual assassin or murderer.

brä'vō, *interj.* [It.] Well done; an exclamation of approval or applause. The word is an Italian adjective, and the correct usage is to say *bravo* to a male singer or actor, *brava* to a female, and *bravi* to a company.

bra-vū'ra, *n.* [It., bravery, spirit.] An air in music characterized by minute divisions, giving several notes to a syllable, and requiring great force and spirit in the singer; a style written to show the natural gifts and acquired skill of a performer.

braw, *a.* [Scot.] 1. Well-groomed; smart; brave; applied both to persons and their attire.

2. Fine; pleasant; as, a *braw* day.

brawl, *v.i.*; brawled, *pt.*, *pp.*; brawling, *ppr.* [ME. *brallen*, to cry out, vociferate; *braulen*, to quarrel; D. *brallen*, to boast; Dan. *bralle*, to jabber, chatter.]

1. To quarrel or speak noisily and indecently.

2. To roar, as water; to make a noise.

brawl, *n.* 1. Noise; quarrel; scurrility; uproar; loud or angry contention.

2. Formerly, a kind of dance, said to resemble the modern cotillion. [Obs.]

brawl'ēr, *n.* A noisy fellow; a wrangler.

Common brawler; a brawling fellow indictable at common law as a nuisance.

brawl'ing, *n.* The act of quarreling.

brawl'ing, *a.* Quarreling; quarrelsome.

brawl'ing-ly, *adv.* In a quarrelsome manner.

brawn, *n.* [ME. *braun*, *brawn*, muscle, boar's flesh; OFr. *braon*, a piece of flesh; O.H.G. *brato*, a piece of flesh for roasting.]

1. The fleshy, protuberant, muscular part of the body, especially of the arm or leg; hence, bulk; muscular strength.

2. The arm, from its muscles or strength. [Rare.]

3. The flesh of the boar or the hog, especially prepared by being pressed, boiled, spiced, and pickled.

4. A boar. [Obs.]

brawned, *a.* Brawny; strong. [Obs.]

brawn'ēr, *n.* A boar killed for the table.

brawn'i-ness, *n.* The quality of being brawny; strength; hardiness.

brawn'y, *a.* Muscular; strong; stout; big.

Syn.—Athletic, bulky, stout, muscular, powerful, robust, sinewy, stalwart, strong, vigorous.

brax'y, *n.* [As the disease is in some parts called also *braik*, *bracks*, the name is probably derived from the verb to *break*; compare AS. *broc*, disease, misery; G. *brechen*, vomiting, and *brechen*, to break.]

1. A disease peculiar to sheep, usually consisting of a carbuncular fever. [Scot.]

2. A sheep affected with this disease, or mutton from such a sheep.

brāy, *v.t.*; brayed, *pt.*, *pp.*; braying, *ppr.* [ME. *brayen*; OFr. *breier*, to pound, bray; M.H.G. *brechen*, to break.] To pound, beat, or grind small; as, to *bray* a fool in a mortar.

brāy, *v.i* [ME. *brayen*; OFr. *braire*; LL. *bragire*, *bragare*, to cry, squall.]

1. To make a harsh sound, as an ass.

2. To make a harsh, disagreeable, grating sound.

brāy, *v.t.* To make with a rough, harsh sound; as, to *bray* discords.

brāy, *n.* The harsh sound or roar of an ass; a harsh, grating sound.

bray, *n.* See *Brae*.

brāy'ēr, *n.* 1. One who brays like an ass.

2. In printing, a hand-roller to spread ink.

brāy'ing, *n.* 1. The noise of an ass.

2. Roar; noise; clamor.

brāze, *v.t.*; brazed, *pt.*, *pp.*; brazing, *ppr.* [ME. *brasen*; OFr. *braser*, to solder; Ice. *brasa*, to harden by fire.]

1. To solder with an alloy of brass and zinc.

2. To harden to impudence; to harden, as with brass.

3. To put a covering or ornamentation of brass upon.

brāzed, *a.* See *Braced*.

brā'zen, *a.* [ME. *brasen*; AS. *bræsen*, from *bræs*, brass.]

1. Made of brass; as, a *brazen* helmet.

2. Pertaining to brass; proceeding from brass; as, a *brazen* din.

3. Impudent; shameless; having a front like brass; as, he put on a *brazen* face.

Brazen age, or *age of brass*; in mythology, the age which succeeded the silver age, when men had degenerated from primitive purity.

Brazen sea; in Jewish antiquity, a huge vessel of brass, cast on the plain of Jordan, and placed in Solomon's temple. It was designed for the priests to wash themselves in, before they performed the service of the temple.

brā'zen, *v.t.*; brazened, *pt.*, *pp.*; brazening, *ppr.* To face, act, or maintain with effrontery; as, to *brazen* it out.

brā'zen-browed, *a.* Shamelessly bold.

brā'zen-face, *n.* An impudent person; one remarkable for effrontery.

brā'zen-faced (-fāst), *a.* Impudent; bold to excess; shameless.

brā'zen-ly, *adv.* In a bold, impudent manner.

brā'zen-ness, *n.* 1. Appearance like brass; brassiness.

2. Impudence; excess of assurance.

brā'ziēr, *n.* See *Brasier*.

bra-zil', **bra-zil'-wood**, *n.* [ME. *brasil*, *brasyle*; OFr. *bresil*; Sp. and Port. *brasil*; LL. *brasilium*, *bresillum*; originally, a dyewood found in the East, and later in Brazil; the country received its name from the wood.]

1. A very heavy wood, of a red color, growing in Brazil and other tropical countries, and used in dyeing. It is the product of *Cæsalpinia echinata*.

2. Originally, the wood of *Cæsalpinia Sappan*; sapan-wood.

braz-i-let'tō, *n.* [Port. *brazilete*; It. *brasiletto*, dim. of *brasil*, brazil-wood.] A kind of red dyewood, inferior to brazil, brought from Jamaica; obtained from two trees, *Cæsalpinia Brasiliensis* and *Cæsalpinia crista*. [See *Brazil*.]

Bra-zil'ian (-yan), *a.* Pertaining to Brazil.

Bra-zil'ian, *n.* A native or inhabitant of Brazil.

braz'i-lin, **braz'i-line**, *n.* A crystalline substance extracted from sapan-wood and brazil-wood. When pure, it is white; when combined with alkalis, it has a crimson color. Also written *brasilin*, *brasiline*, *breziline*.

bra-zil'-nut, *n.* A seed of the fruit of *Bertholletia excelsa*, a tree of the family *Myrtaceæ*, a native of Guiana, Venezuela, and Brazil. The fruit is nearly round and about six inches in diameter, having a hard shell about one-half inch thick. When the fruits are ripe they are split open and the seeds taken out and packed in baskets for transportation. Besides being used as an article of dessert, a bland oil, used by watchmakers and others, is expressed from them.

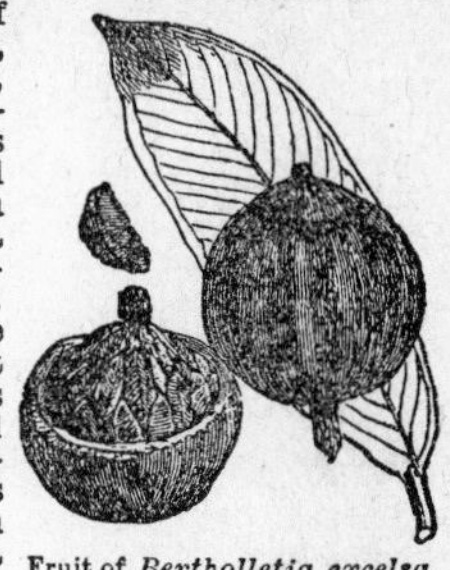

Fruit of *Bertholletia excelsa*.

bra-zil'-wood, *n.* See *Brazil*.

brēach, *n.* [ME. *breke*, *breche*; AS. *brice*, *bryce*, *gebrece*, from *brecan*, to break.]

1. The act of breaking, or state of being broken; a rupture; a break; a gap; the space between the several parts of a solid body parted by violence; as, a *breach* in stonework or in a fortification.

2. The violation of a law; the violation or nonfulfilment of a contract; the nonperformance of a moral duty; nonperformance of duty being a *breach* of obligation as well as a positive transgression or violation.

Every *breach* of the public engagements is hurtful to public credit. —Hamilton.

3. Separation between friends by means of enmity; difference; quarrel.

4. Infraction; injury; invasion; as, a *breach* upon kingly power.

5. An inrush or surging of waters, as over a pier-head; the waves themselves.

6. A contusion or wound.

7. In medicine, a rupture.

A clear breach; among sailors, the rolling of waves over a vessel without breaking; it is *a clean breach* when everything movable on deck is swept away.

Breach of arrest; in military life, the offense committed by an officer under technical arrest, of leaving without permission the limits within which he has been ordered to remain. The offense is punishable by dismissal from the service.

Breach of faith; the breaking of a promise, expressed or implied.

Breach of the peace; a violation of the public peace, as by a riot, affray, or any tumult which is contrary to law, and destructive to the public tranquillity; disorderly conduct.

Breach of privilege; an act in violation of the rules, order, privileges, or dignity of a legislative body. It may occur either within or without the precincts of the assembly.

Breach of promise; failure to fulfil one's word; specifically, failure to keep a promise to marry.

Breach of trust; violation by fraud or omission of any duty or confidence lawfully imposed on a trustee, executor, or other person in a position of trust.

Syn.—Break, chasm, gap, opening, rent.—A *breach* and a *gap* are the consequence of a violent removal, which destroys the connection; a *break* and a *chasm* may arise from the absence of that which would form a connection. A *breach* and a *chasm* always imply a larger opening than a *break* or *gap*.

brēach, *v.t.*; breached, *pt.*, *pp.*; breaching, *ppr.* To make a break, gap, or opening in; as, to *breach* the gate of the citadel.

brēach, *v.i.* To break the surface of water by jumping from it; said of a whale or porpoise.

brēach'y, *a.* Inclined to break out of pasture-fields; as, *breachy* horses.

bread (bred), *n.* [ME. *breed*, *bred*; AS. *bread*; D. *brood*; Ice. *braudh*, bread; from the root of *breowan*, to brew.]

1. An article of food made by moistening, kneading, and raising or fermenting the flour or meal of some species of grain, and baking it in an oven, usually in the form of loaves, or as biscuits, rolls, etc.

2. Food in general; as, give us this day our daily *bread*.

3. Support of life in general; maintenance.

Aerated bread; bread raised by charging dough with gas instead of yeast or baking powder.

Black bread; rye bread, particularly the kind made in Germany; pumpernickel.

Bread and butter; figuratively, means of livelihood; as, he earns his *bread and butter*.

Brown bread; (a) bread made of unbolted wheat flour, often called Graham bread; (b) bread made of rye flour and corn meal.

Corn bread; bread made of corn-meal.

Raised bread; bread made with yeast, and raised or fermented, as distinguished from bread in which the flour or meal is mixed with water and salt only, which is *unleavened bread*.

To break bread; (a) to partake of a meal; (b) to partake of the sacrament of the Holy Eucharist; to attend a communion service.

To know on which side one's bread is buttered; to be aware and careful of one's own interests.

A bread-and-butter miss; a youthful, immature girl; a schoolgirl.

A bread-and-butter candidate; one impelled or actuated by need, or mercenary reasons.

bread, *v.t.* To spread. [Obs.]

bread, *v.t.* In cookery, to dress (meat, fish, etc.,) with bread-crumbs before cooking; as, to *bread* veal.

bread'bȧs"ket, *n.* The stomach. [Slang.]

bread'chip"pẽr, *n.* One who chips or slices bread. [Obs.]

bread'-corn, *n.* Any grain or cereal of which bread in some form is made, as wheat, rye, etc.

bread'-crumb (-krum), *n.* 1. Bread crumbled for use in cookery.

2. The soft part of bread within the crust.

bread'ed, *a.* Braided. [Obs.]

bread'en, *a.* Made of bread. [Rare.]

bread'fruit, *n.* 1. The edible fruit of a tree, *Artocarpus incisa*, found particularly in the Pacific islands. The fruit is a large, roundish, starchy mass and when baked is thought to resemble fresh bread, whence its name.

2. The breadfruit-tree, which is about the size of the apple-tree, and has large, lobed leaves. The bark is made into cloth and the wood is in common use among the natives. Called also *bread-tree*.

Breadfruit (*Artocarpus incisa*).

bread'-knife (-nīf), *n.* A knife for cutting bread.

bread'less, *a.* Without bread; destitute of food.

bread'nut, *n.* The nut of a moraceous tree, *Brosimum Alicastrum*, found in the West Indies and Mexico; it is roasted, ground into a flour, and made into bread.

bread'-room, *n.* A storeroom for bread, particularly one on board a ship.

bread'root, *n.* The starchy, edible root of a leguminous plant, *Psoralea esculenta*, found on the western plains near the Rocky Mountains; called also *prairie-turnip*.

bread'stuff, *n.* Any grain, flour, or meal of which bread is made; in the plural, as a commercial term, such materials collectively; as, *breadstuffs* were higher.

breadth (bredth), *n.* [ME. *bredthe*, *bredethe*, *brede*; AS. *brædu*, breadth, from *brad*, broad.]

1. The measure or extent of any surface or thing from side to side, or at right angles to the length; width.

2. In the fine arts, the quality which creates an impression of largeness, simple grandeur, and liberality of treatment, produced by the artistic handling of color and a masterly arrangement of objects; as, to secure *breadth* of effect.

3. Liberality of thought or sentiment; freedom from narrowness in opinion; as, a man of intellectual *breadth*.

4. A piece of goods of the full width; as, two *breadths* of silk.

breadth'less, *a.* Having no breadth.

breadth'wāys, *adv.* Breadthwise.

breadth'wīse, *adv.* Along the line of the breadth.

bread'win"nẽr, *n.* That member of a family by whose labor it is supported; a provider or producer; one who works for his living; something by which a livelihood is earned.

brēak, *v.t.*; broke (brake, *obs.*), *pt.*; broken (broke, *obs.*), *pp.*; breaking, *ppr.* [ME. *breken*; AS. *brecan*; D. *breken*; L.G. *breken*, *bræken*; G. *brechen*; Goth. *brikan*, to break.]

1. To part or divide by force and violence, as a solid substance; to rend apart; as, to *break* a band; to *break* a thread or a cable.

2. To burst or lay open by force; as, to *break* a package of goods.

3. To divide by piercing or penetrating; to burst forth; as, the light *breaks* through the clouds.

4. To make breaches or gaps by battering, as in a wall.

5. To destroy, crush, weaken, or impair, as the human body or constitution.

6. To sink; to appal or subdue; as, to *break* the spirits or the passions.

7. To tame; to train to obedience; to make tractable; as, to *break* a horse.

8. To make bankrupt; as, to *break* a bank.

9. To discard, dismiss, or cashier; as, to *break* an officer.

10. To crack, to part, or divide, as the skin; to open, as an abscess.

11. To violate, as a contract or promise, either by a positive act contrary to the promise, or by neglect or nonfulfilment.

12. To infringe or violate, as a law or any moral obligation, either by a positive act, or by an omission of what is required.

13. To stop; to interrupt; to cause to cease; as, to *break* conversation; to *break* sleep.

14. To intercept; to check; to lessen the force of; as, to *break* a fall, or a blow.

15. To separate; to part; as, to *break* ranks.

16. To dissolve, as a union; sometimes with *off*; as, to *break off* a connection.

17. To cause to abandon; to reform, or cause to reform; as, to *break* one of bad habits or practices.

18. To lay open, as a purpose; to propound, as something new; to make a disclosure of, as information or opinions; as, to *break* one's mind; to *break* the news.

19. To destroy the completeness of; to take a part from; as, to *break* a set.

20. To destroy the arrangement or order of; as, the cavalry charge failed to *break* the enemy's line.

21. To exchange for other coins or currency of smaller denominations; as, to *break* a ten-dollar bill.

22. To destroy the firmness, strength, or consistency of; as, to *break* flax.

23. To shatter to pieces; to reduce to fragments.

24. In electricity, to open or interrupt, as a circuit.

To break the back; (a) to strain or dislocate the vertebræ with too heavy a burden; to disable totally; (b) to get through the worst part of; as, *to break the back* of an undertaking.

To break bulk; to begin to unload.

To break cover; to come forth from a lurking-place, as game when hunted.

To break ground; (a) to plow; (b) to dig; to open trenches; and hence, figuratively, to commence an undertaking; (c) among sailors, to release the anchor.

To break the heart; to afflict grievously; to cause great sorrow or grief; to depress with sorrow or despair.

To break the ice; to overcome first difficulties; to make a start; to introduce a subject.

To break in; (a) to force in; as, *to break in* a window or door; (b) to train, to tame; as, *to break in* a horse.

To break jail; to escape from jail by any means.

To break a lance; to engage in a tilt; figuratively, to engage in a contest of any kind.

To break of; to free from; to cause to forsake; as, to *break* one *of* a habit.

To break off; (a) to put a sudden stop to; to discontinue; (b) to sever; to divide; as, *to break off* a twig.

To break a path, road, etc.; to make a way, in spite of difficulties.

To break sheer; in nautical language, to be forced by wind or current out of a position in which an anchored ship can keep clear of the anchor.

To break up; to dissolve or put an end to; as, *to break up* housekeeping.

To break upon the wheel; to stretch and break the bones by torture upon a wheel.

To break a will; to nullify or secure the nullification of a will.

Syn.—Batter, burst, demolish, crack, rend, split, fracture, rupture, shatter, shiver, destroy, tame, curb, tear asunder, sever, smash, subdue, violate, infringe.

brēak, *v.i.* 1. To part; to separate; to divide in two; as, a rope *breaks*.

2. To burst; as, a storm or deluge *breaks*.

3. To burst by dashing against something; as, a wave *breaks* upon a rock.

4. To open, as a bubble or a tumor.

5. To open, as the morning; to show the first light; to appear; to dawn; as, the day begins to *break*.

6. To burst forth; to utter or exclaim.

7. To fail in trade or other occupation; to become bankrupt; as, to *break* and come to poverty.

8. To decline in health and strength; to begin to lose the natural vigor.

9. To issue out with vehemence.

10. To make way with violence or suddenness; to rush; often with a preposition; as, *to break in*; *to break in upon*, as calamities; to *break over*, as a flood; to *break out*, as a fire; to *break forth*, as light or a sound.

11. To terminate friendship; to fall out.

Be not afraid to *break* with traitors.
—B. Jonson.

12. To make a sudden change; to change the gait; as, to *break* into a run or gallop.

13. To lose musical quality; as, a singer's voice *breaks* when a tone is not completed.

To break away; (a) to disengage oneself abruptly; (b) to dissolve or dissipate, as fog or clouds.

To break forth; to issue out suddenly.

To break from; to disengage from; to depart abruptly, or with vehemence.

To break in; to enter by force; to enter unexpectedly; to intrude.

To break into; to enter by force; as, *to break into* a house.

To break in upon; to approach violently or unexpectedly; to enter abruptly.

To break loose; to get free by force; to escape from confinement by violence; to shake off restraint.

To break off; to become parted or divided; also, to desist suddenly.

To break off from; to part from with violence.

To break out; (a) to issue forth; to discover itself by its effects; to arise or spring up; as, a fire, sedition, or a fever *breaks out*; (b) to appear in eruptions, as pustules; to have pustules or an efflorescence on the skin; as, a child *breaks out* with measles; (c) to throw off restraint and become dissolute.

To break up; to dissolve and separate; to disperse; as, a company *breaks up*; a fog *breaks up*.

To break with; to part from in enmity; to cease to be friends; as, *to break with* a friend or companion.

brēak, *n.* 1. An opening made by force; a state of being open; the act of separating; an open place; as, a *break* in a fence.

2. A pause; an interruption; as, a *break* in the conversation.

3. The first appearance of light in the morning; the dawn; as, the *break* of day.

4. In architecture, any abrupt change in appearance, as in style, color, or form.

5. In fortification, a sudden change in the direction of a curtain.

6. On board ship, the place where a deck terminates or its continuity is broken; as, the *break* of the quarter-deck or of the forecastle.

7. A large four-wheeled carriage, having a straight body, calash top; light wagonette.

8. In telegraphy, (a) an instrument for changing the direction of an electrical current; a commutator; (b) an opening in the circuit interrupting the current; as, a *break* in the circuit.

9. In music, the point where a tone changes, or where a tone is produced imperfectly or with difficulty; also, the point where one register or quality of voice changes to another, as soprano to alto

10. In the game of billiards, (a) the first play, or (b) a number of successful shots; as, a good *break*. In pool, the first shot.

11. In geology, a sudden change in the uniformity of the stratum; a fault.

12. In commercial and speculative use, a sudden decline in quotations.

13. A starting out; as, a *break* for liberty.

14. An unfortunate remark or ill-advised action; as, he made a bad *break*. [Colloq.]

15. In printing, the gap between paragraphs.

brēak'ȧ-ble, *a.* Capable of being broken.

brēak'āge, *n.* The act of breaking; that which is broken; also, an allowance for things broken in transportation or use.

brēak'ax, brēak'axe, *n.* Any one of several kinds of extremely hard wood found in Jamaica and Mexico, especially *Sloanea Jamaicensis*.

brēak'-cir"cuit (-kit), *n.* A device to change the direction or break the circuit of a current of electricity.

brēak'down, *n.* 1. The act or result of breaking down or collapsing, as a carriage; downfall.

2. A spirited, noisy, shuffling dance.

brēak'ẽr, *n.* 1. One who breaks anything; a violator or transgressor; as, a *breaker* of the law.

2. A machine for crushing rocks or coal; or a building containing such machinery.

3. A rock which breaks the waves; the wave itself which breaks against a rock, sand-bank, or shore; a ship drifted toward *breakers*.

4. A pier or other solid structure placed in a river or lake, to break floating ice; called also *ice-breaker*.

5. Among sailors, a small water-cask suitable for use in small boats.

6. A separation point between two trolley-wires, dividing electrical power currents derived from distinct power-houses.

Syn.—Billow, surge, wave.

break'fȧst (brek'), *n.* [ME. *brekefast*, *break fast*; *breke*; AS. *brecan*, to break; *fast*, from *fasten*, to observe, fast.]

1. The first meal in the day; or the food eaten at the first meal.

2. Any meal with which a fast is broken.

break'fȧst, *v.t.*; breakfasted, *pt.*, *pp.*; breakfasting, *ppr.* To furnish with the first meal in the morning.

break'fȧst, *v.i.* To eat breakfast.

brēak'ing, *n.* In philology, a digraph resulting from the change of one vowel to two before certain consonants, as in Anglo-Saxon *earm*. Old

Saxon *arm*; Friesic *earm*, Old Friesic *arm*, *erm*, an arm; AS. *eorthe*, Old Saxon *ertha*, earth.

break'ing-frāme, *n.* An apparatus used in wool-carding which joins the ends of the slivers and places them ready for spinning.

break'ing-in, *n.* The act of subduing and training to labor.

break'măn, *n.* See *Brakeman.*

break'neck, *n.* 1. A fall that breaks the neck.
2. A steep place endangering the neck.

break'neck, *a.* Endangering the neck or likely to break it; as, *breakneck* speed.

break'staff, *n.* The handle of a blacksmith's bellows.

break'stōne, *n.* A name applied to plants growing in stony places, as saxifrage, parsley-piert, the dewcup, or the pimpernel.

break'-up, *n.* A dismemberment or disruption of anything; as, the *break-up* of a company.

break'wa"tĕr, *n.* Any structure or contrivance, as a mole, mound, or wall, placed at the mouth of a river, estuary, or harbor to break the force of waves and protect shipping, docks, etc.; or a structure devised to form an artificial harbor.

brēam, *n.* [ME. *breem*, *breme*; OFr. *bresme*; O.H.G. *brahsima*, *brahsina*; D. *brasem*; Dan. *brasen*, a bream.]
1. A fresh-water cyprinoid fish, *Abramis brama*, or carp-*bream* of Europe, which sometimes attains the weight of twelve to fourteen pounds; also, other species of *Cyprinidæ*, as the white *bream*, *Abramis blicca*.
2. Any of the perch-like fishes of the genus *Lepomis* or any allied genus, as the blue *bream*, *Lepomis pallidus*.
3. The common name applied to several marine sparoid food-fishes of the genera *Diplodus* and *Pagellus*, and to species of the genus *Labrus*, family *Labridæ*. The common sea-*bream* is *Pagellus centrodontus*.

brēam, *v.t.*; breamed, *pt.*, *pp.*; breaming, *ppr.* [Etymology doubtful.] In nautical language, to clear a ship's bottom of shells, seaweed, ooze, etc., by scraping or applying burning reeds or furze.

Breaming.

breast (brest), *n.* [ME. *brest*, *breest*; AS. *breost*; Ice. *brjost*, the breast.]
1. One of a pair of yielding, hemispherical, glandular bodies attached anteriorly to the thorax in females, for the secretion of milk during lactation; commonly, the bosom, especially that of a woman.

> How sweet unto that *breast* to cling.—Burns.

2. The fore part of the thorax, or the fore part of the body between the neck and the belly, in man and beast.

> My Eustace might have sat for Hercules;
> So muscular he spread, so broad a *breast.*
> —Tennyson.

3. Figuratively, the seat of the affections and emotions; the repository of consciousness, designs, and secrets; the affections; the heart.

> Each in his *breast* his secret sorrow kept.
> —Rowe.

4. The power of singing. [Obs.]
5. Anything resembling the breast in position or form; as, (a) the front of a moldboard; (b) the wall between a window and the floor; (c) the lower surface of a hand-rail, rafter, or beam; (d) the face of coal or other mineral workings; (e) the front of a (mining) furnace.
To make a clean breast of; to disclose all one's secrets, especially guilty secrets; to lay bare the mind and heart; to confess.

breast, *v.t.*; breasted, *pt.*, *pp.*; breasting, *ppr.* To meet in front boldly or openly; to oppose with the breast; to act with the breast upon; to bear the breast against; to stem.

> (Who) *breasts* the blows of circumstance,
> And grapples with his evil star.—Tennyson.

To breast up a hedge; to trim on one side, baring the stalks and making the hedge breast-shaped.

breast'band, *n.* A nautical term for a strap, rope, or band, especially a band of canvas, passed round the body of the man who heaves the lead in sounding, and fastened to the rigging to prevent his falling; called also *breast-rope.*

breast'bēam, *n.* 1. The cloth-beam of a loom.
2. The forward connecting-rod of a locomotive.

breast'bōne, *n.* The bone of the breast; the sternum.

breast'-deep, *a.* As deep as the breast is high; up to the breast; as, a stream is *breast-deep.*

breast'-drill, *n.* A hand-driven drillstock held up to the work by the driller's breast, pressed against a suitable breast-piece.

breast'ed, *a.* Having a breast; used especially in composition; as, a double-*breasted* coat.

breast'fast, *n.* A line or hawser used to hold a ship alongside a wharf or another vessel; one which passes from the waist of the ship, as distinguished from *bow-* and *stern-fasts.* Called also *breastline.*

breast'height (-hīt), *n.* A sloping bank on the inner side of the parapet in a fortification.

breast'-high (-hī), *a.* As high as the breast.

breast'hook, *n.* A thick, knee-shaped timber, placed directly across the stem of a ship to strengthen the fore part and unite the bows on each side.

breast'ing, *n.* The closely-fitting channel of a water-wheel, confining the water so as to take advantage of its momentum and weight.

breast'knot (-not), *n.* A knot of ribbons worn on the breast.

breast'line, *n.* See *Breastfast.*

breast'pin, *n.* A pin worn for a fastening, or for ornament, on the breast.

breast'plāte, *n.* 1. Armor for the breast.
2. A strap that runs across a horse's breast.
3. In Jewish antiquity, a part of the vestment of a high priest, consisting of a folded piece of the rich embroidered stuff of which the ephod was made. It was set with twelve precious stones, on which were engraved the names of the twelve tribes.
4. A plate built on a drillstock or like tool, to allow the workman to press the tool up to the work with his breast.

breast'plow, *n.* A plow, driven by the breast, used to cut or pare turf.

breast'rāil, *n.* A top rail about breast-high, as the upper rail of the breastwork on a ship's quarter-deck.

breast'rōpe, *n.* See *Breastband.*

breast'sum"mĕr, *n.* A beam or girder built in to carry part of a wall above it. The girder or beam extends continuously from one side wall to the other, and is flush with the front wall it supports; also written *brestsummer.* [Rare.]

breast'weed, *n.* The lizard's-tail, *Saururus cernuus*; used as a remedy for inflammation of the breasts.

breast'-wheel (-hwēl), *n.* A water-wheel on which the stream of water strikes neither so high as in the overshot wheel, nor so low as in the undershot, but at an intermediate point between.

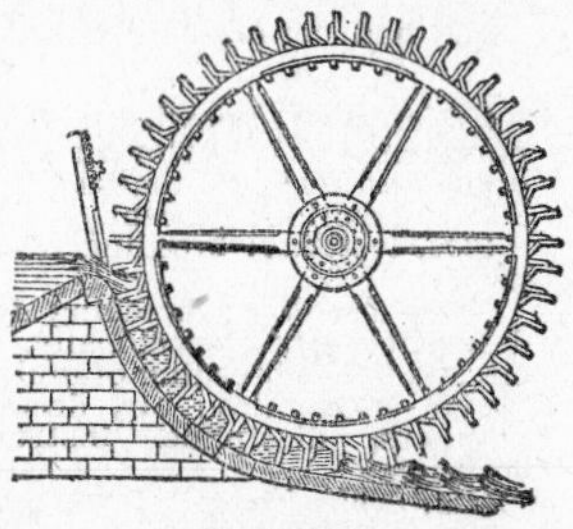
Breast-wheel.

breast'-wood, *n.* Shoots branching from fruit-trees trained against a wall.

breast'wŏrk, *n.* 1. In fortification, a work thrown up for defense; a parapet.
2. A railing on a vessel, either as a division or a guard.

breath (breth), *n.* [ME. *breeth*, *breth*; AS. *bræth*, breath, odor; O.H.G. *bradam*; G. *brodem*, vapor, exhalation.]
1. The air inhaled and exhaled in the respiration of animals.
2. The power of breathing; life.

> No man has more contempt than I of *breath.*
> —Dryden.

3. The state or power of breathing freely; opposed to a state of exhaustion from violent action; as, I am out of *breath*; I am scarce in *breath.*
4. Respite; pause; time to breathe; as, let me take *breath*; give me some *breath.*
5. Breeze; air in gentle motion.

> Calm and unruffled as a summer's sea,
> When not a *breath* of wind flies o'er its surface.
> —Addison.

6. A single respiration; as, he swears at every *breath.*
7. An instant; the time of a single respiration; a single act.

> He smiles and he frowns in a *breath.*
> —Dryden.

8. A slight thing; a mere trifle; the faintest indication; as, a *breath* of suspicion.

> A *breath* can make them, as a *breath* has made.
> —Goldsmith.

9. Odor; exhalation; as, the *breath* of the violet.
Out of breath; breathless.
Under the breath; in a very low tone; in a whisper.
Syn.—Respiration, inspiration, expiration, inhalation, exhalation.

brēath'ȧ-ble, *a.* Capable of being breathed.

brēath'ȧ-ble-ness, *n.* State of being breathable.

brēathe, *v.i.*; breathed, *pt.*, *pp.*; breathing, *ppr.* [ME. *brethen*, to breathe, blow, from *breth*; AS. *bræth*, breath, odor.]
1. To respire; to inspire and expire air; hence, to live.
2. To take breath; to rest from action; as, let them have time to *breathe.*
3. To pass, as air; to move gently; to give forth, as fragrance.

> To whose foul mouth no wholesome air *breathes* in.
> —Shak.

4. To take one regular respiration; as, to *breathe* twenty times per minute.

brēathe, *v.t.* 1. To inhale, as air, into the lungs, and expel it; to respire.
2. To inject by breathing; to infuse; followed by *into.*

> And the Lord God *breathed into* his nostrils the breath of life.
> —Gen. ii. 7.

3. To expire; to eject by breathing; followed by *out*; as, to *breathe out* one's life.
4. To exercise, to keep in breath.

> The greyhounds are as swift as *breathed* stags.
> —Shak.

5. To inspire or blow into; to cause to sound by breathing; as, to *breathe* the flute.
6. To exhale; to emit, as breath; as, the flowers *breathe* odors or perfume.
7. To utter softly or in private; as, to *breathe* a vow.
8. To express; to manifest.

> Other articles *breathe* the same severe spirit.
> —Milner.

9. To exhaust by over-exercise; to put out of breath.
10. To give an opportunity to recover normal breathing; to give rest to.
11. In phonology, to produce or emit an unvoiced sound.
To breathe again; to feel a sense of relief, as from care or danger.
To breathe one's last; to die.

brēathe, *v.t.* [W. *brathu*, to pierce.] To give air or vent to; to open; as, to *breathe* a vein.

brēath'ĕr, *n.* 1. One who breathes or lives; one who utters; an inspirer; one who animates or inspires.
2. That which makes one breathless; used in reference to violent exercise. [Colloq.]

breath'fụl, *a.* Full of breath; full of odor; pleasing to the sense of smell. [Obs.]

brēath'ing, *n.* 1. Respiration; the act of inhaling and exhaling air.
2. Air in gentle motion; applied also, figuratively, to a gentle influence or operation; as, the *breathings* of the Spirit.
3. Aspiration; secret prayer.
4. A breathing-place; a vent. [Obs.]
5. In phonetics, accent; aspiration; also, the mark indicating the aspiration, or the aspirate ('); as, a rough *breathing.*
6. Exercise to assist or improve the respiration.
7. Communication by speech.
8. An intermission in a pursuit or business.
Rough breathing; in Greek, the aspirate ('), a mark indicating that the sound of *h* is to precede the vowel so marked.
Smooth breathing; in Greek, a mark (') denoting the absence of the aspirate sound.

brēath'ing-märk, *n.* In music, a mark in the score indicating where the vocalist is to draw breath.

brēath'ing-plāce, *n.* 1. A pause.
2. A vent.

brēath'ing-tīme, *n.* Pause; relaxation; time to recover one's breath.

breath'less (breth'), *a.* 1. Out of breath; spent with labor or violent action.
2. Dead; as, a *breathless* body.
3. Tense with expectation, fear, or interest; intensely eager, as if so wrought up as to refrain from breathing.

breath'less-ly, *adv.* In a breathless or intent manner.

breath'less-ness, *n.* The state of being exhausted or empty of breath.

breath'y, *a.* 1. Pertaining to breath; like breath.
2. Decidedly aspirated; especially in vocal music.

brec'ciȧ (bret'chȧ), *n.* [It., a breach, fragments of stone.] In geology, an aggregate composed of angular fragments of the same rock or of different rocks united by a matrix or cement.

Osseous breccia; a breccia composed largely of bones.

brec′ci-ā-ted (bret′chi-ā-ted), *a.* Consisting of angular fragments cemented together.

bred, *v.*, past tense and past participle of *breed.*

brēde, *n.* A braid. [Rare.]

Spoilt all her silver mail and golden *brede.*
—Keats.

brēde, breede, *n.* Breath. [Obs.]

breech, *n.* [ME. *breech, breche*; AS. *broc,* breech, pl. *brec, brœc,* breeches.]
1. The lower part of the body behind.
2. Breeches. [Obs.]
3. The hind part of anything.
4. The large, thick end of a cannon or other firearm; in breech-loading artillery, the metal part behind the entrance to the chamber; the distance from the hind part of the base ring to the bore.
5. In shipbuilding, the outer angle of a knee-timber.

breech, *v.t.*; breeched, *pt., pp.*; breeching, *ppr.*
1. To put into breeches.
2. To whip on the breech. [Obs.]
3. To fasten with a breeching.
4. To equip with a breech.

breech′block, *n.* A strong metal block, bolt, or wedge, closely shutting the breech of a breech-loading firearm at the time of firing. It is removably mounted to enable the breech to be opened for loading.

breech′çloth, breech′çlout, *n.* A cloth worn about the loins by savage or semicivilized peoples.

breech′eş (brich′ez), *n.pl.* [AS. *brec,* breeches.] A garment worn by men, covering the body from the waist to the knees, or in some instances only to mid-thigh, and divided so as to incase each leg separately; colloquially used in the sense of trousers or pantaloons.

To wear the breeches; to usurp a husband's prerogatives or authority; said of a wife.

breech′eş-buoy (-boi), *n.* An apparatus used in rescuing persons from wrecks, consisting of a pair of canvas breeches, secured to a ring of buoyant material, in which the person is conveyed to the shore or other place of safety by a sheaved traveler, carrying the slings supporting the *breeches-buoy,* and traveling on a line run from the shore to some high place on the wreck. Hauling lines lead to the ship and the shore to move the traveler.

breech′eş-pipe, *n.* A pipe branching out into two, usually parallel, pipes.

breech′ing (brich′ing), *n.* 1. That part of a harness which comes round the breech of a horse.
2. A flogging administered on the breech; the act of administering it.
3. A stout, short length of hawser passing through the cascabel of a broadside gun and shackled to the ship's side, to stop the movement of the gun inboard upon recoil, and also used to secure the gun at sea. The *breeching* is not used in modern warships, having been superseded by various mechanical devices, such as compression chambers.
4. The sheet-iron smoke-box fitted to the ends of boilers to carry off smoke from the flues.

breech′lōad″ẽr, *n.* A gun or cannon that is loaded at the breech.

breech′-lōad″ing, *a.* Fitted for being loaded at the breech; as, a *breech-loading* rifle.

breech′-pin, *n.* A strong plug or screw used to close the bottom of the bore of a muzzle-loading smallarm, or forming the bottom of the chamber in a breechloader.

breech′-sçrew, *n.* A breech-pin.

breech′-sight (-sīt), *n.* The rear sight of a gun, mounted on the breech; it is usually adjustable for different ranges, and is brought in line with the front sight when the piece is aimed.

breed, *v.t.*; bred, *pt., pp.*; breeding, *ppr.* [ME. *breden*; AS. *bredan,* to nourish, cherish, keep warm, from *brod,* brood; D. *broeden*; O.H.G. *bruoten*; G. *brüten,* to brood, hatch.]
1. To generate; to engender; to hatch; to produce, as the young of any animal.
2. To produce within or upon the body; as, to *breed* teeth. [Obs.]
3. To cause; to occasion; to produce; to originate.
4. To contrive; to hatch; to produce by plotting.

Had he a heart and a brain to *breed* it in?
—Shak.

5. To give birth to; to be the native place of; as, a pond *breeds* fish; a northern country *breeds* a race of stout men.
6. To educate; to instruct; to form by education; as, to *breed* a son to an occupation; a man *bred* at a university.
7. To bring up; to nurse and foster; to take care of in infancy, and through the age of youth; to provide for, train, and conduct; to instruct the mind and form the manners of in youth.

To bring thee forth with pain, with care to *breed.*
—Dryden.

8. To produce by special selection of parents or progenitors; also, to raise (such products of special breeding).
9. To raise, as live stock; as, to *breed* cattle for the market.

Well bred; of good extraction; having a good pedigree.

breed, *v.i.* 1. To produce a fetus; to bear and nourish, as in pregnancy.
2. To be formed in the parent or dam; to be generated, or to grow, as young before birth; as, children or young *breed* in the matrix.
3. To have birth; to be produced; as, fish *breed* in rivers.
4. To raise a breed; as, to choose the best species of cattle to *breed* from.

To breed in and in; to breed from animals of the same stock that are closely related.

breed, *n.* 1. A race or progeny from the same parents or stock.
2. A caste; a kind; a race of animals which have an alliance by nativity, or some distinctive qualities in common; as, a *breed* of horses or sheep; also applied to inanimate things or attributes.
3. A number produced at once; a hatch; a brood. [Obs.]

breed′bāte, *n.* One who breeds or originates quarrels. [Obs.]

breede, *n.* See *Brede.*

breed′ẽr, *n.* 1. One who breeds, procreates, or produces young; formerly, often used distinctively of the female that breeds or produces, whether human or other animal.
2. The person who educates or brings up; that which brings up.

Italy and Rome have been the best *breeders* of worthy men.
—Ascham.

3. One who or that which produces.

Time is the nurse and *breeder* of all good.
—Shak.

4. One who breeds; one who raises a particular breed or breeds, as of horses or cattle.

breed′ing, *n.* 1. The act of generating or producing.
2. The raising of a breed or breeds; especially with reference to the proper selection of breeds for mating; as, the farmer attends to the *breeding* of sheep.
3. Nurture; education; instruction; formation of manners.

She had her *breeding* at my father's charge.
—Shak.

4. Manners; knowledge of ceremony; deportment or behavior in social life. Hence, *good breeding* is politeness.
5. Extraction; descent. [Obs.]

Close breeding; breeding from closely-related parents.

Cross breeding; breeding from parents of different stocks; specifically, of different species, as in the breeding of mules.

Syn.—Education, air, decorum, demeanor, manners, discipline, instruction, nurture, training.

breeks, *n.pl.* [Scot.] Breeches.

breeşe, *n.* The breeze-fly.

breeze, breeze′-fly̆, *n.* [ME. *brese*; AS. *breosa, briosa,* a gadfly; named from the sound it makes in flying.] One of certain buzzing insects of the family *Tabanidæ*; a gadfly or horsefly; the most noted is *Tabanus bovinus,* the great horsefly. Written also *breese* and *brise.*

breeze, *n.* [ME. *brize*; Fr. *brize, brise,* a breeze; Port. *briza,* a northeast wind.]
1. A light, gentle wind.

From land a gentle *breeze* arose at night.
—Dryden.

2. A shifting wind, that blows from the sea or from the land, for a certain time, by night or by day. Such *breezes* are common in the tropical regions, and to a great degree regular. The wind from the sea is called a *sea-breeze,* and that from the land, a *land-breeze.* In general the sea-*breeze* blows in the daytime and the land-*breeze* at night. Similar *breezes* are common, in the summer months, in the temperate latitudes.
3. A flurried state of feeling; excitement; a slight disturbance. [Colloq.]
4. A vague intimation; a rumor.

breeze, *n.* [Fr. *braise,* live coals, embers.]
1. The cinders made as a by-product of the manufacture of charcoal or coke.
2. Refuse fuel resulting from the process of brickburning.
3. A fuel consisting of any fine sweepings of coal, or coke, or cinders, left as a refuse material in any industrial process involving the use of fuel; also applied to screenings.

breeze, *v.i.* To blow gently. [Rare.]

breeze′less, *a.* Motionless; destitute of breezes.

breeze′-ŏv″en, *n.* A furnace in which breeze is used as fuel; also, an oven in which coke is manufactured

breez′i-ness, *n.* The condition of being breezy.

breez′y, *a.* 1. Fanned with gentle winds or breezes; as, the *breezy* shore.
2. Subject to frequent breezes.
3. Brisk; blithe; lively. [Colloq.]

breg′mȧ, *n.*; *pl.* **breg′mȧ-tȧ.** [Gr. *bregma,* the front of the head.] The point where the coronal and sagittal sutures of the skull unite; the fontanel.

breg-mat′iç, *a.* Relating to the bregma.

brē′hŏn, *n.* [Ir. *breitheamh,* from *brath,* a decision.] An ancient Irish judge.

Brehon laws; in ancient times, the general laws of Ireland, unwritten, like the common law of England. These laws were abolished by statute of Edward III. —Blackstone.

bre-loque′ (-lok′), *n.* [Fr.] A seal or locket serving to adorn a watch-chain or necklace.

brēme, *a.* Same as *Brim.*

bren, brenne, *v.t.* and *v.i.* [AS. *bœrnan,* to burn.] To burn. [Obs.]

bren, *n.* Bran. [Obs.]

bren′nāge, *n.* [OFr. *brenage,* from *bren,* bran.] In the middle ages, a tribute which tenants paid to their lord, in lieu of bran, which they were obliged to furnish for his hounds.

brenne, *v.t.* and *v.i.* See *Bren.*

bren′ning-ly, *adv.* Ardently; zealously. [Obs.]

brent, brant, *a.* 1. Steep; high. [Obs.]
2. Smooth; void of wrinkles. [Scot.]

brent, *n.* The brent-goose or brand-goose, *Bernicla brenta,* found throughout the northern hemisphere; it has a black neck, and a white collar or line around it.

brent, *v.*, past tense and past participle of *bren.* [Obs.]

breq′uet-chāin (brek′et-), *n.* [After a French watchmaker, *Briguet,* but influenced by Fr. *briquet,* a little chain.] A short watch-guard or chain to which the key is usually attached; a fob-chain.

brēre, *n.* A brier. [Obs.]

brest, breast, *n.* In architecture, the member of a column usually called torus. [Obs.]

brest, breste, *v.t.* and *v.i.* To burst. [Obs.]

brest′sum″mẽr, *n.* Same as *Breastsummer.*

bret, *n.* A local name of the turbot. [Eng.]

bret, *n.* See *Birt.*

bret-esse′, *n.* [OFr. *bretesse,* the battlements of a wall.] A name common to several wooden, crenelated, and roofed erections, used in the middle ages for military purposes. The *bretesse* over a hotel-de-ville was sometimes used as a convenient place from which to read proclamations or address the public.

Bretesse, Council-house, Constance.

bret′fu̇l, *a.* Brimful. [Obs.]

breth′ren, *n.*, pl. of *brother.* [ME. *brether, bretheren,* pl. of *brother,* brother.] Used in solemn and scriptural language in the place of *brothers.*

Bret′ŏn, *a.* and *n.* [Fr.]
I. *a.* Pertaining to Brittany in France, or its people or language.
II. *n.* An inhabitant of Brittany; also, the old language of the Bretons; Armoric.

brett, *n.* Same as *Britzska.*

bret′tice, *n.* Same as *Brattice.*

Bret′wa̤l-dȧ, *n.* [AS. *bretwalda, bryten walda,* a powerful ruler.] The name or title sometimes given to an Anglo-Saxon chieftain or king of acknowledged power or supremacy.

bret′zel, *n.* See *Pretzel.*

brēve, *n.* [It. *breve,* from L. *brevis,* short.]
1. In music, a note or character of time, equivalent to two semibreves or four minims. When dotted, it is equal to three semibreves.
2. In law, any sealed writ issued out of court; a brief.
3. In printing, a curved sign (˘) to mark the short quality of a vowel; in poetry, to mark the short quantity of syllables.
4. In zoölogy, the Sumatra ant-thrush, *Pitta gigas,* a tropical bird, whose favorite food consists of ants. It somewhat resembles the American ground-thrush, but has a very short tail, whence the name.

brē-vet′, *n.* [ME. *brevet*; OFr. *brievet,* a commission, license; dim. of *brief,* a writing.]
1. Before the French Revolution, a document without seal or a warrant by which the king granted a favor, privilege, title, or dignity.
2. A commission to an officer which entitles him to an honorary rank in the army above his actual rank and pay. Thus a *brevet* major serves as a captain and receives pay as such.

brē-vet′, *v.t.*; brevetted, *pt., pp.*; brevetting, *ppr.* To confer brevet rank upon.

brē-vet′, *a.* Pertaining to rank conferred by brevet; as, a *brevet* captain.

brē-vet′cy, *n.* The condition of brevet rank. [Rare.]

brev′i-. A combining form from L. *brevis*, short, and meaning brief, short, little.

brē′vi-ā-ry, *n.* [L. *breviarium*, an abridgment, from *brevis*, short.]

1. An abridgment; a compend; an epitome.

2. A book containing the daily service of the Roman Catholic church. It consists of prayers or offices to be used at the canonical hours.

3. A similar book used in the Greek church.

brē′vi-āte, brē′vi-at, *n.* [L. *breviatum*, from *breviare*, to shorten; *brevis*, short.]

1. A short compend; a summary.

2. The brief of a lawyer. [Rare.]

brē′vi-āte, *v.t.* [Obs.] See *Abbreviate.*

brē′vi-ā-tūre, *n.* [Obs.] See *Abbreviature.*

brev-i-çau′dāte, *a.* [*Brevi-*, and L. *cauda*, a tail.] Having a short caudal appendage.

brē-vièr′, *n.* [So called from being used in printing breviaries; G. *brevier*; L. *breviarium*, a breviary; *brevis*, short.] A small kind of printing-type, in size between bourgeois and minion. In the modern interchangeable system of type gradation, it is known as eight-point, and runs nine lines to an inch.

This line is set in brevier.

brev-i-lin′guăl (-gwăl), *a.* [*Brevi-*, and L. *lingua*, tongue.] Having a short tongue; as, a *brevilingual* bird.

bre-vil′ō-quence, *n.* [L. *breviloquentia*, from *breviloquens* (*-entis*), short speaking; *brevis*, short, and *loquens*, ppr. of *loqui*, to speak.] A brief and pertinent mode of speaking.

brev′i-ped, *a.* and *n.* [*Brevi-*, and L. *pes*, *pedis*, foot.]

I. *a.* Having short legs, as certain birds.

II. *n.* A bird having short legs.

brev′i-pen, *n.* [*Brevi-*, and L. *penna*, a wing.] A short-winged bird.

brev-i-pen′nāte, *a.* [*Brevi-*, and L. *pennatus*, from *penna*, a wing.] Having short wings; a term applied to a family of grallatory birds, *Brevipennes*, which are unable to fly, as the cassowary.

brev-i-ros′trāte, brev-i-ros′trăl, *a.* [*Brevi-*, and L. *rostratus*, beaked, from *rostrum*, a beak.] Short-beaked; having a short bill; said of a bird.

brev′i-ty, *n.* [L. *brevitas*, from *brevis*, short.]

1. Shortness, applied to time; as, the *brevity* of human life.

2. Shortness; conciseness; contraction into few words; applied to discourses or writings.

Brevity is the soul of wit. —Shak.

Syn.—Conciseness, pointedness, shortness, succinctness, terseness, pithiness, laconism.

brew, *v.t.*; brewed, *pt.*, *pp.*; brewing, *ppr.* [ME. *brewen*; AS. *breówan*, to brew; D. *brouwen*; O.H.G. *briuwan*; Ice. *brugga*, to brew.]

1. To concoct; to boil; to mix.

2. To prepare from malt and hops or other materials, by steeping, boiling, and fermentation, as ale, beer, or other similar liquor.

3. To prepare for use by steeping; as, to *brew* a pot of tea.

4. To contrive; to plot; as, to *brew* mischief.

5. To put in a state of preparation.

brew, *v.i.* 1. To be in a state of preparation; to be mixing, forming, or collecting; as, a storm *brews* in the west.

2. To perform the business of brewing or making beer; as, she can *brew*, wash, and bake.

brew, *n.* The mixture formed by brewing; that which is brewed.

brew′āge, *n.* Malt liquor; drink which has been brewed.

brew′ēr, *n.* One whose occupation is to prepare malt liquors; one who brews.

brew′ēr-y, *n.* A brewhouse; an establishment in which brewing is carried on.

brew′house, *n.* A brewery; a house appropriated to brewing.

brew′ing, *n.* 1. The act or process of preparing liquors from malt and hops.

2. The quantity brewed at once.

3. The act of making a mixture.

4 Among seamen, a collection of black clouds portending a storm.

brew′is, *n.* [ME. *brewes*; OFr. *broues*; LL. *brodum*, gravy, broth; O.H.G. *brod*, broth.]

1. Bread soaked in gravy, broth, or pottage of any kind.

2 Broth; pottage. [Obs.]

brew′stēr-ite, *n.* [Named after Sir David *Brewster* (1781-1868).] A rare hydrous mineral of the zeolite section, having monoclinic crystals of pearl-like luster.

brez′i-lin, *n.* Same as *Brazilin.*

bri′ăr, *n* Same as *Brier.*

Bri-ā′rē-ăn, *a.* Hundred-handed; reaching in many directions; from Briareus, a fabled giant with a hundred hands.

brib′ā-ble, *a.* Capable of being bribed.

brībe, *n.* [OFr. *bribe*, a piece of bread, usually that given to beggars; a gift, present; LL. *briba*, a scrap of bread.]

1. A price, reward, gift, or favor bestowed or promised to induce one to commit a wrong or illegal act; as to decide a cause, give testimony, or perform some act in violation of law, either moral or civil.

2. That which seduces or allures.

brībe, *v.t.*; bribed, *pt.*, *pp.*; bribing, *ppr.* [ME. *briben*, to steal; OFr. *briber*, to beg.]

1. To give or promise a reward or consideration to, with a view to pervert the judgment or corrupt the conduct; to hire for bad purposes; to corrupt, as a judge, a witness, or a legislator.

2. To gain by a bribe.

3. In familiar language, to induce, in a good sense; as, to *bribe* a child to take a medicine.

brībe, *v.i.* To offer or give bribes.

The bard may supplicate, but cannot *bribe.* —Goldsmith.

brībe′less, *a.* Not to be bribed; not bribed.

brīb′ēr, *n.* One who bribes, or pays for corrupt practices.

brīb′ēr-y, *n.* [OFr. *briberie*, theft, robbery.] The act or practice of giving or taking rewards for corrupt practices; the act of paying or receiving a reward for a false judgment or testimony, or for the performance of that which is known to be illegal or unjust. It is applied both to him who gives and to him who receives the bribe, but especially to the giver.

brīb′ēr-y-ōath, *n.* An oath sometimes required to be taken by a voter, declaring that he was not bribed. [Eng.]

briç′-à-braç, *n.* [Fr.] Curiosities and works of art of miscellaneous pattern and assortment, used for decorating and as shelf ornaments.

brick, *n.* [ME. *bryke*; OFr. *brique*, a brick, plate, wedge of metal; D. *bricke*, *brigke*, a tile, brick.]

1. A hardened block of clay, formed in a mold, dried and baked or burned in a kiln; used in buildings and walls. It is usually rectangular in form.

2. In a collective sense, used for the plural; as, a car of *brick.*

3. Any mass in the form of an oblong rectangular solid; as, a *brick* of ice-cream.

4. A jolly good fellow; a trustworthy friend; as, the guardian is a *brick.* [Slang.]

Brick tea; a small brick made of refuse tea, tea-leaves, and twigs, mixed with fat, steamed, and pressed into shape.

Pressed brick; bricks that are put into a press and perfected before burning.

brick′bat, *n.* A piece of a brick.

brick′field, *n.* A yard where bricks are made.

brick′kiln (-kil), *n.* A kiln, or furnace, in which bricks are baked or burned, or a pile of bricks, laid loose, with arches underneath to receive the fuel for burning them.

brick′lāy-ēr, *n.* One whose occupation is to build with bricks.

brick′lāy″ing, *n.* The art or trade of constructing walls, etc., with bricks and mortar or cement; the act of laying bricks.

brig′kle, *a.* [ME. *brekil*, from AS. *brecan*, to break.] Brittle; easily broken. [Obs.]

brig′kle-ness, *n.* Brittleness. [Obs.]

brick′māk″ēr, *n.* One whose occupation is to make bricks.

brick′māk″ing, *n.* The art or act of making bricks.

brick′nog″ging, *n.* In building, a filling of brickwork between the wooden framework.

brick′-trim″mēr, *n.* In architecture, a brick arch abutting against a wooden trimmer in front of a fireplace to guard against accidents by fire.

brick′wŏrk, *n.* Work done with bricks.

brick′y, *a.* Full of bricks, or formed of bricks.

brick′yärd, *n.* A place where bricks are made.

bri-çōle′, *n.* [Fr.] 1. In medieval times, a kind of machine for throwing missiles and darts against an enemy.

2. A kind of harness for men who move guns in situations where the use of horses is impossible.

3. In court-tennis, a side-stroke; also, the rebound of the ball.

4. In billiards, a stroke by which the cue-ball is driven against the cushion before striking an object-ball; commonly called a *bank-shot.*

brid, *n.* An obsolete form of either *bird* or *bride.*

brīd′ăl, *a* Belonging to a bride, or to a wedding; nuptial; connubial; as, *bridal* ornaments.

brīd′ăl, *n.* [ME. *bridale*; AS. *brydealo*, bridal, bride-ale, bride-feast; *bryd*, bride, and *ealo*, ale, in comp. feast.] The nuptial festival; a wedding.

brīd′ăl-ty, *n.* Celebration of the nuptial feast. [Obs.]

brīd′ăl-wrēath (-rēth), *n.* A plant, *Spiræa hypericifolia*, having long slender branches and clusters of white blossoms; also called *St. Peter's-wreath.*

brīde, *v.t.* To take a woman in marriage. [Obs.]

brīde, *n.* [ME. *bride*, *bryde*; AS. *bryd*, a bride.]

1. A woman newly married; applied also to a woman at the marriage festival, before she is married, as well as after the ceremony; occasionally used of a woman espoused, or contracted to be married.

2. Figuratively, something dearly loved; as, the church is his *bride.*

3. A loop that connects or ties in lace or needlework.

4. A bridle. [Obs.]

Bride of the Sea; a distinctive figurative name of the city of Venice, Italy.

War bride; a term applied to the bride of a soldier in the World War, particularly when the nuptials were hastened by reason of the soldier leaving for the service.

brīde′-āle, *n.* 1. An old form of *bridal.*

2. Mulled ale sometimes served to guests at a wedding. [Eng.]

brīde′bed, *n.* The marriage bed.

brīde′çāke, *n.* The cake which is made for the guests at a wedding; commonly called *wedding-cake.*

brīde′chăm″bēr, *n.* The nuptial apartment.

brīde′grōōm, *n.* [ME. *bridegome*, *bridgume*; AS. *brydguma*, *brydiguma*; *bryde*, genit. of *bryd*, bride, and *guma*, man.] A man newly married; or a man about to be married.

brīde′knot (-not), *n.* A wedding favor of ribbons.

brīde′ṣ′-lā″ceṣ, *n.pl.* A popular name for either the common dodder or for ribbon-grass, *Phalaris arundinacea.*

brīdeṣ′māid, brīde′māid, *n.* An unmarried woman who attends a bride at her wedding.

brīdeṣ′măn, brīde′măn, *n.* A man who attends a bridegroom and bride at a wedding; generally called *best man.*

brīde′stāke, *n.* A stake or post set in the ground to dance round, especially at a wedding.

brīde′well, *n.* A house of correction for the confinement of disorderly persons; so called from the palace built near St. Bride's (or Bridget's) well in London, which was turned into a workhouse.

brīde′wŏrt, *n.* The common meadowsweet, *Spiræa salicifolia.*

bridge (brij), *n.* [ME. *brigge*, *brugge*; AS. *brycg*, *bricg*; D. *brug*; O.H.G. *brucca*; G. *brücke*, a bridge; Ice. *bryggja*; Sw. *brygga*, a pier, landing-place.]

1. Any structure of wood, stone, brick, or iron raised to afford convenient passage over a river, pond, lake, railroad, ravine, or any other obstacle.

2. The upper, bony part of the nose.

3. The part of a stringed musical instrument by which the strings are raised and their vibrations transmitted.

4. In steamships, an elevated platform standing transversely amidships, upon which the pilot or deck-officer stands; a hurricane-deck; a bridge-deck.

5. In gunnery, the two pieces of timber which go between the two transoms of a gun-carriage.

6. Any one of a variety of structures or objects resembling a bridge in appearance or use,

Suspension Bridge.

the essential idea being that it affords means of passage over an obstacle or from one elevation to another.

7. In electricity, a device employed to measure an unknown electric resistance. [See *Wheatstone's bridge*, below.]

8. The game of bridge whist.

9. Figuratively, a means of surmounting difficulty; as, I will cross that *bridge* when I come to it.

Asses' bridge; see under *Ass.*

Bridge crane; a crane which is movable upon a bridge, or tramway.

Bridge of Sighs; the popular name of an elevated passageway from a palace in Venice to a prison on the opposite side of the street.

Cantaliver bridge; see *Cantaliver.*

Flying bridge; (a) a bridge constructed for temporary use, as one rapidly built for the passage of troops and then removed or destroyed; (b) a kind of ferry anchored by a strong cable upstream and so placed and handled as to be carried across by the force of the stream.

Lattice bridge; a bridge of wood or iron

constructed with cross-framing, like lattice-work.

Pontoon bridge; see *Pontoon*.

Skew bridge; a bridge by which a road or railway is carried over an opening at some other than a right angle, so as better to maintain the continuity of the road or track.

Tubular bridge; a bridge built in the form of a great rectangular tube, through which the roadway or railway passes.

Wheatstone's bridge; an electric apparatus, invented by Sir Charles Wheatstone, for measuring resistance by means of a bridge, or wire carrying a current between two points, and including a galvanometer whose needle indicates no current when the resistances in the two arms of the instrument are equal. The resistance in one of these arms is known by means of the resistance-box of which it mainly consists, while that in the other is the resistance sought.

bridġe, *v.t.*; bridged, *pt.*, *pp.*; bridging, *ppr.* 1. To build a bridge over; to make a passage on or through, as by a bridge or bridges; as, to *bridge* a river.

2. To get over or surmount; to overcome; usually followed by *over*; as, to *bridge over* a difficulty.

bridġe′ bōard, *n.* 1. A board supporting the steps and risers of stairs.

2. Any plank serving as a bridge or passage-way.

bridġe′head (-hed), *n.* In fortification, a work covering that end of a bridge which is nearest the enemy.

bridġe′less, *a.* Having no bridge.

bridġe′ pot, *n.* The adjustable socket or bearing in which the spindle of a millstone rests.

bridġe′tree, *n.* In a grinding-mill, the beam supporting the shaft of the rotating millstone.

bridġ′ing, *n.* A system of braces used between floor-joists or other beams to distribute weight or hold them apart.

bridġ′ing-joist, *n.* In architecture, a joist in a double-framed floor which is laid transverse to the girder, and to which the flooring-boards are nailed.

bridġ′y, *a.* Having many bridges, or like a bridge.

brī′dle, *n.* [AS. *bridel*; OFr. *bridel*; D. *breidel*; O.H.G. *bridel*, *britel*, a bridle.]

1. The head-harness with which a horse is governed and restrained by a rider or driver; consisting of a headstall, a bit, and reins, with other appendages, according to its particular form and uses.

2. A restraint; a curb; a check.

3. That part of a gunlock which covers and holds in place the tumbler and sear, being itself held by the screws on which they turn.

4. In seamanship, a Y-shaped arrangement of two lines, cables, hawsers, or the like, meeting in a point to which the pull is applied or transmitted; as, the *mooring-bridle*, formed of two lengths of chain, each of which is secured inboard and which meet forward of the bow in a swivel or shackle; a *towing-bridle*, enabling the towline to adapt itself to the yawing of the tow; a *bowline-bridle*, distributing the pull of the bowline to two points of the leech of a top-sail or course.

Scolding bridle; a device like a gag formerly used for the correction of scolding women; branks.

brī′dle, *v.t.*; bridled, *pt.*, *pp.*; bridling, *ppr.* [ME. *bridlen*, *bridelen*; AS. *gebridlian*, to bridle, restrain, from *bridel*, a bridle.]

1. To put a bridle on; as, to *bridle* a horse.

2. To restrain, guide, or govern; to check, curb, or control; as, to *bridle* the passions; to *bridle* a muse.

brī′dle, *v.i.* To throw up the head, and hold in the chin, as from vexation, indignation, pride, or disdain; generally used with *up*; as, she *bridled up* at the insinuation.

brī′dle-hand, *n.* The hand in which the bridle is held while riding, i.e., the left hand.

brī′dle-ī″ron (-ūrn), *n.* A metal strap bent into the shape of a stirrup and used to hold the end of a horizontal beam.

brī′dle-pȧth, brī′dle-wāy, *n.* A path used by or set apart for saddle-horses or pack-animals.

brī′dle-pōrt, *n.* In a ship, especially a warship, the foremost port on each side of the bows, generally on the main deck, so called because the legs of a mooring or towing bridle may be passed through them.

brī′dlẽr, *n.* One who bridles; one who restrains and governs.

bri-dọọn′, *n.* [Fr. *bridon*, from *bride*, a bridle, check.] In a military bridle, a light snaffle-bit, in addition to the principal bit, and having a distinct rein.

brïēf, *a.*; *comp.* briefer; *superl.* briefest. [OFr. *bref*, *brief*; It. *breve*; Sp. *breve*; L. *brevis*; Gr. *brachys*, short.]

1. Short; not lasting; ending quickly; as, a *brief* respite from work.

2. Concise; of few words; compact in expression; as, a *brief* letter.

3. Short in manner; of scant courtesy; abrupt; somewhat rude.

4. Of limited length or extent; as, a *brief* stretch of ground; also, in colloquial use, unusually short; as, a girl in *brief* petticoats.

5. Prevalent; widespread. [Prov. Eng.]

In brief; briefly; in a few words.

Syn.—Condensed, concise, laconic, short, succinct, curt, transitory.

brïēf, *adv.* In brief; in short; soon; in a short time. [Obs.]

brïēf, *n.* 1. An epitome; a short or concise writing; any summary or brief statement.

2. A letter patent, from proper authority, sanctioning the collection of money in the churches for some particular purpose. [Eng.]

3. In music, a breve. [Obs.]

4. In the Roman Catholic church, a letter or communication from the pope to an individual or community. It differs from a bull in contents, being less solemn (consisting often of merely a friendly message or congratulatory letter to a person of high rank), and in form, being shorter, written on paper in Roman letters, and sealed in red wax with the ring of the fisherman.

5. In law, (a) an abridgment of a client's case, made out for the instruction of counsel in a trial at law; (b) a statement in writing of the points of an argument and the authorities cited; (c) a writ issued by any court; a breve.

6. In Scots law, same as *Brieve*.

Brief of title; a summary of the deeds and all other instruments bearing upon the ownership of property; an abstract of title.

brïēf, *v.t.* To make a summary of; to shorten or condense.

brïēf′less, *a.* Without a brief; hence, lacking clients; applied to lawyers.

brïēf′ly, *adv.* Concisely; in a few words.

brïēf′măn, *n.* One who makes out an abstract or brief; also, one who makes a transcript of a manuscript.

brïēf′ness, *n.* The state or quality of being brief.

brī′ẽr, brī′ăr, *n.* [ME. *brere*; AS. *brer*, *brær*, a bramble; Ir. *briar*, a prickle, thorn, pin.]

1. In general, any shrub or bush having prickles or little thorns along its stems; in particular, a plant of the genera *Rosa*, *Rubus*, or others of the rose family; as the sweet*brier* and wild *brier*.

2. Figuratively, anything sharp or cutting; a disagreeable or painful circumstance.

3. A pipe made from the wood of brier-root; as, he smokes a French *brier*.

brī′ẽred, *a.* Set with briers.

brī′ẽr-rọọt, *n.* The root of *Erica arborea*, a tree common in southern Europe, from which tobacco-pipes are made.

brī′ẽr-y, *a.* Full of briers; rough; thorny.

brī′ẽr-y, *n.* A place where briers grow.

brïēve, *n.* [A Scot. form of *brief*; Fr. *bref*, a writing.] In Scots law, a writ issuing from the chancery, directed to any judge ordinary, commanding and authorizing that judge to call a jury to inquire into the case, and upon their verdict to pronounce sentence.

brig, *n.* [Contr. of *brigantine*.]

1. A vessel with two masts, square-rigged, or rigged nearly like a full-rigged ship's mainmast and foremast. The term, however, is loosely applied to various kinds of sailing-vessels.

2. The place on board a man-of-war where prisoners are kept.

Hermaphrodite brig; a brig having the mainmast rigged fore-and-aft.

Brig.

bri-gāde′, *n.* [Fr. *brigade*; It. *brigata*, a troop, company, from *brigare*, to contend; *briga*, strife, quarrel.]

1. A party or division of troops, consisting of cavalry, infantry, artillery, or a combination of these branches, commanded by a brigadier. It may consist of an indeterminate number of regiments, squadrons, or battalions. In the United States army formation, three regiments ordinarily constitute a *brigade*, and three *brigades* a division.

2. Any organized body of persons acting under authority; as, a fire *brigade*.

bri-gāde′, *v.t.*; brigaded, *pt.*, *pp.*; brigading, *ppr.* To form into a brigade, or into brigades.

bri-gāde′-mă″jŏr, *n.* An officer appointed by a brigadier to assist him in the management and ordering of his brigade.

brig-ȧ-dïēr′, *n.* [Fr. *brigadier*, from *brigade*, a brigade.] The general officer who commands a brigade, whether of horse or foot; in rank next below a major-general, and next above a colonel. In the United States army, designated as *brigadier-general*.

brig′ănd, *n.* [Fr. *brigand*; It. *brigante*, a brigand, pirate, from *brigare*, to strive for, contend; *briga*, quarrel, trouble.]

1. A robber; a freebooter; a bandit; a lawless fellow who lives by plunder.

2. A soldier of some irregular band. [Obs.]

brig′ănd-āġe, *n.* [Fr., from *brigand*, a brigand, robber.] Theft; robbery; plunder; methods and habits of, or resembling those of, brigands.

brig′ăn-dine, brig′ăn-tine, *n.* [OFr. *brigandine*, from *brigand*, a foot-soldier.] Anciently, a coat of mail. It consisted of thin, jointed scales of plate, fastened to leather or cloth, making the coat pliant and easy to the body.

brig′ănd-ish, *a.* Brigand-like; like a robber.

brig′ănd-iṣm, *n.* Robbery; plunder; brigandage.

brig′an-tīne (*or* -tin), *n.* [Fr. *brigantin*; It. *brigantino*, a brigantine, pirate vessel; *brigante*, a brigand, pirate; from *brigare*, to contend for, struggle; *briga*, trouble, quarrel.]

1. A two-masted vessel, square-rigged like a brig, excepting the mainsail, which is fore-and-aft; occasionally the term is applied to a hermaphrodite brig.

2. A light sailing vessel formerly much used by pirates. [Obs.]

3. See *Brigandine*.

brigge, *n.* A bridge. [Obs.]

brīght (brīt), *a.* [ME. *bright*, *briht*; AS. *bryht*, *briht*, *beorht*; O.H.G. *beraht*, *bereht*; Goth. *bairhts*, bright; Sans. root *bhraj*, to shine.]

1. Giving forth, shedding, or reflecting, much light; radiant; shining; as, a *bright* sun or star; a *bright* metal.

2. Clear; transparent, as liquors.

3. Of active mind; discerning; clever; keen-witted; as, a *bright* scholar.

4. Characterized by cheerfulness and gaiety; lively; pleasant; as, *bright* memories.

5. Giving promise of prosperity or happiness; favorable; auspicious; as, a *bright* outlook.

6. Illustrious; glorious; as, the *brightest* period of a kingdom.

7. Sparkling; animated; as, *bright* eyes.

8. Of brilliant hue or color; as, a *bright* blue; the *bright* poppy.

9. Resplendent with charms; having attractive qualities; as, a *bright* beauty.

10. Evident; clear; manifest to the mind, as light is to the eyes.

> The evidence of this truth is *bright*.—Watts.

Syn.—Sparkling, shining, clear, luminous, gleaming, radiant, brilliant, clever, witty, sunny, limpid, pellucid, resplendent, translucent, lustrous, glittering.

brīght, *v.i.* Same as *Brite*.

brīght, *n.* Brightness; brilliancy.

> Dark with excessive *bright* thy skirts appear.
> —Milton.

brīght, *adv.* Brightly; with brightness. [Poet.]

> The moon shines *bright*. —Shak.

brīght′en (brīt′), *v.t.*; brightened, *pt.*, *pp.*; brightening, *ppr.* 1. To make bright or brighter; to make to shine; to add to the color or luster of.

2. To cheer; to make gay or cheerful; to drive away the darkness or gloom of; as, to *brighten* sorrow.

3. To make illustrious or more distinguished; as, to *brighten* a character.

4. To make acute or witty.

brīght′en, *v.i.* To grow bright, or more bright; to clear up; to be relieved of darkness or gloom; as, the sky *brightens*; our prospects *brighten*.

brīght′en-ing, *n.* In assaying, the flash of light seen when the last of the oxid of lead or copper leaves the surface of gold or silver in the process of cupellation; called also *ful′guration*.

brīght′-hăr″nessed (-nest), *a.* Having glittering armor.

brīght′ly, *adv.* 1. Splendidly; with luster.

2. Intelligently; sharply; alertly; keenly.

brīght′ness, *n.* Splendor; luster; brilliancy; the condition or quality of being bright in any sense.

Brīght's dis-ēaṣe′. [From Dr. Richard *Bright*, the physician who first diagnosed it.] A disease of the kidneys characterized by a granular condition. The urine contains albumin, and is of less specific gravity than in normal health. The disease, in its advanced stages, is accompanied with uneasiness or pain in the loins, pale or cachectic countenance. disordered digestion, frequent urination, and dropsy. The blood contains urea, and is deficient in albumin and hæmatosin. Progressive blood-poisoning induces other visceral diseases, and in the end gives rise to the cerebral disturbance which is the frequent cause of death. Called also *granular degeneration of the kidneys*.

brīght′sōme, *a.* Bright; shining; cheerful.

bri-gōse′, *a.* Contentious. [Obs.]

brïgue (brēg), *n.* [Fr.] A cabal; intrigue; faction; contention. [Obs.]

brïgue, *v.i.* To canvass; to solicit. [Obs.]

brike, *n.* [AS. *brice*, a fracture, breaking.] A breach; a break; peril; ruin. [Obs.]

brill, *n.* [Corn. *brilli*, mackerel, contr. of *brithelli*, from *brith*, spotted, speckled.] One of the flatfishes, in general form resembling the turbot, but inferior to it both in size and quality.

brïl-län′te, *adv.* [It.] In music, in a gay and lively manner.

bril′liănce (-yăns), **bril′liăn-cy** (-yăn-), *n.* Splendor; glitter; great brightness; used in both a literal and a figurative sense.

bril′liănt, *a.* [Fr. *brillant*, sparkling, ppr. of *briller*, to glitter, sparkle; from L. *beryllus*, *berillus*, a precious stone, beryl.]

1. Sparkling with luster; glittering; as, a *brilliant* gem; a *brilliant* dress.

2. Splendid; remarkable; illustrious; as, a *brilliant* achievement.

3. Having unusual powers; possessing striking abilities or conspicuous attainments; applied to persons with reference to mental qualifications; as, a *brilliant* orator; a *brilliant* writer.

Syn.—Beaming, effulgent, flashing, glorious, luminous, lustrous, radiant, shining, sparkling.

bril′liănt, *n.* 1. A diamond of the finest cut, formed into facets so as to reflect the light, by which it is rendered more glittering.

2. In the manège, a brisk, high-spirited horse, with a stately carriage.

3. The smallest size of type manufactured; 3½ point.

This line is set in brilliant.

4. A figured cotton fabric.

bril′liăn-tïne, *n.* [Fr.] 1. A preparation for the hair, to make it smooth and glossy.

2. A dress material somewhat resembling, but superior to, alpaca; both sides have a hard and smooth finish.

bril′liănt-ly, *adv.* Splendidly; with brilliance, in a brilliant manner.

bril′liănt-ness, *n.* Brilliancy; splendor; glitter.

brills, *n.pl.* [G *brille*, spectacles.] The hair on the eyelids of a horse.

brim, *n.* [AS. *brim*; Ice. *brim*, the surf, sea; Dan. *bræmme*; G. *bräme*, the edge, border; AS. *bremman*, to roar; Gr. *bremein*, to roar especially as the waves; Sans. *bhram*, to whirl, wander.]

1. The rim, lip, border, or upper edge of any vessel or hollow article; as, the *brim* of a cup or glass.

2. The edge or brink of any body of water; the verge.

3. The top or surface of any liquid near the edge; that part next to the border at the top.

4. The rim of a hat, as distinct from the crown.

Syn.—Border, brink, edge, margin, rim, verge.

brim, *a.* [AS. *bryme*, celebrated, famous.]

1. Public; well known; celebrated. [Obs.]

2. Fierce; cruel. [Obs.]

brim, *v.t.*; brimmed, *pt.*, *pp.*; brimming, *ppr.* To fill to the brim, upper edge, or top.

brim, *v.i.* To be full to the brim.

brim′fụl, *a.* Full to the top; completely full; as, a glass *brimful*; a heart *brimful* of sorrow.

brim′fụl-ness, *n.* Fullness to the top.

brim′ing, brim′ming, *n.* [AS. *bryme.*] A condition of the sea at night characterized by a phosphorescent glow and sometimes due to the presence of shoals of herrings. [Eng.]

brim′less, *a.* Having no brim.

brimmed, *a.* 1. With a brim; used in composition; as, a broad-*brimmed* hat.

2. Full to or level with the brim.

brim′mẽr, *n.* A bowl full to the top; a bumper.

brim′ming, *a.* Full to the top or brim; as, a *brimming* pail.

brim′ming, *n.* See *Briming*.

brim′stōne, *n.* [ME. *brimston*, *brinston*, *bernston*, from *brin-*, *bren-*, from *brinnen*, *brennen*, to burn, and *ston*, stone.]

1. Sulphur; especially, sulphur in a solid state. [See *Sulphur.*]

2. In zoölogy, a species of butterfly, *Gonopteryx rhamni.*

brim′stōne, *a.* Made of or relating to brimstone; as, *brimstone* pills.

brim′stōne-wŏrt, *n.* Same as *Sulphurwort*.

brim′stō-ny, *a.* Full of brimstone, or containing it; resembling brimstone; sulphurous.

brin, *n.* [Fr.] One of the smaller sticks forming the frame of a fan.

brin′ded, *a.* [A variant of *branded*, from AS. *brinnan*, *byrnan*, to burn.] Marked with spots; tabby; having different colors; brindled. [Rare.]

brin′dle, *n.* 1. The state of being brindled; spottedness.

2. A color or mixture of colors of which gray is the base, with bands of a darker gray or black color.

3. A brindled animal.

brin′dle, *a.* Brindled; as, a *brindle* cow.

brin′dled (-dld), *a.* [A dim. of *brinded*, brindled.] Spotted; variegated with spots of different colors.

brïne, *n.* [AS. *bryne*, a burning, salt liquor, from *brinnan*, *byrnan*, to burn.]

1. Water containing as much salt as possible; pickle.

2. The ocean or sea.

3. Tears; so called from their saltness.

brïne, *v.t.*; brined, *pt.*, *pp.*; brining, *ppr.* To steep in brine, as corn, to prevent smut; also, to mix salt with; as, to *brine* hay.

brïne′=flȳ, *n.* A fly of the genus *Ephydra*, so called because its larvæ are found in brine and in salt lakes.

brïne′=gāuġe, *n.* An instrument which measures the amount of salt in a liquid.

brïne′=pan, *n.* A pit of salt water, where, by the action of the sun, salt is formed by crystallization.

brïne′=spit, *n.* A salt spring or well, from which water is taken to be boiled or evaporated for making salt.

brïne′=pump, *n.* A pump which cleans the brine from the boilers of a steamship.

brïne′=shrimp, *n.* A minute crustacean, *Artemia salina*, which lives in the strong brines of salt-works and in salt lakes.

brïne′=spring, *n.* A spring of salt water.

brïne′=worm (-wẽrm), *n.* Same as *Brine-shrimp*.

bring, *v.t.*; brought, *pt.*, *pp.*; bringing, *ppr.* [ME. *bringen*; AS. *bringan*; Sw. *bringa*; Dan. *bringe*; D. *brengen*; G. *bringen*; Goth. *briggan*, to bring.]

1. To fetch; to bear, convey, or lead from a distant to a nearer place, or to a person; as, *bring* me a book from the shelf; *bring* me a morsel of bread. In this sense, it is opposed to *carry*; and it is applied to the person bearing or leading, in opposition to sending or transmitting by another.

2. To produce; to procure as a cause; to draw to; as, nothing *brings* a man more honor than to be invariably just.

3. To attract or draw along; as, in distillation the water *brings* over with it another substance.

4. To cause to come; to cause to proceed from a distant place, in company, or at the same time; as, to *bring* a boat over a river; to *bring* a horse or carriage; to *bring* a cargo of dry-goods.

5. To obtain in exchange; to sell for; as, what does coal *bring?* This is the sense of *fetch*.

6. To cause to come to a point, by moral influence; used of the mind, and implying previous remoteness, aversion, alienation, or disagreement; as, to *bring* the mind to assent to a proposition; to *bring* a man to terms by persuasion or argument.

To bring about; to bring to pass; to effect; to accomplish; to bring to the desired issue.

To bring by the lee; to incline so rapidly to leeward of the course, when a ship sails large, as to bring the lee side suddenly to the windward, and, by laying the sails aback, expose her to the danger of capsizing.

To bring down; to cause to come down; also, to humble or abase; as, *to bring down* from a high horse; in hunting or warfare, to kill or wound; as, *to bring down* a bird, or an enemy.

To bring forth; to produce, as young or fruit; also, to bring to light, that is, to make manifest, to disclose.

To bring home; (a) to bring to one's residence; (b) to prove against one; as, *to bring home* a charge of murder; (c) to cause to understand by experience; (d) in navigation, to bring to its place on a vessel, as a boat or chain.

To bring in; to import; to introduce; to bear from a remote place within a certain precinct; to place in a particular condition; to collect things dispersed; to reduce within the limits of law and government; to produce, as income, rent, or revenue; to induce to join; to render, as a verdict, or a report.

To bring off; to bear or convey from a distant place; as, *to bring off* men from an isle; also, to procure to be acquitted; to clear from condemnation; to cause to escape.

To bring on; to cause to begin; as, *to bring on* an action; also, to originate or cause to exist; as, *to bring on* a disease; also, to bear or convey from a distance; as, *to bring on* a quantity of goods; also, to attend or to aid in advancing; as, *to bring* one *on* his way.

To bring out; to expose; to detect; to bring to light from concealment; as, *to bring out* an accomplice or his crimes; the place of concealment was *brought out* at the trial.

To bring over; to bear across; as, *to bring over* dispatches; *to bring over* passengers in a boat; also, to convert by persuasion or other means; to draw to a new party; to cause to change sides, or an opinion.

To bring to; in navigation, to check the course of a ship, by arranging the sails in such a manner that they shall counteract each other, and keep her nearly stationary. She is then said to *lie to*. Also, to restore to life or consciousness, as a half-drowned or fainting person.

To bring under; to subdue; to repress; to restrain; to reduce to obedience.

To bring up; to nurse; to educate; to instruct; to feed and clothe; to form the manners and furnish the mind with knowledge. The phrase may comprehend all these particulars. Also, to introduce to practice; as, *to bring up* a fashion or ceremony; also, to cause to advance near; as, *to bring up* forces or a body of reserves; also, to bear or convey upward; in navigation, to cast anchor; to stop.

To bring up the rear; to be at the end.

Syn.—Fetch, procure, convey, carry, bear, adduce, import, produce, cause, induce.—The primary sense of *bring* is to *lead, draw*, or *cause to come*; the sense of *conveying* or *bearing* is secondary. In general, the word implies motion from a place remote, either in a literal or figurative sense.

bring′ẽr, *n.* One who brings or conveys to.

Bringer in; one who introduces (a bill, etc.).

Bringer up; an instructor; one who feeds, clothes, and educates; also, one who is in the rear of an army.

bring′ing=fōrth, *n.* Production.

brïn′i-ness, *n.* The quality of being briny; saltness.

brïn′ish, *a.* Like brine; somewhat salt; saltish.

brïn′ish-ness, *n.* Saltness; the quality of being saltish.

brin′jąl, brin′jąul, *n.* A term used in India for the fruit of the eggplant, *Solanum Melongena*.

brin-jar′ree, brin′jar-ry, *n.* [Anglo-Ind.] 1. In India, a traveling dealer in grain, etc.

2. A kind of East Indian hound.

brin̄k, *n.* [ME. *brink*, edge; LG. *brink*, brink, margin, edge; Sw *brink*, a declivity, hill; Ice. *brekka*, a slope.] The edge, margin, or border of a steep place, as of a precipice, or the bank of a river; also used figuratively; as, to be on the *brink* of failure.

brïn′y, *a.* Pertaining to brine, or to the sea; partaking of the nature of brine; salt, as, a *briny* taste; the *briny* flood.

brï-ōçhe′, *n.* [Fr.] A soft cake or roll served as a breakfast dish.

brï-ō-lette′, *n.* [Fr., from *brillant*, a brilliant.] A pear-like shape given to a diamond or other precious stone; also, the stone which is so shaped.

brī′ō-ny, *n.* See *Bryony*.

brï-quet′, brï-quette′ (-ket′) *n.* [Fr. *briquette*, dim. of *brique*, brick.]

1. A molded, brick-like block of compressed coal-dust, peat, etc., used for fuel.

2. A brick-shaped piece of artificial stone, used for street paving.

3. A molded lump of cement or mortar used as a sample to show the strength of the material.

4. Generally, any brick-shaped piece of material which has obtained its form by pressure.

brï-ṣé′ (-zā′), *a.* [Fr.] Broken; in music, broken off short, as a chord.

bri-sin̄′goid, *a.* [L. *Brisinga*, from Ice. *Brisinga-men*, the name of a necklace of Freya, and Gr. *eidos*, form.] In zoölogy, pertaining to the genus *Brisinga*, which includes some species of deep-sea starfishes.

brisk, *a.* [W. *brysg*, from *brys*, haste; Gael. *briosg*, quick, lively; Ir. *briosg*, a start, jerk.]

1. Lively; active; nimble; gay; sprightly; vivacious; as, a *brisk* young man; a *brisk* movement.

2. Stimulating; effervescing; as, *brisk* air.

3. Burning freely; as, a *brisk* fire.

Syn.—Animated, spirited, vivacious, sprightly, alert, active, nimble, quick.

brisk, *v.t.* and *v.i.*; brisked, *pt.*, *pp.*; brisking, *ppr.* To make lively; to enliven; to animate; to come up with life and speed; to take an erect or bold attitude; generally with *up*; as, to *brisk up* a horse, or a servant.

bris′ket, *n.* [ME. *bruskette*; OFr. *bruschet*; Bret. *bruched*, *brusk*, the breast, chest, of a bird; W. *brysced*, the breast of a slain animal.]

1. The breast of an animal; that part of the breast that lies next to the ribs; or a joint cut from this portion of the animal.

2. The forepart or breast of a horse, from the shoulder down to the fore legs.

brisk′ly, *adv.* Actively; vigorously; with life and spirit.

brisk′ness, *n.* Liveliness; vigor in action; quickness; gaiety; vivacity; effervescence of liquors.

bris′tle (bris′sl), *v.t.*; bristled, *pt.*, *pp.*; bristling, *ppr.* 1. To stiffen the bristles of; to erect in defiance or anger, like the bristles of a hog; as, to *bristle* the crest.

2. To attach a bristle to; as, to *bristle* a piece of cotton thread.

bris′tle, *v.i.* 1. To rise or stand erect; as, the hair *bristles*.

2. To raise the head and show anger or defiance; as, a man *bristles* up.

3. To seem as though hidden by bristles; as, the hill *bristled* with bayonets.

bris′tle, *n.* [OE. *bristel, brustel*; AS. *bristl, byrst*, a bristle; O.H.G. *burst*; G. *borste*, a bristle, brush; Sans. *bhrshti*, an edge, point.]

1. A stiff, glossy hair of swine, especially one of those growing on the back, used for making brushes; also, a similar hair on other animals.

2. A species of pubescence on plants, in the shape of a stiff, roundish hair.

bris′tle=bēar″ing, *a.* Having bristles.

bris′tle=līke, *a.* Stiff as a bristle.

bris′tle=point″ed, *a.* Needle-pointed, as some leaves; terminating in a bristle.

bris′tle=rat, *n.* The hedgehog-rat, a West Indian rodent.

bris′tle=shāped (-shāpt), *a.* Of the thickness and length of a bristle, as a leaf.

bris′tle-tāil, *n.* An insect belonging to the *Thysanura*, particularly one which has bristlelike abdominal appendages.

bris′tli-ness (bris′sli-), *n.* The state of having bristles.

bris′tlings (bris′slingz), *n.pl.* Small fish, found in European waters, that are packed in oil for the market.

bris′tly (bris′sli), *a.* Thickset with bristles, or with hairs like bristles; rough.

bris′tŏl=bōard, *n.* [Named after the city of Bristol, Eng.] A fine calendered pasteboard used in drawing, in printing, etc.

bris′ūre (*or* bri-ṣūr′), *n.* [Fr., from *briser*, to break.]

1. Any part of a parapet or rampart out of line with the general direction of a fortification.

2. In heraldry, a mark of cadency; a device designating the son by whom a paternal shield is borne.

brit, britt, *n. sing.* and *pl.* 1. A fish of the herring kind, from one to four inches long, found, at some seasons, in immense numbers on the coast of New England; the sprat.

2. A general name for the minute animals upon which the right or whalebone whale feeds.

Bri-tan′ni-ȧ, *n.* [From L. *Britannia*, Great Britain.]

1. A poetic name for Great Britain.

2. A metallic compound or alloy, consisting chiefly of block-tin, with some antimony and a small proportion of copper and brass, used for tableware.

Bri-tan′niç, *a.* [L. *Britannicus*, from *Britannia*, Great Britain.] Pertaining to Great Britain; British; applied almost exclusively to the title of the king; as, His *Britannic* Majesty.

brīte, bright (brīt), *v.i.* [Prov. Eng.] To be or become overripe, as wheat, barley, or hops.

Brit′i-çism, *n.* A British characteristic or mode of speech, or a word, phrase, idiom, etc., peculiar to Great Britain or to the British; as, his speech was full of *Briticisms*.

Brit′ish, *n. sing.* and *pl.* [ME. *Britissh, Brytisc*; AS. *Bryttisc*, from *Bryttas, Brettas*, the Britons.]

1 The people of the United Kingdom of Great Britain and Ireland and of the British dominions beyond the seas.

2. The language of the ancient Britons, to which the Welsh and Cornish, as now spoken, bear a strong resemblance.

3. The original inhabitants of Britain; the ancient Britons.

Brit′ish, *a.* Pertaining to the United Kingdom of Great Britain, etc., or its people; as, the *British* empire; a *British* ambassador.

British gum; a substance of a brownish color and very soluble in cold water, formed by heating dry starch at a temperature of about 600° Fahr. It corresponds, in its properties, with dextrin, and is used in solution, as a substitute for gum, in stiffening fabrics.

British lion; the emblem of Great Britain.

Brit′ish-ẽr, *n.* 1 An Englishman; a subject of Great Britain; a term used colloquially or humorously by Americans and by Englishmen settled in the United States.

2. A term, peculiar to the Revolutionary period, for a British soldier.

Brit′ŏn, *n.* 1. A native of Great Britain.

2. One of the ancient inhabitants of Britain.

Brit′ŏn, *a.* British. [Obs.]

brits′kȧ, *n.* See *Britzska.*

britt, *n.* See *Brit.*

brit′tle, *a.* [ME. *britel, brutel*, from AS. *breotan*, to break.] Easily broken, or easily breaking short, without splinters or loose parts; fragile; as, *brittle* stone or glass.

brit′tle-ly, *adv.* In a brittle manner.

brit′tle-ness, *n.* Aptness to break; fragility.

brit′tle-stär, *n.* Any species of sand-star; so called from its fragility.

britz′skȧ, *n.* A long carriage with a calash top, and so constructed as to give space for reclining at night, when used on a journey; especially used in Russia and in Poland, where it originated. Also written *britska.*

brīze, *n.* The gadfly [Obs. See *Breeze.*]

brōach, *n.* [ME. *broche*, a pin, peg, spit; OFr. *broche*; LL. *brocca*, a spit, sharp stake; Gael. *brog*, a shoemaker's awl, from *brog*, to spur, goad.]

1. A spit. [Obs.]

2. An awl; a bodkin. [Prov. Eng.]

3. Same as *Brooch.*

4. A start like the end of a spit, on the head of a young stag.

5. A rod used in candle-making to dip the wicks.

6. A stonecutter's broad chisel.

7. In architecture, a spire built on a tower without an intermediate parapet; a term peculiar to certain parts of England.

8. The pin or projection in a lock that enters the barrel of a key.

9. A reamer, or tapering tool for enlarging and smoothing holes in metal.

10. A borer for sampling casks of wine, etc.

11. A metal-worker's tool with file teeth, used for dressing holes where rotating tools cannot reach.

Broach.

brōach, *v.t.*; broached (brōcht), *pt., pp.*; broaching, *ppr.* [ME. *brochen*; OFr. *brocher*, from *broche*, a spur, spit.]

1. To spit; to pierce as with a spit. [Obs.]

2. To tap; to pierce, as a cask in order to draw the liquor; hence, to shed, as blood.

3. To open, as a storehouse, or as a case of goods.

4. To utter; to give out; to publish first; to introduce in conversation; as, he *broached* the subject at dinner.

5. In masonry, to chisel roughly into shape, as a block of stone.

6. To use a broach in enlarging or dressing (a hole).

To broach to; in navigation, to incline suddenly to windward, so as to lay the sails aback and expose the vessel to the danger of upsetting.

brōach′ẽr, *n.* 1. A spit. [Obs.]

2. One who broaches, opens, or publishes first.

brọad, *a.*; *comp.* broader; *superl.* broadest. [ME. *brood, brod*; AS. *brad*; Ice. *breidhr*; D. *breed*; Sw. *bred*; Dan. *bred*; Goth. *braids*, broad.]

1. Wide; extended in breadth, or from side to side, as distinguished from *long*, opposed to *narrow*.

2. Wide; extensive; as, the *broad* ocean.

3. Liberal; not limited; as, *broad* statesmanship.

4. Open; clear; as, in *broad* sunshine.

5. Coarse; gross; tending to obscenity; as, a *broad* comment.

6. Comprehensive; catholic; tolerant; as, he was too *broad* to be orthodox.

7. Evident; plain; as, a *broad* hint.

8. Strongly marked; very noticeable; as, he has a *broad* accent.

9. Characterized by a full utterance; as, the *broad* sound of a vowel

As broad as it is long; equal upon the whole; amounting to the same thing in the end.

Broad Church; the liberal or moderate portion or division of the Church of England, standing between the High Church and Low Church parties or factions.

Syn.—Ample, extensive, large, wide.

brọad, *n.* 1. The broad part of anything.

2. A turning-lathe for cylinders.

3. A broadened fen at flood. [Prov. Eng.]

4. An English gold coin of the time of James II., worth twenty shillings.

brọad, *adv.* Broadly; completely; as, to be *broad* awake.

brọad′=ar″rōw, *n.* 1. An arrow with a broad head.

2. A mark on English government stores of every description, to obliterate or deface which is a felony. In English surveying, the mark cut by the officers of the ordnance department conducting the trigonometrical survey, to note the points from which their several measurements are made.

Broad-arrow.

brọad′ax, brọad′axe, *n.* 1. A battle-ax.

2. An ax for hewing timber.

brọad′bill, *n.* 1. A wild duck frequenting the eastern coast of the United States in autumn; the scaup-duck.

2. The shoveler-duck, *Spatula clypeata.*

3. One of several species of birds belonging to the family *Eurylæmidæ*, and found in the East Indies.

brọad′brim, *n.* 1. A hat with a very wide brim, as those worn by the Society of Friends.

2. A Quaker. [Colloq.]

brọad′=brimmed, *a.* Having a wide brim.

brọad′ċast, *v.t.* 1. To scatter widely.

2. In radiotelegraphy or telephony, to send

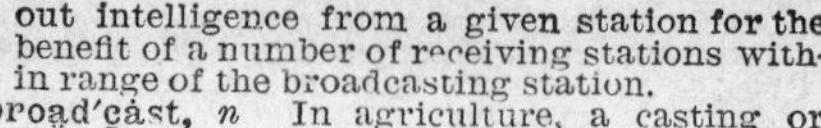

out intelligence from a given station for the benefit of a number of receiving stations within range of the broadcasting station.

brọad′ċast, *n.* In agriculture, a casting or throwing seed from the hand for dispersion in sowing.

brọad′ċast, *adv.* In a scattering manner, as by throwing at large from the hand.

brọad′ċast, *a.* Cast or dispersed, as seed in sowing; widely diffused.

brọad′çlọth, *n.* A fine, smooth, woolen cloth, used in making tailored garments; so called because it was originally made of greater width than ordinary woolens.

brọad′en, *v.i.* To grow broad.

brọad′en, *v.t.*; broadened, *pt., pp.*; broadening, *ppr.* To make broad or broader; to render more comprehensive.

brọad′=gāuġe, *a.* 1. A railroad term applied to the distance between rails and signifying of wider gauge than the standard, which is fifty six and one-half inches.

2. Liberal-minded; as, a *broad-gauge* man.

brọad′hqrn, *n.* A flat-bottomed river freight boat.

brọad′=hqrned, *a.* Having widespread horns.

brọad′ish, *a.* Rather broad.

brọad′lēaf, *n.* A Jamaican tree, *Terminalia latifolia*, which furnishes wood for building purposes; also called *almond-tree.*

brọad′ly, *adv.* In a broad manner; liberally.

brọad′mouth, *n.* A passerine bird of the East Indies, family *Eurylæmidæ*; a broadbill.

brọad′ness, *n.* The state or condition of being broad.

brọad′pīēce, *n.* An old English gold coin. [See *Broad.*]

brọad′=sēal, *n.* The public seal of a country or state.

brọad′sēal, *v.t.* To stamp with a broad-seal; to set the stamp of authority upon.

brọad′sīde, *n.* 1. The simultaneous discharge of all the guns on one side of a ship above and below; also, all the guns so placed.

2. The whole of a vessel's side above the water-line from bow to quarter.

3. In printing, a sheet of paper containing one large page, or printed on one side only; especially, such a sheet containing an attack upon a person and intended for circulation.

4. Figuratively, a volley of invective or abuse. [Colloq.]

brọad′spread (-spred), *a.* Widespread.

brọad′spread″ing, *a.* Spreading widely.

brọad′stōne, *n.* Same as *Ashler.*

brọad′swōrd (-sōrd), *n.* A sword with a broad blade and a cutting-edge.

brọad′tāil, *n.* Any parrot of the genus *Platycercus*, with broad tail-feathers.

brọad′thrōat, *n.* A book-name of birds of the family *Eurylæmidæ.*

brọad′=tread (-tred), *a.* Having a wide face; as, a *broad-tread* car-wheel.

brọad′wīse, *adv.* In the direction of the breadth.

brob, *n.* A specially shaped spike used to hold an abutting timber in place.

Brob-ding-nag′i-ăn, Brob-dig-nag′i-ăn, *a.* and *n.* [From *Brobdingnag*, a country of giants, in Swift's "Gulliver's Travels."]

I. *a.* Gigantic; of great height.

II. *n.* A giant; a marvel for size.

brō-çāde′, *n.* [Sp. *brocado*, from LL. *brocare*, to embroider, stitch.] A fabric, usually of silk, satin, or velvet, variegated with gold and silver, or raised and enriched with flowers, foliage, and other ornaments.

brō-çād′ed, *a.* 1. Woven or worked, as brocade.

2. Dressed in brocade.

brō-çāde′=shell, *n.* A party-colored cone-shell, *Conus geographicus.*

brō′çāġe, *n.* See *Brokerage.*

broç′ärd, *n.* [OFr., from *Brocard*, French for Burchhard, bishop of Worms, who published a collection of ecclesiastical canons.]

1. A brief maxim, rule, or proverb in philosophy, ethics, or law.

2. A pointed jest; a sneer or gibe.

brō′çȧ-tel, brō′çȧ-telle, *n.* [Fr. *brocatelle*; It. *broccatello*, dim. of *broccato*, brocaded.]

1. A calcareous stone or marble, having a yellow ground, flecked with white, gray, and red.

2. A kind of coarse brocade, used chiefly for tapestry.

broç′çō-li, *n.* [It. *broccoli*, sprouts; pl. of *broccolo*, a sprout, cabbage-sprout; dim. of *brocco*, LL. *brocca*, a spit, sharp-pointed thing.] A variety of the common cabbage, *Brassica oleracea*, closely resembling the cauliflower

broch, *n.* [Scot.] A circular stone tower of ancient and unknown origin; found in ruins in the Orkney and Shetland islands and the northern part of Scotland.

brō′chăn-tīte, *n.* [After *Brochant* de Villiers, French mineralogist.] A basic sulphate of copper, occurring in emerald-green crystals.

brōche, *n.* [Obs.] Same as *Broach.*

brō-çhé′ (-shā′), *a.* [Fr., from *brocher*, to stitch, sew.]

1. Ornamentally woven; brocaded.
2. Stitched, as a pamphlet or unbound book.

brō-çhette′, *n.* [Fr., dim. of *broche*, a spit.] A skewer; a small spit.

brō-çhid′ō-drōme, *a.* [Gr. *brochis*, dim. of *brochos*, a loop, and *dromos*, a running.] Having loops; applied to nervation in leaves, when loops are formed within the blade.

brō-çhụre′, *n.* [Fr., from *brocher*, to stitch.] A brief treatise, sketch, or essay, in pamphlet form.

brock, *n.* [AS. *broc*; Ir. *broc*; W. *broch*, a badger.] A badger.

brock, *n.* A broken portion; a fragment. [Prov. Eng. and Scot.]

brock, *n.* A cart-horse; sometimes a cow. [Prov. Eng.]

brock, *v.t.* and *v.i.* [ME. *brokken*, from *brekken*, to break.]
I. *v.t.* To break in pieces; to crumble. [Scot.]
II. *v.i.* To break into epithets; to complain. [Rare.]

brock′āge, *n.* 1. Coin rejected as having been imperfectly minted.
2. Articles broken or damaged.

brock′et, *n.* [ME. *broket*; Fr. *brocart*, *broquart*, a brocket; OFr. *broc*, a spit, tine of a stag's horn.]
1. A red deer two years old; a pricket.
2. Any South American deer of the genus *Cariacus*.

brock′et, *a.* Party-colored; variegated; chiefly used of cattle. [Scot.]

brock′ish, *a.* Bestial; cruel. [Obs.]

brōde′kin, brōde′quin (-kin), *n.* [Fr.] A buskin or half-boot. [Obs.]

brog, *n.* A sharpened prodding instrument, as a needle, pin, or awl. [Scot. and Prov. Eng.]

brog, *v.t.* To pierce or prick with or as with a brog. [Scot. and Prov. Eng.]

brō′gan (*or* brō-gan′), *n.* [Gael.] A stout, coarse shoe; a brogue.

brog′gēr-īte (brĕg′-), *n.* [Named after W. C. *Brögger*.] A rare mineral of the nature of uraninite or pitchblende, from which the gas helium has been obtained, and composed to a great extent of uranium oxid.

brog′gle, *v.i.* To fish for eels; to sniggle with a brog. [Prov. Eng. and Scot.]

brōgue (brōg), *n.* [Gael. and Ir. *brog*, a shoe.]
1. A stout, coarse shoe. In the Highlands of Scotland, it was formerly made of horsehide or deerskin with the hair on. The Irish *brogues* were made of rawhide.
2. A peculiar dialect or manner of pronunciation; specifically, the Irish pronunciation of English.
3. [*pl.*] Breeches. [Obs.]

Irish Brogues.

broid, *v.t.* To braid. [Obs.]

broid′ēr, *v.t.* [ME. *broiden*, *brouden*; Fr. *broder*, *border*, from *bord*, a border, edge, welt.] Literally, to work on the edge; to embroider.

> A robe, a *broidered* coat, and a girdle.
> —Ex. xxviii. 4.

broid′ēr-ēr, *n.* One who embroiders. [Rare.]

broid′ēr-y, *n.* [ME. *broiderie*; OFr. *broderie*, from *broder*, *border*, to border, edge.] Embroidery; ornamental needlework wrought upon cloth.

broil, *n.* [Fr. *brouiller*, to mix, confuse, quarrel; LL. *brogilus*, *broilus*, a thicket, wood.] A tumult; a noisy quarrel; contention; discord, either between individuals or in the community.

Syn.—Affray, altercation, feud, fray, quarrel, contest, uproar.

broil, *v.t.*; broiled, *pt.*, *pp.*; broiling, *ppr.* [ME. *broilen*; OFr. *bruiller*, to broil, roast; from *bruir*; M.H.G. *brüen*, to scald, burn.] To cook over coals, before the fire; especially upon a gridiron over coals; to cook by direct, intense heat of any kind.

broil, *v.i.* To be subjected to the direct action of heat, like meat over the fire; to be greatly heated, or to perspire with heat.

> Where have you been *broiling?* —Shak.

broil′ēr, *n.* One who excites broils or engages in brawls.

broil′ēr, *n.* 1. One who cooks by broiling.
2. A broiling gridiron.
3. A bird suitable for broiling.

broil′ing, *a.* Extremely hot.

broil′ing, *n.* The operation of cooking by direct application of heat.

brō′kāge, *n.* Same as *Brokerage*.

brōke, *v.i.*; broked, *pt.*, *pp.*; broking, *ppr.* To transact business for another in trade; to act as agent in buying and selling, and other commercial business; to transact business through an agent. [Rare.]

brōke, *v.*, past tense of *break*.

brōke, *a.* Broken; bankrupt; without money or resources. [Colloq.]

To go broke; to lose one's money or estate; to exhaust one's resources; to become bankrupt. [Colloq.]

brō′ken, *a.* [Pp. of *break*; ME. *broken*; AS. *brocen*, from *brecan*, to break.]
1. Parted by violence into two or more pieces or fragments; as, a *broken* beam; a *broken* cable; a *broken* dish.
2. Uneven; rough; as, a *broken* surface; opened up with the plow; as, *broken* ground.
3. Intersected with hills and valleys; as, *broken* country.
4. Uttered disjointedly; ejaculated; as, *broken* speech caused by emotion; *broken* words at parting.
5. Not fluent; with foreign accent; as, *broken* English.
6. Interrupted; incomplete; as, *broken* sleep.
7. Violated; unfulfilled; as, *broken* laws; *broken* promises.
8. Unsettled; as, *broken* weather.
9. Ruined in resources, estate, or fortune; as, a *broken* bank.
10. Weakened; enfeebled; made infirm; as, *broken* health; a *broken* constitution.
11. Crushed; humbled; as, a *broken* spirit.
12. Subdued; tamed; trained; as, a *broken* colt.
13. In music, arranged for several instruments, or in parts.
14. In painting, applied to a tone or tint produced by unblended primary colors or harmonious degrees of those colors.
15. In entomology, abruptly bent at an angle; as, *broken* antennæ.
16. Fractional; not integral; as, *broken* numbers.

Broken breast; abscess of the glands of the breast, causing a breaking down of the tissue.

Broken meat; fragments of food; broken victuals.

Broken wind; a disease in horses, commonly called *heaves*.

brō′ken-backed, *a.* 1. Having a broken back.
2. In nautical language, hogged. A *broken-backed* ship is one which is so weakened in her frame as to droop at each end.

brō′ken-down, *a.* Worn out; disintegrated; disheartened; broken in health or spirit.

brō′ken-heärt″ed, *a.* Having the spirits depressed or crushed by grief or despair.

brō′ken-ly, *adv.* In a broken, interrupted manner; without a regular series.

brō′ken-ness, *n.* 1. The state of being broken; unevenness.
2. Abject misery; as, *brokenness* of heart.

brō′ken-wind″ed, *a.* Having short breath, as a horse.

brō′kēr, *n.* [ME. *broker*, *brokour*, from AS. *brucan*, to use, possess, enjoy.]
1. An agent or negotiator who is employed on a commission basis.
2. One who deals in money, notes, bills of exchange, etc.; a money-lender; a pawnbroker.
3. One who deals in old household goods. [Eng.]

Broker's note; a voucher and memorandum of particulars of a contract existing between a broker and his principal; also, a note that has been bought and sold.

Curbstone broker or *street broker*; a broker, not a member of an exchange, who transacts his business on the street or by calling at various offices.

Exchange broker; one who makes a specialty of dealing in uncurrent money or in exchanges relating to money.

Insurance broker; one whose business is to write insurance.

Ship broker; one who buys and sells ships and procures cargoes, etc., for others.

brō′kēr-āge, *n.* 1. The business or employment of a broker.
2. The fee, reward, or commission given or charged for transacting business as a broker.

brō′kēr-ly, *a.* Mean; servile. [Obs.]

brō′kēr-y, *n.* The business of a broker. [Obs.]

brō′king, *n.* The business or occupation of a broker.

brō′mȧ, *n.* [Gr. *broma*, food, from *bibrōskein*, to eat.]
1. In medicine, aliment; solid food.
2. A preparation made from cacao seeds or beans; used in making a beverage.

brō′măl, *n.* [*Brom*ine and *al*cohol.] An oily, colorless fluid obtained by the action of bromine on alcohol.

brō′māte, *n.* A bromic-acid salt.

brō′māte, *v.t.*; bromated, *pt.*, *pp.*; bromating, *ppr.* To impregnate or saturate with bromine; to brominate.

brō-mȧ-tog′rȧ-phy, *n.* [Gr. *broma* (*-atos*), food, and *-graphia*, from *graphein*, to write.] The subject of foods treated scientifically; bromatology.

brō-mȧ-tol′ō-ġist, *n.* An expert in bromatology.

brō-mȧ-tol′ō-ġy, *n.* [Gr. *broma* (*-atos*), food, and *-logia*, from *legein*, to speak.] The science which treats of alimentation; bromatography.

brōme, *n.* Same as *Bromine*.

brōme′-grȧss, *n.* A name common to different species of coarse forage grass belonging to the genus *Bromus*.

Brō-mē′li-ȧ, *n.* [Named after Olaf *Bromel*, Swedish botanist.] A genus of tropical American plants, including the wild pineapple, *Bromelia Pinguin*, belonging to the order *Bromeliaceæ*.

Brō-mē-li-ā′cē-æ, *n.pl.* A natural order of plants remarkable for the hardness and dryness of their gray foliage. They abound in tropical America, commonly growing on trees or rocks.

brō-mē-li-ā′ceous, *a.* Belonging to or resembling the *Bromeliaceæ*.

brō′mē-lin, *n.* A digestive ferment present in the juice of the pineapple.

brō′miç, *a.* Pertaining to bromine; having bromine in its composition.

Bromic acid; a compound of oxygen, bromine, and hydrogen.

brō′mide (*or* -mīd), **brō′mid**, *n.* A compound formed by the union of bromine with another element or an organic radical.

Bromide paper; a paper sensitized with bromide of silver, used in printing photographs.

brō-mi-drō′sis, *n.* [L., from Gr. *brōmos*, a stench, and *hidrōs*, sweat.] A disease of the sweat glands, attended by an offensive odor; osmidrosis.

brō′mi-nāte, *v.t.* Same as *Bromate*.

brō′mine, *n.* [L. *brominium*, from Gr. *brōmos*, stench.] A nonmetallic element, found in sea-water and in saline springs. It is one of the halogens and, in combination with a metal, forms a salt. Its color is deep red, or reddish-brown, and its odor very offensive.

brō′mism, brō′min-ism, *n.* A disorder of body and mind produced by the excessive use of bromine or bromides.

brō′mīte, *n.* Same as *Bromyrite*.

brō′mīze, *v.t.*; bromized, *pt.*, *pp.*; bromizing, *ppr.* To treat or impregnate with bromine or a bromide, as chemicals and plates used in photography.

brom′līte, *n.* [From *Bromley* Hill, Alston, Eng.] A carbonate of barium and calcium occurring in white, gray, and pink crystals; also called *alstonite*.

brō′mō-. A combining form used in names of chemical compounds in which bromine is a principal ingredient.

brō′mō-fọrm, *n.* A liquid similar to chloroform and producing similar effects, made by bromine and caustic potash acting upon wood-spirits or alcohol.

brō-mō-ġel′ȧ-tin, *n.* [*Bromo-*, and Fr. *gelatine*, from L. *gelare*, to congeal.] An emulsion formed of bromides, silver nitrate, and gelatin, used for preparing photographic dry plates.

brō-mog′rȧ-phy, *n.* See *Bromatography*.

brōm′ū-ret, *n.* An obsolete form of *bromide*.

Brō′mus, *n.* [L., from Gr. *bromos*, oats.] A genus of coarse grasses similar to oats; the brome-grasses.

brōm′y-rīte, brō′mīte, *n.* [*Bromine*, from Gr. *bromos*, a stench, and *argyros*, silver.] A rare native silver bromide, of a yellowish-green color.

broṅ′chī, *n.*, pl. of *bronchus*.

broṅ′chi-ȧ, *n.pl.* [LL., from Gr. *bronchia*, the bronchial tubes.] The subdivisions or ramifications of the trachea in the lungs.

broṅ′chi-ăl, *a.* Belonging to the bronchia.

Bronchial arteries; branches from the superior part of the descending aorta, accompanying the bronchia, and which supply the lung substance with blood.

Bronchial glands; lymphatic glands, lying along the bronchia, whose uses are unknown.

Bronchial membrane; the mucous membrane which lines the bronchia.

Bronchial tubes; the minute ramifications of the bronchia, terminating in the bronchial cells, or air-cells of the lungs.

broṅ′chiç, *a.* Same as *Bronchial*.

broṅ′chi-ōle, *n.* A very small bronchial tube.

broṅ-chit′iç, *a.* Relating to bronchitis.

broṅ-chī′tis, *n.* [Gr. *bronchia*, the bronchia, and *-itis*.] An inflammation of any part of the bronchial membrane.

broṅ′chō, *n.* See *Bronco*.

broṅ′chō-. A combining form from Gr. *bronchos*, the windpipe, and used in medicine and anatomy to designate relation to the bronchi; as, *broncho*-pneumonia.

broṅ′chō-cēle, *n.* [Gr. *bronchokēlē*; *bronchos*, the windpipe, and *kēlē*, a tumor.] An enlarged thyroid gland; a tumor on the fore part of the neck; goiter.

broṅ-choph′ō-ny (-kof′), *n.* [*Broncho-*, and Gr. *phōnē*, voice.] The sound of the voice as heard through the stethoscope applied over a healthy bronchus, an indication of disease if heard elsewhere.

broṅ″chō-pneū-mō′ni-ȧ, *n.* [*Broncho-*, and Gr. *pneumonia*, from *pneumōn*, pl. *pneumones*, the lungs.] Bronchitis accompanied by inflammation of the lungs; catarrhal pneumonia.

broṅ′chō-tōme, *n.* [*Broncho-*, and Gr. *tomos*,

from *temnein*, to cut.] A surgical instrument used for making an incision in the bronchial tubes.

bron-chot'ō-my, *n.* [*Broncho-*, and Gr. *tomia*, from *temnein*, to cut.] An incision into the windpipe or larynx, between the rings; called also *tracheotomy*, or *laryngotomy*.

bron'chus, *n.*; *pl.* **bron'chī**. [L., from Gr. *bronchos*, the windpipe.] One of the two primary branches of the windpipe.

bron'có, bron'chō, *n.* [Sp. *bronco*, rough, rude, crabbed, morose.] A small horse, broken or unbroken, native to the plains of the United States and Mexico; a mustang.

brond, *n.* A sword; a brand. [Obs.]

bron'tō-. A combining form from Gr. *brontē*, thunder. In paleontology, it usually denotes hugeness.

bron'tō-graph, *n.* [*Bronto-*, and Gr. *graphein*, to write.] An instrument that makes a record of thunderstorms; also, the record made.

bron'tō-lith, bron'tō-līte, *n.* [*Bronto-*, and Gr. *lithos*, a stone.] A meteoric rock or stone; an aerolite; a thunderstone.

bron-tol'ō-gy, *n.* [*Bronto-*, and Gr. *-logia*, from *legein*, to speak.] A discourse or dissertation upon thunder.

bron-tom'e-tēr, *n.* Same as *Brontograph*.

bron-tō-sau'rus, *n.* [*Bronto-*, and Gr. *sauros*, a lizard.] A gigantic lizard, once inhabiting North America, but now only found in fossil form.

Bron-tō-thē'ri-um, *n.* [*Bronto-*, and Gr. *thērion*, a wild beast.] A genus of extinct rhinoceros-like animals that grew to the size of the elephant, and at one time inhabited North America. Their remains are found in the Miocene strata.

bron-tō-zō'um, *n.* [*Bronto-*, and Gr. *zōon*, an animal.] A huge, extinct, three-toed animal, the tracks of which are found in Mesozoic sandstone in the Connecticut valley. It is undecided whether it was a reptile or a bird.

bronze, *n.* [Fr. *bronze*; It. *bronzo*; from *bruno*; O.H.G. *brūn*; AS. *brun*, brown.]

1. A compound of copper and tin, to which other metallic substances are sometimes added, especially zinc. It is brittle, hard, and sonorous, and used for statues, bells, and cannon, the proportions of the respective ingredients being varied to meet the particular requirements.

2. A shade of brown; the hue of bronze.

3. A prepared pigment used for the purpose of imitating the typical bronze color; also, various decorative pigments, similar to bronze, having a gold or silver effect; as, aluminium *bronze*, which is compounded of aluminium and copper and is of a pale gold color; *phosphor bronze* and *silicium bronze*, tenacious alloys formed by adding phosphorus and silicon respectively to the ordinary bronze.

4. Among antiquarians, a term applied to figures of men or beasts, urns, or other pieces of sculpture, which the ancients made of bronze; also, any copy of these.

5. Among medalists, any copper medal.

6. Effrontery; boldness; brass.

Bronze age; the prehistoric period which followed the stone age, as evidenced by the discovery of bronze and copper in its geological strata.

bronze, *v.t.*; bronzed, *pt.*, *pp.*; bronzing, *ppr.*

1. To give the color of bronze to, by means of copper dust or leaf fastened on the outside, as gold leaf in gilding.

2. To harden, or make like brass.

3. To make of the color of bronze.

4. To make hard-hearted or unsympathetic; to brazen.

bronze'-liq"uŏr (-lik"ēr), *n.* A solution of chlorid of antimony and sulphate of copper, used for bronzing gun-barrels, etc.

bronze'-pow"dēr, *n.* A metallic powder, mixed with oil-paint, for coloring objects in imitation of bronze. The yellow is composed of pulverized brass and the red of pulverized copper.

bronze'wing, *n.* One of several species of Australian pigeons, chiefly of the genus *Phaps*, distinguished by the bronze color of their plumage.

bronz'ine, *n.* and *a.* I. *n.* A metal treated to look like bronze; an imitation of bronze.

II. *a.* Having the appearance of bronze.

bronz'ing, *n.* 1. The act or art of imparting to any substance the appearance of bronze, by means of copper dust or leaf, or by any other method.

2. Any preparation for giving a bronze color.

bronz'ist, *n.* A collector of or dealer in bronzes; a worker in bronze.

bronz'ite, *n.* A ferriferous variety of enstatite, having nearly the luster of bronze, and allied to hypersthene. It is regarded as a distinct species of the pyroxene family, being a silicate of magnesia and iron.

bronz'y, *a.* Similar to bronze.

brōoch (*or* brōch), *n.* [ME. *broche*, a pin, peg, spit; OFr. *broche*; LL. *brocca*, a spit, sharp stake.]

1. An ornamental pin or clasp used for fastening the dress or merely for display. It is now worn mostly by women, and on the breast; but formerly *brooches* were also worn by men, and on the cap or hat.

> Honor's a good *brooch* to wear in a man's hat at all times. —B. Jonson.

2. In art, a painting of one color only; a monotint.

brōoch, *v.t.* To adorn or furnish with or as with a brooch. [Rare.]

brood, *n.* [ME. *brood*; AS. *brod*; D. *broed*; O.H.G. *bruot*, a brood.]

1. Offspring; progeny; all the young children of one mother; formerly used of human beings, but now more generally used in contempt.

2. A hatch; (a) the young birds hatched at one time; as, a *brood* of chickens or of ducks; (b) the young of bees before they issue from the brood cells; (c) the pupæ of ants.

3. That which is bred; species; that which is produced.

> Libya's *broods* of poison. —Addison.

4. In mining, any heterogeneous mixture found in copper and tin ores.

brood, *v.i.*; brooded, *pt.*, *pp.*; brooding, *ppr.*

1. To sit on and cover eggs, for the purpose of warming and hatching them, or as a hen over her chickens, to warm and protect them.

2. To sit on or spread over anything; as, darkness is *brooding* over the vast abyss.

3. To remain a long time in anxiety or solicitous thought; to have the mind uninterruptedly dwell a long time on a subject; with *on* or *over*; as, to *brood over* one's wrongs.

brood, *v.t.* 1. To sit over, cover, and cherish; as, a hen *broods* her chickens.

2. To cherish. [Rare.]

3. To meditate upon moodily.

> You'll *brood* your sorrows on a throne. —Dryded.

brood, *a.* 1. Having young; kept for breeding; as, a *brood*-mare.

2. Having a tendency to sit, or sitting, on eggs; as, a *brood* hen.

brood'-bud, *n.* 1. In botany, same as *bulbil*.

2. A soredium.

brood'ēr, *n.* A covered apparatus or structure, artificially heated, for protecting chicks reared without a hen.

brood'-gem"ma, *n.* In botany, a gemma or leaf-bud. [See *Gemma*.]

brood'i-ness, *n.* The state or quality of being broody.

brood'ing, *a.* 1. Warming.

> The *brooding* heat. —Tennyson.

2. Deeply thoughtful; pondering; regardful; as, *brooding* eyes; a *brooding* look.

3. Subjective; dwelling upon; as, a *brooding* spirit.

brood'ing-ly, *adv.* In a brooding manner.

brood'-māre, *n.* A mare kept for breeding purposes.

brood'-pouch, *n.* A pouch or sac in which eggs are carried during the hatching process, as in many species of crustaceans.

brood'y, *a.* Having an inclination to brood; inclined to sit, as a hen, on eggs.

brook, *n.* [ME. *brook*, *brok*; AS. *broc*, a stream; D. *brock*; LG. *brook*, a marsh; G. *bruch*, a marsh; from the root to break, in the sense of a stream bursting forth.] A small natural stream of water, or a current flowing from a spring or fountain less than a river.

brook, *v.t.*; brooked (brookt), *pt.*, *pp.*; brooking, *ppr.* [ME. *brook*, *brok*; AS. *brucan*, to use, enjoy, as food; LG. *bruken*, to use; O.H.G. *bruhhan*, to use, need; Goth. *brukjan*; Sans. root *bhuj*, to enjoy, especially food.]

1. To bear; to endure; to tolerate; as, young men cannot *brook* restraint.

2. To deserve or merit; to earn. [Obs.]

3. To enjoy; to be in possession of. [Obs.]

brook'ite, *n.* [Named after H. J. *Brooke*, an English mineralogist.] A yellowish or reddish-brown mineral whose chief constituent is titanic oxid. It crystallizes in the orthorhombic system.

brook'let, *n.* A small brook.

brook'lime, *n.* A plant (*Veronica Beccabunga*) with blue flowers in loose lateral spikes; also, the European speedwell, the water speedwell or lesser *brooklime*, and the American *brooklime* (*Veronica Americana*).

brook'-mint, *n.* The water-mint, *Mentha aquatica*.

brook'side, *n.* The side or bank of a brook.

brook'-trout, *n.* The common speckled trout found in the rivers of eastern North America.

brook'weed, *n.* A herb, *Samolus valerandi*, growing in marshy ground, bearing a small white flower; called also the *water pimpernel*.

brook'y, *a.* Abounding with brooks.

broom, *n.* [AS. *brōm*; LG. *brām*, broom; D. *brem*, broom, furze; closely allied to *bramble*, both being, according to Max Müller, from same root as Sans. *bhram*, to whirl, to be confused.]

1. The popular name of various plants. The common broom (*Cytisus scoparius*) is a leguminous shrub growing abundantly on sandy pastures and heaths in Britain and throughout Europe. Its twigs when bound together are suitable for making *brooms*. It is distinguished by having large, yellow flowers, leaves in threes, and single, and the branches angular.

2. A besom, or brush with a long handle, for sweeping floors, etc., so called because formerly made of the twigs of the broom-plant. *Brooms* are now made chiefly of broom-corn and of some species of wood splintered. A *broom* at the masthead of a vessel indicates that she is for sale, probably from the old custom of displaying boughs at shops and taverns.

Butcher's broom; a shrub, *Ruscus aculeatus*, which receives its name from the fact that it is commonly used by butchers to clean their blocks.

Spanish broom; see under *Spanish*.

broom, *v.t.*; broomed, *pt.*, *pp.*; brooming, *ppr.* To sweep or remove with a broom.

broom, *v.t.* Same as *Bream*.

broom'-corn, *n.* *Sorghum saccharatum*, a variety of corn native to India, with a jointed stem like a reed or the stem of maize, rising to the height of eight or ten feet, bearing panicles of which brooms are made.

broom'-grass, *n.* Same as (a) *Broom-sedge*; (b) *Brome-grass*.

broom'-rāpe, *n.* A parasitic plant of the genus *Orobanche*. The term is also applied to various other plants allied to this genus, as *Aphyllon uniflorum*.

broom'-sedge (-sej), *n.* Any one of several species of grass of the genus *Andropogon*, as *Andropogon scoparius*.

broom'staff, *n.* A broomstick. [Obs.]

broom'stick, *n.* The handle of a broom.

broom'-tree, *n.* A shrub of Jamaica, *Baccharis scoparia*, having thickly clustered branches almost devoid of leaves.

broom'y, *a.* Pertaining to or resembling a broom; covered with broom; as, *broomy* land.

brōse, *n.* [Scot.] A thick porridge made by mixing boiling liquid with meal; called water *brose*, milk *brose*, chicken *brose*, beef *brose*, etc., according to the kind of liquid used.

brot'an, *n.* *Artemisia abrotanum*, a variety of wormwood. [See *Southernwood*.]

brot'á-ny, *n.* Brotan.

brot'el, *a.* Brittle. [Obs.]

brot'el-ness, *n.* Brittleness. [Obs.]

broth, *n.* [AS. *broth*; Ice. *brodh*; O.H.G. *brot*, *brod*, broth.] Fluid food; a thin soup in which meat, and usually vegetables, are boiled and macerated; as, beef *broth*.

broth'el, *n.* [ME. *brothel*, *brethel*, a prostitute, worthless fellow; AS. *breothan*, to ruin, frustrate.] A house of lewdness; a house appropriated to the purposes of prostitution; a bawdy-house; a stew.

broth'el-ēr, *n.* One who frequents brothels.

broth'el-ry, *n.* Lewdness; obscenity; a brothel.

brŏth'ēr, *n.*; *pl.* **brŏth'ērs** or **breth'ren**. [ME. *brother*; AS. *brothor*, *brother*, brother; D. *broeder*; G. *bruder*; Ice. *brodhir*; Sw. *broder*; Goth. *brothar*; L. *frater*; Gr. *phratēr*; Sans. *bhrātar*, brother.]

1. A human male in his relation to another person born of the same father and mother. He is a *half-brother*, or *brother* of the half-blood, if there is but one parent in common.

2. Any male person closely united to another by some common interest, as of occupation, class, profession, membership in a lodge or society, manner of living, etc.; an associate; more generally, a fellow-creature; as, a band of *brothers*; a *brother* in distress.

3. One who resembles another in manners or disposition; that which possesses qualities characteristic of anything of the same denomination.

> He also that is slothful in his work is *brother* to him that is a great waster. —Prov. xviii. 9.

In Scripture, the term *brother* is applied to a kinsman by blood more remote than a son of the same parents; as in the case of Abraham and Lot, Jacob and Laban.

Brother-german; a brother by the father's and mother's side; a full brother.

Brother Jonathan; an appellation humorously, but generally respectfully, applied to the citizens of the United States collectively, or the government; probably originating from Washington's allusions to Jonathan Trumbull, governor of Connecticut, the most generous financial supporter of the government in the early years of its existence.

Christian Brothers; in the Roman Catholic church, a well-known order devoted to education; also known as *Brothers of the Christian Schools*.

brŏth'ēr, *v.t.* To make a brother of; to designate as a brother; to admit to brotherhood.

brŏth'ẽr-hood, *n.* 1. The state or quality of being a brother or brothers.
2. An association of men for any purpose, as a society of monks; a fraternity.
3. A class of men of the same kind, profession, or occupation; as, the legal *brotherhood*; the *brotherhood* of iron-workers.
4. A class of individuals or objects of a like kind.

A *brotherhood* of lofty elms.—Wordsworth.

Syn.—Fraternity, association, fellowship, society, sodality.

brŏth'ẽr-in-law, *n.*; *pl.* **brŏth'ẽrs-in-law.** The brother of one's husband or wife; the husband of one's sister; in the United States, the husband of the sister of one's wife.

brŏth'ẽr-less, *a.* Without a brother.

brŏth'ẽr-like, *a.* Characteristic of or befitting a brother.

brŏth'ẽr-li-ness, *n.* The state of being brotherly.

brŏth'ẽr-ly, *a.* Pertaining to brothers; such as is natural for brothers; befitting brothers; kind; affectionate; as, *brotherly* love.
Syn.—Kind, affectionate, fraternal, loving, tender, devoted.

brŏth'ẽr-ly, *adv.* In a brotherly manner.

I speak but *brotherly* of him. —Shak.

brŏth'ẽr-wŏrt, *n.* Wild thyme.

broud, *v.t.* To braid; to embroider. [Obs.]

broud'ed, *a.* Braided. [Obs.]

broud'ing, browd'ing, *n.* Embroidery. [Obs.]

brough (brok *or* bruf), *n.* [Scot.] 1. A ring or halo about a luminous body, as the moon.
2. One of the two circles with a common center about the tee in the Scotch game of curling.
3. Same as *Broch.*

brough'ăm (bro'ăm *or* brōm), *n.* [Named after the first Lord *Brougham.*] A four-wheeled close carriage adapted to either two or four persons, having a curved opening underneath the driver's seat in front, admitting of turning within a narrow space.

brought (brot), *v.,* past tense and past participle of *bring.*

Brous-sō-nē'ti-ȧ (-shi-ȧ), *n.* [From *Broussonet,* a French naturalist.] A genus of trees of the nettle family, including the paper-mulberry.

brow, *n.* [ME. *browe, bruwe;* AS. *bru,* brow, *brǣw, breaw,* the eyelid; G. *braue,* the eyebrow; Ice. *bra;* Sans. *bhru,* the eyebrow.]
1. The prominent ridge over the eye, forming an arch above the orbit.
2. The hair that covers the *brow,* forming an arch, called the *eyebrow.*
3. The forehead; hence, the general air of the countenance; as, his *brow* was sad.
4. The edge of a steep place, as of a precipice; as, the *brow* of a hill.
To knit the brow; to frown.

brow, *v.t.* To bound; to limit; to form the edge or border of. [Rare.]

brow'bēat, *v.t.*; browbeat, *pt.*; browbeaten, *pp.*; browbeating, *ppr.* To subdue or silence with stern looks, or arrogant speech; to bear down by impudent treatment; to bully; as, to *browbeat* a witness.

brow'bēat"ẽr, *n.* One who browbeats.

brow'bēat"ing, *n.* A subduing by overbearing speech or manners.

brow'bound, *a.* Crowned; having the head encircled as with a diadem. [Poet.]

browed, *a.* Possessing a brow (of a peculiar kind); as, low-*browed*; dark-*browed.*

browd'ing, *n.* See *Brouding.*

brow'less, *a.* Without shame. [Rare.]

brown, *a.* [ME *brown, brun;* AS. *brun;* O.H.G. *brun;* Ice. *brunn;* Sw *brun;* Dan. *brun;* Lith. *brunas;* Sans *bhru,* brown.] Dusky; of a dark or dusky color, inclining to redness.
Brown coal; see *Lignite.*
Brown hematite; see *Limonite.*
Brown paper; coarse, dark wrapping paper, made of unbleached stock.
Brown study; a condition of deep concentration of the mind; abstraction; reverie.
Brown thrush; the brown thrasher, *Harporhynchus rufus,* a common songster of America related to the mocking-bird.
To do up brown; to accomplish in a thorough manner.

brown, *n.* A dark or dusky color obtained by mixing black, red, and yellow.

brown, *v.t.*; browned, *pt., pp.*; browning, *ppr.* 1. To make brown or dusky.
2. To give a bright brown color, as to articles of iron, such as gun-barrels, by forming a thin, uniform coat of oxid on their surface.
3. To render brown by subjecting to heat, either natural or artificial; as, to *brown* bread; to *brown* the skin.

brown, *v.i.* To turn brown, as bread in the oven.

brown'back, *n.* Same as *Dowitcher.*

brown'-bess, *n.* A smoothbore, bronzed flintlock musket, formerly the regulation arm of the British service.

brown'bill, *n.* A kind of halbert formerly used by the English foot-soldiers.

Brown'i-ăn, *a.* Relating to Dr. Robert Brown (1757-1831) or to his demonstration of the rapid oscillation of minute particles of certain substances, as carmine, when suspended in water; as, the *Brownian* movement.

brown'ie, *n.* [So called from its supposed color.] In Scottish superstition, a good-natured sprite, who was supposed to perform important services about the house by night, such as thrashing, churning, etc.

brown'ing, *n.* 1. The act or operation of giving a brown color to articles of iron, as gun-barrels, etc.
2. In masonry, a coat of brown mortar forming the foundation for the last coat of plaster.
3. A preparation of sugar, port wine, spices, etc., for coloring and flavoring meat and made dishes.

brown'ish, *a.* Somewhat brown; inclined to brown.

Brown'ism, *n.* 1. The doctrines or religious creed of the Brownists, or followers of Robert Brown, a Puritan dissenter, who, in the sixteenth century, maintained that any body of professing Christians, united under one pastor, or communing together, constituted a church independent of any other. The Independent or Congregational sect of English dissenters was developed from *Brownism.*
2. The Brunonian theory of medicine.

Brown'ist, *n.* A follower of Robert Brown. [See *Brownism.*]

brown'ness, *n.* The quality of being brown.

brown'-spär, *n.* A sparry or crystallized variety of dolomite, colored a reddish-brown from the presence of a small portion of oxid of iron and manganese.

brown'stōne, *n.* A brownish-red variety of sandstone extensively used in modern building.

brown'-stout, *n.* A superior kind of porter.

brown'wŏrt, *n.* The *Scrophularia vernalis,* or yellow figwort, with brown stalks.

brown'y, *a.* Brown or brownish; as, *browny* locks. [Obs.]

brow'pōst, *n.* A crossbeam.

browse, *v.t.*; browsed, *pt., pp.*; browsing, *ppr.* [OFr. *brouster,* to browse, from *broust,* a sprout, shoot.]
1. To feed on, as the ends or branches of trees and shrubs, or the young shoots; said of cattle, deer, and some other animals.
2. To pasture on; to nibble off; to graze on.

browse, *v.i.* 1. To feed on the tender branches or shoots of shrubs and trees, as cattle, sheep, etc.
2. To nibble; to graze.

browse, *n.* [OFr. *broust,* a bud, shoot; M.H.G. *broz,* a bud.] The tender branches or twigs of trees and shrubs, fit for the food of cattle and other animals.

browse, *n.* [Origin unknown.] An imperfectly smelted mass of metallic ore, slag, etc.

brows'ẽr, *n.* Any animal that browses or feeds on green vegetation.

browse'wood, *n.* Shrubs and bushes upon which animals browse. [Rare.]

brows'ing, *n.* 1. Tender green growths on which animals browse.
2. A place where such growths abound.

brow'spot, *n.* The interocular gland of a toad or frog; a round organ between the eyes of toads, supposed to give rise to the fiction of their jeweled heads.

brṳ'ang, *n.* [Native name.] The sun-bear of the Malayan archipelago.

Brṳ'chi-dæ, *n.pl.* A family of herbivorous beetles.

Brṳ'chus, *n.* [LL., a field-cricket, from Gr. *brouchos,* a locust without wings.] 1. A genus in entomology typical of *Bruchidæ.*
2. [b—] A weevil-like beetle; a locust without wings.

Bruchus pisi.
(Natural size and magnified.)

brṳ'ci-nȧ, *n.* Same as *Brucine.*

brṳ'cine, brṳ'cin, *n.* [From James *Bruce,* a Scottish traveler.] A vegetable alkaloid of great power, found in the seeds of various species of *Strychnos,* chiefly in the *Nux-vomica.* In its crude state it is found together with strychnine, but is less powerful than that drug.

brṳ'cite, *n.* Native hydrate of magnesium; a white, pearly mineral, having a thin, foliated structure, like talc. It was named in honor of Dr. A. Bruce, of New York. The name *brucite* has also been given, by American mineralogists, to chondrodite. [Rare.]

bruck'eled, *a.* Draggled; grimy. [Obs.]

bruh, *n.* [Native name.] A species of European monkey, the *Rhesus nemestrinus.*

brṳ'in, *n.* [D. *bruin;* O.H.G. *brun,* brown.] A familiar name given to a bear, because of its typical color.

brṳise, *v.t.*; bruised, *pt., pp.*; bruising, *ppr.* [ME. *broosen, brisen,* from AS. *brysan,* to break, bruise; and influenced by OFr. *bruser, bruiser,* to break.]
1. To crush by beating or pounding with an instrument not edged or pointed.
2. To injure by a blow or by pressure without laceration.
Syn.—Break, crush, pound, squeeze.

brṳise, *v.i.* To strike with the fists in boxing or fighting.

brṳise, *n.* A contusion; a hurt upon the flesh of animals, plants, fruit, or other bodies, by a blunt or heavy instrument, or by collision or squeezing.

brṳised, *a.* Crushed; hurt or broken by violent impact.

brṳis'ẽr, *n.* 1. A concave tool for grinding lenses or specula.
2. A pugilist or fighting bully; one who bruises.
3. A machine for crushing or bruising grain, as for fodder.

brṳise'wŏrt, *n.* Any plant whose preparations are considered healing in case of bruises, as soapwort, the comfrey, the daisy, etc.

brṳis'ing, *n.* In popular language, a beating or boxing.

brṳit, *n.* [Fr. *bruit,* noise, uproar, rumor, from *bruire,* rustle, roar.] Report; rumor; fame.

brṳit (*Fr pron.* brwē), *n.* In medicine, an abnormal sound, varying in kind and pathological significance, and made manifest by auscultation.

brṳit, *v.t.*; bruited, *pt., pp.*; bruiting, *ppr.* To make known to the public; to tell abroad.

Brṳ-māire', *n.* [Fr., from L. *bruma,* winter.] The second month in the calendar of the first French republic, being the first month after the autumnal equinox.

brṳ'măl, *a.* [L. *brumalis,* from *bruma,* winter.] Belonging to the winter.

brṳme, *n.* [Fr., mist, fog, from L. *bruma,* winter.] Mist; fog; vapors.

brum'mȧ-ġem, *a.* [From *Birmingham,* formerly *Bromwycham,* Eng., where much cheap jewelry and gilt toys are manufactured.] Showy but worthless; sham; fictitious.

brṳ'mous, *a.* Characterized by fog or mist.

brun, *n.* [Scot.] A brook or small stream. [Rare. See *Burn.*]

brṳ-nette', *n.* [Fr. f. dim. of *brun,* brown.] A girl or woman with dark hair, eyes, and skin.

brṳ-nette', *a.* Characterized by dark hair, eyes, and skin.

brun'iŏn (-yun), *n.* [Fr. *brugnon,* from L. *prunum,* a plum.] A nectarine.

Brṳ-nō'ni-ăn, *a.* Pertaining to any individual by the name of Brown; Brownian.
Brunonian movement; same as *Brownian movement.*
Brunonian theory; a system of medicine proclaimed by Dr. John Brown of Edinburgh (1735-1788), who classified and treated diseases according to his theory as to whether they were caused by too much or too little excitement.

Brṳ-nō'ni-ăn, *n.* 1. An adherent of the Brunonian medical theory.
2. A student or graduate of Brown University.

brunt, *n.* [ME. *brunt, bront,* a shock, impetus, from Ice. *bruna,* to rush.]
1. The heat, or utmost violence, of an onset; the strength or violence of any contention; as, the *brunt* of a battle.
2. The force of a blow; violence; shock of any kind.

brush, *n.* [ME. *brusshe;* OFr. *broche, broce, brosse,* a bush, brushwood; LL. *brustia, bruscia,* from O.H.G. *brusta, burst,* a bristle.]
1. An implement made of animal hairs, bristles, feathers, or vegetable fibers, disposed in various ways to suit particular purposes, usually mounted on a wooden back, or bound in suitable bundles and provided with a handle for manipulation, and used in sweeping over material, either for removing dirt or undesirable matter, or for depositing paint, colors, medicines, or acids.
2. Branches of trees cut off; brushwood.
3. The small trees and shrubs of a wood; or a thicket of small trees; also, a region covered with thickets of shrubs and trees.
4. A skirmish; a slight encounter; also, an assault; a shock, or rude treatment, from collision; similarly, any brief trial of respective merits; a short race or contest.
5. A bushy tail; as, the *brush* of a fox.
6. The performance of brushing; as, giving the hat a *brush*; hence, any light, passing touch, as one vessel grazing another; we had a *brush* as the car went by.
7. In electrical machinery, an attachment made of flexible wires, wire webbing, or plates, used for the machine terminals of a dynamo or motor circuit to supply current to or take it off the commutator.
8. Divergent rays of a brush-like appearance,

(a) from an electrical ball serving as a conductor, or (b) as seen in the polarized light of certain crystals.

brush, *v.t.*; brushed (brusht), *pt., pp.*; brushing, *ppr.* [ME *bruschen*; OFr. *brosser*, to beat the brush for game; from *brosse*, a brush, thicket.]

1. To sweep or rub with a brush; as, to *brush* a hat.

2. To strike as with a brush; to strike lightly, by passing over the surface without injury or impression; as, to *brush* the arm in passing.

3. To paint with a brush.

4. To remove by brushing, usually followed by *off*; as, to *brush off* dust; also, to carry away by an act like that of brushing, or by passing over lightly, as by wind.

To brush aside; to sweep from one's way.

To brush away; to remove or drive away by brushing.

To brush up; to clean up; to make presentable; to furbish.

brush, *v.i.* To move nimbly in haste; to move so lightly as scarcely to be perceived; to move or skim over, with a slight contact, or without much impression; as, to *brush* by.

brush'=bŭrn, *n.* An injury to the flesh similar to a burn or scald, resulting from great friction, as from sliding down a pole, rope, or the like.

brush'ĕr, *n.* One who or that which brushes.

brush'i-ness, *n.* A condition or appearance characteristic of a brush.

brush'ing, *n.* A rubbing or sweeping.

brush'ing, *a.* 1. Brisk; light; as, a *brushing* gallop.

2. Used or made to brush with.

brush'ite, *n.* A colorless, white, or gray monoclinic crystal formed by calcic phosphate; named after George J. Brush, an American mineralogist.

brush'like, *a.* Resembling a brush.

brush'=tŭr"key, *n.* A large bird found in Australia and New Guinea, making its habitat in the brush; several species are known by this name, but it is especially applied to the *Talegalla lathami*.

Brush-turkey (*Talegalla lathami*).

brush'=wheel (-hwēl), *n.* A revolving circular brush used for polishing by silversmiths, lapidaries, turners, etc.; a cogless wheel which, in light machinery, turns a like wheel by the friction of a rubbing surface of bristles, rubber, buff-leather, etc.

brush'wood, *n.* Brush; a thicket or coppice of small trees and shrubs; also, branches of trees cut off.

brush'y, *a.* 1. Resembling a brush; rough; shaggy; having long hair.

2. Characterized by brushwood.

brusk, brusque (brusk), *a.* [Fr. *brusque*, from It. *brusco*, tart, sour, rude.] Lacking polish in social or business intercourse; bluff; blunt; as, he had a *brusk* way of speaking.

brusk'ness, brusque'ness, *n.* Bluntness; the quality of being blunt or plain.

Brus'sels, *n.* A city of Belgium, noted for its manufacturing industries, whence originate the names of a number of manufactures that were first introduced from there and largely produced there.

Brussels carpet; a strong, handsome carpet having a foundation of linen thread and interwoven with looped worsted yarn, the yarn alone showing on the upper surface and forming the pattern.

Brussels ground; the network ground of genuine Brussels lace, always made by hand.

Brussels lace; a delicate and expensive lace, made in several varieties, as Brussels ground, Brussels wire ground, Brussels point. [See *Point-lace*.]

Brussels net; a machine-made imitation of Brussels ground.

Brussels wire ground; a lace ground made of silk, having partly straight and partly arched meshes.

Brussels sprouts; the popular name of a delicate variety of cabbage. They consist of small green heads, each a cabbage in miniature, of about one or two inches in diameter, which sprout forth from an upright stem or stalk.

brus'tle (-sl), *v.i.*; brustled, *pt., pp.*; brustling, *ppr.* [ME. *brustlien*; AS. *brastlian, bærstlian*, to crackle, burst.] To crackle; to make a small, crackling noise; to rustle, as a silk garment; to bristle up, as a bully. [Obs.]

brus'tle, *n.* A bristle. [Obs.]

brut, *v.i.* [Fr. *brouter*, to browse.] To browse. [Obs.]

brut, *n.* Same as *Birt*.

Brū'tà, *n.* Same as *Edentata*.

brū'tăl, *a.* [LL. *brutalis*, from L. *brutus*, heavy, dull, irrational.]

1. Pertaining to a brute; as, *brutal* nature.

2. Savage; cruel; inhuman; brutish; unfeeling, like a brute; merciless; as, *brutal* courage; *brutal* manners.

Syn.—Savage, inhuman, rude, unfeeling, merciless, ruthless, brutish, barbarous, sensual, beastly, ignorant, stolid, dense, cruel, violent, vindictive, bloodthirsty, intemperate.

brū'tăl-ism, *n.* A brutal state or quality; brutality.

brū-tal'i-ty, *n.* 1. Inhumanity; savageness; churlishness; insensibility to pity or shame.

2. An act of brutal character.

brū"tăl-i-zā'tion, *n.* The act or process of making inhuman or brutal.

brū'tăl-ize, *v.t.*; brutalized, *pt., pp.*; brutalizing, *ppr.* 1. To make brutal, churlish, or inhuman; to deaden the humane feelings or sensibilities of.

> All cruel punishments *brutalize* the heart.
> —Z. Swift.

2. To treat with brutality.

brū'tăl-īze, *v.i.* To become brutal, inhuman, or coarse and beastly. [Rare.]

brū'tăl-ly, *adv.* Cruelly; inhumanly; in a coarse, churlish, or brutal manner.

brūte, *a.* [Fr. *brut*, from L. *brutus*, senseless, irrational.]

1. Unconscious; having no life; inanimate in character and origin; as, the *brute* earth.

2. Irrational; senseless; not gifted with reason; as, a *brute* beast.

3. Bestial; resembling the beasts; having the nature or characteristics of beasts; brutal; ferocious; also, gross or carnal; as, *brute* violence.

4. Uncivilized; insensible; as, a *brute* philosopher. [Rare.]

5. Having the animal faculties developed far beyond the human; rough; coarse; unrefined.

brūte, *n.* 1. A beast; any animal destitute of reason; the word comprehends all animals except man, but is applied mostly to the larger quadrupeds.

2. A brutal person; a savage in heart or manners; an inhuman person; also, a sensual person; a low-bred, unfeeling man.

brūte, *v.t.* [Obs.] Same as *Bruit*.

brūte'ly, *adv.* In a rude manner.

brūte'ness, *n.* 1. Brutality. [Obs.]

2. Insensibility.

brū'ti-fȳ, *v.t.*; brutified, *pt., pp.*; brutifying, *ppr.* [Fr. *brutifier*, from L. *brutus*, senseless, irrational, and *-ficare*, from *facere*, to make.] To make a brute of; to make senseless, stupid, or unfeeling.

brū'tish, *a.* Like a brute or beast in qualities and attributes; as, *brutish* men.

Syn.—Savage, ferocious, brutal, gross, carnal, bestial, base, beastly, animal, coarse, sensual, swinish, vile.

brū'tish-ly, *adv.* In the manner of a brute; grossly; irrationally; stupidly; savagely.

brū'tish-ness, *n.* Stupidity; insensibility; brutality; savageness; the qualities of a brute.

brū'tism, *n.* The characteristic qualities or actions of a brute; extreme stupidity, or beastly vulgarity.

Brū'tus, *n.* A style of hair-dressing supposed to be in imitation of Lucius Brutus, and consisting chiefly of a brushing of the hair back from the forehead.

Brȳ-ā'cē-æ, *n.pl.* [L., from Gr. *bryon*, moss, lichen, and *-aceæ*.] The principal family of small cryptograms; the true mosses. It embraces about 150 genera and 3,000 species, among which are practically all the common varieties except the peat-mosses.

brȳ-ā'ceous, *a.* Belonging to the *Bryaceæ*.

Brȳ'ăn-īte, *n.* See *Bible Christians*, under *Bible*.

brȳ-ō-log'ic-ăl, *a.* Relating to bryology.

brȳ-ol'ō-gist, *n.* One who is interested or skilled in bryology.

brȳ-ol'ō-gȳ, *n.* [Gr. *bryon*, moss, lichen, and *-logia*, from *legein*, to speak.] In botany, the study of mosses.

brȳ'ō-nin, *n.* An alkaloid obtained from the root of the white bryony, *Bryonia alba*. It is a yellowish-brown, bitter substance, and is emetic and cathartic.

brȳ'ō-ny, brī'ō-ny, *n.* [L. *bryonia*; Gr. *bryōnia*, from *bryein*, to swell.] A name common to the different species of the genus *Bryonia*. The root of the rough or *white bryony* is a strong, irritating cathartic. The *black bryony*, so called on account of the color of its roots, is a species of the yam family, botanically known as *Tamus communis*.

Brȳ-oph'y-tà, *n.pl.* [L., from Gr. *bryon*, moss, and *phyton*, plant.] In botany, a subdivision of the *Cryptogamia*, or plants which propagate from spores, comprising the mosses, the scale-mosses, and the liverworts.

brȳ'ō-phȳte, *n.* Any member of the *Bryophyta*.

Brȳ-ō-zō'à, *n.pl.* [L., from Gr. *bryon*, moss, and *zōon*, an animal.] In zoölogy, a class of minute mollusks, mostly marine, which propagate by budding; called also the *Polyzoa*.

brȳ-ō-zō'ăn, *a.* and *n.* I. *a.* Pertaining to the *Bryozoa*.

II. *n.* Any member of the *Bryozoa*.

brȳ-ō-zō'um, *n.* An individual of a bryozoan colony.

bū-an-sū'ăh, *n.* The native name for the *Cyon primævus*, the wild dog of northern India; thought to be the prototype of the domestic dog; also, the dhole.

bū'at, *n.* [Scot.] 1. A hand-lantern.

2. The moon.

bū'āze, *n.* The fiber of an African climbing shrub of the milkwort family; also, the native name for the shrub itself.

bub, *n.* Malt liquor that is strong. [Slang.]

bub, *n.* A familiar term of address to a small boy or young brother. [Colloq.]

bub, *v.t.* To throw out in bubbles. [Obs.]

bū'bà-lē, *n.* Same as *Bubalis*.

bū'bà-line, *a.* [L. *bubalinus*, from *bubalus*, the buffalo.] In zoölogy, relating to a buffalo; also, bovine.

Bubaline antelope; same as *Bubalis*.

bū'bà-lis, *n.* [Gr. *boubalis*, the antelope.] A large antelope found in northern Africa.

bub'ble, *n.* [D. *bobbel*; Dan. *boble*; Sw. *bubbla*, a bubble.]

1. A vesicle of water or other fluid inflated with air or gas; as, a soap-*bubble*.

2. A small spherical or spheroidal mass of air or gas contained in a liquid or a transparent solid; as, the *bubbles* in glass or champagne.

3. The act or state of bubbling; also, the sound made by *bubbles*, as in boiling a liquid.

4. Anything that wants firmness or solidity; a vain project; that which is more specious than real. Hence, a false show; a cheat or fraud; similarly, a delusive scheme or speculation; an empty project to raise money on imaginary grounds; as, the South Sea *bubble*.

5. A person deceived by an empty project. [Obs.]

The South Sea bubble; a stock company organized in England by the Earl of Oxford to trade with South America. The shares had an immense sale at greatly inflated values, which caused financial distress throughout England when the company failed in 1720.

Syn.—Trifle, toy, fancy, conceit, vision, dream, froth, trash.

bub'ble, *v.i.*; bubbled, *pt., pp.*; bubbling, *ppr.* 1. To rise in bubbles, as liquors when boiling or agitated; to contain bubbles.

2. To run with a gurgling noise; as, a *bubbling* stream.

3. To warble in singing, as a nightingale.

4. To be in a ferment; to be unable to contain news, excitement, or good spirits; to effervesce; usually followed by *over*; as, she *bubbled over* with joy.

bub'ble, *v.t.* 1. To cause to effervesce; to produce bubbles in.

2. To utter with a bubbling sound.

3. To cheat; to deceive or impose on.

bub'blĕr, *n.* 1. One who cheats.

2. A fish found in the Ohio river and its tributaries; so named because it makes a bubbling noise; called also *drumfish*.

bub'ble=shell, *n.* A univalve sea-shell of the genus *Bulla*; so called from its general resemblance in form to a bubble.

bub'bling=jock, *n.* The wild turkey-cock; it makes a gurgling or gobbling sound; hence, also called the *gobbler*.

bub'bly, *a.* Full of bubbles; bubbling.

bub'by, *n.* 1. A familiar colloquial address to a small boy. [See *Bub*.]

2. A woman's breast. [Vulgar.]

bū'bō, *n.*; *pl.* **bū'bōes**. [L. *bubo*, a swelling in the groin, from Gr. *boubōn*, the groin.] An inflammation, with enlargement, of a lymphatic gland, particularly in the groin.

Bū'bō, *n.* [L., an owl.] A genus of large owls, including the great owl or eagle-owl, the largest of the nocturnal birds, and the horned owl of Virginia; typical of the subfamily *Buboninæ*.

Bubo.
Head of Virginia horned owl.

bū-bon'ic, *a.* In pathology, pertaining to a bubo; accompanied by buboes.

Bubonic plague; an infectious disease of extremely severe nature, characterized by buboes, particularly in the groin, neck, and armpits.

Bū-bō-nī'næ, *n.pl.* [L., from *bubo, bubonis*, and *-inæ*.] A subfamily of *Strigidæ*, of which *Bubo* is the type.

bū-bon'ō-cēle, *n.* [Gr. *boubōnokēlē*; *boubon*, the groin, and *kēlē*, a tumor.] A bubonic tumor in the groin, formed by a prolapsus of the intestines to the groin; called also *inguinal rupture.*

bū'bū-kle, *n.* A red pimple. [Rare.]

bū'bū-lin, *n.* [L. *bubulus*, pertaining to cattle; from *bos, bovis*, an ox.] A chemical reagent obtained from the excrement of cattle; used in calico-printing.

buc'ăn, buc'căn, *n.* [Fr. *boucan*, from a native Carib word.] A gridiron for smoking meat, or a place for drying coffee or cocoa.

buc'ăn, buc'căn, *v.t.* To prepare and smoke (meat), after the manner of the Caribs and bucaneers of the West Indies.

buc-ȧ-neer', buc-cȧ-neer', *n.* [Fr. *boucanier*, a curer of wild meat, a pirate; *boucan*, a place for smoking meat.] Primarily, one who dried and smoked flesh or fish after the manner of the Indians. The name was first given to the French settlers in Haiti or Hispaniola, whose business was to hunt wild cattle and hogs. It was afterward applied to the piratical adventurers, chiefly English and French, who combined to make depredations on the Spaniards in America. It is now applied to any depredating pirate, freebooter or sea-robber. Also spelled *bucanier.*

buc-ȧ-neer', *v.i.*; bucaneered, *pt., pp.*; bucaneering, *ppr.* To serve as a bucaneer; to live as a sea-robber.

buc-ȧ-neer'ish, *a.* Having the attributes of a bucaneer; pertaining to a freebooter or rover of the sea.

bù'cā-rō, *n.* [Sp.] A water-jug of rough, porous earthenware, used in Spain and South America.

buc'căl, *a.* [L. *bucca*, the cheek.] Pertaining to the cheek. The *buccal* glands are the small salivary glands situated on the inside of the cheeks, between the mucous membrane of the mouth and the muscles.

buc'cāte, *a.* [L. *bucca*, the cheek.] In zoölogy, having distended cheeks; as certain flies.

bùc-che'rō, *n.* [It.] An ancient variety of rough earthenware, most frequently found as jugs or bottles, rudely fashioned and of a dark color, without glazing or painting, but often ornamented with figures in relief, representing an early stage of the Etruscan ceramic art.

buc'ci-năl, *a.* [L., a trumpet.] Having a shape or sound like a trumpet.

buc'ci-nā-tŏr, *n.* [L., from *buccinare*, to blow a trumpet; *buccina*, a trumpet.] A muscle of the cheek aiding in mastication; so called from its use in blowing the trumpet.

buc'ci-nīte, *n.* A fossil or petrifaction of the shells called *Buccinum.*

buc'ci-noid, *a.* [L. *buccinum*, shell-fish, from *buccina*, a trumpet, and Gr. *eidos*, form.] Pertaining to or bearing a resemblance to the genus *Buccinum*, a family of marine mollusks.

Buc'ci-num, *n.* [L.] A genus of large univalve mollusks, of which the common whelk is a species.

Buc'cō, *n.* [L. *bucco*, one with distended cheeks, a babbler, blockhead.] A genus of birds of about fifteen species, typical of the family *Bucconidæ*, whose distinguishing feature is a very broad bill, giving the appearance of distended cheeks.

buc-cō-lā'bi-ăl, *a.* Relating to both the cheek and lip; as, the *buccolabial* nerve.

Buc-con'i-dæ, *n.pl.* The puff-birds; a family of picarian birds allied to the jacamars. The group is small and confined to America.

bū-cen'taur, *n.* [Gr. *bous*, ox, and *kentauros*, centaur.]

1. A mythical beast, half ox and half man.
2. [B—] The state barge of Venice.

Bū'cē-ros, *n.* [L., from Gr. *boukerōs*, *boukeraos*, horned like an ox; *bous*, ox, and *keras*, horn.] A genus of birds inhabiting the warmer countries of Africa and Asia. The name *hornbill* is common to the different species. The rhinoceros hornbill, or horned Indian raven, is common in the East Indies.

buch'ōl-zite, *n.* [From *Bucholz*, a German chemist.] A fibrous silicate of alumina, the structure of which sometimes consists of irregular columns. It is of a gray or pale yellow color, and is also called *fibrolite* or *sillimanite.*

bū'chū, *n.* [Native name.] Any one of several species of shrubs or plants found chiefly in Cape Colony, of the genus *Barosma*. The leaves have an aromatic taste and spicy odor and are medicinally used in diseases of the stomach and kidneys.

buck, *n.* [Ir. and Gael. *buac*, cow-dung, used in bleaching, bleaching liquor; Gael. *bo*, a cow.]

1. Lye in which clothes are soaked in bleaching; also, the liquid in which clothes are washed.
2. The clothes soaked or washed in lye. [Obs.]

buck, *v.t.*; bucked (bukt), *pt., pp.*; bucking, *ppr.* [ME. *boucken*; L.G. *büken*; M.H.G. *buchen*; G. *bauchen*; Sw. *byka*, to wash in lye.]

1. To soak, steep, or boil in lye, as in the process of bleaching.
2. To wash or cleanse by beating in water, with a bat, especially on stones in running water.

buck, *v.t.* To break into small bits or pulverize, as ore with a hammer. [Eng. Dial.]

buck, *n.* [ME. *bucke*, *buk*; AS. *bucca*, *buc*, a he-goat; D. *bok*; G. *bock*; Ir. *boc*; W. *bwch*; Sans. *bukka*, a goat.]

Buck of Fallow-deer.

1. The male of the deer, the goat, the sheep, the rabbit, and the hare.
2. A gay, dashing young fellow; a young blood.
3. A full-grown male negro or Indian. [Colloq. U.S.]
4. The mark of a cuckold. [Obs.]

The word *buck* is often used in connection with the names of antelopes; as, bush*buck*, spring-*buck*, etc.

Great buck; a roebuck at least six years old.

Water buck; an antelope of South Africa.

buck, *v.i.* 1. To copulate, as bucks and does.

2. To leap from the ground, as an unruly horse or mule, while keeping the fore legs stiff, the back arched, and the head as low as possible, the object being to throw off a pack or unseat a rider.

buck, *v.t.* 1. To inflict punishment by tying the wrists together, putting the arms over the bended knees, and forcing a stick under the knees and across the elbow joints.

2. To throw or attempt to throw (a rider) by bucking; as, the bronco *bucked* him out of the saddle.

buck, *n.* 1. A sawhorse or framework upon which wood is sawed.

2. The beech-tree.
3. The body or front part of the box of a wagon. [Prov. Eng.]
4. The plunge or leap given by a vicious horse or mule for the purpose of unseating its rider.

buck'=bȧs"ket, *n.* A basket in which clothes are carried to the wash.

buck'=bēan, *n.* See *Bog-bean.*

buck'bōard, *n.* A four-wheeled vehicle in which elastic boards or slats, extending from axle to axle and upon which the seat rests, take the place of the ordinary springs; called also *buck-wagon.*

buck'ẽr, *n.* 1. One who bucks or pulverizes ore.

2. A hammer with a broad face used in bucking ore.
3. A bucking horse or mule.

buck'et, *n.* [ME. *boket*; AS. *buc*, a bucket, water-pot; Ir. *buicead.*]

1. A vessel of wood or other material in which water is dipped or drawn from any source, or which is used for containing or conveying water, or other liquids.
2. One of the V-shaped troughs of a water-wheel.
3. A tub or scoop for hoisting coal, grain, earth, etc.
4. The piston of a lifting-pump, with a valve opening upward.

buck'et, *v.t.*; bucketed, *pt., pp.*; bucketing, *ppr.*

1. To draw, dip, catch, or carry (water, etc.) in a bucket or as in a bucket.
2. To saturate from a bucket.
3. To ride (a horse) furiously or cruelly.

To kick the bucket; to die. [Slang.]

buck'et, *v.i.* To move fast, as the body in the swinging motion incident to rowing or horseback riding.

> He sprang into the saddle, and *bucketed* back at a hand-gallop. —Dickens.

buck'et=en"gine, *n.* A series of buckets running on an endless chain and operated by a waterfall.

buck'et-ful, *n.* As much as a bucket will hold.

buck'et=shop, *n.* An office or exchange where people may gamble on the prevailing prices of stocks, grains, etc., without actually dealing in the commodities or securities. [U. S.]

buck'et-y, *n.* [A corrupted form of *buckwheat.*] Paste used for dressing webs in weaving.

buck'eye, *n.* 1. Any one of several species of American trees and shrubs of the genus *Æsculus*, including the horse-chestnut; as, the Ohio or fetid *buckeye*, *Æsculus glabra.*

2. A native of Ohio. [Colloq.]
3. A small schooner used chiefly for oyster fishing, and peculiar to Chesapeake Bay.
4. A species of butterfly, *Junonia cœnia.*

Buckeye state; Ohio; so named because of the many buckeye-trees growing there.

buck'=eyed (-īd), *a.* A horse-dealer's epithet for horses which have bad or speckled eyes.

buck'=fē"vẽr, *n.* Nervous agitation such as amateur sportsmen experience when suddenly coming upon a deer or other game. [Colloq.]

buck'finch, *n.* The chaffinch.

buck'=flȳ, *n.* A buck-moth.

buck'hōrn, *n.* The prepared horn of the deer; used for cane heads, knife handles, buttons, etc.

buck'hound, *n.* A small hound used in hunting deer.

buck'ie, *n.* A Scotch name for such species of marine shells as the common whelk. [See *Buccinum.*]

buck'ing, *n.* A vice peculiar to the horses of the western American plains, and to mules; as, a bronco addicted to *bucking.*

buck'ing, *n.* 1. The act or process of soaking cloth in lye for bleaching; also, the lye or liquid used.

2. A wash or washing.
3. The act of crushing or pulverizing ores.

buck'ing=ī"ron (-ūrn), *n.* A hammer used in bucking ores.

buck'ing=kiēr, *n.* A large bleaching boiler.

buck'ing=stool, *n.* A washing-block.

buck'ish, *a.* Pertaining to a buck, or gay young fellow; foppish.

buck'jump, *v.i.* Same as *Buck*, v.i., 2.

buck'jump"ẽr, *n.* A horse or mule that bucks.

buc'kle, *n.* [ME. *bocle*, a buckle, boss of a shield; OFr. *bocle*, *bucle*, the boss of a shield, a ring, a buckle; LL. *bucula*, *buccula*, a beaver, a shield; L. *buccula*, a little cheek, a beaver, dim. of *bucca*, a cheek.]

1. A device, usually made of some kind of metal, and consisting of a ring or rim with a chape and tongue, used for fastening harness, belts, or parts of dress together.
2. A curl, or a state of being curled or crisped, as hair.
3. In coats of arms, a token of the surety, faith, and service of the bearer.
4. A distortion; deformity; a bend, as in a beam, or a kink or bulge, as in a metal plate.
5. A contorted expression. [Rare.]

buc'kle, *v.t.*; buckled, *pt., pp.*; buckling, *ppr.* [ME. *buclen*, *boclen*; OFr. *boucler*, to buckle; from *bocle*, *bucle*, the boss of a shield, ring, buckle.]

1. To fasten with a buckle, or buckles.
2. To prepare for action; usually followed by the reflexive pronoun; as, he *buckled himself* to his task.
3. To join in battle. [Obs.]
4. To confine or limit. [Rare.]

> A span *buckles* in his sum of age. —Shak.

buc'kle, *v.i.* 1. To bend; to bow; as, to *buckle* under life.

2. To give way; to yield.
3. To bend out of original form or position, as, a beam *buckles.*

To buckle down; to apply oneself earnestly, as to hard work.

To buckle to; to bend to; to apply with vigor; to engage with zeal.

To buckle with; to encounter with embrace; to join in close combat.

To buckle up; to marry. [Scot.]

buc'klẽr, *n.* [OFr. *bocler*, so named from the *bocle* or boss in its center.]

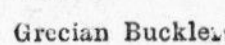

Grecian Buckler.

1. A kind of shield, a piece of defensive armor anciently used in war, and worn on the left arm. *Bucklers* varied considerably in size, form, and materials in different ages and nations. In early times they were of wicker-work, or of wood covered with leather, and ornamented with metal plates, and during the middle ages they were made entirely of metal.

2. A block of wood or piece of steel to fit into the portholes in a vessel's side, or the holes through which the ropes pass, to keep the water out when the vessel pitches or rolls.
3. A shell-like plate found on many ganoid fishes; the anterior segment of the carapace or shell in trilobites.

Blind buckler; a buckler with no opening.

Riding buckler; a buckler with an opening for a rope or cable.

buc'klẽr, *v.t.* To shield; to defend. [Obs.]

buc'klẽr=head"ed (hed"), *a.* Having a head like a buckler.

buc'kling, *n.* A bending or warping, usually from pressure; a tendency to bend or warp.

buc'kling, *a.* Curling; waving, as hair.

buck'=log, *n.* A beech log.

buck'=mack"ẽr-el, *n.* The scad (*Trachurus trachurus*). [Scot.]

buck'=māst, *n.* The nuts of the beech-tree.

buck'=mōth, *n.* A moth appearing in the fall, belonging to the genus *Bombyx.*

buck'rä, *n.* 1. A white man; a superior being; a master.

2. Among the negroes of the Calabar coast, a powerful and superior being.

buck′rȧ, *a.* White; belonging or pertaining to the white man; hence, good and strong.

buck′răm, *n.* [ME. *bokeram, bockrom*; OFr. *boqueran*; LL. *boquerannus*; M.H.G. *buckeram*, buckram; from *boc*, a goat.]

1. A coarse linen cloth, stiffened with glue-size, used in garments to keep them in the form intended, for wrappers to cover cloths and other merchandise, and in bookbinding.

2. The ramson or wild garlic, *Allium ursinum*.

3. Preciseness or stiffness of manner.

buck′răm, *a.* Made of buckram, or resembling buckram; hence, stiff; precise; formal.

buck′răm, *v.t.* To stiffen or strengthen with buckram; hence, figuratively, to make stiff or formal.

buck′=saw, *n.* A framed saw used for sawing wood on a sawhorse.

buck's′=horn, *n.* A species of plantain, *Plantago Coronopus*, having forked or branched leaves; also, *Lobelia coronopifolia*.

buck′shot, *n.* A coarse grade of lead shot used in killing large game.

buck′skin, *n.* 1. The skin of a buck.

2. A soft, strong, yellowish-gray leather, originally made from deerskins, but later chiefly from sheepskins.

3. One clad in *buckskin*, especially a soldier of the American Revolution; a native or pioneer American.

4. [*pl.*] Trousers made of *buckskin*.

buck′stall, *n.* A toil or net to take deer.

Buck′tail, *n.* One of a political faction formed in New York State about 1815, which opposed the administration of Governor DeWitt Clinton. They were given this name because some of the Tammany society, which held the same political views, wore the tails of bucks in their hats.

buck′thorn, *n.* The popular name of any shrub or small tree of the genus *Rhamnus*. The common *buckthorn* grows to the height of twelve or fourteen feet, and bears a black berry.

buck′=tooth, *n.* A tooth that protrudes noticeably.

buck′wheat (-hwēt), *n.* [Scot. from AS. *boc*, beech, and *whæt*, wheat; so called from the resemblance of the fruit to beechnuts.] The name commonly given to a plant, *Fagopyrum esculentum*, or *Polygonum fagopyrum*, natural order *Polygonaceæ*, and also to its seeds. It is a native of central Asia, but is naturalized both in Europe and the United States. It is cultivated as food for horses, cattle, and poultry, but is also much used for human food, especially in the form of flour for griddle-cakes.

False buckwheat; a North American plant that has seeds resembling buckwheat.

buck′wheat=tree, *n.* A small evergreen shrub, *Cliftonia nitida*.

bū-col′iç, bū-col′iç-ăl, *a.* [L. *bucolicus*; Gr. *boukolikos*; from *boukolos*, a herdsman; *bous*, an ox.] Pastoral; relating to country affairs and to a shepherd's life and occupation.

bū-col′iç, *n.* 1. A pastoral poem; usually in the plural; as, the *bucolics* of Theocritus and Virgil.

2. A writer of pastorals. [Rare.]

bū′crāne, *n.* [Fr.] Same as *Bucranium*. [Rare].

bū-crā′ni-um, *n.*; *pl.* **bū-crā′ni-ȧ**. [LL., from Gr. *boukranion*, an ox-head; *bous*, an ox, and *kranion*, head, skull.] A sculptured ornament representing an ox-skull adorned with wreaths or other ornaments, which was employed to decorate the frieze of the entablature in the Ionic and Corinthian orders of architecture.

bud, *n.* [ME. *budde*; D. *bot*, a bud, eye, shoot; OFr. *boton*, a bud, button.]

1. A shoot of a plant; a small protuberance containing the rudiments of a flower; a receptacle of the leaves of plants or of a flower, which will unfold in summer, and which is covered with scales to defend the inclosed rudiments from harm. *Buds* are of three kinds: those containing the flower, the leaves, and both flower and leaves.

2. An unexpanded flower; as, the *bud* of a rose.

3. A small protuberance, either attached or free, on low types of vegetables and animals, that expands into a new organism.

4. An undeveloped thing or person; as, a *bud* of a horn; a *bud* of a girl.

bud, *v.i.*; budded, *pt., pp.*; budding, *ppr.* [ME. *budden*; D. *botten*, from *bot*, a bud, eye, shoot.]

1. To put forth or produce buds.

2. To be in the condition of a bud; to sprout; to begin to grow or to issue from a stock in the manner of a bud, as a horn.

3. Figuratively, to be young and undeveloped, as a bud, or a young girl.

Syn.—Germinate, sprout, shoot.

bud, *v.t.* To ingraft, as a plant; to insert the bud of a plant in (another plant or tree).

Bụd′dhȧ (-dȧ), *n.* [Sans., the enlightened, wise, sage, from *budh*, to know.] The deity of Buddhism: the great teacher and reformer; the perfectly enlightened one, the apotheosis of self-abnegation.

Bụd′dhism, *n.* A system of religion in eastern Asia, embraced by more than one-third of the human race. It teaches that life on earth can never be anything but a mixed round of cares, fleeting joys, and pain, and that complete forgetfulness of self is the only cure; the transmigration of souls from lower to higher and back and forth is part of the belief. It also declares that at distant intervals, a deity, called Buddha, appears to rescue the world from ignorance and decay, then to sink into a state of non-existence, or rather, perhaps, of bare existence. This state, called Nirvana, is regarded as the supreme good, and the highest reward of virtue among men. The last Buddha, Gautama Sakyamuni, a prince of the Sakya tribe, became incarnate about 600 years before Christ.

Buddha, from a Burmese Bronze.

Bụd′dhist, *n.* A follower of Buddha or a believer in his doctrine.

Bụd′dhist, *a.* Pertaining to Buddhism, Buddha, or the Buddhists.

Bụd-dhis′tiç, *a.* Same as *Buddhist*.

bud′ding, *n.* 1. Bud production.

2. Asexual reproduction, as when a portion of the parent animal or vegetable develops into a new organism; gemmation.

3. The insertion of a bud of one tree under the bark of another, for propagation; a form of grafting.

Budding.

bud′ding=knife (-nīf), *n.* A knife used by gardeners in budding.

bud′ding-ness, *n.* State of budding.

bud′dle, *n.* In mining, a large, square frame of boards, used in washing stamped ore.

bud′dle, *v.i.*; buddled, *pt., pp.*; buddling, *ppr.* [Origin unknown.] Among miners, to wash ore.

budge (buj), *v.i.* and *v.t.*; budged, *pt., pp.*; budging, *ppr.* [Fr. *bouger*, to stir, move; Pr. *bolegar*; It. *bulicare*, from L. *bullire*, to boil.]

I. *v.i.* To move; to stir; to give way.

II. *v.t.* To cause to move a little; to change the position of.

budġe, *n.* [ME. *bowge*, a bag; OFr. *bouge*, from L. *bulga*, a leather bag.]

1. The dressed skin or fur of lambs, tanned with the wool on, and formerly much used for trimming scholastic habits or gowns.

2. A leather bag. [Obs.]

3. Intoxicating liquor; spirits; booze. [U. S. Slang.]

budġe, *a.* Brisk; stirring; jocund. [Obs.]

budġe, *a.* 1. Trimmed with budge in scholastic fashion; as, *budge* robes.

2. Pompous or stiff.

Budge bachelors; a company of men clothed in long gowns lined with budge fur, the members of which formerly accompanied the lord mayor of London at his inaugural procession.

budġe′=bar″rel, *n.* A kind of powder-barrel, having at one end a leather covering drawn close by strings, like a purse.

budġe′ness, *n.* Sternness; severity. [Obs.]

budġ′ẽr, *n.* One who moves or stirs from his place.

budġe′rō, budġe′rōw, *n.* [Anglo-Ind.] A roomy boat without keel, used by travelers on the Ganges.

budġ′et, *n.* [Fr. *bougette*, dim. of OFr. *bouge*, a bag.]

1. Originally, a pouch or small bag with its contents; hence, a collection or supply; as, a *budget* of news.

2. The annual statement respecting the finances of the British nation, presented by the chancellor of the exchequer in the House of Commons. The term is also applied to annual official financial statements made in other countries.

3. Any detailed report by a treasurer or financial agent.

4. Plan of affairs; arrangement for the day.

To open the budget; to lay before a legislative body the financial estimates and plans of the executive government.

budġ″y, *a.* Consisting of fur. [Obs.]

bud′let, *n.* A little bud springing from a parent bud.

bud′mash, *n.* [Hind. *badm'āsh*; Per. *bad*, evil, and Ar. *m'āsh*, means of living; *'āsh*, to live.] A disreputable character; a worthless fellow. [India.]

buff, *n.* [ME. *buff*, *buffle*; Fr. *buffle*, a buffalo.]

1. Buff-skin; a sort of leather, prepared from the skin of the buffalo, dressed with oil, like chamois; also, the skins of deer, elks, and the like, prepared in the same way. Called also *buff-leather*.

2. A military coat made of buff-skin or similar leather.

3. The color of buff-skin; a light or brownish yellow.

4. In medicine, a yellow, viscid coat, formed on the surface of blood under certain circumstances. [See *Buffy coat*, under *Buffy*.]

5. In the manufacture of cutlery and other metallic goods, a polishing-wheel or stick covered with leather or cloth.

6. The naked skin. [Colloq.]

7. A buffalo. [Obs.]

buff, *a.* 1. Made of buff-skin.

2. Of the color of buff-skin; brownish yellow.

buff, *v.t.*; buffed (buft), *pt., pp.*; buffing, *ppr.* To polish with a buff-stick or -wheel.

buff, *v.t.* To strike. [Obs. See *Buffet*, v.t.]

buff, *n.* A buffet; a push or jolt; now used only in the name of a game for children, blindman's *buff*.

buff, *a.* [Origin unknown.] Steady; firm; as, to stand *buff* against a shock or collision.

bụf′fä, *n.* [It.] The comedy actress in an opera.

bụf′fä, *a.* In music, comic; farcical; as, aria *buffa*; opera *buffa*. [See *Opera bouffe*, under *Opera*.]

buf′fȧ-lō, *n.* [Sp. *bufalo*; It. *bufalo*, *bubalo*; LL. *bufalus*, *buffalus*; L. *bubalus*, the wild ox; Gr. *boubalos*, an African species of antelope; *bous*, an ox.]

1. A species of the bovine genus, the *Bos bubalus*, originally from India, but now found in the warmer countries of the eastern hemisphere. It is larger and not so tractable as the common ox.

1. Head of Indian buffalo (*Bubalus buffelus*). 2. Head of Cape buffalo (*Bubalus caffer*).

2. A species of the same genus (*Bos* or *Bubalus caffer*), found in South Africa and commonly called the Cape *buffalo*; it is savage and of large size.

3. An improper though common name for the bison of North America, formerly found in immense herds on the prairies of western United States, but now almost extinct.

4. A lap-robe; more commonly called a *buffalo-robe*.

5. The buffalo-fish.

buf′fȧ-lō=ber″ry, *n.* A shrub of the upper Missouri valley (*Shepherdia argentea*), bearing sour red berries.

buf′fȧ-lō=bīrd, *n.* The African oxpecker, or any other species of the genus *Sturnopastor*.

buf′fȧ-lō=clō″vẽr, *n.* A kind of clover (*Trifolium reflexum*) found in the old herding grounds of the American bison.

buf′fȧ-lō=cod, *n.* A large marine fish (*Ophiodon elongatus*) esteemed as food on the north Pacific coast; also called *blue cod* and *cultus-cod*.

buf′fȧ-lō=fish, *n.* A fish of the family *Catostomidæ*, found in the Mississippi valley.

buf′fȧ-lō=fly, *n.* A small, biting, two-winged insect, which infests the lower sections of the Mississippi valley, often causing heavy losses among horses and cattle.

buf′fȧ-lō=gnat, *n.* See *Buffalo-fly*.

buf′fȧ-lō=grȧss, *n.* A kind of grass which grows on the prairies east of the Rocky Mountains.

buf′fȧ-lō=nut, *n.* The oily fruit of the *Pyrularia oleifera* of North America; also, the bush itself.

buf′fȧ-lō=pērch, *n.* 1. The fresh-water drum-fish.

2. A buffalo-fish.

buf′fȧ-lō=rōbe, *n.* The skin of the North American bison, prepared with the hair on; formerly, a popular sleigh or carriage rug for winter use.

buf′fel=duck, *n.* See *Buffle-duck*.

buff′ẽr, *n.* 1. A cushion, fender, or apparatus with strong springs, to deaden the concussion between a moving body and one on which it strikes, as at the ends of a railroad-car or the end of a track; sometimes called *buffing apparatus*.

2. Any thing or any one standing between another and a blow, literally or figuratively; as, the major always acted as a good *buffer* between his wrath and the colonel's ire.

3. A wheel for buffing; a buff.

4. One who uses a buff in polishing.

5. A rather dull, but good-tempered person; as, a good old *buffer*. [Colloq.]

buff'ẽr-head (-hed), *n.* The cushion or head of a buffer; the part which receives the shock or concussion, as in railroad-cars.

buf'fet (*or Fr.* boo-fā'), *n.* [Fr. *buffet*, a sideboard, refreshment-room.]

1. A cupboard or set of shelves for plates, glass, and china. It was formerly, and is still in some places, a closet or apartment on one side of a room; but usually it takes the form of a sideboard.

2. A refreshment-room; a railway-station restaurant; a bar or barroom.

3. The part of an organ in which the pipes are placed.

buf'fet, *n.* [OFr. *buffet*, a blow in the face, a pair of bellows; from *buffe*, *bufe*, a blow.]

1. A blow with the hand; a box on the ear or face; a slap; a cuff.

2. A blow of whatever sort, or anything producing an effect like a blow; a stroke of adversity; anything that harasses.

Fortune's *buffets* and rewards. —Shak.

3. A low stool or footstool; a hassock.

buf'fet, *v.t.*; buffeted, *pt.*, *pp.*; buffeting, *ppr.* [From Fr. *buffe*, *bufe*, a blow, a box.]

1. To strike with hand or fist; to box; to beat.

2. To beat against; to struggle through; as, to *buffet* the storm.

buf'fet, *v.i.* 1. To exercise at boxing.

2. To progress by blows.

Strove to *buffet* to land in vain.—Tennyson.

buf'fet-ẽr, *n.* A boxer; one who buffets.

buf'fet-ing, *n.* 1. A striking with the hands.

2. A succession of blows; strife; opposition; adversity.

buf'fin, *n.* A sort of coarse stuff; as, *buffin* gowns. [Obs.]

buf'fing, *n.* 1. In leather manufacturing, the cutting away or trimming of a hide; or, the portion so removed.

2. The process of polishing metal goods, such as cutlery, with a buff.

buff'ing-ap-pa-rā'tus, *n.* A pad protecting a fender. [See *Buffer*.]

buf'fle, *n.* [Fr.] The buffalo. [Obs.]

buf'fle, *v.i.* To puzzle; to be at a loss. [Obs.]

buff'-leath"ẽr, *n.* See *Buff*, n.1.

buf'fle-duck, buf'fel-duck, *n.* The buffle-headed duck (*Anas bucephala*), a bird with a short, blue bill and a head whose apparent size is greatly increased by the fullness of its feathers.

buf'fle-head (-hed), *n.* One who has a large head; a blockhead.

buf'fle-head"ed, *a.* Having a large head, like a buffalo; dull; stupid; foolish. [Obs.]

buf'fle-horn, *n.* A small, rubiaceous South African tree with a strong tough wood.

buf'fō, *n.* [It.] The comic actor in an opera.

buf'font, *n.* [Fr. *bouffant*, ppr. of *bouffer*, to puff out.] A puffed-out, gauzy covering, sometimes made of linen, worn over the breast by women in the eighteenth century.

Buffont.

buf-foon', *n.* [Fr. *bouffon*; It. *buffone*, a jester; *buffa*, a jest, a mocking.]

1. One who tries to amuse others by low tricks and vulgar pleasantries; a droll; a mimic.

2. One who uses indecent raillery.

buf-foon', *a.* Characteristic of a buffoon.

buf-foon', *v.t.* and *v.i.* I. *v.t.* To make ridiculous.

II. *v.i.* To indulge in buffoonery.

buf-foon'ẽr-y, *n.* The arts and practices of a buffoon; low jests; ridiculous pranks; vulgar tricks and postures.

buf-foon'ish, *a.* Like a buffoon; consisting in low jests or gestures.

buf-foon'ism, *n.* The practices of a buffoon.

buf-foon'ly, *a.* Buffoonish. [Rare.]

buff'-stick, *n.* A stick covered with soft material, used in polishing.

buff'-wheel (-hwēl), *n.* A wheel of soft material used in polishing glass and metals.

buf'fy, *a.* 1. Resembling the buff of the blood in color and texture.

2. Relating to the buff of the blood.

Buffy coat; the coagulated fluid of the blood, after the red corpuscles have sunk; especially noticeable in certain diseased conditions.

Bū'fō, *n.* [L. *bufo*, a toad.] A genus of tailless batrachians comprehending the true toads.

bū'fon-ite, *n.* Toadstone, considered as a fossil tooth of the *Anarrhichas* or sea-wolf, formerly much esteemed for its imaginary virtues, and worn in rings. It was named from an opinion that it was found in the head of a toad.

bug, *n.* [ME. *bugge*; W. *bwg*, *bwgan*, a specter, hobgoblin.]

1. An object of terror; a bugbear. [Obs.]

2. An insect of the genus *Cimex*, especially the bedbug. In common language, the name of a vast multitude of insects, which infest houses and plants. In zoölogy, this word is applied to the insects arranged under the genus *Cimex*, of which several hundred species are described. They belong to the order *Hemiptera*, and are furnished with an inflected rostrum or beak, and with antennæ longer than the thorax. The wings are folded together crosswise, the back is flat, the throat margined, and the feet are formed for running. Some species have no wings.

3. One of various coleopterous insects, as the lady*bug* or potato-*bug*; commonly, any of the *Coleoptera*.

4. One of various kinds of *Entomostraca*; or more generally, certain crustaceans; as, the sow*bug* and pill*bug*.

bug-a-boo', *n.* A bugbear.

bug'bāne, *n.* [*Bug*, and ME. *bane*, destruction; AS. *bana*, murderer.] A tall plant, *Cimicifuga Americana*, flowering in long racemes; or any allied genus, as *Cimicifuga fœtida*, efficacious against vermin.

bug'beãr, *n.* [W. *bwg*, *bwgan*, a specter.] Something that causes needless terror.

Syn.—Hobgoblin, goblin, gorgon, ghoul, spirit, spook, specter, ogre, scarecrow.

bug'beãr, *v.t.* To alarm or frighten with idle phantoms. [Rare.]

bug'fish, *n.* The menhaden, an American fish belonging to the herring family.

bug'ga-low, *n.* See *Baggala*.

bug'gẽr, *n.* A sodomite.

bug'gẽr-y, *n.* Sodomy.

bug'gi-ness, *n.* The state of being infested with bugs.

bug'gy, *a.* Abounding with bugs.

bug'gy, *n.*; *pl.* **bug'gies**. [Anglo-Ind., from Hind. *baggi*, *bagghi*, a gig, buggy; *bag*, to move.]

1. A light vehicle, either with or without a top, generally with but one seat, and drawn by one or two horses.

2. In England, a light one-horse, two-wheeled vehicle without a hood.

Buggy cultivator; a riding cultivator.

Buggy plow; a riding or sulky plow.

bū'gle, *n.* [OFr. *bugle*, a wild ox; L. *buculus*, dim. of *bos*, an ox.]

1. A hunting-horn.

2. A wind-instrument consisting of a seamless tube of metal, generally in one coil, ending in a bell, used for sounding military signals; in military bands, etc., now virtually superseded by the cornet.

3. A sort of wild ox. [Obs.]

bū'gle, *n.* [LL. *bugulus*, an ornament; G. *bugel*, a bent piece of metal.] An elongated glass bead, of various colors, though more commonly black.

bū'gle, *a.* Having the color of a glass bugle; jet-black.

bū'gle, *n.* [Fr. *bugle*, from LL. *bugillo*, a plant.] A name common to different species of plants, of the genus *Ajuga*, natives of Europe.

Yellow bugle; the variety *Ajuga Chamæpitys*.

bū'gled, *a.* Ornamented with bugles.

bū'gle-horn, *n.* 1. A musical instrument, the bugle.

2. A drinking-vessel of horn. [Obs.]

bū'glẽr, *n.* One who plays a bugle; specifically, a soldier whose duty is to convey the commands of the officers by sounding a bugle.

bū'gle-weed, *n.* A plant of the mint family, *Lycopus Virginicus*, valued as a remedy for hemoptysis or spitting of blood.

bū'gloss, *n.* [Fr. *buglosse*; L. *buglossa*, *buglossus*; Gr. *buglōssos*, *bugloss*, oxtongue; *bous*, an ox, and *glōssa*, a tongue.] The popular name of a plant, *Anchusa officinalis*, used in dyeing and coloring, and of similar plants of different genera. The small wild *bugloss* is *Asperugo procumbens*, and the viper's-*bugloss*, *Echium vulgare*. The Spanish *bugloss* is the alkanet or oxtongue.

bug'seed, *n.* A low, branching, chenopodiaceous, annual herb, native to north temperate regions. So called from having oval seeds.

bug'wŏrt, *n.* Same as *Bugbane*.

bühl (böl), *n.* [Named after André Charles *Boule*, a celebrated French woodworker.] A name given to light and complicated figures of brass, unburnished gold, etc., set, as ornaments, into surfaces of ebony or other dark wood, or of tortoise-shell. Called also *boule*, *buhlwork*.

buhl'buhl, *n.* Same as *Bulbul*.

bühr'stōne (bũr'-), *n.* See *Burstone*.

build (bild), *v.t.*; built, builded, *pt.*, *pp.*; building, *ppr.* [ME. *bilden*, *bylden*; AS. *byldan*, to build, from *bold*, a house; *buan*, to dwell.]

1. To frame, construct, and raise, as a house, vessel, or wall; to unite into a structure.

2. To raise by art; to frame or shape into a particular form; to fabricate; as, to *build* up a headdress.

3. To raise on a support or foundation; as, to *build* our hopes on air.

4. To increase and strengthen; to cement and knit together; to settle or establish, and preserve; usually followed by *up*; as, to *build up* a reputation.

Syn.—Construct, erect, establish, found, frame.

build (bild), *v.i.* 1. To exercise the art or practise the business of building.

2. To construct, rest, rely, or depend, as on a foundation; as, to *build* on the opinions of others.

build, *n.* Style of construction; general figure; as, a person of large *build*.

build'ẽr, *n.* 1. One who builds; that which builds; specifically, one whose business is the erection or supervision of the erection of buildings, as an overseeing contractor.

2. A creator; as, God the *builder* of the universe.

build'ing, *n.* 1. The act, art or business of constructing, erecting, or establishing.

2. A fabric or edifice constructed; the thing built, as a house, a church, and the like.

Syn.—Edifice, architecture, construction, erection, fabric, structure.

built, *n.* Form; shape; general figure of a structure; as, the *built* of a ship. [Obs.]

built, *a.* 1. Constructed; made; formed; used frequently in compounds; as, strongly *built*; clipper-*built*; union-*built*.

2. Built-up.

built'-up, *a.* Consisting of a number of parts so fitted as to give strength or solidity; as, a *built-up* spar.

buïre (bwēr), *n.* [Fr.] A jug with handle and spout.

buis-son', *n.* [Fr.] A closely-pruned fruit-tree trained on a low stem.

buk'shish, *n.* Same as *Backsheesh*.

bū'lau, *n.* [Native name.] A rat-like insectivorous animal, *Gymnura rafflesi*, resembling a hedgehog, a habitant of the East Indies.

bulb, *n.* [Fr. *bulbe*; L. *bulbus*; Gr. *bolbos*, a bulbous root.]

1. In botany, a scaly body formed on a plant, above or beneath the surface of the ground, emitting roots from its base, and a stem from its center—as in the meadow-lily, onion, tulip, etc.—formed of imbricated scales. A *bulb* is never solid, differentiating from a *corm*.

2. Any protuberance or expansion resembling a *bulb*, especially an expansion at the end of a stalk or long and slender body; as, the *bulb* of a thermometer; the *bulb* of a hair; the *bulb* of the aorta.

Bulb of a hair; the thickened portion at the root of a hair.

Bulb of a tooth; the enlargement of a tooth filling the pulp-cavity.

Bulb of the eye; the ball of the eye.

Bulb of the spinal cord; the medulla oblongata.

bulb, *v.i.* To swell; to be protuberant.

bul-bā'ceous, *a.* Bulbous.

bulb'ăr, *a.* [L. *bulbus*, a bulb.] Pertaining to a bulb; as, in pathology, *bulbar* paralysis, affecting the medulla oblongata.

bulbed, *a.* Round-headed.

bulb'el, bulb'il, *n.* [Dim. from L. *bulbus*, a bulb.] A bulblet; a reproductive secondary bulb.

bul-bif'ẽr-ous, *a.* [L. *bulbus*, a bulb, and *ferre*, to bear.] Producing bulbs; as, *bulbiferous* stems.

bul-bil'lȧ, *n.*; *pl.* **bul-bil'læ**. [From L. *bulbus*, a bulb.] In zoölogy, a hydroid bud capable of reproduction.

bulb'let, *n.* A small bulb formed above ground on some plants, as on the lily or onion.

bul'bōse, *a.* Bulbous.

bul'bō-tū"bẽr, *n.* A corm, as a turnip. [See *Corm*.]

bulb'ous, *a.* [L. *bulbosus*, from *bulbus*, a bulb.]

1. Containing bulbs or a bulb, growing from bulbs.

2. Containing a knob, or protuberant part; swelling out; presenting rounded elevations.

bul'bul, *n.* [Per. *bulbul*, a nightingale.] The Persian nightingale, *Pycnonotus jocosus*, rendered familiar in English poetry by Moore, Byron, and others. The same name is also given in southern and southwestern Asia to sundry other birds.

bul'būle, *n.* [LL. *bulbulus*, dim. of L. *bulbus*, a bulb.] A bulblet, or small bulb.

bul'chin, *n.* [ME. *bulchin*, dim. of *bul*, a bull.] A bull calf; in a personal sense, applied contemptuously. [Obs.]

bulge, *n.* [ME. *bulge*, a swelling, lump; Sw. *bulgja*, to swell; AS. *belgan*, to swell.]

1. The protuberant or most convex portion

of a thing; a part that swells out; as, the *bulge* of a cask; the *bulge* of a shield.

2. In a ship, the *bilge*.

3. The whirling eddy, or swirl, made by salmon in coming to the surface.

To get the bulge on; to get the better of; to obtain an advantage. [Slang.]

bulge, *v.i.*; bulged, *pt., pp.*; bulging, *ppr* 1. To swell out; to be protuberant.

2. To bilge, as a ship.

bulg'ēr, *n.* In golf, a driving club having a convex face.

bul'gy, *a.* Swollen; unduly protuberant; bending or having a tendency to bend outward.

bū-lim'i-à, *n.* [Gr. *boulimia*; *bous*, ox, and *limos*, hunger.] A voracious appetite; a disease in which the patient has an insatiable appetite for food; also written *bulimy*.

Bū-lim'i-dæ, *n.pl.* A group of gasteropods, of which *Bulimus* is the type.

Bū'li-mus, *n.* [L. *bulimus*; Gr. *boulimos*, great hunger; *bous*, ox, and *limos*, hunger, famine.] An extensive genus of pulmoniferous gasteropodous mollusks, allied to the genus *Helix*; the type of *Bulimidæ*. In the tropical forests some of the species are of large size, and their eggs might almost be taken for those of small birds.

bulk, *n.* [ME. *bulke*, *bolke*, a heap; Ice. *bulki*, a cargo of a ship.]

1. Magnitude; dimension; size; as, an ox or ship of great *bulk*.

2. The gross; the main mass; the main fabric; as, the *bulk* of a debt; the *bulk* of a nation.

3. A ship's capacity for the stowage of goods.

4. The body. [Obs.]

A sale by bulk; a sale of goods as they are, without weight or measure.

In bulk; in a mass, or solid state; as, pork *in bulk*, or bulk pork, i.e., pork not cut up.

Laden in bulk; having the cargo loose in the hold.

To break bulk; in seamen's language, to unload.

Syn.—Size, magnitude, greatness, largeness, extent, majority.

bulk, *n.* A part of a building protruding from the rest. [Obs.]

bulk, *v.i.*; bulked (bulkt), *pt., pp.*; bulking, *ppr.* 1. To grow large; to swell.

2. To appear large or important; as, the question *bulked* large in his sight.

bulk'ēr, *n.* A nautical term for one who measures goods for shipment to ascertain the proper freightage.

bulk'head (-hed), *n.* 1. A nautical term for the partition in a vessel that forms a compartment, or a water-tight chamber.

2. A built structure to confine or restrain something pressing from without, as water or earth.

Bulkhead line; a line along a coast marking the limit to which wharves may be built.

bulk'i-ness, *n.* Greatness in bulk, size, or stature.

bulk'y, *a.* Large; of great dimensions.

Syn.—Massive, massy.—*Bulky* refers to prominence or excess of figure or size; *massive* or *massy* designates what is both large and weighty without implying such excess.

bull, *n.* [ME. *bul*, *bole*; G. *bulle*; D. *bul*, a bull.]

1. The male of any bovine quadruped, or of the different species of the genus *Bos*; also, the male of other large animals, particularly the whale.

2. [B—] Taurus, one of the twelve signs of the zodiac.

3. In finance, one who operates in order to effect a rise in the price of stocks or in the quotations on commodities; the opposite of a *bear*.

Bull in a china-shop; one who, from total lack of judgment, commits great havoc, presumably in a delicate situation.

Bull Moose; a member of the Progressive Party, formed under Theodore Roosevelt as leader in 1912.

John Bull; a humorous appellation for the British people.

To take the bull by the horns; to grapple with a difficulty, as to seize a bull.

bull, *n.* [ME. *bulle*; OFr. *bulle*; It. *bulla*; LL. *bulla*, a papal edict; L. *bulla*, a stud, knob, boss.] A letter, edict, or rescript of the pope, containing some decree or decision. If indicating justice, the seal is hung by a hempen cord; if indicating grace, by a silken thread. The leaden seal is impressed on one side with the heads of St. Peter and St. Paul, on the other with the name of the pope and the year of his pontificate.

The Golden Bull; an edict or imperial constitution, made by the Emperor Charles IV. (1356), containing the fundamental law of the old German empire; so called from its golden seal.

bull, *n.* A blunder or contradiction; more exactly, an apparent congruity, but real incongruity, of ideas; an inconsistency.

bull, *v.t.*; bulled, *pt., pp.*; bulling, *ppr.* To buy on a large scale in a determined endeavor to raise market or stock exchange prices in order to sell out at a profit.

To bull the market; to endeavor to raise the price of any marketable commodity.

bull, *v.i.* To show sexual desire, as a cow in heat.

bul'là, *n.*; *pl.* **bul'læ**. [L. *bulla*, bubble.]

1. A bleb; a vesicle, or an elevation of the cuticle containing a transparent watery fluid.

2. In anatomy, the egg-shaped inflated part of the osseous external meatus of the ear. Also called *bulla ossea*.

Leaden Bulla of Pope Alexander IV.

3. A leaden seal for a document; used especially in reference to the round, leaden seal used by the pope and attached to the papal bulls.

4. [B—] A genus of univalvular hard-shelled *Mollusca*.

bul'lāce, *n.* [ME. *bolas*, *bolace*; OFr. *beloce*; Gael. *bulaistear*, a bullace.]

1. The wild plum, a species of *Prunus* (*Prunus insititia*); a native of Asia Minor.

2. A West Indian tree, *Melicocca bijuga*, which bears an egg-shaped fruit of pungent flavor, known as the *bullace-plum*.

3. The American grape of southern United States; also called the *muscadine*.

bul'là-hoo, *n.* Same as *Ballahoo*.

bul-lan'tic, *a.* [LL. *bullans* (-*antis*), ppr. of *bullare*, to attach the seal; *bulla*, a seal.] Designating certain Gothic letters, used in apostolic bulls.

bul'là-ry, *n.* [LL. *bullarium*, from *bulla*, a papal bull.] A collection of papal bulls.

bul'là-ry, *n.* A place for the preparation or boiling of salt; a salt-house; a boilery.

bul'lāte, *a.* [L. *bullatus*, from *bulla*, bubble.] Having elevations like blisters; inflated; puckered. In botany, a *bullate* leaf is one the membranous part of which rises between the veins in elevations like blisters.

bull'=bāit"ing, *n.* An old English sport, now prohibited, of infuriating bulls by setting dogs to attack, worry, and excite them.

bull'=bee, *n.* The bullfly; the gadfly.

bull'=beef, *n.* The flesh of a bull; coarse, sinewy beef. [Colloq.]

bull'beg"gär, *n.* A hobgoblin; a bugbear; something terrible or frightful, especially to children or weak-minded persons.

bull'ber"ry, *n.* The buffalo-berry.

bull'bri"ēr, *n.* A species of greenbrier or smilax, with very stout thorns, growing on the Atlantic coast, from New Jersey to the Gulf of Mexico, and in southern portions of the United States; called also *China brier* and *bamboo brier*.

bull'cŏmb"ēr (-kōm"ēr), *n.* A scaraboid beetle, or one whose antennæ terminate in scales called lamellæ; especially, the English beetle, *Typhœus vulgaris*.

bull'dog, *n.* 1. One of a breed of dogs of remarkable courage, ferocity, and tenacity of grip; so named, probably, from being formerly employed in baiting bulls, or from the size of the head.

2. A refractory material used as a lining for puddling-furnaces and converters; produced by calcining slag from the furnace of a rolling-mill.

3. A short, powerful pistol of large caliber; often called a *bulldog revolver*.

4. A large Australian ant, which is both aggressive and venomous; also called *bull ant*.

bull'dog, *a.* Having the characteristics of a bulldog; as, *bulldog* courage.

Bulldog bat; a bat of the genus *Nyctinomus*; so named because the shape of its face is similar to that of a bulldog.

bull'dōze, *v.t.*; bulldozed, *pt., pp.*; bulldozing, *ppr.* To restrain or coerce by intimidation or violence; originally used in the southern part of the United States in connection with the intimidation of negro voters, said to have been derived from *bull-whack*, the name of a heavy whip used in western Louisiana and Texas to drive stubborn beasts. [Colloq.]

bull'dō-zēr, *n.* One who bulldozes. [Colloq.]

bulled, *a.* Swollen. [Obs.]

bul'len-bul"len, *n.* The native Australian name for the lyre-bird; so named because of its cry.

bul'len=nail, *n.* A short lacquered nail with a large round head, used chiefly by upholsterers.

bul-les'cence, *n.* [L. *bullescens*, from *bulla*, a bubble.] In botany, the state of being bullate.

bul'let, *n.* [Fr. *boulet*, dim. of *boule*, a ball.]

1. A small ball.

2. A projectile, spherical, conical, conoid, or elongated in form, to be discharged from a small firearm. It is usually made of lead.

3. A cannon-ball; a sling missile. [Obs.]

4. A fetlock.

5. In heraldry, a black circle, representing a bullet or cannon-ball.

bul'le-tin, *n.* [Fr. *bulletin*, a ballot, news; It. *bulletino*, *bulleta*, dim. of LL. *bulla*, a papal edict.]

1. A report of a state of facts, issued by authority, for the information of the public, as of military operations, political events, or of the health of some distinguished personage.

2. In a wider sense, any public notice or announcement, especially of news recently received.

3. A publication issued periodically, especially one which chronicles the proceedings of a society.

bul'le-tin=bōard, *n.* A board conspicuously placed on which announcements of news are posted, particularly at newspaper offices, hotels, clubs, telegraph offices, etc.

bul'let=proof, *n.* Any substance or material that is capable of resisting the force of a bullet; something not penetrable by a bullet.

bul'let=proof, *a.* Not susceptible to entrance or injury by a bullet.

bul'let=tree, *n.* Same as *Bully-tree*.

bull'fāced (-fāst), *a.* Having a large, threatening face.

bull'fēast, *n.* A bullfight. [Obs.]

bull'fight, bull'fight"ing (-fit-), *n.* A combat in an arena between men and bulls; a popular sport among the Spaniards, Portuguese, and Latin Americans.

bull'fight"ēr, *n.* One who fights with a bull to furnish sport for spectators; a toreador.

bull'finch, *n.* A European bird allied to the grosbeak, whose breast, cheeks, and throat are of a crimson color. It is popular as a cage-bird.

Bullfinch.

bull'fist, bull'fice, *n.* [*Bull*, and Prov. Eng. *feist*, *foist*, wind from the anus.] A variety of fungus filled with dustlike spores; called also *puffball*.

bull'fly, *n.* A gadfly; a breeze-fly; any large fly troublesome to cattle or horses.

bull'frog, *n.* The *Rana catesbiana*, a large species of frog, found in North America, of a dusky-brown color, mixed with a yellowish-green, and spotted with black. These frogs utter a loud, croaking sound, from which they receive their name.

Bullfrog (*Rana catesbiana*).

bull'head (-hed), *n.* 1. Any one of several varieties of fish having a broad, massive, bull-like head; (a) the American catfish (*Amiurus melas*), found chiefly in the eastern sections of the United States; (b) the miller's-thumb of the United States and England; (c) the sculpin, or cottoid, a river *bullhead* of Great Britain; (d) the kingfish of Florida; (e) the goby of New Zealand, and (f) the Tasmanian shark.

2. A stupid fellow; a blockhead.

3. A small, black water-vermin.

4. The black-bellied plover (*Squatarola helvetica*); sometimes called *beetlehead*; also, the *golden plover*, *Charadrius dominicus*.

Bullhead kelp; in botany, the bladder-kelp, a large seaweed, or wrack.

bull'head"ed (-hed"ed), *a.* Having a head like a bull's; figuratively, headstrong.

bull'ing, *n.* The process of blasting rock by exploding gunpowder or dynamite in its fissures.

bul'lion (-yun), *n.* [OFr. *bouillon*, a stud, boss; LL. *bullio*, *bullionis*, a mass of gold or silver.]

1. Uncoined gold or silver in the mass; the precious metals when smelted and not perfectly refined, or when refined, but in bars, ingots, or in any form uncoined, as in plate.

2. In political economy, gold and silver both coined and uncoined.

3. Coin which is base or uncurrent, and therefore of only metallic value. [Obs.]

bul'lion, *n.* 1. A boss or bright ornament of metal used to decorate bridles, saddles, etc. [Obs.]

2. A thick, heavy fringe, sometimes of gold or silver wire and used for epaulets, etc.

bul'liŏn-ism, *n.* The doctrine that all currency should be metallic, or if paper, at all times convertible into gold or silver.

bul'liŏn-ist, *n.* One who advocates or is a believer in bullionism.

bul'li-rag, *v.t.* Same as *Bullyrag.*

bull'ish, *a.* Of the nature of a bull or laughable blunder.

bull'ish, *a.* 1. Like a bull in nature and characteristics.

2. Having a tendency to rise in price; said of stocks, etc.; as, a *bullish* market.

bull'ist, *n.* A writer of papal bulls. [Rare.]

bul-li'tion (-lish'un), *n.* [Obs.] See *Ebullition.*

bull'-necked (-nekt), *a.* Having a short, thick, coarse neck, resembling that of a bull.

bull'nut, *n.* The mocker-nut, *Carya tomentosa*, a species of hickory.

bul'lŏck, *n.* [ME. *bullok*; AS. *bulluca*, a young bull.]

1. A young bull or a full-grown beef-ox.

2. Any beef-animal fatted for market. [Eng.]

bul'lŏck, *v.t.* To abuse or bully. [Obs.]

bul'lŏck's-eye, *n.* 1. A small, thick glass or skylight, in a covering or roof.

2. A garden plant, *Sempervivum tectorum*, of the houseleek family.

bul'lŏck's-heärt, *n.* The custard-apple, *Anona reticulata.*

bul'lon, *n.* [W. Ind.] The *Scarus croicensis*, or West Indian parrot-fish.

bul'lous, *a.* [L. *bulla*, a bubble, boss.] Characterized by or partaking of the nature of bullæ or blebs; vesicular.

bull'-pŏll, *n.* A kind of hair-grass, *Aira cæspitosa*, with very slender leaves or branches.

bull'pout, *n.* A bullhead, or species of *Amiurus.*

bull'-rōar"ēr, *n.* A rude toy, consisting of a long, narrow piece of wood attached to a string; it produces a roaring noise when whirled in the air; widely used under different names. Among some races, a similar instrument is used in religious rites. Also called *tundun.*

bull's'-eye, *n.* 1. Among seamen, a ring of hard wood, spliced into or seized onto rigging, used in reeving ropes or stays.

2. [B—] In astronomy, Aldebaran, a star in the constellation Taurus, the Bull.

3. Among seamen, a small, obscure cloud, ruddy in the middle, supposed to portend a storm; hence, a severe storm.

4. In architecture, a small circular or elliptical opening or window.

5. A small, thick disk of glass inserted in various parts of a ship to admit light.

6. A lantern provided with a convex lens on one side for focusing light on any object; applied also to the lens itself.

7. In archery or marksmanship, the center of a target; also, a shot which reaches it.

8. A thick protuberance left on crown glass by the end of the blowpipe.

bull's'-nōse, *n.* In joinery, the external angle of a polygon, or of two lines which meet at an obtuse angle.

bull'-ter"ri-ēr, *n* One of a breed of dogs obtained by a cross between the bulldog and the terrier, and combining the courage and fierceness of the one with the activity of the other.

bull'-trout, *n.* 1. A large species of European salmon-trout, either *Salmo cambricus* or *Salmo trutta*; the sea-trout, which, like the salmon, ascends rivers periodically to spawn.

2. The Dolly Varden trout, *Salvelinus malma*, found on the Pacific coast of North America.

3. The huso, *Acipenser huso*, or Danube salmon.

bull'weed, *n.* Knapweed.

bull'wŏrt, *n.* Bishop's-wood, *Ammi majus.*

bul'ly, *n.* [L.G. *bullerjaan*, *bullerbäk*, a noisy, blustering fellow; AS. *belgan*, to bellow.]

1. A noisy, blustering, overbearing fellow, more distinguished for insolence and empty menaces than for courage, and disposed to provoke quarrels.

2. A dashing, popular fellow. [Obs.]

bul'ly, *a.* 1. Popular; dashing. [Obs.]

2. First-rate; fine. [Slang.]

bul'ly, *v.t.*; bullied, *pt., pp.*; bullying, *ppr.* To insult and overbear with noise and blustering menaces.

bul'ly, *v.i.* To be noisy and quarrelsome.

bul'ly, *n.* [Fr. *bouilli*, boiled meat, from Fr. *bouillir*, to boil.] Pickled beef; canned beef; also called *bully-beef.* [Colloq.]

bul'ly-rag, *v.t* To bully; to insult; to intimidate with noisy threats.

bul'ly-rook, *n.* A bully. [Rare.]

bul'ly-tree, *n.* [Corruption of *balata*, the native name.] Any one of several sapotaceous trees native to the West Indies and the American tropics, as *Mimusops globosa*, of Guiana, which yields a substance very like gutta-percha.

bul'rush, *n.* [ME. *bulryshe*, *bolroysche*, *bole*, stem of a tree, and AS. *risc*, a rush; L. *ruscum*, a butcher's-broom.] A large kind of rush growing in wet land or water. The name *bulrush* is applied, in England, to the *Scirpus lacustris* and also to the *Typha latifolia*, and *Typha angustifolia*; in America, to the *Juncus effusus*, etc.

bulse, *n.* [Anglo-Ind.] 1. A certain quantity of diamonds; a measure.

2. A purse or jewel-bag.

bul'tel, *n.* A bolter or bolting-cloth; also, bran. [Obs.]

bul'ti, *n.* Same as *Bolty.*

bul'tong, *n.* Same as *Biltong.*

bul'tōw, *n.* [*Bull*, large, and *tow*, from AS. *teon*, to draw.] A mode of trawling with many hooks strung on one line; used by fishermen on the banks of Newfoundland; also, the line and hooks used.

bul'wärk, *n.* [ME. *bulwerk*; D. *bolwerk*; G. *bollwerk*; Sw. *bolverk*; Dan. *bulvark*, a rampart.]

1. In fortification, a bastion; a rampart; a mound of earth round a place, capable of resisting cannon-shot, and formed with bastions, curtains, etc.

2. Any means of defense; as, a navy is the *bulwark* of a nation.

3. That which secures against an enemy or external annoyance; a screen or shelter; means of protection and safety.

4. [*pl.*] The sides of a vessel above the upper deck.

Syn.—Rampart, defense, barrier.

bul'wärk, *v.t.*; bulwarked, *pt., pp.*; bulwarking, *ppr.* To fortify with a rampart; to secure by a fortification; to protect.

bum, *n.* 1. An inebriate; a mendicant; a tramp; a loafer. [Slang.]

2. A buzzing sound; a hum. [Rare.]

bum, *n.* [Contr. of *bottom.*] The buttocks. [Vulgar.]

bum, *v.i.*; bummed, *pt., pp.*; bumming, *ppr.* 1. To make a buzzing or humming noise.

2. To loaf; to dissipate; to sponge on others. [Colloq.]

bum, *v.t.* 1. To travel without expense to oneself by begging or stealing food and lodging; as, a tramp *bums* his way from town to town. [Slang.]

2. To importune; to dun. [Prov. Eng.]

bum-bāil'iff, *n.* [Corruption of *bound-bailiff.*] In England, an under-bailiff; a term of contempt.

bum'bärd, *n.* and *v.* [Obs.] See *Bombard.*

bum'bärge, *n.* Same as *Bumboat.*

bum'bast, *n.* [Obs.] See *Bombast.*

bum-bāze', *v.t.* To amaze; to confuse; to perplex. [Scot.]

bum'bē-lō, *n.* Same as *Bombolo.*

bum'ble, *n.* 1. A bittern. [Prov. Eng.]

2. A bungle. [Prov. Eng.]

3. A bumblebee. [Scot.]

bum'ble, *v.i.* [ME. *bumblen*, freq. of *bummen*, to hum; L.G. *bummeln*; D. *bommelen*, to hum.]

1. To make a humming sound, as a bee.

2. To cry out, as a bittern.

bum'ble-bee, *n.* [L. *bombus*, a buzzing.] A large, hairy, social bee of the genus *Bombus*, of which there are more than sixty species in America; also called *humblebee.*

bum'ble-foot, *n.* 1. A suppurative disease of the feet of domestic fowls.

2. A clubfoot.

bum'ble-pup"py, *n.* 1. Whist played regardless of rules.

2. The game of nineholes.

bum'bōat, *n.* [D. *bumboot*, a fishing-boat; *bum*, *bun*, a cauf, a fish-cauf, and *boot*, a boat.] A small boat for carrying provisions to a ship at a distance from shore.

Bū-mē'li-à, *n.* [L., from Gr. *boumelia*, a large kind of ash; *bous*, ox, large, and *melia*, ashtree.] A genus of trees and shrubs of the natural order *Sapotaceæ*, native in eastern United States, the West Indies, and Central America, and including the southern buckthorn, bastard bully-tree, etc.

bum'kin, **boom'kin**, *n.* [D. *boomkin*, dim. of *boom*, a tree, bar.]

1. A short boom projecting from each side of the bow of a ship, to extend the clew of the foresail to windward.

2. A small outrigger over the stern of a boat, to extend the mizzen.

3. A projecting spar on each quarter of a ship, to which the brace-blocks are fastened.

bum'mà-lō, *n.* [E. Ind.] A small, ravenous, teleostean fish of the size of a smelt, abounding on the southern coast of Asia; when dried and salted, it is relished as a food in Europe and India; humorously called *Bombay duck.*

bum'mēr, *n.* A dissolute sponger. [Slang.]

bum'me-ry, *n.* [Obs.] See *Bottomry.*

bump, *n.* 1. A swelling or protuberance.

2. A thump; a heavy blow.

3. A collision; a running into; specifically, in England, the act of running the prow of a racing-boat against the stern of the boat ahead.

4. In phrenology, one of the protuberant lumps on the cranium which are associated with distinct traits of character.

bump, *n.* [Imitative of the sound.] A booming, hollow noise; as, the bittern's *bump.*

bump, *v.t.*; bumped (bumpt), *pt., pp.*; bumping, *ppr.* To strike, as with or against anything large or solid; to thump; as, to *bump* the head against a wall.

bump, *v.i.* 1. To make a loud, heavy, or hollow noise, as the bittern; to boom.

2. To come into sudden contact with something.

bump'ēr, *n.* [Corruption of *bombard*, a drinking-vessel.]

1. A cup or glass filled to the brim, or till the liquor runs over.

2. A crowded house at a theater, etc., in honor of some favorite performer.

3. A buffer; anything that modifies the force of a bump or shock; as, a *bumper* on a car or ship.

4. Anything or any one that bumps or causes a bump.

bump'kin, *n.* [D. *boomkin*, a short tree; dim. of *boom*, a tree; in allusion to the short, blocky build of the countryman.] An awkward, heavy rustic; a clown or country lout.

bump'tious, *a.* Impertinent; conceited; self-assertive. [Colloq.]

bump'tious-ly, *adv.* In a bumptious manner.

bump'tious-ness, *n.* The quality of being bumptious.

bum'wood, *n.* Same as *Burnwood.*

bun, **bunn**, *n.* [Scot.] A kind of cake or sweetened roll; a raised biscuit glazed and sugared on top.

bun, *n.* [Gael. *bun*, stock, stump, root.]

1. A pet name for a rabbit or squirrel; a bunny.

2. A rabbit's or hare's tail. [Obs.]

bunch, *n* [ME. *bunche*, a hump; Ice. *bunki*; Sw. *bunke*, a heap, pile.]

1. A protuberance; a hunch; a knob or lump; as, the *bunch* on a camel's back.

2. A cluster; a number of the same kind growing together; as, a *bunch* of grapes.

3. A number of things tied together; as, a *bunch* of keys; a *bunch* of rods.

4. A collection of things; a knot; as, a *bunch* of hair; a *bunch* of trees.

5. In mining, a small mass of ore.

Bunch of fives; the closed fist. [Slang.]

bunch, *v.i.*; bunched (buncht), *pt., pp.*; bunching, *ppr.* To swell out in a protuberance; to be protuberant or round.

bunch, *v.t.* To form or tie in a bunch or bunches.

bunch'-backed, *a.* Having a bunch on the back; crooked.

bunch'ber"ry, *n.* In botany, the dwarf cornel, *Cornus Canadensis*, bearing clusters or bunches of edible berries.

bunch'flow"ēr, *n.* A plant, *Melanthium Virginicum*, of the lily family, bearing a panicle of greenish flowers; found in the eastern and southern parts of the United States.

bunch'-grȧss, *n.* One of various pasture-grasses that usually grow in clumps, as the Californian *Atropis tenuifolia.*

bunch'i-ness, *n.* The quality of being bunchy, or growing in bunches.

bunch'y, *a.* 1. Growing or swelling out in bunches; like a bunch; having knobs or protuberances.

2. In mining, yielding irregularly; said of a mine where the vein is not continuous.

bun'çō, *n.*, *a.* and *v.t.* See *Bunko.*

bun'çombe (-kum), **bun'kum**, *n.* Anything said for mere show; inflated or bombastic speechmaking for the gratification of constituents or to gain applause; empty talk. [Colloq.]

The word originated near the close of the debate on the Missouri Question in the Sixteenth Congress. Felix Walker, an old North Carolina mountaineer, whose district included the county of Buncombe, rose to speak. Several members begged him to desist, but he persevered, declaring that his constituents expected it and that he was bound to talk "for *Buncombe.*"

bund, *n.* [G.] A league; a federation; especially, the confederation of states in the German Empire.

bund, *n.* [Anglo-Ind.] An embankment or dike to prevent inundation.

bun'dēr, *n.* [Per. *bandar*, a landing-place.]

1. A landing-place; a dock.

2. A Bombay surfboat or raft used in the landing of passengers or goods; called also *bunder-boat.*

bun'dēr, **bhun'dŏr**, *n.* [Hind. *bandar*, a monkey, ape.] An East Indian monkey of various species, as the rhesus, etc.

Bun'des-räth (-rät), *n.* [G. *bundes*, genit. of *bund*, a league, and *rath*, a council.]

1. The federal council of the German Empire, which shares with the Reichstag the legislative power. It consists primarily of two members from each state in the empire, and is presided over by the imperial chancellor.

2. The federal council of Switzerland, composed of seven members, who exercise executive

and administrative functions. They are chosen by the united congress and headed by the president of the republic.

bun'dle (-dl), *n.* [ME. *bundel*; AS. *byndel*, from *bindan*, to bind.]

1. A number of things fastened or tied together.

2. A roll; anything bound or rolled into a convenient form for conveyance; as, a *bundle* of lace; a *bundle* of hay.

3. In biology, an aggregation of one or more elementary tissues traversing other tissues.

4. A definite quantity of certain things; as, a *bundle* of linen thread, or twenty hanks of 3,000 yards each; a *bundle* of paper, or two reams.

5. A number or group of immaterial objects considered as related; as, a *bundle* of objections.

bun'dle-pil"lăr, *n.* In architecture, a column having other columns of smaller dimensions clustering about it.

bun'dle, *v.t.*; bundled, *pt., pp.*; bundling, *ppr.* 1. To tie or bind in a bundle or roll; often followed by *up*; as, to *bundle up* clothes.

2. To send off in a hurry, or without ceremony; as, they *bundled* me into a coach.

To bundle off; to send away abruptly; as, to *bundle* a boy *off* to school.

To bundle oneself up; to wrap oneself up warmly, or in cumbrous garments.

bun'dle, *v.i.* 1. To set off hurriedly or without ceremony; to make ready for departure.

2. To lie or sleep on the same couch without undressing; formerly a practice of lovers or of engaged couples in Wales, in Pennsylvania, the region of the lower Hudson in New York State, and parts of New England.

bun'dō-bust, *n.* [Anglo-Ind.] Systematic regulation of one's affairs; discipline.

bung, *n.* [ME. *bunge*; W. *bwnge*, an orifice, a bung; Ir. *buinne*, a tap, spigot.]

1. The stopper of the orifice in the bilge of a cask.

2. The hole in a cask through which it is filled; the bunghole.

3. A pickpocket or sharper. [Obs.]

4. One who serves out grog on board ship. [Slang.]

bung, *v.t.*; bunged, *pt., pp.*; bunging, *ppr.* To stop up or close with a bung; to close up.

To bung up; to use up or exhaust; to incapacitate for further action. [Slang.]

buṅ'gȧ-lōw, *n.* [Anglo-Ind.] In India, a house

Bungalow.

or cottage, commonly thatched or tiled, consisting usually of one story and surrounded by a wide veranda.

buṅ'gȧ-rum, *n.* [From native name, *bungar.*] A venomous snake of India, related to the cobra, but having no hood.

bung'hōle, *n.* The hole or orifice in the bilge of a cask by means of which it is filled; sometimes shortened into *bung.*

buṅ'gle (-gl), *v.i.*; bungled, *pt., pp.*; bungling, *ppr.* [Derivation uncertain.] To perform in a clumsy, awkward manner; as, to *bungle* in making shoes.

buṅ'gle, *v.t.* [Sw. *bangla*, to work ineffectually.] To make or mend clumsily; to botch; to manage awkwardly; sometimes with *up.*

buṅ'gle, *n.* A botch; a gross blunder; a clumsy performance.

buṅ'glẽr, *n.* A clumsy, awkward workman; one who bungles.

Syn.—Botcher, clown, lubber, fumbler, novice.

buṅ'gling, *a.* Clumsy; awkwardly done; as, a *bungling* workman; a *bungling* job.

buṅ'gling-ly, *adv.* Clumsily; awkwardly.

buṅ'gō, *n.* A Central or South American canoe; also, a boat used in southern United States.

bung'-sēat, *n.* A metal bushing around a bunghole; it is usually screwed in.

bung'-stärt"ẽr, *n.* A wooden mallet, of a peculiar form, for starting the bung out of a cask.

bung'-stāve, *n.* The stave of a barrel which contains the bunghole.

bung'-vent, *n.* A small hole in a bung, to allow gases to escape during fermentation, or to admit air to increase the flow of liquid through the faucet.

bun'iŏn, bun'yŏn, *n.* [It. *bugnone*, a knob, boil; OFr. *bugne, bune*; Ice. *bunga*, an elevation.] A painful enlargement and swelling, or distortion of the bony structure of the foot, usually on the great toe.

buṅk, *n.* [Ice. *bunki*, a heap, pile; Dan. *bunke*, a cargo stowed in the hold of a ship.]

1. A case, shelf, or box of boards used for a bed, especially in crowded quarters, as in a car or ship.

2. One of a number of berths or bed-places arranged one above another.

3. A bed or anything used for a bed. [Colloq.]

4. A piece of lumber so arranged across a lumber-sled as to support the ends of logs; also, the sled so arranged. [Colloq.]

buṅk, *v.i.*; bunked (bunkt), *pt., pp.*; bunking, *ppr.* 1. To go to bed; to sleep; especially, to go to bed or to sleep in a bunk. [Colloq.]

2. To be off; as, I must *bunk* now. [Eng. Slang.]

buṅk'ẽr, *n.* [Scot.] 1. A large bin or receptacle for various things, as coal, etc.

2. A sort of box or chest, the lid forming a seat, as in a window.

3. In golf, any rough, hazardous ground; more strictly, a sand-pit.

buṅ'kẽr, *n.* In zoölogy, the mossbunker; the menhaden.

buṅ'kō, buṅ'çō, *n.* [Corruption of Sp. *banco*, a bank, money-changer's stall; *banca*, a game of cards.] A swindle or swindling game by which two or more confederates decoy a stranger to some place for the purpose of robbing him by means of cards, a sham lottery, or other scheme; a confidence game.

buṅ'kō, buṅ'çō, *a.* Swindling; having a swindling nature; as, a *bunko* game.

buṅ'kō, buṅ'çō, *v.t.*; bunkoed, *pt., pp.*; bunkoing, *ppr.* To swindle or rob by a bunko game, or any similar piece of trickery.

buṅ'kō-joint, *n.* A haunt of bunko-men, or a place to which their victims are steered.

buṅ'kō-man, *n.* A swindler who practises bunko games.

buṅ'kō-steer"ẽr, *n.* One who acts as a decoy to lure intended victims to a place where a bunko game is proposed or in progress.

buṅ'kum, *n.* See *Buncombe.*

bunn, *n.* See *Bun.*

bun'niăn (-yun), *n.* [Obs.] Same as *Bunion.*

bun'ny, *n.* In mining, a mass of ore, as distinguished from a vein.

bun'ny, *n.* [Dim. of *bun*; Gael. *bun*, a stock, a short, thick person or animal.] A familiar or pet name for a rabbit or squirrel.

bū'nō-dont, *a.* [Gr. *bounos*, hill, mound, and *odous, odontos*, a tooth.] In zoölogy, having tuberculated molar teeth; pertaining to the *Bunodonta.*

bū'nō-dont, *n.* One of the *Bunodonta.*

Bū-nō-don'tȧ, *n.pl.* A group of nonruminant artiodactyl mammals, including the hogs and hippopotami; so called because the teeth are tuberculated.

Bun'sen bat'tẽr-y. See under *Battery.*

Bun'sen bũrn'ẽr. See under *Burner.*

bunt, *n.* [Sw. *bunt*; Dan. *bundt*; G. *bund*, a bundle.] The middle part, cavity, or belly of a sail.

bunt, *v.i.*; bunted, *pt., pp.*; bunting, *ppr.* 1. To swell out; as, the sail *bunts.*

2. In baseball, to hit the ball so slowly within the infield that it cannot be fielded in time to retire the batsman. Also used transitively; as, he *bunted* the ball.

3. To come together; to collide; as, they *bunted* into each other.

bunt, *v.t.* To strike or push with the head or horns; to butt; as, the goat *bunted* the boy.

bunt, *n.* 1. A push or shove; a butt.

2. In baseball, the act of bunting the ball; as, he made a *bunt.*

bunt, *n.* A fungus, *Tilletia caries*, destructive to cereals in Europe; a species of smut.

bunt, *n.* The tail of a hare or rabbit.

bun'tẽr, *n.* A female ragpicker; a low, vulgar woman. [Slang.]

bun'ting, *n.* [G. *bunt*, variegated, motley; Scot. *buntlin*; LL. *puntus*, pricked, dotted; L. *punctus*, pierced, pricked.] A name common to various fringilline birds of the genus *Emberiza* and related genera; as, the English or common *bunting*, the snow-*bunting*, and the rice-*bunting*, or bobolink, etc.

bun'ting, bun'tine, *n.* [G. *bunt*, streaked, or of different colors.] A thin woolen stuff, of which colors, flags, and the signals of ships are made; a flag; hence, collectively, a display of flags, colors, etc.; as, the ship showed all her *bunting.*

bun'ting, *n.* A strong, heavy timber; a support for machinery, etc.

bun'ting-i"ron (-ũrn), *n.* In glass-making, a blower's rod for handling hot glass; a pontil.

bunt'line (*or* -lin), *n.* [ME. *bunt*, the middle part of a sail, and *line*, a rope.] A rope fastened to a cringle on the bottom of a square sail, to haul it up.

bun'tons, *n.pl.* [Origin unknown.] In mining, horizontal timbers in a shaft, dividing it into compartments and supporting the guides.

bun'yȧ, *n.* [Anglo-Ind.] In India, especially in Bengal, a grain-dealer.

bun'yȧ-bun"yȧ, *n.* [Native name.] A tall Australian evergreen tree, *Araucaria Bidwillii*, bearing edible seeds. The latter are highly prized by the aborigines as an article of food, and in one large district the trees are protected by law.

bun'yŏn, *n.* See *Bunion.*

buoy (boy, bwoi *or* bọ̈i), *n.* [D. *boei*; OFr. *buie*, a chain, fetter; L. *boia*, a leather collar for the neck; Gr. *boeios*, made of leather; *bous*, an ox.]

1. A floating object anchored in a position to indicate channels or dangerous rocks, bars, etc.

2. Any apparatus or buoyant object which keeps a person or thing afloat in the water.

Anchor buoy; a buoy fastened to an anchor and marking its position.

Bell buoy; a large buoy supporting a bell, to

Buoys.

1. Can buoy. 2. Nun buoy. 3. Bell buoy. 4. Mooring buoy.

be rung in warning by the action of the waves.

Cable buoy; a buoy consisting of an empty cask, used to support a cable in rocky anchorage.

Can buoy; a hollow buoy of sheet iron or boiler-iron, resembling a can.

Life buoy; a buoy, usually consisting of a ring or belt of cork covered with canvas, intended to support persons who have fallen or been cast into the water until other aid can reach them.

Improved Life buoy.

Nut or *nun buoy*; a buoy bulging in the middle and tapering toward each end.

To stream the buoy; to drop the anchor buoy into the water by the ship's side, before dropping the anchor.

Whistling buoy; a buoy supporting a whistle to be sounded by the action of the waves.

buoy, *v.t.*; buoyed, *pt., pp.*; buoying, *ppr.* 1. To keep afloat in a fluid; to bear up, or keep from sinking in a fluid, as in water or air; with *up.*

2. To support or sustain; to keep from sinking into ruin or despondency.

3. To fix buoys in, as a direction to mariners; as, to *buoy* a channel.

4. To indicate the position of with a buoy; as, to *buoy* an anchor.

buoy, *v.i.* To float; to rise by specific lightness.

buoy'āge, *n.* A series of buoys to indicate a channel or course for ships or boats; the providing of such buoys; buoys collectively.

buoy'ănce, *n.* Buoyancy. [Rare.]

buoy'ăn-cy, *n.* 1. The quality of floating on the surface of water or in the atmosphere; specific lightness.

2. In physics, the upward pressure by any fluid on a body partly or wholly immersed therein; it is equal to the weight of the floating body, which, in turn, is equal to the weight of the fluid displaced.

3. The power or tendency of any fluid, etc., to support or buoy up a body.

4. Figuratively, ability to withstand or overcome depression of any kind; as, *buoyancy* of temperament.

Syn.—Animation, elasticity, cheerfulness, life, vivacity, liveliness, sprightliness.

buoy'ănt, *a.* 1. Floating; light; having the quality of rising or floating in a fluid.

2. Bearing up, as a fluid; sustaining another body.

3. Cheerful; gay; light-hearted.

4. Rising, or tending to rise; as, a *buoyant* market.

Syn.—Sprightly, spirited, vivacious, lively, light, floating, hopeful, cheerful, elastic, joyous.

buoy'ănt-ly, *adv.* In a buoyant manner.

bū-pres'ti-dăn, *n.* A coleopterous insect, or beetle, distinguished by its bright metallic coloring; an individual of the genus *Buprestis.*

Bū-pres′tis, *n.* [L., from Gr. *bouprestis*, a poisonous beetle causing swelling in cattle; *bous*, an ox, and *prethein*, to blow up, swell up.] The typical genus of the *Buprestidæ*, a family of beetles distinguished by their brilliant colors and metallic luster. The larvæ bore into the bark and timber of trees, often doing great damage.

bũr, bũrr, *n.* [ME. *burre*, a bur; Dan. *burre*, a burdock, bur; Sw. *borre*, a sea-urchin.]

1. A rough, prickly covering of the seeds of certain plants, as of the chestnut and burdock; also, the plant burdock, or a similar plant bearing *burs*.

Rude *burs* and thistles. —Milton.

2. In engraving, a slight ridge of metal raised on the edges of a line engraved either by the burin or the dry-point, and which is generally removed by a scraper, as it retains superfluous ink in printing a plate, and has the effect of a smear.

3. The rough neck left on a bullet in casting.

4. The round knob of a horn next a deer's head.

5. The lobe or lap of the ear.

6. A triangular chisel used to clear the corners of mortises.

7. A small circular saw.

8. A broad ring of iron adjusted to a lance behind the place for the hand.

9. The sweetbread.

10. A partially vitrified brick; a clinker.

11. The guttural pronunciation of the rough *r* common in some of the northern counties of England; often called the Northumberland, Newcastle, or Tweedside *bur*.

12. Anything put under a wheel to impede its motion.

13. The opening leading to the tympanum of the ear. [Obs.]

bũr, bũrr, *v.i.*; burred, *pt.*, *pp.*; burring, *ppr.* 1. To speak with a bur; to pronounce the letter *r* roughly or gutturally, as in the north of England.

2. To murmur hoarsely.

bu′ran, *n.* [Russ.] A snowstorm, particularly one accompanied by high winds.

bũr′bärk, *n.* The fibrous bark of certain shrubs found in India, Ceylon, the West Indies, etc.

bũr′bōlt, *n.* [Obs.] See *Birdbolt*.

bũr′bot, bũr′bōlt, *n.* [A corruption of Fr. *barbote*, a burbot, from *barbe*, L. *barba*, a beard.] A fish, *Lota maculosa*, shaped like an eel, but shorter and thicker, with a flat head; on the nose it has two small barbels, and another on the chin; called also *eelpout*, *ling*, etc.

bũr-dē-lāis′ (-lā′), *n.* [Fr. *bourdelais*.] A sort of grape. [Obs.]

bũr′den, *n.* [ME. *burden*, *birden*, *birthen*; AS. *byrthen*; O.H.G. *burdin*, *burthin*, a burden, load.]

1. That which is borne or carried; a load.

2. That which is borne with labor or difficulty; that which is grievous, wearisome, or oppressive; as, my *burden* is greater than I can bear.

3. A birth. [Obs.]

4. A fixed quantity of certain commodities; as, a *burden* of gad-steel, i.e., 120 or 180 pounds.

5. The contents of a ship; the quantity or number of tons a vessel will carry; as, a ship of a thousand tons *burden*.

6. In metallurgy, the charge of a blast-furnace.

7. A customary or prescribed load. [Obs.]

Beast of burden; an animal which habitually carries burdens.

Burden of proof; the obligation to prove an assertion, especially to prove the plaintiff's case in a court of law.

Syn.—Weight, load, encumbrance, impediment, cargo.

bũr′den, *n.* [ME. *burdoun*, the bass in music, the refrain; *bourdon*, a humming, buzzing; LL. *burdo*, *burdonis*, a drone, an organ-pipe.]

1. The verse repeated in a song, or the return of the theme at the end of each verse; the chorus; the refrain.

2. That which is often repeated; a subject on which one dwells; as, the *burden* of a speech.

3. The drone of certain musical instruments, as the bagpipe.

bũr′den, *v.t.*; burdened, *pt.*, *pp.*; burdening, *ppr.* 1. To load; to lay a heavy load on; to encumber with weight.

2. To oppress with anything grievous; as, to *burden* a nation with taxes.

3. To surcharge; as, to *burden* the memory.

bũr′den-ẽr, *n.* One who loads; an oppressor.

bũr′den-ous, *a.* 1. Grievous; heavy to be borne; oppressive. [Obs.]

2. Cumbersome; useless. [Obs.]

bũr′den-sōme, *a.* Heavy; grievous to be borne; causing uneasiness or fatigue; oppressive.

bũr′den-sōme-ly, *adv.* In a burdensome manner.

bũr′den-sōme-ness, *n.* The quality of being burdensome; heaviness; oppressiveness.

bũr′dock, *n.* [ME. *bur*, a bur, and AS. *docce*, a dock.] The common name of the *Arctium Lappa*, a coarse, troublesome weed, bearing burs that adhere tenaciously to clothing, and to the hair of cattle, horses, dogs, etc.

bū′reau (-rō), *n.* [Fr. *bureau*, a writing-table or desk, an office, the people engaged in an office; OFr. *bureau*, a coarse brown cloth with which writing-tables were covered, from *burel*, a coarse cloth.]

1. A desk or table for writing, having drawers to hold papers, etc.

2. A chest of drawers for keeping clothing, etc., and commonly provided with a mirror.

3. A department for the transaction of business by a public functionary. On the continent of Europe, the highest departments, in most countries, have the name of *bureau*; as, the *bureau* of the minister of foreign affairs. In the United States and England, the term is confined to subordinate departments; as, the *bureau* of animal industry in the department of agriculture; the weather *bureau*, etc.

Bureau Veritas; an institution for the uniform inspection and rating of ships of all nationalities, in the interest of marine underwriters. It was established in Brussels in 1828, moved to Paris in 1830, and returned to Brussels in 1870.

Weather bureau; a popular name for the signal-service bureau, which has charge of meteorological observations in the United States, and publishes weather predictions based upon them.

bū-reau′crȧ-cy (-rō′), *n.* [Fr. *bureaucratie*, *bureau*, and Gr. *kratein*, to be strong; *kratos*, strength.]

1. A system in which the business of government is carried on in departments, each under the control of a chief, in contradistinction to a system in which the officers of government have a coördinate authority.

2. Government officials considered as a body.

bū′reau-crat (-rō-), *n.* An official of a bureau; particularly, an official who prefers to conduct his business through a system of bureaus and thus avoid personal responsibility.

bū-reau-crat′iç, bū-reau-crat′iç-ăl, *a.* Pertaining to or resembling a bureaucracy.

bū-reau′crȧ-tist, *n.* One who advocates or supports bureaucracy; a bureaucrat.

bũr′el, *n.* Same as *Burrel*.

bu-re′ō, *n.* [Sp., from Fr. *bureau*, a bureau.] In Spanish law, a court in which persons belonging to the royal household are tried.

bū-rette′, *n.* [Fr., dim. of OFr. *buire*, a flagon, from *buire*, to drink.]

1. In chemistry or physics, a graduated glass tube for measuring small quantities of liquids. It is of even bore, stands vertically, with a small aperture below, and is fitted with a stopcock.

2. A decorated or valuable cruet.

bũr′fish, *n.* A fish found along the Atlantic coast of North America, capable of expanding its body, which, being covered with spines, presents the appearance of a chestnut-bur, whence the name; called also *balloon-fish*, *swell-fish*, and *porcupine-fish*.

bũrg, *n.* [ME. *burgh*; AS. *burh*, *burg*, a fortified town.] Originally, a fortified town of Great Britain; now a colloquial name for a town; as, a thrifty *burg*; frequently used as a terminal in names of towns; as, Pitts*burg*.

bũr-gāde′, *n.* [Obs.] See *Bourgade*.

bũrg′āge, *n.* [ME. *burgage*, from *burg*, a town.] In English law, a kind of tenure of real estate, held at a fixed rate of rent payable in money or in services; socage.

bũr′gall, *n.* [Local U. S.] A small sea-fish, the cunner, blue perch, or nibbler.

bũr′gȧ-mot, *n.* Same as *Bergamot*.

bũr′gȧ-net, bũr′gō-net, *n.* [Sp. *borgoñota*; OFr. *bourguignote*, a Burgundian helmet, from *Burgogne*, Burgundy.] A kind of helmet; the Spanish morion.

Burganet.

bũr′ġee, *n.* [Origin unknown.]

1. A sort of small coal for firing furnaces.

2. A flag or pennant ending in two points.

bũr-ġeois′ (-jois′), *n.* Same as *Bourgeois*.

bũr′ġeŏn, *n.* [ME. *burgen*, *burgeon*; OFr. *borjon*, a bud; O.H.G. *burjan*, to raise, lift up.] A leaf-bud at the extremity of a branch.

bũr′ġeŏn, *v.i.*; burgeoned, *pt.*, *pp.*; burgeoning, *ppr.* To commence growth in the bud; to form a bud.

bũr′ġess, *n.* [OFr. *burgeis*; LL. *burgensis*, a citizen; *burgus*, a borough, town; O.H.G. *burc*, a fortified town.]

1. An inhabitant of a borough, or walled town, or one who possesses a tenement therein; a citizen or freeman of a borough.

2. A representative of a borough in the British parliament.

3. A magistrate of certain corporate towns.

4. Before the Revolution, a representative in the popular branch of the legislature of Maryland or Virginia, which bore the title *house of burgesses*; now called *house of delegates*.

5. A citizen of a Scotch burgh who is eligible to vote at municipal elections.

Burgess oath; a solemn oath of allegiance formerly taken by the burgesses of Great Britain.

bũr′ġess-ship, *n.* The state or office of a burgess.

bũrg′grāve, *n.* [Fr. *burggrave*; LL. *burggravius*; O.H.G. *burggravo*; *burg*, *burc*, a town, and *gravjo*, *gravo*, a count, earl.] In Germany, a title applied originally to one appointed to the command of a burg; but afterward it became hereditary, with a domain attached. Some of the *burggraves* were immediate members of the old German Empire.

bũrgh (bũrg), *n.* An incorporated town; a borough. [Scot.]

bũrgh′ăl, *a.* Pertaining to a burgh.

bũrgh′bōte, *n.* [AS. *burgbōte*; *burg*, *burh*, a borough, and *bōt*, compensation, boot.] In old law, a contribution toward the building or repairing of castles, or walls for the defense of a city or town.

bũrgh′brēch, *n.* In old English law, a fine imposed on a burgh, for a breach of the peace.

bũrgh′ẽr, *n.* [D. *burger*; M.H.G. *burgære*, *burger*; G. *bürger*, a citizen; *burgh*, a town.]

1. An inhabitant of a burgh or borough who enjoys the privileges of the borough of which he is a free citizen.

2. [B—] A member of that section of the Scotch Seceders which recognized the legality of the burgess oath, the opposing parties being called Anti*burghers*.

bũrgh′ẽr-mȧs″tẽr, *n.* Same as *Burgomaster*.

bũrgh′ẽr-ship, *n.* The state or privilege of a burgher.

bũrgh′mȧs″tẽr, *n.* 1. A burgomaster.

2. An officer in tin mines who directs and lays out the boundaries for the workmen; called also *bailiff* and *barmaster*. [Eng.]

bũrgh′mōte, *n.* The court of a burgh or borough.

bũr′glăr, *n.* [OFr. *burg*, from LL. *burgus*, a town, and OFr. *lere*, from L. *latro*, a thief.] One guilty of committing a burglary.

bũr′glăr-ȧ-lärm″, *n.* A contrivance designed to give an alarm if a building is entered by an intruder, usually by ringing a bell or turning on a light.

bũr-glā′ri-ăn, *n.* A person guilty of burglary. [Obs.]

bũr-glā′ri-ous, *a.* Pertaining to burglary; constituting the crime of burglary.

To come down a chimney is held a *burglarious* entry. —Blackstone.

bũr-glā′ri-ous-ly, *adv.* With an intent to commit burglary; in the manner of a burglar.

bũr′glȧ-ry, *n.* The act or crime of nocturnal housebreaking, with an intent to commit a felony. To constitute this crime, the act must be committed in the night, or when there is not daylight enough to discern a man's face. It must be in a dwelling-house, or in an adjoining building which is a part or parcel of the dwelling-house. —Blackstone.

In many states, the term has been amplified to include the breaking and entering of any building by day as well as by night, with the intention of committing crime. Many degrees of the crime are defined by law. Raising a latch or obtaining entrance by trick or threat is construed as a breaking-in.

bũr′gō-mȧs″tẽr, *n.* [D. *burgemeester*; *burg*, borough, and *meester*, master.]

1. A burghmaster; a magistrate, or one employed in the government of a city; a chief magistrate of the cities of Holland and Germany.

2. An aquatic bird, the glaucous gull (*Larus glaucus*), common in arctic regions, which domineers over smaller birds.

bũr′gō-net, *n.* See *Burganet*.

bũr′goo, bũr′göut (-gö), *n.* [A corruption of ME. *burgood*, yeast.]

1. A sailor's name for oatmeal pudding or thick gruel.

2. In some parts of the United States, a kind of soup or stew served especially at open-air feasts.

bũr′grȧss, *n.* A kind of grass that grows in sand and bears burs; a species of *Cenchrus*.

bũr′grāve, *n.* Same as *Burggrave*.

bũr′gun-dy, *n.* A full-bodied red or white wine, produced in Burgundy, a province of France.

Burgundy pitch; a resinous product of the Norway spruce, *Abies excelsa*, and other pines. It is in reality turpentine from which the essential oil has been distilled, with the addition of water. It is used in medicine as a stimulating plaster.

bũrh, *n.* An early English form of *borough*.

bũr′hel, bũrr′hel, *n.* [E. Ind.] The wild sheep of the Himalayas, *Ovis burrhel*; the blue sheep.

bur′i-ăl (ber′-), *n.* [ME. *burial*, *beriel*; AS.

byrgel, a tomb, a grave, from *byrgan*, to bury.]

1. The act of burying a deceased person; sepulture; interment; the act of depositing a dead body in the earth, in a tomb or vault, or in the water.

2. The act of placing anything under earth or water.

3. A grave or tomb. [Obs.]

Burial service; the service performed at the interment of the dead, or that portion of a liturgy read at a burial.

bur′i-ăl-căse, *n.* A casket or coffin.

bur′i-ăl-ground, *n.* A tract of land set apart for a cemetery or graveyard.

bur′i-ẽr (ber′), *n.* One who buries a deceased person; that which covers or buries.

bū′rin, *n.* [Fr. *burin*, a graver's chisel.]

1. A graver; an instrument for engraving on metal. It is made of hard steel, the cutting end being ground to a diamond-shaped point.

Burin.

2. The style of an engraver's work; as, a soft *burin*; a brilliant *burin*.

3. A tool for engraving on stone.

bū′rin-ist, *n.* One who uses the burin; an engraver.

bū′ri-ŏn, *n.* [Origin unknown.] The red-breasted sparrow or house-finch, native to California (*Carpodacus frontalis*).

bũrke, *v.t.*; burked, *pt.*, *pp.*; burking, *ppr.* [From the name of the first criminal executed for the act, Edinburgh, 1829.]

1. To murder (a person) in such a way as to produce no incriminating marks, usually by suffocation, and with the intention of selling the body for dissection.

2. To get rid of in a hidden or disguised manner; to suppress or postpone; as, to *burke* a legislative measure or inquiry.

bũrk′ing, *n.* The crime of murdering persons in order to sell their bodies to doctors or medical schools.

bũrl, *v.t.*; burled, *pt.*, *pp.*; burling, *ppr.* 1. To dress, as in finishing cloth.

2. To pick knots and loose threads from, as cloth.

Burling iron; a kind of nippers used for picking the knots from woolen cloth.

bũrl, *n.* [ME. *burle*; OFr. *bouril*, *bourril*, flocks or ends of threads, from *bourre*; LL. *burra*, coarse hair.]

1. A kink in thread; a knot in a woven fabric.

2. A knot overgrown by bark, or a similar projection on a tree; also, the veneer made from such a knot.

bũr′lap, *n.* [Origin unknown.] A cloth of coarse texture made of jute or hemp, and used for wrapping. A finer variety of the same material is used for wall-hangings, curtains, and in upholstery. Mostly used in the plural, *burlaps*.

bũrl′ẽr, *n.* A dresser of cloth.

bũr-lesque′ (-lesk′), *a.* [Fr. *burlesque*; It. *burlesco*, from *burla*, a jest, mockery.] Jocular; tending to excite laughter by ludicrous images, or by a contrast between the subject and the manner of treating it, as when a trifling subject is treated with mock gravity.

bũr-lesque′, *n.* 1. Ludicrous representation; a contrast between the subject and the manner of treating it, which tends to excite laughter or ridicule; satirical exaggeration.

2. A literary or dramatic composition in which a trifling subject or low incident is treated with much gravity, as a subject of great dignity or importance; or one in which the contrast between the subject and the manner of considering it renders it ludicrous or ridiculous; specifically, in theatrical parlance, an extravaganza; a travesty of a serious play or subject, usually interspersed with music.

3. Any gross or ludicrous copy, travesty, caricature, or perversion.

Syn.—Farce, mimicry, mockery, travesty, extravaganza.

bũr-lesque′, *v.t.*; burlesqued, *pt.*, *pp.*; burlesquing, *ppr.* To turn into ridicule; to make ludicrous by the manner of representation, as by treating a low or trifling subject with mock gravity.

bũr-lesque′, *v.i.* To use burlesque.

bũr-les′quẽr (-kẽr), *n.* One who burlesques or turns to ridicule; a burlesque actor or actress.

bũr-let′tȧ, *n.* [It.] A comic opera; a musical farce.

bũr′li-ness, *n.* Bulk; bluster; the quality of being burly.

bũr′ly, *a.* [O.H.G. *burlih*, high, elevated; *bor*, an elevation.]

1. Great in size; bulky; now applied chiefly to human beings, but formerly to animals that were tall and handsome, and to inanimate things of huge size.

2. Overbearing; coarse; boisterous.

Bũr′măn, *n.*; *pl.* **Bũr′măns.** A member of one of the four main racial divisions inhabiting Burma; applied also to any inhabitant of Burma.

Bũr′măn, *a.* Of or pertaining to Burma or the Burmans.

Bũr-man-ni-ā′cē-æ, *n.pl.* [Named after Johannes *Burmann*, a Dutch botanist.] An order of monocotyledonous plants containing ten genera and about sixty species. They grow chiefly in the tropics and bear regular flowers.

bũr-man-ni-ā′ceous, *a.* Pertaining to the *Burmanniaceæ*.

Bũr-mēse′ (*or* -mēz′), *a.* Of or relating to Burma or its people.

Bũr-mēse′, *n. sing.* and *pl.* A native or natives of Burma; also, the language of the country.

bũrn, *v.t.*; burned *or* burnt, *pt.*, *pp.*; burning, *ppr.* [ME. *bernen*, *bærnan*, *brennan*; AS. *bærnan*, *beornan*; L.G. *brennen*; Ice. *brenna*, to burn.]

1. To consume with fire; to reduce to ashes by the action of heat or fire; frequently with *up*; as, to *burn up* wood.

2. To subject to the action of fire, to improve the matter treated or for the benefit of the user: (a) in surgery, to apply an actual cautery to; to cauterize; (b) to heat or dry; as, to *burn* colors; (c) to expel the volatile parts and reduce to charcoal; as, to *burn* wood into charcoal; (d) to calcine; to expel the volatile matter from substances, so that they are easily pulverized; as, to *burn* oyster shells, or limestone; (e) to cleanse of soot; to inflame; as, to *burn* a chimney; (f) to harden; to bake or harden; as, to *burn* bricks.

3. To injure by changing the condition of, by exposure to or application of fire or heat: (a) to scorch; to affect by heat; as, to *burn* the clothes by the fire; to *burn* meat or bread in cookery; (b) to dry up or dissipate, with *up*; as, to *burn up* tares; (c) to dry excessively; to cause to wither by heat; as, the sun *burns* the grass or plants.

4. To produce or effect by burning; as, to *burn* a name on a box; to *burn* a hole in a blanket.

5. To produce a sensation or effect in or upon, similar to that of heat: (a) to heat or inflame; to affect with excessive stimulus; as, ardent spirits *burn* the stomach; (b) to affect with excess of heat; as, fever *burns* a patient; (c) to impair, or to destroy partially the tissue of, as if by burning; as, to *burn* with lye or acid.

6. To consume or use as a heating or illuminating agent; as, to *burn* coke; to *burn* kerosene.

7. In chemistry, to combine with oxygen or other gas; to cause the oxidation of; to oxidize.

To burn a bowl or *curling-stone*; in the game of bowls or in curling, to displace by accident a bowl or curling-stone.

To burn a hole in one's pocket; to be on one's mind continually until taken out and spent; said of money.

To burn daylight; to illuminate artificially before it is dark; hence, to do that which is unnecessary or useless.

To burn one's fingers; to get into trouble, as by meddling or taking part in any matter not properly concerning one.

To burn one's bridges; to destroy all means or hope of retreat.

To burn the candle at both ends; to be extravagant; especially, to waste one's energy by combining business with dissipation or an exhausting round of pleasures.

To burn together, or *to burn on*; to unite two pieces of like metal (usually a piece to be added to a casting) by raising both parts to an intense heat, just short of the melting-point, and pouring on them around the place of juncture a quantity of fused metal of the same kind.

bũrn, *v.i.* 1. To be on fire; to flame; as, the mount *burned* with fire.

2. To shine; to sparkle.

> O prince! O wherefore *burn* your eyes?
> —Rowe.

3. To be inflamed with passion or desire; as, to *burn* with anger or love.

4. To be in commotion; to rage with destructive violence.

> The groan still deepens and the combat *burns*. —Pope.

5. To be affected with a sensation of heat, pain, or acidity; as, the heart *burns*.

6. To feel excess of heat; to be in a glow; as, her face *burns*; a patient *burns* with a fever.

7. In chemical reactions, to combine with the evolution of much heat.

8. In certain games, to get near a result sought or a thing hidden, either in a progression of guesses, or by actual personal proximity; hence, to come near to the truth or the solution of anything. [Colloq.]

To burn down; to burn to the ground.

To burn out; to burn till the fuel is exhausted, and the fire ceases.

To burn up; to be consumed.

Syn.—Ignite, kindle, brand, consume, cauterize, cremate, incinerate, rage, glow, smolder, blaze, flash.

bũrn, *n.* A small stream; a brook. [Scot.]

bũrn, *n.* 1. A hurt or injury of any part of the body, caused by burning; the result of burning or of undue exposure to heat.

2. A burning or that which results from it as, a good *burn* of bricks.

3. A disease of plants, the brand.

bũrn′ȧ-ble, *a.* Capable of being burned.

bũrned, *a.* Same as *Burnt*.

bũrn′ẽr, *n.* 1. One who or that which burns.

2. The part of an apparatus for illuminating, heating, or cooking which emits, controls, and modifies the flame.

Bude burner; a burner of two or more concentric Argand lamps fitted with a tube by which air or oxygen is supplied.

Bunsen burner; a kind of gas-burner invented by Professor R. W. Bunsen, of Heidelberg, and consisting of a short, straight tube provided with air-holes, through which air is drawn by the heated column, thus supplying the oxygen to the illuminating gas coming from the main. It produces a feebly luminous but extremely hot flame.

Regenerative burner; a gas-burner in which the waste heat of the escaping gas is utilized and applied to the gas just entering the burner.

Rose or *rosette burner*; a kind of gas-burner producing a rose-shaped flame by a circle of jets.

bũr′net, *n.* [ME. *burnet*; OFr. *brunete*, *brunette*, the name of a plant.] One of several plants, all perennial, of the genus *Poterium*, specifically *Poterium Sanguisorba*, the common or garden *burnet*.

Canadian burnet; a plant, *Poterium Canadense*, growing in marshes.

bũr′net-mọth, *n.* Any moth of the genera *Zygæna* or *Anthrocera*; specifically, a European moth, *Zygæna filipendulæ*, having six crimson spots on its wings.

bũr′net-sax″i-frage, *n.* A name common to different species of plants of the genus *Pimpinella*.

bũr′nett-īze, *v.t.*; burnettized, *pt.*, *pp.*; burnettizing, *ppr.* [Named after Sir William *Burnett*, the inventor of the process.] To preserve from decay by saturating with Burnett's liquid, a solution of chlorid of zinc, as wood, dead bodies, etc.

bũrn′ie, *n.* A burn or small brook. [Scot.]

bũrn′ing, *a.* 1. Being on fire; much heated; scorching.

> The *burning* plains of India. —Smith.

2. Causing excitement or strong emotion; intense; vehement; exciting; as, a *burning* shame; a *burning* question.

Syn.—Ardent, earnest, fervent, impassioned, intense, glowing, hot, fiery, consuming.

bũrn′ing, *n.* 1. Combustion; the act of expelling volatile matter and reducing to ashes; a fire; inflammation; the heat or raging of passion.

2. In surgery, actual cautery; cauterization.

3. The state of burning or of being much heated; the act of baking or firing pottery, etc.

4. A batch of articles, such as bricks or pottery, fired at one time.

bũrn′ing-bush, *n.* 1. Any one of several shrubs or plants bearing crimson foliage or flowers; as, (a) the wahoo, *Euonymus atropurpureus*; (b) the strawberry-bush, *Euonymus Americanus*; (c) the fraxinella, *Dictamnus Fraxinella*; (d) the artillery-plant, *Pilea serpyllifolia*.

2. The emblem adopted by the Presbyterian churches of Scotland in memory of the persecutions of the seventeenth century, and in allusion to the appearance of God to Moses in the blazing bush. The legend is *Nec tamen consumebatur*, "yet not consumed."

bũrn′ing-flū″id, *n.* Any inflammable fluid, especially one composed of oil of turpentine and alcohol, formerly used in lamps.

bũrn′ing-glȧss, *n.* A convex glass, which, when exposed to the direct rays of the sun, focuses them, producing an intense heat.

bũrn′ing-house, *n.* A furnace in which tin ores are heated, to extract the arsenic and sulphur from the pyrites; a kiln.

bũrn′ing-mir″rŏr, *n.* A single concave mirror, or a combination of plane mirrors, of much greater power than a burning-glass.

bũr′nish, *v.t.*; burnished (burnisht), *pt.*, *pp.*; burnishing, *ppr.* [OFr. *brunir*, *burnir*, to make brown, to polish.]

1. To make smooth, bright, and glossy; to polish, especially by friction; as, to *burnish* steel.

2. To make bright or resplendent; to cause to glow; as, the sunset *burnished* the hill.

bũr′nish, *v.i.* To grow bright or glossy; also, to thrive; to increase.

bũr′nish, *n.* Gloss; brightness; luster.

bũr′nish-ẽr, *n.* 1. One who burnishes or polishes.

2. Anything which burnishes or polishes:

specifically, a tool of metal or bone, with a smooth surface, used for various purposes.

bŭr-nọọse′, bŭr-nọ̈us′ (*or* bŭr′ nōs), *n.* [Fr. *burnous*; Sp. *al-bornoz*, a Moorish cloak; Ar. *burnus*, a high-crowned cap.]

1. An outer cloak or garment, worn by the Arabs, having a hood attached, the whole being usually made in one piece.

Burnoose.

2. A combination hood and cloak, or a loose outer cloak, of various materials, worn by women in England and America at different periods. Also written *bornouse, burnouse, bernouse, bournous*.

bŭrn′sīdeṣ, *n.pl.* The popular name for a style of wearing the beard adopted by General Burnside, a well-known commander of the United States army during the Civil War. The chin is shaved and the mustache and whiskers are worn.

bŭrn′stic̦-kle, *n.* Same as *Stickleback*.

bŭrnt, *a.* Affected by fire or heat; consumed; parched; charred.

Burnt offering; an offering burned on an altar, as an atonement for sin; specifically, the sacrifice made by the Jews in ancient times of some animal known as clean under the Mosaic law, as an atonement for sin. In cases of poverty, a bird was sometimes substituted, and in rare cases, vegetables and fruits were burned. Also called *burnt sacrifice*.

bŭrnt′=ēar, *n.* A disease in grain, by which the seed is rendered abortive, and its coat covered with a black powder.

bŭrn′wood, *n.* Coral-sumac, *Rhus Metopium*, of Florida and the West Indies; called also *bumwood*.

bŭr′=pump, *n.* A kind of pump used on board ship, in which a cup-shaped cone of leather nailed on the end of a pump-rod serves instead of a box, its sides collapsing as the rod descends, and expanding with the weight of the water as it ascends; a bilge-pump.

bŭrr, *n.* See *Bur*.

bŭrr, *v.i.* See *Bur*.

bŭr-rȧ-mun′di, *n.* Same as *Barramunda*.

bŭr′rȧs=pīpe, *n.* [*Burras*, an obsolete form of *borax*, and *pipe*.] An instrument or vessel used by surgeons to keep corroding powders in.

bŭr′rȧ-wang, *n.* [Native name.] In botany, one of the species of the nut-bearing Australian *Macrozamia*.

bŭr′rel, *n.* [Fr *beurre*, butter-pear, from *beurre*, butter; OFr. *burel*, reddish.] A sort of pear, called also the *red butter pear*, from its smooth, delicious, soft pulp.

bŭr′rel, *n.* [OFr. *burel*, reddish, a kind of coarse, reddish cloth; LL. *burra*, a shaggy garment; L. *burras*, red; Gr. *pyrros*, red, flame-colored; *pyr*, fire.] A coarsely woven cloth of brownish or russet color, formerly much used for poorer kinds of garments; also, a garment made of this cloth. Also written *borrel, borel, burel*.

bŭr′rel=flȳ, *n.* The oxfly, gadfly, or breeze. [Rare.]

bŭr′rel=shot, *n.* [Fr. *bourreler*, to torment, and *shot*.] Small shot, nails, stones, pieces of old iron, etc., put into cases, to be discharged at short range. [Obs.]

bŭrr′hel, *n.* [E. Ind.] In zoölogy, a species of wild sheep peculiar to the Himalayas (*Ovis burrhel*); also written *burhel, burrel*.

bŭrr′ing=mȧ-c̤hïne″, *n.* A machine for taking burs, seeds, and other substances out of wool.

bŭr′rō, *n.* [Sp.] A western United States name for a donkey.

bŭr′rŏck, *n.* [AS. *beorg, burg*, a hill, and dim. *-ock*.] A small weir or dam laid in a river to aid in catching fish.

bŭr′rōw, *n.* [Obs.] See *Borough*.

bŭr′rōw, *n.* [ME. *borow, borur*, a hole for shelter, a mound; AS. *beorh*, a mound, *burh*, a fortified place.]

1. A hollow place in the earth, where small animals lodge and sometimes deposit their provisions.

2. In mining, a heap of dirt or rubbish; a mound; particularly, the dump or dumps of refuse from mines.

bŭr′rōw, *v.i.*; burrowed, *pt., pp.*; burrowing, *ppr.* 1. To excavate a hole in the earth, especially one to lodge in.

2. To lodge in a hole excavated in the earth, as rabbits. In a more general sense, to lodge in any deep or concealed place.

Burrowing owl; a small owl, *Speotyto cunicularia*, which inhabits holes in the ground, as those of the western prairie-dog.

bŭr′rōw, *v.t.* To excavate or dig holes in; to make burrows through.

bŭr′rōw=duck, *n.* A sheldrake.

bŭr′rōw-ẽr, *n.* One who or that which burrows.

bŭrr′=pump, *n.* See *Bur-pump*.

bŭr′ry, *a.* Full of burs; resembling burs.

bŭr′sȧ, *n.*; *pl.* **bŭr′sæ**. [LL., a purse, sac.] In anatomy, a kind of sac; as, *bursa* mucosa, a sac situated at a joint and containing the synovial fluid.

bŭr′săl, *a.* In anatomy, pertaining to a bursa.

bŭr′sȧr, *n.* [LL. *bursarius*, a treasurer, from *bursa*, a purse.]

1. A treasurer, or keeper of cash; as, the *bursar* of a college, or of a monastery; a purser.

2. A student to whom a stipend is paid out of a burse or fund appropriated for that purpose.

bŭr′sȧr-ship, *n.* The office of a bursar.

bŭr′sȧ-ry, *n.* 1. The treasury of a college or monastery.

2. A grant or fund established in a college or university for the collegiate expenses of impecunious, deserving students.

bụrsch, *n.*; *pl.* **bụrsch′en**. [G., from M.H.G. *bürse*, a society of students; a common purse; LL. *bursa*, a purse.] A youth; especially, a student in a German university.

bŭrse, *n.* [Fr. *bourse*, a purse, exchange; LL. *bursa*, a purse.]

1. A purse; a pouch; a pod or bladder. [Obs.]

2. A fund or foundation for the maintenance of poor scholars in their studies; a bursary.

3. A public exchange or bourse. [Obs.]

4. In the Roman Catholic church, a receptacle for the corporal and chalice-cover. It is square and flat, made of cardboard covered with rich silk or cloth of gold, embroidered and studded with jewels, open on one side only, and placed over the chalice-veil when the sacred vessels are carried to the altar by the celebrant.

Bŭr′sē-rȧ, *n.* [Named after Joachim *Burser*, a German botanist.] A genus of tropical trees or shrubs, exuding aromatic gums, resins, and balsams, and typical of the family *Burseraceæ*.

Bŭr-sē-rā′cē-æ, *n.pl.* [LL.] A family of tropical trees and shrubs, usually with small flowers and alternate compound leaves, and furnishing many valuable balsams and aromatic gums.

bŭr-sē-rā′ceous, *a.* In botany, pertaining to the *Burseraceæ*.

bŭr-sic̦′ū-lāte, *a.* [From L. *bursa*, a purse, bag.] In botany, pouch-shaped; subspherical; bursiform.

bŭr′si-fọrm, *a.* Same as *Bursiculate*.

bŭr-sī′tis, *n.* [LL. *bursa*, a purse, bag, and *-itis*.] In medicine, inflammation of a bursa.

bŭrst, *v.i.*; burst, *pt., pp.*; bursting, *ppr.* [ME. *bersten, bristen*; AS. *berstan*; D. *bersten*; O.H.G. *brestan*; Ice. *bresta*, to burst, break asunder.]

1. To fly or break open with force, or with sudden violence; to suffer a violent disruption; to explode; to be suddenly liberated; to have a sensation of rending; to be surcharged with emotions; as, to *burst* from a prison; the heart *bursts* with grief.

2. To come or fall upon suddenly or with violence; to rush upon unexpectedly; as, a sound *bursts* upon our ears.

3. To break forth into action suddenly; as, to *burst* into tears.

4. To break or rush in with violence; as, to *burst* into a house or a room.

5. To open spontaneously, as an abscess.

6. To become suddenly manifest; as to *burst* into view.

bŭrst, *v.t.* 1. To break or rend by force or violence; to open suddenly; as, to *burst* a chain or a door; to *burst* a cannon.

2. To effect by bursting.

Syn.—Break, split, explode, rend, fracture, rive, disrupt, crack, separate.

bŭrst, *n.* 1. A sudden breaking forth; a disruption; a violent rending; more appropriately, a sudden explosion or shooting-forth; as, a *burst* of thunder; a *burst* of applause; a *burst* of passion.

2. A brief, intense effort; a spurt; as, a *burst* of brilliant imagery; a *burst* of speed.

3. A sudden appearance; an unexpected disclosure of a view.

4. A rupture or hernia. [Obs.]

bŭrst′en, *a.* Affected with hernia. [Obs.]

bŭrst′en, *v.*, past participle of *burst*. [Obs.]

bŭrst′ẽr, *n.* One who or that which bursts.

bŭrst′ing=chärg̤e, *n.* 1. In gunnery, a quantity of explosive placed in a shell to cause it to burst upon impact.

2. In blasting, an ignitive charge placed about the fuse in a blasting charge and usually of quick-burning powder, serving to insure the explosion of the blasting charge, especially where electric fuses are used.

bŭr′stōne, bŭrr′stōne, bŭhr′stōne, *n.* [ME. *bur*, a whetstone, and *stone*, a stone.] A subspecies of silex or quartz occurring in amorphous masses, compact like hornstone, but containing irregular cavities; it is used for millstones.

bŭrst′wŏrt, *n.* The *Herniaria glabra*, a plant which, in former times, was supposed to be efficacious in the cure of rupture or hernia.

bŭrt, *n.* [Prov. Eng.] A flatfish of the turbot kind.

bŭr′then, *n.* and *v.* Same as *Burden*.

bŭr′tŏn, *n.* A nautical term for a small tackle formed by two blocks or pulleys, used to set up or tighten the topmost shrouds, and for various other purposes.

bụr′y (ber′i), *n.* A variant of *burg, burh, borough*, signifying a house, habitation, or castle; retained in many names of places, as in Shrews*bury*, Dan*bury*, Aldermanb*ury*, etc.

bụr′y (ber′i), *v.t.*; buried, *pt., pp.*; burying, *ppr.* [ME. *beryen, buryen, byrien*; AS. *byrgan*, to bury, inter; *beorgan*, to protect, shelter, save.]

1. To inter; to place (a deceased person) in the earth or in the sea; to entomb.

2. To cover from sight by placing anything on; to hide; to conceal; to overwhelm; as, to *bury* one in the ruins of a house.

3. To withdraw or conceal in retirement; as, to *bury* oneself in a monastery; hence, in the past participle, to be wholly absorbed in; as, he is *buried* in thought.

4. To hide in oblivion; as, to *bury* an injury.

To bury the hatchet; in the striking metaphorical language of American Indians, to lay aside the instruments of war, forget injuries, and make peace.

Syn.—Entomb, inter, conceal, inhume, hush, repress, compose, cancel, obliterate, suppress.

bụr′y-ing=bee″tle, *n.* A beetle belonging to the genus *Necrophorus*; also called *sexton-beetle*.

bụr′y-ing=ground, *n.* A place appropriated to the sepulture of the dead; a graveyard.

bus, *n.* [Contr. of *omnibus*.] An omnibus or public conveyance. [Colloq.]

Bus bars, bus rods, and *bus wires*; in electricity, terms applied to conductors of large area, receiving the main current from the brushes in a dynamo, or generally from distributing points of an electric circuit; the conducting apparatus for a powerful electric current.

buṣ′by, *n.*; *pl.* **buṣ′bieṣ** (-biz). A fur cap or headgear used in the British army, sometimes having a bag marked with the distinguishing colors of the regiment hanging from the top over the right side.

Busby.

bus′c̦ärl, *n.* A mariner; a sailor. [Obs.]

bus′c̦ŏn, *n.* [Sp. *buscon*, from *buscar*, to search.] A miner who works on the basis of a certain percentage of extracted ore.

bụsh, *n.* [ME. *bussh, bosch, bosk*, a bush, thicket; O.H.G. *busc*; Dan. *busk*, a bush, shrub.]

1. A shrub; particularly, a shrub with branches rising from or near the root; a thick shrub; a cluster of shrubs.

2. A thicket or place abounding in trees or bushes. This was the original sense of the word, as in the Dutch *bosch*, a wood. In this sense, the word is extensively used in South Africa, Australia, and Canada; as, to live in the *bush*.

3. A tavern sign; a bush or bough natural or pictured, hung outside a tavern; hence, the tavern itself.

Good wine needs no *bush*. —Old proverb.

4. A shrub or shrubby branch of a tree, used as a prop; as, a *bush* for pease.

5. In hunting, a fox's tail or brush.

To beat about the bush; to suggest or hint at anything; to approach a subject indirectly.

bụsh, *v.i.* To grow thick or bushy.

bụsh, *v.t.*; bushed, *pt., pp.*; bushing, *ppr.* 1. To prop up with bushes; to place bushes for; as, to *bush* pease.

2. To cover (seeds) with earth by means of a bush-harrow; as, to *bush* a garden.

bụsh, *n.* [G. *büsshe*; D. *bos*, a box.] The lining of any piece of mechanism, used as a protection against the wear of friction, as around the keyhole of a watch, the center of a cart-wheel, etc.; a bushing; often called a *box*.

bụsh, *v.t.* To line with a bush in order to protect from friction, or to render the opening smaller.

bụsh′=bēan, *n.* A variety of bean growing in bushlike form; a dwarf bean.

bụsh′boy, *n.* See *Bushman*.

bụsh′buck, *n.* [D. *boschbok*; *bosch*, a bush, and *bok*, a buck.] A handsome antelope, *Tragelaphus sylvaticus*, found in the South African bush.

bụsh′c̦at, *n.* An African wildcat; the serval.

bụsh′chat, *n.* A bird of the thrush family, as the whinchat or stonechat.

bụsh′=clō̤″vẽr, *n.* Japan clover.

bụsh′=dog, *n.* 1. A small wild dog of South America, *Icticyon venaticus*.

2. The lemuroid potto of West Africa.

bụshed, *a.* Lost in the bush.

bụsh′el, *n.* [ME. *busshel, buschel*; OFr. *bussel*,

boissel; LL. *bussula*, a little box, dim. of *bustia*, from L. *pyxis*, a box.]

1. A dry measure, containing eight gallons or four pecks. The standard *bushel* of the United States is founded on the old Winchester *bushel*, which was the standard in England from Anglo-Saxon times to the year 1826, when it was succeeded in that country by the imperial *bushel*. The capacity of the United States or Winchester *bushel* is 2150.42 cubic inches, the English or imperial *bushel* containing 2218.192 cubic inches. Many of the American states have established equivalent weights for the *bushel* of various commodities, the weights varying considerably in different states.

2. A measure or vessel of the capacity of a *bushel*.

3. A quantity that would fill a *bushel* measure; as, a *bushel* of potatoes.

4. A large quantity; used indefinitely; as, a *bushel* of money. [Colloq.]

5. A tailor's thimble.

bụsh'el, *v.t.* and *v.i.*; busheled, *pt.*, *pp.*; busheling, *ppr.* To renovate or mend (men's clothes).

bụsh'el-āge, *n.* A duty payable on commodities by the bushel. [Eng.]

bụsh'el-ēr, *n.* A bushelman.

bụsh'el-măn, *n.* [Local U. S.] A tailor's assistant who repairs or alters men's clothes; a busheler.

bụsh'et, *n.* A thicket; a copse; shrubbery; also, a small bush.

bụsh'fight"ēr (-fīt"ēr), *n.* One accustomed to fighting under cover of bushes, etc.

bụsh'fight"ing, *n.* A mode of fighting in which the combatants fire from behind the shelter of trees and bushes.

bụsh'gōat, *n.* Same as *Bushbuck*.

bụsh'ham"mēr, *n.* Any one of various hammers used by masons for shaping and dressing stone. The most important form of *bushhammer* is composed of a bunch of thin steel bars arranged in rows, bolted together, and having pyramidal or sharply grooved points. Another form consists of a solid head with a face cut into rows having such points.

bụsh'ham"mēr, *v.t.*; bushhammered, *pt.*, *pp.*; bushhammering, *ppr.* To trim or dress (stone) with a bushhammer; as, to *bushhammer* a block of granite; to *bushhammer* a millstone.

bụsh'-har"rōw, *n.* A frame to which is attached brush and branches, used to cover grass-seed.

bụsh'-hog, *n.* A wild hog of South Africa, *Potamochœrus africanus*; the boschvark; called also *bush-pig* and *river-hog*.

bụsh'i-ness, *n.* The state or quality of being bushy.

bụsh'ing, *n.* 1. The process of lining a pivot-hole, axle-bearing, etc., with a bush to reduce friction and guard against wear.

2. The lining or bush thus applied.

3. A hollow, circular block fitted into the bore of a breech-loading cannon, and forming the foundation of the breechblock.

bụsh'-lạw"yēr, *n.* The common name for *Rubus australis*, a blackberry of New Zealand.

bụsh'less, *a.* Devoid of bushes; bare.

> O'er the long backs of the *bushless* downs.
> —Tennyson.

bụsh'măn, *n.*; *pl.* **bụsh'men**. 1. In Australia, one who dwells in the bush or interior, as distinguished from inhabitants of cities and towns; a bush-farmer; a bush-settler.

2. [B—] One of an unclassified, aboriginal tribe in South Africa, inferior to the Hottentots, and in recent times mostly dwarfed and stunted nomads living in desert regions; so named by the Dutch of South Africa. Called also *Bosjesman*.

bụsh'mȧs"tēr, *n.* A large venomous serpent, *Lachesis mutus*, of the family *Crotalidæ*, allied to the rattlesnake, and found in tropical South America; also called *curucucu* and *surucucu*.

bụsh'ment, *n.* 1. A thicket; a cluster of bushes. [Obs.]

2. An ambush or ambuscade. [Obs.]

bụsh'-pēa, *n.* A kind of pea that needs to be supported or bushed.

bụsh'răn"ġēr, *n.* One who lives and roams for freedom, safety, robbery, or profit, in the bush. In Australia, the term implies a fugitive from justice taking refuge in the bush.

bụsh'răn"ġing, *n.* The act or practice of living as a bushranger.

bụsh'-shrike, *n.* A South American passerine bird of the family *Formicariidæ*, and subfamily *Thamnophilinæ*; especially, the tropical American ant-thrush of the genus *Thamnophilus*.

bụsh'-tit, *n.* A small passerine bird belonging to the genus *Psaltriparus*, of which several species are found in western United States and Mexico.

bụsh'whack"ēr, *n.* 1. One who is accustomed to range through woods and among bushes; hence, during the Civil War many deserters and desperate characters who carried on guerrilla warfare were stigmatized as *bushwhackers*.

2. A country clown; an awkward fellow.

3. A kind of scythe for cutting down or trimming bushes; also, one who wields it.

bụsh'whack"ing, *n.* 1. The act of grasping bushes on the bank of a river or stream, to serve as leverage in working a boat along.

2. Guerrilla warfare or the depredations committed by bushwhackers.

3. The act or practice of using a bushwhacker in cutting bushes.

bụsh'y, *a.* 1. Overgrown or covered with bushes; full of shrubbery.

2. Having many close twigs and branches; low and shrubby.

3. Resembling a bush or bushes; thick and spreading; shaggy; as, a *bushy* tree; a *bushy* beard; *bushy* eyebrows.

buṣ'i-ly (biz'), *adv.* In a busy manner; earnestly; steadily; unceasingly.

buṣi'ness (biz'nes), *n.* [ME. *business*, *bysiness*, labor, diligence, from *busy*, busy.]

1. Employment; occupation; profession; calling; vocation; means of livelihood; that which occupies the time, attention, and labor of men, for the purpose of profit or improvement; as, his *business* was that of a merchant; the *business* of a banker.

2. Mercantile concerns, or traffic in general; as, a good knowledge of *business*.

3. In a theatrical sense, the work determined upon and arranged by the stage manager for the action of a play.

> Consider what scope the *business* of the scene gives to the actor's purpose.—Irving.

4. Concern; right or power of interference; as, it was none of his *business*.

5. Anxiety; care. [Obs.]

6. The state of being busy or actively employed. [Obs.]

7. Serious engagement; important occupation, as distinguished from trivial affairs; as, *business* before pleasure; life is a serious *business*.

To make it one's business; to take the management of; to consider and act upon as a personal affair.

To mean business; to be determined; to be in earnest.

To mind one's own business; to confine oneself to one's own affairs; to refrain from interference with the affairs of others.

Syn.—Employment, calling, vocation, occupation, trade, profession, office, affair, matter, transaction.

buṣi'ness-līke (biz'), *a.* Practical; systematic; methodical; as, to do a thing in a *businesslike* manner.

busk, *n.* [Fr. *busc*, *busque*, busk.]

1. A strip of steel, whalebone, or other material, that strengthens and shapes the front of a woman's corset; a corset-stay.

2. The entire corset when made of stiffened material.

busk, *v.t.*; busked, *pt.*, *pp.*; busking, *ppr.* [ME. *busken*; Ice. *buask*, to get oneself ready; *bua*, to prepare, live, dwell, and *sik*, self.]

1. To prepare; to equip; to fit out; to make ready.

2. To dress; to array; to apparel. [Scot. and OE.]

> *Busk* ye, *busk* ye, my bonny, bonny bride.
> —Hamilton.

3. To employ; to use or make use of.

busk, *v.i.* 1. To go; to hurry; to guide or direct one's course. [Obs.]

2. To dress; to get ready.

3. Among seamen, to cruise or beat about; to stand off and on shore; to cruise, as a pirate.

busk, *n.* A harvest-feast, or feast of first fruits, among certain tribes of American Indians, especially the Creeks.

busked (buskt), *a.* Wearing a busk.

bus'ket, *n.* 1. A small bush; a bouquet. [Obs.]

2. A shrubbery in a garden. [Rare.]

bus'kin, *n.* [D. *broosken*, a buskin, dim. of *broos*, a buskin, a purse.]

1. A half-boot or high shoe, worn for protection against thorns, mud, etc., which reaches half-way to the knee, being laced or strapped to the ankle and calf of the leg.

> The hunted red-deer's undressed hide
> Their hairy *buskins* well supplied. —Scott.

1. Buskin of Diana.
2. Buskin of Bacchus.

2. A similar covering worn by actors in tragedy among the ancients in contradistinction to the *sock* worn by comedians. The stage *buskins* had very thick soles to give an appearance of elevation to the stature of the actor.

3. Hence, tragedy or the tragic drama, as opposed to comedy.

> He was a critic upon operas, too,
> And knew all niceties of the sock and *buskin*.
> —Byron.

4. A woman's laced shoe or half-boot.

5. In the Roman Catholic church, a kind of stocking of rich stuff, as satin, cloth of gold, or silk embroidered, worn by bishops when celebrating mass, being the first vestment assumed.

bus'kined, *a.* 1. Dressed in buskins.

2. Relating to tragedy; having buskins on the feet, as actors on the stage.

busk'y, *a.* Same as *Bosky*.

buss, *n.* [G. *bus*, a kiss; Ir. and Gael. *bus*, a mouth, a lip.] A smacking kiss; a salute with the lips.

buss, *v.t.*; bussed, *pt.*, *pp.*; bussing, *ppr.* To kiss; to smack with the lips.

> We *buss* our wantons, but our wives we kiss.
> —Herrick.

buss, *n.* [OFr. *busse*; LL. *bussa*, *buscia*, a small boat, a box; L. *buxus*, a box.] A small vessel of from fifty to seventy tons, carrying two masts, and two sheds or cabins, one at each end; long used in the herring fishery.

bụs'ṣụ, *n.* [Native name.] A short palm, *Manicaria saccifera*, with leaves longer than the trunk or stem, and spreading spathes used for bags or thatch. It thrives in the swamps of the Amazon. Also called **bussu-palm**.

bust, *n.* [Fr. *buste*; It. *busto*; LL. *bustum*, the trunk of the body.]

1. In sculpture, the figure of a person in relief, showing only the head, shoulders, and breast.

> Can storied urn or animated *bust*,
> Back to its mansion call the fleeting breath?
> —Gray.

2. The chest or thorax; the trunk of the human body.

bus'tȧrd, *n.* [OFr. *bistard*, *oustarde*; Pr. *aus tarda*; L. *avis tarda*, slow bird.] A large grallatorial bird of the genus *Otis*, natural order *Cursores*, but approaching the waders. The great bustard, *Otis tarda*, is the largest European bird, the male often weighing thirty pounds, with a breadth of wing of six or seven feet. It inhabits the temperate regions of Europe, and parts of Asia and Africa. It runs fast, taking flight with difficulty. *Otis tetrax*, the little bustard, inhabits southern Europe and Morocco. There are about twenty species.

Great Bustard (*Otis tarda*).

bus'ted, *a.* Ruined financially; without funds; bankrupt; broken. [Slang.]

bus'tēr, *n.* 1. Something remarkable or great. [Slang.]

2. A drunken carousal; a spree. [Slang.]

3. In Australia and New Zealand, a cutting, violent wind; a gale. [Slang.]

bus'tle (bus'sl), *v.i.*; bustled, *pt.*, *pp.*; bustling, *ppr.* [Ice. *bustla*, to bustle, splash; *bustl*, a splashing, turmoil.] To stir quickly; to be active; to be quick in motion; often with rudeness, noise, or commotion.

bus'tle, *n.* Hurry; noise; fuss; tumult; agitation.

> All would have been well without this *bustle*.
> —Spectator.

bus'tle, *n.* A pad worn by women on the back part of the body below the waist, to fill out the figure.

bus'tlēr (bus'lēr), *n.* An active, stirring person.

bus'tling (bus'ling), *a.* Stirring; moving actively, with noise or agitation; as, a *bustling* throng.

bus'tō, *n.*; *pl.* **bus'tōeṣ**. [It.] A bust; a statue. [Rare.]

buṣ'y (biz'i), *a.* [ME. *bisy*, *bysy*, *busy*; AS. *bysig*, busy, occupied; D. *bezig*; L.G. *besig*, active, busy.]

1. Employed with constant attention; active in business; not idle; full of business; as, a man is *busy* posting his books.

> My mistress is *busy*, and cannot come.—Shak.

2. Filled with business; characterized by business activity; as, a *busy* town; a *busy* day.

3. Continually active or at work; as, the *busy* bee; *busy* thoughts; *busy* feet.

4. Officiously or foolishly active; meddling; as, a *busy* gossiper.

5. Solicitous; cautious. [Obs.]

buṣ'y (biz'i), *v.t.*; busied, *pt.*, *pp.*; busying, *ppr.* To employ with attention; to keep engaged; to make busy; as, to *busy* oneself with books.

> To be *busied* with genus and species.—Locke.

buṣ'y-bod"y, *n.* A meddling person; one who

officiously concerns himself with the affairs of others.

bus′y-ness (biz′i-), *n.* The state of being busy. [Rare.]

but, *n.* The outer room of a cottage having but two apartments; the kitchen of such a house. The house is spoken of as having a *but* and a ben. [Scot.]

but, *n.* A boundary; a butt.

but, *n.* See *Butt.*

but, *n.* A condition; an objection or exception; as, there are too many ifs and *buts* in this contract.

but, *v.i.* and *v.t.* To abut.

but, *prep.* [ME. *but, bote, bute, buten*; AS. *butan, buton,* without, outside; *be,* by, and *utan,* out, from without; *ut,* out; *butan* is primarily an adverb.]

1. Except; barring; besides; save.

Who can it be, *but* perjured Lycon?—Smith.

2. To the but or outer room of; as, gae (go) *but* the house. [Scot.]

3. Except; besides; in this sense, similar to the conjunctional use and not easily distinguished from it.

4. Without; unless with.

Touch not a cat *but* a glove.—Scotch saying.

but, *adv.* 1. Only; not other than; merely; just; as, there is *but* one man present.

A formidable man *but* to his friends.—Dryden.

If they kill us, we shall *but* die.—2 Kings vii.4.

2. In the outer apartment, or to the outer room of a cottage having a but and a ben; as, to gae (go) *but*; this is the primary adverbial use of the word. [Scot.]

3. Outside; without. [Obs.]

but, *conj.* 1. Except; unless; with exception of the fact that; excepting that; unless it were that; as, most classes joined in the demonstrations, *but* the Poles refrained.

2. More; further; however; yet; still.

Now abideth faith, hope, charity, these three; *but* the greatest of these is charity.
—1 Cor. xiii. 13.

3. Before; at the time that; at which time; immediately thereafter; than; when; as, I had not left the room *but* he commenced to betray me; no sooner conceived, *but* done.

4. Otherwise than that; in any other way except that; exceeding that; beyond that; as, none are so bad *but* there is some good left in them; we cannot *but* believe that death does not end all.

5. On the contrary; on the other hand; as, the spirit is willing, *but* the flesh is weak.

Syn.—Except, excepting, however, nevertheless, notwithstanding, save, still, yet.

bū′tāne, *n.* [L. *butyrum,* butter.] An inflammable gaseous compound contained in petroleum, belonging to the paraffin series, and formed by the action of zinc on ethyl iodide.

butch′ẽr, *n.* [ME. *bocher*; OFr. *bochier, bouchier,* one who kills and sells he-goats; OFr. *boc,* a he-goat.]

1. One who slaughters animals for market; one whose occupation is to kill animals for the table; also, one who cuts up and sells meat.

2. One who kills men, or commands troops to kill them; one who sheds, or causes to be shed, human blood in abundance; applied to commanders and conquerors, who delight in war or are remarkable for destroying human life.

3. A mutilator of any good work; hence, a poor workman; a poor performer; a bungler.

butch′ẽr, *v.t.*; butchered, *pt., pp.*; butchering, *ppr.* 1. To kill or slaughter (animals) for food or for market.

2. To murder; specifically, to murder with unusual cruelty, or under circumstances of uncommon barbarity.

3. To spoil; to cut up; to mutilate; to bungle.

butch′ẽr-bīrd, *n.* The shrike; a name common to different birds of the genus *Lanius.* They derive the name from their habit of suspending the uneaten portions of their prey upon thorns, as a butcher hangs meat upon hooks, for consumption at their leisure. The great northern shrike, *Lanius borealis,* and the white-rumped shrike or loggerhead, *Lanius ludovicianus,* are common in America.

butch′ẽr-ing, *n.* 1. The act of needless and cruel killing; wanton slaughtering.

2. The business of slaughtering animals, or selling meat.

butch′ẽr-li-ness, *n.* A cruel, savage, butcherly manner.

butch′ẽr-ly, *a.* Cruel; savage; murderous; grossly and clumsily barbarous.

butch′ẽr′ṣ-broom, *n.* A plant, the *Ruscus aculeatus*; called also *kneeholly.*

butch′ẽr′ṣ-meat, *n.* Flesh of domestic animals slaughtered for food and kept for sale by butchers, as distinguished from game or other animal food.

butch′ẽr-y, *n.* 1. The business of slaughtering cattle for the table or for market. [Rare.]

2. Murder, especially murder committed with unusual barbarity; great slaughter.

3. The place where animals are killed for market; a shambles, or slaughterhouse; also, a place where blood is shed. [Obs.]

Syn.—Slaughter, murder, carnage, massacre.

Bū′tē-ȧ, *n.* A genus of East Indian leguminous trees, named after the Earl of Bute (1713-92). *Butea frondosa* yields butea gum or Bengal kino.

bū′tēne, *n.* Same as *Butylene.*

but′lẽr, *n.* [Fr. *bouteillier,* from *bouteille,* a bottle, i.e., the bottler.]

1. A manservant employed to take charge of the wine-cellar, plate, and dining-room arrangements and generally to have supervision of other servants.

2. Formerly, an officer attached to a royal court, usually intrusted with the supply of wine for the royal table.

but′lẽr-āġe, *n.* A duty of two shillings formerly levied on every tun of wine imported into England by foreigners or merchant strangers. So called because originally paid to the king's butler for the king.

but′lẽr-ship, *n.* The place or duties of a butler.

but′ment, *n.* Same as *Abutment.*

but′ment-cheek, *n.* One of the sides of a mortise.

Bū-tō-mā′cē-æ, *n.pl.* [L., from Gr. *boutomos,* a kind of water-plant.] A small order of endogens, the type of which is *Butomus umbellatus* or flowering-rush.

bū-tō-mā′ceous, *a.* Relating to the *Butomaceæ.*

butt, but, *n.* [ME. *but, butte,* a goal, mark; OFr. *but, butte,* a goal, mark to shoot at; from *buter, boter,* to push, butt, strike; O.H.G. *bozen,* to beat, strike.]

1. Literally, end; furthest point; hence, a mark to be shot at; a target; the point where a mark is set or fixed to be shot at.

2. The point to which a purpose or effort is directed.

3. The object of aim; the thing against which an attack is directed.

4. The person at whom ridicule, jest, or contempt is directed; as, the *butt* of ridicule.

5. A push or thrust given by the head of an animal; as, the *butt* of a ram; also, a thrust in fencing.

6. The larger or thicker end of anything; as, the *butt* of a rifle or of a fishing-rod.

7. The end of a plank in a ship's side or bottom.

8. A particular kind of double hinge for doors; called also *butt-hinge.*

9. A small portion of unplowed land at the sides or end of a field.

10. A joint where two ends meet without being grooved into each other.

11. The square end of a shaft or connecting-rod to which a boxing or bushing is attached. In the cut, *b* represents the *butt.*

12. The thickest part of tanned hides, used for sole-leather; also called *back.*

13. The metal ring at the end of a hose, to which a nozzle or another length of hose may be screwed.

14. A shelter for the target attendant at a rifle-range.

15. A pile of earth, etc., behind a target to stop the projectiles that miss or go through the target; in the plural, *butts,* a range for rifle or artillery practice.

16. A goal; a bound; a limit; an abuttal; as, the *butts* and bounds of an estate.

A butt's length; the ordinary distance from the place of shooting to the butt, or mark.

Butts and bounds, contraction of abuttals and boundaries. In ordinary rectangular lands, the *butts* are the ends and the *bounds* are the sides, as they were once termed in conveyancing.

Butt and butt; end to end, as timbers joined without overlapping.

Full butt; headfirst with much force, or without warning; full tilt.

butt, *n.* [AS. *butte, butt.*]

1. A large cask to contain wine.

2. A wine measure whose contents are 126 gallons of wine, or two hogsheads; called also a *pipe.*

3. A leathern bottle. [Obs.]

butt, *v.i.*; butted, *pt., pp.*; butting, *ppr.* [ME. *butten,* to push, throw; OFr. *buter, boter,* to push, strike.] To thrust the head forward; to strike by thrusting the head against, as a goat.

butt, *v.t.* To bump; to push with the head.

butt′-chain, *n.* A chain attached to the end of a tug, in harness.

butte, *n.* [Fr.] A high detached hill or ridge rising abruptly from a plain, especially in the Rocky Mountains and vicinity.

but′ted, *a.* Having a butt; as, heavy-*butted.*

butt′-end, *n.* The stoutest or blunt end of any object; as, the *butt-end* of a musket or of a log.

but′tẽr, *n.* [ME. *butter, butere*; AS. *butere*; D. *boter*; L.G. *botter*; O.H.G. *butra*; It. *burro, butiro*; L. *butyrum*; Gr. *boutyron,* butter; *bous,* ox, cow, and *tyros,* cheese.]

1. An oily substance obtained from cream or milk by churning. Agitation separates the fat or oily part of milk from the thin and curdy part, called buttermilk.

2. Any substance resembling *butter* in consistence, etc.; as, apple-*butter*; especially, one of the fat concrete vegetable oils, sometimes called *vegetable butter*; as, cacao-*butter.*

3. In the old chemistry, a name given to some of the chlorids, from their soft, butyraceous consistence, when recently prepared; as, *butter* of antimony, now called the sesquichlorid of antimony.

Butter and eggs; one of many species of plants which have flowers in different shades of yellow, as the toadflax, *Linaria vulgaris.*

Creamery butter; butter made at a public creamery.

Dairy butter; butter from a private butter-making establishment or direct from the farm.

but′tẽr, *v.t.*; buttered, *pt., pp.*; buttering, *ppr.* 1. To smear or cover with butter.

2. In gambling, to raise (the stakes) at every throw or every game. [Slang.]

but′tẽr, *n.* One who or that which butts.

but′tẽr-ball, *n.* The spirit- or buffle-duck.

but′tẽr-bēan, *n.* The Lima bean, *Phaseolus lunatus.*

but′tẽr-bīrd, *n.* A name given in Jamaica to the bobolink.

but′tẽr-bōat, *n.* A small dish for serving melted butter, etc.; often boat-shaped.

but′tẽr-bump, *n.* [*Butter,* a dial. form of *bittern,* and *bump,* the sound made by the bittern.] The bittern.

but′tẽr-bũr, but′tẽr-bũrr, *n.* [So called from the leaves being used to wrap butter.] A European plant, *Petasites vulgaris,* growing in wet land; the sweet coltsfoot.

but′tẽr-çŏl″ŏr, *n.* A preparation used to color butter, butterin, or similar products in imitation of the rich yellow of butter.

but′tẽr-çup, *n.* A plant, and its flower, of the genus *Ranunculus,* more especially *Ranunculus bulbosus,* which has bright yellow cup-shaped flowers; called also *butterflower, golden-cup,* and *kingcup,* and by Shakspere the *cuckoobud.*

but′tẽr-fin″gẽred, *a.* Liable to let things slip through one's fingers, or to let things fall; slippery, as though smeared with butter; careless.

but′tẽr-fin″gẽrṣ, *n.* One who lets drop anything he should hold; specifically, in games, one who muffs. [Slang.]

but′tẽr-fish, *n.* A name given to several species of fish because of their slippery coating, as *Stromateus triacanthus,* the dollar-fish, and the West Indian food-fish, *Enneacentrus punctatus.*

but′tẽr-flow″ẽr, *n.* The buttercup.

but′tẽr-flȳ, *n.*; *pl.* **but′tẽr-flieṣ.** [ME. *butterflye, boterflye*; AS. *buttorfleoge, buturfleoge,* a butterfly, white moth; *butere,* butter, *fleoge,* a fly; probably first applied to the yellow variety.]

1. The common name of all the diurnal lepidopterous insects, corresponding to the original Linnean genus *Papilio,* in their last and fully developed state.

2. Figuratively, one who leads an idle, gay life; an idler; a trifler.

Butterfly cock; a butterfly valve.

Butterfly damper; a valve consisting of a disk which turns on its axis across a pipe.

Butterfly valve; a pair of clack-valves arranged back to back; used in pumps.

Butterfly Valve.

but′tẽr-flȳ-fish, *n.* Any one of various fishes, such as the European blenny, the flying gurnard, or the angel-fish.

but′tẽr-flȳ-plant, *n.* A West Indian orchid having flowers resembling butterflies; also, an East Indian orchid having similar flowers.

but′tẽr-flȳ-shell, *n.* A shell belonging to the genus *Voluta*; also, a pteropod.

but′tẽr-flȳ-weed, *n.* A common weed, *Asclepias tuberosa,* of the milkweed family; the pleurisy-root, said to be of use in medicine.

but′tẽr-in, but′tẽr-ine, *n.* [*Butter,* and *-ine.*] A substitute for butter made from oleomargarin, or animal fat, with milk, coloring matter, etc. It is now an article of great commercial importance, being widely used as a substitute for butter. In many states its sale is regulated by statute. [See *Oleomargarin.*]

but′tẽr-is, but′trice, *n.* [Forms of *buttress,* from Fr. *bouter,* to push.] An instrument of steel set in wood, used for paring the hoof of a horse.

but′tẽr-milk, *n.* That part of milk which remains after the butter is extracted.

but′tẽr-nut, *n.* 1. The edible fruit of an American tree, *Juglans cinerea*, so called from the oil it contains; also, the tree itself; sometimes called *oilnut* or *white walnut.*

2. The nut of the *Caryocar nuciferum*, a native of South America; called also the *souari nut.*

3. The brown color from the dye of the *butternut*; sometimes used attributively; as, *butternut* jeans.

but′tẽr-print, *n.* A block of carved wood for molding butter; also called *butter-stamp.*

but′tẽr-scotch, *n.* A kind of crisp, sticky candy made of butter and sugar.

but′tẽr-tooth, *n.* A broad front tooth.

but′tẽr-tree, *n.* A tree belonging to the genus *Bassia*, found in Africa, and yielding a substance like butter.

but′tẽr-tri″ẽr, *n.* An instrument used in sampling butter, as from a firkin.

but′tẽr-weed, *n.* A plant, *Senecio lobatus*, found in southern United States.

but′tẽr-weight (-wāt), *n.* A term signifying overweight, because it was once the custom to sell eighteen ounces of butter to the pound.

but′tẽr-wŏrt, *n.* A plant, *Pinguicula vulgaris*, growing on bogs or soft ground.

but′tẽr-y, *a.* Having the qualities or appearance of butter.

but′tẽr-y, *n.*; *pl.* **but′tẽr-ieṣ.** 1. A room in a house, originally for the keeping of bottles; now, a pantry.

2. In some English colleges, a room where liquors, fruit, and refreshments are kept for sale to the students.

3. A cellar or underground place where butts of wine are stored.

but′tẽr-y-hatch, *n.* A hatch or half-door giving entrance to a buttery.

butt′-hinge, *n.* See *Butt*, 8.

but′thorn, *n.* A starfish, *Asterias rubens*, common in European waters.

but′ting, *n.* Anything that abuts; a boundary; an abuttal.

but′tŏck, *n.* [ME. *buttok*, *bottok*; *butt*, limit, extremity, and dim. *-ock*.]

1. One of the rounded parts of the gluteal region; plurally, the rump.

2. The round part of a ship abaft, from the wing transom to the upper water-line.

but′tŏn, *n.* [ME. *boton*, *botoun*; OFr. *boton*, a button, bud; from *boter*, to push out, butt.]

1. A knob or flattened piece of some substance, such as metal, bone, china, etc., with or without a covering of cloth; attached to material by means of holes or a shank on the under side, and commonly fitted into a buttonhole or slit in a corresponding part of the material; made in various forms and often used for ornamental purposes only.

2. Any knob or ball fastened to another body; a small protuberant body; as, a push-*button*; the *button* of a fencing-foil, etc.

3. A bud; a knob-like swelling on a plant. [Prov. Eng.]

4. A flat, usually oblong, piece of wood or metal, turning on a pivot, used to fasten a door, window, etc.

5. A small, round mass of metal found at the bottom of a crucible, after fusion, or which remains on the cupel in the process of assaying.

6. An ornamental knob worn on the hat in China and indicating rank; as, a red-*button* mandarin.

7. [*pl.*] A page; so called from the rows of gilt buttons which adorn his jacket. [Colloq.]

To hold by the button; to persist in conversation; to bore with talk.

but′tŏn, *v.t.*; buttoned *pt.*, *pp.*; buttoning, *ppr.* [ME. *botonen*, to button, from *boton*, a button.]

1. To fasten with a button or buttons; to inclose or make secure with buttons; often followed by *up*; as, to *button up* a coat.

2. To dress or clothe. [Obs.]

but′tŏn, *v.i.* To be capable of being buttoned; as, the glove *buttons* with difficulty.

but′tŏn-ball, *n.* Same as *Buttonwood.*

but′tŏn-bush, *n.* The popular name of the *Cephalanthus occidentalis*, a shrub of the madder family that bears a spherical head of flowers.

but′tŏn-hōle, *n.* The hole or loop in which a button is caught.

but′tŏn-hōle, *v.t.*; buttonholed, *pt.*, *pp.*; buttonholing, *ppr.* To interview; implying detention.

but′tŏn-hook, *n.* A small metal hook for drawing a button through a buttonhole; used chiefly for fastening shoes and gloves.

but′tŏn-mōld, *n.* A knob or disk of hard material to be covered with leather or cloth to form a button.

but′tŏn-shell, *n.* A marine gasteropod of the genus *Rotella*, the shell of which is small and polished.

but′tŏn-snake″root, *n.* A popular name for a plant of the composite genus *Liatris*, from the shape of its flowers; also, a perennial plant of southern and western United States, the leaves of which are parallel-veined and bristly along the margins, and the flowers white and spherical.

but′tŏn-tree, *n.* The popular name of the *Conocarpus*, a genus of trees native to tropical America and western Africa; called also *buttonwood.*

but′tŏn-weed, *n.* The popular name of various plants of the genera *Spermacoce* and *Diodia*, and others of the madder family.

but′tŏn-wood, *n.* The *Platanus occidentalis*, or western plane-tree, a large tree producing rough balls, from which it is named; known also as the *buttonball* and the *sycamore*; also, a dwarf evergreen tree of the genus *Conocarpus* growing in the West Indies.

but′tŏn-y, *a.* Trimmed with numerous buttons.

but′tress, *n.* [ME. *buttrace*, *butterasse*; OFr. *bouterets*, a buttress, from *bouter*, to thrust.]

1. A wall or abutment, built on the outside and serving to support another wall which is very high, or loaded with a heavy superstructure; used also for decorative purposes, especially to produce symmetrical effects.

2. Any prop or support, material or figurative; as, the *buttress* of a good cause.

Flying buttress; see under *Flying.*

Buttress.

but′tress, *v.t.*; buttressed, *pt.*, *pp.*; buttressing, *ppr.* To strengthen or brace by means of a buttress; to support; to uphold.

but′trice, *n.* See *Butteris.*

butt′-shaft, *n.* A blunt-headed arrow often used in shooting at a target.

butt′strap, *v.t.*; buttstrapped, *pt.*, *pp.*; buttstrapping, *ppr.* To weld (the ends of two pieces of metal) to form a butt.

butt′-weld, *n.* A joint made by the abutting of two pieces of metal, welded into a butt-joint when at a white heat.

butt′weld, *v.t.*; buttwelded, *pt.*, *pp.*; buttwelding, *ppr.* To join by means of a butt-weld.

but′ty, bud′dy, *n.* [Shortened form of Early Modern Eng. *boty-felowe*, a partner; *boty*, property shared, and *felowe*, a fellow.] In mining, one who takes a contract for working out coal or ore at a specified price per ton.

2. In English dialect, a chum or associate.

but′ty-gang, *n.* A number of men working together as a body, on contract, and sharing the profits jointly.

bū′tyl, *n.* [*Butyric*, and *-yl.*] A compound radical, C_4H_9, existing only in combination.

bū′tyl-am-ine, *n.* [*Butyl*, and *amine.*] The hydrocarbon $C_4H_9NH_2$; a colorless alkaline fluid, formed by bacterial action.

bū′ty-lēne, *n.* Any of the three isomeric modifications of the gaseous hydrocarbon C_4H_8.

bū-ty-rā′ceous, *a.* Having the qualities of butter; resembling butter.

bū′ty-rāte, *n.* A salt of butyric acid.

bū-tyr′iç, *a.* [From L. *butyrum*, butter.] Of, pertaining to, or obtained from butter.

Butyric acid; a volatile, liquid compound, $C_4H_8O_2$, found in butter; having the smell of rancid butter, and an acrid taste, with a sweetish aftertaste, like that of ether.

bū′ty-rin, *n.* A peculiar oily matter, existing in butter, associated with olein and stearin; a butyrate of glycerin.

bū-ty-rom′e-tẽr, *n.* [L. *butyrum*, butter, and *metrum*, Gr. *metron*, measure.] An instrument by which the quantity of butter-fat present in milk can be ascertained.

bū′ty-rōne, *n.* The colorless liquid ketone of the butyric series; produced by distilling calcium butyrate.

bū′ty-rous, *a.* Same as *Butyraceous.*

bux′ē-ous, *a.* [L. *buxeus*, from *buxus*, a boxtree.] Belonging to the box-tree.

bux′in, bux′ine, *n.* An alkaloid obtained from the leaves of the common box-tree.

bux′ŏm, *a.* [ME. *buxom*, *boxom*, pliable, obedient, from *bugan*, to bend, and *-sum.*]

1. Obedient; obsequious; pliable; ready to obey; meek; humble. [Obs.]

2. Gay; lively; brisk; large and hearty; evidencing the possession of good health and spirits; comely and stout; as, a *buxom* dame; a *buxom* lass.

bux′ŏm-ly, *adv.* In a buxom manner.

bux′ŏm-ness, *n.* The state or quality of being buxom.

Bux′us, *n.* [L., box-tree.] A genus of trees of the family *Euphorbiaceæ*, the various species of which yield the valuable hardwood called boxwood. The best-known specimen is the common box-tree, the *Buxus sempervirens.*

buȳ (bī), *v.t.*; bought, *pt.*, *pp.*; buying, *ppr.* [ME. *buyen*, *byen*, *biggen*; AS. *bycgan*, to buy.]

1. To acquire the ownership, right, or title, to (anything), by paying a consideration or an equivalent in money.

2. To procure by a consideration given, or by something that is deemed worth the thing bought; to procure at a price; as, to *buy* pleasure with pain; to *buy* favor with flattery.

3. To bribe; to corrupt or pervert; to obtain by illegal or dishonorable means; as, to *buy* a seat in the legislature.

Buying in; on the stock exchange the purchasing of stock for the purpose of meeting a "short" or returning borrowed stocks.

To buy in; to purchase a commodity for the owner, as at an auction; also, to buy stock in any corporation.

To buy off; to influence to compliance; to cause to bend or yield by some consideration; as, to *buy off* conscience; to detach by a consideration given; as, to *buy off* one from a party.

To buy on credit; to purchase a thing on a promise in fact or in law, to make payment at a future day.

To buy out; (a) to buy off, or detach from; (b) to purchase the share or shares of a person in a stock, fund, or association, by which the seller leaves the company, the purchaser taking his place; as, A *buys out* B.

To buy the refusal; to give money for the right of purchasing, at a fixed price, at a future time.

Syn.—Purchase, acquire, obtain, secure, procure.

buȳ, *v.i.* To negotiate, or treat about a purchase.

I will *buy* with you and sell with you.
—Shak.

buȳ′ẽr, *n.* One who purchases anything for a money consideration; a purchasing agent who buys anything merchantable for his principal.

buz, *v.* and *n.* [Obs.] See *Buzz.*

buzz, *v.i.*; buzzed, *pt.*, *pp.*; buzzing, *ppr.* [An onomatopoetic word.]

1. To make a low, humming sound, as bees; to make the sound of *z* with an expiration of breath between the tongue and the roof of the mouth or upper teeth.

2. To whisper; to speak with a low, humming voice.

buzz, *v.t.* 1. To whisper; to spread, as report, by whispers, or to spread secretly.

2. To communicate, as a secret, in a buzzing tone.

buzz, *n.* 1. The noise of bees; also, a whisper or murmuring sound as heard in a confused conversation.

2. Anything of a buzzing character, as a cautiously communicated secret reported in low soft tones, or the mingling of soft sibilants in conversation.

buz′zărd, *n.* [ME. *busard*, *bosarde*, *busart*; OFr. *busart*, *buzart*, from *buse*, *buze*, a buzzard.]

1. A large raptorial bird, genus *Buteo*, of the falcon family, marked by a short curved bill, hooked at the tip, long wings, long tarsi, and short, weak toes. *Buteo borealis*, from feeding upon poultry, is commonly called the *hen-hawk*, as is *Buteo lineatus*. *Buteo vulgaris* is the common buzzard of Europe.

2. A blockhead; a dunce.

Bald buzzard; same as *Fishhawk.*

Honey buzzard; the *Pernis apivorus*, named from its feeding upon bees and their larvæ, though it also takes other insects and even reptiles.

Rough-legged buzzard; the *Archibuteo lagopus*, having its legs partially covered with feathers.

buz′zărd, *a.* Senseless; stupid. [Obs.]

buz′zărd-et, *n.* [Dim. of *buzzard.*] A species of hawk, described by Pennant, but not clearly identified.

buzz′ẽr, *n.* A whisperer; one who is busy in telling tales secretly; anything that buzzes.

buzz′ing-ly, *adv.* In a buzzing manner.

buzz′-saw, *n.* A circular saw, so named because of the sound it makes when in rapid motion.

bȳ, *prep.* [ME. *by*, *bi*, *be*; AS. *bi*, *big*, *be*, near to, by, of, from, according to; G. *bei*; O.H.G. *bi*; Goth. *bi*, by, about.]

1. Through or with; as, a city is destroyed *by* fire; to take *by* force.

2. By the way of; on; upon; as, journeys *by* land and *by* sea.

3. Through; passing from one to another; as, day *by* day; *by* the space of seven years.

4. At; as, *by* this time the sun had risen.

5. According to; as, it thus appears *by* his own account; these are good rules to live *by.*

6. Against. [Obs.]

By is properly used in such situations as the following: (a) before a word defining method of measurement or designating direction; as, he sells *by* the pound, but buys *by* the bushel; (b) the vessel is sailing north *by* west; (c) in expressing rectangular dimensions; as, an 8 *by* 10 pane of glass; (d) in expressing the operation of combining two factors; as, multiply 4 *by* 5.

By all means; certainly; most assuredly; without fail.

By and by; a phrase denoting nearness in time; in a short time after; presently; soon.

When persecution ariseth because of the word, *by and by* he is offended.
—Matt. xiii. 21.

By the by; in passing; before proceeding; noting something interposed in the progress of a discourse which is distinct from the main subject.

By the head; in nautical terms, drawing most water forward.

By the lee; drifting so as to let the wind strike the sails on the wrong side.

By the run; to let a vessel go without attempting to slack off.

By the stern; drawing most water aft.

By the way; (a) along the way; as, they conversed *by the way*; (b) a phrase used to introduce a subject just brought to mind, or to interpolate a new thought.

By the wind; sailing with the yards all drawn in so as to go as near into the wind as possible; closehauled.

To come by; to obtain; to get possession of.

To do by; to assist; to behave favorably toward; to do for.

To stand by; to stand near; to support; approve; defend.

bȳ, *adv.* 1. Present; near; in the vicinity.

2. Aside; as, to lay *by*.

3. Beyond; over; passing near; going past, as a bird flying *by*.

By and large; from all standpoints; in every way; on and off the wind, as a ship sails.

bȳ, *a.* Side; secondary; used only in composition; as, *by*path; *by*play; *by*-street, etc.

bȳ, bȳe, *n.* 1. That which is not of primary importance; not in use except in the phrase *by the by*.

2. In games, as hide-and-seek or prisoner's base, a goal.

3. In cricket, a run made on a ball not struck by the batsman, but which the wicket-keeper and long-stop have failed to stop.

4. In contests between paired contestants, the condition of being left without a competitor, as in tennis.

5. In golf, any hole or holes remaining to be played at the conclusion of the match.

bȳ, *n.* [ME. *by*, *bi*; AS. *by*, from *buan*, to dwell; Dan. *by*, a town, village.] A dwelling-place; a town; used only terminally in names of places; as, Rug*by*.

bȳ'ärd, *n.* A piece of leather crossing the breast, used by men who drag sledges in coal-mines.

bȳ'=bid"dẽr, *n.* A confederate who bids in behalf of an owner or auctioneer at an auction, not to purchase, but simply to raise the prices.

bȳ'=blōw, *n.* 1. A side or incidental blow.

2. A bastard child. [Obs.]

bȳ'book, *n.* A book for memoranda; a notebook.

bȳ'=cor"nẽr, *n.* A private corner.

bȳ'=dē-pend"ence, *n.* An appendage; that which is accessory.

bȳ'=drink"ing, *n.* A drinking outside of regular meal hours. [Obs.]

bȳe, *n.* See first *By*, n.

bȳe, *n.* [AS.] See second *By*, n.

bȳ'=ē-lec"tion, *n.* An election held at a time apart from the regular one.

bȳ'=end, *n.* Private end; secret purpose or advantage.

bȳ'=fel"lōw, *n.* A student of an English university not elected to full fellowship.

bȳ'gone, *n.* Something past, or gone by.

Let bygones be bygones; let the past be forgotten.

bȳ'gone, *a.* Past; gone by.

bȳ'=in"tẽr-est, *n.* Self-interest; private advantage.

bȳ'land, *n.* A point or peninsula. [Obs.]

bȳ'lănd-ẽr, *n.* [Obs.] See *Bilander*.

bȳ'=lāne, *n.* A private lane, or one branching off the usual road.

bȳ'=law, *n.* [Dan. *bylov*; Sw. and Dan. *bylag*; Ice. *bæjar-lög*, a town-law; *byjar*, genit. of *by*, a town and *lög*, a law.]

1. A town law; the local or subordinate law of a city, town, or private corporation.

2. One of a number of subordinate laws usually drawn up by societies or corporations for the government of their members or stockholders.

bȳ'=mat"tẽr, *n.* Something incidental.

bȳ'=nāme, *n.* A nickname; an epithet.

bȳ'nāme, *v.t.* To give a nickname to. [Obs.]

bȳ'=pȧss, *n.* An auxiliary pipe leading around a valve or chamber, preventing a complete cessation of the flow when the valve or chamber is closed.

bȳ'=pas"sāge, *n.* A passage aside from the main course; a byway.

bȳ'=pȧst, *a.* Past; gone by.

bȳ'pȧth, *n.*; *pl.* **bȳ'pȧths**. A private path; an obscure way.

bȳ'=plāce, *n.* A place apart or retired.

bȳ'plāy, *n.* On the stage, a scene which is carried on aside, and commonly in dumb show; anything accessory to the main action.

bȳ'=prod"uct, *n.* Something produced in a specific process apart from the main result; as, the *by-product* of arsenic in iron-smelting.

bȳre, *n.* A cow-house. [Scot.]

bȳ'=rē-spect", *n.* Private end or view. [Obs.]

byr'law, *n.* [Ice. *bæjar-lög*, a town-law.] A local system of popular government, which formerly existed in northern England and Scotland, and according to which the rights of parties were determined by their neighbors; also, the district in which such a court had jurisdiction; also written *birlaw*, *burlaw*.

byr'nie (-ni), *n.* [AS. *byrne*; O.H.G. *brunna*; Ice. *brynja*; Dan. *brynje*, a corselet, coat of mail.] A coat of mail used in the middle ages by Norwegians, Icelanders, and others.

bȳ'rōad, *n.* A private or obscure road.

Bȳ-ron'iç, *a.* Pertaining to Lord Byron, or to the literary style characteristic of his poems.

bȳ'=room, *n.* A private room or apartment.

bȳ'=speech, *n.* An incidental or casual speech, not relating directly to the main issue.

bȳ'=spell, *n.* [ME. *bispel*; AS. *bispell*, *bigspell*, a parable, example, story; *bi*, by, and *spell*, a story.] A proverb; a parable.

bys-sā'ceous, *a.* [L. *byssus*, Gr. *byssos*, a fine flax or linen.] Resembling a byssus; consisting of fine silky filaments.

bys'săl, *a.* Relating to a byssus.

bys-sif'ẽr-ous, *a.* [L. *byssus*, byssus, and *ferre*, to bear.] Bearing a byssus or tuft.

bys'sin, *n.* See *Byssus*, n. 1.

bys'sine, *a.* [L. *byssinus*; Gr. *byssinos*, from *byssos*, byssus.] Made of silk; having a silky or flax-like appearance.

bys'soid, *a.* Byssaceous.

bys'sōl-ite, *n.* [Gr. *byssos*, fine flax, and *lithos*, stone; so called from its resemblance to flax.] A variety of hornblende occurring in short silky fibers.

bys'sus, *n.*; *pl.* **bys'sī**. [L. *byssus*; Gr. *byssos* fine linen, or cotton.]

1. Among the ancients, a cloth of exceedingly fine texture.

2. One of the *Byssi*, a name formerly given by botanists to a heterogeneous collection of filamentous cryptogamic plants.

3. In zoölogy, a long, delicate, lustrous, and silky bunch of filaments, secreted by the foot, and by means of which the *Mytilus*, *Pinna*, and other bivalve mollusks are attached to fixed objects.

Pinna flabellum.
a, Byssus.

bȳ'stand"ẽr, *n.* One who stands near; a spectator; one who has no concern with the business being conducted.

Syn.—Looker-on, spectator, observer, beholder, gazer, witness.

bȳ'=street, *n.* A separate, private, or obscure street.

bȳ'=strōke, *n.* An incidental or sly stroke.

bȳ'=tŭrn"ing, *n.* An obscure road.

bȳ'=view (-vū), *n.* Private view; self-interested purpose.

bȳ'=walk, *n.* A secluded or private walk.

bȳ'=wăsh, *n.* A conduit or by-pass to carry off superfluous water from a reservoir or dam.

bȳ'wāy, *n.* A secluded path; a private or obscure way.

bȳ'=wīpe, *n.* A secret stroke or sarcasm. [Obs.]

bȳ'word (-wũrd), *n.* 1. A common saying; a proverb; a saying that has a general currency; a nickname.

2. A laughingstock.

bȳ'work (-wũrk), *n.* A secondary business; employment aside from regular work.

byz'ănt, *n.* Same as *Bezant*.

By-zan'tine, *a.* and *n.* [LL. *Byzantinus*, from *Byzantium*; Gr. *Byzantion*, *Byzantium*, from *Byzas*, said to have been its founder.]

I. *a.* Relating to Byzantium.

II. *n.* One native to or residing in Byzantium, the former name of the city of Constantinople.

Byzantine architecture; the style of architecture prevalent at Byzantium while the capital

Byzantine Capitals.
1. From the Apse of Murano. 2. From the Casa Loredan, Venice.

of the Greek empire; characterized by incrustation, surface ornament, and sculpture, the leading forms being the arch, circle, cross, and dome.

Byzantine church; the Greek church.

Byzantine empire; the Greek empire, flourishing from A.D. 395 to 1453.

C

C (sē.) The third letter and the second consonant of the English alphabet. It came into the English from the Latin, where it had the sound of *k*, through the French. The Latin got it from the Greek alphabet where it was represented by gamma, γ, in the sound of hard *g*. The Greeks in turn got it from the Phenicians.

C serves to represent two perfectly distinct sounds, namely, the guttural sound pertaining to *k* and the hard or thin sound of *s*, the former being that which historically belongs to it; while it also forms with *h* the digraph *ch*. The former sound it has before the vowels *a*, *o*, and *u*, the consonants *l*, *r*, *s*, *t*, and when final; the latter before *e*, *i*, and *y*. The digraph *ch* has three different sounds, the first nearly equivalent to *tsh*, as in *church*; the second equivalent to *sh*, as in *machine*; and the third in words from the Greek, equivalent to *k*, as in *chord*. To these the Scotch adds a fourth, as in the word *loch*, where the sound of *ch* is the same as in German. As an initial sound *c* occurs either alone or before the consonants *l* and *r*; as a final it is found chiefly or only in words of foreign origin, in purely English words being followed by *k* when in this position. In the Latin alphabet *c* had the *k*-sound, and this was the sound which belonged to the letter in Anglo-Saxon in all positions, *cicen*, a chicken, being pronounced *kiken*, and *cild*, a child, *kild*. The old sound is now often represented by *k* or *ck*; in many words it has been softened, and is now represented by *ch*, this digraph being borrowed from the French. In *ajar*, *knowledge*, the *k*-sound first changed to the *ch*-sound, and latterly to the sound of *j*.

C, c, *as a symbol.* As a numeral, *C* stands for 100; *CC* for 200; etc.

In music, *C* after the clef is the mark of common time, in which each measure is a semibreve, corresponding to $\frac{4}{4}$. *C* is also the name of a note in the scale; the keynote major, and the third minor, of the natural scale.

As an abbreviation, *c.* stands for cent, or centime; chapter; *C.* for Centigrade, etc.

ça, çaa, *v. t.* [Scot.] To drive; impel; knock.

But *ca* them out to park or hill. —Burns.

çaa'ing=whāle, *n.* [Scot. *caa*, to drive, and *whale*; so called from their being driven in herds.] A porpoise-like cetacean. *Globicephalus svineval*, frequenting the shores of the Orkney, Shetland, and Faroe islands, and Iceland, appearing in large herds.

çaa'mȧ, *n.* A name given to the hartbeest; also, a South African fox, *Vulpes caama*.

çab, *n.* [Abbrev. of *cabriolet*.]

1. A covered carriage with two or four wheels, usually drawn by one horse.

2. The covered part of a locomotive in which the engineer and fireman are stationed.

çab, *n.* [Heb. *kab*, a hollow, from *kabab*, to hollow out.] A Hebrew dry measure, variously estimated to contain from one to two quarts.

çȧ-bal', *n.* [Fr. *cabale*, an intrigue, club, society; LL. *cabbala*, a cabala; Heb. *qabbālāh*, reception, mysterious doctrine; *qābal*, to take, receive.]

1. A number of persons united in some close design; usually to promote their private views in church or state by intrigue; a junto. It is sometimes synonymous with faction, but a *cabal* usually consists of fewer men than a party, and the word generally implies close union and secret intrigues. This name was

given to the ministry of Charles II., Clifford, Ashley, Buckingham, Arlington, and Lauderdale, the initials of whose names compose the word.

2. Intrigue; secret artifices of a few united in a close design.

3. Something hidden or secret.

4. The cabala. [Obs.]

Syn.—Party, faction, combination, conspiracy, intrigue, junto, plot.

ça-bal′, *v.i.*; caballed, *pt.*, *pp.*; caballing, *ppr.* To unite in a small party to promote private views by intrigue; to intrigue; to unite in secret artifices to effect some design.

çab′ȧ-lȧ, kab′ȧ-lȧ, *n.* [LL. *cabbala*; Heb. *qabbālāh*, a reception, mysterious doctrine, from *qābal*, to receive, take.]

1. Tradition, or a mysterious kind of science among Jewish rabbis, pretended to have been delivered to the ancient Jews by revelation, and transmitted by oral tradition; serving for the interpretation of the hidden sense of Scripture.

2. Secret science in general; mystic art.

çab′ȧ-lişm, *n.* 1. The science of the cabalists.

2. Superstitious religious devotion. [Rare.]

çab′ȧ-list, *n.* One who professes faith in the cabala.

çab-ȧ-lis′tiç, çab-ȧ-lis′tiç-ăl, *a.* Pertaining to the cabala; mystic; occult.

çab-ȧ-lis′tiç-ăl-ly, *adv.* In the manner of the cabalists.

çab′ȧ-līze, *v.i.* To use the manner or language of the cabalists. [Rare.]

çȧ-bal′lẽr, *n.* One who cabals.

çä-bäl-le-rī′ȧ (-lyä-rē′ȧ), *n.* [Sp., from *caballo*, L. *caballus*, a horse.] A Spanish land measure, now varying from thirty-three to one hundred and ninety-four acres, formerly granted to a horseman who had seen military service.

çä-bäl-le′rō (-lyā′rō), *n.* [Sp., from *caballo*, L. *caballus*, a horse.]

1. A Spanish cavalier or gentleman.

2. A grave and stately Spanish dance.

çab′ăl-line, *a.* [L. *caballinus*, from *caballus*, a horse.] Pertaining to a horse.

Caballine aloes; horse aloes, *Aloe caballina*.

Caballine spring; same as *Hippocrene*.

çä-bäl′lō (-lyō), *n.* A Spanish-American name for a horse.

çä-bän′, *n.* [Sp., prob. a native name.] A Philippine grain measure of about 1 bu. 2.4 pk. Spelled also *cavan*.

çab′ȧ-ret, *n.* [Fr.] 1. A tavern; a house where liquors are retailed.

2. A set or service, as for tea or coffee.

3. A vaudeville performance given in restaurants for the diners.

çä′bȧs (-bä), *n.* [Fr.] A fig basket; also, a lady's flat workbasket or hand-bag.

çȧ-bas′sŏu, *n.* Same as *Kabassou*.

çab′bāġe, *v.t* or *v.i.*; cabbaged, *pt.*, *pp.*; cabbaging, *ppr.* [Fr. *cabasser*, to put into a basket; OFr. *cabas*, a basket.] To purloin or embezzle, as pieces of cloth after cutting out a garment.

çab′bāġe, *v.i.* To form a head in growing.

çab′bāġe, *n.* [ME. *cabbish*; OFr. *cabus*, *caboche*, cabbage; It. *capuccio*, a little head, from *capo*, L. *caput*, head.]

1. The popular name of some species of *Brassica*, especially applied to the plane-leaved, hearting, garden varieties of *Brassica oleracea*, cultivated for food. The kinds most cultivated are the common *cabbage*, the savoy, the broccoli, and the cauliflower.

2. An esculent terminal bud occurring in certain palms.

Thousand-headed cabbage; Brussels sprouts.

çab′bāġe, *n.* Cloth purloined by one who cuts out garments; hence, anything stolen.

çab′bāġe-ā″phis, *n.* [*Cabbage*, and New L. *aphis*, a louse, insect.] The cabbage plant-louse.

çab′bāġe-bug, *n.* A bright-colored insect, *Murgantia histrionica*, destructive to cabbages, that has invaded the United States from Central America.

çab′bāġe-but″tẽr-flȳ, *n.* A butterfly of the genus *Pieris*, the larvæ of which destroy cabbage and other plants; also, the native American species.

çab′bāġe-flēa, *n.* A beetle, as *Haltica consobrina*, having larvæ subsisting upon cabbages.

çab′bāġe-flȳ, *n.* A fly, *Anthomyia brassicæ*, the larvæ of which feed upon cabbage roots.

çab′bāġe-head (-hed), *n.* 1. The compact leaves of a cabbage, usually approaching a globular form.

2. A stupid or foolish person. [Slang.]

çab′bāġe-mag″gŏt, *n.* A cabbage-worm.

çab′bāġe-mŏth, *n.* The *Mamestra* or *Noctua brassicæ*, or pot-herb moth.

çab′bāġe-pälm (päm), *n.* See *Cabbage-tree*.

çab′bāġe-pal-met″tō, *n.* A palmetto of southern United States.

çab′bāġe-rōşe, *n.* A species of rose, *Rosa centifolia*, of many varieties, used in the manufacture of rose-water and attar; called also *Provence rose*.

çab′bāġe-tree, *n.* 1. The common name of a number of palms having a succulent bud terminally on the stem; as, *Sabal Palmetto*, of southern United States; *Oreodoxa* or *Areca oleracea*, the cabbage-palm of the West Indies; the Australian fan-leafed palm, *Livistona australis*.

2. Any tree of the genus *Andira*, the bark of which is used as a vermifuge.

Cabbage-palm (*Areca oleracea*).

çab′bāġe-worm (-wẽrm), *n.* The cabbage-butterfly, -fly, or -moth when in the larval stage.

çab′ble, *v.t.*; cabbled, *pt.*, *pp.*; cabbling, *ppr.* [Origin unknown.] In metallurgy, to break (flat masses of partially finished iron) into pieces, to be again heated in a furnace and wrought or hammered into bar iron.

çab′blẽr, *n.* One employed at cabbling.

çȧ-be′çȧ, çȧ-besse′, *n.* [Port., head, chief; L. *caput*, head.] The Portuguese name for the highest grade of silk imported from India.

çā′bẽr, *n.* [Gael. *cabar*, a pole, stake.] A pole; a beam; specifically, in Highland games, a long undressed stem of a tree, used for tossing or turning over.

çȧ-bes′trō, *n.* [Sp., a halter.] A hair rope or lariat.

çab-e-zon′, *n.* [Sp., from *cabeza*, head.] A Californian fish, *Scorpænichthys marmoratus*.

çȧ-bï′ai, *n.* Same as *Capibara*.

çab′in, *n.* [ME. *caban*; OFr. *cabane*; LL. *capanna*, a cabin; W. *caban*, dim. of *cab*, a booth, hut.]

1. A small room; an inclosed place.

2. A cottage; a hut or small house.

3. Any covered place for a temporary residence.

4. An apartment in a ship for officers and passengers; the saloon.

çab′in, *v.i.*; cabined, *pt.*, *pp.*; cabining, *ppr.* To live in a cabin; to lodge.

çab′in, *v.t.* To confine in a cabin.

çab′ined, *a.* Inclosed in or furnished with a cabin. [Rare.]

çab′i-net, *n.* [Fr. *cabinet*, dim. of *cabine*, *cabane*, a cabin, hut.]

1. A closet; a small room or apartment.

2. A private room in which consultations are held.

3. The select council of the chief executive of a government; specifically, (a) in the United States, the heads (taken collectively) of the ten executive departments, being the Secretaries of State, Treasury, War, Navy, Interior, Agriculture, Commerce, Labor, the Postmaster-General, and the Attorney-General; (b) in Great Britain, the committee of ministers, from twelve to seventeen in number, under the leadership of the Prime Minister, who take charge of the government.

4. A piece of furniture, consisting of a chest with drawers and doors.

5. Any close place where things of value are deposited for safe-keeping.

6. A hut; a cottage; a small house. [Obs.]

7. In printing, a closed stand for job-type, leads, cuts, etc., with or without a galley-top.

Cabinet photograph; a standard size photograph printed from a plate 4½ x 6½ inches.

Kitchen cabinet; an epithet applied to certain friends of President Jackson who were supposed to have influenced his official actions to a large extent.

çab′i-net, *a.* Pertaining to a cabinet; specifically, small; tasty.

çab′i-net, *v.t.* To shut in or inclose. [Rare.]

çab′i-net-māk″ẽr, *n.* One whose occupation is to make cabinets, tables, bureaus, bedsteads, and similar furniture.

çab′i-net-māk″ing, *n.* The business or trade of a cabinetmaker.

çab′i-net-work″(-wẽrk″), *n.* Fine joinery or similar work.

Çab-i-rē′ăn, *n.* One of the Cabiri.

Çȧ-bī′rī, *n.pl.* [L., from Gr. *Kabeiroi*.] Divinities worshiped in the ancient Greek islands of Lemnos, Imbros, and Samothrace, and also on the neighboring coast of Troy in Asia Minor.

Çȧ-bir′i-ăn, Çȧ-bir′iç, *a.* Pertaining to the Cabiri or their worship.

Çab-i-rit′iç, *a.* Same as *Cabirian*.

çā′ble (-bl), *n.* [ME. *cable*, *cabel*; OFr. *cable*; LL. *capulum*, a cable, rope, from *capere*, to take hold.]

1. Any large, strong rope or chain designed to support a heavy weight or stand a powerful strain; specifically, (a) a ship's hawser; (b) a wire rope; as of a *cable*-railway, suspension-bridge, or gravel-plow of a construction-train.

2. In electricity, a conductor, usually consisting of several insulated and protected wires and designed for submarine, underground, or aerial purposes.

3. Colloquially, a cablegram.

4. In architecture, (a) a kind of wreathed convex molding in the form of a rope; (b) a molding representing a spiral scroll.

Stream cable; a hawser or rope, smaller than the bower cables, to moor a ship in a place sheltered from wind and heavy seas.

To pay out, or *to veer out the cable*; to slacken it that it may run out of the ship.

To serve the cable; to bind it round with ropes, canvas, etc., to prevent its being worn or galled in the hawse.

To slip the cable; to let it run out end for end; colloquially, to die.

çā′ble, *v.t.* and *v.i.*; cabled, *pt.*, *pp.*; cabling, *ppr.* To send (a message) by submarine cable.

çā′ble, *v.t.* 1. To make fast with a cable.

2. To ornament with cabling.

çā′bled (-bld), *a.* 1. Fastened with a cable.

2. Having the architectural ornament called a cable.

çā′ble-gram, *n.* [Fr. *cable*, a cable, rope, and Gr. *gramma*, from *graphein*, to write. A word formed on the analogy of *telegram*, *chronogram*, etc.] A message sent by cable.

çā′ble-lāid, *a.* 1. Formed of three three-stranded ropes twisted into one.

2. Twisted in the manner of a cable.

çā′ble-mōld″ing, *n.* See *Cable*, n. 4.

çā′ble-rāil″rōad, *n.* A railway in which the motive power is furnished by an endless cable moving in a tunnel beneath the track.

çā′ble-rōad, *n.* A cable-railroad.

çā′ble's-length, *n.* A measure of length on the sea, either 120 fathoms, 720 feet, or one-tenth of a nautical mile, 600 feet.

çā′blet, *n.* A little cable; specifically, one having a circumference of less than ten inches.

çā′ble-tiẽr, *n.* The place in a vessel where the cables are coiled away.

çā′ble-wāy, *n.* A cable-railroad.

çā′bling, *n.* 1. The cables used in decorating; any cable-molding, or moldings.

2. Transmission by cable.

çab′măn, *n.* The driver of a cab.

çȧ-bob′, *n.* [Anglo-Ind. from Per. *kab*, an ox.]

1. An Oriental dish, consisting generally of a neck or loin of mutton cut in pieces and roasted on a wooden spit, dressed with onions, eggs, spices, and sauce.

2. Roast leg of mutton with stuffing of herbs and herrings.

çȧ-bob′, *v.t.* To roast or prepare for a cabob. [Rare.]

çȧ-boçhed′, *a.* Caboshed.

çȧ-bō-çhon′, *n.* [Fr.] A precious stone cut in such a manner as to leave a convex surface instead of the usual facets.

Çȧ-bom′bȧ, *n.* [Native Guiana name.] A small genus of the water-lily family, nearly identical with the water-shields, found in the still waters of southern United States, having the submerged leaves dissected and those at the surface peltate.

çȧ-boo′dle, *n.* [A corruption of *kit and boodle*; *kit*, *kith*, family, relations, and *boodle*, D. *boedel*, property, possessions.] A slang term meaning lot or number, used mostly in the phrase, *the whole caboodle*.

çȧ-boose′, *n.* [D. *kabuis*, *kombuis*, a ship's galley, booth, hut; Fr. *cambuse*; Dan. *kabys*, a little room, hut.]

1. The cook-room of a merchant vessel; the galley.

2. A serviceable car, usually having a lookout, attached to a freight- or construction-train for the use of conductor and rear brakemen.

çȧ-boshed′ (-bosht′), *a.* [OFr. *caboche*, the head; It. *capocchia*, from *capo*, L. *caput*, head.] In heraldry, showing full-faced, with none of the neck visible; said of an animal's head used as a bearing.

çab′ō-tāġe, *n.* [Fr. *cabotage*, from *caboter*, to coast, go from cape to cape; Sp. *cabo*, a cape.] Navigation along a coast; coasting-trade.

ca-bré (brā′) *n.* [Fr.] In aviation, a flying attitude in which the angle of incidence is greater than normal; tail down.

çȧ-brer′ite, *n.* [Named from the Sierra *Cabreras*, in Spain, where it was first found.] A green hydrous arseniate of cobalt, nickel, and magnesia, found native in fibrous masses.

çȧ-bril′lȧ (*Sp. pron.* kä-brēl′yä), *n.* [Sp.] A name generally applied to many serranoid fishes, habitants of the Mediterranean Sea, the Californian coast, and other warm waters, as the kelp-salmon, the rock-bass.

çab′ri-ōle, *n.* A leap or caper.

çab-ri-ō-let′ (-lā′), *n.* [Fr., dim. of *cabriole*, a leap, caper; It. *capriola*, from L. *caper*, a he-goat.] A two-wheeled, one-horse carriage.

çab′rit, *n.* A North American antelope; the pronghorn; also written *cabree*, *cabret*, etc.

çab′ūrns, *n. pl.* [Origin unknown.] Small lines made of spun-yarn, to bind cables, seize tackles, and the like.

çȧ-çā′in, *n.* Theobromine.

çȧ-çā′ō, *n.* [Sp., from Mex. *cacauatl*, the cacao.]

The chocolate-tree, *Theobroma Cacao*, a native of the West Indies. This tree grows about twenty feet high, bearing pods which are oval and pointed. The nuts or seeds are numerous, lodged in a white, pithy substance, and furnish the cocoa and chocolate of commerce.

Cacao (*Theobroma Cacao*).

çaçh'ȧ-lot, *n.* [Fr.] The sperm-whale.

çaçhe, *n.* [Fr., from *cacher*, to hide, conceal.] A hole in the ground for secreting and preserving provisions which it is inconvenient to carry.

çȧ-çhec'tiç, çȧ-çhec'tiç-ăl, *a.* [L. *cachecticus*; Gr. *kachektikos*, from *kachexia*, cachexy.] Having cachexy; pertaining to cachexy.

çaçhe'pot, *n.* [Fr., from *cacher*, to hide, and *pot*.] A casing of ornamental design to hide an ordinary flowerpot.

çaçh-et' (kash-ā'), *n.* [Fr., from *cacher*, to hide.] A seal.

Lettre de cachet; in French history, a sealed letter of state; particularly, one authorizing the imprisonment or execution of a person without a trial and on a trifling pretext. *Lettres de cachet* were abolished at the Revolution.

çȧ-çhex'y, çȧ-çhex'i-ȧ, *n.* [Gr. *kachexia*, from *kakos*, bad, and *hexis*, habit, from *echein*, to have.] A morbid state of the bodily system, the result of disease, as the venereal, or of intemperate habits.

çaçh'i-böu, *n.* [Fr., from a native West Indian name.] A tree of the myrrh family, growing in tropical North America; also, the aromatic resin obtained from it; also called *chibou*.

çaçh-in-nā'tion, *n.* [L. *cachinnatio*, from *cachinnare*, to laugh loudly; an imitative word.] Noisy and mirthless laughter; often a symptom of dementia or hysteria.

çȧ-çhin'nȧ-tō-ry, *a.* Of or pertaining to cachination or immoderate laughter.

çȧ-çhi'ri, *n.* An intoxicant manufactured in Cayenne from the root of the manioc.

çaçh'ō-long, *n.* [Fr. *cacholong*; *Cach*, the name of a river in Bokhara, and *cholon*, a Kalmuck word for stone.] A mineral of the quartz family, a variety of opal, and often called *pearl-opal*, usually milk-white, sometimes grayish- or yellowish-white, opaque or slightly translucent at the edges.

çȧ-çhöu', *n.* [Fr.] An aromatic pill or tablet for perfuming the breath.

çȧ-chü'chȧ, *n.* [Sp.] An Andalusian dance or piece of dance-music in three-four time, similar to the Spanish bolero.

çȧ-chün'de, *n.* [Sp.] A pastil compounded of drugs and aromatics, highly esteemed in China and India as a perfume and a medicine to correct stomach troubles.

çȧ-çique' (kȧ-sēk'), *n.* [Sp., from a Haitian word.] The name given by the Spanish discoverers to a native chief of the West Indies or America.

çack, *v.i.* [ME. *cakken*; D. *kakken*; L. *cacare*; Gr. *kakkān*, from *kakkē*, ordure, dung.] To void excrement.

çack'ẽr-el, *n.* A fish which is said to void excrements when pursued, or a fish whose flesh produces laxness of the bowels. [Obs.]

çaç'kle, *v.i.*; cackled, *pt.*, *pp.*; cackling, *ppr.* [ME. *cakelen*; G. *kakeln*, to cackle. Imitative word.]

1. To utter a noisy cry such as that made by a hen on leaving the nest.

2. To laugh with a broken noise, like the cackling of a goose; to giggle.

3. To prate; to prattle; to tattle; to talk in a silly manner.

çaç'kle, *n.* 1. The cackling of a goose or hen.

2. Idle talk; silly prattle.

çaç'klẽr, *n.* One who or that which cackles; sometimes, a telltale.

çaç'kling, *n.* The broken noise of a goose or hen.

çaç'ō-. A combining form from Gr. *kakos*, bad, evil, and used principally in medicine; as, *caco*plastic, *caco*phony.

çaç-ō-çhym'i-ȧ, çaç'ō-çhym-y, *n.* [*Caco-*, and Gr. *chymos*, juice.] A vitiated state of the humors of the body, especially of the blood.

çaç'ō-çhym-iç, çaç-ō-çhym'iç-ăl, *a.* Having the fluids of the body vitiated, especially the blood.

çaç-ō-dē'mŏn, *n.* [Gr. *kakodaimōn*; *kakos*, bad, evil, and *daimōn*, spirit.]

1. An evil spirit.

2. A medical term for nightmare.

çaç-ō-dox'iç-ăl, *a.* Heretical; heterodox.

çaç'ō-dox-y, *n.* [*Caco-*, and Gr. *doxa*, opinion.] Heresy. [Rare.]

çaç'ō-dyl, çaç'ō-dyle, *n.* [Gr. *kakōdēs*, ill-smelling; *kakos*, bad, and *ozein*, to smell, and *hylē*, matter.] Dimethyl arsine; alkarsin.

çaç-ō-dyl'iç, *a.* Pertaining to cacodyl.

Cacodylic acid; a colorless crystalline arsenic compound, obtained by the oxidation of cacodyl. It is odorless, and said not to be actively poisonous.

çaç'ō-e-py, *n.* [Gr. *kakoepeia*, incorrect language; *kakos*, bad, and *epos*, word.] Faulty pronunciation; the opposite of *orthoepy*.

çaç-ō-ē'thēṣ, *n.* [L., from Gr. *kakoēthēs*, a bad habit; *kakos*, bad, and *ēthos*, habit, custom.]

1. A bad custom or habit; a bad disposition.

2. In medicine, a bad quality or disposition in disease; an incurable ulcer.

Cacoethes loquendi; a propensity for talking or making speeches.

Cacoethes scribendi; a passion for writing; an inordinate or insane desire to see oneself in print.

çaç-ō-gas'triç, *a.* [*Caco-*, and Gr. *gastēr*, *gastros*, stomach.] Dyspeptic. [Rare.]

çaç-ō-graph'iç, *a.* Pertaining to cacography; written or spelled incorrectly.

çȧ-çog'rȧ-phy, *n.* [*Caco-*, and Gr. *-graphia*, from *graphein*, to write.] Illegible writing or incorrect spelling.

çaç'cō-let (-lā), *n.* [Fr.] A pack-saddle fitted with folding chairs or a litter, by means of which travelers or feeble persons may be carried on a mule's back in the mountains. A military mule-litter, for carrying the sick and wounded, was first used by the French in the Crimean War.

Cacolet, or Mule-chair.

çȧ-çol'ō-ġy, *n.* [Gr. *kakologia*, evil speaking, abuse; *kakos*, bad, and *legein*, to speak.] Poor diction; a bad use of words.

çȧ-çō-mix'l, çȧ-çō-mix'le, *n.* [Mex.] A racoon-like, carnivorous animal, *Bassaris astuta*, or allied species; a habitant of Mexico and southwestern United States.

çaç'ō-nym, *n.* [*Caco-*, and Gr. *onyma*, name.] In zoölogy, an undesirable name.

çaç-ō-nym'iç, *a.* Relating to a caconym.

çȧ-çoon', *n.* [African name.] A commercial name for the large beans of the *Entada scandens*, used for making snuffboxes, purses, etc.

çaç-ō-phon'iç, çaç-ō-phon'iç-ăl, *a.* Having a harsh sound.

çȧ-çoph'ō-ny, *n.* [Gr. *kakophōnia*, from *kakophōnos*, harsh-sounding; *kakos*, bad, evil, and *phōnē*, voice.]

1. In rhetoric, an uncouth or disagreeable sound of words, proceeding from the meeting of harsh letters or syllables.

2. In medicine, a depraved voice; an altered state of the voice.

3. In music, a combination of discordant sounds.

çaç-ō-plas'tiç, *a.* [*Caco-*, and Gr. *plastikos*, from *plassein*, to form.] In pathology, susceptible of only a low degree of organization, as the indurations resulting from low or chronic inflammation, cirrhosis, etc.

çaç'ō-teçh-ny, *n.* [*Caco-*, and Gr. *technē*, art.] A corrupt state of art.

çȧ-çox'ēne, çȧ-çox'e-nīte, *n.* [Gr. *kakoxenos*, unfriendly to strangers; *kakos*, bad, and *xenos*, stranger, guest.] A mineral occurring in yellowish, radiating tufts, and consisting of phosphoric acid with alumina, fluoric acid, and water; hydrous phosphate of iron.

Çaç-tā'cē-æ, *n.pl.* [L., from *cactus*, a prickly plant, and *-aceæ*.] A natural order of dicotyledonous plants, the cactus or Indian-fig order. The species are succulent shrubs, with minute scale-like leaves, except in the genus *Pereskia*, and with clusters of spines on the stems. They are natives of America, but are naturalized throughout the world.

Sharp-angled Cactus (*Echinocactus oxygonus*).

çaç-tā'ceous, *a.* Belonging to or resembling the cactus or the order *Cactaceæ*.

çaç'tus, *n.* [L., from Gr. *kaktos*, a prickly plant.] The old name of a group of plants once considered to form a single genus, but now divided into several, and constituting the natural order *Cactaceæ*.

çaç'tus-bīrd, *n.* Any oscine bird of the genus *Cactornis*.

çaç'tus-wren (-ren), *n.* Any one of the genus of birds, *Campylorhynchus*.

çȧ-çū'mi-năl, *a.* [L. *cacumen* (*-inis*), the top or summit, and *-al*.] Pertaining to a top or summit; specifically, pertaining to the top of the palate; as, a *cacuminal* letter.

çȧ-çū'mi-nāte, *v.t.* To make sharp or pointed. [Obs.]

çad, *n.* [An abbrev. of *cadet*.]

1. A slang term of contempt applied originally to various classes of persons of a low grade, as hangers-on about innyards, conductors of omnibuses, messengers or errand-boys, and the like. [Eng.]

2. A coarse, vulgar fellow; also, a snob; an overbearing arrogant fellow.

çȧ-das'tẽr, çȧ-das'tre (-tẽr), *n.* [Fr. *cadastre*; LL. *capitastrum*, a poll-tax register, from L. *caput*, head.] A detailed survey of lands, their extent, subdivisions, etc.; in most countries executed by the government as the basis of taxation.

çȧ-das'trăl, *a.* [Fr.] Relating to a cadaster or survey.

çȧ-dā'vẽr, *n.* [L., from *cadere*, to fall.] A corpse.

çȧ-dav'ẽr-iç, *a.* Resembling or pertaining to a corpse, or to the changes resulting from death.

çȧ-dav'ẽr-ous, *a.* [L. *cadaverosus*, corpse-like; *cadaver*, a corpse.]

1. Having the appearance or color of a dead human body; pale; hollow; wan; ghastly; as, a *cadaverous* look.

2. Having the qualities of a dead body.

Syn.—Ghastly, deathlike, pale, pallid, wan.

çȧ-dav'ẽr-ous-ly, *adv.* In a cadaverous form.

çȧ-dav'ẽr-ous-ness, *n.* The quality of being cadaverous.

çad'bāit, *n.* The larva of the caddis-fly.

çad'die, *n.* [Scot.] 1. A boy employed to run errands; specifically, one who attends a golfer.

2. A cadet. [Obs.]

çad'dis, çad'dice, *n.* [Prov. Eng. *caddy*; G. *käder*, *käderle*, bait.]

1. A kind of ribbon or tape. [Obs.]

2. A kind of wadding or cotton wool; also, a cloth resembling serge. [Obs.]

çad'dis, çad'dice, *n.* The caddis-worm.

çad'dis-flȳ, çad'dice-flȳ, *n.* A phryganeid insect of the order *Neuroptera*, commonly called the May-fly, the larva or grub of which forms a case of small stones, grass-roots, shells, etc., and lives under water till ready to emerge from the pupa state.

Caddis-fly and Worms.

1. Caddis-fly. 2. Larva in case formed of straw or dry grass-stalks. 3. In case formed of small stones. 4. In case formed of grass-roots. 5. In case formed of shells.

çad'dish, *a.* Like a cad; ill-bred; vulgar.

çad'dis-wŏrm, çad'dice-wŏrm, *n.* The larva of the caddis-fly. [See *Caddis-fly*.]

çad'dōw, *n.* A jackdaw. [Prov. Eng.]

çad'dy, *n.* [Corruption of *catty*, from Malay *kati*, a weight equivalent to one and one-half pounds.] A small box for keeping tea; a tea-canister.

çāde, *a.* [Of doubtful origin, perhaps from Ice. *kād*, a new-born child.] Tame; bred by hand; domesticated; as, a *cade* lamb.

çāde, *v.t.* [ME. *cade*, *cad*, a lamb.] To bring up or nourish by hand, or with tenderness. [Obs.]

çāde, *n.* [ME. *cade*; L. *cadus*; Gr. *kados*, a jar, liquid measure.] A barrel or cask; a measure containing five hundred herrings or a thousand sprats.

çāde, *n.* [Fr.] Juniper.

Oil of cade; see *Cade-oil*.

çȧ-delle', *n.* [Fr.] The larva of a horny-headed beetle, *Trogosita mauritanica*, very destructive to grain in the bin.

çā'dence, *n.* [ME. *cadence*; L. *cadentia*, a falling, from *cadere*, to fall.]

1. A fall; a decline; a state of sinking.

2. A fall of the voice in reading or speaking, as at the end of a sentence; also, the falling of the voice in the general modulation of tones in reciting.

3. The general tone or modulation of the voice in reading or reciting, especially in reading or reciting verse.

4. Tone; sound; as, hoarse *cadence*.

5. Any regularity and uniformity of beat or measure, as in marching or dancing.

6. In horsemanship, an equal measure or

proportion observed by a horse in all his motions.

7. In heraldry, same as *marks of cadency.*

8. In music, (a) in general, the close of a musical passage or phrase; (b) specifically, a vocal or instrumental shake or trill, run, or division, introduced as an ending or as a means of return to the first subject; (c) same as *Cadenza.*

Imperfect cadence; one consisting of the chord of the tonic followed by that of the dominant.

Perfect cadence; one composed of the chord of the dominant, followed by that of the tonic, likewise of the chord of the dominant seventh, followed by that of the tonic.

çā′dence, *v.t.*; cadenced, *pt., pp.*; cadencing, *ppr.* To regulate by musical measure.

çā′den-cy, *n.* The various steps in the descent of a family.

Marks of cadency; in heraldry, marks intended to show the descent of a younger branch of a family from the main stock.

çȧ-dēne′, *n.* [Fr. *cadene*; Sp. *cadena*, a chain, the warp in weaving; L. *catena*, a chain.] A species of inferior carpet imported from the Levant.

çā′dent, *a.* [L. *cadens* (*-entis*), ppr. of *cadere*, to fall.] Falling; sinking; applied specifically in astrology to planets.

çȧ-den′zȧ, *n.* [It.] An instrumental or vocal flourish preceding the close or division of a movement.

çāde′=oil, *n.* An oil used in Germany and France for veterinary purposes, made of the fruit of the *Juniperus communis*, called in those countries *cada.*

çȧ-det′, *n.* [Fr. *cadet*, a younger brother; a dim. from L. *caput*, head.]

1. The younger of two brothers; the youngest son.

2. A gentleman who carries arms in a regiment, as a private, with a view to acquire military skill, and obtain a commission.

3. A young man in training for the rank of an officer in the army or navy, or in a military school; specifically, a student at either the United States Military or Naval Academy or a similar institution.

çȧ-det′ship, *n.* The commission given a cadet.

çȧ-dew′, çāde′wŏrm, *n.* A caddis-worm.

çadġe (kaj), *n.* A round frame on which to carry hawks for sale. [Obs.]

çadġe, *v.t.* and *v.i.*; cadged, *pt., pp.*; cadging, *ppr.* [Prov. Eng. and Scot.] 1. To carry, especially to carry for sale; to hawk or peddle.

2. To sponge on another.

çadġ′ẽr, *n.* [OFr. *cagier*, one who carried about falcons or other birds in a cage for sale.]

1. An itinerant huckster; a truck-peddler.

2. One who gets his living by trickery; a beggar; a sponger. [Prov. Eng. in both senses.]

çadġ′ẽr, *n.* One who carries hawks.

çadġ′y, *a.* [Dan. *kaad*; Ice. *kātr*, merry, cheerful.] Lively; frolicsome; cheerful; also, loose. [Prov. Eng.]

çā′di, *n.* See *Kadi.*

çad′ie, *n.* [Obs.] See *Caddie.*

çā-di-les′kẽr, *n.* See *Kadilesker.*

çȧ-dil′laç, *n.* [Fr., named from *Cadillac*, a town in France.] A sort of pear.

çad′is, *n.* See *Caddis*, n. 2.

Çad-mē′ăn, *a.* Relating to Cadmus, a legendary prince of Thebes, in Greece, who is said to have introduced into Greece the sixteen simple letters of the alphabet—α, β, γ, δ, ε, ι, κ, λ, μ, ν, ο, π, ρ, σ, τ, υ, which are therefore called *Cadmean* letters.

Cadmean victory; a proverbial phrase of uncertain origin, for a victory in which the victors suffer as much as the vanquished.

çad′mi-ȧ, *n.* [L. *cadmia*; Gr. *kadmeia*, calamin.]

1. A name given by old writers to calamin.

2. An oxid of zinc which collects on the sides of furnaces where zinc happens to be present in an ore and is sublimed.

çad′miç, *a.* Containing, relating to, or derived from cadmium.

çad′mi-um, *n.* [From L. *cadmia*, calamin.] A metal discovered by Stromeyer, in 1817, in carbonate of zinc. It is of a white color; is ductile and malleable, and, when fused, crystallizes in octahedrons. It melts below a red heat, and suffers but slight change in air. *Cadmium* is comparatively rare, occurring in some zinc ores.

Cadmium yellow; cadmium sulphid, used as a pigment.

çad′răns, *n.* [Fr. *cadran*, a quadrant.] An instrument for measuring the angles in cutting and polishing gems, and keeping the gems at the proper angle during the process.

çā′dre (-d′r), *n.* [Fr. *cadre*, a frame; L. *quadrum*, a square.] A nucleus; a framework; the skeleton of a thing; specifically, in France, the officers of a regiment about which may be grouped the rank and file.

çȧ-dū′çȧ-ry, *a.* [L. *caducarius*, from *caducum*, property without a master, from *cadere*, to fall.] In old law, of, relating, or pertaining to escheat.

çȧ-dū′cē-ăn, *a.* Belonging to Mercury's wand.

çȧ-dū′cē-us, *n.* [L.] In antiquity, Mercury's rod; a wand entwisted by two serpents surmounted by two wings and borne by Mercury, messenger of the gods, as an ensign of office.

Caduceus.

çȧ-dū′ci-ā-ry (-shi-), *a.* 1. Caducary.

2. In Scots law, not acquired by succession.

çȧ-dū-ci-brañ′çhi-āte, *a.* [L. *caducus*, falling, and *branchiæ*, gills.] In zoölogy, a term applied to tailed amphibians, such as the newts, which lose the gills before attaining maturity.

çȧ-dū′ci-ty, *n.* [LL. *caducitas*, from L. *cadere*, to fall.] Tendency to fail; senility; decrepitude. [Rare.]

çȧ-dū′çous, *a.* Having a tendency to fall or decay; specifically in biology, applied to organs that early drop off, as branchiæ, floral envelopes, etc.

çȧ-dūke′, *a.* Transitory; fleeting; short-lived. [Obs.]

çā′dy, *n.* A slang term for a hat.

çad′y, *n.* Same as *Caddie.*

çæ′çȧ (sē′kȧ), *n.*, pl. of *cæcum.*

çæ′çăl, *a.* Of, relating, or pertaining to the cæcum; specifically, bag-shaped; as, the *cæcal* extremity of a duct.

çæ′ci-ăs, *n.* [L. *cæcias*; Gr. *kaikias*, the northeast wind.] A wind from the northeast.

Çæ-cil′i-æ, *n.* See *Ophiomorpha.*

çæ-cil′i-ăn, *a.* and *n.* [L. *cæcus*, blind.]

I. *a.* Pertaining to the *Cæciliæ.*

II. *n.* One of the *Cæciliæ.*

çæ′çum, *n.*; *pl.* **çæ′çȧ.** [L. *cæcus*, blind, invisible, concealed.] In comparative anatomy, a blind process in the alimentary canal of various animals. In fishes they are often numerous and long, and birds have generally two near the termination of the intestine. Mammals have commonly only one *cæcum.*

çæ-lom′e-tẽr, *n.* [L. *cælum*, *cœlum*, heaven, and *metrum*, Gr. *metron*, a measure.] An instrument employed in illustrating astronomic principles.

Çæ-nō-ġæ′ȧ (sē-nō-jē′ȧ), *n.* [L., from Gr. *kainos*, new, and *gaia*, land.] One of several proposed primary zoögeographical divisions, including the Nearctic, Palearctic, and Oriental provinces; its complement being *Eogæa.*

Çæ-nō-ġæ′ăn, *a.* Pertaining to the *Cænogæa.*

çæ-nō-ġen′e-sis, *n.* Same as *Kenogenesis.*

çæ″nō-ġē-net′iç, *a.* Same as *Kenogenetic.*

Çæ-nō-zō′iç, Çē-nō-zō′iç, *a.* In geology, exhibiting recent life-forms; applied to the Tertiary age or to the Tertiary and the Quaternary ages.

Çæs-al-pin′i-ȧ (ses-), *n.* [Named after Andreas *Cæsalpinus*, an Italian botanist.] A genus of trees of the bean family bearing showy flowers, and found in the tropics of both hemispheres. Brazil-wood comes from *Cæsalpinia echinata*, and the species *Sappan* furnishes the sapanwood of India.

Çæ′ṣãr, *n.* [L.] 1. In ancient Rome, a title of the emperor, adopted by the Julian family, after it had been made famous by the dictator, Caius Julius Cæsar. Later, it was applied to the heir presumptive.

2. Figuratively, any powerful ruler or autocrat; an emperor.

3. Formerly, an emperor of Germany, or of the Holy Roman Empire; in this sense, now replaced by the German word *Kaiser*; first assumed by Charlemagne.

Çæ-ṣā′rē-ăn, Çæ-ṣā′ri-ăn (sē-), *a.* Pertaining to or characteristic of Cæsar or the Cæsars; imperial; autocratic.

Cæsarean section or *operation*; extraction of the fetus by an abdominal incision; said to have been employed to effect the delivery of Julius Cæsar.

Çæ′ṣãr-iṣm, *n.* A system of government in which the power rests with a single person; autocracy; imperialism.

çæ′ṣi-ous, *a.* [L. *cæsius*, bluish-gray.] Pale blue, bluish-gray, or lavender.

çæ′ṣi-um, *n.* [Neut. of L. *cæsius*, bluish-gray.] A rare element, one of the alkali metals, the first to be discovered by spectrum analysis; named from the two blue lines in its spectrum.

çæs′pi-tōse (ses′), *a.* Same as *Cespitose.*

çæs′pi-tōse-ly, *adv.* Same as *Cespitosely.*

çæ-ṣū′rȧ, *n.* See *Cesura.*

çæ-ṣū′răl, *adv.* See *Cesural.*

çȧ-fé′ (-fā′), *n.* [Fr., coffee, a coffeehouse.]

1. Coffee.

2. A coffeehouse; sometimes a place where liquors as well as food are served.

Café au lait; [Fr.] coffee with milk.

Café noir; [Fr.] strong, black coffee; coffee without milk; usually served at the close of a meal.

çȧf′e-net, çȧ′fe-neh (-nā), *n.* [Turk. *qahveh-khāneh*, a coffeehouse.] A Turkish coffeehouse and resting-place for travelers; an inn.

çȧ′fē-tăl, çȧ-fē-tȧ′lē, *n.* [Sp. Am.] A coffee-plantation.

çaf-e-tē′ri-ȧ, *n.* An eating-house where customers serve themselves.

çaf′fȧ, *n.* [Native name.] 1. A rich cloth probably silk, in use during 16th century.

2. A cotton cloth, ornamented with painting, formerly made in India.

çaf-fē′iç, *a.* [Fr. *caféique*, from *café*, coffee.] Obtained from or pertaining to coffee.

Caffeic acid; a peculiar vegetable acid, $C_9H_8O_4$, found in coffee tannin.

çaf-fē′in, çaf-fē′ine (*or* çaf′), *n.* [Fr. *caféine*, from *café*, coffee.] A slightly bitter, highly azotized substance, crystallizing in slender, silk-like needles, found in coffee-beans, tea-leaves, Paraguay tea, guarana, etc.

çaf-fē-in′iç, *a.* Pertaining to or derived from caffein.

çaf′fē-in-iṣm, *n.* A morbid condition characterized by nervousness, sleeplessness, etc., brought on by the excessive use of coffee.

çaf-fē-tan′niç, *a.* Obtained from or pertaining to tannin and caffein.

Caffetannic acid; caffeic acid.

çaf′fi-lȧ, çä′fi-läh, *n.* See *Kafila.*

Çaf′fre (-fẽr), *n.* See *Kafir.*

çaf′tăn, kaf′tăn, *n.* [Ar. *qaftan*, a kind of garment.] A garment consisting of a long, wide-sleeved gown usually fastened by a belt or sash, worn by men in Oriental countries.

çag, *n.* [Obs.] See *Keg.*

çāġe, *n.* [ME. *cage*; OFr. *caige*; O.H.G. *chevia*; Port. and Sp. *gavia*; L. *cavea*, a hollow place.]

1. A box or inclosure, made of boards, or with latticework of wood, wicker, wire, or metal, for confining animals.

2. A prison for petty criminals; any place of confinement.

3. In carpentry, an outer work of timber, inclosing another within it; as, the *cage* of a windmill, or of a staircase.

4. In machinery, any cage-like contrivance or framework, as the frame used to confine a ball-valve; or, a wire guard used in pumps and pipes to prevent the passage of solids.

5. The platform, box, or car of an elevator, inclosed by gratings.

6. In mining, the trundle-wheel or whim on which the rope winds in a hoisting apparatus.

7. In baseball, the wire mask worn by the catcher.

8. A glass cup, in the hollow of which liquids may be placed for microscopic examination.

çāġe, *v.t.*; caged, *pt., pp.*; caging, *ppr.* To confine in a cage; to shut up or confine.

çāġe′ling, *n.* A poetic term for a bird confined in a cage, especially a young bird.

çā′ġit, *n.* A green parrot of the Philippine Islands.

çag′mag, *n.* [Prov. Eng.] 1. A tough, old goose, sent to market; hence, poor food, offal.

2. A kind of inferior sheep.

Çȧ-gōt′ (-gō′), *n.* [Fr.] One of a degraded race inhabiting the valleys of the Pyrenees in France and Spain. Although they obtained civil rights by the Revolution, they are still despised socially.

Çȧ-hens′ly-iṣm, *n.* A plan to regulate the policy of the Roman Catholic church in the appointment of its bishops and priests, and especially those in America, suggested to Pope Leo XIII., in 1891, by P. P. Cahensly, a member of the German parliament. Its main provision was that every bishop and pastor should be of the same nationality as the majority of his flock. Other measures were suggested for the continuance, among the various races represented in the United States, of the use of their mother tongues, and for the preservation of their national traditions.

çȧ-hiẽr′ (*or* kä-yā′), *n.* [Fr. *cahier*; OFr. *caier*, *quayer*; It. *quaderno*; LL. *quaternus*, four each.]

1. In bookbinding, a section. [Rare.]

2. A report of the proceedings of any body, as a legislature; a memorial, or similar document.

çȧ-hiñ′çȧ=rọot, *n.* The root of a shrub, *Chiococca racemosa*, found in Florida and the American tropics; also written *cainca-root.*

çȧ-hin′çiç, *a.* Pertaining to the cahinca-root.

çȧ-họọt′, *n.* [Prob. from Fr. *cahute*, a cabin.] Partnership; company; as, to go in *cahoot* with any one; used also in plural, *cahoots.* [Slang.]

çȧ-how′, *n.* See *Cohow.*

çä-iç′, *n.* See *Caique.*

çāi-mȧ-çam′, *n.* See *Kaimakam.*

çāi′măn, *n.* See *Cayman.*

çȧ-iñ′çȧ=rọot, *n.* Same as *Cahinca-root.*

çȧ′ing=whāle, *n.* Same as *Caaing-whale.*

Çāin′ite, *n.* 1. A descendant of Cain.

2. One of a strange sect of fanatical heretics of the second century, who professed to venerate Cain, Korah, Dathan, and Abiram, and the Sodomites.

Çāi-nō-zō′iç, *a.* Same as *Cænozoic.*

çä-ïque′, (kä-ēk′) *n.* [Fr. *caique*, from Turk. *qayik*, a boat.] A small skiff or rowboat; especially a light skiff used in the Bosporus; also, a vessel of the Levant of larger size.

Çȧ ï-rä′. [Fr.; lit., "It (the revolution) shall

go on."] The burden of a French revolutionary song composed about 1789.

çaird, *n.* [Gael. *ceard*, a tinker, smith.] An itinerant tinker; a vagrant or gipsy. [Prov. Eng.]

çairn, *n.* [Scot., from Gael. *carn*, a heap.] A heap of stones; specifically, (a) certain piles of stones of a rounded or conical form, erected by the early inhabitants of the British isles, apparently as sepulchral monuments; (b) a stone mound for a landmark, or to indicate a specified site.

çairn′gorm, *n.* A yellow or brown variety of rock-crystal, or crystallized quartz, found in the mountain of Cairngorm, in Scotland.

çais′sŏn, *n.* [Fr. from *caisse*, a chest, box.]

1. A military term for, (a) an ammunition-chest; formerly, the ammunition-wagon itself; (b) a subterranean box containing explosives to be fired when the enemy approaches.

2. In architecture, the sunk panels in flat or vaulted ceilings, or in soffits generally.

3. In civil engineering, (a) a vessel in the form of a boat used as a flood-gate in docks; (b) an apparatus on which vessels may be raised and floated; (c) a water-tight box or casing used in founding and building structures in water too deep for the coffer-dam, such as piers of bridges, quays, etc.

Pneumatic caisson; one resembling an inverted box, into which air is forced, allowing workmen to enter.

çāi′tiff, *n.* [OFr. *caitif*, a captive, wretched man; L. *captivus*, a captive, from *capere*, to take.]

1. A mean villain; a despicable knave.

2. A miserable or unfortunate person. [Obs.]

3. One held captive. [Obs.]

çāi′tiff, *a.* 1. Belonging to a caitiff; base; vile.

2. Wretched; enslaved. [Obs.]

Çȧ-jā′nus, *n.* [Malay *kachany*.] A genus of East Indian leguminous shrubs. *Cajanus Indicus*, or angola-pea, is the most extensively cultivated species.

çaj′ē-put, çaj′u̇-put, *n.* [Malay *kāyūputīh*, from *kāyū*, tree, and *putīh*, white.] An essential oil from the East Indies, resembling that of cardamoms, obtained from the leaves of a small tree, *Melaleuca Cajuputi*.

çȧ-jōle′, *v.t.*; cajoled, *pt.*, *pp.*; cajoling, *ppr.* [Fr. *cajoler*, to coax, to wheedle.] To flatter; to coax; to deceive or delude by flattery.

Syn.—Coax, flatter, wheedle.

çȧ-jōle′ment, *n.* Cajolery; the act of cajoling.

çȧ-jōl′ẽr, *n.* A flatterer; a wheedler.

çȧ-jōl′ẽr-y, *n.*; *pl.* **çȧ-jōl′ẽr-ieṣ**. [Fr. *cajolerie*, from *cajoler*, to coax, wheedle.] Flattery; a wheedling to delude.

çā′jun, *n.* [A corruption of *Acadian*.] An appellation applied to a person in Louisiana supposed to be of Acadian French descent.

çaj′u̇-put, *n.* See *Cajeput*.

çaj′u̇-put-ēne, *n.* An aromatic compound obtained from cajeput.

çāke, *n.* [ME. *cake*; Sw. *kaka*, a cake.]

1. A mass of fine light dough baked, and generally sweetened or flavored with various ingredients, or a composition of flour, butter, sugar, or other ingredients, baked in a mass.

2. Something made or concreted in the form of a *cake*; a mass of matter in a solid form relatively thin and extended; as, a *cake* of soap.

To have one's cake dough; to meet with disappointment or failure.

To take the cake; to be superior in; to excel; to outdo.

çāke, *v.i.*; caked, *pt.*, *pp.*; caking, *ppr.* To concrete or become formed into a hard mass.

çāke, *v.t.* To form into a cake or mass.

çāke, *v.i.* To cackle. [Prov. Eng.]

çāke′=ŭr″chin, *n.* A name popularly applied to sea-urchins having a discoid shape.

çāke′=wạlk (-wạk), *n.* A characteristic dance of the negroes in southern United States, so named from the fact that a cake was originally given to the couple adjudged the most graceful walkers.

çal, *n.* [Prov. Eng.] See *Wolframite*.

çal′ȧ-bȧ, *n.* [Native name.] A tree, *Calophyllum Calaba*, of the West Indies, furnishing resin and valuable timber.

Çal′ȧ-bär, *a.* [W. African word.] Denoting a region of western Africa, adjacent to a river of the same name.

çal′ȧ-bär-in, çal′ȧ-bär-ine (*or* -ine), *n.* An alkaloid existing in the Calabar bean.

çal′ȧ-bash, *n.* [Fr. *calebasse*; Port. *calabaca*, a calabash; Ar. *qar*, a gourd, and *yābis*, *aybas*, dry.]

Calabashes.

1. A vessel made of a dried gourd-shell, or of the shell of a calabash-tree, used for containing liquors, or goods, as pitch, resin, and the like.

2. A popular name of the gourd plant.

3. The fruit of the calabash-tree.

çal′ȧ-bash=tree, *n.* 1. The popular name of an American tree belonging to the genus *Crescentia*.

2. A name also given to *Adansonia digitata*, the baobab of Africa.

çal″ȧ-bä-zil′lȧ (-sēl′yȧ), *n.* [Mex., from Sp. *calabaza*, gourd.] A large-rooted, Californian squash, *Cucurbita perennis*, yielding a soap-like substance.

çal-ȧ-bọọse′, *n.* [Corruption of Sp. *calabozo*, prison.] A prison; a jail. [Local U. S.]

çal′ȧ-bŭr=tree, *n.* A West Indian tree, *Muntingia Calabura*, yielding a cordage-fiber.

çȧ-lāde′, *n.* [Fr.] The slope of a rising manège-ground down which a horse is ridden in training him.

Çȧ-lā′di-um, *n.* 1. A genus of tropical plants of the order *Araceæ*, much valued for their foliage and cultivated because of it. They have tuberous roots and sagittate leaves, sometimes spotted or variegated.

2. [c—] Any plant of this genus.

çal′ā-ite, *n.* [L. *callais*; Gr. *kallais*, *kalais*, a sea-green stone.] A name given to the turquoise.

Çal″ȧ-mȧ-gros′tis, *n.* [L., from Gr. *kalamos*, a reed, and *agrōstis*, a sort of grass.] A genus of grasses allied to *Arundo*. The species are mere weeds, found chiefly in damp woods.

çal-ȧ-man′ço, *n.* [LL *calamancus*, from Gr. *kamelaukion*, a head-dress.] A woolen stuff, of a fine gloss and checkered in the warp.

çal′ȧ-man-dẽr=wood, *n.* A beautiful species of wood, the product of *Diospyros quæsita*, a native of Ceylon; it resembles rosewood, but is much harder.

Çal-ȧ-mā′ri-æ, *n.pl.* [L., from *calamarius*, pertaining to a reed; *calamus*, a reed.] One of the principal families of plant-life of the Carboniferous age.

çal-ȧ-mā′ri-ăn, *a.* Pertaining to the *Calamariæ*.

çal′ȧ-mā-ry, çal′ȧ-mär, *n.* [L. *calamarius*, from *calamus*, a reed, pen; Gr. *kalamos*, a reed.] The general name for decapod cuttlefishes of the order *Dibranchiata*, but properly used to designate those of the genus *Loligo*. They have the power of discharging a black fluid from an ink-bag; called also *squid*.

çal′ȧm-bac, *n.* [Fr., from Per. *kalambak*, a fragrant wood.] See *Agallochum*.

çal′ȧm-bŏur, *n.* [Fr., *calambour*; Sp. *cabambuco*; Per. *kalambak*.] A species of agallochum, or aloes-wood, of a dusky or mottled color, of a light, friable texture, less fragrant than calambac; used by cabinetmakers and inlayers.

çal-ȧ-mif′ẽr-ous, *a.* [L. *calamus*, reed, and *ferre*, to bear.] Bearing reeds; reedy.

çȧ-lam′i-fọrm, *a.* [L. *calamus*, a reed, and *forma*, form.] Reed-like in form.

çal′ȧ-min, çal′ȧ-mine, *n.* [Fr. *calamine*; LL. *calamina*, a corruption of L. *cadmia*, calamin.] The native silicious hydrous oxid of zinc, an important ore.

çal′ȧ-mint, *n.* A plant of the genus *Calamintha*.

Çal-ȧ-min′thȧ, *n.* [LL. *calamintha*; L. *calaminthe*; Gr. *kalaminthē*, a kind of mint; *kalos*, beautiful, and *mintha*, mint.] A genus of plants of the mint family, comprising about forty species.

çal′ȧ-mist, *n.* [L. *calamus*, a reed.] A player upon a pipe or reed. [Obs.]

çal-ȧ-mis′trāte, *v.t.* To curl (the hair). [Obs.]

çal-ȧ-mis′trum, *n.*; *pl.* **çal-ȧ-mis′trȧ**. [L., a curling-iron, from *calamus*, a reed.] One of the short, curved, spiny bristles disposed in two rows along the upper surface of the sixth joint of the hind legs of certain spiders; used in forming the thread of the web.

çal′ȧ-mite, *n.* [L. *calamus*, a reed.] A variety of tremolite, occurring in imperfect or rounded prismatic crystals, of a vitreous luster, longitudinally striated, and sometimes resembling a reed.

Çal-ȧ-mī′tēṣ, *n.* [Gr. *kalamitēs*, reed-like, from *kalamos*, a reed.] A genus of the most common coal-plants, found in the form of jointed fragments, having a stem and branch marked with ribs and furrows; referred by some to the order *Equisetaceæ*.

çȧ-lam′i-tous, *a.* 1. Very miserable; involved in deep distress; oppressed with infelicity; wretched from misfortune.

2. Producing distress and misery; making wretched; as, a *calamitous* event.

3. Full of misery; distressful; wretched.

çȧ-lam′i-tous-ly, *adv.* In a calamitous manner.

çȧ-lam′i-tous-ness, *n.* Deep distress; wretchedness; misery; the quality of producing misery.

çȧ-lam′i-ty, *n.*; *pl.* **çȧ-lam′i-tieṣ**. [Fr. *calamité*; L. *calamitas*, damage, misfortune.]

1. Any great misfortune or cause of misery; generally applied to events producing extensive evils either to persons or communities.

2. A condition of distress; a time of adversity; misery.

The deliberations of *calamity* are rarely wise.
—Burke.

Syn.—Disaster, misfortune, mischance, mishap.—A *calamity* is a great *disaster* or *misfortune*; a *misfortune* a great *mischance* or *mishap*; whatever is attended with destruction is a *calamity*; whatever occasions mischief to the person, defeats or interrupts plans, is a *disaster*; whatever is accompanied with a loss of property, or the deprivation of health, is a *misfortune*; whatever diminishes the beauty or utility of objects is a *mischance* or *mishap*.

çal′ȧ-mus, *n.*; *pl.* **çal′ȧ-mī**. [L., from Gr. *kalamos*, a stalk, a reed, stubble; Sans. *kalamas*, a stalk, stem, straw.]

1. The sweet-flag or sweet-rush, *Acorus Calamus*, the pungent and aromatic root of which is used medicinally, especially in disorders of the stomach.

2. In Scripture, an aromatic substance obtained from some kind of reed or cane, probably Indian lemon-grass, or sweet-flag.

3. [C—] A genus of tropical East Indian palms, the stems of the different species of which are the rattan-canes of commerce.

4. In the Roman Catholic church, a tube of precious metal, anciently used by communicants when partaking of the contents of the chalice in the eucharist.

5. The quill or horny part of a feather.

6. A reed; a cane.

7. A flute made of a reed.

8. In classical antiquity, (a) a split reed used as an instrument for writing; (b) a Pan's pipe; (c) a Greek measure of length, equal to ten feet.

çȧ-lan′dō, *a.* and *adv.* [It., ppr. of *calare*, to decrease.] In music, more slowly and decreasing in volume of tone.

çȧ-lan′drȧ, *n.* [Fr. *calandre*; LL. *calandra*; Gr. *kalandra*, a kind of lark.]

1. A thick-billed lark, *Melanocorypha calandra*, a habitant of the Mediterranean countries.

2. [C—] A genus of weevils, as the corn-weevil, *Calandra granaria*.

Corn-weevil (*Calandra granaria*), natural size and magnified.

çȧ-lan′gāy, *n.* [Native name.] A hook-billed cockatoo of the Philippine Islands.

çȧ-lash′, *n.* [Fr *caleche*; G. *kelesche*; Bohem. *kalesha*; Russ. *kolyaska*, a calash; Russ. *koleso*, a wheel.]

1. A light, low-wheeled pleasure or traveling carriage, having an adjustable top or hood. The Canadian *calash* has a U-shaped body, folding top, seat for two, and driver's seat between the main and second dashboards, two wheels, and is drawn by a single horse.

2. The adjustable top of any hooded vehicle.

3. A lady's hood supported by hoops projecting over the face. [Obs.]

çal-ȧ-thid′i-um, çȧ-lā′thi-um, *n.* [L., dim. of *calathus*, a basket.] In botany, a name applied to the flower-head of a composite plant.

çȧ-lath′i-fọrm, *a.* [L. *calathus*, a basket, and *forma*, form.] Concave; cup-shaped.

çȧ-lā′thi-um, *n.* Same as *Calathidium*.

çal′ȧ-thus, *n.*; *pl.* **çal′ȧ-thī**. [L., from Gr. *kalathos*, a basket.] An ancient, lily-shaped basket in which Greek and Roman women kept their work. It is often represented on monuments, and frequently as a symbol of maidenhood.

çȧ-lȧ-ve′rite, *n.* A tellurid of gold, discovered in Calaveras county, California. It occurs massive without crystalline structure, and is of a bronze-yellow color.

çal-çā′nē-ăl, *a.* In anatomy, pertaining to the calcaneum, or great bone of the heel.

çal-çā′nē-ō-. A combining form from L. *calcaneum*, the heel; used in anatomy to denote relation to the calcaneum; as, *calcaneo*-fibular, pertaining to the calcaneum and the fibula.

çal-çā′nē-um, *n.* [L., the heel.] In anatomy, the largest bone of the tarsus; the heel-bone; called also *fibulare*.

çal′çär, *n.*; *pl.* **çal-çā′ri-ȧ**. [L. *calcar*, a spur, from *calx*, the heel.]

1. In botany, a basal spur or spur-like projection from a petal or sepal.

2. In anatomy, the smaller of the two projections on the floor of the lateral ventricles of the brain of some mammals, including man; the hippocampus minor or *calcar* avis.

3. In zoölogy, (a) the spur of a bird; (b) an eminence on the tarsus of bats, acting as a support to the interfemoral web.

çal′çär, *n.* [L. *calcaria*, a lime-kiln.]

1. In glassmaking, a kind of oven or reverberatory furnace, used to calcinate sand and potash, and convert them into frit.

2. An oven for annealing metals.

çal′çȧ-rāte, çal′çȧ-rā-ted, *a.* [L. *calcar*, a

spur.] In biology, provided with a spur; as, a *calcarate* corolla.

çal-çā′rē-ō-. A combining form from L. *calcarius*, pertaining to lime, and indicating the presence of lime in connection with the other element of the word.

çal-çā″rē-ō-är-ġil-lā′ceous, *a.* Having or containing lime and clay; said of earths.

çal-çā″rē-ō-bi-tū′mi-nous, *a.* Having lime and bitumen in combination, or consisting of both.

çal-çā″rē-ō-si-li′cious (-lish′us), *a.* Containing lime and silica, or consisting of both.

çal-çā″rē-ō-sul′phūr-ous, *a.* Containing lime and sulphur, or consisting of both.

çal-çā′rē-ous, *a.* [L. *calcarius*, pertaining to lime, from *calx, calcis*, lime.] Partaking of the nature of lime; having the qualities of lime; containing lime; as, *calcareous* earth or stone.

Calcareous spar; see *Calcite*.

çal-çā′rē-ous-ness, *n.* The quality of being calcareous.

çal-çā′ri-ȧ, *n.*, pl. of *calcar*.

çal-çȧ-rif′ẽr-ous, *a.* [L. *calcarius*, from *calx*, lime, and *ferre*, to bear.] Yielding calcite or lime.

çal-çar′i-fọrm, *a.* [L. *calcar*, a spur, and *forma*, form.] Spur-shaped.

çal′çȧ-rine, *a.* 1. Calcaneal.

2. Pertaining to the calcar avis.

çal-çȧ-vel′lȧ, *n.* [Named from *Carcavelhos*, the district in Portugal where it is made.] A kind of superior sweet wine from Portugal; written also *carcavelhos* and *calcavellos*.

çal′cē-ā-ted, *a.* [L. *calceatus*, pp. of *calceare*, to shoe; *calceus*, a shoe.] Shod; wearing shoes.

çalced (kalst), *a.* [L.] Shod; wearing shoes; as, a *calced* Carmelite. [See *Discalced*.]

çal′cē-dŏn, *n.* A foul vein, like chalcedony, found in some precious stones.

çal-cē-don′iç, çal-cē-dō′ni-ăn, *a.* Same as *Chalcedonic*.

çal-ced′ō-ny, *n.* See *Chalcedony*.

çal′cē-i-fọrm, *a.* [L *calceus*, a shoe, and *forma*, form.] In botany, having the form of a shoe or slipper, as the corolla of *Calceolaria*; calceolate.

Çal″cē-ō-lā′ri-ȧ, *n.* [L. *calceolarius*, from *calceolus*, a slipper, dim. of *calceus*, a shoe; so called from the shape of the corolla.] Slipperwort, a genus of ornamental herbaceous or shrubby plants of the natural order *Scrophulariaceæ*. The roots of *Calceolaria arachnoidea*, the parent of many hybrids, are used for dyeing woolen cloth crimson, under the name relbun.

Calceolaria.

çal′cē-ō-lāte, *a.* Same as *Calceiform*.

çal′cēş, *n.*, pl. of *calx*.

çal′ciç, *a.* [L. *calx, calcis*, lime.] Of or pertaining to lime; containing calcium; as, *calcic* chlorid.

çal-cif′ẽr-ous, *a.* [L. *calx, calcis*, lime, and *ferre*, to bear.] Producing or containing lime, especially when in considerable quantity; as, *calciferous* strata; *calciferous* sandstone.

Calciferous epoch; that epoch in the Lower Silurian system following the Cambrian period.

çal-cif′iç, *a.* [L. *calx, calcis*, lime, and *ficus*, from *facere*, to make.] Calciferous; calcic.

çal″cif-i-çā′tion, *n.* A changing into lime; the process of changing into a stony substance by the deposition of salts of lime, as in the formation of teeth.

çal′ci-fīed, *a.* Calcareous.

çal′ci-fọrm, *a.* [L. *calx, calcis*, lime, and *forma*, form.] In the form of chalk or lime.

çal-cif′ū-gous, *a.* [L. *calx, calcis*, lime, and *fugere*, to flee.] In botany, avoiding calcareous soils; said of certain lichens.

çal′ci-fȳ, *v.i.*; calcified, *pt., pp.*; calcifying, *ppr.* [L. *calx, calcis*, lime, and *ficare*, from *facere*, to make.] To become gradually changed into a stony condition by the deposition or secretion of lime, as in the formation of teeth.

çal′ci-fȳ, *v.t.* To make stony by depositing lime.

Calcifying segment; a thick glandular sac or dilatation in the lower part of the oviduct of birds, often, but erroneously, called the uterus, which secretes the shell of the egg

çal-ciġ′e-nous, *a.* [L. *calx, calcis*, lime, and *-genus*, producing.] Yielding calx on oxidation, as certain minerals.

çal-ciġ′e-rous, *a.* [L. *calx, calcis*, lime, and *gerere*, to bear.] Lime-producing, as certain cells of the teeth.

çal′ci-mine, *n.* [L. *calx, calcis*, lime.] A wash for walls and ceilings, the base of which is whiting. It is made in various tints and applied in the same manner as whitewash; incorrectly spelled *kalsomine*.

çal′ci-mine, *v.t.*, calcimined, *pt., pp.*; calcimining, *ppr.* To apply calcimine to.

çal′ci-mī-nẽr, *n.* A person who calcimines.

çal-ci-mū′rite, *n.* [L. *calx*, lime, and *muria*, salt water.] A species of earth of a blue or olive-green color, of the consistency of clay. It consists of calcareous earth and magnesia tinged with iron.

çal-cin′ȧ-ble, *a.* Capable of calcination.

çal′ci-nāte, *v.t.* To calcine. [Rare.]

çal-ci-nā′tion, *n.* [LL. *calcinatio*, from *calcinare*, to calcine.] The act or process of calcining.

çal-cin′ȧ-tō-ry, *n.* A calcination-vessel.

çal′cine (*or* çal-cīne′), *v.t.*; calcined, *pt., pp.*; calcining, *ppr.* [Fr. *calciner*; LL. *calcinare*, to reduce to lime or calx; L. *calx, calcis*, lime.]

1. To reduce to a powder, or to a friable state, by the action of heat; or to expel from a substance some volatile matter combined with it, as the carbondioxid from limestone.

2. To oxidize, as a metal; to reduce to a metallic calx. [Obs.]

çal′cine (*or* çal-cīne′), *v.i.* To be converted into a powder or friable substance, or into a calx, by the action of heat.

çal′ci-nẽr, *n.* 1. One who calcines.

2. A calcining or roasting furnace.

Çal-ci-spon′ġi-æ, *n.pl.* [L. *calx, calcis*, lime, and *spongia*, a sponge.] A division of the sponges having three-rayed calcareous needles or spicules.

çal′cite, *n.* [L. *calx, calcis*, lime.] A term applied to various minerals, all of which are modifications of the rhombohedral form of calcium carbonate. It includes limestone, all the white and most of the colored marbles, chalk, Iceland spar, etc.

çal′ci-trănt, *a.* Kicking; obstinate.

çal′ci-trāte, *v.t.* [L. *calcitratus*, pp. of *calcitrare*, to kick, be stubborn; *calx*, a heel.] To kick.

çal-ci-trā′tion, *n.* The act of kicking.

çal′ci-um, *n.* [L. *calx, calcis*, lime.] The metallic basis of lime, and the most widely diffused of the alkaline metals. It is of a light yellow color, very ductile and malleable, and rapidly changes into the oxid or quicklime in the air.

Calcium light; an intensely white light produced by the oxyhydrogen flame on lime; the Drummond light; commonly called *lime-light*.

çal-civ′ō-rous, *a.* [L. *calx*, lime, and *vorare*, to devour.] Eating into or living on limestone; as, *calcivorous* plants.

çal-çog′rȧ-phẽr, *n.* One who draws with chalk.

çal-çō-graph′iç-ăl, *a.* Pertaining to calcography.

çal-çog′rȧ-phy, *n.* [L. *calx*, lime, chalk, and Gr. *-graphia*, from *graphein*, to write.] Drawing with chalk.

çalç′-sin″tẽr, *n.* [G. *kalk-sinter*; *kalk*, from L. *calx, calcis*, lime, and *sinter*, a stalactite.] Calcareous sinter; stalactitic carbonate of lime.

çalç′-spär, *n.* [L. *calx, calcis*, lime, and AS. *spær*, spar.] Calcareous spar, or crystallized carbonate of lime.

çalç′-tuff, *n.* [L. *calx*, lime, and It. *tufa*, L. *tofus*, tuff-cone.] A form of calcite; also called *calc-tufa* and *calcareous tufa*.

çal′çū-lȧ-ble, *a.* That may be calculated or ascertained by calculation.

çal′çū-lā-ry, *n.* [L. *calcularius*, pertaining to calculation, from *calculus*, a pebble, a reckoning.] A congeries of little stony knots dispersed through the soft portion of the pear and other fruits.

çal′çū-lā-ry, *a.* Relating to calculi or stones in the bladder.

çal′çū-lāte, *v.t.*; calculated, *pt., pp.*; calculating, *ppr.* [L. *calculatus*, pp. of *calculare*, to reckon; *calculus*, a pebble, a reckoning.]

1. To ascertain by computation; to compute; to reckon up; to estimate; as, to *calculate* the cost of a house.

2. To make the necessary or usual computations regarding; as, to *calculate* eclipses or nativities.

> A cunning man did *calculate* my birth.—Shak.

3. To fit or prepare by the adaptation of means to an end; to make suitable; generally in past participle in this sense.

> This letter was admirably *calculated* to work on those to whom it was addressed. —Macaulay.

4. To intend; to count on; as, to *calculate* to go; in this sense, an Americanism.

5. To think; to suppose; to guess; as, to *calculate* it will rain. [New England.]

Syn.—Compute, estimate, reckon, count. *Calculate* is generic, referring to the operation as a whole; *compute* relates to the obtaining of a gross sum or amount; *reckon* and *count* to the details in so doing.

çal′çū-lāte, *v.i.* To make a computation; to arrive at a conclusion after weighing all the circumstances; to estimate by calculation; to deliberate.

> The strong passions, whether good or bad, never *calculate*. —Robertson.

çal′çū-lā-ted, *a.* 1. Relating to something which may be or has been subjected to calculation; as, a *calculated* plot.

2. Designed or suitable for; as, a machine *calculated* for rapid work. [Colloq.]

çal′çū-lā-ting, *a.* 1. Having the power or habit of making mathematical calculations; quick at such calculations.

2. Given to forethought and calculation; especially given to look ahead with thoughtful regard to self-interest; deliberate and selfish; scheming.

> With his cool *calculating* disposition he easily got the better of his rival. —Godwin.

çal′çū-lā-ting, *n.* The act of estimating or computing.

çal′çū-lā-ting-mȧ-çhïne″, *n.* Any machine by which mathematical calculations may be made; a term including the more complicated machines, as one designed to multiply and divide, down to a simple abacus.

çal-çū-lā′tion, *n.* 1. The art or practice of calculating or computing; the result so obtained; as, a geometrical *calculation*.

2. A forecast or estimate; as, weather *calculations*.

3. A state of mind marked by careful plans or schemes; as, a general of aggressive *calculation*.

Syn.—Estimation, consideration, balance, apportionment, investigation, reckoning, computation, anticipation, forethought, regard, circumspection, watchfulness, vigilance, caution, care.

çal′çū-lā-tive, *a.* Pertaining to calculation; tending to calculate.

çal′çū-lā-tŏr, *n.* [L. from *calculare*, to calculate.] One who or that which calculates.

çal′çū-lā-tō-ry, *a.* Belonging to calculation.

çal′çūle, *n.* Reckoning; computation. [Obs.]

çal′çūle, *v.t.* To calculate. [Obs.]

çal′çū-li, *n.*, pl. of *calculus*.

çal′çū-lous, *a.* 1. Stony; gritty; hard, like stone; as, a *calculous* concretion.

2. Arising from calculi or stones in the bladder; caused by calculi; as, a *calculous* disorder.

3. Affected with the gravel or stone; as, a *calculous* person.

çal′çū-lus, *n.* [L. *calculus*, a small stone or pebble; dim. of *calx, calcis*, a stone.]

1. A small stone or pebble.

2. Any hard solid concretion, formed in any part of the body; as, a stone in the bladder or kidneys, called urinary *calculus*, or a gallstone, called biliary *calculus*.

3. Any branch of mathematics which may involve or lead to calculation; embracing the whole science excepting pure geometry; when used without a qualifying word, differential *calculus* is usually understood, or, more broadly, infinitesimal *calculus*.

Barycentric calculus; in geometry, the designation of a point by both weight and position.

Calculus of finite differences; that branch of mathematics dealing with the changes of functions due to finite changes in the variables involved; hence, without assumption of continuity; E, Δ, and Σ being important symbols.

Calculus of functions; that branch of mathematical analysis which investigates the form of a function and not its value in any particular case, nor the conditions under which it may have a particular value.

Calculus of operations; a systematic method of treating problems by operating algebraically upon symbols of operation.

Calculus of probability; the science of calculating the mathematical likelihood of probability of events or chances.

Calculus of variations; that branch of analysis which seeks the laws of changes attending a slight alteration in the form of the function, or in the transformation of one function into another.

Differential calculus; the arithmetic of the infinitely small differences of variable quantities; the method of differencing quantities or of finding an infinitely small quantity, which, being taken infinite times, shall be equal to a given quantity. This coincides with the doctrine of fluxions.

Imaginary calculus; a method of investigating the nature of imaginary quantities required to fulfil apparently impossible conditions, using $\sqrt{-1}$ as a unit.

Integral calculus; the inverse of differential calculus, being the deduction, from the ratio of the infinitely small changes of two or more magnitudes, of the magnitudes themselves.

çal-dā′ri-um, *n.*; *pl.* **çal-dā′ri-ȧ.** [L.] One of the rooms in the Roman thermæ, in which the hot baths were taken.

çal-de′rȧ, *n.* [Sp.] A deep, caldron-like cavity found at the summit of an extinct volcano.

Çal-de-rä′ri, *n. pl.* [It., coppersmiths.] A politico-religious sect in Italy set on foot during the reign of Murat in opposition to the Carbonari.

çal′drŏn, çaul′drŏn, *n.* [ME. *caldron, caudron*;

OFr. *caudron, chaudron*; L. *caldaria*, a kettle for hot water, from *calidus*, hot, *calere*, to be hot, warm.] A large metallic kettle or boiler having a movable handle or bail.

çāle′çan-nŏn, *n.* [AS. *caul*; L. *caulis*, cabbage.] An Irish dish consisting of several vegetables, mainly potatoes and cabbage, stewed together.

çȧ-lèçhe′, *n.* See *Calash.*

Çal-ē-dō′ni-ȧ, *n.* [L.] Scotland.

Çal-ē-dō′ni-ăn, *a.* Of or pertaining to Caledonia.

Çal-ē-dō′ni-ăn, *n.* A native or inhabitant of Caledonia, or Scotland.

çȧ-led′ō-nite, *n.* [Named from *Caledonia*, where it is found.] A mineral of a green color, a cupreous sulphato-carbonate of lead.

çal-e-fā′cient, *a.* [L. *calefaciens* (*-entis*), ppr. of *calefacere*, to make warm; *calere*, to be warm, and *facere*, to make.] Warming; heating. [Rare.]

çal-e-fā′cient, *n.* That which warms or heats, as mustard applied to the body.

çal-e-fac′tion, *n.* [L. *calefactio*, from *calefacere*, to make warm.]

1. The act or operation of warming or heating; the production of heat in a body by the action of fire, or by the communication of heat from other bodies or substances.

2. The state of being heated.

çal-e-fac′tive, çal-e-fac′tō-ry, *a.* Having the quality of producing or communicating heat or warmth.

çal-e-fac′tō-ry, *n.* 1. A sitting-room in a monastery, containing a stove or fireplace.

2. A warming-pan or dish containing live coals or hot water, placed on the altar to warm the priest's hands in cold weather.

çal′e-fȳ, *v.i.*; calefied, *pt., pp.*; calefying, *ppr.* [L. *calefio*, to become warm or hot; *calere*, to be warm, and *fieri*, to become.] To grow hot or warm; to be heated.

çal′e-fȳ, *v.t.* To make warm or hot.

çal′em-böur, çal′em-böurg, *n.* [Fr., from a German Count *Kalemberg*, noted for his blunders in the French language.] A pun.

çal′e-mēş, *n.* Same as *Camenes.*

çal′en-dăr, *n.* [ME. *calendar*; L. *calendarium*, an account-book; from *calendæ, kalendæ*, the calends.]

1. A series of tables giving in tabulated form the days of the week and month, usually with certain astronomical information; an almanac; specifically, such information concisely prepared for handy reference; as, a wall- or desk-*calendar.*

2. Any concise and systematic arrangement of facts, observances, etc., generally in chronological order; as, a church or school *calendar*; a bar *calendar*; a *calendar* of sporting events.

3. One of a number of systems of chronology; as, the Julian *calendar.*

Calendar months; see under *Month.*

Gregorian calendar; see under *Gregorian.*

Julian calendar; see under *Julian.*

Perpetual calendar; an adjustable calendar showing any month or year.

Republican calendar; that of the first French republic. [See *Vendémiaire.*]

çal′en-dăr, *v.t.*; calendared, *pt., pp.*; calendaring, *ppr.* To enter or write in a calendar.

çal′en-dăr-clock, *n.* A clock showing the day of the week and month as well as the hour of the day.

çal-en-dā′ri-ăl, *a.* Calendary.

çal′en-dā-ry, *a.* [L. *calendarius, kalendarius*, from *calendarium*, a calendar.] Of or pertaining to a calendar.

çal′en-dẽr, *n.* [Fr. *calendre*; LL. *calendra*; L. *cylindrus*: Gr. *kylindros*, a roller, cylinder.]

1. A machine consisting of two or more cylinders, generally steam-heated, revolving so nearly in contact with each other that cloth or paper passing through between them is smoothed and even glazed by their pressure.

2. A calendering establishment.

3. One who calenders. [Obs.]

çal′en-dẽr, *v.t.*; calendered, *pt., pp.*; *calendering*, *ppr.* To press between rollers, for the purpose of making smooth, glossy, and wavy, as various cloths, papers, etc.

çal-en-dog′rȧ-phẽr, *n.* [L. *calendarium*, a calendar, and Gr. *graphein*, to write.] A calendar-maker. [Rare.]

çal′en-drẽr, *n.* A person who calenders cloth.

çȧ-len′driç, çȧ-len′driç-ăl, *a.* Pertaining to a calendar. [Rare.]

çal′endş, kal′endş, *n.pl.* [AS. *calend*, a month; L. *calendæ, kalendæ*, the first of the month; from *calare*, Gr. *kalein*, to call.] Among the Romans, the first day of each month.

The Greek calends; figuratively, a time that will never come, the Greeks having no calends.

Çȧ-len′dū-lȧ, *n.* [Dim. from L. *calendæ*, the first day of the month; so called from its producing flowers during almost the entire year.] A genus of plants, natural order *Compositæ* with yellow or orange flowers, with a powerful but not pleasant odor, natives of the Mediterranean region; the marigolds.

çȧ-len′dū-lin, çȧ-len′dū-line, *n.* A mucilaginous substance derived from the marigold.

çal′en-tūre, *n.* [Fr. *calenture*; Sp. *calentura*, heat, a calenture, from *calentar*; L. *calere*, to be warm, hot.] A kind of delirium, sometimes caused within the tropics, especially on board ship, by exposure to excessive heat.

çal′en-tūre, *v.i.* To have illusions like those of the delirium of calenture. [Poet.]

çȧ-les′cence, *n.* [L. *calescens*, ppr. of *calescere*, to grow warm or hot; *calere*, to be warm or hot.] Intensifying heat.

çȧlf (kȧf *or* käf), *n.*; *pl.* **çȧlveş** (kȧvz *or* kävz). [ME. *calf*; AS. *cealf*; Ice. *kalfr*; Dan. *kalv*; OHG. *calb*; D. *kalf*, a calf.]

1. The young of the cow, or of the bovine genus of quadrupeds; applied also to the young of other mammals, as the elephant, whale, etc.

2. Leather prepared from calfskin, commonly used in making shoes and, when especially prepared, in bookbinding.

3. A small island situated near a large one.

4. A fragment of ice detached from the submerged part of an iceberg, and floating near it.

5. In contempt, a dolt; an ignorant, stupid person; a weak or cowardly man. [Colloq.]

Calf's-foot jelly: a jelly made by sweetening and flavoring the gelatinous matter obtained from calves' feet by boiling.

çȧlf, *n.* The thick, fleshy part of the leg behind, below the knee.

çȧlf's′-foot, *n.* In botany, the common wake-robin, *Arum maculatum*, of Europe.

çȧlf's′-head (-hed), *n.* The pitcher-plant of California.

çȧlf′skin, *n.* The hide or skin of a calf, or leather made of the skin.

çal′i-bẽr, çal′i-bre, *n.* [Fr. *calibre*, perhaps from L. *qua libra*, what pound, weight, size.]

1. The diameter of a body; as, the *caliber* of a column or of a bullet; usually and specifically, the diameter of the bore of a firearm.

In small firearms, *caliber* is expressed by the diameter of the bore in hundredths of an inch; in cannon, by the diameter of the bore in inches or by the weight of the projectile.

2. Figuratively, mental capacity or endowment; personal ability.

çal′i-bẽr-çŏm″pȧss, *n.* Same as *Calipers.*

çal′i-bẽr-rūle, *n.* Gunner's calipers, an instrument used to determine, from a ball's weight, its diameter or caliber, and vice versa.

çal′i-brāte, *v.t.*; calibrated, *pt., pp.*; calibrating, *ppr.* To find the caliber of and to graduate, as a thermometer-tube; to adjust to scale or standard, any graduated instrument.

çal-i-brā′tion, *n.* The act or process of calibrating; particularly applied to determination of thermometer-calibers.

çal′ice, *n.* Same as *Chalice.*

çȧ-li′çhe, *n.* [Sp., from *cal*, L. *calx*, lime.] The name by which the impure native nitrate of soda of Peru, or Chile saltpeter, is known throughout Spanish-American countries.

çal′i-çle (-k'l), *n.* [L. *caliculus*, a small cup; dim. of *calix, calicis*, a cup.] In zoölogy, same as *Calycle.*

çal′i-çō, *n.*; *pl.* **çal′i-çōeş** or **çal′i-çōş**. [From *Calicut*, India, whence it was first imported.]

1. A kind of cotton cloth. In the United States, the word is applied only to cotton cloth printed with a figured design on one side. In England, any plain or unprinted white cotton cloth is called *calico*. Originally, *calico* was an East Indian fabric, and its importation into Europe seems to have begun in the early seventeenth century.

çal′i-çō, *a.* Made of or resembling calico; in the latter sense, often applied colloquially in the United States to animals having a mixed, spotted, or variegated coloring; as, a *calico* pony.

Calico bass; a common variety of fresh-water fish, the *Pomoxys sparoides*, frequent in the waters of western United States. It has a variegated coloring and is called by numerous names, such as the calicoback, strawberry bass, grass-bass, etc.

çal′i-çō-back, *n.* 1. The calico bass.

2. The *Murgantia histrionica*, an insect known also as the calico-bug and the harlequin cabbage-bug, which destroys cabbages and other vegetables.

3. The turnstone, a bird allied to the plover; so called from its spotted plumage.

çal′i-çō-bug, *n.* The cabbage-bug. [See *Calicoback.*]

çal′i-çō-bush, *n.* A poisonous shrub, better known as the mountain-laurel; the *Kalmia latifolia.*

çal′i-çō-print″ing, *n.* The process of producing the colored designs on calico, by printing; extended sometimes to include the dyeing.

çal′i-çō-wood, *n.* A small American tree, *Halesia tetraptera*, yielding a soft, light brown wood; called also the silverbell- or snowdrop-tree, from its white bell-shaped flowers.

çȧ-liç′ū-lȧ, *n.*; *pl.* **çȧ-liç′ū-læ.** In botany, same as *Calycle.*

çȧ-liç′ū-lăr, çȧ-liç′ū-lāte, *a.* [L. *caliculus*, dim. of *calix*, a cup.] Shaped like a cup.

çal′id, *a.* [L. *calidus*, from *calere*, to be hot.] Hot; burning; ardent. [Obs.]

çȧ-lid′i-ty, *n.* Heat. [Obs.]

çal′i-duçt, *n.* [L. *calere*, to be warm, and *ductus*, from *ducere*, to lead, conduct.] A pipe to convey hot air or steam. [Rare.]

çā′lif, çā′liph, *n.* [Fr. *calife*; Ar. *khalifa*, a calif, successor, from *khalafa*, to succeed.] A successor or vicar; a representative of Mohammed. Among the Mohammedans, one who is vested with supreme dignity and power in all matters relating to religion and civil policy; a title borne by the sultan of Turkey; also spelled *kalif, khalif.*

çāl′i-fāte, çāl′i-phāte, *n.* The office or dignity of a calif; the government of a calif.

Çal-i-fọr′ni-ăn, *a.* and *n.* I. *a.* Pertaining to California; as, *Californian* wines.

II. *n.* An inhabitant or native of California.

çal′i-gā-ted, *a.* See *Laminiplantar.*

çal-i-gā′tion, *n.* [L. *caligatio*, from *caligare*, to be dark, *caligo*, dark.] Darkness; dimness; cloudiness. [Rare.]

çȧ-lig-i-nos′i-ty, *n.* Darkness, obscurity. [Rare.]

çȧ-lig′i-nous, *a.* Dim, obscure; dark. [Rare.]

çȧ-lig′i-nous-ly, *adv.* Obscurely. [Rare.]

çȧ-lig′i-nous-ness, *n.* Dimness; obscurity. [Rare.]

çȧ-lī′gō, *n.* [L., darkness.] Impairment of the sight.

çal-i-graph′iç, *a.* See *Calligraphic.*

çȧ-lig′rȧ-phy, *n.* See *Calligraphy.*

çā′lin, *n.* [Fr., prob. from Malay *kelang*, tin.] A compound metal of which the Chinese make tea-canisters, etc., probably composed of lead and tin.

çal-i-pash′, *n.* [A form of *calabash*, with sense of *carapace*; Fr. *carapace*, the shell of a turtle.] That part of a turtle adhering to the upper shell, a fatty substance esteemed in cookery.

çal-i-pee′, That part of a turtle adhering to the lower shell, similar to calipash.

çal′i-pẽrş, *n.pl.* [Corruption of *caliber.*] An instrument having a graduated scale for the measurement of diameters, generally resembling a pair of compasses in form; called also *caliber-* or *caliper-compasses.*

Vernier calipers; see *Vernier.*

çal′i-pẽr-square, *n.* A square designed for uses similar to that of calipers, having a graduated scale and adjustable jaws.

çā′liph, *n.* See *Calif.*

çāl′i-phāte, *n.* See *Califate.*

çā′liph-ship, *n.* A califate.

Çȧ-lip′piç, *a.* Relating to Calippus, a Greek astronomer.

Calippic period; a period of 27,759 days, equal to 940 lunar months or 76 years, suggested by Calippus as an improvement on the Metonic cycle.

çal-i-sā′yȧ, *n.* [S. Am.] Cinchona bark, especially *Cinchona Calisaya*, having astringent properties and used as a tonic and in malaria.

çal-is-thē′nē-um, *n.* See *Callisthenium.*

çal-is-then′iç, *a.* See *Callisthenic.*

çal-is-then′içs, *n.* See *Callisthenics.*

çal′i-vẽr, *n.* [A corruption of *caliber.*] A kind of hand-gun, musket, or harquebus. [Obs.]

çā′lix, *n.*; *pl.* **çal′i-çēş.** A cup. [See *Calyx.*]

Çȧ-lix′tine, *n.* [LL. *Calixtini*, from L. *calix* (*-icis*), a cup.] One of a Hussite sect, who in the fifteenth century demanded the right to receive the cup in the eucharist; called also *Utraquist.*

çalk, çaulk (kak), *v.t.*; calked, *pt., pp.*; calking, *ppr.* [ME. *cauken*, to tread; OFr. *cauquer*, to tread, tread in; L. *calcare*, to tread; from *calx*, a heel.]

1. To drive tarred oakum into the seams of (a ship, or other vessel), to prevent their admitting water; also, to treat the cracks between stone slabs in a similar manner.

2. To force the edge of (one metal plate against the edge of another) in order to make a tight seam, as in boilermaking, shipbuilding, etc.

çalk, *v.t.* [Fr. *calquer*, to chalk, trace; It. *calcare*; from L. *calx, calcis*, chalk.] To copy, as a design or drawing, by tracing with a stylus on the print itself, the back of which has been treated with prepared chalk.

çalk, *n.* [AS. *calc*, shoe, hoof; L. *calx, calcis*, a heel; *calcar*, a spur.]

1. A sharp-pointed piece of iron on the shoe of a horse or other draft animal, to prevent slipping.

2. An instrument with sharp points worn on the sole of a shoe or boot to prevent slipping.

çalk, *v.t.* 1. To fit or furnish with calks; as, to *calk* a horse or shoe.

2. To injure or wound with a calk; as, a horse *calks* himself by interfering.

çalk′ẽr, *n.* One who calks; sometimes, a calk or pointed iron on a horseshoe.

çalk′in, *n.* A calk.

çalk′ing-ī″ron (-ŭrn), *n.* An instrument resembling a chisel, used in calking ships.

çall, *v.t.*; called, *pt., pp.*; calling, *ppr.* [ME

çallen, kallen; AS. ceallian, to call, speak; D. kallen, to speak, say; Ice. *kalla*, to say, call, name.]

1. To name; to denominate or give a name to

And God *called* the light Day, and the darkness he *called* Night. —Gen. i. 5.

2. To pronounce the name of.

Answer as I *call* you. —Shak.

3. To designate or characterize as; to affirm to be.

Call you that backing of your friends? A plague upon such backing. —Shak.

He was a grave personage, about my own age (which we shall *call* about fifty). —Scott.

4. To invite or command to come; to summon; to convoke; as, to *call* a messenger; to *call* a meeting; often with *together*; as, the president *called* the cabinet *together*.

5. To select or appoint, as for an office, duty, or employment.

Paul, *called* to be an apostle. —Rom. i. 1.

6. To invoke or appeal to.

I *call* God for a record upon my soul. —2 Cor i. 23.

7. To arouse, as from sleep; to awaken.

You must wake, and *call* me early, *call* me early, mother dear. —Tennyson.

8. To proclaim; to utter the name of in a loud voice.

Nor parish clerk who *calls* the psalm so clear. —Gay.

9. To lure (animals), particularly birds, by uttering a call similar to their own.

To call a bond; to make it known that the holder of a bond will be paid the amount upon presentation of the bond for redemption on a certain date.

To call a card; in the game of whist, to demand that a person play a card as a penalty for certain violations of the rules, as for leading out of turn, etc.

To call a party; in law, to summon by crying, as a witness.

To call attention; to direct attention to something definite and important.

To call back; to direct the return of; to recall; to revoke or retract; to repeat.

To call down; (a) to invoke; to pray for; (b) to take to task; to rebuke; in latter case, slang.

To call forth; to bring into play; as, to *call forth* one's entire resources.

To call in; (a) to collect, as debts; (b) to withdraw from circulation, as coin or bonds; (c) to invite, as neighbors to one's house for assistance or company; (d) to request the coöperation or assistance of; as, *to call in* a physician for consultation.

To call in question; to challenge as to truthfulness, soundness, or veracity.

To call into play; to employ in an active way, as a fire-engine at the time of a fire.

To call names; to designate any one by abusive or opprobrious names, particularly if done in direct address.

To call out; to challenge, as to a fight; to summon into action, as the militia.

To call to order; (a) to announce authoritatively that order is to be maintained or that business is to be commenced; (b) to inform a person that he is out of order; particularly, that he is violating the rules governing debates.

To call to the bar; to admit as a practitioner of law.

To call up; (a) to revive the memory of; (b) to take necessary steps to bring up for action or discussion, as in a meeting or council; to demand the consideration of; (c) to communicate with any one by means of a telephone or speaking-tube; (d) to call upon for payment of amounts due, especially of profits or dividends on stock.

Syn.—Bid, invite, convoke, summon, name, designate, term, denominate, assemble.—*Call* is generic; *summon* and *convoke* imply some right or authority; as, to *summon* a witness or *convoke* an assembly; to *bid* supposes superiority; as, to *call* a servant and *bid* him do something.

çall, *v.i.* 1. To speak in a loud tone; to shout out; to utter a loud sound, or to address by name; to utter the name; sometimes with *to*

The angel *called to* Hagar. —Gen. xxi. 17.

2. To address; to address by name; to utter the name; sometimes with *to* or *for*.

3. To address oneself to, in request, entreaty, or command; to demand; to require; to give notice by voice, by sounding an instrument, or by visual signal; as, the tocsin is *calling* to arms; go where duty *calls*.

4. To stop, without intention of staying; to make a short stop; as, to *call* at the inn.

5. In poker, to demand (a) that opposing hands be shown; (b) a sight.

To call for; to demand or require specifically; as, the order *calls for* one hundred tons of coal; to order, as a meal at a restaurant; to stop for in passing; as, he *called for* his parcel at the store.

To call on or *upon*; (a) to visit; to present a request or a business proposition; (b) to invoke or implore; (c) to demand payment or assistance from, with a right to do so; (d) to invoke the Deity; to pray to, especially for some particular purpose; to solemnly invoke or request to witness.

To call out; to make an outcry, as of one in distress.

To call off; (a) to divert one's attention; to summon away from; (b) to postpone a proposed or promised event or function, or to declare that it never is to take place; to revoke; (c) to read aloud from a list or enumeration; as, *to call off* the names of the eligible candidates.

To call over; (a) to enumerate, as a list of figures or names; (b) to itemize; to recite the items of.

To call to account; to demand an explanation or examination of.

To call to mind; to recall to memory; to revive the recollection of.

çall, *n.* 1. The sound of calling, made either vocally or by instrument; as, I did not hear you *call*; the *call* of the bugle.

2. The act of calling by voice, signal, instrument, messenger, or writing, or in any manner of notifying the public, the individual, or the creature that is called; as, the riot-*call*; the president's *call* for volunteers.

3. The sound of any instrument (as well as the instrument itself) used for the purpose of attraction or of warning; as, the seaman's whistle for summoning the sailors to duty, the hunter's horn for inciting his hounds, or his imitating cry to decoy the game.

4. Any moral obligation imposed; as, the *call* of humanity for charity; the *call* to religious service, as of Abraham or of St. Paul; the *call* of a clergyman to preach the gospel.

5. A formal invitation to a minister to accept a pastorate.

6. In broker's parlance, a demand that grain or stock be delivered within a certain time and at a stated price.

7. A short visit, either social or in the interest of business.

8 In law, a term applied to some natural mark, object, line, or direction, mentioned in the descriptive part of a deed, grant, or conveyance.

9. In poker, a demand, sanctioned by the rules of the game, for a show of opposing hands.

10. A demand for the payment of subscription instalments or of cash, to meet losses.

11. Any notification or announcement; as, the last *call* for dinner or for a bid at auction.

At call or *on call*; payable on demand without previous notice; as, a sum of money deposited in a bank *at call*.

Call of the house; the reading aloud of the names of the members of a legislative assembly to ascertain who is absent, or for purposes connected with the business of the house; specifically, for the purpose of obtaining the ayes and nays of the members present.

Close call; a narrow escape from disaster or death. [Colloq.]

Çal'lȧ, *n.* [L. *calla*, a plant mentioned by Pliny.]

1. A genus of plants, natural order *Orontiaceæ*. The known species are few and of widely different habitats. The common calla-lily, *Richardia Æthiopica*, was formerly included in this genus, and is still sometimes called *Calla Æthiopica*.

2. [c—] Any plant of this genus.

çall'-bell, *n.* A bell by which attendants are called or signals given.

çall'-bird, *n.* A bird trained to decoy other birds by sounding its call.

çall'-boy, *n.* 1. A boy whose duty it is to call actors onto the stage at the proper moment.

2. The boy who repeats the orders of the captain of a steamboat to the steward.

3. A bell-boy.

çall'-but"tŏn, *n.* A button for closing the circuit of an electric current which causes a call-bell to ring.

çall'-duck, *n.* A decoy duck.

çalle, *n.* [Obs.] See *Caul*.

çall'ẽr, *n.* One who calls.

çal'lẽr, *a.* [Scot.] 1. Refreshing; cool; reviving; as, *caller* breezes.

2. Fresh; not stale; as, *caller* fish.

çal'let, çal'lat, *n.* A trull; a strumpet; a scolding or gossiping woman. [Obs.]

çal'let, *v.i.* To rail; to scold. [Obs.]

çal'lid, *a.* [L. *callidus*, expert, shrewd.] Skilful; cunning; crafty. [Rare.]

çal-lid'i-ty, *n.* Skill; shrewdness. [Rare.]

çal-lig'rȧ-phẽr, çȧ-lig'rȧ-phẽr, *n.* One skilled in calligraphy; an excellent penman.

çal-li-graph'iç, çal-i-graph'iç, *a.* Pertaining to calligraphy.

çal-li-graph'iç-ăl, çal-i-graph'iç-ăl, *a.* Same as *Calligraphic*.

çal-lig'rȧ-phist, çȧ-lig'rȧ-phist, *n.* A calligrapher.

çal-lig'rȧ-phy, çȧ-lig'rȧ-phy, *n.* [Gr. *kalligraphia*, from *kalligraphos*; *kalos*, beautiful, and *graphein*, to write.] Beautiful or expert handwriting.

My *calligraphy*, a fair hand
Fit for a secretary. —B. Jonson.

çall'ing, *n.* 1. The act of one who or that which calls; crying; shouting; naming; summoning, etc.

A *calling* of the sea. —Tennyson.

2. Divine summons; state of being divinely called; call.

3. A vocation; profession; trade; occupation or employment.

4. A body of persons following any profession.

Not to impose celibacy on whole *callings*. —Hammond.

5. One's name, title, or designation. [Obs.]

Syn.—Business, vocation, pursuit, function, occupation, concern, employment, office, duty, work.

çall'ing-drop, *n.* An indicating-drop on a telephone switchboard.

çall'ing-hāre, *n.* See *Pika*.

Çal-lī'ō-pē, *n.* [L., from Gr. *Kalliopē*, the beautiful-voiced; *kalos*, beautiful, and *ops*, *opos*, voice.]

1. In Greek and Roman mythology, the muse that presided over eloquence and heroic poetry.

2. [c—] A musical instrument consisting of a number of steam-whistles toned to different notes and played by a keyboard.

3. [c—] The specific name of a Californian humming-bird of the genus *Stellula*.

Calliope, from antique statue in Vatican.

çal-li-pash', *n.* Same as *Calipash*.

çal-li-pee', *n.* Same as *Calipee*.

çal'li-pẽrş, *n.pl.* Same as *Calipers*.

çal-li-seç'tion, *n.* [L. *callere*, to be insensible, and *sectio*, from *secare*, to cut.] Vivisection made painless by use of anæsthetics; antonym of *sentisection*.

çal-lis-then'iç, çal-is-then'iç, *a.* Pertaining to callisthenics.

çal-lis-then'içs, çal-is-then'içs, *n.* [Gr. *kalos*, beautiful, and *sthenos*, strength.] A system of light gymnastic exercises, adapted to the promotion of health and cultivation of gracefulness.

çal-lis-thē'ni-um, *n.*; *pl.* **çal-lis-thē'ni-ȧ**. A hall or gymnasium devoted to the practice of callisthenics; also spelled *calisthenium*.

çal'li-thump, çal'i-thump, *n.* A noisy and boisterous mock serenade; a charivari, intended either as a joke or as a hostile demonstration. [U. S.]

çal-li-thump'i-ăn, *a.* and *n.* [U. S.] I. *a.* Pertaining to a callithump.

II. *n.* A callithump; sometimes, a participant in such a demonstration.

Çal'li-tris, *n.* [L., from Gr. *kalos*, beautiful.] A genus of conifers. The wood of *Calitris quadrivalvis* is used by the Turks for floors and ceilings of mosques. It supplies the aromatic gum-resin called sandarac.

çall'-lōan, *n.* A loan of money payable on demand of the lender before close of banking hours of the day on which the call is made.

çall'-nōte, *n.* The note used by a bird or animal to call its mate or young.

çall'-num"bẽr, *n.* 1. The number given a library book to show the division, case, and shelf assigned to it.

2. The distinctive number of a telephone.

çal-lō'săl, *a.* In anatomy, pertaining to the corpus callosum.

çal'lōse, *a.* [L. *callosus*, hard-skinned, from *callum*, *callus*, hardened skin.] In botany, having hard, protuberant spots; callous.

çal-los'i-ty, *n.*; *pl.* **çal-los'i-tieş** (-tiz). 1. The state or quality of being hardened or indurated.

2. In a concrete sense, any thickened or hardened part on the surface of the human body or that of any other animal.

3. In botany, any part of a plant unusually hard.

çal-lō'sum, *n.* Same as *Corpus callosum*.

çal'lot, *n.* Same as *Calotte*.

çal'lous, *a.* [L. *callosus*, from *callum*, *callus*, hard skin.]

1. Hard, hardened; indurated, as an ulcer, or the skin on some part of the body, from exposure to continuous pressure or friction.

The patient rustic came, whose *callous* hand. —Goldsmith.

2. Hardened in mind or feelings; insensible; unfeeling.

And *callous*, save to crime. —Byron.

Syn.—Hard, hardened, indurated, insensible, unfeeling, obdurate, unsusceptible.

cal′lous-ly, *adv.* In a hardened or unfeeling manner.

cal′lous-ness, *n.* The quality of being callous.

cal′lōw, *a.* [ME. *calowe, calu*; AS. *calu*; O.H.G. *calo*; D. *kaal*, bald, bare.]

1. Destitute of feathers; naked; unfledged.

2. Immature; without experience; youthful; as, *callow* love.

cal′lōw, *n.* A species of duck, the old-squaw.

cal′lus, *n.* [L. *callus, callum*, hard skin.]

1. In anatomy, (a) a callosity; (b) the new growth of osseous matter between the extremities of fractured bones, serving to unite them.

2. In horticulture, the tissue that forms on an end of a slip or cutting before it roots.

cälm (käm), *a.*; *comp.* calmer; *superl.* calmest. [Fr. *calme*; LL. *cauma*, the heat of the sun; Gr. *kauma*, from *kaiein*, to burn; probably due to the period of rest, during midday.]

1. Still; quiet; being at rest; undisturbed; not agitated; not stormy.

Calm is the morn without a sound. —Tennyson.

2. Undisturbed by passion; not agitated or excited; quiet; tranquil, as the mind, temper, or attention.

People are generally *calm* at the misfortunes of others. —Goldsmith.

Syn.—Tranquil, placid, quiet.—*Calm*, when applied to the mind, implies that the person remains unagitated, even though there may be considerable care and anxiety; *tranquil* implies that the mind is serene and free from anxiety. *Quiet*, when applied to the disposition, implies that the person is naturally silent and undemonstrative. It implies also that one is free from external annoyances; as, leave him *quiet*. *Placid* is nearly allied in sense to *tranquil*, but denotes a more cheerful and settled state.

cälm, *n.* Freedom from motion, agitation, or disturbance; stillness; tranquillity; quiet.

The soul as even as a *calm*. —Shak.

A dead, stark, or *flat calm*; terms used by seamen to denote the greatest possible calm.

Region of calms, or *calm latitudes*; the tracts in the Atlantic and Pacific oceans on the confines of the trade-winds, where calms of long duration prevail.

cälm, *v.t.*; calmed, *pt., pp.*; calming, *ppr.* 1. To still; to quiet, as the wind or elements.

2. To allay or pacify, as the mind or passions.

cälm′ẽr, *n.* One who or that which calms.

cälm′ly, *adv.* In a calm manner; quietly.

cälm′ness, *n.* The state of being calm; repose.

Cal′muck, *n.* Same as *Kalmuck*.

cälm′y, *a.* Calm; quiet; peaceful; tranquil. [Rare.]

Cal-ō-chor′tus, *n.* [L., from Gr. *kalos*, beautiful, and *chortos*, grass.] A genus of bulbous plants of Mexico and California, natural order *Liliaceæ*, nearly allied to the fritillary and tulip.

cal′ō-mel, *n.* [Gr. *kalos*, beautiful, and *melas*, black.] Mercurous chlorid, Hg_2Cl_2, much used in medicine, prepared by sublimation of corrosive sublimate and mercury. It is tasteless, inodorous, insoluble in water, turning gray on exposure to the light.

Cal-ō-phyl′lum, *n.* [L., from Gr. *kalos*, beautiful, and *phyllon*, leaf.] A genus of tropical, guttiferous timber-trees, *Calophyllum Calaba* being the calaba-tree.

cal-ō-res′cence, *n.* [L. *calor*, heat.] The change of invisible into visible heat; a name first used by Tyndall.

cȧ-lor′ic, *n.* [L. *calor*, heat.] The name given to a supposed subtle imponderable fluid to which the sensation and phenomena of heat were formerly attributed; loosely, heat.

cȧ-lor′ic, *a.* Pertaining to heat.

Caloric engine; a hot-air engine.

Caloric paradox; same as *Spheroidal state*.

cal-ō-ric′i-ty, *n.* The faculty given to animals of producing the heat necessary for the maintenance of life, and of controlling this heat so as to produce an almost constant temperature of the body.

cȧ-lor′i-duct, *n.* [L. *calor*, heat, and *ductus*, from *ducere*, to lead.] A tube or passage for conveying heat. [See *Caliduct*.]

cal′ō-rie, *n.* See *Calory*.

cȧ-lor-i-fā′cient, *a.* [L. *calor*, heat, and *faciens*, ppr. of *facere*, to make.] Heat-producing; also written *calorificient, calorifiant, calorifient*.

cȧ-lor-i-fi′ănt, *a.* Same as *Calorifacient*.

cal-ō-rif′ic, *a.* Capable of producing heat; causing heat; heating.

Calorific rays; the invisible, heating rays which emanate from the sun, and from burning and heated bodies.

cȧ-lor″i-fi-cā′tion, *n.* The production of heat, especially animal heat.

cȧ-lor-i-fi′cient (-fish′ent), *a.* See *Calorifacient*.

cal-ō-rif′ics, *n.* The science treating of heat and heating appliances.

cȧ-lor-i-fi′ent, *a.* Same as *Calorifacient*.

cal-ō-rim′e-tẽr, *n.* [L. *calor*, heat, and *metrum*, Gr. *metron*, a measure.] An apparatus for measuring absolute quantities of heat or the specific or latent heat of bodies, as an instrument for measuring the heat given out by a body in cooling from the quantity of ice it melts or from the rise of temperature it produces in water around it.

cȧ-lor-i-met′ric, cȧ-lor-i-met′ric-ăl, *a.* Of or pertaining to calorimetry.

cȧ-lor-i-met′ric-ăl-ly, *adv.* By means of a calorimeter; according to calorimetry.

cal-ō-rim′e-try, *n.* The science and practice of measuring the specific or latent heat in bodies.

cȧ-lor-i-mō′tŏr, *n.* [L. *calor*, heat, and *motor*, from *movere*, to move.] An electric battery having very large contact-surfaces in the electrodes, low internal resistance, and producing a current of high heating effect.

cal′ō-ry, *n.* [Fr. *calorie*, from L. *calor*, heat.] In physics, the quantity of heat necessary to raise one degree centigrade the temperature of a given volume of water (one kilogram, in the case of the great or kilogram *calory*, or a gram, in that of the small, or gram *calory*).

Cȧ-lot′rō-pis, *n.* [L., from Gr. *kalos*, beautiful, and *tropis*, a ship's keel.] In botany, a genus of tropical fiber-producing plants of the milkweed family, of which *Calotropis gigantea* and *Calotropis procera* yield the valuable fiber known as mudar, and a bark having strong medicinal properties.

cȧ-lotte′, cal′lot, *n.* [Fr. *calotte*, dim. of OFr. *cale*, a kind of cap.]

1. A close-fitting cap worn by the Roman Catholic clergy.

2. The part of any headdress which fits close to the head.

3. In architecture, a round cavity or depression, in form of a cup or cap, lathed and plastered, used to diminish the elevation of a chapel, cabinet, alcove, etc.

4. In ornithology, a colored, hood-like eminence on the head of a bird.

To assume the calotte; to be ordained as a priest.

cal′ō-type, *n.* [Gr. *kalos*, beautiful, and *typos*, impression, type.] An old process of photography invented by Fox Talbot; also called *Talbotype*.

cȧ-loy′ẽr, *n.* [Fr., from Gr. *kalogeros*, a monk; *kalos*, beautiful, good, and *gēras*, old age.] A monk of the Greek church, especially one belonging to the order of St. Basil.

cal′pac, *n.* [Turk.] A large, black, cap-like headgear worn by Armenians, and various Oriental peoples.

calque, *v.t.* Same as second *Calk*, v.t.

cal′sŏns, *n.pl.* Hose; drawers. [Obs.]

cal′trŏp, cal′trăp, *n.* [ME. *caltrap, calletrappe*, a caltrop, star-thistle; AS. *coltræppe, calcatrippe*, a star-thistle, caltrop; LL. *calcatrippa*; *calx*, heel, and *trappa*, a snare.]

1. An obsolete military instrument with four iron points disposed in a triangular form, such that, three of them being on the ground, the other points upward. These were formerly scattered on the ground, where an enemy's cavalry were to pass, to impede their progress by endangering the horses' feet.

Caltrop.

2. In botany, any one of several herbaceous plants, so called because their stout spines resemble the military *caltrop*; as, (a) the star-thistle, *Centaurea Calcitrapa*; (b) the water-*caltrop*, *Trapa natans*; (c) the land-*caltrop*, *Tribulus terrestris*.

cȧ-lum′bȧ, *n.* Same as *Columbo*.

cȧ-lum′bin, *n.* Same as *Columbin*.

cal′ū-met, *n.* [Fr. *calumet*, a reed-pipe; dim. of OFr. *chalemel*; LL. *calamellus*, dim. of L. *calamus*, a reed.] Among the American Indians, a pipe used for smoking tobacco, having a bowl made of soft red stone and a long reed for the stem, usually ornamented with many feathers. It is used as a symbol of peace and war, to seal compacts, and as a mark of welcome to strangers.

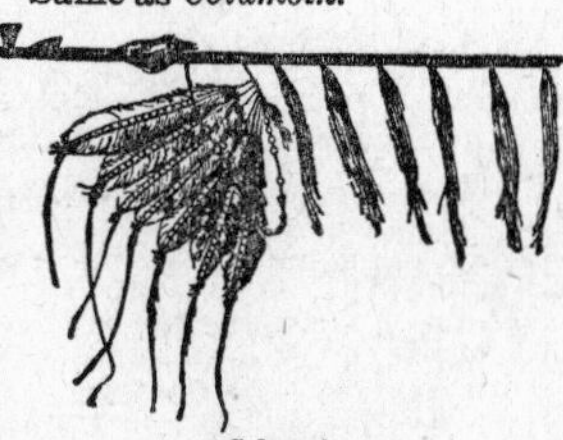

Calumet.

cȧ-lum′ni-āte, *v.t.*; calumniated, *pt., pp.*; calumniating, *ppr.* [L. *calumniatus*, pp. of *calumniari*, to slander; *calumnia*, slander.] To accuse or charge one falsely and knowingly with some crime, offense, or something disreputable; to slander.

cȧ-lum′ni-āte, *v.i.* To misrepresent intentionally; to utter calumny; to gossip.

cȧ-lum-ni-ā′tion, *n.* False accusation of a crime or offense, or a malicious and false representation of the words or actions of another, with a view to injure his good name.

cȧ-lum′ni-ā-tŏr, *n.* One who calumniates.

cȧ-lum′ni-ȧ-tō″ry, *a.* Slanderous.

cȧ-lum′ni-ous, *a.* Slanderous; bearing or implying calumny; injurious to reputation.

cȧ-lum′ni-ous-ly, *adv.* Slanderously.

cȧ-lum′ni-ous-ness, *n.* Slanderousness.

cal′um-ny, *n.* [Fr. *calomnie*; L. *calumnia*, trickery, slander; from *calvi*, to deceive.] Slander; false accusation of a crime or offense, knowingly or maliciously made or reported, to the injury of another; false representation of facts reproachful to another, made by design, and with knowledge of its falsehood; sometimes followed by *on*.

Neglected *calumny* soon expires. —Tacitus.

Syn.—Traducement, aspersion, slander, defamation, detraction, libel, backbiting, opprobrium, lying, falsehood.

cal-vā′ri-ȧ, *n.*, pl. of *calvarium*.

cal-vā′ri-ăn, *a.* Of or pertaining to the calvarium.

cal-vā′ri-um, *n.*; *pl.* **cal-vā′ri-ȧ.** [Neut. of L. *calvaria*, a skull, from *calva*, the scalp without hair; f. of *calvus*, bald.] The upper part of the cranium; the skullcap.

Cal′vȧ-ry, *n.* [L. *calvaria*, a skull, from *calva*, a scalp without hair.]

1. The place where Christ was crucified on a small hill west of Jerusalem; Golgotha.

Calvary, formerly on Mont Valerian, Paris.

2. [c—] A series of pictures or statues, representing the fourteen stations of the cross or phases of the Passion of Christ, placed in a church or chapel; also, the church or chapel containing such a representation.

3. [c—] A representation of the Crucifixion, consisting of the three crosses erected in the open air, often upon an elevation.

cȧlve (kȧv), *v.i.*; calved, *pt., pp.*; calving, *ppr.* [ME. *calven*; AS. *cealfian*, from *cealf*, a calf.]

1. To give birth to a calf; also applied contemptuously to birth in the human species.

2. To produce; to throw off from or out of itself; as, a glacier *calves* in producing an iceberg.

cal′vẽr, *v.t.* 1. To cut in slices. [Obs.]

2. To crimp; to gash, as fish, to render it firm and crisp when cooked.

cal′vẽr, *v.i.* [Origin unknown.] To be in right condition or of native fitness for clean, crisp cooking.

cȧlves′′-snout, *n.* The snapdragon, *Antirrhinum majus*; so called from the appearance of its seed-vessels.

Cal′vin-ism, *n.* The theological tenets or doctrines of Calvin (1509-64), who was born in Picardy, France, and in 1536 chosen professor of divinity, and minister of a church in Geneva. The distinguishing doctrines of this system are predestination, particular redemption, total depravity, irresistible grace, and the certain perseverance of the saints.

Cal′vin-ist, *n.* A follower of Calvin: one who embraces the theological doctrines of Calvin.

Cal-vin-is′tic, Cal-vin-is′tic-ăl, *a.* Pertaining to Calvin or to his opinions in theology.

Cal′vin-ize, *v.t.* To convert to Calvinism.

cȧlv′ish, cȧlf′ish, *a.* Like a calf.

cal-vi′ti-ēs (-vish′i-ēz), *n.* [L., from *calvus*, bald.] A medical term for baldness.

cal′vi-ty, *n.* Baldness. [Obs.]

calx, *n.*; *pl.* **calx′ēs** or **cal′cēs.** [L. *calx*, a small stone, lime.]

1. Lime or chalk.

2. The substance of a mineral which remains after calcination by heat, or solution by acid, and is capable of being reduced to a fine powder. Metallic *calxes* are now called oxids.

3. Glass fragments or refuse, returned to the melting-pot.

Cal″y-can-thā′cē-æ, *n.pl.* [L., from Gr. *kalyx, kalykos*, a cup, and *anthos*, a flower.] An order including two genera of shrub-like plants, having two seed-lobes, with large sweet-scented blossoms, with a perfume like wild strawberries. These plants grow in eastern Asia and the United States.

cal″y-can-thā′ceous, *a.* Of or pertaining to the order *Calycanthaceæ*.

cal-y-can′the-mous, *a.* [Gr. *kalyx (-ykos)*, a calyx, and *anthemon*, a flower.] Having petaloid sepals.

cal-y-can′the-my, *n.* The conversion, wholly or partially, of sepals into petals.

Cal-y-can′thus, *n.* 1. A genus of North American shrubs having two species, *Calycanthus floridus* being the Carolina allspice.

2. [c—] Any plant of this genus.

cal′y-cāte, *a.* [L. *calyx, calycis*, a calyx.] Provided with a calyx.

cal-y-cif′ẽr-ous, *a.* Calyx-bearing.

cȧ-lyc-i-flō′răl, cȧ-lyc-i-flō′rous, *a.* Calyciflorate.

cȧ-lyc-i-flō′rāte, *a.* [L. *calyx, (-ycis)*, a calyx, and *flos, floris*, a flower.] Having the calyx bearing the petals and stamens.

cȧ-lyc′i-form, *a.* In biology, calyx-shaped; resembling a calyx.

cȧ-lyc′i-năl, cal′y-cine, *a.* Relating to a calyx; situated on, adjacent to, or having a resemblance to a calyx.

cal′y-cle (-kl), *n.* [L. *calyculus*, dim. of *calyx*, a calyx.]

1. In botany, an outer accessory calyx, or set of leaflets or bracts looking like a calyx, as in the pink.

2. In zoölogy, a term applied to the small cuplike prominences, containing each a polyp, covering the surface of many corals.

Cal′y-coid, cal-y-coid′ē-ous, *a.* [L. *calyx*; Gr. *kalyx (-ykos)*, a calyx, cup, and Gr. *eidos*, form.] In biology, resembling a calyx in any manner.

Cal″y-cō-zō′ȧ, *n.pl.* [L., from Gr. *kalyx (-ykos)*, a calyx, cup, and *zōon*, an animal.] A group of animals of the lowest form of life, the *Lucernaria*, characterized by cup-shaped bodies, having little differentiation of the archenteric cavity.

cȧ-lyc′ū-lăr, *a.* Pertaining to a calycle.

cȧ-lyc′ū-lāte, cȧ-lyc′ū-lā-ted, *a.* Having calyx-shaped bracts.

cal′y-cūle, *n.* Same as *Calycle*.

cȧ-lyc′ū-lus, *n.*; *pl.* **cȧ-lyc′ū-lī**. See *Calycle*.

Cȧ-lym′e-nē, *n.* [Gr. *kekalymmenē*, concealed; pp. of *kalyptein*, to conceal.] A genus of fossil trilobites found in the Silurian rocks.

cȧ-lym′nȧ, *n.* [Gr. *kalymma*, a covering, from *kalyptein*, to hide.] The adhering, jelly-like covering of the protoplasmic body of radiolarians.

cal′yōn, *n.* Pebbles or flint. [Obs.]

Cȧ-lyp′sō, *n.* [L., from Gr. *Kalypsō*, a nymph in Greek mythology.]

1. A genus of orchidaceous plants remarkable for their beauty. It has one species, *Calypso borealis*, a small tuberous plant found in high latitudes throughout the northern hemisphere.

2. [c—] Any plant of this genus.

cȧ-lyp-tō-blas′tic, *a.* [Gr. *kalyptos*, covered, and *blastos*, a shoot, germ.] Pertaining to a suborder of hydroids characterized by capsular inclosing hydranths.

cȧ-lyp′trȧ, *n.* [Gr. *kalyptra*, a veil, from *kalyptein*, to cover.] A hood-like covering; specifically, in botany, the hood of the theca or capsule of mosses.

cȧ-lyp′tri-form, *a.* [L. *calyptra*, a hood, and *forma*, form.] Having the form of a calyptra.

cȧ-lyp′trō-gen, *n.* [Gr. *kalyptra*, a veil, covering, and *genēs*, producing.] In botany, the cell from which the rootcap develops.

cā′lyx, *n.*; *pl.* **cā′lyx-eṣ** or **cal′y-cēṣ**. [L. *calyx*; Gr. *kalyx*, a calyx, cup.]

1. The outer covering of a flower, or perianth external to the corolla, which it incloses, and consisting of verticillate leaves called sepals, united by their margins (mono- or gamosepalous), or distinct (poly- or dialysepalous), usually of a green color and less delicate texture than the corolla. In endogens the venation of the sepals is parallel, in exogens reticulated. The *calyx*, as thus defined, corresponds to the perianth of Linnæus.

2. In anatomy, a membranous sac, inclosing each papilla of the kidney, opening at its apex into the pelvis of the kidney; called also infundibulum. In this sense the plural form, *calyces*, is commonly used.

cal′zoonṣ, cal′ṣöundṣ, *n.pl.* Calsons. [Obs.]

cam, *n.* [ME. *camb*; AS. *camb*; D. *kam*; G. *kamm*, a comb, ridge.]

1. A ridge or long elevation of earth. [Prov. Eng.]

2. The projecting part of a wheel or curved plate, so shaped as to cause an eccentric or alternating motion of any required velocity or direction in another piece engaging or meeting it.

cam, kam, *a.* [Gael. and Ir. *cam*, crooked.] Awry; bent; crooked. [Obs.]

cȧ-mā′ieu, *n.* [Fr.]

1. A stone or an onyx engraved in relief; a cameo.

2. In the fine arts, monochrome painting or painting with a single color, varied only by the effect of chiaroscuro. Pictures in two or three tints where the natural hues of the objects are not copied may also be called *en camaieu*.

3. A method of printing pictures to make them resemble drawings.

Cams.

1. Elliptical cam, used for giving motion to the levers of punching and shearing machines. 2. The heart-cam or heart-wheel, much used in cotton machinery to produce a regular ascent and descent of the rail on which the spindles are situated. 3. Form of cam much used in ironworks for setting in motion the tilt-hammers.

cȧ-māil′, *n.* [Fr.] 1. In ancient armor, a guard for the neck, hanging from the headpiece and made of chain mail.

2. A furred tippet formerly worn by the Roman Catholic clergy.

Cȧ-mal′dō-lite, *n.* A member of a nearly extinct fraternity of monks founded in the Vale of Camaldoli in the Apennines in 1018, by St. Romuald, a Benedictine monk.

Cam-al-dū′li-ăn, Cȧ-mal-dūle′, *n.* Same as *Camaldolite*.

cam′ȧ-rȧ, *n.* [From native Guiana name.] A durable wood obtained from the tonka-bean tree or others of the same genus.

cȧ-mȧ-rȧ-de-riē′, *n.* [Fr., from *camarade*, a comrade.] Intimate, loyal, and spontaneous comradeship; good-fellowship.

Cam″ȧ-rȧ-sau′rus, *n.* [L., from Gr. *kamara*, a vaulted chamber, and *sauros*, a lizard.] A genus of huge Jurassic (American) *Dinosauri* characterized by cavities in the vertebræ.

Cam-ȧ-rā′tȧ, *n.pl.* [Neut. pl. of L. *camaratus*, vaulted.] A genus of immense reptiles, remains of which are found in the Dakotan Cretaceous group.

cam-ȧ-ril′lȧ (*or* -ril′yȧ), *n.* [Sp.] 1. The audience-chamber of a monarch.

2. Secret advisers; a cabal or clique.

cam′ȧss, *n.* The Indian name for the *Camassia esculenta*, a blue-flowered lily of the northwestern states; also, its bulb.

Cȧ-mas′si-ȧ, *n.* A genus of North American plants, resembling the lily and having bulbed roots; called also *Quamasia*.

cȧ-mā′tȧ, *n.* The trade name for the half-grown acorns of the *Quercus Ægilops*, which are imported for tanning.

cam-bāye′, *n.* [Named from *Cambay*, in India.] A kind of Indian cotton cloth.

cam′bẽr, *n.* [Fr. *cambrer*, to arch, to vault, to bend; L. *camerare*, from *camera*, an arch, vault.] In architecture, the convexity of a beam on its upper surface.

cam′bẽr, *v.t.* To arch; curve, as a beam.

cam′bẽr, *v.i.* To curve or arch upward.

cam′bẽr-bēam, *n.* A beam arched or curved upward.

cam′bẽr-deck, *n.* A deck which is higher in the middle, or arched.

cam′bẽr-keeled, *a.* Having the keel slightly arched, but not hogged.

cam′bẽr-win″dōw, *n.* A window arched or curved at the top.

cam′bi-ăl, *a.* [LL. *cambialis*, from *cambire*, to exchange.]

1. Belonging to exchanges in commerce.

2. In botany, pertaining to cambium.

cam-bi-ā′lē, *n.* A bill of exchange.

cam′bi-form, *a.* [LL. *cambium*, exchange, and *forma*, form.] Resembling in shape cambium cells.

cam″bi-ō-ġe-net′ic, *a.* [LL. *cambium*, exchange, cambium, and L. *genesis*, from Gr. *gignesthai*, to beget.] Yielding or secreting cambium.

cam′bist, *n.* [Fr. *cambiste*; It. *cambista*, from L. *cambire*, to exchange.] A banker; one who deals in exchange, or is skilled in the science of exchange or finance.

cam′bist-ry, *n.* The science of exchange, weights, measures, etc.

cam′bi-um, *n.* 1. In botany, a viscid secretion, which, in the spring, separates the alburnum of an exogenous plant from the liber, or inner bark.

2. In law, exchange of property.

3. A fancied nutritious humor that was formerly supposed to repair waste of tissue. [Obs.]

cam′blet, *n.* See *Camlet*.

cam-bōġe′, *n.* See *Gamboge*.

cam-bōose′, *n.* See *Caboose*.

cam′brȧ-ṣīne, *n.* [Fr.] A fine linen made in Egypt.

cam′brel, *n.* See *Gambrel*.

Cam′bri-ăn, *a.* 1. Pertaining to Wales.

2. In geology, of or pertaining to an extensive series of gritstones, sandstones, and slates, often metamorphosed into chlorite and mica schists, and gneiss, and lying under the lower Silurian beds or identified with them.

Cam′bri-ăn, *n.* 1. A native or inhabitant of Wales.

2. In geology, the Cambrian group.

cām′bric, *n.* [From *Cambrai*, a town in France.]

1. A kind of very white linen cloth.

2. A cotton imitation of such a cloth; sometimes, a kind of stiff lining; as, paper *cambric*.

cām′bric-grȧss, *n.* The Chinese ramie-plant.

Cam′brō-Brit″ŏn, *n.* A native of Wales.

cam-bū′cȧ, *n.* [LL.] A pastoral staff; also, a golf-club.

cāme, *v.*, past tense of *come*.

cāme, *n.* [Scot. *came, caim*, comb.] In glazing, a slender rod of metal, as turned lead, used as a sash-bar in stained glass windows.

cam′el, *n.* [OFr. *camel*; L. *camelus*; Gr. *kamēlos*; Heb. *gāmāl*, a camel.]

1. A name given to two animals, *Camelus dromedarius*, the ordinary or Arabian *camel*, and *Camelus bactrianus*, or Bactrian *camel*. It is a hornless, long-necked animal having broad elastic feet; one (or two) adipose humps on the back, and pouches in the paunch to store up water. It is valuable as a beast of burden especially in sandy countries.

Camel (*Camelus bactrianus*).

2. A device used for raising ships so that they may sail in shallow water or over shoals.

cam′el-backed (-bakt), *a.* Having a back like a camel; humpbacked.

cam′el-bīrd, *n.* The African ostrich.

cam′el-cāde, *n.* A body of persons mounted on camels. [Humorous.]

cam′el-cōrps (-kōr), *n.* A military cavalcade mounted on camels.

cam′el-crick″et, *n.* The camel-insect.

cam-el-eer′, *n.* The driver of a camel.

cam′el-grȧss, *n.* A sweet-scented grass or hay, *Andropogon Schœnanthus*, or an allied species.

Cam-e-lī′nȧ, *n.* [L., irregularly formed from Gr. *chamai*, on the ground, and *linon*, flax.] A genus of cruciferous plants of which the species *sativa* is the gold-of-pleasure.

cam′e-line, *n.* A plant belonging to the genus *Camelina*.

cam′el-in″sect, *n.* The camel-cricket; the mantis.

Cȧ-mel′li-ȧ, *n.* [Named after George Joseph Kamel, a Moravian Jesuit.]

1. A genus of trees or shrubs, natural order *Ternstrœmiaceæ*, with showy flowers and laurel-like leaves, nearly allied to the plants which yield tea.

2. [c—] Any plant of this genus; specifically, *Camellia Japonica*.

Camellia (*Camellia Japonica*).

cȧ-mel′ō-pärd (*or* cam′el-ō-pärd), *n.* [LL. *camelopardus*; L. *camelopardalis*; Gr. *kamēlopardalis*; *kamēlos*, a camel, and *pardalis*, a pard, leopard.]

1. The giraffe.

2. An imaginary beast of heraldic creation, formed by the addition of two long horns, slightly curved backward, on the head of the camelopard.

3. [C—] A northern constellation situated between Cepheus, Perseus, Ursa Major and Minor, and Draco, and contains thirty-two stars.

cāme′lot, *n.* Camlet. [Obs.]

cam′el-ry, *n.* 1. Troops having camels for mounts.

2. A depot for the handling of goods to be transported by camels.

cam′el's-hāir, *n.* The hair of the camel, used chiefly for the manufacture of shawls, carpets, and fine brushes for drawing and painting.

Camel's-hair cloth; a material for cloaks and dresses, made of camel's-hair, or in imitation of it.

Camel's-hair pencil; a fine brush for artists, now often made of the tail hairs of the Siberian squirrel.

Camel's-hair shawl; another name for a cashmere shawl.

çam'el's-thorn, *n.* A spiny leguminous plant, *Alhagi camelorum*, of which the camel is very fond, and which yields a manna-like exudation from its leaves and branches.

çam'en-ēs, *n.* In logic, a mnemonic word to express a syllogism in the fourth figure having one universal affirmative and one universal negative premise and a universal negative conclusion.

çam'ē-ō, *n.* [It. *cameo*, *cammeo*, from LL. *cammæus*, a cameo; a word of uncertain origin.] A general name for all stones cut in relief, in contradistinction to those hollowed out, or *intaglios*; more particularly, a stone composed of several different colored layers having a subject in relief cut upon one or more of the upper layers, an under layer of a different color forming the ground.

çam'ē-ō-conch, *n.* Any shell used in cutting cameos, as the queen conch.

çam'e-rȧ, *n.*; *pl.* **çam'e-rȧs**, **çam'e-ræ** (-rē). [L. *camera*, *camara*, a vault; Gr. *kamara*, a vaulted chamber.]

1. A chamber; specifically, (a) in English law, a judge's room; (b) in anatomy, any chambered or vaulted organ.

2. A photographic *camera*, the essentials of which are a light-proof box, a lens, or combination of lenses, and means for holding a sensitized plate or film so as to receive and record rays of light passing through the lens, thus fixing an image of the object or scene in focus.

Bellows camera; one in which the focus can be changed by means of a bellows-like adjustment.

Camera lucida; a small instrument depending upon internal reflection, serving to take the outline of any object. In the figure, the rays

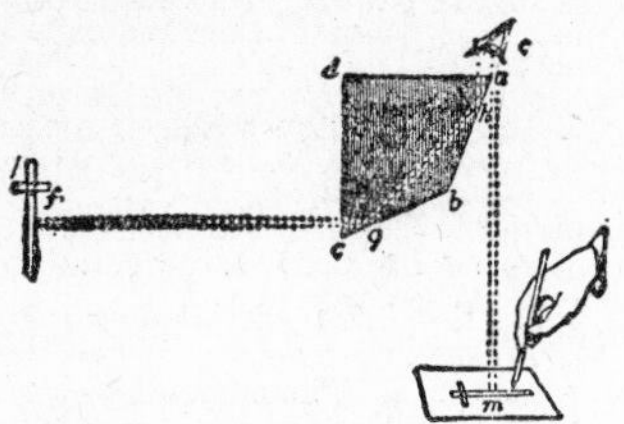

Camera Lucida.

from the image, *f*, to the eye, *e*, undergo two reflections, one at *g*, in the side *bc*, and the other at *h*, in the side *ab*; thus, the apparent image shows at *m* where it may be traced.

Camera obscura; a form of camera in which images of external objects are received upon a plane surface to be traced. In the illustration,

Camera Obscura.

the rays *a* are reflected from the mirror *m* upon the ground glass *n*, where the object may be drawn.

Panoramic camera; one having a wide-angled lens for taking a landscape picture in the form of a panorama.

Photographic camera; see *Camera*, 2.

çame'rade, *n.* A comrade. [Obs.]

çam"e-rȧ-lis'tiç, *a.* [Fr. *caméralistique*, from It. *camerale*; LL. *camera*, a chamber; L. *camera*, a vault.] Pertaining to finance and public revenue.

çam"e-rȧ-lis'tiçs, *n.* The science of finance, or public revenue, comprehending the means of raising and disposing of it.

çam'er-a-phōne, *n.* A machine combining the cinematograph and phonograph.

çam'ĕr-āte, *v.t.*; camerated, *pt.*, *pp.*; camerating, *ppr.* [L. *cameratus*, pp. of *camerare*, to arch over; from *camera*, a vault.] To build in vaults or chambers; to arch. [Rare.]

çam-ĕr-ā'tion, *n.* An arching, or vaulting.

çam-ĕr-lin'gō, *n.* [It., a chamberlain, from L. *camera*, a chamber.] The highest officer in the papal household; the chamberlain. He is clergy in the persecuting times of Charles II.

Cam-ĕ-rō'ni-ăn, *n.* One of the followers or Richard Cameron, in Scotland, who refused to accept the indulgence granted the Presbyterian

çȧ-mes'trēs, *n.* In logic, one of the nineteen valid moods of a syllogism, its special nature being indicated by each letter of the word.

çam'i-on, *n.* [Fr. *camion*, dray or truck.] A truck for the transportation of heavy ordnance and ordnance stores.

çam'is, **çȧ-mïse'**, **çȧ-mēse'**, *n.* [OFr. *camise*; LL. *camisia*, a shirt, tunic.] A loose Oriental shirt or tunic; a morning gown. [Obs.]

çam-i-sāde', **çam-i-sā'dō**, *n.* [Fr. *camisade*, from OFr. *camise*, a shirt.]

1. A shirt worn by soldiers over their armor in a night attack to enable them to recognize each other. [Obs.]

2. A surprise attack at night or break of day, when the enemy is supposed to be in bed, properly by soldiers wearing the *camisade* [Obs.]

Cam'i-sărd, *n.* [Fr.] One of the French Calvinists of the Cevennes in revolt, 1688-1705.

çam'i-sā-ted, *a.* Wearing an outer shirt. [Obs.]

çam'i-sōle, *n.* 1. A short light garment worn by ladies when dressed in negligee.

2. A straitjacket.

çam'let, *n.* [Fr. *camelot*; LL. *camelotum*; Ar. *khamlat*, camlet, from *khaml*, pile, plush.] A stuff originally made of camel's-hair. It is now made, sometimes of wool or silk, sometimes of hair, especially that of goats, with wool or silk.

çam'măs, *n.* The camass.

çam'mŏck, *n.* [AS. *cammoc*, a plant.] A plant, *Ononis arvensis*; known as rest-harrow.

çam'ō-mile, **cham'ō-mile**, *n.* [OFr. *camamille*; L. *chamomilla*; Gr. *chamaimēlon*, earth apple; *chamai*, ground, and *mēlon*, an apple.] The common name of a genus of herbs, of the aster family, having flowers of a strong fragrance and a bitter taste; used as a tonic or an emetic, according to the strength of doses. There are several varieties of the genus, the most common being *Anthemis nobilis*.

Camomile (*Anthemis nobilis*).

Cȧ-mor'rȧ, *n.* [It.] An Italian secret society, organized ostensibly for political purposes, but largely for extortion and violence.

Cȧ-mor'rist, *n.* A member of the Camorra, or one who believed in its principles and procedures.

çȧ-möu-flage' (fläjh), *n.* [Fr. *camoufler*, to disguise.] The blind or cover of a ship, camp, battery, etc., by paint, shrubbery, etc., to screen military movements from the enemy. In its fullest sense, camouflage is the art of reducing the visibility of objects and of deceiving as to their true nature, its main principle being the destruction of outline; hence, any deceit.

çȧ-möu-flage', *v.t.*; camouflaged, *pt.*, *pp.*; camouflaging, *ppr.* To disguise by paint, screen or other artifice.

çȧ-möu-fleur (-flūr') *n.* One employed or skilled in camouflage.

çȧ-möu'flet (-flā), *n.* [Fr.] A military term denoting a mine with a charge so small as not to produce any crater; also called a *stifler*.

çā'mous (-mus), *a.* [OFr. *camus*, flat-nosed; Gael. *cam*, crooked.] Flat; depressed; applied only to the nose. [Obs.]

çamp, *v.i.*; camped, *pt.*, *pp.*; camping, *ppr.* 1. To rest or lodge, as an army; to pitch tents, or to live in them, often used with *out*.

2. To play camp, an English football game.

çamp, *v.t.* To supply with lodging accommodations, as travelers or an army.

çamp, *n.* [Fr. *camp*, a camp; L. *campus*, a field.

1. The ground upon which tents are pitched for the lodging of an army, or a smaller body of people, such as lumbermen, miners, etc.

2. A scene of preparation for war.

3. Any collection of persons lodging in tents.

4. Any unconventional place of lodging.

5. A rough shelter; as, a hunter's *camp*.

6. A mound of earth for the storage and protection of vegetables. [Prov. Eng.]

7. A form of English football.

To pitch camp; to erect the tents for an army, or other body of men.

To strike camp; to take down the tents forming a camp and pack them for transportation.

Çam-pä'gnȧ (-nyä), *n.* [It., from L. *campus*, field.] A champaign.

çȧm-pȧ-gnol' (-nyol'), *n.* [Fr., from *campagne*, field.] A species of field-rat or vole, the *Arvicola arvalis* or *agrestis*.

çam-pāign' (-pān'), *n.* [Fr. *campaigne*, *campagne*, an open field, military expedition; LL. *campania*, level country; L. *campus*, a field.]

1. An open field; a champaign. [Obs.]

2. The time, or the operations of an army during the time it keeps the field in one season

3. Operations preceding a political election; a canvass for votes.

4. The time during which a blast furnace is continuously operated; also called the *run*.

çam-pāign', *v.i.*, campaigned, *pt*, *pp*; campaigning, *ppr.* To serve in a campaign.

çam-pāign'ĕr, *n.* One who has served in an army during several campaigns; a veteran.

çam-pā'nȧ, *n.* [LL. and It. *campana*, a bell.]

1. A church-bell.

2. A bell-like dish or cover used in making sulphuric acid.

3. In botany, the pasqueflower.

4. In archæology, one of the drops or guttæ of the Doric architrave.

çam-pāne', *n.* [Fr. *campane*; LL. *campana*, a bell.] In heraldry, a bell.

çam-pāned', *a.* In heraldry, bearing bells.

çam-pȧ-nē'rō, *n.* [Sp., a bellman, from *campana*, a bell.] The South American bell-bird.

çam-pā'ni-ȧ, *n.* [LL. *campania*, level country.] A champaign. [Obs.]

çam-pan'i-fŏrm, *a.* [L. *campana*, a bell, and *forma*, form.] Shaped like a bell.

çam-pȧ-nï'le, *n.*; *pl.* **çam-pȧ-nï'leṣ**, **çam-pȧ-nï'li**. [It. *campanile*, from LL. *campana*, a bell, said to be from *Campania*, in Italy, where bells were first used in divine service.] In archæology, a bell-tower; a term applied especially to detached buildings in some parts of Italy, erected for the purpose of containing bells; also, to such structures as the two western towers of St. Paul's cathedral, London, St. Peter's, at Rome, etc.

Campanile, Church of San Andrea, Mantua.

çam-pȧ-nil'i-fŏrm, *a.* Campaniform.

çam-pȧ-nol'ō-gist, *n.* A bell-ringer; one practised in campanology.

çam-pȧ-nol'ō-ġy, *n.* [LL. *campana*, a bell, and Gr. *logia*, from *legein*, to speak.] The art of ringing bells; also a treatise on the art.

Çam-pan'ū-lȧ, *n.* [LL. *campanula*, dim. of *campana*, a bell.]

1. A genus of plants bearing bell-shaped flowers.

2. [c—] Any plant of this genus.

Çam-pan-ū-lā'cē-æ, *n. pl.* The bellworts, a natural order of monopetalous dicotyledonous plants.

çam-pan-ū-lā'ceous, *a.* Pertaining to the *Campanulaceæ*.

Çam-pan-ū-lā'ri-ȧ, *n. pl.* A genus of zoöphytes in which the polyp-cells assume a bell-shape and are terminal on the footstalk.

çam-pan-ū-lā'ri-ăn, *n.* One of the *Campanulariidæ*.

Çam-pan"-ū-lȧ-rī'i-dæ, *n. pl.* A family of hydroid hydrozoans having the polyps protected by a campanulate calycle.

çam-pan'ū-lāte, *a.* [L. *campanula*, dim. of *campana*, a bell.] In biology, bell-shaped.

çamp'=bed, *n.* A bed having a light folding frame, adapted to camp life.

Çamp'bell-ite (kam'), *n.* 1. A member of the denomination more properly called Christians or Disciples of Christ.

2. A follower of Rev. John McLeod Campbell, deposed from the ministry in 1831 for teaching universal atonement. [Scot.]

çamp'ceil"ing, *n.* In architecture, a ceiling formed by an inclination of the wall on each side toward the plane surface in the middle, so as to form something like a coved ceiling.

çamp'=chāir, *n.* A light chair, easily packed, often with canvas seat and back.

çamp'ĕr, *n.* One who camps.

çam-pes'trăl, **çam-pes'tri-ăn**, *a.* [L. *campestris*, from *campus*, a field.] Pertaining to an open field; growing in a field, or on open ground.

çamp'fight, *n.* In English law, a duel fought to decide a case.

çamp'=fire, *n.* 1. The fire used for cooking, etc., in a tented camp.

2. A soldier's reunion, especially one of veterans of the Civil War.

Camp-fire Girl; a member of The Camp-fire Girls of America, an organization aiming to develop girls in character through outdoor activities and to invest home duties with real interest.

camp'=fol"lōw-ẽr, *n.* One who follows or attaches himself or herself to a camp or army without serving, such as a sutler.

cam'phēne, cam'phīne (*or* kam-fēn'), *n.* [From *camphor*.]

1. The generic name for the volatile oils or hydrocarbons, isomeric or polymeric with oil of turpentine, as oil of bergamot, cloves, copaiba, hops, juniper, orange, pepper, etc. Many *camphenes* exist ready formed in plants.

2. The commercial term for purified oil of turpentine, obtained by distilling the oil over quicklime to free it from resin.

cam'phīre, *n.* Camphor. [Obs.]

cam'phō-gen, *n.* [LL. *camphora*, camphor, and *-genus*, producing.] A colorless liquid, $C_{10}H_{14}$, produced by distilling camphor with phosphorous pentoxid. This hydrocarbon is better known under the name of *cymene*.

cam'phŏl, *n.* Borneo camphor; also called *borneol*.

cam-phol'ic, *a.* Relating to camphol.

Campholic acid; a volatile substance, white in color, obtained chiefly by the sublimation of camphor over potash-lime brought to a red heat.

cam'phŏr, *v.t.* To impregnate or wash with camphor. [Rare.]

cam'phŏr, *n.* [ME. *camfere*; Fr. *camphre*; Sp. *canfor*; LL. *canfora*, *camphora*; Ar. *kāfūr*; Sans. *karpūra*, camphor.]

1. A solid concrete substance obtained from different species of the laurel family, especially the *Laurus camphora* of Linnæus. It is a whitish, translucent, volatile and resinous gum, of a granular fracture and somewhat unctuous to the touch. It has an aromatic taste and a fragrant smell, being also a powerful diaphoretic, stimulant, and sedative.

2. Any one of a number of substances resembling *camphor*; as, borneol, peppermint-*camphor*, or cedar *camphor*.

cam-phō-rā'ceous, *a.* Of the nature of camphor; partaking of camphor.

cam'phŏr-āte, *v.t.*; camphorated, *pt.*, *pp.*; camphorating, *ppr.* To impregnate or treat with camphor.

cam'phŏr-āte, *n.* Salt formed by the combination of camphoric acid with a base.

cam'phŏr-āte, cam'phŏr-ā-ted, *a.* Pertaining to camphor, or impregnated with it.

cam-phor'ic, *a.* Pertaining to camphor, or partaking of its qualities.

Camphoric acid; a crystallized acid, produced by the action of hot nitric acid on camphor.

cam'phŏr=lau"rel, *n.* The camphor-tree.

cam'phŏr=oil, *n.* Any one of various oleaginous products of the camphor-tree.

cam'phŏr=tree, *n.* 1. A Japanese tree, *Cinnamomum camphora*, of the laurel family, yielding common or commercial camphor.

2. An immense tree, *Dryobalanops aromatica*, growing in Borneo and Sumatra, producing borneol.

cam'phŏr=wood, *n.* The wood of the camphor-tree.

cam-phret'ic, *a.* Relating to or obtained from camphor. [Rare.]

Camphor-tree (*Cinnamomum camphora*).

cam'phyl, *n.* The monad radical $C_{10}H_{17}$.

cam'pi-ŏn, *n.* [Prob. from L. *campus*, a field, a plain.] The popular name of certain plants belonging to the genera *Lychnis* and *Silene*. Bladder-*campion*, having a bladder-like calyx, is *Silene inflata*; red *campion* or adder's flower, *Lychnis dioica*; rose-*campion*, a handsome garden flower, *Lychnis coronaria* or *Lychnis Flos-Jovis*, etc.

camp'=meet"ing, *n.* A religious out-door gathering or series of meetings, for preaching, public worship, and revival work.

cam'pō, *n.* [Sp. and It., from L. *campus*, a field.]

1. An expanse of level country.

2. An Italian measure of land, equivalent to about an acre.

cam'=pump, *n.* A pump in which a cam imparts motion to the valves.

camp'=stool, *n.* A folding seat or stool.

camp'tō-drōme, *a.* [Gr. *kamptos*, from *kamptein*, to bend, and *dromos*, course.] Pertaining to a system of venation in which the veinlets inosculate after curving near the margin of the leaf.

cam'pus, *n.* [L. *campus*, a field.] The space or grounds belonging to or inclosed by the buildings of an American college or university; the college yard.

cam'py-lō-drōme, *a.* [Gr. *kampylos*, curved, and *dromos*, course.] In botany, having a nerve-curvature, as in leaves of the ribworts, the primary ribs of which are marked by a uniform curve from the insertion to the apex of the blade.

cam"py-lō-spẽr'mous, *a.* [Gr. *kampylos*, curved, and *sperma*, a seed.] In botany, having the albumen of the seed curved at the margin so as to form a longitudinal furrow, as in the fruits of some umbelliferous plants, as sweet cicely.

cam-py-lot'rō-păl, *a.* [Gr. *kampylos*, curved, and *tropē*, a turning.] In botany, a term applied to curved ovules in which the nucleus is folded over upon itself in the form of the letter U; also written *campylotropous*.

cam'us, *n.* A camis; a thin dress. [Obs.]

cam'=wheel, *n.* A wheel formed so as to move eccentrically and produce a reciprocating rectilineal and interrupted motion in some other part of machinery connected with it. [See *Cam*.]

cam'wood, *n.* Same as *Barwood*.

can, *v.*, an obsolete form of *began*, past tense of *begin*, occasionally found in old poetry. [See *Gan*.]

> With gentle words he *can* her fairly greet.
> —Spenser.

can, *n.* [AS. *canne*; D. *kan*; G. *kanne*, a can, mug.] A rather indefinite term applied to various vessels of no great size, now more especially to vessels made of sheet metal, for containing liquids, preserves, etc.

can, *v.t.*; canned, *pt.*, *pp.*; canning, *ppr.* To put into a can or cans; as, to *can* meat.

Canned goods; in the United States, a general name for fruit, vegetables, meat, or fish, preserved in hermetically sealed cans; in England, called *tinned goods*.

can, *v.t.* 1. To know. [Obs.]

> I *can* but small grammere. —Chaucer.

2. To have ability; to be capable of accomplishing. [Obs.]

> In evil the best condition is not to will, the second not to *can*. —Bacon.

can, *v.i.*; could, *pt.* [AS. *can*, *cann*, pres. ind. of *cunnan*, to know, be able; D. *kunnen*; G. *können*, to know.] To be able physically, mentally, morally, legally, or the like; to possess the qualities, qualifications, or resources necessary for the attainment of any end or the accomplishment of any purpose.

Syn.—May.—*Can* denotes possibility, *may* liberty and probability. He who has sound limbs *can* walk; but he *may* not walk in places which are prohibited.

Cā'năan-īte, *n.* 1. An inhabitant of the land of Canaan; specifically, one of the inhabitants before the return of the Israelites from Egypt; any person descended from Canaan, the son of Ham.

2. An enthusiast; a fanatic.

Cā'năan-ī-tish, *a.* Pertaining to the country or people of Canaan.

cà-ñā'dà (kà-nyä'dà), *n.* [Sp.] A small or narrow canon; a valley resembling a cañon.

Cà-nā'di-ăn, *a.* Pertaining to Canada.

Canadian period; a term formerly employed in geologic nomenclature to include the Chazy, Quebec, and Calciferous epochs.

Cà-nā'di-ăn, *n.* An inhabitant or native of Canada.

cà-năi'gre (-gēr), *n.* A species of Texan dock, *Rumex hymenosepalus*, the root of which yields an acid used in tanning.

cà-năille', *n.* [Fr. *canaille*, a mob, pack of dogs; from L. *canis*, a dog.]

1. The lowest class of people; the rabble; the vulgar.

2. Shorts, especially of an inferior grade.

can'à-kin, *n.* A little can or cup.

> And let me the *canakin* clink. —Shak.

cà-nal', *n.* [Fr. *canal*, from L. *canalis*, a channel, from the same root as Sans. *khan*, to dig.]

1. An artificial water-course, particularly one constructed for the passage of boats or ships.

2. In architecture, a channel; a groove or a flute.

3. In anatomy, any cylindrical or tubular cavity in the body through which solids, liquids, or certain organs pass; a duct; as, the vertebral *canal* containing the spinal cord; the intestinal or alimentary *canal*.

4. In zoölogy, a groove observed in different parts of certain univalve shells, and adapted for the protrusion of the long cylindrical siphon or breathing tube possessed by those animals.

cà-nal'=bōat, *n.* A boat used on canals, usually drawn by horses.

ca'năl=cōal, *n.* A corruption of *cannel-coal*.

can-à-lic'ū-lăr, *a.* [L. *canaliculus*, dim. of *canalis*, a channel, canal.] Canal-shaped; specifically, in anatomy, canaliculate.

can-à-lic'ū-lāte, can-à-lic'ū-lā-ted, *a.* [L. *canaliculatus*, from *canaliculus*, little pipe, dim. of *canalis*, a channel, pipe.] Channeled; furrowed; specifically, relating to a canaliculus.

can-à-lic'ū-lus, *n.*; *pl.* **can-à-lic'ū-lī.** [L., dim. of *canalis*, a channel, pipe.] The anatomical name for a minute canal or tube.

can-à-lif'ẽr-ous, *a.* Grooved; furrowed.

cà-năl-i-zā'tion, *n.* The building of a canal or a system of canals. [Rare.]

cà-närd' (*or* ka-när'), *n.* [Fr., a duck, a false newspaper report.] A hoax; especially, an untruthful report in a newspaper or other medium, for the purpose of deceiving the public.

Can-à-rēse', Kan-à-rēse' (*or* -rēz'), *n.* A native or inhabitant of a district in the southwestern part of India, called Canara; the language spoken in that district; sometimes used attributively.

can'à-rin, can'à-rīne, *n.* A dye for imparting a permanent bright yellow to various fabrics, prepared by the oxidation of potassium sulphocyanide and potassium sulphate while subjected to hydrochloric and sulphuric acids.

Cà-nā'ri-um, *n.* [L., from *canari*, an E. Ind. name.] A genus of plants, natural order *Amyridaceæ*, consisting of lofty trees which exude resin or balsam, that of the species *strictum* resembling copaiba.

cà-nā'ry, *a.* Of or pertaining to the color of a canary; of a bright yellow color.

cà-nā'ry, *n.*; *pl.* **cà-nā'ries.** [Sp. *canario*, a bird, a dance; from L. *Canaria insula*, Canary island, so called from its large dogs; L. *canis*, a dog.]

1. Wine made in the Canary Islands.

2. An old dance. [Obs.]

3. The canary-bird or its characteristic color.

4. A word put by Shakspere in its singular and plural forms in the mouth of Mrs. Quickly (*Merry Wives*), and which commentators differ in explaining. It is probably a blunder for *quandary*.

cà-nā'ry, *v.i.* To dance; to frolic; to perform the old dance called a canary. [Obs.]

cà-nā'ry=bird, *n.* An insessorial singing bird, a kind of finch, from the Canary Islands, the *Carduelis canaria*, or *Fringilla canaria*, of the finch family, much esteemed as a household pet, being one of the most common cage-birds.

Canary-bird (*Carduelis canaria*).

Canary-bird flower; same as *Canary-vine*.

cà-nā'ry=finch, *n.* See *Canary-bird*.

cà-nā'ry=grass, *n.* A plant, *Phalaris canariensis*, the seeds of which are valued for canary-birds.

cà-nā'ry=moss, *n.* A name given to various lichens from which a rich violet dye is obtained; also called *canary-weed*.

cà-nā'ry=stōne, *n.* A very beautiful and somewhat rare variety of carnelian; so named from its yellow color.

cà-nā'ry=vīne, *n.* A tropical climbing or trailing plant, *Tropæolum peregrinum*, bearing yellow flowers; called also *canary-creeper*, *canary-bird flower*.

cà-nā'ry=wood, *n.* The wood of the trees *Persea Indica* and *Persea Canariensis*, light orange in color and having a straight, coarse grain; called also *Madeira mahogany*.

cà-nas'tẽr, *n.* [Fr. *canastre*; L. *canastrum*; Gr. *kanastron*, a wicker basket.]

1. The rush basket in which tobacco is packed in South America.

2. An imported tobacco for smoking, consisting of the dried leaves, coarsely broken.

can'can, *n.* [Fr.] A kind of dance characterized by suggestive and lascivious postures, high kicking, and extravagant movements, performed in low resorts.

can'cel, *v.t.*; canceled *or* cancelled, *pt.*, *pp.*; canceling *or* cancelling, *ppr.* [Fr. *canceller*; L. *cancellare*, to make like a lattice; to strike out a writing by drawing lines across.]

1. To inclose with latticework or a railing. [Obs.]

2. To draw lines across (something written) so as to deface; to blot out or obliterate.

3. To annul or destroy; to throw aside; as, to *cancel* an obligation or a debt.

> Know then, I here forget all former griefs,
> *Cancel* all grudge. —Shak.

4. Specifically, (a) in mathematics, to strike out a common factor, as from the numerator and denominator of a fraction; as, by *canceling* 2 in the fraction $\frac{4}{6}$ we obtain the equivalent fraction $\frac{2}{3}$; (b) in printing, to throw aside any portion of a printed work, as single leaves or whole sheets, etc., and print it afresh.

Syn.—To blot out, obliterate, deface, erase, efface, expunge, annul, abolish, revoke, abrogate, repeal, destroy, do away, set aside.

can'cel, *n.* [Sp. *cancel*; L. *cancelli* (pl.), latticework, grating.]

1. Latticework, or one of the crossbars in latticework; hence, a barrier; a limit. [Obs.]

2. In printing, the suppression and reprinting

of a page or more of a work; the part so suppressed.

çan-cel-ā'tion, çan-cel-lā'tion, *n.* The act of canceling; specifically, in mathematics, that part of the science treating of the elimination of common factors.

çan-cel-eer', çan-cel-iēr', *v.i.* [OFr. *canceler*, to waver, to cross the legs so as not to fall.] In falconry, to turn two or three times on the wing before seizing, as a hawk in stooping, especially when it misses. [Obs.]

çan-cel-eer', çan-cel-iēr', *n.* The canceleering of a hawk. [Obs.]

çan-cel-lā'rē-ăn, *a.* [LL. *cancellarius*, a chancellor, an officer in charge of records.] Relating to a chancellor, or his official position. [Rare.]

çan-cel-lā'rē-āte, *a.* Same as *Cancellarean.*

çan'cel-lāte, *a.* [L. *cancellatus*, pp. of *cancellare*, to make like a lattice.]

1. Consisting of a network of veins, without intermediate parenchyma, as the leaves of certain plants.

2. In zoölogy, marked with lines crossing each other; marked latticewise.

çan'cel-lā-ted, *a.* Cancellate.

çan-cel-lā'tion, *n.* See *Cancelation.*

çan-cel'lī, *n.pl.* [L., a lattice.] Latticework; specifically, (a) in churches, the latticework partition between the choir and the body of the church, so constructed as not to intercept the view; (b) in anatomy, the lattice-like cellular or spongy texture of bones.

çan'cel-lous, *a.* Cancellate.

Çan'cēr, *n.* [L. *cancer, cancri*, a crab, an ulcer; Gr. *karkinos*, a crab.]

1. The crab genus, a genus of ten-footed, anomural or short-tailed crustaceans, now including only the common edible crab.

2. In astronomy, one of the twelve signs of the zodiac, represented by the form of a crab, and limiting the sun's course northward in summer; hence, the sign of the summer solstice.

3. [c—] In medicine, a morbid growth or structure which can extend itself nd form again after removal. *Scirrhous cancer* is a firm, incompressible, and nodulated mass. *Encephaloid cancer* is a soft, elastic tumor. *Colloid cancer* occurs most frequently in the stomach and intestinal canal and consists of fibers. *Epithelial cancer* occurs on the skin and mucous membrane, beginning as a hard little tubercle and ending like all the others in an ulcer with an ichorous discharge.

çan'cēr-āte, *v.i.* To grow into a cancer; to become cancerous.

çan-cēr-ā'tion, *n.* A growing cancerous, or into a cancer.

çan'cēr-cell, *n.* In pathology, a cell characterized by its large nucleus, bright nucleolus, and the irregular form of the cell itself; it frequently occurs in malignant tumors.

çan'cēr-īte, *n.* [L. *cancer*, a crab.] A fossil crab.

çan'cēr-ous, *a.* [LL. *cancerosus*, from *cancer*, a crab.] Like a cancer; having the qualities of a cancer.

çan'cēr-ous-ly, *adv.* In the manner of a cancer.

çan'cēr-ous-ness, *n.* The state of being cancerous.

çan'cēr-root, *n.* A name given in the United States to several species of low herbs of the broom-rape family, parasitic on the roots of trees.

çan'cēr-weed, *n.* See *Rattlesnake-root.*

çan'cēr-wŏrt, *n.* A plant, toadflax.

çan-chă-lä'guä, *n.* [Sp.] The herbaceous plant *Erythræa Chilensis* of Chile; sometimes extended, taking in other plants, as *venusta*, of the same genus.

çañ'cri-form, *a.* [L. *cancer, cancri*, a crab, cancer, and *forma*, form.]

1. Cancerous

2. Having the form of a cancer or crab.

çañ'crine, *a.* Having the qualities of a crab.

çañ'cri-nite, *n.* [Named after Count *Cancrin*, a Russian minister of finance.] A silicate closely resembling nephelite.

çañ-cri-sō'ciăl, *a.* [L. *cancer, cancri*, a crab, cancer, and *socialis*, from *socius*, a companion.] Social or associated with crabs, as the sea-anemone.

çañ-criv'ō-rous, *a.* [L. *cancer, cancri*, a crab, and *vorare*, to eat.] Living on crabs or similar crustaceans.

çañ'croid, *a.* [L. *cancer, cancri*, a crab, and Gr. *eidos*, form.]

1. Pertaining to the crab family.

2. Like cancer; applied to morbid growths somewhat like cancer but not really cancerous.

çañ-croph'ă-gous, *a.* Same as *Cancrivorous.*

çand, *n.* [Corn.] A miner's term for fluor-spar.

çan-dă-reen', *n.* A name given to a Chinese monetary value equal to 1.4 cents; also, to a weight equal to about 5.8 grains troy.

çan-de-lā'brum, *n.*; *pl.* **çan-de-lā'bră.** [L. *candelabrum*, from *candela*, a candle, torch.]

1. In antiquity, (a) a tall candlestick often highly ornamented; (b) a stand for supporting lamps, either standing on broad disks or pendent from branches.

2. A branched, highly ornamental candlestick; a chandelier.

Candelabra.

çan'dent, *a.* [L. *candens (-entis)*, ppr. of *candere*, to be white-hot.] Very hot; heated to whiteness; glowing with heat.

çan'de-ros, *n.* [E. Ind.] An East Indian gum, of the appearance of amber, but white and pellucid; sometimes made into toys of various kinds.

çan-des'cence, *n.* Incandescence. [Rare.]

çan-des'cent, *a.* [L. *candescens (-entis)*, ppr. of *candescere*, to become white or hot.] Incandescent. [Rare.]

çan'di-cănt, *a.* Growing white. [Obs.]

çan'did, *a.* [L. *candidus*, white, pure, sincere, from *candere*, to be white or hot.]

1. White. [Obs.]

2. Fair; open; frank; ingenuous; free from undue bias; disposed to think and judge according to truth and justice, or without partiality or prejudice.

> A *candid* judge will read each piece of wit
> With the same spirit that its author writ.
> —Pope.

Syn.—Fair, open, frank, ingenuous.—A man is *fair* when he puts things on a just or equitable footing; he is *candid* when he looks impartially on both sides of a subject, doing justice especially to the motives and conduct of an opponent; he is *open* and *frank* when he declares his sentiments without reserve; he is *ingenuous* when he does this from regard for truth.

çan'di-dă-cy, *n.* The state of being a candidate for any preferment or elective office.

çan'di-dāte, *n.* [L. *candidatus*, a candidate, white robed, from *candidus*, white; those who sought office in Rome wore white gowns.] A person who aspires or is put forward by others as an aspirant to an office or honor; one who offers himself, or is proposed for preferment, by election or appointment; usually followed by *for*; as, a *candidate for* the office of sheriff.

çan'di-dāte, *v.i.* To be an aspirant or candidate; specifically, to preach on trial with a view toward appointment as a clergyman.

çan'di-dāte-ship, *n.* Same as *Candidacy.*

çan'di-dă-tūre, *n.* Same as *Candidacy.*

çan'did-ly, *adv.* Openly; frankly; without trick or disguise; ingenuously.

çan'did-ness, *n.* The state or quality of being candid.

çan'died (kan'did), *a.* 1. Preserved with sugar, or incrusted with it; covered with crystals of sugar or ice, or with matter resembling them; as, *candied* raisins.

2. Wholly or partially converted into sugar; as, *candied* honey.

3. Figuratively, honeyed; flattering; blandishing; as, a *candied* tongue.

çan'di-fȳ, *v.t.* or *v.i.* To make or become white, or candied; to candy. [Rare.]

Çan'di-ot, *a.* and *n.* I. *a.* Pertaining to Candia or Crete.

II. *n.* An inhabitant or native of Candia.

çan'dīte, *n.* A kind of spinel found at Candy, Ceylon; called also *ceylonite.*

çan'dle, *n.* [ME. *candel, candele*; AS. *candel*; L. *candela*, a light, torch, from *candere*, to shine, be bright.]

1. A taper; a cylindrical body of tallow, wax, spermaceti, or other fatty material, formed on a wick composed of linen or cotton threads, woven or twisted loosely, used for a portable light.

2. A candle-power.

Electric candle; two parallel carbons insulated by some heat-resisting material, as kaolin, an alternating current being passed in and out of the blunt end of the carbons, whereby a voltaic arc is formed at the pointed ends; called also *Jablochkoff candle.*

Excommunication by inch of candle; a form of excommunication which gives the offender the length of time it takes a candle to burn out to repent or be excommunicated.

Not worth the candle; not worth the pains requisite for attainment.

Rush candle; one made of the pith of certain rushes, peeled except on one side, and dipped in grease.

Sale by inch of candle; an auction sale in which persons are allowed to bid only till a small piece of candle burns out.

Standard candle; one used as the basis of photometric measurement, producing a light of fixed and definite brightness, burning two grains of spermaceti per minute.

To curse by bell, book, and candle; see under *Bell.*

çan'dle-ber"ry, *n.* The fruit of the candleberry-tree.

çan'dle-ber"ry-tree, *n.* 1. The *Myrica cerifera*, or wax-myrtle; a shrub common in North America, the drupes of which are covered with a greenish-white wax (popularly called bayberry-tallow), of which candles are made. The wax is collected by boiling the drupes in water and skimming off the surface. It is afterward melted and refined, a bushel of berries yielding from four to five pounds of wax.

Candleberry or Wax-myrtle (*Myrica cerifera*).

2. A tree, *Aleurites triloba*, found in the Pacific islands, the nuts of which are dried and used for candles.

çan'dle-bomb (-bom *or* -bum), *n.* A small glass bubble, filled with water, placed in the wick of a candle, where it bursts with a report.

çan'dle-çōal, *n.* See *Cannel-coal.*

çan'dle-fish, *n.* 1. A large edible fish, the *Anoplopoma fimbria*, somewhat resembling the pollack.

2. A sea-fish of the salmon family, the *Thaleichthys pacificus*, frequenting the northwestern shores of America, of about the size of the smelt. It takes its name from the fact that a wick may be passed through it and ignited, the whole acting as a candle.

çan'dle-flȳ, *n.* 1. The lantern-fly.

2. A moth. [Obs.]

çan'dle-foot, *n.* A photometric unit of illumination; being that produced by a standard candle at a distance of one foot.

çan'dle-hōld"ēr, *n.* One who or that which holds a candle; specifically, a menial.

çan'dle-līght (-līt), *n.* The light of a candle.

Çan'dle-măs, *n.* [ME. *candelmasse*; AS. *candelmæsse*; *candel*, a candle, and *mæsse*, a mass.] An ecclesiastical festival held on the second day of February in honor of the purification of the Virgin Mary. This feast in the medieval church was remarkable for the number of lighted candles borne about in processions and placed in churches.

çan'dle-nut, *n.* The fruit of the candleberry-tree.

çan'dle-pow"ēr, *n.* The illuminating power of any agent compared with the illuminating power of a standard candle.

çan'dle-stick, *n.* [AS. *candelsticca.*] An instrument or utensil to hold a candle.

çan'dle-tree, *n.* 1. A tree, *Parmentiera cerifera*, growing on the isthmus of Panama and bearing fruit resembling a candle.

2. A catalpa-tree of the United States, bearing long, round pods.

çan'dle-wast"ēr, *n.* One who wastes or consumes candles; a hard student, or one who studies by candlelight; a spendthrift.

çan'dle-wood, *n.* A name given to certain resinous trees; as those of the genus *Fouquiera*; the West Indian rhodeswood, etc.

çan'dock, *n.* A local name for one or more species of *Equisetum*, or horsetails, given because some of the kinds are employed in polishing tin cans and other vessels.

çan'dŏr, çan'dŏur, *n.* [L. *candor*, whiteness, radiance, openness, from *candere*, to be white, to shine.]

1. Openness of heart; frankness; ingenuousness of mind; a disposition to treat subjects with fairness; freedom from prejudice or disguise; sincerity.

2. Clearness; brilliancy. [Obs.]

Syn.—Fairness, ingenuousness, frankness, openness, sincerity, impartiality.

çan'droy, *n.* [Origin unknown.] A machine used in preparing cotton cloths for printing.

çan'dy, *v.t.*; candied, *pt., pp.*; candying, *ppr.*

1. To conserve or dress with sugar; to boil in sugar.

2. To form into congelations or crystals.

3. Figuratively, to cover or incrust with congelations, or crystals of ice.

çan'dy, *v.i.* [Fr. *candir*; It. *candire*, to candy; from *candi*, candy.] To form into crystals or become congealed; to take on the form of candied sugar.

çan'dy, *n.* [Fr. *candi*; It. *candi*, from Ar. *qandi*, made of sugar; from Sans. *khanda*, a piece sugar in pieces, from *khand*, to break.] A species of confectionery, or compound of sugar with some other substance; as, sugar *candy*; molasses *candy*, etc.

çan′dy, kan′dy, *n.* [Tamil *kandi*, a measure of weight; Sans. *khanda*, a portion, piece, from *khand*, to break.]
1. An Eastern measure of weight, equal to 500 pounds in some places, but varying, in different towns, up to 821¼ pounds.
2. In Malabar, a measure of length equivalent to 28¼ inches.

çan′dy-tuft, *n.* [From *Candia*, the ancient Crete.] The popular name of plants of the genus *Iberis*, especially *Iberis umbellata*, a tufted flower brought from the island of Candia.

çāne, *n.* [ME. *cane, canne*; OFr. *cane, canne*; It. *canna*; L. *canna*, a reed, cane; Gr. *kanna*; Heb. *qāneh*, a reed.]
1. A term applied popularly and commercially to the stems of some palms, grasses, and other plants, such as the bamboo, rattan, and sugar-*cane*.
2. A walking-stick.
3. A lance or dart made of cane.
4. A linear measure, in several countries of Europe.

çāne, *v.t.*; caned, *pt., pp.*; caning, *ppr.* 1. To beat with a cane or walking-stick.
2. To plait a mesh of cane or rattan; as, to *cane* chairs.

çāne′brāke, *n.* A thicket of canes.

çāned, *a.* [Prov. Eng.] Mothery; said of vinegar.

Çȧ-nel′lȧ, *n.* [LL. *canella*, dim. of *canna*, a cane, reed.]
1. One of the genera of the order *Canellaceæ*, ornamental aromatic trees.
2. [c—] Any tree of this genus, particularly *Canella alba*, the wild cinnamon of the West Indies and Florida.
3. [c—] The bark of *Canella alba*.

çāne′=mill, *n.* A mill in which sugar-cane is ground.

çan′e-phōre, *n.* [L. *canephora*; Gr. *kanēphoros*, a basket-bearer; *kaneon*, a wicker basket, and *-phoros*, from *pherein*, to bear.]
1. One of the bearers of the baskets containing the implements of sacrifice, in the processions of the Dionysia, Panathenæa, and other ancient Grecian festivals, an office of honor much coveted by the virgins of antiquity.
2. In architecture, a term applied to a figure bearing a basket on the head.

Canephore, from terra-cotta in British Museum.

çȧ-neph′ō-ros, *n.*; *pl.* **çȧ-neph′ō-ri.** [L.] A canephore.

çȧ-nes′cent, *a.* [L. *canescens (-entis)*, ppr. of *canescere*, to become white or hoary; *canus*, white or hoary.] Growing white or hoary.

çāne′=trash, *n.* The refuse after grinding sugar-cane.

çangue (kang), *n.* [Port. *cangue*, a wooden collar, from Chinese *kang*, to bear on the shoulders, and *kia*, a wooden collar.] A wooden collar worn by Chinese criminals as a penalty.

çan′=hook, *n.* A rope with hooks at each end for raising casks by the projecting ends of the staves.

Çȧ-niç′ū-lȧ, *n.* [L. *canicula*, a little dog, dim. of *canis*, a dog.] A star in the constellation of Canis Major, called also the dog-star, or Sirius.

çȧ-niç′ū-lȧr, *a.* [L. *canicularis*, from *canicula*, a little dog, the dog-star.] Pertaining to the star Canicula.
Canicular days; same as *Dog-days*.
Canicular year; the Egyptian natural year, which was reckoned from one heliacal rising of Canicula to the next.

Çan′i-çūle, *n.* Same as *Canicula*. [Obs.]

çȧ-nī′nȧl, *a.* Canine. [Obs.]

çȧ-nīne′ (*or* **çā′nīne**), *a.* [L. *caninus*, from *canis*, a dog.]
1. Pertaining to dogs; having the properties or qualities of a dog.
2. Pertaining to the pointed teeth between the incisors and the premolars.
Canine appetite; morbid voracity for food.
Canine letter; the letter R.
Canine madness; hydrophobia.
Canine teeth; the sharp, pointed teeth between the incisors and grinders; so named from their resemblance to a dog's teeth.

çȧ-nīne′ (*or* **çā′nīne**), *n.* 1. In anatomy, a canine tooth.
2. A dog. [Colloq.]
3. One of the genus *Canis*.

çȧ-nin′i-fọrm, *a.* [L. *caninus* (supply *dens*, a tooth), canine, and *forma*, form.] Formed like a canine tooth.

çan′iŏn (-yun), *n.* See *Cannon*, n. 5.

Çā′nis, *n.* [L.] 1. A genus of digitigrade carnivorous mammals, including the dog, wolf, fox, and jackal.
2. A constellation of the northern heavens.
Canis Major; the Greater Dog; a constellation of the southern hemisphere, under the feet of Orion; including Sirius or the dog-star.
Canis Minor; the Lesser Dog; a constellation of the northern hemisphere, just below Gemini, including Procyon, a star of the first magnitude.

çan′is-tēr, *n.* [L. *canistrum*, a wicker basket; Gr. *kanistron*, from *kanna*, a reed.]
1. A small basket made of reeds, twigs, or the like. [Obs.]
2. A case for tea, coffee, spices, etc.
3. Canister-shot.

çan′is-tēr=shot, *n.* Metal cases containing bullets which scatter after leaving the gun; also called *case-shot*.

çan′kēr, *n.* [ME. *canker, kankir*; AS. *cancer*; D. *kanker*; from L. *cancer*, a crab, cancer.]
1. A disease incident to trees, which causes the bark to rot and fall.
2. Ulceration; particularly, one of a group of ulcers in the mouth, particularly of children. They are generally covered with a whitish slough.
3. A virulent, corroding ulcer; or anything that corrodes, corrupts, or destroys.

> Sacrilege may prove an eating *canker*.
> —Atterbury.

4. A kind of rose, the dogrose.
5. In farriery, a running thrush of the worst kind, a disease in horses' feet, discharging a fetid matter from the cleft in the middle of the frog.

çan′kēr, *v.t.*; cankered, *pt., pp.*; cankering, *ppr.* 1. To eat, corrode, corrupt, consume, in the manner that a cancer affects the body.
2. To infect or pollute.

çan′kēr, *v.i.* 1. To grow corrupt; to be or become infected, ill-conditioned, or malignant.

> And as with age his body uglier grows,
> So his mind *cankers*. —Shak.

2. To decay or waste away; to grow rusty or discolored by oxidation, as a metal. [Obs.]

çan′kēr-ber″ry, *n.* 1. The fruit of the wild dogrose of England, *Rosa canina*.
2. The berry of a Jamaican nightshade, *Solanum Bahamense*.

çan′kēr=bīrd, *n.* The cedar-bird.

çan′kēr=bit, *a.* Cankered, as by an envenomed tooth. [Obs.]

çan′kēr=blọọm, *n.* The flower of the dogrose.

çan′kēr=blos″sŏm, *n.* A flower eaten by canker; also, the cause of such attack. [Obs.]

çan′kēred, *a.* Infected with or as with canker, either literally or figuratively; as, a *cankered* tree; a *cankered* temper.

çan′kēred-ly, *adv.* In a cankered or cross manner.

çan′kēr-flȳ, *n.* Any fly preying on fruit.

çan′kēr-ous, *a.* Relating to or corroding like canker.

çan′kēr=rash, *n.* Scarlet fever.

çan′kēr=rọọt, *n.* A name given to a number of plants having astringent roots; as the marshrosemary, the three-leaved goldthread, the common sorrel, etc.

çan′kēr=weed, *n.* Ragwort. [Obs.]

çan′kēr=wŏrm, *n.* A worm or larva destructive to trees or plants; specifically, the fall worm, *Anisopteryx pometaria*, and the spring species, *Anisopteryx vernata*. These geometrid spanworms attack the foliage of shade and fruit trees, consuming the leaves for food, and are found throughout the United States generally.

çan′kēr-y, *a.* 1. Cankered; corroded; rusty.
2. Ill-natured; crabbed; venomous; vexing.

çan′nȧ, *n.* [It.] A fathom.

Çan′nȧ, *n.* [L., a cane, reed.] A genus of plants, of which there are several species known by the name of Indian shot, from their round seeds.
Canna Indica, a common garden plant having red, yellow, or variegated flowers; is valued for foliage and summer flowering.

Canna (*Canna Indica*).

çan′nȧ-bēne, *n.* [L. *cannabis*, hemp, and *-ene*.] A white, volatile oil, one of the constituents of Indian hemp.

çan′nȧ-biç, *a.* [L. *cannabis*, hemp.] Relating to hemp; obtained from hemp.

çan′nȧ-bin, çan′nȧ-bīne, *n.* A resinous substance, the active constituent of Indian hemp.

çan′nȧ-bīne, *a.* [L. *cannabinus*, from *cannabis* hemp.] Pertaining to hemp; hempen.

Çan′nȧ-bis, *n.* [L.] A genus of plants of the nettle family, having the single species, hemp.
Cannabis Indica; Indian hemp; hasheesh.

çan′nel=çōal, *n.* A fossil coal of a black color, sufficiently hard and solid to be cut and polished. It burns readily, with a clear yellow flame, and on this account has been used as a substitute for candles; also called *candle-coal*.

çan′ne-lūre, *n.* [Fr., from *canneler*, to groove, flute.] A groove or channel on the surface of anything, as the fluting on Doric columns, or on a conical bullet or projectile.

çan′ne-lūred, *a.* Grooved; fluted.

çan′ne-quin (-kin), *n.* [Fr.] White cotton cloth from the East Indies.

çan′nēr-y, *n.* A factory for canning food products for the market.

çan′ni-băl, *n.* [Fr. *cannibale*; G. *canibale*; Sp. *canibal*, a savage, cannibal; a corruption of *Caribal*, a Carib, a word used by Columbus but later changed to *canibal*, as if from L. *canis*, a dog.]
1. A human being that eats human flesh; a man-eater or anthropophagite.
2. An animal that eats its own or similar species.

çan′ni-băl, *a.* Denoting cannibals or cannibalism.

çan′ni-băl-işm, *n.* 1. The act or practice of eating human flesh by mankind; also, the act of an animal eating its own kind.
2. Murderous cruelty; barbarity.

çan′ni-băl-ly, *adv.* In the manner of a cannibal.

çan′ni-kin, *n.* A small cup or can.

çan′ni-ly, *adv.* [Scot.] In a canny manner.

çan′ni-ness, *n.* [Scot.] Careful, conservative management.

çan′nŏn, *n. sing.* and *pl.*; also, *pl.* **çan′nŏns.** [Fr. *canon*, a gun, barrel of a gun; LL. *canon*, a tube, pipe, gun; L. *canna*; Gr. *kanōn*, from *kanē, kannē*, a reed.]
1. A large military engine for throwing projectiles by the force of gunpowder, or more powerful explosives; a big gun or piece of ordnance. Guns of this kind are made of iron, brass, bronze, or steel, and of different sizes, carrying balls from a few pounds in weight up to a ton or more, and are classified as guns, howitzers, carronades, and mortars; also as field, mountain, coast, sea, and siege guns.
2. In mechanics, a hollow spindle or shaft having a motion of its own, while permitting independent motion of a shaft through its diameter; as the part *a* of the wheel *A*, loose on the shaft *b*.

A a b

3. In printing, a size of type; also spelled *canon*.
4. In billiards, a carom. [Eng.]
5. An ornamental bottom of a breeches-leg, in style in the sixteenth and seventeenth centuries. [Obs.]

çan′nŏn, *v.i.*; cannoned, *pt., pp.*; cannoning, *ppr.* 1. To bombard or cannonade.
2. To carom. [Eng.]
3. To strike, as in a collision.

çan-nŏn-āde′, *n.* [Fr. *canonnade*, from *canon*, a cannon.] The act of discharging cannon and throwing balls, for the purpose of destroying an army, or battering a town, ship, or fort; usually implying an attack of some continuance; also used figuratively; as, a *cannonade* of hail.

çan-nŏn-āde′, *v.t.*; cannonaded, *pt., pp.*; cannonading, *ppr.* To attack with cannon.

çan-nŏn-āde′, *v.i.* To discharge cannon.

çan′nŏn=ball, *n.* Any missile or projectile adapted for use in a cannon.

çan′nŏn=bōne, *n.* The single metacarpal or metatarsal bone of certain animals, as the horse and all ruminants; also spelled *canon-bone*.

çan′nŏn=bul″let, *n.* [Obs.] See *Cannon-ball*.

çan′nŏn=çrack″ēr, *n.* A loud-sounding firecracker.

çan′nŏned, *a.* Supplied with cannon.

çan-nŏn-eer′, çan-nŏn-ïer′, *n.* [Fr. *canonnier*, from *canon*, a cannon.] A man who manages cannon; a gunner.

çan-nŏn-eer′ing, *n.* The act of using cannon.

çan′nŏn=met″ăl, *n.* Same as *Gun-metal*.

çan′nŏn=pin″iŏn (-yun), *n.* In watchmaking, a squared tubular piece on the arbor of the center-wheel, to hold the minute-hand and enable it to be turned by means of the watch-key.

çan′nŏn=prọọf, *a.* Able to resist cannon-shot.

çan′nŏn-ry, *n.* Cannon, collectively; also, a cannonade.

çan′nŏn=shot, *n.* A ball for cannon; also, the range or distance a cannon will throw a ball.

çan′not. *Can* and *not*.—These words are usually united, but without any very good reason.

çan′nū-lȧ, çan′ū-lȧ, *n.* [L., dim. of *canna*, a reed, pipe.] In surgery, a tube used for withdrawing fluids from the body, generally fitted with a pointed rod for puncturing the skin.

çan′nū-lăr, çan′ū-lăr, *a.* [L. *cannula*, dim. of *canna*, a reed.] Tubular; having the form of a tube.

çan′nū-lāte, *v.t.*; cannulated, *pt.*, *pp.*; cannulating, *ppr.* [L. *cannula*, dim. of *canna*, a reed, pipe.] To make cannular; also spelled *canulate.*

Cannulated needle; a surgical needle hollow its whole length, permitting the passage of a thread.

çan′ny, çan′nie, *a.* [Scot., from *can*, knowledge, ability; Ice. *kœnn*, wise, clever, skilful.—A Scotch and Northern English word whose meanings are exceedingly various, being used in different localities in different senses.]

1. Cautious; prudent; knowing; wary; watchful.

> Whate'er he wins I'll guide with *canny* care.
> —Ramsay.

2. Skilled; expert.

> His wife was a *cannie* body, and could dress things very well. —Scott.

3. Moderate, as in charges, exactions, treatment, and the like; not extortionate or severe.

4. Gentle; quiet in disposition; tractable.

5. Easy; comfortable.

6. Possessed of supernatural power; skilled in magic.

No canny; dangerous through supernatural powers. [Scot.]

çȧ-nöe′, *n.*; *pl.* **çȧ-nöeṣ′.** [Sp. *canoa*, from the Carib name.] Any light boat, narrow in the beam, and propelled by paddles. The name was originally given to boats used by rude nations, especially to such as are formed of the body or trunk of a tree, excavated by cutting or burning into a suitable shape; but *canoes* are also constructed of bark—as among the North American Indians—and similar boats are now commonly used for pleasure-boats, being of light construction and often fitted for sailing.

Canoe of Carib Indians.

çȧ-nöe′, *v.i.*; canoed, *pt.*, *pp.*; canoeing, *ppr.* To propel or ride in a canoe.

çȧ-nöe′ing, *n.* The act or sport of managing or riding in a canoe.

çȧ-nöe′ist, *n.* One who manages or rides in a canoe.

çȧ-nöe′măn, *n.*; *pl.* **çȧ-nöe′men.** A canoeist.

çan′ŏn, *n.* [AS. *canon*, a rule; OFr. *canone*; LL. *canon*, from L. *canon*, a measuring-line, rule; Gr. *kanōn*, from *kanē*, *kannē*, a reed, rod.]

1. A law or rule in general.

2. Ecclesiastically, any governing law or rule, enacted by a council and confirmed by authority; a decision of matters in religion, or a regulation of policy or discipline by a general or provincial council.

3. The books of the Holy Scriptures universally received as genuine by Christian churches.

4. The rules of a religious order, or of persons devoted to a strictly religious life, as monks and nuns; also, the book in which such rules are written.

5. The catalogue of members of the chapter of a cathedral or collegiate church. [Eng.]

6. A dignitary who possesses a prebend or revenue allotted for the performance of divine service in a cathedral or collegiate church. [Eng.]

7. A catalogue of saints acknowledged and canonized in the Roman Catholic church. [Eng.]

8. The secret words of the mass from the preface to the pater, in the middle of which the priest consecrates the host. The people are to rehearse this part of the service on their knees, and in an almost inaudible tone of voice.

9. In music, a kind of perpetual fugue, in which the different parts, beginning one after another, repeat incessantly the same air.

10. In geometry and algebra, a general rule for the solution of cases of a like nature.

11. In pharmacy, a rule for compounding medicines.

12. In surgery, an instrument used in sewing up wounds.

13. In printing, one of the largest kinds of type or letter used; supposed to be so named because it was used in the printing of *canons.*

14. A device for supporting a b[illegible].

15. In billiards, a carom.

Apostolic canons; see under *Apostolic.*

Augustinian or *black canons*; see under *Augustinian.*

Canon capitular or *residentiary*; one officiating in a canonry.

Canon law; see under *Law.*

Canon of the mass; see *Canon*, 8.

Honorary canon; one not obliged to keep the hours and serving without emolument.

Minor canon; in the Church of England, one of a lower rank assisting in the performance of the daily choral service in a cathedral.

Regular canon; in the Roman Catholic church, one living an ascetic life, in monasteries or in community, and who, to the practice of the rules, has added the profession of vows.

Secular or *lay canon*; in the Roman Catholic church, a layman living outside a monastery, but keeping the hours.

çañ′ŏn, çan′yŏn (kan′yun), *n.* [Sp. *cañon*, from *caña*, a tube, funnel, cannon; L. *canna*, a reed, cane.] A term applied originally by the Spanish Americans to long and narrow mountain gorges or deep ravines with precipitous and almost perpendicular sides, occurring frequently in the Rocky Mountains, and the great western plateaus of the United States.

çan′ŏn-bit, *n.* That part of a bit held in a horse's mouth.

çan′ŏn-bōne, *n.* See *Cannon-bone.*

çan′ŏn-ess, *n.*, feminine of *canon.*

Regular canoness; one who has taken all the vows.

Secular canoness; a woman living after the manner of a secular canon.

çȧ-non′iç, *a.* Same as *Canonical.*

çȧ-non′iç-ăl, *a.* [LL. *canonicalis*; L. *canonicus*, from *canon*, a rule.] Pertaining to a canon or rule; according to a canon or canons, or to the canon.

Canonical books or *canonical Scriptures*; those books of the Bible which are admitted by the canons of the church to be of divine origin. The Roman Catholic church admits the books of the Apocrypha; the Protestants reject them.

Canonical epistles; see *Catholic epistles.*

Canonical form; in mathematics, the most concise form of expression for functions of the same class.

Canonical hours; certain stated times of the day, fixed by the ecclesiastical laws and appropriated to the offices of prayer and devotion; in the Roman Catholic church being the seven periods of daily prayer, viz., matins with lauds, prime, tierce, sext, nones, evensong or vespers, and complin. In England, the same name is also given to the hours from eight a. m. to three p. m., before and after which marriage cannot be legally performed in a parish church.

Canonical letters; letters which anciently passed between the orthodox clergy, as testimonials of their faith, to keep up the catholic communion and to distinguish them from heretics.

Canonical life; the method or rule of living prescribed by the ancient clergy who lived in community; a course of living prescribed for clerks, less rigid than the monastic, and more restrained than the secular.

Canonical obedience; submission to the canons of a church, especially the submission of the inferior clergy to their bishops, and of religious orders to their superiors.

Canonical punishments; those the church may inflict, as excommunication, degradation, penance, etc.

Canonical sins; in the ancient church, those for which capital punishment was inflicted, as idolatry, murder, adultery, heresy, etc.

çȧ-non′iç-ăl-ly, *adv.* In a manner agreeable to the canons.

çȧ-non′iç-ăl-ness, *n.* The quality of being canonical.

çȧ-non′iç-ălṣ, *n.pl.* The full dress of the clergy, worn when they officiate.

çȧ-non′i-çāte, *n.* [LL. *canonicatus*, canonical, from L. *canon*, a rule.] The office of a canon.

çan-ŏn-iç′i-ty, *n.* The state of belonging to the canon, or genuine books of Scripture.

çȧ-non′içs, *n.* In theology, the scientific analysis of the canon of the Scriptures.

çan′ŏn-ist, *n.* A professor of canon law; one skilled in the study and practice of ecclesiastical law.

çan-ŏn-is′tiç, *a.* Having the knowledge of a canonist; pertaining to a canonist.

çȧ-non′i-zănt, *n.* [From *canonize*, and *-ant.*] In algebra, a function used in the transformation of quantics into canonical form.

çan″ŏn-i-zā′tion, *n.* 1. In the Roman Catholic church, the act of declaring a man a saint; the act of ranking a deceased person in the catalogue of saints called a canon. This act is preceded by beatification, and by an examination into the life and miracles of the person, after which the pope decrees the *canonization.*

2. The state of being sainted.

çan′ŏn-īze, *v.t.*; canonized, *pt.*, *pp.*; canonizing, *ppr.* [LL. *canonizare*, to put into the catalogue of saints, from *canon*, a canon.]

1. To enroll (a deceased person) in the canon or list of saints; to declare one a saint.

2. To sanction as canonical.

3. To raise to the highest rank of honor and glory, as if enrolled in the canon.

çan′ŏn-ry, *n.*; *pl.* **çan′ŏn-rieṣ.** The office held by a canon; in England, the benefice filled by a canon.

çan′ŏn-ship, *n.* A canonry.

Çȧ-nop′iç, *a.* Of or pertaining to Canopus, a city of ancient Egypt.

Canopic vases; vases used by Egyptian priests to hold the entrails of embalmed bodies.

Çȧ-nō′pus, *n.* [L., from Gr. *Kanōpos*, *Kanōbos*, a town in Egypt.]

1. A star of the first magnitude in the rudder of the constellation Argo.

2. [c—] An Egyptian jar.

çan′ō-py, *n.*; *pl.* **çan′ō-pieṣ.** [OFr. *conopée*; L. *conopeum*; Gr. *kōnōpeion*, a pavilion, or net spread over a bed to keep off gnats; *kōnōps*, a gnat.]

1. A covering fixed above a throne or a bed; a covering held over a person's head as an honor.

2. In architecture, a decoration serving as a hood or cover suspended over an altar, throne, chair of state, pulpit, and the like; also, the ornamented projecting head of a niche or tabernacle. The label-molding or dripstone which surmounts the head of a door or window, if ornamented, is similarly named.

Niche with Canopy, Norwich Cathedral.

çan′ō-py, *v.t.*; canopied, *pt.*, *pp.*; canopying, *ppr.* To cover with or as with a canopy.

çȧ-nō′rous, *a.* [L. *canorus*, from *canere*, to sing.] Musical; tuneful.

çȧ-nō′rous-ness, *n.* State of being melodious.

çan′stick, *n.* A candlestick. [Obs.]

çant, *n.* [OFr. *cant*, a corner, angle, edge; LL. *cantus*, a side, corner; L. *canthus*, the tire of a wheel; Gr. *kanthos*, the corner of the eye, the felly of a wheel.]

1. A corner or niche; an angle. [Obs.]

2. An external or salient angle.

3. One of the segments forming a sidepiece in the head of a cask.

4. A segment of the rim of a wooden cogwheel.

5. An inclination from a horizontal line; as, to be on the *cant.*

6. A wooden block attached to a vessel's deck for any purpose, as for a bulkhead-support.

7. A toss, thrust, or push with a sudden jerk; as, to give a ball a *cant.*

çant, *v.t.*; canted, *pt.*, *pp.*; canting, *ppr.* 1. To turn about or over by a sudden push or thrust; as, to *cant* over a pail or cask.

2. To toss; as, to *cant* a ball.

3. To cut off an angle, as of a square piece of timber.

4. Nautically, to turn (anything) so as to be no longer fair or square; to give a ship an inclination to one side so as to prepare her for being careened.

çant, *n.* [OFr. *cant*, singing, in allusion to the tone of voice assumed by beggars; L. *cantus*, pp. of *canere*, to sing.]

1. A whining or singing manner of speech; specifically, the whining speech of beggars, as in asking alms and making complaints of their distresses.

2. The language or jargon spoken by gipsies, thieves, professional beggars, and the like, and containing many words different from ordinary English; a kind of slang or argot.

3. The words and phrases peculiar to or characteristic of a sect, party, or profession; the dialect of a sect or set of people.

> Of all the *cants* which are canted in this canting world, though the *cant* of hypocrisy may be the worst, the *cant* of criticism is the most tormenting. —Sterne.

4. A pretentious assumption of a religious character without sincerity.

çant, *a.* Of the nature of cant or slang; as, a *cant* word or phrase.

çant, *v.i.* [L. *cantare*, freq. of *canere*, to sing.]

1. To speak with a whining voice or in an affected or assumed tone; hence, to beg.

2. To make a hypocritical pretense of great goodness; to advocate a cause, as religion, in a whining manner.

3. To talk in a certain special jargon; to use the words and phraseology peculiar to a particular sect, party, profession, and the like.

çant, *n.* [Prov. Eng.] An auction.

çant, *v.t.* [Prov. Eng.] To bid or sell at auction.

çȧn′t. A colloquial contraction of *cannot.*

Çan′tab, *n.* and *a.* A colloquial abbreviation of *Cantabrigian.*

ċȧn-tä′bĭ-le, *a.* and *n.* [It.] I. *a.* In music, executed in an easy, flowing style.

II. *n.* Music characterized by an easy, flowing, singing style; also called *cantilena.*

Ċan-tā′brĭ-ăn, *a.* Pertaining to Cantabria, on the Bay of Biscay, in Spain.

Ċan-tȧ-brĭġ′ĭ-ăn, *n.* [LL. *Cantabrigiensis,* pertaining to Cambridge; *Cantabrigia,* Cambridge.] One native to or resident of Cambridge, England; also, a student or graduate of the university of Cambridge; often abridged into *Cantab.*

ċan′tȧ-lev-ẽr, *n.* Same as *Cantaliver.*

ċan′tȧ-liv-ẽr, ċan′tȧ-lev-ẽr, ċan′ti-lev-ẽr, *n.* [Origin doubtful; compare OFr. *cant,* an angle, and *lever,* to raise.]

Cantaliver.

1. In architecture, a kind of bracket of stone, iron, or wood, projecting from a wall, and carrying moldings, eaves, balconies, etc.

2. In engineering, a structure or arm projecting from a pier and forming one side of the span of a bridge, a similar structure projecting toward it from the opposite side; used also adjectively; as, a *cantaliver* bridge.

ċan′tȧ-lōup, *n.* [From *Cantalupo,* near Rome, where they were first grown in Europe.] A small round variety of muskmelon, globular, ribbed, of pale green or yellow color, and of a very delicate flavor; written also *cantaloupe, cantaleup,* etc.

ċan-tan̄′kẽr-ous, *a.* [ME. *conteck, contak,* contention, quarreling.] Ill-natured, cross; contentious; disputatious. [Colloq.]

ċan-tan̄′kẽr-ous-ly, *adv.* In a cantankerous manner.

ċan-tan̄′kẽr-ous-ness, *n.* The state or quality of being cantankerous.

ċan′tär, ċan-tȧ′rō, *n.* [It. *cantaro;* Turk. *qantār;* Ar. *qintār;* L. *centenarius,* consisting of a hundred, from *centum,* a hundred.] A measure of weight and capacity used in many countries, and varying greatly in extent. Thus the weight in Turkey is about 125 pounds; in Egypt, 98 pounds; in Malta, 175 pounds, etc. The Spanish wine measure is equal to about 3½ gallons.

ċȧn-tä′tȧ, *n.* [It., from *cantare,* L. *cantare,* to sing.] In music, originally a composition intermixed with recitatives and airs, intended for a single voice; now, a composition in the form of an oratorio, but shorter; a story or poem set to music.

Ċan-tā′tē, *n.* [L., 2d pers. pl. imper. of *cantare,* to sing.] The 98th Psalm; so called from the first words of the Latin version, *Cantate Domino.*

ċan-tā′tion, *n.* A singing. [Obs.]

ċant′ȧ-tō-ry, *a.* [L. *cantator,* a singer, from *cantare,* to sing.] Having a singsong, whining, or canting manner. [Rare.]

ċan-tȧ-trĭ′ce (-che), *n.*; *pl.* **ċan-tȧ-trĭ′cĭ** (-chē) [It.] A female singer.

ċant′-dog, *n.* Same as *Cant-hook.*

ċant′ed, *a.* 1. Sloping; slanting; tilted up.

2. Having cants or angles; as, a *canted* ornament.

Canted column; a polygonal column; one whose flutes are formed in cants instead of curves.

ċan-teen′, *n.* [Fr. *cantine,* from It. *cantina,* a wine-cellar, a vault, from *canto,* an angle, a corner.]

1. A flask used by soldiers for carrying water, liquor, or other drink; in the United States, a canvas-covered tin vessel holding three pints.

2. A sort of sutler's shop in barracks, camps, garrisons, etc., where provisions, etc. (sometimes beer or other liquors), are sold to soldiers, under regulations prescribed by the authorities; also, a post exchange.

3. In the British service, a square box, fitted up with compartments, containing an officer's cooking outfit.

ċan′tel, *n.* Same as *Cantle.*

ċan-te-leup, ċan′te-lōup, *n.* Same as *Cantaloup.*

ċan′tẽr, *n.* [Abbrev. of *Canterbury-gallop.*]

1. A moderate gallop; a Canterbury-gallop.

> The *canter* is to the gallop very much what the walk is to the trot, though probably a more artificial pace. —Youatt.

2. A hasty skimming or passing over.

> A rapid *canter* in the Times over all the topics of the day. —Stephen.

ċan′tẽr, *v.i.*; cantered, *pt., pp.*; cantering, *ppr.* To move in a moderate gallop, raising the two fore feet nearly at the same time, with a leap or spring; said of horses.

ċan′tẽr, *v.t.* To cause (a horse or other animal) to move at a gentle gallop.

ċant′ẽr, *n.* 1. One who cants or whines.

2. One who talks cant.

ċan′tẽr-bur-y (-ber-i), *n.* [Named from *Canterbury,* England, where it is made.] A receptacle for music, portfolios, loose papers, etc., being a stand with divisions.

ċan′tẽr-bur-y-bell′, *n.* The popular name of the bellflower, *Campanula Trachelium,* given to it by Gerard because it is abundant around Canterbury; also, other flowers of the same genus.

Ċan′tẽr-bur-y-gal″lop, *n.* The moderate gallop of a horse, commonly abbreviated to *canter;* said to be derived from the pilgrims riding to Canterbury at this pace.

ċant′-frāmeṣ, *n.pl.* In a ship, those ribs situated at the ends of the vessel; cant-timbers.

ċan-thar′i-dăl, *a.* Relating to or obtained from cantharides.

Ċan-thar′i-dēṣ, *n.pl.* 1. The family of beetles to which the Spanish fly belongs. [See *Cantharis.*]

2. [c—] A pharmacopœial preparation of Spanish flies.

ċan-thȧ-rid′iċ, ċan-thar′iċ, *a.* Pertaining to or derived from cantharidin.

ċan-thar′i-din, ċan-thar′i-dine, *n.* That peculiar substance which causes vesication, existing in the Spanish fly. It is a volatile crystalline body, very soluble in ether, alcohol, and essential oils.

Ċan′thȧ-ris, *n.* [L., from Gr. *kantharis,* a blistering fly, from *kantharos,* a kind of beetle.] A genus of coleopterous insects having the head separated from the thorax by a neck; the type of the family *Cantharidæ.* The best-known species is that which is sold under the name of the Spanish or blistering fly, *Cantharis vesicatoria.* It is of a shining green color mixed with azure, has a nauseous smell, and is, when bruised, extensively used as the active element in blistering plasters.

Cantharis vesicatoria.

ċan′thȧ-rus, *n.*; *pl.* **ċan-thȧ′rī.** [L., from Gr. *kantharos,* a tankard, pot.]

1. In classical antiquity, a large wide-mouthed drinking-cup, having two handles rising above the brim.

2. A fountain or basin in the courtyard before ancient churches, where persons could wash before entering the church.

ċan′thī, *n.,* pl. of *canthus.*

ċant′-hook, *n.* A wooden lever with an iron hook at the end, for canting or turning over heavy logs.

ċan′thō-plas-ty, *n.* [Gr. *kanthos,* a corner of the eye, and *plastos,* from *plassein,* to form, mold.] The operation of enlarging the opening between the eyelids by slitting the outer canthus.

ċan′thus, *n.*; *pl.* **ċan′thī.** [Gr. *kanthos,* corner of the eye.] An angle of the eye; a cavity at the extremities of the eyelids; the greater is next to the nose, the lesser near the temple.

ċan′ti-ċle (-kl), *n.* [ME. *canticle;* L. *canticulum,* dim. of *canticum,* a song; from *cantus,* a singing, *canere,* to sing.]

1. An unmetrical hymn of a poetical character taken from Scripture, arranged for chanting, and so used in church service.

2. [C—*pl.*] The Songs, Song of Songs, or Song of Solomon, one of the books of the Old Testament.

3. A canto; a division of a song or poem. [Obs.]

4. A song, especially a little song. [Obs.]

ċan′tile, *v.t.* Same as *Cantle.*

ċan-tĭ-le′nä, *n.* [It.] See *Cantabile.*

ċan′ti-lev-ẽr, *n.* See *Cantaliver.*

ċan′til-lāte, *v.t.* [L. *cantillare,* to sing, hum; dim. of *cantare,* to sing.] To chant; to recite with musical tones.

ċan-til-lā′tion, *n.* A chanting; recitation with musical modulations.

ċan-tine′, *n.* Same as *Canteen.*

ċant′ing, *n.* 1. The use of cant.

2. The language of cant.

ċant′ing, *a.* Affectedly pious; whining; as, a *canting* hypocrite; a *canting* tone of voice.

Canting arms; in heraldry, arms containing charges which allude to the name of the bearer.

ċant′ing-ly, *adv.* In a canting manner.

ċant′ing-ness, *n.* The quality of employing cant.

ċan-tĭ-nière′ (-nyâr′), *n.* [Fr.] A female sutler to a regiment; a vivandière.

ċan′tion, *n.* A song or verses. [Obs.]

ċan′tle, *n.* [OFr. *cantel,* a corner, piece; LL. *cantellus,* dim. of *cantus,* a side, corner.]

1. A fragment; a corner or edge of anything; a piece or part.

2. The hind bow of a saddle; also written *cantel.*

ċan′tle, *v.t.* To cut into pieces; to cut out a piece. [Obs.]

ċant′let, *n.* A piece; a little corner; a fragment.

ċan′tō, *n.*; *pl.* **ċan′tōṣ.** [It. *canto;* L. *cantus,* a song, from *canere,* to sing.]

1. A part or division of a long poem, answering to what in prose is called a book.

2. In music, the highest voice part in concerted music; soprano; also, the melody or air in choruses.

Canto fermo [It., firm song]; (a) plain song or choral song in unison or octave, with the notes all of one length; a sort of grave measured chant in use in the early Christian church; (b) any theme written in imitation of plain song, and treated contrapuntally.

ċan′ton, *n.* [Obs.] See *Canto.*

ċan′tŏn, *n.* [Fr. *canton;* LL. *canto,* a region, district; from L. *cantus,* a corner.]

1. A portion of territory; in Switzerland, a state; in France, a subdivision embracing a number of communes.

2. In heraldry, a part of the design on a shield occupying the upper left corner; also, the part of a flag occupying the same relative position, as the blue field studded with stars in the flag of the United States.

Canton.

3. In architecture, a corner adorned with a pilaster, an angular column, rustic quoins, or any projection.

Canton crape; a kind of fragile soft silk fabric used by ladies for scarfs, etc.

Canton flannel; a heavy twilled cotton fabric with a long glossy nap on one side; called also *cotton flannel.*

ċan′tŏn, *v.t.*; cantoned, *pt., pp.*; cantoning, *ppr.* 1. To divide into small parts or districts, as territory; to divide into distinct portions.

2. To allot, as separate quarters, to different parts or divisions of an army or body of troops.

ċan′tŏn-ăl, *a.* Pertaining to a canton; divided into cantons.

ċan′tŏned, *a.* Having a canton or cantons; used specifically in heraldry and architecture; as, a *cantoned* shield; a *cantoned* corner.

ċan′tŏn-īze, *v.t.*; cantonized, *pt., pp.*; cantonizing, *ppr.* To canton, or divide into small districts.

ċan′tŏn-ment, *n.* A part or division of a town or village, assigned to a particular body of troops; separate quarters.

ċan-tọọn′, *n.* [Origin unknown.] A species of cotton fabric with a satin-like surface on one side and finely corded on the other.

ċan′tŏr, *n.* [L., a singer, from *canere,* to sing.] A singer, usually the leader of a choir; a leader of singing.

ċan′tŏr-ăl, *a.* Relating to a leader of singing.

ċan-tō′ris, *a.* [L., genit. of *cantor,* a singer.] Of or relating to a cantor; specifically, on the left side of the choir as one faces the altar.

ċan′tred, *n.* [ME. *cantrede,* from W. *cantref, cant,* a hundred, and *tref, tred,* a dwelling-place, town.] A hundred villages, as in Wales.

ċan′trip, ċan′trap, *n.* [Scot.] An incantation or spell; mischief artfully performed.

ċant′-tim″bẽr, *n.* In shipbuilding, one of the timbers at the end of a ship, which are canted, that is, rise obliquely from the keel; in the plural, same as *cant-frames.*

ċan′tus, *n. sing.* and *pl.* [L., a song.] A church song or chant; the melody in a chorus.

Cantus firmus; same as *Canto fermo* under *Canto.*

ċan′ty, *a.* [Scot.] Full of cheer; characterized by sprightliness and good feeling; applied to persons and things.

Ċȧ-nuck′, *n.* A slang term for a Canadian; by extension, a kind of Canadian pony or sinewy small horse.

ċan′văs, *n.*; *pl.* **ċan′văs-eṣ, ċan′văss-eṣ.** [ME. *canvas;* OFr. *canevas;* LL. *canabacius,* hempen cloth, canvas; L. *cannabis;* Gr. *kannabis,* hemp.]

1. A coarse cloth made of hemp or flax, used for tents, sails of ships, painting, and other purposes.

2. A clear, unbleached cloth, woven regularly in little squares, used for working tapestry with the needle.

3. The rough draft or model on which an air or piece of music is composed, and given to a poet as a guide to his part of the composition. [Rare.]

4. Nautically, cloth in sails, or sails in general; as, to spread as much *canvas* as the ship will bear.

5. By metonymy, anything wholly or partly made of *canvas,* as a painting or paintings, a ship, etc.

> Touched by the glowing *canvas,* into life. —Addison.

ċan′văs, *a.* Made of canvas; as, a *canvas* sack; a *canvas* sail.

ċan′văs-back, *n.* A kind of duck, the *Aythya vallisneria,* highly esteemed for the delicacy of its flesh, plentiful in the rivers of Chesapeake Bay, and deriving its name from the color of its back.

ça̤n′văss, *v.t.*; canvassed, *pt.*, *pp.*; canvassing, *ppr.* [OFr. *canabasser*, to beat out, shake, examine; from LL. *canabacius*, hempen cloth, canvas.]

1. To discuss; literally, to beat or shake out; to open by beating or shaking; as, to *canvass* a subject, or the policy of a measure.

2. To examine; to search or scrutinize; as, to *canvass* the votes for senators.

3. To go through in the way of solicitation; as, to *canvass* a district for votes.

ça̤n′văss, *v.i.* 1. To seek or go about to solicit votes or interest; to use efforts to obtain; to arouse sentiment in favor of; followed by *for*; as, to *canvass for* an office, or preferment; to *canvass for* a friend.

2. To solicit orders for some commodity or privilege; as, to *canvass for* life insurance.

Syn.—Question, investigate, challenge, test, dispute, solicit, sift, examine, discuss, request.

ça̤n′văss, *n.* 1. Examination; close inspection to know the state of; as, a *canvass* of votes.

2. Discussion; debate; thorough investigation.

3. A seeking, solicitation, or effort to obtain.

ça̤n′văss-ẽr, *n.* One who canvasses or solicits; also, an examiner of voting returns.

çān′y, *a.* 1. Consisting of cane, or abounding in a growth of canes; as, a *cany* marsh.

2. Made of canes; as, *cany* wagons.

ça̤n′yŏn, *n.* Same as *Cañon*.

ça̤n-zō′nȧ, ça̤n-zō′ne, *n.* [It., from L. *cantio*, *cantionis*, a singing, from *canere*, to sing.] In music, (a) a song or air in two or three parts, with passages of fugue and imitation; (b) an instrumental composition similar to the earlier forms of the sonata.

ça̤n-zō-net′, *n.* [It. *canzonetta*, dim. of *canzona*, from L. *cantio*, a singing.] In music, (a) a little or short song, shorter and less elaborate than the *aria* of oratorio or opera; (b) a short concerted air; a madrigal.

ça̤öut′chin, ça̤öut′chine (kö′), *n.* A distillation of caoutchouc isomeric with the terpenes.

ça̤öut′chöuc, *n.* [Fr. *caoutchouc*, from native S. Am. name, *cahuchu*.] India-rubber, an elastic gum, the dried juice of numerous tropical plants of the dogbane, spurge, and nettle families, as *Siphonia elastica*, *Ficus elastica*, etc. It is extremely elastic and is impervious to water and to nearly all other fluids.

Mineral caoutchouc; see under *Mineral*.

Caoutchouc (*Siphonia elastica*).

ça̤öut′chöu-cin, *n.* Same as *Caoutchin*.

ça̤p, *n.* [ME. *cappe*, *coppe*; AS. *cæppe*, a cap, cape, hood; LL. *cappa*, *capa*, a cape, hooded cloak.]

1. A part of dress made to cover the head; a term very widely applied, but generally to head-coverings of softer material and less definite form than a hat, and without a brim.

2. The badge or ensign of some dignity; specifically, of a cardinalate.

> He'll make his *cap* coequal with the crown. —Shak.

3. The top or chief; the acme.

> Thou art the *cap* of all the fools alive. —Shak.

4. An act of respect made by uncovering the head.

> Give a *cap* and make a leg in thanks. —Fuller.

5. A certain size of paper. *Full cap* is 14 x 17 inches; *double cap*, 17 x 28; *legal cap* is 13 x 16. [See *Foolscap*.]

6. Anything resembling a *cap* in appearance, position, or use. In this sense, the word has a great number of specific uses, of which the following are among the principal: (a) in architecture, the congeries of moldings which form the head of a pier or pilaster; (b) in botany, the pileus of an agaric; (c) in carpentry, the uppermost of any assemblage of parts; (d) in heraldry, the figure of a cap used in charges, and as part of a crest or an accessory in a coat of arms, sometimes of very conventional shape; (e) the inner case which covers the movement of some kinds of watches, etc.; (f) a percussion-cap; (g) nautically, either a block of wood variously used, or a tarred canvas cover for the end of a rope; (h) in mining, a streak of poor matter overlying good ore.

Cap and bells; the bauble carried by a professional fool or jester, denoting his calling.

Cap of a cannon; the vent-cover or apron of a fieldpiece.

Cap in hand; cringingly obedient; in a servile manner.

Cap of liberty; a liberty-cap.

Cap of maintenance; an ornament of state, carried before the kings of England at the coronation. It is also carried before the mayors of some cities.

To set one's cap for; to indulge in blandishments to win a man in marriage.

ça̤p, *v.t.*; capped, *pt.*, *pp.*; capping, *ppr.* 1. To put a cap on; to cover with a cap or as with a cap; to cover the top or end of; as, to *cap* a dunce at school; to *cap* a gun.

> The cloud-*capped* towers. —Shak.

2. To complete; to consummate; to crown; to follow up with something more remarkable than what has previously been done; as, he *capped* this exploit by another still more audacious.

3. To deprive of the cap. [Obs.]

To cap texts or *proverbs*; to quote texts or proverbs alternately in emulation or contest.

> I will *cap* that *proverb* with, "There is flattery in friendship." —Shak.

To cap verses; to name alternately verses beginning with a particular letter or having a corresponding rime.

ça̤p, *v.i.* To uncover the head in reverence or civility. [Obs.]

çä′pȧ, *n.* [Sp.] 1. An overgarment.

2. A fine quality of tobacco used in making wrappers for Cuban cigars.

çā-pȧ-bil′i-ty, *n.* 1. The quality of being capable; capacity; capableness.

2. [*pl.*] Undeveloped attainments or power of being converted to any use; as, a theme possessing great *capabilities*.

çā′pȧ-ble, *a.* [Fr. *capable*; LL. *capabilis*, from L. *capere*, to take, seize.]

1. Able to hold or contain; able to receive; sufficiently capacious; often followed by *of*; as, the room is not *capable of* receiving the company.

2. Endued with power sufficient for an act; as, a man is *capable* of judging.

3. Possessing mental powers; intelligent; able to understand, or to receive into the mind; having a capacious mind; as, a *capable* judge; a *capable* instructor.

4. Susceptible; as, *capable* of pain or grief.

5. Qualified for; as, a thing is *capable* of long duration; or, it is *capable* of being colored or altered.

6. Having legal power or capacity; as, a minor is not *capable* of voting.

Syn.—Able, adequate, competent, equal, qualified, suitable, fitted, efficient, clever, gifted, skilful, susceptible, impressible.

çā′pȧ-ble-ness, *n.* The state or quality of being capable; capacity; power of understanding; knowledge.

çȧ-pac′i-fy, *v.t.* To qualify. [Obs.]

çȧ-pā′cious, *a.* [L. *capax*, *capacis*, from *capere*, to take, hold, contain.]

1. Wide; large; capable of holding much; as, a *capacious* vessel.

2. Extensive; comprehensive; able to take a wide view; as, a *capacious* mind.

Syn.—Commodious, extensive, spacious, ample, roomy, large, broad, wide, great.

çȧ-pā′cious-ly, *adv.* In a capacious manner or degree.

çȧ-pā′cious-ness, *n.* The state or quality of being capacious.

çȧ-pac′i-tāte, *v.t.*; capacitated, *pt.*, *pp.*; capacitating, *ppr.* To make capable; specifically, in law, to furnish with legal powers; as, to *capacitate* one for an office.

çȧ-pac-i-tā′tion, *n.* The act of making capable. [Rare.]

çȧ-pac′i-ty, *n.* [L. *capacitas*, from *capax* (-*acis*), from *capere*, to take, hold, contain.]

1. The power of receiving or containing; specifically, the power of containing a certain quantity exactly; cubic contents.

> Had our great palace the *capacity*
> To camp this host, we all would sup together. —Shak.

2. The extent or comprehensiveness of the mind; the power of receiving ideas or knowledge; passive mental capability; the receptive faculty; as, instruction should be adapted to the *capacity* of the pupil.

3. Active power; ability; productive amount; output; applied to men or things; as, a factory having a *capacity* of a thousand pieces a day.

4. Ability in a moral or legal sense; legal qualification; legal power or right; as, a corporation may have a *capacity* to hold estate.

> He had been restored to his *capacity* of governing by renouncing the errors of Popery. —Brougham.

5. Character; profession; occupation; as, in the *capacity* of teacher.

Capacity for heat; the quantity of heat absorbed by a body rising in temperature through a given range, as from zero to 1° centigrade.

Syn.—Capability, power, faculty, skill, ability.

ça̤p-ȧ-pïe′, ça̤p-ȧ-pē′, *adv.* [OFr. *de cap a pie*, from head to foot.] From head to foot; all over; as, armed *cap-a-pie*.

çȧ-par′i-sŏn, *n.* [OFr. *caparason*; Sp. *caparazon*, a cover for a saddle or coach; from LL. *cappa*, *capa*, a cape, hooded cloak.]

1. A cloth or covering laid over the saddle or furniture of a horse, especially a horse equipped for a state occasion.

War-horse caparisoned, from seal of Philip of Burgundy.

2. Figuratively, clothing, especially gay clothing.

çȧ-par′i-sŏn, *v.t.*; caparisoned, *pt.*, *pp.*; caparisoning, *ppr.* 1. To cover with a cloth, as a horse.

2. To dress pompously; to adorn with rich dress.

çȧ-pär′rō, *n.* [Native name.] A large South American monkey, *Lagothrix humboldti*.

ça̤p′çāse, *n.* A kind of covered case for carrying clothing. [Obs.]

çāpe, *n.* [Fr. *cap*, a cape, headland, from L. *caput*, a head.]

1. A piece of land jutting into the sea or a lake beyond the rest of the coast-line; a headland; a promontory.

2. [C—] A kind of wine from the Cape of Good Hope.

Cape jasmine; see under *Jasmine*.

Cape pigeon; a small sea-bird, *Daption capense*, common about the Cape of Good Hope.

çāpe, *v.i.*; caped, *pt.*, *pp.*; caping, *ppr.* [Fr. *cap*, a cape, head of a ship.] Nautically, to keep in a certain direction or course; as, she *capes* north by northeast.

çāpe, *n.* [OFr. *cape*; LL. *capa*, *cappa*, a cape, hooded cloak.] A short garment without sleeves, worn over the shoulders, chiefly for protection against rain or snow, sometimes double, and attachable to a coat.

çāpe, *v.i.*, obsolete form of *gape*.

çā′pel, çā′ple, *n.* [Ice. *kapall*; L. *caballus*.] A horse. [Obs.]

çā′pel, çā′ple, *n.* [Prov. Eng.] In mining, a lode-wall.

ça̤p′e-line, ça̤p′el-line, *n.* [Fr., from LL. *capella*, dim. of *capa*, *cappa*, a cape, hooded cloak.] In the middle ages, a kind of iron skull-cap worn by archers.

Çȧ-pel′lȧ, *n.* [L., dim. of *capra*, a goat.] A bright fixed star in the left shoulder of the constellation Auriga.

ça̤p′el-lāne, *n.* One having the care of a chapel. [Obs.]

ça̤p′el-let, *n.* [Fr. *capelet*; LL. *capelletum*, a little cape, dim. of *capella*, from *capa*, *cappa*, a cape.] A kind of swelling, like a wen, growing on the heel of the hock on a horse, or on the point of the elbow.

çȧ-pell′meis-tẽr, *n.* Same as *Kapellmeister*.

çā′pẽr, *v.i.*; capered, *pt.*, *pp.*; capering, *ppr.* [Fr. *cabriole*; It. *capriola*, from L. *caper*, *capra*, a goat.] To leap; to skip or jump; to prance; to spring.

çā′pẽr, *n.* A leap; a skip; a spring; as in dancing or mirth, or in the frolic of a goat or lamb.

To cut a caper; to leap and dance in a frolicsome manner; to do something ridiculous.

çā′pẽr, *n.* [D. *kaper*, from *kapen*, to take, seize.] A Dutch privateer of the seventeenth century.

çā′pẽr, *n.* [Fr. *capre*; L. *capparis*; Gr. *kapparis*, a caper.]

1. A plant, *Capparis spinosa*, a low shrub, generally growing from the joints of old walls, from fissures in rocks, and amongst rubbish, in the southern part of Europe.

Caper (*Capparis spinosa*).

2. The flower-bud or unexpanded flower of the caper-bush, much used for pickling.

Caper sauce; a kind of sauce flavored or seasoned with capers.

Wild caper; the caper-spurge.

ca′pēr-ber″ry, *n.* The fruit of the caper-bush.

ca′pēr-bush, *n.* The caper.

cā-pēr-cail′lie, ca′pēr-cail-zie (-yē), *n.* [Scot.] The Scotch wood-grouse, *Tetrao urogallus*, the largest gallinaceous bird of Europe, found in the northern part of the continent, especially in Norway and Sweden. It had become extinct in the British Isles, but has been reintroduced and is now an ornament of the British fauna. The male is called the cock-of-the-woods. Also written *capercalye*, *capercally*, etc.

Capercaillie (*Tetrao urogallus*).

ca′pēr-claw, cap′pēr-claw, *v.t.* To treat with abuse; to torture. [Obs.]

ca′pēr-ēr, *n.* One who or that which capers.

Cā-pēr′nā-ite, *n.* A native or an inhabitant of Capernaum; by extension, a believer in transubstantiation.

Cā-pēr-nā-it′ic, *a.* Of or pertaining to the Capernaites.

ca′pēr-spūrge, *n.* A noxious weed, *Euphorbia Lathyris*, sometimes called *wild caper*.

Cā-pē′tiăn, *a.* Of or relating to Hugh Capet or the dynasty founded by him A.D. 987 in France.

cā-pe-ū′nā, *n.* [Braz.] A tropical food-fish, the white grunt.

cāpe′weed, *n.* 1. A lichen, *Roccella tinctoria*, of the Cape Verde Islands.

2. An Australian composite plant resembling the marigold.

cap′ful, *n.*; *pl.* **cap′fuls.** As much as fills a cap; a small quantity; specifically, in nautical language, a light flaw of wind which suddenly careens a vessel and passes off.

cā′pi-as, *n.* [L. *capias*, you take; 2d pers. sing. pres. subj. of *capere*, to take.] In law, a document issued by a court commanding an officer to arrest a person.

cap-i-bä′rä, *n.* [Sp. *capibara*, from the native name.] The largest known rodent quadruped, *Hydrochœrus capibara*, of aquatic habits, native to South America. It is more than three feet in length, heavy-bodied, and its flesh is edible. Called also *water-hog* and *water-cavy*. Written also *capybara*.

Capibara (*Hydrochœrus capibara*).

cap-il-lā′ceous, *a.* [L. *capillaceus*, hairy.] Having long filaments; resembling a hair.

cap-il-laire′, *n.* [Fr. *capillaire*, the maidenhair fern, and a syrup from it, from L. *capillaris*, capillary.] Originally, a kind of syrup prepared with maidenhair fern, but now applied to any simple syrup, as of sugar or honey, flavored with orange flowers, or orange-flower water.

cā-pil′lā-ment, *n.* [L. *capillamentum*, from *capillus*, the hair.] A filament or thread-like fiber. [Obs.]

cap″il-lā-rim′e-tēr, *n.* [L. *capillaris*, from *capillus*, hair, and *metrum*, Gr. *metron*, a measure.] A tester for liquids used in determining their properties by means of capillary attraction.

cap′il-lā-ri-ness, *n.* The state of being capillary.

cap-il-lar′i-ty, *n.* 1. The state or condition of being capillary.

2. Capillary attraction; the force that produces capillary attraction.

cap′il-lā-ry (*or* **cā-pil′lā-ry**), *a.* [L. *capillaris*, from *capillus*, hair, from *caput*, head.]

1. Resembling a hair, fine, minute, small in diameter though long; filiform; as, a *capillary* tube or pipe; a *capillary* vessel in animal bodies, such as the ramifications of the blood-vessels.

2. In botany, resembling hair in the manner of growth; applied in this sense by Ray, Boerhaave, and others, to ferns.

3. Pertaining to *capillary* tubes, or to the *capillary* vessels, or capillaries, in animals; as, *capillary* action.

4. In physics, of or relating to certain phenomena, as the rise of fluids in tubes and fissures, drop-formation in fluid substances, etc., caused by the forces cohesion and adhesion acting at minute distances.

Capillary attraction and *repulsion*; terms denoting the cause which determines the ascent or descent of a fluid in a capillary tube or on a surface, above or below the level of the surrounding fluid, when the tube or surface meets that fluid.

Capillary tubes; tubes with very small bores, of which the diameter is only a half, a third, a fourth, etc., of a line. If a tube of this sort has an end immersed in water, the water will rise within the tube to a sensible height above the surface of the water in the vessel, owing to capillary attraction.

Capillary vessels; in anatomy, the capillaries.

cap′il-lā-ry, *n.*; *pl.* **cap′il-lā-ries.** 1. A tube with a small bore; specifically, a minute blood-vessel constituting the termination of an artery or vein; one of the minute vessels which intervene between the terminal arteries and veins.

2. In botany, a fern; especially applied to such ferns as grow like tufts of hair on walls. [Obs.]

cap-il-lā′tion, *n.* A blood-vessel like a hair. [Obs.]

cā-pil′lā-tūre, *n.* The act of dressing the hair. [Obs.]

cā-pil′li-form, *a.* In the shape or form of a hair, or of hairs.

cap-il-li′ti-um (-lish′i-um), *n.* [L. *capillus*, a hair.] In botany, a kind of purse or net in which the sporules of some fungi are retained.

cap′il-lōse, *a.* Hairy; having abundant hair. [Rare.]

cā-pis′trāte, *a.* [L. *capistratus*, pp. of *capistrare*, to halter; *capistrum*, a halter.] In ornithology, having a hood of distinct color.

cap′i-taine, *n.* [Fr.] The Florida hogfish.

cap′i-tăl, *a.* [OFr. *capital*; L. *capitalis*, relating to the head, dangerous, preeminent, from *caput*, head.]

1. Relating to the head; on the head.

> Needs must the serpent now his *capital* bruise
> Expect with mortal pain. —Milton.

2. First in importance; chief; principal; notable; metropolitan; as, a *capital* requisite; a *capital* instance.

3. Affecting the head or life; incurring the forfeiture of life; punishable with death; as, treason and murder are *capital* offenses or crimes.

4. Very good; excellent; first-class; as, a *capital* singer or player; a *capital* dinner.

> When the reading was over, nobody said *capital*, or even good, or even tolerable. —Hook.

5. In writing and printing, the term applied to such letters as are used to begin sentences, proper names, etc., distinguished from lower-case letters by different form and larger size; sometimes abbreviated to *cap*; as, a *cap* A.

Small capitals or *caps*; in printing, letters having the form of capitals and the height of lower-case letters.

Syn.—Chief, principal, leading, prominent, notable, essential, important, excellent, first-class, splendid.

cap′i-tăl, *n.* [ME. *capital*; It. *capitello*; LL. *capitellum*, the head of a column or pillar; dim. of *caput* (*-itis*), head.]

1. The head or uppermost member of any part of a building; but generally applied in a restricted sense to the uppermost part of a column, pillar, or pilaster, serving as the head or crowning, and placed immediately over the shaft, and under the entablature. In classical architecture, the different orders have their respective appropriate *capitals*, but in Egyptian, Indian, Moorish, Norman, and Gothic architecture they are endlessly diversified.

Egyptian Capital.

Moorish Capital, Alhambra.

Gothic Capital, Salisbury Cathedral.

2. In fortification, the line which bisects the salient angle of a ravelin.

cap′i-tăl, *n.* That city, town, or village from which any political division is governed; as, Washington, the *capital* of the United States; Chicago, the *capital* of Cook county.

cap′i-tăl, *n.* 1. Money or wealth in some shape employed in trade, in manufactures, or in any business; stock in trade; specifically, in political economy, the product of industry which remains either in the shape of national or of individual wealth, after a portion of what is produced is consumed, and which is still available for further production.

> This accumulated stock of the product of former labor is termed *capital*. —Mill.

2. Figuratively, stock of any kind, whether physical or moral; means of influence or of increasing one's power; as, to make *capital* of the fact that a competitor had failed.

Active capital; any property immediately convertible into money; ready cash.

Capital stock; the sum of money which a merchant, banker, or manufacturer embarks in any undertaking, or which he contributes to the common stock of a partnership; his capital invested.

Fixed capital; wealth in a permanent form which is used in the course of production and exchange, as lands and buildings.

cap′i-tăl, *n.* A subdivision of a book. [Obs.]

cap′i-tăl-ism, *n.* The state of owning or controlling capital, especially when tending to monopoly; the power of capital so held.

cap′i-tăl-ist, *n.* A man who has a capital or stock in trade, usually denoting a man of large property, which is or may be employed in business.

cap-i-tăl-is′tic, *a.* Of, relating, or pertaining to capital or capitalists.

cap′i-tăl-i-zā′tion, *n.* The use of capital letters.

cap′i-tăl-i-zā′tion, *n.* The act of capitalizing; (a) the act of applying as capital to the purposes of trade; (b) the act of computing or realizing the present value of a periodical payment.

cap′i-tăl-īze, *v.t.*; capitalized, *pt.*, *pp.*; capitalizing, *ppr.* To write or set with a capital letter or letters.

cap′i-tăl-īze, *v.t.* To convert into capital: (a) to apply as capital to the purposes of trade; (b) to compute or realize the present value of a periodical payment for a definite or indefinite length of time; as, to *capitalize* a pension; to *capitalize* rents.

cap′i-tăl-ly, *adv.* 1. In a capital or excellent manner; nobly; finely.

2. In a way involving the loss of life; as, to punish *capitally*.

cap′i-tăl-ness, *n.* The state or quality of being capital. [Rare.]

cap′i-tāte, *a.* [L. *capitatus*, from *caput*, a head.] In botany, growing in a head; having a rounded head; pin-like; applied to a flower or stigma.

cap-i-tā′tim, *a.* Of a certain sum per head; as, a *capitatim* assessment.

cap-i-tā′tion, *n.* 1. Numeration by the head; a numbering of persons. [Obs.]

2. A tax or imposition upon each head or person; a poll-tax.

cap′i-tē, *n.* See *Tenant in capite*, under *Tenant*.

cap-i-tel′lāte, *a.* [L. *capitellum*, dim. of *caput*, a head.] In botany, growing in small heads; capitular.

cap-i-tel′lum, *n.*; *pl.* **cap-i-tel′lā.** [L.] See *Capitulum*, 1.

Cap″i-ti-bran-chi-ā′tā, *n.pl.* [L. *caput* (*-itis*), a head, and *branchia*, gills.] The *Cephalobranchia*.

Cap′i-tŏl, *n.* [Fr. *capitole*; L. *capitolium*, from *caput*, the head.]

1. The temple of Jupiter, in Rome, and a fort or castle, on the Mons Capitolinus, in which the senate of Rome anciently assembled.

2. The edifice occupied by the Congress of the United States; by extension, a statehouse, or house in which the legislature holds its sessions.

Cap′i-tō-line, Cap-i-tō′li-ăn, *a.* [L. *Capitolinus*, from *Capitolium*, the Capitol.] Pertaining to the Capitol in Rome.

Capitoline games; annual games instituted by Camillus in honor of Jupiter Capitolinus, and in commemoration of the preservation of the Capitol from the Gauls, and other games instituted by Domitian, and celebrated every five years.

cā-pit′ū-lā, *n.*, pl. of *capitulum*.

cā-pit′ū-lăr, cā-pit′ū-lā-ry, *n.* 1. An act passed in a chapter, as of knights or canons.

2. The body of laws or statutes of a chapter or of an ecclesiastical council. This name is also given to the laws, civil and ecclesiastical, made by Charlemagne and other princes in general councils and assemblies of the people. They are so called because they are divided into chapters or sections.

3. The member of a chapter.

cā-pit′ū-lăr, *a.* [LL. *capitularis*, pertaining to a chapter, from L. *capitulum*, a chapter, dim. of *caput*, a head.]

1. Pertaining to a chapter, as of a cathedral.
2. In botany, growing in a head or capitulum.
3. In anatomy, relating to a capitulum; as, the *capitular* process of a bone.

ça-pit'ū-lär-ly, *adv.* In the form of an ecclesiastical chapter.

ça-pit'ū-lā-ry, *a.* Relating to the chapter of a cathedral.

çà-pit'ū-lāte, *a.* Headed; capitular.

çà-pit'ū-lāte, *v.i.*; capitulated, *pt., pp.*; capitulating, *ppr.* [LL. *capitulatus*, pp. of *capitulare*, to draw up in heads or chapters, to arrange conditions, from L. *capitulum*, a chapter, from *caput*, a head.]

1. To draw up a writing in chapters, heads, or articles. [Obs.]
2. To surrender, as an army or garrison, to an enemy, by treaty, in which the terms of surrender are specified and agreed to by the parties.

çà-pit'ū-lāte, *v.t.* To surrender (an army or garrison) conditionally. [Rare.]

çà-pit-ū-lā'tion, *n.* 1. The act of capitulating and surrendering to an enemy, upon stipulated terms or conditions.
2. The treaty or instrument containing the conditions of surrender.
3. A reducing to heads; a formal agreement.

çà-pit'ū-lā-tŏr, *n.* One who capitulates.

çap'i-tūle, *n.* A summary.

çà-pit'ū-lum, *n.*; *pl.* **çà-pit'ū-là.** [L. *capitulum*, dim. of *caput*, a head.]

1. In anatomy, the head of a bone.
2. In botany, a close head of sessile flowers (as in the *Compositæ*); also, a term vaguely applied among fungi to the receptacle, pileus, or peridium.

çà-pi'vi, *n.* See *Copaiba.*

çā'ple, *n.* See *Capel.*

çap'lin, *n.* [Fr. *caplan, capelan*, a kind of fish.] A fish, the *Salmo arcticus* or *Mallotus villosus* of the smelt family. Its chief value is as bait for cod. This fish frequents the shores of Greenland, Iceland, Newfoundland, and Labrador in immense shoals. Also written *capelan, caplan, kibling*, etc.

Caplin (*Mallotus villosus*).

çap'lin, *n.* The end of the handle of a flail where the swingel is attached.

çap'nō-man-cy, *n.* [Gr. *kapnos*, smoke, and *manteia*, divination.] Divination by the ascent or motion of smoke.

çap'nō-mọr, *n.* [Gr. *kapnos*, smoke, and *moira*, a part, from *meiresthai*, to divide.] A transparent, colorless, oil-like fluid, obtained from the smoke of organic bodies or wood-tar.

çā'poc, *n.* [Hind. *kapas*, cotton.] A kind of short fine cotton used in Oriental countries as a stuffing for mattresses, cushions, and the like.

çà-pōçh', *n.* and *v.t.* See *Capouch.*

çā'pŏn, *n.* [ME. *capon*; AS. *capun*; It. *cappone*; L. *capo*; Gr. *kapōn*, a capon, from *koptein*, to cut.]

1. A castrated cock; a cock-chicken castrated for the purpose of improving the flesh for table.
2. A letter. It is said to have got this application from letters being often conveyed inside fowls. [Rare.]

çā'pŏn, *v.t.*; caponed, *pt., pp.*; caponing, *ppr.* To castrate, as a cock.

çā'pŏn-et, *n.* A young capon. [Obs.]

çap-ō-niēre', *n.* [Fr., from Sp. *caponera*, a coop for capons, a covered lodge; *capon*, a capon.] In fortification, (a) a defensive work constructed in or across a ditch, generally in the form of a single or double row of palisades, sometimes covered overhead, serving as a kind of blockhouse or lodgment for soldiers. When there is a stockade on one side only, it is called a demi-*caponiere*. A double *caponiere* is arranged for firing in two directions. (b) A passageway, covered or otherwise, protected by walls or parapets on each side, between two parts of a work.

çā'pŏn-īze, *v.t.* To castrate a fowl.

çà-pot', *n.* [Fr.] A winning of all the tricks at the game of piquet.

çà-pot', *v.t.* To win all the tricks at piquet; to win a capot from.

çà-pōte', *n.* [Fr. *capote*, from LL. *cappa*, a cape.] A kind of long, coarse cloak, especially one with a hood, but of various forms and for both sexes.

çà-pōuçh', çà-pōçh', *n.* [Fr. *capuche*; It. *capuccio*; LL. *capuccium, caputium*, a cowl, from *capa, cappa*, a cape, hood.] A monk's cowl or hood, especially one of pointed form worn by Capuchin monks; also, the hood of a cloak; written also *capuche.*

çà-pōuçh', çà-pōçh', *v.t.* To hood. [Obs.]

çap'pà-dine, *n.* [Origin unknown.] Waste silk flock sheared from the silkworm's cocoon after the good silk has been reeled off; used for shag in rugmaking.

çap'-pā"pēr, *n.* 1. A coarse paper, so called from being used to make caps to hold commodities.
2. A kind of writing-paper in large sheets, usually called foolscap.

Çap"pà-ri-dā'cē-æ, *n.pl.* [From L. *capparis* (*-idos*), the caper-bush, caper, and *-aceæ.*] A natural order of dicotyledonous, polypetalous, herbaceous plants, sometimes shrubs or trees—the caper family. Plants of this family, which includes about twenty-three genera and three hundred species, are found in tropical and subtropical regions.

çap-pà-ri-dā'ceous, *a.* Pertaining or belonging to the *Capparidaceæ.*

Çap'pà-ris, *n.* [L., the caper-bush, caper.] A large genus of plants and shrubs, typical of the family *Capparidaceæ*, including the *Capparis spinosa*, which yields the common caper.

çap'pēak, *n.* The vizor of a cap.

çap'pēr, *n.* 1. One who makes or sells caps.
2. A device for fitting percussion-caps to cartridges or shells.
3. One employed as a stool-pigeon or decoy by gamblers, or as a deceptive by-bidder by auctioneers. [Slang.]

çap'ping-plāne, *n.* A plane for slightly rounding the upper surface of hand-rails, as of staircases.

Çā'prà, *n.* [L., a she-goat.] A genus of ruminants having hollow horns, belonging to the family *Bovidæ*, typified by the common goat, and including several other species.

çap'rāte, *n.* [*Capric* and *-ate.*] A salt formed by the union of capric acid with a base.

çap'rē-ō-lā-ry, *a.* [L. *capreolus*, a wild goat, tendril, from *caper*, a goat.] In anatomy, capreolate; in the form of tendrils; pampiniform.

çap'rē-ō-lāte (*or* kà-prē'ō-lāt), *a.* 1. In botany, having tendrils, or filiform spiral claspers, by which plants fasten themselves to other bodies, as in vines.
2. In anatomy, resembling a tendril.

çap'rē-ō-line, *a.* [L. *capreolus*, wild goat.] Of or pertaining to the subgenus *Capreolus.*

çà-prē'ō-lus, *n.*; *pl.* **çà-prē'ō-lī.** [L., dim. from *caper*, a goat.]

1. The tendril of a plant. [Obs.]
2. A buck.
3. [c—] A subgenus of deer, family *Cervidæ.*

çap'riç, *a.* [L. *caper*, a goat.] Of or pertaining to a goat; resembling or derived from a goat.

Capric acid; a peculiar acid, $C_{10}H_{20}O_2$, first discovered in the butter of cow's milk, in which it exists along with butyric and caproic acids, as well as in the milk of the goat, in cocoanut-oil, and in several kinds of fusel-oils; called also *rutic acid.*

çà-priç'cio (-prit'chō), *n.* [It., freak, whim.]

1. A loose irregular kind of music, in which the composer is more guided by fancy than by rule, allowing full scope to his imagination.
2. Any caprice, whim, or expression of fancy in art or in actual events.

çà-priç-ciō'sō (-prit-chō'zō), *adv.* [It.] In music, in a free, fantastic style.

çà-priçe', *n.* [Fr. *caprice*; It. *capriccio*, whim, freak, fancy, originally a fantastical goat-leap, from L. *caper*, f. *capra*, a goat.]

1. A sudden start of the mind; a sudden change of opinion or humor; a whim, freak, or particular fancy; as, the *caprice* or whim of a bishop; the *caprices* of a poor appetite.
2. Capriciousness.

> Everywhere I observe in the feminine mind something of beautiful *caprice*.
> —De Quincey.

3. Same as *Capriccio*, 1.

Syn.—Vagary, whim, freak, fancy, humor, conceit, inclination, crotchet.

çà-prich'iō, *n.* Capriccio. [Obs.]

çà-pri'cious (-prish'us), *a.* Governed by or showing caprice; unsteady; changeable; fickle; fanciful; as, a man of a *capricious* temper.

Syn.—Wayward, whimsical, changeable, fanciful, fickle, fitful, unsteady, crotchety, inconstant.

çà-pri'cious-ly, *adv.* In a capricious manner; whimsically.

çà-pri'cious-ness, *n.* The quality of being capricious.

Çap'ri-çorn, *n.* [L. *capricornus*, from *caper*, a goat, and *cornu*, a horn.]

1. One of the twelve signs of the zodiac, which the sun enters at the winter solstice, about December 21; represented on ancient monuments by the figure of a goat, or a figure having the fore part like a goat, and the hind part like a fish.
2. A zodiacal constellation between Sagittarius and Aquarius, anciently represented on monuments by the figure of a goat.
3. [c—] An ibex.

Capricorn beetles; beetles of the family *Cerambycidæ*; long-horned beetles, the larvæ of which are destructive to trees and shrubbery.

çap'rid, *a.* Relating to that tribe of ruminant mammals, of which the genus *Capra* is the type.

çap"ri-fi-çā'tion, *n.* [L. *caprificatio*, from *caprificare*, to ripen figs by caprification; *caprificus*, a fig-tree.]

1. A process intended to hasten the ripening of figs and to improve the quality of the fruit, the practice being to suspend above the cultivated figs branches of the wild fig covered with cynips, a species of small insects which spread themselves over the whole tree, distributing the pollen of the male flowers and puncturing the fruit, thus producing the alleged beneficial effects mentioned. Although of great antiquity, the practice in recent times has been declared not only useless but injurious.
2. The fecundation of the female date-palms by shedding over them the pollen from the male plant.

çap'ri-foil, *n.* A plant of the honeysuckle family.

çap'ri-fōle, *n.* Caprifolium. [Obs.]

Çap-ri-fō-li-ā'cē-æ, *n.pl.* [LL. *caprifolium*, the honeysuckle, woodbine, and *-aceæ.*] A natural order of monopetalous dicotyledons, allied to the *Rubiaceæ*, including a number of erect or twining shrubs and herbaceous plants, among which are the honeysuckle, elder, viburnum, and snowberry. The characteristics of the order are opposite leaves without stipules, free anthers, epipetalous stamens, and fruit not splitting open when ripe.

çap-ri-fō-li-ā'ceous, *a.* Of, pertaining to, or resembling the family *Caprifoliaceæ.*

çap-ri-fō'li-um, *n.* [LL., the honeysuckle.] Honeysuckle; woodbine.

çap'ri-fọrm, *a.* [L. *caper, capri*, a goat, and *forma*, form.] Having the form of a goat.

çà-prig'e-nous, *a.* [L. *caper, capri*, a goat, and *genus*, producing.] Produced by or formed like a goat.

çap'rin, çap'rine, *n.* A substance found in butter, which, with butyrin and caprone, gives it its peculiar taste and odor. It is a compound of capric acid and glycerin, or a caprate of glycerin.

çap'rine, *a.* [L. *caprinus*, from *caper*, a goat.] Of or pertaining to the *Caprinæ*; hircine; goatlike.

çap'ri-ōle, *n.* [Fr., from It. *capriola*; L. *capreolus*, a wild goat; from *caper*, a goat.]

1. In the manège, an upward leap made by a trained horse in which he does not advance, but, when at the height of the leap, flings out his hind legs evenly and close together.
2. A frolicsome leap or caper.

çap'ri-ōle, *v.i.* To leap; to caper; to execute a capriole.

> Far over the billowy sea of heads may be seen Rascality *caprioling* on horses from the royal stud.
> —Carlyle.

çap'ri-ped, *a.* [L. *caper, capri*, a goat, and *pes, pedis*, a foot.] Having feet like those of a goat.

çap'ri-zănt, *a.* [Fr. *caprisant*; LL. *caprizans* (*-antis*), from L. *caper*, a goat.] A term used in regard to the pulse when it seems to leap, one imperfect dilatation of the artery being succeeded by a fuller one.

çap'rō-āte, *n.* A salt of caproic acid.

çà-prō'iç, *a.* Of or pertaining to a goat; derived from a goat.

Caproic acid; the sixth in the series of fatty acids, $C_6H_{12}O_2$, a clear mobile oil which may be produced from butter, from cocoanut-oil, and from various other sources. It is extremely fluid, colorless, inflammable, and has a very acid and penetrating taste.

çap'rōne, *n.* [*Capric* and *-one.*] A clear colorless oil obtained from butter, to which the butter in part owes its peculiar flavor.

çap'ryl, *n.* See *Octyl.*

çap'ry-lāte, *n.* A salt of caprylic acid.

çà-pryl'iç, *a.* Of, pertaining to, or derived from capryl, or octyl.

çap-sā'i-cin, *n.* [L. *capsicum*, Cayenne pepper; *capsa*, a box.] A colorless, active irritant, $C_9H_{14}O_2$, obtained from Cayenne pepper.

çap'shēaf, *n.* 1. The top bundle of a stack or shock of grain; the crowner.
2. Figuratively, the summit or finishing part.

çap'si-cin, çap'si-cine, *n.* An alkaloid, the active principle of the capsules of *Capsicum*. It has a resinous aspect and a burning taste. It is soluble in alcohol, and forms crystallizable salts with acetic, nitric, and sulphuric acids.

Çap'si-çum, *n.* [L. *capsa*, a box; so named from the shape of the seed-pods.] A genus of South American and Asiatic annual subshrubby plants, of the nightshade family. Many of the species are cultivated for their fruit, which in some reaches the size of an orange, is fleshy and variously colored, and contains capsicin, present also in the seed. The fruit or pod is used for

Capsicum annuum.

pickles, sauces, etc., and also in medicine, both externally and internally. Cayenne pepper consists of the ground pods of various species, especially *Capsicum fastigiatum*, the African or Guinea pepper, or spur-pepper, and of the common red pepper of the garden, *Capsicum annuum*. *Capsicum baccatum* is bird-pepper, *Capsicum fruticosum*, goat-pepper. *Capsicum grossum*, or bell-pepper, is an East Indian species with large capsules.

çap-size′, *v.t.*; capsized, *pt.*, *pp.*; capsizing, *ppr.* [Perhaps a corruption of Sp. *capuzar*, to sink a vessel by the head, from L. *caput*, a head.] To upset; to overturn, as a boat or a vehicle.

çap-size′, *v.i.* To be upset or overturned; as, take care, or the boat will *capsize*.

çap-size′, *n.* The act of capsizing; an overturn.

çap′=squâre (-skwâr), *n.* In gunnery, one of the strong plates of iron which pass over the trunnions of a cannon and keep it in the carriage.

çap′stan, *n.* [Fr. *cabestan*; Sp. *cabestrante*, *cabrestante*, *cabra*, a goat, a machine for throwing stones, and *estante*, a shelf, crossbeam; from L. *stans*, ppr. of *stare*, to stand.] An apparatus consisting of a cylinder adjusted on an upright axis, which is turned round by means of horizontal bars or levers, so that a rope is thus wound round it and a weight raised or moved. It is chiefly used for weighing anchor, hoisting sails, moving buildings, etc. When it is employed to draw coal from pits, it is usually called a *gin*, and when worked by horses it is called a *whim-gin*. Sometimes written *capstern*.

Capstan.

To come up with the capstan; to turn it the contrary way.

To heave in at the capstan; to go round with it by pushing with the breast against the bars.

To pawl the capstan; to fix the pawls to prevent it from recoiling.

To surge the capstan; to slacken the rope wound round it.

çap′stan=bär, *n.* A lever or bar used in turning a capstan.

çap′stōne, *n.* 1. A crowning stone at the summit of a wall, turret, tower, or other structure.

2. A name given to a fossil echinite (sea-urchin) of the genus *Conulus*, from its resemblance to a cap.

çap′sū-lăr, **çap′sū-lā-ry**, *a.* Hollow, like a chest; pertaining to, resembling, or of the nature of a capsule.

Capsular ligament; in anatomy, the ligament which surrounds every movable articulation, and contains the synovia like a bag.

çap′sū-lāte, **çap′sū-lā-ted**, *a.* Inclosed in a capsule, or as in a chest, or box.

çap′sūle, *n.* [Fr. *capsule*; L. *capsula*, a little chest, dim. of *capsa*, a chest, from *capere*, to take, contain.]

1. In botany, a dry fruit, either membranous or woody, which dehisces by regular valves corresponding in number to the carpels, or twice as many.

2. In chemistry, (a) a small saucer made of clay for roasting samples of ores, or for melting them; (b) a small shallow vessel made of Berlin ware, platinum, etc., for evaporations, solutions, and the like.

3. In anatomy, a membranous envelope inclosing a part like a bag; as, the *capsule* of the crystalline lens.

4. A small gelatinous shell or envelope for nauseous medicines.

5. The thin metallic seal or cover for closing a bottle.

6. A thin cuplike metallic shell, as of a cartridge, percussion-cap, etc.

Atrabiliary capsule; the suprarenal capsule.

Bowman's capsule; the membrane forming the commencement of uriniferous tubules and insheathing a tuft of blood vessels in the kidney: the cap of a Malpighian body of the kidney.

Glisson's capsule; a fibrous envelope which protects or insheaths the portal vessels in their course through the liver.

çap′tain (-tin), *n.* [ME. *captain*; OFr. *capitaine*; LL. *capitaneus*, pertaining to the head; L. *caput*, the head.]

1. One who is at the head of or has authority over others; a chief; a leader; a commander, especially in military affairs. In the Bible, the term is applied to a king or prince, to a general or commander of an army, to the governor of a province; as, "anoint him *captain* over my people;" "*captain* of the host of the Lord;" "*captain* over thousands," etc.

2. The military officer who commands a company, whether of infantry, cavalry, or artillery; the officer next in rank above a lieutenant and below a major.

3. In the United States navy, an officer commanding a ship of war, who ranks next below a commodore and above a commander, and who is equal in rank to a colonel in the army. The title is sometimes conferred by courtesy upon a commander or lieutenant-commander when in temporary command of a ship. The heads of small parties or gangs of men in a ship of war are also called captains, as of the forecastle, maintop, foretop, guns, etc.

4. The commander or master of a merchant or other vessel.

5. In some occupations, the title given to an overseer, foreman, or superintendent; as, the *captain* of a mine.

6. A man skilled in war, or military affairs; as, Napoleon was a great *captain*.

7. A leader; an organizer; one having authority over persons acting in concert; as, the *captain* of a football team, of a baseball nine, of a cricket eleven, of a boat's crew, of a political club, etc.

çap′tain, *a.* Chief; valiant; superior; suited for leadership. [Rare.]

çap′tain, *v.t.*; captained, *pt.*, *pp.*; captaining, *ppr.* To act as a leader of; to conduct as a captain of; to manage; to control. [Rare.]

çap′tain-cy, *n.*; *pl.* **çap′tain-cieş**. 1. The rank, post, or commission of a captain.

2. The jurisdiction of a captain, or commander, as in Spanish military and colonial government.

çap″tain-cy=ġen′ẽr-ăl, *n.* 1. The office, rank, or jurisdiction of a captain-general.

2. In Spain, one of the principal military divisions.

çap″tain=ġen′ẽr-ăl, *n.* 1. The commander-in-chief of an army, or of the militia.

2. In Spain, the governor of a colony, or of one of the chief military divisions.

çap″tain=pȧ-shä′, *n.* In Turkey, the high admiral. [See *Pasha*.]

çap′tain-ry, *n.* Power or command over a certain district; chieftainship. [Obs.]

çap′tain-ship, *n.* 1. The condition or post of a captain; captaincy.

2. The command of a clan, or government of a certain district. [Obs.]

çap-tā′tion, *n.* [L. *captatio*, from *captare*, to reach after, desire.] The act or practice of courting favor or applause, by flattery or adroit appeals. [Obs.]

çap′tion, *n.* [L. *captio*, a taking, seizing, fraud, from *capere*, to seize, take.]

1. A catch; a trick; an imposition. [Obs.]

2. Caviling; cavil. [Obs.]

3. The act of taking or apprehending by a judicial process. [Rare.]

4. In law, the certificate of execution of a warrant, commission, or indictment stating the time and place of execution and such other particulars as are necessary to make it legal and valid.

5. The heading of a chapter, section, or page in a book or document.

çap′tious, *a.* [L. *captiosus*, from *captio*, a seizing, fraud, deceit, from *capere*, to take.]

1. Disposed to find fault or raise objections; apt to cavil; as, a *captious* man; a *captious* criticism.

2. Fitted to catch or insnare; insidious; as, a *captious* question.

Syn.—Cross, fretful, peevish, petulant, caviling, splenetic.—*Captious* marks a readiness to be offended; *cross* indicates a readiness to offend others; *peevish* expresses a strong degree of crossness; *fretful* a complaining impatience; *petulant* a quick or sudden impatience; *caviling* indicates a willingness to find fault on trivial grounds.

çap′tious-ly, *adv.* In a captious manner.

çap′tious-ness, *n.* Disposition to find fault; inclination to object; peevishness.

çap′ti-vāte, *v.t.*; captivated, *pt.*, *pp.*; captivating, *ppr.* [L. *captivatus*, pp. of *captivare*, to take captive; *captivus*, a captive; from *captus*, pp. of *capere*, to take.]

1. To take prisoner; to seize by force; to subdue, as an enemy in war. [Obs.]

2. To overpower and gain through excellence or beauty; to charm; to engage the affections of; to bind in love.

Syn. — Fascinate, entrance, enchant, charm, overpower, bewitch, capture, subdue, enslave.

çap′ti-vāte, *a.* Taken prisoner; insnared; captivated.

çap′ti-vā-ting, *a.* Having power to engage the affections.

çap′ti-vā-ting-ly, *adv.* In a captivating manner.

çap-ti-vā′tion, *n.* The act of captivating; the state of being captivated.

çap′tive, *n.* [L. *captivus*, from *captus*, pp. of *capere*, to take.]

1. A prisoner taken by force or stratagem in war, by an enemy; followed by *to*; as, a *captive to* the victor.

2. One who is charmed or subdued by beauty or excellence; one held by love.

çap′tive, *a.* 1. Made prisoner in war; kept in bondage or confinement; as, *captive* souls.

2. Holding in confinement; as, *captive* chains.

3. Enslaved, as by passion or affection.

çap′tive, *v.t.*; captived, *pt.*, *pp.*; captiving, *ppr.* To take prisoner; to bring into subjection. [Rare.]

çap-tiv′i-ty, *n.* [Fr. *captivité*; L. *captivitas*, from *captivus*, a captive.]

1. The state of being a prisoner, or of being in the power of an enemy by force or the fate of war.

2. Subjection; a state of being under control.

To lead captivity captive; in Scripture, to subdue those who have held others in slavery or captivity.

Syn. — Bondage, enthralment, confinement, subjection, imprisonment, slavery, servitude, thraldom.

çap′tŏr, *n.* [L. *captor*, from *capere*, to take.] One who takes by force, as a prisoner or a prize; specifically, one who takes a prize at sea.

çap′tūre, *n.* [Fr. *capture*; L. *captura*, from *capere*, to take.]

1. The act of taking or seizing; seizure; arrest; as, the *capture* of an enemy, of a ship, or of booty, by force, surprise, or stratagem; the *capture* of a criminal or debtor.

2. The thing taken; a prize.

Syn.—Seizure, arrest, detention.

çap′tūre, *v.t.*; captured, *pt.*, *pp.*; capturing, *ppr.* To take or seize by force, surprise, or stratagem, as an enemy or his property; to take by force under the authority of a commission; as, to *capture* a ship or a fortress.

çȧ-puç′ciō (-put′chō), *n.* [It.] A capuchin or hood. [Obs.]

çȧ-pūçhe′, *n.* A capouch. [Obs.]

çap′ū-chin (*or* -shēn′), *n.* [Fr. *capucin*, a monk who wears a cowl, from *capuce*, It. *cappuccio*, a cowl.]

1. A garment worn by women, consisting of a cloak and hood, made in imitation of the dress of Capuchin monks.

2. [C—] A monk of the order of St. Francis, so called from the capouch, a stuff cap or cowl, the distinguishing badge of the order. The order, which is most austere, was founded by Matteo di Bassi, in 1526 or 1528.

3. A kind of pigeon with a range of inverted feathers on the back part of the head, like the cowl of a monk.

4. A South American monkey, *Cebus capucinus*, having a bare and wrinkled forehead and hair growing like a monk's cowl; also, other monkeys of the same genus.

Capuchin nun; one of the Franciscan nuns, whose order, established by Maria Longa, espoused Capuchin rule in 1538.

çap′ū-cine, *n.* A monkey, the capuchin.

çap′ū-let, *n.* Same as *Capellet*.

çap′ū-lin, *n.* The Mexican cherry.

çā′put, *n.*; *pl.* **çap′i-tȧ**. [L., the head.]

1. In anatomy, the head or any head-like protuberance or rounded extremity.

2. In law, a citizen; one's status as such.

3. The council of Cambridge University, England, previous to 1856.

Caput mortuum; in old chemistry, the residuum of distillation or sublimation; therefore, any worthless residue.

çap-y-bä′rȧ, *n.* Same as *Capibara*.

çär, *n.* [OFr. *car*; LL. *carrus*, a two-wheeled vehicle; L. *carrus*, *currus*, from *currere*, to run.]

1. A small vehicle moved on wheels, either four-wheeled or two-wheeled, but usually the latter, drawn by a single horse; an automobile.

2. A vehicle, mounted on trucks, for use on a railroad; a vehicle for running on rails.

3. In poetical language, any vehicle of dignity or splendor; a chariot of war or of triumph.

4. The cage or box of an elevator.

5. The basket of a balloon, for the occupancy of the aeronaut and his passengers.

6. A perforated box floating in water for keeping live fish.

7. [C—] The constellation called Charles's Wain, the Great Bear, or the Great Dipper; the Northern Car.

çar′ȧ-bid, *a.* Pertaining to the *Carabidæ*.

çar′ȧ-bid, *n.* Any one of various species of the *Carabidæ*.

Çar-ab′i-dæ, *n.pl.* [L., from Gr. *karabos*, a horned beetle.] A family of beetles or coleopterous insects, of the section *Pentamera* of Latreille. There are more than 6,000 known species. The celebrated bombardier beetle, *Brachinus crepitans*, belongs to this family.

çar′ȧ-bine, *n.* Same as *Carbine*.

çar″ȧ-bi-neer′, *n.* Same as *Carbineer*.

çar′ȧ-boid, *a.* Pertaining to or resembling the genus *Carabus*.

Çar′ȧ-bus, *n.* [L., from Gr. *karabos*, a horned beetle.]

1. The type genus of *Carabidæ*.

2. [c—] A beetle belonging to this genus.

çar′ăç, *n.* [Obs.] See *Carack*.

çar′ȧ-çal, *n.* [Fr. *caracal*; Turk. *qara qulaq*; *qara*, black, and *qulaq*, ear.] A lynx, the *Lynx caracal*, a native of northern Africa and southwestern Asia. Its color is a uniform reddish-brown; its ears black externally, and tipped with long, black hairs.

çä-rà-çä′rȧ, *n.* [Named in imitation of their cry.] The name given to the birds of the subfamily *Polyborinæ*, an aberrant one belonging to the *Falconidæ*. They resemble the vultures in appearance, are habitants of tropical America, and subsist on carrion.

çar′ăck, çar′răck, *n.* [ME. *caracke*; OFr. *carraque*; LL. *carraca*, a ship of burden, from L. *carrus*, a car.] A galleon; a large Portuguese or Spanish merchant vessel, usually carrying guns, formerly employed in trade with the East Indies and America.

çar′ȧ-çōle, *n.* [Fr. *caracole*, a snail, winding staircase, a caracole.]

1. In the manège, a semi-round, or half-turn, which a horseman makes, either to the right or left.

2. In architecture, a staircase in a helix or spiral form.

çar′ȧ-çōle, *v.i.*; caracoled, *pt.*, *pp.*; caracoling, *ppr.* To move in a caracole; to wheel.

çar′ȧ-çol-y, çar′ȧ-çol-i, *n.* [Origin unknown.] An alloy of gold, silver, and copper, of which cheap jewelry and ornaments are made.

çar-ȧ-çō′rȧ, *n.* [Malay *karakura*, a kind of boat.] A long, narrow, sailing boat or canoe, notable for swiftness, used by the inhabitants of Borneo and by the East Indian Dutch.

çȧ-răfe′, çȧ-răffe′, *n.* [Fr. *carafe*; It. *caraffa*, a vessel for liquids; Ar. *ghirāf*, a vessel.] A glass bottle or decanter commonly used for water.

Çar-ȧ-gā′nȧ, *n.* [L., from *caragan*, the Mogul name.] A genus of leguminous Asiatic trees, several species of which are cultivated for ornament; commonly called *pea-trees*.

çar′ȧ-geen, çar′ȧ-gheen, *n.* Same as *Carrageen*.

çȧ-rā-ï′pï, *n.* [S. Am.] The pottery-tree, *Moquilea utilis*, of South America. Its pulverized bark is valuable as an ingredient in clay mixtures in the manufacture of pottery.

Çā′rȧ-ïte, *n.* Same as *Karaite*.

çȧ-ram′bō-lȧ, *n.* [E. Ind.] An East Indian tree, *Averrhoa Carambola*, of the geranium family; also, the acutely-angled, acid fruit of this tree, eaten by the natives.

çar′ȧ-mel, *n.* [Fr. *caramel*, burnt sugar.]

1. Anhydrous or burnt sugar; a black, porous, shining substance, obtained by heating sugar to a high temperature. It is soluble in water, which it colors a dark brown, and is used for coloring spirits, etc.

2. A kind of very sweet, hard candy, usually made in small cubes and of different flavors.

çȧ-ran′goid, *a.* Of or pertaining to the *Carangidæ*, a family of acanthopterygian fishes represented by the genus *Caranx*, related to the mackerels, and embracing numerous species of tropical fishes, as the cavallies, pompanos, and pilot-fish.

çȧ-ran′nȧ, *n.* See *Carauna*.

Çar′anx, *n.* [Sp. *carangue*, *caranga*, a W. Ind. flatfish.]

1. A genus of fishes typical of the family *Carangidæ*, inhabiting the Atlantic coast and including the yellow or golden mackerel and the horse-mackerel.

2. [c—] A fish of this genus.

Çar′ȧ-pȧ, *n.* [Fr. *caraipi*, a native Guiana name.] A small genus of tropical trees of the bead-tree family, species of which are found in Africa and South America. The wood of these trees is valuable and their numerous oily nuts yield a bitter oil having medicinal properties, which sometimes is also used for illuminating purposes.

çar′ȧ-pāce, *n.* [Fr. *carapace*; Sp. *carapacho*, a gourd.] The upper shell of crabs, lobsters, or other crustaceans.

çä-rȧ-pä′tō, *n.* [From *carrapato*, the Port. name.] A tick of the genus *Amblyomma*, common to South America.

çar′ȧ-pax, *n.* Same as *Carapace*.

çar′ăt, *n.* [Fr. *carat*; Ar. *qirat*, a pod, husk, the weight of four grains; Gr. *keration*, the fruit of the locust-tree, a weight; dim. of *keras*, a horn.]

1. The weight of four grains, used by goldsmiths and jewelers in weighing precious stones and pearls.

2. The weight that expresses the fineness of gold. The whole mass of gold is divided into twenty-four equal parts, and as many twenty-fourth parts as it contains of pure gold, determine the number of *carats* by which it shall be called; as, gold of twenty-two parts of pure metal is gold of twenty-two *carats*.

çȧ-rau′nȧ, *n.* [From native name.] A resinous gum having an aromatic flavor, the product of various South American trees, used sometimes as a medicine.

çar′ȧ-van, *n.* [Fr. *caravane*; Sp. *caravana*; Ar. *kairawan*; Per. *karwan*, a caravan.]

1. A company of travelers, pilgrims, or merchants, marching or proceeding in a body over deserts, as in Oriental countries, or in regions infested with robbers.

2. A large close carriage on springs, for conveying wild beasts when carried round as a show.

3. A covered wagon for transporting furniture; commonly abbreviated into *van*.

çar″ȧ-van-eer′, *n.* [Fr. *caravanier*, from *caravane*, a caravan.] The leader or driver of a caravan.

çar-ȧ-van′sȧ-ry, *n.* [Fr. *caravanserai*; Turk. *kerwānseray*; Per. *kārwānserāi*; from *kārwān*, a caravan, and *serāi*, a place, an inn.] A place

Interior of Caravansary at Aleppo.

for loading caravans; a kind of Oriental inn, where caravans stop for the night, being a large square building with a spacious court in the center; written also *caravanserai* and *caravansera*.

çar′ȧ-vel, *n.* [Sp. *caravela*, *carabela*, dim. of *caraba*, a small vessel; LL. *carabus*, from Gr. *karabos*, a kind of light ship, a beetle, crawfish.]

1. A fifteenth-century sailing boat such as used by Columbus, having its origin in Spain and Portugal. It had broad bows, with high poop, and was four-masted.

2. A later boat of the same type used for bearing despatches.

3. A frigate or man-of-war belonging to the Turkish navy.

Caravel of the fifteenth century.

4. A small French boat used in the fisheries.

çar′ȧ-wāy, *n.* [From Sp. *alcarahueya*, caraway; *al*, the, and *karwiya*, from Gr. *karon*, caraway.]

1. A biennial plant, *Carum Carui*, a native of Europe, having a taper root like a parsnip.

2. The seed of the plant, having an aromatic smell and semipungent taste. They are used in cookery and confectionery; also in medicine, as an antispasmodic.

3. A pastry in which *caraway* is an ingredient.

çär-bam′iç, *a.* [*Carbo*nic and *am*ide and *-ic.*] Relating to carbamic acid.

Carbamic acid; an acid in which the amido group has taken the place of the nonacid hydrogen, occurring as a salt in ammonium carbonate; called also *amido-formic acid*.

çär-bam′ide (*or* -id), *n.* [*Carb*on and *amide.*] The name given in chemistry to urea.

çär-bam′ine, *n.* A liquid compound of cyanogen with a hydrocarbon radical.

çär′bȧ-nil, *n.* A liquid salt of isocyanic acid.

çär′bȧ-zōl, *n.* [*Carb*on and *az*ote and *-ol.*] A coal-tar product; white, and crystalline in form.

çär-baz′ō-tāte, *n.* Picrate, a salt derived from picric acid.

çär-bȧ-zot′iç, *a.* [*Carb*on and *az*ote and *-ic.*] Relating or allied to carbon and nitrogen.

Carbazotic acid; see *Picric acid.*

çär′bide (*or* -bid), *n.* [*Carb*on and *-ide.*] A compound of carbon, in which the carbon is negative and the other elements positive.

çär′bi-mide (*or* -mid), *n.* [*Carb*on and *imide.*] The name given in chemistry to isocyanic acid or any of the salts formed from it.

çär′bïne, *n.* [Fr. *carabin*; OFr. *calabrin*, from *calabre*, an engine of war used in besieging.]

1. A light firearm discharged by hand, used in the fifteenth and sixteenth centuries. [Obs.]

2. A short musket used more particularly by cavalry.

çär-bi-neer′, *n.* [Fr. *carabinier*, from *carabine*, a carbine.] A soldier having a carbine for equipment.

çär′bi-nōl, *n.* Methyl alcohol, or other alcohol, a derivative thereof, formed by replacing with an alcohol radical the element hydrogen in the methyl group.

çär-bō-hȳ′drāte, *n.* [*Carbo*n and *hydrate.*] One of a number of groups of carbon compounds, the general formula of which is 5, 6, or 12 parts of carbon to 5, 6, or 11 parts of H_2O.

çär-bō-hȳ′dride (*or* -drid), *n.* See *Hydrocarbon.*

çär-bol′iç, *a.* [L. *carbo*, coal, and *oleum*, oil.] Relating or allied to carbon and oil, or coal-tar oil.

Carbolic acid; an acid found in coal-tar; when pure, as a colorless crystalline substance, but usually as an oily liquid, colorless, with a burning taste and the odor of creosote. It is much employed as a disinfectant; called also *phenol*.

çär′bō-līze, *v.t.*; carbolized, *pt.*, *pp.*; carbolizing, *ppr.* To use carbolic acid in the treatment of; to apply carbolic acid to as a wash or disinfectant.

çär′bŏn, *n.* [Fr. *carbone*, from L. *carbo*, coal.]

1. In chemistry, an element, one of the nonmetals, common to all organic substances. Symbol C, atomic weight 12, specific gravity (diamond) 3.52. It is one of the most common elements, of the utmost value in the arts, familiar forms being charcoal (of which it forms the basis), graphite, and the diamond. It readily combines with oxygen to form *carbon* dioxid, called carbonic acid or carbonic oxid; when united with hydrogen it forms hydrocarbons.

2. In electricity, an essential part of an arc light, the pencil of *carbon* used in producing an arc; also, a plate of *carbon* used in various forms of batteries.

3. Impure forms of *carbon* known as bort or carbonado.

Carbon compounds; compounds the principal constituent of which is carbon, distinguished from metallic compounds; called also *organic compounds*.

Carbon dioxid; see *Carbonic acid.*

Carbon monoxid; see *Carbonic oxid.*

Gas carbon; one of the by-products of gas manufacture used in making pencils for the arc light or plates for batteries.

çär-bō-nā′ceous, *a.* Pertaining to, or containing, or composed of, carbon; as, *carbonaceous* matter.

çär′bō-nāde, *n.* [Fr. *carbonade*; It. *carbonata*, from L. *carbo*, a coal.] In cookery, flesh, fowl, or the like, cut across, seasoned, and broiled on coals.

çär-bō-nāde′, çär-bō-nā′dō, *v.t.* To cut or hack, either for cooking or, figuratively, as in an encounter. [Obs.]

çär-bō-nā′dō, *n.*; *pl.* **çär-bō-nā′dōeṣ.** [Sp. *carbonada*, from L. *carbo*, coal.] A form of carbon found in Brazil as a fragmentary, imperfectly crystallized, intensely hard form of rock, known as *black diamond.* It is used to tip diamond drills and similar boring instruments. As *bort*, it is often reduced to powder and used in cutting and polishing precious stones.

Çär-bō-nä′riṣm, *n.* Anything pertaining or relating to the Carbonari.

Çär-bō-nä′rō, *n.*; *pl.* **Çär-bō-nä′rï.** [It., a charcoal-burner.] One belonging to an Italian secret society organized at the beginning of the nineteenth century. The members of the organization met originally in the mountains to plot against the government of Naples (1808), but soon became identified with the party of "Young Italy," and fifty years later were at the height of their influence with an Italian republic as their object and Garibaldi and Mazzini for their leaders.

çär′bŏn-āte, *n.* A salt formed by the union of carbonic acid with a base; as, the *carbonate* of lime; *carbonate* of copper.

çär′bŏn-ā-ted, *a.* Combined with carbonic acid.

Carbonated waters; such mineral waters as are impregnated with carbonic acid.

çär-bŏn-ā′tion, çär″bŏn-ā-tā′tion, *n.* A purifying process in sugar-making in which the lime salts are precipitated from the juice by means of carbon dioxid.

çär′bōne, *v.t.* To cook over coals. [Obs.]

çär-bō-ne′rō, *n.* [Sp., a charcoal-burner.] A fish of the family *Carangidæ*, having markings of a dark color, common to West Indian waters.

çär-bon′iç, *a.* [Fr. *carbonique*; Sp. *carbonico*, from L. *carbo*, coal.] Relating to or derived from carbon.

Carbonic acid; in chemistry, CO_2, a heavy gas without odor or color, produced in nature by fermentation and decomposition, and given off by respiration. It is used for various manufacturing purposes, as for example in the making of aerated waters. In common with other gases it may be liquefied or solidified by cold and pressure.

Carbonic oxid or *carbonous oxid*; CO, a gas formed by deoxidizing CO_2, having as its characteristics many of the properties of the oxid but burning with a pale blue flame. Known also as *carbon monoxid*.

çär′bŏn-īde, *n.* [Rare.] See *Carbide.*

çär-bŏn-if′ẽr-ous, *a.* [L. *carbo* (*-onis*), coal, and *ferre*, to bear.]

1. Producing or containing carbon or coal.

2. [C—] In geology, relating to the *Carboniferous* age.

Carboniferous age; the age following the Devonian and preceding the Jurassic age, in which a luxuriant land vegetation flourished, forming the present beds of coal.

Carboniferous formation; the collective formation of rocks embracing the strata of the Carboniferous age.

çär″bŏn-i-zā′tion, *n.* The act or process of carbonizing.

çär′bŏn-īze, *v.t.*; carbonized, *pt., pp.*; carbonizing, *ppr.* 1. To convert into carbon by combustion or the action of fire, or by other means, as by the action of concentrated acids on animal and vegetable substances.

2. To cover with a coating of carbon or one of the carbon compounds.

3. To prepare with carbon; as, to *carbonize* a battery by adding carbon plates.

çär″bŏn-ō-hȳ′drous, *a.* Composed of carbon and hydrogen.

çär-bŏn-om′e-tẽr, *n.* [L. *carbo* (*-onis*), coal, and *metrum*, Gr. *metron*, a measure.] An instrument for determining the presence of carbon or carbon dioxid, and measuring the amount.

çär′bŏn-ous, *a.* Same as *Carbonic.*

çär′bŏn-pā″pẽr, *n.* A thin paper used for manifolding, having one side coated with a composition of lampblack.

çär′bŏn-point, *n.* A pencil of carbon used in the arc-light.

çär′bŏn-tis″sūe, *n.* A gelatin paper having suitable coloring material, for use in autotype photography.

çär′bŏn-yl, *n.* The organic radical CO, of common occurrence, but found only combined, as in urea.

Carbonyl chlorid; a gas, $COCl_2$, marked by its strong odor. It is colorless, formed in numerous ways, and has also been termed *phosgene gas* and *carbon oxychlorid.*

çär-bō-run′dum, *n.* A compound of carbon and silicon made by electric fusion and having uses similar to emery.

çär-bō-stȳ′ril, *n.* A phenol derived from alkaloids and coal-tar; written also *oxyquinolin.*

çär-box′id (*or* -īd), *n.* Carbon and oxygen in combination with some radical, as potassium *carboxid.*

çär-box′yl, *n.* [*Carb*on and *ox*ygen, and *-yl.*] The radical CO.OH, common to all oxygen acids of carbon.

cär′boy, *n.* [Per. *qarāba*, a large bottle.] A large, globular bottle of green glass, inclosed in basketwork or securely boxed for protection; used especially for carrying corrosive liquors, as sulphuric acid.

Carboy.

çär′bun-cle (-buñk-l), *n.* [L. *carbunculus*, a little coal, a gem, from *carbo*, a coal.]

1. An inflammatory tumor; a painful gangrenous boil or ulcer; in pathology, called an *anthrax.*

2. A beautiful gem, of a deep red color, called by the Greeks *anthrax*; found in the East Indies. Its usual size is nearly a quarter of an inch in length, and two-thirds of that in diameter. The *carbuncle* of the ancients is supposed to have been a garnet.

3. In heraldry, a charge or bearing consisting of eight radii, four of which make a common cross, and the other four, a saltier.

çär′bun-cled (-buñk-ld), *a.* Set with carbuncles; spotted.

çär-bun′cū-lăr, *a.* Belonging to a carbuncle; resembling a carbuncle; red; inflamed.

çär-bun-cū-lā′tion, *n.* The blasting of the young buds of trees or plants, by excessive heat or cold.

çär′bū-ret, *n.* A combination of carbon with some other substance, the resulting compound not being an acid or base. More exactly, a compound of carbon with a basic substance, in which the carbon is the electro-negative ingredient. Also called *carbide.*

çär′bū-ret, *v.t.*; carbureted, *pt., pp.*; carbureting, *ppr.* Same as *Carburize.*

çär′bū-ret-ănt, *n.* A volatile hydrocarbon that increases the illuminating power of gas.

çär′bū-ret-ed, çär′bū-ret-ted, *a.* Combined with carbon in the manner of a carburet; as, *carbureted* hydrogen gas.

Carbureted hydrogen gas; a term applied to various gaseous compounds of carbon and hydrogen.

Heavy carbureted hydrogen; a colorless inflammable gas, C_2H_4, one of the constituents of coal-gas; ethylene.

Light carbureted hydrogen; a compound of carbon and hydrogen, CH_4, formed in stagnant pools and mines; marsh-gas; fire-damp.

çär′bū-ret-ẽr, çär′bū-ret-ŏr, *n.* 1. An apparatus by which gas is carbureted.

2. Same as *Carburetant.*

çär″bū-ri-zā′tion, *n.* The process and result of carburizing.

çär′bū-rīze, *v.t.*; carburized, *pt., pp.*; carburizing, *ppr.* To add volatile hydrocarbons to, in the improvement of the illuminating power of gas or in the making of cement-steel from iron.

çär′ca-jöu, *n.* [Fr., from native name.] The wolverene; sometimes confused with the Canadian lynx and the American badger.

çär′ca-net, *n.* [A dim. from Fr. *carcan*, the collar of a criminal, a carcanet; LL. *carcannum*, the throat.] A jeweled chain, circlet, or other like ornament.

çär′căss, çär′çāse, *n.* [Fr. *carcasse*; It. *carcassa*, a bomb, shell; OFr. *carquais*, from Per. *tarkash*, a quiver.]

1. The body of an animal; usually, the body when dead. It is not applied to the living or dead body of the human species, except in low or ludicrous language.

2. The decaying remains of a bulky thing, as of a boat or ship.

3. The frame or main parts of a thing, unfinished or without ornament.

4. An iron case or hollow vessel, about the size of a bomb, of an oval figure, filled with combustible and other substances, as saltpeter, gunpowder, sulphur, broken glass, turpentine, etc., to be thrown from a mortar as an ignitor.

Carcass.

çär-ca-vel′hōs (-yōs), *n.* [Port., from *Carcavelhos*, a village in Portugal.] A sweet wine produced in Portugal.

çär′cel, *n.* [Named after *Carcel*, a French inventor.] A standard of illuminating effect, used in France, equal to nine and one-half candle-power, or the light of a *Carcel* lamp.

Carcel lamp; a lamp in which the oil is raised through tubes by clockwork, producing a very brilliant light.

çär′cel-āge, *n.* [L. *carcer*, a prison.] Prison fees. [Obs.]

çär′cẽr, *n.* [L.] A starting-post; a prison.

çär′cẽr-ăl, *a.* Belonging to a prison.

Çär-çhar′ō-don, *n.* [L., from Gr. *karcharodōn*, with sharp, jagged teeth; *karcharos*, sharp, and *odous*, *odontos*, tooth.] A genus of nearly extinct man-eating sharks of great size; the only living species is *Carcharodon rondeleti.*

çär-çhar′ō-dont, *a.* 1. Pertaining to the genus *Carcharodon.*

2. Having pointed teeth, as a serpent.

çär′ci-noid, *a.* [Gr. *karkinos*, crab, and *eidos*, form.] Pertaining to a crab.

çär″ci-nō-log′iç-ăl, *a.* Pertaining to carcinology.

çär-ci-nol′ō-ġy, *n.* [Gr. *karkinos*, a crab, and *-logia*, from *legein*, to speak.] A branch of zoölogy relating to lobsters and crabs, or the crustaceans; called also *crustaceology.*

çär-ci-nō′mȧ, *n.* [Gr. *karkinōma*, a cancer, from *karkinoun*, to affect with a cancer, from *karkinos*, a crab, cancer.] In the strict pathological sense, a cancer. Some varieties, such as carcinoma scirrhosum, are hard, while others are of a soft consistency; the latter are most rapid and fatal.

çär-ci-nom′ȧ-tous, *a.* Cancerous; like a cancer, or tending to it.

Çär″ci-nō-mor′phȧ, *n.pl.* [Gr. *karkinos*, a crab, and *morphē*, form.] A group of crustaceans embracing the common crab: called also *Brachyura.*

çär″ci-nō-mor′phiç, *a.* Pertaining to or resembling the crab.

çär-ci-nō′sis, *n.* [Gr. *karkinos*, cancer.] Any form or development of carcinoma.

çär′-çoup″ling, çär′-çoup″lẽr (-kup″), *n.* Any device for connecting cars.

çärd, *n.* [Fr. *carte*, a card, ticket, chart; LL. *carta*, *charta*, a card, paper; L. *charta*, a leaf of paper, tablet; Gr. *chartē*, a leaf of paper, layer of papyrus.]

1. A piece of paper or pasteboard prepared for various purposes.

2. A piece of cardboard bearing figures, a picture, or printed matter; as, a calendar *card*; a playing-*card* in games.

3. A piece of cardboard with one's name, etc., written, engraved, or printed on it, used in visiting, and generally for indicating the name of the person presenting it; as, a visiting-*card*; a business *card*, etc.

4. The chart on which the points of the compass are printed; the dial of a compass.

5. A piece of pasteboard on which is engraved an invitation to a public or private entertainment.

6. A slang term applied to an eccentric person, or any one who has some notable peculiarity.

> Such an old *card* as this, so deep, so sly.
> —Dickens.

7. A note published by some one in the papers, containing a brief statement, explanation, or request.

8. That part of a Jacquard loom which guides the threads.

9. A piece of pasteboard bearing exact and concise information respecting a book or some particular subject. [See *Card catalogue* under *Catalogue.*]

10. A *card* issued to a member of a club, certifying to his membership and admitting him to the privileges thereof.

11. [*pl.*] Any game or games played with *playing-cards*, fifty-two *cards* of which constitute a pack, arranged in four suits of thirteen *cards*, each suit comprehending ten spot-*cards*, having spots varying in number from one to ten, the one-spot being known as the *ace*, and three coat-*cards*, the king, queen and knave or jack. The black suits are clubs and spades; the red, hearts and diamonds. An extra card known as the *joker* is used in some games.

Card is used in numerous self-evident compounds; as, Christmas-*card*, calling-*card*, *card*-basket, *card*-table, *card*-party, playing-*cards*, etc.

On the cards; originally a fortune-teller's phrase, now signifying likely to occur; as, it is quite *on the cards* that he will appear.

To have the cards in your own hands; to be in possession of the means for successful accomplishment in any matter; to be master of the situation.

To play one's cards well; so to employ one's abilities and control one's circumstances as to gain a desired end. It implies shrewdness and tact rather than intellectual ability.

To show one's cards; to expose one's plans; to divulge that which has previously been guarded as a secret.

To speak by the card; to speak accurately and from exact knowledge.

çärd, *v.i.* To play much at cards; to game.

çärd, *n.* [ME. *carde*; Fr. *carde*; Sp. *carda*; It. *carda*; LL. *cardus*, a card, thistle, from L. *carere*, to card.]

1. An instrument for combing, opening, and breaking wool or flax, freeing it from the coarser parts, and from extraneous matter. The primitive device was made by inserting bent teeth of wire in a thick piece of leather, and nailing this to an oblong piece of board, to which a handle is attached. This work is now done by machinery.

2. Fiber in strands or rolls after going through the carding process, ready for the bobbins.

çärd, *v.t.*; carded, *pt., pp.*; carding, *ppr.* 1. To comb or open, as wool, flax, or hemp, with a card, for the purpose of cleansing it of extraneous matter, separating the coarser parts and making it fine and soft for spinning.

2. To clean out, as with a card. [Obs.]

3. To mix, mingle, or unite (one quality) with another, as a good grade with a poor one. [Obs.]

Çär′dȧ-mīne, *n.* [L. *cardamina*, Gr. *kardaminē*, from *kardamon*, a kind of cress.] A genus of herbs of which lady's-smock, cuckoo-flower, and meadow-cress are popularly known varieties.

çär′dȧ-mŏm, *n.* [L. *cardamomum*; Gr. *kardamōmon*, cress.]

1. A plant of the genus *Amomum*, and its seeds, a native of India. The seeds of this plant are used in medicine and as a condiment.

2. A plant which yields *cardamoms*, particularly *Elettaria Cardamomum* and various species of *Amomum.*

Çär-dan′iç, *a.* Relating to or named after Cardan, a celebrated mathematician and physician of Italy, living in the sixteenth century.

Cardanic suspension; a manner of suspending an object by which it may move freely in any direction, as by expanding the limitations of ordinary gimbals.

çärd′bōard, *n.* A more or less stiff variety of pasteboard, smooth or unglazed, used in making boxes, tickets, price-cards, and the like.

çärd′çāse, *n.* A case for holding visiting-cards, made of almost any material from leather to mother-of-pearl and gold; any kind of case in which cards are held.

çärd′-çlŏth″ing, *n.* A covering for the main cylinder and doffers of a carding-machine, formed of wire teeth of varying size set on a card back and cut in convenient strips.

çär′de-çū, *n.* [A corruption of Fr. *quart d'écu.*] A former French coin of silver worth a quarter of a crown. [Obs.]

çärd′ed, *a.* Combed; opened; cleansed with cards, as wool or cotton.

çärd′ẽr, *n.* One who cards wool, cotton, or any other fibrous material; also, one who plays much at cards.

çärd′ẽr-bee, *n.* A name applied to a bee of the genus *Bombus*, which has a peculiar habit of carding or smoothing out certain mosses for use in building a nest.

çär′di-ȧ, *n.* [Gr. *kardia*, the heart.]

1. The heart.

2. The cardiac orifice of the stomach, the point

where it is entered by the esophagus, being to the left and in the vicinity of the heart.

çär′di-aç, *a.* [L. *cardiacus*; Gr. *kardiakos*, pertaining to the heart; *kardia*, the heart.]

1. Pertaining to the heart; in the region of the heart.

2. Exciting action in the heart, through the medium of the stomach; having the quality of stimulating action in the system.

3. Figuratively, producing strength, cordiality, or heartiness.

Cardiac dullness; the area over the heart marked by a dull sound under percussion and corresponding to the part uncovered by the lung.

Cardiac passion; a form of heartburn; gastric neuralgia; called also *gastralgia* and *cardialgia*.

Cardiac wheel; same as *Heart-wheel*.

çär′di-aç, *n.* A medicine which excites action in the stomach, and animates the spirits.

çär-dī′ȧ-çăl, *a.* Cardiac.

çär′di-ȧ-grȧph, *n.* See *Cardiograph*.

çär-di-al′ġi-ȧ, çär′di-al-ġy, *n.* [Gr. *kardialgia*, heartburn; *kardia*, heart, and *algos*, pain.] The heartburn, a violent sensation of heat and acrimony in the upper or left orifice of the stomach, seemingly at the heart, but rising into the esophagus.

çär′di-fọrm, *a.* [LL. *cardus*, a card, and L. *forma*, shape.] In appearance resembling a wool card, as the teeth of certain fishes.

çär′di-găn, *n.* [Named after Lord *Cardigan*.] A jacket of knitted worsted; a warm waistcoat or vest having long sleeves.

Çär-dī′i-dæ, *n.pl.* [From L. *cardia*, heart, and *-idæ*.] The family of headless mollusks, including the cockles, shaped like a heart and having two central or cardinal teeth in each valve.

çär′di-năl, *a.* [L. *cardinalis*, from *cardo*, hinge, that on which something turns or depends.] Chief, principal, preëminent, or fundamental; as, the *cardinal* virtues.

Cardinal numbers; the numbers *one, two, three*, etc., in distinction from *first, second, third*, etc., which are called *ordinal* numbers.

Cardinal points; in cosmography, the four intersections of the horizon with the meridian, and the prime vertical circle, or north and south, east and west. In astrology, the *cardinal points* are the rising and setting of the sun, the zenith and nadir.

Cardinal signs; in astronomy, Aries, Libra, Cancer, and Capricorn.

Cardinal teeth; the teeth in the center of a bivalve shell.

Cardinal veins; the two veins which in embryos traverse each side of the vertebral column, sending the blood back to the heart. Certain fishes retain them through life.

Cardinal virtues; chief virtues, as prudence, justice, temperance, and fortitude.

Cardinal winds; those which blow from the cardinal points of the compass, north, south, east, and west.

çär′di-năl, *n.* [Fr. *cardinal*; It. *cardinale*; LL. *cardinalis*, a cardinal, from L. *cardo*, a hinge, that on which something important depends.]

1. An ecclesiastical prince in the Roman Catholic church, who has a voice in the conclave at the election of a pope, the latter being chosen from their number. The cardinals are divided into three classes or orders, containing six bishops, fifty priests, and fourteen deacons, making seventy. These constitute the Sacred College, and compose the pope's council. Originally, they were subordinate in rank to bishops; but they have now the precedence. The dress of a cardinal is a red soutane or cassock, a rochet, a short purple mantle, and a red hat.

2. A deep red color, something between scarlet and crimson, the color of a *cardinal's* vestments.

3. A mulled drink made chiefly of claret.

4. A woman's short cloak, scarlet in color and worn in the eighteenth century.

Cardinal's hat; a red hat with a low crown and broad brim, forming a part of a cardinal's state dress. From each side hangs a cord, and at the end of each cord are fifteen tassels. The figure is used as a cardinal's heraldic charge.

Cardinal's Hat.

çär′di-năl-āte, *n.* The office, rank, or dignity of a cardinal.

çär′di-năl-bird, *n.* The grosbeak; an American song-bird, *Cardinalis cardinalis*, or *Cardinalis virginianus*, belonging to the finch family. It has a brilliant red plumage and a noticeable crest. The male birds have a clear, musical whistle. Popularly called the *redbird*.

çär′di-năl-flow″ẽr, *n.* A plant, native of North America, the *Lobelia cardinalis*; so called from its brilliant red flowers.

çär′di-năl-īze, *v.t.* To make a cardinal, or give anything the distinctive color of his vestments.

çär′di-năl-ship, *n.* Same as *Cardinalate*.

çärd′ing, *n.* 1. The act of breaking or cleaning with cards; as, the *carding* of wool or cotton preparatory to spinning it into yarn.

2. A spool of combed material taken direct from the carding-machine.

çärd′ing-mȧ-chïne″, çärd′ing-en″ġine, *n.* A machine for combing, breaking, and cleansing wool and cotton. It consists of cylinders, thick set with teeth, and is moved by water, steam, or other mechanical power.

çär′di-ō-. A combining form from Gr. *kardia*, the heart, and used in anatomy, medicine, etc., to indicate relation to the heart; as, *cardiometer, cardiology*.

çär′di-ō-gram, *n.* [*Cardio-*, and Gr. *gramma*, a writing.] The record traced by a cardiograph.

çär′di-ō-grȧph, *n.* [*Cardio-*, and Gr. *graphein*, to write.] An instrument which records the force and intervals of heart-beats.

çär″di-ō-graph′iç, *a.* Pertaining to or recorded by a cardiograph.

çär′di-oid, *n.* [Gr. *kardioeidēs*, heartshaped; *kardia*, heart, and *eidos*, form.] A figure consisting of two combined curves, so called from its resemblance to a heart.

çär′di-oid, *a.* Characteristic of the *Cardiidæ*.

çär″di-ō-in-hib′i-tō-ry, *a.* [*Cardio-*, and LL. *inhibitorius*; *in*, in, and *habere*, to have, hold.] Curbing or stopping the heart's action.

çär-di-ol′ō-ġy, *n.* [*Cardio-*, and Gr. *-logia*, from *legein*, to speak.] The science which treats of the heart.

çär-di-om′e-tẽr, *n.* [*Cardio-*, and Gr. *metron*, measure.] An instrument for ascertaining and measuring the strength of the heart's action and of the pulse.

çär-di-om′e-try, *n.* [*Cardio-*, and Gr. *-metria*, from *metron*, a measure.] Measurement of the heart, as by sounding or tapping on the chest.

çär-di-op′ȧ-thy, *n.* [*Cardio-*, and Gr. *-patheia*, from *pathein*, to suffer.] Any disorder of the heart.

çär″di-ō-per″i-çär-dī′tis, *n.* [*Cardio-*, and Gr. *perikardion*, the pericardium.] Inflammation of the heart extending to the pericardium or membrane surrounding it.

çär″di-ō-sphyg′mō-grȧph, *n.* A cardiograph and sphygmograph in one.

çär-dī′tis, *n.* [From Gr. *kardia*, the heart, and *-itis*.] Inflammation of the fleshy substance of the heart.

Çär′di-um, *n.* [L., from Gr. *kardia*, heart.] The true cockles, the type genus of the family *Cardiidæ*.

çär′dō, *n.*; *pl.* **çär′di-nēş.** [L., a hinge.] The connecting joint of an insect's maxilla; also, the connecting ligament or hinge of a double shell.

çär′dol, *n.* An oleaginous yellow liquid obtained from the shell of the cashew-nut; of service for blistering purposes.

çär-dọọn′, *n.* [ME. *cardoun*; OFr. *cardon*; Sp. *cardon*, a cardoon, thistle; LL. *cardo*; L. *carduus*, a thistle.] A species of *Cynara*, resembling the artichoke, but larger.

Çär′dū-us, *n.* [L., a thistle.] The thistles; a botanical genus of the natural order *Compositæ*, containing numerous species, freely distributed over the northern portions of the globe.

Carduus benedictus; an old term for the herb *blessed thistle*.

çâre, *n.* [ME. *care*; AS. *cearu, caru*, sorrow, anxiety; O.H.G. *kara, chara*, a lament.]

1. Concern; anxiety; solicitude; noting some degree of pain in the mind, from apprehension of evil; as, oppressed with the *care* of many things.

2. Caution; a looking to; regard; attention, or heed, with a view to safety or protection; as, to take *care* of yourself.

3. Charge or oversight, implying concern for safety and prosperity; as, he was under the *care* of a physician.

4. The object of *care*, or watchful regard and attention; as, she is his constant *care*.

Care Sunday; see *Carl*, n. 3.

Syn.—Anxiety, solicitude, concern, attention, caution, trouble, precaution, forethought, heed, regard, management, oversight.—*Care* belongs primarily to the intellect, and becomes painful from overburdening thought; *anxiety* is a state of painful uneasiness from the dread of evil; *solicitude* and *concern* express the same feeling in diminished degrees.

çâre, *v.i.*; cared, *pt., pp.*; caring, *ppr.* [ME. *carien, caren*; AS. *cearian*, to be anxious, from *cearin*, anxiety, sorrow.]

1. To be anxious or solicitous; to be concerned about.

> Master, *carest* thou not that we perish?
> —Mark iv. 38.

2. To be inclined or disposed; to have regard to; with *for* before a noun, and *to* before a verb; as, he does not *care for* dancing; he does not *care to* dance.

To care for; to guard against danger or trouble; to have regard for; to have friendship or love for another.

çâre′-çrāzed, *a.* Broken or disordered by care or solicitude; as, a *care-crazed* mother.

çȧ-reen′, *v.t.*; careened, *pt., pp.*; careening, *ppr.* [Fr. *carener*, to careen, from *carene, carine*; L. *carina*, the keel of a ship.] In nautical language, to heave or bring (a ship) so as to lie on one side, for the purpose of calking, repairing, cleansing, or the like.

çȧ-reen′, *v.i.* To incline to one side, as a ship under a press of sail.

çȧ-reen′, *n.* 1. The act of careening.

2. The position of being inclined to one side.

3. A rolling movement.

çȧ-reen′āġe, *n.* 1. Cost of careening vessels.

2. A place where vessels are careened for the purpose of making repairs.

çȧ-reen′ing, *n.* The act of heaving down on one side, or inclining, as a ship.

çȧ-reer′, *n.* [Early modern Eng. *careere, carreer*; Fr. *carriere*, a road, race-course; OFr. *carier*, to carry by wagon; L. *carrus*, a wagon.]

1. A course; a race, or running; a rapid running; speed in motion; as, a horse in full *career*.

2. The course of life, whether of business activity or purposeless leisure; the general course of experience or conduct in life; in particular, a professional or public course of life.

3. In horsemanship, (a) the ground on which a race is run; (b) in the manège, the ring inclosed with a barrier.

4. In falconry, a flight or tour of the hawk, about one hundred and twenty yards.

Syn.—Course, success, walk, line, progress, history, way or experience of life, passage, race.

çȧ-reer′, *v.i.*; careered, *pt., pp.*; careering, *ppr.* To move or run rapidly, as a sailing vessel.

çâre′fụl, *a.* [ME. *careful*; AS. *cearful, carful*, from *cearu*, anxiety, and *full*, full.]

1. Full of care; anxious; solicitous. [Obs.]

2. Provident; attentive to support and protect; generally with *of*; as, *careful of* her health.

3. Watchful; cautious; giving good heed; as, be *careful* to maintain good works.

4. Filling with care or solicitude; exposing to concern, anxiety, or trouble; full of cares.

> By him that raised me to this *careful* height.
> —Shak.

Syn.—Attentive, solicitous, thoughtful, heedful, anxious, watchful, provident, circumspect.

çâre′fụl-ly, *adv.* 1. With care, anxiety, or solicitude.

2. Heedfully; watchfully; attentively; cautiously.

çâre′fụl-ness, *n.* 1. Anxiety; solicitude.

> Drink thy water with trembling and with *carefulness*. —Ezek. xii. 18.

2. Heedfulness; caution; vigilance in guarding against evil and providing for safety.

çâre′less, *a.* 1. Having no care; heedless; negligent; unthinking; inattentive; regardless; unmindful; followed by *of* or *about*; as, a mother, *careless of* or *about* her children, is an unnatural parent.

2. Free from care or anxiety; whence, undisturbed; cheerful.

> Thus wisely *careless*, innocently gay.—Pope.

3. Done or said without care; unconsidered; as, a *careless* throw; a *careless* expression.

4. Not regarding with care; unmoved by; unconcerned for; as, *careless of* money; *careless of* consequences.

5. Contrived without art; spontaneous; easy; also untidy; as, *careless* attire; *careless* habits.

Syn.—Heedless, inattentive, incautious, inconsiderate, negligent, thoughtless, unconcerned, unmindful.

çâre′less-ly, *adv.* In a careless manner; negligently; heedlessly; inattentively; without care.

çâre′less-ness, *n.* Heedlessness; inattention; negligence.

çȧ-rēne′, *n.* [LL. *carena*, a corruption of *quarentena*, from L. *quadraginta*, forty.] A fast lasting forty days. [Obs.]

çȧ-ress′, *v.t.*; caressed, *pt., pp.*; caressing, *ppr.* [Fr. *caresser*, from *caresse*, a caress.] To treat with fondness, affection, or kindness; to fondle; to embrace with tender affection, as a parent a child; to touch or speak to with affection.

Syn.—Embrace, fondle, salute, pet, coddle, pamper.

çȧ-ress′, *n.* [Fr. *caresse*; L. *carus*, dear, precious; from Sans. root *kam*, to love, desire.] An act of endearment; any act or expression of affection; as, conjugal *caresses*; his very words were *caresses*.

Syn.—Endearment, blandishment, fondling, wheedling.

çȧ-ress′ing-ly, *adv.* In a caressing manner.

çā′ret, *n.* [L. *caret*, there is wanting; from *carere*, to want.] In writing and proofreading, this mark, ∧, which shows that something, omitted in the line, is interlined above or inserted in the margin, and should be read in the place thus indicated.

çā′ret, *n.* [Sp. *careta*, a pasteboard mask; dim. of *cara*, the face.] A species of sea-turtle called the *hawkbill*.

çär-ette′, *n.* A small omnibus with a low body. [Local, U. S.]

çāre′-tūned, *a.* Tuned by care; mournful.

çāre′wōrn, *a.* Harassed, tired, or burdened with care; having the appearance caused by worry or anxiety.

Çā′rex, *n.* [L., a sedge, rush.]

1. A widespread genus of perennial herbaceous plants of which the sedge is the type, and *Cyperaceæ* the order.

2. [c—*pl.* çā′ri-çēs.] A sedge-grass of this order.

çärf, *v.*, past tense of *carve*. [Obs.]

çär′gȧ-ṣŏn, *n.* A cargo. [Obs.]

çär′gō, *n.* [Sp. *cargo*, *carga*, burden, load, from *cargar*, to load, charge, impose taxes.] The lading or freight of a ship; the goods, merchandise, or whatever is conveyed in a ship or other merchant vessel. The lading within the hold is called the inboard *cargo*, in distinction from horses, cattle, and other things carried on deck.

çär′gọọse, *n.* [Gael. and Ir. *cir*, *cior*, a crest, comb, and *goose*.] A fowl belonging to the genus *Colymbus*; called also the *crested grebe*. [Local, Eng.]

çar′i-ȧ-çöu, çar′jȧ-çöu, *n.* [S. Am.] A deer of the genus *Cariacus*.

Çȧ-rī′ȧ-çus, *n.* [L., from *cariacou*.] A genus of deer smaller than animals of the genus *Cervus*, and of which the white-tailed or Virginia deer is a good example.

çȧ-rï-ä′mȧ, *n.* [Native name.] A South American bird of large size having remarkably long legs. It is the *Cariama cristata* which lives on small reptiles. [See *Seriema*.]

Çar′ib, *n.* [W. Ind. *Carib*, a valiant man.] A term applied in particular to any member of a native tribe living in the northern parts of South America, in Central America, and the West Indies. *Caribs* were the native inhabitants encountered by Columbus and other Spanish explorers, but are now almost extinct.

Çar-ib-bē′ăn, *a.* Relating to the Caribs, to their islands, or to the Caribbean sea.

Çar′ib-bee, *n.* A Carib.

çar′i-bē, *n.* [Sp., a cannibal.] A voracious fresh-water fish of South America, belonging to the genus *Serrasalmo*, having a scaly body and a naked head. When encountered in schools they are dangerous, as they will even attack and kill a human being.

çar′i-böu, çar′i-bọọ, *n.* [Canadian Fr.] The reindeer of North America, including those found in wild woodlands, *Rangifer caribou*, also those of the barren lands of the Arctic regions, or barren-ground *caribou*.

Çar′i-çȧ, *n.* [L., a fig.] A genus of American trees found for the most part in the tropics, one species of which is popularly called *papaw*; it is the type of the family *Caricaceæ*.

Çar-i-çā′cē-æ, *n.pl.* [From L. *carica*, a fig, and *-aceæ*.] A family of dicotyledonous trees found in the tropics of America.

çar′i-çȧ-tūre, *n.* [Fr. *caricature*; It. *caricatura*, a satirical picture, from *caricare*, to load, exaggerate.]

1. A picture or description in which beauties are concealed and blemishes exaggerated, but still bearing a resemblance to the object.

2. The exaggeration of defects in anything, with a view of ridiculing it.

Syn.—Burlesque, exaggeration, farce, imitation, mimicry, parody, travesty.

çar′i-çȧ-tūre, *v.t.*; caricatured, *pt.*, *pp.*; caricaturing, *ppr.* To make or draw a caricature of; to represent, as by a caricature.

çar′i-çȧ-tūr-ist, *n.* One who caricatures others.

çar-i-çog′rȧ-phy, *n.* [L. *carex* (*-icis*), a sedge, and Gr. *graphein*, to write.] A description of the plants of the genus *Carex*, or sedge.

çar-i-çol′ō-ġist, *n.* One versed in the botany of the sedges.

çar′i-çous, *a.* [L. *carica*, a fig.] Resembling a fig; an epithet given to tumors that resemble a fig, such as occur often in the piles.

çā′ri-ēṣ, *n.* [L.] 1. The mortification of a bone piecemeal; an ulcer of a bone; as, *caries* of the teeth.

2. In botany, a wasting disease of vegetable tissue.

çar′il-lŏn, *n.* [Fr., a chime of bells, originally composed of four.] A little bell; also, a simple air in music, adapted to the performance of bells, etc.; a set of bells for playing tunes.

çȧ-rī′nȧ, *n.*; *pl.* **çȧ-rī′næ.** [L., the keel of a ship.]

1. The keel of the blossom, or the united petals of certain leguminous plants, which envelops the organs of fructification; also, a keel-like ridge on the glumes or husks of grass-seeds.

2. In zoölogy, the keel or ridge of a bird's breastbone.

3. [C—] One of the divisions of the constellation Argo.

Çar-i-nā′ri-ȧ, *n.* [L. *carina*, the keel of a ship, and *-aria*; so called from their shape.] A genus of marine heteropods, the nucleus and gills of which are covered with a thin glassy shell, not unlike a bonnet in shape.

Çar-i-nā′tæ, *n.pl.* A grand division of birds which includes all the living varieties except those belonging to the ostrich family, whose breasts are flat rather than keel-like.

çar′i-nāte, çar′i-nā-ted, *a.* [L. *carinatus*, from *carina*, a keel.] In botany, shaped like the keel of a ship; having a longitudinal prominence on the back, like a keel; applied to a calyx, corol, or leaf.

çar′i-ōle, *n.* [Fr.] A small open carriage; a covered cart; a kind of calash.

çar-i-op′sis, *n.* See *Caryopsis*.

çā-ri-os′i-ty, *n.* [L. *cariosus*, from *caries*, decay, and *-ity*.] The condition of suffering from caries, or of being carious.

çā′ri-ous, *a.* [L. *cariosus*, from *caries*, decay.] Mortified; ulcerated, as a bone.

çärk, *n.* [ME. *cark*, care, anxiety; AS. *carc*; W. *carc*, care, anxiety.] Care; anxiety; concern; solicitude; distress. [Obs.]

çärk, *v.i.* To be careful, anxious. [Obs.]

çärk, *v.t.* To annoy, worry, burden, make anxious, or vex. [Obs.]

çär′kȧ-net, *n.* See *Carcanet*.

çärk′ing, *a.* Distressing; perplexing.

çärl, *n.* [ME. *carl*, *carle*; AS. *ceorl*, a man, a churl.]

1. A rude, rustic, rough, brutal man; a churl.

2. A seed-bearing hemp-plant; called also *carl-hemp*.

3. [*pl.*] A dish of gray peas steeped in water and then fried in butter or fat, eaten on *Carl* or *Carling Sunday*, the second Sabbath before Easter; also written *carlings*.

çär′lin, *n.* [Ice. *karlinna*, a woman.] In Scotland, the name for an aged woman.

çär′line, çär′ling, *n.* [Fr. *carlingue*, Sp. *carlinga*, a timber of a ship.] A piece of timber in a ship, ranging fore and aft, from one deck beam to another, directly over the keel, serving as a foundation for the body of the ship.

Carline knees; timbers in a ship, lying across from the sides to the hatchway and serving to sustain the deck.

çär′line, *n.* A thistle-like plant of the genus *Carlina*.

Carline thistle; the popular name of a prickly plant found in Asia and Europe. It was used by Charlemagne's army as a cure for the plague and thus derived its name.

çär-lï′nō, çär′line, *n.* [It. *carlino*; named from *Charles VI.*] An Italian silver coin varying from four to sixteen U. S. cents; also, a Sardinian gold coin worth about $28, U. S. money.

çärl′ish, *a.* Rude; boorish; churlish.

Çär′list, *n.* An adherent to the claims of Don Carlos of Spain or Charles X. of France.

çär′lōad, *n.* 1. The capacity of a railroad car, or the weight which it can safely carry.

2. Specifically, in the United States, the capacity or carrying-weight of a freight-car: (a) in weight, from 20,000 to 30,000 pounds; (b) in various products and manufactures, approximately 9,000 feet of boards, 20 head of cattle, 300 bushels of corn, 300 sacks or 150 barrels of flour, 50 head of hogs, 70 barrels of salt, 430 bushels of potatoes, and 340 bushels of wheat.

Used also adjectively; as, he made his purchase in *carload* lots.

çär′lock, *n.* [Fr., from Russ. *karlukŭ*.] A sort of isinglass from Russia, made of the sturgeon's bladder, and used in clarifying wine.

çär′lot, *n.* A countryman; a carl. [Obs.]

Çär-lō-vin′ġi-ăn, *a.* Pertaining to Charlemagne; as, the *Carlovingian* race of kings.

Çär-lō-vin′ġi-ăn, *n.* A member of the Frankish imperial dynasty founded by Charlemagne; also written *Carolingian*.

çär-mȧ-gnōle′ (-nyōl′), *n.* [Fr., from *Carmagnola*, in Piedmont.]

1. [C—] A popular song and dance much enjoyed during the French Revolution, and taking its name from the garments worn by the revolutionists.

2. The costume worn by the French revolutionists.

3. A bombastic report issued by a French revolutionist, or other incendiary.

çär′măn, *n.* A man whose employment is to drive a cart, or to convey goods and other things in a cart.

Çär′mel-in, *a.* and *n.* Same as *Carmelite*.

Çär′mel-īte, *n.* and *a.* I. *n.* A monk or a nun of the order established on Mount Carmel, Syria, in the twelfth century, and known as the Order of Our Lady of Mount Carmel.

II. *a.* Belonging to the order of Carmelites.

çär′mi-nāte, *n.* A salt of carminic acid.

çär′mi-nā-ted, *a.* Combined or impregnated with carmine; as, *carminated* coke, a pigment used in painting.

çär-min′ȧ-tive, *a.* Expelling wind from the body; warming; antispasmodic.

çär-min′ȧ-tive, *n.* [L. *carminatus*, pp. of *carminare*, to card, to cleanse; from *carere*, to card.] A medicine which tends to expel wind, or to remedy colic and flatulencies.

Carmelite.

çär′mine (*or* -mīn), *n.* [Fr. *carmin*; Sp. *carmin*; LL. *carmesinus*, purple color, crimson; from *kermes*; Ar. *qirmizī*, *qirmiz*, crimson; Sans. *krimija*, produced by an insect; *krimi*, an insect, and *jan*, to produce.]

1. A powder or pigment, of a beautiful red or crimson color, bordering on purple. It is prepared by dissolving cochineal in an alkaline lye, and precipitating it by alum. This is properly a *lake*, or a combination of the coloring principle of cochineal with alumina.

2. The pure coloring matter or coloring principle of cochineal; precipitated, by spontaneous evaporation, from the alcoholic tincture of cochineal, in the form of crystals of a fine red color.

3. Carminic acid.

Burnt carmine; a pigment, reddish purple in color, obtained by burning cochineal carmine.

çär-min′iç, *a.* Pertaining to carmine.

Carminic acid; a purple compound, $C_{17}H_{18}O_{10}$.

çär′mot, *n.* In alchemy, a name signifying the supposed material of the philosopher's stone.

çär′nāġe, *n.* [Fr. *carnage*; It. *carnaggio*; LL. *carnaticum*, a tribute of animals; L. *caro*, *carnis*, flesh.]

1. Literally, flesh or heaps of flesh, as in shambles.

2. Slaughter; great destruction of men; havoc; massacre.

Syn.—Slaughter, massacre, butchery.—*Carnage* has reference to the number of dead bodies; *slaughter* respects the act of taking away life, and the circumstances of the agent; *massacre* and *butchery* refer to the circumstances of the objects who are the sufferers of the action.

çär′năl, *a.* [L. *carnalis*, from *caro*, *carnis*, flesh.]

1. Pertaining to flesh; fleshly; sensual; as, *carnal* pleasure.

2. Being in the natural state; unregenerate.

> The *carnal* mind is enmity against God.
> —Rom. viii. 7.

3. Lecherous; lustful; libidinous; given to sensual indulgence.

4. Bloody; cruel. [Obs.]

5. Related by natural descent or blood. [Obs.]

Carnal knowledge; sexual intercourse.

çär′năl-iṣm, *n.* The indulgence of carnal appetites.

çär′năl-ist, *n.* One given to the indulgence of sensual appetites.

çär-nal′i-ty, *n.* 1. Fleshly lust or desires, or the indulgence of those lusts; sensuality.

2. Grossness of mind or desire; love of sensual pleasures.

çär′năl-īze, *v.t.*; carnalized, *pt.*, *pp.*; carnalizing, *ppr.* To make carnal; to debase to carnality.

çär′năl-līte, *n.* [Named after Von *Carnall*, a Prussian.] A chemical compound sometimes occurring with rock salt; a hydrous chlorid of magnesium and potassium.

çär′năl-ly, *adv.* In a carnal manner; according to the flesh; in a manner to gratify the flesh or sensual desire.

çär′năl-mīnd″ed, *a.* Worldly-minded.

çär′năl-mīnd″ed-ness, *n.* Grossness of mind.

çär′nȧ-ry, *n.* [L. *carnarium*, from *caro*, *carnis*, flesh.] A charnel house or vault used for keeping human bones which have been disinterred.

çär-nas′si-ăl, *a.* [Fr. *carnassier*, carnivorous; from L. *caro*, flesh.] Fitted for flesh-eating; as, the *carnassial* tooth; particularly the last premolar in carnivorous animals.

çär′nāte, *a.* [L. *carnatus*, from *caro*, *carnis*, flesh.] Having flesh.

çär-nā′tion, *n.* [L. *carnatio*, fleshiness, from *caro*, *carnis*, flesh.]

1. Flesh color; [*pl.*] parts of a picture which are naked or without drapery, exhibiting the natural color of the flesh.

2. The popular name of a species of the genus of plants called *Dianthus*, so named from the color of the flower.

3. A tropical leguminous shrub, known also as the *Spanish bean.*

çär-nā'tioned, *a.* Having a carnation, flesh, or pink color.

Two varieties of Carnation.

çär-nau'bȧ, *n.* [Braz.] The wax-palm of Brazil.

çär-nēl'iăn, *n.* [Fr. *cornaline*; It. *cornalina*, a dim. from L. *cornu*, a horn.] A silicious stone, a variety of chalcedony, of a deep-red, flesh-red, or reddish-white color. It is tolerably hard, capable of a good polish, and used for seals. Also spelled *cornelian.*

çär'nē-ous, *a.* [L. *carneus*, from *caro, carnis*, flesh.] Fleshy; having the qualities of flesh.

çär'ney, *n.* [L. *carneus*, fleshy, from *caro, carnis*, flesh.] A disease of horses, in which the mouth is so furred that they cannot eat.

çär'niç, *a.* [L. *caro*, flesh.] Pertaining to flesh. *Carnic acid*; a soluble acid derived from muscular tissue.

çär'ni-fex, *n.* [L. *caro, carnis*, flesh, and *facere*, to make.] An executioner; primarily, the public executioner of the lowest criminals in ancient Rome; hence, applied as a term of degradation.

çär"ni-fi-çā'tion, *n.* A turning to flesh, as the tissues of the vital organs in certain diseases.

çär'ni-fȳ, *v.i.* [Fr. *carnifier*; It. *carnificare*; L. *carnificare*; *caro, carnis*, flesh, and *facere*, to make.] To form flesh; to receive flesh in growth.

çär'nin, çär'nine, *n.* [L. *caro, carnis*, flesh.] A chemical salt found in meat-extract; it is white, crystalline, and contains nitrogen.

çär'ni-văl, *n.* [Fr. *carnaval*; It. *carnovale*; from LL. *carnelevamen*, for *carnis levamen*; *carnis*, genit. of *caro*, flesh, and *levamen*, solace, mitigation, from *levare*, to lighten.]

1. A festival celebrated with merriment and revelry in Roman Catholic countries, during the week before Lent.

2. Any festival, especially when accompanied by a masquerade, of an excessive or riotous nature.

Syn.—Revel, rout, festivity, masquerade.

Çär-niv'ō-rȧ, *n.* [L., neut. pl. of *carnivorus*; *caro, carnis*, flesh, and *vorare*, to eat.] An order of mammals having large, sharp teeth and powerful jaws, adapted to flesh-eating. Some, however, such as bears, live also on vegetable food.

çär"niv-ō-rac'i-ty, *n.* Greediness of appetite for flesh.

çär'ni-vōre, *n.* A flesh-eating animal or an insect-eating plant.

çär-niv'ō-rous, *a.* Eating or feeding on flesh; an epithet applied to animals which naturally seek flesh for food; to insectivorous plants; to caustics or other substances which destroy flesh.

çär-nos'i-ty, *n.* [Fr. *carnosité*; LL. *carnositas*, from *caro, carnis*, flesh.]

1. Fleshiness. [Obs.]

2. An abnormal growth of flesh upon any portion of the body.

çär'nous, çär-nōse', *a.* 1. Fleshy; pertaining to flesh.

2. In botany, of a fleshy character; as, *carnous* leaves.

çar'ŏb, *n.* [Fr. *caroube*, from It. *carrubo*, from Ar. *kharrūb*, bean-pods.] A leguminous evergreen tree, *Ceratonia Siliqua*, native of southern Europe and northern Africa. The long, flat pods which grow on this tree are fed to animals, and are sometimes eaten by people. Also called *St. John's bread, carob bean*, and *algaroba bean.*

çȧ-rōche', *n.* A carriage of pleasure. [Obs.]

çȧ-rōched' (-rōcht'), *a.* Placed in a caroche. [Obs.]

çar'oigne (-oin), *n.* [OFr. *caroigne*; LL. *caronia*, a carcass, from L. *caro*, flesh.] A dead body; carrion. [Obs.]

çar'ŏl, *n.* [ME. *carol, carole*; OFr. *carole*, a kind of dance, a Christmas song.]

1. A song of joy, rapture, or gladness; as, the *carol* of birds.

2. A religious song; a hymn of praise; as, a Christmas *carol.*

3. A merry song or lively music.

çar'ŏl, *v.t.*; caroled *or* carolled, *pt., pp.*; caroling *or* carolling, *ppr.* 1. To celebrate or praise with song.

2. To sing in joyful notes.

çar'ŏl, *v.i.* To sing with joy; to warble.

çar'ŏl, çar'rŏl, *n.* [OFr. *carole*, a circular space.]

1. Formerly, a cell or stall built against a window on the inner side, as a study; a bay-window.

2. A stall in a cloister.

3. A chain, generally of flowers or stones. [Obs.]

çar'ō-lī, *n.*, pl. of *carolus.*

çar'ō-lin, *n.* [LL. *Carolinus*, from *Carolus*, Charles.] A current gold coin of Sweden, worth about two dollars; a German gold coin formerly worth about five dollars.

Çar'ō-line (*or* -lin), *a.* [LL. *Carolinus*, from *Carolus*, Charles.] Relating to Charles, especially those of that name belonging to the royal families of England and Spain; as, the *Caroline* age of England; the *Caroline* islands, etc.

çar'ŏl-ing, *n.* A song of praise or devotion.

Çar-ō-lin'gi-ăn, *a.* Carlovingian.

Çar-ō-lin'i-ăn, *a.* Pertaining to the Carolinas.

Çar-ō-lin'i-ăn, *n.* A native or inhabitant of the Carolinas.

çar-ō-lit'iç, *a.* In architecture, decorated with branches.

çar'ō-lus, *n.*; *pl.* **çar'ō-lus-eş, çar'ō-lī.** [LL. *Carolus*, Charles.] An English gold coin first struck during the reign of Charles I., and valued at twenty shillings.

çar'ŏm, *n.* [Corruption of Fr. *caramboler*, to carom; *carambolage*, a carom; *carambole*, the red billiard ball.] A shot in billiards in which the cue-ball strikes successively two or more balls; also, the stroke used in making such a shot, termed in England a *cannon.* Also spelled *carrom.*

çar'ŏm, *v.i.*; caromed, *pt., pp.*; caroming, *ppr.* To make a carom, as in billiards.

çar'ō-mel, *n.* See *Caramel.*

çar-ō-tel', çar-ō-teel', *n.* [E. Ind.] A bundle, tierce, or cask of dried fruits weighing about 700 pounds; used in East Indian commerce.

çȧ-rot'iç, *a.* [Sp. *carótico*; Gr. *karōtikos*, stupefying; from *karoun*, to stupefy; *karos*, stupor, heavy sleep.]

1. Characterized by or pertaining to stupor.

2. In anatomy, carotid; a flow of blood to the brain through the *carotic* or *carotid* arteries, caused by compression or otherwise, was thought to produce stupor.

çȧ-rot'id, çȧ-rot'id-ăl, *a.* Pertaining or adjacent to the carotids; as, a *carotid* canal.

çȧ-rot'id, *n.* [Gr. *karōtis*, pl. *karōtides*, the two great arteries of the neck; from *karoun*, to plunge into sleep or stupor; so called from the belief that sleep was caused by the blood flowing through them.] One of the two carotid arteries which convey the blood from the aorta to the head.

çȧ-rō'tin, *n.* [L. *carota*, the carrot.] A tasteless red crystalline compound extracted from carrots, of which it is the coloring matter.

çȧ-rouş'ăl, *n.* [Fr. *carrousel*, a tilting-match; It. *carosello*, from *garosello*, dim. of *garoso*, quarrelsome, from *gara*, strife, contention.] A rough, noisy feast or festival; a revel.

Syn.—Banquet, feast, festival, orgies, revel, festivity, wassail.

çȧ-rouşe', *v.i.*; caroused, *pt., pp.*; carousing, *ppr.* To drink hard; to guzzle; to participate in a carousal.

çȧ-rouşe', *v.t.* To drink deeply or boisterously; as, he *caroused* many a cup of wine. [Obs.]

çȧ-rouşe', *n.* [OFr. *carous, carousse*, a drinking-bout; G. *garaus*, all out, a finishing stroke; *gar*, quite, completely, and *aus*, out.] A drinking-bout; a full draught of liquor.

çȧ-rouş'el, *n.* A merry-go-round.

çȧ-rouş'ēr, *n.* A drinker; a toper; a noisy reveler or bacchanalian.

çȧ-rouş'ing-ly, *adv.* In a carousing manner.

çärp, *v.i.*; carped, *pt., pp.*; carping, *ppr.* 1. Literally, to snap or catch at, or to pick. Hence, to censure, cavil, or find fault, particularly without reason, or petulantly; followed by *at.*

2. To prattle; to talk. [Obs.]

çärp, *v.t.* [ME. *carpen*, to tell, say; Ice. *karpa*, to boast, brag; associated with L. *carpere*, to snatch, envy, slander.] To tell; to say; to censure; to find fault with. [Obs.]

çärp, *n.* [Fr. *carpe*; LL. *carpa*, a carp.] A long large-scaled fresh-water fish, genus *Cyprinus*, that is largely used as food and bred in ponds. It breeds rapidly, grows to a large size, and lives to a great age. Several varieties have been propagated by pisciculture, including the *leather-carp* and the *mirror-carp.* The *carp-sucker* is a species common to the United States.

çär'păl, *a.* [L. *carpus*, the wrist.] Pertaining to the carpus or wrist.

Carpal angle; the angle at the joint nearest the body in the folded wing of a bird; when the wing is measured for length, the distance is taken from this angle to the tip of the longest quill.

çär-pā'lē, *n.*; *pl.* **çär-pā'li-ȧ.** A bone of the carpus or wrist, particularly one articulating with the metacarpals.

Çär-pā'thi-ăn, *a.* Pertaining to a range of mountains between Poland, Hungary, and Transylvania.

çär'pel, çär-pel'lum, *n.* [From Gr. *karpos*, fruit.] In botany, a small seed-vessel or pericarp, that is, one of a group produced by a single flower.

çär'pel-lā-ry, *a.* Belonging to carpels, or containing them.

çär'pen-tēr, *n.* [ME. *carpenter*; OFr. *carpentier*; LL. *carpentarius*, a carpenter, wagon-maker, from L. *carpentum*, a two-wheeled carriage, a cart.] An artificer who works in timber; a framer and builder of houses, ships, etc.

çär'pen-tēr-ant, *n.* Any ant whose habit is to excavate a habitation in the wood of dead trees; specifically, *Formica pennsylvanica.*

çär'pen-tēr-bee, *n.* Any bee of the genus *Xylocopa* (literally, woodcutters), which makes its nest and habitation by boring elongated chambers in dry, sound wood.

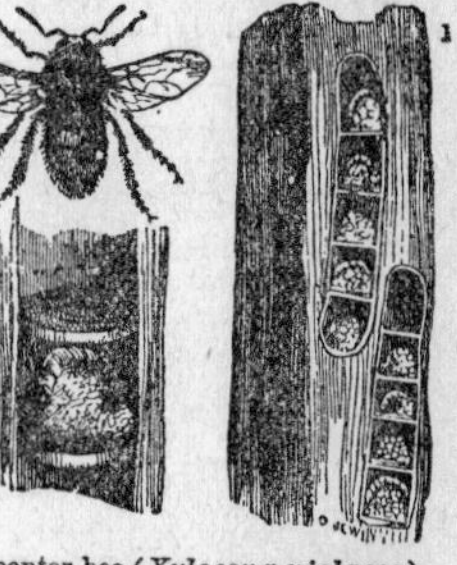

Carpenter-bee (*Xylocopa violacea*), one-half the natural size.
1. A piece of wood bored by the bee, and grubs and food deposited in the cells.
2. Two of the cells drawn larger in order to show the partitions.

çär'pen-tēr-bird, *n.* A bird that makes holes or openings in the wood of dead trees; specifically, the *Melanerpes formicivorus* of California, distinguished for picking holes in trees and depositing in them acorns which become the home of the larvæ of insects, thus furnishing food for the bird.

çär'pen-tēr-ing, *n.* The art, the vocation, or the work of a carpenter.

çär'pen-tēr-mŏth, *n.* A moth whose larvæ, called *carpenter-worms*, subsist by boring beneath the bark of trees; any moth of the subfamily *Cossinæ.*

çär'pen-tēr's-hērb, *n.* A herb whose application was supposed to heal wounds made by edge-tools; specifically, the *Brunella vulgaris.*

çär'pen-tēr-wŏrm, *n.* See *Carpenter-moth.*

çär'pen-try, *n.* 1. The art of cutting, framing, and joining timber, in the construction of buildings.

2. The constructive work of a carpenter, such as buildings or portions of them.

çärp'ēr, *n.* One who carps; a caviler.

çär'pet, *v.t.*; carpeted, *pt., pp.*; carpeting, *ppr.* To cover with a carpet; to spread with carpets; to cover as with a carpet; as, nature *carpets* the lawn with green.

çär'pet, *n.* [ME. *carpette*; OFr. *carpite*, a carpet, a kind of cloth; LL. *carpita, carpeta*, a kind of thick woolen cloth, from L. *carpere*, to card, to pluck.] A pliant covering for floors or stairs; figuratively, any covering resembling *carpet*; as, nature's soft *carpet* of moss.

Brussels carpet; see under *Brussels.*

To be on the carpet; to be under consideration; to be the subject of deliberation.

çär'pet-bag, *n.* A traveler's bag made of carpet; any capacious bag for holding one's personal belongings while traveling.

çär'pet-bag"gēr, *n.* A newcomer, especially an adventurer; originated in the United States and applied as a contemptuous epithet to Northern office-holders in the South during the period of reconstruction after the Civil War.

çär'pet-bee"tle, çär'pet-bug, *n.* The *Anthrenus scrophulariæ*, a beetle whose larvæ infest and feed upon carpets and other woolen fabrics; also called *buffalo-bug.*

çär'pet-ing, *n.* The act of laying carpet; the material of which carpets are made.

çär'pet-knight (-nīt), *n.* A knight who spends his time in luxury rather than in the strenuous labors of a true knight; an effeminate hero of the drawing-room.

çär'pet-mŏn"gēr, *n.* 1. A carpet dealer.

2. An effeminate gallant; one fond of ease.

çär'pet-mŏth, *n.* Same as *Carpet-beetle.*

çär'pet-snāke, *n.* Same as *Diamond-snake.*

çär'pet-sweep"ēr, *n.* A mechanical device for sweeping carpets, consisting essentially of rotating brushes which carry the dust into a covered receptacle.

çär'pet-wāy, *n.* A grassy strip left unplowed around the margin of a field.

çär'pet-weed, *n.* A low prostrate herbaceous plant which makes a carpet-like covering on the ground in southern climates, belonging to the pink family; specifically, *Mollugo verticillata.*

çär-phō-lō'gi-ȧ, çär-phol'ō-gy, *n.* Same as *Floccillation.*

çärp'ing, *n.* and *a.* I. *n.* The act of caviling; a cavil; unreasonable censure.

II. *a.* Caviling; captious; censorious.

çärp'ing-ly, *adv.* Captiously; in a carping manner.

çär-pin-te'rō, *n.* See *Carpenter-bird.*

cärp′=louse, *n.*; *pl.* **cärp′=lice.** A crustaceous parasite of the family *Argulidæ*, which is found upon the carp and other species of fish.

cär′pō-. A combining form from L. *carpus*, the wrist, and used in medicine and anatomy to indicate relation to the wrist.

cär′pō-. A combining form from Gr. *karpos*, fruit, and used in botany and zoölogy; as, *carpophore*, *Carpophaga*.

cär-pō-bal′sȧ-mum, *n.* [*Carpo-*, and Gr. *balsamon*, balsam.] The balsamiferous dried fruit of the *Balsamodendron Gileadense*, or balm-of-Gilead tree of the Orient; also, the fragrant oil yielded by that fruit.

Cär-pō-crā′tiăn, *n.* and *a.* I. *n.* A believer in the doctrines of Carpocrates, a Gnostic of Alexandria living in the second century.

II. *a.* Related in any way to Carpocrates or to his teachings; specifically, having the essential quality of the doctrines of Carpocrates, i.e., the transmigration of the soul and the humanity of Christ, the latter purified, elevated, and strengthened in a superlative degree by his recollection of a previous state of exaltation.

cär-pō-gen′ic, cär-pog′e-nous, *a.* [*Carpo-*, and Gr. *genesis*, origin, birth.] Producing fruit; opposed to *sterile*.

cär-pō-gō′ni-um, *n.*; *pl.* **cär-pō-gō′ni-ȧ.** [*Carpo-*, and Gr. *-gonos*, from *gignesthai*, to beget, produce.] The unfructified swollen part of the female productive organ of certain algæ, which, after fertilization, develops a sporocarp.

cär′pō-līte, *n.* [*Carpo-*, and Gr. *lithos*, a stone.] The fossil of any kind of fruit, usually of a nut or hard seed; written also *carpolith*.

cär-pō-log′ig-ăl, *a.* Relating in any way to carpology.

cär-pol′ō-gist, *n.* One who makes a specialty of carpology.

cär-pol′ō-gy, *n.* [*Carpo-*, and Gr. *-logia*, from *legein*, to produce.] A description of fruits; more strictly, that division of botany which relates to the structure of seeds and seed-vessels, or of the fruit.

Cär-poph′ȧ-gȧ, *n.pl.* [Gr. *karpophagos*, fruit-eating; *karpos*, fruit, and *phagein*, to eat.]

1. Fruit-eating marsupials; specifically, *Phalangistidæ*.

2. Fruit-eating pigeons; specifically, *Carpophaginæ*.

cär-poph′ȧ-gous, *a.* Pertaining to the *Carpophaga*.

cär′pō-phōre, *n.* [Gr. *karpophoros*, bearing fruit; *karpos*, fruit, and *pherein*, to bear.] In botany, generally, the organ that supports the carpels; specifically, a very much elongated part of the receptacle, which is usually discoid.

cär′pō-phyl, *n.* [*Carpo-*, and Gr. *phyllon*, a leaf.] A carpel or modified leaf.

cär′pō-phȳte, *n.* [*Carpo-*, and Gr. *phyton*, a plant.] A cryptogamous plant, as the red seaweed, which upon fertilization bears spores and true fruit.

cär-pop′ō-dite, *n.* [*Carpo-*, and Gr. *pous*, *podos*, a foot.] That part of a crustacean's leg which most nearly answers to the wrist in man; counting from the body, the fifth division of a crustacean's leg.

cär′pos, *n.* [Gr. *karpos*, the wrist.] The distinguishing division of the carpopodite.

cär′pō-spērm, *n.* [*Carpo-*, and Gr. *sperma*, seed.] The oösphere of the red seaweed changed by fertilization.

cär′pō-spōre, *n.* [*Carpo-*, and *spora*, a sowing, generation.] A minute spore in the sporocarp of the red seaweed.

cär-pō-spōr′ic, *a.* Related in any way to a carpospore.

cär′pō-stōme, *n.* [*Carpo-*, and Gr. *stoma*, a mouth.] The opening through which the carpospores are discharged from the cystocarp of the red seaweed.

cärp′=suck″ēr, *n.* Any one of several varieties of North American fresh-water fishes belonging to the genus *Carpiodes* and related genera; called also *quillback* and *buffalo-fish*.

cär′pus, *n.* [L.] 1. In anatomy, that part of the skeleton forming the wrist, consisting of eight small bones, arranged in two rows.

2. In crustaceans, the carpos.

car′răck, *n.* Same as *Carack*.

car′rȧ-geen, car′rȧ-gheen (-gēn), *n.* [From *Carrageen*, near Waterford, Ireland.] A kind of cartilaginous edible seaweed, *Chondrus crispus*, found along rocky coasts; when dried known as *Irish moss*.

car-ran′chȧ, *n.* The Brazilian caracara, *Polyborus brasiliensis*.

car′rȧ-wāy, *n.* Same as *Caraway*.

car′rel, *n.* [Obs.] See *Carol*.

car′rel, *n.* [OFr. *carrel*, *quarrel*; LL. *quadrellus*, a square tile, a dart; L. *quadrum*, a square.]

1. An arrow with a four-pointed head used in a crossbow; a quarrel.

2. A fabric of the seventeenth century composed of silk and worsted.

3. A closet for study in a monastery.

car-re-lāge′ (-läzh′), *n.* [Fr., from OFr. *carrel*, *quarrel*, a square tile, dart.] Tiling; especially, patterned and variegated tiling laid in a floor; diamond-shaped tiling; called also *encaustic tile*.

car-re′tȧ, *n.* [Sp. Am.] A long, two-wheeled conveyance used chiefly in southwestern United States.

car′ri-ȧ-ble, *a.* Capable of being carried.

car′riage (-rij), *n.* [ME. *cariage*, baggage, transport; OFr. *cariage*, a cart, carriage, from *carier*, to carry.]

1. The act of carrying, bearing, transporting, or conveying; as, the *carriage* of goods.

2. The act of taking by an enemy; conquest; acquisition. [Obs.]

3. That which carries; a wheeled vehicle; any conveyance for carrying persons or things.

4. In mechanics, any solid, parallel portion of a machine which carries another part; as, the *carriage* of a typewriter.

5. The price or expense of carrying; transportation, whether by land or sea.

6. That which is carried; burden; baggage; tonnage. [Rare.]

7. In a moral sense, the manner of carrying oneself; behavior; conduct; deportment; personal manners.

8. Measures; practices; management.

Syn.—Bearing, behavior, demeanor, deportment, conduct, gait, manner, mien, pace, walk.

car′riage-ȧ-ble, *a.* Fit for the passage of a carriage, as a road or driveway; also, carriable, as a package or trunk.

car′riage=pōrch, *n.* A roofed structure over a driveway leading to the entrance of a house, for the protection of a carriage and its occupants.

car′ri-boo, *n.* Same as *Caribou*.

car′rick, *n.* [Scot.] The game of shinny; also, the ball used in the game.

car′rick, *n.* Same as *Carack*.

car′rick=bend, *n.* A particular kind of knot used in connecting hawsers.

car′rick=bitt, *n.* In a ship, one of the bitts which support the windlass.

car′ri-ēr, *n.* 1. One who or that which carries; a messenger.

2. One who or that which is employed to carry goods for compensation.

3. A person who carries disease germs in his system but himself remains immune; likewise any animal or thing which disseminates disease germs.

4. In machinery, any part which does the work of carrying; as, the lathe-*carrier*.

Common carrier; one who or a corporation which undertakes, for hire, to transport or carry persons or goods from one place to another, as a railroad or steamship company, etc. Such a carrier having the necessary accommodation is bound to perform the service of carrying for all persons without discrimination, upon the fixed or stipulated price being tendered, and in the case of a carrier of goods or freight is liable for all losses and injuries to the goods, except those which are unavoidable, i.e., not the fault of the carrier.

car′ri-ēr=pig″eŏn, *n.* A pigeon trained to fly between points which it has previously visited, carrying messages attached to the neck, leg, or wing.

car′ri-ēr=shell, *n.* In zoölogy, a univalve that conceals its shell by incrusting it with bits of shell, coral, and stones, the *Xenophora conchylophora*, family *Phoridæ*.

car′ri-ŏn, *n.* [ME. *carion*, *caryon*, *caraigne*; OFr. *caroigne*; LL. *coronia*, a carcass, from L. *caro*, flesh.]

1. The dead and putrefying body or flesh of animals; flesh so corrupted as to be unfit for food.

2. A worthless person; a term of reproach. [Obs.]

car′ri-ŏn, *a.* Relating to dead and putrefying carcasses; feeding on carrion; as, a *carrion*-crow.

car′ri-ŏn=bee″tle, *n.* A beetle which makes a habit of feeding on or depositing its eggs in decaying flesh.

car′ri-ŏn=buz″zărd, *n.* A name given to various scavenger-birds representing several genera and species; they are natives of South America.

car′ri-ŏn=crōw, *n.* The European crow, and other carrion-eating birds, as the black vulture, *Catharista atrata*.

car′ri-ŏn=flow″ēr, *n.* A name applied to any plant whose flowers have a putrid odor, as species of *Stapelia*.

car′ritch, car′ritch-es, *n.* [Scot.] In Scotland, the catechism; a scolding or catechizing.

To give one his carritch; to catechize or scold a person.

car-roc′ciō (-roch′iō), *n.* [It.] A war-chariot on which was borne the standard of a medieval Italian state.

car′roch, *n.* Same as *Carroccio*.

car′rŏl, *n.* Same as *Carol*.

car′rŏm, *n.* Same as *Carom*.

car-rŏn-āde′, *n.* [Named from *Carron*, in Scotland, where it was first made.] A short piece of ordnance, having a large caliber and a chamber for the powder, like a mortar; carried on the upper deck of a vessel for use in naval engagements at short range.

car′rŏn=oil, *n.* A liniment for burns and scalds made of linseed- or cottonseed-oil and lime-water, first used at the iron-works in Carron, Scotland, whence the name.

Carronade.

car′rŏt, *n.* [Fr. *carotte*; L. *carota*; Gr. *karōton*, a carrot.]

1. The fusiform edible root of the *Daucus Carota*, a plant of the family *Umbelliferæ*; the common carrot.

2. Any plant of the genus *Daucus* made edible by cultivation.

3. Any one of several other umbelliferous plants, some of them poisonous; as, the *Thapsia Garganica*, or deadly *carrot* of northern Africa, used in making plasters for the cure of rheumatism.

4. Figuratively, anything resembling a *carrot* in shape; as a twist or roll of tobacco leaves.

car′rŏt-i-ness, *n.* The characteristic color of the carrot, especially as applied to the hair.

car′rŏt-y, *a.* Like a carrot in color; an epithet applied to yellowish-red hair.

car′rōw, *n.* In Ireland, a strolling gamester.

car′ry, *v.t.*; carried, *pt.*, *pp.*; carrying, *ppr.* [ME. *carien*; OFr. *carier*, from *car*; L. *carrus*, a car, cart.]

1. To bear, convey, or transport, by sustaining and moving the thing carried, either by bodily strength, upon a beast, in a vehicle, or in any kind of water-craft; as, to *carry* home a basket of fruit; a car *carries* the mail; a pigeon *carries* a message; a boat *carries* provisions. Generally, to transport a commodity from one place to another.

2. To effect; to accomplish; to achieve; to succeed in; to win; to subdue; as, to *carry* a point, measure, or resolution; to *carry* a fort.

3. To bear out; to face through.

4. To urge, impel, lead, or draw, noting moral impulse; as, passion *carries* a man too far.

5. To have with one continuously; as, he *carries* a wound in his arm; she *carries* sunshine wherever she goes.

6. To be the means or instrument of moving or accomplishing; as, sound is *carried* by the atmosphere; the audience was *carried* by his eloquence; a gun *carries* a projectile to a great distance.

7. To endure; to suffer; as, to *carry* the weight of a great sorrow.

8. To prolong or to extend in space or in time; as, to *carry* an edifice higher; to *carry* a reader along in a narrative; to *carry* a joke too far.

9. To show; to make manifest; as, he *carries* an air of distinction; a work of art *carries* the marks of patient labor.

10. To convey to the mind; to indicate; as, your arguments *carry* conviction; the carnage of battle *carries* horror; the prisoner's conduct *carries* a suspicion of guilt.

11. In commerce, to assume or to become responsible for; as, to *carry* for one his indebtedness until he becomes able to pay.

Carry arms; the command given when an officer in the army wishes each man to grasp his gun with the right hand holding the guard, arm hanging down, gun-stock forward, barrel almost vertical and resting against the hollow of the shoulder. The soldier is then standing at a *carry*.

To be carried away; to be deeply moved or enraptured; as, the convention *was carried away* by the eloquence of the speaker.

To carry arms; to bear arms or to serve in the army or navy.

To carry all before one; to overcome all resistance in any undertaking; to meet with success after success.

To carry away; in nautical parlance, to lose by breaking off; as, our foretopmast was *carried away*.

To carry coals; to bear injuries meekly. [Rare.]

To carry coals to Newcastle; to take things to a place where they already abound; to lose one's labor.

To carry off; to remove to a distance; also, to kill; as, the epidemic *carried off* thousands; to take from the possible possession of a competitor; as, he *carried off* the prize.

To carry on; to prosecute or promote; as, he *carries on* an extensive business.

To carry out; to complete to a successful termination what has been undertaken either by oneself or by another; as, the vice-president *carries out* the policy of the late president whose place he occupies.

To carry through; to support to the end; to succeed in; to sustain, or keep from failing, or from being subdued; as, he *carried* his project *through* in spite of opposition.

To carry up; in law, to remove to a higher court; in architecture, to extend upward.

To carry weight; to be influential; to be hampered by weight, as in a horse-race where a horse is compelled to carry a certain weight in order to enter the race.

Syn.—Convey, transport, transfer, transmit, move, support, sustain, bear, deport.

çar′ry, *v.i.* 1. To act as a bearer; as, the horse was *carrying* double, that is, had two persons mounted on it.

2. In hunting, to run on ground, or hoarfrost, which sticks to the feet, as a hare.

3. To bear the head in a particular manner, as a horse.

4. In falconry, to escape with the quarry; said of a hawk.

5. To convey; to propel; as, a gun or mortar *carries* well.

To carry on; to conduct oneself in a wild, reckless manner; to frolic; as, he *carries on* at a great rate. [Colloq.]

çar′ry, *n.*; *pl.* **çar′rieṣ** (-riz). 1. A transportation, as of boats or stores, from one navigable water to another; the way of such carriage; a portage.

2. In military terms, (a) range, as of a projectile or gun; (b) the act in obedience to the command *carry arms*; as, to bring arms to the *carry*.

çar′ry-ạll, *n.* [Corrupted from *cariole.*] A light vehicle for one horse, having usually four wheels, and designed to carry a number of persons.

çar′ry-ing, *n.* Transportation.

çar′ry-ing=plāce, *n.* A portage.

çar′ry-ing=trāde, *n.* Freightage, especially by water, as, rivals in the *carrying-trade.*

çar′ryk, *n.* A carack. [Obs.]

çar′ry=tāle, *n.* A talebearer. [Obs.]

çärse, *n.* [Scot.] Low, fertile land, adjacent to a river.

çär′=sēal, *n.* A seal to prevent a freight-car door from being opened while in transit, consisting of a soft metal clasp which connects the ends of a wire passing through the lock.

çärt, *n.* [ME. *cart, kart*; AS. *cræt*; Ir. *cairt*, dim. of *car*, a car.]

1. A general name inclusive of a number of vehicles differing in construction and use, as, (a) a heavy vehicle for rough work, usually two-wheeled and fitted for one horse; (b) a light, two-wheeled pleasure carriage, with or without a top; (c) colloquially, any wheeled vehicle, as a delivery-*cart*.

2. A cart-load; as, two *carts* of sand.

To put the cart before the horse; to make a mistake by inverting facts or ideas logically dependent.

çärt, *v.t.*; carted, *pt., pp.*; carting, *ppr.* 1. To carry or convey on a cart; as, to *cart* hay.

2. Formerly, to expose in a cart, by way of punishment.

çärt, *v.i.* To carry anything in a cart; to be engaged in the business of a carter.

çärt′āge, *n.* 1. The act of carrying in a cart.

2. The price paid for carting.

çär′tȧ-ret, *n.* [From a proper name.] A sleeping-cot.

çärt′bōte, *n.* In old English law, wood to which a tenant was entitled for making and repairing carts and other instruments of husbandry.

çärte, *n.* [Fr., a card.]

1. The bill of fare; as, a dinner *à la carte*, one ordered from the bill of fare.

2. Abbreviated form of *carte-de-visite.*

Carte blanche; a blank paper; a paper duly authenticated with signature, etc., and intrusted to a person to be filled up, as he pleases; hence, unconditional terms; unlimited power to decide; usually with *gave* or *given*; as, at his departure upon the special mission, the president *gave* him *carte blanche.*

çärte, *n.* [Fr. *quarte*, from L. *quartus*, fourth.] A movement in fencing consisting in throwing the hand as far as possible on the inside, with the point of the sword toward an adversary's breast; written also *quarte.*

çärte′=de=vi-ṣite′, *n.*; *pl.* **çärtes′=de=vi-ṣite′** (kärt′). [Fr.] Literally, a visiting card; a term generally applied to a photograph on a small card.

çär-tel′, *n.* [Fr. *cartel*; It. *cartello*; LL. *cartellus*, a dim. from L. *carta, charta*, a piece of paper or papyrus; a writing.]

1. A writing or agreement between states at war, for the exchange of prisoners, or for some mutual advantage.

2. A letter of defiance or challenge; a challenge to single combat. [Obs.]

çär-tel′, çär-tel′=ship, *n.* A ship employed in the exchange of prisoners, or in carrying propositions to an enemy; formerly written *chartel.*

çär′tel, *v.t.* To defy. [Obs.]

çärt′ẽr, *n.* 1. One who drives a cart, or whose occupation is to drive a cart.

2. In zoölogy, (a) the daddy-longlegs; (b) an English flatfish, the whiff.

Çär-tē′ṣiăn, *a.* [From Renatus *Cartesius*, a Latinized form of René *Descartes*; the first element of the word, *Des*, is a removable prefix.] Pertaining to the philosopher René Descartes (1596-1650), or to his philosophy.

Cartesian coördinates; in geometry, intersecting straight lines to which points are referred to determine their relative position.

Cartesian devil; a hydrostatic toy consisting of a hollow figure partly filled with air, which may be induced to float at various depths in a tube of water by compression of the air in the tube; called also *bottle-imp.*

Cartesian oval; the locus of a describing point having a distance from two fixed points equal to a given constant.

Çär-tē′ṣiăn, *n.* One who adopts the philosophy of Descartes.

Çär-tē′ṣiăn-iṣm, *n.* The philosophy of Descartes; a belief in the duality of mind and body.

Çär-thȧ-ġin′i-ăn, *a.* Pertaining to ancient Carthage, situated about twelve miles from the modern Tunis.

Çär-thȧ-ġin′i-ăn, *n.* An inhabitant or native of Carthage.

çär′thȧ-min, çär′thȧ-mine, *n.* An astringent bitter principle obtained from the flowers of the *Carthamus tinctorius*, or safflower. It is a beautiful red pigment, and is used in silk-dyeing and rouge-making.

Çär-thū′ṣiăn, *n.* One of an order of monks, remarkable for their austerity, founded in 1086, under Benedictine rule, by St. Bruno, and deriving their name from some place associated with their origin (not the Chartreuse, Grenoble). Their first monastery was built near the village of Chartrousse.

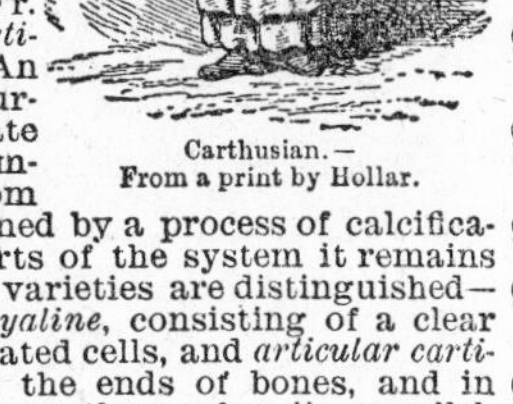

Carthusian.—From a print by Hollar.

Çär-thū′ṣiăn, *a.* Pertaining to the order of monks above named.

çär′ti-lāġe, *n.* [Fr. *cartilage*; L. *cartilago*, gristle.] An elastic tissue occurring in vertebrate animals, and forming the tissue from which bone is formed by a process of calcification. In some parts of the system it remains permanent. Two varieties are distinguished—*true cartilage* or *hyaline*, consisting of a clear matrix with nucleated cells, and *articular cartilage*, which coats the ends of bones, and in which the cells near the surface lie parallel, while the deep cells lie vertical to the surface. *Yellow* or *reticular cartilage* is found especially in the epiglottis.

çär′ti-lāġe=bōne, *n.* Ossified cartilage.

Çär″ti-lȧ-ġin′e-ī, *n.pl.* [From L. *cartilago* (*-inis*), gristle.] The cartilaginous fishes; also called *Chondropterygii.*

çär″ti-lȧ-ġin′e-ous, *a.* [Obs.] See *Cartilaginous.*

çär″ti-lȧ-ġin″i-fi-çā′tion, *n.* [L. *cartilago* (*-inis*), gristle, and *facere*, to make.] The act or process of converting into cartilage.

çär-ti-laġ′i-nous, *a.* Pertaining to or resembling a cartilage; gristly; consisting of cartilage; as, *cartilaginous* fishes.

Çär′tist, *n.* [Sp. and Port. *carta*, a charter.] A Spanish or Portuguese supporter of the constitutional charter.

çärt′lōad, *n.* As much as a cart will hold.

çärt′măn, *n.*; *pl.* **çärt′men.** A driver of a cart; a teamster.

çär-tō-graph′iç, çär-tō-graph′iç-ăl, *a.* Pertaining to cartography.

çär-tō-graph′iç-ăl-ly, *adv.* By cartography.

çär-tog′rȧ-phy, *n.* [Fr. *cartographie*, from L. *charta*, Gr. *chartēs*, a leaf of paper, and *-graphia*, from *graphein*, to write.] The art or practice of making charts or maps.

çär′tō-man-çy, *n.* [LL. *carta*, a card, and Gr. *manteia*, divination.] The use of playing-cards to tell fortunes; divination by cards.

çär′tŏn, *n.* [Fr.] 1. A thin kind of pasteboard.

2. A box made from such pasteboard.

3. A cartoon.

4. In rifle practice, a white disk fixed on the bull's-eye of a target.

çär′tŏn-nāge, *n.* [Fr., from *carton*, pasteboard.]

1. Pasteboard.

2. A kind of material used for mummy-casings, by the ancient Egyptians, consisting of layers of linen cloth fixed together with glue, stucco being often added as a coating.

çär-tọn′=pierre′ (-pyãr′), *n.* [Fr., lit. stone-paper.] A composition resembling papier-maché, largely used in making statuettes, moldings, etc.

çär-tọọn′, *n.* [Fr. *carton*; It. *cartone*, pasteboard, a cartoon; L. *charta*, a paper, writing.]

1. In painting, a design drawn on strong paper, to be afterward calked through and transferred on the fresh plaster of a wall to be painted in fresco; also, a design colored for working in mosaic, tapestry, etc.; as Raphael's famous *cartoons*, which were designs for tapestry to be made in Flanders.

2. A pictorial representation or caricature designed to influence public opinion; usually a drawing of a sketchy character appearing in a newspaper or periodical, most of the large daily journals of this country publishing each day a *cartoon* dealing with events or persons in the public eye.

çär-tọọn′ist, *n.* A drawer of cartoons.

çär-tọụche′, çär-tọụch′, *n.* [Fr. *cartouche*; OFr. *cartoche*, from It. *cartoccio*, a cartridge, a roll of paper, from *carta*, paper; L. *charta*, paper; Gr. *chartēs*, a leaf of paper.]

Cartouche of Ptolemy.

1. A case of wood filled with shot to be fired from a cannon; a roll of paper containing a charge; a cartridge.

2. A portable box for charges for firearms.

3. A case for holding cannon-balls.

4. A military pass given to a soldier going on furlough.

5. The name given by Champollion to the ovals on ancient Egyptian monuments and in papyri, containing groups of characters expressing the names or titles of kings.

6. In architecture, (a) a sculptured ornament in the form of a scroll unrolled, often appearing on the cornices of columns, used as a field for inscriptions, etc.; (b) a kind of ornamental block used in the cornices of house interiors.

7. In heraldry, the oval escutcheon of the pope or of a churchman.

çär′tridġe (-trij), *n.* [Formerly also *cartrage*, a corruption of *cartouche.*] A charge for a firearm or for blasting purposes.

Blank cartridge; one containing powder but no shot or ball.

Center-fire cartridge; one having the primer in the center of the shell-base, as opposed to a *rim-fire cartridge*, in which the fulminate is contained in the rim of the shell-base.

çär′tridġe=bag, *n.* In gunnery, a bag made of serge or some similar material, in which the charge of cannon is contained.

çär′tridġe=belt, *n.* A belt for the waist or to go over the shoulder, having pockets for cartridges.

çär′tridġe=box, *n.* A portable case or box for carrying cartridges.

çär′tridġe=çāse, *n.* 1. A cartridge-box.

2. The tube in which the powder of a cartridge is contained.

çär′tridġe=pā″pẽr, *n.* A thick sort of paper originally manufactured for soldiers' cartridges, but extensively used in the arts—its rough surface giving it an advantage for drawing upon—and for other purposes.

çär′tū-lȧ-ry, *n.*; *pl.* **çär′tū-lȧ-rieṣ.** [LL. *cartularium, chartularium*, from L. *charta*, paper.]

1. A register or record, as of a monastery.

2. The officer who has the care of the monastic records.

çärt′wāy, *n.* A roadway for carts or other vehicles.

çärt′=wheel (-hwēl), *n.* 1. A large wheel, as that of a cart.

2. A large coin; usually applied to the United States dollar. [Colloq.]

3. A kind of somersault; as, the boys turned *cart-wheels* on the grass.

çärt′wright (-rīt), *n.* An artisan whose business is making or repairing carts.

çar′ū-çāġe, *n.* [LL. *carrucagium*, from LL. *carruca*, a plow; L. *carruca*, a coach.]

1. Act of plowing.

2. A duty or tax on the plow. [Obs.] Also written *carrucage.*

çar′ū-çāte, *n.* Formerly as much land as one team could plow in the year, varying according to the nature of the soil and practice of husbandry in different districts.

Çā′rum, *n.* [From Gr. *karon*, caraway.] A considerable genus of plants, natural order *Umbelliferæ. Carum Carui* is the caraway-plant, the fruit of which is caraway-seeds.

çar′un-çle, çȧ-run′çū-lȧ, *n.* [L. *caruncula*, dim. from *caro*, flesh.]

1. A small fleshy excrescence, either natural or morbid; specifically, a fleshy excrescence on the head of a fowl, as the comb of a cock, the wattles of a turkey.

2. In botany, a protuberance surrounding the hilum of a seed.

çȧ-run′çū-lăr, çȧ-run′çū-lous, *a.* Resembling or pertaining to a caruncle; having caruncles.

çȧ-run′çū-lāte, çȧ-run′çū-lā-ted, *a.* Caruncular.

çā′rus, *n.* [Gr. *karos*, heavy sleep, torpor.] Complete insensibility, which no stimulus can remove; the last degree of coma.

ca-rụ'tō, *n.* [S. Am. name.] 1. A dye of a deep blue-black obtained from genipap.
2. The genip-tree, *Genipa Americana*.

cär'vȧ-crŏl, *n.* [Fr. *carvi*, caraway, and L. *acer, acris*, sharp, and *oleum*, oil.] A derivative of oil of caraway and similar oils, being an oleaginous liquid with an odor and taste like those of creosote.

cärve, *v.t.*; carved, *pt., pp.*; carving, *ppr.* [ME. *kerven*; AS. *ceorfan*, to carve, cut; G. *kerben*; Gr. *graphein*, to inscribe.]
1. To cut into small pieces or slices, as meat at table.
2. To cut (wood, stone, or other material) into some particular form, with an instrument, usually a chisel; to engrave.
3. To make or shape by cutting; to hew; as, to *carve* an image out of wood or stone.
4. To apportion; to distribute; to provide at pleasure; to select and take, as to oneself, or to select and give to another.
To carve out; to cut out or to lay out, by design; to plan.

cärve, *v.i.* 1. To cut up meat; followed sometimes by *for*; as, to *carve for* all the guests.
2. To exercise the art of a sculptor or an engraver.

cärve, *n.* A carucate. [Obs.]

cärved, *a.* Cut or divided; engraved; formed by carving.

cär'vel, *n.* 1. A small vessel.
2. The *Urtica marina*, or sea-blubber.

cär'vel-built (-bilt), *a.* In shipbuilding, joining the planks flush at the seams; distinguished from *clinker-built*, in which the joints lap.

cär'ven, *a.* Carved; made by carving; embellished by carvings, as fine woodwork or objects of art.

cär'ven, *v.*, old past participle of *carve*; generally used in a poetic sense.

cär'vēne, *n.* [Fr. *carvi*, caraway.] A substance of an oily nature, virtually odorless and tasteless, obtained from oil of caraway.

cärv'ēr, *n.* 1. One who cuts meat at table; a sculptor; one who apportions or distributes at will, or one who takes or gives at pleasure.
2. A large table knife for carving.

cärv'ing, *n.* 1. The act of cutting, as meat; the act or art of cutting figures in wood or stone.
2. A piece of decorative work artistically designed and cut in stone, wood, marble, ivory, or other material.
3. Decorative sculpture of any kind or period, as distinguished from more pretentious work generally designated as *statuary*.

cär'vist, *n.* In falconry, a hawk which is of proper age and training to be carried on the hand; supposed to be a corruption of *carry-fist*.

cär'vŏl, *n.* [Fr. *carvi*, caraway, and L. *oleum*, oil.] An aromatic oil, much like carvacrol, being one of a series of such oils.

cär'-wheel (-hwēl), *n.* A wheel of iron, steel, or other material, with a flange on the inside to keep it on a track; used on the trucks of railroad and other traction cars.

car-y-at'ic, car-y-at'id, *a.* Pertaining to a caryatid or characterized by caryatids.

car-y-at'id, *n.* [From L. pl. *caryatides*; Gr. *karyatides*, priestesses of the temple of Diana at Karyai.] In architecture, a sculptured female figure, fully draped, which takes the place of a column or pilaster in supporting an entablature.

Caryatid, from British Museum.

car-y-at'i-dēs, *n.*, Latin pl. of *caryatid*.

Ca-rȳ'ō-cär, *n.* [Gr. *karyon*, a nut, and *kara*, a head.] A genus of plants, natural order *Rhizobolaceæ*, consisting of ten species of lofty trees, natives of tropical America. They produce good timber, and their fruits contain three or four large kidney-shaped seeds, called souari or butternuts, which have a pleasant, nutty flavor and yield a soothing oil.

Car″y-ō-phyl-lā'cē-æ (-fil-lā'sē-ē), *n.pl.* [From Gr. *karyophyllon*, the clove-tree; *karyon*, a nut, and *phyllon*, a leaf.] The pink tribe, a natural order of plants, consisting of more than a thousand species of bland herbs. The species comprise chick-weed, spurrey, sandwort, etc., also the pink, carnation, sweet-william, etc.

car″y-ō-phyl-lā'ceous, *a.* Pertaining to the *Caryophyllaceæ*; especially applied to flowers having five petals with long claws in a tubular calyx.

car-y-ō-phyl'lic, *a.* Pertaining to caryophyllin.

car″y-ō-phyl'lin, car″y-ō-phyl'line, *n.* A crystalline substance obtained from cloves by treating them with alcohol.

car-y-oph'yl-lous, *a.* Same as *Caryophyllaceous*.

car-y-op'sis, *n.* [Gr. *karyon*, a nut, and *opsis*, an appearance.] In botany, a small one-seeded, dry, indehiscent fruit, in which the seed adheres to the thin pericarp throughout, so that the fruit and seed are incorporated into one body, as in wheat and other kinds of grain.

cȧ sä'bȧ melon, [From Kassaba, Smyrna, Asia Minor, whence the melon was introduced.] A type of winter muskmelon, having a yellow rind and a sweetish, white, watery flesh.

cā'sal, *a.* In grammar, pertaining to case.

cas'cȧ-bel, *n.* [Sp. *cascabel*, a little bell, a button or knob at the end of a cannon.] The rear part of a cannon; the part which is behind the base ring, and includes the base and knob.

cas-cāde', *n.* [Fr. *cascade*; It. *cascata*, from *cascare*, to fall.]
1. A waterfall; a steep fall or flowing of water over a precipice, in a river or natural stream; or an artificial fall in a garden. The word is applied to falls that are less than a cataract.
2. In electricity, the charging of a number of connected Leyden jars; known variously as charged in *cascade*, charging by *cascade*, or discharged in *cascade*.
Cascade amplification; in radiotelegraphy, the building up of received signals by means of several vacuum tubes, each in turn amplifying the sound and passing it on to the next tube.

cas-cāde', *v.i.* 1. To fall like a cascade or in the form of a cascade.
2. To vomit. [Colloq.]

cas-cal'hō (-yō), *n.* [Port.] In Brazil, a deposit of pebbles, gravel, and ferruginous sand, in which the diamond is usually found.

cas'cȧ-rȧ, *n.* [Sp.] The bark of certain trees.
Cascara buckthorn; bearwood growing on the Pacific coast of the United States.
Cascara sagrada; bark from the cascara buckthorn; used as a mild laxative.

cas-cȧ-ril'lȧ, *n.* [Sp. dim. of *cascara*, peel, bark.] The aromatic, bitter bark of *Croton Eleuteria*, a small tree of the natural order *Cinchonaceæ*, and closely allied to cinchona, cultivated chiefly in Eleuthera, one of the Bahamas. This bark is imported in small, thin fragments and brittle rolls like quills, and is sometimes employed as a substitute for cinchona, but is inferior in tonic and febrifuge qualities.

Cascarilla Plant (*Croton Eleuteria*).

cas-cȧ-ril'lin, cas-cȧ-ril'line, *n.* The active principle of cascarilla, being a white, crystalline, bitter substance but little soluble in water.

cas'cō, *n.* [Sp.] A boat of the Philippines, almost of rectangular form, very flat and durable, and much used at Manila for conveying freight to and from ships.

cāse, *n.* [ME. *case*; OFr. *casse*; L. *capsa*, a box, chest, from *capere*, to take, contain, hold.]
1. A covering, box, or sheath; that which incloses or contains; as, a *case* for knives.
2. The skin of an animal. [Obs.]
3. The exterior portion of a building; an outer coating for walls.
4. A box and its contents; as, a *case* of wine.
5. In printing, the receptacle for the types, from which the compositor gathers them; commonly, a wooden frame divided into boxes.
6. In mining, a small fissure which lets water into the workings.

cāse, *v.t.*; cased, *pt., pp.*; casing, *ppr.* 1. To cover with a case; to surround with any material that shall inclose or defend.
2. To put in a case or box.
3. To remove the skin of. [Obs.]

cāse, *n.* [ME. *cas, case*; OFr. *cas*, an event, chance; L. *casus*, a falling, accident, from *cadere*, to fall.]
1. Literally, that which falls, comes, or happens; an event; hence, the particular state, condition, or circumstances that befall a person, or in which he is placed.
2. An individual occurrence or specific instance, pathologically speaking; as, a *case* of fever.
3. A question; a state of facts involving a question for discussion or decision; as, the lawyer stated the *case*.
4. A cause or suit in court; as, the *case* was tried at the last term, *cause* being the more technical term.
5. One of the forms in the declension of a noun, pronoun, or adjective; as, the genitive *case*. The *cases*, except the nominative, are called *oblique cases*.
Action on the case; in law, an action in which the whole cause of complaint is set out in the writ. [Obs.]
A hard case; a person who is past reform.
Case lawyer; one well acquainted with reports of cases.
Case stated or *agreed on*; a submission of facts upon which disputants agree, to a court or board of arbitration.
In any case; anyhow; anyway.
In case; in the event or contingency; if it should so fall out or happen.
In good case; in good physical health.
To make out one's case; to prove an assertion.
To put a case; to suppose an event or a certain state of things.
Syn.—Situation, condition, state, circumstance, plight, predicament.

cāse, *v.i.* To put cases; to give illustrations. [Obs.]

cā'sē-āte, *n.* A salt resulting from the union of caseic acid with a base.

cā-sē-ā'tion, *n.* 1. Precipitation of casein during the coagulation of milk.
2. In medicine, conversion of tissue into caseic matter.

cāse'-bāy, *n.* 1. In architecture, the space between two girders.
2. A joist framed between two girders.

cāse'-bind″ing, *n.* A method of bookbinding in which the cover is finished separately before being fastened to the book for which it is intended.

cāse'härd″en, *v.t.*; casehardened, *pt., pp.*; casehardening, *ppr.* To harden the outer part or surface of, as of iron, by converting it into steel.

cāse'härd″ened, *a.* Having the outside hardened, as tools; having no sense of shame or honor; brazenfaced.

cāse'härd″en-ing, *n.* The process by which the surface of iron is converted into steel, while the interior retains the softness and toughness of malleable iron. This may be done by putting the iron into an iron box with vegetable or animal charcoal and cementing it by exposing it for some hours to a red heat.

cā'sē-ic, *a.* [L. *caseus*, cheese.] Of or pertaining to cheese.

cā'sē-in, cā'sē-ine, *n.* That ingredient in milk which is neither coagulated spontaneously like fibrin, nor by heat, like albumen, but by the action of acids alone, and constituting the chief part of the nitrogenized matter contained in it. Cheese made from skimmed milk and well pressed is nearly pure casein. It is identical with legumin, and occurs in many vegetables.

cāse'-knife (-nīf), *n.* 1. A knife carried in a case or sheath.
2. A large table-knife.

cāse'-māte, *n.* [Fr. *casemate*, from It. *casamatta*, a casemate; *casa*, a house, and *matto*, foolish, dull, dim, dark.]
1. In fortifications, (a) a vault of stone or brickwork, usually built in the thickness of the rampart of a fortress, and pierced in front with embrasures, through which artillery may be fired; (b) a shellproof vault of stone or brick to protect the troops, ammunition, etc.
2. In architecture, a hollow molding, chiefly used in cornices; called also a *cavetto*.

cāse'mā-ted, *a.* Furnished with a casemate.

cāse'ment, *n.* 1. A glass frame or sash forming a window or part of a window; commonly any window.

> I released
> The *casement*, and the light increased
> With freshness in the dawning east.
> —Tennyson.

2. An old English name for a deep hollow molding.

cāse'ment-ed, *a.* Having casements.

cā'sē-ous, *a.* [L. *caseus*, cheese.] Pertaining to cheese; like cheese; having the qualities of cheese.
Caseous degeneration; a gradual change of tissue or other animal matter into a cheese-like substance, considered an evidence of scrofula or consumption.

cȧ-sērn', *n.* [Fr. *caserne*; Port. *caserna*, from L. *casa*, a hut, cottage, barrack.] A lodging for soldiers in garrison towns, usually near the ramparts; barracks.

cāse'-shot, *n.* Any projectile made of an inclosing case and small balls; called also *canister-shot*.

cā'sē-um, *n.* Same as *Casein*.

cāse'-weed, *n.* The flower, shepherd's-purse.

cāse'-wŏrm, *n.* The caddis-worm.

cash, *n.* [Fr. *caisse*, a box, case, money-box, cash; OFr. *casse*; from L. *capsa*, a box, chest, from *capere*, to take, contain.]
1. A receptacle for money; a money-box. [Obs.]
2. Money; primarily, ready money; money in chest or on hand, in bank or at command.
3. In numismatics, (a) a thin coin of a very base alloy of copper, perforated and strung on a thread, used by the Chinese as small change, commonly called by Europeans, a *li*; (b) one of various coins current in Madras, Pondicherry, and throughout Sumatra.

çash, *v.t.*; cashed, *pt.*, *pp.*; cashing, *ppr.* 1. To turn into money, or to exchange for money; as, to *cash* a note or an order.

2. To pay money for; as, the clerks of a bank *cash* notes when presented.

çash, *v.t.* To discard. [Obs. See *Cashier*.]

çash'-aç-çount", *n.* That part of bookkeeping which constitutes a record of cash received and paid out.

çash'book, *n.* A book in which is kept a register or account of money received or paid.

çash'boy, *n.* A boy who carries money received from a customer by a salesman to the cashier, and brings back the goods bought and change. [U. S.]

çash'-çred"it, *n.* An account with a bank by which, security having been given for repayment, the bank may be drawn upon to an agreed amount; called also *cash-account* and *bank-credit*.

çȧ-shew', *n.* [A corruption of Fr. *acajou*, *cajou*, from Hind. *kaju*, the cashew-nut.] A tree of the West Indies, *Anacardium occidentale*, bearing a kidney-shaped nut. The receptacle is as large as an orange, and full of an acid juice, which is often used to make punch.

çȧ-shew'-bïrd, *n.* The Jamaica tanager.

çȧ-shew'-nut, *n.* A nut at one extremity of the fruit of the cashew-tree, containing a black liquor much used in marking linen.

Anacardium occidentale. 1, 1, 1. Cashew-nuts.

çash-iēr', *n.* [Fr. *caissier*, from *caisse*, a money-box, money.] One who has charge of money; a cash-keeper. In a banking institution, the *cashier* is the officer who superintends the books, payments, and receipts of the bank. He also signs or countersigns the notes, and superintends all the transactions, under the order of the directors.

çash-iēr', *v.t.*; cashiered, *pt.*, *pp.*; cashiering, *ppr.* [OFr. *casser*, to discharge, cashier, from L. *cassare*, to bring to naught, destroy; *cassus*, empty, void.]

1. To dismiss from an office or place of trust, by annulling the commission; to break, as for malconduct, and therefore with reproach; as, to *cashier* an officer of the army.

2. To dismiss or discard from service or from society.

3. To reject; to annul or vacate.

çash-iēr'ēr, *n.* One who rejects, discards, or breaks; as, a *cashierer* of monarchs. [Rare.]

çash'-keep"ēr, *n.* One intrusted with the keeping of money; a cashier.

çash'mēre, *n.* 1. A rich and costly kind of shawl; so called from the country where first made.

2. A rich material first made from the fine soft wool which grows at the roots of the hair of goats native to Cashmere, Thibet, and the adjacent regions.

3. A dress-fabric of fine wool.

çash-mē-rette', *n.* [Dim. of *cashmere*.] A dress-fabric having a fine glossy surface, made in imitation of cashmere.

çȧ-shọọ', *n.* See *Catechu*.

çash'-reg"is-tēr, *n.* A machine for containing and registering the amounts of cash received.

çash'-sāle, *n.* A sale of goods made for cash and immediate delivery.

çās'ing, *n.* 1. A covering; a case; either ornamental or useful, in the latter case usually to prevent the loss of heat by radiation.

2. The frame round a window or door.

çā'singş, *n.pl.* Cattle manure dried and used as fuel. [Prov. Eng.]

çȧ-sï'nō, *n.* [It., dim. of *casa*, L. *casa*, a house, cottage.]

1. A club-house or building used for social meetings, having rooms for public amusement, reading-rooms, etc.

2. A small country dwelling.

3. A game of cards played by two, three, or four persons, the object being to make as many points as possible, as follows: The most cards taken in scores three points; the most spades, one point; big casino (the ten of diamonds), two points; little casino (the two of spades), one point; each ace, one point; each sweep (the taking in of all the cards on the table), one point. The play is started by dealing one card to each player, and one, face up, on the board.

çȧsk, *n.* [Fr. *casque*; Sp. *casco*, a cask, helmet, from *cascar*, to break in pieces, burst.]

1. A close vessel for containing liquors, formed by staves, headings, and hoops. This is a general term, comprehending the pipe, hogshead, butt, barrel, etc.

2. Same as *Casque*. [Obs.]

3. The quantity held by a cask.

4. A jewel box; a casket. [Obs.]

çȧsk, *v.t.* To inclose in a cask.

çȧs'ket, *n.* [ME. *casket*; OFr. *cassette*, dim. of *casse*, a box, chest.]

1. A small chest or box, for jewels or other small articles.

2. Anything intended as a receptacle for something highly prized or of great value, as the tomb containing the remains of some one well-beloved, a book containing choice selections.

3. A special kind of burial case often handsomely finished; a coffin.

çȧs'ket, *v.t.*; casketed, *pt.*, *pp.*; casketing, *ppr.* To put into a casket or little chest.

çasque, çȧsk, *n.* [Fr. *casque*; It. *casco*; Sp. *casco*, a helmet, skull.]

1. A headpiece; a helmet; a piece of defensive armor, to cover and protect the head and neck in battle.

2. In zoölogy, (a) the cone or helmet-shaped protuberance or shield on the upper bill of certain birds of the *Icteridæ* family, as of the cassowary; (b) a process on the upper jaw of certain insects, as of beetles.

çȧs'quet-el (-ket-), *n.* A small cap of steel or an open visorless helmet much like a casque, and provided with a jointed neckpiece.

Casquetel (Edward IV.), side and back view.

çass, *v.t.* [Fr. *casser*; L. *quassare*, to break, to quash.] To quash; to defeat; to annul. [Obs.]

ças-sä'dȧ, ças-sä'dō, *n.* See *Cassava*.

ças'sȧ-reep, *n.* [S. Am. name.] A seasoning obtained from the juice of the cassava root.

ças'sāte, *v.t.* [L. *cassatus*, pp. of *cassare*, to annul.] To vacate, annul, or make void. [Obs.]

ças-sā'tion, *n.* The act of annulling. In France, the *Court of Cassation* is the highest court of appeal, having power to break (*casser*) or reverse the decisions of the courts below.

ças-sä'vȧ, *n.* [Fr. *cassave*; Sp. *casabe*, from the Haytian *kasabi*.]

1. A shrub or plant belonging to the genus *Manihot*, producing large thick roots from which a nutritious starch is obtained; it is found in tropical and subtropical Africa and America. Also known as *manioc*.

2. The edible starch obtained from the *cassava*, which by drying is made into the tapioca of commerce and domestic use.

Cassava Plant (*Manihot utilissima*).

ças-sä'vȧ-wood, *n.* The drumwood; the *Turpinia occidentalis*, a tree belonging to the soap-berry family found in the West Indies.

ças-sē'nȧ, *n.* [Of N. Am. Indian origin.] An evergreen shrub, *Ilex Cassine*, found in the southern states. A decoction is made from its leaves; also called the *yaupon*.

çasse'-pā"pēr, *n.* [Fr. *cassé*, pp. of *casser*, to break, and *paper*.] Spoiled paper, wrinkled or injured in making and not sold as perfect stock.

ças'se-rōle, *n.* [Fr. *casserole*, a saucepan, dim. of OFr. *casse*, a basin.]

1. A vessel of earthenware, porcelain, or the like, usually with a cover, and either a handle or a separate holder of metal, in which food may be baked and served. Also food served in such a dish.

2. In chemistry, a small dish ordinarily made of porcelain, with a handle attached, and used for heating or boiling compounds, etc.

3. In cookery, a hollow form or shell made of pastry, rice, potatoes, or the like, being eaten with a filling made of meat or vegetables.

çasse'-tête' (-tāt'), *n.* [Fr., from *casser*, to break, and *tête*, head.] A bludgeon; a club; specifically, a war-club used by savages, having a particularly hard stone fastened to a wooden handle.

ças-sette' (-set'), *n.* [Fr., dim. of *casse*, a case.]

1. In photography, a plate-holder.

2. A casket, in the sense of a receptacle for trinkets, etc.

3. A mold or shell of clay and sand completely inclosing porcelain when the latter is being baked; called also a *seggar*.

Ças'siȧ (kash'iȧ), *n.* [L., from Gr. *kasia*, *kassia*, cassia.]

1. A genus of plants belonging to the *Leguminosæ*, containing many species, among which is the senna.

2. A species of *Laurus*, the bark of which usually passes under the name of cinnamon, differing from real cinnamon chiefly in the strength of its qualities.

3. [c—] The bark or cinnamon obtained from this tree; also called *Chinese cinnamon*.

4. [c—] In medicine, the pulp made from the pods of the *Cassia Fistula*, found in the tropics, particularly in the East Indies, and used as a laxative.

ças'siȧ-bärk, *n.* Same as *Cassia*.

ças'siȧ-budş, *n.pl.* The dried buds of *Cinnamomum Cassia* and of several kindred cinnamon species.

ças'siȧ-oil, *n.* An aromatic oil obtained from cassia-buds and cassia-bark.

ças'si-çăn, *n.* [From L. *cassis*, a helmet.] A species of oriole belonging to the genus *Cassicus*, found in North America, also called *cacique* or *crested oriole*.

ças-sid'ē-ous, *a.* [L. *cassis* (-*idis*), a helmet.] In botany, helmet-shaped; a term applied to an irregular corol, having the upper petal dilated into a broad, helmet-shaped leaf, as in aconite.

ças'si-dō-ny, *n.* [Fr. *cassidoine*; LL. *cacedonius*, *chalcedonius*, from *Chalcedon*, a town in Bithynia.] In botany, the popular name of a species of *Gnaphalium*, cottonweed, cudweed, or goldilocks; also, of *Lavandula Stœchas*, or French lavender.

ças'si-mēre, *n.* [Fr. *casimir*; Sp. *casimiro*; Turk. *qāzmir*, cassimere.] A thin, twilled, woolen cloth.

ças-si-nette', *n.* [From *cassimere*.] A cloth made of a cotton warp, and the woof of very fine wool, or wool and silk.

Ças-sin'i-ăn, *a.* Pertaining to or named from the Cassini family, members of which were astronomers and mathematicians famous in France for four generations.

Cassinian oval; a closed plane curve forming the locus of a point the sum of whose distances from two fixed points does not vary.

ças-sï'nō, *n.* See *Casino*.

ças'si-ō-ber"ry, *n.* [Am. Ind. origin.] The black edible fruit of the shrub *Viburnum obovatum*, growing in southeastern United States and a member of the honeysuckle family.

Ças"si-ō-pē'iȧ (-pē'yȧ), *n.* A constellation in the northern hemisphere, situated near Cepheus, as the fabulous Cassiopeia was wife to Cepheus, king of Ethiopia.

ças-sit'ēr-īte, *n.* [L. *cassiterum*; Gr. *kassiteros*, tin.] Dioxid of tin in the natural state (SnO_2); it is the chief natural tin compound and usually occurs as a brown or black lustrous crystal.

ças'sius (kash'us), *n.* [Named after the discoverer, A. *Cassius*.] A beautiful purple color obtained from the chlorid of gold by means of tin; much valued for the beautiful color which it gives to glass or enamel.

ças'sŏck, *n.* [Fr. *casaque*, a cassock; It. *casacca*, a greatcoat, a house; L. *casa*, a house.]

1. A close garment, resembling a long frock coat, worn by clergymen of the Roman Catholic and Episcopal churches, under the surplice or gown.

2. A cloak or gown worn over the other garments. [Obs.]

ças'sŏcked, *a.* Clothed with a cassock; as, the *cassocked* priest.

ças-sō-lette', *n.* [Fr.] A vase or box, with small holes in the lid for the diffusion of perfumes; an incense-burner.

ças-sŏn-āde', *n.* [Fr., from OFr. *casson*, a large chest, brown sugar, so called from its being shipped in casks.] Cask-sugar; sugar not refined; especially, sugar coming from Brazil.

ças'sō-wā-ry, *n.*; *pl.* **ças'sō-wā-rieş** (-riz). [Malay *kassuwaris*, cassowary.] A large fleet-footed East Indian bird of the genus *Casuarius*, much resembling an ostrich, though of stouter build and not so tall; the wings, armed with several long, sharp spines, are very small. The head is surmounted with a horny protuberance consisting of plates or scales. The common species of this bird is found principally on the largest and least densely inhabited islands of the East Indian Archipelago, such as Borneo and New Guinea. Several other species are found in Australia and New Guinea.

Crested Cassowary (*Casuarius galeatus*).

ças-sụ-mū'när, ças-sụ-mū'ni-är, *n.* [E. Ind.] A tonic and stimulant obtained from an East Indian aromatic root, *Zingiber Cassumunar*, having a bitter, pungent taste.

çȧst, *v.t.*; cast, *pt.*, *pp.*; casting, *ppr.* [ME. *casten*; Ice. *kasta*; Dan. *kaste*, to throw.]

1. To project; to fling, throw, or thrust; as, to *cast* a stone.

2. To shed or throw off, as a serpent its skin.

3. To drop or let fall; as, to *cast* anchor.

4. To put or set in a particular state; as, he was *cast* into a deep sleep.

5. To distribute (the parts of a play) among the actors; as, the play is *cast*; to assign (an actor) to a part; as, I am *cast* for Lear.

6. To get the better of in a contest of strength.

7. To emit; to throw out or forth, as perfume from flowers.

8. To dig, raise, extend, or form, as a trench or rampart.

9. To throw, as dice or lots.

10. To throw upon the ground, as a man in wrestling.

11. To direct or turn; as, to *cast* a glance.

12. To found; to form into a particular shape by pouring liquid metal into a mold; as, to *cast* cannon. Sometimes in a figurative sense, to shape.

13. To spread over; to communicate; as, to *cast* light on a topic.

14. To cause to preponderate; to throw into one scale; as, to *cast* the balance in some one's favor; to give in favor of; as, they *cast* three votes for the candidate.

15. To throw together, as the items, circumstances, or facts; as, to *cast* accounts; to *cast* one's destiny.

16. To give; to intrust to; as, he *cast* the responsibility upon her.

17. To place; to distribute; to group; as, to *cast* a speech under several heads.

18. To bring forth (young) prematurely.

19. In printing, to make an electrotype or stereotype of.

To cast a shoe; to drop or strike off a shoe, as a horse does.

To cast aside; to reject as useless or undesirable.

To cast away; to throw aside; also, to wreck a ship.

To cast down; to deject or depress the mind.

To cast in one's lot with; to risk one's fortune with that of another.

To cast in the teeth of; to upbraid one face to face; to charge one with something.

To cast off; to disburden; to drive away; among huntsmen, to leave behind or free, as dogs; among sailors, to loose; to untie.

To cast off copy; to ascertain how many printed pages will be made by a manuscript.

To cast up; (a) to compute; to calculate; (b) to vomit; (c) to remind in an accusing way.

To cast the draperies; to arrange the folds of a model's garments, for painting or sculpture.

To cast the lead; to take a sounding of the depth of water by dropping a lead at the end of a line.

çȧst, *v.i.* 1. To turn or revolve something in the mind; to contrive; usually with *about*; as, he *cast about* in his mind for some plan of relief.

2. To throw a fly or artificial bait in fishing; to throw a line in angling.

3. To warp; to twist from regular shape.

4. In nautical language, to fall off or incline, so as to bring the side of a ship to the wind; applied particularly to a ship riding with her head to the wind, when the anchor is first weighed.

5. To throw up food; to vomit.

Syn.—Throw, abandon, forego, discontinue, give, distribute.

çȧst, *n.* 1. A throw; the thing thrown, as in angling and fly-fishing.

2. The space through which a thing thrown generally passes; as, a stone's *cast*.

3. A touch; a stroke; as, a *cast* of politics. [Obs.]

4. A motion or turn of the eye.

5. A throw of dice; hence, a state of chance or hazard.

It is an even *cast*, whether the army should march this way or that way. —South.

6. Form; shape.

7. A slight coloring; a shade of color; a slight deviation from natural appearance; as, a *cast* of green.

8. Manner; air; mien.

9. A flight; a number of hawks released at once.

10. An impression in plaster; a small statue of bronze, plaster, or other material.

11. Among founders, a tube of wax, fitted into a mold, to give shape to metal.

12. A cylindrical piece of brass or copper, slit in two lengthwise, to form a canal or conduit, in a mold, for conveying metal.

13. Whatever is cast in a mold.

14. An assignment of the parts of a play to the several actors; also, the actors themselves to whom the parts are assigned.

15. A plot or design. [Obs.]

16. In zoölogy, refuse; anything thrown off as useless; as the skin of a snake, excrement of an earthworm, the indigestible matter ejected from the stomach of a bird of prey, etc.

17. In brewing, the quantity of water necessary to make a given quantity of beer.

18. An after-swarm of bees.

19. A certain quantity of food for an animal; as, a *cast* of hay.

20. A family; a breed; a race. [Obs.]

Bridling cast; a parting drink.

Cast in the eye; strabismus; a partial squint.

Renal cast; a microscopic body in the urine of a person suffering from kidney disease.

Syn.—Mold, stamp, kind, figure, form, aspect, mien, air, style, manner, character.

Ças-tā'li-ȧ, *n.* A genus of aquatic plants of the water-lily family including the common lily of the United States.

Ças-tā'li-ăn, *a.* Pertaining to Castalia, a mythical spring on Mount Parnassus, sacred to the Muses; as, *Castalian* fountain.

Ças-tā'nē-ȧ, *n.* [L., a chestnut, from Gr. *kastanon*.] A genus of trees having two species and typified by the common chestnut.

ças-tā'nē-ous, *a.* Relating to or having the color of a chestnut.

ças'tȧ-net, *n.* [Sp. *castañeta*, L. *castanea*, chestnut.] One of a pair of small, concave shells of ivory or hard wood, shaped like spoons, placed together, fastened to the thumb, and struck with the middle finger. They are used principally by the Spaniards, Moors, and Bohemians, as an accompaniment to their dances and guitars.

Castanets.

çȧst'ȧ-wāy, *n.* 1. An outcast from home or society; a profligate or abandoned person.

2. In nautical phraseology, one who is adrift on sea or shore.

çȧst'ȧ-wāy, *a.* Rejected; useless; of no value.

çaste, *n.* [Fr. *caste*; Port. *casta*, breed, race, caste, from L. *castus*, pure, chaste.]

1. In Hindustan, a name given first by the Portuguese to the several classes into which society is divided, with fixed occupations, which have come down from the earliest ages. The original *castes*, called in Sanskrit *varnas*, or *colors*, are four, viz., the Brahmans, or sacred order; the Kshatriyas, or soldiers and rulers; the Vaisyas, who are husbandmen and merchants; and the Sooders, Sudras, or laborers and mechanics. Numerous mixed classes, or *castes*, have sprung up in the progress of time.

2. A separate and fixed order or class in society; the term is now used to express high social standing.

3. In biology, the diversity in form or type of classes of individuals belonging to the same species. Instances are common in bees. It is supposed to be produced at will by differences in feeding while at the larval stage. Other instances of *caste* are seen in some butterflies and flowers.

To lose caste; to suffer loss of social standing.

Syn.—Order, class, rank, lineage, race, blood, respect.

çȧs'tel-lăn, *n.* [ME. *castellain*; OFr. *castellain*; LL. *castellanus*, keeper of a castle; from L. *castellum*, a castle.] A governor or constable of a castle.

çȧs'tel-lā-ny, *n.* The lordship belonging to a castle; or the extent of its land and jurisdiction.

çȧs'tel-lā-ted, *a.* 1. Inclosed in a building, as a fountain or cistern. [Obs.]

2. Adorned with turrets and battlements, like a castle.

çȧs-tel-lā'tion, *n.* The act of fortifying a house, and transforming it into a castle or a castle-like structure.

çȧs'tel-let, *n.* A small castle; also written *castlet*.

çȧst'ẽr, *n.* 1. One who throws or casts, or who makes castings in metal, etc.; one who computes; a calculator; one who casts fortunes.

2. A small phial or vessel for the table; as, a set of *casters*.

3. A stand for holding small bottles or cruets for the table.

4. A small wheel on a swivel, on which furniture is rolled on the floor in any direction. This word is sometimes, but incorrectly, written *castor*.

ças'ti-gāte, *v.t.*; castigated, *pt.*, *pp.*; castigating, *ppr.* [L. *castigatus*, pp. of *castigare*, to purify, chastise, from *castus*, pure.] To chastise; to punish by stripes; to correct; to chasten; to check.

ças-ti-gā'tion, *n.* 1. Punishment; correction; penance; discipline; emendation; restraint.

2. Correction; alteration. [Obs.]

ças'ti-gā-tŏr, *n.* One who corrects.

ças'ti-gȧ-tō-ry, *a.* Tending to correction; corrective; punitive.

ças'ti-gȧ-tō-ry, *n.* A device formerly used to punish and correct arrant scolds; called also a *ducking-stool* or *trebucket*.

Ças-til'iăn, *a.* Pertaining to Castile, in Spain.

Ças-til'iăn, *n.* 1. An inhabitant or native of Castile, in Spain.

2. The purest of Spanish; originally, the language of Castile.

çȧst'ing, *n.* 1. The act of throwing; as a line in fishing, or dice in gambling.

2. That which is cast in a mold; anything formed by pouring a liquid in a hollow form and allowing it to harden or solidify.

3. The act or process of so making a *casting*.

4. Computation, especially of an arithmetical sum.

5. Assignment, making up, or distribution, as of parts in a play; a plan or estimate, as for a house; a pattern or copy to be followed.

6. The warping of a board.

7. The thing cast out or off; also, the act of so throwing; as animal excremental matter or regurgitation.

Casting of draperies; see under *Cast*, v.t.

çȧst'ing-line, *n.* The gut at the end of a fishing line to which the fly and hook are attached; sometimes the unreeled part of a line is so called.

çȧst'ing-net, *n.* A net which is cast and drawn, in distinction from a net that is set and left.

çȧst'ing-vōte, *n.* The vote of a presiding officer, in an assembly or council, which decides a question, when the votes are equally divided between the affirmative and negative.

çȧst'ing-weight (-wāt), *n.* A weight of such heaviness as to tip the beam of a balance.

çȧst'-ī''ron (-ūrn), *a.* 1. Formed of iron that has been cast.

2. Rigid; set; strong.

çȧst'-ī''ron (-ūrn), *n.* See *Iron*.

çȧs'tle (kȧs'l), *v.t.*; castled, *pt.*, *pp.*; castling, *ppr.* In the game of chess, to cover (the king) with a castle, by a certain move.

çȧs'tle, *n.* [ME. *castle*, *castel*, a castle; AS. *castel*, a village; OFr. *castel*, from L. *castellum*, dim. of *castrum*, a fort.]

1. A house fortified for defense against an enemy; a fortress. The term often includes the house and the walls or other works around it. In old writings, the word is used for a town or village fortified.

Château de Coucy (13th Century).

In the foreground, the esplanade; *a*, the fosse, twenty yards broad; *b*, the gateway, approached by two swing bridges, defended by two guardrooms, *c*; *d*, inner bailey or courtyard; *e*, covered buildings for the men defending the walls or curtains; *f*, apartments for the family, entered by the grand staircase, *g*; *h*, great hall; *i*, donjon or keep, the strongest part of the castle; *k*, a postern leading from the donjon and communicating with an outer postern and drawbridge; *l*, *m*, *n*, *o*, towers or bastions flanking the walls.

2. A modern house characterized by size, imposing structure, and resemblance to an ancient *castle*.

3. Any place of security, or structure of defense; as, a floating *castle* (a heavily armed war-ship).

4. In the game of chess, a name of one of the pieces resembling a *castle*; called also a *rook*.

5. A helmet.

A man's castle; his home; the place where he may rest without being disturbed.

Castle in the air, *castle in Spain*; a visionary project; a scheme having no solid foundation; a day-dream.

çȧs'tle-build''ẽr (-bild''ẽr), *n.* One who forms visionary schemes.

çȧs'tle-build''ing, *n.* Indulgence in day-dreams; a reverie.

çȧs'tled (-ld), *a.* 1. Having or bearing a castle.

2. Having protection after the manner of castles.

çȧs'tle-guärd, çȧs'tle-wärd, *n.* 1. A feudal tenure, or knight service, which obliged the tenant to perform service within the realm, without limitation of time.

2. Those upon whom the defense of a castle devolved.

3. In old English law, a levy on buildings within a certain radius of a castle.

ças'tle-ry, *n.* The government of a castle.

càs'tlet, *n.* Same as *Castellet.*

càs'tle-wàrd, *n.* Same as *Castle-guard.*

càst'ling, *n.* An abortion. [Obs.]

càst'ling, *n.* In chess, a combined move in which the king and castle take part.

càst'-off, *a.* No longer in use or no longer wanted; as, *cast-off* garments.

càst'-off, *n.* 1. A useless or rejected article or person.

2. In printing, the computation in type of any manuscript.

3. The off-set of a gun-stock.

càs'tŏr, *a.* [L. *castor*, the beaver.] Of a light brown color; applied generally throughout the commercial world to hats, gloves, and coats.

càs'tŏr, *n.* [L. *castor*; Gr. *kastōr*, a beaver.]

1. Same as *Castoreum.*

2. [C—] A genus of rodents characterized by a resemblance to the beaver, including some species now extinct.

3. Formerly, a hat made of the fur of the beaver; any hat.

4. A broadcloth a grade lighter than beaver, used for overcoats and ladies' jackets.

5. A wooden tablet, serving as money, formerly used by the Hudson Bay Company in their trade with the Indians.

càs'tŏr, *n.* A color; a kind of buff; a shade very well known throughout the commercial world.

càs'tŏr, *n.* 1. See *Castorite.*

2. [C—] In Greek mythology, one of the twin sons of Jupiter and Leda.

Castor and Pollux; (a) a globular electric glow which is sometimes seen on some parts of the rigging of a ship; so called when a double flame, when single called *Helena*; (b) the two most luminous stars in the zodiacal constellation, the Twins; (c) in classic mythology, the twin sons of Jupiter and Leda.

càs'tŏr-bēan, *n.* The oily seed of the castor-oil plant.

ças-tō'rē-um, *n.* [L.] A substance having a strong, penetrating smell, obtained from the preputial follicles of the beaver; also, the follicles themselves together with their contents; formerly much used in medicine as a stimulant and antispasmodic, now chiefly known as a perfume.

càs'tō-rin, *n.* A constituent of castoreum, white and forming in crystals

ças'tŏr-īte, *n.* A mineral, silicate of aluminium and lithium, and a variety of petalite; also called *castor.*

càs'tŏr-oil, *n.* A purgative oil very generally known, obtained from the castor-bean.

Castor-oil plant; the plant, *Ricinus communis*, or palma-Christi.

Nut of Castor-oil Plant.

ças″trà-mē-tā'tion, *n.* [LL. *castrametari*, to pitch a camp; L. *castra*, a camp, and *metari*, to measure, lay out.] The art or act of encamping; the marking or laying out of a camp.

ças'trāte, *v.t.*; castrated, *pt., pp.*; castrating, *ppr.* [L. *castratus*, pp. of *castrare*, to castrate, to prune.]

1. To geld; to deprive of the testicles; to emasculate.

2. To cut out or revise, as the obscene parts of a writing; figuratively, to take the life out of (anything).

3. In botany, to take away the anthers from (a flower).

ças'trāte, *a.* 1. In botany, destitute of anthers, or deprived of them.

2. Gelded; emasculated.

ças-trā'tion, *n.* The act of castrating, in any of its senses.

càs-trä'tō, *n.*; *pl.* **càs-trä'tī.** [It.] A man emasculated when young so as to retain his soprano voice for singing.

ças'trel, *n.* See *Kestrel.*

ças-tren'siăl, ças-tren'siăn, *a.* [L. *castrensis*, from *castra*, a camp.] Belonging to a camp.

çaş'ū-ăl, *a.* [Fr. *casuel*; Sp. *casual*; LL. *casualis*, by chance, from L. *casus*, chance, event.]

1. Falling, happening, or coming to pass without volition and without being foreseen or expected; accidental; fortuitous; coming by chance; as, the parties had a *casual* meeting.

2. Occasional; coming at certain times, without regularity, in distinction from stated or regular; as, *casual* expenses.

3. Taking place, or beginning to exist, without an efficient intelligent cause, and without design.

Atheists assert that the existence of things is *casual.* —Dwight.

Syn.—Accidental, fortuitous, incidental, occasional.—*Casual* and *fortuitous* are substantially the same; a thing is *accidental* when not planned or sought, as a meeting; *incidental* when it falls in as secondary, or out of the regular course of things, as a remark; *occasional* when it occurs only now and then.

çaş'ū-ăl, *n.* A pauper; one who receives relief temporarily.

çaş'ū-ăl-işm, *n.* The theory that all things occur by chance.

çaş'ū-ăl-ist, *n.* A believer in casualism.

çaş'ū-ăl-ly, *adv.* Accidentally; fortuitously; without design; by chance.

çaş'ū-ăl-ness, *n.* Accidentalness; the quality of being casual.

çaş'ū-ăl-ty, *n.* 1. Accident; that which comes by chance or without design, or without being foreseen; contingency.

2. Any injury of the body from accident, whether resulting in death or not; and by a metonymy, death, or other misfortune, occasioned by an accident.

In military returns, the head of *casualties* embraces all men who die, desert, or are dismissed.

3. In Scots law, an emolument due from a vassal to his superior, beyond the stated yearly duties, upon certain casual events.

Casualty ward; a hospital ward for the treatment of persons injured accidentally; an emergency ward.

Syn.—Chance, accident, hazard, contingency, fortuity, misfortune.

Çaş″ū-à-rī'nà, *n.* [From L. *casuarius*, the cassowary; so called from the resemblance of the twigs to the feathers of the cassowary.] A genus of trees chiefly found in Australia, having no leaves and with drooping, reed-like branches. Those which are large furnish a heavy, hard timber known as beefwood and she-oak.

Caş-ū-ar-i-nā'cē-æ, *n.* A small family of trees, growing mostly in Australia, and having but one genus, *Casuarina.*

çaş-ū-ar-i-nā'ceous, *a.* Relating to or like the *Casuarinaceæ.*

çaş'ū-ist, *n.* [Fr. *casuiste*, from L. *casus*, a case, fall.] One who studies and resolves cases of conscience.

The judgment of any *casuist* or learned divine is not sufficient to give him confidence. —South.

çaş'ū-ist, *v.i.* To play the part of a casuist.

çaş-ū-is'tiç, çaş-ū-is'tiç-ăl, *a.* Relating to cases of conscience or to cases of doubtful propriety.

çaş'ū-ist-ry, *n.* 1. The science or doctrine of cases of conscience; the science of resolving cases of doubtful propriety, or of deducing a standard of morality from the laws of society or from equity and natural reason.

2. False reasoning about morals and duties; sophistry.

çaş'ū-là, çaş'ūle, *n.* Same as *Chasuble.*

çā'sus, *n.* [L.] A case; an occurrence; an accident.

Casus belli; the cause of war, real or alleged.

Casus fœderis; whatever comes under the terms of a treaty.

Casus fortuitus; an unpreventable accident.

Casus omissus; a case for which the statutes make no provision.

çat, *v.t.* To haul up to the cathead, as an anchor.

çat, *n.* [AS. *cat*; D. *kat*; LL. *catus*; Hind. *katās*; Turk. *qadi*, a cat.]

1. A name applied to certain species of carnivorous quadrupeds, of the genus *Felis.* The domestic cat includes many distinct varieties, such as the *Angora cat*, the *Maltese* (or *blue*) *cat*, the *Manx cat*, and the *Persian cat.* The wild cat is much larger than the domestic breed.

2. A ship formed on the Norwegian model, having a narrow stern, projecting quarters, and a deep waist. It is strongly built, from four to six hundred tons burden, and employed in the coal and timber trades.

3. A strong tackle or combination of pulleys, to hook and draw an anchor perpendicularly up to the cathead of a ship.

4. An old game called *tipcat*; the thick, short stick pointed at each end, with which it was played; also, a ball-game, commonly known as *one, two,* or *three old cat.*

5. A tripod having six feet; called a *cat* because it always lands on three feet, however placed.

6. A colloquial term for a gossiping woman.

A cat in the meal; a figure drawn from one of Æsop's fables; a hidden danger.

Cat and dog life; a life of fighting and backbiting, like a cat and a dog; a quarrelsome time.

Enough to make a cat laugh; something very astonishing or absurd.

To let the cat out of the bag; to tell a secret before the time is ripe.

To wait to see which way the cat jumps; to postpone action until one sees what turn things are going to take or how others are going to act.

çat'à-. A prefix from Gr. *kata*, and signifying down, downward, under, against, contrary to, according to, and sometimes merely intensive; final *a* is sometimes dropped, and frequently becomes *cath-* for the sake of euphony, as *cat*opter, *cath*artic, *cath*ode.

çat-à-bap'tist, *n.* [Late Gr. *katabaptistēs*, from *katabaptizein*, to dip down or into; *kata*, down, *baptizein*, to dip.] One who opposes baptism.

çat-à-bā'sion, *n.* [Gr. *katabasion*; *kata*, downward, and *bainein*, to go.] A chamber in a Greek church, under the altar, where relics are kept.

çà-tab'à-sis, *n.*; *pl.* **çà-tab'à-sēş.** [Gr. *katabasis*, a going down; *kata*, down, and *bainein*, to go.] The act of descending; hence, in medicine, the abating of a disease.

çat-à-bat'iç, *a.* [Gr. *katabatikos*, from *katabainein*, to go down; *kata*, down, and *bainein*, to go.] Slowly yielding; abating.

çat″à-bī-ot'iç, *a.* [*Cata-*, and Gr. *bios*, life.] Having the effect of living organisms or structures on adjacent cells and the harmonious development of the latter.

çat-à-bol'iç, *a.* Relating to catabolism.

çà-tab'ō-lişm, *n.* [Gr. *katabolē*, a throwing down; from *kata*, down, and *ballein*, to throw.] Destructive metabolism, in which complex living bodies are broken down into less complex waste bodies; the opposite of *anabolism.*

çat-à-çaus'tiç, *a.* [*Cata-*, and Gr. *kaustikos*, from *kaiein*, to burn.] Produced by reflection; as, *catacaustic* curves, in geometry.

çat-à-çaus'tiç, *n.* In optics, a caustic curve resulting from the reflection of rays of light.

çat-à-çhrē'sis, *n.* [L., from Gr. *katachrēsis*, the misuse of a word, from *katachrēsthai*; *kata*, against, and *chrēsthai*, to use.] An abuse of a trope, or of words; a figure in rhetoric, when one word is put for another, or when a word is too far wrested from its true signification; as, a voice *beautiful* to the *ear.*

çat-à-çhres'tiç, çat-à-çhres'tiç-ăl, *a.* [Gr. *katachrēstikos*, misused, misapplied.] Belonging to a catachresis; forced; far-fetched.

çat-à-çhres'tiç-ăl-ly, *adv.* In a forced manner.

çat'à-çlaşm, *n.* [Gr. *kataklasma*, from *kata*, down, and *klaein*, to break.] Disruption; a breaking down or apart on a large scale.

çat-à-çli'năl, *a.* [Gr. *kataklinēs*, sloping, from *kata*, down, and *klinein*, to bend.] Descending according to the incline of the strata; as, a *cataclinal* valley. Opposed to *anaclinal.*

çat'à-çlyşm, *n.* [L. *cataclysmos*; Gr. *kataklysmos*; from *kataklyzein*; *kata*, down, and *klyzein*, to wash.]

1. A deluge, or overflowing of water; particularly, the flood in Noah's days. In geology, used to denote various inundations or deluges, supposed to have occurred at different periods, and to have deposited different formations of diluvium or drift.

2. Any violent and widespread disturbance of the order of nature, such as the eruption of Mt. Pelee over Martinique in 1902.

3. Any extraordinary and violent change, such as a sudden and complete revolution.

çat-à-çlyş'măl, çat-à-çlyş'miç, *a.* Pertaining to a cataclysm.

çat-à-çlyş'mist, *n.* A believer in the production of great geological changes by cataclysms.

çat'à-çōmb (-kōm), *n.* [It. *catacomba*; LL. *catacumba*; a sepulchral vault; Gr. *kata*, down, and *kymbē*, a hollow, a cavity.] A cave, grotto, or subterraneous place for the burial of the dead; originally applied to the chapel of St. Sebastian, in Rome, where, the ancient Roman calendars say, the body of St. Peter was deposited; now applied to a vast number of subterranean sepulchers, about three miles from Rome, in the Appian Way; supposed to be the cells and caves in which were deposited the bodies of the primitive Christian martyrs. Each catacomb is three feet broad, and eight or ten high; along the side walls are sepulchral niches, closed with thick tiles, or pieces of marble. Catacombs are found also at Naples, and in other places.

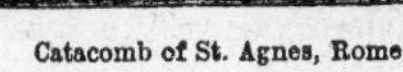

Catacomb of St. Agnes, Rome.

çat″à-çō-rol'là, *n.* [*Cata-*, and L. *corolla*, dim. of *corona*, a crown.] In botany, a second corolla within or outside the true one; also, an abnormal growth of petals inside the true corolla.

çat-à-çous'tiçs, *n.* [*Cata-*, and Gr. *akoustikos*,

from *akouein*, to hear.] That part of acoustics, or the doctrine of sounds, which treats of reflected sounds; cataphonics.

çat-à-crot′iç, *a.* [*Cata-*, and Gr. *krotos*, a beating, knocking.] Pertaining to a kind of sphygmogram, or pulse-tracing, in which the descending part of the curve shows secondary elevations.

çat″à-di-op′triç, çat″à-di-op′triç-ăl, *a.* Reflecting light.

çat″à-di-op′triçs, *n.* [*Cata-*, and Gr. *dioptrika*; *dia*, through, and the root of *opsomai*, I shall see.] The science of the reflection of light, and of the correct use of instruments for observing its phenomena.

çat′à-drōme, *n.* [Gr. *katadromos*, a race-course.]
1. A race-track.
2. A crane for lifting great weights.

çà-tad′rō-mous, *a.* [Gr. *katadromos*, overrun; *kata*, down, and *dramein*, to run.]
1. In botany, a term used of branching ferns, in which the inferior fronds rise from the posterior of the pinnæ; the opposite of *anadromous*.
2. In ichthyology, said of certain fishes which descend rivers or streams in the spawning season.

Çà-tad′y-sās, *n.* [Gr. *katadysis*, a dipping under water; *kata*, down, and *dyein*, to enter, dive.] The type genus of the family *Catadysidæ*.

Çat-à-dys′i-dæ, *n.pl.* A North American family of spiders with only two pulmonary sacs and the fangs directed in a vertical direction.

çat′à-falque (-falk), **çat-à-fal′çō,** *n.* [Fr. *catafalque*; It. *catafalco*, a funeral canopy, stage.] A temporary resting place or platform for a corpse, draped and canopied; chiefly used for exposing the remains of eminent persons to public view, and, when mounted on wheels, for conveying them to the burial place.

çat-ag-mat′iç, *a.* [Gr. *katagma* (*-atos*), a breakage; from *kata*, intens., and *agnynai*, to break.] Having the quality of consolidating broken parts; promoting the union of fractured bones.

çat′à-grȧph, *n.* [Gr. *katagraphē*, a drawing, outline.] The first draft of a picture; a profile.

Çà-tāi′ăn, Çà-thāi′ăn, *n.* A native of China, formerly called *Cathay*; a Chinese barbarian; hence, by early writers, used in the sense of a villain, a blackguard, etc.

Çat′à-lăn, *n.* A native of Catalonia, a former province of Spain, or one of Catalonian descent; also, the language of Catalonia, allied to the Provençal.

Çat′à-lăn, *a.* Pertaining to Catalonia, its people or language.

çat-à-leç′tiç, *a.* [LL. *catalecticus*; Gr. *katalēktikos*, a leaving off, incomplete; from *katalēgein*; *kata*, intens., and *lēgein*, to leave off, cease.] In prosody, wanting a syllable at the end, or terminating in an imperfect foot; as, a *catalectic* verse.

çat′à-lep-sy, çat-à-lep′sis, *n.* [LL. *catalepsis*; Gr. *katalēpsis*, a seizing, grasping, from *katalambanein*; *kata*, down, and *lambanein*, to take, seize.] A sudden suppression of motion and sensation, in which the patient is speechless, senseless, and fixed in one posture, with his eyes open, without seeing or understanding. While there is a suspension of animation, there is a continued action of the lungs and heart.

çat-à-lep′tiç, *a.* Pertaining to catalepsy; as, a *cataleptic* fit.

çat-à-lep′ti-fọrm, *a.* Having the nature of catalepsy.

çat-à-lex′is, *n.* [Gr. *katalēxis*, an ending, termination, from *katalēgein*, to leave off, cease; *kata*, down, and *lēgein*, to cease.] In prosody, the state of being catalectic; an incomplete foot at the end of a verse, or, more generally, any incomplete foot.

Çat-al-laç′tà, *n.pl.* [From Gr. *katallassein*, to exchange, change.] A class or division of *Protozoa*, with pear-shaped cells and with stems meeting in the center of spherical colonies.

çat-al-laç′tiçs, *n.* [Gr. *katallaktikos*, changeable, easy to reconcile, from *katallassein*, to exchange, reconcile; *kata*, down, and *allassein*, to exchange, from *allos*, other.] In political economy, the science of commercial exchanges.

çat′à-lō-ġize, *v.t.* To insert in a catalogue. [Rare.]

çat′à-logue (-log) or **çat′à-log,** *n.* [Fr. *catalogue*; LL. *catalogus*; Gr. *katalogos*, a list, register, from *katalegein*, to reckon, count up; *kata*, down, completely, and *legein*, to say.] A list or enumeration of the names of men or things, disposed in a certain order, often alphabetically; as, a *catalogue* of the students of a college, of books, of merchandise, or of the stars.

Card catalogue; a catalogue, usually of books, in which items are entered on separate cards, these cards being methodically arranged in cases either by subjects or authors, or alphabetically.

Catalogue raisonné [Fr.]; a catalogue of books classed according to their subjects.

çat′à-logue, or **çat′à-log,** *v.t.*; catalogued, *pt.*, *pp.*; cataloguing, *ppr.* To make a list of; to insert in a catalogue.

çat′à-log-uẽr, *n.* One who makes or compiles catalogues.

Çà-tal′pà, *n.* [Am. Ind.] A genus of large trees, having spotted white flowers and long cylindrical pods. They are found in many parts of North America, notably in the Mississippi valley, and in Japan, China, and the East Indies.

çà-tal′y-sis, *n.*; *pl.* **çà-tal′y-sēş.** [Gr. *katalysis*, dissolution; *kata*, down, and *lyein*, to loose.]
1. Dissolution; decay; deterioration.
2. In chemistry, a decomposition and new combination produced among the proximate and elementary principles of one or more compounds, by virtue of the mere presence of a substance or substances which do not of themselves enter into combination.

çat-à-lyt′iç, *a.* Relating to catalysis; as, *catalytic* force.

çat-à-lyt′iç, *n.* A counteracting agent employed in catalysis to arrest morbid influences in the blood.

çat″à-mà-ran′, *n.* [E. Ind.] 1. A kind of long, narrow raft, made of logs or floats, fastened together; used for fishing and landing goods on the coasts of India and South America, and in the waters of the East and West Indies.

Catamaran.

2. A vessel having twin hulls; particularly, a pleasure-boat so built, which is noted for its speed and safety.
3. A kind of raft used to send fire or torpedoes into an enemy's fleet.
4. A petulant or scolding woman; a vixen. [Colloq.]

çat-à-mē′ni-à, *n.pl.* [Gr. *katamēnia*, neut. pl. of *katamēnios*, monthly; *kata*, according to, and *mēn*, a month.] The monthly flowings of females; menstruation.

çat-à-mē′ni-ăl, *a.* Pertaining to the catamenia.

çat′à-mount, *n.* Cat of the mountain, the European wildcat; the cougar; also applied to the lynx.

çat-à-nad′rō-mous, *a.* [Gr. *kata*, down, *ana*, up, and *dromos*, a course, a running.] In ichthyology, passing annually from salt water to fresh, and returning.

çat′à-paşm, *n.* [Gr. *katapasma*, a powder.] A powder formerly used for sprinkling the body.

çat-à-pel′tiç, *a.* [Gr. *katapeltikos*, from *katapeltēs*, a catapult.] Pertaining to the catapult.

çat-à-pet′ăl-ous, *a.* [*Cata-*, and Gr. *petalon*, a leaf.] A term applied to petals of a flower when held together by stamens, which grow to their bases, as in the mallow.

çat-à-phā′şi-à, *n.* A mental affection which shows itself in a derangement of the speech, one or more words being repeated continuously in reply to a question.

çat-à-phon′iç, *a.* Pertaining to cataphonics.

çat-à-phon′içs, *n.* [*Cata-*, and Gr. *phōnē*, sound.] The science of reflected sounds, a branch of acoustics; catacoustics.

çat″à-phō-rē′sis, *n.* [Gr. *kataphora*, a lethargic attack, a bringing down, from *katapherein*; *kata*, down, and *pherein*, to bring.] The introduction of a liquid, usually medicinal, into bodily tissue by means of an electric current; commonly called *electric osmose*.

çat′à-phraçt (-frakt), *n.* [L. *cataphracta*; Gr. *kataphraktēs*, a coat of mail, from *kataphrassein*, to cover with mail; *kata*, against, and *phrassein*, to fence.]
1. A piece of heavy, defensive armor, formed of cloth or leather, strengthened with scales or links, used to defend the breast, or whole body, or even the horse, as well as the rider.
2. A horseman in complete armor.
3. The natural armor or covering of certain fishes.

çat′à-phraçt-ed, *a.* In zoölogy, covered with a hard callous skin, or with horny or bony plates or scales, closely joined together, like those of the Roman soldiers called cataphracti; hence the term.

çat-à-phraç′tī, *n.pl.* [L., from Gr. *kataphraktos*, mailed.]
1. The body of soldiers introduced into the Roman army in the fourth century armored with the cataphract, or any soldiers thus protected.
2. [C—] A group of spiny-finned fishes whose faces or cheeks are covered with large, strong plates.

çat-à-phraç′tiç, *a.* Pertaining to or resembling a cataphract.

çat-à-phyl′lum, *n.*; *pl.* **çat-à-phyl′là.** [*Cata-*, and Gr. *phyllon*, a leaf.] In botany, an elementary leaf or scale, generally of a fungaceous character.

çat-à-phyş′iç, çat-à-phyş′iç-ăl, *a.* [*Cata-*, and Gr. *physis*, nature.] Unnatural; not according to nature.

çà-tap′là-sis, *n.* [Gr. *kataplassis*; *kata*, down, and *plassein*, to form.] The natural period of decline in organic or germ development.

çat′à-plaşm, *n.* [Gr. *kataplasma*, from *kataplassein*, to anoint, spread over.] A poultice; a soft and moist substance to be applied to some part of the body, to excite or repel heat, or to relax the skin.

çat-à-pleç′tiç, *a.* Pertaining to cataplexy.

çat′à-plex-y, *n.* [Gr. *kataplēx*, stricken; *kata*, down, and *plessein*, to strike.] A sudden nervous shock resulting in paralysis.

çat′à-pūce, *n.* [Fr.] The herb spurge. [Obs.]

çat′à-pult, *n.* [L. *catapulta*; Gr. *katapeltēs*, an engine for throwing stones, from *kata*, down, and *pallein*, to toss, whirl.]
1. A military engine used by the ancient Greeks and Romans for throwing stones, darts, and arrows. Later, the engine assumed the form of a gigantic crossbow and was called a *ballista*. The annexed cut shows a simple form of the *catapult*.

Catapult.

F, end of lever; A, windlass; EE, prongs of fork which holds the object to be thrown. When the lever is relieved it bounds suddenly upward, the centrifugal force causing the loop C to slip off the hook, D, whereupon the object on the fork is liberated. B, rings of iron or lead, increasing the rebound.

2. A toy consisting of a forked stick to which is attached an elastic band, used for throwing small missiles; popularly known as a *sling-shot*.

çat-à-pul′tiç, *a.* Pertaining to a catapult.

çat′à-raçt, *n.* [L. *cataracta*; Gr. *katarraktēs*, a waterfall, portcullis, from *katarrēgnynai*; *kata*, down, and *rēgnynai*, to break.]
1. A great fall of water over a precipice; a cascade upon a great scale.
2. In medicine and surgery, an opacity of the crystalline lens, or its capsule; a disorder in the eye, by which the pupil, which is usually black and transparent, becomes colored and opaque.
3. In mechanics, a hydraulic brake which regulates or modifies the action of pumping engines and other machines; also called a *dash-pot*.

çat-à-raç′tine, *a.* Pertaining to a cataract (waterfall), or similar to it.

çat-à-raç′tous, *a.* Partaking of the nature of a cataract in the eye.

çà-tärrh′ (-tär′), *n.* [L. *catarrhus*; Gr. *katarrhoos*, from *katarrhein*, to flow down; *kata*, down, and *rhein*, to flow.] An inflammatory affection of the mucous membranes, more particularly of the throat and head, accompanied by an undue secretion of mucus; as, nasal *catarrh*; *catarrh* of the stomach.

çà-tärrh′ăl, *a.* Pertaining to catarrh, produced by it, or attending it; as, a *catarrhal* fever.

Çat-ăr-rhī′nà, *n.pl.* A division of Old World *Quadrumana* with narrow heads and nostrils, the latter being turned downward.

çat′ăr-rhine (*or* -rin), *n.* [Gr. *katarrhis*; *kata*, down, and *rhis*, *rhinos*, nose.] One of the *Quadrumana* belonging to the *Catarrhina*.

çà-tärrh′ous, *a.* Same as *Catarrhal*.

çat-à-stal′tiç, *a.* [Gr. *katastaltikos*, fitted for checking, from *katastellein*, to keep down, to check; *kata*, down, and *stellein*, to send.] In medicine, astringent or styptic; effective in checking morbid evacuations.

çà-tas′tà-sis, *n*; *pl.* **çà-tas′tà-sēş.** [Gr. *katastasis*, an arranging, setting forth, from *kathistanai*; *kata*, down, and *histanai*, to set up, cause to stand.]
1. In ancient times, that part of the Greek drama which prepared for or intensified the catastrophe.
2. In rhetoric, something explanatory of the main action or subject matter.
3. In medicine, a settled or normal habit of body.
4. In anatomy, the replacement of bones to their normal position after a dislocation.

çat′ȧ-stāte, *n.* [Gr. *kathistanai*, to settle down.] One of the series of substances produced by a catabolic process; written also *katastate.*

çȧ-tas′tēr-işm, *n.* [Gr. *katasterismos*, from *katasterizein*, to place among the stars; *kata*, down, and *asterizein*, to make into a star, from *astēr*, a star.] A constellation; a placing among the stars; an enumeration of the stars.

çȧ-tas′tō-mid, *a.* and *n.* See *Catostomid.*

çȧ-tas′tō-moid, *a.* See *Catostomoid.*

çȧ-tas′trō-phē, *n.* [L. *catastropha*; Gr. *katastrophē*, an overthrowing, from *katastrephein*, to overturn; *kata*, down, and *strephein*, to turn.]

1. The unraveling or denouement of a plot; the final event of a dramatic piece. The ancients divided a play into the protasis, epitasis, catastasis, and *catastrophe*—the introduction, continuance, heightening, and development or conclusion.

2. A final event; conclusion; generally, an unfortunate conclusion, calamity, or disaster.

3. In geology, a supposed change in the globe from sudden physical violence, causing elevation or subsidence of the solid parts, or a cataclysm of the waters.

Syn.—Revolution, disaster, calamity, misfortune, misadventure, reverse, blow, visitation, denouement.

çat-ȧ-stroph′iç, *a.* Pertaining to a catastrophe.

çȧ-tas′trō-phişm, *n.* The theory that geological changes are the result of sudden and violent physical causes.

çȧ-tas′trō-phist, *n.* A believer in the doctrine of catastrophism.

Çȧ-tạw′bȧ, *n.* [Named from the *Catawba* river in South Carolina, where it was first raised.]

1. A variety of American grape.

2. A light colored wine made from the Catawba grape.

çat′-back, *n.* A small rope which plays upon the hoisting block of the anchor.

çat′-bēam, *n.* The longest beam of the boat, terminating in the cathead, which, in turn, supports the anchor.

çat′bīrd, *n.* In ornithology, (a) an American mimic bird, *Galeoscoptes carolinensis*, allied to the thrush, and less perfect in its imitative qualities than the mocking-bird; (b) an Australian bird, *Ptilonorhynchus smithii.* In both varieties the cry of alarm resembles the mewing of a cat.

çat′-block, *n.* The block by which the anchor is hoisted to the cathead.

çat′bōat, *n.* A one-masted sailboat which has its mast placed far forward.

çat′çall, *n.* A derisive cry, not unlike that of a cat, sometimes made in public places; also, an instrument for imitating such a noise.

çat′çall, *v.t.* To deride by making the sounds known as catcalls; as, they *catcalled* the actor.

çatch (kach), *v.t.*; caught (kạt), *pt.*, *pp.*; catching, *ppr.* [ME. *catchen*, *cachen*; OFr. *cacher*, *cachier*; LL. *captiare*, from L. *captare*, intens. of *capere*, to take.]

1. To seize or lay hold on with the hand; carrying the sense of pursuit.

2. To seize, in a general sense; as, to *catch* a ball.

3. To seize, as in a snare or trap; to insnare; to entangle.

4. To attack; to communicate to; as, the fire *caught* the adjoining building.

5. To seize the affections of; to engage and attach to; as, to *catch* the fair.

6. To take or receive by contagion or infection; as, to *catch* the measles.

7. To snatch; to take suddenly; as, to *catch* a book out of the hand.

8. To be acted upon by; as, the sails *catch* the breeze.

9. To seize with the senses or mind; to apprehend; as, to *catch* a melody; to *catch* the meaning of a remark.

10. To get possession of; to attain.

11. To come upon unexpectedly; as, to *catch* one in the act of stealing.

12. To reach in time; as, to *catch* a train.

To catch fire; to become ignited.

To catch one's eye; to attract one's attention.

To catch on; to grasp the situation; to understand. [Colloq.]

To catch one on the hip; to gain the advantage.

To catch one up; to call one's attention abruptly to a mistake; to interrupt while speaking.

Syn.—Grasp, clutch, capture, entrap, insnare, discover, apprehend.

çatch, *v.i.* 1. To communicate; to spread by infecting; as, a disease will *catch* from man to man.

2. To desire a thing; as, to *catch* at hope.

3. To attain possession. [Obs.]

4. To be impeded by slight obstruction, as a door; to become entangled, as a book.

To catch up with; to overtake.

çatch, *n.* 1. Seizure; the act of seizing.

2. Anything that seizes or takes hold, as a hook.

3. The posture of seizing; a state of preparation to catch, or of watching an opportunity to seize; as, to lie upon the *catch.* [Obs.]

4. The thing caught, considered as an object of desire; profit; advantage.

> Hector shall have a great *catch.* —Shak.

5. A snatch; a short interval of action.

> It has been writ by *catches.* —Locke.

6. An artful plan to entrap; as, there is a *catch* in your query.

7. In music, a fugue in the unison, wherein, to humor some conceit in the words, the melody is broken, and the sense is interrupted in one part, and caught and supported by another, or a different sense is given to the words; or a piece for three or more voices, one of which leads and the others follow in the same notes.

8. A sudden advantage taken.

9. The quantity of fish taken at one time.

10. A sudden and painful stoppage of the breath; as, a *catch* in the side.

Syn.—Detention, seizure, capture, arrest, apprehension.

çatch′ȧ-ble, *a.* That may be caught. [Rare.]

çatch′ạll, *n.* A receptacle for various articles, as a basket or a bag.

çatch′-bā″sin, *n.* A vault near the intersection of the gutter outlet and the sewer, for retaining solid matter likely to clog the sewer.

çatch′drāin, *n.* A ditch or drain on the side of a hill to catch the surface water; also, a ditch on the side of a canal, to catch the surplus water.

çatch′ēr, *n.* One who catches; that which catches, or in which anything is caught; in baseball, the player behind the batter.

çatch′flȳ, *n.* A plant of the genus *Lychnis*, of the pink family. The joints of the stem, and sometimes other portions, give out a sticky exudate to which insects adhere. Called also *campion.*

çatch′ing, *a.* 1. Communicating, or that may be communicated, by contagion; infectious; as, a disease is *catching.*

2. Captivating.

Catching bargain; a bargain made with an heir expectant for the purchase of his expectancy, at an inadequate price.

Syn.—Contagious, infectious, pestilential.

çatch′-līne, *n.* A line of fine type between two lines of large type; or, in manuscript, any line at the bottom or the top of the page, which directs attention to what follows or precedes.

çatch′-mead″ōw (-med″ō), *n.* A meadow which is irrigated by water from a spring or rivulet on the declivity of a hill.

çatch′ment, *n.* Ground on which water may be caught and retained; drainage.

Area of catchment; in hydraulic engineering, the available area from which water may be caught or drawn to supply any given locality.

çatch′pen″ny, *n.* and *a.* I. *n.* Something worthless, particularly a book or pamphlet, adapted to the popular taste, and intended to gain money in market.

II. *a.* Contrived with the object of obtaining small amounts from the unwary or uninformed; as, a *catchpenny* affair.

çatch′-pōle, *n.* A pole provided with metal bars and strong springs, used chiefly by medieval officers for the purpose of catching criminals, or by foot-soldiers to unhorse knights.

çatch′pōll, *n.* [ME. *catchepoll*, a bailiff, taxgatherer; OFr. *chacipol*, *chassipol*, a tax-gatherer; *cacier*, *cacher*, to catch, and E. *poll*, head.] A bailiff's assistant, so called by way of reproach.

çatch′up, çat′sup, *n.* [E. Ind. *kitjap.*] A sauce from tomatoes, walnuts, mushrooms, etc.; written also *ketchup.*

çatch′wạ″tēr, *n.* See *Catchdrain.*

çatch′weed, *n.* Any one of various herbaceous plants, distinguished by stiff spines on the stems and fruits; also called *cleavers.*

çatch′weight (-wāt), *adv.* A race-course term, signifying without a handicap.

çatch′wŏrd, *n.* 1. Among actors, the last word of the preceding speaker, which reminds one that he is to speak next.

2. A word designed to express something in a pleasing or striking manner, so that, for a while at least, it may be generally adopted.

3. A word of direction or information, either on the printed or manuscript page, which indicates the continuance of a sentence or subject.

çatch′wŏrk, *n.* A system of irrigation for hilly and meadow land, for catching water and distributing it from the higher to lower levels.

çatch′y, *a.* Lightly attractive; changeable; as, a *catchy* song; a *catchy* wind.

çāte, *n.* [From OFr. *acat*, a purchase.] Rich or delicate food; usually used in the plural; as, he fed on *cates.* [Obs.]

çat-ē-çhet′iç, çat-ē-çhet′iç-ăl, *a.* [Gr. *katēchētikos*, from *katēchētēs*, an instructor; *katēchein*, to instruct, teach by word of mouth.]

1. Relating to oral instruction, and particularly in the first principles of the Christian religion.

2. Relating to or consisting in asking questions and receiving answers, according to the old manner of teaching pupils.

çat-ē-çhet′iç-ăl-ly, *adv.* By question and answer; in the way of oral instruction.

çat-ē-çhet′içs, *n.* The art of instruction by questions and answers.

çat′e-chin, çat′e-chine, *n.* A white crystal extracted from catechu; known also as *catechuic acid.*

çat″ē-çhi-şā′tion, *n.* See *Catechization.*

çat′ē-çhīşe, *v.t.* See *Catechize.*

çat′ē-çhīş-ēr, *n.* See *Catechizer.*

çat′ē-çhişm, *n.* [LL. *catechismus*, from Gr. *katēchizein*, to catechize.]

1. A form of instruction by means of questions and answers, particularly in the principles of religion.

2. An elementary book containing a summary of principles in any science or art, but especially in religion, reduced to the form of questions and answers.

çat-ē-çhiş′măl, *a.* Having an arrangement of questions and answers, like a catechism.

çat′ē-çhist, *n.* One who instructs *viva voce*, or by question and answer; a catechizer; one appointed by the church to instruct in the principles of religion.

çat-ē-çhis′tiç, çat-ē-çhis′tiç-ăl, *a.* Pertaining to a catechist or catechism.

çat″ē-çhi-zā′tion, *n.* The act of examining by the putting of questions; also spelled *catechisation.*

çat′ē-çhīze, çat′ē-çhīşe, *v.t.*; catechized, *pt.*, *pp.*; catechizing, *ppr.* 1. To instruct by asking questions, receiving answers, and offering explanations and corrections.

2. To question; to interrogate; to examine or try by questions, sometimes with a view to elicit condemnatory answers.

3. To question concerning the doctrines of the Christian religion; to examine (pupils) and give instruction in the principles of religion.

çat′ē-çhīz-ēr, *n.* One who catechizes; one who instructs by question and answer, and particularly in the rudiments of the Christian religion.

çat′e-çhōl, *n.* Same as *Pyrocatechin.*

çat′e-chū, *n.* A dry, brown, astringent extract, obtained by decoction and evaporation from the *Acacia Catechu*, in India. It contains a large portion of tannin or tannic acid.

çat-e-chū′iç, *a.* Pertaining to catechu.

Catechuic acid; an acid soluble in boiling water, contained in that portion of catechu which is insoluble in cold water. It was at first considered a base.

çat-ē-çhū′men, *n.* [LL. *catechumenus*; Gr. *katēchoumenos*, one instructed, ppr. of *katēchein*, to instruct.] One who is in the first rudiments of Christianity; one who is receiving instruction and preparing himself for baptism; anciently the child of believing parents, or of pagans not fully initiated in the principles of the Christian religion. Such were admitted to this state by the imposition of hands, and the sign of the cross.

çat-ē-çhū′men-āte, *n.* The condition of a catechumen, or the period during which one is a catechumen.

çat″ē-çhū-men′i-căl, *a.* Belonging to catechumens.

çat-ē-çhū′men-ist, *n.* A catechumen.

çat-ē-gor-ē-mat′iç, *a.* [Gr. *katēgorēma* (-*atos*), a predicate.] In logic, applied to a word which is capable of being employed by itself as a term or predicate of a proposition.

çat-ē-gor′iç-ăl (-i-kal), *a.* [LL. *categoricus*; Gr. *katēgorikos*, from *katēgoria*, a category.]

1. Pertaining to a category.

2. Absolute; positive; express; not relative or hypothetical; as, a *categorical* answer is requested.

çat-ē-gor′iç-ăl-ly, *adv.* Absolutely; directly; expressly; positively; as, to affirm *categorically.*

çat-ē-gor′iç-ăl-ness, *n.* The quality of being categorical, absolute, or positive.

çat′ē-gō-rist, *n.* One who compiles or classifies a category.

çat′ē-gō-rize, *v.t.*; categorized, *pt.*, *pp.*; categorizing, *ppr.* To classify in a category; to catalogue. [Rare.]

çat′ē-gō-ry, *n.* [L. *categoria*; Gr. *katēgoria*, from *katēgorein*, to accuse, assert, predicate; *kata*, against, and *agoreuein*, to declaim, address an assembly; *agora*, an assembly.]

1. In logic, a series or order of all the predicates or attributes contained under a genus. The school philosophers distributed all the objects of our thoughts and ideas into genera or classes. Aristotle made ten *categories*, viz., substance, quantity, quality, relation, action, passion, time, place, situation, and habit.

2. Class; condition; predicament; as, to put a person in the same *category* with another.

Syn.—Class, inventory, predicament.—*Category* and *predicament* are both used to express the idea of *condition* or *situation*, but with this difference, that *predicament* supposes it to be a bad or unfortunate one.

çat′el, *n.* [ME. *catel*; OFr. *catel*; LL. *captale, capitale*, property, goods.] Property or chattels; used by old English writers as the opposite of *income*.

çat-ē-leç′trōde, *n.* [*Cata-*, and Gr. *ēlektron*, amber, and *hodos*, way.] A negative electrode; the negative pole of a galvanic battery.

çat-ē-leç-trō-ton′iç, *a.* Pertaining to or distinguished by catelectrotonus.

çat″ē-leç-trot′ō-nus, *n.* [*Cata-*, and Gr. *ēlektron*, amber, and *tonos*, tension.] The increased tension produced in a nerve near the cathode or negative pole of a voltaic battery, when an electric current passes through it.

çȧ-tē′nȧ, *n.*; *pl.* **çȧ-tē′næ.** [L. *catena*, a chain.] A chain of connected things or subjects, especially relating to polemic theology.

çat′ē-nā-ry, çat-ē-nā′ri-ăn, *a.* [L. *catenarius*, from *catena*, a chain.] Relating to a chain; like a chain.

çat′ē-nā-ry, *n.*; *pl.* **çat′ē-nā-rieṣ.** In geometry, the curve formed by a perfectly flexible cord or chain, of uniform density, hanging freely between two points of suspension, whether the points are horizontal or not.

çat′ē-nāte, *v.t.*; catenated, *pt.*, *pp.*; catenating, *ppr.* To chain, or rather to connect in a series of links or ties.

çat′ē-nāte, çat′ē-nā-ted, *a.* Connected, as links in a chain.

çat-ē-nā′tion, *n.* Connection of links, union of parts, as in a chain; regular connection. [See *Concatenation*.]

çȧ-ten′ū-lāte, *a.* [L. *catenula*, dim. of *catena*, a chain.]

1. Consisting of little links or chains.

2. In natural history, presenting, on the surface, a series of oblong tubercles, resembling a chain.

çā′tēr, *v.i.*; catered, *pt.*, *pp.*; catering, *ppr.* [ME. *catour*, a purchaser, caterer; OFr. *acator*, from *acater*, to buy, provide; from LL. *accaptare*; *ad*, to, and *captare*, to strive, seize; intens. of L. *capere*, to take.]

1. To provide refreshments; followed by *for*; as, to *cater for* a large company.

2. To give what is wanted or required; followed by *for* or *to*; as, to *cater to* public ideas.

çā′tēr, *v.t.* To cut in a diagonal direction. [Obs.]

çā′tēr, *n.* A provider; a caterer. [Obs.]

çā′tēr, *n.* [Fr. *quatre*, from L. *quattuor*, four.] The four of cards or dice.

çat′e-ran, *n.* A Highland robber or freebooter; a sort of irregular soldier. [Scot.]

çā′tēr-çor″nēred, *a.* Diagonal. [Colloq.]

çā′tēr-çouṣ″in (-kuz″n), *n.* [Fr. *quatre*; L. *quattuor*, four, and *cousin*.] A quater-cousin; a remote relation; hence, a friend.

çā′tēr-ēr, *n.* A provider, buyer, or purveyor of provisions.

çā′tēr-ess, *n.* A woman who caters; a female provider of food.

çat′ēr-pil-lăr, *n.* [ME. *catyrpel*, a corruption of OFr. *chatepelouse*, *catepelue*, from *chate*, a she-cat, and *pelouse*, hairy; LL. *catus*, a cat, and *pilosus*, from *pilus*, a hair.]

1. The colored and often hairy larva of lepidopterous insects. This term is also applied to the larvæ of other insects, such as the *Tenthredo*, or sawfly, but is more generally confined to the lepidopters. *Caterpillars* are produced immediately from the egg. They contain the embryo of the perfect insect, inclosed within a muscular envelope, which is thrown off when the insect enters the nymph or chrysalis state, in which it remains for some time as if inanimate. It then throws off its last envelope and emerges a perfect insect.

2. A plant belonging to the genus *Scorpiurus*, having pods not unlike caterpillars in appearance.

çat′ēr-pil-lăr-çatch″ēr, *n.* A bird of the shrike family, which devours caterpillars.

çat′ēr-pil-lăr-ēat″ēr, *n.* 1. A caterpillar-catcher.

2. A worm bred in the body of a caterpillar, and which eats its way out.

çat′ēr-pil-lăr-fun″gus, *n.* A fungus of the genus *Cordyceps*, which infests the larvæ of insects; especially, the *Cordyceps Robertsii* of New Zealand.

çat′ēr-pil-lăr-hunt″ēr, *n.* One of several species of the *Carabidæ*, which feed upon caterpillars.

çat′ēr-wąul, *v.i.*; caterwauled, *pt.*, *pp.*; caterwauling, *ppr.* To cry or waul, as cats in rutting time; to make a harsh, offensive noise.

çat′ēr-wąul, *n.* A caterwauling.

çat′ēr-wąul-ing, *n.* The cry of cats; a harsh, disagreeable noise or cry.

çā′tēr-y, *n.* The place where provisions are deposited. [Obs.]

çāteṣ, *n.pl.* [ME. *acate*, *achate*, provisions, from OFr. *acator*, a caterer, from *acater*, to buy provisions, from LL. *accaptare*, to buy, provide; L. *ad*, to, and *captare*, to take, seize.] Provisions; viands; delicacies.

çat′-eyed (-īd), *a.* Having eyes like a cat.

çat′fąll, *n.* In ships, a rope used in hoisting the anchor up to the cathead.

çat′fish, *n.* 1. The wolf-fish.

2. A common name for the naked-skinned fishes of the family *Siluridæ*, embracing five genera. *Amiurus melas*, the common bullhead, found especially in muddy waters of the middle West, is an inferior food-fish having eight erectile barbels. Other species of this genus are found throughout the United States, *Amiurus ponderosus*, reaching an immense size.

3. Any fish resembling the *catfish*.

çat′-foot, *n.* A stubby foot, with arched toes, like that of a cat.

çat′-foot″ed, *a.* Having feet like a cat; hence, sly; stealthy.

çat′gut, *n.* 1. The intestines of sheep and other animals, dried and twisted, used for strings of violins and other instruments.

2. A sort of linen or canvas, with wide interstices.

Çath′ȧ-rī, *n.pl.* [From Gr. *katharos*, pure.]

1. The pure; hence, the members of such sects as protested against corruption in life or doctrine. The name was applied especially to the Novatians of the third century, who claimed to be the true church, because they refused to reinstate the *lapsi*, or those who had back-slidden.

2. A sect of the middle ages which included the Bogomiles, the Albigenses, and other bodies which accepted dualism and were composed of the religionists known as the *perfecti*, or perfect.

çath′ȧ-rine-wheel, çath′ēr-ine-wheel, *n.* [So called from St. *Catharine* of Alexandria, who is represented with a *wheel* in connection with her martyrdom.]

1. In Gothic architecture, an ornamented window, or compartment of a window, of a circular form, with rosettes or radiating divisions or spokes; known also as *rose-window* or *wheel-window*.

2. A revolving piece of fireworks similar in form to the window of the same name.

3. In heraldry, the figure of a hooked wheel symbolic of St. Catharine's martyrdom.

çath′ȧ-riṣm, *n.* 1. The act or process of making a surface chemically clean.

2. [C—] The doctrine or principles of the Cathari.

Çath′ȧ-rist, *n.* [Gr. *katharos*, pure.] One who pretends to more purity than others possess; a puritan; specifically, one of the Cathari.

çath′ȧ-rīze, *v.t.*; catharized, *pt.*, *pp.*; catharizing, *ppr.* [Gr. *katharizein*, to cleanse, from *katharos*, pure.] To make clean, as a surface, by the use of chemicals.

çat′-härp″in, çat′-härp″ing, *n.* [Origin unknown.] A rope serving to brace in the shrouds of the lower masts behind their respective yards, to tighten the shrouds, and give more room to draw in the yards, when the ship is close-hauled.

çȧ-thär′sis, *n.* [Gr. *katharsis*, purification, from *kathairein*, to purify.] Purgation; alvine discharges; evacuation.

Çȧ-thär′tēṣ, *n.* [Gr. *kathartēs*, a cleanser, from *kathairein*, to purify.] A genus of vultures which gives its name to the family *Cathartidæ*; now restricted to the turkey-buzzards.

çȧ-thär′tiç, çȧ-thär′tiç-ăl, *a.* [Gr. *kathartikos*, from *kathairein*, to purify; *katharos*, pure.]

1. Purging the bowels; promoting alvine discharges.

2. Pertaining to the purgative principle of senna; as, *cathartic* acid.

çȧ-thär′tiç, *n.* A medicine that promotes alvine discharges, and thus cleanses the stomach and bowels; a purge; a purgative, less effective than a *drastic* and more so than a *laxative*.

çȧ-thär′tiç-ăl-ly, *adv.* In the manner of a cathartic.

çȧ-thär′tiç-ăl-ness, *n.* The quality of promoting discharges from the bowels.

çȧ-thär′tin, *n.* A doubtful alkaloid, the active purgative principle of different species of *Cassia*, popularly known as *senna*; it is a glucoside, having the nature of a weak acid; known also as *cathartic acid* and *cathartina*.

çat′-hąw, *n.* [Prov. Eng.] The berry of the hawthorn; the haw.

çat′head (-hed), *n.* A strong beam projecting horizontally over a ship's bows, carrying two or three sheaves, about which a rope, called the catfall, passes, and communicates with the cat-block.

çath′ē-drȧ (*or* **çȧ-thē′drȧ**), *n.* [L. *cathedra*; Gr. *kathedra*, a seat, bench; *kata*, down, and *hedra*, from *hezesthai*, to sit.] A chair; especially, the official chair or throne of a bishop, or the professional chair of any one entitled to teach with authority or possessed of high dignity; hence, *ex cathedra*, from the chair of authority; as, he speaks *ex cathedra*.

çȧ-thē′drăl, *n.* [LL. *cathedralis* (supply *ecclesia*), from L. *cathedra*; Gr. *kathedra*, a seat,

Cathedra at Torcello.

bench.] The see or seat of a bishop; the principal church in a diocese; so called because it possesses the cathedra or official chair of the bishop.

çȧ-thē′drăl, *a.* 1. Pertaining to the church which is the bishop's seat, or head church of a diocese; containing the see of a bishop; as, a *cathedral* church; *cathedral* service.

2. Resembling the aisles of a cathedral; as, *cathedral* walks.

3. Emanating from the official chair, as of a pope or bishop; authoritative.

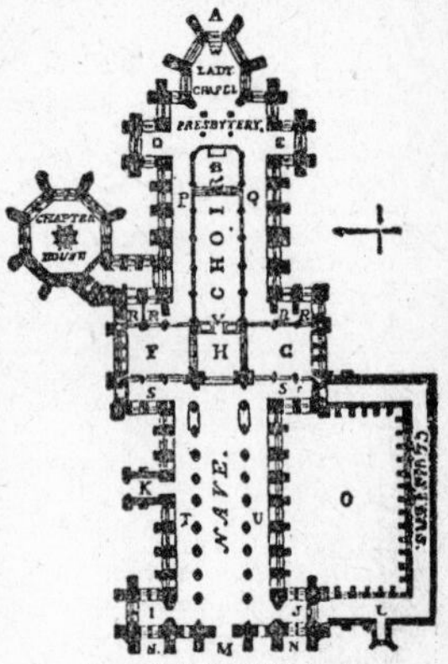

Plan of Wells Cathedral.

A, apse or apsis. B, altar, altar-platform, and altar-steps. D E, eastern or lesser transept. F G, western or greater transept. H, central tower. I J, western towers. K, north porch. L, library or register. M, principal or western doorway. N N, western side-doors. O, cloister-yard or garth. P Q, north and south aisles of choir. R S, east and west aisles of transept. T U, north and south aisles of nave. R R, chapels. V, rood-screen or organ-loft. W, altar of lady chapel.

çath-ē-dral′iç, *a.* Cathedral. [Rare.]

çath′ē-drā-ted, *a.* Relating to the authority of the chair or office of a teacher. [Obs.]

çath-ē-ret′iç, *n.* [Gr. *kathairetikos*, from *kathairein*, to destroy.] A caustic of mild nature used to reduce warts, moles, and similar growths.

çath′ēr-ine-wheel, *n.* See *Catharine-wheel*.

çath′e-tăl, *a.* [Gr. *kathetos*, a perpendicular line.] Of or pertaining to a cathetus.

çath′e-tēr, *n.* [LL. *catheter*; Gr. *kathetēr*, a catheter, a plug; from *kathienai*, to let down, thrust in; *kata*, down, and *hienai*, to send.] In surgery, a tubular instrument, usually made of silver, to be introduced into the bladder, to draw off the urine, when the natural discharge is suppressed; a sound to search for the stone, or a bougie made of silver or elastic gum; a tubular instrument designed to pass through other canals.

Eustachian catheter; a catheter introduced into the Eustachian tube in order to reach the middle ear.

çath′e-tēr-iṣm, çath″e-tēr-i-zā′tion, *n.* The operation of introducing a catheter.

çath′e-tēr-ize, *v.t.*; catheterized, *pt.*, *pp.*; catheterizing, *ppr.* To accomplish the act of catheterism in.

çath-e-tom′e-tēr, *n.* [Gr. *kathetos*, perpendicular, and *metron*, a measure.]

1. An instrument designed to ascertain with precision small differences in the height of the same column at various moments and under different conditions; also, to determine how much higher one column of mercury or some liquid is than another column. It consists of a telescope, or telescopes, sliding on a graduated rod.

2. A similar instrument in which the bar may be either vertical or horizontal.

çath′e-tus, *n.*; *pl.* **çath′e-ti,** [L., from Gr. *kathetos*, perpendicular, a perpendicular line.]

1. In geometry, a line or radius falling perpendicularly on another. Thus, the *catheti* of a right-angled triangle are the two sides that include the right angle. [Obs.]

2. In architecture, a perpendicular line, supposed to pass through the middle of a cylindrical body; also, the axis of the Ionic volute.

çath′ō-dăl, *a.* [Gr. *kathodos*, a descent; *kata*, down, and *hodos*, a way.]

1. Pertaining to a cathode.

2. In botany, situated underneath or on the lower side. [Rare.]

çath′ōde, *n.* [Gr. *kathodos*, going down; *kata*, down, and *hodos*, way.] In electro-chemistry, the way by which the electric current leaves substances through which it passes, or the surface at which the electric current passes out of the electrolyte; opposed to *anode*, and equivalent to *negative pole*.

Cathode ray; a kind of ray caused by the discharge of electricity in a vacuum vessel and generated at the cathode.

çȧ-thod′iç, *a.* [Gr. *kathodos*, going down.] A term given to the outward or efferent course of the nervous impulses; also, pertaining to a cathode; emanating from or having its origin in a cathode.

çȧ-thod′ō-grȧph, *n.* [Gr. *kathodos*, going down, and *graphein*, to write.] An image showing the internal appearance of an opaque body, produced by the Röntgen rays; called also a *radiograph*.

çat′=hōle, *n.* A hole in the stern of a boat for the play of a hawser or cable.

çath′ō-liç, *a.* [L. *catholicus*, universal, general; Gr. *katholikos*; *kata*, down, completely, and *holos*, whole.]

1. Universal or general; as, the *catholic* church. Originally this epithet was given to the Christian church in general, but is now applied more particularly to the Roman Catholic church. The term is sometimes set in opposition to *heretic*, *sectary*, or *schismatic*.

2. Liberal; not narrow-minded, partial, or bigoted; as, a *catholic* man; *catholic* principles.

3. [C—] Pertaining to or affecting the Roman Catholics; as, *Catholic* emancipation.

Catholic epistles; the epistles of the apostles, which are addressed to all the faithful, and not to a particular church; as, James, Peter, and Jude, and usually the three epistles of John.

Catholic majesty; the title of an Asturian prince in the eighth century, and subsequently of Spanish monarchs in recognition of their devotion to the Roman Catholic church.

Çath′ō-liç, *n.* 1. An adherent of the Roman Catholic church.

2. One who accepts the creeds received in common by all sects of the orthodox Christian church.

Old Catholics; the name adopted by those Roman Catholics who seceded from the Church of Rome in 1870. In that year, Pope Pius IX. promulgated the doctrine of papal infallibility, which they declined to accept as an article of faith. The *Old Catholics* also refuse to recognize that the decisions of the Vatican council are binding on the whole Roman Catholic church. They differ from Roman Catholics on no other points than these mentioned.

çȧ-thol′i-çăl, *a.* Catholic. [Obs.]

Çȧ-thol′i-çīse, *v.t.* and *v.i.* See *Catholicize*.

Çȧ-thol′i-çişm, *n.* 1. The doctrines of the Roman Catholic church; adherence to these doctrines. The Roman Catholic church teaches that the Pope is the vicar of Christ on earth; maintains the worship of the Virgin Mary and the saints; claims for its priesthood the right of binding and loosing for all eternity in the confession and absolution; teaches that besides heaven and hell there is a purgatory; upholds the real presence in the consecrated host; and holds that, with one exception, the teachings it ordains have never changed since Peter became the first bishop of Rome. The admitted exception is the doctrine of papal infallibility, proclaimed in 1870 by Pope Pius IX. There is still a striking similarity between the Greek church (the national church of Russia) and the Roman Catholic church on almost every point, although the schism occurred in the ninth century.

2. [c—] Liberality; universality; catholicity; as, his *catholicism* was a marked trait.

Çath-ō-liç′i-ty, *n.* 1. The system of doctrine, discipline, and worship held by the Church of Rome.

2. The system of doctrine, discipline, and worship held in common by all denominations of the orthodox Christian church.

3. [c—] Universality; as, the *catholicity* of a doctrine.

4. [c—] The quality of being catholic; freedom from prejudice; liberality of sentiments.

Çȧ-thol′i-çīze, *v.i.* and *v.t.* To become or cause to become a Roman Catholic, or convert to Roman Catholicism. [Rare.]

çath′ō-liç-ly, *adv.* Generally; in a catholic manner.

çath′ō-liç-ness, *n.* Universality.

çȧ-thol′i-çon, *n.* [Gr. *katholikon*, neut. of *katholikos*, universal.] A remedy for all diseases; a universal remedy; a remedy supposed to be efficacious in purging away all humors; a panacea; a kind of soft purgative electuary, so called.

Çȧ-thol′i-ços, *n.* The spiritual head of the Armenian church, who ordains bishops and consecrates the sacred oil used in religious ceremonies.

çat′=hook, *n.* A strong hook fitted to the cat-block.

Çat″i-li-nā′ri-ăn, *a.* Resembling Catiline, the noted Roman conspirator, or his conspiracy.

Çat″i-li-nā′ri-ăn, *n.* One who resembles Catiline.

Çat′i-lin-işm, *n.* The practices of Catiline; conspiracy. [Obs.]

çat′i-on, *n.* [Gr. *katiōn*, going down, ppr. of *katienai*; *kata*, down, and *ienai*, to go.] A name given by Faraday to an electropositive element which appears at the cathode in electrolysis; opposed to *anion*.

çat′kin, *n.* [A dim. of *cat*, from its resemblance to a cat's tail.] In botany, a scaly spike, the flowers of which are incomplete and the inflorescence falling off in a single piece after flowering or ripening, as in the flowers of the willow and birch; called also an *ament*.

Hazel Catkin.

çat′līke, *a.* Like a cat; vigilant; watchful; stealthy.

çat′ling, *n.* 1. A dismembering knife, used by surgeons.

2. The down or moss growing about walnut-trees, resembling the hair of a cat.

3. A little cat; a kitten.

4. Catgut; the string of a lute, violin, etc. [Obs.]

çat′lin-īte, *n.* [Named after George *Catlin*, an American traveler.] A red clay-stone used by the North American Indians for making pipes, etc.

çat′=nap, *n.* A very brief sleep or nap.

çat′nip, çat′mint, *n.* A plant of the genus *Nepeta*, somewhat resembling mint, and used in medicine. Cats are fond of it, hence the name.

çat″ō-çȧ-thär′tiç, *a.* and *n.* [Gr. *katō*, downward, and *kathartikos*, purging.]

I. *a.* Purging; producing alvine discharges.

II. *n.* A medicine that purges; a cathartic.

Çat′ō-don, *n.* [Gr. *katō*, down, and *odons*, *odontos*, tooth.]

1. A genus of cetaceans, including the sperm-whale, *Physeter macrocephalus*, the type of the family *Catodontidæ*. It has this name from the fact of its having teeth in the lower jaw only. Now usually called *Physeter*.

2. The typical genus of the *Catodonta*.

çat′ō-dont, *a.* 1. Pertaining to the *Catodonta*; having teeth in the lower jaw only; as, a *catodont* serpent or cetacean.

2. Pertaining to whales of the genus *Catodon*.

Çat-ō-don′tȧ, *n.pl.* A suborder of the *Ophidia*, including the family *Stenostomidæ*.

Çat-ō-don′ti-dæ, *n.pl.* A family of whales, the typical genus of which is *Catodon* or *Physeter*.

Çā-tō′ni-ăn, *a.* Pertaining to either of the two great Romans, Cato the Censor or Cato Uticensis, both remarkable for severity of manners; hence, grave; severe; inflexible.

çat=ō′=nine′=tāilş, *n.* 1. An instrument of punishment, consisting of nine pieces of line or cord fastened to a piece of thick rope, and having three knots at intervals, used to flog offenders.

2. Same as *Cattail*.

çȧ-top′tẽr, çȧ-top′tron, *n.* [Gr. *katoptron*, a mirror.] A reflecting optical glass or instrument; a mirror.

çȧ-top′triç, çȧ-top′triç-ăl, *a.* Relating to catoptrics, or vision by reflection; as, a *catoptric* telescope.

Catoptric dial; a kind of dial that shows the hours by means of a piece of mirror-plate adjusted to reflect the solar rays upward to the ceiling of a room on which the hour-lines are marked.

Catoptric light; a light in which the rays are concentrated by a series of concave mirrors and reflected in one parallel beam, so as to render it visible at a great distance.

çȧ-top′triçs, *n.* [Gr. *katoptrikos*, from *katoptron*, a mirror.] That branch of the science of optics which explains the properties of incident and reflected light, and particularly that which is reflected from mirrors or polished bodies.

çȧ-top′trō-man-çy, *n.* [Gr. *katoptron*, a mirror, and *manteia*, divination.] A species of ancient divination for the benefit of the sick, which was performed by letting down a mirror into water. If the patient's countenance appeared distorted and ghastly, it was an ill omen; if fresh and healthy, it was favorable.

çȧ-top′tron, *n.* See *Catopter*.

çȧ-tos′tō-mid, *a.* and *n.* I. *a.* Of or pertaining to the *Catostomidæ*.

II. *n.* One of the *Catostomidæ*.

Çā-tos-tom′i-dæ, *n.pl.* [From Gr. *katō*, down, and *stoma*, mouth, and *-idæ*.] A family of eventognathous fishes, including the suckers and buffalo-fish of North America.

çȧ-tos′tō-moid, *a.* and *n.* Same as *Catostomid*.

çat′pipe, *n.* Same as *Catcall*.

çat′=rigged, *a.* Having the sails and rigging of a catboat.

çat′s=sạlt, *n.* A sort of salt beautifully granulated, formed out of the bittern or leach-brine, used for making hard soap.

çat′s′=çrā″dle, *n.* A child's game played by looping a string on the fingers so as to produce a symmetrical figure supposed to resemble a cradle.

çat′s′=eȳe, *n.* A variety of quartz or chalcedony, used as a gem, and exhibiting yellowish, opalescent reflections from within, especially apparent when cut with a convex surface. These reflections resemble those observable in the eye of a cat.

çat′s′=foot, *n.* A plant of the genus *Nepeta*, ground-ivy, or gill; also called *cat's-paw*.

çat′s′=head (-hed), *n.* A kind of large apple.

Çats′kill, *a.* An epithet applied by geologists to the closing period of the Devonian age in America; from the *Catskill* mountains, where the rocks of this period are quite prominent.

çat′sō, *n.* [It. *cazzo*.] A rogue; a cheat; a base fellow. [Obs.]

çat′s′=pạw, *n.* 1. A dupe; the instrument which another uses to accomplish his designs and screen himself. This application of the term is derived from the story of the monkey which, to save its own paw, used the paw of the cat to draw the roasting chestnuts out of the fire. Also written *catspaw*.

2. A nautical term, signifying, (a) a light air perceived in a calm by a rippling of the surface of the water; (b) the ripple so made; (c) a turn in the bight of a rope, to hook a tackle on.

3. In botany, same as *cat's-foot*.

çat′s′=tāil, *n.* See *Cattail*.

çat′stick, *n.* A stick or bat used in playing tipcat.

çat′stitch, *v.t.* In needlework, (a) to join (two edges) with a cross-stitch; also called *fagot-stitch*; (b) to turn down the edge of and sew with a zigzag stitch.

çat′sup, *n.* See *Catchup*.

çat′tāil, *n.* 1. A name given to the tall reed-like aquatic plant, *Typha latifolia*, often popularly called *bulrush* and *cat-o'-nine-tails*.

2. Any grass of the genus *Phleum*.

3. A catkin.

çat-ti-man′dọọ, *n.* [Native E. Ind. name.] A resinous cement obtained from the juice of the East Indian plant, *Euphorbia Cattimandoo*; written also *kattimundoo*.

çat′tish, *a.* Resembling a cat; feline.

çat′tle, *n.pl.* [ME. *catel*, *katel*; OFr. *catel*; LL. *captale*, *capitale*, property, goods, stock; L. *capitalis*, principal, chief, from *caput* (-*itis*), head.]

1. Beasts or quadrupeds in general that serve for agricultural or other labor, and for food to man. In its primary sense, the word includes horses, asses, all the varieties of domesticated horned beasts of the bovine genus, sheep of all kinds, camels, goats, and perhaps swine. In this general sense it is constantly used in the Scriptures.

2. Specifically, beasts of the genus *Bos*.

3. Human beings, used in contempt or reproach; as, such *cattle* have no right to vote.

çat′tle=guärd, *n.* A trench or other device at a level- or grade-crossing of a railroad, so constructed as to prevent cattle from straying upon the track.

çat′tle=louse, *n.* Any one of several species of parasites that infest cattle, some of which devour the hair, while others suck the blood.

çat′tle-măn, *n.* One who raises or cares for cattle.

çat′tle=plāgue (-plāg), *n.* Any contagious disease destructive to cattle; particularly the form of typhoid called in Germany the *rinderpest*, and in Russia, the *steppe disease*.

çat′tle=ranch, *n.* A cattle-range.

çat′tle=rānge, çat′tle=run, *n.* A large space or district used for the grazing and breeding of cattle; as, the immense *cattle-ranges* of the West.

çat′tle=shōw, *n.* An exhibition of domestic animals for prizes or the encouragement of breeding fine stock; in the United States, usually held in connection with state or county fairs.

Çat′tlē-yȧ, *n.* A genus of orchids bearing many-colored flowers, which are among the most beautiful known in horticulture; named after William Cattley, an English botanical collector. *Cattleya maxima* is the largest and handsomest species.

çat′ty, *n.* [Malay *kati*, a pound.] An Asiatic weight varying somewhat; in China equal to sixteen taels or one kin, equivalent to 1.33 pounds avoirdupois.

Çạu-çā′siăn (-shăn), *a.* 1. Pertaining to the Caucasus mountains or the region thereabout, forming a division of the Russian empire, and lying between the Black and Caspian seas.

2. Of or pertaining to the white race of mankind.

Çạu-çā′siăn, *n.* 1. Any one of the white division of human beings, so called because the people about the Caucasus mountains were taken as the highest type of the human family;

it includes nearly all Europeans, the Circassians, Jews, Armenians, Hindus, and Persians.

2. Any native or inhabitant of the region about the Caucasus, as the Georgians, Circassians, etc.

ça̤u′cus, *n.* [Etymology uncertain. The word seems, however, to have been used early in the eighteenth century. Writing in 1774, Dr. William Gordon said of Boston that, more than fifty years before, Samuel Adams's father and others "used to meet and make a *caucus*," and lay plans for introducing certain persons into places of trust and power. The meetings of a *caucus* club, which held *caucuses* in a Boston garret in 1763, are referred to by John Adams in his *Diary*. This club seems to have possessed the features of secrecy and conviviality, and some have suggested that its name may have been derived from LL. *caucus*, Gr. *kaukos*, a drinking-vessel. Other writers profess to find the origin of the word in *calkers' meetings*, a Tory term applied in derision to meetings held in Boston about 1770 to protest against certain acts of the British troops, but the use of the word in John Adams's *Diary* for 1763 militates against this supposition. It has been well suggested (by Dr. J. H. Trumbull, in 1872) that the word originated in the Algonquin *cau′-cau-as′u*, one who promotes or advises, Indian names having been frequently adopted for New England political societies. It appears to be certain that the word was first used in Boston or its vicinity, and that it was applied in its present sense long before the Revolution. Its introduction into England is of comparatively recent date.]

1. In a general sense, a private or secret meeting of members of a political or other organization for the purpose of choosing candidates for election to office, deciding upon joint action on pending public measures, or discussing and deciding questions of policy.

> This day learned that the *Caucus* club meets, at certain times, in the garret of Tom Dawes, the adjutant of the Boston regiment. . . . There selectmen, assessors, collectors, warders, fire-wards, and representatives are regularly chosen before they are chosen in the town. . . . Captain Cunningham says they have often solicited him to go to those *caucuses*.
> —John Adams's *Diary*, Feb., 1763.

2. A meeting of voters of a particular party, to select delegates to a nominating convention, or to select candidates for office; a primary election, often called for short a *primary*.

In some states of late years the voters of each party select their candidates for local offices at a primary election or *caucus*, and the nominating convention is done away with as far as those offices are concerned.

3. A private meeting of members of a particular party in Congress; a deliberative body to settle questions of party policy; as, to abide by the decision of the Democratic *caucus*.

4. A secret meeting of any persons associated in a common cause or by common interests; as, a *caucus* of bank presidents or of street railway employes.

5. In English politics, a local party committee having power to select candidates, settle questions of local policy, etc., and conduct election campaigns; the *caucus* first appeared in England at Birmingham, where it was adopted as a form of organization by the Liberal party.

ça̤u′cus, *v.i.*; caucused, *pt.*, *pp.*; caucusing, *ppr.* To hold or gather in a caucus or caucuses.

ça̤u′dȧ, *n.*; *pl.* **ça̤u′dæ**. [L., a tail.] A tail or tail-like appendage.

Cauda galli; a plume-shaped fossil of the Devonian period; supposed to have been a seaweed.

ça̤u′dad, *adv.* [L. *cauda*, a tail, and *ad*, to.] Toward the caudal extremity or posterior part; backward.

ça̤u′dăl, *a.* [L. *cauda*, a tail.] Pertaining to a tail; having an appendage resembling a tail; opposed to *cephalic*.

Caudal fin; the tail-fin of a fish; sometimes written *caudal*.

Ça̤u-dā′tȧ, *n.pl.* [L. *cauda*, tail.] An order of amphibians having a long caudal appendage; called also the *Urodela*.

ça̤u′dāte, ça̤u′dā-ted, *a.* [L. *cauda*, a tail.] Having a tail; having a long termination like a tail.

ça̤u′dex, *n.*; *pl.* **ça̤u′di-cēṣ** or **ça̤u′dex-eṣ**. [L. *caudex*, the stem of a tree.] In botany, the stem of a tree; generally used of a tree stem without branches, as a palm.

ça̤u′di-çle, ça̤u-diç′ū-lȧ, *n.* [Dim. of L. *caudex*, stem.] The thin pliable stalk in orchids, on which the mass of pollen accumulates.

ça̤u-dis′ō-nănt, *a.* [L. *cauda*, a tail, and *sonans* (*-antis*), ppr. of *sonare*, to sound.] Making a sound with the tail, as do rattlesnakes.

ça̤u′di-trunk, *n.* [L. *cauda*, tail, and *truncus*, trunk.] The trunk and tail, or the body behind the head, in fishes or pisciform mammals.

ça̤u′dle, *n.* [ME. *caudel*; OFr. *caudel*, from L. *calidus*, *caldus*, warm.] A kind of warm drink; a mixture of wine and other ingredients prepared for the sick.

ça̤u′dle, *v.t.*; caudled, *pt.*, *pp.*; caudling, *ppr.* To make into caudle; also, to serve with caudle; to refresh.

ça̤uf, *n.* [A corruption of *corf*, *corb*, L. *corbis*, a basket.] A chest with holes for keeping fish alive in water.

ça̤u′fle, *n.* Same as *Coffle*.

ça̤ught (kạt), *v.*, past tense and past participle of *catch*.

ça̤uk, *n.* [Prov. Eng. *cauk*, limestone.] A compact variety of sulphate of baryta; written also *cawk*.

ça̤uk′y, *a.* Pertaining to or resembling cauk; written also *cawky*.

ça̤ul, *n.* [ME. *calle*, *kalle*; OFr. *cale*, a kind of cap; Ir. *calla*, a veil, hood.]

1. In anatomy, a membrane in the abdomen, covering the greatest part of the lower intestines, called, from its structure, *reticulum*, a net, but more generally the *great omentum*; also, a little membrane sometimes encompassing the head of a child when born, forming part of the amnion; as, to be born with a *caul*.

2. A kind of net in which women sometimes inclose their hair; the hinder part of a cap.

3. Any kind of net or thin membrane.

To be born with a caul; to be born lucky; the superstitious regarded the *caul* as a protection against drowning.

ça̤ul, *n.* [Fr. *cale*, wedge; G. *keil*; O.H.G. *chil*, a wedge.] A wooden clamp used to hold veneers together until the glue has set.

ça̤ul′drŏn, *n.* See *Caldron*.

Ça̤u-lẽr′pȧ, *n.* [L. *caulis*; Gr. *kaulos*, a stem, and *herpein*, to creep.] A peculiar genus of single-celled algæ peculiar to warm climates.

ça̤u-les′cent, *a.* [L. *caulis*, a stem, and *-escent*.] In botany, having a herbaceous stem, which bears both leaves and fruit.

ça̤u′li-çle, *n.* [L. *cauliculus*, dim. of *caulis*, a stem.] In botany, a little stem or rudimentary stem; applied to the neck of the embryo to distinguish it from the cotyledons or seed-leaves. The term is also applied to those small stems which proceed from buds formed at the neck of a plant without the previous production of a leaf.

ça̤u′li-çōle, *n.* Same as *Cauliculus*.

ça̤u-liç′ō-lous, *a.* [L. *caulis*, stem, and *colere*, to inhabit.] In botany, parasitic on the stem or stalk, as certain fungi.

ça̤u′li-çūle, *n.* A caulicle.

ça̤u-liç′ū-lus, *n.*; *pl.* **ça̤u-liç′ū-lī**. [L., dim. of *caulis*, a stem.]

1. In architecture, the name given to the little twists or volutes under the flower on the abacus in the Corinthian capital, representing the twisted tops of the acanthus stalks. Also written *Caulicole*.

2. In botany, same as *Caulicle*.

ça̤u-lif′ẽr-ous, *a.* Same as *Caulescent*.

ça̤u′li-flow-ẽr, *n.* [L. *caulis*, cabbage, a stem, and *flower*.]

1. A variety of *Brassica oleracea* or cabbage, the inflorescence of which is condensed while young into a depressed fleshy head, which is highly esteemed as a table vegetable.

2. The edible portion of a cauliflower plant, forming a compact, fleshy, cream-colored mass.

ça̤u′li-fọrm, *a.* [L. *caulis*, a stem, and *forma*, form.] Having the form of a caulis or stem, either in architectural decoration or botany.

ça̤u-liġ′e-nous, *a.* Carried on a stem.

ça̤u′line, *a.* [L. *caulis*, a stalk.] In botany, growing immediately on a caulis.

ça̤u′lis, *n.*; *pl.* **ça̤u′lēṣ**. [L. from Gr. *kaulos*, a stock, stem.]

1. A herbaceous stem, bearing both leaves and fruit.

2. In architecture, one of the main stems or leaves which springs from the angle of a Corinthian capital.

ça̤ulk, *n.* and *v.t.* See *Calk*.

ça̤u-lō-cär′pous, *a.* [Gr. *kaulos*, a stem, and *karpos*, fruit.] In botany, a term applied to such plants as produce flowers and fruit on their branches annually without perishing, as trees or shrubs.

ça̤u′lōme, *n.* [Gr. *kaulos*, a stem, and *-ome*.] The stem of a plant, or its axial portion.

ça̤u-lom′iç, *a.* Pertaining to the caulome.

ça̤u′mȧ, *n.* [Gr. *kauma*, heat.] In medicine, burning heat; febrile heat; a simple inflammatory fever. [Rare.]

ça̤u′pō-nāte, *v.i.* [L. *cauponatus*, pp. of *cauponari*, to traffic.] To keep a victualing-house. [Obs.]

ça̤u-pō-nā′tion, *n.* Low trafficking; huckstering. [Obs.]

ça̤u′pō-nize, *v.i.* To sell wine or victuals. [Obs.]

ça̤uṣ′ȧ-ble, *a.* That may be caused, produced, or effected.

ça̤uṣ′ăl, *a.* [L. *causalis*, from *causa*, cause, reason.] Relating to a cause or causes; implying or containing a cause or causes; expressing a cause.

> *Causal* propositions are where two propositions are joined by *causal* words, as *that* or *because*. —Watts.

ça̤uṣ′ăl, *n.* In grammar, a word that expresses a cause or introduces the reason.

ça̤u-ṣal′i-ty, *n.* 1. The agency of a cause; the action or power of a cause, in producing its effect.

2. In phrenology, the faculty of tracing effects to their causes.

ça̤uṣ′ăl-ly, *adv.* According to the order or series of causes; as a cause.

ça̤uṣ′ăl-ty, *n.* [Origin unknown.] In mining, the lighter, earthy parts of ore, carried off by washing.

ça̤u-ṣā′tion, *n.* The act of causing or producing; the act or agency by which an effect is produced; the doctrine as to the connection of causes and effects.

Law of causation; the law that every event or phenomenon results from an adequate antecedent cause.

ça̤u-ṣā′tion-ist, *n.* A believer in universal causation.

ça̤uṣ′ȧ-tive, *a.* [L. *causativus*, from *causa*, a cause, reason.]

1. Expressing a cause or reason.

2. Effecting as a cause.

ça̤uṣ′ȧ-tive, *n.* A word expressing or suggesting a cause.

ça̤uṣ′ȧ-tive-ly, *adv.* In a causative manner.

ça̤u-ṣā′tŏr, *n.* [LL. *causator*, from L. *causare*, to cause.] One who causes or produces an effect. [Rare.]

ça̤uṣe, *n.* [ME. *cause*; OFr. *cause*; L. *causa*, a cause, reason.]

1. A suit or action in court; any legal process which a party institutes to obtain his demand, or by which he seeks to realize his claim. This is a legal, scriptural, and popular use of the word, coinciding nearly with *case*.

> The *cause* of both parties shall come before the judges. —Ex. xxii. 9.

2. That which produces an effect; that which impels into existence, or produces what did not before exist; that by virtue of which anything is done; that from which anything proceeds, and without which it would not exist.

> *Cause* is a substance exerting its power into act, to make a thing begin to be. —Locke.

3. The reason or motive that urges, moves, or impels the mind to act or decide; as, *cause* for joy; *cause* for anger.

> And David said, Is there not a *cause?* —1 Sam. xvii. 29.

4. Sake; account. [Obs.]

> I did it not for his *cause* that had done the wrong. —2 Cor. vii. 12.

5. That which a person, party, or nation pursues; or rather, pursuit, prosecution of an object; as, Bible societies are engaged in a noble *cause*. Hence the word *cause* is used to denote that which a person or thing favors; that to which the efforts of an intelligent being are directed; as, to promote religion is to advance the *cause* of God. In all its applications, *cause* retains something of its original meaning—struggle, impelling force, contest, effort to obtain or to effect something.

6. Any matter as a subject of discussion.

Efficient cause; the power or agent that effects a result.

Final cause; the purpose or end for which anything is produced.

First cause; the prime mover in anything.

For cause; in law, for good and sufficient reason.

Formal cause; the plan according to which any thing or event is produced or brought about.

Material cause; the material upon which an efficient cause operates to produce anything.

The Great First Cause; God; the Creator, who was himself uncaused and the original source of all life and power.

To make common cause with; to join in securing some definite object; to side with; to form an alliance with.

Syn.—Incitement, inducement, motive, origin, reason, source, purpose, object.

ça̤uṣe, *conj.* Abbreviation of *because*. [Obs.]

ça̤uṣe, *v.t.*; caused, *pt.*, *pp.*; causing, *ppr.* [Fr. *causer*, from *cause*; L. *causa*, a cause, reason.]

1. To produce; to bring into existence.

2. To effect by agency, power, or influence.

> I will *cause* it to rain on the earth forty days. —Gen. vii. 4.

ça̤uṣe, *v.i.* To assign cause; to make excuse. [Obs.]

ça̤uṣe′fụl, *a.* Having a sufficient cause. [Obs.]

ça̤uṣe′less, *a.* 1. Having no cause or producing agent.

2. Without just ground, reason, or motive; as, *causeless* hatred; *causeless* fear.

çause'less-ly, *adv.* Without cause or reason.

çause'less-ness, *n.* The state of being causeless.

çaus'ẽr, *n.* One who causes; the agent by which an effect is produced.

çau-șeușe' (kō-zūz'), *n.* [Fr.] A seat for two persons; a tête-a-tête.

çause'way, çau'șey, *n.* [ME. *cauci, cauchie*; OFr. *cauchie*; LL. *(via) calceata*, from *calciare*, to make a road; from L. *calx, calcis*, lime, limestone.] A road or path raised above the natural level of the ground by stones, earth, timber, fascines, etc., serving as a dry passage over wet or marshy ground, or as a mole to confine water to a pond or restrain it from overflowing lower ground; a sidewalk or path at the side of a street or road raised above the carriageway.

The other way Satan went down
The *causey* to hell-gate. —Milton.

Giants' Causeway; a noted projection of basaltic columns from the northern coast of Ireland, at Antrim, resembling a gigantic causeway into the sea.

çause'wāyed, çau'șeyed, *a.* Having a causeway.

çau-sid'i-căl, *a.* [L. *causidicalis*, pertaining to an advocate or pleader, *causidicus*, a pleader; *causa*, a cause, and *dicere*, to say.] Pertaining to an advocate or to the maintenance and defense of suits.

çaus'son, *n.* See *Cavezon.*

çaus'tiç, *n.* 1. In medicine, any substance which, applied to living animals, acts like fire in burning and corroding the part and dissolving its tissue; called also an *escharotic*.

2. In optics, the name given to the curve or surface to which rays of light, reflected or refracted by another curved surface, are tangents. *Caustics* are consequently of two kinds, *catacaustics* and *diacaustics*, the former being *caustics* by reflection and the latter *caustics* by refraction.

Lunar caustic; a name given to nitrate of silver when cast into sticks for medical use.

çaus'tiç, çaus'tiç-ăl, *a.* [L. *causticus*; Gr. *kaustikos*, from *kaustos*, burning; *kaiein*, to burn.]

1. Capable of burning, corroding, or destroying the texture of animal substances.

2. Figuratively, severe; cutting; as, a *caustic* speech.

Caustic potash (potassium hydrate); a powerful potash used in medicine and the arts, for cauterizing and cleansing purposes, and in the manufacture of soft soap.

Caustic silver; lunar caustic.

Caustic soda (sodium hydrate); similar in properties and uses to caustic potash, the soaps made with it, however, being hard.

Syn.—Stinging, cutting, pungent, searching.

çaus'tiç-ăl-ly, *adv.* In a cutting or sarcastic manner.

çaus-tic'i-ty, *n.* 1. The quality of being caustic.

2. Figuratively, severity; a cutting remark.

çaus'tiç-ness, *n.* Causticity.

çau'tel, *n.* [L. *cautela*, from *cavere*, to take care.]

1. Caution. [Obs.]

2. Duplicity; deceit; craft. [Obs.]

çau'te-lous, *a.* 1. Cautious; wary; provident. [Obs.]

2. Cunning; treacherous; wily. [Obs.]

çau'te-lous-ly, *adv.* 1. Cunningly; slyly; treacherously.

2. Cautiously; warily. [Obs.]

çau'te-lous-ness, *n.* Cautiousness. [Obs.]

çau'tẽr, *n.* [LL., from Gr. *kautēr*, a burner; *kaiein*, to burn.] A cauterizing-iron.

çau'tẽr-ănt, *n.* A substance which cauterizes.

çau'tẽr-ișm, *n.* The application of a cautery.

çau″tẽr-i-zā'tion, *n.* 1. In surgery, the act of cauterizing or searing some morbid part, by the application of a hot iron or of caustics, etc.

2. The effect of the application of a cautery or caustic.

çau'tẽr-ize, *v.t.*; cauterized, *pt., pp.*; cauterizing, *ppr.* [LL. *cauterizare*, from Gr. *kautēriazein*, from *kautērion*, *kautēr*, a burning or branding iron, from *kaiein*, to burn.]

1. To burn or sear with fire or a hot iron or with caustics, as morbid flesh.

2. To sear, in a figurative sense.

The more *cauterized* our conscience is, the less is the fear of hell. —Jer. Taylor.

çau'tẽr-y, *n.* [L. *cauterium*; Gr. *kautērion*, dim. of *kautēr*, a branding iron.]

1. A burning or searing, as of morbid flesh, by a hot iron, or by caustic substances that burn, corrode, or destroy any solid part of an animal body. The burning by a hot iron is called *actual cautery*; that by caustic medicines, *potential cautery*.

2. The instrument or drug employed in cauterizing.

çau'tion, *n.* [L. *cautio (-onis)*, from *cavere*, to be on one's guard, to take care.]

1. Provident care; prudence in regard to danger; wariness, consisting in a careful attention to the probable effects of a measure, and a judicious course of conduct to avoid failure or disaster.

2. Security for; nearly the sense of the French *caution*, bail. [Rare.]

The Parliament would give his majesty sufficient *caution* that the war should be prosecuted. —Clarendon.

3. Provision or security against; measures taken for security; as, the rules and *cautions* of government. [Obs.]

4. Precept; advice; injunction; warning; exhortation, intended as security or guard against evil.

5. A warning, or reason for caution; as, the way he beat him was a *caution*. [Slang.]

Syn.—Care, forethought, forecast, heed, prudence, vigilance, watchfulness, circumspection, warning, admonition.

çau'tion, *v.t.*; cautioned, *pt., pp.*; cautioning, *ppr.* To give notice of danger; to warn; to exhort to take heed.

You *cautioned* me against their charms. —Swift.

çau'tion-ā-ry, *a.* 1. Containing caution or warning to avoid danger; as, *cautionary* advice.

2. Given as a pledge or in security; as, a *cautionary* town.

3. Cautious. [Obs.]

çau'tion-ẽr, *n.* 1. One who cautions or advises.

2. In Scots law, the person who is bound for another to the performance of an obligation.

çau'tion-ry, *n.* In Scots law, the act of giving security for another, or the obligation by which one person becomes engaged as security for another, that he shall pay a sum of money or perform a deed.

çau'tious, *a.* Wary; watchful; careful to avoid evils; attentive to examine probable effects and consequences of measures, with a view to avoid danger or misfortune; prudent; circumspect.

Syn.—Wary, circumspect, careful, watchful, prudent. — *Cautious* expresses less than *wary*; we must be *cautious* on all occasions where there is danger, but we must be *wary* where there is great danger. *Cautious* and *wary* are used in reference to practical matters, or the common matters of business, where the senses or bodily powers are more exercised than the mind; *circumspect* is used in reference to matters of theory or contemplation, when the mind is principally employed.

çau'tious-ly, *adv.* With caution.

çau'tious-ness, *n.* The quality of being cautious.

çav'ăl-çāde, *n.* [Fr. *cavalcade*; It. *cavalcata*, a troop of horsemen, from *cavalcare*, to ride; *cavallo*, L. *caballus*, a horse.] A procession of persons on horseback; a formal, pompous march of horsemen by way of parade, or to grace a triumph; the public entry of a person of distinction, etc.

çav-ȧ-lē'rō, çav-ȧ-liē'rō, *n.* [Sp. *cavallero*, *caballero*, a cavalier, knight.] A cavalier; a gay military man; a gallant.

çav-ȧ-liẽr', *n.* [Fr., from LL. *caballarius*, a knight, horseman, from L. *caballus*, a horse.]

1. A horseman, especially an armed horseman; a knight.

2. A gay, sprightly, military man.

3. [C—] The appellation of the party of Charles I. of England.

4. In fortification, an elevation of earth, situated ordinarily in the gorge of a bastion, bordered with a parapet, with embrasures.

5. In the manège, one who understands horsemanship; one skilled in the art of riding.

çav-ȧ-liẽr', *a.* 1. Gay; warlike; brave; generous.

2. Haughty; disdainful.

3. [C—] Pertaining to the party of Charles I. of England.

çav-ȧ-liẽr'ish, *a.* Pertaining to a cavalier.

çav-ȧ-liẽr'ișm, *n.* The practice or principles of cavaliers.

çav-ȧ-liẽr'ly, *adv.* Haughtily; arrogantly; disdainfully.

çav-ȧ-liẽr'ness, *n.* Haughtiness; a disdainful manner.

çȧ-val'ly, çȧ-văl'li, *n.* [Port. *cavalla*, from *cavallo*, a horse.] The horse-mackerel.

çav'ăl-ry, *n.* [Fr. *cavalerie*; It. *cavalleria*, cavalry, from *cavaliere*, a horseman, knight.] A body of military troops on horses; a general term, including light-horse, dragoons, and other bodies of men serving on horseback.

çav'ăl-ry-măn, *n.*; *pl.* **çav'ăl-ry-men.** A mounted soldier.

çȧ-vȧ-sī'nȧ, *n.* [Origin unknown.] A fish of California, *Seriola dorsalis*; called also *yellowtail.*

çȧ-vass', *n.* In Turkey, a police officer or an official military attendant; also spelled *kavass*.

çā'vāte, *v.t.* [L. *cavatus*, pp. of *cavare*, to make hollow; *cavus*, hollow.] To dig out; to make hollow.

çȧ-vȧ-tī'nȧ, *n.* [It.] In music, a melody of simpler character than the *aria*, and without a second part and a *da capo* or return part. The term is also applied to short, simple airs of any kind.

çā-vā'tion, çā-vā'zion, *n.* [It. *cavazione*; L. *cavatio (-onis)*, from *cavare*, to make hollow, excavate; *cavus*, hollow.] In architecture, the underdigging or hollowing of the earth, for the foundation of a building, or for cellarage.

çāve, *n.* [Fr. *cave*; L. *cavea*, cavity, from *cavus*, hollow.]

1. A hollow place in the earth; a subterranean cavern; a den, either natural or artificial.

2. Any hollow. [Obs.]

3. [C—] A name given to a party in the British parliament who seceded from the Liberals on the reform bill introduced by them in 1866. [See *Adullamite.*]

çāve, *v.t.* [L. *cavare*, to make hollow.] To make hollow. [Obs.]

çāve, kāve, *v.t.* To toss up or pitch; especially to winnow (grain) from chaff by tossing with a rake or by threshing. [Prov. Eng.]

çāve, *v.i.* 1. To dwell in a cave. [Obs.]

2. To fall in, as the sides of a mine or well.

To cave in; a slang expression indicating to yield or submit.

çā'vē-ȧ, *n.* [L., a cave, cage.] In ancient architecture, a term applied to the dens or stables for wild beasts, under the seats and around the arches of an amphitheater; the amphitheater itself.

çȧ-vēach', *n.* [W. Ind.] West Indian fish, especially mackerel, seasoned and pickled.

çȧ-vēach', *v.t.* To prepare (mackerel) after the West Indian method.

çā'vē-at, *n.* [L. *caveat*, let him beware, 3d sing. pres. subj. of *cavere*, to beware, take heed.]

1. In law, a process in a court to stop proceedings until the party interested may appear and object.

2. Intimation of caution; hint; warning; admonition.

3. In the patent laws of the United States, a description of some invention, designed to be patented, lodged in the office before the patent right is taken out. It operates as a bar to other applications respecting the same invention.

Caveat emptor; let the purchaser beware; that is, let him examine the quality of what he buys, since the risk lies with him.

çā'vē-at, *v.i.* 1. To enter a caveat.

2. In fencing, to shift the sword from one side of the adversary's to the other.

çā'vē-ā-tŏr, *n.* One who enters a caveat.

çāve'-bēar, *n.* A fossil bear of the Quaternary epoch contemporaneous with the cave-dwellers.

çāve'-dwel″lẽr, *n.* 1. One who dwells in caves.

2. A prehistoric man who dwelt in natural caves and subsisted on shellfish and wild animals.

çāve'-hȳ-ē″nȧ, *n.* A species of fossil hyena found in the caves of Great Britain.

çav'el, çav'il, kev'el, *n.* 1. A part or share; especially, an allotment of land. [Prov. Eng. and Scot.]

2. A gag or a horse's bit.

3. A ship's cleat.

4. An ax for trimming stone.

çāve'-lī″ŏn, *n.* A fossil lion found in European caves.

çav'en-dish, *n.* [From the proper name *Cavendish.*] Tobacco which has been softened, sweetened and pressed into plugs; also called *negro-head.*

Cut cavendish; cavendish tobacco cut into small shreds.

çav'ẽrn, *n.* [L. *caverna*, from *cavus*, hollow.] A deep, hollow place in the earth; a cavity; a den.

çav'ẽrned, *a.* 1. Full of caverns or deep chasms; having caverns.

2. Inhabiting a cavern.

çav-ẽr-nic'ō-lous, *a.* [L. *caverna*, cave, and *colere*, to live in.] Living in caves.

çav'ẽrn-ous, *a.* 1. Hollow; full of caverns; filled with small cavities.

2. Having a resonant sound produced by a cavity.

Cavernous body; a body made up of erectile tissue, as is found in the penis and clitoris.

Cavernous respiration; an unnatural respiratory sound heard distinctly in auscultation, over morbid interspaces in the lungs.

çȧ-vẽr'nū-lous, *a.* Full of little cavities; as, *cavernulous* metal.

çav'es-sŏn, *n.* See *Cavezon.*

çȧ-vet'tō, *n.* [It., dim. of *cavo*; L. *cavus*, hollow.]

1. A concave molding much employed in the cornices of classic structures.

2. In decorative art, a pattern which is sunken; opposed to *relief.*

çav'e-zŏn, *n.* [Fr. *cavesson*; It. *cavezzone*, from *cavezza*, a halter; from L. *caput*, head.] A noseband used to facilitate the breaking of a horse.

çav-i-ăr', çā-viăre', *n.* [Fr. *caviar*; It. *caviale*, from Turk. *havyār*, caviar.] The roe of certain large fish, prepared and salted. The best is made from the roe of the sterlet, sturgeon, sevruga, and beluga, caught in the lakes or rivers of Russia.

çav'i-çorn, *a.* and *n.* [L. *cavus*, hollow, and *cornū*, horn.]

I. *a.* Hollow-horned, or relating to the *Cavicornia.*

II. *n.* One of the cavicorn ruminants.

Çav-i-çor'ni-ȧ, *n.pl.* [L. *cavus*, hollow, and *cornū*, a horn.] A family of ruminants, characterized by hollow horns.

çav'il, *v.i.*; caviled *or* cavilled, *pt.*, *pp.*; caviling *or* cavilling, *ppr.* [OFr. *caviller*; L. *cavillari*, to jeer, mock, quibble; *cavilla*, a jeering, mocking.] To raise captious and frivolous objections; to find fault without good reason.

çav'il, *v.t.* To receive with objections. [Obs.]

çav'il, *n.* A false or frivolous objection.

çav'il, *n.* See *Cavel.*

çav'il-ēr, çav'il-lēr, *n.* One who cavils.

çav'il-ing, *a.* Having a disposition to cavil.

çav'il-ing-ly, *adv.* In a caviling manner.

çav-il-lā'tion, *n.* The act of caviling. [Obs.]

çav'il-ous, çav'il-lous, *a.* [L. *cavillosus*, from *cavilla*, a mocking, jeering.] Captious; unfair in argument; apt to object without good reason. [Rare.]

çav'il-ous-ly, *adv.* In a cavilous manner. [Rare.]

çav'il-ous-ness, *n.* Captiousness.

çav'in, *n.* [Fr., from L. *cavus*, hollow.] A hollow way, or natural hollow, adapted to cover troops, and facilitate their approach to a place.

çāv'ings, *n.* Chaff, screenings, etc. [Prov. Eng.]

çȧ-vin'nȧ-wood, *n.* A species of rosewood from *Dalbergia nigra*, a Brazilian tree.

çav'i-tā-ry, *a.* In zoölogy, containing a cavity; specifically, applied to a class of entozoic worms.

çav'i-ty, *n.*; *pl.* **çav'i-ties** (-tiz). [Fr. *cavité*, from L. *cavus*, hollow.] A hole; a hollow place; hollowness; an opening; as, the abdominal *cavity*; a *cavity* in a tooth.

çä'vō-ri-lie'vō, çä'vō-rē-lie'vō (-lyä'vō), *n.* [It.] In sculpture, relief made by cutting into a flat surface, so that no part of the design stands above the plane of the original stone.

çȧ-vort', *v.i.*; cavorted, *pt. pp.*; cavorting, *ppr.* [Prob. corruption of *curvet.*] To prance about in a showy manner, as a horse; figuratively, to bustle about ostentatiously; in the latter sense, a slang expression.

çā'vy, *n.*; *pl.* **çā'vies.** [From Braz. name *cabiai.*] A rodent of the family *Caviidæ*, as the guinea-pig.

Giant or *water-cavy*; the capibara.

çaw, *v.i.*; cawed, *pt.*, *pp.*; cawing, *ppr.* [Imitative.] To cry like a crow, rook, or raven; also written *kaw.*

çaw, *n.* The cry of the crow, raven, or rook.

çawk, *n.* See *Cauk* and *Chalk.*

çawk'ēr, *n.* Same as *Calker.*

çawk'y, *a.* See *Cauky.*

çax'ŏn, *n.* [Sp. *caxa*, from L. *capsa*, a chest.]

1. In mining, a chest of ores of any metal that has been burnt, ground, and washed, and is ready to be refined.

2. A wig used in the eighteenth century.

Çax'tŏn, *n.* 1. Any book from the press of Wm. Caxton, who introduced the printer's art into England in the latter half of the fifteenth century.

2. The style of type used by Caxton, or one in imitation of it.

çāy, *n.* [Sp. *cayo*, a shoal, rock.] A sandy shoal, reef of rocks, or small island common in the Gulf of Mexico. [See *Key*, n. 7.]

çāy-enne', *n.* [Named from *Cayenne*, a town in Fr. Guiana.] Cayenne pepper.

Cayenne pepper; the ground pods of various species of *Capsicum.*

Çāy'lēy-ăn, *n.* A complex curve in higher mathematics, named from Arthur Cayley, an English mathematician.

çāy'măn, *n.* [Sp. *caiman*, from the native Guiana name.] Any alligator common to tropical America, especially *Caiman palpebrosus* and *Caiman trigonatus.*

çāy'nȧrd, *n.* A cowardly knave; written also *kaynard.* [Obs.]

Çā-yū'gȧs, *n.pl.* A tribe of American Indians of the Iroquois stock, originally located in western New York.

çā-ūse', *n.* In northwestern United States, a bronco or Indian pony, originally bred by the Cayuse Indians; sometimes, any riding-horse of little value.

çȧ-zïque', çȧ-zïç', *n.* See *Cacique.*

çä'zō (kä'thō), *n.* [Sp.] A kettle for reducing silver by the amalgamation process.

Cē-ȧ-nō'thus, *n.* [From Gr. *keanōthos*, a kind of thistle.]

1. A genus of large shrubs of the buckthorn family, common to North America and bearing various colored flowers.

2. [c—] A plant belonging to this genus.

çēase, *v.i.*; ceased, *pt.*, *pp.*; ceasing, *ppr.* [ME. *ceesen, cessen*; OFr. *cesser*; L. *cessare*, to loiter, cease, give way; freq. of *cedere*, to go away, yield, withdraw.]

1. To stop moving, acting, or speaking; to leave off; to give over.

2. To fail; to be wanting; to be at an end; as, the wonder *ceases*; the storm has *ceased.*

çēase, *v.t.* To put a stop to; to put an end to.

Cease this impious rage. —Milton.

Syn.—Desist, discontinue, leave off, quit, stop.

çēase, *n.* Extinction; cessation. [Obs.]

çēase'less, *a.* Without a stop or pause; incessant; continual; without intermission.

çēase'less-ly, *adv.* Incessantly; perpetually.

ceb-ȧ-dil'lȧ, *n.* Same as *Cevadilla.*

Cē-bi'næ, *n.pl.* A subfamily of South American monkeys, with broad noses and prehensile tails, including the spider- and the squirrel-monkeys.

cē'bine, *a.* and *n.* [Gr. *kēbos*, a monkey.]

I. *a.* Relating to the *Cebinæ*, a family of monkeys.

II. *n.* A member of the family *Cebinæ.*

cē'boid, *a.* and *n.* Same as *Cebine.*

Cec"i-dō-mȳ'i-ȧ, *n.* [From Gr. *kekis* (*-idos*), a gallnut, and *myia*, a fly.]

1. A genus of flies, producing galls for the protection and food of the larvæ or laying its eggs in various grains. The Hessian-fly is a well known variety.

2. [c—] A member of the genus.

cec"i-dō-mȳ'i-ăn, *a.* Pertaining to the genus *Cecidomyia.*

cec"i-dō-mȳ'i-id, *a.* and *n.* I. *a.* Relating to the genus *Cecidomyia.*

II. *n.* A member of the genus *Cecidomyia.*

cē'ci-ty, *n.* [L. *cæcitas*, from *cæcus*, blind.] Blindness. [Rare.]

Cē-crō'pi-ȧ, *n.* [Named after *Cecrops*, first king of Athens.]

1. In botany, an extensive genus of moraceous tropical trees, the products of which find numerous uses in the arts and manufactures.

2. [c—] In zoölogy, a moth of the family *Bombycidæ*, or silkworm family.

cē-çū'tien-cy (-shien-cy), *n.* Tendency to blindness. [Rare.]

cē'dăr, *n.* [ME. *ceder, cedre*; OFr. *cedre*; L. *cedrus*; Gr. *kedros*, a cedar-tree.]

1. An evergreen tree that grows to a large size and is remarkable for the durability and fragrance of its wood. The name is also given to the *deodar* and to many trees which have no relation to the true cedar, as the Bermuda cedar, *Juniperus Bermudiana*, used for making pencils, the red cedar, *Juniperus Virginiana*, the Honduras, or bastard Barbados cedar, *Cedrela odorata*, and the red cedar of Australia, *Cedrela Australis*, used in making cigar-boxes. It is applied further to the genus *Cedrus.*

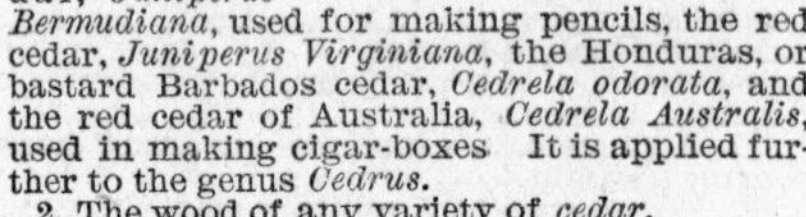

Cedar.

2. The wood of any variety of *cedar.*

cē'dăr, *a.* Relating to cedar.

cē'dăr-ap"ple, *n.* A parasitic outgrowth forming on twigs of the red cedar-tree. When fully grown it presents a number of slim arms extending from a central mass, the whole being of a bright orange-color.

cē'dăr-bird, *n.* A name given the American waxwing, *Ampelis cedrorum*, from its food, cedar-berries and the like, and from its frequenting cedar-trees.

cē'dăred, *a.* Covered or furnished with cedars.

cē'dărn, *a.* Pertaining to the cedar. [Rare.]

cēde, *v.t.*; ceded, *pt.*, *pp.*; ceding, *ppr.* [Fr. *céder*, from L. *cedere*, to withdraw, yield.] To yield; to surrender; to give up; to resign; as, to *cede* a fortress, a province, or country, by treaty.

cē'dent, *n.* [L. *cedens* (*-entis*), ppr. of *cedere*, to yield, withdraw.] An assignor in a lawsuit.

cē-dil'lȧ, *n.* [Fr. *cédille*; Sp. *cedilla*, dim. of *zeda*; Gr. *zēta*, the Greek name of the letter *z*; so called because *z* was written after *c*, to give the sound of the letter *s*.] A mark used on the French *c* (thus *ç*), to show that it is to be sounded like *s.*

cē'drāte, cē'drat, *n.* [Fr.] A species of citron-tree.

Cē-drē'lȧ, *n.* [L. *cedrelate*; Gr. *kedrelatē*, a cedar-fir tree; *kedros*, a cedar, and *elatē*, fir-tree.]

1. A genus of large tropical trees of both hemispheres; *Cedrela Toona*, an East Indian species, and *Cedrela odorata*, of Honduras and the West Indies, are examples.

2. [c—] A tree belonging to this genus.

cē'drēne, *n.* [L. *cedrus* cedar, and *-ene.*] Any hydrocarbon expressed by the general formula $C_{15}H_{24}$, especially those obtained from the oil of sage or red cedar.

cē'drin, *n.* The principle giving the intensely bitter taste to cedron.

cē'drine, *a.* [L. *cedrinus*; Gr. *kedrinos*, from *kedros*, cedar.] Pertaining to cedar.

cē'dri-ret, *n.* Same as *Cerulignone.*

cē'drŏn, *n.* [From L. *cedrus*, cedar.] A tree, *Simaba Cedron*, and its fruit. It is of the natural order *Simarubaceæ*, growing in tropical America; the seeds are employed as a remedy for serpent-bites, hydrophobia, and intermittent fever.

Cē'drus, *n.* [L., from Gr. *kedros*, cedar.] A genus of trees closely allied to the genus *Larix.* It includes only three species or varieties, the *Cedrus Libani*, or cedar of Lebanon; *Cedrus Deodara*, or deodar, and *Cedrus Atlantica*, or Mount Atlas cedar.

cē'dry, *a.* Resembling cedar. [Rare.]

ced'ū-lȧ, *n.* [Sp.] A promissory note issued by any of the South American republics.

ced'ūle, *n.* [OFr.] A scroll; a writing. [Obs. See *Schedule.*]

ced'ū-ous, *a.* Fit to be felled. [Obs.]

cē'i-ba (*or Sp. pron.*, thā'i-bȧ), *n.* [Sp., from native name.] The silk-cotton tree of the tropics; also called the *God-tree.* [See *Bombax.*]

cēil, *v.t.*; ceiled, *pt.*, *pp.*; ceiling, *ppr.* [Fr. *ciel*, heaven, canopy, from L. *cælum*, heaven, vault, covering; Gr. *koilos*, hollow.]

1. To overlay or cover the inner roof of (a room or building); to provide with a ceiling.

2. To line inside, as with sheathing, stone, or plaster, or some similar finishing substance.

cēil'ing, *n.* 1. The upper covering of an apartment, opposite the floor. It is commonly of boards, lath and plastering, steel or other metal, but may be of any substance adapted to the purpose.

2. Lining similar to the foregoing, but taking in the sides as well, as in an apartment, ship, or car.

3. In nautical affairs, the inner woodwork or other finishing of a ship.

ceint, *n.* A cincture. [Obs.]

ceiṅ-tūre' (saṅ-), *n.* [Fr.] A cincture; a girdle.

cel'ȧ-don, *n.* [Fr.] 1. The color sea-green (grayish green).

2. Fine pottery or porcelain of a sea-green color.

cel'ăn-dīne, *n.* [ME. *celidoine, celydon*; OFr. *celidoine*; L. *chelidonia*; Gr. *chelidonion*, swallow-wort, from *chelidōn*, a swallow.] A name given to two plants native to England, now introduced in America, the greater *celandine* and the lesser *celandine* (the swallow-worts). The former is *Chelidonium majus*, and the latter *Ficaria Ranunculoides*, or pile-wort. The species of *Bocconia* from the West Indies are called *tree-celandines.*

cē-lā'rent, *n.* A mnemonic name given to one of the moods in logic.

Cel-as-trā'cē-æ, *n.pl.* [*Celastrus* and *-aceæ.*] An order of polypetalous exogens, consisting of shrubs or trees, sometimes spinous or climbing, with a beautiful scarlet aril to the seeds, found principally in warm latitudes. Among the members of this order is the *Euonymus* or spindle-tree. The species number about 400 in forty genera.

cel-as-trā'ceous, *a.* Of, relating, or pertaining to the order *Celastraceæ.*

Cē-las'trus, *n.* [Gr. *kēlastros*, an evergreen.] A small genus of low shrubs or climbing vines of the family *Celastraceæ.* *Celastrus paniculata* of the East Indies is an example of this genus. Called also *staff-tree* and *climbing bittersweet.*

cē-lā'tion, *n.* [L. *celatio* (*-onis*), from *celare*, to conceal.] In medical jurisprudence, a term applied to the concealment of pregnancy.

cel'ȧ-tive, *a.* [L. *celatio*, concealment.] Having the style of coloration of an animal, tending to effect its partial or complete concealment.

cel'ȧ-tūre, *n.* [L. *cælatura*, from *cælare*, to engrave, carve.]

1. The act or art of engraving or embossing.

2. That which is engraved. [Obs.]

cel'ē-brănt, *n.* [L. *celebrans* (*-antis*), ppr. of *celebrare*, to frequent, celebrate.] One who performs a public religious rite; applied particularly to the officiating priest in the Roman Catholic church.

cel'ē-brāte, *v.t.*; celebrated, *pt.*, *pp.*; celebrating, *ppr.* [L. *celebratus*, pp. of *celebrare*, to frequent, go in great numbers, honor, from *celeber*, frequented, populous.]

1. To praise; to extol; to commend; to give praise to; to make famous; as, to *celebrate* the name of the Most High.

2. To distinguish by solemn rites; to keep holy; to observe in due form; to honor or distinguish by ceremonies and marks of joy and respect; as, to *celebrate* Thanksgiving or the Fourth of July.

3. To perform or solemnize with reverence or veneration, as a religious ceremony.

Syn.—Praise, extol, commemorate, glorify, honor.—*Extol* is stronger than *praise*; we *commemorate* events which we desire to cherish in affectionate remembrance by appropriate rites; we *celebrate* by demonstrations of public joy, processions, etc.

cel′ē-brā-ted, *a.* Having celebrity; distinguished; well-known.

cel′ē-brā-tēr, cel′ē-brā-tŏr, *n.* One who celebrates.

cel-ē-brā′tion, *n.* The act of celebrating; also, the time and manner of celebrating.

cē-lē′bri-ous, *a.* Famous; renowned. [Obs.]

cē-leb′ri-ty, *n.* [L. *celebritas*, a multitude, fame, from *celeber*, frequented, populous, famous.]

1. Fame; renown; the distinction or honor publicly bestowed on a nation or person because of noted character or exploits; the distinction bestowed on whatever is great or remarkable, and manifested by praises or eulogies; as, the *celebrity* of Lincoln.

2. A person who has won distinction.

3. Celebration. [Obs.]

Syn.—Fame, honor, glory, reputation, distinction, renown, notability, eminence, notoriety.

cel′ē-ō-morph, *n.* [Gr. *keleos*, woodpecker, and *morphē*, form.] One of the family of woodpeckers.

cel″ē-ō-mor′phic, *a.* Of, pertaining, or relating to the woodpeckers.

cē-lē′ri-ac, *n.* [From *celery*.] A variety of celery, called also the *turnip-rooted celery*.

cē-ler′i-ty, *n.* [L. *celeritas*, from *celer*, swift, quick.] Rapidity of motion; swiftness; speed.

Syn.—Quickness, rapidity, speed, speediness, swiftness, fleetness, velocity.

cel′ẽr-y, *n.* [Fr. *céleri*; It. *seleri*; L. *selinon*, parsley; Gr. *selinon*, parsley.] A plant, *Apium graveolens*, much cultivated for the table, the blanched stalks being used in salads and as a relish.

cē-les′tiăl, *a.* [OFr. *celestial*; L. *cœlestis*, from *cœlum*, heaven.]

1. Heavenly; belonging or relating to heaven; dwelling in heaven; as, *celestial* spirits; *celestial* joys.

2. Belonging to the upper regions, or visible heaven; as, *celestial* signs; the *celestial* globe.

3. [C—] Pertaining to the Chinese empire or its inhabitants.

Celestial Empire; China, so called because the first emperors are fabled to have been deities.

Syn.—Heavenly, ethereal, atmospheric, supernal, angelic, radiant, eternal, immortal, seraphic, divine, godlike, elysian.

cē-les′tiăl, *n.* 1. An inhabitant of heaven.

2. [C—] A person born in China.

cē-les′tiăl-ize, *v.t.* To make celestial. [Rare.]

cē-les′tiăl-ly, *adv.* In a heavenly or transporting manner.

cē-les′ti-fȳ, *v.t.* To communicate something of a heavenly nature to; to make heavenly. [Obs.]

Cel′es-tine, Cel-es-tin′i-ăn, *n.* 1. One of a Benedictine order founded by Pope Celestine in the thirteenth century.

2. A Pelagian, especially a supporter of Cælestius, an early adherent to Pelagianism.

cel′es-tite, *n.* [L. *cœlestis*, of heaven, and *-ite*.] A white or bluish translucent mineral which occurs in tabular to prismatic orthorhombic crystals, fibrous and cleavable masses, and rarely, granular. It is notably heavy and resembles barite. Also written *celestine*.

cē′li-ac, cœ′li-ac, *a.* [L. *cœliacus*; Gr. *koiliakos*, from *koilia*, the belly, *koilos*, hollow.] Pertaining to the abdominal cavity or, in former times, to affections of the bowels; as, *celiac* passion (diarrhea).

Celiac artery; the artery which issues from the aorta below the diaphragm.

Celiac vein; a vein of the intestinum rectum.

cel′i-bá-cy, *n.* [L. *cœlibatus*, from *cœlebs* (*-itis*), a single life.] An unmarried state; a single life; particularly that of a person bound by solemn vows to remain single.

cel′i-bāte, *n.* 1. A single life; celibacy; chiefly used when speaking of the single life of the Roman Catholic clergy.

2. A person who is unmarried; particularly one pledged not to marry.

cel′i-bāte, *a.* [L. *cœlibatus*, from *cœlebs*, a single life.] Not married.

cel′i-bá-tist, *n.* One who lives in an unmarried state. [Rare.]

cel-i-dog′rá-phy, *n.* [Gr. *kelis* (*-idos*), a spot, and *graphia*, from *graphein*, to write.] A description of apparent spots on the disk of the sun, or on planets.

cell, *n.* [ME. *celle*; OFr. *celle*; L. *cella*, a small room, hut.]

1. A small or close apartment, as in a convent or prison.

2. A small religious house subordinate to a greater.

3. Any small hollow space.

4. In architecture, the hollow space between the ribs of a vaulted roof.

5. In biology, the mass of protoplasm which is the fundamental element of all organisms.

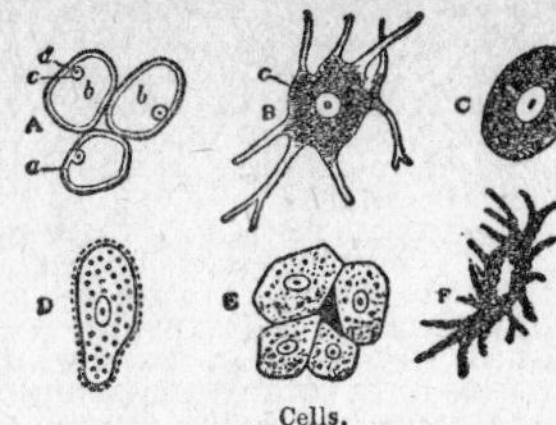

Cells.

A, A few cells from the chorda dorsalis of the lamprey. *a*, Cell-wall; *b*, cell-contents; *c*, nucleus; *d*, nucleolus. B, multipolar nerve-cell (with many processes), from human spinal cord; *c*, nucleus and nucleolus. C, An oval nerve-cell. D, Cartilage-cell. E, Hepatic or liver cells. F, Pigment or color-cell, from skin of frog. (All magnified.)

6. In zoölogy, (a) a cuplike cavity inclosing the zoöids of certain hydroids, as in corals; (b) a protective covering for the eggs or young of insects; (c) one of the spaces outlined by the veins in the wing of an insect.

7. In electricity, the means for producing a voltaic current, consisting of two dissimilar conductors, usually metals, or a metal and carbon, called the electrodes, and at least one substance which can be decomposed electrolytically by the electric current. The combination of the electrodes and the electrolyte in a containing vessel constitutes a cell. The electrode from which the current flows *inside* the cell is called the positive electrode or *anode*; the one toward which the current flows is the negative electrode or *cathode*. With reference to the external circuit, the cathode is positive and the anode negative. The origin of the electromotive force of such a cell is not surely known; the energy of the electric current which the cell can give out is rendered available by the chemical actions which go on in the cell. When the electrodes are eaten away or the electrolyte wholly decomposed, the cell is said to be "run down," and can serve as a source of current only after its elements have been renewed. When the products of chemical decomposition are gaseous, these gases collect on the electrodes and reduce the area of the plate that is in contact with the liquid, increasing the resistance of the cell. The gases, by their tendency to reunite, set up an electromotive force which is opposed in direction to the electromotive force of the current actually flowing. These two actions are covered by the term polarization. In cells which polarize, certain substances or devices may be added, which, by chemical combination with the gases, or by mechanical means, prevent the accumulation of the gases on the electrodes. Such substances or devices are called depolarizers. Electric cells may be divided into two classes, (a) primary and (b) secondary, or storage cells, sometimes called accumulators. [See *Primary cell*; *Secondary cell*.]

Bunsen cell; one in which carbon forms the negative electrode, zinc the positive, and nitric acid is used in a porous cup with the carbon, while sulphuric acid is in the outer vessel with the zinc.

Daniell cell; one in which the anode is zinc, the cathode copper. The zinc plate is surrounded by a porous cup filled with dilute sulphuric acid, or a zinc sulphate solution; the copper electrode is immersed in a solution of copper sulphate. The zinc enters into combination with the acid to form zinc sulphate and liberates the hydrogen from the acid. The hydrogen replaces the copper of the copper sulphate, forming sulphuric acid, the copper so replaced is deposited on the cathode and the acid attacks the zinc. The copper sulphate acts as the depolarizer. Energy of chemical combination is transformed in the consumption of the zinc into electrical energy which accompanies the current when the external circuit is closed. This is typical of all cells.

Gravity cell; a modification of the Daniell, in which the two fluids are separated by their difference in specific gravity, so that the porous septum is dispensed with.

Grove cell; one in which platinum replaces the carbon of the Bunsen cell.

Latimer-Clark standard cell; one noted for the uniformity of its electromotive force; zinc being the anode, metallic mercury the cathode, the electrolyte being zinc sulphate and the sulphate of mercury.

Leclanché cell; one having a zinc rod for its anode, immersed in a sal ammoniac solution (the electrolyte); while the cathode is a carbon plate surrounded by powdered dioxid of manganese and carbon (the depolarizer). This cell is very much used for bell and annunciator circuits.

Primary cell; one which is always in condition to give an electric current, upon mere assemblage of its elements.

Secondary or *storage cell*; one which of itself can give no current until it has been acted upon electrolytically by a current from some outside source. The *secondary* or *storage cell* consists, in its ordinary form, of two lead electrodes, made in the form of a grid to increase the effective surface and immersed in a ten per cent solution of sulphuric acid. While the charging current is passing, the water is broken up into hydrogen and oxygen, the hydrogen passing to the cathode and thence off into the air, while the oxygen goes to the anode and attacks the lead, changing it first to the oxid of lead, then to the peroxid. The cathode remains pure lead. In charging, electrical energy has been transformed into chemical energy. When the charging current is interrupted and the electrodes of the cell are metallically connected, a current passes in a direction opposite to that of the charging current, and the lead peroxid of the anode is reduced to lead oxid, while the pure lead cathode is oxidized to lead oxid. Energy of chemical combination is thus transformed back into electrical energy. When the electrodes are both lead oxid the cell is discharged.

Single-fluid cell; a cell using but one liquid, the electrolyte, and either a mechanical or an air depolarizer, or none whatever.

Two-fluid cell; a cell, such as the Daniell, in which two liquids are used.

cell, *v.t.*; celled, *pt.*, *pp.*; celling, *ppr.* To shut up in a cell. [Rare.]

cel′lȧ, *n.* [L.] The inclosed part of a temple.

cel′lăr, *n.* [L. *cellarium*, a pantry, storeroom, from *cella*, a small room, hut.] A room under a house or other building, used as a repository for liquors, provisions, or goods of any kind.

cel′lăr-āge, *n.* 1. The room for a cellar; a cellar or cellars.

2. Charge for storage in a cellar.

cel′lăr-ẽr, cel′lăr-ist, *n.* [L. *cellarius*, a steward, butler, from *cellarium*, a pantry.] An officer in a monastery who has the care of the cellar, or the charge of procuring and keeping the provisions; also, an officer in chapters who has the care of the temporals, and particularly of distributing bread, wine, and money to canons on account of their attendance in the choir.

cel′lăr-et, *n.* A case of cabinetwork for holding bottles of liquors.

celled (seld), *a.* Furnished with a cell or cells: commonly used as the terminal element of a compound adjective; as, single-*celled*.

Cel-lep′ō-rȧ, Cel-lip′ō-rȧ, *n.* [L. *cella*, a cell, and *porus*, Gr. *poros*, a passage.] A genus of corals belonging to the class *Polyzoa*, composed of minute distinct cells arranged like fringes in longitudinal rows.

cel-lif′ẽr-ous, *a.* [L. *cella*, a cell, and *ferre*, to bear.] Bearing or producing cells.

cel′list (chel′), *n.* An abbreviated form of *violoncellist*.

cel′lō (chel′), *n.*; *pl.* **cel′lōs** or **cel′lï** (chel′). An abbreviation for *violoncello*.

cel′lū-lȧ, *n.* [L. *cellula*, dim. of *cella*, a room, hut.] A small cell; same as *Cellule*.

cel′lū-lăr, *a.* Made up of cells; pertaining to cells.

Cellular plants; plants having no spiral vessels, as mosses, lichens, etc.

Cellular or *cell theory*; the doctrine that all animal and vegetable bodies consist of either a cell or cells, and that all cells develop from other cells.

Cellular tissue; (a) in anatomy, the ordinary connective tissue made up of cells with large interspaces; (b) in botany, parenchyma, or vegetable pulp.

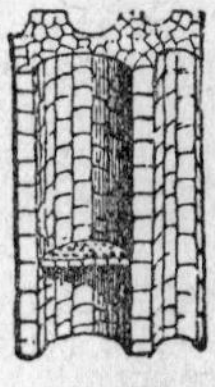

Cellular Tissue in Plants.

cel′lū-lăr, *n.* A plant having no spiral vessels, and bearing no flowers, as lichens and mosses.

cel′lū-lā-ted, *a.* Having a cellular structure.

cel′lūle, *n.* A small cell, as on the wings of *Neuroptera*, or in the parenchyma of plants.

cel-lū-lif′ẽr-ous, *a.* [L. *cellula*, a little cell, and *ferre*, to bear.] Bearing or producing little cells.

cel-lū-lī′tis, *n.* [L. *cellula*, a dim. of *cella*, a cell, and *-itis*.] Inflammation of cellular or connective tissue.

cel′lū-loid, *n.* [*Cellulose*, and *-oid*.] An artificial substance, composed chiefly of cellulose or vegetable fibrin, and much used as a substitute for ivory, bone, coral, etc.

cel′lū-lōse, *a.* [L. *cellula*, dim. of *cella*, a room, hut.] Containing or made up of cells.

cel′lū-lōse, *n.* In botany, the substance of which the permanent cell-membranes of plants are always composed.

Starch cellulose; the frail skeleton of cellulose remaining after the dissolution of the starch-granules in pepsin or saliva.

Cē-lō′si-ȧ, *n.* [Gr. *kēlos*, dry, burned, from the burned-like appearance of the flowers of some species.] A genus of annual plants, generally native to the tropics, order *Amarantaceæ*. The cockscomb, *Celosia cristata*, so common in cultivation, is perhaps the best known variety.

cē-lot′ō-my, *n.* [Gr. *kēlotomia*; *kēlē*, a tumor, and *-tomia*, from *temnein*, to cut.] In surgery, a term for the operation of removing the stricture in strangulated hernia by cutting.

cel′si-tūde, *n.* [L. *celsitudo*, from *celsus*, high.] Height; elevation of rank; excellency. [Obs.]

Cel′si-us, *n.* A thermometer invented by the Swedish astronomer, Anders Celsius; the *centigrade thermometer.* [See under *Centigrade.*]

Celt, Kelt, *n.* [L. *Celtæ*, pl.; Gr. *Keltoi*, Celts; W. *celt*, a covert, *celtiad*, one that dwells in a covert, from *celu*, to hide.] One of the earliest Aryan inhabitants of the south and west of Europe. Of the Celts there are two great branches, viz., the Gadhelic, comprising the Highlanders of Scotland, the Irish and Manx, and the Cymric, comprising the Welsh and Bretons.

celt, *n.* [LL. *celtis*, a chisel, a celt.] In archæology, an implement, sometimes made of stone and sometimes of metal, found in ancient tumuli and barrows of the Celtic period in Great Britain, Ireland, and on the continent of Europe.

Celts.

Celt-i-bē′ri-ăn, *a.* [L. *Celtiberi*, compounded of *Celtæ*, Celts, and *Iberi*, Iberians, the supposed original inhabitants of Spain.] Pertaining to Celtiberia and its inhabitants, the Celtiberi, an ancient people of Spain.

Celt-i-bē′ri-ăn, *n.* An inhabitant of Celtiberia, the name given in ancient times to central Spain.

Celt′iç, Kelt′iç, *a.* [L. *Celticus*; Gr. *Keltikos*, from *Keltoi*, Celts.] Pertaining to the Celts, or to their language; as, *Celtic* tribes; *Celtic* tongues.

Celt′iç, Kelt′iç, *n.* The language or group of dialects spoken by the Celts, including Welsh, Armoric or Breton, Irish, Gaelic, and Manx.

Celt′i-cişm, Kelt′i-cişm, *n.* 1. The manners and customs of the Celts.

2. A Celtic expression or mode of expression.

Celt′i-cīze, Kelt′i-cīze, *v.t.* and *v.i.* I. *v.t.* To render Celtic.

II. *v.i.* To become Celtic.

Celt′is, *n.* [L., an African species of lotus.] A genus of trees of several species, natural order *Urticaceæ*; the nettle-trees. *Celtis occidentalis*, the hackberry, is the principal North American species.

cem′bá-lō, *n.* [It.] An antique name for the harpsichord; the dulcimer.

cē-ment′ (*or* sem′ent), *n.* [OFr. *cement*, *ciment*; L. *cæmentum*, rough stone, chippings, from *cædere*, to cut.]

1. Any substance capable of uniting bodies in close cohesion, as mortar, glue, solder, etc. In building, cement denotes a stronger kind of mortar than that which is ordinarily used.

2. Bond of union; that which unites firmly, as persons in friendship, or men in society.

3. The substance in which iron, glass, etc., is packed, as in pots and crucibles, in the process of cementation; also, a minutely divided metal obtained by precipitation.

4. In placer and hydraulic mining, a firmly compacted mass of detrital auriferous gravel, held together by clay or silica.

5. A kind of mortar, or calcined mixture of lime and clay, which hardens under water; hence, called *hydraulic cement.*

6. In anatomy, the tissue forming the outer crust of the fangs or root of the teeth; crusta petrosa; called also *cementum.*

Portland cement; a hydraulic cement made by the burning of limestone with some clayey or chalky substance; much used in buildings and such structures as cisterns and water-tanks.

Rubber cement; pure rubber mechanically mixed with sulphur and dissolved in some such hydrocarbon as benzine; used for coating cloth, belting, etc.

cē-ment′, *v.t.*; cemented, *pt., pp.*; cementing, *ppr.* 1. To unite or cause to adhere by the application of glutinous substances, by mortar which hardens, or other matter that produces cohesion of bodies.

2. Figuratively, to unite firmly or closely; as, to *cement* friendship.

3. To coat with cement, as a cellar or a cistern.

cē-ment′, *v.i.* To unite or become solid; to cohere.

cē-ment′ăl, *a.* Pertaining to cement, as of a tooth.

cem-en-tā′tion, *n.* 1. The act of cementing; the act of uniting by a suitable substance.

2. In chemistry, the process by which a solid substance is caused to enter into or combine with another at a high temperature without fusion of either; specifically, the conversion of iron into steel by heating the iron in a mass of ground charcoal, and thus causing it to absorb a certain quantity of the charcoal; known as carburization by *cementation.*

cē-ment′á-tō-ry, *a.* Cementing; having the quality of uniting firmly.

cē-ment′ēr, *n.* One who or that which cements.

cem-en-ti′tious (-tish′us), *a.* [L. *cæmentitius*, pertaining to quarried stones; from *cæmentum*, rough stone, stone chippings.] Pertaining to cement; having the quality of cementing; of the nature of cement.

cem-ē-tē′ri-ăl, *a.* Pertaining to a cemetery or burial. [Rare.]

cem′ē-ter-y, *n.* [LL. *cœmeterium*; Gr. *koimētērion*, a sleeping-place, cemetery, from *koiman*, to put to sleep.] A place set apart for burial or interment; a graveyard; a necropolis.

cē-nan′thy, *n.* [Gr. *kenos*, empty, and *anthos*, flower.] In botany, the abnormal suppression or absence of the stamens and pistils, or essential organs of flowers.

cē-nā′tion, *n.* [L. *cenatio*, from *cenare*, to dine, eat.] The act of dining or supping. [Obs.]

cen′á-tō-ry, *a.* Pertaining to dinner or supper. [Rare.]

> The Romans washed, were anointed, and wore a *cenatory* garment. —Browne.

ceṅ′ċhrus, *n.*; *pl.* **ceṅ′ċhrī.** [Gr. *kenchros*, millet.]

1. An insect of the family *Tenthredinidæ*; a kind of saw-fly.

2. In entomology, one of the two little marks on the last segment of the thorax, usually white.

3. [C—] A small genus of grasses, including the species commonly known as *burgrass* and *hedgehog-grass.*

cen′dal, *n.* Same as *Sendal.*

cen′ō-bite, *n.* [LL. *cœnobita*, from *cœnobium*; Gr. *koinobion*, a convent, neut. of *koinobios*; *koinos*, common, and *bios*, life.] One of a religious order living in a convent or in community; in opposition to an *anchoret*, or hermit, who lives in solitude.

cen-ō-bit′iç, cen-ō-bit′iç-ăl, *a.* Living in community, as men belonging to a convent.

cen′ō-bī-tişm, *n.* The state of being a cenobite; the principles or practice of a cenobite; the theory of conventual life.

ce-nō′bi-um, *n.*; *pl.* **ce-nō′bi-á.** 1. Same as *Cenoby.*

2. Same as *Cœnobium.*

cen′ō-by, *n.* A place where persons live in community; a monastery or conventual abode.

cē-nog′á-my, *n.* [Gr. *koinos*, common, and *gamos*, marriage.] The state of having husbands or wives in common, as in certain primitive tribes or communistic societies; written also *cœnogamy.*

cen-ō-gen′e-sis, *n.* See *Kenogenesis.*

cen″ō-ġē-net′iç, *a.* See *Kenogenetic.*

cē-nos′i-ty, *n.* [L. *cœnositas*, from *cœnosus*, filthy.] Uncleanness; filthiness; squalor.

cen′ō-taph, *n.* [L. *cenotaphium*; Gr. *kenotaphion*, an empty tomb; *kenos*, empty, and *taphos*, a tomb.] An empty tomb erected in honor of some deceased person; a monument erected to one who is buried elsewhere; as, a *cenotaph* in Westminster abbey.

Cenotaph of Burns, Banks of Doon.

> A *cenotaph* his name and title kept.—Dryden.

cen′ō-taph-y, *n.* Same as *Cenotaph.*

Cē-nō-zō′iç, *a.* See *Cœnozoic.*

cens (säṅs), *n.* [Fr.] In French-Canadian law, the annual payment, apart from rent, exacted from a tenant by the owner of an estate, as a token of the latter's superiority and a formal acknowledgment of his title.

cense, *n.* [OFr. *cens*, *cense*; L. *census*, a registering, rating of property, tax.]

1. A public rate or tax. [Obs.]

2. Condition; rank. [Obs.]

3. A census. [Obs.]

cense, *v.t.*; censed, *pt., pp.*; censing, *ppr.* [Abbrev. from *incense.*] To perfume with odors from burning substances, as gums or spices.

> The Salii sing, and *cense* his altars round. —Dryden.

cense, *v.i.* To scatter incense; as, *censing* about the altar.

cen′sēr, *n.* [A shortened form for *incenser.*] A vase or pan in which incense is burned; a vessel for burning and wafting incense. *Censers* are used in the Roman Catholic church at mass, vespers, and other offices, in the Greek, some Anglican, and other churches.

cen′sō (*or Sp. pron.*, then′sō), *n.* [Sp.] 1. In Spanish-American law, a ground-rent; an annual ground-rent charged upon specific property.

2. The right to an annuity out of a specific fund or estate.

cen′sŏr, *n.* [L. *censor*, from *censere*, to tax, value, judge.]

1. An officer in ancient Rome whose business was to draw up a register of the citizens and the amount of their property, for the purposes of taxation; to keep watch over the morals of the citizens, for which purpose they had power to censure vice and immorality by inflicting a public mark of ignominy on the offender; and to superintend the maintenance and improvement of all public works.

2. In several European countries, one who is empowered to examine all manuscripts and books before they are published, and to see that they contain nothing deemed heretical or immoral, or libelous to royalty and the government.

3. One who censures, blames, or reproves; one who is given to censure; one who is addicted to perpetual fault-finding; as, ill-natured *censors* of the present age.

4. In schools, a pupil appointed to keep the register of all who attend, to mark those who are absent each day on meeting, to report faults, etc.

5. One who reviews; a critic.

cen′sŏr-āte, *n.* A body or board of censors, as in governmental or official life in China.

cen-sō′ri-ăl, cen-sō′ri-ăn, *a.* 1. Belonging to a censor or to the correction of public morals; as, *censorial* power.

2. Full of censure; censorious.

cen-sō′ri-ous, *a.* [L. *censorius*, from *censor*, a magistrate, judge.]

1. Addicted to censure; apt to blame or condemn; severe in making remarks on others, or on their writings or manners; as, a *censorious* critic.

2. Implying or expressing censure; as, *censorious* remarks.

Syn.—Fault-finding, hypercritical, captious, severe, carping, caviling.

cen-sō′ri-ous-ly, *adv.* In a censorious manner.

cen-sō′ri-ous-ness, *n.* The quality of being censorious; disposition to blame and condemn; the habit of censuring or reproaching.

cen′sŏr-ship, *n.* The office, dignity, or power of a censor; the time during which a censor holds office.

cen′su̦-ăl (-shu̦-ăl), *a.* [L. *censualis*, from *census*, a census.] Relating to or containing a census.

cen′su̦r-á-ble (-shu̦r-), *a.* Deserving of censure; blamable; culpable; reprehensible; faulty; as, a *censurable* person, or *censurable* conduct.

cen′su̦r-á-ble-ness, *n.* Blamableness; fitness to be censured.

cen′su̦r-á-bly, *adv.* In a manner deserving of blame.

cen′su̦re (-shu̦r), *n.* [L. *censura*, the office of a censor, judgment, opinion, from *censere*, to judge, tax.]

1. An estimate or judgment without implying disapprobation. [Obs.]

2. The act of blaming or finding fault and condemning as wrong; blame; reproof; reprehension; reprimand.

3. Judicial sentence; judgment that condemns. An ecclesiastical *censure* is a sentence of condemnation or penalty inflicted on a member of a church for malconduct, by which he is deprived of the communion of the church, or debarred from the sacerdotal office.

Syn.—Blame, condemnation, invective, rebuke, reproach, remonstrance, reprimand, stricture, reproof.

cen′su̦re (-shu̦r), *v.t.*; censured, *pt., pp.*; censuring, *ppr.* 1. To find fault with and condemn as wrong; to blame; to express disapprobation of; as, to *censure* a man.

2. To condemn by a judicial sentence, as in ecclesiastical affairs.

3. To estimate; to form or express an opinion of. [Obs.]

Syn.—Accuse, blame, carp, cavil, condemn, reproach, reprove, upbraid.

cen′su̦re, *v.i.* To judge; to form or express an opinion. [Obs.]

cen′su̦r-ēr, *n.* One who criticizes or censures.

cen′sus, *n.* [L., from *censere*, to enroll, tax, assess.]

1. In ancient Rome, an authentic enumeration of the people, with special reference to the value of their property and estates, for the purpose of determining the rate of taxation; usually made every five years.

2. An official enumeration of the people of a nation, state, district, or city, together with the collecting of statistics concerning their property, nativity, age, sex, occupation, etc. In the United States, a general or federal census has been taken at the end of every ten years since 1790, an intermediate census being taken by some of the states and cities.

cent, *n.* [OFr. *cent*; L. *centum*, a hundred.]

1. A hundred. In commerce, *per cent* denotes a certain rate by the hundred; as, ten *per cent* is ten in the hundred, whether profit or loss.

2. In the United States, a coin formerly made of copper, but later of copper with a five per cent alloy of tin and zinc, the value of which is the hundredth part of a dollar; a penny.

3. An old game of cards, resembling piquet, in which 100 was the game.

cent'āge, *n.* Rate by the cent or hundred; percentage.

cen'tăl, *n.* A hundredweight, or one hundred pounds avoirdupois.

cen'tăl, *a.* Pertaining to a hundred.

cen'tāre, *n.* [Fr. *centiare*, from L. *centum*, hundred.] In the metric system, one square meter, or about one and one-fifth square yards the hundredth part of an are; a measure of area.

cen'taur, *n.* [L. *centaurus*; Gr. *kentauros*.]

1. In mythology, a fabulous being, supposed to be half man and half horse. It has been supposed that this fancied monster originated among the Lapithæ, a tribe in Thessaly, who first invented the art of breaking horses. But the origin of the fable and of the name is doubtful.

2. [C—] The constellation of the southern hemisphere, situated between Argus and Scorpio.

Centaur.—Antique statue in Vatican Museum.

Cen-tau-rē'ă, *n.* [L. *centauria*; Gr. *kentaureion*, centaury, from *kentauros*, a centaur.] An extensive genus of herbaceous plants, natural order *Compositæ*. The species are annual or perennial herbs. They are found in Europe, western Asia, and north Africa. The annuals, *Centaurea Cyanus* (cornbluebottle), *Centaurea moschata* (purple or white sultan), and *Centaurea suaveolens* (yellow sultan), are sometimes cultivated in gardens.

cen'taur-ize, *v.i.* To perform the acts of or to be like a centaur; to be a man, and act like a brute. [Rare.]

cen'taur-like, *a.* Having the nature or appearance of a centaur.

cen-tau-rom'ă-chy, *n.* [L. *centauromachia*; Gr. *kentauromachia*; *kentauros*, a centaur, and *machē*, battle.] A fight between centaurs, or between centaurs and men; a theme much used by sculptors in rilievo-work.

cen'tau-ry, *n.* [L. *centauria*; Gr. *kentaureion*, centaury, from *kentauros*, a centaur.] The popular name of various plants. The lesser *centaury* is a species of *Erythræa*.

cen-tä'vō (*Sp. pron.* then-), *n.* [Sp., from L. *centum*, hundred.] In some Central and South American countries, a small nickel or copper coin; the hundredth part of a dollar or peso.

cen-ten' (*Sp. pron.* then'tān), *n.* [Sp., from L. *centeni*, pl., a hundred each.] A Spanish gold coin of Porto Rico, valued at $5.02.

cen-tō-nā'ri-ăn, *n.* and *a.* I. *n.* A person a hundred years old or upward.

II. *a.* Pertaining to a centenary or centenarian.

cen'te-nā-ry, *n.*; *pl.* **cen'te-nā-ries**. [L. *centenarius*, from *centum*, a hundred.]

1. What consists of or comprehends a hundred; the space of a hundred years.

2. The commemoration of any event, as the birth of a great man, which occurred a hundred years before; as, the *centenary* of Burns; the *centenary* of Emerson.

cen'te-nā-ry, *a.* Relating to or consisting of a hundred; relating to a hundred years; as, a *centenary* festival or celebration.

cen-ten'ni-ăl, *a.* [L. *centum*, a hundred, and *annus*, a year.]

1. Pertaining to, consisting of, or lasting a hundred years; as, a *centennial* epoch; a *centennial* address.

> That opened through long lines
> Of sacred ilex and *centennial* pines.
> —Longfellow.

2. Happening every hundred years; as, a *centennial* celebration.

3. Aged a hundred years.

cen-ten'ni-ăl, *n.* The commemoration or celebration of any event which occurred a hundred years before; as, the *centennial* of American independence; the *centennial* of the Louisiana Purchase; first applied to the *Centennial* Exhibition, at Philadelphia, in 1876.

cen-ten'ni-ăl-ly, *adv.* Once in every hundred years; as, to celebrate an event *centennially*.

cen'tēr, cen'tre, *n.* [OFr. *centre*; L. *centrum*; Gr. *kentron*, a sharp point, goad, spur, the point round which a circle is described; from *kentein*, to prick, goad.]

1. A point equally distant from the extremities of a line, figure, or body; the middle point or place of anything.

2. The middle or central object of anything.

3. The point, object, or place to which things converge; the nucleus about which they are gathered or concentrated; a point of attraction; as, the *center* of interest; the *center* of power.

4. In ancient astronomy, the middle point of the earth. [Obs.]

5. One of the points in a lathe-spindle on which the object to be turned is placed; or one of two similar points for holding an object to be operated on by some other machine, as a planing-machine, and enabling the object to be rotated on its axis.

6. In the French and German legislative assemblies especially, the title given to members of moderate views, intermediate between the right and left; in Germany called the *Clerical party*.

7. A temporary structure which supports the materials of a vault or arch while the work is in process of construction. [See *Centering*.]

8. In football, the player in the middle of the forward or rush line; called also *center-rush*.

9. In rifle practice, or marksmanship, (a) the part of a target next the bull's-eye; (b) a shot striking the target within the circle or square next the bull's-eye.

10. In anatomy and pathology, the concentration of special and similar organs or morbid processes; as, a nervous *center*; a *center* of inflammation.

11. In military terms, (a) that portion of an army, in line of battle, between the wings; (b) that portion of a fleet between the van and the rear, or (when sailing) between the weather and the lee.

Center of attraction of a body; that point into which, if all its matter were collected, its action upon any remote particle would be the same as before; or the point to which bodies tend in consequence of the action of gravity.

Center of a bastion; a point in the middle of the gorge of a bastion, whence the capital line commences, which is generally at the angle of the inner polygon.

Center of buoyancy; the mean center of that part of a ship which is immersed in the water; also called the *center of cavity*, *center of immersion*, and *center of displacement*.

Center of a conic section; that point which bisects any diameter, or that point in which all the diameters intersect each other.

Center of a curve of the higher kind; the point where two diameters concur.

Center of conversion; a point in a body about which it turns, or tends to turn, when a force is applied to any part of it; as when a bar of iron lies horizontally, and is struck at one end perpendicularly to its length, one point in the rod remains at rest, as a center about which all the other points tend to revolve.

Center of gravity; in mechanics, the point about which all the parts of a body exactly balance each other, so that when that point is supported, the whole body is supported.

Center of gyration; the point at which, if the whole mass of a revolving body were collected, the rotary effect would remain unaltered.

Center of inertia; that point in a body which is so situated that the force requisite for producing motion in the body, or bringing it to rest, is equivalent to a single force applied at this point. It is the same with the center of gravity.

Center of motion; the point which remains at rest, while all the other parts of a body move round it.

Center of oscillation; the point of a body suspended by an axis, at which, if all the matter were concentrated, the oscillations would be performed in the same time.

Center of percussion; the point at which, if a moving body encountered an immovable obstacle, the motion would be arrested without producing any strain on the axis. It coincides with the center of oscillation when the percutient body moves about a fixed point; and with the center of gravity when the body moves in a straight line.

Center of population; the geographical point about which the entire population of a country or district is supposed to balance.

Center of pressure; in hydrostatics, that point on the surface of a body subjected to pressure which would be in equilibrium if an equal counter-pressure were exerted in the same line.

Center of similitude; in geometry, the point at which either the direct or crosswise tangents of two circles intersect.

Center of vision; the point in the retina from which the radial line in perspective starts.

cen'tēr, cen'tre, *v.i.*; centered, centred, *pt.*, *pp.*; centering, centring, *ppr.* 1. To be placed in a center or in the middle.

2. To be collected to one point; to be concentrated or united in one; as, our hopes must *center* in ourselves alone.

> Life's choicest blessings *centre* all in home.
> —Cowper.

cen'tēr, cen'tre, *v.t.* 1. To place on a center; to fix on a central point.

2. To collect to a point.

> Thy joys are *centered* all in me alone.—Prior.

3. In mechanics, to form an indentation or supply with a center.

cen'tēr-bär, *n.* An arbor, or mandrel of a circular saw or turning lathe.

cen'tēr-bit, *n.* An instrument turning on a center, for boring circular holes.

cen'tēr-bōard, *n.* A movable or shifting keel passing through a slot in the bottom of a vessel and swinging on a pin at the forward lower corner. It consists of a broad slab of wood or metal, and may be raised or lowered as occasion requires; when lowered it acts as a projecting keel, increasing the area of lateral resistance, and when raised is completely housed in the boat, reducing her draft to that of the keel proper.

cen'tēr-fire, *a.* Having the fulminating charge of powder in the center of the base; said of cartridges.

cen'tēr-ing, *n.* The framing of timber by which the arch of a bridge or other structure is supported during its erection. The same name is given to the woodwork or framing on which

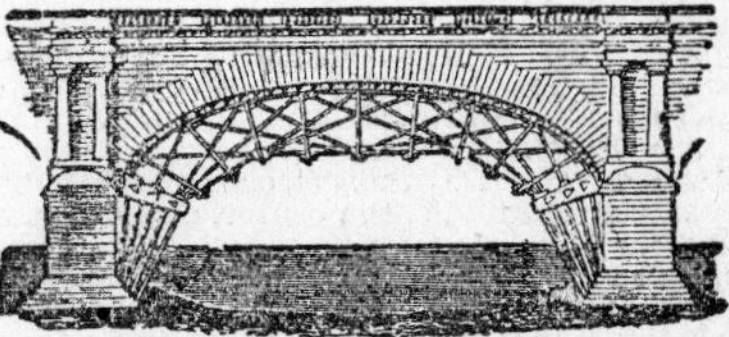

Centering, Waterloo Bridge, London.

any vaulted work is constructed. The *centering* of a bridge has to keep the stones or voussoirs in position till they are keyed in; that is, fixed by the insertion of the requisite number of stones in the center. Written also *centring* and *center*.

cen'tēr-piēce, *n.* A central ornament, as of a table, ceiling, etc., or a decorative article or figure between other ornaments.

cen'tēr-sec"ŏnd, *a.* Having the second-hand mounted on the same arbor as the minute and hour hands, as in a watch.

cen-tes'i-măl, *a.* and *n.* I. *a.* The hundredth.

II. *n.* The next step of progression after decimal in the arithmetic of fractions.

cen-tes-i-mā'tion, *n.* [L. *centesimare*, to take out every hundredth, from *centesimus*, hundredth; *centum*, a hundred.] A military punishment for desertion, mutiny, or the like, where one person in every hundred is selected for execution.

cen-tes'i-mō, *n.*; *pl.* **cen-tes'i-mï**. [It. and Sp., from L. *centesimus*, hundredth.] A copper coin of Italy and Spain; the equivalent of a *centime*, and the hundredth part of various units of money.

cen'tesm, *n.* [L. *centesimus*, hundredth.] The hundredth part of an integer or thing.

cen-tet'id, *n.* A member of the family *Centetidæ*.

Cen-tet'i-dæ, *n.pl.* [Gr. *kentētēs*, one who pierces, from *kentein*, to pierce.] A subgenus of insectivores, of which there are several species, including the little tenrecs of Madagascar.

cen'ti-. A combining form from L. *centum*, hundred, and signifying hundred; as, *centi*ped, *centi*folious. In the metric system it is used to signify hundredth part; as, *centi*meter, *centi*gram.

cen'ti-āre, *n.* See *Centare*.

cen-ti-cip'i-tous, *a.* [L. *centiceps* (*-ipitis*); *centum*, hundred, and *caput*, head.] Having a hundred heads.

cen-tif'i-dous, *a.* [L. *centifidus*; *centum*, hundred, and *findere*, to split.] Divided into a hundred parts.

cen-ti-fō'li-ous, *a.* [L. *centifolius*; *centum*, hundred, and *folium*, leaf.] Having a hundred leaves.

cen'ti-grāde, *a.* [Fr., from L. *centum*, hundred, and *gradus*, a degree.] Consisting of a hundred degrees; graduated into a hundred divisions or equal parts.

Centigrade thermometer; a thermometer having the distance between the freezing and boiling points of water divided into 100 degrees; called also *Celsius thermometer*.

cen'ti-gram, cen'ti-gramme, *n.* [*Centi-*, and Fr. *gramme*, a weight; Gr. *gramma*, a writing.] In the metric system, the hundredth part of a gram.

cen'ti-lï-tēr, cen'ti-lï-tre, *n.* [*Centi-*, and Fr. *litre*; Gr. *litra*, a silver coin.] The hundredth part of a liter, equals .338 of a fluid ounce or a little more than 6-10 of a cubic inch, dry measure.

cen-til′ō-quy, *n.* [L. *centum*, a hundred, and *loqui*, to speak.] A hundredfold discourse.

cen-time′ (sän-teem′), *n.* [Fr.] The hundredth part of a franc.

cen′ti-mē-tēr, cen′ti-mē-tre, *n.* [*Centi-*, and Fr. *mètre*, Gr. *metron*, a measure.] In French measure, the hundredth part of a meter, or .3937+ of an inch.

cen′ti-nel, *n.* [Obs.] Same as *Sentinel*.

cen′ti-nōde, cen-tin′ō-dy, *n.* [L. *centinodia*; *centum*, hundred, and *nodus*, a knot.] Knotgrass, *Polygonum aviculare*; also, a weed, *Illecebrum verticillatum*.

cen′ti-ped, cen′ti-pēde, *n.* [L. *centipeda*; *centum*, a hundred, and *pes*, *pedis*, a foot.] A general term applied to insects having a great number of feet and belonging to the order *Chilopoda*.

cen′ti-stēre, *n.* [*Centi-*, and Fr. *stere*, from Gr. *stereos*, solid.] A cubic centimeter, equal to .353 of a cubic foot, or a hundredth part of a stere.

cent′nēr, *n.* [L. *centenarius*, from *centum*, a hundred.]

1. In metallurgy and assaying, a weight divisible first into a hundred parts, and then into smaller parts.

2. The name in several European countries for a hundredweight.

cen′tō, *n.* [L. *cento*, patchwork.] A composition formed by combining the work of several authors or artists in a new form; specifically, in art, a pasticcio; in music, a medley or olio.

cen′tō-nism, *n.* The act or practice of arranging borrowed literary, artistic, or musical features in a new order, thus forming a patchwork composition.

cen′trad, *adv.* [L. *centrum*, center, and *ad*, to.] Toward the middle, the center, or the interior of a body or organ.

cen′trăl, *a.* [L. *centralis*, from *centrum*, center.] Relating to the center; placed in the center or middle; containing the center, or pertaining to the parts near the center.

Central forces; in mechanics, the two antagonistic forces (the centripetal and centrifugal), by whose united action bodies are caused to revolve round a central point.

Central particle; same as *Centrosome*.

Central Powers; the term applied during the World War to Austria-Hungary and Germany. Sometimes used to include their allies, Bulgaria and Turkey.

cen′trăl, *n.* A telephone exchange. [Colloq.]

cen-trā′lē, cen′trăl, *n.* [L. *centralis*, central.] One of the middle bones of the eight composing the wrist of man, or of the seven forming his ankle. In animals, one of the bones between the antibrachium and the fore foot; or between the tibia and metatarsus.

cen′trăl-ism, *n.* 1. The state or condition of being in the center; the bringing of several portions into one body; centralization.

2. The system of centralizing power, as in government; centralization in a political sense.

cen-tral′i-ty, *n.*; *pl.* **cen-tral′i-ties.** The state of being central or inclining toward a center.

cen″trăl-i-zā′tion, *n.* The act or process of centralizing; the state of being centralized; the combining or concentrating of several parts into a whole.

cen′trăl-īze, *v.t.*; centralized (-īzd), *pt.*, *pp.*; centralizing, *ppr.* To draw to a central point; to bring to a center; to bring under one authority or control.

cen′trăl-ly, *adv.* With regard to the center; in a central manner.

cen′tre (-tēr), *n.* and *v.* Same as *Center*.

cen′tric, cen′tric-ăl, *a.* [Gr. *kentrikos*, from *kentron*, center.] Placed in the center or middle.

cen′tric-ăl-ly, *adv.* In a central position.

cen′tric-ăl-ness, *n.* Situation in the center.

cen-tric′i-ty, *n.* The state or quality of being centric.

cen-trif′ū-găl, *a.* [L. *centrum*, center, and *fugere*, to flee.]

1. Tending to recede from the center; as, the *centrifugal* force by which comets tend to fly from their parent bodies; opposed to *centripetal*.

2. In botany, expanding first at the summit, and later at the base, as a flower.

Centrifugal inflorescence; in botany, that kind of inflorescence in which the terminal or central flower is the first to open. The elder and valerian furnish examples. Called also *determinate* or *definite inflorescence*.

Centrifugal machine; a machine with a whirling motion designed to drive moisture out of damp articles, separate fluids of different densities, raise water, ventilate mines, etc.

cen-trif′ū-găl, *n.* A centrifugal machine with a drum-like part in which is a revolving cylinder.

cen-trif′ū-gence, *n.* The property of receding from the center, or the centrifugal tendency.

cen′tring, *n.* Same as *Centering*.

cen-trip′e-tăl, *a.* [L. *centrum*, center, and *petere*, to move toward, seek.]

1. Tending toward the center; as, the *centripetal* force by which planets and satellites tend to revolve around their parent bodies.

2. In botany, expanding first at the base of the inflorescence, and later at the summit, as a flower; as, *centripetal* inflorescence.

3. Progressive changing from the outside toward the center; as, in pathology, *centripetal* calcification.

cen-trip′e-tence, cen-trip′e-ten-cy, *n.* [L. *centrum*, center, and *petens* (*-entis*), ppr. of *petere*, to seek.] Inclination or tendency toward the center.

cen-tris′coid, *a* [Gr. *kentriskos*, a kind of fish, and *eidos*, form.] Pertaining to the genus *Centriscus*.

Cen-tris′cus, *n.* [Gr. *kentriskos*, a kind of fish, dim. of *kentron*, a spine.] A genus of fishes comprising the bellows-fish, trumpet-fish, seasnipe, etc.

cen′trō-. A combining form from L. *centrum*, center; Gr. *kentron*, a horn, point, sting, center.

cen-trō-bar′ic, *a.* [*Centro-*, and Gr. *baros*, weight.] Pertaining to the center of gravity, or to the means of finding it.

Centrobaric method; a method enabling the surface or volume of a solid to be measured by means of a line or surface rotating about a fixed axis.

cen′troid, *n.* [Gr. *kentron*, center, and *eidos*, form.] The center of gravity or mass-center of a body or combination of bodies.

cen-trō-lec′i-thăl, *a.* [*Centro-*, and Gr. *lekithos*, yolk of an egg.] Having the food-yolk in the center of the ovum, with regular or unequal segmentation.

cen-trō-lin′ē-ad, *n.* [*Centro-*, and L. *linea*, a line.] An instrument used in perspective drawing, for drawing lines converging toward a point.

cen-trō-lin′ē-ăl, *a.* [*Centro-*, and L. *linea*, a line.] Converging to a center.

cen′trō-sōme, *n.* [*Centro-*, and Gr. *sōma*, the body.] A central particle or oval body appearing near the nucleus of a cell, and thought to be the center of attraction or motive force during the indirect division and primary development of the cell.

cen′trum, *n.* [L., from Gr. *kentron*, center.]

1. A central mass.

2. Specifically, (a) in anatomy, the body of a vertebrate or the mass of a cranial segment; (b) in geology, the focus or place of origin of an earthquake-shock.

cen′try, *n.* [Obs.] Same as *Sentry*.

cen-tum′vir, *n.*; *pl.* **cen′tum-virs** or **cen-tum′vi-rī.** [L. *centumvir*; *centum*, hundred, and *vir*, a man.] A name given to certain judges in ancient Rome, appointed by the pretor, to decide common causes among the people. At first, three were taken from each of the thirty-five tribes, making 105, though, for the sake of the round number, they were called *centumviri*. The number was afterward increased to 180, without a change of their title.

cen-tum′vi-răl, *a.* Pertaining to the centumvir.

cen-tum′vi-rāte, *n.* The office of a centumvir.

cen-tum′vi-rī, *n.* Latin plural of *centumvir*.

cen′tū-ple, *a.* [Fr., from L. *centuplex*, hundredfold; *centum*, hundred, and *plicare*, to fold.] Increased by a hundredfold.

cen′tū-ple, *v.t.*; centupled, *pt.*, *pp.*; centupling, *ppr.* To multiply a hundredfold.

cen-tū′pli-cāte, *v.t.*; centuplicated, *pt.*, *pp.*; centuplicating, *ppr.* To make a hundredfold. [Rare.]

cen-tū′ri-ăl, *a.* 1. Relating to a century, or a hundred years; as, a *centurial* sermon.

2. Divided into hundreds or centuries; as, the *centurial* military organization of the Roman army; a *centurial* history.

cen-tū′ri-āte, *v.t.* [L. *centuriatus*, pp. of *centuriare*, to divide into hundreds; *centuria*, a hundred.] To divide into hundreds. [Obs.]

cen-tū′ri-āte, *a.* Pertaining to centuries or divided into hundreds. [Rare.]

cen-tū′ri-ā-tōr, cen′tū-rist, *n.* [From L. *centuriare*, to divide into hundreds.] A historian who distinguishes time by centuries, as in the Universal Church History of Magdeburg.

cen-tū′ri-ŏn, *n.* [L. *centurio* (*-onis*), from *centuria*, a company of a hundred.] Among the Romans, a military officer who commanded a hundred men, a century, or company of infantry, answering to the captain in modern armies.

cen′tū-ry, *n.*; *pl.* **cen′tū-ries.** [L. *centuria*, from *centum*, a hundred.]

1. In a general sense, a hundred; anything of a hundred in number.

2. In antiquity, a division of the Roman people for the purpose of electing magistrates and enacting laws, the people voting by *centuries*; also, a company consisting of a hundred men; one of the sixty companies composing a legion of the army.

3. A period of a hundred years. This is the most common signification of the word; and as we begin our modern computation of time from the incarnation of Christ, the word is generally applied to some term of a hundred years subsequent to that event; as, the *first century*, A. D. 1—100; the *nineteenth century*, A. D. 1801—1900, both inclusive. If we intend to apply the word to a different era, we use an explanatory adjunct; as, the third *century* before the Christian era, or after the reign of Cyrus.

4. In sports, a hundred; in cricket, a hundred runs; in bicycling, a hundred miles.

The Centuries of Magdeburg; a title given to an ecclesiastical history, arranged in thirteen centuries, compiled by a great number of Protestants at Magdeburg.

cen′tū-ry-plant, *n.* A name sometimes given to the American aloe, *Agave Americana*, which was formerly supposed to flower only once in a century.

ceorl, *n.* [AS.] A freeman of the lowest rank among the Anglo-Saxons; a churl. [Obs.]

cē-pā′ceous, *a.* [L. *cepa*, *cæpa*, the onion.] Characteristic of an onion; smelling like an onion; alliaceous.

cē-pev′ō-rous, *a.* [L. *cepa*, an onion, and *vorare*, to devour.] Feeding or subsisting upon onions. [Rare.]

Ceph-ȧ-ē′lis, *n.* [*Cephal-*, and Gr. *eilein*, to compress.] A large genus of herbs or shrubs, natural order *Rubiaceæ*, found in the tropical parts of America.

cē-phal-, ceph′ȧ-lō-. Combining forms from Gr. *kephalē*, head, and used to signify connection with, or relation to, the head; as, *cephale*tron, *cephalo*branchia.

ceph′ȧ-lad, *adv.* [From Gr. *kephalē*, head, and L. *ad*, toward.] Toward the head; in the opposite direction from *caudad*.

ceph-ȧ-lal′gi-ȧ, ceph′ȧ-lal-gy, *n.* [Gr. *kephalalgia*, headache; *kephalē*, head, and *algos*, pain.] Headache.

ceph-ȧ-lal′gic, *a.* and *n.* I. *a.* Pertaining to or afflicted with headache.

II. *n.* A cure for headache; also, one who suffers from headache.

ceph-ȧ-lan′thi-um, *n.* Same as *Anthodium*.

Ceph-ȧ-las′pis, *n.* [*Cephal-*, and Gr. *aspis*, a shield.] A genus of fossil fishes found in the Devonian formation. The head, which is very large, is covered by a protecting plate shaped like a buckler, and prolonged backward into a point on either side.

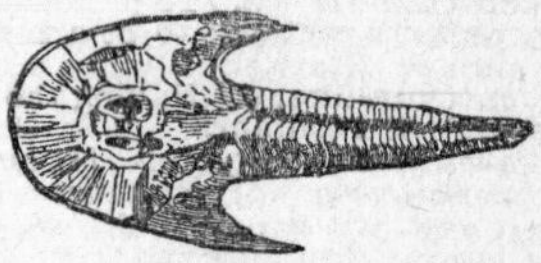

Cephalaspis lyelli.

Ceph-ȧ-lā′tȧ, *n.pl.* [From Gr. *kephalē*, head.] An order of mollusks with specially developed head, comprising the pteropods, gasteropods, and scaphopods, but not the bivalves.

ceph′ȧ-lāte, *a.* Possessing a head; applied to certain mollusks.

ceph-ȧ-le′tron, *n.* [*Cephal-*, and Gr. *ētron*, abdomen.] The head or anterior division of the body of some crustaceans, as the king-crab.

cē-phal′ic, *a.* [L. *cephalicus*; Gr. *kephalikos*, from *kephalē*, head.] Pertaining to the head; as, *cephalic* medicines, remedies for headache.

Cephalic index; the proportion of the greatest width of the skull to its greatest length.

Cephalic vein; a large vein which runs along the arm; so named because the ancients used to open it for disorders of the head.

cē-phal′ic, *n.* A medicine for headache, or other disorder in the head.

ceph′ȧ-lism, *n.* [Gr. *kephalē*, head.] The development of the skull, as characteristic of the different races of mankind.

ceph-ȧ-lī′tis, *n.* Same as *Phrenitis*.

ceph″ȧ-li-zā′tion, *n.* In biology, the term proposed by Prof. Dana to denote a tendency in the development of animals toward the location of important parts in the neighborhood of the head, as by the transfer of locomotive members or limbs to the head, as in the *Cephalopoda*.

ceph′ȧ-lō-. See *Cephal-*.

Ceph″ȧ-lō-bran′chi-ȧ, *n.* [*Cephalo-*, and Gr. *branchia*, gills.] A subdivision of *Annelida*, characterized by gills borne upon or near the head.

ceph″ȧ-lō-cēr′căl, *a.* [*Cephalo-*, and Gr. *kerkos*, tail.] In anatomy, extending from head to tail; cephalocaudal.

Ceph″ȧ-lō-chor′dȧ, *n.pl.* [*Cephalo-*, and Gr. *chordē*, a string, cord.] The lancelets, *Amphioxus*, considered as a division of vertebrates.

ceph″ȧ-lō-chor′dăl, *a.* Relating to the *Cephalochorda*, or vertebrates, in which the notochord continues into the head.

ceph′ȧ-lō-cōne, *n.* [*Cephalo-*, and Gr. *kōnos*, a cone.] A cone-shaped organ on the head of a pteropod; an inferior tentacle.

ceph″ȧ-lō-con′ic, *a.* Pertaining to a cephalocone.

ceph-ȧ-lō′di-um, *n.*; *pl.* **ceph-ȧ-lō′di-ȧ,** [Gr

kephalōdēs, like a head; *kephalē*, head, and *eidos*, form.] A convex development on the thallus of a lichen, containing algal cells.

ceph′ȧ-loid, *a.* [Gr. *kephalē*, head, and *eidos*, form.] Having the shape of a head; spherical.

ceph-ȧ-lol′ō-gy̆, *n.* [*Cephalo-*, and Gr. *-logia*, from *legein*, to speak.] The scientific study of the head; a treatise on the head.

ceph′ȧ-lō-man″cy, *n.* [*Cephalo-*, and Gr. *manteia*, divination.] Prediction by means of a head.

ceph′ȧ-lō-mēre, *n.* [*Cephalo-*, and Gr. *meros*, part.] A serial division or segment of the head of arthropods.

ceph-ȧ-lom′e-tēr, *n.* [*Cephalo-*, and Gr. *metron*, measure.] An instrument for measuring a fetal head in parturition.

ceph″ȧ-lō-met′riç, *a.* Pertaining to cephalometry or craniometry; craniometric.

ceph-ȧ-lom′e-try, *n.* The art of measuring skulls; craniometry.

ceph′ȧ-lon, *n.* [Gr. *kephalē*, the head.] In zoölogy, the head.

Ceph-ȧ-loph′ō-rȧ, *n.pl.* Same as *Cephalata*.

ceph′ȧ-lō-pod, ceph′ȧ-lō-pōde, *n.* One of the *Cephalopoda*.

Ceph-ȧ-lop′ō-dȧ, *n.pl.* [*Cephalo-*, and Gr. *pous*, *podos*, a foot.] A class of the *Mollusca*, the highest in organization in that division of the animal kingdom, characterized by having the organs of prehension and locomotion, called tentacles, attached to the head. They are divided into two sections, *Tetrabranchiata* and *Dibranchiata*. The nautilus, and several fossil genera belong to the *Tetrabranchiata*, in which the animal has an external shell. The dibranchiate group includes the argonaut, the octopus or eight-armed cuttlefishes, and the ten-armed forms, as the calamaries, the fossil belemnites, etc. The shell is in all these internal, in some rudimentary. The fossil *Cephalopoda* are multitudinous.

ceph-ȧ-lop′ō-dăn, *n.* A cephalopod.

ceph-ȧ-lop′ō-dous, ceph″ȧ-lō-pod′iç, *a.* Belonging to the cephalopods.

Ceph-ȧ-lop′te-rȧ, *n.* [*Cephalo-*, and Gr. *pteron*, wing.] A genus of rays including the gigantic devilfish, *Manta birostris*.

ceph′ȧ-lō-sōme, *n.* [*Cephalo-*, and Gr. *sōma*, body.] The anterior part or head of insects, crustaceans, etc.

ceph′ȧ-lō-sty̆le, *n.* [*Cephalo-*, and Gr. *stylos*, a pillar.] The anterior part of the notochord, or that part of it which is situated in the head.

ceph″ȧ-lō-thē′çȧ, *n.* [*Cephalo-*, and Gr. *thēkē*, a case.] In entomology, the head-case of an insect-pupa.

ceph″ȧ-lō-thē′çăl, *a.* Pertaining to a cephalotheca.

ceph″ȧ-lō-thō′rax, *n.* [*Cephalo-*, and Gr. *thōrax*, a breastplate.] A united head and thorax, such as is found in the higher crustaceans.

ceph′ȧ-lō-tōme, *n.* [*Cephalo-*, and Gr. *tomē*, a cutting.] An instrument used in obstetrics for dividing the head of a fetus so as to make delivery possible.

ceph-ȧ-lot′ō-my, *n.* 1. In anatomy, dissection of the head.

2. In obstetrics, the act or practice of operating with the cephalotome.

ceph′ȧ-lō-tribe, *n.* [*Cephalo-*, and Gr. *tribein*, to bruise.] In obstetrics, an instrument for crushing the head of the fetus in the womb when delivery is otherwise impossible.

ceph′ȧ-lō-trip-sy, *n.* The operation of using a cephalotribe.

ceph′ȧ-lō-troch, *n.* [*Cephalo-*, and Gr. *trochos*, a wheel.] The ciliated band on the head of the larvæ of certain annelids, as the marine worms.

Ceph-ȧ-lot′rō-chȧ, *n.* [*Cephalo-*, and Gr. *trochos*, a wheel.] A group of annelids whose larvæ have a ciliated band on the head.

ceph-ȧ-lot′rō-chăl, *a.* Relating to the *Cephalotrocha*.

ceph′ȧ-lous, *a.* [Gr. *kephalē*, the head.] Possessing a head; cephalate.

Cē′pheūs (-fūs), *n.* [L., from Gr. *Kepheus*, in classical mythology, the name of a king of Ethiopia, and husband of Cassiopeia, placed among the stars after his death.] In astronomy, a constellation in the northern hemisphere, surrounded by Cassiopeia, Ursa Major, Draco, and Cygnus.

cē-rā′ceous, *a.* [L. *cera*, wax.] Wax-like; partaking of the nature of wax.

cē-rā′gō, *n.* [L. *cera*, wax.] Beebread; a substance consisting chiefly of the pollen of flowers, used by bees as food.

cē′răl, *a.* In ornithology, pertaining to a cere.

Cō-rā-mi-ā′cē-æ, *n.pl.* [Gr. *keramion*, a jar, pitcher; so called from the shape of the filaments.] The rose-tangles, a natural order of cellular seaweeds, *Algæ*, consisting of thread-like jointed plants of a red or brown-red hue.

cē-rā-mi-ā′ceous, *a.* Pertaining or belonging to the *Ceramiaceæ*.

cē-ram′iç, *a.* [Gr. *keramikos*, from *keramos*, potter's clay, a jar.] Of or belonging to the fictile arts or pottery; pertaining to the manufacture and decoration of porcelain and earthenware; as, the *ceramic* art.

cē-ram′içs, *n.* 1. The potter's art; the process of manufacturing pottery, etc.

2. [*pl.*] Articles of pottery.

cer-ȧ-mid′i-um, *n.*; *pl.* **cer-ȧ-mid′i-ȧ**. [Gr. *keramidion*, dim. of *keramos*, potter's clay, pottery, a jar.] One of the conical or ovate capsules of the *Ceramiaceæ* or rose-spored algæ. They generally open by a terminal pore for the escape of the spores.

Cē-rā′mi-um, *n.* [Gr. *keramion*, dim. of *keramos*, potter's clay, an earthen vessel.] The typical genus of the rose-tangle family of seaweeds, *Ceramiaceæ*.

cē-rär′ġy-rīte, *n.* [Gr. *keras*, a horn, and *argyritēs*, of silver; *argyros*, silver.] Native silver chlorid, a mineral nearly white when fresh, but changing to brown when exposed to light. It crystallizes in the isometric system and is found both massive and in cubic crystals. It looks somewhat like wax, and is easily cut; also called *horn silver*.

cer′as, *n.*; *pl.* **cer′ȧ-tȧ**. A horn. [See *Cerata*.]

cer′ȧ-sin, *n.* [L. *cerasus*, a cherry-tree.]

1. A kind of gum which exudes from the cherry and plum tree. It is distinguished from gum-arabic by being insoluble in cold water.

2. A crude precipitate from tincture of choke-cherry.

cer′ȧ-sine, *a.* [Gr. *keras*, horn.] Corneous.

cē-ras′i-nous, *a.* [L. *cerasinus*, from *cerasus*; Gr. *kerasos*, a cherry.]

1. Of, pertaining to, or containing cerasin.

2. Having the color of a cherry; deep-red. [Rare.]

cer′ȧ-sīte, *n.* [L. *cerasus*, cherry-tree, and *-ite*.]

1. A petrifaction resembling a cherry.

2. A variety of Japanese iolite.

Cē-ras′tēs, *n.* [L. *cerastes*; Gr. *kerastēs*, a horned serpent, from *keras*, a horn.] In zoölogy, a genus of poisonous African serpents having two little horns formed by the scales above the eyes; hence, called *horned vipers*.

Cerastes horridus.

Cē-ras′ti-um, *n.* [From Gr. *keras*, a horn, so called from the horn-shaped capsules of many of the species.] Mouse-ear chickweed, a genus of plants, natural order *Caryophyllaceæ*, consisting of many pubescent herbs with small leaves and white flowers, forming common weeds in all temperate and cold regions.

Cerastium aquaticum (Water Mouse-ear Chickweed).

cer′at-, cer′ȧ-tō-. Combining forms from Gr. *keras*, *keratos*, a horn, and used to signify relation or likeness to a horn; as, *cerato*saurus, *cerato*stoma.

cer′ȧ-tȧ, *n.pl.* [Gr. *keras*, *keratos*, a horn.] In zoölogy, the notal projections or papillæ of the *Ceratobranchia*.

cē′rāte, *n.* [L. *ceratus*, pp. of *cerare*, to wax; *cera*, wax.] A thick kind of ointment composed of wax, lard, or oil, with other ingredients, applied externally in various diseases.

cē′rāte, *a.* In zoölogy, possessing a cere.

cē′rā-ted, *a.* [L. *ceratus*, pp. of *cerare*, to cover with wax; *cera*, wax.] Covered with wax.

cer′ȧ-tin, cer′ȧ-tine, *n.* [Gr. *keras*, horn, and *-in*.] In chemistry, a substance consisting of carbon, hydrogen, nitrogen, sulphur, and oxygen, which forms the basis of the epidermis of animals, of hair, wool, silk, feathers, nails, claws, hoofs, horns, scales, etc. Also spelled *keratin*.

cer-ȧ-tī′tis, *n.* [Gr. *keras* (-*atos*), a horn.] In pathology, inflammation of the cornea.

cē-rā′ti-um (-shi-um), *n.*; *pl.* **cē-rā′ti-ȧ**. [Gr. *keration*, dim. of *keras*, *keratos*, a horn.] In botany, a pod or capsule resembling a silique, but having no dividing wall.

cer′ȧ-tō-. See *Cerat-*.

cer′ȧ-tō-blast, *n.* [*Cerato-*, and Gr. *blastos*, a sprout.] In zoölogy, a cell which secretes ceratin, as in sponges; a cell which secretes the material of the horny fiber.

Cer″ȧ-tō-brañ′chi-ȧ, *n.pl.* [*Cerato-*, and Gr. *branchia*, gills.] A group of mollusks, having gills situated on the back or sides and without protecting shell or covering.

cer″ȧ-tō-brañ′chi-ăl, *a.* A term applied to the lower of the two bony pieces which form the branchial arches in fishes.

Cer-ȧ-tō′dȧ, *n.pl.* Same as *Ceratospongiæ*.

cer′ȧ-tōde, *n.* [Gr. *keras*, *keratos*, a horn.] The skeletal substance of certain sponges.

cē-rat′ō-dont, *a.* Pertaining to *Ceratodus*.

Cē-rat′ō-dus, *n.* [Gr. *keras*, *keratos*, a horn, and *odous*, *odontos*, a tooth.] A genus of dipnoan fishes of which the Australian salmon or barramunda is typical.

cer-ȧ-toġ′e-nous, *a.* [*Cerato-*, and Gr. *-genes*, producing.] Horn-secreting or producing; as, a *ceratogenous* cell.

cer″ȧ-tō-hy̆′ăl, *a.* and *n.* [*Cerato-*, and Gr. *hyoeidēs*, from the letter Y, and *eidos*, form.]

I. *a.* In anatomy, pertaining to the smaller and anterior cornu of the hyoid bone.

II. *n.* In mammals, the lesser cornu of the hyoid bone.

cer′ȧ-toid, *a.* [Gr. *keratoeidēs*, hornlike; *keras*, a horn, and *eidos*, form.] Horny; ceratose.

Cer-ȧ-toi′dē-ȧ, *n.pl.* Same as *Ceratospongiæ*.

cer′ȧ-tōme, *n.* [Gr. *keras*, a horn, and *tomē*, a cutting, from *temnein*, to cut.] A surgical instrument for cutting the cornea; spelled also *keratome*.

cer″ȧ-tō-nyx′is, *n.* [*Cerato-*, and Gr. *nyxis*, a puncture.] In surgery, an operation for removing cataract with a needle; written also *keratonyxis*.

Cer″ȧ-tō-phyl-lā′cē-æ, *n.pl.* [*Cerato-*, and Gr. *phyllon*, a leaf.] A natural order of plants, containing a single genus with only one species, *Ceratophyllum demersum* (hornwort). It is common in pools or slow streams over a great part of the world.

cer-ȧ-toph′yl-lous, *a.* Having linear leaves resembling horns; pertaining to the *Ceratophyllum*.

Cer″ȧ-tō-phyl′lum, *n.* [*Cerato-*, and Gr. *phyllon*, a leaf.] A genus of aquatic plants belonging to the natural order *Ceratophyllaceæ*.

cer′ȧ-tō-phy̆te, *n.* [*Cerato-*, and Gr. *phyton*, a plant.] In zoölogy, a coral having an interior axis of horny fibers.

Cer-ȧ-tō′sȧ, *n.pl.* Same as *Ceratospongiæ*.

cer″ȧ-tō-sa̤u′rus, *n.* [*Cerato-*, and Gr. *sauros*, a lizard.] An American species of the *Dinosauria*, whose skull exhibits a bony horn-core.

cer′ȧ-tōse, *a.* [Gr. *keras*, *keratos*, a horn.]

1. Horny.

2. Pertaining to the *Ceratosa*.

cer′ȧ-tōse, *n.* Same as *Ceratode*.

Cer″ȧ-tō-spon′ġi-æ, *n.pl.* [*Cerato-*, and Gr. *spongos*, a sponge.] An order of sponges, distinguished by their soft flexible skeleton of horn, of which the bath-sponge is the type.

cer-ȧ-tos′tō-mȧ, *n.*; *pl.* **cer″ȧ-tō-stom′ȧ-tȧ**. [*Cerato-*, and Gr. *stoma* (-*atos*), mouth.] In botany, the long-necked and narrow-mouthed receptacle containing the fructification in certain fungi.

cer′ȧ-tō-stōme, *n.* Same as *Ceratostoma*.

cē-ra̤u′niçs, *n.* [Gr. *keraunos*, a thunderbolt, thunder and lightning.] That branch of natural philosophy which deals with heat and electricity, and their phenomena.

cē-ra̤u′nō-sçōpe, *n.* [Gr. *keraunos*, thunder and lightning, and *skopein*, to view.] An apparatus used in ancient mysteries for the purpose of imitating thunder and lightning.

Cēr-bē′re-ăn, Cēr-bē′ri-ăn, *a.* Relating to or resembling Cerberus.

> Wide *Cerberian* mouths. —Milton.

Cēr′be-rus, *n.* [L.] 1. In mythology, a monster in the shape of a dog, the offspring of the giant Typhaon and the serpent-woman Echidna, guarding the entrance into the infernal regions, and described by different ancient writers as having three, fifty, and even a hundred heads; usually portrayed with three heads and a serpent's tail, and with serpents round his neck.

2. Figuratively, any rough vigilant guardian; as, a *Cerberus* of the stage-door.

3. A subgenus of serpents (ophidians) which have nearly the whole of the head covered with small scales, as the bokadam of the East Indies.

Cerberus.—Antique bronze.

cēr′căl, *a.* [Gr. *kerkos*, tail.] Pertaining to the tail.

cēr-çā′ri-ȧ, *n.*; *pl.* **cēr-çā′ri-æ**. [Gr. *kerkos*, a tail.] In zoölogy, the second larval stage of a trematode worm or fluke. It is a tadpole-like body, which becomes encysted, and gives rise to the sexual forms. The larvæ are chiefly found in the bodies of mollusks, the adults in vertebrated animals, as birds.

cēr-çā′ri-ăn, *a.* and *n.* I. *a.* Pertaining to or resembling a cercaria.

II. *n.* A larva in the cercarian stage.

cēr′cō-pod, *n.* [Gr. *kerkos*, tail, and *pous*, *podos*, a foot.] In zoölogy, one of the jointed anal appendages of certain insects and crustaceans, as those of the genus *Apus*.

cẽr′çus, *n.*; *pl.* **cẽr′ci̇.** Same as *Cercopod.*

cēre, *n.* [L. *cera*, wax, from its appearance.] The naked skin that covers the base of the bill in some birds, as in those of the hawk tribe, parrots, etc.

cēre, *v.t.*; cered, *pt.*, *pp.*; cering, *ppr.* [L. *cerare*, from *cera*, wax.] To wax or cover with wax, or with a cerecloth.

Then was the body *cered.* —Hall.

cē′rē-ăl, *a.* and *n.* [L. *Cerealis*, pertaining to *Ceres*, goddess of agriculture.]

I. *a.* Pertaining to or producing edible grain, such as wheat, barley, maize, oats, rice, rye, millet; as, *cereal* grasses; *cereal* crops.

II. *n.* Any edible grain, or grain-plant, such as wheat, oats, barley, rye, etc.

Cē-rē-ā′li-ȧ, *n.pl.* 1. The systematic name for that group of the *Gramineæ* or grasses which comprises the edible grains or cereals.

2. In Roman antiquities, festivals in honor of Ceres, the goddess of agriculture.

cē′rē-ȧ-lin, *n.* A nitrogenous substance resembling diastase, contained in bran.

cer′ē-bel, *n.* The cerebellum. [Obs.]

cer-ē-bel′lăr, cer-ē-bel′lous, *a.* Relating to the cerebellum.

cer-ē-bel′lum, *n.* [L. *cerebellum*, dim. or *cerebrum*, the brain.] The lobe of the brain which is the posterior of the medullary masses comprising the brain in vertebrates and underlying the great cerebral mass; the little brain. It is the principal organ of the central nervous system. [See *Brain.*]

cer′ē-brăl, cer′ē-brine, *a.* [L. *cerebrum*, brain.] Pertaining to the cerebrum, or brain.

Cerebral apoplexy; see *Apoplexy.*

cer′ē-brăl, *n.* [A mistranslation of Sans. *mūrdhanya*, head-sounds.] In Sanskrit, one of the lingual consonants; called in English philology, a *cerebral letter.*

cer′ē-brăl-iṣm, *n.* The theory that psychical phenomena result solely from the activity of the brain.

cer′ē-brăl-ist, *n.* One who believes in the theory or doctrine of cerebralism.

cer′ē-brāte, *v.i.*; cerebrated, *pt.*, *pp.*; cerebrating, *ppr.* To manifest mental activity; to work with the brain.

cer′ē-brāte, *v.t.* To perform by means of the action of the brain.

cer-ē-brā′tion, *n.* Exertion or action of the brain, conscious or unconscious.

Unconscious cerebration; the action of the brain in arriving at intellectual results without conscious effort; latent thought.

cer′ē-briç, *a.* Relating to or obtained from the brain.

Cerebric acid; an old name for *cerebrin.*

cer-ē-briç′i-ty, *n.* The power of the brain. [Rare.]

ce-reb′ri-fọrm, *a.* [L. *cerebrum*, brain, and *forma*, form.] Brain-shaped.

cer-ē-brif′ū-găl, *a.* [L. *cerebrum*, brain, and *fugere*, to flee.] Transmitting cerebral impulses outward; applied to nerve fibers proceeding from the brain to the spinal cord.

cer′ē-brin, *n.* [L. *cerebrum*, the brain, and *-in.*] A name given to several nitrogenous substances obtained chemically from the brain.

cer-ē-brip′e-tăl, *a.* [L. *cerebrum*, the brain, and *petere*, to seek.] Transmitting sensations to the brain inward; applied to nerve fibers proceeding from the spinal cord to the brain.

cer-ē-brī′tis, *n.* [L. *cerebrum*, the brain, and *-itis.*] An inflamed condition of the brain; encephalitis.

cer′e-bro-, cer′e-br-. Combining forms from L. *cerebrum*, the brain, and used in medicine and anatomy to indicate connection with, or relation to, the brain; as, *cerebro*spinal; *cerebro*scopy.

cer′ē-broid, *a.* [L. *cerebrum*, brain, and Gr. *eidos*, form.] Resembling the brain.

cer-ē-brol′ō-ġy, *n.* [*Cerebro-*, and Gr. *-logia*, from *legein*, to speak.] The science or study of the brain.

cer-ē-brop′ȧ-thy, *n.* [*Cerebro-*, and Gr. *pathos*, suffering.] A morbid condition, usually accompanied by melancholia, caused by anxiety or overwork; brain-fag or brainsickness.

cer-ē-bros′çō-py, *n.* [*Cerebro-*, and Gr. *-skopia*, from *skopein*, to view.] The examination of the condition of the brain, especially by means of ophthalmoscopy, in the diagnosis of brain-disease.

cer′ē-brōse, *n.* A substance resembling sugar, obtained by the decomposition of cerebrin.

cer′ē-brōse, cer′ē-brous, *a.* [L. *cerebrosus*, from *cerebrum*, the brain.] Brainsick; mad; wilful; passionate. [Rare.]

cer″ē-brō-spī′năl, *a.* [*Cerebro-*, and L. *spina*, the spine.] In anatomy, pertaining to the brain and spinal cord together; consisting of the brain and spinal cord; as, the *cerebrospinal* axis or system.

Cerebrospinal fever, cerebrospinal meningitis; an acute, infectious disease characterized by inflammation of the meninges of the brain and spinal cord, with the involvement of the superficial layers of nerve-substance.

Cerebrospinal fluid; a fluid between the arachnoid and the pia mater, membranes investing the brain and spinal cord.

cer′ē-brous, *a.* Cerebrose.

cer′ē-brum, *n.* [L.] The front and larger part of the brain; the center of the reasoning faculties. It occupies the whole upper part of the cranium.

cēre′clọth, *n.* [L. *cera*, wax, and *cloth.*] A cloth smeared with melted wax, or with some gummy or glutinous matter; a cerement.

cēre′ment, *n.* [L. *cera*, wax.]

1. A cloth dipped in melted wax, with which a dead body is wrapped when embalmed.

2. [*pl.*] Graveclothes in general.

cer-ē-mō′ni-ăl, *a.* [LL. *cærimonialis*, from L. *cærimonia*, ceremony.]

1. Relating to ceremony, or external rite; ritual; according to the forms of established rites; as, *ceremonial* exactness. It is particularly applied to the forms and rites of the Jewish religion; as, the *ceremonial* law, or worship, as distinguished from the *moral* and *judicial* law.

2. Formal; observant of old forms; exact; precise in manners. [In this sense *ceremonious* is preferable.]

Syn.—Official, ministerial, functional, pompous, imposing, sumptuous, scenic.

cer-ē-mō′ni-ăl, *n.* 1. Outward form; external rite, or established forms, or rites, including all the forms prescribed; a system of rules and ceremonies, enjoined by law, or established by custom, whether in religious worship, in social intercourse, or in the courts of princes.

2. The order for rites and forms in the Roman Catholic church, or the book containing the rules prescribed to be observed on solemn occasions.

cer-ē-mō′ni-ăl-iṣm, *n.* Esteem for ceremonial forms; adherence to ritualism.

cer-ē-mō′ni-ăl-ly, *adv.* According to rites and ceremonies; as, a person *ceremonially* unclean; an act *ceremonially* unlawful.

cer-ē-mō′ni-ăl-ness, *n.* The quality of being ceremonial.

cer-ē-mō′ni-ous, *a.* 1. Consisting of outward forms and rites; as, the *ceremonious* part of worship. [In this sense, *ceremonial* is preferable.]

2. Full of ceremony, or solemn forms.

3. According to the rules and forms prescribed, or customary; civil; formally respectful; as, *ceremonious* phrases.

4. Formal; according to the rules of civility; as, to take a *ceremonious* leave.

5. Formal; exact; precise; too observant of forms.

cer-ē-mō′ni-ous-ly, *adv.* In a ceremonious manner; formally; with due forms.

cer-ē-mō′ni-ous-ness, *n.* The use of customary forms; the practice of too much ceremony; great formality in manners.

cer′ē-mō-ny, *n.*; *pl.* **cer′ē-mō-nieṣ.** [L. *cærimonia*, sacredness, a sacred rite.]

1. Outward rite; external form in religion.

2. Forms of civility; rules established by custom for regulating social intercourse; behavior governed by strict etiquette.

3. Outward forms of state; the forms prescribed or established by order or custom, serving for the purpose of civility or magnificence, as in levees of princes, the reception of ambassadors, etc.

4. A crown, scepter, or other symbol of ceremony. [Obs.]

5. A portent or prodigy. [Obs.]

Master of ceremonies; an officer who superintends the reception of ambassadors; a person who regulates the forms to be observed by the company, or attendants, on a public occasion.

Not to stand on ceremony; to be frank, familiar, or outspoken.

Ceres.—Antique statue in the Louvre.

cē′rē-ous, *a.* [L. *cereus*, from *cera*, wax.] Waxen; like wax.

Cē′rēṣ, *n.* [L.] 1. In classic mythology, the goddess of corn and harvests. The daughter of Saturn and Ops or Rhea, sister of Jupiter, and mother of Proserpine; the Roman name applied to the Greek *Demeter.*

2. One of the asteroids or small planets revolving between the orbits of Mars and Jupiter. It was discovered by M. Piazzi, at Palermo, in Sicily, in 1801, and was the first of the asteroids to be observed.

cer′ē-sin, *n.* [L. *cera*, wax.] A white wax, used as a substitute for beeswax; made from ozocerite by a bleaching and purifying process.

Cē′rē-us, *n.* [L., a wax candle.] A large genus of plants of the cactus family, chiefly tropical, but found growing from California to Chile. Though several species producing large tubular nocturnal blossoms have the name night-blooming cereus, this name is specially applied to *Cereus grandiflorus*, which is extensively cultivated for its beautiful, short-lived flowers. *Cereus giganteus*, native to Arizona, New Mexico, and Texas, has a columnar trunk which often rises to a height of sixty feet.

cẽrġe, *n.* A wax candle used in religious rites; written also *cierge, serge.*

cer′i-ăl, *a.* An obsolete form of *cerrial.*

cē′riç, *a.* Pertaining to cerium; as, *ceric* compounds.

cē-rif′ẽr-ous, *a.* [L. *cera*, wax, and *ferre*, to produce.] Yielding wax.

cē-rig′ẽr-ous, *a.* Same as *Ceriferous.*

cē′rin, *n.* [L. *cera*, wax, and *-in.*]

1. A peculiar substance which precipitates, on evaporation, from alcohol which has been digested on grated cork.

2. The part of common wax, usually about seventy per cent, which dissolves in boiling alcohol.

3. A variety of the mineral allanite.

Cē-rin′thi-ăn, *n.* One of a sect of heretics, the earliest of the Gnostic sects, so called from Cerinthus, one of the first heresiarchs in the church. They denied the divinity of Christ.

cer′iph, *n.* Same as *Serif.*

ce-rïṣe′, *a.* [Fr., a cherry.] Of a light, clear red; cherry-colored; applied to silk and other fine textiles.

cē′rīte, *n.* The silicious oxid of cerium, a rare mineral, of a brownish or cherry-red color, with a tinge of yellow.

cē′ri-um, *n.* A metal discovered in Sweden, in the mineral cerite, and so called from the asteroid Ceres. It is of a great specific gravity; its color a grayish-white, and its texture lamellar.

cẽr′nū-ous, *a.* [L. *cernuus*, stooping.] In botany, having the top curved downward; pendulous; drooping; said of a bud, flower, or fruit.

cē′rō, *n.* [Sp. *sierra*; L. *serra*, a saw.] A large and valuable fish of the genus *Scomberomorus*; related to the Spanish mackerel, but much larger. Two species are found in the West Indies and on the Atlantic coast.

cē′rō-grȧph, *n.* [Gr. *kēros*, wax, and *graphein*, to write.] A representation of any kind made on wax; anything written or engraved on wax; also spelled *kerograph.*

cē-rō-graph′iç, cē-rō-graph′iç-ăl, *a.* Pertaining to the art of making cerographs.

cē-rog′rȧ-phist, *n.* One who is skilled in, or who practises, cerography.

cē-rog′rȧ-phy, *n.* 1. A writing on wax.

2. The art of engraving on wax, spread on a sheet of copper, from which a stereotype plate is taken.

cer′ō-līte, *n.* [Gr. *kēros*, wax, and *lithos*, stone.] Silicated magnesium occurring in waxlike masses of a greenish-yellow color; also spelled *kerolite.*

ce-rō′mȧ, *n.* [L., from Gr. *kērōma*, a wax tablet, salve, from *kēros*, wax.]

1. In ancient architecture, that part of the ancient baths and gymnasia in which bathers and wrestlers used to anoint themselves with a composition of oil and wax.

2. An unguent made of oil and wax, used by wrestlers among the ancient Romans.

3. In ornithology, the waxlike sheath at the base of a bird's bill, especially that of birds of prey.

cer′ō-man-cy, *n.* [Gr. *kēros*, wax, and *manteia*, divination.] Divination by dropping melted wax in water.

cē-rọọn′, *n.* Same as *Seroon.*

cē-rō-plas′tiç, *a.* [G. *kēroplastikos*, from *kēros*, wax, and *plassein*, to mold.] Having any relation to the art of wax-modeling; as, a *ceroplastic* statuette.

cē-rō-plas′tiçs, cē′rō-plas-ty, *n.* The art of making models in wax.

cer′ō-sin, *n.* [L. *cera*, wax.] A delicate crystalline wax extracted from sugar-cane bark, having a lamellar crystallization.

cē′rōte, *n.* [Obs.] See *Cerate.*

cer′ō-tēne, *n.* [L. *cerotum*, a pomade.] A solid white wax similar to paraffin; obtained from Chinese wax, also from cerotin, by distillation.

cē-rot′iç, *a.* [Gr. *kērotē*, a salve, cerate, from *kēros*, wax.] Relating to Chinese wax or beeswax; as, *cerotic* acid, a wax compound.

cer′ō-tin, *n.* A substance derived from Chinese wax, of a crystalline structure, and regarded as belonging to the marsh-gas series of alcohols; called also *cerotic alcohol* and *ceryl alcohol.*

cer′ō-tyl, *n.* Same as *Ceryl.*

cē′rous, *a.* Pertaining to a cere.

cer′ri-ăl, *a.* Pertaining to the cerris, or bitter oak.

cer′ris, *n.* [L. *cerrus*, a kind of oak.] The bitter oak, *Quercus cerris.*

cẽr′tain (-tin), *a.* [Fr. *certain*, from L. *certus*, determined, fixed, settled, pp. of *cernere*, to distinguish, decide, resolve.]

1. Sure; true; undoubted; unquestionable; that cannot be denied; existing in fact and truth.

2. Assured in mind; having no doubts; followed by *of*, before a noun.

To make her *certain of* the sad event.
—Dryden.

3. Unfailing; always producing the intended effect; as, we may have a *certain* remedy for a disease.

4. Stated; fixed; determinate; regular; as, a *certain* rate of interest.

5. Particular, but not specified; as, a *certain* man whom I shall not mention.

For certain; most surely; without any doubt.

Syn.—Sure, undeniable, unquestionable, indisputable, indubitable, incontrovertible, unfailing.

cẽr′tain, *n.* 1. Obsolete in the sense of *certainty.*

2. One or more.

Certain of your own poets have said.
—Acts xvii. 28.

cẽr′tain, *adv.* [Obs.] See *Certainly.*

cẽr′tain-ly, *adv.* 1. Without doubt or question; in truth and fact; as, *certainly* he was a good man.

2. Without failure; as, he will *certainly* return.

cẽr′tain-ness, *n.* Certainty; the condition of being certain.

cẽr′tain-ty, *n.*; *pl.* **cẽr′tain-ties.** 1. A fixed or real state; truth; fact.

2. Full assurance of mind; exemption from doubt.

3. Exemption from failure.

4. Regularity; settled state.

Of a certainty; assuredly; without doubt.

cẽr′tēs, *adv.* Certainly; in truth; verily. [Obs.]

cẽr-tif′i-cāte, *n.* [LL. *certificatus*, pp. of *certificare*, to certify; L. *certus*, certain, and *facere*, to make.]

1. A written testimony not sworn to; a declaration in writing, signed by the party, and intended to verify a fact.

2. The written declaration, under the hand or seal, or both, of some public officer, to be used as evidence in a court, or to substantiate a fact.

Certificate of deposit; a bank's written acknowledgment that a stated sum has been deposited to the credit of the person named.

Certificate of merit; a certificate granted by the President of the United States, to an enlisted man who has distinguished himself in military service. It is issued upon recommendation of his regimental or corps commander and entitles him to extra pay.

Gold and silver certificates; bills issued by the United States government as a portion of its currency, redeemable in gold and silver, and certifying to that fact.

Trial by certificate; a case in which the evidence of the person certifying is the only proper criterion of the point in dispute.

cẽr-tif′i-cāte, *v.t.*; certificated, *pt.*, *pp.*; certificating, *ppr.* 1. To give a certificate to, acknowledging one to be a parishioner, a teacher, an engineer, or one competent and reliable in any occupation.

2. To verify or attest by certificate.

cẽr″ti-fi-cā′tion, *n.* The act of certifying.

cẽr′ti-fī-ẽr, *n.* One who certifies, or assures.

cẽr′ti-fȳ, *v.t.*; certified, *pt.*, *pp.*; certifying, *ppr.* [OFr. *certifier*; LL. *certificare*; L. *certus*, certain, and *facere*, to make.]

1. To testify to in writing; to make a declaration in writing, under hand, or hand and seal; to make known or establish a fact.

2. To give certain information to; as, we have *certified* the king.

3. To give certain information of. It is followed by *of*, after the person, and before the thing told; as, I *certified* you *of* the fact.

Certified check; a bank check which shows its validity on its face, having the word "good" or its equivalent stamped or written across it, with the signature of the cashier or the paying teller of the bank on which it is drawn.

Syn.—Acknowledge, aver, attest, vouch, avow, avouch, testify, declare, demonstrate, prove, evidence, inform, assure.

cẽr″ti-ō-rā′rī (sẽr″shi-ō-rā′rī), *n.* [LL. *certiorari*, from L. *certior*, comp. of *certus*, certain.] A writ issuing out of chancery, or a superior court, to call up the records of an inferior court, or remove a cause there pending to a higher court. This writ is obtained upon complaint of a party, that he has not received justice, or that he cannot have an impartial trial in the inferior court.

cẽr′ti-tūde, *n.* [LL. *certitudo*, from L. *certus*, certain.] Certainty; assurance; freedom from doubt.

cer′ūle, *a.* [L. *cæruleus*, dark blue.] Blue. [Obs.]

cē-rū′lē-ăn, *n.* Of a deep, clear blue, as of the sky; azure; sky-blue.

cē-rū′lē-in, *n.* A dye-product of coal-tar used in giving to fabrics a brownish-green color; written also *cærulein.*

cē-rū′lē-ous, *a.* Sky-colored; blue.

cer-ū-les′cent, *a.* [L. *cæruleus*, dark blue.] Approximating a sky-blue color; light blue.

cer-ū-lif′iç, *a.* Producing a blue or sky-color. [Rare.]

cē-rū-lig′nōne, *n.* [L. *cæru*leus, sky-blue, and *lig*num, wood, and Eng. quin*one.*] A compound crystalline substance obtained from wood-tar; written also *cœrulignone.*

cē-rū′men, *n.* [L. *cera*, wax.] The wax or yellow matter secreted by the ear.

cē-rū′mi-nous, *a.* Relating to cerumen; secreting cerumen.

cē′rūse, *n.* [L. *cerussa*, white lead, from *cera*, wax.]

1. White lead; a carbonate of lead, produced by exposing the metal, in thin plates, to the vapor of vinegar. Lead is sometimes found native in the form of *ceruse.*

2. A cosmetic made chiefly of white lead.

cē′rūse, *v.t.*; cerused, *pt.*, *pp.*; cerusing, *ppr.* To wash with a cosmetic of white lead.

cē′rū-sīte, cē′rūs-sīte, *n.* [L. *cerussa*, white lead and *-ite.*] A massive, compact mineral, white or yellowish; native carbonate of lead; a lead ore.

cẽr′vȧ-lat, cẽr′vē-lat, *n.* [Fr. *cervelat*, a kind of sausage.] An old-fashioned wind-instrument with a tone like that of a bassoon.

cẽr′van-tīte, *n.* [Named from *Cervantes*, a town in Spain.] The gray ore of antimony.

cẽr′vē-lat, *n.* See *Cervalat.*

cẽr-ve-liere′ (-lyăr′), *n.* [Fr., from *cervelle*, brain.] A close-fitting steel cap for the defense of the head, worn in medieval times.

cẽr′vi-çăl, *a.* [L. *cervix* (*-icis*), the neck.] Belonging to the neck; as, the *cervical* nerves.

cẽr′vi-cide, *n.* [L. *cervus*, deer, and *cædere*, to kill.] Deer-killing. [Rare.]

cẽr′vi-çō-. A combining form from L. *cervix*, *cervicis*, and used to indicate connection with, or relation to, the neck; as, *cervico*branchia.

cẽr″vi-çō-braçh′i-ăl, *a.* [*Cervico-*, and L. *brachium*, the arm.] Relating to both the neck and the arm.

Cẽr″vi-çō-brañ′çhi-ȧ, *n.* [*Cervico-*, and Gr. *branchia*, gills.] A suborder of gasteropods with a conical shell and cervical gills.

cẽr″vi-çō-brañ′çhi-āte, *a.* Pertaining to the *Cervicobranchia.*

cẽr′vi-çorn, *a.* [L. *cervus*, deer, and *cornu*, horn.] Having horns like the antlers of a deer; having the appearance of antlers.

cẽr-viç′ū-lāte, *a.* [L. *cervicula*, dim. of *cervix*, neck.] Having a neck like that of a deer; with a small or slim neck.

Cẽr′vi-dæ, *n.pl.* [From L. *cervus*, a deer.] A family of ruminants, the males generally being antlered, which now excludes the chevrotains of Asia and Africa. Its type is *Cervus*, which was formerly coextensive with the family

cẽr′vine, *a.* [L. *cervinus*, from *cervus*, a deer.] Pertaining to the deer, or to animals of the family *Cervidæ.*

cẽr′vix, *n.*; *pl.* **cẽr′vix-eṣ.** [L., neck.] Of vertebrates, the part between the thorax and the head; the neck; any neck-like part or appendage.

cẽr′void, *a.* Same as *Cervine.*

Cẽr′vus, *n.* [L., a deer.] A genus of ruminants, formerly including all species of deer; now confined to the red deer and related species.

cē′ryl, *n.* [L. *cera*, wax, and *-yl.*] A chemical radical, said to be obtained from Chinese wax, beeswax, etc.

Ceryl alcohol; see *Cerotin.*

cē′ṣȧ-rē, *n.* In logic, a mnemonic word designating a syllogism with a universal negative major premise, a universal affirmative minor, and a universal negative conclusion; as, x is not y; y is z; therefore x is not z.

Cē-ṣā′rē-ăn, *a.* Same as *Cæsarean.*

Cē′ṣăr-iṣm, *n.* Same as *Cæsarism.*

cē′ṣi-ous, *a.* Same as *Cæsious.*

ces′pi-tine, *n.* [L. *cæspes* (*-itis*), a turf.] An oil distilled from peat.

ces-pi-ti′tious (-tish′us), *a.* [L. *cæspes* (*-itis*), a turf.] Pertaining to turf; made of turf.

ces′pi-tōse, *a.* In botany, growing in tufts.

ces′pi-tōse-ly, *adv.* In a cespitose manner.

ces′pi-tous, *a.* Pertaining to turf; turfy; as, a *cespitous* plant.

ces-pit′ū-lōse, *a.* Growing in little bunches, as the tufted grasses.

cess, *n.* [For *sess*, from *assess.*]

1. An assessment; a tax on land. [Prov. Eng.]

2. A boundary; a limit; an estimate. [Obs.]

cess, *v.t.*; cessed (sest), *pt.*, *pp.*; cessing, *ppr.* To levy a tax; to make an assessment; contraction of *assess.*

cess, *v.i.* [ME. *cessen*; OFr. *cesser*; L. *cessare*, to cease.] To relinquish a legal duty. [Obs.]

ces′sănt, *a.* [L. *cessans* (*-antis*), ppr. of *cessare*, to cease.] Ceasing; intermitting action.

ces-sā′tion, *n.* [L., *cessatio*, from *cessare*, to cease.] A ceasing; a stop; the act of discontinuing motion or action of any kind, whether temporary or final.

A cessation of arms; an armistice or truce agreed to by the commanders of armies, to give time for a capitulation, or for other purposes.

Syn.—Stop, rest, pause, intermission.—*Stop* is generic; *cessation* is a ceasing from action, either temporary or final; *pause* is a temporary stopping; *rest* is a stopping for the sake of relief or repose; *intermission* is a stopping at intervals to recommence.

ces-sā′vit, *n.* [L., he has ceased; third person sing. perf. ind. act. of *cessare*, to cease.] In law, formerly a writ given by statute, to cover lands, when the tenant or occupier had ceased for two years to perform the service which constituted the condition of his tenure, and had not sufficent goods or chattels to be distrained, or the tenant had so inclosed the land that the lord could not come upon it to distrain.
—Blackstone.

ces′sẽr, *n.* [OFr. *cesser*, a ceasing] A ceasing; a neglect to perform services or make payment for two years. —Blackstone.

ces-si-bil′i-ty, *n.* The act of giving way or receding. [Obs.]

ces′si-ble, *a.* Giving way; yielding; easy to give way. [Obs.]

ces′sion (sesh′un), *n.* [L. *cessio* (*-onis*), from *cessare*, to yield.]

1. The act of giving way; a yielding to force or impulse.

2. A yielding or surrender, as of property or rights, to another person; particularly, a surrender of conquered territory to its former proprietor or sovereign, by treaty.

3. In the civil law, a voluntary surrender of a person's effects to his creditors, to avoid imprisonment.

4. In ecclesiastical law, the leaving of a benefice without dispensation or being otherwise qualified. When an ecclesiastical person is created a bishop, or when the parson of a parish takes another benefice, without dispensation, the benefices are void by cession, without resignation.

ces′sion-ā-ry, *a.* Having surrendered effects; as, a *cessionary* bankrupt.

cess′ment, *n.* An assessment or tax. [Obs.]

ces′sŏr, *n.* [L. *cessare*, to cease.]

1. In law, he that neglects, for two years, to perform the service by which he holds lands, so that he incurs the danger of the writ of cessavit.

2. An assessor or taxer.

cess′pipe, *n.* A pipe which drains water from a cesspool or sink.

cess′pool, *n.* A cavity sunk in the earth, to receive and retain the sediment of water conveyed in drains.

cest, *n.* [L. *cestus*, a girdle.] A lady's girdle.

Ces′ti-dæ, *n.pl.* An invertebrate family with ribbon-like bodies, the type and only genus of which is *Cestum.*

Ces-tō′dȧ, *n.* See *Cestoidea.*

ces′tōde, *a.* and *n.* I. *a.* Having reference to the group of worms *Cestoidea.*

II. *n.* An individual belonging to the *Cestoidea.*

ces′toid, *a.* and *n.* Same as *Cestode.*

Ces-toid′ē-ȧ, *n.pl.* [Gr. *kestos*, girdle, and *eidos*, form.] A group of worms having a flat body containing numerous joints, in each of which may be found a complete set of reproductive organs. They belong to the class *Platyhelmintha.* The tapeworm is the most common species. Written also *Cestoda.*

ces-toid′ē-ăn, *n.* An individual of the group *Cestoidea.*

Ces-trā′ci-on, *n.* [From Gr. *kestra*, a poleax, a kind of fish.] Formerly, the generic name for the *hammer-headed shark*, now given to the *Port Jackson shark.*

ces-trā′ci-ont, *n.* and *a.* [Gr. *kestra*, a hammer or weapon.]

I. *n.* A shark of the now nearly extinct genus *Cestracion* and similar genera, the back teeth of which form a series of plates for crushing the shellfish on which they feed. Among the living species are the Port Jackson shark and another found along the coast of California.

II. *a.* Characteristic of the genus *Cestracion.*

ces′trum, *n.*; *pl.* **ces′trȧ**, [L., from Gr. *kestron*, from *kentein*, to prick.] In encaustic painting, a metal tool for fusing the wax and fixing the colors.

ces′tui, **ces′tuy** (ses′twi), *n.* [OFr.] A law term meaning a person, the one who; as, *cestui que trust*, one who is a beneficiary of a trust; *cestui que use*, one who has a right to a use.

ces′tum, *n.* [L. *cestus*, a girdle.] In zoölogy, a genus of *Ctenophora*, the only genus of the family *Cestidæ*. Venus's-girdle, *Cestum veneris*, a typical Mediterranean species, is ribbon-like in form and several feet long.

ces′tus, *n.* [L.] 1. The girdle of Venus, or marriage-girdle, among the Greeks and Romans.

2. [C—] In zoölogy, same as *Cestum*.

ces′tus, cæs′tus, *n. sing.* and *pl.* [L. *cæstus*, *cestus*; Gr. *kestos*, a girdle.] Among the Romans, a kind of leather mitten or band worn on the hands of pugilists and often loaded with lead or other metal to give effect to the blows.

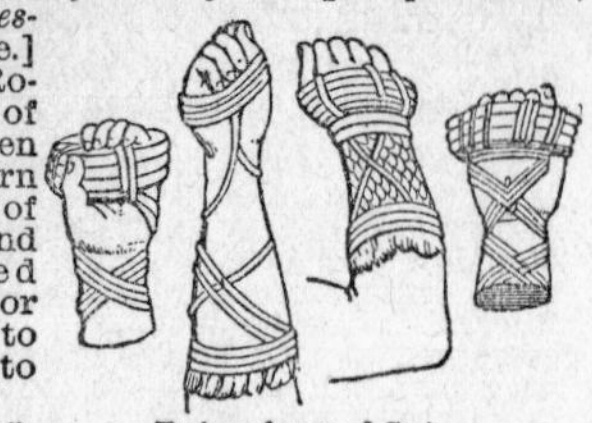

Various forms of Cestus.

ces′tuy (-twi), *n.* See *Cestui*.

cē-sū′rȧ (*or* -sū′rȧ), *n.*; *pl.* **cē-sū′rȧs** or **cē-sū′ræ**. [L. *cæsura*, from *cædere*, to cut off.] A metrical pause in verse, so introduced as to aid the recital, and render the versification more melodious, as well as to express more clearly the meaning. It divides a verse or line into equal or unequal parts. The following is an example of the use of the *cesura* at the end of the second foot:

Man nev | er is, ‖ but al | ways to | be blest.
—Pope.

Feminine cesura; a cesura following a metrically unaccented syllable.

Masculine cesura; a cesura following a metrically accented syllable.

cē-sū′răl, *a.* Of, relating, or pertaining to a cesura.

Cē′tȧ, *n.pl.* Same as *Cete*.

Cē-tā′cē-ȧ, *n.pl.* [L. *cetus*; Gr. *ketos*, a whale.] An order of mammals of fishlike form, including the whales of the suborders *Mysticete*, or whalebone-whales, *Denticete*, embracing the sperm-whale and dolphin, and the *Zeuglodontia*. The last-named is extinct.

cē-tā′ceăn (-shiăn), *n.* An animal of the whale kind.

cē-tā′ceous, *a.* Pertaining to the *Cetacea*; belonging to the whale kind.

Cē′tē, *n.pl.* [Gr. *kētē*, *kētea*, pl. of *kētos*, any sea-monster, especially a whale.] A division of mammals including the whale.

cē′tē, *n.* A whale.

cē′tēne, *n.* A hydrocarbon product of spermaceti; also called *cetylene*.

cet′e-rach, *n.* [Fr. *ceterac*; It. *cetracca*.] A trivial name of a species of fern, *Asplenium Ceterach*, found in Europe and western Asia.

cet′e-wāle, *n.* [Obs.] Same as *Zedoary*.

cē′tiç, *a.* Pertaining to the whale.

Cetic acid; a pearly substance in the form of starlike crystals obtained from the spermaceti.

cē′tin, *n.* The essential part of spermaceti.

cē-tō-log′iç-ăl, *a.* Pertaining to cetology.

cē-tol′ō-gist, *n.* One who is versed in the natural history of the whale and kindred animals.

cē-tol′ō-gy, *n.* [Gr. *kētos*, a whale, and *-logia*, from *legein*, to speak.] The science or natural history of cetaceous animals.

cē-trar′iç, *a.* [L *cetra*, *cætra*, a Spanish shield.] Obtained from or pertaining to *Cetraria Islandica*, or Iceland moss.

cet′rȧ-rin, *n.* A vegetable principle extracted by alcohol from several lichens, as *Cetraria Islandica*, and *Sticta pulmonacea*. It forms a white powder very bitter to the taste.

cē′tyl, *n.* [L. *cetus*, a whale, and *-yl*.] In chemistry, a radical corresponding in structure to the ethyl compounds. It is formulated as $C_{16}H_{33}$, and is derived from spermaceti.

cē-tyl′iç, *a.* [*Cetyl* and *-ic*.] Relating to or containing spermaceti; as, *cetylic* acid.

Cetylic alcohol; a solid crystalline form of alcohol derived from spermaceti, and in composition corresponding to ethal; often called *cetyl alcohol*.

cev-ȧ-dil′lȧ, ceb-ȧ-dil′lȧ, *n.* [Sp., dim. of *cevada*, *cebada*, from *cebar*; L. *cibare*, to feed; *cibus*, food.] In medicine, the seeds of a bulbous plant growing in Central America and Mexico, and belonging to the lily family; also, the plant itself. Written also *Sabadilla*.

cēy′lan-ite, *n.* See *Ceylonite*.

Cēy-lon-ēse′ (*or* -ēz′), *a.* and *n.* I. *a.* Relating to the island of Ceylon or its people.

II. *n. sing.* and *pl.* An inhabitant or the inhabitants of Ceylon.

cēy′lon-ite, *n.* A dingy blue variety of spinel; also called *pleonaste*.

c. g. s. In physics, an abbreviation of centimeter-gram-second, and used to designate a unit of energy, the factors of which are the centimeter, the gram, and the second; as, a force that will move a mass of one gram a distance of one centimeter in one second of time is a *c. g. s.* unit of force.

chab, *n.* The Carolina woodpecker, *Melanerpes carolinus*; called also *red-bellied woodpecker*.

chab′ȧ-zite, chab′ȧ-site, *n.* [Gr. *chabazios*, a species of stones mentioned in a poem ascribed to Orpheus.] A mineral classed with the zeolites, occurring in oblique, glassy crystals (rhombohedrons), having nearly the form of the cube. It is either colorless or tinged with red or a shade of yellow.

Chȧ-blis′ (-blē′), *n.* [Fr.] A white wine, so named because made near Chablis, France.

chȧ-bouk′, chȧ-buk′, *n.* [Hind. *chābuk*, a whip.] A whip of unusual length, used in Oriental countries for the infliction of corporal punishment.

Chā′çȧ, *n.* 1. A genus of East Indian catfishes, family *Chacidæ*.

2. [c—] A fish of this genus; also spelled *chaka*.

chāce, *v.* and *n.* [Obs.] See *Chase*.

chä-chä-lä′çȧ, *n.* [Imitative of the bird's cry.] A gallinaceous bird, the guan, of Texas, capable of domestication; also written *chiacalaca*.

chack, *v.t.*; chacked, *pt.*, *pp.*; chacking, *ppr.* 1. To toss or jerk (the head), as a horse does to relieve the strain of the reins.

2. To pinch or bruise, as in a door. [Scot.]

chaç′mȧ, *n.* Native name for a large species of South African baboon, *Cynocephalus porcarius*; called also the *ursine baboon*.

chaç′ō, *n.* [S. Am.] An edible earth, eaten in Bolivia with chocolate.

chȧ-çonne′, chȧ-çōne′, *n.* [Fr., from Sp. *chacona*, a dance.] An old dance, having a moderate movement, and much used by classical composers as a theme for musical variations.

chad, *n.* A kind of fish; the shad. [Obs.]

chæt-, chæto-. Combining forms from Gr. *chaitē*, long, flowing hair, a mane, and used to signify connection with or relation to hair, a bristle or seta; as, *chæto*gnatha, *chæti*ferous.

chæ′tȧ (kē′tȧ), *n.*; *pl.* **chæ′tæ**. [Gr. *chaitē*, hair.] In biology, a bristle or stiff hair; called also a *seta*.

chæ-tif′ēr-ous, *a.* [*Chæto-*, and L. *ferre*, to bear.] Bearing bristles or stiff hairs.

chæ′tō-dont, *n.* and *a.* [*Chæt-*, and Gr. *odous*, *odontos*, a tooth.]

I. *n.* A salt-water fish of the family *Chætodontidæ*, having a wide, thin, and brightly colored body.

II. *a.* Having any relation to a chætodont or to the *Chætodontidæ*.

chæ′tog-nath, *n.* and *a.* I. *n.* One of the *Chætognatha*.

II. *a.* Having some relation to the *Chætognatha*.

Chæ-tog′nȧ-thȧ, *n.pl.* [*Chæto-*, and Gr. *gnathos*, jaw.] An order of transparent marine worms of bright color, so called on account of having cephalic setæ. The genus *Sagitta* belongs to this order.

chæ-toph′ō-rous, *a.* [*Chæto-*, and Gr. *pherein*, to bear.] Bearing stiff hairs, or setæ.

chæ′tō-pod, *a.* and *n* I. *a.* Having relation to the *Chætopoda*.

II. *n.* An individual of the *Chætopoda*.

Chæ-top′ō-dȧ, *n.pl.* [*Chæto-*, and Gr. *pous*, *podos*, foot.] A large order of earth and marine worms, *Annelida*, having spines on most of their segments. The principal groups are the *Oligochæta* and the *Polychæta*.

chæ′tō-tax-y, *n.* [*Chæto-*, and Gr. *taxis*, arrangement.] The distinguishing arrangement of the bristles of an insect.

chāfe, *v.t.*; chafed, *pt.*, *pp.*; chafing, *ppr.* [ME. *chaufen*; OFr. *chauffer*, to warm; L. *calefacere*, to make warm; *calere*, to be warm, and *facere*, to make.]

1. To excite heat or inflammation in by friction; as, to *chafe* the skin; also, to fret and wear by rubbing; as, to *chafe* a cable.

2. To excite heat in the mind of; to excite passion in; to inflame; to make angry; to cause to fret; to provoke or incense; as, her words sorely *chafed* him.

3. To excite violent action in; to cause to rage; as, the wind *chafes* the ocean.

chāfe, *v.i.* 1. To be excited or heated; to rage; to fret; to be in violent action.

The troubled Tiber *chafing* with his shores.
—Shak.

2. To be fretted and worn by rubbing; as, a cable *chafes*.

chāfe, *n.* 1. Heat excited by friction.

2. Violent agitation of the mind or passions; heat; fret; passion.

3. Wear or damage sustained by friction.

chāfed (chāft), *a* Heated or fretted by rubbing; worn by friction.

chāf′ēr, *n.* 1. One who chafes.

2. A small furnace or water-heater; a chafing-dish.

chāf′ēr, *n.* [AS. *ceafor*, *ceafer*; D. *kever*, a beetle, chafer.] An insect, a species of *Scarabæus*, or beetle; called also the *cockchafer* or *rose-chafer*.

chāf′ēr-y, *n.* [From *chafe*.] In iron works, a forge in which the metal is subjected to a welding heat.

chāfe′wax, chaff′wax, *n.* In England, a chancery officer, who fitted the wax for the sealing of writs.

chāfe′weed, *n.* A weed used as a remedy for chafing; called also *cudweed*, *Gnaphalium Germanicum*.

chȧff, *n.* [ME. *chaf*, *caffe*; AS. *ceaf*, chaff.]

1. The husk or dry calyx of corn and grasses; usually applied to the husks when separated from the grain by threshing or winnowing.

2. Hay or straw cut small for the food of cattle.

3. Refuse; worthless matter; especially that which is light.

4. Banter; jesting; good-natured raillery.

5. In botany, dry scales or bracts, as those on the receptacle subtending the flowers in the heads of certain *Compositæ*.

chȧff, *v.i.*; chaffed, *pt.*, *pp.*; chaffing, *ppr.* To banter or jest.

chȧff, *v.t.* To quiz or make fun of; as, he *chaffed* the hackman.

chȧff′=cut″tēr, *n.* Same as *Straw-cutter*.

chȧf′fēr, *v.i.*; chaffered, *pt.*, *pp.*; chaffering, *ppr.* [ME. *chaffaren*, *cheffaren*, to bargain, negotiate, from *chaffare*, *chapfare*, *cheapfare*, a bargaining, merchandise; *cheap*, *chep*, a bargain, trade, and *fare*, a going, journey.]

1. To treat about a purchase; to bargain; to haggle; to negotiate; as, to *chaffer* for preferments.

2. To talk idly; to chatter lightly.

chȧf′fēr, *v.t.* To buy; to exchange. [Obs.]

chȧf′fēr, *n.* Merchandise. [Obs.]

chȧf′fēr-ēr, *n.* One who chaffers; a bargainer; a buyer.

chȧf′fēr-y, *n.* Traffic; buying and selling. [Obs.]

chȧff′finch, *n.* [So called on account of eating chaff or grain.] A common European finch (*Fringilla cœlebs*) belonging to the *Fringillidæ*, which is admired for its singing.

chȧff′ing, *n.* Raillery; banter; talk of a jesting character.

chȧff′seed, *n.* A perennial herb, *Schwalbea Americana*, bearing seeds with loose seed coverings like chaff; found along the Atlantic coast.

chȧff′weed, *n.* A plant of the genus *Centunculus*, a low annual, common in America and Europe.

chȧff′y, *a.* 1. Like chaff; full of chaff; light; as, *chaffy* straws; *chaffy* opinions.

2. In botany, covered with light, dry scales; resembling chaff.

chāf′ing, *n.* The state of being irritated by friction; the act of rubbing to produce heat, restore circulation, etc.

chāf′ing=dish, *n.* 1. A metal dish or vessel for the cooking of light dishes at the table, or for keeping food warm; it is usually set upon a stand furnished with a small heating apparatus,' the term *chafing-dish* being frequently applied to the whole device.

2. A portable grate for coals.

chāf′ing=gear, *n.* Among seamen, anything used to protect sails, ropes, etc., from friction.

chȧ-green′, *n.* Same as *Shagreen*.

chȧ-grin′ (*or* -grēn′), *n.* [Fr. *chagrin*, grief, sorrow, vexation, from *chagrin*, a kind of roughened leather used for rasping wood.] Ill-humor; mortification; vexation; peevishness; fretfulness; disappointment mingled with shame.

Syn. — Vexation, mortification. — *Vexation* springs from a sense of loss, disappointment, etc.; *mortification* from wounded pride; *chagrin* may spring from either, and is not usually so keen or lasting.

chȧ-grin′, *v.t.*; chagrined, *pt.*, *pp.*; chagrining, *ppr.* To excite ill-humor in; to vex; to mortify.

chȧ-grin′, *v.i.* To be vexed or mortified.

chȧ-grin′, *a.* Peevish; fretful. [Rare.]

chāin, *n.* [ME. *chaine*, *cheine*; OFr. *chaine*, *chæne*, from L. *catena*, a chain.]

1. A series of links or rings connected, or fitted into one another, usually of some kind of metal; as, a *chain* of gold or of iron. Chains are used often for an ornament about the person; as, a watch-*chain*; a *chain* of beads; a *chain* of coral.

2. That which binds; that which restrains, confines, or fetters; as, a prisoner held in *chains*.

3. Bondage; slavery; also, affliction; as, my *chain* is heavy.

In despotism the people sleep soundly in their *chains*. —Ames.

4. A series of things linked together; a series of things connected or following in succession; as, a *chain* of causes, of ideas, or events; a *chain* of mountains.

5. In surveying, an instrument formed of a series of links and used in measuring land. The *chain* in general use is *Gunter's chain*, which has 100 links, each 7.92 inches in length, making the total length of the chain 66 feet or 4 rods.

6. A land measure of length, etc., a *linear chain* being 66 feet long, and a *square chain* being 16 square rods or one-tenth of an acre.

7. In weaving, the warp.

8. [*pl.*] In shipbuilding and nautical language, strong links or plates of iron, bolted at the lower end to the ship's side, used to contain the blocks called *dead-eyes*, by which the shrouds of the mast are extended; also, called the *channel-plates* or the *chain-plates*.

Chain cable; a cable made like a chain, usually of iron.

Closed chain, open chain; terms used to describe the diagrammatic representation of chemical compounds as they are supposed to be constituted in respect to saturation.

Endless chain; a chain having its ends united by a link so as to form a belt, usually called a *chain-belt*; also applied figuratively to any succession of actions, circumstances, or events without end.

chāin, *v.t.*; chained, *pt.*, *pp.*; chaining, *ppr.* 1. To fasten, bind, or connect with a chain; to fasten or bind with anything in the manner of a chain.

2. To enslave; to keep in slavery.

3. To guard with a chain, as a harbor or passage.

4. To unite closely and strongly; to attach.

O Warwick, I do bend my knee with thine,
And in this vow do *chain* my soul to thine.
—Shak.

5. In surveying, to measure with a chain.

chāin'=beăr"ẽr, *n.* Same as *Chainman.*

chāin'=belt, *n.* In mechanics, a chain used for transmitting power.

chāin'=bōat, *n.* Same as *Anchor-hoy.*

chāin'=bōlt, *n.* 1. The bolt which fastens the chain-plate to the side of the ship.

2. A bolt with chain attached by which it may be withdrawn.

chāin'=bond, *n.* A metal chain or bar, as well as a wooden beam, built into masonry to bind it together.

chāin'=bridġe, *n.* A suspension-bridge swung upon chains.

chāin'=ċor"ăl, *n.* A fossil coral, the parts of which are so placed as to resemble the uniformly joined links of a chain.

chāin'=ċoup"ling (-kup"), *n.* A chain used for a supplementary coupling of railroad cars.

chāin'=gang, *n.* A number of convicts chained together.

chāin'=hook, *n.* A hook for drawing chain-cables about the deck of a ship.

chāin'less, *a.* 1. Having no chain; as, a *chainless* bicycle.

2. Incapable of being chained; unfettered.

chāin'let, *n.* A little chain.

chāin'măn, *n.* In surveying, the man who carries the chain; called also the *chain-bearer.*

chāin'=mōld"ing, *n.* A Norman style of architectural molding resembling a chain.

chāin'=piẽr, *n.* A pier extending into the sea and suspended by chains in the manner of a suspension-bridge.

chāin'=pipe, *n.* An opening in the deck through which a chain-cable is stowed away.

chāin'=plāte, *n.* One of the iron plates on the ship's side to which the shrouds are fastened.

chāin'=pul"ley, *n.* A pulley with depressions or projections in its wheel to fit the links of a chain; called also a *sprocket-wheel.*

chāin'=pump, *n.* A pump with an endless chain passing over a wheel at the top and entering a tube below the level of the water. It is fitted with disks or buckets by means of which the water is raised.

chāin'=rule, *n.* An arithmetical rule by which, when a series of equivalents is given, the last of each being of the same kind as the first of the next, a relation of equivalence is established, by the employment of compound proportion, between numbers of the first and last kind involved.

chāin'=shot, *n*, A projectile consisting of two cannon-balls or two halves of a cannon-ball, connected by a short chain, and formerly used in firing into an enemy's rigging.

chāin'=stitch, *n.* An ornamental stitch used in crocheting, etc.; also a kind of stitch made by a sewing-machine.

chāin'=tim"bẽr, *n.* Same as *Bond-timber.*

chāin'=wāle, *n.* See second *Channel*, n.

chāin'=wheel, *n.* A sprocket-wheel; a chain-pulley.

chāin'wŏrk, *n.* 1. Work linked together after the fashion of a chain.

2. In sewing, chain-stitch work.

chāir, *n.* [ME. *chaire, chaere*; OFr. *chaiere, chaere*, from L. *cathedra*, Gr. *kathedra*, a chair, seat.]

1. A seat, usually movable, for a single person; a seat with a back and with or without arms; originally, a stool, and anciently, a kind of pulpit in churches.

2. A seat of justice or of authority; as, a *chair* of state.

3. A seat for a professor, or his office; as, the *chair* of English literature.

4. The seat for a speaker or presiding officer of a public council or assembly; as, the speaker's *chair*; and, by a metonymy, the speaker himself; as, to address the *chair.*

5. The framework in which criminals are electrocuted; as, death by the *chair*; it consists of a seat furnished with straps for the confinement of the condemned person, and with the necessary electrical apparatus.

6. A sedan; a vehicle on poles borne by men.

7. A two-wheeled carriage, drawn by one horse; a gig. [Obs.]

8. Supreme office or magistracy; as, General Smith was installed in the gubernatorial *chair.*

9. An iron block used to support and secure the rails of a railway-track.

Curule chair; an ivory seat, placed on a car, used by the prime magistrates of Rome.

To put into the chair; to elect as presiding officer; to make president.

To take the chair; to undertake the duties of chairman of a meeting.

chāir, *v.t.*; chaired, *pt.*, *pp.*; chairing, *ppr.* 1. To place in a chair; to install.

2. To carry publicly in a chair in triumph; as, in England, a candidate for office who has gained his election, or is otherwise popular, is *chaired* by his constituents.

chāir'=dāyṣ, *n.pl.* Old age; decline. [Poet.]

chāir'măn, *n.* 1. The presiding officer or speaker of an assembly, association, or company; particularly of a legislative house; also, the president or senior member of a committee.

2. Formerly, one whose business was to carry a sedan-chair.

chāir'măn-ship, *n.* The office of a chairman or presiding officer.

ċhaiṣe, *n.* [Fr. *chaise*, a seat or chair.]

1. A two-wheeled carriage for two persons, drawn by one horse and generally furnished with a hood or top that can be let down.

2. Loosely, any light carriage.

3. A gold coin current in France from 1346 to 1430, varying in value at different periods. It was named from the *chaise* in which the figure was represented as sitting. *Chaises* were also coined in England in the reign of Edward III.

chaise longue (shaz long) *n.* [Fr. lit. long chair.] An elongated seat or couch which usually has a support for the back at one end only.

chä'jȧ (*or* chä'hȧ), *n.* Brazilian name for the crested screamer. [See *Screamer.*]

ċhä'kȧ, *n.* Same as *Chaca.*

ċhä'ki, *n.* A silk-and-cotton fabric made in Egypt.

ċhȧ-lā'zȧ, ċhȧ-lāze', *n.*; *pl.* **ċhȧ-lā'zæ.** [Gr. *chalaza*, hail, pimple.]

1. In botany, that part of the ovule or seed where the integuments cohere with each other and with the nucleus.

2. In zoölogy, one of the two membranous twisted cords which bind the yolk-bag of an egg to the lining membrane at the two ends of the shell and keep it near the middle as it floats in the albumen, so that the germinating point is always uppermost, and consequently nearest the source of heat during the process of incubation.

ċhȧ-lā'zăl, *a.* Related in any way to a chalaza; as, the *chalazal* end of an ovule.

ċhȧ-lā'zi-ȧ, *n.*, pl. of *chalazion.*

ċhal-ȧ-zif'ẽr-ous, *a.* Chalaza-bearing; as, the *chalaziferous* membrane.

ċhȧ-lā'zi-on, ċhȧ-lā'zi-um, *n.*; *pl.* **ċhȧ-lā'zi-ȧ.** [Gr. *chalazion*, dim. of *chalaza*, hail, a pimple.] A small tubercle on the eyelid, commonly called a sty.

ċhal-can'thite, *n.* [L. *chalcanthum*; Gr. *chalkanthon*, a solution of blue vitriol; *chalkos*, bronze, and *anthos*, flower.] Mineral copper sulphate, or blue vitriol.

ċhal-cē-don'iç, *a.* Pertaining to chalcedony.

ċhal-ced'ō-ny (*or* ċhal'cē-dō-ny), *n.* [L. *chalcedonius*; Gr. *chalkēdōn*, a precious stone found at *Chalkēdōn*, a Greek town in Asia Minor.] An uncrystallized, translucent variety of quartz, having a whitish color and a luster nearly like wax. It is found covering the sides of cavities in amygdaloid, forming stalactites in these cavities, and is a deposit from infiltrated siliceous waters; also written *calcedony.*

ċhal-ced'ō-nyx, *n.* A variety of agate, in which white and gray layers alternate.

chal-chi-huitl' (-wētl'), *n.* The Mexican name of turquoise.

ċhal'cid, *n.* Same as *Chalcidian.*

ċhal-cid'i-ăn, *n.* [L. *chalcis*; Gr. *chalkis*, a lizard.] A lizard of the tropical family *Chalcididæ*, characterized by having merely rudimentary legs and a snake-like body.

Ċhal-cid'i-ăn, *a.* and *n.* I. *a.* (a) Relating to the *Chalcididæ*; (b) relating to the city Chalcis or to its inhabitants.

II. *n.* (a) An individual of the *Chalcididæ*; (b) a native or resident of the Greek city Chalcis, in Eubœa.

Chalcidian alphabet; the alphabet from which the Roman alphabet is derived, being that of the Chalcidians, who came from Chalcis, in Eubœa, and formed colonies in Sicily and adjacent parts of Italy.

ċhal-cid'i-çum, *n.*; *pl.* **ċhal-cid'i-çȧ.** [L. *chalcidicum*; Gr. *chalkidikos*, from *Chalkis*, a Greek city.] An entrance in the form of a room or porch; a vestibule to a basilica or to a modern church.

Ċhal-cid'i-dæ, *n.pl.* [Gr. *chalkis*, a kind of lizard, from *chalkos*, bronze.]

1. A parasitic family of insects, the members of which attach themselves chiefly to the larvæ or eggs of insects. Their bodies are hard and have brilliant metallic colors.

2. A family of lizards found chiefly in tropical America, including various species, by many referred to the family *Teiidæ.*

ċhal'cō-cīte, *n.* [Gr. *chalkos*, bronze.] A vitreous crystalline mineral copper sulphid (Cu_2S).

ċhal-ċog'rȧ-phẽr, ċhal-ċog'rȧ-phist, *n.* An engraver on copper and brass.

ċhal-ċog'rȧ-phy, *n.* [Gr. *chalkos*, bronze, and *-graphia*, from *graphein*, to write, engrave.] The act or art of engraving on copper or brass, particularly for printing purposes.

ċhal-cō-pyr'īte, *n.* [Gr. *chalkos*, bronze, and *pyritēs*, from *pyr*, fire.] A yellow crystalline compound of copper, iron, and sulphur ($CuFeS_2$), known as copper pyrites.

ċhal-cō-stib'īte, *n.* [Gr. *chalkos*, bronze, and *stibi*, antimony.] A lead-gray mineral compound of sulphur, antimony, and copper; called also *wolfsbergite* from its occurrence at Wolfsberg in the Harz mountains.

Ċhal-dā'iç, *a.* Pertaining to Chaldea, anciently a country on the Euphrates in Asia, called in Scripture *Shinar.* Of this, Babylon was the principal city.

Ċhal-dā'iç, *n.* The language or dialect of the Chaldeans; Chaldee.

Ċhal'dā-iṣm, *n.* An idiom or peculiarity in the Chaldee dialect.

Ċhal-dē'ăn, *n.* An inhabitant of Chaldea.

Ċhal'dee, *a.* and *n.* I. *a.* Pertaining to Chaldea.

II. *n.* The language or dialect of the Chaldeans; the Aramaic of Chaldea.

Chaldee paraphrase; a translation of some portion of the Old Testament into Chaldee.

ċhal'dẽr, *n.* 1. A dry measure of capacity, formerly used in Scotland.

2. A chaldron. [Local Eng.]

3. Same as *Chaldrick.*

ċhal'drick, *n.* A bird with red feet and bill and black-and-white plumage, called *oyster-catcher* from its feeding upon small mollusks. The American oyster-catcher is the *Hæmatopus palliata.*

ċhal'drŏn, *n.* [OFr. *chaldron*; L. *caldaria*, a pot for boiling, from *caldus*, hot.]

1. A measure for coke or coal, varying in weight in the United States between 2500 and 2900 pounds.

2. See *Chaudron.*

ċhȧ-let' (-lā'), *n.* 1. A Swiss herdsman's summer-hut in the mountains.

2. A Swiss summer-cottage; any country cottage built in the Swiss style.

ċhal'ice, *n.* [OFr. *chalice, calice*; L. *calix* (*-icis*), a cup.] A drinking-cup or bowl; particularly, a communion-cup.

Chalice, from Treasury in Mayence Cathedral.

ċhal'ice=cell, *n.* Same as *Goblet-cell.*

ċhal'iced, *a.* Having a cell or cup; similar to a chalice.

ċhal'ice=veil, *n.* A covering for the chalice, made of silk or other fine material, and of a different color for each of the ecclesiastical seasons; used in the Roman Catholic and in the Anglican churches.

ċhal-i-cō'sis, *n.* A disease of the lungs, caused by inhaling stone-dust.

ċhalk (chąk), *n.* [ME. *chalk*; AS. *cealc*, chalk, lime; L. *calx, calcis*, limestone, chalk.]

1. A common calcareous earthy substance, of an opaque white color, soft, and admitting no polish. It is a variety of limestone, calcium carbonate ($CaCO_3$).

2. In the fine arts, etc., a fine quality of artificial *chalk* molded into a convenient shape for use as a drawing implement; the name is also applied by extension to any chalk-like compound used for a similar purpose; a crayon; as, a drawing in *chalk.*

Black chalk; a kind of bluish-black mineral; a chalk colored with carbonaceous matter.

By a long chalk; by a long way. [Slang.]

Chalk drawing; a picture made wholly with crayons.

French chalk; soapstone or steatite, a soft magnesian mineral used by tailors, etc., for marking on cloth, or for removing grease-stains.

Red chalk; an indurated clayey ocher used by painters and artificers.

To walk a chalk-line; among sailors, etc., to prove one's sobriety by walking straight along a chalk-mark without staggering to the right or left; hence, figuratively, to keep in order; to keep in the line of strict discipline; to obey punctiliously.

chalk, *v.t.*; chalked (chakt), *pt.*, *pp.*; chalking, *ppr.* 1. To rub with chalk; to mark with chalk.

2. To manure with chalk, as land.

3. To bleach; to make white or pale by the use of chalk.

To chalk out; from the use of chalk in marking lines, a phrase signifying to lay out, draw out, or describe; as, *to chalk out* a plan of procedure.

chalk′cut″tēr, *n.* A man who digs chalk.

chalk′i-ness, *n.* The state of being chalky.

chalk′-line, *n.* A cord covered or rubbed with chalk so that when held taut and snapped against any surface it will leave a straight line marked upon it; also, the mark so made.

chalk′-pit, *n.* A pit in which chalk is dug.

chalk′stōne, *n.* 1 In medicine, a concretion in the hands and feet of persons violently affected by the gout, once supposed to be of a chalky nature, but now known to be composed chiefly of uric acid in combination with soda.

2. A lump of chalk.

chalk′y, *a.* 1. Resembling chalk; as, a *chalky* taste.

2. White with chalk; consisting of chalk; as, *chalky* cliffs.

3. Impregnated with chalk; as, *chalky* water.

chal′lenge, *n.* [ME. *chalenge*; OFr. *chalenge*, *chalonge*, *calenge*, *calonge*, an accusation, claim, dispute; L. *calumnia*, a false accusation.]

1. A calling upon one to fight in single combat; an invitation or summons, verbal or written, to decide a controversy or give satisfaction for an insult by a duel; also, the letter or message containing the summons.

2. An invitation to a contest of any kind; as, a *challenge* to a public debate.

3. The act of a sentry, who salutes those who appear at his post.

4. A claim or demand made of a right or supposed right. [Obs.]

5. Among hunters, the opening and crying of hounds at first finding the scent of their game.

6. In law, an exception to jurors; the claim of a party that certain jurors shall not sit in trial upon him or his cause; that is, a calling them off. The right of challenge is given, both in civil and criminal trials, for certain causes which are supposed to disqualify a juror to be an impartial judge.

The right of challenge extends either to the whole panel or array, or only to particular jurors, called *a challenge to the polls*. A *principal challenge* is that which the law allows without cause assigned. A *challenge to the favor* is when the party alleges a special cause. In criminal cases, a prisoner may challenge a limited number of jurors without assigning a cause. This is called *a peremptory challenge*. —Blackstone.

7. In elections, an exception to a person as not legally qualified to vote, exception being taken when the person offers to vote.

chal′lenge, *v.t.*; challenged, *pt.*, *pp.*; challenging, *ppr.* [ME. *chalengen*; OFr. *chalengier*; L. *calumniari*, to attack with false accusations.]

1. To call, invite or summon to a contest, controversy, debate, or similar affair; especially, to invite to a duel.

2. To claim as due; to demand as a right; as, truth *challenges* our admiration.

3. To accuse; to call to answer; to censure. [Obs.]

4. In military affairs, to demand the countersign of.

5. To object to (a person or thing); to take exception to; to call in question; as, to *challenge* the accuracy of a solution or demonstration.

6. In law, to object or demand the rejection of; as, to *challenge* a juror.

7. In the United States, to make a formal protest against (one's exercising suffrage), under the claim of disqualification.

chal′lenge, *v.i.* 1. To make known a right. [Obs.]

2. In hunting, to cry when the scent of game is first discovered; said of a hound.

Syn.—Defy, summon, dare, question, brave.

chal′lenge-ȧ-ble, *a.* Liable or subject to challenge.

chal′len-gēr, *n* One who challenges.

chal′lis, **chal′ly** (shal′ly), *n.* [Fr.] A fine woolen fabric, used for ladies' dresses.

chä′lon, *n.* A coverlet; a blanket. [Obs.]

chȧ-lu-meau′ (-mō′), *n.* [Fr.] 1. A kind of clarinet, now obsolete.

2. The four lowest notes of a clarinet.

Chȧ-lyb′ē-ăn, *a.* Pertaining to the Chalybes, an ancient people of Asia famed as workers in iron and steel; hence, as applied to steel, well-tempered.

chȧ-lyb′ē-āte, *a.* [L. *chalybs*; Gr. *chalyps* (-*ybos*), steel; called from the *Chalybes*.] Impregnated with particles of iron; as, *chalybeate* waters.

chȧ-lyb′ē-āte, *n.* Any water or liquid in which iron is contained in solution.

chȧ-lyb′ē-ous, *a.* Looking like tempered steel; steel-blue; a zoölogical term.

chal′y-bite, *n.* An anhydrous metacarbonate of iron, existing abundantly under the names of spathic, sparry iron, or siderite.

cham, *n.* The sovereign prince of Tartary. [Obs. See *Khan*.]

cham, *v.t.* [Obs.] See *Champ*.

chȧ-māde′, *n.* [Fr., from It. *chiamata*, from *chiamare*; L. *clamare*, to call out.] In war, a signal inviting an armistice.

Cham-æ-cyp′ȧ-ris, *n.* [Gr. *chamai*, on the ground, and *kyparissos*, cypress.] A genus of trees of the pine family, valuable for their woods; evergreens; *Chamæcyparis thyoides*, the common white cedar, and *Chamæcyparis Nutkaensis*, the yellow or Alaska cedar, are species of the genus.

Chȧ-mæ′rops, *n.* [L., from Gr. *chamairhōps*; *chamai*, on the ground, and *rhōps*, a bush, shrub.] A genus of palms consisting of dwarf trees with fan-shaped leaves borne on prickly petioles. They are natives of the northern hemisphere. The leaves are employed in making hats, baskets, and various other products used in the arts.

chä′măl, *n.* [Native name.] The angora goat.

chām′bēr, *v.i.*; chambered, *pt.*, *pp.*; chambering, *ppr.* 1. To reside in or occupy a chamber.

2. To be wanton; to indulge in lewdness or licentiousness. [Obs.]

chām′bēr, *v.t.* 1. To shut up in, or as in, a chamber.

2. To make chambers in, as a gun; or to place or fit into, as a cartridge in a piece.

chām′bēr, *n.* [ME. *chamber*; OFr. *chambre*, *cambre*; LL. *camera*, a chamber, room; L. *camera*; Gr. *kamara*, anything with an arched cover, a vault.]

1. A room or apartment in the upper part of a house, especially a sleeping-room; a bedroom.

2. Furnished rooms hired for residence in the house of another; lodgings.

A bachelor life in *chambers*. —Thackeray.

3. The place where an assembly meets, a court sits, or a sovereign gives audience; and, by metonymy, the body (if collective) itself; as, the senate *chamber*; the *chamber* of commerce.

4. A compartment or inclosed space; a hollow or cavity in the body of an animal or plant; as, the *chamber* of the eye; the *chamber* of a flower.

And all the secret of the Spring
Moved in the *chambers* of the blood.
—Tennyson.

5. [*pl.*] A room where professional men, as lawyers, conduct their business; especially, the room in which judges sit for the disposing of points of practice and other matters not sufficiently important to be heard and argued in court; as, judges' *chambers*.

6. In mechanics, an air-tight room or a hollow part of an instrument or mechanism, examples of which are: (a) the space between the gates of a canal-lock; (b) the part of a pump in which the bucket or plunger works; (c) that part of the chase of a firearm where the powder lies; (d) a receiver for cartridges in a revolver; (e) a fixing-room for printed fabrics.

7. In military affairs, (a) a cavity in a mine, generally of a cubical form, where the powder is confined; (b) a short piece of ordnance without a carriage but standing on its breach; formerly used chiefly for celebrations and theatrical purposes.

8. A pot for urine.

Chamber of commerce; a board to protect the interests of commerce, chosen from among the merchants and business men of a city.

To sit at chambers; to despatch summary business in chambers; said of a judge.

chām′bēr-coun″cil, *n.* Private or secret council.

chām′bēr-coun″sel-ŏr, **chām′bēr-coun″sel**, *n.* A counsel or person learned in the law who gives his opinion in private, but does not plead cases in court.

chām′bēred, *a.* Provided with a chamber or chambers; as, a *chambered* shell.

chām′bēr-ēr, *n.* 1. One who intrigues or indulges in wantonness; a gallant. [Rare.]

2. One who attends in a chamber; a chambermaid. [Obs.]

chām′bēr-fel″lōw, *n.* One who sleeps in the same apartment as another; a chum.

chām′bēr-hang″ings, *n.* Tapestry or hangings for a chamber.

chām′bēr-ing, *n.* Wanton behavior; lewdness. [Obs.]

chām′bēr-lain (-lin), *n.* [OFr. *chamberlain*; LL. *camarlingus*, *camerlengus*; O.H.G. *chamarlinc*, *chamarling*, from *chamara*, a chamber; L. *camera*, a vault.]

1. A person charged with the direction and management of a chamber or chambers.

2. A head-waiter or upper chambermaid at an inn. [Obs.]

3. An officer charged with certain of the higher duties in connection with the household of a monarch or other great personage; therefore, in Europe a superior officer at court.

4. A receiver of rents and revenues; as, the *chamberlain* of a municipality.

The lord chamberlain of England; an officer who has the government of the palace of Westminster, superintends the fitting up of Westminster Hall for coronations, banquets, and trials, attends the sovereign when visiting parliament, and is the official head of the royal household.

chām′bēr-lain-ship, *n.* The post or dignity of a chamberlain.

chām′bēr-lye, *n.* Urine.

chām′bēr-māid, *n.* 1. A woman who has the care of chambers, making the beds, and cleaning the rooms.

2. A female attendant. [Obs.]

chām′bēr-mū″sic, *n.* Vocal or instrumental compositions suitable for performance in a chamber, as opposed to a concert-hall.

Chām-ber-tin′ (shäṅ-ber-taṅ′), *n.* A superior sort of red Burgundy wine, named after the place where the grapes from which it is made grow.

cham′brāy, *n.* [Fr., from *Cambray*, a town in France where it was made.] A kind of gingham or plain-colored dress-goods, with linen finish.

cham′brel, *n.* See *Gambrel*.

chȧ-meck′, *n.* [Braz.] A Brazilian monkey, genus *Ateles*, subfamily *Cebinæ*, having the head round and small, limbs long and slender.

chȧ-mē′lē-ŏn, *n.* [L. *chamæleon*; Gr. *chamaileōn*; *chamai*, on the ground, and *leōn*, lion.] A lizard of the genus *Chamæleo*, having a naked body, a prehensile tail, four feet suited for grasping branches, and the eye covered by a single circular eyelid with an aperture in the center. The best known species is *Chamæleo africanus* or *Chamæleo vulgaris*, a native of Africa. The faculty which the chameleon possesses of changing its color is due to the presence of clear or pigment-bearing contractile cells placed at various depths in the skin, their contractions and dilatations being under the influence of the nervous system.

Chameleon mineral; potassium manganate, produced by fusing oxid of magnesia with niter or potash. When dissolved in water it assumes a variety of colors, passing rapidly from green to blue, purple, and red.

chȧ-mē′lē-ŏn-īze, *v.t.* To change into various colors. [Rare.]

cham′fēr, *n.* [Fr. *chanfrein*, a chamfer.]

1. In carpentry, a small gutter or furrow cut in wood or other hard material.

2. A bevel or slope; the corner of anything originally right-angled cut aslope equally on the two sides which form it.

cham′fēr, *v.t.*; chamfered, *pt.*, *pp.*; chamfering, *ppr.* 1. In carpentry, to cut a furrow in; to flute; to channel.

2. To cut or grind in a sloping manner, as the edge of anything square, so as to form a bevel.

cham′fret, *n.* and *v.* [Obs.] See *Chamfer*.

cham′frŏn, *n.* [OFr. *chamfrein*, chamfron.] The defensive armor for the fore part of the head of a war-horse; written also *chanfrin*.

chä-mi-sal′, *n.* [Sp. Am.] A chaparral of chamiso.

chȧ-mï′sō, *n.* [Sp. Am.] A small, close, densely growing shrub, *Adenostoma fasciculatum*, of the rose family.

cham′let, *n.* [Obs.] See *Camlet*.

cham′ois (sham′i *or* shȧ-moi′), *n.* [Fr. *chamois*: Sp. *camuza*, *gamuza*; from O.H.G. *gamz*, chamois.]

1. A species of goat-like or capriform antelope, *Antilope rupicapra* or *Rupicapra tragus*, inhabiting high inaccessible mountains in Europe and the west of Asia. Its size is about that of a goat, and it is so agile that it can clear at a bound crevices sixteen or eighteen feet wide.

2. A kind of soft leather made from various skins dressed with fish-oil; so called because first prepared from the skin of the *chamois*; called also *chammy*.

cham′ō-mile, *n.* See *Camomile*.

champ, *v.t.*; champed, *pt.*, *pp.*; champing, *ppr.* [OE. *cham*, to chew; connected with Sw. dial. *kämsa*, to chew.]

1. To bite with repeated action of the teeth; as, a horse *champs* the bit.

2. To bite into small pieces; to chew; to masticate; to devour.

champ, *v.i.* To chew; to perform the action of biting by repeated motion of the teeth; as, to *champ* upon the bit.

champ, *n.* The act of working the jaws loudly.

champ, *n.* The native name given to a valuable kind of timber produced in the East Indies by *Michelia excelsa*.

champ, champe, *n.* [Fr. *champ*, from L. *campus*, a field.] In architecture, the field or ground on which carving is raised.

cham′paç, *n.* See *Champak.*

çham-pāgne′ (-pān′), *n.* [From *Champagne*, an old province of France.]

1. Wine, including several sparkling and still varieties, either white or red.

2. A highly effervescent, amber-colored wine, the effervescence being caused by fermentation in the bottle and the consequent generation of carbon-dioxid gas.

çham-pāign′ (-pān′), *a.* and *n.* [OFr. *champaigne*, from *campaigne*, from L. *campus*, a field.]

I. *a.* Flat; open; level.

II. *n.* A flat, open country.

cham′pak, *n.* [Sans. *champaka.*] A beautiful Indian tree, *Michelia Champaca*, much esteemed by Brahmans and Buddhists, who regard it as sacred. Images of Buddha are made of its wood, which is also used for more common purposes.

cham′pär-ty, *n.* See *Champerty.*

champ′ẽr, *n.* One who champs, or bites.

cham′pẽr-tŏr, *n.* One who is guilty of champerty.

cham′pẽr-ty, *n.* [Fr. *champart*, field-rent, from L. *campi pars*; *campi*, genit. of *campus*, a field, and *pars, partis*, a part.]

1. An agreement with a litigating party to meet the expense of a suit for a share in the award.

2. Joint power; partnership in authority. [Obs.]

çham-pi′gnŏn (-pin′yŏn), *n.* [Fr., from L. *campus*, a field.] A mushroom; the French name for mushrooms in general.

cham′pi-ŏn, *n.* [OFr. *champion*; LL. *campio* (*-onis*), a gladiator; from L. *campus*, a field, place for games.]

1. One who comes forward in defense of any cause; one who defends or maintains; a protector or vindicator; especially, one who engages in combat for the cause of another.

2. The victor having acknowledged superiority in certain matters decided by public competition, as prize-fighting, pedestrianism, rowing, or contest of any kind; one open to contend with all comers, or otherwise required to resign the title; as, the old-time *champion* of the prize-ring.

cham′pi-ŏn, *a.* Holding superiority or first prize over all competitors. [See *Champion*, n. 2.]

cham′pi-ŏn, *v.t.*; championed, *pt., pp.*; championing, *ppr.* 1. To challenge to a combat. [Obs.]

2. To maintain or support, as a cause or individual; to advocate; to protect; to vindicate; to act as champion for.

cham′pi-ŏn-ess, *n.* A female champion. [Rare.]

cham′pi-ŏn-ship, *n.* The state of being a champion; the honor or supremacy gained by a champion.

Çham-plāin′, *n.* [Named from the beds near Lake *Champlain.*] The geological term for that epoch that follows in rotation the Glacial epoch; the deposits made at that time.

Çham-plāin′, *a.* Of or pertaining to Champlain.

çhamp-le-vé′ (-vā′), *n.* [Fr., pp. of *champlever*; *champ*, a surface, and *lever*, to lift.] A style of enamel having part or all of the pattern cut out of the surface; also, the process of so enameling.

chânce, *n.* [ME. *chance, chaunce*; OFr. *cheance*, a chance, risk; LL. *cadentia*, that which falls out; L. *cadens* (*-entis*), ppr. of *cadere*, to fall.]

1. A supposedly existing force not subject to any recognized law; destiny; fortune; often used personified; as, *chance* could not rule the world.

2. That which is regarded as determining the course of events in the absence of ordinary causation or providence; absence of assignable cause; accident; as, to meet a person by *chance.*

> That power
> Which erring men call *chance.* —Milton.

3. The effect of either of the agents given above.

4. Possibility of an occurrence; uncertainty; hazard.

> I would set my life on any *chance.* —Shak.

5. In logic and mathematics, the ratio of probability of a thing happening to its not happening; as, in drawing from a pack of cards there is one *chance* in fifty-two of drawing a given card.

6. Opportunity; favorable circumstances; as, now is my *chance.*

Absolute chance; an expression originating in the Aristotelian philosophy, indicative of an operating force absolutely devoid of control; a cause not subject to law.

The last chance; the only hope remaining.

The main chance; a colloquial phrase meaning the direction pointed out by self-interest.

Theory of chances; a branch of mathematics treating of the probability of events under given exact conditions.

To mind one's chances; to take advantage of all opportunities.

Syn.—Accident, fortuity, hazard, haphazard, fortune, random, casualty, luck.

chânce, *v.i.*; chanced, *pt., pp.*; chancing, *ppr.* To happen; to fall out; to come or arrive without design or expectation.

> Ah, Casca, tell us what hath *chanced* to-day. —Shak.

This verb is sometimes used impersonally, as in the expression, "how chances it." Sometimes the "it" is omitted.

chânce, *v.t.* To risk or hazard.

chânce, *a.* Happening by chance; casual; as, a *chance* comer.

chânce, *adv.* By chance.

chânce′ȧ-ble, *a.* Accidental; fortuitous. [Obs.]

chânce′ȧ-bly, *adv.* Casually; by chance. [Obs.]

chânce′fụl, *a.* Hazardous. [Obs.]

chan′cel, *n.* [OFr. *chancel, cancel*; LL. *cancellus*, a chancel; L. *cancelli*, pl., lattices, crossbars.] That part of a church between the altar or communion table and the balustrade or railing that incloses it, or the portion where the altar is placed, reserved for the officiating clergy; formerly inclosed with lattices or crossbars, as now with rails. In modern architecture, all that part of a cruciform church beyond the nave and transepts; the choir. In churches other than the Roman Catholic and Anglican, a space including the pulpit, separated from the auditorium by a rail.

Chancel aisle; the aisle on either side of or around the chancel.

Chancel arch; the arch spanning the main opening leading to the chancel.

Chancel casement; the main window in a chancel.

Chancel table; the communion table.

chân′cel-lẽr-y, *n.* Chancellorship; the office or dignity of a chancellor; a foreign ministry.

chân′cel-lŏr, *n.* [OFr. *chanceler*; LL. *cancellarius*, a chancellor, an officer in charge of records who stood behind latticework; L. *cancelli*, latticework.]

1. A judicial officer of high rank, who presides in a court of chancery or equity. In England and in the United States, a chancery court is distinctively a court with equity jurisdiction, and its president, or chief justice, is a *chancellor.* In certain states of the United States, chancery jurisdiction is given to common-law courts; in others, separate chancery courts are established by statute, the judges of which are *chancellors.*

2. Originally, a chief notary or scribe, under the Roman emperors; but, in later times, an officer invested with judicial powers, and particularly with the superintendence of all charters, letters, and other official writings of the crown that were to be solemnly authenticated. Hence, this officer became the keeper of the great seal. From the Roman Empire, this office passed to the church, and hence every bishop had his chancellor.

3. In France, a secretary, particularly of an embassy.

4. In the German Empire, the *chancellor* (*reichskanzler*) is the president of the federal council, and has the general conduct of the imperial administration.

5. In the Scriptures, a master of the decrees, or president of the council.

Chancellor of a bishop or *of a diocese*; the vicar-general to the bishop, who holds his courts and directs and assists him in matters of ecclesiastical law.

Chancellor of a cathedral; an officer who arranges the celebration of religious services, hears lessons and lectures in the church; by himself or his vicar, applies the seal, writes letters of the chapter, keeps the books, etc.

Chancellor of a university; the highest honorary official in the university, from whom the degrees are regarded as proceeding.

Chancellor of the Duchy of Lancaster; an officer who presides either in person or by deputy in the court of the Duchy of Lancaster.

Chancellor of the exchequer; the highest finance minister of the British government.

Chancellor of the Order of the Garter (and other military orders); an officer who seals the commissions and mandates of the chapter and assembly of the knights, keeps the register of their proceedings, and delivers their acts under the seal of their order.

The lord high chancellor of Great Britain, or *keeper of the great seal*; the highest officer of the crown, and after the princes of the blood royal the first lay subject. He is a cabinet minister and privy councilor by his office, and prolocutor of the House of Lords by prescription. To him belongs the appointment of all justices of the peace; he is keeper of the sovereign's conscience, visitor of all hospitals and colleges founded by the king, guardian of all charitable uses, and judge of the High Court of Chancery.

chân′cel-lŏr-ship, *n.* The office of a chancellor; the time during which one is chancellor.

chânce′-med″ley, *n.* [From *chance* and *medley*; OFr. *meslee*, a fray, a *mêlée* or mellay.]

1. In law, originally a term signifying a casual affray or riot, accompanied with violence, and without deliberate or preconceived malice, but applied at present to a particular kind of homicide, viz., the killing of another in self-defense, upon a sudden and unpremeditated encounter.

2. Haphazard mixture.

chân′cẽr, *v.t.*; chancered, *pt., pp.*; chancering, *ppr.* To adjudicate or settle equitably, as in a court of chancery. [Obs.]

chân′cẽr-y, *n.* [Contr. from *chancelery*; OFr. *chancellerie*; LL. *cancellaria*, a chancery court, record office of a chancellor.]

1. In the United States, a court of equity, as distinguished from a common-law court; a court having jurisdiction in cases of rights, recognized and protected by municipal jurisprudence, where a plain and adequate remedy cannot be obtained in courts of common law; equity or proceedings in equity.

2. In England, formerly the highest court of justice next to parliament, but since 1873 a division of the High Court of Justice, which is itself one of the two departments of the Supreme Court of Judicature.

In chancery; in boxing, having the head of an opponent under one's arm and able to administer punishment; by extension, in a helpless condition.

Inns of chancery; see under *Inn.*

çhan′çre (-kẽr), *n.* [Fr.] A sore or ulcer which arises from the direct application of the venereal virus; also, an initial syphilitic lesion.

Hard chancre; a venereal ulcer preceding constitutional syphilis; called also *Hunterian, indurated, infecting, nonsuppurating*, or *true chancre.*

Soft chancre; chancroid.

çhan′çroid, *n.* A local infective process characterized by ulceration, local glandular involvement, and often suppuration.

çhan′çrous, *a.* Ulcerous; having the qualities of a chancre.

chân′cy, *a.* [Scot.] 1. Lucky.

2. A colloquial term meaning risky.

çhan-de-liēr′, *n.* [Fr. *chandelier*; Pr. *candelier*; LL. *candelarius*, a candlestick; L. *candela*, a candle.]

1. A branching frame, often ornamental in design, suspended from a ceiling to support lights; it may be equipped to hold candles or lamps, or have fixtures for the burning of gas or for electric lights.

2. In fortification, a movable parapet, serving to support fascines to cover pioneers. [Obs.]

chân-delle′, *n.* [Fr. lit. Roman candle.] In aviation, a very sudden and steep leap upward.

chan′dlẽr, *n.* [ME. *chandeler*; OFr. *chandelier*; LL. *candelarius*, a candle-maker, a candlestick; L. *candela*, a candle.]

1. A general term for a dealer, the particular meaning being determined by a prefix, as, tallow-*chandler*, ship-*chandler*, etc.

2. One who makes or sells candles.

chan′dlẽr-ly, *adv.* Like a chandler.

chan′dlẽr-y, *n.* The commodities sold by a chandler.

chan-doo′, *n.* [Malay.] An extract of opium, obtained by dissolving it in water and evaporating, used by the Chinese for smoking.

chan′dry, *n.* A place where candles are kept.

chan′frin, *n.* 1. The fore part of a horse's head.

2. Same as *Chamfron.*

chānge, *v.t.*; changed, *pt., pp.*; changing, *ppr.* [ME. *changen*; OFr. *changier*; LL. *cambiare*, from L. *cambire*, to exchange, barter.]

1. To cause to turn or pass from one state to another; to alter or make different; to vary in external form or in essence; as, to *change* the shape of a thing; to *change* the countenance.

2. To substitute another thing or things for; to shift; as, to *change* one suit of clothes for another.

3. To give or procure another kind of money for; to give away for a money equivalent of a different kind; as, to *change* a bill.

> He called me aside, and requested I would *change* him a twenty-pound bill. —Goldsmith.

4. To give and take reciprocally; to barter; to exchange.

> Those thousands with whom thou would'st not *change* thy fortune and condition. —Jer. Taylor.

To change hands; to change ownership.

To change one's tune; to become less sanguine; to show less confidence or boastfulness. [Colloq.]

chānge, *v.i.* 1. To be altered; to undergo variation; to be partially or wholly transformed; as, men sometimes *change* for the better.

2. To begin a new revolution, or to pass from

one phase to another, as the moon; as, the moon will *change* on Friday.

Syn.—Alter, vary, innovate, diversify, shift, veer, turn.

chānge, *n.* 1. Any variation or alteration in form, state, quality, or essence; or a passing from one state or form to another; as, a *change* of countenance; a *change* of habits or principles.

The sky is changed! And such a *change!*
—Byron.

2. Sometimes, in a special sense, the passing from life to death; death; as, her *change* was very peaceful.

3. A succession of one thing in the place of another; as, a *change* of seasons.

4. The beginning of a new monthly revolution; the passing from one phase to another; as, a *change* of the moon.

5. Alteration in the order of a series; permutation.

Four bells admit twenty-four *changes* in ringing. —Holder.

6. That which makes a variety or may be substituted for another; as, a *change* of clothing.

7. Small money, which may be given for larger pieces or bills.

Wood buys up our old halfpence, and from thence the present want of *change* arises.
—Swift.

8. The balance of money paid beyond the price of goods purchased; as, here is your purchase and *change*.

9. A place where merchants and others meet to transact business; a building appropriated for mercantile transactions; in this sense, an abbreviation for *exchange*, and often written *'change*.

10. Exchange. [Obs.]

Give us a prince of the blood in *change* of him.
—Shak.

11. A public-house; a change-house. [Scot.]

They call an ale-house a *change*. —Burt.

12. A round in dancing; as, the first *change* of a quadrille.

Change of life; the physiologic cessation of the menses, usually occurring between forty-five and fifty years of age; also called *menopause* or *climacteric*.

To ring the changes on; to present a subject in varied lights and in a prolix manner.

Syn.—Variety, variation, alteration, modification, deviation, transformation, mutation, transition, vicissitude, innovation, novelty, transmutation, revolution, reverse.

chānge-ȧ-bil′i-ty, *n.* Changeableness.

chānge′ȧ-ble, *a.* 1. Liable to change; subject to alteration; fickle; inconstant; mutable; variable; as, a person of a *changeable* mind.

2. Having the quality of undergoing alteration of external appearance; as, *changeable* silk.

Syn.—Fickle, inconsistent, mutable, uncertain, unstable, unsteady, variable, wavering, whimsical.

chānge′ȧ-ble-ness, *n.* The quality of being changeable; fickleness; inconstancy.

chānge′ȧ-bly, *adv.* Inconstantly.

chānge′fụl, *a.* Full of change; inconstant; mutable; fickle; uncertain.

chānge′fụl-ly, *adv.* In a changeful manner.

chānge′fụl-ness, *n.* The state of being changeful.

chānge′less, *a.* Constant; not admitting alteration.

chānge′less-ness, *n.* The state of being changeless.

chānge′ling, *n.* 1. A child left or taken in the place of another; a child supposed to be exchanged by fairies.

2. An idiot; a fool.

3. One apt to change; a waverer.

4. Anything changed and put in the place of another.

chānge′ling, *a.* 1. Substituted; changed.

2. Subject to change; fickle.

chān′gẽr, *n.* 1. One who alters the form of anything.

2. One who is employed in changing and discounting money; a money-changer.

3. One given to change or fickleness.

chānge′=wheel, *n.* One of a series of interchangeable cogwheels of fine pitch used to transmit motion from the mandrel of a lathe-head to the guide screw, for the cutting of screws of various pitches.

chañk, chañk=shell, *n.* [Sans. *çankha*, a conch-shell.] The common conch-shell, *Turbinella pyrum*, which is fished up by divers in the Gulf of Manar and other places; used for ornaments and bangles.

chan′nel, *n.* [ME. *chanel*; OFr. *chanel, canel*; L. *canalis*, a water-pipe, canal.]

1. The bed of a stream of water; the hollow or course in which a stream flows.

2. The deeper part of an estuary, bay, etc., where the current flows, or which is most convenient for the track of a ship.

3. A strait or narrow sea between two continents or between a continent and an island; as, the British *channel*.

4. That by which something passes or is transmitted; means of passing, conveying or transmitting; as, the news was conveyed to us by different *channels*.

5. A furrow or groove; as, the *channels* of a fluted column.

chan′nel, *n.* [A corruption of *chain-wale*.] In nautical parlance, one of the pieces of plank of considerable thickness projecting horizontally from the vessel's sides, nearly abreast of the masts, and hence, named respectively the main, fore, and mizzen *channels*. The chain-plates are carried through notches on their outer edge in order to extend the shrouds of the lower rigging and keep them clear of the gunwale. They are also called *chain-wales* or *channel-boards*.

Shrouds extended on the Channels.

chan′nel, *v.t.*; channeled or channelled, *pt.*, *pp.*; channeling or channelling, *ppr.* 1. To form a channel or cut channels in; to groove; as, to *channel* a field or a column.

2. To bring through or over, as though employing a channel.

chan′nel=bär, *n.* See *Channel-iron*.

chan′nel=bȧss, *n.* The redfish or red bass of southern waters.

chan′nel=bill, *n.* An Australian cuckoo, *Scythrops novæ-hollandiæ*, of unusually large size.

chan′nel=gọọse, *n.* The white gannet.

chan′nel-ing, *n.* 1. The act of making a channel or channels.

2. A channel; channels collectively.

chan′nel=ī″ron (-ũrn), *n.* A flanged iron beam whose section is that of three sides of a parallelogram, used for structural purposes generally; called also *channel-bar*.

çhan′sŏn, *n.* [Fr.] A song.

çhan-sŏn-nette′, *n.* [Fr.] A short song or chanson.

chȧnt, *v.t.*; chanted, *pt.*, *pp.*; chanting, *ppr.* [ME. *chanten*; OFr. *chanter, canter*; L. *cantare*, freq. of *canere*, to sing.]

1. To sing; to utter with a melodious voice.

The cheerful birds do *chant* sweet music.
—Spenser.

2. To celebrate in song; as, to *chant* praises.

3. To sing after the manner of a chant.

To chant horses; to praise highly in making a sale; hence, to cheat.

chȧnt, *v.i.* 1. To sing; to make melody with the voice.

2. To sing after the manner of a chant.

chȧnt, *n.* [Fr. *chant*; L. *cantus*, a song, from *cantare*, to sing.]

1. A song or singing; melody.

2. A short musical composition consisting generally of a long reciting-note, on which an indefinite number of words may be intoned, and a melodic phrase or cadence.

Ambrosian chant; see under *Ambrosian*.

Chant royal; in old French poetry, a composition consisting of five stanzas, each having eleven lines, and a concluding stanza, each of these parts in turn closing with a common refrain.

Gregorian chant; see under *Gregorian*.

chȧn′tȧnt (*or Fr. pron.* shäṅ-täṅ′), *a.* and *n.* [Fr. *chantant*, ppr. of *chanter*, to sing.]

I. *a.* Singing.

II. *n.* Instrumental music of an easy, smooth, and singing style.

chȧnt′ẽr, *n.* 1. One who chants; a singer.

2. The chief singer, or priest of the chantry.

3. The pipe which sounds the tenor or treble in a bagpipe.

4. The hedge-warbler.

çhȧn-te-relle′, çhȧn-tȧ-relle′, *n.* [Fr.] The *Cantharellus cibarius*, an edible mushroom; also, other mushrooms of the same genus.

çhȧn-te-relle′, *n.* [Fr.] The highest string of a musical instrument, as a guitar.

chȧnt′ey, *n.* A song, common among sailors when heaving, to enliven the work by marking rhythm.

chan′ti-çleer, *n.* A cock, so called from the clearness or loudness of his voice in crowing.

chȧnt′ing, *n.* The act of singing or uttering after the manner of a chant.

chȧnt′ŏr, *n.* One who chants; a chanter.

chȧnt′ress, *n.* A female singer.

chȧnt′ry, *n.*; *pl.* **chȧnt′rieṣ**. [OFr. *chanterie*, from *chanter*, to sing.]

1. An endowed chapel where one or more priests daily sing or say mass for the souls of the donors, or such as they appoint.

2. An endowment for chanting masses and offering prayers in such a chapel.

çhā′ō-man-çy, *n.* [Gr. *chaos*, chaos, and *manteia*, divination.] Divination by means of aerial visions.

çhā′os, *n.* [L. *chaos*; Gr. *chaos*, empty space, abyss, from *chainein*, to yawn, gape.]

1. That confusion, or confused mass, in which matter is supposed to have existed, before it was separated into its different kinds, and reduced to order.

2. Any mixed mass, without due form or order; as, a *chaos* of materials.

3. Confusion; disorder; a state in which the parts are indistinguishable.

4. An empty, immeasurable space.

çhā-ot′iç, *a.* Resembling chaos; confused; as, the earth was originally in a *chaotic* state.

çhā-ot′iç-ăl-ly, *adv.* In a chaotic way or state; in complete confusion.

chap, *v.t.*; chapped *or* chapt, *pt.*, *pp.*; chapping, *ppr.* 1. To cause to crack or break in chinks and slits; as, a cold wind *chaps* the skin.

2. To strike, especially with a hammer or the like; to beat. [Scot.]

chap, *v.i.* 1. To crack open; to break in slits; as, the lips or hands *chap*.

chap, *n.* 1. A crack, chink, or cleft, as in the hands or lips or in the earth's surface.

2. A stroke of any kind; a blow. [Scot.]

chăp, chop, *n.* [Scot. *chaft*; Ice. *kjaptr*; Dan. *kjæft*, a jaw, chap.]

1. The upper or lower part of the mouth; the jaw; commonly in the plural.

2. [*pl.*] The mouth of a channel. In this sense always written *chops*.

3. A jaw of a clamp or vise.

chap, *n.* [An abbrev. of *chapman*, a merchant.]

1. A buyer; a chapman. [Obs.]

2. A man or boy; a youth; used familiarly; as, poor old *chap*; little *chap*.

chap, *v.i.* [AS. *ceápian*, from *ceáp*, a bargain, price.] To buy or sell; to trade; to traffic; to bargain. [Obs.]

chap, *v.t.* To fix upon (any person or thing) by selection; to select and claim. [Scot.]

chȧ-par-ral′, *n.* [Sp., from *chaparro*, an evergreen oak.]

1. A grove of low evergreen oaks.

2. A clump or thicket formed by thorny shrubs; sometimes a thick tangle of cacti. [Western U. S.]

chȧ-par-ral′=çock, chȧ-par-ral′=hen, *n.* A bird common in chaparrals. It is a species of cuckoo, *Geococcyx californianus*; also called *ground-cuckoo* and *road-runner*.

chȧ-pä′ti, *n.* See *Chupatty*.

chap′book, *n.* [*Chap*, abbrev. of *chapman*, and *book*.] A cheap form of book, containing a short story, verses or the like, sold throughout the country by peddlers, and once common in the British Isles and American colonies.

chāpe, *n.* [Fr. *chape*, a cope, a cover, chape; LL. *cappa*, cape, hooded cloak.]

1. The catch of anything, as the hook of a scabbard, or the catch of a buckle, by which it is held to the back-strap.

2. A brass or silver tip, or case that strengthens the end of a scabbard.

3. The cross-guard of a sword for the protection of the hand.

4. In casting, the outer jacket or case holding together a bronze mold.

5. In military terms, an outer case protecting a gunpowder barrel.

çhȧ-peau′ (-pō′), *n.*; *pl.* **çhȧ-peaux′** (-pōz′). [Fr., from OFr. *chapel*, from LL. *capellus*, a hat headdress.]

1. A hat; specifically in the United States, a military hat that may be folded flat and carried under the arm; called also a *chapeau bras*.

2. In heraldry, a cap of maintenance. [See under *Cap*.]

Chapeau bras; a small three-cornered hat, capable of being folded flat and carried under the arm; worn chiefly by gentlemen in the latter half of the eighteenth century, and a modification of which is still worn by general and staff officers in the United States army.

chāped (chāpt), *a.* Furnished with a chape or chapes. [Obs.]

chap′el, *n.* [OFr. *chapele, capele*, from LL. *capella*, dim. of *cappa*, a cope, cape; originally a sanctuary in which the *cappa* or cope of St. Martin was preserved; then, any sanctuary.]

1. A secondary place of worship usually attached to a large church or cathedral, separately dedicated, and devoted to special services.

2. A building subsidiary to a parish church; as, a parochial *chapel*; a mission *chapel*.

3. In England, a place of worship used by dissenters from the Church of England; a meetinghouse; in Scotland and Ireland, a Roman Catholic church.

4. A place of worship connected with some public institution; as, a college *chapel*; hospital *chapel*; prison *chapel*.

5. A choir or an orchestra connected with a nobleman's establishment or a prince's palace.

6. A printing-office, said to be so called because Caxton, the pioneer English printer, first conducted an establishment of that kind in a *chapel* attached to Westminster Abbey. [Obs.]

7. The body of journeyman compositors in a printing-office.

Chapel of ease; in England, originally a chapel for the ease or accommodation of the parishioners that dwell too far away to be able to attend the parish church.

Chapel royal; a chapel attached to a royal palace.

To hold a chapel; to have a meeting of the journeymen printers of a printing-office.

chap'el, *v.t.*; chapeled, *pt.*, *pp.*; chapeling, *ppr.*

1. To place or bury in a chapel. [Rare.]

2. To turn (a ship) round in a light breeze, when closehauled, so that she will lie the same way as before.

chāpe'less, *a.* Having no chape or scabbard-tip; said of a sword.

chap'e-let, *n.* [Fr., a chaplet, a stirrup-leather.]

1. A pair of stirrup-leathers, with stirrups, joined at the top in a sort of leather buckle, by which they are made fast to the framework of the saddle, after they have been adjusted to the length and bearing of the rider.

2. A dredging or water-raising machine, consisting of a chain provided with buckets or with pallets traversing in a trough.

3. A metallic contrivance, or chuck, for holding a cannon against the turning-lathe in the process of centering the barrel.

chap'el-lā-ny, *n.* [Fr. *chapellenie*; LL. *capellania*, a chaplaincy, from *capellanus*, a chaplain; *capella*, a chapel.] A chapel or small building connected with a large church; an ecclesiastical foundation subordinate to some other.

chap'el-mäs"tẽr, *n.* Same as *Kapellmeister*.

chap'el-ry, *n.* [OFr. *capelerie*; LL. *capellaria*, from *capella*, a chapel.] The bounds of jurisdiction of a chapel.

chap'ẽr-ōn, *n.* [Fr., a hood, shoulder-knot, coping; from *chape*, a cope.]

1. A hood or cap worn by the Knights of the Garter in their habits. It was anciently worn by men, women, nobles, and populace; afterward confined to doctors and licentiates in colleges. The name then passed to certain devices placed on the foreheads of horses which drew the hearse in pompous funerals.

2. A married or elderly lady who accompanies young unmarried ladies to public places as a guide and mentor.

chap'ẽr-ōn, *v.t.*; chaperoned, *pt.*, *pp.*; chaperoning, *ppr.* To attend (a lady) to public places in the capacity of a chaperon.

chap'ẽr-ōn-āge, *n.* The protection and care of a chaperon.

chap'fall-en (-fal'n), *a.* Having the lower chap depressed; hence, dejected; dispirited; silenced.

chā'pin, *n.* Same as *Chopine*.

chap'i-tẽr, *n.* [A corruption of OFr. *chapitel*; LL. *capitellum*, a capital; L. *capitulum*, a chapter, a capital.]

1. The upper part or capital of a column or pillar. [Obs. See *Capital*.]

2. That which is delivered by the mouth of the justice in his charge to the inquest.

3. Articles, or a schedule of matters that are to be introduced at any session before the justice of the peace, assize, or eyre.

chap'lain (-lin), *n.* [OFr. *chapelain*; LL. *capellanus*, from *capella*, a chapel.]

1. An ecclesiastic who has a chapel, or who performs service in a chapel.

2. A clergyman who belongs to a ship of war, to a regiment of land forces, or to some public institution, for performing divine service.

3. A clergyman who is retained to perform divine service in a family.

chap'lain-cy, *n.* The office or station of a chaplain.

chap'lain-ship, *n.* 1. The office or business of a chaplain.

2. The possession or revenue of a chapel.

chap'less, *a.* Without a lower jaw; without flesh. [Rare.]

chap'let, *n.* [OFr. *chapelet*, a headdress, wreath, dim. of *chapel*, a headdress, cap.]

1. A garland or wreath to be worn on the head; a crown.

2. A string of beads used by the Roman Catholics, by which they count the number of their prayers. They are made sometimes of coral, of wood, of diamonds, etc., and are called *paternosters*.

3. In architecture, a little molding, carved into round beads, pearls, olives, or the like.

4. In horsemanship, same as *chapelet*.

5. A tuft of feathers on a peacock's head.

6. A contrivance of bent sheet iron for keeping a core in position in a mold.

chap'let, *v.t.* To embellish with flowers, beads, or chaplets.

chap'măn, *n.*; *pl.* **chap'men.** [ME. *chapman*, *chepman*; AS. *ceápman*, a buyer, seller, merchant; *ceáp*, a bargain, trade, and *man*.]

1. A cheapener; a peddler.

> Their *chapmen* they betray. —Dryden.

2. A market-man; a tradesman.

chä-pō'te, *n.* [Mex.] The black persimmon of Mexico.

chā-pöur'net, *n.* [Fr. *chaperonnet*, dim. of *chaperon*, a hood, cope.] In heraldry, a chief divided by a curved line.

Chapournet.

chap'py, chap'pie, *n.* 1. A little fellow; used in much the same way as *chap*.

2. A dude or dandy.

chap'py, *a.* Full of chaps; cleft.

chapt, *v.*, past tense and past participle of *chap*.

chap'tẽr, *n.* [Fr. *chapitre*; L. *capitulum*, a head, a chapter of a book, dim. of *caput*, a head.]

1. A division of a book or treatise; as, Genesis contains fifty *chapters*.

2. In ecclesiastical polity, a society or community of clergymen, belonging to a cathedral or collegiate church; as, the dean and *chapter* of Westminster; a community of canons and canonesses; a meeting of a religious body for business purposes; a bishop's council.

3. An organized branch of some society or fraternity, as of the Freemasons, etc.

4. A place where delinquents receive discipline and correction.

5. A decretal epistle.

6. A house where a *chapter* meets; a chapter-house.

Chapter of accidents; a number of chance happenings.

To read one a chapter; to reprimand severely; or, using another phrase, to deliver one a lecture.

To the end of the chapter; throughout; to the end of a series of actions or of life.

chap'tẽr, *v.t.* 1. To form into chapters.

2. To tax with; to correct. [Obs.]

chap'tẽr-house, *n.* A house where a chapter meets.

chap'trel, *n.* [Dim. of *chapiter*, from OFr. *chapitel*, a chapter, capital.] The top of a pillar on which an arch rests. [See *Impost*.]

chãr, *n.* [ME. *charren*, *cherren*; AS. *cerren*, *cerran*, to turn, return.] In England, work done by the day, job, or task. In the United States, the old form *chore* is more commonly used. [See *Chore*.]

chär, chärr, *n.* [Gael. *ceara*; Ir. *cear*, blood-colored, blood.] A fish of several species, found in deep, mountainous lakes of Europe; so called from its red belly. Brook-trout in the United States is sometimes called *char*.

chär, chäre, *n.* [Fr.] A chariot. [Obs.]

chär, *v.t.* [AS. *cerran*, *cyrran*, to turn.] To hew, as granite.

chär, *v.t.*; charred, *pt.*, *pp.*; charring, *ppr.* [ME. *charren*, to turn, return. The meaning is influenced by *char* in *charcoal*.]

1. To turn into charcoal by the action of heat.

2. To burn partially.

3. To expel all volatile substances from (earth or stone) by heat.

chãr, *v.i.* [AS. *cerran*, *cyrran*, to turn, return.] To work by the day and at odd jobs without being a regularly hired servant.

Chā'rȧ, *n.* [Gr. *chara*, delight, from *chairein*, to rejoice.] A genus of plants growing in damp places, without flowers.

chär-ȧ-bănc' (shär-ä-bäṅ'), *n.*; *pl.* **chärs-ȧ-bănc'.** [Fr.] A light vehicle with seats arranged like those of a jaunting car, i.e., with a knife-board in the middle and seats lengthwise down each side facing outward.

Chā-rā'cē-æ, *n.pl.* [*Chara* and *-aceæ*.] A family of chlorophyl-bearing plants allied to the algæ.

chā-rā'ceous, *a.* Relating to or like the *Characeæ*.

char-ȧ-cin'oid, *a.* [From Gr. *charax* (*-akos*), a sea-fish, and *eidos*, form.] Pertaining to the family of the *Characinidæ*, numerous fresh-water fishes in Africa and tropical America.

char'act, *n.* An inscription. [Obs.]

char'ac-tẽr, *n.* [L. *character*; Gr. *charaktēr*, from *charassein*, engrave.]

1. A mark made by cutting or engraving, as on stone, metal, or other hard material; hence, a mark or figure made with a pen or style, on paper or other material used to contain writing; a letter or figure used to form words and communicate ideas. Characters are *literal*, as the letters of an alphabet; *numeral*, as the arithmetical figures; *emblematical* or *symbolical*, which express things or ideas; and *abbreviations*, or contractions.

2. A mark or figure made by stamping or impression, as on coins.

3. The manner of writing; the peculiar form of letters used by a particular person.

> You know the *character* to be your brother's. —Shak.

4. The peculiar qualities impressed by nature or habit on a person, which distinguish him from others; hence, a *character* is not formed when the person has not acquired stable and distinctive qualities.

5. An account, description, or representation of anything, exhibiting its qualities and the circumstances attending it; as, to give a bad *character* to a town.

6. A person; as, the assembly consisted of various *characters*; all the *characters* in the play appeared to advantage.

> The friendship of distinguished *characters*. —Roscoe.

7. By way of eminence, distinguished or good qualities, those which are esteemed and respected; as, he is a man of *character*.

8. Adventitious qualities impressed by office or station; the qualities that, in public estimation, belong to a person in a particular station; as, his *character* as a judge was high.

9. The peculiar qualities or properties by which one thing is distinguished from another, as animals, plants, and minerals.

> These properties, when employed for the purpose of discriminating minerals, are called *characters*. —Cleaveland.

10. Distinctive quality of any kind strongly marked, particularly energy or force; as, a man is said to have no *character*, or a great deal of *character*.

11. A written testimonial as to competency or behavior, usually given to a subordinate. [Colloq.]

Dominant characters; in heredity, the predominating characteristics which are transmitted by either parent to the offspring with little or no variation, and which form the prevailing characters.

Recessive characters; characters found in the offspring which may be referred to one or the other of the parental forms, but which are not the prevailing characters. In subsequent generations the *recessive characters* never produce dominants.

Syn.—Symbol, letter, nature, type, disposition, temperament, cast, estimation, repute, office, species, mark, figure, record.

char'ac-tẽr, *v.t.* 1. To engrave; to inscribe.

2. To describe; to distinguish by particular marks or traits. [Obs.]

char'ac-tẽr-ism, *n.* 1. Distinction of character.

2. A particular aspect or configuration of the heavens.

char"ac-tẽr-is'tic, char"ac-tẽr-is'tic-ăl, *a.* That constitutes the character; that marks the peculiar distinctive qualities of a person or thing; as, generosity is often a *characteristic* virtue of a brave man.

Characteristic triangle of a curve; in geometry, a rectilinear right-angled triangle, whose hypotenuse makes a part of the curve, not sensibly different from a right line.

char"ac-tẽr-is'tic, *n.* 1. That which constitutes a character; that which characterizes; that which distinguishes a person or thing from another.

> Invention is the *characteristic* of Homer. —Pope.

2. In grammar, the principal letter of a word, which is preserved in most of its tenses, in its derivatives and compounds; also called *characteristic letter* or *stem-character*.

Characteristic of a logarithm; its index or exponent.

Syn.—Distinction, peculiarity, diagnosis, idiosyncrasy, specialty, individuality, personality, singularity.

char"ac-tẽr-is'tic-ăl-ly, *adv.* In a manner that distinguishes character.

char"ac-tẽr-is'tic-ăl-ness, *n.* The state or qualities of being characteristic.

char"ac-tẽr-i-zā'tion, *n.* Act of characterizing.

char'ac-tẽr-ize, *v.t.*; characterized, *pt.*, *pp.*; characterizing, *ppr.* [LL. *characterizare*; Gr. *charaktērizein*, to designate by a mark; from *charactēr*, a mark, character.]

1. To give a character, or an account of the personal qualities of (one); to describe by peculiar qualities.

2. To distinguish; to mark or tell the character of; to exhibit the peculiar qualities of (a person or thing); as, humility *characterizes* the true Christian.

> The system of mediation has *characterized* the entire scheme of divine dispensation. —Thodey.

3. To engrave or imprint. [Obs.]

4. To mark with a peculiar stamp or figure.

> European, Asiatic, and African faces are all *characterized*. —Arbuthnot.

char'ac-tẽr-less, *a.* Destitute of any peculiar character.

char'ac-tẽr-y, *n.* 1. Impression; mark; distinction. [Obs.]

2. A system of signs or characters; symbolism.

3. The meaning; the import. [Obs.]

çhȧ-rāde′, *n.* [Fr.] A character-sketch, sometimes in complete costume, in which a chosen word of two or more syllables is acted out syllable by syllable and then as a whole, it being necessary for each syllable to be mentioned in the words spoken, during the representation or game, at the end of which the word must be guessed by those who listen or look on.

chär′bō-ġle, *n.* [Obs.] Same as *Carbuncle.*

chär′çōal, *n.* [Lit., turn-coal; ME. *charren*, to turn, and *cole*, coal; i.e., wood turned to coal.]

1. Coal made by charring wood; the remains of wood burned by a process of smothered combustion to exclude air, and from which all watery and other volatile matter has been expelled by heat. It makes a strong heat, and is used in furnaces and forges.

2. Fine *charcoal* in small pencils, for drawing.

Animal charcoal; charcoal obtained by calcining bones, used for filtering and disinfecting.

Mineral charcoal; called by miners *mother-of-coal*, and taking the form of layers of fine charcoal between beds of bituminous coal.

chär′çōal-black, *n.* A pigment made from burnt ivory, cork, etc.

chär′çōal-drạw″ing, *n.* Formerly a preliminary drawing made with charcoal; recently finished drawings have been so made.

chär′çōal-ī″ron (-ūrn), *n.* Iron smelted in furnaces heated with charcoal.

chär′çōal-point, *n.* The carbon pencil in an arc light.

chärd, *n.* [Fr. *carde*; L. *carduus*, a thistle, artichoke.] The leaves of artichokes blanched for table use.

Chards of beet; plants of white beet transplanted, producing great tops, having a large, white, main shoot, esteemed as a table delicacy.

chāre, *n.* and *v.* Same as first and sixth *Char.*

chärġe, *v.t.*; charged, *pt.*, *pp.*; charging, *ppr.* [ME. *chargen*; OFr. *charger*; LL. *carricare*, to load a wagon, from L. *carrus*, a car, wagon.]

1. To rush on; to fall on; to attack, especially with fixed bayonets; as, an army *charges* the enemy.

2. To load, as a musket or cannon; to thrust powder, or powder and ball or shot into.

3. To load or burden; to throw on or impose that which oppresses; as, to *charge* the stomach with indigestible food; or to lay on, or to fill, without oppressing; as, to *charge* the mind with facts.

4. To set or lay on; to impose, as a tax, or as a task; often followed by *with*; as, he *charged* the officer *with* the execution of the plan.

> The gospel *chargeth* us *with* piety toward God. —Tillotson.

5. To put or lay on, often implying superfluity; as, to *charge* a building with ornaments.

6. To intrust to; followed by *with*; as, an officer is *charged with* despatches.

7. To set to, as a debt; to place on the debit side of an account; as, to *charge* a man with the price of goods sold to him.

8. To load or lay on, in words, something wrong, reproachful, or criminal; to impute to; as, to *charge* a man with theft; to *charge* a crime on the offender; to *charge* his friend rashly.

9. To lay on, give, or communicate, as an order, command, or earnest request; to enjoin; to exhort; as, he *charged* his son not to act rashly.

10. To give directions to; to instruct authoritatively; as, the judge *charged* the grand jury to inquire respecting breaches of the peace.

11. To communicate electric force to, as to an electric battery.

12. To make or ask as a price; as, he *charged* ten dollars for it.

13. To put on, as a bearing in heraldry.

Syn.—Accuse, arraign, impeach, indict.

chärġe, *v.i.* 1. To set a price on; as, they *charge* very high.

2. To make a sudden rush; as, he *charged* on ahead.

3. To lie on the belly and four feet, as a trained dog when a sportsman orders him to *charge.*

chärġe, *n.* [Fr. *charge*; LL. *carricare*, to load; *carrus*, a car, wagon.]

1. That which is laid on or in; in a general sense, any load or burden.

2. The quantity of powder, or of powder and ball or shot, used, or proper to be used, in loading a musket, cannon, or other like weapon; or the quantity of electricity which a battery requires.

3. An onset; a rushing on an enemy; attack.

4. An order; injunction; mandate; command; as, the officer gave *charge* concerning the prisoner.

5. That which is enjoined, committed, intrusted, or delivered to another, implying care, custody, oversight, or duty to be performed by the person intrusted; generally followed by *of* or *over*; as, she was placed in *charge of* the boy; she was given *charge over* him.

6. The person or thing committed to another's custody, care, or management; a trust.

> The starry guardian drove his *charge* away
> To some fresh pasture. —Dryden.

7. Instructions given by a judge to a jury, by a bishop to his clergy, or, among certain religious denominations, by a member of an ordaining council to one who is set as pastor over a congregation, or to the congregation itself. The word may be used as synonymous with *command*, *direction*, *exhortation*, or *injunction*, but always implies solemnity.

8. Imputation in a bad sense; accusation; as, do not lay this crime to my *charge.*

9. That which constitutes debt, in commercial transactions; an entry of money, or the price of goods, on the debit side of an account.

10. Cost; expense; as, the *charges* of the war.

11. Imposition on land or estate; rent, tax, or whatever constitutes a burden or duty.

12. In military affairs, a signal to attack; as, to sound the *charge.*

13. The posture of a weapon fitted for an attack or combat.

14. Among farriers, a preparation of the consistence of a thick decoction, or between an ointment and a plaster, used as a remedy for sprains and inflammations.

15. In heraldry, that which is borne upon the color; or the figures represented on the escutcheon.

16. Anxiety; trouble; care; heed. [Obs.]

17. In painting, *charge*, or *overcharge*, is an exaggeration of character in form, color, or expression.

Charge and discharge; formerly a method of taking accounts before a master of chancery.

To sound the charge; to give the signal to make an attack.

çhär-ġé′ (shär-zhā′), *n.* [Fr.] A diplomatic representative from one country or court to another, ranking below a minister or ambassador; or a temporary representative, intrusted with diplomatic affairs and interests such as in a more important post, or ordinarily, would be in care of an ambassador or minister; a *chargé d'affaires.*

chärġe′ȧ-ble, *a.* 1. Capable of being charged, set, laid or imposed; as, a duty of forty per cent is *chargeable* on wine.

2. Subject to be charged; as, wine is *chargeable* with a duty of forty per cent.

3. Expensive; costly; as, a *chargeable* family.

4. Laying or bringing expense; as, the bill was *chargeable* to him.

5. Imputable; that may be laid or attributed as a crime, fault, or debt; as, a fault *chargeable* on a man.

6. Subject to be charged or accused; as, a man *chargeable* with a fault or neglect.

chärġe′ȧ-ble-ness, *n.* Expensiveness; cost.

chärġe′ȧ-bly, *adv.* Expensively; at great cost.

chär′ġeȧnt, *a.* [Fr.] Onerous; oppressive. [Obs.]

çhär-ġé′ d'af-fāires′ (shär-zhā′ daf-fâr′), *n.*; *pl.* **çhär-ġés′ d'af-fāires′.** See *Chargé.*

chärġe′fụl, *a.* Expensive; costly. [Obs.]

chärġe′house, *n.* A schoolhouse. [Obs.]

chärġe′less, *a.* Not expensive; free from expense.

chär′ġeous (-jus), *a.* Onerous. [Obs.]

chär′ġẽr, *n.* 1. One who or that which charges.

2. An instrument used to measure or insert a charge.

3. A large dish. [Obs.]

4. A war-horse.

chärġe′-sheet, *n.* The daily record kept in a police station of all arrests made and charges preferred.

çhär-ġé′ship (-zhā′), *n.* The office of a chargé d'affaires.

chär′i-ly, *adv.* Carefully; warily; frugally.

chär′i-ness, *n.* Caution; care; nicety; scrupulousness.

char′i-ŏt, *n.* [OFr. *chariot*, dim. of *char*, *car*, a car, from L. *carrus*, a car, wagon.]

1. A half coach; a carriage with four wheels, and one seat behind, used for convenience and pleasure.

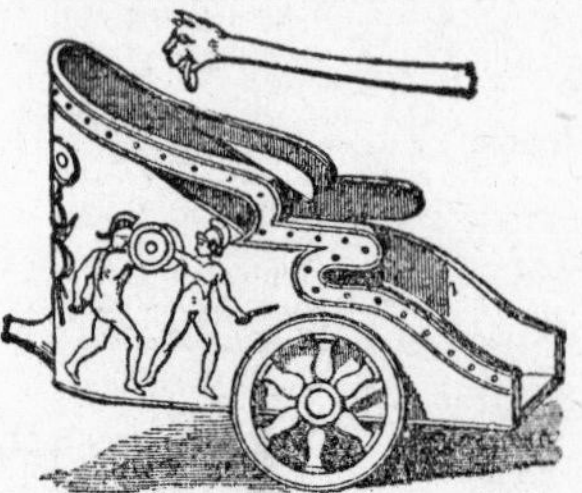

Grecian Chariot.

2. A car or vehicle, used formerly in war, drawn by two or more horses and conveying two men each. These vehicles were sometimes armed with hooks or scythes.

char′i-ŏt, *v.t.*; charioted, *pt.*, *pp.*; charioting, *ppr.* To convey in a chariot.

char″i-ŏt-ee′, *n.* A light, four-wheeled pleasure-carriage having two seats and a top.

char″i-ŏt-eer′, *n.* 1. The person who drives or conducts a chariot. It is used in speaking of military chariots, and those in the ancient games, but not of modern drivers.

2. [C—] In astronomy, a constellation in the northern hemisphere, and known also as *Auriga* and *Wagoner.*

char′i-ŏt-man, *n.* The driver of a chariot.

char′i-ŏt-rāce, *n.* A race with chariots; a sport in which chariots were driven in contest for a prize.

çhā′rịsm, çhā-rịṣ′mȧ, *n.*; *pl.* **çhā-rịṣ′mȧ-tȧ.** [Gr. *charisma*, a gift, from *charizesthai*, to favor, gratify; *charis*, favor, grace.] An extraordinary power, as of working miracles or speaking many tongues, etc., said to be possessed by some of the early Christians.

çhar-is-mat′iç, *a.* Pertaining to charism.

char′i-tȧ-ble, *a.* 1. Benevolent and kind; as, a *charitable* disposition.

2. Liberal in benefactions to the poor, and in relieving them in distress; as, a *charitable* man.

3. Pertaining to charity; springing from charity, or intended for charity; benevolent; as, a *charitable* institution; a *charitable* purpose.

4. Formed on charitable principles; favorable; dictated by kindness; as, a *charitable* construction of words or actions.

5. Liberal in judgment of others; given neither to severe criticism nor to evil construction of motives.

Syn.—Benevolent, generous, liberal, forgiving, benign, indulgent, lenient.

char′i-tȧ-ble-ness, *n.* 1. The disposition to be charitable, or the exercise of charity.

2. Liberality to the poor.

char′i-tȧ-bly, *adv.* Kindly; liberally; benevolently; with a disposition to help the poor; favorably.

char′i-ty, *n.* [OFr. *charite*, from L. *caritas* (*-atis*), dearness, affection, high regard, from *carus*, dear.]

1. In a general sense, love, benevolence, good-will; that disposition of heart which inclines men to think favorably of their fellow-men, and to do them good. In a theological sense, it includes supreme love to God, and universal good-will to men.

2. In a more particular sense, love, kindness, affection, tenderness, springing from natural relations; as, the *charities* of father, son, and brother.

3. Liberality to the poor, consisting in almsgiving or benefactions, or in gratuitous services to relieve them in distress.

4. Alms; whatever is bestowed gratuitously on the poor for their relief.

5. Liberality in gifts and services to promote public objects of a religious nature, as the founding and supporting of Bible societies, missionary societies, and the like.

6. Candor; liberality in judging of men and their actions; a disposition which inclines men to think and judge favorably, and to put the best construction on words and actions which the case will admit.

> The highest exercise of *charity* is *charity* toward the uncharitable.—Buckminster.

7. Any act of kindness or benevolence; as, the *charities* of life.

8. A charitable institution, especially for the relief of the helpless or unfortunate in mind or body.

9. [*pl.*] In law, grants or devises, which include relief of the poor and friendless, education, religious culture, and public institutions.

Sisters of Charity; in the Roman Catholic church, an order or society of women whose office is to attend the sick and poor.

Syn.—Alms, benevolence, good-will, kindness, liberality.

char′i-ty-sçhọol, *n.* A school maintained by voluntary contributions for educating poor children.

çhā-ri-vä′ri, *n.* [Fr.] A mock serenade of discordant noises made on kettles, tin horns, etc., designed to annoy and insult. It was at first directed against widows who married a second time, at an advanced age; but is now extended to unpopular persons of any age, and in some rural districts to any persons newly married.

chärk, *v.t.* [Abbrev. from *charcoal.*] To burn to a coal; to char. [Obs. See *Char.*]

chärk, *n.* A cinder. [Obs.]

çhär′lȧ-tăn, *n.* [Fr., from It. *ciarlatano*, a quack, from *ciarlare*, to prate.] One who prates much in his own favor, and makes unwarrantable pretensions; a quack; an empiric; a mountebank; an impostor.

çhär-lȧ-tan′iç, çhär-lȧ-tan′iç-ăl, *a.* Quackish; making undue pretensions; pertaining to a charlatan.

çhär-lȧ-tan′iç-ăl-ly, *adv.* After the manner of a charlatan.

çhär′lȧ-tăn-iṣm, *n.* [Fr. *charlatanisme.*] Charlatanry.

çhär′lȧ-tăn-ry, *n.* Undue pretensions to skill; quackery; wheedling; deception by fair words.

Chär′ley, Chär′lie (-li), *n.* 1. Familiar form of *Charles.*

2. An old English name for a night-watchman.

3. A short pointed beard.

4. A fox; a term used in fables, etc.

chär′lock, *n.* [ME. *carlok*; AS. *cerlic,* charlock.] The wild mustard, *Brassica Sinapistrum,* a troublesome weed which does much damage in grain-fields; also written *carlick.*

Jointed or *white charlock*; a noxious weed, *Raphanus Raphanistrum*; the wild radish.

çhär′lŏtte, *n.* [Fr.] A baked delicacy in the form of a light pudding.

Apple charlotte; slices of bread and butter and apple mixed with milk, sugar, etc., and baked.

Charlotte russe, charlotte à la russe; a delicacy consisting mainly of whipped cream inclosed in a cup of sponge-cake.

chärm, *n.* [Fr. *charme*; L. *carmen,* a song, poem, charm.]

1. A word, character, or other thing imagined to possess some occult or unintelligible power; hence, a magic power or spell; an enchantment; an incantation.

2. That which has power to subdue opposition, and gain the affections; that which can please irresistibly; that which delights and attracts the heart; a fascinating or alluring quality; in the plural, the beauties of a woman's form and face; as, she iufluenced many by her *charm.*

3. A song or melody. [Obs.]

4. Any object worn or carried in the hope of bringing good fortune, or averting evil; as, he wore a *charm* against seasickness.

5. An ornament worn on the person; as, a watch-chain and its *charm.*

Syn.—Spell, incantation, enchantment, fascination, attraction, allurement.

chärm, *v.t.*; charmed, *pt., pp.*; charming, *ppr.* 1. To subdue or control by incantation or secret influence; as, to *charm* a serpent.

2. To subdue by secret power, especially by that which pleases and delights the mind; to allay or appease; to soothe.

Music the fiercest grief can *charm.* —Pope.

3. To give exquisite pleasure to the mind or senses of; to fascinate; to enchant; to delight; as, we were *charmed* with the conversation.

4. To fortify with charms against evil.

5. To make powerful by charms.

6. To summon by incantation.

7. To tune or make music upon. [Obs.]

chärm, *v.i.* 1. To sound harmonically. [Obs.]

2. To use charms or practise magic.

3. To please; to attract; to act as a charm.

Syn.—Attract, bewitch, captivate, delight, enchant.

chärmed, *a.* Subdued or defended by charms; delighted; enchanted.

I bear a *charmed* life, which must not yield. —Shak.

chärm′ẽr, *n.* 1. One that charms or has power to charm; one that uses or has the power of enchantment; a magician.

2. One who delights and attracts the affections.

chärm′ẽr-ess, *n.* An enchantress. [Rare.]

çhär-meuse′ (mūz), *n.* [Fr.] A dull, soft, clinging satin.

chärm′fụl, *a.* Abounding with charms.

chärm′ing, *a.* Pleasing in the highest degree; delighting; fascinating; of attractive character and personality; as, a *charming* maid; a *charming* song.

Syn.—Delightful, amiable, lovely, pleasing.

chärm′ing-ly, *adv.* Delightfully; in a manner to charm, or to give delight.

She smiled very *charmingly.* —Addison.

chärm′ing-ness, *n.* The power to please.

chärm′less, *a.* Destitute of charms.

chär′nē-cō, chär′ni-cō, *n.* [Named from *Charneco,* a village near Lisbon.] A sort of sweet wine. [Obs.]

chär′nel, *a.* [OFr. *charnel, carnel*; LL. *carnale,* neut. of *carnalis,* of flesh; L. *caro, carnis,* flesh.] Containing flesh or carcasses; containing dead bodies; as, *charnel* vaults.

chär′nel, *n.* A charnel-house.

chär′nel-house, *n.* A place of sepulture; a mortuary; a tomb or vault; a cemetery; originally, a depository for the bones of the dead when removed from their graves for any purpose.

chär′ni-cō, *n.* See *Charneco.*

Chā′ron, *n.* [Gr. *Charōn.*]

1. In mythology, the son of Erebus and Nox,

Charon and Spirits of the Deceased.

whose office was to ferry the souls of the deceased over the Styx, a river of the infernal regions.

2. By humorous analogy, a ferryman.

chär′-ŏv″en, *n.* A furnace or kiln for burning turf to an ash.

çhär′pie (-pi), *n.* [Fr., pp. of *charpir,* to pick to pieces, from L. *carpere,* to seize.] In medicine, lint obtained from old linen used for dressing wounds.

chär′poy, *n.* [Hindu *chārpāi,* a couch.] A pallet or small bed used in India.

chär′quī (-kē), *n.* [Sp.] Jerked beef; beef cut into strips and dried in the sun.

chärr, *n.* See second *Char,* n.

chär′răs, *n.* Same as *Churrus.*

chär′ry, *a.* Pertaining to charcoal; like charcoal.

chärt, *n.* [Fr. *charte*; L. *charta,* a leaf of paper, a writing, tablet; Gr. *chartē,* a leaf of paper, layer of papyrus bark.]

1. A hydrographic or marine map; a draft or projection on paper of some part of the earth's surface, with the coasts, islands, rocks, banks, channels, or entrances into harbors, rivers, and bays, the points of compass, soundings or depth of water, etc., to regulate the courses of ships and aid navigation. The term *chart* is applied to a marine map; *map* is applied to a draft of some portion of land.

2. A sheet giving information or facts, usually in tabular form; as, a genealogical, historical, or statistical *chart.*

3. A charter or written deed. [Obs.]

Globular chart; a chart made on a globular projection.

Heliographic chart; a chart showing the sun and its spots.

Hydrographic chart; a marine chart used by navigators.

Mercator's chart; a chart made on the plan of projection adopted in the sixteenth century by the Flemish cartographer Mercator, in which the meridians and parallels of latitude are projected in straight lines.

Physical chart; a chart showing the physical geography of a section of the earth's surface.

Plane chart; a chart of some part of the earth's surface in which its globular form is not considered and the meridians and parallels are projected as straight lines.

Selenographic chart; a chart of the moon and its spots.

Topographic chart; a chart showing in detail the topographic features of a particular place or a district of limited size.

chärt, *v.t.*; charted, *pt., pp.*; charting, *ppr.* To map out in a chart; to delineate; as, to *chart* a part of the ocean; to *chart* a coast.

çhär′tȧ, *n.*; *pl.* **çhär′tæ.** [L.] 1. An instrument under which a grant is conveyed; a deed; a conveyance. [See *Magna Charta.*]

2. In law, a parchment or paper upon which documents, books, etc., are inscribed.

3. In medicine, the paper used in wrapping up powders.

Magna Charta; the great charter of the liberties of England, *Magna Charta Libertatum,* granted by King John at Runnymede, June 15, 1215. It is held to be the foundation of the personal and political liberties enjoyed by the English people. It provided that no freeman should be kept under arrest without proper trial, that he should not be convicted save by the judgment of his peers or in accordance with the law of the land, and that no taxes should be levied except by the common council of the kingdom. The term *Magna Charta* is now applied to any constitutional guarantee of personal rights or privileges.

çhär-tā′ceous, *a.* [L. *chartaceus,* from *charta,* a leaf of paper.] Resembling paper; having a paper-like texture; quite opaque, like most leaves.

Çharte, *n.* [Fr.] The constitution or fundamental law of the French monarchy, as established on the restoration of Louis XVIII., in 1814.

chär′tẽr, *n.* [ME. *chartre, chartere*; OFr. *chartre, cartre*; L. *chartula,* dim. of *charta,* a sheet of paper, a writing, tablet.]

1. An instrument, executed with due forms, given as evidence of a grant, contract, or whatever is done between man and man. In its more usual sense, it is the instrument of a grant conferring powers, rights, and privileges, as from a state or other sovereign power; the act of a legislature empowering a corporation to do business as a legal entity is called a *charter.*

2. Any instrument, executed with form and solemnity, bestowing rights or privileges, such as is issued by a grand lodge to subordinate lodges, in fraternal societies, etc.

3. Privilege; immunity; exemption.

My mother,
Who has a *charter* to extol her blood.—Shak.

4. The hiring or leasing, as of a vessel, by contract; also, the contract itself; as, the ship was under *charter* to proceed to Europe.

Charter member; an original member of an order, corporation, society, etc., particularly one having to do with organizing it; one whose name appears in the charter of an organization.

Charter oak; a historical oak-tree at Hartford, Conn., first used as a place of safe-keeping for the charter of the colony in 1687. The tree was destroyed by a gale in 1856.

Charter school; one of the free schools founded in Ireland in 1733, by the Protestants.

Great Charter; *Magna Charta*; see under *Charta.*

chär′tẽr, *v.t.*; chartered, *pt., pp.*; chartering, *ppr.* 1. To establish by charter.

2. To hire or let as a ship, by charter.

chär′tẽred, *a.* 1. Granted by charter; invested with privileges by charter; as, *chartered* rights; *chartered* power.

2. Hired or let, as a ship.

chär′tẽr-ẽr, *n.* One who charters; especially, one who charters a vessel.

Chär′tẽr-house, *n.* A noted public school and charitable institution established in London in 1611; founded in a building before used as a Carthusian monastery or *Chartreuse,* of which *Charterhouse* is considered a probable corruption, as those educated at the school are called *old Carthusians.*

Chär′tẽr-ist, *n.* Same as *Chartist.*

chär′tẽr-land, *n.* In old English law, land held by charter; freehold land.

chär′tẽr-pär″ty, *n.* An instrument of contract, between the owner of a vessel and a shipper of freight, etc., for the leasing of the vessel or a portion of it. The instrument was originally cut in two and half given to each of the contractors. The word *party* was originally the French *partie,* divided, whence the name.

Chärt′iṣm, *n.* [Fr. *charte,* a charter, and *-ism.*] In English history, the principles of a political party which stood for universal suffrage, the vote by ballot, annual parliaments, and other reforms.

Chärt′ist, *n.* One who upheld the principles of Chartism.

chärt′less, *a.* Without a chart; of which no chart has been made; vague; unknown; as, the *chartless* main.

çhär-tog′rȧ-phẽr, çär-tog′rȧ-phẽr, *n.* One skilled in the art or science of map-making.

çhär-tō-graph′iç, çär-tō-graph′iç, *a.* Pertaining to the making of maps.

çhär-tog′rȧ-phy, çär-tog′rȧ-phy, *n.* [LL. *carta*; L. *charta,* a map, and Gr. *-graphia,* from *graphein,* to write.] The art or science of map-making.

çhär′tō-man-cy, *n.* Same as *Cartomancy.*

çhär-tom′e-tẽr, *n.* [L. *charta,* a map, and *metrum,* a measure.] An instrument for computing distances on charts and maps.

Çhar-treuṣe′, *n.* [Fr.] 1. A monastery of Carthusians, especially the original house, *La Grande Chartreuse,* near Grenoble, France.

2. [c—] A liqueur or cordial made largely of Alpine nettles, at *La Grande Chartreuse.*

çhär′tū-lā-ry, çär′tū-lā-ry, *n.* [LL. *chartularium, cartularium,* from *chartula,* a charter, a record.] A monasterial room where a schedule of property is kept; the schedule itself or the official who keeps such record.

chär′wom″ăn (-woom″), *n.*; *pl.* **chär′wom″en** (-wim″). [ME. *char,* a chore, and *woman.*] A woman who is hired to do domestic work by the single day or by the piece.

chā′ry, *a.* [AS. *cearig,* careful; *cearu,* to care.] Careful; wary; frugal; saving.

Chȧ-ryb′dis, *n.* [L., from Gr. *Charybdis.*] A whirlpool on the coast of Sicily, opposite Scylla, on the Italian coast. [See *Scylla.*]

Between Scylla and Charybdis; figuratively, in a position of danger or difficulty; having dangers or difficulties on either hand.

chās′ȧ-ble, *a.* Capable of being chased; fit for hunting; also spelled *chaseable.*

chāse, *v.t.*; chased (chāst), *pt., pp.*; chasing, *ppr.* [ME. *chasen, chacen*; OFr. *chacier, cacier,* from L. *captare,* to strive to seize, from *capere,* to take.]

1. Literally, to drive, urge eagerly, press forward with vehemence; hence, to pursue for the

purpose of taking, as game; to hunt; as, to *chase* a deer.

2. To pursue or drive, as a defeated or flying enemy.

3. To follow or pursue, as an object of desire; to pursue for the purpose of overtaking; as, to *chase* a ship.

chase, *v.t.* [A contr. of *enchase.*]

1. To embellish by such means as embossing and cutting away.

2. To cut like a screw-thread.

chāse, *v.i.* To look for; to hunt; to follow; to hasten.

chāse, *n.* 1. Vehement pursuit; a running or driving after, as game in hunting.

2. Pursuit with an ardent desire to obtain, as pleasure, profit, or fame.

3. The act of chasing; the hunt; as, beasts of the *chase.*

4. That which is pursued or hunted; as, seek some other *chase.*

5. In law, a driving of cattle to or from a place.

6. In England, an open ground, or place of retreat for deer and other wild beasts; differing from a forest, which is not private property, and is invested with privileges, and from a park, which is inclosed.

7. In court-tennis, the place where a ball falls beyond which the player must strike his ball or lose a point.

Wild-goose chase; a fruitless errand; a mission with an indefinite or unattainable object.

chāse, *n.* [OFr. *chasse*, a frame, shrine, from *casse*, a box, chest, from L. *capsa*, a box, chest.

1. A strong rectangular iron frame, used by printers to impose and lock up type when set in columns or pages, and otherwise ready for electrotyping, stereotyping, or the press.

2. A wide groove or channel; a trench, as for the holding of a drain-tile.

3. The forward portion of a gun, from the trunnions to the swell of the muzzle.

4. A joint, as at the ends of a clinker-built boat, in which an overlapping joint merges into one that is flush.

chāse′ȧ-ble, *a.* See *Chasable.*

chāse′-gun, *n.* In a battleship, a gun used in chasing an enemy or in defending a ship when pursued.

chāse′-pōrt, *n.* The port of a chase-gun.

chās′ẽr, *n.* 1. One who chases; a pursuer; a driver; a hunter.

2. A term applied to guns at the head and stern of a vessel, for firing when in chase or being pursued; called also *chase-gun.*

3. A mild drink following a strong one. [Colloq.]

chās′ẽr, *n.* 1. One skilled in the art of enchasing or engraving.

2. A finishing-tool for screw-threads, having several points that bear on work revolving on a lathe.

chas′i-ble, *n.* See *Chasuble.*

Chas-i-dē′ăn, *n.* See *Assidean.*

chās′ing, *n.* The act or art of embossing on metals.

chasm, *n.* [L. *chasma*; Gr. *chasma*, a yawning hollow, gulf, from *chainein*, to yawn, to gape.]

1. A deep cleft; a fissure; a gap; properly, an opening made by disrupture, as a breach in the earth or a rock.

2. A void space; a vacuity; a gap.

Bloody chasm; an expression formerly much used in the United States in description of the Civil War.

Syn.—Abyss, gorge, depth, gulf, breach.

chas′mȧ, *n.* [Gr. *chasma*, from *chainein*, to yawn, gape.] In pathology, an abnormal spell of yawning.

chasmed, *a.* Having gaps or a chasm.

chas-mog′ȧ-my, *n.* [Gr. *chasma*, an opening, chasm, and *gamos*, marriage.] In botany, the opening of the perianth of a flower for the purpose of fertilization; opposed to *clistogamy.*

chas′my, *a.* Abounding with chasms. [Rare.]

chȧs-sé′ (-sā′), *n.* [Fr., from *chasse*, pp. of *chasser*, to chase.] A dancing movement, as a glide across to right or left.

chȧs-sé′ (-sā′), *v.i.*; chasséd, *pt.*, *pp.*; chasséing, *ppr.* To glide, as in a chassé; as, we *chasséd* right and left.

chȧsse (shȧs), *n.* [Fr., from *chasser*, to chase.] A light, spirituous drink, served after the coffee; called also *chasse-café.*

chas′se-las, *n.* [Named from the French village of *Chasselas*, where it is grown.] A white variety of fine table-grape.

chȧsse′-mȧ-rée′ (-rā′), *n.* [Fr., from *chasser*, to chase, and *marée*, tide.] A small sailing vessel used in the French coasting-trade; a lugger.

chȧsse′pōt (-pō), *n.* [Fr., named after the inventor, A. A. *Chassepot.*] A breech-loading needle-gun, or center-fire rifle, formerly used by the French, especially during the Franco-Prussian war of 1870-71.

chȧs-sēur′, *n.* [Fr., a huntsman, from *chasser*, to hunt, chase.]

1. In military affairs, one of a body of cavalry, light and active, trained for rapid movements.

2. A semi-military attendant upon Europeans of rank or wealth.

3. A hunter.

chas′sis, *n.* [Fr., from *chasse*, a frame.]

1. In ordnance, the movable base frame which conveys the carriage of a barbette- or casemate-gun back and forth.

2. The under framework of the automobile, on which the body is mounted, and the wheels and machinery.

3. The under framework of an aeroplane, to which the motor is attached, usually fitted with wheels to run along the ground when starting or landing.

chāste, *v.t.* To chasten. [Obs.]

chāste, *a.* [OFr. *chaste*, *caste*, from L. *castus*, pure, chaste; Gr. *katharos*, pure.]

1. Pure from all unlawful sexual intercourse; true to the marriage vows.

2. Free from obscenity; pure in thought and act; innocent; modest.

3. Unmarried. [Obs.]

4. In literature, architecture, or the arts, indicative of simplicity and refinement; free from vulgarisms, affectations, or extravagancies; as, a *chaste* essay; the building or the statue was *chaste* in design.

Syn.—Immaculate, incorrupt, modest, pure, simple, unaffected, uncontaminated, undefiled, virtuous.

chāste′-eyed (-īd), *a.* Having modest eyes.

chāste′ly, *adv.* In a chaste manner; without obscenity; purely; without barbarisms or unnatural phrases.

chās′ten (chās′n), *v.t.*; chastened, *pt.*, *pp.*; chastening, *ppr.* [ME. *chastien*; OFr. *chastier*, from L. *castigare*, to punish, chastise; *castus*, pure, and *agere*, to lead, drive.]

1. To correct by punishment; to punish; to inflict pain upon, in order to reclaim; to discipline; as, to *chasten* a son with a rod.

2. To afflict by other means.

3. To purify from errors or faults.

Syn.—Chastise, discipline, correct, punish, purify.

chās′tened (chās′nd), *a.* Corrected; punished; afflicted for correction; purified from faults.

chās′ten-ẽr, *n.* One who punishes for the purpose of correction.

chāste′ness, *n.* 1. Chastity; purity.

2. Specifically, in literature and the arts, freedom from vulgarisms, extravagancies, and mannerisms; the quality of being both simple and refined.

chās′ten-ing, *n.* Correction; suffering inflicted for the purpose of reclaiming.

chāste′-tree, *n.* The agnus castus, or *Vitex*; a Mediterranean tree that grows to the height of eight or ten feet, whose aromatic properties were said to be productive of chastity.

chas-tiṣ′ȧ-ble, *a.* Deserving of chastisement.

chas-tiṣe′, *v.t.*; chastised, *pt.*, *pp.*; chastising, *ppr.* [ME. *chastisen*, an extended form of *chastien*, to chasten, punish.]

1. To correct by punishing; to punish; to inflict pain upon, by blows or otherwise, for the purpose of punishing an offender and recalling him to his duty.

2. To reduce to order or obedience; to restrain; to awe; to repress.

3. To correct; to purify by expunging faults; as, to *chastise* a poem.

Syn.—Punish, chasten, afflict, correct, discipline.—*Punish* and *chastise* differ in the object aimed at. The former is designed to uphold law by the infliction of penalty; the latter to prevent the repetition of faults and reclaim the offender.

chas′tiṣe-ment, *n.* Correction; punishment; pain inflicted for punishment and correction, either by stripes or otherwise; as, he suffered *chastisement* for his sins.

chas-tiṣ′ẽr, *n.* One who chastises; a punisher; a corrector.

chas′ti-ty, *n.* [ME. *chastite*, *chastete*; OFr. *chastete*, *chasteit*; L. *castitas* (*-atis*), from *castus*, chaste, pure.]

1. Purity of the body; freedom from all unlawful commerce of sexes.

2. Freedom from obscenity, as in language or conversation.

3. Freedom from bad mixture; purity in words and phrases; simple refinement of design.

4. Purity; unadulterated state; as the *chastity* of the gospel.

5. Celibacy. [Obs.]

chas′ū-ble, *n.* [OFr. *chasuble*; LL. *casubula*, *casubla*, *casula*, a hooded garment; from L. *casa*, a hut, cottage.] In the Roman Catholic and Greek churches, an outward vestment worn by the priest in saying mass, having a large embroidered or gilt cross on the back, and a pillar in front, designed to be emblematical of Christ's sufferings. It consists of two pieces, front and back, hanging low and connected at the shoulders only; also written *chasible*, or *chesible.*

chat, *v.i.*; chatted, *pt.*, *pp.*; **chatting**, *ppr.* [Shortened from *chatter.*]

1. To talk in a familiar manner; to talk without form or ceremony.

2. To talk idly; to prate.

chat, *v.t.* To talk of. [Obs.]

chat, *n.* 1. Free, familiar talk; informal conversation; idle talk; gossip.

2. A bird of the genus *Icteria*, related to the warblers, the best known varieties being the yellow-breasted chat, a fluent songster common in the United States, and the long-tailed chat. The name is also applied to several European birds of the family *Saxicolidæ*, including the stonechat, whinchat, and wheatear.

A, Ancient form of Chasuble: 1. Apparel of the neck. 2 2 2 2. Chasuble. 3 3. Orphreys of the Chasuble. 4. The stole. 5 5. The alb. 6. Apparel of the alb. 7. The maniple.
B, Modern form of Chasuble.

chat, *n.* 1. A twig or little stick; also called a *chit.*

2. [*pl.*] Poor ore freely mixed with small stones.

3. A little potato. [Colloq.]

chȧ-teau′ (-tō′), *n.*; *pl.* **chȧ-teaux′** (-tōz′). [Fr., from OFr. *chastel*, *castel*, from L. *castellum*, a castle.]

1. In France, a castle or a fortress.

2. Generally, any manor-house, imposing country residence, or royal residence outside a city; specifically, in France, a country residence.

Chateau en Espagne; a castle in Spain; figuratively, a castle in the air, Spain being regarded as the country of romance.

chat′e-lāine, *n.* [Fr. *chatelaine*, a wife of a castellan, a chatelaine chain, f. of *chatelain*; LL. *castellanus*, a keeper of a castle, from L. *castellum*, a castle.] A brooch or clasp fastened at a lady's waist upon which are hung various articles, both ornamental and useful; used also adjectively; as, a *chatelaine* bag.

chat′e-let, *n.* See *Castellet.*

chat′el-lā-ny, *n.* See *Castellany.*

chȧ-tī′, *n.* [S. Am.] A wildcat, *Felis mitis*, or tiger-cat, of South America, small and spotted.

chȧ-toy′ăn-cy, *n.* The condition or quality of being chatoyant.

chȧ-toy′ănt, *a.* [Fr. *chatoyant*, ppr. of *chatoyer*, to change luster like the eye of a cat; *chat*, a cat.] Having a changeable, undulating luster or color, like that of a cat's eye in the dark.

chȧ-toy′ănt, *n.* A hard stone, which, being cut smooth, presents on its surface and in the interior an undulating or wavy light.

chȧ-toy′ment, *n.* Changeableness of color, in a mineral; play of colors, as in a cat's eyes.

chat′täh, *n.* [Anglo-Ind.] In India, an umbrella.

chat′tel (chat′l), *n.* [ME. *chatel*; OFr. *chatel*; LL. *captale*, *capitale*, capital, property, goods; neut. of L. *capitalis*, chief, head, from *caput* (*-itis*), head.] Primarily, any article of movable goods. In modern usage, the word chattels comprehends all goods, movable or immovable, except such as have the nature of freehold. Chattels are real or personal, the term being more comprehensive than either goods or effects.

Chattel mortgage; a mortgage on personal property, as distinguished from one on real estate.

Chattel personal; movable property in general.

Chattel real or *interest*; a limited leasehold in real estate, although in some portions of the United States the ninety-nine-year leasehold, renewable at pleasure, is excluded from this classification.

chat′tel-iṣm, *n.* The condition of holding chattels or of being a chattel.

chat′tẽr, *v.i.*; chattered, *pt.*, *pp.*; chattering, *ppr.* [Imitative in origin.]

1. To utter sounds rapidly and indistinctly, as a magpie or a monkey.

2. To make a noise by collision of the teeth: as, the teeth *chatter* when one is chilly.

3. To talk idly, carelessly, or rapidly.

4. In machinery, to make a chattering noise, as a cutting tool or a wide scraping tool when

not held with sufficient firmness, or when the tool itself is too flexible.

chat′tēr, *v.t.* To utter, as rapid indistinct sounds; as, to *chatter* nonsense; to gibber; to jabber, as birds or monkeys.

chat′tēr, *n.* 1. Sounds like those of a magpie or monkey; idle talk.

2. Noise made by clicking the teeth together.

chat-tēr-ā′tion, *n.* The act of habitual or excessive chattering. [Colloq.]

chat′tēr-box, *n.* One who talks incessantly.

chat′tēr-ēr, *n.* 1. A prater; an idle talker.

2. A name given to some species of dentirostral birds, from their loud and monotonous notes; especially, the waxwing.

chat′tēr-ing, *n.* Rapid, inarticulate sounds, as of birds; idle talk; rapid striking of the teeth, as in chilliness.

chat′ter-mark, *n.* 1. One of the fine undulations formed on the surface of work by a cutting tool which chatters.

2. (*Geol.*) A short crack on the surface of rock planed smooth by a glacier.

chat′=thrush, *n.* An Oriental bird, especially of India, related to the starling family and possessing the imitative qualities of the magpie; called also *mina* or *mino.*

chat′ti-ness, *n.* The disposition to talk lightly and agreeably; the act of so doing.

chat′ty, *a.* Given to free conversation; talkative.

chat′ty, *n.* [Anglo-Ind.] A porous earthen pot or jar for cooling water by evaporation; used in the East Indies.

chat′wood, *n.* Little sticks for fuel.

ċhaud′=med″ley (shōd′-), *n.* [Fr. *chaud-mêlée;* *chaud,* hot, and *mêler, medler,* to mingle.] Unpremeditated homicide committed in passion but not in self-defense; when committed in self-defense, it is known as *chance-medley.*

ċhau′drŏn, ċhal′drŏn, *n.* Entrails. [Obs.]

ċhauf′fēr, *n.* [Fr. *chauffer,* to heat.] In chemistry, a small furnace, a cylindrical box of sheet iron, open at the top, with a grate near the bottom.

ċhauf-fēur′ (shō-fēr′), *n.* [Fr. *chauffeur,* a stoker, from *chauffer,* to heat, get up steam.] A professional expert in the management of an automobile.

ċhauf′feuse (shō′fös,) *n.* [Fr.] A female chauffeur.

ċhaul-mū′grȧ, ċhaul-mau′grȧ, *n.* [E. Ind.] A tree of the East Indies belonging to the Indian plum family; it yields a large succulent fruit, from the seeds of which a medicinal oil is obtained that is used in the treatment of leprosy and other skin diseases.

ċhau-mon-telle′ (shō-), *n.* [Fr.] A sort of pear.

chaun, *n.* A gap. [Obs.]

chaun, *v.i.* To open; to yawn. [Obs.]

chaunt, *n.* and *v.* See *Chant.*

chaunt′ēr, *n.* See *Chanter.*

ċhā′us, *n.* An animal of Asia and Africa like a lynx; called also the *jungle-cat.*

ċhaus-sé′ (shō-sā′), *a.* [Fr.] A heraldic term, which, in the common acceptation, signifies *shod,* and in blazon denotes a section in base.

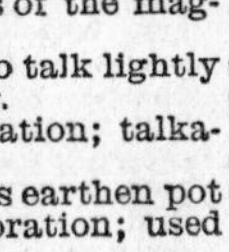

A Wreath, the Base Chaussé.

ċhaus′ses (shō′ses, *or, Fr. pron.,* shōs), *n.pl.* [Fr.] Trousers covering the hips, legs, and feet, worn in Europe in medieval conflicts; also, flexible armor for the same parts.

ċhau′vin-iṣm (shō′), *n.* [Fr. *chauvinisme,* from Nicolas *Chauvin,* a soldier of Napoleon I., who, in 1815, acquired much notoriety by his grotesque and threatening displays of attachment to the fallen Napoleon and the imperial cause.] Absurd, unreasoning, and vainglorious patriotism; the quality of being wildly extravagant, demonstrative, and often childish and silly, in regard to national glory and honor; blind devotion to a fallen leader or an obsolete cause.

ċhau′vin-ist (shō′), *n.* A ranter on the subject of patriotism.

ċhau-vin-is′tic (shō-), *a.* Pertaining to the qualities of chauvinism.

chav′en-dēr, *n.* [Fr. *chevin;* OFr. *chevesne,* a chub.] A species of short, thick carp; also called *chub* or *cheven.*

ċhav′i-ċhȧ, *n.* A name given the Columbia salmon by the Alaskan Indians.

chaw, *v.t.*; chawed, *pt., pp.*; chawing, *ppr.* [A variant of *chew.*]

1. To grind with the teeth; to masticate, as food in eating; to ruminate, or to chew, as the cud. [Vulgar.]

2. To ruminate in thought; to revolve and consider. [Obs.]

chaw, *n.* A cud, as of tobacco; as much as is put in the mouth at once. [Vulgar.]

chaw′=bā″cŏn, *n.* A country bumpkin; a lout; an uncouth rustic. [Colloq. Eng.]

chaw′=tooth, *n.* A molar or grinder. [Vulgar.]

chāy′=root, *n.* [Tamil *chaya,* a root, and *root.*] The root of the *Oldenlandia umbellata,* used in giving the beautiful red to the Madras cottons; also called *shaya-root, chaya-root,* and *choy-root.*

chēap, *a.*; *comp.* cheaper; *superl.* cheapest. [Shortened from *good cheap,* good bargain.]

1. Having a low price in market; capable of being purchased at a low price; that is, at a price at low or lower than the usual price of the article or commodity, or at a price less than the real value.

2. Being of small value; common; not respected; as, *cheap* beauty.

Syn.—Common, inexpensive, uncostly, mean, vile, worthless, low-priced.

chēap, *n.* [ME. *cheep, cheap;* AS. *ceáp,* trade, traffic, price, cattle.] Bargain; purchase; as in the phrases good *cheap,* better *cheap.* [Obs.]

chēap, *adv.* In a cheap manner; cheaply. [Obs.]

chēap, *v.i.* To bargain. [Obs.]

chēap′en, *v.t.*; cheapened, *pt., pp.*; cheapening, *ppr.* [ME. *cheapien, chepen;* AS. *ceápian,* to trade, buy.]

1. To attempt to buy; to ask the price of (a commodity); to chaffer. [Obs.]

2. To lessen the value of; to make common.

chēap′en-ēr, *n.* One who cheapens or bargains.

chēap′=jack, chēap′=john, *n.* One who hawks or sells cheap goods on the streets; also, one who ostensibly fixes a price and gradually reduces it to effect a sale.

chēap′ly, *adv.* At a small price; at a low rate.

chēap′ness, *n.* Lowness in price, considering the usual price or real value.

chēar, *n.* and *v.* An obsolete form of *cheer.*

chēat, *v.t.*; cheated, *pt., pp.*; cheating, *ppr.* [ME. *cheten,* to confiscate, seize; a contr. of *escheten,* escheat.]

1. To deceive and defraud in a bargain; to deceive for the purpose of gain in selling.

2. To impose on; to trick. It is followed by *of* or *out of,* and colloquially by *into;* as, to *cheat* a child *into* a belief that a medicine is palatable.

Syn.—Defraud, trick, fleece, delude, cozen, juggle, overreach, swindle, dupe, beguile, deceive, deprive, hoodwink, prevaricate, gull, dissemble, shuffle, inveigle.—One *cheats* by direct and gross falsehood or artifice; one *defrauds* by a settled plan or contrivance; one *tricks* by a sudden invention.

chēat, *v.i.* To practise trickery or fraud; to act dishonestly; as, to *cheat* in business or at cards.

chēat, *n.* 1. A fraud committed by deception; a trick; imposition; imposture.

2. A person who cheats; one guilty of fraud by deceitful practices.

3. A weedy grass which grows among grain; also called *chess.*

4. In law, the obtaining of another's property by intentional and persistent misrepresentation.

Syn.—Artifice, deception, imposture, chicanery, swindle, deceit, fraud, delusion, trick, imposition, guile, stratagem.

chēat′ȧ-ble, *a.* Liable to be defrauded.

chēat′ȧ-ble-ness, *n.* Liability of being cheated.

chēat′=bread (-bred), *n.* English wheaten bread next in grade to the finest, the latter being called *manchet.*

chēat′ēr, *n.* 1. One who practises a fraud in commerce.

2. An escheater. [Rare.]

chēat′ing, *a.* Defrauding by deception; imposing on.

chēat′ing, *n.* The act of defrauding by deceitful arts.

chēat′ing-ly, *adv.* In a cheating manner.

Chē-bag′cō=boat, *n.* [From *Chebacco,* a river in Massachusetts, where such vessels were built.] A two-masted boat, with a broad bow and a narrow stern, formerly used in the Newfoundland cod and mackerel fisheries; also called *pinkstern, pinkie,* and *chebec.*

chē-bec′, *n.* [Imitative word.] The least flycatcher, a small American bird, *Empidonax minimus.*

check, *v.t.*; checked, *pt., pp.*; checking, *ppr.*

1. To stop; to restrain; to hinder or repress; to curb; to moderate.

2. To rebuke; to chide or reprove.

3. To compare (any paper) with its counterpart or with a cipher, with a view to ascertain its authenticity; to control by a counter-register.

4. To mark, as names in going over a list.

5. In seamanship, to ease off (a little of a rope, which is too stiffly extended); also, to stopper (the cable).

6. To make cracks in; to cause to crack; as, heat *checks* timber.

Syn.—Control, curb, inhibit, govern, rebuke, repress, reprove, restrain, stop.

check, *v.i.* 1. To stop; to make a stop; with *at.*

The mind *checks at* any vigorous undertaking.
—Locke.

2. To clash or interfere. [Rare.]

3. To strike with repression. [Rare.]

4. To crack, as wood subjected to heat, or varnish in drying.

5. In falconry, to turn or to abandon the chase of proper game for other birds that cross the course; said of a hawk.

check, *n.* [ME. *chek, chekke;* OFr. *eschek, eschec, eschac,* a check at chess, repulse, defeat; from Per. *shāh,* king, the principal piece in a game of chess.]

1. A stop; hindrance; rebuff; sudden restraint, or continued restraint; curb; control; government.

2. That which stops or restrains, as reproof, reprimand, rebuke, slight, or disgust, fear, apprehension, a person; any stop or obstruction.

3. A mark put against names in going over a list.

4. A ticket or token given, (a) on railroads, to identify the claimant of baggage; (b) in places of amusement, to identify those who wish to leave temporarily; (c) at restaurants, to indicate the cost of the meal.

5. In falconry, the forsaking by a hawk of her proper game, to follow rooks, pies, or other fowls that cross her flight.

6. The correspondent cipher of a bank note; a corresponding indenture; any counter-register.

7. An order for money, drawn on a banker or on the cashier of a bank, payable to a person named, or his order, or to bearer.

8. A term in chess, when one party obliges the other either to move or guard his king.

9. In popular use, checkered cloth; a checkerboard square.

Certified check; see *Certify.*

Clerk of the check; (a) an official of Great Britain who controls and has a checking register of the members of the royal household; (b) a similar official who superintends those connected with the royal navy at the port where he is stationed.

To take check; to be hurt; to take offense.

check, *a.* Patterned in squares; checkered.

check′āġe, *n.* The act of checking, as an item in a catalogue.

check′=book, *n.* A book formed of a number of blank checks, each attached to a stub on which a record may be kept.

check′ēr, *v.t.*; checkered, *pt., pp.*; checkering, *ppr.* 1. To variegate with cross lines; to form into little squares, like a chess-board, by lines or stripes of different colors.

2. To diversify; to variegate with different qualities, scenes, or events; to subject (one) to sudden reversals of fortune; as, later events sadly *checkered* his career.

check′ēr, *n.* 1. One who checks or restrains; a rebuker.

2. A chess-board; a checker-board.

3. Work varied alternately as to its colors or materials; work consisting of cross lines.

4. A design in checks, or a single check.

5. One of the pieces used in playing the game of checkers or draughts; also spelled *chequer.*

check′ēr-ber″ry, *n.* The wintergreen plant, *Gaultheria procumbens,* and its fruit.

check′ēr=bōard, *n.* A board on which the game of checkers or draughts is played. It is laid out in sixty-four squares of alternate colors.

check′ēred, *a.* 1. Diversified; variegated in a marked manner.

2. Patterned in alternate squares of color or material.

check′ērṣ, *n.pl.* Draughts; a common game on a checkered board. It is played by two persons, each having twelve men, or *checkers,* which are moved diagonally across the squares, the object of each player being to take all his opponent's men or force them into a position where they cannot be moved without being taken.

check′ēr-wŏrk, *n.* 1. Any article exhibiting different colors, alternating and arranged in squares.

2. A condition or situation presenting diversified features, especially relating to misfortunes.

check′=hook, *n.* 1. A hook on the saddle of a horse's harness over which the checkrein is caught.

2. A device on a hoisting-machine calculated to check too high speed.

check′lȧ-tŏun, *n.* Same as *Ciclaton.*

check′less, *a.* That cannot be checked or restrained.

check′=list, *n.* A list or catalogue used for verifying or checking.

check′māte, *n.* 1. The movement in the game of chess, which stops all further moving, and ends the game.

2. Figuratively, defeat; overthrow.

check′māte, *v.t.*; checkmated, *pt., pp.*; checkmating, *ppr.* To make a move, in chess, which stops all further moving of (the opponent); hence, to arrest and defeat.

check′=nut, *n.* In mechanics, a nut which screws down upon the primary nut to secure it; called also a *lock-nut.*

check′rein, *n.* 1. A strap looped around the check-hook to prevent a horse from lowering his head; also called *bearing-rein.*

2. A rein or line which connects the

driving-rein of one horse of a double team with the bit of the other.

check′rōll, *n.* A list of employes in a palace or household.

check′string, *n.* A cord by which a person in a conveyance may signal to the driver or person in charge.

check′=valve, *n.* A valve placed in the feed-pipe of the boiler for preventing the return of the feed-water.

check′y, *a.* Arranged in checker-like form. In heraldry, applied to the checker-like design of the border or field of an armorial bearing.

Checky Field.

cheek, *n.* [ME. *cheke*, *cheoke*, *choke*; AS. *ceace*, *ceoce*, the cheek; L.G. *koek*; D. *kaak*, cheek, jaw.]

1. The side of the face below the eyes on each side.

2. [*pl.*] In mechanics, those pieces of a machine which form corresponding sides, or which are double and alike; as, the *cheeks* of a printing-press; the *cheeks* of a turner's lathe.

3. In founding, one of the side parts of a flask consisting of more than two parts.

4. A branch of a horse's bit.

5. Brazen impudence; cool self-possession. [Slang.]

6. Portion; share; allowance. [Colloq.]

I have drunk to my own *cheek* above two quarts between dinner and breakfast.
—Trollope.

Butment cheek; see *Butment-cheek*.

Cheek by jowl; extremely intimate.

cheek, *v.t.* 1. To assail with impudent or insulting language; also, to face; to confront in a bold or impudent manner. [Slang.]

What does he come here *cheeking* us for?
—Dickens.

2. To bring up to the cheek. [Obs.]

His pike *cheek'd*, to guard the tun
He must not taste. —Cotton.

cheek′=bōne, *n.* The bone of the cheek.

cheeked, *a.* With cheeks; used in compound forms; as, red-*cheeked* apples.

cheek′=pouch, *n.* A bag situated in the cheek of a monkey, by means of which it is enabled to stow away and carry off food for future consumption.

cheek′=tooth, *n.* A molar tooth or grinder.

cheek′y, *a.* Presumptuous; self-confident. [Colloq.]

cheep, *v.i.*; cheeped, *pt.*, *pp.*; cheeping, *ppr.* To chirp as a bird.

cheep, *v.t.* To utter in a chirping or puling tone; to pipe.

cheep, *n.* A squeak, as of a mouse; a chirp; a creak.

Come, screw the pegs in tunefu' *cheep*.
—Burns.

cheer, *v.i.*; cheered, *pt.*, *pp.*; cheering, *ppr.* 1. To grow cheerful; to become gladsome or joyous.

At sight of thee my gloomy soul *cheers* up.
—Phillips.

2. To utter a cheer or shout of acclamation or joy.

3. To fare; to prosper; to be influenced. [Obs.]

cheer, *v.t.* 1. To salute with shouts of joy, cheers, stamping or other expressions of approval.

2. To dispel gloom, sorrow, or apathy from; to cause to rejoice; to gladden; to make cheerful; as, to *cheer* a lonely desert; to *cheer* the heart.

3. To infuse spirit or animation in; to incite; to encourage; as, to *cheer* the hounds.

Syn.—Inspire, encourage, comfort.

cheer, *n.* [ME. *chere*, the face, look, demeanor, welcome; OFr. *chere*, *chiere*, from LL. *cara*, the face; Gr. *kara*, the head; Sans. *ciras*, the head.]

1. A shout of joy; as, they gave three *cheers*; also stamping, or other expressions of applause.

2. A state of gladness or joy; a state of animation; mirth; gaiety; jollity.

3. Entertainment; that which makes cheerful; provisions for a feast.

The table was loaded with good *cheer*.
—Irving.

4. The air of the countenance, noting a greater or less degree of cheerfulness. [Obs.]

His words their drooping *cheer*
Enlightened. —Milton.

Syn.—Hope, happiness, comfort, hospitality, plenty, conviviality.

cheer′ẽr, *n.* One who cheers; he or that which gladdens.

cheer′fụl, *a.* Animated; having good spirits; full of life; gay; joyful.

Syn.—Lively, gay, bright, happy, bonny, merry, joyful, pleasant, buoyant, sunny, enlivening, sprightly, blithe, joyous.

cheer′fụl-ly, *adv.* In a cheerful manner.

cheer′fụl-ness, *n.* Life; animation; good spirits; a state of moderate joy or gaiety; alacrity.

Syn.—Gaiety, mirth, merriment, blithesomeness, gladness, jollity, liveliness, sprightliness, vivacity.—*Cheerfulness* is a habit of mind; *gaiety* is an occasional excitement of animal spirits; *mirth* or *merriment* are noisy gaiety.

cheer′i-ly, *adv.* With cheerfulness; with spirit.

cheer′i-ness, *n.* Cheerfulness.

cheer′ing-ly, *adv.* In a cheerful manner.

cheer′ish-ness, *n.* State of cheerfulness. [Rare.]

cheer′less, *a.* Without joy, gladness, or comfort; gloomy; destitute of anything to enliven or animate the spirits.

cheer′less-ly, *adv.* In a cheerless manner.

cheer′less-ness, *n.* State of being destitute of cheerfulness or comfort.

cheer′ly, *a.* Gay; cheerful; not gloomy. [Obs.]

cheer′ly, *adv.* Cheerfully; briskly. [Obs.]

cheer′y, *a.* Gay; sprightly; having power to make gay.

cheeṣe, *n.* [ME. *chese*; AS. *cese*, *cysa*; LL. *casius*; L. *caseus*, cheese.] 1. The curd of milk, coagulated usually by rennet, separated from the serum or whey, and pressed in a vat, hoop, or mold. It consists of casein, together with water, fat, and a small per cent of mineral matter. Soft or cream cheese does not keep long in any temperature, but hard cheese may be kept for a considerable time. There are numerous varieties of cheese, in many cases receiving their names from the place of their original manufacture.

2. A mass of pomace or ground apples placed on a press.

3. The unripe fruit of dwarf mallow, somewhat resembling a cheese. [Colloq.]

4. A low bow, in which the skirts are inflated and assume the shape of a cheese, as the bower sinks toward the floor.

American cheese; a rich, rather strong cheese made in large molds, and of varying shades of yellow, according to the amount of coloring matter added.

Brickbat cheese; an English cheese made from new milk and pressed into a form like a brick.

Brie cheese; a rich cream cheese, salted, made in Brie, France.

Camembert cheese; a finely flavored cream cheese of a pale yellow color, made in the Norman village from which the name is derived.

Cheddar cheese; a large, rich cheese, originally made in Cheddar, England, but now imitated in the United States.

Cottage cheese; pressed curds, into which cream is worked, without rennet. It is variously called *Dutch cheese*, *pot-cheese*, and *smeer-kaas*.

Cream cheese; a soft cheese made of unskimmed milk, with or without the addition of cream.

Double-cream cheese; cheese from a certain quantity of unskimmed milk with the addition of cream from a like quantity of milk.

Dunlop cheese; a soft cheese similar to single Gloucester, made in Ayrshire, Scotland.

Dutch cheese; (a) a hard cheese made from skimmed milk pressed into round molds the size of the head and smaller, the outside being colored a reddish tint with a preparation of madder; (b) same as *Cottage cheese*.

Edam cheese; a hard, mild cheese made in Holland.

Filled cheese, a kind of cheese made from skim-milk; so called because a fatty filling, as lard or oleomargarin, is used as a substitute for the cream.

Gloucester cheese; a rich English cheese of mild flavor. It is called *double* or *single Gloucester*, as there is more or less cream in its composition.

Gruyère cheese; a cheese made in France and Switzerland, intermediate between hard and soft, yellow, and of an open structure; takes its name from Gruyère, Switzerland.

Limburger cheese; a soft cheese originally made near Limburg, Belgium, and now in the United States. It is kept until putrefaction begins, hence its strong odor and taste.

Lincolnshire cheese; an English cheese made in small molds from new milk and cream.

Neufchâtel cheese; a delicate cream cheese made in small molds at Neufchâtel-en-Bray, France.

Parmesan cheese; a hard, dry cheese of delicate flavor, and colored with saffron. It is made in Italy.

Pineapple cheese; a hard, deep yellow cheese of strong taste molded in the form of a pineapple.

Pont l'Evêque cheese; a cream cheese, similar to Neufchâtel, made in Normandy, near Pont l'Evêque.

Roquefort cheese; a hard cheese made at Roquefort, in Guienne, France, from ewes' milk. When the cheeses are somewhat solid and dry they are placed in caves in which the temperature remains at 40° F. Here they take on a reddish color, and when they have reached the proper tint, are ready for use.

Sage or *green cheese*; cheese to which have been added leaves of the sage to impart a green color and a delicate flavor.

Slipcoat cheese; a rich cheese made from milk while it still retains its natural warmth. It is soft and resembles uncolored butter.

Stilton cheese; a rich, double-cream cheese, of strong taste, originally made at Stilton, England.

cheeṣe′=cāke, *n.* 1. A cake filled with a jelly made of soft curds, sugar, and butter.

2. A small cake made in various ways and with a variety of different ingredients; as, lemon *cheese-cake*, orange *cheese-cake*, apple *cheese-cake*, etc.

cheeṣe′=clọth, *n.* A thin cotton cloth used for wrapping cheese, and many other purposes, such as draperies, women's dresses, etc.

cheeṣe′=flȳ, *n.* A small black dipterous insect bred in cheese, the *Piophila casei*, of the family *Muscidæ*, the same to which the house-fly, blow-fly, etc., belong. It has a very extensible ovipositor, which it can sink to a great depth in the cracks of cheese, laying its eggs therein. The maggot, well known as the *cheese-hopper*, is furnished with two horny claw-shaped mandibles, which it uses both for digging into the cheese and for moving itself, having no feet.

Cheese-hopper (*Piophila casei*). *a*, Maggot extended. *b*, *c*, In leaping position. *d*, *e*, Fly (nat. size).

cheeṣe′=hop″pẽr, *n.* See *Cheese-fly*.

cheeṣe′lep, *n.* [AS. *cyslybb*, rennet.] Rennet; also a bag in which it is kept.

cheeṣe′=mīte, *n.* A mite or arachnidan of the group *Acarida*, which infests cheese. It is also found in flour, and called the *flour-mite*, and in milk, when it is called the *milk-mite*.

cheeṣe′mŏn″gẽr, *n.* One who deals in or sells cheese.

cheeṣe′pār″ing, *a.* and *n.* I. *a.* Meanly economical; parsimonious; as, a *cheeseparing* policy.

II. *n.* A paring of the rind of cheese; figuratively, parsimony.

cheeṣe′=press, *n.* A press or apparatus for pressing curd in the making of cheese.

cheeṣe′=ren″net, *n.* A name given to the yellow lady's-bedstraw, *Galium verum*, used for coagulating milk.

cheeṣe′=vat, *n.* The vat or case in which curds are confined for pressing.

cheeṣ′i-ness, *n.* The quality of being cheesy or resembling cheese in consistency.

cheeṣ′y, *a.* Having the nature, qualities, taste, odor, or form of cheese; resembling cheese in any respect; caseous; as, a *cheesy* substance.

chee′tȧ, chee′tȧh, *n.* See *Chetah*.

chee′tạl, *n.* [Hind. *chītal*.] The spotted or axis deer of India.

çhef, *n.* [Fr.] A head or chief; particularly, a head cook.

çhef=d'œuvre′ (shā-dûvr′), *n.*; *pl.* **çhefs=d'œuvre′** (shā-). [Fr.] A masterpiece, as in art, literature, etc.

cheg′ōe, *n.* Same as *Chigoe*.

Chei-lan′thēṣ, *n.* [Gr. *cheilos*, a lip, and *anthos*, a flower, so called from the form of the indusium.] A genus of polypodiaceous ferns, distinguished by the small sori at the ends of the free veins, and covered by the bent-over margin of the frond.

çheir, *n.* An abbreviated form of *Cheiranthus*. The wild *cheir* is the wallflower.

Chei-ran′thus, *n.* [Gr. *cheir*, the hand, and *anthos*, a flower.] A genus of plants, natural order *Cruciferæ*, consisting of pubescent herbs or small shrubs with large yellow or purple sweet-scented flowers. The wallflower, *Cheiranthus cheiri*, is the best known species.

chek′mak, *n.* A Turkish silk and cotton fabric.

çhē′lȧ, *n.*; *pl.* **çhē′læ**. [Hind. *chelā*, a pupil, a disciple, a slave.] A pupil; a disciple; especially, a Buddhist novice.

çhē′lȧ, *n.*; *pl.* **çhē′læ**. [Gr. *chēlē*, a claw.] One of the prehensile claws with which some of the limbs are terminated in certain crustaceans, as the crab, lobster, etc.

çhē′lāte, *a.* Having a claw like a forceps or a chela; applied especially to the joint.

çhel-e-ryth′rin, çhel-e-ryth′rine, *n.* [Gr. *chelidonion*, celandine, and *erythros*, red, and *-in*.] A colorless, crystalline, acrid, poisonous narcotic obtained from the root and unripe fruit of the celandine.

çhē-lic′ẽr-ȧ, *n.*; *pl.* **çhē-lic′ẽr-æ**. [Gr. *chēlē*, a claw, and *keras*, a horn.] A name given to the prehensile claws of the scorpion and spider, which are the homologues of antennæ.

Chel′i-don, *n.* [Gr. *chelidōn*, the swallow.]

1. A genus of swallows, of which the house swallow, *Chelidon urbica*, is the type.

2. [c—] The hollow in the arm at the bend of the elbow.

chel-i-don'ic, *a.* [Gr. *chelidonion*, the celandine.] Pertaining to celandine.

Chelidonic acid; an acid that crystallizes in silky needles, obtained from celandine.

chel'i-fēr, *n.* The book-scorpion.

chē-lif'ēr-ous, *a.* [L. *chele*, a claw, and *ferre*, to bear.] Furnished with chelæ, as a lobster, a crab, etc.

chel'i-form, *a.* [L. *chele*, a claw, and *forma*, form.] Having the form of a chela or prehensile claw, like that of the lobster.

Chē-lō'nē, *n.* [Gr. *chelōnē*, a tortoise.]

1. A genus of turtles, represented by the green turtle.

2. A genus of plants in which the corolla resembles the head of a tortoise.

Chē-lō'ni-ȧ, *n.pl.* An order of reptiles, distinguished by the body being inclosed in a double shell, out of which the head, tail, and four extremities protrude, including the various species of tortoise and turtle.

chē-lō'ni-ăn, *a* and *n.* I. *a.* Pertaining to or designating animals of the tortoise kind.

II. *n.* A member of the order *Chelonia*.

Chē-lū'rȧ, *n.* [Gr. *chēlē*, a claw, and *oura*, a tail.] A genus of marine shrimps destructive to timber by boring tunnels under the surface; called also the *wood-shrimps*.

chē'ly, *n.* A chela. [Obs.]

chem'ic, *n.* [Fr. *chimique*; LL. *alchimicus*, from *alchimia*, alchemy.]

1. An alchemist; a chemist. [Obs.]

2. A solution of chlorid of lime for bleaching purposes.

chem'ic, *a.* Having chemical properties.

chem'ic-ăl, *a.* 1. Pertaining to chemistry; as, a *chemical* laboratory.

2. Resulting from the operation of the principles of bodies by decomposition, combination, etc.; as, *chemical* changes; according to the principles of chemistry; as, a *chemical* combination.

Chemical attraction; see *Attraction*.

chem'ic-ăl, *n.* A substance used in a chemical operation or the product of such an operation.

chem'ic-ăl-ly, *adv.* According to chemical principles; by chemical process or operation.

chem-i-glyph'ic, *a.* [*Chemic*, and Gr. *glyphein*, to engrave.] Engraved by means of chemical action.

chem-i-loon', *n.* [*Chemi*se, and panta*loon*.] A woman's undergarment in which the chemise and drawers are in one piece.

chē-mīṣe', *n.* [Fr. *chemise*; LL. *camisia*, a shirt, tunic.]

1. A shirt, shift, or undergarment, worn by women.

2. A wall that lines the face of any earthwork.

chem-i-sette', *n.* [Fr.] An undergarment, worn over the chemise.

chem'iṣm, *n.* Chemical power or influence: also chemical effects.

chem'ist, *n.* 1. One versed in chemistry; one who practises chemistry, especially analytical chemistry; an analyst; one who compounds or sells drugs.

2. In England, a druggist.

Pharmaceutical chemist; a chemist whose practice is confined to the preparation of drugs and medicines; an apothecary.

chem'is-try, *n.* [From *chemist*, shortened form of *alchemist*, from *alchemy*, *alchymy*; OFr. *alchemie*, from Ar. *al*, the, and *kimia*, from Late Gr. *chēmeia*, *chymeia*, a fusion, pouring, from *cheein*, to pour.]

1. The science which investigates the composition of all substances, together with the combinations and decompositions resulting from their action upon one another under the influence of chemical force.

2. A work or treatise setting forth the science defined above.

3. Alchemy. [Obs.]

Inorganic chemistry; that division of chemistry treating of elements other than carbon.

Organic chemistry; a division of chemistry treating of the vast number of carbon compounds or of the elements which compose animal and vegetable structure.

Physiological chemistry; the chemistry of the body and its processes.

Practical or *applied chemistry*; the chemistry of the arts and manufactures.

Pure chemistry; a consideration of the laws which govern chemical actions, and of the bearing of these upon the general theories of matter, irrespective of any practical application.

chem'i-type, *n.* [*Chemic*al and *type*; Gr. *typos*, form, impression.]

1. A process of obtaining casts in relief from engravings, particularly adapted for producing maps.

2. The finished plate resulting from this process.

chē-mol'y-sis, *n.* [*Chemic*al, and Gr. *lysis*, a loosing.] Chemical analysis.

chē-mō'sis, *n.* [Gr. *chēme*, a yawning, and *-osis*.] An affection of the eye in which the conjunctiva is elevated above the transparent cornea.

chem-os-mō'sis, *n.* [*Chem*ical, and *osmosis*, from Gr. *ōsmos*, a pushing, impulsion.] Osmose of a chemical nature.

chem-os-mot'ic, *a.* Pertaining to chemosmosis.

chem-ō-tax'is, *n.* Movement of living cells.

chem-ō-ther'ȧ-py, *n.* That science devoted to the discovery of drugs capable of killing organisms which produce a disease.

chē-mot'ic, *a.* Pertaining to chemosis.

cheng, *n.* [Chinese.] A Chinese musical instrument, consisting of a series of tubes having free reeds. This instrument is the forerunner of the accordion, harmonium, and similar instruments; called also *sang*.

A Cheng.

che-nille', *n.* [Fr., a caterpillar.] A tufted cord of silk or worsted, somewhat resembling a caterpillar, used for making trimmings, fringes, laces, etc.

Chē-nō-mor'phæ, *n.pl.* [Gr. *chēn*, a goose, and *morphē*, shape.] An ornithological division including ducks, geese, swans, etc.

Chē-nō-pō-di-ā'cē-æ, *n.pl.* [After the typical genus *Chenopodium*, and *-aceæ*.] An order of apetalous exogens, consisting of more or less succulent herbs or shrubs, and embracing about eighty genera and 600 species. They are mostly useless weeds, but several are employed as pot-herbs, such as spinach and beet, and others for the manufacture of soda.

chē-nō-pō-di-ā'ceous, *a.* Relating to the order *Chenopodiaceæ*.

Chē-nō-pō'di-um, *n.* [Gr. *chēn*, *chēnos*, a goose, and *pous*, *podos*, a foot.] A genus of variable herbs, natural order *Chenopodiaceæ*. They are known by the names of *goosefoot*, *pigweed*, etc.

chep'stēr, *n.* A local English name for the starling.

cheque, *n.* See *Check*.

cheq'uēr, *n.* See *Checker*.

chē-quin' (-kēn'), *n.* A sequin. [Obs.]

cher'if, *n.* [Fr.] Same as *Sherif*.

cher-i-moy'ēr, *n.* [Fr. *chérimolier*, a corruption of *cherimoles*, the name of the fruit in Peru.]

1. The fruit of *Anona Cherimolia*, a native of Peru; it is heart-shaped with a scaly exterior and numerous seeds, buried in a delicious pulp.

2. The tree bearing this fruit.

cher'ish, *v.t.*; cherished, *pt.*, *pp.*; cherishing, *ppr.* [ME. *cherischen*, *cherisen*, from OFr. *cheris-*, the stem of *cherir*, to hold dear, cherish; *cher*, from L. *carus*, dear.]

1. To treat with tenderness and affection; to take care of; to foster; to nurture; to support and encourage; to comfort.

2. To hold as dear; to indulge and encourage in the mind; to harbor; to cling to; as, to *cherish* the principles of virtue.

Syn.—Foster, harbor, indulge, nourish, nurture.—To *foster* is to sustain and nourish with care and effort. To *cherish* is to hold and treat as dear. To *harbor* is to provide with shelter and protection. To *indulge* is to treat with gentleness and consideration.

cher'ish-ēr, *n.* One who cherishes; an encourager; a supporter.

cher'ish-ment, *n.* Encouragement; comfort. [Obs.]

Chēr'mēs, *n.* 1. A genus of bark-lice found chiefly on firs and larches.

2. [c—] Same as *Kermes*.

chēr'nȧ, *n.* [Sp.] A name applied to several fishes of the family *Serranidæ*, including the red grouper.

Cher-o-kee', *n.* A member of a tribe of American Indians formerly inhabiting northern Georgia; now settled in the Indian Territory.

che-root', *n.* [Hind. *churut*, a cigar.] A form of cigar having blunt ends, and thicker at one end than at the other; originally made at Manila.

cher'ry, *n.*; *pl.* **cher'ries.** [ME. *chery*, *chere*; AS. *ciris*, *cyrs*; LL. *ceresia*; L. *cerasus*; Gr. *kerasos*, a cherry-tree, from *keras*, a horn, from the hardness of the wood.]

1. The fruit of various trees of the genus *Prunus*.

2. Any tree or shrub producing *cherries*; specifically, (a) the cultivated varieties of *Prunus Cerasus* and *Prunus avium*, having fruit which is a pulpy drupe inclosing a one-seeded smooth stone; (b) *Prunus Virginiana*, the wild choke-cherry, and *Prunus serotina*, the wild black cherry, bearing a smaller and sharper tasting drupe; (c) a section of evergreens, *Prunus Lauro-Cerasus*, having a diminutive tasteless fruit.

3. The wood of the various cherry-trees, especially that of the black cherry, valuable for its hardness and susceptibility to polish.

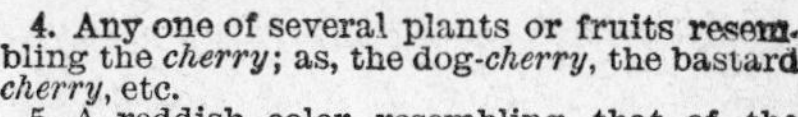

4. Any one of several plants or fruits resembling the *cherry*; as, the dog-*cherry*, the bastard *cherry*, etc.

5. A reddish color resembling that of the *cherry*.

Barbados cherry; a tree growing in the West Indies, a species of *Malpighia*, fifteen feet high, and producing a pleasant tart fruit.

Cherry bounce; an old popular drink, consisting of burned brandy and sugar, in which cherries had been steeped.

Cherry brandy or *cordial*; a brandy or cordial made of cherries or syrup of cherries; similar to cherry bounce.

cher'ry, *a.* Like a red cherry in color; red; ruddy; blooming; as, *cherry* lips; *cherry* cheeks.

cher'ry-bird, *n.* A bird whose chief food is cherries, such as the Carolina cedar-bird, the California house-finch, and the European oriole.

cher'ry-lau"rel, *n.* The English name of *Prunus Lauro-Cerasus*, natural order *Rosaceæ*, a native of Asia Minor. The distilled water from the leaves is used in medicine in the same way as diluted hydrocyanic or prussic acid.

cher'ry-pep"pēr, *n.* A species of capsicum, whose fruit is small and cherry-shaped.

cher'ry-pit, *n.* 1. A cherry-stone.

2. A child's game played with cherry-stones.

cher'ry-stōne, *n.* The seed of the cherry.

chēr'sō-nēṣe, *n.* [Gr. *chersonēsos*; *chersos*, dry land, and *nēsos*, an island.] A peninsula; a tract of land nearly surrounded by water; as, the Tauric *Chersonese*, or Crimea.

chērt, *n.* [Ir. *ceart*, a stone.] A variety of quartz, called also hornstone, or rock flint. It is less hard than common quartz; its fracture usually conchoidal and dull, sometimes splintery.

chērt'y, *a.* Like chert; full of chert; flinty.

cher'ub, *n.*; *pl.* **cher'ubs** or (*Heb.*) **cher'ū-bim.** [LL. *cherub*; Heb. *kerūb*, a cherub.]

1. One of an order of angels variously represented, but generally as winged spirits with a human countenance, and distinguished by their knowledge from the seraphs, whose distinctive quality is love. In the celestial hierarchy, cherubs are represented as spirits next in order to seraphs.

2. A beautiful child; so called because artists have generally represented cherubs as beautiful winged children. [In this sense the plural is always *cherubs*.]

che-rū'bic, che-rū'bic-ăl, *a.* Pertaining to or resembling cherubs; angelic.

cher'ū-bim, *n.*, Hebrew plural of *cherub*.

cher-ū-bim'ic, *a.* Pertaining to cherubim.

cher'ū-bin, *a.* Cherubic; angelic. [Obs.]

cher'ū-bin, *n.* An obsolete form of *cherub*, used both in the singular and plural.

cher'up, *v.t.* and *v.i.*; cheruped, *pt.*, *pp.*; cheruping, *ppr.* [Of imitative origin.] To chirrup; to chirp.

cher'up, *n.* A chirrup; a chirp.

chēr'vil, *n.* [AS. *cerfille*; OFr. *cherfuel*; Sp. *cerafolio*; L. *cærafolium*, *cerafolium*; Gr. *chairephyllon*, chervil; *chairein*, to rejoice, and *phyllon*, a leaf.] The popular name of various umbelliferous plants, as *Myrrhis odorata*, sweet chervil; *Scandix Pecten-Veneris*, needle-chervil; *Anthriscus sylvestre*, cow-chervil; but especially, *Anthriscus Cerefolium*, garden chervil, used in salads.

chēṣe, *v.t.* To choose. [Obs.]

ches'i-ble, *n.* See *Chasuble*.

chess, *n.* [ME. *ches*, *chesse*; OFr. *esches*, *eschas*; from Per. *shah*, a king, the most important piece in the game.] An ancient game of skill played by two persons with different pieces, on a board divided into sixty-four squares, alternately light and dark. Each player has eight principal pieces, called a king, a queen, two bishops, two knights, and two rooks, or castles; also eight pawns. The object of each player is to capture or checkmate his opponent's king. The origin of the game is lost in obscurity. It is played in all civilized countries, and has been known to the Chinese for many centuries.

chess, *n.* An American stalked plant, *Bromus secalinus*, resembling oats, often growing with wheat; also called *cheat*.

chess'-ap"ple, *n.* A species of service-tree, *Pyrus Aria*, common to Europe.

chess'bōard, *n.* The checkered board upon which the game of chess is played.

ches'sel, *n.* [From *cheese* and *well*.] A mold or vat in which cheese is formed.

chess'eṣ, *n.pl.* [Fr. *chassis*, a frame, sash.] The boards used for the flooring of a temporary military bridge; sometimes used in the singular, *chess*.

chess'man, *n.*; *pl.* **chess'men.** One of the pieces used in the game of chess.

ches'sŏm, *n.* A kind of sandy and clayey earth. [Obs.]

chess'tree, *n.* A nautical name for a piece of wood bolted perpendicularly on the side, to confine the clews of the mainsail.

ches'sy-lite, *n.* [From *Chessy*, a town near Lyons, in France, where the mineral occurs,

and Gr. *lithos*, a stone.] Azurite; also called *Chessy copper.*

chest, *n.* [ME. *chest, chist*; AS. *cist, cyst, cest*, a box, coffin; L. *cista*; Gr. *kistē*, a box, chest.]

1. A box of wood, or other material, in which goods are kept or transported; usually of considerable dimensions, and provided with a hinged cover, and sometimes with compartments for various kinds of personal property; often used in composition; as, tool-*chest*; treasure-*chest.*

2. A packing-case for the transportation of goods; as, a tea-*chest.*

3. A measure of quantity, often indefinite; as, a *chest* of tea.

4. The thorax; the part of the body containing the heart, the lungs, and the mediastinal structures.

5. In mechanics, a tight box; a closely fitted receptacle; as, a steam-*chest.*

Chest of drawers; an arrangement of drawers in a box-like frame; usually called a bureau.

chest, *v.t.*; chested, *pt., pp.*; chesting, *ppr.*

1. To deposit in a chest; to hoard.

2. To coffin. [Obs.]

chest, *n.* [ME. *chest*; AS. *ceast*, strife, contention.] Debate; quarrel; strife; enmity. [Obs.]

chest′ed, *a.* Having a special kind of chest; used chiefly in composition; as, broad-*chested*; narrow-*chested.*

ches′ten, *n.* The chestnut-tree or its nut. [Obs.]

Ches-tēr-fiēld′i-ăn, *a.* Resembling the fourth earl of Chesterfield (1694-1773), who was distinguished for his courtliness; hence, extremely polite; polished.

ches′tēr-līte, *n.* [Named after *Chester* county, Pennsylvania, where it is found.] A variety of orthoclase, or feldspar.

ches′teyn, *n.* [Obs.] See *Chestnut.*

chest′=found″ēr, *n.* Rheumatism of the chest; a disease of horses.

chest′nut (ches′), *n.* [For *chesten-nut*; ME. *chesten, chestein*, a chestnut; AS. *cisten* in *cisten-beam*, a chestnut; L. *castanea*; Gr. *kastanea*, a chestnut, from *Kastana*, a city in Pontus, where chestnuts grew in abundance.]

Chestnut (*Castanea vesca*).

1. The fruit, seed, or nut of a tree belonging to the genus *Castanea.* It is inclosed in a prickly pericarp, which contains two or more seeds.

2. *Castanea vesca*, the tree which produces the *chestnut.* It grows to a great size, with spreading branches, being one of the most valuable of the timber-trees.

3. The wood of the chestnut-tree.

4. The color of the husk of a *chestnut*; a reddish-brown color.

5. A name given to certain trees or plants of other genera, or their fruit, as the horse-chestnut, *Æsculus Hippocastanum*; the wild chestnut, *Brabejum stellatum* of South Africa; the Tahiti, Otaheite, or Fiji chestnut, *Inocarpus edulis*, of the islands of the Pacific.

6. A callous excrescence composed of horny layers, on the inner side of a horse's leg.

7. A trite expression or worn-out joke or stale story. [Slang, U. S.]

chest′nut, *a.* Of a reddish-brown color resembling the chestnut.

chest′nut=būr, *n.* The prickly hull or bur of a chestnut.

chest′nut=çōal, *n.* A size of hard coal which has passed through screen meshes about an inch square.

chest′=voice, *n.* In phonetics, sound uttered with resonance of the vocal cords, and not with a mere emission of breath; sonant utterance.

chest′y, *a.* Vain; puffed up; arrogant. [Slang.]

chē′tăh, chee′tȧ, chee′tăh, *n.* [Hind. *chīta*, a leopard.] The hunting leopard of India, *Guepardа jubata.*

chet′vērt, *n.* [Russ.] A Russian grain measure, equal to about six bushels.

çhev′ȧ-çhiē, *n.* An expedition with cavalry. [Obs.]

chē′vāġe, *n.* [Obs.] Same as *Chiefage.*

çhe-val′, *n.*; *pl.* **çhe-vaux′** (-vō′). [Fr.] 1. A horse.

2. In composition, a support or frame; as, a *cheval*-glass.

À cheval; on each side so as to command any intermediate space. Troops are arranged *à cheval* when they command two roads, or both sides of a river.

çhe-val′=de=frīṣe, *n.*; *pl.* **çhe-vaux′=de=frīṣe** (-vō′-). 1. Same as *Chevaux-de-frise.*

2. A kind of trimming in a cross line pattern.

çhe-val′=glȧss, *n.* A mirror mounted so as to swing in a frame, and large enough to reflect the whole figure.

çhev-ȧ-liēr′, *n.* [Fr., from *cheval*, a horse.]

1. A horseman; a knight; a cavalier.

2. In heraldry, a horseman armed at all points.

3. A member of certain orders; as, a *chevalier* of the Legion of Honor.

Chevalier d'industrie; one who gains a living by dishonest means; a sharper; a swindler; a thief.

çhev-ȧ-liēr′=bīrd, *n.* A bird of the genus *Totanus*, commonly called *yellowlegs.*

çhev-ȧ-liēr′=crab, *n.* An ocypodian, commonly called *horseman.*

çhev′ăl-ry, *n.* Chivalry. [Obs.]

çhe-vaux′ (-vō′), *n.*, pl. of *cheval.*

çhe-vaux′=de=frīṣe (-vō′-), *n.pl.* [Fr. *cheval*, a horse, pl. *chevaux*, and *Frise*, Friesland, because said to have been first employed at the siege of Gröningen.] Pieces of timber traversed with wooden spikes, pointed with iron, five or six feet long, or the whole made of iron, used to defend a passage, stop a breach, form an obstacle to the advance of cavalry, etc.

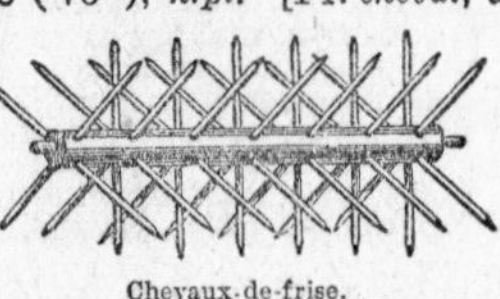

Chevaux-de-frise.

chēve, *v.i.* See *Chieve.*

çheve-lūre′, *n.* [Fr., head of hair.]

1. In astronomy, the coma of a comet or other nebulous body.

2. The hair of the head.

chev′en, *n.* [OFr. *chevesne*, a chub.] The chub. [Obs.]

chev′en-teīn, *n.* A chieftain. [Obs.]

chev′ēr-el, chev′ēr-il, *n.* [OFr. *chevrel*, a kid, dim. of *chevre*; L. *capra*, a goat.] Soft leather made of kid-skin; hence, a yielding disposition. [Obs.]

chev′ēr-el, chev′ēr-il, *a.* Made of cheverel; hence, yielding; pliable. [Obs.]

chev′ēr-il-īze, *v.t.* To make as pliable as kid-leather. [Obs.]

çhe-vet′ (-vā′), *n.* [Fr., the head of a bed, dim. of *chef*, a head.] In architecture, the eastern end of the apse, especially in French Gothic churches. The chevet is always inclosed by an open screen of columns on the ground floor, and opens into an aisle, which again opens into three or more apsidal chapels.

Chevet, east end of Westminster Abbey.

Chev′i-ŏt, *n.* [From the *Cheviot* Hills in Scotland.]

1. A variety of sheep noted for their large size and valuable wool.

2. [c—] A kind of loosely woven cloth made from the wool of the Cheviot sheep.

çhev′i-ṡănce, *n.* [Fr., from *chevir*, to come to an end, prevail; from *chef*, head, extremity.]

1. Achievement; deed; performance. [Obs.]

2. In old law, a making of contracts; a bargain; also, an unlawful agreement or contract.

3. An agreement between a creditor and his debtor. [Obs.]

çhev-rette′, *n.* [Fr., from *chèvre*, L. *capra*, a goat.] A machine formerly used in handling heavy guns or mortars. [Obs.]

çhev′rŏn, *n.* [Fr., a rafter, chevron, from LL. *capro*, a rafter; L. *caper*, a goat.]

1. In heraldry, an honorable ordinary, representing two rafters of a house meeting at the top.

2. In architecture, an ornament in the form of zigzag work; zigzag molding.

3. A distinguishing mark on the sleeves of a noncommissioned officer's coat.

Chevron.

çhev′rŏn=bōne, *n.* One of the arched bones branching from the vertebral column in cetaceans, etc.

çhev′rŏned, *a.* Having a chevron, or the form of it; worked with a pattern chevron-wise.

çhev′rŏn-el, *n.* In heraldry, a half-chevron; a small chevron, half as wide as the ordinary chevron.

çhev′rŏn-wīṣe, *adv.* In heraldry, in the manner of a chevron.

çhev-rō-tāin′, *n.* [Fr., from OFr. *chevrot*, dim. of *chevre*, a goat.] The *Tragulus pygmæus*, a small animal resembling the musk-deer, but with projecting upper teeth, without horns, and classified with the genus *Tragulus*, family *Tragulidæ.*

chev′y, chiv′y, *v.t.* To chase; to hunt; to worry. [Eng. Slang.]

chew (chū), *v.t.*; chewed, *pt., pp.*; chewing, *ppr.* [ME. *chewen, cheowen*; AS. *ceowan*, to chew.]

1. To bite and grind with the teeth; to masticate.

2. To ruminate in the thoughts; to meditate; as, to *chew* revenge.

3. To champ; to bite, hold, or roll about in the mouth; as, to *chew* tobacco.

To chew the cud; to ruminate; to chew the food a second time, as a ruminating animal; figuratively, to meditate.

chew, *v.i.* To champ; to ruminate.

Old politicians *chew* on wisdom past.—Pope.

chew, *n.* That which is chewed; that which is held in the mouth at once; a cud or quid. [Colloq.]

chew′ēr, *n.* One who chews.

chew′et, *n.* 1. A kind of pie made of chopped substances.

2. A chough, or red-legged crow; figuratively, a chatterer. [Obs.]

chew′ing=gum, *n.* A masticatory in popular use, consisting of a natural gum resin, as spruce-gum, or an artificial preparation of chicle, paraffin, etc.

chē-wink′, *n.* [Imitative of its note.] An American finch; the towhee bunting, *Pipilo erythrophthalmus.*

Çhey-enne′, *n.* One of a tribe of the Algonkian family of Indians, formerly inhabiting Wyoming, but now settled in the Indian Territory.

çhe-yō′te, *n.* The native name of a Cuban fruit, the plant producing it being of the gourd family; botanically, *Sechium edule*; also known as *choco.*

chī′ȧ, *n.* [Sp.] A name used in Arizona and Mexico for several species of *Salvia*, especially *Salvia Columbariæ* which produces edible seeds.

Chī′ăn, *a.* Pertaining to Chios, an isle in the Levant.

Chian earth; a dense, compact kind of earth, from Chios, used anciently as an astringent and a cosmetic.

Chian or *Cyprus turpentine*; a turpentine procured from the *Pistacia Terebinthus.* It is of the consistence of honey, clear, and of a yellowish white.

Çhī-an′ti, *n.* An Italian red wine.

çhī-ä″rō=os-çū′rō, *n.* See *Chiaroscuro.*

çhī-ä-ros-çū′rist, *n.* An artist who lays stress upon chiaroscuro.

çhiä-rō-sçū′rō, çhī-ä″rō=os-çū′rō, *n.* [It., literally, clear dark; L. *clarus*, clear, and *obscurus*, dark.] In the fine arts, that department of painting which relates to light and shade; the art of judiciously distributing the lights and shadows in a picture.

çhī′aṣm, çhī-aṣ′mȧ, *n.* [Gr. *chiasma*, two lines crossed, from *chiazein*, to mark with the letter χ.] In anatomy, the central body of nervous matter formed by the junction and decussation of the optic nerves.

çhī-aṣ′măl, *a.* Pertaining to the chiasm.

çhī-aṣ′mus, *n.* In rhetoric, a comparison made by placing words in reversed parallel form; as, do not live to eat, but eat to live.

çhī-as′tō-līte, *n.* [Gr. *chiastos*, marked with a letter χ, and *lithos*, stone.] A mineral of the cyanite family, generally regarded as a variety of andalusite and also called *macle*; remarkable for the diagonal arrangement of its crystals as seen when the stone is cut transversely.

chib′băl, *n.* [Obs.] See *Cibol.*

chi-bouk′, chi-bouque′ (-bök′), *n.* [Turk. *chibuq*, a pipe.] A form of pipe used by the Turks, Persians, Arabs, etc., having a long, straight, wooden stem, bowl of red clay, and amber mouthpiece.

çhiç, *a.* Stylish and original; effective in style; elegant; knowing; cunning.

çhiç, *n.* [Fr. slang.] 1. Elegance and originality in attire; cleverness of style.

2. Knowingness; cunning.

3. In the fine arts, skill and facility combined; the faculty of producing effective works easily and rapidly.

4. Easy elegance; grace.

chī′çȧ, *n.* [Sp.] 1. An orange-red coloring matter obtained from the *Bignonia Chica*, a climbing plant of South America.

2. An old Spanish dance, from which the fan dango and bolero are said to have developed.

chī-çȧ-lō′te, *n.* [Mex.] A prickly poppy of California, *Argemone platyceras.*

çhi-çāne′, *n.* [Fr., from Per. *chaugān*, the game of polo, which was introduced into France in the middle ages under this name. The various senses are figurative of the methods of the game. Some derive the word from OFr. *chic*, small.] The art of protracting a contest or discussion by the use of evasive stratagems or mean and unfair tricks and artifices; trickery; sophistry; chicanery.

chi-cāne′, *v.i.* [Fr. *chicaner*, to use trickery.] To use shifts, cavils, or artifices.

chi-cān′ẽr, *n.* One who employs chicanery.

chi-cān′ẽr-y, *n.* Sophistry; mean or unfair artifices used in contest or discussion; chicane.

Syn.—Sophistry, caviling, quibble, trickery, stratagem.

chic′ō-ry, *n.* See *Chicory*.

chich, *n.* [Fr. *chiche*, from L. *cicer*, chick-pea.] The dwarf pea or chick-pea.

chi′chȧ, *n.* Same as *Chica*.

chiche′vȧche, *n.* [Fr. *chiche*, lean, and *vache*, cow.] A cow of great size which in fable fed upon patient wives, and was consequently very lean.

chich′ling, **chich′ling-vetch**, *n.* Same as *Chickling*.

chick, *v.i.* To sprout, as seed in the ground; to vegetate.

chick, *n.* 1. See *Chicken*.

2. An endearing term for a child or person of tender years.

chick′ȧ-bid-dy, *n.* 1. A fowl; a chick.

2. A playful name for a child.

chick′ȧ-dee, *n.* [Imitative of its note.] The blackcap titmouse, *Parus atricapillus*.

chick′ȧ-ree, *n.* [Imitative of its cry.] The American red squirrel, *Sciurus hudsonius*.

Chick′ȧ-saw, *n.* One of a tribe of North American Indians, formerly occupying the eastern portions of the lower Mississippi valley, but now settled in Indian Territory.

chick′en, *n.* [ME. *chiken*, *chekin*; AS. *cicen*, dim. of *coc*, a cock.]

1. The young of any breed of the common domestic fowl, particularly a fowl less than one year old; loosely, a fowl of any age; also its meat.

2. A child, or a young and inexperienced person; often used with the negative; as, she is no *chicken*.

Chicken cholera; see under *Cholera*.

chick′en-breast″ed, *a.* Having a narrow, projecting chest, the result of a forward curvature of the vertebral column.

chick′en-heärt″ed, *a.* Timid; fearful; cowardly.

chick′en-pox, *n.* A mild, contagious, eruptive disease, generally appearing in children.

chick′en-weed, *n.* 1. Same as *Chickweed*.

2. The canary-moss.

chick′ling, *n.* A small chick or chicken.

chick′ling, *n.* A vetch or pea, *Lathyrus sativus*, used in Germany for food; also called *chichling*.

chick′-pēa, *n.* [For *chich-pea*; OFr. *chiche*, from L. *cicer*, the chick, chick-pea.]

1. The popular name of *Cicer arietinum*, a native of Spain, but now found all over southern Europe, and in many parts of Africa and Asia. It is smaller than the common pea.

2. The seed of the plant which is used for food and when roasted is the common parched pulse of the East.

chick′weed, *n.* The popular name of several species of the pink family, especially *Stellaria media*, the common *chickweed* much used as a food for birds.

chick′y, *n.* A chicken; a term much used in calling fowls.

chic′le (chik′l), *n.* [Sp. Am.] A gum obtained from the milky juice of the sapodilla, *Achras Sapota*, and much used as a base in the manufacture of chewing-gum.

chic′ō-ry, *n.* [Fr. *chicorée*, *cichorée*; L. *cichorium*; Gr. *kichora*, *kichoreia*, chicory.] The popular name of *Cichorium Intybus*, a composite plant common in Europe, Asia, and America. The roots have been extensively employed as a substitute for coffee, or to mix with coffee. The blanched leaves are sometimes used as a salad.

Chicory (*Cichorium Intybus*).

chīde, *v.t.*; chid, *pt.*; chidden *or* chid, *pp.*; chiding, *ppr.* [ME. *chiden*; AS. *cīdan*, to chide, blame.]

1. To fret at or chafe against; as, the waves *chide* the shore.

2. To scold at; to reprove; to rebuke; as, to *chide* one for his faults.

3. To blame; to reproach; as, to *chide* folly or negligence.

To chide from, or *chide away*; to drive away by scolding or reproof.

Syn.—Reprimand, scold, rebuke, reprove, censure, blame.

chīde, *v.i.* 1. To scold; to clamor; to find fault; to contend in words of anger; sometimes followed by *with*.

The people did *chide with* Moses.—Ex. xvii. 2.

2. To quarrel.

3. To make a rough, clamorous, roaring noise; as, the flood *chides*.

chīde, *n.* Murmur; gentle noise. [Rare.]

chīd′ẽr, *n.* One who chides, clamors, reproves, or rebukes.

chīd′ẽr-ess, *n.* A female who chides. [Obs.]

chīde′stẽr, *n.* A scolding female. [Obs.]

chīd′ing, *n.* A scolding or clamoring; rebuke; reproof.

chīd′ing-ly, *adv.* In a scolding or reproving manner.

chiēf, *a.* [ME. *cheef*, *chefe*, the head man; OFr. *chef*, leader, commander; L. *caput*, head.]

1. Highest in office or rank; principal; as, a *chief* priest; the *chief* butler.

2. Principal or most eminent, in any quality or action; most distinguished; having most influence; commanding most respect; taking the lead; most valuable; most important; as, agriculture is the *chief* employment of men.

3. First in affection; most dear and familiar; as, my *chief* friend. [Rare.]

Chief justice; the presiding justice; particularly the presiding judge of the Supreme Court of the United States, and also of the supreme court in some of the states.

chiēf, *n.* 1. A commander; particularly a military commander; the person who heads an army or other considerable body of soldiers; equivalent to the modern terms *commander*, *general*, etc.

2. The principal person of a tribe, family, or clan.

3. The principal officer of a department of administration or branch of military service, etc.; as, a *chief* of police; *chief* of a fire department; *chief* of staff; *chief* of engineers; *chief* of ordnance, etc.

4. In heraldry, the upper part of the escutcheon, divided into three *chiefs*, dexter, middle, and sinister.

Chief.

5. The principal one or ones; primarily an adjective and denoting *chief person* or *persons*; as, the *chief* among ten thousand; the *chief* of the officers that were over Solomon's work.

6. The principal part; the most or largest part of one thing or of many; as, the *chief* of the debt remains unpaid.

In chief; (a) in or of the highest rank; as, commander-*in-chief*; (b) in law, original, principal; as, examination-*in-chief*; (c) in heraldry, borne in the upper part of the escutcheon.

Syn.—Chieftain, commander, leader.—A *chief* has the preëminence or rule in civil matters; as, the *chief* of police or of a tribe; a *chieftain* and *commander* occupy high military stations; a *leader* takes the direction of enterprises.

chiēf′āge, *n.* [Fr. *chevage*.] A tribute by the head. [Obs.]

chiēf′dŏm, *n.* Sovereignty. [Rare.]

chiēf′est, *a.* Old superlative of *chief*.

chiēf′-jus′tice-ship, *n.* The office of chief justice.

chiēf′less, *a.* Without a chief or leader.

chiēf′ly, *adv.* 1. Principally; eminently; in the first place; as, it *chiefly* concerns you.

2. For the most part.

In the parts of the kingdom where the estates of the dissenters *chiefly* lay.—Swift.

chiēf′ry, **chiēf′rie**, *n.* 1. A small rent paid to the lord paramount.

2. The domain or system of government of a lord or chief, especially of ancient Ireland.

chiēf′tain (-tin), *n.* [ME. *chefetain*; OFr. *chevetaine*; LL. *capitanus*, a commander, from L. *caput*, head.] A captain, leader, or commander; a chief; the head of a troop, army, or clan; most commonly used in the latter sense. The *chieftains* of the Highland clans, in Scotland, were the principal noblemen and gentlemen.

chiēf′tain-cy, **chiēf′tain-ship**, *n.* Headship; captaincy; the state of a chieftain.

chiēv′ānce, *n.* [OFr. *chevance*, gain, from *chevir*, to attain.] An unlawful bargain; traffic in which money is extorted. [Obs.]

chiēve, *v.i.* and *v.t.* To come or bring to an end; to prosper or accomplish. [Obs.]

chiff′-chaff, *n.* The whitethroat, *Sylvia rufa*, an English songbird; so called from its note. Also called *pettychaps*.

chif′fŏn (*or Fr. pron.*, shē-fōṅ′), *n.* [Fr.] 1. Any ornamental trifle worn by women, as a knot of ribbon, etc.

2. A light, gauzy material extensively used in millinery and dressmaking.

chif-fŏn-niēr′, *n.* [Fr. *chiffonnier*, a ragpicker, a chiffonnier (furniture), from *chiffonner*, to rumple.]

1. A kind of small sideboard; a cabinet.

2. A ragpicker; in this sense used by English writers only as a French word; its feminine form is *chiffonnière*.

chif′fre (-fr), *n.* [Fr. *chiffre*, a cipher.] In music, a character indicating the harmony, as in figured bass.

chi′gnoṅ (-nyoṅ) *n.* [Fr. *chignon*; OFr. *chaïgnon*, the nape of the neck, from *chaine*, a chain.] A term applied to ladies' back hair when raised and folded up, usually round a pad, in a sort of roll on the back part of the head and nape of the neck; sometimes a fashionable mode of hairdressing.

chig′ōe, **cheg′ōe**, **chig′re** (-ẽr), *n.* [Native name.] A curious insect, *Pulex penetrans*, closely resembling the common flea, but smaller, found in the West Indies and South America. It burrows beneath the skin of the foot and often causes great irritation and even troublesome sores. Also called *jigger*.

Chigoe (*Pulex penetrans*).
1. Male (nat. size). 2. Male, magnified. 3. Female, full of eggs (nat. size), as taken from a human toe.

chī-kä′rȧ, *n.* [East Indian origin.] A goat-like antelope found in Bengal, the male having four horns; also called *chousingha*.

chil′blāin, *n.* [Prov. Eng., from AS. *cele*, cold, and *blegen*, a sore.] A blain or sore produced by cold, affecting the hands and feet, accompanied with inflammation, itching, and sometimes ulceration.

chil′blāin, *v.t.* To produce chilblains in.

chīld, *n.*; *pl.* **chil′dren.** [ME. *child*, *childe*, pl. *childre*; AS. *cild*, pl. *cild*, *cildru*, child, children.]

1. A son or a daughter; a male or female descendant, in the first degree; the immediate progeny of parents; applied to the human race, and chiefly to a person when young. In law, a legitimate son or daughter.

2. One weak in knowledge, experience, judgment, or attainments; as, he is a mere *child*.

3. One who is born again, spiritually renewed and adopted; as, a *child* of God.

4. That which is the product or effect of something else.

This noble passion, *child* of integrity.—Shak.

5. A native of a country; as, a *child* of Italy.

6. In the plural, the descendants of a man, however remote; as, the *children* of Israel.

7. Same as *Childe*. [Obs.]

Child study; a scientific inquiry into the laws of growth and development governing the mind and body from the time of birth to maturity.

Child's play; something easily accomplished; a trivial matter.

To be with child; to be pregnant.

chīld′beār″ing, *a.* Bearing or producing children.

chīld′beār″ing, *n.* The act of producing or bringing forth children; parturition; gestation.

chīld′bed, *n.* The state of a woman bringing forth a child or being in labor; parturition.

chīld′birth, *n.* The act of bringing forth a child; travail; labor; as, the pains of *childbirth*.

chīld′-crōw″ing, *n.* An inflammatory affection of the trachea; false or spasmodic croup.

Chīlde, *n.* In England, a cognomen formerly prefixed to his name by the oldest son, until he succeeded to the titles of his ancestors, or gained new honors by his own prowess; as, *Childe* Harold; *Childe* Rowland.

Chil′dẽr-mȧs-dāy, *n.* [AS. *cilda mæsse-dæg*; *cild*, child, *mæsse*, mass, *dæg*, day.] An anniversary of the Church of England, held on December 28, in commemoration of the children of Bethlehem slain by Herod; called also *Innocents' Day*.

chīld′hood, *n.* [ME. *childhod*; AS. *cildhād*, childhood; *cild*, a child, and *hād*, state.] The state of a child; the time in which persons are children, including the time from birth to puberty; in a more restricted sense, the state or time from infancy to boyhood and girlhood, or to puberty.

chīld′ing, *a.* Bearing children; fruitful. [Rare.]

chīld′ish, *a.* 1. Belonging to a child or to childhood; trifling; puerile.

When I became a man, I put away *childish* things. —1 Cor. xiii. 11.

2. Pertaining to a child; as, *childish* sports.

3. Like a child; ignorant; silly; weak; as, *childish* fear.

Syn.—Childlike, foolish, imbecile, infantine, paltry, petty, puerile.

chīld′ish-ly, *adv.* In the manner of a child.

chīld′ish-ness, *n.* The state or quality of being childish; puerility; simplicity; harmlessness; weakness of intellect; generally used in a disparaging sense.

child'less, *a.* Destitute of children or offspring.
child'less-ness, *n.* The state of being without children.
child'like, *a.* Resembling a child, or that which belongs to children; becoming a child; meek; submissive; dutiful; as, *childlike* obedience.
child'ly, *a.* Childish.
child'ly, *adv.* In the manner of a child.
child'ness, *n.* The character or nature of a child. [Obs.]
chil'dren, *n.*, pl. of *child.*
child'ship, *n.* The condition of being a child. [Rare.]
chil'e (i) chil'e-con-car'ne (nē) *n.* A pungent Mexican dish of beans, chopped meats and pepper sauces.
chil'e, *n.* See *Chilli.*
Chil'ē-ăn, *a.* and *n.* I. *a.* Pertaining to Chile. II. *n.* A native or inhabitant of Chile; also written *Chilian.*
chil'i, *n.* See *Chilli.*
chil'i-ad, *n.* [Gr. *chilias*, the number 1,000, from *chilioi*, a thousand.]
1. A thousand; a collection or sum, containing a thousand individuals or particulars.
2. The period of a thousand years.
chil''i-ă-ē'drŏn, chil''i-ă-hē'drŏn, *n.* [Gr. *chilioi*, a thousand, and *hedra*, a base.] A solid figure of a thousand sides or faces.
chil'i-ă-gon, *n.* [Gr. *chiliagōnos*, with a thousand angles; *chilioi*, a thousand, and *gōnia*, a corner.] A plane figure of a thousand angles and sides.
Chil'i-ăn, *a.* See *Chilean.*
chil'i-ărch, *n.* [Gr. *chiliarchēs*, the commander of a thousand men, from *chilioi*, a thousand, and *archos*, a leader, from *archein*, to lead.] In Greek history, the commander or chief of a thousand men.
chil'i-ărch-y, *n.* A body consisting of a thousand men.
chil'i-așm, *n.* [Gr. *chiliasmos*, from *chiliazein*, to be a thousand years old; *chilioi*, a thousand.]
1. The millennium.
2. The doctrine that Christ will personally reign on earth during the millennium.
chil'i-ast, *n.* One who believes in the doctrine of chiliasm; a millenarian.
chil-i-as'tic, *a.* Millenarian.
chill, *n.* [ME. *chil*, *chile*; AS. *ciele*, *cele*, chill, from *calan*, *celan*, to be cold.]
1. A shivering with cold; the cold fit that sometimes precedes a fever; a sensation of cold in an animal body; chilliness.
2. A moderate degree of cold; chilliness in any body; that which gives the sensation of cold.
3. Figuratively, a check to feelings of joy or sociability; as, a *chill* came over the assembly.
4. In foundry practice, an iron mold designed to cool suddenly and harden the surface of an iron casting; also, the surface thus hardened.
Chills and fever; fever and ague.
chill, *a.* 1. Cool; moderately cold; tending to cause shivering; as, the *chill* vapors of night.
2. Shivering with cold.
3. Cool; distant; formal; dull; not warm, enthusiastic, animated, or affectionate; as, a *chill* reception.
4. Depressed; dispirited; dejected; discouraged.
chill, *v.t.*; chilled, *pt.*, *pp.*; chilling, *ppr.* 1. To cause a shiver in; to affect with a chill.
2. To make cold, or cool; as, the evening air *chills* the earth.
3. To check the life or action of; to depress; to deject; to discourage, as, to *chill* the gaiety of the spirits.
4. To cool rapidly and thus harden, as the surface of molten iron.
chill, *v.i.* To become hardened at the surface by rapid cooling; said of cast iron.
chilled, *a.* 1. Hardened on the surface by chilling; as, *chilled* iron.
2. In painting, applied to the varnish of a picture when the cloudiness or dimness called blooming appears on the surface.
chil'li, chil'ly, chil'i, chil'e, *n.* [From a native name.] The pod or fruit of the *Capsicum annuum* or Guinea pepper; used in making sauces, etc.
chill'i-ness, *n.* 1. A sensation of shivering; the state of being chill.
2. A moderate degree of coldness; as, the *chilliness* of the air, which tends to cause a shivering.
3. Lack of enthusiasm or warmth of feeling; formality.
chill'ing, *a.* Cooling; causing to shiver; discouraging; cold; as, a *chilling* wind or reply.
chill'ing-ly, *adv.* In a chilling manner.
chill'ness, *n.* Coolness; coldness; a shivering.
chill'y, *a.* Cool; moderately cold, such as to cause shivering; as, a *chilly* day, night, or air.
chi'log-nath, *n.* One of the *Chilognatha.*
Chi-log'nă-thă, *n.pl.* [L., from Gr. *cheilos*, lip, and *gnathos*, jaw.] An order of myriapods, represented by the hairy worms or millipeds, in which the two mandibles and the tongue are united to form a large lower lip.
chī-lō'mă, *n.* [Gr. *cheilōma*, lip.] In zoölogy, the upper lip or muzzle of a quadruped, when tumid and continued uninterruptedly from the nostril, as in the camel.
chī'lō-plas-ty, *n.* [Gr. *cheilos*, the lip, and *plassein*, to form, to mold.] In surgery, the term for the operation of supplying deficiencies of the lip, by appropriating a sufficient quantity of the healthy surrounding surface.
chī'lō-pod, *n.* One of the *Chilopoda.*
Chī-lop'ō-dă, *n.pl.* [L., from Gr. *cheilos*, lip, and *pous*, *podos*, foot.] One of the two orders of *Myriapoda*, represented by the centipeds, in which a pair of mandibles, or large jaws with small palpi, two pairs of maxillipeds or foot-jaws, and a lower lip, are developed.
Chī-lō-stom'ă-tă, *n.pl.* [Gr. *cheilos*, lip, and *stoma*, mouth.] A suborder of funnel-shaped marine *Polyzoa*, characterized by having the orifice of the cell filled with a thin membranous or calcareous plate, and a curved mouth furnished with a movable lip.
chī-lō-stom'ă-tous, *a.* Pertaining to the *Chilostomata.*
chil'vēr, *n.* A ewe lamb or ewe mutton. [Prov. Eng.]
Chi-mæ'ră, *n.* 1. A genus of cartilaginous fishes, of which the best known species is the *Chimæra monstrosa*, which inhabits the northern seas, and is sometimes called *king of the herrings*, and, from its two pairs of large teeth, *rabbit-fish.*

Chimæra monstrosa.

2. Same as *Chimera.*
chi-mæ'roid, *a.* Pertaining to or resembling the *Chimæra.*
chi-man'gō, *n.* [A native name.] The carrion-buzzard, *Milvago chimango*, one of the South American caracaras.
Chi-maph'i-lă, *n.* [Gr. *cheima*, winter, and *philos*, loving.] A genus of perennial plants, of which *Chimaphila umbellata*, the pipsissewa, is the type.
chimb (chīm), *n.* See second *Chime*, n.
chimb (chīm), *v.t.* See second *Chime*, v.t.
chime, *n.* [ME. *chimbe*, *chymbe*; AS. *cimbal*, *cimbala*; L. *cymbalum*; Gr. *kymbalon*, a cymbal, a bell.]
1. The consonant or harmonic sound of corresponding instruments.

> Instruments that made melodious *chime.* —Milton.

2. Correspondence of sound.

> Love harmonized the *chime.* —Dryden.

3. The musical sound of a set of bells struck with hammers.
4. Correspondence of proportion or relation.
5. A kind of periodical music, or tune of a clock, etc., produced by an apparatus attached.
6. A set of bells (generally five to twelve) which ring in harmony, and are usually placed in the belfry of a church or in a tower; often used in the plural; as, the *chimes* are silent tonight.
chime, *v.i.*; chimed, *pt.*, *pp.*; chiming, *ppr.* 1. To sound in consonance or harmony, as bells; to accord.

> To make the rough recital aptly *chime.* —Prior.

2. To correspond in relation or proportion; to agree; to suit with.

> Father and son, husband and wife, correlative terms, do readily *chime.* —Locke.

3. To agree; to fall in with; to join in a conversation, etc.; followed by *in* or *in with.*

> He often *chimed in with* the discourse. —Arbuthnot.

4. To jingle; to clatter; to have a jingling sound, as some rimes.
chime, *v.t.* 1. To move, strike, or cause to sound in harmony.
2. To recite harmoniously; as, a child *chiming* verse.
chime, chimb, *n.* [ME. *chymbe*, edge, brim; AS. *cim-*, in composition, *cim-stān*, the base of a column.]
1. The edge or rim of a cask, barrel, etc., being the part formed by the projection of the stave ends.
2. The chamfered end of a stave.
chime, chimb, *v.t.* To make the chime in (a cask, barrel, or tub); to chamfer the ends of (staves) in order to make a chime.
chim'ēr, *n.* One who chimes.
chi-mē'ră, chi-mæ'ră, *n.* [L. *chimæra*; Gr. *chimaira*, a goat, a monstrous beast.]
1. In mythology, a monster vomiting flames, represented with the head of a lion, the body of a goat, and the tail of a dragon; supposed to represent a volcanic mountain in Lycia, whose

Chimera—Lycian terra-cotta, British Museum.

top was the resort of lions, the middle that of goats, and the foot that of serpents.
2. In modern usage, a vain or idle fancy; a creature of the imagination; an absurdity or impossible conceit.
chi-mēre', *n.* [OFr. *chamarre*, from Sp. *chamarra*, a shepherd's coat made of sheepskin.] The upper robe worn by a bishop, to which lawn sleeves are usually attached.
chi-mer'ic, *a.* Chimerical.
chi-mer'ic-ăl, *a.* Merely imaginary; fanciful; fantastic; wildly or vainly conceived; that has or can have no existence except in the imagination; as, *chimerical* plans.
chi-mer'ic-ăl-ly, *adv.* Wildly; vainly; fancifully; fantastically.
chim'i-nāge, *n.* [Fr. *chemin*; Sp. *camino*, a way.] In old law, a toll for passage through a forest. [Obs.]
chim'is-try, *n.* Chemistry. [Obs.]
chim'ney, *n.*; *pl.* **chim'neyș.** [ME. *chimny*, *chymney*; OFr. *cheminee*, chimney; LL. *caminata*, a fireplace; L. *caminus*, a furnace, a flue; Gr. *kaminos*, an oven, a furnace.]
1. In architecture, a body of brick, stone, etc., erected in a building, containing a flue or flues, to convey smoke and other volatile matter through the roof from the stove, furnace, hearth, or fireplace where fuel is burned.
2. A fireplace; a hearth. [Obs.]
3. A tall tube of glass, etc., to surround the flame of a lamp or gas-jet, and promote draft and protect the flame.
4. A shaft of brick, iron, or other material, containing flues for the promotion of draft through a furnace, and to carry away smoke, gases, etc.; sometimes forming part of the building containing the fire or furnace, sometimes apart from it though connected by flues; as, a city of tall *chimneys.*

Elizabethan Chimney, East Barsham, Norfolk.

5. The stack of a steam-boiler.
6. In mining, any vertical mass of rich ore in a vein.
chim'ney-bōard, *n.* A fireboard.
chim'ney-breast (-brest), *n.* The projection of a wall inclosing a chimney; especially, the projection inside a building.
chim'ney-cap, *n.* A device, often ornamental, placed on the top of a chimney to improve the draft, or to keep out rain and snow.
chim'ney-cor''nēr, *n.* 1. The corner of a fireplace, or a space between the fire and the sides of the fireplace.
2. In an enlarged sense, the fireside, or a place near the fire.
chim'ney-hook, *n.* A hook in old fireplaces on which to hang pots and kettles.
chim'ney-mŏn''ey, *n.* A duty formerly paid in England for each chimney in a house; also called *hearth-money.*
chim'ney-pieçe, *n.* An ornamental structure of wood or stone set round a fireplace; a mantelpiece.
chim'ney-pot, *n.* A cylinder of earthenware, etc., placed at the top of chimneys to increase the draft.
chim'ney-shaft, *n.* The part of a chimney above the roof.
chim'ney-swal''lōw, *n.* An American bird which lives in chimneys, *Chætura pelagica*; also, the common English swallow, *Hirundo rustica.*
chim'ney-sweep, chim'ney-sweep''ēr, *n.* 1. One whose occupation is to sweep and scrape the soot from chimneys and flues.
2. A mechanical device for cleaning chimneys.
chim'ney-swift, *n.* Same as *Chimney-swallow.*
chim-pan'zee, *n.* [Fr. *chimpanzé*, from a native name.] An animal of the ape kind, *Troglodytes niger*, more nearly resembling man than any other animal; it attains a height of nearly five feet.
chin, *n.* [ME. *chin*; AS. *cin*, chin.] The lowest extremity of the face, below the mouth; the

point of the under jaw in man, or a corresponding part in other animals.

Up to the chin; deeply involved; generally used in connection with something disagreeable.

Chimpanzee (*Troglodytes niger*).

chin, *n.* Talk; chatter; especially, unwelcome talk. [Slang.]

chin, *v.t.* To talk to incessantly and impudently; as, he *chinned* the stranger unmercifully. [Slang.]

chin, *v.i.* To talk. [Slang.]

chī′nȧ, *n.* A fine kind of earthenware, originally made in China and brought thence in the sixteenth century; also called *chinaware*, and *porcelain*. [See *Porcelain*.]

Blue china; a kind of Chinese porcelain decorated in blue beneath the glazing.

China aster; a plant cultivated for its handsome flowers.

chī′nȧ-clāy, *n.* Clay suitable for making porcelain; also called *kaolin*.

Chī′nȧ-măn, *n.*; *pl.* **Chī′nȧ-men.** A Chinese; a man born of Chinese parents.

chi-när′, *n.* [Hind.] The plane-tree of India, *Platanus orientalis*.

chī′nȧ-rọọt, *n.* The rootstock of *Smilax China*, formerly used in medicine as a purgative. It is native to China and Japan.

chī′nȧ-shop, *n.* A store in which chinaware, porcelain, or crockery is sold.

chī′nȧ-stōne, *n.* An old name for *kaolin* or *china-clay*.

chī′nȧ-tree, *n.* A shade-tree, *Melia Azedarach*, sometimes called *pride of India*, widely cultivated in warm countries.

Wild china-tree; the soapberry, *Sapindus marginatus*, found in southern United States, Mexico, and the West Indies.

chī′nȧ-wāre, *n.* 1. Porcelain; pottery made of china-clay. [See *China*.]

2. Crockery, especially the finer kinds.

chiñ′cȧ-pin, *n.* See *Chinkapin*.

chinch, *n.* [Sp. *chinche*, chinch-bug; L. *cimex*, a bug.]

1. A kind of bug of a disgusting odor, which does great injury to wheat and other grains; the *Blissus leucopterus*; called also *chinch-bug*.

2. The *Cimex lectularius*, or bedbug.

chin′chȧ, *n.* [Native name.] A rodent of South America, *Lagidium cuvieri*.

chin′che, chin′chȧ, *n.* [Native Am. name.] The American skunk, *Mephitis mephitica*.

chinch′ẽr-y, *n.* Stinginess. [Obs.]

chin-chil′lȧ, *n.* [Sp.] 1. A small animal of South America, producing a beautiful fur. It is native to Chile and Peru and is of the size of a large squirrel.

2. The fur of the animal.

3. A heavy woolen cloth with a long nap.

Chinchilla lanigera.

Chin-chō′nȧ, Chin-cō′nȧ, *n.* Same as *Cinchona*.

chin′-cough (-kọf), *n.* [Obs.] Same as *Whooping-cough*.

chine, *n.* [ME. *chine, chyne*; OFr. *eschine*, the spine.]

1. The backbone or spine of an animal.

2. A piece of the backbone of an animal, with the adjoining parts, cut for cooking.

chine, *n.* [ME. *chine, chyne*; AS. *cinu*, a crack, chink.] A cleft; a deep ravine. [Prov. Eng. See *Chink*.]

chine, *n.* A common but corrupt form of *chime*, the edge of a cask, etc.

chīne, *v.t.*; chined, *pt.*, *pp.*; chining, *ppr.* To cut through the backbone, or into chine-pieces.

chīne, *v.t.* [Corrupt form of *chime, chimb*.] To chamfer the ends of (staves) to form a chine.

chī-nē′ (-nā′), *a.* [Fr.] Dyed or woven after the fashion of Chinese fabrics; applied to dress-goods, etc.

chined, *a.* 1. Pertaining to the back.

2. Back-broken. [Obs.]

Chī-nēṣe′ (*or* chī-nēs′), *a.* Pertaining to China; made in China.

Chinese fire; a composition used in fireworks to produce colored light.

Chinese wax; the secretion of certain Chinese insects, bleached white and resembling wax; it is used in China for a high class of candles.

Chī-nēṣe′, *n. sing.* and *pl.* 1. A native or natives of China.

2. [*sing.*] Any one of the monosyllabic dialects or languages spoken by Chinamen.

chiñ′gle, *n.* Gravel free from dirt; an old form of *shingle*.

chiñk, *n.* [ME. *chine*; AS. *cinu, cine*, a crack.] A small aperture lengthwise; a cleft, rent, or fissure of greater length than breadth; a gap or crack; as, the *chinks* of a wall.

chiñk, *n.* [Imitative.] 1. A metallic sound; as, the *chink* of coins.

2. Cash; money. [Slang.]

chiñk, *v.i.* To crack; to open.

chiñk, *v.t.* 1. To cause to part and form a fissure.

2. To fill up holes or chinks in; to fill (cracks).

chiñk, *v.t.*; chinked, *pt.*, *pp.*; chinking, *ppr.* To cause to sound, by shaking, as coins or small pieces of metal, or by bringing small, sonorous bodies in collision; as, to *chink* a purse of money.

chiñk, *v.i.* To make a small, sharp sound, as by the collision of little pieces of money, or other sonorous bodies.

chiñ′kȧ-pin, chiñ′cȧ-pin, *n.* [Am. Indian origin.] A small North American tree, *Castanea pumila*, akin to the chestnut, and bearing small, sweet, edible nuts; also written *chinquapin*.

chiñk′y, *a.* Full of chinks or fissures; gaping; opening in narrow clefts.

chinned, *a.* Having a chin; used in compounds; as, long-*chinned*.

Chī′nō-. A combining form signifying connection with China or the Chinese; as, *Chino*-Russian affairs.

chi-noid′ine, *n.* A by-product of cinchona bark in the form of a brown and brittle resinous compound precipitated by ammonia.

Chi-noiṣe′rie (-nwäẓ′ri), *n.* [Fr.] Anything made by or peculiar to the Chinese.

chin′ō-line, *n.* An alkaloidal distillation obtained from a combination of quinine with potash; also written *quinoline*.

Chi-nọọk′, *n.* [Am. Indian.] 1. A Flathead Indian, so called from a tribal custom of flattening the skull when young. The tribe is located in the state of Washington.

2. A dialect consisting of a jargon of Indian, English, French, and other words and phrases, used in intercourse between Indians of various tribes, traders, and others, in the northwestern states. It contains many words from the language of the Chinook Indians, hence its name.

3. [c—] In Montana and neighboring territory on the eastern slope of the Rockies, a warm, dry wind from the west or north; probably so called because coming from the direction of the Chinook country.

chiñ′quȧ-pin (-kȧ-), *n.* See *Chinkapin*.

chinse, *v.t.*; chinsed, *pt.*, *pp.*; chinsing, *ppr.* [Nautical term, U. S.] Among seamen, to thrust oakum into (the seams or chinks of a ship) with a chisel or point of a knife, as a temporary expedient for calking.

chins′ing-ī″ron (-ūrn), *n.* A small chisel used in chinsing.

chintz, *n.* [Hind. *chhint*, chintz; Sans. *chitra*, spotted, bright.] A kind of cloth, printed with flowers and other devices, in a number of different colors and usually glazed.

chiop-pīne′ (chop-), *n.* See *Chopine*.

chip, *n.* [ME. *chip, chippe*, a chip; AS. *cyp, cypp*; L. *cippus*, a stake, post.]

1. A piece of wood, stone, or other substance, separated from a mass by a cutting instrument, as an ax, chisel, or the like.

2. A fragment or piece broken off; a small piece.

3. A material composed of slips of wood, palm-leaf, or straw, plaited into a convenient form for the manufacture of hat and bonnet shapes.

4. Anything regarded with contempt, as lifeless, withered, spoiled, or useless.

5. A counter used in games, especially in the game of poker.

6. The nautical name for the quadrant-shaped piece of wood fastened at the end of a log-line; called also the *log*.

7. In nautical parlance, a carpenter; generally used in the plural.

A chip of the old block; a colloquial term applied to a child who exhibits characteristics similar to those of his father.

Brother chip; a brother carpenter; hence, a fellow workman in any trade. [Colloq.]

Buffalo chips; the dried dung of the buffalo, sometimes used in the prairie states as fuel.

Chip bonnet, chip hat; a bonnet or hat shape, manufactured of chip.

Saratoga chips; very thin slices of potato fried to a chip, that is, fried crisp.

chip, *v.t.*; chipped (chipt), *pt.*, *pp.*; chipping, *ppr.* 1. To cut into small pieces or chips; to diminish by cutting away a little at a time or in small pieces; to hew.

2. To break open by degrees; as, the chickens *chipped* their shells.

3. In poker, to put up, as a stake.

4. To break off a small piece from; as, to *chip* crockery.

To chip in; to contribute; to add to a common fund; to share the expense of. [Colloq.]

chip, *v.i.* To break or fly off in small pieces, as earthenware.

chip′-ax, *n.* A small ax for chipping wood.

chip′-bĩrd, *n.* A bird of the *Fringillidæ* family, *Spizella socialis*, widely distributed in North America, and also known as the *chipping-sparrow*, or *chippy*.

chip′muñk, chip′mŏñk, *n.* [Am. Indian origin.] A small animal, *Tamias striatus*, resembling a squirrel, and common in the United States; called also *ground-squirrel, striped squirrel, chipping-squirrel*, etc.

chip′pẽr, *v.i.* To chirp or chirrup. [Prov. Eng.]

chip′pẽr, *a.* Lively; cheerful; talkative. [Colloq.]

Chip′pe-wāyṣ, *n.pl.* [Am. Indian.] The Ojibways, an Indian tribe formerly living on the shores of Lake Superior.

chip′ping, *n.* 1. A chip; a piece cut off or separated by a cutting or graving instrument; a fragment.

2. The flying or breaking off in small pieces of the edges of earthenware and porcelain.

3. The act of cutting or breaking off small pieces, as in dressing stone or timber.

chip′ping-bĩrd, *n.* Same as *Chip-bird*.

chip′ping-squir″rel, *n.* Same as *Chipmunk*.

chip′py, *a.* Dry, like chips; abounding in chips

chip′py, *n.* Same as *Chip-bird*.

chī-rā′grȧ, *n.* [Gr. *cheiragra*, gout in the hand; *cheir*, hand, and *agra*, seizure.] Gout in the hand.

chī-rag′riç-ăl, *a.* Having the gout in the hand, or subject to that disease.

chī-ret′tȧ, *n.* [Hind. *chiraeta, chiraita*, a kind of gentian.] A herb of the gentian family found in northern India and used in medicine as a tonic, etc.

chĩrk, *a.* Lively; cheerful; in good spirits; in a comfortable state. [Colloq., New Eng.]

chĩrk, *v.i.* [ME. *chirken*, to make a noise, as a bird; AS. *cearcian*, creak, crack.]

1. To chirp like a bird. [Obs.]

2. To screech; to shriek. [Obs.]

chĩrk, *v.t.* To enliven; to cheer; with *up*; as, to *chirk* a man *up*. [Colloq., New Eng.]

chĩrm, *v.i.* [ME. *chirmen*; AS. *cirman*, to cry out, make a loud noise.] To sing or cry mournfully, as birds before a storm. [Obs.]

chī′rō-. A combining form from Greek *cheir* the hand.

chī-rog′nō-my, *n.* [*Chiro-*, and Gr. *gnomē*, understanding.] The reading of character by the appearance or lines of the hand; palmistry.

chī′rō-grȧph, *n.* [*Chiro-*, and Gr. *graphein*, to write.]

1. Formerly, a writing which, requiring a counterpart, was engrossed twice on the same piece of parchment, with a space between, in which was written the word *chirographum*, or other word or words, through which the parchment was cut, and one part given to each party. It answered to what is now called a *charter-party*.

2. A written voucher of a debt, signed by the debtor's own hand.

3. Any written instrument; an autograph.

chī-rog′rȧ-phẽr, *n.* 1. One who exercises or professes the art or business of writing.

2. A palmist; one who professes to tell fortunes by the hand.

chī-rō-graph′iç, chī-rō-graph′iç-ăl, *a.* Pertaining to chirography.

chī-rog′rȧ-phist, *n.* A chirographer.

chī-rog′rȧ-phy, *n.* [Gr. *cheirographos*, hand writing; *cheir*, the hand, and *graphein*, to write.]

1. The art of writing, or a writing with one's own hand; as, let me see his *chirography*.

2. The art of fortune-telling by the hand.

chī-rō-ġym′nast, *n.* [*Chiro-*, and Gr. *gymnastēs*, a trainer of athletes, from *gymnazein*, to train.] A device by means of which pianists may exercise their fingers.

chī-rō-loġ′iç-ăl, *a.* Pertaining to chirology.

chī-rol′ō-ġist, *n.* One who communicates thoughts by signs made with the hands and fingers.

chī-rol′ō-ġy, *n.* [*Chiro-*, and Gr. *logos*, description, from *legein*, to speak.] The art or practice of communicating thoughts by signs made by the hands and fingers; a substitute for language or discourse, much used by the deaf and dumb, and by others who communicate with them; a manual alphabet. [See *Dactylology*.]

chī′rō-man-cẽr, *n.* [*Chiro-*, and Gr. *manteia*, divination.] One who professes to foretell future events, or to tell the fortunes and dispositions of persons, by inspecting the hands; a palmist.

chī'rō-man-cy, *n.* Divination by the hand; palmistry; the art or practice of attempting to foretell events, or to discover the disposition of a person, by inspecting the lines and lineaments of his hand.

chī-rō-man'tic, chī-rō-man'tic-ăl, *a.* Pertaining to chiromancy, or divination by the hand.

chī'rō-man-tist, *n.* Same as *Chiromancer.*

chī-rō-nom'ic, *a.* Relating to chironomy.

chī-ron'ō-my, *n.* [*Chiro-*, and Gr. *nemein*, to manage, wield.] The science of pantomimic gesticulation, especially in musical directing as practised by the choir-masters of the early Western church.

chī'rō-plast, *n.* [*Chiro-*, and Gr. *plastos*, formed, from *plassein*, to form.] An instrument to guide and train the hand when playing on the piano.

chī-rop'ō-dist, *n.* [*Chiro-*, and Gr. *pous*, *podos*, foot.] Literally, one who handles the feet; a surgeon for the hands or feet. The term is usually applied to one who treats or removes corns and bunions.

chī-rop'ō-dy, *n.* The art of treating the diseases and excrescences of the hands and feet.

chī-rō-prac'tics, *n.* [Gr *cheir*, hand+*praktikos*, active, practical.] A system of healing which treats disease by the manipulation of the spinal column.

chī-rō-prac'tor, *n.* One skilled in chiropractics.

chī-rop'tėr, *n.* A mammal of the order *Chiroptera.*

Chī-rop'tē-rȧ, *n.pl.* [L., from Gr. *cheir*, hand, and *pteron*, wing.] An order of mammals, the bats. They are characterized by the elongation of all the fingers, save the thumb, for the support of a membrane which stretches along the sides of the body, and is attached to the posterior limbs. They have thus the power of sustained flight. [See *Bat.*]

chī-rop'tē-rous, *a.* Belonging to or having the characteristics of the *Chiroptera.*

chī-rop-tē-ryġ'i-um, *n.* [*Chiro-*, and Gr. *pteryx*, wing.] The hand-like fore limb of certain vertebrates.

chī-ros'ō-phist, *n.* [*Chiro-*, and Gr. *sophos*, wise.] A fortune-teller by means of palmistry; a chiromancer.

chī-ros'ō-phy, *n.* Same as *Chiromancy.*

chī-rō-thē'ri-um, *n.* [L., from Gr. *cheir*, hand, and *therion*, a wild animal.] In geology, a name given to the great unknown and extinct animal that formed the larger footsteps upon the slabs of the Trias, which resemble a human hand.

chī-rot'ō-ny, *n.* [Gr. *cheirotonia*, a stretching-out of the hands; *cheir*, hand, and *teinein*, to stretch.]

1. A voting or electing by a show of hands, as in ancient Greece. [Rare.]

2. A laying-on of hands, as in the ordination of a priest.

chirp, *v.i.*; chirped, *pt.*, *pp.*; chirping, *ppr.* [Imitative.] To make the noise of certain small birds or of certain insects; as, a *chirping* lark.

chirp, *v.t.* To utter in a high, cheerful tone of voice. [Rare.]

chirp, *n.* The sharp, cheerful note of certain birds or insects.

chirp'ėr, *n.* One who chirps, or is cheerful.

chirp'ing, *n.* The noise of certain small birds and insects.

chirp'ing-ly, *adv.* In a chirping manner.

chirp'y, *a.* Inclined to chirp; lively; talkative. [Colloq.]

chirr, chirre, *v.i.* [AS. *ceorran*, to murmur.] To coo, as a pigeon; to utter a trilling sound, as a grasshopper or cricket.

chir'rup, *v.t.*; chirruped, *pt.*, *pp.*; chirruping, *ppr.* To cherup; to quicken or animate by chirping; as, to *chirrup* one's horse.

chir'rup, *v.i.* To chirp.

chir'rup, *n.* The sound of a chirp; the act of chirping.

chir'rup-y, *a.* Joyful; cheerful; chirpy.

chī-rūr'ġeon, *n.* [L. *chirurgus*; Gr. *cheirourgos*, a surgeon, one who operates with the hand; *cheir*, the hand, and *ergos*, work.] A surgeon. [Obs.]

chī-rūr'ġeon-ly, *adv.* In the manner of a chirurgeon; surgically.

chī-rūr'ġėr-y, *n.* [Gr. *cheirourgia.*] Surgery. [Obs.]

chī-rūr'ġic, chī-rūr'ġic-ăl, *a.* Surgical. [Obs.]

chis'el, *n.* [ME. *chisel*, *chysel*; OFr. *cisel*, chisel; LL. *cisellus*, forceps, from L. *cæsus*, pp. of *cædere*, to cut.] An instrument of iron or steel, used in carpentry, cabinetwork, masonry, sculpture, etc., for paring, hewing, or gouging. It consists of a metal blade with a cutting-edge at one end, and a handle at the other to which the pressure is generally applied by a mallet or hammer, the hand or a machine. There are many forms of *chisels*, which take their names either from their shape or from their uses, as calking-chisel, turning-chisel, tooth edged chisel etc.

chis'el, *v.t.*; chiseled *or* chiselled, *pt.*, *pp.*; chiseling *or* chiselling, *ppr.* 1. To cut, pare, gouge, or engrave with a chisel.

2. To fashion by means of a chisel; as, to *chisel* a statue.

3. Figuratively, to drive a sharp bargain with; to get the better of by shrewd deceit; to cheat. [Slang.]

chis'el-draft, *n.* The dressed edge of a stone, serving as a guide in cutting the other edges and sides.

chis'eled, chis'elled, *a.* Fashioned with a chisel; resembling work done by a chisel; clear-cut; statuesque.

chis'el-tooth, *n.* One of the incisors of a rodent, having a chisel-shaped edge.

Chis'leu (-lū), *n.* [Heb. *Kisleu.*] Formerly, the ninth, now the third, month of the Jewish ecclesiastical year, answering to part of November and part of December.

chis'ley, *a.* [AS. *ceosel*, *ceosl*, gravel, sand.] Formed by pebbles, containing chiefly gravel and sand; having a sandy and clayey character; applied to soils.

chit, *n.* [AS. *cith*, a shoot or twig.]

1. A shoot or sprout; the first shooting or germination of a seed or plant.

2. A child or babe; a pert young person, especially, a girl. [Colloq.]

3. A freckle; a wart; an excrescence. [Obs.]

chit, *n.* A note or short letter; any memorandum or brief writing; used chiefly in Japan and China; in India also called *chitty.*

chit, *v.i.* To sprout; to shoot, as a seed or plant.

chit'ăl, *n.* [Hind. *chītal*, spotted, a spotted snake; *chītal*, a spotted deer.]

1. The axis, or Indian spotted deer, *Axis maculata.*

2. A venomous sea-serpent found off the coasts of India, and belonging to the genus *Hydrophis.*

chit'chat, *n.* Prattle; familiar or trifling talk.

chī'tin, chī'tine, *n.* [Gr. *chitōn*, a tunic.] In chemistry, a hard, amorphous compound, the chief constituent of the external covering or integument of crustaceans and insects; also called *entomolin.*

chī"ti-ni-zā'tion, *n.* The act or process of assuming a chitinous form.

chī-ti-nog'e-nous, *a.* [Gr. *chitōn*, a tunic, and *-genēs*, producing.] In biology, producing, or coated with chitin.

chī'ti-nous, *a.* Pertaining to, formed of, or containing chitin.

chit'lings, chit'lins, *n.pl.* Same as *Chitterlings.*

chī'ton, *n.* [Gr. *chitōn*, a woolen undergarment.]

1. An undergarment or shirt worn by the ancient Greeks; a kind of tunic.

2. [C—] In zoölogy, a genus of gasteropods having an armored shell composed of eight pieces.

chit'rȧ, *n.* [Native Indian name.] The Indian spotted hog-deer; also spelled *chittra.*

chit'tăm-wood, *n.* In botany, *Rhus cotinoides*, the smoketree of southern United States; also, the wood of the tree, which furnishes an orange-colored dyestuff.

chit'tėr, *v.i.* [ME. *chiteren*, to chirp, an imitative word.]

1. To twitter; to whistle tremulously, as a bird. [Obs.]

2. To chatter, as the teeth; to shiver with cold. [Scot.]

chit'tėr-ling, *n.* The wrinkled frill to the breast of a shirt. [Obs.]

chit'tėr-lings, *n.pl.* [ME. *chitterlinge*, entrail; compare G. *kutteln*, entrails.] The smaller intestines of swine, etc., fried for food.

chit'trȧ, *n.* See *Chitra.*

chit'ty, *a.* 1. Full of chits or sprouts.

2. Childish. [Obs.]

3. Having warts or pimples. [Obs.]

chit'ty, *n.* [Hind. *chit hee*, a letter.] In India, a short letter, memorandum, or certificate. [See *Chit.*]

chiv'ā-chē, chiv'ā-chiē, *n.* [Obs.] See *Chevachie.*

chiv'ăl-ric, *a.* Partaking of the character of chivalry; knightly; gallant; chivalrous.

chiv'ăl-rous (-rus), *a.* [ME. *chivalrous*; OFr. *chevalereus*, bold, gallant; *chevalier*, a knight.] Pertaining to chivalry or knight-errantry; warlike; bold; gallant; brave.

Syn.—Courageous, generous, knightly, gallant, heroic, valiant, high-minded.

chiv'ăl-rous-ly, *adv.* In a chivalrous manner; boldly; gallantly.

chiv'ăl-ry, *n.* [ME. *chivalrie*; OFr. *chevalerie*, knighthood, from *cheval*, a horse; L. *caballus*, horse, nag.]

1. Knighthood; a military dignity, founded on the service of soldiers on horseback, called knights; a service formerly deemed more honorable than service in infantry.

2. The qualifications of a knight, as valor and dexterity in arms.

3. The system of knighthood; the privileges, characteristics, or manners of knights; the practice of knight-errantry, or the knightly defense of life and honor.

4. An adventure or exploit. [Obs.]

5. The body or order of knights.

6. In old English law, a tenure of lands by knight's service; that is, by the condition of performing some service on horseback, or of performing some noble or military service to the lord.

Age of chivalry; the period when chivalry flourished, from the tenth to the fourteenth century.

Court of chivalry; a court, formerly held before the lord high constable and earl marshal of England, having cognizance of contracts and other matters relating to deeds of arms and war.

chīve, *n.* [Obs.] 1. In botany, a filament; a blade.

2. A slice or a piece; as, a *chive* of bread.

chīve, *n.* See *Cive.*

chiv'y, *v.t.*; chivied, *pt.*, *pp.*; chivying, *ppr.* [Origin obscure.] To goad; to hunt; to drive; to chase. [Slang, Eng.]

chlam'y-dāte, *a.* [L. *chlamydatus*, dressed in a cloak, from *chlamys*, Gr. *chlamys*, a cloak.] In zoölogy, having a hood, as certain gasteropods.

chlȧ-myd'ē-ous, *a.* [Gr. *chlamys*, cloak.] In botany, pertaining to the floral envelope of a plant.

chlam'y-dēs, *n.*, L. pl. of *chlamys.*

Chlam-y-doph'ō-rus, *n.* [Gr. *chlamys*, a cloak, and *phoros*, bearing, from *pherein*, to bear.] A genus of small South American armadillos, covered with a shell or coat of mail, like a cloak.

chlam'y-dō-spōre, *n.* [Gr. *chlamys*, cloak, and *sporos*, a sowing.]

1. In biology, a spore furnished with protective envelopes.

2. One of certain protected spores generated in certain fungi.

chlā'mys, *n.*; *pl.* **chlā'mys-ēs** or **chlam'y-dēs.** [L., from Gr. *chlamys*, a military cloak.]

1. A tunic or loose coat, worn by the ancient Greeks over the vest or doublet.

2. One of the pontifical vestments.

Typical Chlamys.

chlō-aṣ'mȧ, *n.* [Gr. *chloazein*, to be or become green.] In medicine, a disease of the skin characterized by yellow patches.

chlōr-. A combining form from Gr. *chloros*, green; used in scientific compounds.

chlōr-ā-cē'tic (*or* -cet'ic), *a.* [*Chlor-*, and L. *acetum*, vinegar.] In chemistry, pertaining to or obtained from chlorin and acetic acid.

Chloracetic acid; an acid formed by the action of chlorin on acetic acid.

chlō'răl, *n.* [*Chlor-* and *al*cohol.]

1. An oleaginous liquid compound, $CCl_3.CHO$, obtained by the action of chlorin on alcohol, and by other methods. It has a pungent odor and a dry, bitter taste. Also called *anhydrous chloral.*

2. In medicine, chloral hydrate, a white crystalline substance, used internally or hypodermically as a soporific.

chlō'răl-ism, *n.* A low and unhealthy condition of the system produced by excessive use of chloral; also, the habit of using chloral.

chlōr-al'um, *n.* A disinfectant and antiseptic containing chlorid of aluminium, of which it is an aqueous solution.

chlōr-an'il, *n.* [*Chlor-* and *aniline*, from Ar. *an-nil*, the indigo-plant.] A yellow crystalline compound, obtained by the action of chlorin on phenol and other benzene derivatives, as aniline.

Chlō-ran-thā'cē-æ, *n.pl.* A family of tropical aromatic plants and small trees, of which *Chloranthus* is typical.

Chlō-ran'thus, *n.* [*Chlor-*, and Gr. *anthos*, flower.] A small genus of perennial plants of the family *Chloranthaceæ*, natives of Asia, and having spicy and tonic qualities. The roots and seeds of some of the species are used in medicine.

chlō-ran'thy, *n.* See *Chlorosis.*

chlō'rāte, *n.* A salt of chloric acid.

chlōr-hȳ'dric, *a.* Same as *Hydrochloric.*

chlōr-hȳ'drin, *n.* [*Chlor-*, and Gr. *hydōr*, water.] Any one of a class of compounds formed by the substitution of chlorin for one to three hydroxyl groups in glycerin, etc.

chlō'ric, *a.* Pertaining to chlorin, or obtained from it; as, *chloric* acid.

Chloric acid; that acid of chlorin and oxygen which contains the greatest proportion of the oxygen.

Chloric ether; a compound made by subjecting alcohol to the action of hydrochloric acid; ethylchlorid. The name is also given to spirits of chloroform.

çhlō′rid, çhlō′ride, *n.* A nonacid compound of chlorin with another element; formerly called *muriate.*

Chlorid of lime; bleaching-powder. It is also used as a disinfectant.

çhlō′ri-dāte, *v.t.* Same as *Chloridize.*

çhlō-rid′iç, *a.* Relating to or containing a chlorid.

çhlō′rid-īze, *v.t.;* chloridized, *pt., pp.;* chloridizing, *ppr.* To subject to or sensitize with a chlorid; as, in photography, to *chloridize* a plate with chlorid of silver.

çhlō-rim′e-try, *n.* See *Chlorometry.*

çhlō′rin, çhlō′rine, *n.* [Gr. *chlōros,* pale green, greenish-yellow.] An elementary gaseous substance contained in common salt. As commonly isolated it is a greenish, highly poisonous, liquefiable gas, with an offensive, suffocating odor. It is two and a half times as heavy as air and can be liquefied by cold and pressure. The extraordinary affinity of chlorin for hydrogen enables it to decompose compounds containing that element, which makes it of the greatest value as a disinfecting, bleaching, and oxidizing agent.

çhlō′rin-āte, *v.t.;* chlorinated, *pt., pp.;* chlorinating, *ppr.* To combine with chlorin; to treat or impregnate with chlorin.

çhlō-ri-nā′tion, *n.* The act or process of chlorinating, or subjecting anything to the action of chlorin. In mining, *chlorination* is used for the extraction of gold by exposing the ore to chlorin gas, the resulting gold chlorid being then dissolved in water, from which the precious metal is precipitated.

çhlŏr-ī-od′iç, *a.* Compounded of or containing chlorin and iodine.

çhlŏr-ī′ō-dine, *n.* A compound of chlorin and iodine; chloriodic acid. [Rare.]

çhlō′rite, *n.* [L. *chloritis;* Gr. *chlōritis,* a light green stone, from *chlōros,* light green.] A soft, olive-green mineral, consisting of minute scales, and somewhat soapy to the touch. It is allied to mica and talc, but contains also silica, magnesia, and alumina.

Chlorite slate; a slablike rock, a subspecies of chlorite.

çhlō′rite, *n.* A salt formed of chlorous acid and a base.

çhlō-rit′iç, *a.* Pertaining to or containing chlorite; as, *chloritic* sand.

çhlō′ri-toid, *n.* A chloritic mineral, shading from dark gray to greenish black in color and found in scales easily broken or split. It is a hydrous silicate of alumina, iron and magnesia; also called *brittle mica.*

çhlō′rō-. A combining form, from Gr. *chlōros,* pale green; used in chemistry to indicate that chlorin is part of the compound named.

çhlō″rō-çär-bon′iç, çhlō-rō-çär′bŏn-ous, *a.* [*Chloro-,* and L. *carbo,* coal.] Consisting of a compound of chlorin and carbonic oxid, formed by exposing a mixture of the two gases to the direct solar rays.

çhlō-rō-çrụ′ō-rin, *n.* [*Chloro-,* and L. *cruor,* blood.] A green coloring matter supposed to produce the green tinge of the blood in certain worms.

çhlō′rō-dȳne, *n.* A powerful anodyne remedy formerly much used, containing opium, chloroform, Indian hemp, etc.

çhlō′rō-fọrm, *n.* [*Chloro-,* and *formyl,* from L. *formica,* an ant.] Trichlormethane, or formyl trichlorid, $CHCl_3$; a colorless, volatile liquid of a sweetish taste and fragrant odor, formed by distilling together alcohol, water, and chlorid of lime. It is in general use as an anesthetic in surgical operations, and is also applied externally to relieve pain. Formerly called *chloric ether.*

çhlō′rō-fọrm, *v.t.;* chloroformed, *pt., pp.;* chloroforming, *ppr.* To administer chloroform to, or to place under its influence; to treat with chloroform.

çhlō-rō-leū′cite, *n.* Same as *Chloroplastid.*

çhlō-rō′mȧ, *n.* [Gr. *chlōros,* yellowish green.] A fleshy tumor of a greenish color, occurring usually in the membranes of the skull.

çhlō-rom′e-tẽr, *n.* [*Chloro-,* and Gr. *metron,* a measure.] An instrument for testing the decoloring or bleaching powers of chlorid of lime.

çhlō-rom′e-try, *n.* The process for testing the bleaching power of any combination of chlorin.

çhlō-rō′pȧl, *n.* [*Chloro-,* and L. *opalus,* opal; Gr. *opallios,* a rock, stone, precious stone.] A greenish, earthy mineral, consisting of silica and oxid of iron, with eighteen to twenty per cent of water.

çhlō′rō-phāne, *n.* [*Chloro-,* and Gr. *-phanēs,* evident; from *phainein,* to show.]

1. A variety of fluor spar, from Siberia. When placed on a heated iron it gives a beautiful emerald-green light.

2. The pigment in the inner portion of the cones of the retina, yellowish green in color.

Çhlō-rō-phyc′ē-æ (-fis′ē-ē), *n.pl.* [*Chloro-,* and Gr. *phykos,* seaweed.] A large group of green algæ, or seaweeds; the group comprises the orders *Volvocineæ, Siphoneæ, Protococcaceæ,* and *Confervoideæ.*

çhlō-rō-phy′ceous (-fish′us), *a.* Pertaining to the *Chlorophyceæ.*

çhlō′rō-phyl, çhlō′rō-phyll, *n.* [Fr. *chlorophylle;* Gr. *chlōros,* green, and *phyllon,* leaf.] The green coloring matter contained in plants; leaf-green; also a granular matter formed in the cells of those parts of plants which are exposed to the light and by means of which all regular absorption and digestion of plant food is made.

Chlorophyl.

a, Spiral bands of Chlorophyl in Spirogyra. *b,* Irregular mass in Zygnema. *c,* Granules in cells of the leaf.

çhlō-rō-phyl′li-ăn, *a.* Pertaining to chlorophyl or containing it; as, *chlorophyllian* granules; *chlorophyllian* cells.

çhlō″rō-phyl-lif′ẽr-ous, *a.* Chlorophylligerous.

çhlō″rō-phyl-lig′e-nous, *a.* [L., from Gr. *chlōros,* green, and *phyllon,* a leaf, and *-genēs,* producing.] Producing chlorophyl; produced by chlorophyl.

çhlō″rō-phyl-lig′ẽr-ous, *a.* Containing or resembling chlorophyl.

çhlō-roph′yl-loid, *a.* [*Chloro-,* and Gr. *phyllon,* leaf, and *eidos,* form.] Resembling chlorophyl.

çhlō-roph′yl-lous, *a.* Same as *Chlorophylligerous.*

çhlō-rō-piç′rin, *n.* [Gr. *chlōros,* a greenish color, and *pikros,* sharp.] A colorless liquid, with a strong penetrating odor, formed by the action of picric acid on chlorid of lime.

çhlō′rō-plast, *n.* Same as *Chloroplastid.*

çhlō-rō-plas′tid, *n.* [*Chloro-,* and Gr. *plastos,* formed, from *plassein,* to form.] A granule of chlorophyl; also called *chloroleucite.*

çhlō″rō-plȧ-tin′iç, *a.* Designating an acid, compounded of chlorin, platinum, and hydrochloric acid, produced in the form of reddish-brown crystals, and largely used as a reagent.

çhlō-rō′sis, *n.* [Gr. *chlōros,* green.]

1. The green sickness, a disease of young women, characterized by a pale or greenish hue of the skin, weakness, palpitation, dyspepsia, etc.

2. In botany, (a) a disease of plants caused by lack of iron, by which they turn to a pale, sickly hue; (b) the transformation of most of the organs or normally-colored parts of a flower into green leaves; chloranthy.

çhlō-rot′iç, *a.* 1. Pertaining to chlorosis; as, *chlorotic* affections.

2. Affected by chlorosis.

çhlō′rous, *a.* Relating to or consisting of an acid of chlorin and oxygen which contains the smallest proportion of oxygen.

çhlō′rụ-ret, *n.* [Gr. *chlōros,* green, and *-uret.*] A compound of chlorin; a name formerly given to a *chlorid.* [Obs.]

chōak, *v.* An obsolete form of *choke.*

çhō′ȧ-nȧ, *n.; pl.* **çhō′ȧ-næ.** [Gr. *choanē,* funnel.]

1. In anatomy, a funnel-like opening; specifically, one of the funnel-like nasal cavities.

2. The collar-like rim encircling the flagellum of some kinds of *Infusoria.*

çhō′ȧ-nāte, *a.* Relating to or formed like a choana.

çhō′an-ite, *n.* A zoöphyte of the Chalk; also called *petrified anemone.*

çhō′ȧ-noid, *a.* [Gr. *choanē,* a funnel, and *eidos,* form.] Having the shape of a funnel; specifically applied to a hollow muscle attached to the ball of the eye in a number of reptiles and mammals.

çhō-ȧ-noph′ō-rous, *a.* [Gr. *choanē,* a funnel, and *pherein,* to bear.] Possessed of a collar, as certain infusorians; choanate.

Chō′cärd, *n.* A kind of crow; the chough; called also the *red-legged crow.*

chock, *v.t.;* chocked (chokt), *pt., pp.;* chocking, *ppr.* To make fast or to stop, with a block or wedge; as, to *chock* a wheel or a barrel.

chock, *v.i.* [From *choke;* ME. *choken;* AS. *ceocian,* to choke, fill up.]

1. To fill up a cavity; as, the woodwork exactly *chocked* into the joints.

2. To encounter. [Obs.]

chock, *n.* 1. A wedge, or something to confine a cask or other body, by chocking into the space around it.

2. An encounter. [Obs.]

3. In shipbuilding, a metal casting, having two short horn-shaped projections curving inward, between which ropes or hawsers are passed during the acts of hauling or warping.

chock, *adv.* Among seamen, completely; thoroughly; as, *chock* aft; *chock* out, etc.

chock′ȧ-block, *a.* Lifted as far as the tackle will allow, the blocks being brought together, thus preventing further motion; jammed, said of a tackle, or a thing being hoisted.

chock′=fụll, *a.* Full as possible; quite full; also written *choke-full.*

choc′ō-lāte, *n.* [Fr. *chocolat;* Sp. and Port. *chocolate;* Mex. *chocolatl,* chocolate; *choco,* cacao, and *latl,* water.]

1. A paste or cake composed of the roasted kernel of the cacao, with other ingredients, such as sugar, cinnamon, or vanilla.

2. The beverage made by dissolving chocolate in boiling water or boiling milk.

choc′ō-lāte, *a.* 1. Made of or flavored with chocolate; as, *chocolate* cake.

2. Of the color of chocolate; as, a *chocolate* livery.

choc′ō-lāte=rọọt, *n.* See *Geum.*

Choc′tạws, *n.pl.* One of the civilized tribes of North American Indians now living in the Indian Territory.

chog′set, *n.* See *Cunner.*

choice, *n.* [ME. *chois, choise;* OFr. *chois, choix,* choice, from *choisir,* to choose.]

1. The act of choosing; the voluntary act of selecting or separating from two or more things that which is preferred; or the determination of the mind in preferring one thing to another; election.

2. The power of choosing; option; as, he had the *choice* of two evils.

3. Care in selecting; judgment or skill in distinguishing what is to be preferred, and in giving a preference. [Rare.]

> I imagine Cæsar's apophthegms were collected with judgment and *choice.*—Bacon.

4. The person or thing chosen; that which is approved and selected in preference to others; selection.

> Nor let thy conquests only be her *choice.* —Prior.

5. The best part of anything; that which is preferable, and properly the object of choice.

> In the *choice* of our sepulchers bury thy dead. —Gen. xxiii. 6.

6. The act of electing to office by vote; election.

7. A number large enough to furnish a *choice.*

Hobson's choice; a choice without an alternative; the expression is said to have originated in the practice of a livery-stable keeper by that name who would only allow a patron to take the horse nearest the stable door.

Syn.—Election, option, preference, selection.

choice, *a.; comp.* choicer; *superl.* choicest. 1. Worthy of being preferred; select; precious.

> My *choicest* hours of life are lost. —Swift.

2. Holding dear; preserving or using with care, as valuable; frugal; as, to be *choice* of time, or of advantages.

3. Selecting with care and due attention to preference; as, to be *choice* of one's company.

choice′=drạwn, *a.* Selected with particular care. [Rare.]

choice′fụl, *a.* Fickle. [Obs.]

choice′less, *a.* Not having the power of choosing; not free. [Rare.]

choice′ly, *adv.* 1. With care in choosing; with exact choice; as, a band of men *choicely* collected.

2. Valuably; excellently; preferably; curiously.

3. With great care; carefully; as, a thing *choicely* preserved.

choice′ness, *n.* Valuableness; particular value or worth; as, the *choiceness* of a plant, or of wine.

choil, *n.* The part of a knife-blade between the cutting-edge and the tang.

çhoir (kwīr), *n.* [ME. *queer, quere;* OFr. *cuer,* a choir; L. *chorus;* Gr. *choros,* a band of dancers and singers.]

1. A collection of singers, especially in divine service, in a church.

2. Any collection of singers.

3. That part of a church appropriated for the singers.

çhoir′=ọr″găn, *n.* A part of the full church-organ, complete in itself, and specially suited for choir accompaniments.

çhoir′=screen, *n.* A screen, in old churches, usually of handsomely carved woodwork, dividing the choir from the aisles.

çhoir′=sẽrv″ice, *n.* A religious observance in which the services of a choir are used.

chōke, *v.t.;* choked (chōkt), *pt., pp.;* choking *ppr.* [ME. *choken, cheken;* AS. *ceocian,* to choke; probably imitative.]

1. To obstruct the respiration of, by filling the windpipe or compressing the neck; used to express a temporary or partial stoppage, or an entire stoppage that causes death; to suffocate; to strangle.

2. To stop by filling; to obstruct; to block up; as, to *choke* the entrance to a harbor.

3. To hinder by obstruction or impediments;

to hinder or check the growth, expansion, or progress of; as, to *choke* the spreading of the fruit.

4. To smother or extinguish, as fire.

5. To suppress or stifle; usually with *down*; as, he *choked down* his rising emotions.

6. To offend; to cause to take an exception; as, I was *choked* at this word.

7. To affect with a sense of choking, as in anger.

8. To narrow (the bore of a gun) at the muzzle.

To choke off; figuratively, to obstruct by decisive action; as, by their loud shouts the audience *choked off* the speaker.

chōke, *v.i.* 1. To have the windpipe stopped; as, cattle are apt to *choke* when eating.

2. To be offended; to take exceptions.

3. To stick, as if by choking; as, the words *choked* in his throat.

Syn.—Suffocate, stifle, strangle, constrict, throttle.

chōke, *n.* 1. The act of choking; the noise or stoppage in the windpipe, as in strangulation.

2. The constriction, or part of smallest caliber, in the bore of a choke-bored gun.

3. The neck of a rocket, where the stick is attached.

4. The tie at the end of a nonmetallic cartridge.

5. The filamentous or capillary part of the artichoke.

Choke coil; a coil so wound that when in the path of an alternating current it possesses great self-induction or exerts a choking effect. Used in radiotelegraphy.

chōke, *n.* [Hind. *chauk*, a square, market-place.] In India, the principal street or an open area in a town or village.

chōke′ber″ry, *n.* An American shrub, *Pyrus arbutifolia*, which belongs to the rose family and grows in damp thickets; also, its fruit, a small, red or purple, apple-shaped or pear-shaped, astringent berry.

chōke′-bōre, *n.* A gun with the bore narrowing toward the muzzle to keep the charge of shot from spreading; also, the bore of a gun, so narrowed.

chōke′-bōre, *v.t.* To bore with a choke or gradually narrowing caliber.

chōke′-cher″ry, *n.* The popular name of a species of wild cherry, *Prunus Virginiana*, of North America; also, its fruit, remarkable for its astringent properties.

chōke′-damp, *n.* Noxious vapor (carbonic acid gas) in wells, coal mines, and other pits; called also *black-damp*.

chō′ke-där, *n.* Same as *Chokidar*.

chōke′-full, *a.* Same as *Chock-full*.

chōke′-peär, *n.* 1. A kind of pear that has a rough, astringent taste, and is therefore swallowed with difficulty.

2. Hence, anything that stops the mouth; an unanswerable argument; an aspersion or sarcasm by which a person is put to silence. [Low.]

chōk′ẽr, *n.* 1. One who or that which chokes; that which irritates with a sense of strangulation: something difficult to swallow.

> He had left a glass of water just tasted. I finished it. It was a *choker*.—Thackeray.

2. That which puts another to silence; that which cannot be answered. [Colloq.]

3. A neckcloth; a stiff wide cravat formerly worn on dress occasions; as, a white *choker*. [Slang.]

4. In military engineering, a chain used to compress and measure fascines.

chōke′-strap, *n.* In saddlery, a strap passing from the lower portion of the collar to the belly-band, to keep the collar in place when an animal is descending a hill or backing.

chōke′weed, chōke′wŏrt, *n.* A name given to several weeds of different genera; to some because they choke the growth of other plants, to others because when swallowed they produce a choking sensation in the throat.

chō′ki-där, chō′ke-där, *n.* [Hind. *chaukidar*, a watchman, policeman; *chauki*, watch, and *-dar*, holding.] In India, a watchman or policeman.

chōk′ing, *a.* 1. Causing suffocation; tending to choke or suffocate; as, a *choking* cloud of dust.

2. Obstructed or indistinct in utterance; gasping; as, to speak with a *choking* voice.

chōk′y, chōk′ey, *a.* 1. That tends to suffocate, or has power to suffocate.

2. Inclined to choke; affected as if being choked; as, he felt *choky*.

chō′ky, *n.* [Hind. *chauki*, a guard.]

1. In India, a station, applied in various senses, as a prison or lockup, a customs station, a palanquin station, etc.

2. The act of watching or keeping guard.

ċhol-, ċho′lo-. Combining forms, from Gr. *cholē*, the bile, used in scientific compounds.

ċhō-læ′mi-à, *n.* [L., from Gr. *cholē*, bile, and *haima*, blood.] In medicine, a disease caused by the presence of bile in the blood, and producing extreme nervousness; also written *cholemia*.

ċhol′à-gogue (-gog), *n.* [Gr. *cholagōgos*, carrying off bile; *cholē*, bile, and *agōgos*, leading, from *agein*, to lead.] A medicine that has the specific quality of evacuating the bile.

ċho-lal′iç, *a.* Same as *Cholic*.

ċhō′lāte, *n.* A salt of cholic acid.

ċhol′ē-cyst, ċhol-ē-cys′tis, *n.* [L. *cholecystis*, the gall-bladder; Gr. *cholē*, bile, gall, and *kystis*, bladder.] The gall-bladder.

ċhol″ē-cys-tot′ō-my, *n.* [Gr. *cholē*, bile, *kystis*, bladder, and *tomē*, a cutting, from *temnein*, to cut.] The surgical operation of opening the gall-bladder by incision, as for the removal of gallstones.

ċhol-ē-dol′ō-ġy, *n.* [Gr. *cholē*, bile, and *logos*, a description.] A medical treatise relating to bile or the secretion of bile.

ċhō-lē′iç, *a.* [Gr. *cholē*, bile.] Pertaining to or derived from bile.

ċhō-lē′mi-à, *n.* See *Cholæmia*.

ċhol′ẽr, *n.* [ME. *coler, colere*; OFr. *colere*, anger, bile; L. *cholera*; Gr. *cholera*, a disease of the bile; *cholē*, bile.]

1. The bile. Anger was formerly supposed to be produced by excess or disturbance of this fluid.

2. Hence, anger; wrath; irritation of the passions.

ċhol′ẽr-à, *n.* [Gr. *cholera*, a disease of the bile, from *cholē*, bile.]

1. A name given to several acute diseases characterized mainly by copious discharges of fluid material from the bowels, vomiting, and collapse.

2. An acute, infectious disease, specific, highly malignant, and often rapidly fatal, existing in India and the tropics of Asia during the entire year, and occasionally spreading as an epidemic over large areas. It is generally preceded by a diarrhea and is characterized by vomiting, alvine discharges resembling flocculent rice-water, severe cramps, especially in the legs and abdominal walls, and profound collapse. The rate of mortality varies from ten to sixty-six per cent, the average being over fifty per cent. The cause is the comma bacillus of Koch, which is always found in the rice-water discharges. The germs commonly gain entrance into the system by means of drinking water; specifically called *Asiatic cholera*.

Chicken cholera; an infectious diarrheal, and usually fatal, disease peculiar to fowls, but really bearing no resemblance to cholera.

Cholera bacillus; see *Comma bacillus*.

Cholera infantum; the "summer complaint" of infants and young children; an acute disease occurring in warm weather, and characterized by pain, vomiting, purgation, fever, and prostration. The cause of the disease is probably micro-organic, and is favored by the prolonged action of heat, together with errors in diet and hygiene. The disease is of short duration, death frequently ensuing in from three to five days. It is especially fatal in large cities, owing to bad air, poor milk, unhealthy surroundings, and congestion of population in the poorer districts.

Cholera morbus; an acute catarrhal inflammation of the mucous membrane of the stomach and intestines, with pain, purging, vomiting, spasmodic contractions of the muscles, etc. It is a disease appearing in hot weather, frequently being caused by errors in diet, and is very similar to Asiatic cholera in its symptoms.

Hog cholera; a contagious disease affecting swine, characterized by a high fever, inflammation of the digestive and respiratory organs, diarrhea, cough, and the effusion of blood into the mucous membranes and skin; called also *swine-plague*.

Sporadic cholera; same as *Cholera morbus*.

ċhol-ẽr-ā′iç, *a.* Pertaining to cholera; resulting from cholera.

ċhol′ẽr-iç, *a.* [ME. *colerik*; OFr. *colerique*; L. *cholericus*, bilious, choleric; Gr. *cholerikos*, resembling the cholera, from *cholera*, cholera.]

1. Abounding with choler.

2. Easily irritated; irascible; inclined to anger; as, a *choleric* man.

3. Angry; indicating anger; excited by anger; as, a *choleric* speech.

Choleric temperament; the bilious, irritable temperament.

ċhol′ẽr-iç-ly, *adv.* In a choleric manner; irascibly; angrily.

ċhol′ẽr-iç-ness, *n.* Irascibility, anger; peevishness.

ċhol′ẽr-i-form, *a.* Resembling cholera.

ċhol-ẽr-iġ′e-nous, *a.* Producing or generating cholera.

ċhol′ẽr-ine, *n.* 1. A mild form of Asiatic cholera, also, the initial diarrheal stage of epidemic cholera.

2. The precursory symptoms of cholera; the morbific agent which formerly was believed to cause cholera.

ċhol′ẽr-oid, *a.* Pertaining to cholera.

ċhō-les-ter′iç, *a.* Pertaining to cholesterin, or obtained from it; as, *cholesteric* acid.

ċhō-les′tẽr-in, ċhō-les′tẽr-ine, *n.* [Gr. *cholē*, bile, and *stereos*, solid.] A white crystalline substance, found in blood, brain, egg-yolks, gallstones, and in various plant and animal products and tissues, but especially in bile and biliary secretions.

ċhō′li-amb, ċhō-li-am′biç, *n.* [L. *choliambus*, choliambic; Gr. *chōliambos*, lame iambus, from *chōlos*, lame, and *iambos*, an iambus.] A verse in poetry having an iambic foot in the fifth place, and a spondee in the sixth or last.

ċhol′iç, *a.* [Gr. *cholē*, bile.] Pertaining to or derived from the bile.

Cholic acid; a compound found in the acids of the bile which may be chemically extracted as resinous crystals.

ċhō′line, ċhō′lin, *n.* [Gr. *cholē*, bile.] A basic alkaline compound found most abundantly in bile, from which it was originally extracted. It is also obtained from the yolk of eggs, nervous tissue, and other parts of the animal organism.

ċhol′ō-ċhrōme, *n.* [*Cholo-*, and Gr. *chrōma*, color.] A bile-pigment of any kind; called also *bilirubin*.

ċhō-loid′iç, *a.* Pertaining to bile; as, *choloidic* acid.

ċhol-ō-phæ′in, *n.* [*Cholo-*, and Gr. *phaios*, dusky, gray.] Same as *Bilirubin*.

chōl′try, chōul′try, *n.* [Anglo-Ind. from Malayalam *chawati*, an inn.] A Hindu caravansary or empty house, for the use of travelers.

chomp, *n.* See *Champ*. [Colloq.]

ċhondr-, ċhon′drō-, Combining forms signifying a grain, granular, cartilaginous, from Gr. *chonaros*, cartilage, corn, grain.

ċhon′drăl, *a.* [Gr. *chondros*, cartilage, grain.] Pertaining to cartilage; cartilaginous.

ċhon″dri-fi-ċā′tion, *n.* [*Chondr-*, and L. *facere*, to make.] The process of being converted into cartilage; the state of being chondrified.

ċhon′dri-fȳ, *v.t.* and *v.i.*; chondrified, *pt.*, *pp.*; chondrifying, *ppr.* I. *v.t.* To convert into cartilage.

II. *v.i.* To be converted into cartilage.

ċhon′dri-ġen, *n.* [*Chondr-* and Gr. *-genēs*, producing.] The substance of hyaline cartilage from which chondrin is obtained after long boiling in water.

ċhon-driġ′e-nous, *a.* [*Chondr-*, and Gr. *-genēs*, producing.] Yielding chondrin.

ċhon′drin, ċhon′drine, *n.* [Gr. *chondros*, cartilage.] A transparent substance similar to gelatin, without taste, odor, or color, obtained by long boiling of cartilaginous tissue with water. It is largely used as an ingredient of commercial gelatin.

ċhon′drite, *n.* [Gr. *chondritēs*, made of groats or coarse meal.] A meteoric stone having chondrules in its composition.

ċhon-drit′iç, *a.* Granular in structure; having the peculiar granular structure characteristic of the meteorites called chondrites.

ċhon-drī′tis, *n.* Inflammation of cartilage or cartilaginous tissue.

ċhon′drō-. See *Chondr-*.

ċhon′drō-blast, *n.* [*Chondro-*, and Gr. *blastos*, a bud, shoot.] A cell that produces cartilage.

Ċhon-drō-den′dron, *n.* [*Chondro-*, and Gr. *dendron*, a tree.] A small genus of woody vines or high-climbing shrubs, with large leaves, indigenous to Brazil and Peru. The root of *Chondrodendron tomentosum* yields pareira brava, a drug formerly much esteemed for diseases of the bladder.

ċhon′drō-dite, *n.* [Gr. *chondros*, a grain of wheat, cartilage.] A light yellow, brittle mineral, occurring disseminated through primary limestone. Regular crystals can rarely be distinguished. It is sometimes brownish, reddish or apple-green. *Chondrodite* consists of silica, fluorine, and magnesia. Also called *brucite*.

Ċhon″drō-gà-noi′dē-à, *n.pl.* [*Chondro-*, and Gr. *ganoidea*, from *ganos*, brightness, and *eidos*, form.] A suborder of ganoid fishes including the sturgeon and many fossil forms; so called from having a cartilaginous skeleton. The living representatives are referable to the orders *Chondrostei* and *Selachostomi*.

ċhon′drō-ġen, *n.* Same as *Chondrigen*.

ċhon-drō-ġen′e-sis, *n.* [*Chondro-*, and Gr. *genesis*, origin, source.] The formation or development of cartilage; the morbid conversion of parts into cartilage; also written *chondrogeny*.

ċhon-droġ′e-ny, *n.* Same as *Chondrogenesis*.

ċhon′droid, *a.* [Gr. *chondros*, cartilage, and *eidos*, appearance.] Resembling cartilage.

ċhon-drol′ō-ġy, *n.* [Gr. *chondros*, a cartilage, and *logos*, description.] The history of cartilages; the anatomy or scientific knowledge of cartilages.

ċhon-drō′mà, *n.*; *pl.* **ċhon-drō′mà-tà.** [*Chondro-*, and Gr. *-ōma*, signifying a morbid condition.] A tumor which consists of cartilage.

ċhon-drom′e-tẽr, *n.* [*Chondro-*, and Gr. *metron*, a measure.] A device like a steelyard for weighing grain.

chon-drop-tẽr-yġ'i-ăn, *n.* [*Chondro-*, and Gr. *pterygion*, dim. of *pteryx*, a wing, fin.] One of the *Chondropterygii.*

chon-drop-tẽr-yġ'i-ăn, *a.* Pertaining to the *Chondropterygii*; gristly finned; having a cartilaginous skeleton.

Chon-drop-te-ryġ'i-ī, *n.pl.* [L., from Gr. *chondros*, cartilage, and *pterygion*, a fin, dim. of *pteryx*, a wing.] A group of fishes including the sturgeon, shark, ray, and lamprey, distinguished from the fishes with true bone by the cartilaginous or gristly substance of which the skeleton is composed.

chon-drō-skel'e-tŏn, *n.* The cartilaginous skeleton.

Chon-dros'tē-ī, *n.pl.* [L., from Gr. *chondros*, cartilage, and *osteon*, bone.] An order of ganoid fishes, including the sturgeons, having the skeleton partly cartilaginous and partly bony.

chon-drot'ō-my, *n.* [*Chondro-*, and Gr. *tomē*, a cutting, from *temnein*, to cut.] In surgery and anatomy, the cutting and the dissection of cartilages.

chon'drūle, *n.* The English form of *chondrus.*

chon'drus, *n.*; *pl.* **chon'drī.** [L. *chondrus*; Gr. *chondros*, a grain, cartilage.] A peculiar spherical crystal, mineral grain, or composite glassy mass found imbedded in meteoric stones.

chooṣe, *v.t.*; chose, *pt.*; chosen, chose [obs.], *pp.*; choosing, *ppr.* [ME. *cheosen*, *chesen*; AS. *ceosan*, to choose.]

1. To pick out; to select; as, refuse the evil and *choose* the good.

2. To wish; to be inclined or have an inclination for; as, he did not *choose* to go.

chooṣe, *v.i.* 1. To select; to make a choice; to decide; to exercise the power of choice; as, do as you *choose.*

2. To do as one pleases. [Obs.]

Cannot choose but; cannot do otherwise than.

Syn.—Select, pick out, prefer, cull, elect, adopt, follow.

chooṣ'ẽr, *n.* One who chooses; one who has the power or right of choosing; an elector.

chooṣ'ing, *n.* The act of making a choice.

chooṣ'ing-ly, *adv.* By choosing or preference. [Rare.]

chooṣ'ing-stick, *n.* A divining-stick. [Prov. Eng.]

chop, *v.t.*; chopped (chopt), *pt.*, *pp.*; chopping, *ppr.* [ME. *choppen*, *chappen*; G. and D. *kappen*, to chop; origin obscure.]

1. To cut into small pieces; to mince; often with *up*; as, to *chop up* meat; to *chop* straw.

2. To sever or separate with a sharp instrument; with *off*, *down*, etc.; as, to *chop off* a head; to *chop down* a tree.

3. To grind and mince with the teeth; to devour eagerly; to gobble; with *up*; as, to *chop up* a dinner. [Obs.]

4. To cause to cleave or open into chinks or fissures; to crack; in this sense usually *chap.*

To chop a fox; in fox-hunting, to seize a fox before he has had time to escape from cover; said of a hound.

chop, *v.i.* 1. To catch or attempt to seize; to do something with sudden, unexpected motion; to make a hasty movement; to strike. [Obs.]

2. To make a cutting stroke, or repeated strokes, with an ax, knife, or other sharp instrument.

3. To utter words abruptly; to interrupt by remarking; with *in* or *out.*

chop, *v.t.* [D. *koopen*, to buy.]

1. To barter; to truck.

2. To exchange; to put one thing in the place of another.

To chop logic; to dispute or argue in a sophistical manner, or with an affectation of logical terms or methods.

chop, *v.i.* 1. To bargain; to buy by way of truck.

2. Among seamen, to turn, vary, change, or shift suddenly; as, the wind *chops*, or *chops* about.

3. To bandy words; to dispute.

> Let not the counsel at the bar *chop* with the judge. —Bacon.

chop, *n.* A turn of fortune; change; vicissitude; also written *chap.*

Chops and changes; vicissitudes of fortune; ups and downs.

chop, *n.* 1. The act of chopping.

2. A piece chopped off; a slice, particularly of meat; as, a mutton-*chop*; usually in the plural.

chop, *n.* [Ice. *kjaptr*, the jaw.]

1. The chap; the jaw; usually in the plural. [See *Chap.*]

2. A movable jaw, as of a carpenter's vise.

3. [*pl.*] The mouth or entrance to a channel; as, the *chops* of the English channel.

chop, *n.* [Hind. *chhāp*, a brand.]

1. An official mark on weights and measures to show their accuracy; an Eastern customhouse stamp or seal on goods that have paid duty; a permit or clearance.

2. A word used in China to signify quality; as, silk or tea of the first *chop*; hence, the colloquial phrase, *first chop* (first rate).

3. The entire bulk of a certain kind of tea brought to market, or of the quantity made.

4. The hulk of a boat remodeled and anchored for storage or residence.

The grand or *red chop*; a ship's clearance certificate given in Chinese ports, indicating a compliance with all the customs regulations, the official seal being of a vermilion color.

chop'bōat, *n.* In China, a licensed lighter for carrying either passengers or freight.

chop'chūrch, *n.* In old English law, an exchange or an exchanger of benefices for money.

chop'-dol"lăr, *n.* In certain Asiatic ports, a coin bearing the stamp of a trading-company to attest its genuineness.

chop'fạll-en (-fạl'n), *a.* See *Chapfallen.*

chop'house, *n.* A restaurant whose specialty is the serving of meats.

chop'in, *n.* [ME. *chopyn*; OFr. *chopine*, a liquid measure.] A liquid measure formerly used in France and Great Britain, the capacity of which varied in different localities, ranging from half a pint to nearly a wine quart.

chō-pīne', *n.* [OFr. and Sp. *chapin*, a sock, pump.] An unusually high clog or patten, in some cases resembling a short stilt, formerly worn by ladies under their shoes to elevate them from the ground and make them appear taller; introduced into the West from Turkey; written also *chioppine.*

Chopines.

chop'-log"iç, *n.* 1. An argumentative person.

2. Pretentious and hair-splitting disputation.

chop'ness, *n.* A kind of shovel or spade. [Eng.]

chop'pẽr, *n.* One who or that which chops.

chop'ping, *a.* Stout; lusty; plump. [Obs.]

chop'ping, *a.* Having tumbling broken waves which dash against each other with a short, quick motion; also, veering or shifting suddenly as the wind.

chop'ping, *n.* The act of cutting by a stroke or series of strokes.

chop'ping-block, *n.* A solid block of wood on which anything may be chopped.

chop'ping-knife (-nīf), *n.* A knife with a curved blade, or blades, fixed to a handle, for mincing cooking-materials.

chop'py, *a.* Full of clefts or cracks.

chop'py, *a.* Characterized by small, rough, tumultuous waves; as, a *choppy* sea.

chop'sticks, *n.pl.* Small tapering sticks, usually of wood or ivory, held by the Chinese between the thumb and fingers, and used, in pairs, to convey food to the mouth.

chop-sü'ey, chop-sō'oy, *n.* [Chinese *sap*, to enter the mouth, and *sui*, small bits.] A Chinese dish consisting of sliced meats and various vegetables flavored with sesame oil and served in their juices. It is eaten with noodles, rice, etc.

chō-rag'iç, *a.* Pertaining to or connected with a choragus; as, a *choragic* monument.

Choragic monument; in Greek antiquities, a monument erected in honor of the choragus who gained the prize (a bronze tripod) by the exhibition of the best musical or theatrical entertainment at the festival of Bacchus; the prize itself was displayed on the *choragic monument.*

chō-rā'gus, *n.*; *pl.* **chō-rā'gī.** [L. *choragus*; Gr. *chorēgos*, the leader of a chorus, from *choros*, chorus, and *hēgeisthai*, to lead.] In Greek antiquities, the leader or superintendent of a chorus or of a theatrical representation; especially, one who provided at his own expense the choruses for tragedies and comedies, and for the various religious festivals at Athens. Figuratively, therefore, any leader of an organization or festival of a choragic nature.

chō'răl, *a.* [LL. *choralis*, pertaining to a chorus, from L. *chorus*, Gr. *choros*, chorus.] Pertaining to a choir, concert, or chorus; as, *choral* service; opposed to *instrumental.*

chō'răl, *n.* A psalm or hymn-tune sometimes sung in unison by a congregation, the organ supplying the harmony; written also *chorale.*

chō'răl-ist, *n.* One who sings or composes chorals; a member of a choir.

chō'răl-ly, *adv.* In the manner of a chorus; so as to suit a choir.

chord, *n.* [L. *chorda*; Gr. *chordē*, the string of a musical instrument.]

1. The string of a musical instrument.

2. In music, the simultaneous combination of different sounds, consonant or dissonant.

3. In geometry, a right line, drawn, or supposed to extend, from one end of an arc of a circle to the other. Hence, the chord of an arc is a right line joining the extremities of that arc. Thus AC and AB are the chords of the arcs AC and ACB.

4. In anatomy, a cord; a tendon; written, scientifically, *chorda.*

5. In engineering, an important member of the truss of a bridge, generally horizontal, which withstands compression or tension.

Chord of curvature; a chord drawn from any point of a curve within the osculating circle of the curve for that point.

chord, *v.t.*; chorded, *pt.*, *pp.*; chording, *ppr.* To furnish with chords or musical strings; also, to bring into harmony; to tune.

chord, *v.i.* To be in accord; to harmonize; as, the violin *chords* with the piano.

chor'dȧ, *n.*; *pl.* **chor'dæ.** [L.] 1. In anatomy, a tendon.

2. [C—] In botany, a genus of algæ. One species, *Chorda filum*, is known by the name of sea-lace.

Chorda dorsalis; the notochord or dorsal cord, a term applied to a gelatiniform, transparent cord found in the embryonic stage of all vertebrate animals.

chor'dăl, *a.* Pertaining to a chord.

Chor-dā'tȧ, *n.pl.* A subclassification of the animal kingdom, embracing those having a notochord.

chor-dee', *n.* [Fr. *cordé*, pp. of *corder*, to twist.] A painful erection of the penis in which it is more or less curved downward, especially at night. It usually attends gonorrhea.

chor-dō-tō'năl, *a.* [Gr. *chordē*, chord, and *tonos*, tone, measure.] Affected by or responsive to sound-vibrations, as certain auditory organs in the legs of insects; pertaining to or designating such organs.

chōre, *n.* [ME. *cheer*, *char*, a turning; AS. *cerr*, *cyrr*, turn, occasion, from *cerran*, *cyrran*, to turn.] Small work of a domestic kind, as distinguished from the principal work of the day, either indoors or outdoors; generally used in the plural. [U. S.]

chōre, *v.i.*; chored, *pt.*, *pp.*; choring, *ppr.* To perform chores. [U. S.]

chōre, *n.* A choir; a chorus. [Obs.]

chō-rē'ȧ, *n.* [L. *chorea*; Gr. *choreia*, a dance.] St. Vitus's dance; a nervous affection accompanied by convulsive motions of the limbs, occasioning strange and involuntary gesticulations.

chō-ree', *n.* A rare form of *trochee*; also written *choreus.*

chō-rē-graph'iç, chō-rē-graph'iç-ăl, *a.* See *Chorographic.*

chō-reg'ră-phy, *n.* See first *Chorography.*

chō-rē'gus, *n.* Same as *Choragus.*

chō-rē'iç, *a.* Having the nature of, or relating to, chorea; characterized by convulsions.

chō-rē-ō-mā'ni-ȧ, *n.* Same as *Choromania.*

chō-rē-pis'cō-păl, *a.* Pertaining to the jurisdiction and power of a chorepiscopus.

chō-rē-pis'cō-pus, *n.*; *pl.* **chō-rē-pis'cō-pī.** [LL., from Gr. *chōra*, place, spot, and *episkopos*, an overseer; *epi*, over, and *skopein*, to examine.] A local or suffragan bishop; a bishop appointed in the early Christian church by the ordinary bishop of a diocese to assist him in taking charge of the country lying around the city in which he himself lived.

chō-rē'us, chō-ree', *n.* [L. *choreus*; Gr. *choreios*, in prosody, the trochee.] In prosody, (a) a foot of two syllables, the first long and the second short; a trochee; (b) with later prosodists, a tribrach; a foot consisting of three short syllables.

chō'ri-. A combining form from Greek *chōris*, apart.

chō'ri-amb, *n.* [Gr. *choriambos*, a choriambus, from *chorios*, a choreus or trochee, and *iambos*, an iambus.] In ancient poetry, a foot consisting of four syllables, of which the first and last are long, and the others short; that is, a choreus or trochee and an iambus united; as, *nōbĭlĭtās*, *ānxĭĕtās.*

chō-ri-am'bī, *n.*, pl. of *choriambus.*

chō-ri-am'biç, *n.* A choriamb.

chō-ri-am'biç, *a.* Pertaining to a choriamb.

chō-ri-am'bus, *n.* See *Choriamb.*

chō'riç, *a.* [Gr. *chorikos*, belonging to a choral dance.] Pertaining to a chorus.

chō'ri-on, *n.* [Gr. *chorion*, leather, skin.]

1. In anatomy, the outer membrane which surrounds the fetus of the higher vertebrates, attaching it to the uterus; the cell-wall of the original ovum.

2. A membrane or covering like a *chorion* which invests various ova, as of insects or of seeds, at certain stages of development.

3. The corium or true skin; the cutis.

chō-ri-pet'ăl-ous, *a.* [Gr. *chōris*, apart, and *petalon*, leaf.] Polypetalous; having unconnected or separate petals.

chō-riph'yl-lous, *a.* [Gr. *chōris*, asunder, apart, and *phyllon*, leaf.] Having the leaves distinct and separate, as a perianth.

chō-ri-sep'ăl-ous, *a.* [Gr. *chōris*, apart, and L. *sepalum*, sepal.] Polysepalous; having unconnected sepals.

chō'ri-sis, *n.* [Gr. *chōrisis*, a separation, from *chōrizein*, to separate.] In botany, the separation of a lamina from one part of an organ, so as to form a scale, or a doubling of the organ; it may be either transverse or collateral.

çhō'rist, *n.* [Fr. *choriste*, a chorist, from L. *chorus*, choir.] One who sings in a choir. [Rare.]

çhō-ris'tāte, *a.* Affected with chorisis.

çhor'is-tẽr, *n.* [From *chorus*, *choir*.]

1. Literally, a singer; one of a choir; a singer in a concert.

2. One who leads a choir in church music.

3. A songster; as, a feathered *chorister*.

çhō-ris'tiç, *a.* Choral; choric. [Rare.]

çhō'rō-grȧph, *n.* [Gr. *chōros*, place, and *graphein*, to describe.] An instrument to construct, by mechanical means, two similar triangles on two given straight lines, their angles being given. It is especially important in marine surveying.

çhō-rog'rȧ-phẽr, *n.* 1. One who describes a particular region or country; or one who forms a map or maps of particular regions or countries.

2. A student of geographical antiquity.

çhō-rō-graph'iç, **çhō-rō-graph'iç-ăl**, *a.* Pertaining to chorography.

çhō-rō-graph'iç-ăl-ly, *adv.* In a chorographical manner.

çhō-rog'rȧ-phy, *n.* [Gr. *choreia*, dance, and *graphein*, to describe.] The art of reproducing dancing, or figures in dancing, by written signs, as music is represented by notes.

çhō-rog'rȧ-phy, *n.* [Gr. *chōros*, place, and *graphein*, to describe.] The art or practice of making a map or description of a particular region, country, or province; or of marking its limits, bounds, or position.

çhō'roid, *a.* In anatomy, a term applied to several investing membranes similar to the chorion.

Choroid membrane; one of the membranes of the eye of a very dark color situated between the sclerotic and the retina, and terminating anteriorly at the great circumference of the iris.

Choroid plexus; one of the membranous and vascular duplicatures of the pia mater or inner membrane investing the brain.

çhō'roid, *n.* [Gr. *chorion*, skin, membrane, and *eidos*, shape.] In anatomy, a membrane resembling the chorion; more especially, the choroid membrane of the eye.

çhō-roid'ăl, *a.* Pertaining to the choroid coat, as of the eye.

çhō-roid-ī'tis, *n.* Inflammation of the choroid coat, involving the iris.

çhō-rol'ō-ġy, *n.* [Gr. *chōros*, place, and *logos*, description.]

1. Same as second *Chorography.*

2. The science which treats of the laws governing the geographical distribution of plants and animals.

çhō-rō-mā'ni-ȧ, *n.* [Gr. *choros*, a dance, and *mania*, madness.] A disease in which those afflicted dance to exhaustion under great religious excitement; the dancing mania; written also *choreomania.*

çhō-rom'e-try, *n.* [Gr. *chōros*, place, and *metron*, measure.] The art of land-surveying.

chor'tle, *v.i.* To laugh long and noisily.

çhō'rus, *n.*; *pl.* **çhō'rus-es**. [L. *chorus*; Gr. *choros*, a dance in a ring, a chorus.]

1. A number of singers; a concert company, or a selection rendered by it. The composition is usually in four vocal parts; when in eight parts it is called a *double chorus.*

2. In Greek drama, the persons supposed to behold what passed in the acts of a tragedy, and to sing their sentiments between the acts.

3. The song between the acts of a tragedy.

4. Verses of a song in which the company joins the singer; or the union of a company with a singer, in periodically repeating certain couplets or verses.

5. A musical composition of two or more parts.

6. Among the ancient Greeks, a band of singers and dancers.

7. The joining of a company in any noisy exhibition; as, a *chorus* of yells.

8. An old musical instrument somewhat resembling a bagpipe, consisting chiefly of a bag made from the skin of an animal and two pipes. The Welsh crwth was known by this name. The term was also applied in Scotland to a trumpet with a harsh, loud tone.

Chorus (ninth century).

çhō'rus, *v.t.*; chorused, *pt., pp.*; chorusing, *ppr.*

1. To sing or join in the chorus of.

2. To exclaim or call out in concert.

Oh, do let the Swiper go in, *chorus* the boys.
—T. Hughes.

chōṣe, *v.*, past tense and obsolete past participle of *choose.*

chōse, *n.* [Fr. *chose*, a thing; OFr. *cose*, *cosa*; LL. *causa*, a thing; L. *causa*, cause]. In law, property; a right to possession, or that which may be demanded and recovered by suit or action at law.

Chose in action; an incorporeal right to a sum of money or a thing not actually in possession, but legally recoverable; also, a written obligation, as a note or bond, upon which suit may be legally brought.

Chose in possession; a piece of personal property in actual and legal possession, as distinguished from a legal evidence of debt or obligation, or a chose in action.

Chose local; anything annexed to a place, as a mill or the like.

Chose transitory; a piece of property which is portable or movable.

chō'ṣen, *v.*, past participle of *choose.*

chō'ṣen, *a.* Selected from a number; picked out; elect; choice.

Chosen freeholder; see *Freeholder.*

The chosen people; the Israelites.

Chöu'ăn (*or Fr. pron.* shö-on'), *n.* [Fr. *chat-huant*, a screech-owl.] One of a band of insurgent royalists of Brittany who rose in 1792 against the French republic, and carried on a bitter guerrilla warfare.

chough (chuf), *n.* [ME. *choughe*, *cheo*; AS. *ceó*, a chough or jackdaw.] A bird belonging to the genus *Fregilus*, of the crow family, but nearly allied to the starlings.

Cornish chough; in heraldry, a chough, once a heraldic emblem of numerous Cornish families.

chöu'i-chȧ, *n.* Same as *Chavicha.*

choul, *n.* [Obs.] Same as *Jowl.*

chōul'try, *n.* See *Choltry.*

chouse, *v.t.*; choused, *pt., pp.*; chousing, *ppr.* To cheat, trick, defraud; followed by *of* or *out of*; as, to *chouse* one *out of* his money. [Colloq.]

chouse, *n.* [Turk. *cha'ush*, *chaush*, an interpreter; Ar. *khawas*; Hind. *khawas*, an attendant. The word is said to have been adopted because in 1609 a Turkish interpreter swindled several London merchants.]

1. One who is easily gulled.

2. An imposition; a trick.

3. A rogue; a swindler.

chou'sing-hä, *n.* [Hind.] Same as *Chikara.*

chout, *n.* [Hind. *chauth*, a fourth of the revenue.] In the East Indies, a fourth part of the clear revenue, formerly exacted by the Mahrattas; hence, extortion of any kind.

chow, *n.* In China, a subordinate district or its principal city.

chow'=chow, *a.* [Pidgin Eng.] A Chinese term signifying mixed; as, *chow-chow* sweetmeats, preserved fruits of various kinds mingled together.

Chow-chow chop; the last lighter, containing the small sundry packages of a ship's cargo.

chow'=chow, *n.* A Chinese term for any mixture, but elsewhere confined generally to mixed pickles.

chow'dẽr, *n.* [Prob. from Fr. *chaudière*, a caldron.]

1. A stewed dish of fish or clams containing salt pork, biscuits, potatoes, onions, etc.

2. A picnic at which the making and serving of *chowder* is the chief feature.

chow'dẽr, *v.t.*; chowdered, *pt., pp.*; chowdering, *ppr.* To make into a chowder.

chow'dẽr=beer, *n.* A beverage made by boiling black spruce in water and mixing it with molasses.

chow'ry, *n.* [Hind.] In the East Indies, a whisk to keep off flies, often made of the tail of a yak.

chow'tẽr, *v.i.* To grumble like a froward child. [Obs.]

choy'=root, *n.* Same as *Shaya-root.*

çhrē-mȧ-tis'tiç, *a.* Pertaining to chrematistics.

çhrē-mȧ-tis'tiçs, *n.* [Gr. *chrēmatistēs*, one who carries on business, from *chrēmatizein*, to transact business.] The science of wealth; a name given to that part of political economy relating to the manipulation of property and wealth.

çhrē-ō-teçh'niçs, *n.* [Gr. *chreios*, useful, and *technē*, art.] The useful arts; specifically, agriculture, manufactures, and commerce. [Rare.]

çhres-tō-math'iç, **çhres-tō-math'iç-ăl**, *a.* Pertaining to chrestomathy.

çhres-tom'ȧ-thy, *n.* [Gr. *chrēstos*, useful, and *manthanein*, to learn.] A name given to books of extracts from a foreign language, with notes, intended to be used in acquiring the language.

çhriṣm, *n.* [ME. *chrisme*; AS. *crisma*; LL. *chrisma*, chrism oil; Gr. *chrisma*, an unguent, from *chriein*, to rub, anoint.]

1. Olive oil or unguent, consecrated by a bishop and used in the administration of baptism, confirmation, ordination, and extreme unction. In the Greek and Roman Catholic churches, it is prepared on Holy Thursday with much ceremony, and in some cases mixed with balsam.

2. See *Chrisom.*

çhriṣ'mȧ, *n.* See *Chrismon.*

çhriṣ'măl, *a.* Pertaining to chrism.

çhriṣ-mā'tion, *n.* The act of applying the chrism, or consecrated oil. In ordination, it is usually styled *unction.*

çhriṣ'mȧ-tō-ry, *n.* A vessel in the shape of a cruet in which the chrism is held. In the Roman Catholic churches there are usually three distinct *chrismatories*; one containing the oil for baptism, another that for confirmation, and the third that for the use of the sick.

Chrismatory.

çhriṣ'mon, *n.* A monogram formed of the first two letters in the Greek name of Christ.

çhriṣ'ŏm, *n.* A child that dies within a month after baptism; so called from the chrisom-cloth, a linen cloth anointed with holy oil, which was formerly laid over a child's face when it was baptized; also, the cloth itself. [Obs.]

Çhrist, *n.* [ME. *Crist*; AS. *Crist*; L. *Christus*, Christ; Gr. *Christos*, Christ, lit. the Anointed, from *chriein*, to anoint.] The Anointed; an appellation given to Jesus of Nazareth, and synonymous with the Hebrew Messiah. It was a custom of antiquity to consecrate persons to the sacerdotal and regal offices by anointing them with oil.

Çhris-tȧ-del'phi-ăn, *n.* [Gr. *Christos*, Christ, and *adelphos*, brother.] A member of a small religious sect founded in the United States about 1833 by John Thomas, M. D., and later extending to England and other countries. They reject the Trinity, deny infant baptism, etc.; also called *Brothers of Christ* and *Thomasites.*

Çhrist'=child, *n.* The representation of Christ as a child, especially by the Germans during their Christmas festivities.

çhrist'çross (kris'), *n.* 1. The mark of the cross cut, printed, or stamped on any object. It was sometimes placed on a dial for the figure XII., that is, as the sign of 12 o'clock.

2. The beginning and end; the Alpha and Omega.

çhrist'çross=rōw, *n.* An old term for the alphabet, probably from the cross anciently set before it, or from a superstitious custom of writing it in the form of a cross by way of charm.

çhris'ten (kris'n), *v.t.*; christened, *pt., pp.*; christening, *ppr.* [ME. *christenen*; AS. *cristenian*, *cristnian*, to christen, from *Cristen*, a Christian; L. *Christianus*; Gr. *Christianos*, a Christian.]

1. To give a name in baptism; as, the child was *christened* Edith.

2. To baptize (a person) as a religious rite.

3. To name; to denominate; applied to things.

4. Colloquially, to use for the first time; as, to *christen* a house.

5. To convert to Christianity. [Obs.]

Çhris'ten-dŏm (kris'n-dum), *n.* [ME. *cristendom*; AS. *cristendom*, Christianity, from *Cristen*, Christian, and *dōm*, domain, jurisdiction, from *dōn*, to do.]

1. The profession of faith in Christ by baptism; hence, adoption of faith in Christ; personal Christianity. [Obs.]

2. The territories, countries, or regions chiefly inhabited by Christians or those who profess to believe in the Christian religion.

3. The whole body of Christians.

4. [c—] The name received at baptism; hence, any personal name or epithet. [Obs.]

çhrist'en-ing, *n.* The act of conferring baptism, especially when accompanied by a naming of the baptized.

Çhris'tiăn (kris'chăn), *n.* [ME. *Cristen*; AS. *Cristen*, *Cristena*; L. *Christianus*; Gr. *Christianos*, a Christian, from *Christos*, Christ.]

1. A believer in the religion of Christ; one who follows his teachings in practice.

2. One who formally professes his belief in the religion of Christ.

3. In a general sense, the word *Christians* includes all who are born in a Christian country or of Christian parents.

4. In church history, (a) a member of a sect which is the offshoot of three other churches, which reject creeds, accept the Bible literally, and believe in open communion and immersion; (b) one belonging to a similar sect founded by Thomas and Alexander Campbell also called *Disciples of Christ* or *Campbellites.*

Çhris'tiăn, *a.* 1. Pertaining to Christ, taught by him, or received from him; as, the *Christian* religion; *Christian* doctrines.

2. Professing the religion of Christ; as, a *Christian* friend.

3. Belonging to the religion of Christ; relating to Christ, or to his doctrines, precepts, and examples; as, *Christian* profession and practice.

4. Pertaining to the church; ecclesiastical; as, a *Christian* court.

5. Showing the spirit of the teachings of Christ; as, *Christian* charity.

Christian Brothers; see under *Brother*.

Christian commission; see under *Commission*.

Christian court; see *Ecclesiastical courts*, under *Ecclesiastical*.

Christian era; the period of time from the birth of Christ to the present time.

Christian name; the baptismal name.

Christian Science; a Christian religion discovered and founded by Mary Baker G. Eddy and fully set forth in her book, "Science and Health with Key to the Scriptures." Its interpretation of Bible truths reduces them to a science whose adoption and application, it is claimed, heals the body by mental or spiritual regeneration. [See further definition under *Science*.]

Çhris'tiăn-ism, *n.* 1. The Christian religion. [Obs.]

2. The nations professing Christianity. [Obs.]

çhris'tiăn-ite, *n.* [After Prince *Christian* Frederick of Denmark.] A mineral, a product of Mount Vesuvius. Its primitive form is that of an oblique rectangular prism; its colors brown, yellow, or reddish.

Çhris-tian'i-ty, *n.* 1. The religion of Christians, or the system of doctrines and precepts taught by Christ and recorded by the evangelists and apostles.

2. Adherence to the Christian faith; conformity to the laws and precepts of the Christian religion.

3. Christendom. [Obs.]

Çhris″tiăn-i-zā'tion, *n.* The act or process of converting to Christianity.

Çhris'tiăn-ize, *v.t.*; Christianized, *pt.*, *pp.*; Christianizing, *ppr.* 1. To make Christian; to convert to Christianity; as, to *Christianize* pagans.

2. To inspire with Christian principles.

Çhris'tiăn-ize, *v.i.* To become Christian.

Çhris'tiăn-ly, *adv.* In a Christian manner; in a manner becoming the principles of the Christian religion, or the profession of that religion.

Çhris'tiăn-ly, *a.* Becoming in a Christian.

Çhris'tiăn-ness, *n.* The state or quality of being in accord with Christian doctrines. [Obs.]

Çhrist'less, *a.* Having no interest in Christ; without the spirit of Christ.

Çhrist'like, *a.* Bearing resemblance to Christ in nature.

Çhrist'like-ness, *n.* The state of being Christlike.

Çhrist'ly, *a.* Like Christ.

Çhrist'măs, *n.* [ME. *Cristmas*, *Cristmes*, from *Christ*, and *mass*, from AS. *mæssa*, a church festival, from L. *missus*, pp. of *mittere*, to send.] The festival of the Christian church observed annually on the 25th day of December, in memory of the birth of Christ, and celebrated by a particular church service, by the giving of gifts, and by general hospitable cheer.

Christmas box; a box in which presents are deposited at Christmas; hence, a Christmas gift.

Christmas carol; a carol suitable for Christmas; a song or hymn in celebration of the nativity of Christ.

Christmas eve; the evening of the day before Christmas.

Christmas fern; a fern, *Aspidium acrostichoides*, used for decorative purposes in winter.

Christmas rose or *Christmas flower*; a plant, *Helleborus niger*, so called from its open rose-like flower, which blossoms during the winter months.

Christmas tree; an evergreen tree or large branch with offshoots set up at Christmas, from which are hung presents, generally with the names of the recipients inscribed on them.

Christmas rose (*Helleborus niger*).

Çhrist'măs-tide, *n.* The season of Christmas; specifically, from Christmas eve until Epiphany, January 6.

Çhris-tō-cen'triç, *a.* [L. *Christus*, Christ, and *centrum*, center.] Grouping all things in history and religion about Christ as a center.

Çhris-tol'ō-ġy, *n.* [Gr. *Christos*, Christ, and *logos*, description.] A discourse or treatise concerning Christ.

Çhris-toph'ȧ-ny, *n.* [Gr. *Christos*, Christ, and *phainein*, to appear.] The appearance of Christ after his death, as recorded in the New Testament.

Çhrist's'-thorn, *n.* One of several thorny shrubs, as *Paliurus aculeatus*, supposed to have been the variety of which the crown of thorns for Christ was made.

çhrōm-, çhrō'mȧ-, çhrō'mȧ-tō-. Combining forms from Greek *chrōma*, color.

çhrō'mȧ-sçōpe, *n.* [*Chroma-*, and Gr. *skopein*, to view.] An instrument for showing the various optical effects of color and colored light.

çhrō'māte, *n.* A salt formed by chromic acid, producing compounds used in dyeing and as pigments.

çhrō-mat'iç, *a.* [L. *chromaticus*; Gr. *chrōmatikos*, suited for color, from *chrōma*, color.]

1. Relating to color.

2. In music, relating to a peculiar movement which proceeds by several semitones in succession; the intermediate tones were formerly written in colors, hence the application of the word.

Chromatic aberration; see *Aberration*, 3.

Chromatic interval; in music, a difference of a semitone in pitch.

Chromatic printing; any method of color-printing; specifically, the use of several plates printing different colors so as to blend and produce varying tints.

Chromatic scale; in music, the scale embracing the tones and semitones.

Chromatic semitone; the difference in pitch between a note and its sharp or flat.

Chromatic sign; in music, an accidental.

çhrō-mat'iç-ăl, *a.* Same as *Chromatic*.

çhrō-mat'iç-ăl-ly, *adv.* In a chromatic manner.

çhrō-mat'içs, *n.* The science of colors.

çhrō'mȧ-tin, *n.* [Gr. *chrōma*, color, and *-in*.] In biology, that part of a cell, as a nucleus or ovum, which is most subject to the action of dyes.

çhrō'mȧ-tişm, *n.* [Gr. *chrōmatismos*, coloring, from *chrōmatizein*, to color.]

1. Chromatic aberration.

2. In botany, abnormal coloration.

çhrō'mȧ-tō-. See *Chrom-*.

çhrō-mȧ-toġ'e-nous, *a.* [*Chromato-*, and Gr. *-genēs*, producing.] Yielding color.

çhrō'mȧ-tō-grȧph, *n.* [*Chromato-*, and Gr. *graphein*, to write.] An instrument designed to show the synthetical production of white light by the rotation of a circular disk bearing the colors of the spectrum.

çhrō-mȧ-tog'rȧ-phy, *n.* [*Chromato-*, and Gr. *graphē*, a representation, from *graphein*, to write.] A treatise on colors.

çhrō-mȧ-tol'ō-ġy, *n.* [*Chromato-*, and Gr. *logos*, a description.] Chromatography.

çhrō-mȧ-tom'e-tẽr, *n.* [*Chromato-*, and Gr. *metron*, a measure.] An arrangement of various colors which serve by comparison to classify other colors; a scale for colors.

çhrō'mȧ-tō-phōre, *n.* [*Chromato-*, and Gr. *-phoros*, bearing, from *pherein*, to bear.]

1. In zoölogy, a pigment-cell capable of contraction and expansion with consequent change of color, as shown by the chameleon.

2. In botany, one of an aggregate of protoplasmic particles.

3. In biology, a plastid having coloring matter in its composition.

çhrō'mȧ-tō-sçōpe, *n.* [*Chromato-*, and Gr. *skopein*, to view.]

1. In astronomy, a reflecting and revolving telescope by which the observer views a star as a ring of light instead of a point. It is used in the study of star-scintillation.

2. A chromatograph.

çhrō-mȧ-tos'çō-py, *n.* The study of color or of star-scintillation by means of the chromatoscope.

çhrō'mȧ-trōpe, *n.* [*Chroma-*, and Gr. *tropē*, a turn, from *trepein*, to turn.]

1 An instrument consisting of disks on which circular arcs of brilliant colors are so arranged as, when rotated rapidly, to present the appearance of streams of colors flowing to or from their center.

2. A kaleidoscopic attachment for a magic lantern.

çhrō'mȧ-tȳpe, *n.* See *Chromotype*.

çhrōme, *v.t.*; chromed, *pt.*, *pp.*; chroming, *ppr.* To treat with a compound of chromium, as potassium dichromate, used in dyeing and oxidizing.

çhrōme, *n.* [L. *chromium*, from Gr. *chrōma*, color.] Chromium.

çhrōme'-al″um, *n.* A crystallizable double salt formed from the sulphate of chromium and potassium.

çhrōme'-green, *n.* A dark green pigment prepared from oxid of chromium.

çhrōme'-red, *n.* A beautiful red pigment prepared from red lead. It is a basic chromate of lead.

çhrōme'-yel″lōw, *n.* A name given to chromate of lead, from its color. It is a brilliant yellow pigment much used in the arts.

çhrō'miç, *a.* Relating to or derived from chromium; designating compounds of chromium in its higher valence.

Chromic acid; a term at one time loosely applied to chromium trioxid, but now applied to a red crystalline compound, known mostly through its salts which have an important place in the arts as dyes and oxidizing agents.

Chromic anhydrid; the trioxid of chromium, the most important of the oxids of this metal. It exists as crimson-red, prismatic crystals readily forming chromic acid.

çhrō'mid, *n.* A fish of the family *Chromides*.

Çhrom'i-dēş, Çhrom'i-dæ, *n.pl.* [Gr. *chromis*, a kind of sea-fish, and *eidos*, resemblance.] A family of teleostean fishes, generally inhabiting the fresh waters of hot climates, allied to the *Labridæ*, or true wrasses.

çhrō-mid'i-um, *n.*; *pl.* **çhrō-mid'i-ȧ**. [Dim., from Gr. *chrōma*, color.] In algæ, one of the asexually produced propagative cells.

çhrō-mi-drō'sis, *n.* [Gr. *chrōma*, color, and *hidrōs*, sweat.] A disease characterized by colored perspiration.

çhrō'mişm, *n.* See *Chromatism*.

çhrō'mite, *n.* A mineral, the chief source of chromium, almost infusible, insoluble when crystalline, and imparting hardness to steel.

çhrō'mi-um, *n.* [L., from Gr. *chrōma*, color.] A metal which forms very hard steel-gray masses; it never occurs native, but may be obtained by reducing the oxid. In its highest degree of oxidation it forms a salt of a ruby-red color. It takes its name from the various and beautiful colors which its compounds communicate to minerals into whose composition they enter. Its salts find important use in dyeing, paint-making, as oxidizing agents, and in batteries and photography. Also called *chrome* and sometimes *chromion*.

çhrō'mō, *n.* A contraction of *chromolithograph*.

çhrō'mō-. Same as *Chrom-*.

çhrō'mō-blast, *n.* [*Chromo-*, and Gr. *blastos*, a bud, shoot.] A pigmented connective-tissue cell, as in the skin of snakes.

çhrō'mō-ġen, *n.* [*Chromo-*, and Gr. *-genēs*, producing.]

1. Any matter in vegetation serving to impart a color to it other than green.

2. Any matter in nature having color due to the presence of chromophores.

çhrō-mō-ġen'iç, *a.* Pertaining to chromogen.

çhrō'mō-grȧph, *n.* [*Chromo-*, and Gr. *graphein*, to write.] A hectograph.

çhrō-mō-leū'cite, *n.* [*Chromo-*, and Gr. *leukos*, white.] A chromoplastid.

çhrō-mō-lith'ō-grȧph, *n.* A picture obtained by means of chromolithography.

çhrō″mō-li-thog'rȧ-phẽr, *n.* One who practises chromolithography.

çhrō″mō-lith-ō-graph'iç, *a.* Relating to or producing chromolithography.

çhrō″mō-li-thog'rȧ-phy, *n.* [*Chromo-*, and Gr. *lithos*, a stone, and *graphein*, to write.] A method of producing a colored lithographic picture, by using various stones having different portions of the picture drawn upon them with inks of various colors and so arranged as to blend into a complete picture.

çhrō'mō-phan, *n.* [*Chromo-*, and Gr. *phainein*, to appear.] The coloring matter of the retinal cones of certain animals.

çhrō-moph'i-lous, *a.* [*Chromo-*, and Gr. *philos*, friendly.] Readily stained or colored.

çhrō'mō-phōre, *n.* Any chemical group which, aside from its chemical action, imparts a color to the compounds of which it is a constituent.

çhrō-mō-phō'tō-grȧph, *n.* [*Chromo-* and *photograph*, from Gr. *phōs*, light, and *graphein*, to write, to represent.] Any photograph reproducing colors.

çhrō-mō-phō-tō-lith'ō-grȧph, *n.* A photolithograph which is printed in colors.

çhrō-mō-plas'tid, *n.* [*Chromo-*, and Gr. *plasma*, anything formed, from *plassein*, to form.] A colored granule of protoplasm not green.

çhrō-mop-tom'e-tẽr, *n.* [*Chromo-*, and Gr. *optikos*, of seeing, and *metron*, a measure.] A device for determining the keenness of the color-sense.

çhrō'mō-sōme, *n.* [*Chromo-*, and Gr. *sōma*, the body.] In biology, one of the minute divisions into which the chromatin separates at the beginning of indirect cell-division.

çhrō'mō-sphēre, *n.* [*Chromo-*, and Gr. *sphaira*, a sphere.] The name of the gaseous envelope surrounding the body of the sun, through which the light of the photosphere passes.

çhrō-mō-spher'iç, *a.* Relating to the chromo sphere.

çhrō'mō-tȳpe, çhrō'mȧ-tȳpe, *n.* [*Chromo-*, and Gr. *typos*, an impression.]

1. A print made by any color-process.

2. A chromophotograph.

çhrō'mous (-mus), *a.* Relating to or denoting chromium, especially in its lower valence.

çhrō-mō-xȳ'lō-grȧph (-zī'), *n.* [*Chromo-*, and Gr. *xylon*, wood, and *graphein*, to write, represent.] A color-picture printed from a number of blocks of wood.

çhrō'mūle, çhrō'myle, *n.* [Gr. *chrōma*, color, and *hylē*, matter.] Any coloring substance other than green which enters into the composition of plants. [Obs.]

çhron'iç, *a.* [ME. *cronike*, *cronyke*; L. *chronicus*; Gr. *chronikos*, chronic, of or for the time, from *chronos*, time.]

1. Pertaining to time; having reference to time.

2. Continuing a long time, as a disease.
Chronic disease; one which is inveterate or of long continuance, in distinction from an *acute* disease, which speedily terminates.
çhron'iç, *n.* A chronicle. [Obs.]
çhron'iç-ăl, *a.* [Rare.] See *Chronic.*
çhron'i-çle (-kl), *n.* [ME. *cronicle*, a chronicle, from Gr. *chronos*, time.] A historical account of facts or events disposed in the order of time; a history, more especially one of a simple, unpretentious character.

Irish *chronicles* which are most fabulous and forged. —Spenser.

Book of Chronicles; two books of the Old Testament, consisting mainly of the annals of the kingdom of Judah.
Syn.—Record, register, annals.
çhron'i-çle, *v.t.*; chronicled, *pt.*, *pp.*; chronicling, *ppr.* To record in history or chronicle; to record; to register.
çhron'i-çlẽr, *n.* A writer of a chronicle; a recorder of events in the order of time; a historian.
çhrō-nïque' (-nēk'), *n.* [Obs.] See *Chronic*, n.
çhron'ō-. A combining form from Gr. *chronos*, time.
çhron'ō-gram, *n.* [*Chrono-*, and Gr. *gramma*, a letter or writing, from *graphein*, to write.] An inscription in which a certain date or epoch is expressed by numeral letters, as in the motto of a medal struck by Gustavus Adolphus in 1632:

ChrIstVs DVX; ergo trIVMphVs.

çhron″ō-gram-mat'iç, çhron″ō-gram-mat'iç-ăl, *a.* Belonging to a chronogram, or containing one.
çhron-ō-gram'mȧ-tist, *n.* A writer of chronograms.
çhron'ō-grȧph, *n.* [*Chrono-*, and Gr. *graphein*, to write, describe.]
1. A chronogram.
2. The name given to various devices for measuring and registering very minute portions of time with extreme precision.
çhrō-nog'rȧ-phẽr, *n.* [*Chrono-*, and Gr. *graphein*, to write, describe.] One who writes concerning time or the events of time; a chronologer.
çhron-ō-graph'iç, *a.* Relating to chronography.
çhrō-nog'rȧ-phy, *n.* [*Chrono-*, and Gr. *graphein*, to write]. The description or investigation of past events; chronology. [Rare.]
çhrō-nol'ō-ġẽr, *n.* One versed in chronology; a person who investigates the dates of past events and transactions.
çhron-ō-loġ'iç, çhron-ō-loġ'iç-ăl, *a.* Relating to chronology; containing an account of events in the order of time; according to the order of time.
çhron-ō-loġ'iç-ăl-ly, *adv.* In a chronological manner.
çhrō-nol'ō-ġist, *n.* See *Chronologer.*
çhrō-nol'ō-ġy, *n.*; *pl.* **çhrō-nol'ō-ġieş.** [Gr. *chronos*, time, and *logos*, a description, from *legein*, to describe.] The science of ascertaining the true periods or years when past events took place; and arranging them in their proper order according to their dates.

If history without *chronology* is dark and confused, *chronology* without history is dry and insipid. —A. Holmes.

çhrō-nom'e-tẽr, *n.* [*Chrono-*, and Gr. *metron*, a measure.]
1. Any instrument that measures time; specifically, a compact timekeeper of the highest possible accuracy.
2. A metronome, or mechanism for measuring time in music.
To rate a chronometer; see *Rate*, v.t.
çhron-ō-met'riç, çhron-ō-met'riç-ăl, *a.* Pertaining to a chronometer; measured by a chronometer.
çhrō-nom'e-try, *n.* The art of measuring time; the measuring of time by periods or divisions.
çhron'ō-phẽr, *n.* [*Chrono-*, and Gr. *pherein*, to carry.] An electrical instrument for signaling time between distant points.
çhron'ō-sçōpe, *n.* [*Chrono-*, and Gr. *skopein*, to view.] A chronograph; specifically, one used in measuring the velocity of projectiles or other rapidly moving bodies.
çhrys-, çhrys'ō-. Combining forms, from Gr. *chrysos*, gold.
çhrys'ăl, *n.* In archery, a small crack in the bow; written also *crysal.*
çhrys'ȧ-lid, *a.* Pertaining to a chrysalis.
çhrys'ȧ-lid, *n.* See *Chrysalis.*
çhrys'ȧ-lis, *n.*; *pl.* **çhry-sal'i-dēş.** [L. *chrysallis*; Gr. *chrysallis*, the chrysalis of a butterfly, from *chrysos*, gold.] A form which butterflies, moths, and most other insects assume when they change from the state of larva, or caterpillar, and before they arrive at their winged or perfect state.
çhrys-an'i-line, *n.* [*Chrys-* and *aniline.*] A derivative of rosaniline used in dyeing silk a golden-yellow.
Çhrys-an'thē-mum, *n.* [L. *chrysanthemum*; Gr. *chrysanthemon*, the marigold, lit. the gold flower; *chrysos*, gold, and *anthemon*, a flower.]
1. A large genus of composite plants, consisting of herbs or shrubs with single large-stalked flowers or with many small flowers.
2. [c—] Any plant or flower of this genus.

1, 2. Chrysalis of the White Butterfly-moth: *a*, Palpi or feelers; *b b*, wing-cases; *c*, sucker; *ee*, eyes; *x x*, antennæ. 3. Chrysalis of the Oak Egger-moth.

çhrys-ȧ-rō'bin, *n.* [L., from *chrys-*, and *araroba*, a native name of Goa powder.] The essential ingredient of Goa powder; an acrid, yellow powder yielding chrysophanic acid, by which name it was formerly known.
çhrys″el-e-phan'tine, *a.* [Gr. *chryselephantinos*, made of gold and ivory; *chrysos*, gold, and *elephas*, ivory.] Composed or partly composed of gold and ivory; a term specially applied to statues overlaid with gold and ivory.
çhrȳ'sēne, *n.* [Gr. *chrysos*, gold.] A hydrocarbon, which occurs in the least volatile portion of crude anthracene. It is crystalline, yellow, and without taste or smell.
çhrys'ō-. See *Chrys-.*
Çhrys-ō-bal'ȧ-nus, *n.* [*Chryso-*, and Gr. *balanos*, an acorn.] A genus of trees or shrubs, natives of tropical America and Africa, natural order *Rosaceæ.* The species *Icaco* is the cocoa-plum.
çhrys'ō-ber-yl, *n.* [*Chryso-*, and Gr. *beryllos*, beryl.] A pale green or nearly yellow mineral, crystallizing in the orthorhombic system. It is extremely hard, and the varieties, alexandrite and cat's-eye, are used as gems.
çhrys'ō-çhlōre, *n.* [*Chryso-*, and Gr. *chlōros*, a pale green.] A species of South African mole, the fur of which reflects metallic hues of green and gold.
çhrys'ō-çhrous (-krus), *a.* [*Chryso-*, and Gr. *chrōa*, color.] Of a golden-yellow color.
çhrys-ō-çol'lȧ, *n.* [Gr. *chrysokollos*, inlaid with gold; *chrysos*, gold, and *kolla*, glue, from *kollān*, to weld.] A silicate of the protoxid of copper of a fine emerald-green color, apparently produced from the decomposition of copper ores, which it usually accompanies.
çhry-sog'rȧ-phy, *n.* [Gr. *chrysos*, gold, and *graphein*, to write.]
1. The art of writing in letters of gold.
2. The writing itself thus executed.
çhry-soi'dine, *n.* [Gr. *chrysos*, gold, and *eidos*, form.] A crystalline dyestuff producing a bright yellow.
çhrys-ō-lep'iç, *a.* [*Chryso-*, and Gr. *lepis*, scale.] Having or appearing to have golden scales or flakes.
çhrys'ō-līte, *n.* [*Chryso-*, and Gr. *lithos*, stone.] A mineral composed of silica, magnesium, and iron. Its prevailing color is some shade of green. It is often transparent, sometimes only translucent.
çhry-sol'ō-ġy, *n.* [*Chryso-*, and Gr. *logos*, discourse.] That branch of political economy which relates to the production of wealth.
çhrys'ō-phan, *n.* A glucoside, orange in color and of bitter taste, obtained from rhubarb; when decomposed it yields chrysophanic acid.
çhrys-ō-phan'iç, *a.* [*Chryso-*, and Gr. *phainein*, to show, appear.] Relating to or derived from chrysophan.
Chrysophanic acid; a crystalline compound found in the lichen *Parmelia parietina*, in senna-leaves, rhubarb, etc.; called also *rhein*, *rheic acid*, *parietic acid*, etc.
çhrys'ō-prāşe, *n.* [*Chryso-*, and Gr. *prason*, a leek.] A kind of quartz, a variety of chalcedony, apple-green in color and sometimes used as a gem.
çhry-sop'ra-şus, *n.* Same as *Chrysoprase.*
Çhrȳ'sops, *n.* [L., from Gr. *chrysos*, gold, and *ōps*, eye.] A genus of dipterous insects of the family *Tabanidæ*; the clegs or gadflies. Their larvæ are useful to the farmer in destroying aphids, and are called *aphislions.*

Chrysops cæcutiens, Common Cleg (female).

çhrys'ō-spẽrm, *n.* [*Chryso-*, and Gr. *sperma*, seed.] A means of producing gold. [Obs.]
çhrys'ō-tile, *n.* [Gr. *chrysōtos*, gilded, from *chrysoun*, to gild.] A fibrous variety of serpentine, resembling true asbestos and used as a substitute.
çhrys'ō-tȳpe, *n.* [*Chryso-*, and Gr. *typos*, impression.] A photographic process, the chief agent of which is chlorid of gold; also, the solution employed and the picture produced.
chthōn'i-ăn (thōn'), *a.* Underground; subterranean; relating to the underworld; as, the *chthonian* deities.
chthon'iç (thon'), *a.* Same as *Chthonian.*
chthon-ō-phā'ġi-ȧ, chthon-oph'ȧ-ġy, *n.* [Gr. *chthōn*, earth, and *phagein*, to eat.] A disease, the victims of which have an impulse to eat clay or other soil.
chub, *n.* [Ice. *kubbr*, *kumbr*, a block, stump.]
1. A European fresh-water fish, called also *cheven*, of the family *Cyprinidæ*, the carps.

Chub (*Cyprinus* (*Leuciscus*) *cephalus*).

2. One of various other fishes found in the United States and elsewhere; as the fallfish, *Semotilus bullaris*; the tautog; the chub-sucker; the spot, *Liostomus xanthurus*; the marine food-fish, *Pimelepterus boscii*, of Bermuda, and the Bermuda bream, *Diplodus sargus.*
chub'bed, *a.* Chubby. [Rare.]
chub'bed-ness, *n.* The condition of being chubby.
chub'by, *a.* [Sw. *kubbug*, fat.] Resembling a chub; short and thick; plump; rounded; as, a *chubby* infant.
chub'=fāced (-fāst), *a.* Having a plump, round face.
chub'=mack″ẽr-el, *n.* A kind of mackerel, *Scomber colias*, found irregularly on the Atlantic coast; called also *bull mackerel*, *big-eyed mackerel*, etc.
chub'=suck″ẽr, *n.* The creekfish, *Erimyzon sucetta.*
chuck, *v.i.*; chucked, *pt.*, *pp.*; chucking, *ppr.* [ME. *chukken*, an imitative word.]
1. To make a noise resembling that of a hen when she calls her chickens.
2. To laugh in a quiet manner; to chuckle. [Rare.]
chuck, *v.t.* To call, as a hen her chickens.
chuck, *n.* 1. The cluck or call of a hen.
2. A sudden, small noise.
3. A word of endearment, corrupted from *chick.*
chuck, *v.t.* [From *shock*, to strike; AS. *scacan*, *sceacan*, to shake, strike.]
1. To strike or give a gentle blow; as, to *chuck* one under the chin.
2. To throw, with quick motion, a short distance; to pitch. [Colloq.]
3. In mechanics, to adjust in a chuck, or hold in place by means of a chuck.
chuck, *n.* 1. A slight blow or gentle tap under the chin.
2. A short throw or pitch.
3. Any game of pitch-and-toss, as pitch-farthing.
4. A mechanical contrivance designed to hold a piece of wood, metal, or other material in place so that it may be rotated, as upon the mandrel of a lathe.
Elliptic chuck; a chuck on which there is an eccentric circle and a slider, used in turning objects having an elliptic cross-section.
chuck, *n.* 1. A small pebble; also called *chuckstone.* [Scot.]
2. [*pl.*] A child's game played with pebbles chucked or thrown in the air. [Scot.]
chuck, *n.* Part of a beef carcass from between the neck and the collar-bone.
chuck'=fär″thing, *n.* A game in which coins are pitched at a mark.
chuck'=hōle, *n.* A depression in a rut made by wagon-wheels.
chuç'kle, *v.i.*; chuckled, *pt.*, *pp.*; chuckling, *ppr.* [Frequentative of *chuck*, to cluck.] To laugh in a suppressed or broken manner; to express inward triumph, exultation, or ridicule.
chuç'kle, *v.t.* 1. To call together, as a hen calls her brood. [Obs.]
2. To caress. [Obs.]
chuç'kle, *n.* A short, half-suppressed laugh expressive of exultation or ridicule.
chuç'kle-head (-hed), *n.* A thick-headed fellow; a blockhead; a numskull; also, one having a large head.
chuç'kle-head″ed, *a.* Thick-headed; stupid; possessing a large head.
chuç'klẽr, *n.* [Anglo-Ind.] In some parts of India, a member of a low caste including tanners, cobblers, and shoemakers; specifically, a shoemaker.
chuck'stōne, *n.* See *Chuck.*
chuck'=will'ş=wid″ōw, *n.* One species of a group of birds called goatsuckers, *Antrostomus carolinensis*, found in southern United States and named from its note.
chud, *v.t.* To champ; to bite. [Obs.]
chud'dẽr, chud'dȧ, chud'dȧh, *n.* [Anglo-Ind., from Hind. *chadar*, *chaddar*, sheet, tablecloth, cover; Per. *chadar*, a sheet, pavilion.]
1. A sheet or square of cloth thrown over the head of Moslem and Hindu women in India, and reaching to the ground.

2. A cashmere shawl or the material of which it is made.

Chu'di, *n.pl.* [Russ.] The Russian name for the Mongolian races in western and northwestern Russia, the Finns and Lapps being the best known types.

Chu'dic, *a.* Of or pertaining to the Chudi.

chu'et, *n.* [Obs.] See *Chewet*.

chu'fa, *n.* [Sp.] 1. A species of sedge, *Cyperus esculentus*, bearing edible tubers, and widely cultivated.

2. The edible tuber of the plant; also called *earth almond*.

chuff, *n.* A coarse, heavy, dull fellow; a surly person. [Obs.]

chuff, *a.* 1. Chuffy; swollen. [Obs. See *Chuffy*.]

2. Surly; ill-tempered. [Prov. Eng.]

chuff'i-ly, *adv.* In a rough, surly manner; clownishly.

chuff'i-ness, *n.* Surliness.

chuff'y, *a.* [Prob. from Sw. *kubbug*, fat, plump.]

1. Originally, fat or swelled out, especially in the cheeks; as, a *chuffy* lad.

2. Figuratively, surly; angry; churlish.

Chuffy brick; a brick when swollen by air or steam in the process of burning.

chuff'y-cheeked (-chēkt), *a.* Having plump or chubby cheeks.

chu'lan, *n.* [Chinese, from *chu*, pearl, and *lan*, a name given to plants of an orchideous character.] A Chinese plant, the *Chloranthus inconspicuus*, the spikes of whose flowers are used to scent tea.

chum, *n.* [Of doubtful origin, perhaps a corruption of *comrade*.] A close companion; a friend; a roommate, especially at a school or college.

chum, *v.i.*; chummed, *pt.*, *pp.*; chumming, *ppr.* To occupy the same room with another, especially at college; to chum with some one.

chum, *v.t.* To put into the same room or rooms with another.

chum, *n.* [Origin obscure.] Bits of fish, used as bait for bluefish.

chum, *v.i.*; chummed, *pt.*, *pp.*; chumming, *ppr.* To use chum for bait in fishing.

chum, *n.* [Origin unknown, perhaps from Ice. *kumbr*, a log, block.] In the manufacture of pottery, the block on which an unburned piece of ware is placed for turning purposes.

chum'mage, *n.* The act or condition of chumming; specifically, the proportionate share of expenses paid by each chum.

> Your *chummage*-ticket will be on twenty-seven, in the third. —Dickens.

chum'my, *a.* Familiarly sociable; companionable. [Colloq.]

chump, *n.* [Origin uncertain, compare Ice. *kumbr*, a block.]

1. A short and heavy block of wood.

2. A stupid person; one who lets his opportunities pass unimproved. [Slang.]

chump'-end, *n.* The thick end; usually applied to a loin of veal or mutton.

chump'ish, *a.* Boorish; clownish; stubborn. [Rare.]

chum'ship, *n.* The condition of chumming; confidential intimacy. [Rare.]

chu-nam', *n.* [Anglo-Ind.; Tamil, *chunnam*; Hind. *chūnā*, lime, from Sans. *chūrna*, meal.]

1. In the East Indies, a name given to lime, or a mixture made of lime, as stucco, or the lime prepared from shells to be chewed with the betel-leaf.

2. In northern India, a weight of gold equal to six grains troy.

chu-nam', *v.t.*; chunammed, *pt.*, *pp.*; chunamming, *ppr.* To cover or plaster with chunam.

chunk, *n.* [Prob. a variant of *chump*.] A short, thick piece; hence, a thickset human being or animal. [Colloq.]

chunk'y, *a.* Short and thickset; as, a *chunky* boy. [Colloq.]

chu-pat'ty, *n.* [Anglo-Ind., from Hind. *chapati*, *cha pata*, an unleavened cake.] In India, unleavened bread or cake, made of flour, water, and salt.

church, *v.t.*; churched, *pt.*, *pp.*; churching, *ppr.* To perform with (any one) the office of returning thanks in the church, after any signal deliverance, as from the dangers of childbirth.

church, *n.* [ME *chirche*, *cherche*; AS. *circe*, *cyrce*; Late Gr. *kyriakon*, a church, from Gr. *kyriakē* (supply *dōma*, house), the Lord's house, from *kyriakos*, belonging to the Lord or Master; *kyrios*, lord, master; *kyros*, supreme power, authority.]

1. An edifice consecrated to worship, specifically for Christian worship.

2. The collective body of Christians or *church universal*, composed of three great branches, the Roman Catholic, Protestant, and Greek communions.

> Probably we Christians are too familiarized with the presence of the *church* to do justice to her as a world-embracing institution. —Liddon.

3. A particular body of Christians united under one form of ecclesiastical government, in one creed, and using the same ritual and ceremonies; as, the Greek *church*; the Anglican *church*; the Roman Catholic *church*; hence, ecclesiastical authority and influence; as, the union of *church* and state.

4. The organized body of Christians in any particular district, city, state, or country; as, the *church* at Ephesus.

> The American *church* at large did not do its whole duty in the conflict with slavery. —Jos. Cook.

5. Any edifice dedicated to religious worship other than Christian. [Rare.]

6. The worshipers of Jehovah or the true God before the advent of Christ; as, the Jewish *church*.

7. The body of Christians who have made a public profession of their faith, as distinguished from those who have not; as, to join the *church*.

8. Any organized body of Christians occupying the same edifice for religious worship; a congregation; as, a pastor and his *church*.

9. The profession of the Christian ministry; as, he has gone into the *church*.

10. In England, specifically, a place of public worship belonging to the established church or Church of England, the term chapel or meeting-house being applied to the places of worship of Dissenters.

Church militant; the church on earth, distinguished from the *church triumphant*; the visible church in conflict with the powers of evil

Church triumphant; the collective body of saints now glorified in heaven.

Church of England; the Protestant Episcopal church in England, established and endowed by law as the national church.

Eastern church; the Greek church.

Western church; the Church of Rome.

church, *a.* Pertaining to the church or to ecclesiastical matters; as, *church* music.

Church festival; a day or several days on which special religious services are held by the churches to pay honor to, and commemorate events in the life of Jesus Christ, or in the lives of his apostles, or of various later saints.

Church government; the polity and discipline of any church body in regard to its members; or the enforcement of its regulations by the heads or officers of a church.

Church living; a benefice in an established church.

Church service; the order of any religious observance held in a church; in the Anglican church, a prescribed form of service, and the book containing it.

Church text; a rather thin pointed style of blackletter, something like early English, much used in engraved texts and ornamental lettering for ecclesiastical purposes.

church'-ale, *n.* In England, a specially strong ale formerly brewed for church festivals; also, the festival itself at which the ale was served, [Obs.]

church'dom, *n.* [AS. *circe*, church, and *dom*, jurisdiction.] The government or authority of the church. [Rare.]

church'-garth, *n.* A churchyard.

church'gō"er, *n.* One who attends church.

church'gō"ing, *a.* 1. Usually attending church.

2. Calling to church.

> The sound of the *churchgoing* bell.—Cowper.

church'-haw, *n.* A churchyard. [Obs.]

church'-house, *n.* A building connected with a church and used for parish, diocesan, or general purposes according to the denomination.

church'ism, *n.* Sectarianism; narrow adherence to ritual and forms.

church'less, *a.* Without a church, or unattached to a church.

church'like, *a.* Becoming the church or a churchman.

church'li-ness, *n.* Consideration for the church and its polity.

church'ly, *a.* Ecclesiastical; appropriate for a church.

church'man, *n.* 1. An ecclesiastic or clergyman; one who ministers in sacred things.

2. In England, an Episcopalian, as distinguished from a Dissenter; as, he was a strict *churchman*.

church'man-ly, *a.* Befitting a churchman.

church'man-ship, *n.* The state of being a churchman, or of belonging to the established church. [Eng.]

church'-mem"ber, *n.* A communicant having membership in some church.

church'-mem"ber-ship, *n.* Communicants of a church, considered collectively; also, membership in a church.

church'-mouse, *n.* A mouse formerly supposed to run about churches and live on nothing.

Poor as a church-mouse; poor as can be; having nothing to eat.

church'-rate, *n.* A rate formerly levied in England by the vestries on all parishioners.

church'reeve, *n.* [ME. *chirche-reve*; AS. *circe*, church, and *gerēfa*, steward.] A warden or steward of a church. [Obs.]

church'ship, *n.* Institution as a church.

church'ward"en, *n.* [ME. *chirchewardein*, *kirkewardein*, a warden of the church; AS. *ciric*, church, and *weard*, a keeper.]

1. A keeper or guardian of an English or Episcopal church, and a representative of the parish. *Churchwardens* are appointed by the minister, or elected by parishioners, to superintend the church, its property and concerns, and the behavior of the parishioners.

2. A long clay pipe. [Colloq., Eng.]

church'ward"en-ship, *n.* The office of a churchwarden.

church'-work, *n.* 1. Work on a church building.

2. Work to promote the religious interests of the church.

3. Work that drags, or is slowly performed.

> This siege was *church-work*, and therefore went on slowly. —Fuller.

church'-writ, *n.* A writ issued from a court which deals with ecclesiastical affairs.

church'y, *a.* Attaching extreme importance to church forms and rules.

church'yard, *n.* [ME. *chirchezeard*; AS. *cirice*, church, and *geard*, yard.] The ground adjoining a church, in which the dead are buried; a cemetery.

chu'ri-a, *n.* [Native Mex. name.] The chaparral-cock; an appellation common among the Mexicans.

churl, *n.* [ME. *churl*, *cherl*; AS. *ceorl*, a man, a countryman of the lowest rank.]

1. A rude, surly, ill-bred man.

2. A rustic; a countryman, or laborer.

3. A miser; a niggard.

4. In early English history, a freeman of low rank.

churl, *a.* See *Churlish*.

churl'ish, *a.* 1. Like a churl; rude; surly; austere; sullen; rough in temper; unfeeling; uncivil.

2. Selfish; narrow-minded; avaricious.

3. Unpliant; unyielding; unmanageable; said of things; as, *churlish* metal.

churl'ish-ly, *adv.* Rudely; roughly; in a churlish manner.

churl'ish-ness, *n.* Rudeness of manners or temper; sullenness; austerity; indisposition to kindness or courtesy.

churl'y, *a.* Rude; boisterous.

churm, *n.* An obsolete form of *chirm*.

churn, *n.* [ME. *cherne*, *chirne*; AS. *cyrin*, a churn.] A vessel in which cream or milk is agitated, for the purpose of separating the oily parts from the caseous and serous parts to make butter.

churn, *v.t.*; churned, *pt.*, *pp.*; churning, *ppr.*

1. To stir or agitate (cream) for making butter.

2. To shake or agitate with violence or continued motion; as, the steamer *churned* the sea into foam.

churn, *v.i.* 1. To perform the act of churning cream or milk in butter-making.

2. To be agitated or in a state of agitation; as, water *churning* over the shoals.

churn'ing, *n.* 1. The operation of making butter from cream by agitation; a shaking or stirring.

2. The quantity of butter produced at one operation.

churr, *n.* [An imitative word.]

1. A name given to the whitethroat, *Sylvia cinerea*, and other trilling birds.

2. A whirring note of certain birds and insects.

chur'rus, *n.* [Hind. *charas*.] A gum resin which oozes from the Indian hemp. It is a narcotic and intoxicant. [See *Bhang*.]

churr'worm, *n.* [AS. *cyrran*, to turn, and *wyrm*, worm.] An insect that turns about nimbly; called also *mole-cricket* and *fan-cricket*.

chuse, *v.* An obsolete spelling of *choose*.

chute, *n.* [Fr. *chute*; OFr. *cheute*, a fall, declivity.]

1. An inclined framework, trough, or conduit by means of which objects are made to slide from a higher to a lower level; a shoot; as, a water *chute*, a coal *chute*, etc. [See *Shoot*.]

2. An opening in a dam for the passage of timber, etc., by flotation with the current.

3. In the lower Mississippi region, a narrow channel between islands or between an island and the shore; a side channel; a bayou.

4. The natural or artificial inclined plane of a toboggan-slide.

chut'ney, **chut'nee**, *n.* [Hind. *chatni*.] A spicy relish or seasoning composed of sweets, acids, and fruits; originally popular in India, its manufacture and sale are now widespread.

chy-lā'ceous, *a.* Having the properties of chyle; consisting of chyle.

chy-lā'quē-ous (-kwē-), *a.* [L., from *chylus*, chyle, and *aqua*, water.] A term applied to the watery, chylaceous, circulating fluid of some inferior animals, as the starfishes, etc.

chyle, *n.* [L. *chylus*; Gr. *chylos*, juice, humor, chyle, from *chein*, to pour.] In physiology, a nutritive milky fluid containing the fatty matter of the food in a condition of emulsion, produced during digestion by the action of the pancreatic juices and the bile on the chyme. After absorption by the lacteals it is carried into the circulation by the thoracic duct.

chyle′-blad″dẽr, *n.* See *Chylocyst.*

chy̆′li-. Same as *Chylo-.*

chyl-i-fac′tion, *n.* [*Chyli-*, and L. *factio*, a making, from *facere*, to make.] The act or process by which chyle is formed from food in animal bodies.

chyl-i-fac′tive, *a.* Forming or changing into chyle; having the power to make chyle.

chy̆-lif′ẽr-ous, *a.* [*Chyli-*, and L. *ferre*, to bear.] Transmitting chyle; as, *chyliferous* vessels.

chy̆-lif′ic, *a.* Chylifactive; applied especially to any portion of the digestive tract concerned in the production of chyle; as, in insects, the *chylific* ventricle, or last stomach

chyl-i-fi-cā′tion, *n.* The formation of chyle; chylifaction.

chy̆-lif′i-cȧ-tō-ry, *a.* Producing chyle; chylifactive.

chy̆′li-fy̆, *v.t.* and *v.i.* To convert, or to be converted into chyle.

chy̆′lō-, chy̆′li-, chy̆l-. [L. *chylus*; Gr. *chylos*, juice, chyle, from *chein*, to pour.] Combining forms denoting relation to or connection with chyle; as *chylo*poietic, *chyli*fication, *chyl*uria, etc.

chy̆′lō-cyst, *n.* [*Chylo-*, and Gr. *kystis*, bladder.] In physiology, the reservoir at the lower end of the thoracic duct into which the lymphatic vessels convey the chyle; also called *chyle-bladder.*

chy̆″lō-pō-et′ic, *a.* Same as *Chylopoietic.*

chy̆″lō-poi-et′ic, *a.* [*Chylo-*, and Gr. *poiētikos*, capable of making, from *poiein*, to make.] Helping to make chyle; connected with chyle; as, the *chylopoietic* organs.

chy̆-lō′sis, *n.* Same as *Chylifaction.*

chy̆′lous, *a.* Consisting of, relating to, or similar to chyle.

chy̆-lū′ri-ȧ, *n.* [*Chyl-*, and Gr. *ouron*, urine.] An abnormal milky condition of the urine when it contains chyle or fatty matter.

chy̆-mā′quē-ous (-kwē-), *a.* [LL. *chymus*, chyle, juice, and L. *aqua*, water.] A term applied to the watery circulating fluid of some polyps, which contains chyme.

chyme, *n.* [LL. *chymus*; Gr. *chymos*, juice, from *chein*, to pour.] The particular form or modification which food assumes after it has undergone the action of the stomach, and is partly digested; it is a thin, pulpy substance which passes into the small intestine, where the process of digestion is completed by its conversion into chyle and by excretion.

chym′ic, chym′ist, chym′is-try. [Obs.] See *Chemical, Chemist, Chemistry.*

chy̆-mif′ẽr-ous, *a.* [LL. *chymus*, chyme, and L. *ferre*, to bear.] Containing or conveying chyme.

chym″i-fi-cā′tion, *n.* [LL. *chymus*, chyme, and L. *facere*, to make.] The process of becoming or of forming chyme; the first stage of digestion.

chym′i-fied, *a.* Formed into chyme.

chym′i-fy̆, *v.t.* and *v.i.* To form, or to be formed into, chyme.

chy̆′mous, *a.* Relating to chyme.

chy̆-om′e-tẽr, *n.* [Gr. *chy-*, the root of *chein*, to pour, and *metron*, a measure.] An instrument formerly used for measuring liquids. It was a device consisting mainly of a syringe with a graduated piston.

ci-bā′ri-ăn, *a.* [L. *cibarius*, pertaining to food, from *cibus*, food.]

1. Pertaining to food; cibarious. [Rare.]

2. In zoölogy, pertaining to the organs of the mouth; as, the *cibarian* system of classifying insects and crustaceans.

ci-bā′ri-ous, *a.* Pertaining to food; useful for food; edible.

ci-bā′tion, *n.* [L. *cibatio*, a feeding, from *cibare*, to feed.]

1. The act of taking nourishment.

2. In alchemy, the act of supplying the contents of a crucible with new essentials.

cib′ōl, *n.* [ME. *chibolle*, *chebole*; Fr. *ciboule*, an onion, from L. *cæpa*, *cepa*, an onion.] A sort of small onion used in cookery; the shallot; also the Welsh onion, *Allium fistulosum.*

ci-bō′ri-um, *n.*; *pl.* **ci-bō′ri-ȧ.** [L. *ciborium*, a drinking-vessel; Gr. *kibōrion*, a drinking-cup made like the large pod of the Egyptian bean.]

1. In architecture, an insulated building, composed of an arched vault on four columns.

2. In the Roman Catholic church, the coffer or case containing the host.

3. The tomb of a martyr, when sculptured and used as an altar.

4. Any insulated tabernacle, as a canopy covering a high altar, etc.; a baldachin.

ci-cā′dȧ, *n.*; *pl.* **ci-cā′dȧs** or **ci-cā′dæ.** [L. *cicada*, the cicada, or tree-cricket.]

1. Any one of many species of insects, genus *Cicada*, living on trees, shrubs, etc., and having a characteristically sharp chirp produced by muscular action upon a tightly stretched membrane beneath the abdomen. The best known American species is *Cicada septendecim* or seventeen-year locust.

2. One of the species of hemipterous insects that make a chirping sound, as the cricket, etc.

3. [C—] The genus of insects of which the seventeen-year locust is a type.

ci-cā′lȧ, *n.* [It., from L. *cicada.*] A cicada.

cic′ȧ-trice, *n.* [ME. *cicatrice*; Fr. *cicatrice*; L. *cicatrix*, a scar.] A scar, whether in animal or vegetable substances; a cicatrix.

cic-ȧ-tri′ciăl (-trish′ăl), *a.* Pertaining to or characteristic of a cicatrice.

cic′ȧ-tri-cle (-kl), *n.* [Fr. *cicatricule*; L. *cicatricula*, dim. of *cicatrix*, a scar.] The germinating or fetal point in the embryo of a seed or the yolk of an egg; as, a germinating *cicatricle.*

cic′ȧ-tri-cōse, *a.* Covered with scars or markings like scars, as animal tissue or the surface of certain insects.

cic′ȧ-trī-sive, *a.* Tending to promote the formation of a cicatrice; beneficial to the healing of a wound.

ci-cā′trix, *n.*; *pl.* **cic-ȧ-trī′cēs.** [L. *cicatrix*, a scar.]

1. In surgery, the thin film of new tissue which forms on a wounded or ulcerated part, and thus effects the healing. It finally contracts and turns white, remaining as a scar.

2. Any scar-like marking, as the point of attachment of the adductor muscle of a bivalve to the shell, or of a leaf to the stalk.

cic′ȧ-tri-zant, *n.* A medicine or application that promotes the formation of a cicatrice, and the healing of the wounded part.

cic″ȧ-tri-zā′tion, *n.* The process of healing or forming a cicatrice; the state of being healed or cicatrized.

cic′ȧ-trīze, *v.t.*; cicatrized, *pt.*, *pp.*; cicatrizing, *ppr.* [L. *cicatrix*, scar.] To heal or induce the formation of a cicatrice in, as in wounded or ulcerated flesh; to apply medicines to for that purpose.

cic′ȧ-trīze, *v.i.* To heal or be healed; to have new tissue or skin over an injured part; as, wounded flesh *cicatrizes.*

cic′ȧ-trīzed, *a.* Healed, as wounded flesh; having a cicatrix formed.

cic′ȧ-trōse, *a.* Same as *Cicatricose.*

cic′e-ly, *n.* [L. *seselis*; Gr. *seselis*, hartwort, seseli.] A popular name of several umbelliferous plants. The sweet *cicely* of Europe is *Myrrhis odorata*, the sweet *cicely* of New England *Osmorrhiza longistylis.*

Wild cicely; an umbelliferous European herb, *Chærophyllum sylvestre.*

cic-e-rō′nē (*or* chē-chä-rō′ne), *n.*; *pl.* **cic-e-rō′nī.** [It., from L. *Cicero*, the famous Roman orator; so called from the usual loquacity of guides.] A guide; one who shows strangers the curiosities of a place.

Cic-e-rō′ni-ăn, *a.* [L. *Ciceronianus*, from the orator, *Cicero.*] Resembling Cicero, either in style or action; in style, diffuse and flowing; in manner, vehement.

Cic-e-rō′ni-ăn-işm, *n.* Imitation of or resemblance to the style or action of Cicero.

Ci-chō-ri-ā′cē-æ, *n.pl.* [L., from *cichorium*, chicory.] A group of composite plants, including the chicory, dandelion, etc.

ci-chō-ri-ā′ceous, *a.* Relating or akin to the *Cichoriaceæ.*

Ci-chō′ri-um, *n.* [L. *cichorium*; Gr. *kichōrion*, chicory, endive.] A genus of *Cichoriaceæ*, the species being found in Europe and the Mediterranean countries; it includes the chicory, endive, etc.

cich′-pēa, *n.* [Obs.] See *Chick-pea.*

ci-cis′bē-işm, *n.* The state or condition of a cicisbeo.

ci-cis′bē-ō, *n.* [It.] 1. A dangler about women; the professed admirer of a married woman.

2. Formerly, a piece of silk knotted to a fan, cane, etc. [Obs.]

cic′lȧ-tŏn, cic′lȧ-tŏun, *n.* [ME. *ciclatoun*, *ciclatun*; OFr. *ciclaton*, *singlaton*, a kind of robe; L. *cyclas*; Gr. *kyklas*, a robe worn chiefly by women.] A costly medieval fabric, usually of silk and worn by men and women; also written *checklaton*, *chekelatoun.*

cic′ō-nine, *a.* [L. *ciconia*, stork.] Relating to or belonging to the stork family, *Ciconiidæ.*

cic′ū-rāte, *v.t.* [L. *cicur*, tame, from *cicurare*, to tame.] To tame; to reclaim from wildness. [Obs.]

cic-ū-rā′tion, *n.* The act of taming wild animals. [Obs.]

Ci-cū′tȧ, *n.* [L. *cicuta*, the hemlock.] A genus of plants containing several poisonous species, one European and the others American. It includes the water-hemlock or cowbane, *Cicuta maculata*, the root of which is a deadly poison.

cic-ū-tox′in, *n.* [L. *cicuta*, hemlock, and *toxicum*, poison.] A poisonous substance extracted from the root of the water-hemlock, *Cicuta maculata.*

Cid, *n.* [Sp., from Ar. *seid*, lord.]

1. Leader, or commander-in-chief; the Spanish appellation for Ruy Diaz, Count de Bivar, who was a champion of Christianity, and upholder of the royal house of Spain during the Moorish wars of the eleventh century.

2. The title of a well known Spanish epic poem exploiting the deeds of Ruy Diaz.

cid′ȧ-ris, *n.*; *pl.* **cid′ȧ-rēş.** [L. *cidaris*; Gr. *kidaris*, a turban.] The royal headdress of ancient Persian kings; also, of the Jewish high priest; a miter.

cī′dẽr, *n.* [ME. *cidre*, *cyder*; OFr. *sidre*, *cidere*, cider; L. *sicera*; Gr. *sikera*; Heb. *shekar*, a sweet fermented liquor, from *shakar*, to be intoxicated.] The expressed juice of apples, used as a beverage. The word was formerly used to signify the juice of other fruits, and other kinds of strong liquor, though not wine; but it is now applied only to the juice of apples, before and after fermentation.

Hard cider; cider after fermentation.

Sweet cider; cider before fermentation.

cī′dẽr-bran′dy, *n.* A brandy distilled from cider; called also *apple-jack.*

cī′dẽr-ist, *n.* A maker of cider. [Obs.]

cī′dẽr-kin, *n.* Weak cider made by steeping the refuse from a cider-press. [Eng.]

cī′dẽr-mill, *n.* A mill in which cider is produced.

cī′dẽr-press, *n.* A press for crushing apples in a cider-mill.

cī′dẽr-tree, *n.* An Australian tree, growing in the swamps, from the gum of which a cider is sometimes made.

cī′dẽr-vin′ē-găr, *n.* Sour cider, or vinegar made from cider.

ci-dē-vaṅt′ (-voṅ′), *a.* [Fr., from *ci*, from *ici*, here, *de*, of, and *avant*, before.] Former; previous; used to designate men who have been in office and retired.

cï-e-nä′gȧ, *n.* [Sp., a quagmire, from *cieno*, mud, from L. *cœnum*, mud.] A morass, swamp, or marsh, in dry surroundings.

cierge, *n.* Same as *Cerge.*

ci-gär′, *n.* [Fr. *cigare*: Sp. *cigarro*, a cigar, originally the name of a variety of Cuban tobacco.] A small roll of tobacco, so formed as to be tubular; used for smoking, and consisting, in the cheaper qualities, of a binder, filler, and wrapper. The best *cigars* are made of tobacco-leaf with wrappers of the same material.

cig-ȧ-rette′ (-ret′), *n.* [Fr., dim. of *cigare*, cigar.] A small quantity of fine tobacco rolled in paper (usually rice-paper), tubular in shape, for smoking.

cig-ȧ-rette′-bee″tle, *n.* See *Tobacco-beetle.*

ci-gär′-fish, *n.* A fish found in the Gulf of Mexico and the Caribbean sea, resembling the mackerel.

ci-gär′-plant, *n.* A Mexican plant having a red and black corolla somewhat resembling a cigar in shape.

cil′ẽr-y, *n.* The drapery or foliage carved on the heads of columns.

cil′i-ȧ, *n.*, pl. of *cilium.*

cil′iȧ-ry (-yȧ-ry *or* cil′i-ā-ry), *a.* [L. *cilia*, the eyelashes.]

1. Pertaining to the eyelashes, or related parts of the eye; as, the *ciliary* gland.

2. Pertaining to the cilia in animals or plants.

Ciliary muscle; the muscle attached to the eyeball which adjusts the crystalline lens to the required focus.

Cil-i-ā′tȧ, *n.pl.* [L. *ciliata*, neut. pl. of *ciliatus*, with cilia, from *cilium*, an eyelid.] An order of *Infusoria* distinguished by having cilia.

cil′i-āte, cil′i-ā-ted, *a.* [L. *ciliatus*, with cilia, from *cilia*, the eyelashes.] In botany, furnished or surrounded with parallel filaments, or bristles resembling the hairs of the eyelids; as, a *ciliate* leaf, etc.

Ciliate Leaf.

cil′ice, *n.* [L. *cilicium*; Gr. *kilikion*, a garment made of goat's hair, from *Kilikia*, Cilicia, a region in Asia Minor, noted for its goats.] A rough undergarment of haircloth, formerly worn by monks, etc., as an act of penance; also, the coarse cloth itself, sometimes made of goat's hair.

Ci-li′ciăn (-lish′ăn), *a.* Relating to Cilicia, a country in Asia Minor.

Ci-li′ciăn, *n.* A native or inhabitant of Cilicia.

ci-li′cious (-lish′us), *a.* [L. *cilicium*; Gr. *kilikion*, haircloth.] Made or consisting of hair; as, a *cilicious* garment. [Obs.]

cil-i-el′lȧ, *n.*; *pl.* **cil-i-el′læ.** [L., dim. of *cilium*, eyelid.] In entomology, a fringe composed of fine hairs.

ci-lif′er-ous, *a.* Having or bearing cilia; ciliate.

cil′i-i-fọrm, *a.* [L. *cilium*, an eyelid, and *forma*, form.] Extremely fine; slender like cilia; having the form of cilia.

cil′i-ō-grāde, *n.* [L. *cilium*, the eyelash, and *gradi*, to step, walk.] An animal that moves by means of cilia.

cil′i-ō-grāde, *a.* Moving by the aid of cilia; as, the *ciliograde Medusæ.*

cil′i-ō-lāte, *a.* Having ciliola.

cil-lī′ō-lum, *n.*; *pl.* **cil-lī′ō-lȧ.** A very small cilium.

cil′i-um, *n.*; *pl.* **cil′i-ȧ.** [L., an eyelid.]

1. In botany, a long hair upon the margin of a vegetable body.

2. In zoölogy, a very minute filament, which projects from animal membranes, and is endowed with the power of vibratory motion.

cil′lō, *n.* [L., from *cilium*, an eyelid.] A convulsive trembling or quivering of the upper eyelid.

cil-lō′sis, *n.* Same as *Cillo.*

cī′mȧ, *n.* Same as *Cyme.*

ci-mär′, *n.* See *Simar.*

cī-mär-rōn′, *n.* [Sp. Am.] The Rocky Mountain sheep; the bighorn.

cim′bāl, *n.* A kind of cake. [Obs.]

cim′bi-ȧ, cim′i-ȧ, *n.* [Sp. *cimbra*, an arched frame, a cincture.] In architecture, a strengthening band or cincture around a pillar.

Cim′brī, *n.pl.* [L. *Cimber*, pl. *Cimbri.*] An ancient tribe of northern Europe. [See *Cimbric.*]

Cim′bri-ăn, *a.* Of or relating to the Cimbri.

Cim′bri-ăn, *n.* One of the Cimbri.

Cim′brig, *a.* [L. *Cimbricus*, from *Cimbri*, the Cimbrians.] Pertaining to the Cimbri, the ancient inhabitants of Jutland, in Denmark, which was anciently called the *Cimbric Chersonese.*

Cim′brig, *n.* The language of the Cimbri.

ci-mē′li-ärch, *n.* [Gr. *keimēliarchēs*, a treasurer; *keimēlion*, treasure, and *archein*, to rule.] A superintendent or keeper of valuable things belonging to a church. [Obs.]

cim′e-tēr, *n.* See *Simitar.*

Cī′mex, *n.* [L., a bug.] 1. A genus of hemipterous insects, the bedbugs.

2. [c—; *pl.* cim′i-cēs.] A bedbug.

cim′i-ȧ, *n.* See *Cimbia.*

ci-mic′ic, *a.* Pertaining to the genus *Cimex.*

Cimicic acid; a yellow substance obtained from the oil of a species of cimex.

cim′i-cid, *n* A bug of the family *Cimicidæ.*

Ci-mic′i-dæ, *n.pl.* [L., from *cimex*, a bug.] A family of insects which includes the typical genus *Cimex.*

cim′i-cine, *n.* The substance which is productive of the odor characteristic of the bedbug.

cī′miss, *n.* [L. *cimex*, a bug.] The bedbug. [Obs.]

Cim-mē′ri-ăn, *a.* 1. Pertaining to Cimmerium, a town at the mouth of the Palus Mæotis. The ancients pretended that this country was involved in darkness; whence the phrase *Cimmerian darkness*, to denote a deep or continual obscurity.

2. Pertaining to the mythical Cimmerii.

3. Without light; dark as night.

Cim-mē′ri-ăn, *n.* One of the mythical or ancient Cimmerii, first prominently mentioned by Homer; written also *Kimmerian.*

cim′ō-līte, *n.* [L. *cimolia* (supply *creta*, clay); Gr. *kimōlia* (supply *gē*, earth), the Cimolian earth; so named from *Kimolus* in the Cyclades.] A species of clay used by the ancients as a remedy for erysipelas and other inflammations. It is white, of a loose, soft texture, and is useful in taking spots from cloth.

cinch, *n.* [Sp. *cincha*; L. *cingula*, a girdle.]

1. A broad saddle-girth, usually made of canvas or horsehair; used especially in the western states.

2. A hold; a tight grip; a certainty or sure thing. [Colloq.]

cinch, *n.* [From Sp. *cinco*, five.] A game of cards; also called *pedro* and *high-five*, in which the leading cards are the five of trumps, called right pedro, and the other five of the same color, called left pedro, each counting five in the score.

cinch, *v.t.*; cinched, *pt.*, *pp.*; cinching, *ppr.* 1. To gird tightly; to fasten a cinch around.

2. To force into a tight place; to get a tight hold upon. [Slang.]

Cin-chō′nȧ, *n.* [So named from the Countess del *Chinchon*, wife of a Peruvian viceroy of the seventeenth century, who was cured of a fever by the use of the bark.]

1. A genus of evergreen trees, natural order *Rubiaceæ*, native to South America. Several species furnish the valuable Peruvian bark, the cinchona of commerce, and quinine. These trees are now extensively cultivated in the East Indies. *Cinchona succirubra* furnishes red cinchona bark; *Cinchona Calisaya* affords calisaya, or the yellow bark, and the ordinary Peruvian bark is obtained from *Cinchona officinalis.*

Cinchona (*Cinchona succirubra*).

2. [c—] The bark of any species of *Cinchona* which possesses medicinal properties; also called *Jesuits' bark*, from its early use by Jesuit missionaries of South America.

cin-chō-nā′ceous, *a.* Pertaining to or resembling cinchona or the trees producing it.

cin-chō′ni-ȧ, *n.* See *Cinchonine.*

cin-chon′ic, *a.* Derived from or belonging to cinchona.

cin-chon′i-cine, *n.* An alkaloid obtained from cinchonine.

cin-chō-nid′i-ȧ, *n.* Same as *Cinchonidine.*

cin-chon′i-dine, *n.* An alkaloid resembling quinine, obtained especially from red cinchona bark.

cin′chō-nine, cin-chō′ni-ȧ, *n.* A quinine alkaloid obtained from the bark of several species of *Cinchona*, and one of the medicinal active principles of the bark.

cin′chō-nism, *n.* An abnormal condition caused by excessive use of quinine; its symptoms are deafness, roaring in the ears, vertigo, and temporary loss of sight.

cin′chō-nize, *v.t.*; cinchonized, *pt.*, *pp.*; cinchonizing, *ppr.* To dose with quinine or cinchona so as to bring about cinchonism.

cin-cin′nāl, *a.* Of, pertaining to, or like a cincinnus.

cin-cin′nus, *n.* [L. *cincinnus*; Gr. *kikinnos*, a curl of hair.] In botany, a form of alternate branching in flower-clusters.

cinc′tūre, *n.* [L. *cinctura*, a girdle, from *cingere*, to surround, to gird.]

1. A belt, a girdle, or something worn round the body.

2. That which encompasses or incloses.

3. In architecture, a ring or list at the top and bottom of a column, separating the shaft, at one end, from the base; at the other, from the capital.

cinc′tūred, *a.* Having a cincture or girdle.

cin′dēr, *n.* [ME. *cinder*, *sinder*; AS. *sinder*, dross of iron, cinder; L. *cinis*, ashes.]

1. A small hot coal or particle of fire mixed with ashes; an ember; as, emptying a grate of *cinders.*

2. Small particles of fuel or other matter, remaining after combustion, in which fire is extinct; as, the *cinders* of a forge.

3. A scale cast off in forging metal.

4. A fragment of scoriaceous substance cast up by a volcano in eruption, together with lava.

5. The slag or scoria of a furnace.

cin′dēr-cōne, *n.* A cone-shaped hill composed of successive deposits of volcanic cinders.

cin′dēr-frāme, *n.* A wire device fixed in front of the tubes of a locomotive to prevent the escape of cinders.

cin′dēr-notch (-noch), *n.* In a blast-furnace, the opening for the removal of slag.

cin′dēr-pȧth, *n.* A path, walk, or track laid with cinders; specifically, a track for athletes.

cin′dēr-pig, *n.* Pig-iron composed of slagged ore.

cin′dēr-wool, *n.* A fibrous substance made from molten slag; generally called *mineral wool.*

cin′dēr-y, *a.* Resembling or composed of cinders; full of cinders.

cin-ē-fac′tion, *n.* [L. *cinis*, ashes, and *factus*, pp. of *facere*, to make.] Reduction to ashes. [Obs.]

cin-ē-mat′ic, cin-ē-mat′ic-āl, *a.* Same as *Kinematic*, etc.

cin-ē-mat′ō-grȧph, *n.* [Gr. *kinēma*, motion, and *graphein*, to write.]

1. A machine for taking in rapid succession, photographs of moving objects, upon a continuous film, to be used in reproducing the appearance of actual motion.

2. One of the many forms of apparatus used in producing moving, animated, or life-motion pictures by projection upon a screen; other names for such an apparatus are *kinetoscope*, *cineograph*, *optigraph*, *kinodrome*, etc.

ci-nen′chy-mȧ, *n.* [Gr. *kinein*, to move, and *enchyma*, infusion.] In botany, laticiferous tissue.

cin-en-chym′ȧ-tous, *a.* Pertaining to cinenchyma.

cin-e-rā′ceous, *a.* [L. *cinereus*, ashy, from *cinis*, ashes.] Like ashes; having the color of the ashes of wood.

Cin-e-rā′ri-ȧ, *n.* [L. *cinerarius*, pertaining to ashes, from *cinis*, ashes.] A genus of plants of the aster family, cultivated for their yellow flowers.

Cineraria (garden variety).

cin′e-rā-ry, *a.* [L. *cinerarius*, of or for ashes; *cinerarium*, a receptacle containing the ashes of the dead, from *cinis*, ashes.] Pertaining to ashes; a term applying especially to the sepulchral urns used by the ancients to preserve the ashes of bodies which had been burned.

cin-e-rā′tion, *n.* [L. *cinis*, ashes.] The reducing of anything to ashes by combustion.

ci-nē′rē-ȧ, *n.* [L., from *cinereus*, ashy.] In anatomy, the gray or cellular nerve-tissue, as distinguished from the white or fibrous.

Cinerary Urns.

ci-nē′rē-āl, *a.* Relating to the cinerea.

ci-nē′rē-ous, *a.* [L. *cinereus*, ashy; *cinis*, ashes.] Having the color of ashes; ash-gray; ashen; like ashes.

cin-ēr-es′cent, *a.* [LL. *cinerescens*, ppr. of *cinerescere*, to become ashes, from L. *cinis*, ashes.] Somewhat resembling the color of wood ashes; turning gray.

cin-e-ri′tious (-rish′us), *a.* [L. *cinis*, ashes.] Having the color or consistence of ashes.

ci-ner′ū-lent, *a.* Full of ashes. [Obs.]

Cin-gȧ-lēse′, Sin-ghȧ-lēse′, *n.* and *a.* [Sans. *Sinhalam*, Ceylon.]

I. *n.* [*sing.* and *pl.*] A native or natives of Ceylon.

II. *a.* Pertaining to Ceylon or its people.

cin′gle (-gl), *n.* [L. *cingula*, a girdle, from *cingere*, to gird.] A girth. [Rare. See *Surcingle.*]

cin′gū-lāte, *a.* [L. *cingula*, girdle.] Having bands of color, as an insect.

cin′gū-lum, *n.* 1. A band or girdle, as the raised spiral line seen on certain univalve shells, the zone of a tooth near the gum, or the clitellus of earthworms.

2. A bundle of fibers in the substance of the brain.

cin′nȧ-bär, *n.* [Fr. *cinabre*; L. *cinnabaris*; Gr. *kinnabari*, cinnabar, vermilion.]

1. Red sulphid of mercury or quicksilver. It occurs native, in brilliant red crystals, and also in amorphous masses of different shades of red and brown. It is very heavy, and gives out fumes of quicksilver when heated.

2. In the arts, a pigment; also called *vermilion.*

Hepatic cinnabar; an impure cinnabar of a liver-brown color and submetallic luster.

cin-nȧ-bar′ic, *a.* Pertaining to cinnabar; consisting of cinnabar, or containing it; as, *cinnabaric* sand.

cin-nȧ-bar′ine, *a.* Same as *Cinnabaric.*

cin′nȧ-mēne, *n.* A compound obtained from cinnamic acid; also called *styrolene* and *cinnamole.*

cin-nam′ic, *a.* [From L. *cinnamomum*, cinnamon.] Obtained from or pertaining to cinnamon; also spelled *cinnamomic.*

Cinnamic acid; a white crystalline substance, derived from benzene. It was formerly obtained from oil of cinnamon.

cin-nȧ-mom′ic, *a.* Same as *Cinnamic.*

Cin-nȧ-mō′mum, *n.* [L., from Gr. *kinnamōmon*, cinnamon.] A genus including several varieties of the laurel family, including the common cinnamon tree and the cassia tree.

cin′nȧ-mŏn, *n.* [ME. *cinamome*; L. *cinnamomum*; Gr. *kinnamōmon*; Heb. *qinnamon*, cinnamon.]

1. The inner bark of *Cinnamomum Zeylanicum* of Ceylon, prepared by drying. It is an aromatic condiment in common use, of a light yellowish-brown color, and has a sweetish, characteristic taste. The name is also given to the inferior bark of *Cinnamomum Cassia* of China.

2. Any tree yielding *cinnamon.*

Cinnamon (*Cinnamomum Zeylanicum*).

Oil of cinnamon; an oil obtained from different trees of the genus *Cinnamomum*, consisting chiefly of cinnamic aldehyde.

cin′nȧ-mŏn-stōne, *n.* A Ceylonese garnet of a cinnamon color.

cin′nȧ-myl, *n.* In organic chemistry, the radical, C_8H_7CO, of cinnamic compounds.

cinque (sink), *n.* [Fr., OFr. *cinc*; L. *quinque*, five.] A five; a word used in games.

Cinque ports; originally, five ports on the southern shore of England, viz., Hastings, Romney, Hythe, Dover, and Sandwich, others being added afterward. These were deemed of so much importance that they received particular privileges, on condition of providing a certain number of ships in war.

cin-que-cen′tist (chin-kwe-chen′tist), *n.* [It. *cinquecentista*, a writer of the sixteenth century, from *cinquecento*, lit. 500, used for **the**

sixteenth century.] Any one connected with the Italian revival in arts and letters known as the cinquecento.

cin-que-cen′tō (chĭn-kwe-chen′tō), *n.* and *a.* A term employed in reference to the decorative art and architecture introduced soon after the beginning of the sixteenth century in Italy; also applied to the literary revival of that period; as, *cinquecento* architecture; *cinquecento* writers; the *cinquecento*.

cinque′foil (sink′foil), *n.* [Fr. *quintefeuille*; It. *cinquefoglie*; L. *quinte*, five, and *folium*, a leaf.]

1. In architecture, an ornament in the pointed

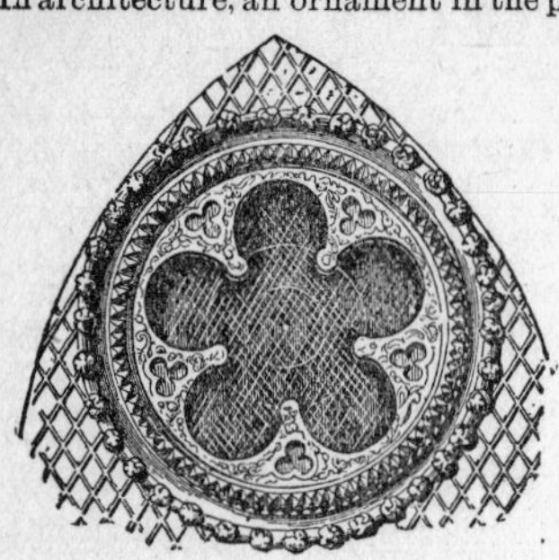

Cinquefoil Window, Lincoln Cathedral.

style of architecture, consisting of five cuspidated divisions. Circular windows frequently have this form.

2. The common name of several plants of the genus *Potentilla*, from their quinate leaves; also called *fivefinger*.

Marsh cinquefoil; a purple-flowered plant, *Potentilla palustris*, growing in marshes inland.

cinque′-pāce (sink′-), *n.* [Fr., from *cinque*, five, and *pas*, pace.] A kind of dance, the steps of which were regulated by the number five.

cinque′-spot″ted (sink′-), *a.* Having five spots.

cin′tēr, *n.* An obsolete form of *center*.

Ci-nū′rȧ, *n.pl.* [L., from Gr. *kinein*, to move, and *oura*, tail.] A group of insects of the family *Thysanura*, whose long, flexible tails end in bristles; the species are known as *bristletails*.

cī′phēr, *n.* [ME. *ciphre*; OFr. *cifre*; LL. *cifra*; Ar. *sifr*, *sefr*, a cipher, nothing, from *safara*, to be nothing.]

1. In arithmetic, a character of this form, 0, which, standing by itself, expresses nothing, but increases or diminishes the value of other figures, according to its position. In whole numbers, when placed at the right hand of a figure it increases its value tenfold; but in decimal fractions, placed at the left hand of a figure, it diminishes the value of that figure tenfold.

2. Figuratively, something of no value or consequence; especially a person of no weight, influence, usefulness, or decided character.

> Here he was a mere *cipher*, there he was lord of the ascendant. —Irving.

3. An intertexture of letters, as the initials of a name, engraved, stamped, or written on something, as on a seal, plate, coach, tomb, picture, etc.; a literal device; a monogram.

4. A secret or disguised manner of writing; certain characters arbitrarily invented and agreed on by two or more persons, to stand for letters or words, and understood only by the persons who invent or agree to use them; also, the matter so written.

cī′phēr, *a.* Useless; having no influence; without weight.

cī′phēr, *v.i.*; ciphered, *pt., pp.*; ciphering, *ppr.* In popular language, to use figures, or to practise arithmetic.

cī′phēr, *v.t.* 1. To write in occult characters.

2. To designate; to characterize. [Obs.]

3. To find out by ciphering; as, to *cipher* the cost.

4. To make out; to interpret; to decipher. [Obs.]

cī′phēr-ēr, *n.* One who ciphers or uses a cipher.

cī′phēr-hood, *n.* The state of being nothing. [Rare.]

cī′phēr-kēy, *n.* A key for deciphering secret writings.

cip′ō-lin, *n.* [It. *cipollino*, a granular limestone, from *cipolla*, an onion; so named on account of its being stratified or veined like an onion.] A green marble containing white zones. It consists chiefly of carbonate of lime, with quartz, schist, and a small portion of iron.

cip′pus, *n.*; *pl.* **cip′pī**. [L., a stake, post, a gravestone.] A small pillar or column, usually having an inscription, used by the ancients for various purposes, often as a funeral monument, or to mark distances.

cirç, *n.* An ancient stone circle. [Rare.]

cir′çȧ, *adv.* [L.] About; around; generally combined with dates or numerals to express approximation and lack of absolute certainty; as, *circa* A. D. 800.

cir-çär′, *n.* See *Sircar*.

Cir-ças′siăn (-kash′ăn), *n.* [L., from Russ. *Zemlya Cherkesovŭ*, the land of the Circassians; *Zemlya*. land, and *Cherkesŭ*, a Circassian.]

1. A native or inhabitant of Circassia, a Russian district, situated on the Black sea.

2. [c—] Same as *Circassienne*.

Sepulchral Cippus.

Cir-ças′siăn, *a.* Pertaining to Circassia.

cir-ças-si-enne′, *n.* [Fr.] A variety of cashmere, made of mohair and silk.

Cir-cē′ăn, *a.* [L. *Circe*; Gr. *Kirkē*, Circe.] Pertaining to or resembling Circe, the fabled daughter of Sol and Perseis, who was supposed to possess great knowledge of magic and venomous herbs, by which she was able to charm and fascinate her victims, and then change them into beasts; hence, pleasing, but harmful; fascinating, but degrading; as, the *Circean* spells of opium.

cir-cen′siăn (-shăn), **cir-cen′siăl** (-shăl), *a.* [L. *circensis*, pertaining to the circus, from *circus*, circus.] Pertaining to the *circenses*, the athletic games held in the Circus Maximus, Rome.

cir′ci-năl, *a.* Same as *Circinate*.

cir′ci-nāte, *a.* [L. *circinus*; Gr. *kirkinos*, a pair of compasses, from *kirkos*, a circle.] Rolled in spirally downward, the tip occupying the center; a term used of foliation or leafing, as in ferns.

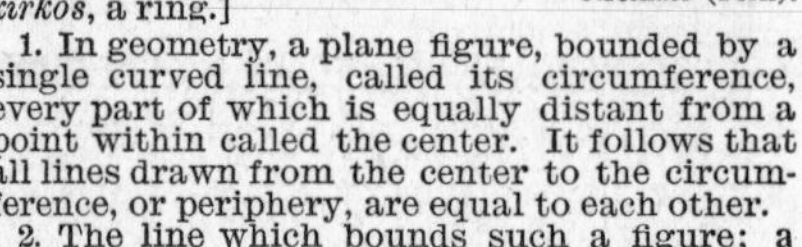

Circinate (Fern).

cir′ci-nāte, *v.t.* To make a circle upon, or to encircle with a compass. [Obs.]

cir-ci-nā′tion, *n.* 1. An orbicular motion. [Obs.]

2. In botany, the quality of being circinate; as, the rings or *circinations* of onions.

cir′cle (-kl), *n.* [ME. *cercle*, *sercle*; OFr. *cercle*; AS. *circul*; L. *circulus*, a circle, dim. of *circus*; Gr. *kirkos*, a ring.]

1. In geometry, a plane figure, bounded by a single curved line, called its circumference, every part of which is equally distant from a point within called the center. It follows that all lines drawn from the center to the circumference, or periphery, are equal to each other.

2. The line which bounds such a figure; a ring.

3. A sphere; the earth; any round body.

4. Compass; circuit; inclosure; as, the *circle* of the forest.

5. An assembly surrounding a principal person; a ring; hence, any company or assembly; as, a *circle* of friends, or of beauties.

6. Any number of persons of a particular character, whether associated or not; as, a political *circle*.

7. A series ending where it begins, and perpetually repeated; a going round.

> Thus in a *circle* runs the peasant's pain. —Dryden.

8. Circumlocution; indirect form of words; as, talking in a *circle*.

9. In logic, an inconclusive form of argument, i.e., when unproved statements are used to prove one another; as, heavy bodies descend by gravity, since gravity is a quality by which a heavy body descends; otherwise called *argument in a circle*.

10. In some European countries, a territorial division or district.

Circle of altitude; same as *Almucantar*.

Circle of latitude; in astronomy, a great circle perpendicular to the plane of the ecliptic, passing through its poles.

Circle of longitude; in astronomy, a lesser circle parallel to the ecliptic.

Circle of perpetual apparition; at any given place, the boundary of that space around the elevated pole, within which the stars never set. Its distance from the pole is equal to the latitude of the place.

Circle of perpetual occultation; at any given place, the boundary of that space around the depressed pole, within which the stars never rise.

Circle of Willis; in anatomy, a circle of arteries at the base of the brain; named after Thomas Willis, an English anatomist, who described it.

Circles of the Empire; the provinces or principalities of the former German Empire, which had a right to be represented at the diets.

Circles of the sphere; either great circles, which divide the sphere into equal parts, as the equator, etc., or small circles, which divide it into unequal parts, as the polar circles.

Diurnal circle; the apparent daily circle described by a heavenly body on account of the rotation of the earth.

Dress circle; a section of a theater, generally containing the better and more costly seats.

Druidical circles; see under *Druidical*.

Horary circle; on dials, the lines which indicate the hour.

Syn.—Sphere, orb, globe.—The *sphere* is a round body, conceived to be formed according to the rules of geometry by the circumvolution of a *circle* round about its diameter; hence, the whole frame of the world is denominated a *sphere*. An *orb* is any body which describes a *circle*; hence, the heavenly bodies are termed *orbs*; a *globe* is any solid body, the surface of which is in every part equidistant from the center; of this description is the terrestrial *globe*.

cir′cle, *v.t.*; circled, *pt., pp.*; circling, *ppr.* 1. To move round; to revolve round.

> And other planets *circle* other suns.—Pope.

2. To encircle; to encompass; to surround; to inclose.

To circle in; to confine; to keep together.

cir′cle, *v.i.* To move circularly; to circulate; as, the bowl *circles*; the *circling* years.

cir′cled, *a.* Having the form of a circle; round; as, the moon's *circled* orb.

cir′clēr, *n.* An itinerant poet; also one of the cyclic poets, or those whose subjects were chosen from a series or circle of early Greek legends. [Obs.]

cir′clet, *n.* 1. A little circle.

2. A bracelet, ring, or other personal ornament in the form of a circle.

3. A sphere; an orb.

cir′cō-cēle, *n.* See *Cirsocele*.

cir′cuit (-kit), *n.* [ME. *circuit*; OFr. *circuit*; L. *circuitus*, a going round, a circuit; from *circum*, around, and *itus*, pp. of *ire*, to go.]

1. The act of moving or passing round; as, the periodical *circuit* of the earth round the sun, or of the moon round the earth.

2. The space inclosed in a circle, or within certain limits.

3. Any space or extent measured by traveling around; as, the *circuit* of the United States; the narrow *circuit* of a country town.

4. Anything which encircles, such as a ring or diadem. [Rare.]

5. The regular route of judges in the holding of court; as, the judge is on *circuit*.

6. The extent of territory in which the same judge or judges hold court and administer justice.

7. The district traveled by an itinerant Methodist preacher.

8. A roundabout manner of speech; circumlocution. [Obs.]

9. The perimeter of any area; as, the *circuit* of the diamond, in baseball.

10. A number of theaters or other places of amusement under the same management and successively engaging the same performers.

11. In electricity, the path of a current; as, to complete a *circuit*.

Circuit court; a court empowered to sit at different places within certain prescribed limits. In the United States, there are two kinds: (a) the circuit courts established by statute in certain individual states, and (b) the United States circuit courts. The state circuit judges have general jurisdiction in matters of state cognizance, and may hold court successively at different places within their district. Each of the United States circuit courts has a district comprising several states, is presided over by a judge of the Supreme Court or a specially appointed circuit judge, who sits with the federal judge of the district, and takes cognizance of all matters coming within the scope of federal jurisdiction, also deciding appeals from the federal district courts. It is the principal federal court below the Supreme Court.

To make a circuit; to go around; to go by a roundabout route.

Voltaic or *galvanic circuit*; the flow of electricity from one pole of a battery to another.

cir′cuit, *v.i.* To move in a circle; to go round.

cir′cuit, *v.t.* To move or go round. [Obs.]

cir-cuit-eer′, *n.* A rare form of *circuiter*.

cir′cuit-ēr, *n.* One who makes or travels a circuit, as a circuit preacher or circuit judge.

cir-cū-i′tion (-ish′un), *n.* [L. *circuitio*, a going round.] The act of going round; compass; circumlocution. [Rare.]

cir-cū′i-tous, *a.* [L. *circuitus*, pp. of *circumire*, to go round.] Going round in a circuit; not direct; as, a *circuitous* road; a *circuitous* way of doing things.

Syn.—Winding, roundabout, sinuous, tortuous, devious, erratic, eccentric.

cir-cū′i-tous-ly, *adv.* In a circuitous or roundabout way.

cir-cū′i-tous-ness, *n.* Indirection.

cĩr-çū'i-ty, *n.* [L. *circuitus*, a circuit.] A going round; a course not direct; a roundabout method or manner.

Circuity of action; in law, an unnecessary length of procedure, or other means taken, with a view of delaying direct legal action.

cĩr'çū-là-ble, *a.* Capable of being circulated.

cĩr'çū-lăr, *a.* [LL. *circularis*, in the form of a circle, from L. *circulus*, a circle.]

1. In the form of a circle; round; circumscribed by a circle; as, the sun appears to be *circular*.
2. Successive in order; always returning. [Rare.]
3. Related to the circle; as, *circular* points.
4. Ending in itself; used of a paralogism, where the second proposition at once proves the first, and is proved by it; illogical; not conclusive.
5. Addressed to a circle, or to a number of persons having a common interest; as, a *circular* letter.
6. Complete. [Obs.]
7. Cyclic; treating of a limited cycle of legends; said of certain early Greek, or cyclic, poets.

Circular arc; part of the circumference of a circle.

Circular insanity; insanity in which there are recurrences of melancholy and exaltation.

Circular instrument; a mathematical instrument having a complete circle of graduation from 1 to 360 degrees; used in measuring angles.

Circular line; a straight line pertaining to the circle, as a sine, tangent, or secant.

Circular note; in diplomacy, a note on a matter of common interest addressed in identical terms to several governments or their representatives.

Circular number; a number whose powers terminate in the same digit as the root itself; as 5, whose square is 25.

Circular sailing; the method of sailing by the arc of a great circle.

cĩr'çū-lăr, *n.* [LL. *circularis*, circular; L. *circulus*, a circle.]

1. A circular letter or paper, usually printed; a document addressed to a number of persons or to the public; a form of advertisement.
2. A loose round cloak, without sleeves, worn by women.

cĩr-çū-lar'i-ty, *n.* The state of being circular; a circular form.

cĩr'çū-lăr-īze, *v.t.* 1. To give a round shape to.
2. To advertise in, with circulars; as, they *circularized* the entire city.

cĩr'çū-lăr-īz-ẽr, *n.* One who distributes circulars.

cĩr'çū-lăr-ly, *adv.* In a circular manner; in the form of a circle.

cĩr'çū-lā-ry, *a.* Roundabout; illogical; as, *circulary* remarks. [Rare.]

cĩr'çū-lāte, *v.i.*; circulated, *pt.*, *pp.*; circulating, *ppr.* [L. *circulatus*, pp. of *circulari*, to form a circle.]

1. To move in a circle; to move or pass round; to move round and return to the same point; as, the blood *circulates* in the body.
2. To pass from place to place, from person to person, or from hand to hand; to be diffused; as, money *circulates* in the country.

cĩr'çū-lāte, *v.t.* To cause to pass from place to place, or from person to person; to put about; to spread; as, to *circulate* a newspaper.

Syn.—Diffuse, disseminate, spread, propagate, scatter.

cĩr'çū-lā-ting, *a.* Moving or passing round; passing from one to another.

Circulating decimal; see *Decimal*.
Circulating library; see *Library*.
Circulating medium; see *Medium*.

cĩr-çū-lā'tion, *n.* [L. *circulatio*, a circular course; *circulari*, to form a circle.]

1. The act of moving round, or in a circle, or in a course which brings or tends to bring the moving body to the point where its motion began; as, the *circulation* of steam through pipes.
2. A series in which the same order is preserved, and things return to the same state.
3. The act of going and returning, or of passing from place to place, or from person to person; as, the *circulation* of money.
4. Currency; circulating coin, or representatives of it; the combined mediums of exchange, of a monetary character; as, the *circulation* of the country.
5. The measure of diffusion, as of a newspaper.
6. The circuitous action by which the life-giving fluid of animals and plants pursues a regular course; as, the *circulation* of the blood; the *circulation* of sap.

Collateral circulation; the passage of the blood from one part to another of the same system of vessels by collateral communicating channels; it is much more frequent in the veins than in the arteries.

cĩr'çū-lā-tive, *a.* Promoting or causing circulation; circulating. [Rare.]

cĩr'çū-lā-tŏr, *n.* [L. *circulator*, a peddler; *circulari*, to form a circle.]

1. One who or that which circulates; specifically applied to a circulating decimal fraction.
2. An employee of a newspaper or periodical publication who superintends the details of its distribution or circulation.

cĩr"çū-là-tō'ri-ous, *a.* Traveling in a circuit, or from house to house. [Obs.]

cĩr'çū-là-tō-ry, *a.* 1. Circular; as, a *circulatory* letter.
2. Circulating; going in a circuit; as, *circulatory* travels.
3. Affecting the organs of circulation; as, *circulatory* diseases.

Circulatory system; the system in the animal organism through which the blood circulates, made up of the heart, arteries, capillaries, and veins.

cĩr'çū-là-tō-ry, *n.*; *pl.* **cĩr'çū-là-tō-rieș**. In old chemistry, a vessel consisting of two parts, unequally exposed to heat, in which fluids were repeatedly distilled.

cĩr'çū-let, *n.* A ring; a circlet. [Obs.]

cĩr'çū-line, *a.* Circular; especially applied to motion. [Obs.]

cĩr'çum-. A combining form from L. *circum*, round, about, on all sides.

cĩr-çum-aġ'i-tāte, *v.t.* To agitate on all sides.

cĩr-çum-am'bi-en-cy, *n.* The quality of being circumambient; the act of surrounding or encompassing. [See *Ambient*.]

cĩr-çum-am'bi-ent, *a.* Surrounding; encompassing; inclosing or being on all sides; used particularly of the air about the earth.

cĩr-çum-am'bū-lāte, *v.i.* [*Circum-*, and L. *ambulare*, to walk.] To walk round about.

cĩr-çum-am-bū-lā'tion, *n.* The act of walking round.

cĩr-çum-bend'i-bus, *n.* A roundabout course or method; circumlocution. [Humorous.]

Cĩr-çum-cel'liŏn (-yun), *n.* [*Circum-*, and L. *cella*, a cell.] In church history, one of a set of fanatic Donatists in the fourth century, who roved through northern Africa seeking death by committing deeds of violence, so as to gain the glory of martyrdom; hence, any vagrant monk.

cĩr'çum-cen"tẽr, *n.* [*Circum-*, and L. *centrum*, center.] In mathematics, the center of a circumscribed circle; the *circumcenter* of a triangle is the center of the circle circumscribed about it.

cĩr'çum-cīșe, *v.t.*; circumcised, *pt.*, *pp.*; circumcising, *ppr.* [ME. *circumcisen*; L. *circumcidere*, to cut around; *circum*, and *cædere*, to cut.]

1. To cut off the prepuce of (a male or males); a ceremony or rite in the Jewish and Mohammedan religions and among Abyssinian Christians. The word is applied also to the performance of an analogous operation upon females.
2. To put off the sins of (the flesh); to make spiritual or holy; a metaphorical and scriptural use.
3. To cut round; the literal meaning of the word. [Obs.]

cĩr'çum-cīșed, *a.* Having the prepuce cut off; spiritually purified.

cĩr'çum-cī-șẽr, *n.* One who performs circumcision.

cĩr-çum-ci'șion, *n.* 1. The act or custom of cutting off the prepuce or foreskin of human males or (rarely) the internal labia of females. The practice of male circumcision was enjoined upon the Jews by the Mosaic law, finds favor also among the Mohammedans and Abyssinian Christians, and is employed in individual instances, for remedial purposes, by surgeons in all civilized countries.
2. Rejection of the sins of the flesh; spiritual purification, and acceptance of the Christian faith.
3. The Jews, as distinguished from Gentiles, the former being a circumcised people.

> They that were of the *circumcision* contended with him. —Acts xi. 2.

4. A festival observed in the Anglican, Roman Catholic, and Greek churches on January 1, the octave of Christmas day, in commemoration of the circumcision of Christ.

cĩr-çum-clū'șion, *n.* [L. *circumcludere*, to inclose on every side.] The act of inclosing on all sides. [Rare.]

cĩr-çum-çũr-sā'tion, *n.* [*Circum-*, and L. *cursare*, to run.] The act of running about; roundabout language. [Obs.]

cĩr-çum-den-ū-dā'tion, *n.* [*Circum-*, and L. *denudare*, to uncover.] In geology, denudation around an object so as to expose it or elevate it; as, hills of *circumdenudation*.

cĩr-çum-dūçe', *v.t.* Same as *Circumduct*, 3.

cĩr-çum-duçt', *v.t.* [L. *circumducere*, to lead around; *circum*, and *ducere*, to lead.]

1. To contravene; to nullify; a term of civil law. [Rare.]
2. To lead about; to lead astray. [Rare.]
3. In Scots law, to deny the admission of (further evidence).
4. To revolve (as a line) round an axis, as in describing a cone.

cĩr-çum-duç'tion, *n.* 1. A leading about. [Rare.]
2. In old English law, an annulling or cancelation. [Rare.]
3. In physiology, the moving of a limb round an axis so as to describe an imaginary cone.

cĩr"çum-ē-sō-phaġ'ē-ăl, *a.* [*Circum-*, and L. *œsophagus*, the esophagus.] In anatomy, surrounding the esophagus.

cĩr-çum-fẽr', *v.t.* To bear or carry round. [Obs.]

cĩr-çum'fẽr-ence, *n.* [ME. *circumference*; L. *circumferens*, ppr. of *circumferre*, to carry round.]

1. The line that goes round or encompasses a figure; a periphery; applied particularly to the line that goes round a circle, sphere, or similar figure.
2. The space included in a circle.
3. An orb; a circle; anything circular or orbicular, as a shield.

> The broad *circumference*
> Hung on his shoulders like the moon.
> —Milton.

4. The external surface of any orbicular body or sphere.
5. The distance around a circle or globe, or anything approaching these in form; circuit; compass; as, a chest-*circumference* of thirty-six inches.

cĩr-çum'fẽr-ence, *v.t.* To include in a circular space. [Obs.]

cĩr-çum-fẽr-en'tiăl (-shăl), *a.* Pertaining to the circumference.

cĩr-çum-fẽr-en'tiăl-ly, *adv.* After the manner of a circumference.

cĩr-çum-fẽr-en'tŏr, *n.* 1. An instrument used by surveyors for taking angles; a surveyor's compass. It consists of a compass with magnetic needle and dial graduated into 360 degrees, mounted on a horizontal brass bar at the ends of which are the sighting-slits.
2. A small wheel used for measuring the length of tires for larger wheels; a graduated wheel.

Circumferentor, with rackwork adjustment.

cĩr'çum-flant, *a.* Blowing about or around. [Obs.]

cĩr'çum-fleçt, *v.t.*; circumflected, *pt.*, *pp.*; circumflecting, *ppr.* [L. *circumflectere*; *circum*, and *flectere*, to bend.]

1. To bend around.
2. To place a circumflex accent on (a word). [Rare.]

cĩr-çum-fleç'tion, **cĩr-çum-flex'ion**, *n.* The act or condition of assuming a curved form or taking a winding course.

cĩr'çum-flex, *n.* [L. *circumflexus*, pp. of *circumflectere*; *circum*, and *flectere*, to bend.]

1. A wave of the voice, embracing both a rise and fall on the same syllable.
2. A character, or accent, denoting a rise and fall of the voice on the same long syllable.

cĩr'çum-flex, *v.t.*; circumflexed, *pt.*, *pp.*; circumflexing, *ppr.* To mark or pronounce with a circumflex accent.

cĩr'çum-flex, *a.* 1. Moving or bending round; circuitous. [Rare.]
2. Curved in a circular manner; said of certain arteries and veins of the hip, thigh, or shoulder, and of a nerve of the shoulder.
3. Indicative of the tone called circumflex; as, the *circumflex* accent.

cĩr-çum-flex'ion, *n.* See *Circumflection*.

cĩr-çum'flū-ence, *n.* [L. *circumfluens*, ppr. of *circumfluere*; *circum*, and *fluere*, to flow.] A flowing round on all sides; an inclosure of waters.

cĩr-çum'flū-ent, *a.* Flowing round; surrounding as a fluid; as, *circumfluent* waves.

cĩr-çum'flū-ous, *a.* Flowing round; encompassing as a fluid; circumfluent.

cĩr"çum-fō-rā'ne-ăn, **cĩr"çum-fō-rā'ne-ous**, *a.* [L. *circumforaneus*, about the market-place; *circum*, around, and *forum*, a market-place.] Going about; walking or wandering from house to house; as, a *circumforaneous* fiddler.

cĩr-çum-ful'ġent, *a.* [*Circum-*, and L. *fulgere*, to shine.] Shining around.

cĩr-çum-fūșe', *v.t.* [L. *circumfusus*, pp. of *circumfundere*; *circum*, and *fundere*, to pour.]

1. To pour round; to spread round, as a fluid.
2. To spread round; to surround.

cĩr-çum-fū'șile, *a.* [*Circum-*, and L. *fusilis*, fluid.] That may be poured or spread round; as, *circumfusile* gold.

cĩr-çum-fū'șion, *n.* The act of pouring or spreading round; the state of being poured round.

cĩr"çum-ġes-tā'tion, *n.* A carrying about. [Obs.]

cir-cum-gy̆′rāte, *v.t.* To roll or turn round.

cir″cum-gy̆-rā′tion, *n.* [*Circum-*, and L. *gyrus*, Gr. *gyros*, a circle.] The act of turning, rolling, or whirling round; as, the *circumgyration* of the planets.

cir-cum-gy̆′rȧ-tō-ry, *a.* Moving in a circular manner or around.

cir-cum-gȳre′, *v.i.* To roll or turn round; to circumgyrate. [Obs.]

cir″cum-in-ces′sion, *n.* [*Circum-*, and L. *incessus*, a going, walking, from *incedere*, to advance, to walk.] In theology, the intercommunion of persons, as of the Trinity of the Godhead.

cir-cum-in′sū-lăr, *a.* Surrounding or around an island; in anatomy, around the island of Reil, a frontal lobe of the brain.

cir-cum-jā′cence, *n.* The state of bordering on every side, or of being circumjacent.

cir-cum-jā′cent, *a.* [L. *circumjacens*, ppr. of *circumjacere*; *circum*, and *jacere*, to lie.] Lying round; bordering on every side.

cir-cum-jō′vi-ăl, *n.* and *a.* I. *n.* One of Jupiter's satellites or moons.

II. *a.* Moving or revolving around Jupiter.

cir″cum-li-gā′tion, *n.* [L. *circumligare*; *circum*, and *ligare*, to tie, bind.] The act of binding round; the bond with which anything is encompassed.

cir-cum-lit′tō-răl, *a.* [*Circum-*, and L. *litus*, *litoris*, shore.] Adjacent to the shore.

cir″cum-lō-cū′tion, *n.* [L. *circumlocutio*, circumlocution; *circum*, and *locutio*, a speaking, from *loqui*, to speak.] A circuit or compass of words; a periphrase; the use of a number of words to express an idea, when a suitable term is not at hand, or when a speaker chooses to avoid the use of a single term.

Circumlocution office; a depreciative or sarcastic term applied to a public office in which it is difficult to expedite business by reason of having to deal with many officials and formalities.

cir″cum-lō-cū′tion-ăl, *a.* Pertaining to circumlocution.

cir-cum-loc′ū-tō-ry, *a.* Pertaining to circumlocution; consisting of or contained in an unnecessarily large compass of words.

cir″cum-me-rid′i-ăn, *a.* [*Circum-*, and L. *meridies*, midday.] About, or in close proximity to, the meridian.

cir-cum-mūre′, *v.t.* [*Circum-*, and L. *murus*, wall.] To surround with a wall. [Rare.]

cir-cum-nav′i-gȧ-ble, *a.* That may be sailed round.

cir-cum-nav′i-gāte, *v.t.*; circumnavigated, *pt.*, *pp.*; circumnavigating, *ppr.* To sail round; to pass round by water; as, to *circumnavigate* the globe.

cir-cum-nav-i-gā′tion, *n.* The act of sailing round.

cir-cum-nav′i-gā-tŏr, *n.* One who sails round.

cir-cum-nū′tāte, *v.i.* To go through the motions of circumnutation.

cir″cum-nū-tā′tion, *n.* [*Circum-*, and L. *nutare*, to nod.] The act or inclination of the tendrils of climbing plants to bend in various directions.

cir-cum-oc′ū-lăr, *a.* Around or near the eye.

cir-cum-ō′răl, *a.* [*Circum-*, and L. *os*, genit. *oris*, mouth.] Being situated near, or encircling, the mouth.

cir″cum-pli-cā′tion, *n.* [L. *circumplicare*; *circum*, and *plicare*, to fold.] A folding, winding, or wrapping round; a state of being inwrapped.

cir-cum-pō′lăr, *a.* About the pole; an appellation given to stars which are so near either pole as to revolve around it without setting; as, *circumpolar* stars; *circumpolar* sea.

cir″cum-pō-si′tion, *n.* The act of placing in a circle, or the state of being so placed.

cir-cum-rō′tȧ-ry, *a.* Turning, rolling, or whirling round.

cir-cum-rō′tāte, *v.t.* and *v.i.* To revolve; to rotate, as on an axis.

cir″cum-rō-tā′tion, *n.* The act of rolling or revolving round, as a wheel; circumvolution; the state of being whirled round.

cir-cum-rō′tȧ-tō-ry, *a.* Same as *Circumrotary*.

cir-cum-scis′sile, *a.* [*Circum-*, and L. *scissilis*, easily cut, from *scissus*, pp. of *scindere*, to cut.] A term applied to a mode of dehiscence in botany, occurring by a transverse, circular separation of the sides of the ovary.

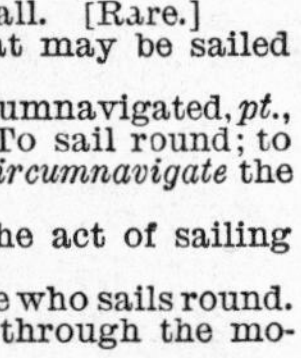

Circumscissile Dehiscence.

cir-cum-scrib′ȧ-ble, *a.* Capable of being circumscribed.

cir-cum-scribe′, *v.t.*; circumscribed, *pt.*, *pp.*; circumscribing, *ppr.* [ME. *circumscrive*; L. *circumscribere*, to draw a line around.]

1. Literally, to draw a line around.

2. To inclose within a certain limit; to limit, bound, confine.

3. To write around. [Rare.]

Syn.—To bind, restrain, restrict, narrow.

cir-cum-scrībed′, *a.* 1. Drawn around, as a line; limited; confined.

2. In geometry, applied to a figure which is drawn around another figure, so that all the sides of the former are tangent to the latter.

cir-cum-scrib′ẽr, *n.* A person or object that circumscribes.

cir-cum-scrip′ti-ble, *a.* Capable of being circumscribed or limited by bounds.

cir-cum-scrip′tion, *n.* [L. *circumscriptio*, an encircling, boundary, from *circumscribere*, to draw a line around; *circum*, and *scribere*, to draw, write.]

1. The line that limits; limitation; bound; confinement.

2. The termination or limits of a body; the exterior line which determines the form or magnitude of a body.

3. A circular inscription.

cir-cum-scrip′tive, *a.* Defining the external form; marking or inclosing the limits or superficies of a body.

cir-cum-scrip′tive-ly, *adv.* In a limited manner.

cir-cum-script′ly, *adv.* Narrowly; in a slavishly literal sense. [Rare.]

cir-cum-sō′lăr, *a.* Revolving around, or surrounding the sun.

cir′cum-spect, *a.* [L. *circumspectus*, pp. of *circumspicere*, to look about; *circum*, and *specere*, to look.]

1. Literally, looking on all sides; looking round.

2. Cautious; prudent; watchful on all sides; examining carefully all the circumstances that may affect a determination, or a measure to be adopted.

Syn.—Cautious, discreet, prudent, careful, scrupulous.

cir-cum-spec′tion, *n.* Caution; attention to all the facts and circumstances of a case, and to the natural or probable consequences of a measure, with a view to a correct course of conduct, or to avoid unfavorable results.

cir-cum-spec′tive, *a.* Looking round in every direction; cautious; careful of consequences; watchful of danger.

cir-cum-spec′tive-ly, *adv.* Cautiously; vigilantly; heedfully; with watchfulness to guard against danger.

cir′cum-spect-ly, *adv.* With caution and watchfulness; with attention to guard against surprise or danger.

cir′cum-spect-ness, *n.* Caution; circumspection; vigilance in guarding against evil from every quarter.

cir′cum-stance, *n.* [L. *circumstantia*, a standing around, condition, from *circumstare*; *circum*, and *stare*, to stand.]

1. Literally, that which stands around or near.

2. Something attending, appendant, or relative to a fact, or case; a particular thing, which, though not essential to an action, in some way affects it; applied to a moral action in the same way as is the word *accident* to a material object; as, the *circumstances* of time, place, and persons are to be considered.

3. One of the adjuncts of a fact, which makes it more or less criminal, or makes an accusation more or less probable; accident; something adventitious; incident; event.

4. When used in the plural, meaning condition in regard to worldly estate; state of property; as, a man in easy *circumstances*.

5. Detail; circumlocution. [Obs.]

Under the circumstances; when everything is considered.

Syn.—Fact, event, incident, position, situation.—A *fact* is a thing done; an *event* a thing which turns up or occurs; an *incident* something that falls in with some general course of events. A *circumstance* is some adjunct thereto which more or less affects it.

cir′cum-stance, *v.t.*; circumstanced, *pt.*, *pp.*; circumstancing, *ppr.* To place relatively, or in a particular situation.

cir′cum-stanced (-stanst), *a.* 1. Placed in a particular manner, with regard to attending facts or incidents; as, *circumstanced* as we were, we could not escape.

2. Governed by circumstances or conditions.

cir′cum-stant, *a.* and *n.* I. *a.* Surrounding. [Obs.]

II. *n.* A spectator. [Obs.]

cir-cum-stan′tiȧ-ble (-shȧ-bl), *a.* Capable of being circumstantiated. [Obs.]

cir-cum-stan′tiăl (-shăl), *a.* 1. Attending; relating to, but not essential.

2. Pertaining to circumstances, or to particular incidents.

> The usual character of human testimony is substantial truth under *circumstantial* variety. —Paley.

3. Incidental; casual.

4. Abounding with circumstances, or exhibiting all the circumstances; minute; particular; as, a *circumstantial* account or recital.

Circumstantial evidence; in law, that class of evidence deduced from circumstances, which necessarily or usually attend facts of a particular nature, from which arises presumption. —Blackstone.

cir-cum-stan′tiăl, *n.* Something incident to the main subject, but of less importance; opposed to *essential*; generally used in the plural; as, the *circumstantials* rather than the *essentials* of history.

cir-cum-stan-ti-al′i-ty (-shi-al′), *n.* 1. The quality or state of being modified by circumstances.

2. The quality of presenting circumstances; as, the *circumstantiality* of the description was vivid.

cir-cum-stan′tiăl-ly, *adv.* 1. According to circumstances; not essentially; accidentally.

2. Minutely; exactly; in every circumstance or particular.

cir-cum-stan′ti-āte (-shi-āt), *v.t.* 1. To place in particular circumstances; to invest with particular accidents or adjuncts.

2. To prove or confirm by presenting circumstances.

3. To place in a particular condition with regard to power or wealth. [Rare.]

4. To describe minutely.

cir″cum-tẽr-rā′nē-ous, *a.* [*Circum-*, and L. *terra*, earth.] Around the earth.

cir-cum-un′dū-lāte, *v.t.* [*Circum-*, and L. *undulatus*, waved, from *unda*, a wave.] To flow round, as waves. [Rare.]

cir-cum-val′lāte, *v.t.* To surround with a rampart.

cir-cum-val′lāte, *a.* 1. Inclosed by a wall.

2. In anatomy, surrounded by a ridge.

cir″cum-val-lā′tion, *n.* [L. *circumvallare*, to surround with a rampart; *circum*, and *vallum*, a rampart.]

1. In the art of war, a surrounding with a wall or rampart; also, a wall, rampart, or parapet with a trench, surrounding the camp of a besieging army.

2. The rampart or fortification surrounding a besieged place.

cir-cum-vec′tion, *n.* [L. *circumvectio*, a carrying around; *circum*, and *vehere*, to carry.] A carrying about.

cir-cum-vent′, *v.t.* [L. *circumventus*, pp. of *circumvenire*, to come round, encircle; *circum*, and *venire*, to come.] To gain advantage over by stratagem or deception; to delude; to impose on.

cir-cum-ven′tion, *n.* 1. The act of prevailing over another by artifice or fraud; deception; imposture; delusion.

2. Prevention; preoccupation. [Obs.]

cir-cum-vent′ive, *a.* Deceiving by artifice; deluding.

cir-cum-vent′ŏr, *n.* A person who accomplishes his purpose by cunning.

cir-cum-vest′, *v.t.* To cover round, as with a garment. [Obs.]

cir-cum′vō-lănt, *a.* Flying about.

cir″cum-vō-lā′tion, *n.* [L. *circumvolare*; *circum*, and *volare*, to fly.] The act of flying round. [Rare.]

cir″cum-vō-lū′tion, *n.* [*Circumvolutus*, pp. of *circumvolvere*, to roll round; *circum*, and *volvere*, to turn.]

1. The act of rolling round; the state of being rolled; also, the thing rolled round another.

2. In architecture, a turn in the spiral line of the Ionic capital.

3. Indirection.

cir-cum-volve′, *v.t.*; circumvolved, *pt.*, *pp.*; circumvolving, *ppr.* To roll round; to cause to revolve; to put into a circular motion.

cir-cum-volve′, *v.i.* To roll round; to revolve.

cir′cus, *n.*; *pl.* **cir′cus-eṣ.** [L. *circus*, a circle, ring, race-course; Gr. *kirkos*, a circle.]

1. In antiquity, a long, oval edifice, used for games and exhibitions. The Roman *circus* was encompassed with porticos, and furnished with rows of seats, rising one above another, for the accommodation of spectators. The *Circus Maximus* was nearly a mile in circumference.

2. The open area, or space inclosed, in which were exhibited such sports as wrestling, fighting with swords, staffs, or pikes, running or racing, dancing, and quoits.

3. In modern times, a circular inclosure for the exhibition of feats of horsemanship and various performances; also, the company of performers, or the exhibition given.

4. Any inclosed space. [Rare.]

5. Uproarious fun; sport. [Slang.]

cirl′-bun″ting, *n.* [It. *zirlo*, the whistling of a thrush; *zirlare*, to whistle like a thrush.] An Italian bird about the size of a sparrow.

cirque (sẽrk), *n.* [Fr., from L. *circus*, a ring, circus.]

1. A circus; a circular arrangement or inclosure.

2. A circular space in a mountain surrounded by precipitous cliffs.

cir′rāte, *a.* [L. *cirratus*, having ringlets or

tendrils, from *cirrus*, a ringlet.] Having curling tendrils about an organ.

cir-rhō′sis, *n.* [L., from Gr. *kirrhos*, tawny.] A disease of the liver, in which the organ becomes inflamed, the cells waste away, and the tissues become thick and fibrous; also applied to other organs similarly affected.

cir-rhot′iç, *a.* Caused by, affected with, or resembling cirrhosis.

cir′ri, *n.*, pl. of *cirrus*.

cir′ri-, cir′rō-. Combining forms from L. *cirrus*, a curl, tendril, ringlet, signifying having curls or tendrils; as, *cirri*gerous, *cirro*stomatous.

Cir″ri-braṅ″chi-ā′tȧ, *n.pl.* [*Cirri-*, and Gr. *branchia*, gills.] An order of mollusks having slender cirriform gills.

cir-rif′ẽr-ous, *a.* [*Cirri-*, and L. *ferre*, to bear.] Producing tendrils or cirri, as a plant.

cir′ri-fọrm, *a.* [*Cirri-*, and L. *forma*, form.] With a tendril-like form.

cir-riġ′ẽr-ous, *a.* [*Cirri-*, and L. *gerere*, to carry.] Having curled locks of hair or hairlike appendages.

cir′ri-grāde, *a.* [*Cirri-*, and L. *gradi*, to walk.] Being moved, or moving, by means of cirri, or hairlike tendrils.

cir′ri-ped, cir′ri-pēde, *n.* [*Cirri-*, and L. *pes*, *pedis*, foot.] An animal belonging to the subclass *Cirripedia*.

Cir-ri-pē′di-ȧ, *n.* A crustacean order, including barnacles. The feet are long, slender, and curved, having the appearance of fine tendrils, or cirri.

Cir″rō-braṅ″chi-ā′tȧ, *n.* See *Cirribranchiata*.

cir″rō-çū′mū-lus, *n.* [*Cirro-*, and L. *cumulus*, a heap.] See under *Cloud*.

cir′rōse, *a.* [L. *cirrus*, a tendril.] Having or resembling tendrils or cirri; applied to plants, birds, beetles, etc. [See *Cirrus*.]

cir-rō-stom′ȧ-tous, *a.* Relating to the *Cirrostomi*; written also *cirrostomous*.

Cir-ros′tō-mī, *n.pl.* [*Cirro-*, and Gr. *stoma*, mouth.] An order of vertebrates, having cirri around the mouth and forming the lowest group, the leptocardians.

cir-ros′tō-mous, *a.* Same as *Cirrostomatous*.

cir″rō-strā′tus, *n.* [*Cirro-*, and L. *stratus*, pp. of *sternere*, to spread out.] In meteorology, a cloud having the characters of the stratus in its main body, but of the cirrus on its margin.

cir′rous, *a.* See *Cirrose*.

cir′rus, *n.*; *pl.* **cir′rī.** [L., a lock, curl, tendril.]

1. In meteorology, a name given to one of the four fundamental clouds, from its fibrous appearance resembling carded wool.

2. A fossil turbinated shell of the chalk.

3. An external organ of copulation found in some species of worms and mollusks, particularly the trematodes.

4. A tendril or clasping appendage found on many plants.

5. A yielding tendril-like process found on the external fold of many species of mollusks, and on the lateral appendage of many worms.

6. In ornithology, a bunch of curly feathers on the head.

Cirrus or Tendril.

Cir′si-um, *n.* [L., from Gr. *kirsion*, a kind of thistle, said by the ancients to cure varicocele.] In botany, the same as *Cnicus*.

cir′sō-cēle, *n.* [Gr. *kirsos*, an enlarged vein, varicocele, and *kēlē*, a tumor.] A varix, or dilatation of the spermatic vein.

cir′soid, *a.* [Gr. *kirsos*, an enlarged vein, and *eidos*, form.] Enlarged; varicose.

Cirsoid aneurism; an arterial disease, in which the affected part is extended and swollen.

cir-sot′ō-my, *n.* [Gr. *kirsos*, an enlarged vein, and *tomē*, from *temnein*, to cut.] A surgical operation for removing varicose veins and tumors by cutting.

cis-. A prefix from the L. prep. *cis*, signifying on this side of, within.

cis-al′pine, *a.* On this side of the Alps, with regard to Rome; that is, on the south of the Alps; opposed to *transalpine*.

cis-at-lan′tiç, *a.* Being on the hither side of the Atlantic Ocean.

cis′çō, *n.* [Origin unknown.] A food fish very abundant in the Great Lakes of North America; called also the *lake-herring*.

ci-ṣe-lūre′, *n.* [Fr., from *ciseler*, to carve.] Metal chased work; also, the art of metal-chasing.

cis-lei′thăn, *a.* Situated on the side of the river Leitha toward Vienna; Austrian as opposed to Hungarian.

cis-mon′tāne, *a.* Situated on this side of the mountains. [See *Ultramontane*.]

cis′pȧ-dāne, *a.* [*Cis-*, and L. *Padus*, the river Po.] Situated on this side of the Po, with regard to Rome; that is, on the south side.

cis′soid, *n.* [Gr. *kissoeidēs*, like ivy; *kissos*, ivy, and *eidos*, form.] In geometry, a curve of the second order, invented by Diocles. In the diameter, A B, of a circle described about C, take B M = A N, and erect the ordinates M Q = N R, and join A Q; the locus of the point P, in which the line A Q cuts the ordinate N R, is the *cissoid*. To find its equation, let A N = x, P N = y, A C = a, then since

$$\frac{PN = y}{AN = x} = \frac{QM = \sqrt{2ax - x^2}}{AM = 2a - x}$$

the equation is $y^2(2a - x) = x^3$. The curve has an equal branch on the other side of A B; the two branches meet in a cusp at point A, and have the line H K as an asymptote. The area included between the curve and the asymptote is three times the area of the generating circle. In the *cissoid* of Diocles the generating curve is a circle; but this term has been applied in later times to all curves described in a similar manner, where the generating curve is not a circle.

cist, *n.* [L. *cista*; Gr. *kistē*, a chest.]

1. In architecture and sculpture, a chest or basket; usually applied to the baskets employed in processions connected with the Eleusinian mysteries.

Cist.

2. A place of interment of an early or prehistoric period, consisting of a stone chest formed of two parallel rows of stones fixed on their ends, and covered by similar flat stones. Such cists are found in barrows or mounds inclosing bones.

3. A round or oval bronze box, generally engraved and having ornamental castings for the handles and feet.

4. An urn for holding the ashes of the dead.

Cis-tā′cē-æ, *n.* [L., from Gr. *kistos*, *kisthos*, the rockrose.] A natural order of polypetalous exogens, consisting of low shrubby plants or herbs, with entire leaves, and crumpled, generally ephemeral, showy flowers. Some species exude a balsamic resin.

Cistercian.

cis-tā′ceous, *a.* Resembling or belonging to the order *Cistaceæ*.

cist′ed, *a.* Inclosed in a cist.

Cis-tẽr′ciăn, *n.* [Fr. *Cistercien*, from LL. *Cistercium*, Fr. *Cîteaux*, the original convent.] An order of monks that separated from the Benedictines in 1098 and was established at Cîteaux, France.

Cis-tẽr′ciăn, *a.* Belonging or pertaining to the Cistercians.

cis′tẽrn, *n.* [ME. *cisterne*; OFr. *cisterne*; L. *cisterna*, a reservoir for water, from *cista*, Gr. *kistē*, a chest, box.]

1. An artificial reservoir or receptacle for holding water, beer, or other liquids, as in dwellings, distilleries, and breweries.

2. A natural reservoir; a hollow place containing water, as a fountain or lake.

cist′iç, *a.* Same as *Cystic*.

cis-tin′ē-ous, *a.* Same as *Cistaceous*.

Cis′tus, *n.* [L., from Gr. *kistos*, or *kisthos*, the rockrose.] The rockrose, a genus of plants, natural order *Cistaceæ*, of many species, most of them natives of the southern parts of Europe. Some of them are beautiful evergreen, flowering shrubs, and ornamental in gardens.

çist′vāen, *n.* Same as *Cist*, 2.

cit, *n.* [Contracted from *citizen*.] A citizen; an inhabitant of a city; a pert townsman; a cockney; a pragmatic trader. [Colloq.]

cit′ȧ-ble, *a.* Capable of being cited or quoted.

cit′ȧ-del, *n.* [Fr. *citadelle*; LL. *civitatella*, a small city, from L. *civitas*, citizenship, a state or city.] A fortress or castle, in or near a city, intended for its defense; a place of arms.

cit′ăl, *n.* 1. Reproof; impeachment. [Rare.]

2. Summons; citation; quotation. [Rare.]

ci-tā′tion, *n.* [ME. *citacion*, from L. *citare*, to arouse, summon.]

1. A summons; an official call or notice, given to a person to appear in a court and answer to a demand; a call or notice to appear, in various other cases; also, the paper containing such notice or call.

2. Quotation; the act of citing a passage from a book, or from another person in his own words; also, the passage or words quoted.

3. Enumeration; mention.

4. In law, a reference to a previous case, or decision regarding it.

ci-tā′tŏr, *n.* The person who cites. [Rare.]

ci′tȧ-tō-ry, *a.* Citing; calling; having the power or form of citation; as, letters *citatory*.

cite, *v.t.*; cited, *pt.*, *pp.*; citing, *ppr.* [Fr. *citer*, to summon; L. *citare*, to arouse, summon.]

1. To call upon officially or authoritatively; to summon; to give legal or official notice, as to a defendant to appear in court, to answer or defend.

2. To enjoin; to direct; to summon; to order or urge.

3. To quote; to name or repeat; as, to *cite* a passage from Scripture; to *cite* the very words a man utters.

4. To call or name, in support, proof, or confirmation; as, to *cite* an authority in law.

5. To call for. [Obs.]

6. To summon into court.

Syn.—Summon, call, quote, mention, name, adduce.

cit′ẽr, *n.* 1. One who cites or summons into court.

2. One who quotes a passage or the words of another.

cit′ess, *n.* A city woman. [Obs. See *Cit*.]

cith′ȧ-rȧ, *n.* [L. *cithara*; Gr. *kithara*, a kind of lyre, harp.] A musical instrument of antiquity, resembling the modern guitar.

Egyptian Cithera.

Cith-ȧ-rex′y-lum, *n.* [L., from Gr. *kithara*, a lyre, and *xylon*, wood.] A genus of shrubs and trees, natives of tropical America; valuable for building-material because of the hardness and durability of their wood; often called *fiddlewood*.

cith-ȧ-ris′tiç, *a.* [Gr. *kitharistikos*, pertaining to the lyre; *kithara*, a lyre.] Pertaining to or adapted to the harp.

cith′ẽrn, cit′tẽrn, *n.* [ME. *gitterne*; L. *cithara*; Gr. *kithara*, a kind of lyre, harp.]

1. A stringed musical instrument, among the ancients, the precise form of which is not known, but it bore some resemblance to the modern guitar.

2. A modern modification of the instrument; also called *cither*, *zither*.

cith′ẽrn-head (-hed), *n.* A stupid person, so called because there was usually a carved head on the handle of a cithern.

Cithern.

cit′i-ciṣm, *n.* [From *cit*.] The manners of a cit or a citizen.

cit′ied (-id), *a.* 1. Belonging to a city. [Rare.]

2. Resembling a city.

3. Having many cities.

cit′i-fīed, *a.* Having city style and manners; following city ways; as, his dress was *citified*, and so were his manners. [Colloq.]

Cit-i-grā′dȧ, *n. pl.* [L., from *citus*, rapid, and *gradi*, to walk.] A family of spiders which catch their prey by swift running. It includes the European tarantula and the wolf-spiders.

cit′i-grāde, *a.* Relating to the *Citigrada*.

cit′i-nẽr, *n.* A city-born or city-bred person. [Obs.]

cit′i-zen (-zn), *n.* [ME. *citizen*; OFr. *citeein*, a citizen, from L. *civitas*, genit. *civitatis*, a state, city.]

1. The native of a city, or an inhabitant who enjoys the freedom and privileges of the city in which he resides; the freeman of a city or town, as distinguished from a foreigner, or one not entitled to its franchises.

2. An inhabitant of or dweller in any city, town, or place.

3. In a general sense, a native or permanent resident in a city or country; as, the *citizens* of Philadelphia; the *citizens* of the United States.

4. In the United States, a person, native or naturalized, who has the privilege of exercising the elective franchise.

> If the *citizens* of the United States are not free and happy, the fault will be entirely their own. —Washington.

cit′i-zen, *a.* 1. Having the qualities of a citizen; as, *citizen* soldiery.

2. Town-bred; effeminate. [Obs.]

cit′i-zen-ess, *n.* A female citizen. [Rare.]

cit′i-zen-ship, *n.* The state of being vested with the rights and privileges of a citizen.

cit′ōle, *n.* [OFr. *citole*, from L. *cithara*, a cithern.] An instrument resembling a dulcimer, used in the middle ages. [Obs.]

cit-rȧ-çon′iç, *a.* Pertaining to or derived from plants of the genera *Citrus* and *Aconitum*.

Citraconic acid; a bibasic acid prepared from citric acid; also called *pyrocitric acid*.

cit'rāte, *n.* [L. *citrus*, the citron-tree.] In chemistry, a salt formed by a union of citric acid with a base.

cit're-ăn, *a.* Same as *Citrine*.

cit'rēne, *n.* A crystalline compound obtained from the oil of lemon.

cit'riç, *a.* Belonging to lemons or limes; as, *citric* acid.

Citric acid; an acid obtained from the juice of many fruits, especially lemons.

cit'ril, *n.* [It. *citrinella*, dim. of *citrina*, the yellowhammer, citril, from LL. *citrinus*, yellow; L. *citrus*, the citron.] A beautiful songbird of Italy, *Fringilla citrinella*; the European yellowhammer.

cit-ri-nā'tion, *n.* The turning to a yellow-green color.

cit'rine, *a.* Like a citron or lemon; of a lemon color; yellow or greenish-yellow.

Citrine ointment; an ointment containing mercury, and so named from its yellow color.

cit'rine, *n.* 1. A yellow, pellucid variety of quartz.

2. In chromatography, citron-color.

cit'rŏn, *n.* [Fr. *citron*; L. *citreum* (supply *malum*, apple), a citron; Gr. *kitron*, a citron.]

1. The fruit of the citron-tree, resembling a lemon.

2. The tree itself, *Citrus medica*.

3. A variety of watermelon, having a particularly solid and white interior; used in making preserves.

cit-rŏn-el'lȧ, *n.* A grass found in southern Asia, which yields the fragrant *citronella*-oil.

cit'rŏn-tree, *n.* The tree, *Citrus medica*, which produces the citron.

cit'rŏn-wa"tēr, *n.* A liquor distilled from the rind of citrons.

cit'rŏn-wood, *n.* The wood of the Barbary pine or sandarac-tree, *Callitris quadrivalvis*.

cit'rul, *n.* The watermelon, *Citrullus vulgaris*.

Cit'rus, *n.* [L., the citron-tree.] A large genus, primarily indigenous to southern Asia, including the citron, orange, lemon, and lime trees.

cit'tērn, *n.* See *Cithern*.

cit'y, *n.* [ME. *cite, citee*; OFr. *cite, citet*, city; L. *civitas*, citizenship, from *civis*, a citizen.]

1. In a general sense, a large town; a large number of houses and inhabitants, established in one place.

2. Specifically, a corporate town; a town or collective body of inhabitants, incorporated and governed by particular officers, as a mayor and aldermen. This is the sense of the word in the United States. In Great Britain, a borough or town corporate, which is or has been the seat of a bishop, or the capital of his see, is called a *city*.

3. The collective body of citizens, or the inhabitants of a city; as, the *city* voted to establish a market.

cit'y, *a.* Pertaining to a city; as, a *city* council.

City article; in England, an editorial in a metropolitan newspaper, summarizing the commercial or financial news of the day.

City council; see *Common council*, under *Council*.

City editor; in the United States, the editor in charge of the local news department of a newspaper; in England, the editor on a London newspaper staff who superintends the preparation of the city, or commercial, article.

City fathers; the aldermen of a city.

cīve, *n.* [Fr. *cive*; L. *cepa*, onion.] A perennial herb, *Allium Schœnoprasum*, of the same genus as the leek and onion, and cultivated in gardens; also written *chive*.

civ'et, *n.* [Fr. *civette*; It. *zibetto*; Ar. *zabbad*, the civet.]

1. A substance of the consistence of butter or honey secreted by the anal glands of the civet-cat. It is of a clear yellowish or brownish color, and is used as a perfume.

Civet (*Viverra civetta*).

2. The animal that produces *civet*; the civet-cat, *Viverra civetta*. This animal is of a cinereous color, tinged with yellow, marked with dusky spots disposed in rows. It inhabits northern Africa and Asia.

civ'et, *v.t.* To scent with civet.

civ'et-cat, *n.* See *Civet*, n. 2.

civ'iç, *a.* [L. *civicus*, civil, from *civis*, a citizen.] Literally, pertaining to a city or citizen; relating to civil affairs or honors.

Civic crown; a crown, wreath, or garland of oak-leaves and acorns, anciently given as a mark of public approbation to any Roman soldier who had in battle saved the life of a citizen.

civ'i-cism, *n.* Government based on citizenship.

civ'içs, *n.* The science that treats of civil government, citizenship, and civil affairs.

civ'il, *a.* [Fr. *civil*; L. *civilis*, pertaining to a citizen, from *civis*, a citizen.]

1. Relating to the community, or to state policy and the government and rights of the citizen; as, *civil* rights; *civil* government; *civil* privileges; *civil* war; *civil* justice; opposed to *criminal*, and distinguished from *ecclesiastical* and *military*.

2. Reduced to order, rule, and government; under a regular administration; not savage or wild; as, *civil* life; *civil* society.

3. Civilized; courteous; complaisant; gentle and obliging; well-bred; affable; kind; having the manners of a citizen of a civilized community.

> Where *civil* speech and soft persuasion hung. —Prior.

Civil action; any suit or action at law other than a criminal prosecution.

Civil architecture; the architecture which is employed in constructing buildings for the purposes of civil life, in distinction from *military* and *naval architecture*.

Civil engineering; see under *Engineering*.

Civil law; see under *Law*.

Civil liberty; the natural liberty of the individual, regulated by law only so far as may be necessary for the public good.

Civil list; in England, formerly, a list of the entire expenses of the civil government; hence, in the United States, the officers of civil government, who are paid from the public treasury; also, the revenue appropriated to support the civil government. The *civil list* in England now embraces only the expenditures of the reigning monarch's household and the sovereign's allowances.

Civil remedy; remedy obtainable by a civil action.

Civil rights; the rights or privileges of citizenship.

Civil service; (a) that branch of the public service relating to civil affairs, as distinguished from military; (b) the system of appointment and promotion by merit in the civil departments of public service.

Civil service reform; a system of appointment to office under which government positions are subject to competitive examinations, and under which successful candidates receive appointments according to merit, which also is the ruling factor in future promotion.

Civil state; the whole body of citizens not included under military, maritime, and ecclesiastical institutions.

Civil war; a war between factions of the same nation, state, or city; opposed to *foreign war*.

Civil year; the legal year, or annual period established by a government, as distinguished from the *natural year*.

Syn.—Courteous, obliging, well-bred, polite, affable, complaisant.

ci-vil'ian (-yăn), *a.* Relating to or characteristic of the state of civil life; as, in *civilian* costume.

ci-vil'ian, *n.* [ME. *civilian*, a civilian; L. *civilis*, pertaining to a citizen.]

1. One who is skilled in the Roman law; a professor or doctor of civil law.

2. In a more extended sense, one who is versed in law and government.

3. A student of the civil law at a university.

4. One whose pursuits are those of civil life, not military or ecclesiastical.

civ'il-ist, *n.* A civilian. [Rare.]

ci-vil'i-ty, *n.* [ME. *civylite*; OFr. *civilite*, civility; L. *civilitas*, the art of government, from *civilis*, civil.]

1. The state of being civilized, as applied especially to nations. [Obs.]

2. Good breeding; politeness; complaisance; courtesy. *Civility* respects manners or external deportment, and, in the plural, *civilities* are acts of politeness.

civ'i-lī-zȧ-ble, *a.* Capable of becoming civilized.

civ"il-i-zā'tion, *n.* The act of civilizing; the state of being civilized or refined in manners.

> *Civilization* is the humanization of man in society. —M. Arnold.

Syn.—Humanization, decency, refinement, polish.

civ'il-ize, *v.t.*; civilized, *pt., pp.*; civilizing, *ppr.* [Fr. *civiliser*, to civilize; L. *civilis*, civil.] To reclaim from a savage state; to introduce enlightened manners and customs among.

civ'il-ized, *a.* Reclaimed from savage life and manners; instructed in learning, in morality, and in civil manners.

> Such sale of conscience and duty in open market is not reconcilable with the present state of *civilized* society. —J. Quincy.

civ'il-īz-ēr, *n.* 1. One who civilizes; one who reclaims others from an unenlightened life, and teaches them the rules and customs of civilized society.

2. That which reclaims from savageness.

civ'il-ly, *adv.* 1. In a manner relating to government, or to the individual as a member of the community.

2. In a manner relating to private rights; opposed to *criminally*; as, to proceed against a man *civilly*.

3. Not naturally, but in law; as, a man *civilly* dead.

4. Politely; complaisantly; gently; with due decorum; courteously; as, we were *civilly* treated.

civ'ism, *n.* [L. *civis*, a citizen.] Citizenship; devotion to a city or country. [Rare.]

ciz'ārs, *n.pl.* Scissors. [Obs.]

clab'bēr, *n.* See *Bonnyclabber*.

clab'bēr, *v.i.*; clabbered, *pt., pp.*; clabbering, *ppr.* To curdle; to become thick, as milk when souring.

clach'ăn, *n.* [Scot.] In Scotland, a hamlet of which a church is the center; or, the village church itself.

clack, *v.i.*; clacked, *pt., pp.*; clacking, *ppr.* [ME. *clacken*, to clack; an imitative word.]

1. To make a sudden, sharp noise, as by striking or cracking; to clink; to click.

2. To utter words rapidly, noisily, and thoughtlessly.

clack, *v.t.* 1. To strike together in such a manner as to make a cracking sound; to clap.

2. To utter in a rapid, noisy, or indiscreet manner; to babble.

clack, *n.* 1. A sharp, abrupt sound, continually repeated, such as is made by striking an object, or by bursting or cracking.

2. The instrument that strikes the hopper of a gristmill, to facilitate the discharge of the grain; sometimes applied to a bell that rings when more grain is required.

3. Continual and heedless talk; prattle.

clack'-box, *n.* The chamber in which a clack-valve works.

clack'-dish, *n.* A dish or money-box with a movable lid, formerly carried by beggars, who attracted attention by clacking the lid.

clack'-dōor, *n.* An adjustable cover to an aperture in the side of a clack-box.

clack'ēr, *n.* One who or that which clacks; especially the clapper of a mill.

clack'-goose, *n.* The barnacle-goose. [See *Barnacle*.]

clack'-valve, *n.* A valve in pumps, with a single flap, hinged at one edge, and consisting of a plate of leather a little larger than the valve aperture; also called *clapper*.

Clack-valve.

clad, *v.*, past tense and past participle of *clothe*.

clad, *v.t.* To clothe. [Obs.]

clad'ine, *a.* Same as *Cladose*.

clȧ'dō-. A combining form from Gr. *klados*, a shoot, branch, signifying branched or having branches; as, *Cladocera*.

Clad-ō-cär'pī, *n.pl.* In botany, a division of mosses having cladocarpous fruit.

clad-ō-cär'pous, *a.* [*Clado-*, and Gr. *karpos*, fruit.] Having the fruit at the end of a lateral shoot; said of mosses.

Clȧ-doc'e-rȧ, *n.pl.* [*Clado-*, and Gr. *keras*, horn.] An order of ostracoid entomostracans, having a bivalve shell covering the body but not the head, and branched antennæ; it includes the water-fleas; found mostly in fresh water.

clad'ōde, clȧ-dō'di-um, *n.* [*Clado-*, and Gr. *eidos*, form.] In botany, a branch having the shape and apparently the functions of a leaf, as those of the broom, *Ruscus*, and of the smilax, *Myrsiphyllum*; also called *cladophyl*.

clad'ō-dont, *a.* [*Clado-*, and Gr. *odous*, tooth.] Same as *Hybodont*.

clȧ-dog'e-nous, *a.* Same as *Cladocarpous*.

clad'ō-phyl, *n.* Same as *Cladode*.

clā-dōse', *a.* [L. *cladus*; Gr. *klados*, a branch.] In zoölogy, branched, as a sponge-spicule; having many branches.

Clad'ō-thrix, *n.* [*Clado-*, and Gr. *thrix*, a hair.] A genus of thread-like bacteria, found on plants in a variety of forms.

clag'gy, *a.* [Scot. *clag*, a clog, impediment.] Sticky, adhesive; said, in mining, of a wall to which coal adheres. [Eng.]

clāik, clāik'-goose, *n.* The barnacle-goose. [See *Barnacle*.]

clāim, *v.t.*; claimed, *pt., pp.*; claiming, *ppr.* [ME. *claimen*; OFr. *claimer*, to call, cry out, claim; L. *clamare*, to cry out; Gr. *kalein*, to call, cry out.]

1. To call for; to ask or seek to obtain, by virtue of authority, right, or supposed right; to challenge as a right; to demand as due; as,

to *claim* a debt; to *claim* obedience or respect.

2. To assert as a fact; to state; as, he *claims* to speak good French; to assert or maintain as a right; as, he *claims* the position of expert. [Colloq.]

3. To have a right or title to; as, the heir *claims* the estate by descent.

4. To proclaim. [Obs.]

5. To call, or name. [Obs.]

Syn.—Ask, demand, insist, require, request, maintain.

çlāim, *v.i.* 1. To be entitled to; to have a claim; to derive a right; as, he *claims* by royal descent.

2. To make an assertion; to maintain or express an opinion. [Colloq.]

3. To call; to cry out. [Obs.]

çlāim, *n.* 1. A demand of a right or supposed right; a calling on another for something due or supposed to be due; as, a *claim* of wages for services. A *claim* implies a right, or supposed right, in the claimant to something which is in another's possession or power. A *claim* may be made in words, by suit, or by other means.

2. A right to demand; a title to any debt, privilege, or other thing in possession of another; as, a prince has a *claim* to the throne.

3. The thing claimed or demanded, or to which one intends to establish a right; as, a settler's *claim*; a miner's *claim*.

4. A loud call. [Obs.]

Syn.—Pretension, right, title, preëmption, assertion, statement.

çlāim′ȧ-ble, *a.* Capable of being demanded as due.

çlāim′ănt, *n.* 1. A person who claims; one who, justly or unjustly, demands anything as his right.

2. A person who has a right to demand.

çlāim′ẽr, *n.* A claimant; one who demands as due.

çlāim′less, *a.* Having no claim. [Rare.]

çlāir-au′di-ence, *n.* [Fr. *clair*, clear, and *audience*, hearing.] The supposed ability to hear or perceive sounds not within reach of the ear in the natural waking state, or under ordinary conditions; attributed especially to persons in a mesmeric trance; also, the exercise of this power or the alleged act of hearing or perceiving such sounds.

çlāir-au′di-ent, *a.* and *n.* I. *a.* Relating to or having the nature of clairaudience.

II. *n.* One who is alleged to possess the power of clairaudience.

çlāire′-çōle, çlēar′-çōle, *n.* [Fr. *claire colle*, clear glue.] A kind of size used in house-painting and in applying gold-leaf.

çlāir′-ŏb-sçūre′, *n* See *Chiaroscuro.*

çlāir-voy′ănce, *n.* [Fr. *clair*, clear, and *voyant*, ppr. of *voir*, to see.] Literally, clear-sightedness; a power, attributed to persons in a mesmeric trance, of discerning objects which are not present to the normal senses.

çlāir-voy′ănt, *a.* Discerning objects which are not present to the senses; pertaining to clairvoyance.

çlāir-voy′ănt, *n.* [Fr. *clairvoyant*, lit clear-seeing.] One having, or pretending to have, the gift of clairvoyance.

çlāke, çlāke′-gooṣe, *n.* The barnacle-goose. [See *Barnacle.*]

çlam, *n.* [AS. *clam, clom*, a band, fetter, clamp.]

1. The popular name of certain bivalvular shellfish, of many species, and especially of those of an edible kind. The name is said to have been first given to the giant clam of the East Indies, *Tridacna gigas*, and is now applied to such bivalve mollusks of North America as the long, soft, or bait-clam, *Mya arenaria*; the round or hard clam, or quahog, *Venus mercenaria*; the black clam, surf-clam, or hen-clam, *Spisula solidissima*, and numerous other species. The first two are highly esteemed as food.

çlam, *n.* 1 A wooden vise or clamp.

2. [*pl.*] Strong pincers or forceps, used by shipcarpenters.

çlam, *n.* A cold dampness; clamminess. [Rare.]

çlam, *n.* Same as *Clamp*, first n. 5.

çlam, *n.* [Abbrev. of *clamor.*] The medley of sounds made by the simultaneous ringing of all the bells in a chime; a crash or clangor, as in a wedding peal. [Prov. Eng.]

çlam, *v.t.*; clammed, *pt., pp.*; clamming, *ppr.* [From the same root as AS. *beclemman*, to fasten, stick, *clæman*, to clam, smear.] To clog with glutinous or viscous matter.

çlam, *v.t.* and *v.i.* In bell-ringing, to produce a clam or clangor with (bells); to sound all the bells at once. [Prov. Eng.]

çlam, *v.i.* To be moist or sticky; to stick; to adhere. [Rare.]

çlā′mănt, *a.* [L. *clamans*, ppr. of *clamare*, to cry out.] Crying for help; beseeching with clamor; urgent.

çlȧ-mā′tion, *n.* [LL. *clamatio*, from L. *clamare*, to cry out.] The act of crying or calling out. [Obs.]

Çlam-ȧ-tō′rēṣ, *n.pl.* [L. *clamator*, pl. *clamatores*, a bawler, from *clamare*, to cry out.]

1. A suborder of passerine birds, including the nonoscine forms, which have poorly developed vocal muscles and so have little singing power.

2. The *Gallinæ*, including the common domestic fowls, pheasants, grouse, quail, etc.; so called from the crowing or clamoring of the males, especially among the domestic species.

çlam-ȧ-tō′ri-ăl, *a.* Pertaining to the *Clamatores.*

çlam′bāke, *n.* 1. The cooking of clams on hot stones between layers of fresh damp seaweed, as practised in the United States on the Atlantic coast, especially in the New England states.

2. A picnic-party or outdoor feast of which a *clambake* is the principal feature.

çlam′bẽr, *v.i.*; clambered, *pt., pp.*; clambering, *ppr.* [ME. *clambren*, to clamber; origin doubtful, perhaps from Ice. *klambra*, to pinch closely together.]

1. To climb with difficulty, or with both hands and feet.

2. Figuratively, to mount upward in a laborious manner.

> The narrow street that *clambered* toward the mill. —Tennyson.

çlam′bẽr, *v.t.* To ascend by climbing, with difficulty or arduous effort, using hands and feet; as, he *clambered* the wall. [Rare.]

çlam′bẽr, *n.* The act of clambering.

çlam-jam′fe-ry, *n.* See *Clanjamfrie.*

çlam′mi-ly, *adv.* In a cold, sticky manner; in a clammy way.

çlam′mi-ness, *n.* The state of being clammy or viscous; stickiness; tenacity of a soft substance.

çlam′my, *a.* [ME. *clam*, moist, clammy.] Thick; viscous; adhesive; soft and sticky; glutinous; tenacious.

> Cold sweat, in *clammy* drops, his limbs o'erspread. —Dryden.

çlam′ŏr, *n.* [ME. *clamour*; OFr. *clamour*; L. *clamor*, a loud call, from *clamare*, to cry out.]

1. A great outcry; noise; exclamation; vociferation, made by a loud human voice continued or repeated, or by a multitude of voices. It often expresses complaint and urgent demand.

2. Figuratively, any loud and continued noise, as of a river or other inanimate things.

3 A prolonged exhibition of discontent; violent agitation by a mob.

çlam′ŏr, *v.t.*; clamored, *pt., pp.*; clamoring, *ppr.* 1. To stun with noise. [Rare.]

2. To salute loudly. [Rare.]

3. To utter loudly or repeatedly; to assent vehemently.

To clamor bells; to multiply the strokes, so as to produce a loud clang.

çlam′ŏr, *v.i.* To utter loud sounds or outcries; to talk loudly; to vociferate, as an individual; to cry aloud, as a multitude; to complain; to make importunate demands; as, the crowd *clamored* for bread.

çlam′ŏr-ẽr, *n.* One who clamors.

çlam′ŏr-ous, *a.* Talking loudly and continuously; noisy; vociferous; loud; turbulent.

çlam′ŏr-ous-ly, *adv.* In a clamorous manner.

çlam′ŏr-ous-ness, *n.* The state or quality of being clamorous.

çlamp, *n.* [AS. *clam, clom*, a band, bond, fetter.]

1. In general, something rigid that fastens or binds; a piece of wood or metal fastening two pieces together.

2. In nautical terms, (a) a thick plank on the inner part of a ship's side used to sustain the ends of the beams; (b) any plate of iron made to turn or open and shut so as to confine a spar or boom.

3. In joinery, (a) an instrument of wood or metal used for holding pieces of timber closely together until the glue hardens; (b) a piece of wood fixed to another with a mortise and tenon, or groove and tongue, so that the fibers of the piece thus fixed cross those of the other, and thereby prevent it from casting or warping.

4. One of a pair of movable cheeks of lead or copper covering the jaws of a vise, and enabling it to grasp without bruising.

5. A pile of bricks laid up for burning, in which the end of one brick is laid over another, spaces being left for the ascent of the fire; also, a pile of ore for roasting, or of coal for coking; a pile of turnips, etc. Called also *clam.*

çlamp, *v.t.*; clamped, *pt., pp.*; clamping, *ppr.* To fasten with clamps; to fix a clamp on.

çlamp, *n.* [Imitative; compare *clank, clink.*] A heavy footstep or tread; a tramp.

çlamp, *v.i.* To tread heavily.

çlamp′ẽr, *n.* A metal plate having sharp prongs, designed to be fastened to the shoe or boot, so as to enable a person to walk safely on ice; also called *creeper* and *calk*

çlamp′-ī″ron (-ūrn), *n.* One of several irons attached to the ends of fireplaces to prevent the fuel from falling.

çlamp′-nāil, *n.* A short, stout, large-headed nail for fastening clamps in ships.

çlan, *n.* [Gael. *clann*; Ir. *clann, cland*, offspring, children, a tribe, prob. from W. *plant*, offspring; L. *planta*, offshoot.]

1. A race; a family; a tribe; an association of persons under a chieftain. Among the Highlanders of Scotland, a clan consisted of the common descendants of the same progenitor.

2. A clique, sect, society, or body of persons closely united by some common interest or pursuit; in this sense used contemptuously.

çlañ′çū-lăr, *a.* Clandestine; secret; private; concealed. [Obs.]

çlañ′çū-lăr-ly, *adv.* Privately; secretly. [Obs.]

çlan-des′tine (-tin), *a.* [Fr. *clandestin*; L. *clandestinus*, secret, hidden.] Secret; private; hidden; withdrawn from public view; generally implying craft, deception, or evil design; as, *clandestine* meetings.

Syn.—Concealed, secluded, unseen, unknown, private, covert.

çlan-des′tine-ly, *adv.* Secretly; privately; in secret.

çlan-des′tine-ness, *n.* Secrecy; a state of concealment.

çlan-des-tin′i-ty, *n.* Privacy or secrecy. [Rare.]

çlang, *n.* [An imitative word; compare O.H.G. *chlang*; L. *clangor*, clang, clangor.]

1. A loud sound produced from solid bodies, especially that produced by the collision of metallic bodies; a clank; clangor; as, the *clang* of arms.

2. In music, timbre.

çlang, *v.i.*; clanged, *pt., pp.*; clanging, *ppr.* To give out a clang; to clank; to resound.

> The wood which grides and *clangs.* —Tennyson.

çlang, *v.t.* To cause to sound with a clang.

> They *clanged* their sounding arms.—Prior.

çlañ′gŏr, *n.* [L.] A sharp, shrill, harsh sound.

çlañ′gŏr-ous, *a.* Sharp or harsh in sound.

çlañ′gous, *a.* Making a clang, or a shrill or harsh sound. [Obs.]

çlang′-tint, *n.* [*Clang*, and *tint*, from L. *tinctus*, pp. of *tingere*, to dye.] The quality of a compound tone; also called *clang-color.*

çlan-jam′frie, çlan-jam′fry, *n.* Rubbish or trumpery; persons who are collectively worthless; a vulgar herd; a rabble; a mob; canaille; also written *clamjamfery.* [Scot.]

çlañk, *n.* [An imitative word.] The loud, shrill, sharp sound made by a collision of metallic or other sonorous bodies; a sound less resonant than a clang, and more resonant than a clink.

çlañk, *v.t.*; clanked, *pt., pp.*; clanking, *ppr.* To cause to sound with a clank; to strike with a sharp sound; as, the prisoners *clank* their chains.

çlañk, *v.i.* To sound with a clank.

çlañk′less, *a.* Without a clank; not clanking.

çlan′nish, *a.* Closely united, like a clan; disposed to adhere closely, as the members of a clan.

çlan′nish-ly, *adv.* In a clannish manner.

çlan′nish-ness, *n.* Close adherence or disposition to unite, as a clan.

çlan′ship, *n.* A state of union, as in a family or clan; an association under a chieftain.

çlanṣ′măn, *n.*; *pl.* **çlanṣ′men.** A member of a clan.

çlap, *v.t.*; clapped, *pt., pp.*; clapping, *ppr.* [ME. *clappen*; AS. *clæppian*, to clap, knock; prob. imitative in origin.]

1. To strike with a quick motion; to slap; to tap; as, to *clap* one on the shoulder.

2. To thrust; to drive together; to shut hastily; followed by *to*; as, to *clap to* the door or gate.

3. To place or put, by a hasty or sudden motion; as, to *clap* the hand to the mouth; to *clap* a board over a pit.

4. To manifest approbation of by striking the hands together; as, to *clap* a performance on the stage.

To clap hands; to strike the hands together, (a) in token of the conclusion of an agreement; (b) as a mark of applause or delight.

To clap up; (a) to make or complete hastily; as, to *clap up* a peace; (b) to imprison without formality or delay.

çlap, *v.i.* 1. To come together suddenly with noise; to make a noise by rapping or tapping; to clack.

> The doors around me *clapt.* —Dryden.

2. To begin or set to work with alacrity and briskness. [Obs.]

3. To strike the hands together in applause.

4. To knock, as at a door. [Obs.]

5. To chatter; to prattle or prate continually or noisily. [Obs.]

çlap, *n.* 1. A collision of bodies with noise; a bang; a slap.

2. A sudden act or motion; generally in the phrase *at a clap*, that is, all at once.

> What, fifty of my followers *at a çlap*!—Shak.

3. A burst or peal of thunder.

4. A striking of hands to express approbation,

3. In falconry, the nether part of the beak of a hawk.

çlap, *n.* [OFr. *clapoir*, a venereal sore.] A venereal disorder; gonorrhea.

çlap′bōard (klab′ōrd), *n.* 1. A thin overlapping board used for rough outside work, as for boarding up a house.

2. A roughly made board for roofing.

3. In England, a cask-stave.

çlap′bōard, *v.t.*; clapboarded, *pt.*, *pp.*; clapboarding, *ppr.* To put on or cover with clapboards.

çlap′=bread, çlap′=çāke, *n.* A kind of oatmeal cake rolled out thin and baked hard.

çlap′=dish, *n.* A clack-dish.

çlāpe, *n.* The yellow-hammer or flicker.

çlap′match (-mach), *n.* A fur-bearing female seal.

çlap′=net, *n.* A net in hinged sections for taking small birds.

çlap′pẽr, *n.* 1. A person who claps, or applauds by clapping.

2. That which strikes, as the tongue of a bell, or the piece of wood that strikes a mill-hopper.

3. A burrow or inclosure. [Obs.]

çlap′pẽr-çlaw, *v.t.* 1. To fight and scratch.

2. To scold; to abuse with the tongue; to revile.

çlap′pẽr=rāil, *n.* A species of rail, *Rallus crepitans*, found in eastern United States.

çlapse, *v.t.* Clasp. [Obs.]

çlap′trap, *n.* 1. A contrivance for clapping in theaters. [Obs.]

2. Figuratively, an artifice or device to elicit applause or gain popularity.

çlap′trap, *a.* Designing or designed merely to catch applause.

çlaque (klak), *n.* [Fr., from *claquer*, to clap the hands, to applaud.] A name applied collectively to a set of men, who, in theaters, are regularly hired to applaud the piece or the actors.

çlȧ-queūr′ (klȧ-kẽr′), *n.* [Fr.] A member of a claque.

çlar-ȧ-bel′lȧ, *n.* [L. *clarus*, clear, and *bellus*, beautiful.] A stop in an organ, with open wood pipes, which produces a soft, melodious tone.

Çlāre, *n.* A nun of the order of St. *Clare*.

çlar′ence, *n.* [From the proper name *Clarence*.] A close four-wheeled carriage, with one seat inside and a driver's seat.

Çlar′en-cieūx, Çlar′en-ceūx (-sū), *n.* See *King-at-arms*.

çlar′en-dŏn, *n.* [From *Clarendon*, the proper name.] In printing, one of the common heavy condensed type-faces.

This line is set in clarendon.

çlāre′=ŏb-sçūre′, *n.* Same as *Chiaroscuro*.

çlar′et, *n.* [ME. *claret*; OFr. *claret*, clear, claret; L. *clarus*, clear.] A red wine; also, formerly, a wine amber in color; originally made at Medoc, in France, but the name now includes the red Bordeaux and similar wines made in California and elsewhere. The red wines were first called *claret* in England, but the name is not used in the same sense in France.

çlar′et=çup, *n.* A summer drink, consisting of claret, brandy, and flavoring ingredients, with the addition of chipped ice.

çlar-i-bel′lȧ, *n.* Same as *Clarabella*.

çlar′i-çhord, *n.* [L. *clarus*, clear, and *chorda*, a string.] A medieval musical instrument, in the form of a spinet; called also *manichord*.

çlar″i-fi-çā′tion, *n.* [LL. *clarificatio*, glorification, from L. *clarus*, clear, and *facere*, to make.] The act of clearing; the process of clarifying; as, the *clarification* of impure alcohol.

çlar′i-fī-ẽr, *n.* That which clarifies or purifies, specifically, in the manufacture of sugar; (a) a heater purifying the expressed juice by means of lime; (b) a rapidly revolving drum for separating impurities from the juice.

çlar′i-fȳ, *v.t.*; clarified, *pt.*, *pp.*; clarifying, *ppr.* 1. To make clear; to purify from feculent matter; to defecate; to fine; as, to *clarify* wine or syrup.

2. To make clear; to brighten or illuminate; applied to the mind or reason.

3. To make glorious. [Obs.]

çlar′i-fȳ, *v.i.* 1. To clear up; to grow clear or bright.

> His understanding *clarifies*, in discoursing with another. —Bacon.

2. To grow or become clear or fine; to become pure, as liquors; as, cider *clarifies* by fermentation.

çlar′i-gāte, *v.i.* To declare war formally. [Obs.]

çlar′i-net, *n.* [Fr. *clarinette*; It. *clarinetto*, from L. *clarus*, clear.] A musical wind-instrument made of wood, and similar in shape to the oboe, but of larger size. It has a fixed mouthpiece, containing a reed, which forms the upper joint of the instrument. The compass of the clarinet is about three octaves and a half from E in the third space of the bass, including all the intermediate semitones. The spelling *clarionet* is obsolete.

çlȧ-rī′nō, *n.* [It., from L. *clarus*, clear.] An organ-stop having reed pipes, generally of four feet pitch and sounding like a trumpet; also written *clarion*.

çlar′i-ŏn, *n.* [ME. *clarioun*; OFr. *clarion*; LL. *clario*, a trumpet; L. *clarus*, clear.] A kind of trumpet, having a tube narrower and a tone more acute and shrill than that of the common trumpet.

çlar″i-ō-net′, *n.* [Obs.] See *Clarinet*.

çlȧ-ris′ō-nous, *a.* [L. *clarus*, clear, and *sonus*, a sound.] Having a clear sound. [Obs.]

Çlȧ-rïsse′, *n.* [Fr.] The name given to a member of a Franciscan order of nuns, from the founder of the order, St. Clare, who died A. D. 1253.

çlȧ-rïs′si-mō, *n.* A title given to a noble in Venice. [Obs.]

çlar′i-tūde, *n.* Clearness; splendor. [Obs.]

çlar′i-ty, *n.* Clearness; brightness; splendor. [Obs.]

Çlär′ki-ȧ, *n.* [Named after William *Clarke*, the explorer.] A small herbaceous genus of annual plants characterized by showy purplish flowers. They are of the natural order *Onagraceæ*.

çlä′rō=ob-sçū′rō, *n.* See *Chiaroscuro*.

çlar-ré′ (-rā′), *n.* [Fr.] Wine mixed with honey and spices, and afterward strained till it is clear. [Obs.]

çlärt, *v.t.* To daub, smear, or spread. [Prov. Eng.]

çlärt′y, *a.* Wet; slippery. [Prov. Eng.]

çlär′y, *v.i.* To make a loud or shrill noise. [Obs.]

çlā′ry, *n.* [Fr. *sclarée*; LL. *sclarea*, clary.] A plant of the genus *Salvia*, or sage, *Salvia Sclarea*.

Wild clary; *Salvia Verbenaca*, a wild English variety, often called *vervain clary*.

çlā′ry=wa″tẽr, *n.* A composition of brandy, sugar, clary-flowers, and cinnamon, with a little ambergris dissolved in it; formerly much used as an aid to digestion.

çlash, *v.i.*; clashed (klasht), *pt.*, *pp.*; clashing, *ppr.* [An imitative word.]

1. To strike against; to drive against with force; making a jumble of metallic sounds.

2. To meet in opposition; to be contrary; to act in a contrary direction; to interfere as to immaterial things; as, the opinions of men *clash*; *clashing* interests.

> Independent jurisdictions could not fail to *clash*. —Dwight.

çlash, *v.t.* To strike sharply against, with resonance, as cymbals.

çlash, *n.* 1. A meeting of bodies with violence; a striking together with noise; as, the *clash* of arms.

2. Opposition; contradiction; as between differing or contending interests, views, purposes, etc.

çlash′ing-ly, *adv.* With clashing.

çlȧsp, *v.t.*; clasped, *pt.*, *pp.*; clasping, *ppr.* [ME. *claspen*, to grasp firmly, from AS. *clam*, *clom*, a band, bond, fetter.]

1. To shut or fasten together with a clasp; to furnish with a clasp; as, to *clasp* a book.

2. To catch and hold by twining or embracing; to surround and cling to; to embrace closely; to catch with the arms or hands; to grasp; as, the mother *clasped* her child to her breast.

3. To inclose or encompass with the fingers; to infold mutually; as, they *clasped* each other's hands; they were *clasped* in each other's arms.

çlȧsp, *n.* 1. A catch, to hold something together; a hook for fastening; a hook to hold together the covers of a book, or the different parts of a garment, of a belt, etc.

2. A clinging, grasping, or embracing; a close embrace.

çlȧsp′ẽr, *n.* 1. One who or that which clasps; in botany, applied specifically to tendrils.

2. In zoölogy, (a) a portion of the male reproductive organ used in a clasping manner, as by certain insects; (b) one of the organs appendant to the ventral fins, used in sexual union, developed in some male fish-like vertebrates, as the sharks and rays.

çlȧsp′ẽred, *a.* Furnished with tendrils or claspers.

çlȧsp′=knīfe (-nīf), *n.* A knife commonly used in hunting, having a folding blade which, when open, is generally held firmly by a catch so as not to close and cut the hand.

çlȧsp′=lock, *n.* A lock in which the catch fastens itself automatically.

çlȧss, *n.* [Fr. *classe*; L. *classis*, a class or division of the Roman people; Gr. *klēsis*, a calling, summons, from *kalein*, to call.]

1. An order or rank of persons; a number of persons in society, supposed to have some resemblance or equality in rank, education, property, talents, and the like; as in the phrase, all *classes* of men in society.

> The readers of poetry may be distinguished into three *classes*, according to their capacity of judging. —Dryden.

2. A number of students in a college or school, of the same standing, or pursuing the same studies.

3. Scientific division or arrangement; a set of beings or things having something in common, as in ethnology or biology.

4. A group of objects, truths, or happenings possessing general properties in common; a set; a variety; as, a *class* of ideas; a *class* of beliefs.

5. In the Methodist church, a section of the congregation under leadership of one of their number, having the betterment of the church in view.

Class of a curve; a geometrical term denoting the number of tangential lines which may be passed through a given point to a given curve. Thus, two lines may be drawn from a point tangent to a circle; consequently a circle is a curve of the second class.

Class of a surface; a geometrical term denoting the number of tangential planes which may be passed through a given line to a given surface.

Syn.—Order, rank, degree, category, grade, division, genus, kind, group.—*Class* and *order* are said of the persons who are distinguished; *rank* and *degree* of the distinction itself; men belong to a certain *class* or *order*; they hold a certain *rank*; they are of a certain *degree*.

çlȧss, *v.t.*; classed, *pt.*, *pp.*; classing, *ppr.* 1. To arrange in a class or classes; to rank together; to refer to a class or group; to classify.

2. To place in ranks or divisions, as students that are pursuing the same studies; to form into a class or classes.

çlȧss, *v.i.* To be grouped or arranged in classes. [Rare.]

çlȧss′i-ble, *a.* Adapted to arrangement in classes; capable of being classed.

çlȧs′siç, çlȧs′siç-ăl, *a.* [L. *classicus*, relating to the classes of the Roman people, from *classis*, a class.]

1. Belonging to or associated with the first or highest class, especially in literature; hence, primarily and more specifically, (a) relating to Greek and Roman authors of the first rank or estimation; (b) pertaining to writers of the first rank among the moderns; being of the first order; constituting the best model or authority, as an author.

2. Pertaining to ancient Greece or Rome; relating to places associated with the ancient Greek and Latin writers, or to the ancient localities of Greece and Rome famous in history.

> And still I seem to tread on *classic* ground. —Addison.

3. In literature and the fine arts, pure; chaste; correct; refined; as, a *classical* taste; a *classical* style; a *classical* work of art.

> At Liverpool Roscoe is like Pompey's column at Alexandria, towering alone in *classic* dignity. —Irving.

4. In some Reformed churches, relating to a classis or class. [See *Classis*, 2.]

Classic orders; in architecture, the Doric, Ionic, and Corinthian orders.

çlȧs′siç, *n.* 1. An author of the first rank; a writer whose style is pure, correct, and refined; primarily, a Greek or Roman author of this character; but the word is applied to similar writers of any nation.

2. One versed in the classics.

çlȧs′siç-ăl-işm, *n.* 1. A classic idiom or style; classicism.

2. In art, close adherence to the rules of Greek or Roman art.

çlȧs′siç-ăl-ist, *n.* 1. A devoted admirer of classicalism.

2. In art, one who scrupulously adheres to the canons of Greek or Roman art.

çlȧs-siç-al′i-ty, çlȧs′siç-ăl-ness, *n.* The quality of being classical.

çlȧs′siç-ăl-ly, *adv.* 1. In the manner of classes; according to a regular order of classes or sets.

2. In a classical manner; according to the manner of classical authors or artists.

çlȧs′si-çişm, *n.* A classic idiom or style.

çlȧs′si-cist, *n.* One versed in or an advocate of the classics.

çlȧs′si-fī-ȧ-ble, *a.* Capable of being arranged in classes.

çlȧs-sif′iç, *a.* Constituting or characterizing a class or classes; noting classification, or the order of distribution into sets.

çlȧs″si-fi-çā′tion, *n.* The act of forming into a class or classes; distribution into sets, sorts, or ranks; kind; class.

Syn.—Order, species, nature, character, cast, stamp, group, kind, section, sect, category, assortment, designation, description, genus.

çlȧs′si-fi-çā-tō-ry, *a.* Pertaining to classification; admitting of classification.

çlȧs′si-fī-ẽr, *n.* One engaged in classification.

çlȧs′si-fȳ, *v.t.*; classified, *pt.*, *pp.*; classifying, *ppr.* [L. *classis*, a class, and *facere*, to make.] To place in a class or classes; to distribute into classes; to arrange in sets according to some common properties or characters.

çlas'sis, *n.* [L. *classis*, a class.]

1. Class; order; sort.

2. In church affairs, an ecclesiastical body, convention, or assembly; specifically, in some Reformed churches, a judicatory corresponding to a presbytery.

çlàss'măn, *n.*; *pl.* **çlàss'men**. 1. A classmate.

2. In English universities, a candidate for graduation in arts who has passed an examination of special severity in one of the departments in which honors are conferred, and who is placed according to merit in one of several classes.

çlàss'māte, *n.* A fellow-member in a class at school or college.

çlas'tiç, *a.* [Gr. *klastos*, broken in pieces, from *klān*, to break.]

1. Characterized by a separation into parts, or the ability to be so separated.

2. In mineralogy, scaly; fragmental; composed of irregular parts.

çlatch (klach), *n.* [Scot., from Norw. *kleksa*, to daub, smear.]

1. Soft mud.

2. Slipshod or botched work; hence, a slattern.

çlath'rāte, *a.* [L. *clathri*; Gr. *klēthra*, a trellis, grate.] Latticed; divided like latticework; a term in biology; also written *clathroid*.

çlath'rōse, *a.* Barred or latticed, sometimes at right angles; a term in entomology.

çlat'tēr, *v.i.*; clattered, *pt., pp.*; clattering, *ppr.* [ME. *clateren*, to clatter; AS. *clatrung*, a clattering; imitative in origin.]

1. To make rattling sounds; to make repeated sharp sounds, as by striking sonorous bodies; as, to *clatter* on a shield.

2. To talk fast and idly; to run on; to rattle with the tongue.

çlat'tēr, *v.t.* To strike so as to produce a rattling noise from.

çlat'tēr, *n.* 1. A rapid succession of abrupt, sharp sounds, made by the collision of metallic or other sonorous bodies; rattling sounds.

2. Tumultuous and confused noise; a repetition of abrupt, sharp sounds.

3. Idle gossip; tattle. [Prov. Eng.]

çlat'tēr-ēr, *n.* One who clatters; a babbler.

çlat'tēr-ing-ly, *adv.* With a clattering noise.

çlau'dent, *a.* [L. *claudens*, ppr. of *claudere*, to shut.] Shutting; confining; drawing together; as, a *claudent* muscle. [Rare.]

çlau'di-çănt, *a.* [L. *claudicans*, ppr. of *claudicare*, to limp.] Halting; limping. [Rare.]

çlau-di-çā'tion, *n.* A halting or limping. [Rare.]

çlauṣe, *n.* [ME. *clause*; OFr. *clause*; LL. *clausa*, a clause; L. *clausula*, a clause, close of a period, from *clausus*, pp. of *claudere*, to close.]

1. In grammar, a member of a compound sentence containing both a subject and its predicate.

2. An article in a contract or other writing; a distinct part of a contract, will, agreement, charter, commission, or the like; a distinct stipulation, condition, proviso, etc.

Syn.—Portion, paragraph, stipulation, provision, article, condition, chapter, section, passage.

çlauṣe, *a.* Close. [Obs.]

çlaus'trăl, *a.* [L. *claustrum*, a fastening, an inclosed place, from *claudere*, to close.] Relating to a cloister or religious house; as, a *claustral* prior.

çlaus'trum, *n.*; *pl.* **çlaus'trȧ**. [L. *claustra*, neut. pl., a bar, lock.] A thin layer of the cortical part of each cranial hemisphere in man.

çlau'sū-lăr, *a.* Consisting of or having clauses.

çlau'ṣūre, *n.* [ME. *clausure*; L. *clausura*, an inclosure, from *claudere*, to close.] The act of shutting up or confining; confinement. [Rare.]

çlā'vȧ, *n.*; *pl.* **çlā'væ**. [L. *clava*, a knotty branch or club.] The blunt, knobbed end of the antenna in some insects.

çlā'văl, *a.* Pertaining to or resembling a clavus or clava.

çlā'vāte, **çlā'vā-ted**, *a.* [L. *clava*, a club.] Club-shaped; having the form of a club; growing gradually thicker toward the top, as certain parts of a plant.

çlāve, *v.*, past tense of *cleave*. [Obs.]

çlav'e-cin, *n.* Same as *Harpsichord*.

çlā'vel, *n.* Same as *Clevis*.

çlav'el-lāte, *a.* Same as *Clavate*.

çlav'el-lā-ted, *a.* A term applied to potash and pearlash, from the billets of wood from which they were produced by burning.

çlav'ēr, *n.* An obsolete form of *clover*.

çlav'ēr, *v.i.* [Scot.] To talk idly and foolishly; to talk much and at random.

çlav"i-ȧ-tūr', *n.* [D. *claviatuur*, from L. *clavis*, a key.]

1. The part of a piano or organ occupied by the keys.

2. A system of fingering adapted to a musical keyboard.

çlav'i-çhọrd, *n.* [L. *clavis*, a key, and *chorda*, a string.] See *Clarichord*.

çlav'i-çle (-kl), *n.* [L. *clavicula*, dim. of *clavis*, a key or lock.] The collar-bone, forming one of the elements of the pectoral arch in vertebrate animals. In man and sundry quadrupeds there are two clavicles or collar-bones, each joined at one end to the scapula or shoulder-bone, and at the other to the sternum or breastbone. In many quadrupeds the clavicles are absent or rudimentary, while in birds they are united in one piece, popularly called the *wishbone*.

çlav'i-çọrn, *a.* and *n.* [L. *clava*, a club, and *cornu*, a horn.]

I. *a.* Having the antennæ club-shaped.

II. *n.* One of the family *Clavicornia*.

çlav-i-çọr'nāte, *a.* Clavicorn.

Çlav-i-çọr'ni-ȧ, *n.pl.* [L., from *clava*, a club, and *cornu*, a horn.] A family of pentamerous beetles, so named from the antenna, which terminates in a club-shaped enlargement.

çlȧ-viç'ū-lăr, *a.* Pertaining to the collar-bone or clavicle.

çlav'i-fọrm, *a.* Clavate.

çlav'i-gēr, *n.* [L. *clavis*, a key, and *gerere*, to carry.] One who keeps the keys of a place.

çlav'i-gēr, *n.* [L. *claviger*, a club-bearer; *clava*, a club, and *gerere*, to bear.] A bearer of a club.

çlȧ-viġ'ēr-ous, *a.* 1. Bearing a club.

2. Bearing a key or keys.

çlā'vis, *n.*; *pl.* **çlā'vēṣ**. [L.] A key, as to a book or cipher.

çlav'ō-lȧ, *n.*; *pl.* **çlav'ō-læ**. [L., dim. of *clava*, a club.] The knobbed end of an antenna.

çlav'ū-lȧ, *n.*; *pl.* **çlav'ū-læ**. One of the club-like spines numerous on sea-urchins.

çlā'vus, *n.*; *pl.* **çlā'vī**. [L. *clavus*, a nail.]

1. A nail-like growth; a corn.

2. The thickened portion of the fore-wings of certain bugs.

çlaw, *n.* [ME. *claw*; AS. *clawu*, a claw, hoof.]

1. The sharp, hooked nail of an animal; or more generally, a hooked extremity belonging to any animal member or appendage.

> The maxillary palps in the spiders are long jointed appendages, terminated in the females by pointed *claws*.—H. A. Nicholson.

2. The whole leg or foot of such animals (crustaceans, spiders, etc.) as have curved jointed legs usually terminating in a sharp point; in a special sense applied to the pincers of certain shellfish, as the lobster and crab.

3. The hand; in contempt.

4. Anything shaped like the claw of an animal, as the crooked forked end of a hammer, used for drawing nails.

5. In botany, the narrow base of a petal, especially when it is long, as in the pink and wallflower.

çlaw, *v.t.*; clawed, *pt., pp.*; clawing, *ppr.* [ME. *clawen*; AS. *clawian*, to claw, scratch.]

1. To tear, scratch, pull, or seize with, or as with, claws or nails.

> Like wild beasts shut up in a cage, to *claw* and bite each other to their mutual destruction. —Burke.

2. To relieve, as if by scratching; to scratch, as an itching part, with intent to gratify.

> Look, whether the wither'd elder hath not his poll *claw'd* like a parrot. —Shak.

3. To fawn on; to flatter.

> Rich men they *claw*, soothe up, and flatter; the poor they contemn and despise. —Holland.

To claw off, to claw away; to rail at; to scold. [Obs.]

çlaw, *v.i.* 1. To use the claws.

2. A nautical term meaning to beat to windward, to prevent falling on a lee shore or on another vessel; with *off*; hence, to get off; to escape.

çlaw'back, *n.* and *a.* I. *n.* One who flatters; a sycophant; a wheedler. [Obs.]

II. *a.* Flattering. [Obs.]

çlaw'back, *v.t.* To flatter. [Obs.]

çlawed, *a.* Furnished with claws.

çlaw'-ham"mēr, *n.* A hammer divided into two claws, for drawing nails out of wood.

Claw-hammer coat; a colloquial term for a full-dress or swallow-tail coat; sometimes contracted to *claw-hammer*.

çlaw'less, *a.* Destitute of claws.

çlaw'-sick"ness, *n.* Foot-rot, a disease of cattle and sheep.

çlāy, *n.* [ME. *clay*, *cley*; AS. *clæg*, clay.]

1. The name common to various viscous earths, compounds of silica and alumina, sometimes with lime, magnesia, soda or potash, and metallic oxids. All the varieties are characterized by being firmly coherent, weighty, compact, and hard when dry, but stiff, viscid, and ductile when moist; smooth to the touch; not readily diffusible in water, and when mixed not readily subsiding in it. They contract by heat, absorb water readily, and become soft, but are so tenacious as to be molded into any shape, and hence they are the raw materials used in the manufacture of brick and tile, pottery, etc.

2. In poetry and the Scriptures, earth in general, especially as the material of the human body.

> I also am formed out of the *clay*.—Job xxxiii. 6.

Fatty clay; any clay having a greasy feeling, as halloysite.

Fire-brick clay; a clay having no fusible constituents.

Porcelain clay; see *Kaolin*.

Potter's clay; any clay, including kaolin, suitable by reason of its composition for the making of earthenware.

çlāy, *a.* Formed or consisting of clay; as, a *clay* soil.

çlāy, *v.t.*; clayed, *pt., pp.*; claying, *ppr.* 1. To cover or manure with clay.

2. To purify and whiten with clay, as sugar.

3. To puddle with clay.

çlāy'-çōld, *a.* Cold as clay or earth; lifeless.

çlāyeṣ, *n.pl.* [Fr. *claie*; OFr. *cloie*, a hurdle; of Celtic origin.] In fortification, wattles or hurdles made with stakes interwoven with osiers, to cover lodgments.

çlāy'ey, *a.* Consisting of clay; abounding with clay; partaking of clay; like clay.

çlāy'ish, *a.* Partaking of the nature of clay, or containing particles of it.

çlāy'-märl, *n.* A whitish, smooth, chalky clay.

çlāy'mōre, *n.* [Gael. *claidheamhmor*, a great sword; *claidheamh*, a sword, and *mor*, great; comp. L. *gladius*, a sword, and *magnus*, great.] Formerly, the large two-handed sword of the Scotch Highlanders; now a basket-hilted, double-edged broadsword.

çlāy'-pit, *n.* A pit from which clay is dug.

çlāy'-slāte, *n.* A rock consisting of clay which has been hardened and otherwise changed, for the most part extremely fissile and often producing good roofing slate.

Çlāy-tō'ni-ȧ, *n.* [From John *Clayton*, a Virginia botanist.] A genus of low, smooth herbs of the family *Portulacaceæ*; the spring-beauties.

-cle. A dim. suffix from L. *-culus*, *-cula*, *-culum*, occurring in such words as arti*cle*, parti*cle*, mus*cle*, corpus*cle*, etc.

çlēad'ing, *n.* [Prov. Eng. and Scot. form of *clothing*.]

1. In engines, the jacket or outer covering of the cylinder; also, a casing of a locomotive engine and firebox; the covering put on steam-pipes to prevent the radiation of heat.

2. Any kind of plank covering, such as the slating-boards of a roof, the boards of a floor, the plank lining of a pit-shaft, the planking of a cofferdam, etc.

çlēan, *a.* [ME. *clene*, *clæne*; AS. *clæne*, clean, bright.]

1. Clear of dirt or filth; having all uncleanness removed; unmixed with matter foreign to the substance itself; unadulterated; pure.

2. Free from what is injurious; without fault, imperfection, or defect; as, a *clean* garden; *clean* timber; a *clean* copy; a *clean* proof.

3. Clean-limbed; well-proportioned; shapely; lithe.

> Thy waist is straight and *clean*. —Waller.

4. Free from awkwardness; not clumsy or bungling; dexterous; adroit; as, a *clean* boxer; a *clean* leap; a *clean* trick.

5. Free from limitation or any modifying quality or circumstance; entire; complete.

6. In whale-fishing, having no fish or oil aboard; as, the ship returned *clean*; that is, came back without having captured whales or seals.

7. Free from moral impurity, guilt, or blame; innocent; sinless; holy; as, a *clean* man.

8. Among the Jews, (a) applied to persons free from ceremonial defilement; (b) to animals and things not causing ceremonial defilement; specifically to animals not forbidden by the ceremonial law for use in sacrifice and for food.

9. Completely cleared or swept free of something, or effecting such clearance; as, a *clean* sweep.

10. Free from vulgarism or indecency; as, *clean* literature.

Clean bill of health; an official document issued by a health officer or consul to the master of a ship, certifying that the vessel is free from contagion, and sails from a port free from infectious disease; also, a similar certificate that a person or thing is free from infection or disease.

To make a clean breast of; see under *Breast*.

To show a clean pair of heels; to make one's escape effectually by sudden or rapid flight.

Syn.—Clear, spotless, pure, purified, cleansed, untarnished.

çlēan, *adv.* 1. Quite; perfectly; wholly; entirely; fully.

> The people passed *clean* over Jordan. —Josh. iii. 17.

2. Without miscarriage; dexterously.

> Pope came off *clean* with Homer.—Henley.

çlēan, *v.t.*; cleaned; *pt., pp.*; cleaning, *ppr.* To make clean; to remove all foreign matter from; to purify; to cleanse; as, to *clean* a ship's bottom; to *clean* a house; to *clean* a field or garden.
To clean out; to deprive of all available means; to exhaust the pecuniary resources of. [Colloq.]

çlēan′=bred, *a.* Well-bred; of selected parentage.

çlēan′=çut, *a.* Formed as with artistic or skilful neatness; well-shaped; precise; clear-cut; definite; as, a *clean-cut* face; a *clean-cut* statement.

çlēan′ēr, *n.* One who or that which cleans.

çlēan′=hand″ed, *a.* 1. Having clean hands.
2. Figuratively, free from moral taint or suspicion; as, he went out of court *clean-handed*.

çlēan′=hand″ed-ness, *n.* The state or quality of being clean-handed.

çlēan′=heärt″ed, *a.* Having a pure heart.

çlēan′ing, *n.* 1. The act of making clean.
2. The afterbirth of cows, ewes, etc.

çlean′li-ly (klen′), *adv.* In a cleanly, neat manner.

çlēan′=limbed (-limd), *a.* Having well-proportioned, symmetrical limbs; lithe; lissome; as, a *clean-limbed* athlete.

çlean′li-ness (klen′), *n.* The state or quality of being cleanly; freedom from dirt, filth, or any foul, extraneous matter; neatness of person or dress; purity.

çlean′ly (klen′), *a.*; *comp.* cleanlier; *superl.* cleanliest. 1. Free from dirt, filth, or any foul matter; neat; carefully avoiding filth.
2. Free from injurious or polluting influence; pure; innocent.
3. Cleansing; making clean; as, *cleanly* powder. [Obs.]
4. Nice; artful; dexterous; adroit; as, a *cleanly* play; a *cleanly* evasion. [Obs.]

çlēan′ly, *adv.* 1. In a clean manner; neatly; without filth; as, he was *cleanly* dressed.
2. Purely; innocently.
3. Cleverly; adroitly; dexterously. [Obs.]

çlēan′ness, *n.* The state or quality of being clean; specifically, (a) freedom from dirt, filth, and foreign matter; neatness; (b) freedom from ceremonial pollution; (c) exactness, purity, justness, correctness; said of language or style; (d) purity, innocence.

çleanș′ȧ-ble (klenz′), *a.* Capable of being cleansed.

çleanșe (klenz), *v.t.*; cleansed, *pt., pp.*; cleansing, *ppr.* 1. To purify; to make clean; to free from filth, impurity, guilt, infection, or whatever is unseemly, noxious, or offensive.

Cleanse thou me from secret faults.—Ps. xix. 12.

2. To remove; to purge away.

Not all her odorous tears can *cleanse* her crime. —Dryden.

çleanș′ēr (klenz′), *n.* One who or that which cleanses; in medicine, a detergent.

çleanș′ing (klenz′), *a.* Adapted to cleanse and purify.

çleanș′ing (klenz′), *n.* The act of purifying or purging.

çleanș′ing=dāyș, *n.pl.* Ash Wednesday and the three following days.

çleanș′ing=week, *n.* The week beginning with Quinquagesima Sunday; also called *chaste week*.

çlēan′skin, çlēar′skin, *n.* In Australia, an unbranded bullock or heifer; called a *maverick* in the United States.

çlēan′=tim″bēred, *a.* Well-proportioned; symmetrical in shape; clean-limbed. [Poet.]

I think Hector was not so *clean-timbered*. —Shak.

çlēan′=up, *n.* 1. A general domestic or personal cleaning. [Colloq.]
2. In mining, the gathering together of gold after the process of washing or stamping; hence, the gold so gathered.

çlēar, *a.* [ME. *clere, cler*; OFr. *cler, clair*; L. *clarus*, clear, bright.]
1. Free from darkness or opacity; brilliant; light; luminous; unclouded; not obscured.
2. Bright-colored; gay; showy; magnificent. [Obs.]

Him that is clothed with *clear* clothing. —Wickliffe.

3. Free from that which would dim the transparency or bright color of a thing; as, *clear* water; a *clear* complexion; *clear* sand.

The stream is so transparent, pure, and *clear*. —Denham.

4. Free from that which confuses; specifically, (a) not confused or dull; having the power of perceiving or comprehending quickly; sharp; acute; discriminating; as, a *clear* intellect; (b) easily seen or comprehended; free from obscurity; easily intelligible; perspicuous; distinct; lucid; as, a *clear* statement.
5. Evident; manifest; indisputable; undeniable.

Remained to our Almighty foe *clear* victory. —Milton.

6. Free from that which perturbs; undisturbed by care or passion; unruffled; serene.

To whom the Son with calm aspect and *clear*. —Milton.

7. Free from guilt or blame; morally unblemished; irreproachable.

Duncan hath been so *clear* in his great office. —Shak.

8. Free from entanglement or embarrassment; free from accusation or imputation, distress, imprisonment, or the like; followed by *of* or *from*.

To get *clear of* all the debts I owe. —Shak.

9. Free from impediment or obstruction; unobstructed; as, a *clear* view.
10. Sounding distinctly; distinctly audible; canorous; as, his voice was loud and *clear*.
11. Without diminution or deduction; in full; net; as, *clear* profit or gain.
Clear breach; see under *Breach*, n.
Clear days (preceded by a numeral, as four, five, or nine *clear days*); in law, days reckoned exclusively of those on which any proceeding is commenced or completed.
Clear stuff; lumber free from knots.
Syn.—Lucid, bright, vivid, apparent, distinct, evident, free, guiltless, manifest, obvious, perspicuous, plain, pure.—*Clear* expresses less than *lucid*, *lucid* less than *bright*, and *bright* less than *vivid*; a mere freedom from stain or dullness constitutes *clear*; the return of light, and consequent removal of darkness, constitute *lucid*; *bright* supposes a certain strength of light; *vivid* a freshness combined with the strength, and even a degree of brilliancy.

çlēar, *n.* In carpentry and architecture, the space between any two bodies where no other intervenes, or between their nearest surfaces; used in the phrase *in the clear*.

çlēar, *adv.* 1. Clearly; plainly; not obscurely; manifestly.
2. Clean; quite; entirely; wholly, as to go *clear* through; indicating entire separation, as to cut a piece *clear* off; to go *clear* away.

çlēar, *v.t.*; cleared, *pt., pp.*; clearing, *ppr.* 1. To remove whatever diminishes the brightness, transparency, or purity of color from; as, to *clear* liquors; to *clear* a mirror; to *clear* the sky.
2. To free from obscurity, perplexity, or ambiguity; often followed by *up*; as, to *clear* a question or theory; to *clear up* a case.

Let a god descend, and *clear* the business to the audience. —Dryden.

3. To free from obstructions; to free from any impediment or encumbrance, or from anything noxious or injurious; as, to *clear* the sea of pirates; to *clear* land of trees; to *clear* the voice; often used with *off*, *away*, etc.; as, to *clear off* debts; to *clear away* rubbish.
4. To free; to liberate or disengage; as, to *clear* a man from debt, obligation, or duty.
5. To free from the charge or imputation of guilt; to justify or vindicate; to acquit.

That will by no means *clear* the guilty. —Ex. xxxiv. 7.

6. To gain or profit beyond all expenses and charges; to net.

He *clears* but two hundred thousand crowns a year. —Addison.

7. To leap over or pass by without touching; as, to *clear* a fence, hedge, or ditch; to *clear* a rock at sea.
8. In maritime affairs, to pay the customs on, or connected with; to obtain permission to sail for, by procuring the necessary documents, giving the requisite bonds, etc.; as, to *clear* a cargo; to *clear* a ship at the custom-house.
To clear a ship for action, or *to clear for action*; to remove all encumbrances from the decks and prepare for an engagement.
To clear hawse; to disentangle twisted cables.
To clear the land; to gain such a distance from shore as to have open sea-room and be out of danger from the land.
Syn.—Exculpate, exonerate, absolve, acquit, relieve, justify, whitewash, release, set free, extricate, vindicate.

çlēar, *v.i.* 1. To become free from clouds or fog; to become fair; to pass away or disappear from the sky; often followed by *up*, *off*, or *away*; as, the mist *clears off* or *away*.

So foul a sky *clears* not without a storm. —Shak.

Advise him to stay till the weather *clears up*. —Swift.

2. To be disengaged from encumbrances, distress, or entanglements; to become free or disengaged. [Obs.]
3. In banking, to exchange checks and bills and settle balances, as in clearing-houses.
4. In navigation, to leave a port; often followed by *out* or *outward*; as, several vessels *cleared* yesterday; the ship will *clear out* or *outward* to-morrow.
To clear out; to take oneself off; to run away; to remove; to depart. [Colloq.]

çlēar′āge, *n.* The act of removing anything; a clearing. [Rare.]

çlēar′ănce, *n.* 1. The act of clearing; as, the *clearance* of land from trees; the *clearance* of an estate from unprofitable tenantry.
2. Clear or net profit; profit over all expenses.
3. A certificate that a ship or vessel has been cleared at the custom-house; permission to sail.
4. In steam-engines, the distance between the piston and the cylinder-cover, when the former is at the end of its stroke; in machinery generally, the distance by which one moving part or body clears another, as the least distance between the points of a cogwheel's teeth and the bottom of the slots between the teeth of the wheel which it engages.

çlēar′=çōle, *n.* See *Claire-cole*.

çlēar′=çut, *a.* 1. Formed with clear, sharp, or delicately defined outlines, as if by cutting, as opposed to molding.

A cold and *clear-cut* face. —Tennyson.

2. Distinctly and exactly stated.

çlēar′ed-ness, *n.* The state or quality of being cleared. [Rare.]

çlēar′ēr, *n.* 1. One who or that which clears.
2. A fine-toothed comb or tool on which hemp is finished for lines and twines, especially those used by sailmakers.

çlēar′=ēyed (-īd), *a.* Having bright, clear eyes; keen of sight or perception.

çlēar′=head″ed (-hed″), *a.* Clear in understanding; not confused or mentally clouded; quick to perceive and understand.

çlēar′=head″ed-ness, *n.* The quality of being clear-headed; intelligence.

çlēar′ing, *n.* 1. The act of clearing; the process of making clear or freeing from anything; as, the *clearing* of land; the *clearing* of a statement.
2. The act of defending, vindicating, or justifying oneself.
3. In banking, the act of exchanging drafts on various institutions and settling the differences. A clerk from each bank attends the clearing-house daily with the checks and bills he may have on the others, and distributes them in drawers allotted to the several banks. They then make out balance-sheets, entering on the one side the sum each bank owes them and on the other side the sum they owe each bank.
4. [*pl.*] The sum total of the balances paid through a clearing-house in any given time; as, the bank *clearings* last month.
5. In English railway management, the act of distributing among the different companies the proceeds of the through traffic passing over several railways, the necessary calculations being made in the railway clearing-house in London.
6. A place or tract of land cleared of wood and underbrush for cultivation; a common use of the word in the United States.

çlēar′ing=house, *n.* The place where the operation termed *clearing* in banks and railways is carried on; an office maintained by the bankers of a city, where their clerks meet daily to exchange checks and drafts and adjust balances.

çlēar′ly, *adv.* 1. In a clear manner; plainly; evidently; fully; as, the fact is *clearly* proved.
2. Without obstruction; luminously; as, to shine *clearly*.
3. With clear discernment; as, to understand *clearly*.
4. Without entanglement or confusion.
5. Plainly; honestly; candidly.

Deal *clearly* and impartially with yourselves. —Tillotson.

6. Without reserve, evasion, or subterfuge.
Syn.—Plainly, distinctly, obviously, palpably, evidently, lucidly, perspicuously, explicitly.

çlēar′ness, *n.* 1. The state or quality of being clear; freedom from anything that diminishes brightness, transparency, or purity of color; as, the *clearness* of water or other liquid; *clearness* of skin.
2. Freedom from obstruction or encumbrance; as, the *clearness* of the ground.
3. Discernment; perspicuity; as, *clearness* of understanding.
4. Distinctness; perspicuity; luminousness; as, the *clearness* of views, of arguments, of explanations.

He does not know how to convey his thoughts to another with *clearness* and perspicuity. —Addison.

5. Plainness or plain dealing; sincerity; honesty; fairness; candor. [Obs.]

Their good faith and *clearness* of dealing made them almost invincible. —Bacon.

6. Freedom from imputation or suspicion of ill.

I require a *clearness.* —Shak.

7. In painting, that peculiar quality in a picture which is realized by a skilful arrangement of colors, tints, and tones, and for the satisfactory attainment of which a knowledge of chiaroscuro is requisite.

Syn.—Perspicuity, transparency.—*Clearness* is either physical or mental. In the latter case, it is a quality of thought, as *perspicuity* is of language; for example, *clearness* of thought; *perspicuity* of phraseology. *Transparency* is physical and moral. The *transparency* of the heavens, of strict integrity, or of a pure literary style.

çlēar′=see″ing, *a.* Having a clear sight or understanding.

çlēar′=shin″ing, *a* Shining with brightness or unobstructed splendor.

çlēar′=sight″ed (-sit″ed), *a.* Seeing with clearness; having acuteness of sight; discerning; perspicacious; as, *clear-sighted* reason; a *clear-sighted* judge.

çlēar′=sight″ed-ness, *n.* The state or quality of being clear-sighted; acute discernment.

çlēar′skin, *n.* Same as *Cleanskin.*

çlēar′stärch, *v.t.*; clearstarched, *pt.*, *pp.*; clearstarching, *ppr.* To stiffen and dress with clear or colorless starch; as, to *clearstarch* muslin.

çlēar′stärch′ẽr, *n* One who clearstarches.

çlēar′stärch″ing, *n.* The act of stiffening with starch, and then clearing by clapping with the hands.

çlēar′stō″ry, çlēre′stō″ry, *n.* The upper story of a cathedral or other church, perforated by a range of windows, which form the principal means of lighting the central portions of the building. It is immediately over the arches of the side aisles and the triforium, or, where there is no triforium, it rests immediately on the arches.

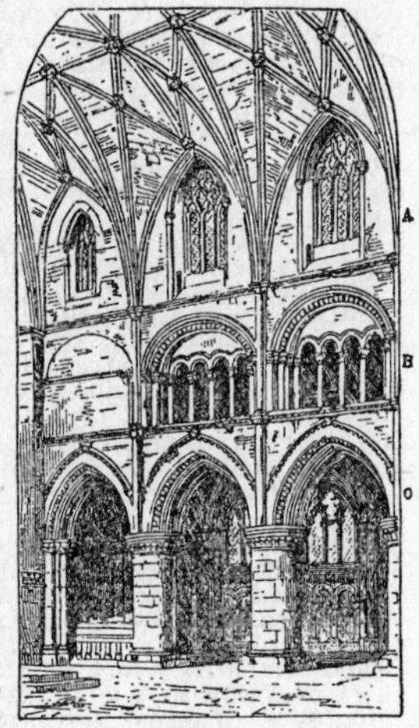

A B C

Part of Malmsbury Abbey.
A, Clearstory B, Triforium C, Arches of the Nave.

çlēar′weed, *n.* A variety of nettle, *Pilea pumila*, with a smooth pellucid stem, found in cool, moist soil.

çlēar′wing, *n.* An insect or sphinx-moth of the family *Ægeriadæ*, having wings transparent or partially transparent in the middle; the currant and peach-tree borers are examples.

çlēat, *n.* [ME. *clete, clyte*, a wedge; from same root as D *kloot*, a ball; G *kloss*, lump, clod.]

1. A piece of wood or iron used in a ship to fasten ropes upon. It is formed with one arm or two, or with a hollow to receive a rope, and is made fast to some part of a vessel. There are several kinds of cleats on board vessels, such as belaying-cleats, deck-cleats, and thumb-cleats.

1 2 3

1. Cleat. 2. Deck-cleat. 3. Thumb-cleat.

2. A piece of iron worn on a shoe.

3. In joinery, a piece of wood nailed transversely or otherwise fastened, and used as a strengthener or support.

4. A trunnion-bracket on a gun-carriage.

5. In coal-mining, the principal set of planes or facings in the natural cleavage of coal.

çlēat, *v.t.*; cleated, *pt.*, *pp.*; cleating, *ppr.* To furnish with a cleat or cleats, so as to prevent warping or slipping; to strengthen.

çlēav′ȧ-ble, *a.* Capable of being cleaved or divided.

çlēav′āge, *n.* 1. The act of cleaving or splitting; the act of separating or dividing off.

2. The property observed in crystals of undergoing mechanical division in certain fixed directions.

3. In mineralogy and geology, the manner in which substances regularly cleave or split. It is used in relation to the fracture of minerals which possess a regular structure. Certain rocks, as slate-rocks in the strictest sense, may be cleft into an indefinite number of thin laminæ which are parallel to each other, but which are not necessarily parallel to the planes of the natural strata. *Cleavage* is the result of an operation which is subsequent to, and entirely independent of, the original stratification of the rocks.

In reference to mineral crystals, *cleavage* is called basal, cubic, diagonal, lateral, peritomous, or prismatic, according as it is parallel to the base of a crystal, to the faces of a cube, to a diagonal plane, to the lateral planes, or to a vertical prism.

Cell cleavage; in biology, increase of cells by the process of fission.

çlēave, *v.i.*; cleaved *or* clave, *pt.*; cleaving, *ppr.*; cleaved, *pp.* [ME *cleven, cleovien*; AS. *cleofian, clifian*, to stick, cleave.]

1. To stick; to adhere; to be attached; used both in a literal and figurative sense.

If any blot hath *cleaved* to mine hands.
—Job xxxi. 7.

2. To unite aptly; to fit closely; to assimilate. [Rare.]

New honors,
Like our strange garments, *cleave* not to their mold
But with the aid of use. —Shak.

3. To unite or be united closely in interest or affection; to adhere with strong attachment.

Who loved one only and *clave* to her
—Tennyson.

çlēave, *v.t.*; cleft, clove, *or* clave, *pt.*; cleaving, *ppr.*; cleft, cloven, *or* cleaved, *pp.* [ME. *cleven, cleoven*; AS. *cleofan*, to split, divide.]

1. To part or divide by force; to split or rive; to sever forcibly; to hew; to cut; as, to *cleave* wood; to *cleave* a rock.

His heart was *cleft* with pain and rage,
His cheeks they quivered, his eyes were wild.
—Coleridge.

2. To part or open naturally.

Every beast that parteth the hoof, and *cleaveth* the cleft into two claws.—Deut. xiv. 6.

çlēave, *v.i.* To part; to open; to crack; to separate as parts of cohering bodies; as, the ground *cleaves* by frost.

çlēave′lănd-ite, *n.* [After Professor Parker *Cleaveland.*] A mineral, generally of a white or grayish-white color, sometimes blue, or bluish, or reddish; called also *silicious feldspar*, or *albite.*

çlēav′ẽr, *n.* 1. One who or that which cleaves.

2. Specifically, a butcher's instrument for cutting carcasses into joints or pieces.

çlēav′ẽrṣ, çliv′ẽrṣ, *n.* [From *cleave*, to stick.] A plant, *Galium Aparine*, with a square, rough, jointed stem, the joints being hairy at the base, and each joint having eight or ten narrow leaves; its hooked prickles adhere to whatever they come in contact with; called also *goosegrass.*

çlēav′ing, *n.* The act of forcibly separating a body into parts, particularly wood in the direction of its fibers.

çle-çhé′, çle-çhée′ (-shā′), *a.* [Fr. *cléché, cléchée*, from L. *clavis*, a key.] In heraldry, a term applied to any ordinary voided or pierced throughout, and so much perforated that the chief substance is taken from it, leaving nothing visible but the edges. Thus a cross *cleché* is a cross with the inside taken out, leaving only an edge; it is more commonly blazoned a cross *voided.*

Cross cleché.

çleck, *v.t.* or *v.i.* [Scot. and Prov. Eng., from ME. *cleken*; Ice. *klekja*, to hatch.] To hatch; to litter.

çledġe (klej), *n.* [AS. *clæg*, clay.] In mining, the upper stratum of fuller's earth.

çledġ′y, *a.* In agriculture, a term applied to stubborn, tenacious soils, or those mixed with clay.

çlee, *n.* A claw. [Obs.]

çlee, *n.* The redshank.

çleek, *v.* and *n.* Same as *Cleik.*

çlef, *n.* [Fr. *clef*; OFr. *cle, clef*; L. *clavis*, a key.] A character in music, placed at the beginning of a staff, to determine the degree of elevation occupied by that staff, and to determine the names of the notes according to their position on the staff. There are three clefs: the *treble*, or G clef, 𝄞; the *mean*, or C clef, 𝄡; and the *bass*, or F clef, 𝄢. The mean clef is now seldom used.

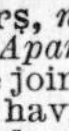

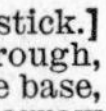

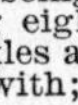

çleft, *v.*, past tense and past participle of *cleave.*

çleft, *a.* 1. Divided or partly divided; split; parted asunder.

2. In botany, divided half way down or further; as, a *cleft* leaf.

çleft, *n.* [ME. *clift, clyft*, a cleft; AS. *cleofan*, to cut.]

1. A space or opening made by splitting; a crack; a crevice; as, the *cleft* of a rock.

2. A disease in horses; a crack on the bend of the pastern.

3. A piece made by splitting; as, a *cleft* of wood.

Syn.—Fissure, crack, crevice, chink, opening, chasm.

çleft′=foot″ed, *a.* Having cleft or cloven feet.

çleft′grȧft, *v.t.* To ingraft a plant in (another) by cleaving the stock and inserting a scion.

çleg, *n.* [Scot. and Prov. Eng. *gleg*; Ice. *kleggi*, a horsefly.] A name applied to various insects, the females of which are troublesome to horses, cattle, and even man, from their blood-sucking habits; as the great horsefly or breeze, *Tabanus bovinus*, also called the gadfly; the *Chrysops cæcutiens*, and in Scotland the *Hæmatopota pluvialis*, a smaller grayish-colored fly.

çlei′dō-. See *Clido-.*

çlei′dō-man-cy, *n.* Same as *Clidomancy.*

çlēik, çleek, *v.t.* and *v.i.* [Scot.] I. *v.t.* To hook; to snatch; to seize; to catch, as by a hook; also, to steal.

II. *v.i.* To take a person's arm; to link together.

çlēik, çleek, *n.* [Scot.] 1. A large iron hook.

2. The arm.

3. A club with an iron head, used for driving in the game of golf.

çleiṡ′tō-. See *Clisto-.*

çleith′răl, *a.* See *Clithral.*

çlem, *v.t.* To cause to perish of hunger; to starve. [Prov. Eng.]

What! will he *clem* me? —B. Jonson.

çlem, *v.i.* To die of hunger; to starve. [Prov. Eng.]

Çlem′ȧ-tis, *n.* [L., from Gr. *klēmatis*, brushwood, clematis, from *klēma*, a vine, twig.] A genus of woody climbing plants, natural order *Ranunculaceæ.* There are many species, natives of temperate climates. *Clematis vitalba* is the common European traveler's-joy, which runs over the hedges. Improved cultivated varieties are much in favor as garden vines; called also *virgin's-bower.*

çlem′ence, *n.* Clemency. [Obs.]

çlem′en-cy, *n.* [L. *clementia*, mildness, from *clemens*, merciful.]

1. Mildness of temper, as shown by a superior to an inferior; disposition to spare or forgive; mercy; leniency.

I pray thee that thou wouldest hear us of thy *clemency* a few words. —Acts xxiv. 4.

2. Softness or mildness of the elements; as, the *clemency* of the weather.

Syn.—Mercy, lenity, compassion, mildness, gentleness, tenderness.

çlem′ent, *a.* [Fr. *clement*; L. *clemens*, mild, calm.]

1. Mild in temper and disposition; gentle; lenient; merciful; kind; tender; compassionate.

2. Of the weather, calm; soft and mild.

Çlem′ent-ine (*or* -in), *a.* Pertaining to St.Clement, or to his reputed compilations; or to the constitutions of Pope Clement V.

Çlem′ent-ine, *n.* 1. One of a series of compilations ascribed to St. Clement, a contemporary of St. Paul, but now believed to be apocryphal.

2. A decretal of Pope Clement V.

çlem′ent-ly, *adv.* With mildness of temper; mercifully.

çlench, çlinch, *v.t.*; clenched, *pt.*, *pp.*; clenching, *ppr.* [ME. *clenchen*, to clench, from same root as AS. *beclencan*, to fasten, knit.]

1. To gripe with the hand; to make fast by bending over, folding, or embracing closely; as, to *clench* a hammer; to *clench* the fist; to *clench* a nail.

2. To shut or bring together tightly; as, to *clench* the teeth.

3. To fix or fasten; to make firm; as, to *clench* an idea.

çlench, çlinch, *n.* 1. The act of holding or grasping firmly; that which serves to hold fast; a clutch; a clasp; a grip; as, to have a *clench* of an opponent, or of a sword; to hold with convulsive *clenches.*

2. A mode of securing a nail, a staple, etc., by turning over a portion of it and hammering it into the wood.

3. In nautical language, the part of a cable which is fastened to the ring of an anchor; also, the kind of knot used to fasten a cable to the ring of an anchor.

4. A pun; a witty reply; a play on words [Rare.]

Comick wit, degenerating into *clenches.*
—Dryden.

çlench′ẽr, *n.* 1. That which clenches; a cramp or piece of iron bent down to fasten anything; one who clenches.

2. One who makes a smart reply. [Rare.]

3. A decisive argument, or reply that puts an end to a controversy.

Çlē-ō′mē, *n.* [LL. *cleome*, an unidentified plant.] A large genus of herbaceous and shrubby plants, natural order *Capparidaceæ*, natives of tropical and warm regions of both hemispheres. A few of the species are cultivated for ornament, and others yield medicinal substances and condiments.

çlēpe, *v.t.* and *v.i.* [ME. *clepen*; AS. *cleopian*, to call, cry out.] To call or name; to cry out; to appeal. [Obs.]

Çlep′si-nē, *n.* [L., from Gr. *klepsia*, theft, from *kleptein*, to steal.]

1. A genus of fresh-water leeches typical of *Clepsinidæ*, having an elongated proboscis and feeding mostly on worms and mollusks.

2. [c—] A leech of this genus.

Çlep-sin′i-dæ, *n.pl.* A family of leeches characterized by a protractile proboscis; the type is *Clepsine*.

çlep′sy-drȧ, *n.*; *pl.* **çlep′sy-drȧṣ** or **çlep′sy-dræ.** [L. *clepsydra*; Gr. *klepsydra*, a water clock; *kleptein*, to steal, and *hydōr*, water.]

1. A device used by the Greeks and Romans, which measured time by the discharge of a certain quantity of water.

2. A chemical vessel.

1. Clepsydra, from an antique seal. 2. Clepsydra, medieval form.

çlep-tō-mā′ni-ȧ, klep-tō-mā′ni-ȧ, *n.* [L., from Gr. *kleptein*, to steal, and *mania*, madness.] A form of moral obliquity or mania characterized by an irresistible desire to steal, irrespective of personal requirements or the individual appropriateness of the articles selected.

çlep-tō-mā′ni-aç, klep-tō-mā′ni-aç, *n.* One affected with cleptomania.

çlēre′stō″ry, *n.* See *Clearstory*.

çlẽr′ġi-ăl, çlẽr′ġi-căl, *a.* Pertaining to the clergy; learned; clerkly. [Obs.]

> Oure termes ben so *clergial*, and queynte. —Chaucer.

çlẽr′ġi-on, *n.* [Fr., dim. of *clerc*, a clergyman, scholar.] A young chorister or choir-boy.

> A litel *clergion*, sevene yere of age.—Chaucer.

çlẽr′ġy, *n.* [ME. *clergie*; OFr. *clergie*, the office or dignity of a clergyman; LL. *clericus*, a clergyman, from Gr. *klēros*, a lot; lit. that which is assigned by lot.]

1. The body of men set apart, and formally consecrated to the service of the Christian church; the body of ecclesiastics, in distinction from the laity.

2. The privilege or benefit of *clergy*. [Obs.]

> If convicted of a clergyable felony, he is entitled equally to his *clergy* after as before conviction. —Blackstone.

3. A learned profession; learning. [Obs.]

Benefit of clergy; in English law, originally, the exemption of the persons of clergymen from criminal process before a secular judge; a privilege which was extended to all who could read, such persons being, in the eye of the law, *clerici*, or clerks. But this privilege was abridged and modified by various statutes, and was repealed in 1827.

çlẽr′ġy-ȧ-ble, *a.* Entitled to or admitting the benefit of clergy; as, a *clergyable* felony.

çlẽr′ġy-măn, *n.*; *pl.* **çlẽr′ġy-men.** A man in holy orders; a man regularly authorized to preach the Christian gospel, and administer its ordinances; in England, commonly restricted to a minister of the Established church.

çler′iç, *n.* 1. A clerk; a scholar. [Rare.]

2. A clergyman.

çler′iç, *a.* Same as *Clerical*.

çler′iç-ăl, *a.* 1. Relating or pertaining to the clergy.

2. Relating to a clerk, writer, or copyist.

Clerical error; an error inadvertently made by a person in writing out a document.

çler′iç-ăl-iṣm, *n.* Clerical power or influence, especially the undue influence of the clergy; sacerdotalism.

çler-ic′i-ty, *n.* The state or quality of being a clergyman. [Rare.]

çler′i-sy, *n.* 1. A body of clerks or learned men; the literati. [Rare.]

> The *clerisy* of a nation, that is, its learned men, whether poets, philosophers, or scholars. —Coleridge.

2. The clergy, as opposed to the laity. [Rare.]

çlẽrk, *n.* [ME. *clerc*, *clærk*; AS. *clerc*; LL. *clericus*, a clergyman, priest, from Gr. *klēros*, the clergy, lit. a lot, or that which is chosen by lot.]

1. A clergyman, or ecclesiastic; a man in holy orders. [Obs.]

2. A man who can read; a man of letters; a scholar. [Obs.]

3. The layman who leads in reading the responses in the service of the Episcopal church.

4. One who is employed in an office, public or private, or in a shop, store, or warehouse, for keeping records and accounts; as, a lawyer's *clerk*; a railroad *clerk*.

5. An assistant in a shop or store, who sells goods; a retail salesman; as, a grocery *clerk*.

6. An officer of a legislature, court, municipal corporation, or other body, whose duty is to keep its records and maintain its routine; as, the *clerk* of the Senate; the *clerk* of a district court; a city *clerk*; the *clerk* of a school-board, etc.

çlẽrk′-āle, *n.* In England, a feast for the benefit of the parish clerk; also, the ale provided for it. [Obs.]

çlẽrk′less, *a.* Ignorant; unlearned. [Obs.]

çlẽrk′like, *a.* Like a scholar; learned. [Obs.]

çlẽrk′li-ness, *n.* Clerkly skill; scholarship. [Obs.]

çlẽrk′ly, *a.* Of or pertaining to a clerk.

çlẽrk′ly, *adv.* In a learned manner. [Obs.]

çlẽrk′ship, *n.* 1. The state of being in holy orders.

2. Scholarship.

3. The office or business of a clerk or writer.

Çlē-rō-den′dron, *n.* [L., from Gr. *klēros*, lot, chance, and *dendron*, tree.] A large genus of trees and shrubs found in the tropical and subtropical climates of both hemispheres. They are allied to the genus *Verbena*.

çler′ō-man-cy, *n.* [Gr. *klēros*, lot, and *manteia*, divination.] Divination by throwing dice or beans, and observing the points or marks turned up.

çlē-ron′ō-my, *n.* [Gr. *klēronomia*, an inheritance, from *klēros*, lot, and *nemesthai*, to possess.] That which is given as his lot to any one; inheritance; heritage or patrimony.

çlē′ruçh, *n.* [Gr. *klērouchia*, the allotment of land in a foreign country; *klēros*, lot, and *echein*, to hold.] In Grecian history, an Athenian citizen colonized in a conquered country, without losing his citizenship.

çlē-ru′çhi-ăl, *a.* Of or pertaining to a cleruch, or the system of colonization by cleruchs.

Çlē′thrȧ, *n.* [Gr. *klēthra*, alder, which these plants resemble in foliage.] A genus of plants, natural order *Ericaceæ*, natives of the Americas. They are shrubs or trees, with alternate serrate leaves. One species, *Clethra alnifolia*, a native of Virginia and the Carolinas, is widely cultivated, and is one of the most beautiful of flowering shrubs.

çleugh, çleuçh (klụk), *n.* [Scot.] A cleft or gorge in a hill; a ravine; also, a cliff or side of a ravine.

> When in the *cleugh* the buck was ta'en. —Sir W. Scott.

çlēve, *n.* An old form of *cliff*.

çlēve′ite, *n.* A kind of uraninite found in Norway; named after Cleve, a Swedish mineralogist.

çlev′ẽr, *a.* [Etymology doubtful; probably of provincial origin.]

1. Performing or acting with skill or address; having the art of doing or devising anything readily; possessing ability of any kind, especially such as involves quickness of intellect or mechanical dexterity; as, a *clever* workman or speaker.

2. Indicative of or exhibiting cleverness; said of things; as, a *clever* speech; a *clever* trick.

3. Fit; suitable; convenient; proper; commodious. [Obs. or Prov. Eng.]

> These *clever* apartments. —Cowper.

4. Well-shaped; active-looking; tight; handsome. [Prov. Eng.]

5. Good-natured; obliging; possessing an agreeable mind or disposition. [Colloq.]

Syn.—Skilful, expert, dexterous, adroit.—One is *clever* who executes well without much instruction; one is *skilful* who understands both the theory and practice; he is *dexterous* when skilled as to handiwork; he is *adroit* if, by a quick, sudden, and well-directed movement, he effects the object he has in view.

çlev′ẽr-ish, *a.* Somewhat clever.

çlev′ẽr-ly, *adv.* In a clever or adroit manner.

çlev′ẽr-ness, *n.* 1. The quality of being clever; dexterity; adroitness; skill.

2. Mildness or agreeableness of disposition; obligingness; good nature. [Colloq.]

çlev′is, çlev′y, *n.* [From ME. *cleven*; AS. *cleofan*, to split.] An iron bent to the form of a horseshoe, with the two ends perforated to receive a pin, used on the end of a plow or wagon tongue to attach it to a whiffletree, etc.

çlew, *n.* and *v.* Same as *Clue*.

çlew′-gär″net, *n.* Same as *Clue-garnet*.

Çlī-an′thus, *n.* [L., from Gr. *kleos*, fame, glory, and *anthos*, a flower.] A genus of handsome shrubs of the bean family, *Leguminosæ*, two species being in cultivation, *Clianthus Dampieri*, or glory-pea, of Australia, and *Clianthus puniceus*, or parrot's-bill, of New Zealand.

çlī-çhé′ (-shā′), *n.* [Fr., pp. of *clicher*, to stereotype; OFr. *cliquer*, to clap.] An electrotype or stereotype plate.

Cliché casting; a method of casting a woodcut, etc., by suddenly pressing or striking the mold upon semimolten metal.

çlick, *v.i.*; clicked, *pt.*, *pp.*; clicking, *ppr.* [An imitative word.]

1. To make a small, sharp noise, or a succession of small, sharp sounds, as by a gentle striking.

> The solemn death-watch *clicked*. —Gay.

2. In farriery, to make a clicking noise with the shoes; said of horses.

çlick, *v.t.* To move with the sound of a click, or cause to make a click or clicks.

> When merry milkmaids *click* the latch. —Tennyson.

çlick, *v.t.* To snatch or snap up. [Prov. Eng.]

çlick, *n.* A pawl, detent, or small piece of iron, falling into a notched or ratchet wheel, attached to a winch, etc., to prevent backward motion.

çlick, *n.* 1. A small, sharp sound; as, the *click* of billiard-balls.

2. The latch of a door. [Prov. Eng.]

3. An articulation employed by Hottentots and other natives of South Africa, produced by the sudden withdrawal of the tip or side of the tongue from the teeth or palate; a cluck. There are several variations of this *click* or cluck, forming part of the native language.

çlick′-bee″tle, *n.* A beetle of the family *Elateridæ*, so named because of the clicking noise which it makes while righting itself, after being placed on its back. [See *Elater*.]

çlick′ẽr, *n.* 1. One who stands at a shop door to invite customers. [Eng. Slang.]

2. In printing, as sometimes conducted, the member of a companionship of compositors who distributes copy, makes up, and has general charge of the work.

3. In shoemaking, one who cuts out the leather and distributes the work.

çlick′et, *n.* The knocker of a door. [Prov. Eng.]

çlick′ing, *n.* A small, sharp noise.

çlick′y, *a.* Full of clicks or clucks; as, their *clicky* language.

Çlī-das′tēs, *n.* [L., from Gr. *kleis*, a key.] A remarkable genus of marine reptiles now extinct. The specimens found in the North American Cretaceous deposits vary from twelve to forty feet in length.

çlī′dō-, çleī′dō-. Combining forms from L. *clavis*, Gr. *kleis*, a key, signifying by means of or pertaining to a key; as, *clido*mancy; or, in anatomy, of or pertaining to the clavicle; as, *clido*mastoid.

çlī′dō-man-cy, çleī′dō-man-cy, *n.* [*Clido-*, and Gr. *manteia*, divination.] Divination by means of a key fastened into a book, especially the Bible, the object being to determine who is to be one's sweetheart.

çlī-dō-mas′toid, *a.* Pertaining to the clavicle and the mastoid process; as, the *clidomastoid* muscle.

çlī-dō-stẽr′năl, *n.* Pertaining to the clavicle or collar-bone and the sternum or breast-bone.

çlī′en-cy, *n.* The state of being a client.

çlī′ent, *n.* [OFr. *client*; L. *cliens*, a client, from *cluere*, to hear oneself called.]

1. Among the ancient Romans, a citizen who placed himself under the protection of a man of distinction and influence, who was called his patron.

2. One who applies to a lawyer or counselor for advice and direction in a question of law, or commits his cause to his management in prosecuting a claim, or defending a suit or criminal charge, in a court of justice.

3. A dependent; one under the protection of another.

çlī′ent-āġe, *n.* 1. The condition or relation of a client.

2. Clients or patrons in the aggregate.

çli-en′tăl, *a.* Dependent; relating to clients or clientage.

çlī′ent-ed, *a.* Supplied with clients. [Rare.]

çlī-en′te-lāġe, *n.* Clientele.

çlī-en-tele′ (*or* -tēl′), *n.* [Fr.] 1. The condition or office of a client. [Obs.]

2. Those who depend on any patron.

3. Clients collectively.

çlī′ent-ship, *n.* The condition of a client; a state of being under the protection of a patron.

çliff, *n.* [ME. *clif*, *clef*; AS. *clif*, a cliff.]

1. A steep bank or rugged face of rock; a headland; as, the *cliffs* of Dover.

2. A high and steep rock; any precipice.

çliff, *n.* In music, a clef. [Obs.]

clĭff'-brāke, *n.* A species of fern found on cliffs and old walls.

clĭff'-dwell"ẽr, *n.* One of the race of Indians living in Mexico or the southwestern portion of the United States, who dwelt in the sides of cliffs.

clĭff'-līme"stōne, *n.* A limestone found in the cliffs of the Ohio and Mississippi valleys, being of mixed Devonian and Silurian origin.

clĭff'-swäl"lōw, *n.* The eaves-swallow of North America, *Petrochelidon lunifrons.*

clĭff'y, *a.* Having cliffs; broken; craggy.

clĭft, *n.* A precipice; a cliff. [Obs.]

clĭft, *n.* A cleft or fissure. [Obs.]

clĭft'ed, *a.* Broken.

clī-mac'tẽr, *n.* [Obs.] See *Climacteric.*

clī-mac'tẽr-ic, *n.* [L. *climactericus*; Gr *klimaktērikos*, from *klimaktēr*, the step of a staircase, round of a ladder, from *klimax*, a ladder.] A critical period in human life, or a period in which some great change is supposed to take place in the human constitution. The critical periods are supposed, by some persons, to be the years produced by multiplying 7 into the odd numbers, 3, 5, 7, and 9; to which others add the 81st year. The 63d year is called the *grand climacteric.* It has been supposed that these periods are attended with some remarkable change in respect to health, life, or fortune.

clī-mac'tẽr-ic, clī-mac-ter'ic-ăl, *a.* Pertaining to a climacteric.

clī-mac'tic, *a.* Tending or relating to a climax.

clī'mȧ-tăl, *a.* A rare form of *climatic.*

clī-mȧ-tär'chic, *a.* [Gr. *klima*, a region, and *archein*, to rule.] Presiding over climates. [Obs.]

clī'māte, *n.* [ME. *climat*; OFr. *climat*; L. *clima*; Gr. *klima*, a region, zone.]

1. In old geography, one of thirty zones into which the surface of the earth was supposed to be divided from the equator to each pole. They were measured by lines parallel to the equator.

2. The condition of a place in relation to the various phenomena of the atmosphere, as temperature and moisture; as, a warm or cold *climate*; a favorable *climate*; a genial *climate.*

3. Any distinct portion of the earth's surface; a region; a clime.

clī'māte, *v.i.* To dwell; to reside in a particular region. [Poet.]

clī-mat'ic, clī-mat'ic-ăl, *a.* Pertaining to a climate or climates; limited by a climate.

clī-mȧ-tic'i-ty, *n.* The property of climatizing.

clī'mȧ-tīze, *v.t.*; climatized, *pt.*, *pp.*; climatizing, *ppr.* To accustom to a new climate, as a plant; to acclimatize.

clī'mȧ-tīze, *v.i.* To become accustomed to a new climate; as, plants will *climatize* in foreign countries.

clī-mȧ-tog'rȧ-phy, *n.* [Gr. *klima*, a region, zone, and *graphein*, to write.] An explanation or demonstration of the subject of climate.

clī"mȧ-tō-log'ic-ăl, *a.* Relating to climatology.

clī-mȧ-tol'ō-gist, *n.* A person who is expert in the science of climatology.

clī-mȧ-tol'ō-gy, *n.* [Gr. *klima*, climate, and *logos*, description.] The science of climates; the study of the causes on which the climate of a place depends.

clī'mȧ-tūre, *n.* A climate or region. [Obs.]

clī'max, *n.* [LL. *climax*, a climax, from Gr. *klimax*, a ladder, from *klinein*, to slope.]

1. Gradation; ascent; a figure of rhetoric, in which a sentence or series of sentences rises, as it were, step by step; or in which the expression which ends one member of the period begins the second, and so on, to the culmination.

2. The highest attainment or degree; the culminating point; the acme; as, the *climax* of one's fortunes.

To cap the climax; to attain the highest degree, whether of excellence or absurdity.

climb (klīm), *v.i.*; climbed, *pt.*, *pp.*; climbing, *ppr.* [ME *climben*; AS. *climban*, to climb.]

1. To creep up by little and little, or step by step; to mount or ascend, by means of the hands and feet.

2. To mount or ascend with labor and difficulty.

3. To mount or ascend by means of tendrils or adhesive fibers; applied to plants.

climb, *v.t.* 1. To ascend by means of the hands and feet, implying labor, difficulty, and slow progress; as, to *climb* a wall or a steep mountain.

2. Figuratively, to mount or ascend, with labor or a slow motion; as, to *climb* the ladder of fame.

Syn.—Clamber, ascend, arise, rise.

climb, *n.* A climbing; a distance which has been, or may be, climbed; as, it was a long *climb.*

climb'ȧ-ble, *a.* Capable of being climbed.

climb'ẽr, *n.* 1 One who climbs, mounts, or rises, by the hands and feet; one who rises by labor or effort.

2. A plant that creeps and rises on some support.

3. One of an order of birds that climb, as the woodpecker.

climb'ẽr, *v.i.* To climb; to mount with effort. [Obs.]

climb'ing, *n.* The act of ascending.

climb'ing-fẽrn, *n.* A fern of the genus *Lygodium*, widely distributed; a climbing and decorative plant.

climb'ing-fish, *n.* An amphibious fish, *Anabas scandens*, which travels or hops over the land and climbs trees by means of the spiny coverings of its gills. [See *Anabas.*]

climb'ing-ī"rons (-ūrnz), *n.pl.* A device consisting of iron hooks with sharp points, attached by a framework to the feet or legs, to assist in climbing telegraph-poles, etc.; also called *creepers.*

climb'ing-pẽrch, *n.* Same as *Climbing-fish.*

clime, *n.* [L. *clima.*] A climate; a tract or region of the earth. [Poet.]

> Whatever *clime* the sun's bright circle warms.
> —Milton.

clī-nā'men, *n.*; *pl.* **clī-nā'mi-nȧ.** [L. *clinamen*, an inclination, from *inclinare*, to bend; Gr. *klinein*, to bend.] Curve; turn; bend; bias.

clī-nan'dri-um, *n.* [L., from Gr. *klinē*, bed, and *anēr*, genit. *andros*, man.] A cavity in the column of some orchids in which the anthers rest; also called *androclinium.*

clī-nan'thi-um, clī-nan'thus, *n.* [L., from Gr. *klinē*, bed, and *anthos*, flower.] The flower-receptacle or clinium of a composite plant.

clinch, *n.* and *v.* See *Clench.*

clinch'ẽr-built, cliñk'ẽr-built (-bilt), *a.* Having the sides constructed with each strip, plank, or plate, overlapping the one beneath, like slates on the roof of a house; especially applied to boats or ships.

clinch'ẽr-wŏrk, *n.* In shipbuilding, etc., work which is clincher-built; opposed to *carvel-work*, in which the joints are flush.

cling, *v.i.*; clung, *pt.*, *pp.*; clinging, *ppr.* [ME. *clingen*, to adhere closely, to shrivel, shrink; AS. *clingan*, to shrink, shrivel.]

1. To adhere closely; to stick; to hold fast, especially by winding round or embracing; as, the tendril of a vine *clings* to its support.

2. To adhere or stick, as a viscous substance.

3. To adhere closely and firmly, in interest or affection; as, men of a party *cling* to their leader.

cling, *v.t.* 1. To dry up; to wither. [Obs.]

> Till famine *cling* thee. —Shak.

2. To cause to fasten or adhere closely, as by embracing. [Rare.]

> I *clung* my legs as close to his sides as I could.
> —Swift.

Syn.—Adhere, clasp, cleave, hang, hold, stick.

cling, *n.* The act of holding fast; attachment; devotion; clasp; an embrace. [Rare.]

cling'fish, *n.* Any species of gobioid fish that has a sucking-disk on the nether side of the body by which it adheres to rocks.

cling'stōne, *n.* A variety of peach, whose pulp adheres closely to the stone.

cling'y, *a.* Apt to cling; adhesive. [Rare.]

clin'ic, *n.* [Fr. *clinique*; LL. *clinicus*, a bed-ridden person, from Gr. *klinikos*, pertaining to the bed; *klinē*, a bed.]

1. Medical instruction given at the bedside, or in the presence of the patient whose symptoms are studied and whose treatment is considered.

2. A gathering of instructors, students, and patients, for the study and treatment of disease.

3. One confined to bed by sickness. [Rare.]

4. Formerly, one who received baptism on a sick-bed.

clin'ic, *a.* Same as *Clinical.*

clin'ic-ăl, clin'ic, *a.* 1. Pertaining to a clinic.

2. Pertaining to a sick-bed.

Clinical baptism; baptism upon a sick-bed or death-bed.

Clinical convert; one converted on his death-bed.

Clinical lecture; a discourse delivered by a medical instructor to students at the bedside of a patient, or in his presence.

Clinical surgery or *medicine*; that form of surgical or medical instruction which is imparted to the student at a clinic.

clin'ic-ăl-ly, *adv.* In a clinical manner; by the bedside.

clī-ni'ciăn (-nish'un), *n.* One skilled in practical medicine or surgery.

clī-nid'i-um, *n.*; *pl.* **clī-nid'i-ȧ.** [L., from Gr. *klinein*, to incline.] In botany, a filament that bears a spore, found in the follicle of some lichens.

clī-nique' (-nēk'), *n.* [Fr.] In medicine, same as *clinic.*

clin'i-um, *n.* Same as *Clinanthium.*

cliñk, *v.t.*; clinked, *pt.*, *pp.*; clinking, *ppr.* [An imitative word.] To ring or jingle; to cause to make a sharp sound or succession of such sounds; as, to *clink* glasses in drinking a toast.

cliñk, *v.i.* 1. To give forth a sharp, tinkling sound.

2. To jingle or rime in a humorous manner

cliñk, *n.* 1. A sharp sound, made by the collision of small sonorous bodies.

2. Money; chink. [Scot.]

cliñk, *n.* A jail; a prison. [Eng. Slang.]

cliñk, *v.t.* To hold fast; to clench. [Scot.]

clin'kănt, *a.* See *Clinquant.*

cliñk'ẽr, *n.* [D. *klinker*, a vitrified brick, which makes a sonorous sound when struck.]

1. Vitreous matter which collects in furnaces, grates, and stoves where coal is used.

2. A very hard kind of brick, sometimes called *Dutch clinker.*

3. A mass caused by the running together of bricks in a kiln.

4. A scale of black oxid of iron formed when iron is heated to redness in the open air.

cliñk'stōne, *n.* See *Phonolite.*

clī'nō-. A combining form from Gr. *klinein*, to bend or slope, signifying bent or inclined; as, *clino*diagonal; used principally in mineralogy and botany.

clī-nō-ax'is, *n.* Same as *Clinodiagonal.*

clī"nō-cē-phal'ic, *a.* Pertaining to clinocephaly.

clī-nō-ceph'ȧ-ly, *n.* [*Clino-*, and Gr. *kephalē*, head.] A flatness or slightly hollow condition of the cranium.

clī'nō-chlōre, *n.* [*Clino-*, and Gr. *chlōros*, yellowish green.] Same as *Ripidolite.*

clī"nō-dī-ag'ō-năl, *n.* [*Clino-*, and L. *diagonalis*; Gr. *diagōnios*, diagonal.] In crystallography, that diagonal or lateral axis in monoclinic crystals which forms an oblique angle with the vertical axis.

clī"nō-dī-ag'ō-năl, *a.* Pertaining to or in the direction of a clinodiagonal.

clī'nō-dōme, *n.* [*Clino-*, and Gr. *dōma*, a house.] A plane or dome in a monoclinic crystal that is parallel to the inclined lateral axis.

clī-nō-graph'ic, *a.* [*Clino-*, and Gr. *graphein*, to write.] Relating to the mode of projection in drawing in which the rays of light are supposed to fall obliquely on the plane of projection.

clī'noid, *a.* [Fr. *clinoide*, from Gr. *klinē*, a bed, and *eidos*, form.] Bed-like; in anatomy, applied to the four processes which are arranged like posts of a bedstead on the inner side of the sphenoid bone.

clī-nom'e-tẽr, *n.* [*Clino-*, and Gr. *metron*, a measure.] An instrument for measuring the dip of mineral strata, the inclination of an embankment, or the degree of a slope.

clin-ō-met'ric, clin-ō-met'ric-ăl, *a.* 1. Measured by or relating to the clinometer.

2. Relating to the measurement of oblique crystalline forms, or to solids having oblique angles between the axes.

clī-nom'e-try, *n.* The science of measuring the inclination or dip of rock-strata, or the slope of an embankment, etc.

clī-nō-pin'ȧ-coid, *n.* [*Clino-*, and Gr. *pinax*, a tablet, and *eidos*, form.] In crystallography, one of the two planes that are parallel to the vertical and inclined lateral axes of a monoclinic crystal.

clī'nō-prism, *n.* [*Clino-*, and Gr. *prisma*, a prism.] A variety of prism in a monoclinic crystal.

clī-nō-pyr'ȧ-mid, *n.* [*Clino-*, and Gr. *pyramis*, a pyramid.] A pyramid of a monoclinic crystal between the zone of unit pyramids and the clinodomes.

clī-nō-rhom'bic (-rom'), *a.* [*Clino-*, and Gr. *rhombos*, a rhombus.] In crystallography, monoclinic.

clī"nō-spō-ran'gi-um, *n.*; *pl.* **clī"nō-spō-ran'gi-ȧ.** [*Clino-*, and Gr. *sporos*, a sowing, and *angeion*, a vessel.] A conceptacle in lichens which contains filaments bearing clinospores.

clī'nō-spōre, *n.* [*Clino-*, and Gr. *sporos*, a sowing.] A spore produced at the summit of a clinidium, or spore-bearing filament, in a clinosporangium.

clī'nō-stat, *n.* [*Clino-*, and Gr. *statos*, verbal adj. from *istasthai*, to stand.] A device employed in the study of plant physiology, and consisting of a revolving disk controlled by clockwork.

clin'quănt (-kănt), *n.* [Fr., tinsel; D. *klinken*, tinsel.] Tinsel; false glitter; also written *clinkant.*

clin'quănt, *a.* Glittering; dressed in tinsel finery.

Clin-tō'ni-ȧ, *n.* A genus of North American plants of the lily family, named after the American statesman, DeWitt Clinton. They bear large lily-shaped flowers on a short peduncle.

Clī'ō, *n.* [L., from Gr. *Kleiō*, Clio, from *kleiein*, to celebrate; *kleos*, fame, glory.] In mythology, the Muse who presided over history and epic poetry. [See illus. p. 314.]

Clī-ō'nē, *n.* [L., from Gr. *Kleiō*, Clio.] A genus of pteropods without gills, constituting a favorite food for whales. *Clione papilionacea* occasionally appears on the eastern coast of the United States.

Clī-on'i-dæ, *n.pl.* [L., from Gr. *Kleiō*, Clio.]

The family of pteropods of which *Clione* is the type. They swim near the surface of the water by means of wing-like appendages at the sides of the head.

clip, *v.t.*; clipped *or* clipt, *pt.*, *pp.*; clipping, *ppr.* [ME. *clippen*; Ice. *klippa*, to clip, shear.]

1. To cut off with shears or scissors; to separate by a sudden stroke; as, to *clip* wool; to *clip* hair.

2. To diminish (coin) by paring the edge.

3. To curtail; to cut short, as words; as, to *clip* one's speech.

To *clip* the divine prerogative. —South.

Clio.—Antique statue, Villa Borghese, Rome.

To clip the wings; literally, to cut a bird's wings short, so as to deprive it of the power of flight; figuratively, to put a check on one's ambition; to render one less able to execute his schemes or realize his aspirations.

clip, *v.t.* [ME. *clippen*; AS. *clyppan*, to embrace.]

1. To confine; to hug; to embrace. [Rare.]

2. To fasten or hold together by pressure, as with a spring or a screw.

clip, *v.i.* To speed or move swiftly, as a horse, a falcon, or a boat.

Clips it down the wind. —Dryden.

clip, *n.* 1. A blow or stroke with the hand; as, he hit him a *clip*. [Colloq.]

2. An embrace. [Obs.]

3. A sheep-shearing.

4. The product of sheep-shearing; as, there will be a large *clip* this year.

5. A device for holding papers by means of a spring.

6. A metal clasp to hold the hook of a whiffletree.

7. In farriery, a projecting flange on the upper surface of a horseshoe, which partially embraces the wall of the hoof; also called *toe-clip*.

8. A device for closing a vent in a machine.

9. A rapid gait. [Slang.]

10. [*pl.*] Sheep-shears. [Scot.]

clip'pẽr, *n.* 1. One who clips; especially, one who clips off the edges of coin.

2. An apparatus or machine for clipping hair; clipping-shears.

3. A vessel with sharp, forward-raking bows, and masts raking aft, built and rigged for fast sailing; a name originally given to the Baltimore *clippers* which became famous for quick runs. Called also *clipper-ship*.

4. An Australian warbler; as, the wag-tail *clipper*.

5. The larva of a neuropter, used as angling-bait.

6. A person or animal that runs swiftly, or looks capable of running swiftly; a very smart person; something first-rate. [Colloq.]

clip'pẽr-built (-bilt), *a.* Built after the clipper type.

clipp'fish, *n.* [Dan. *klipfisk*.] Stockfish.

clip'ping, *n.* 1. The act of cutting off, curtailing, or diminishing; as, the *clipping* of coins.

2. That which is clipped off; a piece separated by clipping; as, a newspaper *clipping*.

clipt, *v.*, past tense and past participle of *clip*.

clique (klēk), *n.* [Fr.] A narrow circle of mutually-interested persons; a party; used commonly in a bad sense; as, a *clique* of corrupt politicians.

clique, *v.i.*; cliqued (klēkt), *pt.*, *pp.*; cliquing, *ppr.* To combine in a clique; to join a clique. [Colloq.]

cli'quish (-kish), *a.* Pertaining to a clique; disposed to be clannish.

cli'quish-ness, *n.* Disposition to associate with a clique or in cliques.

cli'quism (-kizm), *n.* The spirit or tendency of cliques; cliquishness.

clish'-clash, *n.* [Scot.] Chatter; gossip; silly talk.

clis'tō-. A combining form from Gr. *kleistos*, verbal adj. of *kleiein*, to close, signifying shut, closed; as, *clistocarp*.

clis'tō-cärp, cleis'tō-cärp, *n.* [*Clisto-*, and Gr. *karpos*, fruit.] In botany, a form of ascocarp, in which asci or spore-cases develop, and from which they are liberated by bursting the walls of the cell.

Clis-tō-cär'pē-æ, Cleis-tō-cär'pē-æ, *n.pl.* A group of cryptograms or mosses, the fruit of which usually opens by decay, thus discharging the spores.

clis-tō-cär'pous, cleis-tō-cär'pous, *a.* Of or pertaining to the *Clistocarpeæ*.

clis-tō-gam'ic, cleis-tō-gam'ic, *a.* [*Clisto-*, and Gr. *gamos*, marriage.] A term applied to certain flowers borne by many plants, as the dog-violet and wood-sorrel, remarkable for their small size and because they do not open.

clis-tog'ȧ-mous, cleis-tog'ȧ-mous, *a.* Same as *Clistogamic*.

clis-tog'ȧ-my, cleis-tog'ȧ-my, *n.* In botany, the state or condition of being clistogamous; opposed to *chasmogamy*.

clis-tog'e-nous, *a.* Same as *Clistogamic*.

clite, *n.* [ME. *clide*, *clete*; AS. *clite*, coltsfoot.] The goose-grass, *Galium Aparine*; the burdock, *Arctium Lappa*.

cli-tel'lum, cli-tel'lus, *n.* [L. *clitellæ*, a pack-saddle.] A part of the body of a full-grown earthworm, consisting of glands which have grown thick, various segments being joined together in a changed form for reproduction.

clith'răl, cleith'răl, *a.* [Gr. *kleithron*, a bar, from *kleiein*, to close.] In Greek architecture, having a roof that forms a complete covering; said of temples.

clith-rid'i-āte, *a.* [Gr. *kleithria*, a keyhole, from *kleiein*, to close.] In zoölogy, shaped like a keyhole.

cli'tō-ris, *n.* [L., from Gr. *kleitoris*, clitoris, from *kleiein*, to close, hide.] In anatomy, a small elongated organ of the female pudendum, concealed by the labia majora.

cliv'ẽrs, *n.* See *Cleavers*.

clives, *n.* [From ME. *cliven*; AS. *othclifan*, to adhere.] A hook having a spring tongue to close it to prevent unfastening.

cliv'i-ty, *n.* Inclination; ascent or descent. [Rare.]

clō-ā'cȧ, *n.*; *pl.* **clō-ā'cæ**. [L. *cloaca*, a sewer, from Early L. *cluere*, to cleanse.]

1. A common sewer.

2. A sink; a privy.

3. In birds, reptiles, amphibians, and many fishes, the common sewer of the body, into which are discharged the intestinal, urinary, and genital products.

clō-ā'căl, *a.* Pertaining to the cloaca.

clōak, *n.* [ME. *cloke*; OFr. *cloke*, a cloak; LL. *cloca*, a cloak.]

1. A loose outer garment worn over other clothes, both by men and women; properly, a garment without sleeves.

2. A cover; that which conceals; a disguise or pretext; an excuse; a fair pretense; as, a *cloak* for his faults.

clōak, *v.t.*; cloaked (klōkt), *pt.*, *pp.*; cloaking, *ppr.* 1. To cover with a cloak.

2. To hide; to conceal; to use a mask for.

clōak, *v.i.* To put on a cloak; also, to intrigue.

Syn.—Conceal, disguise, mask, veil, hide, cover, palliate, screen, mitigate, extenuate.

clōak'-bag, *n.* A bag in which a cloak or other clothes are carried; a portmanteau.

clōak'ed-ly, *adv.* In a concealed manner.

clōak'ing, *n.* 1. The act of covering with a cloak, or of concealing anything.

2. Material for cloaks.

clōak'room, *n.* A room in a place of public resort, as a theater, where wraps may be temporarily deposited.

cloam, clōme, *n.* [AS. *clām*, mud.] Earthenware or clay; crockery. [Prov. Eng.]

cloche, *n.* [Fr.] A bell-glass used by a gardener.

clō'chẽr, *n.* [Fr.] A bell-tower or belfry. [Obs.]

clock, *n.* [ME. *clock*, clock, bell; LL. *clocca*, bell.] An instrument for the measurement of time by the motion of its parts, and indicating the hours, minutes, and often seconds, by hands which move upon a dial-plate. It usually consists of a frame containing a train of toothed wheels operated by springs or weights and regulated by a pendulum or balance-wheel. It is most commonly constructed so as to signal the hour by the stroke of a hammer on a bell, and differs from a watch in not being adapted to be carried on the person.

The time will seem longer without a *clock* or hour-glass than with it. —Bacon.

A-clock; a corruption of *o'clock* used by some of the older English poets.

Astronomical clock; see under *Astronomical*.

Electric clock; a clock regulated by electricity, or one which is connected with an electromagnetic apparatus for recording the time.

O'clock; a contraction of the old form *of the clock*; as, What *o'clock?* It is twelve *o'clock*.

Ship's clock; a clock which strikes from one to eight bells, at intervals of a half-hour, in accordance with the divisions of a ship's watches.

clock, *n.* A figure or figured work in the ankle or side of a stocking.

clock, *n.* A large beetle; in particular, the European dung beetle, *Scarabæus stercorarius*. [Eng.]

clock, *v.* An obsolete form of *cluck*.

clocked, *a.* Ornamented with clocks or embroidered figures; as, *clocked* stockings.

clock'-māk"ẽr, *n.* One who makes clocks.

clock'-set"tẽr, *n.* One who regulates clocks.

Old Time the *clock-setter*. —Shak.

clock'wīse, *adv.* In the same direction as the hands move around the dial of a clock.

clock'wŏrk, *n.* 1. The machinery and movements of a clock, or any similar mechanism.

2. Figuratively, any well-regulated system by which work progresses regularly and smoothly.

clod, *n.* [ME. *clodde*; AS. *clott*, a round mass.]

1. A hard lump of earth or clay; a mass of earth and turf.

2. Turf; the ground. [Rare.]

3. That which is earthy, base, and vile, as the body of man compared to his soul. [Poet.]

4. A dull, gross, stupid fellow; a dolt.

5. A cut of beef from the fore-shoulder.

6. In coal-mining, indurated clay; bind. [Eng.]

7. A lump or mass in general.

8. A clot; as, *clods* of blood. [Obs.]

clod, *v.i.*; clodded, *pt.*, *pp.*; clodding, *ppr.* To collect into concretions, or a thick mass; as, *clodded* in clayey lumps.

clod, *v.t.* 1. To pelt with clods.

2. To throw in a violent manner; to hurl. [Scot.]

clod'dish, *a.* Having the characteristics of clods; earthy; base; gross; low; boorish; stupid.

clod'dish-ness, *n.* The state of being cloddish; boorishness.

clod'dy, *a.* 1. Consisting of clods; abounding with clods.

2. Earthy; mean; gross.

clod'hop"pẽr, *n.* A clown; a dolt; a rude or rustic fellow; a boor.

clod'hop"ping, *a.* Rude; boorish; clumsy; loutish.

clod'pāte, *n.* A stupid fellow; a dolt; a numskull.

clod'pāt"ed, *a.* Stupid; dull; doltish.

clod'pōll, *n.* A stupid fellow; a blockhead.

cloff, clough (klof), *n.* [Origin unknown.] Originally, in commerce, an allowance of two pounds made in every three hundredweight of certain goods; now, a small deduction of any kind from the original weight. [Eng.]

clog, *v.t.*; clogged, *pt.*, *pp.*; clogging, *ppr.* 1. To load or fill with something that retards or hinders motion; as, to *clog* the channel of a river.

2. To put on anything that hinders the action of; to shackle; as, to *clog* a steer.

3. To load with anything that encumbers; to burden; to embarrass; as, to *clog* commerce with impositions or restrictions.

clog, *v.i.* 1. To become loaded or encumbered with extraneous matter.

2. To coalesce; to unite and adhere in a cluster or mass.

clog, *n.* [ME. *clogge*, a lump, block; Scot. *clag*, an impediment, clog; AS. *clæg*, clay.]

1. Anything put upon an animal to hinder action, as a piece of wood fastened to its leg.

2. An encumbrance; that which hinders motion, or renders it difficult; hindrance; impediment.

Slavery is the greatest *clog* to speculation. —Swift.

3. [*pl.*] A term formerly applied to overshoes with thick soles of leather or wood for wet weather, now superseded by india-rubber overshoes; also, shoes with wooden soles now worn in clog-dancing.

4. A clog-dance.

5. A wooden sandal with an iron ring beneath, worn by women to protect the feet from wet; also called *patten*. [Eng.]

6. Same as *Clog-almanac*.

clog'-al"mȧ-nac, *n.* A rough form of almanac, kept by cutting notches and figures on a clog, or block of wood, bone, etc.; formerly much used in England.

clog'-dance, *n.* A dance performed in clogs or shoes with wooden soles.

clog'gi-ness, *n.* The state of being clogged.

clog'ging, *n.* Anything which clogs.

clog'gy, *a.* Capable of clogging or having power to clog; thick; gross.

cloi'sŏn, *n.* [Fr.] A dividing band or partition; especially, a band used in cloisonné work.

cloi-sŏn-né' (-nā'), *a.* [Fr., partitioned; *cloison*, a partition, from L. *claudere*, to close.] Having partitions; partitioned; a term applied to a form of enamel decoration, in which the parts are separated by wire bands, the interstices being afterward filled in with paste.

clois'tẽr, *n.* [ME. *cloister*, *cloyster*; OFr. *cloistre*, a cloister; L. *claustra*, that which closes, a bolt, a place shut in, from *claudere*, to close.]

1. Literally, a close; a close or inclosed place. Hence, a place of retirement; a monastery or nunnery; a house inhabited by monks or nuns.

2. In architecture, (a) an arcade or colonnade around an open court; (b) an arched way or covered walk running round the walls of certain portions of ecclesiastical, monastic, and college buildings; originally intended as a place for exercise and recreation.

Quiet *cloisters* and gardens. —Macaulay.

Syn.—Monastery, nunnery, convent, abbey, priory.—*Cloister* is generic, being a place of seclusion from the world; a *monastery* is usually for monks; a *nunnery* is always for women; a *convent* is a community of recluses; an *abbey*

and a *priory* are named from their heads, an abbot or prior

Part of the Cloister, Westminster Abbey.

lois'tēr, *v.t.*; cloistered, *pt., pp.*; cloistering, *ppr* 1. To confine in a cloister or monastery.

2. To shut up; to confine closely within walls; to immure; to shut up in retirement from the world.

lois'tēr-ăl, *a.* [Obs.] See *Cloistral.*

lois'tēred, *a* 1. Solitary; retired from the world.

2. Built around, as a court; inclosed.

lois'tēr-ēr, *n* One belonging to a cloister.

lois'tēr=gärth, *n.* The garden or yard surrounded by a cloister

lois'trăl, *a.* Pertaining to a cloister; resembling a cloister; also, secluded; retired.

lois'tress, *n.* A nun; a woman who has vowed religious retirement [Rare.]

lōke, *n.* An obsolete form of *cloak.*

lōmb (klōm), *v.*, past tense and past participle of *climb.* [Obs or Poet.]

long, çlonge, *v.*, past tense and past participle of *cling.* [Obs.]

lon'iç, *a.* [L *clonicus*, clonic, from Gr. *klonos*, any violent motion.] Shaking; convulsive; irregular; as, *clonic* spasm.

Clonic spasm, a spasm in which the muscles or muscular fibers contract and relax alternately, in quick succession, producing the appearance of agitation, as in epilepsy; used in contradistinction to *tonic spasm.*

lō'nus, *n.* [L., from Gr. *klonos*, any violent motion.] Irregular, violent contractions and relaxations of the muscles, symptomatic of certain nervous diseases

loom, *v.t* To close with glutinous matter. [Obs.]

loop, *n* [Imitative.] The sound made when a cork is drawn from a bottle, or an imitation of it

loot, *n.* [Scot.] The whole or part of a cloven hoof.

loot'ie, *n.* [Scot.] 1. A small hoof.

2. [C—] A name for the devil, in reference to the cloven hoofs.

lōṣe, *v.t.*; closed, *pt., pp.*; closing, *ppr.* [ME. *closen*, to shut; AS. *clysung*, a closing; L. *clausus, clusus*, pp. of *claudere, cludere*, to close.]

1. To shut; to make fast by pressing together, or by stopping an open place, as to intercept a passage; as, to *close* the eyes; to *close* a gate, door, or window.

2. To end; to finish; to conclude; to complete; to bring to a period; as, to *close* a speech, a bargain, or contract.

3 To unite, as the parts of a breach or fracture; to make whole; often followed by *up*; as, he *closed up* the wound.

4. To move or bring together; to unite separate bodies or parts of; as, to *close* the ranks of an army.

5. To bring into contact; to make continuous; as, to *close* an electric circuit; to sew or stitch together, as the parts of a shoe.

6. To come into conflict with; as, to *close* the enemy. [Obs]

Closed shop; see under *Shop*, n.

lōṣe, *v.i.* 1 To unite; to coalesce; to come together; often followed by *on* or *upon*; as, the shades of night *close upon* us.

2. To end; to terminate, or come to a period; as, the debate *closed* at six o'clock.

3. To begin a conflict or struggle; to come to close quarters; to grapple with an antagonist.

> If I can *close* with him, I care not for his thrust. —Shak.

4. To cover; to inclose; to encompass; to overwhelm; generally followed by *upon, over*, or *about.*

> The depths *closed* me round *about.* —Jonah ii. 5.

5. To agree; to come to an agreement.

To close on or *upon*; to agree on; to come to a mutual agreement.

To close with; to accede to; to consent or agree to; also, to come to an agreement with.

To close with the land; in nautical language, to approach the land.

çlōṣe, *n.* 1. Conclusion; termination; final end; as, the *close* of life; the *close* of day or night.

2. The manner of shutting; junction. [Obs.]

> The doors of plank were; their *close* exquisite. —Chapman.

3. A grapple, as in wrestling.

4. In music, the conclusion of a strain, or of a musical period.

çlōse, *n.* [ME. *clos, close*, a yard, bounds.]

1. An inclosed place; any place surrounded by a fence, wall, or hedge; specifically, the precinct of an abbey or cathedral.

2. In law, a piece of land held as private property, whether actually inclosed or not.

3. A narrow passage, leading from the street to a court and tenements; as, a *close* in Marylebone. [Eng.]

çlōse, *a.* [ME. *close, clos*; OFr. *clos*, from *clore*, to shut.]

1. Shut fast; tight; made fast, so as to have no opening; as, a *close* box.

2. Having parts firmly united; compact; dense, applied to solid substances of any kind; as, the *close* texture of wood or metal.

3. Having parts firmly adhering; viscous; tenacious, as oil, or glue. [Rare.]

4. Confined; stagnant; oppressive; without ventilation or motion; applied to the air or weather.

5. Confined; secluded from communication; retired; as, a *close* prisoner

6. Hidden; private; secret; as, to keep a purpose *close.*

7. Confined within narrow limits; narrow; as, a *close* alley.

8. Near; within a small distance; as, a *close* fight or action.

9. Joined; in contact, or nearly so; crowded; as, to sit *close.*

10. Compressed, as thoughts or words; hence, brief; concise; opposed to *loose* or *diffuse.*

> When the original is *close*, no version can reach it in the same compass. —Dryden.

11. Very near, in place or time; adjoining, or nearly so.

> Some dire misfortune follows *close* behind. —Pope.

12. Having the quality of keeping secrets, thoughts, or designs; cautious; reticent; as, a *close* minister.

13. Intimate; familiar; confidential; as, a *close* friend.

14. Having an appearance of concealment; implying craft or wariness; as, a *close* aspect.

15. Intent; fixed; attentive; careful; as, to give *close* attention.

> Keep your mind *close* to the business. —Locke.

16. Pressing; earnest; warm; as, a *close* debate.

17. Nearly equal; almost evenly balanced; as, a *close* vote.

18. Short; as, to clip hair or grass *close.*

19. Tied up; scarce; difficult to get; tight; as, money is *close.* [Colloq.]

20. Niggardly; penurious; parsimonious; stingy; as, a *close* man.

21. Adhering closely to an original; literal; exact; strict; as, a *close* copy; a *close* translation.

22. Fitting tightly, or snugly; as, a *close* cap.

23. In heraldry, (a) having the wings lying close to the body; said of birds; (b) having the vizor of a helmet down.

Close communion; see under *Communion.*

Close corporation; a corporation in which the vacancies are filled by the corporation itself.

Close harmony; see under *Harmony.*

Close vowel; a vowel which is pronounced with partially closed lips or with a contraction of the cavity of the mouth.

To come to close quarters; to come into direct contact, especially with an enemy.

Syn.—Compact, compressed, dense, miserly, niggardly, firm, narrow.

çlōse, *adv.* At a little distance; near; closely; secretly; pressingly.

> Behind her Death
> *Close* followed, pace for pace. —Milton.

Close to the wind; in nautical language, with the head directed as nearly as possible to the point from which the wind blows; close-hauled; said of a vessel under sail.

çlōse'=band"ed, *a.* In close order; closely united.

çlōse'=bärred, *a.* Made close by bars; firmly closed.

çlōse'=bod"ied (-id), *a.* Fitting the body exactly, as a garment.

çlōse'=cŏm-paçt"ed, *a.* In compact order; compact.

çlōse'=cŭr"tained (-tind), *a.* Inclosed or surrounded with curtains.

çlōse'=fīghts, *n.pl.* Strong bulkheads or barriers of wood formerly used in a ship for defense when it was boarded; called also *close-quarters.*

çlōse'fist"ed, *a.* Extremely covetous or niggardly.

çlōse'hand"ed, *a.* Covetous; penurious.

çlōse'hand"ed-ness, *n.* Covetousness.

çlōse'hauled, *a.* In seamanship, having the sails drawn close to windward, and the sheets hauled close aft, in sailing near the wind, i. e., near that point from which the wind blows.

çlōse'ly, *adv.* 1. In a close, compact manner.

2. Nearly; with little space intervening; applied to space or time; as, to follow *closely* at one's heels; one event follows *closely* upon another.

3. Intently; attentively; with the mind or thoughts fixed; as, to look or attend *closely.*

4. Secretly; privately. [Rare.]

5. With near affection, attachment, or interest; intimately; as, men *closely* connected by friendship.

6. Strictly; within close limits; without communication abroad; as, a prisoner *closely* confined.

7. With strict adherence to the original; as, to translate *closely.*

çlōse'mouthed, *a.* Reticent; wary; uncommunicative.

çlōs'en, *v.t.* To make close or closer. [Rare.]

çlōse'ness, *n.* The state or quality of being close, according to the nature of the thing to which the word is applied.

Syn.—Nearness, narrowness, strictness, stinginess, intimacy, literalness.

çlōse'=pent, *a.* Shut close.

çlōse'=quar"tērṣ, *n.* See *Close-fights.*

çlōṣ'ēr, *n.* 1. One who or that which closes or concludes; a finisher.

2. A clencher; a settler. [Colloq.]

3. In building, the last stone or brick in a horizontal row, of smaller size than the others and fitted to close the row.

4. In shoemaking, one who or that which closes or sews the seams in boots or shoes.

çlōse'reef, *v.t.* To take in all the reefs of; to reef closely; said of sails.

çlōse'=sēa"ṣŏn, *n.* Certain months of the year during which it is unlawful to kill or catch certain game, fish, etc.; also called *close-time.*

çlōse'=stool, *n.* A box with a tight cover containing a chamber vessel, for the convenience of the sick and infirm.

çloṣ'et, *n.* [ME. *closet*; OFr. *closet*, a small inclosure, dim. of *clos*, an inclosed place.]

1. A small room or apartment for retirement; any room for privacy; as, a dressing-*closet.*

2. A small, close apartment, or recess, in the side or corner of a room for depositing or storing articles; as, a china-*closet*; a clothes-*closet.*

3. A small room used as a lavatory; a privy; a water-closet.

4. In heraldry, a diminutive of the bar, having one-half of its width.

çloṣ'et, *v.t*; closeted, *pt., pp.*; closeting, *ppr.*

1. To shut up in a closet; to conceal, as in a closet.

2. To admit or take into a private room for consultation; to admit to a confidential conversation.

çloṣ'et, *a.* Suitable to, performed in, or admitted to privacy; as, a *closet* picture; *closet* devotions; a *closet* friend.

çlōse'=time, *n.* See *Close-season.*

çlōse'tŏngued (-tungd), *a.* Secretive; cautious in speaking; closemouthed.

çlosh, *n.* [Fr. *clocher*; OFr. *clochier*; L. *claudere*, to limp.] A disease in the feet of cattle; laminitis; also called *founder.*

çlosh, *n.* A bowling-game wherein nine pins are used instead of ten; the game of ninepins. [Obs.]

çlō'ṣure (klō'zhūr), *n.* [OFr. *closure*; L. *clausura*, a closing, from *claudere*, to close.]

1. The act of shutting; a closing; as, the *closure* of a manufactory.

2. That which closes, or shuts; that by which separate parts are fastened or made to adhere.

3. Inclosure; that which confines.

4. Conclusion. [Obs.]

5. In parliamentary practice, a method, first adopted in the British House of Commons, in 1882, for closing a debate so that a vote could be taken upon the measure before the House without any delay. This mode of procedure was originally known by the French word *clôture.* It is similar in effect to putting the previous question.

çlot, *n.* [ME. *clot, clotte*; AS. *clott*, a round mass.] A concretion or coagulation, particularly of soft or fluid matter, which forms into a mass or lump; as, a *clot* of blood. *Clod* and *clot* appear to be radically the same word; but we usually apply *clod* to a hard mass of earth, and *clot* to a mass of softer substances, or fluids concreted.

çlot, *v.i.*; clotted, *pt., pp.*; clotting, *ppr.* To concrete; to coagulate, as soft or fluid matter, into a thick, inspissated mass; as, milk or blood *clots.*

clot, *v.t.* To make into, or cover with clots.

clot'bŭr, *n.* [G. *klette.*]
1. Burdock.
2. The cocklebur.

clōte, *n.* [ME. *clote, cloothe*; AS. *clāte*, the burdock.] The burdock or clotbur. [Obs.]

cloth (*or* kloth), *n.* [ME. *cloth*; AS. *clāth*, cloth.]
1. A manufacture or stuff of wool or hair, or of cotton, flax, hemp, or other vegetable filaments, formed by weaving or intertexture of threads, and used for garments or other covering, and for various other purposes; as, woolen *cloth*, linen *cloth*, cotton *cloth*, hair*cloth*. But *cloth*, as a commercial term, is often used for a fabric of wool, in contradistinction to that made of other material.
2. The covering of a table; usually called a *tablecloth*.
3. The finished canvas which is used as a drop-curtain in a theater, or the scene rolls.
4. A texture or covering put to a particular use; as, a *cloth* of state.
5. Dress; raiment. [Obs. See *Clothes.*]
Cloth measure; the standard measure of length and width by which cloth is sold. When used for measuring cloth, the standard yard is divided into quarters and nails, there being 4 nails of 2¼ inches each to a quarter yard.
Cloth of gold; a cloth, the threads of which are wholly or partially of gold.
Cloth paper; paper of a coarse nature used in pressing woolen cloths.
Cloth shearer; one who shears cloth and removes the nap from its surface.
The cloth; familiarly used for the clerical profession or clergy; as, a credit to *the cloth*; it is also used in a general way for the special dress of any of the professions.

clōthe, *v.t.*; clothed *or* clad, *pt., pp.*; clothing, *ppr.* [ME. *clothen*; AS. *clāthian*, to clothe.]
1. To put garments on; to invest with raiment; to cover with dress, for concealing nakedness and defending the body from cold or injuries.

> The Lord God made coats of skin and *clothed* them. —Gen. iii. 21.

2. To cover with something; to dress.

> Embroidered purple *clothes* the golden beds. —Pope.

3. To put on; to invest; to cover, as with a garment; as, to *clothe* thoughts with words.
4. To invest; to give to by commission; as, to *clothe* with power or authority.
5. In nautical language, to rig, as a mast.

clōthe, *v.i.* To wear clothes. [Rare.]

> Care no more to *clothe* and eat. —Shak.

clōthes, *n.pl.* [ME. *clothes*; AS. *clāthas*, clothes, pl. of *clāth*, a garment.]
1. Covering for the human body; dress; vestments; vesture; a general term for whatever covering is worn, or made to be worn, for decency or comfort.
2. The covering of a bed; bedclothes.
Syn.—Apparel, array, attire, dress, garments, raiment, vesture, habit, garb, habiliments.

clōthes'-bȧs"ket, *n.* A large basket for holding or carrying clothes.

clōthes'-brush, *n.* A brush for removing dust, etc., from clothes.

clōthes'-horse, *n.* A framework on which to hang clothes; usually so constructed that it may be either folded or expanded.

clōthes'-line, *n.* A rope or wire on which clothes are hung to dry or to be aired.

clōthes'-moth, *n.* A moth belonging to the genus, *Tinea*, the larvæ of which feed on furs, woolen goods, etc. They construct tubular cases from the material upon which they feed, and live in them.

Clothes-moths.
a, *Tinea tapetzella*, the woolen clothes-moth; *b*, the case of the caterpillar, *Tinea pellionella*, which infests furs.

clōthes'pin, *n.* A device for securing clothes on a line; made in the form of a forked piece of resilient wood or of a small spring clamp.

clōthes'press, *n.* A case or closet in which clothes are kept; a wardrobe.

clōth'iėr, (-yĕr), *n.* A person who makes or sells clothes; one who dresses or fulls cloth.

clōth'ing, *n.* [ME. *clothing*, from AS. *clāth*, cloth.]
1. Garments in general; clothes; dress; raiment; covering.
2. The art or practice of manufacturing cloth. [Rare.]

> The king took measures to instruct the refugees from Flanders in the art of *clothing*. —Ray.

3. A jacket of nonconducting material for a boiler, engine-cylinder or pipe to prevent radiation of heat.
4. Strips of wire-toothed card used on carding machines as a cover for the cylinders. [See *Card-clothing.*]

Clō'thō, *n.* [L., from Gr. *Klōthō*, one of the three Fates, the spinster, from *klōthein*, to spin.] In classic mythology, she, of the three Fates, who holds the distaff and spins the thread of life.

clot'hred (-ērd), *v.*, pp. of *clotter*. [Obs. Same as *Clottered.*]

clot'pōll, *n.* A thickskull; a blockhead. [See *Clodpoll.*]

clot'ted, *a.* Concreted into a mass; inspissated; adhering in a lump.
Clotted cream; cream obtained by warming new milk.

clot'tēr, *v.i.*; clottered *or* clothred, *pt., pp.*; clottering, *ppr.* To concrete or gather into lumps. [Obs.]

clot'ty, *a.* Full of clots, or small, hard masses; full of concretions, or clods.

clō-tūre', *n.* [Fr.] See *Closure.*

cloud, *n.* [ME. *cloud, cloude*, a cloud; AS. *clud*, a mass of rock.]
1. A collection of visible vapor, or watery particles, suspended in the atmosphere at an average height of about two miles. A like collection of vapors near the earth is usually called *fog*. *Clouds* are distributed into four fundamental classes, depending on their prevailing forms, viz., *cumulus, stratus, cirrus*, and *nimbus*; and three subordinate varieties, composed of mixtures of the others, viz., *cirro-cumulus, cirro-stratus*, and *cumulo-stratus*.
Cumulus; this form appears in great masses and piles with curved edges, often looking like mountains of cotton.
Stratus; a form which presents the appearance of horizontal layers.
Cirrus; a thin, drawn-out cloud, called *cat's-tail* by sailors and *mare's-tail* by landsmen. It lies at the highest altitude of the four.
Nimbus; popularly known as *rain-cloud*. It is gray and ragged, and covers the sky during storms.
Cirro-cumulus; popularly called *mackerel-sky*, resembles cirrus, but is somewhat rounded and divided into regular formation.
Cirro-stratus; this variety has the general appearance of cirrus, but is arranged in layers like stratus.
Cumulo-stratus; a cross between cumulus and stratus, which often presents a blue-black tint at the horizon.
Storm-scud; a formless cloud, driven rapidly near the earth by the wind.

Cumulus.

Stratus.

Cirrus.

Nimbus.

2. A collection of smoke, or a dense collection of dust, rising or floating in the air; as, a *cloud* of dust.
3. A vein or spot of lighter or darker color than the area surrounding it, as in stones, yarn, varnish, etc.
4. A great multitude; a vast collection; as, a *cloud* of witnesses.
5. Figuratively, a state of obscurity, darkness, or danger; as, amidst the *clouds* of wa[r]; a *cloud* hung over his character; there was [a] *cloud* thrown over their prospects.
6. A soft loosely-knitted woolen scarf, wor[n] by women as a wrap for the head and neck.
Cloud on a (or *the*) *title*; an unexplained o[r] obscure connection in a title to property whic[h] can often be cleared up by action in a court o[f] chancery or by appeal to a legislative body.
In the clouds; visionary; to soar in fancy o[r] imagination.
To be under a cloud; to be an object of sus[picion] or out of favor.

cloud, *v.t.*; clouded, *pt., pp.*; clouding, *ppr.*
1. To overspread with a cloud or clouds; as, th[e] sky is *clouded*.
2. To obscure; to darken; as, to *cloud* th[e] rays of truth or reason.
3. To darken in veins or spots; to variegat[e] with colors; as, to *cloud* yarn.
4. To make of a gloomy aspect; to give th[e] appearance of sullenness.

> What sullen fury *clouds* his scornful brow. —Pope.

5. To sully; to tarnish.

cloud, *v.i.* To grow cloudy; to become obscur[e] with clouds; sometimes followed by *over*; as, the sky *clouds over*.

cloud'āge, *n.* Prevalence of clouds. [Rare.]

cloud'ber"ry, *n.* A plant, called also *knotberry*, *Rubus chamæmorus*.

Cloudberry (*Rubus chamæmorus*).

cloud'-built (-bilt), *a.* Located in or built of clouds; hence, imaginary.

cloud' bŭrst, *n.* A sudden downpour of rain, accompanied sometimes by violent wind, as though a cloud had burst; often very destructive to life and property.

cloud'-capped, cloud'-capt, *a.* Capped with clouds; touching the clouds; lofty.

cloud'-cŏm-pel"ler, *n.* He that collects clouds; Jove. [Poet.]

cloud'-cŏm-pel"ling, *a.* Collecting clouds; o[r] driving clouds; as, *cloud-compelling* Jove.

cloud'ed, *a.* Overcast; overspread with clouds; obscured; darkened; rendered gloomy o[r] sullen; variegated with colored spots or veins; as, the *clouded* sky; *clouded* marble.

cloud'i-ly, *adv.* With clouds; darkly; obscurely.

cloud'i-ness, *n.* 1. The state of being overcas[t] with clouds; as, the *cloudiness* of the atmos[phere].
2. Darkness of appearance; variegation o[f] colors in a fossil or other body.

cloud'ing, *n.* 1. A clouded appearance, espe[cially] like that imparted to ribbons and silks i[n] the process of dyeing.
2. A variety of colors in yarn, appearing a[t] regular intervals.

cloud'land, *n.* The realm of clouds and shad[ows]; the land of fancy and dreams.

cloud'less, *a.* Without a cloud; unclouded; clear; bright; luminous; as, *cloudless* skies.

cloud'less-ly, *adv.* Without clouds.

cloud'less-ness, *n.* The condition of bein[g] clear; the state of being without clouds.

cloud'let, *n.* A little cloud.

cloud'y, *a.* 1. Overcast with clouds; obscure[d] with clouds; as, a *cloudy* day.
2. Consisting of a cloud or clouds.

> The *cloudy* pillar descended.—Ex. xxxiii. 9.

3. Obscure; dark; indistinct; not easily un[der]stood; as, *cloudy* notions.
4. Having the appearance of gloom; indica[ting] gloom, anxiety, sullenness, or ill-nature; not open or cheerful; as, *cloudy* looks.
5. Marked with veins or spots of dark or va[rious] hues, as marble.
6. Lacking clearness or luster; as, a *cloudy* diamond.

clough (kluf), *n.* [ME. *clough*; Ice. *klofi*, a clef[t] or rift in a hill, from *kljufa*, to split.]
1. A cleft, ravine, or valley in a hill-side; [a] small wooded hollow. [Prov. Eng.]
2. A kind of sluice for letting off water, em[ployed] in the operation of improving land by flooding it with muddy water; in this sens[e] also *clow*.

clough (kluf), *n.* Same as *Cloff.*

clour, *n.* [Scot.] 1. A blow.
2. An indentation produced by a blow, or a raised lump produced by a blow on the person.

clout, *n.* [ME. *clout, clut*; AS. *clūt*; W. *clwt*, [a] patch.]
1. A patch; a piece of cloth or leather, etc. used to mend something.

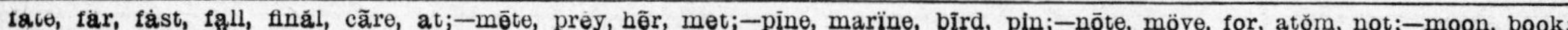

2. Any piece of cloth, especially a worthless piece; sometimes, a swaddling-band; a dish-clout.

3. In archery, the nail fixed in the center of the target at which archers are shooting.

He'll ne'er hit the *clout*. —Shak.

4. An iron plate on an axletree to keep it from wearing.

5. A blow with the hand. [Prov. Eng.]

clout, *v.t.* 1. To patch; to mend by sewing on a clout or patch.

2. To cover with a piece of cloth.

3. To join clumsily.

4. To strike; to beat. [Prov. Eng.]

5. To stud or fasten with clout-nails.

clout'ed, *a.* 1. Patched; mended clumsily; covered with a clout.

2. Studded, strengthened, or fastened with clout-nails.

3. Clotted; as, *clouted* cream. [Prov. Eng.]

clout'-nail, *n.* 1. A short, large-headed nail worn in the soles of shoes.

2. A nail for securing clouts or small patches of iron, as to the axletree of carriages; called also simply *clout*.

clōve, *n.* [D. *klove*, *kloof*, a cleft.] A ravine; a mountain pass; a gully.

clōve, *n.* [ME. *clowe*; Sp. *clavo*, a clove, from L. *clavus*, a nail; so called from its shape.] A biting fragrant spice, the dried flower-buds of *Caryophyllus aromaticus*, a tree growing in the West Indies, British India, Ceylon, and Mauritius, and belonging to the myrtle tribe.

Clove (*Caryophyllus aromaticus*).

clōve, *n.* [ME. *clove*; AS. *clufe* (pl., sing. not used), clove, from *cleofan*, to cleave.]

1. One of the small bulbs formed in the axils of the scales of a mother bulb, as in garlic.

2. A provincial English term for a weight of about seven pounds, used in weighing cheese or wool.

clōve, *v.*, past tense of *cleave*.

clōve'-gil'ly-flow"ēr, clōve'-piṅk, *n.* Any carnation having a sweet odor; in particular, the large, deep red, almost claret-colored, flower having a particularly clovelike scent.

clōve'-hitch, *n.* See under *Hitch*.

clōve'-hook, *n.* One of a pair of overlapping hooks; sometimes called a *sister-hook*.

clō'ven, *a.* [ME. *cloven*; AS. *clofen*, pp. of *cleofan*, to cleave.] Divided; parted.

To show the cloven hoof; to exhibit signs of an evil nature or bad intention, the devil being supposed to have cloven hoofs.

clō'ven, *v.*, past participle of *cleave*.

clō'ven-foot"ed, clō'ven-hoofed, *a.* 1. Having the foot cleft or divided into two parts, as the hog; bisulcate.

2. Satanic; devilish.

clō'vēr, *n.* [ME. *clover*; AS. *clafre*, clover.] A plant of the various species of the genus *Trifolium*, order *Leguminosæ*. The species, of which there are about 150, are low herbs, chiefly found in the temperate regions of the northern hemisphere. Some species are merely weeds, but many are valued as food for cattle. The *red clover*, *Trifolium pratense*, is generally cultivated for fodder and for enriching land. The *white clover*, *Trifolium repens*, is also excellent food for cattle, either green or dry, and its blossoms an important source of honey supply. *Alsike clover* is in high repute, and *Italian* or *crimson clover*, *Trifolium incarnatum*, is also cultivated for ornament and recommended by authorities as yielding a heavy crop. The name *clover* is often applied to plants cultivated for the same purpose and belonging to the same natural order, although not of the same genus.

In clover, or *to live in clover*; to be in most enjoyable circumstances; to live luxuriously.

clō'vēred, *a.* Covered with clover.

clō'vēr-wee"vil, *n.* A kind of weevil, genus *Apion*, different species of which feed on the seeds of the clover, as also on tares and other leguminous plants.

clō'vēr-wōrm, *n.* A moth, *Asopia costalis*, the larvæ of which are very destructive to clover hay.

clow, *n.* Same as *Clough*.

clowe'-gi-lof"re (-ēr), *n.* The spice-clove. [Obs.]

clown, *n.* [ME. *cloune*; Ice. *klunni*, a clumsy, boorish fellow.]

1. A countryman; a rustic.

2. One who has the manners of a rustic; a churl; a man of coarse manners; an ill-bred man.

3. The fool or buffoon in a circus or like entertainment.

clown, *v.i.* To behave like a clown. [Obs.]

clown'age, *n.* The manners of a clown. [Obs.]

clown'ēr-y, *n.* Ill-breeding; rustic behavior; rudeness of manners.

clown'heal, *n.* A plant supposed to heal wounds; called also *clown's woundwort*.

clown'ish, *a.* Pertaining to or resembling clowns; of rough manners; ill-bred; awkward.

Syn.—Boorish, bucolic, awkward, clumsy, rude.

clown'ish-ly, *adv.* In a clownish manner; rudely.

clown'ish-ness, *n.* The manners of a clown; rusticity; coarseness or rudeness of behavior; incivility; awkwardness.

cloy, *v.t.*; cloyed, *pt.*, *pp.*; cloying, *ppr.* [Fr. *clouer*, to nail; *clou*, a nail; L. *clavus*, a nail.]

1. Strictly, to fill; to choke up; to obstruct.

2. To glut; to satisfy, as the appetite; to satiate.

Who can *cloy* the hungry edge of appetite
By bare imagination of a feast? —Shak.

3. Figuratively, to fill to loathing; to surfeit.

4. To spike, as a gun; to drive a spike into, as a vent.

5. In farriery, to prick or lame (a horse) in shoeing. [Obs.]

6. To claw. [Obs.]

cloy'less, *a.* Not cloying; not filling to satiety.

cloy'ment, *n.* Surfeit; repletion beyond the demands of appetite. [Obs.]

club, *n.* [ME. *club*, *clubb*, a club; Ice. *klubba*, *klumba*, a club, a mass of anything.]

1. A stick or piece of wood, with one end thicker and heavier than the other, and no larger than can be wielded with the hand; in golf, the implement with which the ball is struck; a policeman's billy.

2. The name of one of the suits of cards; so named from its figure; in the plural, the suit of *clubs*.

3. An association of persons who meet under certain self-imposed regulations, for the promotion of some common object, as literature, science, goodfellowship, politics, etc.

4. An association for the support of a clubhouse.

5. The dividend of expense at a *club* or some meeting; as, to pay one's *club*.

Indian clubs; see under *Indian*.

club, *v.i.*; clubbed, *pt.*, *pp.*; clubbing, *ppr.* 1. To join, as a number of individuals, to the same end; to contribute separate powers to one end, purpose, or effect.

Till grosser atoms, tumbling in the stream
Of fancy, madly met, and *clubbed* into a
dream. —Dryden.

2. To pay an equal proportion of a common reckoning or charge, or by contribution.

3. To be driven along by a current, with an anchor out; a nautical term.

club, *v.t.* 1. To unite for the accomplishment of a common end; as, to *club* exertions.

2. To raise by a proportional assessment; as, to *club* the expense.

3. To strike with a club or with anything used as a club; said of policemen in the United States when they use their billies.

4. To throw, or permit to fall, into disorder; said in reference to a company of soldiers.

club'a-ble, club'ba-ble (-bl), *a.* A colloquial word denoting possession of qualities that fit a person to be a member of a club; sociable.

clubbed, *a.* Shaped like or used as a club.

club'bēr, *n.* 1. A person or the thing that clubs.

2. A member of a party, club, or association. [Rare.]

club'bish, *a.* Rough; ill-mannered; rustic. [Obs.]

2. Disposed to associate together; clubable.

club'bist, *n.* One who belongs to or frequents clubs. [Rare.]

club'fist, *n.* 1. A strong, brawny fist.

2. A coarse brute; a ruffian. [Obs.]

club'fist"ed, *a.* Having a large fist.

club'foot, *n.* A short, twisted foot, usually existing at birth; also, the deformity or disease of having such a foot.

club'foot"ed, *a.* Having a clubfoot.

club'hand, *n.* A twisted hand; also, the deformity itself.

club'haul, *v.t.*; clubhauled, *pt.*, *pp.*; clubhauling, *ppr.* To tack (a ship) by letting go the lee-anchor as soon as the wind is out of the sails; this brings the ship's head to wind, and as soon as she pays off the cable is cut and the sails trimmed.

club'house, *n.* The home of a club.

club'-law, *n.* 1. Government by clubs or violence; the use of arms or force in place of law; anarchy.

2. In the game of loo and some other games of cards, a rule compelling every player to play when clubs are trumps.

club'-moss, *n.* The common name of the plants of the order *Lycopodiaceæ*, or more particularly of the genus *Lycopodium*.

club'root, *n.* A disease attacking cabbage, ruining the heads and twisting the roots in irregular growths.

club'-rush, *n.* Any plant of the genus *Scirpus*; also, the cattail.

club'-sand"wich, *n.* A combination of three layers of toast, roast fowl, and fried bacon served with lettuce, etc.

club'-shāped, *a.* In biology, same as *clavate*.

club'-top"sāil (*or* -sl), *n.* An accessory sail; a kind of gaff-topsail.

cluck, *v.i.*; clucked (klukt), *pt.*, *pp.*; clucking, *ppr.* [ME. *clokken*; AS. *cloccian*, to cluck; an imitative word.] To utter the call or cry of a hen with chicks.

cluck, *v.t.* To call or assemble by clucking.

cluck, *n.* 1. A sound uttered by a hen.

2. A kind of articulation employed by the natives of South Africa, especially by the Kaffirs and Hottentots, when talking.

cluck'ing, *n.* The noise of a hen when she calls her chickens.

clūe, clew (klū), *n.* [ME. *clewe*; AS. *cliwen*, *clywen*, a ball, a ball of thread.]

1. A ball of thread.

2. The thread that forms a ball.

3. From the mythological story that Theseus was guided by a clue of thread through the Cretan labyrinth, anything that guides or directs one in an intricate case; a hint or suggestion.

4. Among seamen, the lower corner of a square sail, and the aftmost corner of a fore-and-aft sail.

5. One of the set of cords by which a hammock is suspended.

clūe, clew, *v.t.*; clued, clewed, *pt.*, *pp.*; cluing, clewing, *ppr.* 1. In seamanship, to truss up to the yard by means of clue-garnets or clue-lines.

2. To direct, as by a clue or thread. [Rare.]

clūe'-gär"net, *n.* A sort of tackle or rope and pulley fastened to the clues of the mainsail and foresail to truss them up to the yard.

clūe'-ī"ron (-ūrn), *n.* An iron loop with thimbles for use at the corner of a sail.

clūe'-line, *n.* The same tackle, and used for the like purpose, as a clue-garnet, but applied to the smaller square sails.

clum, *interj.* Be silent; hush! [Obs.]

clum'bēr, *n.* [So named from *Clumber*, the Duke of Newcastle's estate.] A species of field-spaniel having a stocky body with short legs. It is characterized by its still work.

clump, *n.* [From AS. *clympre*, a lump of metal; compare Dan., Sw. *klump*, a clump, lump.]

1. A thick, short piece of wood or other solid substance; a shapeless mass.

2. A cluster of trees or shrubs.

3. The compact layers of clay found in coal strata.

clump, *v.t.*; clumped (klumpt), *pt.*, *pp.*; clumping, *ppr.* To shape into a clump; to arrange in masses or groups.

clump, *v.i.* To walk clumsily or heavily; to clamp. [Prov. Eng.]

clump'ēr, *v.t.* To form into clumps or masses. [Obs.]

clumps, *n.* A game or amusement in which questions are asked so that the questioners may be able to detect the thing or word that has been previously chosen by two persons of the company, whose duty it is to answer the questions. The game derives its name from the fact that the players divide into two clumps or groups, and the clump which guesses the word wins the game.

clump'y, *a.* Formed of clumps; heavy; unshapely.

clum'si-ly, *adv.* In a clumsy manner; awkwardly.

clum'si-ness, *n.* The quality of being clumsy.

clum'sy, *a.*; *comp.* clumsier; *superl.* clumsiest. [ME. *clumsid*, *clomsed*, pp. of *clumsen*, to benumb; Sw. dial. *klummsen*, to benumb with the cold; Norw. *klumsa*, speechless, palsied.]

1. Stiffened with cold; benumbed. [Obs.]

2. Moving heavily, slowly, or awkwardly; as, *clumsy* fingers.

3. Awkward; ungainly; unhandy; artless; without readiness, dexterity, or grace; as, a *clumsy* fellow.

4. Ill-made; badly constructed; as, a *clumsy* garment; *clumsy* verse.

Syn.—Awkward, bungling, inexpert, ungraceful, lubberly, vexatious, troublesome.

clunch, *n.* [Origin obscure, prob. from same root as AS. *clympre*, a lump of metal.]

1. Among miners, indurated clay, found in coalpits next to the coal.

2. A soft limestone.

clung, *v.*, past tense and past participle of *cling*.

clung, *a.* Shrunken. [Obs.]

Clū'ni-ac, *a.* and *n.* I. *a.* Relating to the monks of Cluny.

II. *n.* One of an order of Benedictine monks founded in the tenth century, taking their name from the town of Cluny, France.

Clū"ni-ā-cen'siăn, *a.* Cluniac.

clū'pē-i-fōrm, *a.* [L. *clupea*, a small river-fish,

herring, and *forma*, form.] Like a herring in form.

çlū'pē-oid, *a.* [L. *clupea*, a small river-fish, and Gr. *eidos*, shape.] In zoölogy, characteristic of the herring family.

çlus'tẽr, *n.* [ME. *cluster*; AS. *cluster*, a cluster.]
1. A bunch; a number of things of the same kind growing or joined together; a knot; as, a *cluster* of raisins.
2. A number of individuals or things collected or gathered into a close body; as, a *cluster* of bees; a *cluster* of people.

çlus'tẽr, *v.i.*; clustered, *pt., pp.*; clustering, *ppr.* To grow in clusters; to gather or unite in a bunch, or bunches; as, *clustering* grapes.

çlus'tẽr, *v.t.* To collect into a bunch or close body.
Clustered column; see under *Column.*

çlus'tẽr-çup, *n.* One of a number of cup-like capsules surrounding spores common to certain parasitic fungi.

çlus'tẽr-ing-ly, *adv.* In clusters.

çlus'tẽr-y, *a.* Growing in clusters; full of clusters.

çlutch (kluch), *n.* 1. A griping or pinching with the fingers; seizure; grasp; as, to make a *clutch* at a thing.
2. In machinery, the medium by which a temporary connection is made between separate spindles or parts of a shaft.
3. The paw or talon of a rapacious animal or bird.

> It was the hard fortune of a cock to fall into the *clutches* of a cat. —L'Estrange.

4. The hand; often in the plural and figurative sense of power or absolute disposal; as, to fall into the *clutches* of an enemy.

> I must have . . . little care of myself if I ever more come near the *clutches* of such a giant. —Stillingfleet.

5. The number of eggs upon which a bird sits.

çlutch, *v.t.*; clutched (klucht), *pt., pp.*; clutching, *ppr.* [ME. *clucchen*, to clutch; Scot., *cleuk*, a claw, talon; origin doubtful.]
1. To close tightly; to clench.
2. To seize, clasp, or grip with the hand; as, to *clutch* a dagger.

çlutch, *v.i.* To reach after.

çlut'tẽr, *n.* [W. *cludair*, a heap, pile; *cludeirio*, to pile up; *cludo*, a heap.]
1. A heap or assemblage of things lying in confusion; confusion; litter.

> He saw what a *clutter* there was with huge pots, pans, and spits. —L'Estrange.

2. Confused noise; bustle; clamor.

> Prithee, Tim, why all this *clutter?*
> Why ever in these raging fits? —Swift.

çlut'tẽr, *v.t.*; cluttered, *pt., pp.*; cluttering, *ppr.* To crowd together in disorder; to fill with things in confusion; as, to *clutter* a room.

> The law of a history, which *clutters* not praises together upon the first mention of a name. —Bacon.

çlut'tẽr, *v.i.* To bustle; to fill with confusion.

çlut'tẽr, *v.t.* To clot. [Obs.]

çlyp'ē-. A combining form from Latin *clipeus, clypeus*, a shield, signifying like a shield, or furnished with a shield; as, *Clype*astridæ.

Çlyp-ē-as'tẽr, *n.* A genus of sea-urchins typical of *Clypeastridæ.*

Çlyp-ē-as'tri-dæ, *n.pl.* [L., from *clipeus*, a shield, and Gr. *astēr*, a star.] A subfamily of sea-urchins, of a rounded form, having the mouth and vent on the under side, the mouth being in the center of the body and toothed.

çlyp-ē-as'troid, *a.* and *n.* [*Clype-*, and Gr. *astēr*, a star, and *eidos*, form.]
I. *a.* Pertaining to the genus *Clypeaster.*
II. *n.* A sea-urchin of this genus.

çlyp'ē-āte, *a.* In entomology, shaped like or furnished with a shield.

çlyp'ē-i-fọrm, *a.* [*Clype-*, and L. *forma*, form.] Clypeate.

çly-pē'ō-lȧ, *n.*; *pl.* **çly-pē'ō-læ.** [L., dim. of *clipeus, clypeus*, a shield.] A modified leaf bearing spores; a sporophyl.

çlyp'ē-us, *n.*; *pl.* **çlyp'ē-ī.** [L. *clipeus, clypeus*, a shield.] In entomology, that part of an insect's head which lies in front of the frons or forehead, therefore in front of the eyes, and behind the labrum.

çlyṣ'mi-ăn, *a.* Relating to the deluge, or to any cataclysm; as, *clysmian* changes. [Rare.]

çlyṣ'miç, *a.* [Gr. *klysma*, a liquid used for washing out, from *klyzein*, to wash.] Washing; cleansing.

çlys'tẽr, *n.* [OFr. *clistere*; L. *clyster*; Gr. *klystēr*, a clyster pipe, syringe, from *klyzein*, to wash.] In medicine, a rectal injection; an enema.

cnē'mi-ăl (nē'), *a.* [Gr. *knēmē*, the tibia.] Pertaining to the shin-bone, or tibia.

Cnī'çus (nī'), *n.* [L. *cnicus*; Gr. *knēkos*, a plant of the thistle kind.] In botany, a genus of thistle-like composites, with hard-spined involucres, including the genus *Cirsium.*

cnī'dȧ, *n.*; *pl.* **cnī'dæ** (nī'). [L. *cnide*; Gr. *knidē*, a nettle, from *knizein*, to scrape.] One of the urticating cells whereby many cœlenterate animals obtain their power of stinging; called also *thread-cells.*

Cni-dā'ri-ȧ (nī-), *n.pl.* [L., from Gr. *knidē*, a nettle.] The *Cœlenterata*, excepting the sponges.

cnī'dō-blast (nī'), *n.* [L. *cnide*; Gr. *knidē*, a nettle, and *blastos*, a germ.] A cell developing, or which has developed, a cnida.

cnī'dō-cil (nī'), *n.* [L. *cnide*, a nettle, and *cilium*, an eyelid.] The thread of a cnida.

cnī'dō-phōre (nī'), *n.* [L. *cnide*; Gr. *knidē*, a nettle, and *-phoros*, carrying, from *pherein*, to bear.] Any part or organ developing cnidoblasts.

çō-, *prefix.* A combining form from L. *cum*, with, and signifying with, together, jointly, mutually, at the same time; *co-* becomes *con, com*, or *cor*, before certain consonants for the sake of euphony.

çō-, *prefix.* In mathematics, an abbreviation of Latin *complementum*, that which completes, the complement; signifying of the complement; as, *co*sine, *co*secant.

çō-ȧ-cẽr'vāte, *v.t.* [L. *coacervatus*, pp. of *coacervare*, to heap together.] To heap up; to pile. [Rare.]

çō-ȧ-cẽr'vāte, *a.* Heaped; raised into a pile; collected into a crowd; accumulated. [Rare.]

çō-ac-ẽr-vā'tion, *n.* The act of heaping, or state of being heaped together. [Rare.]

çōach, *n.* [Fr. *coche*; Hung. *kocsi*, a coach, so called from *Kocsi* (now *Kitsee*), in Hungary, where the coach was invented and first used.]
1. A vehicle drawn by horses, and designed for the conveyance of passengers; more particularly a four-wheeled closed vehicle of considerable size.
2. An old name of an apartment in a large ship of war, near the stern and beneath the poop-deck, usually occupied by the captain.
3. A private tutor, generally employed to prepare a person for a specific examination; also, a trainer in athletics, as for a race.
4. In railroading, a car run in passenger trains; generally with a qualifying word; as, a passenger-*coach*; a baggage-*coach.*

çōach, *v.t.* 1. To carry in a coach.
2. To prepare for an examination by private instruction. [Colloq.]

çōach, *v.i.* To ride or travel in a coach.

çōach'=box, *n.* The seat on which the driver of a coach sits.

çōach'=dog, *n.* A dog of Dalmatian breed, of handsome form, and generally white, spotted with black, kept as an attendant upon carriages.

çōach'ee, *n.* A coach-driver. [Colloq.]

çōach'fel"lōw, *n.* 1. A horse which draws a coach along with another; a yokefellow.
2. One intimately connected with another; a close companion.

çōach'măn, *n.* 1. The person who drives a coach.
2. A fish, *Dules auriga*, frequenting waters of the tropics, named from its spine, which resembles a whip; called also *charioteer.*

çōach'măn-ship, *n.* Skill in driving coaches.

çōach'whip (-hwip), *n.* A whip used in coach-driving.
Coachwhip bird; an Australian name for the passerine bird, *Psophodes crepitans*, from its note; also called *coachman* and *whipbird.*
Coachwhip snake; an innoxious snake of the genus *Masticophis*, having a tail resembling in its markings the strands of a braided whiplash. It is found in southern United States.

çōach'wood, *n.* A large tree, *Ceratopetalum apetalum*, of the saxifrage family, found in Australasia, and valued for its compact, fine-grained wood.

çō-açt', *v.t.* and *v.i.* To force together; to act together. [Obs.]

çō-aç'tion, *n.* [L. *coactio*, a collecting, from *coactus*, pp. of *cogere*, to drive together, collect.] Force; compulsion, either in restraining or impelling.

çō-aç'tive, *a.* 1. Forcing; compulsory; having the power to impel or restrain.
2. Acting in concurrence.

çō-aç'tive-ly, *adv.* In a compulsory manner.

çō-aç-tiv'i-ty, *n.* The state of being coactive.

çō-ad-ap-tā'tion, *n.* [*Co-* and *adaptation*, from L. *adaptare*, to, fit to; *ad*, to and *aptare*, to fit.] Reciprocal or mutual adaptation.

çō-ȧ-dapt'ed, *a.* Mutually adapted.

çō-ad'jū-ment, *n.* Mutual assistance.

çō-ad-just'ment, *n.* Mutual help, aid, or assistance. [Rare.]

çō-ad'jū-tănt, *a.* and *n.* [*Co-*, and L. *adjutans*, ppr. of *adjutare*, to help.]
I. *a.* Helping; mutually assisting or operating.
II. *n.* One who assists.

çō-ad'jū-ting, *a.* Mutually helping. [Obs.]

çō-ad'jū-tive, *a.* Rendering mutual assistance; coadjutant. [Rare.]

çō-ad-jū'tŏr, *n.* 1. One who aids another; an assistant; a fellow-helper; an associate in occupation.
2. One who is empowered or appointed to perform the duties of another.
3. The assistant of a bishop or other prelate.
Syn.—Assistant, helper, ally, associate, fellow-worker, partner, colleague.

çō-ad-jū'tŏr-ship, *n.* State of a coadjutor; joint assistance.

çō-ad-jū'tress, çō-ad-jū'trix, *n.* [*Co-*, and L. *adjutrix*, a female assistant.] A female assistant.

çō-ad'jū-văn-çy, *n.* Joint help; assistance; concurrent aid; coöperation. [Rare.]

çō-ad'jū-vănt, *a.* Coöperating with; assisting.

çō-ad'jū-vănt, *n.* [*Co-*, and L. *adjuvans*, ppr. of *adjuvare*, to help.] In medicine, an ingredient in a prescription designed to aid some other ingredient.

çō-ad'nāte, *a.* Same as *Adnate.*

çō-ad'ū-nāte, *a.* [LL. *coadunatus*, pp. of *coadunare*, to unite together; L. *co-*, together, *ad*, to, and *unus*, one.] In botany, united at the base; adnate, as leaves.

çō-ad-ū-nā'tion, *n.* Union of constituent parts.

çō-ad-ū-ni'tion (-nish'un), *n.* Coadunation. [Rare.]

çō-ad-ven'tūre, *n.* and *v.i.* I. *n.* An adventure having two or more participants.
II. *v.i.* To share with others in an adventure or venture. [Rare.]

çō-ad-ven'tūr-ẽr, *n.* A fellow-adventurer.

çō-af-for'est, *v.t.* To convert (land) into a forest.

çō-ā'gen-çy, *n.* Joint agency.

çō-ā'gent, *n.* An assistant or associate in an act.

çō-ag-ment', *v.t.* To congregate or heap together. [Obs.]

çō-ag-men-tā'tion, *n.* Collection into a mass or united body; union; conjunction. [Obs.]

çō-ag"ū-lȧ-bil'i-ty, *n.* The capacity of being coagulated.

çō-ag'ū-lȧ-ble, *a.* Having the property of coagulation.

çō-ag'ū-lănt, *n.* That which produces coagulation.

çō-ag'ū-lāte, *a.* Coagulated. [Obs.]

çō-ag'ū-lāte, *v.t.*; coagulated, *pt., pp.*; coagulating, *ppr.* 1. To curdle; to congeal; to change from a fluid into a curd-like or inspissated solid mass; as, to *coagulate* blood; rennet *coagulates* milk.
2. To crystallize. [Obs.]

çō-ag'ū-lāte, *v.i.* [L. *coagulatus*, pp. of *coagulare*, to curdle.] To become clotted or congealed.

çō-ag'ū-lā-ted, *a.* Exhibiting coagulation.
Coagulated proteid; a proteid readily converted into a peptone by the action of the gastric juice in an alkaline medium, or of pancreatic juice in an alkaline medium.

çō-ag-ū-lā'tion, *n.* [L. *coagulatio*, coagulation, from *coagulare*, to coagulate.]
1. The act of changing from a fluid to a thickened curd-like state, well exemplified by the clotting of blood; the state of being coagulated.
2. The mass or result of such change.

çō-ag'ū-lā-tive, *a.* Possessing a tendency to become coagulated.

çō-ag'ū-lā-tŏr, *n.* That which causes coagulation.

çō-ag'ū-lā-tō-ry, *a.* Coagulative.

çō-ag'ū-lum, *n.*; *pl.* **çō-ag'ū-lȧ.** [L. *coagulum*, a means of coagulation, rennet.] A coagulated mass, as curd, a clot of blood, etc.; the thick precipitate produced when albuminous matter coagulates.

çō-ai'tȧ, *n.* [Native name.] A South American monkey, *Ateles paniscus*, about eighteen inches in length; the black spider-monkey.

çōak, *n.* See *Coke.*

çōak, *n.* [Origin uncertain.]
1. In ship-carpentry, a small cylinder of hard wood let into the ends of pieces of wood intended to be joined, by which means the joining is rendered more secure.
2. In nautical language, the metal hole in a sheave through which the pin runs.

çōak, *v.t.* In ship-carpentry, to unite together, as two pieces of wood in the center, by means of coaks or hard-wood pins.

çōaks, *n.pl.* Cinders; also spelled *cokes.* [Prov. Eng.]

çōal, *n.* [ME. *cole, col*; AS. *col*, coal.]
1. A piece of wood or other combustible substance ignited, burning, or charred; charcoal; a cinder.
2. A solid, opaque, inflammable substance found in the earth, largely employed as fuel, and formed from vast prehistoric deposits of vegetable matter. It is generally divided into three chief kinds—*anthracite* or *glance* or *hard coal, bituminous* or *soft coal*, and *brown coal* or *lignite*; under which divisions are included many varieties.
3. The broken mineral *coal*, burned in grates; used in England, both in the plural as well as the singular, as a collective noun.
Anthracite or *glance coal*; see under *Anthracite.*
Bituminous coal; see under *Bituminous.*
Blind coal; see under *Blind.*

Brown coal or *lignite*; see *Lignite.*

çōal, *v.t.*; coaled, *pt., pp.*; coaling, *ppr.* 1. To burn to coal or charcoal; to char. [Rare.]

2. To mark or delineate with charcoal.

3. To supply with coal; as, the admiral *coaled* his ships at sea.

çōal, *v.i.* To take in coal; as, the ship *coaled* at Honolulu.

çōal′=bed, *n.* Geologically, a formation in which there are strata of coal; the deposit of coal itself.

çōal′=black, *a.* Black as a coal; very black.

çōal′=breāk″ēr, *n.* 1. A machine or building used in the process of breaking coal.

2. One who breaks coal.

çōal′ēr-y, *n.* A colliery. [Obs.]

çō-ȧ-lesce′ (-les′), *v.i.*; coalesced (-lest), *pt., pp.*; coalescing, *ppr.* [L. *coalescere*, to grow together; *co-*, together, and *alescere*, to grow up, from *alere*, to nourish.]

1. To grow together; to unite, as separate bodies, or separate parts, into one body; as, the brooks *coalesce* to form a river; parts separated by a cut *coalesce* in healing.

2. To unite and adhere in one body or mass, by natural attraction; as, gases *coalesce.*

3. To unite in a community or society; to combine or blend, as individuals, parties, or nations; as, the Populists *coalesced* with the Democrats.

çō-ȧ-les′cence, *n.* The act of growing together; the act of uniting by natural affinity or attraction; the state of being united; union; concretion.

çō-ȧ-les′cent, *a.* Growing together; uniting.

çōal′=field, *n.* A field for mining coal; a bed of mineral coal.

çōal′fish, *n.* 1. A species of *Gadus* or cod, named from the dark color of its back.

2. One of various other fishes, as the eulachon, the cobia, etc.

çōal′=gas, *n.* 1. The gas thrown off by burning coal.

2. Ordinary illuminating-gas; a variety of carbureted hydrogen, distilled from bituminous coal and purified for lighting, cooking, and heating purposes.

çōal′gōose, *n.* The cormorant. [Prov. Eng.]

çōal′=heāv″ēr, *n.* One who is employed in carrying coal, and especially in discharging it from coal-ships.

çō′ȧ-līte, *v.t.* To cause to coalesce. [Obs.]

çō′ȧ-līte, *v.i.* To coalesce. [Obs.]

çō′ȧ-līte, *a.* [L. *coalitus*, pp. of *coalescere*, to grow together.] Coalesced; grown together.

çō-ȧ-li′tion (-lish′un), *n.* 1. The act of coalescing; the state of being joined by coalescence.

2. Union of atoms or particles in a mass; coalescence.

3. A combination of persons, parties, or states, for a temporary or particular purpose; especially, of those whose interests are usually diverse; an international or political alliance; as, the *coalitions* of European powers against France.

Syn.—Alliance, combination, confederacy, conspiracy, league, union.

çō-ȧ-li′tion-ist, çō-ȧ-li′tion-ēr, *n.* One who joins or promotes a coalition.

çō=al-lȳ′, *n.*; *pl.* **çō=al-lies′.** A joint ally; as, the army of a *co-ally.*

çōal′=meas″ūreṣ (-mezh″ūrz), *n.pl.* Strata of coal with the attendant rocks; a geological division of the Carboniferous series.

çōal′=mē″tēr, *n.* In England, an official appointed to measure coal.

çōal′=mīne, *n.* A mine or pit containing mineral coal.

çōal′mouse, çōle′mouse, *n.* A small species of titmouse, with a black head; called also *coaltit.*

çōal′=oil, *n.* Same as *Kerosene.*

çōal′=pȧss″ēr, *n.* On board steamships, one who carries coal from the bunkers to the furnaces.

çōal′=pīpe, *n.* In geology, the figure of a tree in sandstone or other rock, sometimes found standing upright in coal-mines.

çōal′pit, *n.* 1. A pit or mine from which coal is dug.

2. A place where charcoal is made.

çōal′=plant, *n.* A fossil plant of the Carboniferous era.

çōal′=sack, *n.* 1. A bag for carrying coal.

2. A dark space in the heavens; especially, one in the Milky Way, near the Southern Cross; so called by sailors.

çōal′=tär, *n.* A thick, black, viscid, opaque liquid which condenses in the pipes when gas is distilled from coal. It is a compound of many different liquid and solid substances, and the separation of these into useful products is now an important branch in manufacturing chemistry. Among these products may be named paraffin, naphtha, benzol, creosote, etc. The basic oil of coal-tar is the most abundant source of the beautiful aniline colors, their various hues being due to the oxidation of aniline by means of acids, etc. Coal-tar is a chief ingredient in printer's ink, in the shape of lampblack. It is also made into asphalt for pavements, and, with coal-dust, forms by pressure an excellent artificial fuel.

çōal′tit, *n.* See *Coalmouse.*

çōal′=whip″pēr, *n.* In England, one who or that which raises coal out of the hold of a ship; a coal-heaver.

çōal′=wŏrks, *n. sing.* or *pl.* A colliery; a place where coal is dug, including the machinery for raising the coal.

çōal′y, *a.* Like coal; containing coal; of the nature of coal.

çōam′ing, *n.* [From ME. *comb*; AS. *camb*, a comb.] A nautical device, one of the raised borders or edges of the hatches, made to prevent water from running into the lower apartments from the deck; written also *combing.*

çō-an-nex′, *v.t.* To annex with something else. [Rare.]

çō-apt′, *v.t.* To fit together; also written *coaptate.* [Rare.]

çō-ap-tā′tion, *n.* [LL. *coaptatio*, from *coaptare*, to fit together.] The adaptation or adjustment of parts to each other; specifically, in surgery, bone-setting.

çō-ärb′, *n.* [Ir. *comharba*, a successor, abbot.] The abbot of a monastery; also called *comarb.*

çō-ärçt′, *v.t.* To crowd; to restrain; also spelled *coarctate.* [Obs.]

çō-ärç′tāte, *a.* [L. *coarctatus*, pp. of *coarctare*, to compress; *co-*, together, and *artare*, to press.] Crowded; pressed together; applied specifically, in entomology, to the abdomen of certain insects.

Coarctate pupa; a pupa inclosed by the stiffened larval skin.

çō-ärç-tā′tion, *n.* 1. Confinement; restraint to a narrow space; restraint of liberty. [Obs.]

2. Pressure; contraction; specifically, in medicine, the contraction or lessening of the diameter of a canal, as the intestinal canal or the urethra.

çōarse, *a.*; *comp.* coarser; *superl.* coarsest. [Formerly written *course*, *cowrse*, and believed to be the same word as *course.* A thing *of course*, or *in course*, is what is natural, ordinary, common, and hence probably the development of the meaning.]

1. Wanting in fineness of texture or structure, or in elegance of form; composed of large parts or particles; thick and rough in texture; of ordinary or inferior quality; as, *coarse* thread; *coarse* hair; *coarse* sand; *coarse* glass; *coarse* features.

> Eat, also, tho' the fare is *coarse.*—Tennyson.

2. Rude; rough; unrefined; uncivil; unpolished; as, *coarse* manners.

3. Gross; indelicate; as, he indulged in *coarse* language.

Syn.—Bluff, brutish, large, thick, blunt, uncouth, immodest, vulgar.

çōarse′=grāined, *a.* 1. Consisting of large particles or constituent elements; as, *coarse-grained* granite or wood.

2. Wanting in refinement or delicacy; vulgar; as, a *coarse-grained* nature.

çōarse′ly, *adv.* In a coarse manner.

çōars′en, *v.t.* To render coarse or wanting in refinement; to make vulgar; as, to *coarsen* one's nature. [Rare.]

çōarse′ness, *n.* The state or quality of being coarse in all its senses.

çō-är-tiç-ū-lā′tion, *n.* In anatomy, the fitting together of bones to form a joint.

çō=as-sess′ŏr, *n.* A joint assessor.

çōast, *n.* [ME. *coste*, *coost*, coast; OFr. *coste*, a rib, hill, shore, coast; L. *costa*, a rib, a side.]

1. The exterior line, limit, or border, of a country. [Rare.]

2. The edge or margin of the land next to the sea; the seashore; also, the country near the seashore; as, populous towns along the *coast.*

3. The side of an object. [Obs.]

4. A slide downhill, as on a sled; a ride down an incline without using propelling power, as on a bicycle.

The coast is clear; a proverbial phrase, signifying, the danger is over; the enemy has left the coast open.

Coast and geodetic survey; see under *Survey.*

çōast, *v.i.*; coasted, *pt., pp.*; coasting, *ppr.* 1. To sail near a coast; to sail by or near the shore, or in sight of land.

> The ancients *coasted* only in their navigation.
> —Arbuthnot.

2. To sail from port to port in the same country.

3. To ride downhill without using force to propel the vehicle, as on a bicycle or sled.

4. To approach. [Obs.]

çōast, *v.t.* 1. To sail by or near to; as, to *coast* the American shore.

2. To draw near; to approach; to follow. [Obs.]

3. To conduct along a river-bank or coast; as, the guides *coasted* us along the river.

çōast′ăl, *a.* Pertaining to a coast. [Rare.]

çōast′ēr, *n.* 1. One who sails near the shore; one who coasts, as on a sled.

2. A vessel employed in sailing along a coast, or in trading from port to port in the same country.

3. A tray used for passing a decanter at table; a decanter-stand.

4. A sled, etc., suitable for coasting.

çōast′=guärd, *n.* 1. In the United States, the organized life-saving service, distributed along the coast.

2. In England, the coast police, originally organized to prevent smuggling.

3. One employed to guard the coast in any capacity.

çōast′ing, *a.* Sailing along or near a coast; as, a *coasting* schooner.

çōast′ing, *n.* 1. The act of sailing along or near a shore.

2. The sport of sliding down a hillside, upon sleds or sledges, in winter; the act of riding down an incline without propelling power, as on a bicycle.

Coasting trade; the trade which is carried on between the different ports of the same country, as distinguished from *foreign trade.*

çōast′=rat, *n.* A small mammal, *Bathyergus maritimus*, of South Africa. It is about the size of a rabbit, and is also called *mole-rat* or *sand-mole.* Its burrows are exceedingly large.

çōast′=wāit″ēr, *n.* In England, a customs officer who oversees the loading and landing of goods in the coasting trade; also called *land-waiter.*

çōast′wīse, çōast′wāyṣ, *adv.* By way of or along the coast.

çōat, *n.* [ME. *cote*, *coote*; OFr. *cote*, a coat; LL. *cota*, *cotta*, a tunic.]

1. A garment for the upper part of the body, especially an outer garment worn by men, though the word is also used of a woman's outer garment.

2. A petticoat; a garment worn by infants or young children. [Obs.]

3. The habit or vesture of an order of men, indicating the order or office.

> Men of his *coat* should be minding their prayers. —Swift.

4. External covering, as the fur or hair of a beast, the skin of serpents, the wool of sheep, etc.

5. A tunic of the eye; a membrane that serves as a cover; a tegument; as, the *coat* of the eye.

6. A cover; a layer of any substance covering another; as, a *coat* of tar, pitch, or varnish; a *coat* of tinfoil.

Coat of arms; originally, a light-weight garment worn over the armor, often decorated with heraldic bearings; hence, the heraldic bearings of an individual or family.

Coat of mail; a piece of armor, in the shape of a coat, made of links or scales; chain mail.

Coats of Mail.—1. Roman. 2. Greek.

çōat, *v.t.*; coated, *pt., pp.*; coating, *ppr.* 1. To cover or spread over with a layer of any substance; as, to *coat* a retort; to *coat* a ceiling.

2. To cover with cloth or canvas; as, to *coat* a mast, or a pump.

3. To envelop with a coat.

çōat′=är″mŏr, *n.* 1. An outer coat worn over the armor-bearing heraldic devices. [Obs.]

2. A coat of arms; an escutcheon with crest, motto, etc.

çōat′=çärd, *n.* The king, queen, or knave among playing cards; a face-card; usually called *court-card.*

çōat-ee′, *n.* A coat with short flaps.

çō′ȧ-ti, *n.* [Native name.] An animal of South America, resembling the racoon, but with a longer body and neck.

çōat′ing, *n.* 1. The act of covering; any substance spread over for cover or defense; as, the *coating* of a retort.

2. Cloth for coats; as, an assortment of *coatings.*

çōat′=link, *n.* Studs or buttons joined by a link; also, a loop and button, for fastening a coat.

çōax, *n.* One who is easily deceived; a simpleton; also written *cokes.* [Obs.]

çōax, *v.t.*; coaxed (kōxt), *pt., pp.*; coaxing, *ppr.* [From *coax*, a fool; origin obscure.] To wheedle; to flatter; to soothe, appease, or persuade by flattery and fondling.

Syn.—Wheedle, cajole, flatter, entice, persuade.

çō-ax-ā′tion, *n.* [L. *coaxare*, to croak as a frog; Gr. *koax*, the croaking of a frog.] Croaking. [Rare.]

çōax′ẽr, *n.* A wheedler; a flatterer; one who coaxes.

çō-ax′i-ăl, *a.* Having an axis, or axes, in common.

çōax′ing, *n.* The act of wheedling or leading on by kind treatment; managing.

çōax′ing-ly, *adv.* By coaxing; in a coaxing manner.

çob, *n.* [Origin obscure; the primary idea doubtless being that of head; compare G. *kopf*; AS. *cop, copp*, head.]

1. The top or head. [Obs.]
2. The tough core on which the kernels of corn grow; a corncob.
3. A sea-gull; the sea-cob.
4. A ball or pellet for feeding fowls.
5. A spider.
6. A close-built, strong, hardy kind of horse.
7. Clay mixed with straw, as in cobwalls, which are used in constructing cottages in some parts of England.
8. A large stone, lump of coal, or round mass of any material.
9. A leader, particularly if rich and grasping. [Obs.]
10. A Spanish coin worth about a dollar. [Obs.]
11. A newly hatched herring.
12. A small fresh-water fish, the miller's-thumb.
13. A large hazelnut; the cobnut.
14. A beating or spanking with a piece of wood or a strap; also written *cobb*.
15. A swan of the male sex.
16. A wheat-ear.

çob, çobb, *v.t.* 1. To punish by striking on the buttocks with a flat piece of wood, or with a board.

2. To break with a hammer, as in mining ores.

Çō-bæ′ȧ, *n.* [Latinized form from Barnabas *Cobo*, a Spanish naturalist.] A genus of Mexican and South American climbers of rapid growth.

çō′bạlt, *n.* [G. *kobalt*; the name is probably derived from *kobold*, a goblin, the demon of the mines, applied to cobalt by the miners, when they did not know its value, because it was troublesome.] A metal of a reddish-gray or grayish-white color, very brittle, of a fine, close grain, compact, but easily reducible to powder. It is never found in a pure state, but usually as an oxid, or combined with arsenic or its acid, with sulphur, iron, etc. The great use of cobalt is to give a permanent blue color to glass and enamels upon metals, porcelain, and earthenware.

Cobalt blue; a pigment of dark blue; called also *cobalt ultramarine*.

Cobalt green; a pigment made from the oxids of zinc and cobalt.

Cobalt yellow; the double nitrite of potassium and cobalt which yields a permanent yellow pigment much used by artists.

çō′bạlt-bloom, *n.* An arseniate of cobalt coming in needle-shaped crystals; also called *erythrite*.

çō′bạlt-crust, *n.* An earthy kind of erythrite.

çō′bạlt-glance, *n.* Same as *Cobaltite*.

çō-bạlt′iç, *a.* Pertaining to cobalt, resembling cobalt, or containing it.

çō-bạlt-if′ẽr-ous, *a.* Containing or yielding cobalt.

çō′bạlt-īte, *n.* A mineral of a silver or yellowish color, composed chiefly of the arseniate and sulphid of cobalt; also called *cobalt-glance*.

çō-bạlt′ous (-us), *a.* Containing or of the nature of cobalt.

Cobaltous chlorid; a crystalline substance used in solution as an ink, the writing being almost colorless after drying, but becoming a bright blue upon the application of heat.

çō′bang, *n.* A Japanese gold coin; written also *kobang*.

çob′bing, *n.* A beating on the buttocks with a flat piece of wood, etc.

çob′bing, *a.* Vulgar; tawdry; purse-proud. [Obs.]

çob′ble (-bl), *n.* [Scot.] A small fishing-boat.

çob′ble, *n.* [Dim. of *cob*.]

1. A cobblestone.
2. A lump of coal from the size of an egg to that of a football.

çob′ble, *v.t.*; cobbled, *pt., pp.*; cobbling, *ppr.* [Of uncertain origin.]

1. To make or mend coarsely, as shoes; to botch.
2. To make or do clumsily or unhandily; as, to *cobble* rimes.
3. To use cobblestones in paving.

çob′blẽr, *n.* 1. A mender of shoes.

2. A clumsy workman.
3. A mean person.
4. A cooling beverage; as, a sherry *cobbler*.

çob′blẽr-fish, *n.* A fish found in the Atlantic; so called from its thread-like dorsal fin-rays.

çob′ble-stōne, *n.* A roundish stone; a pebble; supposed to be a fragment rounded by the attrition of water. The name is given to stones of various sizes, from that of a hen's egg or smaller to that of large paving-stones. These stones are called by the English *copplestones*, and *bowlder-stones*, or *bowlders*.

çob′by, *a.* 1. Stout; brisk. [Obs.]

2. Self-willed; obstinate. [Obs.]

çob′-çōal, *n.* Same as *Cobble*, n. 2.

çō-bel-lig′ẽr-ent, *a.* Carrying on war in conjunction with another power; ordinarily, in accordance with some previous arrangement or stipulation.

çō-bel-lig′ẽr-ent, *n.* A nation or state that carries on war in connection with another.

çob′head (-hed), *n.* The young of the goldeneye duck.

çō′bi-ȧ, *n.* [West Indian origin.] The crab-eater, or bonito; a large fish with a wide, flattened head; also called *sergeant-fish*.

çob′ī″ron (-ŭrn), *n.* An andiron with a knob at the top.

çō-bish′ŏp, *n.* A joint or coadjutant bishop.

çob′le, *n.* [ME. *coble*; W. *ceubal*, a ferryboat, from *ceuo*, hollow.] A boat having a flat bottom and a lug-sail, first used off the coast of Yorkshire, England.

çob′-lōaf, *n.* A crusty loaf of bread with a round lump on the top.

çob′-mŏn″ey, *n.* Gold and silver money, used during the eighteenth century in Spanish South America.

çob′nut, *n.* A child's game, or a hazelnut so called, used in play.

çō′brȧ, *n.* Same as *Copra*.

çō′brȧ, *n.* See *Cobra-de-capello*.

çō′brȧ-de-çȧ-pel′lō, *n.* [Port., a hooded snake; *cobra*, a snake, adder, *de*, from, of, *capello*, a hood.] A venomous snake, found in India, which has the power of expanding its neck, thus giving it a hooded appearance.

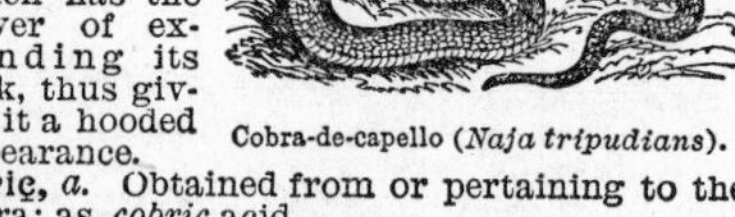

Cobra-de-capello (*Naja tripudians*).

çō′briç, *a.* Obtained from or pertaining to the cobra; as, *cobric* acid.

çob′stōne, *n.* Same as *Cobblestone*.

çob′swăn, *n.* The head or leading swan.

çō′bŭrg, *n.* [Named from *Coburg*, in Germany.] A mourning-fabric for women's wear, made of worsted and silk or cotton.

çob′wạll, *n.* A wall made of unburned clay, mixed with straw.

çob′web, *n.* [ME. *copweb*; *cop*, abbrev. of AS. *attercoppe*, a spider, and *web*, from AS. *web*, from *wefan*, to weave.]

1. The line, thread, or filament which a spider spins from its abdomen; the network spread by a spider to catch its prey.
2. Any snare, implying insidiousness and weakness. In this sense, it is used adjectively, or in composition, for thin; flimsy; slender; feeble; as, a *cobweb* law.
3. The spotted flycatcher of Europe; also called *cobweb-bird*.

Cobweb lawn; a linen of very fine texture made in the seventeenth century.

çob′webbed, *a.* 1. In botany, covered thickly with downy hairs.

2. Covered with cobwebs.

çob′web-by, *a.* Covered with cobwebs; resembling a cobweb.

çob′wŏrk, *n.* A structure of logs laid horizontally and securely held by dovetailing the ends where they meet. Sometimes the logs are used to inclose stones or other material, as in breakwaters, etc.

çō′çȧ, *n.* [S. Am. name.] A highly stimulating narcotic, the dried leaf of the *Erythroxylon Coca*, a plant found wild principally in the mountainous districts of Bolivia, and cultivated in various sections of South America.

Çōç-āgne′ (-āne′), *n.* See *Cockaigne*.

çō′çȧ-ine, *n.* A powerful white crystalline alkaloid extracted from coca-leaves and much used as an anæsthetic and narcotic. Its habitual use is very deleterious both mentally and physically.

çō-çärde′, *n.* [Fr.] One of the bright red lobed vesicles in the thorax of certain beetles.

Çoç-cē′iăn (-yăn), *n.* [Latinized form of *Koch*.] An adherent of the theology of the Covenants founded by Johannes Koch or Cocceius (1603-1669), professor of theology at Leyden.

Çoç-cē′iăn-işm, *n.* The doctrine of the Cocceians.

çoç′ci-. See *Cocco-*.

çoç′cid, *a.* and *n.* I. *a.* Pertaining to the family *Coccidæ*.

II. *n.* One of the *Coccidæ*.

Çoç′ci-dæ, *n.pl.* [L., from *coccum*; Gr. *kokkos*, a kind of berry, now known to be the cochineal insect, found upon the scarlet dye oak.] A family of scale-insects that live on plants.

çoç-cif′ẽr-ous, *a.* [*Cocci-*, and L. *ferre*, to bear.] Bearing or producing berries; as, *cocciferous* trees or plants.

Çoç-ci-nel′lȧ, *n.* [L., from *coccinus*; Gr. *kokkinos*, scarlet, from *kokkos*, a berry, especially the kermes-insect, once thought to be a berry, used to dye scarlet.] A genus of beetles that feed on plant-lice, including the ladybirds or ladybugs.

çoç′cō-, çoç′ci-. Combining forms from L. *coccum*, Gr. *kokkos*, a berry, the kermes-insect.

çoç″cō-baç-tē′ri-um, *n.*; *pl.* **çoç″cō-baç-tē′ri-ȧ.** [*Cocco-*, and L. *bacterium*, a bacterium, from Gr. *bakterion*, *baktron*, a staff.] A kind of bacterium that occurs in either rodlike or spheroidal form.

çoç′cō-līte, *n.* [*Cocco-*, and Gr. *lithos*, a stone.] A variety of pyroxene, usually green in color. It is composed of granular, distinct concretions, easily separable, some of which present the appearance of crystals whose angles and edges have been obliterated; called also *granuliform pyroxene*.

çoç′cō-lith, *n.* [*Cocco-*, and Gr. *lithos*, a stone.] A minute organism abounding in the depths of the North Atlantic ocean and probably one of the *Algæ*.

Çoç-col′ō-bȧ, *n.* [*Cocco-*, and Gr. *lobos*, a pod.] A genus of polygonaceous plants of the American tropics. It includes, *Coccoloba ovifera*, the seaside grape of the West Indies.

çoç′cō-sphēre, *n.* [*Cocco-*, and Gr. *sphaira*, a sphere.] A spheroidal aggregation of coccoliths found in the ooze of the North Atlantic ocean.

Çoç-cos′tē-us, *n.* [*Cocco-*, and Gr. *osteon*, a bone.] A genus of fish of the Devonian period having berrylike tubercles on the body and cranial plates.

Çoç′ cū-lus, *n.* [L., dim. of *coccus*, a berry.] A genus of East Indian menispermaceous plants, consisting of climbers, whose leaves are usually more or less heart-shaped and the flowers small. The species are generally powerful, bitter febrifuges.

Cocculus Indicus; the fruit of the *Anamirta cocculus*, a narcotic, emetic, and cathartic; not infrequently used in the early period of brewing.

çoç′cus, *n.*; *pl.* **çoç′cī.** [L., from *coccum*, Gr. *kokkos*, a berry, the kermes-insect found upon the scarlet dye oak, supposed by the ancients to have been a berry.]

1. A globular variety of bacteria.
2. In botany, a single-celled seed-vessel; one of the parts of a compound carpel in fruit.
3. [C—] A genus of insects including the cochineal and scale insects.

çoç-cyġ′ē-ăl, *a.* Pertaining to the coccyx.

Coccygeal gland; a gland located at the base of the tail of a bird and containing an oily fluid used in dressing the feathers; also called the *uropygial gland*. A similar gland exists in man, near the coccyx, but its function is unknown.

çoç-cyġ′ē-ous, *a.* Same as *Coccygeal*. [Rare.]

çoç′cyx, *n.*; *pl.* **çoç-cȳ′ġēş.** [L., from Gr. *kokkyx*, a cuckoo, so called from the cuckoo's beak which it resembles.] In anatomy, a vertebrate process at the lower extremity of the *os sacrum*, or caudal end of the spine.

çō′chin, *n.* [From *Cochin-China*.] A variety of domestic fowl of large size, full-breasted, and with heavily feathered legs.

çō′chin-chī′nȧ, *n.* A variety of large domestic fowl originally brought from Cochin-China or Anam, in Indo-China. From these have been bred the *brahma* and *cochin* varieties.

çoch′i-nēal, *n.* [Sp. *cochinilla*, cochineal; L. *coccineus*, *coccinus*, scarlet, from *coccum*; Gr. *kokkos*, a berry, especially the kermes-insect.] An insect, the *Coccus cacti*, a native of the warmer climates of America, particularly of Oaxaca, in Mexico. It is found on several species of cactus, particularly on that called nopal or Indian fig-tree. The female, which alone is valued for its color, is ill-shaped, tardy, and stupid; the male is small, slender, and active. It is of the size of a tick. At a suitable time, the insects are gathered and put in a pot, where they are confined for some time, and then killed by the application of heat, either dry or in the form of steam. When subjected to this process, they form a substance which is primarily a dyestuff, the *cochineal* of commerce. It is used in dyeing, especially crimson and scarlet, and for making carmine. It has been also used in medicine, as a cardiac, sudorific, and febrifuge.

Cochineal-fig (*Nopalea cochinillifera*) and Insect.

çoch′i-nēal-fig, *n.* A plant of the cactus family, *Nopalea cochinillifera*, upon which the cochineal insect thrives. It is widely cultivated in the American tropics

çoch′lē-ȧ, *n.*; *pl.* **çoch′lē-æ.** [L. *coclea*, or

cochlea; Gr. *kochlias*, a snail, from *kochlos*, a shellfish.]

1. The anterior division of the internal ear. In man and most other mammals it consists of a gradually tapering spiral tube, the inner wall of which is formed by a central column or modiolus, around which it winds.

2. In botany, any body or organ of a spiral form, especially a spiral legume.

çoch′lē-ăn, *a.* Same as *Cochleate.*

çoch′lē-ăr, *a.* 1. Of or relating to the cochlea; as, the *cochlear* duct; the auditory duct.

2. In botany, spoon-shaped.

çoch′lē-ăr, *n.*; *pl.* **çoch-lē-ā′ri-ȧ.** [L. *coclear*, *cochlear*, a spoon, from *coclea*, *cochlea*, a snail.]

1. In the Greek church, the eucharistic spoon in which the consecrated elements are administered to communicants; also called *labis.*

2. In ancient Rome and Greece, a measure for medicine; a spoonful.

çoch-lē-ā′rē, *n.* [L. *coclear*, *cochlear*, spoon; from *coclea*, *cochlea*, a snail.] In medicine, a spoon; a spoonful.

Çoch-lē-ā′ri-ȧ, *n.* [L. *coclear*, *cochlear*, a spoon, from the shape of the leaves.] A genus of cruciferous plants, including the horse-radish and common scurvy-grass. The plants are perennial herbs with simple or pinnate leaves and small white flowers. They have pungent and antiscorbutic properties.

çoch-lē-ar′i-fōrm, *a.* [L. *coclear*, *cochlear*, a spoon, and *forma*, shape.] Having the form of a cochleare or spoon; spoon-shaped.

çoch′lē-ā-ry, *a.* Cochleate.

çoch′lē-āte, çoch′lē-ā-ted, *a.* [L. *cocleatus*, *cochleatus*, spiral, from *coclea*, *cochlea*, a snail.] Spiral; used especially in botany, and applied to leaves, pods, seeds, etc.; written also *cochlean.*

çoch-lē′i-fōrm, *a.* [L. *coclea*, *cochlea*, a snail, and *forma*, form.] Having the form of a snail's shell.

çoch′lē-ous, *a.* Spiral in form; cochleate.

Çoch-lō-spẽr′mum, *n.* [L., from Gr. *kochlos*, a shellfish, and *sperma*, seed.] A genus of small trees or shrubs found in the tropics of both hemispheres. They have palmately-lobed leaves, large yellow flowers, and pear-shaped fruits.

çock, *n.* [ME. *cock*, *cok*; AS. *coc*, *cocc*, a cock; a word of imitative origin.]

1. The male of birds, particularly of gallinaceous or domestic fowls. The word is often used adjectively, as, a *cock* sparrow; and occasionally to signify the male of certain animals other than birds; as, a *cock* lobster. In composition it is sometimes applied to birds without regard to sex; as, pea*cock*, wood*cock*, etc.

2. A weathercock; a vane shaped like a cock.

3. A valve, for permitting or arresting the flow of fluids through a pipe, usually taking its special name from its peculiar use or construction; as, a feed-*cock*, gauge-*cock*, etc.

4. The style or gnomon of a dial.

5. The needle of a balance.

6. The piece which covers the balance in a clock or watch.

7. A prominent portion of the lock of a firearm; in the old flintlock, the part that held the flint; in a percussion lock, the hammer.

8. A leader; a chief among men or boys; as, the *cock* of the school. [Colloq. Eng.]

9. A canard; a cock-and-bull story.

10. A familiar appellation; as, a jolly old *cock.* [Colloq.]

11. The act of turning up or setting up, or the effect or form produced by such an act; as, a *cock* of the head, eye, nose, etc.

At cock, at full cock; in firearms, having the hammer fully raised.

At half cock; having the hammer pulled halfway back.

Cock-and-bull story; a fictitious or exaggerated story; a canard.

Cock of the plains; the largest kind of American grouse, *Centrocercus urophasianus*; also called *sage-cock.*

Cock of the rock; a beautiful bird, *Rupicola aurantia*, of South America. It is about as large as a pigeon, orange colored, with black on the wings and tail. It forms the type of the genus *Rupicola.*

Cock of the walk or *loft*; a man or boy who is the leader or hero of a particular set or circle.

To go off at half cock; to act before one is fully ready; to act precipitately.

çock, *v.t.*; cocked (kokt), *pt.*, *pp.*; cocking, *ppr.*

1. To set erect; to turn up; as, to *cock* the eye, nose, or ears; to set up with an air of pertness; as, to *cock* the brim of a hat.

2. To set or draw back the cock of (a gun) in order to fire.

çock, *v.i.* 1. To hold up the head; to strut; to look big, pert, or menacing.

2. To train or use fighting cocks. [Rare.]

çock, *n.* [Dan. *kok*, a heap, a pile.] A small conical pile of hay.

çock, *v.t.*; cocked (kokt), *pt.*, *pp.*; cocking, *ppr.* In haymaking, to put into cocks or piles.

çock, *n.* [It. *cocca*, the nock of an arrow.] The notch of an arrow or crossbow.

çock, *v.t.* To calk or furnish (a horseshoe) with sharp points of iron to prevent slipping in frost.

> Cautious men when they went on the roads
> had their horses' shoes *cocked.*—Trollope.

çock, *n.* [ME. *cokboot*, cockboat; OFr. *coque*, a boat; L. *concha*, a shell.] A small boat.

> Yond tall anchoring bark
> Diminished to her *cock*, her *cock* a buoy
> Almost too small for sight. —Shak.

çock-āde′, *n.* [Fr. *cocarde*, a cockade, from *coq*, a cock, on account of its resemblance to the crest of a cock.] A knot of ribbon, leather, or the like, worn on the hat; especially, a rosette of leather worn by uniformed or liveried servants on the side of their hats; as, a coachman's *cockade.*

çock-ā′ded, *a.* Wearing a cockade.

çock′=ȧ=hōōp′, *a.* [Fr. *coq à huppe*, cock with a crest.]

1. Strutting like a cock; triumphant; jubilant.

2. Intoxicated; tipsy. [Scot.]

çock′=ȧ=hōōp′, *adv.* In a triumphant or jubilant manner; boastingly.

Çock-āigne′, Çoc-āgne′ (-ān′), *n.* [ME. *cockaigne*; OFr. *cocaigne*, profit, luxury, prob. from L. *coquere*, to cook; an imaginary place of luxury and idleness.]

1. An imaginary country of idleness and luxury.

2. The land of cockneys; London and its suburbs; used in a humorous sense; also written *Cockayne.*

çock′ăl, *n.* [Of doubtful origin.]

1. An old English game of chance, played with the ankle-bones of sheep instead of dice. [Obs.]

2. A bone used in playing the game. [Obs.]

çock-ȧ-lee′kie (-ki), *n.* [Scot.] In Scotland, a soup made of a capon boiled with leeks, etc.; also written *cockieleekie* and *cockyleeky.*

çock′ȧ-pẽrt, *a.* Impudent; saucy. [Obs.]

çock-ȧ-teel′, *n.* The Australian cockatoo.

çock-ȧ-tōō′, *n.* [Hind. *kakatua*, a cockatoo.]

1. A name common to numerous birds of the parrot kind, chiefly inhabiting Australia and the Indian islands, distinguished from all others and from one another by their crests, which are composed of a tuft of elegant feathers, and which the birds can raise or depress at pleasure. There are several species, as the broad-crested cockatoo, *Cacatua cristata*; the great sulphur-crested cockatoo, *Cacatua galerita*; the red-vented cockatoo, *Cacatua philippinarum*; the tricolor-crested or Leadbeaters' cockatoo, *Cacatua leadbeateri.*

Cockatoo (*Cacatua leadbeateri*).

2. In Australia, a name for a small farmer; called also *cockatoo squatter.* [Colloq.]

çock′ȧ-trice (*or* -tris), *n.* [ME. *cocatryse*, *kokatrice*; OFr. *cocatrice*, *cocatris*, a cockatrice, a corruption of L. *crocodilus*, a crocodile.]

1. A basilisk, a fabulous serpent, supposed to have been produced from a cock's egg hatched by a serpent. Its breath and glance were believed to be fatal to any who came within their influence.

Cockatrice.

2. In Scripture, a venomous serpent. [Obs.]

3. Figuratively, anything venomous or deadly. [Obs.]

4. In heraldry, a basilisk combed, wattled, and spurred, like the cock, and with a serpentine tail.

Çock-āyne′, *n.* Same as *Cockaigne.*

çock′bill, *v.t.* To place acockbill, as a ship's yards or anchor. [See *Acockbill.*]

çock′bōat, *n.* A small boat, especially a small ship's boat.

çock′=brāined, *a.* Rash; giddy; flighty. [Obs.]

çock′=brọth, *n.* Broth made by boiling down a cock; cockaleekie.

çock′chāf″ẽr, *n.* [*Cock*, for Scot. *clock*, a beetle, and *chafer*, from AS. *ceafor*, *ceafer*, the cockchafer.] The May-bug, or dorbeetle, *Melolontha vulgaris*; also, a species of *Scarabæus.*

çock′crōw, çock′crōw″ing, *n.* The time at which cocks crow; early morning; as, I rose at *cockcrow.*

çock-ee′, *n.* [Scot.] The mark aimed at in curling; the tee.

çock′ẽr, *v.t.* [ME. *cockeren*, to fondle; of uncertain origin.] To fondle; to indulge; to treat with tenderness; to pamper.

çock′ẽr, *n.* 1. One who follows cockfighting as a business, or as a sport.

2. A spaniel resembling the field-spaniel, but smaller, having short legs, long pendant ears, and an acute sense of smell. It is noted for its agility and keen instinct. *Cockers* are black, liver-colored, liver and white, or black and white.

Cocker.

çock′ẽr, *n.* [OE. *coker*, boot.] A half-boot worn by farmers. [Obs.]

çock′ẽr-el, *n.* A young cock.

çock′ẽr-ing, *n.* Indulgence.

çock′et, *a.* Brisk; pert. [Obs.]

çock′et, *n.* [ME. *coket*, a seal; of uncertain origin.]

1. In England, formerly a seal of the customhouse; a royal seal; a scroll of parchment, sealed and delivered, by the officers of the customhouse, to merchants, as a warrant that their merchandise is entered.

2. The office of entry in a customhouse. [Eng.]

3. A bread-measure. [Obs.]

4. Bread of inferior grade. [Obs.]

çock′et=bread (-bred), *n.* In England, a former variety of wheat bread, second in quality to the finest.

çock′eȳe (-ī), *n.* 1. A squinting eye.

2. The socket in a millstone.

çock′fīght (-fīt), *n.* A match or contest of gamecocks.

çock′fīght″ing, *n.* The pitting of gamecocks against each other.

çock′head (-hed), *n.* The point of the spindle of a millstone, on which it is balanced.

çock′hōrse, *n.* 1. A child's toy horse, usually set on rockers.

2. Any horse of unusual height. [Rare.]

çock′hōrse, *a.* On horseback; exalted; exulting; as, a *cockhorse* general.

çock-ie-lee′kie, *n.* Same as *Cockaleekie.*

çock′ing, *n.* Cockfighting.

çock′ing=māin, *n.* A match of fighting-cocks, consisting of several bouts.

çock′=lāird, *n.* In Scotland, a landowner in a small way.

çoc′kle (kok′l), *n.* [ME. *cockle*, *cockel*; AS. *coccel*, tares.] A plant or weed that grows among grain, as the corn-rose or corn-*cockle.* A name also applied to *Lolium temulentum* or darnel.

çoc′kle, *n.* [ME. *cokel*, dim. of *cocke*, a shell; OFr. *coquille*, a shell, cockle; L. *conchylium*; Gr. *konchylion*, a shellfish, *konchē*, a mussel.]

1. A small testaceous shell, or rather a genus of shells, the *Cardium.* The general characteristics are: shells nearly equilateral and equivalvular; hinge with two small teeth, one on each side near the beak, and two larger remote lateral teeth, one on each side; prominent ribs running from the hinge to the edge of the valve. A name also applied to similar shells belonging to other genera.

2. A mineral; a name given by the Cornish miners to black tourmalin; also called *shirl*, or *schorl.*

3. A young cock. [Obs. See *Cockerel.*]

4. The part of a furnace containing the fire. [Eng.]

5. A kiln used for drying hops.

6. The rounded top of a hot-air furnace.

7. In zoölogy, a small edible European mollusk, *Cardium edule*; also, any similar bivalve, of the same or a related genus.

çoc′kle, *v.i.* or *v.t.*; cockled, *pt.*, *pp.*; cockling, *ppr.* To contract into wrinkles; to shrink, pucker, or wrinkle, as cloth.

çoc′kle-bũr, *n.* The clotbur, a coarse weed with a prickly fruit.

çoc′kled (-kl′d), *a.* 1. Inclosed in a shell.

2. Contracted into wrinkles, shrunk and puckered, as cloth.

çoc′kle=hat, *n.* A hat decorated with a cockle-shell, formerly worn by pilgrims.

çoc′klẽr, *n.* One who deals in cockles.

çoc′kle-shell, *n.* 1. One of the shells of the *Cardium edule.*

2. A small skiff; a frail boat.

çoc′kle=stāirṣ, *n.pl.* Winding or spiral stairs.

çock′lọft, *n.* The top loft; the upper room in a house or other building; a lumber-room.

çock′mȧs″tẽr, *n.* One who breeds gamecocks.

çock′match (-mach), *n.* A match of cocks; a cockfight; a cocking-main.

çock′ney, *n.* [ME. *cockney*, *cocknaye*, a spoiled child; etym. uncertain.]

1. A native or resident of London; used

humorously or colloquially, especially of the uneducated and their ways.

2. An effeminate, cockered, or spoiled child or youth.

A young heir or *cockney*, that is his mother's darling. —Nash.

çock'ney, *a.* Pertaining to or resembling the cockneys of London; characteristic of cockneys; as, a *cockney* song; a *cockney* dialect.

çock'ney-dŏm, *n.* A term applied humorously to London and its environs; the abode or realm of cockneys; cockneys as a class, or taken collectively.

çock'ney-fȳ, *v.t.*; cockneyfied, *pt., pp.*; cockneyfying, *ppr.* To impart the peculiarities of a cockney to.

çock'ney-ish, *a.* Like cockneys.

çock'ney-işm, *n.* The condition, qualities, manners, or dialect of a cockney.

çock'pāi"dle, *n.* A name applied to the lumpfish or the lumpsucker.

çock'pit, *n.* 1. A pit or area, where gamecocks fight.

2. A term formerly applied to the English privy council room at Westminster, because built on the *cockpit* of Whitehall palace.

3. In ships of war, a room or apartment in which wounded men are treated by the surgeons; formerly situated near the after-hatchway, under the lower gun-deck. The fore-cockpit in old war-ships was a place leading to the magazine-passage and the storerooms of the boatswain, gunner, and carpenter.

4. In small yachts, etc., an open space lower than the deck, admitting to the cabin.

çock'rōach, *n.* [Sp. *cucaracha*, a wood-louse, a cockroach.] The popular name of *Blatta*, a genus of insects of several species of which *Blatta orientalis* is the type. They have four semicrustaceous wings, and resemble the beetle; the head is deflected toward the breast; the feelers are hard like bristles; the elytra and wings are plain, and resemble parchment. They are the especial pests of housekeepers, infesting food and clothing, and having a very unsavory odor.

çocks'cōmb (-kōm), *n.* 1. The caruncle or comb of a cock.

2. A plant, the name given to the *Celosia cristata*, the *Pedicularis* or lousewort, and the *Rhinanthus Crista-galli* or yellow rattle.

3. A fop, or vain, silly fellow. [See *Coxcomb.*]

çocks'cōmbed (-kōmd), *a.* Flattened and laterally widened; banded or compacted together; as, *cockscombed* strawberries.

çocks'foot, *n.* The orchard grass, *Dactylis glomerata*; also called *cocksfoot-grass.*

çocks'head (-hed), *n.* A plant, *Onobrychis sativa* or sainfoin, having small spiny-crested pods.

çock'shut, *n.* 1. The close of the day, when fowls go to roost. [Obs.]

2. A net used for catching woodcock. [Obs.]

çock'shȳ, *n.* 1. A game in which toys or trinkets are set up as targets at a picnic booth, to be shied or thrown at, and usually given as prizes to those who hit them; so named from the old sport of shying or throwing sticks at cocks.

2. Any object to be thrown at; hence, one who is a butt or target.

çock'spŭr, *n.* 1. Virginia hawthorn, a species of medlar, having long, straight thorns; also called *cockspur-thorn, Cratægus Crus-galli.*

2. One of the sharp spines on the leg of a cock.

3. In ceramics, a small, flat piece of clay to separate pieces of pottery, especially while they are being glazed.

çock'ṣūre (-shūr), *a.* Absolutely certain. [Colloq.] The term is metaphorically derived from the *cock* of a firearm, as being much more *sure* to fire than the match of the old matchlock.

çock'swāin (*or* kox'en), *n.* [From poss. of *cock*, OFr. *coque*, a boat, and *swain*, from AS. *swein*, a youth.] A minor officer on board of a ship, who has the care of a boat and the boat's crew; the steersman of a boat; spelled also *coxswain.*

çock'tāil, *n.* 1. A special American drink; an iced beverage concocted of whisky, gin, brandy, or some other form of spirits, liqueurs, or sometimes wine, with bitters, sweetened, and aromatically flavored.

2. In stock-breeding, an underbred horse; generally one having one-eighth or one-sixteenth outside blood in his veins; hence, a person of inferior breeding.

3. A kind of rove-beetle with an elevated tail; also called the *devil's coach-horse.*

çock'up, *n.* A large predatory serranoid fish of India, highly esteemed for its food qualities; sometimes called *begti.*

çock'weed, *n.* A plant, called also *dittander* and *peppergrass.*

çock'y, *a.* Pert or forward; conceited; snobbish. [Slang.]

çock-y-ol'y-bird, *n.* The yellowhammer, a European bird; also, an Anglo-Indian name for any small bird.

çō'çoa (kō'kō), **çō'çō,** *n.* [Sp. and Port. *coco*, cocoa; Gr. *kouki*, the cocoa-tree.] A name given to a simple preparation of the ground kernels of the cacao or chocolate-tree. The name applies also to the beverage made from cocoa or cocoa-shells.

çō'çoa-nut, çō'çō-nut, *n.* The large nut or fruit of the cocoa-tree, the interior of which contains a milky liquid, and is lined with a solid white meat much in request as a food and for making oil.

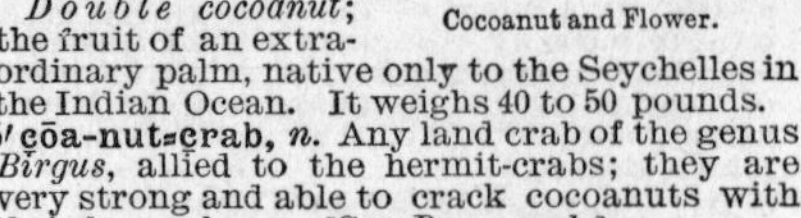

Cocoanut and Flower.

Double cocoanut; the fruit of an extraordinary palm, native only to the Seychelles in the Indian Ocean. It weighs 40 to 50 pounds.

çō'çoa-nut-çrab, *n.* Any land crab of the genus *Birgus*, allied to the hermit-crabs; they are very strong and able to crack cocoanuts with their large claws. [See *Purse-crab.*]

çō'çoa-nut-pälm (-päm), **çō'çoa,** *n.* A palm belonging to the genus *Cocos*, producing the cocoanut. The cocoanut-palm, *Cocos nucifera*, is everywhere cultivated in tropical regions. It has a cylindrical stem rising to a height of from 60 to 90 feet, and surmounted by a crown of feather-like leaves 18 to 20 feet long. The fruits are in bunches of twelve to twenty; they are of a subtriangular ovoid form, 12 inches long by 6 broad. They have each a single seed inclosed in a very hard shell, and surrounded by a thick fibrous rind or husk.

Cocoanut-Palm (*Cocos nucifera*).

çō'çoa-plum, *n.* A tree, *Chrysobalanus Icaco*, belonging to the rose family, which yields an edible fruit like a plum. It is native to tropical America, but grows as far north as southern Florida; also called *Icaco plum* and *incense-tree.* The name also applies to its fruit.

çō'çō-bō-lō, çō'çō-bō-lăs, *n.* [Sp.] A beautiful hard wood which grows in the West Indies. It is largely used in fine cabinetwork and for ornamental and useful articles, including the handles of fine tools.

ço-çoon', *n.* [Fr. *cocon*, dim. of *coque*, a shell, the shell of an egg, a cocoon; L. *concha*, a shellfish, shell.]

1. An oblong ball or case in which the silkworm involves itself during the chrysalis state. It is formed by the threads which compose the silk of commerce and which are spun by the worm just before leaving the larval state.

2. The case constructed by any insect to envelop its larva; also, the silken case produced by spiders for the protection of their eggs, and the mucous cases made by earthworms, leeches, etc., for the same purpose.

ço-çoon'ẽr-y, *n.* A building or apartment for silkworms when feeding and forming cocoons.

çoç'ti-ble, *a.* Capable of being boiled or baked.

çoç'tile, *a.* [L. *coctilis*, burned, baked, from *coctus*, pp. of *coquere*, to cook.] Made by baking or exposing to heat, as a brick.

çoç'tion, *n.* [L. *coctio*, from *coquere*, to cook.]

1. The act of boiling or exposing to heat in liquor.

2. In medicine, that alteration in the crude matter of a disease, which fits it for digestion and elimination. [Obs.]

çō'çum, *n.* [Prob. from native name.] A thick oil extracted from an East Indian tree, *Garcinia Indica*, used chiefly as an adulterant in the melted butter of India, and in the drug trade; also called *corcopali, cocum-butter*, and *cocum-oil.*

çō'çus-wood, *n.* A close-grained wood of the West Indies, sometimes known as *American ebony*, which is used in the manufacture of musical instruments.

çod, *n.* [ME. *cod, codde*; AS. *cod, codd*, a bag, pouch, cod.]

1. Any husk, envelope, or case, containing the seeds of a plant; a pod.

2. A bag; the scrotum.

3. A pillow. [Scot.]

çod, çod'fish, *n.* [Origin uncertain.]

1. A species of edible fish, of the genus *Gadus*, inhabiting northern seas, but particularly the banks of Newfoundland and the shores of New England. It is the basis of an important industry, being taken in great numbers, salted and dried, and widely used for food. *Cod* are named from the place where found, the nature of their food, etc.; as, *shore cod, bank cod, rock cod, George's cod, clam cod*, etc.

Cod (*Morrhua vulgaris*).

2. Any one of several fishes inhabiting Australasian waters; as, (a) in Australia, the Murray River cod, *Oligorus maquariensis*; (b) in New Zealand, the serranoid, *Polyprion prognathus*; also a chiroid, the cultus cod, *Ophiodon elongatus*, on the Pacific coast of North America.

Cod fishery; the cod-fishing industry.

çō'dȧ, *n.* [It., from L. *coda, cauda*, tail.] In music, a separate passage appended to the natural termination of a composition for the sake of forming a marked and usually rather extended close; the finale of a sonata movement or of a fugue.

çō-dam'ine, çō-dam'in, *n.* [From *cod*eine and *amine.*] A white crystalline alkaloid, found in the aqueous extract of opium; isomeric with laudanine.

çod'ded, *a.* Inclosed in a cod or pod.

çod'dẽr, *n.* A gatherer of cods or pease. [Obs. or Prov. Eng.]

çod'ding, *a.* Wanton; lustful. [Obs.]

çod'dle, *v.t.*; coddled, *pt., pp.*; coddling, *ppr.* [Ice. *kvotla*, to dabble.]

1. To boil partly; to soften by hot water. [Rare.]

2. To treat with excessive care; to spoil; to pamper; to fondle.

çod'dy, *a.* Husky. [Obs.]

çod'dy-mod"dy, *n.* A gull in its first plumage.

çōde, *n.* [Fr. *code*, a code; L. *codex*, the trunk of a tree, a wooden tablet covered with wax for writing.]

1. In modern jurisprudence, a complete and coördinated body of law, approved by legislation and arranged under public authority, in which the laws enacted and to be specifically applied by the courts are set forth in a brief manner and according to their relation to each crime or condition. There is neither deviation nor latitude. Thus a true *code* is not only a concise arrangement of existing laws, but it also substitutes new provisions and brief instructions for those existing laws which have seemed contradictory or inefficient.

In Roman law, *The Code* is the distinctive title which, by way of eminence, is applied to the collection of laws and constitutions of the Roman emperors, made by order of Justinian, containing twelve books.

2. Any accepted system of rules and regulations pertaining to a given subject; as, the *medical code*, which governs the professional ethics of physicians; the *naval code*, a system of rules governing the flying of signals at sea; a *cipher code*; the *telegraphic code*, etc.; also, a system of rules and regulations governing the conduct in particular cases; as, the *social code*; the *code of honor*, etc.

Code Napoleon, or *Code Civil*; a system of laws established in France in 1803 and 1804, compiled under the direction of Napoleon I., dealing with the rights of persons and of property, and being largely a reënactment of the Justinian code.

Mosaic code; the religious, social, and civil laws which were codified by Moses in the Pentateuch.

çō-dē'ine, *n.* [Gr. *kōdeia*, a poppy-head.] An alkaloid, obtained from opium, and one of its active medicinal principles; similar to morphine, but feebler in its effects.

çō-det'tȧ, *n.* [It., dim. of *coda*, a tail; L. *coda, cauda*, a tail.] A short passage in music joining two sections, but not belonging to either; a short coda.

çō'dex, *n.* [L.] 1. A manuscript; a book; a code.

2. A digest or code of laws.

3. An ancient manuscript of the Scriptures or of certain parts of them, especially of the New Testament; also an old manuscript of certain classics; as, the *Codex Ambrosianus* of the Iliad.

4. A collection of canons or formulas, especially those relating to medicine.

çod'fish, *n.* The cod; the flesh of the cod prepared as food; also used adjectively; as, *codfish* balls.

Codfish aristocracy; pretentious, newly-rich people; often so called in derision, especially when they give themselves airs inconsistent with their origin or real merits; first said of certain rich New Englanders who made their money out of the codfish industry.

çodġ'ẽr (koj') *n.* [Prov. Eng. and Scot., from ME. *cachen*; Scot. *cache*, to toss, drive.]

1. A rustic; a clown; a miserly man.

2. A peculiar person. [Colloq.]

Çō-di-æ'um, *n.* [L., origin uncertain, perhaps from Gr. *kōdeia*, head, because the leaves were used in making wreaths for the head.] A small genus of shrubs and trees, found in the islands of the Pacific, and valued for their beautiful foliage; also called *Croton.*

çod′i-çăl, *a.* Pertaining to a code, or to a codex.

çod′i-çil, *n.* [L. *codicillus*, a small tablet, a short writing, note, dim. of *codex*, a writing-tablet.] A writing by way of supplement to a will.

çod-i-çil′là-ry, *a.* Of the nature of a codicil.

çō″di-fi-çā′tion, *n.* The act or process of reducing laws to a code or system.

çō′di-fī-ẽr, *n.* One who forms a code or reduces to codical form.

çō′di-fȳ (*or* çod′i-fȳ), *v.t.*; codified, *pt., pp.*; codifying, *ppr.* To reduce to a code or digest, as laws.

çō-dil′là, *n.* [LL. *codicula*, dim. of L. *coda*, *cauda*, tail.] The coarsest part of hemp or flax, which is sorted out by itself.

çō-dille′ (-dil′), *n.* [Fr. *codille*; Sp. *codillo*, the knee, a joint, dim. of *codo*, the elbow; L. *cubitus*, the elbow, cubit.] A term at ombre, when the game is won.

çō′dist, *n.* [Rare.] See *Codifier*.

çod′le, *v.t.* See *Coddle*.

çod′=line, *n.* An eighteen-thread line of hemp or cotton, used in cod-fishing.

çod′ling, çod′lin, *n.* An apple coddled, i. e., boiled or stewed; one suitable for coddling.

çod′ling, *n.* A young codfish.

çod′ling=moth, *n.* A small moth, which in the larval state lives in apples; called also the *apple-worm*.

çod′=liv″ẽr, *n.* The liver of the cod and allied species.

Cod-liver oil; an oil obtained from the liver of the codfish; used medicinally to fatten or build up the tissues in cases of malnutrition.

çod′piēce, *n.* The front flap of old-fashioned breeches.

çod′=wŏrm, *n.* A caddis- or case-worm.

cœ-çil′i-ăn (sē-), *a.* See *Cæcilian*.

çō-ed-ū-çā′tion, *n.* [*Co-*, and L. *educare*, to educate.] Literally, an educating together; but in a special sense, as now used, the education of young men and young women together in the same classes, under the same instructors, in the same institution; especially applied to collegiate or university education; the opposite of *segregation*, in college life.

çō-ed-ū-çā′tion-ăl, *a.* Relating to or having coeducation.

çō-ef′fi-çà-çy, *n.* [*Co-*, and L. *efficax*, powerful, from *efficere*, to do.] Joint efficacy; the power of two or more things acting together to produce an effect.

çō-ef-fi′cien-çy (-fish′en-cy), *n.* Coöperation; joint power of two or more things or causes acting to the same end.

çō-ef-fi′cient (-fish′ent), *a.* Coöperating; acting in union to the same end.

çō-ef-fi′cient, *n.* 1. That which unites in action with something else to produce the same effect.

2. In algebra, a number or known quantity put before letters, or quantities, known or unknown, and into which it is supposed to be multiplied; as, in $3x$ and ax, 3 and a are the *coefficients* of x.

3. In fluxions, the *coefficient* of any generating term is the quantity which arises from the division of that term by the generated quantity.

4. In aviation, the relation of surface to speed and curve, for sustaining effect.

çō-ef-fi′cient-ly, *adv.* By coöperation.

çōe′hŏrn, *n.* [From Baron *Coehorn*, the inventor.] A small military howitzer or mortar with two handles, by which it may be carried short distances; also written *cohorn*.

cœl- (sēl- *or* sel-). A combining form. [See *Cœlo-*.]

cœ′là, *n.*, pl. of *cœlum*.

cœl′à-çanth (sel′), *a.* [*Cœl-*, and Gr. *akantha*, spine.] A term applied to some ganoid fishes because of their hollow spines.

cœ-lā′ri-um (sē-), *n.*; *pl.* **cœ-lā′ri-à**. [L., from Gr. *koilos*, hollow.] The surface-layer of cells in the cœloma.

cœl′el-minth (sel′), *n.* A member of the *Cœlelmintha* division of *Entozoa*.

Cœl-el-min′thà (sel-), *n.pl.* [*Cœl-*, and Gr. *helmins*, a worm.] A large group of parasitic worms infesting the cavities of the body; they are entozoans, having an intestinal canal, and include the threadworms.

Cœ-len′te-rà, Cœ-len-te-rā′tà (sē-), *n.pl.* [*Cœl-*, and Gr. *enteron*, intestine.] A group of invertebrates, mostly marine, having one cavity for the stomach and abdomen.

cœ-len′tẽr-āte (sē-) *a.* and *n.* I. *a.* Relating to the *Cœlentera*.

II. *n.* A member of the *Cœlentera*.

cœ-len′te-ron, *n.* The intestine of an animal having no body-cavity; also the alimentary part of an embryo.

cœ-les′tine (sē-), *n.* See *Celestite*.

cœ-les′tine, *n.* A modified pianoforte or harpsichord of the eighteenth century.

cœ′li-à (sē) *n.* [L., from Gr. *koilia*, a cavity, *koilos*, hollow.] A cavity, as a ventricle of the brain.

cœ′li-aç, *a.* See *Celiac*.

cœ′lō- (cœl-, before vowels). A combining form from Gr. *koilos*, hollow, signifying hollow, with a cavity; as, *cœlo*blastula.

cœl-ō-blas′tū-là, *n.* [*Cœlo-*, and Gr. *blastos*, a shoot.] An embryo having a large cavity in the center.

cœ′lō-dont, *a.* and *n.* [*Cœlo-*, and Gr. *odous*, *odontos*, tooth.]

I. *a.* Said of a group of lizards with hollow teeth.

II. *n.* One of a group of hollow-toothed lizards.

cœl-ō-gas′trū-là, *n.* [*Cœlo-*, and Gr. *gastēr*, belly.] A gastrula possessed of an opening directly into the cavity in the form of a blastopore.

Cœ-loġ′y-nē (sē-), *n.* [*Cœlo-*, and Gr. *gynē*, a woman.] A large genus of handsome orchids, natives of the East Indies and the Malay archipelago.

cœ-lō′mà, cœ′lom, *n.* [L., from Gr. *koilōma*, a hollow, from *koiloun*, to make hollow.] The body-cavity of a metazoan, as distinguished from the intestinal cavity.

cœ-lō′māte, *a.* and *n.* I. *a.* An anatomical and zoölogical term, which signifies having a cœloma.

II. *n.* An animal which has a cœloma.

cœ-lom′iç, *a.* Relating to the cœloma.

cœl-ō-plan′ū-là, *n.* [*Cœlo-*, and L. *planula*, dim. of *planum*, a plain.] A cœlogastrula without a blastopore.

cœl-ō-spẽr′mous, *a.* [*Cœlo-*, and Gr. *sperma*, a seed.] Having hollow seeds.

cœ′lum, *n.*; *pl.* **cœ′là**. [L., from Gr. *koilos*, a hollow.] A cavity of the body. [See *Cœloma*.]

çō-emp′tion, *n.* [L. *coemptio*; *co-*, together, and *emere*, to buy.] The act of purchasing the whole quantity of any commodity.

cœn-. Combining form. [See *Cœno-*.]

cœ-nan′thi-um (sē-), *n.*; *pl.* **cœ-nan′thi-à**. [*Cœn-*, and Gr. *anthos*, a flower.] Same as *Clinanthium*.

çō-en′dọọ, *n.* [Native name.] The porcupine of Brazil, noted for its prehensile tail.

cœ-nen′çhy-mà, cœ-nen′çhym (sē-), *n.* [*Cœn-*, and Gr. *enchyma*, an infusion, from *enchein*, to infuse; *en*, in, and *chein*, to pour.] The soft, or partly ossified, tissue which joins the polyps of a compound coral.

cœn-es-thē′sis (sēn-), *n.* [*Cœn-*, and Gr. *aisthesis*, perception.] General sensation in the body, as distinguished from the special or local sensations ascribed to separate organs.

çō-en-joy′, *v.t.* To enjoy together. [Rare.]

cœ′nō-. A combining form from Gr. *koinos*, common, signifying in common; common; as, *cœno*bium.

cœ′nō-bīte, *n.* See *Cenobite*.

cœ-nō′bi-um, *n.* [LL. from Gr. *koinos*, common, and *bios*, life.]

1. A monastery; a monastic community under one roof, governed by the same regulations.

2. The conglomerate mass of a compound protozoan.

cœ-nœ′ci-um (se-nē′), *n.* [*Cœno-*, and Gr. *oikos*, a dwelling.] The tissue which covers the common organization of hydroid hydrozoans.

cœ-nog′à-my, *n.* [*Cœno-*, and Gr. *gamos*, marriage.] See *Cenogamy*.

cœn′ō-särç (sēn′), *n.* [*Cœno-*, and Gr. *sarx*, flesh.] The soft tissues joining the organizations of a composite zoöphyte in one living basis.

cœn′ō-sīte, *n.* [*Cœno-*, and Gr. *sitos*, food.] One who eats with another, or (as in zoölogy and botany) an animal or a plant living in the same environment.

cœ-nū′rus, *n.* [*Cœno-*, and Gr. *oura*, tail.] A tapeworm which in the larval period infests the brains of sheep, causing a fatal disease called vertigo, staggers, or water-brain.

çō-ē′quăl, *a.* [*Co-*, and L. *æqualis*, equal.] Equal with another person or thing; of the same rank, dignity, or power.

çō-ē′quăl, *n.* One who is equal to another.

çō-ē-quăl′i-ty, *n.* The state of being equal with another; equality in rank, dignity, or power.

çō-ē′quăl-ly, *adv.* With joint equality.

çō-ẽrce′, *v.t.*; coerced (kō-ẽrst′), *pt., pp.*; coercing, *ppr.* [OFr. *coercer*, to coerce; L. *coercere*, surround; *co-*, together, and *arcere*, to confine.]

1. To restrain by force; to keep from acting or transgressing, particularly by moral force, as by law or authority; to repress.

2. To compel; to constrain.

3. To obtain by force.

Syn.—Compel, force, constrain.—*Coerce* had at first only the negative sense of checking or restraining by force; as, to *coerce* subjects within the bounds of law; it has now also gained a positive sense, that of driving forward or compelling; as, to *coerce* the performance of a contract.

çō-ẽr′ci-ble (-bl), *a.* Capable of being restrained or compelled; condensible; as, a *coercible* gas.

çō-ẽr′ci-ble-ness, *n.* The state of being coercible.

çō-ẽr′cion (-shun), *n.* 1. Restraint; hindrance, particularly by law or authority; compulsion; force.

2. In law, the application to another of moral or physical force. Thus when *coercion* is physical, the person coerced is not responsible; when moral, the responsibility is divided according to the degree of moral influence.

çō-ẽr′ci-tive, *a.* Same as *Coercive*.

çō-ẽr′cive, *n.* and *a.* I. *n.* That which has power to restrain, particularly by moral force, as of law or authority.

II. *a.* Compulsory; constraining; forcing.

çō-ẽr′cive-ly, *adv.* By constraint.

çō-ẽr′cive-ness, *n.* The quality of being coercive.

cœ-rū′lē-in (sē-), *n.* See *Cerulein*.

cœ-rū-lig′nōne, *n.* See *Cerulignone*.

çō-es-sen′tiăl, *a.* [*Co-*, and L. *essentia*, the being or essence of a thing.] Partaking of the same essence.

> We bless and magnify that *coessential* Spirit, eternally proceeding from the Father and Son. —Hooker.

çō-es-sen-ti-al′i-ty (-shi-al′i-ty), *n.* The quality of being coessential.

çō-es-sen′tiăl-ly (-shăl-ly), *adv.* In a coessential manner.

çō-es-tab′lish-ment, *n.* Joint establishment.

çō-es-tāte′, *n.* An estate or state of equal rank; a joint estate.

çō-ē-tā′nē-ăn, *n.* One who lives at the same time as another; a contemporary. [Rare.]

çō-ē-tā′nē-ous, *a.* [LL. *coætaneus*, of the same age; L. *co-*, together, and *ætas*, age.] Of the same age with another; beginning to exist at the same time; with *to* or *with*. This word is sometimes used as synonymous with *contemporary*; but *coetaneous* seems properly to denote contemporary in origin, rather than contemporary in existence at any other period. It may, however, be used in both senses.

çō-ē-tā′nē-ous-ly, *adv.* Of or from the same age or beginning.

çō-ē-tẽr′năl, *a.* Equally eternal with another.

çō-ē-tẽr′năl-ly, *adv.* With joint eternity.

çō-ē-tẽr′ni-ty, *n.* [LL. *coæternus*, coexistent from eternity; L. *co-*, together, and *æternitas*, eternity.] Existence from eternity equally with another being; joint eternity.

cœur (kẽr), *n.* [Fr.] In heraldry, the heart of the shield E, otherwise called the *center* or *fesse-point*.

Cœur.

çō-ē′văl, *a.* [LL. *coævus*, of the same age; L. *co-*, together, and *ævum*, age.] Of the same period; existing at the same time; of equal age; followed by *with*.

çō-ē′văl, *n.* One of the same age; one who begins to exist at the same time; a contemporary.

çō-ē′vous (-vus), *a.* Coeval. [Obs.]

çō-ex-eç′ū-tŏr (-egz-ek′), *n.* A joint executor.

çō-ex-eç′ū-trix (-egz-ek′), *n.* A joint executrix.

çō-ex-ist′ (-eg-zist′), *v.i.*; coexisted, *pt., pp.*; coexisting, *ppr.* To exist at the same time with another; followed by *with*.

çō-ex-ist′ence, *n.* Existence at the same time with another; followed by *with*.

çō-ex-ist′ent, *a.* and *n.* I. *a.* Existing at the same time with another.

II. *n.* That which coexists with another.

çō-ex-ist′ing, *a.* Existing at the same time with another; regularly followed by *with*.

çō-ex-tend′, *v.i.*; coextended, *pt., pp.*; coextending, *ppr.* To extend through the same space or duration with another; to extend equally; as, one line *coextends* with another.

çō-ex-tend′ing, *a.* Extending through the same space or duration with another.

çō-ex-ten′sion, *n.* The act of extending equally, or the state of being equally extended.

çō-ex-ten′sive, *a.* Equally extensive; having equal extent.

çō-ex-ten′sive-ly, *adv.* Of equal extent.

çō-ex-ten′sive-ness, *n.* Equal extension or extent.

çō-feof-fee′ (-fef-), *n.* [*Co-*, and OFr. *feoffé*, a feoffee.] Any one of two or more individuals to whom a feoffment is granted jointly.

çof′fee (*or* kof′fē), *n.* [From Turk. *quahwe*; Ar. *qahwa*, *qahwe*, coffee.]

1. The berry of a tree belonging to the genus *Coffea*, growing in Arabia, Persia, and in other warm climates of Asia and America. It will grow to the height of 16 or 18 feet, but its growth is generally restricted to 5 feet, for the convenience of gathering the fruit. The stem is upright, and covered with a light-brown bark; the branches are horizontal and opposite

Coffee Plant (*Coffea Arabica*).

appear; *com-*, with, and *parere*, to appear.] In Scots law, to appear in court either in person or by attorney.

çom-peer′, *n.* [ME. *compeer, compere*; L. *compar*, equal, an equal; *com-*, with, and *par*, equal.] An equal; a companion; an associate; a mate.

çom-peer′, *v.t.* To equal; to match; to be equal with. [Obs.]

çom-peer′, *v.i.* See *Compear.*

çŏm-pel′, *v.t.*; compelled, *pt., pp.*; compelling, *ppr.* [ME. *compellen*; OFr. *compellir*; L. *compellere*, to compel; *com-*, together, and *pellere*, to drive.]

1. To drive or urge with force, or irresistibly; to constrain; to oblige; to necessitate, either by physical or moral force; as, circumstances *compel* us to practise economy.

2. To take by force or violence; to seize. [Rare.]

The subjects' grief
Comes through commissions, which *compel* from each
A sixth part of his substance. —Shak.

3. To drive together; to gather; to unite in a crowd or company. [A Latinism.]

4. To seize; to overpower; to hold.

And easy sleep their weary limbs *compelled.* —Dryden.

5. To call forth. [Obs.]

Syn.—Constrain, coerce, oblige, drive, force.

çŏm-pel′, *v.i.* To use irresistible force; as, if necessity *compels*, I will submit.

çŏm-pel′lȧ-ble, *a.* Capable of being driven, forced, or constrained.

çŏm-pel′lȧ-bly, *adv.* By compulsion.

çom-pel-lā′tion, *n.* [L. *compellatio*, an accosting, from *compellare*, to address, rebuke.] A ceremonious appellation; the word of salutation; as, the *compellation* of the kings of France was *Sire.*

çŏm-pel′lȧ-tive, *n.* and *a.* I. *n.* A descriptive name; a proper name; an appellative.

II. *a.* Denoting address; applied to grammatical forms.

çŏm-pel′lȧ-tō-ry, *a.* Capable of compelling; tending to compel or constrain; compulsory. [Rare.]

çŏm-pel′lẽr, *n.* One who compels or constrains.

çom′pend, *n.* Same as *Compendium.*

çŏm-pen-di-ā′ri-ous, *a.* Short; contracted; compendious. [Obs.]

çŏm-pen′di-āte, *v.t.* To add or collect together. [Obs.]

çŏm-pen′di-ous, *a.* [L. *compendiosus*, short, from *compendium*, a weighing together; abridgment.] Short; succinct; abridged; comprehensive; containing the substance or general principles of a subject or work in a narrow compass; as, a *compendious* system of chemistry.

çŏm-pen′di-ous-ly, *adv.* In a short or brief manner; summarily; in brief; in epitome; as, *compendiously* written.

çŏm-pen′di-ous-ness, *n.* Shortness; brevity; comprehension within a narrow compass.

çŏm-pen′di-um, *n.* [L. *compendium*, a weighing together, an abridgment, from *compendere*, to weigh together; *com-*, together, and *pendere*, to weigh.] A composition containing the substance of a larger work, or the leading features of a subject; a summary; an abridgment.

çom′pen-sāte (*or* çŏm-pen′), *v.t.*; compensated, *pt., pp.*; compensating, *ppr.* [L. *compensatus*, pp. of *compensare*, to weigh together, or weigh one thing against another; *com-*, with, and *pensare*, to weigh.]

1. To give equal value to; to recompense; as, to *compensate* a laborer for his work.

2. To be equivalent in value or effect to; to counterbalance; to make amends for.

The length of the night and the dews do *compensate* the heat of the day. —Bacon.

çom′pen-sāte, *v.i.* To make amends; to supply an equivalent; followed by *for*; as, nothing can *compensate for* the loss of a good reputation.

Syn.—Recompense, remunerate, reward, indemnify, requite, countervail, counterbalance.

çom-pen-sā′tion, *n.* [L. *compensatio*, a weighing together, a compensation, from *compensare*, to weigh together, compensate.]

1. That which is given or received as an equivalent for services, debt, want, loss, or suffering; amends; remuneration; recompense.

All other debts may *compensation* find. —Dryden.

2. That which supplies the place of something else, or makes good a deficiency.

3. The act of compensating.

4. In law, a set-off; the payment of debt by a credit of equal amount.

5. An equivalent, for which provision is made in real-estate transactions, acting as a safeguard against errors in descriptions of property.

6. In mechanics, any means employed to counteract the effect upon the precision of a piece of mechanism of such exterior forces as temperature and electricity.

Compensation balance; a balance-wheel or pendulum in the construction of which are employed several varieties of metal varying in degrees of expansibility, thereby providing for uniformity of movement in all temperatures.

Compensation bars; bars formed of two or more metals of different expansibilities, used to produce perfect equality of motion in the balances of watches and chronometers and the pendulums of clocks.

Syn.—Remuneration, amends, recompense, indemnity, requital, satisfaction, set-off.

çŏm-pen′sȧ-tive, *a.* Making amends or affording compensation.

çŏm-pen′sȧ-tive, *n.* Compensation. [Rare.]

çom′pen-sā-tŏr, *n.* 1. One who or that which compensates.

2. A name given to a number of mechanical devices for equalizing pressure and the effects of temperature, electricity, magnetism, etc.

3. On iron ships, a magnet or sheet of iron placed in proximity to a compass in order to counteract the local attraction on the magnetic needle.

4. An automatic appliance to regulate the pressure of gas in the cylinders of gas-works or in the mains.

çŏm-pen′sȧ-tō-ry, *a.* Serving as compensation; making amends.

çŏm-pense′, *v.t.* To recompense. [Obs.]

çom-pe-ren′di-nāte, *v.t.* To delay. [Obs.]

çom-pesce′, *v.t.* [L. *compescere*, to restrain; *com-*, with, and *pes*, foot.] To restrain. [Rare.]

çŏm-pēte′, *v.i.*; competed, *pt., pp.*; competing, *ppr.* [L. *competere*, to strive together, compete; *com-*, together, and *petere*, to seek.] To seek or strive for the same thing as another; to carry on competition or rivalry.

The sages of antiquity will not dare to *compete* with the inspired authors. —Milner.

çom′pē-tence, çom′pē-ten-cy, *n.* [L. *competens*, ppr. of *competere*, to strive together, be fit, suitable.]

1. Capacity equal to requirement; adequate fitness or ability; the state of being competent.

2. Property or means of subsistence sufficient to furnish the necessaries and conveniences of life, without superfluity.

Happy years of health and *competence.* —Tennyson.

3. In law, legal capacity or qualifications; fitness; as, the *competence* of a witness to testify; the *competence* of a judge to try a case.

çom′pē-tent, *a.* [OFr. *competent*, competent; L. *competens*, ppr. of *competere*, to be sufficient, strive for.]

1. Answering all requirements; suitable; fit; convenient; hence, sufficient; fit for the purpose; adequate; as, a *competent* force.

2. Having ability or capacity; duly qualified; as, a *competent* workman.

3. Incident; belonging to, by right; followed by *to.*

That is the privilege of the infinite Author of things, but is not *competent to* any finite being. —Locke.

4. In law, having legal capacity or power; as, a *competent* judge or court; a *competent* witness.

A *competent* judge is one who has jurisdiction in the case. —Johnson.

çom-pē-ten′tēş, *n.pl.* [LL., from L. *competens*, ppr. of *competere*, to be competent, to compete.] In the early church, such neophytes as, after having received a course of instruction, had applied to be baptized.

çom′pē-tent-ly, *adv.* Sufficiently; adequately; suitably; reasonably; as, the fact has been *competently* proved; a church is *competently* endowed.

çom-pē-ti′tion (-tish′un), *n.* [L. *competitio*, an agreement, rivalry, from L. *competitus*, pp. of *competere*, to compete.]

1. The act of seeking or endeavoring to gain that for which another is also striving; rivalry; strife for superiority; as, the *competition* of two candidates for an office. Formerly sometimes followed by *to*, now always by *for*, before the thing sought.

2. A trial of skill, as a test of superiority or of fitness.

Syn.—Emulation, rivalry, contention, controversy.

çŏm-pet′i-tive, *a.* Relating to or denoting competition; inducing competition; as, a *competitive* examination.

çŏm-pet′i-tŏr, *n.* [L. *competitor*, a rival, from *competitus*, pp. of *competere*, to compete.]

1. One who endeavors to obtain what another seeks; one who claims what another claims; a rival; one who competes.

They cannot brook *competitors* in love. —Shak.

2. An opponent.

3. A zealous and friendly associate in the same cause. [Obs.]

çŏm-pet′i-tō-ry, *a.* Rivaling; acting or done in competition.

çŏm-pet′i-tress, çŏm-pet′i-trix, *n.* A female competitor.

çom-pi-lā′tion, *n.* [Fr. *compilation*, compilation; L. *compilatio*, a pillaging, plundering; hence, contemptuously of a collection of documents, a compilation, from *compilatus*, pp. of *compilare*, to plunder, pilfer.]

1. The act of compiling or collecting from different sources; a gathering or piling up; a collection.

2. That which is compiled or collected from different sources, as a collection of material from various publications, to form a separate work.

çom′pi-lā-tŏr, *n.* A compiler. [Obs.]

çŏm-pile′, *v.t.*; compiled, *pt., pp.*; compiling, *ppr.* 1. To collect (material) from different sources and put in a new form; especially, to prepare, as a written or printed work, by collecting and collating literary material; as, to *compile* a gazetteer; to *compile* a history of the world.

2. To write; to compose.

3. To put together; to build. [Obs.]

4. To contain; to comprise. [Obs.]

çŏm-pile′ment, *n.* The act of putting or piling together; compilation. [Rare.]

çŏm-pi′lẽr, *n.* [ME. *compilour*; OFr. *compileor*; L. *compilator*, a compiler, from *compilare*, to snatch together.] One who compiles; one who gathers literary material from different sources for publication in a new form.

çŏm-pinġe′, *v.t.* To confine; to compress; to close up. [Obs.]

çŏm-plā′cence, çŏm-plā′cen-cy, *n.* [L. *complacens*, ppr. of *complacere*, to be very pleasing; *com-*, with, and *placere*, to please.]

1. Pleasure; satisfaction; gratification; self-satisfaction.

Others proclaim the infirmities of a great man with satisfaction and *complacency.* —Addison.

2. The cause of pleasure or joy. [Rare.]

3. Complaisance; civility; disposition to please.

Every moment of her life brings me fresh instances of her *complacency* to my inclinations. —Steele.

çŏm-plā′cent, *a.* 1. Accompanied with a sense of quiet enjoyment; displaying complacence; gratified; satisfied; as, a *complacent* look or smile.

They look up with a sort of *complacent* awe to kings. —Burke.

2. Kindly; complaisant.

çom-plā-cen′tiăl (-shăl), *a.* Marked by complacence; accommodating.

çŏm-plā′cent-ly, *adv.* In a complacent manner.

çŏm-plāin′, *v.i.*; complained, *pt., pp.*; complaining, *ppr.* [ME. *complaynen*; OFr. *complaindre*, to complain; L. *com-*, with, and *plangere*, to strike.]

1. To utter expressions of grief; to lament; followed by *of*; as, he *complained* tearfully *of* his condition.

2. To utter expressions of censure or resentment; to murmur; to find fault; as, he *complained* bitterly of his treatment.

3. To utter expressions of uneasiness or pain; as, he *complains* of thirst; he *complains* of a headache.

4. In law, to accuse formally of an offense; to present an accusation against a person to a proper officer.

Syn.— Bewail, bemoan, deplore, murmur, grumble, grieve, repine.

çŏm-plāin′ȧ-ble, *a.* That may be complained of. [Rare.]

çŏm-plāin′ănt, *n.* 1. One who makes a complaint; a complainer.

2. A prosecutor; one who prosecutes by complaint, or commences a legal process against another; a plaintiff.

çŏm-plāin′ẽr, *n.* One who complains, expresses grief, or laments; one who finds fault; a murmurer.

çŏm-plāin′fụl, *a.* Full of complaint. [Rare.]

çŏm-plāin′ing, *n.* The expression of regret, sorrow, or injury; a complaint.

çŏm-plāint′, *n.* 1. Expression of grief, regret, pain, censure, or resentment; lamentation; murmuring.

2. The cause or subject of complaint or murmuring.

The poverty of the clergy hath been the *complaint* of all who wish well to the church. —Swift.

3. The cause of pain and uneasiness; a malady; a disease; usually applied to disorders not violent; as, his physical *complaints* were aggravated by his mental troubles.

4. In law, a charge made by a private person

in legal form; a plaintiff's pleading in a civil suit.

çŏm-plāint′fụl, *a.* Prone to complain; complainful. [Rare.]

çom′plāi-ṣănce, *n.* [Fr. *complaisance,* complaisance, from *complaire;* L. *complacere,* to please.]

1. A pleasing deportment; courtesy; that manner of address and behavior, in social intercourse, which gives pleasure; kind and affable treatment; acts of civility; as, the gentleman received us with *complaisance.*

2. Condescension; acquiescence; obliging compliance with the wishes or humors of others.

In *complaisance* poor Cupid mourned.—Prior.

çom′plāi-ṣănt, *a.* [Fr. *complaisant,* pleasing, ppr. of *complaire;* L. *complacere,* to please.] Pleasing in manners; courteous; obliging; desirous to please; as, a *complaisant* gentleman.

Syn.—Affable, gracious, benign, condescending, benignant, urbane, courteous.

çom′plāi-ṣănt-ly, *adv.* In a complaisant manner.

çom′plāi-ṣănt-ness, *n.* Civility; complaisance. [Rare.]

çom′plă-nāte, *a.* 1. Flat or laminate; having thin plates. [Rare.]

2. In botany, lying in the same plane, as the leaves of certain mosses.

çom′plă-nāte, *v.t.* [L. *complanatus,* pp. of *complanare,* to make level; *com-,* together, and *planum,* a plain.] To make level; to reduce to an even surface. [Rare.]

çŏm-pleçt′, *v.t.* 1. To place the arms around; to embrace. [Obs.]

2. To weave together.

çŏm-pleçt′ed, *a.* Pertaining to the complexion; of a certain complexion; as, a light-*complected* man. [Colloq.]

çom′plē-ment, *n.* [L. *complementum,* that which fills up or completes, from *complere,* to complete; *com-,* intens., and *plere,* to fill.]

1. Full quantity or number, full amount; as, a company has its *complement* of men; a ship has its *complement* of stores.

2. Perfect state; fullness; completeness.

3. What is wanted to complete or fill up some quantity or thing; difference.

4. In music, the interval wanting to complete an octave; as, the *complement* of a third is a sixth; that of a fourth, a fifth; of a fifth, a fourth.

5. In optics, a color producing white when united or blended with another color.

6. That which is added, not as necessary, but as ornamental; outward show; an accessory. [Obs.]

7. Compliment. [Obs.]

Arithmetical complement of a number; the difference between a number and the power of ten next in series; as, 2 is the complement of 8, and 24 of 76.

Complement of an arc or *angle;* in geometry, the difference between an arc and a quadrant or between an angle and a right angle; specifically, in the figure, the arc D B is the complement of either the arc A B or B E. Similarly, the angle B C D is the complement of the angles A C B or B C E; hence, to find the complement of any given angle expressed in degrees, minutes, and seconds, subtract it from 90° if acute, but if obtuse subtract 90° from it.

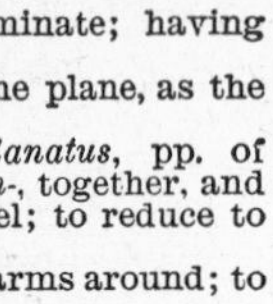

Complement of a parallelogram; in geometry, referring to the figure, opposite parallelograms at the point I (any point in the diagonal D B) are complements of the parallelogram A B C D.

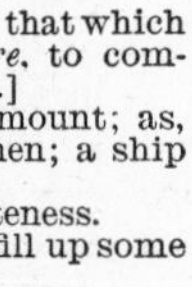

çom′plē-ment, *v.t.* 1. To make good a deficiency in; to add a complement to.

2. To flatter. [Obs.]

çom-plē-men′tăl, *a.* 1. Filling; supplying a deficiency; completing; forming a complement.

2. Flattering; courteous. [Obs.]

Complemental air; the amount of air which the lungs will hold in addition to an ordinary inspiration.

Complemental males; a term applied by Darwin to imperfect organisms, such as are found in cirripeds, which are in reality rudimentary males, perfect male animals being abundant. They are parasitic on hermaphrodites.

çom-plē-men′tă-ry, *n.* 1. Anything which complements.

2. One skilled in compliments. [Obs.]

çom-plē-men′tă-ry, *a.* Helping to fill out; aiding completion.

Complementary colors; see under *Color,* n.

çŏm-plēte′, *a.* [ME. *compleet;* OFr. *complet,* complete, full, from L. *completus,* pp. of *complere,* to fill up, complete; *com-,* intens., and *plere,* to fill.]

1. Having no deficiency; perfect.

2. Finished; ended; concluded; as, the edifice is *complete.*

3. In botany, furnished with all the normal parts; as, a *complete* flower is one having calyx, corolla, stamens, and pistils.

4. Perfect in kind or quality.

çŏm-plēte′, *v.t.;* completed, *pt., pp.;* completing, *ppr.* 1. To finish; to end; to perfect; as, to *complete* an edifice; to *complete* an education.

2. To fulfil; to accomplish; to realize; as, to *complete* one's desires.

Syn.—Perform, execute, terminate, conclude, finish, end, achieve, realize, effect, consummate, accomplish.

çŏm-plēte′ly, *adv.* Fully; perfectly; entirely.

çŏm-plēte′ment, *n.* The act of completing; a finishing. [Obs.]

çŏm-plēte′ness, *n.* The state of being complete; perfection.

çŏm-plē′tion, *n.* [LL. *completio,* a filling up, from L. *complere,* to fill up.]

1. Fulfilment; accomplishment.

There was a full, entire harmony and consent in the divine predictions, receiving their *completion* in Christ. —South.

2. The act of completing; the state of being complete; utmost extent; perfect state; as, the *completion* of an education.

çŏm-plē′tive, *a.* Filling; making complete. [Rare.]

çom-plē-tō′ri-um, *n.; pl.* **çom-plē-tō′ri-ȧ.** [LL., from L. *completus,* pp. of *complere,* to fill up, complete.]

1. The last canonical or daily public prayer of the Roman Catholic breviary; the complin.

2. In the Ambrosian ritual, an evening song of praise.

çŏm-plē′tō-ry, *a.* and *n.* I. *a.* Tending or serving to complete; fulfilling. [Obs.]

II. *n.* Same as *Complin.*

çom′plex, *a.* [L. *complexus,* pp. of *complecti,* to encircle, embrace; *com-,* with, and *plectere,* to weave, braid.]

1. Composed of two or more parts; composite; not simple; as, a *complex* being.

2. Involved; perplexing; difficult; as, a *complex* subject.

Complex fraction, number, etc.; see under the nouns.

Syn.—Abstruse, complicated, composite, confused, conglomerate, entangled, heterogeneous, intricate, involved.

çom′plex, *n.* A more or less complicated collection or system of related things or parts.

Complex of lines; in geometry, the entire collection of straight lines which fulfil given requirements.

çom′plexed, *a.* 1. Complex; intricate. [Obs.]

2. In heraldry, spiral or serpentine in form; annodated.

çŏm-plex′ed-ness, *n.* Complexity; the state or quality of being complex; as, the *complexedness* of moral ideas.

çŏm-plex′iŏn (-plek′shun), *n.* [ME. *complexion;* OFr. *complexion,* complexion, constitution; L. *complexio,* a combination, connection, from *complexus,* pp. of *complecti,* to entwine.]

1. The temperament, habitude, or natural disposition of the body or mind; the peculiar cast of the constitution; physical character; nature.

Shylock knew the bird was fledged; and then it is the *complexion* of them all to leave the dam. —Shak.

2. The color or hue of the skin, particularly of the face.

3. The general appearance of anything; aspect.

Men judge by the *complexion* of the sky
The state and inclination of the day.
—Shak.

4. The state of being complex; complexity; involution. [Obs.]

çŏm-plex′iŏn-ăl, *a.* Depending on or pertaining to complexion; constitutional; as, *complexional* prejudices. [Rare.]

çŏm-plex′iŏn-ăl-ly, *adv.* By complexion; constitutionally. [Rare.]

çŏm-plex′iŏn-ā-ry, *a.* Pertaining to the complexion, or to the care of it. [Rare.]

çŏm-plex′iŏned (-shund), *a.* 1. Having a certain temperament or state. [Rare.]

2. Having a certain tint or hue, especially of the skin; used in composition; as, a dark-*complexioned* man.

çŏm-plex′i-ty, *n.* 1. The state of being complex; complexness.

2. That which is fashioned complexly; as, the palace was a network of *complexities.*

çom′plex-ly, *adv.* In a complex manner; not simply.

çom′plex-ness, *n.* The state of being complex.

çŏm-plex′us, *n.* [L. *complexus,* an encircling, surrounding, from *complexus,* pp. of *complecti,* to encircle.]

1. An aggregation of involutions or complications.

2. In anatomy, the large muscle connecting the upper vertebræ with the head and chiefly governing its motions.

çŏm-plī′ȧ-ble, *a.* Capable of bending or yielding.

çŏm-plī′ănce, *n.* [From L. *complere,* to fill up.]

1. The act of complying; a yielding, as to a request, wish, desire, demand, or proposal; concession; submission.

Let the king meet *compliance* in your looks,
A free and ready yielding to his wishes.
—Rowe.

2. A disposition to yield to others; complaisance.

He was a man of few words and great *compliance.* —Clarendon.

Syn.—Acquiescence, assent, concession, consent, execution, obedience, performance, submission.

çŏm-plī′ăn-cy, *n.* Same as *Compliance.*

çŏm-plī′ănt, *a.* 1. Yielding; pliant; bending; as, the *compliant* boughs.

2. Yielding to request or desire; civil; obliging.

çŏm-plī′ănt-ly, *adv.* In a yielding manner.

çom′pli-çȧ-çy, *n.* A state of being complex or intricate. [Rare.]

çom′pli-çănt, *a.* Folding over; applied to the anterior wings of beetles.

çom′pli-çāte, *v.t.;* complicated, *pt., pp.;* complicating, *ppr.* [L. *complicatus,* pp. of *complicare,* to fold together; *com-,* together, and *plicare,* to fold, weave.] To fold or twist together; to entangle; to intertwine; to interweave; to render complex or intricate; to involve; as, to *complicate* matters, he was suddenly taken ill.

çom′pli-çāte, *a.* 1. Complex; composed of two or more parts united.

2. In botany, folded together, as the valves of the glume or chaff in some grasses.

çom′pli-çāte-ly, *adv.* In a complex manner.

çom′pli-çāte-ness, *n.* The state of being complicated.

çom-pli-çā′tion, *n.* 1. The act of interweaving or involving two or more things or parts; the state of being interwoven, involved, or intimately blended.

2. A mass or collection of many things involved or interwoven, or mutually united.

By admitting a *complication* of ideas, the mind is bewildered. —Watts.

3. In medicine, a combination of diseases or morbid conditions, coexistent, but not necessarily correlative.

çom′plice, *n.* [Obs.] Same as *Accomplice.*

çŏm-pliç′i-ty, *n.* [LL. *complex,* genit. *complicis,* a participant, from L. *complicare,* to fold together, involve.] The state or condition of being an accomplice.

çŏm-plī′ẽr, *n.* One who complies, yields, or obeys; a person of ready compliance and yielding temper.

çom′pli-ment, *n.* [Fr. *compliment;* It. *complimento,* a compliment, an expression of civility; L. *complementum,* that which fills up or completes, from *completus,* pp. of *complere,* to fill up; *com-,* intens., and *plere,* to fill.] An expression of civility, respect, or regard; delicate flattery; commendation; praise; as, my best *compliments* to you; to lavish *compliments.*

Compliments of congratulation are always kindly taken, and cost one nothing but pen, ink, and paper. —Chesterfield.

Left-handed compliment; an expression ostensibly complimentary, but not so in fact; an uncomplimentary expression.

To stand on compliment; to treat in a ceremonious manner.

çom′pli-ment, *v.t.;* complimented, *pt., pp.;* complimenting, *ppr.* To praise; to flatter by expressions of approbation, esteem, or respect, to congratulate or pay a compliment to.

She *compliments* Menelaus very handsomely. —Pope.

Syn.—Congratulate, flatter, felicitate, praise.

çom′pli-ment, *v.i.* To pass compliments; to use ceremony or ceremonious language. [Rare.]

çom-pli-men′tăl, *a.* Expressive of civility or respect; implying compliments. [Obs.]

çom-pli-men′tăl-ly, *adv.* In the nature of a compliment; by way of civility or ceremony. [Obs.]

çom-pli-men′tăl-ness, *n.* The tendency to be complimentary. [Obs.]

çom-pli-men′tȧ-ry, *a.* Expressing civility, regard, or praise; conveying a compliment; as *complimentary* remarks; *complimentary* tickets.

çom-pli-men′tȧ-tive, *a.* Complimentary.

çom′pli-ment-ẽr, *n.* One who compliments; one given to compliments; a flatterer.

çom′plin, çom′pline, *n.* [ME. *complyn;* OFr. *complie;* LL. *completa,* the complin, from f. of L. *completus,* pp. of *complere,* to fill up.] The last of the seven canonical hours; the last prayer at night, to be recited after sunset; so called because it closes the service of the day.

çom′plot, *n.* [Fr. *complot*, a plot, conspiracy; OFr. *complot*, a crowd, a battle, a plot, from L. *complicatus*, pp. of *complicare*, to confuse, fold together.] A plotting together; a joint plot; a plot; a confederacy in some evil design; a conspiracy.

> I know their *complot* is to have my life. —Shak.

çŏm-plot′, *v.t.*; complotted, *pt.*, *pp.*; complotting, *ppr.* To plot together; to contrive.

çŏm-plot′, *v.i.* To form a plot; to join in a secret design, generally criminal; to conspire.

çŏm-plot′ment, *n.* A plotting together; conspiracy. [Rare.]

çŏm-plot′tẽr, *n.* One joined in a plot; a conspirator.

çŏm-plot′ting-ly, *adv.* By complotting.

Çom-plū-ten′siăn, *a.* Designating the copy of the Bible first published in 1522 by Cardinal Ximenes, and printed at Complutum, or Alcala de Henares, a city near Madrid.

çom-plụ̈′vi-um, *n.*; *pl.* **çom-plụ̈′vi-ȧ.** [L., from *compluere*, to flow together, in raining; *com-*, together, and *pluere*, to rain.] A large unroofed space over the court of an ancient Roman house for the admittance of light and air, and through which rain fell into the cistern or impluvium.

çŏm-plȳ′, *v.i.*; complied, *pt.*, *pp.*; complying, *ppr.* [L. *complere*, to fill up, supply, satiate.]

1. To fulfil; to perfect or carry into effect; to complete; to perform or execute; as, to *comply* with a promise; to *comply* with one's wishes.

2. To yield; to yield in compliance; to accord; to suit; often followed by *with*; as, to *comply with* a request.

3. To be formally polite. [Obs.]

Syn.—Accede, assent, concur.

çŏm-plȳ′, *v.t.* 1. To fulfil; to bring into conformity. [Obs.]

2. To inwrap; to embrace. [Obs.]

çom-pōne′, *v.t.* To compose; to settle. [Obs.]

çom-pō′né (-nā), çom-pō′ny, *a.* [Fr. *componé*, composed, from L. *componere*, to place together.] In heraldry, composed of small squares of two tinctures alternately in one row; said of a bordure, bend, or other ordinary.

Bordure Componé.

çŏm-pō′nent, *a.* [L. *componens*, ppr. of *componere*, to place together, compose; *com-*, together, and *ponere*, to place.] Composing; constituting; forming a constituent part; as, the *component* parts of a vegetable substance; the *component* parts of society.

çŏm-pō′nent, *n.* A constituent part.

çŏm-pōrt′, *v.i.*; comported, *pt.*, *pp.*; comporting, *ppr.* [Fr. *comporter*, allow, admit of; L. *comportare*, bring together; *com-*, together, and *portare*, to bring.] Literally, to bear; to carry; hence, to agree or suit; to accord; followed by *with*; as, charity should *comport with* prudence; his behavior does not *comport with* his station.

çŏm-pōrt′, *v.t.* 1. To behave; to conduct; with the reflexive pronoun. [Rare.]

> It is curious to observe how Lord Somers *comported himself* on that occasion.—Burke.

2. To bear; to endure. [Obs.]

çom′pōrt, *n.* Behavior; conduct; manner of acting; deportment. [Obs.]

> I knew them well, and marked their rude *comport*. —Dryden.

çŏm-pōrt′ȧ-ble, *a.* Suitable; consistent. [Obs.]

çŏm-pōrt′ănce, *n.* Behavior; deportment. [Obs.]

çom-pŏr-tā′tion, *n.* An assemblage. [Obs.]

çŏm-pōrt′ment, *n.* Behavior; demeanor; manner of acting; deportment. [Obs.]

çom′pō-sănt, *n.* Same as *Corposant.*

çŏm-pōşe′, *v.t.*; composed, *pt.*, *pp.*; composing, *ppr.* [OFr. *composer*, to compose, adjust, settle; L. *componere*, to put together, arrange; *com-*, together, and *ponere*, to put, place.]

1. To form by uniting two or more things; to put together; to form, frame, or fashion.

> A casque *composed* by Vulcan's skill.—Shak.

2. To form by being combined or united; to form the substance or constituents of; to constitute; to make; as, levies of raw soldiers *compose* his army.

3. To write as an author; to become the author of; as, to *compose* a sermon or a book; to *compose* a sonata for the piano.

4. To calm; to quiet; to appease.

> *Compose* thy mind;
> Nor frauds are here contrived, nor force design'd. —Dryden.

5. To settle; to adjust; as, to *compose* differences.

6. To place in proper form or in a quiet state.

> In a peaceful grave my corpse *compose*. —Dryden.

7. To dispose; to put in a proper state or temper for any purpose.

> *Compose* yourself to the situation.—Dickens.

8. In the fine arts, to arrange the leading features of; as, to *compose* a painting.

9. In printing, to put into type; to arrange in the composing-stick.

Syn.—Construct, form, frame, fashion, make, constitute, arrange, write, draw up, soothe, calm, pacify, allay, quiet.

çŏm-pōşe′, *v.i.* 1. To come to terms; to arrange. [Obs.]

2. To engage in composition of a literary or musical character; as, she *composes* well.

çŏm-pōşed′, *a.* Calm; sedate; quiet; tranquil; free from agitation.

çŏm-pōş′ed-ly, *adv.* Calmly; seriously; sedately.

çŏm-pōş′ed-ness, *n.* The state of being composed; calmness; sedateness; tranquillity.

çŏm-pōş′ẽr, *n.* 1. One who composes; one who writes an original work, as distinguished from a *compiler*; an author; especially an author of music; as, Mozart, the great *composer*.

2. One who or that which quiets or calms; one who adjusts a difference.

çŏm-pōş′ing, *a.* 1. Pertaining to composition.

2. Quieting; soothing; as, a *composing* draught.

çŏm-pōş′ing-frāme, *n.* In printing-offices, a working-stand of wood or metal for holding cases of type when in use by a compositor.

çŏm-pōş′ing-rụ̈le, *n.* In printing, a thin strip of steel or brass by the aid of which type is set and handled after setting. It is used in the composing-stick, the type being arranged against it; also called *setting-rule.*

çŏm-pōş′ing-stick, *n.* Among printers, an instrument in which type is set from the cases. It is usually made of metal, has one side open and one end adjustable to various lengths of line. It is held by the compositor in his left hand.

Composing-stick.

Çom-pos′i-tæ, *n.pl* [L., from *compositus*, composite, pp. of *componere*, to put together, compose.] The largest natural order of plants, containing over 12,000 described species of herbs or shrubs distributed all over the world. The flowers are generally numerous and sessile, forming a close head on the dilated top of the receptacle, and surrounded by an involucre of whorled bracts. Many varieties are common weeds, as the daisy, dandelion, and thistle, while many are cultivated in gardens, such as the aster, marigold, etc.

çom-pos′ite, *a.* [L. *compositus*, compound, composite, pp. of *componere*, to put together; *com-*, together, and *ponere*, to put.]

1. Made up of distinct parts, elements, or substances; compounded; as, a *composite* language.

> Happiness, like air and water, is *composite*. —Landor.

2. [C—] In architecture, a term applied to the last of the five classical orders; so called because the capital belonging to it is composed of the other orders, borrowing a quarter-round from the Tuscan and Doric, a row of leaves from the Corinthian, and volutes from the Ionic. Called also the *Roman* or *Italic* order.

Composite Order.

3. In shipbuilding, having a wooden skin on an iron framework; as, a vessel built on the *composite* principle.

4. In botany, belonging to the order *Compositæ*; having the characters of this order; as, a *composite* plant; *composite* flowers.

Composite carriage; in England, a railway-carriage made up of compartments of different classes, as first, second, and third.

Composite numbers; such as can be measured exactly by a number exceeding unity, as 6 by 2 or 3, so that 4 is the lowest *composite number*.

Composite photograph; a photographic picture formed by the combination of a number of distinct photographs in such manner that their principal points or features correspond and blend.

çom-pos′ite, *n.* Anything made up of separate parts; a compound.

çom-pō-şi′tion, *n.* [ME. *composicion*; OFr. *composition*; L. *compositio*, a putting together, (in rhetoric) a proper arrangement of words, from *compositus*, pp. of *componere*, to put together, arrange; *com-*, together, and *ponere*, to put.]

1. The act of composing or compounding, or the state of being composed or compounded; the act of producing some literary or musical piece.

2. The act of writing for practice in English or a foreign language; as, to learn Latin and Greek *composition*.

3. Adjustment; orderly disposition; regulation. [Obs.]

4. The act of coming to an agreement or arrangement; specifically, the act of making a mutual agreement for the discharge of a debt; as, a bankrupt is cleared by *composition* with his creditors.

5. In the fine arts, that combination of the several parts whereby a subject or object is agreeably presented to the mind, as the arrangement of figures, trees and vessels, in a painting or piece of sculpture, or of doors, windows, piers, columns, pilasters, and cornices in a building, with the view of setting off the whole to the best advantage.

6. In grammar, the act of forming compound words.

7. In printing, the act of setting type.

8. The result of an act of composing or compounding; applied to persons and things; as, the *composition* of a man of business; the *composition* of marble; a literary, musical, or artistic *composition*; a *composition* with creditors.

9. Relation in a group; the state of being placed together. [Obs.]

10. Consistency; congruity. [Rare.]

> There is no *composition* in those news,
> That gives them credit. —Shak.

11. Synthesis.

Composition cloth; a material made from long flax, and dressed with a solution which renders it waterproof.

Composition deed; the agreement between an insolvent creditor and those having claims against him.

Composition face or *plane*; the common plane in a twin crystal.

Composition metal; a kind of brass made of copper, zinc, etc., used instead of copper, which is dearer, as sheathing for vessels.

Composition of forces; the union or assemblage of several forces or motions that are oblique to one another, into an equivalent force or motion in another direction.

Composition of proportion; in mathematics, the substitution, in a series of four proportionals, of the sum of the first and second terms for the first term, and the sum of the third and fourth for the fourth, the same equality of proportion subsisting in the second series as in the first.

Syn.—Compound, conformation, structure, mixture, combination, compromise, adjustment, settlement, commutation.

çŏm-pos′i-tive, *a.* Compounded; having the power of compounding or composing. [Rare.]

çŏm-pos′i-tŏr, *n.* [L *compositor*, an arranger, or disposer, from *compositus*, pp. of *componere*, to arrange, put together.]

1 In printing, one who sets type, a typesetter; a printer.

2. One who composes or settles.

çŏm-pos′i-tous, *a.* Composite; denoting one of the *Compositæ*. [Rare.]

çom′pos men′tis. [L *compos mentis*, lit., having control of one's mind; *compos*, having control of, and *mens*, genit., *mentis*, mind.] Possessed of mind; of sound mind; used commonly to denote a sane and responsible person as distinguished from one who is insane and irresponsible.

çom-pos′si-ble, *a.* Consistent. [Rare.]

çom′pōst, *n.* [ME. *compost*; OFr. *composte*, a condiment, pickle; It. *composta*, a mixture, conserve, from L. *compositus*, pp. of *componere*, to bring together.]

1. In agriculture, a mixture or composition of various manuring substances for fertilizing land.

2. A plastering composition.

3. A compound. [Rare.]

çom′pōst, *v.t.*; composted, *pt.*, *pp.*; composting, *ppr.* To treat with a farm compost.

çom-pos′tūre, *n.* Soil; manure. [Obs.]

çŏm-pō′şūre, *n.* [From L. *compositus*, pp. of *componere*, to compose, put together.]

1. The act of composing, or that which is composed; a composition; as, a form of prayer of public *composure*; a hasty *composure*. [Obs.]

> In the *composures* of men, remember you are a man. —Watts.

2. Composition; combination; arrangement; order. [Rare.]

From the various *composures* of these corpuscles, happen all the varieties of bodies formed out of them. —Woodward.

3. The form, adjustment or disposition of the various parts; as, the *composure* of the body.
4. Frame; make; temperament. [Obs.]

His *composure* must be rare indeed,
Whom these things cannot blemish.—Shak.

5. A settled state of the mind; sedateness; calmness; tranquillity.

When the passions are silent, the mind enjoys its most perfect *composure*. —Watts.

6. Combination; bond. [Obs.]

It was a strong *composure* a fool could disunite. —Shak.

Syn.—Self-possession, tranquillity, sedateness, serenity, calmness, repose.

çom-pō-tā′tion, *n.* [L. *compotatio*, a drinking together; *com-*, together, and *potatio*, a drinking, from *potare*, to drink.] The act of drinking or tippling together. [Rare.]

çom′pō-tā-tŏr, *n.* One who drinks with another. [Rare.]

çom′pōte, *n.* [Fr.] 1. A preparation of fruit preserved in syrup so as to retain the form.
2. Same as *Compotier*.

çom-pō-tier′ (-tyā′), *n.* [Fr.] A dish in which compote is served.

çŏm-pound′, *v.t.*; compounded, *pt., pp.*; compounding, *ppr.* [M.E. *compounen*; OFr. *compondre*, to arrange, direct; L. *componere*, to arrange, put together; *com-*, together, and *ponere*, to put.]
1. To mix or unite (various ingredients) in one mass or body; as, to *compound* drugs.
2. To unite or combine.

We have the power of altering and *compounding* images into all the varieties of picture. —Addison.

3. To compose; to constitute. [Obs.]
4. In grammar, to unite (two or more words); to form (one word) of two or more.
5. To settle amicably; to adjust by agreement, as a difference or controversy.

I pray, my lords, let me *compound* this strife. —Shak.

6. To pay by agreement; to discharge, as a debt, by paying a part, or giving an equivalent different from that stipulated or required; as, to *compound* debts.
7. To change by combining with something else.
To compound a felony; to agree, for a consideration, not to prosecute for a crime committed. [See *Theftbote*.]

çŏm-pound′, *v.i.* 1. To agree upon concession; to come to terms of agreement, by abating something of the first demand; followed by *for* before the thing accepted or remitted.

They were glad to *compound for* his bare commitment to the Tower. —Clarendon.

2. To bargain in the lump; to agree; followed by *with*.

Compound with this fellow by the year.—Shak.

3. To come to terms, by granting something on each side; to agree.

Cornwall *compounded* to furnish ten oxen for thirty pounds. —Carew.

4. To settle with a creditor by agreement.

çom′pound, *a.* [M.E. *compouned*, compound, from *compounen*, to put together, compound.] Composed of two or more elements, parts, or ingredients; not simple.
Compound addition, subtraction, etc.; the addition, subtraction, etc., of compound numbers.
Compound crystal; see under *Crystal*.
Compound engine; one utilizing exhaust steam by using it in a low-pressure cylinder or cylinders, where it does work by expansion.
Compound ether; see under *Ether*.
Compound flower; the flower of a plant of the order *Compositæ*.
Compound fraction, fracture; see the nouns.
Compound householder; in England, one who makes an agreement with his landlord to include his rates in the rent.
Compound interest, larceny; see the nouns.
Compound leaf; a leaf composed of several leaflets on one petiole called a common petiole.
Compound microscope, motion; see the nouns.
Compound numbers; quantities consisting of more than one denomination, as 16 days, 8 hours, 7 minutes, 6 seconds; also called *denominate numbers*.
Compound pier; see *Clustered column* under *Column*.
Compound quantities; in algebra such quantities as are joined by the sign + or − (plus or minus), and expressed by more letters than one or by the same letters unequally repeated. Thus $a + b - c$ and $b^2 - b$ are *compound quantities*.
Compound radical; see under *Radical*.
Compound ratio; one which the product of the antecedents of two or more ratios has to the product of their consequents.
Compound rest; the tool-carrier of an engine-lathe, having a longitudinal and transverse movement.
Compound screw; two or more screws on the same axis. They may vary in size, or run in different directions.
Compound sentence; see *Sentence*.
Compound time; in music, time in which the bar is divided into two or more groups of simple measures, as $\frac{6}{8}$ or $\frac{9}{8}$.
Compound word; a word composed of two or more words either consolidated or connected by a hyphen, as *ink-well, writing-desk, table-cloth, housetop*.

çom′pound, *n.* Something produced by compounding two or more ingredients, parts, or elements; a word made up of two or more separate words.

Man is a *compound* of flesh and spirit.—South.

Many words that are really compound have lost the appearance of *compounds*, and look like simple words. —Bain.

Binary compound; see under *Binary*.
Carbon compounds; see under *Carbon*.
Syn.—Amalgamation, combination, mixture, medley.

çom′pound, *n.* [Malay *campong*, an inclosure.] In the East Indies, the inclosure in which isolated houses stand.

çŏm-pound′ȧ-ble, *a.* Capable of being compounded.

çŏm-pound′ẽr, *n.* 1. One who compounds or mixes.
2. One who attempts to bring parties to terms of agreement. [Rare.]
3. One who compounds with a debtor or felon.
4. One at an English university who pays extraordinary fees, according to his means, for the degree he is to take.
5. In English history, a member of one of the two divisions of the Jacobite party soon after the Revolution, wishing a restoration accompanied by amnesty and constitutional guarantees.

çom-prä-dōr′, *n.* [Port. and Sp. *comprador*; LL. *comparator*, a buyer; L. *comparatus*, pp. of *comparare*, to prepare, provide.] In the Chinese ports, as Canton, etc., a native trading manager for European merchants or residents.

çom-prē-çā′tion, *n.* A praying together. [Obs.]

çom-prē-hend′, *v.t.*; comprehended, *pt., pp.*; comprehending, *ppr.* [ME. *comprehenden*; OFr. *comprendre*; L. *comprehendere*, to seize, lay hold of, comprehend; *com-*, with, and *prehendere*, or *prendere*, to catch hold of, seize.]
1. To take in or include within a certain scope; to include by implication or signification; to embrace; to comprise; to imply; as, the United States *comprehends* Alaska and the Philippines.
2. To take into the mind; to grasp by the understanding; to possess or have in idea; to understand; to conceive or imagine.

Fantasies that apprehend more than cool reason ever *comprehends*. —Shak.

Syn.—Include, comprise, embody, embrace, encompass, contain, involve, understand, apprehend, conceive, discern, perceive, grasp.

çom-prē-hen-si-bil′i-ty, *n.* The quality of being comprehensible; comprehensibleness.

çom-prē-hen′si-ble, *a.* [L. *comprehensibilis*, comprehensible, from *comprehensus*, pp. of *comprehendere*, to lay hold of, comprehend.]
1. Capable of being comprehended or included.
2. Capable of being understood; intelligible; conceivable.

çom-prē-hen′si-ble-ness, *n.* Capability of being understood.

çom-prē-hen′si-bly, *adv.* In a comprehensive manner.

çom-prē-hen′sion, *n.* [L. *comprehensio*, a seizing, laying hold of, comprehension, from *comprehensus*, pp. of *comprehendere*, to lay hold of.]
1. The act of comprehending, including, or embracing; a comprising, inclusion.
2. That which comprehends or contains within itself; a summary; an epitome.
3. The act of taking into the mind; capacity of the mind to understand; power of the understanding to receive and contain ideas; capacity of knowing.
4. In rhetoric, a trope or figure, by which the name of a whole is put for a part, or that of a part for a whole, or a definite number for an indefinite.
5. In logic, all those attributes which make up the notion signified by a general term; all those attributes which are essential to the existence of an object as such.

Body, in its *comprehension*, takes in solidity, figure, quantity, mobility. —Watts.

Syn.—Understanding, knowledge, capacity, conception, perception, summary, epitome.

çom-prē-hen′sive, *a.* [LL. *comprehensivus*, comprehensive, from L. *comprehensus*, pp. of *comprehendere*, to comprehend.]
1. Having the quality of comprising or comprehending much; extensive in scope; said of mental and moral attributes; as, a *comprehensive* charity; a *comprehensive* mind.
2. In biology and zoölogy, synthetic.

çom-prē-hen′sive-ly, *adv.* In a comprehensive manner.

çom-prē-hen′sive-ness, *n.* The quality of being comprehensive, or of having a large scope; as, the *comprehensiveness* of a view.

Compare the beauty and *comprehensiveness* of legends on ancient coins. —Addison.

çom-prē-hen′sŏr, *n.* One who has obtained knowledge. [Obs.]

çŏm-press′, *v.t.*; compressed, *pt., pp.*; compressing, *ppr.* [L. *compressus*, pp. of *comprimere*, to press together, squeeze; *com-*, together, and *premere*, to press.]
1. To press together; to force, urge, or drive into a smaller compass; to condense; as, the air was *compressed*.
2. To embrace sexually. [Obs.]
Syn.—Crowd, press, squeeze, condense.

çom′press, *n.* 1. In surgery, a soft mass formed of tow, lint, or soft linen cloth, so contrived as by the aid of a bandage to make due pressure on any part.
2. An apparatus for further compressing bales of cotton.

çŏm-pressed′ (-prest′), *a.* 1. Pressed into narrow compass; condensed.
2. Flattened laterally or lengthwise; having the two opposite sides plane or flat; as, a *compressed* stem; the *compressed* bill of a bird; chiefly used in botany and zoölogy.
Compressed-air engine; see under *Engine*.

çŏm-press-i-bil′i-ty, *n.* The quality of being compressible; as, the *compressibility* of elastic fluids.

çŏm-press′i-ble, *a.* Capable of being forced or driven into a narrower compass; as, elastic fluids are *compressible*.

çŏm-press′i-ble-ness, *n.* Compressibility; the quality of being compressible.

çŏm-pres′sion, *n.* [L. *compressio*, a pressing together, from *compressus*, pp. of *comprimere*, to press or squeeze together.] The act of compressing, or the state of being compressed.

çŏm-press′ive, *a.* Having power to compress.

çŏm-press′ŏr, *n.* [L., from *compressus*, pp. of *comprimere*, to squeeze, compress.] One who or that which compresses. Specifically, (a) in anatomy, a name given to those muscles which press together the parts on which they act; as, the *compressor naris*, a muscle of the nose; (b) in surgery, a name given to instruments of various forms, used for compressing different parts of the body; (c) an appendage to a microscope, used for compressing objects with the view of rendering the examination of them more complete; (d) in gunnery, a mechanism for compressing a gun-carriage to its slide or platform during recoil; (e) in pneumatics, a machine for compressing air.

çŏm-pres′sūre (-presh′ūr), *n.* Compression; pressure. [Rare.]

çom-print′, *v.t.* and *v.i.* In law, to print (a work belonging to another) surreptitiously. [Rare.]

çom′print, *n.* The surreptitious printing of a work belonging to another; a work thus printed. [Obs.]

çŏm-pris′ăl, *n.* The act of comprising or comprehending; a compendium. [Rare.]

çŏm-prīşe′, *v.t.*; comprised, *pt., pp.*; comprising, *ppr.* [Fr. *compris*, pp. of *comprendre*, to comprehend, include; L. *comprehensus*, or *comprensus*, pp. of *comprehendere*, to comprehend, comprise.] To comprehend; to contain; to include; as, the German empire *comprises* a number of separate states.

Friendship does two souls in one *comprise*. —Roscommon.

Syn.—Embrace, include, comprehend, contain, encircle, inclose, involve, imply.

çom′prō-bāte, *v.i.* To agree or concur in testimony. [Obs.]

çom-prō-bā′tion, *n.* 1. Proof; joint attestation. [Obs.]
2. Joint approval or approbation. [Obs.]

çom′prō-mīşe, *n.* [Fr. *compromis*; LL. *compromissum*, a compromise, originally a mutual promise, from L. *compromissus*, pp. of *compromittere*, to make a mutual promise, to abide by the decision of an arbiter; *com-*, together, and *promittere*, to promise.]
1. A mutual promise or contract of two parties in controversy, to refer their differences to the decision of arbitrators.
2. An amicable agreement between parties in

controversy, to settle their differences by mutual concessions; mutual agreement; adjustment.

3. Submission to objectionable acts or opinions; as, it was a *compromise* of character.

4. Something which partakes of different characters or qualities; followed by *between*; as, it was a *compromise between* right and wrong.

Missouri compromise; a compromise between the advocates and opponents of slavery, incorporated in the congressional act by which Missouri was admitted into the Union as a slave state (1820), and by which in all the territory of the United States north of 36° 30′ north latitude slavery was prohibited; repealed in 1854.

çom′prō-mīse, *v.t.*; compromised, *pt.*, *pp.*; compromising, *ppr.* 1. To adjust and settle (a difference) by mutual agreement, with concessions of claims by the parties; to compound.

2. To agree; to accord.

3. To commit; to pledge in some manner or form; to put to hazard, or endanger (one's character, reputation, etc.), by an action that cannot be revoked.

çom′prō-mīse, *v.i.* 1. To come to terms; to yield partially for the sake of peace.

2. To agree. [Obs.]

çom′prō-mī-sẽr, *n.* One who compromises.

çom″prō-mis-sō′ri-ăl, *a.* Relating to a compromise. [Rare.]

çom-prō-mit′, *v.t.*; compromitted, *pt.*, *pp.*; compromitting, *ppr.* [ME. *compromytte*; L. *compromittere*, to make a mutual promise.]

1. To pledge or engage, by some act or declaration, which may not be a direct promise, but which renders necessary some future act.

2. To put to hazard, by some previous act or measure, which cannot be recalled; to compromise; as, to *compromit* the honor or the safety of a nation.

çom-prō-vin′ciăl (-shăl), *n.* and *a.* I. *n.* One belonging to the same province or archiepiscopal jurisdiction. [Obs.]

II. *a.* Relating to or emanating from the same province.

Çomp-sog′nā-thus, *n.* [Gr. *kompsos*, elegant, and *gnathos*, jaw.] A genus of extinct reptiles, of the order *Dinosauria*, having some characteristics of birds.

çompt (kount), *n.* [Fr. *compte*, from L. *computo*.] Account; computation. [Obs.]

çompt, *v.t.* To compute. [Obs. See *Count*.]

çompt, *a.* Neat; spruce. [Obs.]

çompt′ẽr, *n.* [Obs.] Same as *Counter*.

çompt′i-ble (kount′), *a.* Accountable. [Obs.]

çompt′ly, *adv.* Neatly. [Obs.]

çompt′ness, *n.* Neatness. [Obs.]

çompt′ō-grăph (kount′), *n.* [Fr. *compter*; L. *computare*, to compute, count, and Gr. *graphein*, to write.] An adding-machine that automatically makes a record of the results obtained.

çomp-tom′e-tẽr (kom-), *n.* [Fr. *compter*; L. *computare*, to compute, and *metrum*, a measure.] A machine for calculating figures; an arithmometer.

çomp-trōl′ (kon-), *n.* and *v.* See *Control*.

çomp-trōl′lẽr (kon-), *n.* See *Controller*.

çŏm-pul′sȧ-tive, *a.* Compulsory. [Rare.]

çŏm-pul′sȧ-tive-ly, *adv.* By constraint or compulsion. [Rare.]

çŏm-pul′sȧ-tō-ry, *a.* Compelling; forcing; constraining; operating by force. [Rare.]

çŏm-pul′sion, *n.* [LL. *compulsio*, compulsion, from L. *compulsus*, pp. of *compellere*, to force, drive together, compel; *com-*, together, and *pellere*, to strike.]

1. The act of driving or urging by force, physical or moral; constraint of the will; the application of a force that is irresistible.

> If reasons were as plenty as blackberries, I would give no man a reason on *compulsion*. —Shak.

2. The state of being compelled or urged by violence; the condition of being subject to a compelling power.

Syn.—Coercion, constraint, force, restraint, urgency, necessity, violence, obligation.

çŏm-pul′sive, *a.* Having power to compel; driving; forcing; constraining; applying force; as, uniformity of opinions cannot be effected by *compulsive* measures.

çŏm-pul′sive-ly, *adv.* By compulsion; by force.

çŏm-pul′sive-ness, *n.* Force; compulsion.

çŏm-pul′sō-ri-ly, *adv.* In a compulsory manner; by force or constraint.

çŏm-pul′sō-ry, *a.* 1. Having compelling power; applying such force as to overcome resistance; constraining.

2. Prescribed by proper authority; obligatory; required; as, *compulsory* studies.

çŏm-punçt′, *a.* Stricken by conscience, or with compunction. [Obs.]

çŏm-punç′tion, *n.* [LL. *compunctio*, a sticking or pricking; L. *compunctus*, pp. of *compungere*, to prick, sting; *com-*, intens., and *pungere*, to prick.]

1. Literally, a pricking; stimulation; irritation. [Obs.]

2. A pricking of heart; poignant grief or remorse proceeding from a consciousness of guilt; the sting of conscience.

> He acknowledged his disloyalty to the king, with expressions of great *compunction*. —Clarendon.

Syn.—Contrition, penitence, regret, remorse, repentance, sorrow.

çŏm-punç′tion-less, *a.* Having no compunction.

çŏm-punç′tious, *a.* Pricking the conscience; causing or actuated by compunction.

çŏm-punç′tious-ly, *adv.* With a feeling of compunction.

çŏm-punç′tive, *a.* 1. Causing remorse. [Obs.]

2. Sensitive to remorse; capable of repentance; conscientious.

çom-pũr-gā′tion, *n.* [LL. *compurgatio*, a purifying, from L. *compurgatus*, pp. of *compurgare*, to purge, purify; *com-*, intens., and *purgare*, to purge, purify.]

1. In law, the act or practice of justifying a man by the oath of others, who swear to their belief in his veracity; called also *wager of law*; specifically, in early English law, the privilege by which the accused could call upon twelve witnesses to swear to such belief.

2. Testimony of a vindicatory nature; exculpation.

çom′pũr-gā-tŏr, *n.* One who bears testimony or swears to the veracity or innocence of another.

çŏm-pũr-gȧ-tō′ri-ăl, *a.* Pertaining to compurgation, or to those who swear to it; as, *compurgatorial* testimony.

çom-pũr′sion, *n.* Drawing up or wrinkling of the features; as, *compursion* of the mouth. [Rare.]

çŏm-pūt′ȧ-ble, *a.* Capable of being computed, numbered, or reckoned.

çom-pū-tā′tion, *n.* [L. *computatio*, a reckoning, from *computare*, to compute, reckon.]

1. The act of computing, numbering, reckoning, or estimating; the process by which different sums or items are numbered, estimated, or compared; as, a *computation* of the time required to do a certain thing; a *computation* of the quantity of provisions required to support an army for a year.

2. The sum, quantity, or amount ascertained by computing or reckoning.

> We pass for women of fifty: many additional years are thrown into female *computations* of this nature. —Addison.

çŏm-pūte′, *v.t.* and *v.i.*; computed, *pt.*, *pp.*; computing, *ppr.* I. *v.t.* To number; to count; to reckon; to cast together (several sums or particulars); to ascertain the amount, aggregate, or other result of; as, to *compute* the quantity of water that will fill a vessel of certain dimensions; to *compute* the expenses of a campaign.

II. *v.i.* To cast or estimate in the mind; to estimate the amount by known or supposed data; to calculate; as, to *compute* by tens.

Syn.—Calculate, appraise, estimate, number, cast up, reckon, count, value, rate.

çŏm-pūte′, *n.* Computation. [Rare.]

çŏm-pūt′ẽr, *n.* One who computes; a reckoner; a calculator.

çom′pū-tist, *n.* A computer. [Obs.]

çom′rade (*or* răd), *n.* [ME. *comered*; Fr. *camerade*, a company, society, comrade; Sp. *camarada*, a chamber-mate; L. *camera*, a chamber.] A fellow, a mate, or companion; an associate in occupation or pleasure; used especially of soldiers; as, *comrades* in arms.

çom′rade-ry, *n.* Comradeship. [Rare.]

çom′rade-ship, *n.* The state of being comrades; good-fellowship; intimacy,

çom′rōgue (-rōg), *n.* A fellow-rogue. [Obs.]

çomte (koṅt), *n.* [Fr.] In France, a count; a hereditary title of nobility.

Çom′ti-ăn (koṅ′), *a.* Pertaining to Auguste Comte, a French metaphysician of the eighteenth century, or to his system of philosophy. [See *Positivism*.]

Çom′tişm (koṅ′), *n.* The system of reasoning taught by Comte; positivism.

Çom′tist (koṅ′), *n.* A student or adherent of Comte's philosophy; a positivist.

çon-. A prefix from L. *com-*, or *con-*, with, together, from the L. prep. *cum*, with, and signifying with, together, or sometimes adding merely intensive force; also written *co-*, *col-*, *com-*, *cor-*, for the sake of euphony.

çon, *adv.* and *n.* [An abbrev. of L. *contra*, against.]

I. *adv.* In opposition; in the phrase *pro and con*, for and against, *con* denotes the negative.

II. *n.* A person who is in the negative, or an argument for the negative; as, the *pros* and *cons*.

çon, *v.t.*; conned, *pt.*, *pp.*; conning, *ppr.* [ME. *cunnen*; AS. *cunnian*, to try, test.]

1. To know. [Obs.]

> Of muses, Hobbinol, I *conne* no skill. —Spenser.

2. To peruse or study carefully; to gaze at steadfastly; to memorize; to learn; as, to *con* a speech.

çon, *v.t.* [A dialectical form of *can*, to be able.] To direct the course or steering of (a ship); as, he *conned* the ship from the main rigging.

çon-ā′çre (-kẽr), *v.t.* and *n.* I. *v.t.* To let on the conacre system.

II. *n.* In Ireland, the custom of letting land in small portions to poor people for a single crop, the rent being paid in money or in labor.

çon-ā′çre, *a.* Relating to the custom of conacre, or of letting land in that way; as, the *conacre* system.

çon ä-mō′re. [It.] With love or pleasure; as, in music, to play or sing *con amore*.

çō-nā′ri-um, *n.* [L., from Gr. *kōnarion*, the pineal gland, dim. of *kōnos*, a cone.] In anatomy, the pineal gland, or pineal body of the brain.

çō-nā′tion, *n.* [L. *conatio*, an attempt, from *conari*, to undertake, attempt.] The faculty of impelling or directing muscular or mental effort; a philosophical term embracing the voluntary powers; voluntary agency.

çō′nȧ-tive, *a.* Relating to the faculty of conation.

> The exertive or *conative* powers.—Hamilton.

çō-nā′tus, *n.* A tendency simulating an effort on the part of a plant or animal to supply a want; a nisus; an effort; an impulse.

çon-ax′i-ăl, *a.* See *Coaxial*.

çon-çam′ẽr-āte, *v.t.*; concamerated, *pt.*, *pp.*; concamerating, *ppr.* [L. *concameratus*, pp. of *concamerare*, to arch over.]

1. To arch over; to vault; to lay a concave over. [Rare.]

2. In zoölogy, to separate into chambers or cavities.

çon-çam-ẽr-ā′tion, *n.* 1. An arching; an arch or vault; an arched chamber. [Rare.]

2. A chamber or cell, as of some shells.

çon-çat′e-nāte, *v.t.*; concatenated, *pt.*, *pp.*; concatenating, *ppr.* [LL. *concatenatus*, pp. of *concatenare*, to link together.] To link together; to unite in a successive series or chain, as things depending on each other; as, all the affairs of human life are *concatenated*.

çon-çat-e-nā′tion, *n.* 1. A series of links united; a successive series or order of things connected or depending on each other; as, a *concatenation* of causes.

2. The condition of being concatenated.

çon-çau-les′cence, *n.* [L. *con-*, with, and *caulis*, a stalk.] In botany, the gradual approach and union of axes, or of an organ and an axis.

çon-çause′, *n.* Joint cause. [Rare.]

çon-çȧ-vā′tion, *n.* The act of making concave.

çon′çāve, *a.* [Fr. *concave*; L. *concavus*, hollow; *con-*, intens., and *cavus*, hollow.]

1. Hollow, and arched or rounded, as the inner surface of a spherical body; opposed to *convex*; as, a *concave* lens; a *concave* mirror.

2. Arched or curved, in a general sense; as, the *concave* shores of the Tiber. [Rare.]

3. In botany, hollow like a dish; as, a *concave* leaf.

Concave or Plano-concave Lens.

Concave lens; a lens which has either one or both sides arched in toward the center, or hollow; if both, the lens is said to be *double concave*, or *concavo-concave*.

çon′çāve, *n.* 1. A hollow; an arch, or vault; as, the *concave* of the heavens.

2. Any portion of a machine which has a concave surface.

çon′çāve, *v.t.*; concaved, *pt.*, *pp.*; concaving, *ppr.* To make hollow or incurved.

çon′çāved, *a.* Arched; shaped like an arch.

çon′çāve-ness, *n.* Hollowness.

çon-çav′i-ty, *n.* [LL. *concavitas*, concavity; L. *concavus*, hollow.] Hollowness; the internal surface of a hollow curved body; the space within such body.

çon-çā′vō-çon′çāve, *a.* Concave or hollow on both surfaces; usually applied to lenses.

Concavo-concave Lens.

çon-çā′vō-çon′vex, *a.* Concave on one side, and convex on the other.

Concavo-convex lens; in optics, a lens in which the convex face has a slighter curvature than the concave.

çon-çā′vous, *a.* Concave. [Obs.]

çon-çā′vous-ly, *adv.* In a concave manner; so as to show a concave surface; concavely.

çŏn-çēal′, *v.t.*; concealed, *pt.*, *pp.*; concealing, *ppr.* [ME. *concelen*; L. *concelare*, to hide; *con-*, together, and *celare*, to hide.]

Concavo-convex Lens.

1. To keep close or secret; to forbear to disclose; to withhold from utterance or declaration; as, to *conceal* one's thoughts or opinions.

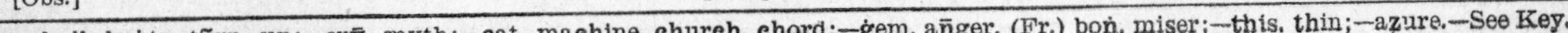

2. To hide; to withdraw from observation; to cover or keep from sight; as, a party of men *concealed* themselves behind a wall; a mask *conceals* the face.

Syn.—Cover, disguise, dissemble, withhold, secrete, hide, mask, palliate, screen, veil, cloak, bury.

çŏn-çēal′á-ble, *a.* Capable of being concealed, hidden, withheld, or kept close.

çŏn-çēaled′, *a.* Kept close or secret; hidden; withdrawn from sight; covered.

Concealed weapons; weapons, such as fire-arms or knives, hidden upon the person, but ready for use, to carry such being a violation of law.

çŏn-çēal′ed-ly, *adv.* So as not to be detected; secretly.

çŏn-çēal′ed-ness, *n.* The state of being concealed.

çŏn-çēal′ẽr, *n.* One who hides or withholds knowledge of; as, the *concealer* of a crime.

çŏn-çēal′ment, *n.* 1. Forbearance of disclosure; a keeping close or secret; as, the *concealment* of opinions or passions.

2. The act of hiding, covering, or withdrawing from sight; as, the *concealment* of the face by a mask; the *concealment* of a person in a house.

3. The state of being hidden or concealed; privacy; as, a project formed in *concealment.*

4. The place of hiding; a secret place; retreat from observation; cover from sight; as, his *concealment* was a deep forest.

5. Secret knowledge; a secret. [Obs.]

6. In law, the suppression of truth to the injury or prejudice of another; the withholding of knowledge which one is bound in justice to reveal.

çŏn-çēde′, *v.t.*; conceded, *pt., pp.*; conceding, *ppr.* [L. *concedere*, to yield, grant; *con-*, with, and *cedere*, to go, cede, grant.]

1. To yield; to admit as true, just, or proper; to grant; to let pass undisputed; as, the advocate *concedes* the point in question.

We *concede* that their citizens were those who lived under different forms. —Burke.

2. To grant; to bestow on request; to yield to application; as, when asked, he readily *conceded* the use of the property.

3. To make a concession of; to grant as a privilege; to yield up; to grant, to allow; to surrender; as, the Egyptian government *conceded* to a Frenchman the privilege of cutting the Suez canal.

çŏn-çēde′, *v.i.* To assent, yield, permit, or make concession.

Syn.—Yield, admit, grant, suffer, permit, allow, acquiesce, assent, surrender.

çŏn-çēit′, *n.* [ME. *conceit, conseit*; OFr. *concept*, conceit, from L. *conceptus*, a collecting, taking, from *concipere*, to take, lay hold of, perceive.]

1. Conception; that which is conceived, imagined, or formed in the mind; idea; thought; image; as, his *conceit* of happiness was vague indeed. [Rare.]

2. Understanding; power or faculty of conceiving; apprehension; as, a man of quick *conceit.* [Obs.]

3. Opinion; notion; fancy; imagination; estimation; fantastic notion.

Seest thou a man wise in his own *conceit?* there is more hope of a fool than of him. —Prov. xxvi. 12.

4. A witty, happy, or ingenious thought or expression; something witty, amusing, or well-conceived; a quaint or humorous fancy; as, it was a happy *conceit.*

5. Favorable or self-flattering opinion; a lofty or vain conception of one's own person or accomplishments; self-consciousness.

By a little study and a great *conceit* of himself, he has lost his religion. —Bentley.

6. A trifling article, ingeniously contrived; a fanciful device; a pretty or attractive trifle.

Out of conceit with; not having a favorable opinion of; no longer pleased with; as, a man is *out of conceit with* his neighbor.

Syn.—Conception, thought, image, apprehension, fancy, device, whim, idea, vagary, vanity, egotism, pride.

çŏn-çēit′, *v.t.* and *v.i.* I. *v.t.* To conceive; to imagine; to think; to fancy. [Obs.]

The strong, by *conceiting* themselves weak, are thereby rendered inactive. —South.

II. *v.i.* To conceive an idea; to have an image; to picture to oneself. [Obs.]

çŏn-çēit′ed, *a.* 1. Endowed with fancy or imagination. [Obs.]

2. Entertaining a flattering opinion of oneself; having a vain conception of one's own person or accomplishments; vain; self-conscious; self-opinionated; commonly followed by *of* before the object of conceit.

The Athenians were *conceited of* their own wit, science, and politeness. —Bentley.

3. Ingeniously contrived; curiously designed. [Obs.]

Syn.—Egotistical, opinionated, proud, self-important, vain.

çŏn-çēit′ed-ly, *adv.* In a conceited manner; fancifully; whimsically.

Conceitedly dress her. —Donne.

çŏn-çēit′ed-ness, *n.* The state of being conceited; conceit; vanity; an overweening sense of one's own importance

çŏn-çēit′less, *a.* Of dull conception; stupid; dull of apprehension. [Obs.]

çŏn-çēiv′á-ble, *a.* [Fr. *concevable.*]

1. Capable of being imagined or thought.

If it were possible to contrive an invention, whereby any *conceivable* weight may be moved by any *conceivable* power.—Wilkins.

2. Capable of being understood or believed.

It is not *conceivable* that it should be the very person, whose shape and voice are assumed. —Atterbury.

çŏn-çēiv′á-ble-ness, *n.* The quality of being conceivable.

çŏn-çēiv′á-bly, *adv.* In a conceivable or intelligible manner.

çŏn-çēive′, *v.t.*; conceived, *pt., pp.*; conceiving, *ppr.* [ME. *conceiven, conceyven*; OFr. *concever, conciver*; L. *concipere*, to take in, receive; *con-*, together, and *capere*, to take.]

1. To receive into the womb, and breed; to begin the formation of the embryo or fetus of.

Elizabeth, she hath also *conceived* a son in her old age. —Luke i. 36.

2. To form in the mind; to imagine; to devise; as, to *conceive* a plan of escape.

3. To form an idea concerning; to understand; to comprehend; as, we cannot *conceive* the manner in which spirit operates upon matter.

4. To think; to imagine; to apprehend; to believe or suppose.

You can hardly *conceive* this man to have been bred in the same climate. —Swift.

5. To become possessed with; as, to *conceive* a violent hatred of any one.

çŏn-çēive′, *v.i.* 1. To have a fetus formed in the womb; to breed; to become pregnant.

Thou shalt *conceive* and bear a son. —Judges xiii. 3.

2. To think; to have a conception or idea; used with *of.*

Conceive of things clearly and distinctly in their own natures. —Watts.

Syn.—Engender, originate, formulate, comprehend, apprehend, perceive, suppose, understand, think.

çŏn-çēiv′ẽr, *n.* A person who conceives or comprehends.

çon-çel′ē-brāte, *v.t.* To celebrate together. [Obs.]

çŏn-çent′, *n.* [L. *concentus*, harmony, from *concinere*, to sing, play, or sound together; *con-*, together, and *canere*, to sing.]

1. Concert of voices; concord of sounds; harmony; as, a *concent* of notes. [Rare.]

2. Consistency; accordance; as, in *concent* to a man's own principles. [Obs.]

çŏn-çen′tẽr, çŏn-çen′tre, *v.i.*; concentered or concentred, *pt., pp.*; concentering or concentring, *ppr.* [Fr. *concentrer*, to center; L. *con-*, together, and *centrum*, center.] To come to a point, or to meet in a common center; used of converging lines, or other things that meet in a point.

All these are like so many lines drawn from several objects, that in some way relate to him, and *concenter* in him. —Hale.

çŏn-çen′tẽr, çŏn-çen′tre, *v.t.* To draw or direct to a common center; to bring to a point, as lines or arguments.

All is *concentered* in a life intense.—Byron.

çŏn-çent′fụl, *a.* Harmonious. [Obs.]

çŏn-çen′trāte (*or* kon′), *v.t.*; concentrated, *pt., pp.*; concentrating, *ppr.* 1. To bring to a common center, or to a closer union; to cause to approach nearer to a point, or center; to bring nearer to each other; as, to *concentrate* the troops in an army; to *concentrate* rays of light into a focus.

2. To increase the specific gravity of a body; to intensify in strength by evaporation, etc.; as, to *concentrate* acid.

3. To intensify or purify, as by removing foreign substances from ore or deleterious and weakening elements from liquid compounds.

çŏn-çen′trāte, *v.i.* 1. To gather toward a common center; to become solidified or compacted; as, the army will *concentrate* at Manila.

2. To become pure or unmixed, as ores or chemicals.

Syn.—Converge, congregate, assemble, muster, convene, conglomerate, draw, condense, localize, centralize, intensify.

çŏn-çen′trāte, *a.* and *n.* I. *a.* Increased in strength by concentration; purified by chemical action.

II. *n.* The resultant of a process of reduction; the chemical or ore thus purified.

çŏn-çen′trā-ted, *a.* 1. Brought to a point or center; brought to a closer union; reduced to a narrow compass; collected into a closer body.

2. Intensified in strength or purity by a process of concentration.

çon-çen-trā′tion, *n.* [From L. *con-*, together, and *centrum*, a center.]

1. The act of concentrating; the act of bringing nearer together; collection at a central point; compression into a narrow space; the state of being brought to a point.

2. In chemistry, the volatilization of part of a liquid, in order to increase the strength of the remainder.

3. In mining, the act or process of separating waste matter, as earth and rock, from ore, as by washing, or chemical action in a reduction-mill.

4. The result of concentrating.

çŏn-çen′trā-tive, *a.* Inclining to or distinguished by concentration.

çŏn-çen′trā-tive-ness, *n.* The quality or faculty of concentrating; specifically, in phrenology, the power by which mental concentration (or the centering of the mentality upon one object) is assured.

çon′çen-trā-tŏr, *n.* 1. One who or that which concentrates.

2. In mining, a machine or device for concentrating ore.

3. A device used by trap-shooters and others to prevent the scattering of shot.

çon-çen′triç, çon-çen′triç-ăl, *a.* 1. Having a common center; as, the *concentric* coats of an onion; the *concentric* orbits of the planets.

2. In military language, concentrated upon a given point; as, *concentric* fire.

çon-çen′triç, *n.* Anything which has a common center with another thing. [Rare.]

Its peculiar relations to its *concentrics.* —Coleridge.

çon-çen′triç-ăl-ly, *adv.* In a concentric manner.

çon-çen-tric′i-ty, *n.* The state of being concentric; the state of having a center in common with another body or figure.

çon-çen′tū-ăl, *a.* [L. *concentus*, harmony, from *concinere*, to play or sing together.] Harmonious; accordant. [Rare.]

çon′çept, *n.* [L. *conceptus*, a collecting, gathering, a thought, from *concipere*, to take in, conceive; *con-*, and *capere*, to take.] The subject of a conception; the object conceived by the mind; an abstract conception.

The modern distinction between *percept* and *concept*, the one sensuous, the other intellectual. —Max Müller.

çŏn-çep′tā-çle, *n.* 1. That in which anything is contained; receptacle.

2. In botany, a follicle; a pericarp of one valve, opening longitudinally on one side and having the seeds loose in it. The term has also been applied to the cases containing the reproductive organs of such plants as ferns.

Conceptacle of an Alga, embedded in cellular tissue.

çŏn-çep-ti-bil′i-ty, *n.* That which is capable of conception; conceivableness.

çŏn-çep′ti-ble, *a.* Conceivable; intelligible; as, attributes easily *conceptible* by us.

çŏn-çep′tion, *n.* [ME. *conceptioun*; L. *conceptio*, a comprehending, a conception, from *conceptus*, pp. of *concipere*, to conceive.]

1. The act of conceiving; the first formation of the embryo of an animal; figuratively, origin; source; beginning.

2. The act or power of conceiving in the mind; that which is conceived in the mind; a product of the imaginative or inventive faculty. When an object is seen with the eyes, there is a *perception* of it; when the same object is presented to the mind in idea only, or in memory, there is a *conception* of it.

3. In philosophy, that mental act or combination of acts by which an absent object of perception is brought before the mind by the imagination.

4. Thought, notion, or idea, in the general sense; as, you have no *conception* how clever he is.

5. A conceit; a fanciful thought; a fantastic thought or figure of speech. [Obs.]

6. The formation in the mind of a plan or design; a plan thought out beforehand; a mental picture; an image; an idea; as, an architect's *conception* of a building.

False conception; a conception in which an abnormal, fleshy mass, as a tumor or mole, is produced, instead of a normally developed fetus.

Immaculate conception; see *Immaculate.*

Order of the Conception; an order formed in the German and Italian states during the seventeenth century by princes of the Holy Roman Empire.

Syn.—Apprehension, comprehension, concept, image, imagination, thought, notion, idea, sentiment, view.

çŏn-cep′tion-ăl, *a.* Relating to a conception or image.

çŏn-cep′tion-ăl-ist, *n.* Same as *Conceptualist.*

çŏn-cep′tious (-shus), *a.* Apt to conceive; fruitful; pregnant. [Obs.]

çŏn-cep′tive, *a.* Capable of conceiving; used in a physical and also in a figurative sense.

çŏn-cep′tū-ăl, *a.* Pertaining to conception, mental or physical.

çŏn-cep′tū-ăl-iṣm, *n.* In metaphysics, a doctrine in some sense intermediate between realism and nominalism, viz., that the mind has the power, inherent in itself, of formulating concepts, to which there are no corresponding concrete universals.

çŏn-cep′tū-ăl-ist, *n.* One who holds the doctrine of conceptualism.

çŏn-cẽrn′, *v.t.*; concerned, *pt., pp.*; concerning, *ppr.* [Fr. *concerner*, to concern; LL. *concernere*, to mix, mingle as in a sieve; L. *con-*, and *cernere*, to separate, sift.]

1. To relate or belong to.

> Preaching the kingdom of God and teaching those things which *concern* the Lord Jesus Christ. —Acts xxviii. 31.

2. To relate or belong to, in an emphatic manner; to affect the interest of; to be of importance to.

3. To interest or affect the mind of; to take an interest in; to engage by feeling or sentiment; as, a good prince *concerns* himself in the happiness of his subjects.

4. To disturb; to make uneasy; as, to be much *concerned* for the safety of a friend.

Syn.—Pertain, relate to, affect, disturb, belong to, interest, impress, trouble, move, touch.

çŏn-cẽrn′, *n.* 1. That which busies or occupies one's thoughts; that which relates or pertains to one; business; matter; interest; affair; as, each one has his own *concerns* to attend to.

2. That which pertains to or affects in any way one's interests, welfare, or happiness; a matter of importance.

> 'Tis all mankind's *concern* that he should live. —Dryden.

3. Compassionate or affectionate regard; solicitude; anxiety; agitation or uneasiness of mind; disturbed state of feeling.

> Why all this *concern* for the poor? We want them not. —Swift.
>
> O Marcia, let me hope thy kind *concerns*,
> And gentle wishes, follow me to battle.
> —Addison.

4. An establishment or firm for the transaction of business; a manufacturing or commercial establishment; as, two banking *concerns* closed their doors at noon.

5. Loosely applied to objects generally, especially to those that are large and somewhat clumsily constructed; a contrivance. [Colloq.]

> The hackney-coach, a great, lumbering, square *concern.* —Dickens.

Syn.—Matter, affair, business, interest, regard, moment, importance, care, solicitude, anxiety.

çŏn-cẽrned′ *a.* 1. Interested; engaged; having a connection with; as, A is *concerned* with B in the East India trade.

2. Regarding with care; solicitous; anxious; as, we are *concerned* for the fate of our fleet.

çŏn-cẽrn′ed-ly, *adv.* With affection or interest.

çŏn-cẽrn′ing, *prep.* Pertaining to; regarding; about; having relation to; as, he spoke only good *concerning* the man.

çŏn-cẽrn′ing, *a.* Affecting the interests; important. [Obs.]

çŏn-cẽrn′ing, *n.* A matter of concern, interest, or importance. [Obs.]

çŏn-cẽrn′ment, *n.* 1. The thing in which one is concerned or interested; concern; affair; business; interest.

> The great *concernment* of men is with men. —Locke.

2. Importance; moment.

> Experimental truths are matters of great *concernment* to mankind. —Boyle.

3. Concern; interposition; meddling; as, the father's *concernment* in the marriage of his daughter was slight.

4. Emotion of mind; solicitude; as, their ambition is manifest in their *concernment.*

çŏn-cẽrt′, *v.t.*; concerted, *pt., pp.*; concerting, *ppr.* [Fr. *concerter*; It. *concertare*; L. *concertare*, to contend, contest; *con-*, and *certare*, to strive.]

1. To contrive and settle by mutual communication of opinions or propositions; to settle or adjust, as a plan or system to be pursued, by conference or agreement of two or more parties; as, to *concert* a scheme; to *concert* a plan of operations.

2. To arrange; to plan.

çŏn-cẽrt′, *v.i.* To act in conjunction; to plan or arrange after consultation or agreement.

çon′cẽrt, *n.* [Fr. *concert*; It. *concerto*, an agreement, union, from *concertare*, to contest together; L. *concertare*, to strive.]

1. Agreement of two or more in a design or plan; union formed by mutual communication of opinions and views; accordance in a scheme; harmony; as, the allies acted in *concert.*

2. A public or private musical entertainment at which a number of vocalists or instrumentalists, or both, perform singly or combined.

3. Any public musical entertainment.

4. In music, concord; harmony.

Concert grand; a loud-toned grand piano, for orchestral use.

Concert pitch; see under *Pitch.*

çon-cẽr-tan′tē (*or It. pron.*, kon-chär-tän′te), *n.* and *a.* [It., ppr. of *concertare*, to form a concert.] A term applied in the eighteenth century to compositions for the orchestra in which there were special parts for solo instruments, and occasionally to compositions for solo instruments without the orchestra. It is now generally used as an adjective, indicating certain prominent solo parts in an orchestral composition, which are spoken of as *concertante* parts.

çon-cẽr-tā′tion, *n.* Strife; contention. [Obs.]

çŏn-cẽr′tȧ-tive, *a.* Contentious; quarrelsome. [Obs.]

çŏn-cẽrt′ed, *a.* 1. Mutually planned or contrived; as, a *concerted* scheme.

2. In music, arranged in parts for several voices or instruments, as a trio, a quartet, etc.

çon-cẽr-tī′nȧ, *n.* [It., from *concerto*, a concert.] A portable musical instrument, the principle of which is similar to that of the accordion. It is composed of a bellows, with two faces or ends, generally polygonal in shape, on which are placed the various stops or studs, by the action of which air is admitted to the free metallic reeds which produce the sounds. The *concertina* varies somewhat, in different countries, as to the number of finger-stops and the general compass of the instrument.

çon-cẽr-tī′nō, *n.* [It., dim. of *concerto.*] A short, solo composition for the orchestra.

çŏn-cẽr′tion, *n.* Concert; contrivance; adjustment. [Rare.]

çon′cẽrt-mȧs″tẽr, *n.* In an orchestra, the principal violinist; the assistant conductor.

çon-cẽr′to (*or It. pron.*, kon-chär′tō), *n.* [It.] A piece of music for a concert; originally, a composition in which many performers played in unison, but in which one or two instruments took the lead; but now a species of composition, usually in a symphonic form, written for one principal instrument, with accompaniments for a full orchestra, designed for displaying the ability of a solo performer.

çŏn-ces′sion, *n.* [Fr. *concession*; L. *concessio*, a concession, from *concessus*, pp. of *concedere*, to concede, grant.]

1. The act of granting or yielding; usually implying a demand, claim, or request from the party to whom it is made, and thus distinguished from *giving*, which is voluntary or spontaneous.

> The *concession* of these charters was in a parliamentary way. —Hale.

2. The thing granted or yielded; as, in the treaty of peace, each power made large *concessions*; a *concession* of land.

3. In rhetoric, the yielding, granting, or allowing to the opposite party, some point of fact that may bear dispute, with a view of obtaining something which cannot be denied, or to show that, even admitting the point conceded, the cause is not with the adverse party, but can be maintained by the advocate on other grounds.

4. Any privilege or right granted; as, a *concession* for the construction of a public building, railroad, canal, etc.

çŏn-ces′sion-ā-ry, *a.* Yielding by indulgence or allowance. [Obs.]

çŏn-ces′sion-ā-ry, *n.*; *pl.* **çŏn-ces′sion-ā-rieṣ.** A concessioner.

çŏn-ces′sion-ẽr, *n.* [Fr. *concessionnaire.*] One who receives or holds a concession, as for the construction of public buildings, ships, canals, etc.

çŏn-ces′sion-ist, *n.* One who is in favor of making concessions.

çŏn-ces′sive, *a.* Implying concession; as, a *concessive* conjunction.

çŏn-ces′sive-ly, *adv.* By way of concession or yielding.

çŏn-ces′sō-ry, *a.* Conceding; yielding; permissive. [Rare.]

çon-cet′ti, *n.*, pl. of *concetto.*

çon-cet′tiṣm, *n.* [It. *concetto*, conceit.] The use of affected wit or concetto.

çon-cet′tō, *n.*; *pl.* **çon-cet′ti.** [It.] Affected wit; a conceit. [Obs.]

çonch, *n.* [L. *concha*; Gr. *konchē*, a mussel, shell.]

1. A marine shell, especially that of the *Strombus gigas*, or fountain-shell, found in the West Indies, and of great size.

> Orient pearls which from the *conchs* he drew. —Dryden.

2. A spiral shell used by the mythological divinities called Tritons as a trumpet, and often depicted in works of art.

3. The external portion of the ear, more especially the hollow part of it; also called *concha.*

4. In architecture, the semidome of an apse, or the apse itself; also called *concha.*

5. An inhabitant of the Bahamas and other neighboring islands; so called by way of nickname from the abundance of the conch-shell there.

6. Any large shell used as a horn or instrument for calling.

çon′chȧ, *n.* [L. *concha*; Gr. *konchē*, a shell.]

1. In architecture, same as *conch.*

2. The external ear. [See *Conch*, n. 3.]

çon′chăl, *a.* Pertaining to the external ear.

çon′chi-fẽr, *n.* [L. *concha*, a shell, and *ferre*, to bear.] An animal that produces or is covered with a shell, as the tortoise; applied specifically to bivalve mollusks.

Çon-chif′e-rȧ, *n.pl.* [L., from *concha*, a shell, and *ferre*, to bear.] The large class of acephalous molluscous animals commonly known as bivalves, and including the *Lamellibranchiata* and the *Brachiopoda.*

çon-chif′ẽr-ous, *a.* Pertaining to the *Conchifera*; producing or having shells.

çon′chi-fọrm, *a.* [L. *concha*, a shell, and *forma*, shape.] Having the form of a shell.

çon-chi′ō-lin, *n.* The organic base of mollusk shells.

çon′chite, *n.* A fossil or petrified conch or shell. [Obs.]

çon-chit′iç, *a.* [Gr. *konchitēs*, a shelly marble, from *konchē*, a shell.] Composed of or containing shells; applied to limestones and marbles in which the remains of shells are a noticeable feature.

çon′chō-grȧss, *n.* The millet of Texas, *Panicum Texanum.*

çon′choid, *n.* [Gr. *konchē*, a shell, and *eidos*, form.] The name of a curve of the fourth degree, given to it by its inventor Nicomedes.

çon-choid′ăl, *a.* In mineralogy, having curved elevations or depressions, in form like a bivalve shell; applied only to a surface produced by fracture; the fracture, when of the kind described, is said to be *conchoidal*, as in obsidian and chalcedony.

çon-chō-log′iç-ăl, *a.* [*Conch*, and Gr. *logos*, a discourse.] Pertaining to conchology.

çon-chol′ō-ġist, *n.* One versed in conchology; one who studies the nature, properties, and habits of shells and their included animals.

çon-chol′ō-ġy, *n.* [Gr. *konchē*, a shell, and *logos*, a description.] The science of shells; that department of zoölogy which treats of the nature, formation, and classification of the shells with which the bodies of many mollusks are protected; also, a knowledge of the animals themselves; also called *malacology.*

çon-chom′e-tẽr, *n.* [Gr. *konchē*, a shell, and *metron*, a measure.] An instrument for measuring shells or the angle of their spire.

çon-chom′e-try, *n.* The practice or art of measuring shells; the use of the conchometer.

çon-chō-spi′răl, *n.* A variety of spiral curve existing in many univalve shells.

çon-chy-lā′ceous, çon-chyl-i-ā′ceous, *a.* [L. *conchylium*; Gr. *konchylion*, dim. of *konchē*, a shell.] Pertaining to shells; resembling a shell; as, *conchylaceous* impressions.

çon-chy-lif′ẽr-ous, *a.* Same as *Conchiferous.*

çon-chyl-i-ol′ō-ġy, *n.* [Obs.] See *Conchology.*

çon-chyl-i-om′e-try, *n.* Same as *Conchometry.*

çon-chyl′i-ous, *a.* Pertaining to *Conchifera* or their shells; conchylaceous.

çon-chyl′i-um, *n.*; *pl.* **çon-chyl′i-ȧ.** [L. *conchylium*; Gr. *konchylion*, dim. of *konchē*, a shell.] Any shell of a mollusk; a conch.

çon′ci-ā-tŏr, *n.* [It. *conciatore*, from *conciare*, to fit, adorn, from L. *comptus*, adorned, elegant, pp. of *comere*, to dress, adorn.] In glass-works, one who weighs, proportions, works, and tempers the materials used.

çon-cierge′ (-siärzh′), *n.* [Fr.] A doorkeeper to a hotel, house, prison, or public or private edifice of any kind; a janitor or janitress.

çŏn-cil′i-ȧ-ble, *n.* A small assembly. [Obs.]

çŏn-cil′i-ȧ-ble, *a.* [From L. *conciliare*, to conciliate.] Capable of being conciliated.

çon-cil′i-ȧ-būle, *n.* [L. *conciliabulum*, a place of assembly, from *conciliare*, to call together, conciliate.] A private ecclesiastical assembly; an obscure council. [Rare.]

çŏn-cil'i-ăr, çŏn-cil'i-ā-ry, *a.* [L. *concilium*, a council.] Pertaining to a council.

çŏn-cil'i-āte, *v.t.*; conciliated, *pt.*, *pp.*; conciliating, *ppr.* [L. *conciliatus*, pp. of *conciliare*, to call or bring together, to win over, from *concilium*, a meeting, assembly.]

1. To lead or draw to, by moral influence or power; to win, gain, or engage, as the affections, favor, or good-will.

2. To reconcile, or bring to a state of friendship; to pacify; to soothe.

Syn.—Win, gain, engage, propitiate, reconcile, appease, pacify.

çŏn-cil-i-ā'tion, *n.* The act of conciliating or state of being conciliated.

çŏn-cil'i-ȧ-tive, *a.* Conciliatory; reconciling; pacific.

çŏn-cil'i-ā-tŏr, *n.* One who conciliates or reconciles.

çŏn-cil'i-ȧ-tō-ry, *a.* Tending to conciliate or reconcile; tending to make peace between persons at variance; pacific; as, the general made *conciliatory* propositions to the insurgents.

Syn.—Pacific, winning, engaging.

çŏn-cin'nāte, *v.t.* To unite becomingly; to adapt; to connect fitly; to clear; to purify. [Obs.]

çŏn-cin'ni-ty, *n.*; *pl.* **çŏn-cin'ni-tieș.** [L. *concinnitas*, fitness, elegance.] Fitness; suitableness; neatness. [Rare.]

> An exact *concinnity* and evenness of fancy. —Howell.

çŏn-cin'nous, *a.* Fit; suitable; agreeable; becoming; pleasant; as, a *concinnous* interval in music; a *concinnous* system. [Rare.]

çon'ciō-nāte (-shiō-), *v.i.* To preach. [Obs.]

çon'ciō-nā-tive (-shiō-), *a.* Pertaining to preaching or public speaking. [Rare.]

çon'ciō-nā-tŏr, *n.* [L. *contionator*, a haranguer, from *contio*, an assembly.]

1. A preacher.

2. In old English law, a common-councilman; a freeman. [Obs.]

çon'ciō-nā-tō-ry, *a.* [Obs.] See *Concionative.*

çŏn-cise', *a.* [L. *concisus*, cut off, brief, from *concidere*, to cut off; *con-*, and *cædere*, to cut.] Brief; short, applied to language or style; containing few words; comprehensive; employing as few words as possible; as, in Genesis there is a *concise* account of the creation.

Syn.—Succinct, brief, condensed.

çŏn-cise'ly, *adv.* Briefly; in few words.

çŏn-cise'ness, *n.* Brevity in speaking or writing; as, the *conciseness* of Demosthenes.

çŏn-ci'șiŏn (-sizh'un), *n.* 1. A schism; a faction; a division; a sect. [Obs.]

2. Conciseness.

> His wonted vigor and *concision.*—Brougham.

çon-ci-tā'tion, *n.* The act of stirring up, exciting, or putting in motion. [Obs.]

çon-cite', *v.t.* To excite. [Obs.]

çon-clȧ-mā'tion, *n.* [L. *conclamatio*, from *conclamare*; *con-*, and *clamare*, to cry out.] An outcry or shout of many together. [Rare.]

çon'clāve, *n.* [ME. *conclave*; OFr. *conclave*; L. *conclave*, a room or closet; *con-*, with, and *clavis*, a key.]

1. A private apartment, particularly that in which the cardinals of the Roman Catholic church meet in privacy for the election of a pope.

2. The secret assembly or meeting of the cardinals for the election of a pope; hence, the college of cardinals.

3. A private meeting; a close assembly.

> In close recess and secret *conclave* sat. —Milton.

çon'clȧ-vist, *n.* [It. *conclavista.*] An ecclesiastical attendant whom a cardinal is allowed to take with him into the conclave for the choice of a pope.

çŏn-clūde', *v.t.*; concluded, *pt.*, *pp.*; concluding, *ppr.* [ME. *concluden*, to conclude; L. *concludere*, to shut up closely, inclose; *con-*, together, and *claudere*, to shut.]

1. To shut. [Obs.]

2. To include; to comprehend. [Obs.]

> The Scripture hath *concluded* all under sin. —Gal. iii. 22.

3. To arrive at by reasoning; to infer, as from premises; to close (an argument) by inferring.

> Therefore we *conclude*, that a man is justified by faith without the deeds of the law. —Rom. iii. 28.

4. To decide; to determine; to make a final determination concerning; as, we have *concluded* not to go.

5. To end; to finish.

> I will *conclude* this part with the speech of a counselor of state. —Bacon.

6. To stop or restrain, or, as in law, to estop from further argument or proceedings; to oblige or bind, as by authority, or by one's own argument or concession; generally in the passive; as, the defendant is *concluded* by his own plea.

7. To settle or arrange finally; as, to *conclude* a bargain; to *conclude* a peace.

Syn.—Infer, decide, determine, close, finish, terminate, end, arrange, settle.

çŏn-clūde', *v.i.* 1. To settle an opinion; to form a final judgment.

> Can we *conclude* upon Luther's instability? —Atterbury.

2. To end; to terminate.

> A train of lies,
> That, made in lust, *conclude* in perjuries. —Dryden.

çŏn-clūd'en-cy, *n.* Inference; logical deduction from premises. [Obs.]

çŏn-clūd'ent, *a.* Bringing to a close; decisive. [Obs.]

çŏn-clūd'ẽr, *n.* One who concludes.

çŏn-clūd'ing, *a.* Final; ending; closing; as, the *concluding* sentence of an essay.

çŏn-clūd'ing-ly, *adv.* Conclusively; with incontrovertible evidence. [Obs.]

çŏn-clū'si-ble, *a.* Capable of being concluded or inferred; determinable. [Obs.]

çŏn-clū'șion, *n.* 1. The end; the close; the last part; as, the *conclusion* of an address.

2. The close of an argument, debate, or reasoning; inference that ends the discussion; final result.

> Let us hear the *conclusion* of the whole matter: Fear God, and keep his commandments; for this is the whole duty of man. —Eccles. xii. 13.

3. Determination; final decision; as, after long debate, Congress came to this *conclusion.*

4. In logic, consequence; inference; that which is collected or drawn from premises; particularly deduction from propositions, facts, experience, or reasoning.

5. The result of experiments; experiment. [Obs.]

> We practice all *conclusions* of grafting and inoculating. —Bacon.

6. In law, (a) the formal end of a pleading or deed; (b) an estoppel; (c) a finding or result; as, a *conclusion* of law or fact.

7. Something concluded or accomplished; as, a foregone *conclusion.*

Conclusion of fact; a conclusion from testimony as to the verity of an alleged fact.

Conclusion of law; the decision or decree of a court as to the law applying to a given state of facts.

Conclusion to the country; in law, the formal end of a pleading, demanding a trial by jury, or putting oneself "upon the country."

Foregone conclusion; something decided upon in advance that cannot be changed by argument or influence; a thing prearranged.

In conclusion; finally; lastly; in short.

To try conclusions; to make a trial of strength; to determine superiority; to make an experiment.

Syn.—Decision, determination, inference, deduction, result, consequence, end.

çŏn-clū'șion-ăl, *a.* Concluding; final. [Obs.]

çŏn-clū'sive, *a.* 1. Final; decisive; expressing a final determination; as, a *conclusive* answer to a proposition.

2. Decisive; concluding the question; putting an end to debate; convincing; leaving no room for doubt; as, a *conclusive* argument.

Conclusive evidence; evidence which legally establishes a fact beyond question or doubt.

Conclusive presumption; a presumption which the law does not permit to be called in question by evidence of any nature whatever.

Syn.—Convincing, decisive, final, ultimate, unanswerable.

çŏn-clū'sive-ly, *adv.* In a conclusive manner; decisively; with final determination; as, the point of law is *conclusively* settled.

çŏn-clū'sive-ness, *n.* The quality of being conclusive, or decisive; as, the *conclusiveness* of evidence, or of an argument.

çŏn-clū'sō-ry, *a.* Conclusive. [Rare.]

çŏn-çoct', *v.t.*; concocted, *pt.*, *pp.*; concocting, *ppr.* [L. *concoctus*, pp. of *concoquere*, to boil together, prepare; *con-*, together, and *coquere*, to cook.]

1. To digest by the stomach; to turn food to nutriment. [Obs.]

> The vital functions are performed by general and constant laws; the food is *concocted.* —Cheyne.

2. To purify chemically; to refine by separation. [Obs.]

3. To ripen. [Obs.]

> Fruits and grains are half a year in *concocting* their products. —Bacon.

4. Figuratively, to form and prepare in the mind; to plan; as, to *concoct* a scheme.

5. To prepare from raw materials, or by mixing different ingredients, as food, medicine, or beverages; as, to *concoct* a new dish; to *concoct* a cocktail.

çŏn-çoct'ẽr, *n.* A person who concocts.

çŏn-çoc'tion, *n.* 1. Digestion or solution in the stomach; the process by which food is turned into nutriment. [Obs.]

2. Maturation; the process by which morbid matter was supposed to be separated from the bodily fluids, preparatory to being thrown off. [Obs.]

3. A ripening. [Obs.]

4. The act of concocting or preparing from raw materials, or by mixing a variety of ingredients.

5. The result of concocting; anything produced by concocting; as, a medical *concoction.*

6. The act of turning over or digesting in the mind; as, the *concoction* of a scheme.

çŏn-çoct'ive, *a.* Digestive; having the power of digesting or ripening.

çŏn-çŏl'ŏr, *a.* Of one color; having the same coloration. [Rare.]

çŏn-çŏl'ŏr-ous, *a.* In zoölogy, having a uniform color throughout; concolor.

çŏn-çom'i-tănce, çon-çom'i-tăn-cy, *n.* [Fr. *concomitance*, from L. *con-*, together, and *comitari*, to accompany; *comes*, a companion.]

1. A being together, or in connection with another thing; the state of accompanying.

2. The doctrine maintained in the Roman Catholic church that both the body and blood of Christ exist in each element of the eucharist, so that both are partaken of or received by communicating in one element only.

çŏn-çom'i-tănt, *a.* Accompanying; conjoined with; concurrent; attending; as, decency is *concomitant* to virtue.

çŏn-çom'i-tănt, *n.* 1. A companion; a person or thing that accompanies another, or is collaterally connected; seldom, however, applied to persons.

> Reproach is a *concomitant* to greatness. —Addison.

2. Any algebraic function the relations of which to a given quantic are unchanged by linear transformation of the variables which the function represents.

Syn.—Accompaniment, attendant, addition, circumstance, incident.

çŏn-çom'i-tănt-ly, *adv.* In company with others; concurrently.

çon'çord, *n.* [L. *concordia*, agreement, union, from *concors*, genit. *concordis*, of the same mind; *con-*, together, and *cor*, heart.]

1. Agreement between persons or things; union in opinions, sentiments, views, or interests; peace; harmony.

> What *concord* hath Christ with Belial? —2 Cor. vi. 15.

2. In music, consonance of sounds; harmony; the relation between two or more sounds which are agreeable to the ear.

> The true *concord* of well-tuned sounds.—Shak.

3. A compact; an agreement by stipulation; a treaty. [Obs.]

4. In old English law, an agreement between the parties in a fine, made by leave of the court.

5. In grammar, agreement of words in construction, as adjectives with nouns in gender, number, and case, or verbs with nouns or pronouns in number and person.

Form of concord; in ecclesiastical history, a Lutheran document containing a system of doctrines to be subscribed as a condition of communion, prepared at Torgau in 1577.

Syn.—Agreement, harmony, accordance, concurrence, conformity, consonance, uniformity unison.

çŏn-çord', *v.i.* and *v.t.* [L. *concordare*, to agree.]

I. *v.i.* To coöperate; to agree; to accord. [Obs.]

II. *v.t.* To reconcile; to bring into harmony. [Obs.]

çŏn-çord'ȧ-ble, *a.* Capable of according; agreeing; harmonizing.

çŏn-çord'ȧ-bly, *adv.* With agreement.

çŏn-çord'ănce, *n.* [ME. *concordaunce*; OFr. *concordance*, agreement, a concordance, from L. *concordans*, ppr. of *concordare*, to agree.]

1. Agreement; accordance; the state of being concordant.

2. In grammar, concord. [Obs.]

3. A book in which the principal words used in any work, as the Scriptures, Shakspere, Milton, Tennyson, etc., are arranged alphabetically, and the book, chapter, and verse, or act, scene, line, or other subdivision in which each word occurs, are noted; designed to assist an inquirer in finding any passage by means of any leading word which he can recollect.

> His knowledge of the Bible was such that he might be called a living *concordance.* —Macaulay.

cŏn-çord′ăn-cy, *n.* Agreement. [Obs.]

cŏn-çord′ănt, *a.* [L. *concordans*, ppr. of *concordare*, to agree.] Agreeing; agreeable; correspondent; harmonious.

cŏn-çord′ănt-ly, *adv.* In a concordant manner.

çon-çor′dat, *n.* [L. *concordatus*, pp. of *concordare*, to agree.]

1. In papal history, an agreement made by a temporal sovereign or secular power with the papal see relative to ecclesiastical matters; as, the *concordat* between Napoleon Bonaparte, then first consul, and Pope Pius VII., in 1801.

2. In canon law, a compact, covenant, or agreement concerning some beneficiary matter, as a resignation, promotion, and the like.

3. An agreement, compact, or convention concerning any matter; generally used, however, in the special senses noted above.

cŏn-çord′ist, *n.* The compiler of a concordance.

çon-çor′pō-rāte, *v.t.* and *v.i.* To unite different things in one mass or body; to incorporate. [Obs.]

çon-çor′pō-rāte, *a.* United in the same body; incorporated. [Obs.]

çon-çor-pō-rā′tion, *n.* Union of things in one mass or body. [Rare.]

çon′çōurse, *n.* [Fr. *concours*, from L. *concursus*, a running together, from *concurrere*, to run together.]

1. A moving, flowing, or running together; confluence; as, a *concourse* of matter.

2. A meeting; an assembly of people; an assemblage of things; a collection formed by a voluntary or spontaneous moving and meeting in one place.

3. The place or point of meeting; the point of junction of two or more bodies. [Rare.]

4. The point of meeting of two or more roads, at which the roadways are widened to form a large, clear space, similar to a plaza or square; as, a *concourse* in a park.

5. A working together; concurrence. [Obs.]

6. In Scots law, concurrence by a person having legal qualification to grant it; as, the lord advocate's *concourse* to a libel.

çon-çrē-āte′, *v.t.* To create with or at the same time. [Rare.]

çon-çrē-mā′tion, *n.* The act of burning different things together. [Obs.]

çon′çrē-ment, *n.* A growing together; the collection or mass formed by concretion, or natural union. [Obs.]

çŏn-çres′cence, *n.* [L. *concrescentia*, a growing together, from *concrescere*, to grow together; *con-*, together, and *crescere*, to grow.]

1. Growth or increase; the act of growing or increasing by spontaneous union, or the coalescence of separate particles; increment.

2. In biology, a joining or growing together of two or more individual cells or other organisms; conjugation.

3. In botany, cementation, or the growing together of hyphæ.

çŏn-çres′ci-ble, *a.* Capable of growing together or changing or being changed from a liquid to a solid state.

çŏn-çres′cive, *a.* Growing together. [Rare.]

çon′çrēte, *a.* [L. *concretus*, pp. of *concrescere*, to grow together, to be solid; *con-*, together, and *crescere*, to grow.]

1. United in growth; hence, formed by coalition of separate particles in o one body; forming a mass; united in a solid form.

> The first *concrete* state or consistent surface of the chaos. —Burnet.

2. In logic, a term applied to an object as it exists in nature, invested with all its attributes, or to the notion of such an object; also, a term applied to the names of such objects.

> *Concrete* is opposed to *abstract*. The names of individuals are *concrete*, those of classes *abstract*. A *concrete* name is a name which stands for a thing; as, *this table*; an *abstract* name is a name which stands for the attribute of a thing; as, this table is *square*. —Mill.

3. Made of concrete; as, a *concrete* floor. [See *Concrete*, n.]

Concrete number; a number which expresses or denotes a particular object, as *three* men; when used without reference to a particular object, as *three* or *five*, it is an *abstract number*.

Concrete science; a science dealing with concrete matter or things, as opposed to one dealing with abstract laws.

Concrete sound; a gliding sound or movement of the voice, as distinguished from a *discrete* movement, in which the transition from one pitch to another is abrupt.

çon′çrēte, *n.* 1. A compound; a mass formed by concretion, spontaneous union, or coalescence of separate particles of matter in one body; as, gold is a porous *concrete*.

2. A mass of sand, stone chippings, pebbles, etc., bound together with hydraulic cement or mortar, or sometimes by a tarry cement, asphalt, or the like; used as a building material, particularly in sea-walls, breakwaters, and the foundations of bridge-piers, and in paving, foundations of buildings, etc.

3. In logic, a concrete term; a term that includes both the quality and the subject in which it exists, as *negro*, a black man.

çŏn-çrēte′, *v.i.*; concreted, *pt.*, *pp.*; concreting, *ppr.* To unite or coalesce, as separate particles, into a mass or solid body by cohesion, growing together, or other natural process; as, saline particles *concrete* into crystals.

çŏn-çrēte′, *v.t.* 1. To form into a mass by the cohesion or coalescence of separate particles.

2. To construct or cover with concrete; as, to *concrete* a roadway.

3. To unite so as to form a specific notion; as, to *concrete* color with figure.

çŏn-çrēte′ly, *adv.* In a concrete manner; not abstractly.

çŏn-çrēte′ness, *n.* The state of being concrete; coagulation.

çŏn-çrē′tion, *n.* [L. *concretio*, a uniting, condensing, from *concretus*, pp. of *concrescere*, to grow together; *con-*, together, and *crescere*, to grow.]

1. The act of concreting; the process by which soft or fluid bodies become thick, consistent, solid, or hard; the act of growing together, or of uniting, by other natural process, the small particles of matter into a mass.

2. The mass or solid matter formed by growing together, by congelation, condensation, coagulation, or induration; a clot; a lump; a solidification.

> *Concretions* of slime. —Bacon.

3. In geology, a nodule formed by molecular aggregation as distinct from crystallization.

4. In logic, the act of regarding in the concrete or as existing in nature; opposed to *abstraction*.

çŏn-çrē′tion-ăl, *a.* Concretionary.

çŏn-çrē′tion-ā-ry, *a.* Pertaining to or made up of concretions; producing concretions.

çon-çrē′tive, *a.* Causing to concrete; having power to produce concretion; as, *concretive* juices.

çŏn-çrē′tive-ly, *adv.* In a concretive manner.

çŏn-çrē′tūre, *n.* A mass formed by concretion. [Obs.]

çon-çrew′, *v.i.* To grow together. [Obs.]

çon-çrim-i-nā′tion, *n.* A joint accusation.

çŏn-çū′bi-nā-cy, *n.* The practice of cohabiting without marriage. [Obs.]

çŏn-çū′bi-nāġe, *n.* [Fr. *concubinage*, from *concubine*, a concubine.]

1. The act or practice of cohabiting as man and wife, without a legal marriage; the state of being a concubine.

2. In old law, an exception against a woman suing for dower, on the ground that she was the concubine and not the wife of the man of whose land she seeks to be endowed.

3. An inferior kind of marriage allowed in some countries, performed with less solemnity than a true or formal marriage; or marriage with a woman of inferior condition, to whom the husband does not convey his rank or quality. This was the sense of the word in Roman law.

çŏn-çū′bi-năl, *a.* Pertaining to concubinage.

çŏn-çū-bi-nā′ri-ăn, *a.* and *n.* Concubinary.

çŏn-çū′bi-nā-ry, *a.* and *n.* I. *a.* Relating to concubinage; living in concubinage.

II. *n.* One living in concubinage. [Rare.]

çŏn-çū′bi-nāte, *n.* Concubinage. [Obs.]

çon′çū-bine, *n.* [ME. *concubine*; OFr. masc. *concubin*, f. *concubine*; L. masc. *concubinus*, f. *concubina*, one who lives in concubinage, from *concumbere*, to lie together or with; *con-*, with, and *cubare*, to lie down.]

1. A paramour, male or female. [Obs.]

2. A woman who cohabits with a man without being legally married to him; a kept mistress.

> I know I am too mean to be your queen,
> And yet too good to be your *concubine*.—Shak.

3. A wife of inferior condition; a lawful wife, but not united to the man by the usual ceremonies; as, Hagar and Keturah, the *concubines* of Abraham.

çŏn-çul′çāte, *v.t.* To tread on; to trample under foot. [Obs.]

çon-çul-çā′tion, *n.* A trampling under foot. [Obs.]

çŏn-çū′pis-cence, *n.* [ME. *concupiscence*; Fr. *concupiscence*; LL. *concupiscentia*, an eager desire; L. *concupiscens*, ppr. of *concupiscere*, to desire eagerly; *con-*, together, and *cupere*, to desire.] Lust; unlawful or irregular desire for sexual pleasure; inclination for unlawful enjoyments.

> We know even secret *concupiscence* to be sin. —Hooker.

çŏn-çū′pis-cent, *a.* Desirous of unlawful pleasure; libidinous; lustful.

çŏn-çū-pis-cen′tiăl (-shăl), *a.* Relating to concupiscence. [Obs.]

çŏn-çū-pis-cen′tious, *a.* Concupiscent. [Obs.]

çŏn-çū′pis-ci-ble, *a.* Liable to be affected by concupiscence or carnal desire; concupiscent; lustful.

çŏn-çū′pis-ci-ble-ness, *n.* The state or quality of being concupiscible; concupiscence. [Rare.]

çon′çū-py, *n.* A contraction of *concupiscence* used by Shakspere in "Troilus and Cressida."

çŏn-çūr′, *v.i.*; concurred, *pt.*, *pp.*; concurring, *ppr.* [L. *concurrere*, to run together; *con-*, together, and *currere*, to run.]

1. To run together; to meet in the same point. [Obs.]

2. To agree, join, or unite, as in one action or opinion; to meet, mind with mind; used absolutely or followed by *with*; as, they *concurred* in the challenge; Mr. Burke *concurred with* Lord Chatham in opinion.

3. To assent; with *to*. [Rare.]

4. To unite or be conjoined; to meet together; to be combined.

> In whom all these qualities do *concur*. —Whitgift.

5. To unite in contributing to a common object; as, various causes may *concur* in the changes of temperature.

6. To coincide; to have points of agreement.

Syn.—Agree, join, unite, combine, meet, conjoin, coincide, approve.

çŏn-çūr′rence, *n.* [L. *concurrens*, ppr. of *concurrere*, to run together; *con-*, together, and *currere*, to run.]

1. Agreement in opinion; union in design, implying joint approbation.

2. A meeting or conjunction, whether casual or intended; combination of agents, circumstances, or events; as, the *concurrence* of great historical events.

3. Agreement or consent, implying joint aid or contribution of power or influence.

4. A meeting, as of claims or power; joint rights, implying equality in different persons or bodies; as, a *concurrence* of jurisdiction in two different courts.

5. In ecclesiastical language, the falling together in part or in whole of two or more festivals.

Syn.—Agreement, bargain, compact, stipulation, covenant.

çŏn-çūr′ren-cy, *n.* Concurrence.

çŏn-çūr′rent, *a.* 1. Meeting; uniting; accompanying; acting in conjunction; agreeing in the same act; contributing to the same event or effect; operating with.

> A *concurrent* cause of this reformation. —Davies.

2. Conjoined; associate; concomitant; joint and equal; existing together and operating on the same objects; as, the federal and state courts have, in some cases, *concurrent* jurisdiction.

3. In geometry, meeting in a point; passing through the same point.

çŏn-çūr′rent, *n.* 1. That which concurs; joint or contributory cause; as, the *concurrents* to wealth are usually shrewdness and industry combined.

2. One who concurs or agrees with another in opinion, etc.

3. One who is aiming at the same object as another; hence, a rival. [Obs.]

4. The day or days in excess of fifty-two weeks in any one year; so called because they concur with the solar cycle.

çŏn-çūr′rent-ly, *adv.* With concurrence; unitedly.

çŏn-çūr′rent-ness, *n.* Concurrence.

çŏn-çūr′ring, *a.* Agreeing; uniting in action; contributing to the same event or effect; consenting.

Concurring figure; in geometry, a figure which, being laid on another, corresponds with it in every part.

çon-çūr′sō, *n.* [Sp., Port., from L. *concursus*, a running together, from *con-*, together, and *currere*, to run.] A civil law process by which each creditor may maintain his right to payment out of the assets of a debtor without regard to the claims of the other creditors.

çŏn-çuss′, *v.t.* [L. *concussus*, pp. of *concutere*, to shake together; *con-*, together, and *quatere*, to shake.]

1. To shake, jar, or agitate; especially, to shock (the brain). [Rare.]

2. In law, to compel the surrender of (something) or the performance of (an act) by force or threats. [Rare.]

çon-çus-sā′tion, *n.* A violent shock or agitation. [Obs.]

çŏn-çus′sion, *n.* [L. *concussio*, a violent shock, from *concutere*, to shake violently, shake together; *con-*, together, and *quatere*, to shake.]

1. The act of violently shaking or agitating by the stroke or impulse of another body.

2. The state of being shaken or shocked by impact with another body; as, *concussion* of the brain; the *concussion* of the earth.

3. In civil law, extortion by intimidation.

çŏn-çus′sion-fūşe, *n.* A shell-fuse which ignites

upon the concussion of the shell with some solid.

çŏn-cus′sive, *a.* Having the power or quality of shaking by sudden or violent shock.

çŏn-cyç′lic, *a.* [*Con-*, and Gr. *kyklos*, a circle.] Located in the same circumference, or possessing parallel cyclic planes.

çond, *v.t.* [Obs.] See second *Con*, v.t.

çŏn-demn′ (-dem′), *v.t.*; condemned, *pt.*, *pp.*; condemning, *ppr.* [L. *condemnare*, to condemn, doom, blame; *con-*, intens., and *damnare*, to harm, condemn.]

1. To pronounce utterly wrong; to utter a sentence of disapprobation against; to censure; to blame. The word often expresses more than *censure* or *blame*, conveying the idea of utter rejection; as, to *condemn* heretical opinions; to *condemn* one's conduct.

2. To witness against; to show or prove to be wrong, or guilty.

3. To pronounce guilty; to sentence to a fine or other punishment; to utter sentence against judicially; to doom; with *to* before the penalty; as, the judge *condemned* him *to* death.

4. To judge or pronounce to be unfit for use, or service; as, the ship was *condemned* as unseaworthy.

5. To pronounce to be forfeited; as, the ship and her cargo were *condemned*.

6. To exercise the right of eminent domain in or take for public use; as, they *condemned* the land for the use of the railroad.

Syn.—Blame, censure, upbraid, convict, sentence, adjudge, reprove, doom, reprobate, reproach.

çŏn-dem′nȧ-ble, *a.* Fit to be condemned; blamable; culpable.

çon-dem-nā′tion, *n.* [LL. *condemnatio*, condemnation, from L. *condemnare*, to condemn.]

1. The act of condemning; the judicial act of declaring one guilty, and sentencing him to punishment.

2. The state of being condemned; as, the *condemnation* of the wicked.

3. The cause or reason of a sentence of guilt or punishment.

This is the *condemnation*. —John iii. 19.

4. Blame; disapprobation.

çŏn-dem′nȧ-tō-ry, *a.* Condemning; bearing condemnation or censure; as, a *condemnatory* sentence or decree.

çŏn-demned′, *a.* 1. Censured; pronounced to be wrong, guilty, worthless, or forfeited; adjudged or sentenced to punishment; as, the *condemned* criminal.

2. Intended for persons under sentence of death; as, the *condemned* cell.

çŏn-dem′nẽr, *n.* One who condemns.

çŏn-den-sȧ-bil′i-ty, *n.* Capability of being condensed.

çŏn-den′sȧ-ble, *a.* Capable of being condensed or of being compressed into a smaller compass; as, vapor is *condensable*.

çŏn-den′sāte, *v.t.* and *v.i.*; condensated, *pt.*, *pp.*; condensating, *ppr.* I. *v.t.* To condense; to compress into a closer form; to cause to take a more compact state; to make more dense. [Rare.]

II. *v.i.* To become more dense, close, or compact. [Rare.]

çŏn-den′sāte, *a.* Made more dense or compact; condensed.

çon-den-sā′tion, *n.* [LL. *condensatio*, condensation, from L. *condensare*, to condense.]

1. The act of making dense or compact; the process of condensing.

2. In physics, the act or process of reducing a vapor or gas to a denser form, as steam to water, or a liquid to a solid or semisolid.

3. In chemistry, the rearrangement of atoms so as to form a molecule of greater density and weight; as, the *condensation* of oxygen into ozone.

4. The result or product of condensing.

Condensation product; in chemistry, a substance obtained by increasing the molecular weight of another substance, or by uniting two or more substances so as to increase their density.

Surface condensation; a method of condensing steam by contact with cold metallic surfaces instead of by the injection of cold water.

çŏn-den′sȧ-tive, *a.* Having power or tendency to condense.

çŏn-dense′, *v.t.*; condensed, *pt.*, *pp.*; condensing, *ppr.* 1. To make more close, thick, or compact; to cause to unite more closely, either by attraction, affinity, or mechanical force; as, to *condense* steam into water by the application of cold air; to *condense* milk.

2. To compress into a smaller compass, or into a close body; to abridge; as, to *condense* ideas; to *condense* a speech.

Condensing engine; a steam-engine so constructed that the steam is condensed into water after having been admitted to the cylinder.

Syn.—Compress, squeeze, abridge, contract, epitomize, reduce.

çŏn-dense′, *v.i.* 1. To become more dense or compact, as the particles of a body; to approach or unite more closely; to grow thick.

2. In physics and chemistry, to become reduced to a denser form, as gas to a liquid.

çŏn-dense′, *a.* Close in texture or composition; compact; firm; dense. [Rare.]

çŏn-densed′ (-denst), *a.* Made more dense; contracted.

Condensed milk; see under *Milk*.

Condensed type; a type-founder's name for tall and slender styles of type, thinner than compressed type.

çŏn-dens′ẽr, *n.* 1. One who or that which condenses.

2. An apparatus in which air or other elastic fluids may be compressed. It consists of a cylinder, in which is a movable piston to force the air into a receiver, and a valve to prevent the air from escaping.

3. An apparatus for reducing aqueous or spirituous vapors to a liquid form, by the application of cold, as in the distillation of spirits; the worm of a still.

4. An apparatus forming part of a steam-engine, in which the exhaust steam is condensed into water by the action of cold water or air.

5. An apparatus for concentrating electricity by the effect of induction between conducting plates separated by a nonconductor, as tinfoil sheets separated by oiled paper or silk.

6. A lens or set of lenses in a microscope, stereopticon, etc., for concentrating rays of light and illuminating the object observed or to be projected.

7. In cloth-manufacturing, (a) an apparatus (part of a cotton-gin) for compressing lint; (b) a device for forming carded wool into rolls.

8. In the manufacture of illuminating gas, a condensing device by which the gas is freed from impurities.

Achromatic condenser; in optics, an achromatic lens employed to concentrate rays.

Bull's-eye condenser; a lens of short focus used as a condenser of light.

Injection condenser; a condenser in which steam comes in contact with a jet of cold water; called also *jet condenser* and *siphon condenser*.

Musical condenser; an apparatus connected with a telephone transmitter for the better reproduction of musical sounds.

Surface condenser; in steam-engines, an apparatus for condensing the exhaust steam by bringing it into contact with cold metallic surfaces.

çŏn-den′si-ble, *a.* Condensable.

çŏn-den′si-ty, *n.* The state of being condensed; denseness; density. [Obs.]

çond′ẽr, *n.* A lookout; same as *conner*.

çon-dē-scend′, *v.i.*; condescended, *pt.*, *pp.*; condescending, *ppr.* [ME. *condescenden*; OFr. *condescendre*; LL. *condescendere*, let oneself down, condescend; *con-*, together, and *descendere*, to come down; *de-*, from, and *scandere*, to climb.] To descend from the privileges of superior position, rank, or dignity; to submit or yield, as to an inferior, implying an occasional relinquishment of distinction; frequently used ironically with the implication of an assumption of superiority; as, pray *condescend* to notice me.

çon-dē-scend′ence, *n.* The act of condescending. [Rare.]

çon-dē-scend′en-cy, *n.* Condescension. [Obs.]

çon-dē-scend′ing, *a.* Yielding, as to inferiors; stooping; courteous; obliging.

çon-dē-scend′ing-ly, *adv.* In a condescending manner; courteously.

çon-dē-scen′sion, *n.* Voluntary descent from rank, dignity, or just claims; relinquishment of strict right; submission to inferiors in granting requests or performing acts which strict justice does not require; courtesy.

çŏn-dign′ (-dīn′), *a.* [L. *condignus*, very worthy.]

1. Deserved; suitable; as, the prisoner has suffered *condign* punishment.

2. Worthy; merited; as, *condign* praise. [Obs.]

çŏn-dig′ni-ty, *n.* [L. *condignus*, very worthy; *con-*, intens., and *dignus*, worthy.]

1. Merit; desert.

2. The merit of human actions, which claims reward on the score of justice.

çŏn-dign′ly, *adv.* According to merit.

çŏn-dign′ness, *n.* Agreeableness to deserts; suitableness. [Obs.]

çon′di-ment, *n.* [Fr. *condiment*; L. *condimentum*, a spice, seasoning, from *condire*, to pickle.] Seasoning; sauce; that which is used to give relish to meat or other food.

çon-dis-ci′ple, *n.* A schoolfellow; a pupil in the same school, or under the same instructor. [Rare.]

çŏn-dite′, *v.t.* To prepare and preserve with sugar, salt, spices, or the like; to pickle. [Obs.]

çon′dite, *a.* Pickled; preserved. [Obs.]

çŏn-di′tion (-dish′un), *n.* [ME. *condicion*; OFr. *condicion*; L. *condicio*, an agreement, stipulation, condition, situation, from *condicere*, to speak with, agree; *con-*, together, and *dicere*, to speak.]

1. State of being; situation in relation to environment or to physical or mental soundness; social position.

2. Quality; property; attribute.

3. A prerequisite; a set of terms provided as the ground of something else; that which is established, or to be done, or to happen, as requisite to another act; as, I will lend you a sum of money on *condition* that you will refund it.

4. A clause in a contract, agreement, or other document which provides that the principal obligation may be qualified or nullified, under stated circumstances.

Conditions of sale; the terms of a sale, especially of a sale at auction, contained in an instrument setting forth the agreement; also, the instrument itself.

On or *upon condition*; a phrase used in the sense of *if* in a sentence containing a condition; followed by *that*.

çŏn-di′tion, *v.i.*; conditioned, *pt.*, *pp.*; conditioning, *ppr.* 1. To make terms; to stipulate; as, to *condition* is not always to perform.

2. To ascribe to an object relations which are claimed to be essential for thought and knowledge.

çŏn-di′tion, *v.t.* 1. To contract; to stipulate.

2. To place conditions upon.

3. In the United States, to require (a student) to take another examination after he has failed to pass one.

4. To test.

çŏn-di′tion-ăl, *a.* 1. Containing or depending on a condition or conditions; made with limitations; not absolute; made or granted on certain terms; as, a *conditional* promise; a *conditional* fee.

2. In grammar and logic, expressing a condition or supposition; as, a *conditional* word, mode, or tense; a *conditional* syllogism.

çŏn-di′tion-ăl, *n.* 1. A limitation. [Rare.]

2. A word, clause, or proposition expressing a condition.

çŏn-di-tion-al′i-ty, *n.* The quality of being conditional, or limited; limitation by certain terms.

çŏn-di′tion-ăl-ly, *adv.* With certain limitations; subject to particular terms or stipulations; not absolutely or positively.

çŏn-di′tion-āte, *a.* Conditional; established on certain terms. [Obs.]

çŏn-di′tion-āte, *v.t.* 1. To qualify; to regulate. [Obs.]

2. To make subject to conditions.

çŏn-di′tioned, *a.* 1. Stipulated; containing terms to be performed.

2. Having a certain state or qualities; usually preceded by some qualifying term; as, *well-conditioned*, *ill-conditioned*, *best-conditioned*.

3. Opposite of *absolute*; determined by other things.

çŏn-di′tioned, *n.* In philosophy or metaphysics, that which depends upon or is determined by something else; used with the definite article; opposed to *the absolute*.

çon′di-tō-ry, *n.* [L. *conditorium*, a place where anything is put away, from *condire*, to preserve, put aside.] A repository for holding things.

çŏn-dō′lȧ-tō-ry, *a.* Expressing condolence.

çŏn-dōle′, *v.i.*; condoled, *pt.*, *pp.*; condoling, *ppr.* [LL. *condolere*, to condole; *con-*, with, and *dolere*, to grieve.] To feel pain, or to grieve, at the distress or misfortunes of another; as, to *condole* with friends.

çŏn-dōle′, *v.t.* To lament or grieve over with another. [Rare.]

çŏn-dōle′ment, *n.* Grief; pain of mind at another's loss or misfortune; sorrow; mourning.

çŏn-dō′lence, *n.* The expression of sympathy excited by the distress or misfortune of another.

çŏn-dōl′ẽr, *n.* One who condoles.

çon-dō-min′i-um, *n.* Joint or concurrent dominion or jurisdiction, especially as applied to nations.

çon-dō-nā′tion, *n.* [L. *condonatio*, a giving away, pardoning, from *condonare*, to give as a present, to pardon.]

1. The act of pardoning. [Rare.]

2. In law, the act of pardoning or overlooking marital infidelity by either husband or wife, either directly by words, or indirectly by continuing the marital relation.

çŏn-dōne′, *v.t.*; condoned, *pt.*, *pp.*; condoning, *ppr.* [L. *condonare*, to give up, pardon; *con-*, and *donare*, to give.]

1. To pardon.

2. To forgive or overlook (marital infidelity).

çon′dor, *n.* [Sp., from Peruv. *cuntur*, condor.]

1. A large bird, *Sarcorhamphus gryphus*, found in the most elevated parts of the Andes, in South America.

2. A vulture resembling the true *condor*, found in California.

3. A current Chilean gold coin, stamped with a condor's figure, and worth about $7.30.

çon-dot-tie′re (-tyā′), *n.*; *pl.* **çon-dot-tie′ri.** [It., from L. *conducti*, mercenary soldiers, from *conductus*, pp. of *conducere*, to hire.] In Italian history, one of the soldiers of fortune who, in the fourteenth and fifteenth centuries, made a practice of selling their services and those of their military followers to warring states or factions.

Condor (*Sarcorhamphus gryphus*).

çŏn-dūce′, *v.i.*; conduced (-dūst), *pt.*, *pp.*; conducing, *ppr.* [OFr. *conduire*; L. *conducere*, to lead, draw or bring together, hire, conduce; *con-*, together, and *ducere*, to lead.] To lead or tend; to contribute to a result; followed by *to*; as, virtue *conduces to* the welfare of society.

> They may *conduce to* further discoveries for completing the theory of light.—Newton.

çŏn-dūce′, *v.t.* To conduct; to bring about. [Obs.]

çŏn-dūce′ment, *n.* A leading or tending to; tendency. [Obs.]

çŏn-dū′cent, *a.* Tending or contributing to.

çŏn-dū-ci-bil′i-ty, *n.* The state of contributing to an end.

çŏn-dū′ci-ble, *a.* Leading or tending to; conducive.

çŏn-dū′ci-ble-ness, *n.* The quality of leading or contributing to any end.

çŏn-dū′ci-bly, *adv.* In a manner to promote.

çŏn-dū′cive, *a.* Capable of conducing or contributing; having a tendency to promote.

> An action, however *conducive* to the good of our country, will be represented as prejudicial to it. —Addison.

çŏn-dū′cive-ness, *n.* The quality of conducing.

çon′duçt, *n.* [L. *conductus*, pp. of *conducere*, to bring together, collect.]

1. The act of leading; guidance; administration; management; command; as, the *conduct* of a campaign.

2. Skilful management; good generalship.

3. Guard on the way; convoy; escort. [Obs.]

4. Personal behavior; deportment; course of action.

5. In ethics, the voluntary control and direction of one's actions toward moral or spiritual development.

6. A conveyor; conduit; a carrier; an instrument; that which conducts. [Obs.]

7. Construction; action; plot; literary or dramatic development; as, the *conduct* of a novel.

Syn.—Deportment, behavior, demeanor, management, guidance.

çŏn-duçt′, *v.t.*; conducted, *pt.*, *pp.*; conducting, *ppr.* [L. *conductus*, pp. of *conducere*, to bring or lead together; *con-*, together, and *ducere*, to lead.]

1. To introduce; to escort; to attend; to usher; to guide; to lead; as, to *conduct* a lady to a seat.

2. To direct; to manage; to command; as, to *conduct* an orchestra; to *conduct* one's affairs.

3. To behave; used with the reciprocal pronoun; as, to *conduct oneself* properly.

4. In physics, to serve as a transmitting medium for.

çŏn-duçt′, *v.i.* 1. To act as a conveyor, transmitter, or conductor, as of electricity, heat, etc.

2. To behave; to act. [Rare.]

3. To act as musical conductor; as, A *conducts* to-night.

çŏn-duçt′ănce, *n.* In electricity, the capacity of conduction.

çon′duçt-book, *n.* In the United States navy, an official register of the character and conduct of members of a crew.

çŏn-duçt-i-bil′i-ty, *n.* 1. Capability of being conducted; as, the *conductibility* of the electric current.

2. The power of receiving and transmitting; but improperly so used; as, the *conductibility* of copper wire.

çŏn-duçt′i-ble, *a* Capable of being transmitted.

çŏn-duç′tion, *n.* 1. The act of training up. [Obs.]

2. Transmission of any kind; specifically, in physics, the transmission of some force through the agency of a continuous medium.

çŏn-duçt′ive, *a.* Having the power of conducting; resulting from conduction.

çon-duç-tiv′i-ty, *n.* The power of conducting heat, electricity, or sound; the property of being conductive.

Thermal conductivity; the volume of heat which in unit time passes through a plate whose surfaces are one degree apart in temperature, with unit area and thickness.

Thermometric conductivity; thermal conductivity, under the condition that the raising of a unit volume one degree be adopted as the unit of heat.

çon′duçt-mŏn″ey, *n.* A portion withheld from a seaman's wages, its final payment depending upon good conduct.

çŏn-duçt′ŏr, *n.* [L. *conductor*, a lessee, a contractor, from *conducere*, to lead, bring together.]

1. A leader; a guide; one who goes before or accompanies, and shows the way.

2. A chief; a commander; one who leads an army or a people. [Obs.]

3. A director; a manager; a superintendent; as, the *conductor* of an enterprise.

4. In surgery, a grooved staff which serves to direct the knife.

5. In physics, a substance which forms a medium for the transmission of some other substance, fluid, or force, particularly of heat, sound, or electricity.

6. The official in charge of a railroad-train, a street-car, etc.

7. The leader of a band of musicians; as, the *conductor* of an orchestra.

Prime conductor; the largest of the conductors in an electrical apparatus, which collects and retains the electricity.

çŏn-duçt′ō-ry, *a.* Having the property of conducting. [Rare.]

çŏn-duçt′ress, *n.* A woman who leads or directs; a directress.

çon′duit (-dit), *n.* [ME. *conduit*; OFr. *conduit*, conduct, guidance, from L. *conductus*, pp. of *conducere*, to bring or lead together, conduct.]

1. In ancient architecture, a narrow passage, usually underground, for the purpose of secret communication between apartments.

2. A canal, pipe, or passageway for the conveyance of water, electric wires, etc. Conduits are made of various materials and may be either above or below the surface.

3. In the physical structure, any medium of transmission, as the nerves (*conduits* of sensation) and the blood-vessels.

> The *conduits* of my blood. —Shak.

çon-dū′pli-çāte, *a.* Doubled or folded over or together, as the leaves of a bud; in botany, applied to leaves that are folded lengthwise through the middle, the halves of the lamina coming together face to face.

çon-dū′pli-çāte, *v.t.* [L. *conduplicatus*, pp. of *conduplicare*, to double, fold together; *con-*, together, and *duplicare*, to double.] To double; to fold together.

Section of Conduplicate leaf.

çon-dū′pli-çā-ted, *a.* Doubled; folded together.

çon-dū-pli-çā′tion, *n.* A doubling; a duplication.

çon-dū-ran′gō, *n.* See *Cundurango*.

çon-dur′rite, *n.* A form of domeykite; an arsenide of copper, taken from the Condurrow mine in Cornwall, England.

çon′dy-lăr, *a.* Pertaining to or resembling a condyle.

Condylar foramen; see under *Foramen*.

Çon-dy-lăr′thrȧ, *n.pl.* [L., from Gr. *kondylos*, a knuckle, and *arthron*, a joint.] An extinct order of Eocene mammals characterized by possessing a third femoral trochanter and a peculiar articulation of the ankle-bone with the tibia.

çon″dy-lăr-thrō′sis, *n.* In anatomy, a form of movable joint of which the articular surfaces are spheroidal, permitting angular motion in any direction; condylar articulation.

çon′dyle (*or* -dil), *n.* [L. *condylus*; Gr. *kondylos*, a knob, knuckle, joint.]

1. Any rounded eminence, such as occurs in the joints of many of the bones, especially the femur, humerus, and lower jaw.

2. A rounded part of the hard integument covering the joints of the limbs in arthropods.

çon′dy-loid, *a.* Pertaining to or resembling a condyle.

Condyloid process; in anatomy, the posterior protuberance at the extremities of the lower jaw; an oblong rounded head, which is received into the fossa of the temporal bone, forming a movable articulation.

çon-dy-lō′mȧ, *n.*; *pl.* **çon-dy-lō′mȧ-tȧ.** [L., from Gr. *kondylos*, a knob, knuckle, and *-ōma*, from *ōmos*, raw, like a tumor.] A wart-like growth or tumor on the epidermis or adjacent mucous membrane of the anus or genitals.

çon′dy-lōpe, *n.* [Obs.] See *Condylopod*.

çon-dyl′ō-pod, *n.* [L. *condylopus*, from Gr. *kondylos*, a knuckle, and *pous*, *podos*, a foot.] A general term applied by Cuvier to insects, crustaceans, and spiders, in allusion to the fact that they are articulated animals with jointed feet; an arthropod.

çōne, *n.* [Fr. *cone*; L. *conus*; Gr. *kōnos*, a wedge, peak, cone.]

1. In geometry, a solid body or figure having a circle for its base, and its top terminated in a point or vertex.

2. In botany, the conical fruit of several evergreen trees, as of the pine, fir, and spruce. It is composed of woody scales, usually opening, and has a pair of naked seeds upon each scale.

3. Any form of matter having the shape of a geometrical *cone*, as the mass of slaggy lava piled up in a conical shape about the crater of a volcano.

4. A shell belonging to the genus *Conus*; a cone-shell.

5. In spinning, one of the tapering drums in the headstock of a mule.

Cone of rays; in optics, all the rays of light which proceed from a radiant point and fall upon a given flat surface.

Cones of the retina; the crystalline cones of the eye.

Oblique or *scalene cone*; a cone the axis of which is inclined to the plane of its base, the sides being unequal.

Right cone; a cone of which the axis is perpendicular to the plane of its base, the sides being equal.

çōne, *v.t.*; coned, *pt.*, *pp.*; coning, *ppr.* To shape or bevel like a cone.

çōne′-beăr″ing, *n.* A bearing in which a cone-like end supports the revolving part.

çōne′flow″ẽr, *n.* Any one of the composite plants belonging to the genus *Rudbeckia*, with flowers forming a cone, as the dark brown daisy, *Rudbeckia hirta*.

çōne′-in-çōne′, *a.* In geology, a term applied to a structural peculiarity found in such aqueous rocks as limestone, giving the mass the appearance of being made of an infinite number of hollow cones inserted within each other.

çō-nē′ine, *n.* See *Conine*.

çō-nen′çhy-mȧ, *n.* [L., from Gr. *kōnos*, a cone, and *enchyma*, an infusion.] Plant or vegetable tissue found in the form of conical cells.

çōne′-nōse, *n.* Any one of the hemipterous insects belonging to the genus *Conorhinus*, having a cone-shaped head.

çō′ne-patl, çō′ne-pāte, *n.* The Mexican popular name of an animal of the weasel kind, resembling the skunk in form and size, and in its fetid stench.

çōne′-pul″ley, *n.* A pulley made in sections of graduating diameters, giving it the shape of a cone.

çō′ney, *n.* See *Cony*.

çon′fab, *n.* [Colloq. for *confabulation*.] Familiar and easy conversation.

çŏn-fab′ū-lāte, *v.i.*; confabulated, *pt.*, *pp.*; confabulating, *ppr.* [L. *confabulatus*, pp. of *confabulari*, to talk together.] To talk familiarly together; to chat; to prattle.

çŏn-fab-ū-lā′tion, *n.* Familiar talk; easy, unrestrained, unceremonious conversation; familiarly abridged into *confab*.

çŏn-fab′ū-lā-tō-ry, *a.* Pertaining to familiar talk or confabulation; colloquial. [Rare.]

çon′fȧ-lon, *n.* [OFr. *gonfanon*; O.H.G. *gundfano*, a standard, from *gund*, battle, and *fano*, banner.] One of a Roman Catholic order of seculars, called also *Penitents*, who were erected into a confraternity by Pope Clement IV., in 1267, their principal object originally being to deliver Christian prisoners from the Saracens.

çon-far-rē-ā′tion, *n.* [L. *confarreatio*, from *confarreare*, to connect in marriage by an offering of bread; *con-*, together, and *farreus*, of grain, from *far*, grain, spelt.] The highest form of marriage among the Romans, by a ceremony in which the bridegroom and bride tasted a cake made of flour, with salt and water, in presence of the high priest and at least ten witnesses.

çon-fāte′, *v.t.* To decree or determine together with something else; to fate or decree at the same time; only in the passive; as, happiness is *confated* with good deeds. [Rare.]

çon-fāt′ed, *a.* Decreed together with something else. [Rare.]

çŏn-feçt′, *v.t.*; confected, *pt.*, *pp.*; confecting, *ppr.* 1. To make into sweetmeats. [Obs.]

> Saffron *confected* in Cilicia. —Browne.

2. To put together; to construct; to compose; to form. [Obs.]

çon′feçt, *n.* Something prepared, with sugar or honey, as fruit, herbs, roots, and the like; a confection; a comfit; a sweetmeat. [Obs.]

çŏn-feç′tion, *n.* [ME. *confection*, *confeccioun*; OFr. *confection*, *confession*, a confection, preparation, from L. *confectus*, pp. of *conficere*, to prepare, put together; *con-*, together, and *facere*, to make.]

1. Anything prepared or preserved with sugar, as fruit; a sweetmeat.

2. A composition or mixture. [Obs.]

3. A composition of drugs.

> The *confection* which I gave him for a cordial. —Shak.

4. In medicine, an electuary; a conserve; a medicinal substance combined with honey, syrup, sugar, etc.

5. In trade, a ready-made article of women's wear, as a cloak, etc., of fashionable make; as, the season's new *confections*. [Fr.]

çŏn-feç′tion-ā-ry, *n.*; *pl.* **çon-feç′tion-ā-rieṣ.** 1. A confectioner.

2. A confection; a sweetmeat.

çŏn-feç′tion-ā-ry, *a.* Relating to or consisting of confections; as, *confectionary* wares.

The biscuit, or *confectionary* plum.—Cowper.

çŏn-feç′tion-ẽr, *n.* 1. One who manufactures or deals in confections, such as candies, bonbons, cakes, ice-cream, comfits, etc.

2. One who compounds drugs, such as conserves, electuaries, etc. [Obs.]

çŏn-feç′tion-ẽr-y, *n.* 1. A place where sweetmeats and similar things are made or sold; a confectioner's store or shop.

2. Sweetmeats in general; things prepared or sold by a confectioner.

çŏn-feç′tō-ry, *a.* and *n.* I. *a.* Pertaining to the art of making sweetmeats. [Obs.]

II. *n.* A place where confections are made; a confectionery. [Obs.]

çŏn-feç′tūre, *n.* [Obs.] Same as *Confiture*.

çŏn-fed′ẽr, *v.i.* [Obs.] See *Confederate*.

çŏn-fed′ẽr-ā-cy, *n.*; *pl.* **çŏn-fed′ẽr-ā-cieṣ.** [ME. *confederacie*; OFr. *confederacie*, a league, from LL. *confœderatus*, pp. of *confœderare*, to league together; L. *con-*, together, and *fœdus*, a league.]

1. A contract between two or more persons, bodies of men, or states, combined in support of each other, in some act or enterprise; a league; compact; alliance.

The friendships of the world are oft
Confederacies in vice. —Addison.

2. The persons, states, or nations united by a league.

3. In law, a combination of two or more persons to commit an unlawful act; a conspiracy.

Southern Confederacy; in American history, the Confederate States. [See under *Confederate*, a.]

Syn.—Alliance, league, association, combination, union, covenant, confederation.

çŏn-fed′ẽr-āte, *a.* 1. United in a league; allied by treaty; engaged in a confederacy; pertaining to a confederacy.

All the swords
In Italy, and her *confederate* arms,
Could not have made this peace. —Shak.

2. [C—] Of or pertaining to the Confederate States of America; as, the *Confederate* Congress.

Confederate States of America; the name assumed by the league of eleven southern or slave-holding states of the American Union, which seceded in the following order: South Carolina, Mississippi, Florida, Alabama, Georgia, Louisiana, Texas, Virginia, Arkansas, Tennessee, and North Carolina. This action was taken on the election of Abraham Lincoln, the Abolitionist candidate, to the presidency in November, 1860, and led to a great civil war, which terminated in 1865 in the dissolution of the Confederacy.

çŏn-fed′ẽr-āte, *n.* 1. One who is united with others in a league; a person or nation engaged in a confederacy; an ally; an accomplice.

2. [C—] Specifically, one who sided with the Confederate States in the American Civil War (1861-1865), especially, a soldier or sailor of the southern forces, as distinguished from a *Federal* or *Union* soldier or sailor.

Syn.—Friend, companion, associate, accomplice, accessory, abetter, ally.

çŏn-fed′ẽr-āte, *v.t.*; confederated, *pt.*, *pp.*; confederating, *ppr.* To cause to unite in a league; to ally.

çŏn-fed′ẽr-āte, *v.i.* To unite in a league; to join in a mutual contract or covenant; as, the colonies of America *confederated* in 1776; the southern states *confederated* in 1861-1865.

çŏn-fed′ẽr-ā-tẽr, çŏn-fed′ẽr-ā-tŏr, *n.* A confederate. [Obs.]

çŏn-fed-ẽr-ā′tion, *n.* 1. The act of confederating; a league; a compact for mutual support; an alliance.

2. The parties to a league, especially states or nations united by a confederacy.

Articles of Confederation; in United States history, the constitution adopted by the Continental Congress in 1777, which expired on March 4, 1789, under the provisions of the present Constitution.

çŏn-fed′ẽr-ā-tive, *a.* Of or belonging to a confederation.

çŏn-fed′ẽr-ā-tŏr, *n.* Same as *Confederater*.

çŏn-fẽr′, *v.t.*; conferred, *pt.*, *pp.*; conferring, *ppr.* [OFr. *conferer*; L. *conferre*, to bring together, compare, confer; *con-*, together, and *ferre*, to bring.]

1. To compare; to examine by comparison; to collate. [Obs.]

2. To give or bestow; followed by *on* or *upon*.

Coronation *confers on* the king no royal authority. —South.

3. To bring or carry to; hence, to contribute; to conduce. [Obs.]

çŏn-fẽr′, *v.i.* To consult together; to compare opinions; to carry on a discussion or deliberation; formerly often simply to discourse, to talk, but now implying conversation on some serious or important subject, in distinction from mere light talk or familiar conversation.

When they had commanded them to go aside out of the council they *conferred* among themselves. —Acts iv. 15.

Syn.—Bestow, give, grant, consult, discuss, converse, advise, discourse.

çon-fẽr-ee′, *n.* 1. One who participates in a conference; one who is conferred with.

2. One upon whom something, as an honor, a title, a gift, or the like, is conferred.

çon′fẽr-ence, *n.* [Fr. *conférence*, conference, from L. *conferens*, ppr. of *conferre*, to compare, bring together.]

1. Comparison; examination of things by comparison. [Obs.]

The mutual *conference* of all men's collections and observations. —Hooker.

2. The act of conferring or consulting together; a meeting for consultation, discussion, or instruction; an interview and statement or interchange of opinions; as, we held a *conference* as to how we should proceed.

3. In diplomacy, a meeting of the representatives of different foreign countries for discussion and recommendation. It has been held that the difference between a *conference* and a *congress* is that the latter has the power of making final decision.

4. A meeting of the two branches of a legislature, by their committees, to adjust differences respecting bills, etc.

5. In the Methodist Episcopal church, a stated meeting of ministerial and lay delegates for the transaction of ecclesiastical business; as, the quadrennial or general *conference*; the annual *conference*; the district *conference*.

6. In the Congregational church, a voluntary local assembly, representing the several churches of a district.

7. In the Roman Catholic church, an assembly of priests for the discussion of theological questions.

8. Discourse; oral discussion; talk; conversation.

To have some *conference* with your grace. —Shak.

çon-fẽr-en′tiăl (-shăl), *a.* Of or relating to conference. [Rare.]

çŏn-fẽr′ment, *n.* The act of conferring; as, the *conferment* of a title or a degree.

çŏn-fẽr′rȧ-ble, *a.* Capable of being conferred.

çŏn-fẽr′rẽr, *n.* One who confers; one who consults; also, one who bestows.

çon-fer-rū′mi-nāte, çon-fer-rū′mi-nā-ted, *a.* [L. *conferruminatus*, pp. of *conferruminare*, to solder together; *con-*, together, and *ferruminare*, to solder, from *ferrumen*, solder, cement; *ferrum*, iron.] Soldered together. In botany, united together, so as to be separated with difficulty.

Çon-fẽr′vȧ, *n.* [L. *conferva*, an aquatic plant.] A genus of algæ, consisting of marine and a few fresh-water species. The plants consist of simple hair-like filaments, formed of oblong cells, filled with granular endochrome. They are reproduced by zoöspores formed from the cell contents.

Conferva (*Cladophora nuda*); *a*, branched filament magnified.

çon-fẽr′vȧ, *n.*; *pl.* **çon-fẽr′væ.** An alga of the genus *Conferva*.

Çon-fẽr-vā′cē-æ, *n.pl.* A family of marine or fresh-water algæ having green fronds which are composed of articulated filaments, simple or branched. The cells are shortish, cylindrical, and not reproduced by conjugation but by zoöspores. *Conferva* is the type genus.

çon-fẽr-vā′ceous, *a.* Of or belonging to the *Confervaceæ*; having the characters of the *Confervaceæ*.

çon-fẽr′văl, *a.* and *n.* I. *a.* Of or allied to the genus *Conferva*.

II. *n.* A plant of the family *Confervaceæ*.

çon-fẽr′vite, *n.* A fossil plant, occurring chiefly in the Chalk formation, apparently allied to the aquatic confervæ.

çon-fẽr′void, *a.* [L. *conferva*, and Gr. *eidos*, form.] In botany, formed of a single row of cells; or having articulations like a conferva. In a more general sense, resembling a conferva, or partaking of its character.

Çon-fẽr-voi′dē-æ, *n.pl.* A name often employed for the green-spored algæ or *Chlorospermeæ*, the lowest order of water plants.

çon-fẽr′vous, *a.* Conferval.

çŏn-fess′, *v.t.*; confessed (-fest), *pt.*, *pp.*; confessing, *ppr.* [ME. *confessen*; OFr. *confesser*, to confess; L. *confessus*, pp. of *confiteri*, to confess, own; *con-*, together, and *fateri*, to acknowledge.]

1. To own, acknowledge, or avow; to make avowal or admission of, as of a crime, a fault, a charge, a debt, or something that is against one's interest or reputation; to own to.

And there *confess*
Humbly our faults, and pardon beg.—Milton.

2. Specifically, (a) to acknowledge (sins) to a priest in private with a view to absolution; sometimes with the reflexive pronoun; as, he hath *confessed himself*; (b) to hear or receive the confession of, as a priest that of a penitent.

I have *confessed* her and I know her virtue. —Shak.

3. To acknowledge as having a certain character or certain claims; to recognize; to own; to avow; to declare belief in.

Whosoever therefore shall *confess* me before men, him will I *confess* also before my Father which is in heaven. —Matt. x. 32.

4. To grant; to admit; not to dispute.

5. To show by the effect; to prove; to attest; to reveal.

The lovely stranger stands *confessed*
A maid in all her charms. —Goldsmith.

Syn.—Acknowledge, own, reveal, concede, avow, admit, attest, accept, grant, assent, recognize, prove, exhibit.

çŏn-fess′, *v.i.* To make confession or avowal; to disclose faults; specifically, to make known one's sins or the state of the conscience to a priest; as, he went to the priest to *confess*.

çŏn-fess′ănt, *n.* One who confesses to a priest. [Obs.]

çŏn-fess′ȧ-ry, *n.* One who makes a confession. [Obs.]

çŏn-fessed′ (-fest′), *a.* Admitted; avowed; undeniable; clear; patent; as, a *confessed* thief.

çŏn-fess′ed-ly, *adv.* By one's own confession or acknowledgment; by general confession or admission; admittedly; without denial.

çŏn-fess′ẽr, *n.* One who confesses.

çŏn-fes′sion (-fesh′un), *n.* [ME. *confession*; OFr. *confession*; L. *confessio*, confession.]

1. The act of confessing; especially, the acknowledgment of anything adverse to one's interest or reputation.

2. The act of making an avowal; profession.

3. A disclosing of sins or faults to a priest; the disburdening of the conscience privately to a confessor; in the Roman Catholic church, part of the sacrament of penance; often called *auricular confession*.

4. A formulary which comprises the articles of faith; a creed to be assented to or signed as a preliminary to admission into a church; usually called a *confession of faith*.

5. In law, (a) the acknowledgment of a debt, by a debtor, before a justice of the peace, or other court, on which judgment is entered and execution issued; (b) an acknowledgment of guilt; as, a judicial *confession*, which is one made before a magistrate or in court; or an extra-judicial *confession*, which is one made out of court, whether to an official or a non-official.

Confession and avoidance; in law, a form of pleading, as when a party confesses the facts in the declaration to be true, but presents some new matter by way of avoiding the legal effect.

General confession; the joint confession of sins by a number of persons, as in public worship.

çŏn-fes′sion-ăl, *n.* [L. *confessio*, confession.] A compartment or cell in which a priest sits to hear confessions, having a small opening or window at each side through which the penitent, kneeling without, makes confession.

Confessional, Cathedral of St. Gudule, Brussels.

Many *confessionals* are constructed in three divisions, the central division having a seat for the priest, and some are elaborately carved.

Called also *confession-chair, shriving-pew,* and *confessionary.*

çŏn-fes′sion-ăl, *a.* Of or pertaining to a confession, especially to a confession of faith.

çŏn-fes′sion-ăl-iṣm, *n.* Extreme adherence to the letter of a particular creed or confession of faith. [Rare.]

çŏn-fes′sion-ăl-ist, *n.* A priest who sits in the confessional; a confessor.

çŏn-fes′sion-ā-ry, *n.* and *a.* I. *n.* [Obs.] See *Confessional.*

II. *a.* Pertaining to auricular confession.

çŏn-fes′sion-ist, *n.* 1. One who makes a profession of faith.

2. A term applied to the Lutherans who held to the Augsburg formulary.

çŏn-fess′ŏr, *n.* 1. One who confesses; one who acknowledges a crime, fault, or sin.

2. One who makes a profession of his faith in the Christian religion; specifically, one who avows his religion in the face of danger, or adheres to it in defiance of persecution and torture.

3. One who hears confessions; specifically, a priest who hears confession and grants absolution.

çŏn-fess′ŏr-ship, *n.* The state of suffering martyrdom or being persecuted on account of religious faith.

çŏn-fest′, *v.,* old past tense and past participle of *confess.*

çŏn-fest′ly, *adv.* See *Confessedly.*

çon-fi-dant′, *n. masc.;* **çon-fi-dante′,** *n. fem.* [Fr.] A person intrusted with the confidence of another; one to whom secrets are confided; a confidential friend.

çŏn-fīde′, *v.i.;* confided, *pt., pp.;* confiding, *ppr.* [L. *confidere,* to trust; *con-,* together, and *fidere,* to trust.] To trust; to rely; to believe; followed by *in;* as, the prince *confides in* his ministers.

çŏn-fīde′, *v.t.* To intrust; to commit to the charge of, with reliance on the trustworthiness of the party to whom the thing is committed; followed by *to;* as, to *confide* a valuable or a secret *to* a friend; the common interests of the United States are *confided to* Congress.

> Congress may, under the Constitution, *confide to* the circuit court jurisdiction of all offenses against the United States.—Story.

Syn.—Trust to, rely on, depend on.

çon′fi-dence, *n.* [L. *confidentia,* confidence, trust, from *confidens,* ppr. of *confidere,* to trust.]

1. An assurance of mind or firm belief in the trustworthiness of another, or in the truth and reality of a fact; trust; reliance; usually followed by *in.*

> A cheerful *confidence in* the mercy of God. —Macaulay.

2. Reliance on one's own abilities, fortune, or circumstances; belief in one's own competency; self-reliance; assurance.

3. That in which trust is placed; ground of trust; he who or that which supports.

> The Lord shall be thy *confidence.*—Prov. iii. 26.

4. Boldness; courage; defiance of danger.

> But *confidence* then bore thee on. —Milton.

5. A secret; a private or confidential communication; often in the plural; as, the two were soon so friendly as to exchange *confidences.*

Confidence game; a swindling operation, in which the swindlers first gain the confidence of the victim.

Confidence man; one who swindles by a confidence game; a bunko-steerer.

To take a person into one's confidence; often specifically, to communicate some private matter or matters to another.

Syn.—Trust, faith, reliance, belief, assurance, self-reliance.

çon′fi-dent, *a.* 1. Having full belief; fully assured.

2. Confiding; not entertaining suspicion or distrust.

3. Relying on oneself; full of assurance; bold; dogmatical; sometimes overbold, impudent, or presumptuous.

> The fool rageth and is *confident.*—Prov. xiv. 16.

> As *confident* as is the falcon's flight
> Against a bird, do I with Mowbray fight. —Shak.

4. Giving occasion or ground for confidence. [Rare.]

> The cause was more *confident* than the event was prosperous. —Taylor.

5. Trustworthy; as, a *confident* servant. [Obs.]

6. Confidential. [Scot.]

Syn.—Positive, assured, sure, certain, sanguine, bold, impudent.

çon′fi-dent, *n.* [Obs.] Same as *Confidant.*

çon-fi-den′tiăl, *a.* [Fr. *confidentiel,* from L. *confidentia,* confidence.]

1. Enjoying the confidence of another; trusty; capable of being trusted; as, a *confidential* friend.

2. Having a secret character; kept in confidence; private; as, a *confidential* matter.

Confidential communication; see *Privileged communication* under *Communication.*

Confidential creditor; see *Preferred creditor* under *Creditor.*

Confidential debt; see *Preferred debt* under *Debt.*

çon-fi-den′tiăl-ly, *adv.* In confidence; in reliance on secrecy.

çon′fi-dent-ly, *adv.* With firm trust; with strong assurance; without doubt or wavering of opinion; positively; as, to believe *confidently;* to assert *confidently.*

çon′fi-dent-ness, *n.* Confidence; the quality or state of having full reliance.

çŏn-fīd′ẽr, *n.* One who confides; one who trusts in or intrusts to another.

çŏn-fīd′ing, *a.* Trusting; reposing confidence; trustful; credulous; as, a person of a most *confiding* disposition.

çŏn-fīd′ing-ly, *adv.* In a confiding manner; trustfully.

çŏn-fīd′ing-ness, *n.* The quality of being trustful; confidence; confiding disposition; trustfulness.

çŏn-fig′ūr-āte, *v.i.;* configurated, *pt., pp.;* configurating, *ppr.* [L. *configuratus,* pp. of *configurare,* to form after something; *con-,* together, and *figurare,* to form, from *figura,* a form, figure.] To exhibit uniformity of plan or balance of parts. [Rare.]

> The whole structure doth *configurate.* —Jordan.

çŏn-fig-ū-rā′tion, *n.* 1. External form, figure, or shape of a thing as resulting from the disposition and shape of its parts; external aspect or appearance; shape or form.

2. In astrology, relative position or aspect of the planets; the face of the horoscope, according to the relative positions of the planets at any time; in modern astronomy, the position of the stars in regard to each other, which may help in identification.

3. Resemblance of one figure to another. [Rare.]

çŏn-fig′ūre, *v.t.;* configured, *pt., pp.;* configuring, *ppr.* To form; to dispose in a certain form, figure, or shape.

çŏn-fīn′ȧ-ble (-bl), *a.* Capable of being confined or limited.

çon′fīne, *n.* [Fr. *confin;* OFr. *confin,* a border, boundary; L. *confinis,* bordering on, from *confinium,* a boundary, border; *con-,* with, and *finis,* an end, limit.]

1. Border; edge; exterior part; frontier; borderland; the part of any territory which is at or near the end or extremity; used generally in the plural, and applied chiefly to physical boundaries of considerable extent, although often applied figuratively; as, the *confines* of France; the *confines* of death or the grave.

2. Cell; prison; place of restraint. [Obs.]

> Confines, wards, and dungeons. —Shak.

çon′fīne, *v.i.* To border; to touch the limit; to be adjacent or contiguous, as one territory, kingdom, or state, to another; usually followed by *on;* sometimes by *with;* as, England *confines on* Scotland; Connecticut *confines on* Massachusetts, New York, Rhode Island, and the Sound. [Obs.]

çŏn-fīne′, *v.t.;* confined, *pt., pp.;* confining, *ppr.*

1. To bound or limit; to restrain within limits; to imprison; to shut up; to restrain from forcible escape; as, to *confine* horses or cattle to an inclosure; to *confine* water in a pond; to *confine* a garrison in a town; to *confine* a criminal in prison.

2. To immure; to keep close, by a voluntary act; to be much in retirement; as, a man *confines* himself to his studies, or to his house.

3. To limit or restrain voluntarily, in some act or practice; with the reflexive pronoun and *to;* as, a man may *confine himself to* the use of animal food.

4. To restrain by a moral force; as, to *confine* men by laws; the Constitution of the United States *confines* the states to the exercise of powers of a local nature.

To be confined; to be kept to the house, or bed, especially because of childbirth.

Syn.—Imprison, incarcerate, immure, restrict, bound, limit, circumscribe, inclose.

çŏn-fīned′, *a.* Restrained within limits; imprisoned; limited; secluded; close.

çŏn-fīne′less, *a.* Boundless; without end.

çŏn-fīne′ment, *n.* 1. The state of being confined; restraint within limits; any restraint of liberty by force or other obstacle or necessity; imprisonment.

> The mind hates restraint, and is apt to fancy itself under *confinement,* when the sight is pent up. —Addison.

2. Restraint from going abroad by sickness, particularly by childbirth; the lying-in of a woman.

çŏn-fīn′ẽr, *n.* One who or that which limits or restrains.

çon′fi-nẽr, *n.* A borderer; one who lives on confines, or near the border of a country; a neighbor.

> The senate hath stirr'd up the *confiners.* —Shak.

çon-fin′i-ty, *n.* [L. *confinis,* bordering upon.] Contiguity; nearness; neighborhood. [Rare.]

çŏn-fīrm′, *v.t.;* confirmed, *pt., pp.;* confirming, *ppr.* [ME. *confermen;* OFr. *confermer;* L. *confirmare,* to make firm, strengthen; *con-,* together, and *firmare,* to strengthen, from *firmus,* firm, strong.]

1. To make firm, or more firm; to add strength to; as, health is *confirmed* by exercise.

2. To settle or establish.

> I *confirm* thee in the high priesthood, and appoint thee ruler. —Maccab. xi. 57.

3. To make certain; to give new assurance of truth or certainty; to put past doubt; to assure; to verify; as, my suspicions are now fully *confirmed.*

4. To sanction; to ratify; as, to *confirm* an agreement, promise, covenant, or title; the Senate *confirms* or rejects the appointments brought before it by the President of the United States.

5. To strengthen in resolution, purpose, or opinion.

> *Confirmed* then I resolve
> Adam shall share with me in bliss or woe. —Milton.

6. In ecclesiasticism, to admit to the full privileges of a Christian, by the imposition of hands; to administer the rite of confirmation to.

Syn.—Corroborate, establish, substantiate, settle, strengthen, fix, ratify.

çŏn-fīrm′ȧ-ble, *a.* 1. Capable of being confirmed, established, or ratified; capable of being made more certain; as, the statement is *confirmable* by instances which may be deduced.

2. Corroboratory. [Rare.]

> *Confirmable* in their declaration as witnesses. —Parke.

çŏn-fīrm′ănce, *n.* Confirmation; establishment of confidence. [Obs.]

> For their *confirmance,* I will therefore now
> Slepe in our black barke. —Chapman.

çon-fīr-mā′tion, *n.* 1. The act of confirming; the act of establishing; a fixing, settling, establishing, or making more certain or firm; establishment.

2. That which confirms or corroborates; that which gives new strength or assurance; additional evidence; proof; convincing testimony.

3. In ecclesiasticism, the act or ceremony of laying on of hands by a bishop in the admission of baptized persons to the Christian church.

4. In law, an assurance of title, by the conveyance of an estate or right *in esse* from one man to another, by which a voidable estate is made sure or unavoidable, a particular estate is increased, or a possession made perfect. —Blackstone.

çŏn-fīrm′ȧ-tive, *a.* Having the power of confirming; tending to establish; confirmatory; as, what you say is quite *confirmative* of my statement.

çŏn-fīrm′ȧ-tive-ly, *adv.* In a confirmative manner; so as to confirm.

çon′fīr-mā-tŏr, *n.* One who or that which confirms.

çŏn-fīrm′ȧ-tō-ry, *a.* 1. Serving to confirm; giving additional strength, force, or stability, or additional assurance or evidence.

2. Pertaining to the rite of confirmation.

> The *confirmatory* usage in the synagogues. —Compton.

çŏn-fīrm′ed-ly, *adv.* In a confirmed manner; with confirmation.

çŏn-fīrm′ed-ness, *n.* The state or quality of being confirmed.

çon-fīr-mee′, *n.* In law, one to whom anything is confirmed.

çŏn-fīrm′ẽr, *n.* One who or that which confirms, establishes, or ratifies; one who produces new evidence; an attester.

çŏn-fīrm′ing-ly, *adv.* In such a manner as to strengthen or corroborate.

çŏn-fis′çȧ-ble, *a.* Capable of being confiscated; liable to forfeiture.

çon′fis-çāte (*or* -fis′kāt), *v.t.,* confiscated, *pt., pp.,* confiscating, *ppr.* [L. *confiscatus,* pp. of *confiscare,* to lay up in a chest, to seize for the public treasury, confiscate; *con-,* together, and *fiscus,* a wicker basket, a money basket or chest, the public treasury.]

1. To adjudge to be forfeited to the public treasury, as the goods or estate of a traitor or

other criminal, by way of penalty; to appropriate, as a penalty, to public use.

It was judged he should be banished, and his whole estate *confiscated* and seized.—Bacon.

2. More generally, to appropriate under legal authority as forfeited; as, a railway company has power to *confiscate* a pass or season-ticket found in the possession of any one other than the person in whose name it was issued; police magistrates have power to *confiscate* weapons.

çon'fis-çāte, *a.* 1. Forfeited and adjudged to the public treasury, as the goods of a criminal.

Thy lands and goods
Are by the laws of Venice *confiscate.*—Shak.

2. Appropriated under legal authority as forfeited.

çon-fis-çā'tion, *n.* The act of condemning as forfeited, and adjudging to the public treasury, as the goods of a criminal who has committed a public offense; also, the act of alienating private property as forfeited under the law.

çon'fis-çā-tŏr, *n.* One who confiscates.

çŏn-fis'çà-tō-ry, *a.* Consigning to forfeiture; relating to confiscation.

çon'fit, *n.* A sweetmeat; confection; comfit. [Obs.]

çon'fi-tent, *n.* [L. *confitens*, pp. of *confiteri*, to confess.] One who confesses his sins and faults. [Obs.]

Çon-fit'ē-ọr, *n.* [L., I confess, first pers. sing. pres. ind. of *confiteri*, to confess.] In the Roman Catholic church, a form of public confession, in Latin, used at the beginning of the mass; so called from its initial word.

çon'fi-tūre, *n.* 1. The act of making confections. [Obs.]

2. A sweetmeat; confection; comfit. [Obs.]

3. A composition, as of various drugs. [Obs.]

çŏn-fix', *v.t.*; confixed (-fixt), *pt.*, *pp.*; confixing, *ppr.* To fasten or fix firmly. [Obs.]

çŏn-fix'ūre, *n.* The act of fastening. [Obs.]

çŏn-flā'grănt, *a.* Burning together in a common flame. [Rare.]

çon'flà-grāte, *v.t* and *v.i.*; conflagrated, *pt.*, *pp.*; conflagrating, *ppr.* [L. *conflagratus*, pp. of *conflagrare*, to burn together; *con-*, together, and *flagrare*, to burn.]

I. *v.t.* To burn up utterly; to consume.

Conflagrating the poor man himself into ashes and caput mortuum. —Carlyle.

II. *v.i.* To burn or blaze with flame.

Civil war *conflagrating* universally over France. —Carlyle.

çon-flà-grā'tion, *n.* A great fire, or the burning of any great mass of combustibles; as, the *conflagration* of a city or of a forest.

çon'flà-grā-tive, *a.* Tending to produce or causing a conflagration.

çŏn-flāte', *v.t.*; conflated, *pt.*, *pp.*; conflating, *ppr.* [L. *conflatus*, pp. of *conflare*, to blow together, kindle; *con-*, together, and *flare*, to blow.]

1. To blow together; to waft together from several sources; to bring together; to collect.

2. To combine into a composite text or reading from various sources, as extracts from old manuscripts; used in the passive.

3. To melt together; to fuse; to join. [Obs.]

çŏn-flāte', *a.* 1. Blown together; brought together from several sources.

2. Formed by combining different readings, as a composite text.

çŏn-flā'tion, *n.* [LL. *conflatio*, a blowing together, from *conflare*, to blow together.]

1. The act of fusing or combining variant readings into a text.

2. A blowing together, as of many instruments in a concert, or of many fires in melting metals. [Rare.]

çon'fleçt, *a.* [*Con-*, and L. *flectere*, to bend.] In entomology, clustered thickly; as, *conflect* hairs on an insect.

çŏn-flex'ūre, *n.* A bending. [Obs.]

çon'fliçt, *n.* [L. *conflictus*, a striking together, a contest, from *confligere*, to strike together; *con-*, together, and *fligere*, to strike.]

1. A fighting or struggling for mastery; a combat; a battle; a striving to oppose or overcome; active opposition; contention; controversy; strife.

In our last *conflict*, four of his five wits went halting off. —Shak.

2. A striking or dashing together, as of two moving bodies in opposition; violent collision of substances; as, a *conflict* of armies; a *conflict* of the elements.

Conflict of laws; the opposition between the municipal laws of different countries, in the case of an individual who may have acquired rights or become subject to duties within the limits of more than one nation or state.

Irrepressible conflict; a phrase once very common in the United States to indicate the unavoidable conflict over the slavery question; first used by Wm. H. Seward in 1859.

Syn.—Contention, contest, fight, struggle, combat, encounter.

çŏn-fliçt', *v.i.*; conflicted, *pt.*, *pp.*; conflicting, *ppr.* 1. To strike or dash against; to meet and oppose; as, *conflicting* waves or elements.

2. To contend; to fight; to strive or struggle to resist and overcome; as, a man should *conflict* with great difficulties, in hope of a mighty reward.

3. To be in opposition; to be contrary; as, the evidence given by the second witness *conflicted* with that given by the first.

çŏn-fliçt'ing, *a.* Being in opposition; contrary; contradictory; incompatible; as, *conflicting* jurisdiction; the evidence was very *conflicting*.

çŏn-flic'tion, *n.* The act of conflicting or clashing; the state of being in conflict with; want of harmony. [Rare.]

çŏn-fliçt'ive, *a.* Tending to conflict; clashing; conflicting; as, *conflictive* systems of theology.

çon'flū-ence, *n.* [LL. *confluentia*, a flowing together.]

1. A flowing together; the meeting or junction of two or more streams of water, or other fluid; also, the place of meeting; as, the *confluence* of the Ohio and Mississippi.

2. The running together of people; the act of meeting and crowding in a place; a crowd; a concourse.

3. In philology, the tendency by which words become similar in form, or figuratively run together.

çon'flū-ent, *a.* 1. Flowing together; meeting in their course, as two streams.

2. In anatomy, united, blended, or grown together, as two bones which originally were separate; connate.

3. In botany, united at some part; as, *confluent* leaves, that is, leaves united at the base; *confluent* lobes.

4. In pathology, (a) running together; as, *confluent* pustules; (b) characterized by *confluent* pustules; as, *confluent* smallpox.

çon'flū-ent, *n.* 1. A tributary stream.

2. The place of joining or confluence of two streams. [Obs.]

çon'flū-ent-ly, *adv.* In a flowing or blending manner.

çon'flux, *n.* 1. A flowing together; a meeting of two or more currents of a fluid.

2. A collection; a crowd; a multitude collected; as, a general *conflux* of people.

çŏn-flux-i-bil'i-ty, *n.* The tendency of fluids to run together. [Rare.]

çŏn-flux'i-ble, *a.* Having a tendency to flow or run together.

çŏn-flux'i-ble-ness, *n.* Same as *Confluxibility.*

çŏn-fō'çăl, *a.* [*Con-*, and L. *focus*, a hearth, in modern sense, a center.] In mathematics, having the same focus; as, *confocal* quadrics; *confocal* conics; *confocal* surfaces.

çon-fō-rā'nē-ous, *a.* [*Con-*, and L. *forum*, market-place.] Of the same market-place. [Obs.]

çŏn-fọrm', *a.* Conformable.

çŏn-fọrm', *v.t.*; conformed, *pt.*, *pp.*; conforming, *ppr.* [ME. *conformen*; OFr. *conformer*; L. *conformare*, to fashion, form.]

1. To make of the same form or character; to make like; with *to*; as, to *conform* anything *to* a model.

2. To bring into harmony or correspondence; to make agreeable; to adapt; to submit; often with reflexive pronouns.

Demand of them why they *conform* not *themselves* unto the order of the church. —Hooker.

çŏn-fọrm', *v.i.* 1. To act in conformity to or compliance with; to obey; with *to*; as, to *conform to* the fashion or *to* the custom.

2. Specifically, in English ecclesiasticism, to comply with the usages of the Established church; in this sense often used absolutely.

There was a Puritan gentleman who served under Cromwell, but afterward *conformed.* —George Eliot.

çŏn-fọrm-à-bil'i-ty, *n.* 1. The state or quality of being conformable.

2. In geology, the relation of two strata, one of which reposes on the other and is parallel to it.

çŏn-fọrm'à-ble, *a.* [From L. *conformare*, to conform.]

1. Corresponding in form or shape, character, moral qualities, manners, opinions, etc.; resembling; like; similar.

The Gentiles were not made *conformable* to the Jews, in that which was to cease at the coming of Christ. —Hooker.

2. In harmony or conformity; agreeable; suitable; consistent; as, nature is *conformable* to herself.

3. Compliant; ready to follow directions; submissive; obsequious; peaceable; disposed to obey.

I have been to you a true and humble wife,
At all times to your will *conformable.*—Shak.

[In all the foregoing senses generally followed by *to*, sometimes by *with.*]

4. In proper form; convenient.

5. In geology, lying in parallel or nearly parallel planes; having the same dip and changes of dip; said of strata or groups of

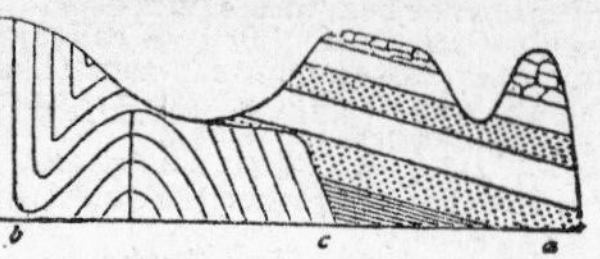

Conformable and Unconformable Strata.

strata; opposed to *unconformable.* Thus in the figure, the groups of strata *a* and *b* are *conformable* each by itself, but *unconformable* in reference to each other where they meet at the point *c.*

çŏn-fọrm'à-ble-ness, *n.* The state of being conformable.

çŏn-fọrm'à-bly, *adv.* In a conformable manner; in conformity with; suitably; agreeably.

çŏn-fọrm'ănce, *n.* Conformity. [Rare.]

çŏn-fọrm'āte, *a.* Having the same form. [Rare.]

çon-fọr-mā'tion, *n.* [L. *conformatio*, a forming, fashioning, conforming, from *conformare*, to conform.]

1. The manner in which a body is formed; the particular texture or structure of a body, or disposition of the parts which compose it; form; structure.

2. The act of conforming; the act of producing suitableness or conformity; with *to*; as, the *conformation* of our lives *to* the dictates of true religion.

çŏn-fọrm'ẽr, *n.* One who conforms; one who complies with established forms or doctrines.

çŏn-fọrm'ist, *n.* One who conforms or complies; specifically, one who complies with the worship of the Church of England, or the Established church, as distinguished from a dissenter or nonconformist.

çŏn-fọrm'i-ty, *n.* 1. Correspondence in form or manner; resemblance; agreement; congruity; likeness; correspondence; harmony; in this and the following meaning followed by *to* or *with* before the object with which another agrees, and *in* before the matter in which there is agreement; as, a ship is constructed in *conformity to* or *with* a model; *conformity in* shape.

2. Correspondence with the decrees or dictates of; submission; accordance.

We cannot be otherwise happy but by our *conformity to* God. —Tillotson.

3. Specifically, in ecclesiasticism, compliance with the usages or principles of the Anglican church.

A proclamation requiring all ecclesiastical and civil officers to do their duty by enforcing *conformity.* —Hallam.

Syn.—Consistency, harmony, similitude, resemblance, accordance, agreement.

çon-fọr-tā'tion, *n.* The act of giving strength. [Obs.]

çŏn-found', *v.t.*; confounded, *pt.*, *pp.*; confounding, *ppr.* [ME. *confounden*; OFr. *confondre*; L. *confundere*, to pour or mingle together, confuse, confound; *con-*, together, and *fundere*, to pour.]

1. To mingle and blend so that forms or natures cannot be distinguished; to throw into disorder.

Let us go down, and there *confound* their language. —Gen. xi. 7.

2. To mistake one for another; to make a mistake between; to regard as identical though different.

3. To throw into consternation; to perplex with terror, surprise, or astonishment; to stupefy with amazement; to abash.

4. To destroy; to overthrow; to ruin; hence such interjectional phrases as, *confound* it! *confound* the fellow!

Which infinite calamity shall cause
To human life, and household peace *confound.* —Milton.

5. To waste or spend uselessly, as time. [Obs.]

Syn.—Abash, astonish, baffle, confuse, defeat, dismay, intermingle, mix, terrify.

çŏn-found'ed, *a.* A mild colloquial invective signifying detestable, execrable, huge; as, a *confounded* nuisance.

çŏn-found'ed-ly, *adv.* Colloquially, in a confounded manner.

çŏn-found'ed-ness, *n.* The state of being confounded.

çŏn-found'ẽr, *n.* One who or that which confounds.

çon'fraçt, *a.* Broken. [Obs.]

çon-frà-gōse', *a.* Broken; uneven. [Obs.]

çon-frà-tẽr'ni-ty, *n.*; *pl.* **çon-frà-tẽr'ni-ties.** [LL. *confraternitas*, brotherhood.]

1. A brotherhood; a society or body of men united for some purpose or in some profession; as, a *confraternity* of artists.

2. Specifically, in the Roman Catholic and Episcopal churches, an organization of laymen for religious or charitable purposes.

çon-frère′ (-frâr′), *n.* [Fr.] A colleague; a fellow-member; an associate in something.

çon-frī′ăr, çon-frī′ẽr, *n.* An associate of the same religious order. [Obs.]

çon-frī-cā′tion, *n.* [LL. *confricatio*, from L. *confricare*, to rub together.] A rubbing against; friction. [Obs.]

çon-frī′ẽr, *n.* [Obs.] See *Confriar.*

çŏn-frŏnt′, *v.t.*; confronted, *pt.*, *pp.*; confronting, *ppr.* [Fr. *confronter*, to confront; L. *con-*, together, and *frons*, forehead.]

1. To stand facing; to face; to stand in front of.

He spoke and then *confronts* the bull. —Dryden.

2. To stand in direct opposition to; to meet in hostility; to oppose.

Strength match'd with strength, and power *confronted* power. —Shak.

3. To set face to face; to bring into the presence of, as an accused person and a witness, in court, for examination and discovery of the truth; followed by *with*; as, the witness was *confronted with* the accused.

4. To set together for comparison; to compare (one thing with another); with *with*. [Rare.]

When I *confront* a medal *with* a verse I only show you the same design executed by different hands. —Addison.

çon-frŏn-tā′tion, *n.* The act of confronting.

çoṅ-frŏn-té′ (-tā′), *a.* Same as *Affronté.*

çŏn-frŏnt′ẽr, *n.* One who or that which confronts.

çŏn-frŏnt′ment, *n.* The act of confronting. [Rare.]

Çŏn-fū′ciăn (-shăn), *a.* and *n.* I. *a.* Relating to Confucius (551-478 B. C.)

II. *n.* A follower of or believer in the teachings of Confucius.

Çŏn-fū′ciăn-ism, *n.* The doctrines or system of morality taught by Confucius, which has been long adopted in China as the basis of jurisprudence and education. It inculcates civil, family, and social duties, but provides for the worship of no god, and can scarcely therefore be called a religion. The synonymous Chinese term is *Yu-Kiao*, the system of the learned.

Çŏn-fū′ciăn-ist, *n.* A Confucian.

çŏn-fūṣ-ȧ-bil′i-ty, *n.* Liability to be perplexed.

çŏn-fūṣ′ȧ-ble, *a.* Liable to be perplexed.

çŏn-fūṣe′, *a.* Mixed; confounded. [Obs.]

çŏn-fūṣe′, *v.t.*; confused, *pt.*, *pp.*; confusing, *ppr.* [L. *confusus*, pp. of *confundere*, to pour together, confuse; *con-*, together, and *fundere*, to pour.]

1. To mix up without order or clearness; to bring disorder among; to throw together indiscriminately; to disorder; to jumble; as, the accounts were *confused.*

2. To perplex or derange the mind or ideas of; to embarrass; to disconcert; to cause to lose self-possession; to confound.

The want of arrangement and connexion *confuses* the reader. —Whately.

Syn.—Derange, disorder, jumble, involve, abash, disconcert, confound, embarrass, distract.

çŏn-fūṣ′ed-ly, *adv.* In a confused manner.

çŏn-fūṣ′ed-ness, *n.* The state of being in confusion.

çŏn-fūṣe′ly, *adv.* Confusedly. [Obs.]

çŏn-fū′ṣion, *n.* 1. A state in which things are so confused or mixed as to cause perplexity or obscurity; an indiscriminate or disorderly mingling; disorder; tumultuous condition; as, the *confusion* of the crowd; a *confusion* of ideas.

2. Perturbation of mind; embarrassment; distraction.

Confusion dwelt in every face. —Spectator.

3. Abashment; shame.

We lie down in our shame, and our *confusion* covereth us. —Jer. iii. 25.

4. Overthrow; defeat; ruin.

Ruin seize thee, ruthless king!
Confusion on thy banners wait. —Gray.

5. One who confuses; a confounder.

Confusion of goods; the intermixing of the goods of different persons so that the ownership is in doubt.

çŏn-fū′sive, *a.* Having a tendency to confusion.

çŏn-fūt′ȧ-ble, *a.* Capable of being confuted.

çŏn-fūt′ănt, *n.* A confuter.

çon-fū-tā′tion, *n.* [L. *confutatio*, from *confutare*, to confute.] The act of confuting or proving to be false.

çŏn-fūt′ȧ-tive, *a.* Adapted or designed to confute.

çŏn-fūte′, *v.t.*; confuted, *pt.*, *pp.*; confuting, *ppr.* [L. *confutare*, to confute.]

1. To disprove; to prove to be false, defective, or invalid; to overthrow; as, to *confute* arguments.

2. To prove to be wrong; to convict of error, by argument or proof; as, to *confute* an advocate at the bar; to *confute* a writer.

çŏn-fūte′ment, *n.* Confutation; disproof. [Obs.]

çŏn-fūt′ẽr, *n.* One who confutes.

çong, *n.* In medicine, an abbreviation of *congius*, a gallon.

çoṅ-ġé′ (-zhā′), *n.* [ME. *congie, congey*, leave, departure; OFr. *congie, congiet*, leave, permission to depart; L. *commeatus*, a leave of absence, furlough.]

1. Leave to depart; farewell; dismissal; generally in such phrases as to take one's *congé*; to give one his *congé.*

2. A bow or courtesy, especially when leaving.

The captain salutes you with *congé* profound. —Swift.

3. In architecture, same as *apophyge.*

Congé d'élire; in ecclesiastical affairs, the sovereign's license or permission to a dean and chapter to choose a bishop. [Eng.]

çon′ġē, *v.i.*; congeed, *pt.*, *pp.*; congeing, *ppr.* To take leave with the customary civilities; to bow or courtesy.

çon′ġē-ȧ-ble, *a.* In old English law, allowable; permissible. [Obs.]

çŏn-ġeal′, *v.t.*; congealed, *pt.*, *pp.*; congealing, *ppr.* [L. *congelare*, to cause to freeze together, to thicken; *con-*, together, and *gelare*, to freeze.]

1. To change from a fluid to a solid state, as water in freezing, liquid metal or wax in cooling, blood in stagnating or cooling, etc.; to harden, as into ice.

(The island of Sal) hath its name from the abundance of salt that is naturally *congealed* there. —Dampier.

2. To check the flow of; to make run cold.

Sadness hath *congealed* your blood. —Shak.

çŏn-ġeal′, *v.i.* To grow hard, stiff, or thick, from loss of heat; to pass from a fluid to a solid state; to concrete into a solid mass; to be chilled; as, melted lead *congeals*; water *congeals*; blood *congeals.*

çŏn-ġeal′ȧ-ble, *a.* Capable of being congealed.

çŏn-ġeal′ȧ-ble-ness, *n.* Capability of congealing.

çŏn-ġeal′ed-ness, *n.* The state of being congealed.

çŏn-ġeal′ment, *n.* 1. A clot or concretion; that which is formed by congelation. [Obs.]

2. Congelation.

çon′ġee, *n.* and *v.* [Obs.] See *Conge.*

çon-ġee′, *n.* [Hind. *kanji*; Pali, *kanjikam*, rice-water.]

1. In the East Indies, boiled rice.

2. An East Indian jail; a regimental lockup; also called *congee-house.*

çon-ġee′-wa″tẽr, *n.* In India, rice-water.

çon-ġē-lā′tion, *n.* [L. *congelatio*, a congealing, from *congelatus*, pp. of *congelare*, to congeal.]

1. The act or process of congealing; the state of being congealed; the process of passing, or the act of converting, from a fluid to a solid state; concretion.

The capillary tubes are obstructed either by outward compression or *congelation* of the fluid. —Arbuthnot.

2. What is congealed or solidified; a concretion; as, a *congelation* of blood.

çon′ġē-nẽr, *n.* [L., of the same race; *con-*, together, and *genus*, genit. *generis*, race, kind.] A thing of the same kind or nearly allied; specifically, in biology, a plant or animal belonging to the same or an allied genus.

çon-ġē-ner′iç, çon-ġē-ner′iç-ăl, *a.* [L. *con-*, together, and *genus*, kind, race.] Being of the same kind or nature; belonging to the same genus or one allied to it.

çon-ġen′ẽr-ous, *a.* Congeneric. [Obs.]

çon-ġen′ẽr-ous-ness, *n.* The quality of being congenerous. [Obs.]

çŏn-ġēn′iăl (-yăl), *a.* [L. *con-*, together, and *genialis*, of the same nature or birth, from *genus*, kind.]

1. Partaking of the same nature or natural characteristics; kindred; sympathetic; suited for each other; as, *congenial* souls.

Smit with the love of sister arts we came
And met *congenial.* —Pope.

2. Naturally suited or adapted; as, *congenial* work.

çŏn-ġē-ni-al′i-ty, *n.* The state of being congenial; participation of the same nature; natural affinity; suitableness.

çŏn-ġēn′iăl-ize, *v.t.* To make congenial. [Rare.]

çŏn-ġēn′iăl-ly, *adv.* In a suitable or congenial manner.

çŏn-ġēn′iăl-ness, *n.* Congeniality.

çŏn-ġēn′ious (-yus), *a.* Congeneric. [Obs.]

çŏn-ġen′i-tăl, *a.* [L. *congenitus*, born together with; *con-*, together, and *genitus*, pp. of *gignere*, to bear.] Belonging or pertaining to an individual from birth; as, a *congenital* disease; a *congenital* deformity.

çŏn-ġen′i-tăl-ly, *adv.* In a congenital manner.

çŏn-ġen′ite, *a.* Congenital. [Obs.]

çoṅ′gẽr, *n.* [L. *conger*; Gr. *gongros*, the sea-eel.] The conger-eel.

çoṅ′gẽr-eel, *n.* 1. The sea-eel, *Conger vulgaris*, a large voracious eel, pale brown above and grayish-white below, sometimes ten feet in length and weighing one hundred pounds.

2. A local American name for either the eel-pout or the *Sidera mordax* of the coast of California.

çon-ġē′ri-ēṣ, *n.* [L. *congeries*, that which is brought together, a pile, from *congerere*, to bring together.] A collection of several particles or bodies in one mass or aggregate.

çŏn-ġest′, *v.t.*; congested, *pt.*, *pp.*; congesting, *ppr.* [L. *congestus*, pp. of *congerere*, to bring together.]

1. To collect or gather into a mass or aggregate.

2. In medicine, to become congested.

çŏn-ġest′ed, *a.* 1. Crowded very closely; overcrowded with inhabitants; obstructed by crowding or massing together.

2. In medicine, affected with congestion, as of blood.

çŏn-ġes′tion (-chun), *n.* 1. The act of gathering or heaping together; aggregation.

2. Crowded condition; condition of obstruction from crowding; as, *congestion* of risks in fire-insurance.

3. In medicine, an excessive accumulation of blood in an organ, with disorder of its functions.

çŏn-ġest′ive, *a.* Pertaining to congestion.

çon′ġi-ā-ry, *n.*; *pl.* **çon′ġi-ā-rieṣ.** [L. *congiarium* (supply *donum*, gift), a gift to the people consisting of a congius for each one.]

1. A largess or distribution of corn, oil, or wine, afterward of money, among the people or soldiery of ancient Rome.

2. A coin struck in commemoration of the Roman *congiaries* or largesses.

çon′ġi-us, *n.* [L.] 1. A measure of capacity among the Romans, the eighth part of the amphora, and equal to about six pints.

2. In medicine, a gallon; often abbreviated to *cong.*

çŏn-glā′ci-āte (-shi-), *v.i.* To turn to ice; to freeze. [Obs.]

çŏn-glā-ci-ā′tion, *n.* [L. *conglaciatus*, pp. of *conglaciare*, to turn to ice, freeze; *con-*, together, and *glaciare*, to freeze.] The act of changing into ice, or the state of being converted to ice; a freezing; congelation.

çŏn-glō′bāte, *a.* [L. *conglobatus*, from *conglobare*; *con-*, together, and *globare*, to collect, or to make round; *globus*, a ball.] Formed or gathered into a ball or small spherical body; combined into one mass.

çŏn-glō′bāte, *v.t.*; conglobated, *pt.*, *pp.*; conglobating, *ppr.* To collect or form into a ball.

çŏn-glō′bāte-ly, *adv.* In a round or roundish form.

çon-glō-bā′tion, *n.* The act of forming into a ball; or the body so formed.

çŏn-glōbe′, *v.t.*; conglobed, *pt.*, *pp.*; conglobing, *ppr.* To gather into a ball; to collect into a round mass.

çŏn-glōbe′, *v.i.* To collect, unite, or coalesce in a round mass.

Tho' something like moisture *conglobes* in my eye. —Burns.

çŏn-glob′ū-lāte, *v.i.* To gather into a little round mass or globule. [Rare.]

çŏn-glom′ẽr-āte, *a.* [L. *conglomeratus*, pp. of *conglomerare*, to roll together, wind up; *con-*, together, and *glomerare*, to gather into a ball, from *glomus*, a ball.]

1. Gathered into a ball or round body; crowded together; clustered.

The beams of light when they are multiplied and *conglomerate* generate heat. —Bacon.

2. In botany, collected in parcels, each of which has a roundish figure.

3. In geology, denoting rocks composed of smaller rock-particles united.

çŏn-glom′ẽr-āte, *v.t.*; conglomerated, *pt.*, *pp.*; conglomerating, *ppr.* To gather into a ball or round body; to collect into a round mass.

çŏn-glom′ẽr-āte, *n.* 1. An aggregate or mixture of ingredients.

2. In geology, a rock composed of rounded fragments of various rocks cemented together by siliceous or other matter; called also *pudding-stone.* [See *Breccia.*]

çŏn-glom-ẽr-ā′tion, *n.* The act of gathering into a ball; the state of being thus collected; collection; accumulation; a conglomerated mass.

çon-glū'tin, *n.* One of the proteids found in pease, beans, almonds, wheat, etc.

çon-glū'ti-nănt, *a.* Gluing; uniting; healing. [Obs.]

çon-glū'ti-nănt, *n.* A medicine that heals wounds. [Obs.]

çon-glū'ti-nāte, *v.t.*; conglutinated, *pt., pp.*; conglutinating, *ppr.* [L. *conglutinatus*, pp. of *conglutinare*, to glue together; *con-*, together, and *glutinare*, to glue, from *gluten*, glue.]

1. To glue together; to unite by some glutinous or tenacious substance.

2. To heal; to unite (the separated parts of a wound) by a tenacious substance.

çon-glū'ti-nāte, *v.i.* To coalesce; to unite.

çon-glū'ti-nāte, *a.* Glued together; united by a tenacious substance.

çon-glū-ti-nā'tion, *n.* The act of gluing together; a joining by means of some tenacious substance; coalescence.

çon-glū'ti-nā-tive, *a.* Conglutinant.

çon-glū'ti-nā-tŏr, *n.* A medicine having the power of uniting wounds.

çon'gō-eel, *n.* A corruption of *conger-eel*.

çon'gō-snāke, *n.* A name given to one or two of the amphibians of the family *Amphiumidæ*.

çon'gōu, *n.* [Chinese *kung-fu*, labor.] The second lowest quality of black tea, being the third picking from a plant during the season.

çon-grat'ū-lănt, *a.* Rejoicing with another.

çon-grat'ū-lāte, *v.t.*; congratulated, *pt., pp.*; congratulating, *ppr.* [L. *congratulatus*, pp. of *congratulari*, to wish joy; *con-*, together, and *gratulari*, to manifest joy; wish joy.]

1. To address with expressions of sympathetic pleasure on some piece of good fortune happening to the party addressed; to compliment upon an event deemed happy; to wish joy to; as, to *congratulate* the nation on the restoration of peace.

2. To welcome; to hail with expressions of pleasure.

To congratulate oneself; to have a lively sense of one's good fortune; to rejoice or exult at it.

çon-grat'ū-lāte, *v.i.* To express or feel sympathetic joy; followed by *with*. [Rare.]

> I cannot but *congratulate with* my country, which hath outdone all Europe in advancing conversation. —Swift.

çon-grat-ū-lā'tion, *n.* The act of congratulating; also, words used in congratulating.

Syn.—Felicitation.—*Congratulation* implies an actual feeling of pleasure in another's happiness or good fortune, while *felicitation* rather refers to the expression on our part of a belief that the other is fortunate, *felicitations* being complimentary expressions intended to make the fortunate person well pleased with himself.

çon-grat'ū-lā-tŏr, *n.* One who offers congratulation.

çon-grat'ū-lā-tō-ry, *a.* Expressing joy for an event.

çon-grēe', *v.i.* To agree. [Obs.]

çon-grēet', *v.i.* To salute mutually. [Obs.]

çoṅ'grē-gāte, *v.t.* and *v.i.*; congregated, *pt., pp.*; congregating, *ppr.* [L. *congregatus*, pp. of *congregare*, to collect into a flock, congregate; *con-*, together, and *gregare*, to collect into a flock, to gather, from *grex*, a flock.]

I. *v.t.* To collect into an assemblage; to bring into one place, or into a crowd or united body; as, to *congregate* men or animals.

II. *v.i.* To come together; to assemble; to meet.

> Equals with equals often *congregate*. —Denham.

çoṅ'grē-gāte, *a.* Collected; compact; close. [Rare.]

çoṅ-grē-gā'tion, *n.* 1. The act of congregating; the act of bringing together or assembling; as, by *congregation* of the separate particles.

2. A collection or assemblage of separate things; as, a *congregation* of animals.

3. An assembly of persons, especially one meeting at a stated time and place for the holding of religious services.

4. Used in various specific senses; as, (a) in Scripture, an assembly of rulers among the Jews; (b) an assembly of ecclesiastics or cardinals appointed by the pope, to which is intrusted the management of some important branch of the affairs of the church; (c) a fraternity of religious persons forming a subdivision of a monastic order; (d) at Oxford and Cambridge, the assembly of masters and doctors which confers degrees; (e) in Scotland, an appellation assumed by the adherents of the reformed faith about the middle of the sixteenth century.

çoṅ-grē-gā'tion-ăl, *a.* 1. Of, relating or pertaining to a congregation; as, *congregational* music.

2. Of, relating or pertaining to congregationalism; as, *congregational* methods.

3. [C—] Designating the denomination of the Congregationalists; as, a *Congregational* church.

çoṅ-grē-gā'tion-ăl-iṣm, *n.* 1. That system of church government which vests all ecclesiastical power in the assembled brotherhood of each local church, as an independent body.

2. [C—] The doctrinal belief and mode of government of the Congregational denomination.

çoṅ-grē-gā'tion-ăl-ist, *n.* 1. One who believes in congregationalism.

2. [C—] A member of one of the evangelical Trinitarian churches holding it to be a duty to worship and work together as a church, being Congregational through the admission of similar churches to the general body. This denomination has grown steadily, extending from the New England states. In point of liberality it lies between the Methodist and Unitarian churches.

çoṅ'gress, *n.*; *pl.* **çoṅ'gress-eṣ.** [L. *congressus*, a meeting, an interview, a hostile encounter, from *congredi*, to come together; *con-*, together, and *gradi*, to step, walk, from *gradus*, a step.]

1. A meeting together of individuals in private or social intercourse. [Obs.]

> That ceremony is used as much in our adieus as in the first *congress*. —Digby.

2. A meeting of two or more persons in a contest; an encounter; a conflict. [Obs.]

> Here Pallas urges on, and Lausus there;
> Their *congress* in the field great Jove withstands. —Dryden.

3. A sudden encounter of things; a collision; a shock. [Obs.]

> From these laws may be deduced the rules of the *congresses* and reflections of bodies. —Cheyne.

4. Sexual intercourse.

5. An assembly of envoys, commissioners, deputies, etc.; particularly, a meeting of sovereign princes or of the representatives of several courts, for the purpose of arranging international affairs.

6. [C—] The legislative branch of the United States government, comprising the Senate and the House of Representatives. The Senate consists of two members chosen by the legislature of each state for a period of six years, one-third of whom are elected every two years. The members of the House of Representatives are chosen by the direct vote of the people of the several states, for a term of two years, the terms of all Representatives beginning and ending at the same time, being coincident with a single Congress. By the Twentieth Amendment, the so-called "Lame Duck" Amendment, effective October 15, 1933, each Congress meets at least once every year, beginning Jan. 3. Before 1934 each Congress began on the first Monday in December of each odd-numbered year succeeding, the second session being termed the short session. To find the number of any Congress, subtract 1789 from the year of meeting, divide by 2 and add 1. Thus, the Congress which convened Jan. 3, 1935, was the 74th Congress.

7. The lower house of various legislative bodies, as of the South American republics, and of Spain.

Congress boot or *gaiter*; a shoe having an elastic gore inserted at the side so as to hold the shoe snugly on the foot.

Congress water; a mineral water from the Congress spring at Saratoga, New York.

Continental Congress; a convention first meeting in 1774, and at intervals thereafter during the War of the Revolution, to take such steps as were deemed for the good of the American Colonies.

Federal Congress; a body first meeting in 1781, in compliance with the Articles of Confederation. The last session was in 1789, which year saw the beginning of Congress in its present form.

çon-gres'sion, *n.* 1. A coming together; as, sexual *congression*. [Obs.]

2. A bringing together for comparison. [Obs.]

çon-gres'sion-ăl, *a.* 1. Of or pertaining to congress.

2. [C—] Of or designating the Congress of the United States.

Congressional district; a division of a state entitled, by reason of its population, to one representative in Congress.

çon-gres'sive, *a.* Coming together, as in sexual intercourse. [Obs.]

çoṅ'gress-măn, *n.*; *pl.* **çoṅ'gress-men.** A member of either house of Congress, especially the lower branch.

çoṅ'grid, *n.* An eel of the family *Congridæ*.

Çoṅ'gri-dæ, *n.pl.* [L., from *conger*; Gr. *gongros*, the conger.] A family of eel-like fishes, the type of which is the genus *Conger*.

çoṅ'groid, *a.* and *n.* [L. *conger*; Gr. *gongros*, the conger, and *eidos*, form, resemblance.]

I. *a.* Belonging or pertaining to the *Congridæ*.

II. *n.* One of the *Congridæ*.

çon-grūe', *v.i.* To agree. [Obs.]

çoṅ'grū-ence, *n.* [L. *congruentia*, agreement, from *congruens*, ppr. of *congruere*, to run together, agree.]

1. Suitableness of one thing to another; agreement; consistency.

2. In mathematics, a relation between three numbers, such that the difference between two of them, which are said to be congruous, is divisible by the third, which is called the modulus.

çoṅ'grū-en-cy, *n.* Congruence.

Congruency of lines; see *Complex of lines* under *Complex*.

çoṅ'grū-ent, *a.* [L. *congruens*, ppr. of *congruere*, to run together, agree.]

1. Characterized by agreement; suitable; corresponding.

2. In mathematics, designating a quantity which has the same remainder when divided by a modulus.

3. In logic, dealing with the same subject; having a difference although true of the same state of things.

4. In geometry, applying to figures or solids which fill exactly the same space, or concur.

çon-grū'i-ty, *n.*; *pl.* **çon-grū'i-tieṣ.** [ME. *congruite*; OFr. *congruite*, congruity, agreement, from L. *congruus*, suitable, agreeing, from *congruere*, to agree.]

1. The state or quality of being congruous; agreement between things; suitableness; fitness; pertinence; consistency; propriety; as, *congruity* of opinions.

2. In school divinity, the performance of good actions for which it is supposed meet and equitable that God should confer grace on those who perform them.

3. In geometry, coincidence.

çoṅ'grū-ous, *a.* 1. Having harmonious relation; accordant; well-adapted; appropriate.

2. In mathematics, having congruence.

çoṅ'grū-ous-ly, *adv.* In a congruous manner.

çon-hȳ'drine, *n.* [From *conium* and *hydrogen*.] A narcotic alkaloid contained in the flowers and seeds of hemlock, from which it is obtained by a complicated process of distillation.

çō'ni-ȧ, *n.* Same as *Conine*.

çon'iç, çon'iç-ăl, *a.* [Gr. *kōnikos*, conic, from *kōnos*, a peak or cone.] Having reference to a cone; cone-shaped; coniform; peaked.

Conic sections; the five figures formed by the cutting of a cone by a plane, corresponding to the different positions of the cutting plane with respect to the cone. When the cutting plane passes through the apex of the cone, and coincides with the axis, or passes through the apex and any part of the base, the section is a triangle, as in fig. 1. When the plane cuts the axis of a right circular cone at right angles, the section is a circle, as in fig. 2. When the plane cuts the axis obliquely, and passes through both sides of the cone, the section is an ellipse or oval, as in fig. 3. When the plane cuts the axis in a line parallel to one side of the cone, the section is a parabola, as in fig. 4. When the section is parallel to the axis, or so as to make a greater angle with the base than that which it makes with the side of the cone, it will be a hyperbola, as in fig. 5. The term *conic sections* is applied more peculiarily to the last three figures, and the doctrines of their several properties constitute one of the principal branches of geometry.

Conical projection; a method of representing part of a sphere upon a plane surface, employed in the construction of some maps.

Conical surface; the surface of a cone.

Conical valve; the puppet or T valve, first used by Watt in the construction of his engines. It consists of a circular plate of metal having a beveled edge accurately fitted to a seat.

Conical Valve.

çon'iç, *n.* A conic section.

çon-i-çal'i-ty, *n.* Conicalness.

çon'iç-ăl-ly, *adv.* In the form of a cone.

çon'iç-ăl-ness, *n.* The state or quality of being conic.

çon'i-çoid, *n.* A quadric surface.

çon'içs, *n.* That part of geometry which treats of the cone and the curves which arise from its sections; conic sections.

çō-nid'i-ȧ, *n.*, pl. of *conidium*.

çō-nid'i-ăl, çō-nid'i-oid, *a.* Resembling or pertaining to a conidium.

çō-nid'i-ō-phōre, *n.* [L. *conidium*, the conidium, from Gr. *konis*, dust, and *-phoros*, bearing, from *pherein*, to bear.] One of the branches in fungi which bear conidia.

ço-nid′i-ō-spōre, *n.* [Obs.] See *Conidium.*

ço-nid′i-um, *n.*; *pl.* **ço-nid′i-å.** [L., from Gr. *konis*, dust.] In botany, one of the simple dust-like, asexual, reproductive cells produced on some lichens and fungi.

çō′ni-fēr, *n.* [L.] A plant producing cones; one of the *Coniferæ.*

Çō-nif′e-ræ, *n.pl.* [L. *conifer*, cone-bearing; *conus*, a cone, and *ferre*, to bear.] A natural order of gymnospermous exogens, consisting of trees or shrubs, found throughout the world, especially in cold regions. The wood is composed of a uniform woody fiber marked with circular disks. The plants abound with resinous juice, and they yield turpentine, pitch, tar, succinic acid, etc. The leaves are usually alternate, awl- or needle-shaped, and entire. The naked flowers are monœcious or diœcious, the male flowers being in deciduous catkins, the female, in cones.

çō-nif′ēr-in, *n.* A glucoside crystallizing in needle-shaped crystals, a constituent of the sap of coniferous trees.

çō-nif′ēr-ous, *a.* 1. Cone-bearing.

2. Relating to the order *Coniferæ.*

çō′ni-form, *a.* Cone-shaped; conical.

çō-nī′ine, *n.* See *Conine.*

çon′i-må, *n.* [Native name.] A medicinal resin obtained from a tropical American tree, the incense-tree.

çō′nine, *n.* [Gr. *kōneion*, the hemlock.] A volatile alkaloid, discovered in *Conium maculatum*, or hemlock, of which it is the active and poisonous principle; called also *coniine* and *coneine.*

çō-ni-ros′tēr, *n.* A bird of the suborder *Conirostres.*

çō-ni-ros′trăl, *a.* 1. Having a thick, conical beak, as crows and finches.

2. Belonging or pertaining to the *Conirostres.*

Çō-ni-ros′trēş, *n.pl.* [L., from *conus*, a cone, and *rostrum*, beak.] A suborder of perching, walking birds, having a conical bill, including the crows, finches, sparrows, linnets, larks, starlings, hornbills, birds of paradise, etc.

çon-i-şor′, *n.* [Obs.] See *Cognizor.*

çō′nite, *n.* [From Gr. *konis*, dust.] A variety of magnesian carbonate of lime, occurring massive or in stalactites. It contains three parts of carbonate of magnesia to one of carbonate of lime.

Çō-nī′um, *n.* [L., from Gr. *kōneion*, hemlock.] In botany, a genus of poisonous biennial plants belonging to the parsley family, *Umbelliferæ.* The most widely known species is the white hemlock, *Conium maculatum*, which is cultivated in this country for medicinal purposes.

çŏn-jeçt′, *v.t.* and *v.i.* I. *v.t.* To throw together, or to throw. [Obs.]

II. *v.i.* To guess. [Obs.]

çŏn-jeçt′ŏr, *n.* One who guesses or conjectures. [Obs.]

çŏn-jeç′tūr-å-ble, *a.* Capable of being guessed or conjectured.

çŏn-jeç′tūr-ăl, *a.* Depending on conjecture; done or said by guess; as, a *conjectural* opinion.

çŏn-jeç′tūr-ăl-ist, *n.* One who conjectures; a conjecturer. [Rare.]

çŏn-jeç-tūr-al′i-ty, *n.* The quality of being conjectural. [Rare.]

çŏn-jeç′tūr-ăl-ly, *adv.* Without proof or evidence; by conjecture; by guess; as, this opinion was given *conjecturally.*

çŏn-jeç′tūre, *n.* [L. *conjectura*, a putting together, a guess, an inference, from *conjectus*, pp. of *conjicere*, to throw or bring together, to guess.]

1. Literally, a casting or throwing together of possible or probable events; a casting of the mind to something future, or something past but unknown; a guess formed on a supposed possibility or probability of a fact, or on slight evidence; preponderance of opinion without proof; surmise; as, the *conjecture* is that he is ashamed of his past life.

2. Idea; notion.

> *Conjectures*, fancies, built on nothing firm.
> —Milton.

çŏn-jeç′tūre, *v.t.*; conjectured, *pt.*, *pp.*; conjecturing, *ppr.* To guess; to judge by guess, or by the probability or the possibility of a fact, or by very slight evidence; to form an opinion regarding; to surmise; as, he *conjectured* that some misfortune had happened.

çŏn-jeç′tūre, *v.i.* To make guesses; to surmise, infer, or imagine.

Syn.—Surmise, guess, suppose, imagine.

çŏn-jeç′tūr-ēr, *n.* One who guesses; a guesser; one who forms or utters an opinion without proof.

çŏn-job′ble, *v.t.* To settle; to concert. [Vulgar.]

çŏn-join′, *v.t.*; conjoined, *pt.*, *pp.*; conjoining, *ppr.* [ME. *conjoignen*; OFr. *conjoindre*; L. *conjungere*, to join together.]

1. To join together; to unite, as two or more persons or things in close connection; as, to *conjoin* friends.

2. To associate or connect.

> Let that which he learns next be nearly *conjoined* with what he knows already.
> —Locke.

çŏn-join′, *v.i.* To unite; to join; to league.

çŏn-joined′, *a.* Joined to or with; united; associated; in heraldry, touching or joined together.

çŏn-joint′, *a.* United; connected; associated.

Conjoint degrees, tetrachords; same as *Conjunct degrees, tetrachords* under *Conjunct.*

çŏn-joint′, *n.* In law, one associated with another in interest or obligation; specifically, in the plural, *conjoints*, married persons.

çŏn-joint′ly, *adv.* Jointly; in union; together.

çŏn-joint′ness, *n.* State of being joined or united.

çŏn-jū′bi-lănt, *a.* Jubilant together. [Rare.]

çon′jū-găl, *a.* [L. *conjugalis*, relating to marriage, conjugal, from *conjunx*, husband or wife, from *conjungere*, to unite, to join together; *con-*, together, and *jungere*, to unite.]

1. Belonging to marriage; matrimonial; connubial; as, the *conjugal* relation; *conjugal* ties.

2. Suitable to the married state; becoming a husband in relation to his wife, or a wife in relation to her husband; as, *conjugal* affection.

çon-jū-gal′i-ty, *n.* 1. The married state.

2. In phrenology, the faculty that gives desire for matrimony.

çon′jū-găl-ly, *adv.* Matrimonially; connubially.

Çon-jū-gā′tæ, *n. pl.* [L., f. pl. of *conjugatus*, pp. of *conjugare*, to join, unite.] In botany, a class of algæ, the *Chlorophyceæ*, embracing several families of fresh-water plants which reproduce by the conjugation of stationary cells.

Conjugatæ, showing the spores formed by the union of the endochromes of two contiguous cells.

çon′jū-gāte, *v.t.*; conjugated, *pt.*, *pp.*; conjugating, *ppr.* 1. To join; to unite in marriage. [Obs.]

2. In grammar, to distribute the parts or inflections of (a verb) into the several voices, modes, tenses, numbers, and persons, so as to show their connections, distinctions, and modes of formation. In English, as the verb undergoes few variations, conjugation consists chiefly in combining the words which unitedly form the tenses in the several persons.

çon′jū-gāte, *v.i.* In biology, to unite in conjugation, as among the lower plants and animals.

çon′jū-gāte, *n.* 1. A word agreeing in derivation with another, and therefore generally resembling it in signification.

> We have learned, in logic, that *conjugates* are sometimes in name only, and not in deed.
> —Bramhall.

2. In chemistry, a complex radical, as one acid or a radical acting with another to form a single radical only.

çon′jū-gāte, *a.* 1. Joined in pairs; coupled.

2. In botany, composed of two leaflets, said of a pinnate leaf.

3. In chemistry, containing two or more radicals acting as a single one. [Rare.]

4. In mathematics, paired and having reciprocal properties; used with reference to two points, quantities, axes, etc., capable of being interchanged.

5. In grammar, related in meaning and origin; said of words with a common derivation.

Conjugate axis; see under *Axis.*

Conjugate diameter; one of the two diameters of an ellipse or hyperbola, so related that the tangents at the ends of either diameter parallel the other.

Conjugate hyperbola; one whose transverse axis is the minor axis of the given hyperbola.

Conjugate lines on a surface; in geometry, lines whose directions at any point are those of conjugate diameters of the indicatrix at the same point.

Conjugate mirrors; in optics, two mirrors so arranged that rays reflected from the focus of one meet at the focus of the other.

Conjugate point; in geometry, an acnode. [See *Acnode.*]

çon′jū-gāte-pin′nāte, *a.* In botany, conjugate, with both parts pinnate.

çon-jū-gā′tion, *n.* 1. The act of uniting or combining; union; assemblage; conjunction.

2. A pair; as, a *conjugation* of nerves. [Obs.]

3. In grammar, the distribution of the several inflections or variations of a verb, in their different voices, modes, tenses, numbers, and persons: a connected scheme of all the derivative forms of a verb.

4. A biological term for the process by which new spores or germs are produced among some lower animals and plants by fusion of the contents of cells or a union of individuals.

çon-jū-gā′tion-ăl, *a.* Pertaining to conjugation.

çŏn-jū′gi-ăl, *a.* [Rare.] Same as *Conjugal.*

çon-jū′gi-um, *n.* [L., a connection, union, the married state.] The matrimonial bond.

çŏn-juñçt′, *a.* [L. *conjunctus*, pp. of *conjungere*, to join together.] Conjoined; united; concurrent.

Conjunct degrees; in music, notes which follow each other immediately in the scale.

Conjunct tetrachords; in music, two tetrachords, or fourths, where the same note is the highest of one and the lowest of the other.

çŏn-juñç′tion, *n.* 1. Union; connection; association by treaty or otherwise.

2. In astronomy, the meeting of two or more stars or planets in the same degree of the zodiac; as, the *conjunction* of the moon with the sun, or of Jupiter and Saturn. Heavenly bodies are said to be in *conjunction* when they are seen in the same part of the heavens, or have the same longitude. The *inferior conjunction* of a planet is its position when in conjunction on the same side of the sun with the earth; the *superior conjunction* is its position when on the side of the sun most distant from the earth.

3. In grammar, a connective or connecting word; an indeclinable word which serves to unite sentences or the clauses of a sentence and words, joining two or more simple sentences into a compound one; as, this book cost one dollar *and* ten cents.

4. The copulation of the sexes.

çŏn-juñç′tion-ăl, *a.* Pertaining to a conjunction.

çon-juñç-tī′vå, *n.*; *pl.* **çon-juñç-tī′væ.** The mucous membrane lining the inner surface of the eyelids and the outer surface back of the eyeballs.

çon-juñç-tī′văl, *a.* 1. Connective; uniting.

2. Relating to the conjunctiva.

çon-juñç′tive, *a.* 1. Closely united.

2. Uniting; serving to unite.

3. In grammar, the *conjunctive* mode is that which follows a conjunction, or expresses some condition or contingency; more generally called the *subjunctive mode.*

4. Intimately joined. [Obs.]

çŏn-juñç′tive-ly, *adv.* In conjunction or union; together.

çŏn-juñç′tive-ness, *n.* The quality of conjoining or uniting

çŏn-juñç-ti-vī′tis, *n.* An inflammation of the conjunctiva.

çŏn-juñçt′ly, *adv.* In union; jointly; together.

çŏn-juñç′tūre, *n.* 1. A joining; a combination or union, as of causes, events, or circumstances; as, an unhappy *conjuncture* of affairs.

2. An occasion; a critical time, proceeding from a union of circumstances; as, at that *conjuncture* peace was very desirable.

çon-jū-rā′tion, *n.* [ME. *conjuracioun*; OFr. *conjuration*; L. *conjuratio*, a swearing together, conspiracy, in LL. enchantment, adjuration, from *conjuratus*, pp. of *conjurare*, to swear together, combine; *con-*, together, and *jurare*, to swear.]

1. The act of using certain words or ceremonies with a view of obtaining the aid of a superior being; the act of summoning in a sacred name; the practice of mysterious arts in the performance of acts alleged to be supernatural.

2. A conspiracy. [Obs.]

çon′jū-rā-tŏr, *n.* [LL.] A conspirator; one who enters into an oath-bound agreement with others.

çŏn-jūre′, *v.t.*; conjured, *pt.*, *pp.*; conjuring, *ppr.* To call on or summon by a sacred name, or in a solemn manner; to implore with solemnity.

> I *conjure* you! let him know,
> Whate'er was done against him, Cato did it.
> — Addison.

çŏn-jūre′, *v.i.* To bind two or more by an oath; to unite in a common design. Hence, to conspire. [Obs.]

çŏn′jure, *v.t.* To effect, in some manner, by mysterious arts, as by invoking the Supreme Being, or by the use of certain words, characters, or ceremonies; to engage (supernatural influence); as, to *conjure* up evil spirits; to *conjure* down a tempest; to *conjure* the stars.

To conjure up; to raise up or bring into existence without reason, or by alleged unnatural means; as, *to conjure up* a phantom; *to conjure up* a story.

çŏn′jure, *v.i.* To practise the arts of a conjurer; to use alleged arts of magic in order to perform some extraordinary act.

çŏn-jūre′ment, *n.* Serious injunction solemn demand.

çŏn′ jūr-ẽr, *n.* [OFr. *conjureur*; LL. *conjurator*, one bound with an oath, a conjurer, from *conjurare*, to swear together.]

1. One who practises conjuration; one who pretends to the secret art of performing things supernatural or extraordinary, by the aid of superior powers; an impostor who pretends, by unknown means, to discover stolen goods, etc.; a prestidigitator.

2. Ironically, a man of shrewd conjecture; a man of sagacity. [Obs.]

çŏn-jūr′ẽr, *n.* One who conjures or implores; one who entreats, charges, or appeals solemnly. [Rare.]

çon-jū′rŏr, *n.* [L. *conjuratus*, pp. of *conjurare*, to swear together; *con-*, together, and *jurare*, to swear.] In law, one who is bound by an oath taken with others. [Obs.]

çŏn′jū-ry, *n.* The art or practice of conjuring or magic; enchantment. [Rare.]

çonn, *v.t.* See second *Con*, v.t.

çon-nas′cence, çon-nas′cen-cy, *n.* [LL. *connascens*, pp. of *connasci*, to be born at the same time; L. *con-*, together, and *nasci*, to be born.]

1. The common birth of two or more at the same time; production of two or more together. [Rare.]

2. A being born or produced with another.

3. The act of growing together, or at the same time. [Obs.]

çon-nas′cent, *a.* Growing together; born or produced at the same time.

çon′nāte, *a.* [LL. *connatus*, pp. of *connasci*, to be born at the same time; L. *con-*, together, and *nasci*, to be born.]

1. Born with another; being of the same birth; as, *connate* notions.

2. Existing together from birth; congenital.

3. In botany, united in origin; growing from one base, or united at their bases; united into one body; as, *connate* leaves or anthers.

Connate Leaves.

çon′nāte-pẽr-fō′li-āte, *a.* Connate at the base and about the stem, so as to produce a broad body through which the stem passes, as opposite sessile leaves.

çon-nā′tion, *n.* Connection by birth; natural union.

çon-nat′ū-rǎl, *a.* [L *con-*, together, and *naturalis*, natural, from *natura*, nature.]

1. Connected by nature; united in nature; born with another.

These affections are *connatural* to us.
—L'Estrange.

2. Participating in the same nature.

And mix with our *connatural* dust.
—Milton.

çon-nat-ū-ral′i-ty, *n.* Participation in the same nature; natural union.

çon-nat′ū-rǎl-īze, *v.t.*; connaturalized, *pt.*, *pp.*; connaturalizing, *ppr.* To connect by nature. [Rare.]

çon-nat′ū-rǎl-ly, *adv.* By the act of nature; originally.

çon-nat′ū-rǎl-ness, *n.* Participation in the same nature; natural union.

çon-nā′tūre, *n.* Likeness or identity in nature or character. [Rare.]

çŏn-neçt′, *v.t.*; connected, *pt.*, *pp.*; connecting, *ppr.* [L *connectere*, to bind together.]

1. To link or join together; to tie or fasten together; to combine; to unite; to bring into correlation.

2. To associate.

çŏn-neçt′, *v.i.* To join, unite, or cohere; to have a close relation; to be associated.

Syn.—Attach, attribute, associate.

çŏn-neçt′ed-ly, *adv.* By connection; in a connected manner.

çŏn-neçt′ing-link, *n.* 1. A movable link used to connect one chain with another.

2. Figuratively, any circumstance, fact, or thought which may be used to complete a logical chain.

çŏn-neçt′ing-rod, *n.* A rod or bar connecting two or more moving parts, as the rod connecting the driving-wheels of a locomotive.

çŏn-neç′tion, çon-nex′iŏn, *n.* 1. The act of joining, or state of being joined; a state of being knit or fastened together; union.

2. That which connects or unites; a tie; a bond.

3. A relation by blood or marriage.

4. A religious sect or united body; as, the Methodist *connection*.

Syn.—Kinsman, relation, relative.

çŏn-neçt′ive, *n.* and *a.* I. *n.* That which connects; specifically, in grammar, a word that connects other words and sentences; a conjunction; in botany, the portion of a filament that connects cells, lobes, etc.

II. *a.* Having the power of connecting.

Connective tissue; tissue derived from mesoblast, including fat, cartilage, bone, and mucous membrane; it is gelatinous and fibrous in composition and forms the framework of the body in which the cells are sustained and connected.

çŏn-neçt′ive-ly, *adv.* In union or conjunction; jointly.

çŏn-neçt′ŏr, *n.* 1. One who connects; a connective.

2. A contrivance for connecting the ends of a conducting wire.

3. A rubber tube used in pneumatics by which glass tubes are connected.

çŏn′nẽr, *n.* [Etym. obscure.]

1. The *Crenilabrus melops*, a fish found in European waters.

2. The American cunner.

çon′nẽr, *n.* [From ME. *cunnen*; AS. *cunnian*, to try, test, examine.] An examiner; one who inspects or tests.

çon′nẽr, *n.* A lookout on shore or on shipboard.

çon′nex, *v.t.* To link together; to join. [Obs.]

çŏn-nex′ion, *n.* See *Connection.*

çŏn-nex′ive, *a.* Connective. [Obs.]

çon′ning-tow″ẽr, *n.* The ironclad pilot-house on a modern battleship.

çŏn-nīv′ănce, *n.* [Fr. *connivence*; L. *conniventia*, connivance, from *connivere*, to wink, connive.]

1. Properly, the act of winking; hence, figuratively, voluntary blindness to an act; intentional forbearance to see a fault or other act, generally implying consent to it.

Every vice interprets a *connivance* to be approbation.
—South.

2. Knowledge of wrongdoing by another, without making an effort to prevent the transgression.

Syn.—Collusion, combination, conspiracy.

çŏn-nīve′, *v.t.*; connived, *pt.*, *pp.*; conniving, *ppr.* To feign ignorance of. [Obs.]

çŏn-nīve′, *v.i.* [L. *connivere*, to wink, wink at, overlook.]

1. To wink; to close and open the eyelids rapidly. [Obs.]

2. In a figurative sense, to close the eyes upon a fault or other act; to pretend ignorance or blindness; to overlook a fault or other act, and suffer it to pass unnoticed, uncensured, or unpunished, as, the father *connives* at the vices of his son.

çŏn-nīv′en-cy, *n.* Connivance. [Obs.]

çŏn-nīv′ent, *a.* 1. Shutting the eyes; forbearing to see. [Rare.]

2. In anatomy, the *connivent* valves are those wrinkles, cellules, and vascules which are found on the inside of the intestines.

3. In botany, closely united; converging together.

çŏn-nīv′ẽr, *n.* One who connives.

çon-nois-seūr′ (-nis-sūr′ *or* -nis-sẽr′), *n.* [Fr *connaisseur*, formerly *connoisseur*; OFr. *conoisseor*, a judge, one well versed in anything, from *conoistre*; L. *cognoscere*, to know.] A person well versed in any subject; a skilful or knowing person; a critical judge or master of any art, particularly of painting and sculpture; one with ripe experience and knowledge.

çon-nois-seūr′ship, *n.* The skill of a connoisseur.

çon′nō-tāte, *v.t.* To designate with something else; to imply. [Rare.]

çon-nō-tā′tion, *n.* [L. *con-*, together, and *notare*, to mark, note.] The act of making known or designating with something; implication of something beside itself; inference.

çon-nō′tă-tive, *a.* 1. Suggesting something to be added.

2. Suggesting a quality.

Connotative term; one which states a subject and gives its attributes by implication.

çon-nō′tă-tive-ly, *adv.* In the manner of connotation.

çŏn-nōte′, *v.t.*; connoted, *pt.*, *pp.*; connoting, *ppr.* 1. To make known together; to imply; to denote or designate; to include.

2. In logic, to suggest as an attribute.

çŏn-nū′bi-ǎl, *a.* [L. *connubialis*, pertaining to marriage, from *connubium*, marriage; *con-*, together, and *nubere*, to veil, marry.] Pertaining to marriage; nuptial; belonging to the state of husband and wife; as, *connubial* rites; *connubial* love.

çŏn-nū-bi-al′i-ty, *n.* A quality or act characteristic of marriage.

çon-nū-mẽr-ā′tion, *n.* A reckoning together. [Rare.]

çon′nu-sănce, *n.* [Obs.] See *Cognizance.*

çon′nu-sănt, *a.* [Obs.] See *Cognizant.*

çon-nu-sor′, *n.* [Obs.] See *Cognizor.*

çon-nū-tri′tious (-trish′us), *a.* 1. Fed or reared together. [Obs.]

2. Taken in with one's food; applied to diseases which are contracted from a nurse or owing to a kind of food.

çon′ny, *n.* [Obs.] See *Cony.*

çō′nō-dont, *n.* [Gr. *kōnos*, a cone, and *odous*, a tooth.] A peculiar fossil, occurring especially in carboniferous rocks, having the form of a tooth, but being more likely the jaw of an annelid.

çō′noid, *n.* [Gr. *kōnoeidēs*, cone-shaped.]

1. In geometry, a solid formed by the revolution of a conic section about its axis. If the conic section is a parabola, the resulting solid is a parabolic conoid, or paraboloid; if a hyperbola, the solid is a hyperbolic conoid, or hyperboloid; if an ellipse, an elliptic conoid, a spheroid, or an ellipsoid.

2. In anatomy, a gland in the third ventricle of the brain, resembling a cone or pineapple, and called the pineal gland.

3. Anything having the form of a cone.

çō′noid, *a.* Same as *Conoidal.*

çō-noid′ǎl, *a.* Nearly but not exactly conical.

Conoidal ligament; a ligament, conical in form, which serves to protect the collar-bone and to hold it in place at its distal end.

çō-noid′iç, çō-noid′iç-ǎl, *a.* Pertaining to a conoid; having the form of a conoid.

çō-nom-i-nee′, *n.* One nominated in conjunction with another; a joint nominee.

çō′nō-sçōpe, *n.* [Gr. *kōnos*, a cone, and *skopein*, to view.] A kind of polariscope for the examination of crystals in converging rays of light.

çon-quăd′rāte, *v.t.* [L. *conquadratus*, pp. of *conquadrare*, to make square; *con-*, and *quadrare*, to make square.] To bring into a square.

çon-quas′sāte, *v.t.* To shake. [Obs.]

çon-quas-sā′tion, *n.* An agitation. [Obs.]

çoṅ′quẽr (-kẽr), *v.t.*; conquered, *pt.*, *pp.*; conquering, *ppr.* [ME. *conqueren*; OFr. *conquerre*, to conquer, seek after; L. *conquirere*, to seek after, procure.]

1. To subdue; to reduce, by physical force, till resistance is no longer made; to gain by force; to win; to take possession by violent means; to gain dominion or sovereignty over.

2. To subdue (opposition or resistance of the will) by moral force; to overcome by argument, persuasion, or other influence; as, Luther went forth to reform and to *conquer* evil.

3. To overcome, as difficulties; to surmount, as obstacles; to subdue (whatever opposes); as to *conquer* the passions; to *conquer* reluctance.

4. To gain or obtain by effort; as, to *conquer* freedom; to *conquer* peace.

çoṅ′quẽr (-kẽr), *v.i.* To overcome; to gain the victory.

The champions resolved to *conquer* or to die.
—Waller.

Syn.—Beat, crush, defeat, discomfit, down, humble, master, overcome, overmaster, overmatch, overpower, overthrow, prevail over, reduce, rout, subdue, subject, subjugate, surmount, vanquish, win, worst.

çoṅ′quẽr-ȧ-ble, *a.* Capable of being conquered, overcome, or subdued.

çoṅ′quẽr-ȧ-ble-ness, *n.* A state of being conquerable.

çoṅ′quẽr-ess, *n.* A female who conquers; a victorious female.

çoṅ′quẽr-ing-ly, *adv.* By conquering; in a conquering manner.

çoṅ′quẽr-ŏr, *n.* One who conquers.

The Conqueror; an epithet applied to William I., as expressing his conquest of England in 1066. As originally applied, however, the name was not exactly synonymous with *conqueror* in the modern sense.

çoṅ′quest (-kwest), *n.* [ME. *conquest*; OFr. *conquest*; L. *conquisitus*, pp. of *conquirere*, to seek for; *con-*, and *quærere*, to seek.]

1. The act of conquering; the act of overcoming or vanquishing opposition by force, physical or moral; victory; success in arms; subjugation.

In joys of *conquest* he resigns his breath.
—Addison.

2. That which is conquered; possession gained by force, physical or moral; as, Jamaica was a valuable *conquest* for England.

3. In a feudal sense, acquest; acquisition; the acquiring of property by other means than by inheritance.

4. The act of gaining or regaining by effort; as, the *conquest* of liberty or peace.

Syn.—Victory, triumph, mastery, reduction, subjugation, subjection, achievement.

çoṅ-quis′tȧ-dōr, *n.* [Sp.] A term applied to any one of the conquerors of Spanish America.

çon-saṅ-guin′ē-ǎl (-gwin′), *a.* Consanguineous.

çon-saṅ′guined, *a.* Related by blood. [Rare.]

çon-saṅ-guin′ē-ous, *a.* [L. *consanguineus*; *con-*, and *sanguis*, blood.] Of the same blood; related by birth; descended from the same parent or ancestor.

çon-saṅ-guin′i-ty, *n.* The relation of persons by blood; the relation or connection of persons descended from the same stock or common ancestor, in distinction from affinity or relation by marriage.

çon-sär-ci-nā′tion, *n.* [L. *consarcinatus*, pp. *consarcinare*, to patch together.] The act of patching together. [Obs.]

çon′science (-shens), *n.* [Fr. *conscience*, from L. *conscientia*, a joint knowledge, feeling, from *conscire*; *con-*, together with, and *scire*, to know.]

1. Internal or self-knowledge, or judgment of

right and wrong; or the faculty, power, or principle within a person which decides on the lawfulness or unlawfulness of his actions and affections, and approves or condemns them.

Conscience is first occupied in ascertaining our duty, before we proceed to action; then in judging of our actions when performed. —J. M. Mason.

2. Consciousness; knowledge of our own actions or thoughts. [Obs.]

The sweetest cordial we receive, at last, Is *conscience* of our virtuous actions past. —Denham.

3. The estimate or determination of *conscience*; justice; honesty.

What you require cannot, in *conscience*, be deferred. —Milton.

A matter of conscience; a matter in which one is bound to act according to the dictates of conscience.

Court of conscience; in England, formerly, a court for the recovery of small debts.

Conscience clause; a clause in a law exempting certain persons from doing certain things prescribed for others, when they have conscientious scruples against performing such acts, as taking oaths, rendering military service, etc.

Conscience money; money paid secretly in settlement of claims evaded by fraud, or in atonement for theft, etc. Such money is frequently sent to the United States treasury by persons who have evaded customs duties, etc., and is placed in a fund called the conscience fund.

In all conscience; in all reason or reasonableness.

con'scienced (-shenst), *a.* Having conscience. [Rare.]

con'science-less, *a.* Having no conscience; unscrupulous.

con'scient, *a.* Conscious. [Rare.]

con-sci-en'tious (-shi-en'shus), *a.* 1. Influenced by conscience; governed by a strict regard to the dictates of conscience, or by the known or supposed rules of right and wrong; as, a *conscientious* judge.

2. Regulated by conscience; according to the dictates of conscience; as, a *conscientious* probity.

con-sci-en'tious-ly, *adv.* According to the direction of conscience; faithfully; with a strict regard to right and wrong; as, a man may err *conscientiously*.

con-sci-en'tious-ness, *n.* A scrupulous regard to the decisions of conscience; a sense of justice, and strict conformity to its dictates.

con'sciŏn-å-ble (-shun-), *a.* According to conscience; reasonable; just.

Let my debtors have *conscionable* satisfaction. —Wotton.

con'sciŏn-å-ble-ness, *n.* Reasonableness; equity.

con'sciŏn-å-bly, *adv.* In a manner agreeable to conscience; reasonably; justly.

con'scious (-shus), *a.* [L. *conscius*, knowing, aware, from *conscire*, to know with, be cognizant of; *con-*, with, and *scire*, to know.]

1. Possessing the faculty or power of knowing one's own thoughts or mental operations; as, man is a *conscious* being.

2. Knowing from memory, or without extraneous information; as, I am not *conscious* of the fact.

3. Knowing by consciousness, or internal perception or persuasion; as, I am not *conscious* of having given any offense; *conscious* of innocence, or of crime.

Syn.—Aware, sensible, felt, known, cognizant, apprised.

con'scious-ly, *adv.* With knowledge of one's own mental operations or actions.

con'scious-ness, *n.* 1. The knowledge of sensations and mental operations, or of what passes in one's own mind; the state of being conscious.

2. Feeling or internal sense or knowledge of guilt or innocence; as, a man may betray his *consciousness* of guilt by his countenance.

3. Certain knowledge from observation or experience; as, the *consciousness* of external objects.

Syn.—Feeling, attention, sensation.

cŏn-scrībe', *v.t.* To force to do military service; to draft; to conscript. [Obs.]

cŏn-script', *v.t.*; conscripted, *pt., pp.*; conscripting, *ppr.* [L. *conscriptus*, pp. of *conscribere*, to enroll; *con-*, together with, and *scribere*, to write.] To draft for military service; to enlist by force; to enroll in a compulsory manner.

con'script, *a.* Written; enrolled; as, *conscript* fathers, the senators of ancient Rome, so called because their names were written in the register of the senate.

con'script, *n.* One taken by lot from a conscription list, or enrolled by force, and compelled to serve as a soldier or sailor.

cŏn-scrip'tion, *n.* 1. An enrolling or registering.

2. A compulsory enrolment of men of a certain age, held liable to be drafted for military or naval service; a system which existed among the Romans, and has long been in vogue in France, Germany, and other countries.

cŏn-scrip'tion-ăl, *a.* Relating to or of the nature of a conscription.

con'sē-crāte, *v.t.*; consecrated, *pt., pp.*; consecrating, *ppr.* [L. *consecratus*, pp. of *consecrare*, to dedicate; *con-*, together, and *sacrare*, to consecrate, devote to a divinity, from *sacer*, sacred.]

1. To make or declare to be sacred, by certain ceremonies or rites; to appropriate to sacred uses; to set apart, dedicate, or devote to the service and worship of God; as, to *consecrate* a church; to *consecrate* a bishop.

2. To canonize; to exalt to the rank of a saint; to enroll among the gods, as a Roman emperor.

3. To set apart and bless, as the elements in the eucharist.

4. To render venerable; to make respected; as, customs or principles *consecrated* by time.

5. To devote to a sacred or high purpose; to hallow; as, he *consecrated* his life to the glory of his country; *consecrated* by the blood of patriots.

con'sē-crāte, *a.* Sacred; consecrated; devoted; dedicated. [Obs. or Poet.]

They were assembled in that *consecrate* place. —Bacon.

con'sē-crā-ted-ness, *n.* The state of being consecrated.

con-sē-crā'tion, *n.* The act of consecrating; the state of being consecrated; dedication.

con'sē-crā-tŏr, *n.* One who consecrates.

con'sē-crā-tō-ry, *a.* Making sacred.

con-sec-tā'nē-ous, *a.* Following or deducible as a matter of course.

con'sec-tā-ry, *a.* [L. *consectarius*, from *consectari*, to follow after; *con-*, with, and *sectari*, to follow.] Following; consequent; consequential; deducible. [Rare.]

con'sec-tā-ry, *n.* That which follows; consequence; a deduction from premises; a corollary. [Rare.]

con'sē-cūte, *v.t.* To follow closely after; to pursue. [Obs.]

con-sē-cū'tion, *n.* [L. *consecutio*, from *consequi*, to follow; *con-*, and *sequi*, to follow.]

1. A following or sequel; a train of consequences from premises; a series of deductions.

2. Succession; a series of things that follow each other; as, a *consecution* of colors. [Rare.]

Consecution month; in astronomy, the lunar month.

cŏn-sec'ū-tive, *a.* 1. Following in a train; succeeding one another in a regular order; successive; uninterrupted in course or succession; as, fifty *consecutive* years.

2. Following; consequential; succeeding; used with *to*; as, the actions of men are *consecutive to* volition.

Consecutive chords; a succession or repetition of musical chords having the same interval.

Consecutive combination; a chemical process by which a series of salts are formed from one another.

Consecutive symptoms; in medicine, symptoms appearing on the cessation of a disease or during convalescence, but having neither direct nor evident connection with the primary ailment.

cŏn-sec'ū-tive-ly, *adv.* In a consecutive manner; in regular succession; successively.

cŏn-sec'ū-tive-ness, *n.* The state of being consecutive.

cŏn-sen'sion, *n.* [Fr. *consension*; L. *consensio*, from *consentire*, to be of one opinion, to agree.] Agreement; accord. [Rare.]

cŏn-sen'sū-ăl, *a.* In law, formed or existing by mere consent; as, a *consensual* marriage; a *consensual* contract, etc.

Consensual motions; in physiology, a term applied to two or more simultaneous motions, of which the secondary or more remote motions are independent of the will. Thus the iris contracts when the eye is open to admit the light.

cŏn-sen'sus, *n.* Unanimity; agreement; concord; a general accord of a number of people upon a subject admitting of a diversity of views.

cŏn-sent', *n.* [L. *consensus*, from *consentio*, to be of one mind, to agree; *con-*, and *sentire*, to think, feel, or perceive.]

1. Unity of opinion; agreement in sentiment; accord of minds; concord.

They all with one *consent* began to make excuse. —Luke xiv. 18.

2. A yielding of the mind or will to that which is proposed; voluntary allowance or acceptance of something done or proposed; concurrence; compliance; acquiescence; as, he gave his *consent* to the marriage of his daughter.

3. Agreement; coherence; correspondence in parts, qualities, or operation. [Rare.]

Such is the world's great harmony that springs
From union, order, full *consent* of things. —Pope.

4. In physiology, an agreement or sympathy, by which one affected part of the system affects some distant part.

5. In law, intelligent concurrence in the terms of a contract or agreement, of such a nature as to bind the party consenting. *Consent* of parties is implied in all legal and binding documents; hence, persons legally incapable of giving *consent*, as idiots, cannot be parties to a contract. *Consent* is null where it proceeds on essential error, or where obtained by fraud, or by force and fear.

Syn.—Concord, assent, compliance, concurrence, agreement, approval, permission.

cŏn-sent', *v.i.*; consented, *pt., pp.*; consenting, *ppr.* 1. To agree in mind or will; to yield to what one has the power, right, or inclination to withhold or refuse to grant; to yield, as by persuasion or influence; to acquiesce; to approve or give permission; as, I cannot *consent* to the request.

2. To be of the same opinion; to agree or accord. [Rare.]

Syn.—Accede, agree, assent, comply, yield, allow, permit, approve.

cŏn-sent', *v.t.* To give assent to; to acknowledge or admit; to grant. [Obs.]

cŏn-sent'å-ble, *a.* Established by common consent; agreed upon; applied in Pennsylvania law to a property boundary line.

con-sen-tā-nē'i-ty, *n.* Mutual agreement. [Rare.]

con-sen-tā'nē-ous, *a.* Agreeable; accordant; consistent; suitable.

A good law and *consentaneous* to reason. —Howell.

con-sen-tā'nē-ous-ly, *adv.* Agreeably; consistently; suitably.

con-sen-tā'nē-ous-ness, *n.* Agreement; accordance; consistency.

cŏn-sent'ănt, *a.* Giving consent. [Obs.]

cŏn-sent'ẽr, *n.* One who consents.

cŏn-sen'tient (-shent), *a.* Agreeing in mind; accordant in opinion.

The *consentient* judgment of the church. —Pearson.

cŏn-sent'ing-ly, *adv.* In a consenting manner.

con'sē-quence, *n.* [Fr. *consequence*; L. *consequentia*, from *consequens* (*-entis*), ppr. of *consequi*, to follow after; *con-*, with, and *sequi*, to follow.]

1. That which follows from any act, cause, principle, or series of actions; an event or effect produced by some preceding act or cause; a result.

Shun the bitter *consequence*. —Milton.

2. In logic, a proposition collected from the agreement of other previous propositions; a conclusion which results from reason or argument; inference; deduction; consequent.

3. Connection of cause and effect; consecution. [Rare.]

4. Power to produce results; importance in influence or effect; significance; applied to things; as, a matter of little *consequence*.

5. Importance; extensive influence; distinction; applied to persons; as, a man of great *consequence* in society.

In consequence; as a result; for this reason; hence; therefore.

In consequence of; as the effect of; because of; through.

Syn.—Effect, result, outgrowth, end, consequent, issue.

con'sē-quence, *v.i.* To draw inferences; to form deductions. [Obs.]

Moses condescends to such a methodical and school-like way of defining and *consequencing*. —Milton.

con'sē-quent, *a.* 1. Following as the natural effect; often used with *on*, *upon*, or *to*; as, favorable weather and *consequent* abundant crops; distress *consequent on* the war.

The right was *consequent to*, and built on, an act perfectly personal. —Locke.

2. Following by necessary inference or rational deduction; as, a proposition *consequent* to other propositions.

3. Logical; marked by correct reasoning; as, the argument is very *consequent*.

Consequent poles or *points*; points along a magnetic bar having an abnormally high attraction.

con'sē-quent, *n.* 1. Effect; that which follows a cause; result. [Rare.]

2. In logic, that which follows from propositions by rational deduction; especially, (a) that member of a hypothetical proposition

which contains the conclusion; (b) the conclusion of a syllogism.

3. In mathematics, the second of the two terms of a ratio, or that with which the antecedent is compared.

çon-sē-quen′tiăl (-shăl), *a.* 1. Following as the natural effect; proceeding from a cause or logical antecedent; resulting; consequent; as, a *consequential* failure.

2. Having the consequence justly connected with the premises; conclusive. [Obs.]

3. Assuming the air of a person of consequence; pompous; applied to persons; as, a very *consequential* delegation.

4. Important; far-reaching; applied to things; as, a *consequential* event. [Rare.]

Consequential losses or *damages*; in law, such losses or damages as arise out of a man's act, for which, according to a fundamental principle in law, he is answerable if he could have avoided them.

çon-sē-quen′tiăl-ly, *adv.* 1. With just deduction of consequences; with right connection of ideas.

2. By consequence; not immediately; eventually.

3. In a regular series; in the order of cause and effect.

4. With assumed importance; with conceit.

çon-sē-quen′tiăl-ness, *n.* 1. The state or quality of being consequential or consecutive, as in discourse.

2. Conceit; pompousness; the assumption of dignity or importance.

çon′sē-quent-ly, *adv.* By consequence; by necessary connection of effects with their causes; therefore; accordingly.

çon′sē-quent-ness, *n.* Regular connection of propositions following each other; consecution of discourse; the quality or condition of being consequential, in any sense. [Obs.]

çon-sẽr′tion, *n.* [L. *consertio*, from *conserere*, to put together.] Junction; adaptation. [Rare.]

çŏn-sẽrv′ȧ-ble, *a.* Capable of being kept or preserved from decay or injury.

çŏn-sẽrv′ăn-cy, *n.* The act of preserving; conservation; preservation from injury or improper use; as, the *conservancy* of fisheries or forests.

çŏn-sẽrv′ănt, *a.* Conserving; having the power or quality of preserving from decay or destruction.

çon-sẽr-vā′tion, *n.* [L. *conservatio*, from *conservare*, to keep; *con-*, together, and *servare*, to keep, save.] The act of preserving, guarding, or protecting; preservation from loss, decay, injury, or violation; the keeping (of a thing) in a safe or entire state; as, the *conservation* of bodies from perishing; the *conservation* of the peace of society; the *conservation* of privileges.

Conservation of areas; the theory that a planetary radius vector traverses equal areas in equal times.

Conservation of energy or *of force*; the theory that the aggregate of energy in any material system is a constant quantity, transformable in countless ways, but never increased or diminished.

çon-sẽr-vā′tion-ăl, *a.* Tending toward conservation; having the power of keeping sound; preservative.

çŏn-sẽrv′ȧ-tiṣm, *n.* 1. The practice of preserving what is established; disposition to oppose change or innovation.

2. [C—] The political principles and opinions maintained by the Conservative party of either Great Britain or Canada.

çŏn-sẽrv′ȧ-tive, *a.* 1. Preservative; having power to preserve in a safe or entire state, or from loss, waste, or injury.

2. Respecting old institutions, methods, customs, and the like; adhering to what is old or established; not given to change merely for the sake of change; said of persons and their principles; as, a *conservative* physician.

3. In a political sense, having a tendency to uphold and preserve entire existing institutions, both civil and ecclesiastical; opposed to radical changes or innovations in church or state.

> The slow progress which Sweden has made in introducing needful reforms, is owing to the *conservative* spirit of the nobility and the priesthood. —Bayard Taylor.

4. [C—] Pertaining to the English or Canadian Conservatives or their principles.

Conservative system; any material system exemplifying the principle of the conservation of energy; any system the total energy of which is constant, whatever form or forms that energy may take.

çŏn-sẽrv′ȧ-tive, *n.* 1. A person or thing tending to preserve from ruin or injury; a conserver.

2. One who aims to preserve from innovation or radical change; one who wishes to maintain an institution, or form of government, in its present state.

3. [C—] One of an English political party which advocates the support and preservation, by every constitutional means, of the existing institutions of the country, both ecclesiastical and civil, and the opposition of such measures and changes as it believes have a tendency either to destroy or to impair these institutions.

4. [C—] One of a Canadian political party.

çŏn-sẽrv′ȧ-tive-ness, *n.* A preference for existing conditions; conservatism; the state or quality of being conservative.

çon-ser-va-toire′ (-twär′), *n.* [Fr.] A school for special instruction, especially in art or music; a conservatory.

çon′sẽr-vā-tŏr, *n.* [L.] A preserver; one who or that which preserves from injury or violation; as, a *conservator* of the public peace.

2. In Connecticut, a person appointed to superintend idiots, lunatics, etc., manage their property, and preserve it from waste.

çŏn-sẽrv′ȧ-tō-ry, *a.* Having the quality of preserving from loss, decay, or injury.

çŏn-sẽrv′ȧ-tō-ry, *n.* 1. A preservative; as, a *conservatory* of life. [Obs.]

2. A place for preserving anything from loss, decay, waste, or injury; particularly, a greenhouse for the growing of exotics or the protection of any tender plants.

3. A place of instruction and training in some special branch of study, usually art or science. On the continent of Europe, the term is applied to certain public institutions teaching music and declamation; in America and England, it is loosely used of numerous private schools teaching various special subjects.

çon-sẽr-vā′trix, *n.* [L.] A female conservator.

çŏn-sẽrve′, *v.t.*; conserved, *pt.*, *pp.*; conserving, *ppr.* [L. *conservare*, to keep, preserve.]

1. To keep in a safe or sound state; to save; to preserve from loss, decay, waste, or injury; to defend from violation; as, to *conserve* the peace of society.

2. To preserve with sugar, in order to prevent decay, as fruits, herbs, etc.

çon′sẽrve, *n.* 1. A sweetmeat made from fruits, etc., and sugar; a preserve; in general, anything that is conserved.

2. A pharmaceutical preparation of vegetable substances and sugar; a confection or electuary.

3. A conservatory. [Obs.]

çŏn-sẽrv′ẽr, *n.* One who conserves; one who keeps from loss or injury; one who lays up for preservation.

çŏn-ses′sion, *n.* A sitting together. [Obs.]

çŏn-ses′sŏr, *n.* One who sits with others. [Obs.]

çŏn-sid′ẽr, *v.t.*; considered, *pt.*, *pp.*; considering, *ppr.* [ME. *consideren*; OFr. *considerer*; L. *considerare*, to look at closely, observe; *con-*, and *sidus*, *sideris*, a star.]

1. To fix the mind on, with a view to a careful examination; to think on with care; to ponder; to study; to meditate on; as, the commissioners met to *consider* the matter.

2. To view attentively; to observe and examine.

3. To attend to; to regard with care.

4. To respect; to hold in high estimation; to honor; as, the men in his department *consider* him highly.

5. To take into view in examination, or into account in estimates; to make allowance for; as, *consider* hereditary tendencies when judging character.

6. To requite; to reward, particularly for gratuitous services; as, she was careful to *consider* the servants.

7. To regard in a particular light; to judge to be; to esteem; to think; to hold as an opinion; to estimate; as, I *consider* him a rascal; we *consider* that it is a question of honor.

Syn.—Deliberate, ponder, reflect, contemplate, examine, regard.

çŏn-sid′ẽr, *v.i.* 1. To think seriously, maturely, or carefully; to reflect; as, take time to *consider* well.

2. To doubt; to hesitate. [Rare.]

çŏn-sid′ẽr-ȧ-ble, *a.* [Fr. *considérable*; L. *considerabilis*, from *considerare*, to observe closely, consider.]

1. Deserving to be observed, remarked, or attended to. [Obs.]

2. Respectable; deserving of notice; of some distinction; important; applied to persons.

> Men *considerable* in all worthy professions, eminent in many ways of life. —Spratt.

3. Worthy of consideration on account of its amount; more than a little; moderately large; somewhat important or valuable; as, a man of *considerable* influence; a *considerable* estate; a body of a very *considerable* thickness.

çŏn-sid′ẽr-ȧ-ble-ness, *n.* Some degree of importance, moment, or dignity; a degree of value or importance that deserves notice. [Rare.]

çŏn-sid′ẽr-ȧ-bly, *adv.* In a degree deserving notice; in a degree not trifling or unimportant.

çŏn-sid′ẽr-ănce, *n.* Consideration; reflection; sober thought. [Obs.]

çŏn-sid′ẽr-āte, *a.* 1. Given to consideration or to sober reflection; thoughtful; serious; discreet; not hasty or rash; not negligent.

> Æneas is patient, *considerate*, and careful of his people. —Dryden.

2. Having respect for; regardful; as, *considerate* of praise. [Rare.]

3. Characterized by consideration or regard for another's circumstances and feelings; not rigorous or exacting; accommodating; charitable; as, a *considerate* master; *considerate* treatment.

Syn.—Careful, cautious, prudent, thoughtful, serious, kind, unselfish, charitable.

çŏn-sid′ẽr-āte-ly, *adv.* 1. With deliberation; with due consideration; calmly; prudently.

2. Kindly; with regard for others; accommodatingly; charitably.

çŏn-sid′ẽr-āte-ness, *n.* The state or quality of being considerate.

çŏn-sid-ẽr-ā′tion, *n.* 1. The act of considering; mental view; regard; notice; as, let us take into *consideration* the consequences of a hasty decision.

2. Mature thought; serious deliberation.

> Let us think with *consideration*. —Sidney.

3. Contemplation; meditation.

> The love you bear to Mopsa hath brought you to the *consideration* of her virtues. —Sidney.

4. Some degree of importance; claim to notice or regard; a moderate degree of respectability.

> Lucan is an author of *consideration* among the Latin poets. —Addison.

5. That which is considered; motive of action; influence; ground of conduct.

> He was obliged, antecedent to all other *considerations*, to search an asylum.—Dryden.

6. Reward for trouble or for services; as, he will do it for a *consideration*.

7. In law, the reason which moves a contracting party to enter into an agreement; the material cause of a contract; the price or motive of a stipulation. In all contracts, each party gives something in exchange for what he receives.

8. Respect or regard; used with *for*; as, *consideration for* the feelings of others.

Syn.—Attention, friendliness, motive, prudence, reflection.

çŏn-sid′ẽr-ȧ-tive, *a.* Taking into consideration; careful; thoughtful. [Rare.]

çŏn-sid′ẽr-ā-tŏr, *n.* One who considers. [Obs.]

çŏn-sid′ẽr-ẽr, *n.* A thinker; one who considers; a man of reflection. [Rare.]

çŏn-sid′ẽr-ing, *prep.* Having regard to; taking into account; making allowance for.

çŏn-sid′ẽr-ing-ly, *adv.* With consideration or deliberation.

çŏn-sīgn′ (-sīn′), *v.t.*; consigned, *pt.*, *pp.*; consigning, *ppr.* [Fr. *consigner*, present, deliver; L. *consignare*, to seal, attest, register; *con-*, together, and *signare*, to sign, mark; *signum*, a mark, sign.]

1. To give, send, or set over; to transfer or deliver into the possession of another, or into a different state, with the sense of fixedness in that state, or permanence of possession; as, at death the body is *consigned* to the grave.

> At the day of general account, good men are to be *consigned* over to another state. —Atterbury.

2. To deliver or transfer, as a charge or trust.

3. To forward (goods) in trust for sale.

4. To assign; to appropriate; to apply.

5. To put into a certain form for the purpose of preserving permanently.

6. To impress or stamp, as with a seal. [Obs.]

Syn.—Commit, intrust, make over, transfer, deliver, resign.

çŏn-sīgn′, *v.i.* To submit to the same terms with another; also, to sign; to agree or consent. [Obs.]

çŏn-sig′nȧ-tȧ-ry, *n.* The person to whom goods are consigned; a consignee. [Obs.]

çon-sig-nā′tion, *n.* 1. The act of consigning; the act of delivering or committing to another person, place, or state.

> Despair is a certain *consignation* to eternal ruin. —Taylor.

2. Ratification; attestation; the act of confirming or establishing. [Obs.]

3. The act of consigning. [Obs.]

4. In Scots law, the depositing in the hands of a third party of a sum of money about which there is either a dispute or a competition.

5. In the Greek and other churches, the act of consecrating by marking with the sign of the cross.

çŏn-sig′nȧ-tō-ry, *n.* One of two or more to sign jointly.

çŏn-sig′nȧ-tūre, *n.* Full signature; joint signing or stamping. [Rare.]

çon′signe (-sin), *n.* [Fr. *consigne*, from *consigner*, to confine, put under orders.] A military term for an order or instruction given to a sentinel; a countersign; a password.

çŏn-sĭ-gnĕ′ (-nyä′), *n.* [Fr.] A person who is commanded to keep within certain limits, as an army officer under arrest.

çon-sign-ee′, *n.* The person to whom goods or other things are delivered in trust, for sale or superintendence; a factor.

çon-sig-nif′i-çănt, *a.* Expressing the same meaning or significance; synonymous.

çon-sig″ni-fi-çā′tion, *n.* Joint signification. [Rare.]

çon-sig-nif′i-çā-tive, *a.* Having a like signification, or jointly significative. [Rare.]

çŏn-sig′ni-fȳ, *v.t.*; consignified, *pt.*, *pp.*; consignifying, *ppr.* To signify in conjunction with something else; to signify secondarily. [Rare.]

çŏn-sign′ment (-sīn′), *n.* 1. The act of consigning or shipping; consignation; the act of sending or committing, as a charge for safe-keeping or management; the act of depositing with, as goods for sale.

2. The thing consigned or shipped; the goods sent or delivered to an agent or factor for sale; as, A received a large *consignment* of goods from B.

3. The writing by which anything is consigned.

çŏn-sīgn′ŏr, çon-sīgn′ẽr, *n.* The person who consigns; one who consigns or delivers goods to another in trust, for carriage or for sale; a shipper of goods.

çŏn-sil′i-ā-ry, *a.* [L. *consiliarius*, from *consilium*, counsel.] Of or pertaining to counsel or advice; of the nature of advice.

çŏn-sil′i-ence, *n.* [L. *con-*, together, and *salire*, to leap.] A coincidence; the act of concurring.

çon-sim′i-lăr, *a.* Having common resemblance. [Obs.]

çon-si-mil′i-tūde, *n.* Resemblance. [Rare.]

çon-si-mil′i-ty, *n.* Common resemblance.

çŏn-sist′, *v.i.*; consisted, *pt.*, *pp.*; consisting, *ppr.* [L. *consistere*, to stand together, stand still; *con-*, together, and *sistere*, to stand, cause to stand; caus. of *stare*, to stand.]

1. To stand together; to be in a fixed or permanent state, as a body composed of parts in union or connection; hence, to be; to exist; to subsist; to be supported and maintained.

> He is before all things, and by him all things *consist*. —Col. i. 17.

2. To have as a foundation, substance, or character; to be contained; followed by *in*; as, the beauty of letter-writing *consists in* ease and freedom.

3. To be composed or made up; followed by *of*; as, a landscape should *consist of* a variety of scenery.

4. To agree; to be in accordance (with); to be compatible; to harmonize.

5. To insist; followed by *on*. [Obs.]

çŏn-sist′ence, çon-sist′en-cy, *n.* 1. A standing together; a being fixed in union, as the parts of a body; that state of a body, in which its component parts remain fixed; firmness; solidity; as, the *consistence* of wood or iron.

> The *consistency* of bodies is divers; dense, rare, tangible, pneumatic, volatile, etc. —Bacon.

2. A degree of density or spissitude, but indefinite.

> Let the juices or liquor be boiled into the *consistence* of a syrup. —Arbuthnot.

3. Substance; make; firmness of constitution or character; as, friendship of a lasting *consistency*; resolutions of durable *consistence*.

4. Agreement or harmony of all parts of a complex thing among themselves, or of the same thing with itself at different times; congruity; uniformity; as, the *consistence* of laws, regulations, or judicial decisions.

> There is harmony and *consistency* in all God's works. —J. Lathrop.

5. Anything which stands together as a whole; a combination; as, the whole *consistence* of orders and members in the church of God. [Obs.]

çŏn-sist′ent, *a.* 1. Fixed; firm; solid; not fluid; as, the *consistent* parts of a body, distinguished from the fluid.

2. Standing together or in agreement; compatible; congruous; uniform; not contradictory or opposed; as, two opinions or schemes are *consistent*; let a man be *consistent* with himself; the law is *consistent* with justice and policy.

3. Conducting oneself in harmony with one's belief or profession; as, a *consistent* Methodist.

Syn.—Accordant, consonant, changeless.

çon-sis-tent′ēs, *n.pl.* The third or highest order of penitents in the early church. They were permitted to be present at the celebration of sacraments, but were not allowed either to join in making oblations or to receive the holy communion. Called also *standers* or *by-standers*.

çŏn-sist′ent-ly, *adv.* In a consistent manner; in agreement; agreeably; as, to command confidence a man must act *consistently*.

çon-sis-tō′ri-ăl, *a.* Pertaining to a consistory, or ecclesiastical court; as, *consistorial* laws.

çon-sis-tō′ri-ăn, *a.* Consistorial.

çŏn-sis′tō-ry, *n.* [L. *consistorium*, a place of assembly, a council, from *consistere*, to stand together.]

1. A place of meeting; a council-house, or place of justice; hence, any assembly or council.

2. In the English church, a spiritual court; the court of every diocesan bishop, held in the cathedral churches, for the trial of ecclesiastical causes arising within the diocese.

3. In the Roman Catholic church, an assembly of prelates; the college of cardinals at Rome.

> Pius was then hearing causes in *consistory*. —Bacon.

4. A place of residence. [Obs.]

5. In some religious bodies, as the Dutch Reformed church, the lowest tribunal, corresponding to a church session, or one composed of ministers and elders, corresponding to a presbytery.

6. A civil court or seat of justice. [Obs.]

çŏn-sō′ci-āte (-shi-āt), *n.* An associate; a partner or confederate; an accomplice.

çŏn-sō′ci-āte, *v.t.*; consociated, *pt.*, *pp.*; consociating, *ppr.* [L. *consociatus*, pp. of *consociare*, to unite, associate; *con-*, together, and *sociare*, from *socius*, joined with.]

1. To unite; to join; to associate.

2. To unite in an assembly or convention, as pastors and messengers, or delegates of churches.

çŏn-sō′ci-āte, *v.i.* 1. To unite; to coalesce.

2. To unite, or meet in a body; to form a consociation of pastors and messengers; said of the Congregationalists.

çŏn-sō-ci-ā′tion, *n.* 1. Intimate union of persons; fellowship; alliance; companionship; union of things; association.

2. An assembly of the pastors and delegates of the Congregational churches within a certain district, forming a court of appeal from the decisions of the churches.

çŏn-sō-ci-ā′tion-ăl, *a.* Pertaining to a consociation.

çŏn-sōl′ā-ble, *a.* That admits comfort; capable of receiving consolation.

çon′sō-lāte, *v.t.* [Obs.] See *Console*.

çon-sō-lā′tion, *n.* [L. *consolatio*, from *consolari*, to console.]

1. Comfort; alleviation of misery, or distress of mind; refreshment of mind or spirits.

> Against such cruelties,
> With inward *consolations* recompensed.
> —Milton.

2. That which comforts or refreshes the spirits; the cause of comfort; as, the *consolation* of Israel.

Syn.—Alleviation, comfort, condolence, relief, solace, support.

çon′sō-lā-tŏr, *n.* One who comforts.

çŏn-sol′ā-tō-ry, *a.* [L. *consolatorius*.] Tending to give comfort.

çŏn-sol′ā-tō-ry, *n.* A speech or writing containing topics of comfort.

çŏn-sōle′, *v.t.*; consoled, *pt.*, *pp.*; consoling, *ppr.* To comfort; to cheer (the mind) in distress or depression; to alleviate (grief), and give refreshment to (the mind or spirits); to give (some one) contentment or moderate happiness, by relieving from distress.

> We *console* our friends when they meet with affliction. —Crabb.

Syn.—Comfort, solace, soothe, cheer, sustain, encourage, support.

çon′sōle, *n.* [Fr., origin unknown.]

1. In architecture, strictly, the French term for a bracket, or for an ancon, but applied by English writers to a bracket or corbel of any kind in classical architecture. It is a projecting ornament, having for its contour generally a curve of contrary flexure, generally employed to support a cornice, bust, vase, or the like. It is frequently, however, used merely as an ornament, as on the keystone of an arch.

Cornice supported by Consoles.

2. In a breech-loading cannon, a platform for supporting a withdrawn breech-piece.

çŏn-sōl′ẽr, *n.* A comforter.

çon′sōle-tā″ble, *n.* A table supported by consoles.

çŏn-sol′i-dȧ, *n.* A consound. [Obs.]

çŏn-sol′i-dănt, *a.* Tending to consolidate or make firm; specifically, in medicine, having the quality of uniting wounds, or forming new flesh.

çŏn-sol′i-dănt, *n.* A medicine designed to heal or unite the parts of wounded flesh.

çŏn-sol′i-dāte, *v.t.*; consolidated, *pt.*, *pp.*; consolidating, *ppr.* [L. *consolidatus*, pp. of *consolidare*; *con-*, together, and *solidare*, to make solid, from *solidus*, solid.]

1. To make solid; to unite or press together (loose or separate parts), and form a compact mass; to harden or make dense and firm.

> He fixed and *consolidated* the earth.—Burnet.

2. To unite (the parts of a broken bone, or the lips of a wound), by means of applications.

3. In a more general sense, to unite (various particles) into one mass or body; as, to *consolidate* the forces of an army; to *consolidate* various funds.

çŏn-sol′i-dāte, *v.i.* To grow firm and hard; to unite and become solid; as, moist clay *consolidates* by drying.

> In hurts and ulcers of the head, dryness maketh them more apt to *consolidate*. —Bacon.

Syn.—Unite, combine, harden, compact, condense, compress.

çŏn-sol′i-dāte, *a.* Formed into a solid mass; a poetical use.

> *Consolidate* in mind and frame.—Tennyson.

çŏn-sol′i-dā-ted, *a.* 1. Made solid, hard, or compact; united.

2. In botany, adnate.

Consolidated annuities; same as *Consols*.

Consolidated fund; in 1816 the exchequers of Great Britain and Ireland, which had previously been kept separate, were by act of Parliament consolidated into one, and an act was at the same time passed consolidating certain portions of the joint revenue of Great Britain and Ireland into one fund, hence called the *consolidated fund*, and providing for its indiscriminate application to the payment of the interest on the national debt, the civil list, and other specified expenses.

çŏn-sol-i-dā′tion, *n.* 1. The act of making, or process of becoming, solid; the act of forming into a firm, compact mass, body, or system, or the uniting of several particulars into one body; as, a *consolidation* of the funds.

2. Annexing of one bill to another in parliament or legislation.

3. In law, the combining of two benefices in one.

4. In botany, adnation.

çŏn-sol′i-dā-tive, *a.* Tending to consolidate; healing.

çŏn-sōl′ing, *a.* Adapted to console or comfort; as, *consoling* news.

çon′sols (*or* -solz′), *n.pl.* [Contr. of *consolidated annuities*.] The government securities of Great Britain, including a large part of the national debt, consisting originally of public securities in great variety, these being consolidated in 1751 into a single three per cent stock. Reductions in interest have since been made; in 1889 to two and three-fourths per cent and in 1903 to two and one-half per cent.

çon-som-mé′ (-mā′), *n.* [Fr. perf., from *consommer*; L. *consummare*, to finish, make perfect.] A clear, meat soup made rich by long and slow cooking.

çon′sō-nănce, çon′sō-năn-cy, *n.* [Fr. *consonance*; L. *consonantia*, from *consonans* (*-antis*), ppr. of *consonare*, to sound together with; *con-*, with, and *sonare*, to sound; *sonus*, a sound.]

1. In music, accord or agreement of sounds; an accord of sounds, simultaneously produced, which creates an agreeable sensation in the ear, as the third, fifth, and eighth.

2. Agreement; accord; congruity; consistency.

3. Friendship. [Obs.]

Syn.—Agreement, accord, consistency, unison, harmony, congruity, suitableness, agreeableness.

çon′sō-nănt, *a.* 1. Agreeing; according; congruous; consistent; followed generally by *to*; sometimes by *with*.

2. In music, composed of consonances; as, *consonant* intervals.

3. Like in sound.

4. Of or pertaining to consonants; consonantal.

çon′sō-nănt, *n.* A letter or element of speech, having either no vocality, as *p* and the other mutes, or only an imperfect vocality, as *b*, *l*, etc. For this reason, *consonants* are only sounded in connection with a vowel, hence the name. The *consonants* are better called *articulations*, as they are the names given to the several closings or junctions of the organs of speech, which precede and follow the openings of the organs with which the vowels are uttered. These closings are *perfect*, and wholly intercept the voice, as in the syllables *ek*, *ep*, *et*, or *imperfect*, and admitting some slight sound, as in *em, en.* Hence, some articulations are called *mutes*, and others *semi-vowels*. The *consonants* begin or end syllables, and their use is to determine the manner of beginning or ending the vocal sounds. These closings or configurations of the organs, being various, serve to diversify the syllables, as in uttering *ba, da, pa,* or *ab, ad, ap;* and, although *b* and *p* may be considered as representing no sounds at all, yet they so modify the utterance of *ab, ap,* or *ba, pa,* that the slight difference between these articulations may be perceived as far as the human voice can be distinctly heard.

çon-sō-nan′tăl, *a.* Having the characteristics of, or pertaining to, a consonant or consonants.

çon′sō-nănt-ize, *v.t.*; consonantized, *pt., pp.*; consonantizing, *ppr.* To use as a consonant; to make (a vowel) into a consonant.

çon′sō-nănt-ly, *adv.* Consistently; in agreement.

çon′sō-nănt-ness, *n.* Agreeableness; consistency.

çon′sō-nous, *a.* [L. *consonus*, sounding together.] Agreeing in sound; symphonious.

çŏn-sō-pi-ā′tion, *n.* A lulling asleep. [Obs.]

çon′sō-pīte, *v.t.* [L. *consopitus*, pp. of *consopire*, to lull to sleep.] To compose; to lull to sleep. [Obs.]

çon′sō-pīte, *a.* Calm; composed. [Obs.]

çon′sọrt, *n.* [OFr. *consort*; L. *consors* (*consortis*), a partner, neighbor; *con-*, with, and *sors* (*sortis*), a lot.]

1. A companion; a partner; an intimate associate; particularly, a partner of the bed; a wife or husband.

2. An assembly or association of persons, convened for consultation. [Obs.]

3. Union; conjunction; concurrence.

4. A symphony; a concert. [Obs.]

5. In navigation, any vessel keeping company with another.

Prince consort; the husband of a queen who rules alone.

Queen consort; the wife of a king, as distinguished from a *queen regnant*, who rules alone, and a *queen dowager*, the widow of a king.

çŏn-sọrt′, *v.i.*; consorted, *pt., pp.*; consorting, *ppr.* To associate; to unite in company; to keep company; followed by *with*.

> Which of the Grecian chiefs *consorts with* thee? —Dryden.

çŏn-sọrt′, *v.t.* 1. To join; to marry.

> With his *consorted* Eve. —Milton.

2. To unite in company.

> He begins to *consort* himself with men. —Locke.

3. To accompany. [Obs.]

çŏn-sọrt′ȧ-ble, *a.* Suitable. [Obs.]

çŏn-sọr′tion, *n.* Fellowship. [Obs.]

çon′sọrt-ism, *n.* In biology, physiological partnership or vital association between organisms of different kinds; symbiosis.

çon′sọrt-ship, *n.* Fellowship; partnership.

çon′sound, *n.* [A corruption of Fr. *consoude*, from L. *consolida*, a comfrey; *consolidare*, to make solid.] The former name of a large number of plants, among them Saracen's, middle, less, and comfrey *consound*, respectively, *Senecio saracenicus, Ajuga reptans, Bellis perennis*, and *Symphytum officinale*.

çon-spē-cif′iç, *a.* Of or pertaining to the same species.

çon-speç-tū′i-ty, *n.* Sight; view. [Obs.]

çŏn-speç′tus, *n.* [L.] A view; an abstract, sketch, or draft.

çŏn-spērse′, *a.* [L. *conspersus*, pp. of *conspergere*, to sprinkle; *con-*, and *spargere*, to scatter, sprinkle.] Having irregular blotches or dots; applied to the eggs of certain birds.

çŏn-spēr′sion, *n.* A sprinkling. [Rare.]

çon-spi-çū′i-ty, *n.* Conspicuousness; brightness. [Rare.]

çŏn-spiç′ū-ous, *a.* [L. *conspicuus*, open to view, from *conspicere*, to look at, observe.]

1. Open to the view; obvious to the eye; manifest; as, to stand in a *conspicuous* place.

> Or come I less *conspicuous*. —Milton.

2. Obvious to the mental eye; clearly or extensively known, perceived, or understood; hence, eminent; famous; distinguished; as, a man of *conspicuous* talents.

Syn.—Eminent, famous, distinguished, illustrious, prominent, celebrated, noted.

çŏn-spiç′ū-ous-ly, *adv.* In a conspicuous manner.

çŏn-spiç′ū-ous-ness, *n.* 1. Openness or exposure to the view; a state of being visible at a distance; as, the *conspicuousness* of a tower.

2. Eminence; fame; celebrity; renown; a state of being extensively known and distinguished; as, the *conspicuousness* of an author.

çŏn-spir′ȧ-çy, *n.* [ME. *conspiracie*; OFr. *conspiracie*, from L. *conspirare*, to breathe together, conspire, agree; *con-*, together, and *spirare*, to breathe.]

1. A combination of men for an evil purpose; an agreement, between two or more persons, to commit some crime in concert; a plot.

> More than forty had made this *conspiracy*. —Acts xxiii. 13.

2. In law, an agreement between two or more persons to commit an illegal act or acts.

3. A concurrence; a general tendency of two or more causes to one event.

Syn.—Combination, plot, cabal, collusion, connivance.

çŏn-spir′ănt, *a.* Conspiring; plotting. [Obs.]

çon-spi-rā′tion, *n.* Conspiracy; agreement or concurrence of things to one end. [Rare.]

çŏn-spir′ȧ-tŏr, *n.* 1. One who conspires; one who engages in a plot to commit a crime, particularly treason.

2. In law, one who agrees with another or others to commit an illegal act or acts; specifically, one party to an agreement falsely and maliciously to indict an innocent person of felony.

çŏn-spīre′, *v.i.*; conspired, *pt., pp.*; conspiring, *ppr.* 1. To agree, by oath, convenant, or otherwise, to commit a crime; to plot; to hatch treason.

> The servants of Amon *conspired* against him, and slew the king in his own house. —2 Kings xxi. 23.

2. In law, to be guilty of conspiracy.

3. To agree; to concur to one end.

Syn.—To unite, concur, combine, confederate, league.

çŏn-spīre′, *v.t.* To unite against; to scheme; to plot.

çŏn-spīr′ēr, *n.* One who conspires or plots; a conspirator.

çŏn-spīr′ing-ly, *adv.* In the manner of a conspiracy; by conspiracy.

çon-spis-sā′tion, *n.* [L. *conspissatio*, from *conspissare*, to thicken.] The act of making thick or viscous; thickness. [Rare.]

çon-spūr′çāte, *v.t.* [L. *conspurcatus*, pp. of *conspurcare*, to defile.] To make impure. [Obs.]

çon-spūr-çā′tion, *n.* The act of defiling; defilement; pollution. [Obs.]

çŏn′stȧ-ble, *n.* [ME. *constable, conestable*; OFr. *conestable*; L. *conestabulus, comistabuli*, a constable, from *comes stabuli*, a count of the stable; *comes*, a count, and *stabulum*, a stable.]

1. A town or village official, usually elected by vote of qualified electors, though sometimes an appointive officer. His duties embrace the policing of his district, the serving of writs, execution of warrants, etc.

2. In England, formerly, an officer having power of arrest and detention, execution of warrants, etc., now superseded by the police.

3. An officer of high rank in several of the medieval monarchies.

Lord High Constable of England; anciently, the seventh officer of the crown. He had the care of the common peace, in deeds of arms, and matters of war; he was also a judge of the court of chivalry.

Special constable; one sworn in for special duty.

To outrun the constable; (a) to escape from the subject in dispute when one's arguments are exhausted; (b) to live beyond one's means. In this latter sense written also, *to overrun the constable*. [Colloq.]

çŏn′stȧ-blēr-y, *n.* The body or jurisdiction of constables. [Obs.]

çŏn′stȧ-ble-ship, *n.* The office of a constable.

çŏn′stȧ-bless, *n.* A constable's wife. [Obs.]

çŏn′stȧ-ble-wick, *n.* The district to which a constable's power is limited. [Obs.]

çon-stab′ū-lā-ry, *a.* Pertaining to constables; consisting of constables.

çŏn-stab′ū-lā-ry, *n.* 1. The body of constables of a district, city, or country; a police force.

2. A district under a constable.

3. The office of a constable.

çŏn-stab′ū-lȧ-tō-ry, *n.* Same as *Constabulary*.

çon′stăn-çy, *n.* [ME. *constance*; OFr. *constance*; L. *constantia*, firmness, unchangeableness, from *constans*, ppr. of *constare*; *con-*, together, and *stare*, to stand.]

1. The state or condition of being constant, invariable, or immutable; fixedness; immutability; unalterable continuance; permanent state.

2. Fixedness or firmness of mind; persevering resolution; steady, unshaken determination; particularly applicable to firmness of mind under sufferings, to steadiness in attachments, and to perseverance in enterprise; stability in love or friendship.

> *Constancy* and contempt of danger.—Prescott.

3. Certainty; veracity; reality. [Obs.]

Syn.—Fixedness, stability, firmness, steadiness, permanence, steadfastness, resolution.

çon′stănt, *a.* 1. Fixed; firm; opposed to *fluid*. [Obs.]

> To turn two fluid liquors into a *constant* body. —Boyle.

2. Fixed; not varied; unchanged; permanent; immutable.

> The world's a scene of changes, and to be *Constant*, in nature, were inconstancy. —Cowley.

3. Fixed or firm in mind, purpose, affection, or principle; as, a *constant* friend or lover.

4. According to logic; consistent. [Obs.]

5. In natural history, always present.

6. In mathematics and physics, unchanging; not variable; as, a *constant* quantity; a *constant* resistance.

Syn.—Fixed, steadfast, unchanging, permanent, unalterable, immutable, invariable, perpetual, continual, resolute, firm, unshaken, determined.

çon′stănt, *n.* That which remains unchanged or invariable; specifically, (a) in mathematics, a quantity which remains the same throughout a calculation; (b) in physics, the numerical expression of a physical property of a body, determined under uniform conditions.

Absolute constant; in mathematics, one never varying, as a cardinal number.

Arbitrary constant; one to which any reasonable value may be assigned at pleasure, as the coefficient of any term containing a variable, in an algebraic equation.

Constant of aberration; that one constant by the determination of which the aberration is obtained from its known laws at any given time.

Constant of integration; in mathematics, the introduced, new, unknown quantity in each integration.

Gravitation constant; the unit for calculating the acceleration of a body, being the algebraic expression of unit force acting upon unit mass at unit distance.

Çŏn-stan′ti-ȧ (-shi-ȧ), *n.* A kind of wine, both white and red, from the farms around Constantia, Cape of Good Hope, renowned as the best liqueur wine after Tokay.

Çŏn-stan″ti-nō-pol′i-tăn, *a.* Relating to Constantinople, the capital of the Ottoman empire.

Constantinopolitan creed; the creed adopted by a council at Constantinople in A.D. 381, which was a revision of the Nicene creed; called also *Niceno-Constantinopolitan creed*.

çon′stănt-ly, *adv.* In a constant manner.

çon′stat, *n.* [L., it appears.]

1. A certificate given by the auditors of the exchequer to a person who intends to plead or move for a discharge of anything in that court, showing what appears upon the record respecting the matter in question. [Eng.]

2. An exemplification under the great seal of the enrolment of any letters patent. [Eng.]

çŏn-stāte′, *v.t.* [Fr. *constater*, to verify, take down; L. *constatus*, pp. of *constare*; *con-*, together, and *stare*, to stand.] To find out; to determine; to verify.

çon′stel-lāte, *v.i.* To join luster; to shine with united radiance or one general light. [Obs.]

çon′stel-lāte, *v.t.* 1. To unite (several shining bodies) in one splendor. [Rare.]

2. To furnish or embellish with stars; as, the *constellated* vistas of light.

çon-stel-lā′tion, *n.* [Fr. *constellation*; L. *constellatio*, a collection of stars, from *constellatus*, set with stars; *con-*, and *stellare*, to shine; *stella*, a star.]

1. A group of the fixed stars to which a definite name has been given. These names have mostly their origin in the mythology of the Greeks, derived and modified from the Egyptians and the East; and the stars forming each configuration are ranged and named in order of brilliancy by letters of the Greek alphabet being attached to them, *e.g.*, we have α Ursæ Majoris, β Orionis, etc. The districts of the heavens thus mapped out and designated are entirely arbitrary, and in general correspond to no natural subdivision or grouping of the stars. The *constellations* are about ninety in number, and are divided into northern, southern, and zodiacal.

2. An assemblage of splendors or excellences; a gathering of persons distinguished for unusual gifts; as, a season noted for *constellations* of singers.

çon-stēr-nā′tion, *n.* [L. *consternatio*, from *consternare*, intens. form of *consternere*, to throw down, bestrew; *con-*, together, and *sternere*, to strew.] Amazement or horror that confounds; excessive terror, wonder, or surprise.

Syn.—Dismay, alarm, terror, panic, overwhelming fear, horror.

çon′sti-pāte, *v.t.*; constipated, *pt., pp.*; constipating, *ppr.* [L. *constipatus*, pp. of *constipare*, to press or crowd together; *con-*, together, and *stipare*, to cram, pack.]

1. To crowd into a narrow compass; to condense. [Obs.]

2. To stop (any passage) by filling to such an extent as to prevent motion in; as, to *constipate* capillary vessels; specifically, to crowd (the intestinal canal), and make costive.

çon-sti-pā′tion, *n.* 1. The act of crowding anything; condensation; as, a close *constipation* of particles. [Obs.]

2. A crowding of the intestinal canal, from defective excretion; a morbid condition of the bowels in which there is unnatural retention of the fecal matter or difficult evacuations; costiveness.

çŏn-stit′ū-en-cy, *n.*; *pl.* **çon-stit′ū-en-cieş.** 1. A body of constituents; particularly, those who appoint or elect representatives to any office, generally municipal or legislative.

2. Any body of persons having common interests and representation; the body of supporters or followers to whom one is in a measure answerable; as, his literary *constituency* was not large.

çŏn-stit′ū-ent, *a.* 1. Constituting or existing as an essential component or ingredient; forming, composing, or making as an essential part; component; elementary; as, oxygen and hydrogen are the *constituent* parts of water.

Body, soul, and reason are the three *constituent* parts of a man. —Dryden.

2. Having electoral or appointive powers.

A question of right arises between the *constituent* and representative body.—Junius.

çŏn-stit′ū-ent, *n.* 1. One who or that which constitutes. [Obs.]

2. That which constitutes or composes, as a part, or an essential part.

The lymph in those glands is a necessary *constituent* of the aliment. —Arbuthnot.

3. One who elects or assists in electing another as his representative in a deliberative or administrative assembly; as, the representative took up the claims of his *constituents.*

4. One who empowers another to transact business for him; one who appoints another as his agent; a principal; as, the agent said he could do nothing till he consulted his *constituent.*

çon′sti-tūte, *v.t.*; constituted, *pt.*, *pp.*; constituting, *ppr.* [L. *constitutus*, pp. of *constituere*, to set up, establish; *con-*, together, and *statuere*, to set.]

1. To set; to fix; to enact; to establish.

We must obey laws appointed and *constituted* by lawful authority, not against the law of God. —Taylor.

2. To form or compose; to give formal existence to; as, perspicuity *constitutes* the prime excellence of style.

Truth and reason *constitute* that intellectual gold that defies destruction. —Johnson.

3. To appoint, depute, or elect to an office or employment; to make and empower; as, the people *constitute* a sheriff a conservator of the peace; A has *constituted* B his attorney or agent.

Constituted authorities; the magistrates or officers of a nation, people, municipality, etc.

çon′sti-tūte, *n.* An established law. [Obs.]

çon′sti-tū-tẽr, *n.* One who constitutes or appoints.

çon-sti-tū′tion, *n.* [Fr. *constitution*; L. *constitutio*, from *constituere*, to establish; from *con-*, together, and *statuere*, to set.]

1. The act of constituting, enacting, establishing, or appointing.

2. The state of being, in regard to make-up or composition; that form of being, or peculiar structure and connection of parts, which makes or characterizes a system or body; applied especially to the particular frame or temperament of the human body; as, a robust *constitution*; an irritable *constitution.*

3. The established form of government in a civil state; a system of fundamental rules, principles, and ordinances, for the government of a state or nation, of society, of a corporation or any organized body of men. A *constitution* may be embodied in written documents, as is that of the United States, or established by prescriptive usage, as that of Great Britain.

4. A particular law, ordinance, or regulation, made by the authority of any superior, civil or ecclesiastical; as, the *constitutions* of the churches; the *constitutions* of Justinian.

5. A system of fundamental principles for the behavior of rational and social beings.

The New Testament is the moral *constitution* of modern society. —Grimke.

çon-sti-tū′tion-ăl, *a.* 1. Of, pertaining to, or inherent in, the constitution, or in the natural frame of body or mind; as, a *constitutional* infirmity; *constitutional* ardor or dullness.

2. Consistent with the constitution; authorized by the constitution or fundamental rules of a government; legal; as, a *constitutional* measure; *constitutional* privileges.

3. Relating to or arising from a constitution; as, *constitutional* interpretation.

The ancient *constitutional* traditions of the state. —Macaulay.

4. Based upon a constitution; established or operating by virtue of a constitution; as, a *constitutional* government or organization.

5. Beneficial to or having a tendency to benefit the constitution; as, a *constitutional* walk. [Colloq.]

Constitutional law; the branch of law relating to the fundamental rules and principles of a political government, or dealing with matters involved under the constitution, as distinguished from the common or the statutory law.

çon-sti-tū′tion-ăl, *n.* A popular name of some form of exercise, particularly a walk, taken for health. [Colloq.]

çon-sti-tū′tion-ăl-işm, *n.* The theory or principle of a constitution; constitutional rule or principles; adherence to a constitution.

çon-sti-tū′tion-ăl-ist, *n.* 1. An adherent to the constitution of the government of a country.

2. An innovator on or reformer of old constitutions; specifically, a framer or advocate of the French constitution of 1791.

çon-sti-tū-tion-al′i-ty, *n.* 1. The quality of being constitutional; the state of being inherent in the natural frame; as, the *constitutionality* of disease.

2. The state of being consistent with the constitution or frame of government, or of being authorized by its provisions; as, all question of *constitutionality* has been removed.

çon-sti-tū′tion-ăl-ly, *adv.* 1. In accordance with the constitution or laws of government.

2. With reference to the natural condition of body or mind; in agreement with the physical constitution; as, they were *constitutionally* strong and brave.

çon-sti-tū′tion-ist, *n.* One who adheres to the constitution of the country.

çon′sti-tū-tive, *a.* 1. Entering into composition or formation; elemental; essential.

2. Having power to enact, establish, or create; instituting.

çon′sti-tū-tive-ly, *adv.* In a constitutive manner.

çon′sti-tū-tŏr, *n.* [L. *constitutor*, from *constituere*, to establish; *con-*, together, and *stare*, to stand.]

1. A person or thing that constitutes.

2. In law, a person who makes himself responsible for another's debt.

çŏn-strāin′, *v.t.*; constrained, *pt.*, *pp.*; constraining, *ppr.* [ME. *constrainen*; OFr. *constraindre*; L. *constringere*, to bind together, to draw together; *con-*, together, and *stringere*, to draw tight.]

1. In a general sense, to exert force, physical or moral, on, either in urging to action or in restraining it; to press; to urge; to drive.

2. To compel or force; to urge with irresistible power.

I was *constrained* to appeal to Cæsar. —Acts xxviii. 19.

3. To confine by force; to restrain from escape or action; to repress; to bind or confine.

My sire in caves *constrains* the winds. —Dryden.

4. To force; to ravish. [Obs.]

5. In mechanics, to control or limit the motion of (a body or mass) to some particular direction or manner.

Syn.—Necessitate, compel, force, oblige, urge, drive, restrain, repress.

çŏn-strāin′ȧ-ble, *a.* Able to be constrained, forced, or repressed; liable to constraint, or to restraint.

çŏn-strāined′, *a.* 1. Urged irresistibly or powerfully; compelled; produced by force.

2. Resulting from or exhibiting unusual constraint; repressed; unnatural; embarrassed; as, a *constrained* voice; the meeting was awkward and *constrained.*

çŏn-strāin′ed-ly, *adv.* In a constrained manner; with embarrassment.

çŏn-strāin′ẽr, *n.* One who constrains.

çŏn-strāint′, *n.* [OFr. *constrainte*, pp. of *constraindre*, to constrain.]

1. Irresistible force, or its effect; any force or power, physical or moral, which compels to act or to forbear action, or which urges so strongly as to produce its effect upon the body or mind; compulsion; restraint.

Not by *constraint*, but by my choice, I came. —Dryden.

2. The condition of being compelled or restrained.

3. Unnatural repression of emotions; awkwardness of manner; embarrassment.

Syn.—Necessity, coercion, compulsion, violence, reserve, restraint.

çŏr-strāint′ive, *a.* Having power to compel. [Rare.]

çŏn-striçt′, *v.t.*; constricted, *pt.*, *pp.*; constricting, *ppr.* [L. *constrictus*, pp. of *constringere*, to draw together, draw tight; *con-*, together, and *stringere*, to draw tight, bind together.] To draw together; to bind; to cramp; to draw into a narrow compass; to contract or cause to shrink.

çŏn-striçt′ed, *a.* 1. Drawn together; bound; contracted.

2. In botany, contracted or irregularly small at some places; as, a *constricted* pod.

çŏn-striç′tion, *n.* 1. A drawing together or contraction, by means of some inherent power, or by spasm, as distinguished from *compression*, the pressure of extraneous bodies; as, the *constriction* of a muscle or fiber.

2. The condition of being constricted; the result of constricting or binding; a constricted or compressed part.

çŏn-striçt′ive, *a.* Constricting; tending to contract or compress.

çŏn-striçt′ŏr, *n.* 1. That which draws together or contracts.

2. In anatomy, a muscle which compresses an organ, draws parts together, or closes an orifice of the body; as, the *constrictor labiorum*, a muscle of the lips.

3. In zoölogy, any one of several large serpents which crush their prey in their folds, as the boa *constrictor.*

çŏn-stringe′, *v.t.*; constringed, *pt.*, *pp.*; constringing, *ppr.* [L. *constringere*, to draw together; *con-*, together, and *stringere*, to draw together, to bind.] To draw together; to strain into a narrow compass; to cause constriction in.

çŏn-strin′ġent, *a.* Having the quality of contracting, binding, or compressing; causing constriction; astringent.

çŏn-struçt′, *v.t.*; constructed, *pt.*, *pp.*; constructing, *ppr.* [L. *constructus*, pp. of *construere*, to heap together, build; *con-*, together, and *struere*, to heap or pile up.]

1. To put together the parts of, in their proper place and order; to build; to form; as, to *construct* an edifice; to *construct* a telescope.

2. To devise and put into orderly arrangement; to form by the mind; to originate or invent; as, to *construct* a plausible story; to *construct* a system of classification.

3. To interpret or construe. [Obs.]

4. To draw (a figure, plan, sketch, etc.,) to meet certain requirements; as, to *construct* a regular hexagon.

Syn.—Make, erect, build, form, compose, fabricate, invent.

çon′struçt, *a.* Relating to construction; expressing the genitive relation.

Construct state or *form*; in Hebrew and other Semitic languages, that form of a noun used when it is followed by a second noun which bears the genitive relation to it; annexion.

çŏn-struçt′ẽr, *n.* Same as *Constructor.*

çŏn-struç′tion, *n.* [L. *constructio*, from *construere*, to heap together, build; *con-*, together, and *struere*, to heap, pile up.]

1. The act or process of building, or of devising and forming; fabrication; erection.

2. The form of building; the method of formation; the way in which a thing is made or put together; structure; organization; as, a machine of intricate *construction.*

3. In grammar, the arrangement and connection of words in a sentence; syntax; as, involved *constructions* are seldom necessary in ordinary writing.

4. Sense; meaning; interpretation; explanation; the manner of understanding the arrangement of words, or of explaining facts; as, give the sentence the proper *construction*; what *construction* shall we put upon his conduct?

5. In geometry, the manner of drawing a figure to fulfil certain conditions; also, the figure so constructed; as, the *construction* of an equilateral triangle is simple.

Construction of an equation; in algebra, linear representation of an equation.

Steel construction; in architecture, that form of building which consists of a framework of steel raised upon deep foundations, all the steel parts being securely bolted and riveted together, and the whole faced or veneered with stone or brick.

çŏn-struç′tion-ăl, *a.* Pertaining to construction; deduced from construction or interpretation.

çŏn-struç′tion-ist, *n.* One who puts a construction upon a law, a paper, or public document, or advocates a certain construction thereof; as, a broad *constructionist* of license laws.

Strict constructionist; a term used specifically for one who advocates a rigid construction of the Constitution of the United States, particularly in regard to federal and state rights, favoring the limitation of the former to the express stipulations of the Constitution.

çŏn-struç′tion-trāin, *n.* In railroad building and operation, a train for the transportation of men and materials needed in construction or repair work.

çŏn-struçt′ive, *a.* 1. By construction; created or deduced by construction or interpretation;

not directly expressed, but inferred; as, *constructive* treason.

> Stipulations, expressed or implied, formal or *constructive*. —Paley.

2. Having the power or ability to construct; engaged in the work of construction; as, the *constructive* genius of Ericsson.

3. Pertaining to or involving construction; as, *constructive* architecture.

Constructive crimes; acts of a character analogous to those forbidden by statute or the common law; as, *constructive* treason.

Constructive notice; in law, the knowledge one should have or is supposed to have, as knowledge of an order of court or of a new enactment by a legislature, when the official forms of notice have been complied with.

Constructive trust; a legal relation which the law regards as equivalent to an express trust, whether so understood and considered by the person or persons holding it or not.

cŏn-struct′ive-ly, *adv.* In a constructive manner; by construction or interpretation; by fair inference.

> A neutral must have notice of a blockade, either actually by a formal information, or *constructively* by notice to his government. —Kent.

cŏn-struct′ive-ness, *n.* 1. The ability or proclivity to make, devise, or construct; especially, mechanical ability.

2. In phrenology, the faculty that leads a person to construct.

cŏn-struct′ŏr, con-struct′ẽr, *n.* [L. *constructor*, from *construere*, to heap together, build; *con-*, together, and *struere*, to heap, pile up.]

1. One who constructs; a maker of things; a builder; as, a naval *constructor*.

2. One who construes. [Obs.]

cŏn-struc′tūre, *n.* An edifice; pile; fabric. [Obs.]

con′strūe, *v.t.*; construed, *pt.*, *pp.*; construing, *ppr.* [ME. *construen*, to interpret, construe; L. *construere*, to heap up, bring together; *con-*, together, and *struere*, to heap, or pile up.]

1. To arrange the words of in a natural order; to reduce from a transposed to a natural order, so as to discover the sense of a sentence; hence, to interpret, and, when applied to a foreign language, to translate; to render into English; as, to *construe* Greek, Latin, or French.

2. To interpret; to explain; to show or to understand the meaning of.

> Thus we are put to *construe* and paraphrase our own words. —Stillingfleet.

con′stū-prāte, *v.t.* [L. *constupratus*, pp. of *constuprare*; *con-*, and *stuprare*, to ravish; *stuprum*, dishonor.] To violate; to debauch. [Obs.]

con-stū-prā′tion, *n.* The act of ravishing; violation; defilement. [Obs.]

con-sub-stan′tiăl (-shăl), *a.* [L. *consubstantialis*; *con-*, together, and *substantialis*, from *substantia*, material, substance.]

1. Having the same substance or essence; coessential.

2. Of the same kind or nature.

con-sub-stan′tiăl-ism, *n.* The doctrine of consubstantiation.

con-sub-stan′tiăl-ist, *n.* One who believes in consubstantiation.

con-sub-stan-ti-al′i-ty (-shi-al′), *n.* The existence of more than one in the same substance.

con-sub-stan′tiăl-ly, *adv.* In a consubstantial manner. [Rare.]

con-sub-stan′ti-āte (-shi-āt), *v.t.*; consubstantiated, *pt.*, *pp.*; consubstantiating, *ppr.* [L. *con-*, and *substantia*, substance.] To unite in one common substance or nature. [Rare.]

con-sub-stan′ti-āte, *v.i.* To profess consubstantiation.

con-sub-stan′ti-āte, *a.* Consubstantial.

con-sub-stan-ti-ā′tion, *n.* The theory of impanation or actual presence of the body of Christ in the sacramental elements, bread and wine, after consecration; opposed to *transubstantiation*.

con′suē-tūde (-swē-), *n.* [ME. *consuetude*; L. *consuetudo* (*-tudinis*), custom, habit; from *consuescere*, to accustom; from *consuere*, to, and *suere*, to be accustomed; from *suus*, one's own.] Custom; usage. [Rare.]

con-suē-tū′di-năl, *a.* Customary. [Rare.]

con-suē-tū′di-nā-ry, *a.* Customary; habitual.

con-suē-tū′di-nā-ry, *n.*; *pl.* **con-suē-tū′di-nā-ries**. A ritual of devotions common to any particular diocese or religious order.

con′sul, *n.* [L. *consul*, from *consulere*, to deliberate, take counsel.]

1. One of the chief magistrates of the ancient Roman republic, invested with regal authority for one year. There were two consuls annually chosen in the Campus Martius. In the first ages of Rome they were elected from patrician families or noblemen, but in the year 366 B. C. the people obtained the privilege of electing one of the consuls from their own body, and sometimes both were plebeians.

2. In French history, the title given to the three supreme magistrates of the French republic after the dissolution of the Directory in 1799.

3. In international law, a duly commissioned officer of a nation, residing abroad to represent the commercial and associated interests of his country.

4. A senator. [Obs.]

con′sul-āge, *n.* [Obs.] See *Consulate*.

con′sū-lăr, *a.* Pertaining to a consul; as, *consular* power; *consular* dignity or privileges.

con′sū-lā-ry, *a.* [Obs.] See *Consular*.

con′sū-lāte, *n.* [L. *consulatus*, from *consul*, a consul.]

1. The office of a consul; also, a consul's term of office.

2. The jurisdiction or extent of a consul's authority.

3. The dwelling or locality occupied by a consul.

4. [C—] Consular government, as that in France, which was established after the revolution of the eighteenth Brumaire, and lasted to the coronation of Napoleon I.

con′sul-gen′ẽr-ăl, *n.* A chief consul.

con′sul-ship, *n.* The office of a consul; or the term of his office.

cŏn-sult′, *v.i.*; consulted, *pt.*, *pp.*; consulting, *ppr.* [L. *consultare*, freq. of *consulere*, to deliberate, consider, ask advice.]

1. To seek the opinion or advice of another, by a statement of facts and suitable inquiries, for the purpose of directing one's own judgment; followed by *with*.

2. To take counsel together; as, they *consulted* some time.

cŏn-sult′, *v.t.* 1. To ask advice of; to seek the opinion of, as a guide to one's own judgment; as, to *consult* a friend or parent.

2. To seek information or facts from, as by examining books or papers; as, to *consult* official documents.

3. To regard; to have reference or respect to, in judging or acting; to decide or to act in favor of.

> Ere fancy you *consult*, *consult* your purse. —Franklin.

4. To plan, devise, or contrive. [Obs.]

> Thou hast *consulted* shame to thy house, by cutting off many people. —Hab. ii. 10.

Syn.—Interrogate, canvass, question, deliberate, confer, advise with, regard, consider, care for, promote.

cŏn-sult′, *n.* 1. The act of consulting; the effect of consultation; determination.

2. A deliberating assembly; a council. [Obs.]

cŏn-sult′ȧ-ry, *a.* Relating to consultation.

Consultary response; the opinion on a special case by a court.

con-sul-tā′tion, *n.* 1. The act of consulting; deliberation of two or more persons, with a view to some decision.

2. A meeting of persons to consult together; a council for deliberation, as of legal counsel retained in a cause, or of physicians in a dangerous disease.

Writ of consultation; in English law, a writ awarded by a superior court, to return a cause which had been removed by prohibition from the court Christian to its original jurisdiction; so called, because the judges, on *consultation*, find the prohibition ill-founded.

cŏn-sult′ȧ-tive, *a.* Having the privilege of consulting; of or pertaining to consultation.

cŏn-sult′ȧ-tō-ry, *a.* Advisory; pertaining to consultation.

cŏn-sult′ẽr, *n.* One who consults, or asks counsel or information.

cŏn-sult′ing, *a.* Asking advice; seeking information; deliberating and inquiring mutually.

Consulting physician; one called in by the attending physician for counsel.

cŏn-sult′ive, *a.* Pertaining to consultation; thoroughly considered.

cŏn-sūm′ȧ-ble, *a.* That may be consumed; possible to be destroyed, dissipated, wasted, or spent; as, asbestos is not *consumable* by fire.

cŏn-sūme′, *v.t.*; consumed, *pt.*, *pp.*; consuming, *ppr.* [ME. *consumen*; OFr. *consumer*; L. *consumere*, to eat, use up, destroy; *con-*, together, and *sumere*, to take; *sub*, under, and *emere*, to buy, take.]

1. To destroy by separating the parts of (a thing), as by decomposition, by fire, or by eating, devouring, and annihilating the form of (a substance); as, fire *consumes* wood, coal, stubble; animals *consume* flesh and vegetables.

2. To destroy by dissipating or by use; to expend; to waste; to squander; as, to *consume* an estate.

3. To spend; to cause to pass away, as time; as, to *consume* the day in idleness.

4. To cause to disappear; to waste slowly.

5. To destroy; to bring to utter ruin; to exterminate.

Syn.—Destroy, swallow up, ingulf, absorb, waste, exhaust, spend, expend, squander, lavish, dissipate, burn.

cŏn-sūme′, *v.i.* To waste away slowly; to be exhausted.

cŏn-sūm′ed-ly, *adv.* Immoderately; to an excessive degree. [Slang.]

cŏn-sūm′ẽr, *n.* 1. One who consumes, spends, wastes, or destroys; that which consumes.

2. In political economy, one who uses a product or commodity; opposed to *producer*.

cŏn-sūm′ing-ly, *adv.* In a destructive manner.

cŏn-sum′māte, *v.t.*; consummated, *pt.*, *pp.*; consummating, *ppr.* [L. *consummatus*, pp. of *consummare*, to sum up, finish; *con-*, together, and *summa*, a sum.]

1. To end; to finish by completing (what was intended); to perfect; to bring or carry to the utmost point or degree.

2. In law, to complete, as a marriage, by cohabitation.

cŏn-sum′māte, *a.* Complete; perfect; carried to the utmost extent or degree; as, *consummate* greatness or felicity.

cŏn-sum′māte-ly, *adv.* Completely; perfectly.

con-sum-mā′tion, *n.* Completion; end; perfection of a work, process, or scheme; the act of consummating.

Consummation of marriage; in law, the completion of marriage by copulation.

cŏn-sum′mȧ-tive, *a.* Of or pertaining to consummation; final.

cŏn-sump′tion, *n.* [L. *consumptio*, a consuming, wasting, from *consumere*, to consume, destroy.]

1. The act of consuming; waste; destruction; as, the *consumption* of fuel, of food, of time, etc.

2. The state or process of being wasted or diminished.

> Etna and Vesuvius have not suffered any considerable diminution or *consumption*. —Woodward.

3. In medicine, a wasting or emaciation of the body; specifically, (a) pulmonary tuberculosis; (b) tuberculosis of the bowels.

4. In political economy, the use or expenditure of the products of industry, or of all things having an exchangeable value.

> The distinction of productive and unproductive is applicable to *consumption* as well as to labor. —Mill.

Syn.—Decay, decline, waste, destruction.

cŏn-sump′tive, *a.* 1. Destructive; wasting, exhausting; having the quality of consuming, or dissipating; as, a long, *consumptive* war.

2. Affected with or having a tendency to the disease consumption; as, a *consumptive* person.

cŏn-sump′tive, *n.* A person afflicted with consumption.

cŏn-sump′tive-ly, *adv.* In a way tending to consumption.

cŏn-sump′tive-ness, *n.* A state of being consumptive, or a tendency to consumption.

cŏn-sūte′, *a.* [L. *consutus*, pp. of *consuere*, to stitch together; *con-*, together, and *suere*, to sew.] In entomology, having stitch-like markings, as the elytra of some beetles.

con-tȧ-bes′cence, *n.* 1. In medicine, disease marked by a wasting away, as atrophy, consumption, etc.

2. In botany, a contabescent condition.

con-tȧ-bes′cent, *a.* [L. *contabescens* (*-entis*), pp. of *contabescere*, to waste away.]

1. Wasting away; applied specifically in medicine.

2. In botany, having defective anthers and pollen lifeless or wanting.

con-tab′ū-lāte, *v.t.* [L. *contabulatus*, pp. of *contabulare*, to cover with boards; *con-*, together, and *tabula*, a board, table.] To floor with boards. [Obs.]

con-tab-ū-lā′tion, *n.* The act of laying with boards, or of flooring. [Obs.]

con′tact, *n.* [L. *contactus*, from *contingere*, to touch, seize; *con-*, together, and *tangere*, to touch.]

1. A touching; touch; the relation of being in touch; close union or junction.

2. In mathematics, tangency; coincidence.

3. In mining, the plane marking the limit of an ore-producing vein.

Contact series; in electricity, a series of metals so arranged as to produce positive electricity by adjacent contact.

con′tact-breāk″ẽr, *n.* Any device for interrupting a circuit, as in an induction-coil.

cŏn-tac′tion, *n.* The act of touching. [Obs.]

con′tact-lev″el, *n.* An appliance used in determining minute length-differences by means of a transversely-pivoted spirit-level.

con-tȧ-dī′nȧ, *n.*; *pl.* **con-tȧ-dī′ne.** [It.] A peasant woman of Italy.

con-tȧ-dī′nō, *n.*; *pl.* **con-tȧ-dī′nī.** [It.] A peasant of Italy.

cŏn-tā′giŏn, *n.* [L. *contagio* (*-onis*), a touching, from *contingere*; *con-*, together, and *tangere*, to touch.]

1. Literally, a touching; hence, the communication of a disease by contact, direct or indirect.

2. The specific germ producing *contagion*; contagium.

3. That which communicates some state or condition (generally evil) from one to another; infection; that which propagates mischief; as, the *contagion* of vice or of bad example.

4. Pestilential influence; venomous exhalations. [Obs.]

Syn.—Infection.—Properly speaking, *contagion* is the communication of disease by contact either with the diseased person or the effluvia or excretions given off by such person, while *infection* is the result of general conditions, as the malarial *infection* of the low lands of the South. This distinction, however, is frequently disregarded, the two words being confounded.

çŏn-tā′ġiŏned, *a.* Affected by contagion.

çŏn-tā′ġiŏn-ist, *n.* One who believes in the contagious character of certain diseases.

çŏn-tā′ġious, *a.* 1. Containing or generating contagion; catching; that may be communicated by contact, direct or indirect; as, a *contagious* disease.

2. Poisonous; pestilential; containing contagion; as, *contagious* air; *contagious* clothing.

3. Figuratively, communicating anything from one to another or to others.

Syn.—Epidemical, pestilential, infectious, catching.

çŏn-tā′ġious-ly, *adv.* By contagion.

çŏn-tā′ġious-ness, *n.* The quality of being contagious.

çŏn-tā′ġi-um, *n.*; *pl.* **çŏn-tā′ġi-ȧ.** [L.] 1 The specific virus or morbific matter which communicates disease; as, the *contagium* of diphtheria.

2. Contagion.

çŏn-tāin′, *v.t.*; contained, *pt., pp.*; containing, *ppr.* [ME. *containen*; OFr. *contenir*; L. *continere*, to hold, keep together; *con-*, together, and *tenere*, to hold.]

1. To hold within fixed limits; to comprehend; to comprise; to include; to hold.

> Behold, the heaven and heaven of heavens cannot *contain* thee. —1 Kings viii. 27.

2. To be capable of holding; as, this vessel *contains* two gallons.

3. To comprise, as a writing; to have for contents.

> A sonnet *containing* her affection unto Benedick. —Shak.

4. To put constraint on; to restrain; to retain. [Obs.]

> Others, when the bagpipe sings i' the nose,
> Cannot *contain* their urine. —Shak.

[In this last sense still used reflexively; as, he could not *contain himself* for joy.]

Syn.—Comprise, embrace, inclose, include.

çŏn-tāin′, *v.i.* To live in continence or chastity. [Obs.]

çŏn-tāin′ȧ-ble, *a.* That may be contained or comprised.

çŏn-tāin′ȧnt, *n.* A container. [Obs.]

çŏn-tāin′ẽr, *n.* Anything which contains.

çŏn-tāin′ment, *n.* All a thing contains. [Obs.]

çon-tam′i-nȧ-ble, *a.* Capable of contamination.

çon-tam′i-nāte, *v.t.*; contaminated, *pt., pp.*; contaminating, *ppr.* [L. *contaminatus*, pp. of *contaminare*, to defile; *contamen*, contact, contagion, from *contingere*; *con-*, together, and *tangere*, to touch.] To corrupt; to pollute; figuratively, to sully; to tarnish; to taint; as, lewdness *contaminates* character; cowardice *contaminates* honor.

> Shall we now
> *Contaminate* our fingers with base bribes?
> —Shak.

çŏn-tam′i-nāte, *a.* Polluted; defiled; corrupted; contaminated. [Rare.]

çŏn-tam-i-nā′tion, *n.* The act of polluting; pollution; defilement; taint.

çŏn-tam′i-nȧ-tive, *a.* Adapted to contaminate.

çŏn-tan′gō, *n.* [Of doubtful origin.] In English stockjobbing, a sum of money paid to a seller for accommodating a buyer, by carrying the engagement to pay the price of shares bought over to the next settling-day. In reality *contango* is interest paid for the loan of money for fourteen days, that is, for the interval between settling-days.

çon′teck, çon′tek, *n.* [OFr. *contek*, contention.] Quarrel; contention. [Obs.]

çŏn-teç′tion, *n.* [L. *contectio*, from *contegere*, to cover.] A covering. [Obs.]

çŏn-temn′ (-tem′), *v.t.*; contemned, *pt., pp.*; contemning (-tem′ning *or* -tem′ing), *ppr.* [L. *contemnere*, to despise; *con-*, intens., and *temnere*, to scorn, despise.]

1. To despise; to consider and treat as mean and despicable; to scorn.

> In whose eyes a vile person is *contemned*.
> —Ps. xv. 4.

2. To slight; to neglect as unworthy of regard; to reject with disdain.

> Wherefore doth the wicked *contemn* God?
> —Ps. x. 13.

Syn.—Scorn, despise, disdain, spurn, slight, neglect, underrate, overlook.

çŏn-tem′nẽr (*or* -tem′ẽr), *n.* One who contemns; a despiser; a scorner.

çŏn-tem′ning-ly (*or* -tem′ing-li), *adv.* In a contemptuous manner; slightingly.

çŏn-tem′pẽr, *v.t.* [L. *contemperare*, to temper, mix; *con-*, together, and *temperare*, to mix, temper.] To moderate; to temper. [Obs.]

> The leaves qualify and *contemper* the heat.
> —Ray.

çŏn-tem′pẽr-ȧ-ment, *n.* Proportion. [Obs.]

çŏn-tem′pẽr-āte, *v.t.* To contemper. [Obs.]

çŏn-tem-pẽr-ā′tion, *n.* The act of moderating or tempering. [Obs.]

çŏn-tem′pẽr-ȧ-tūre, *n.* Proportionate temperature. [Obs.]

çon-tem′plănce, *n.* [OFr.] An observance; meditation. [Obs.]

çŏn-tem′plănt, *a.* Meditative; contemplative. [Rare.]

çon′tem-plāte (*or* -tem′plāte), *v.t.*; contemplated, *pt., pp.*; contemplating, *ppr.* [L. *contemplatus*, pp. of *contemplari*, to gaze attentively, observe; lit., to mark out an augural temple; *con-*, with, and *templum*, temple.]

1. To view or consider with continued attention; to gaze upon; to behold; to view or regard mentally; to meditate on; to study; to ponder on.

> *Contemplate* all this work of time.—Tennyson.

2. To consider or have in view in reference to a future act or event; to intend.

> If a treaty contains any stipulations which *contemplate* a state of future war.—Kent.

Syn.—Study, ponder, muse, meditate on, dwell on, consider, intend, design, plan, purpose.

çon′tem-plāte, *v.i.* To think studiously; to study; to muse; to meditate; as, he delights to *contemplate* on the works of creation.

çon-tem-plā′tion, *n.* 1. The act of the mind in considering with attention; meditation; study; continued attention of the mind to a particular subject.

2. Holy meditation; attention to sacred things. [Obs.]

3. The act of looking forward to or purposing; expectation.

çŏn-tem′plȧ-tist, *n.* One who contemplates. [Rare.]

çŏn-tem′plȧ-tive, *a.* 1. Given to contemplation, or continued application of the mind to a subject; studious; thoughtful; as, a *contemplative* philosopher or mind.

2. Having the power of thought or meditation; as, the *contemplative* faculty of man.

çŏn-tem′plȧ-tive, *n.* A religious person of either sex devoted to contemplation and prayer.

çŏn-tem′plȧ-tive-ly, *adv.* In a contemplative manner; attentively; thoughtfully.

çŏn-tem′plȧ-tive-ness, *n.* The condition of being contemplative or thoughtful; meditativeness.

çon′tem-plā-tŏr, *n.* One who contemplates; one employed in study or meditation; an inquirer after knowledge.

çŏn-tem″pō-rȧ-nē′i-ty, *n.* The condition of being contemporaneous, or existing at the same time.

çŏn-tem-pō-rā′nē-ous, *a.* Living or being at the same time.

çŏn-tem-pō-rā′nē-ous-ly, *adv.* At the same time with some other event.

çŏn-tem-pō-rā′nē-ous-ness, *n.* The state or quality of being contemporaneous.

çŏn-tem′pō-rā-ri-ness, *n.* Existence at the same time.

çŏn-tem′pō-rā-ry, *a.* [L. *con-*, with, and *temporarius*, pertaining to time, from *tempus*, time.]

1. Living at the same time; contemporaneous.

> Framed by *contemporary* historians.—Lewis.

2. Done or caused by those living at the same time; belonging to the same times; existing at the same point of time.

> Bring ages past and future together and make them *contemporary*. —Locke.

3. Coeval. [Rare.]

çŏn-tem′pō-rā-ry, *n.*; *pl.* **çŏn-tem′pō-rā-rieş.** One who lives at the same time with another; as, Socrates and Plato were *contemporaries*.

çŏn-tempt′ (-temt′), *n.* [L. *contemptus*, scorn, from *contemnere*, to despise, scorn; *con-*, and *temnere*, to despise.]

1. The act of despising; the act of viewing or considering and treating as mean, vile, and worthless; disdain; hatred of what is mean or deemed vile.

> Nothing, says Longinus, can be great, the *contempt* of which is great. —Addison.

2. The state of being despised; shame; disgrace.

> Some shall awake to everlasting *contempt*.
> —Dan. xii. 2.

3. In law, disobedience to the rules, orders, or process of a court or legislative assembly, or a disturbance or interruption of its proceedings. *Contempts* committed out of court are punishable by attachment, and *contempts* done before the court may be punished or repressed in a summary way, by commitment or by fine. The power of enforcing their process, and of vindicating their authority against open obstruction or defiance, is incident to all superior courts.

Syn.—Disdain, scorn, derision, mockery, contumely, neglect, disregard, slight.

çŏn-tempt-i-bil′i-ty, *n.* Contemptibleness.

çŏn-tempt′i-ble, *a.* 1. Worthy of contempt; that deserves scorn or disdain; despicable; mean; vile; said of persons and things.

> Man groweth daily more *contemptible* in his own eyes. —Taylor.

2. Despised; neglected.

> There is not so *contemptible* a plant that does not confound understanding. —Locke.

3. Apt to despise; contemptuous. [Obs.]

Syn.—Despicable, abject, vile, mean, base, paltry, worthless, sorry, pitiful, scurril.

çŏn-tempt′i-ble-ness, *n.* The state of being contemptible, or of being despised; despicableness; meanness; vileness.

çŏn-tempt′i-bly, *adv.* In a contemptible manner; meanly.

çŏn-temp′tū-ous, *a.* 1. Manifesting or expressing contempt or disdain; scornful; as, *contemptuous* language or manner; a *contemptuous* opinion.

2. Apt to despise; haughty; insolent; as, a nation proud, severe, *contemptuous*.

Syn.—Haughty, insolent, insulting, scornful, supercilious, contumelious.

çŏn-temp′tū-ous-ly, *adv.* In a contemptuous manner; with scorn or disdain; despitefully.

> The apostles and most eminent Christians were poor, and treated *contemptuously*.
> —Taylor.

çŏn-temp′tū-ous-ness, *n.* Disposition to contempt; act of contempt; insolence; scornfulness; haughtiness.

çŏn-tend′, *v.i.*; contended, *pt., pp.*; contending, *ppr.* [L. *contendere*, to stretch out, strive after; *con-*, together, and *tendere*, to stretch, extend.]

1. To strive; to vie; to combat; to quarrel; to encounter.

2. To struggle; to use earnest efforts, as to obtain, or to defend and preserve; usually with *for*.

> You sit above, and see vain men below
> *Contend for* what you only can bestow.
> —Dryden.

3. To debate; to argue; to wrangle; to dispute.

Syn.—Antagonize, battle, combat, compete, contest, cope, dispute, fight, grapple, oppose, strive, vie.

çŏn-tend′, *v.t.* To dispute; to contest. [Rare.]

> Carthage shall *contend* the world with Rome.
> —Dryden.

çŏn-tend′ent, *n.* An antagonist or opposer.

çŏn-tend′ẽr, *n.* One who contends.

çŏn-tend′ress, *n.* A woman who contends.

çon-ten′ē-ment, *n.* That which is held with a tenement, as contiguous land; appurtenance.

çŏn-tent′, *a.* [Fr. *content*; L. *contentus*, pp. of *continere*, to hold in, contain; *con-*, together, and *tenere*, to hold.] Literally, held; contained within limits; hence, quiet; not disturbed; having a mind at peace; easy; satisfied, so as not to repine, object, or oppose.

> *Content* with science in the vale of peace.
> —Pope.

çon′tent, *n.*; *pl.* **çon′tents.** 1. The capacity of a thing; all contained in a certain limit; usually in the plural; as, the *contents* of a barrel or a room.

2. In geometry, included space; area; used both in the singular and plural: as, the *content* of an octagon; circular *contents*.

3. Size; capacity. [Obs.]

Table of contents; a summary arranged so as to show the consecutive order of topics in a book or books; also called *contents*.

çŏn-tent′, *v.t.*; contented, *pt., pp.*; contenting, *ppr.* 1. To satisfy the mind of; to make quiet, so as to stop complaint or opposition; to appease; to make easy in any situation; generally having the reflexive use.

> Do not *content yourselves* with obscure and confused ideas. —Watts.

2. To pay or reward.

Syn.—Satisfy, appease, favor, gratify, humor, please.

çŏn-tent′, *n.* 1. Rest or quietness of the mind in the present condition; satisfaction.

A wise *content* his even soul secured.—Smith.

2. Satisfaction without examination. [Obs.]

The style is excellent;
The sense they humbly take upon *content*.
—Pope.

3. That which gives *content*; wish; as, they ate to their hearts' *content*.

4. The term used in the House of Lords to express assent to a bill or motion; hence, a peer who votes *content*; an assenting or affirmative vote.

çon-ten-tā′tion, *n.* Content. [Obs.]

çŏn-tent′ed, *a.* Satisfied; quiet; easy in mind; not complaining.

Syn.—Satisfied, comfortable, satiated, willing, ready, resigned, passive.

çŏn-tent′ed-ly, *adv.* In a contented manner.

çŏn-tent′ed-ness, *n.* The state or quality of being content.

çŏn-tent′ful, *a.* Full of contentment. [Obs.]

çŏn-ten′tion, *n.* [L. *contentio*, from *contendere*; *con-*, and *tendere*, to stretch.]

1. Strife; struggle; a violent effort to obtain something; contest; quarrel.

A tumult raised by *contention* among the partisans of the several colors. —Adam.

2. Strife in words or debate; quarrel; angry contest; controversy; as, *contention* over property.

3. Zeal; ardor; vehemence of endeavor.

An end worthy of our utmost *contention*.
—Rogers.

4. Something contended for in a debate or other argument; the argument in support of it.

Syn.—Struggle, contest, litigation, controversy, quarrel, conflict, feud, dissension, variance, disagreement, debate, competition, emulation, discord.

çŏn-ten′tious, *a.* 1. Apt to contend; given to angry debate; quarrelsome; perverse.

A continual dropping in a rainy day, and a *contentious* woman, are alike.
—Prov. xxvii. 15.

2. Relating to or characterized by contention, or strife; involving contention; as, *contentious* crimes.

3. In law, having power to decide causes between contending parties; as, a court of *contentious* jurisdiction.

çŏn-ten′tious-ly, *adv.* In a contentious manner; perversely.

çŏn-ten′tious-ness, *n.* The state or condition of being contentious.

çŏn-tent′less, *a.* Discontented. [Rare.]

çŏn-tent′ly, *adv.* In a contented way. [Obs.]

çŏn-tent′ment, *n.* 1. Content; a resting or satisfaction of mind without disquiet; acquiescence.

Contentment, without external honor, is humility. —Grew.

2. Gratification; diversion. [Obs.]

At Paris the prince spent a day, to give his mind some *contentment*. —Wotton.

Syn.—Comfort, satisfaction, repose, acquiescence, gratification.

çon-tẽr′min-ȧ-ble, *a.* Limited or terminated by the same bounds; terminating at the same point, whether of space or time. [Rare.]

çon-tẽr′mi-năl, *a.* Same as *Conterminous*.

çon-tẽr′mi-nănt, *a.* Conterminate. [Obs.]

çon-tẽr′mi-nāte, *a.* Having the same bounds. [Obs.]

çon-tẽr′mi-nous, *a.* [L. *conterminus*, bordering upon.] Bordering upon; touching at the boundary; contiguous; as, a people *conterminous* to the Roman territory.

çon-tẽr-rā′nē-ăn, çon-tẽr-rā′nē-ous, *a.* [L. *conterraneus*; *con-*, together, and *terra*, land.] Being of the same country. [Obs.]

çŏn-tes-sẽr-ā′tion, *n.* Assembly; collection. [Obs.]

çŏn-test′, *v.t.* contested, *pt.*, *pp.*; contesting, *ppr.* [Fr. *contester*, to contest; L. *contestari*, to call to witness, to bring action; *con-*, and *testari*, to bear witness, from *testis*, a witness.]

1. To dispute; to strive earnestly to hold or maintain; to struggle to defend; as, the troops *contested* every inch of ground.

2. To dispute; to argue in opposition to; to controvert; to oppose; as, the advocate *contested* every point.

None have *contested* the proportion of these ancient pieces. —Dryden.

3. To litigate; to call in question; as, to *contest* a will.

Contested election; one in which the result is disputed in court on the ground of illegality.

çŏn-test′, *v.i.* 1. To strive; to contend; followed by *with*.

The difficulty of an argument adds to the pleasure of *contesting with* it. —Burnet.

2. To vie; to emulate.

Of man, who dares in pomp *with* Jove *contest*.
—Pope.

Syn.—Dispute, controvert, debate, litigate, oppose, argue, contend.

çon′test, *n.* 1. Strife; struggle for victory, superiority, or in defense; struggle in arms or athletic ability; as, all Europe engaged in the *contest* against France; the *contest* was furious.

2. Dispute; debate; violent controversy; strife in argument.

Leave all noisy *contests*, all immodest clamors, and brawling language. —Watts.

Syn.—Conflict, combat, battle, feud, broil, dispute, altercation, debate, controversy, difference, fray.

çŏn-test′ȧ-ble, *a.* That may be disputed or debated; disputable; controvertible.

çŏn-test′ȧ-ble-ness, *n.* The state or quality of being contestable.

çŏn-test′ănt, *n.* One who disputes or contests; a litigant; one who claims what another has received; particularly one who contests a will or election.

çon-tes-tā′tion, *n.* 1. The act of contesting; strife; dispute. [Obs.]

2. Testimony; proof by witnesses. [Obs.]

3. Ecclesiastically, the preface to the eucharistic service in the Gallican church.

çŏn-test′ing-ly, *adv.* In a contending manner.

çŏn-tex′, *v.t.* To weave together. [Obs.]

çon′text, *n.* [L. *contextus*, from *contexere*, to weave together.] The general series or composition of a discourse; more particularly, the parts of a discourse which precede or follow the sentence quoted; the passages of Scripture which are near the text, either before it or after it; as, a foreign word understood by the *context*.

çŏn-text′, *a.* Knit or woven together; close; firm. [Obs.]

çŏn-text′, *v.t.* To knit together. [Obs.]

çŏn-tex′tūr-ăl, *a.* Pertaining to contexture.

çŏn-tex′tūre, *n.* [Fr. *contexture*, from L. *contextus*, pp. of *contexere*; *con-*, together, and *texere*, to weave.]

1. The interweaving of several parts into one body; the disposition and union of the constituent parts of a thing, with respect to each other; composition of parts; constitution; as, a silk of admirable *contexture*.

2. In Scots law, a mode of industrial accession taking place when things belonging to one are wrought into another's cloth, and are carried therewith as accessory.

çŏn-tex′tūred, *a.* Woven; formed into texture. [Rare.]

çon′ti-cent, *a.* [L. *conticens*, pp. of *conticere*, to be silent.] Hushed; quiet; silent. [Rare.]

çon-tig-nā′tion, *n.* [L. *contignatio*, from *contignari*, to join with beams.]

1. A frame of beams; a story.

2. The act of framing together, or uniting beams in a fabric.

çŏn-tig′ū-āte, *a.* Contiguous. [Obs.]

çon-ti-gū′i-ty, *n.* 1. Actual contact of bodies; a touching; a continuity.

2. In psychology, one of the associating principles of the mind.

çŏn-tig′ū-ous, *a.* [L. *contiguus*, touching, from *contingere*; *con-*, together, and *tangere*, to touch.] Touching; meeting or joining at the surface or border; close together; neighboring; bordering or adjoining; as, two *contiguous* bodies, houses, or countries; usually followed by *to*.

Contiguous angles; in geometry, such as have one leg or side common to both angles; adjacent angles.

Syn.—Adjoining, adjacent, touching.

çŏn-tig′ū-ous-ly, *adv.* In a manner to touch; without intervening space.

çŏn-tig′ū-ous-ness, *n.* A state of contact; close union of surfaces or borders; close proximity.

çon′ti-nence, çon′ti-nen-cy, *n.* [Fr. *continence*; L. *continentia*, from *continere*, to hold back or together.]

1. The restraint which a person imposes upon his desires and passions; specifically, moderation in the indulgence of sexual enjoyment.

Chastity is either abstinence or *continence*; abstinence is that of virgins or widows; *continence*, that of married persons.
—Taylor.

2. Continuity; uninterrupted course. [Obs.]

çon′ti-nent, *a.* 1. Refraining from unlawful sexual commerce, or moderate in the indulgence of lawful pleasure; chaste.

2. Restrained; moderate; temperate.

Have a *continent* forbearance. —Shak.

3. Opposing; restraining. [Obs.]

4. Continuous; connected; not interrupted; as, a *continent* fever. [Obs.]

çon′ti-nent, *n.* 1. That which contains anything. [Obs.]

2. In physical geography, one of the larger divisions of land of the globe, distinguished from an island by size and surface configuration. North and South America comprise the western, and Europe, Asia, Africa, and Australia the eastern *continent*, though each of the named divisions is commonly reckoned a separate *continent*, as sometimes are smaller divisions, as Greenland.

3. [C—] By restriction, Europe, distinguished from the British Isles; as, to go from London to the *Continent*.

4. Land in general; terra firma. [Obs.]

çon-ti-nen′tăl, *a.* 1. Pertaining or relating to a continent; specifically, [C—] pertaining to the Continent, Europe; as, *continental* borders; *Continental* diplomacy.

2. [C—] In United States history, of or designating the states held together by the Articles of Confederation; as, the *Continental* Congress.

Continental money; paper money issued by the Continental Congress during the Revolutionary period. It soon depreciated, eventually reaching nil.

Continental system; the celebrated plan of the Emperor Napoleon for excluding the merchandise of England from all parts of the Continent.

çon-ti-nen′tăl, *n.* 1. A native or inhabitant of a continent; specifically, [C—] of the Continent of Europe.

2. [C—] A soldier on the side of the colonies during the Revolutionary war.

Not worth a Continental; worthless; as was the paper Continental money at the close of the Revolutionary war.

Çon-ti-nen′tăl-ẽr, *n.* [Obs.] See *Continental*, 2.

çon-ti-nen′tăl-ist, *n.* 1. Same as *Continental*, 1.

2. [C—] In United States history, a believer in a close political union of the separate states at the close of the Revolution.

çon′ti-nent-ly, *adv.* In a continent manner; chastely; moderately; temperately.

çŏn-tin′ġence, *n.* Contingency.

çŏn-tin′ġen-cy, *n.*; *pl.* **çŏn-tin′ġen-cies**. 1. The quality of being contingent or casual; a happening, or the possibility of coming to pass.

We are not . . . to build certain rules upon the *contingency* of human actions.—South.

2. Casualty; accident; a contingent event.

3. Contact. [Obs.]

Syn.—Casualty, accident, chance.

çŏn-tin′ġent, *a.* [L. *contingens* (*-entis*), ppr. of *contingere*, to touch, meet, happen; *con-*, together, and *tangere*, to touch.]

1. Dependent on an uncertain issue; of doubtful occurrence; incidental; casual; conditional.

Things of their own nature *contingent* and mutable. —Hooker.

2. In logic, a term applied to the matter of a proposition when the terms of it in part agree and in part disagree.

3. In law, depending upon some possible future event; as, a policy payable *contingent* on loss by burglary.

Syn.—Incidental, accidental, casual, fortuitous.

çŏn-tin′ġent, *n.* 1. A fortuitous event; that which comes without design, foresight, or expectation; a contingency.

2. That which falls to one in a division or apportionment among a number; a quota; specifically, the share or proportion of troops to be furnished by one of several contracting states or powers; as, the Vermont *contingent* in the Revolutionary war.

çŏn-tin′ġent-ly, *adv.* Accidentally; without design or foresight.

çŏn-tin′ġent-ness, *n.* The state of being contingent; fortuitousness.

çŏn-tin′ū-ȧ-ble, *a.* That may be continued. [Rare.]

çŏn-tin′ū-ăl, *a.* [Fr. *continuel*, from L. *continuus*, continuous.]

1. Proceeding without interruption or cessation; unceasing; not intermitting; continuous.

2. Very frequent; often repeated; as, the business man has *continual* applications for subscriptions.

3. Perpetual.

Continual proportionals; see *Continued proportionals* under *Continued*.

Syn.—Constant, continuous, perpetual, unintermitted, incessant, uninterrupted, unceasing, invariable, regular, unbroken, unvarying.

çŏn-tin′ū-ăl-ly, *adv.* 1. Without pause or cessation; unceasingly; as, the ocean is *continually* in motion.

2. Very often; in repeated succession; from time to time.

çŏn-tin′ū-ăl-ness, *n.* Permanence.

çŏn-tin′ū-ănce, *n.* 1. A holding on or remaining in a particular state; constancy; perseverance; a state of lasting; as, the *continuance* of rain or fair weather for a day or a week.

2. Abode; residence; as, during our *continuance* in Paris.

3. Succession uninterrupted; continuation;

a prolonging of existence; as, the brute regards the *continuance* of his species.

4. In law, adjournment or putting off, as of a case, from day to day or from term to term; also, the complete record of such adjournment.

5. Continuity; resistance to a separation of parts; a holding together. [Obs.]

çŏn-tin′ū-ănt, *a.* Characterized by continuance.

çŏn-tin′ū-ănt, *n.* A letter having a sound that may be drawn out; a prolonged sound.

çŏn-tin′ū-āte, *v.t.* To join closely together. [Obs.]

çŏn-tin′ū-āte, *a.* 1. Immediately united; holding together. [Rare.]

2. Uninterrupted; unbroken. [Rare.]

çŏn-tin′ū-āte-ly, *adv.* With continuity; without interruption. [Obs.]

çŏn-tin-ū-ā′tion, *n.* 1. Extension of existence in a series or line; succession uninterrupted; the state of being continued.

> These things must be works of Providence for the *continuation* of the species.—Ray.

2. Extension or carrying on to a further point or space; production; a carrying on in length; as, the *continuation* of a line in surveying.

çŏn-tin′ū-ȧ-tive, *n.* 1. In logic, an expression denoting continuance, permanence, or duration.

> To these may be added *continuatives*; as, Rome remains to this day; which includes at least two propositions, viz., Rome was, and Rome is. —Watts.

2. In grammar, an indefinite connective; a conjunction.

çŏn-tin′ū-ȧ-tive, *a.* Continuing. [Rare.]

çŏn-tin′ū-ā-tŏr, *n.* One who or that which continues, as a series or succession.

çŏn-tin′ūe, *v.i.*; continued, *pt., pp.*; continuing, *ppr.* [ME. *continuen*; OFr. *continuer*; L. *continuare*, to join, unite, make continuous, from *continuus*, continuous, from *continere*; *con-*, together, and *tenere*, to hold.]

1. To remain in a state or place; to abide for any time indefinitely; to stay.

2. To last; to be durable; to endure; to be permanent.

3. To persevere; to be steadfast or constant in any course; to persist; to abide; as, to *continue* in good works.

çŏn-tin′ūe, *v.t.* 1. To protract; not to cease from or to terminate; to persevere in; as, to *continue* the same diet.

2. To extend from one thing to another; to produce or draw out in length; as, *continue* the line from A to B; let the line be *continued* to the boundary.

3. To hold to or unite. [Obs.]

4. To retain; to allow or permit to remain; to allow to live.

> And how shall we *continue* Claudio.—Shak.

çŏn-tin′ūed, *a.* 1. Drawn out; protracted; produced; extended in length; extended without interruption.

2. Continual; unceasing.

Continued bass; in music, thorough-bass.

Continued fever; a fever which runs its course without interruption.

Continued fractions; in arithmetic, a species of fractions which have acquired great value by their application to the solution of numerical equations and of problems in the indeterminate analysis. A fraction whose denominator is an integer with a fraction, which latter fraction has for its denominator an integer with a fraction, and the same for this last fraction again, and so on to any extent.

Continued or *continual proportionals*; a series of three or more quantities compared together, so that the ratio is the same between every two adjacent terms, viz., between the first and second; the second and third; the third and fourth, etc., as 1, 2, 4, 8, 16, etc., where the terms continually increase in a double ratio. Such quantities are also said to be in *continued proportion*, and a series of *continued proportionals* is also called a *progression*.

Continued or *continuous voyage*; one prosecuted to the objective port, no account being made of intermediate stoppages.

çŏn-tin′ūed-ly, *adv.* Continuously; without interruption; without ceasing.

çŏn-tin′ū-ẽr, *n.* One who continues; one who has the power of perseverance.

çon-ti-nū′i-ty, *n.*; *pl.* **çon-ti-nū′i-tieṣ.** Connection uninterrupted; cohesion; close union of parts; unbroken texture; as, philosophers talk of the solution of *continuity*.

Law of continuity; the principle that nothing passes from one state to another, without passing through all the intermediate states.

çon-ti′nū-ō, *n.* [It.] Continued bass; thorough-bass.

çŏn-tin′ū-ous, *a.* [L. *continuus*, from *continere*, to hold together; *con-*, together, and *tenere*, to hold.]

1. Joined without intervening space; without cessation or interruption; unbroken; constant; continual; as, *continuous* depth.

2. In botany, being uniform throughout; devoid of joints or articulations.

Continuous brake; a series of car-brakes, as the common air-brake, capable of operation at any point of its extent.

Continuous current; in electricity, one produced under the influence of a constant electro-motive force; opposed to *alternating current*.

Continuous impost; in architecture, the moldings of an arch continued along the pillar that supports it down to the ground without any member to mark the impost-point, that is, the point at which the arch and pillar meet.

Continuous Impost.

Continuous waves; (Abbrev. C. W.) a form of electro-magnetic wave extensively used in radiotelegraphy, as they possess a constant amplitude and no damping effect.

Syn.—Incessant, continual, perpetual.

çŏn-tin′ū-ous-ly, *adv.* In a continuous manner.

çŏn-tin′ū-ous-ness, *n.* The state or quality of being continuous.

çont′line, *n.* A nautical term for (a) the space between the strands on the outside of a rope or hawser; (b) the space between casks resting side by side, their bilges being in contact.

çon′tō, *n.* [Port.] An elliptical term for 1,000,000 reis; $1,080; in Brazil, $546.

çŏn-tor′ni-āte, *a.* Having edges appearing as if turned in a lathe; applied to medals.

çŏn-tor′ni-āte, çŏn-tor-ni-ā′tō, *n.* [Fr. *contorniate*; It. *contorniato*, from *contorno*, a circuit, circumference, from LL. *contornare*; *con-*, intens., and *tornare*, to turn.] A species of medal or medallion in bronze, having a curved furrow on each side, supposed to have been struck in the days of Constantine the Great and his successors, and to have formed tickets of admission to the public games of the circus of Rome and of Constantinople.

çŏn-tor′sion, *n.* Contortion. [Obs.]

çŏn-tort′, *v.t.*; contorted, *pt., pp.*; contorting, *ppr.* [L. *contortus*, pp. of *contorquere*, to whirl, to twist; *con-*, together, and *torquere*, to twist.] To twist together or out of shape; to distort; as, disease *contorted* his limbs.

çŏn-tort′ed, *a.* 1. Twisted; distorted.

2. In botany, convolute.

çŏn-tor′tion, *n.* 1. A twisting; a writhing; a wresting; a twist; wry motion; as, the *contortion* of the muscles of the face.

2. In medicine, a twisting or wresting of a limb or member of the body out of its natural situation; partial dislocation.

çŏn-tor′tion-ist, *n.* An athlete whose specialty is contorted poses or acts of contortion.

çŏn-tor′tive, *a.* Causing or exhibiting contortion.

çon-tor-tū′pli-çāte, *a.* [L. *contortuplicatus*; *contortus*, twisted, and *plicatus*, pp. of *plicare*, to fold, double up.] In botany, spiral and having a lengthwise plait, as certain buds.

çon-tōur′ (*or* kon′tör), *n.* [Fr. *contour*, a circuit, circumference, from LL. *contornare*, to go around; *con-*, and *tornare*, to turn; *tornus*, a lathe; Gr. *torsios*, a tool to make a circle with.] The outline of a figure or body; the line that defines or bounds a body, its form being determined by the shape of the body; the periphery considered as distinct from the object; the word is rarely used except when speaking of rounded or sinuous bodies; specifically, (a) in the fine arts, a line or lines representing the outline of any figure; (b) in fortification, the horizontal outline of works of defense; (c) in surveying, the outline of the surface of the ground with regard to its undulations.

çon-tōur′, *v.t.*; contoured, *pt., pp.*; contouring, *ppr.* To make a contour of; to make an outline of (a figure or of a country), in the latter case having reference only to its heights and depressions.

çon-tōur′-feath″ẽrs (feth) *n.pl.* The outer plumage of a bird; pennæ.

çon-tōur′-line, *n.* A line or level carried along the surface of a country or district at a uniform height above the sea-level, and then laid down on a map or plan, so that an approximately true outline of its contour is presented, the degree of accuracy depending on the number of lines or levels taken between the sea-level and the highest point in the region.

çon-tōur-né′ (-nā′), *a.* [Fr.] A term in heraldry, used when a beast is represented standing, passant, courant, etc., with its face to the sinister side of the escutcheon.

çon-tōur′ni-āte, çon-tōur′ni-ā-ted, *a.* Contorniate.

çon′trȧ-. A prefix, from Latin *contra*, a preposition and adverb, signifying against, contrary, opposite; as, *contra*diction, *contra*bass.

çon′trȧ-band, *a.* [It. *contrabbando*, from L. *contra*, against, and LL. *bandum, bannum*, a proclamation.] Prohibited or excluded by proclamation, law, or treaty.

çon′trȧ-band, *n.* 1. Illegal or prohibited traffic.

> Persons most bound to prevent *contraband*. —Burke.

2. Articles by law prohibited to be imported or exported.

3. In United States history, any negro refugee within the lines of the Union army; from the decision of General B. F. Butler in 1861, declaring such negroes "*contraband* of war," later shortened to *contraband*.

Contraband of war; such goods as are prohibited to be imported or exported, either by the laws of a particular state or nation, or by the law of nations, or by special treaties. In time of war, arms and munitions of war are not permitted by one belligerent to be transported by neutrals to the other, but are held to be contraband and liable to capture and condemnation.

çon′trȧ-band, *v.t.* To declare prohibited; also, to smuggle. [Obs.]

çon′trȧ-band-iṣm, *n.* Illegal traffic.

çon′trȧ-band-ist, *n.* One who traffics illegally.

çon-trȧ-băss′, *a.* Of deep tone; specifically, of an octave lower than any other instrument of its class.

çon-trȧ-băss′, *n.* A viol having the lowest tone of any instrument of its class.

çon-trȧ-bas′sō, *n.* [It., from L. *contra*, opposite, and *basso*, L. *bassus*, low.] A contrabass.

çŏn-traçt′, *v.t.*; contracted, *pt., pp.*; contracting, *ppr.* [L. *contractus*, pp. of *contrahere*, to draw together, make a bargain; *con-*, together, and. *trahere*, to draw.]

1. To draw together or nearer; to draw into a less compass, either in length or breadth; to shorten; to abridge; to narrow; to lessen; as, to *contract* an inclosure; to *contract* the faculties; to *contract* the period of life; to *contract* the sphere of action.

2. To draw (the parts) together; to wrinkle; as, to *contract* the brow.

3. To betroth; to affiance; as, A *contracted* his daughter to B.

4. To draw to; to bring on; to incur; to gain; as, we *contract* debt by extravagance.

5. To shorten by omission of a letter or syllable; as, to *contract* a word.

6. To epitomize; to abridge; as, to *contract* an essay.

çŏn-traçt′, *v.i.* 1. To shrink; to become less in area, extent or body; as, iron *contracts* on cooling.

2. To bargain; to make a mutual agreement, as between two or more persons; as, we have *contracted* for a load of flour.

3. To betroth in marriage.

> Young folks can *contract* against their parents' will. —Taylor.

Syn.—Abbreviate, shorten, abridge, epitomize, narrow, lessen, condense, reduce, confine, incur, assume.

çŏn-traçt′, *a.* Contracted. [Obs.]

çon′traçt, *n.* 1. An agreement or covenant between two or more persons, in which each party binds himself to do or forbear some act, and each acquires a right to what the other promises; a mutual promise upon lawful consideration or cause which binds the parties to a performance; a bargain; a compact.

2. The act by which a man and woman are betrothed each to the other.

3. The writing which contains the agreement of parties with the terms and conditions, and which serves as a proof of the obligation.

Syn.—Covenant, agreement, compact, stipulation, bargain, arrangement, obligation, promise, engagement.

çŏn-traçt′ănt, *n.* A person who contracts.

çŏn-traçt′ed, *a.* 1. Drawn together, or into a shorter or narrower compass; shrunk.

> To whom the angel with *contracted* brow. —Milton.

2. Bargained for; betrothed.

3. Incurred; as, a debt improperly *contracted*.

4. Narrow; mean; selfish; as, a man of a *contracted* soul or mind.

Contracted vein; in hydraulics, a term denoting the diminution which takes place in the diameter of a stream of water issuing from a vessel at a short distance from the discharging aperture owing to the particles nearest the periphery experiencing greater attrition than the rest, and being thus retarded; called also *vena contracta*.

çŏn-traçt′ed-ly, *adv.* In a contracted manner.

çŏn-traçt′ed-ness, *n.* The state of being contracted; narrowness; meanness; excessive selfishness.

çŏn-traçt-i-bil′i-ty, *n.* Possibility of being contracted; quality of suffering contraction; as, the *contractibility* and dilatability of air.

çŏn-traçt′i-ble, *a.* Capable of contraction.

çŏn-traçt′i-ble-ness, *n.* The quality of suffering contraction; contractibility.

çŏn-traçt′ile, *a.* Tending to contract; having the power of shortening or of drawing into smaller dimensions; as, the *contractile* force of certain elastic bodies.

Contractile vacuole; a minute **air-cell** having a regular dilation, as in the *Protozoa*.

çon-traç-til′i-ty, *n.* 1. The inherent quality or force by which bodies shrink or contract.

2. The contracting or shortening power possessed by fibers of living muscles.

çŏn-traç′tion, *n.* 1. The act of drawing together or shrinking; the act of shortening, narrowing, or lessening extent or dimensions, by causing the parts of a body to approach nearer to each other; the state of bein contracted.

> Oil of vitriol will throw the stomach into involuntary *contractions*. —Arbuthnot.

2. The act of shortening, abridging, or reducing within a narrower compass by any means; as, improvement by omissions or *contractions*.

3. In grammar, the shortening of a word, by the omission of a letter or syllable, as *can't* for *cannot*.

4. A contract; marriage contract. [Obs.]

5. In surgery, an abnormal and permanent alteration in the relative position and forms of parts, arising from various causes, as in ankylosis, distortion, clubfoot, wryneck.

6. In mathematics, the abridgment of an operation.

7. The act of contracting; as, the *contraction* of malaria.

çŏn-traçt′ive, *a.* Relating to contraction; having a tendency to contract.

çŏn-traçt′ŏr, *n.* 1. One who contracts; one of the parties to a bargain, one who covenants to do anything for another; specifically, one who makes a business of executing work according to contract.

2. In anatomy, a constrictor.

çŏn-traç′tūre, *n.* Permanent muscle-shortening.

çon′trȧ-dȧnce, *n.* [Fr. *contredanse*; *contre*, opposite, and *danse*, dance.] A country-dance; also, the music for such a dance.

çon-trȧ-diçt′, *v.t.*; contradicted, *pt.*, *pp.*; contradicting, *ppr.* [L. *contradictus*, pp. of *contradicere*; *contra*, against, and *dicere*, to speak.] To oppose by words; to assert the contrary of; to deny, as an affirmation.

> It is not lawful to *contradict* a point of history known to all the world. —Dryden.

çon-trȧ-diçt′, *v.i.* To utter a contradiction; to deny.

Syn.—Oppose, gainsay, deny, resist, impugn, correct, rectify, retract, recall, recant.

çon-trȧ-diçt′ȧ-ble, *a.* That is capable of contradiction.

çon-trȧ-diçt′ẽr, *n.* One who contradicts or denies; an opposer.

çon-trȧ-diç′tion, *n.* 1. An assertion of the contrary to what has been said or affirmed; denial; contrary declaration.

2. Direct opposition or repugnancy; complete inconsistency; incongruity or contrariety of things, words, thoughts, or propositions; as, these theorems involve a *contradiction*.

> If we perceive truth, we thereby perceive whatever is false in *contradiction* to it. —Grew.

Principle of contradiction; the axiom that truth and falsity are never inherent in the same thing simultaneously in the same sense.

çon-trȧ-diç′tion-ăl, *a.* Inconsistent; opposing. [Rare.]

çon-trȧ-diç′tious, *a.* 1. Filled with contradictions; inconsistent. [Obs.]

2. Inclined to contradict; disposed to deny or cavil. [Obs.]

çon-trȧ-diç′tious-ness, *n.* Self-contradiction. [Rare.]

çon-trȧ-diçt′ive, *a.* Containing contradiction.

çon-trȧ-diçt′ive-ly, *adv.* By contradiction.

çon-trȧ-diçt′ŏr, *n.* One who contradicts.

çon-trȧ-diçt′ō-ri-ly, *adv.* In a contradictory manner.

çon-trȧ-diçt′ō-ri-ness, *n.* Direct opposition; contrariety in assertion or effect.

çon-trȧ-diçt′ō-ry, *a.* 1. Affirming the contrary; implying a denial of what has been asserted; as, *contradictory* assertions.

2. Inconsistent; opposite; contrary; as, *contradictory* schemes.

Syn.—Adverse, alien, incompatible, inconsistent, opposite, repugnant, contrary.

çon-trȧ-diçt′ō-ry, *n.*; *pl.* **çon-trȧ-diçt′ō-ries**. A proposition which denies or opposes another in all its terms; contrariety; inconsistency.

> It is common with princes to will *contradictories*. —Bacon.

çon″trȧ-dis-tinçt′, *a.* [*Contra-*, and L. *distinctus*, pp. of *distinguere*, to distinguish.] Distinguished by opposite qualities.

çon″trȧ-dis-tinç′tion, *n.* Distinction by opposite qualities.

> We speak of sins of infirmity, in *contradistinction* to those of presumption.—South.

çon″trȧ-dis-tinç′tive, *a.* Distinguishing by opposites.

çon″trȧ-dis-tinç′tive, *n.* That which contradistinguishes.

çon″trȧ-dis-tin′guish (-gwish), *v.t.*; contradistinguished, *pt.*, *pp.*; contradistinguishing, *ppr.* To distinguish not merely by differential, but by opposite qualities.

çon″trȧ-fȧ-got′tō, *n.* [It.] The double bassoon; also, an organ-stop having a similar pitch.

çon-trȧ-fis′sūre (-fish′ŭr), *n.* [*Contra-*, and L. *fissura*, from *findere*, to cleave.] In surgery, a fissure or fracture in the cranium, on the side opposite to that which received the blow, or at some distance from it.

çon-trȧ-grē′di-ent, *a.* In mathematics, denoting the relation of one system of variables to another when one is subject to undergo linear substitution simultaneously with the other, but of a different kind.

çon′trȧ-hent, *a.* Contracting; agreeing. [Obs.]

çon-trȧ-in′di-çănt, *n.* A symptom that forbids to treat a disorder in the usual way

çon-trȧ-in′di-cāte, *v.t.*; contraindicated, *pt.*, *pp.*; contraindicating, *ppr.* [*Contra-*, and L. *indicatus*, pp. of *indicare*, to point out; *in*, in, and *dicare*, to proclaim.] In medicine, to indicate (some method of cure) the contrary of, i. e., what the general tenor of the disease requires; or to forbid to be done, as what the main scope of the malady points out.

çon-trȧ-in-di-çā′tion, *n.* A contraindicant symptom or phase of a disease.

çŏn-tral′tō, *n.* [It.] 1. In music, the highest voice of a male adult, or the lowest of a woman or a boy, called also the *alto*, or when possessed by a man *counter-tenor*. It is next below the treble and above the tenor, its easy range being from tenor G to treble C.

2. The person who sings with this voice; also, the part sung; as, she is a splendid *contralto*; the *contralto* was poorly sung.

çŏn-tral′tō, *a.* Pertaining to or possessed of the quality of contralto; as, a *contralto* voice.

çon′trȧ-mūre, *n.* Same as *Countermure*.

çon-trȧ-nat′ū-răl, *a.* Opposed or contrary to nature. [Rare.]

çon-trȧ-ni′ten-çy, *n.* [*Contra-*, and L. *nitens*, ppr. of *niti*, to strive.] Reaction; resistance to force. [Obs.]

çon′trȧ-oç-tāve, *n.* [*Contra-*, and L. *octava*, an eighth, from *octo*, eight.] That octave on the piano which begins with lowest C; the corresponding octave on other instruments.

çon′trȧ-plex, *a.* See *Duplex*.

çon-trȧ-pōṣe′, *v.t.*; contraposed, *pt.*, *pp.*; contraposing, *ppr.* [*Contra-*, and L. *positus*, pp. of *ponere*, to place.]

1. To set in opposition. [Obs.]

2. In logic, to transpose (the terms of a proposition) by contraposition.

çon″trȧ-pō-ṣi′tion (-zish′un), *n.* 1. A placing over against; opposite position.

2. In logic, conversion, in particular negative propositions, effected by separating the word *not* from the copula and attaching it to the predicate; without which the change would in English be impracticable.

çon-trȧ-pun′tăl, *a.* [It. *contrappunto*, counterpoint.] Pertaining to counterpoint, or conforming to its rules.

çon-trȧ-pun′tăl-ly, *adv.* In a manner conformable to the rules of counterpoint.

çon-trȧ-pun′tist, *n.* One skilled in counterpoint.

çon-trȧ-pun′tō, *n.* Same as *Counterpoint*.

çon″trȧ-rē-mon′strănt, *n.* One who remonstrates against a remonstrance.

çŏn-trā′ri-ănt, *a.* [Fr., from L. *contrarians*, ppr. of *contrariare*, to contradict, from *contrarius*, opposite; *contra*, against.] Contradictory; opposite; inconsistent; opposing. [Rare.]

çŏn-trā′ri-ănt, *n.* In general, a contrariant person, applied particularly, in English history, to Thomas, earl of Lancaster, and the barons who took part with him against King Edward II., because on account of their great power it was not politic to call them rebels or traitors.

çŏn-trā′ri-ănt-ly, *adv.* In a contrary manner. [Obs.]

çon-trȧ-rī′e-ty, *n.*; *pl.* **çon-trȧ-rī′e-tieṣ**. [L. *contrarietas*, from *contrarius*, opposite, opposed; *contra*, against.]

1. The condition of being opposed in fact, essence, quality, or principle; the quality of being contrary; lack of agreement; inconsistency; repugnance.

> There is nothing more common than *contrariety* of opinions. —Locke.

2. An inconsistency; any quality or thing contrary or opposed to another; as, political *contrarieties*.

Syn.—Disagreement, discrepancy, dissimilarity, inconsistency, antagonism.

çon′trā-ri-ly, *adv.* In a contrary manner.

çon′trā-ri-ness, *n.* The state or quality of being contrary.

çŏn-trā′ri-ous, *a.* Contrary; opposing. [Rare.]

çŏn-trā′ri-ous-ly, *adv.* Contrarily; oppositely. [Rare.]

çon′trā-ri-wīṣe, *adv.* 1. On the contrary; oppositely; on the other hand.

> Not rendering evil for evil, or railing for railing; but *contrariwise* blessing. —1 Pet. iii. 9.

2. Conversely; in reverse order.

çon″trȧ-rō-tā′tion, *n.* Rotation in a direction opposite to another motion.

çon′trā-ry, *a.* [L. *contrarius*, opposite, opposed, from *contra*, against.]

1. Opposite; adverse; in an opposite direction or position; as, *contrary* winds.

2. Opposite; contradictory; not merely different, but inconsistent or repugnant; conflicting; antagonistic; as, an idea *contrary* to accepted theories.

3. Disposed to contrariness; characterized by habitual opposition; perverse; as, an exasperatingly *contrary* person.

4. Having qualities which are opposite; unlike in the extreme; applied to terms which, while belonging to the same class or category, are the most widely different of all that belong to the class; as, good, bad; wise, foolish; also, mutually opposed; applied in logic to two propositions, one of which denies every possible case of the other; as, all men are mortal; no men are mortal.

Contrary motion; a musical phrase designating oppositeness of progression of parts, as when one ascends while another descends.

Syn.—Dissimilar, unlike, opposite, opposed, conflicting, antagonistic.

çon′trā-ry, *n.*; *pl.* **çon′trā-rieṣ**. 1. A thing that is contrary or of opposite qualities; one of two related but contrary propositions, facts, conditions, or qualities; an opposite.

> No *contraries* hold more antipathy
> Than I and such a knave. —Shak.

2. An opposer; an antagonist. [Obs.]

On the contrary; in opposition; on the other side.

To the contrary; to an opposite purpose or effect.

çon′trā-ry, *v.t.* To contradict or oppose. [Obs.]

çŏn-trȧst′, *v.t.*; contrasted, *pt.*, *pp.*; contrasting, *ppr.* [Fr. *contraster*; LL. *contrastare*, to stand opposed to, withstand; *contra*, against, and *stare*, to stand.]

1. To set in opposition (different things or qualities) to show the comparative excellences of, or the differences between; to compare by differences; as, to *contrast* night and day.

2. In painting and sculpture, to place in such relation of opposition that one figure shall heighten the effect of the other.

> The figures of the groups must *contrast* each other. —Dryden.

çŏn-trȧst′, *v.i.* To stand in contrast or opposition; to present differences or dissimilarity when compared.

> The joints which divide the sandstone *contrast* finely with the divisional planes which separate the basalt into pillars. - Lyell.

çon′trȧst, *n.* 1. The act or process of contrasting; the placing together in view or in juxtaposition things of the same category or class but widely differing from each other, in order to render the difference more vividly marked; comparison by contrariety of qualities; opposition of things or qualities; unlikeness; difference; as, the *contrast* between a well-bred man and a clown; the sky seemed light in *contrast* with the water.

2. In painting, sculpture, and other arts, the opposition or dissimilarity of figures, colors, etc., by which one heightens the effect of the other.

çon-trȧ-stim′ū-lănt, *a.* and *n.* I. *a.* Having the properties of or acting as a contrastimulant.

II. *n.* A remedy or treatment tending to counteract the effects of a stimulant or an excessive use of stimulants.

çon′trāte, *a.* [From L. *contra*, opposite, against.] Bearing on the rim cogs parallel to the axis; applied to clockwork-wheels.

çon′trȧ-ten″ŏr, *n.* [It.] In music, a middle part between the tenor and treble; contralto; counter-tenor; also, a singer having such a voice.

çon′trāte-wheel, *n.* Same as *Crown-wheel*.

çon″trȧ-val-lā′tion, *n.* [Fr. *contrevallation*, from L. *contra*, against, and *vallum*, a rampart.] In fortification, a trench guarded with a parapet, formed by the besiegers between their camp and the place besieged, to secure themselves and check sallies of the besieged garrison.

çon-trȧ-vā'ri-ănt, *n.* A function which stands in the same relation to the primitive function from which it is derived as any of its linear transforms to an inversely derived transform of its primitive.

çon-trȧ-vēne', *v.t.*; contravened, *pt., pp.*; contravening, *ppr.* [LL. *contravenire*; *contra*, against, and *venire*, to come.]

1. To come against; to oppose in principle or effect; to contradict; to obstruct in operation; as, such a ruling will *contravene* all precedent.

2. To act so as to violate; to transgress; as, we must not *contravene* the law.

Syn.—Oppose, run counter to, contradict, nullify, thwart, defeat.

çon-trȧ-vēn'ēr, *n.* One who opposes or contravenes.

çon-trȧ-ven'tion, *n.* The act of contravening, opposing, or transgressing; violation; opposition; as, the proceedings of the allies were in *contravention* of the treaty.

çon-trȧ-vēr'sion, *n.* [L. *contraversus*; *contra*, against, and *versus*, pp. of *vertere*, to turn.] A turning to the opposite side; antistrophe. [Rare.]

çon-trȧ-yēr'vȧ, *n.* [L., from Sp. *contrayerba*, a counter-herb, antidote; L. *contra*, against, and *herba*, a herb.] In botany, a South American plant, *Dorstenia Contrayerva*, which possesses an aromatic root having medicinal qualities.

çon'tre-çoup (kon'tr-kö), *n.* [Fr. *contre*, L. *contra*, against, and *coup*, a blow.] In surgery, shock-transmission from the point struck to an opposite point of the body or part.

çon-trec-tā'tion, *n.* [L. *contrectatio*, from *con-* and *trectare*, to handle, touch.] A touching or handling. [Rare.]

çon-tre-temps' (kon-tr-täṅ'), *n.* [Fr., from L. *contra*, against, and *tempus*, time.]

1. An unexpected accident, which throws everything into confusion; an embarrassing occurrence.

2. In music, variation from the written time.

cŏn-trib'ū-tȧ-ble, *a.* Able to be contributed.

cŏn-trib'ū-tȧ-ry, *a.* Tributary; jointly contributing. [Obs.]

> It was situated on the Ganges, at the place where this river received a *contributary* stream. —D'Anville.

cŏn-trib'ūte, *v.t.*; contributed, *pt., pp.*; contributing, *ppr.* [L. *contributus*, pp. of *contribuere*, to throw together, unite; *con-*, together, and *tribuere*, to grant, assign.] To give or grant in common with others; to give to a common stock or for a common purpose; to pay a share of or make a gift toward; as, to *contribute* money to a famine fund.

> England *contributes* much more than any other of the allies. —Addison.

cŏn-trib'ūte, *v.i.* To give a part; to lend a portion of power, aid, or influence; to have a share in any act or effect; to assist; as, he *contributed* to the success of the evening.

> There is not a single beauty in the piece, to which the invention must not *contribute*. —Pope.

Syn.—Add, subscribe, give, coöperate, assist, supply, tend, conduce.

çon-tri-bū'tion, *n.* 1. The act of giving to a common stock, or in common with others; the act of lending a portion of power or influence to a common purpose; the payment of each man's share of some common expense.

2. That which is given to a common stock or purpose, either by an individual or by many; as, the *contribution* of one person, or the *contribution* of a society.

3. In a military sense, an imposition paid by a frontier country, to secure itself from being plundered by the enemy's army; or an imposition upon a country in the power of an enemy, which is levied for the support of the army.

4. In law, the share of a common loss, obligation, or benefit, paid or to be paid by each of the persons interested.

çon-tri-bū'tion-ăl, *a.* Of or pertaining to a contribution; making contributions.

cŏn-trib'ū-tive, *a.* Tending to contribute; contributing.

cŏn-trib'ū-tŏr, *n.* One who contributes; in particular, one who supplies material to a magazine or joint literary work.

cŏn-trib'ū-tō-ry, *a.* Contributing to the same stock or purpose; promoting the same end; bringing assistance to some joint design, or increase to some common stock.

Contributory negligence; in law, negligence on the part of an injured person, which helped to bring about the cause of the injury, and therefore precludes him from recovery in an action for damages.

cŏn-trib'ū-tō-ry, *n.*; *pl.* **cŏn-trib'ū-tō-ries.** A person or thing that contributes; a contributor.

cŏn-trist', *v.t.* To make sorrowful; to sadden. [Obs.]

cŏn-tris'tāte, *v.t.* [L. *contristatus*, pp. of *contristare*, to make sad.] To make sorrowful. [Obs.]

çon-tris-tā'tion, *n.* The act of making sad; sadness; dejection; sorrowfulness. [Obs.]

çon'trīte, *a.* [L. *contritus*, pp. of *conterere*, to bruise, rub; *con-*, together, and *terere*, to rub.]

1. Worn or bruised. [Obs.]

2. Broken-hearted for sin; deeply affected with grief and sorrow for having done wrong; humbled; penitent; as, a *contrite* sinner.

> A broken and a *contrite* heart, O God, thou wilt not despise. —Ps. li. 17.

çon'trīte, *n.* One who is thoroughly penitent.

çon'trite-ly, *adv.* In a contrite manner; with penitence.

çon'trite-ness, *n.* Contrition; deep sorrow and penitence for sin.

cŏn-tri'tion (-trish'un), *n.* 1. Attrition; the act of grinding or rubbing to powder. [Obs.]

2. Penitence; deep sorrow for sin; grief of heart for having done wrong.

Syn.—Penitence, sorrow, repentance, compunction, remorse.

çon-trit'ū-rāte, *v.t.*; contriturated, *pt., pp.*; contriturating, *ppr.* To pulverize or reduce to small particles; to triturate.

cŏn-trīv'ȧ-ble, *a.* Able to be contrived; capable of being planned, invented, or devised.

> Perpetual motion may seem easily *contrivable*. —Wilkins.

cŏn-trīv'ănce, *n.* 1. The act of inventing, devising, or planning.

> There is no work impossible to these *contrivances*. —Wilkins.

2. The thing invented or planned; disposition of parts or causes by design; arrangement; plan; scheme; artifice.

> Our bodies are made according to the most orderly *contrivance*. —Glanville.

Syn.—Appliance, mechanism, invention, project, device, design, ruse, trick.

cŏn-trīve', *v.t.*; contrived, *pt., pp.*; contriving, *ppr.* [ME. *contriven*, *controven*; OFr. *controver*, to find out, contrive; *con-*, and *trover*, to find.]

1. To invent; to devise; to plan; to project.

2. To carry to completion or success by scheming or using ingenuity; to manage; as, he *contrived* to pull through.

Syn.—Invent, form, arrange, frame, design, devise, scheme, plot.

cŏn-trīve', *v.i.* To form a plan; to scheme.

cŏn-trīve'ment, *n.* Contrivance; invention; scheme. [Obs.]

cŏn-trīv'ēr, *n.* An inventor; one who plans or devises; a schemer.

cŏn-trōl', *n.* [Fr. *contrôle*; OFr. *contrerole*; LL. *contrarotulum*, a counterroll or register; L. *contra*, against, and *rotula*, a roll.]

1. A counter-register; a duplicate book of account. [Obs.]

2. The act of controlling; the power which controls, regulates or guides; as, out of one's *control*; a board of *control*.

Syn.—Regulation, check, restraint, ascendancy, dominion, influence.

cŏn-trōl', *v.t.*; controlled, *pt., pp.*; controlling, *ppr.* 1. To keep under check by a counter-register or double account. [Obs.]

2. To exercise such an influence over (something) as to guide, direct, manage or restrain (it); to have under command; to check; as, to *control* a delegation; *control* the will.

> I feel my virtue struggling in my soul;
> But stronger passion does its power *control*. —Dryden.

Syn.—Restrain, rule, govern, direct, check, curb, overpower, counteract.

çon-trōl'-ex-per''i-ment, *n.* One of two or more similar experiments used as a verifier.

çon-trōl-lȧ-bil'i-ty, *n.* The quality of being controllable; controllableness.

cŏn-trōl'lȧ-ble, *a.* That may be controlled, checked, or restrained; subject to command.

> Passion is the drunkenness of the mind, and not always *controllable* by reason. —South.

cŏn-trōl'lȧ-ble-ness, *n.* Controllability.

cŏn-trōl'lēr, *n.* 1. A keeper of counterrolls. [Obs.]

2. One who controls or restrains; one that has the power or authority to govern or control.

> The great *Controller* of our fate
> Deigned to be man, and lived in low estate. —Dryden.

3. An officer having specified duties in connection with the management of financial affairs of any corporation, as a trust company or a city or state government. Three *controllers* are authorized by the national government, and a number of the states and larger cities have a similar officer; in this sense wrongly spelled *comptroller*.

4. In mechanics, any controlling device or part; (a) popularly, the current-interrupter of an electric car; (b) nautically, a block engaging links of a cable paying out from the locker to the hawse-hole.

çon-trōl'lēr-ship, *n.* The office of a controller.

çon-trōl'ment, *n.* 1. The power or act of controlling; the state of being restrained; control; restraint.

2. Opposition; resistance. [Obs.]

çon-trō-vēr'săl, *a.* Inclined or faced opposite ways; disputatious. [Obs.]

çon-trō-vēr'sȧ-ry, *a.* Disputatious. [Obs.]

çon'trō-vērse, *n.* Controversy. [Obs.]

çon'trō-vērse, *v.t.* To controvert. [Obs.]

çon'trō-vēr-sēr, *n.* One who disputes. [Obs.]

çon-trō-vēr'siăl (-shăl), *a.* Relating to disputes; as, a *controversial* discourse.

çon-trō-vēr'siăl-ist, *n.* One who carries on a controversy; a disputant.

çon-trō-vēr'siăl-ly, *adv.* In a controversial manner.

çon-trō-vēr'sion, *n.* Controversy. [Obs.]

çon'trō-vēr-sŏr, *n.* A disputant. [Obs.]

çon'trō-vēr-sy, *n.*; *pl.* **çon'trō-vēr-sies.** [L. *controversia*, from *controversus*, turned in an opposite direction; *contra*, against, and *versus*, pp. of *vertere*, to turn.]

1. A suit in law; contention incident to such suit.

2. A prolonged discussion or dispute, as one of a literary, scientific, or theological character; a disputation in writing; as, *controversy* over the Philippine friar question.

> *Controversies* engendered *controversies*. —Macaulay.

Syn.—Dispute.—A *dispute* is commonly oral, and is generally of short continuance. It may be defined as a temporary debate, and in its colloquial usage involves the idea of heat. A *controversy* may be oral, but is commonly in writing, and is frequently continued for a long period of time, many persons taking part in it.

çon'trō-vērt, *v.t.*; controverted, *pt., pp.*; controverting, *ppr.* [L. *contravertere*, to turn in an opposite direction; *contra*, against, and *vertere*, to turn.] To dispute; to oppose by reasoning; to contend against in words or writings; to deny and attempt to disprove or confute; to agitate or argue against; as, to *controvert* opinions or principles; to *controvert* the justness of a conclusion.

çon'trō-vēr-tēr, *n.* One who controverts; a controversial writer.

çon-trō-vēr'ti-ble, *a.* Capable of being disputed; disputable; not too evident to exclude difference of opinion; as, this is a *controvertible* point of law.

çon-trō-vēr'ti-bly, *adv.* In a controvertible manner.

çon'trō-vēr-tist, *n.* One who controverts; a disputant; one versed in or given to controversy or disputation.

> How unfriendly is the spirit of the *controvertist* to the discernment of the critic! —Campbell.

çon-tū'bēr-năl, çon-tū-bēr'ni-ăl, *a.* [L. *contubernalis*, from *contubernium*, companionship in a tent; *con-*, together, and *taberna*, a tent.] Having fellowship in a mess or lodging; living together familiarly. [Rare.]

çon-tū-mā'cious, *a.* [L. *contumax*, from *con-*, and *tumere*, to swell.]

1. Literally, swelling against; haughty; hence, obstinate; perverse; stubborn; inflexible; unyielding; disobedient; as, a *contumacious* child.

2. In law, wilfully disobedient to the orders of a court.

Syn.—Obstinate, obdurate, stubborn, disobedient, perverse, unyielding, headstrong.

çon-tū-mā'cious-ly, *adv.* Obstinately; stubbornly; perversely; in disobedience of orders.

çon-tū-mā'cious-ness, *n.* Obstinacy; perverseness; stubbornness; contumacy.

çon'tū-mȧ-cy, *n.* [L. *contumacia*, from *contumax*, haughty, stubborn; *con-*, and *tumere*, to swell up.]

1. Stubbornness; unyielding obstinacy; perverseness; inflexibility.

2. In law, a wilful contempt of, and disobedience to, any lawful summons or order of court, as a refusal to appear in court when legally summoned, or disobedience to its rules and orders.

Syn.—Stubbornness, obstinacy, perverseness, obduracy.

çon-tū-mē'li-ous, *a.* [L. *contumeliosus*, from *contumelia*, abuse, reproach.]

1. Haughty and contemptuous; disposed to utter reproach, or to insult; insolent; proudly rude; as, a *contumelious* person.

2. Reproachful; shameful; ignominious. [Obs.]

çon-tū-mē'li-ous-ly, *adv.* In a contumelious manner.

çon-tū-mē′li-ous-ness, *n.* Reproach; rudeness; contempt.

çon′tū-mē-ly, *n.* [L. *contumelia*, reproach, abuse.] Rudeness or reproach compounded of haughtiness and contempt; contemptuousness; insolence; contemptuous language or conduct.

> The oppressor's wrong, the proud man's *contumely* —Shak.

çŏn-tūşe′, *v.t.*; contused, *pt.*, *pp.*; contusing, *ppr.* [L. *contusus*, pp. of *contundere*, to bruise, beat together.]

1. To beat together; to bray. [Obs.]

2. To deface or injure, as by a blow, either with or without rupture of the enveloping membrane.

Contused wound; one in which the skin is broken; distinguished from a *contusion*.

çŏn-tū′şion, *n.* 1. The act of beating and bruising, or the state of being bruised; also, pulverization, as by braying.

2. In surgery, a bruise; a hurt or injury to the flesh or some part of the body by a blunt instrument, or by a fall, producing no breach or apparent wound.

çō-nun′drum, *n.* [Probably a corruption of L. *conandum*, a thing to be attempted, from *conari*, to attempt.]

1. A sort of riddle in which some odd resemblance is proposed for discovery between things quite unlike; a puzzling question asked in jest, the answer often involving a pun.

2. Any question or thing of a perplexing nature; as, life is full of *conundrums*.

çō-nūre′, *n.* [L. *conurus*, from Gr. *kōnos*, a cone, and *oura*, a tail.] One of several species of American parrots, genus *Conurus*, so named from their tapering tails, as the Carolina parrakeet.

çō′nus, *n.*; *pl.* **çō′nī**. [L.] 1. A cone or cone-shaped organ.

2. [C—] A genus of mollusks of the family *Conidæ*, having cone-shaped shells.

çon′ū-sȧ-ble, *a.* Liable to be tried or judged. [Obs.]

çon′ū-sănt, *a.* In law, knowing; having knowledge of; cognizant. [Obs.]

çon-ū-sor′, *n.* See *Cognizor*.

çon-vȧ-lesce′, *v.i.*; convalesced, *pt.*, *pp.*; convalescing, *ppr.* [L. *convalescere*, to begin to grow strong; *con-*, intens., and *valescere*, incept. of *valere*, to be strong.] To grow better after sickness; to recover health.

çon-vȧ-lesced′ (-lest′), *a.* Same as *Convalescent*. [Rare.]

çon-vȧ-les′cence, çon-vȧ-les′cen-cy, *n.* Renewal of health; the insensible recovery of health and strength after disease; the state of a body renewing its vigor after sickness or weakness; also, the period occupied in such recovery or renewal.

çon-vȧ-les′cent, *a.* 1. Recovering health and strength after sickness or debility.

2. Relating to convalescence.

çon-vȧ-les′cent, *n.* One recovering from illness or regaining strength.

çon-vȧ-les′cent-ly, *adv.* In the manner of one convalescing; with gradually increasing strength.

çon-val-lȧ-mā′rin, *n.* [*Convall-*, from *Convallaria*, and L. *amarus*, bitter.] In chemistry, a bitter, poisonous compound extracted from the lily-of-the-valley.

Çon-văl-lā′ri-ȧ, *n.* [L., from *convallis*, a valley inclosed on all sides; *con-*, together, and *vallis*, a valley.]

1. In botany, a genus of herbs of the lily family, *Liliaceæ*, having only one species, the lily-of-the-valley, *Convallaria majalis*.

2. [c—] The lily-of-the-valley.

çon-val-lā′rin, *n.* In chemistry, an acrid, crystalline glucoside extracted from the *Convallaria*.

çŏn-vec′tion, *n.* [L. *convectio*, from *convehere*, to bring together.] The act of carrying or conveying; specifically, the transference of heat by means of the upward motions of the particles of a liquid or gas which is heated from beneath. *Convection*-currents are thus produced, and the liquid or gas is soon heated all through. Electricity also is transferred or transmitted by means of such currents.

çŏn-vec′tive, *a.* Resulting from or caused by convection; as, a *convective* discharge of electricity.

çŏn-vec′tive-ly, *adv.* In a convective manner.

çŏn-vel′lent, *a.* [L. *convellens* (*-entis*), ppr. of *convellere*, to tear up, rend away; *con-*, together, and *vellere*, to pluck.] Having a tendency to uproot. [Obs.]

çon′vēn-ȧ-ble, *a.* In accord with convenance. [Obs.]

çŏn-vēn′ȧ-ble, *a.* That may be convened or assembled.

çon′vē-nănce, *n.* [Fr.] That which is proper, suitable, or in accordance with established customs.

çŏn-vēne′, *v.i*; convened, *pt.*, *pp.*; convening, *ppr.* [L. *convenire*, to come together, fit, join.]

1. To come together; to meet; to unite, as things. [Rare.]

> The rays of light converge and *convene* in the eyes. —Newton.

2. To come together; to meet in the same place; to assemble, implying publicity and a common purpose, as persons; as, the meeting *convened* in the schoolhouse.

Syn.—Meet, assemble, congregate.

çŏn-vēne′, *v.t.* 1. To cause to assemble; to call together; to convoke; as, to *convene* Congress.

2. To summon judicially to meet or appear.

çŏn-vēn′ēr, *n.* 1. One who convenes or meets with others. [Obs.]

2. One who convenes or calls a meeting; in Scotland, one appointed to call an organized body together, as a committee, of which he is generally chairman.

çŏn-vēn′ience (-yens), **çŏn-vēn′ien-cy**, *n.* [L. *convenientia*, from *convenire*, to come together, join, suit.]

1. The state or quality of being convenient; suitableness; appropriateness of place or of time; as, money returnable at one's *convenience*.

2. Absence of that which annoys or discommodes; freedom from difficulty; ease; as, a garment having more *convenience* than style.

3. That which gives ease or comfort; accommodation; that which is suited to wants or necessity; a handy adjunct; as, a flat with modern *conveniences*.

> A man alters his mind as the work proceeds, and will have this or that *convenience* more. —Dryden.

4. A meeting or coming together. [Obs.]

çŏn-vēn′ient, *a.* 1. Fit; suitable; proper.

> Some arts are peculiarly *convenient* to particular nations. —Tillotson.

2. Giving certain facilities or accommodation; as, a very *convenient* staircase.

3. Opportune; as, a *convenient* season.

4. At hand; handy. [Colloq.]

> Obstinate heretics used to be brought thither *convenient* for burning hard by. —Thackeray.

Syn.—Fit, suitable, adapted, fitted, suited, commodious.

çŏn-vēn′ient-ly, *adv.* In a convenient manner; without trouble or difficulty.

çon′vent, *n.* [Fr. *couvent*; L. *conventus*, from *convenire*, to come together, assemble.]

1. A gathering; a meeting. [Obs.]

2. An assembly of persons devoted to religion; a body of monks or nuns.

3. A house for persons devoted to religion; an abbey; a monastery; a nunnery.

çŏn-vent′, *v.t.* To call before a judge or judicature. [Obs.]

çŏn-vent′, *v.i.* To meet; to concur; also, to be handy. [Obs.]

çon-vent′iç-ăl, *a.* Of, relating, or pertaining to a convent.

çŏn-ven′ti-çle, *n.* [L. *conventiculum*, dim. of *conventus*, an assembly.]

1. A small gathering; an assembly; specifically, a small (often secret) meeting for religious worship.

2. In Great Britain, (a) originally, the schools of Wyclif; (b) later, the Dissenters from the Establishment in Queen Elizabeth's time, but not commonly used till the passing of the Uniformity Act in 1662, when nonconformist gatherings in England and the Covenanters in Scotland remaining separated from the established churches were so called.

3. The meeting-place of such a body.

çŏn-ven′ti-çle, *v.i.* To belong to a conventicle. [Rare.]

çŏn-ven′ti-çlēr, *n.* One who supports or frequents conventicles.

çŏn-ven′tion, *n.* [L. *conventio*, from *convenire*, to come together.]

1. The act of coming together; union; coalition.

2. A formal, recognized, or statutory meeting or assembly of men for civil or ecclesiastical purposes; particularly, an assembly of delegates or representatives for consultation on important concerns, civil, political, or ecclesiastical; specifically, (a) in the United States, a body of delegates convened for some political purpose, as to write or revise a constitution, or to nominate candidates and fix upon a platform; (b) [C—] in French history, the governing body of France which abolished royal rule (1792-1795).

3. One of the tacit rules of common conduct going to make up established procedure; a conventionality.

> An open condemnation of worldly *conventions*. —Coleridge.

4. In diplomacy, an agreement or contract between two parties; an agreement previous to a definitive treaty; as, a military *convention*.

5. In civil law, an agreement of persons to act in common.

çŏn-ven′tion-ăl, *a.* [LL. *conventionalis*, pertaining to an agreement, from *conventio*, an assembly, agreement.]

1. Stipulated; formed by agreement.

> *Conventional* services reserved by tenures on grants, made out of the crown or knights service. —Hale.

2. Arising out of custom or tacit agreement; as, a *conventional* use of language.

3. In the fine arts, (a) depending on accepted models or traditions, irrespective of the true principles of art, (b) conventionalized, as for decoration.

Syn.—Customary, usual, ordinary, stipulated, prevalent, social.

çŏn-ven′tion-ăl-işm, *n.* 1. That which is received or established by convention or agreement.

2. Clinging to conventional customs and rules; formalism.

3. In the fine arts, the theory or exemplification of conventional methods.

çŏn-ven′tion-ăl-ist, *n.* 1. One who is faithful to a treaty or agreement.

2. An adherent of the conventional.

çŏn-ven-tion-al′i-ty, *n.*; *pl.* **çŏn-ven-tion-al′i-tieş**. 1. The state or quality of being conventional; artificiality.

2. A conventional observance; a convention.

> It is strong and sturdy writing; and breaks up a whole legion of *conventionalities*. —Lamb.

çŏn-ven″tion-al-i-zā′tion, *n.* The practice or result of conventionalizing.

çŏn-ven′tion-ăl-īze, *v.t.*; conventionalized, *pt.*, *pp.*; conventionalizing, *ppr.* 1. To render conventional; to bring under the influence of conventional rules; to render observant of the conventional rules of society.

2. In the fine arts, to render or represent in accordance with conventional rules.

çŏn-ven′tion-ăl-ly, *adv.* In a conventional manner.

çŏn-ven′tion-ā-ry, *a.* Acting under contract; as, *conventionary* tenants. [Obs.]

çŏn-ven′tion-ēr, *n.* One who belongs to a convention.

çŏn-ven′tion-ist, *n.* One who makes a contract.

çŏn-ven′tū-ăl, *a.* Belonging to a convent; monastic; as, *conventual* priors.

Conventual church; one associated with a convent.

çŏn-ven′tū-ăl, *n.* 1. One who lives in a convent; a monk or nun.

2. [C—] In church history, one of a section of the Franciscan order, consisting of those members who consented to modify somewhat the severe discipline of the founder. They formed a separate organization in 1368.

çŏn-vērġe′, *v.t.*; converged, *pt.*, *pp.*; converging, *ppr.* To cause to tend to one point; to make to incline and approach nearer together; to refract to a common focal point.

çŏn-vērġe′, *v.i.* [LL. *convergere*, to incline together; *con-*, together, and *vergere*, to turn, bend.] To tend to one point; to incline and approach nearer together, and come to a focus; opposed to *diverge*.

> The mountains *converge* into a single ridge. —Jefferson.

çŏn-vēr′ġence, çŏn-vēr′ġen-cy, *n.* The quality of converging; tendency to one point.

çŏn-vēr′ġent, *a.* Tending to one point; approaching each other, as they proceed or are extended.

çŏn-vēr′ġi-nērved, *a.* In botany, a term used in describing the venation of leaves, to denote cases where the ribs form a curve, and meet at the point, as in *Plantago lanceolata*.

Converginerved Leaf.

çŏn-vēr′ġing, *a.* Tending to one point; approaching each other, as lines extended.

Converging rays; in optics, those rays of light, which, proceeding from different points of an object, tend toward a single point.

Converging series; in mathematics, a series of numbers proceeding without end, and having terms which gradually diminish in such a manner that no number whatsoever of them added together will be as great as a certain given number.

çŏn-vērs′ȧ-ble, *a.* Qualified for conversation; disposed to converse; sociable; free in discourse; affable.

çŏn-vērs′ȧ-ble-ness, *n.* The state or quality of being conversable.

çŏn-vērs′ȧ-bly, *adv.* In a conversable manner.

çon′vēr-sănce, *n.* Disposition to associate; habit of familiarity. [Rare.]

çon′vēr-sănt, *a.* [L. *conversans* (*-antis*), ppr. of *conversari*, to live with, converse, freq. of *convertere*; *con-*, together, and *vertere*, to turn.]

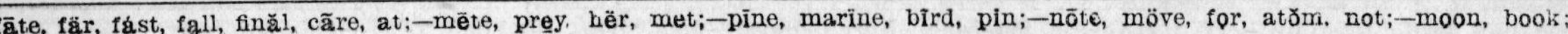

1. Having frequent or customary intercourse; intimately associating; well acquainted; followed by *with*; as, a student *conversant with* his instructors.

Never to be infected with delight,
Nor *conversant with* ease and idleness.—Shak.

2. Acquainted by familiar use or study; having a thorough understanding; proficient; followed by *with* or *among*; as, one *conversant with* politics.

3. Concerning; having concern or relation to; having for its object; followed by *about* or *with*.

Education is *conversant about* children.
—Wotton.

con-vērs'ănt, *n.* A converser.

con'vēr-sănt-ly, *adv.* In a conversant or familiar manner.

con-vēr-sā'tion, *n.* [Fr. *conversation*; L. *conversatio*, intercourse, conversation.]

1. General behavior; deportment. [Rare.]
2. Close fellowship or association; intimacy. [Rare.]
3. Carnal commerce, legitimate or illegitimate, but most usually the latter; as, criminal *conversation*.
4. A conversazione.
5. Familiar discourse; general intercourse of sentiments; chat; unrestrained talk, opposed to a formal conference.

What I mentioned in *conversation* was not a new thought. —Swift.

Syn.—Talk, intercourse, communion, communication, discourse, conference, colloquy.

con-vēr-sā'tion-ăl, *a.* Pertaining to conversation; done in mutual discourse or talk.

con-vēr-sā'tion-ăl-ist, *n.* One who excels in conversation.

con-vēr-sā'tioned, *a.* Having a certain behavior or deportment. [Obs.]

con-vēr-sā'tion-ism, *n.* A conversational term; a colloquialism.

con-vēr-sā'tion-ist, *n.* One who excels in or is given to conversation; a talker.

I must not quite omit the talking sage,
Kit-Cat, the famous *conversationist*.—Byron.

con-vēr'sȧ-tive, *a.* Conversable; social in habits; establishing intercourse.

con-ver-sȧ-zi-ō'ne, *n.*; *pl.* **con-ver-sȧ-zi-ō'nī** (-sät-si-ō'). [It.] A meeting for conversation, particularly on literary subjects.

con-vērse', *v.i.*; conversed, *pt.*, *pp.*; conversing, *ppr.* [ME. *conversen*; OFr. *converser*; L. *conversari*, to dwell, keep company with, freq. of *convertere*; *con-*, together, and *vertere*, to turn.]

1. To associate; to hold intercourse and be intimately acquainted; followed by *with*; as, to *converse with* nature.
2. To have sexual commerce. [Obs.]
3. To talk familiarly; to have free intercourse in mutual communication of thoughts and opinions; to convey thoughts reciprocally; followed by *with* before the person addressed, and *on* before the subject.

So she goes by him attended,
Hears him lovingly *converse*. —Tennyson.

Syn.—Talk, commune, communicate, confer, discourse, chat, speak.

con'vērse, *n.* 1. Conversation; familiar discourse or talk; free interchange of thoughts or opinions.

Formed by thy *converse* happily to steer
From grave to gay, from lively to severe.
—Pope.

2. Friendly intercourse; association; communion.
3. Sexual union. [Obs.]

con'vērse, *a.* Reversed; reciprocal; having the first and last parts transposed.

con'vērse, *n.* [L. *conversus*, pp. of *convertere*, to turn around; *con-*, together, and *vertere*, to turn.]

1. A part answering or corresponding to another, but differing from it in nature and required to make it complete; a reciprocating part; the complement; the counterpart; as, the hollows in a mold in which a medal has been cast are the *converse* of the parts of the medal in relief; often used incorrectly in the sense of the opposite, the contrary, the reverse.

2. In logic and mathematics, an opposite proposition; thus, after drawing a conclusion from something supposed, we invert the order, making the conclusion the supposition or premises, and draw from it what was first supposed; as, "truth is the best guide," would be the *converse* of "the best guide is truth"; and, "the area of a circle equals πR^2," would be the *converse* of "πR^2 equals the area of a circle."

con'vērse-ly, *adv.* With change of order; in a contrary order; reciprocally.

con-vērs'ēr, *n.* One who converses.

con-vēr'si-ble, *a.* Capable of conversion; reversible.

con-vēr'sion, *n.* 1. In general, a turning or change from one state to another; transmutation; as, a *conversion* of water into ice, or of food into chyle or blood.

2. In military affairs, (a) a change of front, as of a body of troops attacked on the flank; (b) an alteration, as of arms from one bore or style of bore to another.

3. In theology, the change of belief and life, either immediate or gradual, manifested by one forsaking unbelief, either active or apathetic, to take up the worship of God; change of heart.

4. A change in which one believes or advocates views at variance with those held in the past; particularly, a change from beliefs considered erroneous to those accepted as right.

That *conversion* will be suspected that apparently concurs with interest. —Johnson.

5. In law, the act of appropriating to private use; as, in trover and *conversion*.

Conversion of equations; in algebra, the reduction of equations by multiplication, or the manner of altering an equation when the quantity sought or any member of it is a fraction; the reducing of a fractional equation into an integral one.

Conversion of proportions; in mathematics, a term expressing the condition when of four proportionals it is inferred that the first is to its excess above the second as the third is to its excess above the fourth; and the four terms, when thus arranged, are said to be proportionals by conversion.

Conversion of propositions; in logic, a changing of the subject into the place of the predicate, and still retaining the quality of the proposition. [See *Converse*, n. 2.]

Conversion of St. Paul; a festival commemorative of St. Paul's conversion, held January 25, by the Anglican and Roman Catholic churches.

con-vēr'sive, *a.* Capable of being converted or changed; convertible. [Rare.]

con-vēr'sive, *a.* Conversable; social. [Rare.]

con-vērt', *v.t.*; converted, *pt.*, *pp.*; converting, *ppr.* [L. *convertere*, to turn round, turn toward; *con-*, together, and *vertere*, to turn.]

1. To turn; to move. [Obs.]
2. To change or turn into another substance or form; as, to *convert* gases into water, or water into ice.
3. To change from one state to another; as, to *convert* a barren waste into a fruitful field; to *convert* a wilderness into a garden; to *convert* rude savages into civilized men.
4. In theology, to effect the conversion of or change of heart in.
5. To change or turn from one belief to another, or from one party or sect to another; as, to *convert* one to socialism; to *convert* a bigot to liberalism.
6. To turn from one use or destination to another; as, to *convert* liberty into an engine of oppression.
7. To appropriate or apply to one's own use or personal benefit, implying dishonesty or illegality; as, to *convert* public property to one's own use.
8. In logic, to transform by conversion.
9. In ordnance, to transform, as the bore of a gun.
10. To turn into another language. [Obs.]

Converted iron; iron or steel which has been submitted to carburization by cementation.

con-vērt', *v.i.* To turn or be changed; to undergo a change.

The love of wicked friends *converts* to fear;
That fear, to hate. —Shak.

con'vērt, *n.* 1. A person who is converted from one opinion or practice to another; a person who renounces one creed, religious system, or party, and embraces another.

2. In theology, one who is turned from sin to holiness.

3. In monasteries, a lay friar or brother, admitted to the service of the house, without orders, and not allowed to sing in the choir.

Syn.—Disciple, neophyte, proselyte, apostate, renegade.

con-vēr-tend', *n.* Something to be converted; specifically, in logic, a proposition to undergo, or that has undergone, conversion.

con-vērt'ēr, *n.* 1. One who converts; one who makes converts.

2. In the Bessemer process, the vessel employed for the production of steel directly from cast-iron. It is a pear-shaped vessel lined with refractory material, axially swiveled upon trunnions, so as to pour out the molten steel when the process is complete; also spelled *convertor*.

3. In electricity, a transformer.

4. In the cotton trade, a wholesale dealer who has the gray goods converted into the finished cloth at his own risk and expense.

con-vērt-i-bil'i-ty, *n.* The quality or condition of being convertible.

con-vērt'i-ble, *a.* 1. That may be changed; susceptible of change; transmutable; transformable.

Minerals are not *convertible* into another species, though of the same genus.—Harvey.

2. So much alike that one may be used for another; interchangeable.
3. In logic, capable of conversion.
4. In commerce, exchangeable for gold, as currency; by extension, exchangeable for money, as bonds.

con-vērt'i-ble-ness, *n.* Convertibility.

con-vērt'i-bly, *adv.* Reciprocally; with interchange of terms.

con'vērt-ite, *n.* A convert. [Obs.]

con'vex, *a.* [L. *convexus*, vaulted, arched; pp. of *convehere*, to bring together; *con-*, together, and *vehere*, to bring.] Rising or swelling on the exterior surface into a spherical or round form; opposed to *concave*; as, a *convex* mirror or lens.

con'vex, *n.* A convex body; the rounded form of a convex body.

con'vexed (-vext) *a.* Made convex; protuberant in a spherical form.

Convex or Plano-convex Lens.

con-vex'ed-ly, *adv.* In a convex form.

con-vex'ed-ness, *n.* Convexity.

con-vex'i-ty, *n.*; *pl.* **con-vex'i-ties**. 1. The rounded surface of a convex body.

2. The state of being convex.

con'vex-ly, *adv.* In a convex form; as, a body *convexly* conical.

con'vex-ness, *n.* Convexity.

con-vex'ō-con'cāve, *a.* Convex on one side and concave on the other; having the hollow on the inside corresponding to the convex surface.

con-vex'ō-con'vex, *a.* Convex on both sides; also called *double-convex*.

Convexo-concave Lens.

con-vex'ō-plāne, *a.* Plano-convex.

con-vey', *v.t.*; conveyed (-vād), *pt.*, *pp.*; conveying, *ppr.* [ME. *conveyen*, *conveien*; OF. *conveier*, to escort, convoy; LL. *conviare*, to accompany on the way; *con-*, together, and *via*, way.]

1. To carry, bear, or transport, either by land or water or in air.

Convexo-convex Lens.

There was one *conveyed* out of my house yesterday in this basket.
—Shak.

2. To pass or cause to pass; to transmit; as, to *convey* a right or an estate from father to son.

3. In law, to transfer; to pass (a title to anything) from one person to another, as by deed, assignment, or otherwise; as, to *convey* lands by bargain and sale.

4. To carry as a medium; as, air *conveys* sound; words *convey* ideas.

Full well the busy whisper, circling round,
Convey'd the dismal tidings when he frown'd.
—Goldsmith.

5. To manage; to carry on. [Obs.]

I will *convey* the business as I shall find means.
—Shak.

6. To impart; to communicate.

To *convey* our thoughts in ardent and intense phrases. —Addison.

7. To steal; synonymous with *lift* in the Scotch phrase, to lift cattle. [Obs.]

Convey, the wise it call. Steal!—foh, a fico for the phrase. —Shak.

con-vey', *v.i.* To play the thief. [Old Slang.]

con-vey'ȧ-ble, *a.* That may be conveyed or transferred

con-vey'ănce, *n.* 1. The act of conveying; transportation; carriage; transference.

2. The means, instrument, or vehicle in which anything is conveyed or transported from one place to another; a carriage.

Bethink you of some *conveyance*. —Shak.

3. In law, (a) assignment of property by deed or otherwise; (b) the instrument of such transfer; specifically, a deed.

4. The act of removing; removal; conduct; convoy. [Obs.]

Mad'st quick *conveyance* with her good aunt Anne. —Shak.

5. Management; artifice; secret practices [Obs.]

Since Henry's death, I fear there is *conveyance*.
—Shak.

con-vey'ăn-cēr, *n.* One whose occupation is to draw conveyances of property, deeds, etc.

con-vey'ăn-cing, *n.* The act or practice of drawing deeds, leases, or other writings for transferring the title to property from one person to another, of investigating the title of the vendors and purchasers of property, and of drawing deeds and contracts for the definition and protection of the rights or liabilities of individuals.

çŏn-vey′ẽr, *n.* 1. One who or that which conveys; specifically, in mechanics, any appliance used to move substances or objects from one place to another: also spelled *conveyor.*

2. A tricky fellow; a thief. [Obs.]

çŏn-vi′ci-āte (-vish′i-), *v.t.* To reproach. [Obs.]

çon-vi-cin′i-ty, *n.*; *pl.* **çon-vi-cin′i-tieṣ.** Neighborhood; vicinity.

çŏn-vi′cious (-vish′us), *a.* Railing; reproaching. [Obs.]

çŏn-viçt′, *v.t.*; convicted, *pt., pp.*; convicting, *ppr.* [L. *convictus*, pp. of *convincere*, to overcome, conquer; *con-*, intens., and *vincere*, to conquer.]

1. To prove or find guilty of a crime charged; to determine or decide to be guilty, as by the verdict of a jury, by confession, or other legal decision; as, the jury *convicted* the prisoner of felony.

2. To convince of sin; to prove or determine to be guilty, as by the conscience.

3. To confute.

4. To show by proof or evidence. [Obs.]

çŏn-viçt′, *a.* Proved or found guilty. [Obs.]

çon′viçt, *n.* A person proved or found guilty of a crime alleged against him, either by the verdict of a jury or other legal decision; in popular language, commonly a person undergoing penal servitude.

Syn.—Malefactor, culprit, felon, criminal.

çŏn-viçt′i-ble, *a.* Capable of being found guilty or convicted.

çŏn-viç′tion, *n.* 1. The act of proving, finding, or determining to be guilty of an offense; specifically, in law, the act of finding or the state of being found guilty of crime before any legal tribunal, as a jury.

2. Strong belief on the ground of satisfactory evidence, without any implication of previous error; the state of having such belief; also, a proposition sought to make up such belief; as, a *conviction* of right; laboring under wrong *convictions.*

3. In theology, the awakening of conscience preceding conversion; as, under *conviction* of sin.

4. The act of convincing of error or the truth of what is alleged; confutation. [Rare.]

çon′viçt-iṣm, *n.* Any system of disposition of convicts.

çŏn-viçt′ive, *a.* Having the power to convince or convict. [Rare.]

çŏn-viçt′ive-ly, *adv.* In a convincing manner.

çŏn-viçt′ive-ness, *n.* Power of convicting.

çŏn-viç′tŏr, *n.* [L. *convictor*, from *convivere*, to live together.] A messmate; a table associate.

çŏn-vince′, *v.t.*; convinced, *pt., pp.*; convincing, *ppr.* [L. *convincere*, to overcome, convict of error; *con-*, intens., and *vincere*, to conquer.]

1. To persuade or satisfy by evidence; to subdue the opposition of (the mind) to truth, or to what is alleged, and compel (it) to yield assent; as, to *convince* a man of his errors; or to *convince* him of the truth.

> Proofs as might enable them to *convince* others. —Atterbury.

2. To convict. [Obs.]

3. To prove; also, to overpower. [Obs.]

Syn.—Persuade.—To *convince* a person is to satisfy his understanding as to the truth of a certain statement; to *persuade* him is to influence his feelings or will.

çŏn-vince′ment, *n.* Conviction. [Rare.]

çŏn-vin′cẽr, *n.* One who or that which convinces.

çŏn-vin′ci-ble, *a.* 1. Capable of conviction.

2. Capable of being disproved or refuted. [Obs.]

çŏn-vin′cing-ly, *adv.* In a convincing manner.

çŏn-vin′cing-ness, *n.* The power of convincing.

çŏn-viv′ăl, *a.* Convivial. [Obs.]

çŏn-vive′, *v.i.* To feast. [Obs.]

çon′vive, *n.* One entertained. [Obs.]

çŏn-viv′i-ăl, *a.* [L. *convivialis*, from *convivium*, a feast, from *convivere*; *con-*, together, and *vivere*, to live.] Relating to a feast or entertainment; implying mirth and good-fellowship; festal; social; jovial; as, a *convivial* meeting.

çŏn-viv′i-ăl-ist, *n.* One of convivial habits.

çŏn-viv-i-al′i-ty, *n.*; *pl.* **çŏn-viv-i-al′i-tieṣ.** 1. The good humor or mirth indulged in at entertainments of a convivial character.

2. A convivial spirit or disposition.

çŏn-viv′i-ăl-ly, *adv.* In a convivial manner.

çon′vō-çāte, *v.t.*; convocated, *pt., pp.*; convocating, *ppr.* [L. *convocatus*, pp. of *convocare*, to call together; *con-*, together, and *vocare*, to call.] To convoke; to call or summon to meet; to assemble by summons. [Obs.]

çon-vō-çā′tion, *n.* 1. An assembly.

2. The act of calling or assembling by summons.

3. [C—] In the Church of England, an assembly of the clergy, by their representatives, to consult on ecclesiastical affairs.

House of Convocation; in the University of Oxford, the assembly which enacts and amends laws and statutes, elects burgesses, many professors, and other officers, etc.

Syn.—Meeting, assembly, congregation, congress, diet, convention, synod, council.

çon-vō-çā′tion-ăl, *a.* Pertaining to a convocation. [Rare.]

çon-vō-çā′tion-ist, *n.* In the Church of England, one who supports Convocation; an advocate of Convocation; one favorable to the revival of its powers.

çŏn-vōke′, *v.t.*; convoked, *pt., pp.*; convoking, *ppr.* [L. *convocare*, to call together; *con-*, together, and *vocare*, to call.] To call together; to summon to meet; to assemble by summons.

Syn.—Summon, assemble, convene, call, collect, muster.

çon′vō-lūte, çon′vō-lū-ted, *a.* [L. *convolutus*, pp. of *convolvere*, to roll together.] Rolled together, or one part on another, as the sides or margins of nascent leaves in plants, or as the petals and stigmas in *Crocus.*

çon-vō-lū′tion, *n.* 1. The act of rolling or winding together, or one thing on another; a winding motion.

> O'er the calm sky in *convolution* swift
> The feathered eddy floats. —Thomson.

2. The state of being rolled upon itself or rolled or wound together; a turn or winding; a fold; as, the *convolutions* of the brain, of the intestines, of a vine.

> The *convolutions* of a smooth-lipped shell. —Wordsworth.

3. In anatomy, a fold, twist, or coil of any organ; specifically, one of the convex parts of the brain marked off by furrows.

çŏn-volve′, *v.t.*; convolved, *pt., pp.*; convolving, *ppr.* [L. *convolvere*, to roll together.] To roll or wind together; to roll (one part) on another.

Çon-vol-vū-lā′cē-æ, *n.pl.* [L. *convolvulus*, from *convolvere*, to roll together, and *-aceæ*.] A natural order of monopetalous exogens, consisting of herbs or shrubs. About a thousand species have been described from temperate and tropical countries.

çon-vol-vū-lā′ceous, *a.* Of or pertaining to the *Convolvulaceæ.*

çŏn-vol′vū-liç, çŏn-vol-vū-lin′iç, *a.* Specifying or pertaining to plants of the genus *Convolvulus.*

çŏn-vol′vū-lin, *n.* A colorless, transparent resin contained in jalap-root.

Çŏn-vol′vū-lus, *n.* [L., from *convolvere*, to roll together.]

1. Bindweed, a genus of plants, natural order *Convolvulaceæ*, consisting of slender, twining herbs, with milky juice.

2. [c—] Any plant of this or an allied genus.

The Jalap Convolvulus (*Exogonium purga*).

çŏn-voy′, *v.t.*; convoyed, *pt., pp.*; convoying, *ppr.* [Fr. *convoyer*; OFr. *convoier*, to escort, convoy; LL. *conviare*, to accompany on the way; *con-*, with, and *via*, way.]

1. To accompany for protection, either by sea or land; as, ships of war *convoyed* the Jamaica fleet.

2. To convey. [Obs.]

çon′voy, *n.* 1. A protecting force accompanying ships or property on their way from place to place, either by sea or land; (a) by sea, a ship or ships of war which accompany merchantmen for protection from an enemy; (b) by land, any body of troops which accompany provisions, ammunition, or other property, for protection.

2. The ship or fleet conducted and protected; that which is conducted by a protecting force; that which is convoyed.

3. The act of attending for defense.

4. Conveyance. [Obs.]

5. A carriage-brake.

çŏn-vul′sănt, *a.* and *n.* I. *a.* Causing convulsions.

II. *n.* Anything that produces convulsions.

çŏn-vulse′, *v.t.*; convulsed (-vulst), *pt., pp.*; convulsing, *ppr.* [L. *convulsus*, pp. of *convellere*, to tear up, wrench away; *con-*, together, and *vellere*, to pluck, pull.]

1. To draw or contract, as the muscular parts of an animal body; to affect by irregular spasms; as, the whole frame may be *convulsed* by agony, or by laughter.

2. To shake; to affect by violent, irregular action.

> *Convulsing* heaven and earth. —Thomson.

Syn.—Agitate, disturb, shake, tear, rend.

çŏn-vul′sion, *n.* 1. In medicine, an unnatural, violent, and involuntary contraction of the muscular parts of an animal body.

2. Any violent and irregular motion; a great agitation; tumult; commotion; as, political *convulsions.*

Syn.—Agitation, commotion, tumult, disturbance, turmoil, tremor, perturbation, throe.

çŏn-vul′sion-ăl, *a.* Subject to convulsions; convulsionary. [Rare.]

çŏn-vul′sion-ā-ry, *a.* and *n.* I. *a.* Pertaining to convulsion; convulsive.

II. *n.* [C—] In church history, one of a body of French fanatics of the eighteenth century, who experienced convulsive spasms under alleged supernatural influence.

Çŏn-vul′sion-ist, *n.* 1. A Convulsionary.

2. [c—] In geology, a catastrophist.

çŏn-vul′sive, *a.* Causing, resulting from, or characterized by convulsions; as, *convulsive* strife; *convulsive* rage; *convulsive* motions.

çŏn-vul′sive-ly, *adv.* With violent shaking or agitation; in a convulsive manner.

çō′ny, *n.*; *pl.* **çō′nieṣ.** [ME. *cony, conyng, conig*; OFr. *conin, counin*, from L. *cuniculus*, a rabbit.]

1. A rabbit; especially, the *Lepus cuniculus* of Europe.

2. The daman, or *cony* of Scripture.

> The high hills are a refuge for the wild goats; and the rocks for the *conies.* —Ps. civ. 18.

3. The little chief hare or pika, *Lagomys princeps.*

4. The fur of rabbits or *conies*, formerly much used in England.

5. A simpleton; a dupe. [Obs.]

6. In heraldry, the representation of a rabbit used as a bearing.

7. Any one of various fishes, as the *Epinephelus apua*, or hind, of the West Indies, and, in England, the burbot. Also spelled *coney* and *conny.*

çō′ny-çatch, *v.i.* In the slang of thieves, to cheat; to bite; to trick. [Obs.]

çō′ny-çatch″ẽr, *n.* A thief; a cheat. [Obs.]

çō′ny-çatch″ing, *n.* Banter. [Obs.]

çon′y-lēne, *n.* [*Conine* and *acetylene.*] A pungent and oily hydrocarbon, C_8H_{14}, resembling conine.

çon′y-rine, *n.* A derivative of conine, being an oily compound without color.

çōō, *v.i.*; cooed, *pt., pp.*; cooing, *ppr.* [Imitative of the sound.]

1. To cry, or make a low sound, like the repeated calls of pigeons or doves.

2. To act in an affectionate way; as, they bill and *coo* like youthful lovers.

çō″-ob-li-gŏr′, *n.* In law, one jointly obligated with another.

çōō′ee, çōō′ey, *n.* A peculiar, penetrating cry or call of the Australian aborigines, an imitation being in general use among Australian colonists, as a means of attracting attention or signaling. The last syllable is prolonged and the call carries a great distance in the bush.

çōō′ee, çōō′ey, *v.i.*; cooeed *or* cooeyed, *pt., pp.*; cooeeing *or* cooeying, *ppr.* To call out *cooee* after the manner of the natives, as a signal or to attract attention. [Australian.]

çōō′ing, *a.* Uttering a low sound, as a dove.

çōō′-in-new′, *n.* [Australian.] An Australian tree, the *Gmelina Leichhardtii*, yielding a fine-grained timber much used for flooring and decking.

çook, *v.t.*; cooked (kookt), *pt., pp.*; cooking, *ppr.* [ME. *coken*, from L. *coquere*, to cook.]

1. To prepare, as food for the table, by boiling, roasting, baking, broiling, stewing, frying, etc.; to dress, as meat or vegetables, for eating.

2. To prepare for any purpose; hence, to tamper with; to alter or garble; as, to *cook* a report; often with *up*; as, to *cook up* a story. [Colloq.]

To cook one's goose; to spoil one's plans; to circumvent; to destroy or ruin. [Slang.]

çook, *v.i.* To make food ready for the table; to do the work of a cook; as, to *cook* for a living.

çōōk, *v.t.* To pitch; to throw. [Prov. Eng. Obs.]

çōōk, *v.i.* To make the noise of the cuckoo. [Rare.]

çook, *n.* 1. One whose occupation is to prepare food for the table; one who dresses or cooks meat or vegetables for eating.

2. In zoölogy, the European fish called the red wrasse, *Labrus mixtus*; also called the *cook-conner* and *cook-wrasse.*

çook′book, *n.* A book containing directions for cooking, recipes for various dishes, and other useful information for cooks.

çook′ee, *n.* [Colloq.] 1. A female cook. [Rare.]

2. An assistant to the cook in a lumber camp. [Local, U. S.]

çook′ẽr-y, *n.* 1. The art or the practice of dressing and preparing food for the table; as, *cookery* has become an art.

2. Cooked dishes; cooking. [Rare.]

3. A dainty or delicacy. [Obs.]

4. Material for cooking. [Obs.]

5. A place for cooking.

çook′ey, çook′ie, *n.* See *Cooky.*

çook′house, *n.* A ship's galley.

çook′ing, *a.* and *n.* I. *a.* Of or pertaining to cookery; as, a *cooking* utensil.

II. *n.* The art or process of preparing food for

consumption; cookery; as, good *cooking* is true economy.

çook′māid, *n.* A female servant or maid who dresses provisions.

çook′rṑom, *n.* A room for cookery; a kitchen; in ships, a galley or caboose.

çook′shop, *n.* An eating house; a place where cooked food is sold.

çook′y, *n.*; *pl.* **çook′ieṣ.** [D. *koekje*, dim. of *koek*, a cake.] A thin, crisp cake, usually sugared or spiced and cut in fancy or circular shapes before baking.

çṑol, *a.*; *comp.* cooler; *superl.* coolest. [ME. *cool*, *cole*; AS. *cōl*, cool, from *calan*, to be cold.]

1. Moderately cold; of a temperature between hot and cold; as, *cool* winds; *cool* water.

2. Not ardent or zealous; not angry; not fond; not excited by passion of any kind; indifferent; self-possessed; as, a *cool* friend; a *cool* temper; a *cool* lover.

3. Not hasty; deliberate; as, a *cool* purpose; a *cool* deception.

4. Impudent in a deliberate way; selfish; ignorant or negligent of matters of propriety; as, *cool* behavior.

5. Not retaining heat; light; as, a *cool* dress.

6. Exhibiting a cold demeanor, indifference, or dislike; as, a *cool* manner.

7. A term applied to money, values, etc., to emphasize their amount; as, he lost a *cool* million; her costume cost a *cool* thousand. [Colloq.]

Syn.—Calm, dispassionate, self-possessed, repulsive, composed, frigid, alienated, impudent, cold, fresh.

çṑol, *v.t.*; cooled, *pt.*, *pp.*; cooling, *ppr.* 1. To allay heat in; to make cool or cold; to reduce the temperature of; as, ice *cools* water.

> Send Lazarus, that he may dip the tip of his finger in water, and *cool* my tongue.
> —Luke xvi. 24.

2. To moderate excitement or intensity of; to allay, as passion of any kind; to calm or abate; to moderate; to render indifferent; as, to *cool* his ire.

To cool one's heels; to wait long for admission or notice; to be detained in attendance. [Colloq.]

çṑol, *v.i.* 1. To become less hot; to lose heat.

2. To lose the heat of excitement or passion; to become less ardent, angry, zealous, or affectionate; to become more moderate; as, let your temper *cool*.

çṑol, *n.* A moderate state of cold; moderate temperature between hot and cold; as, the *cool* of the day; the *cool* of the morning or evening.

çṑol′-çup, *n.* A beverage that is cooling.

çṑol′ẽr, *n.* 1. That which cools; anything which abates heat or excitement.

2. Any vessel, receptacle, or apparatus in which liquids or other things are cooled; as, a water-*cooler*.

3. A prison; a jail. [Slang.]

çṑo′ley, çṑo′lie, *n.* Same as *Coulee*.

çṑol′-head″ed, *a.* Having a temper not easily excited; free from passion.

çṑol′-head″ed-ness, *n.* The state or quality of being cool-headed.

çṑo′lie, çṑo′ly, *n.*; *pl.* **çṑo′lieṣ.** [Anglo-Ind.] In the East Indies, a porter or carrier. The term is also extended to emigrant laborers from India, China, and other eastern countries, who are introduced into the West India islands, British Guiana, Mauritius, and other European colonies.

çṑol′ing, *a.* Adapted to cool and refresh; as, a *cooling* drink.

Cooling card; a setback; hence, figuratively, something to dampen one's hopes or ardor.

çṑol′ish, *a.* Somewhat cool.

çṑol′ly, *a.* Same as *Coolish*. [Obs.]

çṑol′ly, *adv.* 1. Without heat or sharp cold.

2. In a cool or indifferent manner; not cordially; without passion or ardor; as, he was *coolly* received at court.

3. Without haste; calmly; deliberately; as, the design was formed *coolly*, and executed with firmness.

4. Nonchalantly; audaciously; impudently; as, he *coolly* stepped by the servant at the door. [Colloq.]

çṑol′ness, *n.* 1. A moderate degree of cold; a temperature between cold and heat; as, the *coolness* of the summer evening; a moderate degree, or a want of passion, ardor, or zeal; indifference; want of affection or cordiality; as, they parted with *coolness*.

2. Calmness; deliberateness; self-possession.

3. Quiet and unabashed impudence. [Colloq.]

çṑol′-tank″ărd, *n.* An old English spiced beverage of various composition.

çṑo′lung, *n.* The native name of the East Indian crane; also spelled *coolen*.

çṑol′weed, *n.* Richweed or clearweed.

çṑol′wŏrt, *n.* A perennial herb of the United States, more commonly known as *false miterwort*.

çṑo′ly, *n.* Same as *Coolie*.

çṑom, *n.* [Scot. and Prov. Eng.] Dust; refuse; soot; also, the greasy matter that works out of the naves or boxes of carriage wheels.

çṑomb, *n.* See fourth *Comb*.

çṑon, *n.* 1. An American abbreviation of racoon.

2. A negro. [Slang.]

çṑon′tie, çṑon′ty, *n.* [Am. Ind.] The only plant of the cycad family native to the United States. It is found in Florida, also the West Indies, and yields a kind of sago from its stems.

çṑop, *n.* [ME. *coop*, *coppe*, a cup; D. *kuip*, a tub; M.H.G. *kuofe*; G. *kufe*, a coop, tub; L. *copa*, *cupa*, a tub, vat, cask; Gr. *kypē*; Sans. *kūpa*, a pit, well, vat.]

1. A pen; an inclosed place for small animals, particularly, a box with slats or netting used to confine fowls, or a hen while her brood is allowed to range.

2. A shanty; a rickety dwelling or room. [Colloq.]

3. A barrel or cask for liquors. [Obs.]

4. A tumbrel, or close cart. [Scot.]

çṑop, *v.t.*; cooped (köpt), *pt.*, *pp.*; cooping, *ppr.* 1. To put in a coop; to confine in a coop; hence, to shut up or confine in a narrow compass; usually followed by *up* or *in*.

> They are *cooped in* close by the laws of the country.
> —Locke.

2. To repair, as a cooper. [Obs.]

Syn.—Cage, inclose, imprison, confine, hem in.

çṑo-pee′, *n.* Same as *Coupee*. [Obs.]

çṑop′ẽr, *n.* 1. One whose occupation is to make and repair barrels, hogsheads, butts, tubs, and casks of various kinds.

2. A popular English beverage, consisting of one-half stout and one-half porter.

çṑop′ẽr, *v.t.*; coopered, *pt.*, *pp.*; coopering, *ppr.* To do the work of a cooper upon; to mend or put in order, as casks, barrels, etc.

çṑop′ẽr-āġe, *n.* 1. The work or business of a cooper.

2. A place where coopers' work is done.

3. The price paid for coopers' work.

çō-op′ẽr-ănt, *a.* Acting together; coöperating.

çō-op′ẽr-āte, *v.i.*; coöperated, *pt.*, *pp.*; coöperating, *ppr.* [LL. *cooperatus*, pp. of *cooperari*, to work together, *co-*, with, and *operari*, to work, from *opus*, *operis*, work.]

1. To act or operate jointly with another or others, to the same end; to work or labor with mutual efforts to promote the same object; as, Russia *coöperated* with Great Britain, Austria, and Prussia, to reduce the power of Bonaparte.

2. To act together; to unite in producing the same effect; as, natural and moral events often *coöperate*.

Syn.—Aid, assist, help, work together.

çō-op-ẽr-ā′tion, *n.* 1. The act of working or operating together to one end; joint operation; concurrent effort or labor; as, the *coöperation* of the understanding and the will.

2. In political economy, the association of any number of individuals for the purpose of engaging in the production or distribution of commodities, thus enabling the members of such organization to save for themselves the profits that would otherwise go to the employer.

çō-op′ẽr-ā-tive, *a.* Operating jointly to the same end.

Coöperative society; a joint-stock, limited-liability society, formed for the purpose of providing the members with genuine goods at prime cost, with the simple cost of management added. Such societies have a store or stores, the profits of which are divided among the members in proportion to the amount of their purchases.

çō-op′ẽr-ā-tŏr, *n.* One who works jointly with others to promote the same end.

2. A member of a coöperative society.

çṑop′ẽr-ing, *n.* The manufacturing or repairing of casks, barrels, etc.; cooperage.

çṑop′ẽr's-wood, *n.* A wood much used for barrel staves, etc., obtained from Australian trees of the buckthorn family, particularly the *Alphitonia excelsa*.

çṑop′ẽr-y, *a.* Pertaining to a cooper; made by a cooper. [Obs.]

çṑop′ẽr-y, *n.* A cooper's trade.

çō-opt′, *v.t.*; coöpted, *pt.*, *pp.*; coöpting, *ppr.* [L. *cooptare*, to choose, elect; *co-*, *cum*, with, and *optare*, to choose.] To choose by united action; to elect into some body of which the electors are members.

çō-op′tāte, *v.t.* To coöpt; to select by common choice. [Rare.]

çō-op-tā′tion, *n.* 1. Adoption; assumption. [Obs.]

2. Selection; mutual choice; election; particularly, the election of a person to some body by the members thereof.

çō-or-dāin′, *v.t.*; coördained, *pt.*, *pp.*; coördaining, *ppr.* To appoint together with another.

çō-or′di-năn̄ce, *n.* Joint ordinance.

çō-or′di-nāte, *a.* 1. Being of equal order, or of the same rank or degree; not subordinate; as, two courts of *coördinate* jurisdiction

2. In mathematics, pertaining to, or involving a system of coördinates.

çō-or′di-nāte, *v.t.*; coördinated, *pt.*, *pp.*; coördinating, *ppr.* [LL. *coordinatus*, pp. of *coordinare*, to arrange together; *co-*, with, and *ordinare*, from *ordo* (*ordinis*), order.]

1. To place in the same rank; to make of equal value.

2. To arrange (a set of things), as in proper and relative order; to harmonize; to combine for a common action or purpose.

> The founders of universities held the theory that . . . the business of philosophy was to interpret and *coördinate* these two.
> —Huxley.

çō-or′di-nāte, *n.* 1. A person or thing of the same rank with another, and working or employed to the same end.

2. In mathematics, a member of a system of lines, to which points under consideration are referred, and by means of which their position is determined. *Coördinates* determine the position of a point either in space or in a plane which is understood to contain all the figure under consideration. They determine position by straight lines only, or by a straight line and angles; in the latter case they are called *polar coördinates*. When *coördinates* are at right angles to each other they are called rectangular, and when they make any other angle with each other they are called oblique. In plane geometry, one of the *coördinates* is called the abscissa, and the other the ordinate. In the figure, C D and B A are coördinates, the first being an abscissa, to which, through the point D, is drawn the ordinate B A. The *coördinates* of a star are its distances from the pole of the heavens and from the meridian of the place of observation, measured in degrees of the respective circles.

Geographical coördinates; latitude and longitude; also, the height above the sea-level regarded as a third coördinate.

Spherical coördinates; the distances from two great circles of a sphere which locate a point on its surface; quantities corresponding to latitude and longitude.

Trilinear coördinates; the distances of a point from the sides of a triangle, called the fixed triangle of reference.

çō-or′di-nāte-ly, *adv.* In a coördinate manner.

çō-or′di-nāte-ness, *n.* The state of being coördinate; equality of rank and authority.

çō-or-di-nā′tion, *n.* 1. The state of holding equal rank, or of standing in the same relation to something higher or lower; the condition of being coördinate.

> In the high court of Parliament there is a rare *coördination* of power.
> —Howell.

2. The act or process of making coördinate; the act of arranging a set of things, each in its relative order.

çō-or′di-nā-tive, *a.* Indicating coördination.

çṑo′rong, *n.* The native name of a tree of the pine family found in Australia; the *Frenela robusta*. Its wood is valuable for the construction of fine furniture, etc., and is much used for veneers, especially the wood of the root.

çō-os′si-fȳ, *v.i.*; coössified, *pt.*, *pp.*; coössifying, *ppr.* [*Co-*, and Fr. *ossifier*, from L. *os* (*ossis*), a bone.] To become united by ossification; to form one bone; as, several bony elements *coössify* in man to form the sphenoid bone.

çṑot, *n.* [ME. *coote*; D. *koet*; W. *cwtiar*; *cwta*, bobtailed, and *iar*, a hen.]

Common Coot (*Fulica atra*).

1. A water fowl of the genus *Fulica*, found in most parts of the world, frequenting lakes and other still waters. The common *coot* has an extension of the culmen of the bill, a black body, and lobated toes, and is about fifteen inches in length. It makes its nest among rushes, with grass and reeds, floating on the water. The common European and Asiatic species is the bald *coot*, the *Fulica atra*; the North American *coot* being recognized as a distinct species, the *Fulica americana*.

2. A sea-duck of the genus *Œdemia*, a scoter.

3. The guillemot.

4. A foolish person; a dolt. [Colloq.]

çṑot′ẽr, *n.* [Local, U. S.] A term applied to various tortoises, especially the common box-tortoise, the snapping turtle, and a fresh-water terrapin of Florida, the *Pseudemys concinna*.

çṑot′foot, *n.* The popular name of the phalarope.

çṑo-thāy′, *n.* [Ind. name.] A satin showing stripes, manufactured in India.

çṑo′tie, *n.* A body-louse. [Soldiers' slang.]

çop, *n.* [ME. *cop*, top, head; AS. *cop*, top, summit.]

1. The head or top of a thing, especially the top of a hill. [Obs.]

2. A tuft on the head of birds.

3. The conical ball of thread formed on the spindle of a wheel or spinning-frame; sometimes called *coppin*.

4. The tube used in a spinning machine to wind silk thread or yarn upon.

5. A merlon or portion of a battlement.

çop, *n.* A policeman; sometimes also called *copper*. [Slang.]

çō-pāi′bȧ, çō-pāi′vȧ, *n.* [Sp. and Port. from the Braz. name.] The balsam, or liquid, resinous juice flowing from incisions made in the stem of plants of the genus *Copaifera*, growing in South America. This juice is clear, transparent, of a whitish or pale yellowish color, an agreeable smell, and a bitterish, pungent taste. It is of the consistence of oil, or a little thicker. It is used in medicine, especially in affections of the mucous membranes. Written also *copayva* and *capivi*.

Copaiba Plant (*Copaifera officinalis*).

çō-pāi′viç, *a.* Derived from copaiba.

çō-pāi′yé-wood (-yā-), *n.* [*Copaiye*, native name.] The wood obtained from a tree native to British Guiana, the *Vochysia Guianensis*.

çō′păl, *n.* [Sp. from Mex. *copalli*, a generic name of resins.] The resinous product of several different tropical trees, hard, shining, transparent, citron colored, and odoriferous. When dissolved in linseed-oil and diluted with spirit of turpentine it forms a beautiful transparent varnish, which when properly applied and slowly dried is exceedingly durable and hard, and is susceptible of a fine polish. The most valuable *copal* is obtained from trees of eastern Africa, although large quantities are secured in South America and the East Indies.

çō-pal′chē, çō-pal′chi, *n.* [Native name.]

1. A Brazilian tree, the bark of which has medicinal properties, the *Strychnos Pseudo-Quina*.

2. A shrub native to Mexico, the *Croton niveus*. The bark is used medicinally.

çō-păl-if′ẽr-ous, *a.* [*Copal*, and L. *ferre*, to bear.] Productive of copal.

çō′păl-in, çō′păl-ine, *n.* A fossil resin found in roundish lumps in the blue clay of Highgate Hill, London, resembling copal resin in appearance and some of its characteristics; called also *copalite*.

çō′pälm (-päm), *n.* [Etymology unknown.] The North American sweet-gum tree, the *Liquidambar Styraciflua*; also, the balsam obtained from it.

çō-pär′ce-nā-ry, *n.* Partnership in inheritance; joint heirship; joint right of succession or joint succession to an estate of inheritance.

çō-pär′ce-nẽr, *n.* [*Co-*, and Fr. *parcener*, *parcenier*, from L. *partitio*, a sharing, distribution; *pars*, a part.] A coheir; one who has an equal portion of the inheritance of his or her ancestor with others.

çō-pär′ce-ny, *n.* An equal share of an inheritance.

çō-pärt′, *v.t.* To share. [Obs.]

çō-pärt′ment, *n.* Compartment. [Obs.]

çō-pärt′nẽr, *n.* [*Co-*, and *partner*, for *parcener*; influenced by *part*.]

1. One who has a share in a common stock for transacting business, or who is jointly concerned with one or more persons, in carrying on business; a partner; an associate.

2. In a general sense, a sharer; a partaker; as, *copartners* of our joys.

çō-pärt′nẽr-ship, *n.* The state of having a joint share or concern in some common undertaking or interest; partnership.

çō-pärt′nẽr-y, *n.* The state of being copartners in any undertaking. [Rare.]

çop′ȧ-tāin, *a.* [OFr. *copitain*, captain, from LL. *capitaneus*, pertaining to the head.] Pointed at the top; high-crowned; applied to hats. [Obs.]

çō-pā′tri-ŏt, *n.* A joint patriot; a compatriot.

çōpe, *n.* [ME. *cope*; OFr. *cape*; from L. *cappa*, *capa*, a cape, cope.]

1. Anything used as a covering for the head. [Obs.]

2. An ecclesiastical vestment resembling a cloak.

3. Anything spread or extended over the head; the arch or concave of the sky; the roof or covering of a house; the arch over a door, etc.

4. An ancient tribute due to the king or lord of the soil, out of the lead-mines in some parts of Derbyshire, England.

5. In founding, the top part of a mold.

çōpe, *v.t.* and *v.i.*; coped, *pt.*, *pp.*; coping, *ppr.*

I. *v.t.* To cover with or as with a cope; to furnish with a coping.

II. *v.i.* In architecture, to form a cope; to bend, as an arch or vault.

çōpe, *v.t.* and *v.i.* [ME. *copen*, to buy, pay for, from D. *koopen*, to buy.]

I. *v.t.* To barter for; to make return for; to reward. [Obs.]

II. *v.i.* To bargain or barter; to make return. [Obs.]

çōpe, *v.t.* [ME. *copen*, from OFr. *coup*, *colp*; LL. *colpus*, a blow, stroke, from *colaphus*, Gr. *kolaphos*, from *kolaptein*, to peck, strike.] To meet; to engage against; to match against.

> I love to *cope* him in these sullen fits.—Shak.

çōpe, *v.i.* 1. To strive or contend on equal terms, or with equal strength; to equal in combat; to match; to oppose with success; often followed by *with*.

> Their generals have not been able to *cope with* the troops of Athens. —Addison.

2. To contend; to strive or struggle; to combat; to meet.

> Host *coped* with host; dire was the din of war. —Philips.

çōpe, *v.t.* To pare the beak or talons of, as a hawk.

çōpe′-chis″el, *n.* A chisel used to cut grooves, the blade being particularly narrow.

çō′peck, kō′peck, *n.* [Russ. *kopieika*, from *kopati*, to cut, dig.] A Russian coin, the hundredth part of a ruble, equivalent to about half of a United States cent.

çōped (kōpt), *a.* Covered with a cope.

Çop-ē-lā′tæ, Çop-ē-lā′tȧ, *n.pl.* [L., from Gr. *kōpelatēs*, a rower.] In zoölogy, an order of tunicates, more generally known as *Larvalia*.

çōpe′măn, *n.* A merchant; a peddler; a hawker. [Obs.]

çop′ē-pod, *a.* and *n.* I. *a.* Pertaining or belonging to the order *Copepoda*.

II. *n.* A crustacean of the *Copepoda*.

Çō-pep′ō-dȧ, *n.pl.* [L., from Gr. *kōpē*, an oar, and *pous*, *podos*, a foot.] An order of minute entomostracous fresh-water and marine crustaceans, so named because their five pairs of feet are mostly used for swimming.

çōp′ẽr, *n.* [From D. *koopen*, to buy, bargain.] A peddler; a seller. [Eng.]

Çō-pẽr′ni-căn, *a.* Pertaining to Copernicus, or his theory regarding the solar system. This theory, called the *Copernican* system, which considers the sun as the center around which the earth and the planets revolve, was promulgated in 1543, and is the theory now accepted.

çōpes′māte, *n.* A friend; an associate or partner. [Obs.]

çōpe′stōne, *n.* [AS. *cop*, top, summit, and Eng. *stone*.] The top or head stone; the stone used for coping.

çō-phō′sis, *n.* [L., from Gr. *kophōsis*, deafness, from *kōphos*, deaf.] Deafness; inability to hear.

çop′i-ȧ-ble, *a.* Capable of being copied.

çō′pi-ȧ-pīte, *n.* [From *Copiapo*, in Chile, where it is found, and *-ite*.] A hydrated iron sulphate, found massive or in crystalline scales. Also known as *yellow copperas* and *misy*.

çop′i-ẽr, *n.* One who copies; one who writes or transcribes from an original or form; a transcriber; an imitator; also, a plagiarist; formerly spelled *copyer*.

çōp′ing, *n.* [From AS. *cop*, top, summit.] The top course or cover of a wall, usually made sloping to carry off the water.

çō′pi-ous, *a.* [ME. *copious*, from L. *copiosus*, plentiful, from *copia*, abundance.]

1. Abundant; plentiful; in great quantities; full; ample; furnishing full supplies.

> The tender heart is peace,
> And kindly pours its *copious* treasures forth.
> —Thomson.

2. Showing or employing an abundance, as of words, ideas, etc.; as, a *copious* argument.

Syn.—Abundant, plenteous, rich, fruitful, ample, overflowing, full.

çō′pi-ous-ly, *adv.* 1. Abundantly; plentifully; in large quantities.

2. Largely; fully; amply; diffusely.

> The remains of antiquity have been *copiously* described by travelers. —Addison.

çō′pi-ous-ness, *n.* 1. Abundance; plenty; great quantity; full supply.

2. Diffusiveness of style or manner of treating a subject; as, the *copiousness* of Tolstoi.

çop′ist, *n.* A copier. [Obs.]

çō-plān′ȧr, *a.* In mathematics, lying or situated in the same plane.

çop′land, *n.* A piece of ground terminating in a cop or acute angle.

çō-pōr′tion, *n.* Equal share. [Obs.]

çopped (kopt), *a.* [ME. *cop*; AS. *cop*, a summit, head.] Rising to a point or head; peaked; conical.

çop′pel, *n.* and *v.* Same as *Cupel*.

çop′pẽr, *n.* [ME. *coper*; LL. *cuper*, *cuprum*, contr. of *cyprium*, in *Cyprium æs*, Cyprian brass, from Gr. *Kyprios*, the island where the best copper was produced.]

1. One of the metallic elements, specific gravity 8.95. It is very malleable, ductile, and tenacious; an excellent conductor of heat and electricity, and is acted upon by moist air, forming the green carbonate. It is widely diffused in the mineral kingdom, as native ore of Lake Superior or as the sulphid, oxid, or carbonate. It is industrially prepared by refining, by a complicated roasting and refining process, by reduction and by lixivating methods or electrolytic deposition. *Copper* finds extensive use in the arts, particularly those connected with electricity, in sheathing for ships, for coins, etc. Its compounds are many and poisonous, its green salts being used as pigments or insect-destroyers. The alloys of *copper* are especially important.

2. A vessel made of *copper*, particularly a large boiler; specifically, a boiler of a ship's galley.

3. A small copper coin, as a cent; collectively, small change.

> My friends filled my pockets with *coppers*.
> —Franklin.

4. In faro, a coin or object resembling a coin, used to copper a card.

5. A butterfly, the copperwing.

6. In technics, a reel for wire as it leaves the drawplate.

7. The stomach or digestive apparatus. [Slang.]

çop′pẽr, *a.* Like copper; made of copper; as, a *copper* wire.

çop′pẽr, *v.t.*; coppered, *pt.*, *pp.*; coppering, *ppr.*

1. To cover or sheathe with sheets of copper; as, to *copper* a ship.

2. In faro, to denote (the card a player wishes to bet against) by placing chips or other token upon such card; by extension, to bet against.

çop′pẽr-ăs, *n.* [ME. *coperose*; OFr. *couperose*; from L. *cupri*, genit. of *cuprum*, copper, and *rosa*, rose.] Sulphate of iron or ferrous sulphate, $FeSO_4$, a green, efflorescent, soluble salt prepared from iron pyrites or as a by-product in galvanizing iron. The term *copperas* was formerly synonymous with *vitriol*, and included the green, blue, and white vitriols, or the sulphates of iron, copper, and zinc.

çop′pẽr-bel″ly, *n.* The common water-snake of America.

çop′pẽr-bot″tŏmed, *a.* Having a bottom covered with or made of copper.

çop′pẽr-fāced, *a.* Faced or covered with copper, as some type.

çop′pẽr-fas″tened (-nd), *a.* Fastened with copper bolts; said of ship-planking.

çop′pẽr-finch, *n.* See *Chaffinch*.

çop′pẽr-head (-hed), *n.* 1. The common venomous snake, *Ancistrodon contortrix*, of a hazel color marked with blotches. It strikes without warning.

2. An opprobrious name given by the Unionists to southern sympathizers in the North during the Civil War.

çop′pẽr-ing, *n.* A copper covering; the act of facing or covering with copper.

çop′pẽr-ish, *a.* Containing copper; like copper, or partaking of it.

çop′pẽr-nick″el, *n.* Niccolite.

çop′pẽr-plāte, *n.* 1. A plate of polished copper on which lettering or a design is engraved, the sunken lines being filled with prepared ink. On the plate being cleaned an impression may be taken in a suitable press.

2. A print or impression from a *copperplate*.

çop′pẽr-rōse, *n.* [Prov Eng.] The scarlet field-poppy; also written *coprose*, *cuprose*.

çop′pẽr-smith, *n.* One whose occupation is to manufacture copper utensils.

çop′pẽr-wing, *n.* A butterfly of the family *Lycænidæ*.

çop′pẽr-wŏrks, *n. sing.* and *pl.* A place where copper is wrought or manufactured.

çop′pẽr-wŏrm, *n.* One of various pests; as, (a) the teredo; (b) a clothes-moth; (c) an itch-mite.

çop′pẽr-y, *a.* Mixed with copper; containing copper, or made of copper; like copper.

çop′piçe, çopse, *n.* [OFr. *copeiz*, wood newly cut, from *coper*, *copper*, to cut, from *cop*, *colp*; LL. *colpus*, from *colaphos*, Gr. *kolaphos*, a blow, from *kolaptein*, to peck, strike.] A wood of small growth, or consisting of underwood or brushwood; a wood cut at certain times for fuel or other purposes.

çop′piçe, *v.t.* To copse.

çop′pin, *n.* A cone of thread; a cop.

çop′ple, *n.* An elevation; a conical hill.

çop′ple-crown, *n.* A tuft of feathers on the head of a fowl; sometimes, a hen having such crest.

çop′pled, *a.* [From *copple*, dim. of *cop*, a hill, summit.] Rising to a point; conical. [Obs.]

çop′ple-dust, *n.* Cupel-dust.

çop'ple-stōne, *n.* [Obs.] Same as *Cobblestone.*
çopps, *n.* [Obs.] Same as *Copse.*
çō'prȧ, *n.* [Malay *koppara.*] The dried kernel of the cocoanut, from which the oil is extracted; also written *cobra, coprah, copperah.*
çō-præ'mi-ȧ, çō-prē'mi-ȧ, *n.* [L., from Gr. *kopros,* dung, and *haima,* blood.] Blood-poisoning caused by chronic constipation.
çop'rō-līte, *n.* [Gr. *kopros,* dung, and *lithos,* stone.] Petrified dung of carnivorous reptiles.
çop-rō-lit'iç, *a.* Containing or resembling coprolites.
çō-proph'ȧ-găn, *n.* A dung-eating beetle of the *Coprophagi.*
Çō-proph'ȧ-gī, *n.pl.* [L., from Gr. *koprophagos; kopros,* dung, and *phagein,* to eat.] A section of lamellicorn beetles, which live in and upon the dung of animals. It contains the scarabæus of the ancients, and the shard-borne beetles.
çō-proph'ȧ-gous, *a.* Feeding on excrements.
çō-proph'i-lous, *a.* Dung-eating; also, growing from or upon dung, as fungi.
çop'rōşe, *n.* [Fr.] The copper-rose.
çops, *n.* The hook for connecting parts of a harrow. [Prov. Eng.]
çopse, *n.* A wood of small growth. [See *Coppice.*]
çopse, *v.t.*; copsed (kopst), *pt., pp.*; copsing, *ppr.* 1. To preserve, as underwoods.
2. To clip or trim down, as small trees or brushwood.
çopse'wood, *n.* Coppice.
çops'y, *a.* Having a copse or copses.
Çopt, *n.* [LL. *Cophti;* Ar. *Qobt, Kibti,* probably from *-gypt* in Gr. *Aigyptos,* Egypt.] A descendant of the ancient Egyptian race, belonging to the Jacobite sect of Monophysite Christians, who have for eleven centuries been in possession of the patriarchal chair of Alexandria.
Çop'tiç, *a.* and *n.* [L. *Copticus,* from *Cophti,* Copts.]
I. *a.* Pertaining to the Copts.
II. *n.* A Copt; also, the language of the Copts.
çop'ū-lȧ, *n.* [L. *copula,* a band, link, for *co-apula; co-,* together, and *apere,* to join.]
1. In grammar and logic, the word which unites the subject and predicate of a proposition.
2. The coupler of an organ.
3. In anatomy, a part serving as a coupler.
4. In law, sexual intercourse.
çop'ū-lāte, *a.* Joined. [Obs.]
çop'ū-lāte, *v.t.* [L. *copulatus,* pp. of *copulare,* to unite, couple, from *copula,* a band, bond.] To unite. [Obs.]
çop'ū-lāte, *v.i.* To unite; specifically, to embrace sexually.
çop-ū-lā'tion, *n.* The act of coupling; specifically, the sexual act; coition.
çop'ū-lȧ-tive, *a.* 1. Coupling; having the property of joining.
2. Relating to copulation.
Copulative conjunction; in grammar, one joining coördinate clauses.
çop'ū-lȧ-tive, *n.* 1. A copulative conjunction.
2. Connection. [Obs.]
çop'ū-lȧ-tive-ly, *adv.* In a copulative manner.
çop'ū-lȧ-tō-ry, *a.* Copulative; specifically, in zoölogy, designating the organs of copulation.
çop'y, *n.*; *pl.* **çop'ies.** [OFr. *copie,* abundance, transcript, copy; L. *copia,* plenty; LL., copy; *co-,* together, and *opes,* riches.]
1. Abundance [Obs.]
2. Copyhold; also, copyright. [Obs.]
3. A reproduction, either legitimate or as an imitation, of a prototype; one thing like another; a duplicate; as, a *copy* of a letter, mortgage, or work of art.
5. A pattern to be followed in producing a duplicate, or for instruction; a model; as, a penmanship *copy.*
6. An individual book or set of books or other literary work; as, a circulation of 950 *copies.*
7 Any matter to be reproduced in printing; as, *copy* for the compositor or lithographer.
8. A size of writing paper measuring 16 x 20 inches.
Certified or *office copy;* in law, a transcript attested by the officer having legal care of the original.
çop'y, *v.t.*; copied, *pt., pp.*; copying, *ppr.* [ME. *copien;* OFr. *copier,* from LL. *copiare,* to copy, from *copia,* a copy; L., abundance.]
1. To make (a thing or things) like another; to make a reproduction or imitation of, as in the arts; sometimes with *out;* as, to *copy* a pattern of a machine; to *copy out* a page of a book.
2. To imitate or attempt to duplicate; to follow after; to ape; as, to *copy* the habits of the rich.
çop'y=book, *n.* A book containing examples of penmanship to be imitated by students.
çop'y-ēr, *n.* A copier.
çop'y-grȧph, *n.* [LL. *copia,* copy, and Gr. *graphein,* to write.] A hectograph.
çop'y-hōld, *n.* In England, (a) a tenure of estate by copy of court roll; or a tenure for which the tenant has nothing to show, except the rolls made by the steward of the lord's court; (b) land so held.
çop'y-hōld"ēr, *n.* One who is possessed of land in copyhold.
çop'y=hōld"ēr, *n.* 1. A proofreader's assistant.
2. Any device for holding copy on the printer's frame typesetting-machine, or typewriter.
çop'y-ing=ink, *n.* An ink used in printing or writing which may be reproduced in the copying-press.
çop'y-ing=pā"pēr, *n.* Tissue paper for use in a copying-press.
çop'y-ing=pen"çil, *n.* A pencil the lead of which makes a copiable mark.
çop'y-ing=press, *n.* An appliance used in the duplication of matter produced by any copiable medium, as in copying-ink or pencil. The paper to receive the duplicate is dampened and pressure applied.
çop'y-ing=rib"bŏn, *n.* A typewriter-ribbon charged with copying-ink.
çop'y-ist, *n.* One who copies.
çop'y-right (-rīt), *n.* The exclusive right of publication granted an author or artist, for a certain term of years, embracing the right to issue his specified (literary or artistic) work as desired; to transfer such right to any individual, firm or corporation; to protect himself under the law against any infringement. In the United States copyright may be secured for a term of twenty-eight years, renewable for twenty-eight years, by filing a copy of the title of the book or other work with the Librarian of Congress, Washington, D. C.; forwarding two copies of the work with a recording fee of fifty cents (a certificate, if desired, costing fifty cents additional), and placing the required imprint on each copy of the published work.
International copyright; an arrangement between different countries giving special copyright privileges to citizens of such countries as are in the copyright union.
çop'y-right, *v.t.*; copyrighted, *pt., pp.*; copyrighting, *ppr.* To secure by copyright; as, a *copyrighted* book.
çoque (kok), *n.* [Fr.] A small loop or bow of ribbon used in trimming.
çoque'li-çot, çoque'li-çō (kok'lē-kō), *n.* [Fr.] Wild poppy; hence, the color of wild poppy, a mixture of orange and scarlet.
çō-quet' (-ket'), *v.t.*; coquetted, *pt., pp.*; coquetting, *ppr.* [Fr. *coqueter,* to coquet, flirt, to strut like a cock, from *coquet,* a little cock.] To attempt to attract notice, admiration, or love of, from vanity; to treat with an appearance of tenderness or regard, with a view to deceive and disappoint.

You are *coquetting* a maid of honor.—Swift.

çō-quet', *v.i.* To trifle in love; to treat a person with an appearance of favor, but with a design to deceive and disappoint.
çō'quet-ry, *n.*; *pl.* **çō'quet-ries.** Attempts to attract admiration, notice, or love, from vanity; affectation of amorous advances; trifling in love.
çō-quette' (-ket'), *n.* [Fr. *coquette,* f. of *coquet,* a beau, flirt, lit., a little cock.]
1. A vain girl or woman who endeavors to attract amorous advances and rejects them when offered; a jilt; a flirt.

A *coquette* and a tinder-box are spark-led.
—Pope.

2. One of a group of crested humming-birds.
çō-quet'tish, *a.* Practising or displaying coquetry.
çō-quet'tish-ly (ko-ket'ish-ly), *adv.* In a coquettish manner.
çō-quil'lȧ=nut (-kwil'), *n.* [Port. *coquilho;* Sp. *coquillo,* dim. of *coco,* a cocoanut.] The seed of the palm *Attalea funifera,* one of the cocoanut group, a native of Brazil. The nuts are three or four inches long, oval, of a rich brown color and very hard.
çō-quil'lō, *n.* [Sp., dim. of *coco,* a cocoanut.] The physic-nut.
çō-quim'bite (-kim'), *n.* An astringent, hydrous, iron sulphate, first found in the province of Coquimbo, Chile.
çō-quī'nȧ (-kē'), *n.* [Sp., shellfish, cockle.] A rock made up of shell-fragments. It is used as a building-stone, particularly in Florida.
çō-quī'tō (-kē'), *n.* [Sp.] The *Jubæa spectabilis,* a very beautiful palm of Chile, allied to the cocoanut, growing to the height of forty or fifty feet.
çor-. A prefix, from L. *cum,* which becomes *con-, com-, cor-,* etc., for euphony, and meaning with, together with.
çor, *n.* [Heb. *kor.*] A Hebrew measure of capacity containing 11⅛ bushels; a homer; also *chor.*
çō'rȧ, *n.* The Arabian gazel.
çor'ȧ-çine, *n.* [L. *coracinus;* Gr. *korakinos,* from *korax,* a raven, so named from its black color.] A fish, thought to be *Chromis chromis,* of the river Nile. [Obs.]
çor'ȧ-çle, *n.* [From W. *corwgl,* a coracle, from *corwg,* a frame, boat.] A boat used in Wales by fishermen, made by covering a wicker frame with leather or oilcloth, being so light as to be easily carried on the back. A similar boat was used by the ancient Egyptians.

Fisherman with Coracle

çor'ȧ-çō-. A combining form from *coracoid,* used in anatomy and medicine to indicate connection with, or relation to the coracoid bone or process; as, *coraco*-acromial, pertaining to the coracoid and acromion; *coraco*-costal.
çor'ȧ-çoid, *n.* [L. *coracoides,* from Gr. *korakoeidēs,* like a raven; *korax,* a raven, and *eidos,* form.] A small, sharp process of the scapula, shaped like a crow's beak.
çor'ȧ-çoid, *a.* 1. Shaped like a crow's beak.
2. Of or pertaining to the coracoid.
çō-rad'i-çāte, *a.* In philology, derived from the same root.
çor'āge, *n.* Courage. [Obs.]
çō'rȧh, *a.* and *n.* [Hind. *korā,* new, plain.]
I. *a.* Of the natural color, as silk.
II. *n.* Undyed silk; also, a silk handkerchief.
çor'ăl, *a.* Made of coral; resembling coral.
çor'ăl, *n.* [OFr. *coral;* LL. *corallum;* Gr. *korallion,* coral.]
1. A general term for the hard, calcareous skeleton secreted by the marine cœlenterate polyps for their support and habitation. These zoöphytes are usually compound animals, young buds sprouting from the body of the parent polyp and remaining connected with it on the same spot even after it is dead; so that a piece of coral may be regarded as the abode either of one compound animal or of a multitude of individuals.
2. A piece of *coral,* used by children as a plaything.
3. Unimpregnated lobster-eggs, resembling *coral* when boiled.
Coral reefs; coralline structures occasionally branching not unlike a shrub, sometimes spreading like a fan, or assuming the appearance of a brain, a flower, a mushroom, etc. These structures sometimes, as in the Pacific and southern parts of the Indian Ocean, form reefs from twenty yards to several miles in breadth trending for hundreds of miles along the coasts, and also the peculiar coral islands known as atolls.

Red Coral (*Corallium rubrum*).

çor'ăl=ber"ry, *n.* The tree, *Symphoricarpus vulgaris,* the Indian currant.
çor'ăled, çor'ălled, *a.* Having corals; of the color of coral.
çor'ăl=fish, *n.* A fish of the family *Chætodontidæ* or *Pomacentridæ,* frequenting coral reefs.
çor'ăl=in"seçt, *n.* One of the polyps by which coral is produced.
çor-ăl-lā'ceous, *a.* Resembling coral.
çō-ral'li-ăn, *n.* A coral-rag.
çor-ăl-lif'ēr-ous, *a.* Containing or consisting of coral; producing coral.
çor'ăl-li-form, *a.* Resembling coral; forked and crooked.
Çor-ăl-liġ'e-nȧ, *n.pl.* Same as *Anthozoa.*
çor-ăl-liġ'e-nous, *a.* [L. *coralligenus; corallum,* coral, and *-genus,* producing.] Producing coral.
çor-ăl-liġ'ēr-ous, *a.* Same as *Coralliferous.*
çor'ăl-lin, *n.* [Named from its resemblance to coral-red; L. *corallinus,* from *corallum,* coral.] A red dye prepared by the action of sulphuric and oxalic acids on phenol; also spelled *coralline.*
Çor-ăl-lī'nȧ, *n.* A genus of rose-spored algæ with calcareous jointed fronds. The spores are borne in urn-shaped conceptacles.
çor'ăl-line, *a.* [LL. *corallinus,* coral-red, from *corallum,* coral.] Consisting of coral; like coral; containing coral; specifically, resembling coral in color.
çor'ăl-line, *n.* 1. A name popularly applied to the seaweeds with rigid, calcareous fronds, from their resemblance to coral. [See *Corallina.*]
2. An animal belonging to the zoöphytes or *Polyzoa.*
3. See *Corallin.*
çor'ăl-lin-ite, *n.* Fossil coral.
çor'ăl-līte, *n.* 1. Corallinite.
2. A fossil polypidom of the corallines.
çor'ăl-loid, *n.* A name formerly given to several of the *Polyzoa.*

çor′ăl-loid, çor-ăl-loid′ăl, *a.* [LL. *corallum*, coral, and Gr. *eidos*, form.] Having the form of coral; branching like coral.

çō-ral′lum, *n.* [LL.] A coral; coral.

çor′ăl-plant, *n.* An East Indian plant, *Jatropha multifida*, having deeply cut foliage and beautiful scarlet flowers.

çor′ăl-rag, *n.* A provincial term for the highest member of the middle Oölitic series, a variety of limestone containing an abundance of petrified corals.

çor′ăl-root, *n.* A British plant, having thick, fleshy roots, with much-branched fibers. The flowers are borne on a spike, and are of a yellowish color.

çor′ăl-snāke, *n.* One of various snakes having coral-like markings.

çor′ăl-stitch, *n.* A stitch in embroidery so worked as to give the appearance of finely-branched coral.

çor′ăl-sū″mach, *n.* Poison-wood.

çor′ăl-tree, *n.* A genus of plants, *Erythrina*, of several species, natives of Africa and America. They are all shrubby, flowering plants, adorned chiefly with trifoliate or three-lobed leaves, and scarlet spikes of papilionaceous flowers.

çor′ăl-wood, *n.* A fine-grained cabinet wood, yellow when first cut, but afterward becoming a coral-red.

çor′ăl-wŏrt, *n.* Coral-root.

çor′ăl-zōne, *n.* The sea-depth at which corals flourish.

çor′ȧ-nach, *n.* See *Coronach.*

çō-rant′, çō-ran′tō, *n.* A dance; the courant.

çorb, *n.* [O.H.G. *corb*, from L. *corbis*, a basket.] A basket used in coal-mines.

çorb, *n.* A corbel.

çor′ban, *n.* [Heb. *korbān*, an offering, sacrifice, from *karab*, to approach, offer.]

1. In Jewish antiquity, a gift or present made to God or to the temple, usually to fulfil a vow.

2. A corbana. [Obs.]

3. The host of the Coptic liturgy.

çor-bā′nȧ, *n.* In the early church, the treasury, being the place where money-offerings were deposited.

çorbe, *a.* Crooked. [Obs.]

çor′beil (-bel), *n.* [Fr. *corbeille*, from LL. *corbicula*, dim. of L. *corbis*, a basket.]

1. In fortification, a little basket, to be filled with earth and set upon a parapet, to shelter men from the fire of besiegers.

2. In architecture, a carved basket with sculptured flowers and fruits.

çor′bel, *n.* [OFr. *corbel*, dim. from L. *corbis*, a basket.]

1. In architecture, a form of bracket used in the Gothic style for the purpose of supporting

Corbel.

Corbel.

the ends of the timbers, arches, parapets, floors, cornices, etc. It consists of a projecting block of stone, usually carved in a fantastic manner and having a receding face.

2. The vase or drum of the Corinthian column; so called from its resemblance to a basket.

çor′bel, *v.t.*; corbeled, *pt.*, *pp.*; corbeling, *ppr.* To furnish with a corbel; to form like a corbel.

çor′bel-steps, *n.pl.* Steps into which the sides of gables, from the eaves to the apex, are broken; also called *corbie-steps, crow-steps.*

çor′bel-tā″ble, *n.* A projecting course; a parapet; a tier of windows; an arcade; an entablature; any architectural arrangement requiring the support of a number of corbels.

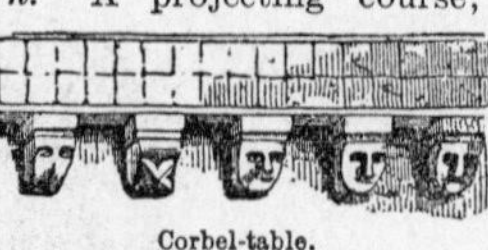
Corbel-table.

çor′bet, *n.* A corbel. [Obs.]

Çor-biç′ū-lȧ, *n.* [LL. *corbicula*, a little basket, dim. of *corbis*, a basket.]

1. A genus of bivalve mollusks similar to the clam.

2. [c—] A corbiculum.

çor-biç′ū-lum, *n.*; *pl.* **çor-biç′ū-lȧ.** A pollen-basket.

çor′bie, çor′by, *n.* [Scot.] A crow; a raven.

çor′bie-crōw, *n.* The carrion crow.

çor′bie-steps, *n.pl.* Corbel-steps.

Çor′chō-rus, *n.* [L., from Gr. *korchoros*, a wild plant of bitter taste.]

1. A genus of tropical plants of the linden family. The species *capsularis* and *olitorius* of this genus furnish jute.

2. [c—] A Japanese shrub, *Kerria Japonica*, cultivated for its rose-like flower.

çor′cle, çor′cūle, *n.* [L. *corculum*, dim. of *cor*, heart.] The heart or embryo of a seed. [Obs.]

çord, *n.* [OFr. *corde*; L. *chorda*, from Gr. *chordē*, catgut, chord, cord.]

1. A string, or small rope, composed of several strands twisted together.

2. Anything resembling a *cord*, as the string of an instrument; specifically, in anatomy, (a) any string-like part; (b) the umbilical *cord.*

3. A measure of cubic contents, 128 cubic feet, equivalent to a pile 4x4x8 feet.

4. In fabrics, (a) corduroy; (b) the ribs of woven goods having a raised surface.

5. Any influence that binds and holds; as, the *cords* of love.

çord, *v.t.*; corded, *pt.*, *pp.*; cording, *ppr.* 1. To bind with a cord or rope; to fasten with cords.

2. To pile (wood or other material) for measurement and sale by the cord.

çord′āge, *n.* [Fr. *cordage*, from *cord* and *-age.*]

1. Ropes or cords collectively.

2. The ropes or rigging of a ship.

Çor-dȧ-i′tēş, *n.* [Named after *Corda*, a German botanist.] A genus of immense, arborescent trees of the Carboniferous epoch belonging to the cycad family, their remains going to make up coal-formations.

çord′ăl, *n.* [OFr. *cordal, cordail*, from *corde*, a cord.] In heraldry, a string of the mantle or robe of estate, made of silk and gold threads interwoven like a cord, with tassels at the ends.

çor′dāte, *a.* [From L. *cor*, *cordis*, a heart.] Having the form of a heart; heart-shaped; as, a *cordate* leaf. Hence, *cordate*-oblong, heart-shaped, lengthened; *cordate*-lanceolate, heart-shaped, gradually tapering toward the extremity, like the head of a lance; *cordate*-sagittate, heart-shaped, but resembling the head of an arrow.

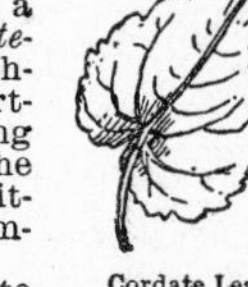
Cordate Leaf.

çor′dāte-ly, *adv.* In a cordate form or manner.

çord′ed, *a.* 1. Bound or fastened with cords.

2. Piled in a form for measurement by the cord.

3. Made of cords; furnished with cords. [Obs.]

4. Striped or furrowed, as by cords.

5. In heraldry, represented as bound about or wound with cords. Bales, etc., when bandaged or bound with cords, are blazoned *corded.*

Çor-de-liēr′, *n.* [Fr. *cordelière*, a cord or girdle worn by the order, from *corde*, a cord.]

1. The name applied in France to the strictest branch of Franciscan friars, on account of their wearing a girdle of knotted cord.

2. [*pl.*] The name given one of the Parisian political clubs in the time of the Revolution, which numbered Danton and Marat among its chief members, from their holding their sittings in an old convent of the *Cordeliers.*

çor′del-ing, çor′del-ling, *a.* [Fr. *cordeler*, to twist.] Twisting.

çor-delle′, *n.* [Fr. *cordelle*, dim. of *corde*, a cord.]

1. A twisted cord; a tassel.

2. A towline. [West. U. S.]

Çor′di-ȧ, *n.* [Named after *Cordus*, a German botanist.] A large genus of plants of the borage family, consisting of some 200 species scattered over the warm regions of the world, especially in America. They are trees or shrubs with alternate simple leaves. The fruit is drupaceous, and that of some species, as sebesten, is eaten. Some species yield a good timber.

çor′diăl (-jăl *or* -di-ăl), *a.* [Fr. *cordial*; LL. *cordialis*, from *cor*, *cordis*, heart.]

1. Relating to the heart. [Obs.]

2. Proceeding as from the heart (the ancients believing the heart the source of affection); hearty; sincere; not hypocritical; warm; affectionate; as, we give our friends a *cordial* reception.

> With looks of *cordial* love. —Milton.

3. Reviving the spirits; cheering; invigorating; giving strength or spirits; as, *cordial* waters.

çor′diăl, *n.* 1. That which revives the spirits; an exhilarant; specifically, an exhilarating draught; a refreshing medicine.

2. Liqueur.

çor-dial′i-ty (-jal′i-ti), *n.* 1. Relation to the heart. [Obs.]

2. Sincerity; freedom from hypocrisy; sincere affection and kindness; as, our friends were received with *cordiality.*

çor′diăl-ize (-jăl-īz), *v.t.*; cordialized, *pt.*, *pp.*; cordializing, *ppr.* 1. To make into a cordial.

2. To make cordial or warm in feeling or manner; to render genial or hearty.

çor′diăl-ize, *v.i.* To feel or show cordiality. [Rare.]

çor′diăl-ly, *adv.* In a cordial manner.

çor′diăl-ness, *n.* Cordiality; hearty good-will.

çor′di-ĕr-ite, *n.* [Named after *Cordier*, a French geologist.] A mineral, iolite.

çor′di-form, *a.* [L. *cor*, *cordis*, the heart, and *forma*, form.] Heart-shaped; having the form of the human heart.

çor-dil′lēr-ȧ, *n.* [Sp., from OSp. *cordilla*, *cordiella*, dim. of *cuerda*, a rope, string, from L. *chorda*, a cord, string.] A ridge or chain of mountains; first applied to the ranges of the Andes in South America, and then also to their continuation into Mexico and further north. Now the term is used generally for any mountain ranges bordering a continent.

çor′di-nēr, *n.* A cordwainer. [Obs.]

çor′dite, *n.* A smokeless high explosive made in the form of a cord, hence its name. It is of a brown color and composed principally of nitroglycerin, guncotton, and vaseline. It has been adopted in the English military and naval service for small arms and cannon.

çord′lēaf, *n.* A plant of the order *Restiaceæ.*

çor′dŏn, *n.* [Fr. and Sp. *cordon*; It. *cordone*, from LL. *corda*, L. *chorda*, a cord, string.]

1. In fortification, a row of stones jutting before the rampart and the basis of the parapet; or a row of stones between the wall of a fortress which lies aslope, and the parapet, which is perpendicular; serving as an ornament, and used only in fortifications of stonework.

2. In military language, a line or series of military posts or sentinels, inclosing or guarding any particular place; as, a *cordon* of troops.

3. A ribbon or cord worn as the badge of any order or of honor.

4. A tasseled lace or string of a mantle on state and installation robes.

5. In architecture, the edge of a stone on the exterior of a building, indicating a division of stones.

6. In heraldry, a baldric or ribbon worn across the breast by knights of the first class or order.

7. In horticulture, a tree pruned of branches to force fruit of fine quality.

Cordon bleu; (a) the blue ribbon worn as a scarf or badge of the order of the Holy Ghost, the highest order of the old French chivalry; (b) one entitled or fitted to wear a badge of the highest honor; any person of great eminence in his profession or calling; a first-class cook, able journalist, expert marksman, etc.

Cordon sanitaire or *sanitary cordon*; a line of troops or military posts on the borders of a district of country infected with disease, to cut off communication, and thus prevent the disease from spreading.

çor-don-net′ (-nā′), *n.* A raised edge or border of a point-lace pattern.

çor-dō-nette′ (-net′), *n.* [Fr., dim. of *cordon*, a cord.] An edging of small cord or piping.

çor′dō-văn, *n.* [Sp. *cordoban*, from *Cordoba*, in Spain.]

1. Cordwain.

2. Leather made from horsehide. [Eng.]

çor′dū-roy, *n.* [Of doubtful origin.]

1. A stout, ribbed, cotton fabric, made with a pile, so cut as to leave a surface ridged in the direction of the warp.

2. A corduroy road.

3. [*pl.*] Trousers made of *corduroy.*

Corduroy road; a road constructed with logs laid transversely and in contact. It is used in swampy places, and derives its name from its ribbed appearance, resembling corduroy.

çor′dū-roy, *v.t.*; corduroyed, *pt.*, *pp.*; corduroying, *ppr.* To construct of logs, in the manner of a corduroy road.

çord′wāin, *n.* [ME. *cordwane*; OFr. *cordowan*; Sp. *cordoban*, from *Cordova*, in Spain.] Spanish leather; goatskin tanned and dressed.

çord′wāin-ēr, *n.* A worker in cordwain; a shoemaker.

Çor′dy-ceps, *n.* [L., from Gr. *kordylē*, a club, and L. *-ceps*, from *caput*, head.] A genus of ascomycetous fungi. Some species grow upon decaying leaves and branches on plants affected by ergot, others on living insects. A wasp in the West Indies is thus attacked, and the caterpillar of a New Zealand ghost-moth.

çōre, *n.* [ME. *core*; OFr. *cor*, *coer*; L. *cor*, heart.]

1. The heart or inner part of a thing; particularly, the central part of fruit, containing the kernels or seeds; as, the *core* of an apple.

2. The inner part of an ulcer or boil.

3. In architecture, the interior part of a column or wall.

4. A disorder of sheep, occasioned by worms in the liver.

5. The center or innermost part of any open space. [Obs.]

> In the *core* of the square she raised a tower of a furlong high. —Raleigh.

6. Figuratively, the deepest or most essential part of anything; as, the *core* of a question.

> This obscure belief lies at the very *core* of our spiritual nature. —J. A. Froude.

7. In molding, the internal mold which forms a hollow in the casting of metals, as the bore of a tube or pipe.

8. The bony center of a ruminant's horn.

9. In electrodynamics, an iron bar or collection of thin iron plates around which a helix or spiral conductor is wound.

10. In ethnological archæology, a piece of flint or other similar material from which stone implements have been chipped.

11. In telegraphy, the cord of insulated conducting wires in the heart of a cable.

çōre, *v.t.*; cored, *pt., pp.*; coring, *ppr.* 1. To remove the core of, as of an apple or other fruit.

2. To mold or cast by means of a core.

3. To roll in salt and prepare for drying, as herrings.

çōre, *n.* [Phonetic spelling of Fr. *corps*, a body.] A body; party; company. [Obs.]

çōre, *n.* [A corruption of *chore.*] In mining, the number of hours, generally from six to eight, each party of miners works at a time before being relieved. The miner's day is thus usually divided into three or four *cores.*

çōre′=bar″rel, *n.* A vertical iron tube or pipe, wrapped with straw and covered with sand and clay, used in casting guns.

çōre′=box, *n.* A divisible box in which clay is rammed to form cores for molding.

çō-rec′tōme, *n.* [Gr. *korē*, the pupil, and *ektomos*, from *ektemnein*, to cut out; *ek*, out, and *temnein*, to cut.] An instrument for cutting through the iris to form an artificial pupil.

çōre′=disk, *n.* A disk cut or stamped out of sheet-iron and used for the laminated core of any dynamo-electric apparatus.

çō-rē′gent, *n.* A joint regent or ruler.

Çō-reg′ō-nus, *n.* [Origin unknown.] A genus of fishes, separated from the salmons by having the first dorsal fin further forward than the ventrals, the scales large, and the teeth either minute or wanting.

Çō-rē′i-dæ, *n.pl.* [L., from Gr. *koris*, a bug, and *-idæ.*] A family of insects of the suborder *Heteroptera*, abounding chiefly in tropical regions, remarkable for their size and grotesque shapes.

çō-re-lā′tion, *n.* Corresponding relation.

çōre′less, *a.* 1. Having no core.

2. Figuratively, without pith or stamina; weak.

çō-rē-lig′ion-ist, *n.* One of the same religion or sect as another.

çō-rel′là, *n.* [L., dim. of *cora*; Gr. *korē*, a girl, doll.] A beautiful yellow-crested parrakeet, *Nymphicus novæ-hollandiæ*, of Australia.

Çō-rē-op′sis, *n.* [L., from Gr. *koris*, a bug, and *opsis*, appearance, in allusion to the form of the seed which has two little horns at the end.] A genus of plants, natural order *Compositæ.* Most of the species are herbaceous perennials, with opposite leaves and yellow or party-colored rays. The fruit is an achene, flat on one side and convex on the other, slightly winged, and with two awns. The species are natives of North America and South Africa.

çōre′=print, *n.* A projecting piece on a pattern for molding, forming a hole in the mold to receive the end of the core, by which it is sustained in the mold in proper position relatively to the object cast.

çōr′ẽr, *n.* An instrument for removing the core from fruit; as, an apple *corer.*

çōr′e-sēs, *n.pl.* [L., from Gr. *koris*, a bug, pl. *koreis*; named from the resemblance to a bug.] Dark red, broad, discoid bodies found beneath the epicarp of grapes.

çō-rē-spond′ent, *n.* In law, one who is made a joint respondent with another in a suit; especially one who is charged with adultery with the wife or husband of the plaintiff, and made a party to a suit for divorce.

çō′ret, *n.* A pond-snail of the genus *Planorbis.*

Çō′re-us, *n.* [L., from Gr *koris*, a bug.] The typical genus of *Coreidæ.*

çōre′=wheel, *n.* A wheel having a rim furnished with cavities to receive cogs.

çorf, *n., pl.* **çoṙves.** [A variant of *corb.*] A basket, box, or low-wheeled vehicle for carrying coal and other minerals in a mine. [Eng.]

çorf′=house, *n.* In Scotland, a temporary shed where the nets and other material used in salmon-fishing are stored, and where the fish are cured.

Çor′fi-ōte, Çor′fūte, *n.* A native or inhabitant of Corfu, one of the Ionian islands.

çō-ri-ā′ceous, *a.* [L. *coriaceus*, from *corium*, leather.]

1 Consisting of leather, or resembling leather; tough; as, *coriaceous* concretions.

2. In botany, stiff, like leather or parchment.

çō-ri-an′dẽr, *n.* [Fr. *coriandre*; L. *coriandrum*, from Gr *koriannon, korion*, the coriander; perhaps from *koris*, a bug, on account of the smell of its leaves.] The popular name of an umbelliferous plant, *Coriandrum sativum.* The fruit (commonly called coriander seeds) is pleasantly aromatic, and is used in cooking for flavoring, and in medicine is considered as stomachic and carminative.

Çō-ri-an′drum, *n.* A genus of plants, natural order *Umbelliferæ*, containing two species. They are slender annual herbs with white flowers, natives of the Mediterranean region. *Coriandrum sativum*, the officinal coriander, is cultivated on account of its seeds, or rather fruit.

Coriander (*Coriandrum sativum*).

Çō″ri-à-ri′ē-æ, *n.pl.* [L. *coriarius*, from *corium*, leather; so named from the crustaceous covering of the fruit.] A small natural order of polypetalous exogens, consisting of six known species of shrubs included in a single genus, *Coriaria.* The best known species is the *myrtifolia*, of southern Europe, employed by dyers for staining black.

çō′ri-dine, *n.* [From L. *corium*, leather.] A colorless liquid, $C_{10}H_{15}N$, obtained from coal-tar, Dippel's oil, etc., having an odor like new leather.

çō-rin′don, *n.* Corundum. [Obs.]

çō-rinne′ (-rin′), *n.* [From Fr. *corinnes*, the gazel.]

1. A variety of the common gazel.

2. A humming-bird having a long lance-like bill and very brilliant coloration.

çor′inth, *n.* [From *Corinth*, a famous city of Greece near which the fruit grows.] A small dried grape; a currant. [Obs.]

Çō-rin′thi-aç, *a.* Corinthian; of or pertaining to Corinth.

Çō-rin′thi-ăn, *a.* 1. Pertaining to Corinth, a celebrated city of Greece; as, *Corinthian* column; *Corinthian* brass.

2. Licentious; dissipated; wild.

3. Amateur; applied especially to a yacht-race in which only amateurs participate.

Corinthian order; the most ornate of the various orders of classical architecture. The Grecian Corinthian, like the Ionic, consists of stylobate, column and entablature, the first being harmoniously molded in an ornate style. The column consists of base, shaft, and capital, and is ten diameters in height, the cone of the capital being a perfect cylinder banded by a row of waterleaves one-sixth of the whole height, and another of the leaves of the acanthus with flowered buttons attaching them to the cylinder. The entablature is two and two-sevenths diameters in height and much ornamented. The Roman Corinthian differs mainly from the Grecian in the proportions observed.

Corinthian Order.

Çō-rin′thi-ăn, *n.* 1. An inhabitant of Corinth.

2. A gay, licentious person. [Obs.]

3. A member of the aristocracy. [Eng. Slang].

4. An amateur yachtsman.

5. [*pl.*] Two epistles written by St. Paul to the Church of Corinth, about A. D. 57 or 58.

Çō′ris, *n.* [L., from Gr. *koris*, a bug.] A genus of plants of the natural order *Primulaceæ.* There is only one species, the blue maritime *coris*, which grows in the Mediterranean region. It is a thyme-like plant, with a dense terminal raceme of purplish flowers.

çō′ri-um, *n.* [L.] 1. A kind of body armor, composed of scales or small plates of leather, worn by the Roman soldiers. In England it continued in use until the reign of Edward I.

2. The innermost layer of the skin in mammals, the *cutis vera* or true skin.

3. In entomology, the main portion of the hemelytron of a heteropterous insect.

Roman Corium.

çō-ri′văl, *n.* A rival or fellow-rival; a competitor.

çō-ri′văl, *v.t.* To rival; to pretend to equal.

çō-ri′văl-ry, çō-ri′văl-ship, *n.* Joint rivalry.

çork, *n.* [ME. *cork*, from Sp. *corcho*, cork; L. *cortex, corticis*, bark, rind.]

1. A glandiferous tree, a species of oak, *Quercus Suber*, growing in Spain and Portugal, having a thick, rough, fungous, cleft bark.

2. The outer bark of this tree, of which stoppers for bottles, floats, insoles for shoes, etc., are made.

3. Anything made of *cork*; as, (a) a fishing-float; (b) a bottle-stopper; (c) a shoe-sole.

4. The subereous layer of the bark of any tree when greatly developed.

çork, *v.t.*; corked (korkt), *pt., pp.*; corking, *ppr.* 1. To stop with a cork, as bottles or casks; to confine or make fast with or as with a cork.

2. To make of or fit with cork.

3. To blacken with burnt cork.

çork, *n.* and *v.* Same as *Calk.* [U. S.]

çork′āge, *n.* A charge made by hotel-keepers for keeping over wines, liquors, etc., and reserving from partly emptied bottles.

çorked (korkt), *a.* 1. Stopped with a cork.

2. Fitted with or raised on cork.

> A *corked* shoe or slipper. —Huloet.

3. Having acquired the taste of cork; as, *corked* wine.

çork′ẽr, *n.* 1. One who or that which corks.

2. A conclusive argument. [Slang.]

çork′=fos″sil, *n.* A kind of hornblende; so named from its lightness.

çork′ing=pin, *n.* A pin of a large size. [Obs.]

çork′=jack″et, *n.* A jacket lined with cork for the purpose of sustaining the wearer on the surface of the water.

çork′screw, *n.* A screw to draw corks from bottles.

çork′screw, *v.t.* To make in a twisting way; as, to *corkscrew* one's way [Colloq.]

çork′screw, *a.* Formed like a corkscrew; as, *corkscrew* stairs; a *corkscrew* curl.

çork′=tree, *n.* Same as *Cork*, 1.

çork′wing, *n.* A fish, *Crenilabrus melops*, commonly called *goldfinny.*

çork′wood, *n.* Any one of several kinds of trees having light and porous wood, as the *Anona palustris* or the *Ochroma lagopus.*

Corkwood cotton; the cottony or silky covering of the seeds of the bombaceous tropical tree, *Ochroma lagopus.*

çork′y, *a.* Consisting of cork; resembling cork; dry and tough like cork.

> Bind fast his *corky* arms. —Shak.

çorm, *n.* [L. *cormus*; Gr. *kormos*, the trunk of a tree with the boughs lopped off, from *keirein*, to cut, to shear.]

1. In botany, a bulb-like subterranean stem, differing from a bulb in being solid, and from a tuber, in its oval figure.

2. In biology, same as *cormus.*

Corm of Crocus *sativus.*

çorme, *n.* In botany, the same as *service* or *service-tree.*

çorm′el, *n.* [Dim. of *corm.*] A small corm.

çor′mī, *n.*, pl. of *cormus.*

çor-mid′i-um, *n.*; *pl.* **çor-mid′i-à.** [L., dim. from Gr. *kormos*, the trunk of a tree.] In zoöphytology, a group of zoöids budding from a medusa, the individuals of which are heteromorphic.

çor-mog′e-ny, *n.* [Gr. *kormos*, trunk, and *-genēs*, producing.] In biology, the history of the development of races, communities, families, etc. [Rare.]

çor″mō-phȳ-log′e-ny, *n.* [Gr. *kormos*, the trunk of a tree, and *phylon*, race, tribe, and *genesis*, birth, descent.] In biology, the historical investigation of living organisms taken in the aggregate, also written *cormophyly.* [Rare.]

Çor-moph′y-tà, *n.pl.* [L., from Gr. *kormos*, a trunk, and *phyton*, plant.] A former name given to a class of acrogens, in which there is a distinct axis of growth, or stem and root symmetrically clothed with leaves. They comprise the ferns, mosses, equisetums, etc.

çor′mō-rănt, *n.* [ME. *cormerawnt*; OFr. *cormoran*; L. *corvus marinus*, sea-crow.]

1. A large, web-footed bird of the pelican family. The common species, *Phalacrocorax carbo*, has the head and neck black; the coverts of the wings, the scapulars, and the back, of a deep green, edged with black, and glossed with blue. This bird occupies the cliffs by the sea, feeds on fish, and is extremely voracious. Called also *searaven, coalgoose.*

Common Cormorant (*Phalacrocorax carbo*).

2. A greedy fellow; a glutton.

> Light vanity, insatiate *cormorant*, soon preys upon itself. —Shak.

çor′mō-rănt, *a.* Having the qualities of a cormorant; greedy; rapacious.

If thou be still human and not *cormorant*.
—Carlyle.

çor'mus, *n.*; *pl.* **çor'mī.** [L. from Gr. *kormos*, the trunk of a tree with the leaves lopped off.]

1. In botany, a corm.

2. In biology, a colony of persons; a common aggregate of individuals of a compound animal.

çorn, *n.* [AS. *corn*, a grain, seed, corn; D. *koren*; O.H.G. *koren*; Ice. and Sw. *korn*; Goth. *kaurn*, grain.]

1. A single seed of certain plants, as wheat, rye, barley, and maize; a grain.

2. The seeds of the cereal, *Zea Mays*, or maize, one of the leading farm products of the United States, used when in the milk as a vegetable and, when ripened and hardened as a grain, ground into flour. As a stock-food it is unequaled, being rich in oil and a good producer of fat. It is fed on the cob, ground, or mixed with other grain, particularly oats.

3. The seeds of the small grains, wheat, oats, rye or barley. [Eng.]

4. Oats. [Scot.]

5. The plants which produce *corn*; when growing in the field, the stalks and ears, or the stalks, ears, and seeds, after harvesting and before shelling or threshing.

6. A small, hard particle. [Rare.]

Calico corn; a variety of corn usually dwarfish, having a small cob and variegated kernels; not raised as a field product.

Corn bread; any bread made of the flour of Indian corn.

Corn fritter; a fritter made of green corn.

Corn laws; in England, legislative enactments and restrictions relating to the exportation and importation of grain. The English *corn laws* were repealed in 1846, and foreign grain admitted on payment of a nominal duty, which was repealed in 1869.

Corn pone; a hard baked cake or bread made of corn-meal.

Dent corn; a variety of corn having the kernel furrowed or depressed at the large end; the common kind.

Flint corn; corn having a pearly-white, hard, smooth grain, commonly dented.

Indian corn; maize; common corn.

Pop corn; a dwarf variety used for popping; also, the popped corn itself; also written *pop-corn*.

Sweet corn; a table variety, the grain of which is esculent when green; distinguished from *field corn*.

White corn; the variety usually raised in the southern states, the long season giving it time to ripen. It has a large cob, and long, compact, white kernels.

Yellow corn; the common northern variety, having a yellow grain ripening before the fall frosts.

çorn, *v.t.*; corned, *pt.*, *pp.*; corning, *ppr.* 1. To preserve and season with salt in grains; to sprinkle with salt; as, to *corn* beef.

2. To granulate; to form into small grains.

3. To feed with oats, as a horse. [Scot.]

4. To intoxicate. [Colloq.]

çorn, *n.* A local thickening of the skin, usually painful when subjected to pressure, most common on the feet, being caused by friction or compression.

Çor-nā'cē-æ, *n.pl.* [L. *cornus*, the dogwood, and *-aceæ*.] An order of epigynous exogens, the dogwood family, mostly trees or shrubs, having twelve genera, found in Europe, Asia, and America.

çor-nā'ceous, *a.* Of or pertaining to the *Cornaceæ*.

çor'nāġe, *n.* [OFr. *cornage*, a horn-blowing, from *corne*, L. *cornus*, a horn.] An ancient tenure of lands, which obliged the tenant to give notice of an invasion by blowing a horn.

çor'nȧ-mūte, *n.* A cornemuse. [Obs.]

çorn'=ball, *n.* Popped corn held together by a sticky syrup and made into a ball; a pop-corn ball.

çorn'=bee"tle, *n.* A minute beetle, *Cucujus testaceus*, having a larva destroying wheat in the bin; the wheat-beetle.

çorn'=bells, *n.* A fungoid growth, *Cyathus vernicosus*, attacking growing grain.

çorn'bind, *n.* One of several twining weeds, as (a) bindweed; (b) the climbing buckwheat.

çorn'=clēan"ēr, *n.* A fanning-mill for corn.

çorn'çob, *n.* The spike bearing the kernels of Indian corn.

çorn'=çoç"kle, *n.* A weed, *Lychnis Githago*, growing in small grain. It has a purple, bell-shaped flower and hard black seeds; often called *cockle*.

çorn'=çrack"ēr, *n.* 1. A nickname for a Kentuckian.

2. A corncrake.

çorn'çrāke, *n.* [*Corn* and *crake*, Ice. *kraka*, a crow.] A bird common in Europe, frequenting grain-fields and meadows, and noted for the peculiar call of the male; also called *landrail*. [See *Crake*.]

çorn'çrib, *n.* A granary for holding Indian corn before shelling, usually of slats and set up somewhat from the ground.

Corncrake (*Crex pratensis*).

çorn'çut"tēr, *n.*

1. A cornshredder.

2. A hooked or machete-like knife for cutting corn by hand; also, a corn-harvester.

çorn'dodġ"ēr (-doj"), *n.* A hard-baked cake of corn-meal. [Southern U. S.]

çor'nē-ȧ, [L. f. sing. of *corneus*, horny, from *cornu*, a horn.]

1. In anatomy, the strong, horny, transparent membrane in the fore part of the eye.

2. In entomology, the exterior of a compound eye.

çor'nē-ăl, *a.* Of or pertaining to a cornea.

çor'nel, *n.* [OFr. *cornille*; LL. *cornolium*, the *cornel*-tree; from L. *cornus*, a cornel-tree; from *cornu*, a horn, in allusion to the hardness of the wood.]

1. The cornelian cherry or dogwood, the popular name of *Cornus mascula*, of the dogwood family, a European and Asiatic shrub having a branching stem, small yellowish-green flowers and cherry-like fruit.

2. Any plant of the genus *Cornus*; also called *cornel-tree*, *cornelian-tree*.

çor-nel'i-ăn, *n.* The carnelian.

çorne'mūse, *n.* A bagpipe. [Obs.]

çor"nē-ō-çal-çā'rē-ous, *a.* [L. *corneus*, horny, and *calcareus*, pertaining to lime.] Made up of horny and calcareous matter, either, (a) in mixture, as in certain shells, or (b) in layers, as in the opercula of certain turbinal shells.

çor'nē-ous, *a.* [L. *Corneus*, from *Cornu*, a horn.] Horny; hard; consisting of some substance resembling horn.

çor'nēr, *n.* [ME. *corner*, *cornier*; OFr *corniere*; LL. *cornerium*, from *corne*, a corner, angle; from *cornu*, a horn, projecting-point.]

1. The point of meeting of two lines; the line or point of meeting of two or more planes or surfaces; an angle, whether plane, spherical, or solid. *Corners* may be outside or inside, coinciding with angles.

2. The space between two converging lines or walls which meet in a point; as, a number in the *corner*; a piano in the *corner* of the room.

3. An inclosed place; a secret or retired place.

This thing was not done in a *corner*.
—Acts xxvi. 26.

4. Indefinitely, any part; a part; as, they searched every *corner* of the forest; all *corners* of the country.

5. In surveying, a witness-mark determining the *corner* of a surveyed tract.

6. (a) A bookbinder's tool for corner ornamentation; (b) a device for protecting the *corners* of book-covers, or any other *corner*, while in transportation.

7. Monopoly of a certain product or commodity, so as to be able to regulate the supply at will; as, a *corner* in corn.

8. The end, extremity, or limit. [Obs.]

9. Direction. [Obs.]

çor'nēr, *v.t.*; cornered, *pt.*, *pp.*; cornering, *ppr.*

1. To force into a corner.

2. To force or drive into a difficult or embarrassing position; as, to *corner* a witness.

3. To obtain control of (any commodity) for the purpose of fixing the price; as, to *corner* wheat.

çor'nēr, *v.i.* To meet at a corner or angle; as, the lot *corners* on Wisconsin street.

çor'nēr-çap, *n.* The chief embellishment or ornament. [Obs.]

çor'nēred, *a.* 1. Having corners; having three or more angles.

2. Driven into a corner, or into a difficult or embarrassing position.

çor'nēr-ēr, *n.* One who corners, especially one who controls a commodity so as to fix the price.

çor'nēr=stōne, *n.* 1. The stone which lies at the corner of two walls, and unites them; the principal stone, and especially the stone which forms the corner of the foundation of an edifice.

2. Something fundamental or of primary importance.

çor'nēr=teeth, *n.pl.* The four teeth of a horse, between the middle teeth and the tushes, two above and two below, on each side of the jaw, which shoot when the horse is four and a half years old.

çor'nēr-wīse, *adv.* Diagonally; with the corner in front; not parallel.

çor'net, *n.* [OFr. *cornet*; LL. *cornetum*, a horn, bugle, a kind of hood, from *corneta*, a kind of hood; L. *cornu*, a horn.]

1. In music, (a) the smallest of the wind-instruments of the trumpet kind, consisting of a variously curved metal tube with a cup-shaped, removable mouthpiece, three slides controlled by keys, and terminating in a bell. It has a penetrating and somewhat harsh tone and a range of two octaves; also called *cornet-à-pistons*; (b) a loud organ-stop, now rare; (c) an instrument resembling the oboe, now no longer used.

2. In costumes, (a) a mortar-board cap; (b) a woman's headdress worn about the sixteenth century.

3. In military affairs, (a) a flag; (b) an officer, having charge of such flag; (c) a company of cavalry. [All meanings Obs.]

4. A little cap of paper in which retailers inclose small wares.

5. A cornette.

çor'net, *n.* In farriery, a coronet.

çor'net=ȧ=pis'tŏnş, *n.*; *pl.* **çor'nets=ȧ=pis'tŏnş.** [Fr., a cornet with pistons.] A musical instrument, the cornet. [See *Cornet*, n. 1.]

çor'net-cy, *n.* The commission or rank of a cornet.

çor'net-ēr, *n.* One who blows a cornet.

çor'nette, *n.* The little tube of gold left when the alloy of silver and gold taken from the cupel is rolled and boiled in nitric acid to remove the former metal.

çor-net'tist, *n.* A cornet-player.

çor'neūle, *n.* [Fr., dim. of *cornée*, the cornea.] The cornea of an ocellus.

çorn'fiēld, *n.* A field where corn is grown.

çorn'=flag, *n.* The popular name of a genus of plants, the *Gladiolus*, of several species, bearing red or white flowers.

çorn'flōor, *n.* A floor for threshing corn.

çorn'flow"ēr, *n.* A flower or plant growing among corn, as the bluebottle, wild poppy, etc.

çorn'=här"vest-ēr, *n.* A machine built similar to a self-binder, for cutting and binding corn.

çorn'husk, *n.* One of the tough, fibrous leaves acting as an envelope for an ear of Indian corn.

çorn'=husk"ing, *n.* A husking-bee.

çor'niç, *a.* Pertaining to cornin.

çor'nice, *n.* [OFr. *cornice*; It. *cornice*; L. *cornix*, *coronix*, from *coronis*, a curved line, a flourish with a pen at the end of a book; Gr. *korōnis*, a wreath, garland.]

1. In architecture, any molded projection which crowns or finishes the part to which it is affixed; specifically, the highest part of an entablature resting on the frieze. When the crowning course of a wall is plain it is called a *coping*.

2. A molding for pictures; a picture-cornice.

çor'niced (-nist), *a.* Provided with a cornice.

çor'nice=ring, *n.* The ring on a cannon next behind the muzzle-ring.

çor'ni-çle, *n.* [L. *corniculum*, dim. of *cornu*, a horn.] A little horn. [Obs.]

çor-niç'ū-lăr, *n.* A secretary; a clerk. [Obs.]

çor-niç'ū-lāte, *a.* [LL. *corniculatus*, from *corniculum*, dim. of *cornu*, a horn.]

1. Horned; having horns.

2. In botany, producing horned pods; bearing a little spur or horn.

çor-niç'ū-lum, *n.*; *pl.* **çor-niç'ū-lȧ.** [L. *corniculum*, dim. of *cornu*, a horn.] A hornlike process, as one of the cartilaginous bodies of the larynx.

çor-nif'ēr-ous, *a.* [L. *cornu*, a horn, and *ferre*, to bear.] Horn-bearing; specifically, in geology, designating the lower Devonian rocks.

Çor-nif'ēr-ous, *n.* The Corniferous period.

çor-nif'iç, *a.* [L. *cornu*, a horn, and *-ficus*, from *facere*, to make.] Producing horn.

çor"ni-fi-çā'tion, *n* The transformation into a hornlike substance.

çor'ni-fied, *a.* Transformed into horn.

çor'ni-fọrm, *a.* [L. *cornu*, a horn, and *forma*, form.] Having the form of a horn.

çor-nig'ēr-ous, *a.* [L. *corniger*; *cornu*, a horn, and *gerere*, to bear.] Horned; having horns; as, *cornigerous* animals. [Obs.]

çor'nin, *n.* A crystalline bitter substance extracted from the root of *Cornus florida*; cornic acid.

çorn'ing=house, *n.* A house or place where powder is granulated.

çor'ni-plūme, *n.* [L. *cornu*, a horn, and *pluma*, a feather.] A horn of feathers; a term in ornithology.

Çor'nish, *a.* and *n.* I. *a.* Pertaining to Cornwall, in England

II. *n.* The language of Cornwall.

Cornish chough; see under *Chough*.

Cornish engine; an old form of walking-beam, single-acting engine, first used for pumping in the Cornwall mines, now sometimes used for pumping.

çor'nist, *n.* [Fr. *corniste*, from *corne*, a horn.] A performer on the cornet or horn.

çorn'=jūice, *n.* Whisky. [Slang.]

çorn'=land, *n.* Land appropriated or suitable to the production of corn.

çorn'loft, *n.* An apartment for corn; a granary.

çorn'=mar"i-gōld, *n.* A variety of marigold growing in Italy.

çorn'=meal, *n.* Meal of Indian corn; in Scotland, oatmeal.

çorn′-mil″dew, *n.* Rust, attacking wheat.

çorn′-mill, *n.* A gristmill; specifically, one grinding corn on the cob.

çorn′-mōth, *n.* A small moth, *Tinea granella*, destructive to wheat in the shock or bin.

çorn′mūşe, *n.* A cornemuse. [Obs.]

çor-nō′pē-ăn, *n.* The cornet-à-pistons. [Obs.]

çorn′-plant″ẽr, *n.* An implement for planting corn, either by hand or horse-power.

çorn′-pop″py, *n.* A red poppy, *Papaver Rhœas*, growing in grain-fields.

çorn′-rōşe, *n.* The corn-cockle.

çorn′-sal″ăd, *n.* The common name of *Fedia* or *Valerianella olitoria*, a European plant.

çorn′shel″lẽr, *n.* An implement for shelling corn from the cob.

çorn′shred″dẽr, *n.* A machine for preparing corn for fodder or the silo.

çorn′shuck, *n.* A cornhusk. [Colloq.]

çorn′-smut, *n.* A fungus destroying the growth of corn on the cob by attacking the ear, replacing it by a growth of smut.

çorn′-snāke, *n.* A non-poisonous North American serpent, *Scotophis guttatus*.

çorn′stạlk (-stọk), *n.* 1. A stalk of corn.

2. A native of Australia having white parents. [Colloq. Australia.]

Cornstalk disease; a generally fatal disease, attacking cattle and sometimes horses and sheep after pasturing in corn-fields. Its cause is undetermined but thought to come from corn-smut.

çorn′stärch, *n.* Starch from Indian corn; (a) laundry starch; (b) a meal used as the base of blancmangé, puddings, etc.

çorn′-thrips, *n.* [*Corn* and *thrips*; Gr. *thrips*, a woodworm.] A minute insect, *Phlœothrips cerealium*, found attacking young grain and grass.

çor′nū, *n.*; *pl.* **çor′nū-ȧ.** [L.] 1. A horn.

2. That which resembles a horn; in anatomy, a hornlike part; in conchology, an ammonite.

çor-nū-çō′pi-ȧ, *n.*; *pl.* **çor-nū-çō′pi-æ.** [L. *cornu copiæ*, horn of plenty.]

1. The horn of plenty, an emblem of abundance; also, any representation of such horn, as a cone for holding confectionery.

2. [C—] A genus of grasses having spikes resembling the *cornucopia* in form.

Çor′nus, *n.* A genus of plants of the cornel or dogwood family, consisting of shrubs, trees, or rarely herbs, with small, white or yellowish flowers and ovoid drupes. Fifteen of the twenty-five species are found in the United States.

çor-nūte′, *v.t.* [L. *cornutus*, from *cornu*, a horn.] To give horns to; to cuckold. [Obs.]

çor-nūte′, çor-nūt′ed, *a.* 1. Grafted with horns; horned; also, horn-shaped.

2. Cuckolded. [Obs.]

çor-nū′tō, *n.* [It.] Cuckold. [Obs.]

çor-nū′tŏr, *n.* A cuckold-maker. [Obs.]

çorn′-vī″ō-let, *n.* A species of *Campanula*.

çorn′-wee″vil, *n.* An insect, as *Sphenophorus zeæ*, attacking roots of growing corn, or *Calandra granaria*, which destroys grain in the bin.

çorn′y, *a.* [L. *corneus*, horny, from *cornu*, a horn.] Horny.

çorn′y, *a.* 1. Producing corn; containing corn.

2. Intoxicated. [Slang.]

çor′ō-çōre, *n.* [Native name.] An East Indian boat, sometimes masted. Those of the Celebes are propelled by oars.

çor′ō-dy, *n.*; *pl.* **çor′ō-dieş.** [LL. *corrodium*, *corredium*, furniture, provision, equipment.] Anciently, in English law, an allowance of meat, drink, or clothing, due to the king from an abbey or other religious house, for the sustenance of such of his servants as he thought good to place there for maintenance; also written *corrody*.

çor′ŏl, *n.* A corolla.

çō-rol′lȧ, *n.* [L. *corolla*, a little crown, dim. of *corona*, a crown, wreath.] In botany, the inner covering of a flower. The *corolla* surrounds the parts of fructification, and is composed of one or more flower leaves, called petals. It is distinguished from the perianth by the fineness of its texture and the gayness of its colors.

a a, Many petaled or leaved Corollas. *b b*, Single petaled or leaved Corollas.

çor-ŏl-lā′ceous, *a.* Pertaining to a corolla; inclosing and protecting like a wreath.

çor′ŏl-lā-ry, *n.*; *pl.* **çor′ŏl-lā-rieş.** [LL. *corollarium*, additional inference, corollary, from L. *corolla*, dim. of *corona*, a crown.]

1. A consequent truth which follows immediately from some preceding truth or demonstration.

2. Anything in excess; a surplus. [Obs.]

çor′ŏl-lāte, çor′ŏl-lā-ted, *a.* Like a corolla; having corollas.

çor′ŏl-let, *n.* [Dim. of *corolla*.] One of the partial flowers which make a compound one.

çor-ŏl-lif′ẽr-ous, *a.* Corolla-bearing.

Çō-rol-li-flō′ræ, *n.pl.* One of the great subdivisions of exogenous plants, distinguished by the corolla being gamopetalous, inserted below the ovary, and by the stamens being inserted on the corolla. The primrose, heath, gentian, verbena, etc., are included in this division.

çō-rol-li-flō′răl, çō-rol-li-flō′rous, *a.* [L. *corolla*, a little wreath, and *flos*, *floris*, a flower.] Of or pertaining to the *Corollifloræ*.

çor′ŏl-line, *a.* Relating to a corolla.

çō-rol′lū-lȧ, *n.*; *pl.* **çō-rol′lū-læ.** The corolla of a diminutive flower.

Çor-ō-man′del-wood, *n.* Calamander-wood.

çō-rō′nȧ, *n.*; *pl.* **çō-rō′nȧş,** *or* **çō-rō′næ.** [L., a crown.]

1. A crown bestowed by the Romans as a reward for distinguished military service.

2. In architecture, a member of a cornice, situated between the bed-molding and the cymatium; the drip.

3. In anatomy and zoölogy, any crown or crown-like part.

4. In botany, (a) the margin of a radiated composite flower; (b) an appendage of the corolla or petals attached basally to the limb; (c) the appendage at the top of seeds enabling them to disperse.

5. In astronomy, (a) a halo or luminous circle around one of the heavenly bodies, as in a total eclipse of the sun; (b) a phase of the aurora borealis characterized by luminous radiations from one point.

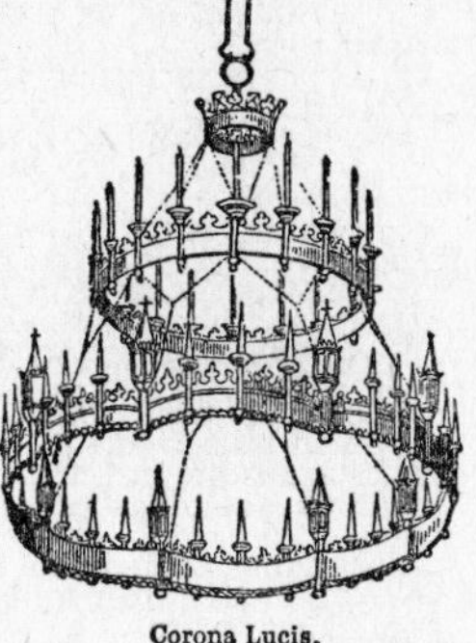

Corona Lucis.

6. Ecclesiastically, the stripe passing horizontally about the lower edge of a miter.

7. A *corona* lucis.

8. In music, a hold, (𝄐).

Corona lucis; a chandelier hung in the vaulting or roof of a church, having the lights arranged in one or more circles and illuminated only on ceremonial occasions; called also *corona*.

çor′ō-naçh, çor′ȧ-naçh, *n.* A dirge or lamentation of the Irish or Scotch for the dead.

çor′ō-năl, *a.* [LL. *coronalis*, from L. *corona*, a crown.]

1. Pertaining or belonging to a crown or to coronation. [Rare.]

2. Of or pertaining to the crown or top of the head; as, the *coronal* suture; following the direction of the *coronal* suture; as, a *coronal* section.

3. In general, of or pertaining to a corona.

Coronal cell; a crowning cell.

Coronal suture; that suture of the skull between the frontal and the parietal bones; the frontoparietal suture.

çor′ō-năl, *n.* 1. A crown; a wreath; a garland; anything resembling a crown.

2. The coronal suture; also, occasionally, the frontal bone.

3. The head of a jousting lance, constructed to unhorse but not to wound a knight; sometimes, the lance itself. Formerly written in these senses, *coronel*.

4. In biology, a crowning or coronal cell.

çor-ō-nā′men, *n.* [LL. *coronamen*, a wreathing, crowning, from L. *coronare*, to crown; *corona*, a crown.] The superior margin of a hoof, called in veterinary surgery the *coronet*.

çor′ō-nā-ry, *a.* [L. *coronarius*, from *corona*, a crown.] Pertaining to a crown or wreath; resembling a crown; placed as a crown; encircling; as, *coronary* vessels, ligaments, etc.

Coronary suture; same as *Coronal suture*.

çor′ō-nā-ry, *n.*; *pl.* **çor′ō-nā-rieş.** The small pastern-bone, constituting the second phalanx of a horse's foot.

çor′ō-nāte, çor′ō-nā-ted, *a.* [L. *coronatus*, pp. of *coronare*, to crown, from *corona*, a crown.] Wearing a crown; having some appendage or process resembling a crown; crowned; particularly, (a) in botany, having a corona; (b) in ornithology, crested, with conspicuous coronal feathers; (c) in zoölogy, surmounted with rows of spines, tubercles, etc., as are certain spiral shells.

çor-ō-nā′tion, *n.* 1. The act or solemnity of crowning a sovereign; the act of investing a prince with the insignia of royalty, on his succeeding to the sovereignty.

2. The pomp or assembly of a coronation.

çor′ō-nel (*or* kūr′nel), *n.* A colonel. [Obs.]

çor′ō-nel, *n.* [Obs.] See *Coronal*, 3.

çor′ō-nẽr, *n.* [ME. *coroner*; OFr. *coroneor*; LL. *coronator*, a coroner, crowner, from L. *coronare*, to crown; *corona*, a crown.]

1. A county officer whose principal duty is to investigate the cause of death of a person who is known or supposed to have died a violent death, or who dies in prison. He also usually acts as sheriff when that officer is disqualified. In some places the office of *coroner* is superseded by that of medical examiner.

2. In England, formerly, an officer having charge of the private property of the crown; hence, the early form of the word, *crowner*, now in disuse.

çor′ō-net, *n.* [OFr. *coronette*, *coronete*, a little crown, dim. of *corone*; L. *corona*, a crown.]

1. A crown worn by noblemen and princes of rank inferior to that of sovereign. In England the *coronet* of a duke is adorned with strawberry leaves; that of a marquis has leaves with pearls interposed; that of an earl raises the pearls above the leaves; that of a viscount is surrounded with pearls only; that of a baron has only four pearls.

1. Coronet of Prince of Wales; 2. Of younger children of the Sovereign; 3. Of a Duke; 4. Of a Marquis; 5. Of an Earl; 6. Of a Viscount; 7. Of a Baron.

2. An ornamental headdress; a coronal.

3. The margin around the upper part of the hoof of a horse, where the skin joins the horn; called also *coronamen*.

4. Same as *Coronal*, n. 3.

5. In zoölogy, a row of spines or hair-like processes encircling some part, generally near its end.

çor′ō-net-ed, *a.* Wearing, or entitled to wear, a coronet.

çō-rō′ni-fọrm, *a.* [L. *corona*, a crown, and *forma*, form.] Having the form of a crown.

Çor-ō-nil′lȧ, *n.* [L., from *corona*, a crown.] A genus of annual or perennial plants of the bean family, having stalked umbels of yellow flowers. The leaves of some species have important medicinal properties.

çō-rō′nis, *n.* [Gr. *korōnis*, a curved line or stroke.]

1. In Greek grammar, the sign (ʼ) of the contraction of two vowels into a long vowel or a diphthong, the first vowel ending a word and the second beginning the succeeding word.

2. A double flourish used in ancient manuscripts to indicate the end of a section or chapter; hence, the end. [Rare or Obs.]

çō-rō′ni-um, *n.* An element, known only through its spectrum, supposed to exist in a gaseous state in the sun's corona.

çor′ō-noid, *a.* [Gr. *korōnē*, a crow, and *eidos*, form.] In anatomy, (a) like the beak of a crow; applied to certain processes of the bones; as, the *coronoid* process of the lower jaw; (b) pertaining to a *coronoid* process.

çor′ō-nūle, *n.* [L. *coronula*, dim. of *corona*, a crown.] A coronet or little crown of a seed; the downy tuft on seeds.

çō-roune′, çō-roun′, *n.* and *v.* [Obs.] Same as *Crown*.

çō-rō′zō, çō-rōs′sō, *n.* [S. Am.] 1. The seed of a tropical American palm, the *Phytelephas Macrocarpa*, whose hardened albumen, under the name of vegetable ivory, is used for the manufacture of small ornamental articles; called also *ivory-nut*.

2. The *Attalea Cohune*; a palm of Central America, the nuts of which are oil-producing.

çor′pō-rȧ, *n.*, pl. of *corpus*.

çor′pō-rāce, *n.* A kind of cloth. [Obs. See *Corporal*.]

çor′pō-răl, *n.* [Corrupted from Fr. *caporal*; It. *caporale*, a corporal, from *capo*, the head; L. *caput*, the head.]

1. A noncommissioned officer next below a sergeant; the lowest officer in a company. He has charge over one of the divisions of the company, a squad; places and relieves sentinels, etc.

2. A popular name for the fish *Semotilus bullaris* or *corporalis*; known also as the *fallfish*, the *silver chub*, etc.

Corporal's guard; a small detachment of soldiers under command of a corporal, as assigned to guard duty, etc.; also, a small number of followers or adherents.

Ship's corporal; an officer under the master-at-arms, having various petty duties.

çor′pō-răl, *a.* [L. *corporalis*, from *corpus*, body.]

1. Belonging or relating to the body; physical; opposed to *mental*; as, *corporal* punishment.

2. Corporeal; material; not spiritual. [Rare.]

3. In zoölogy, pertaining to the body or trunk, as separate from appendages, such as the head, limbs, etc.

çor′pō-răl, *n.* [OFr. *corporal*; LL. *corporale* (*pallium*, pall, understood), neut. of *corporalis*, from *corpus*, *corporis*, body.] A fine linen cloth, used in the celebration of the eucharist to cover the altar. The sacred vessels are placed on it, one end being thrown back over the paten; called also *corporal-cloth*, *corporale*, and, formerly, *corporace*, *corporas*.

Corporal oath; a solemn oath; so called from the ancient usage of touching the *corporal*, or cloth that covered the consecrated elements, while taking an oath.

çor-pō-rā′le, *n.*; *pl.* **çor-pō-rā′li-ȧ.** Same as third *Corporal*.

çor-pō-ral′i-ty, *n.*; *pl.* **çor-pō-ral′i-tieṣ.** 1. The state of having a body or being embodied; opposed to *spirituality*.

2. A gild or corporation. [Obs.]

çor′pō-răl-ly, *adv.* Bodily; in or with the body; as, to be *corporally* present.

çor′pō-răl-ship, *n.* A corporal's office or command.

çor′pō-răs, *n.* A cloth, the corporal. [Obs.]

çor′pō-rāte, *a.* [L. *corporatus*, pp. of *corporare*, to make into a body, from *corpus*, *corporis*, a body.]

1. United in a legal body, as a number of individuals who are empowered to transact business as an individual; formed into a corporation; incorporated; as, a *corporate* town.

2. Belonging or pertaining to a corporation; as, *corporate* interests.

3. United; general; collectively one.

They answer in a *corporate* voice. —Shak.

Corporate member; a voting member of a corporation; an active member as distinguished from an honorary member.

çor′pō-rāte, *v.t.* and *v.i.* [Obs.] Same as *Incorporate*.

çor′pō-rāte-ly, *adv.* 1. In a corporate capacity.

2. Bodily; in, or with regard to the body.

çor′pō-rāte-ness, *n.* The state of being a corporate body.

çor-pō-rā′tion, *n.* [Fr. *corporation*; LL. *corporatio*, the assumption of a body, from *corporare*, to form into a body, from *corpus*, a body.] A body politic or corporate, formed and authorized by law to act as a single person; a society having the capacity of transacting business as an individual.

Corporation aggregate; a corporation consisting of two or more persons united in a society, which is preserved by a succession of members, either forever, or until the corporation is dissolved by the power that formed it, by the death of all its members, by surrender of its charter or franchises, or by forfeiture. Such corporations are the mayor and aldermen of cities, the head and fellows of a college, the dean and chapter of a cathedral church, the stockholders of a bank or insurance company, etc.

Close corporation; see under *Close*.

Corporation sole; a corporation consisting of one person at a time, as a king or bishop, who among other legal rights has that of official succession.

Public or *municipal corporation*; a corporation formed for political purposes, such as a town, county, etc.

Private corporation; a corporation which is not public.

çor′pō-rā-tŏr, *n.* A member of a corporation; particularly, a member at the time of incorporation; an original incorporator.

çor′pō-rā-tūre, *n.* The state of being embodied. [Obs.]

çor-pō′rē-ăl, *a.* [L. *corporeus*, from *corpus*, *corporis*, a body.]

1. Having a body; consisting of material substance; material; opposed to *spiritual* or *immaterial*; as, our *corporeal* frame; *corporeal* substance.

2. Of a physical nature; pertaining to the body; bodily; opposed to *mental*; as, *corporeal* powers.

Corporeal property; in law, property that is tangible, that can be perceived by the senses, as distinguished from incorporeal property.

çor-pō′rē-ăl-iṣm, *n.* The principles of a corporealist; materialism. [Rare.]

çor-pō′rē-ăl-ist, *n.* One who denies the existence of spiritual substances; one who believes in materialism.

çor-pō-rē-al′i-ty, *n.*; *pl.* **çor-pō-rē-al′i-tieṣ.** The state of being corporeal.

çor-pō′rē-ăl-ly, *adv.* In body; in a bodily form or manner.

çor-pō′rē-ăl-ness, *n.* Corporeality.

çor-pō-rē′i-ty, *n.* The state of having a body, or being embodied; materiality; corporeality.

The one attributed *corporeity* to God. —Stillingfleet.

çor-pō′rē-ous, *a.* [Obs.] Same as *Corporeal*.

çor-por″i-fi-çā′tion, *n.* The act of giving body or palpability to. [Obs.]

çor-por′i-fy, *v.t.* To embody; to form into a body. [Obs.]

çor′pō-ṣănt, *n.* [Port. *corpo santo*, from L. *corpus sanctum*, holy body.] A name given by seamen to a luminous appearance often beheld, in dark, tempestuous nights, about the decks and rigging of a ship, but particularly at the mastheads and yardarms, supposed to be electrical; St. Elmo's fire.

çorps (kōr; *pl.* kōrz), *n. sing.* and *pl.* [Fr. *corps*, from OFr. *corps*, the body; L. *corpus*, the body.]

1. Any body of persons associated in some common work or interest; as, a *corps* of artists; a *corps* of teachers.

2. In military usage, a body of men; an organized part of an army; particularly, (a) the tactical unit next larger than a division; an army-*corps*; (b) any branch of the military service which, while related to an army, has its own organization; as, a *corps* of engineers; a signal *corps*.

3. A society formed by the students of a German university.

4. A body of laws. [Obs.]

5. A dead body; a corpse. [Obs.]

Diplomatic corps; the entire body of official representatives from foreign countries.

çorpse, *n.* [Fr. *corps*, from L. *corpus*, a body.]

1. The dead body of a human being; figuratively, anything divested of life.

2. A living body; body in opposition to the soul. [Obs.]

3. The land from which an ecclesiastical endowment is derived. [Obs.]

çorpse′=căn″dle, *n.* 1. A candle used at ceremonious watchings of a corpse before interment.

2. A name popular in England for a phosphorescent light, an ignis fatuus, sometimes seen in graveyards.

çorpse′=gāte, *n.* A covered gateway at the entrance to churchyards, intended to shelter the burial procession from rain; called also *lichgate*.

çorpse′=light, *n.* 1. St. Elmo's fire.

2. A corpse-candle.

çorpse′=plant, *n.* The Indian-pipe.

çor′pū-lence, çor′pū-len-cy, *n.* 1. Fleshiness; excessive fatness; a state of being unduly loaded with flesh; bulkiness of figure.

2. Density or solidity of matter. [Obs.]

çor′pū-lent, *a.* [Fr. *corpulent*, from L. *corpulentus*, fleshy, fat, from *corpus*, a body.]

1. Fleshy; having a great or excessive quantity of fat or flesh; obese; stout; bulky.

2. Solid; dense; opaque. [Obs.]

Syn.—Fat, portly, fleshy, stout.

çor′pū-lent-ly, *adv.* In a corpulent manner.

çor′pus, *n.*; *pl.* **çor′pō-rȧ.** [L.] 1. Any body, living or dead; matter of whatever kind; the substance as distinguished from the spirit.

2. The material substance of a thing; the entire matter or body; in law, a corporeal thing.

3. In anatomy, the whole body; or some part, often designated by a qualifying term.

4. A collection of objects, facts, etc., taken as a whole; also, a statement or account thereof.

Corpora quadrigemina (L., fourfold bodies); four tubercles or eminences, within which is gray matter, situated behind the third ventricle of the brain; the optic lobes. In animals lower than mammals only two of these bodies are developed; they are known as *corpora bigemina*.

Corpus callosum (L., callous body); the transverse commissure uniting the two hemispheres of the brain.

Corpus Christi (L., body of Christ); a festival of the church of Rome, observed on the first Thursday after Trinity Sunday, in honor of the eucharist.

Corpus Christi cloth; the veil which covers the pyx; usually called *pyx-cloth*.

Corpus delicti (L., body of the crime); in law, fundamental proof of the commission of the crime; in a murder case, the production of the body itself.

Corpus luteum (L., yellow body); a firm substance, of a reddish-yellow color, formed in a Graafian follicle after it has been ruptured in the discharge of an ovum.

Corpus striatum (L., striate body), one of two pear-shaped masses of ganglionic cells, situated at the base of the brain, partly imbedded in the white substance of the cerebral hemispheres.

çor′pus-cle (-sl), *n.* [L. *corpusculum*, dim. of *corpus*, body.]

1. A minute particle or molecule of matter.

2. In anatomy, a cell; an exceedingly minute body of matter. *Corpuscles* may be fixed in more or less solid substance, as those of bone and connective tissue or they may be free to move, as those of blood.

Red blood corpuscles; disks which are circular in the blood of man and most mammals. In birds, reptiles, etc., they are oval and occasionally spherical. Human *red blood corpuscles* are non-nucleated, doubly concave disks, averaging about $\frac{1}{3300}$ of an inch in diameter. The cell-wall is colorless, one of the principal constituents of the body matter, hæmoglobin, giving them their color. Red corpuscles tend to adhere in long rolls like piles of coins.

White corpuscles; nucleated blood-cells, somewhat larger than red corpuscles, and much fewer in number. They are composed chiefly of free protoplasm, are irregular in shape, and have certain contractile and locomotive powers.

çor-pus′çū-lăr, *a.* [Fr. *corpusculaire*, from L. *corpusculum*, dim. of *corpus*, a body.] Pertaining to corpuscles; consisting of corpuscles or small particles; molecular.

The corpuscular philosophy; that system of philosophy that attempts to account for the phenomena of nature, by the motion, figure, rest, position, etc., of the minute particles of matter.

Corpuscular theory; a theory for explaining the nature of light, adopted and advocated by Newton, but now rejected for the undulatory theory. According to this theory, the sun and all other luminous bodies have the property of emitting exceedingly minute particles of their substance with prodigious velocity, and these particles entering the eye produce the sensation of vision. It has also been termed the *Newtonian theory*.

çor-pus-çū-lā′ri-ăn, *a.* Corpuscular.

çor-pus-çū-lā′ri-ăn, *n.* An advocate of or believer in the corpuscular philosophy.

çor-pus′çūle, *n.* Same as *Corpuscle*. [Obs.]

çor-pus′çū-lous, *a.* Same as *Corpuscular*.

çor-rāde′, *v.t.*; corraded, *pt.*, *pp.*; corrading, *ppr.* [L. *corradere*, to scrape together; *con-*, together, and *radere*, to scrape, rub.]

1. To rub off; to fret or consume. [Obs.]

2. In geology, to wear away, erode, or disintegrate by the action of running water.

çor-rā′di-ăl, *a.* Radiating from one center; converging to one point. [Rare.]

çor-rā′di-āte, *v.t.*; corradiated, *pt.*, *pp.*; corradiating, *ppr.* [L. *con-*, together, and *radiatus*, pp. of *radiare*, to beam; *radius*, a staff, spoke.] To converge or focus to a single point.

çor-rā-di-ā′tion, *n.* A conjunction of rays in one point.

çor-ral′, *n.* [Sp. *corral*, a pen or inclosure, for cattle, from *corro*, a circle or ring; L. *currere*, to run.]

1. A pen or inclosure for horses or cattle.

2. An inclosure formed of wagons, employed by emigrants as a means of defense and for confining the horses and other grazing animals.

3. A strong stockade or inclosure for capturing wild elephants in Ceylon.

çor-ral′, *v.t.*; corralled, *pt.*, *pp.*; corralling, *ppr.* 1. To form into a corral; to form a corral or inclosure by means of; as, to *corral* wagons; also, to drive into a corral or inclosure; as, to *corral* animals.

2. To secure or capture; to seize or take possession of; as, to *corral* thieves.

3. To cut off from escape; to corner, particularly in argument.

çor-rā′ṣion, *n.* [L. *corradere*; *con-*, together, and *radere*, to scrape, rub off.] The wearing away of rocks, etc., through the action of running water, either by solution or attrition; one of the processes of erosion.

çor-rā′sive, *a.* [Obs.] Same as *Corrosive*.

çor′rē-ăl, *a.* [LL. *correus*, an accomplice; *con-*, together, and *reus*, one accused; *res*, a thing, case.] Relating to, or having joint obligation.

çŏr-rect′, *a.* [L. *correctus*, pp. of *corrigere*; *con-*, together, and *regere*, to lead straight, direct.] Set right, or made straight; right; conformable to truth, rectitude, or propriety, or conformable to a just standard; not faulty; free from error; as, *correct* measurements; *correct* manners.

Syn.—Right, proper, faultless, exact, precise, accurate.

çŏr-rect′, *v.t.*; corrected, *pt.*, *pp.*; correcting, *ppr.* 1. To make right; to rectify; to bring to the standard of truth, justice, or propriety; as, to *correct* manners or principles.

2. To amend; to point out or remove faults or errors in; to set right; as, to *correct* a manuscript; to *correct* a student's work.

3. To bring back or attempt to bring back to propriety in morals; to punish for faults or deviations from moral rectitude; to chastise;

to discipline; to reprove or rebuke; as, a child should be *corrected* for lying.

Correct thy son, and he shall give thee rest. —Prov. xxix. 17.

4 To obviate or remove (something wrong or inconvenient), to reduce or change the qualities of; to counteract; to remedy; to rectify or destroy; as, to *correct* the acidity of the stomach by alkaline preparations; to *correct* errors and abuses.

Syn.—Amend, improve, reform, rectify, reprove, punish.

çŏr-reçt′ȧ-ble, çŏr-reçt′i-ble, *a.* Open to correction; able to be corrected or made right.

çŏr-reçt′i-fȳ, *v.t.* To set right. [Obs.]

çŏr-reç′tion, *n.* 1. The act of correcting; the act of pointing out errors, mistakes, etc., or of setting right according to a just standard, as to truth, rectitude, justice, or propriety; rectification; amendment; as, the *correction* of opinions or manners.

2. That which is substituted or suggested in the place of what is wrong; a change or amendment; as, the *corrections* in his manuscripts were few.

3. That which is intended to rectify or to cure faults; the act of punishing or reproving; a reprimand or rebuke; discipline; chastisement.

4. Abatement of noxious qualities; the act or process of counteracting or removing what is inconvenient or hurtful in its effects; as, the *correction* of acidity in the stomach.

5. In mathematics and physics, a quantity which must be considered in the solution of a problem or the use of an instrument, to secure exact results; as, a compass *correction*; a *correction* for temperature.

House of correction; a house where disorderly persons are confined; a bridewell.

Under correction; open to correction.

çŏr-reç′tion-ăl, *a.* Tending to or intended for correction.

çŏr-reç′tion-ẽr, *n.* One that has been, or is, in the house of correction. [Obs.]

çŏr-reç′tion-line, *n.* In the United States' survey, one of the parallels of latitude taken as a new base-line, thus partially correcting the convergence of north and south lines.

çŏr-reçt′ive, *a.* 1. Having the power to correct; as, *corrective* penalties.

Mulberries are pectoral, *corrective* of bilious alkali. —Arbuthnot.

2. Limiting; restrictive.

çŏr-reçt′ive, *n.* 1. That which has the power of correcting; that which has the quality of altering or removing what is wrong or injurious; counteractive; as, alkalis are *correctives* of acids; penalties are *correctives* of immoral conduct.

2. Limitation; restriction. [Obs.]

çŏr-reçt′ly, *adv.* In a correct manner; accurately; without fault or error.

çŏr-reçt′ness, *n.* The state or quality of exactness or precision; as, the *correctness* of manners, of taste, in writing or speaking.

Syn.—Accuracy, exactness, precision, propriety.

çŏr-reçt′ŏr, *n.* 1. One who corrects.

2. That which corrects; as, a *corrector* of wrongs; an alkali is a *corrector* of acids.

çŏr-reçt′ō-ry, *a.* and *n.* I. *a.* Tending to correct.

II. *n.* A corrective.

çŏr-reçt′ress, *n.* A feminine corrector.

çor-reġ′i-dor (*or Sp. pron*, -rā′hē-dōr), *n.* [Sp., a corrector, from *corregir*, to correct.]

1 In Spain, the mayor of a town.

2. In Spanish America, a magisterial officer.

çor-reġ″i-mi-en′tō (*or Sp. pron.*, -rā-hē-mē-än′-tō), *n.* [Sp., from *corregir*, to correct.] In Spanish America, the authority or jurisdiction of a corregidor.

çor′rei (kor′i), *n.* Same as *Corrie.*

çor-rē-lāt′ȧ-ble, *a.* That can be correlated; as, *correlatable* divisions.

çor′rē-lāte, *n.* [L. *con-*, together, and *relatus*, related, pp. of *referre*, to bear back.] One who or that which stands in a reciprocal relation to something else, as father and son.

çor-rē-lāte′, *v.i.*; correlated, *pt., pp.*; correlating, *ppr.* To have a reciprocal relation; to be reciprocally related, as father and son.

çor-rē-lāte′, *v.t.* To place in reciprocal relation; to institute a comparison or parallelism between; to determine the relations between, as between several objects or phenomena bearing a resemblance to one another.

çor-rē-lā′tion, *n.* 1. Reciprocal relation; corresponding similarity or parallelism of relation or law.

2. In geometry, the reciprocal relation between propositions, figures, etc., derivable from each other by interchanging the words *point* and *plane*, or *point* and *line.*

Correlation of energy or *of forces*; in physics, the theory that all the forces of nature—heat, light, electricity, magnetism, chemical affinity, and motion—are mutually convertible.

çor-rē-lā′tion-ist, *n.* A believer in correlation.

çŏr-rel′ȧ-tive, *a.* Having a reciprocal relation; reciprocal: as, father and son, husband and wife, are *correlative* terms.

çŏr-rel′ȧ-tive, *n.* 1. That which is correlative; that of which the existence implies the existence of something else; thus, "master" and "servant" are *correlatives.*

2. In grammar, the antecedent to a pronoun.

çŏr-rel′ȧ-tive-ly, *adv.* In a correlative relation.

çŏr-rel′ȧ-tive-ness, *n.* The state of being correlative.

çor-rē-liġ′iŏn-ist, *n.* A coreligionist.

çor-rep′tion, *n.* [L. *correptio*, from *corripere*, to seize upon, reproach.] Chiding; reproof; reprimand. [Obs.]

çor-re-spond′, *v.i.*; corresponded, *pt., pp.*; corresponding, *ppr.* [Fr. *correspondre*, from L. *con-*, together, and *respondere*, to answer.]

1. To be correspondent or congruous; to be adapted to; to be suitable to; to be adequate or proportionate to; to agree; to fit; used absolutely or followed by *with* or *to*; as, his words and actions do not *correspond*; levity of manners does not *correspond with* the clerical character.

2. To communicate by letters sent and received; to hold intercourse with a person at a distance by sending and receiving letters.

Not for three years to *correspond* with home. —Tennyson.

3. To hold communion. [Obs.]

Magnanimous to *correspond* with heaven. —Milton.

Syn.—Suit, agree, fit, answer.

çor-re-spond′ence, *n.* 1. Relation; fitness; congruity; mutual adaptation of one thing to another; as, *correspondence* of two theories.

2. Intercourse between persons at a distance, by means of letters sent and answers received; as, a *correspondence* on the subject of commerce.

3. The letters which pass between correspondents; as, the *correspondence* of Washington and Jefferson.

4. Friendly intercourse; reciprocal exchange of offices or civilities; connection.

Let military persons hold good *correspondence* with the other great men in the state. —Bacon.

çor-re-spond′en-cy, *n.* Same as *Correspondence.*

çor-re-spond′ent, *a.* Suitable; fit; congruous; agreeable; answerable, adapted.

çor-re-spond′ent, *n.* 1. One who corresponds, one with whom an intercourse is carried on by letters or messages

2. One who furnishes information to a newspaper or magazine either by mail or telegraph.

3. In commerce, (a) one having charge of the correspondence of a firm; (b) a firm in the same or a similar line of business as another, with whom business correspondence is regularly held; as, country banks have *correspondents* in the cities.

çor-re-spond′ent-ly, *adv.* In a corresponding manner.

çor-re-spond′ing, *a.* Carrying on intercourse by letters; answering; agreeing; suiting.

Corresponding member; a member of a society residing at a distance, who is invited to hold intercourse with the society, and aid in carrying out its designs.

çor-re-spond′ing-ly, *adv.* In a corresponding manner.

çor-re-spon′sion, *n.* Correspondence. [Rare.]

çor-re-spon′sive, *a.* Answerable; adapted; conformable.

çor-re-spon′sive-ly, *adv.* In a corresponsive manner.

çor′ri-dor, *n.* [Fr., from It. *corridore*, a gallery, corridor, runner, from L. *currere*, to run.]

1. In architecture, a gallery or open communication round a building, leading to several chambers at a distance from each other.

2. In fortification, the covered way lying round the whole compass of the fortifications of a place.

çor′rie, çor′ri (kor′i), *n.* [Scot.] A hollow in a side hill, often sheltering game; spelled also *correi.*

çor-ri-ġen′dum, *n.*; *pl.* **çor-ri-ġen′dȧ.** [L., gerund of *corrigere*, to correct.] A thing to be corrected.

çor′ri-ġent, *n.* [L. *corrigens (-entis)*, ppr of *corrigere*, to correct.] In medicine, a substance used to modify the taste or effect of another ingredient.

çor′ri-ġent, *a.* Corrective; modifying.

çor″ri-ġi-bil′i-ty, *n.* Corrigibleness.

çor′ri-ġi-ble, *a.* [Fr., from L. *corrigere*, to correct.]

1. That may be set right, or amended; as, a *corrigible* defect.

2. That may be reformed; submissive.

3. Punishable; that may be chastised for correction. [Obs.]

4. Corrective. [Obs.]

çor′ri-ġi-ble-ness, *n.* The quality of being corrigible.

çor-ri′văl, *n.* 1. A fellow-rival; a competitor.

2. A companion. [Obs.]

çor-ri′văl, *a.* Competitive; rivaling.

çor-ri′văl, *v.i.* and *v.t.* To rival.

çor-ri′văl-ry, *n.* Competition. [Rare.]

çor-ri′văl-ship, *n.* Competition. [Rare.]

çor′ri-vāte, *v.t.* [L. *corrivatus*, pp. of *corrivare*, to corrivate.] To draw water out of several streams into one. [Obs.]

çor-ri-vā′tion, *n.* The running of different streams into one. [Obs.]

çŏr-rob′ō-rănt, *a.* Strengthening; having the power or quality of giving strength; as, a *corroborant* medicine.

çŏr-rob′ō-rănt, *n.* A medicine that strengthens; a tonic.

çŏr-rob′ō-rāte, *v.t.*; corroborated, *pt., pp.*; corroborating, *ppr.* [L. *corroboratus*, pp. of *corroborare*, to strengthen; *con-*, together, and *roborare*, from *robur*, *roboris*, strength.]

1. To strengthen; to make strong, or to give additional strength to. [Obs.]

2. To confirm; to make more certain; as, to *corroborate* a suspicion.

çŏr-rob′ō-rāte, *a* Confirmed. [Obs.]

çŏr-rob-ō-rā′tion, *n* 1. The act of strengthening or confirming; addition of strength, assurance, or security; confirmation; as, the *corroboration* of an argument, or of intelligence.

2. Whatever corroborates.

çŏr-rob′ō-rȧ-tive, *a.* Having the power of giving strength, or additional strength; tending to confirm.

çŏr-rob′ō-rȧ-tive, *n.* A medicine that strengthens; a corroborant.

çŏr-rob′ō-rȧ-tō-ry, *a.* Having a tendency to strengthen; corroborative.

çor-rob′ō-ree, çor-rob′ō-ry, *n.* [Native name.] The war-dance of the Australian aborigines.

çor-rob′ō-ree, çor-rob′ō-ry, *v.i.* To participate in a corroboree.

çŏr-rōde′, *v.t.*; corroded, *pt., pp.*; corroding, *ppr.* [L. *corrodere*, to gnaw to pieces; *con-*, together, and *rodere*, to gnaw.]

1. To eat away by degrees; to wear away or diminish by gradually separating small particles from a body, in the manner an animal gnaws a substance; as, nitric acid *corrodes* copper

2. To wear away by degrees; to prey upon; to impair; to consume or diminish by slow degrees, as, jealousy and envy *corrode* the constitution.

çŏr-rōde′, *v.i.* To act, or be acted on, corrosively, used literally and figuratively.

Syn.—Canker, gnaw, rust, waste, attack.

çŏr-rōd′ent, *a.* Corroding. [Rare.]

çŏr-rōd′ent, *n.* A corrosive

çŏr-rō′di-āte, *v.t.* [Obs.] Same as *Corrode.*

çŏr-rō-di-bil′i-ty, *n.* The quality of being corrodible. [Rare.]

çŏr-rōd′i-ble, *a.* That may be corroded.

çor′rō-dy, *n.* Same as *Corody.*

çŏr-rō-si-bil′i-ty, *n.* Same as *Corrodibility.*

çŏr-rō′si-ble, *a.* Same as *Corrodible.*

çŏr-rō′si-ble-ness, *n.* The quality of being corrosible.

çŏr-rō′sion, *n.* [LL. *corrosio (-onis)*, from L. *corrodere*, to corrode, gnaw to pieces.] The action of eating or wearing away by slow degrees, as by the action of acids on metals, by which the substance is gradually changed.

çŏr-rō′sive, *a.* 1. Eating; wearing away; having the power of gradually wearing, consuming, or impairing; as, *corrosive* care; a *corrosive* ulcer.

2. Having the quality of fretting or vexing.

Corrosive sublimate; the bichlorid of mercury, $HgCl_2$, prepared by subliming an intimate mixture of equal parts of common salt and mercuric sulphate; it is a white crystalline solid, and is an acrid poison of great virulence.

çŏr-rō′sive, *n.* 1. That which has the quality of eating or wearing gradually.

2. That which has the power of fretting.

çŏr-rō′sive-ly, *adv.* In a corrosive manner.

çŏr-rō′sive-ness, *n.* The quality of corroding, eating away, or wearing; acrimony.

çor-rō′văl, *n.* A variety of curari, used by the Indians of South America as an arrow-poison. [See *Curari.*]

çor-rō′vȧ-line, *n.* A poisonous alkaloid derived from corroval; curarine.

çor′rụ-gănt, *a.* Having the power of contracting into wrinkles.

çor′rụ-gāte, *v.t.*; corrugated, *pt., pp.*; corrugating, *ppr.* [L. *corrugatus*, pp. of *corrugare*; *con-*, together, and *rugare*, to wrinkle; from *ruga*, a wrinkle, fold.] To wrinkle; to draw or contract into alternate ridges and furrows; purse up; as, to *corrugate* the brow.

Corrugated iron; sheet iron pressed into wrinkles or folds, so as to give it greater stiffness.

çor′rụ-gāte, *a.* Wrinkled.

çor-ru̇-gā′tion, *n.* A wrinkling; contraction into wrinkles; the act of corrugating.

çor′ru̇-gā-tŏr, *n.* [L., from *corrugare*, to wrinkle.] A muscle which contracts the skin of the forehead into wrinkles.

çor-ru̇′gent, *a.* In anatomy, contracting; drawing together. [Obs.]

çor-rump′, *v.t.* [Obs.] Same as *Corrupt.*

çor-rump′ȧ-ble, *a.* [Obs.] Same as *Corruptible.*

çŏr-rupt′, *v.t.*; corrupted, *pt., pp.*; corrupting, *ppr.* [L. *corruptus*, pp. of *corrumpere*, to destroy, spoil, bribe; *con-*, together, and *rumpere*, to break in pieces.]

1. To change from a sound to a putrid or putrescent state; to separate the component parts of (a body), as by a natural process, which is accompanied by a fetid smell.

2. To vitiate or deprave; to change from good to bad.

3. To waste, spoil, or consume.

4. To pervert or vitiate, as integrity; to bribe; as, to *corrupt* a judge.

5. To debase or render impure, by alterations or innovations; to falsify; to infect with errors; as, to *corrupt* a manuscript.

çŏr-rupt′, *v.i.* 1. To become putrid; to putrefy; to rot.

2. To become vitiated; to lose purity.

çŏr-rupt′, *a.* 1. Changed from a sound to a putrid state, as by natural decomposition; spoiled; tainted; vitiated; unsound.

> *Corrupt* and pestilent bread. —Knolles.

2. Changed from the state of being correct, pure, or true to a worse state; depraved; vitiated; perverted.

> At what ease
> Might *corrupt* minds procure knaves as *corrupt*
> To swear against you. —Shak.

3. Debased; rendered impure; changed to a worse state; as, *corrupt* language.

4. Ready to be influenced by a bribe; as, a *corrupt* judge; a *corrupt* constituency.

5. Not genuine; infected with errors or mistakes; as, the text is *corrupt.*

çŏr-rupt′ẽr, *n.* One who or that which corrupts.

çŏr-rupt′fụl, *a.* Vitiating. [Rare.]

çŏr-rupt-i-bil′i-ty, *n.* Corruptibleness.

çŏr-rupt′i-ble, *a.* 1. That may be corrupted; that may become putrid; subject to decay and destruction; as, our bodies are *corruptible.*

2. That may be vitiated in qualities or principles; susceptible of degeneration.

çŏr-rupt′i-ble, *n.* That which decays. [Obs.]

çŏr-rupt′i-ble-ness, *n.* Susceptibility of corruption; corruptibility.

çŏr-rupt′i-bly, *adv.* In a corruptible manner.

çŏr-rup′tion, *n.* 1. The act of corrupting, or state of being corrupt or putrid; the destruction of the natural form of bodies by the separation of the component parts or by disorganization in the process of putrefaction; physical deterioration, however produced.

2. Putrid matter; pus.

3. Depravity; wickedness; perversion or deterioration of moral principles; loss of purity or integrity.

> Having escaped the *corruption* that is in the world through lust. —2 Pet. i. 4.

4. Debasement, taint, or tendency to a worse state.

> Keep mine honor from *corruption.* —Shak.

5. Impurity; vitiation; debasement; as, a *corruption* of language.

6. A perverting or vitiating influence; more specifically, bribery.

> *Corruption* in elections is the great enemy of freedom. —J. Adams.

7. In law, taint; specifically, in old English law, impurity of blood in consequence of an act of attainder of treason or felony, by which a person is disabled from inheriting lands from an ancestor, and can neither retain those in his possession nor transmit them by descent to his heirs.

> *Corruption* of blood can be removed only by act of Parliament. —Blackstone.

Syn.—Putrescence, putrefaction, pollution, defilement, contamination, depravation, debasement, adulteration, depravity, taint, bribery.

çŏr-rup′tion-ist, *n.* One who or that which corrupts; one guilty of corruption.

çŏr-rupt′ive, *a.* Having the quality of corrupting, tainting, or vitiating.

> It should be endued with some *corruptive* quality. —Ray.

çŏr-rupt′less, *a.* Not susceptible of corruption or decay.

çŏr-rupt′ly, *adv.* In a corrupt manner; by means of bribery.

çŏr-rupt′ness, *n.* The state of being corrupt.

çŏr-rupt′ress, *n.* A female who corrupts others.

çọr′saç, *n.* See *Corsak.*

çọr′sȧge, *n.* [Fr. *corsage*, a bust, trunk; OFr. *cors*, a body.] A bodice; the waist of a woman's dress; as, an openwork *corsage.*

çọr′sāir, *n.* [Fr. *corsaire*; Pr. *corsari*; Sp. *corsario*, a corsair; Pr. *corsa*, a cruise, course; from L. *cursus*, a running; *currere*, to run.]

1. A pirate; one who cruises or scours the ocean with an armed vessel, without a commission from any sovereign or state, seizing and plundering merchant vessels or making booty on land; also, the vessel so used.

> He left a *corsair's* name to other times. —Byron.

2. A fish, *Sebastichthys rosaceus*, of the Pacific coast.

çọr′sak, çọr′saç, *n.* [Native name.] A species of yellowish fox or dog found in Tatary and India, the *Vulpes, Canis*, or *Cynalopex corsak.* It is gregarious, prowls by day, burrows, and lives on birds and eggs.

çọrse, *n.* [OFr. *cors, corps*, from L. *corpus*, a body.]

1. A corpse; the dead body of a human being; a poetical word.

2. The living body; bodily frame. [Obs.]

çọrse′let, *n.* [Fr. *corselet*, dim. of OFr. *cors*, a body.]

1. A small cuirass, or armor to cover and protect the body, worn formerly by pikemen. In England it was enacted in 1558 that all persons having estates of £1000 or upwards should, along with other descriptions of armor, keep forty *corselets.*

2. That part of a winged insect to which the wings and legs are attached; the thorax.

Corselet (*a*), with Morion or head-piece (*b*), and Tassets or armor for the thighs (*c*).

çọrse′let, *v.t.* To encircle with a corselet. [Rare.]

çọrse′pres″ent, *n.* In old English law, a present paid at the interment of a dead body.

çọr′set, *n.* [Fr. *corset*, dim. of OFr. *cors*, a body.]

1. A woman's close-fitting bodice or waist, consisting of two parts made of cloth stiffened by whalebone and steel, when worn being hooked in front and laced behind, and used to form or support the figure; often in the plural *corsets.*

2. A snugly fitting garment of the middle ages. [Obs.]

3. A quilted garment of defense; a gambeson of metal. [Obs.]

çọr′set, *v.t.*; corseted, *pt., pp.*; corseting, *ppr.* To inclose in a corset.

Çọr′si-çan, *a.* and *n.* I. *a.* Of or pertaining to Corsica, an island south of Italy, belonging to France.

II. *n.* A native or inhabitant of Corsica; the Corsican language.

çọrs′let, *n.* A corselet. [Obs.]

çọrs′ned, *n.* [AS. *corsnæd*; *cor-*, from *coren, ceósan*, to choose, and *snæd*, a piece cut off; from *snidan*, to cut.] Consecrated bread used by the Anglo-Saxons as an ordeal, supposed to choke the guilty. [Obs.]

çọr-tége′ (-tāzh′), *n.* [Fr., from It. *corteggio*, a retinue, from *corte*, a court.] A train of attendants.

Çọr′tes, *n.pl.* [Sp. and Port., pl. of *corte*, a court.] The national legislative bodies of Spain and Portugal.

çọr′tex, *n.*; *pl.* **çọr′ti-çēṣ.** [L.] 1. Bark, as of a tree; by extension, any external envelope.

2. In medicine, Peruvian bark.

3. In anatomy, a membrane forming a covering or envelope for any part of the body.

Cortex cerebri; the cortical substance or external part of the brain.

çọr′ti-çăl, *a.* [From L. *cortex, corticis*, bark of a tree.]

1. Of, relating, or pertaining to a cortex.

2. External.

Çọr-ti-çā′tȧ, *n.pl.* [L., neut. pl. of *corticatus*, from *cortex, corticis*, bark.] The barked corals; the *Alcyonaria.*

çọr′ti-çāte, çọr′ti-çā-ted, *a.* 1. Having a bark, rind, or other bark-like covering.

2. Of or relating to the *Corticata.*

çọr-tic′i-fẽr, *n.* [L. *cortex, corticis*, bark, and *ferre*, to bear.] One of the *Corticata.*

çọr-ti-cif′ẽr-ous, *a.* [L. *cortex, corticis*, bark, and *ferre*, to bear.] Producing bark, or that which resembles it.

çọr-tic′i-fọrm, *a.* [L. *cortex, corticis*, bark, and *forma*, form.] Resembling bark.

çọr′ti-cine, *n.* 1. An alkaloid derived from the bark of the *Populus tremula.*

2. A floor-covering resembling linoleum.

çọr′ti-çōle, çọr-tic′ō-lous, *a.* Growing on bark, as certain fungi.

çọr′ti-çōse, çọr′ti-çous, *a.* Barky; full of bark; applied in botany to hard woody pods, as those of the *Cassia fistula.*

çọr′tile, *n.* [It., from *corte*, a court.]

1. In architecture, a small court, inclosed by the divisions or appurtenances of a building.

2. The area or courtyard of a dwelling-house.

çọr-ti-nȧ, *n.* [LL. *cortina*, a curtain, small court, from *cortis*, court.] A term used, in describing fungi, to denote that portion of the veil which adheres to the margin of the pileus in fragments.

çō-run′dum, *n.* [L., from Hind. *kurand*, corundum.] Native crystalline alumina, used when pulverized in grinding and polishing gems. Emery is impure *corundum.* Also called *diamond-spar.* [See *Alumina.*]

çō-rus′çănt, *a.* Flashing; glittering by flashes.

çọr′us-çāte, *v.i.*; coruscated, *pt., pp.*; coruscating, *ppr.* [L. *coruscatus*, pp. of *coruscare*, to move quickly, glitter.] To flash; to lighten; to glitter.

Syn.—Glisten, gleam, sparkle, radiate, shine.

çọr-us-çā′tion, *n.* 1. Any sudden flash of light.

2. Figuratively, intellectual brilliancy; as, the *coruscations* of genius.

Syn.—Flash, glitter, blaze, radiation, gleam, sparkle.

çọrve, *n.* A corf.

çọr-vée′ (-vā′), *n.* [Fr., from LL. *corvata* from *corrogare*, to bring together by entreaty; *con-*, together, and *rogare*, to ask.] In feudal law, an obligation on the inhabitants of a district to perform certain services, as the repair of roads, etc., for the sovereign or the feudal lord.

çọr-vette′, *n.* [Fr., from Sp. *corveta, corbeta*; L. *corbita*, a slow-sailing ship of burden, from *corbis*, a wicker basket.] A flush-decked vessel, ship-rigged, but without a quarter-deck, and having only one tier of guns; a sloop-of-war.

çọr-vet′tō, *n.* A curvet.

çọr′vi-fọrm, *a.* Resembling a crow; crowlike.

çọr-vī′nȧ, *n.* [L. *corvinus*, from *corvus*, a raven.] A Californian bluefish, *Cynoscion parvipinnis*, allied to the weakfish.

çọr′vine, *a.* [L. *corvinus*, from *corvus*, a raven.] Pertaining to the crow family.

çọr′vō-rănt, *n.* [Obs.] Same as *Cormorant.*

Çọr′vus, *n.* [L., a raven.]

1. In astronomy, a constellation of the southern hemisphere, containing nine stars; the Crow or Raven.

2. [c—] A name given to several ancient military war-engines because of a fancied resemblance to a crow's beak.

3. In zoölogy, a genus of conirostral birds, including the crow, jackdaw, raven, and rook.

Çọr′y-bant, *n.*; *pl.* **Çọr′y-bants** *or* **Çọr-y-ban′tēṣ.** [L. *Corybas* (-*antis*); Gr. *Korybas.*] A priest of Cybele who celebrated the mysteries with frenzied dances to the sound of drum and cymbal.

çọr-y-ban′ti-ăn, *a.* Of or pertaining to the Corybants.

çọr-y-ban′tiç, *a.* Madly agitated; frenzied, as the Corybants.

çọr′y-bant-iṣm, çọr-y-ban′ti-aṣm, *n.* In pathology, mania marked by apparitions.

çō-ryd-ȧ-lī′nȧ, çō-ryd′ȧ-line, *n.* A vegetable base found in the roots of the plants *Corydalis bulbosa* and *Corydalis fabacea.*

Çō-ryd′ȧ-lis, *n.* [L., from Gr. *korydallis*, a lark; the spur of the flower resembling the crest of the lark; *korys*, a helmet.] A genus of dicotyledonous plants of the fumitory family. The species are mostly small glaucous herbs, with ternate or pinnated leaves, and fusiform tuberous or fibrous roots.

Çọr′y-lus, *n.* [L., from Gr. *korylos*, a hazel or filbert tree, from *korys*, a helmet, in allusion to the shape of the involucre.] A genus of shrubs or small trees, the hazels, the species *Americana*, yielding the wild hazelnut, common as an undergrowth in the United States.

çọr′ymb, *n.* [L. *corymbus*; Gr. *korymbos*, the uppermost point, a cluster of fruit or flowers, from *korys*, a helmet.] In botany, that form of inflorescence in which the flowers, each on its own pedicel of different lengths, are so arranged along a common axis as to form a flat, broad mass of flowers with a convex or level top, as in the hawthorn and candytuft.

Corymb.

çọr′ymbed, *a.* Corymbose.

çō-rym′bi-āte, çō-rym′bi-ā-ted, *a.* [LL. *corymbiatus*, from *corymbus*, a cluster, corymb.] Garnished with clusters of berries or blossoms in the form of corymbs.

çọr-ym-bif′ẽr-ous, *a.* Producing corymbs; bearing fruit or berries in clusters, or producing flowers in clusters.

çō-rym′bōse, çō-rym′bous, çō-rym′bū-lous, *a.* Consisting of or resembling corymbs.

çō-rym′bōse-ly, *adv.* In a corymbose manner.

çọr-y-phæ′ī, *n.*, pl. of *coryphæus.*

çọr-y-phæ′noid, *a.* Of or pertaining to the genus *Coryphæna*, a family of fishes popularly called the dolphins.

çor-y-phæ′us, çor-y-phē′us, *n.*; *pl.* **çor-y-phæ′i, çor-y-phē′i.** [L. *coryphæus*; Gr. *koryphaios*, the leader of a chorus, from *koryphē*, the head.]

1. The leader of the ancient dramatic chorus; in modern usage, a leader of a chorus or band of musicians.

2. Any leader or chief.

. . . *corypheus* of the Independent faction. —South.

çō-ry-phée′ (-rē-fā′), *n.* [Fr.] 1. A ballet-dancer.

2. An African bird of the genus *Thamnobia.*

çor′y-phēne, *n.* A book-name for any coryphænoid fish.

Çō-ryph′ō-don, *n.* [L., from Gr. *koryphē*, head, summit, and *odōn*, tooth.] A genus of extinct animals, forming a link between the elephants and tapirs; so named because the ridges of the molars are developed into points; found in the Eocene of England and the United States.

çō-ryph′ō-dont, *a.* Of or pertaining to the genus *Coryphodon.*

çō-rȳ′zȧ, *n.* [L., from Gr. *koryza*, catarrh.] Catarrh of the nose.

ços-cin′ō-man-çy, *n.* [Gr. *koskinon*, a sieve, and *manteia*, divination.] Divination by using a sieve suspended on a pair of shears; still practised in voodooism.

ços-çō-rō′bȧ, *n.* A native name for a white South American duck resembling a swan.

çō-sē′çant, *n.* [Abbrev. of L. *complementi secans*, secant of the complement.] In trigonometry, the secant of an arc which is the complement of another to 90°; or the *cosecant* of an arc or angle is the secant of its complement, and vice versa. Thus in the figure let A C B be an angle measured by the arc A B, and let B C D be its complement, measured by the arc B D; then C L, which is the secant of the complement B C D or B D, is the *cosecant* of A C B or A B. In like manner C H, the secant of A C B or A B, is the *cosecant* of the complement B C D or B D.

çō-seis′măl, *a.* [*Co-*, and Gr. *seismos*, earthquake, from *seiein*, to shake.] Denoting the points, line, or area experiencing simultaneous earthquake shocks.

çō-sen′tient (-shent), *a.* [*Co-*, and L. *sentiens* (*-entis*), ppr. of *sentire*, to know, perceive.] Perceiving together.

çō′şey, *a.* Cozy.

çosh′ẽr, *v.t.* [Ir. *cosair*, a feast.] To levy (exactions), as formerly Irish landlords did on their tenants.

çosh′ẽr, *v.t.* or *v.i.* To treat with dainties; to feed with delicacies; to treat kindly and fondly; to fondle; to pet. [Colloq.]

Thus she *coshered* up Eleanor with cold fowl and port wine. —Trollope.

çosh′ẽr-ẽr, *n.* One who coshers.

çosh′ẽr-ing, *n.* In Ireland, an old feudal custom whereby the lord of the soil was entitled to lie and feast himself and his followers at a tenant's house.

çoʹşiẽr (-zhẽr), *n.* A botcher; a cobbler. [Obs.]

çō-sig′nȧ-tō-ry, *a.* [*Co-*, and L. *signatorius*, from *signare*, to sign.] Signing any document, especially a treaty, along with others.

çō-sig′nȧ-tō-ry, *n.* One who signs a document, especially a treaty, along with others.

çō-sig′ni-tā-ry, *a.* and *n.* Cosignatory.

çō′şi-ly, *adv.* Cozily.

çŏş′in-āġe, *n.* [OFr. *cosinage*, *cousinage*, from *cosin*, *cousin*, a cousin, kinsman.] In law, (a) anciently, a writ to recover possession of an estate in lands, when a stranger has entered and abated, after the death of the tresayle, or the grandfather's grandfather, or other collateral relation; (b) now, blood-relation; consanguinity.

çō′sine, *n.* [For *co-sinus*, abbrev. of *complementi sinus*, sine of the complement.] In trigonometry, the sine of an arc which is the complement of another to 90°; or the *cosine* of any arc or angle is the sine of its complement, and vice versa.

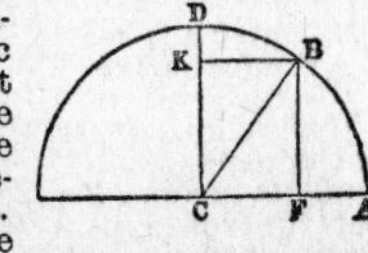

Thus, let D C B, or the arc D B, be the complement of A C B or A B; then K B, which is the sine of D C B or D B, is the *cosine* of A C B or A B. Also F B, the sine of A C B or A B, is the *cosine* of D C B or D B.

çoş-met′iç, çoş-met′iç-ăl, *a.* [Gr. *kosmētikos*, from *kosmein*, to decorate, adorn; *kosmos*, order, adornment.] Beautifying; improving beauty, particularly the beauty of the skin.

çoş-met′iç, *n.* Any external application that renders the skin soft, pure, and white, and helps to beautify and improve the complexion.

çoş′miç, çoş′miç-ăl, *a.* [Gr. *kosmikos*, from *kosmos*, order, universe.]

1. Relating to the universe and to the laws by which its order is maintained.

2. Harmonious, as the universe; orderly.

The dark chaotic dullard, who knows the meaning of nothing *cosmic* or noble. —Carlyle.

3. Designating the solar system as a whole.

4. In astronomy, rising or setting with the sun; not acronycal.

5. Of inconceivably great or prolonged duration; immensely protracted.

A result of the play between organism and environment through *cosmic* ranges of time. —Tyndall.

Cosmic dust; pulverized matter supposed to have an extra-terrestrial source and to form the dust sometimes found on snow in the arctic regions.

çoş′miç-ăl-ly, *adv.* In a cosmic manner; as, a star is said to rise or set *cosmically*, when it rises or sets with the sun.

çoş-mog′ō-năl, çoş-mō-gon′iç, çoş-mō-gon′iç-ăl, *a.* Of or pertaining to cosmogony.

çoş-mog′ō-nist, *n.* One who treats of the origin or formation of the universe; one who is versed in cosmogony.

çoş-mog′ō-ny, *n.*; *pl.* **çoş-mog′ō-nieş.** [Gr. *kosmogonia*, the creation or origin of the world; from *kosmogonos*; *kosmos*, order, universe, and *-gonos*, from the root of *gignesthai*, to produce.] The generation, origin, or creation of the world or universe; the doctrine or science of the origin or formation of the universe.

çoş-mog′rȧ-phẽr, *n.* [Gr. *kosmographos*; *kosmos*, universe, and *graphos*, from *graphein*, to write.] One who describes the world or universe, including the heavens and the earth; one who is versed in cosmography.

çoş-mō-graph′iç, çoş-mō-graph′iç-ăl, *a.* Relating or pertaining to cosmography.

çoş-mō-graph′iç-ăl-ly, *adv.* In a manner corresponding to cosmography.

çoş-mog′rȧ-phy, *n.*; *pl.* **çoş-mog′rȧ-phieş.** A description of the world or universe; or the science which teaches the constitution of the whole system of worlds, or the figure, disposition, and relation of all its parts.

çoş′mō-lābe, *n.* [Gr. *kosmos*, universe, and *lambanein*, to take.] An ancient instrument resembling the astrolabe used in astronomical observations.

çoş-mol′ȧ-try, *n.* [Gr. *kosmos*, universe, and *latreia*, worship.] The worship paid to the world or its parts by heathens.

çoş′mō-line, *n.* [*Cosm*etic, and L. *oleum*, oil.] A hydrocarbon mixture, the residuum of petroleum distillation, used as vaseline, which it resembles.

çoş-mō-log′iç-ăl, *a.* Relating or pertaining to cosmology.

çoş-mol′ō-gist, *n* One who describes the universe; one who is versed in cosmology.

çoş-mol′ō-ġy, *n.* [Fr. *cosmologie*, from Gr. *kosmos*, universe, and *-logia*, from *legein*, to speak.] The science of the world or universe; or a treatise relating to the structure and parts of the system of creation, the elements of bodies, the modifications of material things, the laws of motion, and the order and course of nature.

çoş-mom′e-try, *n.* [Gr. *kosmos*, the world, and *-metria*, from *metron*, a measure.] The art of measuring the world, as by degrees and minutes.

çoş-mō-plas′tiç, *a.* [Gr. *kosmoplastēs*, the framer of the world; *kosmos*, universe, and *plassein*, to form.] World-forming; pertaining to the formation of the universe.

çoş-mō-pol′i-tăn, çoş-mop′ō-lite, *n.* [Gr *kosmopolitēs*, a citizen of the world; *kosmos*, world, and *politēs*, a citizen.]

1. A person who has no fixed residence; one who is nowhere a stranger, or who is at home in every place; a citizen of the world.

2. An animal or a plant found in or migrating to many parts of the world.

çoş-mō-pol′i-tăn, çoş-mop′ō-lite, *a.* 1. Without limit as regards distribution; found in all parts of the world; universal.

Capital is becoming more and more *cosmopolitan.* —Mill.

2. Not provincial; not having or showing narrowness of views; liberal.

3. Designating or characterizing a citizen of the world.

4. Having a wide range or distribution, as a genus of plants or animals.

çoş-mō-pol′i-tăn-işm, *n.* Citizenship of the world; cosmopolitism.

çoş-mop′ō-lite, *a.* and *n.* Cosmopolitan.

çoş″mō-pō-lit′iç-ăl, *a.* Universal.

çoş-mop′ō-li-tişm, *n.* [From Gr. *kosmopolitēs*, a citizen of the world, and *-ism.*] The state or quality of being cosmopolitan; cosmopolitanism.

çoş-mō-rä′mȧ, *n.* [Gr. *kosmos*, the world, and *horama*, from *horān*, to see.] An exhibition in which illuminated views are so disposed as to be reflected by mirrors placed opposite to them diagonally, and seen through a convex lens placed in front of each mirror; also, any similar exhibition.

çoş-mō-ram′iç, *a.* Pertaining to a cosmorama.

çoş′mos, *n.* [Gr. *kosmos*, order, harmony, ornament. hence the world as an orderly system.]

1. Order; harmony.

2. The universe as an embodiment of order and harmony; the system of order and harmony combined in the universe.

. . . first received the title of "*cosmos*," or "beautiful order." —Trench.

3. The doctrine or description of the universe as an orderly and beautiful system; as, Humboldt's *Cosmos.*

4. [C—] A small genus of American composite plants.

çoş′mō-sphēre, *n.* [Gr. *kosmos*, the world, and *sphaira*, a sphere.] An apparatus for showing the position of the earth, at any given time, with respect to the fixed stars. It consists of a hollow glass globe, on which are depicted the stars forming the constellations, and within which is a terrestrial globe.

çoş′mō-thē-işm, *n.* [Gr. *kosmos*, world, and *theos*, god.] Same as *Pantheism.* [Rare.]

çoş-mō-thet′iç, *a.* [Gr. *kosmos*, world, and *thetikos*, from *tithenai*, to fix, set up.] Believing in the real and substantial existence of matter, but denying that the phenomenal world of which we are directly conscious has any existence external to our minds.

çō-söv′ẽr-eign (-in), *n.* A joint sovereign; a king or queen consort.

çoss, *n.* A word used only in the phrase, *Rule of Coss*, an early name for algebra.

çoss, *n.* [Anglo-Ind.] In India, a road-measure of variable extent, ranging between one and one-half and two miles.

Ços′sack, *n.* [Russ. *Kozakŭ.*] One of a warlike people, very expert on horseback, inhabiting the steppes in the south of Russia, about the Don. They became united to Russia in 1654, and now form a valuable portion of its army, being especially useful as light horsemen.

ços′săş, *n.pl.* [E. Ind.] Plain India muslin. of various qualities and breadths.

ços′set, *n.* [Etymology uncertain.] A lamb brought up by hand, or without the aid of the dam; a pet.

ços′set, *v.t.*; cosseted, *pt.*, *pp.*; cosseting, *ppr.* To pet; to fondle.

çoş′siç, çoş′siç-ăl, *a.* Relating to algebra. [Obs.]

Ços′sus, *n.* [L., a kind of larvæ.] A genus of moths of the family *Epialidæ.* The larva of one of the species, *Cossus ligniperda*, emits a very strong and disagreeable odor, from which it receives the name of goat-moth.

Goat-moth (*Cossus ligniperda*).

çost, *n.* [L. *costa*, rib, side.]

1. A side or rib; a coast.

2. In heraldry, a cottise.

çost, *n.* 1. The price, value, or equivalent of a thing purchased; the amount in value paid, charged, or engaged to be paid for anything bought or taken in barter; any outlay, as of time, labor, or money.

What they had fondly wished, proved afterwards, to their *costs*, over true.—Knolles.

2. [*pl.*] In law, the sum fixed by law, or allowed by the court, for charges of a suit, usually awarded against the party losing.

çost, *v.t.*; cost, *pt.*, *pp.*; costing, *ppr.* [ME. *costen*; OFr. *coster*; LL. *costare*, contr. of L. *constare*, to stand together. stand at, cost; *con-*, together, and *stare*, to stand.]

1. To require to be given or expended in barter or purchase; to be bought for; as, the book *cost* a dollar.

2. To require to be borne or suffered; as, our sins *cost* us many pains.

To cost dear; to occasion great expenditure.

çost-. See *Costo-*.

ços′tȧ, *n.* [L., a rib.] In biology, a rib, or part resembling a rib; specifically, (a) the midrib of a leaf; (b) the anterior marginal rib of an insect's wing; (c) the ridge of a shell; (d) a transverse section of a trilobite.

çost′āġe, *n.* Cost. [Obs.]

ços′tăl, *a.* [Fr. *costal*, from L. *costa*, a rib.] In biology, pertaining to a costa or rib; specifically, in anatomy, denoting the ribs or the side of the body.

Costal margin; the costa of an insect.

ços′tăl-nẽrved, *a.* Branching from the costa, as the nerves of a leaf.

ços′tărd, *n.* [ME. *costard*, a ribbed apple, from L. *costa*, a rib.] An apple; also, a head. [Obs.]

ços′tărd-mŏn″gẽr, *n.* A costermonger. [Obs.]

ços′tāte, ços′tā-ted, *a.* [L. *costatus*, from *costa*, rib.] Ribbed; having ribs or the appearance of ribs.

ços'tēan, *v.i.* [Corn. *cothas*, dropped, and *stean*, tin.] To prospect for a lode by sinking pits to the bedrock. [Eng.]

ços'tēan-ing, *n.* The process of prospecting by means of pits. [Eng.]

ços-tel'lāte, *a.* [L. *costellatus*, from *costellum*, dim. of *costa*, a rib.] Having fine ribs; costate.

ços'tẽr, *n.* A costermonger.

ços'tẽr-mŏn"gẽr, *n.* An apple-seller; applied to hawkers and peddlers who sell fruit; a fruiterer; formerly written *costardmonger*.

ços'ti-. See *Costo-*.

ços-tif'ẽr-ous, *a.* [L. *costa*, a rib, and *ferre*, to bear.] Bearing ribs; applied to vertebræ.

ços'ti-fọrm, *a.* [L. *costa*, a rib, and *forma*, form.] Formed like a rib or costa.

ços'tive, *a.* [OFr. *costevé*, from L. *constipatus*, pp. of *constipare*, to cram, stuff; *con-*, together, and *stipare*, to crowd, press together.]

1. Dry and hard; also, cold; formal. [Obs.]

2. Having difficult or rare evacuation of the bowels; constipated.

ços'tive-ly, *adv.* With costiveness.

ços'tive-ness, *n.* 1. Closeness. [Obs.]

2. Constipation.

çost'less, *a.* Costing nothing.

çost'lew, *a.* Costly [Obs.]

çost'li-ness, *n.* Expensiveness.

çost'ly, *a.*; *comp.* costlier; *superl.* costliest. Of a high price; sumptuous; expensive, purchased at a great expense; as, a *costly* habit; *costly* furniture.

Syn.—Choice, gorgeous, precious, expensive.

çost'mā-ry, *n.* [L. *costus*: Gr. *kostos*, an Oriental aromatic plant, and *Maria*, Mary] *Tanacetum Balsamita*, a perennial plant of the natural order *Compositæ*, a native of the south of Europe; alecost.

ços'tō-, ços'ti-, çost-. Combining forms from L. *costa*, a rib, used in anatomy to express relation between a rib and the thing designated; as, *costo*tome

ços'tō-tōme, *n.* A dissecting-instrument used to sever the ribs.

ços'trel, *n.* [W. *costrel*, a cup, flagon.] An eared bottle or flask used by British laborers in the harvest-field.

Costrels.

1. Ancient, of earthenware. 2. Ancient, of leather. 3. Modern, of earthenware.

ços'tūme (*or* -tūm'), *n.* [Fr *costume*; LL. *costuma*; L. *consuetudo*, custom.]

1. In art or literature, local color.

2. Apparel; dress in general.

3. Dress appropriate to a certain age, class, or occasion; as, a medieval *costume*; a theatrical *costume*; a masquerade *costume*.

ços'tūm-ẽr, *n.* A costume-maker or dealer.

ços'tus-rọọt, *n.* The root of a Cashmerian plant, *Saussurea Lappa* (*Aucklandia Costus*), gathered for the East Indian market.

çō-sū-prēme', *n.* A partaker of supremacy.

çō-sūre'ty (-shūr'), *n.*; *pl.* **çō-sūre'tieṣ.** One who is surety with another.

çō'ṣy, *a.* Cozy.

çot, *n.* [ME. *cot*; AS. *cot*, a cot, cottage, hut.]

1. A cottage; a hut; a mean or humble habitation; now generally a poetical word.

Mine be a *cot* beside the hill. —Rogers.

2. A protective cover, as for a sore finger.

3. A small bed; specifically, a folding, portable bed for temporary use; a cot-bed.

4. Nautically, a sort of bed-frame suspended from the beams.

5. The sleeve-like protection for a drawing-roller in a spinning-frame.

çot, *n.* [Ir. *cot*, a small boat.] A little boat. [Irish.]

çot, *n.* [Abbrev. from *cotquean*.] An effeminate person. [Obs.]

çō-tan'ġent, *n.* [Abbrev. of L. *complementi tangens*; complement, and *tangens*, ppr. of *tangere*, to touch.] In trigonometry, the tangent of an arc which is the complement of another to 90°; or the tangent of the complement of any arc or angle. Thus, let D C B, or the arc D B, be the complement of A C B or A B; then D L, the tangent of D C B or D B, is the *cotangent* of A C B or A B; also A H, the tangent of A C B or A B, is the *cotangent* of D C B or D B.

çō-tär'nine, *n.* [By transposition of *narcotine*.] An organic base, $C_{12}H_{13}NO_3$, found in opium. It is a yellow, crystalline, bitter, soluble, slightly alkaline substance.

çot'-bed, *n.* See first *Cot*, n. 3.

çōte, *n.* [ME. *cote*; AS. *cote*, a cot, cottage, chamber.]

1. A hut; a cot. [Obs.]

2. A small house; used in compounds; as, dove*cote*.

çōte, *v.t.* [Fr. *côtoyer*, to go by the side of; OFr. *costoier*, from L. *costa*, a rib, side.] To pass. [Obs.]

çōte, *v.t.* To quote. [Obs.]

çō-teau' (-tō'), *n.*; *pl.* **çō-teaux'** (-tōz'). [Fr., a little hill.] A divide of land; also, a small plateau.

çō-tem-pō-rā'nē-ous, çō-tem'pō-rā-ry, etc. See *Contemporaneous*, *Contemporary*, etc.

çō-ten'ăn-çy, *n.* Combined tenancy.

çō-ten'ănt, *n.* A tenant in common.

çō-te-rie', *n.* [Fr., from LL. *coteria*, an association of villagers in a landholding, from *cota*, a cottage.] A circle of familiar friends; a meeting, for social or literary intercourse.

çō-tẽr'mi-nous, *a.* Conterminous.

çot'gāre, *n.* Waste wool. [Obs.]

çō'thŭrn, *n.* Same as *Cothurnus*.

çō-thŭr'nāte, çō-thŭr'nā-ted, *a.* [L. *cothurnatus*, from *cothurnus*, a buskin.]

1. Buskined.

2. Tragical; solemn and elevated; applied to style.

çō-thŭr'nus, *n.*; *pl.* **çō-thŭr'nī.** [L.] A Greek and Roman buskin; a kind of shoe, laced high, such as Diana and her nymphs are represented as wearing. The tragic actors also wore them; hence, *cothurnus* is sometimes figuratively used for *tragedy*.

Cothurnus or Buskin.

çō-tiç'ū-lär, *a.* [L. *coticula*, dim. of *cos*, a whetstone.] Pertaining to whetstones; like or suitable for whetstones.

çō-tid'ăl, *a.* Having simultaneous or equal tides.

Cotidal lines; those connecting cotidal points.

çō-til'liŏn (-yun), **çō-til'lọn,** *n.* [Fr., a dance, a petticoat, dim. of OFr. *cote*, a coat.]

1. A dance; (a) a quadrille; (b) an intricate combination of round dances and introduced figures; the german.

2. The music adapted to such a dance.

3. Black and white woolen skirting.

Çō-tin'gȧ, *n.* [L., from S. Am. native name.]

1. A genus of birds, the chatterers.

2. [c—] Any bird of this genus.

çot'ise, *n.* Cottise.

çot'ised (-ist), *a.* Cottised.

çot'land, *n.* Land appendant to a cottage.

Çō-tō-nē-as'tẽr, *n.* [L., from L. *cotonea*, a quince, and *-aster*.] A genus of shrubby trees of the rose family, the species *vulgaris* being British, the others growing in southern Europe and India.

çot'quēan (-kwēn), *n.* [ME. *cot*, a cottage, and *quean*, a woman.]

1. A man who busies himself with the affairs which properly belong to women.

2. A masculine woman; a shrew. [Obs.]

çot-quēan'i-ty, *n.* The qualities of a cotquean.

çō-trus-tee', *n.* A joint trustee.

çots'wōld, *n.* [ME. *cot*, a cottage, and *wold*, AS. *weald*, a wood, forest.] A wold where there are sheepcotes; [C—] the name of a range of hills in Gloucestershire, England.

Cotswold sheep; a breed of sheep remarkable for the length of their wool, formerly peculiar to the counties of Gloucester, Hereford, and Worcester, in England.

çot'tȧ, *n.* [LL.] A surplice, with or without sleeves.

çot'tȧ-bus, *n.* [L., from Gr. *kottabos*.] An ancient Greek game, which consisted in throwing wine from cups, without spilling, into metal basins.

çot'tāġe, *n.* [ME. *cotage*, from *cot*, a cottage.]

1. A hut; a humble dwelling; a cot.

2. A small country residence or detached suburban house, adapted to a moderate scale of living.

3. Any residence used as a summer home or for some similar purpose—without reference to size—distinguished from a permanent residence. [U. S.]

Cottage allotment; in Great Britain, a laborer's allowance of land for his use, gratis.

Cottage cheese; homemade cheese from curdled milk; "Dutch cheese."

çot'tāġed, *a.* Set or covered with cottages.

çot'tāġe-ly, *a.* Rustic. [Obs.]

çot'tā-ġẽr, *n.* 1. One who lives in a cottage.

2. In law, one who lives on the common, without paying any rent, or having land of his own.

çot'tẽr, çot'tär, çot'ti-ẽr, *n.* [ME. *cottier*, from LL. *cota*, a cot.] A cottager; in Scotland, one who inhabits a cot or cottage, dependent upon a farm; sometimes a piece of land is attached to the cot.

çot'tẽr, *n.* [Origin unknown.] A wedge-shaped piece of wood or iron for fastening or tightening; a key. In the figure, *a* is the cotter keying the rod *b* to the rod *c* by means of the U-shaped strap *dd*, serving to adjust the parts to each other.

Cotter.

çot'tẽr, *v.t.*; cottered, *pt.*, *pp.*; cottering, *ppr.* To key by use of a cotter.

çot'tẽr-el, *n.* 1. A key; a cotter.

2. A pot-support in a fire-place. [Prov. Eng.]

çot'tise, çot'ise, *n.* [Fr. *côte*; L. *costa*, a rib.] In heraldry, a diminutive of the bend, containing in breadth one half of the bendlet, and when borne alone always termed a *cost* by English heralds, but when borne in pairs *cottises*.

çot'tised (-tist), *a.* In heraldry, having cottises.

Cottised.

çot'toid, *a* and *n.* [L. *cottus*, a kind of fish, and Gr. *eidos*, form.]

I. *a.* Relating to the genus *Cottus*.

II. *n.* A fish of the genus *Cottus*.

çot-tŏn, *a.* Pertaining to cotton; made of cotton; consisting of cotton; as, *cotton* cloth.

çot'tŏn (kot'n), *n.* [ME. *cotoun*; OFr. *coton*; Sp. *coton*, from Ar. *qutun*, *qutn*, cotton.]

1. A soft, downy substance, resembling fine wool, growing in the capsules or pods of *Gossypium*, the cotton-plant. It is the material of a large proportion of cloth for apparel and furniture.

2. Cotton-plants, collectively; also, a single plant.

3. Cloth, thread, or other material made of *cotton*.

Cotton flannel; see *Canton flannel* under *Canton*.

Cotton velvet; velveteen.

Mineral cotton, see *Mineral wool*, under *Wool*.

çot'tŏn, *v.i.*; cottoned, *pt.*, *pp.*; cottoning, *ppr.*

1. To rise with a nap. [Obs.]

2. To agree; to unite closely. [Obs.]

3. To stick to one as cotton sticks; to take a strong fancy to any one; used with *to*. [Slang.]

çot'tŏn-āde, *n.* A thick, stout cotton fabric.

çot'tŏn-ā-ry, *a.* Cottony. [Obs.]

çot'tŏn-çāke, *n.* A stock-feed, the residue after removing the oil from cotton-seed.

çot'tŏn-ġin, *n.* A device for removing the seed from the fiber of cotton. The original machine, invented by Whitney in 1792, remains unchanged in its essentials.

çot'tŏn-grȧss, *n.* The popular name of a genus of plants, the *Eriophorum*.

Çot-tō'ni-ăn, *a.* Pertaining to Sir Robert Cotton (1571–1631), known mostly through his valuable library, now in the British Museum.

çot'tŏn-mouse, *n.* The *Hesperomys gossypinus*, a field-mouse injuring cotton-plants.

çot'tŏn-ous (-us), *a.* Cottony. [Obs.]

çot'tŏn-plant, *n.* The popular name of several species of *Gossypium*, of the mallow family, producing the well-known cotton. *Gossypium herbaceum* is the common, upland, or short-staple cotton, and *Gossypium Barbadense*, the sea-island or long-staple cotton. Many varieties of these and other species are known; also called *cotton-shrub*.

Cotton-plant (*Gossypium herbaceum*).

çot'tŏn-rat, *n.* A rodent native to the cotton plantations of the United States.

çot'tŏn-rōṣe, *n.* A common name for the composite genus *Filago*.

çot'tŏn-sçāle, *n.* *Pulvinaria innumerabilis*, a louse infesting the bark of the cotton-plant.

çot'tŏn-shrub, *n.* The cotton-plant.

çot'tŏn-stāin"ẽr, *n.* *Dysdercus suturellus*, a bug staining cotton a permanent color.

çot'tŏn-tāil, *n.* *Lepus sylvaticus*, the common rabbit of the United States; a name much used in the South.

çot'tŏn-thiēf, *n.* *Tersiphone paradisea*, the Indian paradise flycatcher with white elongated tail-feathers.

çot'tŏn-this"tle (-sl), *n.* *Onopordon Acanthium*, a Scotch thistle.

çot′tŏn-tree, *n.* The American cottonwood; also, a tree of the genus *Bombax.*

çot′tŏn-wāste, *n.* Refuse cotton in manufacturing, used as box-packing and in wiping machinery.

çot′tŏn-weed, *n.* A plant, cudweed.

çot′tŏn-wood, *n.* One of several trees of the genus *Populus,* as *Populus heterophylla,* of eastern United States; so named from their cottony catkins.

çot′tŏn-wool, *n.* Raw cotton.

çot′tŏn-wŏrm, *n.* *Aletia xylina,* a moth having a larva destructive to growing cotton.

çot′tŏn-y, *a.* Having a nap like cotton; downy.

çot′trel, *n.* See *Cotterel,* 2.

çot′y-lē, *n.*; *pl.* **çot′y-læ, çot′y-lēş.** [Gr. *kotylē,* a hollow, a cup.]

1. In anatomy, an acetabulum; also spelled *cotyla.*

2. In ancient Greece, (a) a drinking-cup; (b) a unit of liquid measure, varying in different localities.

çot-y-lē′dŏn, *n.* [L., from Gr. *kotylēdōn,* from *kotylē,* a hollow or cavity.]

1. In the embryo of a plant or seed, the part nourishing the elementary plant. Plants may have one, two, or more *cotyledons,* being mono-, di-, or polycotyledonous.

Cotyledons.

1. Monocotyledon (seed of *Arum maculatum*). 2. Dicotyledon (seed of *Papaver Rhœas*). 3. Polycotyledon (seed of *Pinus sylvestris*).

2. [C—] A genus of polypetalous herbs of the houseleek family; the navelworts.

3. In anatomy, a villous, placental area.

çot-y-led′ŏn-ăl, *a.* Of, relating, or pertaining to a cotyledon.

çot-y-led′ŏn-ā-ry, *a.* Having a cotyledon or cotyledons.

çot-y-led′ŏn-ous (-us), *a.* Pertaining to cotyledons; having a seed-lobe.

çō-tyl′i-form, *a.* [L. *cotyla;* Gr. *kotylē,* a hollow, and *forma,* form.] Cup-shaped.

çot-y-lig′ėr-ous, *a.* [L. *cotyla,* a cotyle, and *gerere,* to carry.] Possessing cotylæ; having acetabula.

çot′y-loid, *a.* [Gr. *kotylē,* a cup, and *eidos,* form.]

1. Cup-shaped; cupped; as, a *cotyloid* socket.

2. Pertaining to a cotyle.

çöu′çăl, *n.* [Prob. native name.] A tropical cuckoo of the genus *Centropus.*

çouch, *v.t.*; couched, *pt., pp.*; couching, *ppr.* [ME. *couchen;* OFr. *coucher;* Pr. *colcar;* It. *colcare;* L. *collocari,* to place together; *con-,* together, and *locare,* to place; *locus,* a place.]

1. To lay upon a bed or place of rest.

Where unbruised youth, with unstuffed brain,
Doth *couch* his limbs. —Shak.

2. To lay down; to spread on a bed or floor; as, to *couch* malt.

3. To lay close, or in a stratum; to make to stoop and lie close.

The waters *couch* themselves, as close as may
be, to the center of the globe. —Burnet.

4. To hide; also, to inlay. [Obs.]

5. In paper-making, to pass (a pulp-sheet) to a drier, from the mold.

6. To express; to put into language; implying hidden or double meaning; as, to *couch* a proposition skilfully; fair words, yet *couching* a menace.

7. To fix (a spear) in the rest, in the horizontal position of attack.

They *couched* their spears. —Milton.

8. In surgery, to treat (a cataract) by forcing down the lens until it no longer intercepts the line of vision.

çouch, *v.i.* 1. To lie; to lie in a bed. [Rare.]

2. To lie down; to crouch; to hide.

Fierce tigers *couched* around. —Dryden.

3. To bend or stoop, as in pain.

4. In embroidery, to catch the thread on the surface of a material by fine stitches.

çouch, *n.* [ME. *couche,* a lair; OFr. *couche, colche,* a bed, from *coucher,* to lie down.]

1. A bed; a place for rest or sleep; particularly, a long seat, usually upholstered; a lounge.

2. Any resting-place, as an animal's den.

3. In brewing, a frame on which to malt barley; the barley so malted.

4. A preliminary layer, coating, or stratum; specifically, (a) in painting, a ground or coat of color, varnish, or size, covering the canvas, wall, or other surface; (b) a coat of gold or silver leaf laid on any substance to be gilded or silvered; (c) in bookbinding, a layer or single thickness of leather.

çouch′ăn-cy, *n.* The act of lying; repose. [Rare.]

çouch′ănt, *a.* [Fr. *couchant,* ppr. of *coucher,* to lie down.]

1. Lying down; squatting; crouching.

2. In heraldry, lying down with the head raised, which distinguishes the posture of *couchant* from that of *dormant,* or sleeping; applied to a lion or other beast.

Levant and couchant; in law, rising up and lying down; applied to beasts, and indicating that they have been long enough on land not their owner's, to lie down and rise up to feed, or one night at least.

çöu-çhé′ (-shā′), *a.* [Fr., pp. of *coucher,* to lie down.] In heraldry, (a) inclined; reclining partly; (b) lying on the side or sides; as, chevrons *couché.*

çouched (koucht), *a.* In heraldry, couché.

çöu-çhee′, *n.* [Fr., f. of *couché,* pp. of *coucher,* to lie down.] Bedtime, or visits received about bedtime; opposed to *levee.* [Obs.]

çouch′ẽr, *n.* 1. One who couches cataracts.

2. In paper-making, one who couches the pulp on the felt as it comes from the mold in sheets.

çouch′ẽr, *n.* In old English law, a factor; a resident in a country for traffic. [Obs.]

çouch′ẽr, *n.* [From LL. *collectarius,* a factor, money-changer.]

1. A book in which a corporation or religious house registers its acts. [Obs.]

2. A book of services or collects. [Obs.]

çouch′-grȧss, *n.* *Triticum* (or *Agropyrum*) *repens,* a species of grass, a great pest from the rapidity with which it spreads, and the difficulty with which it is eradicated; also called *quitch-grass, cutch-grass,* etc.

çouch′ing, *n.* 1. The act of bending.

2. The act or process of treating a cataract by depressing the crystalline lens.

3. A style of embroidery in which the threads are couched.

çouch′less, *a.* Having no couch or bed.

çöu-de′, *n.* A piece of armor covering the elbow. [See illustration under *armor.*]

çöu′dee, *n.* [Fr. *coudée,* from *coude,* elbow.] A linear measure, the cubit. [See *Cubit.*]

çöu′găr, *n.* [Fr. *couguar;* Sp. *couguardo,* from native S. Am. name, *cuguacuara.*] A large American quadruped of the feline family, the *Felis concolor.* It is about six feet long, including the tail, and is of a uniform tawny color. It is found in most parts of North and South America, and is carnivorous in its habits. It is known by various other names, as puma, panther, catamount, and mountain lion. Spelled also *couguar, cougouar, cuguar.*

Cougar (*Felis concolor*).

çough (kof), *v.i.*; coughed, *pt., pp.*; coughing, *ppr.* [Imitative word.] To make a sudden and somewhat violent effort, accompanied with noise, to expel the air from the lungs, or to force out any matter that irritates the respiratory organs or renders respiration difficult.

çough, *v.t.* 1. To expel from the respiratory organs by a more or less violent and noisy effort; followed by *up;* as, to *cough up* phlegm.

2. To cause (some result) or to bring about (a condition) by coughing; as, to *cough* oneself weak; the patient had *coughed* a rupture in the diaphragm.

To cough down; to silence, as an unpopular or too lengthy speaker, by pretended coughing.

çough, *n.* A sudden expulsion of air from the respiratory organs, which is more or less violent and noisy; caused by some irritation, such as the presence of secreted or foreign matter in the air-passages, or a nervous affection, often a symptom of disease.

çough′ẽr, *n.* One who coughs.

çough′wŏrt, *n.* A herb, coltsfoot.

çöug′năr, *n.* [Malay.] A three-masted Malay boat, rigged with square sails. It is broad, sits low in the water, is decked or not, according to fancy, sails well, and carries a large cargo.

Cougnar.

çou′hāge (-āj), *n.* See *Cowhage.*

çould (kụd), *v.* [ME. *coude;* AS. *cūthe;* the *l* was improperly introduced into this word under the influence of *should* and *would* where the *l* is correct.] Past tense of *can.*

çöu-lée′ (-lā′), *n.* [Fr., f. of pp. of *couler,* to flow.]

1. In geology, a stream of lava, whether flowing or solidified.

2. A ravine or deep gully, draining land only in very wet weather.

çöu-lēur′, *n.* [Fr., color, from L. *color,* color.] In certain French card-games, suit.

Couleur de rose; rose-color; adverbially, full of promise.

çöu-lisse′, *n.* [Fr., a groove, slide, from *couler,* to slide, glide.]

1. A timber with a channel or groove in it, used as a guide.

2. In a theater, one of the side scenes; also, the space between any two wings.

çöu-loir′ (-lwär′), *n.* [Fr., from *couler,* to slide.]

1. A deep ravine or gorge.

2. A dredging-machine employing buckets.

çöu-lomb′ (-lom′), *n.* [From *Coulomb,* a French electrician.] The unit of electric quantity, being that conveyed by a current one ampere in strength during one second of time.

çōul′tẽr, *n.* See *Colter.*

çōul′tẽr-neb, *n.* [AS. *culter,* a plowshare, knife, and *nebb,* head, face.] A bird, the puffin.

çöu-lūre′, *n.* [Fr., a falling, running, from *couler,* to slide, run.] Sterility of fruit-bearing plants caused by the removal of the pollen by rain.

çöu-mar′iç, *a.* Pertaining to or derived from coumarin.

Coumaric acid; an acid, $C_9H_8O_3$, found in coumarin.

çöu′mȧ-rin, çöu′mȧ-rine, *n.* [Fr., from *coumarou,* native name of a S. Am. tree.] A vegetable proximate principle, $C_9H_6O_2$, contained in the tonka bean, formerly used in medicine, now employed in flavoring; spelled also *cumarin.*

çöu′mȧ-röu, *n.* The native name of the tree, *Dipteryx odorata,* which yields the sweet-scented tonka bean. It is a native of French Guiana, where it forms a large forest-tree.

çoun′cil, *n.* [ME. *counceil;* OFr. *concile;* L. *concilium,* an assembly; *con-,* together, and *calare,* to call, convoke.]

1. An assembly of men summoned or convened for consultation, deliberation, and advice; as, a *council* of physicians.

2. In the United States, (a) the upper chamber of the legislature in organized territories; called also *legislative council;* (b) a common *council;* see phrase.

3. In English government, (a) a privy *council;* (b) a colonial body accessory to a governor.

4. Ecclesiastically, (a) an assembly of prelates and doctors, convened for regulating matters of doctrine and discipline in the church; (b) a body of delegates, both clerical and lay, of some Protestant denominations, gathered as a general advisory assembly.

5. Counsel. [Obs.]

Aulic Council; see under *Aulic.*

Cabinet Council; an executive's advisory council.

Common council; the legislative body of a municipal corporation; a city council. It is generally the representative body, composed of one or more aldermen elected from each of the city wards, but is sometimes the designation of a coördinate or lower branch of a municipal legislature. In the latter case the two bodies taken together are called the *city council.*

Council of war; a conference of a commander-in-chief with subordinate officers.

Ecumenical council; in church history, a general council or assembly of prelates and divines, representing the whole church, as the council of Nice.

Executive council; the men designated to act as advisers to a chief executive officer, particularly to the governor of a territory.

Legislative council; the senate of a territorial legislature.

Privy council; a select council for advising a sovereign in the administration of the government.

Syn.—Meeting, conference, assembly, convention, convocation, congress, parliament.

çoun′cil-bōard, *n.* The table round which a council holds consultation; hence, the council itself in deliberation or session.

çoun′cil-fire, *n.* A camp-fire, a feature of American Indian deliberative councils.

çoun′cil-ist, *n.* A councilor. [Obs.]

çoun′cil-măn, *n.*; *pl.* **çoun′cil-men.** One who belongs to a council, particularly a city council.

çoun′cil-ŏr, çoun′cil-lŏr, *n.* 1. A member of a council.

2. An adviser; a counselor.

ç̣oun'cil-tā"ble, *n.* A council-board.

cō-ūne', *v.t.* [L. *con-*, together, and *unus*, one.] To unite. [Obs.]

cō-ū-nite', *a.* Combined; united. [Obs.]

cō-ū-nite', *v.t.* [L. *con-*, together, and *unitus*, pp. of *unire*, to unite.] To unite. [Obs.]

çoun'sel, *n.* [ME. *counseil*; OFr. *conseil*; L. *consilium*, deliberation, counsel, from *consulere*, to consult.]

1. Consultation; mutual interchange of opinions.

We took sweet *counsel* together. —Ps. lv. 14.

2. Deliberation; prudence; examination of consequences; deliberate opinion or judgment, or the faculty or habit of judging with caution.

They all confess that, in the working of that first cause, *counsel* is used, reason followed, and a way observed. —Hooker.

3. Advice; opinion or instruction given for directing the judgment or conduct of another; opinion or direction given upon request or upon deliberation or consultation.

Ill *counsel* had misled the girl. —Tennyson.

4. Purpose; design; will; plan.

To show . . . the immutability of his *counsel*. —Heb. vi. 17.

5. A secret; a private opinion. [Obs.]

6. One who gives legal advice; a lawyer retained to conduct or manage a case in court; also used collectively for any number of attorneys, counselors, or barristers, engaged on the same case; as, the plaintiff's *counsel*, or the defendant's *counsel*.

To keep one's own counsel; to keep one's opinions, purposes, etc., to himself.

To take counsel; to invite consultation; to ask advice; to consult.

Syn.—Advice, suggestion, recommendation, warning, admonition, instruction.

çoun'sel, *v.t.*; counseled *or* counselled, *pt.*, *pp.*; counseling *or* counselling, *ppr.* 1. To give advice to; to advise; to exhort, warn, admonish, or instruct; as, we should *counsel* our children.

They that will not be *counseled* cannot be helped. —Franklin.

2. To advise or recommend; as, to *counsel* submission.

çoun'sel, *v.i.* To deliberate; to seek advice or direction.

çoun'sel-ȧ-ble, çoun'sel-lȧ-ble, *a.* 1. Willing to receive counsel; disposed to follow advice. [Rare.]

2. Wise; expedient. [Obs.]

çoun'sel-ŏr, çoun'sel-lŏr, *n.* [ME. *counselour*, *counseiller*; OFr. *consellier*; L. *consiliarius*, a counselor, adviser, from *consilium*, counsel.]

1. One who gives counsel or advice.

2. One of the members of a council; correctly spelled *councilor*.

3. One who gives advice in relation to a question of law; counsel.

çoun'sel-ŏr-ship, *n.* The office of a counselor.

çount, *v.t.*; counted, *pt.*, *pp.*; counting, *ppr.* [ME. *counten*; OFr. *conter*; It. *contare*, from L. *computare*, to count, compute; *com-*, together, and *putare*, to cleanse, prune, adjust.]

1. To number; to name (the units of) in ascertaining the number in a collection; as, to *count* the days; to *count* the stars.

2. To ascribe or impute; to consider or esteem as belonging; as, tact should be *counted* his portion.

3. To esteem; to reckon; to think, judge, or consider; as, to *count* a day lost.

To count out; (a) in children's games to determine a lot by repeating a jingle or ditty; (b) to keep a legally elected candidate from holding office by manipulation of the ballots.

Syn.—Calculate, number, reckon, compute, enumerate.

çount, *v.i.* 1. To take account. [Obs.]

2. To number; as, to *count* to ten.

3. To have ability to reckon or number; as, he can *count* as well as write.

4. To be of value numerically or otherwise; to be worth taking into account; as, education *counts*.

5. In music, to keep time.

6. To depend; with *on* or *upon*.

7. In law, to plead or argue a case in court.

çount, *n.* 1. Reckoning; the act of numbering; also, the number so reckoned.

2. Account; estimation; value.

3. In law, a particular charge in an indictment, or narration in pleading, setting forth the cause of complaint. There may be different *counts* in the same declaration.

çount, *n.* [OFr. *conte*, *comte*, from L. *comes*, *comitis*, a companion.] A title of foreign nobility, equivalent to the English earl, and whose domain is a county.

Count palatine; (a) formerly, in England, a proprietor of a domain called a county, of which he was sovereign; (b) anciently, in Germany, a palsgrave of the king's court or, later, of a province.

çount'ȧ-ble, *a.* That may be numbered.

çoun'te-nănce, *n.* [OFr. *contenance*; LL. *continentia*, countenance, demeanor, from *continere*; *con-*, together, and *tenere*, to hold.]

1. The face; the visage, particularly as denoting the emotions; as, a man of goodly *countenance*.

2. Manifestation of regard; favor; good-will; kindness; as, to give one's *countenance* to graft.

3. Show; resemblance; appearance. [Obs.]

The election being done, he made *countenance* of great discontent thereat. —Ascham.

In countenance; with assurance.

Out of countenance; confounded; abashed.

To keep the countenance, to preserve a calm, composed, or natural look.

çoun'te-nănce, *v.t.*; countenanced (-nanst), *pt.*, *pp.*; countenancing, *ppr.* 1. To favor; to manifest a regard for; to abet; as, to *countenance* vice.

2. To make a show of. [Obs.]

Each to these ladies love did *countenance*. —Spenser.

çoun'te-năn-cēr, *n.* One who countenances, favors, or supports.

çoun'tēr-. [Fr. *contre-*; L. *contra-*, against, opposite.] A prefix signifying opposite, over against, contrary.

çoun'tēr, *a.* Adverse; opposite; opposing; antagonistic.

Innumerable facts attesting the *counter* principle. —Taylor.

çoun'tēr, *adv.* [Fr. *contre*; L. *contra*, against, opposite.]

1. Contrary; in opposition; in an opposite direction; used chiefly with *run* or *go*; as, to *run counter* to the rules of virtue; he *went counter* to his own interest.

2. In the wrong way; contrary to the right course; contrariwise.

3. In the face, or at the face. [Obs.]

çoun'tēr, *n.* [ME. *countour*; OFr. *contoir*, *comptoir*, a countingroom, or table, of a banker; LL. *computatorium*, from L. *computare*, to compute, count.]

1. A table or board on which money is counted; a table on which goods in a store are laid for examination by purchasers.

2. The name of two former prisons in the city of London and of one which formerly existed in Southwark.

çoun'tēr, *n.* [ME. *countour*; L. *computator*, from *computare*, to count.]

1. One who counts or reckons; an auditor.

2. That which indicates a number; that which is used to keep an account or reckoning, as in games.

What comes the wool to? I can do it without *counters*. —Shak.

3. Money, in contempt. [Obs.]

4. An indicator for a machine used to denote speed or total number of revolutions.

çoun'tēr, *n.* 1. A term in music, formerly given to an under part, to serve for contrast to a principal part, but now used as equivalent to *counter-tenor*.

2. That part of a horse's forehand which lies between the shoulders and under the neck.

3. In a ship, an arched space in the stern between the bottom of the stern and the wing-transoms and buttock.

4. In a shoe, the back part about the heel.

Frame of Ship inside of Stern.
1 1. Pointers. 2 2. Quarter-timbers. 3 3. Counter-timbers. 4. Counter-timber knee. 5. Main transom.

çoun'tēr, *v.i.*; countered, *pt.*, *pp.*; countering, *ppr.* To give a blow while making a parry or receiving a blow.

çoun'tēr, *n.* An encounter. [Obs.]

çoun-tēr-aċt', *v.t.*; counteracted, *pt.*, *pp.*; counteracting, *ppr.* [*Counter-*, and L. *actus*, pp. of *agere*, to lead, drive, do.] To act in opposition to; to hinder, defeat, or frustrate, by contrary agency.

çoun-tēr-aċ'tion, *n.* Action in opposition; hindrance.

çoun-tēr-aċt'ive, *n.* One who or that which counteracts.

çoun-tēr-aċt'ive, *a.* Tending to counteract.

çoun-tēr-aċt'ive-ly, *adv.* By counteraction.

çoun'tēr-ap-prōach", *n.* In fortification, a trench or countermine to aid in resisting besiegers.

çoun'tēr-at-traċ"tion, *n.* Opposite attraction.

çoun'tēr-at-traċt'ive, *a.* Attracting in an opposite way.

çoun'tēr-bal-ănce, *n.* Any force or matter acting in opposition to another; specifically, in mechanics, a definite weight added to a moving mass in order to equalize the forces or moments around a revolving shaft.

çoun'tēr-bal-ănce, *v.t.*; counterbalanced, *pt.*, *pp.*; counterbalancing, *ppr.* [Fr. *contre-balancer*; *contre-*, against, opposite, and *balancer*, to balance, from L. *bilanx*; *bis*, twice, and *lanx*, a scale, plate.] To act against with an equal weight; to equiponderate.

çoun'tēr-bond, *n.* A bond to secure one who has given bond for another.

çoun'tēr-bōre, *n.* 1. In any bore or cylindrical cavity, an enlargement of an orifice, as for the insertion of a head.

2. A drill for making such an enlargement.

çoun-tēr-bōre', *v.t.*; counterbored, *pt.*, *pp.*; counterboring, *ppr.* To furnish, as a cylinder, with a counterbore.

çoun'tēr-brāce, *n.* 1. Nautically, the lee brace of the foretopsail-yard.

2. In engineering, diagonal bracing, as in a girder, giving additional support and relieving the main-brace of stress.

çoun-tēr-brāce', *v.t.*; counterbraced, *pt.*, *pp.*; counterbracing, *ppr.* 1. Nautically, to brace (the yards) in opposite directions.

2. In engineering, to furnish with a counterbrace.

çoun-tēr-buff', *v.t.*; counterbuffed (-buft), *pt.*, *pp.*; counterbuffing, *ppr.* To strike back or in an opposite direction; to drive back; to stop by a blow or impulse in front.

çoun'tēr-buff, *n.* A blow in an opposite direction; a stroke that stops motion or causes a recoil.

çoun'tēr-ċȧst, *n.* Delusive contrivance; contrary cast.

çoun'tēr-ċȧst"ēr, *n.* A caster of accounts; a reckoner; a bookkeeper, in contempt.

çoun'tēr-chānġe, *n.* Exchange; reciprocation.

çoun-tēr-chānġe', *v.t.*; counterchanged, *pt.*, *pp.*; counterchanging, *ppr.* To give and receive; or to cause to change places.

çoun-tēr-chānġed', *a.* [Fr. *contre-changé*; *contre*, opposite, and *changé*, from *changer*, LL. *cambiare*, to exchange, barter.]

1. Exchanged.

2. In heraldry, having a field of two tinctures, metal and color, and a charge upon it partaking of both, the charge, or part of the charge, which lies in the metal, being of color, and vice versa.

Per pale gules and or; a boar passant counterchanged.

çoun'tēr-chārġe, *n.* An opposite charge.

çoun'tēr-chärm, *n.* That which has the power of dissolving or opposing the effect of a charm.

çoun-tēr-chärm', *v.t.*; countercharmed, *pt.*, *pp.*; countercharming, *ppr.* To destroy the effect of (enchantment).

çoun-tēr-check', *v.t.*; counterchecked, *pt.*, *pp.*; counterchecking, *ppr.* To oppose or stop (a check) by some obstacle; to check (a check).

çoun'tēr-check, *n.* One who or that which counterchecks.

çoun'tēr-ċlāim, *n.* An opposing claim, as by a defendant against a plaintiff, made to offset a demand.

çoun-tēr-ċlāim', *v.t.* and *v.i.*; counter-claimed, *pt.*, *pp.*; counter-claiming, *ppr.* To enter a counter-claim.

çoun"tēr-com-pō'ny, *a.* [Fr. *contre-componé*; *contre-*, opposite, and *componé*, from L. *componere*, to place together.] In heraldry, denoting a border, bend, or other ordinary, which is compounded of two ranks of panes, or rows of checkers, of alternate metals and colors.

A bend counter-compony.

çoun"tēr-couch'ănt, *a.* In heraldry, denoting animals borne couchant, and having their heads in contrary directions.

çoun"tēr-çou'rănt, *a.* In heraldry, denoting animals borne running in opposite directions.

Counter-courant.

çoun'tēr-çur-rent, *a.* Running in an opposite direction.

çoun'tēr-çur-rent, *n.* A current in an opposite direction to another current.

çoun'tēr-deed, *n.* A secret writing, either before a notary or under a private seal, which invalidates, destroys, or alters a previous deed.

çoun'tēr-dis-tinc"tion, *n.* Contradistinction.

çoun'tēr-drāin, *n.* A drain parallel to a watercourse, for collecting the soakage.

çoun-tēr-drąw', *v.t.*; counterdrew, *pt.*; counterdrawing, *ppr.*; counterdrawn, *pp.* In painting, to trace; to copy by means of a transparent substance.

çoun"tēr-em-bat'tled (-tld), *a.* In heraldry, denoting an ordinary, embattled on both sides.

Counter-embattled.

coun′tẽr-ev″i-dence, *n.* Opposite evidence; evidence or testimony which opposes other evidence.

coun′tẽr-ex-ten′sion, *n.* In surgery, a means of reducing a fracture by making extension in the opposite direction.

coun′tẽr-fall″ẽr, *n.* In a spinning-mule, a counterweighted wire which is depressed when the faller-wire lowers the row of yarns to wind them on the spindle.

coun′tẽr-feit (-fit), *v.t.*; counterfeited, *pt.*, *pp.*; counterfeiting, *ppr.* 1. To put on the semblance of; to imitate; to mimic; as, to *counterfeit* the mannerisms of an actor.

2. To copy with an intent to pass the copy for an original; to imitate wrongfully; to forge; as, to *counterfeit* money.

coun′tẽr-feit, *v.i.* 1. To feign; to dissemble; to carry on a fiction or deception.

2. To make counterfeits.

coun′tẽr-feit, *a.* [OFr. *contrefait*; LL. *contrafactus*, counterfeit, pp. of *contrafacere*; *contra*, against, opposite, and *facere*, to make.]

1. Forged; false; fabricated without right; made in imitation of something else with a view to defraud by passing the false copy for genuine or original; as, a *counterfeit* coin; a *counterfeit* deed or bond.

2. Assuming the appearance of something; false; hypocritical; as, a *counterfeit* friend.

3. Having the resemblance of; false; not genuine; as, *counterfeit* modesty.

Syn.—Bogus, deceptive, false, fictitious, forged, fraudulent, mock, sham, spurious.

coun′tẽr-feit, *n.* 1. A cheat; an impostor.

2. One thing made like or resembling another; specifically, an imitation without lawful authority, made with intent to defraud by passing the false for the true; as, the note is a poor *counterfeit*.

coun′tẽr-feit-ẽr, *n.* One who or that which counterfeits; specifically, a maker or circulator of counterfeit money.

coun′tẽr-feit-ly, *adv.* By forgery; falsely.

coun-tẽr-fē′ṣance, *n.* [Fr. *contrefaisance*, from *contrefaire*, counterfeit, imitate.] The act of forging; forgery; also written *counterfaisance*. [Obs.]

coun′tẽr-fis″sūre (-fish″ūr), *n.* In surgery, a skull-fracture opposite the point of impact.

coun″tẽr-flō′ry, coun″tẽr-fleū′ré (-rā), *a.* [*Counter-*, and Fr. *fleuré*, from *fleur*, a flower.] In heraldry, denoting that the flowers with which an ordinary is adorned stand opposite to each other alternately.

A double tressure flory and counterflory.

coun′tẽr-foil, *n.* [*Counter-*, and OFr. *foil*, *foille*, a leaf.]

1. Formerly, in the English Exchequer on the court officer's record, a corresponding part, the stock, being given the one lending the king money; counterstock.

2. A complementary memorandum or stub. [Eng.]

coun′tẽr-fōrce, *n.* An opposing or counteracting force.

coun′tẽr-fōrt, *n.* 1. In architecture, a buttress or other support.

2. A projecting crag of a mountain.

coun′tẽr-gāge, *n.* In carpentry, a method used to measure the joints, by transferring the breadth of a mortise to the place where the tenon is to be, in order to make them fit each other.

coun′tẽr-guärd, *n.* In fortification, a redan-shaped work having its faces parallel to the faces of the bastion.

coun-tẽr-in′flū-ence, *v.t.* To hinder by opposing influence. [Rare.]

coun-tẽr-ir′ri-tant, *n.* In medicine, a substance employed to produce an artificial or secondary disease in order to relieve another or primary one.

coun-tẽr-ir′ri-tāte, *v.t.*; counterirritated, *pt.*, *pp.*; counterirritating, *ppr.* To use a counterirritant on.

coun′tẽr-ir-ri-tā″tion, *n.* The effect brought about by a counterirritant.

coun′tẽr-jum″pẽr, *n.* A clerk; especially, a dry-goods salesman; a derisive term. [Slang.]

coun′tẽr-light (-lit), *n.* A light opposite to anything, which makes it appear to disadvantage.

coun′tẽr-măn, *n.* A salesman at a counter. [Eng.]

coun-tẽr-mȧnd′, *v.t.*; countermanded, *pt.*, *pp.*; countermanding, *ppr.* [Fr. *contremander*; L. *contramandare*; *contra*, opposite, and *mandare*, to command.]

1. To revoke (a former command); to direct in opposition to, as an order, which annuls a former command, and forbids its execution; as, to *countermand* orders.

2. To oppose; to contradict the orders of (another).

3. To prohibit. [Obs.]

coun′tẽr-mȧnd, *n.* A contrary order; revocation of a former order or command.

coun-tẽr-mȧnd′á-ble, *a.* Subject to countermand.

coun′tẽr-märch, *n.* 1. A marching back; a returning.

2. Militarily, (a) a movement opposite to a former direction of march; (b) a change of the wings or face of a battalion, so as to bring the right to the left, or the front into the rear.

3. A change of measures; alteration of conduct.

coun-tẽr-märch′, *v.t.* and *v.i.*; countermarched, *pt.*, *pp.*; countermarching, *ppr.* To march back.

coun′tẽr-märk, *n.* 1. A supplementary mark put on a bale of goods belonging to several merchants, that it may not be opened but in the presence of all the owners.

2. The mark of the Goldsmiths' Company (London), added to that of the artificer, to show the metal to be standard.

3. An artificial cavity made in the teeth of horses, that have outgrown their natural mark, to disguise their age.

4. A mark added to a coin to make it pass current in another country or to indicate some change, as of value.

coun-tẽr-märk′, *v.t.*; countermarked, *pt.*, *pp.*; countermarking, *ppr.* To affix a countermark on.

coun′tẽr-mīne, *n.* A stratagem or counterplot designed to meet another plot; specifically, in military affairs, a mine designed to destroy or frustrate the effect of another mine.

coun-tẽr-mīne′, *v.t.* and *v.i.*; countermined, *pt.*, *pp.*; countermining, *ppr.* To frustrate by or as by a countermine.

coun-tẽr-möve′, *v.t.* and *v.i.*; countermoved, *pt.*, *pp.*; countermoving, *ppr.* To move in a contrary direction, or in opposition to another.

coun′tẽr-möve, coun′tẽr-möve-ment, *n.* A movement in opposition to another.

coun′tẽr-mūre, *n.* [Fr. *contremur*; L. *contra*, against, and *murus*, a wall.] A wall raised behind another, to supply its place, when a breach is made. [Rare.]

coun-tẽr-mūre′, *v.t.* To fortify with a wall behind another. [Rare.]

coun′tẽr-nat-ū-răl, *a.* Contrary to nature. [Rare.]

coun′tẽr-noiṣe, *n.* A noise or sound by which another noise or sound is overpowered.

coun′tẽr-ō′pen-ing, *n.* An aperture or vent on the opposite side, or in a different place.

coun′tẽr-pāce, *n.* A step or measure in opposition to another; contrary measure or attempt.

coun′tẽr-pāled, coun′tẽr-pā″ly, *a.* In heraldry, denoting an escutcheon divided into an equal number of pieces palewise by a line fessewise, the two tinctures above and below the fesse line being counterchanged.

coun′tẽr-pāne, *n.* [A corruption of *counterpoint*; OFr. *contrepointe*, a quilt, from LL. *culcita puncta*; *culcita*, a quilt, and *puncta*, f. of pp. of *pungere*, to prick.] The outside quilt of a bed; specifically, a cotton quilt having a raised pattern.

coun′tẽr-pāne, *n.* [OFr. *contrepan*, a pledge, pawn; *contre*, opposite, and *pan*, a pledge, pawn.] One part of an indenture; a counterpart or duplicate.

coun′tẽr-pȧ-rōl″, *n.* In military phraseology, a word in addition to the password, which is given in any time of alarm as a signal.

coun′tẽr-pärt, *n.* 1. The correspondent part; the part that answers to another, as the two papers of a contract or indenture; a copy; a duplicate.

2. A person resembling or corresponding to another.

3. The part which fits another, as the key of a cipher, or a seal to its impression; hence, a thing that supplements another thing or completes it; a complement; hence, a person having qualities wanting in another, and such as make him or her complete.

4. In music, the part to be arranged or used in connection with another; as, the bass is the *counterpart* to the treble.

coun-tẽr-pas′sănt, *a.* [OFr. *contrepassant*; *contre*, opposite, and *passer*, to pass, go over.] In heraldry, going opposite directions, as animals.

coun′tẽr-plēa, *n.* In law, a replication to a plea or request.

coun-tẽr-plēad′, *v.t.* To plead in opposition to; to contradict; to deny.

coun-tẽr-plot′, *v.t.*; counterplotted, *pt.*, *pp.*; counterplotting, *ppr.* To plot against in order to defeat another plot.

coun′tẽr-plot, *n.* A plot or artifice opposed to another.

coun-tẽr-plot′ting, *n.* A plotting in opposition to a stratagem.

coun′tẽr-point, *n.* [Fr. *contrepoint*; It. *contrappunto*, from L. *contra*, against, and *punctum*, a prick, small hole.]

1. An opposite point or course.

2. In music, (a) the art of composition generally; (b) the art of arranging one or more parts in harmony with the melody; (c) the part or parts so added.

coun′tẽr-point, *n.* [OFr. *contrepointe*, *contrepoinct*, a quilt, from LL. *culcita puncta*, a stitched quilt, counterpane.] A coverlet, now commonly called *counterpane*.

coun″tẽr-poin-té′ (-tā′), *a.* In heraldry, a term denoting two chevrons meeting with their points in the center of an escutcheon.

Two chevrons counter-pointé.

coun-tẽr-poiṣe′, *v.t.*; counterpoised, *pt.*, *pp.*; counterpoising, *ppr.* [ME. *counterpeisen*; OFr. *contrepeser*, to counterpoise.]

1. To counterbalance; to act against with equal weight; to be equiponderant to; to equal in weight.

2. To act against with equal power or effect; to balance.

coun′tẽr-poiṣe, *n.* [OFr. *contrepois*; L. *contra*, against, and *pensum*, a weight, pound, from *pendere*, to weigh.]

1. Equal weight acting in opposition to something; equiponderance; a weight sufficient to balance another in the opposite scale; equal balance.

2. Equal power or force acting in opposition; a force sufficient to balance another force.

3. In radiotelegraphy, one or more wires insulated from the earth and usually stretched immediately below the regular aerial. Largely used in aircraft radiotelegraphy where ground connection is impossible.

coun′tẽr-poi-ṣŏn, *n.* An antidote.

coun′tẽr-proj-ect, *n.* A project, scheme, or proposal of one party, given in opposition to that of another, as in the negotiation of a treaty.

coun′tẽr-prọọf, *n.* In engraving, a print taken off from another fresh printed, which, by being passed through the press, gives the figure of the former, but inverted.

coun-tẽr-pröve′, *v.t.*; counterproved, *pt.*, *pp.*; counterproving, *ppr.* To take a counterproof of.

coun″tẽr-rev-ō-lū′tion, *n.* A revolution opposed to a former one, and restoring a former state of things.

coun″tẽr-rev-ō-lū′tion-ist, *n.* One taking part in a counter-revolution.

coun′tẽr-rōll, *n.* In old English law, a counterpart or copy of the rolls relating to appeals, inquests, etc., kept by an officer as a check upon another officer's roll.

coun″tẽr-rōl′ment, *n.* A counter account. [Obs.]

coun′tẽr-round, *n.* A body of officers going to visit and inspect the sentinels.

coun″tẽr-sā′li-ent, *a.* [From Fr. *contre*, opposite, and *saillir*, to leap.] In heraldry, denoting two beasts, borne in a coat of arms, leaping from each other.

coun′tẽr-sçāle, *n.* Counterbalance. [Obs.]

coun′tẽr-sçärp, coun′tẽr-sçärf, *n.* [Fr. *contrescarpe*; *contre*, against, opposite, and *escarpe*, from *escarper*, to cut slopewise, scarp.] In fortification, the exterior talus or slope of the ditch, or the talus that supports the earth of the covered way; sometimes, the whole covered way.

coun″tẽr-sçuf′fle, *n.* Equal contest.

coun′tẽr-sēa, *n.* The disturbed state of the sea after a gale, when, the wind having changed, the sea still runs in its old direction.

coun-tẽr-sēal′, *v.t.*; countersealed, *pt.*, *pp.*; countersealing, *ppr.* To seal with another or others.

coun″tẽr-sē-cūre′, *v.t.* To render more secure by additional guarantee.

coun′tẽr-sē-cū″ri-ty, *n.* Security given to one who has become surety for another.

coun′tẽr-sense, *n.* Opposite meaning.

coun′tẽr-shȧft, *n.* An intermediate shaft working between the main shaft and the machine or machines to be driven.

coun-tẽr-sīgn′, (-sīn′), *v.t.*; countersigned, *pt.*, *pp.*; countersigning, *ppr.* [OFr. *contresigner*; *contre*, against, opposite, and *signer*, to sign.]

1. To attest the genuineness of by adding one's signature.

2. To corroborate. [Rare.]

coun′tẽr-sīgn, *n.* 1. A word or other token given, without which none can pass a sentry; a military watchword.

2. The signature of a secretary or other officer to a writing signed by the principal or superior, to attest its authenticity.

coun′tẽr-sig-năl, *n.* A signal to answer or correspond to another.

coun′tẽr-sig″nā-tūre, *n.* The name of a secretary or other officer countersigned to a writing.

coun-tẽr-sīnk′, *v.t.*; countersunk, *pt.*, *pp.*; countersinking, *ppr.* 1. To form by drilling or turning, as a cavity in timber or other materials for the reception of a bolt or screw, plate of iron, etc., below the surface, either wholly or in part; as, to *countersink* a hole for a screw.

2. To cause to sink in any other body so as to be even with or below its surface.

coun′tẽr-sīnk, *n.* 1. A drill or brace-bit for countersinking.

2. The depression made for receiving a bolt or screw.

çoun′tẽr=slōpe, *n.* Any slope that overhangs.

çoun′tẽr=stand, *n.* Ground for opposition.

çoun′tẽr=stat-ūte, *n.* A contrary statute or ordinance.

çoun′tẽr-step, *n.* An opposite step or procedure; an opposite course of action.

çoun′tẽr-stock, *n.* See *Counterfoil*, 1.

çoun′tẽr-strōke, *n.* A contrary stroke; a stroke returned.

çoun′tẽr=sụre′ty, *n.* A counter-bond, or a surety to secure one that has given security.

çoun′tẽr-swāy, *n.* Contrary sway; opposite influence.

çoun′tẽr=tal-ly, *n.* A tally corresponding to another.

çoun-tẽr=ten′ŏr, *n.* In music, one of the middle parts, between the tenor and the treble; high tenor.

çoun′tẽr-tẽrm, *n.* An antithetical term; an antonym.

çoun′tẽr=tīde, *n.* Contrary tide.

çoun′tẽr-tīme, *n.* 1. In the manège, the defense or resistance of a horse, that interrupts his cadence and the measure of his manège, occasioned by a bad horseman, or the bad temper of the horse.

2. Resistance; opposition. [Obs.]

çoun′tẽr-trip′pănt, *a.* In heraldry, a term applied to two animals in an escutcheon, tripping in opposite directions; also written *counter-tripping.*

çoun′tẽr-tũrn, *n.* An unexpected climax in the plot of a play.

çoun-tẽr-vāil′, *v.t.*; countervailed, *pt., pp.*; countervailing, *ppr.* [OFr. *contrevaleir*; *contre-*, L. *contra*, against, and *valeir*, L. *valere*, to be strong.] To act against with equal force or power; to equal; to act with equivalent effect against anything; to balance; to compensate; as, the profit will hardly *countervail* the inconveniences.

çoun′tẽr-vāil, *n.* Equal weight or strength; compensation; requital.

çoun-tẽr=vāir′y, çoun′tẽr=vāir, *a.* In heraldry, charged with vair (one of the furs), differing from it in having the bells or cups arranged base against base and point against point. The tinctures are or and azure.

Counter-vairy.

çoun′tẽr-view (-vū), *n.* 1. An opposite or opposing view; opposition; a posture in which two persons front each other.

2. Contrast; a position in which two dissimilar things illustrate each other by opposition.

çoun-tẽr-vōte′, *v.t.* To vote in opposition; to outvote.

çoun-tẽr-wāit′, *v.t.* To watch for. [Obs.]

çoun-tẽr-weigh′ (-wā′), *v.t.* To weigh against; to counterbalance.

çoun′tẽr-weight (-wāt), *n.* A counterpoise.

çoun-tẽr-wheel′, *v.t.* To cause to wheel in an opposite direction.

çoun-tẽr-wŏrk′, *v.t.*; counterworked, *pt., pp.*; counterworking, *ppr.* To work in opposition to; to counteract; to hinder any effect by contrary operations.

That *counterworks* each folly and caprice. —Pope.

çount′ess, *n.*; *pl.* **çount′ess-eṣ.** [Fr. *comtesse*; It. *contessa*; Sp. *condesa*, a female associate or companion; from L. *comes, comitis*, a companion.] The wife of an earl or count, or a lady possessed of an earldom in her own right. [Eng.]

çount′ing-house, *n.* The house appropriated by merchants, traders, and manufacturers, to the keeping of their books and the transaction of business.

çount′ing-rọọm, *n.* A room in a counting-house.

çount′less, *a.* Innumerable.

çount′ŏr, *n.* In old English law, an advocate. [Obs.]

çoun′tŏur, *n.* An accountant. [Obs.]

çoun′tre-, *prefix.* Contra-. [Obs.]

çŏun′tri-fied (kun′-), *a.* Rustic; rural; having the appearance and manners of the country.

çŏun′tri-fȳ, *v.t.*; countrified, *pt., pp.*; countrifying, *ppr.* To conform to the country; to make rustic.

çŏun′try, *n.*; *pl.* **çŏun′trieṣ.** [ME. *countre*; OFr. *contree, contrie*; Port. and It. *contrada*; LL. *contrata*, a region, country, that which is before, or over against one; from *contra*, opposite, over against.]

1. A large tract of land or a region, as distinct from other regions by location or people; as, Alaska, an undeveloped *country.*

2. An indefinite tract of land; any extent of ground; as, the train passed through an arid *country.*

3. The land of one's birth; one's region of residence; a permanent place of abode.

4. The inhabitants of any region; as, the whole *country* distrusted him.

5. The rural part or agricultural region distinguished from the city or town; as, a vacation in the *country.*

6. In law, the jury as the representative of the community at large.

7. In mining, the rock or strata in which a metallic lode is found; country-rock.

To put oneself upon the country; to demand a jury trial.

çŏun′try, *a.* 1. Pertaining to the country or territory at a distance from a city; rural; rustic; as, a *country* town.

2. Provincial; rude.

3. National. [Obs.]

çŏun′try=bāse, *n.* A game, prison-base.

çŏun′try=dånce, *n.* A dance in which the partners are arranged opposite to each other in lines.

çŏun′try-măn, *n.*; *pl.* **çŏun′try-men.** 1. One born in the same country with another; as, this man is my *countryman.*

2. One who dwells in the country, as opposed to one living in a town or city; a rustic; a farmer.

3. An inhabitant or native of a region.

çŏun′try=rock, *n.* See *Country*, n. 7.

çŏun′try=sēat, *n.* A dwelling in the country used as a place of retirement from the city.

çŏun′try-sīde, *n.* Neighborhood.

çŏun′try-wom″ăn (-woom″), *n.*, feminine of *countryman.*

çount′=wheel, *n.* The wheel of a clock which causes it to strike correctly.

çoun′ty, *n.*; *pl.* **çoun′tieṣ.** [ME. *countee*; OFr. *counte, contee*; It. *contado*, from LL. *comitatus*, the office or jurisdiction of a count or earl, from L. *comes, comitis*, a companion.]

1. A civil division of a state or country designed to facilitate government and administration in and through such division; specifically, in the United States, a subdivision next below the state, having appropriate officers.

2. The inhabitants of a *county*, taken collectively.

3. The district of an earl or count. [Obs.]

County commissioner; see under *Commissioner.*

County corporate; a city or town having the privilege of being a county by itself, as London. [Eng.]

County court; one having jurisdiction only in a county.

County palatine; a division, now abolished, in which the ruler had kingly powers. [Eng.]

County sessions; the general quarter sessions of the peace for each county. [Eng.]

County town; a county-seat.

çoun′ty=sēat, *n.* The seat of government of a county; a county town.

çoup (kö), *n.* [Fr., a stroke, blow.]

1. A stroke or blow, opportune and of some strength; a master-stroke.

2. In certain tribes of Indians of North America, a stroke or maneuver against an enemy so done as to constitute a deed of bravery.

Coup d'état; a sudden decisive blow in politics; a stroke of policy.

Coup de grâce; the finishing stroke.

Coup de main; a sudden attack or enterprise.

Coup d'œil; (a) general view; glance of the eye; (b) militarily, comprehensive grasp, as of the plan of a battle.

Coup de soleil; a sunstroke.

çou′pȧ-ble, *a.* Culpable. [Obs.]

çou-pé′ (-pā′), *n.* [Fr., pp. of *couper*, to cut.]

1. The front seats of a French diligence; the front compartment of an English first-class railway-carriage, generally seated for three.

2. A four-wheeled carriage carrying two inside, with a seat for the driver on the outside.

3. A two- or three-passenger automobile having an enclosed body.

çouped (kōpt), *a.* In heraldry, denoting that the head or any limb of an animal is cut off from the trunk; in contradistinction to *erased*, which indicates that the head or limb is torn off.

Couped.

çou-pee′, *n.* [Fr., from *couper*, to cut.] A motion in dancing, when one leg is a little bent, and suspended from the ground, and with the other a motion is made forward.

çoupe′=gorge (-gorzh), *n.* [Fr. *coupé*, from *couper*, to cut, and *gorge*, a throat.] Militarily, a position in which troops are unable to resist and must surrender or be annihilated.

çou′ple (kup′pl), *n.* [ME. *couple*; OFr. *cuple, cople*; L. *copula*, a band, bond.]

1. Two of the same species or kind, and near in place, or considered together; as, a *couple* of men.

2. A male and female connected by marriage, betrothed, or otherwise allied; as, a married *couple*; a young *couple.*

3. That which links or connects two things together.

4. In mechanics, two equal and parallel forces acting in opposite directions.

5. In electricity, one of the pairs of plates of two metals which compose a battery.

6. One of a pair of opposite rafters in a roof, nailed at the top where they meet, and connected by a tie at or near their lower ends.

Syn.—Brace, pair, two.

çou′ple, *v.t.*; coupled, *pt., pp.*; coupling, *ppr.* [Fr. *coupler*; L. *copulare*, to couple, from *copula*, band, bond.]

1. To link, chain, or connect (one thing) with another; to sew or fasten together.

2. To marry; to wed; to unite, as husband and wife.

çou′ple, *v.i.* To copulate.

çou′ple=beg″gȧr, *n.* One who makes it his business to marry beggars to each other.

çou′ple=clōṣe, *n.* 1. In heraldry, the fourth of a chevron, never borne but in pairs, except there is a chevron between them.

2. In architecture, couples, collectively.

A chevron between two couple-closes.

çou′ple-ment (kup′pl-), *n.* Union. [Obs.]

çoup′lẽr, *n.* One who or that which couples; as, (a) any device in an organ for depressing another key or keys when one is played; (b) the ring slid along a gripping instrument, as tongs; (c) any coupling device; a coupling.

çoup′let, *n.* [Fr., dim. of *couple*, a couple.]

1. Two lines of verse in immediate succession; a pair of rimes.

2. A pair; as, a *couplet* of doves. [Obs.]

çoup′ling, *n.* 1. A joining; copulation.

2. Any mechanical device or appliance serving to unite two or more parts or things; as, the *coupling* of a roof or train of cars.

Half-lap coupling; a form of permanent coupling having the meeting shafts mortised and keyed in a cylindrical coupling-box.

Half-lap Coupling.

çoup′ling=box, *n.* A means of joining the ends of two shafts by a box-shaped fixture.

çoup′ling=pin, *n.* A pin used for coupling together railroad cars or machinery.

çou′pon, *n.* [Fr., a remnant, from *couper*, to cut, cut off.]

1. An interest certificate, printed at the bottom of transferable bonds (state, railroad, etc.), given for a term of years. There are as many of these certificates as there are payments of interest to be made. At each time of payment one is cut off and presented for payment. Hence its name, *coupon*, or cut off.

2. A portion, generally detachable, of a ticket, which designates a specified privilege, as the right to certain transportation or a certain seat, as in a car or theater.

çoup′stick, *n.* A stick carried by certain North American Indians, with which to execute a coup. [See *Coup*, 2.]

çou′pūre, *n.* [Fr., from *couper*, to cut.]

1. In fortification, (a) an intrenchment or fosse, made behind a breach by the besieged, with a view to defense; (b) a passage cut through the glacis in the reëntering angle of the covered way, to facilitate sallies by the besieged.

2. In the theory of functions, a cutting of a Riemann's surface.

çŏur′āge (kur′), *n.* [OFr. *courage, corage*, mind, heart, spirit, from L. *cor*, heart.]

1. That quality of mind which enables men to encounter danger and difficulties with firmness, or without fear or depression of spirits; bravery.

2. Spirit; desire; temper. [Obs.]

Syn.—Bravery, intrepidity, valor, boldness, resolution, fortitude, firmness, fearlessness, daring, enterprise, hardihood, heroism, gallantry, dauntlessness, mettle, pluck.

çŏur-ā′geous (kur-rā′jus), *a.* [OFr. *corageus*, from *corage*, mind, heart, spirit.] Having or exhibiting courage; brave; daring; as, a *courageous* deed.

çŏur-ā′geous-ly, *adv.* In a courageous manner; bravely.

çŏur-ā′geous-ness, *n.* The state or quality of being courageous.

Syn.—Courage, boldness, bravery, intrepidity, spirit, valor.

çou′rant, *a.* Running; applied, in heraldry, to animals.

çou′rant (*or* **çou-rant′**), *n.* A newspaper. [Obs. except in newspaper titles.]

Courant.

çou-rănt′, çou-răn′tō, *n.* [Fr. *courant*, running, pp. of *courir*, to run.] A piece of music in triple time; also, a kind of ancient dance, consisting of a time, a step, a balance, and a coupee.

çou-rap′, *n.* [E. Ind.] An eruptive disease or itch, especially on the groin, face, breast, and armpits; East Indian scabies.

çourb, *v.i.* [Fr. *courber*.] To bend. [Obs.]

çōurb, *a.* Crooked. [Obs.]

çōur'bä-ril, *n.* [From S. Am. name.] A resin; animé.

çōurçhe, *n.* [Scot.] A kerchief. [Obs.]

çōu'ri-ėr, *n.* [OFr. *courier*, from *courir*, to run; L. *currere*, to run.]

1. A messenger sent express with letters or despatches.

2. A traveling servant whose especial duty is to make all arrangements at hotels and on the journey.

çōur'lăn, *n.* [Fr., from S. Am. name.] Any tropical American rail-like bird of the genus *Aramus*.

çōurse, *n.* [Fr. *course*; OFr. *curs*; L. *cursus*, a running, from *currere*, to run.]

1. In a general sense, a moving or motion forward in any direction; a continuous progression or advance.

When his fair *course* is not hindered.—Shak.

2. The direction of motion; the line in which a body moves; as, what *course* shall the pilot steer?

3. In pedestrianism and horse-racing, the ground or distance walked or run over.

4. The charge of one mounted knight or champion against another in the lists.

5. The continual or gradual advance or progress of anything; as, the *course* of an argument.

Time rolls his ceaseless *course*. —Scott.

6. Order; sequence; turn; succession of one to another in office, property, dignity, etc.

7. Methodical or regulated motion or procedure; customary or established sequence of events; recurrence of events according to certain laws.

Seed time and harvest, heat and hoary frost,
Shall hold their *course*. —Milton.

8. A systematized order of lectures and studies in arts or sciences for illustration or instruction; as, a *course* of lectures in history.

9. Manner of proceeding; way of life or conduct; personal behavior; career; procedure in a certain line of thought or action.

You held your *course* without remorse.
—Tennyson.

10. The part of a meal served at one time; as, the dinner consisted of four *courses*.

11. In architecture, a continued range of stones or bricks of the same height throughout the face or faces of a building.

12. Nautically, one of the sails that hangs from a ship's lower yards; as, the mainsail, foresail, and mizzen.

13. [*pl.*] The menstrual flux; catamenia.

In course; regularly; in sequence.

Matter of course; something to be expected in the natural order of things.

Of course; as a matter of course; certainly.

Syn.—Way, road, route, passage, race, procedure, series, succession, rotation, manner, method, mode.

çōurse, *v.t.*; coursed, *pt., pp.*; coursing, *ppr.* 1. To hunt; to pursue; to chase.

We *coursed* him at the heels. —Shak.

2. To cause to run; to force to move with speed.

3. To run through or over; as, the blood *courses* the arteries.

çōurse, *v.i.* 1. To run; to move with speed; to run or move about; as, the blood *courses*.

2. To hunt game with dogs.

çōursed (kōrst), *a.* Hunted; also, arranged in courses.

çōurs'ėr, *n.* [ME. *courser*; OFr. *corsier*; LL. *cursarius*, from L. *cursus*, a running; *currere*, to run.]

1. A swift horse; a runner; a war-horse.

2. One who hunts; one who pursues the sport of coursing hares.

3. In zoölogy, (a) one of a genus of grallatorial birds of the plover tribe; (b) [*pl.*] an order of birds, the runners, including the ostrich.

çōur'sey, *n.* A narrow aisle in a galley separating slaves from each other.

çōurs'ing, *n.* Pursuit of game by dogs using the sense of sight to follow the quarry.

çōurs'ing-joint, *n.* A joint between two courses of masonry.

çōurt, *n.* [ME. *court, cort*; OFr. *curt, cort*; LL. *cortis*, a courtyard, yard, villa, palace; L. *cors*, contr. of *cohors*, a place inclosed.]

1. A place in front of a house, inclosed by a wall or fence; an uncovered area whether behind or in front of a house, or surrounded by buildings; a courtyard.

2. A palace; the place of residence of a king or sovereign prince.

This our *court*, . .
Shows like a riotous inn. — Shak.

3. All the surroundings of a sovereign in his regal state; specifically, the collective body of persons who compose the retinue or council of a sovereign.

Love rules the *court*, the camp, the grove.
—Scott.

4. The hall, chamber, or place where justice is administered.

5. The persons or judges assembled for hearing and deciding causes, civil, criminal, military, naval, or ecclesiastical, as distinguished from the counsel or jury; as, a *court* of law; a *court* of chancery.

6. Any jurisdiction, civil, military, or ecclesiastical.

The archbishop . . .
Held a late *court* at Dunstable. —Shak.

7. The sitting of a judicial assembly.

8. The meeting of a corporation or the principal members of a corporation; as, the *court* of directors; the *court* of aldermen.

9. Attention directed to a person in power; the art of pleasing; the art of insinuation; civility; flattery; address to gain favor; as, to pay *court* to wealth.

10. A short branch of a public street; a level, smooth plot of ground for playing games, as tennis.

Christian court; an ecclesiastical court.

Court circular; news of the court and sovereign, as furnished by authority to the press. [Eng.]

Court day; the day of a court's sitting.

Court dress; a dress suitable for an appearance at the court of a sovereign.

Court guide; a directory or book containing the addresses of the nobility and gentry. [Eng.]

Court of Arches; see under *Arches*.

Court of audience; see under *Audience*.

Court of Claims; the United States court that has for its object the investigation of claims against the government.

Court of Common Pleas; in the United States, a court both civil and criminal, having jurisdiction over a state or in some cases a county.

Court of equity; see under *Equity*.

Court of error; one having jurisdiction in cases of alleged error.

Court of inquiry; one convened to investigate and report on questions of military or naval law or precedent; generally as a preliminary to a court-martial.

Court of St. James; the British court.

District Court of the United States; a court presided over by a judge whose jurisdiction takes in a certain district, as a state or part of a state, and who tries certain civil, criminal and admiralty causes in his district.

General Court; the legislature of Connecticut and of New Hampshire.

Justice court; a court of a justice of the peace.

Superior Court; (a) in the United States, a local court having jurisdiction intermediate between the lower class of inferior courts and the supreme court; (b) in England, one of the main courts sitting at Westminster.

Supreme Court; generally, the highest court of a state, and (except in New York) the court of last resort. [U. S. Supreme Court, see *Supreme*.]

The courts of the Lord; the temple at Jerusalem; hence, any house of public worship.

çōurt, *v.t.*; courted, *pt., pp.*; courting, *ppr.* 1. To endeavor to gain the favor of or win over by attention and address; to ingratiate oneself with; to flatter; a use of the word derived from the manners of a court.

2. To seek the affections or love of; to woo; to solicit for marriage.

A thousand *court* you, though they court in vain. —Pope.

3. To attempt to gain by address; to solicit; to seek; as, to *court* commendation or applause; said of things as the object.

4. To hold out inducements to; to invite.

A well-worn pathway *courted* us.—Tennyson.

çōurt, *v.i.* 1. To act the courtier; to imitate the manners of a court.

2. To pay one's addresses; to woo; as, he is *courting* at present.

çōurt'-bar"ŏn, *n.* A baron's court. [Obs.]

çōurt'-bred, *a.* Used to the ways of a court; easy; polished.

çōurt'-breed"ing, *n.* The etiquette of a court.

çōurt'-çärd, *n.* A coat-card.

çōurt'-çrȧft, *n.* Intrigue, as at court.

çōurt'-çup"bōard (-kub"ērd), *n.* A sideboard. [Obs.]

çōur'tē-ous, *a.* [ME. *curteous, curteis, corteis*; OFr. *curteis, corteis*, from LL. *cortis*, a court.] Having courtlike or elegant manners; using or characterized by courtesy; well-bred; polite; applied to persons or things; as, a *courteous* gentleman; *courteous* words; a *courteous* manner of address.

Syn.—Civil, polite, obliging, condescending, urbane, affable, conciliating, attentive, respectful.

çōur'tē-ous-ly, *adv.* In a courteous manner.

çōur'tē-ous-ness, *n.* The state or quality of being courteous.

çōur'tē-py, *n.* [D. *kort*, short, and *pije*, a coarse cloth.] A coarse, short coat. [Obs.]

çōurt'ėr, *n.* One who courts.

çōur'tē-ṣăn, *n.* Same as *Courtezan*.

çōur'tē-ṣăn-ship, *n.* Same as *Courtezanship*.

çōur'tē-sy, *n.* [ME. *curtesie*; OFr. *curteisie*, from *curteis*, courteous; LL. *cortis*, a court.]

1. Elegance or politeness of manners; especially, politeness connected with kindness; civility; complaisance; as, a *courtesy* done a stranger.

2. An act of civility or respect, an act of kindness or favor performed with politeness.

3. A motion or posture of reverence, civility, or respect, now only applied to a kind of bow made by a woman, consisting in a sinking or inclination of the body with bending of the knees.

4. A favor; as, to hold upon *courtesy*, that is, not of right, but by indulgence.

Courtesy (or *curtesy*) *of England*; the status of one who marries a woman seized of an estate of inheritance, and has by her issue born alive who is capable of inheriting her estate; in this case, on the death of his wife, he holds the lands for his life, as tenant by courtesy. This law exists in some of the United States.

Courtesy title; a title assumed by an individual or given to him by popular consent, to which he has no valid claim.

Syn.—Urbanity, civility, complaisance, condescension, affability, courteousness, elegance, good-breeding.

çōurte'sy (kūrt'), *v.i.*; courtesied, *pt., pp.*; courtesying, *ppr.* To make a courtesy.

çōurte'sy, *v.t.* To treat courteously.

çōur'tē-zăn, çōur'tē-ṣăn, *n.* [ME. *courtezane*; Fr. *courtesan*, a court-lady; from *corte*, a court.]

1. A courtier of either sex. [Obs.]

2. A woman of the town; a prostitute.

çōur'tē-zăn-ship, *n.* Prostitution.

çōurt'-hand, *n.* The old Gothic or Saxon hand or manner of writing used in English records and judicial proceedings.

çōurt'house, *n.* A building used for the regular holding of a court; also, a county-seat, so called in southern United States.

çōurt'iėr (-yēr), *n.* [OFr. *courtier*, a judge, courtier, from LL. *cortis*, a court, yard, palace.] One who attends or frequents the courts of princes; hence, a flatterer.

çōurt'iėr-y, *n.* Manners of a courtier. [Obs.]

çōurt'-lands, *n.pl.* In English law, lands of domain retained as a homestead.

çōurt'-leet, *n.* In English law, a court of record held once a year, in a particular hundred, lordship, or manor, before the steward of the leet. —Blackstone.

çōurt'like, *a.* Polite; elegant.

çōurt'li-ness, *n.* Elegance of manner; stateliness.

çōurt'ling, *n.* A courtier; a retainer to a court.

çōurt'ly, *a.* 1. Deferential; flattering. [Rare.]

2. Relating or pertaining to a court.

3. Courteous; polite.

çōurt'ly, *adv.* Politely; refinedly.

çōurt'-mär'shăl, *n.* One acting as marshal of a law-court.

çōurt'-mär'tiăl (-shăl), *n.*; *pl.* **çōurts'-mär'-tiăl.** A court made up of military or naval officers convened for trial of military or naval offenses.

çōurt'-mär'tiăl, *v.t.*; court-martialed, *pt., pp.*; court-martialing, *ppr.* To try by court-martial.

çōurt'-plas"tėr, *n.* Fine cloth treated with an adhesive substance, often medicated, to cover slight wounds.

çōurt'-rōlls, *n.pl.* Records of a court.

çōurt'ship, *n.* 1. The act of soliciting favor.

2. The act of wooing in love; solicitation of a woman to marriage.

3. Civility; elegance of manners. [Obs.]

çōurt'yärd, *n.* A court or inclosure round a house.

çōus'çōus, *n.* [W. Afr.] Baobab leaves, millet flour, and meat, mixed and used by West Africans as food; called also by them *lalo*.

çōus'çōu-sōu, *n.* Barbary couscous.

çōuṣ'in (kuz'n), *n.* [OFr. *cousin, cosin*; LL. *cosinus*, contr. of *consobrinus*, the child of a mother's sister, a cousin, relation; from *soror*, a sister.]

1. In a general sense, one collaterally related more remotely than a brother or sister; a relative; a kinsman or kinswoman.

2. The son or daughter of an uncle or aunt. The children of brothers and sisters are usually denominated *cousins* or *cousins-german*. In the second generation they are called *second cousins*.

3. A title given by a king to a nobleman, particularly to one of the council.

çōuṣ'in, *a.* Allied. [Obs.]

çōuṣ'in-āge, *n.* Relationship. [Obs.]

çōuṣ'in-hood, *n.* 1. Relationship.

2. The individuals connected with a family, collectively regarded.

çōuṣ'in-ly, *a.* Like or becoming a cousin.

çōuṣ'in-ry, *n.* Collectively, cousins.

çōuṣ'in-ship, *n.* Same as *Cousinhood*.

çous′si-net, *n.* [Fr., a little cushion.] In architecture, (a) a stone placed on the impost of a pier for receiving the first stone of an arch; (b) that part of the Ionic capital between the abacus and quarter round, which serves to form the volute.

çou-teau′ (-tō′), *n.*; *pl.* **çou-teaux′** (-tōz′). [Fr., a knife.] A dagger; a short knife in use during the middle ages.

çouth, çouthe, *v.* [Past tense and past participle of *can.*] Knew; was able; known. [Obs.]

çou′til, *n.* [Fr.] A linen or cotton cloth of a specially heavy close texture, used in making corsets.

çou-väde′, *n.* [Fr., from *couver*, to brood, hatch, sit.] A custom prevalent in ancient as well as modern times among some of the primitive races in all parts of the world, by which, after the birth of a child, the father takes to bed, and receives the care usually given to a mother.

çou-veuşe′, *n.* [Fr., from *couver*, to hatch, brood.] An apparatus for providing an even temperature and warm breathing-air for an infant prematurely born.

çou′xi-ȧ (-shi-), *n.* [S. Am. name.] The black saki of South America; also, the couxio.

çou′xi-ō (-shi-), *n.* *Pithecia chiropotes*, the red-backed or hand-drinking saki.

çō-vā′ri-ănt, *n.* A function which stands in the same relation to the primitive function from which it is derived, as any of its linear transforms do to a similarly derived transform of its primitive.

çōve, *n.* [AS. *cofa*, a room, chamber; Norw. *kove*, a closet.]

1. A small inlet, creek, or bay; a recess in the shore, where vessels and boats may be sheltered from the winds and waves.

> At length I spied a little *cove* on the right shore of the creek. —Defoe.

2. A narrow recess in a mountain; a secluded hollow or dell.

3. A tongue of prairie-land extending into a forest. [U. S.]

4. In architecture, any kind of concave molding; the concavity of a vault; the curve which is sometimes used to connect the ceiling of a room with the walls, and which springs from above the cornice.

çōve, *v.t.*; coved, *pt.*, *pp.*; coving, *ppr.* In architecture, to arch over.

çōve, *v.t.* [OFr. *cover*, to cover.] To cover; to brood over. [Obs.]

çōve, çōv′ey, *n.* [Gipsy *cova*, a thing, *covo*, that man, *covi*, that woman.] A man; a person, a fellow; often preceded by some adjective; as, a queer *cove.* [Slang.]

çōved, *a.* Forming an arch; arched; curving.

Coved ceiling: a ceiling formed in a coved or arched manner at its junction with the side walls. Such ceilings are frequently highly ornamented with panels enriched with moldings or carvings, according as they are formed of plaster or wood.

Coved Ceiling, Staircase of Palazzo Braschi, Rome.

Coved vault; a vault formed by the meeting in a central point of four sections curving concavely from wall to ceiling.

çō-vel′lin, çō-vel′line, *n.* [Named after *Covelli*, the discoverer.] A native form of copper sulphid, massive, and of an indigo-blue color; called also *indigo-copper* and *covellite.*

çŏv′e-nȧ-ble, *a.* [OFr.] Fit; suitable. [Obs.]

çŏv′e-nȧ-bly, *adv.* Fitly; properly; conveniently. [Obs.]

çŏv′e-nănt, *n.* [OFr. *covenant*, an agreement, from *covenir*; L. *convenire*, to agree, be of one mind, come together; *con-*, together, and *venire*, to come.]

1. A mutual consent or agreement of two or more persons, to do or to forbear some act or thing; a contract; stipulation.

2. In theology, the promise of God to man, usually carrying with it a condition to be fulfilled by man.

3. A solemn agreement between the members of a church, that they will act together in harmony with the precepts of the gospel.

4. In law, (a) a writing, under seal, containing the terms of agreement or contract between parties; also, a clause containing a subordinate agreement or stipulation in a deed or other sealed instrument; (b) a form of action which lies in the case of a party claiming damages for breach of contract under seal.

5. In ecclesiastical history, the stand taken by the Covenanters of Scotland. [See *Covenanter*, 2.]

Syn.—Contract, bargain, stipulation, agreement, promise, engagement.

çŏv′e-nănt, *v.t.* and *v.i.*; covenanted, *pt.*, *pp.*; covenanting, *ppr.* I. *v.t.* To grant or promise by covenant.

II. *v.i.* To enter into a formal agreement; to stipulate; to bind oneself by contract; as, A *covenants* with B to convey to him a certain estate.

çŏv″e-năn-tee′, *n.* The person to whose benefit the stipulations of a covenant are made.

çŏv′e-nănt-ẽr, *n.* 1. A person who makes a covenant.

2. [C—] In Scottish history, a subscriber to the National Covenant (1638), or to the Solemn League and Covenant (1643); also, in a later and more general sense, any one upholding the principles of the Reformed Presbyterian church.

çŏv′e-nănt-ing, *a.* 1. Of or pertaining to a covenant.

2. Relating or belonging to the Scottish Covenanters, or, later, to the Reformed Presbyterian church.

çŏv′e-nănt-ŏr, *n.* The person responsible for the performance of the stipulations of a covenant.

çŏv′e-nous, *a.* See *Covinous.*

çŏv′ent, *n.* [OFr. *covent*, convent, from L. *conventus*, an assembly, agreement.]

1. A convent or monastery. [Obs.]

2. A gathering or assembly; also, an agreement or promise. [Obs.]

çŏv′en-try=bell, *n.* Any one of several bellflowers more commonly called *canterbury-bell.*

çŏv′en-try blūe. Blue thread of a superior dye, made at Coventry, England, and used for embroidery.

çŏv′en-try=rāpe, *n.* A European bellflower, the rampion.

çŏv′ẽr, *v.t.*; covered, *pt.*, *pp.*; covering, *ppr.* [ME. *coveren*; OFr. *covrir*, *couvrir*, from L. *cooperire*; *co-*, intens., and *operire*, to hide.]

1. To overspread the surface of (a thing) with another substance; to lay or set over; as, to *cover* a floor with a carpet.

2. To hide; to conceal by something overspread or intervening; to screen.

> If I say, Surely the darkness shall *cover* me. —Ps. cxxxix. 11.

3. To clothe; as, to *cover* with a robe or mantle; to *cover* nakedness.

4. To overwhelm.

> Let them be *covered* with reproach. —Ps. lxxi. 13.

5. To pardon or remit.

> Blessed is he whose sin is *covered.* —Ps. xxxii. 1.

6. To shelter; to protect; to defend; as, a squadron of horse *covered* the troops on the retreat.

7. To attract to or bring upon (oneself); to invest (oneself) with; as, she *covered* herself with fame and renown.

8. To sit on or brood over; as, a hen *covers* her eggs faithfully.

9. To embrace (the female) sexually; to serve; said of the male, particularly of the lower animals.

10. To put the usual headdress on.

> Nay, pray be *covered.* —Shak.

11. To place within range; to have direct aim at; as, to *cover* an enemy with a rifle; also, to have a superior strategic position in relation to; to occupy a vantage-point which gives command of; as, the battery *covered* the bridge.

12. In commerce, to equal, or be of equal extent to; to be equivalent to or adequate for; to include, comprehend, or comprise; to compensate for or counterbalance; as, the receipts do not *cover* the expenses; this principle will *cover* the majority of cases.

To cover ground or *distance*; to travel over; to pass through.

To cover into; to return or transfer to.

To cover shorts; a phrase used on the stock exchange, meaning to buy property of any kind to fill contracts previously made.

Syn.—Overspread, cloak, shield, protect, shelter, hide, disguise, mark.

çŏv′ẽr, *v.i.* 1. To prepare a table for a banquet. [Obs.]

2. To spread or distribute in such a way as to hide something; applied particularly to paints; as, this paint *covers* better than the other.

3. To put one's hat on.

çŏv′ẽr, *n.* 1. Anything which is laid, set, or spread over another thing.

2. Anything which veils or conceals; a screen; disguise; as, gravity may serve as a *cover* for a deceitful heart.

3. Shelter; defense; protection; as, the troops fought under *cover* of the batteries.

4. The table furniture for the use of one person, such as plate, spoons, knives, and forks, napkin, glasses, etc.; as, *covers* were laid for ten.

5. In hunting, the woods or shrubbery which hide game.

6. The part of a shingle, slate, etc., placed in a roof or other portion of a building, that is covered by the row or course above.

7. The amount of lap of a slide-valve of a steam-engine.

To break cover; to come out from a hiding-place or den; used of game.

Under cover; inclosed in a wrapper or contained in a letter; also, under protection from gun-fire.

çŏv′ẽr-chiēf, *n.* A covering for the head. [Obs.]

çŏv′ẽr-çle (-kl), *n.* [Fr.] A small cover; a lid. [Obs.]

çŏv′ẽr=çlọth, *n.* A piece of cloth forming the outside of a lace-maker's pillow.

çŏv′ẽr-ẽr, *n.* The person or the thing that covers.

çŏv′ẽr=glȧss, *n.* A thin glass slide used to cover specimens prepared for the microscope; called also *cover-slip.*

çŏv′ẽr-ing, *n.* 1. That which covers; anything spread or laid over another, whether for security or concealment.

2. The act of providing a cover for.

çŏv′ẽr-let, *n.* [Fr. *couvre-lit*, a bed-cover; *couvrir*, to cover, and *lit*, from L. *lectus*, a bed.] The cover of a bed; a quilt, usually ornamental, designed to be spread over all the other coverings of a bed.

çŏv′ẽr-lid, *n.* A coverlet.

çŏv′ẽr=point, *n.* 1. In cricket, a fielder backing point; the position he occupies.

2. In lacrosse, a player in front of point.

çō-vẽrsed′ (-vẽrst′), *a.* In trigonometry, denoting the sine of the complement of an arc or angle; only in the phrase *coversed sine.* [See under *Sine.*]

çŏv′ẽr=shāme, *n.* Something used to conceal infamy. [Obs.]

çŏv′ẽr=slip, *n.* See *Cover-glass.*

çŏv′ẽrt, *a.* [OFr. *covert*, *couvert*, pp. of *couvrir*, to cover.]

1. Covered; hid; private; secret; concealed; disguised; insidious.

> Whether of open war, or *covert* guile.—Milton.

2. Sheltered; not open or exposed; as, a *covert* corner or place.

3. In law, under cover, authority, or protection; as, a *feme covert*, a married woman who is considered as being under the influence and protection of her husband.

Syn.—Close, concealed, hidden, secret, disguised, veiled, obscure.

çŏv′ẽrt, *n.* 1. A covering, or covering-place; a place which covers and shelters; a shelter; a defense.

2. A thicket; a shady place; a hiding-place for game.

3. That which hides or disguises; a pretext.

4. In fowling, a flock; a covey.

5. In ornithology, one of the feathers on the under part of the wing or on the tail, which lie over and cover the bases of the quills; generally used in the plural.

çŏv′ẽrt=bar″ŏn, *n.* [Fr. *covert*, pp. of *couvrir*, to cover, and *baron*, a baron.] A woman who is married; a feme covert.

çŏv′ẽrt-ly, *adv.* Secretly; closely; in private; insidiously.

> Among the poets, Persius *covertly* strikes at Nero. —Dryden.

çŏv′ẽrt-ness, *n.* Secrecy; privacy.

çŏv′ẽr-tūre, *n.* [OFr. *coverture*, from LL. *coopertura*, from L. *cooperire*, to cover; *co-*, intens., and *operire*, to cover.]

1. Covering; shelter; defense.

2. In law, the state of a married woman, who is considered as under cover, or the power and protection of her husband, and therefore called a *feme covert* or *femme couvert.*

çŏv′et, *v.t.*; coveted, *pt.*, *pp.*; coveting, *ppr.* [ME. *coveten*; OFr. *coveitier*, from L. *cupidus*, eager, desirous of.]

1. To desire, or wish for, with eagerness; to desire earnestly; in a good sense.

> *Covet* earnestly the best gifts.—1 Cor. xii. 31.

2. To desire inordinately; to long for (that which it is unlawful to obtain or possess); in a bad sense.

> Thou shalt not *covet* thy neighbour's house. —Ex. xx. 17.

çŏv′et, *v.i.* To have or to satisfy an extreme desire.

çŏv′et-ȧ-ble, *a.* That may be coveted.

çŏv′et-ẽr, *n.* One who covets.

çŏv′et-ing-ly, *adv.* With eager desire to possess.

çŏv′et-ise (-is), *n.* Avarice. [Obs.]

çŏv′e-tive-ness, *n.* In phrenology, a name sometimes used for acquisitiveness.

çŏv′et-ous (kuv′et-us), *a.* [ME. *coveitous*; OFr. *covoitous*, from L. *cupidus*, eager, desirous of.]

1. Very desirous; eager to obtain, in a good sense; as, *covetous* of wisdom, virtue, or learning

2. Inordinately desirous; excessively eager to obtain and possess; avaricious; grasping; greedy; miserly; parsimonious.

cŏv'et-ous-ly, *adv.* In a covetous manner.

cŏv'et-ous-ness, *n.* 1. A strong or inordinate desire of obtaining and possessing some supposed good; usually in a bad sense, and applied to an inordinate desire of wealth; avariciousness.

2. Strong desire; eagerness. [Rare.]

cŏv'ey, *n.* [OFr. *coveye, covee*, a brood, flock of birds, from *cover*, to brood, sit on, lie hid; L. *cubare*, to lie down.]

1. A brood or hatch of birds; an old bird with her brood of young; hence, a small flock or number of birds together; applied to game; as, a *covey* of partridges.

2. A company; a set; a party. [Rare.]

cŏv'ey, *v.i.* To sit or brood. [Obs.]

cŏv'ey, *n.* A closet or pantry. [Prov. Eng.]

cŏv'ey, *n.* Same as *Cove*. [Slang.]

cŏv'in, cŏv'ine, cŏv'on, *n.* [OFr. *covine*, a secret agreement, plot, from *covenir*, to come together, agree.] In law, a collusive or deceitful agreement between two or more persons to prejudice a third; a secret agreement; deceit; fraud. [Obs.]

cō'ving, *n.* The projection of the upper stories of houses over the lower ones; formerly a prevalent style of building.

cŏv'in-ous, cŏv'en-ous, *a.* Deceitful; collusive; fraudulent.

cow, *n.*; *pl.* **cows**, *old pl.* **kine**. [ME. *cow, cou, cu*; AS. *cu*; D. *koe*; G. *kuh*; Sw. *ko*; L. *bos*; Gr. *bous*; Per. *koh*; Sans. *go*, a cow, ox.]

1. The female of the bovine genus of animals.

2. The female of various mammals, as the elephant, the whale, walrus, etc.

cow, *v.t.*; cowed, *pt., pp.*; cowing, *ppr.* To depress with fear; to lower the spirits or courage of; to oppress with habitual timidity; to intimidate.

cow, *n.* In mining, a wedge-shaped brake.

cow'āge, *n.* A plant, cowhage.

cow'ăn, *n.* 1. A mason who has picked up the trade without serving an apprenticeship. [Scot.]

2. In Freemasonry, a spy; as, *cowans* and eavesdroppers.

cow'ărd, *a.* Relating to a coward; pertaining to cowardice; timid.

cow'ărd, *n.* [ME. *coward, couard*, from OFr. *coue, coe*, from L. *coda, cauda*, a tail, and the depreciatory suffix *-ard*; originally an epithet of the hare, "short-tailed."]

1. A person who lacks courage to meet danger; a poltroon; a timid or pusillanimous man.

> Where's the *coward* that would not dare
> To fight for such a land. —Scott.

2. In heraldry, a term given to an animal borne in the escutcheon with its tail between its legs.

Syn.—Poltroon, craven, dastard.—A *coward* is, in a general sense, one who is afraid to meet danger, real or imaginary; a *poltroon* is a mean-spirited and contemptible coward; a *craven* is one who shrinks back at the approach of danger; a *dastard* is a vile and despicable coward.

cow'ărd, *v.t.* To frighten. [Obs.]

cow'ărd-ice, *n.* Want of courage to face danger; timidity; pusillanimity; fear of exposing one's person to danger.

> *Cowardice* alone is loss of fame. —Dryden.

cow'ărd-ie, *n.* Cowardice. [Obs.]

cow'ărd-ish, *a.* Cowardly. [Obs.]

cow'ărd-īze, *v.t.* To make cowardly. [Obs.]

cow'ărd-li-ness, *n.* Want of courage.

cow'ărd-ly, *a.* 1. Wanting courage to face danger; timid; timorous; fearful; pusillanimous.

2. Mean; base; befitting a coward; as, a *cowardly* action.

cow'ărd-ly, *adv.* In the manner of a coward; meanly; basely.

cow'ărd-ous, *a.* Cowardly. [Obs.]

cow'ărd-ship, *n.* Cowardice. [Obs.]

cow'bāne, *n.* *Cicuta virosa*, the English water-hemlock, or *Cicuta maculata*, an American plant resembling it.

cow'ber"ry, *n.*; *pl.* **cow'ber"ries**. *Vaccinium Vitis-Idæa*, the red huckleberry.

cow'bīrd, *n.* An American bird frequenting the grounds around grazing cattle. *Molothrus ater* is the common species, but any bird of the genus has the same common name. *Cowbirds* lay their eggs and leave the care of their young to other birds, as does the cuckoo.

Young Cowbird fed by female Yellowthroat.

cow'boy, *n.* 1. A boy cattle-herder.

2. An employee of a ranchman having care of the ranging cattle, mounted and equipped for his work.

3. In the War of the Revolution, one of a plundering band working near New York City.

cow'catch"ẽr (kou'kach"ẽr), *n.* In railroading, a strong frame in front of locomotives for removing obstructions, such as strayed cattle and the like, from the rails; the pilot.

cow'=chẽr"vil, cow'=pärs"ley, *n.* The popular names of *Anthriscus sylvestris*, an umbelliferous European plant found in hedge-banks and woods.

cow'=cress, *n.* *Lepidium campestre*, having a rank growth.

cow'die, *n.* A tree, the kauri.

cow'ẽr, *v.i.*; cowered, *pt., pp.*; cowering, *ppr.* [ME. *couren*; Ice. *kura*; Sw. *kura*, to lie quiet, rest.] To sink by bending the knees; to crouch; to squat; to bend down through fear.

cow'ẽr, *v.t.* To cherish with care. [Obs.]

cow'fish, *n.* One of various cetaceans and fishes; as, (a) the sea-cow; (b) the Californian porpoise; (c) the grampus; (d) the tropical, horned *Ostracion quadricorne*.

cow'=grass, *n.* *Trifolium medium*, a red clover of the Old World.

cow'hāge (-āj), *n.* [Hind. *kawānch, koānch*, cowhage.]

1. The hairs of the pods of a leguminous plant, *Mucuna pruriens*.

2. A single pod; also, the entire plant bearing these hairs.

cow'heärt"ed, *a.* Cowardly.

cow'hẽrb (-ẽrb), *n.* *Saponaria Vaccaria*, a soapwort.

cow'hẽrd, *n.* One whose business is to tend cows.

cow'hide, *n.* 1. The hide of a cow made, or to be made, into leather.

2. A heavy, braided, tapering whip.

cow'hide, *v.t.*; cowhided, *pt., pp.*; cowhiding, *ppr.* To beat or whip with a cowhide.

cow'ish, *a.* Cowardly. [Rare.]

cowl, *n.* [ME. *cowle, cuvel*; AS. *cule*; OFr. *coule*; Pr. *cogula*, from L. *cucullus*, a cap, hood.]

1. A hood, especially one worn by a monk; by extension, the habit of a monk or monks.

2. A vane-like ventilator, placed at the summit of a chimney or shaft.

3. The spark-arrester of a locomotive.

cowl, *n.* A water-vessel to be carried on a pole. [Local Eng.]

cowle, *n.* [Anglo-Ind.] A grant, particularly one giving protection.

cowled, *a.* Wearing a cowl; hooded; in shape of a cowl; as, a *cowled* leaf.

cow'leech, *n.* [*Cow*, and *leech*, a doctor.] A cow-doctor.

cow'leech"ing, *n.* Healing the diseases of cows.

cow'=lick, *n.* A reversed tuft of hair on the human forehead, turned back as if licked by a cow.

cowl'staff, *n.* [OFr. *cuvel*, dim. of *cuve*, a tub, from L. *cupa*, a tub, vat, and *staff*, from AS. *stæf*, stick, staff.] A staff or pole on which a vessel is supported between two persons.

cō-wŏrk'ẽr, *n.* One who works with another; a coöperator.

cow'=pärs"ley, *n.* A plant, cow-chervil.

cow'=pärs"nip, *n.* Any weed of the genus *Heracleum* having some of the characteristics of the parsnip.

cow'pēa, *n.* *Vigna Sinensis*, cultivated in the southern United States, Asia, and Africa.

Cow-pē'ri-ăn, *a.* Of or designating as a discoverer, William Cowper (1666–1709), an anatomist of England.

Cowperian or *Cowper's gland*; one of two minute muciparous glands leading to the male urethra.

cow'=pī"lŏt, *n.* *Pomacentrus saxatilis*, a fish frequenting the coasts of Florida and the West Indies.

cow'pock, *n.* One of the pustules of cowpox.

cow'=poi"sŏn, *n.* *Delphinium trolliifolium*, a larkspur of California.

cow'pox, *n.* A contagious disease of cows, characterized by vesicles containing the virus used in vaccination; vaccinia; called also *cowpock, kinepox*.

cow'quākes (-kwāks), *n.* *Briza media*, quaking-grass.

cow'rie, *n.* A tree, kauri.

cow'ry, cow'rie, *n.*; *pl.* **cow'ries**. [Hind. *kauri*, a cowry.] A small gasteropodous shell, the *Cypræa moneta*, used for coin on the coast of Guinea in Africa, and in many parts of southern Asia; also, any shell of the genus *Cypræa*.

cow'slip, *n.* 1. In the United States, *Caltha palustris*, the marsh-marigold.

2. The popular name of *Primula veris*, a wild-flower found in pastures and hedge-banks of England and in cultivation in the United States. It has umbels of small, buff-yellow, scented flowers on short pedicels.

American cowslip; the shooting-star of the Middle West; a herb of the primrose family.

French cowslip; see *Auricu'a*, 1.

cow'slipped (-slipt), *a.* Growing or bearing cowslips.

cow'=tree, *n.* A name of various trees having an abundance of milky juice, especially of *Brosimum Galactodendron*, a South American tree of the nettle family, common in Venezuela.

Twig and Fruit of Cow tree (*Brosimum Galactodendron*).

cow'weed, *n.* A plant, cow-chervil.

cow'whēat, *n.* The popular name of plants of the genus *Melampyrum*.

cox, *n.* [Obs.] Same as *Coxcomb*.

cox'ȧ, *n.*; *pl.* **cox'æ**. [L.] 1. In anatomy, the hip, haunch, or hip-joint; also, the os coccygis.

2. In entomology, the joint of an insect's limb which is next the body.

cox'ăl, *a.* Of or relating to the coxa.

cox-al'gi-ȧ, *n.* [L., from *coxa*, hip, and Gr. *algos*, pain.] A pain located in the hip.

cox'cōmb (-kōm), *n.* [Corruption of *cockscomb*, cock's comb.]

1. The top of the head; by extension, the head.

2. A strip of red cloth notched like the comb of a cock, which licensed fools wore formerly in their caps; also, the cap itself.

3. A fop; a vain, showy fellow; a superficial pretender to knowledge or accomplishments.

4. A flower, the cockscomb.

cox-cŏmb'ic-ăl, *a.* Resembling or indicating a coxcomb; foppish.

cox-cŏmb'ic-ăl-ly, *adv.* After the manner of a coxcomb; conceitedly.

cox'cōmb-ly, *a.* Like a coxcomb. [Obs.]

cox'cōmb-ry, *n.* The manners of a coxcomb.

cox-cŏm'ic-ăl, *a.* Foppish. [Obs.]

cox-cŏm'ic-ăl-ly, *adv.* Foppishly. [Rare.]

cox-oc'ẽr-īte, *n.* [L. *coxa*, the hip, and Gr. *keras*, a horn.] The first or basal joint of an antenna of a crustacean.

cox-op'ō-dīte, *n.* [L. *coxa*, the hip, and Gr. *pous, podos*, a foot.] The first leg-joint of a crustacean.

cox'swāin, *n.* Same as *Cockswain*.

coy, *a.* [ME. *coy*; OFr. *coi, quoi*, quiet, still, secret; Sp. *quieto*, from L. *quietus*, quiet, calm, still.]

1. Still. [Obs.]

2. Resenting familiarity; reserved or inaccessible in bearing; modest; bashful; applied mostly to women.

> The *coy* maid, half willing to be pressed.
> —Goldsmith.

3. Pretending shyness to attract; coquettish.

Syn.—Shrinking, shy, distant, reserved, modest, bashful, backward.

coy, *v.t.*; coyed, *pt., pp.*; coying, *ppr.* 1. To decoy; to allure. [Obs.]

2. To pet; to stroke.

> Pleasure, being *coyed*, follows us. —Hall.

coy, *v.i.* 1. To act coyly. [Obs.]

2. To cause difficulty. [Obs.]

coy'ish, *a.* Somewhat coy or reserved.

coy'ly, *adv.* In a coy manner.

coy'ness, *n.* Reserve; unwillingness to become familiar; disposition to avoid free intercourse, by silence or retirement.

> When the kind nymph would *coyness* feign,
> And hides but to be found again.—Dryden.

Syn.—Reserve, shrinking, shyness, backwardness, modesty, bashfulness.

coy'ō-te (kī'ō-te, kī'ōt, *or* kō-yō'te), *n.* [Sp. Am., from Mex. *coyotl*.] The prairie-wolf, *Canis latrans*, a carnivorous animal, related to the dog, found in the western part of North America.

coy'pŏu, coy'pū, *n.* *Myopotamus coypus*, a beaver-like rodent of South America, yielding a fur called nutria.

coys'trel, coys'tril, *n.* Same as *Coistril*.

cŏz, *n.* Cousin, implying fondness or familiarity.

cŏz'en, *v.t.*; cozened, *pt., pp.*; cozening, *ppr.* [OFr. *cousiner*, to claim kindred for advantage, to sponge.]

1. To cheat; to defraud.

2. To deceive; to beguile; as, to be *cozened* into knowledge.

cŏz'en, *v.i.* To be a deceiver.

cŏz'en-āge, *n.* Cheating; fraud; deceit.

cŏz'en-ẽr, *n.* One who cheats or defrauds.

cō'ziẽr, *n.* Same as *Cosier*.

cō'zi-ly, *adv.* Snugly; comfortably.

ço'zi-ness, *n.* A cozy condition.

ço'zy, *a.*; *comp.* cozier; *superl.* coziest. [Scot. *cosie, cozie*; Gael. *cosach*, abounding in hollows, snug, sheltered; from *cos*, a hollow.] Snug, implying warmth and comfort; social; as, a *cozy* room; also written *cosy.*

ço'zy, *n.* A padded covering for a teapot to keep in the heat.

çrab, *n.* [ME. *crabbe*; AS. *crabba*, a crab; D. *krab*; Sw. *krabba*; Dan. *krabbe*; perhaps from O.H.G. *chrapfo*, a hook, claw.]

1. A popular name for all the ten-footed, short-tailed crustaceans constituting the suborder *Brachyura*, order *Decapoda*, comprising many genera distinguished from the lobster and other macrurous or long-tailed decapods by the shortness of their tail, which is folded under the body. The common large edible *crab* belongs to the genus *Cancer*; the small edible *crab* to the genus *Carcinus*; the long-armed *crab* to the genus *Corystes*; the hermit-*crab* to the genus *Pagurus*, and the land-*crab* to the genus *Gecarcinus*.

2. [C—] Cancer, the constellation.

3. The crab-louse.

4. [*pl.*] In hazard, the lowest throw.

5. In mechanics, (a) an engine with three claws for launching ships and heaving them in the dock; (b) a pillar used sometimes for the same purpose as a capstan; (c) a kind of portable windlass or machine for raising weights, etc.; (d) a yarn-stretcher used in rope-manufactories.

Crab's claws; in materia medica, the tips of the claws of the common crab; formerly used as absorbents.

Crab's eyes; in materia medica, concretions formed in the stomach of the crawfish, formerly when powdered in much repute as antacids.

To catch a crab; in rowing, to miss a stroke and fall backward.

çrab, *n.* [ME. *crabbe*; Sw. in composition, *krabb-äple*, a crab-apple; prob. from *krabba*, a crab; so called because of its sharp taste.]

1. A small, sour apple having a rather astringent taste and used for pickles, jelly, etc.; also written *crab-apple.*

2. A tree of the genus *Pyrus* bearing this fruit.

3. A stick from a crab-tree; a crabstick.

çrab, *v.i.*; crabbed, *pt., pp.*; crabbing, *ppr.* 1. To fish for or catch crabs; as, poor luck *crabbing.*

2. To recede from a position; to back out; usually with *out*; as, to *crab out* of an agreement. [Colloq. U. S.]

3. Nautically, to drift sidewise.

çrab, *v.t.* 1. To beat. [Prov. Eng.]

2. To make crabbed.

çrab, *v.i.* 1. To be crabbed or cross.

2. To fight by seizing each other, as hawks.

çrab, *a.* Surly; ugly; austere. [Obs.]

çrab'-ap"ple, *n.* See second *Crab*, n. 1.

çrab'bed, *a.* 1. Cross; morose; peevish; cynical.

2. Rough; harsh; applied to things.

3. Difficult; perplexing; as, a *crabbed* author or subject.

4. Very intricate or irregular; as, *crabbed* writing.

çrab'bed-ly, *adv.* In a crabbed manner.

çrab'bed-ness, *n.* The state or quality of being crabbed.

çrab'bẽr, *n.* One who fishes for crabs.

çrab'bing, *n.* Crab-fishing.

çrab'bing, *n.* The thorough cleaning given stuffs before dyeing, as by means of alkali and soap.

çrab'bish, *a.* Inclined to be cross or surly.

çrab'by, *a.* Difficult.

çrab'eat"ẽr, *n.* 1. A fish, the cobia.

2. The least bittern, also certain other herons.

çrā'bẽr, *n.* The water-rat.

çrab'fāced (-fāst), *a.* Of a surly countenance.

çrab'-grȧss, *n.* 1. *Panicum sanguinale*, common finger-grass.

2. *Eleusine Indica*, wire-grass.

çrab'-louse, *n.* *Phthirius pubis*, a body-louse sometimes found in the longer hair, as of the pubes.

çrab'-plov"ẽr, *n.* *Dromas ardeola*, an East Indian bird resembling the plover.

çrab'si"dle, *v.i.* To have a sidewise movement. [Humorous.]

çrab'-spi"dẽr, *n.* 1. A spider of the division *Laterigradæ*, moving laterally.

2. A scorpion.

çrab'stick, *n.* A walking-stick made of the wood of the crab-tree; hence, a stick of any kind.

çrab'-tree, *n.* See second *Crab*, n. 2.

çrab'-wood, *n.* The wood of *Carapa Guianensis*, a South American tree.

çrab'-yaws, *n.* A West Indian disease, being a kind of ulcer on the soles of the feet, with hard callous edges.

çracche (krach), *v.t.* and *v.i.* To scratch. [Obs.]

çrack, *v.t.*; cracked (krakt), *pt., pp.*; cracking, *ppr.* [ME. *crakken, craken*; AS. *cracian*, to crack; Gael. *crac*, a crack, break; an imitative word.]

1. To rend, break, or burst into chinks; to break partially; to break without an entire severance of the parts; as, to *crack* glass or ice.

2. To break in pieces.

3. To break with grief; to affect deeply; to pain; to torture. [Rare.]

> O madam, my old heart is *cracked.* —Shak.

4. To open and drink; as, to *crack* a bottle of wine.

5. To throw out or utter with smartness; as, to *crack* a joke.

6. To snap; to cause to make a sharp sudden noise; as, to *crack* a whip.

7. To break or destroy.

8. To disorder; to make crazy.

To crack a crib; to break into a house; to commit burglary. [Thieves' slang.]

To crack up; to cry up; to extol; to puff. [Colloq.]

çrack, *v.i.* 1. To break into pieces with a sharp sound; to be shattered or shivered.

2. To burst; to open in chinks; to be fractured without quite separating into different parts.

3. To fall to ruin, or to be impaired. [Colloq.]

> Credit . . . *cracks* when little comes in and much goes out. —Dryden.

4. To utter a loud or sharp sudden sound; as, the clouds *crack*; the whip *cracks.*

5. To boast; to brag; that is, to utter vain, pompous, blustering words; with *of.*

> The Ethiops *of* their sweet complexion *crack.* —Shak.

6. To chat; to talk freely and familiarly. [Scot.]

> Gae warm ye and *crack* with our dame. —Ramsay.

çrack, *n.* 1. A disruption; a chink or fissure; a narrow breach; a crevice; a separation of the parts of a substance, either allowing of an opening or not; as, a *crack* in timber, in a wall, or in glass.

2. A burst of sound; the sound of anything suddenly rent; a violent report; as, a loud *crack* of thunder; the *crack* of a whip.

3. The tone of voice when changed at puberty.

> Though now our voices
> Have got the mannish *crack.* —Shak.

4. Craziness of intellect; lunacy; insanity; as, he has a *crack.*

5. A crazy person. [Colloq.]

6. A boast; also, a boaster.

7. A fault, flaw, or blemish; a breach of chastity.

8. A prostitute.

9. A boy; generally a pert, lively boy.

> When he was a *crack* not this high.—Shak.

10. An instant; as, I'll be with you in a *crack.* [Old Eng. and Scot.]

11. Free familiar conversation; a comfortable chat. [Scot.]

çrack, *a.* Excellent; first-rate; having qualities to be proud of. [Colloq.]

> . . . soldiers in a *crack* regiment.—Ruskin.

çrack'-brāined, *a.* Foolhardy; crazy.

çracked (krakt), *a.* 1. Burst or split; rent; broken; partially severed; hence, blemished in reputation.

> Intrigue with such a *cracked* pitcher does me no honour at all. —Smollett.

2. Mentally impaired; crazed; crazy.

çrack'ẽr, *n.* 1. One who or that which cracks; specifically, (a) a firecracker; (b) a grinding-machine for raw rubber; (c) a person who breaks flints; (d) a braggart. [Obs.]

2. A hard-baked biscuit, thin and crisp.

3. One of a class of low whites of southern United States.

çraç'kle (krak'l), *v.i.*; crackled, *pt., pp.*; crackling, *ppr.* [ME. *crakelen*, to crackle, quaver in singing; dim. of *crack.*] To make slight cracks; to make small, abrupt noises, rapidly or frequently repeated; to decrepitate; as, burning thorns *crackle.*

çraç'kle, *n.* 1. A crackling.

2. A minute crack.

3. The network of intersecting cracks which cover the glaze of various ceramic wares; it is produced by the method of drying.

4. In medicine, abnormal breathing marked by a crackling sound.

çraç'kled (-kld), *a.* Marked by numerous intersecting cracks, as china.

çraç'kle-wāre, *n.* Ware presenting a crackled surface.

çraç'kling, *a.* Making slight cracks or abrupt noises.

çraç'kling, *n.* 1. The making of small, abrupt cracks or reports, frequently repeated.

2. The rind of roasted pork.

3. [*pl.*] Lard or tallow scraps made into food for dogs.

çrack'nel, *n.* [ME. *crakenelle*; D. *krakeling*, a cake, crackling, from *kraken*, to crack.]

1. A hard, brittle cake or biscuit.

2. [*pl.*] Pork, in small pieces, fried till crisp.

çracks'măn, *n.*; *pl.* **çracks'men.** A burglar.

Çra-ço'vi-ăn, *a.* Of or pertaining to Cracow, in Poland.

Çra-çō-vi-enne', *n.* [Fr., from *Cracovien*, Cracovian.] The favorite dance of the Polish peasantry around Cracow; also, the music for this dance, written in 2/4 time.

çrā'çōwes, *n.pl.* Long-toed boots or shoes introduced into England in 1384; named from the city of Cracow, where the fashion is supposed to have originated.

Cracowes, from the Harleian MS.

çrā'dle, *n.* [ME. *cradel*; AS. *cradel, cradol*; Gael. *creathall*, a cradle, grade.]

1. A crib or crib-like bed for an infant, usually free to rock or swing.

2. Infancy; also, the place in which infancy was spent and the care incident thereto was given; as, Kansas, the *cradle* of populism.

3. In agriculture, an archaic implement consisting of a frame of wood, with long, bending teeth, to which is fastened a scythe, for cutting and laying grain in a swath.

4. The frame supporting a ship on the ways or in any similar position, as in a canal-lift.

5. In surgery, (a) a supporting-case for a broken or dislocated limb; (b) a frame protecting the body from friction of the bed-clothes.

6. In mezzotint engraving, a grooved instrument, which when rocked back and forth makes a zigzag series of burs upon a printing-plate.

7. In mining, (a) a suspended scaffold; (b) a rocking box for washing out earth holding gold.

8. In carpentry, the ribbing for vaulted ceilings when prepared for plastering.

9. In life-saving apparatus, the crib-like structure running on a line from ship to shore.

10. In hat-making, a circular support having inwardly jutting pegs, supporting hats to be dipped in the dye.

11. A standing bedstead for wounded seamen.

12. A child's game, cat's-cradle.

çrā'dle, *v.t.*; cradled, *pt., pp.*; cradling, *ppr.* 1. To lay in a cradle; to rock in a cradle; to compose or quiet.

> It *cradles* their fears to sleep.—D. A. Clark.

2. To nurse in infancy.

3. To use a cradle for, in various ways; as, to *cradle* grain; to *cradle* pay dirt; to *cradle* a limb.

çrā'dle, *v.i.* To lie or lodge in a cradle.

çrā'dle-hōle, *n.* A rut in a vehicle track, as in snow or softening frozen ground. [U. S.]

çrā'dle-scythe (-sith), *n.* A broad-bladed scythe used in a grain-cradle.

çrā'dling, *n.* 1. The act of using a cradle.

2. In carpentry, same as *Cradle*, 8.

3. In coopering, the cutting of a cask in halves lengthwise in order to make it pass a narrow passage, the parts being afterward joined.

çrȧft, *n.* [AS. *cræft*, art, cunning, power, a craft, bark.]

1. Power; also, any art or device. [Obs.]

2. Cunning, art, or skill, in a bad sense, or applied to bad purposes; artifice; guile; skill or dexterity employed to effect purposes by deceit.

3. Art; skill; dexterity in a particular manual occupation; hence, the occupation or employment itself; manual art; trade; specifically (with the definite article), freemasonry; as, brothers of *the craft.*

> Ye know that by this *craft* we have our wealth. —Acts xix. 25.

4. The members of a trade collectively.

5. Nautically, a vessel; as, she is a tidy *craft*; generally used in a collective sense for vessels of any kind.

Small craft; a term given to small vessels of all kinds, as sloops, schooners, cutters, etc.

çrȧft, *v.i.* To play tricks. [Obs.]

çrȧft'i-ly, *adv.* With craft; cunningly.

çrȧft'i-ness, *n.* Artfulness; cunning; artifice; stratagem.

çrȧft'less, *a.* Free from craft.

çrȧfts'măn, *n.*; *pl.* **çrȧfts'men.** An artificer; a mechanic; one skilled in a manual occupation or trade.

çrȧfts'măn-ship, *n.* Mastery of a craft.

çrȧfts'mȧs"tẽr, *n.* One skilled in his craft or trade.

çrȧft'y, *a.* 1. Dexterous; handy. [Obs.]

2. Versed in deceit; skilful at fraud; artful; fraudulent.

Syn.—Skilful, cunning, wily, sly, astute, insidious, politic, deceitful, subtle, shrewd, cunning.

çrag, *n.* [ME. *crag*; W. *craig*; Gael. *creag*, a rock, crag.]
1. A steep, rugged rock; a rough, broken rock, or point of a rock.
2. In geology, shelly deposits in Norfolk and Suffolk, England, usually of gravel and sand, of the older Pliocene period.
Crag and tail; a form of secondary hills, common in Britain, in which a precipitous front is presented to the west or northwest, while the opposite side is formed of a sloping declivity.

çrag, *n.* [M.D. *krage*, neck, throat; M.L.G. *krage*, neck, throat.] The neck. [Obs.]

çrag′ged, *a.* Full of crags or broken rocks; rough; rugged; abounding with points.

çrag′ged-ness, *n.* Cragginess.

çrag′gi-ness, *n.* The state of being craggy.

çrag′gy, *a.* Cragged.

çragṣ′măn, *n.*; *pl.* **çragṣ′men.** One who scales crags; specifically, one who gathers eggs on cliffs adjoining the sea.

çrāie (krā), *n.* [Obs.] See *Crare.*

çrāig′=floun″dēr, çrāig′=flūke, *n.* [Scot. *craig*, a rock.] The pole-flounder.

çrāil, *n.* Same as *Creel.*

çrāi′ṣey, *n.* The buttercup. [Prov. Eng.]

çrāke, *v.i.*; craked, *pt., pp.*; craking, *ppr.* To utter a sound like that of a corncrake.

çrāke, *v.i.* To crack; to boast. [Obs.]

çrāke, *n.* A boast. [Obs.]

çrāke, *n.* [ME. *crake*; Ice. *kraka*, a crow; imitative, from the noise.]
1. A crow; also the raven.
2. The corn*crake*, *Crex pratensis*, of the British isles; also, any rail-like short-billed bird of the same or an allied genus, as *Porzana carolina*, the sora.

çrāke′ber″ry, *n.* The crowberry.

çrāke′=nee″dleṣ (-dlz), *n.* A plant, crow-needles.

çrāk′ēr, *n.* A boaster. [Obs.]

çram, *v.t.*; crammed, *pt., pp.*; cramming, *ppr.* [ME. *crammen*; AS. *crammian*, to cram, from *crimman*, to press, bruise.]
1. To press or drive, particularly in filling or thrusting one thing into another; to stuff; to crowd; to fill to superfluity; as, to *cram* anything into a basket or bag; to *cram* a room with people.
2. To fill with food to satiety; to stuff.
3. To endeavor to qualify, as a pupil, for examination, in a comparatively short time, by storing the memory with information, not so much with the object of gaining real acquaintance with the subjects as of passing the ordeal; to grind; to coach.
4. To tell lies to; to fill up with false stories. [Slang.]

çram, *v.i.* 1. To stuff oneself with food.
2. To study hurriedly to acquire a fund of information; to dig; as, to spend the time *cramming* for an examination.

çram, *n.* 1. In weaving, a warp having more than two threads in each dent or split of the reed.
2. The act of cramming; facts obtained very hurriedly for an examination or other special purpose.
3. A lie. [Slang.]

çram′bō, *n.* 1. A play in which one person gives a word, to which another finds a rime.
2. A riming word.
Dumb crambo; the game in which the riming word is acted out in pantomime by the guesser.

çram′mēr, *n.* 1. One who crams, especially for an examination or other test.
2. A lie. [Slang.]

çra′moi-ṣie, çra′moi-ṣy, *a.* Crimson. [Obs.]

çramp, *n.* [OFr. *crampe*; D. *krampe*; Dan. *krampe*; Ice. *krappr*, strait, narrow.]
1. A paw. [Obs.]
2. A cramp-iron.
3. A hook-shaped block used by carpenters to hold work; a holdfast.
4. A portable kind of iron press, having a screw at one end and a movable shoulder at the other, employed by carpenters and joiners for closely compressing the joints of framework.
5. A piece of wood shaped like the front of a boot, over which leather is formed in making the upper of a boot or shoe.
6. Restraint; confinement; that which hinders motion or expansion. [Rare.]

çramp, *a.* Difficult; knotty. [Rare.]

çramp, *v.t.*; cramped (krampt,) *pt., pp.*; cramping, *ppr.* 1. To confine; to restrain; to hinder from action or expansion; as, to *cramp* the exertions.
2. To fasten, confine, or hold, as with a cramp or cramp-iron.
3. To form (the upper of a boot or shoe) by use of a cramp.
4. To turn (the fore wheels of a vehicle) so as to be at an angle with the rear wheels; as, to *cramp* a buggy.

çramp, *n.* [ME. *crampe, craumpe*; OFr. *crampe*; D. *krampe*; Sw. *kramp*, a cramp, spasm.]
1. The spasmodic and involuntary contraction of a limb, or some muscle of the body, usually of the legs. It commonly attacks swimmers, especially in cold water.
2. Paralysis of a muscle or set of muscles by reason of their unintermitting use, as writers' or telegraphers' *cramp*.

çramp, *v.t.* To affect with cramp; as, to be *cramped* with rheumatism.

çramp′=bōne, *n.* A sheep's kneepan; formerly thought a charm against cramps.

çram′pet, *n.* See *Crampit.*

çramp′fish, *n.* The torpedo, or electric ray.

çramp′=ī″ron (-ŭrn), *n.* A piece of metal, usually iron, bent at each end, and let into the upper surface of two pieces of stone, when their perpendicular faces are joined, to fasten them securely together.

çram′pit, *n.* 1. A piece of metal at the end of the scabbard of a sword.
2. (a) A cramp-iron; (b) a calk to prevent slipping on ice. [Scot.]

çram′pŏn, çram-pọọn′, *n.* [Fr. *crampon*, a cramp-iron.]
1. An iron instrument fastened to the shoes of a storming party, to assist them in climbing a rampart.
2. A device for raising timbers or stones, consisting of two hooked pieces of iron hinged together somewhat like double calipers.
3. In botany, an adventitious root which serves as a fulcrum or support, as in the ivy.

çram-pō-nee′, *a.* [Fr. *cramponné*, pp. of *cramponner*, to fasten with a clamp; *crampon*, a cramp-iron.] In heraldry, denoting a cross having a cramp or square piece at each end.

çramp′y, *a.* Having or producing cramps.

çran, çrāne, *n.* [Scot.] A measure of capacity containing about 750 fresh herrings.

çrān′āġe, *n.* The liberty of using a crane at a wharf for raising wares from a vessel; also, the money or price paid for the use of a crane.

çran′ber″ry, *n.*; *pl.* **çran′ber″rieṣ.** [So called from its being ripe when the cranes return in the spring.]
1. A fruit of certain species of the genus *Vaccinium*, having a tart taste and used in pies and sauce. *Vaccinium macrocarpon* is the American species, being larger than *Vaccinium Oxycoccus*, the mossberry of Europe.
2. The plant producing this fruit.

çran′dăll, *n.* [From proper name *Crandall.*] A tool with which to dress stone, resembling a hammer in form, the head of which is made up of a number of sharp steel bars.

çran′dăll, *v.t.* To dress, as stone, with a crandall.

çrāne, *n.* [ME. *crane*; AS. *cran*; D. *kraan*, a crane.]
1. A migratory grallatorial or wading bird of the genus *Grus*, family *Gruidæ*. The bill is straight, sharp, and long, with a furrow from the nostrils toward the point; the nostrils are linear, and the feet have four toes, the legs long, as is the neck. The European *crane* is *Grus cinerea*; the Siberian *crane*, *Grus gigantea*; the sand-hill *crane* of America being *Grus canadensis*. The crowned *crane*, by some classed in a separate genus (*Balearica*), is about the size of the common *crane*. It receives its common name from having the occiput crowned with a tuft of slender yellow feathers.

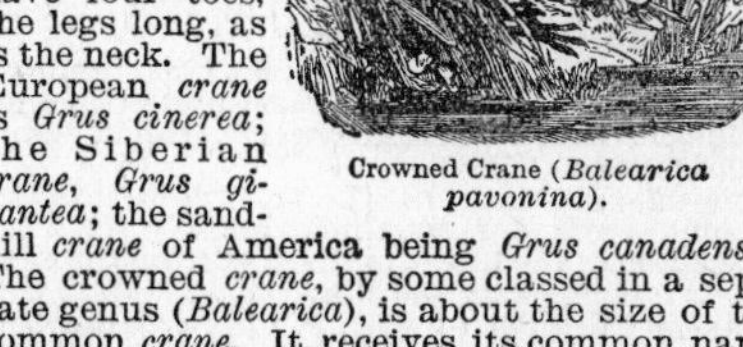
Crowned Crane (*Balearica pavonina*).

2. The popular name wrongly given certain herons, as *Ardea herodias*, and also other large wading birds.

çrāne, *n.* [So called from its resemblance to the neck of a crane; D. *kraan*; L.G. *kran*, a crane (machine).]
1. A machine for raising great weights, and moving them as desired, primarily consisting of an adjustable arm of timber, etc., projecting from a post, furnished with a tackle or pulley, generally modified in its various parts to suit the work to be done.
2. A machine for weighing goods on the principle of the crane for lifting weights. Such machines are common in market towns in Ireland.
3. An arm, the shape of an inverted L, hung in a fireplace as a support for pots and kettles.
4. [*pl.*] Nautically, pieces of iron or timber at a vessel's side for stowing boats or spars upon.
5. A siphon or crooked pipe for drawing liquor out of a cask.

çrāne, *v.t.*; craned, *pt., pp.*; craning, *ppr.* To elongate, as the neck, to obtain a better view.

çrāne, *v.i.* To stretch out one's neck like a crane; hence, in hunting, to look before one leaps; to pull up at a dangerous jump.

çrāne′=flȳ, *n.* An insect of the genus *Tipula.*

çrāne's′=bill, *n.* 1. The geranium.
2. A pair of pincers used by surgeons.

çrang, *n.* Same as *Krang.*

Çrā′ni-ȧ, *n.* [LL. *cranium*, a skull.] A genus of mollusks typical of the family *Craniidæ.*

çrā′ni-ȧ, *n.*, pl. of *cranium.*

çrā″ni-ȧ-çrō′mi-ăl, *a.* [*Cranium*, and Gr. *akrōmion*; *akros*, extreme, and *ōmos*, shoulder.] In anatomy, of or denoting the pectoral girdle or the cranium and shoulder.

çrā′ni-ăl, *a.* [L. *cranialis*, from *cranium*, a skull.] Of or denoting the cranium or skull.

Çrā-ni-ā′tȧ, *n.pl.* Same as *Craniota.*

Çrā-nī′i-dæ, *n.pl.* A family of brachiopod fossil and recent shells, characterized by the absence of a hinge and peduncle, the shells being attached by the lower valve.

çrā′ni-ō-, çrā′ni-. Combining forms from L. *cranium*, Gr. *kranion*, a skull, and used in anatomy to indicate anything having connection with or relation to the skull or cranium; as, *cranio*clast, *cranio*facial.

çrā′ni-ō-çlaṣm, *n.* Same as *Craniotomy.*

çrā′ni-ō-çlast, *n.* [*Cranio-*, and Gr. *klastos*, from *klān*, to break.] Delivery-forceps used in craniotomy.

çrā″ni-ō-fā′ciăl, *a.* [*Cranio-*, and L. *facies*, the face, appearance.] Of or denoting the cranium and face; as, the *craniofacial* angle.

çrā-ni-og′nō-my, *n.* [*Cranio-*, and Gr. *gnōmē*, opinion, judgment.] The science founded on the knowledge of cranium-differences in individuals.

çrā′ni-ō-graph, *n.* [*Cranio-*, and Gr. *graphein*, to write.] An appliance with which to make topographical outlines of the skull.

çrā″ni-ō-log′iç-ăl, *a.* Pertaining to craniology.

çrā-ni-ol′ō-ġist, *n.* One who treats of craniology.

çrā-ni-ol′ō-ġy, *n.* [*Cranio-*, and Gr. *-logia*, from *legein*, to speak.] The study or knowledge of skulls, and their relations to the allied sciences.

çrā-ni-om′e-tēr, *n.* [*Cranio-*, and Gr. *metron*, a measure.] An instrument for measuring the skulls of animals.

çrā″ni-ō-met′riç, çrā″ni-ō-met′riç-ăl, *a.* Pertaining to craniometry.

çrā-ni-om′e-try, *n.* The art of measuring the crania, or skulls, of animals, to discover their specific differences.

çrā-ni-os′çō-pist, *n.* A phrenologist.

çrā-ni-os′çō-py, *n.* [*Cranio-*, and Gr. *skopein*, to view.] Phrenology.

Çrā-ni-ō′tȧ, *n.pl.* [L., from *cranium*; Gr. *kranion*, a skull.] A class of vertebrates comprehending those having a cranium.

çrā-ni-ot′ō-my, *n.* [*Cranio-*, and Gr. *temnē*, from *temnein*, to cut.] In obstetrics, the reduction of the fetal head so as to facilitate delivery.

çrā′ni-um, *n.*; *pl.* **çrā′ni-ȧ.** [L., from Gr. *kranion*, a skull.] The skull of an animal; the assemblage of bones which inclose the brain.

çrañk, *a.* [AS. *cranc*, weak; D. *krank*; Ice. *krankr*, sick, weak.]
1. Nautically, liable to be overset, as a ship when she is too narrow, or has not sufficient ballast, or is loaded too high to carry full sail.
2. Stout; bold; erect; confident; as, a cock crowing *crank*.

> How came they to become so extremely *crank* and confident? —South.

3. Ill; infirm; feeble. [Obs.]

çrañk, *v.i.*; cranked, *pt., pp.*; cranking, *ppr.* To run in a winding course; to bend, wind, and turn.

> See how this river comes me *cranking* in. —Shak.

çrañk, *n.* [This word belongs to the root meaning to twist, turn, bend; D. *krinkel*, *kronkle*, to bend; *crinch* and *cringe* belong to the same group.]
1. An iron axis with the end bent like an elbow, serving as a handle for communicating circular motion; as, the *crank* of a grindstone; or for changing circular into reciprocating motion, as in a sawmill, or reciprocating into circular motion, as in a steam-engine. The bell-*crank* merely changes the direction of a reciprocating motion, as from a horizontal to a vertical line. [See *Bell-crank.*]

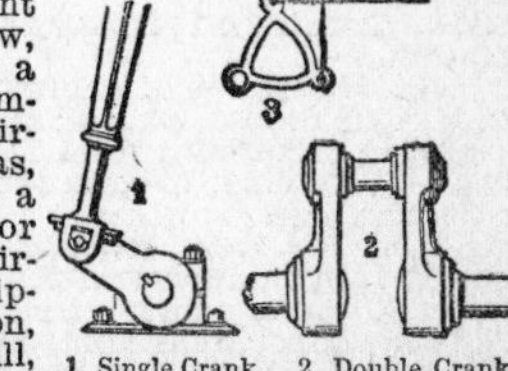

1. Single Crank. 2. Double Crank. 3. Bell-Crank.

2. Any bend, turn, or winding.
3. A twisting or turning in speech; a conceit which consists in a change of the form or meaning of a word.

> Quips, and *cranks*, and wanton wiles.—Milton.

4. A whim; a caprice; also an outburst of temper or passion. [Prov. Eng.]

5. An iron brace for various purposes; such as the braces which support the lanterns on the poop-quarters of vessels.

6. An instrument of prison discipline, consisting of a small wheel, which, on the prisoner turning a handle outside, revolves in a box partially filled with gravel.

7. A person who is wanting in mental poise and has a mind filled with some scheme, project, or crotchet; an extreme faddist, implying impracticability. [Colloq.]

8. A weak person; an invalid. [Obs.]

çrañk′=ax″le (-ak″sl), *n.* 1. In wagon-building, an axle so bent as to allow the box to be hung low.

2. In a locomotive, the driving-axle, when rotated at the center, instead of at the ends.

çrañk′bird, *n.* *Picus minor*, the spotted woodpecker of Europe.

çrañked (krañkt), *a.* Having a bend; formed with a crank; as, a *cranked* shaft.

çrañk′i-ness, *n.* The state of being cranky.

çrañ′kle (krañ′kl), *v.t.* and *v.i.* I. *v.t.* To break into bends, turns, or angles; to crinkle.

> Old Vaga's stream . . .
> *Crankling* her banks. —Philips.

II. *v.i.* To bend, wind, or twist.

çrañ′kle, *n.* A bend or turn; a crinkle.

çrañk′ness, *n.* 1. Liability to be overset, as a ship.

2. Stoutness; erectness.

çrañk′y, *a.*; *comp.* crankier; *superl.* crankiest. 1. Confident; crank.

2. Having whims and crotchets and the characteristics of a crank; crabbed; unreasonable.

3. Liable to be upset, as a vessel.

4. In feeble health; sickly. [Prov. Eng.]

çran′nied (-nid), *a.* Having rents, chinks, or fissures; as, a *crannied* wall.

çran′nog, çran′noge, *n.* [Ir. *crannog*; Gael. *crannag*, a pulpit, top of a mast.] A fortified lake-dwelling, such as remain as ruins from prehistoric times in Scotland and Ireland.

çran′ny, *n.*; *pl.* **çran′nieş.** [ME. *crany*; OFr. *cran*, from L. *crena*, a notch.]

1. A rent; any small, narrow opening, fissure, crevice, or chink, as in a wall, or other substance; a hole; a secret, retired place.

> In a firm building, the cavities ought to be filled with brick or stone, fitted to the *crannies*. —Dryden.

> He peeped into every *cranny*. —Arbuthnot.

2. In glass-making, an iron instrument for forming the necks of bottles.

çran′ny, *a.* Quick; heedless; brisk; thoughtless; sprightly. [Prov. Eng.]

çran′ny, *v.i.*; crannied, *pt.*, *pp.*; crannying, *ppr.* 1. To become intersected with or penetrated by crannies or clefts.

> The ground did *cranny* everywhere. —Golding.

2. To enter by or to frequent crannies.

çran-tä′rȧ, *n.* [Gael. *cranntara*; *crann*, a beam, shaft, and *tair*, reproach, disgrace.] The fiery cross which formed the rallying-symbol in the Highlands of Scotland on any sudden emergency; so called because disobedience to what the symbol implied, inferred infamy.

çrants, *n.* [Ice. *krants*; G. *kranz*, a garland.] A garland carried before the bier of a maiden, and hung over her grave. [Obs.]

çrap, *n.* [ME *crappe*, chaff; OFr. *crape*; LL. *crappa*, siftings.] Buckwheat; also, darnel. [Prov. Eng.]

Çrȧ-paud′ (krȧ-pō′), *n.* [Fr. *crapaud*, a toad.] A whimsical name used in reference to a Frenchman or to the French nation collectively, corresponding to the English name John Bull; usually written *Johnny Crapaud.*

çrap′au-dine, *a.* and *n.* [Fr. *crapaudine*, a socket, sole, step, a toadstone, from *crapaud*, a toad.]

I. *a.* Turning on pivots, as a door, at top and bottom.

II. *n.* Ulceration of a horse's coronet.

çrāpe, *v.t.*; craped, *pt.*, *pp.*; craping, *ppr.* [Fr. *creper*, to crisp, curl, from L. *crispus*, crisped, curled.] To curl, to form into ringlets; as, to *crape* the hair.

çrāpe, *n.* [Fr *crêpe*, *crespe*, crepe, a silk tissue curled into minute wrinkles, from *creper*; L. *crispare*, to crisp, curl; *crispus*, curled, crisped.] A thin, transparent stuff, made of raw silk gummed and twisted on the mill, woven without crossing. In black, it is much used in mourning.

Canton or *oriental crape*; a thin, soft, silk fabric, smoother than the common crape, white or dyed, and used for scarfs, shawls, etc.

çrāpe′fish, *n.* Codfish salted and pressed to hardness.

çrāpe′=myr″tle (-mẽr″tl), *n.* A shrub, *Lagerstrœmia Indica*, native to China and the East Indies, now acclimatized in the United States. Its leaves are like those of the myrtle, and it bears large, beautiful, rose-colored flowers

çrap′nel *n.* A hook or drag. [Obs.]

çrap′ple, *n.* [Origin unknown.] A food-fish, *Pomoxys annularis*, of the Mississippi and tributary waters. It is a handsome fish, mottled green against a shining olive body, and, when mature, is about a foot in length; also called *bachelor.*

çrap′ple, *n.* [A variant of *grapple.*] A claw. [Obs.]

çraps, *n.* A gambling-game, played principally by negroes, employing two dice, the object of the game being to make certain points at a throw.

çrap′ū-lȧ, çrap′ūle, *n.* Same as *Crapulence.*

çrap′ū-lence, *n.* [LL. *crapulentus*, from *crapula*; Gr. *kraipalē*, a drunken sickness, intoxication.] Drunkenness; a surfeit; the sickness caused by overindulgence in food or drink.

çrap′ū-lent, çrap′ū-lous, *a.* 1. Drunk; surcharged with liquor; sick by intemperance.

2. Connected or associated with drunkenness; as, the *crapulous* residence of his father. [Rare.]

çrāp′y, *a.* Like crape; crimped.

çrāre, *n.* [OFr. *craier*; LL. *craiera*, a kind of ship used by the Scandinavians.] An unwieldy trading-vessel; spelled also *crayer*, *cray.* [Obs.]

çrāşe, *v.* and *n.* [Obs.] See *Craze.*

çrash, *v.i.*; crashed (krasht), *pt.*, *pp.*; crashing, *ppr.* [ME. *craschen*, *crasshen*, to crash, break, shatter; imitative of the sound.]

1. To make the loud, clattering sound as of many things falling and breaking at once.

2. To fall or break in with violence, accompanied by a loud report; as, the shell *crashed* through the roof.

çrash, *v.t.* To break; to hurl together violently, with noise and confusion.

çrash, *n.* 1. The loud, mingled sound of many things falling and breaking at once.

2. The collapse of a commercial undertaking; bankruptcy; by extension, commercial depression or panic.

3. A basket or box of broken glass, used in a theater, to imitate the sound of glass breaking.

çrash, *n.* [L. *crassus*, coarse.] A coarse, undyed linen cloth used for furniture covers, towels, and summer clothing.

çrash′ing, *n.* The sound of many things falling and breaking at once.

çrā′sis, *n.* [L., from Gr. *krasis*, a mingling, mixing, from *kerannynai*, to mix.]

1. In medicine, the mixture of the constituents of a fluid, as of the blood; in a more general sense, synonymous with *constitution.*

2. In grammar, a figure by which two different letters are contracted into one long letter or into a diphthong; syneresis; as, *alēthea* into *alēthē*, *teicheos* into *teichous.*

çras-ped′ō-drōme, *a.* [Gr. *kraspedon*, a border, and *dromos*, running.] In botany, denoting a system of nervation in which the nerves of a leaf run to and meet the margin.

Çras-pe-dō′tȧ, *n.pl.* [L., pl. of *craspedotus*, from Gr. *kraspedoun*, to surround with a border; *kraspedon*, a border.] A division of jellyfishes, the *Hydromedusæ.*

çras′pe-dōte, *a.* Relating or pertaining to *Craspedota.*

çrass, *a.* [L. *crassus*, thick, dense.]

1. Gross; thick; coarse; not thin, nor fine; applied to fluids and solids.

2. Gross; stupid; obtuse; as, *crass* ignorance.

çras′sȧ-ment, *n.* [L. *crassamentum*, thickness, thick sediment, from *crassus*, thick, dense.] Thickness. [Obs.]

çras-sȧ-men′tum, *n.* [L., thickness, thick sediment, from *crassus*, thick, dense.] The thick, red part of the blood, as distinct from the serum or aqueous part; the clot.

çras-si-liñ′guăl (-gwăl), *a.* [L. *crassus*, thick, and *lingua*, tongue.] Having the tongue thick.

çras′si-ment, *n.* Crassament. [Obs.]

çras′si-tūde, *n.* [L. *crassitudo*, from *crassus*, thick, dense.] Grossness; coarseness; thickness. [Rare.]

çrass′ness, *n.* Grossness. [Obs.]

Çras′sū-lȧ, *n.* [From L. *crassus*, thick, coarse.] A genus of plants of the natural order *Crassulaceæ*, consisting of herbs and shrubs, natives chiefly of South Africa.

Çras-sū-lā′cē-æ, *n.pl.* [L., from *crassula*, dim. of *crassus*, thick, dense.] The houseleek family, a natural order of polypetalous exogens. It consists of succulent plants, with herbaceous or shrubby stems, and annual or perennial roots, growing in hot, dry, exposed places in the more temperate parts of the world, but chiefly South Africa.

çras-sū-lā′ceous, *a.* Of or pertaining to the *Crassulaceæ.*

çras-ti-nā′tion, *n.* [LL. *crastinatio*, from *crastinus*, of to-morrow; *cras*, to-morrow.] Procrastination. [Obs.]

Çrȧ-tæ′gus, *n.* [L., from Gr. *krataigos*, a flowering thorn.] An extensive genus of hardy, flowering trees and bushes comprehending the hawthorns, oriental thorns, evergreen thorns, small-leaved thorns, etc.

çratch, *n.* [ME. *cratche*, *crecche*; OFr. *creche*, a crib, manger; O.H.G. *crippa*, a crib.] A rack or crib. [Obs.]

çratch′=çrā″dle, *n.* Cat's-cradle.

çratch′eş, *n.pl.* [G. *krätze*, the itch, cratches; *kratzen*, to scratch.] A swelling on the pastern, under the fetlock, and sometimes under the hoof of a horse.

çrāte, *n.* [L. *cratis*, wickerwork.] A wickerwork hamper for preventing the breakage of fragile ware; any case made up of slats to protect goods in transit; also, the amount held by such a case; as, a *crate* of tomatoes.

çrāte, *v.t.*; crated, *pt.*, *pp.*; crating, *ppr.* To place into a crate; as, to *crate* china.

çrā′tẽr, *n.* [L. *crater*, from Gr. *kratēr*, a great cup, a mixing vessel, from *kerannynai*, to mix.]

1. The orifice or mouth of a volcano, which may be either central or lateral, or accompanied by several subsidiary openings.

Crater of Antuco, South America.

2. In classical antiquity, a bowl for the mixing of wine.

3. In military language, the pit of an exploded mine.

4. [C—] In astronomy, an ancient southern constellation of thirty-one stars.

5. In electric lighting, the depression at the point of a positive carbon in the voltaic arc.

çrȧ-ter′i-fọrm, *a.* [L. *crater*, from Gr. *kratēr*, a crater, and *forma*, form.] In botany, having the form of a crater; shaped like a goblet.

çrā′tẽr-ous, *a.* Pertaining to or like a crater.

çräunch, *v.t.*; craunched, *pt.*, *pp.*; craunching, *ppr.* [Imitative of sound.] To crush with the teeth; to chew; to crunch.

çrȧ-vat′, *n.* [Fr. *cravate*, from *Cravate*, a Croat.] A neckcloth; a piece of fine muslin, silk, or other cloth, worn about the neck before neckties came in fashion.

çrāve, *v.t.*; craved, *pt.*, *pp.*; craving, *ppr.* [ME. *craven*; AS. *crafian*, to crave, ask, demand.]

1. To ask with earnestness or importunity; to beseech; to implore; to ask with submission or humility, as a dependent; to beg; to entreat.

> As for my nobler friends, I *crave* their pardons. —Shak.

2. To call for, as a gratification; to long for; to require or demand, as a passion or appetite; as, the stomach or appetite *craves* food.

Syn.—Desire, entreat, beseech, implore, adjure, request, supplicate, solicit, ask.

çrāve, *v.i.* To implore or entreat humbly; to beg; with *for.*

çrā′ven, *n.* [ME. *cravant*, conquered, cowardly; OFr. *cravanté*, pp. of *craventer*, to break, overcome, conquer.] A despicable coward.

çrā′ven, *a.* 1. Vanquished. [Obs.]

2. Cowardly; base.

çrā′ven, *v.t.* To make cowardly. [Obs.]

çrāv′ẽr, *n.* One who craves or begs.

çrāv′ing, *n.* Vehement or urgent desire, or calling for; a longing for.

çrāv′ing-ly, *adv.* In a craving manner.

çrāv′ing-ness, *n.* The state of craving.

çraw, *n.* [Dan. *kro*, the craw; Sw. *kräfva*; D. *kraag*, the neck.] The crop of a bird; by extension, the stomach of any animal.

çraw′fish, çrāy′fish, *n.* [Early ME. *craifish*, *crevis*; OFr. *crevice*, *crevisse*, *ecrevisse*, a crawfish; O.H.G. *chrebiz*, a crab.]

1. *Astacus fluviatilis*, the river lobster, a macrurous, ten-footed crustacean, found in streams of Europe; by extension, any like arthropod of the genera *Astacus* and *Cambarus.* *Cambarus pellucidus*, the blind crawfish, is a habitant of Mammoth Cave.

2. The spiny lobster. [Prov. Eng.]

çrawl, *v.i.*; crawled, *pt.*, *pp.*; crawling, *ppr.* [Ice. *krafla*, to paw, scrabble; Dan. *kravle*, to crawl, creep.]

1. To creep; to move slowly by thrusting or drawing the body along the ground, as a worm; or to move slowly on the hands and knees or feet, as a human being.

2. To move weakly, slowly, or timorously.

3. To move stealthily or clandestinely; to insinuate oneself; to practise servility.

4. To have a sensation as of an insect creeping upon the skin; as, her flesh *crawls* at the sight of a worm.

çrawl, *n.* The act of crawling, slow, creeping motion; as, his walk is little better than a *crawl.*

çrawl, *n.* [D. *kraal*, an inclosure, a cattle-pen.] A pen or inclosure of stakes in which to confine fish or other aquatic animals at the seacoast.

çrawl′ẽr, *n.* One who or that which crawls.

çraw'ley=root, *n.* Same as *Coral-root.*

çrawl'ing-ly, *adv.* In a crawling manner.

çrawl'y, *a.* Marked by a sensation as of the touch of a worm or other crawling thing. [Colloq.]

Çrax, *n.* [L., from Gr. *krazein, kraxein*, to croak like a raven.] The curassows, a genus of gallinaceous birds of the family *Cracidæ.*

çrāy, çrāyer, *n.* See *Crare.*

çrāy'fish, *n.* Same as *Crawfish.*

çrāy'ŏn, *v.t.*; crayoned, *pt., pp.*; crayoning, *ppr.* To sketch or design with a crayon; to sketch or plan, in a general sense.

çrāy'ŏn, *n.* [Fr., from *craie*, chalk, from L. *creta*, chalk, said to be from *creta*, Cretan earth; *Creta*, Crete.]

1. A pencil or cylinder of colored pipe-clay, chalk, or charcoal, used in drawing upon paper. [See *Pastel.*]

2. A composition pencil made of soap, resin, wax, and lampblack, used for drawing upon lithographic stones.

3. The carbon-pencil of an arc lamp.

4. A crayon-drawing.

çrāy'ŏn=bōard, *n.* Prepared cardboard for crayons.

çrāy'ŏn=draw"ing, *n.* The act or art of crayoning; the sketch so produced.

çrāze, *v.t.*; crazed, *pt., pp.*; crazing, *ppr.* [ME. *crasen*, to break, break in pieces; Sw. *krasa*; Dan. *krase*, to break, crackle.]

1. To break. [Obs.]

2. To impair, as an object or the mind, by means of cracks or flaws; as, frost *crazed* the wall.

3. To dement; to make crazy; as, the sight *crazed* him.

çrāze, *v.i.* 1. To burst apart. [Obs.]

2. To split; to be filled with cracks; specifically, in pottery, to crack and peel, as glaze.

3. To become crazy or insane.

çrāze, *n.* 1. A flaw; a defect, particularly, a crack or blister in pottery.

2. Derangement of the intellect.

3. A confirmed or habitual fancy or desire; as, a *craze* for dress.

4. A fad or affectation, generally widespread, and sometimes temporary, for some particular thing; rage; as, a *craze* for rare stamps; the automobile *craze.*

çrāz'ed-ness, *n.* A broken state; decrepitude; an impaired state of the intellect.

çrāze'=mill, çrāz'ing=mill, *n.* [Prov. Eng.] A mill resembling a grist mill, used for grinding tin ore. [Obs.]

çrā'zi-ly, *adv.* In a broken or crazy manner.

çrā'zi-ness, *n.* 1. The state of being broken or weakened; as, the *craziness* of a ship.

2. The state of being broken in mind; imbecility or weakness of intellect; derangement.

çrāz'ing, *n.* In pottery, blistering of the glaze.

çrā'zy, *a.*; *comp.* crazier; *superl.* craziest. 1. Out of order; broken; weak; as, a *crazy* elevator.

2. Broken, weakened, or disordered in intellect; deranged, weakened, or shattered in mind; as, a *crazy* man.

3. Eager to an inordinate degree; ardently desiring; as, he was *crazy* to get home.

Syn.—Insane, mad.

çrā'zy=bōne, *n.* The projection at the elbow, commonly called the *funny-bone.*

çrā'zy=quilt (-kwilt), *n.* A quilt made up of pieces arranged without pattern or order.

çrā'zy=weed, *n.* Same as *Loco-weed.*

çrā'zy=wŏrk, *n.* Patchwork making up a crazy-quilt.

çrē'ȧ-ble, *a.* Creatable. [Obs.]

çreaght (krāt), *n.* [Ir. *graigh*, a herd, flock.] A herd. [Obs.]

çreaght, *v.i.* To graze. [Obs.]

çreak, *v.t.* and *v.i.*; creaked (krēkt), *pt., pp.*; creaking, *ppr.* [ME. *creken*, to make a harsh, grating sound; imitative of the sound.]

I. *v.t.* To cause to creak.

II. *v.i.* To make a sharp, harsh, grating sound, of some continuance, as by the friction of hard substances; as, the hinge of a door *creaks* in turning.

çreak, *n.* A sharp, harsh, grating sound, as that produced by the friction of hard substances; as, the *creak* of an unoiled weather-vane.

çreak'y, *a.* Making or likely to make a creak; as, a *creaky* old bed.

çream, *n.* [ME. *creme*; OFr. *cresme, creme*; LL. *crema, cremum*, cream; *cremor*, thick juice.]

1. In a general sense, any part of a liquor that separates from the rest, rises, and collects on the surface. More particularly, the richer and butyraceous part of milk, which, when the milk stands unagitated in a cool place, rises and forms a scum on the surface. This by agitation forms butter.

2. Anything of a creamy consistency.

3. The best part of a thing; the choice part; as, the *cream* of a jest or story.

> Welcome, O flower and *cream* of knights-errant. —Shelton.

4. A sweetmeat or kind of viand prepared from cream; as, a chocolate *cream.*

5. A name common to the finest liqueurs, as rosolio, maraschino, etc.

6. Oxid of lead formed in shot-making.

Bavarian cream; a dessert made of cream, sugar, gelatin, and eggs.

Cream of lime; lime and water of a creamy consistency.

Cream of tartar; bitartrate of potassium, commercially procured by refining argol. It is used in medicine, baking-powder, etc.

Cream-of-tartar tree; a North Australian tree, *Adansonia Gregorii.* [See *Adansonia.*]

çream, *v.t.*; creamed, *pt., pp.*; creaming, *ppr.* 1. To skim; to take the cream from, by skimming.

2. To put cream with; to make of a consistency like cream; as, to *cream* coffee; to *cream* a sauce.

çream, *v.i.* To gather cream; to gather a covering or scum on the surface; to resemble cream in appearance.

çream'=çāke, *n.* A cake having a custard-like filling made of cream, eggs, sugar, etc.

çream'=cheese, *n.* A soft cheese prepared from curd made with new milk to which a certain quantity of cream is added; also, cheese in general made from unskimmed milk to which extra cream has been added.

çream'çups, *n.* *Platystemon Californicus*, a Californian plant of the poppy family.

çream'ēr, *n.* 1. A cream-separator.

2. A pitcher or jug for cream. [Colloq.]

çream'ēr-y, *n.*; *pl.* **çream'ēr-ies**. A factory where butter is made from cream gathered for the purpose. Usually, as in the Middle West, such a concern churns and markets butter from "raised" cream, though cream separated either by the producer or at the factory is a staple.

çream'=fāced (-fāst), *a.* White; pale; having a coward look.

çream'=fruit, *n.* A plant of the dogbane family growing in western Africa, having a creamy, edible fruit.

çream'=gāuġe, *n.* A test-tube used to determine the percentage of cream in milk.

çream'i-ness, *n.* The state or quality of being creamy.

çream'=nut, *n.* The fruit of the *Bertholletia excelsa* of South America, commonly called *brazil-nut.*

çream'=sep"ȧ-rā-tŏr, *n.* A machine which has a rapidly revolving drum, separating cream from new milk by centrifugal action.

çream'=slice, *n.* A sort of wooden knife used, (a) in skimming milk; (b) in cutting and serving ice-cream.

çream'y, *a.* Containing cream; like cream.

çrē'ănce, *n.* [OFr. *creance*, faith, confidence, from LL. *credentia*; from *credere*, to trust.]

1. Belief; faith; also, credit. [Obs.]

2. In falconry, a fine, small line fastened to a hawk's leash when it is first lured.

çrē'ănce, *v.t.* and *v.i.* To borrow. [Obs.]

çrē'ănt, *a.* [L. *creans* (-*antis*), ppr. of *creare*, to make, create.] Formative; constructive; creative. [Rare.]

çrease, *n.* Same as *Creese.*

çrease, *n.* [Breton *kriz*, a crease, wrinkle; *kriza*, to crease, wrinkle.]

1. A line or mark made by folding or doubling; any mark resembling that of a wrinkle or fold.

2. In the game of cricket, one of certain lines marked on the field.

Bowling crease; in cricket, a line six feet eight inches in length, drawn upon the ground at each wicket, so that the stumps stand in the center.

Popping crease; in cricket, a line four feet in front of the wicket, and parallel with the bowling crease, and at least of the same length.

Return crease; in cricket, one of two short lines drawn at either end of the bowling crease, within which the bowler must be standing when he delivers his ball.

çrease, *v.t.*; creased (krēst), *pt., pp.*; creasing, *ppr.* 1. To make a crease or mark in, by folding, doubling, etc.

2. In hunting, to hit with a bullet in the neck, so as to injure the vertebræ or cut the muscles, and stun without killing.

3. To close or indent (a cartridge-case); to crimp or score.

çreas'ēr, *n.* Any one of various tools used for making creases; as, (a) a tool used in bookbinding to trace depressed lines in the covers; (b) an attachment to a sewing-machine that marks a guide-line for stitching; (c) a device for crimping or turning in the ends of a cartridge-case, so as to hold the charge.

çreas'ing, *n.* In architecture, same as *tile-creasing.*

çrē'ȧ-sōte, *n.* See *Creosote.*

çreas'y, *a.* Having creases; creased; wrinkled.

çrē'at, *n.* [Fr. *créat*; It. *creato*, a servant, pupil; L. *creatus*, pp. of *creare*, to create.] In the manège, an usher to a riding-master.

çrē-āt'ȧ-ble, *a.* Able to be created.

çrē-āte', *a.* Created. [Poet.]

çrē-āte', *v.t.*; created, *pt., pp.*; creating, *ppr.* [L. *creatus*, pp. of *creare*, to make, create. Gr. *krainein*, to accomplish; Sans. *kar*, to make.]

1. To produce; to bring into being from nothing; to cause to exist.

> In the beginning, God *created* the heaven and the earth. —Gen. i. 1.

2. To make or form, by investing with a new character; to appoint; as, to *create* one a peer or baron.

3. To produce; to cause; to be the occasion of; as, long abstinence *creates* uneasiness in the stomach; hurry *creates* confusion.

> Your eye, in Scotland,
> Would *create* soldiers, and make women fight.
> —Shak.

4. To make or produce, by new combinations of matter already existing, and by investing these combinations with new forms, constitutions, and qualities; to shape and organize; as, out of apparently isolated facts, he *created* a system.

5. To bring a certain treatment of into general acceptance; to establish a standard for; as, she *created* the rôle of Portia.

6. To beget; to generate; to bring forth.

Syn.—Constitute, form, make, occasion, originate, produce, generate.

çrē-at'iç, *a.* [Gr. *kreas* (-*atos*), flesh.] Occasioned by or pertaining to animal food; as, *creatic* nausea. Also spelled *kreatic.*

çrē'ȧ-tine, krē'ȧ-tine, *n.* A crystallizable organic substance, $C_4H_9N_3O_2$, obtained from muscular fiber; written also *creatin, kreatin.*

çrē-at'i-nine, çrē-at'i-nin, *n.* An alkaline, crystallizable substance, $C_4H_7N_3O$, obtained by the action of acids on creatine, and also found in the juice of muscular flesh and in urine; written also *kreatinine, kreatinin.*

çrē-ā'tion, *n.* 1. The act of creating from nothing; the act of causing to exist; and especially, the act of bringing this world into existence.

2. The act of making, by new combinations of matter, invested with new forms and properties, and of subjecting to different laws; the act of shaping and organizing; as, the *creation* of a nation.

3. The act of investing with a new character; as, the *creation* of peers in England.

4. The thing or things created; creatures collectively; the world; the universe; nature.

> As subjects then the whole *creation* came. —Denham.

5. Anything produced or caused to exist, in mechanics, science, or art; especially, an unusual product of the mind; as, the master *creations* of art.

> A false *creation*,
> Proceeding from the heat-oppressed brain.
> —Shak.

çrē-ā'tion-ăl, *a.* Pertaining to creation.

çrē-ā'tion-işm, *n.* 1. In philosophy, the doctrine that matter and each new form was created by a direct exercise of the Divine power; opposed to *evolution.*

2. In theology, the doctrine that a new soul is created by a special fiat of God at each new birth, while there was but one creation for the human body; opposed to *traducianism.*

çrē-ā'tive, *a.* Having the power to create, or exerting the act of creation; pertaining to creation; formative; productive; as, *creative* fancy; *creative* power.

çrē-ā'tive-ness, *n.* The state or quality of being creative.

çrē-ā'tŏr, *n.* [L.] 1. The being or person that creates or causes something to exist; particularly, [C—] God, the Maker of all things, the Being that bestows existence or form without any preceding matter.

> Remember now thy *Creator* in the days of thy youth. —Eccles. xii. 1.

2. The thing that creates, produces, or causes; that which acts as a medium in a creative process; as, electricity is to be the *creator* of future mechanical methods.

çrē-ā'tŏr-ship, *n.* The state or condition of being a creator.

çrē-ā'tress, *n.* A woman who creates anything.

çrē-ā'trix, *n.* [L.] Same as *Creatress.*

çrēa'tūr-ăl, *a.* Belonging to a creature; having the qualities of a creature.

çrēa'tūre, *n.* [OFr. *creature*; LL. *creatura*, a creature, creation, from L. *creare*, to create.]

1. That which is created; every being or thing not self-existent.

2. A living being of any kind; most commonly, a beast or domestic animal.

3. A human being, used in contempt or endearment, generally with a qualifying term; as, an idle *creature*; a poor *creature*; a pretty *creature.*

4. A person who owes his rise and fortune to

another; one who is made to be what he is; a dependent; a tool.

> Great princes thus, when favorites they raise,
> To justify their grace, their *creatures* praise.
> —Dryden.

5. A person or a thing considered as produced or controlled by something else; as, a *creature* of accident; intolerance, a *creature* of most religious creeds.

çrēa′tūre, *a.* Pertaining or ministering to the body; as, *creature* comforts.

çrēa′tūre-less, *a.* Alone; solitary. [Obs.]

çrēa′tūre-ly, *a.* Having the qualities of or pertaining to a creature. [Rare.]

çrēa′tūre-ship, *n.* The state of being a creature. [Rare.]

çrēa′tūr-ize, *v.t.* To lower; to make like an animal. [Obs.]

çrēaze, *n.* [Prov. Eng.] In tin-mining, the ore that gathers in the middle of the washing-pit.

çrē-bri-ços′tāte, *a.* [L. *creber*, close, frequent, and *costa*, a rib.] In conchology, having ridges or marks like ribs set closely together.

çrē-bri-sul′çāte, *a.* [L. *creber*, frequent, close, and *sulcus*, a furrow.] In conchology, marked with closely set furrows or grooves, running transversely.

çreb′ri-tūde, *n.* [LL. *crebritudo*, from *creber*, close, frequent.] Frequentness. [Obs.]

çrē′brous, *a.* [L. *creber*, close, frequent.] Frequent. [Rare.]

çrèche (krāsh), *n.* [Fr., from OFr. *creche*, a crib.]
1. A public nursery where babies are left to be cared for during the day.
2. A home for foundlings.

çrē′dence, *n.* [OFr. *credence*; LL. *credentia*, faith, from *credens* (*-entis*), ppr. of *credere*, to believe, put faith in.]

Credence.

1. Belief; credit; reliance of the mind on evidence of facts derived from other sources than personal knowledge; as, we give *credence* to a story related by a man of known veracity.
2. That which gives a claim to credit, belief, or confidence; as, a letter of *credence*.
3. Ecclesiastically, in the Anglican and Roman Catholic churches, a small table near the altar, on which the bread and wine to be used in the eucharist are placed; a prothesis.
4. In medieval times, a sort of buffet or sideboard where the meats were tasted before they were served to the guests, as a precaution against poisoning; later, a kind of china-cupboard.

Syn.—Belief, credit, confidence, trust, faith.

çrē′dence, *v.t.* To believe. [Obs.]

çrē-den′dum, *n.*; *pl.* **çrē-den′dȧ**. [L., neut. gerundive of *credere*, to believe, put faith in.] In theology, a thing to be believed; an article of faith; distinguished from *agendum*, which is a practical duty.

çrē′dent, *a.* [L. *credens* (*-entis*), ppr. of *credere*, to believe.]
1. Believing; giving credit easily; apt to believe. [Rare.]
2. Having credit; not to be questioned. [Obs.]

çrē-den′tiăl, *a.* [From LL. *credentia*, belief, faith, from L. *credere*, to believe, put trust in.] Giving a title to credit; establishing reliability.

çrē-den′tiăl, *n.* 1. That which gives credit; that which gives a title or claim to confidence. [Rare in singular.]
2. [*pl.*] Written testimonials showing that one is entitled to or is vested with authority, as the letters given an ambassador, or the certificate of a public officer.
3. A certificate issued by a passenger association, which conditionally entitles the holder to a rebate after having traveled a specified number of miles on certain railway lines.

çred-i-bil′i-ty, *n.* [Fr. *crédibilité*, from L. *credibilis*, worthy of belief, from *credere*, to believe, put faith in.] The state or quality of being credible.

çred′i-ble, *a.* [L. *credibilis*, from *credere*, to believe, put trust in.]
1. Worthy of credence; believable, as a book or opinion.
2. Entitled to credit or trust; capable of being believed, as a person.

çred′i-ble-ness, *n.* Credibility. [Rare.]

çred′i-bly, *adv.* In a credible manner.

çred′it, *n.* [Fr. *crédit*; L. *creditum*, a loan, neut. of *creditus*, pp. of *credere*, to trust, believe.]
1. Belief; faith; a reliance or resting of the mind on the truth of something said or done; used both subjectively and objectively.

> What though no *credit* doubting wits may give?
> —Pope.

2. Reputation derived from the confidence of others; esteem; estimation; honor; good opinion founded on the belief of a man's veracity, integrity, abilities, and virtue; as, a physician in high *credit* with his brethren.
3. That which procures or is entitled to belief or confidence; authority derived from character or reputation; as, we believe a story on the *credit* of the narrator.
4. One who or that which augments reputation, honor, or fame; as, a *credit* to his family; a *credit* to science.
5. Influence derived from the reputation for veracity or integrity, or from the good opinion or confidence of others; interest; as, the minister has *credit* with the prince; use your *credit* with your friend in my favor.
6. In commerce, (a) trust; transfer of goods in confidence of future payment; (b) the reputation for solvency and probity which entitles a man to be trusted.
7. In bookkeeping, the side of an account in which payment is entered; opposed to *debit*; as, this article is carried to one's *credit* and that to his debit.
8. The notes or bills which are issued by the government or by corporations or individuals, which circulate on the confidence of men in the ability and disposition of those who issue them to redeem them. They are sometimes called *bills of credit*.
9. The time given for payment for lands or goods sold on trust; as, a long *credit*, or a short *credit*.
10. A sum of money due to any person; anything valuable standing on the creditor side of an account; as, A has a *credit* on the books of B; the *credits* are more than balanced by the debits.

Bill of credit; see under *Bill*, n.

Crédit Foncier (krā-dē′ foṅ-syā′); [Fr., lit. land credit.] a peculiar mode of raising money on land in France, the peculiarity of which is that the repayment of the loan is by an annuity terminable at a certain date.

Crédit Mobilier (krā-dē′ mō-bē′lyā); [Fr., lit. personal credit.] a scheme which originated in France in 1852, its object being to undertake trading enterprises of all kinds on the principle of limited liability, and do a general banking business. A similar company was organized in Pennsylvania in 1863.

Letter of credit; a nonnegotiable order given by bankers or others at one place to enable a person to receive money from their agents at another place.

Public credit; the confidence which men entertain in the ability and disposition of a nation to make good its engagements with its creditors; also, a similar confidence on the part of the public toward those in business.

Syn.—Belief, faith, trust, confidence, favor, influence, name, character, reputation, honor.

çred′it, *v.t.*; credited, *pt.*, *pp.*; crediting, *ppr.* [L. *creditus*, pp. of *credere*, to trust, put faith in.]
1. To believe; to confide in the truth of; as, to *credit* a report or the man who tells it.
2. To trust; to sell, or lend in confidence of future payment; as, to *credit* goods or money.
3. To procure credit or honor to; to do credit to; to give reputation or honor to.

> May here her monument stand so,
> To *credit* this rude age. —Waller.

4. To enter upon the credit side of an account; to give credit for; as, to *credit* the amount paid; to *credit* to a man the interest paid on a bond.

çred′it-ȧ-ble, *a.* 1. Believable. [Obs.]
2. Reputable; that may be enjoyed or exercised with reputation or esteem; estimable; as, a *creditable* way of living.

çred′it-ȧ-ble-ness, *n.* The state or quality of being creditable; reputableness.

çred′it-ȧ-bly, *adv.* In a creditable manner.

çred′it-ŏr, *n.* [L. *creditor*, a truster, lender, from *credere*, to trust, put faith in.]
1. One who believes. [Obs.]
2. One to whom a sum of money or other thing is due by obligation, promise, or in law; one who gives credit or has a just claim for money; correlative to *debtor*.

> *Creditors* have better memories than debtors.
> —Franklin.

Preferred creditor; one having legal preference over others.

çred′it-ress, çred′i-trix, *n.* A female creditor.

çrē′dō, *n.* In the Roman Catholic and Anglican churches, the creed; also, the music to which it is sung.

çrē-dū′li-ty, *n.* The quality of being credulous; easiness of belief; readiness to believe without sufficient evidence.

çred′ū-lous, *a.* [L. *credulus*, from *credere*, to trust, put faith in.]
1. Easy of belief; of weak mind; easily imposed upon; unsuspecting; as, *credulous* in matters of belief.
2. Believed too easily. [Obs.]

çred′ū-lous-ly, *adv.* With credulity.

çred′ū-lous-ness, *n.* Credulity.

çreed, *n.* [ME. *crede*; AS. *creda*; from L. *credo*, I believe, the first word of the Latin version of the Apostles' creed; 1st pers. sing. pres. ind. act. of *credere*, to trust, put faith in.]
1. An authoritative summary of the essential points comprising a certain belief, as of a church, political or scientific body, or any organized society; particularly, the confession of faith of a religious body.
2. Belief; particularly, religious belief.

Apostles' creed; see under *Apostle*.
Athanasian creed; see under *Athanasian*.
Nicene creed; see under *Nicene*.

çreed, *v.t.* To believe. [Obs.]

çreed′less, *a.* Without a creed or formula of faith.

çreek, *v.* and *n.* [Obs.] See *Creak*.

çreek, *n.* [ME. *creke*, *crike*, an inlet, cove; Ice. *kriki*, a nook; Sw. *krik*, a bend, cove, creek; D. *kreek*, a bay, creek.]
1. A small inlet, bay, or cove; a recess in the shore of the sea or of a river.
2. Any turn or winding.
3. A small river; a rivulet; a crick.

Çreek, *n.* One of a tribe of Indians now inhabiting Indian Territory, formerly roaming the country which now forms the states of Alabama and Georgia.

çreek′fish, *n.* A fish, the chub-sucker.

çreek′y, *a.* Winding.

çreel, *n.* [Scot., from Gael. *criol*, a chest, coffer.]
1. An osier basket, such as anglers use.
2. In spinning, the bar which holds the paying-off bobbins.
3. A slaughtering-frame for sheep. [Prov. Eng.]

çreel, *v.t.*; creeled, *pt.*, *pp.*; creeling, *ppr.* To place in a creel.

çreep, *v.i.*; crept, *pt.*, *pp.*; creeping, *ppr.* [ME. *crepen*; AS. *creopan*, to creep, crawl; D. *kruipen*; L.G. *krupen*, to creep, crawl.]
1. To move with the belly on the ground, or the surface of any other body, as a worm or serpent without legs, or as many insects with feet and very short legs; to crawl.
2. To move along the ground, or on the surface of any other body, in growth, as a vine; to grow along.

> Oh, a dainty plant is the ivy green,
> That *creepeth* o'er ruins old. —Dickens.

3. To move slowly, feebly, or timorously; as, an old or infirm man, who *creeps* about his chamber.

> We took a little boat to *creep* along the seashore as far as Genoa. —Addison.

4. To move slowly and insensibly, as time.
5. To move secretly; to move so as to escape detection or prevent suspicion; to enter unobserved.

> The sophistry which *creeps* into most of the books of argument. —Locke.

6. To move or behave with extreme servility or humility; to move as if affected with a sense of extreme humiliation or terror.

> Like a guilty thing I *creep*. —Tennyson.

7. To have a sensation such as might be caused by worms or insects creeping on the skin of the body; as, the sight made my flesh *creep*.
8. To have a slow, lengthwise movement; said of rails in a railway-track.

çreep, *n.* 1. The act of creeping.
2. [*pl.*] Shudders; as, to have the *creeps*.
3. In mining, a sinking down of the strata overlying a working, the floor being at the same time pushed up.

çreep′ẽr, *n.* 1. One who creeps; that which creeps; a reptile.
2. In botany, a creeping plant, which moves along the surface of the earth, or attaches itself to some other body, as ivy.
3. An iron used to slide along the grate in kitchens.
4. A kind of patten or clog worn by women; also, an appliance with iron points fixed on a shoe to prevent slipping.
5. An instrument of iron with hooks or claws for dragging the bottom of a well, river, or harbor, and bringing up what may be there. [In this sense used often in the plural.]
6. [*pl.*] Spurred climbers, as those used by telephone linemen.
7. [*pl.*] The popular name of a family of birds, *Certhiidæ*, which strongly resemble the woodpeckers in their habit of creeping on the stems of trees, supporting themselves on the strong quills projecting from the tail-feathers, and of securing their food by an exsertile tongue; also, other birds of similar habits, as the pine-*creepers* and the tree-*creepers*.
8. One of a breed of fowls with legs so short that they jump rather than walk.

çreep′hōle, *n.* A hole into which an animal

may creep to escape notice or danger; also, a subterfuge; an excuse.

çreep'ie, *n.* [Scot.] A kind of low stool.

çreep'i-ness, *n.* A creepy feeling.

çreep'ing, *n.* The act of crawling or using a creeper; specifically, dragging for a submarine cable.

Creeping crowfoot; the popular name of *Ranunculus repens*, a buttercup with long runners, which grows in meadows and pastures.

çreep'ing-ly, *adv.* By creeping; slowly; in the manner of a reptile.

çree'ple, *n.* A reptile; also, a cripple. [Obs.]

çreep'y, *a.* Fearful; producing a chilled and scared sensation.

çreese, krïs, *n.* [From Malay *kris*, a dagger.] A Malay dagger.

çré-māil-lère' (krā-mā-lyãr'), *n.* [Fr.] In fortification, a defensive line of circumvallation traced in the form of a saw, with the view of delivering both oblique and cross fires.

çrē-mas'tẽr, *n.* [L., from Gr. *kremastēr*, a suspender, from *kremannynai*, to hang.]

1. In anatomy, the muscle suspending a testis.

2. In entomology, the abdominal point of the pupa of a lepidopter.

çrem-as-ter'iç, *a.* Pertaining to the cremaster.

çrē'māte, *v.t.*; cremated, *pt., pp.*; cremating, *ppr.* [L. *crematus*, pp. of *cremare*, to burn.] To burn; to dispose of, as a human body, by burning instead of interring.

çrē-mā'tion, *n.* [L. *crematio*, from *cremare*, to burn.] The act or custom of cremating; a burning, as of the dead.

çrē-mā'tion-ist, *n.* An advocate of cremation.

çrē-mā'tōr, *n.* One who or that which cremates.

çrem-ȧ-tō'ri-um, *n.*; *pl.* **çrem-ȧ-tō'ri-ȧ.** A crematory.

çrem'ȧ-tō-ry, *n.*; *pl.* **çrem'ȧ-tō-ries.** [L. *crematorium*, from *cremare*, to burn.] An institution at which bodies are consumed by incineration; the furnace so employed.

çrem'ȧ-tō-ry, *a.* Connected with or relating to cremation.

çrem'ō-çärp, *n.* [Gr. *kremannynai*, to hang, and *karpos*, fruit.] A fruit, as that of umbellifers, consisting of two or more indehiscent, inferior, one-seeded carpels, adhering around a distinct and separable axis.

Çrē-mō'nȧ, *n.* A general name given to violins made at Cremona, the capital of Milan, in the seventeenth century, by the Amati family, and by Stradivarius at the commencement of the eighteenth century.

çrē'mọr, *n.* [L.] Cream; any substance resembling cream.

çrem'ō-sin, *n.* [Obs.] Same as *Crimson*.

çrems, *n.* Same as *Krems*.

çrē'nȧ, *n.*; *pl.* **çrē'næ.** [L., a notch.] In zoölogy, a notch; also, a wrinkle-like projection.

çrē'nāte, çrē'nāt-ed, *a.* [L. *crenatus*, from *crena*, a notch.] Notched; indented; scalloped, as a leaf.

Doubly crenate; having the larger segments with smaller ones upon them.

çrē-nā'tion, *n.* Crenature.

çren'ȧ-tūre, *n.* A tooth of a crenate leaf, or any other part that is crenate.

Crenate Leaf.

Doubly Crenate Leaf.

çrē-nel', *n.* Same as *Crenelle*.

çren'el-āte, *v.t.*; crenelated, *pt., pp.*; crenelating, *ppr.* [OFr. *creneler*, to indent, from LL. *crenellus*, an embrasure, battlement.] To furnish, as a parapet or breastwork, with crenelles; to indent; to notch; written also *crenellate*.

çren'el-ā-ted, *a.* Furnished with crenelles, as a parapet or breastwork; embattled; indented; notched; written also *crenellated*.

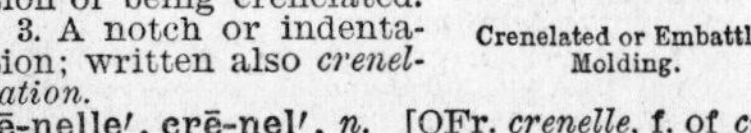
Crenelated or Embattled Molding.

çren-el-ā'tion, *n.* 1. The act of forming crenelles.

2. The state or condition of being crenelated.

3. A notch or indentation; written also *crenellation*.

çrē-nelle', çrē-nel', *n.* [OFr. *crenelle*, f. of *crenel*; LL. *crenellus*, an embrasure, battlement.]

1. Militarily, an embrasure in an embattled parapet.

2. In botany, a crenature.

çrē-nelled', *a.* Same as *Crenelated*.

çren'gle (-gl), **çren'kle,** *n.* Nautically, a cringle.

çrē'niç, *a.* [Gr. *krēnē*, a spring.] Relating to a spring.

Crenic acid; an amorphous product of vegetable molds.

çrē-nit'iç, *a.* [Gr. *krēnē*, a spring.] In geology, pertaining to the upward shifting of matter through the agency of springs.

Crenitic hypothesis; the theory that springs or spring action is responsible for the presence of crystalline rock.

çren'ū-lȧ, *n.*; *pl.* **çren'ū-læ.** [L., dim. of *crena*, a notch.] A small notch or crena.

çren'ū-lāte, çren'ū-lā-ted, *a.* [Dim. of *crenate*.] Having the edge cut into very small notches.

çren-ū-lā'tion, *n.* That which has notches; also, a notched state or condition.

çrē'ōle, *n.* [Fr. *créole*; Sp. *criollo*, a creole; said to be a negro corruption of Sp. *criadillo*, dim. of *criado*, a servant, child; L. *creatus*, pp. of *creare*, to make, create.]

1. In the West Indies and Spanish America, (a) a native of those countries descended from European ancestors; (b) by extension, a native of any color, but not of indigenous blood.

2. In Louisiana, (a) a native of French or Spanish ancestry; (b) a French-speaking white; (c) a native black.

çrē'ōle, *a.* Of or relating to a creole or creoles.

çrē-ō'lē-ăn, *a.* Creole. [Rare.]

çrē-ō'li-ăn, *a.* and *n.* Creole. [Obs.]

çrē'ō-lin, *n.* [Gr. *kreas*, flesh, and L. *oleum*, oil.] A coal-tar product deprived of phenol, used especially in obstetrics as an antiseptic.

çrē-oph'ȧ-gous, *a.* [Gr. *kreophagos*, flesh-eating; *kreas*, flesh, and *phagein*, to eat.] Carnivorous.

çrē'ō-sol, çrē'ȧ-sol, *n.* [*Creo*sote and phen*ol*.] A liquid beech-tar distillate, $C_8H_{10}O_2$.

çrē'ō-sōte, çrē'ȧ-sōte, *n.* [L. *creosota*, from Gr. *kreas*, flesh, and *sōtēr*, from *sōzein*, to save.] A mixture of phenol compounds resulting from wood-tar distillation. Commercial *creosote* is phenol, frequently impure. It has powerful antiseptic properties and has various medicinal uses.

Coal-tar creosote; a coal-tar derivative having many characteristics of true creosote.

çrē'ō-sōte, *v.t.*; creosoted, *pt., pp.*; creosoting, *ppr.* To treat with creosote.

çrē'ō-sōte-bush, *n.* *Laurea Mexicana*, a desert shrub of America.

çrē'pance, çrē'pāne, *n.* [L. *crepare*, to crack, burst.] A wound in a horse's leg, caused by interfering.

çrêpe (krāp), *n.* [Fr.] Same as *Crape*.

çrep-i-taç'ū-lum, *n.*; *pl.* **çrep-i-taç'ū-lȧ.** [L., a rattle, from *crepitare*, freq. of *crepare*, to creak.] In zoölogy, (a) a rattle-like organ, as of the rattle snake; (b) a stridulating organ at the base of the wing, as in katydids.

çrep'i-tănt, *a.* [L. *crepitans* (*-antis*), ppr. of *crepitare*, to rattle.]

1. Relating to the sound of the lungs in pneumonia; crackling.

2. In entomology, able to crepitate.

çrep'i-tāte, *v.i.*; crepitated, *pt., pp.*; crepitating, *ppr.* [L. *crepitatus*, pp. of *crepitare*, to rattle, freq. of *crepare*, to creak, burst.] To crackle; to snap; to burst with a small, sharp, abrupt sound, rapidly repeated, as salt in fire.

çrep-i-tā'tion, *n.* 1. A crackling.

2. In surgery, (a) the grating of fractured bones when moved to ascertain a fracture; (b) the crackling noise produced by pressure upon a cellular membrane when it contains air; (c) one of the sounds detected in the lungs by auscultation; the peculiar rattle of pneumonia.

3. In entomology, a defensive anal ejection, as that of the bombardier beetle.

çrep'i-tus, *n.*; *pl.* **çrep'i-tus.** [L., a rattling, from *crepitare*, freq. of *crepare*, to creak, burst.] Crepitation.

çrē'pon, *n.* [Fr.] A fine stuff, made either of fine wool or of wool and silk, of which the warp is twisted much harder than the weft.

çrept, *v.*, past tense and past participle of *creep*.

çrē-pus'cle (-sl), **çrē-pus'çūle,** *n.* [L. *crepusculum*, twilight, from *creper*, dusky, dark.] Twilight. [Rare.]

çrē-pus'çū-lăr, *a.* 1. Pertaining to twilight; glimmering.

2. In zoölogy, flying or appearing in the twilight or evening, or before sunrise.

çrē-pus'çū-line, *a.* Crepuscular. [Obs.]

çrē-pus'çū-lous, *a.* Glimmering.

çres'cence, *n.* Growth. [Obs.]

çres-cen'dō (kre-shen'dō), *a.* and *adv.* [It., from *crescere*, to increase.] In music, with steadily increasing loudness and fullness of tone.

çres-cen'dō, *n.* (a) A gradually swelling tone in a musical passage; (b) a passage thus rendered.

çres'cent, *a.* [L. *crescens* (*-entis*), ppr. of *crescere*, to grow, increase.]

1. Increasing; growing; as, *crescent* horns.

2. Crescent-shaped.

çres'cent, *n.* 1. The increasing or new moon, which, when receding from the sun, shows a curving rim of light, terminating in points or horns. It is applied to the old or decreasing moon, in a like state, but less properly.

2. The figure or likeness of the new moon, as that borne in the Turkish flag or national standard; the standard itself, and, figuratively, the Turkish power.

Crescent.

3. In heraldry, a bearing in the form of a young or new moon.

4. The name of three orders of knighthood, from the symbol or badge being a crescent—the first instituted by Charles I. of Naples and Sicily in 1268; the second instituted at Angiers in 1464 by René of Anjou, being a revival of the former; and the third instituted by Selim, sultan of Turkey, in 1801, in honor of Lord Nelson.

5. A Turkish military musical instrument with bells or jingles.

6. In architecture, a range of buildings in the form of a crescent or half-moon.

çres'cent, *v.t.* 1. To form into a crescent. [Rare.]

2. To embellish with a crescent or crescents.

çres-cen'tiç, *a.* Shaped like a crescent.

çres'cent-wīṣe, *adv.* In the form of a crescent.

çres'cive, *a.* [From L. *crescere*, to grow, increase.] Increasing; growing.

çrē'sōl, *n.* [Gr. *kreas*, flesh, and L. *oleum*, oil.] One of three metamers having the formula C_7H_8O. It is liquid, prepared from tars, and boils at 203° C.; also called *cresylic acid*.

çrē-sor'çin, *n.* Same as *Isorcin*.

çrē-sot'iç, *a.* Of or designating creosote.

çress, *n.* [ME. *cresse*; AS. *cresse*; OFr. *kerson*, *creson*; LL. *cresso*, *cresco*, the cress.] A name given to various plants, particularly those of the mustard family. *Cardamine rotundifolia* is the American water-*cress*; *Lepidium sativum* is common garden-*cress*; *Nasturtium officinale*, water-*cress*, is used as a salad, and is valued in medicine for its antiscorbutic qualities. The leaves have a moderately pungent taste.

Bitter cress; see under *Bitter*.

Not worth a cress; original form of the phrase, *not worth a curse*. [See *Curse*.]

çres-selle', *n.* A wooden rattle used in some Roman Catholic countries during Passion week instead of bells, to give notice of divine worship.

çres'set, *n.* [OFr. *cresset*, *crasset*, a kind of lamp or torch; D. *kruysel*, a hanging lamp.]

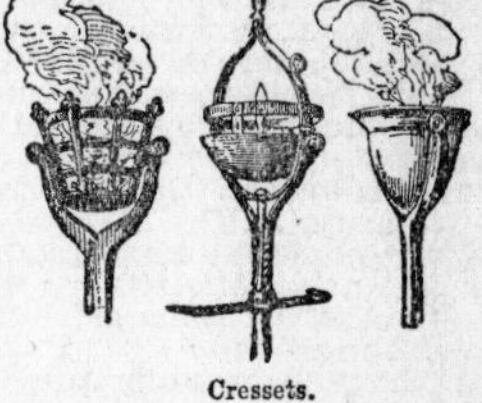
Cressets.

1. In the middle ages, one of various lights; later, a hollow vessel, which held a coil of rope steeped in tar or resin, or other flaming combustibles.

2. An iron frame used by coopers in heating barrels.

3. A chafing-dish.

çress'-rock"et, *n.* The popular name of *Vella pseudocytisus*, a cruciferous plant with yellow flowers.

çress'y, *a.* Abounding in or covered with cresses.

çrest, *n.* [ME. *crest*, *creste*; OFr. *creste*; L. *crista*, a comb or tuft on the head of a bird, a crest.]

1. A tuft, or other excrescence, growing upon the top of an animal's head, as the comb of a cock, the swelling on the head of a serpent, etc.

> Attack his rising *crest* and drive the serpent back.
> —Pitt.

2. Anything resembling, suggestive of, or occupying the same relative position as a *crest*; as, (a) in ancient armor, the plume or tuft affixed to the top of the helmet; hence, the helmet itself; (b) in heraldry, a figure originally intended to represent the ornament of the helmet, but now generally denoting a figure placed upon a wreath, coronet, or cap of maintenance (as in the smaller figure), above both helmet and shield; (c) the foamy, feather-like top of a wave; (d) the summit of a hill or other elevation; (e) in fortification, the top of a slope; (f) in architecture, a cresting.

Crest on a Helmet.

Crest on a Wreath.

> She watched my *crest* among them all.
> —Tennyson.

3. The rising part of a horse's neck.

4. Figuratively, pride; courage; spirit.

çrest, *v.t.*; crested, *pt., pp.*; cresting, *ppr.* 1. To furnish with a crest; to serve as a crest for.

2. To mark with long waving streaks.

çrest, *v.i.* To assume the form of a crest.

çrest'ed, *a.* 1. Wearing a crest; adorned with a crest; as, a *crested* helmet.

2. In biology, having a tuft like a crest.

çrest'fall"en (-fạln), *a.* 1. Dejected; cast down; bowed; dispirited; spiritless.

2. Having the upper part of the neck hanging on one side, as a horse.

çrest'ing, *n.* In architecture, carving or ornamental work, as on the peak of a roof.

çrest'less, *a.* Without a crest; of low birth.

çrest-ol'ȧ-try, *n.* [L. *crista*, a crest, and Gr. *latreia*, worship.] Deference paid on account of rank, station, or wealth; toadyism.

çrest'=tīle, *n.* A tile shaped like an inverted V, covering the ridge of a roof.

çrē'syl, *n.* [From *cre(o)sote* and *-yl*.] An unsaturated hydrocarbon, C_7H_7, of the aromatic series.

çrē-syl'iç, *a.* Pertaining to or derived from cresyl.

Cresylic acid; cresol.

çrē-tā'ceous, *a.* [L. *cretaceus*, from *creta*, chalk.]

1. Chalky; like chalk; abounding with chalk.

2. [C—] In geology, of or relating to the epoch immediately preceding the Eocene and following the Jurassic.

Cretaceous group; the upper strata of the secondary series common to Europe and a part of Asia, consisting chiefly of chalk.

Çrē-tā'ceous, *n.* In geology, the Cretaceous group.

çrē-tā'ceous-ly, *adv.* In a chalky manner.

çrē-tac'iç, *a.* Cretaceous.

Çrē'tăn, *a.* Relating or pertaining to Crete or Candia, an island situated in the Mediterranean.

Çrē'tăn, *n.* A native or inhabitant of Crete.

çrē'tā-ted, *a.* Rubbed with chalk. [Rare.]

Çrēte, *n.* A Cretan.

çrē-te-fac'tion, *n.* Chalk formation.

Çrē'tiăn, *a.* and *n.* Same as *Cretan.*

çrē'tiç, *n.* [L. *Creticus*; Gr. *krētikos* (supply *pous*, foot), a Cretan foot.] In ancient prosody, a poetic foot of three syllables, one short between two long syllables.

Çrē'ti-cism, *n.* Deceit; lying; Cretism.

çrē'tin, *n.* [Fr. *crétin*; origin uncertain.] One afflicted with cretinism.

çrē'tin-ism, *n.* A peculiar endemic disease common in Switzerland, and found also in some other mountainous countries. It resembles rickets in its general symptoms, but is accompanied by mental imbecility from the first.

çrē'tin-ous, *a.* Characteristic of cretin.

Çrē'tism, *n.* [Gr. *Krētismos*, lying, from *Krētizein*, to speak like a Cretan, to lie; *Krēs*, *Krētos*, a Cretan.] A falsehood; from the reputation of the Cretans as liars and deceivers.

çrē-tonne' (-ton'), *n.* [Fr., from *Creton*, the man who first manufactured it.] A cotton cloth having various textures of surface, and pictorial and other patterns printed on one side; used for curtains, draperies, etc.

çrē'tōse, *a.* Chalky. [Obs.]

çreut'zēr (kroit'sēr), *n.* Same as *Kreutzer.*

çreux (krū), *n.* [Fr., hollow.] Intaglio; only in the following phrase:

En creux; cut below the surface, as sculpturing.

çre-vȧl-lé' (-lā'), *n.* [Port. *cavalla*, a fish.] A fish; the cavally.

çre-vȧsse', *n.* [Fr. *crevasse*, a chink, cleft, from *crever*, to break; L. *crepare*, to break, burst, crack.]

1. A rift in a glacier, of some depth and varying widths.

2. A gap in a river embankment occasioned by pressure or high water. [U. S.]

Crevasse in the Alps.

çrev'et, *n.* [A variant of *cruet.*] A melting-pot used by goldsmiths.

çrev'ice, *n.* [ME. *crevace*, *crevasse*; OFr. *crevace*, a chink, cleft, from *crever*, to break; L. *crepare*, to crack, burst, break.] A crack; a cleft; a fissure; a rent; an opening; as, a *crevice* in a wall.

çrev'ice, *v.t.* To crack; to flaw. [Rare.]

çrev'iced (-ist), *a.* Having crevices or clefts.

çrev'is, *n.* The crawfish. [Rare.]

çrew (krö), *n.* [ME. *crewe*, a form of *accrue*, an accession, addition, company; OFr. *acreue*, pp. of *accroître*, to increase, from L. *adcrescere*; *ad*, to, and *crescere*, to grow.]

1. An accrue or reinforcement. [Obs.]

2. A company of persons, implying derogation or ridicule; as, an ill-bred *crew*.

3. Nautically, (a) the company of seamen who man a ship, vessel, or boat; the company belonging to a vessel; (b) the company or gang of a carpenter, gunner, boatswain, etc.

4. Any body of workers assigned to a definite undertaking; as, a threshing *crew*.

Syn.—Band, company, complement, force, gang, set.

çrew, *n.* The shearwater of the Isle of Man.

çrew, *v.*, past tense of *crow*.

çrew'el, *n.* [Dim. of *clew*, a ball of thread.] Two-threaded worsted yarn slackly twisted and used in embroidery.

çrew'els, *n.pl.* [Scot., from Fr. *écrouelles*, scrofula.] Scrofulous swellings of the glands of the neck; written also *cruels*.

çrew'el=stitch, *n.* An embroidery stitch in crewel-work.

çrew'el=wŏrk, *n.* Embroidery done with crewel.

çrew'et, *n.* See *Cruet.*

çrib, *n.* [AS. *crib*, *cryb*; D. *krib*; L.G. *kribbe*; Ice. *krubba*; Dan. *krybbe*, a crib, manger.]

1. A small building; a cottage. [Obs.]

2. An open wooden rack at which live stock feed; a manger; also, a stall.

3. A bin for produce; as, a corn*crib*.

4. A small bed for a child to sleep in.

5. A jail or lockup.

6. A building, particularly a saloon. [Thieves' slang.]

7. A superstructure, as of logs, securely weighted in soft ground or under water, to act as a base for building operations, a *crib*work.

8. A floating foundation, strongly built.

9. A shaft lining; cribbing.

10. A theft, or the thing stolen; specifically, anything copied from an author and not acknowledged; also a literal translation of a classic author for the use of students. [Colloq.]

11. In the game of cribbage, a set of cards made up of two thrown from the hand of each player.

12. A net for fish; a pound.

13. A division of a raft. [Canada.]

çrib, *v.t.*; cribbed, *pt.*, *pp.*; cribbing, *ppr.* 1. To inclose, as in a crib; to confine; to cage; as, *cribbed* in a narrow space.

2. To put away (produce) for future use; as, to *crib* fifty bushels of corn.

3. To steal; also to make use of (a crib) in translating.

4. To furnish a crib for (a shaft).

çrib, *v.i.* 1. To be confined.

2. To use a crib for translating.

3. To do crib-biting, as a horse.

çrib'bāge, *n.* A game at cards, in which the dealer counts the cards of his hand, those of the crib, and a turned card, toward his score. It is played with a full pack, usually by two persons.

çrib'bāge=bōard, *n.* A board having holes supporting pegs with which to score at cribbage.

çrib'bēr, *n.* One who cribs.

çrib'bing, *n.* 1. Crib-biting.

2. A plank lining, as of a well or shaft, keeping the dirt from caving, etc.

çrib'=bīt"ing, *n.* A bad habit of horses in which they bite on some object, simultaneously inhaling the breath; cribbing.

çrib'ble, *n.* [ME. *cribil*; Fr. *crible*, a sieve; LL. *cribellum*, dim. of L. *cribrum*, a sieve.]

1. A coarse sieve or screen.

2. Coarse flour or meal.

çrib'ble, *v.t.*; cribbled, *pt.*, *pp.*; cribbling, *ppr.* To sift; to cause to pass through a sieve or riddle.

çri-bel'lum, *n.*; *pl.* **çri-bel'lȧ.** [LL. *cribellum*, dim. of *cribrum*, a sieve.] A sieve-like spinning organ accessory to the spinneret of certain spiders of the family *Ciniflonidæ*.

çrib'rāte, *a.* [L. *cribratus*, from *cribrum*, a sieve.] Cribriform; cribrose.

çri-brā'tion, *n.* [From L. *cribrare*, to sift; *cribrum*, a sieve.] In pharmacy, separation by sifting.

çrib'ri-fọrm, *a.* Having holes or apertures like those of a sieve; sieve-shaped.

çrib'rōse, *a.* Cribriform.

çrib'wŏrk, *n.* A frame of logs arranged as those of a house, the inclosed space being heavily weighted; a form of construction common for superstructures, especially those in soft land or water.

çriç, *n.* [Fr. *cric*, a jackscrew.] A controller for a lamp having a circular wick.

çrick, *n.* A creak. [Obs.]

çrick, *n.* [ME. *cricke*, *crykke*, a crick in the neck, a twist or bend.] A spasmodic affection of some part of the body, as of the neck or back, rendering it difficult to move the part affected; local spasm or cramp.

çrick, *n.* 1. A cranny or crevice.

2. A rivulet; a creek. [Local, U. S.]

çrick'et, *n.* [ME. *creket*, *crykette*; OFr. *crequet*; Pr. *cricot*, a cricket; M.D. *kriecker*, a cricket, a creaker. Imitative of the sharp sound.] A chirping insect of the genus *Gryllus*, or *Acheta* of some naturalists, belonging to the order *Orthoptera*. There are several species. The American *cricket*, especially common in grain-fields, is *Gryllus niger* or *Gryllus neglectus*; the house-*cricket* is the *Acheta* (*Gryllus*) *domestica*; the mole-*cricket* is the *Gryllotalpa vulgaris*; the New Zealand grand *cricket* is the *Dinacrida heteracantha*. The name is also given to certain locustids.

çrick'et, *n.* [Prob. from OFr. *criquet*, a stick used in a game.]

1 An open-air game played with bats, balls, and wickets, long peculiar to England, but now popular throughout the British empire and occasionally played in the United States.

2. A game played by schoolboys in which a small, doubly pointed, cylindrical piece of wood is alternately pitched and batted from a hole; also, such piece of wood used in the game. [Local, U. S.]

çrick'et, *n.* [AS. *cricc*, *crycc*, a crooked staff, crutch, used in the sense of a stool or wicket.] A footstool.

çrick'et, *v.i.* To play cricket.

çrick'et=bīrd, *n.* The grasshopper-warbler, *Sylvia locustella*, so called from its note resembling that of a cricket.

çrick'et-ēr, *n.* One who plays at cricket.

çrick'et=frog, *n.* *Acris gryllus*, or any similar chirping tree-frog.

çrī'cō-. A combining form, from Greek *krikos*, a ring, circle, and used in anatomy and medicine to indicate relation to the cricoid cartilage; as, *crico*thyroid.

çrī'çoid, *a.* [Gr. *krikos*, a ring, and *eidos*, form.] Ring-like; applied to a round ring-like cartilage of the larynx.

çrī-cō-thȳ'roid, *a.* [*Crico-*, and Gr. *thyreoeidēs*, shield-shaped; *thyreos*, a large shield, and *eidos*, form.] Relating to or connected with both the cricoid and thyroid cartilages.

çried, *v.*, past tense of *cry*.

çrī'ēr, *n.* [ME. *cryour*, *cryar*; OFr. *crieor*, a crier, from *crier*, to cry.] One who cries; one who makes a public proclamation; especially, an officer whose duty is to proclaim the orders or commands of a court, etc.

Town crier; formerly, one who publicly cried notice of sales and other news.

çrīme, *n.* [OFr. *crime*; L. *crimen*, an accusation, fault, crime, from *cernere*; Gr. *krinein*, to decide, judge.]

1. Any important offense against the laws of right; something seriously at variance with morality or general well-doing; iniquity; vice.

2. In law, an act punishable by statute.

Capital crime; a crime punishable with death.

çrīme'fụl, *a.* Criminal; wicked. [Obs.]

çrīme'less, *a.* Free from crime; innocent.

çrim'i-năl, *a.* [LL. *criminalis*, from *crimen*, a crime, fault.]

1. Guilty of a crime; applied to persons.

2. Partaking of the nature of a crime; involving a crime; that violates a law of morality or well-doing; as, theft is a *criminal* act.

> Ornaments only indications of vice, not *criminal* in themselves. —Addison.

3. Relating to crime; opposed to *civil*; as, a *criminal* code; *criminal* law.

Criminal action; see *Penal action* under *Action*, n. 8.

Criminal conversation; adultery.

çrim'i-năl, *n.* 1. One who has committed a crime.

2. One who has been legally convicted of crime.

Syn.—Culprit, malefactor, evil-doer, transgressor, felon, convict.

çrim'i-năl-ist, *n.* An authority in criminal law.

çrim-i-nal'i-ty, *n.* [LL. *criminalitas*, from *criminalis*, pertaining to crime; *crimen*, a crime.] The quality of being criminal, or a violation of law; guiltiness.

> This is by no means the only criterion of *criminality*. —Blackstone.

çrim'i-năl-ly, *adv.* In a criminal manner.

çrim'i-năl-ness, *n.* Criminality. [Rare.]

çrim'i-năl-oid, *a.* [L. *criminalis*, pertaining to crime, and Gr. *eidos*, form.] Having an inherited predisposition toward crime.

çrim'i-năl-oid, *n.* One having an inherited tendency to criminality.

çrim'i-nāte, *v.t.*; criminated, *pt.*, *pp.*; criminating, *ppr.* [L. *criminatus*, pp. of *criminari*, to accuse of a crime; *crimen*, a crime.]

1. To accuse; to charge with a crime; to allege to be guilty of a crime, offense, or wrong.

2. To incriminate; to involve or implicate in a crime.

> Our municipal laws do not require the offender to plead guilty or *criminate* himself.—Scott.

çrim-i-nā'tion, *n.* [L. *criminatio*, from *criminari*, to accuse of a crime; *crimen*, a crime.] The act of accusing; accusation.

çrim'i-nā-tive, *a.* Accusing of crime; criminatory.

crim′i-nȧ-tō-ry, *a.* Of or concerned with crimination or accusation; criminative.

crim-i-nol′ō-gist, *n.* One versed in criminology.

crim-i-nol′ō-gy, *n.* [L. *crimen*, a crime, and Gr. *-logia*, from *legein*, to speak.] The science of crime and its perpetrators.

crim′i-nous, *a.* Very wicked. [Obs.]

crim′i-nous-ly, *adv.* Criminally. [Obs.]

crim′i-nous-ness, *n.* Wickedness; criminality. [Obs.]

crim′ō-sin, *a.* and *n.* [Obs.] See *Crimson.*

crimp, *v.t.*; crimped, *pt.*, *pp.*; crimping, *ppr.* [D. *krimpen*; Dan. *krympe*, to shrink; W. *crimpiaw*, to pinch, crimp, from *crimp*, a sharp edge.]

1. To form into ridges, waves, or curls; as, to *crimp* a ruffle; to *crimp* the hair.

2. To close or indent (a cartridge-case); to crease.

3. To shape, as boot-uppers.

4. To grasp; to seize; by extension, to decoy, as for the army or navy. [Eng.]

5. In cookery, to crimple or cause to contract, as the flesh of a live fish, by gashing it with a knife, to give it greater hardness and make it more crisp.

crimp, *n.* 1. A crimper.

2. [*pl.*] That which is crimped; as, a dress all ruffles and *crimps.*

3. One acting as a stool-pigeon by bringing men to a resort for illegal purposes, particularly a procurer of unwilling recruits for the army or navy.

4. A game at cards. [Obs.]

crimp, *a.* 1. Easily crumbled; friable; brittle. [Rare.]

2. Not consistent.

crimp′āge, *n.* The act of crimping.

crimp′ēr, *n.* One who or that which crimps; a crimping-machine.

crimp′ing-house, *n.* A resort frequented by crimps. [See *Crimp*, n. 3.]

crimp′ing-i″ron (-ūrn), *n.* A curling-iron for the hair; also, an appliance for fluting or waving cloth.

crimp′ing-mȧ-chīne″, *n.* One of various machines used in corrugating, fluting, crimping, etc.

crimp′ing-pin, *n.* A kind of hairpin used to wave the hair.

crim′ple, *v.t.*; crimpled, *pt.*, *pp.*; crimpling, *ppr.* [Dim. of *crimp.*] To contract or draw together; to shrink; to cause to shrink; to curl.

crimp′y, *a.* Having a frizzled or crimped appearance.

crim′sŏn, *n.* [ME. *crimosin*, *cramosin*; OFr. *cramoisyne*; LL. *carmesinus*; from Ar. *qermez*, crimson; from Sans. *krmija*, produced by a worm; *krmi*, a worm, insect, and *jan*, to produce.] A deep red color; a red tinged with blue; also, a red color in general; as, the virgin *crimson* of modesty.

crim′sŏn, *a.* Of a beautiful deep red; as, the *crimson* blush of modesty.

crim′sŏn, *v.t.*; crimsoned, *pt.*, *pp.*; crimsoning, *ppr.* To dye with crimson; to dye of a deep red color; to make red.

crim′sŏn, *v.i.* To become of a deep red color; to be tinged with red; to blush.

crī′nȧl, *a.* [L. *crinalis*, from *crinis*, hair.] Belonging to hair.

crī′nā-ted, *a.* Hairy.

crī′nȧ-tō-ry, *a.* Same as *Crinitory.*

crin′cum, *n.* A cramp; a contraction; a turn or bend; a whimsy. [Colloq.]

crīned, *a.* [Fr. *crin*; L. *crinis*, a hair.] In heraldry, having hair.

crī′nel, *n.* Same as *Crinet.*

crī′net, *n.* [Dim. of Fr. *crin*; L. *crinis*, a hair.] A small, thin feather.

cringe, *v.t.* [AS. *cringan*, *crincan*, to yield, fall.] To contract; to draw together. [Obs.]

cringe, *v.i.* To bow; to bend with servility; to fawn; to make court by truckling or flattery.

Flatterers are always bowing and *cringing.* —Arbuthnot.

Syn.—Crouch, fawn, flatter, grovel, truckle.

cringe, *n.* A crouching, as in servility.

cringe′ling, *n.* One who cringes meanly.

crin′gēr, *n.* One who cringes or flatters.

crin′ging-ly, *adv.* In a cringing or groveling manner.

crin′gle, *n.* [L.G. *kringel*; Ice. *kringla*, a disk, orb, circle.]

1. A withe for fastening a gate. [Eng.]

2. Nautically, a short rope worked into the boltrope of a sail so as to form a ring or eye; written also *crengle* and *crenkle.*

Cringle.

crin-i-cul′tūr-ăl, *a.* [L. *crinis*, hair, and *cultura*, culture.] Relating to the growth of hair. [Rare.]

crī-nig′ēr-ous, *a.* [L. *criniger*, from *crinis*, hair, and *gerere*, to bear.] Covered with hair; hairy. [Rare.]

crī′nīte, *a.* [L. *crinitus*, haired, pp. of *crinire*, to cover with hair; *crinis*, hair.]

1. Having the appearance of a tuft of hair; also written *crinital.*

2. In biology, bearded with long hairs, or having tufts of long weak hairs on the surface.

crī′ni-tō-ry, *a.* Made of or pertaining to hair; spelled also *crinatory.*

crin′kle, *v.t.* and *v.i.*; crinkled, *pt.*, *pp.*; crinkling, *ppr.* [ME. *crenklen*, to bend, turn; D. *krinkelen*, to turn, wind.]

I. *v.t.* To form with short turns or wrinkles; to mold into inequalities; to corrugate.

II. *v.i.* To turn or wind; to bend; to wrinkle; to run in and out in little or short bends or turns; to curl; as, the lightning *crinkles.*

crin′kle, *n.* A wrinkle; a winding or turn; sinuosity.

crin′kle-rọọt, *n.* *Dentaria diphylla*, the pepper-root or toothwort.

crin′kly, *a.* Waved; crimped.

crī′noid, *n.* A member of the *Crinoidea.*

crī′noid, **crī-noi′dăl**, *a.* Belonging or pertaining to the *Crinoidea.*

Crī-noid′ē-ȧ, *n.pl.* [L., from Gr. *krinoeidēs*; *krinon*, a lily, and *eidos*, form.] The encrinites, lily-stars, or sea-lilies, an order of *Echinodermata*, chiefly fossil; so named from the resemblance their rayed bodies have, when closed, to a tulip or lily.

crī-noid′ē-ăn, *n.* A crinoid.

crin′ō-line, *n.* [Fr. *crinoline*, haircloth, crinoline; L. *crinis*, hair, and *linum*, flax.]

1. A stiff cloth, originally made of horsehair, used as a lining for various garments, particularly skirts; now applied loosely to any kind of stiffening-material.

2. A stiff skirt in which *crinoline* or some similar fabric is used; also, a hoop-skirt.

crī′nōse, *a.* Hairy. [Rare.]

crī-nos′i-ty, *n.* Hairiness. [Rare.]

Crī′num, *n.* [L., from Gr. *krinon*, a lily.] A genus of bulbous-stemmed, tropical, greenhouse plants, of the amaryllis family, of which there are many species.

crī′ō-sphinx, *n.* [Gr. *krios*, a ram, and *sphinx*, a sphinx.] One of the three varieties of the Egyptian sphinx, characterized by having the head of a ram, as distinguished from the *androsphinx*, with the head of a human being, and *hieracosphinx* or hawk-headed sphinx.

Criosphinx.

crip′ple, *n.* [ME. *cripel*, *crypel*; L.G. *kropel*; D. *kreppel*; O.H.G. *kruppel*; Ice. *kryppill*, from AS. *creopan*, to creep.]

1. A lame person or animal; one who creeps, halts, or limps; one who has lost, totally or partially, or has never enjoyed, the use of his limbs.

2. A bog; also, a shallow. [U. S.]

crip′ple, *a.* Lame. [Rare.]

crip′ple, *v.t.*; crippled, *pt.*, *pp.*; crippling, *ppr.*

1. To lame; to deprive of the use of the limbs, particularly of the legs and feet.

2. To disable; to deprive of power; to render ineffective; to weaken or impair.

Embarrassments *crippling* the energy of the settlement in the Bay. —Palfrey.

crip′ple-ness, *n.* Lameness. [Rare.]

crip′plēr, *n.* See *Graining-board.*

crip′pling, *n.* One of a number of spars or timbers set up as supports against the side of a building.

crip′ply, *a.* Crippled. [Rare.]

crī′sis, *n.*; *pl.* **crī′sēs.** [L. *crisis*; Gr. *krisis*, a separating, decision, from *krinein*, to decide, separate.]

1. A serious or decisive state of things, or the point of time when an affair must soon terminate or suffer a material change; a turning-point; a critical juncture.

This hour's the very *crisis* of your fate. —Dryden.

2. In medicine, the change of a disease which indicates recovery or death; sometimes used to designate the symptoms accompanying the *crisis.*

crisp, *a.*; *comp.* crisper; *superl.* crispest. [AS. *crisp*, *cirps*, from L. *crispus*, curled, crisp.]

1. Curled; formed into stiff curls or ringlets.

2. Indented; winding; as, *crisp* channels. [Rare.]

3. Brittle; friable; easily broken or crumbled; as, *crisp* crackers.

4. Lively; brisk; sharp or stimulating; as, *crisp* wine or *crisp* air.

5. Fresh; not wilted; as, *crisp* vegetables.

6. Sharp; pointed; witty; short or terse; as, a *crisp* literary style; a *crisp* answer.

7. In botany, curled; applied to a leaf when the border is so much more dilated than the disk that it necessarily becomes crinkled and twisted.

8. In entomology, crispate.

crisp, *v.t.*; crisped, *pt.*, *pp.*; crisping, *ppr.* [ME. *crispen*; L. *crispare*, to curl, from *crispus*, curled, crisp.]

1. To curl; to twist; to contract or form into ringlets, as the hair; to wreathe or interweave, as the branches of trees.

2. To wrinkle or curl into little undulations; to ripple; to cause to be crinkled or wavy.

3. To render crisp; as, to *crisp* potatoes.

crisp, *v.i.* 1. To form little curls or undulations; to curl.

The bubbling runnel *crispeth.* —Tennyson.

2. To snap lightly; to crackle.

cris′pāte, **cris′pā-ted**, *a.* [L. *crispatus*, pp. of *crispare*, to curl, crisp; *crispus*, curled, crisp.] Curled or wavy; particularly, (a) in botany, crisp; (b) in entomology, with an undulating or corrugated edge or margin. In this sense, also *crisp.*

cris-pā′tion, *n.* 1. The act of curling, or state of being curled. [Obs.]

2. In surgery, a slight morbid or natural contraction of any part, as that of the minute arteries of a cut wound when they retract.

3. A minute undulation or quiver on the surface of a liquid caused by vibrations of the containing vessel.

cris′pȧ-tūre, *n.* A curling; the state of being curled.

crisp′ēr, *n.* One who or that which crisps; specifically, a crisping-iron.

Cris′pin, *n.* An appellation given to a shoemaker, from Crispinus, the patron saint of the craft; applied particularly to a member of the shoemakers' trade-union.

crisp′ing-i″ron (-ūrn), *n.* An instrument for curling hair or crimping cloth.

cris-pi-sul′cănt, *a.* Wavy; undulating. [Obs.]

crisp′ly, *adv.* In a crisp manner.

crisp′ness, *n.* A state of being crisp, curled, or brittle.

crisp′y, *a.* 1. Curled; formed into stiff ringlets; as, *crispy* locks.

2. Brittle; easy to break; as, a *crispy* cake.

3. Brisk; fresh; sharp; exhilarating; as, *crispy* air.

cris′sȧ, *n.*, pl. of *crissum.*

cris′săl, *a.* In ornithology, (a) of or pertaining to the crissum; (b) having a crissum that is bright-colored.

criss′cross, *v.t.* and *v.i.*; crisscrossed, *pt.*, *pp.*; crisscrossing, *ppr.* I. *v.t.* To interlace, as lines or threads; to mark with intersecting or crisscross lines; as, *crisscross* the background with various lines.

II. *v.i.* To intersect or interlace, particularly without method or precision.

criss′cross, *adv.* 1. Crosswise; in different or contrary directions; with irregular intersections.

2. Inharmoniously; unpleasingly; contrarily; as, things are going *crisscross.*

criss′cross, *a.* Crossing and recrossing, as lines drawn at random.

criss′cross, *n.* [A corruption of *christcross.*]

1. The cross or other mark made by an illiterate person in lieu of a written signature.

2. A series of lines that intersect one another at different angles.

3. A children's game consisting of a cross of four lines to be filled in, in a certain way, with marks; called also *tit-tat-to.*

criss′cross-rōw, *n.* Same as *Christcross-row.*

cris′sum, *n.*; *pl.* **cris′sȧ.** [L., from *crissare*, to move the thighs.] In ornithology, the under tail-coverts, collectively; also, the region about the anus, particularly that lying between it and the tail.

cris′tȧ, *n.*; *pl.* **cris′tæ.** [L., a crest, tuft on the head of animals.] In anatomy, a prominence of any kind; particularly, a crest or ridge.

Crista acustica; a ridge in the internal passages of the ear, on which the branches of the auditory nerve terminate.

Crista galli; a projection of the mesethnoid to which the outer fibrous covering of the brain is attached.

cris′tāte, **cris′tā-ted**, *a.* [L. *cristatus*, from *crista*, a crest.]

1. In botany, crested; tufted; having an appendage like a crest or tuft, as some anthers and flowers.

2. In zoölogy, (a) having a crest or crest-like process on some part, generally the head; (b) carinate.

crī-tē′ri-ŏn, *n.*; *pl.* **crī-tē′ri-ȧ.** [Gr. *kritērion*, a test, means of judging, from *kritēs*, a judge, from *krinein*, to judge.] A standard of judging; any established law, rule, principle, or fact, by which facts, propositions, opinions, and behavior are compared, in order to discover their truth or falsehood, or by which a correct judgment may be formed; spelled also, rarely, *criterium.*

Syn.—Rule, measure, test, standard.

crī-tē′ri-ŏn-ăl, *a.* Relating to or serving as a criterion. [Rare.]

crith, *n.* [Gr. *krithē*, a barleycorn, a weight.] A name given to the weight of one liter of hydrogen at 0° C. and 760 millimeters' pressure, which is 0.0896 of a gram. This is taken as the unit of weight of gaseous chemical substances.

çrith'ō-man-cy, *n.* [Gr. *krithē*, barley, and *manteia*, divination.] A kind of divination by means of the dough of cakes, and the meal strewed over the victims, in ancient sacrifices.

çrit'iç, *n.* [L. *criticus*; Gr. *kritikos*, from *kritēs*, a judge, discerner, from *krinein*, to judge, to separate, to distinguish.]

1. One who compares, judges, or estimates any person or thing; particularly, one who is able to discern and distinguish the beauties and faults in literature and art; one who estimates the value of works of literature and art, in magazines, reviews, etc.

2. One who judges with severity; one who censures or finds fault; a caviler or carper.

3. The art of criticism; the system of principles on which criticism as a science is based.

4. A critical examination or review. [Obs.]

Syn.—Judge, censor, connoisseur.

çrit'iç, *a.* Critical; relating to criticism, or to a critic or critics.

Critic learning flourished most in France. —Pope.

çrit'iç, *v.i.* To criticize; to play the critic. [Obs.]

çrit'iç-ăl, *a.* 1. Relating to criticism; belonging to the art of a critic; based on or in accordance with the principles of criticism; showing exact knowledge; as, a *critical* dissertation on Homer.

2. Having the skill or ability to pass accurate judgment upon literary and artistic matters.

3. Making nice distinctions; capable of judging with accuracy; accurate; exact; particular; fastidious; as, to be *critical* in rites and ceremonies, or in the selection of books; a *critical* taste.

4. Inclined to find fault, or to judge with severity; carping; criticizing harshly.

5. Pertaining to a crisis; decisive; denoting a time or state on which the issue of things depends; important, as regards the consequences; as, a *critical* time or moment; a *critical* juncture.

6. In medicine, producing a crisis or change in a disease; pertaining to or indicating a crisis; as, a *critical* sweat.

7. Formed or situated to determine or decide; important or essential for determining; as, a *critical* post.

8. In a condition of extreme doubt or danger; attended with danger or risk; perilous; hazardous; as, a *critical* undertaking.

9. Differing in or distinguished by slight details; as, *critical* divisions of a group in botany.

Critical angle; in optics, the smallest angle of incidence giving rise to total reflection of a ray of light.

Critical philosophy; a name sometimes given to the philosophical system of Immanuel Kant, which was based upon a critical examination of the human faculty of reason, in its processes, results, and limitations, particularly in matters of metaphysical speculation.

Critical point; (a) in mathematics, that point at which some two or more values of a function of a complex variable are equal; called also *point of ramification*; (b) in physics, that degree of temperature above which a substance, in gaseous form, will not liquefy, however much pressure may be applied; called also *critical temperature*.

Syn.—Exact, accurate, nice, discriminating, captious, fault-finding, decisive, important, momentous.

çrit'iç-ăl-ly, *adv.* 1. In a critical manner; with nice discernment or scrutiny; accurately; exactly; as, to examine evidence *critically*; to observe *critically*.

2. At the crisis; at an opportune time.

3. In a critical situation, place, or condition, so as to command the crisis; as, a town *critically* situated.

çrit'iç-ăl-ness, *n.* 1. The state of being critical; incidence at a particular point of time.

2. Exactness; accuracy; nicety; minute care in examination.

çrit'iç-as-tẽr, *n.* [L. *criticus*, a critic, and dim. *-aster*.] A small or inferior critic; implying contempt.

çrit'i-çīṣ-ā-ble, çrit'i-çīṣe, çrit'i-çī-ṣẽr. See *Criticizable*, etc.

çrit'i-çiṣm, *n.* 1. The act of criticizing or judging of the merits of a thing; examination of excellences and faults; critical judgment, opinion, or estimate; as, *criticism* presupposes special knowledge.

2. The art or science of judging with propriety of the excellences and faults of a thing, particularly of a literary or artistic production; as, the rules of *criticism*.

3. Adverse judgment; unfavorable comment; a harsh or severe opinion; as, his *criticism* was justifiable.

4. Investigation concerning the source, genuineness, worth, and authenticity of text of documents in literature and history. The branch of such inquiry that deals with the integrity of the text is known as *lower criticism*; that which treats of the history and literary merit of writings as *higher criticism*.

çrit'i-çīz-ā-ble, çrit'i-çiṣ-ā-ble, *a.* Subject to criticism.

çrit'i-çīze, çrit'i-çīṣe, *v.t.*; criticized, *pt.*, *pp.*; criticizing, *ppr.* 1. To make a critical estimate of; to pass judgment on with respect to excellences or defects; to utter or write a critical opinion on the merit of; as, to *criticize* the writings of Milton.

2. To point out the faults in; to judge adversely; to express disapproval of; to censure.

çrit'i-çīze, çrit'i-çīṣe, *v.i.* 1. To judge critically; to express criticisms.

Cavil you may, but never *criticise*. —Pope.

2. To animadvert upon a thing; to utter censure; to find fault; to express harsh and severe judgments.

çrit'i-çī-zẽr, çrit'i-çī-ṣẽr, *n.* A person who utters or writes criticisms.

çri-tïque' (-tēk'), *n.* [Fr. *critique*, from Gr. *kritikos* (supply *technē*, art), critical, from *krinein*, to separate, judge.]

1. A critical analysis or examination of the merits of a production, especially in art or literature; as, Addison's *critique* on "Paradise Lost."

2. The science of criticism; the standard or rules of judging of the merit of any work; also spelled *critic*.

3. A critic. [Obs.]

çri-tïque', *v.t.* and *v.i.* To criticize. [Obs.]

çriz'zle, çriz'zel, *n.* [Prov. Eng.] A kind of roughness on the surface of glass, which clouds its transparency.

çriz'zle, *v.i.*; crizzled, *pt.*, *pp.*; crizzling, *ppr.* To become rough; to have the surface, as of glass or skin, wrinkled or drawn.

çriz'zling, çriz'zel-ing, *n.* Same as *Crizzle*.

çrōak, *v.i.*; croaked, *pt.*, *pp.*; croaking, *ppr.* [ME. *crouken*; AS. *cracettan*, to croak; O.H.G. *chrockezan*, to croak; an imitative word.]

1. To make a low, hoarse noise in the throat, as a frog, crow, or the like; also, to make a sound resembling that of a frog or raven, as the utterance of a person affected with hoarseness.

2. To speak with a low, hollow voice; to cry dismally; to forebode evil; to complain; to grumble.

3. To die; from the gurgling sound in the throat of a dying person. [Slang.]

çrōak, *v.t.* To utter hoarsely; to predict dismally. [Rare.]

çrōak, *n.* The low, harsh sound uttered by a frog or a raven, or a like sound.

çrōak'ẽr, *n.* 1. One who croaks, murmurs, or grumbles; one who complains unreasonably; one who takes a desponding view of everything; an alarmist.

2. Any bird or animal that makes a croaking sound.

3. The name applied to several fishes of the family *Sciænidæ*, as the drum, the queenfish, etc., from the croaking sound they make when caught.

Çrō'at, *n.* 1. A person born or living in Croatia, a province of Austria; especially, a Slavic native.

2. Formerly, a member of a somewhat irregular cavalry force made up in large part of Croats and serving in the Austrian army.

Çrō-ā'tiăn (-shăn), *a.* Relating to the Croats or to Croatia.

Çrō-ā'tiăn, *n.* 1. A Croat.

2. The dialect of the Slavic Croats.

çrō'ceous, *a.* [L. *croceus*, from *crocus*, saffron.] Yellow, like saffron.

çrō'ce-tin, *n.* [L. *crocus*, saffron.] A brilliant yellow dye made from crocin; also, crocin itself.

çrōche, *n.* [OFr. *croche*, f. of *croc*, a hook.] A little bud or knob about the top of a deer's horn.

çrō-chet' (-shā'), *n.* [Fr., dim. of *croc*, a hook.] A kind of knitting in which thread of any material,—silk, wool, or cotton,—is looped and interwoven by means of a needle, the stitches used being generally more elaborate than the regular knitting-stitch.

çrō-chet' (-shā'), *v.t.* and *v.i.*; crocheted, *pt.*, *pp.*; crocheting, *ppr.* I. *v.t.* To form by means of crocheting; as, to *crochet* lace.

II. *v.i.* To do crochet-work.

çrō-chet'=nee"dle (-shā'-), *n.* A hooked needle used in crocheting.

çrō'ci-ā-ry (-shi-), *n.*; *pl.* **çrō'ci-ā-ries.** [ME. *crocer*; OFr. *croce*; LL. *crocea*, *crocia*, a bishop's staff.] A cross-bearer for an archbishop. [Obs.]

çrō-cid'ō-līte, *n.* [Gr. *krokis*, *krokidos*, the nap on cloth, and *lithos*, stone.]

1. A mineral, consisting principally of silicate of iron and soda, occurring in asbestos-like fibers, also massive, in Griqualand, South Africa, and in the region of the Vosges mountains.

2. The tiger-eye.

çrō'cin, *n.* [Gr. *krokos*, saffron.] A red or reddish-yellow coloring-matter obtained from the pods of the *Gardenia grandiflora* of China, and from saffron, *Crocus sativus*; called also *polychroite*.

çrock, *n.* An old sheep. [Scot.]

çrock, *n.* [ME. *crocke*, *crokk*; AS. *crocca*; Ice. *krukka*; Sw. *kruka*; Dan. *krukke*, a crock.]

1. An earthen vessel; especially, a pot or jar.

2. A broken piece of crockery.

çrock, *v.t.*; crocked, *pt.*, *pp.*; crocking, *ppr.* To store or pack in a crock; as, to *crock* butter.

çrock, *n.* A low seat; a stool. [Prov. Eng.]

çrock, *n.* Soot; the black matter collected from combustion, as on pots and kettles, or in a chimney; also, stain or discoloration, as from the coloring in dyed fabrics.

çrock, *v.t.*; crocked (krokt), *pt.*, *pp.*; crocking, *ppr.* To blacken, as with soot; to soil or stain with the coloring-matter of cloth. [Colloq.]

çrock, *v.i.* To give off crock, stain, or smut.

çrock'ẽr, *n.* A maker of crockery. [Obs.]

çrock'ẽr-y, *n.* Earthenware; vessels formed of clay, glazed and baked. The term is applied to the coarser kinds of ware used for domestic purposes.

çrock'et, *n.* [ME. *croket*, a roll, or lock of hair; OFr. *croquet*, *crochet*, dim. of *croc*, a hook.]

1. In architecture, an ornament placed at the angles of pediments, canopies, pinnacles, etc., resembling buds of trees or bunches of foliage.

2. One of the terminal snags on a stag's horn.

3. A woman's coiffure. [Obs.]

Pinnacle decorated with Crockets.

çrock'et-ed, *a.* In architecture, furnished or ornamented with crockets.

çrock'et-ing, *n.* Embellishment of crockets.

çrock'y, *a.* Smutty; sooty.

çroç'ō-dīle, *n.* [L. *crocodilus*; Gr. *krokodeilos*, a kind of lizard, a crocodile.]

1. A genus of saurians, the type of the family *Crocodilidæ*, comprising the largest living forms of reptiles, some species attaining a length of thirty feet. They are oviparous, depositing eggs in the sand. *Crocodilus niloticus* or *vulgaris* is the species frequenting the Nile; *Crocodilus americanus* is found in Florida; the gavial is termed the Ganges *crocodile*.

Crocodile (*Crocodilus niloticus* or *vulgaris*).

2. In logic, a captious and sophistical argument contrived to draw one into a snare.

çroç'ō-dīle, *a.* Of or pertaining to or resembling a crocodile.

Crocodile tears; false or hypocritical tears; a term derived from the fabulous story that crocodiles shed tears over those whom they devour.

çroç'ō-dīle=bïrd, *n.* *Pluvianus ægyptius*, a plover-like bird associated with the crocodile.

Çroç-ō-dil'i-ȧ, *n.pl.* [L., from *crocodilus*; Gr. *krokodeilos*, a lizard, crocodile.] An order of saurian reptiles, found in the Old and New Worlds, including the crocodiles, gavials, alligators, and like animals now extinct.

çroç-ō-dil'i-ăn, *a.* Relating or pertaining to the crocodile.

çroç-ō-dil'i-ăn, *n.* One of the order *Crocodilia*.

Çroç-ō-dil'i-dæ, *n.pl.* A family typical of *Crocodilia*.

çroç-ō-dil'i-ty, *n.* In logic, a false or captious mode of arguing.

çrō'çois-īte, *n.* Same as *Crocoite*.

çrō'çō-īte, *n.* [Gr. *krokoeis*, of a saffron color, from *krokos*, saffron.] A mineral, native chromate of lead or red-lead ore, used as a pigment.

çrō'çon-āte, *n.* A salt of croconic acid.

çrō-çon'iç, *a.* [L. *crocus*; Gr. *krokos*, saffron.] Of, pertaining to, or derived from saffron.

Croconic acid; a yellow crystalline substance, $C_5H_2O_5$, strongly acid and of a yellow color.

çrō'çōse, *n.* [Gr. *krokos*, saffron.] A metamer of glucose, $C_6H_{12}O_6$, derived from crocin.

çrō'çus, *n.* [L. *crocus*; Gr. *krokos*, saffron, also the crocus, from its color.]

1. [C—] A genus of iridaceous herbaceous plants, consisting of many hardy species. They are dwarf herbs with fibrous-coated corms and grass-like leaves appearing after the flowers. *Crocus sativus* is common saffron.

2. Any plant of this genus.
3. In chemistry, a yellow polishing-powder, any metal calcined to a red or deep yellow color.

croft, *v.t.*; crofted, *pt., pp.*; crofting, *ppr.* To subject (linen) to the sun's rays after treatment with an alkaline dye.

croft, *n.* [AS. *croft*, a small inclosed field; D. *kroft*, a hillock; Gael. *croit*, a hump, hillock.] A small field adjoining or near to a dwelling-house, and used for pasture, tillage, or other purposes; any small tract of land; a small farm.

croft'ẽr, *n.* One who cultivates a croft.

crois, *n.* A cross. [Obs.]

croi-sāde', croi-sä'dō, *n.* [Fr. *croisade*, a crusade; OFr. *crois*; L. *crux*, a cross.] A crusade. [Obs.]

croise, *n.* [Fr. *croisé*, a crusader, from OFr. *crois*, a cross.] A crusader.

Croix de Guerre (krwä de gãr) *n.* [Fr.] The French war cross, awarded only for acts of great bravery performed under fire.

crō'ki-nōle, *n.* A parlor game played with small wooden disks on a table; squails.

crom'lech, *n.* [W. *cromlec*; *crom*, bent, bowed, and *llec*, a flat stone.] In archæology, large flat stones laid across others in an upright position; very commonly found in parts of Wales, in Devonshire and Cornwall, and other districts of England, as well as in other countries. They are supposed to have been used for burial purposes. Called also *dolmen*.

Cromlech at Lanyon, Cornwall.

crō-mor'nȧ, *n.* [Fr. *cromorne*; G. *krummhorn*, a crooked horn, cornet; *krumm*, crooked, and *horn*, horn.] A reed-stop of an organ, similar in tone to a clarinet; corruptly written *cremona*.

crōne, *n.* [Ir. *criona*, old; *crion*, dry, withered; *crionaim*, to wither, fade, decay; W. *crina*, to wither.]
1. An old ewe.
2. An old person, commonly a woman; implying depreciation.

crō'nel, *n.* In heraldry, the coronal as a bearing.

crō'net, *n.* [Contr. from *coronet*.]
1. In farriery, a coronet.
2. In heraldry, a cronel.

Crō'ni-ăn, *a.* [L. *Cronius*, neut. *Cronium* (supply *mare*, sea); Gr. *Kronios ōkeanos*, northern or Saturnian sea.] Denoting the Arctic Ocean. [Rare.]

cron'stedt-ite (-stet-), *n.* [Named after A. F. *Cronstedt*, a Swedish mineralogist.] A brilliantly vitreous mineral, found crystalline in hexagonal prisms; a hydrous silicate of iron.

crō'ny, *n.*; *pl.* **crō'nies.** 1. A crone. [Obs.]
2. An intimate companion; a chum.

croo'dle, *v.i.* [Scot.] To coo.

croo'dle, *v.i.* [Prov. Eng.] To cuddle; also, to feel cold.

crook, *n.* [ME. *crok*; Ice. *krokr*, a hook, bend; D. *kroke*, a hook; Sw. *kroka*; Gael. *crocan*, a crook, hook.]
1. Any bend, turn, or curve; as, a *crook* in a stick of timber, or in a river.
2. A curving or crooked part; a turn; as, a cane with a large *crook*.
3. Something having a turn or curve; as, (a) a shepherd's staff, curving at the end; (b) the pastoral staff of a bishop or abbot; (c) in Scotland, a pothook; (d) an accessory tube inserted in a wind-instrument, as a cornet, to change its key.
4. A genuflection.
5. A gibbet or gibbet-like object. [Obs.]
6. An artifice; a trick.
7. A criminal, either habitual or occasional; a swindler; a rogue. [Colloq.]
By hook or crook; by some means; if not one way, then by another.

crook, *v.t.*; crooked (krookt), *pt., pp.*; crooking, *ppr.* 1. To bend; to turn from a straight line; to make a curve or hook in.
2. To turn from rectitude; to pervert.
3. To thwart. [Rare.]

crook, *v.i.* To bend or be bent; to be turned from a right line; to curve; to wind.

crook'back, *n.* A hunchback.

crook'backed (-bakt), *a.* Hunchbacked.

crook'bill, *n.* *Anarhynchus frontalis*, a plover of New Zealand, having a bent bill.

crook'ed, *a.* 1. Not straight; bent; curving; winding.
2. Tricky as regards conduct; not to be trusted; dishonest, as a man; unchaste, as a woman.
3. Made illegally; illicit; as, *crooked* liquor. [Colloq.]
Syn.—Curved, incurvating, curving, winding, bowed, awry, oblique, wry, deformed, perverse, deceitful.

crook'ed-ly, *adv.* In a crooked manner.

crook'ed-ness, *n.* The state or quality of being crooked.

crook'en, *v.t.* To make crooked. [Obs.]

Crookes lay'ẽr. A layer or stratum in the residual atmosphere of a vacuous space, in which the molecules recoiling from a heated or electrified surface do not meet other molecules, but impinge on the inclosing walls.

Crookes tūbe. A glass tube, provided with metallic conductors and capable of being exhausted of air on the air-pump, for the study of the electric discharge in rarefied gases. In the *Crookes tube* the exhaustion of the air is ordinarily not carried as far as in the Roentgen ray tube.

crook'neck, *a.* Designating a form of summer squash having a recurving neck.

croon, *v.i.*; crooned, *pt., pp.*; crooning, *ppr.* [ME. *croynen*, to hum, sing; D. *kreunen*, groan, lament; imitative word.]
1. To roar or bellow. [Rare.]
2. To utter a continuous murmur as if in pain; hence, to hum or sing softly.

croon, *v.t.* To hum or sing in a suppressed voice; to soothe.

croon, *n.* [Scot.] A low, hollow, continued moan; a crooned song.

crop, *n.* [AS. *crop*, *croppe*, craw, top, or head of a plant; D. *krop*, an excrescence, the gullet, craw.]
1. The first stomach of a fowl; the craw.
2. The top or end of a thing. [Obs.]
3. Collectively, plants, grain, or fruit gathered for use; harvest; as, the flax-*crop* of South Dakota; the celery-*crop* of Michigan.
4. Corn and other cultivated plants while growing or being planted; as, *crops* are looking fine; putting in a *crop*.
5. Anything cut off or gathered.
6. Hair cut close or short.
7. A bristly wig.
8. In mining, an outcropping lode.
9. A whip, as for hunting, terminating in a loop instead of a lash.
10. A sole-leather hide, untrimmed.
11. A varying weight for certain produce.
12. An earmark.
13. In architecture, an apex-ornament. [Obs.]

crop, *v.t.*; cropped (kropt), *pt., pp.*; cropping, *ppr.* 1. To cut off the ends of (anything); to eat off; to pull off; to pluck; to mow; to reap; as, to *crop* flowers, trees, or grass.
2. To cut off prematurely.
3. To cause to bear a crop; as, to *crop* a field.
4. To trim or pare, as an animal's ears.

crop, *v.i.* 1. To yield harvest. [Obs.]
2. To become partly visible; to show to some extent; with *up* or *out*; as, troubles will *crop up*; coal *cropped out* in several places.

crop'-ēar, *n.* One having cropped ears.

crop'-ēared, *a.* Having the ears cropped.

crop'ful, *a.* Having a full crop or belly; satiated.

crop'pẽr, *n.* A pigeon, the pouter.

crop'pẽr, *n.* 1. A machine for cloth-facing.
2. A tool for clipping rod- or bolt-ends.
3. Something producing a crop; as, flax is a good *cropper* on new land.
4. A renter on shares.

crop'pẽr, *n.* A fall, as from horseback; hence, failure in an undertaking. [Slang.]

crop'pie, *n.* A fish, the crappie.

crop'pie-crown, *n.* A copple-crown.

crop'sick, *a.* Sick from repletion. [Obs.]

crop'sick"ness, *n.* Sickness from repletion. [Obs.]

crop'weed, *n.* A plant, the knapweed.

crō'quȧnt (-kȧnt), *n.* [Fr., ppr. of *croquer*, to crunch.] A crisp, sweet pastry, often containing almonds.

crō-quet' (-kā'), *n.* [Fr., from *croquer*, to crack; Walloon, *croque*, a blow, fillip.]
1. An open-air game played with mallets, balls, posts, and a series of arches on a prepared lawn, the object of the game being the driving of a ball through the arches, subject to certain rules.
2. The act of forcing an opponent's ball out of position by striking one's own ball, the two balls being in contact at the time of the blow.

crō-quet', *v.t.*; croqueted (-kād'), *pt., pp.*; croqueting, *ppr.* To drive by a croquet.

crō-quette' (-ket'), *n.* [Fr., from *croquet*, a crisp cake, from *croquer*, to crunch.] Meat, fish, potatoes, rice, or other material minced fine, seasoned, molded into regular form, and fried brown.

crō-quis' (-kē'), *n.* [Fr.] The first draft; a rough sketch.

crōre, *n.* [Hind. *kror*, *koti*; Sans. *koti*, ten millions.] In the East Indies, ten millions in number.

crosh'ȧ-bell, *n.* A courtezan. [Obs.]

crō'ṣiẽr (-zhẽr), *n.* See *Crozier*.

cros'let, *n.* See *Crosslet*.

cross, *v.t.*; crossed (krost), *pt., pp.*; crossing, *ppr.* 1. To draw or run (a line), or lay (one thing) across another; as, *cross* your x's in writing; *cross* the arms.
2. To cancel by drawing a cross or line over or through; often with *out* or *off*; as, *cross out* (or *off*) what you have written.
3. To pass from side to side of; to pass, or move, or extend over; to span; as, to *cross* a road; a small bridge *crossed* the river.
4. To cause or require to pass or move over; as, he *crossed* his force in battle array.
5. Reflexively, to make the sign of (the cross).
6. To thwart; to obstruct; to hinder; to embarrass; as, to *cross* a purpose or design.
7. To debar or preclude. [Obs.]
8. To intermix (different breeds); to blend (different varieties); as, to *cross* a Wyandotte with a Cochin, or melons with citrons.
9. Nautically, to raise (a yard) to its proper position on a mast.
10. To pass with or without meeting.
11. In English banking, to write the name of a banker or banking company between two lines drawn across the face of (a check); to indorse.
To cross one's mind; to suggest itself to one.
To cross one's path; to stand in one's way.

cross, *v.i.* 1. To lie across; to intersect; to be athwart of one another; as, two avenues *cross* opposite the gate.
2. To move or pass laterally or from one side toward the other, or from place to place; as, to *cross* from Calais to Dover.
3. To interbreed; to become mixed; as, varieties of plants *cross*.
4. To be wanting in agreement or consistency; as, men's actions do not always *cross* with reason. [Obs.]
5. To meet when moving in opposite directions; as, did our letters *cross*?

cross, *n.* [ME. *cros*, *crosse*, *crois*; OFr. *crois*, *croiz*; Pr. *cros*, *croitz*; L. *crux*, a cross.]
1. A gibbet or ancient instrument of torture, generally made of two pieces of timber placed across each other, either at right angles or obliquely, usually with an upright set in the ground and a horizontal crosspiece below the top of the upright. Upon this, criminals were formerly nailed or bound and left to die from exhaustion.

2 3 1 4 5 6 7 8 9 10 11 12 13 14

Forms of Crosses.

1. *Cross of Calvary*; the three steps are said to signify faith, hope, and charity. 2. *Latin Cross*, or crux capitata. 3. *Tau Cross*, or cross of St. Anthony. 4. *Cross of Lorraine*. 5. *Patriarchal Cross*. 6. *St. Andrew's Cross*, or crux decussata. 7. *Greek Cross*, or Cross of St. George, the national saint of England. 8. *Papal Cross*. 9. *Cross nowy quadrat*. 10. *Maltese Cross*, the badge of the knights of Malta. The eight points are said to symbolize the eight beatitudes. 11. *Cross fourchée*. 12. *Cross formy* or *formée*. 13. *Cross potent* or *Jerusalem Cross*. 14. *Cross patonee*; called also *Cross flory*, from the fleurs-de-lis at its ends.

The *cross* as an instrument of torture and as a symbol of immortality was not unknown to the world before the advent of Christianity, but previous to the crucifixion of Christ the two ideas were in no way associated.
2. The emblem or ensign of the Christian religion; a symbol representing the *cross* on which Christ died.
3. [C—] Christianity; the Christian religion.
4. A mark of a *cross* instead of a signature, used by those unable to write.
5. A monument in the form of a *cross*, or surmounted by a *cross*, set up, particularly in Roman Catholic countries, as a shrine, memorial, landmark, or to designate a market-place.
6. Anciently, in England, a coin stamped with the figure of a *cross*.

Monumental Cross, Eyam, Derbyshire.

7. [C—] In theology, the sufferings of Christ by crucifixion; the atonement.

> That he might reconcile both to God in one body by the *cross*. —Eph. ii. 16.

8. The doctrine of Christ's sufferings and of the atonement, or of salvation by Christ.

The preaching of the *cross* is to them that perish foolishness. —1 Cor. i. 18.

9. A trial or affliction which is looked upon among Christians as a means of grace or as a test of devotion.

If any man would come after me let him deny himself, and take up his *cross* daily, and follow me. —Luke ix. 23.

10. Anything that thwarts, obstructs, or perplexes; hindrance; vexation; misfortune; opposition; trial of patience.

Heaven prepares good men with *crosses*. —B. Jonson.

11. A mixing of breeds in producing animals.
12. The issue resulting from *cross*-fertilization between representatives of the same species; hence, anything, which is an admixture of two opposite elements, or the effect of two counter forces; as, a *cross* between progress and savagery; a *cross* between fear and defiance.
13. A casual electrical contact of two wires by which electricity passes from one to the other.
14. An ornament given as a distinction, or worn as a token of membership in some order or society; as, the *cross* of the Legion of Honor; the Victoria *cross*.
15. Various charges employed in heraldry.
16. A crucifix such as may be attached to a rosary or worn about the neck.
17. A contest decided dishonestly, through one of the parties allowing himself to be beaten, for the sake of gaining money by betting or bribery.

Heraldic Cross.

18. Anything in the form of a *cross*.
19. A crozier, or pastoral staff. [Rare.]
20. A pipe-fitting having two arms at right angles to each other; a four-way joint.
Cross and pile; the ancient English game of heads and tails.
Cross bottony; see under *Bottony*.
Red Cross Society; one of various societies having as an object the relief of sick and wounded soldiers. By international agreement in 1864 at Geneva, Switzerland, members of this society are regarded as neutrals.
Southern cross; see under *Southern*.
Surveyor's cross; an apparatus for determining perpendiculars to the main line.
To be, or *live on the cross*; the opposite of being *on the square*; to be dishonest. [Slang.]

çross, *prep.* Athwart; transversely; over; from side to side; so as to intersect. [Obs. or Colloq.]

And *cross* their limits cut a sloping way. —Dryden.

çross, *a.* 1. Transverse; oblique; intersecting; passing from side to side; falling athwart.
2. Adverse; opposite; obstructing; sometimes with *to*; as, an event *cross to* our inclinations.
3. Peevish; fretful; ill-humored; quick-tempered; applied to persons or things; as, a *cross* person; a *cross* answer.
4. Contrary; contradictory; perplexing.

Contradictions that seem to lie *cross* and uncouth. —South.

5. Interchanged; inverse; reciprocal.
Syn.—Counter, contrary, opposite, morose, sullen, peevish, petulant, perverse, ill-tempered, fractious, crusty, fretful, irritable.

çross'=ac'tion, *n.* In law, an action brought against a plaintiff by a defendant, arising out of the same transaction as occasioned the first suit.

çross'=aisle (-īl), *n.* The aisle in the transept of a cruciform church, meeting the aisles of the nave at right angles.

çross'=ärmed, *a.* 1. With arms across.
2. In botany, brachiate; decussated; having branches in pairs, each at right angles to the next.

çross'=ax"le (-ak"sl), *n.* 1. A device like a windlass, operated by two levers, one at either end.
2. A driving-axle in a steam-engine turned by cranks placed at right angles to one another.

çross'=band"ed, *a.* In architecture, having the grain of the wood crossing that of the rail; applied to hand-rails.

çross'bär, *n.* 1. A bar placed transversely across another, or across something which it is desired to hold firm.
2. A round bar of iron bent at each end, used as a lever to turn the shanks of an anchor.

çross'bärred, *a.* 1. Held fast by bars placed transversely.

Some rich burgher, whose substantial doors, *Crossbarred* and bolted fast, fear no assault. —Milton.

2. Woven or ornamented with lines so crossing each other as to divide the surface into rectangles.

çross'bär=shot, *n.* A shot so constructed that when it left the gun it expanded into the form of a cross with the four quarters of the ball at its radial points. It was formerly used in naval engagements because it was so highly destructive to a ship's rigging.

çross'bēak, *n.* A bird, the crossbill.

çross'bēam, *n.* A girder or member binding the sides or walls of a building; by extension, a similar member in a machine or ship.

çross'=bear"ẽr, *n.* 1. A crociary.
2. In a furnace, a support for grate-bars.

çross'=bed"ding, *n.* Cross-lamination.

çross'=bill, *n.* A bill in an equity suit in which the defendant alleges certain charges against the plaintiff as regards the subject matter of that suit.

çross'bill, *n.* Any passerine bird of the genus *Loxia* and family *Fringillidæ*, having the mandibles of the bill curving oppositely and crossing; the crossbeak. *Loxia curvirostra* is the common species.

çross'=birth, *n.* A birth in which the child lies transversely within the uterus.

çross'=bit, çross'=bitt, *n.* Nautically, a piece of timber bolted across two bits for a rope-fastener.

çross'bīte, *n.* A deception; a cheat. [Obs.]

çross'bīte, *v.t.* To deceive. [Obs.]

çross'=bond, *n.* A bond in bricklaying consisting of headers and stretchers arranged as in the English bond, only the second stretcher breaking joints with the first. [See *Bond*, n. 8.]

çross'=bōne, *n.* 1. In birds, the cartilaginous arch across the lower end of the windpipe.
2. [*pl.*] The representation of two human bones crossing one another, frequently accompanied by a skull, the whole serving as a warning against poison or as an emblem of death.

çross'bōw, *n.* In archery, a weapon used for shooting bolts and arrows, formed by placing a bow athwart a stock. Various forms of the *crossbow* were in use during medieval times, operated by a windlass, wheel, or similar contrivance.

Crossbow with Windlass.

çross'bōw"ẽr, *n.* One who shoots with a crossbow.

çross'bōw"măn, *n.* A soldier armed with a crossbow; an arbalister.

çross'bred, *a.* In stockbreeding, resulting from a commingling of separate breeds.

çross'breed, *n.* 1. A breed produced from the male and female of different breeds.
2. A new variety of plant produced by the union of two distinct species, as by cross-fertilization.

çross'breed"ing, *n.* See *Cross breeding* under *Breeding*.

çross'=bun, *n.* A bun with the form of a Greek cross cut upon its top. It is eaten on Good Friday according to an ancient English custom; commonly called *hot cross-bun*.

çross'=but"tŏck, *n.* A peculiar method of throwing an antagonist, practised by Cornish wrestlers, by which an opponent's guard is broken and he is thrown suddenly; hence, any unlooked-for discouragement or defeat.

çross'=cŏun"try, *a.* Not following the traveled roads, but pursuing a course across fields and over fences; as, a *cross-country* run.

çross'cut, *v.t.*; crosscut, *pt.*, *pp.*; crosscutting, *ppr.* To cut crosswise; to intersect; to take a short way through; as, to *crosscut* a field.

çross'cut, *n.* 1. A short way across or through; a path shorter than the traveled road.
2. In mining, a level driven out from a regular level in search of other lodes.
Crosscut saw; (a) a hand-saw having an edge adapted for cutting across the grain; particularly, one having a handle at either end and used to cut logs and heavy timbers.

çross'=dāyṣ, *n.pl.* Monday, Tuesday, and Wednesday preceding Ascension day; Rogation days.

çrosse, *n.* [Fr. *crosier*, a hockey-stick.] The bent stick used in the game of lacrosse.

çros-sette', *n.* [Fr.] In architecture, a term applied to the small, projecting pieces in arch-stones, which hang upon the adjacent stones; also, the return on the corners of door-cases or window-frames; called also an *ear*, *elbow*, *ancon*, *truss* or *console*.

c c c c, Crossettes.

çross'=ex-am-i-nā'tion, *n.* The examination or interrogation of a witness, called by one party, by the opposite party or his counsel.

çross'=ex-am'ine, *v.t.*; cross-examined, *pt.*, *pp.*; cross-examining, *ppr.* To examine (a witness) by the opposite party or his counsel, as the witness for the plaintiff by the defendant, and vice versa.

The opportunity to *cross-examine* the witness has been expressly waived. —Kent.

çross'=ex-am'in-ẽr, *n.* One who cross-examines.

çross'=eȳe (-ī), *n.* Strabismus.

çross'=eȳed (-īd), *a.* Having one or both eyes turned in toward the nose; squinting.

çross'=fẽr-ti-li-zā'tion, *n.* The fertilization of the ovules of a plant by pollen from another individual of the same species.

çross'=fẽr'ti-lize, *v.t.*; cross-fertilized, *pt.*, *pp.*; cross-fertilizing, *ppr.* To fertilize, as the ovule of a female plant by pollen from a male plant of a related species. The pollen is conveyed either by the wind or by insects, every plant capable of *cross-fertilization* being adapted to one of these means.

çross'=fīle, *n.* A file having two surfaces unequally convex.

çross'=fīre, *n.* Militarily, crossing lines of fire.

çross'fish, *n.* A starfish.

çross'flōw, *v.i.* To flow across.

çross'=frog, *n.* In railroading, a frog permitting the crossing of tracks.

çross'=fŭr"rōw, *n.* A furrow meeting others at an angle, usually for drainage purposes.

çross'=gär"net, *n.* A T-shaped hinge.

çross'grāined, *a.* 1. Having the grain or fibers knotted or irregular, and hence difficult to work.
2. Untractable; perverse; unreasonable.

çross'=guärd, *n.* A defensive guard on a weapon, as at the hilt of a sword or head of a spear.

çross'=hāir, *n.* A spider-line.

çross'hatch, *v.t.*; crosshatched (-hacht), *pt.*, *pp.*; crosshatching, *ppr.* To shade, as a drawing, by the use of crosshatching.

çross'hatch"ing, *n.* Representation of light and shade, as in drawing, by means of parallel intersecting lines.

çross'head (-hed), *n.* In mechanics, a beam or rod stretching across the top of anything, as that part of an engine or pump subject to one or more guide-bars.

çross'ing, *n.* 1. A thwarting; impediment; vexation.
2. The act of crossing or passing across; as, the *crossing* of the Atlantic.
3. The place where something is crossed; as, the *crossings* of streets.
4. Intersection; as, the *crossing* of bars in latticework.
5. The act of making the sign of the cross.
6. In railways, the necessary arrangement of rails to form a communication from one track to another.
7. The practice of crossbreeding.
Grade crossing; a place where a road crosses a railway on the same level.

çross'=in"tẽr-rog'ȧ-tō-ry, *n.*; *pl.* **çross'=in"tẽr-rog'ȧ-tō-rieṣ.** A question asked a witness by a person whose interest is opposed to the one taking the deposition.

çross'jack, *n.* A large square sail extended on the lower yard on the mizzenmast or crossjack yard.

çross'=lam-i-nā'tion, *n.* [*Cross*, and *lamination*, from L. *lamina*, a plate, layer.] A deposit of strata out of parallel to the general dip, effected by the action of water during stratification; called also *cross-bedding* and *false bedding*.

çross'legged, *a.* Having the legs crossed one over the other.

çross'let, çros'let, *a.* [Dim. of *cross*.] In heraldry, relating to a cross the extremities of which are themselves crossed.

çross'let, çros'let, *n.* 1. An alchemist's crucible. [Obs.]
2. In heraldry, a small cross.

Crosslet.

çross'like, *a.* Having the form of a cross.

çross'=lōde, *n.* In mining, a less productive lode intersecting the true lode.

çross'ly, *adv.* 1. Ill-humoredly, peevishly.
2. So as to cross; athwart.

çross'ness, *n.* Peevishness; fretfulness; ill humor; perverseness.

çros-sop-tẽr-yḡ'i-ăn, *a.* and *n.* I. *a.* Pertaining to or having the characteristics of the *Crossopterygii*.
II. *n.* An individual of the *Crossopterygii*.

Çros-sop-te-ryḡ'i-ī, *n.pl.* [L., from Gr. *krossoi*, tassels, fringe, and *pterygion*, dim. of *pteryx*, a wing, fin.] A suborder of ganoid fossil fishes, so called from the fin-rays of the paired fins being arranged so as to form a fringe round a central lobe. They are represented among living forms by the genus *Polypterus*.

çross'patch, *n.* An ill-natured person. [Colloq.]

çross'=pawl, *n.* See *Cross-spale*.

çross'pïēce, *n.* 1. A bar of any material placed crosswise on something else.
2. Nautically, (a) a rail of timber extending over the windlass of a ship, furnished with pins with which to fasten the rigging, as occasion requires; (b) a cross-bit.
3. The cross-guard of a sword and various kinds of daggers.

4. A name infrequently applied to the corpus callosum of the brain.

çross′=pol-li-nā′tion, *n.* Cross-fertilization.

çross′=pûr′pōse, *n.* 1. A purpose or aim at variance with another; an inconsistency.

2. [*pl.*] A game in which questions and answers having no connection are joined to make ridiculous combinations.

To be at cross-purposes; to misunderstand one another, and so to act in a contradictory manner without intending it.

çross′=ques′tiŏn (-kwes′chun), *v.t.*; cross-questioned, *pt.*, *pp.*; cross-questioning, *ppr.* To ask searching questions of; to examine in such a manner as to draw forth facts which the one questioned desires to withhold; to cross-examine.

çross′=rēad′ing, *n.* The reading of the lines of a newspaper directly across the page, through the adjoining columns, thus producing a ludicrous combination of ideas.

çross′=ref′ẽr-ence, *n.* A reference from one place, passage, or subject in a book to something related in another part.

çross′=riv′et-ing, *n.* Riveting in which the rivets of one row are opposite spaces in succeeding rows.

çross′rōad, *n.* 1. A way or road that crosses another, or the place where one road intersects another. In the latter sense, often used in the plural.

2. A by-road connecting main roads; a more direct means of communication than by the highroad.

çross′rōw (-rō), *n.* 1. The alphabet. [See *Christ-cross-row.*]

2. A row that crosses others.

çross′ruff, *n.* In whist, the playing of two partners so that each alternately assists the other to win the trick; also called *seesaw*, and a *double ruff*.

çross′=sēa, *n.* A condition at sea when the waves run contrary to the winds; a choppy sea.

çross′=sec″tion, *n.* The plane cutting a body at right angles to its axis.

çross′=spāle, çross′=spąll, *n.* A horizontal timber used as a temporary brace to support the frame of a ship during its construction; called also *cross-pawl*.

çross′=spring″ẽr, *n.* In groined vaulting, the rib which extends diagonally from the one pier to the other.

çross′=stȧff, *n.* 1. A surveyor's instrument used for sighting at right angles.

2. An early form of the quadrant.

çross′=stitch (-stich), *n.* A kind of fancy stitch in which the thread of one stitch crosses that of the next in the middle.

çross′=stitch, *v.t.* and *v.i.* To embroider with cross-stitch; to do cross-stitch.

çross′=stōne, *n.* A name applied to the minerals andalusite, staurolite and harmotome.

çross′=tāil, *n.* In a marine steam-engine, a strong iron bar connecting the side-lever with the piston-rod.

çross′=tie, *n.* In railroads, a transverse timber supporting the rails.

çross′=tīn″ing, *n.* In agriculture, a mode of harrowing crosswise, or in a direction across the ridges.

çross′tree, *n.* Nautically, one of certain pieces of timber or metal, supported by the cheeks and trestle-trees, at the upper ends of the lower masts, to sustain the frame of the top, and on the topmasts to extend the topgallant shrouds.

çross′=vạult″ing, *n.* Vaulting formed by the intersection of two or more simple vaults.

çross′wāy, *n.* Same as *Cross-road.*

çross′=week, *n.* Rogation week.

çross′=wind, *n.* A side or contrary wind.

çross′=wīre, *n.* A cross-hair.

çross′wīṣe, *adv.* Across; in the form of a cross.

çross′wŏrt, *n.* One of various flowers having parts in fours; as, (a) galium; (b) boneset; (c) the madderwort.

AA, Crosstrees.

çrot′ȧ-lȧ, *n.*, pl. of *crotalum.*

Çrot-ȧ-lā′ri-ȧ, *n.* [L., from Gr. *krotalon*, a rattle.] Rattlewort; a very extensive genus of plants of the order *Leguminosæ*, containing several hundred known species, all natives of warm climates. Bengal and Bombay hemp are made from the inner bark of *Crotalaria juncea.* [See *Sunn.*]

çrot′ȧ-lid, *n.* One of the *Crotalidæ.*

Çrot-al′i-dæ, *n.pl.* [L., from Gr. *krotalon*, a rattle.] A family of venomous serpents, order *Ophidia*, having a large pit on each side of the face, between the eye and nostril, comprehending most of the dangerous snakes of tropical Asia and America.

Çrot-ȧ-lī′næ, *n.pl.* The rattlesnakes, a subfamily of the *Crotalidæ*, characterized by having the tail ending in a rattle.

çrōt′ȧ-line, *a.* Of or relating to the *Crotalinæ*, or rattlesnakes.

çrōt′ȧ-lō, *n.* [Gr. *krotalon*, a rattle, castanet.] A Turkish musical instrument, corresponding to the ancient cymbalum.

çrōt′ȧ-loid, *n.* [Gr. *krotalon*, a rattle, and *eidos*, form.] Any serpent of the family *Crotalidæ.*

çrot′ȧ-lum, *n.*; *pl.* **çrōt′ȧ-lȧ**. [L., from Gr. *krotalon*, a rattle, castanet.]

1. A kind of castanet used by the ancient Egyptians and Greeks.

2. A bell, particularly when small.

Çrōt′ȧ-lus, *n.* [L., from Gr. *krotalon*, a rattle.] The type genus of the subfamily *Crotalinæ.*

çrōt′ȧ-phīte, *a.* [Gr. *krotaphos*, the side of the forehead.] In anatomy, same as *temporal*; sometimes used as a noun. [Rare.]

çrōt-ȧ-phit′iç, *a.* Same as *Crotaphite.*

çrotch, *n.*; *pl.* **çrotch′eṣ**. [ME. *crotche, croche*, a shepherd's crook, from *crotchet*; OFr. *crochet*, dim. of *croc*, a hook.]

1. A fork or forking; the parting of two legs or branches; as, the *crotch* of a tree.

2. Nautically, a crutch.

3. In billiards, a small square at the corner of the table.

çrotched (krocht), *a.* 1. Having a crotch; forked.

2. Cross; peevish. [Prov. Eng.]

çrotch′et, *n.* [OFr. *crochet*, a little hook, dim. of *croc*, a hook.]

1. A hook, especially when small.

2. In entomology, a hook on the prolegs of certain caterpillars; any hooked part.

3. In printing, a bracket. [See *Bracket*, n. 6.]

4. In music, a quarter-note.

5. In fortification, an indentation in a covered way, opposite to a traverse.

6. In military phraseology, disposal of troops in a line forming right angles to the general line of battle.

7. In anatomy, a hook at the anterior extremity of the superior occipitotemporal convolution of the cerebrum.

8. In surgery, a curved instrument with a sharp hook, used to extract the fetus, in the operation of embryotomy.

9. A piece of wood resembling a fork, used as a support in building.

10. A peculiar turn of the mind; a whim, or fancy; a perverse conceit.

Devices and *crotchets* of new inventions.
—Howell.

çrotch′et, *v.i.* To perform music or to sing in quick time. [Obs.]

çrotch′et-ed, *a.* Marked with crotchets.

çrotch′et-i-ness, *n.* The state of being crotchety; eccentricity.

çrotch′et-y, *a.* Having perverse conceits or crotchets of the brain; eccentric; odd.

Çrō′tŏn, *n.* [Gr. *krotōn*, a tick, the plant which bears the castor-oil berry.]

1. A genus of euphorbiaceous plants, comprehending a large number of species, many of which possess important medicinal properties. *Croton Tiglium*, a native of several parts of the East Indies, has violent purgative qualities.

2. [c—] Any foliage plant of this genus.

Croton Tiglium.

çrō′tŏn=bug, *n.* The house cockroach, *Blatta germanica*, common in houses having water-pipes.

çrō-ton′iç, *a.* Of or pertaining to plants of the genus *Croton.*

Crotonic acid; an acid, $C_4H_6O_2$, first found in the seeds of the plant *Croton Tiglium.* It has a pungent and nauseous smell, a burning taste, and is very poisonous.

çrō′tŏn-in, çrō′tŏn-ine, *n.* A vegeto-alkali found in the seeds of *Croton Tiglium.*

çrō′tŏn=oil, *n.* Oil from the *Croton Tiglium.* It is a violent cathartic, one drop being a dose; used where other purgatives fail.

çrō-ton′y-len, çrō-ton′y-lēne, *n.* The unsaturated hydrocarbon, C_4H_6, a constituent of illuminating gas.

çrot′tleṣ (-tlz), *n.pl.* [Gael. *crotal*, a name for lichens.] Certain lichens used as dyestuffs. [Scot.]

çrouch, *v.i.*; crouched (kroucht), *pt.*, *pp.*; crouching, *ppr.* [ME. *crouchen, crouken*, to crouch, bend; *croken*, to crook.]

1. To bend down; to stoop low; to lie close to the ground, as an animal when hunting or in fear.

2. To bend servilely; to stoop meanly; to fawn; to cringe.

çrouch, *v.t.* To cause to stoop. [Rare.]

çrouch, *v.t.* To sign with the cross; to bless. [Obs.]

çrouched (kroucht), *a.* Crossed. [Obs.]

Crouched friars; see *Crutched friars* under *Crutched.*

çroud, *n.* See first *Crowd.*

çrouke, *n.* A jar of earthenware; a crock. [Obs.]

çrōup, *n.* [OFr. *croupe*, the rump; Ice. *kryppa*, a hump.] The rump or buttocks; also, in a horse, the part behind the saddle.

çrōup, *n.* [Scot. *croup, crope, crupe, crowp*, to croak, to cry or speak with a hoarse voice; Goth. *hropyan*; AS. *hreopan*, to call out.] The disease called technically *cynanche trachealis*, an inflammatory affection of the trachea, or larynx and trachea, accompanied by a hoarse voice and a short, constant barking cough and difficult respiration. It mostly attacks infants, and frequently proves fatal by suffocation. The term is applied somewhat loosely, and the severer forms of the disease are not to be distinguished from diphtheria.

False croup; a catarrhal affection of the larynx.

çrōu-pāde′, *n.* [Fr., from *croupe*, the hind quarters.] In the manège, a leap in which the horse pulls up his hind legs, as if drawing them up to his belly.

çrōup′ăl, *a.* Croupous.

çrōup′ẽr, *n.* Same as *Crupper.*

çrōu′pi-ẽr, *n.* [Fr.] 1. One who collects and pays the money at a gaming-table.

2. One who acts as assistant chairman at a public dinner-party.

çrōu-pi-ère′ (-ār′), *n.* [Fr., from *croup*, the hind quarters.] Armor for the buttocks of a horse. [See illustration under *Bard.*]

çrōup′ous, *a.* Relating to or exhibiting the symptoms of croup; having reference particularly to the false membrane which causes the laryngeal spasms in true or membranous croup.

Croupous pneumonia; see under *Pneumonia.*

çrōup′y, *a.* Being affected with or subject to croup; croupous.

çrouṣe, *a.* [Scot.] Brisk; full of heart; courageous; self-satisfied; self-complacent.

çrōu-stāde′, *n.* [Fr., from OFr. *crouste*, a crust.] A dish prepared with crusts of bread.

çrout, *n.* See *Sauerkraut.*

çrōw, *n.* [ME. *crowe, craw*; AS. *crawe*; D. *kraai*; O.H.G. *chraja, chrawa*, a crow.]

1. A large black bird, of the genus *Corvus*; the beak is convex and cultrated, the nostrils are covered with bristly feathers, the tongue is forked and cartilaginous. It utters a strident note, imitatively called a *caw*. The common or carrion crow is the *Corvus americanus*; the raven is the *Corvus corax*; the hooded crow, *Corvus cornix*; the rook, *Corvus frugilegus*; the jackdaw, *Corvus monedula.*

Hooded Crow. Carrion-Crow.

2. A crowbar.

3. The voice of the cock.

4. The mesentery or ruffle of a beast, so called by butchers.

5. One who watches while another commits a theft; a confederate in a robbery. [Thieves' slang.]

6. One of certain birds supposed to resemble the *crow*; as, *Gymnocitta cyanocephala*, the blue *crow.*

As the crow flies; the most direct line between two points.

Red-legged or *Cornish crow*; the chough.

To have a crow to pluck with one; to have something demanding explanation from one; to have a dispute to settle.

çrōw, *v.i.*; crowed, *pt.*, *pp.*; formerly crew, *pt.*, *pp.*; crowing, *ppr.* [ME. *crowen, crawen*; AS. *crawan*, to crow; D. *kraaijen*; G. *krahen*, to crow.]

1. To cry or make a noise as a cock.

2. To boast in triumph; to vaunt; to vapor; to swagger.

3. To express pleasure by a cooing sound, as an infant.

To crow over one; to express elation at a triumph over one; to be exultant at another's expense.

çrōw′bär, *n.* A bar of iron sharpened at one end, formerly used as a lever for raising heavy bodies; now often fitted with a claw for drawing spikes.

çrōw′bellṣ, *n.* A flower; the bluebell; also the daffodil.

çrōw′ber″ry, *n.*; *pl.* **çrōw′ber″rieṣ**. The fruit of *Empetrum nigrum*, also the plant itself, a heath-like evergreen shrub common in Scotland and northern North America; also called *black crowberry, crakeberry*, and *heathberry.*

çrōw′=black′bīrd, *n.* *Quiscalus quiscula,* the American purple grackle, a passerine bird somewhat resembling the crow.

çrowd, *n.* [ME. *crowde, croude;* W. *crwth,* a bulge, crowd, violin; Gael. *cruit,* a violin, harp.] An ancient Irish or Welsh six-stringed violin, four of the strings being bowed and two struck by the thumb in playing; also written *croud, crowth,* and (Welsh) *crwth.*

Crowd.

çrowd, *v.i.* To play the crowd. [Obs.]

çrowd, *n.* [AS. *croda, gecrod,* a crowd; *creodan,* to press, crowd.]

1. A collection; a number of things collected, or closely pressed together.

2. A number of persons congregated or collected into a close body without order; a throng.

3. Colloquially, any company of persons; a set; as, to frequent the fast *crowd.*

4. The common people; the populace.

Syn.—Concourse, confluence, gathering, assembly, throng, group, swarm.

çrowd, *v.t.*; crowded, *pt., pp.*; crowding, *ppr.* [ME. *crowden, cruden;* AS. *creodan,* to crowd, push.]

1. To press; to urge; to drive together.

2. To fill by pressing numbers together without order; as, to *crowd* a room with people.

3. To press upon or out; to come against as a great number; as, the weeds have *crowded* the flowers.

4. Colloquially, to urge; to press by solicitation; as, to *crowd* a debtor.

To crowd out; to cause the omission of, as by a pressure of more urgent or important matter; as, your letter was *crowded out* of our columns.

To crowd sail; nautically, to make all possible speed by spreading all the sails.

çrowd, *v.i.* 1. To press in numbers; as, the multitude *crowded* through the gate.

2. To press; to urge forward; as, the man *crowded* into the room.

çrowd′ẽr, *n.* A crowd-player; a fiddler. [Obs.]

çrowd′ẽr, *n.* One who crowds; a pusher.

çrowd′ie, çrow′dy, *n.* A gruel of meal stirred into cold water or milk. [Scot.]

çrōw′flow″ẽr, *n.* A common name for the buttercup. The older authors applied it to ragged-robin. [See *Crowfoot.*]

çrōw′foot, *n.*; *pl.* **çrōw′feet.** 1. In botany, any species of *Ranunculus* or buttercup, from the leaf being supposed to be in shape like the foot of a crow.

2. Nautically, (a) a number of small cords spreading out from a long block; used to suspend the awnings or to keep the topsails close; (b) in a ship-of-war, a stand for holding mess-kids.

3. Same as *Caltrop.*

4. The zinc of a gravity battery, from its shape; also used adjectively.

çrōw′keep″ẽr, *n.* One who scares crows from a field; also, a scarecrow. [Obs.]

çrōwn, *v.,* past participle of *crow.* [Obs.]

çrown, *n.* [ME. *croun, crone, coroun;* OFr. *corone, coroune;* L. *corona,* a crown, wreath; Gr. *korōnē,* the tip of a bow, anything curved.]

Crown of England.

1. An ornament worn on the head by kings and those having sovereign power, as a badge of their office.

2. Regal power; sovereignty; kingly government or imperial dominion.

3. A wreath or garland. In ancient Rome, crowns, made at first of grass, flowers, twigs of laurel, oak, olive, etc., but later of gold, were awarded to the victors in the public games, and to citizens who had done the state some marked service.

4. Honorary distinction; reward; honor; splendor; dignity.

5. A person having the right to an imperial *crown;* a reigning prince; a sovereign; as, the debts of the *crown* were by this time enormous.

1. Imperial Crown of Charlemagne. 2. Austrian Crown. 3. Russian Crown. 4. French Crown.

6. Completion; accomplishment; highest or most perfect state; acme.

> A sorrow's *crown* of sorrow is remembering happier things. —Tennyson.

7. The top of anything; the highest part; applied variously, as to the summit of a mountain, the crest of a bird, the dome of a furnace, the face of an anvil, etc.

8. The upper part of a rounding or convex surface, as in a bridge, a road, the deck of a ship, etc.

9. The top of the head; also, the head itself.

10. The part of a hat which covers the top of the head.

11. Clerical tonsure in a circular form; a little circle shaved on the top of the head, as a mark of ecclesiastical office or distinction.

12. Nautically, (a) the end of an anchor, or the point from which the arms proceed; (b) one of the loops or bights of a cable when coiled; (c) a kind of knot made at the end of a rope to prevent the strands from raveling.

13. In anatomy, (a) that portion of a tooth which appears beyond the gum; (b) that surface of a molar which meets the tooth above or below it; (c) an artificial cap for a tooth.

14. The top portion of a gem cut in rose shape; the uppermost circle of facets.

15. In architecture, the uppermost member of a cornice; called also the *corona* or *larmier;* also, the top part of an arch or of a lantern made by the meeting of several flying buttresses.

16. In botany, (a) a corona; (b) the topmost part of the root which joins with the stem.

17. A coin generally stamped with the figure of a *crown* or a crowned head. The English *crown* is five shillings sterling, or $1.21 U. S. money.

18. In geometry, the area between two concentric circles.

19. A special size of paper, applied formerly in the United States to a writing-paper 15x19 inches, but now not in general use.

Crown colony; a British colony in which the legislative power remains with the home government.

Crown jewels; the jewels that are owned by a sovereign and pass to his successor.

Crown or *demesne lands;* [Eng.] the lands, estate, or other real property belonging to the crown or sovereign.

Crown law; in England, that part of the common law governing criminal matters.

Crown of aberration; see under *Aberration.*

Crown office; in England, a department of the King's Bench division of the High Court of Justice, which takes cognizance of all criminal causes; commonly called the *crown side* of the court.

Crown prince; the prince-royal who is an apparent successor to a crown.

Crown side; same as *Crown office.*

çrown, *v.t.*; crowned, *pt., pp.*; crowning, *ppr.* [ME. *crownen, corownen;* OFr. *coroner;* L. *coronare,* to crown; *corona,* a crown.]

1. To cover, as with a crown; to cover the top of.

> And peaceful olives *crowned* his hoary head. —Dryden.

2. To invest with a crown or regal ornament; to invest with regal dignity and power.

3. To honor; to dignify; to adorn; to recompense or reward; to bestow an honorary reward or distinction upon; as, to *crown* the victor with laurel.

> Thou . . . hast *crowned* him with glory and honor. —Ps. viii. 5.

4. To terminate or finish; to complete; to perfect.

5. To stand at the top of; to constitute the upper part of; as, an observatory *crowned* the height.

6. Militarily, to secure a foothold in; to gain and hold a position upon.

7. In mechanics, to produce a rounding or bulging in; as, to *crown* the face of a pulley.

8. Nautically, to make a finishing knot on the end of (a rope) by interweaving the strands.

çrown′=ant″lẽr, *n.* The top tine of the antler of a stag. [See *Antler.*]

çrown′=ärch, *n.* A solid arched plate above the fire-box of a boiler.

çrown′=bär, *n.* One of the bars by which the crown-sheet of the fire-box of a steam-boiler is supported.

çrown′bēard, *n.* Any plant of the aster family belonging to the genus *Verbesina.*

çrown′=çrāne, *n.* A bird, the demoiselle.

çrowned, *a.* 1. Invested with a crown, or with regal power and dignity; honored; dignified; rewarded with a crown, wreath, garland, or distinction.

2. In zoölogy, having the head marked in some distinguishing manner, as by a crest or by coloring; crested; coronate.

3. In botany, having a corona.

4. Finished off with a crown knot; said of a rope.

5. Supreme; great. [Obs.]

çrōw′=nee″dleṣ, *n.* A plant, lady's-comb.

çrown′ẽr, *n.* [A corruption of *coroner;* LL. *coronator,* a coroner, crowner, from *coronare,* to crown; *corona,* a crown.] A coroner, who was originally a crown officer. [Obs.]

çrown′ẽr, *n.* One who or that which crowns or completes.

çrown′et, *n.* 1. A coronet. [Rare.]

2. The chief end; result; ultimate reward. [Obs.]

çrown′=gāte, *n.* The head gate in the lock of a canal.

çrown′=head (-hed), *n.* On a checker-board, the king-row.

çrown′=im-pē′ri-ăl, *n.* A liliaceous plant, *Fritillaria imperialis,* cultivated for its beautiful flowers; called also *crown-thistle.*

çrown′ing, *a.* 1. Bulging at the top.

2. Finishing or completing; perfecting; supreme.

> The *crowning* act of a long career. —Buckle.

çrown′ing, *n.* 1. The act of investing with a crown or regal dignity; the state of being so invested; coronation.

> I mean your voice for *crowning* of the king. —Shak.

2. In architecture, the upper termination or finish of a member; particularly, any ornamental work.

3. Nautically, a finishing knot; a crown.

4. In fortification, a position or foothold secured by a besieging force on the top of the glacis.

Crowning cell; the outer cell-wall in certain stages of a developing, segmented ovum; also called *coronal cell.*

çrown′less, *a.* Without a crown.

çrown′let, *n.* [Dim. of *crown.*] A small crown.

çrown′piēce, *n.* The strap of a bridle passing over the top of the horse's head.

çrown′=pōst, *n.* In building, a post which stands upright in the middle of a truss, especially the triangular truss of a roof, coming between two principal rafters; a king-post.

çrown′=saw, *n.* A kind of circular saw formed by cutting the teeth round the edge of a cylinder, as the surgeon's trepan.

çrown′=scab, *n.* A painful sore of a cancerous nature that forms on a horse's hoof.

çrown′=sheet, *n.* The sheet or plate forming the top of the fire-box of a steam-boiler.

çrown′=shell, *n.* See *Acorn-shell,* 2.

çrown′=spar″rōw, *n.* Any bird of the genus *Zonotrichia;* particularly, the Peabody bird.

çrown′=this″tle (-this″sl), *n.* See *Crown-imperial.*

çrown′=tile, *n.* 1. A common roof-tile.

2. A finishing tile resembling a crest-tile.

çrown′=valve, *n.* A crown-shaped valve.

çrown′=wheel, *n.* A wheel with cogs set at right angles with its plane; as in certain watches the wheel that is next the crown and drives the balance. It is also called a *contrate-wheel* or *face-wheel.*

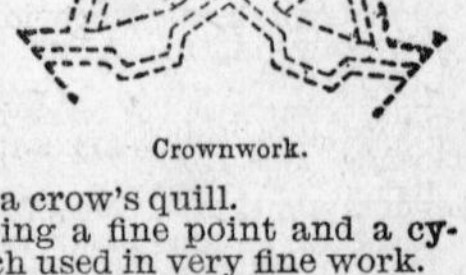

Crown-wheel of Watch.

çrown′wŏrk, *n.* In fortification, an outwork running into the field, consisting of two demi-bastions (*a a*) at the extremes, and an entire bastion (*b*) in the middle, with curtains (*c c*). It is designed to gain some hill or advantageous post, and cover the other works.

Crownwork.

çrōw′=pheaṣ″ănt (-fez″), *n.* A bird, the coucal.

çrōw′=quill (-kwil), *n.* 1. A quill of a crow; also, a pen of a crow's quill.

2. A steel pen having a fine point and a cylindrical shank, much used in very fine work.

çrōw′ṣ′=foot, *n.*; *pl.* **çrōw′ṣ′=feet.** 1. One of the wrinkles which form under the eye and extend from the outer corner radially; most commonly used in the plural.

2. Same as *Caltrop,* 1.

3. A device used for securing a drill-rod as another section is being fitted on.

4. An embroidery-stitch of three points.

çrōw′=shrīke, *n.* A bird, the piping crow.

çrōw′=silk, *n.* Any of the various algæ of the order *Confervaceæ.*

çrōw′ṣ′=nest, çrōw′=nest, *n.* A barrel or box fitted up on the top of a mast of an arctic vessel, or a whaler, for the shelter of the lookout man; called also *bird's-nest.* [See illus. p. 405.]

çrōw′=steps, *n.pl.* Same as *Corbel-steps.*

çrōw′stōne, *n.* The topmost stone in a gable that has corbel-steps on it.

çrowth, *n.* [ME. *crowth, crowd;* W. *crwth,*

bulge, crowd, violin; Gael. *cruit*, a violin harp.] A violin; the crowd. [Obs.]

çrōw'tōe, *n.* 1. [*pl.*] *Lotus corniculatus*, bird's-foot trefoil, a British plant.

2. A plant, probably the crowfoot.

Crow's-nest.

çroyl'stōne, *n.* Crystallized cauk, in which the crystals are small.

çroys, *n.* A cross. [Obs.]

çrōze, *n.* [Origin unknown.] In coopering, the grooving-plane used to channel barrel-staves for insertion of the head; the groove so cut.

çrō'ziēr, çrō'siēr (-zhēr), *n.* [ME. *croser, croyser, crocer*; OFr. *croce, croche*, a bishop's pastoral staff; LL. *crocea, crocia*, a curved stick, bishop's staff.]

1. A staff carried by, or in front of, a bishop or archbishop, on ceremonial occasions. It consists of a hollow staff, that of a bishop ending in a crook, that of an archbishop terminating in a cross or crucifix.

2. A crozier- or cross-bearer. [Obs.]

3. [C—] A constellation of the southern hemisphere, consisting of four stars in the form of a cross; the Southern Cross.

Croziers. 1. From tomb of Archbishop Warham, Canterbury. 2. From drawing in British Museum.

çrō'ziēred, çrō'siēred, *a.* Having a crozier.

çrū'çēs, *n.*, pl. of *crux*.

çrū'ciăl, *a.* [Fr. *cruciale*, from L. *crux, crucis*, a cross.]

1. Cross-shaped; intersecting; cruciform; as, the *crucial* ligaments of the knee-joint.

2. Severe; extreme; torturing.

3. Trying; searching or testing; determining between different suppositions or views; decisive; as, a *crucial* experiment.

çrū'ciăn, çrū'siăn, *n.* [Fr. *carassin*; LL. *coracinus*; Gr. *korakinos*, a fish like a perch.] A short thick broad fish, of a deep yellow color, the German carp, *Carassius carassius*, or *vulgaris*, family *Cyprinidæ*. It inhabits the lakes, ponds, and sluggish rivers in northern Europe and Asia, and differs from the common carp in having no barbels at its mouth; called also *Prussian carp* or *crucian-carp*.

çrū'ci-āte (-shi-āt), *v.t.* [L. *cruciatus*, pp. of *cruciare*, to torture; *crux*, a cross, torture.] To torture. [Rare.]

çrū'ci-āte, *a.* 1. Tormented. [Rare.]

2. Cross-shaped; marked as by a cross; cruciform.

3. In botany, having petals or other parts disposed in the form of a cross, the four arms of which are equal.

Cruciate Flower.

çrū-ci-ā'tion, *n.* 1. Torment. [Obs.]

2. A crossing; decussation.

çrū'ci-ble, *n.* [LL. *crucibulum*, a lamp, a pot for melting metals; OFr. *croche*, an earthen pot; D. *kroes*; Sw. *krus*, a cup, crucible.]

1. A vessel or pot made of clay, black-lead, platinum, or other material, so baked or tempered as to endure extreme heat without fusing. It is used for melting ores, metals, etc.

Various forms of Crucibles.

2. In metallurgy, a hollow place at the bottom of a furnace to receive the melted metal.

3. Figuratively, a severe or searching test; as, his probity was tried in the *crucible* of temptation and poverty.

Hessian crucible; one made of coarse sand and infusible clay, used in reducing metals by the aid of fluxes.

çrū'ci-fēr, *n.* [LL. *crucifer*; *crux, crucis*, a cross, and *ferre*, to bear.] 1. A cross-bearer in religious processions.

2. In botany, any cruciferous herb.

Çrū-cif'e-ræ, *n.pl.* A very extensive natural order of dicotyledonous plants, consisting of annual or perennial herbs with a pungent or acrid watery juice, all having flowers with six stamens, two of which are short, and four sepals and petals, the spreading limbs of which form a Maltese cross. The fruit is a pod divided into two cells. The mustard, water-cress, turnip, cabbage, radish, horseradish, etc., belong to this family.

çrū-cif'ēr-ous, *a.* [LL. *crucifer*, bearing a cross; *crux, crucis*, a cross, and *ferre*, to bear.]

1. Bearing or resembling a cross.

2. In botany, pertaining to or like the order *Cruciferæ*; cruciform.

çrū'ci-fi-ēr, *n.* One who crucifies.

çrū'ci-fix, *n.* [LL. *crucifixum*, a crucifix, neut. of *crucifixus*, pp. of *crucifigere*, to crucify; *crux, crucis*, a cross, and *figere*, to fix, fasten.]

1. A cross, or a representation of a cross, with the figure of Christ crucified upon it.

2. The cross of Christ; hence, figuratively, the religion of Christ. [Rare.]

çrū-ci-fix'iŏn (-fik'shun), *n.* 1. The act of nailing or fastening a person to a cross, for the purpose of putting him to death.

2. The state of being nailed or fastened to a cross; death upon a cross.

3. Intense suffering or affliction; great mental trial.

çrū'ci-form, *a.* [L. *crux, crucis*, a cross, and *forma*, form.] Cross-shaped; applied especially, (a) in botany, to the flowers of the *Cruciferæ*; (b) in anatomy, to the ligament of the atlas.

çrū'ci-fȳ, *v.t.*; crucified, *pt., pp.*; crucifying, *ppr.* [OFr. *crucifier*; LL. *crucifigere, cruci figere*, to fasten to a cross; *crux, crucis*, a cross, and *figere*, to fasten.]

1. To nail to a cross; to put to death by nailing the hands and feet to a cross or gibbet, sometimes anciently by fastening a criminal to a tree with cords.

> But they cried, *Crucify* him, *crucify* him. —Luke xxiii. 21.

2. In Scripture, to subdue; to mortify; to destroy the power or ruling influence of.

> They that are Christ's have *crucified* the flesh with the affections and lusts. —Gal. v. 24.

3. To vex; to torture. [Obs.]

çrū-cig'ēr-ous, *a.* [L. *crux, crucis*, cross, and *gerere*, to bear.] Bearing a cross or cross-shaped marks.

çrud, *v.* and *n.* [Obs.] Same as *Curd*.

çrud'dle, *v.i.* 1. To curdle. [Obs.]

2. To crowd; to huddle. [Prov. Eng.]

çrūde, *a.*; *comp.* cruder; *superl.* crudest. [L. *crudus*, bloody, raw, unripe, from *cruor*, blood.]

1. Raw; not cooked or prepared by fire, heat, or other means; undressed; as, *crude* meat.

2. Not changed from its natural state; not altered or prepared by any artificial process; as, *crude* salt or alum; *crude* ore.

3. Immature; unripe; not mellowed; as, the harsh flavor of *crude* fruit.

4. Rough; coarse; without polish, refinement, or delicacy; as, *crude* manners.

5. Not well formed, arranged, or prepared; characterized by ignorance or unskilfulness; undeveloped; incomplete; imperfect; applied to things; as, a *crude* plan or theory; *crude* work.

6. Lacking knowledge or skill; of undeveloped or limited power; applied to persons; as, a *crude* workman; a *crude* thinker.

çrūde'ly, *adv.* In a crude manner.

çrūde'ness, *n.* 1. The state of being crude; rawness; unripeness; an undigested or unprepared state; as, the *crudeness* of meat.

2. A state of being unformed or imperfect, or of lacking skill or knowledge; immatureness; as, the *crudeness* of a theory.

çrū'di-ty, *n.*; *pl.* **çrū'di-tieṣ.** [L. *cruditas* (*-atis*), from *crudus*, raw, rough, undigested.]

1. Rawness; crudeness.

2. Something in a crude or undigested state; as, the *crudities* of ignorance.

3. Indigestion. [Obs.]

çrū'dle, *v.i.* Same as *Cruddle*.

çrud'y, *a.* Coagulated, thickened or curdled. [Obs.]

çrū'dy, *a.* Raw; rough; crude. [Obs.]

çrū'el, *a.* [Fr. *cruel*; L. *crudelis*, raw, unfeeling, rough.]

1. Disposed to give pain to others, in body or mind; willing or pleased to torment, vex, or afflict; inhuman; destitute of pity, compassion, or kindness; fierce; ferocious; savage; barbarous; hard-hearted.

> They are *cruel*, and have no mercy.—Jer. vi. 23.

2. Causing pain, grief, or distress; exerted in tormenting, vexing, or afflicting; harsh; painful; as, *cruel* words or acts.

Syn.—Barbarous, brutal, ferocious, inhuman, inexorable, merciless, pitiless.

çrū'el, *adv.* Extremely. [Colloq.]

çrū'ell, *n.* [Obs.] Same as *Crewel*.

çrū'el-ly, *adv.* 1. In a cruel or harsh manner; with cruelty; inhumanly; barbarously; without pity.

2. With great suffering; painfully.

3. Exceedingly; in a high degree; very; as, he is *cruelly* strong in body. [Colloq.]

çrū'el-ness, *n.* Inhumanity; cruelty. [Rare.]

çrū'elṣ, *n.pl.* Same as *Crewels*.

çrū'el-ty, *n.*; *pl.* **çrū'el-tieṣ.** [OFr. *cruelte*; It. *crudelita*; L. *crudelitas*, cruelty, barbarity, from *crudelis*, raw, rough, unfeeling.]

1. The quality or characteristic of being cruel; inhumanity; a savage or barbarous disposition or temper, which is gratified in giving unnecessary pain or distress to others; barbarity; applied to persons; as, the *cruelty* of savages.

2. A barbarous deed; any act of a human being which inflicts unnecessary pain; any act intended to torment, vex, or afflict, or which actually torments or afflicts, without necessity; as, the *cruelties* of war.

çrū'en-tāte, *a.* [L. *cruentatus*, pp. of *cruentare*, to make bloody; *cruor*, blood.] Smeared with blood. [Obs.]

çrū-en'tous, *a.* Bloody; cruentate. [Obs.]

çrū'et, *n.* [ME. *cruet, crewet*, dim. of OFr. *cruye, cruie*, a pitcher.]

1. A vial or small glass bottle, particularly, one used on the table for holding vinegar, oil, etc.

2. Ecclesiastically, one of the vessels used for wine or water in the celebration of the eucharist.

çrū'et-stand, *n.* See *Caster*, 3.

çrūise, *n.* Same as *Cruse*.

çrūiṣe, *v.i.*; cruised, *pt., pp.*; cruising, *ppr.* [D. *kruisen*, to move crosswise or in a zigzag course; *kruis*, a cross; OFr. *crois*; L. *crux*, a cross.]

1. To sail back and forth along a coast, as a yacht, or on the high seas, as a war-ship; to sail about in search of an enemy's ships, or for the protection of commerce, or for plunder; as, the admiral *cruised* between the Bahama isles and Cuba; a pirate was *cruising* in the Gulf of Mexico.

2. To wander about on land. [Colloq.]

3. In forestry, to explore or examine forests to estimate the quantity and quality of timber to be cut therefrom.

çrūiṣe, *v.t.* 1. To sail over, about, or through; as, yachts that *cruise* the small lakes.

2. In forestry, to explore, in order to estimate the actual or possible timber-yield; as, to *cruise* a river-valley.

çrūiṣe, *n.* 1. A sailing to and fro, as in search of an enemy's ships, for the protection of merchant-vessels, or for pleasure.

2. A journey of inspection through forest-lands.

çrūiṣ'ēr, *n.* 1. A person or a ship that cruises; particularly, an armed ship that sails to and fro, capturing an enemy's ships or for protecting the commerce of its own country. The word is generally applied to vessels of less size and military power than battleships, but of high speed and adapted to long voyages.

2. An explorer or estimator of standing timber.

çrūis'ken, çrūis'keen, *n.* A small cruse; especially, one containing a dram of whisky.

çruive, *n.* [Scot.] 1. A sty or hovel.

2. A tidal fish-trap of wattles.

çrull, *a.* Curled; crinkly. [Obs.]

çrul'lēr, krul'lēr, *n.* [D. *krullen*, to curl.] A kind of cake cut from a soft, sweet dough, and fried in boiling lard until crisp; a fried-cake.

çrumb, çrum, *n.* [AS. *cruma*, a crumb, from *crummen*, pp. of *crimman*, to break into pieces.]

1. A small fragment or piece; usually, a small piece of bread or other food, broken or cut off; by extension, a small piece of anything.

2. The white inner part of bread.

3. A louse, the grayback. [Local, U. S.]

To a crumb; exactly; with great precision; in every detail.

çrumb, çrum, *v.t.*; crumbed *or* crummed, *pt., pp.*; crumbing *or* crumming, *ppr.* 1. To break into small pieces with the fingers; as, to *crumb* bread into milk.

2. To remove the crumbs from; as, to *crumb* the table.

3. In cooking, to cover with bread or cracker crumbs; as, to *crumb* cutlets.

çrumb'-brush, *n.* A small brush with which to sweep crumbs from a table.

çrumb'çloth, *n.* A cloth protecting a floor or carpet from food-crumbs.

çrum'ble, *v.t.*; crumbled, *pt., pp.*; crumbling, *ppr.* [Dim. of *crumb*.] To break into small pieces; to divide into minute parts.

çrum'ble, *v.i.* 1. To fall into small pieces; to break or part into small fragments.

> If a stone is brittle, it will *crumble* into gravel. —Arbuthnot.

2. To fall to decay; to perish; to dwindle away; to become wasted or scattered; as, the political alliance will soon *crumble*; poor management caused the estate to *crumble*.

çrum'bly, *a.* Brittle; easy to crumble; apt to break.

çrū'men, *n.* [L. *crumena*, a purse.] A larmier or tearpit.

çrū'me-năl, *n.* [L. *crumena*.] A purse. [Obs.]

çrum'mȧ-ble, *a.* Capable of being crumbed.

çrum'my, çrumb'y, *a.* Full of crumbs; soft.

ċrump, *a.* [AS. *crumb*, stooping, bent down; G. *krumm*, crooked.]
1. Crooked.
2. Brittle; crusty; dry-baked; crisp. [Prov. Eng. and Scot.]

ċrump′et, *n.* [W. *crempog*, a pancake, fritter.] A sort of muffin or tea-cake, very light and spongy.

ċrum′ple, *v.t.*; crumpled, *pt.*, *pp.*; crumpling, *ppr.* [ME. *crumplen*, *cromplen*, to make crooked; dim. of *crump*.]
1. To deform. [Obs.]
2. To make wrinkled; to rumple.

ċrum′ple, *v.i.* To become corrugated; to shrink; to shrivel.

ċrump′y, *a.* Easily broken; brittle; crump.

ċrunch, *v.i.*; crunched (krunċht), *pt.*, *pp.*; crunching, *ppr.* [Imitative of the sound.]
1. To craunch; to chew.
2. To press through or against something so as produce a grinding noise; as, to *crunch* through a crust of snow.

ċrunch, *v.t.* To chew noisily with the teeth; to craunch.

ċrunk, ċrunk′kle, *v.i.* [Imitative word.] To cry like a crane. [Obs.]

ċrụ-nō′dăl, *a.* Having a crunode.

ċrụ′nōde, *n.* [L. *crux*, *crucis*, a cross, and *nodus*, a knot.] The point where a curve crosses itself.

ċrụ′ŏr, *n.* [L.] Coagulated blood.

ċrụ′ō-rin, ċrụ′ō-rine, *n.* [L. *cruor*, blood.] The former name of hemoglobin.

ċrup, *a.* [Prov. Eng.] 1. Short; crisp.
2. Snappish; crabbed; testy.

ċrup, *n.* [Fr. *croupe*, crupper, rump.] Same as *Croup*, the buttocks.

ċrup′pẽr, *n.* [Fr. *croupière*, from *croupe*, the buttocks of a horse.]
1. The buttocks of a horse; the rump.
2. The loop in a harness passing under the tail; a similar strap attached to a saddle.

ċrup′pẽr, *v.t.* To put a crupper on; as, to *crupper* a horse.

ċrụ′rȧ, *n.*, pl. of *crus*.

ċrụ′răl, *a.* [L. *cruralis*, from *crus*, *cruris*, the leg.]
1. Of, relating, or pertaining to a crus or crura; as, the *crural* arteries.
2. Shaped like a leg or root.

ċrus, *n.*; *pl.* **ċrụ′rȧ**. [L., the leg.] 1. The part of the leg between the knee and the ankle.
2. In anatomy, one of two leg-like parts; a limb or support.

ċrụ-sāde′, *n.* [Fr. *croisade*; Pr. *crozada*; Sp. *cruzada*, a crusade; It. *crociata*; LL. *cruciata*, a crusade, from L. *crux*, *crucis*, a cross.]
1. A military expedition, such as were undertaken, from 1096 to 1271, by authority of the Christian church for the recovery of the Holy Land from the power of the Mohammedans.
2. An enterprise projected in a spirit of enthusiasm and conducted with earnestness against some social or economic wrong; as, a *crusade* against the slave-trade; a *crusade* against impure milk.

ċrụ-sāde′, *n.* See *Crusado*.

ċrụ-sāde′, *v.i.*; crusaded, *pt.*, *pp.*; crusading, *ppr.* To participate in a crusade; to support or oppose any cause with zeal.

ċrụ-sād′ẽr, *n.* A person engaged in a crusade, particularly, a medieval pilgrim of the crusades.

ċrụ-sād′ing, *a.* Engaged in or relating to the crusades.

> Some gray *crusading* knight. —M. Arnold.

ċrụ-ṣā′dō, ċrụ-zā′dō, *n.* [Port. *cruzado*, marked with a cross, from *cruz*; L. *crux*, a cross.] A Portuguese silver coin valued at fifty-two cents. It was anciently worth about forty-two cents.

ċrụse, *n.* [ME. *cruse*; Ice. *krus*, a pot, tankard; D. *kroes*, a cup, cruse.] A small cup; a bottle or cruet.

ċrụ′set, *n.* [Fr. *creuset*, *cruset*, a melting-pot, crucible.] A goldsmith's crucible or melting-pot.

ċrush, *v.t.*; crushed, (krusht), *pt.*, *pp.*; crushing, *ppr.* [ME. *cruschen*, *crousshen*; OFr. *cruissor*, *croissir*; LL. *cruscire*, to crush, break.]
1. To press and bruise between two hard bodies; to squeeze, so as to force a thing out of its natural shape; to bruise by pressure; as, to *crush* apples for cider.

> The ass *crushed* Balaam's foot against the wall. —Num. xxii. 25.

2. To overwhelm by pressure; to beat or force down by an incumbent weight, with breaking or bruising.

> To *crush* the pillars which the pile sustain. —Dryden.

3. To overwhelm by power; to subdue; to conquer beyond resistance; as, to *crush* one's enemies; to *crush* a rebellion.
4. To oppress grievously.

> Thou shalt be only oppressed and *crushed* alway. —Deut. xxviii. 33.

5. To bruise and break into fine particles by beating or grinding; to comminute.
To crush a cup of wine; to drink in company; to open a bottle together.

ċrush, *v.i.* To be pressed into a smaller compass by external pressure; to have the walls broken in by force from without.

ċrush, *n.* 1. A violent collision, or rushing together, which breaks or bruises the bodies; or a fall that breaks or bruises into a confused mass; as, the *crush* of a large tree, or of a building.

> The wreck of matter and the *crush* of worlds. —Addison.

2. The pressure caused by a crowd of persons or animals; the mass of separate bodies crowded together; as, a person fainted in the *crush*; a *crush* to view a race.

ċrush′ẽr, *n.* 1. One who or the thing which exerts a crushing force.
2. A power machine in which hard substances such as ore and boulders are crushed.
3. Colloquially, anything which bears down with compelling force, as a blow or a reproof.

ċrush′ẽr-gāuġe, *n.* Any appliance for determining the projectile force of a charge in a gun.

ċrush′-hat′, *n.* A soft hat; also, an opera-hat.

ċrush′-rơơm, *n.* A lobby or foyer.

ċrust, *n.* [L. *crusta*, the hard surface of a body, shell, rind.]
1. An external coat or covering of a thing, which is hard or harder than the internal substance; as, the *crust* of bread; the *crust* of snow.
2. A collection of matter into a hard body; an incrustation; specifically, the beeswing of wine. [See *Beeswing*.]
3. A piece of *crust*; a waste piece of bread.

> Give me again a hollow tree,
> A *crust* of bread and liberty. —Pope.

4. A shell, as the hard covering of a crab and some other animals.
5. In cookery, (a) the hard outside part of a loaf of bread, opposed to the *crumb*; (b) the inclosing part of pastry, as of a pie or dumpling.
6. In anatomy, a crusta.
7. In geology, (a) the solid portion of the globe which is accessible to inspection and observation; (b) the shell of hard matter composing the earth's surface, distinguished from the supposedly fused interior.
8. That part of a horse's hoof serving to hold the nails of a shoe.

ċrust, *v.t.*; crusted, *pt.*, *pp.*; crusting, *ppr.* To cover with a hard case or coat; to spread over the surface of, with a substance harder than the matter covered; to incrust; as, to *crust* cake with sugar.

ċrust, *v.i.* To cover with a crust.

ċrus′tȧ, *n.*; *pl.* **ċrus′tæ**. [L., a shell, crust.]
1. A hardened coating; a crust.
2. A medallion or gem to be set in an incrusted surface.
3. In zoölogy, the bony covering of a crustacean; a crust.
4. In botany, a term applied to the brittle crustaceous thallus of lichens.
5. In anatomy, the layer of true bone, *crusta petrosa*, which covers the fang of a tooth, as enamel covers the exposed crown.

Ċrus-tā′ce-ȧ (-shi-ȧ), *n.pl.* [L., from *crusta*, the hard shell of a body, rind, and *-acea*.] One of the three primary divisions or classes into which annulose animals provided with articulated limbs are divided. The higher forms of this class include lobsters, shrimps, crawfish, etc.; the lower animals are of varied forms, as barnacles, wood-lice, fish-lice, etc.

ċrus-tā′ceăn (-shi-ăn), *a.* and *n.* I. *a.* Belonging to or characteristic of the *Crustacea*; crustaceous.
II. *n.* An individual of the *Crustacea*.

ċrus-tā″cē-ō-loġ′iċ-ăl, *a.* Pertaining to crustaceology.

ċrus-tā-cē-ol′ō-ġist, *n.* One versed in crustaceology.

ċrus-tā-cē-ol′ō-ġy, *n.* [L. *crusta*, crust, rind, and *-acea*, and Gr. *-logia*, from *legein*, to speak.] That division of zoölogy which has to do with crustaceans.

ċrus-tā′ceous, *a.* [L. *crustaceus*, from *crusta*, crust, rind.]
1. Pertaining to or of the nature of a crust.
2. In zoölogy, belonging to the *Crustacea*.
3. In botany, (a) brittle, (b) having a brittle thallus, as certain lichens. [See *Crusta*, 4.]

ċrus-tā′ceous-ness, *n.* The quality of being crustaceous.

ċrus′tæ, *n.*, pl. of *crusta*.

ċrust′ăl, *a.* Of the nature of a crust; relating to a crust; crustaceous.

ċrus-tȧ-loġ′iċ-ăl, *a.* Same as *Crustaceological*.

ċrus-tal′ō-ġist, *n.* Same as *Crustaceologist*.

ċrus-tal′ō-ġy, *n.* Same as *Crustaceology*.

ċrus′tāte, ċrus′tā-ted, *a.* [L. *crustatus*.] Covered with a crust; as, *crustate* basalt.

ċrus-tā′tion, *n.* An adherent crust; incrustation.

ċrus-tif′iċ, *a.* Forming or depositing a crust [Rare.]

ċrust′i-ly, *adv.* In a crusty manner; harshly; morosely.

ċrust′i-ness, *n.* 1. Incrustation; hardness.
2. Peevishness; moroseness; surliness.

ċrust′y, *a.* 1. Like crust; of the nature of crust; hard; as, a *crusty* coat.
2. Irritable or cross in manner or speech; lacking gentleness; peevish; testy; petulant; surly.

> Thou *crusty* batch of nature, what's the news? —Shak.

ċrut, *n.* [Fr. *croûte*; L. *crusta*, crust.] The rough, shaggy part of oak-bark.

ċrutch, *n.* [ME. *crutche*, *crucche*; AS. *crycc*; D. *kruk*; Dan. *krykke*; Sw. *krycka*, a crutch.]
1. A staff with a curving crosspiece at the head, to be placed under the arm or shoulder, to support the lame in walking.
2. A forked leg-rest on a sidesaddle.
3. Nautically, (a) a piece of knee-timber placed inside of a ship, for the security of the heels of the cant-timbers abaft; (b) a forked stanchion of wood or iron; any fixture or adjustment with a head or top like that of a crutch.

ċrutch, *v.t.*; crutched (krutcht), *pt.*, *pp.*; crutching, *ppr.* To support on crutches; to prop or sustain, as that which is feeble.

> Fools that *crutch* their feeble sense on verse. —Dryden.

ċrutched, *a.* 1. Supported with crutches.
2. Bearing the sign of the cross; crouched.
Crutched friars; an order of friars founded at Bologna in 1169, so named from their adopting the cross as their special symbol. Called also *crouched* or *crossed friars*.

ċrụth, *n.* See first *Crowd*.

ċrux, *n.*; *pl.* **ċrux′eṣ** or **ċrụ′ċēṣ**. [L. *crux*, a cross.]
1. Anything that puzzles, vexes, or tries, in the highest degree.
2. A cross. [See *Crux ansata*.]
3. [C—] The Southern Cross, a constellation.
Crux ansata; a tau cross surmounted by a circle; an ankh.
Crux criticorum; the greatest difficulty that can occur to critics; an extremely hard nut for the critics to crack.

ċrụ̄y′shāġe, *n.* [Origin unknown.] The porbeagle.

ċrụ-zā′dō, *n.* See *Crusado*.

ċrwth (krōth), *n.* [W.] The crowd; a violin.

ċrȳ, *v.i.*; cried, *pt.*, *pp.*; crying, *ppr.* [ME. *crien*; OFr. *crier*; Pr. *cridar*; LL. *cridare*, to clamor, cry; L. *quiritare*, freq. of *queri*, to lament, complain.]
1. To shout in a loud voice by way of earnest request or prayer, or in giving public notice; to speak, call, or exclaim with vehemence; to call importunately.

> The people *cried* to Pharaoh for bread. —Gen. xli. 55.

2. To call for vengeance or punishment.

> The voice of thy brother's blood *crieth* unto me from the ground. —Gen. iv. 10.

3. To lift up the voice in weeping; to lament.
4. To utter a loud, inarticulate sound, as a dog or a bird.

> In a cowslip's bell I lie;
> There I couch when owls do *cry*. —Shak.

To cry one's eyes out; to shed tears immoderately; to give uncontrolled vent to one's feelings.
To cry out; to shout; to vociferate; to complain loudly; to expostulate.

> And lo, a spirit taketh him, and he suddenly *crieth out*. —Luke ix. 39.

To cry out against; to complain loudly, with a view to censure; to blame; to utter censure.
To cry quits; to declare that all is over; to wind up an affair.
To cry you mercy; to ask your pardon; to beg to be excused.

ċrȳ, *v.t.* 1. To proclaim; to name loudly and publicly for giving notice; as, to *cry* goods; to *cry* a lost child.
2. To reduce to some condition as a result of having uttered cries, or having wept; as, to *cry* oneself hoarse; to *cry* oneself sick.
3. To publish the banns of.
To cry down; (a) to cheapen or belittle anything in the eyes of others; as, *to cry down* goods offered for sale; (b) to condemn.
To cry up; to praise with a view to enhance the value of a thing.
Syn.—Call, shout, exclaim, pray, implore, appeal, clamor, shed tears, sob, weep, proclaim, hawk, advertise.

ċrȳ, *n.*; *pl.* **ċrieṣ**. 1. In a general sense, a loud sound uttered by the mouth of an animal; applicable to the voice of man or beast, and articulate or inarticulate.

2. A loud or vehement sound, uttered in weeping or lamentation, prayer or request.

3. Exclamation of triumph, of wonder, or of other passion; acclamation; expression of popular favor.

The *cry* went once on thee. —Shak.

4. Proclamation; public notice.

At midnight there was a *cry* made. —Matt. xxv. 6.

5. Public reports or complaints, noise; fame.

6. A call by a hawker or peddler announcing the goods he has for sale; as, the characteristic street *cries* of a large city.

7. A pack of hunting-dogs; hence applied in disrespect to a company or party of people.

8. An object for which a political party professes great earnestness for electioneering purposes; a political catchword; as, the party *cry* of the Democrats.

9. The peculiar sound produced by the bending and breaking of pure or block tin.

A far cry; a long distance; a wide separation; as, from anticipation to realization is *a far cry.*

In full cry; a term in hunting signifying that all the hounds have caught the scent and give tongue in chorus; hence, hot pursuit; hard chase.

Syn.—Call, shout, sound, utterance, outcry, tumult, clamor, proclamation, demand, requisition, vociferation, watchword.

çrȳ'ăl, *n.* [W. *cregyr*, a heron, a screamer.] The heron. [Obs.]

çrȳ'ẽr, *n.* 1. A falcon-gentle.

2. Same as *Crier.*

çrȳ'ing, *a.* Calling for vengeance and punishment; notorious; common; great.

Heinous offences are called *crying* sins. —Lowth.

çrȳ'ō-ġen, *n.* [Gr. *kryos*, cold, frost, and *-genēs*, producing.] Any freezing-mixture, as ice and salt.

çrȳ-ō-hȳ'drāte, *n.* [Gr. *kryos*, cold, frost, and *hydōr*, water.] That particular strength of a particular salt, which resists solidification to the lowest temperature.

çrȳ'ō-lite, *n.* [Gr. *kryos*, cold, frost, and *lithos*, stone.] A fluoride of sodium and aluminium found in Greenland. It occurs in masses of a foliated structure, and has a glistening, vitreous luster. It is used in the manufacture of aluminium, soda, and certain grades of glass.

çrȳ-oph'ō-rus, *n.* [L., from Gr. *kryos*, cold, frost, and *-phoros*, from *pherein*, to bear.] An instrument for showing the diminution of temperature in water by evaporation.

Cryophorus.

çrypt, *n.* [L. *crypta*; Gr. *kryptē*, a vault, crypt; from *kryptein*, to hide.]

1. A subterranean cell or cave, especially one constructed for the interment of bodies. [See *Catacomb.*]

2. That part of a basilica or cathedral below the floor, set apart for monumental purposes, and sometimes used as a chapel.

3. In anatomy, a minute tube, gland, or follicle, in the skin or mucous membrane.

çrypt'ăl, *a.* Pertaining to or connected with a crypt; as, the *cryptal* secretion.

çryp'tiç, çryp'tiç-ăl, *a.* [LL. *crypticus*; Gr. *kryptikos*, from *kryptein*, to hide.] Hidden; secret; occult.

çryp'tiç-ăl-ly, *adv.* Covertly; in secret; occultly.

çryp'-ti-dine, *n.* [Gr. *kryptos*, hidden.] A derivative of coal-tar, $C_{11}H_{11}N$; one of the quinoline bases.

çryp'tō-, çrypt-. A combining form from Gr. *kryptos*, hidden, covered, secret; as, *crypto*gram, *crypt*odont.

çryp'tō-bra͞nçh, *a.* and *n.* [*Crypto-*, and Gr. *branchia*, gills.]

I. *a.* Same as *Cryptobranchiate.*

II. *n.* An animal having concealed or internal branchiæ.

Çryp-tō-bra͞n-çhi-ā'tȧ, *n.pl.* A division of animals comprehending those with concealed gills.

çryp-tō-bra͞n'çhi-āte, *a.* In zoölogy, having concealed gills; destitute of distinct gills.

Çryp"tō-Çal'vin-işm, *n.* [*Crypto-*, and *Calvinism.*] An opprobrious epithet applied to the doctrine held by the adherents of Melanchthon, following Luther's death, who accepted Calvin's doctrine of the real presence rather than Luther's.

Çryp"tō-Çal'vin-ist, *n.* One who accepts the doctrine of Crypto-Calvinism.

çryp'tō-çärp, *n.* See *Cystocarp.*

çryp-tō-çeph'ȧ-lous, *a.* [*Crypto-*, and Gr. *kephalē*, head.] Having the head deeply inserted in the thorax.

çryp-toç'ẽr-ous, *a.* [*Crypto-*, and Gr. *keras*, a horn.] Having the antennæ hidden underneath the head.

çryp-tō-çrys'tăl-line, *a.* [*Crypto-*, and Gr. *krystallinos*, from *krystallos*, crystal, ice; *kryos*, cold, frost.] Made up of crystalline particles to be distinguished only under the microscope; applied to minerals.

çryp-tō-di'rous, *a.* [*Crypto-*, and Gr. *deirē*, neck, throat.] Having a retractile neck which, with the head, may be entirely withdrawn beneath the exoskeleton, as in turtles.

çryp'tō-dont, *a.* [*Crypto-*, and Gr. *odous*, *odontos*, tooth.] Having rudimentary tooth-like processes, as certain bivalve mollusks.

çryp'tō-gam, *n.* A plant of the division *Cryptogamia.*

Çryp-tō-gā'mi-ȧ, *n.pl.* [L., from Gr. *kryptos*, hidden, and *gamos*, marriage.] The name given by Linnæus to the large division of plants which do not bear true flowers consisting of stamens and pistils, but grow from spores, which are cells with one or two membranes inclosing a uniform granular substance.

çryp-tō-gā'mi-ăn, çryp-tō-gam'iç, çryp-tog'ȧ-mous, *a.* Pertaining to plants of the division of *Cryptogamia*, including the ferns, mosses, seaweeds, mushrooms, etc.

çryp-tog'ȧ-mist, *n.* One who is skilled in cryptogamic botany.

çryp'tō-gram, *n.* [*Crypto-*, and Gr. *gramma*, a writing, from *graphein*, to write.] A writing in cipher; a cryptograph.

çryp'tō-gräph, *n.* [*Crypto-*, and Gr. *graphein*, to write.]

1. Something written in secret characters or cipher, as a message.

2. A system of secret writing.

çryp-tog'rȧ-phăl, *a.* Same as *Cryptographic.*

çryp-tog'rȧ-phẽr, çryp-tog'rȧ-phist, *n.* One who writes in secret characters.

çryp-tō-graph'iç, çryp-tō-graph'iç-ăl, *a.* Written in secret characters or in cipher, or with sympathetic ink.

çryp-tog'rȧ-phy, *n.* The act or art of writing in secret characters; also, secret characters or cipher.

çryp-tol'ō-ġy, *n.* Secret or enigmatical language.

Çryp-tō-mē'ri-ȧ, *n.* A genus of cypress-like conifers native to China but now grown as ornamental trees in the United States. *Cryptomeria Japonica*, the Japanese cedar, is the only species.

çryp-tō-neū'rous, *a.* [*Crypto-*, and Gr. *neuron*, a nerve.] Without nerves or a nervous system, as the *Acrita.*

çryp'tō-nym, *n.* [*Crypto-*, and Gr. *onyma*, name.] The secret name of an initiate.

çryp'tō-pine, çryp-tō'pi-ȧ, *n.* [*Crypto-*, and Gr. *opion*, poppy-juice.] A colorless, opium alkaloid, $C_{21}H_{23}NO_5$.

çryp-tor'çhis, çryp-tor'çhid, *n.* One having abdominal retention of the testes.

Çryp-tū'ri, *n.pl.* [L., from Gr. *kryptos*, hidden, and *oura*, a tail.] A family of birds, represented by the tinamous of South America. [See *Tinamou.*]

çrys'tăl, *n.* [L. *crystallum*; Gr. *krystallos*, ice, crystal, from *kryos*, cold, frost.]

1. In chemistry and mineralogy, an inorganic body, which, by the operation of affinity, has assumed the form of a regular solid, terminated by a certain number of plane and smooth surfaces, symmetrically arranged.

2. Same as *Rock-crystal.*

3. A kind of heavy, clear glass manufactured from the highest grade of materials; flint-glass. Hence, in a collective sense, all articles, as decanters, cruets, etc., made of this material; cut glass.

4. The thin glass which covers the dial of a watch.

5. A body resembling *crystal* in its qualities, as of clearness, transparency, or purity, as water or other liquid.

Down the liquid *crystal* dropt. —Tennyson.

Compound crystal; a crystal composed of two united crystals.

Iceland crystal; Iceland spar.

çrys'tăl, *a.* Consisting of crystal, or like crystal; clear; transparent; lucid; pellucid.

By *crystal* streams that murmur through the meads. —Dryden.

çrys-tăl-lif'ẽr-ous, *a.* Producing or composed of crystals.

çrys-tăl-lig'ẽr-ous, *a.* [L. *crystallum*, a crystal, ice, and L. *gerere*, to bear.] Bearing or producing crystals; crystalliferous.

çrys'tăl-lin, çrys'tăl-line, *n.* Globulin; also, an old name for aniline.

çrys'tăl-line (*or* -lin), *a.* 1. Consisting of crystal; as, a *crystalline* palace.

2. Relating or pertaining to crystals or crystallography.

3. Formed by crystallization.

4. Resembling crystal; pure; clear; transparent; pellucid; as, a *crystalline* sky.

Crystalline heavens; in ancient astronomy, two spheres imagined between the primum mobile and the firmament, in the Ptolemaic system, which supposed the heavens to be solid and only susceptible of a single motion.

Crystalline lens; the double convex, transparent part of the eye lying behind the iris and in front of the vitreous body of the eye. It serves to refract the various rays of light so as to form a perfect image on the retina.

Crystalline style; a semitransparent cæcal organ of certain bivalves, the use of which is unknown.

çrys'tăl-line, *n.* A crystallized rock, or one only partially crystallized, as granite.

çrys'tăl-lite, *n.* [Gr. *krystallos*, crystal, ice, and *-ite.*]

1. A name given to whinstone, cooled slowly after fusion.

2. A generic name for the various globulites.

çrys'tăl-lī-zā-ble, *a.* That may be crystallized; that may form or be formed into crystals.

çrys"tăl-li-zā'tion, *n.* 1. The act or process by which the parts of a solid body, separated by the intervention of a fluid or by fusion, again coalesce or unite, and form a solid body. If the process is slow and undisturbed, the particles assume a regular arrangement, each substance taking a determinate and regular form, according to its natural laws; but if the process is rapid or disturbed, the substance takes an irregular form. This process is the effect of refrigeration or evaporation.

2. The mass or body formed by the process of crystallizing.

çrys'tăl-līze, *v.t.*; crystallized, *pt., pp.*; crystallizing, *ppr.* To cause to form crystals; figuratively, to cause to assume definite shape; as, to *crystallize* public opinion.

çrys'tăl-līze, *v.i.* To become a crystal or crystalline in form; also used figuratively.

çrys-tal-lō-. A combining form from Greek *krystallos*, crystal, ice.

çrys'tăl-lod, *n.* [Gr. *krystallos*, crystal, and Gr. *od*, from *hodos*, way.] The odic force of crystallization. [See *Od.*]

çrys"tăl-lō-ġen'iç, çrys"tăl-lō-ġen'iç-ăl, *a.* Relating to crystallogeny; pertaining to crystal formation.

çrys-tăl-loġ'e-ny, *n.* [*Crystallo-*, and Gr. *-geneia*, from *-genēs*, producing.] The branch of science which has to do with the formation of crystals.

çrys-tăl-log'rȧ-phẽr, *n.* One who has made a study of crystallography.

çrys"tăl-lō-graph'iç, çrys"tăl-lō-graph'iç-ăl, *a.* Relating to crystallography; as, a *crystallographic* axis.

çrys"tăl-lō-graph'iç-ăl-ly, *adv.* According to the manner of crystallography; by crystallization.

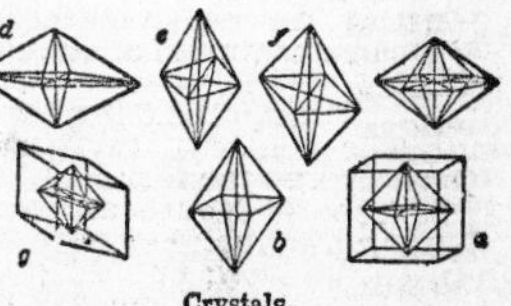

Crystals.

çrys-tăl-log'rȧ-phy, *n.* [*Crystallo-*, and Gr. *-graphia*, from *graphein*, to write.]

1. The doctrine or science of crystallization, teaching the principles of the process, and the forms and structure of crystals. The form of any solid may be determined by referring it to three rectilineal axes, intersecting one another in a single point. In some systems of *crystallography*, however, it is found more convenient to refer the forms of the crystals to four axes. The following are the generally adopted systems: (a) monometric, three rectangular axes all of equal length; (b) dimetric, three rectangular axes, two of equal, the third of different length; (c) hexagonal, four axes, three of equal length, in the same plane, and inclined to each other at an angle of 60°, the fourth of different length and at right angles to the plane of the other three; (d) trimetric or rhombic, three rectangular axes of unequal lengths; (e) monoclinic, three axes, two at right angles to each other, the third perpendicular to one and oblique to the other; (f) diclinic, three axes, two at right angles, the third oblique to both; (g) triclinic, three axes, all oblique to each other.

2. A discourse or treatise on crystallization.

çrys'tăl-loid, *a.* [Gr. *krystallos*, crystal, and *eidos*, form.] Transparent, as crystal; like a crystal in clearness.

çrys'tăl-loid, *n.* 1. The name given by some scientists to a class of crystalline bodies which have the power, when in solution, of passing through animal tissue.

2. A protein-crystal present in some vegetable cells.

çrys-tăl-lol'ō-ġy, *n.* [*Crystallo-*, and Gr. *-logia*, from *legein*, to speak.] A comprehensive term embracing both crystallogeny and crystallography.

çrys'tăl-lō-man-çy, *n.* [*Crystallo-*, and Gr. *manteia*, divination.] An ancient mode of divination through the agency of transparent precious stones and crystal spheres.

çrys-tăl-lom′e-try, *n.* [*Crystallo-*, and Gr. *-metria*, from *metron*, a measure.] The art or process of measuring the forms of crystals.

çrys′tăl-lŭr-ġy, *n.* [*Crystallo-*, and Gr. *ergon*, work.] Formation of crystals; the process of producing crystals.

çrys′tăl-wŏrt, *n.* A plant of the *Hepaticæ* or liverwort family.

cte-nid′i-um (te-), *n.*; *pl.* **cte-nid′i-ȧ.** [L., from Gr. *ktenidion*, dim. of *kteis*, a comb.] The filamentous respiratory organ of a mollusk; a branchia.

cte-nō-. A combining form from Greek *kteis*, *ktenos*, a comb.

cten-ō-brañch, cten-ō-brañ′çhi-āte (ten-), *a.* and *n.* I. *a.* Having comblike gills, as the *Ctenobranchiata.*

II. *n.* One of the *Ctenobranchiata.*

Cten-ō-brañ-çhi-ā′tȧ, Cten-ō-brañ′çhi-ȧ, *n. pl.* A family of mollusks, the *Pectinibranchiata.*

ctē′nō-cyst (tē′), *n.* [*Cteno-*, and Gr. *kystis*, a bladder.] A part, believed to have auditory functions, found in the *Ctenophora.*

cten′ō-dont (ten′), *a.* [*Cteno-*, and Gr. *odous*, *odontos*, a tooth.] Having the teeth ctenoid.

ctē′noid (tē′), *a.* and *n.* [*Cteno-*, and Gr. *eidos*, form.]

I. *a.* Relating to fish of the order *Ctenoidei* or to the comb-shaped scales which characterize them.

II. *n.* A fossil fish of the order *Ctenoidei*; a ctenoidean.

ctē-noid′ē-ăn, ctē-noid′i-ăn, *a.* and *n.* I. *a.* Of or relating to the order *Ctenoidei.*

II. *n.* A ctenoid fish.

Ctē-noid′ē-ī, *n.pl.* [L., from Gr. *kteis*, *ktenos*, a comb, and *eidos*, form.] The third order of fossil fishes, according to the classification of Agassiz, having scales jagged or pectinate like the teeth of a comb.

Ctē-noph′ō-rȧ, *n.pl.* [L., from Gr. *kteis*, *ktenos*, a comb, and *-phoros*, from *pherein*, to bear.] An order of acalephans, of which the genus *Beroe* may be taken as the type. They are gelatinous-like bodies, spherical in form, very delicate and transparent. Eight bands covered with cilia run from pole to pole, by the motion of which cilia the animal moves along. [See *Beroe.*]

cten′ō-phōre, *n.* 1. An individual of the *Ctenophora*

2. One of the motor cilia of the *Ctenophora.*

ctē-noph′ō-rous, cten-ō-phor′iç, *a.* Pertaining to or resembling the *Ctenophora.*

Cten-ō-stom′ȧ-tȧ, *n.pl.* [*Cteno-*, and Gr. *stoma*, *stomatos*, a mouth.] A suborder of marine *Polyzoa*, having the terminal mouths closed by means of a fringe of hair.

çuär-tĭl′lȧ (kwär-tēl′yä), *n.* [Sp., dim. of *cuarta*, fourth.] A Spanish measure; (a) eight liquid pints or one-fourth an arroba; (b) one-fourth a fanega.

çub, *n.* [Ir. *cuib*, a young dog, whelp; *cu*, a dog.]

1. The young of certain quadrupeds, as of the bear and the fox; a puppy; a whelp.

2. A boorish youth; an awkward young person having provincial or uncouth manners.

çub, *v.t.* and *v.i.*; cubbed, *pt.*, *pp.*; cubbing, *ppr.*

I. *v.t.* To bring forth, as a cub or cubs.

II. *v.i.* In contempt, to bring forth young.

çub, *v.t.* To restrain; to confine. [Obs.]

çub, *n.* 1. A stall for cattle. [Obs.]

2. A cubby; a cupboard; a chest. [Obs.]

Çū′băn, *a.* and *n.* I. *a.* Of or relating to the island of Cuba or its people.

II. *n.* A native or citizen of Cuba.

çū′băn-īte, *n.* [So named because first found in Cuba.] A sulphid of iron and copper resembling chalcopyrite.

çū-bā′tion, *n.* [L. *cubatio*, from *cubare*, to lie down.] A reclining. [Obs.]

çū′bȧ-tō-ry, *a.* [LL. *cubator*, one who lies down, from *cubare*, to lie down.] Recumbent. [Rare.]

çū′bȧ-tūre, *n.* [From L. *cubus*, a cube.] Determination of the cubical contents of a body; the contents so found.

çub′bridġe-head (-brij-hed), *n.* [*Cubbord*, cupboard, and *-age* and *head.*] Nautically, a partition made of boards, etc., across the forecastle and half-deck of a ship.

çub′by, *n.* [L.G. *kubje*, a shed.] A secluded nook indoors; a close, snug corner.

çub′by-hōle, *n.* A small inclosed space; a pigeonhole; a recess; by extension, a tiny cottage.

çub′by-yew, *n.* [A corruption of *cobia*, of W. Ind. origin.] A fish, the cobia.

çub′-drawn, *a.* Drawn or sucked by cubs, applied to the bear.

çūbe, *n.* [Fr. *cube*; L. *cubus*; Gr. *kybos*, a cube, die.]

1. In geometry, a regular solid body, with six equal square sides, and containing equal angles.

Cube.

2. In arithmetic, the product of a number multiplied into itself, and that product multiplied into the same number; or it is formed by multiplying any number twice by itself; as, 4×4=16, and 16×4=64, the cube of 4.

Cube root; the number or quantity which, multiplied into itself, and then into the product, produces the cube; or which, twice multiplied into itself, produces the number of which it is the root; thus, 3 is the *cube root* or side of 27, for 3×3=9, and 3×9=27.

çūbe, *v.t.*; cubed, *pt.*, *pp.*; cubing, *ppr.* To raise to the third power, by multiplying a number into itself twice.

çū′beb, *n.* [Sp. *cubeba*; Ar. *kababa*; Hind. *kababa.*] The small, spicy berry of the *Piper Cubeba*, from Java and other East Indian islands, used in diseases of the urinary system, and sometimes smoked for catarrh or bronchial disease.

çū-beb′iç, *a.* Relating to or obtained from cubebs.

çūbe′-ōre, *n.* A mineral, pharmacosiderite.

çūbe′-spär, *n.* A mineral, anhydrite.

çub′hood, *n.* The condition of being a cub.

çū′biç, *a.* [L. *cubicus*; Gr. *kybikos*, from *kybos*, a cube.]

1. Having the form of a cube.

2. Having three dimensions; measured by or capable of being measured by a unit of volume each edge of which is the unit of length having the same name as the unit cube.

3. In mathematics, denoting the third power in a series of geometrical proportionals continued; as, a *cubic* quantity.

Cubic equation; an equation in which the highest or only power of the unknown quantity is a cube.

Cubic number; a number produced by multiplying a number into itself, and that product by the same number.

Cubic parabola; a curve equationally expressed by $y^m=ax^n$, in which one exponent is 3, and greater than the other.

çū′biç, *n.* In mathematics, (a) a cubic expression or equation; (b) a cubic curve.

çū′biç-ăl, *a.* 1. Cubic.

2. Of or pertaining to a cube.

çū′biç-ăl-ly, *adv.* In a cubical method.

çū′biç-ăl-ness, *n.* The state or quality of being cubical.

çū′bi-çle, *n.* [L. *cubiculum*, a bedroom, from *cubare*, to lie down.] A private sleeping-apartment; a chamber; also written *cubicule*, *cubiculo.*

çū-biç′ū-lăr, *a.* Pertaining to a private chamber; as, *cubicular* devotions.

çū′bi-fọrm, *a.* Having the form of a cube.

çū-bi′lē, *n.* [L., a bed, resting-place, from *cubare*, to lie down.] The groundwork or lowest course of stones in a building.

çū′bi-lōse, *n.* The base of edible birds'-nests, a secretion resembling mucilage.

çū′bist, *n.* One of a new school of painters, holding that art shall be an expression of the "soul" of the painter, denying any representation of nature or form of decoration.

çū′bit, *n.* [L. *cubitum*, the elbow, a cubit.]

1. In anatomy, the forearm; the ulna, a bone of the arm from the elbow to the wrist. [Obs.]

2. A measure, originally the distance from the elbow to the extremity of the middle finger. The ancient Egyptian *cubit* measured 20.64 inches, which is the longest known save the Hebrew, which may have exceeded it. The Roman was equal to 17.4 inches and the English *cubit* is a measure of 18 inches.

3. A cubitus.

çū′bit-ăl, *a.* 1. Of the length or measure of a cubit.

2. Pertaining to the cubit or ulna; as, the *cubital* nerve; *cubital* artery; *cubital* muscle.

3. In zoölogy, relating to the cubitus.

çū′bit-ăl, *n.* [L. *cubital*, an elbow-cushion, from *cubitum*, an elbow.]

1. An oversleeve covering the forearm from the wrist to the elbow.

2. A pillow upon which to lean the elbow when in a half-reclining position.

3. In entomology, a cubitus.

çū′bit-ed, *a.* Having the measure of a cubit.

çū′bi-tus, *n.*; *pl.* **çū′bi-tī.** [L. *cubitus*, the elbow.]

1. In entomology, the primary nervure of an insect's wing, lying between the radius and the first anal vein.

2. In anatomy, same as *cubit.*

çub′less, *a.* Having no cubs.

çū-bō-. A combining form from L. *cubus*, Gr. *kybos*, a cube, and employed in mathematical and anatomic terms to signify, (a) relating to a cube, and (b) of or pertaining to the cuboid bone in the foot.

çū″bō-dō″deç-ȧ-hē′drăl, *a.* [*Cubo-*, and Gr. *dōdekaedron*; *dōdeka*, twelve, and *hedra*, a seat, base.] Presenting the two forms, a cube and a dodecahedron.

çū′boid, *n.* [L. *cubus*; Gr. *kybos*, a cube, and *eidos*, form.] In anatomy, the cubical bone on the outer side of the tarsus in man and most of the higher mammals.

çū′boid, çū-boid′ăl, *a.* Having nearly the form of a cube.

çū″bō-oç-tȧ-hē′drăl, *a.* Presenting a combination of the two forms, a cube and an octahedron.

çū″bō-oç-tȧ-hē′drŏn, *n.* [*Cubo-*, and Gr. *oktaedron*, from *oktaedros*, eight-sided; *oktō*, eight, and *hedra*, a seat, base.] A fourteen-sided figure having twelve vertices, being a combination of the cube and octahedron.

çū′çȧ, *n.* See *Coca.*

çuck′ing-stool, *n.* [ME. *cucking-stol*, *kukstole*, *cuck*; Ice. *kuka*, to ease oneself; *kukr*, dung, ordure; from the shape of the chair.] A chair in which an offender, as a refractory woman or defaulting brewer or baker, was placed, usually before her or his own door, to receive the derision and jeers of the populace. The *cucking-stool* has been frequently confounded with the ducking-stool; but the former did not of itself admit of the ducking of its occupant, although in conjunction with the tumbrel it was sometimes used for that purpose.

çuck′ōld, *n.* [ME. *cokolde*, *kukwald*; OFr. *coucol*, *couquiol*; L. *cuculus*, a cuckoo.]

1. A man whose wife is false to his bed; the husband of an adulteress.

2. The horned cowfish, *Ostracion quadricorne.*

3. The cowbird, *Molothrus ater*; so called from its habit of laying its eggs in nests not of its own building.

Cuckold's knot or *neck*; nautically, a knot securing a rope to a spar, the two parts being crossed and seized together.

çuck′ōld, *v.t.*; cuckolded, *pt.*, *pp.*; cuckolding, *ppr.* To make a cuckold of; said of either participant in the crime.

çuck′ōld-ize, *v.t.* Same as *Cuckold.*

çuck′ōld-ly, *a.* Having the qualities of a cuckold; mean; sneaking.

çuck′ōl-dŏm, *n.* The condition of being a cuckold.

çuck′ōld-ry, *n.* The system of debauching other men's wives; the state of being made a cuckold.

çuck′ọọ, *n.* [ME. *cockou*, *cucko*; LL. *cucus*; L. dim. *cuculus*, a cuckoo; Gr. *kokkyx*; Sans. *kokila*, a cuckoo.]

Cuckoo (*Cuculus canorus*).

1. A bird of the family *Cuculidæ*, named in imitation of the call of the male during the mating season. It is of many genera, and is found in most temperate and tropical regions. The typical genus, *Cuculus*, comprises the common European cuckoo, *Cuculus canorus*, a zygodactylous bird about the size of a small pigeon, having an abundance of ashy plumage streaked with white and black. It is parasitical, depositing its eggs generally in the nest of the hedge-sparrow, meadow-pipit, or wagtail, by which birds they are hatched and the young reared. The principal American species are *Coccyzus americanus*, the yellow-billed *cuckoo*, and *Coccyzus erythrophthalmus*, the black-billed *cuckoo*, both species being nonparasitic.

2. An idiot; a fool; used in jest or contempt.

çuck′ọọ-bee, *n.* A bee of any of several genera, as the *Nomada*, *Epeolus*, *Cœlioxys*, etc. It lays its eggs in the nests of other bees, and its larvæ feed upon the food or the larvæ of the bees properly occupying the nest.

çuck′ọọ-bread, çuck′ọọ's-bread (-bred), *n.* [LL. *panis cuculi*, bread of the cuckoo; so called because it blossoms at the time the cuckoo's cry is heard.] A plant, wood-sorrel.

çuck′ọọ-bud, *n.* The buttercup. [Obs.]

çuck′ọọ-clock, *n.* A clock indicating the hours by the note of an automatic cuckoo.

çuck′ọọ-dōve, *n.* A pigeon of the genus *Macropygia*, of the family *Columbidæ.*

çuck′ọọ-fal″çŏn (-fa″k′n), *n.* One of a group of East Indian falconine birds.

çuck′ọọ-fish, *n.* In England, (a) *Trigla cuculus*, the red gurnard; (b) the boarfish; (c) the striped wrasse.

çuck′ọọ-flow″ẽr, *n.* In botany, (a) lady's-smock; (b) ragged-robin.

çuck′ọọ-fly, *n.* A name applied to one of various parasitic insects, as the ichneumon-fly or one of the *Chrysididæ.*

çuck′ọọ-pint, *n.* *Arum maculatum*, the wake-robin.

çuck′ọọ-shrīke, *n.* A bird, the caterpillar-catcher.

çuck′ọọ's-māte, *n.* A name given locally in England to the wryneck.

çuck′ọọ-spit, çuck′ọọ-spit″tle, *n.* A froth or spume found on plants, being a secretion formed by the larvæ of certain small homopterous insects, as the *Aphrophora spumaria* or froghopper; also, any such insect.

çuck′quēan, çuç′quēan, *n.* [*Cuck*old, and *quean*, a woman.] The wife of an unfaithful husband. [Obs.]

çu-çu′jō, *n.* See *Fire-beetle*, 1.

çū-çū′li-fọrm, *a.* [L. *cuculus*, a cuckoo, and *forma*, form.] Resembling a cuckoo, particularly in form; also, cuculine.

çū′çū-line, *a.* [From L. *cuculus*, a cuckoo.] Pertaining or related to the cuckoos; having the characteristics of a cuckoo.

çū′çul-lāte, çū′çul-lā-ted, *a.* [LL. *cucullatus*, from *cucullus*, a hood, cowl.]

1. Hooded; cowled; covered as with a hood.

2. In botany, having the shape or resemblance of a hood; or wide at the top and drawn to a point below, in the shape of a conical roll of paper; as, a *cucullate* leaf.

3. In zoölogy, bearing some process or marking resembling a hood; especially, having the first segment of the thorax raised to cover the head like a hood, as some insects.

çū-çul′lī, *n.*, pl. of *cucullus*.

çū-çul′li-fọrm, *a.* [L. *cucullus*, a hood, and *forma*, form.] Formed like or resembling a hood.

çū-çul′lus, *n.*; *pl.* **çū-çul′lī.** [L.] 1. A cowl or hood worn by the ancient Romans and by monks.

2. In biology, a marking or a part or process, like a hood.

çū′çū-loid, *a.* [L. *cuculus*, a cuckoo, and Gr. *eidos*, form.] Of or pertaining to the typical genus of cuckoos, *Cuculus*; also, resembling the cuckoos.

çū′çum-bẽr, *n.* [ME. *cucumber*, *cocumber*; OFr. *cocombre*; LL. *cucumer*; L. *cucumis*, *cucumeris*, a cucumber.]

1. A name for any of various plants of the genus *Cucumis* or of related genera; also, the fruit of such plants.

2. *Cucumis sativus*, a common garden vegetable. The plant has long rough stalks, creeping or climbing, and yellow flowers. The fruit is fleshy, cylindrical in shape, and edible when unripe. It is also much used for pickling.

Bitter cucumber; the colocynth.

Cool as a cucumber; exceedingly cool; also, composed and self-possessed.

Creeping cucumber; a climbing vine of the southeastern United States; the *Melothria pendula*.

Jamaica or *Jerusalem cucumber*; *Cucumis anguria*, the prickly cucumber, the fruit of which is used for pickles.

Squirting or *wild cucumber*; a cucurbitaceous plant, *Ecballium elaterium*, remarkable for the action of its fruit when ripe in separating from the stem and, by sudden contraction of the rind, forcing out the seeds and juice through the opening left at the point of attachment.

çū′çum-bẽr-bee′tle, *n.* A general name applied to beetles that feed upon the leaves of cucumber, melon, squash, and similar vines; especially, a flea-beetle, *Crepidodera cucumeris*, and the squash-beetle, *Diabrotica vittata*.

çū′çum-bẽr-root, *n.* The Indian cucumber.

çū′çum-bẽr-tree, *n.* 1. A name given to several varieties of magnolia trees cultivated for shade and ornament; especially the *Magnolia acuminata*, which bears a fruit somewhat resembling a small cucumber in shape.

2. The bilimbi of the East Indies.

çū-çū′mi-fọrm, *a.* [L. *cucumis*, a cucumber, and *forma*, form.] Cucumber-shaped.

Çū′çū-mis, *n.* [L., a cucumber.] A genus of plants, natural order *Cucurbitaceæ*, containing about thirty species. They are annual herbs, with hairy stems and leaves, spreading over the ground or climbing. They have yellow flowers, and a roundish, cylindrical, or angular fleshy fruit. The best known species are *Cucumis sativus*, the cucumber; *Cucumis melo*, the muskmelon, and *Cucumis citrullus*, the watermelon.

çū-çũr′bit, çū-çũr′bite, *n.* [Fr. *cucurbite*; L. *curcurbita*, a gourd.]

1. A chemical vessel originally in the shape of a gourd, but sometimes shallow, with a wide mouth. It may be made of copper, glass, tin, or stoneware, and is used in distillation. It constitutes the body of an alembic.

2. Any vessel that is gourd-shaped, as a cupping-glass.

3. A plant belonging to the order *Cucurbitaceæ*.

Çū-çũr′bi-tȧ, *n.* A genus of plants typical of the natural order *Cucurbitaceæ*. There are about a dozen species inhabiting the warmer regions of the world. They are creeping annuals, with lobed, cordate leaves, large yellow flowers, and fleshy, generally very large fruits. The pumpkin and the longneck squashes come from the *Cucurbita Pepo*, and the winter-squash from *Cucurbita maxima*.

Çū-çũr-bi-tā′cē-æ, *n.pl.* A natural order of polypetalous dicotyledonous plants, with the petals more or less united into a monopetalous corolla, consisting of climbing or trailing species with unisexual flowers, scabrous stems and leaves, and a more or less pulpy fruit The order comprehends the melon, gourd, cucumber, pumpkin, squash, colocynth, bryony, and other plants, ranged into more than eighty genera and six hundred species.

çū-çũr-bi-tā′ceous, *a.* Pertaining or belonging to the *Cucurbitaceæ*; having the characteristics of the gourd family.

çū-çũr′bi-tăl, *a.* Of or pertaining to the order *Cucurbitaceæ* or the type genus *Cucurbita*.

çū-çũr-bi-tī′nus, *n.*; *pl.* **çū-çũr-bi-tī′nī.** [L. *cucurbitinus*, like a gourd; *cucurbita*, a gourd.] A segment or joint of a tapeworm.

çū-çũr′bi-tive, *a.* Shaped like the seed of a gourd; a term applied to certain kinds of small worms.

çud, *n.* [ME. *cudde*, *cude*; AS. *cudu*; *cwidu*, cud, from *ceowan*, to chew.]

1. The food which ruminating animals voluntarily bring up into the mouth from the first stomach, and chew at leisure.

2. A portion of tobacco held in the mouth and chewed. [Slang.]

3. The first stomach of ruminants; the rumen.

To chew the cud; to ponder; to reflect; to ruminate; as, *chewing the cud* of sweet and bitter fancy.

çud′beãr, *n.* [A corruption of *Cuthbert*, called after Dr. Cuthbert Gordon, who first brought it into notice.] A purple or violet-colored powder, used in dyeing violet, purple, and crimson, prepared from various species of lichens, especially from *Lecanora tartarea*, growing on rocks in Sweden, Scotland, the north of England, etc.; also the lichen yielding such dye.

Cudbear Plant (*Lecanora tartarea*).

çud′den, *n.* A clown; a low rustic; a dolt. [Obs.]

çud′den, *n.* The coalfish. [Local Eng.]

çud′die, *n.* See third *Cuddy*.

çud′dle, *v.i.*; cuddled (-dld), *pt.*, *pp.*; cuddling, *ppr.* [A corruption of ME. *cuthen*, to cuddle, make known; AS. *cuth*, pp. of *cunnan*, to know.]

1. To snuggle; to lie close or snug.

2. To join in an embrace. [Prov. Eng. and Scot.]

çud′dle, *v.t.* To hug; to fondle.

çud′dle, *n.* A warm embrace.

çud′dy, *n.*; *pl.* **çud′dieṣ.** [Perhaps a contr. of D. *kajuit*, a cabin.]

1. A room or cabin abaft and under the poop-deck of a ship, in which the officers and cabin-passengers take their meals; also, a sort of cabin or cook-room in lighters, barges, etc.

2. A very small apartment; a locker or cupboard.

çud′dy, *n.*; *pl.* **çud′dieṣ.** [Scot.] 1. An ass; a donkey.

2. A stupid fellow; a simpleton or clown.

3. Any lifting device or jack operated by a lever.

çud′dy, *n.*; *pl.* **çud′dieṣ.** [Scot.] A fish of the cod family, the coalfish; written also *cudden*, *cuddie*.

çudġ′el (kuj′el), *n.* [ME. *cuggel*; W. *cogyl*, a club, cudgel.] A short, thick stick of wood, such as may be used as a weapon. It differs strictly from a club, which is larger at one end than the other.

To cross the cudgels; to forbear the contest; to submit; to yield; a phrase borrowed from the practice of cudgel-players, who lay one cudgel over another at the end of a contest.

To take up the cudgels; to make a defense or vindication; to champion some person or cause.

çudġ′el, *v.t.*; cudgeled, cudgelled, *pt.*, *pp.*; cudgeling, cudgelling, *ppr.* To beat with a cudgel or thick stick; to beat, in general.

To cudgel one's brains; to apply one's thoughts to something difficult.

çudġ′el-ẽr, çudġ′el-lẽr, *n.* One who beats with a cudgel.

çudġ′el-plāy, *n.* An encounter with cudgels, especially as a game.

çud′weed, *n.* [Probably corruption of *cottonweed*.] The popular name of various species of *Gnaphalium*, *Filago*, and *Antennaria*, all of which are covered with a soft cottony pubescence; cottonweed.

çūe, *n.* [Fr. *queu*; OFr. *coue*; It. *coda*; L. *coda*, *cauda*, a tail.]

1. The tail; the end of a thing; as the long curl of a wig, or a long roll or braid of hair; written also *queue*.

2. A line of waiting persons, as that formed in front of a ticket-window or in any place where each is served in turn; written also *queue*.

3. Certain words, usually the last, of an actor's speech, or a certain action, which is regarded as a signal for some speech or action by another actor.

4. A hint; an intimation; a short direction.

5. The part which any man is to play; some course of action expedient or necessary under certain circumstances; a particular duty or concern.

Were it my *cue* to fight. —Shak.

6. Humor; turn or temper of mind; as, to be in *cue* for doing a certain thing.

7. The straight rod used in playing billiards and similar games.

8. A support for a lance; a lance-rest.

çūe, *n.* [For *q.*, an abbrev. of L. *quadrans*, a farthing.] A farthing or farthing's worth; the quantity bought with a farthing. [Obs.]

çūe, *v.t.*; cued, *pt.*, *pp.*; cuing, *ppr.* To braid, twist, or curl; to tie in a cue.

çūe′-ball, *n.* In the games of billiards, pool, etc., that ball which is impelled by the cue.

çuer′dȧ (kwer′), *n.* [Sp., a cord, from L. *chorda*, a cord.] A Spanish linear unit, that of Castile being about twenty-three and three-fourths feet.

çuer′pō (kwer′), *n.* [Sp., from L. *corpus*, a body.] The body; the form of the body.

In cuerpo, or *en cuerpo*; Spanish phrases for being without a cloak or upper garment, or without the formalities of full dress; by extension, undressed; unprotected; naked.

çuff, *n.* A blow with the fist, or, more generally, with the open hand; a slap; a box.

çuff, *v.t.*; cuffed, *pt.*, *pp.*; cuffing, *ppr.* [Sw. *kuffa*, to thrust, push; *kufva*, to subdue, oppress.] To strike with the hand, especially with the open hand; to box or slap; also, to beat or buffet.

çuff, *v.i.* To fight; to scuffle.

çuff, *n.* [ME. *cuffe*, *coffe*, a glove or mitten; AS. *cuffie*, cap, hood.]

1. The fold at the end of a sleeve; the part of a sleeve turned back from the hand.

2. Any band of linen, lace, or other material worn at the wrist, either attached to a sleeve or separate from it.

3. That portion of a gauntlet glove which is stiffened and covers the wrist and forearm.

Çuf′fy, *n.* A nickname for a negro. [Slang.]

Çū′fiç, Kū′fiç, *a.* Of or pertaining to Cufa in the province of Bagdad, which contained the most expert and numerous copyists of the Koran; specifically applied to the Arabic alphabet used in the time of Mohammed, and in which the Koran was written; also spelled *Cuphic*.

Çū′fiç, Kū′fiç, *n.* The Cufic series of Arabic characters; as, the manuscript was written in *Cufic*; spelled also *Cuphic*.

çuin′āġe (kwin′), *n.* [Corrupted from *coinage*.] The stamping of pigs of tin, by the proper officer, with the arms of the duchy of Cornwall. [Eng.]

çuī-rȧss′ (kwē-rȧs′), *n.* [Fr. *cuirasse*; L. *coratia*, *coratium*, a breastplate of leather; L. *corium*, skin, leather.]

1. A breastplate; a piece of defensive armor, made originally of leather, later of iron plate, and covering the body from the neck to the girdle both in the front and back.

2. Any hard covering serving as a protection, as the armor of a ship, the carapace of a beetle, etc.

çuī-rȧssed′ (kwē-rȧst′ *or* kwē′rȧst), *a.* Provided with a cuirass; as, a *cuirassed* fish; a *cuirassed* sentry.

çuī-rȧs-siēr′ (kwē-), *n.* A soldier armed with a cuirass, or breastplate; in recent times, employed in the cavalry service only.

çuir-böu′illi, çuir-bouil′ly (kwer-bö′yē), *n.* [Fr. *cuir bouilli*, boiled leather.] Leather that is soaked in hot water or boiled, and pressed into some shape or stamped with a pattern, which is permanently retained when the leather dries and hardens. Formerly used for armor, helmets, etc.; now extensively and effectively employed in decorative art.

çuish (kwis), *n.* [Fr. *cuisse*, the thigh or leg.] Defensive armor for the thighs; generally used in the plural; also written *cuisse*, *quish*.

çuī-ṣine′ (kwē-zēn′), *n.* [Fr., from L. *coquina*, a kitchen; *coquere*, to cook.]

1. The cooking department of an establishment, including the force of cooks; a kitchen.

2. The manner of preparing food for eating; the style of cooking; cookery.

çụ-lasse′, *n.* [Fr., from *cul*, back.] The lower portion of a gem cut as a brilliant; the part between the girdle and the culet.

çulch, *n.* Rubbish; refuse; waste material.

Çul-dee′, *n.* [Gael. *celle*, servant, and *De*, of God.] One of an ancient order of monks who formerly lived in Scotland, Ireland, and Wales, and are supposed to have originated in the sixth century.

çụl′-de-fōur′, *n.*; *pl.* **çụlṣ′-de-fōur′.** [Fr., bottom of an oven.] In architecture, a vault a quarter sphere in form; a semidome.

çụl′-de-saç′, *n.*; *pl.* **çụlṣ′-de-saç′.** [Fr., the bottom of a bag.]

1. A street which is not open at both ends; a place that has no thoroughfare; a blind alley.

2. An ambush; a trap or snare.

3. Militarily, the situation of an army when it is hemmed in behind and at the sides, and has no exit except by the front.

4. In natural history, any natural cavity or bag, or tubular vessel, having but one end open.

5. An inconclusive argument.

çul′ẽr-āge, *n.* [Obs.] Same as *Culrage.*

çū′let, çū-lette′, *n.* [OFr., from *cul,* L. *culus,* the posteriors.]

1. The flat face on the lower side of a gem cut as a brilliant; spelled also *cullet, collet.*

2. [*pl.*] In ancient armor, the overlapping plates from the waist to the hip which protected the back of the knight.

Çū′lex, *n.* [L., a gnat.] The genus of insects regarded as the type of the family *Culicidæ.*

çū′li-cid, *a.* Of or pertaining to the family *Culicidæ;* having characteristics like those of the mosquito family.

çū′li-cid, *n.* An insect of the family *Culicidæ.*

Çū-lic′i-dæ, *n.pl.* [L., from *culex, culicis,* a gnat, and *-idæ.*] A family of insects including about one hundred and fifty species of mosquitos, gnats, etc.

çū-lic′i-fọrm, *a.* [L. *culex, culicis,* a gnat, and *forma,* form.] Of the form or shape of a gnat; resembling a gnat.

çū′li-nā-ri-ly, *adv.* In the manner of cookery, with reference to the process or place of cooking; in relation to a kitchen.

çū′li-nā-ry, *a.* [L. *culinarius,* from *culina,* a kitchen.] Relating to the kitchen, or to the art of cookery; used in kitchens or in the process of cooking; as, *culinary* knowledge; a *culinary* vessel; *culinary* herbs.

çull, *v.t.;* culled, *pt., pp.;* culling, *ppr.* [ME. *cullen,* to gather, pick; OFr. *cuillir, coillir;* L. *colligere,* to collect.]

1. To pick out; to separate one or more things from others; to select and gather together from many; to collect; as, to *cull* flowers.

2. To sort over; to measure and to examine for quality; as, to *cull* lumber.

çull, *n.* Any thing selected from others; something inferior picked out and set aside; applied especially to a timber, plank, or other piece of wood, of poor grade, and to an inferior animal; commonly used in the plural.

çull, *v.t.* [Obs.] Same as *Coll.*

çull, *n.* A cully. [Slang.]

çul′len-dẽr, *n.* See *Colander.*

çull′ẽr, *n.* 1. One who picks or chooses from many.

2. An inspector of commercial staples, especially of lumber.

çul′let, *n.* Broken glass collected to be melted over.

çul′let, *n.* See *Culet.*

çul-li-bil′i-ty, *n.* Credulity; easiness in being gulled. [Obs.]

çul′li-ble, *a.* Gullible. [Obs.]

çull′ing, *n.* 1. The act or process of sorting out or selecting.

2. Anything separated or selected from a mass as inferior; refuse; generally used in the plural.

çul′liŏn (-yun), *n.* [OFr. *couillon, coillon,* a vile fellow, coward, testicle, L. *coleus,* scrotum.]

1. A mean wretch. [Obs.]

2. A round or bulbous root; an orchis.

çul′liŏn-ly, *a.* Mean, base. [Obs.]

çul′lis, *n.* [Fr. *couler,* to strain, to run.]

1. Broth of boiled meat strained. [Obs.]

2. A kind of jelly. [Obs.]

çul′lis, *n.* 1. A trough or gutter in a roof.

2. A groove in which some piece is fitted to run, as a side-scene on the stage of a theater.

çul′ly, *n.; pl.* **çul′lieṣ.** A person who is readily deceived, tricked, or imposed upon, as by a sharper, jilt, or strumpet; a mean dupe; also, fellow or mate. [Slang.]

çul′ly, *v.t.;* cullied, *pt., pp.;* cullying, *ppr.* To deceive, to trick, cheat, or impose on; to jilt. [Slang.]

çul′ly-iṣm, *n.* The state of being a cully. [Slang.]

çulm, *n.* [L. *culmus,* a stock, stem.] In botany, the stalk or stem of grasses, usually jointed and hollow, and supporting the leaves and fructification; generally herbaceous, but becoming solid or woody in some cases, as the bamboo.

çulm, *n.* [ME. *culme, colm,* soot, smoke.]

1. An inferior grade of anthracite coal.

2. Comminuted anthracite coal; coal-dust or refuse from anthracite mines, often used as fuel.

3. A series of rocks of conglomerate composition, found in some parts of Europe in the Carboniferous strata. They consist largely of anthracite shale and are sometimes considered geologically as a lower Carboniferous group.

Culm.

çul′men, *n.* [L., the top, summit.]

1. Top; summit.

2. In ornithology, the ridge running lengthwise down the middle of the upper mandible.

3. In anatomy, a small protuberance on the upper surface of the median lobe of the cerebellum.

çul-miç′ō-lous, *a.* [L. *culmus,* a stock, stem, and *colere,* to inhabit.] Growing on grass-stems; applied to certain fungi.

çul-mif′ẽr-ous, *a.* [L. *culmus,* a stalk, and *ferre,* to bear.] Bearing culms.

çul-mif′ẽr-ous, *a.* [ME. *culm,* soot, smoke, and *ferre,* to bear.] Containing culm; also, abounding in culm.

çul′mi-năl, *a.* [From L. *culmen, culminis,* the top, summit.] Of or pertaining to the summit or culmen; at or belonging to the apex; topmost.

çul′mi-nănt, *a.* Approaching or situated at the highest point; greatest, supreme, dominant.

çul′mi-nāte, *v.i.;* culminated, *pt., pp.;* culminating, *ppr.* [LL. *culminatus,* pp. of *culminare,* from *culmen,* top, summit.]

1. To be vertical, to come to or be on the meridian; to be at the highest or lowest point of altitude; used especially of planets.

2. To rise to the highest point, in any sense; to reach the zenith in any ascending progress; to come to a final result; as, the feeling of dissatisfaction *culminated* in an open protest.

çul′mi-nāte, *a.* Growing upward, as distinguished from a lateral growth; a term applied specifically to the growth of corals.

çul-mi-nā′tion, *n.* 1. The transit of a heavenly body over the meridian; the attainment of the highest or the lowest point of altitude of a planet for any day, the two points being designated as the *upper* and *lower culmination,* respectively.

2. The act of attaining the zenith; the state of being at the apex; the highest point of any ascending progress; the top, summit, acme, height.

çul′pȧ, *n.* [L.] Fault; specifically, negligence; used in law in distinction from *dolus,* intentional and malicious deceit.

çul-pȧ-bil′i-ty, *n.* Blamableness; culpableness.

çul′pȧ-ble, *a.* [L. *culpabilis,* blameworthy, from *culpare,* to find fault with, condemn, *culpa,* a fault, crime.]

1. Blamable; deserving censure, as the person who has done wrong, or the act, conduct, or negligence of the person; as, the man is *culpable;* voluntary ignorance is *culpable.*

2. Guilty; as, *culpable* of a crime. [Obs.]

Syn.—Blamable, blameworthy, censurable, faulty, wrong, criminal, immoral, sinful.

çul′pȧ-ble-ness, *n.* The quality of deserving blame; the state of being censurable, blamableness; guiltiness.

çul′pȧ-bly, *adv.* Blamably; in a faulty manner, in a manner to merit censure.

çul′pȧ-tō-ry, *a.* [L. *culpatus,* pp. of *culpare,* to blame, condemn; *culpa,* a fault, crime.] Censuring or accusing, expressing blame or charging with guilt.

çulpe, *n.* [Fr. *coulpe;* L. *culpa,* fault, crime.] An offense or fault; also, guilt, blameworthiness. [Obs.]

çul′pon, *n.* [ME. *culpe,* a fragment, chip; OFr. *coupon,* from *couper,* to cut.] A piece of something cut, torn, or split off, a slice, shred, or splinter.

çul′prit, *n.* [Corruption of LL. *culpatus,* the accused, pp. of *culpare,* to blame, condemn; *culpa,* a fault, crime.]

1. A person arraigned in court for a crime.

2. Any person convicted of a crime, a criminal; an offender.

çul′rāge, *n.* [ME. *culrage;* OFr. *culrage, curage,* from *cul* (L. *culus*), the posteriors, and *rage,* L. *rabies,* madness.] *Polygonum Hydropiper,* smartweed.

çult, *n.* [Fr. *culte;* L. *cultus,* from *colere,* to cultivate, worship.]

1. Worship; reverential honor; religious devotion.

2. The system of outward forms and ceremonies used in worship; religious rites and formalities.

3. Deep regard for some person or thing; excessive admiration or attention; veneration; homage; as, the Whitman *cult.*

4. The person or thing receiving extensive and devoted attention and admiration, as, the poster is a present *cult* among a certain class of artists.

çultch, *n.* [Origin uncertain.]

1. The various materials, such as shells, gravel, etc., out of which a spawning-bed for oysters is made.

2. The spawn of oysters; a young oyster before it becomes fixed in position; also, young oysters collectively.

çul′tẽr, *n.* [L.] A colter.

çul-ti-ros′trăl, *a.* [L. *culter,* a colter, and *rostrum,* a beak.] Same as *Cultrirostral.*

Çul-ti-ros′trēṣ, *n.pl.* Same as *Cultrirostres.*

çul′ti-vȧ-ble, *a.* Capable of being tilled or cultivated.

çul′ti-vā-tȧ-ble, *a.* Cultivable.

çul′ti-vāte, *v.t.;* cultivated, *pt., pp.;* cultivating, *ppr.* [L. *cultus,* cultivation, from *colere,* to cultivate.]

1. To till; to prepare for crops; to manure, plow, dress, sow, and reap; as, to *cultivate* land; to *cultivate* a farm.

2. To improve by labor or study; to advance the growth of; to refine and improve by correction of faults and enlargement of powers or good qualities; to meliorate, to correct, to civilize; as, to *cultivate* the wild savage; to *cultivate* talents; to *cultivate* a taste for poetry.

3. To seek to become intimate with; to court the friendship or society of, to cherish; to foster.

4. To raise or produce by tillage; as, to *cultivate* corn or grass.

çul-ti-vā′tion, *n.* 1. The art or practice of cultivating or tilling and preparing for crops, husbandry, the management of land for purposes of agriculture, production by tillage.

2. Study, care, and practice directed to improvement, correction, enlargement, or increase; the application of the means of improvement, as, men may grow wiser by the *cultivation* of talents.

3. The state of being cultivated or refined; refinement; culture, improvement of the mind or morals.

Syn.—Civilization, culture, improvement, husbandry, refinement, melioration, advancement.

çul′ti-vā-tọr, *n.* 1. One who cultivates, as, a *cultivator* of land; a *cultivator* of friendship.

2. A farming implement, as a harrow, hoe, etc., used in loosening the soil or ridding it of weeds.

çul′trāte, *a.* [L. *cultratus,* knife-shaped, from *culter,* a knife.] Sharp-edged and pointed; shaped like a pruning knife, as, the beak of a bird is convex and *cultrate.*

çul′trā-ted, *a.* Cultrate.

çul′tri-fọrm, *a.* Cultrate, having the shape of a pruning-knife.

çul-tri-ros′trăl, *a.* [L. *culter,* a knife, and *rostrum,* a beak.] Having a cultrate beak.

Çul-tri-ros′trēṣ, *n.pl.* A family of grallatorial birds distinguished by a bill which is large, long, and strong, as cranes, herons, storks, etc.

çul-triv′ō-rous, *a.* [L. *culter,* knife, and *vorare,* to devour.] Swallowing or pretending to swallow or eat knives. [Rare.]

çul′tūr-ȧ-ble, *a.* Capable of being cultivated or cultured, suitable for cultivation.

çul′tūr-ăl, *a.* Relating to culture, promoting refinement or education, as, the unique *cultural* development of China.

çul′tūre, *n.* [Fr. *culture,* from L. *cultura,* cultivation, care, from *cultus,* pp. of *colere,* to till, to cultivate.]

1. The act or process of tilling and preparing the earth for crops; cultivation.

2. The application of labor or other means to improve, correct, train, or refine man's physical or mental condition, as, the *culture* of the mind, the *culture* of virtue.

3. The state of being cultivated, the result of cultivation, refinement, improvement in man's physical or mental condition, civilization, as, a man of *culture.*

4. In bacteriology, the cultivation or propagation of bacterial or other microorganisms by artificial means; also, the product resulting from such cultivation. In modern science, the word is used in the designation of the various processes and devices employed by bacteriologists, health officers, and others, as, *culture*-fluid, *culture*-medium, *culture*-tube, *culture*-bulb, *culture*-oven, etc.

5. The study of a science or art for the purpose of making amendments or improvements therein.

Gelatin culture, a bacterial growth or development in a jelly-like medium containing gelatin.

Pure culture, a bacterial growth of one species only, not containing bacteria of other varieties.

Solid culture, a bacterial growth in a medium normally solid, which may consist of gelatin or any other suitable preparation, as agar-agar.

çul′tūre, *v.t.;* cultured, *pt., pp.;* culturing, *ppr.* To cultivate, to refine, to educate.

çul′tūre-cell, *n.* A small glass tube or chamber for the development of bacteria for purposes of observation and study.

çul′tūred, *a.* 1. Cultivated; under cultivation or culture, as, *cultured* fields.

2. Possessing refinement and education, having mental and moral excellence, as, *cultured* people.

Syn.—Refined, accomplished, cultivated, learned, erudite, polished.

çul′tūre-flū″id, *n.* Any liquid or semiliquid medium, as meat-broth, often thickened with gelatin, etc., in which bacteria are developed for purposes of study.

çul′tūre-less, *a.* Having no culture.

çul′tūr-ist, *n.* 1. A cultivator.

2. An advocate of culture.

çul′tus, *n.* [L., care, cultivation, from *cultus,* pp. of *colere,* to till, care for.] A state of religious development; a system of religious or ethical belief; a cult.

çul′tus-çod, *n.* [Probably from Chinook *cultus*, worthless.] An edible fish of large size, *Ophiodon elongatus*, found along the northern Pacific coast.

çul′vẽr, *n.* Same as *Culverin.*

çul′vẽr, *n.* [ME. *culver*; AS. *culfre, culufre*, a dove.] A pigeon, or wood-pigeon; a dove.

çul′vẽr-house, *n.* A dovecote.

çul′vẽr-in, *n.* [OFr. *couleuvrine, colouvrine*, a serpent; L. *colubra*, f. of *coluber*, a serpent.] A long, slender cannon of the sixteenth century; an early name for a piece of artillery.

çul-vẽr-in-eer′, *n.* One whose duty it was to load and fire a culverin.

çul′vẽr-key, *n.* [*Culver*, from AS. *culfre*, a dove, and *key*, from AS. *cæg*, key.]

1. An English meadow plant or flower. [Obs.]
2. A bunch of the keys or pods of the ash-tree.

Çul′vẽr's-phys′iç, *n.* The root of *Veronica* (*Leptandra*) *Virginica*, a tall herb having a medicinal use; also, the plant itself. It was used by a Dr. Culver, and named after him.

çul′vẽrt, *n.* [Fr. *coulvir*, a channel or gutter, from *couler*, to drop or trickle; OFr. *coulouere*, a channel.] A passage under a road, railroad or canal, covered with an arch or bridge; an arched drain for the passage of water.

çul′vẽrt-āge, *n.* [OFr. *culvertage*, serfage, from *culvert*, low, mean, a serf, wretch, rascal.] In feudal law, forfeiture of a vassal's holding to the lord of the manor, and his consequent reduction to serfdom.

çul′vẽr-tāil, *n.* In joinery and carpentry, a dovetail.

çul′vẽr-tāiled, *a.* United or fastened, as pieces of timber, by a dovetailed joint.

Çū-mā′cē-ȧ, *n.pl.* [From Gr. *kyma*, a wave.] A group of small crustaceans, resembling the *Schizopoda.*

çū′mȧ-rin, *n.* Same as *Coumarin.*

çum′bent, *a.* [L. *cubere*, to lie down.] Lying down. [Rare.]

çum′bẽr, *v.t.*; cumbered, *pt., pp.*; cumbering, *ppr.* [ME. *cumbren, combren*; OFr. *combrer*, to hinder, obstruct; from L. *cumulus*, a heap.]

1. To overload; to overburden.
2. To check, stop, or retard, as by a load or weight; to make motion difficult; to obstruct.
3. To perplex or embarrass; to distract or trouble.

> Martha was *cumbered* about much serving.
> —Luke x. 40.

çum′bẽr, *n.* Hindrance; obstruction; embarrassment; distress. [Obs.]

çum′bẽr-sōme, *a.* 1. Troublesome; burdensome; embarrassing; vexatious; as, *cumbersome* obedience.

2. Unwieldy; unmanageable; not easily borne or managed; as, a *cumbersome* load; a *cumbersome* machine.

çum′bẽr-sōme-ly, *adv.* In a cumbersome manner.

çum′bẽr-sōme-ness, *n.* Burdensomeness; the quality of being cumbersome.

çum′brănce, *n.* That which obstructs; burden; encumbrance. [Obs.]

Çum′bri-ăn, *a.* [L. *Cumbria*, Cumberland.] Pertaining to Cumbria, an early British kingdom, or to Cumberland, a county in the north of England, formerly part of Cumbria.

Cumbrian system; in geology, the slaty system of rocks, most common in Cumberland. The Cambrian or Silurian system now includes the Cumbrian.

çum′brŏus, *a.* 1. Burdensome; troublesome; rendering action difficult or toilsome; oppressive; as, a *cumbrous* weight or charge.

2. Giving trouble; vexatious. [Obs.]

çum′brŏus-ly, *adv.* In a cumbrous manner.

çum′brŏus-ness, *n.* The state of being cumbrous.

çū′mēne, *n.* One of the hydrocarbons, $C_6H_5.C_3H_7$, prepared from coal-tar; also called *cumol.*

çum′frey, *n.* See *Comfrey.*

çū′miç, *a.* Same as *Cuminic.*

çū′mi-din, çū′mi-dine, *n.* In chemistry, an organic compound obtained from cumene.

çum′in, çum′min, *n.* [ME. *cummin*; AS. *cumin, cymen*; L. *cuminum*; Gr. *kyminon*, the cumin plant.]

1. An annual plant, *Cuminum Cyminum*, whose seeds have a bitterish, warm taste, with an aromatic flavor. It grows wild in Syria, Egypt, and Hindustan.

2. The seeds of this plant used extensively in India as a condiment; also called *cumin-seed.*

Black cumin; the plant *Nigella sativa*; also, its pungent seeds.

Oil of cumin; an oil derived from cumin-seed.

Sweet cumin; the anise *Pimpinella Anisum.*

Wild cumin; *Lagœcia cuminoides*, a European plant of the parsley family.

çū-min′iç, *a.* Pertaining to or derived from cumin; as, *cuminic* acid.

çū′mi-nil, *n.* A yellow crystalline compound, $C_{20}H_{22}O_2$, derived from oil of caraway.

çū′mi-nōl, *n.* A colorless oil, $C_{10}H_{12}O$, derived from oil of caraway.

çum′mẽr-bund, *n.* [Hind. *kamarband*; *kamar*, the loins, and *band, bandh*, a band.] A large, loose girdle or belt for the waist, such as is worn in India; also written *kummerbund, kamarband, cummerband.*

çū′mōl, *n.* Same as *Cumene.*

çum′quăt (-kwăt), *n.* A small Chinese orange, the fruit of the *Citrus Aurantium.* Also written *kumquat.*

çum′shaw, *n.* [Chinese Pidgin-English.] A present; a gift; a tip.

çum′shaw, *v.t.* To give a present to; to tip.

çū′mū-lāte, *v.t.*; cumulated, *pt., pp.*; cumulating, *ppr.* [L. *cumulatus*, pp of *cumulare*, to heap or pile up.]

1. To gather or throw into a heap; to form into a heap; to heap together.

2. In Louisiana law, to unite in one action; as, to *cumulate* actions or causes of actions.

çū-mū-lā′tion, *n.* 1. The act of heaping together; a heap. [See *Accumulation.*]

2. In law, the combination of defenses or causes of action in a single action.

çū′mū-lā-tist, *n.* One who accumulates, gathers, or collects. [Rare]

çū′mū-lā-tive, *a.* 1. Composed of parts in a heap; forming a mass. [Obs.]

2. Increasing or augmenting by addition; as, a *cumulative* action; a *cumulative* argument.

3. In law, (a) augmenting or tending to establish a point already proved by other evidence; (b) applied to a legacy when the legatee is more than once provided for in the same testament.

Cumulative action; in medicine, that property of certain drugs by which repeated doses produce the same effect as though they had been administered at one and the same time.

Cumulative argument; an argument in which the different proofs are complete in themselves, and, not being dependent one on the other, tend to one conclusion.

Cumulative sentence; in law, a sentence in which several punishments are added together and imposed for several similar offenses.

Cumulative voting; a system of voting whereby each voter can record as many votes as there are candidates for election, either giving them all to one candidate or dividing them among the several candidates.

çū′mū-lā-tive-ly, *adv.* In a cumulative manner.

çū′mū-lī, *n.*, pl. of *cumulus.*

çū″mū-lō-çir″rō-strā′tus, *n.* [L. *cumulus*, a heap, *cirrus*, a curl or spiral, *stratus*, pp. of *sternere*, to spread out.] In meteorology, a form of cloud which expands into a crown of cirrus and breaks into a shower; a rain-cloud.

çū″mū-lō-çir′rus, *n.* A fleecy cloud; an alto-cumulus.

çū″mū-lō-nim′bus, *n.* [L. *cumulus*, a heap, and *nimbus*, a cloud.] A rain-cloud having the appearance of a cumulus.

çū′mū-lōse, *a.* Full of heaps.

çū″mū-lō-strā′tus, *n.* [L. *cumulus*, a heap, and *stratus*, pp. of *sternere*, to strew.] A form of cloud having the characteristics of both cumulus and stratus.

çū′mū-lus, *n.*; *pl.* **çū′mū-lī.** [L., a heap.]

1. In meteorology, one of the four fundamental clouds, so called from its structure in convex masses piled one upon another; the common summer cloud.

2. In anatomy, the heap of cells or proligerous disk about a ripe ovum in the Graafian follicle.

çum′yl, *n.* [From L. *cuminum*; Gr. *kyminon*, the cumin plant, and *hylē*, matter.] In chemistry, an organic radical contained in compounds derived from cumin-seed.

çun, *v.t.* To know. [Obs. See *Con.*]

çun, *v.t.* To con or direct the course of (a ship). [Obs.]

çū-nab′ū-lȧ, *n.pl.* [L. *cunabula*, neut. pl., early abode, cradle; dim. of *cunæ*, cradle.]

1. The early abode or birthplace; the beginnings; as, the *cunabula* of anarchism.

2. A term applied to existing copies of the earliest printed books, especially those of the fifteenth century.

çunç-tā′tion, *n.* [L. *cunctatio*, a delay, from *cunctari*, to delay.] Delay; deliberation. [Rare.]

çunç′tā-tive, *a.* Slow-moving; sluggish; dilatory. [Rare.]

çunç-tā′tŏr, *n.* [L. *cunctator*, a loiterer, from *cunctari*, to delay.] One who waits or delays; [C—] in Roman history, a surname of Quintus Fabius Maximus, the Roman general. [Rare.]

çunç-tip′ō-tent, *a.* [L. *cunctus*, all, entire, and *potens*, ppr. of *posse*, to be able, to be powerful.] All-powerful; omnipotent. [Rare.]

çund, *v.t.* 1. To give notice to. [Obs.]

2. To direct or con, as a ship. [Obs.]

çun-dū-ran′gō, *n.* [Native name.] A vine, *Marsdenia cundurango*, of South America; also, its bark, which was once held to be a cure for cancer. Also written *condurango.*

çū′nē-ăl, *a.* [L. *cuneus*, a wedge.] Pertaining to or having the form of a wedge; wedge-shaped.

çū′nē-āte, *a.* [L. *cuneatus*, wedge-shaped, from *cuneus*, a wedge.] Wedge-shaped; in botany, said of a leaf which terminates abruptly with a blunted point and tapers gradually downward or toward the foot-stalk.

Cuneate Leaf.

çū′nē-ā-ted, *a.* Cuneate.

çū′nē-āte-ly, *adv.* In the form of a wedge.

çū-nē-at′iç, *a.* Cuneate. [Rare.]

çū′nē-ā-tŏr, *n.* [From LL. *cuneare*, to shape like a wedge; from L. *cuneus*, a wedge.] Formerly an officer having charge of the dies used in the mints in England.

çū-nē′i-form, *a.* [From L. *cuneus*, genit. *cunei*, a wedge, and *forma*, form.]

1. Shaped like a wedge; particularly applied to (a) one of the wedge-shaped bones of the ankle or of the wrist; (b) the peculiar arrow-headed characters in the inscriptions of the ancient Persians, Babylonians, and Assyrians.

2. Interested in or acquainted with the wedge-shaped characters or the inscriptions in which they are used; as, a *cuneiform* scholar; also written *cuniform.*

çū-nē′i-form, *n.* 1. The peculiar wedge-shaped character found in the inscriptions of the ancient Persians, Babylonians, and Assyrians.

2. In anatomy, a cuneiform bone of the ankle or wrist.

çū-nette′, *n.* [Fr., possibly dim. formed from L. *cuneus*, a wedge.]

1. In fortification, a small trench in the middle of a larger one, for drainage purposes.

2. A deep trench dug along the middle of a dry moat, to add to the difficulty of passing over it.

çū′nē-us, *n.*; *pl.* **çū′nē-ī.** [L. *cuneus*, a wedge.]

1. In zoölogy, a triangular or wedge-shaped portion of the fore wings of certain heteropterous insects.

2. In anatomy, a cuneate or wedge-shaped convolution on the mesial aspect of the occipital lobe.

çū-niç′ū-lăr, *a.* [From L. *cuniculus*, a rabbit; by metonymy, a passage underground.] Relating to or resembling a rabbit or its burrow.

çū-niç′ū-lāte, *a.* In botany, traversed by a long passage open at one end, as the peduncle of the nasturtium.

çū-niç′ū-lous, *a.* Relating to rabbits. [Rare.]

çū-niç′ū-lus, *n.*; *pl.* **çū-niç′ū-lī.** [L., a rabbit; by metonymy, a passage underground.]

1. A small subterranean passage; specifically, one of the ancient subterranean drains about Rome and other districts of Italy.

2. The burrow of the itch-insect.

Çū-nī′lȧ, *n.* [L. *cunila*, a plant.] In botany, a genus of shrubby plants belonging to the family *Labiatæ*; the fragrant herb, *Cunila Mariana*, of eastern United States, commonly called dittany, is the best known species.

çun′nẽr, çŏn′nẽr, *n.* [A local Eng. word; origin obscure.]

1. A small food fish, *Ctenolabrus adspersus*, found along the coast of eastern North America; also called *blue perch, chogset, nipper, burgall*, and *sea-perch.*

2. A shellfish; the limpet. [Local, Eng.]

çun′ning, *a.* [ME. *cunning, connyng*, skilful; AS. *cunnian*, to try, test.]

1. Knowing; skilful; experienced; well instructed.

> Esau was a *cunning* hunter.—Gen. xxv. 27.

2. Wrought with skill; curious; ingenious.

> All the more do I admire
> Joints of *cunning* workmanship.—Tennyson.

3. Artful; shrewd; sly; crafty; astute; designing; hence, deceitful; trickish.

4. Pleasing; having innocent and attractive ways; as, a *cunning* child. [Colloq.]

Syn.—Artful, crafty, designing, sly, astute, subtle, wily, insidious.

çun′ning, *n.* [ME. *cunning, kunnyng*, skill; AS. *cunnung*, trial, test, from *cunnian*, to try or test.]

1. Knowledge; art; skill; dexterity; as, a workman of great *cunning.*

> Let my right hand forget her *cunning.*
> —Ps. cxxxvii. 5.

2. Artfulness; craft; shrewdness; the faculty or act of using stratagem to accomplish a purpose; hence, deceit; fraudulent skill or dexterity.

> Discourage *cunning* in a child; *cunning* is the ape of wisdom. —Locke.

3. Natural wit; instinct; as, the *cunning* of a fox.

çun′ning-ly, *adv.* In a cunning manner.

çun′ning-man, *n.* A man who pretended to tell fortunes, or teach how to recover stolen or lost goods. [Obs.]

çun′ning-ness, *n.* The quality of being cunning.

çun′ning-wom″ăn (-woom″), *n.* A female fortune-teller. [Obs.]

çup, *n.* [ME. *cup, cuppe*; AS. *cuppe*, a cup; LL. *copa, coppa*, a cup; L. *cupa*, a tub, cask.]

1. A small vessel, used commonly to drink out of; as, a pewter *cup*; a wine *cup*; especially, a vessel of pottery usually furnished with a handle and used with a saucer; as, a tea*cup*; a coffee-*cup*.

2. The contents of a *cup*; that which is contained in a *cup*; as, a *cup* of coffee.

3. The chalice from which the sacramental wine is dispensed; also, the wine itself.

4. Suffering or affliction to be endured; that which falls to one's lot; portion.

O my Father, if it be possible, let this *cup* pass from me. —Matt. xxvi. 39.

5. Anything hollow like a *cup*; as, the *cup* of an acorn; an oil *cup*.

6. In surgery, a cupping-glass.

7. [*pl.*] The drinking of intoxicants; noisy festivity; drunkenness.

Thence from *cups* to civil broils. —Milton.

8. A vessel usually shaped like a *cup* or goblet and made of some precious metal, offered as a prize to be contended for in horseracing, yachting, and other sports; as, the America's *cup*.

9. [C—] In astronomy, the constellation Crater.

10. In surgery, a small vessel for receiving and measuring venous blood during venesection.

11. A depression in a boiler-plate to increase the amount of heating surface.

12. In golf, a small hole in the course, usually made by the stroke of a previous player.

13. A mixed drink of wine, etc., usually iced and flavored with fruits; as, claret-*cup*; champagne-*cup*.

Cup and ball; a toy consisting of a cup or hole at the end of a stick to which a ball is attached by a cord. The ball is tossed up and the player seeks to catch it in the cup.

Cup and can; a term applied to familiar companions, the can being the large vessel out of which the cup is filled, and thus the two being constantly associated.

To be in one's cups; to be intoxicated.

çup, *v.t.*; cupped (kupt), *pt., pp.*; cupping, *ppr.* 1. To give cups of liquor to; to make drunk. [Obs.]

2. In surgery, to bleed by scarification and a cupping-glass.

3. In mechanics, to make hollow like a cup; to make concave.

çup, *v.i.* 1. To drink. [Obs.]

2. In surgery, to operate by cupping.

3. In golf, to make a hole or depression in the ground when striking the ball.

çup′bear″ẽr, *n.* 1. An attendant at a feast who conveys wine or other liquors to the guests.

2. Formerly, an official of the household of a prince or noble whose duty it was to taste the wine before handing it to his master or to guests.

For I was the king's *cupbearer*.—Neh. i. 11.

çup′bōard (kub′ẽrd), *n.* 1. A table or shelf for cups to stand on. [Obs.]

2. A small cabinet or inclosure in a room, with shelves to receive cups, plates, dishes, etc.

3. A closet; a larder.

Cupboard love; interested attachment or love.

çup′bōard, *v.t.* To collect into a cupboard; to hoard. [Obs.]

çup′=çor″ăl, *n.* A corallite; coral shaped like a cup.

çū-pee′, *n.* A kind of headdress worn in the early part of the eighteenth century.

çū′pel, *n.* [Fr. *coupelle*, a cupel; LL. *cupella*, a cup; dim. of L. *cupa*, a tub, cask.] A small cup or vessel commonly made of bone-dust, used in refining precious metals; also written *coppel, cuppel.*

çū-pel′, *v.t.*; cupeled *or* cupelled, *pt., pp.*; cupeling *or* cupelling, *ppr.* To purify in a cupel, as gold or silver.

çū′pel=dust, *n.* Powder used in refining metals.

çū-pel-lā′tion, *n.* The process of refining gold, silver, or other metals in a cupel.

çup′fụl, *n.* The contents of a cup; the quantity that a cup will hold.

çup′=gạll, *n.* A peculiar variety of gall, shaped like a cup, found on the leaves of the oak-tree. It is made by the insect *Cecidomyia poculum.*

Çū′phē-ȧ, *n.* [Gr. *kyphos*, a hump, with reference to the protuberant base of the calyx.] A genus of plants, order *Lythraceæ*, found in tropical America and Mexico. *Cuphea platycentra*, the cigar-plant, is widely cultivated.

Çū′phiç, *a.* and *n.* Same as *Cufic.*

Çū′pid, *n.* [L. *Cupido*, the god of love, son of Mercury and Venus; from *cupido*, passion, desire of love; from *cupire*, to desire.] In Roman mythology, the god of love; emblematically represented as a naked boy with wings, and carrying a bow and quiver of arrows, with which he pierced the hearts of lovers, imbuing them with desire; often referred to as blind or blindfolded. The name is also given in art to representations of children without mythological reference; as, a row of painted *Cupids.*

çū-pid′i-ty, *n.* [Fr. *cupidité*; L. *cupiditas*, desire, wish, from *cupire*, to desire.]

1. Inordinate greed for wealth or power; avarice; covetousness.

2. Passionate carnal desire; sexual love. [Obs.]

çū′pi-dōne, *n.* [Fr. *Cupidon*, the name of a flower; L. *Cupido*, Cupid.] In botany, a composite plant bearing blue flowers, *Catananche cœrulea*, native to Mediterranean countries.

Çū-pi-dō′ni-ȧ, *n.* A genus of birds, family *Tetraonidæ*, the pinnated grouse.

çup′=li″çhen, *n.* Same as *Cup-moss.*

çup′=mọss, *n.* In botany, a lichen of the genus *Cladonia*, having a cup-shaped podetium.

Cupid, Townley Marbles, British Museum.

çū′pō-lȧ, *n.* [It. *cupola*, a dome; LL. *cupula*, a cup, dim. of L. *cupa*, a tub, cask.]

1. In architecture, a spherical vault on the top of an edifice; a small dome.

2. The round top of a structure; as, the *cupola* of a furnace.

3. A furnace used in foundries for melting metals; usually of fire-brick cased with iron.

4. A shot-proof turret for the protection of heavy ordnance.

5. In anatomy, the upper part of the cochlea.

çup′pẽr, *n.* 1. One who applies a cupping-glass.

2. A cupbearer. [Obs.]

çup′ping, *n.* In medicine, the act of drawing blood to or from the skin of a body by means of the vacuum created in a cupping-glass.

Dry cupping; cupping without scarification, the aim being to excite action in the part or to extract pus.

Wet cupping; the application of a cupping-glass to a scarified surface.

çup′ping=glȧss, *n.* A small bell-shaped glass used in cupping to produce a vacuum.

çup′ping=mȧ-çhïne″, *n.* In metallic cartridge-making, the first stamping machine employed on cartridge-cases.

çup′=plant, *n.* In botany, a tall, composite American plant, *Silphium perfoliatum*, bearing large, yellow flowers and opposite leaves, the upper pairs curving in cup-shape.

çup′py, *a.* [From Fr. *coupé*, a cut; *couper*, to cut off.] Having hollows resembling a cup; cuplike.

çū′prē-ous, *a.* [LL. *cupreus*, coppery, from *cuprum*, copper, from Gr. *Kypros*, Cyprus island, abounding in copper.] Coppery; consisting of copper; resembling copper, or partaking of its qualities.

çū-pres′sīte, *n.* [From L. *cupressus*, the cypress-tree.] A coniferous fossil plant occurring in the Trias and other formations, and supposed to be allied to the cypress.

Çū-pres′sus, *n.* [L. *cupressus*; Gr. *kyparissos*, the cypress-tree.] In botany, a genus of coniferous evergreen trees having appressed leaves and scaly cones; the cypress; native to Asia and western America.

çū′priç, *a.* [LL. *cuprum*, copper; from Gr. *Kypros*, the island of Cyprus, famous for its copper.] In chemistry, containing, derived from, or pertaining to copper.

çū-prif′ẽr-ous, *a.* [From LL. *cuprum*, copper, and *ferre*, to bear.] Containing or affording copper; as, *cupriferous* silver.

çū′prīte, *n.* [LL. *cuprum*, copper.] In mineralogy, red copper ore, found massive and in isometric crystals.

çū″prō=am-mō′ni-um, *n.* Copperized ammonium.

çū′proid, *n.* [From LL. *cuprum*, copper, and Gr. *eidos*, form.] In crystallography, a solid related to a tetrahedron, and contained under twelve equal triangles.

çup′rōṣe, *n.* The poppy; the coprose.

çū′prous, *a.* Same as *Cupric.*

çū′prum, *n.* [LL.] In chemistry, copper.

çup′seed, *n.* A climbing vine, *Calycocarpum Lyoni*, native to southeastern United States.

çup′=spŏnġe, *n.* A variety of sponge resembling a cup in form.

çū′pū-lȧ, *n.* Same as *Cupule.*

çū′pū-lăr, *a.* Bearing cupules; cup-shaped.

çū′pū-lāte, *a.* Cupular.

çū′pūle, *n.* [Dim. of LL. *cupa*, cup; L. *cupa*, a tub or cask; Gr. *kypē*, anything hollow.]

1. In botany, a cup-shaped part, as the involucre of the acorn.

2. Any small cup-shaped depression in a level surface, as in rock.

3. In zoölogy, an acetabulum or sucking-disk.

çū-pū-lif′ẽr-ous, *a.* [From LL. *cupula*, a cup, and *ferre*, to bear.] Having the form of a cupule; bearing cupules.

çup′=vạlve, *n.* A valve with a seat made to fit a cover in the form of a cup or section of a sphere.

Cup-valve.

çũr, *n.* [ME. *curre, kur*; prob. from Sw. dial. *kurre*, a dog; Ice. *kurra*, to mumble; an imitative word.]

1. A dog of low breed; a mongrel; a scrub; used in depreciation.

2. An ill-disposed or worthless person; a coward; used in contempt.

çūr-ȧ-bil′i-ty, *n.* Capability of being cured.

çūr′ȧ-ble, *a.* Capable of being healed or cured; admitting a remedy; as, a *curable* wound.

çūr′ȧ-ble-ness, *n.* Possibility of being cured.

çụ-rȧ-çaō′ (-sō′), *n.* A liqueur or cordial, flavored with orange-peel, cinnamon, and mace, and deriving its name from the island of Curaçao, north of Venezuela, its place of origin; also written *curaçoa.*

çū′rȧ-cy, *n.* The office, duties, or tenure of a curate.

çū-rä′ri, çụ-rä′rȧ, *n.* [Native S. Am. name.] A black, resinous extract obtained from *Strychnos toxifera* and other trees; it is a deadly poison when injected into the blood, and is used by South American Indians to poison arrow-points, especially those of the arrows used with the blowgun.

çụ′rȧ-rine, *n.* An extremely poisonous alkaloid obtained from curari.

çụ′rȧ-rize, *v.t.*; curarized, *pt., pp.*; curarizing, *ppr.* 1. To poison by administering curari to.

2. To paralyze the motor nerves of, by using curari, as for the purposes of vivisection.

çū-ras′sōw, *n.* [Named from the island of *Curaçao.*] Any bird belonging to the American genera *Crax* and *Pauxi*, family *Cracidæ*. There are a dozen or more species. The crested *curassow, Crax alector*, is native in Guiana, Mexico, and Brazil; called also *curaçao-bird*. Several species of *curassow* are domesticated in South America, being of the size and character of the turkey.

çū′rat, *n.* A breastplate; a cuirass. [Obs.]

çū′rāte, *n.* [ME. *curat*; LL. *curatus*, a priest; L. *curare*, to care for.]

1. In the Church of England and the Roman Catholic church of Ireland, a clergyman who assists a rector or vicar.

2. A guardian or protector. [Obs.]

3. Formerly one who had the cure of souls; a priest or minister.

Perpetual curate; formerly a curate who was independent of a rector, and supported by tithes.

Stipendiary curate; in the Church of England, a curate who is employed by a rector or vicar to assist in the duties of a parish.

çū′rāte-ship, *n.* A curacy.

çū-rā′tion, *n.* The act of healing. [Obs.]

çūr′ȧ-tive, *a.* and *n.* I. *a.* Relating to the cure of diseases; tending to cure.

II. *n.* That which cures; a remedy.

çū-rā′tŏr, *n.* [L. *curator*, a manager, overseer, from *curare*, to care for.]

1. One who has the care and superintendence of anything; a custodian.

2. A guardian appointed by law; a trustee.

çū-rā′tŏr-ship, *n.* The office or position of a curator.

çū-rā′trix, *n.* [LL., f., from L. *curator*, a manager.]

1. A female curator or custodian.

2. A woman who cures. [Rare.]

çũrb, *v.t.*; curbed, *pt., pp.*; curbing, *ppr.* [ME. *courben, kerben*, to bend; OFr. *courber*, to bend or crook; L. *curvare*, to bend or curve, from *curvus*, crooked, curved; same root as L. *circus*, a circle; Gr. *kyrtos*, crooked.]

1. To restrain; to guide and manage, as a horse.

2. To restrain; to check; to hold back; to confine; to keep in subjection; as, to *curb* the passions.

3. To furnish, surround, or protect with a curb, as a well.

4. To bend. [Obs.]

çũrb, *v.i.* To cringe; to crouch. [Obs.]

çũrb, *n.* [ME. *courbe*; Fr. *courbe*, a curve, the knee; L. *curvus*, crooked, from *curvare*, to bend.] A hard callous swelling on a horse's leg, attended with stiffness, and sometimes pain and lameness.

çũrb, *n.* 1. Restraint; check; hindrance; that which checks or controls.

2. A frame or a wall round the mouth of a well; a casing inside a well that is being sunk.

3. A curbstone or row of curbstones; the outer edge of a sidewalk.

4. A bridle attachment, consisting of a chain around the lower jaw, or an enlarged bit, for better control of the horse.

5. A retaining wall to support a bank of earth; the wall-plate at the springing of a dome, etc.

On the curb; in commercial parlance, outside the exchange, or after exchange hours. [Slang.]

çũrb′=bit, *n.* A bit having extended branches

that give the rider or driver a strong leverage on the chain around the horse's lower jaw.

çurb'=chain, *n.* 1. A chain that curbs or checks the motion of machinery.

2. The chain attached to a curb-bit.

çurb'ing, *n.* Curbstones; the material for making a curb.

çurb'less, *a.* Having no curb; unrestrained.

çurb'=pin, *n.* A pin that restrains the balance-wheel of a watch and regulates its vibrations.

çurb'=plāte, *n.* In architecture, any plate that serves as a curb.

çurb'=roof, *n.* In architecture, a gambrel roof; a roof having a double slant.

Curb-roof.

çurb'=send"ẽr, *n.* In submarine telegraphy, an automatic signaling device that sends alternate opposing electric currents, the second curbing the indication produced by the first and making it sharp and distinct.

çurb'stone, *n.* A thin, flat stone set on edge at the margin of a sidewalk, a series of such stones forming the curb.

Curbstone broker; see under *Broker*.

çurch, *n.* A woman's head-covering; an inner linen cap; a kerchief. [Scot.]

çur-çū'li-ō, *n.* [L. *curculio*, a corn-worm.] In entomology, any one of several species of destructive beetles or weevils that infest grain and fruit.

Çur-çū-li-on'i-dæ, *n.pl.* A large family of coleopterous insects, the weevils or snout-beetles, of which there are 1,500 genera and over 10,000 species described. The head is prolonged into a beak or snout, furnished with sharp jaws. They are all found on plants.

çur-çū-li-on'i-dous, *a.* Pertaining to the *Curculionidæ.*

Çur'çū-mȧ, *n.* [Ar. *kurkum*, saffron.] In botany, a genus of plants of the family *Scitamineæ*, having perennial roots and annual stems. *Curcuma longa* yields turmeric.

çur'çū-mȧ=pā"pẽr, *n.* See *Turmeric paper* under *Turmeric*.

çur'çū-min, çur'çū-mine, *n.* [Ar. *kurkum*, saffron.] In chemistry, the coloring matter of turmeric.

çurd, *n.* [Scot. and Eng. dial. *crud*; ME. *curd*; Ir. *cruth*, curds.]

1. The coagulated or thickened part of milk, which is made into various kinds of cheese, or eaten as food; generally in the plural; as, *curds* and whey.

2. Any chemical coagulation.

çurd, *v.t.*; curded, *pt.*, *pp.*; curding, *ppr.* To cause to coagulate; to curdle.

çurd, *v.i.* To become coagulated; to congeal.

çurd'i-ness, *n.* The quality of being curdy.

çur'dle, *v.i.*; curdled, *pt.*, *pp.*; curdling, *ppr.* 1. To coagulate or concrete; to thicken or change into curd; as, milk *curdles* by a mixture of rennet.

2. To thicken; to congeal; as, the blood *curdles* in the veins.

çur'dle, *v.t.* 1. To change into curd; to cause to thicken or coagulate.

2. To congeal or thicken; as, the recital *curdled* my blood.

çurd'less, *a.* Without curd.

çurd'y, *a.* Like curd; full of curd; coagulated.

çūre, *n.* [ME. *cure*; Fr. *cure*, cure; L. *cura*, care.]

1. A healing; the act of healing; restoration to health from disease, and to soundness from a wound.

2. A remedy for disease; a restorative; that which heals.

> Cold, hunger, prisons, ills without a *cure*.
> —Dryden.

3. The care of souls; spiritual charge; curacy.

4. Attention; care. [Obs.]

5. A method or course of remedial treatment for disease; as, the gold-*cure*; the water-*cure*.

çūre, *v.t.*; cured, *pt.*, *pp.*; curing, *ppr.* 1. To heal, as a person diseased, or a wounded limb; to restore to health, as the body, or to soundness, as a limb.

> The child was *cured* from that very hour.
> —Matt. xvii. 18.

2. To subdue, remove, destroy, or put an end to by means of a remedy; to heal, as a disease.

3. To dry; to prepare for preservation; as, to *cure* hay; or to prepare by salt, or in any manner, so as to preserve; as, to *cure* fish or beef.

Syn.—Heal, make well, remedy, restore.

çūre, *v.i.* 1. To become healed; to recover.

2. To bring about a cure; to restore soundness.

3. To heed; to take care. [Obs.]

çu-ré' (-rā'), *n.* [Fr., from L. *curare*, to care for.] A priest or curate; a parson.

çūre'=all, *n.* A remedy for all diseases; a panacea.

çūre'less, *a.* Not admitting of a remedy; incurable; as, a *cureless* disorder.

çūr'ẽr, *n.* 1. A healer; a physician; one who heals.

2. One who prepares meats to be preserved.

çū-rette', *n.* [Fr., a scoop, scraper, from *curer*, to cleanse.] A surgical instrument of various sizes and shapes for removing foreign matter from a cavity, as from the eye, ear, or throat.

çū-rette', *v.t.*; curetted, *pt.*, *pp.*; curetting, *ppr.* To scrape and cleanse with a curette.

çûr'few, *n.* [ME. *curfewe*; OFr. *courfeu*, curfew, contr. of *couvre-feu*, lit. cover-fire; *couvrir* (L. *cooperire*), to hide, and *feu*, fire; L. *focus*, hearth.]

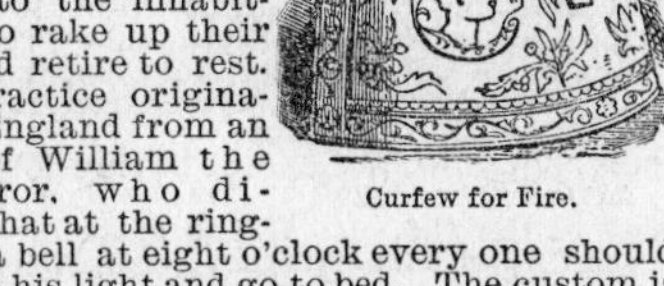

Curfew for Fire.

1. The ringing of a bell or bells at night, as a signal to the inhabitants to rake up their fires and retire to rest. This practice originated in England from an order of William the Conqueror, who directed that at the ringing of a bell at eight o'clock every one should put out his light and go to bed. The custom is still retained in some places as a police regulation.

2. The hour for ringing curfew.

3. The curfew-bell.

4. A cover for a fire. [Obs.]

çū'ri-ȧ, *n.*; *pl.* **çū'ri-æ.** [L.] 1. One of the thirty divisions of the Roman people, established by Romulus.

2. The meeting-place of one of these divisions.

3. The Roman senate house.

4. In the middle ages, the court of a sovereign or feudal lord.

5. In old law, a court of justice.

6. The collective body of officials of the papal government; also called *curia Romana.*

çū'ri-ăl, *a.* [L. *curialis*, pertaining to the curia.]

1. Pertaining to the papal curia

2. Pertaining to an ancient Roman curia; as, *curial* festivals.

çū'ri-ă-lism, *n.* The political doctrines or policy of the Roman Catholic church; ultramontanism.

çū'ri-ă-list, *n.* In the Roman Catholic church, an ultramontanist.

çū"ri-ă-lis'tiç, *a.* Pertaining to a court.

çū-ri-al'i-ty, *n.* The privileges, prerogatives or retinue of a court. [Obs.]

çū'ri-et, *n.* Same as *Curat.*

çūr'ing=house, *n.* 1. A building in which sugar is drained and dried.

2. Any house in which an article of commerce is cured.

çū'ri-ō, *n.* [Abbrev. of *curiosity.*] Any rare or curious article of virtu or bric-à-brac; as, a dealer in *curios.*

çū"ri-ō-log'iç, *a.* [Gr. *kyriologikos*, one who speaks literally, from *kyros*, authority or power, and *legein*, to speak.] Designating a rude kind of hieroglyphics, in which a thing is represented by its picture.

çū-ri-os'i-ty, *n.* [ME. *curiosite*; OFr. *curiosete*; L. *curiositas*, curiosity; *curiosus*, curious.]

1. A desire to gratify the senses with a sight of what is new or unusual, or to gratify the mind with new discoveries; inquisitiveness.

2. Nicety; delicacy. [Obs.]

3. Accuracy; exactness; nice performance; curiousness; as, the *curiosity* of workmanship.

4. That which excites a desire for seeing, or deserves to be seen, as novel and extraordinary; something rare or strange.

çū-ri-ō'sō, *n.*; *pl.* **çū-ri-ō'si.** [It.] An admirer or collector of curiosities; a virtuoso.

çū'ri-ous, *a.* [ME. *curious*, *corious*; OFr. *curious*; L. *curiosus*, careful, diligent, from *cura*, care.]

1. Strongly desirous to see what is novel, or to discover what is unknown; solicitous to see or to know; inquisitive.

2. Accurate; careful not to mistake; solicitous to be correct. [Obs.]

3. Wrought with care and art; elegant; neat; finished; as, a *curious* girdle; *curious* work.

4. Rare; singular; arousing curiosity; as, a *curious* fact.

Syn.—Inquisitive, prying, rare.

çū'ri-ous-ly, *adv.* Attentively; with nice care and art; fantastically; inquisitively.

çū'ri-ous-ness, *n.* Fitness to excite curiosity; the state of being curious.

çûrl, *v.t.*; curled, *pt.*, *pp.*; curling, *ppr.* 1. To turn, bend, or form into ringlets, as the hair.

2. To writhe; to twist; to coil, as a serpent's body.

3. To dress with curls; to adorn.

> The snaky locks
> That *curled* Megæra. —Milton.

4. To raise in waves or undulations; to ripple.

> Seas would be pools, without the brushing air
> To *curl* the waves. —Dryden.

5. To form into a curve, as the rim of a hat.

çûrl, *v.i.* 1. To bend in curves; to take the form of ringlets; to assume a curved or spiral form, to appear curly.

> It'll make your hair *curl.* —Thackeray.

2. To move in waves or undulations; to ripple; to rise in a winding outline; as, *curling* smoke; *curling* waves.

3. To writhe; to twist.

> Then round her slender waist he *curled.*
> —Dryden.

4. To play at the game called curling.

çûrl, *n.* [ME. *crull*, *crulle*, curly, from M.D. *krul*, *krol*, a curl.]

1. A ringlet of hair, or anything of a like form.

2. Undulation; a waving; sinuosity; flexure; a winding, as in the grain of wood.

3. A disease in peach-trees, potatoes, etc., in which the leaves, at their first appearance, seem curled and distorted.

çûrled, *a.* Having curls; wavy.

çûrl'ed-ness, *n.* The state of being curled; curliness. [Rare.]

çûrl'ẽr, *n.* 1. One who or that which curls.

2. One who plays at the game of curling.

çûr'lew, *n* [ME. *curlewe*; OFr. *corlieu*, the curlew bird; name probably formed from the bird's cry.]

European Curlew (*Numenius arquatus*).

1. An aquatic bird, of the genus *Numenius*, and the grallic order. It has a long bill, and the largest species spread more than three feet of wing. It is of the same family as the woodcock and sandpiper, and is widely scattered in Europe and America.

2. A name given to certain wading birds, not of the genus *Numenius*; as, the pygmy *curlew* the stone-*curlew.*

çûr'lew-ber"ry, *n.* The black crowberry, *Empetrum nigrum.*

çûr'lew=jack, *n.* The European whimbrel, *Numenius phæopus.*

çûr'lew=knot (-not), *n.* The curlew-jack.

çûr'lew=sand'pi"pẽr, *n.* A European sand piper, *Tringa ferruginea*, having a bill like a curlew.

çûrl'i-çūe, *n.* Something curled or twisted, as a flourish with a pen or a caper on skates; also written *curlycue.* [Colloq.]

çûrl'i-ness, *n.* The state of being curly.

çûrl'ing, *n.* 1. The act of making curls.

2. A winter amusement, popular among the Scottish people in Europe and America. Contending parties slide large, smooth stones of a circular form and furnished with a handle, along the ice from one mark to another, called the tee. The chief object of each player is to hurl his stone toward the tee with proper strength and precision, and the interest of the game depends on the skill displayed by the players in placing their own stones in favorable positions, or in driving rival stones out of such positions with reference to the tee.

çûrl'ing=ī"rons (-ūrnz), *n.pl.* An instrument for curling the hair.

çûrl'ing-ly, *adv.* In a curling manner.

çûrl'ing=stone, *n.* One of the smooth, round stones used in the game of curling, having a handle attached to the upper side.

çûrl'ing=tongs, *n.pl.* Curling-irons.

çûrl'y, *a.* Having curls; tending to curl; full of ripples.

çûrl'y-çūe, *n.* Same as *Curlicue.*

çûrl'y=head"ed, *a.* Having curly hair; as, a *curly-headed* boy.

çûrl'y=pā"ted, *a.* Curly-headed.

çûr-mudġ'eŏn (-muj'un), *n.* [Corruption of *corn-mudgin*, a dealer in corn; AS. *corn*, corn, and OFr. *muchier*, to hide.] An avaricious, churlish fellow; a miser; a niggard; a churl.

çûr-mudġ'eŏn-ly, *a.* Avaricious; covetous, niggardly; churlish.

çûr-mûr'ring, *n.* [Scot.; formed by imitation of the sound.] A murmuring or rumbling sound; particularly the motion and sound in the bowels caused by flatulence or wind.

çûrn'ber"ry, *n.* A currant. [Prov. Eng.]

çûrr, *v.i.* [Sw. *kurra*, to growl, coo, rumble; a word formed from imitation of the sound.] To coo or purr as a dove or cat. [Scot.]

çur'raçh, çur'ragh (-raçh), *n.* [Gael.] 1. A coracle or light skiff for one person.

2. A small cart made of wickerwork. [Scot.]

çur'rȧ-jong, *n.* [Native name.] An Australian tree, *Plagianthus sidoides*, the fibrous bark of which is used to make cordage; also written *kurrajong.*

çur'rănt, *n.* [ME. *raisins of corans*; Fr. *raisins de Corinth*, raisins of Corinth, from Corinth, their place of origin.]

1. A small kind of dried grape, imported from

the Levant, chiefly from Zante and Cephalonia, and used in cookery.

2. The name given to the fruit as well as the shrubs of several species of *Ribes*, from the berries resembling in size the small grapes from the Levant. The red *currant* is *Ribes rubrum*, of which the white *currant* is a variety; the black *currant* is *Ribes nigrum*, and the flowering *currant* or Missouri *currant* is *Ribes aureum*, which is cultivated for the sake of its flowers.

3. In Australia, one of several species of trees and shrubs bearing fruit resembling the true *currant*.

çur'rănt=bōr"ẽr, *n.* In zoölogy, a clearwing moth, *Ægeria tipuliformis*, the larva of which infests the stems of currant-bushes.

çur'rănt=gạll, *n.* The name given in England to a small, round gall resembling an unripe currant, formed upon the flowers and leaves of the oak-tree by an insect, *Spathegaster baccarum*.

çur'rănt=wŏrm, *n.* In zoölogy, the larva of any insect that devours the currant; especially, *Nematus ventricosus*, a European species of saw-fly; *Pristiphora grossulariæ*, an American sawfly, and *Eufitchia ribearia*, the spanworm.

çur'ren-cy, *n.* [LL. *currentia*, a current, from L. *currens*, ppr. of *currere*, to run.]

1. Literally, a flowing, running, or passing; a continued or uninterrupted course like that of a stream; as, the *currency* of time. [Obs.]

2. The state of being current; a continued course in public opinion, belief, or reception; a passing from person to person, or from age to age.

3. A continual passing from hand to hand, as coin or bills of credit; circulation; as, a report has had a long or general *currency*; the *currency* of cents; the *currency* of bank-bills or of treasury notes.

4. That which is current or in circulation as a medium of trade or exchange; as, a country's *currency*; paper *currency*.

5. Fluency; readiness of utterance. [Obs.]

6. General estimation; the rate at which anything is generally valued.

> He takes greatness of kingdoms according to their bulk and *currency*, and not after intrinsic value. —Bacon.

Fractional currency; coins or paper money of a denomination smaller than the monetary unit; in the United States, currency smaller than a dollar, now issued only in coin.

Metallic currency; the gold, silver, and copper coin in circulation in any country.

Paper currency; that which passes current as a substitute for money or a representative of it; the legal-tender bills or certificates issued by a government, or by a bank on the authority of a government.

çur'rent, *a.* [ME. *currant*, *coraunt*; OFr. *curant*; L. *currens*, ppr. of *currere*, to run, hasten.]

1. Running; flowing; passing. [Rare.]

2. Now passing; present in its course; as, the *current* month or year.

3. Passing from person to person, or from hand to hand; common; general; circulating; as, *current* opinions; *current* coin; *current* notions.

4. Established by common estimation; generally received; as, the *current* value of coin.

5. Passable; that may be accepted or admitted; authentic; genuine.

To pass current; to have acceptance or recognition.

çur'rent, *n.* [LL. *currentia*, current, from L. *currens*, ppr. of *currere*, to run, hasten.]

1. A flowing or passing; a stream; a flow; used of fluids moving continuously in one direction; as, a *current* of air; a *current* of electricity; the *current* of the Gulf Stream.

2. General or main course; progressive motion or movement; continuation; successive course; as, the *current* of time; the *current* of events.

3. The degree of depression given to a roof to cause the water which falls upon it to pass off in a given direction.

Atmospheric currents; disturbances of the atmosphere, from regular or accidental causes, which constitute winds.

Commuted current; in electricity, a current which alternates when generated, but is made to flow continuously in one direction by a commutator.

Direct current; in electricity, a current that flows in one direction and does not alternate.

Electric current; see under *Electric*.

Foucault current; in electricity, a useless current created in a conducting mass by movement through magnetic induction.

Galvanic current; in electricity, a current generated in a voltaic cell or battery.

Make-and-break current; a current in an electric circuit which is made and broken alternately.

Primary current; in electricity, a current which passes through a primary circuit.

Secondary current; in electricity, a current produced in a conductor by changes in currents in a contiguous conductor; a current produced in the secondary circuit of an induction-coil or alternating current converter.

Undulatory current; in electricity, a current whose direction is constant, but whose strength is continuously varying.

Voltaic current; a galvanic current.

Syn.—Flow, stream, course, tide, flux.

çur'rent=den"si-ty, *n.* In electricity, the strength of current which flows in any part of a circuit divided by the cross-section area of that section of the circuit.

çur'rent-ly, *adv.* In a current manner; commonly; as, it is *currently* reported.

çur'rent=mē"tẽr, *n.* An instrument for measuring the strength of an electric current; also, a device for determining the strength and velocity of other currents, as a current in a river, or a current in the ocean.

çur'rent=mill, *n.* A mill having for its motor a current-wheel.

çur'rent-ness, *n.* 1. The state or quality of being current; currency; circulation; general reception.

2. Fluency; easiness of pronunciation. [Obs.]

çur'rent=wheel, *n.* A wheel driven by a current of water or by a tide.

çur'ri-çle, *n.* [L. *curriculum*, a race, a racecourse, from *currere*, to run.]

1. A chaise or carriage with two wheels, drawn by two horses abreast.

2. A short course. [Obs.]

çur-riç'ū-lum, *n.*; *pl.* **çur-riç'ū-lums** or **çur-riç'ū-lȧ**. [L.] 1. A race-course.

2. A course; applied particularly to the course of study in a university, college, or school.

çur'rie, *n.* See *Curry*.

çur'ried (-rid), *a.* 1. Dressed by currying; dressed as leather; cleaned; prepared.

2. Made with curry; as, *curried* chicken.

çur'ri-ẽr, *n.* [ME. *coriour*; OFr. *corier*, *corrier*, a worker in leather; L. *coriarius*, a tanner, from *corium*, leather.] One who dresses and colors leather after it is tanned.

çũr'rish, *a.* Like a cur; having the qualities of a cur; brutal; malignant; snappish; snarling; churlish; intractable; quarrelsome.

çũr'rish-ly, *adv.* In a currish manner.

çũr'rish-ness, *n.* The state or quality of being currish.

çur'ry, *v.t.*; curried, *pt.*, *pp.*; currying, *ppr.* [ME. *curreyen*, *currayan*, to curry a horse, to prepare leather; OFr. *correier*, *coreer*, to put in order, prepare, from *conroy*, *corroi*, preparation, order.]

1. To dress (leather) after it is tanned; to soak, scrape, cleanse, beat, and color (tanned hides), and prepare for use.

2. To rub and clean with a comb; to groom; as, to *curry* a horse.

3. To beat; to thrash.

> By setting brother against brother,
> To claw and *curry* one another. —Butler.

To curry favor; to seek or gain favor by flattery, caresses, kindness, or officious civilities.

çur'ry, *v.t.* To prepare or flavor with curry; as, to *curry* rice.

çur'ry, **çur'rie**, *n.* [Anglo-Ind. word; Tamil *kari*, curry.]

1. A kind of sauce much used in India, containing red pepper and other strong spices. [See *Curry-powder*.]

2. A stew of fowl, fish, etc., cooked with curry.

çur'ry-çōmb (-kōm), *n.* A metal instrument or comb, for grooming and cleaning horses.

çur'ry-çōmb, *v.t.*; currycombed, *pt.*, *pp.*; currycombing, *ppr.* To comb with a currycomb; to curry.

çur'ry=leaf, *n.* The aromatic leaf of an East Indian rutaceous tree, *Murraya Kœnigii*, esteemed as a flavoring for curries.

çur'ry=pow"dẽr, *n.* A condiment used for making curry, composed of turmeric, coriander seed, ginger, and cayenne pepper, to which salt, cloves, cardamoms, pounded cinnamon, onions, garlic, and scraped cocoanut may be added.

çũrse, *v.t.*; cursed *or* curst, *pt.*, *pp.*; cursing, *ppr.* [ME. *cursien*, *cursen*, late AS. *cursian*, to curse.]

1. To utter a wish of evil against; to imprecate evil upon; to call for mischief or injury to fall upon; to execrate.

> Thou shalt not *curse* the ruler of thy people. —Ex. xxii. 28.

2. To excommunicate; to place under an ecclesiastical ban; as, to *curse* by bell, book, and candle.

3. To injure; to subject to evil; to blight with a curse; to vex, harass, or torment with great calamities.

> On impious realms and barbarous kings impose
> Thy plagues, and *curse* 'em with such sons as those. —Pope.

çũrse, *v.i.* To utter imprecations; to affirm or deny with imprecations of divine vengeance; to swear; to blaspheme.

> Then began he to *curse* and to swear. —Matt. xxvi. 74.

çũrse, *n.* [ME. *curs*; AS. *curs*, a curse.]

1. Malediction; the expression of a wish of evil to another; imprecation of evil.

> They entered into a *curse*. —Neh. x. 29.

2. Evil, solemnly or in passion, invoked upon one.

> The priest shall write all these *curses* in a book. —Num. v. 23.

3. That which brings evil or severe affliction; torment; great vexation; a scourge.

> The common *curse* of mankind, folly and ignorance. —Shak.

4. Condemnation; sentence of divine vengeance on sinners. [Rare.]

> Christ hath redeemed us from the *curse* of the law. —Gal. iii. 13.

Not worth a curse; no good; useless; formerly and properly, *not worth a cress*. [See *Cress*.]

The curse of Scotland; in card-playing, the nine of diamonds, probably from its resemblance to the armorial bearings of a detested nobleman, the earl of Stair.

Syn.—Malediction, anathema, execration, imprecation, oath.

çũrs'ed, *a.* Execrable; hateful; odious; abhorred; detestable; blasted by a curse; deserving a curse.

çũrs'ed-ly, *adv.* In a cursed manner; miserably; in a manner to be cursed or detested.

çũrs'ed-ness, *n.* 1. The state of being under a curse, or of being doomed to execration or to evil.

2. Blasphemy; cursing. [Obs.]

3. Shrewishness; contrariness.

çũrs'ẽr, *n.* One who curses.

çũr'ship, *n.* The state of being a cur.

çũr'si-tā-ting, *a.* Changing or moving about. [Rare.]

çũr'si-tŏr, *n.* [L. *cursor*, a runner, from *currere*, to run.]

1. In England, a clerk in the court of chancery, whose business was to make out original writs.

2. A courier. [Obs.]

çũr'sive, *a.* [LL. *cursivus*, running, from *cursus*, a running, course.] Running; flowing.

Cursive hand; in writing, a running hand.

çũr'sive, *n.* 1. A character or letter used in cursive writing.

2. A manuscript written in cursive characters, as distinguished from one in uncials or separate characters.

çũr'sive-ly, *adv.* In a cursive manner.

çũr'sŏr, *n.* [L., a runner, from *currere*, to run.] Any part of a mathematical instrument that slides backward and forward upon another part, as the piece in an equinoctial ring-dial that slides to the day of the month, or the point that slides along a beam-compass, etc.

çũr'sō-rā-ry, *a.* Cursory; hasty. [Obs.]

Çũr-sō'rēṣ, *n.pl.* [L. *cursores*, runners, pl. of *cursor*, a runner.]

1. The runners, an order of birds, so named from their remarkable velocity in running; the *Ratitæ*, or *Brevipennes*. The wings are but little developed and are totally incapable of raising the birds from the ground. The utmost that they can accomplish is to assist the powerful run, which is effected by the strong and highly developed legs. The order comprises the ostrich, cassowary, emu, rhea, and apteryx.

2. A name given to a group of spiders which make no webs, but catch their prey by swift pursuit, such as the wolf-spiders, *Lycosidæ*.

Çũr-sō'ri-ȧ, *n.pl.* [LL., neut. pl. of *cursorius*, running; L. *currere*, to run.] A suborder of insects of the order *Orthoptera*, containing only the cockroaches.

çũr-sō'ri-ăl, *a.* 1. Adapted for running; as, the legs of a dog are *cursorial*.

2. Pertaining to the *Cursores*.

çũr'sō-ri-ly, *adv.* In a running or hasty manner; hastily; without close attention.

çũr'sō-ri-ness, *n.* The quality of being cursory; slightness of attention; superficiality.

Çũr-sō'ri-us, *n.* [LL., running; L. *cursor*, a runner.] A genus of grallatorial birds of the plover tribe, including those birds which, from

Brazen-winged Courser (*Cursorius chalcopterus*).

the limited development of their wings, are unable to fly, but which from the size and strength of their legs possess superior powers of running. To this genus belong the black-bellied courier, the brazen-winged courser, and the cream-colored courser or swift-foot. These birds chiefly inhabit Africa.

çũr'sō-ry, *a.* [L. *cursor*, a runner.]

1. Running; hasty; slight; superficial; careless; not with close attention; as, a *cursory* reading; a *cursory* view.

2. Running about; not stationary. [Obs.]

Syn.—Careless, desultory, hasty, slight, superficial, rapid.

çũrst, *v.*, past tense and past participle of *curse*.

çũrst, *a.* Hateful; froward; tormenting; vexatious; malignant; malicious; snarling. [Obs.]

çũrst'ful-ly, *adv.* Peevishly; ill-naturedly; cursedly. [Obs.]

çũrst'ness, *n.* Peevishness; surliness. [Obs.]

çũr'sus, *n.* [L.] A regular course or order of service in churches; the office of daily prayer; the choir-offices as a whole.

çũrt, *a.* [L. *curtus*, shortened, mutilated.] Rudely short or concise; characterized by brevity; abrupt; as, a *curt* reply.

Syn.—Short, brief, sharp, concise, acute, abrupt.

çũr-tāil', *v.t.*; curtailed, *pt.*, *pp.*; curtailing, *ppr.* [OFr. *courtault*, curtal, from *court*, short (L. *curtus*), and *tailler*, to cut.] To shorten; to cut off the end or a part of; to lessen; as, to *curtail* expenses; to *curtail* an allowance.

Syn.—Reduce, lessen, diminish, abridge, abbreviate, shorten, dock, retrench, decrease.

çũr'tāil, *n.* In architecture, the end of any member when it is shaped like a scroll.

çũr'tāil-dog, *n.* Formerly, a dog whose tail was cut off, according to the forest laws, its owner being hindered from coursing; hence, a dog not meant for sport; a dog that has missed his game.

çũr-tāil'ẽr, *n.* One who curtails; one who cuts off or shortens anything.

çũr-tāil'ment, *n.* The act of curtailing; the result of curtailing; a diminution.

çũr'tāil-step, *n.* The lowest step in a flight of stairs when it is shaped at its outer extremity like a scroll.

çũr'tain (-tin), *n.* [ME. *curteyn*; OFr. *curtine*, a curtain; LL. *cortina*, a small court, a screen of cloth; dim. of *cortis*, a court; L. *cohors*, a court, an inclosed space; Gr. *chortos*, a yard, court.]

1. A hanging cloth or screen round a bed, at a window, or elsewhere, which may be contracted, spread, or drawn aside at pleasure; any hanging fabric intended to conceal from view; specifically, the removable hanging screen before the stage of a theater; also called *drop-curtain*.

2. In fortification, that part of the rampart which is between the flanks of two bastions, bordered with a parapet, behind which the soldiers stand to fire.

3. In mycology, the cortina.

4. A flag or ensign. [Obs.]

Behind the curtain; in concealment; in secret.

The curtain falls; the scene or performance ends; the incident is closed.

The curtain rises; the play or scene begins; light is thrown on the matter.

To draw the curtain; to remove from view; to stop discussion or investigation.

To drop the curtain; to close the scene; to end.

çũr'tain (-tin), *v.t.*; curtained, *pt.*, *pp.*; curtaining, *ppr.* To inclose with curtains; to furnish with curtains.

çũr'tain-an"gle, *n.* In fortification, the angle between curtain and bastion-flank.

çũr'tain-lec"tũre, *n.* A private lecture; a reproof or scolding given to a husband by his wife; originally, behind bed-curtains.

çũr'tăl, *n.* A horse or dog with a docked tail. [Obs.]

çũr'tăl, *a.* [L. *curtus*, short.] Curt; brief; cut off; scant. [Obs.]

çũr'tăl-ax, çũr'tle-ax, *n.* Corrupt forms of *cutlas*.

çũr'tăl-dog, *n.* See *Curtail-dog*.

çũr'tăl-frī"ăr, *n.* A friar who attended the gate of a monastery, or one attired in a short habit.

çũr-tā'nȧ, *n.* Same as *Curtein*.

çũr'tāte, *a.* [L. *curtatus*, pp. of *curtare*, to shorten.] Reduced; shortened.

Curtate cycloid; see *Cycloid*.

Curtate distance (of a planet); in astronomy, the distance from the earth or sun to that point where a perpendicular, let fall from the planet, meets the plane of the ecliptic.

çũr-tā'tion, *n.* [L. *curtatus*, pp. of *curtare*, to shorten.] The interval between a planet's true distance from the sun and the curtate distance.

çũr-tein', *n.* [L. *curtus*, shortened, broken.] The pointless sword displayed before English kings at their coronation, symbolizing mercy, and known as the sword of Edward the Confessor; also called *curtana*.

çũr-tēis', *a.* Courteous. [Obs.]

çũr'tē-sy, *n.* Same as *Courtesy*.

çũr'ti-lāġe, *n.* [OFr. *cortillage*, from *courtil*, a court; L. *cohors*, a yard.] In law, a yard, garden, inclosure, or field, near and belonging to a dwelling.

çũrt'ly, *adv.* Briefly; in a curt manner.

çũrt'ness, *n.* Shortness; the quality of being curt.

çũrt'sy, çũrt'sey, *n.* and *v.* Same as *Courtesy*.

çū'rū-bȧ, *n.* [Corruption of West Indian *culupa*.] The sweet calabash of the West Indies; the fruit of *Passiflora multiformis*.

çū-rū-çū'çū, *n.* See *Bushmaster*.

çū'rū-çui (-kwi), *n.* [Native Brazilian name.] A Brazilian bird, the trogon.

çū'rūle, *a.* [L. *curulis*, pertaining to a chariot, from *currus*, a chariot, car; *currere*, to run.]

1. Belonging to a chariot.

2. Privileged to sit in a *curule* chair; as, a *curule* magistrate.

Curule Chair, from a drawing found in Pompeii.

Curule chair; in ancient Rome, a chair or stool without a back, so made as to be folded up and opened in the manner of a camp-stool; at first plain, but later inlaid with gold, ivory, etc.; used by dictators, consuls, pretors, censors, and ediles, who from this fact were called *curule magistrates*.

çū-rū'rō, *n.* [Native name.] A burrowing rodent of Chile, genus *Spalacopus*.

çũr'văl, *a.* Same as *Curvant*.

çũr'vănt, *a.* In heraldry, bowed or curved.

çũr'vāte, çũr'vā-ted, *a.* [L. *curvatus*, pp. of *curvare*, to bend.] Curved; bent in a regular form.

çũr-vā'tion, *n.* The act of bending or crooking.

çũr'vȧ-tive, *a.* In botany, slightly curved, as the margins of leaves. [Rare.]

çũr'vȧ-tũre, *n.* [L. *curvatura*, a bending, from *curvare*, to bend.]

1. The flexure or bending of a line from a rectilinear direction; a curve.

2. In mathematics, the comparative degree of flexion or bending which takes place near the different points of a curve.

3. The act of curving; the state of being bent.

Aberrancy of curvature; in geometry, the extent of the deviation of a curve from a circle.

Absolute curvature; in a twisted curve, the reciprocal of the radius of the osculating circle.

Angle of curvature; in geometry, an angle which expresses the extent of curvature of a curve.

Chord of curvature; see under *Chord*.

Circle of curvature; a circle which touches a curve in a point, so that no other circle touching it in the same point can pass between it and the curve.

Curvature of the spine; in medicine, an abnormal curving of the spinal column, either angular or lateral.

Radius of curvature; the radius of the circle of curvature.

çũrve, *a.* Bending; crooked; inflected in a regular form and forming part of a circle; as, a *curve* line.

çũrve, *n.* [OFr. *courbe*, curve; L. *curvus*, bent, crooked; Gr. *kyrtos*, curved, bent.]

1. A bending without angles; that which is bent; a flexure.

2. In geometry, a line which changes its direction at every point; a line of which no three consecutive points are in the same direction or straight line.

3. An instrument for making curved figures, used by draftsmen.

4. In baseball, the course traversed by the ball, due to the manner of pitching, and independent of the force of gravity; there are in, out, drop, and up *curves*.

5. Anything bent continuously.

Algebraic curve; see under *Algebraic*.

Axis of a curve; see under *Axis*.

Curve of beauty; a curve of double flexure, to which all beauty of form has been ascribed; also called *line of beauty*.

Curve of population; in statistics, a line drawn from a fixed point to different points of observation whose distances from the axis show the variations in density.

Curve of probability; a transcendental curve representing the probabilities of recurrences of an event.

Plane curve; in geometry, a curve situated in a plane, as distinguished from a *twisted curve*.

çũrve, *v.t.*; curved, *pt.*, *pp.*; curving, *ppr.* [OFr. *curber*; L. *curvare*, to bend, curve.]

1. To bend; to crook; as, to *curve* a pipe or rod; to *curve* a dome.

2. To deflect; as, to *curve* a pitched ball.

çũrve, *v.i.* To bend gradually from a straight line; to assume the form of a curve.

çũrv'ed-ness, *n.* The state of being curved. [Rare.]

çũr'vet, *n.* [It. *corvetta*, a leap, curvet, from *corvare*, to bend, stoop; L. *curvare*, to bend.]

1. In the manège, a leap of a horse in which he raises both his fore legs at once, equally advanced, and, as his fore legs are falling, springs forward with his hind legs, so that all his legs are raised at once.

2. A prank; a frolic.

çũr'vet, *v.i.*; curveted *or* curvetted, *pt.*, *pp.*; curveting *or* curvetting, *ppr.* [It. *corvettare*; Fr. *courbetter*; Sp. *corvetear*.]

1. To leap; to bound; to spring and form a curvet.

2. To leap and frisk.

çũr'vet, *v.t.* To cause to describe a curvet; to cause to leap or prance.

çũr-vi-. A combining form from L. *curvus*, curved.

çũr-vi-çau'dāte, *a.* [*Curvi-*, and L. *cauda*, tail.] In zoölogy, having a bent or curved tail.

çũr-vi-ços'tāte, *a.* [*Curvi-*, and L. *costa*, rib.] Having crooked or curved ribs; marked with small bent ribs.

çũr-vi-den'tāte, *a.* [*Curvi-*, and L. *dens*, tooth.] Having curved teeth.

çũr-vi-fō'li-āte, *a.* [*Curvi-*, and L. *folium*, leaf.] Having curved leaves.

çũr'vi-fọrm, *a.* Having the form of a curve; curved.

çũr-vi-lin'ē-ad, *n.* [*Curvi-*, and L. *linea*, a line.] In geometry, an instrument for making curved lines.

çũr-vi-lin'ē-ăr, çũr-vi-lin'ē-ăl, *a.* [*Curvi-*, and L. *linea*, line.] Consisting of curve lines; bounded by curve lines; as, a *curvilinear* figure.

çũr-vi-lin-ē-ar'i-ty, *n.* The state of being curvilinear, or of consisting of curved lines.

çũr-vi-lin'ē-ăr-ly, *adv.* In a curvilinear manner.

çũr-vi-nẽr'vāte, *a.* [*Curvi-*, and L. *nervus*, nerve.] Having the veins or nervures curved; applied to the leaves of plants and the wings of insects.

çũr'vi-nẽrved, *a.* Same as *Curvinervate*.

çũr-vi-ros'trăl, *a.* [*Curvi-*, and L. *rostrum*, a beak.] In ornithology, (a) having a crooked or decurved beak, as the curlew; (b) having the mandibles curved and crossed, as the crossbill.

Çũr-vi-ros'trēs, *n.pl.* In ornithology, a group of laminiplantar passerines, including the creepers and nuthatches.

çũr-vi-sē'ri-ăl, *a.* [*Curvi-*, and L. *series*, series.] Disposed in a series describing a curve or spiral, as leaves about a stem.

çũr'vi-tăl, *a.* Pertaining to curves.

çũr'vi-ty, *n.* A bending in a regular form; crookedness; curvature; the state of being curved.

çũr'vō-grȧph, *n.* [L. *curvus*; Gr. *kyrtos*, curved, and *graphein*, to write.] In geometry, an arcograph or cyclograph.

çũr'vū-lāte, *a.* Slightly curved.

çus'çus, *n.* [Fr. *couscous*; Ar. *kuskus*.] The rootstock of an Indian grass, *Andropogon muricatus*.

çush, *n.* [Anglo-Ind.] Sorghum; a commercial name.

çush'at, *n.* [ME. *cowscot*, *couscot*; AS. *cuscoet*, *cusceote*, the ringdove; *cwicu*, quick, and *sceotan*, to shoot.] The ringdove or wood-pigeon.

çush'ew-bird, *n.* The galeated curassow.

çush'iŏn (-un), *n.* [ME. *cushone*; OFr. *cuissin*; LL. *cussinus*, cushion; L. *culcita*, a cushion, pillow.]

1. A cloth or leather case or bag, filled with soft material and used as a seat or rest, as in chairs, carriages, etc.; a soft pad.

2. Anything having the appearance or effect of a cushion, especially when used to counteract or prevent sudden shocks or jolts, as in machinery.

3. The padded sides of a billiard table.

4. In architecture, a cushion-capital.

5. A bag of leather filled with sand, used by engravers to support the plate.

çush'iŏn, *v.t.*; cushioned, *pt.*, *pp.*; cushioning, *ppr.* 1. To place on, or as on, a cushion.

2. To cover or furnish with a cushion or cushions; as, to *cushion* a buggy.

çush'iŏn, *v.i.* In billiards, to cause the cue-ball to strike the cushion before or after touching the object-ball.

çush'iŏn-çap"i-tăl, *n.* In architecture, a capital of such form as to appear like a cushion flattened by the weight of the superstructure; very common in Indian buildings; applied, also, to the Norman capital, which consists of a cube rounded off at its base.

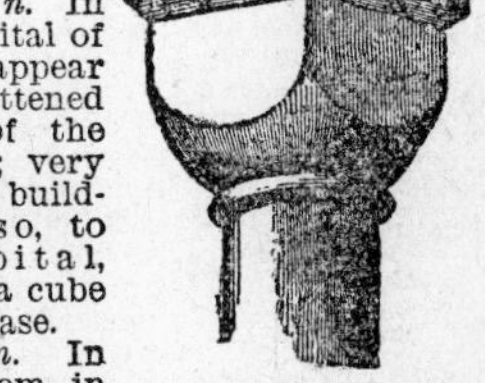

Norman Cushion-capital.

çush'iŏn-car"ŏm, *n.* In billiards, a carom in which the cue-ball touches the cushion before contact with the second object-ball.

çush'ion-dance, *n.* A rustic dance, formerly popular in England and Scotland, in which each dancer, at recurring intervals, dropped before another of the opposite sex a cushion, on which they knelt and exchanged kisses.

çush'ioned (-und), *a.* Supported by cushions; furnished with cushions.

çush'ion-et, *n.* A little cushion.

çush'ion-raft"ẽr, *n.* In architecture, an auxiliary rafter, used to relieve the strain on a principal rafter.

çush'ion-scāle, *n.* In entomology, an insect fruit-pest, *Icerya purchasi*, the females of which are provided with a cushion-shaped ovisac.

çush'ion-stär, *n.* In ichthyology, any one of several species of pentagonal starfish, as the *Goniaster equestris* of Great Britain.

çush'ion-stitch, *n.* In embroidery, a straight, short stitch used in the groundwork of designs intended to imitate painting.

çush'ion-y, *a.* Like a cushion; elastic; soft.

Çush'ite, *a.* and *n.* [Name from *Cush*, the son of Ham.]

I. *a.* Pertaining to the Cushites or to the language spoken by them.

II. *n.* In ethnology, one of a branch of the Hamite family anciently inhabiting Ethiopia.

çush'y, *adj.* Comfortable; easy. [Soldiers' slang.]

çusk, *n.* 1. An English name for the torsk, *Brosmius brosme*.

2. An American name for the burbot, *Lota maculosa*.

çus'kin, *n.* A kind of ivory drinking-cup. [Obs.]

çusp, *n.* [L. *cuspis*, a point.]

1. In astronomy, the point or horn of the crescent moon or other crescent-shaped luminary.

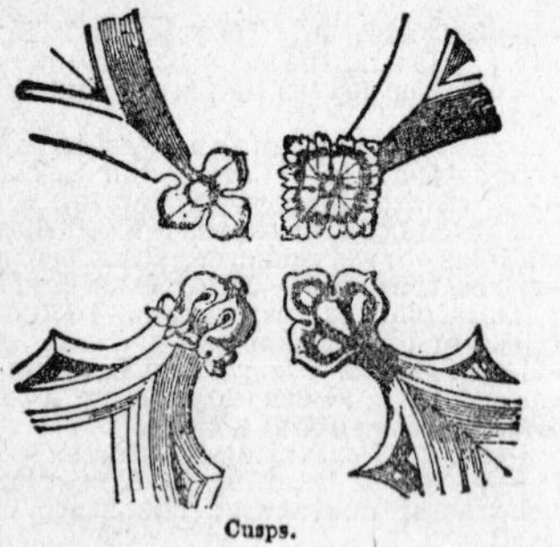

Cusps.

2. In architecture, a projecting point in the foliations of Gothic tracery, arches, panels, etc.

3. In astrology, the initial entrance of a house in the calculation of nativities.

4. In botany, a rigid, sharp point, especially on a leaf.

5. In anatomy, any prominence on the crown of a tooth; a denticle.

6. In geometry, a point on a curve at which a point describing the curve has its motion reversed.

çusp, *v.t.*; cusped, *pt.*, *pp.*; cusping, *ppr.* To decorate or provide with a cusp or cusps.

çus'pā-ted, *a.* Pointed; ending in a point.

çus'pid, *n.* [L. *cuspis*, a point.] In anatomy, a canine tooth.

çus'pi-dăl, *a.* Ending in a point.

çus'pi-dāte, çus'pi-dā-ted, *a.* [L. *cuspidatus*, pp. of *cuspidare*, to make pointed; *cuspis*, a point.] Having a sharp end, like the point of a spear; terminating in a bristly point.

çus'pi-dāte, *v.t.*; cuspidated, *pt.*, *pp.*; cuspidating, *ppr.* To make pointed; to form like a cusp.

çus'pi-dine, *n.* [L. *cuspis*, a point, spear.] In mineralogy, a Vesuvian fluosilicate of calcium, occurring in pale red, spear-shaped crystals.

çus'pi-dọr, çus'pi-dōre, *n.* [Port. *cuspidor*, a spittoon, from *cuspir*, to spit; L. *conspuere*, to spit upon.] A spittoon.

çus'pis, *n.*; *pl.* **çus'pi-dēs**. [L. *cuspis*, a point.] A point; a cusp.

çuss'ed-ness, *n.* Cantankerousness; malignity; meanness. [Colloq.]

çus'sō, *n.* [Abyssinian.] 1. In botany, a rosaceous tree of Abyssinia, *Brayera anthelmintica*.

2. A kind of vermifuge made of the dried flowers of *Brayera anthelmintica*; also written *kousso*.

çus'tärd, *n.* [OFr. *croustade*, pie, pastry; from L. *crustatus*, pp. of *crustare*, to crust, *crusta*, a crust, shell.] A composition of milk and eggs, sweetened, and baked or boiled.

çus'tärd-ap"ple, *n.* A low tree or plant, *Anona reticulata*, growing in the West Indies, whose fruit is of an orange color, and contains a yellowish pulp of the consistence of custard.

çus'tärd-cof"fin, *n.* A crust covering a custard. [Obs.]

çus'tōde, *n.* 1. A custodian.

2. Same as *Custodia*.

çus-tō'di-ȧ, *n.* [L., guard, a prison.] A receptacle for sacred objects.

çus-tō'di-ăl, *a.* Relating to custody or guardianship.

çus-tō'di-ăn, *n.* [L. *custodia*, a watch, guard; *custodire*, to guard.] One who has the care or custody of some public building, etc.; a guardian; a keeper.

çus-tō'di-ăn-ship, *n.* The office of a custodian.

çus-tō'di-ẽr, *n.* Custodian. [Obs.]

çus'tō-dy, *n.* [L. *custodia*, a watch, guard, from *custos*, a watchman; Gr. *keuthein*, to hide, conceal.]

1. A keeping; a guarding; care, watch, inspection, for keeping, preservation, or security; as, in the *custody* of the sheriff.

2. Imprisonment; confinement; restraint of liberty.

çus'tŏm, *n.* [ME. *custom*, *custome*; OFr. *costume*, custom; from L. *consuetudo*, custom, habit; *con*, intensive, and *suere*, to be accustomed, wont.]

1. Frequent or common use, or practice; a frequent repetition of the same act; way; established manner; habitual practice.

2. Any regular tax or tribute; in the plural, *customs*, the legal duties on imports or exports; as, an officer of the *customs*; at the *custom*house.

3. In law, long-established practice, which constitutes the unwritten law, and long consent to which gives it authority; usage; habitude.

4. Frequent or habitual purchase of goods, household supplies, or other things at a particular manufactory, shop, store, etc.; the sum expended in such dealings; as, his *custom* is considerable.

Custom of merchants; the code or unwritten law in commerce which governs contracts, exchange, insurance, etc.

Custom of war; the mode of procedure established by military usage.

Customs duty; the tariff tax imposed by law upon commodities imported from or (sometimes) exported to a foreign country.

Customs union; an international union for the regulation of customs duties; a zollverein.

Syn.—Fashion, habit, manner, practice, habitude, usage, wont.

çus'tŏm-ȧ-ble, *a.* Liable to payment of duties; dutiable.

çus'tŏm-ā-ri-ly, *adv.* In the prevailing manner; ordinarily.

çus'tŏm-ā-ri-ness, *n.* Frequency; commonness; habitual use or practice.

çus'tŏm-ā-ry, *a.* [ME. *customere*; OFr. *costumier*; LL. *custumarius*, subject to tax; *custuma*, custom.]

1. According to custom, or to established or common usage; conventional; usual.

2. Habitual; in common practice; as, *customary* vices.

3. In law, holding by custom; as, *customary* tenants.

çus'tŏm-ā-ry, *n.* [Fr. *coutumier*; OFr. *coustumier*.] A book containing laws and usages, or customs; as, the *customary* of the Normans.

çus'tŏm-ẽr, *n.* [OFr. *costumier*, customer; LL. *custumarius*, toll-gatherer, from *custuma*, tax, custom.]

1. One who frequents any place of sale for the sake of purchasing goods; one who purchases goods or wares; a buyer.

2. One who frequents or visits any place to procure what he wants; as, the *customers* of a mill, a bank, or a restaurant.

3. A toll-gatherer. [Obs.]

An ugly customer; one who is difficult to deal with or to manage. [Colloq.]

çus'tŏm-house, *n.* 1. The house or building where vessels are entered and cleared, and where customs duties are paid.

2. In popular language, the whole establishment or system by means of which the customs revenue is collected and its regulations enforced.

Customhouse broker; an agent or broker who attends to the entering and clearing of vessels and cargoes, payment of customs duties, etc.

çus'tos, *n.* [L. *custos*, a keeper, guardian, from *custodire*, to guard.] A custodian; a keeper. [Obs.]

Custos rotulorum; in English law, the principal justice of the peace in a county, who is keeper of the rolls and records of the sessions of the peace.

çus'trel, *n.* 1. A buckler-bearer.

2. A vessel for holding wine. [Obs.]

çus'tum-ā-ry, *n.* A customary. [Obs.]

çut, *v.t.*; cut, *pt.*, *pp.*; cutting, *ppr.* [ME. *cutten*, *kutten*, to cut; used first about 1200 A. D., prob. of Celtic origin.]

1. To separate or divide the parts of with an edged instrument; to gash; to incise; to wound; to sever; to notch with an edged tool; said of the instrument used or of the agent using it; as, the saw *cuts* the board; the man *cuts* his finger.

2. To sever or divide, as wood for gathering; to mow or reap; as, to *cut* grass or corn.

3. To sever and remove, as the nails or hair; to trim; to dress.

4. To make ready or form by cutting; as, to *cut* a dress; to carve or engrave; as, to *cut* a jewel or an inscription.

5. To intersect; to cross; as, one line *cuts* another at right angles; the ecliptic *cuts* the equator.

6. To divide, as a pack of cards; as, to *cut* and shuffle the pack.

7. To penetrate; to pierce; to affect deeply; as, a sharp rebuke *cuts* her to the quick.

8. To divide; to cleave, by passing through; as, a ship *cuts* the briny deep.

9. To castrate; as, to *cut* a horse.

10. To divide or pass through by means of something resembling an edged instrument, or as an edged instrument does.

11. To curtail; to reduce in quantity or extent; to shorten; often followed by *down*; as, to *cut* expenses; to *cut* or *cut down* a literary composition.

12. To remain away from intentionally; to neglect; as, to *cut* an appointment. [Colloq.]

13. To pass with intentional lack of recognition; to ignore; as, to *cut* an acquaintance on the street. [Colloq.]

14. To dissolve; to mix with closely; as, the acid *cut* the metal; vinegar *cuts* oil.

15. To move forward in the direction desired by successive swinging of the ends sideways; as, to *cut* a safe or other object too heavy to be lifted bodily.

16. In cricket, to bat downward toward the ground on the off side; in tennis, to strike so as to give the ball a whirling motion.

17. To excavate, or make ready by cutting; as, to *cut* a road.

18. To give up; to quit; as, he *cut* the service.

To cut a dash or *figure*; to make an ostentatious display. [Colloq.]

To cut down; (a) to fell; to cause to fall by severing. (b) To reduce; to curtail; as, *to cut down* expenditure; *to cut down* manuscript. (c) Among seamen, to collide with and damage so that a vessel is in danger of sinking; as, the frigate *cut down* the privateer.

To cut loose; to withdraw from.

To cut lots; to draw lots.

To cut off; (a) to separate from other parts; to remove; as, *to cut off* a leg or arm; *to cut off* a letter or syllable. (b) To kill; to put an end to suddenly; as, *cut off* in his prime. (c) To interrupt; to stop; as, *to cut off* communication. (d) To intercept; to stop by the way; as, *to cut off* troops from a ship. (e) To omit from the benefits of a will or testament; to disinherit; as, his father *cut* him *off* with a shilling.

To cut one's wisdom teeth; to reach an age of discretion.

To cut out; (a) to remove a part by cutting or carving. (b) To remove and take the place of, as a rival. (c) To make; to shape. (d) To remove from a collection or number; as, *to cut out* a steer from a drove. (e) To abandon; to quit; to cease; as, he was told *to cut out* his nonsense. [Colloq.] (f) To seize and take away, as a ship from under an enemy's guns.

To cut short; to terminate abruptly or suddenly.

To cut one's stick; to leave hurriedly or secretly. [Slang.]

To cut teeth; to have teeth appear by cutting through the gums.

To cut the Gordian knot; to settle a difficulty by bold or unusual measures.

To cut under; to undersell; to sell at a lower price than a competitor; to cut prices.

To cut up; (a) to cut in pieces; as, *to cut up* beef. (b) To score or criticize harshly; as, *to cut up* a writer or his book.

To have cut one's eyeteeth; to be worldly-wise. [Colloq.]

Syn.—Hew, chop, cleave, sever, gash, incise, dissect, carve.

çut, *v.i.* 1. To be fitted for severing or incising; as, the blade *cuts* well.

2. To be of such a nature as to admit of incision or division; as, lead *cuts* with a metallic luster.

3. To operate by severing, dissecting, or incising; to use a knife or edge-tool; as, the surgeon *cuts* carefully.

4. To divide a pack of cards in order to determine the order of play, to decide the trump or the deal, or to alter the arrangement of the cards to be dealt to the various players.

5. To interfere, as a horse.

6. To strike, as with a whip.

7. To hurry away; as, to *cut* and run. [Colloq.]

8. To pierce through the gums, as teeth.

9. To open a coal-seam transversely in order to blast away a portion of it.

To cut across; to pass by a shorter course, so as to cut off an angle or distance.

To cut and run; to get away quickly; among seamen, to cut the cable and set sail immediately, leaving the anchor behind.

To cut in or *into*; to join, or take part, in anything suddenly and unceremoniously.

To cut up; (a) to play pranks. (b) To be worth when cut up; to turn out; a butcher's phrase sometimes applied to estates, etc.; as, I wonder how he will *cut up*. (c) To give pain to; to wound; to trouble; as, he was much *cut up* by his misfortune. [Colloq.]

To cut up rough; to become quarrelsome or obstreperous; to become dangerous. [Slang.]

çut, *n.* 1. A stroke or blow, with, or as with, a knife or other edged instrument; a cleft; a gash; a notch; a wound; the opening made by an edged instrument.

2. A stroke or blow with a whip.

3. A channel made by cutting or digging; a ditch; a groove; a furrow; a canal.

4. A part cut off from the rest; as, a good *cut* of beef; a *cut* of timber.

5. The surface made by cutting; as, a clean *cut*.

6. A near passage, by which an angle is cut off; as, a short *cut*.

7. An engraving on wood or metal from which an impression is taken in printing; also, the impression itself; as, a half-tone *cut*; a book full of *cuts*.

8. The act of dividing a pack of cards; also, the right to divide; as, whose *cut* is it?

9. The manner in which a thing is cut; form; shape; fashion; as, the *cut* of a garment; the *cut* of one's beard.

10. An intentional failure to recognize the salutation of an acquaintance; as, he gave him a stern *cut*.

11. Anything that wounds one's feelings deeply, as a severe rebuke or stern criticism.

This was the most unkindest *cut* of all. —Shak.

12. A reduction or lowering; as, a *cut* in price.

13. An intentional absence from a college exercise or class. [Colloq.]

14. In cricket, a sharp downward stroke of the bat, which sends the ball to the off side.

15. In tennis, a stroke which imparts to the ball an irregular whirling motion.

16. A gelding. [Obs.]

17. A skein of yarn containing two hanks.

18. A slip of wood, paper, straw, etc., used in drawing lots.

The cut of one's jib; the cast of one's countenance; one's general appearance. [Colloq.]

çut, *a.* 1. Divided or gashed, as by a knife or edge-tool; as, a *cut* finger.

2. Shaped by cutting; hewn or chiseled; carved; polished; dressed; as, *cut* stone; *cut* glass.

3. Castrated.

4. Formed by cutting from a plate of metal; as, *cut* nails.

5. Intoxicated. [Slang.]

6. Separated from the stem or plant; as, *cut* flowers.

Cut and dried; prepared for the occasion; lacking spontaneity; a metaphor from hewn lumber.

Cut terrace; a terrace formed by the erosive action of waves upon a cliff.

çū-tā'nē-ous, *a.* [L. *cutis*, skin.] Belonging to the skin; existing on, or affecting the skin; as, a *cutaneous* disease; *cutaneous* eruption.

çū-tā'nē-ous-ly, *adv.* In a manner to affect the skin.

çut'ȧ-wāy, *n.* A form of coat for men's wear with the skirts cut on a slope away from the waist.

çutch, *n.* Same as *Cultch*.

çutch, *n.* [Anglo-Ind.] Catechu.

çutch, *n.* [*Cutch* or *quitch*, from *quick*; ME. *quik*; AS. *cwic*.] Quitch-grass.

çutch, *n.* In gold-beating, the package of vellum leaves between which gold-leaf is placed to be beaten.

çutch'ẽr, *n.* A cylinder in a paper-making machine around which an endless felt apron is carried.

çutch'ẽr-y, *n.* [Hind. *kachahrī*, a court, court-house.] In India, a court of justice or public office.

çūte, *a.* [Abbrev. for *acute*; L. *acutus*, sharp.]

1. Clever; sharp; cunning; as, a *cute* swindle. [Colloq.]

2. Attractive because of prettiness or cunning ways; bright; usually with the idea of smallness; as, a *cute* little child.

çūte'ly, *adv.* In a cute manner. [Colloq.]

çūte'ness, *n.* The state or quality of being cute. [Colloq.]

çut'=grȧss, *n.* A species of swamp-grass, the blades of which have very sharp edges which cut the flesh readily; spear-grass.

çū'ti-çle, *n.* [L. *cuticula*, dim. of *cutis*, skin.]

1. In anatomy, the outermost thin transparent skin which covers all the surface of the body, except the parts which correspond to the nails; the epidermis or scarfskin.

2. In botany, the thin external covering of the bark of a plant; the outer pellicle of the epidermis.

3. A thin skin formed on the surface of liquor.

çū-tiç'ū-lăr, *a.* Pertaining to the cuticle or external coat of the skin.

çū-tiç"ū-lăr-i-zā'tion, *n.* Same as *Cutinization*.

çū-tiç'ū-lăr-īze, *v.t.* and *v.i.*; cuticularized, *pt.*, *pp.*; cuticularizing, *ppr.* To render cuticular; to give the character, nature, or composition of the cuticle to.

çū'ti-fȳ, *v.i.*; cutified, *pt.*, *pp.*; cutifying, *ppr.* To form skin.

çū'tin, *n.* [L. *cutis*, the skin.] A peculiar modification of cellulose, contained in the epidermis of leaves, petals, and fruits, together with ordinary cellulose, albumen, pectous substances, and fat.

çut'=in, *a.* In printing, applied to a note, heading, etc., that is set in at the side of a page, thus taking up a portion of the space otherwise occupied by the text; as, a *cut-in* headline.

çū"tin-i-zā'tion, *n.* In botany, the change wrought by the presence of cutin in cell-walls, by which they become waterproof.

çū'tin-īze, *v.t.* and *v.i.*; cutinized, *pt.*, *pp.*; cutinizing, *ppr.* To cuticularize.

çū'tis, *n.* The true skin; the layer beneath the epidermis. [See *Derma*.]

çut'lȧs, çut'lȧss, *n.* [Fr. *coutelas*, a cutlas; OFr. *coutel*, a knife, dagger; L. *cultellus*, dim. of *culter*, a knife.] A broad, curving sword used by seamen in the navy; a weapon used when boarding an enemy's ship or repelling boarders.

çut'lȧs=fish, *n.* A long, thin fish, *Trichiurus lepturus*, found in the West Indies; also called *scabbard-fish*, *saber-fish*, and *silver-eel*.

çut'lẽr, *n.* [ME. *coteler*; OFr. *cotelier*; LL. *cultellarius*, a maker of knives; from L. *cultellus*, dim. of *culter*, a knife.]

1. One who manufactures or deals in cutlery.

2. One who sharpens cutlery; a knife-grinder.

çut'lẽr-y, *n.* 1. The occupation of a cutler.

2. Knives or other cutting instruments, collectively.

çut'let, *n.* [Fr. *côtellette*, a chop, dim. of *côte*, rib, side; OFr. *coste*; L. *costa*, a rib.] A small piece of meat, but especially of mutton or veal, for broiling or frying.

çut'ling, *n.* The art of cutlery. [Obs.]

çut'lips, *n.* 1. The stone-toter, *Exoglossum maxillingua*, a cyprinoid fish.

2. The harelipped sucker of the Mississippi valley.

çut'=off, *n.* 1. That which cuts off or shortens, as a short road or path; a short cut.

2. In steam-engines, a contrivance for cutting off the steam from the steam-chest to the cylinder, when the piston has made a part of its stroke, leaving the rest of the stroke to be accomplished by the expansive force of the steam already in the cylinder. It economizes steam, and thus saves fuel.

3. Any arrangement by which a current or stream is or may be diverted or stopped.

4. In plumbing, a connecting pipe.

5. The shorter channel formed when a river or stream cuts through a bend in its course; as, the *cut-offs* of the Mississippi.

6. An arm on a reaping machine which supports the grain as it is about to fall, while that which has fallen on the platform is being removed.

çū'tōse, *n.* [L. *cutis*, skin.] In chemistry, a form of cellulose composing the cuticle that covers the aerial organs of plants.

çut'=out, *n.* 1. In electricity, an apparatus for cutting off part of a circuit.

2. In telegraphy, a device in the form of a switch to divert a current to another circuit or to shorten it.

çut'=pīle, *a.* Having a pile made by cutting the loops of thread, as in some textile fabrics.

çut'pŭrse, *n.* One who cut purses in order to steal them or their contents, a practice said to have been common when men wore purses at their girdles; one who steals from the person; a pickpocket.

çut'tẽr, *v.i.* [Eng. dial. for *quitter*, to speak low.] To speak in a whisper; to murmur, as a dove. [Rare.]

çut'tẽr, *n.* 1. One who cuts or hews; one who shapes or forms by cutting; as, a stone*cutter*. Specifically, one who cuts out cloth for garments according to measurements.

2. That which cuts; an instrument that cuts; as, a straw-*cutter*; a paper-*cutter*.

3. A front tooth that cuts, as distinguished from a grinder; an incisor.

4. A ship's boat of varying size; especially, a man-of-war's boat equipped with sails.

5. A vessel with one mast and a straight running-in bowsprit; rigged nearly like a sloop, but of deeper draft and narrower beam; usually having a mainsail, topsail, foresail, and jib; a favorite rig for yachts.

6. A small steamer or other vessel, armed and often designed for speed, employed in the government service; usually called *revenue cutter*.

7. A small one-horse sleigh.

8. In England, formerly, an officer in the exchequer whose duty it was to provide wood for the tallies, and to cut on them the sums paid.

9. A ruffian; a bravo; a destroyer. [Obs.]

10. A soft, yellow brick, easily cut and used for face work.

11. A colter.

12. In mining, a crack or fissure cutting across the strata; usually in the plural, as in the geological phrase, *backs and cutters*, for jointed structure.

13. In mineralogy, a crack in the substance of a crystal, which destroys or greatly lessens its value.

çut'tẽr=bär, *n.* 1. The bar of a reaping machine which carries the triangular knives or cutters.

2. In mechanics, the bar of a boring machine, in which the cutters or cutting tools are fixed. The cutters are fixed directly in recesses made in the *cutter-bar*, as represented by the figure, in which *a* is the cutter fixed in its place by the key *b*.

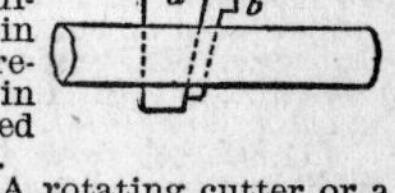

çut'tẽr=head (-hed), *n.* A rotating cutter or a stock to carry cutters, as in a planing machine.

çut'thrōat, *n.* 1. A murderer; an assassin; a ruffian.

2. The mustang grape of Texas, *Vitis candicans*; so called from its acrid taste.

çut'thrōat, *a.* Murderous; cruel; barbarous.

çut'ting, *n.* 1. The act of making a cut in any sense. [See *Cut*, v.t.]

2. Something cut off or made by cutting, as a twig or scion cut off for the purpose of grafting; an excavation through a hill in constructing a railroad, canal, etc.; a clipping from a newspaper.

3. The action of a horse when he strikes the inner and lower part of the fetlock-joint with his hoof while traveling; usually called *interfering*.

4. [*pl.*] In mining, the refuse obtained from washing ore.

5. In coal-mining, the making of openings across a seam for the purpose of separating a portion to be blasted.

çut'ting, *a.* 1. Adapted to cut; serving to sever or divide; as, a *cutting* instrument.

2. Piercing the heart; wounding the feelings; sarcastic; as, a *cutting* remark.

3. Piercing; keen; disagreeably chilling; as, a *cutting* blast.

çut'ting-ly, *adv.* In a cutting manner.

çut'tle, *n.* A knife. [Obs.]

çut'tle, *n.* [ME. *cotul*, *cotull*; AS. *cudele*, the cuttlefish.]

1. A cuttlefish.

2. A foul-mouthed fellow. [Obs.]

çut'tle-bōne, *n.* The internal shell or bone of a cuttlefish, used as a polish, as a food for birds, etc.

çut'tle-fish, *n.* Any one of the *Cephalopoda*, more strictly applied to those of the genus *Sepia*, dibranchiate cephalopodous mollusks, with a depressed body, inclosed in a sac. The shorter arms or feet, eight in number, covered with four rows of raised disks or suckers, are arranged around the mouth, and from the midst of them extend two long tentacles, also furnished with disks. These members the animal uses in walking, for attaching itself to objects, and for seizing its prey. It has the power of ejecting a black ink-like fluid from a bag or sac, so as to darken the water and conceal itself from pursuit.

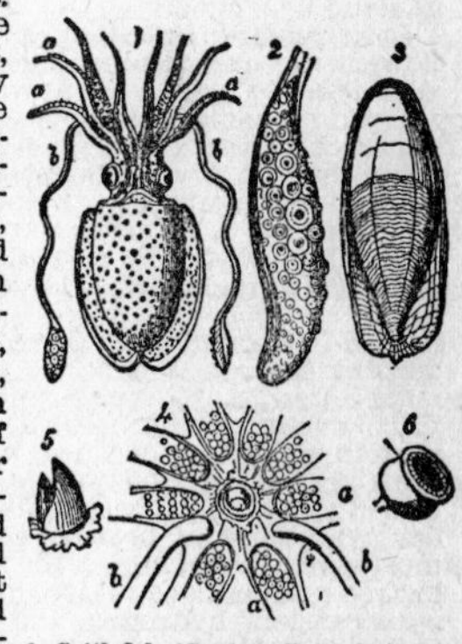

1. Cuttlefish (*Sepia officinalis*): *a a*, arms with suckers; *b b*, tentacles with suckers on the ends. 2. End of one of the tentacles, showing the suckers. 3. Cuttlefish bone—the interior shell. 4. Upper view of central part of animal, showing the mouth (*c*), arms (*a a*), tentacles (*b b*). 5. The beak or mouth. 6. One of the suckers.

çut'tọọ=plāte, *n.* A hood attached to the end of a wagon-axle to protect it from mud.

çut'ty, *a.* [Scot.] Short; as, a *cutty* spoon.

Her *cutty* sark o' Paisley harn. —Burns.

çut'ty, *n.* 1. Anything abbreviated or cut short, as a pipe or spoon.

2. A slatternly woman or girl; a wanton.

çut'ty-stọọl, *n.* Formerly, a small raised seat or gallery in old Scottish churches where female offenders against chastity were seated during three Sundays, and publicly rebuked by their minister.

çut′wąl, *n.* [Per. *kotwal*, chief officer of police.] In the East Indies, the chief police-officer in a city.

çut′wą″tẽr, *n.* 1. The fore part of a ship's prow, which cuts the water.

2. The lower portion of the pier of a bridge, formed with an angle or edge directed up the stream, so as more effectually to resist the action of the water, ice, etc.

3. The razorbill, *Rhynchops nigra.*

çut′weed, *n.* Any one of several varieties of coarse marine algæ, such as *Fucus vesiculosus, Fucus serratus*, and *Laminaria digitata.*

çut′wŏrk, *n.* 1. Formerly, a term for embroidery, in which the pattern is cut out and sewed to the ground.

2. The earliest form of lace.

çut′wŏrm, *n.* A name given to any caterpillar which eats or cuts away the young plants of cabbage, corn, beans, etc.

çū-vette′, *n.* [Fr., dim. of *cuve*, a tub; L. *cupa*, a tub.]

1. A vessel used in glass-works to carry molten glass from the melting-pot to the rolling-table.

2. In fortification, a cunette; a trench or drain dug in the middle of a large dry ditch.

Çū-vi-ē′ri-ăn, *a.* In zoölogy, pertaining to Georges Cuvier, a French naturalist (1769-1832), or to his system of classification.

-cy, *suffix.* [ME. *-cie*; OFr. *-cie*; L. *-cia, -tia*; Gr. *-sia, -teia.*] A suffix of abstract nouns denoting (a) condition, as innocen*cy*, democra*cy*, aristocra*cy*; (b) office, as captain*cy*, cura*cy.*

cȳ-am′e-lide (*or* -lid), *n.* In chemistry, an amorphous inodorous compound, CNOH, supposed to be polymeric with cyanic acid.

cȳ-am′el-lōne, *n.* [From *cyanic*; Gr. *kyanos*, dark blue, and L. *mel*, genit. *mellis*, honey.] A hypothetical compound, $C_9H_3N_{13}$, a derivative of cyanogen, not existing free and found only in its salts. Formerly known as *hydromellonic acid.*

cȳ-an-am′ide, *n.* [Gr. *kyanos*, dark blue, and *ammōniakon*, ammonia.] A crystalline compound, CH_2N_2, resulting from the action of ammonia on cyanogen chlorid.

cȳ′ȧ-nāte, *n.* A salt of cyanic acid.

Ammonium cyanate; a white crystalline compound, NH_4OCN, easily passing into urea.

cy-an-au′rāte, *n.* Same as *Aurocyanide.*

cȳ-ā′nē-ăn, *a.* [Gr. *kyaneos*, dark blue.] Azure-blue; cerulean.

cȳ-ā′nē-ous, *a.* Cyanean.

cȳ-an-hȳ′driç, *a.* [Gr. *kyanos*, dark blue, and *hydōr*, water.] In chemistry, hydrocyanic; prussic.

cȳ-an′iç, *a.* [Gr. *kyanos*, dark blue.]

1. Relating to or containing cyanogen.

2. Relating to blue.

Cyanic acid; a compound, CNHO, of cyanogen and hydrogen.

Cyanic colors; in botany, a series of colors in flowers, having a blue tinge, as opposed to *xanthic colors*, which have a yellow tinge.

cȳ′ȧ-nide (*or* -nid), *n.* In chemistry, a combination of cyanogen with a metallic base; as, the *cyanide* of silver, of copper, etc.

cȳ′ȧ-nin, cȳ′ȧ-nine, *n.* Same as *Anthocyanin.*

cȳ′ȧ-nite, *n.* A mineral occurring usually in long, thin, blade-like crystals, of a clear blue or bluish-white color. It is a silicate of aluminium.

cȳ′an-ō-. A combining form from Gr. *kyanos*, dark blue.

cȳ-an′ō-gen, *n.* [L. *cyano-*, and Gr. *genos*, kind.] A colorless gas, C_2N_2, of a strong odor, resembling that of crushed peach-leaves, and burning with a rich purple flame. It is obtained by heating dry cyanide of mercury. Under a pressure of between three and four atmospheres it becomes a limpid liquid, and is highly poisonous and irrespirable. It unites with oxygen, hydrogen, and most other nonmetallic elements, and also with the metals forming cyanides. The term is also given to the compound radical, CN.

cȳ-ȧ-nom′e-tẽr, *n.* [*Cyano-*, and Gr. *metron*, a measure.] An instrument to ascertain degrees of blueness, or the azure color of the ocean or sky.

cȳ-ȧ-nom′e-try, *n.* The science of measuring the intensity of blue light, particularly that of the sky.

cȳ-ȧ-nop′ȧ-thy, *n.* [*Cyano-*, and Gr. *pathos*, suffering.] Cyanosis; blue jaundice.

Cȳ″ȧ-nō-phyc′ē-æ, *n.pl.* [*Cyano-*, and Gr. *phykos*, seaweed.] A class of algæ of a blue-green color.

cȳ″ȧ-nō-phy′ceous (-fish′us), *a.* Pertaining to the *Cyanophyceæ.*

cȳ-an′ō-phyl, cȳ-an′ō-phyll, *n.* [*Cyano-*, and Gr. *phyllon*, a leaf.] A blue coloring-substance supposed to be a constituent of chlorophyl.

cȳ′ȧ-nōsed, *a.* Affected with or exhibiting cyanosis.

cȳ-ȧ-nō′sis, *n.* [Gr. *kyanos*, dark blue.] A disordered circulation, usually due to malformation of the heart, which causes the skin to assume a livid blue color; the blue jaundice of the ancients.

cȳ-an′ō-site, *n.* [Gr. *kyanos*, dark blue.] Blue vitriol; chalcanthite.

cȳ-ȧ-not′iç, *a.* Pertaining to or affected with cyanosis.

cȳ-ȧ-not′ri-chite, *n.* [*Cyano-*, and Gr. *thrix*, hair.] A hydrous sulphate of copper and aluminium, crystallizing in the orthorhombic system; also called *lettsomite.*

cȳ-an′ō-tȳpe, *n.* [*Cyano-*, and Gr. *typos*, stamp, impression.] A photographic picture obtained by the use of cyanide.

cȳ-an-ū-ram′ide, *n.* See *Melamine.*

cȳ-an′ū-rāte, *n.* A salt of cyanuric acid.

cȳ-an′ū-ret, *n.* An obsolete name for cyanide.

cȳ-ȧ-nū′riç, *a.* [Gr. *kyanos*, dark blue, and *ouron*, urine.] In chemistry, relating to or obtained from cyanic and uric acids.

Cyanuric acid; an acid, $C_3N_3O_3H_3$, the product of the decomposition of the solid chlorid of cyanogen by water, of the soluble cyanates by dilute acids, of urea by heat, of uric acid by destructive distillation, etc. It is colorless, inodorous, and has a slight taste. It is a tribasic acid, and its salts are termed cyanurates.

Cȳ-ath′ē-ȧ, *n.* [Gr. *kyathos*, a cup.] A genus of arborescent ferns, of the order *Polypodiaceæ*, having the spores, which are borne on the back of the frond, inclosed in a cup-shaped indusium. There are many species scattered over the tropical regions of the world. Some have short stems, but in others they reach a height of 40 or 50 feet.

cȳ-ath-ē-ā′ceous, *a.* Pertaining to or characteristic of the genus *Cyathea.*

cȳ-ath′i-fọrm, *a.* [L. *cyathus*; Gr. *kyathos*, a cup, and *forma*, shape.] In the form of a cup or drinking-glass, a little widened at the top.

Cyathiform.

cȳ′ath-oid, *a.* Same as *Cyathiform.*

cȳ-ath′ō-lith, *n.* [Gr. *kyathos*, cup, and *lithos*, stone.] A coccolith shaped like a cup.

Cȳ″ȧ-thō-phyl′li-dæ, *n.pl.* [Gr. *kyathos*, a cup, *phyllon*, a leaf, and *eidos*, form.] A family of fossil stone-corals of the group *Rugosa*, the species of which are called cup-corals.

cȳ″ȧ-thō-phyl′loid, *a.* Pertaining to the family *Cyathophyllidæ.*

cȳ″ȧ-thō-phyl′loid, *n.* A fossil cup-coral belonging to the family *Cyathophyllidæ.*

cȳ″ȧ-thō-zō′oid, *n.* [Gr. *kyathos*, a cup, *zōos*, alive, and *eidos*, form.] An imperfect rudimentary zoöid of certain ascidians, as of those belonging to the genus *Pyrosoma.*

cȳ′ȧ-thus, *n.*; *pl.* **cȳ′ȧ-thī.** [L. *cyathus*; Gr. *kyathos*, a cup.]

1. In Greek antiquity, a small, long-handled ladle or cup used especially for taking wine from the crater or mixing-bowl.

2. An Attic liquid measure, equivalent to about one twenty-fourth of a quart.

3. In botany, a small, conical organ or cavity in some cryptogams.

4. [C—] A genus of nidulariaceous fungi.

Cyb′e-lē, *n.* [L. *Cybele*; Gr. *Kybelē*, the goddess Cybele.] In classic mythology, the name under which the goddess Rhea was worshiped in Phrygia.

cȳ′çad, *n.* Any one of the *Cycadaceæ.*

Cyç-ȧ-dā′cē-æ, *n.pl.* [Gr. *kykas*, the African cocoa-palm.] A peculiar order of gymnosperms, resembling palms in appearance and having affinities with tree-ferns. The order includes nine genera, natives of tropical climates.

cyç-ȧ-dā′ceous, *a.* In botany, belonging to or characteristic of the order *Cycadaceæ.*

cy-çad′ē-ăn, *a.* Cycadaceous.

Cȳ′ças, *n.* [Gr. *kykas*, the African cocoa-palm.] A genus of cycadaceous trees having affinities with the palms and pines. They are natives of Asia, Australia, and Polynesia. From the pith of the trunk of certain species a coarse sago is obtained, and the tree is sometimes called *sago-palm.*

Cyclamen (garden variety).

Cyç′lȧ-men, *n.* [Gr. *kyklaminos*, the cyclamen; *kyklos*, a circle.]

1. A genus of bulbous plants of the order *Primulaceæ.* They are low-growing herbs with very handsome flowers. Several of them are favorite greenhouse plants. The fleshy root-stocks, though acrid, are greedily sought after by swine; hence the vulgar name *sowbread.*

2. [c—] A plant of the genus *Cyclamen.*

cyç′lȧ-min, *n.* The bitter principle of the root of *Cyclamen Europæum.*

Cyç-lan-thā′cē-æ, *n.pl.* [Gr. *kyklos*, circle, and *anthos*, a flower.] A small order of tropical plants having affinities with the palms and the screw pines. The typical genus is *Cyclanthus*, and its species inhabit tropical America.

cyç-lan-thā′ceous, *a.* Belonging to or characteristic of the order *Cyclanthaceæ.*

cȳ′çlas, *n.* 1. In Roman antiquity, an upper garment made of a rich stuff or silk. It was worn by both sexes, was somewhat similar to the surcoat, and was embroidered or interwoven with gold.

2. An outer gown worn by women in the fourteenth century, and also by knights over their armor.

cȳ′çle, *n.* [Fr. *cycle*; LL. *cyclus*; Gr. *kyklos*, a circle.]

1. An imaginary circle or orbit in the heavens.

2. A round of years, or period of time, in which the same course begins again; a periodical space of time; as, the *cycle* of the seasons.

3. Any long period; an age.

> Better fifty years of Europe than a *cycle* of Cathay. —Tennyson.

4. In literature, the aggregate of legendary or traditional matter accumulated round some mythical or heroic event or character, as the siege of Troy or the Argonautic expedition of antiquity, the Round Table, the Cid, and the Nibelungs of medieval times, and embodied in epic or narrative poetry or in romantic prose narrative; as, the ballads of the Arthurian *cycle.*

5. A round of duties. [Obs.]

6. In botany, (a) a term employed in the theory of spiral leaf arrangement to express a complete turn of the spire, which is assumed to exist; (b) an entire circle of leaves.

7. A bicycle, tricycle, or other vehicle of this class; a wheel.

8. A set of equal septa in corals.

9. A repeating or recurrent series; specifically, in physics, a succession of operations by which the original status of a substance is restored.

10. In electricity, a complete alternation of a current that changes from the positive to the negative direction and back again rapidly; also, the time necessary for such an alternation.

Calippic cycle; a period of seventy-six years, or four Metonic cycles.

Cycle of eclipses; a period required for the revolution of the moon's node, about eighteen years eleven days, after which eclipses usually return in a similar order.

Cycle of indiction; a period of fifteen years, at the end of which the Roman emperors imposed an extraordinary tax to pay the soldiers, who were obliged to serve in the army for that period and no longer.

Cycle of the sun, or *solar cycle*; a period of twenty-eight years, which having elapsed, the dominical or Sunday letters return to their former place, and proceed in the former order; that is, the days of the month again fall upon the same days of the week.

Metonic cycle; a period of nineteen years, which being completed, the new and full moon returns at the same time of the year.

cȳ′çle, *v.i.*; cycled, *pt., pp.*; cycling, *ppr.* 1. To recur in cycles.

2. To ride a bicycle, tricycle, or other similar machine.

cȳ′çlẽr, *n.* A cyclist.

cyç′liç (*or* sik′), *a.* 1. Pertaining to or moving in a cycle or circle.

> All the *cyclic* heavens around me spun. —E. B. Browning.

2. Connected with a cycle, in a literary sense; specifically applied to certain ancient Greek poets (sometimes inclusive of Homer) who wrote on the Trojan war and the adventures of the heroes connected with it.

3. In ancient prosody, having a certain shortened measure in which the time of three syllables is occupied instead of four; designating certain dactyls and anapests.

4. Having the parts arranged in the form of a whorl.

Cyclic chorus; the chorus which performed the songs and dances of the dithyrambic odes at Athens, dancing round the altar of Bacchus in a circle.

Cyclic poets; a term applied to certain epic poets who followed Homer, and wrote merely on the Trojan war, keeping within the circle of a single subject.

cyç′liç (*or* sik′), *n.* 1. A poem of the epic cycle.

2. A poem in cyclic meter.

cyc'lic-ăl, *a.* Cyclic.

cy'clide, *n.* In geometry, the envelope of a sphere touching three spheres that are fixed.

cy'cling, *n.* The act or sport of riding a cycle, particularly a bicycle.

cy'clist, *n.* 1. One who rides a cycle, particularly a bicycle.

2. One who believes in the cyclic recurrence of certain events, especially of meteorological phenomena, and of commercial and political crises, attempting to form a connection between them and the sun's spots.

cyc-lī'tis, *n.* Inflammation of the ciliary body.

cy'clō-. [Gr. *kyklos*, circle, wheel.] A combining form meaning, of a wheel or circle; circular.

cy-clō-bran'chi-āte, *a.* [*Cyclo-*, and Gr. *branchia*, gills.] In zoölogy, having the gills arranged in a circlet about the body, as a limpet.

cy-clō-cœ'lic (-sē'lik), *a.* [*Cyclo-*, and Gr. *koilia*, the belly, intestines.] Arranged in coils, as the intestines of certain birds.

cy-clō-gan'oid, *a.* Relating to the *Cycloganoidei.*

cy-clō-gan'oid, *n.* A fish of the order *Cycloganoidei.*

Cy"clō-gă-noi'dē-ī, *n.pl.* [*Cyclo-*, and L. *ganoideus*, from Gr. *ganos*, brightness, and *eidos*, form.] An order of ganoid fishes distinguished by cycloid scales; the species are mostly extinct.

cy'clō-gen, *n.* [*Cyclo-*, and Gr. *genos*, kind.] An exogen. [Rare.]

cy'clō-graph, *n.* [*Cyclo-*, and Gr. *graphein*, to describe.] An instrument for describing the arcs of circles; an arcograph.

cy'cloid, *n.* [Gr. *kyklos*, a circle, and *eidos*, form.] In geometry, a curve generated by a point in the plane of a circle that is rolled along a straight line and kept always in the same plane.

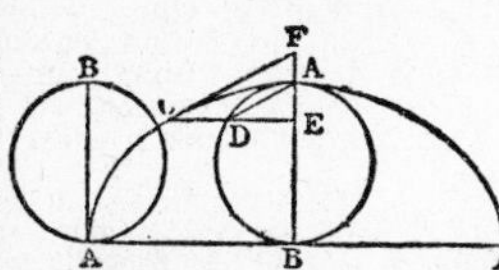

The *common cycloid* is described by a point in the circumference; the *curtate cycloid* is the cycloid described when the generating point lies without the circumference of the circle; the *prolate* or *inflected cycloid* is the cycloid described when the point lies within the circumference. In the figure let the circle B D A, of which the diameter is A B, make one revolution upon the straight line A B A, equal in length to its circumference, then the curved line A C A A, traced out by that point of the circle which was in contact with the point A in the straight line when the circle began to revolve, is called a *cycloid*. The following are some of its properties: If the generating circle be placed in the middle of the *cycloid*, its diameter coinciding with the cycloidal axis A B, and from any point C in the curve there be drawn the tangent C F, the ordinate C D E perpendicular to the axis, and the chord A D be drawn from the upper extremity of the diameter to the point where the ordinate cuts the circle, then C D = the circular arc A D; the cycloidal arc A C = double the chord A D; the semi-cycloid A C A = double the diameter A B; and the tangent C F is parallel to the chord A D.

cy'cloid, *n.* Any one of the *Cycloidei.*

cy'cloid, *a.* Relating to the *Cycloidei.*

cy-cloid'ăl, *a.* Pertaining to or having the shape of a cycloid.

cy-cloi'dē-ăn, *a.* and *n.* I. *a.* Pertaining to the *Cycloidei.*

II. *n.* One of the *Cycloidei.*

Cy-cloi'dē-ī, *n.pl.* [L., from Gr. *kyklos*, circle, and *eidos*, form.] An artificial order of fishes, as classified by Agassiz, having cycloid scales.

cy-clom'e-tẽr, *n.* [*Cyclo-*, and Gr. *metron*, a measure.] An instrument for recording a wheel's revolutions or the number of miles traveled by a wheeled vehicle; much used with automobiles, bicycles, etc.

cy-clom'e-try, *n.* [*Cyclo-*, and Gr. *metron*, a measure.] In geometry, the art of measuring circles.

cy'clōne, *n.* [Gr. *kyklōn*, ppr. of *kykloun*, to whirl around, twist.]

1. In meteorology, a violent, circular storm, having a diameter of 100 to 500 miles, with winds rotating about a calm center of low barometric pressure, that moves forward at a rate of from two to forty miles an hour. Cyclones occur at all hours of the day and night, and are preceded by a great fall of the barometer and a singular calm. They seem to be eddies formed by the meeting of opposing currents of air.

2. Any violent wind-storm having a rotary motion, especially a destructive storm which makes a narrow path, often not wider than 100 feet; a tornado.

cy'clōne-cel"lăr, *n.* An underground place of refuge during a cyclone.

cy-clon'ic, *a.* Pertaining to or resembling a cyclone.

cy-clō-pē'ăn, *a.* [L. *Cyclopeus*; Gr. *Kyklōpeios*, Cyclopean, from *Kyklōps*, Cyclops.]

1. [C—] Pertaining to the Cyclopes, fabulous giants of antiquity; massive; rough; as, *Cyclopean* architecture.

2. Gigantic; vast; as, a *cyclopean* work.

3. In zoölogy, having a single eye in the center of the forehead.

1. Cyclopean Walls at Paleokastron, Greece.
2. Porta Saracenica at Signa, Italy.

cy-clō-pē'di-ă, cy-clō-pæ'di-ă, *n.* [Gr. *kyklos*, a circle, and *paideia*, education.]

1. A book containing a summary of one branch of learning; as, a *cyclopedia* of electricity.

2. In a more comprehensive sense, a book, with subjects alphabetically arranged, containing an extensive account of all branches of knowledge; an encyclopedia.

cy-clō-pē'dic, cy-clō-pæ'dic, *a.* 1. Pertaining to a cyclopedia.

2. Of the nature of a cyclopedia; exhaustive; thorough.

cy-clō-pē'dist, *n.* One who compiles, or assists in compiling, a cyclopedia.

cy-clop'ic, *a.* Pertaining to, or resembling, the Cyclopes; cyclopean.

cy'clō-pid, *n.* In zoölogy, one of the *Cyclopidæ.*

Cy-clop'i-dæ, *n.pl.* [Gr. *Kyklōps*, Cyclops, and *eidos*, form, shape.] A family of minute entomostracans, having but one eye.

cy'clō-poid, *a.* Pertaining to the *Cyclopidæ.*

Cy'clops, *n.*; *pl.* **Cy'clō-pēs.** [L. *Cyclops*, pl. *Cyclopes*; Gr. *Kyklōps*, pl. *Kyklōpes*, Cyclops; *kyklos*, a circle, and *ōps*, eye.]

1. In Greek mythology, a class of giants, the sons of Neptune and Amphitrite, having but one circular eye in the midst of the forehead, who inhabited Sicily, and assisted Vulcan in making thunderbolts for Jupiter.

2. In crustalogy, a typical genus of the *Cyclopidæ.*

3. [c—] A small portable forge.

cy-clō-rä'mă, *n.* [*Cyclo-*, and Gr. *horama*, a view.] A pictorial representation, usually of a battle or landscape, displayed on a circular wall in imitation of natural perspective, and viewed from a central point; a circular panorama.

cy-clō-ram'ic, *a.* Pertaining to a cyclorama.

cy'clō-scōpe, *n.* [*Cyclo-*, and Gr. *skopein*, to look at, view.] An automatic apparatus for measuring velocity of revolution at any given moment.

cy-clō'sis, *n.* [Gr. *kyklōsis*, a surrounding, from *kykloun*, to inclose.] In the animal and vegetable kingdoms, circulation of the life-giving fluids.

Cy-clos'tō-mă, *n.* [*Cyclo-*, and Gr. *stoma*, mouth.] In conchology, a genus of gastropods whose shells have circular apertures; type of the family *Cyclostomidæ.*

Cy-clō-stō'mă-tă, *n.pl.* [*Cyclo-*, and Gr. *stoma*, mouth.]

1. In zoölogy, a genus of gymnolæmatous polyzoans having circular apertures.

2. In ichthyology the order *Marsipobranchii.*

cy'clō-stōme, *a.* and *n.* I. *a.* Same as *Cyclostomous.*

II. *n.* A lamprey; a marsipobranch; one of the *Cyclostomi.*

Cy-clos'tō-mī, *n.pl.* An order of jawless fishes with circular mouths; the *Marsipobranchii.*

cy-clos'tō-mous, *a.* 1. Having a circular mouth.

2. Of or relating to the *Cyclostomi.*

cy-clō-sty'lăr, *a.* 1. Made by, or pertaining to, a cyclostyle.

2. In architecture, resembling or pertaining to the cyclostyle; monopteral.

cy'clō-style, *n.* [*Cyclo-*, and Gr. *stylos*, a pillar.]

1. In architecture, a circular range of columns supporting a roof, without a core or building within; a monopteron.

2. A device for duplicating manuscripts, drawings, etc., by running an inked roller over sensitized paper that has been punctured by a style or typewriter.

cy-clō-tom'ic, *a.* Pertaining to cyclotomy.

cy-clot'ō-my, *n.* [*Cyclo-*, and Gr. *tomē*, a cutting, from *temnein*, to cut.]

1. In geometry, the theory of the division of the circle into aliquot parts.

2. In surgery, an operation for the relief of glaucoma, consisting of an incision through the ciliary body.

cy-dar'i-form, *a.* [L. *cydarum*, a ship, and *forma*, form.] In entomology, globular with truncated ends, as a palpus joint.

cy'dẽr, *n.* [Obs.] See *Cider.*

cy-dō'nin, *n.* [L. *cydonia*, a quince, a Cydonian apple, from Cydonia, a town in Crete.] In chemistry, an amyloid extract of quince-seeds resembling mucilage.

cy-dō'ni-um, *n.* In pharmacy, quince-seed.

cy-ē-si-ol'ō-gy, *n.* [Gr. *kyēsis*, pregnancy, and *legein*, to describe.] In physiology, that branch which treats of gestation.

cy-ē'sis, *n.* [Gr. *kyēsis*, pregnancy.] In medicine, conception; pregnancy.

cyg'nē-ous, *a.* [L. *cycneus*, pertaining to a swan, from *cycnus*, a swan.] In botany, curved to resemble a swan's neck.

cyg'net, *n.* [Fr., dim. of *cygne*, a swan; L. *cycnus*; Gr. *kyknos*, a swan.] A young swan.

Cyg'nus, *n.* [L. *cygnus*; Gr. *kyknos*, a swan.]

1. In astronomy, a northern constellation, the Swan.

2. In ornithology, a genus of anatoid birds typical of *Cygninæ*, the swans.

cyl'in-dẽr, *n.* [ME. *chilindre*, a cylindrical sundial; Gr. *kylindros*, a cylinder, roller, from *kylindein*, to roll.]

1. In geometry, a solid body supposed to be generated by the rotation of a parallelogram round one of its sides; or a long, circular body, of uniform diameter, its extremities forming equal parallel circles. When the axis is at right angles to the planes, it is called a *right cylinder*; otherwise, it is an *oblique cylinder.*

Right Cylinder.

2. Any hollow, round body whose length is greater than its diameter; a term of wide application; as, the *cylinder* of a printing-press; the *cylinder* of a steam-engine; the *cylinder* of an air-pump; the *cylinder* of an electrical machine.

3. A cylindrical stone, bearing a design or inscription, worn by the Babylonians as an amulet or seal, and found in antiquarian research.

cyl'in-dẽr-bit, *n.* In carpentry, the half-round bit.

cyl'in-dẽr-bōre, *n.* A gun having a bore of uniform diameter throughout.

cyl'in-dẽr-cock, *n.* A cock at the end of a steam-cylinder through which water may be blown out or steam blown in.

cyl'in-dẽr-desk, *n.* A roll-top desk.

cyl'in-dẽr-en"gine, *n.* In paper-making, a machine in which the pulp is made into a web upon a cylinder and delivered to the driers in a continuous sheet.

cyl'in-dẽr-pōrt, *n.* An opening in a cylinder for the admission of steam.

cyl'in-dẽr-wrench, *n.* A wrench so formed as to hold cylindrical objects; a pipe-wrench.

cyl-in-drā'ceous, *a.* Approximately cylindrical.

cyl-in-dren'chy-mă, *n.* [Gr. *kylindros*, a cylinder, and *enchyma*, an infusion; *en*, in, and *chein*, to pour.] In botany, plant tissue composed of cylindrical cells, as in the genus *Conferva* and in hairs, etc.

cy-lin'dric, cy-lin'dric-ăl, *a.* Having the shape of a cylinder; like a cylinder.

Cylindrical lens; a lens having cylindrical surfaces, as in spectacles worn to correct astigmatism.

Cylindrical surface; in geometry, a surface described by a straight line moving constantly parallel to itself.

cyl-in-dric'i-ty, *n.* The quality or state of being cylindrical.

cy-lin'dri-cūle, *n.* A small cylinder.

cy-lin'dri-form, *a.* [L. *cylindrus*, a cylinder, and *forma*, shape.] Having the form of a cylinder.

cyl'in-droid, *a.* and *n.* [Gr. *kylindros*, a cylinder, and *eidos*, form.]

I. *a.* Of cylindrical form, with elliptical bases equal and parallel.

II. *n.* A solid body, approaching to the figure of a cylinder, but having the bases or ends elliptical, parallel and equal.

cy-lin-drō-met'ric, *a.* [Gr. *kylindros*, a cylinder, and *metron*, a measure.] Belonging to a scale used in measuring cylinders.

cy'mă, *n.* [Gr. *kyma*, wave, from *kyein*, to swell.]

1. In architecture, a member or molding of the cornice, the profile of which is a curve of contrary flexure. *Cyma recta* is concave at top and convex at bottom, and *cyma reversa*, convex at top and concave at bottom. Also called *cyme* and *zima.*

1. Cyma recta. 2. Cyma reversa.

2. [C—] A genus of crustaceans.

3. In botany, a cyme.

cy'mă-graph, *n.* [Gr. *kyma*, a wave, swell, and *graphein*, to write.] A tracing implement for copying the outlines of architectural moldings or other objects in relief; a pantograph.

cȳ′mȧ-phen, *n.* [Gr. *kyma*, wave, and *phainein*, to show.] A receiving apparatus in a telephone.

cy-mär′, *n.* [Obs.] Same as *Simar.*

cȳ-mā′ti-um (-shi-um), *n.* [L. *cymatium*, a waved molding, from Gr. *kyma*, a wave.] In architecture, a top molding or capping; a cyma.

cym′băl, *n.* [ME. *cimbale, cymbale*; OFr. *cimbale*; L. *cymbalum*; Gr. *kymbalon*, a cymbal, from *kymbe*, a hollow vessel.]

1. One of a pair of concave brass or bronze plates which have handles at the back and make a ringing sound when clashed together.

2. A musical instrument consisting of a triangular wire strung with movable rings.

3. A stop of high pitch in an organ.

cym′băl-ist, *n.* [L. *cymba*; Gr. *kymbē*, a boat, skiff.] One who performs upon cymbals.

cym′bāte, *a.* Shaped like a boat; cymbiform.

cym′bi-fọrm, *a.* [L. *cymba*, a boat, and *forma*, shape.] Having the form of a boat; scaphoid.

cymb′lin, cymb′ling, *n.* Same as *Simlin.*

cym-bō-ceph′ȧ-ly, *n.* [Gr. *kymbē*, a bowl, and *kephalē*, head.] In craniology, a bilobate skull.

cȳme, *n.* [L., from Gr. *kyma*, fetus, a young sprout, from *kyein*, to swell.]

Cyme.

1. In botany, a cluster of flowers composed of several florets on a receptacle, producing all the primary peduncles from the same point, but having the partial peduncles scattered and irregular; all fastigiate, or forming a flat surface at the top.

2. A panicle, the elongation of all the ramifications of which is arrested, so that it has the appearance of an umbel.

3. In architecture, the cyma.

cȳme′let, *n.* Same as *Cymule.*

cȳ′mēne, *n.* [L. *cuminum*; Gr. *kyminon*, cumin.] In chemistry, a colorless oily liquid obtained from oil of cumin, oil of thyme, oil of caraway, camphor, etc.; called also *camphogen* and *cymol.*

cȳ′mē-nōl, *n.* Same as *Carvacrol.*

cȳ′mi-dine, *n.* In chemistry, an oily compound derived from cymene.

cȳ-mif′ẽr-ous, *a.* [L. *cyma*, cyme, and *ferre*, to bear.] In botany, bearing cymes.

cym′lin, *n.* See *Simlin.*

cȳ-mō-bot′ry-ōse, *a.* Thyrsoid.

cȳ-mō-bot′rys, *n.* [L., from Gr. *kyma*, a swell, and *botrys*, a cluster of grapes.] In botany, a thyrse.

cȳ′mō-gēne, *n.* [L. *cuminum*; Gr. *kyminon*, cumin, and *-genēs*, producing.] In chemistry, a volatile liquid mixture of hydrocarbons obtained from petroleum; used as a refrigerant.

cȳ′moid, *a.* Having the form of a cyme.

cȳ′mōl, *n.* See *Cymene.*

cym′ō-phāne, *n.* Same as *Chrysoberyl.*

cȳ-moph′ȧ-nous, *a.* [Gr. *kyma*, a wave, and *phanein*, to appear.] Having a wavy, floating light; opalescent; chatoyant.

cȳ′mōse, cȳ′mous, *a.* Containing a cyme; in the form of a cyme.

Çym′riç, *a.* and *n.* I. *a.* Pertaining to the Cymry.

II. *n.* The language of the Cymry, a division of the Celtic race.

Çym′ry, *n.pl.* [W. *Cymro*, a Welshman, pl. *Cymry*, the Welsh.] A name assumed by the Welsh, and also applied to the division of the Celtic race including the Cornishmen and the Bretons; also written *Kimri, Cymri, Cwmry.*

cȳ′mūle, *n.* In botany, a simple or small cyme; a cymelet.

cȳ-nan′çhē, *n.* [L., from Gr. *kynanche*, a dog-collar, a bad kind of sore throat; *kyōn*, a dog, and *anchein*, to press, choke.] In medicine, any disease of the throat or windpipe attended with inflammation, swelling, and difficulty of breathing and swallowing.

cy-nan′thrō-py, *n.* [Gr. *kyōn*, a dog, and *anthrōpos*, man.] A kind of madness in which the patient believes himself to be a dog, and barks and acts like a dog.

Cyn′ȧ-rȧ, *n.* [L., from Gr. *kynara*, a plant, either the dog-thorn or artichoke.] In botany, a genus of composite herbs allied to the thistle, found in the Mediterranean regions, and including the cultivated artichoke and cardoon.

cyn-ȧ-rā′ceous, *a.* Pertaining to or resembling the genus *Cynara*; cynareous.

cyn-ärç-tom′ȧ-çhy, *n.* [Gr. *kyōn*, a dog, *arktos*, a bear, and *machē*, a fight.] Bear-baiting with a dog.

cy-nā′rē-ous, *a.* Cynaraceous.

cyn-ȧ-roid′, *a.* Cynaraceous.

cyn-ar-rhō′di-um, *n.* [L., from Gr. *kynorodon*, the dogrose; *kyōn*, dog, and *rhodon*, rose.] In botany, a fruit in which the receptacle is deeply concave or urn-shaped, inclosed by the calyx, and bearing numerous bony achenia on its inner surface, as in the rose.

cyn-ar′rhō-don, *n.* Same as *Cynarrhodium.*

cyn-ē-ġet′iċs, *n.* [Gr. *kynēgetēs*, a hunter; *kyōn*, a dog, and *ēgeisthai*, to lead.] The art of hunting with dogs.

cyn′iç, cyn′iç-ăl, *a.* 1. Having the qualities of a surly dog; snarling; captious; surly; currish; austere.

2. Pertaining to the dog-star.

3. Pertaining to the Cynics or their doctrines.

4. Professing unbelief in human rectitude; sarcastic; carping; as, a *cynical* remark.

5. Doglike; canicular.

Cynic spasm; in medicine, a contraction of the muscles of one side of the face, suggesting the movements of a dog's upper lip.

Cynic year; the Sothic or canicular year.

Syn.— Carping, sarcastic, sneering.

cyn′iç, *n.* [L. *cynicus*, cynical; Gr. *kynikos*, doglike, from *kyōn*, a dog.]

1. A man of a canine temper; a surly or snarling man or philosopher; a misanthrope.

2. [C—] One of a sect of Greek philosophers founded by Antisthenes, of whom Diogenes was a disciple.

3. A person of sarcastic disposition; a snarler; especially one who professes to disbelieve in all moral worth and disinterestedness.

cyn′iç-ăl-ly, *adv.* In a snarling, captious, or morose manner.

cyn′iç-ăl-ness, *n.* Moroseness; contempt of riches and amusements.

cyn′i-cism, *n.* [LL. *cynismus*; Gr. *kynismos*, cynicism, from *kynizein*, to be a cynic.] The practice of a cynic; a morose contempt of the pleasures and arts of life.

cyn′i-pid, *a.* and *n.* I. *a.* Pertaining to the *Cynipidæ.*

II. *n.* An insect of the family *Cynipidæ.*

Cy-nip′i-dæ, *n.pl.* [LL. *cyniphes*, a kind of gallfly; Gr. *knips*, a kind of emmet, from *knizein*, to tease.] In entomology, the family of gallflies.

cyn-i-pid′ē-ous, *a.* Cynipidous.

cy-nip′i-dous, *a.* Characteristic of or pertaining to the gallflies or *Cynipidæ.*

cyn′i-poid, *a.* Pertaining to or resembling the *Cynipidæ*; cynipid.

Cȳ′nips, *n.* 1. A genus of hymenopterous insects, type of the family *Cynipidæ.*

2. [c—] An insect of this genus; a gallfly.

cyn-ō-ce-phal′iç, *a.* Pertaining to a cynocephalus; dog-headed; cynocephalous.

cyn-ō-ceph′ȧ-lous, *a.* Cynocephalic.

Cyn-ō-ceph′ȧ-lus, *n.* [L. *cynocephalus*; Gr. *kynokephalos*, the African dog-headed ape; *kyōn*, a dog, and *kephalē*, head.]

1. A genus of baboons of the family *Cynopithecidæ.*

2. [c—] A dog-faced baboon.

Cyn-ō-glos′sum, *n.* [L. *cynoglossus*, a plant named the dog-tongued by Pliny.] A genus of plants of the borage family, having about sixty species, of which six are found in North America. *Cynoglossum officinale*, or hound's-tongue, was formerly used as a remedy for scrofula.

cȳ′noid, *a.* [Gr. *kynōdes*, doglike.]

1. Pertaining to the *Cynoidea.*

2. Canine; doglike.

Cȳ-noi′dē-ȧ, *n.pl.* In zoölogy, the group of the *Carnivora*, including the dog, fox, and wolf, or family *Canidæ.*

cȳ-nop′ō-dous, *a.* [L., from Gr. *kyōn*, a dog, and *pous*, genit. *podos*, foot.] Dog-footed; having feet resembling those of a dog, with blunt, nonretractile claws.

cyn-ō-rex′i-ȧ, *n.* [Gr. *kyōn*, a dog, and *orexis*, appetite; *orexein*, to reach out, desire.] In medicine, a voracious, doglike appetite; insatiable hunger; bulimia.

cȳ-nō-sū′răl (*or* sin′ō-), *a.* Pertaining to a cynosure; strongly attractive.

cȳ′nō-sūre (*or* sin′ō-), *n.* [L. *cynosura*; Gr. *kynosoura*, the Ursa Minor, or Lesser Bear; *kyōn*, dog, and *oura*, tail; the *cynosure* forms the tip of the tail.] Anything which strongly attracts attention; a center of attraction, as the polestar in the constellation *Cynosura*, or Lesser Bear, was for the eyes of ancient mariners.

Where perhaps some beauty lies,
The *Cynosure* of neighb'ring eyes.—Milton.

Cyn′thi-ȧ, *n.* [L., f. adj. from *Cynthus*; Gr. *Kynthos*, a mountain in Delos.]

1. In mythology, a name given to Artemis (Diana), derived from Mount Cynthus, her reputed birthplace.

2. A poetic name for the moon, emblem of Diana.

3. A genus of butterflies, including the painted-lady, *Cynthia cardui*; also, a subgenus of *Ascidiidæ.*

4. A genus of crustaceans.

cȳ′on, *n.* [Obs.] See *Scion.*

Cyp-e-rā′cē-æ, *n.pl.* [L. *cyperos*; Gr. *kypeiron*, a marsh-plant.] In botany, a natural order of rushlike monocotyledonous plants of the sedge family; it contains more than sixty genera and three thousand species.

cyp-ẽr-ā′ceous, *a.* Of or pertaining to the *Cyperaceæ*; resembling the sedges.

Cyp′e-rus, *n.* A genus of herbs of the sedge family, natural order *Cyperaceæ*, embracing seven hundred species, of which more than fifty are found in the United States as annuals or perennials. *Cyperus Papyrus* furnished the papyrus of Egypt.

cȳ′phel, *n.* Same as *Cyphella.*

cȳ-phel′lȧ, *n.*; *pl.* **cȳ-phel′læ.** [L., from Gr. *kyphella*, the hollow of the ear; *kypellon*, a drinking-cup.] A small, cuplike pit on the nether surface of the thallus of some lichens.

cȳ-phel′lāte, *a.* In botany, showing cuplike pits; having cyphellæ.

cȳ′phẽr, *n.* and *v.* [Obs.] See *Cipher.*

cȳ′phon, *n.* An ancient form of pillory.

cyph-ō-nạu′tēṣ, *n.* [L., from Gr. *kyphos*, bent, and *nautes*, a sailor.] In zoölogy, the larva of a bryozoan of the genus *Membranipora*; formerly classed as a distinct genus of the *Rotifera.*

cyph′ŏn-iṣm, *n.* [Gr. *kyphōn*, a kind of pillory.] A species of punishment frequently used by the ancients, consisting in besmearing the criminal with honey, and exposing him to insects; also, punishment by the cyphon.

Cy-præ′ȧ, *n.* [L., from *Cypria*; Gr. *Kypris*, a name for Venus, from the isle of Cyprus, where she was most worshiped.] A genus of gasteropods; the cowries.

cy-præ′id, *n.* One of the *Cypræa*; a cowry.

cy-prēṣ′ (sē-prā′). [OFr. *cyprès*, near to, so near; *cy*, here, *pres*, near; L. *pressus*, pressed, close.] In law, as near as may be; a term applied to an equitable rule for interpreting written instruments containing trusts, charities, etc.

cȳ′press, *n.* [ME. *cipres*; OFr. *cypres*; LL. *cypressus*; L. *cupressus*; Gr. *kyparissos*, the cypress-tree.]

Cypress (*Cupressus sempervirens*, var. *fastigiata*).

1. The popular name of plants or trees of the genus *Cupressus*. The most remarkable are *Cupressus sempervirens*, or common cypress, the evergreen American cypress or white cedar, and *Cupressus disticha*, or deciduous American cypress. The wood of these trees is remarkable for its durability. The coffins in which the Athenian heroes and the mummies of Egypt were deposited are said to have been made of the first species.

2. The emblem of mourning for the dead, cypress-branches having been anciently used at funerals.

3. A name applied to many coniferous trees allied to or resembling the true cypresses.

cȳ′press, *a.* Made of or resembling cypress.

cȳ′press-knee, *n.* A large, hollow tumor or cone-shaped excrescence on the roots of the swamp-cypress, *Taxodium distichum*; adapted for use as beehives.

cȳ′press-vīne, *n.* A Mexican climbing plant, *Ipomœa Quamoclit.*

Cyp′ri-ăn, *n.* [L. *Cyprius*; Gr. *Kyprios*, a Cyprian, from *Kypros*, Cyprus, noted for its temple to Venus; hence L. *Cypria*; Gr. *Kypris*, Venus.]

1. A native of ancient Cyprus; a Cypriote.

2. [c—] A lewd woman; a courtezan.

Cyp′ri-ăn, *a.* 1. Belonging to the island of Cyprus; Cypriote.

2. [c—] Lewd; wanton.

cyp′rine, *a.* 1. In ichthology, pertaining to the *Cyprinidæ*; cyprinoid.

2. In botany, pertaining to the cypress-tree.

Cy-prin′i-dæ, *n.pl.* [L., from Gr. *kyprinos*, a carp, and *eidos*, resemblance.] A family of teleostean fishes, the species of which are distinguished by having the mouth small and generally devoid of teeth, the pharyngeal bones furnished with strong teeth, the branchiostegal rays few in number, and the scales generally of large size. The genus *Cyprinus* is the type of the family, which, besides the carp, contains the goldfish, tench, roach, loach, bleak, barbel, etc.

cy-prin'ō-dont, *a.* and *n.* I. *a.* Pertaining to the *Cyprinodontidæ.*

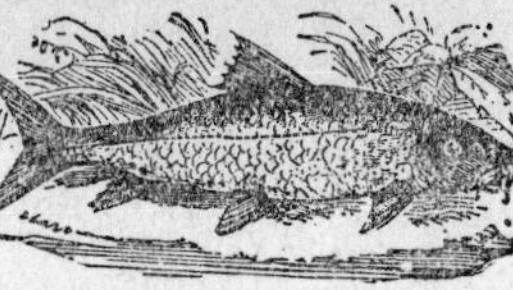
Cyprinoid (*Barbus vulgaris*).

II. *n.* A fish of the family *Cyprinodontidæ.*

Cy-prin-ō-don'ti-dæ, *n.pl.* [L., from Gr. *kyprinos*, a carp, and *odous*, a tooth.] A family of malacopterygious fishes, allied to *Cyprinidæ*, but having the jaws more protractile and toothed; it includes the killifishes, minnows, etc.

cy-prin-ō-don'toid, *a.* and *n.* Same as *Cyprinodont.*

cyp'ri-noid, *a.* and *n.* I. *a.* Carp-like.
II. *n.* One of the carp family.

Cy-prī'nus, *n.* [L. *cyprinus*; Gr. *kyprinos*, a carp.] A genus of fishes typical of the family *Cyprinidæ*; the true carps.

Cyp'ri-ōte, *n.* [L. *Cyprius*, a Cyprian.]
1. An inhabitant of Cyprus.
2. The modern language of Cyprus, a Greek dialect.

Cyp'ri-ōte, *a.* Of or pertaining to the island of Cyprus.

Cyp-ri-pē'di-um, *n.* [L., from Gr. *Kypris*, Aphrodite, and *pedion*, an open plain, dim. of *pedon*, the ground.] A genus of orchids embracing the lady's-slipper, or moccasin-flower.

cy̆'prus, *n.* An old name for a thin, transparent, white or black fabric resembling crape and formerly used for mourning. [Obs.]

cy̆'prus-bird, *n.* [Prov. Eng.] The blackcap of Europe, *Sylvia atricapilla.*

cyp'se-là, *n.* [L., from Gr. *kypselē*, a hollow vessel.] In botany, an achene distinguished by an adnate calyx.

Cyp-sel'i-dæ, *n.pl.* A family of insessorial birds, including the swifts.

cyp-sel'i-form, *a.* [L. *cypsellus*, a swift, and *forma*, form.] In ornithology, pertaining to or resembling the swifts; cypseline.

cyp'se-line, *a.* [L. *cypsellus*, a swift.] Pertaining to the *Cypselidæ* or swifts.

cyp'se-loid, *a.* Same as *Cypseline.*

Cy̆-rē-nā'iç, *a.* [L. *Cyreniacus*; Gr. *Kyrenaikos*, a Cyrenaic, from *Kyrene*, Cyrene.]
1. Pertaining to Cyrene, a Greek colony on the north coast of Africa.
2. Pertaining to the Greek school of hedonistic philosophy founded by Aristippus of Cyrene, a disciple of Socrates.

Cy̆-rē-nā'iç, *n.* A philosopher of the Cyrenaic school, which held that pleasure is the only rational aim in life.

Cy̆-rē'ni-ăn, *n.* 1. Same as *Cyrenaic.*
2. A native or inhabitant of Cyrene.

Cy̆-rē'ni-ăn, *a.* Of or pertaining to Cyrene; Cyrenaic.

Cyr-il-lā'cē-æ, *n.pl.* [LL. *cyrillus*; Gr. *kyrillos*, Cyril.] A natural order of evergreen trees or shrubs, nearly allied to the *Ericaceæ*, and natives of North America or the American tropics.

cyr-il-lā'ceous, *a.* Pertaining to the *Cyrillaceæ.*

Cy-ril'liç, *a.* Pertaining to St. Cyril or to the alphabet invented by him.
Cyrillic alphabet; an old Slavic alphabet based on the Greek, invented by Cyril in the ninth century, and adopted by all the Slavonic peoples belonging to the Eastern church.

cyr"i-ō-log'iç, *a.* [Gr. *kyrios*, chief, and *logos*, discourse.]
1. Pertaining to capital letters.
2. Same as *Curiologic.*

cyr-tom'e-tẽr (sẽr-), *n.* [Gr. *kyrtos*, curved, bent, and *metron*, a measure.] In medicine, an instrument for measuring the circumference of the chest and for exact comparison of one side with the other.

cyr'tō-style (sẽr-), *n.* [Gr. *kyrtos*, curved, and *stylos*, a pillar.] In architecture, a circular portico projecting from the front of a building.

cyst, *n.* [L., from Gr. *kystis*, a bladder, pouch, from *kyein*, to be pregnant.]
1. In pathology, a bag or vesicle which includes morbid matter in animal bodies.
2. In anatomy, any vesicle or sac of membranous tissue.
3. In botany, (a) the envelope surrounding the spores in certain seaweeds; (b) a minute cavity containing oil in the rind of certain fruits; (c) the seed-cells of some cryptogamous plants.

cyst'ed, *a.* Surrounded by a cyst.

cys'tel-minth, *n.* [Gr. *kystis*, a bladder, and *elmins*, a worm.] In zoölogy, any worm inclosing itself in a cyst.

cyst'iç, *a.* 1. Pertaining to a cyst; cysted.
2. Bladdery; resembling a cyst.
Cystic duct; in anatomy, the membranous canal that conveys the bile from the hepatic duct into the gall-bladder.
Cystic worm; in zoölogy, a hydatid, or immature entozoan.

cys-ti-cẽr'cus, *n.* [L., from Gr. *kystis*, a bladder, and *kerkos*, tail.] In zoölogy, a tapeworm in larval form; called also *bladder-worm* or *hydatid.*

cys'ti-cle, *n.* [Dim. from L. *cystis*; Gr. *kystis*, a bladder.] A small cyst.

cys'tid, *n.* [Gr. *kystis*, a sac, bladder.] One of the *Cystidea.*

Cys-tid'ē-à, *n.pl.* Same as *Cystoidea.*

cys-tid'ē-ăn, *a.* and *n.* I. *a.* Pertaining to the *Cystidea.*
II. *n.* A cystic crinoid; one of the *Cystidea.*

cys-ti-cig'ō-lous, *a.* [L. *cystis*; Gr. *kystis*, a bladder, and L. *colere*, to inhabit.] In zoölogy, living in a cyst.

cys-tid'i-um, *n.*; *pl.* **cys-tid'i-à.** [L., dim. of Gr. *kystis*, bladder.] In hymenomycetous fungi, a spherical cell, supposedly sterile, emerging from the basidia and paraphyses, and projecting beyond them.

cys'tin, *n.* [Gr. *kystis*, bladder.] In physiological chemistry, a crystalline compound, contained in minute amounts in urine or in the sediment of urine; a rare urinary calculus.

cys'tis, *n.*; *pl.* **cys'ti-dēs.** Same as *Cyst.*

cys-tī'tis, *n.* In medicine, inflammation of the bladder.

cys-tō-. A combining form from L. *cystis*; Gr. *kystis*, bladder, sac, from *kyein*, to be pregnant.

cys'tō-cärp, *n.* [*Cysto-*, and Gr. *karpos*, fruit.] In botany, a small sac or pericarp containing the spores of reproduction of algæ; called also *sporocarp.*

cys'tō-cēle, *n.* [*Cysto-*, and Gr. *kēlē*, a rupture.] In medicine, a hernia or rupture, causing the urinary bladder to protrude.

cys'toid, *a.* 1. Cystoidean.
2. Resembling a cyst; cystiform.

Cys-toi'dē-à, *n.pl.* [Gr. *kystis*, bladder, and *eidos*, form.] An order of crinoid Paleozoic fossils, having a roundish body inclosed in sutured plates and a lateral orifice closed by jointed plates; called also *Cystidea.*

cys-toi'dē-ăn, *a.* and *n.* I. *a.* Pertaining to the *Cystoidea.*
II. *n.* One of the *Cystoidea.*

cys'tō-lith, *n.* [*Cysto-*, and Gr. *lithos*, stone.] In botany, a peculiar crystalline concretion found in the cells of certain plant-leaves.

cys-tō-lith'iç, *a.* In medicine, pertaining to stone in the bladder.

cys'tō-plast, *n.* [*Cysto-*, and Gr. *plastos*, anything formed or molded, from *plassein*, to form.] In anatomy, a cell consisting of an enveloped nucleus.

Cys'tō-pus, *n.* [*Cysto-*, and Gr. *ōps*, face, appearance.] In botany, a genus of parasitic fungi affecting cruciferous plants.

cys'tōse, *a.* Containing cysts; bladdery; vesicular.

cys'tō-tōme, *n.* [*Cysto-*, and Gr. *tomos*, a cutting, from *temnein*, to cut.] In surgery, an instrument for making incisions in the bladder.

cys-tot'ō-my, *n.* In surgery, cutting into the urinary bladder; the operation of opening cysts.

cy-tas'tẽr, *n.* [Gr. *kytos*, a cavity, and *astēr*, star.] In biology, a radiate shape assumed by the nucleus of a cell.

cyte, *n.* [Gr. *kytos*, a hollow, cavity, from *kyein*, to contain, conceive.] In biology, a cell; especially a nucleated cell.

Cyth-e-rē'ăn, *a.* [L. *Cythereus*, of Cytherea; Gr. *Kythereia*, Venus; so named from *Cythera*, an island south of Greece near which Venus was said to have sprung from the waves.]
1. In astronomy, pertaining to the planet Venus.
2. In mythology, pertaining to the goddess Cytherea (Venus).

cyt'i-ō-blast, *n.* The nucleus of a cell, especially of the cell of certain algæ.

Cyt'i-sus, *n.* [L. *cytisus*, shrubby lucerne, a kind of clover.] A genus of hardy, leguminous shrubs, native to the borders of the Mediterranean. The leaves are usually composed of three leaflets, though some species are leafless. The large flowers are purple, white, or yellow. *Cytisus scoparius* is the broom.

Broom (*Cytisus scoparius*).

cy̆'tō-. A combining form, from Gr. *kytos*, a hollow.

cy̆'tō-blast, *n.* [*Cyto-*, and Gr. *blastos*, a bud, shoot.] Same as *Cytioblast.*

cy̆"tō-blas-tē'mà, *n.* [*Cyto-*, and Gr. *blastēma*, a bud.] In biology, the formative substance which produces cells.

cy̆"tō-chy̆-lē'mà, *n.* See *Cytolymph.*

cy̆-tō-coc'cus, *n.*; *pl.* **cy̆-tō-coc'ci.** [*Cyto-*, and Gr. *kokkos*, a berry.] The nucleus of a cytula.

cy̆'tōde, *n.* [Gr. *kytos*, a hollow, and *eidos*, form.] In biology, a cell; specifically, a cell without a nucleus.

cy̆'tō-dẽrm, *n.* [*Cyto-*, and Gr. *derma*, skin.] In biology, the wall of a cell.

cy̆-tō-gen'e-sis, *n.* [*Cyto-*, and Gr. *genesis*, birth, origin.] The formation or development of cells.

cy̆"tō-ġē-net'iç, *a.* Developing or generating cells; pertaining to cytogenesis.

cy̆-tog'e-nous, *a.* [*Cyto-*, and Gr. *-genēs*, producing.] In anatomy, producing cells; cytogenetic.

cy̆-tog'e-ny, *n.* Same as *Cytogenesis.*

cy̆'toid, *a.* [Gr. *kytos*, a hollow, and *eidos*, form.] In physiology, cell-like; applied to corpuscles, as of chyle, lymph, etc.

cy̆-tol'ō-gy, *n.* [*Cyto-*, and Gr. *logos*, description, from *legein*, to speak.] In biology, that branch of the science which treats of cells.

cy̆'tō-lymph, *n.* [*Cyto-*, and L. *lympha*, water.] In biology, the more liquid portion of protoplasm occurring in a cell; cytochylema.

cy̆'tō-plasm, *n.* [*Cyto-*, and Gr. *plasma*, anything formed, image; from *plassein*, to form.] In biology, the protoplasmic substance of a cell, exclusive of the nucleus.

cy̆-tō-plas'miç, *a.* Pertaining to cytoplasm.

cy̆-tō-py̆'ġē, *n.*; *pl.* **cy̆-tō-py̆'ġæ.** The excretory aperture of a unicellular animal.

cy̆'tō-stōme, *n.* [*Cyto-*, and Gr. *stoma*, mouth.] In biology, the mouth of unicellular organisms.

cyt'ū-là, *n.* [L., from Gr. *kytos*, a hollow.] In biology, the fertilized ovum or parent-cell from which any organism is developed.

czär (zär), *n.* [Russ. *tsare*; O.H.G. *keisar*; L. *Cæsar*, emperor, from the cognomen of Caius Julius *Cæsar*.] A king; a chief; specifically, a title of the emperor of Russia; also spelled *tsar, tzar.*

czär'e-vitch, *n.* [Russ. *tsarevichu*, prince.] A Russian prince of the reigning house; specifically, the eldest son of the czar of Russia; also written *tsarevitch.*

czä-rev'nà, *n.* [Russ. *tsarevna*, *tsesarevna*, princess.] The wife of the czarevitch; also written *tsarevna.*

czä-rī'nà, *n.* [Russ. f. of *czar*.] The wife of the czar of Russia, or a reigning empress of Russia; also written *tsarina.*

Czech (chek), *n.* [Bohem. *Chekh*; named from their chieftain *Czech.*]
1. In ethnology, a member of the most westerly branch of the great Slavic family of races, and inhabiting Bohemia, Moravia, and North Hungary.
2. The language of the Czechs, usually called Bohemian, and allied to the Polish.

Czech'iç (chek'), *a.* and *n.* I. *a.* Relating to the Czechs.
II. *n.* The Czech language.

Czech'ō-Slō väk (chek), *a.* and *n.* I. *a.* Relating to the Czechs and Slovaks or to their language; relating to the people of Bohemia, Moravia and Northwestern Hungary, or to their language.
2. *n.* A member of that race of people.

D

D (dē). The fourth letter and the third consonant of the English alphabet, and a vocal consonant. It holds the same place in the English as in the Chaldee, Syriac, Hebrew, Samaritan, Greek, and Latin alphabets. In the Arabic, it is the eighth; in the Russian, the fifth; and in the Ethiopic, the nineteenth letter.

D is a dental articulation, formed by placing the end of the tongue against the gum just above the upper teeth. It is closely allied to *T*, but is not so close a letter, and in forming the articulation, there is a lingual and nasal sound, which has induced some writers to rank *D* among the lingual letters.

D, d, *as a symbol.* As a numeral in the Roman notation *D* represents 500, and when a dash or stroke is placed over it, thus, *D̄*, it denotes 500,000.

In music, it is, (a) the name given to the second tone of the natural scale of C; (b) a note representing this tone; (c) the tonic of the key of two sharps.

In chemistry, *D* is the symbol for *didymium.*

As an abbreviation, (a) in the English monetary system, penny, from the original name, *denarius*; (b) when placed before a date (as in a biographical list), *died.*

dab, *v.t.*; dabbed, *pt., pp.*; dabbing, *ppr.* [ME. *dabben*, to strike, prob. from OFr. *dauber*, to whiten.]

1. To strike gently with the hand; to slap.

2. To strike gently with some soft or moist substance; as, to *dab* a sore with lint.

3. To strike or stab with a pointed weapon; as, he was *dabbed* in the side.

dab, *n.* 1. A gentle blow with the hand; a peck.

2. A small lump or mass of anything soft or moist.

dab, *n.* An expert man; an adept. [Colloq.]

dab, *n.* A small marine flat fish of several species allied to the flounder, *Pleuronectes limanda.* It averages about a foot in length, is a common food-fish on the British coasts, and derives its name from the rapidity with which it dives into the sand.

Dab (*Pleuronectes limanda*).

dabb, *n.* In zoölogy, *Uromastix spinipes*, a large lizard with a spiny tail found in the northern part of Africa.

dab′bẽr, *n.* One who or that which dabs; specifically, a kind of pad used by engravers, etchers, printers, etc., for dabbing plates and type.

dab′ble, *v.t*; dabbled, *pt., pp.*; dabbling, *ppr.* To dip a little or often; to wet; to moisten; to spatter; to wet by little dips or strokes; to sprinkle.

dab′ble, *v.i.* 1. To play in water; to dip the hands, throw water, and splash about; to play in mud and water.

2. To do anything in a slight or superficial manner; to tamper.

> You have, I think, been *dabbling* with the text. —Atterbury.

dab′blẽr, *n.* 1. One who plays in water or mud.

2. One who dips slightly into anything; a superficial worker or thinker; as, a *dabbler* in politics.

dab′bling-ly, *adv.* In a dabbling manner.

dab′chick, *n.* A water-fowl, a species of grebe remarkable for the rapidity with which it dives.

dä-boy′ȧ, *n.* [E. Ind. name.] *Daboia xanthica*, a large venomous snake of Asia.

dab′stẽr, *n.* One who is skilled; one who is expert; a master of his business; improperly used for *dabbler.* [Colloq.]

dä cä′pō. [It., from the beginning; *de*, L. *de*, from, and *capo*, L. *caput*, head.] In music, from the commencement; a direction to return to, and end with, the first strain; abbreviated to *D. C.*

dāce, *n.* [ME. *darce, darse*; OFr. *dars*, a dart, a dace, so named from its swiftness.] A small cyprinoid fish of Europe, genus *Leuciscus*, gregarious and frequenting fresh waters. The name is also given to various American species of certain allied genera. Called also *dar, dart* and *dare.*

Dace (*Leuciscus vulgaris*).

dachs′hund (-hünt), *n.* [G. *dachs*, badger, and *hund*, dog.] A small dog with a long body and short legs; known also as the *badgerdog.*

Dā′ciăn, *a.* [L. *Dacus*, or *Dacicus*, Dacian, from *Dacia*, Dacia.] Relating to the old Roman province of Dacia or to the Daci.

Dā′ciăn, *n.*; *pl.* **Dā′ci.** A native of Dacia.

dā′cīte, *n.* [From *Dacia*, where the mineral is found.] In mineralogy, a volcanic rock consisting essentially of plagioclase and quartz, together with either hornblende, biotite, or pyroxene.

dack′ẽr (*or* dāk′ẽr), *v.i.* [Eng. dial. and Scot.]

1. To be unsettled; to waver; to be undetermined.

2. To loiter; to walk about carelessly; to saunter.

3. To potter; to work with little purpose.

4. To search, as for smuggled goods.

dack′ẽr, *v.t.* To examine; search for; as, to *dacker* a house. [Scot.]

dȧ-çoit′, *n.* Same as *Dakoit.*

dȧ-çoit′y, dȧ-çoit′āge, *n.* Same as *Dakoity.*

Dȧ-çō′tȧhş, *n.pl.* Same as *Dakotas.*

dac′ry-ō-, dac′ry-. Combining forms from Gr. *dakryon*, a tear.

dac″ry-ō-cys-tī′tis, *n.* [*Dacryo-*, and Gr. *kystis*, a vessel.] Inflammation of the lacrymal sac.

dac′ry-ō-līte, dac′ry-ō-lith, *n.* [*Dacryo-*, and Gr. *lithos*, a stone.] A calculous concretion in the lacrymal passage.

dac′tyl, *n.* [L. *dactylus*; Gr. *daktylos*, a finger, a measure of length, a dactyl.]

1. A poetical foot, consisting of three syllables, the first long or accented, and the others short or unaccented, like the joints of a finger, as *tĕgmĭnĕ, cārmĭnĕ.*

2. A finger or toe; a digit.

3. Same as *Dactylus.*

4. A unit of measure used by the ancients; a finger-breadth; a digit.

dac′tyl-ăr, *a.* 1. Pertaining to a dactyl; reducing from three to two syllables; dactylic.

2. Relating to a finger, toe, or claw.

dac′tyl-et, *n.* A small dactyl. [Obs.]

dac-tyl′ic, *a.* and *n.* I. *a.* Pertaining to or consisting chiefly or wholly of dactyls; as, *dactylic* verses.

II. *n.* 1. A line consisting chiefly or wholly of dactyls.

2. [*pl.*] Meters composed of a repetition of dactyls or equivalent feet.

dac-tyl′i-ō-glyph, *n.* [Gr. *daktylioglyphos*, an engraver of gems; *daktylios*, a finger-ring, from *daktylos*, a finger, and *glyphein*, to cut, engrave.]

1. The inscription of the name of the artist on a finger-ring or gem.

2. One who engraves precious stones for rings and other adornments.

dac-tyl″i-ō-glyph′ic, *a.* Relating to or characteristic of dactylioglyphy.

dac-tyl-i-og′ly-phist, *n.* Same as *Dactylioglyph*, 2.

dac-tyl-i-og′ly-phy, *n.* The art of engraving precious stones.

dac-tyl-i-og′rȧ-phy, *n.* [Gr. *daktylios*, a finger-ring, and *graphein*, to write.]

1. An essay upon engraved gems or finger-rings.

2. The study or science of finger-rings.

dac-tyl-i-ol′ō-gy, *n.* Same as *Dactyliography.*

dac-tyl′i-ō-man-cy, *n.* [Gr. *daktylios*, a finger-ring, and *manteia*, divination.] The pretended art of divining by finger-rings.

dac-tyl′i-ŏn, *n.* [Gr. *daktylos*, a finger.]

1. In surgery, a condition of the fingers or toes, in which they are joined together from birth, or by accident or disease.

2. A device invented by Henri Herz in 1835, for the use of piano-players.

dac′tyl-ist, *n.* One who writes dactylic verse.

dac-tyl-ī′tis, *n.* [Gr. *daktylos*, finger or toe.] In medicine, inflammation of a digit.

dac′tyl-ō-. A combining form from Gr. *daktylos*, a finger or toe.

dac′tyl-oid, *a.* [*Dactylo-*, and Gr. *eidos*, form.] Shaped like a finger.

dac-tyl-ol′ō-gy, *n.* [*Dactylo-*, and Gr. *logos*, description.] The act or art of communicating ideas or thoughts by the fingers; the language of the deaf and dumb. [See *Deaf-mute.*]

dac-tyl-on′ō-my, *n.* [*Dactylo-*, and Gr. *nemein*, to deal out, distribute.] The art of counting or numbering on the fingers.

dac-tyl-op′ō-dīte, *n.* [*Dactylo-*, and Gr. *pous*, genit. *podos*, a foot.] In crustaceans, the terminal segment of a limb.

dac-tyl-op′tẽr-ous, *a.* [*Dactylo-*, and Gr. *pteron*, a wing.] Having the inferior rays of the pectoral fins free, either wholly or in part, as in certain fishes.

dac″ty-lō-thē′cȧ, *n.* [L., from Gr. *daktylos*, finger, and *thēkē*, a case, covering.] The scaly integument of the toes of a bird.

dac″tyl-ō-zō′oid, *n.* [*Dactylo-*, and Gr. *zōon*, an animal.] In zoölogy, an elongated, mouthless appendage of hydrozoans, resembling a worm and having one tentacle.

dac′ty-lus, *n.*; *pl.* **dac′ty-lī.** [L., from Gr. *daktylos*, a finger, toe.]

1. In anatomy, a digit.

2. In zoölogy, (a) the last segment of a crustacean's leg having seven joints; (b) the second tarsal joint or those following the first joint of an insect's leg.

3. *Pholas dactylus*, a European piddock.

dad, *n.* [ME. *dadd, dadde*; Ir. *daid*, imitative of a child's attempt to say father.] A familiar name for father.

dad, daud, *n.* [Prov. Eng. and Scot.]

1. A severe blow.

2. A lump or fragment of anything broken off by a blow.

dad′dle, *v.i.* [Scot.] To do anything slowly; to walk slowly or feebly, like a child or an old man. [Rare.]

dad′dŏck, *n.* [Etym. unknown.] The rotten heart or body of a tree. [Prov. Eng.]

dad′dy, *n.* A diminutive form of dad, a childish name for father.

dad′dy-long′legs, *n.* 1. A name given to a species of the crane-fly, *Tipula oleracea*; called also *father longlegs.*

2. A name given to an arachnid belonging to the genus *Phalangium*, having a small body and eight very long legs; known also as *carter, harvestman*, and *grandfather-longlegs.*

dāde, *v.t.* and *v.i.* I. *v.t.* To hold up or support by leading-strings, as a child learning to walk. [Rare.]

II. *v.i.* To toddle; to move slowly and unsteadily, as a child learning to walk. [Rare.]

dā′dō, *n.*; *pl.* **dā′dōeş.** [It.] In architecture, (a) the die of a pedestal; (b) the finishing of the lower part of the walls in rooms, made somewhat to represent a continuous pedestal, and consisting frequently of a skirting of wood about three feet high, or of a special wall-covering.

Pedestal.—*b*, Dado. *a*, Surbase. *c*, Base.

dā′dō, *v.t.*; dadoed, *pt., pp.*; dadoing, *ppr.* 1. To groove; to furnish with a dado.

2. To insert or fit into a groove.

dæ′dăl, dæ-dal′ĭăn, dæd′ȧ-lous, *a.* See *Dedal, Dedalian*, and *Dedalous.*

dæ′mŏn, *n.* See *Demon.*

dæ-mon′ic, *a.* See *Demonic.*

dȧff, *v.t.* To toss aside; to put off. [Obs.]

dȧff, *n.* A stupid, blockish fellow. [Obs.]

dȧff, *v.i.* To be foolish; to toy; to make sport. [Scot.]

dȧff, *v.t.* To intimidate; to daunt. [Prov. Eng.]

daf′fō-dil, *n.* [ME. *affodylle*; LL. *affodillus*; L. *asphodilus*; Gr. *asphodelos*, the asphodel.] A plant of the genus *Narcissus*, having a bulbous root and beautiful flowers of a deep yellow hue. The genus includes many species. Known also as *daffadilly, daffodilly, daffodowndilly*, etc.

dȧft, *a.* 1. Insane; foolish; thoughtless; giddy.

2. Frolicsome; playful; wanton. [Scot.]

dȧft′ly, *adv.* In a daft manner.

dȧft′ness, *n.* The quality of being daft.

dag, *n.* [OFr. *dague*, a dagger, from *daguer*, to thrust.]

1. A dagger. [Obs.]

2. A hand-gun; pistol. [Obs.]

3. An unbranched antler.

dag, *n.* Dew; thick mist. [Obs.]

dag, *v.t.* and *v.i.* I. *v.t.* To daggle. [Prov. Eng.]

II. *v.i.* To drizzle; to bedew. [Prov. Eng.]

dag, *n.* [ME. *dagge*, an ornamental point on the edge of garments, from OFr. *dague*, a dagger.]

1. A loose end, as of locks of wool.

2. An ornamental cut in the edge of garments, in use as early as the reign of Henry I. [Obs.]

Garment ornamented with Dags.

dag′gẽr, *n.* [ME. *dagger*; W. *dagr*, a dagger; of Celtic origin.]

1. A short sword; a poniard.

2. In fencing schools, a blunt blade of iron with a basket hilt, used for defense.

3. In printing, an obelisk, a mark of reference in the form of a dagger; thus (†).
Double dagger; in printing, a mark of reference, thus (‡).
To look or *speak daggers*; to look or speak sharply or fiercely.

dag′gẽr, *v.t.* To pierce with a dagger; to stab.

dag′gẽr, *n.* [Prob. a corruption of *diagonal.*] In ship-building, any timber resting diagonally in the frame.

dag′gẽr-moth, *n.* A moth of the genus *Apatalea*, the larvæ of which infest fruit trees and their foliage; so named from a dagger-like mark on its fore wing.

Various forms of Daggers.

dag′gẽr-plant, *n.* A plant having leaves with sharp points, belonging to the genus *Yucca.*

dag′gẽrs-draw″ing, *n.* The act of drawing daggers; approach to open attack or to violence; a quarrel. [Obs.]

dag′gle, *v.t.* and *v.i.*; daggled, *pt., pp.*; daggling, *ppr.* [Sw. *dagga*, to bedew.] I. *v.t.* To trail; to befoul, as the lower end of a garment.
II. *v.i.* To run through mud and water; to draggle.

dag′gle-tāil, dag′gle-tāiled, *a.* Having the lower ends of garments defiled with mud. [Obs.]

dag′gle-tāil, *n.* A slatternly woman; a draggle-tail. [Obs.]

dag′lock, *n.* A lock of wool on a sheep that hangs and drags in the wet; a taglock. [Scot.]

dā′gō, *n.* A nickname applied to an Italian, particularly of the lower class. It was originally given to people of Spanish or Portuguese descent by Yankee sailors, in allusion to the fact that the names of several Spanish-American ports contained the sound of *dago*; as, San *Diego*, San*tiago*, hence, *Diegos* and *dago* men. [U.S.]

Ceylonese Dagoba.

dȧ-gō′bȧ, *n.* [Cingalese.] A name given in Buddhist countries to a monumental structure containing relics of Buddha or of some Buddhist saint.

dag′on, *n.* An end: a piece or slip. [Obs.]

Dā′gon, *n.* [L. *Dagon*; Gr. *Dagōn*; Heb. *dag*, a fish.] The national god of the Philistines, represented with the upper part of a man and the tail of a fish. His most famous temples were at Gaza and Ashdod.

Dagon of the Philistines. Bas-relief from Khorsabad.

dag′swāin, *n.* [ME. *daggysweyne*, origin obscure.] A kind of carpet; a rough or coarse mantle to cover a bed.

dag′-tāiled, *a.* [Obs.] Same as *Daggle-tail.*

dȧ-guer′rē-ăn, da-guerre′ī-ăn (dȧ-ger′rē-ăn), *a.* 1. Pertaining to the daguerreotype.
2. [D—] Pertaining to Daguerre, the inventor of the daguerreotype.

dȧ-guerre′ō-tȳpe, *n.* [Fr.] 1. An early photographic process, invented by L. J. M. Daguerre, of Paris, in 1839, by which pictures were produced on plates of silvered copper.
2. A picture produced by such a process.

dȧ-guerre′ō-tȳpe, *v.t.*; daguerreotyped, *pt., pp.*; daguerreotyping, *ppr.* 1. To produce, as a picture, by the daguerreotypic process.
2. To imitate exactly; to impress with great distinctness.

dȧ-guerre′ō-tȳ-pẽr, dȧ-guerre′ō-tȳ-pist, *n.* One who takes pictures by the daguerreotypic process.

dȧ-guerre-ō-typ′ic, *a.* Pertaining to or characteristic of a daguerreotype.

dȧ-guerre-ō-typ′ic-ăl, *a.* Daguerreotypic.

dȧ-guerre′ō-tȳ-pist, *n.* See *Daguerreotyper.*

dȧ-guerre′ō-tȳ-py, *n.* The art of producing photographic pictures by the process invented by Daguerre.

dä-hä-bī′yeh, dä-hä-bī′eh, dä-hä-bē′ȧh, *n.* [Ar. *dahabiya.*] A kind of boat, having one or two masts with a long yard supporting a triangular sail; in use on the Nile for the conveyance of passengers.

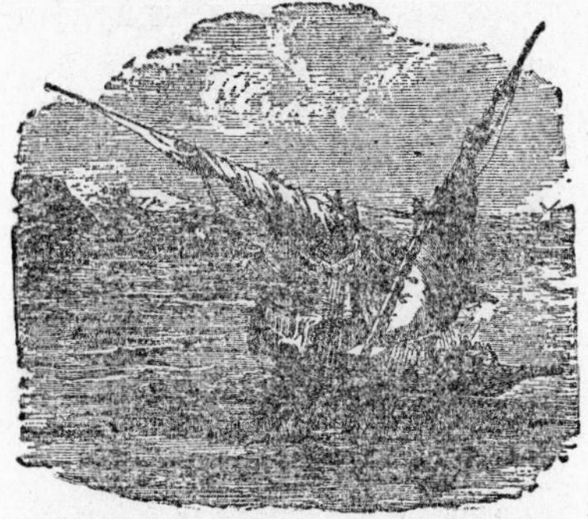

Dahabiyeh.

Däh′liȧ (däl′yȧ *or* dāl′yȧ), *n.* [From *Dahl*, a Swedish botanist.]
1. A genus of composite plants of which several species are known, all natives of Mexico and Central America. *Dahlia variabilis*, one of the species, is extensively cultivated by florists.
2. [d—] Any plant of the genus *Dahlia*, or its flower.
3. [d—] In dyeing, a violet coal-tar pigment obtained from rosaniline; also called *Hoffmann's violet* and *primula.*

däh′lin, *n.* Same as *Inulin.*

dȧ-hoon′, *n.* A small evergreen tree, *Ilex Dahoon*, growing in southern United States, its wood being white, soft and close-grained; called also *dahoon-holly.*

dāik′ẽr, *v.i.* and *v.t.* Same as *Dacker.*

dāi′li-ness, *n.* Daily occurrence. [Rare.]

dāi′ly, *a.* [ME. *dayly*; AS. *dæglic*, daily, from *dæg*, day.] Happening or being every day; done day by day; bestowed or enjoyed every day; diurnal; as, *daily* labor.

dāi′ly, *adv.* Every day; day by day.

dāi′ly, *n.*; *pl.* **dāi′lies.** A newspaper or other publication issued each day.

dāi′mi-ō, *n.* [Japan.] The title of the chief class of feudal lords in Japan.

dāint, *a.* and *n.* I. *a.* Dainty. [Obs.]
II. *n.* Something of exquisite taste; a dainty. [Obs.]

dāin′ti-fȳ, *v.t.* To make dainty or delicate; to render fastidious. [Rare.]

dāin′ti-ly, *adv.* In a dainty manner; nicely; elegantly; delicately; fastidiously; deliciously.

dāin′ti-ness, *n.* The quality or state of being dainty; delicacy; elegance; fastidiousness; squeamishness.

dāin′trel, *n.* [Obs.] Same as *Dainty.*

dāin′ty, *n.* [ME. *daynte*; OFr. *daintie*, worth, value, a delicacy, from L. *dignitas*, worth, dignity.]
1. Something nice and delicate to the taste; that which is exquisitely delicious; a delicacy.
2. A term of fondness; darling. [Obs.]
3. Estimation or value; the pleasure taken in anything. [Obs.]

dāin′ty, *a.* 1. Nice; pleasing to the palate; of exquisite taste; delicious; as, *dainty* food.
2. Delicate; of acute sensibility; nice in selecting what is pleasing; squeamish; soft; luxurious; as, a *dainty* taste or palate.
3. Elegant; tender; soft; pure; neat; effeminately beautiful; as, *dainty* hands or limbs.
4. Nice; affectedly fine; as, a *dainty* speaker.
Syn.—Choice, delicate, elegant, exquisite, fine, neat, nice, rare, refined.

dāi′rī, *n.* 1. The court or palace of the emperor of Japan.
2. A term of respect applied to the mikado.

dāi′ry, *n.* [ME. *deyery*, dairy, from *deye, deie*, a female servant, from Ice. *deija*, a female servant, originally a dough-kneader, from *deig*, dough.]
1. The place, room, or house where milk is set for cream, managed, and converted into butter or cheese.
2. A dairy-farm. [Rare.]
Dairy lunch; a public lunch room where simple dishes are served, those in which dairy products figure being a specialty.

dāi′ry-färm, *n.* A farm devoted to the production of dairy products.

dāi′ry-ing, *n.* The business of conducting a dairy.

dāi′ry-māid, *n.* A female servant whose business it is to milk the cows, and care for milk in the dairy.

dāi′ry-măn, *n.*; *pl.* **dāi′ry-men.** A man who conducts a dairy business.

dā′is, *n.* [ME. *deis, deys*; OFr. *deis, dois*, a high table in a hall; LL. *discus*, a table; L. *discus*, a platter, quoit, discus.]
1. A platform or raised floor at the end or side of a reception-room or hall, on which are placed tables and chairs for specially honored guests; often covered with a canopy.
2. Any raised portion of the floor of a room when set apart for distinguished guests.
3. In Scotland, (a) a long board, seat, or settle erected against a wall, and sometimes so constructed as to serve both for a settee and a table; (b) a seat on the outer side of a country-house, sometimes formed of turf.

Dais in Presence-chamber, Hampton Court, England.

dāi′sied (-zid), *a.* Full of daisies; adorned with daisies.

dāi′sy, *n.* [ME. *daysie, daysy*; AS. *dæges*, the daisy, lit. day's eye, from *dæg*, day, and *eage*, eye.]
1. A common plant of the genus *Bellis*, family *Compositæ*, of which *Bellis perennis* abounds in England, having a yellow disk, with white, pinkish, or rose-colored rays.
2. Any one of several plants popularly called *daisies*, as the oxeye daisy or whiteweed, *Chrysanthemum Leucanthemum*, of North America.
3. Any elegant or excellent person or thing; as, my pony is a *daisy*. [Slang.]
Michaelmas daisy; any one of several species of aster which bloom in England at Michaelmas.

dāi′sy-cut″tẽr, *n.* 1. In the games of baseball and cricket, a batted ball which skims along the ground.
2. A horse that trots with slightly raised feet.

dak, dawk, *n.* [Hind. *dak*, the post, post-office, a relay of men.] The East Indian mail or postal arrangements; a relay of mail-carriers or palanquin-bearers.

dak′-bun′gȧ-lōw, *n.* A hotel at the end of a relay or dak stage.

dā′kẽr, *n.* Same as *Dicker*, 1.

dā′kẽr-hen, *n.* In ornithology, the corncrake or land-rail.

dȧ-koit′, dȧ-coit′, *n.* [Hind. *dakait*, a robber, from *daka*, an attack by robbers.] One of a class of robbers in India and Burma who maraud in bands.

dȧ-koit′y, dȧ-coit′y, *n.* The system of robbery conducted by dakoits, or the crimes committed by them.

Dȧ-kō′tăn, *a.* and *n.* I. *a.* Of or relating to, (a) the Dakota Indians; (b) to the former territory of Dakota; (c) to the present states of North and South Dakota.
II. *n.* An inhabitant of the former territory or the present states.

Dȧ-kō′tȧs, Dȧ-cō′tăhs, *n.pl.* [Am. Indian.] In ethnology, a race of North American Indians of the Sioux stock.

dal, *n.* [Hind. *dal*, a kind of pulse.] In botany, split pulse, an East Indian food; also, a vetch cultivated in East India as a fodder-plant.

Dal-bẽr′gi-ȧ, *n.* [From the name of Nicholas *Dalberg*, a Swedish botanist.] In botany, a large genus of tropical trees and climbing shrubs of the family *Leguminosæ*, that furnish valuable timber, including the rosewoods of Brazil and the East Indies.

dāle, *n.* [ME. *dale*; AS. *dæl*, a dale, valley.]
1. A level or gently undulating space between hills; a dell; a vale.
2. A spout or trough to carry off water.

Dā-lē′ȧ, *n.* [From the name of Samuel *Dale*, an English physician.] In botany, a genus of American herbs or shrubs of the family *Leguminosæ*, having gaudy flowers and pointed leaves; native to western United States and Mexico.

dāle′-land, *n.* Low-lying land.

dāles′măn, *n.* One dwelling in a dale; particularly, one living in the dale-lands of England and Scotland.

dä′li, *n.* [Native name.] In botany, a large tree, allied to the nutmeg-tree, growing in tropical

America; the wood is used in cooperage and the seeds yield an illuminant.

dalk, *n.* A hollow; a hole. [Obs.]

dalle, *n.* [Fr. *dalle*, gutter, tube, trough.]

1. In decorative art, a slab of marble, stone, etc., bearing ornamentations, such as those used in medieval church pavements and walls; any slab or tile.

2. [D—*pl.*] The rapids of a river flowing swiftly over a broad, rock-covered bed, as those of the Columbia river.

Dal′li-ȧ, *n.* [From W. H. *Dall*, an American naturalist.] The type genus of the family *Dalliidæ*. The edible blackfish of Alaska is a well-known species.

dal′li-ănce, *n.* [ME. *daliance*, from *dailyen*, to delay, to dally; AS. *dwalian*, to err, to be foolish.]

1. The act of dallying; delay; a lingering or loitering.

2. Fondling; toying; interchange of caresses.

dal′li-ẽr, *n.* One who fondles; a trifler; as, a *dallier* with pleasant words.

Dal-li′i-dæ, *n.pl.* A family of soft-rayed fishes, fusiform, with flattish head; common to the fresh waters of the Arctic regions and typified by its only genus, *Dallia*.

dal′ly, *v.i.*; dallied, *pt.*, *pp.*; dallying, *ppr.* **1.** To delay; to linger; to wait.

2. To trifle; to lose time in idleness and trifles; to amuse oneself with idle play.

3. To toy and wanton, as man and woman; to interchange caresses; to fondle.

dal′ly, *v.t.* To delay; to defer; to put off; to amuse till a proper opportunity; as, to *dally* off the time. [Rare.]

Dal-mā′tiăn, *n.* and *a.* I. *n.* A member of the Slavic race of Dalmatia or an inhabitant of the Austrian province of that name.

II. *a.* Pertaining to Dalmatia or the Dalmatians.

Dalmatian dog; a white spotted dog, commonly known as the coach-dog.

dal-mat′iç, dal-mat′i-çȧ, *n.* [LL. *dalmatica*, from *Dalmatia*.]

1. In the Roman Catholic church, a long, wide-sleeved, loose-fitting vestment worn by deacons, over the alb and cassock, at communion or mass; worn by bishops under the chasuble and over the tunicle.

2. In medieval history, a senatorial or coronation robe of Dalmatian origin.

Dalmatic, Cathedral of Chartres (twelfth century).

dȧl se′gnō (-nyō). [It., lit. from the sign.] A direction used in music to signify that the performer is to go back to 𝄋 and repeat to the end; abbreviated *D. S.*

Dạl-tō′ni-ăn, *n.* and *a.* I. *n.* A person who cannot distinguish colors; one who is color-blind.

II. *a.* Pertaining to John Dalton, the chemist, or to his atomic theory of chemical combination.

dạl′tŏn-işm, *n.* [Named from John *Dalton*, the chemist, a sufferer from this defect.] Incapacity to distinguish colors, especially red; color-blindness.

dam, *n.* [ME. *damme*, a woman, dame; OFr. *dame*; L. *domina*, a lady, f. of *dominus*, lord, master.]

1. A female parent; used of beasts, particularly of quadrupeds.

2. A human mother, in contempt.

dam, *n.* A crowned man in the game of draughts or checkers. [Local, Eng.]

dam, *n.* [ME. *dam*, *damme*, a dam, from AS. *fordemman*, to stop up.]

1. A mole, bank, or mound of earth, or any wall or framework, raised to obstruct a current of water.

2. The body of water held by a dam.

3. In mining, any contrivance for the exclusion of air, gas, or water.

4. In metallurgy, a wall of firebrick or stone that forms the hearth-front of a blast-furnace.

5. In dentistry, a thin rubber guard stretched tightly around a tooth to exclude moisture during treatment.

6. A buoy displaying a flag by day, a lantern by night.

Floating dam; a caisson used to close the entrance to a dry-dock.

Movable dam; in engineering, a barrage.

dam, *v.t.*; dammed, *pt.*, *pp.*; damming, *ppr.* **1.** To obstruct or stop the current of, as a stream of water; commonly used with *in* or *up*; as, to *dam in*, or to *dam up*, the water.

2. To close up; to stop up; confine; restrain.

To dam out; to keep from coming in, by means of damming; as, to *dam out* water from a mine.

dam′āġe, *n.* [ME. *damage*; OFr. *damage*; L. *damnum*, loss, injury.]

1. Any hurt, injury, or harm to one's person or estate; any loss of property sustained; any hindrance to the increase of property or any obstruction to the success of an enterprise.

2. [*pl.*] In law, money recoverable or recovered as a recompense for injury sustained to person, property, or reputation.

Consequential damages; see under *Consequential*.

Damage feasant; in law, doing injury; trespassing, as cattle.

Exemplary or *vindictive damages*; in law, damages assessed against the defendant with the intent to reimburse the complainant and to be an example or warning to others.

Nominal damages; in law, in a case where no appreciable loss has been inflicted, damages assessed to sustain right of action.

Syn.—Detriment, harm, injury, loss.

dam′āġe, *v.t.* and *v.i.*; damaged, *pt.*, *pp.*; damaging, *ppr.* I. *v.t.* To hurt or harm; to injure; to impair; to lessen the soundness, goodness, or value of.

II. *v.i.* To receive harm; to be injured or impaired in soundness or value.

dam′āġe-ȧ-ble, *a.* 1. Liable to be injured or impaired; susceptible of damage.

2. Hurtful; pernicious. [Rare.]

dam-ȧ-jav′ag, *n.* In dyeing and tanning, the trade name for the extract of chestnut bark and wood; a substitute for gallnuts.

dam′an, dam′on, *n.* [Syrian.] In zoölogy, a small, herbivorous, hoofed mammal of the Syrian genus *Hyrax*; the cony of Scripture.

dam′ăr, *n.* See *Dammar-resin*.

Dam′ăs-cēne, *n.* [ME. *Damascene*; L. *Damascenus*; Gr. *Damaskēnos*, of Damascus, from *Damaskos*, Damascus.]

1. An inhabitant or native of Damascus.

2. [d—] In botany, the damson plum.

Dam′ăs-cēne, *a.* 1. Pertaining to Damascus, in Syria.

2. [d—] Relating to the art of damaskeening.

Damascene work; same as *Damaskeening*.

dam-ăs-cēne′, *v.t.* Same as *Damaskeen*.

Dȧ-màs′cus, *n.* [L. *Damascus*; Gr. *Damaskos*; Heb. *Dameseq*, Damascus.] The chief city in Syria, noted for the fine temper of the blades manufactured there, the metal being imitated in modern times.

Damascus blade; a noted kind of sword or blade formerly made in Damascus of excellent steel, and artistically finished by the process known as damaskeening. [See *Damaskeening*, 2.]

dam′ăsk, *n.* [ME. *damaske*, named from the city of *Damascus*.]

1. A silk stuff, having some parts raised above the ground, representing flowers and other figures, originally from Damascus.

2. A kind of wrought linen, in imitation of damask silks.

3. Red or pink color, from the damask rose.

4. Damascus steel; damaskeening.

5. A mixed modern fabric of cotton, silk, wool, etc., used in upholstery, hangings, etc.

dam′ăsk, *a.* 1. Having a pinkish color, as the damask rose.

2. Of, originating at, or pertaining to, Damascus.

3. Woven with figures like damask; as, a *damask* tablecloth.

Damask plum; a small, purple plum; the damson.

Damask rose; the pink rose of Damascus.

Damask violet; see *Dame's-violet*.

dam′ăsk, *v.t.*; damasked (-ăskt), *pt.*, *pp.*; damasking, *ppr.* To decorate in the style known as damaskeening; to variegate; to diversify.

dam′ăsked (-ăskt), *a.* 1. In heraldry, having an ornamented pattern, as the field. [Rare.]

2. Having a diversified surface, as in damaskeened metal.

dam-ăs-keen′, *v.t.* [Fr. *damasquiner*, to damask, flourish, carve, from *damasquin*, of damask, from *damas*, damask.] To ornament, as articles of metal, by engraving or inlaying with other metals, or by producing damask effects during manufacture; to damask.

dam-ăs-keen′ing, *n.* 1. The act or art of beautifying a metal by engraving or inlaying it with another metal; called also *damascene work*.

2. The effect resulting from welding together iron and steel and applying to the surface an acid, which does not change the iron, but covers the steel with a black coating of carbon. This produced the wavy watered-steel effect of the famous blades of Damascus.

dam′ăs-kin, *n.* A sword made of damask steel; a damaskeened blade. [Obs.]

dam′ăsk-ing, *n.* Same as *Damaskeening*.

dä-mas-sé′ (-sā′), *n.* and *a.* [Fr., pp. of *damasser*, to damask.]

I. *n.* A kind of linen, so woven that the surface resembles damask.

II. *a.* 1. In dress fabrics, woven with a figured or flowered surface, as certain silks.

2. In ceramics, having white ornamentation on a white ground.

dam′ăs-sin, *n.* [From Fr. *damasser*, to damask.] A damask fabric or brocade having threads of gold or silver.

dam′bō-nite, *n.* [From *n′dambo*, the native African name for the tree.] In chemistry, a white crystalline substance found in small percentage in the caoutchouc obtained along the Gaboon river, in West Africa.

dam′bōse, *n.* In chemistry, a kind of sugar obtained from dambonite.

dāme, *n.* [ME. *dame*; OFr. *dame*; L. *domina*, a lady, f. of *dominus*, lord.]

1. In Great Britain, the title borne by the wife or widow of a baronet or knight.

2. A woman of culture, rank, or high social position; a lady.

3. The mistress of a family; a mature woman, married or single; the mistress of a school for children.

4. At Eton college, England, the person with whom the pupils board, whether man or woman.

5. A dam; a mother. [Obs.]

dāme′ș=vī″ō-let, *n.* In botany, a fragrant plant bearing large purple or white flowers, the *Hesperis matronalis*; called also *damask violet*, *damewort* and *rocket*.

dam-i-an′ȧ, *n.* [L., origin uncertain.] In medicine, a drug composed of the leaves of Mexican plants of the genus *Turnera*; used as an aphrodisiac, or tonic.

Dā′mi-ăn-īte, Dā′mi-ăn-ist, *n.* In ecclesiastical history, one of the followers of Damianus, patriarch of Alexandria, in the sixth century, who concentered all the personal attributes of the Father, Son, and Holy Ghost in the one God, and therefore was accused of teaching Sabellianism.

Dam′mă-rȧ, *n.* [L., from Hind. *damar*, resin, pitch.] In botany, a genus of large, coniferous trees of the East Indies and Australasia, having several species, including the dammar-pine, which yields the dammar-resin of commerce; called also *Agathis*.

dam′măr=reṣ″in, *n.* [Hind. *damar*, resin, pitch.] A resinous substance similar to copal, obtained in the East Indies and New Zealand from several species of *Dammara*, trees allied to the pine. The resin or gum is used principally in composition with colorless varnish.

damn (dam), *v.t.*; damned, *pt.*, *pp.*; damning, *ppr.* [ME. *damnen*; OFr. *damner*; L. *damnare*, to condemn, fine, from *damnum*, loss, injury.]

1. In theology, to sentence to punishment in a future state; to curse.

He that believeth not shall be *damned*.
—Mark xvi. 16.

2. To condemn; to decide to be wrong or worthy of punishment; to censure; to reprobate.

3. To condemn by some outward mark of displeasure; as, to *damn* a play.

damn, *v.i.* To swear profanely; to curse; as, to *damn* right and left.

damn, *n.* A word used in profaneness; a term of execration.

Not to care a damn; to be oblivious or indifferent. [Slang.]

dam′nȧ-ble, *a.* 1. Capable of being damned or condemned; deserving damnation; worthy of punishment.

2. Odious, detestable, or pernicious.

dam′nȧ-ble-ness, *n.* The state or quality of deserving damnation.

dam′nȧ-bly, *adv.* 1. In a manner to incur condemnation or punishment; detestably; odiously.

2. Abominably; detestably; used profanely; as, I have been *damnably* cheated.

dam-nā′tion, *n.* 1. In theology, condemnation to future punishment.

2. Condemnation in a general sense; disapprobation; the condition of being doomed to punishment, as by judicial sentence.

dam′nā-tō-ry, *a.* Containing a sentence of condemnation; meriting condemnation; condemnatory.

damned (damd), *a.* **1.** Judicially reprobated; sentenced to future punishment; condemned; used in theology of lost souls.

2. Hateful; detestable; abominable; used in a profane sense.

dam-nif′iç, *a.* Procuring loss or injury; mischievous.

dam′ni-fȳ, *v.t.* To cause loss or damage to; to injure. [Rare.]

damn′ing, *a.* Exposing to damnation or condemnation; as, a *damning* sin.

damn′ing-ness, *n.* Tendency to bring damnation.

dam′num, *n.*; *pl.* **dam′nȧ.** [L. *damnum*, loss, injury.] In law, damage; harm; loss.

Damnum absque injuria; loss without any injury of which the law can take cognizance.

dam′ō-şel, *n.* [Obs.] See *Damsel*.

dam-öur′īte, *n.* [Named from *Damour*, a French chemist.] In mineralogy, a yellowish muscovite or potash mica, holding water in combination.

damp, *a.* [ME. *dampen*, to extinguish.]

1. Moist; humid; moderately wet; as, a *damp* cloth; *damp* air.

2. Dejected; depressed. [Rare.]

damp, *n.* 1. Moist air; humidity; moisture; fog.

2. Dejection; depression of spirits.

3. A gaseous exhalation found in coal-mines and other excavations, as choke-*damp*.

Black damp; in mining, carbonic acid gas, sometimes in combination with fire-damp: also called *choke-damp*.

Damp sheet; in mining, a curtain so arranged in a gallery as to direct air-currents and rid the mine of foul air and gas.

damp, *v.t.*; damped (damt), *pt.*, *pp.*; damping, *ppr.* [ME. *dampen*, to extinguish.]

1. To moisten; to make humid, or moderately wet.

2. To chill; to deaden; to depress or deject; to abate; as, to *damp* the spirits; to *damp* the ardor of passion.

3. To check or restrain, as action or vigor; as, to *damp* industry; to *damp* the vibrations of a harp-string.

damp′en, *v.t.* and *v.i.*; dampened, *pt.*, *pp.*; dampening, *ppr.* I. *v.t.* 1. To make damp or moist.

2. To put a damper on; to check; to depress.

II. *v.i.* To become damp.

damp′ẽr, *n.* 1. That which damps or checks.

2. A valve or sliding plate in a furnace to stop or lessen the quantity of air admitted, and thus to regulate the heat or extinguish the fire.

3. In pianofortes, a felt-covered device for checking vibration.

4. A device to stop the vibrations of a magnetic needle.

5. An Australian unfermented bread, made of flour and water, and baked on a stone or in ashes.

damp′ẽr-ped″ăl, *n.* In pianofortes, the pedal that raises all the dampers from the strings, prolonging vibration; called also *loud pedal*.

damp′ish, *a.* Moderately damp, or moist.

damp′ish-ly, *adv.* In a dampish manner.

damp′ish-ness, *n.* A moderate degree of dampness, or moistness; slight humidity.

dam′-plāte, *n.* An iron plate attached to the front of the dam in a blast-furnace to reinforce it.

damp′ness, *n.* Moisture; fogginess; moistness; moderate humidity; as, the *dampness* of the air.

damp′y, *a.* 1. Dejected; gloomy. [Obs.]

2. In coal-mining, affected by choke-damp, as the underground air.

dam′ṣel, *n.* [ME. *damesele*; OFr. *dameisele*; LL. *domicella*, a young lady, girl, from L. *domina*, a lady.]

1. A young man or woman of noble or genteel extraction; as, *Damsel* Pepin; *Damsel* Richard, prince of Wales. [Obs.]

2. A young unmarried woman; a maiden.

3. In milling, the hopper-shaker, attached to the millstone spindle.

dam′ṣel-fly̆, *n.* In entomology, a dragon-fly.

dam′ṣŏn, *n.* [ME. *damasyn*; L. *Damascenus*, of *Damascus*.] The fruit of a variety of the *Prunus domestica*, a small blue or purple plum; called also *damask plum*.

Bitter or *mountain damson*; in botany, the *Simaruba amara* of Guiana and the West Indies, whose bitter bark has medicinal qualities.

Damson cheese; conserved damsons pressed into the shape of a cheese.

dam′-stōne, *n.* The stone closing the front of the hearth in a blast-furnace, to which the damplate is attached.

dan, *n.* A title of honor formerly equivalent to *don*, *master*, *sir*. [Obs.]

dan, *n.* [Etym. unknown.] In mining, (a) a barrel or tub used in conveying water [Eng.]; (b) a small coal-carrying truck or sled.

dā′nă-ide, *n.* [Named for the *Danaides* of mythology, condemned to dip water with sieves.] In machinery, a tub-wheel, consisting of two tapering shells, one within the other.

dā′nă-ite, *n.* [Named from J. F. *Dana*, an American chemist.] In mineralogy, a variety of cobaltiferous arsenopyrite.

dā′nă-lite, *n.* [Named from J. D. *Dana*, an American mineralogist.] In mineralogy, a silicate of iron, zinc, manganese, and glucinum, containing a small percentage of sulphur, and occurring in crystals.

dan′bŭr-ite, *n.* [Named from *Danbury*, Conn., where first found.] In mineralogy, a white or pale yellow borosilicate of calcium, occurring in crystals.

dȧnce, *v.i.*; danced (dȧnst), *pt.*, *pp.*; dancing, *ppr.* [ME. *dauncen*; OFr. *dancer*, to dance; probably from O.H.G. *danson*, to draw or drag along, *dinsan*, to trail, drag.]

1. To move, leap, or step rhythmically, as when the motions are regulated by music.

2. To leap and frisk about; to move nimbly and gracefully; to caper; as, the little girl fairly *danced* with joy.

To dance on nothing; to dangle from a gibbet; to be hanged.

dȧnce, *v.t.* 1. To perform the steps or figures of, as a waltz.

2. To cause to dance; to move up and down, or back and forth; to dandle; as, to *dance* a child on the knee.

To dance attendance; to wait with obsequiousness; to strive to please and gain favor by assiduous attentions and officious civilities; as, *to dance attendance* at court.

dȧnce, *n.* 1. A leaping or stepping with rhythmical motions of the body, particularly by two or more in concert; a lively, brisk exercise or amusement, in which the movements of the persons are regulated by art, in figure, and by the sound of instruments, in measure.

2. Dance-music by which dancing is regulated, as the minuet, the waltz, the cotillion, etc.

Dance of death; in painting and sculpture, an allegorical illustration of the power of death, in which a skeleton leads a merry group composed of all ages and conditions.

Pyrrhic dance; in ancient Greece, a war-dance symbolizing attack and defense.

Round dance; any dance in which the movements are revolving in nature, as the waltz, polka and schottische.

Square dance; any dance in which the formation of the dancers is in squares, as the quadrille and lancers.

St. Vitus's dance; chorea.

To lead one a dance; figuratively, to cause one trouble or expense, through false hopes; to play on one's credulity or good-nature.

To lead the dance; to take the lead in any movement.

dȧn′cẽr, *n.* 1. One who practises dancing, or is skilful in the performance; particularly, one whose profession is dancing.

2. [D—] In church history, one of an ephemeral sect, who, in the fourteenth century, appeared at Aix-la-Chapelle and danced in honor of their patron, St. John.

Merry dancers; a phrase expressive of the lively motions sometimes seen in a peculiar formation of the northern lights.

dȧn′cẽr-ess, *n.* A female dancer. [Obs.]

dan-cet-té′ (-tā′), *a.* and *n.* [Fr., from OFr. *dent*, L. *dens*, tooth.]

I. *a.* In heraldry, noting a line of division of the same character as indented, but larger, consisting of only three teeth.

II. *n.* In heraldry, a zigzag across the field. A fesse *dancetté* has but three indentations, unless otherwise described.

Dancetté.

dan-cette′, *n.* In architecture, the chevron or zigzag molding peculiar to medieval Norman structures in the Romanesque style.

Dancette.

dȧn′cing, *n.* The act or art of moving in measured step corresponding to the time of the music; leaping; tripping.

dȧn′cing-dis-ēaṣe″, *n.* Same as *Tarantismus*.

dȧn′cing-gīrl, *n.* 1. A professional female dancer; in India, a nautch-girl.

2. In botany, an East Indian plant, *Mantisia saltatoria*, whose purple and yellow flowers bear a fancied likeness to a ballet-dancer.

dȧn′cing-mȧs″tẽr, *n.* One who teaches the art of dancing.

dȧn′cing-sc̶hool, *n.* A school in which the art of dancing is taught.

dan′cy, *a.* Same as *Dancetté*.

dan′dee, *n.* See second *Dandy*, n.

dan′dē-li-ŏn, *n.* [Fr. *dent de lion*, lit. tooth of the lion; from L. *dens* (*dentis*), tooth, *de*, of, and *leo*, lion.] In botany, a common plant, *Taraxacum officinale*, having a milky, perennial root, naked stalk, deeply notched leaves, and a single large, yellow flower.

dan′dẽr, *v.i.* To wander about; to talk incoherently. [Prov. Eng.]

dan′dẽr, *n.* [Corrupted from *dandruff*.]

1. Dandruff; head-scurf.

2. Anger; passion; rage. [Colloq.]

To get one's dander up; to become enraged. [Colloq.]

dan′dẽr, *n.* [Scot. Etym. obscure.] A cinder; refuse from a furnace.

dan′di-ȧ-căl, *a.* Pertaining to or like a dandy; dandified.

Dan′die, *n.* One of a breed of small, hardy terriers; called also *Dandie Dinmont*.

dan′di-fied, *a.* Having the characteristic dress or manners of a dandy; foppish; as, *dandified* ways.

dan′di-fy̆, *v.t.*; dandified, *pt.*, *pp.*; dandifying, *ppr.* To cause to resemble a dandy; to make foppish.

dan′di-prat, *n.* [Etym. obscure.]

1. A little fellow; an urchin; a dapperling; used as a word both of affection and contempt.

2. An English silver coin of the value of three halfpence, coined by Henry VII.

dan′dle, *v.t.*; dandled, *pt.*, *pp.*; dandling, *ppr.* [Comp. Scot. *dandill*, to go about idly; G. *tandeln*, to trifle, dandle.]

1. To shake or jolt on the knee, as an infant; to move up and down in the hand; literally, to amuse by play.

2. To fondle; to amuse; to treat as a child; to toy with.

3. To delay; to protract by trifles. [Obs.]

dan′dlẽr, *n.* One who dandles or fondles.

dan′drụff, dan′driff, *n.* [Origin uncertain; perhaps from W. *ton*, a crust, skin, and AS. *drof*, dirty.] A scurf which forms on the head, and comes off in small scales or particles.

dan′dy, *n.*; *pl.* **dan′dieṣ**. [Fr. *dandin*, a ninny, a silly fellow.]

1. A fastidious dresser; an exquisite; a fop; a coxcomb.

2. In mechanics, (a) a preliminary heating-chamber in a puddling-furnace; (b) in tin-plate making, a portable furnace that permits of access from all sides; (c) an accessory or attachment to a machine; (d) in paper-making, the dandy-roller.

3. Anything fine, dainty, or natty. [Slang.]

4. In medicine, same as *dengue*.

5. A small drinking-glass used in Ireland.

6. In navigation, (a) a sloop-rigged vessel carrying a jigger-mast; (b) a small jigger-mast sail.

dan′dy, dan′dee, *n.* [Hind. *dandi*, a boatman, a rower, from *dand*, an oar, a staff.]

1. A boatman on the Ganges river.

2. A cloth hammock or litter attached to a bamboo staff and carried by bearers.

dan′dy, *a.* 1. Characteristic of or pertaining to a coxcomb or fop.

2. Dainty; exquisite; natty. [Slang.]

dan′dy-cock, *n.* A bantam cock. [Eng.]

dan′dy-fē′vẽr, *n.* Same as *Dengue*.

dan′dy-hen, *n.* A bantam hen. [Eng.]

dan′dy-ish, *a.* Like a dandy; foppish.

dan′dy-iṣm, *n.* The characteristics or dress of a dandy; foppishness.

dan′dy-ize, *v.t.* and *v.i.* I. *v.t.* To make like a dandy; to dandify.

II. *v.i.* To become or be a dandy.

dan′dy-ling, *n.* A little dandy; an absurd or contemptible fop.

dan′dy-nōte, *n.* In Great Britain, a permit from the customs authorities to remove goods.

dan′dy-rōll″ẽr, *n.* In paper-making, a cylinder of wire gauze which compacts, drains, and water-marks the web of paper-pulp; called also a *dandy*.

Dāne, *n.* A native or inhabitant of Denmark.

Great Dane; see *Danish dog* under *Danish*.

Dan′e-brog, Dan′ne-brog, *n.* 1. A Danish order of knighthood, founded in 1219; second in rank and consisting of five classes.

2. The national standard of Denmark, a white cross on a red field.

dāne′-flow″ẽr, *n.* In botany, the pasque-flower, *Anemone Pulsatilla*.

Dāne′geld, Dāne′gelt, *n.* [ME. *Danegeld*, from AS. *Dene*, the Danes, and *geld*, *gild*, a payment, from *gildan*, to pay, yield.] In English history, an annual tax laid, from the tenth into the twelfth century, on the English nation, for maintaining forces to oppose the Danes, or to furnish tribute to procure peace. It was at first one shilling, afterward two, and at last seven, for every hide of land, except such as belonged to the church. At a subsequent period, when the Danes became masters, the *Danegeld* was a tax levied by the Danish princes on every hide of land owned by the Anglo-Saxons.

dāneṣ′blood (-blud), *n.* In botany, the popular English name for the clustered bellflower, the pasque-flower, or the dwarf elder, fancied to have sprung up from the blood of Danes killed in battle.

dāne′weed, *n.* In botany, danewort; also, the plant, *Eryngium campestre*, of the parsley family.

dāne′wŏrt, *n.* In botany, the dwarf elder, *Sambucus Ebulus*, of Europe; danesblood.

dān′gẽr, *n.* [ME. *daunger*; OFr. *danger*, absolute power, from L. *dominium*, right of ownership, power, from *dominus*, a ruler.]

1. Liability to injury or loss; hazard; insecurity; peril; risk.

2. Jurisdiction; power to inflict harm. [Obs.]

3. Hesitation; difficulty. [Obs.]

4. Disdain; coyness. [Obs.]

Syn.—Peril, hazard, risk, jeopardy, venture, exposure.—*Danger* is generic; *peril* is instant or impending danger. *Hazard* arises from something fortuitous or beyond our control; as, the *hazard* of the seas. *Risk* is doubtful or uncertain danger, often incurred voluntarily. *Jeopardy* is extreme danger.

dān′gẽr, *v.t.* To place in danger; to hazard. [Obs.]

dān′gẽr-fụl, *a.* Dangerous. [Obs.]

dān′gẽr-fụl-ly, *adv.* In a dangerous manner. [Obs.]

dān′ġẽr-less, *a.* Devoid of danger. [Rare.]

dān′ġẽr-ous, *a.* 1. Beset with danger; hazardous; perilous; risky; unsafe; as, a *dangerous* experiment.

2. Creating danger; causing menace; as, a *dangerous* man.

3. In danger or peril, as from illness. [Colloq.]

4. Hard to please; critical; haughty; reserved; unaffable. [Obs.]

dān′ġẽr-ous-ly, *adv.* With danger; with risk of evil; hazardously.

dān′ġẽr-ous-ness, *n.* The quality or condition of being dangerous.

dān′ġẽr-sig″nāl, *n.* A sign so placed as to forewarn of danger.

dan′gle, *v.i.*; dangled, *pt., pp.*; dangling, *ppr.* [Dan. *dangle*, to dangle, bob.]

1. To depend loosely and swing to and fro in an irregular or jerky manner; as, to *dangle* on a gibbet.

2. To follow with importunity; used with *after* or *about*; as, to *dangle after* a patron; to *dangle about* a girl.

dan′gle, *v.t.* To cause to move or swing loosely or with a swaying motion; as, he *dangled* the banner before her eyes.

dan′gle-ber″ry, *n.* The blue huckleberry of the United States, with the shrub which bears it; also called *bluetangle*.

dan′gle-ment, *n.* The act of dangling; the condition of being dangled.

dan′glẽr, *n.* One who dangles about or after others; particularly, one who dangles about women; a trifler.

Dān′i-ciṣm, *n.* Any idiom of the Danish language; also written *Danism*.

Dan′i-el (*or* -yel), *n.* [Heb., a divine judge.]

1. One of the books of prophecy contained in the Old Testament, whose authorship is attributed to Daniel, a sagacious and upright Hebrew prophet of the period of the Captivity, a portion (chapters ii. 4 to vii. 28) being written in Aramaic and the remainder in Hebrew.

2. An astute and upright judge; as, a *Daniel* come to judgment.

Dān′ish, *a.* and *n.* I. *a.* Pertaining to Denmark, to the Danes, or to their language.

II. *n.* The language of the Danes.

Danish ax; a battle-ax of peculiar form, with elongated blade.

Danish dog; a large, close-haired dog of a breed reared in Denmark; called also *Great Dane*.

Danish embroidery; (a) a coarse stitch used in making small designs, in crochet work; (b) a white embroidery used on the edges of handkerchiefs.

Dān′iṣm, *n.* 1. Same as *Danicism*.

2. [d—] Lending money at usurious rate. [Obs.]

Dan′ite, *n.* [From *Dan*, signifying in Heb. a judge.]

1. A descendant of Dan, the son of Jacob; a member of the Israelitish tribe of Dan.

2. In the United States, one of a band or secret society formed among the Mormons in the early history of their church, called the *Danites* or Destroying Angels, whose alleged purpose was secret assassination.

dank, *a.* and *n.* [ME. *dank*; Sw. dial. *dank*, a marshy piece of ground.]

I. *a.* Damp; humid; moist; wet.

II. *n.* Humidity; moisture; water.

dank′ish, *a.* Slightly dank; moist.

dank′ness, *n.* The state of being dank; humidity.

danks, *n.* In mining, black shale with a mixture of fine coal.

dän-sēuṣe′ (-sēz′), *n.* [Fr., f. of *danseur*, a dancer, from *danser*, to dance.] A professional female dancer in ballets and divertissements.

Première danseuse; a danseuse who leads in a ballet.

Dansk′ẽr, *n.* A Dane. [Obs.]

dant, *v.t.* [ME. *daunten*; OFr. *danter*, to daunt, subdue; L. *domitare*, to tame, rule.]

1. To intimidate; to daunt.

2. To reduce to a lower temper; as, to *dant* metal. [Prov. Eng.]

dant, *n.* [From Prov. Eng. *dant*, to daunt.]

1. Coal so crushed as to be without value. [North Eng.]

2. A heavy iron weight used as a compress in packing certain articles (as provisions) in casks.

Dan-tē′ăn, *a.* Pertaining to, proceeding from, or similar to the poet Dante or his writings; when applied to literary style, both somber and sublime.

Dan-tesque′ (-tesk′), **Dan-tes′ċăn,** *a.* Same as *Dantean*.

Dan′tist, *n.* An admirer of Dante, or one versed in his writings.

Dan′tŏn-ist, *n.* A political adherent of Georges Jacques Danton, a leader in the French Revolution of 1793.

Dá-nū′bi-ăn, *a.* Pertaining to or situated near the river Danube

Danubian principalities; Moldavia and Wallachia, which were united in 1861 and named Rumania.

dap, *v.i.* [ME. *dabben*, to strike, dab.] In angling, to let the bait fall lightly on the water.

dá-pat′iç-ăl, *a.* Sumptuous in cheer. [Obs.]

daph′nad, *n.* In botany, any plant or shrub of the spurge-laurel family, *Thymeleaceæ*, of which *Daphne* is the typical genus.

Daph′nē, *n.* [L. *daphne*; Gr. *daphnē*, the laurel or bay-tree.]

1. In botany, a genus of shrubs of the natural order *Thymeleaceæ*, including about forty species, mainly evergreens, and bearing fragrant blooms of different colors.

2. [d—] A shrub of the genus *Daphne*.

3. In Greek mythology, a nymph of Diana, daughter of Peneus and Ge, said to have been changed into a laurel-tree while fleeing from Apollo.

daph′ne-tin, *n.* In chemistry, a crystalline substance found in daphnin.

Daph′ni-ȧ, *n.* [L., from Gr. *daphnē*, the laurel-tree.] In crustalogy, a genus of minute entomostracans typical of the *Daphniidæ*; called also *water-flea*.

daph′nid, *a.* and *n.* I. *a.* Pertaining to or resembling the *Daphnia*.

II. *n.* One of the *Daphnia*.

Daph-nī′i-dæ, *n.pl.* A family of minute entomostracans. [See *Cladocera*.]

daph′nin, *n.* In chemistry, a bitter, transparent, crystalline glucoside found in the bark and flowers of various species of *Daphne*.

daph′ni-oid, daph′noid, *a.* [L. *Daphnia*, and Gr. *eidos*, form.] In crustalogy, pertaining to the *Daphniidæ* or to the *Cladocera*.

daph′nō-man-cy, *n.* [Gr. *daphnē*, the laurel-tree, and *manteia*, divination.] Divination by means of the laurel.

dap′i-fẽr, *n.* [L. *daps*, a feast, and *ferre*, to bear.] The steward of a royal or noble household.

dap′pẽr, *a.* [ME. *daper*, pretty, neat; D. *dapper*, brave, valiant.]

1. Active; lively; small.

2. Neat in dress; spruce; trim.

dap′pẽr-ling, *n.* A diminutive person; a dwarf.

dap′ple, *n.* and *a.* [ME. in comp. *dappul-gray*, dapple-gray; Ice. *depill*, a spot, dot, a splash of water, from *dapi*, a pool.]

I. *n.* A spot or patch on the skin of an animal of a different hue from the general color.

II. *a.* Dotted with spots of various colors; as, a *dapple* horse.

dap′ple, *v.t.*; dappled, *pt., pp.*; dappling, *ppr.* To bespot; to variegate with spots.

dap′ple-bāy, *a.* Of a bay color, marked with dapples.

dap′pled (-pld), *a.* Marked with variegated spots.

dap′ple-grāy, *a.* Of a gray color, variegated with dapples.

dãr, *n.* See *Dace*.

dãr′by, *n.*; *pl.* **dãr′bieṣ.** [Prob. from the personal name *Darby* or *Derby*.]

1. A mason's or plasterer's float.

2. [*pl.*] Handcuffs. [Slang.]

Dãr′by-ites, *n.pl.* In church history, the *Plymouth Brethren*; also the *Exclusive Brethren*, a sect founded in England in 1830 by John N. Darby.

Dãr′dăn, *a.* and *n.* I. *a.* Pertaining to Dardanus or to Dardania, a city near ancient Troy.

II. *n.* An inhabitant of Dardania or Troy; a Trojan.

dāre, *n.* 1. Challenge; defiance; disregard; show of resistance.

2. The quality of being venturesome; boldness; intrepidity. [Obs.]

To take a dare; to receive a challenge of any kind without a return, either in words or action.

dāre, *n.* See *Dace*.

dāre, *v.t.*; dared, *pt., pp.*; daring, *ppr.* [ME. *dar, der*; AS. *dear, dearr*, first pers. pres. ind. of *durran*, to dare.]

1. To attempt to accomplish; to have courage to undertake; to venture.

2. To offer provocation to; challenge; defy.

I dare say; likely; I think so.

dāre, *v.t.* and *v.i.* I. *v.t.* To daunt; to terrify.

II. *v.i.* To lie hidden; to lurk. [Obs.]

To dare larks; to catch larks after terrorizing them by hawks, mirrors, etc.

dāre′dev″il, *n.* and *a.* I. *n.* One who fears nothing and is ready to attempt anything.

II. *a.* Daring; reckless; characteristic of a daredevil; as, *daredevil* work.

dāre′dev″il-iṣm, *n.* Daredeviltry.

dāre′dev″il-try, *n.* The conduct of a daredevil; recklessness.

dāre′-dö″ing, der′-dö″ing, *a.* Bold. [Obs.]

dāre′fụl, *a.* Full of defiance. [Rare.]

dār′ẽr, *n.* One who dares or defies.

därg, därgue, *n.* [Scot.] A day's work; also, a certain quantity of work, whether more or less than that supposed to be done in a day.

därg, *v.i.* [Scot.] To be employed by the day.

därg′ẽr, *n.* One employed by the day. [Scot.]

dãr′gle, *n.* [Eng. dial.] A local English term for the coalfish.

dar′iç, *n.* [Gr. *dareikos*, a Pers. gold coin, from *Dareios*, Darius, by whom it was first coined, from Pers. *dara*, a ruler.]

Golden Daric, from British Museum.

1. In antiquity, (a) a gold coin of Darius the Mede weighing about 129 grains, and worth about $5.50; (b) a silver coin of both ancient and modern times, worth about twenty-seven cents; also called the *siglos*.

2. Any coin of very pure gold.

dā′ri-ī, *n.* One of the valid moods in logic. [See *Mood*.]

dãr′ing, *n.* A bold act; a hazardous attempt; boldness; adventurousness; intrepid courage.

dãr′ing, *a.* 1. Bold; courageous; intrepid; fearless; adventurous; brave; stout.

Grieve not, O *daring* prince, that noble heart.
—Pope.

2. Audacious; impudent.

Syn.—Brave, courageous, fearless, intrepid, bold, adventurous, impudent.

dãr′ing-ly, *adv.* In a daring manner.

dãr′ing-ness, *n.* The quality of being daring.

dá′ri-ōle, *n.* A little French sweet cake filled with cream, macaroons, fruit, etc.

därk, *a.* [ME. *dark, derk*; AS. *deorc*, dark.]

1. Destitute of light; neither illuminated nor illuminating; obscure.

The sun to me is *dark*. —Milton.

2. Wholly or partially black; having the quality opposite to white; as, a *dark* color or substance.

3. Gloomy; disheartening; having unfavorable prospects; as, a *dark* time in political affairs.

4. Concealed; mysterious; secret; not easily explained or understood.

The words of the wise, and their *dark* sayings.
—Prov. i. 6.

5. Not enlightened with knowledge; destitute of learning and science; rude; ignorant; as, a *dark* age.

6. Wanting sight; blind. [Obs.]

7. Morally black; atrocious; wicked; sinister; as, *dark* designs.

8. Not fair; said of the complexion; as, a *dark* skin.

Dark ages; a period in European history, extending from about the time of the fall of the Roman Empire of the West (476 A. D.), and the consequent incursion of barbarians, to the period of the Italian Renaissance of the thirteenth century; not synchronous with the *middle ages*, which historians conclude two hundred years later.

Dark heat; in physics, the heat produced by the invisible heat-rays of the spectrum.

Dark horse; in horse-racing, a horse whose capabilities are not generally known, or concerning whose chances of success in a pending race no conclusive information is to be had; hence, applied to any competitor or candidate, especially in politics, about whom nothing certain is known. [Colloq.]

Dark room; in photography, a room from which all actinic light has been excluded, used in the process of sensitizing and developing plates.

Dark space; in physics, a space in an exhausted tube near the cathode or negative pole, which remains obscure while an electric discharge is passing; particularly, that space within the glow of both electrodes; called also *first dark space* or *Crookes' space*.

The dark and bloody ground; a name given to the state of Kentucky, by reason of the many bloody conflicts carried on there by Indians.

To keep dark; to hide or to conceal all information. [Colloq.]

Syn.—Obscure, opaque, dismal, dim, gloomy, mysterious, dusky, shady, somber, black, shadowy, murky.—A corner may be said to be literally *dark* or *obscure*, while some of the passages of ancient writers, for instance, are figuratively so. *Opaque* objects are those which are not transparent, as stained glass. *Dim* expresses a degree of darkness, but it is employed more in relation to the person seeing than to the object seen; as, the eyes grow *dim*.

därk, *v.t.* To darken; to obscure. [Obs.]

därk, *n.* 1. Darkness; obscurity; absence of light; a place deprived of light.

2. Obscurity; secrecy; a state of ignorance; as, we are all in the *dark* concerning his plans, which were formed in the *dark*.

3. In art, a shade or shadow in a picture; as, *darks* and lights are both necessary.

därk′en, *v.t.*; darkened, *pt., pp.*; darkening,

ppr. 1. To make dark; to deprive of light; as, to *darken* a room.

2. To make dim; to deprive of vision; as, deep sorrow *darkened* his mind.

3. To render gloomy; as, sorrow *darkened* the home.

4. To obscure; to perplex; to render less clear or intelligible; as, her foolish words *darkened* the solution of the question.

5. To sully; to make foul; to render less bright.

To darken one's door; to call upon; to visit; usually implying unwelcomeness.

därk'en, *v.i.* To grow dark or darker; also, to grow less white or clear.

därk'en-ẽr, *n.* One who or that which darkens.

därk'en-ing, *n.* Twilight; gloaming. [Scot. and Prov. Eng.]

därk'fụl, *a.* Full of darkness. [Obs.]

därk'=house, *n.* A lunatic asylum; a madhouse. [Obs.]

därk'ish, *a.* Dusky; somewhat dark.

där'kle, *v.i.*; darkled, *pt., pp.*; darkling, *ppr.* To appear dark; to show indistinctly.

därk'ling, *adv.* In the dark; at night; a poetic word.

därk'ling, *a.* 1. Growing dark or gloomy; becoming obscure.

2. Gloomy; dark; obscure.

därk'ly, *adv.* 1. In a dark manner; obscurely; dimly; blindly; uncertainly; with imperfect light, clearness, or knowledge; as, *darkly* seen against the cloudy sky; *darkly* perceived by the clouded mind.

2. With a dark, threatening look.

därk'ness, *n.* 1. Absence of light; obscurity; gloom.

2. Obscurity; want of clearness or perspicuity; that quality or state which renders anything difficult to be understood.

3. A state of being intellectually clouded; ignorance; hence, sin; wickedness.

4. A private place; secrecy; privacy.

What I tell you in *darkness*, that speak ye in light. —Matt. x. 27.

5. Great trouble and distress; calamities; perplexities.

A day of clouds and of thick *darkness*. —Joel ii. 2.

Prince of darkness; the devil.

Syn.—Dimness, obscurity, gloom.—*Darkness* arises from a total, and *dimness* from a partial, want of light. A thing is *obscure* when so overclouded or covered as not to be easily perceived. As the shade or *obscurity* increases, it deepens into *gloom*. When taken figuratively, these words have a like use; as, the *darkness* of ignorance, *dimness* of discernment, *obscurity* of reasoning, and *gloom* of superstition.

därk'sōme, *a.* Dark; gloomy; obscure; as, a *darksome* house.

därk'y, *n.* A negro. [Slang.]

där'ling, *a.* and *n.* [ME. *derling, durling*; AS. *deorling*, a favorite, dim. of *deor*, dear.]

I. *a.* Dearly beloved; favorite; regarded with great kindness and tenderness; as, a *darling* child; a *darling* science.

II. *n.* One much beloved; a favorite.

Där-ling-tō'ni-ȧ, *n.* [Named after Dr. William *Darlington*, an American botanist.] A genus of pitcher-plants with only one species, *Darlingtonia Californica*, found in the northern part of California.

därn, *v.t.*; darned, *pt., pp.*; darning, *ppr.* [W. *darnio*, to piece, break in pieces, tear, from *darn*, a piece, fragment.] To mend (a rent or hole) by imitating the texture of the cloth or stuff with yarn or thread and a needle; to sew together with yarn or thread.

därn, *n.* A place mended by darning.

därn, *v.t.* To damn (used as a euphemistic oath).

där'nel, *n.* [ME. *darnel*; Fr. dial. *darnelle*, the darnel, from OFr. *darne*, stupefied; so called from its supposed stupefying or intoxicating qualities.] Any grass of the genus *Lolium*, particularly *Lolium temulentum*. Its grains are believed to possess narcotic properties, but recent researches have cast some doubt on its reported deleterious qualities. It is sometimes found in the wheat-fields of Europe. The name was formerly given to any weed in grain.

Darnel (*Lolium temulentum*).

därn'ẽr, *n.* One who mends by darning.

där'nex, där'niç, *n.* Same as *Dornick*.

därn'ing, *n.* The act of mending, as a hole in a garment; also, that which is to be darned; as, a bundle of *darning*.

därn'ing=nee"dle, *n.* 1. A needle having an eye large enough to receive yarn, etc., used for darning.

2. A dragon-fly having a slender body.

dȧ-rō'gȧ, dȧ-rō'ghȧ, *n.* [Hind. *daroga*, from Per. *daroga*, a manager, superintendent.] A name given in India to a native chief of any of the various departments; a superintendent; a manager; a chief of police.

dȧ-rọọ', *n.* [Egypt.] *Ficus Sycomorus*, the sycamore of Egypt.

därr, *n.* The black tern of Europe.

dar'raign, dar'rain (*or* dar-rān'), *v.t.* Same as *Deraign*. [Obs.]

dar'rein (-rin), *a.* [OFr. *darrain*, last, from L. *de*, from, and *retro*, back.] In old law, last; as, *darrein* continuance, the last continuance.

därt, *n.* [ME. *dart*; OFr. *dart*, a dart.]

1. A pointed weapon, to be thrown by the hand; a short lance; any missile.

Time shall throw a *dart* at thee. —B. Jonson.

2. That which pierces or wounds; anything characteristic of a *dart*; a piercing look or word.

If there be such a *dart* in princes' frowns. —Shak.

3. The dace.

4. A spear given as a prize in running or other athletic exercises. [Obs.]

5. A sudden movement; as, to make a *dart* at anything.

6. In entomology, the sting of an insect.

7. In dressmaking, a seam uniting two edges from between which a gore has been cut, to make the garment fit the figure.

därt, *v.t.*; darted, *pt., pp.*; darting, *ppr.* To throw with a sudden thrust; as, to *dart* a javelin; to send; to emit; to shoot; as, the sun *darts* his beams on the earth.

därt, *v.i.* 1 To fly or shoot, as a dart; to fly rapidly.

2. To spring and run with velocity; to start suddenly and run; as, the deer *darted* from the thicket.

där'tärş, *n.* [Fr. *dartre*, tetter, ringworm.] A scab or ulcer under the skin of lambs.

därt'ẽr, *n.* 1. One who throws a dart.

2. One who or that which springs or darts forward.

3. *Plotus anhinga*, the snakebird or water-turkey, so named from the way it darts upon its prey.

4. *Toxotes jaculator*, the archer-fish.

5. A small American fresh-water fish of the family *Percidæ*, somewhat resembling the common yellow perch; so named from the rapidity with which it darts from its retreats when disturbed.

därt'ẽr=fish, *n.* Same as *Archer-fish*.

därt'ing-ly, *adv.* Rapidly; like a dart.

där'tle, *v.t.* and *v.i.* To shoot through; to dart repeatedly. [Rare.]

därt'=mọth, *n.* A moth of the genus *Agrotis*, the larvæ of which are cutworms.

där'toid, där-tō'iç, *a.* [Gr. *dartos*, skinned, and *eidos*, form.] Relating to the dartos; as, *dartoid* tissue.

där'tos, *n.* [Gr. *dartos*, skinned, from *derein*, to skin, flay.] A contractile, fibrous layer situated immediately beneath the skin of the scrotum.

där'tre (-tr), *n.* [Fr.] Herpes, or tetter; a term which has been used to designate almost all cutaneous diseases.

där'trous, *a.* [Fr. *dartreux*, scurvy, from *dartre*, tetter, ringworm.] Relating or subject to dartre or tetter; herpetic.

Dartrous diathesis; a diseased condition of the body tending to the development of various cutaneous affections, such as eczema.

därt'snāke, *n.* A serpent-like lizard of the genus *Acontias*, so called from its dartlike motions.

Där-win'i-ăn, *a.* Of or pertaining to Charles Darwin, a celebrated English naturalist.

Darwinian theory; a theory which treats of the evolution of all forms of living organisms from a few forms of primitive life or from one; the keynote of the theory being natural selection, or the survival of the fittest. This theory was propounded and defended by Darwin in 1859, in his work entitled "The Origin of Species," and later (1871) in "The Descent of Man."

Darwinian tubercle; a nodule on the edge of the external ear corresponding to the pointed portion of the ear of quadrupeds.

Där-win'i-ăn, *n.* A believer in the Darwinian theory.

Där-win'i-ăn-iṣm, *n.* Darwinism.

Där'win-iṣm, *n.* The doctrine or theory of evolution propounded and defended by Darwin; also, belief in or support of the Darwinian theory.

dāṣe, *v.t.* [Obs.] See *Daze*.

dash, *v.t.*; dashed (dasht), *pt., pp.*; dashing, *ppr.* [ME. *daschen*, to rush with violence, strike with violence, from Dan. *daske*, to slap, strike, beat.]

1. To throw hastily or violently; as, to *dash* one stone against another; to *dash* water on the head.

2. To strike or throw so as to shatter or destroy.

Thou shalt *dash* them in pieces like a potter's vessel. —Ps. ii. 9.

3. To bespatter; to sprinkle; to suffuse; as, to *dash* a garment with water; her face was *dashed* with blushes.

4. To mix and reduce or adulterate by throwing in another substance; to mingle; followed by *with*; as, to *dash* wine *with* water; the story is *dashed with* fables.

5. To confound; to confuse; to put to shame; to abash; to depress by shame or fear; as, he was *dashed* at the appearance of the judge.

6. To form, sketch, or write hastily; with *off*; as, to *dash off* an article for a newspaper.

7. To erase by a stroke; to strike out; with *out*; as, to *dash out* a line or word.

8. To strike violently and suddenly. [Obs.]

9. To thrust aside or out; to discourage; to frustrate; to blight; as, to *dash* one's hopes.

dash, *v.i.* To move rapidly; to rush violently and furiously; as, the waves *dashed* furiously along; he *dashed* here and there, through thick and thin.

dash, *n.* 1. Collision; a violent striking of two bodies; as, the *dash* of clouds.

2. Infusion; admixture, especially in small proportion; as, the wine has a *dash* of water.

Innocence with a *dash* of folly. —Addison.

3. A rushing, or onset, with violence; a short, quick movement; as, to make a *dash* upon the enemy.

4. A sudden check; frustration; abashment; as, his hopes met with a *dash*.

5. Capacity for prompt action; boldness; hence, spirit; liveliness; vivacity; as, the corps was distinguished for its *dash*.

6. A flourish; blustering parade; as, to make or cut a *dash*.

7. In writing or printing, a horizontal mark or line [—], indicating a break or stop in the sentence or a pause or division of the sentence. *Dashes* are also sometimes used instead of parentheses.

8. In music, (a) a small mark [ꜝ] denoting that the note over which it is placed is to be given the staccato effect; (b) a line drawn through a figure in thorough-bass, directing the note to be raised a semitone.

9. In racing, a single trial of speed; as, a hundred-yard *dash*.

10. A present or gratuity given to an African chief for permission to trade with the natives.

11. A dashboard.

12. In zoölogy, a mark commonly seen on the wings of lepidopterous insects.

dash'bōard, *n.* 1. A board placed on the fore part of a carriage, sleigh, or other vehicle, to protect the occupant from anything thrown by the horse's heels; called also *dasher* or *splash-board*.

2. In ships, (a) the float of a paddle-wheel; (b) a screen at the bow of a steam-tug to throw off the spray; a sprayboard.

dash'ẽr, *n.* 1. One who or that which dashes or agitates, as the float of a paddle-wheel, the plunger of a churn, etc.

2. A dashboard.

3. One who makes an ostentatious parade; a bold, showy man or woman. [Colloq.]

dash'ẽr=block, *n.* In ships, a small block fastened to the end of the spanker-gaff for reeving the ensign-halyards.

dash'guärd, *n.* The dashboard of a street-car which protects the platform from flying water, mud, or snow.

dash'ing, *a.* 1. Spirited; impetuous; as, a *dashing* attack.

2. Showy; ostentatious; as, a *dashing* girl.

dash'ing-ly, *adv.* Ostentatiously; showily. [Colloq.]

dash'iṣm, *n.* The character of being dashing. [Rare.]

dash'=lamp, *n.* A small lamp usually provided with a reflector, hung upon the dashboard of a vehicle.

dash'pot, *n.* In machinery, an apparatus for deadening the blow of any falling weight, and preventing any jar in the machinery, as in the valve-gear of an engine; also an apparatus for regulating the motion of an arc lamp and other electrical appliances.

dash'=rūle, *n.* In printing, a metallic rule for printing a dash.

dash'=wheel, *n.* A name given to two cylinders revolving against each other in water, used for washing calico.

dash'y, *a.* Calculated to catch the eye or to attract attention; showy; dashing. [Colloq.]

das'sy, *n.* [Native name.] *Hyrax capensis*, the southern rock-rabbit of the Cape of Good Hope.

das'tärd, *n.* [ME. *dastard*, a dullard, from Ice. *dæstr*, exhausted.] A coward; a poltroon; one who meanly shrinks from danger; a craven.

das'tärd, *a.* Cowardly; meanly shrinking from danger.

Curse on their *dastard* souls. —Addison.

das′tȧrd, *v.t.* 1. To make cowardly, intimidate; dispirit. [Rare.]

2. To call one dastard. [Rare.]

das′tȧrd-ize, *v.t.* To make cowardly.

das′tȧrd-li-ness, *n.* Cowardliness.

das′tȧrd-ly, *a.* Cowardly; meanly timid; base; sneaking.

das′tȧrd-ness, *n.* Cowardliness; mean timorousness.

das′tȧrd-y, *n.* Cowardliness; base timidity. [Rare.]

dȧs-tūr′, *n.* [Anglo-Ind.] 1. One of the priests, particularly a chief priest, of the Parsees; written also *destour*.

2. The commission or bribe paid to servants by native tradesmen in India, in order to secure the trade of employers or masters; also written *dustoor*.

das′we, *v.i.* [Obs.] See *Daze*.

das′y-. A combining form from Greek *dasys*, hairy, dense, thick.

dȧ-sym′e-tẽr, *n.* [*Dasy-*, and Gr. *metron*, a measure.] An instrument used in testing the density of gases.

das-y-pæ′dăl, *a.* Dasypædic.

Das-y-pæ′dēs, *n.pl.* [*Dasy-*, and Gr. *pais*, *paidos*, a child.] A division of birds, the *Ptilopædes* or the *Præcoces*, including the common fowls and ducks.

das-y-pæ′dic, *a.* Relating to the *Dasypædes*.

Das-y-pod′i-dæ, *n.pl.* A South American family of armadillos, typical of this variety of edentate quadrupeds. It includes four subfamilies, the typical one being *Dasypodinæ*.

dȧ-syp′o-dine, *a.* [*Dasy-*, and Gr. *pous*, *podos*, foot.] Relating to or characteristic of the family *Dasypodidæ*, or the subfamily *Dasypodinæ*.

dȧ-syp′ō-doid, *a.* Same as *Dasypodine*.

das′y-tēs, *n.* [L., from Gr. *dasytēs*, hairiness, roughness, from *dasys*, hairy, rough.] In zoölogy, hairiness.

das′y-ūre, *n.* [*Dasy-*, and Gr. *oura*, tail.] An Australian and Tasmanian animal of the genus *Dasyurus* of which there are several species; especially, *Dasyurus maculatus*, a small spotted marsupial.

das-y-ū′rine, *a.* Pertaining to or characteristic of the dasyures.

dā′tȧ, *n.*, pl. of *datum*.

dāt′ȧ-ble, *a.* Capable of being dated.

dȧ-tā′ri-ȧ, *n.* [LL., from L. *datum*, a date.] The papal office of the chancery at Rome, from which all bulls, favors, and dispensations are issued.

dā′tȧ-ry, *n.* [From LL. *dataria*, the office or business of a datary, from L. *datum*, a date.]

1. A high officer of the chancery of Rome, who affixes the *datum Romæ* (given at Rome) to the pope's bulls.

2. The employment of a datary.

dāte, *n.* [ME. *date*; OFr. *date*, the fruit of the date-palm; L. *dactylus*; Gr. *daktylos*, a date, lit. a finger, so named from its shape.] The fruit of the date-palm, *Phœnix dactylifera*, used extensively as an article of food. In shape it somewhat resembles an olive, and inside is a hard kernel deeply grooved on one side.

dāte, *v.t.*; dated, *pt.*, *pp.*; dating, *ppr.* 1. To write or note the time of, as when a letter is written, or a writing executed; as, to *date* a letter.

2. To note or fix the time of, as of an event or transaction; as, to *date* the fulfilment of a prophecy.

dāte, *v.i.* 1. To reckon.

> We *date* from the late era of about six thousand years. —Bentley.

2. To begin; to have origin.

> The Batavian republic *dates* from the successes of the French arms. —Everett.

3. To have a date; as, the letter *dates* from Chicago.

dāte, *n.* [ME. date; OFr. *date*, date; L. *datum*, neut. of *datus*, pp. of *dare*, to give; the first word in Roman letters or documents, giving the place and time of writing, as *datum Romæ*, given at Rome.]

1. That addition to a writing or inscription which specifies the year, month, and day when it was given or executed. In letters, it names the time when they are written or sent; in deeds, contracts, wills, and other papers, it specifies the time of execution, and, usually, when they are to take effect and operate on the rights of persons. To the *date* is usually added the name of the place where the writing is executed, and this is sometimes included in the term *date*.

2. The time when any event happens, when anything is transacted, or when it is to be done; as, the *date* of a battle; the *date* of Cæsar's arrival in Britain.

3. End; conclusion. [Rare.]

4. Duration; continuance; as, ages of endless *date*.

5. An allotted or assigned period of time; as, his *date* has expired.

6. Age; the period of time during which one has lived or anything has existed; as, his *date* is sixty.

7. A period of time in general; as, at an early *date*.

Out of date; behind the times; old-fashioned.

To bear date; see under *Bear*, v.t.

To make a date; to make an appointment or engagement.

Up to date; brought up to the present; strictly modern.

dāte′less, *a.* Having no date; having no fixed term or limit; incapable of being dated; so old as to be beyond date; neither divisible by dates nor marked by events.

dāte′-line, *n.* An established imaginary boundary-line (180° from Greenwich) on the earth's surface, between neighboring regions, where the reckoning of the calendar day changes.

dāte′-pălm, *n.* The palm which bears the date, and most productive in northern Africa and southwestern Asia. Its stem shoots up to a height of 60 or 80 feet, without branch or division, and of nearly the same thickness throughout its length. From the summit it throws out a magnificent crown of large feather-shaped leaves, and a number of spadices, each of which in the female plant bears a bunch of from 180 to 200 dates, each bunch weighing from 20 to 25 pounds.

Date-palm (*Phœnix dactylifera*).

dāte′-plum, *n.* The edible fruit of various species of the genus *Diospyros*; also, any one of the trees themselves.

dāt′ẽr, *n.* 1. One who or that which dates.

2. [Obs.] See *Datary*.

dāte′-shell, *n.* A bivalve shell of the genus *Lithodomus*, so named from its resemblance to a date.

dāte′-tree, *n.* The date-palm.

dath′ō-līte, *n.* See *Datolite*.

Dȧ-tis′cȧ, *n.* [L.] A genus of tall exogenous herbs of the family *Datiscaceæ*, embracing only two species, *Datisca glomerata* of southern California and *Datisca cannabina* of southern Europe.

dȧ-tis′cin, *n.* [From *Datisca*.] In chemistry, a substance having the appearance of grape-sugar, first extracted by Braconnot from the leaves of *Datisca cannabina*. It has been used as a yellow dye.

dȧ-tī′si, *n.* In logic, one of the valid moods. [See *Mood*.]

dā′tive, *a.* [L. *dativus*, relating to giving; in LL. *casus dativus*, or *dativus* alone, the dative case, from *datus*, pp. of *dare*, to give.]

1. In grammar, a term applied to the case of nouns which usually follows verbs or other parts of speech that express giving, or some act directed *to* an object. In English, this relation is expressed by *to* or *for*.

2. In law, (a) capable of being given or disposed of at pleasure; being in one's gift; (b) removable, in distinction from *perpetual*; said of an officer; (c) given or appointed by a magistrate or court of justice, in distinction from what is given by law or by a testator; as, in Scots law, an executor *dative*, whose office is equivalent to that of an administrator.

dā′tive, *n.* The dative case.

dā′tive-ly, *adv.* As a dative; in the dative case.

dat′ō-līte, dath′ō-līte, *n.* [Gr. *dateisthai*, to divide, and *lithos*, stone.] The siliceous borate of lime, a mineral of two subspecies, the common and the botryoidal.

dat′tŏck, *n.* [W. African name.] *Detarium Senegalense*, a tropical African tree of the bean family. The wood is hard and resembles mahogany in color.

dā′tum, *n.*; *pl.* **dā′tȧ**. [L. *datum*, a gift, present, from neut. of *datus*, pp. of *dare*, to give.]

1. Something given, granted, or admitted; a premise upon which something can be argued or inferred; usually in the plural; as, the problem could not be solved, owing to insufficient *data*.

2. [*pl.*] In mathematics, certain relations or quantities, given or known, from which unknown quantities are determined.

dā′tum-līne, *n.* In civil engineering, the horizontal or base line of a section, from which the heights and depths are reckoned or measured.

dā′tum-plāne, *n.* 1. In craniometry, an assumed horizontal plane, from which measurements of the skull are determined.

2. In engineering, the horizontal plane forming a basis for measuring heights and depths.

Dā-tū′rȧ, *n.* [L., from Hind. *dhatūrā*, a plant.] A genus of poisonous plants of several species, belonging to the nightshade family, and having large funnel-shaped flowers possessing a disagreeable odor. *Datura Stramonium*, the thorn-apple, having strong narcotic properties, is the commonest species.

dā-tū′rine, *n.* A poisonous alkaloid found in the thorn-apple; called also *atropin*.

dąub, *v.t.*; daubed, *pt.*, *pp.*; daubing, *ppr.* [ME. *dauben*, *dawben*, to daub; OFr. *dauber*, to whiten, whitewash; L. *dealbare*, to whiten, whitewash; *de*, intens., and *albus*, white.]

1. To smear with soft, adhesive matter; to plaster; to cover with mud, slime, or other soft substance; to besmear; to soil.

2. To paint coarsely.

> If a picture is *daubed* with many bright colors, the vulgar admire it. —Watts.

3. To cover with something gross or specious; to disguise with an artificial covering.

> So smooth he *daubed* his vice with show of virtue. —Shak.

4. To lay or put on without taste; to deck awkwardly or ostentatiously. [Rare.]

> Let him be *daubed* with lace. —Dryden.

5. To flatter grossly. [Obs.]

dąub, *v.i.* To practise gross flattery; to play the hypocrite.

dąub, *n.* 1. A viscous adhesive application; a smear.

2. A coarse painting.

3. An inferior kind of mortar; plaster made of mud.

4. A smearing stroke. [Scot.]

dąub′ẽr, *n.* 1. One who or that which daubs; particularly, an unskilful painter.

2. A low and gross flatterer.

3. In copperplate printing, a device consisting of rags firmly tied together, and covered with a piece of canvas, for inking plates.

4. One who builds walls with clay or mud mixed with straw.

5. A mud-wasp; so named from the manner in which it daubs mud in building its nest.

dąub′ẽr-y, dąub′ry, *n.* 1. A daubing.

2. Anything artful; trickery. [Obs.]

dąub′ing, *n.* 1. The act of one who daubs; anything daubed.

2. A coat of coarse plaster applied to a wall to give it the appearance of stone.

3. Gross flattery.

4. Coarse painting.

5. In currying, any mixture of an oily nature rubbed into the leather.

dąu-bree′līte, *n.* [From *Daubrée*, a French mineralogist, and Gr. *lithos*, stone.] A metallic sulphid of chromium, a rare mineral of a black color occurring in certain meteoric irons.

dąu-brē′ite, *n.* [Named from G. A. *Daubrée*, a Fr. mineralogist.] Bismuth oxychlorid, found in a free state in nature, occurring either in compact or earthy masses of a yellowish color, in Chile.

dąub′ry, *n.* See *Daubery*.

dąub′y, *a.* Viscous; glutinous; slimy; adhesive.

Dąu′cus, *n.* [L., from *daucus*, *daucum*; Gr. *daukos*, *daukon*, a carrot-like plant growing in Crete.] A genus of umbelliferous plants of several species, with spinous fruit of a somewhat compressed ovate or oblong form. *Daucus carota*, the cultivated carrot, is the best-known species.

dąud, *n.* Same as second *Dad*, n.

dąugh′tẽr (dą′), *n.* [ME. *doughter*; AS. *dohtor*, daughter, prob. from Sans. *duhitar*, daughter, lit. milker, from *duh*, milk.]

1. The female offspring of a man or woman; a female child of any age.

2. A daughter-in-law; a son's wife.

3. A woman; a female descendant of any generation.

> Dinah went out to see the *daughters* of the land. —Gen. xxxiv. 1.

4. A female in relation to her native country; as, a *daughter* of Italy.

5. A term of affection and kindness, as given to a woman by an elder or spiritual teacher.

> *Daughter*, be of good comfort.—Matt. ix. 22.

6. Anything regarded as feminine respecting its origin or function; as, French is the *daughter* of Latin.

Eve's daughters; all women.

dąugh′tẽr, *a.* Having the natural characteristics of a daughter; specifically, in biology, related in the first degree or generation.

dąugh′tẽr-cell, *n.* In biology, one of the cells formed by the division of another cell.

dąugh′tẽr-in-ląw, *n.*; *pl.* **dąugh′tẽrs-in-ląw**. The wife of a son.

daugh'tēr-li-ness, *n.* The state of a daughter; the conduct becoming a daughter.

daugh'tēr-ly, *a.* Becoming a daughter; dutiful; as, *daughterly* affection.

dauk, *v.t.* See *Dawk*.

daun, *n.* An obsolete form of *dan*, a title of respect.

daun'dēr, *v.i.* Same as *Dander*.

däunt, *v.t.*; daunted, *pt.*, *pp.*; daunting, *ppr.* [ME. *daunten*; OFr. *danter*, *donter*, to daunt, subdue, tame, from L. *domitare*, to tame, break in, freq. of *domare*, to tame, subdue.]

1. To repress or subdue courage; to intimidate; to dishearten; to check by fear of danger.

> Some presences *daunt* and discourage us. —Glanville.

2. To conquer; to subdue. [Obs.]

Syn.—Intimidate, dismay, frighten, dishearten, cow, appal, terrify.

däunt'ēr, *n.* One who daunts.

däunt'less, *a.* Bold; fearless; not timid; not discouraged; as, a *dauntless* spirit.

däunt'less-ly, *adv.* In a dauntless manner.

däunt'less-ness, *n.* The state or quality of being dauntless.

dau'phin, *n.* [Fr., from OFr. *dauphin*, *daulphin*, the dauphin, from L. *delphinus*, a dolphin.]

1. A name assumed about the middle of the ninth century by the lord of the French province of Dauphiny, which was bequeathed by Humbert II. to the king of France, in 1349, on condition that the heir of the throne should bear the title of *Dauphin* of Viennois.

2. The eldest son of the king of France prior to the revolution of 1830.

dau'phïne, dau'phin-ess, *n.* The wife of a dauphin.

dauw (da), *n.* [South African D. form of native name.] *Equus burchelli*, one of the South African zebras; Burchell's zebra. It is a very beautiful animal and somewhat resembles the quagga.

dav'en-pōrt, *n.* 1. A kind of small ornamented writing-desk used as an article of furniture in a boudoir or parlor.

2. An upholstered couch with high arms and back.

Dā-vid'ic, Dā-vid'ic-ăl, *a.* Of or pertaining to David, king of Israel.

Dā'vid-ist, *n.* 1. A follower of David of Dirant, Belgium, who held extreme pantheistic views. His book "Quaternuli" was burned in 1209, and his followers scattered.

2. A follower of David George or Joris, of Delft, Holland, who founded an Anabaptist sect in the sixteenth century.

Dā'vid's-rōōt, *n.* The cahinca-root, of Brazil, used for snake-bites.

dav'it (*or* dā'vit), *n.* 1. One of two curved uprights of timber or iron projecting over the side or stern of a vessel, used for suspending, hoisting, or lowering a boat by means of sheave and pulley.

2. A beam formerly used on board ships, as a crane to hoist the flukes of the anchor to the top of the bow, without injuring the sides of the ship; called also a *fish-davit*.

Davits.

dā'vy, *n.* An affidavit. [Slang.]

dā'vy, *n.*; *pl.* **dā'vies**. A lamp invented by Sir Humphry Davy to protect miners from explosions of fire-damp; called also *Davy lamp* and *safety-lamp*.

Dā'vy Jōnes. A humorous name among seamen for the spirit of the sea, or sea-devil.

Davy Jones's locker; the ocean; specifically, the ocean regarded as the grave of all who perish at sea.

dā'vyne, *n.* [From Sir Humphry *Davy*.] A crystalline Vesuvian mineral resembling nephelite.

dā'vy-um, *n.* [From Sir Humphry *Davy*.] A rare metal of the platinum group discovered by Sergius Kern of St. Petersburg, in 1877, in separating the metals rhodium and iridium from some platinum ores.

daw, *n.* [ME. *dawe*; name probably imitative.]

1. A jackdaw, a bird allied to the crows.

2. A sluggard. [Prov. Eng. and Scot.]

3. A simpleton. [Prov. Eng.]

daw, *v.i.* and *v.t.* I. *v.i.* To dawn. [Obs.]

II. *v.t.* 1. To daunt; to frighten. [Obs.]

2. To rouse; to cheer. [Obs.]

daw'dle, *v.i.* and *v.t.*; dawdled, *pt.*, *pp.*; dawdling, *ppr.* [From Scot. *daidle*, to walk with tottering steps, to daddle.]

I. *v.i.* To waste time; to trifle.

II. *v.t.* To waste by trifling; with *away*; as, to *dawdle away* an afternoon.

daw'dle, *n.* A trifler; a dawdler.

daw'dlēr, *n.* One who dawdles; a trifler; an idler.

daw'dy, *n.* Same as *Dowdy*.

dawe, *n.* Day. [Obs.]

daw'ish, *a.* Like a daw.

dawk, *n.* Same as *Dak*.

dawk, *n.* [A variant of *dalk*, from ME. *dale*, *dal*, a hollow; AS. *dæl*, a pit, hole, hollow.] A hollow or incision, as in timber.

dawk, *v.t.* To cut or mark with an incision.

dawm, *n.* [Hind. *dam*.] An East Indian copper coin of the value of one and one-fifth cents.

dawn, *v.i.*; dawned, *pt.*, *pp.*; dawning, *ppr.* [ME. *dawnen*, *dawen*, to become day; AS. *dagian*, to become day, from *dæg*, day.]

1. To begin to grow light in the morning; to grow light; as, the day *dawns*; the morning *dawns*.

2. To begin to open or expand; to begin to show intellectual light, or knowledge; as, the genius of the youth begins to *dawn*.

3. To begin to appear; to begin to become visible in consequence of more light shining upon; as, the truth *dawns* upon me.

dawn, *n.* 1. The break of day; the first appearance of light in the morning.

2. First opening or expansion; first appearance; beginning; rise; as, the *dawn* of a new era; the *dawn* of time.

High dawn; daybreak first seen above a bank of clouds.

Low dawn; daybreak seen near the horizon.

dawn'ing, *n.* Dawn.

daw'pāte, *n.* A simpleton; a fool.

daw'sŏn-ite, *n.* [Named after J. W. *Dawson*, of Montreal.] A hydrous carbonate of aluminium and sodium, crystallizing in the monoclinic system and found chiefly near Montreal and in Italy.

dāy, *n.* [ME. *day*; AS. *dæg*, day.]

1. That part of the time of the earth's revolution on its axis, in which a given area of its surface is presented to the sun; the part of the twenty-four hours when it is light; or the space of time between the rising and setting of the sun; light; sunshine; called the *artificial day*.

2. The whole time or period of one revolution of the earth on its axis, being the interval between two successive transits of the sun over a given meridian, or twenty-four hours; called the *natural*, *astronomical*, or *solar day*. In this sense, the day may commence at any period of the revolution. The Babylonians began the day at sunrise; the Jews, at sunset; the Egyptians, at midnight, as do most of the nations of Europe and America. This day, in reference to civil transactions, is called the *civil day*. Thus the day when a legal instrument is dated begins and ends at midnight.

3. In industry, the number of hours devoted to labor; as, an eight-hour *day*.

4. Time specified; any period of time distinguished from another; age; time with reference to the existence of a person or thing; as, he was a useful man in his *day*.

5. In architecture, the space between mullions in a window.

6. The contest of a *day*; battle; issue of a combat; as, to win the *day*.

Day by day; daily; every day; each day in succession; continually; without intermission of a day.

Day in court; the day for the appearance of parties to a suit.

Day letter; a telegram of more than the usual ten-word length now sent at special low rates, taken by the carrying company subject to delay in transmission.

Days in banc; in English law, set days for return of writs and appearance of parties to suits. [See *Banc*.]

Days of grace; the three days after the date of maturity specified in a note which the law allows for its payment.

Days of obligation; in the Roman Catholic church, festival days on which attendance at mass is obligatory.

Day's work; among seamen, (a) the reckoning of a ship's course and distance covered for twenty-four hours; (b) among landsmen, a day's work is regulated by custom and, in recent years, largely by the action of labor-unions, it being, in the United States, generally covered by a period of eight hours; in the latter sense also called a *working-day*.

From day to day; without certainty of continuance; temporarily.

Independence day; in the United States, the Fourth of July.

Jewish day; the interval from sunset to sunset.

Lunar day; see under *Lunar*.

Rainy day; a day of adversity or misfortune.

Sidereal day; see under *Sidereal*.

The day; contemporaneous time; as, the best thought of *the day*.

Tidal day; see under *Tidal*.

To name the day; to fix the date, especially that of marriage.

To pass the time of day; to greet; as, "Good morning."

Day'ak, *n.* Same as *Dyak*.

dāy'bēam, *n.* The light of the day.

dāy'-bed, *n.* A bed used for idleness, indulgence, or rest during the day; a lounge. [Obs.]

dāy'ber"ry, *n.* In botany, the English popular name for the wild gooseberry.

dāy'-blīnd"ness, *n.* A defect of the eye by which vision is obscured by daylight; called also *night-sight*, and, in medicine, *nyctalopia*.

dāy'book, *n.* A journal of accounts; a book in which are recorded the debits and credits or accounts of the day.

dāy'brēak, *n.* The dawn or first appearance of light in the morning.

dāy'-cōal, *n.* In mining, the upper stratum of coal.

dāy'drēam, *n.* A vision to the waking senses; an air-castle.

dāy'drēam"y, *a.* Addicted to the indulgence of vain fancy or reverie.

dāy'flow"ēr, *n.* The popular name of a genus of plants, the *Commelina*, whose flowers wither in a day.

dāy'flȳ, *n.* In entomology, the popular name of those neuropterous insects which belong to the genus *Ephemera*. They are called *dayflies* because, though they may exist in the larval and pupal state for several years, in their perfect form they exist only from a few hours to a few days, taking no food, but only propagating their species and then dying.

Dayfly (*Ephemera vulgata*).

dāy'-hōle, *n.* In coal mining, a level that opens at the surface.

dāy'-house, *n.* In astrology, the house that is ruled by a planet by day; as, Libra is the *day-house* of Venus, etc.

dāy'-lā"bŏr, *n.* Labor hired or performed by the day.

dāy'-lā"bŏr-ēr, *n.* One who works by the day.

dāy'light, *n.* 1. The light of the day; the light of the sun, as opposed to that of the moon or of a lamp or candle.

2. The beginning of the day; dawn; as, the fire lasted until *daylight*.

3. The American popular name for the sand-flounder or spotted turbot, a fish so thin as to be nearly transparent.

4. The empty space at the top of a drinking-glass, as usually filled, but forbidden in toasts; hence, "no *daylights*" is a call for bumpers. [Slang.]

5. [*pl.*] The eyes. [Slang.]

To let the daylight into or *through one*; to shoot or stab one.

dāy'-lil"y, *n.* In botany, (a) a garden-plant of the genus *Hemerocallis*, whose tawny or yellow flowers last but one day; (b) the common lily-wort of the genus *Funkia*.

dāy'-lōng, *a.* Lasting throughout the day.

dāy'-man, *n.* One who hires by the day; a day-laborer.

dāy'māre, *n.* In medicine, an incubus or chest pressure occurring in the daytime, during waking hours.

dāy'-net, *n.* A net used in catching small birds. [Obs.]

dāy'-nūrs"ēr-y, *n.* A place where small children are cared for during the day.

dāy'-owl, *n.* A hawk-owl, *Surnia ulula*, the most diurnal of the owl family.

dāy'-peep, *n.* The dawn.

dāy'-rōōm, *n.* In penal institutions, the ward for the use of prisoners during the day.

dāy'-schol"ăr, *n.* 1. One who attends a day-school.

2. A pupil of a boarding-school who lodges elsewhere.

dāy'-schōōl, *n.* A school whose sessions are held by day and which does not board the pupils.

dāy'shine, *n.* Daylight. [Rare.]

dāy'-sight, *n.* Night-blindness.

dāys'man, *n.* An umpire or arbiter; a mediator.

dāy'-stär, *n.* 1. The morning star; the star which precedes the morning light.

2. The sun, as the orb of day.

3. Figuratively, an emblem of hope or bright prospects.

dāy'-tāle, *a.* and *n.* I. *a.* Hired by the day.

II. *n.* The work of a day.

dāy'time, *n.* The interval during which the sun is above the horizon.

dāy'-wŏrk, *n.* Work by the day; day-labor.

dāze, *v.t.*; dazed, *pt.*, *pp.*; dazing, *ppr.* [ME. *dasen*, to stupefy; Ice. *dasask*, to become weary.]

1. To confuse, as by a glaring light; to stun, as by a blow; to stupefy, as by liquor.

2. To spoil, as in cooking bread or meat. [Prov. Eng.]

dāze, *n.* 1. The condition of being dazed.

2. In mining, a glittering or shining stone.

daz'zle, *v.t.*; dazzled, *pt.*, *pp.*; dazzling, *ppr.*

1. To overpower with light; to hinder distinct vision of by intense light; to cause to shake; to render unsteady, as the sight.

2. To strike or surprise with a bright or intense light; to dim or blind by a glare of light, or by splendor, in a literal or figurative sense.

daz′zle, *v.i.* 1. To be overpowered by light; to shake or be unsteady; to waver, as the sight.

2. To be intensely bright.

3. To arouse profound admiration, as by brilliant conversation.

daz′zle, *n.* A brilliant light; brightness; display.

daz′zle-ment, *n.* The act, power, or effect of dazzling.

daz′zling-ly, *adv.* In a dazzling manner.

de-, *prefix.* [ME. *de*; OFr. *de*; L. *de*, from, away from, of, concerning.] A combining form of L. origin denoting the departure or separation of an object from a thing to which it was originally attached, signifying from, away from, down from, out of, of, about, concerning, or with a privative force, as in *decompose*.

dēa′çŏn, *n.* [ME. *deken*, *dekyn*; AS. *deacon*; LL. *diaconus*, a deacon; Gr. *diakonos*, a servant, a messenger, a deacon.]

1. A person in the lowest degree of holy orders. The office of *deacon* was instituted by the apostles, Acts vi. 1-6.

2. In the Roman Catholic church, the office of the *deacon* is to assist at the altar.

3. In the Church of England, the lowest of the three orders of priesthood, these being bishops, priests and *deacons*.

4. In the Presbyterian church, the official who attends to secular interests.

5. In the independent churches, the deacon's office is secular, with the addition that he distributes the bread and wine to the communicants.

Deacon, from Cloisters, Liége, 1460.

6. In Scotland, the president of an incorporated trade, who is chairman of its meetings.

dēa′çŏn, *v.t.*; deaconed, *pt.*, *pp.*; deaconing, *ppr.* 1. To ordain as deacon.

2. To read aloud, as two lines of a hymn before the congregation sings it; to line out.

3. To deceive by placing the best uppermost, as fruit in a measure. [Slang.]

4. To adulterate or weaken; as, to *deacon* wine. [Slang.]

5. To kill for food while too young; as, to *deacon* veal. [Slang.]

dēa′çŏn-ess, *n.* [LL. *diaconissa*, f. of *diaconus*, a deacon.]

1. A member of the Institution of Deaconesses, an order devoted to charitable work.

2. In the Congregational church, a woman appointed as a helper or assistant.

3. In the Anglican and Protestant Episcopal churches, a woman church-worker appointed by a bishop.

4. In the primitive church, one of an order of women appointed to minister to the sick and assist in spiritual work.

dēa′çŏn-hood, *n.* The condition of being a deacon; the office and duties of a deacon.

dēa′çŏn-ship, dēa′çŏn′ry, *n.* The office, dignity, or ministry of a deacon or deaconess.

dead (ded), *a.* [ME. *ded*, *deed*; AS. *dead*, dead.]

1. Deprived or destitute of life; in that state in which the organs of motion and life have ceased permanently to perform their functions.

2. Without life; inanimate; lifeless; unproductive; used of both physical and spiritual life; as, a *dead* tree; *dead* faith.

3. Imitating death; deathlike; deep or sound; as, a *dead* sleep.

4. Perfectly still; inert; motionless as death; as, a *dead* calm; a *dead* weight.

5. Incapable of transmitting sound; nonresonant; dull; heavy; as, a *dead* sound; a *dead* floor.

6. Unemployed; useless; unprofitable; unsalable; unproductive; as, *dead* capital; *dead* stock.

7. Dull; gloomy; still; not enlivened; as, a *dead* social season.

8. Dull; without natural force or efficacy; not lively or brisk; as, a *dead* fire.

9. Perfect or complete; assured; unerring; unfailing; as, a *dead* level; a *dead* certainty; a *dead* shot.

10. In printing, type or slugs that are ready for the distributer or melting-pot; as, *dead* matter.

11. In law, cut off from the rights of a citizen; deprived of the power of enjoying the rights of property; as, one banished or imprisoned for life is civilly *dead*.

12. In machinery, not transmitting power or motion; as, a *dead* wire; *dead* steam.

13. Without gloss or luster; dull; as, a *dead* painting; a *dead* color.

Dead ahead; straight ahead.

Dead beat; a contemptible cheat or sponge. [Slang.]

Dead calm; entire absence of wind.

Dead cotton; in dyeing, the unripe cotton fibers that cannot be dyed.

Dead drunk; so drunk as to be helpless.

Dead floor; in architecture, a floor through which sound cannot pass.

Dead freight; in maritime law, the sum paid for unoccupied space in a chartered vessel.

Dead heat; a heat in a race in which the contestants finish even.

Dead horse; work done in payment of debt, as for wages advanced. [Slang.]

Dead language; a language which is no longer spoken or in common use by a people, and known only in writings, as the Hebrew, Greek, and Latin.

Dead letter; (a) an uncalled-for letter sent to the dead-letter office; (b) a statute that is neither enforced nor repealed.

Dead-letter office; the department of the general post-office in which dead letters are opened, and from which they are returned to the writers, if possible.

Dead lift; a lift without mechanical aid; a difficult task.

Dead load; in civil engineering, an unvarying load, such as the weight of a structure, as distinguished from such varying weight as that of traffic, wind-pressure, etc.

Dead men; (a) nautically, an old name for gasket-ends or reef-ends not tucked in when furling the sail; (b) the empty bottles at a banquet's end. [Slang.]

Dead on end; nautically, directly opposing the ship's course; as, the wind is *dead on end*.

Dead set; (a) anxious for or determined upon something, as a journey; (b) the pose of a dog indicating game; (c) a scheme to cheat in a game. [Slang.]

Dead workings; in mining, workings in dead-ground.

Syn.—Deceased, extinct, defunct, inanimate, lifeless.

dead (ded), *n.* 1. One who is dead; those who have died; as, the *dead* lie sleeping.

2. A time of profound gloom or stillness; as, the *dead* of winter; the *dead* of night.

3. Among students, failure in recitation. [Slang.]

4. [*pl.*] In mining, unproductive rock; attle.

dead, *v.t.* and *v.i.* I. *v.t.* To deprive of life, force, or vigor. [Obs.]

II. *v.i.* To lose life or force. [Obs.]

dead, *adv.* In a deathlike degree; absolutely; completely. [Colloq.]

dead′-an″gle, *n.* In fortification, any space that is not visible from the parapet or that cannot be defended from behind it.

dead′bēat, *a.* and *n.* I. *a.* Beating without recoil; free from oscillation.

II. *n.* A deadbeat escapement.

dead′-block, *n.* One of two iron or wooden blocks that serve as buffers at the end of a freight-car.

dead′bọrn, *a.* Stillborn.

dead′-cen″tẽr, *n.* In mechanics, the condition of a steam-engine's connecting-rod and crank-axle being in a straight line; called a *stroke-end* or a *dead-point*.

dead′-clōthes̱, *n.pl.* Clothes appropriate for a corpse.

dead′-cŏl″ŏr-ing, *n.* In painting, the first layer of colors, usually some shade of gray, on which are superimposed the finishing colors which give life and beauty to the picture.

dead′-dip″ping, *n.* The process of giving to brass a dead, pale color, by dipping in acid.

dead′-dōor, *n.* In shipbuilding, a door fitted to the outside of a ship's quarter, to keep out the sea in case the quarter-gallery should be carried off.

dead′en, *v.t.*; deadened, *pt.*, *pp.*; deadening, *ppr.* [ME. *deden*; AS. *dydan*, to kill, deprive of life.]

1. To deprive of a portion of vigor, force, or sensation; to abate (vigor or action); as, to *deaden* the force of a ball; to *deaden* the natural powers or feelings.

2. To girdle with incisions, as a tree; to make nonconductive of sound, as a floor or wall.

3. To retard; to lessen velocity or motion of; as, to *deaden* a ship's way.

4. To diminish spirit; to make vapid or spiritless; as, to *deaden* wine or beer.

5. To deprive of gloss or brilliancy; as, to *deaden* gilding by a coat of size.

dead′en-ẽr, *n.* One who or that which deadens.

dead′eye (ded′ī), *n.* On shipboard, a round, flattish, wooden block, encircled by a rope, or an iron band, and pierced with three holes, to receive the lanyard; used to extend the shrouds and stays, and for other purposes.

dead′fall, *n.* 1. A trap supporting a weight intended to fall upon and crush the game sought.

2. Fallen trees and undergrowth that make a matted mass.

3. A drinking- or gambling-house of bad repute. [Colloq.]

dead′-flat, *n.* In shipbuilding, a ship's widest cross-section; the midship frame.

dead′-ground, *n.* In mining, unproductive ground which must be worked through to reach ore-bearing rock; country-rock.

dead′-hand, *n.* In law, inalienable tenure; mortmain.

dead′head (ded′hed), *n.* 1. In founding, the extra length given to a casting, as a gun; sprue; sullage.

2. The tailstock of a lathe.

3. A rough block of wood used as an anchor buoy.

dead′head, *v.t.* and *v.i.*; deadheaded, *pt.*, *pp.*; deadheading, *ppr.* I. *v.t.* To furnish free admission or transportation; as, to *deadhead* a traveler.

II. *v.i.* To enjoy or use without payment, as hotels, theaters, trains, etc.

dead′head, *n.* One who receives free accommodations for which payment is usually required.

dead′-heärt″ed, *a.* Faint-hearted; listless.

dead′house, *n.* In hospitals, etc., a house or room in which the dead are placed temporarily; a morgue.

dead′latch, *n.* A latch made immovable by a detent, or catch.

dead′light, *n.* On shipboard, a strong shutter fitted to a window or porthole, to shut out water in stormy weather.

dead′-līne, *n.* In a military prison, a line bounding the prisoners' privilege; any line the crossing of which entails penalty, in times of war, often death.

dead′li-ness, *n.* The quality of being deadly.

dead′lock, *n.* 1. A lock so constructed that it must be worked on one side by a handle and on the other by a key.

2. A complete blocking or stoppage, resulting from lack of a majority vote; as, the *deadlock* of a jury or legislature.

dead′ly (ded′ly), *a.* 1. Capable of causing death; mortal; fatal; destructive; as, a *deadly* blow or wound.

2. Implacable; aiming to kill or destroy; as, a *deadly* enemy; *deadly* malice; a *deadly* feud.

3. Liable to death; mortal. [Obs.]

4. Bearing a resemblance to death; deathly.

5. Very great; excessive. [Colloq.]

A *deadly* number of pardons. —Pepys.

Deadly nightshade; see under *Nightshade*.

Syn.—Destructive, fatal, mortal.—*Deadly* is applied to what is productive of death; *mortal* to what terminates in or is liable to death; *fatal* applies not only to death, but to everything which may be of great mischief. A poison is *deadly*; a wound or a wounded part is *mortal*; a step in walking, or a step in one's conduct, may be *fatal*. Things only are *deadly*; creatures are *mortal*. Hatred is *deadly*; whatever has life is *mortal*. There may be remedies sometimes to counteract that which is *deadly*; but that which is *mortal* is past all cure; and that which is *fatal* cannot be retrieved.

dead′ly, *adv.* 1. In a manner resembling death; as, *deadly* pale or wan; mortally.

2. Implacably; destructively.

3. Very; extremely; excessively. [Colloq.]

dead′-man′s̱-hand′, *n.* 1. *Nephrodium Filix-mas*, the male fern.

2. *Laminaria digitata*, the devil's-apron.

dead′-märch, *n.* A piece of solemn music, played at a funeral; as, the *dead-march* from Handel's "Saul."

dead′-men′s̱-fin′gẽrs̱, *n.* 1. *Orchis maculata*, a species of the genus *Orchis*, having pale, hand-like tubers; also, any one of other species of the same genus.

2. *Alcyonium digitatum*, a polyp having a resemblance to the human hand.

dead′-men′s̱-līnes′, *n.* *Chorda filum*, a species of seaweed having cordlike fronds sometimes many feet in length.

dead′-nēap, *n.* The lowest point reached by a neap tide.

dead′ness, *n.* The state of being dead, in any sense.

dead′-net″tle, *n.* A name given to any one of the species of plants of the genus *Lamium*, from the resemblance of their leaves to those of the nettle; they are stingless, however; hence the name.

dead′-oil, *n.* An oil containing naphthalin, carbolic acid, etc., obtained in the distillation of coal-tar, and heavier than water.

dead′-pāy, *n.* In England, the continued pay of a deceased soldier or sailor, fraudulently drawn by the living. [Rare.]

dead′-plāte, *n.* A flat iron plate sometimes attached to the bars of a furnace in order to first coke the bituminous coal before it is finally consumed as fuel.

dead′-pledġe (ded′plej), *n.* A mortgage or pawning of lands or goods, or the thing pawned.

dead′-point, *n.* See *Dead-center*.

dead′-reck″ŏn-ing, *n.* In navigation, the judgment or calculation of a ship's position at sea independent of astronomical observations, and simply from the distance she has run by the log, and the courses steered by the compass, due allowances being made for drift, leeway, etc.

dead′=rīṣe, *n.* In shipbuilding, the distance between the top of the keel and a horizontal line joining the top of the floor-timbers amidships.

dead′=rīṣ″ing, *n.* Same as *Dead-rise.*

deadṣ (dedz), *n.pl.* See *Dead*, n. 4.

dead′=shēave, *n.* In ships, a scored aperture in the heel of a topmast, through which a second top-tackle can be rove.

dead′=shōre, *n.* A piece of wood built up vertically in a wall which has been broken through.

dead′=smạll, *n.* In coal-mining, the smallest screened coal.

dead′=strōke, *a.* and *n.* I. *a.* Without recoil, as certain power-hammers.

II. *n.* A stroke delivered, as by certain power-hammers, in which the recoil is resisted by a spring.

dead′=tŏngue (-tung), *n.* *Œnanthe crocata*, the water-hemlock, an umbelliferous plant of Europe.

dead′=wạ″tẽr, *n.* The water which eddies about the stern of a ship as she passes through the water; also called *eddy-water*.

dead′=weight (-wāt), *n.* 1. A heavy or oppressive burden.

2. A name given to an advance by the Bank of England to the government, on account of half-pay and pensions to retired officers of the army or navy.

3. The lading of a vessel when it consists of heavy goods; that portion of the cargo, as coal, iron, etc., which pays freight according to its weight and not its bulk.

4. In railroading, the weight of the rolling-stock as distinguished from the *live-weight* or load. [See *Dead load* under *Dead*, a.]

dead′=wind, *n.* A wind right against the ship, or that blowing from the very point toward which she is sailing.

dead′wood, *n.* 1. Blocks of timber laid upon the keel of a ship, particularly at the extremities, afore and abaft, to a considerable height one above another, and into which the two half-timbers are secured.

2. Useless material.

3. A buffer-block.

4. In bowling, the pins that have been knocked down.

To get the deadwood on one; to obtain the advantage over one. [Slang.]

dead′=wool, *n.* Wool taken from the skin of sheep which have been slaughtered or have died.

dead′=wŏrk, *n.* Work from which no direct profit is derived, but which is preliminary to that which is profitable; specifically, the work of opening a mine.

dead′wŏrks, *n.pl.* The parts of a ship which are above the surface of the water when the ballast or the cargo is on board; called also *upper works*.

deaf (def *or* dēf), *a.* [ME. *def*, *deef*; AS. *deaf*, deaf.]

1. Not perceiving sounds; not receiving impressions from sonorous bodies through the air; wanting the sense of hearing; having organs which do not perceive sounds; as, a *deaf* ear; a *deaf* man.

2. Not listening, or refusing to listen; not moved, persuaded or convinced; with *to*; as, *deaf to* all entreaties; *deaf to* argument.

3. Stifled; imperfect; obscurely heard. [Rare.]

A *deaf* noise of sounds that never cease. —Dryden.

4. Barren; blasted; as, a *deaf* field. [Obs. or Prov. Eng.]

deaf, *v.t.* To deafen. [Obs.]

deaf′=dumb″ness (-dum″ness), *n.* Dumbness or aphony arising from deafness, whether congenital or occurring during infancy.

deaf′en (def′en *or* dēf′en), *v.t.*; deafened, *pt.*, *pp.*; deafening, *ppr.* 1. To make deaf; to deprive of the power of hearing; to impair the organs of hearing of, so as to render them insensible to sounds.

2. To stun; to render incapable of perceiving sounds distinctly; as, *deafened* with clamor or tumult.

3. In architecture, to render impervious to sound, as a floor or partition, by means of sound-boarding or pugging.

deaf′en-ing, *n.* The act of putting in pugging to prevent the passage of sound through floors, partitions, etc.; also, the pugging itself.

deaf′ly, *adv.* Without sense of sounds; obscurely heard.

deaf′ly, *a.* Lonely. [Prov. Eng.]

deaf′=mūte, *n.* A deaf and dumb person, the dumbness resulting from deafness which has either existed from birth or from a very early period of the person's life.

deaf′=mūt″iṣm, *n.* 1. The condition of being a deaf-mute.

2. Any word, expression, or idiom peculiar to a deaf-mute, usually brought about by a transposition of letters; as, the writing of *stale* for *slate*; *kinfe* for *knife*.

deaf′ness (def′nes *or* dēf′nes), *n.* 1. Incapacity of perceiving sounds; the state of the organs

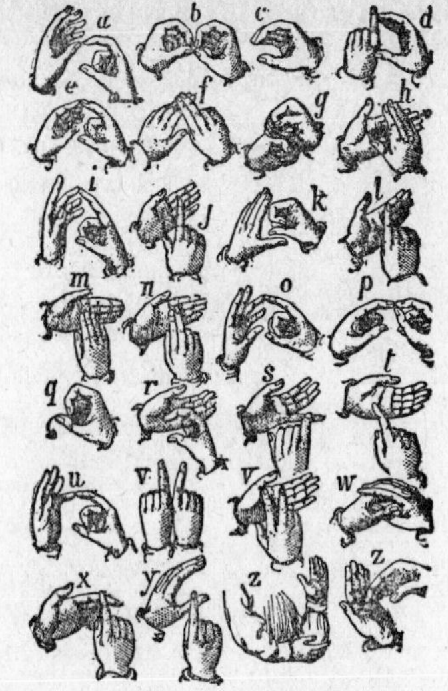

Deaf-mute Manual Alphabet.

which prevents the reception of auditory impressions.

2. Unwillingness to hear and regard; complete rejection of what is addressed to the ear and to the understanding.

Nervous deafness; deafness resulting from some derangement in the nervous system, particularly that of the auditory nerve.

dēal, *v.t.*; dealt (delt), *pt.*, *pp.*; dealing, *ppr.* [ME. *delen*; AS. *dælan*, to divide, share.] To divide; to part; to separate; hence, to divide in portions; to distribute; often followed by *out*.

And Rome *deals out* her blessings and her gold. —Tickell.

dēal, *v.i.* 1. To divide; to distribute in portions, as in card-playing.

2. To traffic; to trade; to do business; as, to *deal* in coffee; to *deal* with a merchant.

They buy and sell, they *deal* and traffic. —South.

3. To act between man and man; to intervene; to transact or negotiate between men.

He that *deals* between man and man, raiseth his own credit with both. —Bacon.

4. To behave well or ill; to act; to conduct oneself in relation to others; as, he *dealt* dishonestly in this matter.

5. To contend, in order to restrain, curb, or correct; as, to *deal* with one's temper.

6. To negotiate secretly and corruptly; to conspire.

dēal, *n.* [ME. *deel*, *dæl*; AS. *dæl*, a part, share.]

1. A division, part, or portion; hence, an indefinite quantity, degree, or extent; as, a *deal* of time and trouble. In general, the word is qualified by *great*; as, a *great deal* of labor. In the phrase, it is a *great deal* better, the true construction is, it is better *by a great deal*, that is, by a great part or difference.

2. The act, art, or practice, of dealing cards.

3. An understanding or scheme, usually of a secret nature, between business men or politicians, whereby a limited circle will profit. [U. S., Slang.]

dēal, *n.* [From D. *deel*, a board, plank, threshing-floor.]

1. The division of a piece of timber made by sawing; a board or plank. The name is chiefly applied to boards about seven inches in width and of various lengths exceeding six feet.

2. Wood from which *deals* are made.

dē-al′bāte, *v.t.* To whiten. [Obs.]

dē-al-bā′tion, *n.* The act of bleaching; a whitening. [Obs.]

dēal′=endṣ, *n.pl.* Boards or planks less than six feet in length. [Eng.]

dēal′ẽr, *n.* One who deals in anything; a trader; a trafficker; a shopkeeper; a broker; a merchant; as, a *dealer* in dry goods.

dēal′fish, *n.* *Trachypterus arcticus*, a fish found occasionally on the coasts of the Orkney and Shetland islands.

dēal′=frāme, *n.* A sawing-machine for cutting deals. [See *Log-frame.*]

dēal′ing, *n.* 1. The act of one who deals.

2. Intercourse in buying and selling; traffic; business; negotiation; any intercourse.

The Jews have no *dealings* with the Samaritans. —John iv. 9.

Double dealing; duplicity; dissimulation; deceitful conduct.

Plain dealing; upright and honest conduct; fairness; openness.

dealt (delt), *v.*, past tense of *deal*.

dealth, *n.* A division; a share. [Obs.]

dēal′=tree, *n.* The fir-tree; so called because deals are commonly made of it.

dē-am′bū-lāte, *v.i.* To walk abroad. [Obs.]

dē-am-bū-lā′tion, *n.* The act of walking abroad; a promenading. [Obs.]

dē-am′bū-lā-tō-ry, *a.* and *n.* I. *a.* Relating to walks; strolling. [Obs.]

II. *n.* A covered place in which to promenade, as a veranda, an aisle, a gallery. [Obs.]

dēan, *n.* [ME. *deen*, *dene*; OFr. *deien*, a dean; LL. *decanus*, one set over ten soldiers, from L. *decem*, ten.]

1. A dignitary, in the Roman Catholic and Anglican churches, subordinate to the bishop; in the early Christian church, governor of the monastery, in the absence of the abbot or provost.

2. In some English universities, an officer who attends to the moral and religious welfare of the students in addition to his other regular duties.

3. The chief or head of a faculty in some universities and colleges.

4. A registrar of the faculty in a department or school of a university; as, *dean* of the theological, medical, or law department.

5. The representative chief of a company or body on formal occasions, because of his long and honorable service; as, the *dean* of the diplomatic corps.

Dean and chapter; the ecclesiastical council to advise with the bishop in affairs of religion and in the temporal concerns of his see.

Dean of a cathedral church; the officer of a chapter having charge of the cathedral and its estates.

Dean of Arches; in England, the chief judicial officer of the ecclesiastical court of appeal, known as the Court of Arches.

Dean of faculty; in Scotland, the president of the faculty of advocates.

Dean of gild; a Scottish magistrate who supervises all matters relative to the erection of new structures.

Dean of peculiars; a dean who sometimes has both jurisdiction and cure of souls, and sometimes jurisdiction only; one not subject to direct diocesan rule.

Monastic dean or *dean of a monastery*; a superior in a monastery over ten monks.

Rural dean; originally, a beneficed clergyman appointed by a bishop to exercise a certain jurisdiction in districts of his diocese remote from his personal superintendence. The duties of *rural deans* are now usually performed by archdeacons.

dēan, *n.* A small, narrow valley. [Obs.]

dēan′ẽr-y, *n.*; *pl.* **dēan′ẽr-ieṣ.** 1. The office or the revenue of a dean.

2. The house of a dean.

3. The jurisdiction of a dean.

Each archdeaconry is divided into rural *deaneries*, and each *deanery* is divided into parishes. —Blackstone.

dē-an′i-măl-īze, *v.t.* [*De-* priv., and L. *animal*, a living being, animal.] To free from animal qualities. [Rare.]

dēan′ship, *n.* The office of a dean.

dēar, *a.*; *comp.* dearer; *superl.* dearest. [ME. *deere*, *dere*; AS. *deore*, beloved, precious, very valuable.]

1. High in price; more costly than usual; expensive.

The cheapest of us is ten groats too *dear*. —Shak.

2. Marked or characterized by scarcity; as, a *dear* season.

3. Of a high value in estimation; greatly valued; beloved; precious; as, a *dear* mother.

4. High in degree; heartfelt; intense; dangerous; as, *dear* speed; *dear* peril. [Obs.]

dēar, *v.t.* To make dear. [Obs.]

dēar, *n.* A darling; a sweetheart; a word denoting tender affection or endearment; as, my *dear*.

dēar, *adv.* Dearly; at a dear rate.

If thou attempt it, it will cost thee *dear*. —Shak.

dēar′bọrn, *n.* A light four-wheeled carriage, named after Dearborn, its inventor.

dēar′=bọught (-bọt), *a.* Dearly bought; as, *dear-bought* experience.

dēare, *v.*, *n.*, and *a.* [Obs.] See *Dere.*

dēar′ie, *n.* Same as *Deary.*

dēar′ling, *n.* A darling. [Obs.]

dēar′=lōved (-luvd), *a.* Greatly beloved.

dēar′ly, *adv.* 1. At a high price; as, he pays *dearly* for his rashness.

2. With great fondness; as, we love our children *dearly*.

3. Richly; exquisitely. [Obs.]

dearn, *n.* In architecture, a doorpost or threshold; written also *dern.*

dear′ness, *n.* 1. Costliness; high price, or a higher price than the customary one; as, the *dearness* of corn.

2. Fondness; nearness to the heart or affections; great value in estimation; preciousness; tender love; as, the *dearness* of friendship.

dearth, *n.* [ME. *derth, derthe,* scarcity, from *deere, dere*; AS. *deore,* dear, of great value.]

1. Famine; privation; want; as, a *dearth* of food.

2. Absence; lack; paucity; barrenness; sterility; as, a *dearth* of workmen; a *dearth* of incident (in a novel).

dē-är-tic′ū-lāte, *v.t.* [*De-* priv., and L. *articulare,* to divide into joints, from *articulus,* a joint.] To disjoint.

dear′y, *n.* [Dim. of *dear.*] One who is dear; a darling.

dē′as, *n.* Dais. [Obs.]

death (deth), *n.* [ME. *deth, deeth*; AS. *death,* death.]

1. Cessation of life; that state of a being, animal or vegetable, in which all vital functions cease permanently.

2. Total extinction; cessation; destruction; as, the *death* of love.

3. The manner of dying; as, let me die the *death* of the righteous.

4. In theology, separation or alienation of the soul from God; a being under the dominion of sin, and destitute of grace or divine life; called *spiritual death.*

To be carnally minded is *death.*—Rom. viii. 6.

5. Destroyer or agent of *death*; as, he will be the *death* of his father.

6. Murder; slaughter; as, a man of *death.*

7. A disease generally fatal; as, the black *death.*

8. Something deemed as dreadful as *death*; as, friendlessness is *death* itself.

Black death; see under *Black,* a.

Civil death; the separation of a man from civil society, or from the enjoyment of civil rights, as by banishment, life imprisonment, etc.

Death knell; the tolling of a bell as a death signal.

Local death; the destruction of a part or parts in animal or plant organisms, by the disassimilative processes of metabolism.

Second death; in theology, the death of the soul.

To be death on; to be superior in doing anything; to have a particular fondness for.

To be in at the death; a phrase taken from fox-hunting, indicating to be present at the conclusion of anything, especially if the action involves a contest.

To put to death; to slay or cause to be slain; to execute.

To the death; to the utmost extremity; to the end.

Syn.—Decease, demise, departure, dissolution, release.—*Death* applies to every form of existence; the other words only to the human race. *Decease* is the term used in law for the removal of a human being out of life; *demise* was formerly confined to the decease of princes, but is now sometimes used of distinguished men; *departure* and *release* are peculiarly terms of Christian affection and hope; *dissolution* refers to the separation of the soul from the body and the disintegration of the earthly personality.

death′=ad″dēr, *n.* In herpetology, the *Acanthophis antarctica,* a venomous Australian snake.

death′=ag″ō-ny, *n.* The final physical struggle accompanying dissolution.

death′bed, *a.* and *n.* I. *a.* Pertaining to mortal illness; as, *deathbed* repentance.

II. *n.* The bed on which one dies; mortal illness.

death′=bell, *n.* 1. A bell whose ringing announces death; the passing-bell.

2. A monotonous tolling sound in either ear, thought by the superstitious, especially the Scottish peasantry, to foretell death.

death′bird, *n.* 1. In ornithology, a small North American owl, *Nyctala richardsoni.*

2. In entomology, the death's-head moth.

death′blōw, *n.* 1. A mortal blow or shock.

2. Figuratively, anything that causes irretrievable loss.

death′=bōd″ing, *a.* Foretokening death.

death′=cord, *n.* The hangman's halter; gallows-rope.

death′=damp, *n.* In pathology, a cold sweat that sometimes precedes death.

death′=dance, *n.* See *Dance of death* under *Dance.*

death′=dāy, *n.* The day on which death comes.

death′=fire, *n.* The ignis fatuus, thought by the superstitious to foretell death.

death′ful, *a.* 1. Full of slaughter; deadly; destructive; sanguinary.

2. Liable to death; mortal.

death′ful-ness, *n.* An appearance as of death; the quality of suggesting death.

death′=grap″ple, *n.* A desperate struggle or grapple upon which life depends.

death′=hunt″ēr, *n.* One who robs the dead on battlefields.

death′less, *a.* 1. Not subject to death; immortal; as, *deathless* beings.

2. Imperishable; unending; as, *deathless* fame.

death′less-ness, *n.* The condition of being deathless; immortality.

death′like, *a.* 1. Having the appearance of death; deathly.

2. Fatal; deadly. [Obs.]

death′li-ness, *n.* Likeness to death.

death′ly, *a.* 1. Having the appearance or nature of death; as, *deathly* pallor.

2. Threatening death; deadly. [Rare.]

death′ly, *adv.* In such manner as to resemble death; as, *deathly* sick.

death′=mask, *n.* A cast (usually of plaster) of a dead person's face.

death′=point, *n.* 1. That degree of cold or heat at which life ceases.

2. The time limit of animal existence in a given degree of heat, the latter being usually fixed at the boiling point of water.

death′=rāte, *n.* The ratio of deaths to population for a specified period.

death′=rat″tle, *n.* A rattling or gurgling sound which sometimes accompanies the breathing of a dying person; in Scotland, called *death-ruckle.*

death′s′head (deths′hed), *n.* 1. The skull of a human skeleton or a figure representing it.

2. In zoölogy, one of the saimiri; the squirrel-monkey of South America.

Death's-head moth; in entomology, a large European moth, *Acherontia atropos,* having on the back of its thorax markings like a human skull.

death′s′hērb, *n.* In botany, the deadly nightshade, *Atropa Belladonna.*

deaths′măn, *n.* A public executioner; a hangman.

death′=thrōe, *n.* The final spasm or struggle in some cases of death.

death′=tick, *n.* In entomology, the deathwatch.

death′=tō″ken, *n.* In medicine, any symptom denoting approach of death.

death′=trance, *n.* In medicine, a deathlike condition, the result of reduced action of the vital organs.

death′=trap, *n.* Any place or structure that especially endangers life, as a railway crossing or an insecure building.

death′wărd, *adv.* Toward death.

death′=wăr″rănt, *n.* 1. In law, an official order directing the execution of a criminal.

2. Figuratively, the death knell of hope.

death′watch, *n.* 1. In entomology, a small beetle, *Anobium tessellatum,* whose ticking is thought by some persons to prognosticate death, but in fact is only the call of the sexes to each other. The beetle produces this ticking sound by raising itself upon its hind legs and rapidly beating its head against woodwork, usually about a dozen times. Called also *death-tick.*

Deathwatch Beetle (*Anobium tessellatum*). 1. Natural size. 2. Magnified. 3. Head, as seen from underneath.

2. A guard set over a condemned criminal during his last hours.

3. The vigil by the dying, or with a corpse before burial.

death′=wound, *n.* A wound that is mortal.

dē-au′rāte, *a.* [*De-,* and L. *auratus,* ornamented with gold; *aurum,* gold.]

1. In entomology, having a golden color.

2. Gilded. [Obs.]

dē-au′rāte, *v.t.* To gild. [Obs.]

deave, *v.t.* and *v.i.* I. *v.t.* To confuse or stun with noise; to deafen. [Scot.]

II. *v.i.* To become deaf.

dē-bac′chāte, *v.i.* To rave and bluster as a bacchanal. [Rare.]

dē-bac-chā′tion, *n.* A raving. [Rare.]

dē-bac′le, *n.* [Fr. *débâcle,* a break-up, overthrow, from *débâcler,* to break up.]

1. In geology, a breaking or bursting forth.

2. An unmanageable rush; a stampede.

dē-bär′, *v.t.*; debarred, *pt., pp.*; debarring, *ppr.* To cut off from entrance; to preclude; to hinder from approach, entry, or enjoyment; to shut out or exclude; used with *from* or *of.*

Syn.—Deprive, exclude, interdict, preclude, prevent.

dē-bärb′, *v.t.* To deprive of the beard. [Obs.]

dē-bärk′, *v.t.* [Fr. *débarquer*; *de,* from, and *barque,* a ship, bark, from LL. *barca,* a bark.] To land from a ship or boat; to remove from on board any water-craft and place on land; to disembark; as, to *debark* artillery.

dē-bärk′, *v.i.* To go ashore from a boat or ship; to disembark.

dē-bär-kā′tion, *n.* The going, or being taken, ashore from a vessel; disembarkation.

dē-bär′ment, *n.* The act of debarring or prohibiting; the state of being debarred; hindrance from approach; exclusion.

dē-bar′rass, *v.t.* To relieve from embarrassment; to disembarrass. [Rare.]

dē-bāse′, *v.t.*; debased (dē-bāst′), *pt., pp.*; debasing, *ppr.* [*De-,* and Fr. *bas*; LL. *bassus,* low.]

1. To reduce from a higher to a lower state in quality or respectability.

2. To reduce or lower in quality, purity, or value; to adulterate; as, to *debase* gold or silver by alloy.

3. To lower or degrade; to make mean or despicable; as, vicious habits *debase* the mind as well as the body.

4. To impair in purity or elegance; to vitiate by meanness; as, to *debase* literary style by vulgar expressions.

Syn.—Abase, corrupt, degrade, impair, lower, taint.

dē-bāsed′ (dē-bāst′), *a.* 1. In heraldry, turned over or downward from its proper position or use; inverted; reversed.

2. Reduced in fineness or purity; adulterated.

3. Corrupted; degraded.

An Escutcheon Debased.

dē-bāse′ment, *n.* The act of debasing; degradation; reduction of purity, fineness, quality, or value; adulteration; a state of being debased; as, *debasement* of character, of coin, of style, etc.

dē-bās′ēr, *n.* One who debases or lowers in estimation or in value; one who degrades or renders mean; that which debases.

dē-bās′ing-ly, *adv.* In such manner as to debase or degrade.

dē-bāt′ȧ-ble, *a.* Capable of being debated; disputable; subject to controversy or contention; as, a *debatable* question.

Debatable land; formerly, a tract of land, situated between the rivers Esk and Sark, claimed by both England and Scotland.

Debatable ground; figuratively, any question or subject open to discussion.

dē-bāte′, *n.* [ME. *debate*; OFr. *debat,* a debate, from *debatre,* to fight, contend, debate.]

1. Contention in words or arguments; discussion for elucidating truth; argument or reasoning, especially between those of diametrical views; dispute; controversy; as, the *debates* in Parliament or in Congress.

2. Strife; contention. [Rare.]

3. Subject of discussion. [Rare.]

Statutes and edicts concerning this *debate.*
—Milton.

dē-bāte′, *v.t.*; debated, *pt., pp.*; debating, *ppr.* To contend for in words or arguments; to strive to maintain by reasoning; to dispute; to discuss; to argue; as, they *debated* the question with vigor.

Syn.—Argue, contest, controvert, dispute.

dē-bāte′, *v.i.* 1. To deliberate; discuss; examine; often followed by *on, upon,* or *in*; as, he *debated upon* the great question of immortality.

2. To dispute.

3. To engage in combat. [Obs.]

dē-bāte′ful, *a.* Contentious; quarrelsome. [Obs.]

dē-bāte′ful-ly, *adv.* With contention. [Obs.]

dē-bāte′ment, *n.* The act of debating; controversy; debate. [Rare.]

dē-bāt′ēr, *n.* One who debates; a disputant; a controvertist.

dē-bāt′ing, *n.* The act of arguing; contention.

Debating society; a society for the purpose of debate and improvement in extemporaneous speaking.

dē-bāt′ing-ly, *adv.* In the manner of a debate.

dē-bauch′, *v.t.*; debauched (dē-bacht′), *pt., pp.*; debauching, *ppr.* [OFr. *desbaucher,* to corrupt, seduce, lit. to hew away; *des-* priv., away from, and *baucher,* to hew, chip.]

1. To corrupt or vitiate; as, to *debauch* a youth; to *debauch* good principles.

2. To corrupt with lewdness; to seduce; as, to *debauch* a woman.

3. To seduce from duty or allegiance; as, to *debauch* an army.

dē-bauch′, *v.i.* To take part in debauchery; to revel.

dē-bauch′, *n.* 1. Excess in eating or drinking; intemperance; drunkenness; gluttony; lewdness.

2. A time or period of debauchery.

dē-bauched′ (-bacht′), *a.* Corrupted; vitiated in habits and character; profligate.

dē-bauch′ed-ly, *adv.* In a profligate manner.

dē-bauch′ed-ness, *n.* The condition of being debauched; intemperance.

deb-au-chee′ (-ō-shē′), *n.* One given to intemperance or bacchanalian excesses; one habitually lewd or profligate.

dē-bauch′ēr, *n.* One who debauches or corrupts others; a seducer from virtue or duty.

dē-bauch′ẽr-y, *n.* 1. Gross intemperance; lustfulness; gluttony.

2. Seduction from duty or allegiance.

dē-bauch′ment, *n.* The act of debauching or corrupting; the act of seducing from virtue or duty.

dē-bauch′ness, *n.* [Obs.] See *Debauchedness.*

dē-bel′, *v.t.* To subdue. [Obs.]

dē-bel′lāte, *v.t.* [Obs.] Same as *Debel.*

deb-el-lā′tion, *n.* The act of conquering or subduing. [Obs.]

dē bē′nē es′sē. [L. *de*, of, for, *bene*, well, *esse*, to be.] Well-being, or conditional allowance. In law, to take an order or testimony *de bene esse* is to take or allow it for the present, but subject to be suppressed or disallowed on a further or full examination.

dē-ben′tūre, *n.* [Fr., from L. *debentur*, 3d pers. pl. ind. pres. of *debere*, to owe; so called because these receipts began with the Latin words *debentur mihi*, there are owing to me.]

1. A writing acknowledging a debt; a writing or certificate signed by a public officer, as evidence of a debt; the amount thus due.

2. A customhouse certificate which states that a person is entitled to a certain sum from the government, on the exportation of specified goods, the duties on which have been paid.

dē-ben′tūred, *a.* Entitled to a drawback; as, *debentured* goods.

deb′ile, *a.* [OFr. *debile*; L. *debilis*, weak; *de-* priv., and *habilis*, able.] Relaxed; weak; feeble.

dē-bil′i-tāte, *v.t.*; debilitated, *pt.*, *pp.*; debilitating, *ppr.* [L. *debilitatus*, pp. of *debilitare*, to weaken, from *debilis*, weak.] To weaken; to impair the strength of; to enfeeble; to make faint or languid; as, excessive indulgence *debilitates* the system.

Syn.—Enervate, enfeeble, impair.

dē-bil-i-tā′tion, *n.* The act of weakening; relaxation.

dē-bil′i-ty, *n.* [ME. *debylite*; OFr. *debilite*, L. *debilitas*, weakness, from *debilis*, weak.] Weakness; feebleness; languor of body; faintness; usually applied to the body; as, his *debility* was extreme.

Syn.—Infirmity, imbecility.—An *infirmity* belongs, for the most part, to individual members, as of the eyes, and is often temporary; *debility* is more general and deeply-seated; *imbecility* is a permanent weakening, and is usually applied to the mind.

deb′it, *n.* [L *debitum*, what is owing, a debt; neut. pp. of *debere*, to owe.]

1. A debt, or an account of debts recorded on account.

2. The debit side of an account.

deb′it, *v.t.*; debited, *pt.*, *pp*; debiting, *ppr.* 1. To charge with a certain sum; as, to *debit* a purchaser

2. To enter an account on the debtor side of a book; as, to *debit* the sum or amount of goods sold.

deb′it-ŏr, *n.* A debtor. [Obs]

dē-bi-tū″mi-ni-zā′tion, *n.* The act of depriving of bitumen.

dē-bi-tū′mi-nīze, *v.t.* To deprive of bitumen.

dé-blāi′ (dā-blā′), *n.* [Fr.] In fortification, the place from which earth is removed in building a parapet.

deb-ō-nāir′, *a.* [ME. *debonaire*; OFr. *de bon aire*, lit. of good mien.] Having an affable manner; easy; attractive.

deb-ō-nāir′i-ty, *n.* The state of being debonair. [Obs.]

deb-ō-nāir′ly, *adv.* In a meek and gentle manner.

deb-ō-nāir′ness, *n.* Gentleness; kindness; unaffected courtesy.

dē-bosh′, dē-bosh′ment, etc. [Obs.] See *Debauch, Debauchment*, etc.

dē-bouch′, *v.i.* [Fr. *deboucher*, to emerge from; *de*, from, and *boucher*, to stop up, from *bouche*, mouth; L. *bucca*, cheek.]

1. To issue or march out of a confined place, or from a defile, as troops.

2. In geography, to issue from a mountain through a defile or gorge; said of a stream.

dé-bou-ché′ (dā-bö-shā′), *n.* [Fr., from *deboucher*, to open up.]

1. An opening in works for the passage of troops.

2. A commercial outlet; a market for goods.

dé-bou-chure′ (dā-bö-shur′), *n.* [Fr.] The outlet of a valley or an extended body of water.

dé-brïde′ment (dā-brēd′mon), *n.* [Fr., from *debrider*, to unbridle; *de-* priv., and *bride*, bridle, from AS. *bridel*, bridle.] In surgery, the operation of removing a stricture or obstacle, or the enlargement of an opening for the passage of pus.

dé-bris′ (dā-brē′), *n.* [Fr. *débris*, fragments, from *desbriser*, to break apart.]

1. Scattered fragments; remains; rubbish; ruins.

2. In geology, any collection of rock fragments, as at the bases of cliffs, or in drift.

dē-brüise′, *v.t.* and *v.i.* To bruise or be bruised. [Obs.]

dē-brüised′, *a.* [ME. *debrusen, debrisen*, to break apart; OFr. *debruiser*, to break, break open; *de*, apart, and *brusier*, to break.] In heraldry, surmounted or partly covered by an ordinary; as, a lion *debruised.*

Debruised.

debt (det), *n.* [ME. *det, dette*; OFr. *dette, debte*, debt, from L. *debitum*, neut. pp. of *debere*, to owe; *de*, from, and *habere*, to have.]

1. That which is due from one person to another, whether goods, money, or services; a due; a liability.

2. The condition of being under obligation to pay money to, or perform services for, another; as, I am in his *debt.*

3. Neglected moral duty; sin; trespass.

Forgive us our *debts.* —Matt. vi. 12.

Action of debt; in law, an action for the recovery of a specified sum of money alleged to be due.

Bonded debt; see under *Bonded.*

Debt of honor; a debt which cannot be collected at law, but whose payment depends on the honor of the debtor.

Debt of nature; death.

Floating debt; the unfunded debt of a corporation or government.

Funded debt; debt which has been converted into bonds or annuities.

National debt; indebtedness of government to the individual creditor, which is funded and based upon public securities.

Preferred debt; a debt of such a character as to have priority of payment

debt′ed (det′ed), *a.* Indebted; bounden; as, he stands *debted* to this gentleman. [Rare.]

debt-ee′, *n.* In law, a creditor.

debt′less, *a.* Free from debt.

debt′ŏr, *n.* [ME. *dettur*; OFr. *detor*; L. *debitor*, a debtor, from *debitus*, pp. of *debere*, to owe.] One who owes goods, money, or services to another; one who is in debt; opposed to *creditor.*

dē-bul′li-āte, *v.i.* To boil over. [Obs.]

deb-ul-li′tion, *n.* A boiling over. [Obs.]

dē-bŭrse′, *v.t.* and *v.i.* To disburse. [Obs.]

dē-bu-scōpe′, *n.* [Named from *Débus*, the inventor, and Gr. *skopein*, to view.] In optics, a modified kaleidoscope, consisting of two polished surfaces, used in producing decorative designs.

dé-but′ (dā-bu′), *n.* [Fr., the first step, first throw, first appearance, from *debuter*, to lead, play first; *de*, from, and *buter*, to throw at a mark, from *but*, a mark, goal.] First appearance or attempt; a beginning; specifically, a first appearance in society or in public; as, the *début* of an actor.

dé-bu-tänt′ (dā-bu-tän′), *n.* [Fr., ppr. of *debuter*, to make one's first appearance.] One, especially a man, who makes a début.

dé-bu-tänte′ (dā-bu-tänt′), *n.* A woman who makes a début, especially on the stage or in society.

dec-a-. A combining form from L. *decem*, Gr. *deka*, ten, signifying ten or a multiplication by ten, as *decachord.*

De-cac′e-rȧ, *n.pl.* [*Deca-*, and Gr. *keras*, horn.] In conchology, an order of cephalopods having five pairs of arms or tentacles; also called *Decapoda.*

de-cac′ẽr-ous, *a.* Pertaining to the *Decacera.*

dec′ȧ-chord, dec-ȧ-chor′dŏn, *n.* [*Deca-*, and Gr. *chordē*, a chord.]

1. A harplike musical instrument of ancient Greece, having ten strings.

2. Something consisting of ten parts.

dec-ȧ-cū′mi-nā-ted, *a.* [L. *de*, from, and *cacumen*, a point.] Having the top cut off. [Rare.]

dec′ad, *n.* [L. *decas*; Gr. *dekas*, the number ten; *deka*, ten.]

1. In ancient philosophy, the Pythagorean quarternary number (ten), considered an elemental factor of the universe.

2. A decade.

Decad ring; a ring having ten bosses on the circumference, used as a rosary; also called *rosary ring.*

dec′ȧ-dăl, *a.* Pertaining to or consisting of tens.

dec′ȧ-dā-ry, *a.* Pertaining to a period of ten days.

dec-ȧ-dā′tion, *n.* In music, the process of modulation by decades.

dec′āde, *n.* [L. *decas*; Gr. *dekas*, the number ten; *deka*, ten.]

1. A period of time covering ten years; a decennium.

2. Any group or set of ten.

3. One of ten parts or divisions of a literary work; as, the third *decade* of Livy.

4. In music, a group of ten acoustically related tones, so arranged as to explain and test harmony.

dē-cā′dence, dē-cā′den-cy, *n.* [Fr. *décadence*, a falling away, from L. *de*, from, and *cadens*, ppr. of *cadere*, to fall.] Decline in force or quality; a falling off in a character or repute, decay; deterioration.

dē-cā′dent, *a.* and *n.* I. *a.* Exhibiting decadence; declining; deteriorating.

II. *n.* One who is below the moral, mental, or social standard of his time.

dec′ȧ-dist, *n.* [From Gr. *deka*, ten.] An author whose writings comprise ten parts or volumes. [Rare.]

dec′ȧ-drachm (-dram), *n.* See *Dekadrachm.*

dec′ȧ-gon, *n.* [*Deca-*, and Gr. *gōnia*, an angle.] In geometry, a plane figure having ten sides and ten angles.

Regular decagon; in geometry, a decagon whose sides and angles are equal.

de-cag′ō-năl, *a.* Pertaining to or resembling a decagon.

dec′ȧ-gram, dec′ȧ-gramme, *n.* [*Deca-*, and Gr. *gramma*, a thing drawn or written.] In the metric system, a weight equal to ten grams, 154.32349 grains, 0.353 ounce avoirdupois, or 0.3215 ounce troy.

dec′ȧ-gyn, *n.* [*Deca-*, and Gr. *gyne*, a woman.] In botany, a plant of the order *Decagynia*, having ten pistils.

Dec-ȧ-gyn′i-ȧ, *n.pl.* [L., from Gr. *deka*, ten, and *gynē*, a woman.] In the Linnæan botanic system, the tenth order in the first thirteen classes, including those plants which have ten styles.

dec-ȧ-gyn′i-ăn, *a.* In botany, belonging to the order *Decagynia.*

de-cag′y-nous, *a.* Same as *Decagynian.*

dec-ȧ-hē′drăl, *a.* In geometry, resembling a decahedron.

dec-ȧ-hē′drŏn, *n.* [*Deca-*, and Gr. *hedra*, a seat, base.] In geometry, a solid having ten plane faces.

dē-cal″ci-fi-cā′tion, *n.* [*De-* priv., and L. *calx* (*calcis*), lime.]

1. In medicine, the removal of calcareous matter.

2. In dentistry, the removal of incrustation or tartar from the teeth.

dē-cal′ci-fȳ, *v.t.*; decalcified, *pt.*, *pp.*; decalcifying, *ppr.* To remove calcareous matter from, as bones or teeth.

dē-cal-cō-mā′ni-ȧ, *n.* [Fr. *décalcomanie*, from *décalquer*, to counterdraw, and Gr. *mania*, madness.] The art of transferring pictures and ornamental designs from paper to china, glass, wood, etc., and fixing them permanently.

dē-cȧ-les′cence, *n.* [*De*, from, and L. *calescere*, to become warm.] In metallurgy, the acceleration of heat absorption in iron at a temperature above 795° C.; opposed to *recalescence.*

dec′ȧ-lī-tẽr, dec′ȧ-lī-tre, *n.* [*Deca-*, and Fr. *litre*, a liter; Gr. *litra*, a pound.] In the metric system, a measure of capacity equal to ten liters or 610.23 cubic inches or 2.64 United States wine gallons.

dē-cal′ō-gist, *n.* A commentator or expounder of the decalogue.

dec′ȧ-logue (-log), *n.* [ME. *decaloge*; LL. *decalogus*; Gr. *dekalogos*, the decalogue; *deka*, ten, and *logos*, word or speech, from *legein*, to speak.] In Scripture, the ten commandments; the precepts received by Moses on Mount Sinai, originally written on two tables of stone; also called *the moral law.*

Dē-cam′e-ron, *n.* [It. *Decamerone*, from Gr. *deka*, ten, and *meros*, part, share.]

1. A collection of tales written by Boccaccio in the fourteenth century.

2. [d—] Any book or literary work divided into ten parts; a decade. [See *Heptameron.*]

Dē-cam-e-ron′ic, *a.* Pertaining to or in the style of the Decameron.

dē-cam′ẽr-ous, *a.* [*Deca-*, and Gr. *meros*, part.] In botany, having the parts in tens; said of flowers; also written *10-merous.*

dec′ȧ-mē-tẽr, dec′ȧ-mē-tre, *n.* [Fr. *décamètre*, a length of ten meters; Gr. *deka*, ten, and *metron*, a measure.] In the metric system, a measure of length containing ten meters; equal to 393.70 inches or 32.81 feet.

dē-camp′, *v.i.*; decamped, *pt.*, *pp*; decamping, *ppr.* [Fr. *décamper*, to break camp; L. *de*, from, and *campus*, a camp.]

1. To depart from a camping-ground; to break camp and resume the march, as troops.

2. To run away; to abscond.

3. To camp. [Rare.]

dē-camp′ment, *n.* Departure from a camp; a sudden departure; a marching off.

dec′ȧ-năl, *a.* 1. Pertaining to a dean or to a deanery.

2. Same as *Decani.*

dec′ȧ-nāte, *n.* [From LL. *decanatus*, the office of a *decanus*, or dean, from L. *decem*, ten.] In astrology, one of the zodiacal divisions of ten degrees in which a planet has its least dignity.

dē-can′dẽr, *n.* In botany, a plant with ten stamens.

Dē-can′dri-ȧ, *n.pl.* [L., from Gr. *deka*, ten, and *anēr* (*andros*), a man.] In botany, the tenth class of plants in the Linnæan system. These plants have ten stamens, and one, two, three, or more pistils, and are classed with the genera *Lychnis, Dianthus, Cerastium, Sedum, Saxifraga, Oxalis*, etc.

dē-çan'drous, dē-çan'dri-ăn, *a.* In botany, pertaining to the genus *Decandria.*

deç'āne, *n.* [From Gr. *deka,* ten.] In chemistry, any one of several isomeric modifications of liquid hydrocarbon; a paraffin contained in coal-tar.

deç-an'gū-lăr, *a.* [*Deca-,* and L. *angulus,* an angle.] Having ten angles.

dē-çā'ni, *a.* [L., genit. of *decanus,* a dean.] Pertaining to a dean; as, the *decani* side of a church, the side on which the dean's stall is located.

Decandria (*Cerastium aquaticum*).

dē-çant', *v.t.*; decanted, *pt., pp.*; decanting, *ppr.* [Fr *décanter,* to pour off from the edge of a vessel; *de,* from, and OFr. *cant,* edge; L. *canthus,* the iron ring round a carriage-wheel.] To pour off gently, as liquor from its sediment; or to pour from one vessel into another; as, to *decant* wine.

dē-çan'tāte, *v.t* [Obs.] See *Decant.*

dē-çan-tā'tion, *n.* The act of pouring off a clear fluid gently from its lees or sediment, or from one vessel into another.

dē-çant'ẽr, *n.* 1. A vessel used to decant liquors, or for receiving decanted liquors; a glass bottle for table service used for holding wine or other liquors.

2. One who decants liquors.

deç-ȧ-pet'ăl-ous, *a.* [*Deca-,* and Gr. *petalon,* a leaf.] In botany, having ten petals.

deç-ȧ-phyl'lous, *a.* [*Deca-,* and Gr. *phyllon,* a leaf.] In botany, having ten leaves.

dē-çap'i-tāte, *v.t.*; decapitated, *pt., pp.*; decapitating, *ppr.* [L. *de,* off, and *caput,* head.]

1. To behead.

2. To remove from office. [Colloq.]

dē-çap-i-tā'tion, *n.* 1. The act of beheading.

2. Dismissal from office.

deç'ȧ-pod, dē-çap'ō-dăl, dē-çap'ō-dous, *a.* Pertaining to the *Decapoda;* having ten arms or feet.

deç'ȧ-pod, *n.* [L. *decapus;* Gr. *dekapous,* with ten feet, used in the sense of ten feet long; *deka,* ten, and *pous* (*podos*), foot.] In crustalogy, one of the *Decapoda:* (a) a ten-footed crustacean, as a crab; (b) a ten-armed cephalopod, as the cuttlefish.

Dē-çap'ō-dȧ, *n.pl.* [L., from Gr. *deka,* ten, and *pous* (*podos*), foot.]

1. In crustalogy, an order of crustaceans having five pairs of legs, including crabs, lobsters, shrimps, etc.

2. The ten-armed cephalopods, including the cuttlefish; also called *Decacera.*

dē-çap'ō-dăl, *a.* Same as *Decapod.*

deç-ȧ-pōd'i-fọrm, *a.* [L. *decapus,* the decapod, and *forma,* shape.] In entomology, having the form of a crawfish or lobster.

dē-çap'ō-dous, *a.* Same as *Decapod.*

dē-çär'bŏn-āte, *v.t.* In chemistry, to free from carbon.

dē-çär"bŏn-i-zā'tion, *n.* Same as *Decarburization.*

dē-çär'bŏn-īze, *v.t.* Same as *Decarburize.*

dē-çär"bū-ri-zā'tion, *n.* The act or process of depriving of carbon.

dē-çär'bū-rīze, *v.t.*; decarburized, *pt., pp.*; decarburizing, *ppr.* To deprive of carbon, wholly or in part, as in making steel; opposed to *carburize.*

dē-çärd', *v.t.* To discard. [Obs.]

dē-çär'di-năl-īze, *v.t.* To remove from the rank of a cardinal.

deç'āre, *n.* [Fr.] In the metric system, a superficial measure equal to ten ares, or one thousand square meters.

deç-ȧ-sep'ăl-ous, *a.* [*Deca-,* and L. *sepalum,* a leaf.] In botany, having ten sepals.

deç'ȧ-stēre, *n.* [Fr. *decastere;* Gr. *deka,* ten, and *stereos,* solid.] In the metric system, ten steres, equivalent to ten cubic meters or about thirteen cubic yards.

deç'ȧ-stiçh, *n.* [*Deca-,* and Gr. *stichos,* a verse.] A poem containing ten lines.

deç'ȧ-stȳle, *a.* [*Deca-,* and Gr. *stylos,* a column.] Having or consisting of ten columns; as, a *decastyle* portico; a *decastyle* temple.

deç"ȧ-syl-lab'iç, *a.* [*Deca-,* and Gr. *syllabē,* a syllable.] Consisting of ten syllables.

deç-ȧ-tō'iç, *a.* In chemistry, relating to or derived from decane.

dē-çau'dāte, *v.t.* [*De-* priv., and L. *cauda,* tail.] To deprive of the tail.

dē-çāy', *v.i.*; decayed, *pt., pp.*; decaying, *ppr.* [OE. *decaye;* OFr. *decair,* decay, decline, from L. *decidere,* to fall down, to fall away; *de,* down, and *cadere,* to fall.] To pass gradually from a sound or prosperous state to one of less perfection; to fail; to decline; to be gradually impaired; to become rotten.

dē-çāy', *v.t.* To cause to fail; to impair. [Rare.]

dē-çāy', *n.* 1. Gradual decadence of health, strength, soundness, prosperity, or any other excellence; tendency toward dissolution or extinction.

2. Putrefaction; rot.

3. Destruction; death. [Obs.]

4. Cause of decay. [Rare.]

Syn.—Decline, decadence, degeneracy, collapse, downfall.

dē-çāyed', *a.* Having deteriorated; impaired; weakened.

dē-çāy'ed-ness, *n.* A state of being impaired; a decayed state.

dē-çāy'ẽr, *n.* That which causes decay. [Rare.]

dē-çēase', *v.i.*; deceased (dē-cēst), *pt., pp.*; deceasing, *ppr.* To depart from this life; to die; as, General Washington *deceased,* December 14, 1799.

dē-çēase', *n.* [ME. *deces, deses;* OFr. *deces,* death, departure, from L. *decessus,* pp. of *decedere,* to depart, go away; *de,* from, and *cedere,* to go, move.] Departure from this life; death.

Syn.—Death, demise, departure, dissolution, release.

dē-çēased' (-sēst'), *a.* Departed from life; dead.

dē-çēde', *v.i.* To depart. [Obs.]

dē-çē'dent, *a.* [L. *decedens,* ppr. of *decedere,* to depart.] Departing; seceding.

dē-çē'dent, *n.* [L. *decedens,* ppr. of *decedere,* to depart.] A deceased person.

dē-çēit', *n.* [ME. *deceite;* OFr. *deceite,* deceit; L. *deceptus,* pp. of *decipere,* to deceive; *de,* from, and *capere,* to take.]

1. The act of catching or ensnaring; the misleading of a person; fraud; fallacy; cheat.

2. The quality of being false and resorting to tricky devices.

3. In law, any trick, device, collusion, shift, or underhand practice, used to defraud another.

Syn.—Deception, double-dealing, cunning, duplicity, fraud, guile, trickery, hypocrisy.

dē-çēit'fụl, *a.* 1. Tending to mislead, deceive, or ensnare; as, *deceitful* words; *deceitful* practices.

2. Full of deceit; tricky; fraudulent; cheating; insincere; as, a *deceitful* man.

dē-çēit'fụl-ly, *adv.* In a deceitful manner; fraudulently.

dē-çēit'fụl-ness, *n.* 1. Tendency to mislead or deceive; as, the *deceitfulness* of sin.

2. The quality of being fraudulent; as, the *deceitfulness* of a man's practices.

3. The disposition to deceive; as, a man's *deceitfulness* may be habitual.

dē-çēit'less, *a.* Free from deceit.

dē-çēiv'ȧ-ble, *a.* 1. Subject to deceit or imposition; capable of being misled or entrapped; as, young persons are very *deceivable.*

2. Subject to or apt to produce error or deception; deceitful. [Obs.]

dē-çēiv'ȧ-ble-ness, *n.* Liability to deceive or be deceived.

dē-çēiv'ȧ-bly, *adv.* In a deceivable manner.

dē-çēive', *v.t.*; deceived, *pt., pp.*; deceiving, *ppr.* [ME. *deceyven;* OFr. *decever;* L. *decipere,* to take down or from, to beguile, deceive; *de,* from, and *capere,* to take.]

1. To mislead; to cause to err; to impose on; to delude; to cheat.

2. To beguile; to divert; to while away. [Poet.]

dē-çēiv'ẽr, *n.* One who deceives; one who leads into error; a cheat; an impostor.

Syn.—Impostor.—A *deceiver* operates by stealth and in private; an *impostor* practises his arts on the community at large. The one succeeds by artful falsehood, the other by bold assumption.

dē-cem-. A combining form from L. *decem,* ten.

Dē-cem'bẽr, *n.* [L. *December,* from *decem,* ten; this being the tenth month among the early Romans, who reckoned from March.]

1. The last or twelfth month of the year, in which the sun enters the tropic of Capricorn, and makes the winter solstice. It has thirty-one days.

2. Figuratively, the period of old age; as, he had reached the *December* of life.

Dē-cem'brist, *n.* One of those who were in conspiracy against Czar Nicholas on his accession to the Russian throne in December, 1825.

dē-cem-den'tāte, *a.* [*Decem-,* and L. *dentatus,* having teeth.] Having ten points or teeth.

dē-cem'fid, *a.* [*Decem-,* and L. *findere,* to divide.]

1. Cleft or divided into ten parts.

2. In botany, separated into ten lobes or segments.

dē-cem-loç'ū-lăr, *a.* [*Decem-,* and L. *loculus,* a small receptacle, dim. of *locus,* a place.] In botany, having ten cells for seeds.

dē-cem-pär'tīte, *a.* Same as *Decamerous.*

dē-cem'pe-dăl, *a.* [LL. *decempedalis,* ten feet in length; L. *decem,* ten, and *pes* (*pedis*), a foot.]

1. Ten feet in length.

2. Same as *Decapod.*

dē-cem-pen'nāte, *a.* [*Decem-,* and L. *penna,* a wing.] In ornithology, having ten developed flight-feathers.

dē-cem'vĭr, *n.*; *pl.* **dē-cem'vĭrs, dē-cem'vi-rī.** [L. *decem,* ten, and *vir,* a man.]

1. One of ten magistrates, who had absolute authority in ancient Rome. The term of office was two years.

2. A member of any official body consisting of ten men.

dē-cem'vi-răl, *a.* Pertaining to the Roman decemvirs.

dē-cem'vi-rāte, *n.* [L. *decemviratus,* the rank or office of the decemvirs.]

1. The office or term of office of the Roman decemvirs.

2. Any body of ten men in authority.

dē-cem'vĭr-ship, *n.* The office, rank, or dignity of a decemvir.

dē'cence, *n.* Decency. [Obs.]

dē'cen-cy, *n.*; *pl.* **dē'cen-cieṣ.** [OFr. *decence;* L. *decentia,* comeliness.]

1. The state or quality of being decent, proper, or becoming.

2. That which is fit or suitable, in words or behavior; proper formality; becoming ceremony; as, *decency* of conduct; *decency* of worship; he discoursed with *decency.*

Syn.—Decorum, propriety, modesty, suitableness, becomingness.

dē-cen'nȧ-ry, *n.*; *pl.* **dē-cen'nȧ-rieṣ.** [L. *decennis,* lasting ten years; *decem,* ten, and *annus,* a year.]

1. A period of ten years.

2. In old English law, a tithing consisting of ten freeholders and their families.—Blackstone.

dē-cen'ni-ăl, *a.* [L. *decem,* ten, and *annus,* a year.] Continuing for ten years; happening every ten years; as, a *decennial* period; *decennial* games.

dē-cen'ni-ăl, *n.* An anniversary observed every ten years.

dē-cen'ni-um, *n.* [L., from *decem,* ten, and *annus,* a year.] A period covering ten years; a decade.

dē-cen'nō-văl, *a.* [LL. *decennovalis,* of nineteen years; L. *decem,* ten, and *novem,* nine.] Pertaining to the number nineteen; designating a period or cycle of nineteen years. [See *Metonic cycle* under *Cycle.*]

dē-cen'nō-vȧ-ry, *a.* Same as *Decennoval.*

dē'cent, *a.* [Fr. *decent;* L. *decens* (*decentis*), comely, fitting, from *decere,* to become, be fitting.]

1. Becoming; fit; suitable, in words, behavior, dress, or ceremony; as, *decent* language; *decent* conduct; *decent* dress.

2. Comely; proper. [Obs.]

A sable stole of Cyprus lawn,
O'er the *decent* shoulders drawn. —Milton.

3. Not indelicate; conforming to the accepted standard of modesty.

4. Moderate, but competent; respectable; as, a *decent* fortune; a *decent* person.

Syn.—Suitable, modest, respectable, befitting, decorous, proper, seemly, becoming.

dē'cent-ly, *adv.* In a decent manner.

dē'cent-ness, *n.* Decency; the quality of being decent.

dē-cen"trăl-i-zā'tion, *n.* The act of decentralizing; the state of being decentralized.

dē-cen'trăl-īze, *v.t.* [L. *de,* from, and *centrum,* center.] To distribute or disperse what has been centralized or concentrated; said especially of public administration.

dē-ceph"ȧ-li-zā'tion, *n.* [*De-* priv., and Gr. *kephalē,* head.] In zoölogy, degeneration or degradation of cephalic parts; opposed to *cephalization.*

dē-ceph'ȧ-līze, *v.t.*; decephalized, *pt., pp.*; decephalizing, *ppr.* To effect decephalization of; to degrade or simplify the cephalic parts of.

dē-cep-ti-bil'i-ty, *n.* The liability or capability of being deceived. [Rare.]

dē-cep'ti-ble, *a.* [From L. *deceptus,* pp. of *decipere,* to deceive.] Capable of being deceived; deceivable. [Rare.]

dē-cep'tion, *n.* 1. The act of deceiving or misleading.

2. The state of being deceived or misled.

3. Artifice; cheat; as, this scheme is all a *deception.*

Syn.—Deceit, fraud, imposition, artifice, cheat, finesse, ruse, stratagem, trick.—*Deception* usually refers to the act and *deceit* to the habit of the mind; hence, a person is spoken of as skilled in *deception* and addicted to *deceit.* An *imposition* is an act of deception practised upon some one to his annoyance or injury; a *fraud* implies the use of stratagem with a view to some unlawful gain or advantage.

dē-cep'tious, *a.* Tending to deceive; deceitful. [Rare.]

dē-cep'tive, *a.* Tending to deceive; having power to mislead, or impress false opinions; as, a *deceptive* appearance.

Deceptive cadence; in music, the close of a phrase on any other chord than that of the tonic preceded by that of the dominant. [See *Perfect* and *Imperfect Cadence* under *Cadence.*]

dē-cep'tive-ly, *adv.* In a deceptive manner.

dē-cep'tive-ness, *n.* The power of deceiving; the tendency or aptness to deceive.

dē-cep-tiv′i-ty, *n.* 1. That which deceives; a sham. [Rare.]

2. The power or tendency to deceive.

dē-cep′tō-ry, *a.* Deceptive. [Rare.]

dē-cer′ē-brize, *v.t.* To remove the cerebrum from. [Rare.]

dē-cērn′, *v.t.* [OFr. *decerner*; L. *decernere*, to decide, judge; *de*, from, and *cernere*, to separate, distinguish.]

1. To discern. [Obs.]

2. In Scots laws, to decree; to pass judgment upon.

dē-cērn′i-tūre, *n.* In Scots laws, a decree or sentence of a court; as, he resolved to appeal against the *decerniture* of the judge.

dē-cērp′, *v.t.* To pluck off; to crop. [Obs.]

dē-cērpt′, *a.* Cropped. [Obs.]

dē-cērp′ti-ble, *a.* Capable of being plucked. [Obs.]

dē-cērp′tion, *n.* [L. *decerpere*, to pluck off; *de*, from, and *carpere*, to pluck.]

1. A pulling or plucking off; a cropping.

2. That which is pulled off or separated; a fragment.

dē-cēr-tā′tion, *n.* [L. *decertare*, to fight, contend; *de*, and *certare*, to fight, contend.] Strife; contest for mastery. [Rare.]

dē-ces′sion (-sesh′un), *n.* Departure; decrease; diminution. [Obs.]

dē-chärm′, *v.t.* To remove the spell or enchantment of; to disenchant.

dé-chaus-sé′ (dā-shō-sā′), *a.* [Fr., pp. of *déchausser*, to remove one's shoes; *de*, from, and *chausse*, a shoe.] In heraldry, dismembered, or the members represented as separated; without claws.

dech′en-ite, *n.* [Named after Von *Dechen*, a German geologist.] In mineralogy, a vanadate of lead found free in nature and occurring in massive form.

dē-chris′tiăn-ize, *v.t.*; dechristianized, *pt.*, *pp.*; dechristianizing, *ppr.* To turn from Christianity; to banish Christian belief and principles from.

dec′i-. A combining form from L. *decimus*, tenth, from *decem*, ten, signifying tenth; used in the metric system.

dec′i-āre, *n.* In the metric system, a measure of surface, one-tenth of an are.

dē-cīd′ȧ-ble, *a* Capable of being decided.

dē-cīde′, *v.t.*; decided, *pt.*, *pp.*; deciding, *ppr.* [ME. *deciden*; OFr. *decider*, to decide; L. *decidere*, to cut off, to decide; *de*, off, from, and *cædere*, to cut.]

1. To cut off; to separate. [Obs.]

2. To bring to an end; to determine, as a question, controversy, or struggle, by some recognized authority; to settle in favor of one side or the other; to determine the issue or result of; as, the court *decided* the case for the plaintiff.

3. To resolve; to come to a decision regarding; as, he *decided* to remain.

Syn.—Determine, resolve, settle, fix, adjust, regulate, arrange.

dē-cīde′, *v.i.* To determine; to form a definite opinion; to come to a conclusion; as, the court *decided* for the plaintiff.

dē-cīd′ed, *a.* 1. Undoubted; free from ambiguity or uncertainty; unquestionable.

2. Resolute; determined; as, a *decided* character.

dē-cīd′ed-ly, *adv.* In a decided or determined manner; clearly; indisputably; in a manner to preclude doubt.

dē-cīd′ed-ness, *n.* The state of being decided.

dē-cīde′ment, *n.* The act of deciding; decision. [Obs.]

dec′i-dence, *n.* A falling off. [Rare.]

dē-cīd′ēr, *n.* One who determines a cause or contest.

dē-cīd′ing-ly, *adv.* In a deciding manner.

dē-cid′ū-ȧ, *n.* [L., f. of *deciduus*, that which falls down, from *decidere*, to fall down.] In physiology, a membrane arising from alteration of the upper layer of the mucous membrane of the uterus, after the reception into the latter of the impregnated ovum, the name being given to it because it is discharged at parturition.

Dē-cid-ū-ā′tȧ, *n.pl.* In zoölogy, the division of mammals throwing off a decidua during parturition.

dē-cid′ū-āte, *a.* 1. Having a decidua; characteristic of the *Deciduata*.

2. Being deciduous.

dē-cid-ū′i-ty, *n.* Deciduousness. [Rare.]

dē-cid′ū-ous, *a.* [L. *deciduus*, that which falls down, from *decidere*, to fall down; *de*, down, and *cadere*, to fall.] Falling; not perennial or permanent; specifically, (a) in botany, applied both to trees whose leaves fall in autumn and to the leaves or other parts of plants which do so fall; (b) in zoölogy, applied to parts which fall off at a certain stage of an animal's existence, as the hair, horns, and teeth of certain animals.

dē-cid′ū-ous-ness, *n.* The quality of being deciduous.

dec′i-gram, dec′i-gramme, *n.* [Fr. *décigramme*, from L. *decimus*, tenth, and *gramma*, a gram.] A French weight of one-tenth of a gram, used in the metric system. It is equivalent to 1.5432 grains.

dec′il, dec′ile, *n.* [Fr., from L. *decimus*, tenth, from *decem*, ten.] An aspect or position of two planets, when they are distant from each other a tenth part of the zodiac.

dec′i-lī-tēr, dec′i-lī-tre, *n.* [Fr. *décilitre*; L. *decimus*, tenth, and *litra*, a liter, from Gr. *litra*, a pound.] A French measure of capacity equal to one-tenth of a liter, used in the metric system, and equivalent to 3.38 United States fluid ounces.

dē-cil′liŏn (-yun), *n.* [*Decem-*, and *million*.] According to the English notation, a million involved to the tenth power, or a unit with sixty ciphers annexed; according to the modern notation of France and the United States, a thousand involved to the eleventh power, or a unit with thirty-three ciphers annexed.

dē-cil′liŏnth (-yunth), *a.* Pertaining to a decillion; having the magnitude or position of one of a decillion equal parts.

dē-cil′liŏnth, *n.* The quotient of unity divided by a decillion; one of a decillion equal parts.

dec′i-mȧ, *n.* 1. In music, an interval of ten diatonic degrees.

2. A Spanish coin worth about five cents.

dec′i-măl, *a.* [OFr. *decimal*; L. *decimus*, tenth, from *decem*, ten.]

1. Relating to decimals; numbered by tens; increasing or diminishing by tens; as, *decimal* fractions; *decimal* coinage.

2. Relating to tithes.

Decimal arithmetic; the common system of arithmetic in which the decimal scale of numbers is used.

Decimal fraction; a fraction whose denominator is ten or some power of ten, as $\frac{7}{10}$, $\frac{40}{100}$, $\frac{50}{1000}$. In the notation of decimals the denominator is usually omitted, and to indicate its value a point is placed to the left of as many figures of the numerator as there are ciphers in the denominator. Should there not be a sufficient number of figures in the numerator, as many ciphers are prefixed as supply the deficiency.

Decimal measure; a measure the unit of which is divided into ten equal parts.

Decimal notation; a system of notation based on powers of ten.

Decimal numeration; naming numbers according to a system of multiples and powers of ten, based on the use of the ten fingers in counting.

Decimal place; the position of a figure after the decimal point.

Decimal point; a point either indicating the value of the fraction or separating the whole number from it.

Decimal system; any system of measuring or reckoning by tenths, tens, or powers of ten; specifically, the *metric system*.

dec′i-măl, *n.* A number or expression given in the scale of tens; a decimal fraction.

Circulating decimal; a recurring decimal which, theoretically, repeats a set of figures indefinitely; also called *circulatory decimal*.

Recurring decimal; a decimal fraction which, theoretically, repeats either one figure or a set of figures indefinitely.

Repeating decimal; a recurring decimal fraction which, theoretically, repeats one figure indefinitely.

dec′i-măl-ism, *n.* The theory or system of reckoning by decimals, as in systems of weights, measures, etc.

dec′i-măl-ist, *n.* One who employs or is an advocate of the decimal system.

dec″i-măl-i-zā′tion, *n.* The act of reducing or causing to conform to the decimal system.

dec′i-măl-ize, *v.t.* To reduce to the decimal system; as, to *decimalize* currency, weights, measures, etc.

dec′i-măl-ly, *adv.* By tens; by means of decimals.

dec′i-māte, *v.t.*; decimated, *pt.*, *pp.*; decimating, *ppr.* [L. *decimare*, from *decem*, ten.]

1. To tithe; to take the tenth part of.

2. To select by lot and punish with death, as every tenth man; as, to *decimate* an army or a collection of prisoners.

3. To destroy a great but indefinite number of; as, the inhabitants were *decimated* by fever.

dec-i-mā′tion, *n.* [L. *decimatio*, from *decimare*, to select the tenth by lot, to pay tithes; from *decimus*, tenth; *decem*, ten.]

1. A tithing. [Obs.]

2. The selecting by lot, as for punishment, every tenth person.

3. The destruction of a great but indefinite proportion of people, as of an army or inhabitants of a country; a heavy loss of life.

dec′i-mā-tŏr, *n.* One who or that which decimates.

de-cime′, *n.* [Fr., from L. *decimus*, tenth.] A French coin, the tenth of a franc, worth about two cents.

dec′i-mē-tēr, dec′i-mē-tre, *n.* [Fr., from *deci-*, and Gr. *metron*, a measure.] A French measure of length in the metric system, equal to the tenth part of a meter, or 3.937 inches.

dec″i-mō-sex′tō, *a.* and *n.* Same as *Sextodecimo*.

dē-cī′phēr, *v.t.*; deciphered, *pt.*, *pp.*; deciphering, *ppr.* [OFr. *de chiffrer*; *de*, from, and *cifre*, a cipher.]

1. To ascertain, as that written in cipher, by discovering and applying the key; as, to *decipher* a cablegram.

2. To read, as that written in obscure, partially obliterated, or badly formed characters; to unfold.

3. To discover or explain the meaning of, as of something that is obscure or difficult to be understood; as, to *decipher* an ambiguous speech.

4. To describe; to delineate.

5. To find out; to detect; to discover; to reveal. [Rare.]

Syn.—Interpret, translate, reveal, unravel, unfold, solve.

dē-cī′phēr-ȧ-ble, *a.* Capable of being deciphered or interpreted.

dē-cī′phēr-ēr, *n.* One who explains what is written in cipher or written obscurely.

dē-cī′phēr-ess, *n.* A female who deciphers.

dē-cī′phēr-ment, *n.* The act of deciphering.

dē-cip′i-um, *n.* [L., from *decipere*, to deceive.] In chemistry, a hypothetical metallic substance intermediate between cerium and yttrium, found in the samarskite of North Carolina; now generally known as *samarium*.

dē-ci′șion (-sizh′un), *n.* [L. *decisio*, a cutting short, a decision, from *decisus*, pp. of *decidere*, to cut short, to decide.]

1. The act of separating or cutting off; detachment of a part. [Obs.]

2. Determination, as of a question or doubt; final judgment, as in a case which has been under consideration; resolution; as, the *decision* of the supreme court.

3. Determination, as of a contest or event; end, as of a struggle; as, the *decision* of a battle.

4. The quality of being decided; prompt determination; as, a man of *decision*.

Syn.—Conclusion, disposal, resolution, determination, opinion.

dē-cī′sive, *a.* 1. Having the power or quality of determining a question, doubt, contest, event, etc.; final; conclusive; as, the judgment of the court is *decisive*; a *decisive* victory.

2. Marked by decision or prompt determination; as, a *decisive* character.

Syn.—Decided, final, conclusive, unquestionable, unmistakable, positive.

dē-cī′sive-ly, *adv.* In a decisive manner.

dē-cī′sive-ness, *n.* The quality of being decisive

dē-cī′sō-ry, *a.* Able to decide or determine.

dec′i-stēre, *n.* [Fr., from *deci-*, tenth, and Gr. *stereos*, solid.] In the metric system, a measure of volume, the tenth part of a stere, equivalent to 3.532 cubic feet.

dē-cit′i-zen-īze, *v.t.* To deprive of citizenship. [Rare.]

dē-civ′i-līze, *v.t.*; decivilized, *pt.*, *pp.*; decivilizing, *ppr.* To reduce from a civilized to a wild or savage state.

deck, *v.t.*; decked (dekt), *pt.*, *pp.*; decking, *ppr.* [ME. *decken*, to cover; M.D. *decken*, to hide.]

1. To cover; to clothe, especially with elegance; to array; to embellish; as, she *decked* herself in all her finery.

> The dew with spangles *decked* the ground.
> —Dryden.

2. To furnish with a deck, as a vessel.

Syn.—Adorn, embellish, array, decorate, ornament, beautify, bedeck, garnish.

deck, *n.* [M.D. *decke*, a cover.]

1. A horizontal platform or floor extending from side to side of a ship; where there is more than one *deck*, various names are applied to indicate their location, construction, or use; as, lower *deck*; flush *deck*; berth-*deck*.

2. In card-playing, (a) the pack required to play any specified game; as, a euchre *deck*; (b) that part of the pack remaining after the players have received their hands.

3. A pile; a heap. [Obs.]

4. In mining, the platform of a cage.

5. The roof of a railroad passenger-car.

Cold deck; a pack of playing-cards arranged before being dealt; a stacked deck. [Slang.]

Flush deck; a continued floor from stem to stern upon which there are no superstructures.

On deck; ready for duty or action; hence, in baseball, next in turn to bat.

Protective deck; in naval ships, a curved steel deck below the water, about three inches thick, serving to protect the machinery.

To clear the decks; to prepare a naval ship for action.

To sweep the deck; (a) to carry away everything movable from the deck, as by a wave; (b) to command all parts of the deck; (c) in card-playing, to take all the stakes on the table.

deck′=bēam, *n.* 1. A strong transverse piece of

timber stretching across a ship from side to side, serving to support a deck and retain the sides at their proper distance.

2. A T-shaped iron beam having a slight enlargement opposite the flange.

deck′-bridge (-brij), *n.* In railroad engineering, a bridge carrying the track upon the top, and not between the girders.

deck′el, *n.* See *Deckle.*

deck′ėr, *n.* 1. One who or that which decks or adorns; a coverer; as, a table-*decker.*

2. A vessel that has a deck or decks; chiefly used in composition; as, a two-*decker.*

deck′-feath″ėr (-feth″ẽr), *n.* In zoölogy, one of the pair of middle tail-feathers which cover those below and form a sort of deck.

deck′-hand, *n.* A sailor whose duty it is to work about the deck.

deck′-hook, *n.* The compass-timber bolted horizontally athwart a ship's bow, connecting the stem, timbers, and deck-planks of the fore part of a ship.

dec′kle (dek′l), *n.* [L.G. *dekkel*, a cover, lid.] In paper-making, (a) a thin frame of wood fitting on the shallow mold in which the paper-pulp is placed, serving to regulate the width of the sheet; (b) the rough or raw edge of paper.

dec′kle-edged (-ejd), *a.* Having the edges rough and untrimmed; uncut; said of books and magazines.

deck′-light, *n.* A thick piece of glass fitted into the deck to light the quarters below.

deck′-tran″sŏm, *n.* In shipbuilding, the transom which supports a deck.

dē-clāim′, *v.i.*; declaimed, *pt.*, *pp.*; declaiming, *ppr.* [ME. *declamen*; L. *declamare*, to cry aloud, declaim; *de-*, intens., and *clamare*, to cry, shout.]

1. To make a formal speech or oration; to harangue; as, the students *declaim* twice a week.

2. To speak or write for rhetorical display; to speak or write pompously or elaborately, without sincerity or sound argument; to rant.

dē-clāim′, *v.t.* 1. To publicly utter in a rhetorical manner.

2. To decry; with *against*; as, he *declaimed against* the evils of society.

3. To speak in favor of; to advocate. [Obs.]

dē-clāim′ănt, *n.* Same as *Declaimer.* [Rare.]

dē-clāim′ẽr, *n.* One who declaims; a speaker in public.

dec-lȧ-mā′tion, *n.* [Fr. *declamation*; L. *declamatio*, declamation, from *declamare*, to speak aloud, declaim.]

1. The act or art of speaking in public.

2. A committed speech or a selection of prose or poetry recited, or for recitation in public.

3. A pompous harangue; bombastic oratory.

4. In singing, a clear and correct enunciation, especially in rendering dramatic compositions.

dec′lȧ-mā-tŏr, *n.* A declaimer. [Rare.]

dē-clam′ȧ-tō-ry, *a.* [L. *declamatorius*, belonging to the exercise of speaking aloud, from *declamare*, to speak aloud.]

1. Pertaining to declamation; treated in the manner of a rhetorician; as, a *declamatory* theme.

2. Appealing to the passions; noisily rhetorical; as, a *declamatory* style.

dē-clār′ȧ-ble, *a.* Capable of being declared or proved.

dē-clār′ănt, *n.* In law, one who declares.

dec-lȧ-rā′tion, *n.* [ME. *declaracion*; L. *declaratio*, a declaration, from *declarare*, to make clear, declare; *de-*, intens., and *clarus*, clear.]

1. An affirmation; a formal statement of facts or opinions; verbal utterance; as, he declared his sentiments, and I rely on his *declaration.*

2. The document setting forth a proclamation; as, the *Declaration* of Independence.

3. In law, the paper filed by the plaintiff demanding judgment and stating his complaint.

Declaration of Independence; see under *Independence.*

Declaration of intention; the statement of an alien, when applying for naturalization under the United States laws, declaratory of his intention to become a citizen.

Declaration of rights; see *Bill of rights* under *Bill.*

Declaration of trust; in law, the creation of a trust in writing, or the declaration thereof.

dē-clar′ȧ-tive, *a.* [LL. *declarativus*, from L. *declarare*, to declare.]

1. Making declaration or proclamation; explanatory; as, the name of a thing may be *declarative* of its form or nature.

2. Shown; set forth.

dē-clar′ȧ-tive-ly, *adv.* By distinct statement; specifically.

dec′lȧ-rā″tŏr, *n.* In Scots law, an action praying for the judicial declaration of some right or interest.

dē-clar′ȧ-tō-ri-ly, *adv.* In a clear, explanatory manner.

dē-clar′ȧ-tō-ry, *a.* Making declaration, explicit manifestation, or exhibition; clearly expressive; as, this clause is *declaratory* of the will of the legislature.

Declaratory act; a statute defining the law.

dē-clāre′, *v.t.*; declared, *pt.*, *pp.*; declaring, *ppr.* [ME. *declaren*; OFr. *declarer*; L. *declarare*, to make clear, to declare; *de-*, intens., and *clarus*, clear.]

1. To clear; to free from obscurity; to make plain. [Obs.]

2. To make known; to tell explicitly; to manifest plainly by words.

3. To assert positively; to avow; to state in an unmistakable manner.

4. To announce the existence of, in an official manner; as, to *declare* that war exists.

5. To make an unreserved statement concerning, as of goods liable to duty, or of taxes due.

6. In law, to state in a solemn manner before witnesses.

To declare off; to recede from a position taken; to announce discontinuance; as, to *declare* a strike *off*; to *declare* the contest *off*. [Colloq.]

To declare oneself; to throw off reserve and avow one's opinion; to show openly what one thinks, or which side he espouses.

dē-clāre′, *v.i.*; declared, *pt.*, *pp.*; declaring, *ppr.*

1. To make a declaration; to proclaim or avow some opinion or resolution; to make known explicitly some determination; with *for* or *against*; as, he *declared for* the allies, whereupon the allies *declared against* the emperor.

2. In law, to recite the cause of complaint against the defendant; as, the plaintiff *declares* in debt or trespass.

dē-clāred′, *a.* Avowed; exhibited; manifested; published; proclaimed; recited.

dē-clār′ed-ly, *adv.* Avowedly; explicitly.

dē-clār′ed-ness, *n.* The state of being declared.

dē-clāre′ment, *n.* Declaration. [Obs.]

dē-clār′ẽr, *n.* One who makes known or publishes; that which exhibits.

dē-clāssed′ (-klāst′), *a.* Having fallen or been forced from one's proper or former place in society; having lost caste.

dē-clen′sion, *n.* [L. *declinatio*, a bending aside, from *declinare*, to bend or turn aside.]

1. In grammar, (a) the inflection of nouns, adjectives, and pronouns; the change of endings undergone by them to express their different relations of gender, person, number, and case; (b) the act of so inflecting words; (c) a group of nouns of the same type thus inflected; as, the third *declension.*

2. The state of declining; descent; slope.

3. Act of declining; a refusal.

4. The process of falling or sinking lower; deterioration; decay; as, the *declension* of learning.

dē-clen′sion-ăl, *a.* Belonging or pertaining to declension.

dē-clin′ȧ-ble, *a.* Capable of being declined; admitting of inflection; as, a *declinable* noun.

dē-clīn′ăl, *a.* Declining; bending or sloping downward.

dec′li-nant, *a.* In heraldry, having the tail vertically pendent; as, a serpent *declinant.*

dec′li-nāte, *a.* Bent downward or aside; used in botany and zoölogy, especially of the stamens of flowers.

dec-li-nā′tion, *n.* [ME. *declinacion*; L. *declinatio*, a bending aside, deflection, from *declinare*, to turn or bend aside.]

1. A leaning; the act of bending down; as, a *declination* of the head.

2. A declining into a lower state; decay; deterioration; gradual diminution of strength, soundness, vigor, or excellence.

3. A deviation from a right line, in a literal sense; oblique motion; as, the *declination* of a descending body.

4. The act or state of declining; refusal.

5. In astronomy, the distance of any object from the celestial equator, either northward or southward.

6. In grammar, declension, or the inflection of a noun through its various terminations.

7. In dialing, an arc of the horizon contained between the vertical plane and the prime vertical circle, if reckoned from the east or west, or between the meridian and the plane, if reckoned from the north or south.

Angle of declination; the angle described by a descending line or plane with one which is horizontal.

Circle of declination; a great circle passing through the poles and cutting the equator at right angles.

Declination compass; in physics, a compass designed to ascertain the variations of the magnetic needle.

Declination of the needle; the angle made by the needle with the true meridian.

dec′li-nā-tŏr, *n.* [L., from *declinare*, to decline.]

1. An instrument for taking the declination or inclination of a reclining plane; an instrument in dialing; also written *declinatory.*

2. A dissentient. [Rare.]

dē-clīn′ȧ-tō-ry, *a.* Pertaining to, conveying, or involving a declination.

Declinatory plea; in old English law, a plea before trial or conviction, intended to show that the party was not liable to the penalty of the law, or was specially exempt from the jurisdiction of the court.

dē-clin′ȧ-tō-ry, *n.* Same as *Declinator.*

dē-clin′ȧ-tūre, *n.* A declining; declension; refusal.

dē-cline′, *v.t.*; declined, *pt.*, *pp.*; declining, *ppr.* [ME. *declinen*; OFr. *decliner*; L. *declinare*, to bend, turn aside.]

1. To bend downward; to bring down; to cause to bend or fall.

2. To shun or avoid; to refuse; as, he *declined* the contest; he *declined* the offer.

3. In grammar, to inflect; to change the termination of, in order to express the different relations of gender, person, number, and case.

4. To cause to decrease. [Obs.]

dē-cline′, *v.i.* 1. To lean downward; to bend over or hang down, as from weakness or despondency; to descend; as, the head *declines* toward the earth; the sun *declines* toward the west.

2. To fail; to be impaired; as, the vigor of youth *declines* in age.

3. To lean from a right line; figuratively, to deviate from the prevailing intellectual or moral standard.

dē-cline′, *n.* 1 A falling off; diminution; deterioration, decay; as, the *decline* of life; the *decline* of agriculture; the *decline* of learning.

2. A gradual decay of health; any wasting disease, especially pulmonary.

3. That period of a disease when the symptoms abate in violence; as, the *decline* of a fever.

Syn.—Decay, consumption.—The first stage of the downward progress is *decline*; *decay* follows, tending to ultimate destruction; *consumption* is steady *decay* from an inward wasting of strength.

dē-clīned′, *a.* In botany, declinate.

dē-clīn′ẽr, *n.* 1 One who rejects or refuses.

2. See *Declining dial* under *Dial.*

dec-li-nom′e-tẽr, *n.* [From L. *declinare*, to decline, and Gr *metron*, a measure.] An instrument for measuring the declination of the magnetic needle.

dē-clīn′ous, *a.* In botany, declinate; bent downward.

dec′li-vănt, *a.* See *Declinant.*

dē-cliv′i-tous, *a.* Same as *Declivous.*

dē-cliv′i-ty, *n.* [L. *declivitas*, a sloping place, declivity, from *declivis*, sloping downward; *de*, down, from, and *clivus*, a slope, a hill.] Declination from a horizontal line; descent; a slope downward; chiefly used of the earth, and opposed to *acclivity.*

dē-clī′vous, *a.* Gradually descending; not precipitous; sloping.

dē-coct′, *v.t.* [ME. *decocten*; L. *decoctus*, pp. of *decoquere*, to boil down; *de*, down, and *coquere*, to cook.]

1. To prepare by boiling; to digest in hot or boiling water.

2. To digest by the heat of the stomach; to concoct.

3. To impart warmth or strength to, as if by boiling. [Rare.]

dē-coct′i-ble, *a.* Capable of being boiled or digested.

dē-coc′tion, *n.* 1. The act of boiling a substance in water, for the purpose of extracting its salient properties.

2. The liquor in which a substance has been boiled; water impregnated with the properties of any animal or vegetable substance which has been boiled in it; as, a strong *décoction* of Peruvian bark.

dē-coc′tūre, *n.* A substance made by decoction. [Rare.]

dē-col′lāte, *v.t.*; decollated, *pt.*, *pp.*; decollating, *ppr.* [L. *decollatus*, pp. of *decollare*, to behead; *de*, from, and *collum*, neck.] To behead.

dē-col′lā-ted, *a.* 1. Beheaded.

2. In conchology, having the head or apex worn off, as certain univalve shells.

dē-col-lā′tion, *n.* 1. The act of beheading; decapitation.

2. In surgery, removal of the head of the child in difficult parturition.

3. A painting representing the beheading of a martyr, or a festival commemorative of such an event; as, the *decollation* of St. John the Baptist.

dé-colle-té′ (dā-kol-tā′), *a.* [Fr., pp. of *décolleter*, to bare one's neck and shoulders; *de*, from, and *cou*, neck; L. *de*, from, down, and *collum*, neck.]

1. Cut low in the neck; low-necked, as a dress.

2. [Feminine, *décolletée.*] Having the neck and shoulders bare; said of a woman wearing a *décolleté* gown.

dē-cŏl′ŏr, *v.t.*; decolored, *pt.*, *pp.*; decoloring, *ppr.* To deprive of color; to bleach; decolorate.

dē-cŏl′ŏr-ănt, *a.* and *n.* I. *a.* Tending to remove color; bleaching.

II. *n.* A substance which removes color, or bleaches.

dē-çŏl′ŏr-āte, *a.* Deprived of color; bleached.

dē-çŏl′ŏr-āte, *v.t.* To remove the color from; to decolor.

dē-çŏl-ŏr-ā′tion, *n.* The removal or absence of color.

dē-çŏl″ŏr-i-zā′tion, *n.* The act or art of removing color.

dē′cŏm-plex, *a.* 1. Freed from complexity; simplified, as ideas.

2. Made up of complex constituents. [Rare.]

dē-çŏm-pōș′ȧ-ble, *a.* Capable of being decomposed or resolved into constituent elements.

dē-çŏm-pōșe′, *v.t.*; decomposed, *pt.*, *pp.*; decomposing, *ppr.* [L. *de-* priv., and *componere*, to put together, to compose; *com-*, together, and *ponere*, to put, place.] To resolve into original elements; to disunite, as particles combined by affinity or chemical attraction; to cause to rot.

dē-çŏm-pōșe′, *v.i.* To become separated into constituents; to decay.

dē-çŏm-pōșed′, *a.* 1. In a state of decomposition; rotten.

2. In ornithology, standing apart; divergent; as, a *decomposed* crest.

dē-çŏm-pō′șẽr, *n.* Anything that causes decomposition.

dē-çŏm-poș′ite, *a.* 1. Compounded a second time; compounded with things already composite.

2. In botany, much divided, as a leaf or stem; decompound.

dē-çŏm-poș′ite, *n.* Anything compounded with things already composite.

dē-com-pō-și′tion (-zish′un), *n.* 1. Analysis; the act of separating the constituent parts of a compound body or substance. *Decomposition* differs from mechanical division, as the latter effects no change in the properties of the body divided, whereas the parts decomposed have properties very different from those of the substance itself.

2. Separation into original elements, especially decay or putrefaction of any organic body.

3. A combination of things already compounded. [Obs.]

Decomposition of forces; the process by which a given force or forces is resolved into several minor forces or motions.

Decomposition of light; separation of a beam of light into the prismatic colors.

Electric decomposition; in physics and chemistry, electrolysis, or the decomposition of a substance by a current of electricity.

dē-çŏm-pound′, *v.t.*; decompounded, *pt.*, *pp.*; decompounding, *ppr.* [L. *de-* priv., and *componere*, to put together.]

1. To compound a second time; to form by a second composition.

2. To decompose. [Rare.]

dē-çŏm-pound′, *a.* 1. Composed of things or words already compounded.

2. In botany, divided into a number of compound divisions; as, a *decompound* leaf or panicle.

Decompound Leaf.

dē-çŏm-pound′, *n.* A decomposite.

dē-çŏm-pound′-ȧ-ble, *a.* Capable of being decompounded.

dē-çŏm-pound′-ly, *adv.* In a decompound manner.

dē-çŏn-cen′-trāte, *v.t.* To scatter from a center; to distribute; to decentralize. [Rare.]

dē-çon-cen-trā′tion, *n.* The act of deconcentrating; the state of being deconcentrated.

dē-çŏn-coct′, *v.t.* To decompose. [Rare.]

dē-çon′sē-crāte, *v.t.* To deprive of sacred character or of the virtue conferred by consecration; to secularize; as, to *deconsecrate* a church.

dē-çon-sē-crā′tion, *n.* The act of deconsecrating or the state of being deconsecrated.

dē-çop″pẽr-i-zā′tion, *n.* The process of freeing from copper.

dē-çop′pẽr-ize, *v.t.* To free from copper.

deç′ō-rȧ-ment, *n.* Ornament. [Obs.]

deç′ō-rāte, *v.t.*; decorated, *pt*, *pp.*; decorating, *ppr.* [L. *decoratus*, pp. of *decorare*, to decorate, adorn, from *decus*, ornament, pride, from *decere*, to befit, become.]

1. To deck with something becoming or ornamental; to adorn; to beautify; to embellish; as, to *decorate* the person; to *decorate* a building.

2. Figuratively, to place an adornment upon, as an honor; as, to *decorate* a knight with the cross of the Legion of Honor.

Decorated style; the second style of English Pointed architecture, flourishing from the end of the thirteenth to the commencement of the fifteenth century, when it was superseded by the Perpendicular.

Syn.—Beautify, adorn, ornament, embellish, bedeck, garnish.

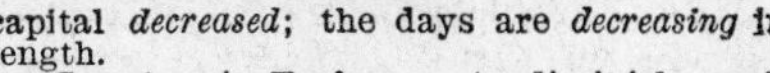

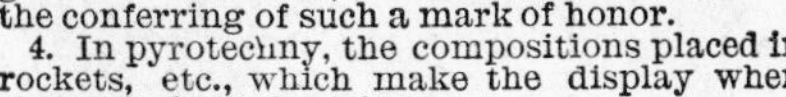

Window, Decorated Style.

deç-ō-rā′tion, *n.* 1. The act of adorning or embellishing; ornamentation.

2. That which decorates or adorns; an ornament.

3. Any badge, as a medal, cross of honor, etc., bestowed for distinguished services; the conferring of such a mark of honor.

4. In pyrotechny, the compositions placed in rockets, etc., which make the display when the explosion takes place.

Decoration day; in the United States, May 30, the day set apart for decorating with flowers the graves of soldiers and sailors who fell in the Civil War; also called *Memorial day.*

deç′ō-rā-tive, *a.* Adorning; suited to embellish.

Decorative art; art which has for its object the mere pleasing of the eye, particularly in the embellishment of the interiors of edifices, both private and public.

deç′ō-rā-tive-ness, *n.* The quality of being decorative.

deç′ō-rā-tŏr, *n.* One who adorns or embellishes; specifically, one whose business it is to decorate the interiors of edifices.

dē-çōre′, *v.t.* To decorate; to honor. [Obs.]

dē-çōre′ment, *n.* Decoration; ornament. [Obs.]

dē-çō′rous (*or* dek′ō-rus), *a.* [L. *decorus*, becoming, from *decor*, comeliness, grace.] Proper; becoming; befitting; as, *decorous* behavior; a *decorous* speech.

dē-çō′rous-ly (*or* dek′ō-), *adv.* In a decorous manner.

dē-çō′rous-ness (*or* dek′ō-), *n.* The quality of being decorous.

dē-çor′ti-çāte, *v.t.*; decorticated, *pt.*, *pp.*; decorticating, *ppr.* [L. *decorticatus*, pp. of *decorticare*, to strip the bark off; *de*, from, and *cortex*, bark.] To strip the bark from; to husk; to remove the cortex or outer covering from; as, to *decorticate* barley, or a tree.

dē-çor-ti-çā′tion, *n.* The act of stripping off the cortex, or outer covering of anything.

dē-çor′ti-çā-tŏr, *n.* A tool for decorticating.

dē-çō′rum, *n.* [L. *decorum*, fitness, propriety, from neut. of *decorus*, fit, proper, from *decor*, grace, ornament, from *decere*, to become.] Propriety of speech or behavior; seemliness; especially formal politeness; as, he both spoke and behaved with great *decorum.*

Syn.—Dignity.—*Decorum* is that which is becoming in outward act or appearance; *dignity* springs from an inward elevation of soul producing a correspondent effect on the manners.

dé-çou-plé′ (dā-kö-plā′), *a.* [Fr. pp. of *découpler*, to uncouple.] In heraldry, uncoupled; parted; as, a chevron *découplé*, i.e., the bars separated.

dē-çoy′, *v.t.*; decoyed, *pt.*, *pp*; decoying, *ppr.* [*De*, from, and OFr. *coi*, *quoi*, to quiet, to coy.] To lead or lure by artifice, as into a snare; to entrap by any means which deceive; as, the fowler *decoys* ducks into a net.

dē-çoy′, *v.i.* To be ensnared by means of a decoy; as, the ducks, *decoying* well, were easily shot.

Syn.—Allure, entice, lure, attract, tempt, draw, seduce, inveigle.

dē-çoy′, *n.* 1. Anything intended to lead into a snare or the power of an enemy.

2. A place into which wild fowls are decoyed in order to be caught.

3. A fowl, or the dummy of one, used to entice other birds into a net or within range of shot; as, a duck was used as a *decoy.*

4. A person employed to lead others into a snare, as in detective operations.

dē-çoy′-bird, *n.* A bird, or a dummy, used to draw others into a decoy.

dē-çoy′-duck, *n.* A duck employed as a decoy-bird; hence, colloquially, a person who decoys.

dē-çoy′ẽr, *n.* A person employed to decoy others.

dē-çoy′-man, *n.*; *pl.* **dē-çoy′-men.** A man employed to decoy and catch fowls.

dē-çras′si-fy̆, *v.t.* To make less crass; to free from grossness.

dē-çrēase′, *v.i.*; decreased (dē̤crēst), *pt.*, *pp.*; decreasing, *ppr.* [ME. *decresen*; OFr. *decresser*; L. *decrescere*, to decrease, become less; *de*, from, away, and *crescere*, to grow, increase.] To become less; to be diminished gradually; as, his capital *decreased*; the days are *decreasing* in length.

dē-çrēase′, *v.t.* To lessen; to diminish gradually or by small deductions; as, dissipation *decreases* one's vitality.

Syn.—Diminish, lessen, abate, minimize, lower, reduce.—Things usually *decrease* by degrees, and from within, or through some cause which is imperceptible. They commonly *diminish* or are *diminished* by an action from without, or one which is apparent.

dē-çrēase′, *n.* 1. The act of decreasing, or the state of being decreased; gradual diminution; as, a *decrease* of revenue.

2. The wane of the moon.

dē-çrēase′less, *a.* Without decrease. [Rare.]

dē-çrēas′ing, *a.* Becoming less; diminishing; waning.

Decreasing series; in mathematics, a series in which each member is less than the one preceding. [See *Arithmetical progression* under *Progression.*]

dē-çrēas′ing-ly, *adv.* In a decreasing manner.

dē-çrē-ā′tion, *n.* The undoing of the act of creation; annihilation. [Rare.]

dē-çree′, *v.t.*; decreed, *pt.*, *pp.*; decreeing, *ppr.* 1. To determine judicially; to resolve by sentence; as, the court *decreed* a restoration of the property.

2. To determine or resolve legislatively; to fix or appoint; to constitute by edict.

> Thou shalt also *decree* a thing, and it shall be established unto thee. —Job xxii. 28.

dē-çree′, *v.i.* To determine; to predetermine immutably; to make an edict; to appoint by edict.

> As my eternal purpose hath *decreed.*—Milton.

Syn.—Ordain, order, determine, decide, command, direct, prescribe, enjoin.

dē-çree′, *n.* [ME. *decre*; OFr. *decret*; L. *decretum*, a decree, neut. of *decretus*, pp. of *decernere*, to decree; *de*, from, and *cernere*, to see, to judge.]

1. An ordinance or order issued by a person or body of persons in authority deciding what is to be done in a certain matter, or what is to take place; an edict; a decision; a command; as, the *decree* of the emperor; an ecclesiastical *decree.*

2. In Roman law, a determination or judgment of the emperor on a suit between parties.

3. A judicial decision, or determination of a litigated cause; as, a *decree* of a court of chancery.

4. The judgment or award of an umpire in a case submitted to him.

5. In theology, the purpose of God concerning future events.

Syn.—Edict, judgment, law, order, ordinance, proclamation.

dē-çree′ȧ-ble, *a.* Capable of being decreed.

dē-çrē′ẽr, *n.* One who decrees.

dē-çreet′, *n.* In Scots law, a decree; a final judgment.

deç′rē-ment, *n.* [LL. *decrementum*, a decrease, from L. *decrescere*, to decrease.]

1. Decrease; waste; the state of becoming gradually less.

> Rocks and mountains suffer a continual *decrement.* —Woodward.

2. The quantity lost by gradual diminution or waste; opposed to *increment.*

3. In mathematics, the small part by which a variable becomes less and less.

4. In crystallography, a successive diminution of the layers of molecules, applied to the faces of the primitive form, by which the secondary forms are supposed to be produced.

5. In heraldry, the wane of the moon.

Equal decrement of life; in the doctrine of annuities, the theory that of a given number of lives there should be an equal annual decrease within a given period.

dē-çrep′it, *a.* [OFr. *decrepit*; L. *decrepitus*, broken down, worn out, very old, from *de-* priv., and *crepare*, to make a noise.] Wasted or worn by the infirmities of old age; being in the last stage of decay.

dē-çrep′i-tāte, *v.t.*; decrepitated, *pt.*, *pp.*; decrepitating, *ppr.* [*De-*, intens., and L. *crepitatus*, pp. of *crepitare*, to crackle, rattle, break with a noise.] To roast or calcine in a strong heat, with a continual bursting or crackling of the substance; as, to *decrepitate* salt.

dē-çrep′i-tāte, *v.i.* To crackle, as salts when roasting.

dē-çrep-i-tā′tion, *n.* The act of decrepitating; the noise made by salt when roasting.

dē-çrep′it-ly, *adv.* In a decrepit manner.

dē-çrep′it-ness, *n.* Decrepitude.

dē-çrep′i-tūde, *n.* [Fr. *décrépitude*, from L. *decrepitus*, decrepit.] The broken state of the body, produced by decay and the infirmities of age.

> From youth to *decrepitude.* —Johnson.

dē-çres-cen′dō (dā-kre-shen′dō), *n.* [It., ppr.

of *decrescere*, to decrease.] In music, a gradual decrease in loudness of tone, indicated upon the staff either by the sign >, or by *decres.*, or *dec.*; also used as an adjective and an adverb. Same as *diminuendo*.

dē-çres′cent, *a.* [L. *decrescens*, ppr. of *decrescere*, to decrease.] Decreasing; becoming less by gradual diminution; as, a *decrescent* moon.

dē-çres′cent, *n.* In heraldry, the moon when declining from the full to the last quarter; used as a bearing.

dē-çrē′tăl, *a.* Appertaining to a decree; containing a decree; as, a *decretal* epistle.

dē-çrē′tăl, *n.* 1. An authoritative order or decree; specifically, a letter of the pope determining some point or question in ecclesiastical law.

2. A book of decrees or edicts; a body of laws; specifically, [C—*pl.*] the second part of the canon law, so called because it contains the decrees of sundry popes.

dē-çrēte′, *n.* A decree. [Obs.]

dē-çrē′tion, *n.* Decrease. [Obs.]

dē-çrē′tist, *n.* [From L. *decretum*, a decree.] One who studies or professes a knowledge of the decretals.

dē-çrē′tive, *a.* Having the force of a decree.

deç-rē-tō′ri-ăl, *a.* Decretory. [Obs.]

deç′rē-tō-ri-ly, *adv.* In a definitive manner.

deç′rē-tō-ry, *a.* 1. Judicial; definitive; established by a decree.

> The *decretory* rigors of a condemning sentence. —South.

2. Critical; determining.

dē-çrew′, *v.i.* To decrease. [Obs.]

dē-çrī′ăl, *n.* A crying down; a clamorous censure; condemnation by censure.

dē-çrī′ēr, *n.* A defamer.

dē-çrown′, *v.t.* To deprive of a crown. [Rare.]

dē-çrus-tā′tion, *n.* The removal of a crust from.

dē-çrȳ′, *v.t.*; decried, *pt.*, *pp.*; decrying, *ppr.* [Fr. *decrier*; OFr. *descrier*, to decry, to cry down; *des*, down, and *crier*, to cry; L. *de*, down, and *queri*, to complain, lament.] To cry down; to censure as faulty or worthless; to clamor against; as, to *decry* a poem.

Syn.—Depreciate, detract, disparage.—*Decry* and *depreciate* refer to the estimation in which a thing is held, the former seeking to cry it down and the latter to run it down in the opinion of others. *Detract* and *disparage* refer to merit or value, which the former assails with caviling, etc., while the latter wilfully underrates and seeks to degrade it. Men *decry* their rivals and *depreciate* their measures. The envious *detract* from the merit of a good action, and *disparage* the motives of him who performs it.

deç-ū-bā′tion (*or* dē-çū-), *n.* [From L. *de*, down, and *cubare*, to lie down, recline.] The act of lying down.

dē-çū′bi-tăl, *a.* Relating to or caused by decubitus; of the nature of a decubitus or bedsore.

dē-çū′bi-tus, *n.* [L., from *decumbere*, to lie down.] In medicine, (a) the attitude of a sick person in bed; (b) a bedsore.

deç′ū-măn, *a.* [L. *decimanus*, or *decumanus*, belonging to the tenth part; *decumus*, tenth; *decem*, ten.]

1. In Roman military antiquity, a term applied to a gate of a Roman camp near which the tenth cohorts of the legions were encamped. The *decuman* gate was the principal entrance to the camp, and was that farthest from the enemy.

2. Of great size; huge; said especially of waves.

deç′ū-măn, *n.* 1. An immense wave supposed to be every tenth in order.

2. In astrology, a tenth division of the ecliptic.

dē-çum′bence, *n.* [L. *decumbens*, ppr. of *decumbere*, to lie down.] The act of lying down; the posture of lying down.

dē-çum′ben-cy, *n.* Decumbence.

dē-çum′bent, *a.* 1. Lying down; reclining; recumbent.

2. In botany, declined or bending down, as a stem which rests on the earth and then rises again.

dē-çum′bent-ly, *adv.* In a decumbent posture.

dē-çum′bi-tūre, *n.* [From L. *decumbere*, to lie down.]

1. The time at which a sick person takes to bed, or during which he is confined to bed.

2. In astrology, the scheme or aspect of the heavens, by which the prognostics of recovery or death were discovered.

deç′ū-ple (-pl), *a.* [L. *decuplus*, tenfold, from *decem*, ten, and *plus*, more.] Tenfold; containing ten times as many.

deç′ū-ple, *n.* A number ten times repeated.

deç′ū-ple, *v.t.*; decupled, *pt.*, *pp.*; decupling, *ppr.* To increase tenfold.

dē-çū′ri-ŏn, *n.* [L. *decurio*, from *decuria*, a company of ten men; *decem*, ten.]

1. An officer in the Roman army, who commanded a decury, or a body of ten soldiers.

2. Any commander or overseer of ten; a tithingman.

dē-çū′ri-ŏn-āte, *n.* The state or office of a decurion.

dē-çur′rence, *n.* A running down; a lapse. [Rare.]

dē-çur′rent, *a.* [L. *decurrens*, ppr. of *decurrere*, to run down; *de*, down, and *currere*, to run.] In botany, extending downward beyond the place of insertion; as, a *decurrent* leaf, having its base extending downward along the stem.

Decurrent Leaf—Thistle.

dē-çur′rent-ly, *adv.* In a decurrent manner.

dē-çūr′sion, *n.* 1. The act of running down, as a stream. [Obs.]

2. In Roman antiquity, a military maneuver or march; a parade. [Obs.]

dē-çūr′sive, *a.* Running down; decurrent.

dē-çūr′sive-ly, *adv.* In a decursive manner.

Decursively pinnate; in botany, a term applied to a leaf having the leaflets decurrent, or running along the petiole.

dē-çūrt′, *v.t.* To shorten by cutting off; to abridge. [Obs.]

dē-çūr-tā′tion, *n.* Abridgment. [Obs.]

dē-çūr-vā′tion, *n.* The act of decurving; the state of being curved downward.

dē-çūr′vā-tūre, *n.* Decurvation.

dē-çūrve′, *v.t.*; decurved, *pt.*, *pp.*; decurving, *ppr.* To curve downward.

deç′ū-ry, *n.*; *pl.* **deç′ū-ries.** [L. *decuria*, from *decem*, ten.] A body of ten men under a decurion.

dē-çus′sāte, *v.t.*; decussated, *pt.*, *pp.*; decussating, *ppr.* [L. *decussatus*, pp. of *decussare*, to divide crosswise in the form of an X, from *decussis*, the figure ten (X), from *decem*, ten.] To intersect so as to make acute angles, thus X; or, in general, to intersect; to cross, as lines, rays of light, leaves, or nerves in the body.

dē-çus′sāte, *a.* 1. Crossed; intersected.

2. In botany, arranged in pairs alternately crossing each other at regular angles; as, *decussate* leaves and branches.

3. In rhetoric, consisting of two rising and two falling clauses, placed in alternate opposition to each other.

Decussate Leaves.

dē-çus′sā-ted, *a.* Decussate.

dē-çus′sāte-ly, *adv.* In a decussate manner.

dē-çus-sā′tion, *n.* [L. *decussatio*, from *decussare*, to cross.] The act of crossing at right or at acute angles; an intersection in the form of X; the state of being so crossed.

dē-çus′sā-tive, *a.* Crossing; intersecting.

dē-çus′sā-tive-ly, *adv.* Crosswise; in the form of an X.

dē′cyl, *n.* [Gr. *deka*, ten, and *hylē*, wood, material.] A monatomic, organic, hydrocarbon radical, $C_{10}H_{21}$.

dē-cyl′iç, *a.* Pertaining to decyl.

dē′dăl, dæ′dăl, *a.* [L. *dædalus*; Gr. *daidalos*, skilfully wrought, from *daidallein*, to work cunningly.]

1. Formed with art; showing artistic skill; ingenious.

2. Artful; crafty.

dē-dā′li-ăn, dæ-dā′li-ăn (-yăn), *a.* Dedal.

ded′á-lous, dæd′á-lous (ded′), *a.* 1. Dedal.

2. In botany, having a margin with various turnings and windings.

de-däns′ (-dän′), *n.* [Fr. *dedans*, the inside.] In court tennis, the space reserved at one end of the tennis court for those looking on.

dede, *a.* [Obs.] See *Dead*.

dē-deç′ō-rāte, *v.t.* To disgrace. [Obs.]

dē-deç-ō-rā′tion, *n.* Disgrace. [Obs.]

dē-deç′ō-rous, *a.* Disgraceful; unbecoming. [Rare.]

dē-den-ti′tion (-tish′un), *n.* The shedding of teeth. [Rare.]

dē′des, *n.* [Javanese.] The perfume obtained from the rasse.

ded′i-cănt, *n.* One who dedicates.

ded′i-cāte, *v.t.*; dedicated, *pt.*, *pp.*; dedicating, *ppr.* [L. *dedicatus*, pp. of *dedicare*, to consecrate, declare.]

1. To set apart and consecrate to a deity or to a sacred purpose; to devote to a sacred use, by a solemn act, or by religious ceremonies; as, to *dedicate* a temple or a church.

2. To appropriate to any person or purpose; to give wholly or earnestly up to.

> No apology for *dedicating* a few pages to discussion. —Macaulay.

3. To inscribe or address to a patron, friend, or public character; as, to *dedicate* a book.

> I *dedicate*, I consecrate with tears—
> These Idylls. —Tennyson.

Syn.—Devote, consecrate, hallow, set apart.

ded′i-cāte, *a.* Consecrated; devoted; appropriated.

ded″i-cā-tee′, *n.* One to whom a thing is dedicated.

ded-i-cā′tion, *n.* 1. The act of consecrating to a deity or to a sacred use, often with religious solemnities; solemn appropriation; as, the *dedication* of Solomon's temple.

2. The act of devoting or giving to; as, the *dedication* of houses or lands to public use by the owner.

3. An address or inscription by the author to a patron, friend, or public character, of a book or other composition.

ded′i-cā-tŏr, *n.* One who dedicates; one who inscribes a composition to some person.

ded″i-cā-tō′ri-ăl, *a.* Of the nature of a dedication; dedicatory.

ded′i-cā-tō-ry, *a.* and *n.* I. *a.* Composing a dedication; as, an epistle *dedicatory*.

II. *n.* A dedication. [Rare.]

ded′i-mus, *n.* [L., we have given, 1st pers. pl. perf. ind. act. of *dare*, to give.] In law, a writ to commission private persons to do some act in place of a judge, as to examine a witness, etc.

dé-dit′ (dā-dē′), *n.* [Fr.] In French and Canadian law, the sum named in the penalty clause of a contract; a forfeit.

dē-di′tion (-dish′un), *n.* [L. *deditio*, a surrender, giving up, from *dedere*, to give up, surrender; *de*, from, and *dare*, to give.] The act of yielding anything; surrender. [Rare.]

ded-i-ti′tiăn-cy (-tish′ăn-cy), *n.* In old Roman law, the state of a freedman denied full citizenship because of gross misbehavior while a slave.

ded′ō-lent, *a.* [L. *dedolens*, ppr. of *dedolere*, to cease to grieve; *de-* priv., and *dolere*, to grieve.] Feeling no compunction or regret. [Rare.]

dē-dūce′, *v.t.*; deduced, *pt.*, *pp.*; deducing, *ppr.* [L. *deducere*, to lead or draw down, to bring away; *de*, down, away, and *ducere*, to lead.]

1. To draw; to bring; to take the subject of.

> O goddess, say, shall I *deduce* my rhymes
> From the dire nation in its early times? —Pope.

2. To draw from, in reasoning; to attain or arrive at, as a truth, opinion, or proposition, from premises; to infer from what precedes; to conclude.

> Reasoning is nothing but the faculty of *deducing* unknown truths from principles already known. —Locke.

3. To lead forth; to transplant. [Obs.]

4. To trace the course of. [Obs.]

dē-dūce′ment, *n.* The conclusion of a deduction; inference.

dē-dū-ci-bil′i-ty, *n.* Deducibleness.

dē-dū′ci-ble, *a.* 1. That may be deduced by reasoning from premises; inferrible; discoverable.

> The properties of a triangle are *deducible* from the complex idea of three lines including a space. —Locke.

2. Capable of being brought down. [Obs.]

dē-dū′ci-ble-ness, *n.* Capability of being deduced; deducibility.

dē-dū′ci-bly, *adv* By means of deduction.

dē-dū′cive, *a.* Performing the act of deduction; inferential.

dē-duçt′, *v.t.*; deducted, *pt.*, *pp.*; deducting, *ppr.* [L. *deductus*, pp. of *deducere*, to lead away; *de*, from, and *ducere*, to lead.]

1. To take away, separate, or remove, in numbering, estimating, or calculating; to subtract; as, from the sum of two numbers *deduct* the lesser number.

2. To reduce; to bring down. [Obs.]

> Do not *deduct* it to days. —Massinger.

3. To lead forth, as a colony; to deduce. [Obs.]

dē-duçt′i-ble, *a.* 1. Capable of being deducted or subtracted.

2. Capable of being deduced; consequential.

dē-duç′tion, *n.* 1. The act or procedure of deducing or inferring.

2. The act of deducting; subtraction.

3. That which is deducted; the sum or amount taken from another; abatement; as, this sum is a *deduction* from the yearly rent.

4. That which is deduced from premises; an inference; a conclusion; as, this opinion is a fair *deduction* from the principles you have advanced.

5. In logic, the form of reasoning by which a specific fact or conclusion is derived or inferred from a general law or principle; opposed to *induction*.

Syn.—Abatement, discount, diminution, inference, consequence, conclusion.

dē-duçt′ive, *a.* Pertaining to deduction; deducible.

dē-duçt′ive-ly, *adv.* By deduction; by way of inference; by consequence.

dē-duç′tŏr, *n.* A cetacean, the caaing-whale.

dē-duit′ (-dwit′), *n.* Delight; sport. [Obs.]

dē-dū-pli-ca′tion, *n.* [*De-*, and L. *duplicare*, to double.] Chorisis.

deed, *a.* Dead. [Obs.]

deed, *n.* [ME. *deed, dede*; AS. *dæd*, a deed, a thing done, from *don*, to do.]

1. That which is done, acted, or effected; an act; a fact; a word of extensive application, including whatever is done, good or bad, great or small.

2. Exploit; achievement; illustrious act.

Whose *deeds* some nobler poem shall adorn. —Dryden.

3. Power of action; agency. [Obs.]

With will and *deed* created free. —Milton.

4. A writing containing some contract or agreement, and the evidence of its execution; particularly, an instrument conveying real estate to a purchaser or donee.

Blank deed; a printed form containing the legal phraseology common to all deeds, with blank spaces for particulars.

Deed of trust; a conveyance of property to one person to be held in trust for another.

Deed poll; a deed not indented, that is, shaved or even, made by one party only.—Blackstone.

In deed; in fact; actually.

Syn.—Action, achievement, accomplishment, exploit, feat.

deed, *v.t.*; deeded, *pt., pp.*; deeding, *ppr.* To convey or transfer by deed; as, to *deed* realty to a wife.

deed′ful, *a.* Filled with deeds; active; stirring. [Rare.]

deed′less, *a.* Inactive; not performing or having performed deeds or exploits.

deed′y, *a.* Industrious; active. [Rare.]

deem, *v.t.*; deemed, *pt., pp.*; deeming, *ppr.* [ME. *demen*; AS. *deman*, to judge, deem, from *dom*, judgment, doom.]

1. To think; to judge; to hold in opinion; to conclude on consideration; as, he *deems* it prudent to be silent.

2. To doom; to judge; to decide. [Obs.]

deem, *v.i.* 1. To be of opinion; to suppose; to think.

deem, *n.* Opinion; judgment; surmise. [Obs.]

deem′stẽr, demp′stẽr, *n.* One of the two judges in the Isle of Man acting as the chief justices of the island.

deep, *a.* [ME. *deep, depe*; AS. *deop*, deep.]

1. Extending or being far below the surface; descending far downward; profound; opposed to *shallow*; as, *deep* water; a *deep* pit or well.

2. Low in situation; being or descending far below the adjacent land; as, a *deep* valley.

3. Entering far; piercing a great way; as, a tree in a good soil takes *deep* root; a spear struck *deep* into the flesh.

4. Far from the outer part; secreted.

A spider *deep* ambushed in her den. —Dryden.

5. Absorbed; engrossed; wholly occupied; as, *deep* in figures; *deep* in love.

6. Not superficial or obvious; hidden; secret; as, *deep* plots or intrigues.

7. Remote from comprehension; hard to penetrate or understand; unintelligible.

O Lord, thy thoughts are very *deep*. —Ps. xcii. 5.

8. Sagacious; profoundly learned; penetrating; having the power to enter far into a subject; as, a man of *deep* thought; a *deep* divine.

9. Artful; contriving; concealing artifice; insidious; designing; as, a friend, *deep*, hollow, treacherous.

10. Grave in sound; low; as, the *deep* tones of an organ.

11. Great in degree; intense; excessive; profound; as, *deep* silence; *deep* darkness; *deep* poverty.

12. Muddy; boggy; slushy; applied to roads.

13. Heartfelt; affecting.

Deep prayers cannot appease thee.—Shak.

14. Reaching back from the front; especially, reaching or extending far back from the front; as, a company six *deep*.

deep, *adv.* Deeply.

Drink *deep*, or taste not the Pierian spring. —Pope.

deep, *n.* [ME. *deepe*; AS. *dype*, the deep sea, from *deop*, deep.]

1. Anything remarkable for depth; specifically, the sea; the abyss of waters; the ocean; any great collection of water.

He maketh the *deep* to boil like a pot. —Job xli. 31.

2. That which is profound, not easily fathomed, or incomprehensible; abyss.

A great free glance into the very *deeps* of thought. —Carlyle.

3. The most still or solemn part; the midst.

The *deep* of night is crept upon your talk. —Shak.

4. Nautically, the space between the marks on a lead-line.

deep′en, *v.t.*; deepened, *pt., pp.*; deepening, *ppr.* 1. To make deep or deeper; to sink lower; as, to *deepen* the channel of a river or harbor; to *deepen* a well.

2. To make dark or darker; to make thicker or more gloomy; as, to *deepen* the shades of night; to *deepen* gloom.

3. To make more poignant or absorbing; as, to *deepen* grief or sorrow.

4. To make graver; as, to *deepen* the tones of an organ.

deep′en, *v.i.* To become deeper; as, the water *deepens* at every cast of the lead.

deep′-fet, *a.* Fetched or brought from a deep place. [Obs.]

deep′-laid, *a.* Laid deep; formed with cunning and sagacity.

deep′ly, *adv.* 1. At or to a great depth; far below the surface; as, a passion *deeply* rooted in our nature; precepts *deeply* engraved on the heart.

2. Profoundly; thoroughly; as, *deeply* skilled in ethics or anatomy.

3. Gravely; as, a *deeply* toned instrument.

4. With profound skill; with art or intricacy; as, a *deeply* laid plot or intrigue.

deep′-mouthed, *a.* Having a hoarse, loud, hollow voice; as, a *deep-mouthed* dog.

deep′ness, *n.* The state of being deep, in all its senses; depth.

deep′-read (-red), *a.* Having fully read; profoundly versed.

deep′-sēa, *a.* Pertaining to or used in the deeper parts of the sea; as, a *deep-sea* lead.

deep′-waist″ed, *a.* Having a deep waist, as a ship when the quarter-deck and forecastle are raised from four to six feet above the level of the main deck.

deer, *n. sing.* and *pl.* [ME. *der*; AS. *deor*, a wild animal.]

1. Any quadruped, particularly if wild. [Obs.]

2. One of the Linnean genus *Cervus*, of ruminant quadrupeds now constituting the family *Cervidæ*, which by some naturalists has been divided into several genera, others regarding the genus and family as coextensive. They are distinguished by solid ramified horns which they shed every year, and eight cutting teeth in the lower jaw and none in the upper. There are many species, generally distinguished by a qualifying word, as musk-*deer*, rein*deer*, or by a specific name, as elk, moose, caribou, etc. *Carius virginianus* is the common American *deer*, *Cervus elaphus* the red *deer* of Europe.

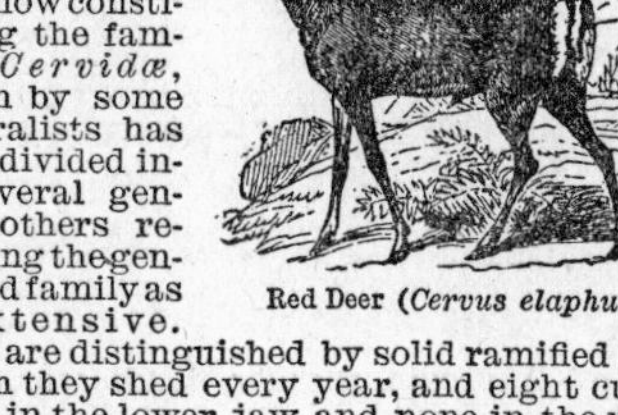

Red Deer (*Cervus elaphus*).

3. Any moschine animal, as the chevrotain.

deer′ber″ry, *n.* *Vaccinium stamineum*, the squaw-huckleberry; also, the wintergreen or the partridge-berry.

deer′grȧss, *n.* Any plant of the genus *Rhexia*, particularly the meadow-beauty.

deer′-hair, *n.* *Scirpus cæspitosus*, heath club-rush.

deer′hound, *n.* A hound for hunting deer; a staghound.

deer′let, *n.* Any small deer, as the chevrotain.

deer′-mouse, *n.* *Hesperomys leucopus* or any other mouse of the same genus.

deer′-neck, *n.* A thin, ill-shaped neck, as of a horse.

deer′skin, *n.* 1. The raw skin of a deer.

2. The dressed leather made of the raw skin; buckskin.

deer′stalk″ẽr, *n.* 1. One who stalks deer.

2. A low-crowned hat. [Eng.]

deer′stalk″ing, *n.* The hunting of deer by stalking instead of pursuit or in the open.

deer′s′-tongue (-tung), *n.* *Liatris odoratissima*, a plant having leaves of a vanilla-like odor.

dees, *n.*, pl. of *die*. [Obs.]

dees, *n.* [Obs.] See *Dais*.

dē-ē′sis, *n.* [Gr. *deēsis*, a supplication.] In rhetoric, an invocation to a deity.

dē′ess, *n.* [Obs.] See *Goddess*.

dē-eth′i-cize, *v.t.* To rid of ethical qualities; to cause to be separated from moral science.

deev, *n.* Same as *Deva*.

dē-face′, *v.t.*; defaced (dē-fāst), *pt., pp.*; defacing, *ppr.* [ME. *defacen*; OFr. *defacier*; L. *de*- priv., and *facies*, face.]

1. To destroy or mar the face or surface of; to injure the beauty of; to disfigure; as, to *deface* a monument; to *deface* an edifice.

2. To injure, destroy, spoil, or mar; to erase or obliterate; as, to *deface* letters or writing; to *deface* a record.

Syn.—Disfigure, deform.—*Deface* expresses more than either *deform* or *disfigure*. To *deface* is an act of destruction; it is the actual destruction of that which has before existed; to *disfigure* is either an act of destruction or an erroneous execution, which takes away the figure; to *deform* is altogether an imperfect execution, which renders the *form* what it should not be. A thing is *defaced* by design; it is *disfigured* either by design or accident; it is *deformed* either by an error or by the nature of the thing. Inanimate objects are mostly *defaced* or *disfigured*, but seldom *deformed*; animate objects are either *disfigured* or *deformed*, but seldom *defaced*.

dē-face′ment, *n.* 1. Injury to the surface or exterior of; erasure; obliteration.

2. That which mars beauty or disfigures.

dē-fā′cẽr, *n.* One who or that which defaces.

dē fac′tō. [L. *de*, of, from; *facto*, ablative of *factum*, a fact, from *facere*, to do.] Actually; in fact; in reality; existing; as, a king *de facto*, distinguished from a king *de jure*, or by right.

dē-fail′, *v.t.* and *v.i.* To fail. [Obs.]

dē-fail′ance, *n.* Failure. [Obs.]

dē-fail′ūre, *n.* Failure. [Obs.]

dē-fal′cāte, *v.t.*; defalcated, *pt., pp.*; defalcating, *ppr.* [LL. *defalcatus*, pp. of *defalcare*, to cut off; L. *de*, from, and *falx*, a sickle.] To cut off; to take away or deduct a part of; used chiefly of money, accounts, rents, income, etc. [Rare.]

dē-fal′cāte, *v.i.* To be guilty of defalcation; to embezzle.

dē-fal-cā′tion, *n.* 1. Misappropriation of money; embezzlement.

2. In law, the reduction of a claim by the allowance of a set-off; abatement.

3. The amount so abated.

def′ăl-cā-tŏr, *n.* An embezzler; a defaulter.

dē-falk′, *v.t.* To defalcate; to cut off. [Obs.]

def-ȧ-mā′tion, *n.* [ME. *diffamacioun*; LL. *diffamatio*, libel, defamation, from L. *diffamare*, to defame.] The uttering of slanderous words or writings; the malicious uttering of falsehood respecting another, which tends to destroy or impair his good name, character, or occupation; aspersion; calumny. *Defamation*, in law, embraces libel and slander.

dē-fam′ȧ-tō-ry, *a.* Calumnious; slanderous; containing defamation; false and injurious to reputation; as, *defamatory* words.

dē-fāme′, *v.t.*; defamed, *pt., pp.*; defaming, *ppr.* [ME. *defamen, diffamen*; L. *diffamare*, to spread an evil report, defame.]

1. To slander by falsely and maliciously circulating statements respecting another which tend to injure his reputation; to speak evil of; to dishonor by false reports; to calumniate.

2. To accuse, especially if the charge be false. [Rare.]

3. To lower the fame of; to bring into disrepute; to make infamous.

The grand old name of gentleman,
Defamed by every charlatan. —Tennyson.

Syn.—Accuse falsely, asperse, calumniate, libel, scandalize, slander, traduce, vilify.

dē-fāme′, *n.* Disrepute. [Obs.]

dē-fām′ẽr, *n.* A slanderer; a detractor; a calumniator.

dē-fām′ing-ly, *adv.* In a calumnious manner.

def′ȧ-mous, *a.* Defamatory; slanderous. [Obs.]

dē-fat′i-gȧ-ble, *a.* [L. *defatigare*, to weary, tire out.] Liable to be wearied. [Rare.]

dē-fat′i-gāte, *v.t.* To weary or tire. [Rare.]

dē-fat-i-gā′tion, *n.* Weariness. [Rare.]

dē-fault′, *v.t.*; defaulted, *pt., pp.*; defaulting, *ppr.* 1. To fail in the performance of. [Obs.]

2. In law, to declare in default, as a defendant, and enter judgment against.

dē-fault′, *v.i.* 1. To fail in fulfilling or satisfying an engagement, claim, contract, or agreement; to fail to appear in court; to let a case go by default.

"Now then!" Mr. P. would say to a *defaulting* lodger, "Pay up!" —Dickens.

2. To offend.

That he 'gainst courtesie so fowly did *default*. —Spenser.

dē-fault′, *n.* [ME. *defaulte*; OFr. *defaute*, a failure, from L. *de*, away, and *fallere*, to fall, to deceive.]

1. A failing or failure; an omission of that which ought to be done; neglect to do what duty or law requires; as, this evil has happened through the governor's *default*.

2. Defect; want; failure; as, in *default* of a meal they went hungry.

3. An offense; fault; wrong act. [Rare.]

4. In law, a failure of appearance in court at a day assigned; said particularly of the defendant in a suit when called to make answer, also of jurors, witnesses, etc.

In default of; through lack or neglect of.

Judgment by default; a judgment rendered against a litigant who fails to plead.

To suffer default; to fail to answer when a case is called for trial.

Syn.—Delinquency, failure, omission, neglect.

dē-fault′ẽr, *n.* 1. One who makes default; one who fails to appear in court when called.

2. One who fails to perform a public duty; particularly, one who fails to account for public money intrusted to his care; an embezzler.

dē-fea′sance, *n.* [OFr. *defeisance*, a rendering void, from *defeisant*, ppr. of *defaire*, to render void, undo.]

1. Defeat. [Obs.]

2. A rendering null; a voiding.

3. In law, a condition relating to a deed, which being performed, the deed is defeated or rendered void; or a collateral deed, made at the same time with a feoffment or other conveyance, containing conditions, on the performance of which the estate then created may be defeated.

dē-fea′sanced, *a.* Liable to be forfeited; subject to defeasance.

dē-fea′si-ble, *a.* That may be defeated or annulled; as, a *defeasible* title.

dē-fea′si-ble-ness, *n.* The quality of being defeasible.

dē-feat′, *v.t.*; defeated, *pt., pp.*; defeating, *ppr.* [ME. *defeten, deffeten*, from OFr. *defait*, pp. of *defaire*, to undo, defeat; L. *de-* or *dis-* priv., and *facere*, to do.]

1. To overcome or vanquish, as an army; to check, disperse, or ruin by victory.

2. To frustrate; to prevent the success of; to disappoint; as, our dearest hopes are often *defeated*.

3. To render null and void; as, to *defeat* a title to an estate.

4. To undo; to destroy. [Obs.]

Syn.—Overpower, overthrow, beat, rout, discomfit, vanquish, subdue, conquer, frustrate, foil, disconcert, baffle.

dē-feat′, *n.* [L. *defectus*, a failure, from *deficere*, to fail.]

1. Overthrow; loss of battle; check, rout, or destruction, as of an army by the victory of an enemy.

2. Frustration by rendering null and void, or by prevention of success; as, the *defeat* of a title; the *defeat* of a plan or design.

3 An undoing; destruction. [Obs.]

de-feat′ism, *n.* The advocacy of the defeat of one's country in war with the pretense that ultimate good will result. In the great World War, usually indicative of sympathy with the aims of Germany.

de-feat′ist, *n.* One desiring or working for the defeat of his country in war, pretending that ultimate good will result.

dē-fea′tūre, *n.* Defeat; also, disguise. [Obs.]

dē-fea′tūre, *v.t.* To change the features of; to disguise. [Rare.]

def′ē-cāte, *a.* Having every impurity removed; cleared; refined.

def′ē-cāte, *v.t.*; defecated, *pt., pp.*; defecating, *ppr.* [L. *defæcatus*, pp. of *defæcare*, to cleanse from dregs, to strain; *de*, from, and *fæx*, grounds, dregs.]

1. To purify; to refine; to clear from dregs or impurities; to clarify; as, to *defecate* liquor.

2. To purify from admixture; to clear; to purge of extraneous matter.

def′ē-cāte, *v.i.* 1. To become clarified.

2. To excrete the feces.

def-ē-cā′tion, *n.* 1. The act of separating from lees or dregs; purification from impurities or foreign matter.

2. Excretion of the feces.

def′ē-cā-tŏr, *n.* One who or that which defecates, as a clarifier for syrup in sugar-making.

dē-fect′, *n.* [ME. *defaicte*; OFr. *defait*, from L. *defectus*, a failure, lack, from *defectus*, pp. of *deficere*, to fail, to lack.]

1. Want or absence of something necessary or useful toward perfection; fault, imperfection; lack; as, a *defect* in the plan.

2. Any natural want or imperfection, whether physical or moral; mistake; blemish; deformity; as, a *defect* in timber; a *defect* of memory.

Syn.—Fault, blemish, flaw, speck, imperfection, spot, stain.—*Defect* is negative, denoting the absence of that which is necessary to a thing's completeness or perfection; *fault* is positive, denoting something improper.

dē-fect′, *v.i.* To be deficient. [Obs.]

dē-fect′, *v.t.* To harm; to injure. [Rare.]

dē-fect-i-bil′i-ty, *n.* Deficiency; imperfection. [Rare.]

dē-fect′i-ble, *a.* Imperfect; deficient. [Rare.]

dē-fec′tion, *n.* [L. *defectio*, a failure, defection, from *defectus*, pp. of *deficere*, to fail.] Want or failure of duty; particularly, a falling away; apostasy; the act of abandoning a person or cause to which one is bound by allegiance or duty, or to which one has attached himself.

dē-fec′tion-ist, *n.* An encourager or inciter of defection.

dē-fec′tious, *a.* Full of imperfections. [Obs.]

dē-fect′ive, *a.* 1. Wanting in substance, quantity, quality, or in anything necessary; imperfect; as, a *defective* limb; *defective* timber; a *defective* copy or book; a *defective* account.

2. In grammar, lacking the full complement of cases, tenses, or forms, as a noun or verb.

Syn.—Imperfect, deficient, incomplete, inadequate, insufficient, faulty, blamable.

dē-fect′ive, *n.* One lacking the full complement of mental, moral, or physical powers.

dē-fect′ive-ly, *adv.* In a defective manner.

dē-fect′ive-ness, *n.* Want; the state of being imperfect; faultiness.

dē-fect-ū-os′i-ty, *n.* Defectiveness [Obs.]

dē-fect′ū-ous, *a.* Full of defects. [Obs.]

def-ē-dā′tion, *n.* Pollution. [Obs.]

dē-fence′, *n.* and *v.t.* See *Defense.*

dē-fend′, *v.t.*; defended, *pt., pp.*; defending, *ppr.* [ME. *defenden*; OFr. *defendre*; L. *defendere*, to ward off, repel; *de*, away, from, and *fendere*, to strike.]

1. To fend or ward off. [Scot.]

2. To forbid; to prohibit. [Obs.]

3. To support by repelling or denying a demand, charge, or accusation; as, he *defended* his case in the courts of law.

4. To repel attacks from; to protect by opposition or resistance, as from anything which assails or annoys; to prevent from being injured or destroyed.

> There arose to *defend* Israel, Tola, the son of Puah. —Jud. x. i.

5. To vindicate; to assert; to uphold; to maintain uninjured by force or by argument; as, to *defend* rights and privileges; to *defend* reputation.

Syn.—Protect.—To *defend* is literally to ward off; to *protect* is to cover over. We *defend* those who are attacked; we *protect* those who are liable to injury or invasion. A fortress is *defended* by its guns, and *protected* by its walls.

dē-fend′, *v.i.* In law, to make opposition; as, the party comes into court, *defends*, and says.

dē-fend′a-ble, *a.* That may be defended.

dē-fend′ant, *a.* 1. Defensive. [Obs.]

2. Making defense; being in the character of a defendant.

dē-fend′ant, *n.* 1. One who defends.

2. In law, the party who opposes a complaint, demand, or charge; one who is summoned into court, and defends, denies, or opposes the demand or charge, and maintains his own right. It is applied to any party of whom a demand is made in court, whether the party denies and defends, or admits the claim and suffers a default.

dē-fen-dee′, *n.* One who is defended. [Rare.]

dē-fend′ẽr, *n.* One who defends by opposition; one who maintains, supports, protects, or vindicates; an asserter; a vindicator, either by arms or by arguments; a champion or an advocate.

Syn.—Advocate, pleader, vindicator, champion.

dē-fend′ress, *n.* A female defender. [Rare.]

dē-fen′sa-tive, *n.* That which serves to defend or protect; a defense; a guard.

dē-fense′, dē-fence′, *n.* [ME. *defense*, L. *defensus*, pp. of *defendere*, to defend.]

1. The act of defending, upholding, or maintaining; support; maintenance; justification; vindication; the state of being defended.

2. Anything that opposes attack, violence, danger, or injury; anything that secures the person, the rights, or the possessions of men; fortification; guard; protection; security

3. Vindication; justification; apology; that which repels or disproves a charge or accusation.

4. In law, the method adopted by a person against whom legal proceedings have been taken for defending himself against them.

5. The science of defending against enemies; military skill; skill in defending from danger; skill, as in fencing, etc.

6. Prohibition. [Obs.]

7. [*pl.*] In heraldry, the natural weapons of an animal, as the antlers of a stag, etc.

Angle of defense; in fortification, the angle formed by the meeting of the line of defense with a diverging flank.

dē-fense′, dē-fence′, *v.t.* To defend by fortification. [Obs.]

dē-fense′less, dē-fence′less, *a.* Being without defense, or without means of repelling assault or injury; unprotected.

dē-fense′less-ness, dē-fence′less-ness, *n.* The state of being defenseless.

dē-fens′ẽr, dē-fenc′ẽr, *n.* A defender. [Obs.]

dē-fen-si-bil′i-ty, *n.* Capability of being defended; defensibleness.

dē-fen′si-ble, *a.* 1. That may be defended; as, a *defensible* city.

2. That may be vindicated, maintained, or justified; as, a *defensible* cause.

3. Capable of defending; contributing to defense. [Obs.]

dē-fen′si-ble-ness, *n.* Defensibility.

dē-fen′sive, *a.* 1. That serves to defend; proper for defense; as, *defensive* armor.

2. Carried on in resisting attack or aggression; as, *defensive* war; opposed to *offensive*.

3. In a state or posture to defend.

dē-fen′sive, *n.* Safeguard; that which defends.

> Wars preventive, upon just fears, are true *defensives*. —Bacon.

To be on the defensive, to stand on the defensive; to be or stand in a state or posture of defense or resistance in opposition to aggression or attack.

dē-fen′sive-ly, *adv.* In a defensive manner; on the defensive.

dē-fen′sŏr, *n.* 1. One who defends; a defender.

2. In law, a defender in court; an advocate.

3. In canon law, the custodian of a church.

dē-fen′sō-ry, *a.* Defensive.

dē-fẽr′, *v.t.*; deferred, *pt., pp.*; deferring, *ppr.* [ME. *differren*; OFr. *differer*; L. *differre*, to carry asunder or different ways, to defer, put off; *dis-*, apart, and *ferre*, to carry.] To delay; to put off; to postpone to a future time; as, to *defer* the execution of a design.

dē-fẽr′, *v.i.* To put off; to delay; to procrastinate.

Syn.—Delay, postpone, procrastinate, prolong, protract, retard, adjourn.

dē-fẽr′, *v.i.* [OFr. *deferer*, from L. *deferre*, to bring down, give, grant; *de*, down, and *ferre*, to bring.] To yield to another's opinion; to submit in opinion; with *to*; as, he *defers to* the opinion of his father.

dē-fẽr′, *v.t.* 1. To offer; to render; to give. [Obs.]

2. To refer; to leave to another's judgment and determination; with *to*.

def′ẽr-ence, *n.* [Fr. *deference*, from L. *deferens*, ppr. of *deferre*, to bring down, to grant; *de*, down, and *ferre*, to bring.] A yielding of opinion; submission of judgment to the opinion or judgment of another; regard; respect.

Syn.—Respect.—*Deference*, usually, but not always, implies *respect*. We may *defer* on some one point to a man who knows better than we do, while we have no general *respect* for his character.

def′ẽr-ent, *a.* 1. Bearing; carrying; conveying; in anatomy and physiology, efferent.

2. Deferential.

def′ẽr-ent, *n.* [L. *deferens*, ppr. of *deferre*, to carry down.]

1. That which carries or conveys.

2. In Ptolemaic astronomy, a circle surrounding the earth, in whose periphery the center of the epicycle was supposed to move round.

def-ẽr-en′tiăl (-shăl), *a.* Expressing deference.

def-ẽr-en′tiăl-ly, *adv.* With deference.

dē-fẽr′ment, *n.* The act of putting off or delaying. [Rare.]

dē-fẽr′rẽr, *n.* One who delays or puts off.

dē-fẽr-ves′cence, *n.* [L. *defervescens*, ppr. of *defervescere*, to cease boiling; *de*, from, and *fervescere*, to begin to boil, from *fervere*, to boil.]

1. Abatement of heat; the state of growing cool; coolness; lukewarmness.

2. In pathology, abatement or decrease of fever or feverish symptoms.

dē-fẽr-ves′cen-cy, *n.* Defervescence.

dē-feu′dăl-ize, *v.t.* To remove the feudal attributes of.

dē-fī′ance, *n.* [ME. *defyaunce*; OFr. *defiance*, distrust, defiance, lack of faith, from L *diffidens*, ppr. of *diffidere*, to distrust, defy; *dis-* priv., and *fidere*, to trust; *fides*, faith.]

1. A daring; a challenge to fight; invitation to combat; a call to an adversary to fight, if he dare; as, Goliath bade *defiance* to the army of Israel.

2. A challenge to meet in any contest; a call upon one to make good any assertion or charge; an invitation to maintain any cause or point.

3. Contempt of opposition or danger; a daring or resistance that implies the contempt of an adversary or of any opposing power; as, *defiance* of authority.

4. Rejection; refusal. [Obs.]

To bid defiance to; see under *Bid.*

dē-fī′ant, *a.* Characterized by defiance, boldness, or insolence; challenging.

dē-fī′ant-ly, *adv.* In a defiant manner.

dē-fī′ant-ness, *n.* The quality of being defiant.

dē-fī′a-tō-ry, *a.* Bidding or bearing defiance. [Obs.]

dē-fī′bri-nāte, *v.t.*; defibrinated, *pt., pp.*; defibrinating, *ppr.* To deprive of fibrin; specifically, to remove fibrin from, as fresh blood by whipping it with rods.

dē-fī-bri-nā′tion, *n.* The act or process of defibrinizing or depriving of fibrin.

dē-fī′bri-nize, *v.t.*; defibrinized, *pt., pp.*; defibrinizing, *ppr.* To defibrinate.

dē-fi′cience, *n.* Deficiency. [Obs.]

dē-fi′cien-cy (-fish′en-cy), *n.*; *pl.* **dē-fi′cien-cies.** [L. *deficiens*, ppr. of *deficere*, to lack, fail; *de*, from, and *facere*, to do.] The state of being deficient; a falling short; imperfection; inadequacy; defect; want; as, a *deficiency* in moral duties; a *deficiency* of means; a *deficiency* of blood.

Deficiency of a curve; in geometry, the number by which its double points fall short of the highest number possible in a curve of the same order.

dē-fi′cient (-fish′ent), *a.* Wanting; defective; imperfect; not sufficient or adequate; not having a full or adequate supply; as, the country may be *deficient* in the means of carrying on war; *deficient* estate; *deficient* strength.

Deficient number; see *Abundant number* under *Abundant*.

Syn.—Defective, inadequate, imperfect, incomplete.

dē-fi′cient-ly, *adv.* In a deficient manner.

dē-fi′cient-ness, *n.* The state of being deficient. [Rare.]

def′i-cit, *n.* [L., 3d pers. sing. pres. ind. of *deficere*, to be wanting, to fail.] Want; deficiency; as, a *deficit* in the taxes or revenue.

dē-fī′ēr, *n.* One who defies or braves; as, a *defier* of the laws.

dē-fig-ū-rā′tion, *n.* A disfiguring. [Obs.]

dē-fig′ūre, *v.t.* To delineate. [Obs.]

dē-fi-lāde′ (*or* def-i-), *v.t.*; defiladed, *pt., pp.*; defilading, *ppr.* [Fr.] In fortification, to erect defensive works, as ramparts, around (a fortification), so as to protect the interior when in danger of being commanded by guns placed on some higher point; as, to *defilade* an exposed side.

dē-fi-lād′ing (*or* def-i-), *n.* That branch of fortification, the object of which is to determine the directions or heights of the lines of rampart or parapet, so that the interior of the work may not be incommoded by a fire directed to it from neighboring eminences.

dē-file′, *v.t.*; defiled, *pt., pp.*; defiling, *ppr.* [*De-*, and AS. *fulian*, to make foul, from *ful*, foul.]

1. To make unclean; to render foul or dirty; to make impure; to render turbid; as, the water or liquor is *defiled*.

2. To soil or sully; to tarnish, as reputation.

> He is among the greatest prelates of the age, however his character may be *defiled* by dirty hands. —Swift.

3. To pollute; to make ceremonially unclean.

> That which dieth of itself, he shall not eat, to *defile* himself therewith. —Lev. xxii. 8.

4. To corrupt the chastity of; to debauch; to violate; to tarnish the purity of character of by lewdness.

> Shechem lay with her, and *defiled* her. —Gen. xxxiv. 2.

5. To taint, in a moral sense; to corrupt; to vitiate; to render impure with sin.

> *Defile* not yourselves with the idols of Egypt. —Ezek. xx. 7.

Syn.—Contaminate, corrupt, pollute, tarnish, taint, vitiate, sully, soil, stain, befoul, debauch.

dē-file′, *v.i.* [OFr. *defiler*, to file off, unravel; *de-* priv., and *filer*, to spin threads, from *fil*, L. *filium*, a thread.] To march off in a line, or file by file; to file off.

dē-file′, *v.t.* To defilade.

dē-file′ (*or* dē′fil), *n.* [Fr. *defilé*, from *fil*, *file*, a thread, a line.]

1. A narrow passage or way, in which troops may march only in a file, or with a narrow front; a long, narrow pass, as between hills.

2. A march in files.

dē-file′ment, *n.* 1. The act of defiling, or the state of being defiled; foulness; dirtiness; uncleanness.

2. Corruption of morals, principles, or character; impurity; pollution by sin.

> The chaste can not rake into such filth without danger of *defilement*. —Addison.

dē-file′ment, *n.* Same as *Defilading*.

dē-fil′ēr, *n.* One who defiles, one who corrupts or violates; that which pollutes.

dē-fil-i-ā′tion, *n.* [*De-* priv., and L. *filius*, a son, *filia*, a daughter.] The act of making childless by abduction. [Rare.]

dē-fīn′ā-ble, *a.* That may be defined; ascertainable; determinable; as, *definable* words; *definable* limits.

dē-fīn′ā-bly, *adv.* In a definable manner.

dē-fīne′, *v.t.*; defined, *pt., pp.*; defining, *ppr.* [ME. *definen*; OFr. *definer*; L. *definire*, to limit, define; *de*, from, and *finire*, to set a limit to, to bound, from *finis*, a boundary.]

1. To determine or describe the end or limit of; to determine with precision; to ascertain; as, to *define* the limits of Alaska.

2. To mark the limit of; to circumscribe; to bound.

3. To determine or ascertain the extent of (the meaning of a word); to ascertain the signification of; to explain, as what a word or term is understood to express; as, to *define* a phrase.

4. To describe; to ascertain or explain, as the distinctive properties or circumstances of a thing; as, to *define* a line or an angle.

5. To settle; to decide. [Obs.]

dē-fīne′, *v.i.* To determine; to decide. [Obs.]

dē-fīne′ment, *n.* The act of defining or describing; definition.

dē-fīn′ēr, *n.* One who or that which defines, as a book of definitions.

def′i-nite, *a.* [L. *definitus*, pp. of *definire*, to define, bound.]

1. Having certain limits; bounded with precision; fixed; determinate; as, a *definite* extent of land; *definite* dimensions; *definite* measure.

2. Having certain limits in signification; determinate; certain; precise; as, a *definite* word, term, or expression.

3. Fixed; determinate; exact; precise; as, a *definite* time or period.

4. In grammar, defining; limiting; pointing out; as, a *definite* article.

5. In botany, (a) of a fixed number not exceeding twenty; applied to stamens; (b) limited in growth; as, a *definite* inflorescence.

Syn.—Bounded, certain, determinate, limited, fixed, precise, positive.

Definite article; in grammar, the article *the*.

Definite inflorescence; see *Centrifugal inflorescence* under *Centrifugal*.

Definite proportions; in chemistry, the relative quantities in which bodies unite to form compounds.

def′i-nite, *n.* A thing defined. [Obs.]

def′i-nite-ly, *adv.* In a definite manner.

def′i-nite-ness, *n.* The state of being definite; precision; certainty of extent.

def-i-ni′tion (-nish′un), *n.* [L. *definitio*, a boundary, a definition, from *definire*, to define.]

1. The act of defining, determining, distinguishing, explaining, or establishing the signification of.

2. A brief description of a thing by its properties; an explanation of the signification of a word or term, or of what a word is understood to express; as, a *definition* of wit; the *definition* of a circle.

3. In logic, the explication of the essence of a thing by its kind and difference.

4. In optics, the ability of a lens to give a distinct image of an object in all its details.

5. Kind; description. [Rare.]

Syn.—Explanation, description.—A *definition* is designed to settle a thing in its compass and extent; an *explanation* is intended to remove some obscurity or misunderstanding, and is, therefore, more extended and minute; a *description* enters into striking particulars with a view to interest or impress by graphic effect.

def-i-ni′tion-ăl, *a.* Pertaining to definition; employed in defining; abounding in definitions.

dē-fin′i-tive, *a.* 1. Limiting the extent; determinate; positive; express; as, a *definitive* term.

2. Limiting; ending; determining; final; as, a *definitive* sentence.

3. In biology, complete in development or formation; as, a *definitive* organ.

dē-fin′i-tive, *n.* In grammar, a defining or limiting word; as, *the, that, some*, etc.

dē-fin′i-tive-ly, *adv.* In a definitive manner.

dē-fin′i-tive-ness, *n.* The state or quality of being definitive.

dē-fin′i-tūde, *n.* Definiteness; precision. [Rare.]

dē-fix′, *v.t.* To fix; to fasten. [Obs.]

def″lā-grā-bil′i-ty, *n.* Combustibility.

dē-flā′grā-ble, *a.* Having the quality of burning with sudden combustion.

def′lā-grāte, *v.t.*; deflagrated, *pt., pp.*; deflagrating, *ppr.* [L. *deflagratus*, pp. of *deflagrare*, to burn, consume; *de-*, intens., and *flagrare*, to burn.] To cause to burn with a sudden and sparkling combustion; as, to *deflagrate* oil or spirit.

def′lā-grāte, *v.i.* To burn rapidly; thus, when a mixture of charcoal and niter is thrown into a red-hot crucible it burns with a kind of explosion, or *deflagrates*.

def-lā-grā′tion, *n.* Combustion.

def′lā-grā-tŏr, *n.* An instrument for producing rapid and powerful combustion, as of metals, by electricity.

dē-flāte′, *v.t.*; deflated, *pt., pp.*; deflating, *ppr.* [L. *de*, from, and *flatus*, pp. of *flare*, to blow.] To remove the air from; to rid of any inflating medium; as, to *deflate* a balloon or pneumatic tire.

dē-flā′tion, *n.* In geology, a wearing away of land by the action of the wind.

dē-fleçt′, *v.t.*; deflected, *pt., pp.*; deflecting, *ppr.* To cause to turn aside; to turn or bend from a right line or regular course; as, to *deflect* the sun's rays.

dē-fleçt′, *v.i.* [L. *deflectere*, to bend aside; *de*, from, and *flectere*, to bend.] To turn away or aside; to deviate from a true course or right line; to swerve; as, the needle *deflects* from the meridian.

dē-fleçt′ā-ble, *a.* Capable of being deflected.

dē-fleçt′ed, *a.* 1. Turned aside, or from a direct line or course.

2. In biology, bending downward archwise.

dē-fleç′tion, *n.* [LL. *deflexio*, a bending aside, from L. *deflexus*, pp. of *deflectere*, to bend aside.]

1. Deviation; the act of turning aside; a turning from a true line or the regular course; used either in a physical or moral sense.

> King David found out the *deflection* and indirectness of our minds. —Montague.

2. Nautically, the departure of a ship from its true course.

3. In optics, same as *diffraction*.

4. In mathematics, a term applied to the distance by which a curve departs from another curve, or from a straight line; and also to any effect, either of curvature or of discontinuous change of direction.

5. In mechanics, the bending of any material exposed to a transverse strain.

6. In electricity, the movement of a needle from its normal position of rest.

dē-fleç″tion-i-zā′tion, *n.* Removal of inflections.

dē-fleç′tion-īze, *v.t.* To rid of inflections.

dē-fleçt′ive, *a.* Causing deflection.

dē-fleç-tom′e-tēr, *n.* [L. *deflectere*, to bend aside, deflect, and *metrum*, a measure.] An appliance for measuring deflection, as that of a bridge under a certain stress.

dē-fleçt′ŏr, *n.* One of various appliances used in producing deflection; as, (a) the diaphragm of the furnace of a boiler; (b) a controller of the nozle of a hydraulic mining machine.

dē-flex′, *v.t.*; deflexed (-flext), *pt., pp.*, deflexing, *ppr.* [L. *deflexus*, pp. of *deflectere*, to turn aside.] To turn aside or down.

dē-flexed′ (-flext′), *a.* Bent down; deflected.

dē-flex′iŏn (-yun), *n.* See *Deflection*.

dē-flex′ūre, *n.* A bending down; a turning aside; deviation.

dē-flō′rāte, *a.* In botany, (a) having cast its pollen, as a flower; (b) having shed its flowers, as a plant.

def-lō-rā′tion, *n.* 1. The act of deflowering; particularly, the act of taking away a woman's virginity.

2. A selection of the flower, or of that which is most valuable. [Rare.]

dē-flour′, *v.t.* See *Deflower*.

dē-flour′ēr, *n.* See *Deflowerer*.

dē-flōw′, *v.i.* To flow down. [Obs.]

dē-flow′ēr, dē-flour′, *v.t.*; deflowered, defloured, *pt., pp.*; deflowering, deflouring, *ppr.* [ME. *deflouren*; OFr. *deflorir*; LL. *deflorare*, to deprive of flowers.]

1. To strip of flowers; by extension, to deprive of that which beautifies or graces; to render worthless.

2. To deprive of virginity; to violate; to ravish; to seduce.

dē-flow′ēr-ēr, *n.* One who deflowers; a ravisher; a seducer.

def′lū-ous, *a.* Flowing down; falling off. [Obs.]

dē-flux′, *n.* A flowing down; a running downward. [Obs.]

dē-flux′iŏn (-fluk′shun), *n.* [LL. *defluxio*, a flowing down, from L. *defluere*, to flow down.] In medicine, a flowing of fluid matter from a superior to an inferior part of the body; properly, an inflammation of a part, attended with increased secretion; sometimes used synonymously with *inflammation*.

def′ly, *adv.* [Obs.] See *Deftly*.

def-œ-dā′tion, *n.* [Obs.] See *Defedation*.

dē-fō′li-āte, *v.t.*; defoliated, *pt., pp.*; defoliating, *ppr.* [*De-* priv., and L. *folium*, a leaf.] To divest or strip of leaves.

dē-fō′li-āte, *a.* In botany, devoid of leaves; having shed the leaves.

dē-fō-li-ā′tion, *n.* The fall of the leaf or shedding of leaves; the time or season of shedding leaves in autumn.

dē-fō′li-ā-tŏr, *n.* That which defoliates, as a leaf-destroying insect.

dē-fōrce′, *v.t.*; deforced, *pt., pp.*; deforcing, *ppr.* [OFr. *déforcer*, to take away by violence; LL. *de*, from, and *fortia*, violence, from L. *fortis*, strong.]

1. In law, to disseize and keep out of lawful possession of (an estate); to withhold the possession of (an estate) from the rightful owner.

2. In Scots law, to resist, as an officer of the law, in the execution of his official duty.

dē-fōrce′ment, *n.* 1. In law, the unjust holding of lands or tenements to which another person has a right.

2. In Scots law, a resisting of an officer in the execution of law.

dē-fōrce′ŏr, *n.* A deforciant. [Obs.]

dē-fōr′ciănt, *n.* In old English law, (a) one who kept out of possession the rightful owner of an estate; (b) one against whom a fictitious action was brought in fine and recovery. [Obs.]

dē-fōr-ci-ā′tion, *n.* Deforcement.

dē-for′est, *v.t.*; deforested, *pt., pp.*; deforesting, *ppr.* To remove the forests from.

dē-for-es-tā′tion, *n.* Removal of forest.

dē-fọrm′, *v.t.*; deformed, *pt., pp.*; deforming, *ppr.* [ME. *deformen*; OFr. *deformer*; L. *deformare*, to put out of shape; *de-* priv., and *forma*, shape.]

1. To change in form; to give a different form to; as, to *deform* the outline of a lake.

2. To mar or injure the form of; to disfigure; as, a hump on the back *deforms* the body.

3. To alter so as to render ugly, displeasing,

or the like; as, to *deform* the face by paint; to *deform* the character by vice.

Syn.—Deface, disfigure, mar, mutilate.

dē-fọrm′, *a.* Deformed. [Obs.]

def-ọr-mā′tion, *n.* [L. *deformatio*, a deforming, disfiguring, from *deformare*, to deform.]

1. The act of deforming; the condition of being deformed.

2. Altered form; transformation.

3. In geology, diastrophism.

dē-fọrmed′, *a.* 1. Injured in form; disfigured; distorted; ugly; wanting natural beauty or symmetry.

> *Deformed*, unfinished, sent before my time
> Into this breathing world. —Shak.

2. Base; disgraceful. [Obs.]

Syn.—Ugly, disfigured, distorted, misshapen, unsightly, ill-favored.

dē-fọrm′ed-ly, *adv.* In a deformed manner.

dē-fọrm′ed-ness, *n.* Ugliness; unnatural form; the state of being deformed.

dē-fọrm′ẽr, *n.* One who deforms.

dē-fọrm′i-ty, *n.*; *pl.* **dē-fọrm′i-tieṣ**. [OFr. *deformete*; L. *deformitas*, unshapeliness, from *deformis*, misshapen, deformed.]

1. Any unnatural state of the shape or form; want of that uniformity or symmetry which constitutes beauty; distortion; irregularity of shape or features; defect; ugliness; as, bodily *deformity*.

2. Anything that destroys beauty, grace, or propriety; irregularity; absurdity; gross deviation from order or the established laws of propriety; as, *deformity* in an edifice; *deformity* of character.

dē-fōrs′ẽr, dē-fōrs′ŏr, *n.* [Obs.] See *Deforciant.*

dē-foul′, *v.t.* To defile; to pollute.

dē-frạud′, *v.t.*; defrauded, *pt.*, *pp.*; defrauding, *ppr.* [ME. *defrauden*; OFr. *defrauder*; L. *defraudare*, to cheat, defraud; *de*, and *fraudare*, to cheat, from *fraus* (*-dis*), deceit, fraud.]

1. To deprive of right, either by obtaining something by deception or artifice, or by taking something wrongfully without the knowledge or consent of (the owner); to cheat; to cozen; followed by *of* before the thing taken; as, to *defraud* a man *of* his right.

> We have corrupted no man, we have *defrauded* no man. —2 Cor. vii. 2.

2. To defeat or frustrate wrongfully.

> By the duties deserted—by the claims *defrauded.* —Paley.

Syn.—Cheat, deceive, rob, cozen, dupe, swindle, trick.

dē-frạu-dā′tion, *n.* The act of defrauding; acquisition by fraud. [Rare.]

dē-frạud′ẽr, *n.* One who defrauds; a cheat; an embezzler; a peculator.

dē-frạud′ment, *n.* Defraudation. [Rare.]

dē-frāy′, *v.t.*; defrayed, *pt.*, *pp.*; defraying, *ppr.* [OFr. *defrayer*, *defraier*, to pay the expense; *de*, from, off, and *frait*, expense, cost.]

1. To satisfy; as, to *defray* anger. [Obs.]

2. To bear, pay, or settle, as costs or charges; to liquidate; as, to *defray* all expenses.

dē-frāy′ăl, *n.* The act of paying or defraying.

dē-frāy′ẽr, *n.* One who defrays expenses.

dē-frāy′ment, *n.* Payment; defrayal.

deft, *a.* [ME. *defte*, simple, meek, from AS. *ge-dæfte*, meek, gentle, from *dæftan*, to prepare, to put in order.]

1. Showing skill and aptness; subtly apt; handy; as, *deft* workmanship; *deft* movements.

2. Modest; also, neat. [Obs.]

def′tẽr-där, *n.* [Turk.] The minister of finance and high treasurer of the Turkish empire.

deft′ly, *adv.* In a deft manner; handily.

deft′ness, *n.* The quality of being deft.

dē-fuṅct′, *a.* and *n.* [L. *defunctus*, pp. of *defungi*, to do, perform, finish anything, finish life, die; *de*, from, off, and *fungi*, to perform.]

I. *a.* Having finished the course of life; dead; deceased.

II. *n.* A dead person; one deceased.

dē-fuṅc′tion, *n.* Death. [Obs.]

dē-fuṅc′tive, *a.* Funereal. [Obs.]

dē-fūṣe′, *v.t.* To diffuse. [Obs.]

dē-fȳ′, *v.t.*; defied, *pt.*, *pp.*; defying, *ppr.* [ME. *defien*, *diffyen*; OFr. *defier*, to distrust, repudiate, defy, from L. *diffidere*, to distrust; *dis-* priv., and *fides*, faith.]

1. To repudiate; to recoil from. [Obs.]

2. To challenge, as to a fight; to provoke by daring to a combat.

> I once again
> *Defy* thee to the trial of mortal fight.—Milton.

3. To dare; to brave; to offer to hazard a conflict by manifesting a contempt of opposition, attack, or hostile force; as, to *defy* the arguments of an opponent.

4. To set at defiance; to baffle; to foil; as, the solution *defies* one.

dē-fȳ′, *n.* A challenge. [Obs.]

deg, *v.t.* and *v.i.*; degged, *pt.*, *pp.*; degging, *ppr.* [Prov. Eng.] To sprinkle.

dé-ga-gé′ (dā-gȧ-zhā′), *a.* [Fr., pp. of *dégager*, to release, redeem.] Unconstrained; unconventional; bohemian.

dē-gär′nish, *v.t.*; degarnished, *pt.*, *pp.*; degarnishing, *ppr.* To strip, as a house of furnishings; to dismantle, as a fort.

dē-gär′nish-ment, *n.* The act of degarnishing.

dē-ġen′dẽr, dē-ġen′ẽr, *v.i.* To degenerate. [Obs.]

dē-ġen′ẽr-ȧ-cy, *n.* 1. A falling off from the qualities proper to things of the same race or kind; a growing worse or inferior; as, the *degeneracy* of a plant.

2. A state or condition of deterioration; lowness; poorness; meanness.

dē-ġen′ẽr-āte, *v.i.*; degenerated, *pt.*, *pp.*; degenerating, *ppr.* [L. *degenerare*, to become unlike one's race, to fall off, to degenerate; *de*, from, and *genus*, race, kind.] To fall off from the qualities proper to the race or kind; to become of a lower type, physically or morally; to pass from a good to a bad or worse state; to lose or suffer a diminution of valuable qualities.

dē-ġen′ẽr-āte, *n.* A person who, in character, qualities, or excellence, has deteriorated from the normal condition or standard.

dē-ġen′ẽr-āte, *a.* Having or exhibiting degeneracy; deteriorated; degraded; corrupt; mean; as, a *degenerate* plant; *degenerate* days.

dē-ġen′ẽr-āte-ly, *adv.* In a degenerate or base manner.

dē-ġen′ẽr-āte-ness, *n.* Degeneracy.

dē-ġen-ẽr-ā′tion, *n.* 1. Degeneracy; specifically, in physiology, the condition of a tissue of which the vitality has become diminished, impaired, or perverted; a gradual falling off or deterioration in any class of animals, or of any particular organ in the animal or vegetable body, from the operation of natural causes.

2. The thing degenerated. [Rare.]

Amyloid degeneration; see under *Amyloid.*
Caseous degeneration; see under *Caseous.*

dē-ġen-ẽr-ā′tion-ist, *n.* One believing that the tendency of all life is toward degeneration; also used adjectively.

dē-ġen′ẽr-ā-tive, *a.* Tending to degenerate; making worse.

dē-ġen′ẽr-ous, *a.* Degenerated. [Obs.]

dē-ġen′ẽr-ous-ly, *adv.* Meanly. [Obs.]

dē-ġẽrm′, *v.t.*; degermed, *pt.*, *pp.*; degerming, *ppr.* In milling, to remove the germs from; as, to *degerm* wheat.

dē-ġẽr-mi-nā′tŏr, *n.* In milling, a machine which crushes grain and removes the germ.

dē-glāze′, *v.t.*; deglazed, *pt.*, *pp.*; deglazing, *ppr.* To remove the glaze from; said of glass.

dē-glō′ry, *v.t.* To dishonor. [Obs.]

dē-glū′ti-nāte, *v.t.*; deglutinated, *pt.*, *pp.*; deglutinating, *ppr.* [L. *deglutinatus*, pp. of *deglutinare*, to unglue; *de-* priv., and *glutinare*, to glue, from *gluten*, glue.]

1. To unglue; to loosen or separate, as substances glued together.

2. To extract gluten from.

dē-glū-ti-nā′tion, *n.* The act or process of deglutinating.

deg-lụ-ti′tion (-tish′un), *n.* [LL. *deglutire*, to swallow down; L. *de*, from, down, and *glutire*, to swallow.] The act or power of swallowing; as, *deglutition* is difficult.

deg-lụ-ti′tious (-tish′us), *a.* Relating to deglutition. [Rare.]

dē-glū′ti-tō-ry, *a.* Acting as an aid to deglutition.

deg′ọr-dẽr, *n.* [*Deg*ree, and *order.*] The pair of numbers signifying the degree and order of any mathematical form.

deg-rȧ-dā′tion, *n.* [LL. *degradatio*, a reducing in rank, from L. *de*, down, and *gradus*, a step.]

1. A reducing in rank; the act of depriving one of a degree of honor, of dignity, or of rank; also, deposition, removal, or dismissal from office; as, the *degradation* of a public or military officer; *degradation* of a priest.

2. The state of being reduced from an elevated or more honorable station to one that is low in fact or in estimation; baseness; degeneracy.

> The descent of Spain, once the first among monarchies, to the lower depths of *degradation.* —Macaulay.

3. Diminution or reduction of strength, efficacy, value, altitude, or magnitude.

4. In painting, a lessening and obscuring of the appearance of distant objects in a landscape, that they may appear as they would to an eye placed at a distance.

5. In geology, the lessening or wearing down of higher lands, rocks, strata, etc., by the action of water, or other causes.

6. In biology, the condition of a type which exhibits degraded forms; degeneration.

> The *degradation* of the species man is observed in some of its varieties. —Dana.

7. In botany, a change consisting of an abstraction, loss, abortion, or nondevelopment of usual organs.

Degradation of energy; dissipation of energy.

Syn.—Debasement, abasement, dishonor, depression, disgrace, degeneracy, baseness, deposition.

dē-grāde′, *v.t.*; degraded, *pt.*, *pp.*; degrading, *ppr.* [ME. *degraden*; OFr. *degrader*; LL. *degradare*, to reduce in rank.]

1. To reduce from a higher to a lower rank or degree; to deprive of any office or dignity by which rank in society is lost; to strip of honors; as, to *degrade* an archbishop or a general officer.

> Prynne was sentenced to be *degraded* from the bar. —Palfrey.

2. To reduce in estimation; to lessen the value of; to lower; to sink; as, vice *degrades* a man; drunkenness *degrades* a man to the level of a beast.

3. In geology, to reduce in altitude or magnitude, as hills or mountains; to wear down, as by the weather.

4. In biology, to reduce or lower in the scale of classification.

Syn.—Depress, humble, debase, lower, sink, bring down, depose, dishonor, disgrace.

dē-grāde′, *v.i.* 1. To degenerate; to become lower in character.

2. In biology, to degenerate in type; to pass from a higher type of structure to a lower; as, a family of plants or animals *degrades.*

3. In a university, to take a lower degree than one is entitled to, or to avoid taking a degree at the proper and usual time. [Eng.]

dē-grād′ed, *a.* 1. Reduced in rank; deprived of an office or dignity; lowered; sunk; reduced in estimation or value; debased; low.

2. In biology, reduced or lowered in the scale of classification.

Cross degraded and conjoined; in heraldry, a plain cross, having its extremities placed upon a step or steps joined to the sides of the shield.

Cross Degraded and Conjoined.

dē-grāde′ment, *n.* Deprivation of rank or office.

dē-grād′ing-ly, *adv.* In a degrading manner.

de-gräs′ (-grä′), *n.* [Fr.] Grease from wool or hides.

deg-rȧ-vā′tion, *n.* The act of making heavy.

dē-gree′, *n.* [ME. *degre*, *degree*; OFr. *degre*, a degree, step, rank; L. *de*, down, and *gradus*, a step, from *gradi*, to walk.]

1. A step; a stair, or set of steps.

2. Figuratively, a step or single movement, upward or downward, toward any end, whether moral or physical; one of a series of progressive advances; as, he is a *degree* worse than his neighbor.

> We have feet to scale and climb
> By slow *degrees.* —Longfellow.

3. Measure of advancement; hence, relative position attained; grade; rank; station; order; quality.

> High was his *degree* in heaven. —Milton.

4. In genealogy, a certain distance or remove in the line of descent, determining the proximity of blood; as, a relation in the third or fourth *degree.*

5. Measure; extent; as, the light is intense to a *degree* that is intolerable; we suffer an extreme *degree* of heat or cold.

6. The 360th part of the circumference of any circle, the circumference of every circle being supposed to be divided into 360 equal parts.

7. In algebra, a term applied to equations, to show what is the highest power under which the unknown quantity appears; thus, if the index of the highest power of the unknown quantity be 3 or 4, the equation is respectively of the 3d or 4th *degree.*

8. In music, an interval of sound marked by a line on the scale.

9. In arithmetic, three figures taken together in numeration; thus, the number 270,360 consists of two *degrees.*

10. A division, space, or interval, marked on a mathematical, meteorological, or other instrument, as on a thermometer or barometer.

11. In grammar, one of the three modifications (positive, comparative, and superlative), by which the adjective or adverb is compared.

12. In United States criminal law, a distinguishing division of crime; as, premeditated murder is of the first *degree.*

13. In secret societies, one of a number of related ceremonials, having a specific name, appropriate rites, and generally, a separate grip, password, and token.

14. In universities, colleges, and certain authorized schools, a mark of distinction conferred on students, members, or distinguished strangers, as a testimony of proficiency in arts and sciences, or as a mark of respect, giving them a kind of rank, and entitling them to certain privileges. The *degrees* are bachelor, master, and doctor; as, bachelor of arts,

philosophy, laws, science, engineering, etc; master of arts, pedagogy, etc.; doctor of divinity, laws, medicine, etc.

Accumulation of degrees; see under *Accumulation*.

By degrees; by moderate advances; step by step.

Degree of a curve; same as *Order of a curve* under *Order*.

Degree of latitude; the distance on any meridian between two parallels of latitude one degree apart.

Degree of longitude; the distance on any parallel of latitude between two meridians of longitude one degree apart.

Prohibited degrees; the degrees of consanguinity within which marriage is prohibited, these varying in different ages and countries.

To a degree; exceedingly; extremely; as, rash *to a degree*.

de'gū, *n.* [Native S. Am. name.] Any South American rodent of the genus *Octodon*.

dē-gum', *v.t.*; degummed, *pt.*, *pp.*; degumming, *ppr.* To rid of gum; to deglutinate; as, to *degum* raw silk.

dē-gust', *v.t.* and *v.i.*; degusted, *pt.*, *pp.*; degusting, *ppr.* [L. *degustare*, to taste of; *de*, and *gustare*, to taste.] To relish or taste.

dē-gus'tāte, *v.t.* To degust.

dē-gus-tā'tion, *n.* [LL. *degustatio*, tasting, from L. *degustare*, to taste.] A tasting.

dē-hisce', *v.i.* [L. *dehiscere*, to gape open; *de*, off, from, and *hiscere*, to gape, yawn.] To gape; specifically, in botany, to open, as the capsules of plants.

Dehiscent Silicle.

dē-his'cence, *n.* 1. A gaping.

2. In botany, the separating into regular parts, or splitting of an organ in accordance with its structure, as the opening of the parts of a capsule or the cells of anthers, etc.

dē-his'cent, *a.* Opening, as the capsule of a plant; exhibiting dehiscence.

dē-hō-nes'tāte, *v.t.* To disgrace. [Obs.]

dē-hon-es-tā'tion, *n.* A disgracing. [Obs.]

dē-hórn', *v.t.*; dehorned, *pt.*, *pp.*; dehorning, *ppr.* To prevent the growth of the horns of (a calf), by cauterization; to remove the horns from (cattle).

dē-hórs', *a.* and *prep.* [Fr. *dehors*; OFr. *defors*, out of doors, outside.] In law, without; foreign to; irrelevant.

dē-hórs', *n.* In fortification, collectively, accessory works without the main fort.

dē-hórt', *v.t.* To dissuade. [Obs.]

dē-hór-tā'tion, *n.* [L. *dehortari*, to dissuade; *de*, from, and *hortari*, to persuade.] Dissuasion; advice or counsel against something.

dē-hórt'ȧ-tive, *a.* Dehortatory. [Rare.]

dē-hórt'ȧ-tō-ry, *a.* Dissuading; belonging or tending to dissuasion.

dē-hórt'ēr, *n.* A dissuader; an adviser to the contrary.

dē-hū'man-ize, *v.t.*; dehumanized, *pt.*, *pp.*; dehumanizing, *ppr.* To divest of those qualities peculiarly human; as, *dehumanizing* theories.

dē-husk', *v.t.* To husk. [Obs.]

dē-hȳ'drāte, *v.t.*; dehydrated, *pt.*, *pp.*; dehydrating, *ppr.* [*De-* priv., and Gr. *hydōr*, water.] To remove the water from; as, alcohol *dehydrates* animal tissue.

dē-hȳ'drāte, *v.i.* To part with water.

dē-hȳ'drā-tēr, *n.* Any dehydrating agent.

dē-hy-drā'tion, *n.* The act of dehydrating; the state of being dehydrated.

dē-hȳ'drō-ġen-āte, *v.t.* To dehydrogenize.

dē-hȳ"drō-ġen-i-zā'tion, *n.* The removal of constituent hydrogen from a compound.

dē-hȳ'drō-ġen-ize, *v.t.*; dehydrogenized, *pt.*, *pp.*; dehydrogenizing, *ppr.* To rid of hydrogen.

dē'i-cīde, *n.* [L. *deus*, a god, and *cædere*, to kill, slay.]

1. The act of putting a deity to death; specifically, the crucifixion of Christ.

2. One concerned in slaying a god; especially, one of the crucifiers of Christ.

deiç'tiç, *a.* [Gr. *deiktikos*, capable of proving, from *deiknynai*, to show, prove.] In logic, direct; applied to reasoning which proves directly, and opposed to *elenchic*, which proves indirectly.

deiç'tiç-ăl-ly, *adv.* With directness and definiteness; pointedly.

dē-if'iç, dē-if'iç-ăl, *a.* [LL. *deificus*, from L. *deus*, god, and *facere*, to make.] Tending to make divine; deifying; as, a *deific* impulse.

dē"i-fi-çā'tion, *n.* 1. The act of deifying; the condition of being deified; apotheosis.

2. In occultism, absorption of the soul by the Deity.

dē'i-fied, *a.* Praised excessively; apotheosized.

dē'i-fi-ēr, *n.* One who deifies.

dē'i-fórm, *a.* [L. *deus*, a god, and *forma*, form.]

1. Like a god; of a godlike form.

2. Conformable to the nature or will of God. [Rare.]

dē-i-fór'mi-ty, *n.* Resemblance to deity. [Obs.]

dē'i-fȳ, *v.t.*; deified, *pt.*, *pp.*; deifying, *ppr.* [ME. *deifien*; OFr. *deifier*; LL. *deificare*, to make divine; L. *deus*, a god, and *facere*, to make.]

1. To make a god of; to exalt to the rank of a deity; to enroll among the deities; as, Julius Cæsar was *deified*.

2. To exalt into an object of worship; to treat as an object of supreme regard; as, to *deify* riches.

3. To make like a god.

deign (dān), *v.t.*; deigned, *pt.*, *pp.*; deigning, *ppr.* [ME. *deignen*; OFr. *deigner*; L. *dignari*, to deem worthy, from *dignus*, worthy.]

1. To think worthy or acceptable. [Obs.]

2. To grant or allow with condescension; to vouchsafe; often having an infinitive object.

> Those who ne'er *deign'd* their Bible to peruse
> Would think it hard to be denied their News.
> —Crabbe.

deign'ous (dān'us), *a.* Arrogant; haughty. [Obs.]

dēil, *n.* [Scot.] 1. The devil.

2. An evil-minded, mischievous, wicked fellow.

Dei'mos, *n.* [Gr. *deimos*, fear, terror, personified by Homer in the Iliad and regarded later by the Greeks as the son of Ares.] A satellite of the planet Mars making a revolution in thirty hours and eighteen minutes; discovered by Asaph Hall, of Washington, D. C., in 1877.

Dei-noc'e-ras, *n.* See *Dinoceras*.

Dei-nór'nis, *n.* See *Dinornis*.

dei'nō-saur, *n.* See *Dinosaur*.

Dei-nō-thē'ri-um, *n.* See *Dinotherium*.

dē-in'tē-grāte, *v.t.* To disintegrate. [Obs.]

dein'tē-ous, dein'tē-vous, *a.* Dainty. [Obs.]

Dē-ip'ȧ-rȧ, *n.* [LL., from L. *deus*, god, and *parere*, to bring forth.] A title of the Virgin Mary, meaning Mother of God. [See *Theotocos*.]

dē-ip'ȧ-rous, *a.* Bearing or bringing forth a god; an epithet applied to the Virgin Mary.

Deip-nos'ō-phist, *n.* [Gr *deipnon*, a dinner, and *sophistēs*, a learned man.] One who discourses learnedly at meals; a table philosopher.

dē'is, *n.* [Obs.] See *Dais*.

dē'işm, *n.* [Fr. *déisme*, from L. *Deus*, God.] The doctrine or creed of a deist; usually, belief in the existence of a Supreme Being as the source of finite existence, to the exclusion of revelation and the supernatural doctrines of Christianity.

dē'ist, *n.* [Fr. *déiste*, from L. *Deus*, God.] One who acknowledges the existence of a God through the evidence of reason, but rejects revealed religion.

dē-is'tiç, dē-is'tiç-ăl, *a.* Pertaining to deism or to deists; embracing deism; as, a *deistic* writer; containing deism; as, a *deistic* book.

dē-is'tiç-ăl-ly, *adv.* In a deistic manner.

dē-is'tiç-ăl-ness, *n.* The state or character of being deistic.

dē'i-tāte, *a.* [Obs.] See *Deified*.

dē'i-ty, *n.* [ME. *deite*; OFr. *deite*; LL. *deitas* (-*atis*), the divinity, from L. *divinitas* (-*atis*), divinity, from *deus*, a god, God.]

1. Godhead; divinity; the nature and essence of the Supreme Being.

2. [D—] God; the Supreme Being, or infinite self-existing Spirit; with the definite article; as, an offense to *the Deity*.

3. Any being vested or held to be vested with a divine nature or powers; a god or goddess; a divinity.

> Even Buddha himself is not worshiped as a *deity*. —Tennent.

dē-jeçt', *v t.*; dejected, *pt.*, *pp.*; dejecting, *ppr.* [L. *dejectus*, pp. of *dejicere*, to throw or cast down.]

1. To throw down; also, to abate. [Obs.]

2. To depress the spirits of; to dispirit; to discourage; to dishearten.

> Nor think, to die *dejects* my lofty mind.—Pope.

dē-jeçt', *a.* Cast down; low-spirited. [Obs.]

dē-jeç'tȧ, *n.pl.* [L., neut. pl. of *dejectus*, pp. of *dejicere*, to throw or cast down.] Excrements.

dē-jeçt'ed, *a.* Cast down; depressed; grieved; discouraged; as, a *dejected* look.

dē-jeçt'ed-ly, *adv.* In a dejected manner.

dē-jeçt'ed-ness, *n.* The state or quality of being dejected.

dē-jeçt'ēr, *n.* One who or that which dejects.

dē-jeç'tion, *n.* 1. The state of being downcast; depression of mind; melancholy; lowness of spirits, occasioned by grief or misfortune.

> Of sorrow, *dejection*, and despair.—Milton.

2. Weakness; as, *dejection* of appetite. [Rare.]

3. In medicine, (a) the act of voiding the excrement; (b) the matter ejected; stool; commonly in the plural.

4. A casting or bowing down. [Rare.]

Syn.—Depression, despondency, gloom, melancholy, sadness.

dē-jeçt'ly, *adv.* Dejectedly. [Obs.]

dē-jeç'tō-ry, *a.* Having power or tending to cast down; specifically, in medicine, purgative.

dē-jeç'tūre, *n.* That which is ejected; specifically, in medicine, dejecta.

dej'ēr-āte, *v.i.* [L. *dejerare*, *dejurare*, to take an oath.] To swear, as in taking an oath. [Obs.]

dej-ēr-ā'tion, *n.* An oath. [Obs.]

dé-jeu-né' (dā-zhē-nā'), *n.* [Obs.] See *Déjeuner*.

dé-jeu-nér' (dā-zhē-nā'), *n.* [Fr.] The first meal of the day; breakfast; corresponding, in France, to our midday meal.

Déjeuner à la fourchette; literally, breakfast with the fork; a repast in the middle of the day, with meat and wine.

dek'ȧ-drachm (-dram), *n.* [Gr. *deka*, ten, and *drachmē*, drachma.] A silver coin of ancient Greece of the value of ten drachms.

dek'ȧ-gram, *n.* See *Decagram*.

dek'ȧ-lī-tēr, *n.* See *Decaliter*.

dek'ȧ-mē-tēr, *n.* See *Decameter*.

dek'ȧ-stēre, *n.* See *Decastere*.

dek'le, *n.* In paper-making, same as *deckle*.

del, *n.* A part or portion. [Obs.]

Del-ȧ-beçh'ē-ȧ, *n.* [Named after *De la Beche*, the English geologist.] A genus of Australian trees, which was formed with the bottle-tree as a sole species, now comprehended by the genus *Sterculia*. [See *Bottle-tree* and *Sterculia*.]

Bottle-tree (*Delabechea* (*Sterculia*) *rupestris*).

dē-lac-ēr-ā'tion, *n.* A tearing in pieces.

dē-laç-ri-mā'tion, dē-laç-ry-mā'tion, *n.* Wateriness of the eyes. [Obs.]

del-aç-tā'tion, *n.* The act of weaning. [Obs.]

dē-laine', *n.* [Fr. *de laine*, of wool; L. *de*, of, from, and *lana*, wool.] A fabric made originally of wool, afterward more commonly of mixed materials and printed.

dē-lam-i-nā'tion, *n.* [L. *de*, from, and *lamina*, a thin piece of metal.] In biology, the process of splitting into separate layers; specifically, the formation of the blastoderm in its division of two, and afterward three layers of cells.

dē-lap-sā'tion, *n.* A falling down; delapsion. [Obs.]

dē-lapse', *v.i.* To fall or slide down; also, to pass down by inheritance. [Obs.]

dē-lap'sion, *n.* [L. *delapsus*, pp. of *delabi*, to fall or sink down; *de*, down, and *labi*, to fall.] A falling down, as of the uterus. [Obs.]

dē-las-sā'tion, *n.* [From L. *delassatus*, pp. of *delassare*, to weary, tire out; *de*, and *lassare*, to tire, weary.] Fatigue; weariness.

dē-lāte', *v.t.*; delated, *pt.*, *pp.*; delating, *ppr.* [L. *delatus*, pp. of *deferre*, to bring or carry down, report, announce, accuse.]

1. To carry; to convey; to transmit. [Obs.]

2. To carry abroad; to make public.

3. To carry on; to conduct; to manage.

4. To bring a charge against; to accuse; to inform against; to denounce.

[In this sense still used in the judicatories of the Scottish church.]

> As men were *delated*, they were marked down for such a fine. —Burnet.

dē-lāte', *v.i.* To allay; to dilute. [Obs.]

dē-lā'tion, *n.* 1. Carriage; conveyance. [Obs.]

2. In law, accusation; act of charging with a crime; information against.

> The accusers were not to be liable to the charge of *delation*. —Milman.

dē-lā'tōr, *n.* An accuser; an informer. [Rare.]

del-ȧ-tō'ri-ăn, *a.* Characteristic of or pertaining to a delator.

Del'ȧ-wāre, *n.* An American hybrid grape. It is of sure growth, reddish in color, and has a sweet flavor.

Del'ȧ-wāreş, *n.pl.* A tribe of American Indians of the Algonkin stock, the greater part of whom now inhabit Indian Territory.

dē-lāy', *v.t.*; delayed, *pt.*, *pp.*; delaying, *ppr.* [ME. *delayen*, *delaien*; OFr. *delaier*, from L. *dilatus*, pp. of *differre*, to carry or bring apart, to delay.]

1. To prolong the time of (acting or proceeding); to put off; to defer; to postpone.

2. To retard; to stop, detain, or hinder for a time; to restrain or retard the motion of; as, the mail is *delayed*.

3. To allay. [Obs.]

Syn.—Defer, postpone, procrastinate, prolong, protract, retard.—To *delay* is simply not to commence action; to *defer* and *postpone* are to fix its commencement at a more distant period; we may *delay* a thing for days, hours, and minutes; we *defer* or *postpone* it for months or weeks. *Delays* mostly arise from the fault of the person *delaying*; they are seldom reasonable or advantageous; *deferring* and *postponing* are discretionary acts, which are justified by the circumstances. *Procrastination* is a culpable *delay* arising solely from the fault of the *procrastinator*. We *delay* the execution of a thing; we *prolong* or *protract* the continuation of a thing; we *retard* the termination of a thing.

dē-lāy′, *v.i.* To linger; to move slowly; to loiter; to stop for a time.

dē-lāy′, *n.* [ME. *delay*; OFr. *delai*, from *delaier*, *delayer*, to delay.] A putting off or deferring; procrastination; hindrance; lingering; stay.

dē-lāy′ẽr, *n.* One who defers; one who lingers.

dē-lāy′ing-ly, *adv.* In a manner to cause delay.

dē-lāy′ment, *n.* Hindrance; loitering. [Obs.]

del crēd′ẽr-e. [It., of belief, or trust; *del*, for *de il*, of the, and *credere*, trust; L. *de*, of, and *credere*, to believe.] A guaranty given by a factor, broker, or mercantile agent, binding him to warrant the solvency of the purchasers of goods which he sells on credit.

dē′lē, *v.t.*; deled, *pt.*, *pp.*; deleing, *ppr.* [L., imper. of *delere*, to blot out, erase.] Blot out; erase; used as a direction to printers, and usually written thus δ.

del′e-ble, del′i-ble, *a.* [L. *delebilis*, from *delere*, to blot out.] Capable of being blotted out; capable of erasure.

dē-lec′tȧ-ble, *a.* [L. *delectabilis*, delightful, from *delectare*, to delight.] Delightful; highly pleasing; that gives great joy or pleasure; as, a *delectable* garden.

dē-lec′tȧ-ble-ness, *n.* Delightfulness.

dē-lec′tȧ-bly, *adv.* Delightfully; charmingly.

dē-lec′tāte, *v.t.* To please; to charm; to delight.

dē-lec-tā′tion, *n.* Great pleasure; enjoyment; delight.

dē-lec′tus, *n.* [L., from *delectus*, pp. of *deligere*, to select, choose.] An elementary text-book in the study of Greek or Latin.

del′ē-gȧ-cy, *n.* 1. The act of delegating or state of being delegated. [Obs.]

2. A delegation. [Obs.]

del′ē-gāte, *n.* [L. *delegatus*, pp. of *delegare*, to appoint.]

1. A person appointed and sent by another with powers to transact business as his representative; a deputy; a commissioner.

2. In the United States, (a) [D—] a person elected or appointed to represent a territory in Congress, having many of the privileges of a representative, but not the power to vote; (b) any duly authorized representative in a convention, as for the nomination of county or state officers, etc.

3. In Great Britain, (a) a commissioner formerly appointed by the crown, to hear and determine appeals from the ecclesiastical courts; (b) an acting committeeman in the University of Oxford.

4. A layman appointed to attend an ecclesiastical council.

Court of delegates; formerly, in England, the great court of appeal in ecclesiastical causes and from the decisions of the admiralty court; now abolished, and its powers and functions transferred to the sovereign in council.

Walking delegate; a member of a trades-union, having different powers in different unions, but usually having the power to call strikes and settle differences with employers.

Syn.—Deputy, representative, commissioner, vicar, attorney, substitute.

del′ē-gāte, *a.* Deputed; sent to act for or represent another; as, a *delegate* judge.

del′ē-gāte, *v.t.*; delegated, *pt.*, *pp.*; delegating, *ppr.* [L. *delegatus*, pp. of *delegare*, to send or remove from one place to another, to appoint, assign; *de*, from, and *legare*, to send, appoint.]

1. To depute; appropriately, to send on an embassy; to send with power to transact business, as a representative.

2. To intrust; to commit; to deliver to another's care and management; as, to *delegate* authority or power to an envoy, representative, or judge.

del-ē-gā′tion, *n.* 1. A sending away; the act of putting in commission, or investing with authority to act for another; the appointment of a delegate.

> These only held their power by *delegation* from the people. —Brougham.

2. A person, or body of persons, deputed to act for another, or for others; specifically, in the United States, the whole number of men representing some political district, as a county or state, in a legislative body.

3. In civil law, the substitution of a person as debtor in place of another.

4. In France, a certificate of shares.

5. One of two legislative bodies of Austria-Hungary, meeting each year by command of the emperor.

6. In banking, a non-negotiable letter of credit or debit.

del′ē-gȧ-tō-ry, *a.* Having a delegated position. [Obs.]

dē-len′dȧ, *n.pl.* [L., neut. pl. of *delendus*, gerundive of *delere*, to erase.] Things to be blotted out or erased.

del-ē-nif′ic-ăl, *a.* [L. *delenificus*, soothing, from *delenire*, to soothe.] Having the virtue to ease or assuage pain. [Obs.]

dē-lēte′, *v.t.*; deleted, *pt.*, *pp.*; deleting, *ppr.* [L. *deletus*, pp. of *delere*, to blot out, destroy.] To blot out; to remove; to cancel; to dele.

del-ē-tē′ri-ous, *a.* [Gr. *dēlētērios*, baneful, destructive, from *dēlētēr*, a destroyer, from *deleisthai*, to injure, to destroy.]

1. Having the quality of destroying or extinguishing life; destructive; poisonous; as, a *deleterious* plant or quality.

2. Injurious; pernicious; unwholesome.

del-ē-tē′ri-ous-ly, *adv.* In a deleterious manner.

del-ē-tē′ri-ous-ness, *n.* The quality of being deleterious.

del′ē-ter-y, *a.* and *n.* I. *a.* Destructive; poisonous. [Obs.]

II. *n.* Any destructive agent. [Obs.]

dē-lē′tion, *n.* 1. The act of blotting out or erasing.

2. An erasure; a passage deleted.

3. Destruction, as by blotting out; extinction; as, the *deletion* of the American Indian.

del-ē-ti′tious (-tish′us), *a.* Permitting erasure, as paper.

del′ē-tive, *a.* Pertaining to deletion; tending to delete or erase. [Rare.]

del′ē-tō-ry, *n.* That which blots out.

delf, *n.* [ME. *delf*, a quarry, a grave; AS. *dælf*, a ditch, from *delfan*, to dig.]

1. Anything the result of digging, as a pit, ditch, mine, etc. [Obs.]

2. A drain, as one on the landward side of a sea-wall.

3. In heraldry, an abatement in the form of a square sod.

delf, delft, *n.* Delftware.

delft′wāre, *n.* A kind of glazed pottery originated at Delft, Holland, in the fourteenth century; by extension, any similar ware.

Del′hi sōre. A cutaneous affection; Aleppo evil.

Dē′li-ăn, *a.* Of or pertaining to Delos, a small island in the Ægean sea, now called *Dili*.

Delian problem; that of the duplication of the cube, so termed from the advice of the oracle of Apollo at Delos, that the plague then raging would cease were the cubical altar doubled.

del′i-bāte, *v.t.* To taste; to take a sip of. [Obs.]

del-i-bā′tion, *n.* A taste; a sip. [Obs.]

del′i-bẽr, *v.t.* and *v.i.* To deliberate. [Obs.]

dē-lib′ẽr-āte, *v.t.*; deliberated, *pt.*, *pp.*; deliberating, *ppr.* [L. *deliberatus*, pp of *deliberare*, to consider, weigh well.] To weigh in the mind; to consider and examine the reasons for and against; to consider; to ponder on; as, to *deliberate* questions of state.

dē-lib′ẽr-āte, *v.i.* To estimate the weight or force of arguments, or the probable consequences of a measure, in order to make a choice or decision; to pause and consider.

> The woman that *deliberates* is lost.—Addison.

dē-lib′ẽr-āte, *a.* 1. Weighing facts and arguments with a view to a choice or decision; carefully considering the probable consequences of a step; circumspect; slow in determining; as, a *deliberate* judge or counselor.

2. Formed with deliberation; well advised or considered; not sudden or rash; as, a *deliberate* opinion; a *deliberate* measure or result.

3. Lacking rapidity; as, a *deliberate* move.

Syn.—Careful, cautious, intentional, purposed, thoughtful.

dē-lib′ẽr-āte-ly, *adv.* With careful consideration or deliberation; circumspectly; not hastily or rashly; slowly; as, a resolution *deliberately* formed.

dē-lib′ẽr-āte-ness, *n.* Calm consideration; circumspection; due attention to the arguments for and against a measure; caution.

dē-lib′ẽr-ā-tẽr, *n.* One who deliberates.

dē-lib-ẽr-ā′tion, *n.* 1. The act of deliberating; the act of weighing and examining the reasons for and against a choice or measure; consideration; reflection.

2. Mutual discussion and examination of the reasons for and against a measure; as, the *deliberations* of a legislative body or council.

3. The act or habit of doing anything coolly or without hurry or excitement and as if with mature reflection; as, a man of *deliberation*.

Syn.—Thoughtfulness, circumspection, reflection, consideration, wariness, caution, coolness, prudence.

dē-lib′ẽr-ȧ-tive, *n.* 1. A discourse in which a question is discussed, or weighed and examined.

2. A mode of rhetoric employed in proving a thing and convincing others of its truth, in order to persuade them to adopt it.

dē-lib′ẽr-ȧ-tive, *a.* 1. Pertaining to deliberation; argumentative; thoughtful; as, a *deliberative* judgment.

2. Proceeding or acting by deliberation, or by mutual discussion and examination; as, the legislature is a *deliberative* body.

dē-lib′ẽr-ȧ-tive-ly, *adv.* By deliberation; in a deliberative manner.

dē-lib′ẽr-ā-tōr, *n.* One who deliberates.

del′i-brāte, *v.t.* To strip, as bark from a tree. [Obs.]

del-i-brā′tion, *n.* The act of delibrating. [Obs.]

del′i-cȧ-cy, *n.*; *pl.* **del′i-cȧ-cieṣ.** 1. The quality of being delicate; exquisite agreeableness to the taste or some other sense; deliciousness; as, *delicacy* of sauces; *delicacy* of perfumes.

2. Fineness of texture; smoothness; softness; tenderness; as, the *delicacy* of the skin; the *delicacy* of a fabric.

3. Lightness or softness of tint; minute accuracy; nicety; as, the *delicacy* of coloring in painting.

4. Fineness; slenderness; minuteness; as, the *delicacy* of a thread.

5. Tenderness, as of constitution; weakness; that quality or state of the animal body which renders it very impressible to injury; as, *delicacy* of constitution or frame.

6. The state or quality of requiring nice handling; niceness; criticalness; as, the *delicacy* of a point or question.

7. Softness, as of manners; civility or politeness proceeding from a nice observance of propriety and a desire to please; tenderness; scrupulousness; the quality manifested in care to avoid offense, or what may cause pain; freedom from grossness; as, *delicacy* of behavior or feeling.

8. Refined discrimination; critical fastidiousness or taste.

9. The quality of being addicted to pleasure; luxuriousness. [Obs.]

10. Pleasure; self-gratification. [Obs.]

del′i-cāte, *n.* 1. A delicacy. [Obs.]

2. A fastidious person.

del′i-cāte, *a.* [ME. *delicate*; L. *delicatus*, giving pleasure, delightful, from *delicere*, to allure; *de*, away, and *lacere*, to draw gently, to charm.]

1. Pleasing to the senses; agreeable; dainty; as, a *delicate* odor.

2. Of a fine texture; fine; soft; smooth; as, a *delicate* fabric.

3. Nice; accurate; fine; soft to the eye; light or softly tinted; as, a *delicate* color.

4. Fine; slender; minute, as, a *delicate* thread.

5. Luxurious; delightful. [Obs.]

6. Nice in perception of what is agreeable to any of the senses; peculiarly sensitive to beauty, harmony, or their opposites; dainty; as, a *delicate* taste; a *delicate* ear for music.

7. Nice in forms; regulated by minute observance of propriety, or by condescension and attention to the wishes and feelings of others; refined; as, *delicate* behavior or manners.

8. Tender; feeble; not able to endure hardship; very susceptible of injury; as, a *delicate* constitution.

> That we can call these *delicate* creatures ours. —Shak.

9. That cannot be handled without injury or danger; that must be approached with care and caution; as, a *delicate* point or topic; a *delicate* question.

del′i-cāte-ly, *adv.* In a delicate manner.

del′i-cāte-ness, *n.* The state of being delicate.

del″i-cȧ-tes′sen, *n.pl.* [G., from Fr. *delicatesse*, a delicacy.] Delicacies for the table; dainties; relishes.

dē-li′ci-āte (-lish′i-āt), *v.i.* To feast. [Obs.]

dē-li′cious (-lish′us), *a.* [ME. *delicious*; L. *deliciosus*, delicious, from *deliciae*, an allurement, charm, from *delicere*, to allure.]

1. Highly pleasing to the taste; most grateful to the senses; affording exquisite pleasure; as, a *delicious* viand; *delicious* fruit or wine.

2. Most pleasing to the mind; yielding exquisite delight; as, a *delicious* entertainment.

3. Pleasure-seeking; effeminate. [Obs.]

Syn. — Delightful. — *Delicious* refers to the pleasure derived from certain of the senses; as, *delicious* food; a *delicious* fragrance; *delightful* may also refer to most of the senses, but has a higher application to matters of taste, feeling, and sentiment; as, a *delightful* abode, conversation, etc.

dē-li′cious-ly, *adv.* In a delicious manner; in a manner to please the taste or gratify the mind; sweetly; pleasantly; delightfully.

dē-li′cious-ness, *n.* 1 The quality of being delicious, or very grateful to the taste or mind; as, the *deliciousness* of a repast.

2. Delight; great pleasure; luxury. [Obs.]

dē-lict′, *n.* [L. *delictum*, a fault, from *delinquere*, to fail, commit a fault; *de*, and *linquere*, to leave.] A misdeed or offense; specifically, in civil and Scots law, a misdemeanor.

del′i-gāte, *v.t.*; delegated, *pt.*, *pp.*; deligating, *ppr.* [L. *deligatus*, pp. of *deligare*, to bind down; *de*, down, and *ligare*, to bind.] In surgery, to bandage; to ligate.

del-i-gā′tion, *n.* [From L. *deligatus*, pp. of *deligare*, to bind down.] In surgery, a binding up; a bandaging.

dē-light′ (-līt′), *n.* 1. A high degree of pleasure or satisfaction of mind; joy.

His *delight* is in the law of the Lord.—Ps. i. 2.

2. That which gives great pleasure; that which affords rapture.

Angels listen when she speaks,
She's my *delight* and mankind's wonder.
—Rochester.

3. Libidinous enjoyment. [Obs.]

Syn.—Rapture, joy, charm, gratification, satisfaction.

dē-light′, *v.t.*; delighted, *pt.*, *pp.*; delighting, *ppr.* [ME. *deliten*; L. *delectare*, to delight.] To affect with great pleasure; to please highly; to give or afford great satisfaction or joy to; as, a beautiful landscape *delights* the eye.

dē-light′, *v.i.* To have or take great pleasure; to be greatly pleased or rejoiced; followed by *in* or an infinitive; as, to *delight in* doing good.

I *delight to do* thy will, O my God.—Ps. xl. 8.

dē-light′ȧ-ble, *a.* Capable of causing delight. [Obs.]

dē-light′ed, *a.* Greatly pleased; full of joy; as, a *delighted* child.

Syn.—Pleased, glad, happy, joyous, joyful, gratified.

dē-light′ed-ly, *adv.* In a delighted manner; with delight.

dē-light′ẽr, *n.* One who takes delight. [Rare.]

dē-light′ful, *a.* Highly pleasing; affording great pleasure and satisfaction; as, a *delightful* thought; a *delightful* prospect.

Syn.—Beautiful, charming, gladsome, lovely, delicious, agreeable, captivating, enjoyable.

dē-light′ful-ly, *adv.* In a delightful manner.

dē-light′ful-ness, *n.* The quality of being delightful.

dē-light′ing, *a.* Giving great pleasure; making glad.

dē-light′ing-ly, *adv.* In a delighting manner.

dē-light′ous, *a.* Full of delight. [Obs.]

dē-light′sōme, *a.* Very pleasing; delightful.

dē-light′sōme-ly, *adv.* Very pleasingly; in a delightful manner.

dē-light′sōme-ness, *n.* Delightfulness.

dē-lig′nāte, *v.t.* To deprive of wood by felling trees. [Rare.]

dē-lim′it, *v.t.* [Fr. *delimiter*, to limit; LL. *delimitare*, to mark out the limits.] To limit; to bound; to mark the boundaries of.

dē-lim-i-tā′tion, *n.* The act of delimiting.

dē-line′, *v.t.* To delineate. [Obs.]

dē-lin′ē-ȧ-ble, *a.* That may be delineated.

dē-lin′ē-ȧ-ment, *n.* Representation by delineation; sketch; picture.

dē-lin′ē-āte, *v.t.*; delineated, *pt.*, *pp.*; delineating, *ppr.* [L. *delineatus*, pp. of *delineare*, to mark out, sketch.]

1. To mark out by lines the form or outline of; to sketch or design; to picture; to portray; as, to *delineate* the form of the earth; to *delineate* a diagram.

2. To represent to the mind or understanding; to exhibit a likeness in words; as, to *delineate* the character of Whitman.

Customs or habits *delineated* with great accuracy. —Walpole.

Syn.—Depict, represent, describe, design, draw, paint, outline, sketch, portray.

dē-lin′ē-āte, *a.* Delineated. [Rare.]

dē-lin-ē-ā′tion, *n.* 1. The act or process of delineating; the act of representing, portraying or describing; as, the *delineation* of a person's features.

2. Representation in words; sketch; description; as, the *delineation* of a character.

Syn.—Sketch, picture, description, outline, figure, design.

dē-lin′ē-ā-tŏr, *n.* 1. One who delineates or sketches.

2. An adjustable pattern used by tailors.

3. A surveying instrument on wheels which makes a record of the distance traversed by it and delineates profiles, as of roads; a perambulator.

dē-lin′ē-ȧ-tō-ry, *a.* Describing; drawing the outline.

dē-lin′ē-ȧ-tūre, *n.* Delineation. [Obs.]

del-i-ni′tion (-nish′un), *n.* The act of smearing. [Obs.]

dē-lin̄′quen-cy (-kwen-), *n.*; *pl.* **dē-lin̄′quen-cieṣ**. [LL. *delinquentia*, a fault, delinquency, from L. *delinquens*, ppr. of *delinquere*, to be wanting, to commit a fault.] Failure or omission of duty; a fault; a misdeed; an offense; a crime.

dē-lin̄′quent, *a.* 1. Failing in duty; offending by neglect of duty.

2. Relating to delinquency; as, *delinquent* taxes.

dē-lin̄′quent, *n.* One who fails to perform his duty; a transgressor; an offender; one who commits a fault or crime.

A *delinquent* ought to be cited in the place or jurisdiction where the delinquency was committed. —Ayliffe.

Syn.—Offender, transgressor, misdoer, culprit, defaulter.

dē-lin̄′quent-ly, *adv.* So as to fail in duty.

del′i-quāte (-kwāt), *v.i.* [L. *deliquatus*, pp. of *deliquare*, to clarify, to strain, to pour off.] To melt or be dissolved.

del′i-quāte, *v.t.* To cause to melt; to dissolve away.

del-i-quā′tion, *n.* A melting.

del-i-quesce′ (-kwes′), *v.i.*; deliquesced (-kwest), *pt.*, *pp.*; deliquescing, *ppr.* [L. *deliquescere*, to melt away, to dissolve.]

1. To melt gradually and become liquid by attracting and absorbing moisture from the air, as certain salts, acids, and alkalis.

2. In vegetable histology, to become liquid by degrees, as a process of regular growth, as the lamellæ of the pileus of mushrooms.

del-i-ques′cence, *n.* Spontaneous liquefaction in the air; a gradual melting or becoming liquid by absorption of moisture from the atmosphere.

del-i-ques′cent, *a.* 1. Liquefying in the air; capable of attracting moisture from the atmosphere and becoming liquid; as, *deliquescent* salts.

2. In botany, branching in such a way that the stem is lost in the branches.

3. In vegetable histology, liquefying gradually; deliquescing.

dē-liq′ui-āte (-lik′we-āt), *v.i.* See *Deliquesce*.

dē-liq-ui-ā′tion, *n.* See *Deliquescence*.

dē-liq′ui-um, *n.* [LL. *deliquium*, a flowing down, from L. *de*, down, and *liquere*, to melt.] Deliquescence, as of a salt; hence, figuratively, a melting or maudlin mood of mind.

Mere unreasoning *deliquium* of love and admiration was not good. —Carlyle.

dē-liq′ui-um, *n.* 1. Cessation of the sun's light, as by an eclipse.

2. In medicine, syncope.

dē-lir′ȧ-cy, *n.* Delirium. [Obs.]

dē-lir′ȧ-ment, *n.* A wandering of the mind; foolish fancy. [Obs.]

dē-lir′ăn-cy, *n.* Delirium. [Obs.]

dē-lī′rănt, *a.* Delirious. [Obs.]

dē-lī′rāte, *v.t.* and *v.i.* To rave, as a madman. [Obs.]

del-i-rā′tion, *n.* A demented state of mind; delirium.

dē-lir′i-ănt, *n.* A poison inducing persistent mental aberration.

dē-lir-i-fā′cient (-fā′shent), *a.* [L. *delirium*, madness, and *faciens* (-*ntis*), ppr. of *facere*, to make.] Causing delirium.

dē-lir-i-fā′cient, *n.* In medicine, any substance tending to produce delirium.

dē-lir′i-ous, *a.* Having delirium; light-headed; disordered in intellect; having ideas that are wild, irregular, and unconnected; insane.

dē-lir′i-ous-ly, *adv.* In a delirious manner.

dē-lir′i-ous-ness, *n.* The state of being delirious; delirium.

dē-lir′i-um, *n.* [L. *delirium*, madness, from *delirare*, to rave, to be crazy, lit. to make the furrow awry in plowing, to deviate from the straight line; *de*, from, and *lira*, a line, furrow.]

1. A temporary disordered state of the mental faculties occurring during illness, either of a febrile or of an exhausting nature; wandering of the mind.

2. Violent excitement; wild enthusiasm; mad rapture.

3. Hallucination.

Delirium tremens; an affection of the brain induced by the excessive and prolonged use of intoxicating liquors.

Syn.—Madness, mania, aberration, frenzy, lunacy, insanity.

dē-līt′, *n.* Delight. [Obs.]

dé-lit′ (dā-lē′), *n.* [Fr.] In law, a mild offense or misdemeanor against penal law.

dē-līt′ȧ-ble, *a.* Delightful; delectable. [Obs.]

del-i-tes′cence, *n.* [L. *delitescens* (-*ntis*), ppr. of *delitescere*, to lie hid, to lurk.]

1. Retirement; obscurity; the state of being concealed.

2. In surgery, the sudden disappearance of inflammatory symptoms or subsidence of a tumor.

del-i-tes′cen-cy, *n.* Delitescence.

del-i-tes′cent, *a.* Concealed; lying hid.

dē-lit′i-gāte, *v.i.* To chide or contend in words. [Obs.]

dē-lit-i-gā′tion, *n.* A chiding; a brawl. [Obs.]

dē-liv′ẽr, *v.t.*; delivered, *pt.*, *pp.*; delivering, *ppr.* [ME. *deliveren*; LL. *deliberare*, to deliver; L. *de*, from, and *liberare*, to set free; *liber*, free.]

1. To free; to release, as from restraint; to set at liberty; to rescue or save; often followed by *from* or *out of*; as, to *deliver* one *from* captivity.

Deliver me, O my God, *out of* the hand of the wicked. —Ps. lxxi. 4.

2. To give or transfer; to put into another's possession or power; to commit; to pass from one to another; as, to *deliver* a letter.

3. To surrender; to yield; to give up; to resign; as, to *deliver* a fortress to an enemy; often followed by *up* or *over*; as, to *deliver up* the city; to *deliver up* stolen goods; to *deliver over* money to an heir.

4. To disburden of a child in childbirth; often followed by *of*; also used figuratively.

5. To utter; to pronounce; to speak; as, to *deliver* a sermon, an address, or an oration.

6. To give forth in action; to discharge; to send forth; as, to *deliver* a broadside; to *deliver* a blow.

7. To make known; to impart, as information. [Obs.]

Syn.—Free, save, rescue, emancipate, release, discharge, give forth, liberate, surrender, utter, pronounce.

dē-liv′ẽr, *v.i.* In molding, to disunite from the mold freely.

dē-liv′ẽr, *a.* Free; nimble; active. [Obs.]

dē-liv′ẽr-ȧ-ble, *a.* That may be or is to be delivered.

dē-liv′ẽr-ănce, *n.* 1. The act of delivering or the state of being delivered; release, as from captivity, slavery, oppression, restraint, or any evil.

2. The act of bringing forth children; parturition; delivery.

3. The act of speaking or pronouncing; utterance; statement; affirmation. In this and in the second sense, *delivery* is now used.

4. In Scots law, the expressed decision of a judge or arbitrator, interim or final. When interim, it is technically called an *interlocutor*.

5. Acquittal of a prisoner by the verdict of a jury.

dē-liv′ẽr-ẽr, *n.* 1. One who delivers; one who releases or rescues; a preserver.

The Lord raised up a *deliverer* to Israel. —Jud. iii. 9.

2. One who relates or communicates. [Rare.]

dē-liv′ẽr-ess, *n.* A female deliverer. [Rare.]

dē-liv′ẽr-ly, *adv.* Nimbly; actively; cleverly. [Obs.]

dē-liv′ẽr-ness, *n.* Nimbleness; agility. [Obs.]

dē-liv′ẽr-y, *n.*; *pl.* **dē-liv′ẽr-ieṣ**. 1. The act of delivering; release; rescue, as from slavery, danger, oppression, or any evil; deliverance.

2. The act of surrendering or giving up; a giving or passing from one to another; as, the *delivery* of goods; the *delivery* of a fort.

3. Utterance, pronunciation, manner of speaking or articulating; as, the speaker has a good *delivery*.

4. The act of giving birth; the expulsion or extraction of the fetus in childbirth.

5. Free motion or use of the limbs. [Rare.]

6. The act of sending forth; discharge; as, the *delivery* of a bowler in cricket; the *delivery* of a blow.

7. Capacity for discharging or pouring out; as, the *delivery* of a pump.

8. In founding, the bevel or free play given to a casting; a draft.

General delivery; the delivery of mail at a post-office, upon application of the person to whom it is to be delivered, according to the address.

dell, *n.* [ME. *dell*; D. *del*, a dale, valley.] A small, narrow valley between two hills; a ravine.

dell, *n.* A girl; a wench. [Obs.]

Del′lȧ Çrus′cȧ. [It., a shortened form of *Accademia della Crusca*, lit. the Academy of Chaff; *della*, of the, and *crusca*, bran, chaff.] The name of an academy founded at Florence, Italy, in 1582, mainly for promoting the purity of the Italian language.

Del-lȧ-crus′căn, *a.* 1. Relating to or characteristic of Della Crusca.

2. A term applied to a school of English poetry started by some Englishmen at Florence toward the close of the eighteenth century.

Del-lȧ-crus′căn, *n.* A member of the Academy Della Crusca, or of the school of English poetry of the same name.

dē-lō′căl-īze, *v.t.* To free from associations or limitations of locality; to widen the scope of.

dē′loo, *n.* [Native North African name.] An antelope, the duykerbok.

dē-lōul′ *n.* Same as *Delul*.

delph, *n.* Same as *Delf*.

Del′phi-ăn, *a.* 1. Relating to Delphi, a town of Phocis in Greece, and to the celebrated oracle of that place.

2. Relating to the priestess of the oracle of Delphi, who in a state of inspiration delivered the responses of the oracle; hence, inspired.

Del′phi-ăn, *n.* An inhabitant of Delphi; particularly, Apollo.

Del′phic, *a.* See *Delphian*.

del′phin, *a.* [L. *delphinus*; Gr. *delphin*, a dolphin.]

1. Pertaining to the dolphin or to the *Delphinidæ*.

2. Pertaining to the dauphin of France; applied particularly to an edition of the Latin classics prepared under Louis XIV. for the dauphin's use. Also spelled *delphine*.

del′phin, *n.* [L. *delphinus*, a dolphin.] One of

the constituents of oils from cetaceans of the genus *Delphinus*.

del′phi-nāte, *n.* A salt of delphinic acid.

del′phine, *a.* See *Delphin.*

del-phin′iç, *a.* [From L. *delphinus*, a dolphin.] Pertaining to an acid discovered by Chevreul, first in dolphin-oil and afterward in the ripe berries of the guelder-rose. It is now known to be identical with valeric acid.

del-phin′iç, *a.* Pertaining to or derived from the larkspur.

Del-phin′i-dæ, *n.pl.* The dolphin tribe, a family of cetaceous animals, characterized by the moderate size of the head, by the presence of teeth in both jaws, and by a dorsal fin.

del′phi-nine, *n.* A vegetable alkaloid discovered in the stavesacre, having a bitter and acrid taste; written also *delphinin, delphinia, delphia, delphin.*

Del-phin′i-um, *n.* [L., from Gr. *delphinion*, the larkspur, so called on account of the resemblance of the nectary to a dolphin; Gr. *delphis, delphin*, a dolphin.] An extensive genus of plants of the crowfoot order, with flowers of a blue, purple, or white color. The genus embraces fifty species found in the north temperate zone. From *Delphinium Staphisagria*, a vegetable alkaloid, delphinine, is obtained.

del′phi-noid, *a* [Gr. *delphis, delphin*, a dolphin, and *eidos*, form.] Pertaining to or characteristic of the dolphin.

del′phi-noid, *n.* Any species of dolphin of the family *Delphinoidea.*

Del-phi-noi′dē-å, *n.pl.* [L., from Gr. *delphin*, a dolphin, and *eidos*, form.] A superfamily of cetaceans, comprising the suborder *Denticete*, excepting only the cachalots.

del-phi-noi′dine, *n.* An alkaloid derived from the seeds of *Delphinium Staphisagria.*

Del-phī′nus, *n.* [L., from Gr. *delphis, delphin*, a dolphin.]

1. The cetacean genus containing the dolphin and kindred species.

2. In astronomy, an ancient constellation situated east of Aquila, the Dolphin.

Del-särte′, *n.* See *Delsartian system* under *Delsartian.*

Del-sär′ti-ăn, *a.* Pertaining to François Delsarte (1811-1871), a French teacher of singing.

Delsartian system or *Delsarte system*; a system of calisthenic exercises formulated by François Delsarte, consisting of graceful and dramatic poses.

del′tå, *n.* [L. *delta*; Gr. *delta*; Heb. *daleth*, the fourth letter of the Gr. and Heb. alphabet; lit., a door.]

1. The fourth letter of the Greek alphabet, Δ, corresponding to the English *D.*

2. A triangular, Δ-shaped tract of alluvial land at the mouth of a river; as, the *delta* of the Nile or of the Mississippi.

3 In anatomy, any triangular surface or space.

del″tå-fi-cā′tion, *n.* [L. *delta*, and *facere*, to make.] The act or process of forming a delta at the mouth of a river.

del-tā′iç, *a.* Pertaining to or resembling a delta.

del′tå-met″ăl, *n.* A nonoxidizing alloy of zinc, copper, and iron; so named because composed of three metals, in allusion to the fact that the Greek letter delta (Δ) is formed by three lines.

del-thy̆′ris, *n.* [Gr. *delta*, delta, and *thyra*, a door.] One of certain fossil brachiopods of the genus *Spirifer.*

del′tiç, *a.* Same as *Deltaic.*

del-tid′i-um, *n.* [L., from Gr. *delta*, the letter delta, Δ.] In zoölogy, the triangular space between the beak and the hinge-bone of brachiopod shells, usually covered by a shelly plate.

del-tō-hē′drŏn, *n.* [Gr. *delta*, delta, and *hedra*, a seat, base.] In crystallography, a hemihedral isometric solid included under twelve quadrilateral faces.

del′toid, *a.* [Gr. *delta*, and *eidos*, form.] Resembling the Greek Δ; triangular; specifically, (a) in anatomy, denoting that muscle of the shoulder which moves the arm forward, upward, and backward; (b) in botany, triangular or trowel-shaped; as, a *deltoid* leaf; more specifically applied to the cross-section of a solid part, as a stem or leaf.

Deltoid Leaf.

del′toid, *n.* In anatomy, the deltoid muscle.

del-toi′dăl, *a.* Triangular; deltoid.

dē-lū′brum, *n.*; *pl.* **dē-lū′brå.** [L. *delubrum*, a shrine, temple, a place of religious purification, from *de*, off, from, and *luere*, to wash.]

1. In Roman antiquity, a temple having a basin or font, where persons coming to sacrifice washed.

2. In ecclesiastical architecture, a church furnished with a font.

3. A font or baptismal basin.

dē-lūd′å-ble, *a.* That may be deluded or deceived; liable to be imposed on.

dē-lūde′, *v.t.*; deluded, *pt., pp.*; deluding, *ppr.* [ME. *deluden*; L. *deludere*, to play false with, to delude, deceive.]

1. To deceive; to impose on; to lead from truth or into error; to mislead the mind or judgment of; to beguile.

> To *delude* the nation by an airy phantom.
> —Burke.

2. To frustrate or disappoint. [Obs.]

Syn.—Deceive, mislead, cheat, beguile, misguide.

dē-lūd′ēr, *n.* One who deceives; a deceiver; an impostor; one who holds out false pretenses.

del′ūġe, *n.* [ME. *deluge*; L. *diluvium*, a flood, deluge, from *diluere*, to wash away; *dis-*, off, from, and *luere*, to wash.]

1. Any overflowing of water; an inundation; a flood; specifically, one of various exterminatory floods shown to have existed, by the traditions or histories of ancient peoples, as that recorded in Genesis vii.

2. Anything resembling an inundation, either in destructiveness or volume; as, a *deluge* of molten lava; a *deluge* of letters.

Syn.—Flood, inundation, submersion.

del′ūġe, *v.t.*; deluged, *pt., pp.*; deluging, *ppr.*

1. To overflow with water; to inundate; to submerge; as, too abundant rains have *deluged* the lowlands.

2. To cover, absorb, or overrun by or as by a deluge; as, the armies *deluged* the country; *deluged* by requests.

dē-lūl′, dē-lōul′, *n.* [Ar.] A female dromedary.

dē-lun′dung, *n.* [Native name.] *Prionodon gracilis*, a catlike quadruped inhabiting Java and Malakka, allied to the civets, but probably forming a connecting link between them and the *Felidæ*, being destitute of scent-pouches.

dē-lū′ṣion, *n.* [L. *delusio*, delusion, from *delusus*, pp. of *deludere*, to cheat, delude.]

1. The act of deluding; deception; a misleading of the mind.

> Under the influence of love's *delusion.*
> —Thackeray.

2. The state of being deluded; false impression or belief; illusion; error or mistake proceeding from false views.

> And fondly mourn'd the dear *delusion* gone.
> —Prior.

Syn.—Illusion, fallacy, deception, error, hallucination.

dē-lū′ṣion-ăl, *a.* Characterized by delusions; afflicted with delusions; as, a *delusional* affection or patient.

dē-lū′ṣion-ist, *n.* One deluded or deluding.

dē-lū′sive, *a.* 1. Apt to deceive; tending to mislead the mind; deceptive; beguiling; as, *delusive* arts; *delusive* appearances.

2. Characterized by delusion; deceptive. [Rare.]

dē-lū′sive-ly, *adv.* In a delusive manner.

dē-lū′sive-ness, *n.* The quality of being delusive; tendency to delude.

dē-lū′sō-ry, *a.* Apt to deceive; deceptive.

delve, *v.t.*; delved, *pt., pp.*; delving, *ppr.* [ME. *delven*; AS. *delfan*, to dig.]

1. To dig; to turn up with a spade.

2. To fathom; to sound; to penetrate.

3. To bury. [Obs.]

delve, *v.i.* 1. To labor with the spade.

2. Figuratively, to make laborious research; to investigate; as, to *delve* amongst Greek roots.

delve, *n.* A place dug; a pit; a pitfall; a ditch; a den; a cave. [Obs.]

Delve of coals; a certain quantity of coal dug from the mine. [Prov. Eng.]

delv′ēr, *n.* One who delves.

dē-mag″net-i-zā′tion, *n.* The act or process of depriving of magnetic or of mesmeric influence.

dē-mag′net-īze, *v.t.*; demagnetized, *pt., pp.*; demagnetizing, *ppr.* 1. To deprive, as a magnet, of magnetism.

2. To deprive of mesmeric influence; to bring from a hypnotic state.

dē-mag′net-ī-zēr, *n.* One who or that which demagnetizes.

dem-å-goġ′iç, dem-å-goġ′iç-ăl, *a.* Relating to or like a demagogue; factious.

dem′å-gog-iṣm, dem′å-gogu-iṣm, *n.* The practice or principles of a demagogue.

dem′å-gogue (-gog), *n.* [Fr. *demagogue*; Gr. *dēmagōgos*, a leader of the people; *dēmos*, the people, and *agōgos*, a leader, from *agein*, to lead.]

1. Anciently, a leader of the people; a person who swayed the people by his oratory.

2. An unprincipled factious orator; one who acquires influence with the populace by pandering to their prejudices or playing on their ignorance; specifically, an agitator for political or mercenary purposes.

> A plausible insignificant word, in the mouth of an expert *demagogue*, is a dangerous and deceitful weapon.
> —South.

dem′å-goġ-y, *n.* Demagogism.

dē-māin′, *n.* [ME. *demayn*; OFr. *demaine*; L. *dominium*, right of ownership, dominion.]

1. Dominion; also, domain. [Obs.]

2. In law, same as *Demesne.* [Obs.]

dē-månd′, *v.t.*; demanded, *pt., pp.*; demanding, *ppr.* [OFr. *demander*, to demand; L. *demandare*, to give in charge, hand over, intrust; *de*, away, from, and *mandare*, to intrust · lit., to put in one's hands, from *manus*, hand, and *dare*, to give.]

1. To ask or call for, as one who has a claim or right to receive what is sought; to claim or seek as due by right; as, the creditor *demands* principal and interest of his debt.

2. To ask by authority; to require; to seek or claim (an answer) by virtue of a right or supposed right in the interrogator, derived from his office, station, power, or authority; as, to *demand* obedience.

3. To require as necessary or useful; as, the execution of this work *demands* great industry and care.

4. To ask; to question; to inquire; to interrogate; as, to *demand* answer.

5. To ask or require, as a seller of goods; as, what price do you *demand?*

6. In law, to summon to court.

Syn.—Ask, request, solicit, seek, inquire.

dē-månd′, *v.i.* To make a demand.

dē-månd′, *n.* 1. An asking with authority; a challenging as due; a request made with authority; as, the *demand* of the creditor was reasonable.

> Confidence to turn his wishes into *demands.*
> —Locke.

2. An asking without right or authority, implying force or penalty; as, the *demands* of a robber or blackmailer.

3. That which is demanded or called for; claim; as, unexpected *demands* on one's resources; *demands* of the body.

4. A desire to obtain; a want; specifically, in political economy, the desire of possession in conjunction with buying power; as, the *demand* for lumber threatens our forests.

5. In law, (a) a valid claim against a person, whether coming from contract, damage, or otherwise; (b) the asking or seeking for what is due or claimed as due, either expressly by words, or by implication, as by seizure of goods or entry into lands.

6. A question; inquiry; interrogation.

Demand and supply; the relation between consumption and production; between the demand of purchasers and the supply of commodities by those who have them to sell.

In demand; called for; especially, for purchase. [See *Demand*, n. 4.]

On demand; on call or presentation; as, a certificate payable *on demand.*

dē-månd′å-ble, *a.* That may be demanded or required.

dē-månd′ănt, *n.* One who demands; the plaintiff in a real action; any plaintiff.

dē-månd′ēr, *n.* One who demands.

dē-månd′ress, *n.* A female demandant.

dē-man′toid, *n.* [G. *demant*, a diamond, from L. *adamas*, Gr. *adamas*, the diamond, and *eidos*, form.] A kind of garnet, emerald-green in color.

dē-mär′çāte, *v.t.*; demarcated, *pt., pp.*; demarcating, *ppr.* [Fr. *demarquer*, to mark off, from L. *de*, off, and O.H.G. *marca*, a boundary.]

1. To mark the limits or boundaries of; to bound.

2. To separate or place, as in a class; as, to *demarcate* electrical phenomena.

dē-mär-çā′tion, *n.* [Fr. *demarcation*, from *demarquer*, to mark off.] The act of marking the limits of; also, separation, as into a class.

dē-märch′, *n.* March; walk; gait. [Obs.]

dē′märch, *n.* [L. *demarchus*, in Rome a tribune of the people; Gr. *dēmarchos*, the head of a deme, or tribe; *dēmos*, a deme, and *archein*, to rule.] The ruler or magistrate of a deme; the mayor of a modern Greek town.

dē-märk′, *v.t.* Same as *Demarcate.*

dē-mär-kā′tion, *n.* See *Demarcation.*

dē-må-tē′ri-ăl-īze, *v.t.* To rid of material elements or attributes.

dē-må-tē′ri-ăl-īze, *v.i.* In spiritualism, to vanish after materialization.

dēme, *n.* [Gr. *dēmos*, a country district, town, the people.]

1. A subdivision of ancient Attica and of modern Greece, a township.

2. In biology, any homogeneous mass of elementary organisms.

dē-mēan′, *v.t.*; demeaned, *pt., pp.*; demeaning, *ppr.* [ME. *demenen*; OFr. *demener*, to drive, lead, conduct, do, from *de*, down, and LL. *minare*, to drive, to drive animals by threatening cries, from L. *minari*, to threaten.]

1. To do; to manage; to guide. [Obs.]

2. To behave; to carry; to conduct; used reflexively; as, they promised to *demean themselves* properly.

> How with so high a nymph he might
> *Demean himself* the marriage-night.—Swift.

dē-mēan′, *n.* 1. Mien; demeanor; behavior; conduct.

2. Conduct; management; treatment. [Obs.]

dē-mēan′, *v.t.* To debase; to lower; wrongly used in this sense.

Demean himself by a marriage with an artist's daughter. —Thackeray.

dē-mēan′, *n.* See *Demain.*

dē-mēan′ănce, *n.* Behavior; demeanor. [Obs.]

dē-mēan′ŏr, dē-mēan′ŏur, *n.* 1. Behavior; carriage; deportment; as, decent *demeanor*; sad *demeanor.*

2. Conduct; treatment; management. [Obs.]

Syn.—Air, bearing, behavior, manner.

dē-mēan′ūre, *n.* Demeanor. [Obs.]

dē-mem-brā′tion, *n.* In Scots law, dismemberment.

dē′men-cy, *n.* Dementia.

dē-ment′, *v.t.* To make insane.

dē-ment′, *a.* and *n.* [L. *demens* (*-ntis*), out of one's mind, mad; *de-* priv., and *mens* (*-ntis*), mind.]

I. *a.* Devoid of reason; dementate. [Rare.]

II. *n.* A demented person; a defective. [Rare.]

dē-men′tāte, *a.* Mad; infatuated; demented.

dē-men′tāte, *v.t.* To dement. [Rare.]

dē-men-tā′tion, *n.* The act of making mad; the state of being demented.

dē-ment′ed, *a.* Devoid of reason; insane.

dē-ment′ed-ness, *n.* The condition of being demented; mental unsoundness.

dē-men′tiȧ (-shiȧ), *n.* [L. *dementia*, madness, insanity, from *demens* (*-ntis*), mad, out of one's mind.] Deterioration or loss of the power of coherent thought; mania; insanity.

dē-meph″i-ti-zā′tion, *n.* The act of purifying from mephitic or foul air.

dē-meph′i-tīze, *v.t.*; demephitized, *pt., pp.*; demephitizing, *ppr.* [*De-* priv., and L. *mephitis*, foul air, ill smell.] To purify from foul, unwholesome air.

dē-mērġe′, *v.t.* To dip; to immerse. [Obs.]

dē-mer′it, *n.* [OFr. *demerite*; LL. *demeritum*, a transgression, from *demerere*, to deserve ill.]

1. That which one merits. [Obs.]

2. That which deserves punishment; the opposite of *merit*; that which is blamable or punishable in moral conduct; vice or crime.

Mine is the merit, the *demerit* thine.—Dryden.

3. A mark denoting deficiency in studies or deportment.

dē-mer′it, *v.t.* 1. To deserve. [Obs.]

2. To depreciate. [Obs.]

dē-mer′it, *v.i.* To be deserving.

dē-mẽrse′, *v.t.* To immerse. [Obs.]

dē-mẽrsed′ (-mẽrst′), *a.* In botany, submersed.

dē-mẽr′sion, *n.* [LL. *demersio*, immersion, from L. *demersus*, pp. of *demergere*, to dip under, plunge into.]

1. Immersion. [Rare.]

2. The state of being overwhelmed. [Rare.]

dē-mes′mẽr-īze, *v.t.* To relieve from mesmeric influence.

dē-mēsne′ (-mēn′), *n.* [ME. *demaine*; OFr. *demaine, domaine*, a right of ownership, from L. *dominium*, property, right of ownership.]

1. Possession; dominion. [Obs.]

2. A manor-house and the land adjacent or near, which a lord keeps in his own hands for immediate occupation or for the use of his family, as distinguished from his tenemental lands, distributed among his tenants, called bookland, or charter-land, and folkland, or estates held in villenage, from which sprung copyhold estates. —Blackstone.

3. Estate in lands.

Ancient demesne; see under *Ancient.*

Demesne lands; in feudal law, lands retained by a noble for his own use.

dē-mēsn′i-ăl (-mē′ni-ăl), *a.* Pertaining to a demesne.

Dē-mē′tẽr, *n.* [Gr. *Dēmētēr*; Doric *Damater*, prob. from Gr. *gē*, Doric *da*, earth, and *mētēr*, mother.] In Greek mythology, a goddess, corresponding in some respects to the Latin Ceres, the goddess of agriculture. She was mother of Bacchus.

demi-. [OFr. *demi-*, half, from L. *dimidius*, half; *dis, di*, apart, and *medius*, middle.] A prefix denoting half; as, *demi*-lion.

dē′mī, *n.* See *Demy*, n. 2.

dem′i-bāin, *n.* See *Demibath.*

dem′i-bas-tiŏn (-chun), *n.* [Fr., from *demi*, half, and *bastion*, a bastion.] In fortification, a bastion that has only one face and one flank.

dem′i-bȧth, *n.* A bath in which only part of the body is immersed.

dem′i-bri-gāde′, *n.* A half brigade.

dem′i-çā-dence, *n.* [*Demi-*, and L. *cadens*, ppr. of *cadere*, to fall.] In music, a half cadence.

dem′i-can-nŏn, *n.* The obsolete name of a sixteenth century piece of ordnance carrying a ball of from thirty to thirty-six pounds in weight.

dem′i-cap-ō-niēre′, *n.* In fortification, a single caponiere. [See *Caponiere.*]

dem′i-cir-cle, *n.* A simple instrument for measuring and indicating angles, having much the same use as the theodolite.

dem′i-çul-vẽr-in, *n.* A heavy cannon. [Obs.]

dem-i-dē′i-fȳ, *v.t.* To deify in part. [Rare.]

dem′i-dis-tănce, *n.* In fortification, the distance between the outward polygons and the flank.

dem′i-dī-tōne, *n.* In music, a minor third.

dem′i-god, *n.* Partly, or, literally, half a god; a fabulous hero, produced by the intercourse of a deity with a mortal.

dem′i-god-dess, *n.* A female demigod.

dem′i-gorġe, *n.* In fortification, that part of the polygon which remains after the flank is raised, extending from the curtain to the angle of the polygon. It is half of the vacant space or entrance into a bastion.

dem′i-grōat, *n.* A half groat.

dem′i-is″lănd (-ī″lănd), *n.* [Obs.] See *Peninsula.*

dem′i-john (-jon), *n.* [Fr. *damejeanne*, a demijohn; Ar. *damagan*, a demijohn, so called from *Damagan*, in northern Persia, once famous for its glass works.] A glass vessel or bottle with a large body and small neck, inclosed in wickerwork.

dem′i-lănce, *n.* A light lance; a short spear; also, one using such a weapon.

dem′i-lī″ŏn, *n.* In heraldry, the upper half of a lion used as a bearing; usually in an upright attitude, rampant.

Demi-lion.

dem′i-lūne, *n.* [Fr., from *demi*, half, and *lune*, moon; L. *luna*, moon.]

1. A crescent.

2. In fortification, an outwork consisting of two faces and two little flanks, constructed to cover the curtain and shoulders of the bastion.

Demilunes of Heidenhain; in physiology, crescentic, protoplasmic bodies present in the salivary glands.

dem′i-man, *n.* A half man.

dem′i-men-ton-nière′ (-nyãr′), *n.* In medieval armor, a half mentonnière attached to the breastplate for the protection of the throat and chin on the left side.

dem′i-monde, *n.pl.* [Fr., from *demi*, half, and *monde*, the world, society, from L. *mundus*, the world.] A class of women not indiscriminately loose in character or favors, but who so conduct themselves as to leave their true character in doubt; by extension, courtezans as a class.

dem′i-par-ăl-lel, *n.* Militarily, a shorter intrenchment thrown up between the main parallels of attack.

dem′i-pīke, *n.* A spontoon.

dem′i-plaç-āte, *n.* A separate or additional piece of armor.

dem′i-quā-vẽr, *n.* In music, a note of half the length of the quaver. [Rare.]

dem′i-rē-lief″, *n.* Same as *Mezzo-rilievo.*

dem′i-rep, *n.* [*Demi-* and *rep*utation.] A woman of suspicious chastity.

dem′i-rē-vet″ment, *n.* In fortification, that form of retaining wall for the face of a rampart which is only carried up as high as cover exists in front of it.

dem′i-rī-lie′vō (-rē-lyā′vō), *n.* [*Demi-*, and It. *rilievo*, relief.] Mezzo-rilievo.

dē-miṣ-ȧ-bil′i-ty, *n.* In law, the state of being demisable.

dē-miṣ′ȧ-ble, *a.* In law, capable of being demised or leased; as, a *demisable* estate.

dē-miṣe′, *n.* [OFr. *demis*, pp. of *demettre*, to resign, from L. *dimittere*, to send away, release, resign; *di*, from, and *mittere*, to send.]

1. Transfer, as by death or otherwise. [Obs.]

2. In law, a conveyance or transfer of an estate for a term of years (the usual sense), or in fee for life.

3. Decease; death; particularly, the death of any distinguished individual.

Demise and redemise; a conveyance where there are mutual leases made from one to another of the same land, or something out of it.

dē-miṣe′, *v.t.*; demised, *pt., pp.*; demising, *ppr.*

1. In law, to transfer or convey, as an estate, for life or for years; to lease.

2. To bequeath; to grant by will.

dē-miṣe′, *v.i.* To descend by bequest or inheritance, as property.

dem′i-sem-i-quā′vẽr (-kwā′), *n.* [*Demi-*, and L. *semi*, half, and ME. *quaveren*, to quiver, shake.] In music, a note of the value of one-fourth of a quaver; a thirty-second note.

dē-miss′, *a.* [L. *demissus*, pp. of *demittere*, to let down, cast down.]

1. Downcast; humble. [Rare.]

2. In botany, depressed.

dē-mis′sion, *n.* A lowering; degradation; depression.

dē-mis′sion, *n.* Resignation, as of an office.

dē-mis′sion-ā-ry, *a.* Tending to degrade or lower.

dē-mis′sion-ā-ry, *a.* Relating to the transfer or demise of an estate.

dē-miss′ive, *a.* Humble. [Rare.]

dē-miss′ly, *adv.* In a humble manner. [Obs.]

dē-mit′, *v.t.*; demitted, *pt., pp.*; demitting, *ppr.* [L. *demittere*, to send or cast down; *de*, down, from, and *mittere*, to send.]

1. To let fall; to depress. [Obs.]

2. To submit; to humble. [Obs.]

dē-mit′, *v.t.* 1. To dismiss. [Obs.]

2. To lay down formally, as an office; to resign; to relinquish; to transfer.

dē-mit′, *n.* In Freemasonry, a dimit.

dem′i-tint, *n.* In painting, a gradation of color between positive light and positive shade; commonly called *half-tint.*

dem′i-tōne, *n.* In music, a semitone. [Rare.]

dem′i-ūrġe, *n.* [L. *demiurgus*; Gr. *dēmiourgos*, a chief magistrate.]

1. Literally, a worker for the people; hence, the maker of the world; the Creator; specifically, the name given by the Gnostics to the creator or former of the world of sense.

2. In some Peloponnesian states of ancient Greece, one of a class of magistrates who did the service of the people. Sometimes they seem to have been the chief executive ministry.

dem-i-ūr′ġiç, dem-i-ūr′ġiç-ăl, *a.* Pertaining to a demiurge or to creative power.

dem′i-vōlt, *n.* [Fr. *demi-volte*, from *demi*, half, and *volte*, a leap.] In manège, one of the seven artificial motions of a horse, in which he raises his fore legs in a particular manner.

dem′i-wolf (-wụlf), *n.* A half wolf; a mongrel between a dog and a wolf.

dē-mō″bi-li-zā′tion, *n.* [Fr. *demobilization*, from *demobilizer*, to demobilize, disband.] In military tactics, the act of disbanding troops; the condition of being demobilized and not liable to be moved on service.

dē-mō′bi-līze, *v.t.*; demobilized, *pt., pp.*; demobilizing, *ppr.* To disarm and dismiss (troops); to disband.

dē-moç′rȧ-cy, *n.*; *pl.* **dē-moç′rȧ-cieṣ**. [OFr. *democratie*; Gr. *dēmokratia*, democracy, popular government, from *dēmos*, the people, and *kratein*, to rule.]

1. Government by the people; a form of government in which the supreme power is lodged in the hands of the people collectively.

2. A state or body politic, the legislative, executive, and judicial power of which is in the hands of the people, either directly or through representatives, as in the various states in the Union.

3. Equality as regards political and legal rights; opposed to *aristocracy.*

4. [D—] The principles, and, collectively, the members of the Democratic party.

5. Collectively, the people, especially those qualified to exercise the right of suffrage.

dem′ō-çrat, *n.* 1. One who adheres to democracy; opposed to *aristocrat.*

2. [D—] In the United States, a member of the Democratic party.

3. A light wagon having several seats and no top.

dem-ō-çrat′iç, *a.* [Gr. *dēmokratikos*, suited to a democracy, from *dēmokratia*, a democracy; *dēmos*, the people, and *kratein*, to rule.]

1. Relating to democracy as a governmental principle.

2. [D— *or* d—] Of, relating to, or denoting the Democratic party.

3. Tending or disposed to equality of rights and privileges; unaffected; approachable; as, a *democratic* disposition.

Democratic party; one of the two leading political parties of the United States, first known as the Anti-Federal party, then as the Republican or Democratic-Republican, and lastly, as now designated.

dem-ō-çrat′iç-ăl, *a.* Democratic.

dem-ō-çrat′iç-ăl-ly, *adv.* In a democratical manner.

dē-moç′rȧ-tiṣm, *n.* Democratic principles or spirit. [Rare.]

dē-moç′rȧ-tist, *n.* A democrat. [Rare.]

dē-moç′rȧ-tīze, *v.t.*; democratized, *pt., pp.*; democratizing, *ppr.* To make democratic.

dē-moç′rȧ-ty, *n.* Democracy. [Obs.]

Dē-mō-gor′gon, *n.* [LL. *Demogorgo*, from Gr. *daimōn*, a demon, and *gorgos*, grim, dreadful.] A mysterious divinity, viewed as an object of terror rather than of worship, by some regarded as the author of creation, and by others as a famous magician, to whose spell all the inhabitants of Hades were subjected.

dē-mog′rȧ-phẽr, *n.* A student of demography.

dem-ō-graph′iç, *a.* Pertaining to demography.

dē-mog′rȧ-phy, *n.* [Gr. *dēmos*, people, and *graphein*, to write.] In ethnology, the study of vital and social statistics.

de-moi-ṣelle′ (de-mwä-zel′), *n.* [Fr.] 1. A damsel; a maid.

2. *Anthropoides virgo*, the Numidian crane.

3. In entomology, the dragon-fly.

4. In ichthyology, (a) any pomacentroid fish; (b) the tiger-shark.

dē-mol′ish, *v.t.*; demolished, *pt., pp.*; demolishing, *ppr.* [L. *demoliri*, to pull down, destroy; *de*, down, and *moliri*, to build, construct, exert oneself, from *moles*, a mass.] To throw or pull down; to raze; to destroy, as a heap or structure; to separate the collected mass, or the connected parts of; to ruin; as, to *demolish* an edifice or a mound.

Syn.—Overturn, overthrow, destroy, dismantle, raze.—That is *overturned* or *overthrown* which had stood upright; that is *destroyed* whose component parts are scattered; that is *demolished* which had formed a mass or structure; that is *dismantled* which is stripped of its covering; that is *razed* which is brought down smooth and level to the ground.

dē-mol′ish-ẽr, *n.* One who or that which demolishes.

dē-mol′ish-ment, *n.* Demolition. [Obs.]

dem-ō-li′tion (-lish′un), *n.* 1. The act of demolishing; ruin; destruction.

2. In French law, abrogation.

dem-ō-li′tion-ist, *n.* A destructionist.

de-mol′ō-gy, *n.* The statistical study of populations and social conditions; demography.

dē′mŏn, *n.* [L. *dæmon*; Gr. *daimōn*, a deity, spirit, one's genius, an evil spirit.]

1. In mythology, (a) a spirit, or immaterial being, holding a middle place between men and the celestial deities; (b) a tutelary spirit.

2. An evil or malignant spirit; a devil.

3. A very cruel, depraved, or wicked person.

dē′mŏn-ess, *n.* A female demon.

dē-mŏn″e-ti-zā′tion, *n.* The act of demonetizing or the condition of being demonetized.

dē-mŏn′e-tize, *v.t.*; demonetized, *pt., pp.*; demonetizing, *ppr.* [*De-* priv., and L. *moneta*, money.] To divest of monetary value, as coin; to deprive of standard value, or value as full legal tender; as, *demonetized* silver.

dē-mō′ni-a̤c, *a.* 1. Pertaining to, produced, or influenced by a demon or demons.

2. Resembling a demon in nature; hence, cruel; as, *demoniac* crimes.

dē-mō′ni-a̤c, *n.* 1. A human being held to be possessed by a demon; one whose volition and other mental faculties are thought to be overpowered, restrained, or disturbed, in their regular operation, by an evil spirit.

2. [D—] In church history, one of a section of the Anabaptists who maintain that the devils will ultimately be saved.

dē-mō-nī′ȧ-ca̤l, *a.* Demoniac.

dē-mō-nī′ȧ-ca̤l-ly, *adv.* In a demoniacal manner.

dē-mō-nī′ȧ-cism, *n.* The state of being demoniac; the practices of demoniacs.

dē-mō′ni-ăl, *a.* Demoniac. [Rare.]

dē-mō′ni-ăn, *a.* Pertaining to or characteristic of a demon.

dē-mō′ni-ăn-ism, *n.* The state of being possessed, supposedly, by a demon. [Rare.]

dē-mō′ni-asm, *n.* Demonianism. [Rare.]

dē-mon′ic, *a.* [Gr. *daimonikos*, demoniac, from *daimōn*, a demon.] Pertaining to demons; demoniac.

dē′mŏn-ism, *n.* The belief in demons or false gods.

dē′mŏn-ist, *n.* One who believes in or worships demons.

dē′mŏn-īze, *v.t.*; demonized, *pt., pp.*; demonizing, *ppr.* [LL. *demonizare*, to make demoniac.] To convert into a demon; to infuse the principles or fury of a demon into.

dē-mŏn-og′rȧ-cy, *n.* [Gr. *daimōn*, a demon, and *kratein*, to rule.] The power or government of demons.

dē-mŏn-og′rȧ-phẽr, *n.* A demonologist.

dē-mŏn-og′rȧ-phy, *n.* [Gr. *daimōn*, a demon, and *graphein*, to write.] Demonology by description. [Rare.]

dē-mŏn-ol′ȧ-tẽr, *n.* One who worships demons.

dē-mŏn-ol′ȧ-try, *n.* [Gr. *daimōn*, a demon, and *latreia*, worship, from *latreuein*, to worship, serve.] The worship of demons or of evil spirits.

dē-mŏn-ol′ō-gẽr, *n.* A demonologist. [Obs.]

dē″mŏn-ō-log′ic, dē″mŏn-ō-log′ic-ăl, *a.* Pertaining to demonology.

dē-mŏn-ol′ō-gist, *n.* One versed in demonology.

dē-mŏn-ol′ō-gy, *n.* [Gr. *daimōn*, a demon, and *logos*, discourse.] The study or science of demons; also, the investigation of legends and superstitions concerning demons.

dē-mŏn-om′ȧ-gy, *n.* [Gr. *daimōn*, a demon, and *magos*, magic.] Magic invoking or requiring the aid of demons.

dē′mŏn-ō-man-cy, *n.* [Gr. *daimōn*, a demon, and *manteia*, divination.] Divination while possessed by the devil or demons.

dē″mŏn-ō-mā′ni-ȧ, *n.* [Gr. *daimōn*, a demon, and *mania*, madness.] A form of insanity in which the patient shows morbid fear of evil spirits and believes himself possessed of devils; demonopathy.

dē-mon′ō-mist, *n.* [Gr. *daimōn*, a demon, and *nŏmos*, law, from *nemein*, to regulate.] One that lives in subjection to the devil, or to evil spirits. [Obs.]

dē-mon′ō-my, *n.* The dominion of demons. [Obs.]

dē-mŏn-op′ȧ-thy, *n.* [Gr. *daimōn*, a demon, and *pathos*, suffering.] Demonomania.

dē′mŏn-ry, *n.* Demoniacal influence.

dē′mŏn-ship, *n.* The state of a demon.

dē-mon-strȧ-bil′i-ty, *n.* Demonstrableness.

dē-mon′strȧ-ble, *a.* Capable of being demonstrated; provable.

dē-mon′strȧ-ble-ness, *n.* The quality of being demonstrable; demonstrability.

dē-mon′strȧ-bly, *adv.* In a manner to preclude doubt; beyond the possibility of contradiction.

dē-mon′strȧnce, *n.* Demonstration. [Obs.]

dem′ŏn-strāte (*or* dē-mon′strāt), *v.t.*; demonstrated, *pt., pp.*; demonstrating, *ppr.* [L. *demonstratus*, pp. of *demonstrare*, to point out, to show; *de*, out, from, and *monstrare*, to show.]

1. To point out; to indicate; to make evident; to exhibit; specifically, in anatomy, to exhibit the parts of when dissected, as a dead body.

2. To show or prove to be certain; to prove beyond the possibility of doubt; to prove in such a manner as to reduce the contrary position to evident absurdity.

Syn.—Evince, manifest, prove.

dem′ŏn-strā-tẽr, *n.* See *Demonstrator.*

dem-ŏn-strā′tion, *n.* 1. The act of demonstrating, or showing forth; an exhibition; a manifestation; a show.

> Did your letters pierce the queen to any *demonstration* of grief? —Shak.

2. The act of exhibiting certain proof, or proof beyond the possibility of doubt.

> From a necessary and universal truth to draw consequences which necessarily follow is *demonstration.* —Fleming.

3. In mathematics, a method of proof by which a result is shown to be the necessary consequence of assumed premises.

4. In logic, syllogistic proof, or the act of employing such proof.

5. In anatomy, the exhibition of parts of a body with lectures or explanations.

6. In military language, an exhibition of warlike intentions; a warlike attempt; an operation of any kind intended as a feint or a menace.

7. A public exhibition by a party, sect, or society of its numbers, principles, etc., as by a parade or mass-meeting.

Direct or *positive demonstration*; a method of proceeding by positive or affirmative propositions, to the correct conclusion.

Indirect or *negative demonstration*; that by which a thing is shown to be true by proving the absurdity of a contrary supposition; called also *reductio ad absurdum.*

dē-mon′strȧ-tive, *a.* 1. Showing or proving by certain evidence; having the power of demonstration; invincibly conclusive; as, a *demonstrative* argument, or *demonstrative* reasoning.

2. Having the power of showing with clearness and certainty; as, a *demonstrative* figure in painting.

3. In rhetoric, laying open or explaining with clearness, force, and beauty.

4. Characterized by or given to the strong exhibition of any feeling or quality; energetically expressive; as, a *demonstrative* manner; a *demonstrative* person.

> May hasn't been too officious about me and too *demonstrative.* —Dickens.

Demonstrative pronoun; in grammar, one that clearly indicates the object to which it refers; as, *this* man; *that* book.

dē-mon′strȧ-tive, *n.* A demonstrative pronoun.

dē-mon′strȧ-tive-ly, *adv.* 1. So as to demonstrate; certainly; clearly; convincingly.

2. In a demonstrative manner, or with the energetic exhibition of any feeling or quality; as, he spoke very *demonstratively.*

dē-mon′strȧ-tive-ness, *n.* The state or quality of being demonstrative.

dem′ŏn-strā-tŏr, *n.* 1. One who demonstrates; one who proves anything with certainty or with indubitable evidence.

2. A teacher of practical anatomy.

3. The index or forefinger.

dē-mon′strā-tō-ry, *a.* Demonstrative. [Rare.]

dē-mor′āge, *n.* Demurrage. [Obs.]

dē-mor″ăl-i-zā′tion, *n.* The act of demoralizing; the state of being demoralized; also spelled *demoralisation.*

dē-mor′ăl-īze, *v.t.*; demoralized, *pt., pp.*; demoralizing, *ppr.* [*De-* priv., and LL. *moralizare*, to have a moral influence, from L. *moralis*, moral, from *mos* (*moris*), custom, morals, manners.]

1. To corrupt or undermine the morals of; to render corrupt in morals.

2. To lower the tone or spirit of; to render distrustful and hopeless; as, hunger and cold *demoralized* the army.

3. To confuse or disorder mentally; as, the examiner's questions *demoralized* the applicant. [Colloq.]

Also spelled *demoralise.*

dē′mos, *n.*; *pl.* **dē′mī.** [Gr. *dēmos*, a deme, the common people.]

1. In Grecian antiquity, the people; the democracy.

2. The common people.

Dem-os-then′ic, *a.* Pertaining to or characteristic of Demosthenes, the Grecian orator.

dē-mot′ic, *a.* [Gr. *dēmotikos*, suiting the people, popular, public, from *dēmos*, the people.] Popular; common; pertaining to the common people; specifically applied to the alphabet used by the people of ancient Egypt, as contradistinguished from that used by the priestly caste, called the *hieratic.*

dē-mount′, *v.i.* To dismount. [Rare.]

dē-mount′ȧ-ble, *a.* Capable of being readily taken apart and reassembled; as a *demountable* aeroplane.

demp′ne, *v.t.* To condemn. [Obs.]

demp′stẽr, *n.* See *Deemster.*

dē-mulce′, *v.t.* [L. *demulcere*, to stroke down, soften.] To soothe; to soften or pacify. [Rare.]

dē-mul′cent, *a.* and *n.* I. *a.* In medicine, soothing; emollient.

II. *n.* A medicine having a soothing or emollient effect.

dē-mul′sion, *n.* [From L. *demulctus*, pp. of *demulcere*, to stroke, soften.]

1. The act of soothing or contenting.

2. That which soothes or comforts; flattery. [Obs.]

dē-mũr′, *v.i.*; demurred, *pt., pp.*; demurring, *ppr.* [OFr. *demorer*; L. *demorari*, to delay; *de*, from, and *morari*, to delay, from *mora*, delay.]

1. To stay; to linger. [Obs.]

2. To pause in uncertainty; to delay determination or conclusion. [Obs.]

3. To have or to state scruples or difficulties; to take exceptions; as, they *demurred* to our proposals.

4. In law, to interpose a demurrer.

dē-mũr′, *v.t.*; demurred, *pt., pp.*; demurring, *ppr.* 1. To delay; to postpone. [Obs.]

2. To hesitate about; as, to *demur* proceedings.

dē-mũr′, *n.* 1. Stop; pause; scruple; suspense of proceeding or decision.

2. Exception taken; objection made.

dē-mūre′, *a.* [ME. *demure*, from OFr *de murs*, of manners, for *de bounes mures*, of good manners.]

1. Sober; grave; modest; downcast; as, a *demure* countenance; a *demure* abasing of the eye.

2. Affecting modesty or decorum; making a pretense of gravity.

dē-mūre′, *v.i.* To seem demure. [Obs.]

dē-mūre′ly, *adv.* With a grave, solemn countenance; with a show of solemn gravity.

dē-mūre′ness, *n.* The state of being demure; gravity of countenance real or affected; a show of modesty.

dē-mũr′i-ty, *n.* Demureness; also, one who acts demurely.

dē-mũr′rȧ-ble, *a.* That may be demurred to; that exception may be taken to.

dē-mũr′rāge, *n.* [OFr. *demorage*, delay, from *demorer*, to delay.]

1. In maritime law, (a) the detention of a vessel by the freighter beyond the time originally stipulated, in loading or unloading; (b) the compensation which the freighter has to pay for such delay or detention.

2. In England, (a) detention of freight-cars, etc.; (b) a discount of 1½d. per ounce, made by the Bank of England in exchanging notes or coin for gold bullion.

dē-mũr′răl, *n.* Hesitation in proceeding or deciding; demur.

dē-mũr′rẽr, *n.* 1. One who demurs.

2. In law, a pleading which takes the ground that, even were the opposing claim allowed, it would be inoperative.

> A demurrer confesses the fact or facts to be true, but denies the sufficiency of the facts in point of law to support the claim or defense. —Blackstone.

Demurrer to evidence; an acknowledgment at trial that the evidence presented by the opposing party is true but inadequate, with a consequent submission of the issue to the court.

dē-mȳ′, *n.*; *pl.* **dē-mīeṣ′.** [Fr. *demi*, half.]

1. A writing paper 16x21 inches in size, in the United States.

2. A half-fellow at Magdalen College, Oxford; also written *demi.*

3. A gold coin issued in 1433 by James I. of Scotland, equivalent at that time to about eighty cents.

dē-mȳ′, *a.* Denoting a certain size of paper. [See *Demy*, n. 1.]

dē-mȳ′ship, *n.* A certain scholarship in Magdalen College, Oxford.

den, *n.* [ME. *den*, *denne*, a den, lair; AS. *denn*, a den, a lair of wild animals.]

1. A cave or hollow place in the earth; usually applied to a cave, pit, or underground recess, used for concealment, shelter, protection, or security; as, a lion's *den*; a *den* of robbers or thieves.

2. Any squalid place of resort or residence; a haunt; used always in a bad sense; as, *dens* of misery; an opium *den.*

3. A small private room or apartment; a close retreat. [Colloq.]

den, *n.* [ME. *dene*; AS. *denu*, a valley, dell.] A narrow glen; a gully; a dell. [Scot.]

den, *v.i.* To dwell in a den.

dē-när″cō-ti-zā′tion, *n.* The state of being denarcotized.

dē-när′cō-tize, *v.t.*; denarcotized, *pt.*, *pp.*; denarcotizing, *ppr.* [*De-*, and *narcotic.*] To deprive of narcotin; as, to *denarcotize* opium.

dē-nā′ri-us, *n.*; *pl.* **dē-nā′ri-ī**. [L. *denarius*, containing ten, from *deni*, ten by ten, from *decem*, ten.] A Roman silver coin worth ten asses, or ten pounds of copper originally, and

Denarius of Tiberius Cæsar.

afterward considered equal to sixteen asses, when the weight of the as was reduced to an ounce on account of the scarcity of silver.

den′ȧ-ry, *a.* [L. *denarius*, containing ten.] Containing ten; tenfold; decimal.

den′ȧ-ry, *n.*; *pl.* **den′ȧ-ries**. 1. The number ten.

2. A tithing; a division into tens.

3. A denarius.

dē-na″tion-ăl-i-zā′tion, *n.* The act of denationalizing or the state of being denationalized.

dē-na′tion-ăl-īze, *v.t.*; denationalized, *pt.*, *pp.*; denationalizing, *ppr.* To divest of national character or rights.

dē-nat′ū-răl-ize, *v.t.*; denaturalized, *pt.*, *pp.*; denaturalizing, *ppr.* 1. To render unnatural; to alienate from nature.

2. To deprive of naturalization or acquired citizenship in a foreign country.

3. To denationalize; to deprive of citizenship.

dē-nā′ture, dē-nā′tur-ize, *v.t.* [L. *de*, away, and nature.] To render unfit for usual use; applied mainly to alcohol, rendering it unfit as beverage or medicine, but valuable as a fuel for various engines, cooking, etc. Is manufactured from nearly all vegetable formation.

dē-nāy′, *n.* Denial; refusal. [Obs.]

dē-nāy′, *v.t.* To deny. [Obs.]

dendr-, den′dri-, den′drō-. Combining forms from Gr. *dendron*, tree.

den′drȧ-chāte, *n.* [*Dendr-*, and Gr. *achatēs*, agate.] Arborescent agate; agate containing the figures of shrubs or parts of plants.

den′drăl, *a.* [From Gr. *dendron*, a tree.] Pertaining to a tree or trees; of the nature of a tree; arboreal. [Rare.]

den′dri-fọrm, *a.* [*Dendri-*, and L. *forma*, form.] Having the form or appearance of a tree; arborescent.

den′drite, *n.* [Gr. *dendritēs*, of or belonging to a tree, from *dendron*, a tree.]

1. A stone or mineral on or in which are the figures of shrubs or trees, produced usually by the presence of hydrous oxid of manganese.

2. Any mineral crystallizing in arborescent form.

den-drit′iç, den-drit′iç-ăl, *a.* 1. Resembling a tree; tree-like; dendriform.

2. Marked by figures resembling shrubs, moss, etc.; said of minerals.

den-drit′iç-ăl-ly, *adv.* In a dendritic manner.

den′drōbe, *n.* An orchid of the genus *Dendrobium.*

Den-drō′bi-um, *n.* [L., from Gr. *dendron*, a tree, and *bios*, life.] An extensive genus of epiphytic orchids, dispersed over the whole of the damp tropical parts of Asia. Over eighty species have been cultivated in hothouses for the beauty of their flowers.

Dendrobium (*Dendrobium Falconeri*).

Den-drō-căl′ȧ-mus, *n.* [*Dendro-*, and Gr. *kalamos*, a reed.] A small genus of arborescent grasses growing in the East Indies, resembling the bamboo, but bearing a berry-like fruit.

Den-drō-cœ′lȧ, *n.pl.* [*Dendro-*, and Gr. *koilos*, hollow.] A division of turbellarian worms characterized by a broad, thin, and flat body; the planarians.

den-drō-cœ′lăn, *n.* A turbellarian worm of the division *Dendrocœla*; a planarian.

den-drō-den′tine, *n.* [*Dendro-*, and L. *dens* (*-ntis*), a tooth.] That modification of the fundamental tissue of the teeth produced by the aggregation of many simple teeth into a mass.

den′drō-dont, *a.* [Gr. *dendron*, a tree, and *odous* (*odontos*), tooth.] Having teeth presenting a dendriform appearance in section, as certain fossil vertebrates.

den′drō-dont, *n.* One of a dendrodont fossil family of vertebrates.

den-drog′rȧ-phy, *n.* [*Dendro-*, and Gr. *graphein*, to write.] Same as *Dendrology.*

den′droid, *a.* [Gr. *dendron*, a tree, and *eidos*, form.] Resembling a shrub or small tree; dendriform.

den-droid′ăl, *a.* Dendroid.

den′drō-līte, *n.* [*Dendro-*, and Gr. *lithos*, a stone.] A petrified or fossil shrub, plant, or part of a plant.

den-drō-log′iç-ăl, *a.* Pertaining to dendrology.

den-drol′ō-gist, *n.* One familiar with dendrology.

den-drol′ō-gous, *a.* Pertaining to dendrology.

den-drol′ō-gy, *n.* [Gr. *dendron*, a tree, and *logos*, description, from *legein*, to speak.] A discourse or treatise on trees; the natural history of trees.

den-drom′e-tēr, *n.* [*Dendro-*, and Gr. *metron*, a measure.] An instrument to measure the height and diameter of trees.

dēne, *n.* A valley; a dean or den. [Obs.]

den′ē-gāte, *v.t.* To deny. [Obs.]

den-ē-gā′tion, *n.* Denial. [Obs.]

dēne′hōle, *n.* [ME. *dene*; AS. *denu*, a valley, and *hol*, a hole.] One of a large number of ancient artificial pits or excavations, often found in the chalk formation in the southeastern part of England.

den′gue, *n.* [Sp. *dengue*, prudery.] A febrile epidemic disease, the symptoms of which resemble those that accompany scarlet fever and rheumatism. It is peculiar to warm climates. This disease, when it first appeared in the British West India islands, was called the *dandy* fever, from the stiffness and constraint which it gave to the limbs and body. The Spaniards of the neighboring islands mistook the term for their word *dengue*, denoting prudery, which might also well express stiffness, and hence the term *dengue* became, at last, the name of the disease.

dē-nī′ȧ-ble, *a.* That may be denied or contradicted.

dē-nī′ăl, *n.* [From L. *denegare*, to deny; *de*, and *negare*, to deny.]

1. The act of denying, contradicting, refusing, or disowning; an assertion that a declaration or fact stated is not true; negation; contradiction; opposed to *affirmation.*

2. Refusal to grant; the negation of a request or petition; as, his request or application met with a direct *denial.*

3. A rejection or refusing to acknowledge; a disowning; a refusing to receive or embrace; as, a *denial* of the faith or the truth.

4. In law, a defense; a formal contradiction of a statement made by the opposing party.

Denial of oneself; a declining of some gratification; restraint of one's appetites or propensities.

Syn.—Disavowal, renunciation, contradiction, dissent, rejection, abnegation.

dē-nī′ănce, *n.* Denial. [Obs.]

dē-nī′ēr, *n.* One who denies.

dē-nïer′, *n.* [OFr. *denier*, from L. *denarius*, lit. containing ten, a denarius.] A small French coin no longer current; the twelfth part of a sou.

den′i-grāte, *v.t.* [L. *denigratus*, pp. of *denigrare*, to blacken; *de*, and *nigrare*, to blacken.] To blacken; to make black. [Obs.]

den-i-grā′tion, *n.* The act of making black; a blackening; aspersion. [Archaic.]

den′i-grā-tŏr, *n.* One who or that which blackens.

den′im, *n.* [Etym. unknown.] A colored cotton drilling largely used for overalls, floorcovering, etc.

dē-nī′trāte, *v.t.*; denitrated, *pt.*, *pp.*; denitrating, *ppr.* To rid of nitric acid.

den-i-trā′tion, *n.* A disengaging of nitric acid.

dē-nī″tri-fi-cā′tion, *n.* The act or process of removing nitrates.

dē-nī′tri-fȳ, *v.t.*; denitrified, *pt.*, *pp.*; denitrifying, *ppr.* To free from nitrogen or nitrates.

den-i-zā′tion, *n.* The act of making one a denizen, subject, or citizen.

dē-nīze′, *v.t.* To make a denizen, subject, or citizen of; to naturalize. [Obs.]

den′i-zen, *n.* [ME. *denesyn*; OFr. *denzein*, one living within a city, from L. *de intus*, from within.]

1. A stranger admitted to residence in a foreign country; specifically, in English law, an alien who is made a subject by the king's letters patent, holding a middle state between an alien and a natural-born subject.

2. A dweller; as, the *denizens* of air.

den′i-zen, *v.t.*; denizened, *pt.*, *pp.*; denizening, *ppr.* To make a denizen of; to admit to residence with certain rights and privileges; to enfranchise.

den″i-zen-ā′tion, *n.* Denization.

den′i-zen-ize, *v.t.* To denizen.

den′i-zen-ship, *n.* The state of being a denizen.

den′net, *n.* [Origin uncertain.] A light, open, two-wheeled carriage for traveling, resembling a gig.

dē-nom′i-nȧ-ble, *a.* Capable of being denominated or named.

dē-nom′i-nănt, *n.* [L. *denominans* (*-ntis*), ppr. of *denominare*, to name.] That which names or denotes a quality; as, boldness is the *denominant* of bold.

dē-nom′i-nāte, *v.t.*; denominated, *pt.*, *pp.*; denominating, *ppr.* [L. *denominatus*, pp. of *denominare*, to name; *de*, and *nominare*, to name, from *nomen*, a name.] To name; to give a name or epithet to; to call; to designate.

Syn.—Name, designate, call, style, entitle.

dē-nom′i-nāte, *a.* In arithmetic, denoting a number which expresses the kind of unit treated of; qualifying; opposed to *abstract*; thus, seven pounds is a *denominate* number, while seven, without reference to concrete units, is *abstract.*

dē-nom-i-nā′tion, *n.* 1. The act of naming.

2. A name or appellation; a specific designation; as, a *denomination* of pounds, hundreds, etc.

3. A society or collection of individuals called by the same name; a sect; as, the Universalist *denomination.*

Syn.—Name, designation, appellation, title, epithet.

dē-nom-i-nā′tion-ăl, *a.* Pertaining to a denomination, or a number of individuals called by the same name; as, *denominational* education.

dē-nom-i-nā′tion-ăl-işm, *n.* Adherence or devotion to a denomination, sect, or policy; specifically, a disposition to maintain sectarian ideas in matters of religion.

dē-nom-i-nā′tion-ăl-ist, *n.* An advocate or believer in denominationalism; a sectarian.

dē-nom-i-nā′tion-ăl-ly, *adv.* In a denominational manner; by denomination or sect.

dē-nom′i-nā-tive, *a.* 1. That may be denominated; namable.

2. That may constitute a distinct designation; appellative.

3. In grammar, drawn from a noun or adjective root; as, a *denominative* verb.

4. In logic, connotative; as, a *denominative* name.

dē-nom′i-nā-tive, *n.* That which has the character of a denomination; specifically, in grammar, a word, especially a verb, formed from a noun, either substantive or adjective.

dē-nom′i-nā-tive-ly, *adv.* By denomination.

dē-nom′i-nā-tŏr, *n.* 1. One who or that which denominates; one from whom or that from which a name is derived.

2. In arithmetic, that number placed below the line in vulgar fractions, which shows into how many parts the integer is divided. Thus, in $\frac{3}{5}$, 5 is the *denominator*, showing that the integer is divided into five parts; and the numerator, 3, shows how many parts are taken; that is, three fifths.

3. In algebra, the expression in a fraction under the line signifying division.

4. Same as *Denominant.*

dē-nōt′ȧ-ble, *a.* That may be denoted or marked.

dē-nō′tāte, *v.t.* To denote. [Obs.]

dē-nō-tā′tion (*or* den-ō-), *n.* [LL. *denotatio*, a marking or pointing out, from L. *denotare*, to mark out, denote.] The act of marking off; separation; distinction, as by name.

dē-nōt′ȧ-tive, *a.* Having power to denote.

dē-nōt′ȧ-tive-ly, *adv.* In a denotative manner.

dē-nōte′, *v.t.*; denoted, *pt.*, *pp.*; denoting, *ppr.* [L. *denotare*, to mark out, denote; *de*, and *notare*, to mark, from *nota*, a mark.]

1. To mark; to signify by a visible sign; to indicate; to express; to designate; as, the sign × *denotes* multiplication.

2. To be the sign or symptom of; to show; to betoken; to indicate; as, a quick pulse *denotes* fever.

Syn.—Mean, indicate, imply, signify, express, show, betoken, mark.

dē-nōte′ment, *n.* Sign; indication. [Rare.]

dē-nōt′ive, *a.* Denoting; indicative.

dé-noüe′ment (dā-nö′moṅ), *n.* [Fr., from *dénouer*, to untie; *dé-* priv., and *nouer*, to tie.] The winding up or catastrophe of a plot, as of a novel, drama, etc.; the solution of any mystery; the issue, as of any course of conduct; the event; the outcome.

dē-nounce′, *v.t.*; denounced, *pt.*, *pp.*; denouncing, *ppr.* [ME. *denouncen*; L. *denuntiare*, to give notice to, threaten, denounce.]

1. To declare solemnly; to announce. [Obs.]

> I *denounce* unto you this day, that ye shall surely perish. —Deut. xxx. 18.

2. To threaten by some outward sign or expression.

> His look *denounced* revenge. —Milton.

3. To inform against; to accuse; as, he was *denounced* to the authorities.

4. To point out in public as deserving of censure or punishment; to stigmatize; to accuse menacingly; as, to *denounce* a man as a thief.

Denounced for a heretic. —More.

5. In Mexican and Spanish mining law, (a) to formally lay claim to (a mine abandoned or inadequately worked); (b) to establish a claim to (a new mine).

dē-nounce′ment, *n.* 1. The declaration of a menace, or of evil; denunciation. [Rare.]

2. In Mexican and Spanish mining law, the act of denouncing. [See *Denounce*, 5.]

dē-noun′cēr, *n.* One who denounces.

dense, *a.* [L. *densus*, thick, close.]

1. Close; compact; having the constituent parts closely united; thick; as, a *dense* body; a *dense* fog.

2. Stupid; dull; thick-headed; as, *dense* ignorance.

3. In photography, intense; opaque, as a negative.

4. Crowded. [Rare.]

dense′ly, *adv.* In a dense manner; compactly.

dense′ness, *n.* Density.

den′shīre, den′shēr, *v.t.* [From *Denshire*, contr. of the proper name *Devonshire*.] To fertilize (land) by burnt refuse. [Prov. Eng.]

den-sim′e-tēr, *n.* [L. *densus*, dense, and *metrum*, a measure.] An instrument for determining the specific gravity or density of a solid or liquid.

den′si-ty, *n.* [L. *densitas*, thickness, from *densus*, thick.]

1. The quality of being dense, close, or compact; closeness of constituent parts; compactness.

2. That quality of a body depending upon the close cohesion of its molecules, measured by the mass of matter per unit of volume. The relative *density* of a substance is generally called its specific gravity.

3. In electricity, the quantity of electricity per unit of volume or area.

dent, *n.* [ME. *dent*, from AS. *dynt*, a stroke or blow.]

1. A stroke; a blow. [Obs.]

2. A mark made by a blow, as a gap or notch; especially, a hollow or depression made on the surface of a solid body; an indentation.

dent, *v.t.*; dented, *pt.*, *pp.*; denting, *ppr.* To make a dent or small hollow in; to indent.

dent, *n.* [Fr. *dent*; L. *dens* (*dentis*), a tooth.] A tooth of a comb, metallic brush, or card; also, a cane or wire of the reed frame of a weaver's loom.

dent, *a.* Marked by an impression; dented; as, *dent* corn. [Colloq.]

den-tag′rȧ, *n.* [L. *dens* (*dentis*), a tooth, and Gr. *agra*, a catching, hunting.]

1. The toothache.

2. A forceps used in drawing teeth.

den′tăl, *a.* 1. Pertaining to the teeth; as *dental* surgery; a *dental* cavity.

2. Relating to dentistry; as, a *dental* saw.

3. In grammar, formed or pronounced by the teeth, with the aid of the tongue; as, *d* and *t* are *dental* letters.

Dental formula; an arrangement of symbols and numbers used to signify the number and kinds of teeth of a mammiferous animal. The *dental formula* of man is: I. $\frac{2-2}{2-2}$, C. $\frac{1-1}{1-1}$, P. M. $\frac{2-2}{2-2}$, M. $\frac{3-3}{3-3}$ = 32. The numerators designate the upper, and the denominators the lower incisors, canines, premolars and molars, respectively.

den′tăl, *n.* 1. An articulation or letter formed by placing the end of the tongue against or close to the upper teeth; as, *t*, *d*, or *th* (as in *th*ose or *th*ink).

2. In zoölogy, a shell of the genus *Dentalium*, resembling a tooth; a tooth-shell.

den′tăl-ite, *n.* A fossil shell of the genus *Dentalium*.

den-tal′i-ty, *n.* The state or quality of being dental.

Den-tā′li-um, *n.* [L., from *dens* (*dentis*), a tooth.] A genus of gasteropodous mollusks, the shell of which consists of a tubular arcuate cone, open at both ends. There are many species known by the common name of tooth-shells.

den″tăl-i-zā′tion, *n.* Change to a dental letter, as the change of *f* in the German *f*ein to *th* in the English *th*in.

Den-tā′ri-ȧ, *n.* [From LL. *dentarius*, pertaining to the teeth, from L. *dens* (*dentis*), tooth.] A genus of cruciferous, ornamental herbs, with creeping scaly rootstocks from which they receive the names of coralroot and *Dentaria* or toothwort. The stem-leaves are opposite or in whorls of three, and the flowers are large and purple. There are about twenty species, natives of temperate countries.

den′tȧ-ry, *n.* The bone in the lower jaw of fishes and reptiles that supports the teeth. It is analogous to the lower jaw of man.

den′tȧ-ry, *a.* Relating to the teeth; bearing teeth; as, the *dentary* bone in fishes.

den-tā′tȧ, *n.* In anatomy, the axis of the vertebral column.

den′tāte, *a.* 1. In botany, toothed; having sharp teeth which project outward; as, a *dentate* leaf.

Dentate Leaf.

2. In zoölogy, having tooth-like processes or points; denticulate.

den′tāte-cil′i-āte, *a.* [L. *dentatus*, toothed, from *dens*, a tooth, and *cilium*, an eyelid.] In botany, having the margin dentate, and fringed or tipped with cilia or hairs.

den′tā-ted, *a.* Dentate.

den′tāte-ly, *adv.* In a dentate manner.

den′tāte-ser′rāte, *a.* In entomology, serrated, and having each denticulation toothed.

den′tāte-sin′ū-āte, *a.* In entomology, having angular teeth separated from each other by incurved spaces.

Part of Dentate-ciliate Leaf.

den-tā′tion, *n.* A dentate state or formation. [Rare.]

dent′ed, *a.* Indented; impressed with little hollows.

dent′ed, *a.* Having teeth; serrated.

den′tel, *n.* See *Dentil*.

den′te-lā-ted, *a.* See *Dentilated*.

den-telle′, *n.* [Fr., lace, edging, from L. *dens*, a tooth.]

1. Lace.

2. In bookbinding, a decoration toothed or lace-like.

den-tel′li, *n.pl.* [It.] Modillions.

den′tex, *n.* [L. *dentix*, a seafish, from *dens* (*dentis*), tooth.] A sparoid marine food-fish of the genus *Dentex*.

den-ti-. A combining form from L. *dens*, genit. *dentis*, a tooth.

Den-ti-cē′tē, *n.pl.* [*Denti-*, and L. *cetus*, any large sea-animal, a whale.] A suborder of *Cetacea* including the dolphins, in which the teeth are more or less permanent.

den′ti-cle, *n.* A small tooth or projecting point.

den-tic′ū-lāte, *a.* 1. Having small teeth; finely dentate; as, a *denticulate* leaf, calyx, or seed.

2. In architecture, formed into dentils.

den-tic′ū-lā-ted, *a.* Denticulate.

den-tic′ū-lāte-ly, *adv.* In a denticulate manner.

den-tic-ū-lā′tion, *n.* 1. The state of being set with small teeth.

2. A denticle; a set of small teeth or notches.

den′ti-cūle, *n.* 1. A dentil.

2. In heraldry, one of an aggregation of dentil-like figures generally arranged as a border.

den′ti-fac-tŏr, *n.* [*Denti-*, and L. *factus*, pp. of *facere*, to make.] A machine for the manufacture of the artificial teeth, gums, and palate used in dental surgery.

den′ti-fọrm, *a.* Having the form of a tooth; of the shape of a tooth or teeth.

den′ti-frice, *n.* [L. *dentifricium*, a tooth-powder, from *dens*, a tooth, and *fricare*, to rub.] A powder or other substance used in cleaning the teeth.

den-tig′ēr-ous, *a.* [*Denti-*, and L. *gerere*, to carry.] Bearing or supporting teeth; supplied with teeth.

den′til, den′tel, *n.* [LL. *dentillus*; L. *denticulus*, dim. of *dens*, a tooth.]

1. In architecture, one of the little cubes into which the square member in the bed-molding of an Ionic, Corinthian, Composite, and occasionally Doric cornice is divided.

Dentils.

2. In heraldry, a tooth or notch.

den-ti-lā′bi-ăl, *a.* and *n.* [*Denti-*, and L. *labium*, lip.]

I. *a.* Articulated by conjunction of the lips and teeth; applied to sounds.

II. *n.* A sound so made.

den′ti-lā-ted, den′te-lā-ted, *a.* Toothed or notched.

den-ti-lā′tion, *n.* Dentition.

den′tile, *n.* [LL. *dentillus*; L. *denticulus*, dim. of *dens* (*dentis*), a tooth.] A small tooth; a denticle.

den-ti-lin′guăl (-gwăl), *a.* and *n.* [*Denti-*, and L. *lingua*, the tongue.]

I. *a.* Formed by inserting the tongue between the teeth, as *th* in *th*ose and *th*ick.

II. *n.* A consonant so formed.

den-ti-lin′guăl-ly, *adv.* In a dentilingual manner.

den-til′ō-quist (-kwist), *n.* One who practises dentiloquy; one who speaks with the teeth closed.

den-til′ō-quy, *n.* [*Denti-*, and L. *loqui*, to speak.] The act or habit of speaking with the teeth closed.

den′tin, den′tine, *n.* [L. *dens* (*dentis*), tooth.] The ivory tissue lying below the enamel and constituting the body of the tooth.

den′ti-năl, *a.* Of or pertaining to dentin.

Dentinal tubes; the minute tubes of the dentin or ivory tissue of the tooth.

den′tine, *n.* See *Dentin*.

den′ti-phōne, *n.* [*Denti-*, and Gr. *phōnē*, voice, sound.] An appliance by which sound waves are collected and conveyed to the auditory nerve through the teeth; an audiphone.

den-ti-ros′tēr, *n.* A bird of the family *Dentirostres*.

den-ti-ros′trăl, *a.* [L. *dens* (*dentis*), a tooth, and *rostrum*, a beak.] Pertaining to or characteristic of the *Dentirostres*.

den-ti-ros′trāte, *a.* Dentirostral.

Den-ti-ros′trēṣ, *n.pl.* A suborder (or tribe) of insessorial birds, characterized by having a notch and tooth-like process on each side of the margin of the upper mandible. The butcher-birds, shrikes, etc., belong to this tribe.

den′ti-scalp, *n.* [*Denti-*, and L. *scalpere*, to scrape.] An instrument for scraping or cleaning the teeth.

den′tist, *n.* [From L. *dens* (*dentis*), a tooth.] One who practises dental surgery and mechanical dentistry.

den-tis′tic, den-tis′ti-căl, *a.* Dental. [Rare.]

den′tist-ry, *n.* The art or profession of a dentist.

den-ti′tion (-tish′un), *n.* [L. *dentitio*, teething, from *dentire*, to cut teeth.]

1. The cutting or protrusion of the teeth; teething.

2. The period of development and cutting of the teeth.

3. In zoölogy, the nature, number, and system of teeth peculiar to an animal.

4. The state of being provided with teeth; denticulation.

den′tīze, *v.i.* [From L. *dentire*, to cut teeth.] To grow or renew the teeth. [Rare.]

den′toid, *a.* Resembling a tooth; shaped like a tooth.

den-tō-lin′guăl (-gwăl), *a.* and *n.* Dentilingual.

den′tūre, *n.* [L. *dens* (*dentis*), a tooth.] In dentistry, a term applied to one or several artificial teeth, or a whole set (a full *denture*).

dē-nū′clē-ā-ted, *a.* Divested of a nucleus.

dē-nū′dāte, *v.t.*; denudated, *pt.*, *pp.*; denudating, *ppr.* [L. *denudatus*, pp. of *denudare*, to strip off; *de*, off, from, and *nudare*, to strip.] To strip; to denude. [Obs.]

dē-nū′dāte, dē-nū′dā-ted (*or* den′ū-), *a.* Nude; naked; denuded.

den-ū-dā′tion, *n.* 1. The act of stripping off covering; a making bare.

2. In geology, the laying bare of rocks by the action of water, frost, weathering, etc.

dē-nūde′, *v.t.*; denuded, *pt.*, *pp.*; denuding, *ppr.* [L. *denudare*, to make bare, strip off.]

1. To strip; to divest of all covering; to make bare or naked.

2. In geology, to subject to denudation.

dē-nū′mēr-ănt, *n.* [L. *denumerans*, ppr. of *denumerare*, to number; *de*, down, from, and *numerare*, to count.] In mathematics, the number denoting how many solutions a given system of equations admits of.

dē-nū-mēr-ā′tion, *n.* In law, payment down; present payment.

dē-nūn′ci-ȧ (-thi-ä), *n.* [Sp., from *denunciar*, to denounce.] In Mexico and Spanish America, (a) the judicial proceedings necessary to denounce a mine; (b) a similar method essential to land-preëmption.

dē-nun′ci-ȧ-ble (-shi-), *a.* Fit or liable to be denounced.

dē-nun′ci-ănt (-shi-), *a.* Denunciative.

dē-nun′ci-āte (-shi-āt), *v.t.* To denounce. [Rare.]

dē-nun-ci-ā′tion, *n.* [L. *denuntiatio*, an announcement, forewarning, from *denuntiatus*, pp. of *denuntiare*, to announce, to denounce; *de*, and *nuntiare*, to announce.]

1. Announcement; proclamation. [Obs.]

2. Solemn or formal declaration accompanied with a menace; or the declaration of intended evil; proclamation of a threat; a public menace; as, a *denunciation* of war or of wrath.

3. In Scots law, the act by which a person who has disobeyed the charge given on letters of horning is proclaimed outlawed or a rebel.

4. In civil law, the filing of information of the commission of a crime, as before a prosecuting attorney.

dē-nun′ci-ā-tive (-shi-), *a.* Denunciatory.

dē-nun′ci-ā-tŏr, *n.* [LL. *denuntiator*, a police office, from L. *denuntiare*, to announce.]

1. One who denounces or threatens.

2. In civil law, one who lays an information against another.

The *denunciator* does not make himself a party in judgment. —Ayliffe.

dē-nun′ci-ȧ-tō-ry, *a.* Relating to or implying denunciation; containing a public threat; comminatory.

dē-nū-tri′tion (-trish′un), *n.* Lack of nutrition.

dē-nȳ′, *v.t.*; denied, *pt.*, *pp.*; denying, *ppr.* [ME. *denyen*; L. *denegare*, to deny, from *de*, and *negare*, to deny.]

1. To contradict; to gainsay; to declare (a statement or position) not to be true; as, to *deny* a proposition.

2. To refuse to grant; to withhold; as, to *deny* aid.

3. To reject; to disown; not to receive or embrace; as, to *deny* revelation.

4. To keep (oneself) alone or secluded; as, he preferred quiet and so *denied* himself all callers.

5. To disprove.

To deny oneself; to decline the gratification of appetites or desires; to refrain from; to abstain.

Syn.—Contradict, disavow, disclaim, disown, oppose, refuse.

dē-nȳ′, *v.i.* To give a negative answer.

dē-nȳ′ing-ly, *adv.* In a manner indicating denial.

dē-ob-struct′, *v.t.*; deobstructed, *pt.*, *pp.*; deobstructing, *ppr.* To remove obstructions or impediments from; as, to *deobstruct* the pores or lacteals.

dē-ob′strụ̈-ent, *a.* and *n.* I. *a.* Removing obstructions; having power to clear or open the natural ducts of the fluids and secretions of the body, resolving viscidities; aperient.

II. *n.* A medicine having the power of removing obstructions.

dē′ō-dand, *n.* [From L. *deodandum*, a thing to be given to God; *Deo*, dat. of *Deus*, God, and *dandum*, neut. of *dandus*, gerundive of *dare*, to give.] Prior to 1846, in old English law, a personal chattel which was the immediate occasion of the death of a rational creature, and for that reason, given to God; that is, forfeited to the king, to be applied to pious uses, and distributed in alms by his high almoner. —Blackstone.

dē-ō-där′, *n.* [L. *deodara*, from Sans. *devadaru*, divine tree; *deva*, divine, and *daru*, wood.] The Indian cedar, *Cedrus Deodara*; also, other trees of the pine family regarded as sacred by the Hindus.

dē′ō-dāte, *n.* An offering to or gift from God. [Obs.]

dē-ō′dŏr-ănt, *n.* [*De-* priv., and *odorans*, ppr. of *odorare*, to smell, from *odor*, a smell.] A deodorizer.

dē-ō″dŏr-i-zā′tion, *n.* The act of removing odor; the condition of being deodorized.

dē-ō′dŏr-īze, *v.t.*; deodorized, *pt.*, *pp.*; deodorizing, *ppr.* To rid or deprive of odor, particularly noxious exhalations.

dē-ō′dŏr-ī-zẽr, *n.* A deodorizing agent, as charcoal or chlorin.

dē-on′ẽr-āte, *v.t.* To unload. [Obs.]

dē-on-tō-lŏg′iç-ăl, *a.* Relating to deontology.

dē-on-tol′ō-ġist, *n.* One versed in deontology.

dē-on-tol′ō-ġy, *n.* [Gr. *deon*, that which is binding, proper, from *dein*, to bind, and *logos*, description.] The science of duty; a term assigned by the followers of Jeremy Bentham to their own doctrine of ethics; by extension, ethics.

dē-ō-pẽr′çū-lāte, *a.* [*De-* priv., and L. *operculum*, a lid, covering.] In botany, a term applied to mosses when the operculum does not separate spontaneously from the spore-cases.

dē-op′pi-lāte, *v.t.* To free from obstructions; to clear a passage in. [Obs.]

dē-op-pi-lā′tion, *n.* The removal of obstructions. [Obs.]

dē-op′pi-lā-tive, *a.* Deobstruent; aperient. [Obs.]

dē-ọr-di-nā′tion, *n.* Disorder. [Obs.]

dē-ọr′găn-īze, *v.t.*; deorganized, *pt.*, *pp.*; deorganizing, *ppr.* To divest of organic character.

dē-os′çū-lāte, *v.t.* To kiss. [Obs.]

dē-os-çū-lā′tion, *n.* A kissing. [Obs.]

dē-os′si-fȳ, *v.t.*; deossified, *pt.*, *pp.*; deossifying, *ppr.* To deprive of bones or bony structure; to make weak.

dē-ox′i-dāte, *v.t.*; deoxidated, *pt.*, *pp.*; deoxidating, *ppr.* To deoxidize.

dē-ox-i-dā′tion, dē-ox-y-dā′tion, *n.* The act or process of reducing from the state of an oxid.

dē-ox″i-di-zā′tion, dē-ox″y-di-zā′tion, *n.* Deoxidation.

dē-ox′i-dīze, *v.t.*; deoxidized, *pt.*, *pp.*; deoxidizing, *ppr.* To deprive of oxygen, or reduce from the state of an oxid; to deoxidate; also spelled *deoxydize*, *deoxidise*.

dē-ox′i-dī-zẽr, *n.* Any agent that removes oxygen.

dē-ox′y-ġen-āte, *v.t.* To deprive of oxygen.

dē-ox″y-ġen-ā′tion, *n.* The act or operation of depriving of oxygen.

dē-ox′y-ġen-īze, *v.t.* To deoxidize.

dē-pāint′, *v.t.* [ME. *depeynten*; OFr. *depeint*, from L. *depingere*, to paint; *de*, and *pingere*, to paint.] To depict or portray, either by painting or by words. [Rare or Obs.]

dē-pāint′ẽr, *n.* A painter. [Obs.]

de-pär′dieux″ (-dyē″), *interj.* [OFr.] In God's name; verily.

dē-pärt′, *v.i.*; departed, *pt.*, *pp.*; departing, *ppr.* [ME. *departen*; L. *dispertire* or *dispartire*, to divide, separate; *dis-*, apart, and *partire*, to divide, from *pars* (*partis*), a part, share.]

1. To share. [Obs.]

2. To separate; to part. [Obs.]

3. To go or withdraw; used absolutely or with *from* before the place or object left.

> He which hath no stomach to this fight
> Let him *depart*. —Shak.

> *Depart from* me, ye cursed, into everlasting fire. —Matt. xxv. 41.

4. To desist; to deviate; as, we cannot *depart* from our rules.

> I have not *departed* from thy judgments. —Ps. cxix. 102.

5. In law, to forsake or abandon the ground assumed in a former pleading and assume a new one.

6. To die; to decease; to leave this world.

> Lord, now lettest thou thy servant *depart* in peace, according to thy word.—Luke ii. 29.

To depart with; to yield. [Obs.]

Syn.—Leave, retire, go, desert, apostatize, deviate, vary, decease, die.

dē-pärt′, *v.t.* 1. To divide. [Obs.]

2. To separate; as, till death us *depart*. [Obs.]

3. To retire from; to leave; to quit.

> Shall I *depart* a spot
> I thus detest? —Crabbe.

dē-pärt′, *n.* 1. Division, as of a compound into its elements. [Obs.]

2. The act of going away; death. [Obs.]

dē-pärt′ȧ-ble, *a.* Divisible; separable. [Obs.]

dē-pärt′ẽr, *n.* 1. One who refines metals by separation.

2. One who departs.

dē-pärt′ment, *n.* [OFr. *departement*, a division, department, from L. *dispartire*, *dispertire*, to divide, depart.]

1. The act of departing; departure. [Obs.]

2. A subordinate division of something having a considerable extent; a distinct branch; a section; a subdivision; as, the *departments* of a college; *departments* of a business.

3. A division of territory; one of the provinces or districts into which a country is divided for governmental or other purposes; as, the military *departments* of the United States; the provincial *departments* of France.

4. A branch of the government or of governmental organization; as, the legislative *department*; the executive *department*; the judicial *department*.

There are nine departments, divisions of and subordinates to the Executive department of the United States, as follows, (1) *Agriculture*; securing, principally by investigation, agricultural knowledge for general dissemination; (2) *Commerce and Labor*; devoted to the promotion of commercial and laboring interests; (3) *Interior*; supervising the Land, Patent, and Pension offices, Bureaus of Indian Affairs and of Education, the census each ten years, and other home affairs; (4) *Justice*; the advisory counsel of the government on law matters; (5) *Navy*; in charge of matters concerning the navy; (6) *Post-office*; in charge of the mails and mail-service; (7) *State*; conducting all foreign negotiations; (8) *Treasury*; in charge of the finances; (9) *War*; in charge of military affairs.

Department store; a large retail store not confined to one line of goods but handling various lines.

dē-pärt-men′tăl, *a.* Pertaining to a department or division.

dē-pär′tūre, *n.* [OFr. *departeure*, from *departer*, to depart.]

1. A separating or parting. [Obs.]

2. The act of going away; a moving from or leaving a place; as, a *departure* from San Francisco.

3. Death; decease; removal from the present life.

> The time of my *departure* is at hand. —2. Tim. iv. 6.

4. A forsaking; abandonment; divergence; as, a *departure* from right.

5. In navigation, (a) change of longitude; (b) the bearing of an object on the coast, taken on starting on a voyage as the point from which dead reckoning begins.

6. In law, the abandonment of the ground taken in a former pleading, and the adoption of another.

To take a departure; to learn the location of a vessel on the beginning of a voyage.

dē-pas′cent, *a.* [L. *depascens*, ppr. of *depascere*, to feed upon; *de*, and *pasci*, to feed.] Feeding. [Rare.]

dē-pȧs′tūre, *v.t.* 1. To eat up; to consume. [Obs.]

2. To pasture; to graze.

dē-pȧs′tūre, *v.i.* To feed; to graze.

dē-pā′tri-āte, *v.t.* To banish. [Obs.]

dē-pā′tri-āte, *v.i.* To leave one's country. [Obs.]

dē-pạu′pẽr-āte, *v.t.* [*De-*, and L. *pauperare*, to make poor, from *pauper*, poor.] To make poor; to impoverish; to deprive of fertility or richness; as, to *depauperate* the soil or the blood.

dē-pạu′pẽr-āte, *a.* Impoverished; made poor; specifically, in botany, imperfectly developed.

dē-pạu′pẽr-īze, *v.t.* To raise from a condition of poverty or pauperism; to free from paupers or pauperism.

dē-pēach′, *v.t.* To acquit; to discharge. [Obs.]

dē-peç′ti-ble, *a.* Tough; thick; pliant. [Obs.]

dē-peç-ū-lā′tion, *n.* A robbing or embezzlement. [Obs.]

dē-peinct′ (-pānt′), *v.t.* To paint. [Obs.]

dē-pend′, *v.i.*; depended, *pt.*, *pp.*; depending, *ppr.* [ME. *dependen*; OFr. *dependre*; L. *dependere*, to hang down from, to depend; *de*, down, and *pendere*, to hang.]

1. To hang; to be sustained by being fastened or attached to something above.

2. To be related to anything, as the cause of its existence or of its operation and effects; to have such connection with anything as a cause, that without it the effect would not be produced; to be contingent or conditioned; followed by *on* or *upon*; as, we *depend on* air for respiration.

3. To serve; to attend. [Obs.]

4. To be in suspense; to be undetermined; as, the suit is still *depending* in court. [See *Pending*.]

5. To rely; to rest with confidence; to trust; to confide; to have full confidence or belief; with *on* or *upon*; as, we *depend on* the word or assurance of our friends; we *depend on* the arrival of the mail.

> A woman will or won't—*depend on*'t.—Hill.

6. To hang over; to impend. [Obs.]

dē-pend′ȧ-ble, *a.* Faithful; reliable; trustworthy.

dē-pend′ȧ-ble-ness, *n.* The state or quality of being dependable.

dē-pend′ănce, *n.* See *Dependence*.

dē-pend′ăn-cy, *n.* See *Dependency*.

dē-pend′ănt, *a.* and *n.* See *Dependent*.

dē-pend′ence, *n.* [L. *dependens*, ppr. of *dependere*, to hang from.]

1. The act of depending; the state of being dependent; the state of hanging from a support.

2. The state of being dependent on, or of being influenced by, something, as a conclusion on a premise; the relation of effect to cause.

3. Connection and support; mutual connection; inter-relation; concatenation.

4. A state of being at the disposal of another; a state of being subject to the power and operation of something external; inability to sustain oneself without the aid of some one else; as, the *dependence* of a child on its parents.

5. Reliance; confidence; trust; as, to place great *dependence* on a person.

6. That on which one depends or relies; as, the son was his mother's chief *dependence*.

7. That which hangs or depends; that which is attached to but subordinate to something else.

> And make a large *dependence* from the bough. —Dryden.

8. A subject of quarrel or controversy. [Obs.]

9. In law, the quality of depending on something else; pendency.

Syn.—Reliance.—*Dependence* is the general term; *reliance* is a species of *dependence*; we *depend* either on persons or things; we *rely* on persons only; *dependence* serves for that which is immediate or remote; *reliance* serves for the future only; we *depend* upon a person for that which we are obliged to receive or led to expect from him; we *rely* upon a person for that which he has given us reason to expect from him.

dē-pend′en-cy, *n.*; *pl.* **dē-pend′en-cieș**. 1. Dependence; the state of being dependent; subjection; reliance; confidence; concatenation; a thing depending.

> Their *dependency* upon the crown of England. —Bacon.

2. That which is connected with and subordinate to something else; particularly, a territory, colony, or state under the control of a power; as, the Philippine islands are *dependencies* of the United States.

3. Something that is not essential; an accident or quality.

> Modes I call such complex ideas . . . which are considered as *dependencies*, or affections of substances. —Locke.

4. An outlying building adjacent to the main building; as, the *dependencies* of a hotel.

Dependence has reference more particularly to the abstract, *dependency*, to the concrete.

dē-pend′ent, *a.* 1. Hanging down; as, a *dependent* leaf.

2. Subject to the power of, or at the disposal of, another; not able to exist or sustain itself without extraneous assistance subordinate; as, the child is *dependent* upon its parent.

3. Contingent upon something external; conditioned, as an effect upon an unknown cause.

4. Requiring assistance from some outside source; poor; as, blind persons are *dependent.*

Dependent clause; in grammar, a clause having no meaning when standing alone; a subordinate clause.

Dependent contract; in law, a contract, invalid until some stipulation has been performed.

Dependent variable; in mathematics, a variable depending for its value on another variable, which is called the *independent variable.*

dē-pend′ent, *n.* 1. One who is at the disposal of another; one who is sustained by another or who relies on another for support or favor; a retainer.

2. That which depends on something else; a consequence; a corollary.

> With all its circumstances and *dependents.*
> —Prynne.

dē-pend′ent-ly, *adv.* In a dependent manner.

dē-pend′ēr, *n.* One who depends; a dependent.

dē-pend′ing-ly, *adv.* In a dependent or subordinate manner.

dē-pēo′ple (-pē′pl), *v.t.* To depopulate. [Rare.]

dē-pēr′dit, *n.* That which is lost or destroyed. [Obs.]

dē-pēr′dite-ly, *adv.* In the manner of one ruined; desperately. [Obs.]

dep-ēr-di′tion (-dish′un), *n.* Loss; destruction. [Obs.]

dē-pēr′sōn-ăl-īze, *v.t.*; depersonalized, *pt., pp.*; depersonalizing, *ppr.* To remove or deny (those characteristics that make up the personality of an individual); to disregard the personality of.

dē-pēr′ti-ble, *a.* Divisible. [Obs.]

dep′hal, *n.* [Bengalese.] *Artocarpus Lakoocha*, an Indian tree of the same genus as the breadfruit and jack, and cultivated for its fruit. The juice is used for birdlime.

dē-phlegm′ (-flem′), *v.t.* To dephlegmate. [Obs.]

dē-phleg′māte, *v.t.*; dephlegmated, *pt., pp.*; dephlegmating, *ppr.* [*De-* priv., and L. *phlegma*, phlegm.] To deprive of superabundant water, as by evaporation or distillation; to rectify; said of spirits or acids.

dē-phleg-mā′tion, *n.* The operation of separating water from spirits and acids, by evaporation or repeated distillation; concentration.

dē-phleg′mā-tōr, *n.* A condensing apparatus for stills, consisting of broad sheets of tinned copper soldered together so as to leave narrow spaces between them.

dē-phleg′mȧ-tō-ry, *a.* Pertaining to or producing dephlegmation.

dē-phlegm′ed-ness (-flem′), *n.* A state of being freed from water. [Obs.]

dē-phlō-gis′ti-cāte, *v.t.*; dephlogisticated, *pt., pp.*; dephlogisticating, *ppr.* [*De-*, and Gr. *phlogistos*, burnt, from *phlogizein*, to burn.] To deprive of phlogiston, formerly the supposed principle of inflammability; as, *dephlogisticated* air was the former term for oxygen.

dē-phlō-gis-ti-cā′tion, *n.* A term applied by the older chemists to certain processes by which they imagined that phlogiston was separated from bodies.

dē-phos″phōr-i-zā′tion, *n.* The act or process of depriving of phosphorus.

dē-phos′phōr-īze, *v.t.*; dephosphorized, *pt., pp.*; dephosphorizing, *ppr.* To deprive of or free from phosphorus.

dē-pict′, *v.t.*; depicted, *pt., pp.*; depicting, *ppr.* [OFr. *depicter*, to depict, from L. *depictus*, pp. of *depingere*, to paint, depict.]

1. To paint; to portray; to form a likeness of in colors; as, to *depict* a lion on a shield.

2. To describe; to represent in words; as, the poet *depicts* the virtues of his hero.

Syn.—Delineate, portray, describe, picture, represent, sketch.

dē-pict′, *a.* Depicted; portrayed.

dē-pict′ēr, *n.* One who depicts.

dē-pic′tion, *n.* A painting or depicting.

dē-pic′tūre, *v.t.*; depictured, *pt., pp.*; depicturing, *ppr.* To paint; to picture; to represent in colors.

dē-pig-men-tā′tion, *n.* The act or process of depigmentizing, or the state of being depigmentized.

dē-pig′ment-īze, *v.t.*; depigmentized, *pt., pp.*; depigmentizing, *ppr.* To take away the pigment from; to make white; to bleach.

dep′i-lāte, *v.t.*; depilated, *pt., pp.*; depilating, *ppr.* [L. *depilatus*, pp. of *depilare*, to deprive of hair.] To strip of hair.

dep-i-lā′tion, *n.* The act or process of removing hair, as from the body or a hide; unhairing.

dep′i-lā-tōr, *n.* An instrument for taking out hairs.

dē-pil′ȧ-tō-ry, *a.* Having the quality or power to remove hair from the skin.

dē-pil′ȧ-tō-ry, *n.*; *pl.* **dē-pil′ȧ-tō-ries.** Any application which is used to remove hair.

dep′i-lous, *a.* Without hair. [Rare.]

dē-plā′nate (*or* dep′lā-nāt), *a.* [LL. *deplanatus*, pp. of *deplanare*, to make level; L. *de*, down, from, and *planus*, flat, level.] In botany, flattened; made level; explanate.

dē-plant′, *v.t.* To remove (plants) from beds; to transplant. [Rare.]

dē-plen′ish, *v.t.* To reduce, exhaust, or deplete.

dē-plēte′, *v.t.*; depleted, *pt., pp.*; depleting, *ppr.* [L. *depletus*, pp. of *deplere*, to empty, from *de-* priv., and *plere*, to fill.]

1. To empty, reduce, or exhaust by draining away, as the strength, vital powers, resources, etc.; as, to *deplete* a country of inhabitants; to *deplete* the treasury.

2. In medicine, to empty or unload (the vessels of the human system), as by bloodletting or saline purgatives.

dē-pleth′ō-ric, *a.* Lacking plethora; anemic.

dē-plē′tion, *n.* 1. The act of emptying or depleting; the state of being depleted.

2. In medicine, the act of depleting the vessels of the body.

dē-plē′tive, *a.* Capable of depleting; causing depletion.

dē-plē′tive, *n.* That which depletes; specifically, any medical agent of depletion.

dē-plē′tō-ry, *a.* Calculated to deplete; depletive.

dep-li-cā′tion, *n.* [*De-* priv., and L. *plicare*, to fold.] An unfolding, untwisting, or unplaiting. [Rare.]

dep-loi-tā′tion, *n.* See *Exploitation.*

dē-plōr-ȧ-bil′i-ty, *n.* Deplorableness. [Rare.]

dē-plōr′ȧ-ble, *a.* [From L. *deplorare*, to deplore, to weep bitterly.] That may be deplored or lamented; lamentable; that demands or causes lamentation; hence, sad; calamitous; grievous; miserable; wretched; pitiable; contemptible; as, the evils of life are *deplorable*; *deplorable* stupidity.

Syn.—Lamentable, sad, dismal, wretched, pitiable, calamitous, grievous, miserable.

dē-plōr′ȧ-ble-ness, *n.* The state of being deplorable; misery; wretchedness; a miserable state.

dē-plōr′ȧ-bly, *adv.* In a manner to be deplored; lamentably; miserably; as, manners are *deplorably* corrupt.

dē-plō′rāte, *a.* Deplorable. [Obs.]

dep-lō-rā′tion (*or* dē-plō-), *n.* The act of lamenting. [Obs.]

dē-plōre′, *v.t.*; deplored, *pt., pp.*; deploring, *ppr.* [L. *deplorare*, to weep bitterly, lament; *de-*, intens., and *plorare*, to weep.]

1. To lament; to bewail; to mourn; to feel or express deep and poignant grief for.

> Thou art gone to the grave! but we will not *deplore* thee. —Heber.

2. To despair of. [Obs.]

3. To complain of. [Obs.]

Syn.—Mourn, lament, bewail, bemoan.—*Mourn* is generic; *lament* denotes an earnest and strong expression of grief; *deplore* marks a deeper and more prolonged emotion; *bewail* and *bemoan* are appropriate only to cases of poignant distress.

dē-plōre′, *v.i.* To lament; to moan. [Rare.]

dē-plōr′ed-ly, *adv.* Lamentably. [Rare.]

dē-plōr′ed-ness, *n.* The state of being deplored. [Rare.]

dē-plōre′ment, *n.* The act of deploring. [Obs.]

dē-plōr′ēr, *n.* One who deplores.

dē-plōr′ing-ly, *adv.* In a deploring manner.

dē-ploy′, *v.t.*; deployed, *pt., pp.*; deploying, *ppr.* [Fr. *déployer*, to unfold, to display; OFr. *desployer*, to unfold, unroll, from L. *de*, from, and *plicare*, to fold.] In military language, to display; to open; to extend in a line of small depth, as an army, a division, or a battalion which has been previously formed in one or more columns.

dē-ploy′, *v.i.* To open; to extend; to form a more extended front or line.

dē-ploy′, *n.* The expansion of a body of troops, previously compacted into a column, so as to present a more extended front.

dē-ploy′ment, *n.* The act of deploying.

dē-plū′māte, *a.* In ornithology, denuded of feathers; deplumed.

dep-lū-mā′tion, *n.* 1. The stripping or falling off of plumes or feathers.

2. In pathology, a disease or swelling of the eyelids in which the eyelashes fall off.

dē-plūme′, *v.t.*; deplumed, *pt., pp.*; depluming, *ppr.* [ME. *deplumen*, from L. *de*, off, from, and *plumare*, to cover with feathers, from *pluma*, a feather.] To strip or pluck feathers from; to deprive of plumage; to pluck; to expose.

dē-pō′lăr-īze, *v.t.* See *Depolarize.*

dē-pō″lăr-i-zā′tion, *n.* The act of depriving of polarity; the removal of the effects of polarity; the result of depolarizing.

dē-pō′lăr-īze, *v.t.*; depolarized, *pt., pp.*; depolarizing, *ppr.* To deprive of polarity; specifically, (a) in optics, to cause (a polarized ray) to reappear before being intercepted by the analyzer; (b) in electricity and magnetism, to rid of polarity.

dē-pō′lăr-ī-zēr, *n.* One who or that which depolarizes; specifically, in electricity, any substance or device used to prevent polarization in a voltaic cell.

dē-pol′ish, *v.t.* To destroy the polish or glaze of by any means.

dē-pol′ish-ing, *n.* The act or process of removing polish or glaze; specifically, in ceramics, the process of removing the glaze from porcelain, which in its deglazed state is called *ivory porcelain.*

dē-pōne′, *v.t.*; deponed, *pt., pp.*; deponing, *ppr.* [L. *deponere*, to lay aside, put down; *de*, from, and *ponere*, to put.]

1. To lay down; to deposit. [Obs.]

2. To lay down as a pledge; to wager. [Obs.]

3. In law, to depose; to testify.

dē-pōne′, *v.i.* In old English and Scots law, to give testimony; to bear witness; to depose.

dē-pō′nent, *a.* [From L. *deponens*, ppr. of *deponere*, to lay aside; *de*, from, and *ponere*, to place, to put.] Laying down.

Deponent verb; in Latin grammar, any one of certain verbs having a passive form with an active signification.

dē-pō′nent, *n.* 1. One who deposes or makes a deposition, especially under oath; one who gives written testimony to be used as evidence in a court of justice, or for any other purpose.

2. In Latin grammar, a deponent verb.

dē-pop′ū-lȧ-cy, *n.* Depopulation. [Obs.]

dē-pop′ū-lăr-īze, *v.t.* To render unpopular. [Rare.]

dē-pop′ū-lāte, *v.t.*; depopulated, *pt., pp.*; depopulating, *ppr.* [L. *depopulatus*, pp. of *depopulari*, to lay waste, devastate; *de*, and *populari*, to lay waste, ravage, ruin, from *populus*, people.] To dispeople; to unpeople; to deprive of inhabitants, whether by death or by expulsion. It is not synonymous with *laying waste* or *destroying*, being limited to the loss of inhabitants; as an army or a famine may *depopulate* a country. It rarely expresses an entire loss of inhabitants, but often a great diminution of their numbers.

dē-pop′ū-lāte, *v.i.* To become dispeopled. [Rare.]

dē-pop-ū-lā′tion, *n.* The act of depopulating or the state of being depopulated.

dē-pop′ū-lā-tōr, *n.* One who depopulates; that which depopulates.

dē-pōrt′, *v.t.*; deported, *pt., pp.*; deporting, *ppr* [OFr. *deporter*, to bear, to suffer, to desist from; L. *deportare*, to carry or bring away; *de*, from, and *portare*, to bring.]

1. To carry; to demean; to behave; with the reflexive pronoun.

> Let an ambassador *deport himself* in the most graceful manner before a prince. —Pope.

2. To transport; to carry away, or from one country to another.

> He told us, he had been *deported* to Spain, with a hundred others like himself.—Walsh.

Syn.—Carry, behave, conduct, demean.

dē-pōrt′, *n.* Behavior; carriage; demeanor; deportment. [Obs.]

dē-pōr-tā′tion, *n.* [Fr. *déportation*; L. *deportatio*, a carrying away, a removal, from *deportare*, to carry or bring away.] A carrying away; a removal from one country to another, or to a distant place; exile; banishment; transportation.

> That sudden transmigration and *deportation.*
> —Stokes.

dē-pōrt′ment, *n.* [OFr. *deportement*, from L. *deportare*, to carry away, to deport; *de*, from, and *portare*, to bring.] Carriage; manner of acting in relation to the duties of life; behavior; demeanor; conduct; management.

> The utmost propriety and dignity of *deportment* prevailed. —Irving.

dē-pōr′tūre, *n.* Deportment. [Obs.]

dē-pōṣ′ȧ-ble, *a.* Capable of being deposed or deprived of office.

dē-pōṣ′ăl, *n.* The act of deposing, or divesting of office.

dē-pōṣe′, *v.t.*; deposed, *pt., pp.*; deposing, *ppr.* [ME. *deposen*, to lay aside, deprive of office, degrade, from OFr. *deposer*, to lay down, deposit; L. *deponere*, to lay down, to lay aside; *de*, down, away, and *ponere*, to place.]

1. To reduce from a throne or other high station; to dethrone; to degrade; to divest of office; as, to *depose* a king or a pope.

2. To state on oath; to bear witness to; to attest; to give (testimony which is committed to writing).

3. To lay down; to let fall; to deposit. [Obs.]

4. To put under oath; to examine on oath. [Rare.]

5. To lay aside; to eject. [Obs.]

dē-pōṣe′, *v.i.* To bear witness.

dē-pōṣ′ēr, *n.* 1. One who deposes or degrades from office.

2. A witness; a deponent.

dē-poṣ′it, *v.t.*; deposited, *pt., pp.*; depositing, *ppr.* [L. *depositus*, pp. of *deponere*, to lay aside; *de*, from, and *ponere*, to place.]

1. To lay down; to lay; to throw down; to put; to place; as, a bird *deposits* her eggs in a nest; an inundation *deposits* soil in a meadow.
2. To lay up; to lay in a place for preservation; to store; as, to *deposit* goods in a warehouse.
3. To lodge in the hands of a person for safekeeping or other purpose; to intrust; to commit to one as a pledge; as, to *deposit* money in a bank; to *deposit* a will with a trust company.
4. To lay aside; to get rid of. [Obs.]

dē-poṣ′it, *v.i.* To be formed by deposition.

dē-poṣ′it, *n.* 1. That which is laid or thrown down; any matter laid or thrown down, or lodged; especially, matter settled by precipitation; as, a *deposit* of sand by a river; a *deposit* of copper in electrolysis.

> The *deposit* already formed affording to the succeeding portions of the charged fluid a basis. —Kirwan.

2. Anything intrusted to the care of another; a pledge; a thing given as security, or for preservation; especially, money placed in a bank for safety or convenience; as, he made a *deposit* of a hundred dollars.
3. A place where things are deposited; a depository. [Rare.]
4. In mining, an occurrence of mineral; as, *deposits* of gold, iron, lead, etc.
5. In law, (a) a sum of money which one puts into the hands of another as a kind of security for the fulfilment of some agreement, or as a part payment in advance; (b) a naked bailment of goods to be kept for the bailor without recompense, and to be returned when the bailor shall require it; (c) in Scots law, same as *depositation.*
6. The state of being deposited for safe-keeping or convenience, as in a bank; as, to place a hundred dollars on *deposit.*

Bank of deposit; see under *Bank.*

In deposit or *on deposit*; in a state of pledge, or for safe-keeping.

dē-poṣ′i-tā-ry, *n.*; *pl.* **dē-poṣ′i-tā-rieṣ.** [LL. *depositarius*, from L. *depositum*, a deposit.]
1. A person with whom anything is left or lodged in trust; one to whom a thing is committed for safe-keeping, or to be used for the benefit of the owner; a trustee; a guardian; also written *depository.*
2. In law, one to whom goods are bailed, to be kept for the bailor without a recompense.

dē-poṣ′i-tā-ry, *a.* Receiving deposits; applied to banks.

dē-poṣ-i-tā′tion, *n.* In Scots law, a contract by which a subject belonging to one person is intrusted to the gratuitous custody of another (called the depositary), to be redelivered on demand.

dep-ō-ṣi′tion (-zish′un), *n.* [OFr. *deposition*; LL. *depositio*, a laying or putting down, from L. *depositus*, pp. of *deponere*, to lay or put down.]
1. The act of laying or setting down; placing; that which is so placed; as, the *deposition* of crystals on cooling; the *deposition* of metals in plating.
2. Presentation. [Obs.]
3. In law, (a) the attested written testimony of a witness to be used in lieu of the actual appearance of such witness in court; (b) same as *deposit*, n. 5.
4. A divesting of sovereignty, or of office and dignity; as, the *deposition* of a king.
5. In surgery of the eye, the downward disposal of the lens in couching.
6. The disposal of a saint's body after death, either by burial or removal to a new resting place; a celebration of such events.

Syn.—Affidavit.—An *affidavit* is simply a declaration under oath; a *deposition* is the testimony of a witness who does not attend on a trial. It must so be taken before a magistrate that both parties have an opportunity to ask questions.

dē-poṣ′i-tŏr, *n.* [LL. *depositor*, from L. *depositus*, pp. of *deponere*, to deposit.] One who deposits; one who has a deposit at a bank.

dē-poṣ′i-tō-ry, *n.*; *pl.* **dē-poṣ′i-tō-rieṣ.** 1. A place where anything is lodged for safekeeping; as, a warehouse is a *depository* for goods.
2. A depositary.

dē-poṣ′i-tum, *n.* [L.] A deposit.

dē-poṣ′i-tūre, *n.* Deposition. [Obs.]

dē′pōt (dē′pō *or* dep-ō′), *n.* [Fr. *dépôt*, a deposit, storehouse; OFr. *depost*, a deposit, pledge, from L. *depositum*, a deposit, from *depositus*, pp. of *deponere*, to lay aside.]
1. A place for storage; a warehouse; as, a flour *depot.*
2. Militarily, a station for drill, supplies, or the like; (b) the distribution-point for the supplies of a regiment; (c) a place of assemblage in the trenches for troops ordered to attack the outworks.
3. A railway building having waiting-rooms for passengers, an office for the station-agent, and often warerooms for freight and express; a railway station.

dep-rȧ-vā′tion, *n.* [L. *depravatio*, a making crooked; a perverting, from *depravare*, to make crooked.]
1. Censure; defamation. [Obs.]
2. The act of making bad or worse; the act of corrupting, impairing, or degenerating.
3. The state of being made bad or worse; degeneracy.

Syn.—Deterioration, degeneracy, corruption, contamination, vitiation.

dē-prāve′, *v.t.*; depraved, *pt.*, *pp.*; depraving, *ppr.* 1. To make bad or worse; to impair the good qualities of; to vitiate; to corrupt; as, to *deprave* manners, morals, government, laws.
2. To defame; to vilify. [Obs.]

Syn.—Contaminate, corrupt, pollute, vitiate.

dē-prāv′ed-ly, *adv.* In a depraved manner.

dē-prāv′ed-ness, *n.* Depravity.

dē-prāve′ment, *n.* Depravity. [Rare.]

dē-prāv′ẽr, *n.* One who depraves; a corrupter.

dē-prāv′ing-ly, *adv.* In a depraving manner.

dē-prav′i-ty, *n.* 1. Corruption; a vitiated state; as, the *depravity* of manners and morals.
2. In theology, a vitiated state of the heart; wickedness; corruption of moral principles; destitution of holiness or good principles.

Total depravity; in theology, the doctrine that man's nature is innately bad and perverse; the original sin of Calvinism. [See *Original sin* under *Original.*]

Syn.—Depravation, corruption.—*Depravity* is a disposition or settled tendency to evil; *depravation* is the act or process of making depraved; as, the *depravation* of morals. *Corruption* applies to anything which is greatly vitiated; as, a *corruption* of morals, of taste, of language, etc.

dep′rē-ċȧ-ble, *a.* Liable to or deserving deprecation.

dep′rē-ċāte, *v.t.*; deprecated, *pt.*, *pp.*; deprecating, *ppr.* [L. *deprecatus*, pp. of *deprecari*, to pray against, to avert by prayer, to pray for; *de*, off, from, and *precari*, to pray.]
1. To pray against; to pray deliverance from; as, to *deprecate* the return of war.
2. To plead or argue earnestly against; to urge reasons against; to express strong disapproval of; said of a scheme, purpose, and the like.

> His purpose was *deprecated* by all around him. —Scott.

3. To implore mercy of. [Obs.]

dep-rē-ċā′ting-ly, *adv.* In a deprecating manner.

dep-rē-ċā′tion, *n.* 1. The act of deprecating; a praying against; a praying that an evil may be removed or prevented; disapprobation.
2. Entreaty; petitioning; an excusing; a begging pardon for.
3. A malediction; a curse. [Obs.]

dep′rē-ċā-tive, *a.* Deprecatory.

dep′rē-ċā-tive-ly, *adv.* In a deprecative manner.

dep′rē-ċā-tŏr, *n.* One who deprecates.

dep′rē-ċȧ-tō-ry, *a.* That serves to deprecate; tending to remove or avert evil by pleading or petition; as, *deprecatory* letters.

dē-prē′ci-āte (-shi-), *v.t.*; depreciated, *pt.*, *pp.*; depreciating, *ppr.* [LL. *depreciatus*, pp. of *depreciare*, to lower the price, to undervalue, from L. *de*, down, and *pretium*, price.]
1. To lessen the price of; to cry down the price or value of.
2. To undervalue; to represent as of little value or merit, or of less value than commonly supposed; to seek to lower in estimation.

Syn.—To disparage, traduce, decry, lower, detract, undervalue, underrate.

dē-prē′ci-āte, *v.i.* To fall in value; to become of less worth; as, a building *depreciates* from year to year.

dē-prē-ci-ā′tion (-shi-ā′shun), *n.* 1. The state or condition of being depreciated.
2. The act of lessening or crying down price or value.
3. The falling of value; reduction of worth.

dē-prē′ci-ȧ-tive (-shi-), *a.* Undervaluing; tending to depreciate.

dē-prē′ci-ȧ-tive-ly, *adv.* In a depreciative manner.

dē-prē′ci-ā-tŏr, *n.* One who depreciates.

dē-prē′ci-ȧ-tō-ry, *a.* Tending to depreciate; depreciative.

dep′rē-dȧ-ble, *a.* Liable to depredation. [Rare.]

dep′rē-dāte, *v.t.*; depredated, *pt.*, *pp.*; depredating, *ppr.* [LL. *deprædatus*, pp. of *deprædare*, to plunder, from L. *de*, and *prædari*, to rob, plunder, from *præda*, booty, prey.] To destroy or prey upon; to devastate, maliciously or for food, to pillage; to plunder; as, to *depredate* a vast area.

dep′rē-dāte, *v.i.* To take plunder or prey; to commit waste; as, the troops *depredated* on the country.

dep-rē-dā′tion, *n.* 1 The act of plundering; a robbing; a pillaging.
2. Waste; consumption.
3 In Scots law, the offense of driving away numbers of cattle or other beasts by the masterful force of armed persons; otherwise called *hership.*

dep′rē-dā-tŏr, *n.* One who plunders or pillages; a spoiler; a waster.

dep′rē-dā-tō-ry, *a.* Characterized by depredation; pillaging; plundering.

dē-pred′i-ċāte, *v.t.* To publish; to proclaim. [Rare.]

dep-rē-hend′, *v.t.*; deprehended, *pt.*, *pp.*; deprehending, *ppr.* [L. *deprehendere* or *deprendere*, to lay hold of, seize; *de*, and *prehendere*, to seize, take.]
1. To catch; to take unawares or by surprise; to seize, as a person committing an unlawful act.
2. To detect; to discover.

dep-rē-hen′si-ble, *a.* That may be caught or discovered. [Obs.]

dep-rē-hen′si-ble-ness, *n.* Capableness of being caught or discovered. [Obs.]

dep-rē-hen′sion, *n.* A catching or seizing; a discovery. [Obs.]

dē-press′, *v.t.*; depressed, *pt.*, *pp.*; depressing, *ppr.* [ME. *depressen*; L. *depressus*, pp. of *deprimere*, to press down.]
1. To press down; to press to a lower state or position; as, to *depress* the end of a tube.
2. To render dull or languid; to limit or diminish; as, to *depress* commerce.
3. To deject; to make sad; as, to *depress* the spirits or the mind.
4. To humble; to abase; as, to *depress* pride.
5. To impoverish; to lower in temporal estate; to bring into adversity; as, misfortunes and losses have *depressed* the merchants.
6. To lower in value; as, to *depress* the price of stock.
7. In algebra, to reduce to a lower degree, as an equation.

To depress the pole; nautically, to cause the pole to appear lower or nearer the horizon, as by sailing toward the equator.

Syn.—Sink, lower, abase, cast down, deject, humble, degrade, dispirit.

dē-press′ănt, *n.* A sedative.

dē-pressed′ (-prest′), *a.* 1. Sad; disheartened.
2. Pressed or forced down; lowered; especially, made level to or sunk below the surface; as, a *depressed* track.
3. In biology, flattened from above, as the body of certain fishes or the growth of some plants.
4. In heraldry, same as *debruised.*

dē-press′ing-ly, *adv.* In a depressing manner.

dē-pres′sion, *n.* [ME. *depressioun*; L. *depressio*, a pressing down.]
1. The act of pressing down, or the state of being pressed down; a low state.
2. A hollow; a sinking or falling in of a surface; a forcing inward; as, roughness consisting in little protuberances and *depressions*; the *depression* of the skull.
3. The act of humbling; abasement; as, the *depression* of pride.
4. A sinking of the spirits; dejection; a state of sadness; want of courage or animation; as, *depression* of the mind.
5. A low state of strength; a state of body succeeding debility in the formation of disease.
6. A state of dullness or inactivity; as, *depression* of trade; commercial *depression.*
7. In astronomy, (a) the sinking of the polar star toward the horizon, as a person recedes from the pole toward the equator; (b) the distance of a star from the horizon below.
8. In surgery, couching, an operation for cataract.
9. In music, the lowering of a tone by flatting.

Angle of depression; the angle by which a straight line drawn from the eye to any object dips below the horizon.

Depression of the dew-point; the difference in degrees between atmospheric temperature at a given time and the dew-point.

Depression of the horizon; see *Dip of the horizon*, under *Dip.*

Syn.—Abasement, reduction, sinking, fall, humiliation, dejection, melancholy.

dē-press′ive, *a.* Able or tending to depress or cast down.

dē-press′ive-ness, *n.* The quality of being depressive.

dē-pres-sō-mō′tŏr, *n.* In medicine, an agent that restrains the motor system; also used adjectively.

dē-press′ŏr, *n.* 1. One who or that which presses down; an oppressor.
2. [*Pl.* dep-res-sō′rēs.] In anatomy, a muscle that depresses or draws down the part to which it is attached.
3. In surgery, an instrument like a curved spatula used for reducing or pushing into place a protruding part.

Depressor nerve; one repressing action at the vasomotor center.

dep′ri-ment, *a.* and *n.* [L. *deprimens*, ppr. of *deprimere*, to press down.]

I. *a.* Serving to depress or lower; as, *depriment* muscles. [Obs.]
II. *n.* Depression. [Obs.]

dē-prī'ṣūre, *n.* Disesteem. [Obs.]

dē-prīv'ȧ-ble, *a.* That may be deprived.

dep-ri-vā'tion, *n.* 1. The act of depriving; a taking away.

2. A state of being deprived; loss; want; bereavement.

3. In ecclesiastical law, the act of divesting a bishop or other clergyman of his spiritual promotion or dignity. This is of two kinds: *a beneficio* and *ab officio*; the former being loss of living or preferment, the latter of an order; otherwise called *deposition* or *degradation*.

dē-prīve', *v.t.*; deprived, *pt.*, *pp.*; depriving, *ppr.* [ME. *depriven*; OFr. *depriver*, to deprive, take away, depose; L. *de*, and *privare*, to deprive, to separate.]

1. To take from; to bereave of something possessed or enjoyed; followed by *of*; as, to *deprive* a man *of* sight; to *deprive* one *of* strength, *of* reason, or *of* property.

2. To hinder from possessing or enjoying; to debar.

3. Ecclesiastically, to depose; to degrade. [See *Deprivation*, 3.]

4. To end. [Obs.]

Syn.—Debar, abridge.—*Deprive* conveys the idea of either taking away that which one has, or withholding that which one may have; *debar* conveys the idea only of withholding; *abridge* conveys that also of taking away. *Depriving* is a coercive measure; *debar* and *abridge* are merely acts of authority. We are *deprived* of that which is of the first necessity; we are *debarred* of privileges; we are *abridged* of comforts, pleasures, etc.

dē-prīve'ment, *n.* Deprivation. [Obs.]

dē-prīv'ẽr, *n.* One who or that which deprives.

dē-pros'trāte, *a.* Very low; mean. [Obs.]

dē-prō-vin'ciăl-īze, *v.t.* To rid of provincialism; as, to *deprovincialize* tastes.

depth, *n.* [ME. *depthe*, depth, from *dep*; AS. *deop*, deep.]

1. Deepness; the distance or measure of a thing from the highest part, top, or surface to the lowest part or bottom, or to the extreme part downward or inward; the measure from the anterior to the posterior part; as, the *depth* of the ocean is unfathomable; the battalion formed a column of great *depth*.

2. A deep place; an abyss; a gulf of infinite profundity.

And sounded all the *depths* and shoals of honor. —Shak.

3. The sea; the ocean.

The *depth* closed me round about. —Jonah ii. 5.

4. The inner, darker, or more concealed part of a thing; the middle, darkest, or stillest part; as, the *depth* of winter; the *depth* of night.

5. Abstruseness; obscurity; that which is not easily explored; as, the *depth* of a science.

6. Immensity; infinity; intensity.

The *depth* of some divine despair. —Tennyson.

7. Profoundness; extent of penetration, or of the capacity of penetrating; as, *depth* of understanding; *depth* of skill.

8. In painting, the manner of treatment of a subject by which richness of shade and tone is brought out.

9. Nautically, the extent of the square sails from the headrope to the footrope.

10. In logic, the essentials of an idea; content.

depth'en, *v.t.* To make deep. [Obs.]

depth'less, *a.* Having no depth.

dē-pū'ce-lāte, dē-pū'di-cāte, *v.t.* To deflower; to rob of virginity. [Obs.]

dē-pulse', *v.t.* To drive away. [Obs.]

dē-pul'sion, *n.* A driving or thrusting away. [Obs.]

dē-pul'sō-ry, *a.* Driving or thrusting away; averting. [Obs.]

dep'ū-rănt, *a.* and *n.* [From *de-*, intens., and L. *purus*, pure.] Depurative; purgative.

dep'ū-rāte, *v.t.*; depurated, *pt.*, *pp.*; depurating, *ppr.* [LL. *depuratus*, pp. of *depurare*, to purify, from L. *de-*, intens., and *purus*, pure.] To purify; to free from impurities, heterogeneous matter, or feculence; to cleanse.

dep'ū-rāte, *a.* Cleansed; pure. [Obs.]

dep-ū-rā'tion, *n.* The act of purifying or freeing from heterogeneous matter; as, the *depuration* of a wound or fluid.

dep'ū-rā-tive, *a.* Purifying; tending to cleanse; depuratory.

dep'ū-rā-tive, *n.* That which purifies, as a medicine.

dep'ū-rā-tŏr, *n.* One who or that which cleanses.

dep'ū-rā-tō-ry, *a.* Cleansing; purifying; or tending to purify. [Obs.]

dep'ū-rā-tō-ry, *n.* That which cleanses or purifies. [Obs.]

dē-pūre', *v.t.* To depurate. [Obs.]

dē-pūr'gȧ-tō-ry, *a.* Serving to purify or cleanse. [Obs.]

dep-ū-ri'tion (-rish'un), *n.* See *Depuration*.

dep'ū-tȧ-ble, *a.* Capable of being deputed; fit to be deputed.

dep-ū-tā'tion, *n.* [ME. *deputation*, from L. *deputatus*, pp. of *deputare*, to cut off, prune down, select; *de*, off, from, and *putare*, to prune, cleanse, think, estimate.]

1. The act of deputing; the state of being deputed; the act of appointing a representative or representatives to act for another or others.

2. The person or persons appointed to represent another or others; delegation; as, the general sent a *deputation* to the enemy to offer terms of peace.

3. In English forestry law, a license giving to a gamekeeper certain privileges and rights.

By deputation, or *in deputation*; by delegation.

dep'ū-tā-tŏr, *n.* A deputy. [Obs.]

dē-pūte', *v.t.*; deputed, *pt.*, *pp.*; deputing, *ppr.* [L. *deputare*, to cut off, prune down, select, depute.]

1. To appoint as a substitute or agent to act for another; to appoint and send with a special commission or authority to transact business in another's name; to delegate; as, the sheriff *deputes* a man to serve a writ.

2. To set aside or apart; to assign. [Obs.]

dē-pūte', *n.* A deputy; as, a sheriff-*depute*. [Scot.]

dep'ū-tīze, *v.t.*; deputized, *pt.*, *pp.*; deputizing, *ppr.* To appoint as a deputy; to empower to act for another; to depute.

dep'ū-tīze, *v.i.* To act as a deputy.

dep'ū-ty, *n.*; *pl.* **dep'ū-ties**. [OFr. *depute*, a deputy, from L. *deputatus*, pp. of *deputare*, to cut off, select.]

1. A person appointed or elected to act for another or others; one who exercises an office in another's right; a delegate; a representative; an agent.

2. One deputed or elected to represent an electorate; as, the Chamber of *Deputies* in France.

Syn.—Agent, delegate, commissioner, ambassador, envoy, proxy, representative, substitute, legate, vicegerent.

dē-quan'ti-tāte, *v.t.* To diminish the quantity of. [Obs.]

dē-rac'i-nāte, *v.t.* [Fr. *déraciner*; OFr. *desraciner*, to root out, uproot; *des-* priv., and *racine*, a root; L. *de-* priv., and *radix* (*-icis*), a root.] To pluck up by the roots; to extirpate. [Rare.]

dē-rac-i-nā'tion, *n.* The act of pulling up by the roots. [Rare.]

dē-rāign', dē-rāin', *v.t.* In old English law, to prove; to justify; to vindicate, as an assertion. [Obs.]

dē-rāign'ment, dē-rāin'ment, *n.* 1. The act of deraigning; proof; justification. [Obs.]

2. A renunciation, as of religious or monastic vows. [Obs.]

dē-rāil', *v.t.*; derailed, *pt.*, *pp.*; derailing, *ppr.* To cause to leave the rails or track; as, to *derail* a railroad train.

dē-rāil', *v.i.* To leave the rails or track.

dē-rāil'ẽr, *n.* An automatic safety device on railways at switches and crossings requiring manipulation before train proceeds, otherwise it is derailed.

dē-rāil'ment, *n.* The act of derailing or the condition of being derailed.

dē-rānge', *v.t.*; deranged, *pt.*, *pp.*; deranging, *ppr.* [Fr. *déranger*; OFr. *desrangier*, to put out of order; *des-* priv., and *ranger*, to put in order, to arrange.]

1. To put out of order; to disturb the regular order of; to throw into confusion; to disarrange; as, to *derange* the plans of a commander, or the affairs of a nation.

2. To put into disorder the natural functions of; to unsettle; as, to *derange* a machine; violent excitement *deranges* the action of the heart.

3. To disorder the intellect of; to unsettle the reason of; as, he is *deranged* by anxiety.

Syn.—Disarrange, confuse, disturb, unbalance, disconcert, disorder, displace.

dē-rānge'ȧ-ble, *a.* That may be deranged; liable to derangement.

dē-rānged', *a.* Disordered in mind; insane.

dē-rānge'ment, *n.* The act of deranging; the state of being deranged; disorder of the mind or reason; insanity.

Syn.—Insanity, lunacy, madness, mania.—*Deranged* persons may sometimes be perfectly sensible in everything but particular subjects. *Insane* persons are sometimes entirely restored. *Lunatics* have their lucid intervals, and *maniacs* their intervals of repose. *Derangement* may sometimes be applied to the temporary confusion of a disturbed mind, which is not in full possession of all its faculties; *madness* may sometimes be the result of violently inflamed passions; and *mania* may be applied to any vehement attachment which takes possession of the mind.

dē-rān'gẽr, *n.* One who deranges.

dē-rāy', *n.* Tumult; disorder; merriment. [Obs.]

dē-rāy', *v.t.* and *v.i.* To derange; to rage. [Obs.]

dẽr'bi-ō, *n.* A large edible fish, *Lichia glauca*, found in the Mediterranean.

Dẽr'by (*in England also* där'bi), *n.*; *pl.* **Dẽr'bieṣ**. 1. A race for three-year-old thorough bred horses, founded in 1780 by the twelfth Earl of Derby, and run annually at Epsom, in Surrey, England. It is the principal horse-race in that country. The name has been adopted for annual races of three-year-old horses at several American race-tracks.

2. [d—] A stiff felt hat having a rounded crown and a curved brim, worn almost exclusively by men.

3. [d—] Same as *Darby*.

Derby day; the day on which the Derby sweepstakes is run at Epsom, which is the Wednesday before Whitsunday.

Dẽr'by-shire spär. Fluoride of calcium; fluor-spar.

der-dō'ing, *a.* [Obs.] See *Daredoing*.

dēre, *v.t.* To hurt. [Obs.]

dēre, *n.* Harm. [Obs.]

dēre, *a.* Dear. [Obs.]

de-re'chō, *n.* [Sp.] In Mexican and Spanish law, (a) right; just claim; (b) in the plural, imposts; taxes.

dē-reine', *v.t.* [Obs.] See *Deraign*.

der'e-lict, *a.* [L. *derelictus*, pp. of *derelinquere*, to forsake utterly, to abandon; *de-*, and *relinquere*, to leave, forsake.]

1. Left; abandoned by the guardian or owner; as, *derelict* property; *derelict* children.

2. Remiss; negligent; unfaithful; as, *derelict* in duty.

Hopelessly *derelict*, and neglectful of his social duties. —Hawthorne.

der'e-lict, *n.* 1. In law, an article of goods, or any commodity thrown away, relinquished, or abandoned by the owner; specifically, a ship abandoned at sea.

2. A tract of land left dry by the sea, and fit for cultivation or use.

der-e-lic'tion, *n.* 1. The act of leaving with an intention not to reclaim or resume; an utter forsaking; abandonment.

2. The state of being left or abandoned.

3. The gaining of land from the water by a change of high-water mark; also, the land thus gained.

4. Neglect; unfaithfulness.

Dereliction of military duties. —Scott.

dē-rē-lig'iŏn-īze, *v.t.* To make irreligious. [Rare.]

dēre'ling, *n.* Darling. [Obs.]

dẽrf, *a.* Brave; bold; powerful. [Obs.]

dẽrf'ly, *adv.* Bravely; boldly. [Obs.]

der'ic, *a.* [From Gr. *deros*, skin.] Ectodermal; opposed to *enteric*.

dē-rīde', *v.t.*; derided, *pt.*, *pp.*; deriding, *ppr.* [L. *deridere*, to mock, laugh at, deride; *de-*, intens., and *ridere*, to laugh.] To laugh at in contempt; to turn to ridicule or make sport of; to mock; to treat with scorn by laughter.

The Pharisees also *derided* him. —Luke xvi. 14.

Syn.—Ridicule, mock, taunt.—A man may *ridicule* without unkindness of feeling; his object may be to correct. He who *derides* is actuated by a severe and contemptuous spirit. To *mock* is stronger, denoting open and scoffing derision; to *taunt* is to reproach with bitter insult.

dē-rīd'ẽr, *n.* One who laughs at another in contempt; a mocker; a scoffer.

dē-rīd'ing-ly, *adv.* By way of derision or mockery.

dē-ris'i-ble, *a.* Open to or worthy of derision.

dē-ri'ṣion, *n.* [LL. *derisio*, derision, from L. *derisus*, pp. of *deridere*, to deride.]

1. The act of deriding or the state of being derided; contempt manifested by laughter; scorn; ridicule.

The Lord shall have them in *derision*. —Ps. ii. 4.

2. An object of derision or contempt; a laughing-stock.

I was a *derision* to all my people.—Lam. iii. 14.

Syn.—Contempt, scorn, disregard, ridicule, mockery, insult, disdain.

dē-rī'sive, *a.* Characterized by or expressing derision; as, *derisive* taunts.

dē-rī'sive-ly, *adv.* With mockery or contempt.

dē-rī'sive-ness, *n.* The state of being derisive.

dē-rī'sō-ry, *a.* Mocking; ridiculing.

dē-rīv-ȧ-bil'i-ty, *n.* The quality of being derivable.

dē-rīv'ȧ-ble, *a.* That may be derived in any sense; as, income *derivable* from land.

All honor *derivable* upon me. —South.

dē-rīv'ȧ-bly, *adv.* By derivation.

der'i-vāte, *a.* Derived. [Rare.]

der'i-vāte, *n.* A word derived from another; a derivative. [Rare.]

der′i-vāte, *v.t.* To derive. [Obs.]

der-i-vā′tion, *n.* [L. *derivatio*, a turning aside into another channel, a derivation, from *derivare*, to divert, derive; *de*, from, and *rivus*, a stream.]

1. The act of deriving, drawing, or receiving from a source, or the state of being derived; as, the *derivation* of an estate from ancestors, or of profits from capital, or of truth or facts from antiquity.

2. A drawing from or turning aside from a natural course or channel; as, the *derivation* of water from its channel by lateral drains. [Obs.]

3. In philology, (a) the drawing or tracing of a word from its original root; as, *derivation* is from the L. *derivare*, to divert; (b) a statement of the origin of a word. [See *Etymology*.]

4. In medicine, a drawing of humors from one part of the body to another, to diminish or remedy inflammation or congestion.

5. The thing derived or deduced; a derivative; a deduction. [Rare.]

6. In mathematics, the operation by which a derivative is deduced from that which precedes it, or from the function itself.

7. In gunnery, the peculiar constant deviation of an elongated projectile from a rifled gun; drift.

8. In biology, descent of organisms from former organisms, the process being accompanied by certain structural changes; the theory of evolution.

der-i-vā′tion-ăl, *a.* Relating to derivation.

der-i-vā′tion-ist, *n.* Same as *Derivatist*.

dē-riv′ȧ-tist, *n.* One who believes in the theory of the derivation or evolution of the human race from inferior antecedent organisms. [Rare.]

dē-riv′ȧ-tive, *a.* [LL. *derivativus*, derivative, from L. *derivatus*, pp. of *derivare*, to derive, to turn aside.]

1. Derived; taken or having proceeded from another or something preceding; secondary; as, a *derivative* perfection; a *derivative* conveyance.

2. In biology, relating to derivation or to the theory of evolution.

3. In medicine, tending to diminish or remedy inflammation or congestion.

Derivative chord; in music, a chord not fundamental, but derived from another by inversion.

Derivative circulation; a circulation existing in certain parts of the body, as the nose and liver, in which the veins receive the blood directly from the arteries.

Derivative conveyance; in law, a secondary deed, as a release, confirmation, surrender, consignment, and defeasance.

Derivative theory; in biology, the theory that species undergo a process of modification by reason of their inherent tendencies, and not by natural selection.

dē-riv′ȧ-tive, *n.* 1. That which is derived; that which is deduced or comes by derivation from another.

2. In grammar, a word which takes its origin from another word, or is formed from it.

3. In music, a chord not fundamental. [See *Derivative chord* under *Derivative*, a.]

4. In medicine, an agent or method for diminishing or remedying inflammation or congestion. [See *Derivation*.]

5. In mathematics, a function expressing the relation between two consecutive states of a varying function; a differential coefficient.

6. In chemistry, a body derived from another, commonly by partial metathesis; as, a monatomic alcohol is a *derivative* of an olefine.

dē-riv′ȧ-tive-ly, *adv.* In a derivative manner; by derivation.

dē-riv′ȧ-tive-ness, *n.* The state of being derivative.

dē-rīve′, *v.t.*; derived, *pt., pp.*; deriving, *ppr.* [ME. *deriven*; L. *derivare*, to turn a stream from its channel, to derive.]

1. To draw from, as in a regular course or channel; to receive from a source or origin by regular conveyance; as, the heir *derives* an estate from his ancestors; we *derive* instruction from books.

2. To turn from its natural course; to divert; as, to *derive* water from the main channel or current into lateral rivulets. [Obs.]

3. To deduce or draw, as from a root or primitive word; as, to *derive* a word from Latin.

4. To trace the derivation of, as a word.

5. To deduce, as from something previously assumed or stated.

6. To communicate from one to another, as by descent. [Rare.]

7. In chemistry, to obtain (one body) from another, as by partial metathesis.

Derived circuit; in electricity, a subsidiary circuit in any part of a circuit where the current divides, some of it flowing in the main circuit and some of it through the subsidiary or shunt; called also *shunt-circuit*.

Derived current; in electricity, a current which flows through a derived circuit.

Syn.—Deduce, trace.—The act of *deriving* is immediate and direct; that of *tracing* a gradual process; that of *deducing* a ratiocinative process. We discover causes and sources by *derivation*; we discover the course, progress, and commencement of things by *tracing*; we discover the grounds and reasons of things by *deduction*.

dē-rīve′, *v.i.* To come or proceed; to have derivation or origin. [Rare.]

dē-rīve′ment, *n.* That which is deduced or derived; an inference. [Obs.]

dē-rīv′ẽr, *n.* One who derives, or draws from a source.

dẽrk, *a.* Dark. [Obs.]

dẽrm, *n.* See *Derma*.

-dẽrm. A suffix from Greek *derma*, skin; much used in anatomy.

dẽr′mȧ, *n.* [L., from Gr. *derma*, skin.]

1. The skin in general.

2. The corium; the true skin; called also *derm, dermis, cutis*, and *enderon*.

dẽrm′ad, *adv.* Same as *Ectad*.

dẽrm′ăl, *a.* 1. Pertaining to skin, or the external covering of the body; consisting of skin.

2. Pertaining to the derma or corium; as, the *dermal* layer.

dẽr-mal′gi-ȧ, *n.* [L., from Gr. *derma*, skin, and *algos*, pain.] A cutaneous affection resulting from nervous disease; neuralgia of the skin; called also *dermatalgia*.

Dẽr-map′te-rȧ, *n.pl.* [L., from Gr. *derma*, skin, and *pteron*, wing.] A group of insects including the earwigs; written also *Dermatoptera, Dermoptera*.

dẽr-map′tẽr-ăn, *a.* Pertaining to the *Dermaptera*.

dẽr-map′tẽr-ăn, *n.* An insect of the *Dermaptera*.

dẽr-map′tẽr-ous, *a.* Pertaining to the *Dermaptera*.

dẽr-mȧ-tal′gi-ȧ, *n.* Same as *Dermalgia*.

dẽr-mat′iç, *a.* Pertaining to the skin; dermal.

dẽr′mȧ-tine, *a.* Dermatic.

dẽr-mȧ-tī′tis, *n.* [L., from Gr. *derma*, skin.] In pathology, inflammation of the skin.

dẽr-mȧ-tō-, dẽr-mat-, dẽr-mō-, dẽrm-. Combining forms from Gr. *derma*, skin, denoting relation to the skin.

Dẽr″mȧ-tō-bran′chi-ȧ, Dẽr″mȧ-tō-bran-chi-ā′tȧ, *n.pl.* Same as *Dermobranchia*.

dẽr-mat′ō-gen, *n.* [*Dermato-*, and Gr. *-genēs*, producing.] In botany, the primordial cellular layer which develops into the epidermis.

dẽr-mȧ-tog′rȧ-phy, *n.* [*Dermato-*, and Gr. *graphein*, to write.] The anatomical description of the skin.

dẽr′mȧ-toid, *a.* [Gr. *derma* (*-matos*), skin, and *eidos*, form.] Resembling skin; skin-like.

dẽr′mȧ-tōl, *n.* [*Dermato-*, and L. *oleum*, oil.] A yellow antiseptic powder used in diseases of the skin and mucous membranes that are associated with excessive secretion; subgallate of bismuth.

dẽr″mȧ-tō-log′iç-ăl, *a.* Relating to dermatology.

dẽr-mȧ-tol′ō-gist, *n.* One versed in dermatology.

dẽr-mȧ-tol′ō-gy, *n.* [*Dermato-*, and Gr. *logos*, discourse.] The branch of physiology which treats of the skin and its diseases.

dẽr-mȧ-tol′y-sis, *n.* [*Dermato-*, skin, and Gr. *lysis*, a loosing, from *lyein*, to loose.] In pathology, an abnormal condition of the skin in which it becomes relaxed and pendulous.

dẽr″mȧ-tō-mȳ-cō′sis, *n.* [*Dermato-*, and Gr. *mykēs*, fungus.] In pathology, any cutaneous disease caused by a vegetable parasite.

dẽr″mȧ-tō-nō′sis (*or* -ton′ō-sis), *n.* [*Dermato-*, and Gr. *nosos*, disease.] Any cutaneous disease.

dẽr″mȧ-tō-path′iç, *a.* [*Dermato-*, and Gr. *pathos*, suffering.] Pertaining to cutaneous diseases or the methods of curing them.

dẽr-mȧ-top′ȧ-thy, dẽr″mȧ-tō-path′i-ȧ, *n.* Any disease of the skin.

dẽr-mat′ō-phȳte (*or* dẽr′mȧ-), *n.* [*Dermato-*, and Gr. *phyton*, a growth, plant.] A parasitic plant, chiefly of the lowest type, infesting the cuticle and epidermis of men and some animals, and giving rise to various forms of skin-disease, as ringworm, sycosis, etc.

dẽr″mȧ-tō-phyt′iç, *a.* Pertaining to or produced by dermatophytes; as, *dermatophytic* diseases.

dẽr′mȧ-tō-plas″ty, *n.* [*Dermato-*, and Gr. *plassein*, to mold, form.] Plastic surgery of the skin.

Dẽr-mȧ-top′te-rȧ, *n.pl.* [L., from Gr. *derma*, skin, and *pteron*, a wing.]

1. In entomology, same as *Dermaptera*.

2. In mammalogy, same as *Dermoptera*.

dẽr″mȧ-tōr-rhē′ȧ, dẽr″mȧ-tōr-rhœ′ȧ, *n.* [L., from Gr. *derma*, skin, and *rhoia*, a flowing, from *rhein*, to flow.] A morbid increase of secretion from the skin.

dẽr″mȧ-tō-sçlē-rō′sis, *n.* [*Dermato-*, and Gr. *sklērōsis*, a hardening.] See *Sclerodermia*.

dẽr-mȧ-tō′sis, *n.* [L., from Gr. *derma*, skin.]

1. In pathology, any cutaneous disease.

2. In anatomy, the condition of having a bony skin, as appearing in the armadillo, turtle, etc.

Dẽr″mȧ-tō-zō′ȧ, *n.pl.*; *sing.* **Dẽr″mȧ-tō-zō′on.** [L., from Gr. *derma*, skin, and *zōon*, a living being, from *zēn*, to live.] A class of parasites infesting the skin.

Dẽr-mes′tēs, *n.* [L., from Gr. *derma*, skin, and *esthiein*, to eat.] A genus of coleopterous insects, the type of the family *Dermestidæ*. The larvæ of this genus are covered with slippery hairs; they devour dead bodies, skins, leather, and other animal substances. One species, *Dermestes lardarius*, is known by the name of bacon-beetle; another, *Dermestes* or *Anthrenus musæorum*, is peculiarly destructive in museums of natural history.

dẽr-mes′tid, *n.* One of the *Dermestidæ*.

dẽr-mes′tid, *a.* Relating to the *Dermestidæ*.

Dẽr-mes′ti-dæ, *n.pl.* [L., from Gr. *derma*, skin, and *esthiein*, to eat.] A family of coleopterous insects, the species of which are for the most part of small size. Their larvæ are covered with hair, and feed upon animal substances.

dẽr-mes′toid, *a.* Characteristic of the genus *Dermestes*; relating to the *Dermestidæ*.

dẽr′miç, *a.* [Gr. *derma*, the skin.]

1. In medicine, pertaining to the skin; as, a *dermic* disease.

2. In anatomy, pertaining to the derma or corium; dermal.

Dermic remedies; remedies which act through the skin.

dẽr′mis, *n.* Same as *Derma*.

dẽr-mō-. A combining form from Gr. *derma*, skin.

Dẽr-mō-bran′chi-ȧ, *n.pl.* [*Dermo-*, and Gr. *branchia*, gills.] A family of gasteropods, comprising those mollusks which respire by means of external branchiæ or gills occurring in the form of thin membranous plates, tufts, or filaments. They are more commonly called *Nudibranchiata*. Called also *Dermobranchiata, Dermatobranchia, Dermatobranchiata*.

Dẽr″mō-bran-chi-ā′tȧ, *n.pl.* Same as *Dermobranchia*.

dẽr-mō-bran′chi-āte, *a.* Relating to the *Dermobranchia*.

dẽr-mō-gas′triç, *a.* [*Dermo-*, and Gr. *gastēr*, stomach.] Relating to the skin and the alimentary canal; connecting the alimentary canal and the skin; as, a *dermogastric* pore.

dẽr-mog′rȧ-phy, *n.* Same as *Dermatography*.

dẽr-mō-hē′măl, dẽr-mȧ-hē′măl, *a.* [*Dermo-*, and Gr. *haima*, blood.] Pertaining to the integument on the hemal side of the body; specifically, applied to the ossified developments of the dermoskeleton in fishes when they form points of attachment for the fins on the ventral or hemal side of the body; written also *dermohæmal, dermahæmal*.

dẽr-mō-hē′mi-ȧ, dẽr-mō-hæ′mi-ȧ, *n.* [L., from Gr. *derma*, skin, and *haima*, blood.] In pathology, hyperemia, or congestion of the skin.

dẽr-mō-hū′mẽr-ăl, *a.* [*Dermo-*, and L. *humerus*, the upper bone of the arm, the humerus.] Relating to or connecting the humerus and skin; specifically, relating to a muscle in certain animals.

dẽr′moid, *a.* See *Dermal*.

Dermoid cyst; a cyst containing elements of the skin, as teeth and hair.

dẽr-mol′ō-gy, *n.* See *Dermatology*.

dẽr-mō-mus′çū-lăr, *a.* Relating to the skin and muscles.

dẽr-mō-neū′răl, *a* [*Dermo-*, and Gr. *neuron*, nerve.] In zoölogy, a term applied to the upper row of spines in the back of a fish, from their connection with the skin and their relation to that surface of the body on which the nervous system is placed.

dẽr-mō-path′iç, *a.* In surgery, relating to dermopathy.

dẽr-mop′ȧ-thy, *n.* [*Dermo-*, and Gr. *pathos*, suffering.] Surgical treatment of cutaneous diseases.

dẽr′mō-phȳte, *n.* See *Dermatophyte*.

Dẽr-mop′te-rȧ, *n.pl.* [L., from Gr. *dermopteros*, having membranous wings like a bat; *derma*, skin, and *pteron*, wing.] A suborder of *Mammalia*, with a membrane connecting the fore and hind limbs and forming a parachute, typified by the colugo, *Galeopithecus volans*, or flying lemur.

dẽr′mop-tēre, *n.* One of the *Dermopteri*.

Dẽr-mop′te-rī, *n.pl.* [L., from Gr. *derma*, skin, and *pteron*, wing.] A subclass of fishes of vermiform shape, in which are included the leptocardians and marsipobranchs; called also *Dermopterygii*.

dẽr-mop′tẽr-ous, *a.* Characteristic of the *Dermopteri*.

Dẽr-mop-te-ryġ′i-ī, *n.pl.* Same as *Dermopteri*.

dẽr-mō-sçlē′rite, *n.* [*Dermo-*, and Gr. *sklēros*, hard.] A mass of spicules which occurs in the tissues of some of the *Actinozoa*.

dẽr-mō-skel′e-tăl, *a.* Pertaining to the dermoskeleton.

dẽr-mō-skel′e-tŏn, *n.* [L., from Gr. *derma*, skin, and *skeleton*.] The coriaceous, crustaceous, testaceous, or osseous integument, such as covers many invertebrate and some vertebrate animals; exoskeleton.

dẽr-mos-tō′sis, *n.* [L., from Gr. *derma*, skin, and *osteon*, a bone.] In physiology, formation of bone in the skin.

dẽr-mot′ō-my, *n.* [*Dermo-*, and Gr. *tomē*, a cutting, from *temnein*, to cut.] The anatomy or dissection of the skin.

dẽrn, *a.* 1. Solitary; sad; cruel. [Obs.]

2. Hidden; secret; private. [Obs.]

dẽrn, *n.* In architecture, same as *Dearn*.

dẽrn *v.t.* and *v.i.* To hide; to conceal; to skulk. [Obs.]

dẽrn, *v.t.* To darn; a colloquial euphemism for *damn*.

dẽrn′fụl, *a.* Solitary; hence, sad; mournful. [Obs.]

dẽr′ni-ẽr (*or Fr. pron.* dãr-nyā′), *a.* [Fr.] Last; final; ultimate; as, in the French phrase, *dernier ressort*, last resort.

dẽrn′ly, *adv.* Secretly; hence, sadly. [Obs.]

der′ō-gănt, *a.* Derogatory. [Rare.]

der′ō-gāte, *v.t.*; derogated, *pt., pp.*; derogating, *ppr.* [L. *derogatus*, pp. of *derogare*, to repeal part of a law, to take away, detract from; *de*, from, and *rogare*, to ask.]

1. To invalidate some part of, as a law or established rule; to annul in part.

> By several contrary customs, many of the civil and canon laws are controlled and *derogated*. —Hale.

2. To lessen the worth of; to disparage.

der′ō-gāte, *v.i.* 1. To detract; to lessen by taking away a part; with *from*; as, to *derogate from* reputation.

2. To act beneath one's rank, place, or birth. [Rare.]

der′ō-gāte, *a.* Diminished in force; degraded. [Rare.]

der′ō-gāte-ly, *adv.* Derogatorily.

der-ō-gā′tion, *n.* 1. The act of derogating; the partial invalidation or abrogation of a law.

> The *derogation* or partial relaxation of that law. —South.

2. The act of taking something from merit, reputation, or honor; a lessening of value or estimation; detraction; disparagement; with *from* or *of*; as, I say not this in *derogation of* my opponent.

3. Change or abatement; a term used on the stock exchange.

dē-rog′ȧ-tive, *a.* Derogatory.

dē-rog′ȧ-tive-ly, *adv.* In a derogative manner. [Rare.]

der′ō-gā-tŏr, *n.* One who derogates; a detractor.

dē-rog′ȧ-tō-ri-ly, *adv.* In a detracting manner.

dē-rog′ȧ-tō-ri-ness, *n.* The quality of being derogatory.

dē-rog′ȧ-tō-ry, *a.* [LL. *derogatorius*, derogatory, from L. *derogare*, to detract from.] Detracting or tending to lessen by taking something from; that lessens the extent, effect, or value; disparaging; as, a *derogatory* statement.

Derogatory clause in a testament; in law, a sentence or secret character inserted by the testator, of which he reserves the knowledge to himself, with a condition that no will he may make hereafter shall be valid, unless this clause is inserted word for word; a precaution to guard against later wills extorted by violence, or obtained by suggestion.

der′rick, *n.* [Originally applied to a gallows; named after *Derrick*, a London hangman, who lived in the 17th century.]

1. An apparatus for hoisting heavy weights, variously constructed, but usually consisting of a boom supported by a central post which is steadied by stays and guys, and furnished with a purchase, either the pulley, or the wheel and axle and pulley combined.

2. In mining or oil-boring, the slim, pyramidal erection over a drill-hole, acting as a support for machinery.

der′rick-crāne, *n.* A form of crane used in hoisting, having a jointed jib so arranged that the inclination, and consequently the sweep of the crane, can be altered as desired.

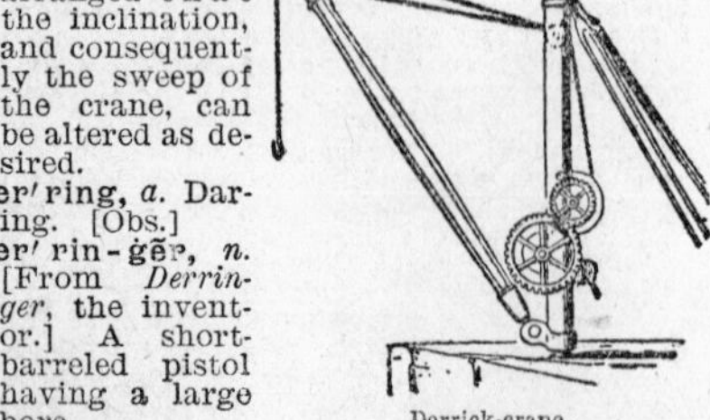

Derrick-crane.

der′ring, *a.* Daring. [Obs.]

der′rin-gẽr, *n.* [From *Derringer*, the inventor.] A short-barreled pistol having a large bore.

dẽrth, *n.* Dearth. [Obs.]

dẽr-trō-thē′cȧ, *n.* [Gr. *dertron*, a vulture's beak, and *thēkē*, a case, sheath.] The outer, terminal investment of the dertrum of a bird.

dẽr′trum, *n.*; *pl.* **dẽr′trȧ.** [Gr. *dertron*, the caul, a vulture's beak, from *derein*, to skin, flay.] The point of the upper mandible of a bird, when characterized by some difference from the remainder of the bill.

dẽr′vish, *n.* [Turk. *dervish*; Ar. *darwish*; Per. *derwesch*, a dervish, from Old Per. *derew*, to beg.]

1. A Mohammedan priest or monk, who professes extreme poverty, and leads an austere life, partly in monasteries, partly itinerant; also written *dervis*, *dervise*.

2. A fanatical Sudanese follower of the Mahdi.

Traveling Dervish of Khorassan.

dẽr′wọrth, *a.* Very valuable. [Obs.]

des′ărt, *a.* and *n.* Desert. [Obs.]

des′cant, *n.* [OFr. *descanter*, to descant, from L. *dis-*, apart, and *cantare*, to sing.]

1. In music, (a) the art of composing music in several parts; (b) an addition of a part or parts to a subject or melody; (c) the air or treble.

2. A song or tune with various modulations.

3. A discourse; discussion; disputation; animadversion; comment, or a series of comments.

des-cant′, *v.i.*; descanted, *pt., pp.*; descanting, *ppr.* 1. To discourse; to comment; to make a variety of remarks.

2. To sing an air or its variation.

des-cant′ẽr, *n.* One who descants.

dē-scend′, *v.i.*; descended, *pt., pp.*; descending, *ppr.* [ME. *descenden*; OFr. *descendre*; L. *descendere*, to climb, go or come down, to fall, descend.]

1. To move or pass from a higher to a lower place; to move, come or go downward; to fall; to sink; to run or flow down; applicable to any kind of motion or of body.

> The rain *descended*, and the floods came. —Matt. vii. 25.

2. To go down, with the view of entering or engaging in.

> He shall *descend* into battle and perish. —1 Sam. xxvi. 10.

3. To come suddenly; to fall violently.

> And on the suitors let thy wrath *descend*. —Pope.

4. Figuratively, to go in; to enter; to retire.

> [He] with holiest meditations fed
> Into himself *descended*. —Milton.

5. To come or go down in a hostile manner; to invade, as an enemy; to fall upon.

> The Grecian fleet *descending* on the town. —Dryden.

6. To proceed from a source or original; to be derived.

7. To proceed, as from father to son; to pass from a preceding possessor, in the order of lineage, or according to the laws of succession or inheritance.

8. To pass, as from general to particular considerations; as, having explained the general subject, we will *descend* to particulars.

9. To come down from a certain moral or social standard; to lower or abuse oneself, morally or socially; as, to *descend* to acts of meanness; to *descend* to an inferior position.

10. To condescend; to stoop.

> *Descending* to play with little children. —Evelyn.

11. In astronomy, to move southward; said of a star.

dē-scend′, *v.t.* To come from a higher part of to a lower; to come down; as, to *descend* a hill.

dē-scend′ănt, *a.* [OFr. *descendant*, from L. *descendens*, ppr. of *descendere*, to descend; *de*, down, and *scandere*, to climb.] Descending; descendent.

dē-scend′ănt, *n.* An individual proceeding from an ancestor in any degree; issue; offspring, in the line of generation, ad infinitum; as, we are all *descendants* of Adam and Eve.

dē-scend′ent, *a.* 1. Descending; falling; sinking.

2. Proceeding from an original or ancestor.

dē-scend′ẽr, *n.* One who or that which descends.

dē-scend-i-bil′i-ty, *n.* The quality of being descendible, or capable of being transmitted from ancestors; as, the *descendibility* of an estate or of a crown.

dē-scend′i-ble, *a.* 1. That may be descended or passed down; as, the hill is *descendible*.

2. That may descend from an ancestor to an heir; as, a *descendible* estate.

dē-scend′ing, *a.* 1. Moving downward; pertaining to descent; marked by downward motion.

2. In heraldry, a term used for a bird, lion, etc., the head of which is turned toward the base of the shield.

Descending.

Descending constellations or *signs*; those through which the planets pass in moving southward.

Descending series; in mathematics, a series in which each term is numerically less than that preceding it.

dē-scend′ing-ly, *adv.* In a descending manner.

dē-scen′sion, *n.* [L. *descensio*, a going down ward, descent, from *descendere*, to go down, descend.] The act of going downward; descent; a falling or sinking; declension; degradation.

Oblique descension; the arc of the equator which descends, with the sign or star, below the horizon of an oblique sphere. [Obs.]

Right descension; the arc of the equator which descends, with the sign or star, below the horizon of a right sphere. [Obs.]

dē-scen′sion-ăl, *a.* Pertaining to descension.

dē-scen′sive, *a.* Descending; tending downward; having power to descend.

dē-scen′sō-ry, *n.* [From L. *descendere*, to descend.] A distillation-vessel used in alchemy. [Obs.]

dē-scent′, *n.* [ME. *descent*; L. *descendere*, to descend.]

1. The act of descending; the act of passing from a higher to a lower place by any form of motion, as by walking, riding, rolling, sliding sinking, or falling.

2. Inclination downward; obliquity; slope; declivity.

3. A sinking or decline, as in station, virtue, quality, or the like; fall from a higher to a lower state or station.

> O foul *descent* . . . into a beast. —Milton.

4. Incursion; invasion, sudden attack.

> A *descent* upon their coasts. —Jortin.

5. In law, a passing from an ancestor to an heir; transmission by succession or inheritance; the hereditary succession of property vested in a person by the operation of law.

6. A proceeding from an original or progenitor; hence, extraction; lineage; pedigree.

> Smile at the claims of long *descent*. —Tennyson.

7. A generation. [Obs.]

8. Offspring; issue; descendants. [Obs.]

9. A rank; a step or degree. [Obs.]

10. Lowest place. [Obs.]

11. In music, a passing from one note or sound to another lower in the scale.

Syn.—Declivity, slope, gradient, fall, degradation, debasement, extraction, pedigree, generation, lineage, assault, invasion, incursion, attack.

dē-scrīb′ȧ-ble, *a.* That may be described; capable of description.

dē-scrībe′, *v.t.*; described, *pt., pp.*; describing, *ppr.* [ME. *descriven*; L. *describere*, to write down or from, to copy, to transcribe, to describe; *de*, from, and *scribere*, to write.]

1. To delineate or mark the form or figure of; to trace out; as, to *describe* a circle by the compasses.

2. To form or trace by motion; as, a star *describes* a circle or an ellipsis in the heavens.

3. To show or represent to others orally or by writing; to give an account of; to depict in words; as, the poet *describes* the Trojan horse; the geographer *describes* countries and cities.

4. To distribute into classes or divisions. [Obs.]

Syn.—Represent, delineate, relate, recount, narrate, express, explain, depict, portray.

dē-scrībe′, *v.i.* To give a clear and vivid exhibition in language; as, Milton *describes* with uncommon force and beauty.

dē-scrīb′ent, *n.* In geometry, the line or surface from the motion of which a surface or solid is supposed to be generated or described.

dē-scrīb′ẽr, *n.* One who describes.

dē-scrī′ẽr, *n.* One who descries.

dē-scrip′tion, *n.* [L. *descriptio*, a marking out, delineation.]

1. The act of delineating, or representing the figure of anything by a plan, to be presented to the eye.

2. The figure or appearance of anything delineated, or represented by visible lines, marks, colors, etc.; as, the *description* of a country.

3. The act of representing a thing by words or by signs, or the passage containing such representation; a representation of names, nature, or properties, that gives to another a view of the thing; as, a *description* of the Nile.

4. The qualities expressed in a representation; the combination of qualities which go to

constitute a class, genus, species, or **individual**; hence, class; species; variety; kind.

A friend of this *description*. —Shak.

Syn.—Account, statement, delineation, representation, sketch, cast, turn, kind, sort.

dē-scrip′tive, *a.* Containing description; tending to describe; having the quality of representing; as, a *descriptive* figure; a *descriptive* narration.

Descriptive anatomy; the study of the separate parts of the body aside from their relation to other parts.

Descriptive geometry; that branch of science in which the situation of points in space is represented by their orthographical projections, on two planes, at right angles to each other, called the planes of projection.

dē-scrip′tive-ly, *adv.* By description.

dē-scrip′tive-ness, *n.* The state of being descriptive.

dē-scrive′, *v.t.* To describe. [Obs.]

dē-scrȳ′, *v.t.*; descried, *pt.*, *pp.*; descrying, *ppr.* [ME. *descryen*, *descrien*; OFr. *descrier*, to proclaim; L. *de*, from, down, and *quiritare*, to cry, freq. of *queri*, to complain.]

1. To espy; to explore; to examine by observation. [Obs.]

The house of Joseph sent to *descry* Bethel. —Jud. i. 23.

2. To detect; to find out; to discover (anything concealed); as, to *descry* a distant foe.

3. To see; to behold; to have a sight of from a distance; as, the seamen *descried* land.

4. To give notice of (something suddenly discovered); to discover.

dē-scrȳ′, *n.* The thing descried, as an army seen at a distance. [Obs.]

des′ē-cāte, *v.t.* To cut off; to mow. [Obs.]

des′ē-crāte, *v.t.*; desecrated, *pt.*, *pp.*; desecrating, *ppr.* [From L. *de-* priv., and *sacrare*, to make sacred, to consecrate, from *sacer*, sacred.] To divest of sacredness; to profane by misapplication; to pervert from a sacred purpose; as, to *desecrate* a holy temple.

des′ē-crā-tēr, *n.* One who desecrates a desecrator.

des-ē-crā′tion, *n.* The act of desecrating or state of being desecrated; profanation; as, the *desecration* of the Sabbath.

des′ē-crā-tŏr, *n.* A desecrater.

dē-seg-men-tā′tion, *n.* The coalescence of anatomical parts, primarily separate, into one; the uniting of segments, as the growing together of the separate bones of an infant's skull.

dē-seg′ment-ed, *a.* Characterized by desegmentation; having the segments reduced in number.

des′ērt, *a.* Uninhabited; untilled; waste; uncultivated; pertaining to or having the appearance of a desert; as, a *desert* island; a *desert* land or country.

des′ērt, *n.* [ME. *desert*; OFr. *desert*, a desert, from L. *desertum*, a desert, neut. of *desertus*, deserted, solitary, waste, pp. of *deserere*, to desert, abandon; *de-* priv., and *serere*, to join, unite.] An uninhabited tract of land; a region in its natural state; a wilderness; a solitude; particularly, a vast sandy, stony, or rocky expanse, almost destitute of moisture and vegetation; as, the *deserts* of Arabia and Africa.

dē-ṣērt′, *n.* [ME. *deserte*; OFr. *deserte*, merit, recompense, from *deservir*, to deserve; L. *de-*, intens., and *servire*, to serve.]

1. A deserving; that which gives a right to reward or demands, or which renders liable to punishment; merit or demerit; good conferred, or evil done, which merits an equivalent return; as, to receive one's just *deserts*.

2. That which is deserved; reward or punishment merited.

Render to them their *desert*.—Ps. xxviii. 4.

Syn.—Merit, worth, excellence, due.

dē-ṣērt′, *v.t.*; deserted, *pt.*, *pp.*; deserting, *ppr.* [L. *deserere*, to desert, abandon.]

1. To forsake; to leave utterly; to abandon; to quit with a view not to return to; as, to *desert* a friend; to *desert* a cause.

2. To leave, without permission; to forsake (the service in which one is engaged), in violation of duty; as, to *desert* the army; to *desert* one's colors; to *desert* a ship.

Syn.—Abandon, abdicate, forsake, leave, quit.

dē-ṣērt′, *v.i.* To run away; to quit a service without permission; as, to *desert* from the army.

dē-ṣērt′ēr, *n.* [Fr. *deserteur*; L. *desertor*, a deserter, from *desertus*, pp. of *deserere*, to desert.] A person who forsakes his cause, his post, or his party or friend; particularly, a soldier or seaman who quits the service without permission, and in violation of his engagement.

dē-ṣērt′fụl, *a.* High in desert; meritorious. [Rare.]

deṣ′ērt-hāre, *n.* A cottontail, *Lepus sylvaticus*, variety *arizonæ*, which inhabits arid portions of Arizona and New Mexico.

dē-ṣēr′tion, *n.* [LL. *desertio*, desertion, from L. *desertus*, pp. of *deserere*, to desert.]

1. The act of forsaking or abandoning, as a party, a friend, the military or naval service, or the like; the act of illegally quitting with an intention not to return.

2. The state of being forsaken by God; spiritual despondency. [Obs.]

3. Desolation; abandonment. [Rare.]

dē-ṣērt′less, *a.* Without merit or claim to favor or reward. [Rare.]

dē-ṣērt′less-ly, *adv.* Undeservedly.

deṣ′ērt-lynx, *n.* The caracal.

deṣ′ērt-mouse, *n.* A variety of American field-mouse.

dē-ṣērt′rice, **dē-ṣērt′rix**, *n.* A female who deserts. [Rare.]

dē-ṣērve′, *v.t.*; deserved, *pt.*, *pp.*; deserving, *ppr.* [ME. *deserven*; OFr. *deservir*, to deserve; from L. *deservire*, to serve diligently; *de-*, intens., and *servire*, to serve.]

1. To be worthy of (either good or ill); to merit; to earn; as, such conduct *deserves* reward; to *deserve* punishment.

2. To benefit by service. [Obs.]

dē-ṣērve′, *v.i.* To merit; to be worthy or deserving; as, he *deserves* well or ill of his neighbor.

dē-ṣērv′ed-ly, *adv.* Justly; according to desert, whether of good or evil.

dē-ṣērv′ed-ness, *n.* The quality of being deserving; meritoriousness.

dē-ṣērv′ēr, *n.* One who deserves.

dē-ṣērv′ing, *a.* and *n.* I. *a.* Worthy of reward or praise; meritorious.

II. *n.* The act of meriting; desert; merit.

dē-ṣērv′ing-ly, *adv.* Meritoriously; with just desert.

des-hȧ-bille′ (des-ȧ-bil′), *n.* See *Dishabille*.

dē-sic′cănt, *a.* and *n.* I. *a.* Tending to dry or desiccate.

II. *n.* A medicine or application that dries a sore.

des′ic-cāte, *v.t.*; desiccated, *pt.*, *pp.*; desiccating, *ppr.* [L. *desiccatus*, pp. of *desiccare*, to dry up completely, to drain; *de-*, intens., and *siccare*, to dry, from *siccus*, dry.] To dry; to exhaust of moisture; especially, to rid of moisture for the purpose of preserving; as, to *desiccate* pork.

des′ic-cāte, *v.i.* To become dry.

des-ic-cā′tion, *n.* The act or process of desiccating, or the condition of being desiccated.

dē-sic′că-tive, *a.* and *n.* I. *a.* Drying; tending to dry.

II. *n.* An application which tends to dry up secretions.

des′ic-cā-tŏr, *n.* 1. One who or that which desiccates or dries.

2. In chemistry, a vessel of glass or earthenware provided with an air-tight cover, in which are contained some chemical absorbent and the substance to be desiccated.

dē-sic′că-tō-ry, *a.* Desiccative.

dē-sid′ēr-ȧ-ble, *a.* Desirable. [Rare.]

dē-sid-e-rā′tȧ, *n.*, pl. of *desideratum*.

dē-sid′ēr-āte, *v.t.*; desiderated, *pt.*, *pp.*; desiderating, *ppr.* [L. *desideratus*, pp. of *desiderare*, to desire.] To want; to feel the need for; to miss; to desire.

Please to insert a *desiderated* stanza. —Wilson.

dē-sid-ēr-ā′tion, *n.* 1. The act of desiderating. [Rare.]

2. The thing desiderated. [Rare.]

dē-sid′ēr-ȧ-tive, *a.* Denoting desire; as, *desiderative* verbs.

dē-sid′ēr-ȧ-tive, *n.* 1. That which is desired.

2. In grammar, a verb formed from another verb, and expressing a desire of doing the action implied in the primitive verb.

dē-sid-e-rā′tum, *n.*; *pl.* **dē-sid-e-rā′tȧ.** [L., from neut. of *desideratus*, pp. of *desiderare*, to desire.] That which is desired; that which is not possessed, but which is desirable.

dē-sid′i-ōse, **dē-sid′i-ous**, *a.* Idle; lazy. [Obs.]

dē-sid′i-ous-ness, *n.* Laziness; indolence. [Obs.]

dē-sight′ (-sīt′), *n.* An unsightly object. [Obs.]

dē-sight′ment, *n.* The act of making unsightly; disfigurement. [Rare.]

dē-ṣign′ (-zīn′ *or* -sīn′), *v.t.*; designed, *pt.*, *pp.*; designing, *ppr.* [OFr. *designer*; L. *designare*, to mark out, to define; *de*, out, from, and *signare*, to mark, from *signum*, a mark, sign.]

1. To plan and delineate by drawing the outline or figure of; to sketch, as in painting and other works of art, as for a pattern or model.

2. To contrive for a purpose; to project with an end in view; to form in idea, as a scheme.

Ask of politicians the end for which laws were originally *designed*. —Burke.

3. To devote to mentally; to set apart in intention; to intend.

One of those places was *designed* by the old man to his son. —Clarendon.

4. To purpose; to intend; as, a man *designs* to write an essay, or to study law.

5. To decide upon and outline the main features of; to plan.

The Roman bridges were *designed* on the same grand scale as their aqueducts. —Fergusson.

6. To mark out by tokens; to indicate; to appoint. [Rare.]

Syn.—Intend, plan, propose, purpose, sketch.

dē-ṣign′, *v.i.* 1. To form plans.

2. To make designs, as an artist, draftsman, or inventor.

dē-ṣign′, *n.* 1. A plan or representation of a thing by an outline; sketch; first idea represented by visible lines, as in painting or architecture; a delineation.

2. A scheme or plan in the mind; purpose; intention; aim; in a bad sense, an evil plan or scheme; plot.

3. The realization of an artistic idea; especially, the emblematic or decorative figuring upon embroidery, medals, fabrics, and the like; as, this carpet is of a fine *design*.

4. Contrivance; the adaptation of means to a preconceived end; as, the evidence of *design* in a watch.

5. In music, the invention and conduct of the subject; the disposition of every part and the general order of the whole.

6. The reason for the existence of something; the purpose for which anything is done.

Arts of design; arts that call into action the inventive and constructive faculties, as architecture, sculpture, engraving, and the like.

School of design; an institution in which persons are instructed in the arts and in the principles of design, especially for manufacturing purposes, and with the view of diffusing a knowledge of and a taste for the fine arts among the people generally.

Syn.—Intention, purpose, aim, plan, scheme. —*Design* has reference to something aimed at; *intention* to the feelings or desires with which it is sought; *purpose* to a settled choice or determination for its attainment.

des′ig-nȧ-ble, *a.* Capable of being designed or marked out; distinguishable.

des′ig-nāte, *a.* Appointed; marked out. [Rare.]

des′ig-nāte, *v.t.*; designated, *pt.*, *pp.*; designating, *ppr.* [L. *designatus*, pp. of *designare*, to mark out, define.]

1. To mark out or show, so as to make known; to indicate by visible lines, marks, description, or something known and determinate; as, to *designate* the limits of a country; to *designate* the place where the troops landed.

2. To point out; to name; to distinguish from others by indication; as, to be able to *designate* every individual who was concerned in a riot.

3. To appoint; to select or distinguish for a particular purpose; to assign; with *for* or *to*; as, to *designate* an officer *for* the command of a station; this captain was *designated to* that station.

Syn.—Name, appoint, indicate, specify, characterize, denominate.

des-ig-nā′tion, *n.* 1. The act of pointing or marking out by signs or objects; a distinguishing from others; indication; as, the *designation* of an estate by boundaries.

2. Appointment; a selecting; assignment; as, the *designation* of an officer to a particular command.

3. That which designates; a distinctive appellation; specifically, an addition to a name, as of a title, trade, occupation or profession, to distinguish the person from others.

4. Import; distinct application, as of a word.

5. In Scots law, the setting apart of manses and glebes for the clergy from the church lands of the parish by the presbytery of the bounds.

des′ig-nā-tive, *a.* Serving to designate or indicate.

des′ig-nā-tŏr, *n.* 1. One who designates or points out.

2. In Roman antiquity, an officer who assigned to each person his rank and place in public shows and ceremonies.

des′ig-nȧ-tō-ry, *a.* Designative. [Rare.]

dē-ṣign′ed-ly, *adv.* By design; purposely; intentionally; opposed to *accidentally*, *ignorantly*, or *inadvertently*.

dē-ṣign′ēr, *n.* 1. One who designs, marks out, or plans; one who frames a scheme or project; a contriver; in a bad sense, a plotter.

2. In manufacturing and the fine arts, one who conceives or forms a design; one who designs figures and patterns for ornamental or artistic purposes.

dē-ṣign′fụl, *a.* Full of design; designing. [Rare.]

dē-ṣign′fụl-ness, *n.* The state or quality of being designful or given to artifice. [Rare.]

dē-ṣign′ing, *n.* The art of making sketches or patterns; the act of scheming.

dē-ṣign′ing, *a.* Artful; intriguing; insidious.

dē-ṣign′less, *a.* Without design. [Obs.]

dē′ṣign′less-ly, *adv.* Without design; inadvertently. [Obs.]

dē-ṣign′ment, *n.* 1. Design; sketch; delineation. [Obs.]

2. Design; purpose; aim. [Obs.]

dē-sil′i-cā-ted, *a.* Freed of silica.

dē-sil″i-ci-dā′tion, *n.* The act or process of removing silicon or siliceous matter from a substance.

dē-si-lic″i-fi-cā′tion, *n.* Desilicidation.

dē-si-lic′i-fȳ, *v.t.* To desiliconize.

dē-sil′i-cŏn-ize, *v.t.* To deprive of silicon.

dē-sil′vẽr, *v.t.* To free from silver, as lead.

dē-sil″vẽr-i-zā′tion, *n.* The act or process of depriving lead of the silver present in its ore.

dē-sil′vẽr-ize, *v.t.* To free from silver, as lead.

des′i-nence, *n.* [L. *desinens*, ppr. of *desinere*, to leave off, cease; *de*, off, from, and *sinere*, to leave.] Ending; close; specifically, in grammar, a formative suffix.

des′i-nent, *a.* Ending; extreme; lowermost. [Obs.]

des-i-nen′tiăl (-shăl), *a.* Desinent. [Obs.]

dē-sip′i-ence, *n.* Trifling; foolishness. [Rare.]

dē-sip′i-ent, *a.* [L. *desipiens* (*-ntis*), ppr. of *desipere*, to lack sense; *de-* priv., and *sapere*, to be wise.] Trifling; foolish. [Rare.]

dē-ṣīr-ȧ-bil′i-ty, *n.* The state or quality of being desirable; desirableness.

dē-ṣīr′ȧ-ble, *a.* [ME. *desirable*; L. *desiderabilis*, worthy of desire, from *desiderare*, to desire.] Worthy of desire; that is to be wished for; calculated or fitted to excite a wish to possess.

dē-ṣīr′ȧ-ble-ness, *n.* The quality of being desirable.

dē-ṣīr′ȧ-bly, *adv.* In a desirable manner.

dē-ṣīre′, *v.t.*; desired, *pt.*, *pp.*; desiring, *ppr.* [L. *desiderare*, to long for, to desire.]

1. To wish for the possession and enjoyment of, with earnestness; to long for; to covet; as, to *desire* wealth.

> Ye *desire* your child to live. —Tennyson.

2. To express a wish to obtain; to ask; to request.

3. To require; to claim. [Obs.]

4. To regret; to miss. [Obs.]

Syn.—Request, wish, covet, solicit, want, long for.—To *desire* is to feel a wish or want; to *request* is to ask for its gratification. A man *desires* food, and *requests* to have it prepared. *Desire* may be used for *request* when the relations of the parties are such that the expression of a *wish* is all that is felt to be necessary. A man *desires* his friend to write often; a merchant *desires* his clerk to be more careful in future. In this latter case, *desire* is stronger than *request*; it implies a command or injunction.

dē-ṣīre′, *n.* [ME. *desire*; L. *desiderium*, desire, longing, appetite, from *desiderare*, to desire.]

1. An emotion directed to the attainment or possession of an object from which pleasure, sensual, intellectual, or spiritual, is expected; a passion excited by the love of an object, or uneasiness at the want of it, and directed to its attainment or possession.

> By this time the Pilgrims had a *desire* to go forward. —Bunyan.

2. A request; a petition; as, a *desire* for aid.

3. That which is desired; an object of longing.

> The *desire* of all nations shall come. —Hag. ii. 7.

4. Appetite; lust.

> Fulfilling the *desires* of the flesh.—Eph. ii. 3.

Syn.—Wish, longing, appetency, hankering, inclination, craving, eagerness.

dē-ṣīre′fụl, *a.* Full of desire. [Rare.]

dē-ṣīre′fụl-ness, *n.* The state of being desireful. [Rare.]

dē-ṣīre′less, *a.* Free from desire.

dē-ṣīr′ẽr, *n.* One who desires or asks; one who wishes.

dē-ṣīr′ous, *a.* Wishing for; wishing to obtain; covetous; solicitous.

dē-ṣīr′ous-ly, *adv.* With earnest desire; longingly.

dē-ṣīr′ous-ness, *n.* The state of being desirous.

dē-sist′ (*or* -zist′), *v.i.*; desisted, *pt.*, *pp.*; desisting, *ppr.* [L. *desistere*, to leave off, to cease; *de*, from, and *sistere*, to set, put, stand.] To stop; to cease to act or proceed; to forbear; frequently with *from*; as, he *desisted from* his purpose.

> Ceres, however, *desisted* not. —Bacon.

Syn.—Cease, stop, discontinue, forbear, abstain.

dē-sist′ănce, dē-sist′ence (*or* -zist′), *n.* A ceasing to act or proceed; a stopping.

dē-sist′ive, *a.* Final; conclusive. [Rare.]

de-si′tion (-sish′un), *n.* End; conclusion. [Obs.]

des′i-tive, *a.* and *n.* I. *a.* Final; conclusive. [Obs.]

II. *n.* In logic, a proposition which relates to a conclusion. [Obs.]

desk, *n.* [ME. *deske*, a desk; L. *discus*; Gr. *diskos*, a round plate, a quoit, anything round like a quoit; hence, a table.] A table, often having a sloping top, for the use of writers and readers; usually made with a box or drawer underneath, and sometimes with a bookcase above; also, a frame or case to be placed on a table for writing purposes. The name is sometimes extended to the whole structure or erection to which such a sloping table is attached, as, in the Church of England, to the raised seat from which the morning and evening service is read, in Scotch churches to the seat of the precentor, and in the United States to the pulpit in a church.

Cylinder or *roll-top desk*; one with a rounded, flexible cover, which can be rolled up and down according as it is necessary to open or close the desk.

desk, *v.t.* To inclose, as in a desk; to treasure. [Rare.]

desk′wŏrk, *n.* Work done at a desk, as by a literary man, bookkeeper, etc.

des′mȧ, *n.*; *pl.* **des′mȧ-tȧ.** [L., from Gr. *desma*, a band, from *dein*, to bind.] In spongology, a spicule with irregular branches.

des′mȧ-ēhȳme, *n.* [Gr. *desma*, a band, and *chymos*, juice.] The connective tissue of sponges.

des′mȧ-cȳte, *n.* [Gr. *desma*, a band, and *kytos*, a hollow.] In spongology, a cell of connective tissue.

des′măn, *n.* [Sw. *desman*, musk.] In zoölogy, an aquatic, insectivorous mammal, found in the southeast of Russia. Another species is found in southwestern Europe.

des′mid, des-mid′i-ăn, *n.* In botany, any one of the plants of the order *Desmidiaceæ*.

Des-mid-i-ā′cē-æ, Des-mid-ī′ē-æ, *n.pl.* [L., from Gr. *desmos*, a band, fetter, from *dein*, to bind.] A natural order of microscopic, unicellular, fresh-water algæ of the class *Conjugatæ*.

des-mid-i-ā′ceous, *a.* Of or pertaining to the order *Desmidiaceæ*.

des′mine, *n.* [Gr. *desmos*, a band, *desmē*, a bundle.] A zeolitic mineral crystallizing in the monoclinic system; stilbite.

des-mī′tis, *n.* [L., from Gr. *desmos*, a band.] In pathology, inflammation of a ligament.

des-mō-. A combining form from Gr. *desmos*, a band, fetter, bond, from *dein*, to bind; signifying a bond, band, ligament.

Des″mō-bac-tē′ri-ȧ, *n.pl.* [L., from Gr. *desmos*, a band, and *bakterion*, a staff.] Same as *Microbacteria*.

Des-mob′ry-ȧ, *n.pl.* [L., from Gr. *desmos*, a band, and *bryon*, moss, lichen.] In botany, ferns in which the fronds are produced from the apex of the caudex, and are adherent to it.

Des-mō′di-um, *n.* [L., from Gr. *desmos*, a band, and *eidos*, form.] A genus of plants, herbs, or shrubs, of the bean family, with leaves of three or five leaflets, or sometimes reduced to a single leaflet. The small flowers are in terminal or lateral racemes, and the pods are flat and jointed. The best known species is *Desmodium gyrans*, remarkable for the peculiar rotatory movements of its leaflets.

Semaphore Plant (*Desmodium gyrans*).

des′mō-dont, *a.* 1. Pertaining to the *Desmodonta*.

2. Pertaining to the *Desmodontes*.

des′mō-dont, *n.* 1. One of the *Desmodonta*.

2. One of the *Desmodontes*.

Des-mō-don′tȧ, *n.pl.* [L., from Gr. *desmos*, a band, and *odous* (*-ontos*), a tooth.] An order of bivalve mollusks having irregular hinge-teeth connected by a ligament.

Des-mō-don′tēs, *n.pl.* In zoölogy, a group of blood-sucking bats found in Central and South America, typified by the genera *Desmodus* and *Diphylla*.

des-mog′nȧ-thiṣm, *n.* [L., from Gr. *desmos*, a band, and *gnathos*, a jaw.] In ornithology, the union of the maxillo-palatine bones, as exhibited by ducks, hawks, herons, and other birds.

des-mog′nȧ-thous, *a.* Pertaining to or exhibiting desmognathism.

des-mog′rȧ-phy, *n.* [*Desmo-*, and Gr. *-graphia*, from *graphein*, to write.] In anatomy, a description of the ligaments.

des′moid, *a.* [Gr. *desmos*, a band, ligament, and *eidos*, form, appearance.] In anatomy, having the appearance or characteristics of a ligament; ligamentous; tendinous; also, fibrous.

des-mol′ō-ġy, *n.* [*Desmo-*, and Gr. *logos*, a description.] That branch of anatomy which treats of the ligaments.

Des″mō-mȳ-ā′ri-ȧ, *n.pl.* [*Desmo-*, and Gr. *mys*, *myos*, muscle, and *-aria*.] A group of tunicates, including the salps.

des-mop′ȧ-thy, *n.* [*Desmo-*, and Gr. *pathos*, suffering.] In pathology, any disease of the ligaments.

des-mō-pel′mous, *a.* [*Desmo-*, and Gr. *pelma*, the sole of the foot.] In ornithology, having the plantar tendons connected by a band, rendering the hind toe incapable of being bent independently.

des′ō-lāte, *a.* 1. Destitute or deprived of inhabitants; deserted; uninhabited; hence, dreary; as, a *desolate* wilderness.

2. Laid waste; in a ruinous condition; neglected; destroyed; as, *desolate* altars; *desolate* towers.

3. Solitary; forsaken; lonely.

> Have mercy upon me, for I am *desolate*. —Ps. xxv. 16.

4. Shameless; dissolute. [Obs.]

5. Destitute. [Obs.]

Syn.—Deserted, lonely, dreary, waste, abandoned, uninhabited.

des′ō-lāte, *v.t.*; desolated, *pt.*, *pp.*; desolating, *ppr.* [ME. *desolaten*; L. *desolatus*, pp. of *desolare*, to leave alone, to forsake, to strip of inhabitants; *de-*, intens., and *solare*, to make lonely, or desolate, from *solus*, alone.]

1. To deprive of inhabitants; to make desert; as, the earth was nearly *desolated* by the flood.

2. To lay waste; to ruin; to ravage; as, an inundation *desolates* fields.

des′ō-lāte-ly, *adv.* In a desolate manner.

des′ō-lāte-ness, *n.* The state of being desolate.

des′ō-lā-tẽr, *n.* See *Desolator*.

des-ō-lā′tion, *n.* 1. The act of desolating; destruction or expulsion of inhabitants; devastation.

2. A place deprived of inhabitants, or otherwise wasted, ravaged, and forsaken.

3. A desolate state; gloominess; destitution; ruin.

Syn.—Devastation, havoc, ruin, destitution, gloom, waste.

des′ō-lā-tŏr, *n.* One who or that which desolates.

des′ō-lȧ-tō-ry, *a.* Causing desolation. [Rare.]

dē-sō-phis′ti-cāte, *v.t.* To clear from sophism or error.

des-ox′ȧ-lāte, *n.* In chemistry, a salt of desoxalic acid.

des-ox-al′iç, *a.* Pertaining to or obtained from oxalic acid.

de-spāir′, *n.* 1. Hopelessness; a hopeless state; a lack of hope or expectation.

2. That which is despaired of; that of which there is no hope.

> The mere *despair* of surgery he cures.—Shak.

Syn.—Desperation, despondency, hopelessness, discouragement.

de-spāir′, *v.i.*; despaired, *pt.*, *pp.*; despairing, *ppr.* [L. *desperare*, to be without hope; *de-* priv., and *sperare*, to hope, from *spes*, hope.] To be without hope; to give up all hope or expectation; often followed by *of*; as, to *despair of* life.

de-spāir′, *v.t.* 1. To give up hope of; to lose confidence in. [Obs.]

2. To cause to despair; to deprive of hope. [Obs.]

de-spāir′ẽr, *n.* One without hope.

de-spāir′fụl, *a.* Hopeless. [Obs.]

de-spāir′ing, *a.* Given to despair; indicating despair.

de-spāir′ing-ly, *adv.* In a despairing manner.

de-spāir′ing-ness, *n.* The state of being despairing.

de-spär′ple, *v.t.* and *v.i.* To scatter. [Obs.]

des-patch′, dis-patch′, *n.* [OFr. *despeche*, haste, riddance, despatch, from *despechier*, to rid, discharge, hasten, despatch.]

1. The act of despatching; a sending or forwarding with promptness and speed; as, the *despatch* of a message or messenger.

2. Speedy execution, as of business; prompt performance; expedition; as, the affair was handled with *despatch*.

3. A communication sent with expedition, as by telegraph; especially, information or instructions sent from one official to another; as, a *despatch* was sent to the admiral.

4. A sending away; a getting rid of or doing away with something; dismissal.

Syn.—Celerity, promptness, speed, haste, expedition.

des-patch′, dis-patch′, *v.t.*; despatched (-pacht), *pt.*, *pp.*; despatching, *ppr.* [OFr. *despechier*, to rid, discharge, hasten, despatch, prob. from L. *dis-* priv., and *pedica*, a snare, trap, fetter, from *pes* (*-dis*), foot.]

1. To execute or transact with promptness, as business; to perform; to accomplish.

> The Three First Books I have already *dispatched*. —Addison.

2. To send off to an appointed place; usually with the implication of promptness or haste; as, to *despatch* a messenger; to *despatch* orders to the general.

3. To send out of the world; to put to death.

The company shall stone them with stones, and *dispatch* them with their swords. —Ezek. xxiii. 47.

4. To free; to rid. [Obs.]

des-patch′, dis-patch′, *v.i.* To make haste; to dispose of a matter; to finish.

Syn.—Accelerate, expedite, conclude, perform, send, kill, slay.

des-patch′-bōat, *n.* A swift vessel for carrying despatches.

des-patch′-box, *n.* A box in which official messages are forwarded.

des-patch′ẽr, dis-patch′ẽr, *n.* One who despatches.

des-patch′fụl, dis-patch′fụl, *a.* Bent on haste; indicating haste; intent on speedy execution of business; as, *despatchful* looks.

dē-spē-cif′i-çāte, *v.t.* [*De-*, intens., and L. *species*, kind, and *facere*, to make.] To alter the specific meaning of; to desynonymize. [Rare.]

dē-spec″i-fi-çā′tion, *n.* Differentiation; discrimination.

dē-spect′, *n.* [L. *despectus*, a looking down upon, properly, pp. of *despicere*, to look down upon.] Despection; contempt. [Rare.]

dē-spec′tion, *n.* A looking down; a despising. [Rare.]

dē-speed′, *v.t.* To send in haste. [Obs.]

dē-spend′, *v.t.* Same as *Dispend*.

des-pẽr-ā′dō, *n.*; *pl.* **des-pẽr-ā′dōs** or **des-pẽr-ā′dōes.** [OSp. *desperado*, from L. *desperatus*, given up, despaired of, desperate.] A desperate, lawless fellow; a furious man; a person urged by furious passions; one having no regard for life.

des′pẽr-āte, *a.* [L. *desperatus*, pp. of *desperare*, to be without hope, to despair of.]

1. Without hope; hopeless. [Obs.]

2. Without regard to danger or safety; extremely reckless; as, a *desperate* man.

3. Done or applied without regard to consequences, or in the last extreme; proceeding from despair; rash; reckless; as, a *desperate* effort.

4. Despaired of; beyond hope of recovery; irretrievable; hopeless; as, *desperate* fortunes; *desperate* conditions.

5. Great in the extreme; hopelessly bad; as, a *desperate* reprobate.

Syn. — Despairing, rash, reckless, furious, hopeless, irretrievable.

des′pẽr-āte, *n.* One who is desperate. [Obs.]

des′pẽr-āte-ly, *adv.* In a desperate manner; furiously; without regard to danger or safety; as, the troops fought *desperately*.

des′pẽr-āte-ness, *n.* Madness; fury; rash precipitance.

des-pẽr-ā′tion, *n.* [L. *desperatio*, hopelessness, despair, from *desperare*, to give up hope, to despair.]

1. A despairing; a giving up of hope.

2. Fury; disregard of safety or danger; the state of being desperate; as, the men fought with *desperation*.

des″pi-çạ-bil′i-ty, *n.* Despicableness. [Rare.]

des′pi-çạ-ble, *a.* [LL. *despicabilis*, contemptible, from L. *despicere*, to despise.] That may be or deserves to be despised; contemptible; mean; vile; worthless; as, a *despicable* man; *despicable* company; a *despicable* gift.

Syn.—Mean, contemptible, pitiful, worthless, base.

des′pi-çạ-ble-ness, *n.* The quality or state of being despicable; meanness; vileness; worthlessness.

des′pi-çạ-bly, *adv.* Meanly; vilely; contemptibly.

des-pi′cience, des-pi′cien-cy (-pish′ence, -en-cy), *n.* [L. *despicio*.] A looking down; a despising. [Obs.]

dē-spīş′ạ-ble, *a.* Despicable; contemptible. [Rare.]

dē-spīş′ạl, *n.* Contempt. [Rare.]

dē-spīşe′, *v.t.*; despised, *pt.*, *pp.*; despising, *ppr.* [ME. *despisen*; OFr. *despiser*, to despise, from L. *despicere*, to look down upon, to despise; *de*, down, from, and *specere*, to look at, behold.] To contemn; to scorn; to disdain; to have a low opinion of; to regard as contemptible.

Syn.—Scorn, disdain, contemn, spurn.

dē-spīş′ed-ness, *n.* The state of being despised.

dē-spīş′ẽr, *n.* One who despises; a scorner.

dē-spīş′ing-ly, *adv.* With contempt.

dē-spīte′, *n.* [ME. *despite*; OFr. *despit*; L. *despectus*, a looking down upon, a despising, contempt, from *despicere*, to look down upon, to despise; *de*, down, from, and *specere*, to look.]

1. Extreme malice; violent hatred; malignity; spite.

2. Defiance, with contempt of opposition; contemptuous defiance.

dē-spīte′, *v.t.* To vex; to offend. [Obs.]

dē-spīte′, *prep.* Against; notwithstanding; as, *despite* his intentions.

dē-spīte′fụl, *a.* Full of spite; malicious; malignant; as, a *despiteful* enemy.

dē-spīte′fụl-ly, *adv.* With despite; maliciously.

dē-spīte′fụl-ness, *n.* Malice; hatred; malignity.

des-pit′ē-ous, dis-pit′ē-ous, *a.* Malicious. [Obs.]

des-pit′ē-ous-ly, *adv.* Despitefully. [Obs.]

dē-spīt′ous, di-spīt′ous, *a.* Despiteous. [Obs.]

dē-spīt′ous-ly, di-spīt′ous-ly, *adv.* Despiteously. [Obs.]

dē-spoil′, *v.t.*; despoiled, *pt.*, *pp.*; despoiling, *ppr.* [ME. *despoilen*; OFr. *despoiller*; L. *despoliare*, to plunder, rob; *de-*, intens., and *spoliare*, to strip, rob, plunder.]

1. To strip; to rob; to plunder; to pillage; often followed by *of*.

Despoiled of innocence, *of* faith, *of* bliss. —Milton.

2. To divest, as of clothing; to strip. [Obs.]

Syn.—Deprive, plunder, pillage, rifle, strip, rob.

dē-spoil′, *n.* Spoil. [Obs.]

dē-spoil′ẽr, *n.* One who strips by force; a plunderer.

dē-spoil′ment, *n.* The act of despoiling; despoliation.

dē-spō-li-ā′tion, *n.* The act of despoiling; a stripping.

dē-spond′, *v.i.*; desponded, *pt.*, *pp.*; desponding, *ppr.* [L. *despondere*, to promise, to pledge, (with or without *animum*, mind, courage), to lose courage, to despair; *de-* priv., and *spondere*, to promise.] To be cast down; to be depressed or dejected in mind; to lose all courage.

Others depress their own minds, and *despond* at the first difficulty. —Locke.

dē-spond′, *n.* Despondency. [Obs.]

dē-spond′ence, *n.* Despondency.

dē-spond′en-cy, *n.* Dejection or depression of spirits; loss of hope.

Let not disappointment cause *despondency*. —Sir T. Browne.

dē-spond′ent, *a.* Losing courage; depressed; disheartened; low-spirited.

dē-spond′ent-ly, *adv.* In a despondent manner.

dē-spond′ẽr, *n.* One who desponds.

dē-spond′ing-ly, *adv.* In a desponding manner; with dejection of spirits.

dē-spon′sāge, *n.* Betrothal. [Obs.]

dē-spon′sāte, *v.t.* To betroth. [Obs.]

des-pon-sā′tion, *n.* A betrothing. [Obs.]

dē-spon′sō-ry, *n.* A written promise of marriage. [Obs.]

des′pot, *n.* [OFr. *despot*; LL. *despotus*; Gr. *despotēs*, a master, lord.] A sovereign or ruler invested with absolute authority, who rules without any restrictions from constitution or laws; hence, a tyrant; an oppressor.

Syn.—Tyrant, autocrat, master, oppressor, dictator.

des′pō-tat, *n.* Government by a despot; the territory governed by a despot. [Rare.]

des-pot′iç, des-pot′iç-ạl, *a.* [From Gr. *despotikos*, of a master, despotic, from *despotēs*, a lord or master.] Absolute in power; unrestrained; arbitrary; tyrannical; characteristic of despotism or a despot; as, a *despotic* sovereign; *despotic* power.

des-pot′iç-ạl-ly, *adv.* With unlimited power; arbitrarily; in a despotic manner.

des-pot′iç-ạl-ness, *n.* Absolute or arbitrary authority.

des-pot′i-çon, *n.* [Gr. *despoticon*, supply *sōma*, body, the body of the Lord.] The most important of the nine parts in the ritual of the Coptic church, into which the host is separated.

des′pō-tişm, *n.* 1. Absolute power; authority unlimited and uncontrolled by constitution or laws, and depending alone on the will of the ruler.

2. An arbitrary government; the rule of a despot; absolutism; autocracy.

3. Figuratively, absolute power or influence of any kind.

Such is the *despotism* of the imagination over uncultivated minds. —Macaulay.

des′pō-tist, *n.* One who upholds or advocates despotism. [Rare.]

des′pō-tize, *v.i.* To be a despot; to act despotically.

des′pū-māte (*or* **dē-spū′**), *v.t.* and *v.i.*; despumated, *pt.*, *pp.*; despumating, *ppr.* [L. *despumatus*, pp. of *despumare*, to skim off; *de*, off, from, and *spumare*, to foam, from *spuma*, foam.] To throw off in foam; to throw off impurities; to froth; to form froth or scum.

des-pū-mā′tion, *n.* The act of despumating; clarification; scumming.

des′quạ-māte (-kwā-), *v.i.*; desquamated, *pt.*, *pp.*; desquamating, *ppr.* [L. *desquamatus*, pp. of *desquamare*, to scale off; *de*, off, *squama*, a scale.] To scale off; to peel off; to exfoliate.

des-quā-mā′tion, *n.* In medicine, the shedding of the superficial epithelium, as of the skin, mucous membranes, and renal tubules.

dē-squam′ạ-tive, *a.* Characterized by desquamation.

dē-squam′ạ-tō-ry, *a.* Desquamative.

dē-squam′ạ-tō-ry, *n.* In surgery, a kind of trepan formerly used for removing the laminæ of exfoliated bones.

dess, *v.t.* [Eng. dial. and Scot., from *dass*; Ice. *des*, a heap, mound.]

1. To place together closely; to pile.

2. To cut out, as a portion of hay or straw from a stack.

dess, *n.* [Prov. Eng. and Scot.]

1. That part of a pile of hay or of a stack of sheaf-grain remaining after a portion has been removed.

2. A portion of hay cut from a stack for use.

desse, *n.* A dais. [Obs.]

deş-şẽrt′, *n.* [Fr., from OFr. *dessert*, dessert, from *desservir*, to clear the table; *des*, *de*, away, from, and *servir*, to serve; L. *de*, from, and *servire*, to serve.] A service of fruits and sweetmeats, at the close of an entertainment or repast; the last course at the table.

deş-şẽrt′-şẽrv″ice, *n.* The dishes used in serving dessert.

deş-şẽrt′-spoọn, *n.* A spoon intermediate in size between a tablespoon and a teaspoon.

des′siá-tine, des′syá-tine, *n.* [Russ. *desiatina*, a tenth.] A land measure in Russia, equal to 2.7 English acres.

des-tem′pẽr, *n.* See *Distemper*.

des′tin, *n.* Destiny. [Obs.]

des′ti-nạ-ble, *a.* Capable of being destined or determined.

des′ti-nạ-bly, *adv.* In a destinable manner.

des′ti-nạl, *a.* Pertaining to destiny; determined by destiny; fated. [Obs.]

des′ti-nāte, *v.t.* To design or appoint. [Obs.]

des′ti-nāte, *a.* Appointed; destined. [Obs.]

des-ti-nā′tion, *n.* [L. *destinatio*, a settlement, appointment, from *destinare*, to fasten down, to secure, to determine, destine; from *de-*, intens., and *stare*, to stand.]

1. The act of destining or appointing.

2. The purpose for which anything is intended or appointed; end or ultimate design; as, every animal is fitted for its *destination*.

3. The place to which a thing is appointed; the predetermined end of a journey or voyage; as, the ship reached her *destination*.

4. In Scots law, (a) the series of heirs called to the succession of heritable or movable property, by the provision of the law or title or by the will of the proprietor; (b) a nomination of successors in a certain order, regulated by the will of the proprietor.

Syn.—Goal, end, appointment, destiny, fate, design, intention, purpose, lot.

des′tine, *v.t.*; destined, *pt.*, *pp.*; destining, *ppr.* [ME. *destenen*; L. *destinare*, to fasten down, to secure, determine.]

1. To set, ordain, or appoint to a use, purpose, state, or place; as, he was *destined* for the ministry.

2. To fix unalterably, as by a divine decree; to doom; to devote; to appoint unalterably.

Syn.—Bound.—We may speak of goods as *destined* to a certain port, and of a ship as *bound* thither. We may also speak of a city as *destined* to become a great commercial emporium; but to say it is *bound* to become so, or that a man is *bound* to succeed in life, is a gross abuse of language. *Bound* always implies some obligation or engagement.

des′ti-nişm, *n.* Fatalism. [Rare.]

des′ti-nist, *n.* A believer in destiny. [Rare.]

des′ti-ny, *n.*; *pl.* **des′ti-nieş.** [ME. *destynie*; OFr. *destinee*, destiny, from L. *destinare*, to make firm, to destine.]

1. State or condition appointed or predetermined; ultimate fate; doom; lot; fortune; destination; as, men are solicitous to know their future *destiny*.

2. Invincible necessity; fate; a necessity or fixed order of things established, as by a divine decree, or by an indissoluble connection of causes and effects.

But who can turn the stream of *destiny*? —Spenser.

3. [D—*pl.*] In classical mythology, the Parcæ or Fates; the supposed powers which preside over human life, spin it out, and determine it.

Destinies do cut his thread of life. —Shak.

Syn.—Fate, doom, lot, fortune.

dē-stit′ū-ent, *a.* Wanting; deficient. [Obs.]

des′ti-tūte, *a.* [ME. *destitute*, from L. *destitutus*, pp. of *destituere*, to forsake, abandon; *de*, down, away, and *statuere*, to set, put, place.]

1. Not having or possessing; wanting; devoid; followed often by *of*; as, *destitute of* virtue or of piety; *destitute of* food and clothing.

Totally *destitute of* all shadow of influence. —Burke.

2. Not possessing the necessaries of life; needy; abject; poor; as, the family has been left *destitute*.

des′ti-tūte, *v.t.* 1. To forsake; to desert; to abandon. [Obs.]

2. To deprive; to divest. [Obs.]

3. To disappoint. [Obs.]

des′ti-tūte-ly, *adv.* In a destitute condition.

des′ti-tūte-ness, *n.* The state of being destitute; destitution. [Rare.]

des-ti-tū′tion, *n.* [L. *destitutio*, a forsaking, deserting, from *destituere*, to forsake.] The state of being destitute or of being deprived of anything; want; poverty; indigence; as, the fire caused much *destitution*.

Syn.—Indigence, poverty, want, privation, distress, need, deficiency, pauperism.

des′tō, *adv.* [It.] In music, in a sprightly manner; briskly.

des-tōur′, *n.* See *Dastur*.

des-trēr′, *n.* A war-horse; written also *destrier*, *dextrer*. [Obs.]

dē-striē′, *v.t.* To destroy. [Obs.]

des′tri-ēr, *n.* [Obs.] See *Destrer*.

de-stroy′, *v.t.*; destroyed, *pt.*, *pp.*; destroying, *ppr.* [ME. *destroyen*; OFr. *destruire*; L. *destruere*, to pull down, to tear to pieces, to destroy; *de-* priv., and *struere*, to build.]

1. To demolish; to pull down; to overthrow; to separate by force the parts of, the union of which is necessary to constitute the thing; as, to *destroy* a house; to *destroy* a city.

2. To ruin; to bring to naught; to annihilate; as, to *destroy* a scheme; to *destroy* a government; to *destroy* one's happiness.

3. To take away the utility, excellence or importance of; to put an end to the existence of; to kill; as, to *destroy* influence.

4. To confute; to disprove.

Syn.—Annihilate, demolish, extirpate, ruin, exterminate, overthrow, devastate, kill, consume, extinguish, dismantle.

de-stroy′ȧ-ble, *a.* Destructible. [Rare.]

de-stroy′ēr, *n.* 1. One who or that which destroys; one who or that which kills, ruins, or makes desolate.

2. A high-speed naval vessel specially designed to overtake and destroy torpedo boats.

dē-struct′, *v.t.* To destroy. [Obs.]

dē-struc-ti-bil′i-ty, *n.* The quality of being destructible.

dē-struc′ti-ble, *a.* Liable to destruction; capable of being destroyed.

dē-struc′ti-ble-ness, *n.* The quality of being destructible.

dē-struc′tion, *n.* [ME. *destruction*; OFr. *destruction*; L. *destructio*, a pulling down, destruction, from *destructus*, pp. of *destruere*, to pull down, to destroy.]

1. The act of destroying; demolition; a pulling down; subversion; ruin; as, the *destruction* of buildings or of towns.

2. The state of being destroyed; ruin.

> So near *destruction* brought. —Waller.

3. Cause of destruction; a consuming plague; a destroyer.

> The *destruction* that wasteth at noonday. —Ps. xci. 6.

Syn.—Devastation, ruin, demolition, extermination, extinction, subversion, downfall, extirpation, eradication.

dē-struc′tion-ist, *n.* 1. One who favors destruction; a destructive.

2. In theology, one who believes in the final complete destruction or annihilation of the wicked; an annihilationist.

dē-struc′tive, *a.* 1. Causing destruction; having the quality of destroying; having a tendency to destroy; ruinous; mischievous; pernicious; with *of* or *to*; as, a *destructive* fire; a *destructive* disposition; intemperance is *destructive of* health; evil examples are *destructive to* the morals of youth.

2. In logic, tending to disprove; refuting; as, a *destructive* dilemma.

Destructive distillation; see under *Distillation*.

Syn.—Ruinous, fatal, mischievous, pernicious, detrimental, deadly.

dē-struc′tive, *n.* One who or that which destroys; a destructionist.

dē-struc′tive-ly, *adv.* In a destructive manner.

dē-struc′tive-ness, *n.* 1. The quality of being destructive.

2. In phrenology, a propensity whose function is to produce the impulse to destroy.

dē-struc′tŏr, *n.* 1. A destroyer; a consumer. [Obs.]

2. An oven or crematory for burning refuse.

dē-struie′, *v.t.* To destroy. [Obs.]

des-ū-dā′tion *n.* [LL. *desudatio*, a very profuse sweating, from L. *desudare*, to sweat violently.] In medicine, a sweating; a profuse or morbid sweating, often succeeded by an eruption of pustules, called heat-pimples.

de-suēte′ (-swēt′), *a.* Out of use; fallen into desuetude. [Rare.]

des′uē-tūde (des′wē-), *n.* [L. *desuetudo*, disuse, from *desuetus*, pp. of *desuescere*, to disuse.] The cessation of use; disuse; discontinuance of practice, custom, or fashion; as, words in every language are lost through *desuetude*.

dē-sul′phūr, *v.t.*; desulphured, *pt.*, *pp.*; desulphuring, *ppr.* To desulphurize.

dē-sul′phū-rāte, *v.t.*; desulphurated, *pt.*, *pp.*; desulphurating, *ppr.* To desulphurize.

dē-sul-phū-rā′tion, *n.* See *Desulphurization*.

dē-sul″phūr-i-zā′tion, *n.* The act or process of depriving of sulphur.

dē-sul′phūr-īze, *v.t.*; desulphurized, *pt.*, *pp.*; desulphurizing, *ppr.* To deprive of sulphur, as an ore, mineral, etc.

des′ul-tō-ri-ly, *adv.* In a desultory manner; without method; loosely.

des′ul-tō-ri-ness, *n.* The character of being desultory; disconnectedness; discursiveness; as, the *desultoriness* of a speaker's remarks.

des-ul-tō′ri-ous, *a.* Desultory. [Obs.]

des′ul-tō-ry, *a.* [L. *desultorius*, pertaining to a vaulter or rider in a circus, from *desultor*, a leaper, vaulter, one who vaulted from one horse to another in the games of the circus, from *desultus*, pp. of *desilire*, to leap down; *de*, down, from, and *salire*, to leap.]

1. Leaping; hopping about. [Obs.]

2. Passing from one thing or subject to another without order or natural connection; disconnected; immethodical; as, a *desultory* conversation.

Syn.—Cursory, rambling, discursive, loose, immethodical, irregular.

dē-sūme′, *v.t.* To take from; to borrow. [Obs.]

dē-syn-on″y-mi-zā′tion, *n.* The act of desynonymizing or depriving of synonymous character.

dē-syn-on′y-mīze, *v.t.*; desynonymized, *pt.*, *pp.*; desynonymizing, *ppr.* To deprive of synonymous character; to give a turn of meaning to (words), so as to prevent from being absolutely synonymous.

dē-tach′, *v.t.*; detached (-tacht′), *pt.*, *pp.*; detaching, *ppr.* [Fr. *détacher*; OFr. *destacher*, to detach, loosen, unfasten.]

1. To separate or disunite; to disengage; to part from; as, to *detach* the coats of a bulbous root from each other; to *detach* a man from a party.

2. To separate for a special purpose or service; used chiefly in a military sense; as, to *detach* a ship from a fleet or a regiment from an army.

Syn.—Separate, withdraw, disengage, disconnect, detail, disunite.

dē-tach′, *v.i.* To become detached or separated; to separate or disunite itself or oneself. [Rare.]

dē-tach-ȧ-bil′i-ty, *n.* The condition of being detachable.

dē-tach′ȧ-ble, *a.* Capable of being detached.

dē-tached′ (-tacht′), *a.* 1. Separated; disunited; disjoined; as, *detached* portions; *detached* territories.

2. Drawn and sent on a separate service; used chiefly in a military sense; as, a *detached* body of infantry.

3. In fire insurance, separated fifty feet or more from an exposure; said of a building.

Detached work; in fortification, a work situated so far from the body of a fort that it is not protected by it, although forming part of the defense.

dē-tach′ment, *n.* [Fr. *détachement*, from *détacher*, to detach.]

1. The act of detaching or separating; the state of being detached.

2. That which is detached; specifically, a body of troops, selected or taken from the main army, and employed on some special service or expedition; or a number of ships taken from a fleet and sent on a separate service.

3. An order detaching an officer from duty at a certain military station.

dē-tāil′, *v.t.*; detailed, *pt.*, *pp.*; detailing, *ppr.* [OFr. *detailler*, to cut up, divide, narrate in particulars; *de*, apart, and *tailler*, to cut; L. *dis-*, apart, and *talea*, a cutting.]

1. To relate, report, or narrate in particulars; to recite the particulars of; to particularize; to relate minutely and distinctly; as, he *detailed* all the facts in due order.

2. In military parlance, to appoint to a particular service, as an officer or a body of troops.

dē-tāil′, *v.i.* To give details about something; to particularize.

dē-tāil′, (*or* dē′tāl), *n.* 1. An individual part; an item; a portion; a particular; as, the account is accurate in all its *details*.

2. A minute account; a narrative or report of particulars; as, he gave a *detail* of all the transaction.

3. In military parlance, a body of troops detailed for a particular service; a detachment.

4. In the fine arts, a minute or particular part, as distinguished from a general conception or from larger parts.

Detail drawing; a drawing showing plainly all parts or details of some portion of a house, machine, etc.

In detail; circumstantially; item by item; individually; part by part.

Syn.—Narrative, narration, account, recital, relation, description.

dē-tāil′ēr, *n.* One who details.

dē-tāin′, *v.t.*; detained, *pt.*, *pp.*; detaining, *ppr.* [L. *detinere*, to hold down or off, to keep back, to detain; *de*, off, from, and *tenere*, to hold.]

1. To keep back or from; to withhold; to keep (what belongs to another).

> *Detain* not the wages of the hireling. —Taylor.

2. To keep or restrain from proceeding; to stay or stop; as, we were *detained* by the rain.

3. In law, to hold in custody.—Blackstone.

dē-tāin′, *n.* Detention. [Obs.]

dē-tāin′dēr, *n.* [Obs. See *Detinue*.]

dē-tāin′ēr, *n.* 1. One who detains.

2. In law, (a) a holding or keeping possession of what belongs to another; detention of what is another's, though the original taking may be lawful; (b) in England, a process lodged with the sheriff, authorizing him to detain a prisoner in custody; specifically, a writ by which a prisoner arrested at the suit of one creditor may be detained at the suit of another.

dē-tāin′ment, *n.* The act of detaining; detention. [Obs.]

dē-tect′, *v.t.*; detected, *pt.*, *pp.*; detecting, *ppr.* [L. *detectus*, pp. of *detegere*, to uncover; *de-* priv., and *tegere*, to cover.]

1. To uncover; to discover; to find out; to bring to light; to ascertain the existence or presence of; as, to *detect* an error in an account; to *detect* a thief.

2. To inform against; to complain of; to accuse. [Obs.]

Syn.—Discover, expose, discern, find out, disclose, ascertain, determine.

dē-tect′ȧ-ble, dē-tect′i-ble, *a.* That may be detected.

> These errors are *detectible* at a glance. —Latham.

dē-tect′ēr, *n.* See *Detector*.

dē-tec′tion, *n.* [LL. *detectio*, a revealing, from L. *detectus*, pp. of *detegere*, to uncover, reveal.] The act of detecting or the state of being detected; the finding out of what was concealed, hidden, or formerly unknown; discovery; as, the *detection* of an error; the *detection* of a thief; the *detection* of fraud or forgery; the *detection* of artifice, device, or a plot.

dē-tect′ive, *a.* 1. Fitted for or skilled in detecting; employed in detecting; as, the *detective* police.

2. Pertaining to detectives; relating to detection; as, a *detective* story; a *detective* bureau.

dē-tect′ive, *n.* One who is employed or detailed to detect and apprehend persons who violate the law.

dē-tect′ŏr, *n.* [LL. *detector*, a revealer, one who detects, from L. *detectus*, pp. of *detegere* to uncover, reveal.]

1. One who or that which detects or brings to light; one who finds out what another attempts to conceal; a revealer; a discoverer.

2. In radiotelegraphy, any device to transform the oscillations received by the antennæ into visible or audible indications.

Bank-note detector; a periodical giving information as to counterfeit and stolen currency.

dē-tect′ŏr-lock, *n.* A lock fitted with a contrivance for indicating any attempt to tamper with it.

dē-ten′ē-brāte, *v.t.* To remove darkness from. [Obs.]

dē-tent′, *n.* [LL. *detentus*, a holding back, from L. *detentus*, pp. of *detinere*, to hold back, detain.] Anything that checks or stops motion, as a lever, pin, or stud forming a check in a clock, watch, tumbler-lock, or other machine. The *detent* in a clock falls into the striking wheel, and stops it when the right number of strokes have been given. The *detent* of a ratchet-wheel prevents back motion.

dē-ten′tion, *n.* [L. *detentus*, pp. of *detinere*, to hold back, detain.]

1. The act of detaining or the state of being detained; confinement; restraint; a keeping of what belongs to another.

2. Delay from necessity; a detaining; as, the *detention* of the mail by bad roads.

dē-ten′tive, *a.* Used in holding or seizing; able to detain.

dē-tēr′, *v.t.*; deterred, *pt.*, *pp.*; deterring, *ppr.* [L. *deterrere*, to frighten from, to deter; *de*, from, and *terrere*, to frighten.] To discourage and stop by fear; to stop or prevent from acting or proceeding, by danger, difficulty, or other consideration which disheartens or countervails the motive for an act; as, we are often *deterred* from our duty by trivial difficulties; a cloudy sky may *deter* a man from undertaking a journey.

> A million of frustrated hopes will not *deter* us from new experiments. —Mason.

Syn.—Discourage, hinder, prevent, restrain.

dē-tērge′, *v.t.*; deterged, *pt.*, *pp.*; deterging, *ppr.* [L. *detergere*, to wipe off, wipe away; *de*, off, from, and *tergere*, to wipe, cleanse.] To cleanse; to purge away, as foul or offending matter from the body, or from an ulcer.

dē-tēr′gence, *n.* The quality of being detergent.

dē-tēr′gen-cy, *n.* Detergence.

dē-tēr′gent, *a.* Cleansing; purging.

dē-tēr′gent, *n.* [L. *detergens* (*-ntis*), ppr. of *detergere*, to wipe off, cleanse.] That which purges or cleanses; a medicine which has the power of cleansing wounds, ulcers, etc.

dē-tē′ri-ō-rāte, *v.t.*; deteriorated, *pt.*, *pp.*; deteriorating, *ppr.* [LL. *deterioratus*, pp. of *deteriorare*, to make worse, from L. *deterior*, worse, inferior.] To make worse; to lower the value of; to reduce in quality; as, to *deteriorate* a race of men, or their condition.

Syn.—Degrade, depreciate, degenerate, impair, corrupt, debase.

dē-tē′ri-ō-rāte, *v.i.* To grow worse; to be impaired in quality; to degenerate.

Under such conditions, the mind rapidly *deteriorates*. —Goldsmith.

dē-tē″ri-ō-rā′tion, *n.* A growing or making worse; the state of growing worse.

dē-tē′ri-ō-rā-tive, *a.* Causing deterioration.

dē-tē-ri-or′i-ty, *n.* Worse state or quality. [Rare.]

dē-tēr′ment, *n.* The act of deterring or the state of being deterred; that which deters.

dē-tēr″mi-nȧ-bil′i-ty, *n.* The quality of being determinable.

dē-tēr′mi-nȧ-ble, *a.* [LL. *determinabilis*, determinable, from L. *determinare*, to determine.]

1. That may be determined, decided, or ascertained with positiveness; as, a *determinable* function.

2. In law, liable to termination; as, a *determinable* lease.

dē-tēr′mi-nȧ-ble-ness, *n.* The quality of being determinable; determinability. [Rare.]

dē-tēr′mi-nă-cy, *n.* Determinateness. [Rare.]

dē-tēr′mi-nănce, *n.* In some old universities, formerly, the degree of bachelor of arts.

dē-tēr′mi-nănt, *a.* Serving to determine; determinative.

dē-tēr′mi-nănt, *n.* 1. That which tends to fix, establish, or decide something

2. In mathematics, the algebraic sum of all the terms found by permuting in every possible way the elements on the principal diagonal of a determinant array, taken in their natural order and with respect to their subscripts only. A determinant array of n^2 elements is arranged as follows:

$$\begin{matrix} a_1' & a_1'' & \cdots & a_{1n} \\ a_2' & a_2'' & \cdots & a_{2n} \\ \vdots & \vdots & & \vdots \\ a_n' & a_n'' & \cdots & a_n^n \end{matrix}$$

The elements on the principal diagonal taken in their natural order, are represented by

$$a_1',\ a_2'',\ a_3''',\ \cdots\ a_n^n.$$

The sign of all terms in the permutation involving even permutations of the subscripts will be positive; of those involving odd permutations of the subscripts, the sign will be negative. The order of a determinant is determined by taking the square root of the number of elements in the determinant array; thus, a determinant array of three rows and three columns, having nine elements, represents a determinant of the third order.

3. In some old universities, one who having graduated as a bachelor of arts, proceeded to take the degree of master of arts.

4. In biology, one of the minute subdivisions of chromatin, beyond the power of the microscope to reveal. It is made up of other theoretical divisions, the biophores. According to Weismann, biophores are united to form determinants, determinants to form ids (chromatin granules), and ids to form idants (chromosomes). These units differ qualitatively and the manner of their combination determines the ultimate development of any cell or group of cells.

dē-tēr′mi-nănt-ăl, *a.* In mathematics, relating to determinants.

dē-tēr′mi-nāte, *v.t.* To bring to an end; to terminate. [Obs.]

dē-tēr′mi-nāte, *a.* [L. *determinatus*, pp. of *determinare*, to determine.]

1. Having defined limits; limited; fixed; definite; specific; as, a *determinate* quantity of matter.

2. Established; settled; positive; as, a *determinate* rule or order.

3. Decisive; conclusive. [Obs.]

4. Resolved on. [Obs.]

5. Fixed; resolute. [Obs.]

6. In botany, characterized by upward growth from side buds, as a plant.

Determinate inflorescence; see *Centrifugal inflorescence* under *Centrifugal*.

Determinate problem; in geometry and analysis, a problem which admits of one solution only, or at least a certain and finite number of solutions; being thus opposed to an *indeterminate problem*, which admits of an infinite number of solutions.

dē-tēr′mi-nāte-ly, *adv.* 1. With certainty; precisely; with exact specification.

2. Resolutely; with fixed resolve.

dē-tēr′mi-nāte-ness, *n.* The state of being determinate, certain, or precise.

dē-tēr-mi-nā′tion, *n.* [ME. *determynation*; L. *determinatio*, a boundary, conclusion, from *determinare*, to bound, limit, determine; *de*, and *terminare*, to bound, limit, from *terminus*, a boundary, limit.]

1. The act of determining or deciding; the state of being determined.

2. An ending; a putting an end to; termination.

A speedy *determination* of that war. —Ludlow.

3. Absolute direction to a certain end.

With a constant *determination* of the will to the greatest apparent good. —Locke.

4. The mental habit of settling upon some line of action with a fixed purpose to adhere to it; adherence to aims or purposes; resoluteness; as, a man of *determination*.

5. Judicial decision; the ending, as of a controversy or suit; as, justice is promoted by a speedy *determination* of causes, civil and criminal.

6. Fixed purpose; resolution; intention.

A *determination* to obtain convictions. —Hallam.

7. In medicine, tendency to flow to, more copiously than is normal; as, *determination* of blood to the head.

8. In physical science, the act, process, or result of determining the nature, quantity, intensity, etc., of anything; as, the *determination* of nitrogen in the atmosphere; the *determination* of the ampere.

9. In logic, the act of defining a notion by adding differentia, and thus rendering it more definite.

10. In natural history, the referring of minerals, plants, etc., to the species to which they belong; classification; as, I am indebted to a friend for the *determination* of the greater part of these shells.

11. In some old universities, a solemn disputation enjoined upon one who has taken the degree of bachelor of arts, preparatory to graduating as master of arts.

Syn.—Decision, resolution.—*Decision* is a cutting short, and supposes energy and promptitude; *determination* is the settling of a thing with a fixed purpose to adhere; *resolution* is a spirit to face danger or suffering in carrying out one's *determinations*

dē-tēr′mi-nȧ-tive, *a.* 1. Having power to determine or direct to a certain end; conclusive.

2. Serving to determine the species; having the power of ascertaining precisely; as, *determinative* tables in the natural sciences, that is, tables arranged for determining the specific character of minerals, plants, etc., and to assist in assigning them to their species.

dē-tēr′mi-nȧ-tive, *n.* That which determines the nature or quality of something else; specifically, (a) in grammar, a demonstrative word; (b) in hieroglyphics, an ideographic sign annexed to a word expressed by a phonetic sign for the purpose of defining its signification.

dē-tēr′mi-nā-tŏr, *n.* One who decides; an arbitrator. [Rare.]

dē-tēr′mine, *v.t.*; determined, *pt.*, *pp.*; determining, *ppr.* [L. *determinare*, to bound, limit, prescribe.]

1. To fix the bounds of; to mark off; to settle; to fix; to establish.

And hath *determined* the times before appointed. —Acts xvii. 26.

2. To set bounds to; to form the limits of; to bound; to confine; as, yonder hill *determines* our view.

The knowledge of man hitherto hath been *determined* by the view or sight. —Bacon.

3. To define the character of; to settle; to direct.

4. To give a direction to; to settle the course of; as, impulse may *determine* a moving body to this or that point.

5. To terminate or decide as a controverted question; to end; as, the court *determined* the cause.

6. To influence the choice of; to cause to come to a conclusion or resolution; as, this circumstance *determined* him to the study of law.

7. To resolve on; to conclude; to come to a decision or resolution concerning; as, he *determined* to remain.

8. To ascertain positively; to settle; to arrive at a definite conclusion respecting the presence, character, or quantity of; as, to *determine* the species of a plant; to *determine* the value of *x* in an equation; to *determine* the altitude of a mountain.

9. In logic, to define or limit by adding differences.

Syn.—Decide, ascertain, define, limit, fix, resolve, settle, conclude.

dē-tēr′mine, *v.i.* 1. To resolve; to conclude; to come to a decision; frequently followed by *on*; as, to *determine on* a course.

He shall pay as the judges *determine*. —Ex. xxi. 22.

2. To come to an end; to terminate. [Obs.]

dē-tēr′mined, *a.* Characterized by determination; resolute; as, a *determined* man.

Syn.—Decided, firm, fixed, immovable, obstinate, resolute, steady.

dē-tēr′min-ed-ly (*or* -mind-ly), *adv.* In a determined manner.

dē-tēr′min-ēr, *n.* One who decides or determines; that which determines.

dē-tēr′min-ism, *n.* In philosophy, the doctrine that man does not possess liberty of action, and that volition is determined by motives and antecedent causes.

dē-tēr′min-ist, *n.* One who believes in determinism.

dē-tēr′min-ist, *a.* Relating to the doctrine of determinism; as, *determinist* principles.

dē-tēr-rā′tion, *n.* [From L. *de*, from, and *terra*, earth.] The uncovering of anything which is buried or covered with earth; a taking out of the earth. [Rare.]

dē-tēr′rence, *n.* That which deters; a hindrance; a deterrent. [Rare.]

dē-tēr′rent, *a.* Having the power or tendency to deter; as, a *deterrent* principle.

dē-tēr′rent, *n.* That which deters or tends to deter.

dē-tēr′sion, *n.* [From L. *detersus*, pp. of *detergere*, to wipe off, cleanse.] The act of cleansing, as a sore.

dē-tēr′sive, *a.* Cleansing; detergent.

dē-tēr′sive, *n.* A detergent.

dē-tēr′sive-ly, *adv.* In a detersive manner.

dē-tēr′sive-ness, *n.* The quality of being detersive.

dē-test′, *v.t.*; detested, *pt.*, *pp.*; detesting, *ppr.* [Fr. *détester*, to detest; L. *detestari*, to invoke a deity by cursing, to execrate, to detest; *de*, and *testari*, to witness; *testis*, a witness.]

1. To abhor; to abominate; to dislike intensely; as, to *detest* crimes or meanness.

And love the offender, yet *detest* th' offense. —Pope.

2. To denounce; to testify against. [Obs.]

Syn.—Hate, abhor, abominate, loathe.—*Hate* is generic. We *abhor* what is repugnant to our sensibilities or feelings; we *detest* what contradicts our moral principles. What we *abominate* does equal violence to our religious and moral sentiments; what we *loathe* is offensive to our nature, and excites unmingled disgust.

dē-test-ȧ-bil′i-ty, *n.* Detestableness.

dē-test′ȧ-ble, *a.* [OFr. *detestable*; L. *detestabilis*, execrable, abominable, detestable.] Extremely hateful; abominable; very odious; deserving abhorrence; as, a *detestable* country.

Syn.—Execrable, abhorred, odious, abominable.

dē-test′ȧ-ble-ness, *n.* The quality of being detestable.

dē-test′ȧ-bly, *adv.* In a detestable manner; abominably.

dē-tes′tāte, *v.t.* To detest. [Obs.]

det-es-tā′tion, *n.* Extreme hatred; abhorrence; loathing; with *of*.

Our *detestation of* civil war. —Burke.

dē-test′ēr, *n.* One who detests.

dē-thrōne′, *v.t.*; dethroned, *pt.*, *pp.*; dethroning, *ppr.* [From L. *de-* priv., and *thronus*, a seat, throne.] To remove or drive from a throne; to depose; to divest of authority and dignity.

The Protector was *dethroned*. —Hume.

dē-thrōne′ment, *n.* Removal from a throne; deposition of a king, emperor, prince, or any supreme ruler.

dē-thrōn′ēr, *n.* One who dethrones.

dē-thrōn-i-zā′tion, *n.* The act of dethroning. [Rare.]

dē-thrōn′ize, *v.t.* To dethrone. [Obs.]

det′i-nūe, *n.* [OFr. *detinu*, pp. of *detenir*, to detain; L. *detinere*, to detain.] In law, formerly, an action whereby a plaintiff sought to recover personal property unlawfully detained.

det′ō-nȧ-ble, *a.* Capable of detonating.

det′ō-nāte, *v.i.*; detonated, *pt.*, *pp.*; detonating, *ppr.* [L. *detonatus*, pp. of *detonare*, to thunder, to make a loud noise; *de-*, intens., and *tonare*, to make a sound.] To explode with a loud noise; as, niter *detonates* with sulphur.

det′ō-nāte, *v.t.* To cause to explode suddenly with a loud report.

det′ō-nā-ting, *a.* Exploding suddenly with a loud report.

Detonating powder; any one of certain chemical compounds, which, on being exposed to heat or suddenly struck, explode with a loud report, owing to one or more of the constituent parts suddenly assuming the gaseous state; called also *fulminating powder*.

det′ō-nā-ting-bulb, *n.* A small glass bulb, shaped like a pear, rendered brittle by cooling in the making. It flies into atoms when scratched by a sharp grain of sand; called also *Prince Rupert's drop.*

det′ō-nā-ting-prīm″ẽr, *n.* A primer for exploding guncotton or other explosive used in blasting. The primer itself is exploded by a fuse.

det′ō-nā-ting-tūbe, *n.* A species of eudiometer, being a stout glass tube used in chemical analysis for detonating gaseous bodies. It is generally graduated into centesimal parts, and perforated by two opposed wires for the purpose of passing an electric spark through the gases which are introduced into it, and are confined within it over mercury and water.

Detonating-Tube.

det-ō-nā′tion, *n.* [From L. *detonare*, to thunder, to make a loud noise.] An explosion or sudden report caused by the combustion of certain combustible bodies, as fulminating gold.

det′ō-nā-tive, *a.* Detonable.

det′ō-nā-tŏr, *n.* That which detonates, as a percussion-cap.

det″ō-ni-zā′tion, *n.* Detonation; the act of exploding, as certain combustible bodies.

det′ō-nize, *v.t.* and *v.i.*; detonized, *pt., pp.*; detonizing, *ppr.* To cause to explode; to detonate.

dē-tor′sion, *n.* Same as *Detortion.*

dē-tort′, *v.t.*; detorted, *pt., pp.*; detorting, *ppr.* [L. *detortus*, pp. of *detorquere*, to turn aside, to turn off; *de*, off, from, and *torquere*, to turn.] To twist; to wrest; to pervert; to turn from the original or plain meaning.

dē-tor′tion, *n.* The act of detorting; a turning or wresting; the state of being detorted.

dē-tour′, *n.* [Fr. *detour*, a turning, an evasion, excuse, from *detourner*, to turn aside, divert, evade.] A turning; a circuitous or roundabout way; a deviation from the direct or shortest path, road, or route; as, the *detours* of a river.

dē-tract′, *v.t.*; detracted, *pt., pp.*; detracting, *ppr.* [L. *detractare*, to draw away from, decline, detract; *de*, from, and *trahere*, to draw.] To depreciate the merit, the motives, or the good deeds of (another); to derogate; with *from.*

> It has been the fashion to *detract* both *from* the moral and the literary character of Cicero. —Knox.

Syn.—Defame, vilify, derogate, slander, decry, depreciate, calumniate.

dē-tract′, *v.i.* To take away a part; hence, specifically, to take away reputation; to defame; often followed by *from.*

> *Detract from* a lady's character. —Addison.

dē-tract′ẽr, *n.* See *Detractor.*

dē-tract′ing-ly, *adv.* In a detracting manner.

dē-trac′tion, *n.* [ME. *detraction*; L. *detractio*, a taking away, drawing off, detraction, from *detractare, detrectare*, to draw away, detract.]

1. A withdrawing; a taking away. [Obs.]

2. The act of taking away from the reputation or worth of another, with the view to lessen him in the estimation of others; a lessening of worth, the act of depreciating another from envy or malice.

Syn.—Slander, defamation, calumny, depreciation, aspersion, derogation.

dē-trac′tious, *a.* Containing detraction; lessening reputation. [Obs.]

dē-tract′ive, *a.* 1. Having the quality or tendency to lessen worth or estimation.

2. Tending to draw or take away. [Obs.]

dē-tract′ive-ness, *n.* The quality of being detractive. [Rare.]

dē-tract′ŏr, *n.* One who detracts; one who takes away or impairs the reputation of another; one who attempts to lessen the worth or honor of another; a defamer; a calumniator.

Syn.—Defamer, calumniator, slanderer, vilifier, derogator.

dē-tract′ō-ry, *a.* Derogatory; defamatory by denial of desert; depreciatory.

dē-tract′ress, *n.* A female detractor.

dē-trāin′, *v.t.* and *v.i.* To remove from or leave a railway train. [Rare.]

dē-trect′, *v.t.* and *v.i.* To refuse. [Obs.]

det′ri-ment, *n.* [OFr. *detriment*; L. *detrimentum*, a rubbing off, loss, damage, from *detritus*, pp. of *deterere*, to rub off, wear away, weaken; *de*, off, from, and *terere*, to rub, wear.]

1. That which causes damage, harm or injury; loss; damage; mischief; diminution; depreciation; a word of very general application; as, *detriment* to interest, property, religion, morals, reputation, etc.

2. In England, a charge made upon barristers and students for repair of damages to the rooms they occupy; a charge for wear and tear.

3. In heraldry, same as *decrement.*

4. In astrology, a sign of mishap, distress, weakness, etc.

Syn.—Injury, harm, evil, loss, hurt, damage, disadvantage.

det′ri-ment, *v.t.* To injure; to harm. [Obs.]

det-ri-men′tăl, *a.* Injurious; hurtful; causing loss or damage.

Syn.—Injurious, damaging, mischievous, disadvantageous, harmful, prejudicial.

det-ri-men′tăl-ly, *adv.* In a detrimental manner.

det-ri-men′tăl-ness, *n.* The quality of being detrimental.

dē-trī′tăl, *a.* In geology, pertaining to or consisting of detritus.

dē-trīte′, *a.* [L. *detritus*, pp. of *deterere*, to rub down, to wear away; *de*, down, from, and *terere*, to rub.] Worn away.

dē-tri′tion (-trish′un), *n.* [From L. *deterere*, to wear or rub away.] A wearing off; the act of wearing away.

dē-trī′tus, *n.* [L. *detritus*, a rubbing away, from *deterere*, to rub or wear away.]

1. In geology, a mass of substances worn off from solid bodies by attrition, and reduced to small portions; as, diluvial *detritus.*

2. Any fragmentary material; waste; disintegrated matter.

dē-trūde′, *v.t.*; detruded, *pt., pp.*; detruding, *ppr.* [L. *detrudere*, to thrust or push down.] To thrust or force down.

dē-trun′cāte, *v.t.*; detruncated, *pt., pp.*; detruncating, *ppr.* [L. *detruncatus*, pp. of *detruncare*, to cut or lop off.] To cut off; to lop; to shorten by cutting.

dē-trun-cā′tion, *n.* [L. *detruncatio*, from *detruncare*, to cut or lop off.] The act of detruncating; in obstetrics, separation of the trunk and head of the fetus.

dē-trụ′sion, *n.* [LL. *detrusio*, a thrusting away, from L. *detrudere*, to drive or thrust away.] The act of thrusting; the act of driving down or out.

dē-trụ′sive, *a.* Tending to detrude.

dē-trụ′sŏr, *n.*; *pl.* **dē-trụ′sō-rēs.** In anatomy, a muscle which expels or ejects.

dette, *n.* Debt. [Obs.]

dette′les, *a.* Free from debt. [Obs.]

dē-tū-mes′cence, *n.* [L. *detumescens*, (*-ntis*), ppr. of *detumescere*, to cease swelling; *de*, from, and *tumescere*, incept. of *tumere*, to swell.] Diminution of swelling. [Rare.]

dē′tūr, *n.* [L. *detur*, lit., let it be given; third pers. sing. pres. subj. pass. of *dare*, to give.] A prize of books annually awarded to a meritorious undergraduate student at Harvard University.

dē-tūrb′, *v.t.* To throw into confusion; to throw down with violence. [Obs.]

dē-tūr′bāte, *v.t.* To evict. [Obs.]

det-ūr-bā′tion, *n.* Eviction. [Obs.]

dē-tūrn′, *v.t.* To turn away. [Obs.]

dē-tūr′pāte, *v.t.* To defile. [Obs.]

det-ūr-pā′tion, *n.* The act of defiling or corrupting; a corruption. [Obs.]

deuce, *n.* [Fr. *deux*; OFr. *deus*; L. *duo*, two.]

1. In gaming, two; a die with two spots; a card with two spots; as, the *deuce* of clubs.

2. In lawn-tennis, that stage of the game when both sides have scored forty, and resumed whenever a tie is made until one side scores two in succession following such tie or *deuce*, which decides the game.

deuce, *n.* [ME. *dewes*; OFr. *Deus*; L. *Deus*, God.] The devil; used in exclamatory or interjectional phrases with or without the definite article; expressive of impatience or annoyance; as, go to *the deuce! deuce* take you!

To play the deuce with; to injure; to damage; to perplex; to annoy; used of persons or things. [Slang.]

deuce′-ace, *n.* A throw of two dice, one of which turns up one and the other two.

deū′ced, *a.* Devilish; excessive; confounded; often used adverbially. [Slang.]

deū′ced-ly, deū′sed-ly, *adv.* Devilishly; confoundedly. [Slang.]

deūse, *n.* See *Deuce*, 2.

deū′sed, *a.* See *Deuced.*

deū′sed-ly, *adv.* See *Deucedly.*

deū″ten-ceph-al′ic, *a.* [From Gr. *deuteros*, second, and *enkephalos*, brain.] Same as *Diencephalic.*

deū-ten-ceph′á-lon, *n.* Same as *Diencephalon.*

deū-tẽr-ō-. A combining form from Gr. *deuteros*, second.

deū″tẽr-ō-cā-non′ic-ăl, *a.* [*Deutero-*, and L. *canon*; Gr. *kanōn*, a rule.] Belonging to a second canon; in the Roman Catholic church, applied to those books of the Bible which were admitted into the canon after the rest.

deū-tẽr-og′á-mist, *n.* One who marries the second time.

deū-tẽr-og′á-my, *n.* [Gr. *deuterogamia*, a second marriage; *deuteros*, second, and *gamos*, marriage] A second marriage after the death of the first husband or wife; the custom of contracting second marriages.

deū″tẽr-ō-gen′ic, *a.* [*Deutero-*, and Gr. *genos*, race.] In geology, of secondary origin; applied to rocks derived from crystalline rocks which are supposed to be formed by the action of fire.

Deū″tẽr-ō-nom′ic, Deū″tẽr-ō-nom′ic-ăl, *a.* Pertaining to the book of Deuteronomy.

Deū-tẽr-on′ō-mist, *n.* The assumed writer or one of the assumed writers of the book of Deuteronomy.

Deū-tẽr-on-ō-mis′tic, *a.* Relating to the Deuteronomist.

Deū-tẽr-on′ō-my, *n.* [L. *deuteronomium*, lit. the second law, Deuteronomy, from Gr. *deuteros*, second, and *nomos*, law.] The second law, or second giving of the law, by Moses; the name given to the fifth book of the Pentateuch.

deū″tẽr-ō-path′i-á, *n.* See *Deuteropathy.*

deū″tẽr-ō-path′ic, *a.* Of or pertaining to deuteropathy.

deū-tẽr-op′á-thy, *n.* [*Deutero-*, and Gr. *pathos*, suffering.] A sympathetic affection of any part of the body, as headache from an overloaded stomach.

deū′tẽr-ō-plasm, *n.* See *Deutoplasm.*

deū-tẽr-os′cō-py, *n.* [*Deutero-*, and Gr. *skopein*, to see.]

1. The second intention; the hidden meaning beyond the literal sense.

2. Prophetic or second sight.

deū-tẽr-os′tō-má, *n.*; *pl.* **deū″tẽr-os-tō′má-tá.** [L., from Gr. *deuteros*, second, and *stoma*, mouth.] A blastopore derived from an archæostoma; a secondary blastopore.

deū″tẽr-ō-zō′oid, *n.* [*Deutero-*, and Gr. *zōon*, an animal, and *eidos*, form.] A zoöid produced by gemmation from a zoöid.

deūt-hy̆-drog′ū-ret, deū″tō-hy̆-drog′ū-ret, *n.* A compound made up of two atoms of hydrogen and a divalent element. [Obs.]

deū-tō-. A combining form, contr. from Gr. *deuteros*, second; used in chemistry to denote the second in order; in some cases equivalent to *bi-* or *di*, as opposed to *mono-.*

deū′tō-plasm, *n.* [*Deuto-*, and Gr. *plasma*, anything formed, from *plassein*, to form.] In biology, that portion of the yolk of ova which furnishes materials for the nourishment of the embryo and its accessories.

deū-tō-plas′mic, *a.* Deutoplastic.

deū-tō-plas′tic, *a.* Of or pertaining to deutoplasm.

deū-tō-scō′lex, *n.* A secondary scolex.

deū-tō-sul′phū-ret, *n.* A disulphid. [Obs.]

deū-tox′id, *n.* [*Deuto-*, and Gr. *oxys*, acid.] A dioxid. [Obs.]

Deut′zi-á (doit′), *n.* [Named after *Deutz*, a Dutch botanist.] In botany, a genus of saxifragaceous shrubs, often cultivated, having ovate leaves and white flowers; native in China and Japan.

de′vá, dev, *n.* [Sans. *deva*, a god, deity.] In Hindu mythology, a deity.

De-vá-nä′gá-ri, *n.* [From Sans. *deva*, god, and *nagari*, one of the alphabets of India, the one in which Sanskrit is usually written, from *nagara*, a city.] The alphabet or script used in Sanskrit sacred books.

dē-vap-ō-rā′tion, *n.* The change of vapor into water, as in the generation of rain.

dē-vast′, *v.t.* To lay waste. [Obs.]

dev′ăs-tāte, *v.t.*; devastated, *pt., pp.*; devastating, *ppr.* [L. *devastatus*, pp. of *devastare*, to lay waste.] To lay waste; to ravage; to desolate; to destroy.

Syn.—Despoil, desolate, ravage, sack, strip.

dev-ăs-tā′tion, *n.* 1. The act of devastating or the state of being devastated; a laying waste; waste; havoc; desolation; as the *devastation* of war.

2. In law, devastavit.

Syn.—Desolation, ravage, waste, havoc, destruction, ruin, overthrow.

dev′ăs-tā-tŏr, *n.* One who or that which devastates.

dev-ăs-tā′vit, *n.* [L., lit. he has laid waste; third pers. sing. perf. ind. act. of *devastare*, to lay waste.] In law, the waste of the property of a deceased person by his executor or administrator.

dēve, *a.* Deaf. [Obs.]

dev′el, *v.t.* [Scot.] To strike with force.

dev′el, *n.* [Scot.] A heavy blow.

dev′el-in, *n.* [Prov. Eng.] The swift, *Cypselus apus.*

dē-vel′ŏp, *v.t.*; developed, *pt., pp.*; developing, *ppr.* [Fr. *développer*; OFr. *desvelopper*, to unfold, unwrap; perhaps from L. *de*, from, and *volutus*, pp. of *volvere*, to roll.]

1. To uncover; to unfold; to lay open; to disclose or make known, as something concealed or withheld from notice; to unravel; as, the general began to *develop* the plan of his operations; to *develop* a plot.

> These serve to *develop* its tenets. —Milner.

2. In photography, to induce such a change in (an exposed sensitized plate or film) as to bring out the latent image preparatory to fixing or printing.

3. In biology, to bring about, as the process of natural evolution from an embryo state or previous stage to that, or toward that, in which the original idea is fully exhibited.

4. In mathematics, to change the form of, as of an algebraic expression, by performing certain operations on it, but without altering its value.

Syn.—Uncover, unfold, disclose, exhibit, unravel, disentangle.

dē-vel′ŏp, *v.i.* 1. To advance from one stage to another by a process of natural or inherent evolution; as, the mind *develops* from year to year; specifically, in biology, to go through a process of gradual evolution; as, the fetus *develops* in the womb; the seed *develops* into the plant.

2. To become visible; to show itself; specifically, in photography, to become visible, as a picture does when undergoing the process of development. [See *Development.*]

dē-vel′ŏp-ȧ-ble, *a.* That may be developed.

Developable surface; in mathematics, a torse.

dē-vel′ŏp-ȧ-ble, *n.* A developable surface.

dē-vel′ŏp-ẽr, *n.* One who or that which develops; specifically, in photography, a chemical or mixture used in the process of developing.

dē-vel′ŏp-ment, *n.* [Fr. *développement*, from *développer*, to develop.]

1. An unfolding; the discovering of something secret or withheld from the knowledge of others; disclosure; full exhibition; the unraveling of a plot.

2. In mathematics, a term in frequent use to denote the transformation of any function into the form of a series; also, the process by which any mathematical expression is changed into another of equivalent value or meaning and of more expanded form.

3. The exhibition of new features; gradual growth or advancement through progressive changes.

> A new *development* of imagination, taste, and poetry. —Channing.

4. Specifically, the term used to express the organic changes which take place in animal and vegetable bodies, from their embryo state until they arrive at maturity.

5. In photography, the process following exposure, by which the image on the plate is rendered visible by the precipitation of new material on that portion of the sensitive surface which has been acted on by light.

Development theory; in biology, the theory of evolution. [See *Evolution.*]

Syn.—Unfolding, unraveling, disentanglement, growth, increase, evolution, progress.

dē-vel-ŏp-men′tăl, *a.* Relating to development; evolutionary.

dev-ē-nus′tāte, *v.t.* To deprive of beauty or grace. [Obs.]

dē-vẽr′ġence, dē-vẽr′ġen-cy, *n.* Divergence; divergency. [Obs.]

dē-vest′, *v.t.*; devested, *pt., pp.*; devesting, *ppr.* [L. *devestire*, to undress; *de-* priv., and *vestire*, to dress, from *vestis*, a dress, garment.]

1. To divest. [Obs.]

2. In law, to alienate, as title or right.

dē-vest′, *v.i.* In law, to be lost or alienated, as a title or an estate.

dē-vex′, *a.* and *n.* I. *a.* Bending down. [Obs.]

II. *n.* Devexity; slope. [Obs.]

dē-vex′i-ty, *n.* [L. *devexitas*, a bending downward, a sloping, from *devehere*, to carry down, to go down.] A bending downward; a sloping; incurvation downward. [Rare.]

dē′vi-ănt, *a.* Deviating. [Obs.]

dē′vi-āte, *v.i.*; deviated, *pt., pp.*; deviating, *ppr.* [LL. *deviatus*, pp. of *deviare*, to turn aside, from L. *devius*, out of the way; *de*, from, and *via*, way, path.] To turn aside or wander from the common or right way, course, or line, either in a literal or figurative sense; to diverge; to differ; as, to *deviate* from the common track or path, or from a true course.

dē′vi-āte, *v.t.* To cause to deflect.

Syn.—Deflect; digress; swerve; wander.

dē-vi-ā′tion, *n.* [LL. *deviatio*, from *deviare*, to deviate.]

1. A wandering or turning aside from the right or usual way, course, or line.

2. A wandering from the path of duty; error; sin.

3. In commerce, the voluntary departure of a ship, without necessity, from the regular and usual course of the specific voyage insured. This discharges the underwriters from their responsibility.

Deviation of a falling body; that deviation from the perpendicular line of descent which falling bodies experience in their descent, in consequence of the rotation of the earth on its axis.

Deviation of the compass; the deviation of a ship's compass from the true magnetic meridian, caused by the near presence of iron.

Deviation of the line of the vertical; deviation of a plumb-line caused by side attraction, as that of an adjacent mountain.

dē′vi-ā-tŏr, *n.* One who or that which deviates.

dē′vi-ā-tō-ry, *a.* Deviating. [Rare.]

dē-vice′, *n.* [ME. *devise*; OFr. *devise, divise*, will, intention, opinion, division, from L. *divisus*, pp. of *dividere*, to divide.]

1. That which is formed by design or invented; scheme; artificial contrivance; stratagem; project; sometimes in a good sense, more generally in a bad sense, as artifices are usually employed for bad purposes.

> His *device* is against Babylon, to destroy it. —Jer. li. 11.

2. Invention; genius; faculty of devising.

> Full of noble *device.* —Shak.

3. Anything fancifully conceived, as a picture, pattern, piece of embroidery, cut or ornament of a garment.

4. An emblem intended to represent a family, person, action, or quality, with a suitable motto; used in painting, sculpture, and heraldry.

5. The motto attached to or suited for such an emblem.

1. Device of Henry VII., (Westminster Abbey). 2. Device of Anne Boleyn.

> A youth, who bore, 'mid snow and ice,
> A banner with the strange *device*,
> Excelsior! —Longfellow.

6. A spectacle; a show.

Syn.—Contrivance, invention, design, scheme, project, stratagem, emblem, motto.

dē-vīce′fụl, *a.* Full of devices; inventive. [Rare.]

dē-vīce′fụl-ly, *adv.* In a curious or skilful manner.

dev′il, *v.t.*; deviled, *pt., pp.*; deviling, *ppr.* 1. To make devilish, or like a devil.

2. To pepper or season excessively and broil; a term used in cookery.

3. To cut up (cloth or rags) by an instrument called a devil.

dev′il, *n.* [ME. *devil*; AS. *deoful*; LL. *diabolus*, the devil; Gr. *diabolos*, the devil, lit. a slanderer, from *dia*, through, across, and *ballein*, to throw.]

1. In theology, an evil spirit or being; specifically, the evil one, represented in Scripture as the traducer, father of lies, tempter, etc., and referred to under the names Satan, Lucifer, Belial, Apollyon, Abaddon, the Man of Sin, the Adversary, etc.

2. A very wicked person; a traitor.

> Have I not chosen you twelve, and one of you is a *devil?* —John vi. 70.

3. Any great evil.

> To be tax'd, and beaten, is the *devil.* —Granville.

4. An expletive expressing wonder, vexation, etc.

> But wonder how the *devil* they got there. —Pope.

5. The name popularly given in Tasmania to a marsupial animal, *Dasyurus ursinus*, of great ferocity.

6. A printer's errand-boy or apprentice; formerly, the boy who took the printed sheets from the tympan of the press.

7. Colloquially, a term usually qualified by *poor* or *little*, synonymous with *fellow*; as, the *poor devil* could hardly walk.

8. The machine through which cotton or wool is first passed to prepare it for the carding machines; a teasing machine; a machine for cutting up rags and old cloth into flock and for other purposes.

9. In cookery, a dish, as a bone with some meat on it, grilled with Cayenne pepper.

Blue devils; see under *Blue.*

Cartesian devil; see under *Cartesian.*

Devil's advocate; in the Roman Catholic church, the official critic of names proposed for canonization; hence, any skeptical critic.

Devil's coach-horse; the wheel-bug; in England, *Ocypus olens*, the rove-beetle.

Devil's darning-needle; (a) the popular name of various species of the dragon-fly, so called from their long cylindrical bodies resembling needles; (b) a flower, Venus's-comb.

Printer's devil; see *Devil*, n. 6.

Tasmanian devil; see *Devil*, n. 5.

The devil's tattoo; a monotonous drumming, as with the hands or feet.

The devil to pay; trouble ahead; bad luck at hand or in store; from the nautical phrase, "*the devil to pay*, and no pitch hot," the devil being a certain seam so called from its awkwardness to calk.

To give the devil his due; to accord deserved credit to one of ill repute.

To play the devil with; to injure; to mismanage; to render inefficient or valueless.

dev′il-bī̇rd, *n.* A bird of the genus *Dicrurus*, native to India; the drongo-shrike.

dev′il-ess, *n.* A she-devil. [Rare.]

dev′il-et, *n.* A devilkin; a little devil. [Rare.]

dev′il-fish, *n.* One of various marine animals, from their appearance; (a) a fish, the angler; (b) a ray, *Manta birostris*; (c) the Californian gray whale.

dev′il-ing, *n.* A young devil.

dev′il-ish, *a.* [ME. *deoflich*; AS. *deoflic*, devilish, from *deoful*, devil.]

1. Partaking of the qualities of the devil; diabolical; very evil and mischievous; malicious; as, a *devilish* scheme; *devilish* wickedness.

2. Excessive; enormous; as, a *devilish* cheat. [Colloq.]

Syn.—Atrocious, diabolical, impious, malicious, satanic, wicked.

dev′il-ish-ly, *adv.* In a manner suiting the devil; diabolically; wickedly.

dev′il-ish-ness, *n.* The qualities of the devil.

dev′il-işm, *n.* The state or doctrine of the devil or devils.

dev′il-īze, *v.t.* To place among devils; opposed to *deify.* [Rare.]

dev′il-kin, *n.* A little devil.

dev′il-māy-çāre′, *a.* Careless; heedless; reckless. [Slang.]

dev′il-ment, *n.* Roguish mischief or trickery without ill intent.

dev′il-ry, *n.*; *pl.* **dev′il-rieş.** 1. Evil conduct; malice; deviltry.

2. Devils or evil spirits collectively.

dev′il′ş-ä″prŏn, *n.* An alga of the genus *Laminaria.*

dev′il′ş-bit, *n.* A plant, blazing-star; also, any plant of the genus *Scabiosa.*

dev′il′ş-clạw, *n.* *Pteroceras scorpio*, a scorpion-shell.

dev′il′ş-cot″tŏn, *n.* *Abroma augusta*, an East Indian fiber-plant.

dev′il′ş-dāi″şy, *n.* The whiteweed.

dev′il′ş-dust, *n.* Shoddy.

dev′il′ş-guts, *n.* *Cuscuta Epithymum*, dodder, a plant parasitic on furze, heath, thyme, and other plants.

dev′il-ship, *n.* The person or character of a devil; a ludicrous title of address, on type of *lordship*, to the devil.

dev′il′ş-shōe″strings, *n.* *Tephrosia Virginiana*, goat's-rue.

dev′il-tree, dev′il′ş-tree, *n.* *Alstonia scholaris*, an evergreen tropical tree of the eastern hemisphere producing dita-bark.

dev′il-try, *n.*; *pl.* **dev′il-trieş.** Conduct in keeping with that of the devil; devilry.

dev′il-wood, *n.* *Osmanthus Americanus*, the American olive, growing in the south Atlantic states. It has a very compact wood.

dev′il-wŏr″ship, *n.* The worship paid to the devil, an evil spirit, a malignant deity, or the personified evil principle in nature, by many of the primitive tribes of Asia, Africa, and America.

dē′vi-ous, *a.* [L. *devius*, out of the way, off the road; *de*, off, from, and *via*, road.]

1. Out of the common way or track; as, a *devious* course.

> The *devious* paths where wanton fancy leads. —Rowe.

2. Following circuitous or winding paths; rambling. [Rare.]

3. Erring; going astray from rectitude or the divine precepts.

> Thoughts of love on a darkened and *devious* spirit. —Longfellow.

Syn.—Circuitous, roundabout, erratic, roving, rambling, erring, straying.

dē′vi-ous-ly, *adv.* In a devious manner.

dē′vi-ous-ness, *n.* Departure from a regular course; wandering.

dē-vir′ġin-āte, *a.* Deflowered. [Obs.]

dē-vir′ġin-āte, *v.t.* To deflower. [Obs.]

dē-vir-ġi-nā′tion, *n.* A deflowering. [Obs.]

dē-viş′ȧ-ble, *a.* 1. That may be bequeathed or given by will.

2. That can be invented or contrived.

dē-viş′ăl, *n.* A devising.

dē-vīşe′, *v.t.*; devised, *pt., pp.*; devising, *ppr.* [ME. *devisen, devysen*; OFr. *deviser*, to distribute, direct, regulate, talk, from L. *divisus*, pp. of *dividere*, to divide.]

1. To invent; to contrive; to form in the mind by new combinations of ideas, new applications of principles, or new arrangement of parts; to plan; to scheme; to project; as, to *devise* an engine or machine; to *devise* a new mode of writing; to *devise* a plan of defense; to *devise* arguments.

> *Devising* their own daughter's death. —Tennyson.

2. In law, to give or bequeath by will, as land or other real estate.

dē-vīşe′, *v.i.* To consider; to contrive; to lay a plan; to form a scheme; as, to plan and *devise.* Formerly followed by *of*; as, let us *devise of* ease.

dē-vīşe′, *n.* 1. Primarily, a dividing or division; hence, the act of giving or distributing real estate by a testator. The term is also sometimes applied, though improperly, to bequest of personal estate.

2. A will or testament.

3. A share of estate bequeathed.
dē-vīse′, *n.* Device. [Obs.]
dev-i-ṣee′, *n.* The person to whom a devise is made; one to whom real estate is bequeathed.
dē-vīṣ′ẽr, *n.* One who contrives or invents.
dē-vīṣ′ŏr, *n.* One who gives by will; one who bequeaths lands or tenements.
dev′i-tȧ-ble, *a.* Avoidable. [Obs.]
dē-vī′tăl-īze, *v.t.* To deprive of vitality or the power to sustain vitality; as, to *devitalize* air or food
dē-vī″tăl-i-zā′tion, *n.* The act of devitalizing or state of being devitalized.
dev-i-tā′tion, *n.* An escaping; a warning off. [Obs.]
dē-vit″ri-fi-cā′tion, *n.* The act of depriving glass of its transparency, and converting it into a gray, opaque substance; the state of being devitrified.
dē-vit′ri-fȳ, *v.t.*; devitrified, *pt.*, *pp.*; devitrifying, *ppr.* To render nonvitreous; to make opaque and hard by subjection to heat.
dē-vō′căl-īze, *v.t.*; devocalized, *pt.*, *pp.*; devocalizing, *ppr.* To deprive of voice; to deprive of the quality of a vowel.
dē-vō″căl-i-zā′tion, *n.* The act of devocalizing or state of being devocalized.
dev-ō-cā′tion, *n.* [L. *devocare*, to call away.] A calling away; seduction. [Rare.]
dē-void′, *a.* 1. Void; empty; vacant. [Obs.]
2. Destitute; not possessing; with *of*; as, *devoid of* understanding.
dē-void′, *v.t.* [ME. *devoiden*, to make empty, to leave; OFr. *desvoidier*, to empty out; *des-*, from, and *voidier*, to make empty; *void*, empty.] To avoid; also, to destroy. [Obs.]
de-voir′ (de-vwär′), *n.*; *pl.* **de-voirṣ′**. [Fr., duty, from *devoir* to owe; L. *debere*, to owe, to be indebted to.] Service or duty; an act of civility or respect; respectful notice due to another; as, we paid our *devoirs* to the ladies.
dev-ō-lū′tion, *n.* [L. *devolutus*, pp. of *devolvere*, to roll down.]
1. The act of rolling down; as, the *devolution* of earth into a valley. [Rare.]
2. Removal from one person to another; a passing or falling upon a successor.
3. Degeneration, as opposed to evolution.
dē-volve′, *v.t.*; devolved, *pt.*, *pp.*; devolving, *ppr.* [L. *devolvere*, to roll down.]
1. To roll down. [Rare.]
2. To move from one person to another; to deliver over or from one possessor to a successor; as, to *devolve* care or power.
dē-volve′, *v.i.* 1. To roll down. [Rare.]
2. To pass from one to another; to fall by succession from one possessor to his successor; as, the command *devolved* on the next officer in rank.
dē-volve′ment, *n.* The act of devolving; devolution.
Dev′ŏn, *n.* A breed of red, hardy, small-sized cattle, valued for the dairy, for beef, and for use under yoke; native to Devonshire, England.
Dē-vō′ni-ăn, *a.* 1. Of or pertaining to Devonshire, England; as, the *Devonian* rocks.
2. In geology, of or pertaining to the *Devonian* age.
Devonian age; in geology, the age of fishes; the formative period between the Silurian and Carboniferous ages, embracing in its strata the old red sandstone of Great Britain, which is rich in fossil fauna.
Dē-vō′ni-ăn, *n.* [AS. *Defenas*, *Defnas*, the inhabitants of Devon or Devonshire, England.] The Devonian age or formation.
dev-ō-rā′tion, *n.* The act of devouring. [Obs.]
dē-vō′tȧ-ry, *n.* A votary. [Obs.]
dē-vōte′, *v.t.*; devoted, *pt.*, *pp.*; devoting, *ppr.* [L. *devotus*, pp. of *devovere*, to vow; *de*, from, and *vovere*, to vow.]
1. To appropriate by vow; to set apart or dedicate by a solemn act; to consecrate.
2. To give up wholly; to addict; to direct the attention wholly or chiefly to; to attach; as, to *devote* oneself to science; to *devote* ourselves to our friends
3. To doom; to consign over; as, to *devote* one to destruction.
4. To execrate; to curse. [Obs.]
Syn.—Dedicate, hallow, destine, consign, doom.
dē-vōte′, *a.* and *n.* I. *a.* Devoted; devout. [Obs.]
II. *n.* A devotee. [Obs.]
dē-vōt′ed, *a.* Appropriated by vow; consecrated; ardent; zealous; strongly attached.
dē-vōt′ed-ly, *adv.* In a devoted manner.
dē-vōt′ed-ness, *n.* The state of being devoted.
dev-ō-tee′, *n.* One who is wholly devoted; particularly, one given wholly to religion; one who is superstitiously given to religious duties and ceremonies; a bigot.
dev-ō-tee′ism, *n.* The state of a devotee; the tendency to become a devotee.
dē-vōte′ment, *n.* The act of devoting; the state of being devoted. [Rare.]
dē-vōt′ẽr, *n.* One who devotes; a worshiper.
dē-vō′tion, *n.* [ME. *devotioun*; OFr. *devotion*; L. *devotio*, a devoting, consecrating, from *devovere*, to vow, devote.]
1. The act of devoting or consecrating; as, the *devotion* of one's talents to God's service.
2. The state of being devoted; observance of any practice or duty, especially of religious duties; devoutness; strong attachment; zeal; ardor; earnestness.

> Whose crime had been a *devotion* too zealous to the interests of his prerogative. —Macaulay.

3. Act of devoutness; act of worship; a religious exercise; prayer; generally used in the plural.

> An aged, holy man,
> That day and night said his *devotion*. —Spenser.

4. Something consecrated; an object of devotion. [Rare.]
5. Disposal; power of disposing. [Obs.]
Syn.—Consecration, devotedness, piety, zeal, ardor, earnestness, devoutness.
dē-vō′tion-ăl, *a.* Pertaining to devotion; used in devotion; as, a *devotional* posture; *devotional* exercises; a *devotional* frame of mind.
dē-vō′tion-ăl-ist, *n.* A devotionist.
dē-vō-tion-al′i-ty, *n.* Devotion as practised by a devotionist. [Rare.]
dē-vō′tion-ăl-ly, *adv.* In a devotional manner; toward devotion; as, *devotionally* inclined.
dē-vō′tion-ist, *n.* A person given to devotion; one superstitiously or formally devout. [Rare.]
dē-vō′tō, *n.* [It.] A devotee. [Obs.]
dē-vō′tŏr, *n.* One who reverences or worships. [Obs.]
dē-vour′, *v.t.*; devoured, *pt.*, *pp.*; devouring, *ppr.* [ME. *devouren*; OFr. *devorer*; L. *devorare*, to devour, to eat greedily; *de-*, intens., and *vorare*, to swallow whole.]
1. To eat up; to eat with greediness; to eat ravenously, as a beast of prey.

> Some evil beast hath *devoured* him. —Gen. xxxvii. 20.

2. To destroy; to consume wantonly and with violence; to annihilate; to waste.

> I waste my life and do my days *devour*. —Spenser.

3. To enjoy with avidity; to gaze upon eagerly.

> *Devour* her o'er and o'er with vast delight. —Dryden.

Syn.—Consume, annihilate, waste, destroy.
dē-vour′ȧ-ble, *a.* Capable of being devoured.
dē-vour′ẽr, *n.* One who or that which devours.
dē-vour′ing-ly, *adv.* In a devouring manner.
dē-vour′ment, *n.* The act or process of devouring.
dē-vout′, *a.* [ME. *devout*; OFr. *devot*, devout; L. *devotus*, pp. of *devovere*, to vow, devote.]
1. Yielding a solemn and reverential devotion to God in religious exercises, particularly in prayer; pious; religious.

> We must be constant and *devout* in the worship of God. —Rogers.

2. Expressing devotion or piety; as, eyes *devout*.
3. Sincere; earnest; as, you have my *devout* wishes for your safety.
Syn.—Holy, pious, religious, reverent, sincere, earnest.
dē-vout′, *n.* 1. A devotee. [Obs.]
2. The whole or a part of a devotional composition. [Obs.]
dē-vout′fụl, *a.* 1. Full of or characterized by devoutness; devout. [Rare.]
2. Sacred. [Rare.]
dē-vout′less, *a.* Destitute of devotion.
dē-vout′less-ly, *adv.* Without devotion.
dē-vout′less-ness, *n.* Want of devotion.
dē-vout′ly, *adv.* 1. In a devout manner; with ardent devotion; piously; religiously; with pious thoughts.
2. Sincerely; solemnly; earnestly.
dē-vout′ness, *n.* The quality or state of being devout.
dē-vōve′, *v.t.* To devote. [Obs.]
dē-vow′, *v.t.* 1. To give up. [Obs.]
2. To disavow; to disclaim. [Obs.]
dē-vul′găr-īze, *v.t.* To deprive of what is vulgar, commonplace, or narrow.
dew (dū), *n.* [ME. *dew*; AS. *deaw*, dew.]
1. The aqueous vapor or moisture which is deposited by condensation from the atmosphere, especially at night, in the form of minute globules, on the surfaces of bodies when they have become colder than the surrounding atmosphere.
2. Anything which falls lightly, or so as to refresh.

> The golden *dew* of sleep. —Shak.

3. Something emblematic of morning, youth, freshness, and vigor.

> Having the *dew* of his youth, and the beauty thereof. —Longfellow.

dew, *v.t.* To wet with or as with dew; to moisten.
dew, *a.* and *n.* Due; duty. [Obs.]
dē-wạn′, *n.* [Hind. *diwan*, a council, minister, a head officer in charge of finance and revenue, from Per. *divan*, an account-book.] In India, (a) a native premier of a state; (b) the principal minister of finance of a state; (c) a native superintendent of certain government institutions; (d) a native confidential chief steward of a house of business.
dē-wạ′ni, dē-wạn′ny, *n.* [Hind.] The office presided over by a dewan.
dew′-bēat″ẽr, *n.* 1. One who takes an early morning walk and brushes off the dew.
2. An oiled shoe.
dew′ber″ry, *n.* 1. The popular name of *Rubus Canadensis*, a low blackberry plant; the fruit of the plant.
2. In England, the popular name of the *Rubus cæsius*, a bramble which grows in woods, thickets, hedges, and the borders of fields; the fruit of the plant.
dew′clạw, *n.* 1. One of the bones or little nails behind the foot of a deer or other ungulate.
2. The uppermost claw in a dog's foot, smaller than the rest, and not touching the ground.
dew′cup, *n.* *Alchemilla vulgaris*, the lady's-mantle.
dew′drop, *n.* A drop of dew.
dew′ey-līte, *n.* [From Chester *Dewey*, an American scientist, and *-lite*.] A hydrous silicate of magnesium found in amorphous masses. It is allied to serpentine.
dew′fạll, *n.* The falling of dew; the early evening when dew begins to fall.
dew′i-ness, *n.* The state of being dewy.
dew′lap, *n.* 1. The fold of skin that hangs from the throat of oxen and cows, which laps or licks the dew in grazing.
2. The flesh on the human throat when flaccid with age. [Humorous.]

> And on the withered *dewlap* pour the ale. —Shak.

dew′lapped (-lapt), *a.* Provided with a dewlap.
dew′less, *a.* Having no dew.
dew′-point, *n.* The temperature at which dew begins to form. It varies with the humidity of the atmosphere.
dew′ret, *v.t.* To rot, as hemp or flax, by subjecting it to the process called dewretting.
dew′ret″ting, *n.* The spreading of hemp or flax on grass to expose it to the action of dew, which expedites the separation of the fiber from the feculent matter.
dew′rot, *v.t.* To dewret.
dew′-shōe, *n.* The lower end of the sheath of a sword.
dew′stōne, *n.* A species of limestone in Nottinghamshire, England, which collects a large quantity of dew on its surface.
dew′try, *n.* The thorn-apple, *Datura Stramonium*.
dew′wŏrm, *n.* Same as *Earthworm*.
dew′y, *a.* 1. Pertaining to, resembling, or characterized by dew; moist with dew; accompanied with dew; abounding in dew.

> A *dewy* mist
> Went up, and watered all the ground. —Milton.

> The sun with orient beams had chased the *dewy* night. —Addison.

2. Falling gently, or refreshing, like dew.

> *Dewy* sleep ambrosial. —Cowper.

3. In botany, appearing as if covered with dew.
dex-i-ō-. A combining form from Gr. *dexios*, on the right side.
dex″i-ō-cär′di-ȧ, *n.* [*Dexio-*, and Gr. *kardia*, heart.] Transposition of the heart from the left to the right side of the thorax.
dex″i-ō-trop′ic, *a.* [*Dexio-*, and Gr. *tropos*, a turning, from *trepein*, to turn.] Turning or turned to the right; dextral, as a shell; opposed to *læotropic*.
dex′tẽr, *a.* [L. *dexter*, on the right side, right.]
1. Pertaining to or situated on the right hand; right, as opposed to left; as, the *dexter* side of a shield.
2. In heraldry, placed on that side of a shield which is toward the right of the wearer, or toward the left of the spectator in front.
Dexter base; in heraldry, the dexter part of the base of the shield.
Dexter base point; in heraldry, a point half way between the base point and the dexter edge of the shield.
Dexter chief; in heraldry, the dexter part of the chief of the shield.
Dexter chief point; in heraldry, a point in the right-hand upper corner of the shield, being in the dexter extremity of the chief, as A in the cut.

A, Dexter Chief Point.

dex-ter′i-ty, *n.* [L. *dexteritas*, skilfulness, handiness, from *dexter*, right, fit, prompt.]

1. Ability to use the right hand more readily than the left; right-handedness. [Rare.]

2. Suppleness; adroitness; activity; expertness; skill; that readiness in performing an action which proceeds from experience or practice, united with activity or quick motion.

Dexterity of hand, even in common trades, cannot be acquired without much practice and experience. —A. Smith.

3. Readiness of mind in managing or controlling a scheme of operations; mental adroitness.

By his incomparable *dexterity*, he raised himself to the first throne of Italy.—Macaulay.

Syn.—Art, ability, expertness, aptness, facility, aptitude, adroitness, skill, tact, cleverness.

dex′tĕr-ous, dex′trous, *a.* [L. *dexter*, right.] 1. Ready and expert in the use of the body and limbs; skilful and active in manual employment; adroit; as, a *dexterous* hand; a *dexterous* workman.

2. Ready in the use of the mental faculties; prompt in contrivance and management; expert; quick at inventing expedients; as, a *dexterous* manager.

Dexterous the craving, fawning crowd to quit. —Pope.

3. Skilful; artful; done with dexterity; as, *dexterous* management.

Syn.—Artful, skilful, clever, adroit, expert, apt, active.

dex′tĕr-ous-ly, dex′trous-ly, *adv.* With dexterity; expertly; skilfully; artfully; adroitly; promptly.

dex′tĕr-ous-ness, dex′trous-ness, *n.* Dexterity; adroitness.

dex′trad, *adv.* Toward the right hand; to the right side; dextrally.

dex′trăl, *a.* 1. Right, as opposed to left.

2. In zoölogy, dextrorse; said of shells which have whorls turning from left to right; opposed to *sinistral.*

dex-tral′i-ty, *n.* 1. The state of being on the right side.

2. Right-handedness.

dex′trăl-ly, *adv.* Toward the right; dextrad.

dex′trăn, dex′trāne, *n.* [From L. *dexter*, right.] A white amorphous gum, $C_6H_{10}O_5$, formed in milk by the action of cocci. It also occurs in unripe beet-root.

dex-trēr′, *n.* [Obs.] See *Destrer.*

dex′trine, dex′trin, *n.* [From L. *dexter*, right, and *-ine.*] The soluble or gummy matter into which the interior substance of starch globules is convertible by diastase or by certain acids. It is remarkable for the extent to which it turns the plane of polarization to the right hand, whence its name. Its composition is the same as that of starch. By the action of hot diluted acids, or of an infusion of malt, dextrine is finally converted into grape-sugar. It is used as a substitute for gum arabic in medicine. Called also *gommeline, British gum, moist gum, starch-gum, Alsace gum, leiocome.*

dex-trō-. A combining form from Latin *dexter*, right.

dex-trō-căr′di-ȧ, *n.* [*Dextro-*, and Gr. *kardia*, the heart.] Same as *Dexiocardia.*

dex′trō-com″pound, *n.* In chemistry, a compound body which causes the plane of a ray of polarized light to rotate to the right, as dextrine, dextroglucose, malic acid, etc.

dex-trog′ĕr-ous, *a.* [*Dextro-*, and L. *gerere*, to carry.] Same as *Dextrogyrate.*

dex-trō-glū′cōse, *n.* Same as *Dextrose.*

dex-trō-gȳ′rāte, *a.* [*Dextro-*, and L. *gyratus*, circular, pp. of *gyrare*, to turn, from *gyrus*, a circle.] Causing to turn toward the right hand; as, a *dextrogyrate* crystal, that is, a crystal which in circular polarization turns rays of light to the right.

dex-trō-gȳ′rous, *a.* [*Dextro-*, and L. *gyrus*, a circle.] Circling to the right.

dex-tron′ic, *a.* Pertaining to dextrose; obtained from dextrose.

Dextronic acid; a compound obtained as a syrupy liquid from glucose, starch, dextrine, etc.; called also *gluconic acid, maltonic acid.*

dex-trō-rō′tȧ-ry, *a.* Same as *Dextrogyrate.*

dex-trō-rō′tȧ-tō-ry, *a.* Same as *Dextrogyrate.*

dex-tror′săl, *a.* See *Dextrorse.*

dex′trorse, *a.* [L. *dextrorsum* or *dextrovorsum*, toward the right; *dexter*, right, and *versus* or *vorsus*, pp. of *vertere* or *vortere*, to turn.] Rising from right to left, as a spiral line, helix, or climbing plant. *Dextrorse* is used in botany by Darwin, Hooker and other scientists as above defined. Linnæus, the De Candolles, and others give it an opposite meaning.

dex′trōse, *n.* A sugar, $C_6H_{12}O_6$, of the glucose group, that rotates the plane of polarization of a ray of light to the right. The solid product is known as grape-sugar, and the syrup, glucose: called also *dextroglucose, grape-sugar*, and *starch-sugar.*

dex-trō-trop′ic, *a.* Same as *Dexiotropic.*

dex-trot′rō-pous, *a.* Dexiotropic.

dex′trous (-trus), *a.* Same as *Dexterous.*

dex′trous-ly, *adv.* Same as *Dexterously.*

dex′trous-ness, *n.* Same as *Dexterousness.*

dey (dā), *n.* [Fr. *dey*; Turk. *day*, a maternal uncle, a friendly title formerly given to middle-aged or old people; in Algiers, given to the commanding officer who frequently became pasha or governor.]

1. A Turkish title of the governor of Algiers before the French conquest in 1830.

2. A former ruler of Tunis or Tripoli.

dey, *n.* [ME. *dey, deye*; Ice. *deigja*, a maidservant.] A dairy servant, usually a woman; any woman-servant.

deye (dā), *v.i.* To die. [Obs.]

deyn′te, deyn′tee (dān′ty), *n.* and *a.* Dainty. [Obs.]

dē-zinc″i-fi-cā′tion, *n.* The act or process of dezincifying.

dē-zinc′i-fȳ, *v.t.*; dezincified, *pt., pp.*; dezincifying, *ppr.* To free from zinc.

dhak (dak), *n.* [Hind.] An East Indian tree, *Butea frondosa.*

dhäl (dol), *n.* Same as *Dholl.*

dhär′mȧ (där′), *n.* [Sans., law.] A Buddhist term for that on which the law of truth and virtue is based; also, the law itself.

dhō′bie, dhō′by (dō′bi), *n.* [Hind. *dhobī*, a washerman, from *dhob*, a washing.] An East Indian term for a manservant who does washing.

dhōle (dōl), *n.* [E. Ind. name.] A wild mountain dog, *Canis dukhunensis*, found in the southeastern part of Asia. It seldom hunts alone, but pursues its prey in packs.

dhōll (dōl), *n.* An East Indian name for the pigeon-pea.

dhō′ney, dhō′ny (dō′), *n.* Same as *Doni.*

dhōur′rȧ, dhūr′rȧ (dūr′), *n.* Same as *Durra.*

dhow (dou), *n.* [Ar.] An Arab vessel, generally with one mast, from 150 to 250 tons' burden, employed in mercantile trading or in the slave-trade; also written *dow.*

Slave Dhow, east coast of Africa.

dhun′chee (dun′chē), *n.* [E. Ind.] A tropical shrub, *Sesbania aculeata*, having a hemp-like fiber.

di-, *prefix.* A combining form from the L. prefix *di-*, Gr. *di-*, two, double, from Gr. *dyo*, two; signifying two, twofold, double.

di-a-, di-, *prefix.* Combining forms from the L. prefix *dia-*, Gr. *dia-*, through, from the prep. *dia*, through; signifying through, right through, throughout, in different directions, from, asunder, between; often with intensive force, as, thoroughly, utterly, absolutely.

dī′ȧ-bāse, *n.* [Fr., from Gr. *diabasis*, a crossing over; *dia*, through, and *bainein*, to go.] A crystalline granular rock, composed of triclinic feldspar, pyroxene, iron oxid, and sometimes apatite or olivin.

dī-ab-ȧ-tē′ri-ăl, *a.* [Gr. *diabatēria* (supply *hiera*), sacrifices, offerings for a happy passage, from *diabainein*, to go across.] Crossing the limits. [Rare.]

dī-ȧ-bē′tēs, *n.* [L., from Gr. *diabētēs*, a pair of compasses, diabetes, from *diabainein*, to make a stride, to stand with the legs apart.] A diseased condition of the system, characterized by an excessive discharge of urine, often saccharine in its nature.

Diabetes mellitus; diabetes in which the urine contains sugar; a disease usually fatal.

Diabetes insipidus; diabetes in which the urine is normal, of low specific gravity, and excessive.

dī-ȧ-bet′ic, dī-ȧ-bet′ic-ăl, *a.* Pertaining to diabetes; affected with diabetes.

Diabetic sugar; a glucose giving the saccharine element to urine in diabetes.

dī-äb′le-rie, dī-äb′le-ry, *n.* [Fr. *diablerie*; OFr. *diablerie*, from *diable*, devil.]

1. Sorcery; magic arts.

2. Devilry; diabolic acts or practices.

dī-ȧ-bol′ic, dī-ȧ-bol′ic-ăl, *a.* [LL. *diabolicus*, devilish, from *diabolus*; Gr. *diabolos*, the devil.] Devilish; pertaining to the devil; hence, extremely malicious; impious; atrocious; nefarious; outrageously wicked; partaking of any quality ascribed to the devil; as, a *diabolical* temper; a *diabolical* scheme or action.

dī-ȧ-bol′ic-ăl-ly, *adv.* In a diabolical manner; very wickedly; nefariously.

dī-ȧ-bol′ic-ăl-ness, *n.* The state of being diabolic.

dī-ȧ-bol′i-fȳ, *v.t.*; diabolified, *pt., pp.*; diabolifying, *ppr.* To ascribe diabolical qualities to.

dī-ab′ō-lism, *n.* 1. The actions of the devil.

2. Possession by the devil.

3. In occultism, black art; sorcery.

dī-ab′ō-līze, *v.t.* To render diabolical. [Rare.]

dī″ȧ-bō-lol′ō-ġy, *n.* [Gr. *diabolos*, the devil, and *logos*, a description, from *legein*, to speak.] The literature, legends, and traditions about the devil; devil-lore.

Dī-ȧ-brot′i-cȧ, *n.* [L., from Gr. *diabrōtikos*, able to eat through; *dia*, through, and *bibrōskein*, to devour.] A large genus of beetles of the *Chrysomelidæ* family, including the common striped cucumber-beetle. They are very destructive to fruit trees, vegetables, etc.

dī″ȧ-cȧ-thol′i-con, *n.* [L., from Gr. *dia*, through, and *katholikos*, universal.] A purgative having a number of constituents, supposed to be of general efficacy.

dī-ȧ-caus′tic, *a.* In mathematics, belonging to a species of caustic curves formed by refraction. If rays P*m*, issuing from a luminous point P, be refracted by the curve A *m* B, so that the sines of incidence are to the sines of refraction in a given ratio; the curve CDH, which touches all the refracted rays, is called the *diacaustic* curve or caustic by refraction.

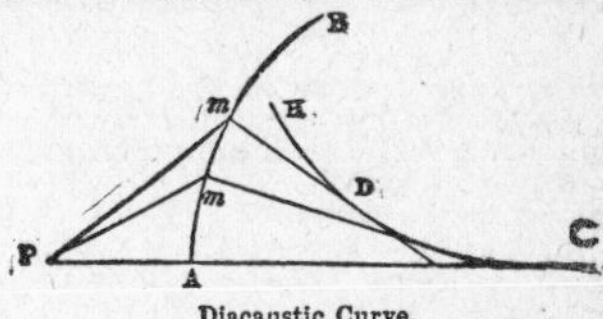

Diacaustic Curve.

dī-ȧ-caus′tic, *n.* 1. A diacaustic curve.

2. In medicine, a double-convex lens sometimes used for cauterization.

dī-ȧ-chē′ni-um, *n.*; *pl.* **dī-ȧ-chē′ni-ȧ.** Same as *Cremocarp.*

dī-ach′y-lon, dī-ach′y-lum, *n.*; *pl.* **dī-ach′y-lȧ.** [L., from Gr. *diachylos*, very juicy; *dia-*, intens., and *chylos*, juice.] A plaster, originally composed of the juices of several plants, whence its name, but now made of an oxid of lead and oil.

dī-ac′id, *a.* Having a valence of two, as a base.

dī-ac′lȧ-sis, *n.* [L., from Gr. *diaklān*, to break in two; *dia*, through, apart, and *klān*, to break.] Refraction.

dī-ȧ-clī′năl, *a.* [*Dia-*, and Gr. *klinein*, to lean.] In geology, transverse, as regards a fold; as, a *diaclinal* fissure.

dī-ȧ-cō′di-um, *n.* [L. *diacodion*, a medicine made from poppy juice, from Gr. *dia*, through, from, and *kōdeia*, a poppy head.] The syrup of poppies.

dī-ac′ō-năl, *a.* [L. *diaconus*, a deacon.] Pertaining to a deacon.

dī-ac′ō-nāte, *n.* 1. The office of a deacon.

2. A board of deacons; deacons collectively.

dī-ac′ō-nāte, *a.* Managed by deacons.

dī-ȧ-con′i-con, dī-ȧ-con′i-cum, *n.*; *pl.* **dī-ȧ-con′i-cȧ.** [L. *diaconicum*; Gr. *diakonikon*, a place for storing the vessels, vestments, etc., from *diakonos*, a servant, a deacon.] In the Greek church, (a) the sacristy; (b) [*pl.*] a deacon's manual.

dī-ac′ō-pē, *n.* [Gr. *diakopē*, a gash, from *diakoptein*, to cut through.]

1. In surgery, a deep cut; a longitudinal fracture. [Rare.]

2. In grammar, same as *tmesis.*

dī-ȧ-cous′tic (*or* -kous′), *a.* [Gr. *diakouein*, to hear through; *dia*, through, and *akouein*, to hear.] Pertaining to the science or doctrine of refracted sounds.

dī-ȧ-cous′tics, *n.* That branch of natural philosophy which treats of the properties of sound refracted by passing through different mediums; called also *diaphonics.*

dī″ȧ-cran-tē′ri-ăn, dī″ȧ-cran-ter′ic, *a.* [*Dia-*, and Gr. *krantēres*, the wisdom teeth, lit. the performers or completers, from *krainein*, to accomplish, complete.] Having the posterior and anterior teeth in rows somewhat apart, as certain serpents.

dī-ȧ-crit′ic, *n.* A diacritical mark.

dī-ȧ-crit′ic-ăl, dī-ȧ-crit′ic, *a.* [Gr. *diakritikos*, able to distinguish, from *diakrinein*, to separate, distinguish; *dia*, between, and *krinein*, to divide, distinguish.] That separates, or distinguishes; distinctive.

Diacritical mark, sign, or *point*; any mark used with a letter or character to distinguish it from another or to indicate how it is pronounced.

dī-ac′tine, dī-ac′ti-năl, *a.* [*Di-*, two, and Gr. *aktis* (*-inos*), a ray.] Tapering at both extremities; having two axes.

dī-ac-tin′ic, *a.* In physics, conducting or able to conduct actinic rays.

Dī-ȧ-del′phi-ȧ, *n.pl.* [Gr. *di-*, twice, and *adelphos*, brother.] A class of plants whose stamens are united into two bodies or bundles by their filaments.

dī-ȧ-del′phous, dī-ȧ-del′phi-ăn, *a.* In botany, having its stamens united in two bundles by their filaments, the bundles being equal or unequal; grouped together in two bundles; as, *diadelphous* stamens. In papilionaceous flowers, out of ten stamens nine are often united, while one (the posterior) is free.

Diadelphous Stamens of *Indigofera tinctoria.*

dī′ȧ-dem, *n.* [ME. *diademe*; OFr. *diademe*; L. *diadema*; Gr. *diadēma*, a band or fillet, from *diadein*, to bind round, encircle; *dia*, through, and *dein*, to bind.]

1. Parthian Diadem. 2. Jeweled Diadem of Constantine.—From ancient coins.

1. In ancient times, a headband or fillet worn by kings as a badge of royalty.

2. A mark or badge of royalty, worn on the head; a crown; figuratively, empire; supreme power.

3. In heraldry, the arch supporting the globe at the top of a crown.

dī′ȧ-dem, *v.t.* To crown.

dī′ȧ-dem-lē″mūr, *n.* A Madagascan ruffed lemur, *Propithecus diadema*, about the size of a cat.

dī′ȧ-dem-spī″dēr, *n.* The common spider, *Epeira diadema.*

Dī-ad′ō-chī, *n.pl.* [L., from Gr. *diadochoi*, pl. of *diadochos*, a successor, from *diadechesthai*, to receive from another, to succeed to; *dia*, through, and *dechesthai*, to take, receive.] The Macedonian generals who divided the empire of Alexander the Great among themselves, after his death.

Dī-ȧ-dō′chi-ăn, *a.* and *n.* I. *a.* Of or pertaining to the Diadochi.

II. *n.* One of the Diadochi.

dī′ȧ-drom, *n.* A course or passing; a vibration; the time in which the vibration of a pendulum is performed. [Obs.]

dī-ær′e-sis (-er′), *n.* Same as *Dieresis.*

dī-æ-ret′ic, *a.* Same as *Dieretic.*

dī-ȧ-ġē-ō-trop′ic, *a.* [*Dia-*, and Gr. *gē*, earth, and *tropos*, a turning, from *trepein*, to turn.] Of the nature of, relating to, or characterized by diageotropism.

dī″ȧ-ġē-ot′rō-pism, *n.* The inclination of the parts of a plant to form a right angle to the direction of gravitation.

dī′ȧ-glyph, *n.* [Gr. *diaglyphein*, to carve through; *dia*, through, and *glyphein*, to carve, hollow out.] An intaglio.

dī-ȧ-glyph′ic, dī-ȧ-glyp′tic, *a.* Depressed; pertaining to or having the characteristics of a diaglyph.

dī-ag-nōse′, *v.t.*; diagnosed, *pt., pp.*; diagnosing, *ppr.* In pathology, to distinguish; to discriminate; to ascertain from symptoms the true nature and seat of (a disease).

dī-ag-nō′sis, *n.* [L., from Gr. *diagnōsis*, a distinguishing, discrimination, from *diagignōskein*, to distinguish, discern between; *dia*, through, between, and *gignōskein*, to know.] Scientific discrimination of any kind; a short distinctive description as of plants; more specifically, in medicine, the discrimination of diseases by their distinctive marks or symptoms; the examination of a person to discover what ailment affects him.

Differential diagnosis; separation of generic diseases or objects in natural history into a specific class.

dī-ag-nos′tic, *a.* Of or pertaining to diagnosis; characteristic.

dī-ag-nos′tic, *n.* [Gr. *diagnōstikos*, able to distinguish.]

1. The sign or symptom by which a disease is known or distinguished from others.

2. In biology, a term or phrase which characterizes or defines.

dī-ag-nos′ti-cāte, *v.t.*; diagnosticated, *pt., pp.*; diagnosticating, *ppr* To diagnose.

dī″ag-nos-ti′ciăn (-tish′un), *n.* One who is skilled in diagnosis.

dī-ag-nos′tics, *n.* That part of medical science which treats of diagnosis; symptomatology.

dī-ȧ-gom′e-tēr, *n.* [From Gr. *diagein*, to conduct; *dia*, through, and *agein*, to lead, and *metron*, a measure.] An electrical apparatus used to determine the relative conductivity of different substances, as of coffee and chicory. It is used to detect adulterants.

dī-ag′ō-năl, *a.* [L. *diagonalis*; Gr. *diagōnios*, from angle to angle, diagonal; *dia*, through, and *gōnia*, an angle, corner.]

1. In geometry, joining, as a line, two nonadjacent angles of a quadrilateral or multilateral figure, and dividing it into two parts.

2. Being in an angular or oblique direction.

Diagonal bond; masonry in which the stones are laid aslant, instead of being bedded flat; herringbone work.

Diagonal scale; a scale upon a flat ruler, in which equidistant parallels are laid down, with oblique lines crossing them. With the aid of the compasses, such a scale facilitates the laying down of lines to the two-hundredth part of an inch.

dī-ag′ō-năl, *n.* 1. A right line joining two nonadjacent angles of a quadrilateral or multilateral figure, and dividing it into two parts.

2. Any oblique or diagonal line, as a row of squares running obliquely on a chessboard; or any member of a framework, running diagonally.

3. A kind of cloth in which the twills or ribs run obliquely.

dī-ag′ō-năl-built (-bilt), *a.* Sheathed in two transverse layers running oppositely, making an angle of forty-five degrees with the keel; applied to a ship.

dī-ag′ō-năl-ly, *adv.* In a diagonal direction.

dī-ȧ-gō′ni-ăl, *a.* Diagonal; opposed diametrically.

dī′ȧ-gram, *n.* [Fr. *diagramme*; L. *diagramma*; Gr. *diagramma*, that which is marked out by lines, a diagram, a scale, from *diagraphein*, to mark out by lines, to draw; *dia*, through, across, and *graphein*, to write.]

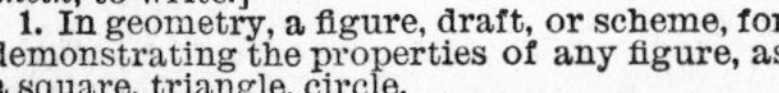

Diagram.

1. In geometry, a figure, draft, or scheme, for demonstrating the properties of any figure, as a square, triangle, circle.

2. Any mechanical drawing, giving only the outlines or essentials, often crude; a map or plan, distinguished from a drawing in perspective; as, a *diagram* of a street-car system.

3. In old music, a scale.

dī′ȧ-gram, *v.t.* To make a diagram of; as, to *diagram* a sentence.

dī″ȧ-gram-mat′ic, *a.* Requiring the use of a diagram; of the nature of or pertaining to a diagram.

dī″ȧ-gram-mat′ic-ăl-ly, *adv.* By the use of a diagram; according to a diagram.

dī′ȧ-grȧph, *n.* [Gr. *diagraphein*, to mark out by lines.]

1. An apparatus by means of which one with no knowledge of drawing or perspective can draw mechanically objects before him.

2. An instrument used in drafting, consisting of a protractor and a scale.

dī-ȧ-graph′ic, dī-ȧ-graph′ic-ăl, *a.* Descriptive.

dī-ȧ-graph′ics, *n.* The art or science of descriptive or mathematical drawing.

dī-ȧ-gryd′i-āte, *n.* [LL. *diagrydium*; Gr. *dia-grydion*, the juice of a purgative plant.] A strong purgative made of scammony and quince juice.

dī-ȧ-hē″li-ō-trop′ic, *a.* Pertaining to diaheliotropism; showing a tendency to turn away from the sun.

dī-ȧ-hē-li-ot′rō-pism, *n.* The tendency of plants or their organs to assume a position transverse to the light.

dī′ăl, *n.* [ME. *dial, dyal*, from LL. *dialis*, daily, from L. *dies*, day.]

1. An instrument for showing the hour of the day from the shadow thrown by a style or gnomon upon a graduated surface. When the shadow is cast by the sun it is called a sundial.

2. The face of a watch, clock, or other timekeeper, on which the time of the day is indicated.

3. A clock; a watch. [Obs.]

He drew a *dial* from his poke. —Shak.

4. A compass for underground surveying. [Eng.]

5. Any plate or face on which a pointer or index revolves, moves backward and forward, or oscillates, marking revolutions, pressure, etc., according to the nature of the machinery of which it forms part; as, the *dial* of a steam-gauge, gas-meter, or telegraphic instrument.

Declining dial; a form of sundial the plane of which intersects that of the horizon in a line not directed to any of the four cardinal points.

dī′ăl, *v.t.*; dialed *or* dialled, *pt., pp.*; dialing *or* dialling, *ppr.* To use a dial, as for testing, measuring, or surveying (something).

dī′ăl-bīrd, *n.* A name given to robin-like birds of the genus *Copsichus*, of India.

dī′ȧ-lect, *n.* [Fr. *dialecte*; L. *dialectus*; Gr. *dialektos*, discourse, discussion, dialect, from *dialegestai*, to discourse, talk; *dia*, between, and *legein*, to choose, talk.]

1. (a) The form or idiom of a language peculiar to a certain district or class of people, consisting chiefly in differences of orthography or pronunciation; a branch of a parent language, with local alterations; as, the Scottish *dialect*; (b) departure from the commonly accepted manner of pronunciation or expression, either as a provincialism, or through lack of familiarity with the language; as, Riley's poems in the Hoosier *dialect*; a play in Swedish *dialect*.

2. Language; speech, or manner of speaking or expression.

Syn.—Language, tongue, speech, idiom, phraseology.

dī-ȧ-lec′tăl, *a.* Having the character of dialect.

dī-ȧ-lec′tăl-ly, *adv.* In the manner or form of dialect.

dī-ȧ-lec′tic, dī-ȧ-lec′tic-ăl, *a.* 1. Pertaining to a dialect or dialects.

2. Pertaining to logic; logical; argumental; pertaining to controversy concerning probabilities, or to scholastic disputation.

dī-ȧ-lec′tic, *n.* 1. The name given to the art of reasoning or disputing, or that branch of logic which teaches the rules and modes of reasoning, or of distinguishing truth from error; the method of investigating the truth by analysis; also, the science of ideas or of the nature and laws of being. Later it came to signify the art of using forms of reasoning so as to make fallacies pass for truth; word-fence; often in the plural; as, the theory of *dialectics*.

2. Efficiency in argument; also written *dialectics.*

dī-ȧ-lec′tic-ăl-ly, *adv.* 1. In the manner of a dialect.

2. Logically.

dī″ȧ-lec-ti′ciăn (-tish′un), *n.* A logician; a reasoner.

dī″ȧ-lec-tol′ō-ġy, *n.* [Gr. *dialektos*, speech, dialect, and *logos*, description.] The branch of the science of language which has to do with dialects.

dī-ȧ-lec′tŏr, *n.* One learned in dialectics.

dī′ăl-ing, dī′ăl-ling, *n.* The science which unfolds the principles of measuring time by dials; or the art of constructing dials.

dī′ăl-ist, *n.* A constructor of dials; one skilled in dialing.

dī-al′lȧ-ġē, *n.* [Gr. *diallage*, a change, from *diallassein*, to change, interchange; *dia*, between, and *allassein*, to make a thing other than it is, to change, from *allos*, other, another.] A rhetorical figure by which arguments are placed in various points of view, and then turned to one point.

dī′ăl-lāġe, *n.* [Gr. *diallage*, a change.] A dark green or bronze-colored laminate mineral, a variety of pyroxene.

dī′ăl-lel, *a.* Intersecting; not parallel. [Obs.]

dī′ăl-lock, *n.* A lock having one or more dials so arranged that until the dials register a certain combination, the mechanism cannot be unlocked.

dī-al′lyl, *n.* See *Allyl.*

dī-ȧ-log′ic, dī-ȧ-log′ic-ăl, *a.* Of the form of or pertaining to a dialogue.

dī-ȧ-log′ic-ăl-ly, *adv.* In the manner of a dialogue.

dī-al′ō-ġism, *n.* [LL. *dialogismos*; Gr. *dialogismos*, a settling of accounts, discourse, from *dialogizesthai*, to settle accounts, to talk, converse.] A feigned speech between two or more.

dī-al′ō-ġist, *n.* A speaker in a dialogue; also, a writer of dialogues.

dī″ăl-ō-ġis′tic, dī″ăl-ō-ġis′tic-ăl, *a.* Having the form of a dialogue.

dī″ăl-ō-ġis′tic-ăl-ly, *adv.* In the manner of a dialogue.

dī-al′ō-ġite, *n.* [Gr. *dialogē*, an argument, doubt.] A rose-red mineral carbonate of manganese; rhodochrosite.

dī-al′ō-ġize, *v.i.* To discourse in dialogue.

dī′ȧ-logue (-log), *n.* [Fr. *dialogue*; L. *dialogus*; Gr. *dialogos*, dialogue, conversation, from *dialegesthai*, to talk, converse; *dia*, between, and *legein*, to talk.]

1. A conversation or conference between two or more persons; particularly, a formal conversation in theatrical performances; also, an exercise in schools, in which two or more persons carry on a discourse.

2. A written conversation, or a composition in which two or more persons are represented as conversing on some topic; as, the *Dialogues* of Cicero.

dī′ȧ-logue, *v.i.* To discourse together; to confer. [Obs.]

dī′ȧ-logue, *v.t.* To express in the form of a dialogue. [Rare.]

dī′ăl-plāte, *n.* 1. The plate of a dial on which the lines are drawn to show the hour or time of the day.

2. The face of a clock or watch, on which the time of the day is shown.

3. Any kind of index-plate.

dī-ȧ-lū′ric, *a.* [*Di-* and *alloxan* and *uric.*] Of, relating, or pertaining to an acid obtained from the action of uric acid on alloxan.

dī-al-y-. A combining form from Gr. *dialyein*, to separate; *dia*, through, and *lyein*, to loose, signifying separate, distinct.

dī″al-y-cär′pous, *a.* See *Apocarpous.*

Dī″al-y-pet′ȧ-læ, *n.pl.* Same as *Polypetalæ.*

dī″al-y-pet′ăl-ous, *a.* Same as *Polypetalous.*

dī-ȧ-lyph′yl-lous, *a.* [*Dialy-*, and Gr. *phyllon*, a leaf.] Having distinct leaves, as a calyx or corolla.

dī″al-y-sep′ăl-ous, *a.* [*Dialy-*, and L. *sepalum*, a sepal.] Having separate sepals making up a calyx; polysepalous.

dī-al′y-sis, *n.*; *pl.* **dī-al′y-sēş.** [Gr. *dialysis*, a separation, dissolution, from *dialyein*, to separate, dissolve; *dia*, apart, and *lyein*, to loose.]

1. In grammar, dieresis; specifically, in Latin grammar, the change of *j* into *i*, and *v* into *u*.
2. In rhetoric, parenthesis or asyndeton.
3. In medicine, debility or loss of strength in the limbs.
4. In surgery, an open cut or wound; a separation of parts normally connected.
5. In chemistry, the act or process of separating mixed substances in solution, as crystalloids and colloids, by means of a membrane through which the crystalloids will pass easily, and the colloids very slowly, if at all.

dī-ȧ-lyt′iç, *a.* 1. Of or pertaining to dialysis.

2. In medicine, laxative.

Dialytic elimination; any method by which the elimination between two or more equations can be made to depend upon the formation of a resultant from a certain system of functions.

Dialytic telescope; a telescope in which the lens for correcting the chromatic aberration is placed in the tube about equally distant from the eye and the crown-glass lens.

dī-al′y-zāte, *n.* A compound to be separated by dialysis; also, the crystalloids after the colloids have been separated from the compound.

dī″ȧ-ly-zā′tion, *n.* Dialysis.

dī′ȧ-lȳze, *v.t.*; dialyzed, *pt.*, *pp.*; dialyzing, *ppr.* To subject to or to separate by dialysis; also written *dialyse*.

dī′ȧ-ly-zẽr, *n.* The means by which chemical dialysis is accomplished.

dī-ȧ-mag′net, *n.* [*Dia-*, and Gr. *magnēs*, a magnet.] Any diamagnetic body.

dī″ȧ-mag-net′iç, *a.* and *n.* I. *a.* Pertaining to or characterized by diamagnetism.

II. *n.* Any substance, as glass, bismuth, zinc, etc., which is diamagnetic in a magnetic field of force.

dī″ȧ-mag-net′iç-ăl-ly, *adv.* In a diamagnetic manner.

dī-ȧ-mag′net-işm, *n.* [*Dia-*, and Gr. *magnēs*, a magnet.]

1. The property possessed by some substances of being repelled by either pole of a magnet and showing a tendency to cross the lines of magnetic force.
2. That division of science treating of diamagnetics.

dī-ȧ-mag-net-om′e-tẽr, *n.* [*Dia-*, and Gr. *magnēs*, a magnet, and *metron*, a measure.] An instrument for measuring the relative diamagnetism of substances.

dī″ȧ-man-tif′ẽr-ous, *a.* [Fr. *diamantifère*, from *diamant*, diamond, and L. *ferre*, to bear, carry.] Yielding or producing diamonds.

dī-ȧ-man′tine, *a.* [Obs.] Same as *Adamantine*.

dī-am′e-tẽr, *n.* [ME. *diametre*; OFr. *diametre*; L. *diametros*; Gr. *diametros*, a diameter; *dia*, through, and *metron*, a measure.]

1. A line passing through the center of a plane figure or solid terminated by the opposite boundaries; the length of a line so described. The term has application especially to circles or spheres. In a cylinder, the *diameter* is that of one of its cross-sections at right angles to the axis.
2. The length of a straight line passing through the center of an object from one side to the other, if elongated, at right angles to the longer axis; thickness; width; as, the *diameter* of the hull of a ship.
3. In architecture, the measure across the lower part of the shaft of a column, which, being divided into sixty parts, forms a scale by which all the parts of the order are measured.

dī-am′e-trăl, *a.* Diametrical; relating or pertaining to a diameter.

Diametral curve; a bisector of parallel chords drawn in a curve.

Diametral plane; a plane which bisects a system of parallel chords drawn in a surface.

dī-am′e-trăl, *n.* The diameter. [Obs.]

dī-am′e-trăl-ly, *adv.* Diametrically.

dī-ȧ-met′riç-ăl, dī-ȧ-met′riç, *a.* 1. Of or pertaining to a diameter.

2. Extreme or remote, as if at opposite ends of a diameter; directly opposed; utmost.

dī-ȧ-met′riç-ăl-ly, *adv.* In a diametrical direction; directly; as, *diametrically* opposite.

dī-am′ide, *n.* [*Di-*, two, ammonia, and *-ide*.] One of a class of compounds formed from a double molecule of ammonia ($(NH_3)_2$), by replacement of hydrogen with a bivalent acid radical.

dī-am′ine, *n.* [*Di-*, two, *ammonia*, and *-ine*.] One of a class of compounds formed from a double molecule of ammonia, by replacement of hydrogen with an alcohol radical or radicals.

dī′ȧ-mŏnd, *n.* [ME. *diamaunde*; OFr. *diamant*, diamond; L. *adamas* (*-antis*); Gr. *adamas*, adamant, the diamond.]

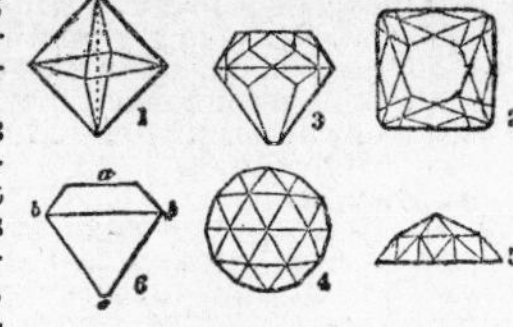

Diamonds, rough and variously cut. 1. Diamond in its rough state; 2. vertical, and 3. lateral appearance of a brilliant; 4. the vertical, and 5. the lateral appearance of a rose-cut diamond; in 6. the flat portion *a* in a cut stone is called the *table*; the part *a b b*, which projects from the setting, is the *front*, the part *b b c*, sunk in the setting, is the *back* or *culasse*, while the line *b b* is the *girdle*.

1. A precious stone, commonly colorless, but noted for its power of refracting light, its beauty as a gem, and its intense hardness, it being the hardest of known substances. Its specific gravity is 3.5 to 3.6. The greater part of the supply of *diamonds* is from South Africa, but some are found in Brazil, India, and Borneo, rarely in the United States.
2. A plane figure made up of four straight lines, the opposite sides equal and parallel, two of the interior angles acute and two obtuse; a lozenge; a rhomb.
3. One of the four suits of playing cards, characterized by a *diamond*-shaped indicator.
4. In baseball, the square having the four bases at its corners.
5. In printing, the smallest type in common use, being between pearl and brilliant.
6. A tool having an uncut face of a *diamond*, used in glass-cutting.

Diamond fret; in architecture, a species of molding consisting of fillets intersecting each other, so as to form diamonds or rhombs.

Diamond Fret.

dī′ȧ-mŏnd, *a.* Containing or consisting of diamonds; of the nature of or like a diamond.

dī′ȧ-mŏnd-back, *n.* The marsh terrapin, *Malaclemmys palustris*, found on the Atlantic coast of the United States.

dī′ȧ-mŏnd-bee″tle, *n.* A weevil, *Entimus imperialis*, native to South America and characterized by its ornamental, sparkling points.

dī′ȧ-mŏnd-bīrd, *n.* An Australian shrike of the genus *Pardalotus*, having brilliant, spangled plumage.

dī′ȧ-mŏnd-çut″tẽr, *n.* A lapidary.

dī′ȧ-mŏnd-drill, *n.* A drill used for boring, the tip of which is set with borts.

dī′ȧ-mŏnd-dust, *n.* Same as *Diamond-powder*.

dī′ȧ-mŏnd-ed, *a.* 1. Furnished, ornamented, or covered with diamonds.

2. Having the form of or marked with the form of a diamond.

dī′ȧ-mŏnd-finch, *n.* The Australian waxbill of the genus *Lagonosticte*, having brilliant plumage of black, white, and carmine.

dī′ȧ-mŏnd-īze, *v.t.* To stud with diamonds; to ornament with or as with diamonds. [Rare.]

dī′ȧ-mŏnd-mor″tăr, *n.* A hardened steel mortar with a close-fitting pestle for pulverizing hard substances.

dī′ȧ-mŏnd-point, *n.* A stylus, having a diamond tip, used by etchers or glaziers.

dī′ȧ-mŏnd-pow″dẽr, *n.* The fine powder resulting in diamond-cutting from cutting one diamond with another; diamond-dust. It is used in cutting and polishing gems, making cameos, etc.

dī′ȧ-mŏnd-shāped (-shāpt), *a.* Having the figure of an oblique-angled parallelogram or rhomb.

dī′ȧ-mŏnd-snāke, *n.* 1. A large boa or python of Australia, *Morelia spilotes*; so called because its skin is marked with diamond-shaped figures.

Diana.—Antique statue in the Louvre.

dī′ȧ-mŏnd-wee″vil, *n.* Same as *Diamond-beetle*.

dī-am′y-lēne, *n.* [*Di-*, and *amylene*.] A polymer of amylene, $C_{10}H_{20}$; an oily, liquid hydrocarbon.

Dī-an′ȧ (*or* **dī-ā′nȧ**), *n.* [L.] 1. In Roman mythology, the goddess of the chase, of chastity, and of marriage. She was worshiped especially by the plebeians and corresponded to the Greek Artemis. Also poetically called *Dian*.

2. [d—] A large monkey, *Cercopithecus diana*, of Africa, having a white beard and a white cross on its forehead.

Dī-an′dri-ȧ, *n.pl.* [L., from Gr. *di-*, two, and *anēr* (*andros*), a man.] A Linnean class of plants having perfect flowers and two distinct stamens.

Diandria.

dī-an′dri-an, dī-an′drous, *a.* Having two stamens; of or relating to the class *Diandria*.

dī″ȧ-nō-et′iç, *a.* [Gr. *dianoetikos*, intellectual, capable of thought, from *dianoeisthai*, to think over, intend; *dia*, through, and *noein*, to think, from *noos*, mind.] Capable of thought; thinking; intellectual; of or pertaining to discursive faculty.

dī″ȧ-noi-al′ō-ġy, *n.* That branch of philosophy which treats of the dianoetic faculties and operations of the mind.

Dī-an′thus, *n.* [L., from Gr. *dios*, divine, and *anthos*, flower.] A large genus of ornamental plants of the pink family, native to the Mediterranean region and the temperate parts of Asia. It embraces the various pinks, the carnation, and sweet-william.

dī-ȧ-pāşe′, *n.* Same as *Diapason*. [Obs.]

dī′ȧ-paşm, *n.* A powder or perfume. [Obs.]

dī-ȧ-pā′şŏn, *n.* [Gr. *diapasōn*, the concord of the first and last notes; *dia*, through, and *pasōn*, genit. pl. of *pas*, all.]

1. In old Greek music, the octave or interval which includes all the tones.
2. The entire range of tones of a voice or instrument.
3. Correct pitch; harmony; concord; often used figuratively.
4. A tuning-fork or the pitch it gives.
5. A stop in an organ, so named because influencing the entire scale of the instrument.

dī″ȧ-pē-dē′sis, *n.* [Gr. *diapēdēsis*, a leaping through, from *diapēdān*, to leap through or across.] The percolation of the white blood-corpuscles into the surrounding tissues through the natural pores of the blood-vessels.

dī″ȧ-pē-det′iç, *a.* Of the nature of, or pertaining to, diapedesis.

Dī-ȧ-pen-si-ā′cē-æ, *n.pl.* [L., from Gr. *dia pente*, by fives.] A small order of plants, allied to the heaths, growing in Europe and America, consisting of prostrate small shrubs with pentamerous gamopetalous flowers, and three-celled erect capsules.

dī-ȧ-pen′te, *n.* [L., from Gr. *dia pente*, by fives.]

1. In old music, a fifth; an interval making the second of the concords, and, with the diatessaron, an octave.
2. In medicine, a composition of five ingredients.

dī′ȧ-pẽr, *n.* [ME. *dyaper*, *diapery*; OFr. *diapre*, a kind of ornamented cloth; LL. *diasprus*, a kind of precious cloth, from L. *jaspis* (*-idis*), jasper.]

1. A figured linen cloth; a cloth woven with flowers or figures and much used for towels or napkins.
2. A form of surface decoration consisting of the regular repetition of a figure or ornament.
3. A napkin or towel. [Obs.]
4. A clout or breech-cloth for an infant.
5. In heraldry, same as *Diapering*, 3.

Diaper, Westminster Abbey.

dī′ȧ-pẽr, *v.t.*; diapered, *pt.*, *pp.*; diapering, *ppr.* To variegate or diversify, as cloth, with figures; to flower.

dī′ȧ-pẽr, *v.i.* To draw flowers or figures, as upon cloth.

dī′ȧ-pẽr-ing, *n.* 1. A diaper pattern or the cloth which it ornaments.

2. In architecture, same as *diaper*, 2.
3. In heraldry, the covering of the surface of a shield with ornament of some kind, independently of the bearing or of the colors. It was much used in the middle ages to give a richness to highly finished work.

Diapering.

dī′ȧ-phāne, *n.* [Gr. *diaphanēs*, transparent, from *diaphainein*, to show through, see through.]

1. A woven silk stuff with transparent and colorless figures.
2. In anatomy, an investing, cortical membrane of a sac or cell. [Rare.]

dī′ȧ-phānd, *a.* Transparent. [Rare.]

dī″ȧ-phȧ-nē′i-ty, *n.* [Gr. *diaphaneia*, transparency, from *diaphanēs*, transparent; *dia*, through, and *phainein*, to show.] The quality of being transparent.

dī-ȧ-phan′iç, *a.* Same as *Diaphanous*.

dī-aph′ȧ-nīe, *n.* The process of ornamenting plain glass with transparent pictures, in imitation of stained glass.

dī″ȧ-phā-nom′e-tẽr, *n.* [Gr. *diaphanēs*, transparent, and *metron*, a measure.]

1. An instrument to determine the relative transparency of atmospheres.

2. A testing-instrument, to determine the purity of liquids by their relative transparency.

dī-ȧ-phan′ō-scōpe, *n.* [Gr. *diaphanēs*, transparent, and *skopein*, to view.] A viewing-box for photographic positives.

dī-ȧ-phan′ō-tȳpe, *n.* [Gr. *diaphanēs*, transparent, and *typos*, an impression.] A picture made by the superposition of a positive having a tinted back upon an uncolored, heavily printed duplicate.

dī-aph′ȧ-nous, *a.* [Gr. *diaphanēs*, transparent, from *diaphainein*, to show through; *dia*, through, and *phainein*, to show.] Having power to transmit rays of light; pellucid; transparent; clear.

dī-aph′ȧ-nous-ly, *adv.* Transparently.

dī-aph-e-met′riç, *a.* [*Dia-*, and Gr. *aphē*, a touch, and *metron*, measure.] Pertaining to the determination of the relative delicacy of the tactile sensibility of different parts of the skin.

dī-ȧ-phon′iç, dī-ȧ-phon′iç-ăl, *a.* [*Dia-*, and Gr. *phonē*, sound.] Same as *Diacoustic.*

dī-ȧ-phon′iȼs, *n.* Same as *Diacoustics.*

dī″ȧ-phō-rē′sis, *n.* [LL. *diaphoresis*, perspiration; Gr. *diaphorēsis*, a carrying away, perspiration, from *diaphorein*, to carry off, throw off by perspiration.] Perspiration, particularly when caused by artificial means.

dī″ȧ-phō-ret′iç, dī″ȧ-phō-ret′iç-ăl, *a.* [Gr. *diaphorētikos*, causing perspiration.] Having the power of producing or increasing perspiration.

dī″ȧ-phō-ret′iç, *n.* A medicine which promotes perspiration; a sudorific. *Diaphoretics* differ from *sudorifics*; the former only increase the insensible perspiration, the latter excite the sensible discharge called sweat.

dī′ȧ-phōte, *n.* Same as *Telephote.*

dī′ȧ-phragm (-fram), *n.* [Gr. *diaphragma*, a partition-wall, the membrane which divides the lungs from the stomach.]

1. In anatomy, the midriff, a muscular, membranous partition separating the chest or thorax from the abdomen in mammals.

2. A partition or dividing substance, commonly with an opening through it.

3. In conchology, the divisional structure or septum found in certain shells.

4. In mechanics, (a) a thin plate, generally free to vibrate; as, the *diaphragm* of a phonograph; (b) an opaque plate or ring, used in optical instruments to cut off marginal portions of a beam of light. In photographic cameras *diaphragms* are often adjustable, commonly by means of separate slides inserted in the lens-tube.

dī″ȧ-phrag-mat′iç, *a.* Of, pertaining to, or resembling a diaphragm.

dī′ȧ-phragm-pump, *n.* A pump which has a pliable diaphragm instead of a piston.

dī-ȧ-phyṣ′i-ăl, *a.* Pertaining to a diaphysis.

dī-aph′y-sis, *n.*; *pl.* **dī-aph′y-sēṣ.** [Gr. *diaphysis*, a growing through; *dia*, through, and *phyesthai*, to grow.]

1. In anatomy, the shaft of a long bone between its two ends; the part of a bone which ossifies first.

2. In botany, an abnormal extension of the center of a flower, or of an inflorescence.

dī-ap-nō′iç, *a.* and *n.* [Gr. *diapnoē*, an outlet, from *dia*, through, and *pnein*, to blow.]

I. *a.* Diaphoretic in a mild degree.

II. *n.* A mild diaphoretic.

dī-ȧ-poph′y-sēṣ, *n.*, pl. of *diapophysis.*

dī″ap-ō-phyṣ′iç-ăl, *a.* Of or relating to a diapophysis.

dī-ȧ-poph′y-sis, *n.*; *pl.* **dī-ȧ-poph′y-sēṣ.** [L., from Gr. *dia*, through, and *apophysis*, outgrowth.] In anatomy, the dorsal or tubercular portion of the transverse process of a vertebra.

dī′ärch-y, *n.* [*Di-*, and Gr. *archos*, a ruler, from *archein*, to rule.] Government (of a country) by two persons.

dī-ā′ri-ăn, dī-ȧ′ri-ăl, *a.* Of, pertaining to, or resembling a diary; journalistic; daily.

dī′ȧ-rist, *n.* One who keeps a diary.

dī-ăr-rhē′ȧ, dī-ăr-rhœ′ȧ (-rē′ȧ), *n.* [LL. *diarrhœa*; Gr. *diarrhoia*, a flowing through, diarrhea, from *dia*, through, and *rhein*, to flow.] A profuse, fluid discharge from the bowels; a lax and morbidly frequent evacuation of the intestines.

dī-ăr-rhē′ăl, dī-ăr-rhœ′ăl, *a.* Pertaining to or having the characteristics of diarrhea; also written *diarrheic, diarrhœic, diarrhetic, diarrhœtic.*

dī-ăr-thrō′di-ăl, *a.* Of or pertaining to diarthrosis.

dī-ăr-thrō′sis, *n.*; *pl.* **dī-ăr-thrō′sēṣ.** [Gr. *diarthrōsis*, a division by joints, from *diarthroun*, to divide by joints.] In anatomy, a joint so articulated as to move freely and in various directions; also, the motion of such a joint.

dī′ȧ-ry, *n.* [L. *diarium*, a daily allowance of food or pay, from *dies*, day.]

1. An account of daily events or transactions; a journal; a register of daily occurrences or observations; as, a *diary* of the weather.

2. A book in which a diary is kept.

dī′ȧ-ry, *a.* Lasting but one day; as, a *diary* fever. [Obs.]

dī-ȧ-skeū′ȧ-sis, *n.* [L., from Gr. *diaskeuazein*, to put in order; *dia*, through, and *skeuazein*, to prepare, make ready, from *skeuos*, an implement.] Revision; critical editing.

dī-ȧ-skeū′ast, *n.* One who revises critically; an editor.

dī-as′pō-rȧ, *n.* [Gr. *diaspora*, a dispersion, from *diaspeirein*, to spread abroad, scatter; *dia*, through, and *speirein*, to scatter, sow.] Biblically, the dispersion spoken of in Peter i. 1, and James i. 1. The former refers to those who were dispersed in the countries of Pontus, Galatia, Bithynia, Asia, and Cappadocia; but the latter more indefinitely addresses the twelve tribes scattered abroad.

dī′ȧ-spōre, *n.* [Gr. *diaspora*, a dispersion; *dia*, throughout, and *speirein*, to scatter.] A variously colored hydrate of aluminium occurring in lamellar masses and orthorhombic crystals. It is infusible, and receives its name from the fact that when exposed to a flame it decrepitates almost instantly and is dispersed.

dī-ȧ-stal′tiç, *a.* [Gr. *diastaltikos*, able to distinguish, dilating, from *diastellein*, to separate, to distinguish; *dia*, apart, and *stellein*, to send.] Dilated; noble; bold; in Greek music, applied to certain intervals, as the major third, major sixth, and major seventh.

dī′ȧ-stāse, *n.* [Gr. *diastasis*, a standing apart, separation, from *dia*, apart, and *histanai*, to stand.] A white, soluble, nitrogenous compound, which has fermentative powers; found in barley, oats, wheat, and potatoes after germination, and in animal fluids, as saliva.

dī-ȧ-stā′siç, *a.* Pertaining to or having the quality of diastase.

dī-as′tȧ-sis, *n.* In surgery, a dislocation; a forcible separation of the bones without breaking them; luxation.

dī-ȧ-stat′iç, *a.* Of, pertaining to, or having the properties of diastase.

dī′ȧ-stem, *n.* Same as *Diastema*, 2.

dī-ȧ-stē′mȧ, *n.*; *pl.* **dī-ȧ-stē′mȧ-tȧ.** [Gr. *diastēma*, an interval, difference, from *dihistanai*, aor. *diastēnai*, to stand apart, divide; *dia*, apart, and *histanai*, to stand.]

1. In anatomy and zoölogy, a space between any two adjacent teeth or series or kinds of teeth.

2. In Greek music, a simple interval.

dī-as′tẽr, *n.* [*Di-*, two, and Gr. *astēr*, a star.] The double group of chromosomes during one of the divergence-periods of cell-division.

dī-as′tō-lē, *n.* [Gr. *diastolē*, distinction, difference, from *diastellein*, to separate, dilate; *dia*, apart, and *stellein*, to send.]

1. A normal and rhythmical dilatation of the heart, auricles, and arteries; opposed to *systole* or contraction.

2. In ancient prosody, the extension of a syllable, or a figure by which a syllable naturally short is made long.

dī-as-tol′iç, *a.* Of, pertaining to, or caused by diastole.

dī-as-troph′iç, *a.* Of or pertaining to diastrophism.

dī-as′trō-phiṣm, *n.* [Gr. *diastrophē*, distortion, from *diastrephein*, to turn aside, distort; *dia*, aside, and *strephein*, to turn.] In geology, the process by which the internal structure and external configuration of the earth's crust are developed by internal forces, producing continents, ocean-beds, mountains, strata, etc.

dī′ȧ-stȳle, *n.* [L. *diastylos*; Gr. *diastylos*, with columns wide apart; *dia*, apart, and *stylos*, column.] See *Intercolumniation.*

dī-ȧ-tes′sȧ-ron, *n.* [L., from Gr. *dia tessarōn*, lit., through four, the interval of a fourth; *dia*, through, and *tessarōn*, genit. pl. of *tessares*, four.]

1. In old music, the interval of a perfect fourth.

2. In old pharmacy, a confection of four medicines in syrup or honey.

3. In theology, a continuous narrative of the four Gospels, to prove their agreement or harmony.

dī-ȧ-thẽr′măl, *a.* Same as *Diathermanous.*

dī-ȧ-thẽr′mănce, dī-ȧ-thẽr′măn-cy, *n.* The state or quality of being diathermanous.

dī-ȧ-thẽr-mȧ-nē′i-ty, *n.* Same as *Diathermance.* [Rare.]

dī-ȧ-thẽr′mȧ-niṣm, *n.* The state or quality of being diathermanous.

dī-ȧ-thẽr′mȧ-nous, *a.* [Gr. *diathermainein*, to heat through; *dia*, through, and *thermainein*, to warm, from *thermos*, heat.] Freely permeable by heat; applied to certain substances, such as transparent pieces of rock-salt, etc., which suffer radiant heat to pass through them; also written *diathermal, diathermous.*

dī″ȧ-thẽr-mom′e-tẽr, *n.* [*Dia-*, and Gr. *thermos*, heat, and *metron*, a measure.] An instrument to measure the comparative power of heat-transmission of various substances.

dī-ath′e-sis, *n.* [Gr. *diathesis*, an arrangement, from *diatithenai*, to arrange; *dia*, apart, and *tithenai*, to place, put.]

1. In medicine, a constitutional susceptibility or liability to certain diseases.

2. A mental or psychical tendency; a predisposition to anything.

dī-ȧ-thet′iç, *a.* Of the nature of or dependent on diathesis; constitutional.

dī′ȧ-tom, *n.* Any plant of the *Diatomaceæ.*

Dī-at′ō-mȧ, *n.* [L., from Gr. *dia*, through, and *tomē*, a cutting, from *temnein*, to cut.] In botany, a genus of *Diatomaceæ* of which the frustules are connected by their angles, forming a zigzag chain.

Diatoma.

Dī″ȧ-tō-mā′cē-æ, *n.pl.* In botany, a natural order of confervoid algæ, consisting of microscopic plants found in fresh, brackish, and salt water, and on moist plants and damp ground. The frond secretes a very large quantity of silex, which is formed in each cell into three portions, two generally symmetrical valves and the connecting hoop. The valves are very various in forms, and covered with beautiful sculpturings, so as to form exquisite objects under the microscope. The species consist of single free cells, or the cells remain attached so as to form linear, flabelliform, circular, or geniculate fronds, or in some cases the cells or frustules are inclosed in a transparent gelatinous sheath or frond. The ordinary method of increase is by cell-division, although in several of the genera it is by sexual conjugation.

dī″ȧ-tō-mā′ceăn, *n.* Any plant of the *Diatomaceæ.*

dī″ȧ-tō-mā′ceous, *a.* Of, pertaining to, or resembling *Diatomaceæ.*

dī-ȧ-tom′iç *a.* [*Di-*, two, and Gr. *atomos*, an atom.] In chemistry, (a) consisting of two atoms; (b) having a valence of two; (c) having two replaceable atoms of hydrogen or other monads.

dī″ȧ-tom-if′ẽr-ous, *a.* [L. *Diatoma*, and *ferre*, to bear.] Bearing or yielding diatoms.

dī-at′ō-min, dī-at′ō-mine, *n.* The buff or brownish pigment of diatoms.

dī-at′ō-mous, *a.* [*Dia-*, and Gr. *tomos*, a cut, from *temnein*, to cut.] In mineralogy, having crystals with one distinct, diagonal cleavage.

dī-ȧ-ton′iç, *a.* [LL. *diatonicus*; Gr. *diatonikon*, or *diatonon* (supply *genos*, kind), the diatonic scale, from *diatonos*, extending through; *dia*, through, and *teinein*, to stretch, from *tonos*, a chord, tone.] In music, designating the natural scale, which, proceeding by degrees, includes both tones and semitones.

Diatonic scale; a major or minor scale of diatonic notes.

dī-ȧ-ton′iç-ăl-ly, *adv.* In a diatonic manner.

dī-at′ō-nous, *a.* [Gr. *diatonos*, extending through; *dia*, through, and *teinein*, to stretch.] Showing on two surfaces; said of a stone extending through a wall.

dī′ȧ-trībe, *n.* [Gr. *diatribē*, a wearing away, waste of time, pastime, from *diatribein*, to rub away, waste.] A continued discourse or disputation; specifically, one of bitter and malicious criticism and abuse.

dī-at′ri-bist, *n.* One who speaks or writes a diatribe.

Dī-ȧ-trȳ′mȧ, *n.* [L., from Gr. *dia*, through and *trymē*, a hole, from *tryein*, to wear out, bore, pierce.] A genus of large fossil birds of the earliest period of the Tertiary age, found in New Mexico.

dī-ạu′los, *n.*; *pl.* **dī-ạu′lī.** [Gr. *diaulos*, a double race-track, a double pipe or channel; *di-*, two, and *aulos*, a pipe, flute.] In ancient Greece, (a) a double track for foot-racing; (b) two flutes controlled by a single mouthpiece; (c) a measure, two stadia.

dī-ȧ-zeūç′tiç, *a.* [Gr. *diazeuktikos*, disjunctive, from *diazeugnynai*, to unyoke, disjoin; *dia*, apart, and *zeugnynai*, to join, yoke.] Disjoining.

Diazeuctic tone; in ancient music, a tone which, like that from F to G in modern music, lay between two tetrachords.

dī-az-ō-. In organic chemistry, a combining form from *di-*, two, and *azote*, nitrogen; used to denote a compound in which only one of the nitrogen atoms is joined to a benzene ring, the other to some radical not benzene, as *diazobenzene.*

dī-ȧ-zō′mȧ, *n.*; *pl.* **dī-ȧ-zō′mȧ-tȧ.** [L., from Gr. *diazōma*, a girdle, partition, from *diazōnnynai*, to gird around; *dia*, through, and *zōnnynai*, to gird, from *zōma*, a girdle.] In the theaters of ancient Greece, a horizontal passageway dividing the auditorium near the middle and crossing the ascending passages.

dī-az′ō-rē-aç′tion, *n.* A chemical reaction in which a diazo-compound takes part in replacement.

dī-az′ō-tīze, *v.t.* To produce (a diazo-compound) by a reaction or series of reactions.

dib, *v.t.* and *v.i.* [ME. *dibben*; AS. *dyppan*, to dip, plunge.] To dip; especially to dip bait into the water, in angling. [Prov. Eng.]

dī-bā′siç, *a.* [*Di-*, and Gr. *basis*, base.] Same as *Bibasic.*

dī-bā′tis, *n.* One of the valid moods. [See *Mood.*]

dib′ble, dib′bēr, *n.* [ME. *dibbille*, from AS. *dyppan*, *dippan*, to dip, plunge.] A pointed instrument, used in gardening and agriculture, to make holes for planting seeds, etc.

Dibble.

dib′ble, *v.t.*; dibbled, *pt.*, *pp.*; dibbling, *ppr.* To plant with a dibble; to make holes in with a dibble.

dib′ble, *v.i.* To dibble or dip, as in angling.

dib′blēr, *n.* One who or that which dibbles.

Dī-bran-ĉhi-ā′tȧ, *n.pl.* [L., from Gr. *di-*, two, and *branchia*, gills.] An order of cephalopods in which the branchiæ are two in number, one situated on each side of the body. The group is divided into two tribes, the decapods and the octopods.

dī-bran′ĉhi-āte, *a.* and *n.* I. *a.* Having two gills; of or belonging to the *Dibranchiata.*

II. *n.* One of the *Dibranchiata.*

dibş, *n.* [Ar.] A Syrian syrup made from concentrated juice of grapes, dates, or figs.

dib′stōne, *n.* One of the bones or stones used in the child's game of jackstones.

dī-bū′tyl, *n.* [*Di-*, and *butyl*, from L. *butyrum*, butter.] A metamer of octane. [See *Octane.*]

dī-çā′cious, *a.* Talkative; saucy; impudent. [Obs.]

dī-çac′i-ty, *n.* [L. *dicacitas*, biting wit, from *dicax* (*-cacis*), witty, sharp in speech, from *dicere*, to speak.] Pertness. [Rare.]

dī-çal′ciç, *a.* Having two atoms of calcium to the molecule.

dī-çär-bon′iç, *a.* Having two carboxyl radicals (CO.OH)$_2$, as a constituent.

dī′çast, *n.* [Gr. *dikastēs*, from *dikazein*, to judge, from *dikē*, right, justice.] In ancient Greece, one of the citizens, chosen annually as officers in a court of justice, who combined the duties of a present-day juror and judge.

dī-ças′tēr-y, *n.* In ancient Greece, a court of justice; dicasts collectively.

dīce, *n.*, pl. of *die*; also the game played with *dice.*

dīce, *v.i.*; diced (dīst), *pt.*, *pp.*; dicing, *ppr.* To play with dice.

dīce, *v.t.* 1. To sew a kind of waved pattern on, as the border of a garment.

2. To weave in or ornament with square or diamond-shaped figures.

3. To cut, as bread, so as to form a cube or cubes.

To dice away; to gamble away, with or as with dice. [Rare.]

dīce′box, *n.* A box from which dice are thrown in gaming.

dīce′-çōal, *n.* Coal which breaks easily into dice-shaped pieces.

dī-cel′lāte, *a.* [Gr. *dikella*, a mattock or pickax with two teeth.] Having two prongs, as a spicule of a sponge.

Dī-cen′trȧ, *n.pl.* [L., from Gr. *dikentros*, with two stings or points.] A genus of herbaceous plants of the order *Fumariaceæ*, widely distributed. They are ornamental and bear heart-shaped flowers. Well-known species are the bleeding-heart, squirrel-corn and Dutchman's-breeches.

dī-ceph′ȧ-lous, *a.* [Gr. *dikephalos*, two-headed.] Two-headed.

dī′çēr, *n.* A player at dice.

dī-cer′i-on, *n.* [Gr. *dikerōs*, two-horned; *di-*, two, and *keras*, a horn.] A symbolic, two-branched candlestick used in ceremonials of the Greek church.

dich, *v.i.* To ditch. [Obs.]

dī-ĉhā′si-um, *n.*; *pl.* **dī-ĉhā′si-ȧ.** [L., from Gr. *dichasis*, a division, from *dichazein*, to divide, from *dicha*, in two.] A cyme having two rays or axes.

dī-ĉhas′tȧ-sis, *n.* [Gr. *dichasis*, a division.] Spontaneous subdivision.

dī-ĉhas′tiç, *a.* Capable of subdividing spontaneously.

dī-ĉhlā-myd′ē-ous, *a.* [*Di-*, and Gr. *chlamys* (*-ydos*), a cloak, mantle.] In botany, having two coverings, a calyx and a corolla.

dī-ĉhlō′rid, dī-ĉhlō′rīde, *n.* Same as *Bichlorid.*

dī-ĉhō-. A combining form from Gr. *dicha*, in two, from *dis*, twice, from *dyo*, two, signifying in two parts, cleft.

dī-ĉhog′ȧ-mous, *a.* Characterized by dichogamy.

dī-ĉhog′ȧ-my, *n.* [*Dicho-*, and Gr. *gamos*, marriage.] In botany, a provision in hermaphrodite flowers to prevent self-fertilization, as where the stamens and pistils within the same flower are not matured at the same time.

dī-ĉhō′rēe, *n.* Same as *Dichoreus.*

dī-ĉhō-rē′us, *n.*; *pl.* **dī-ĉhō-rē′ī.** [L., from Gr. *dichoreios*, a double choreus; *di-*, two, and *choreios*, choreus, from *choros*, dance.] In prosody, a double choreus, or two trochees, considered as a single compound foot; also called *dichoree* and *ditrochee.*

dī-ĉhot′ō-măl, *a.* Pertaining to or situated in a dichotomy.

dī-ĉhot′ō-mist, *n.* One who classifies by division into pairs.

dī-ĉhot′ō-mīze, *v.t.*; dichotomized, *pt.*, *pp.*; dichotomizing, *ppr.* [Gr. *dichotomein*, to cut in two.]

1. To cut into two parts; to divide into pairs.

2. In astronomy, to show (a planet) as if bisected.

dī-ĉhot′ō-mīze, *v.i.* To divide into pairs; to become dichotomous.

dī-ĉhot′ō-mous, *a.* [LL. *dichotomos*; Gr. *dichotomos*, a cutting in two, from *dichotomein*, to cut in two; *dicha*, in two parts, and *temnein*, to cut.]

1. Having or consisting of a pair or pairs; paired; specifically, in biology, regularly dividing by pairs, from top to bottom; as, a *dichotomous* stem; *dichotomous* antlers.

2. In logic, having or exhibiting dichotomy; as, a *dichotomous* division.

Inflorescence of *Valerianella dentata*, showing the Dichotomous Branching.

dī-ĉhot′ō-mous-ly, *adv.* In a dichotomous manner.

dī-ĉhot′ō-my, *n.* [Gr. *dichotomia*, a division into two parts; *dicha*, in two, and *temnein*, to cut.]

1. Division or distribution of things by pairs.

2. In astronomy, that phase of the moon in which it appears bisected, or shows only half its disk, as at the quadratures.

3. In biology, a method of embranchment, characterized by division by pairs or continually recurring forks as shown in the veins of fern leaves, or the foot of a crab; by restriction, a branching-place or fork.

4. In logic, the arrangement of a class into two reciprocally exclusive orders; binary classification, as the Mohammedan division of man into infidels and believers.

dī-ĉhrō′iç, *a.* 1. Of, pertaining to, or characterized by dichroism.

2. Same as *Dichromatic.*

dī′ĉhrō-işm, *n.* [*Di-*, and Gr. *chroia*, color.]

1. The property possessed by some crystals of presenting different colors when viewed in different directions.

2. The characteristic of substances in solution to present colors depending upon the comparative saturation of the menstruum.

dī-ĉhrō-ist′iç, dī-ĉhrō-it′iç, *a.* Same as *Dichroic.*

dī′ĉhrō-īte, *n.* Same as *Iolite.*

dī-ĉhrō′māte, *n.* Same as *Bichromate.*

dī-ĉhrō-mat′iç, *a.* [*Di-*, and Gr. *chrōma*, color.] Having or producing two colors; specifically, in zoölogy, having two different colors, not characteristics of sex or age, at different times; applied to animals such as the screech-owl, exhibiting gray plumage one season and red another.

dī-ĉhrō′mȧ-tişm, *n.* The state or quality of being dichromatic.

dī′ĉhrō-ous, *a.* Same as *Dichroic.*

dī′ĉhrō-sçōpe, *n.* [Gr. *dichroos*, two-colored, and *skopein*, to view.] An instrument to exhibit dichroism, particularly of crystals.

dī-ĉhrō-sçop′iç, *a.* Relating to the dichroscope or to observations made by its use.

dī′çing, *n.* 1. An ornamentation in squares or cubes.

2. Gambling by means of dice.

dī′çing-house, *n.* A gaming-house. [Rare.]

dick-cis′sel, *n.* [U. S.] The black-throated American bunting.

dick′enş, *n.* The devil; the deuce; also used as an interjection. [Colloq.]

dick′ēr, *n.* [ME. *dycer*, from L. *decuria*, a military division of ten, from *decem*, ten.]

1. A number or quantity of ten, particularly ten hides or skins; but applied to other things; as, a *dicker* of gloves, etc. [Obs.]

2. A petty exchange, sale, or negotiation; a barter; a bargain. [Colloq.]

dick′ēr, *v.t.* and *v.i.* To make an insignificant trade or sale; to haggle. [Colloq.]

dick′ey, *n.* See *Dicky.*

Dick-sō′ni-ȧ, *n.* [Named after James *Dickson*, a Scotch botanist.] A genus of tree-ferns with large fronds and the spores inclosed in a coriaceous two-valved indusium. *Dicksonia antarctica* is a great ornament in greenhouses, and is also employed as a bedding plant. It is a native of Australia.

dick′y, dick′ey, *n.* [Dim. of D. *dek*, a cover.]

1. A seat behind the body of a carriage, for servants, etc.

2. A sham bosom of a shirt.

3. The high-standing collar of a shirt.

dick′y-bird, *n.* Any small bird.

dī-çlin′iç, diç′li-nāte, *a.* [*Di-*, and Gr. *klinein*, to incline.] In crystallography, a term applied to crystals in which two of the axes are obliquely inclined, as in the oblique rectangular prism.

dī′çli-nişm, *n.* The quality of being diclinous.

diç′li-nous, *a.* [*Di-*, and Gr. *klinē*, a bed, from *klinein*, to incline, lean.] In botany, having the pistils in one flower and the stamens in another, as in the oak.

dī-çoç′çous, *a.* [*Di-*, and L. *coccum*; Gr. *kokkos*, a berry.] Two-grained; consisting of two cocci.

dī-cœ′lous (-sē′), *a.* [*Di-*, and Gr. *koilos*, hollow.] In anatomy, having both ends concave; amphicœlous; also, possessing two cavities; bilocular.

dī-çō′lȧ, *n.*, pl. of *dicolon.*

dī-çō′liç, *a.* [L., from Gr. *di-*, two, and *kōlon*, a member, a clause.]

1. In prosody, having two cola or members.

2. In rhetoric, having two clauses; as, a *dicolic* sentence.

dī-çō′lon, *n.*; *pl.* **dī-çō′lȧ.** A verse or short division of composition having two cola.

dī-çon-dyl′i-ăn, *a.* [Gr. *dikondylos*, double-knuckled; *di-*, two, and *kondylos*, a knuckle.] Having two cavities in the lower back part of the skull.

dī-çot-y-lē′dŏn, *n.* [*Di-*, and Gr. *kotylēdōn*, a cavity.] A plant whose seeds divide into two lobes in germinating. *Dicotyledons* form the largest and most important class of plants, deriving their name from the embryo. They are further characterized by their netted-veined leaves, the exogenous structure of their stems, and by having the parts of the flower constructed on the plan of five. The class receives also the name of *exogens*, from their stems being formed by additions to the outer parts in the form of rings or zones.

dī-çot-y-led′ŏn-ous, *a.* Of, relating, or pertaining to a dicotyledon or dicotyledons.

Dī-çot′y-lēş, *n.* The type genus of the *Dicotylidæ.*

Dī-çō-tyl′i-dæ, *n.pl.* [L., from Gr. *dikotylos*, with two hollows.] A family of pachydermatous mammalia, the peccaries, found only in America. They possess a curious glandular organ on the back, which secretes a strongly scented fluid which exudes from an orifice.

dī-çrā′noid, *a.* Of or resembling plants of the genus *Dicranum.*

dī-çran-tē′ri-ăn, *a.* Same as *Diacranterian.*

Dī-çrā′num, *n.* [L., from Gr. *dikranos*, two-headed; *di-*, two, and *kranion*, the skull.] A genus of apocarpous operculate mosses, having the teeth of the peristome deeply bifid.

dī-çrot′iç, dī-çrō′tăl, *a.* Pertaining to or characterized by dicrotism.

dī′çrō-tişm, *n.* [Gr. *dikrotos*, double-beating; *di-*, two, and *krotos*, the sound of striking, a beating.] In physiology, a condition showing two waves of the arterial pulse to one heart-beat.

dī′çrō-tous, *a.* Same as *Dicrotic.*

Dī-çrū′ri-dæ, *n.pl.* [L., from Gr. *dikros*, forked, and *oura*, tail.] The drongo-shrikes, a subfamily of dentirostral birds, order *Passeres* and family *Ampelidæ.* In general appearance they resemble crows. The subfamily includes the bee-eater of South Africa. The *Dicruridæ* are found in India, China, Madagascar, and South Africa.

diç′tȧ, *n.* pl. of *dictum.*

diç′tȧ-graph, *n.* A device used for catching sound and transmitting it, inconspicuous in appearance and small in size. Largely used in detective work.

diç-tā′men, *n.* [L. *dictare*, to prescribe, dictate.] A dictate; a saying. [Rare.]

diç′tȧ-ment, *n.* A command; a dictate. [Obs.]

Diç-tam′nus, *n.* [L., from Gr. *diktamnos*, the dittany plant, from *Diktē*, a mountain in Crete, where the plant grows.]

1. A genus of plants of the order *Rutaceæ* found in southern Europe and Asia Minor, of which there is but one species, *Dictamnus Fraxinella*, the fraxinella or dittany. It is cultivated for its beautiful flowers and fragrance.

2. [d—] A plant of this genus.

diç′tȧ-phōne, *n.* A combination of a dictagraph and a telephone.

diç′tāte, *v.t.*; dictated, *pt.*, *pp.*; dictating, *ppr.* [L. *dictatus*, pp. of *dictare*, freq. of *dicere*, to speak.]

1. To deliver orally for another to write down; to compose.

2. To tell with authority; to deliver, as an order, command, or direction.

3. To suggest; to admonish; to direct by impulse on the mind; to instigate.

Syn.—Direct, instruct, order, prescribe.

diç′tāte, *v.i.* 1. To speak as one having authority; to direct.

2. To compose literary productions by communicating orally to another the words to be written.

diç′tāte, *n.* [L. *dictatum*, generally in pl. *dictata* things dictated, lessons, commands, from *dictatus*, pp. of *dictare*, to dictate.]

1. An order delivered; a command.

2. A rule, maxim, or precept, delivered with authority; as, the *dictates* of reason or conscience.

Syn.—Command, injunction, suggestion, admonition, maxim, precept.

diç-tā′tion, *n.* 1. The act of dictating; that which is dictated; specifically, matter, as a letter, dictated to a stenographer or phonograph, to be reproduced in typewriting.

2. The act or habit of giving orders in an arbitrary and overbearing manner.

diç-tā′tŏr, *n.* [L. *dictator*, a commander.]

1. One who prescribes rules for others to follow; one who dictates; as, a *dictator* of fashions.

2. One invested with absolute authority, often for the time being only or during an emergency; as, President Castro was declared *dictator* of Venezuela.

diç-tà-tō′ri-ăl, *a.* 1. Pertaining to a dictator; absolute; unlimited; uncontrollable.

2. Imperious; dogmatic; overbearing; as, the officer assumed a *dictatorial* tone.

diç-tà-tō′ri-ăl-ly, *adv.* In a dictatorial manner.

diç-tà-tō′ri-ăl-ness, *n.* The quality of being dictatorial.

diç-tà-tō′ri-ăn, *a.* Dictatorial. [Obs.]

diç-tā′tŏr-ship, *n.* 1. The office of a dictator; the term of a dictator's office.

2. Authority; imperiousness; dogmatism.

diç′tà-tō-ry, *a.* Dictatorial. [Obs.]

diç-tā′tress, diç-tā′trix, *n.* A woman who dictates or exercises authority.

diç-tā′tūre, *n.* The office of a dictator; dictatorship.

diç′tion, *n.* [L. *dictio*, a saying, delivery, diction, from *dicere*, to speak.] Expression of ideas by words; style or manner of expression.

Syn.—Style, phraseology.—*Style* relates both to language and thought; *diction* to language only; *phraseology* to the mechanical structure of sentences or the mode in which they are phrased.

diç-tion-ā′ri-ăn, *n.* A lexicographer. [Rare.]

diç′tion-ā-ry, *n.* [LL. *dictio*, a word; L. *dictio*, a saying, from *dicere*, to speak.]

1. A book containing the words of a language, arranged in alphabetical order, with explanations of their meanings in the same or another language; a lexicon.

2. A word-book of the terms used in any science, art, or other branch of knowledge or work, or by any class of people; as, a geological *dictionary;* a *dictionary* of slang.

diç′tō-grȧph, *n.* A telephonic device enabling one to give dictation to a stenographer at a distance.

diç′tum, *n.*; *pl.* **diç′tȧ.** [L. *dictum*, something said, a saying, a word, a witty remark, neut. of *dictus*, pp. of *dicere*, to speak.]

1. An authoritative assertion; a positive saying.

2. In law, a nondeliberative opinion expressed by the judge on some point not vital to the case at bar; also called *obiter dictum.*

diç-ty-ō-. A combining form from Gr. *diktyon*, a net, signifying of or like a net.

diç′ty-ō-drōme, *a.* [*Dictyo-*, and Gr. *dromos*, a running.] In botany, having leaves whose veins form a network.

diç′ty-ō-ġen, *n.* [*Dictyo-*, and Gr. *-genēs*, producing.] In botany, the name given by Lindley to a group of monocotyledonous plants, with net-veined leaves, intermediate between the monocotyledons and dicotyledons.

diç-ty-oġ′en-ous, *a.* Of, pertaining to, or resembling the dictyogens.

dī-cȳ′ăn, *n.* Dicyanogen. [Obs.]

dī-cȳ′ȧ-nide, *n.* [*Di-* and *cyano*gen.] A salt having two atoms of cyanogen; called also *bicyanide.*

dī-cȳ-an′ō-ġen, *n.* The double radical, (CN)₂; called also *bicyanogen.*

dī-cy-ē′mid, *a.* and *n.* I. *a.* Of or pertaining to the *Dicyemida.*

II. *n.* One of the *Dicyemida.*

Dic-y-em′i-dȧ, Dī-cȳ-ē′mȧ-tȧ, *n.pl.* [L., from Gr. *di-*, two, and *kyēma*, an embryo, fetus, from *kyein*, to be pregnant.] A genus of parasitic worms, found in the renal organs of cephalopods. Their organism is very simple and the embryos are of two kinds, vermiform and infusoriform.

dī-cyn′ō-dont, *a.* and *n.* [*Di-*, and Gr. *kyōn*, dog, and *odous* (*odontos*), tooth.]

I. *a.* Of or pertaining to the *Dicynodontia.*

II. *n.* One of the *Dicynodontia.*

Dī-cyn-ō-don′tiȧ (-shiȧ), *n.pl.* See *Anomodontia.*

dī-cyn-ō-don′ti-ăn, *a.* and *n.* Dicynodont.

did, *v.*, past tense of *do.*

Did′ȧ-chē, *n.* [Gr. *didachē*, a teaching.] The oldest treatise or manual of Christian teaching, "The Teaching of the Twelve Apostles" (discovered in 1873), by Bryennois, a bishop of the Greek church.

dī-daç′tiç, dī-daç′tiç-ăl, *a.* [Gr. *didaktikos*, apt at teaching, from *didaskein*, to teach.] Adapted to teach; preceptive; containing doctrines, precepts, principles, or rules; intended to instruct; as, a *didactic* poem or essay.

dī-daç′tiç, *n.* A tract on the theory and practice of teaching. [Obs.]

dī-daç′tiç-ăl-ly, *adv.* In a didactic manner; in a form to teach.

dī-daç-ti′ciăn (-tish′un), *n.* A teacher; a student, advocate, or promulgator of didactic principles.

dī-daç′ti-çişm, *n.* The didactic manner, plan, or tendency.

dī-daç-tiç′i-ty, *n.* The characteristic or quality of being didactic.

dī-daç′tiçs, *n.* The art or science of imparting instruction; pedagogics.

dī-daç′tyl, dī-daç′tyle, *a.* and *n.* [Gr. *didaktylos*, two-fingered, from *di-*, two, and *daktylos*, a finger.]

I. *a.* Having but two digits; two-toed or two-fingered.

II. *n.* An animal with only two toes to each foot.

dī-daç′tyl-ous, *a.* Same as *Didactyl*, I.

dī′dăl, *n.* A triangular spade. [Obs.]

dī′dap-pēr, *n.* [ME. *dydoppar*; AS. *dufedoppa*, the diving bird; *dufan*, to dive, and *doppettan*, to dip.] A bird, the dabchick.

dī-das-çal′iç, dī-das′çȧ-lăr, *a.* [Gr. *didaskalikos*, of or for teaching, from *didaskalos*, a teacher, from *didaskein*, to teach.] Didactic; preceptive; giving precepts. [Rare.]

did′dēr, *v.i.* To shake; to tremble. [Prov. Eng.]

did′dle, *v.t.* To overreach; to cheat; to swindle. [Colloq.]

did′dle, *v.i.* 1. To totter, as a child in walking; to toddle. [Prov. Eng. and Scot.]

2. To loiter; to dawdle. [Colloq.]

did′dlēr, *n.* A cheat; a swindler. [Colloq.]

dī-deç-ȧ-hē′drăl, *a.* [*Di-*, and Gr. *deka*, ten, and *hedra*, a seat.] In crystallography, having the form of a decahedral prism, with pentahedral summits.

dī′delph, *n.* A marsupial; one of the *Didelphia.*

Dī-del′phi-ȧ, *n.pl.* [L., from Gr. *di-*, two, and *delphys*, womb.] One of the three subclasses of *Mammalia* (the other two being *Ornithodelphia* and *Monodelphia*) founded on the nature of the female reproductive organs; the *Marsupialia.*

dī-del′phi-ăn, dī-del′phiç, *a.* Of or pertaining to the *Didelphia*; having two wombs.

dī-del′phid, *n.* and *a.* I. *n.* A marsupial; an animal belonging to the *Didelphia.*

II. *a.* Didelphian.

dī-del′phoid, *a.* Same as *Didelphian.*

dī-del′phous, *a.* See *Didelphian.*

Dī-del′phys, *n.* [*Di-*, and Gr. *delphys*, womb.] A genus of marsupial animals, which is confined to America and comprises only the opossums.

Virginian Opossum (*Didelphys virginiana*).

dī′dine, *a.* Pertaining to or resembling the dodo.

did′n't. A contracted form of *did not.*

dī′dō, *n.*; *pl.* **dī′dōş.** [From L. *Dido*, the legendary queen of Carthage, who, in buying as much land as could be covered by the hide of a bull, cut the hide into a long, thin strip and thus inclosed a large tract.] A clever trick; a caper; a prank. [Colloq.]

To cut a dido; to act mischievously; to cut a caper; to play a clever trick.

dī-dō″deç-ȧ-hē′drăl, *a.* [*Di-*, and Gr. *dōdeka*, twelve, and *hedra*, a seat.] In crystallography, having the form of a dodecahedral prism with hexahedral summits.

dī-dō″deç-ȧ-hē′dron, *n.* See *Diploid.*

dī-dō′ni-ȧ, *n.* [L., so named from the trick of Queen *Dido*, with the bull's hide.] In geometry, the curve which incloses the maximum area with a given perimeter and surface.

dī′drachm (-dram), **dī-drach′mȧ,** *n.* [Gr. *didrachmon*, a double drachm; *di-*, two, and *drachmē*, a drachm.] A silver coin of ancient Greece, worth two drachmæ.

didst, *v.*, second person, singular, past tense of *do*, used only with the pronoun *thou* in poetic or religious speech.

dī-duç′tion, dī-dūce′ment, *n.* [L. *diductio*, a leading away, from *diductus*, pp. of *diducere*, to lead or draw away; *di-*, from, and *ducere*, to lead or draw.] Separation or the act of separating into distinct parts.

dī-duç′tive-ly, *adv.* By means of diduction.

dī-dym′i-um, *n.* [L., from Gr. *didymos*, double.] A rare metal, composed of neodymium and praseodymium, found in the oxid of cerium. It never occurs free.

did′y-mous, *a.* [Gr. *didymos*, double.] In botany, growing in pairs or twins.

Did-y-nā′mi-ȧ, *n.* [L., from Gr. *di-*, two, and *dynamis*, power.] The fourteenth class in the Linnean system of plants. The plants have four stamens, of which two are longer than the other two. It is divided into two orders—*Gymnospermia*, having the fruit composed of single-seeded achenes, which Linneus mistook for naked seeds, and *Angiospermia*, with many seeds inclosed in an obvious seed-vessel.

Didynamia.

A, Gymnospermia (*Teucrium Scorodonia*). *c*, Stamina. *d*, Divided ovary. *e*, Section of ditto.
B, Angiospermia (*Antirrhinum majus*). *c*, Stamina. *d*, Capsule. *e*, Section of ditto.

did-y-nā′mi-ăn, did-y-nam′iç, *a.* Same as *Didynamous.*

dī-dyn′ȧ-mous, *a.* Containing four stamens, disposed in pairs, one shorter than the other; of or pertaining to the *Didynamia.*

die, *v.i.*; died, *pt.*, *pp.*; dying, *ppr.* [ME. *dien*, *deyen*; Ice. *deyja*, to die; of Scand. origin.]

1. To cease to live; to be deprived of respiration, of the circulation of blood, and other bodily functions, and rendered incapable of resuscitation, either by natural decay, by disease, or by violence; to expire; to decease; to perish; said of sentient beings and used absolutely or with *of*, *by*, *from*, *for*, and rarely *with*; as, to *die of* consumption; *by* or *with* the sword; *for* one's belief.

2. To lose vital power; to become dead; to wither; said of plants or parts of plants; as, the branch *died* slowly

3. To come to an end, to cease; to be lost; to perish or come to nothing; as, let the secret *die* in your own breast.

4. To sink; to faint.

His heart *died* within him, and he became as a stone. —1 Sam. xxv. 37.

5. To vanish or recede gradually, as if by death; to grow fainter; usually with *away*, *out* or *down*; as, the music *died away.*

6. To become vapid or spiritless, as liquors.

7. In theology, to perish everlastingly; to suffer divine wrath and punishment in the future world.

8. To become indifferent to a thing or to cease to be under its power; as, to *die* to sin.

9. In architecture, to disappear gradually or be merged into another part.

The curious zigzag with which its triangles *die away* is one of the most curious features of the structure. —Ruskin.

10. To desire greatly; to pine, as with love; as, he was *dying* to go; the youths were *dying* for Rebecca. [Colloq.]

To die in the last ditch; to fight to the bitter end; to resist desperately and beyond hope of success; to choose death rather than surrender.

To die in harness; to die in the midst of the usual work; to attend to duties up to the time of death.

To die out; to become gradually extinct; as, the family *died out.*

Syn.—Decease, expire, perish.

die, *n.*; *pl.* **dice, dieş** in senses 3, 4, 5. [ME. *dee*, a die; OFr. *de*, pl. *dez*, a die, dice, from L. *datum*, lit. that which is given or thrown, neut. of *datus*, pp. of *dare*, to give or throw.]

1. A small cube, marked on its faces with spots or indicators from one to six, used variously in games of chance by being thrown from the hand or from a dice-box.

2. Hazard; chance.

Such is the *die* of war. —Spenser.

3. Any cubic body.

4. In architecture, the cubical part of the pedestal, between its base and cornice.

5. A tool or appliance, commonly of hardened steel, used in giving a desired shape to a piece (generally) of metal; as, (a) a female screw for cutting outside screw-threads; (b) a mold or matrix for forging eyes, tress-rod ends, etc.; (c) a suitably engraved stamp for coining or milling blanks; (d) an endless knife for cutting irregular shapes by impression.

The die is cast; the decision is made; the step has been taken and to turn back is impossible.

dī-ē′cious, dī-ē′ciăn, *a.* Same as *Diœcious.*

dī-ē′drăl, *a.* Same as *Dihedral.*

Diēf-fen-bach′i-ȧ, *n.* [L., from *Dieffenbach*, a German botanist.] A small genus of South American and West Indian plants of the order *Araceæ*, cultivated for their beautiful foliage.

dī-ē-ġē′sis, *n.* [L., from Gr. *diēgēsis*, a narration, from *diēgeisthai*, to narrate; *dia*, through, and *ēgeisthai*, to lead.] A narration; a recital of facts.

dī-ē-leç'triç, *a.* and *n.* I. *a.* Allowing electrical induction, but not conduction; said of media.

II. *n.* In electricity, any medium through or across which static induction takes place.

Dī-el'y-trȧ, *n.* [L., from Gr. *di-*, two, and *elytron*, a covering, sheath.] Same as *Dicentra.*

dī'en, *n.* An abbreviation of *diencephalon.*

dī-en-ceph'ȧ-liç, *a.* Of or pertaining to the diencephalon.

dī-en-ceph'ȧ-lon, *n.*; *pl.* **dī-en-ceph'ȧ-lȧ.** [L., from Gr. *dia*, through, and *enkephalos*, brain; *en*, in, and *kephalē*, head.] In anatomy, the middle brain; the thalamencephalon.

dī-er'e-sis, *n.*; *pl.* **dī-er'e-sēṣ.** [LL. *diæresis*; Gr. *diairesis*, a division, from *diairein*, to divide, separate; *dia*, apart, and *hairein*, to take.]

1. The separate pronunciation of two diphthongal or adjacent vowels of a word; also, the separation of one syllable into two.

2. The sign (¨) placed over vowels to be pronounced separately, as in *zoölogy*; in German, the mark of the umlaut.

3. In prosody, the division made in a verse, when the end of a metrical foot is also the end of a word. Also spelled *diæresis.*

dī-ē-ret'iç, dī-æ-ret'iç, *a.* [Gr. *diairetikos*, divisive, from *diairein*, to divide.] Capable of dividing or dissolving; corrosive; said of medicines.

Dī-ēr-vil'lȧ, *n.* [From M. *Dierville*, who sent it from Canada to Tournefort.] A genus of caprifoliaceous plants consisting of erect shrubs of North America, China, and Japan. They are nearly allied to the honeysuckle, but have a funnel-shaped three-cleft corolla and a two-celled capsule. The best known species is *Diervilla Canadensis*, a hardy shrub with yellow flowers which appear early in summer.

dī'ēṣ, *n.* A day, from L. *dies*, day; used only in Latin phrases.

Dies Iræ; the Day of Wrath, the name and first words of a famous song of the medieval church.

Dies juridicus, pl. *dies juridici*; in law, a judicial or court day.

Dies non juridicus, or *dies non*; a day on which courts are not held, and business transacted is not legal, as Sunday.

dīe'sink"ēr, *n.* One who engraves dies.

die'sink"ing, *n.* The process of engraving dies for embossing, milling, etc.

dī'e-sis, *n.* [L. *diesis*; Gr. *diesis*, a sending through, in music a semitone; later a quarter tone; *dia*, through, and *hienai*, to send.]

1. In music, the division of a tone, less than a semitone; or an interval consisting of a less or imperfect semitone.

2. In printing, the reference-mark (‡), the double dagger.

die'stock, *n.* An appliance with two handles for holding the dies used for cutting screws.

dī'et, *n.* [ME. *diete*; OFr. *diete*, diet; LL. *dieta*; L. *diæta*; Gr. *diaita*, a manner of living, a place for living, a summerhouse.]

1. Food and drink, habitually taken; especially considered in relation to quantity, quality, and its effects; fare; as, meat was the chief part of his *diet.*

2. Food regulated by a physician, or by medical or hygienic rules; food prescribed for the prevention or cure of disease, or for attaining a certain physical condition; as, the football team was put on a strict *diet.*

3. Allowance of provision. [Obs.]

> For his *diet* there was a continual *diet* given him by the king. —Jer. lii. 34.

4. Allowance for food or expenses, as of one in the service of the government. [Obs.]

dī'et, *n.* [OFr. *diete*, LL. *dieta*, *diæta*, an assembly, a day's journey, from L. *dies*, day.] An assembly of the states or circles of the empire of Germany and of Poland; a convention of princes, electors, ecclesiastical dignitaries, or other representatives; a council or congress.

dī'et, *v.t.*; dieted, *pt.*, *pp.*; dieting, *ppr.* 1. To feed; to board; to furnish provisions for; as, the master *diets* his apprentice. [Rare.]

2. To regulate or prescribe the food for; as, the physician *dieted* him.

dī'et, *v.i.* 1. To eat according to rules prescribed.

2. To eat; to feed; as, the students *diet* in common. [Rare.]

dī-ē-tā'ri-ăn, *a.* and *n.* I. *a.* Of or pertaining to dieting or a dietary.

II. *n.* One who follows or advocates prescribed rules for diet; one who diets.

dī'et-ā-ry, *n.* A system of diet; an allowance of food, especially in prisons, hospitals, charitable institutions, etc.

dī'et-ā-ry, *a.* Pertaining to diet or the rules of diet.

dī'et-ēr, *n.* One who diets.

dī-ē-tet'iç, dī-ē-tet'iç-ăl, *a.* Pertaining to diet, or to the rules for regulating the kind and quantity of food to be eaten.

dī-ē-tet'iç-ăl-ly, *adv.* In a dietetic manner.

dī-ē-tet'içs, *n.* That part of medicine which relates to diet or food.

dī-ē-tet'ist, *n.* An advocate of dieting; a physician who considers dietetics the most important means of curing disease.

dī-eth-yl-am'ine, *n.* [*Di-* and *ethylamine.*] The liquid hydrocarbon, NH $(C_2H_5)_2$, having a fishlike smell.

dī-et'iç, dī-et'iç-ăl, *a.* Of or pertaining to diet; specifically applied to diseases caused or aggravated by a faulty diet.

dī'et-ine, *n.* [Fr. *diétine*, dim. of *diète*, diet.] A subordinate or local diet; a cantonal convention.

dī'et-ist, dī-e-ti'tiăn (-tish'un), *n.* One who understands the principles of dietetics.

dī'et-kitch"en (-kich"), *n.* A kitchen connected with a dispensary or hospital, which provides food for the sick among the poor, or for patients.

dif-fāme', *v.* and *n.* [Obs.] Same as *Defame.*

dif-far-rē-ā'tion, *n.* [LL. *diffarreatio*, from L. *dis-*, apart, and *farreatio*, the use of the spelt cake in the marriage ceremony, from *far* (*farris*), grain, spelt.] The parting of a cake; a ceremony among the Romans at the divorce of man and wife.

dif'fēr, *v.i.*; differed, *pt.*, *pp.*; differing, *ppr.* [ME. *differen*; L. *differre*, to carry apart, differ, protract; *dis-*, apart, and *ferre*, to bring, carry.]

1. To be unlike, dissimilar, distinct, or various in nature, condition, form, or qualities; followed by *from*; as, a statue *differs from* a picture; wisdom *differs from* folly.

> One star *differeth from* another star in glory. —1 Cor. xv. 41.

2. To disagree; not to accord; to be of a contrary opinion; used absolutely or with *from* or *with*; as, he *differs with* me.

3. To contend; to be at variance; to strive or debate in words; to dispute; to quarrel; followed by *with.*

> We'll never *differ with* a crowded pit.—Rowe.

Syn.—Disagree, dissent, vary, dispute, oppose, contend, quarrel, wrangle.

dif'fēr, *v.t.* 1. To cause to be different; as, his early life *differed* his manners. [Rare.]

2. To cause to quarrel or contend; to divide. [Scot.]

dif'fēr-ence, *n.* [ME. *difference*; OFr. *difference*; L. *differentia*, difference, from *differens* (-*ntis*), ppr. of *differre*, to carry apart, to differ.]

1. The state of being unlike or distinct; distinction; disagreement; want of sameness; variation; dissimilarity, either total or partial, and existing in the nature and essence of things, in the form, the qualities, or degrees.

2. The quality which distinguishes one thing from another; the opposite of resemblance.

3. Dispute; debate; contention; quarrel; controversy.

> What was the *difference?* It was a contention in public. —Shak.

4. The point in dispute; ground of controversy.

5. An evidence or mark of distinction. [Obs.]

> The marks and *differences* of sovereignty. —Davies.

6. Distinction; discrimination; as, a mother makes no *difference* between her children.

> There is no *difference* between the Jew and the Greek. —Rom. x. 12.

7. In commerce, a matured margin.

8. In mathematics, the remainder of a sum or quantity, after a lesser sum or quantity is subtracted.

9. In logic, the differentia.

10. In heraldry, a certain figure added to a coat of arms, serving to distinguish one family from another, or to show how distant a younger branch is from the elder or principal branch.

Syn.—Distinction, dissimilarity, contrariety, dissimilitude, variation, divergence, contention, dispute.

dif'fēr-ence, *v.t.*; differenced, *pt.*, *pp.*; differencing, *ppr.* 1. To cause a difference or distinction in or between, as, his speech *differenced* him from us.

2. In heraldry, to add a difference or distinguishing mark to.

3. In mathematics, to reckon the consecutive differences of (a series of quantities).

dif'fēr-ent, *a.* 1. Distinct; separate; not the same; as, we belong to *different* churches or nations.

2. Of various or contrary natures, forms, or qualities; unlike; dissimilar; as, *different* kinds of drink; *different* states of health; *different* shapes; *different* degrees of excellence.

[*Different from* is more correct than *different to* (as, the things are very *different from* each other), and the latter is to be avoided.]

Syn.—Distinct, diverse, unlike, several, various.

dif-fēr-en'ti-ȧ, *n.*; *pl.* **dif-fēr-en'ti-æ** (-shi-). [L. *differentia*, difference.]

1. In logic, the characteristic attribute of a species, or that by which it is distinguished from other species of the same genus; specific difference.

> The material part, which is called the *genus*, or the formal and distinguishing part, which is called *differentia*. —Whately.

2. A concise cadence peculiar to Gregorian music.

dif-fēr-en'ti-ȧ-ble (-shi-), *a.* Capable of being differentiated.

dif-fēr-en'tiăl (-shăl), *a.* 1. Making a difference or distinction; discriminating; distinguishing; special; as, a *differential* rate.

2. In mathematics, pertaining to a differential or differentials, or to mathematical processes in which they are employed.

3. In mechanics, denoting differences of motion or the results of such differences.

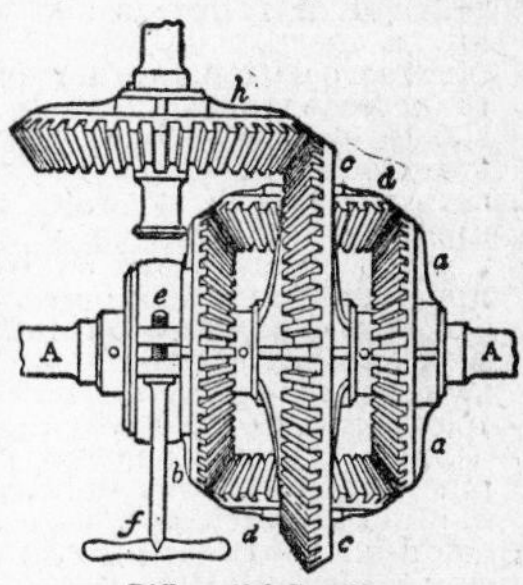

Differential Coupling.

Differential calculus; see under *Calculus.*

Differential coefficient; the ratio of the differential of any function of a variable to the differential of the variable.

Differential coupling; in machinery, a form of slip-coupling applied in light machinery for the purpose of regulating the velocity of the connected shaft at pleasure. In the figure, A is the power-shaft having the wheel *a a* fast, and *b* and *c* loose. The pinions *d d* have their bearings in *c c* and gear in *a a* and *b*. Revolving, A communicates opposite motion to *b*; *c c* remaining at rest until the friction-clutch *e f* is engaged, making the teeth of *b* fulcra to *d d*, carrying *c c*, which, gearing with the wheel *h* on the second shaft, communicates motion to it of any degree of velocity not greater than half that of the driving-shaft.

Differential duties; in political economy, duties which are not levied equally upon the produce or manufactures of different countries.

Differential equation; an equation involving or containing differential quantities.

Differential galvanometer; a needle-galvanometer having two similar coils through which currents are passed in opposite directions, the deflection determining their relative strength.

Differential motion; an adjustment by which a single combination is made to produce such a degree of velocity, as by ordinary arrangements would require a considerable train of mechanism practically to reduce the velocity.

Differential pulley; (a) a portable differential windlass; (b) differential gearing applied to a pulley.

Differential screw; a compound screw producing differential motion; as, in the figure, the pitch of the threads at A and B being different, the jaw C moves a distance equal to the difference in the pitch of A and B at each revolution of A B.

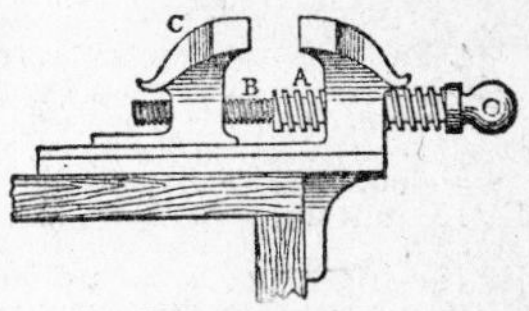

Differential Screw.

Differential thermometer; a U-shaped tube, each end of which terminates in an air bulb, the bend being filled with a colored liquid. A graduated scale measures differing temperatures of the two bulbs.

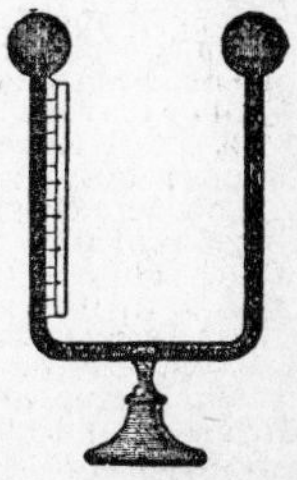

Differential winding; in electricity, the winding of two insulated parallel wires of an instrument so that there is no third current induced when equal currents are passed in opposite directions through them, used in duplex telegraphy, galvanometers, etc.

Differential Thermometer.

Differential or *Chinese windlass*; a means for producing differential motion; shown by the figure, the cylinders A and B having a common axis, in the forward motion of B, A unwinds, communicating a motion to C equal to half the difference of the surface velocities of the two cylinders.

dif-fēr-en'tiăl, *n.* 1. In mathematics, an infinitesimal difference between two states of a variable quantity. In the differential and integral calculus, if two or more quantities are dependent on each other and subject to variations of value, their *differentials* are any other quantities whose ratios to each other are the limits to which the ratios of the variations approximate, as these variations are reduced nearer and nearer to zero.

2. A slight decrease in rates which a competing railroad or railroads allow a member of their tariff association, in order to increase traffic.

3. In electricity, one of two electrified wire coils, acting in such a way upon each other, or on a magnet or armature subject to mutual influence, as to produce opposite polar action.

Differential Windlass.

Partial differential; in mathematics, an increment, infinitesimally small, of a function of two or more variables resulting from a similar increment in only one of the variables.

Total differential; in mathematics, the resultant of simultaneous infinitesimal increments of all of the variables.

dif-fẽr-en′ti-āte (-shi-), *v.t.*; differentiated, *pt.*, *pp.*; differentiating, *ppr.* 1. To make different; to mark with a specific distinction; as, both physical and mental attributes *differentiate* the normal man from the idiot.

2. In logic, to discriminate between, by observing or describing the marks of differentiation, or the differentia.

3. In biology, to cause to change; to render specific functionally or structurally; to modify.

4. In mathematics, to determine the differential of; as, to *differentiate* an algebraic equation.

dif-fẽr-en′ti-āte (-shi-), *v.i.* To become specifically distinct and separate.

dif-fẽr-en-ti-ā′tion (-shi-), *n.* 1. The formation or discrimination of differences or varieties.

> The mode of the *differentiation* of species. —Agassiz.

2. The assignment of a specific agency to the discharge of a specific function, as the assignment of a particular faculty in a university to the study and teaching of a particular branch of knowledge.

> The Faculties arose by process of natural *differentiation* out of the primitive University. —Huxley.

3. In biology, the formation of different parts, organs, species, etc., by the production or acquisition of a diversity of new structures, through a process of evolution or development, as when animals, as they advance in type of organization, acquire, more and more, specific organs for the performance of specific functions, in place of one organ, as in the lower organisms, serving for heart, stomach, lungs, etc.; specialization.

> *Differentiation* is, therefore, a mark of higher organization. —Page.

4. In mathematics, the act of differentiating; the operation of finding the differential of any function.

dif-fẽr-en′ti-ā-tŏr (-shi-), *n.* One who or that which differentiates.

dif′fẽr-ent-ly, *adv.* In a different manner; variously.

dif′fẽr-ing-ly, *adv.* In a different manner.

dif′fi-cile, *a.* Difficult; hard; scrupulous. [Obs.]

dif′fi-cile-ness, *n.* Difficulty of persuasion; stubbornness. [Obs.]

dif′fi-cult, *a.* [L. *difficultas*, difficulty.]

1. Hard to be made, done, or performed; not easy; attended with labor and pains; as, our task is *difficult*; it is *difficult* to persuade men to abandon vice; it is *difficult* to ascend a steep hill or travel a bad road.

2. Hard to be pleased; not easily wrought upon; not readily yielding; not compliant; unaccommodating; rigid; austere; not easily managed or persuaded; as, a *difficult* man; a person of a *difficult* temper.

3. Hard to understand or expound; perplexing; as, a *difficult* problem.

Syn.—Hard, arduous, laborious, toilsome, troublesome, unaccommodating.

dif′fi-cult, *v.t.* To make difficult; to hinder; to impede. [Obs.]

dif′fi-cult-āte, *v.t.* To make difficult. [Obs.]

dif′fi-cult-ly, *adv.* With difficulty. [Rare.]

dif′fi-cult-ness, *n.* Difficulty. [Rare.]

dif′fi-cul-ty, *n.* [ME. *difficultee*; OFr. *difficulte*; L. *difficultas*, difficulty; *dis-* priv., and *facilis*, easy.]

1. Hardness of accomplishment; the state of anything which renders its performance laborious or perplexing; opposed to *easiness* or *facility*; as, the *difficulty* of a task or enterprise; a work of labor and *difficulty*.

2. That which is hard to be performed or surmounted; as, we often mistake *difficulties* for impossibilities.

3. Perplexity; trouble; whatever renders progress or execution of designs laborious; embarrassment of affairs; specifically, of pecuniary affairs and usually in the plural; as, he was in *difficulties* owing to the low state of trade.

4. Objection; obstacle to belief; that which cannot be easily understood, explained, or believed; as, science often raises *difficulties* concerning miracles.

5. An embroilment; a quarrel; a contention.

Syn.—Obstacle, obstruction, impediment, perplexity, trouble, embarrassment.

dif′fi-dence, *n.* [L. *diffidentia*, distrust, from *diffidens* (*-ntis*), ppr. of *diffidere*, to distrust; *dis-* priv., and *fidere*, to trust.]

1. Distrust of oneself; lack of self-reliance; want of confidence in one's own power, ability, correctness, or wisdom; as, fearing the critics he wrote with *diffidence*.

2. Distrust, doubt of the power, ability or disposition of others. [Obs.]

Syn.—Bashfulness, modesty, humility, hesitation, reserve, shyness.

dif′fi-den-cy, *n.* Diffidence. [Obs.]

dif′fi-dent, *a.* Having or showing diffidence.

Syn.—Modest, reserved, retiring, humble, bashful, hesitating, doubtful, suspicious.

dif′fi-dent-ly, *adv.* In a diffident manner.

dif-find′, *v.t.* To split. [Obs.]

dif-fin′i-tive, *a.* Determinate; definitive. [Obs.]

dif-fis′sion (-fish′un), *n.* The act of splitting. [Obs.]

dif-flā′tion, *n.* The act of scattering by a gust of wind. [Obs.]

dif′flū-ence, dif′flū-en-cy, *n.* [L. *diffluo*.] A flowing or falling away on all sides. [Obs.]

dif′flū-ent, *a.* Flowing away on all sides; not fixed.

dif′fọrm, *a.* [L. *deformis*, deformed; *de-*, *dis-* priv., and *forma*, form, shape.] Not uniform; dissimilar.

dif-fọrm′i-ty, *n.* Irregularity of form; lack of uniformity.

dif-fraçt′, *v.t.*; diffracted, *pt.*, *pp.*; diffracting, *ppr.* [L. *diffractus*, pp. of *diffringere*, to break in pieces.] To break or separate into parts, as a ray of light.

dif-fraçt′, *a.* Broken; having distinct areolæ; applied to the thalli of lichens.

dif-fraç′tion, *n.* [L. *diffractus*, pp. of *diffringere*, to break in pieces.] In optics, a modification of light when it passes the edge of a body, or through a small aperture, by which the luminous rays deviate from the straight course, often producing *diffraction* spectra through interference.

Diffraction grating; a means for producing diffraction spectra either by a narrow slit, a series of fine, parallel wires, or parallel ruling on glass or polished metal.

Diffraction spectra; those produced by diffraction instead of other means, as by a prism.

dif-fraç′tive, *a.* Pertaining to or causing diffraction.

dif-fran′chịse, *v.t.* To disfranchise. [Obs.]

dif fran′chịse-ment, *n.* Disfranchisement. [Obs.]

dif-fran-ġi-bil′i-ty, *n.* The state or quality of being diffrangible.

dif-fran′ġi-ble, *a.* [L. *diffringere*, to break in pieces.] Capable of diffraction or causing diffraction.

dif-fū̦ṣ′āte, *n.* In dialysis, the diffusible resultant.

dif-fūṣe′, *v.t.*; diffused, *pt.*, *pp.*; diffusing, *ppr.* [L. *diffusus*, pp. of *diffundere*, to pour in different directions; *dis-*, apart, and *fundere*, to pour.]

1. To pour out and spread, as a fluid; to cause to flow and spread; as, the river *diffused* its waters over the land.

2. To spread; to send out or extend in all directions; to scatter; disseminate; circulate; as, flowers *diffuse* their fragrance.

Syn.—Spread, expand, extend, circulate, proclaim, publish, scatter, disperse.

dif-fūṣe′, *v.i.* To spread freely; to permeate.

dif-fūse′, *a.* 1. Widely spread; dispersed.

2. Copious; prolix; using many words; giving full descriptions; as, Johnson is a *diffuse* writer.

dif-fūṣed′, *a.* Spread abroad; scattered; flowing.

dif-fūṣ′ed-ly, *adv.* In a diffused manner.

dif-fūṣ′ed-ness, *n.* The state or condition of being diffused.

dif-fūse′ly, *adv.* In a diffuse manner.

dif-fūse′ness, *n.* The state or quality of being diffuse; copiousness; prolixity.

dif-fūṣ′ẽr, *n.* One who or that which diffuses.

dif-fū-ṣi-bil′i-ty, *n.* The quality of being diffusible; as, the *diffusibility* of clay in water.

dif-fū′ṣi-ble, *a.* Capable of flowing or being spread in all directions; capable of being dispersed.

dif-fū′ṣi-ble-ness, *n.* Diffusibility.

dif-fū-ṣi-om′e-tẽr, dif-fū-sim′e-tẽr, *n.* [L. *diffusio*, diffusion, and *metrum*, a measure.] An appliance to measure the diffusibility of gases.

dif-fū′ṣion, *n.* [L. *diffusio* (*-onis*), diffusion, from *diffusus*, pp. of *diffundere*, to pour in different directions, to diffuse.]

1. The act or process of diffusing, or the state of being diffused; specifically, the spontaneous mingling of liquids or gases when they come in contact with each other.

2. A spreading or scattering; dispersion; as, a *diffusion* of dust or of seeds.

3. A spreading; extension; propagation; as, the *diffusion* of knowledge or of good principles.

dif-fū′sive, *a.* [L. *diffusus*, pp. of *diffundere*, to diffuse.] Having the quality of diffusing, or spreading by flowing, as liquid substances or fluids; or of dispersing, as minute particles.

dif-fū′sive-ly, *adv.* In a diffusive manner.

dif-fū′sive-ness, *n.* The quality or state of being diffuse.

dig, *v.t.*; dug *or* digged, *pt.*, *pp.*; digging, *ppr.* [ME. *diggen*, *dyggen*, to dig; AS. *dician*, to make a ditch, from *dic*, a ditch.]

1. To excavate; to open and break, or turn up (the earth), with a spade or other sharp instrument.

> Be first to *dig* the ground. —Dryden.

2. To make by excavation; to form by removing earth; as, to *dig* a well.

3. To obtain or draw forth from the earth, by excavation; as, to *dig* gold or potatoes.

4. To break up the earth or force a passage through; usually with *up*; as, the mole *dug up* the garden.

5. To push against; to prod; to poke. [Colloq.]

To dig down; to undermine and cause to fall by digging; as, *to dig down* a wall.

To dig in; to mix in by covering with a layer of earth; as, *to dig in* fertilizers.

To dig up; to obtain something from the earth by opening it, or uncovering the thing with a spade or other instrument, or by forcing out from the earth by a bar; as, *to dig up* a stone.

dig, *v.i.* 1. To work with a spade or other piercing instrument; to do servile work.

2. To study hard and steadily; to plod; to grind. [College Slang.]

dig, *n.* 1. A thrust; a prod; a poke. [Colloq.]

2. One who studies hard and steadily; a plodder. [College Slang.]

3. In mining, same as *gouge*.

dī-gal′liç, *a.* [*Di-* and *gallic*, from L. *galla*, the gallnut.] Of or pertaining to an acid, *digallic* acid, the same as tannic acid.

dig′ȧ-mist, *n.* One who commits digamy. [Rare.]

dī-gam′mȧ, *n.* [Gr. *digamma*, *digammos*, the letter digamma, so called because it resembles two gammas in form; *di-*, two, and *gamma*, gamma.] A letter, F, in the early Greek, having the sound of *w* or *v*. It fell into early disuse except in the Æolic dialect.

dī-gam′mā-ted, dī-gam′māte, *a.* Resembling or using a digamma or its representative sound.

dig′ȧ-mous, *a.* Pertaining to digamy.

dig′ȧ-my, *n.* [*Di-*, and Gr. *gamos*, marriage.] Second marriage. [Obs.]

dī-gas′triç, *a.* [*Di-*, and Gr. *gastẽr*, belly.]

1. Having a double belly; applied to certain muscles, especially to one of the lower jaw.

2. Of or pertaining to a digastric muscle.

Dī-ġē′nē-ȧ, *n.pl.* [L., from Gr. *digenēs*, of two kinds or sexes; *di-*, two, and *genos*, kind.] A division of worms or flukes, parasitic in nature, having alternate characteristics in successive generations.

dī-ġen′e-sis, *n.* [L., from Gr. *di-*, two, and *genesis*, origin, generation.] In biology, alternate generation. [See *Parthenogenesis*.]

dī-ġē-net′iç, *a.* In biology, characterized by digenesis.

dig′e-nous, *a.* [L., from Gr. *di-*, two, and *genos*, kind.] Bisexual.

dig′ẽr-ent, *a.* Digesting. [Obs.]

dī′gest, *n.* [ME. *digest*; LL. *digestum*, a collection of writings arranged under different heads, a code of laws, as that of Justinian, from L. *digestus*, pp. of *digerere*, to distribute, arrange.]

1. [D—] A collection or body of Roman laws, digested or arranged under proper titles by order of the emperor Justinian; the Pandects.

2. Any collection, compilation, abridgment, or summary of laws, disposed under proper heads or titles; as, the *digest* of Comyn.

3. Any compilation, abridgment, or summary of literary, historical, or other writings, arranged systematically.

Syn.—Code, abridgment, abstract, compendium, epitome, summary, synopsis, system.

di-gest′, *v.t.*; digested, *pt.*, *pp.*; digesting, *ppr.* [L. *digestus*, pp. of *digerere*, to carry apart, distribute, set in order, arrange; *dis-*, apart, and *gerere*, to carry.]

1. To distribute into suitable classes, or under proper heads or titles; to arrange in convenient order; to dispose in due method; as,

to *digest* the Roman laws or the common law.

2. To arrange methodically in the mind; to form with due arrangement of parts; as, to *digest* a plan or scheme.

3. To separate or dissolve in the stomach and intestinal canal, as food; to reduce to minute parts fit to enter the lacteals and circulate; to convert into chyme.

4. In chemistry, to prepare by moisture and heat; to expose to a gentle heat in a boiler or matrass, as a preparation for chemical operations.

5. To bear with patience; to brook; to receive without resentment; not to reject; as, say what you will, he will *digest* it.

6. To receive and comprehend in the mind; to dispose in a manner to improve the understanding; as, to *digest* a discourse or sermon.

7. To dispose (an ulcer or wound) to suppurate.

8. In agriculture, to soften and prepare for manure, as plants and other substances.

di-ġest′, *v.i.* 1. In chemistry, to be prepared by heat.

2. To suppurate; to generate pus, as an ulcer or wound.

3. In agriculture, to soften and be prepared for manure, as substances in compost.

4. To undergo digestion; as, cheese does not *digest* easily.

di-ġest′ed-ly, *adv.* In a well arranged manner.

di-ġest′ẽr, di-ġest′ŏr, *n.* 1. One who digests or disposes in order.

2. One who digests his food.

3. A medicine or article of food that aids digestion, or strengthens the digestive power of the stomach.

4. An appliance for softening animal fiber, as in the preparation of gelatin, by subjecting it to the action of superheated water boiling under pressure.

di-ġest-i-bil′i-ty, *n.* The quality of being digestible.

di-ġest′i-ble, *a.* Capable of being digested.

di-ġes′tion, *n.* [ME. *digestioun*; OFr. *digestion*; L. *digestio*, digestion, an orderly distribution.] The act of digesting; the process of digesting; the power or ability to digest; as, *digestion* of food; *digestion* of a scheme; chemical *digestion*.

di-ġest′ive, *a.* [LL. *digestivus*, from L. *digestus*, pp. of *digerere*, to digest.]

1. Of, relating, or pertaining to digestion; as, the *digestive* apparatus; *digestive* powers.

2. Aiding digestion; as, certain foods are considered *digestive*.

di-ġest′ive, *n.* 1. In medicine, any preparation which aids digestion; a stomachic.

2. In surgery, an application which ripens an ulcer or wound, or disposes it to suppurate. [Obs.]

di-ġest′ŏr, *n.* See *Digester*.

di-ġes′tūre, *n.* Concoction; digestion. [Obs.]

diġ′gȧ-ble, *a.* Capable of being dug.

diġ′gẽr, *n.* 1. One who or that which digs.

2. [D—] One of a tribe of inferior Indians of California and Nevada; so called because their chief article of food consists of roots dug from the ground.

diġ′gẽr-wäsp, *n.* Any burrowing wasp of the order *Hymenoptera*.

diġ′ġings, *n.pl.* 1. Locality; neighborhood; vicinity; as, a stranger in these *diggings*. [Colloq.]

2. A location where mining operations are carried on, especially gold-mining.

dight (dit), *v.t.* [ME. *dighten*; AS. *dihtan*, to set in order, arrange, from L. *dictare*, to repeat, pronounce.]

1. To prepare; to put in order; hence, to dress or put on; to array; to adorn.

2. To put into the required condition; to clean.

3. To embrace sexually. [Obs.]

diġ′it, *n.* [L. *digitus*, a finger.]

1. A finger or toe.

2. Any one of the ten Arabic numerals or symbols, 0, 1, 2, 3, 4, 5, 6, 7, 8, 9, by combinations of which all numbers are expressed; so called from counting on the fingers.

3. The measure of a finger's breadth, or three-fourths of an inch.

4. In astronomy, the twelfth part of the diameter of the sun or moon; a term used to express the quantity of an eclipse; as, an eclipse of six *digits* is one which hides one-half of the disk.

diġ′it, *v.t.* To point at or designate with the finger. [Rare.]

diġ′i-tăl, *a.* 1. Of, pertaining to, or resembling a digit or digits.

2. In biology, digitate.

diġ′i-tăl, *n.* 1. A digit. [Rare.]

2. A key of a piano or similar musical instrument.

3. The final articulation of a spider's pedipalp.

diġ-i-tal′i-fọrm, *a.* In botany, like the corolla of *Digitalis*.

diġ′i-tȧ-lin, diġ′i-tȧ-line, *n.* A compound or related group of compounds, the active principle of the foxglove.

Diġ-i-tā′lis, *n.* [L., from *digitalis*, pertaining to the fingers, from *digitus*, a finger.]

1. A genus of plants popularly called *foxglove*.

2. [d—] A medicine prepared from the dried leaves of plants of this genus.

diġ′i-tāte, *v.t.* To point out, as with the finger. [Rare.]

diġ′i-tāte, *a.* 1. In botany, branching into several distinct leaflets or roots like fingers.

2. In zoölogy, having processes resembling a digit or digits.

diġ′i-tā-ted, *a.* Same as *Digitate*, 2.

diġ′i-tāte-ly, *adv.* In a digitate manner.

diġ-i-tā′tion, *n.* A division into fingerlike processes; one of such divisions.

diġ-i-ti-. A combining form from Latin *digitus*, finger or toe.

diġ′i-ti-fọrm, *a.* [*Digiti-*, and L. *forma*, form.] In the shape of a finger or arranged like fingers.

Diġ-i-tiġ′rȧ-dȧ, *n.pl.* [*Digiti-*, and L. *gradi*, to walk.] The second tribe, in Cuvier's arrangement, of *Carnivora*, including those animals which walk on the toes only, such as the lion, tiger, cat, weasel, civet, hyena, etc.; distinguished from *Plantigrada* or bears, which walk on the broad sole of the foot.

Digitigrada.—Hind leg of Lion. *a*, Femur or thigh. *b*, Tibia or leg. *c*, Tarsus or foot. *d*, Calx or heel. *e*, Planta or sole of foot. *f*, Digits or toes.

diġ′i-ti-grāde, *a.* 1. Walking on the toes, rather than the ball of the foot, as carnivorous quadrupeds.

2. Of, relating, or pertaining to the *Digitigrada*.

diġ′i-ti-nẽrved, *a.* [*Digiti-*, and L. *nervus*, nerve.] In botany, having radiate nervation from the apex of the leaf.

diġ″i-ti-pär′tīte, *a.* In botany, parted like the extended fingers.

diġ′i-tīze, *v.t.* To finger; to handle. [Rare.]

diġ-i-tō′ri-um, *n.*; *pl.* **diġ-i-tō′ri-ȧ**. [L., from *digitus*, a finger.] An appliance for piano-practice, having mute keys; a dumb piano.

diġ′i-tūle, *n.* [L. *digitulus*, dim. of *digitus*, a finger.] In zoölogy, a small finger or toe; a digit-like process.

diġ′i-tus, *n.*; *pl.* **diġ′i-tī**. [L.] In entomology, the final articulation of the tarsus.

dī-glā′di-āte, *v.t.* [L. *digladiari*, to fight for life or death.] To fence; to quarrel. [Rare.]

dī-glā-di-ā′tion, *n.* A combat with swords; a quarrel. [Obs.]

dī′glot, *a.* [Gr. *diglōssos*, speaking two languages; *di-*, two, and *glōssa*, tongue.] In two languages; bilingual.

dī-glot′ism, *n.* The use of two languages; bilingualism. [Rare.]

dī′glyph, *n.* [Gr. *diglyphos*, doubly indented; *di-*, two, and *glyphein*, to hollow out, carve, cut.] In architecture, an imperfect triglyph having two channels instead of three.

dig-nā′tion, *n.* The act of believing worthy or of conferring honor. [Obs.]

digne (dīn *or* dēn), *a.* Worthy; proud; disdainful. [Obs.]

dig″ni-fi-cā′tion, *n.* The act of dignifying; exaltation; promotion.

dig′ni-fied, *a.* Having or characterized by dignity; as, a *dignified* bearing.

dig′ni-fȳ, *v.t.*; dignified, *pt.*, *pp.*; dignifying, *ppr.* [OFr. *dignifier*, to dignify, from L. *dignus*, worthy, and *facere*, to make.]

1. To invest with honor or dignity; to exalt in rank; to promote; to elevate to a high office.

2. To honor; to make illustrious; to distinguish by some excellence, or that which gives celebrity.

> Your worth will *dignify* our feast.—Jonson.

Syn.—Exalt, elevate, prefer, advance, honor, adorn, ennoble.

dig′ni-tā-ry, *n.*; *pl.* **dig′ni-tā-ries**. [L. *dignitas*, dignity.] One of high rank, especially an ecclesiastic who is in authority above a priest or clergyman.

dig′ni-ty, *n.* [ME. *dignitee*; OFr. *dignite*; L. *dignitas*, worth, merit, from *dignus*, worthy.]

1. A state of worth or honor; nobleness or elevation of mind; excellence of character.

2. Elevation; nobility; grandeur.

3. Honorable place or rank; an elevated office, civil or ecclesiastical, giving a high rank in society; advancement; preferment, or the rank attached to it.

4. The state or quality calculated to inspire awe, respect, or reverence; impressiveness; stateliness.

5. One high in rank or honor.

6. A general maxim or principle; an axiom. [Obs.]

7. In astrology, an advantage which a planet has on account of its being in some particular place of the zodiac, or in a particular station in respect to other planets.

To stand upon one's dignity; to have or assume an exalted idea of one's own importance, especially if offended.

dig-nō′tion, *n.* Distinguishing mark; distinction. [Obs.]

dī-gō-neū′tiç, *a.* Brooding twice a year; said of insects.

diġ′ō-nous, *a.* [*Di-*, and Gr. *gōnia*, an angle.] In botany, having two angles, as a stem.

dī′gram, *n.* A digraph.

dī′grȧph, *n.* [*Di-*, and Gr. *graphein*, to write.] A union of two characters of which one only is pronounced, as *ea* in *head*, *breath*.

dī-graph′iç, *a.* Of or pertaining to a digraph.

di-gress′, *v.i.*; digressed (-grest), *pt.*, *pp.*; digressing, *ppr.* [L. *digressus*, pp. of *digredi*, to go apart, separate; *dis-*, apart, and *gradi*, to go, step.]

1. Literally, to step or go from the way or road; hence, to depart or wander from the main subject, design, or tenor of a discourse, argument, or narration; used only of speaking or writing.

> Let the student of our history *digress* into whatever other fields he will.—Stephens.

2. To go out of the right way or common track; to deviate. [Rare.]

di-gress′, *n.* A digression. [Obs.]

di-gres′sion (-gresh′un), *n.* [ME. *digression*; L. *digressio*, a parting, separating, from *digressus*, pp. of *digredi*, to go apart, separate.]

1. The act of digressing; a departure from the main subject under consideration; an excursion of speech or writing.

2. Deviation from a regular course; as, the *digression* of a ship.

3. Departure from virtue; transgression. [Rare.]

4. In astronomy, the apparent distance of the inferior planets, Mercury and Venus, from the sun; elongation.

di-gres′sion-ăl, *a.* Pertaining to or consisting in digression; departing from the main purpose or subject.

dī-gress′ive, *a.* Departing from the main subject; partaking of the nature of digression.

di-gress′ive-ly, *adv.* By way of digression.

digue (dig), *n.* A dike. [Obs.]

Dī-ġyn′i-ȧ, *n.pl.* [L., from Gr. *di-*, two, and *gynē*, a woman, a female.] The name given by Linneus, in his artificial system, to such plants as have two styles, or a single style deeply cleft into two parts.

dī-ġyn′i-ăn, diġ′yn-ous, *a.* In botany, having two styles.

dī-hē′drăl, *a.* Having two sides or plane faces; as, a *dihedral* crystal or angle.

Dihedral angle; one formed by the intersection of two planes.

dī-hē′drŏn, *n.* [*Di-*, and Gr. *hedra*, a seat, a base.] A figure with two sides or surfaces.

dī-hex-aġ′ō-năl, *a.* [*Di-*, and Gr. *hexagōnos*, six-cornered; *hex*, six, and *gōnia*, corner.] Twelve-sided; doubly hexagonal.

dī-hex-ȧ-hē′drăl, *a.* In crystallography, having the form of a hexahedral prism with trihedral summits.

dī-hex-ȧ-hē′drŏn, *n.* [*Di-*, and Gr. *hex*, six, and *hedra*, a seat, base.] In crystallography, a dihexahedral prism.

dī-i-amb′, *n.* [Gr. *diiambos*, a diiamb; *di-*, two, and *iambos*, an iambus.] In prosody, a double iambus; a foot consisting of two iambi.

dī-i-am′bus, *n.*; *pl.* **dī-i-am′bī**. Same as *Diiamb*.

dī-i-sat′ō-ġen, *n.* [*Di-*, and *isatine*, and *-gen*.] A red crystalline compound easily transformed into indigo.

dī-jū′di-cănt, *n.* One who dijudicates. [Rare.]

dī-jū′di-cāte, *v.t.* [L. *dijudicatus*, pp. of *dijudicare*, to judge between, decide; *dis-*, apart, and *judicare*, to judge.] To judge or determine. [Rare.]

dī-jū-di-cā′tion, *n.* A judging between; judicial distinction. [Rare.]

dī′kȧ, *n.* [Native West African name.] Dika-bread.

dī′kȧ-bread (-bred), *n.* An oily chocolate-like substance, prepared by the West Africans from the nuts of the tree *Irvingia Barteri*, and used as food.

dik-ȧ-mä′li, *n.* [E. Ind. name.] The native name of a fragrant resinous gum used as a lotion, exuding from the ends of young shoots of *Gardenia lucida*, an East Indian tree.

dike, *n.* [ME. *dike*, *dyke*; AS. *dic*, a ditch, channel, dike.]

1. A ditch; a trench. [Obs.]

2. A bank or wall to prevent an overflow of water on low land; a levee; as, the *dikes* of the Netherlands.

3. A stone or turf fence. [Scot.]

4. In geology, a

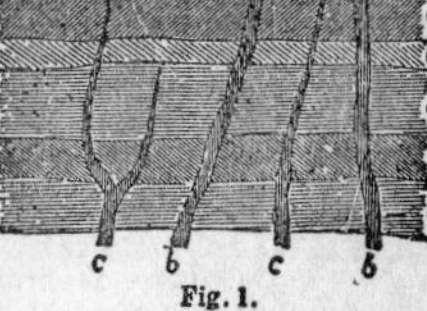

Fig. 1.

vein of basalt, greenstone, or other igneous rock which has been intruded in a melted state into rents or fissures of rocks. When a mass of the unstratified or igneous rocks, such as granite, trap, and lava, appears as if injected into a great rent in the stratified rocks, cutting across the strata, it forms a *dike*. The illustrations show lava dikes in the Val del Bove, on the slopes of Mount Etna. In fig. 1, *a a* are horizontal strata, *b c* dikes of lava forced through the

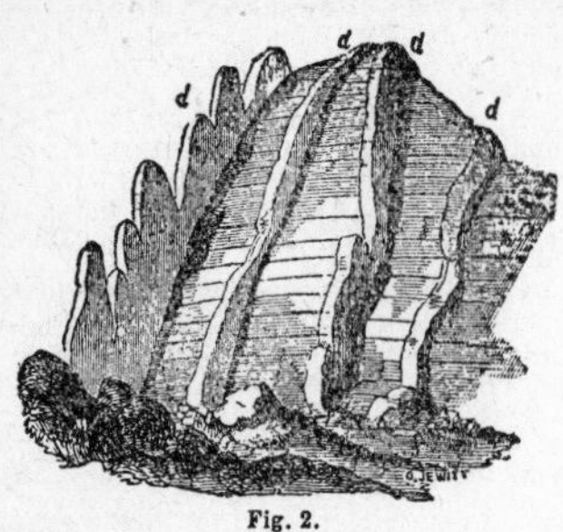

Fig. 2.

strata; *b b* are of equal breadth throughout their entire length, and *c c* decrease upward. In fig. 2, the horizontal strata are shown worn away by the action of the weather, and the vertical veins of lava *d d* (marked *c b* in fig. 1), being harder, have resisted its effects, and consequently remain projecting in the form of walls or dikes.

dīke, *v.t.*; diked (dīkt), *pt., pp.*; diking, *ppr.* 1. To surround or protect with a dike.

2. To drain. [Obs.]

dīke, *v.i.* To dig. [Obs.]

dīke′grāve, *n.* [Holland.] A dike superintendent.

dīk′ẽr, *n.* One who builds dikes or ditches.

dīke′reeve, *n.* [AS. *dic*, a ditch, and *gerefa*, a superintendent.] A superintendent of dikes and ditches. [Eng.]

di-lac′ẽr-āte, *v.t.*; dilacerated, *pt., pp.*; dilacerating, *ppr.* [L. *dilaceratus*, pp. of *dilacerare*, to tear to pieces.] To tear; to rend asunder; to separate by force. [Rare.]

di-lā′ni-āte, *v.t.* [L. *dilaniatus*, pp. of *dilaniare*, to tear in pieces.] To tear; to rend in pieces; to mangle. [Rare.]

di-lā-ni-ā′tion, *n.* A tearing in pieces. [Rare.]

di-lap′i-dāte, *v.t.*; dilapidated, *pt., pp.*; dilapidating, *ppr.* [L. *dilapidatus*, pp. of *dilapidare*, to squander, consume, demolish, scatter like stones; *dis-*, apart, and *lapidare*, to throw stones at, from *lapis* (*-idis*), a stone.]

1. To pull down; to waste or destroy partially; to suffer to go to ruin.

If the bishop, parson, or vicar, etc., *dilapidates* the buildings, or cuts down the timber of the patrimony of the church. —Blackstone.

2. To waste; to squander.

di-lap′i-dāte, *v.i.* To go to ruin; to fall by decay.

di-lap′i-dā-ted, *a.* Having or presenting an appearance of dilapidation.

di-lap-i-dā′tion, *n.* The process of dilapidating or the state of being dilapidated; specifically, ecclesiastical waste or suffering to go to decay of any building in possession of an incumbent.

di-lap′i-dā-tŏr, *n.* One who causes dilapidation.

di-lā-tȧ-bil′i-ty, *n.* The quality of admitting expansion by the elastic force of the body itself, or of another elastic substance acting upon it; opposed to *contractibility*.

di-lāt′ȧ-ble, *a.* [L. *dilatare*, to expand.] Capable of expansion; possessing elasticity; elastic; as, a bladder is *dilatable* by the force of air; air is *dilatable* by heat.

di-lāt′ăn-cy, *n.* That characteristic of matter in granular form, which makes a change of shape result in an increase of volume.

di-lāt′ănt, *a.* Having the property of dilatancy.

di-lāt′ănt, *n.* 1. Any substance which is dilatant in nature.

2. In surgery, any device for dilating a part, as a vaginal speculum.

dil-ȧ-tā′tion, *n.* [ME. *dilatacioun*; LL. *dilatatio*, an extension, expansion, from L. *dilatatus*, pp. of *dilatare*, to expand.]

1. The act of expanding; expansion; a spreading or extending in all directions; the state of being expanded; opposed to *contraction*.

2. An abnormal enlargement of any canal or cavity of the body, especially for medical or surgical treatment.

3. Verbosity; wordiness; as, *dilatation* of speech.

dil-ȧ-tā′tŏr, *n.* Anything that dilates; specifically, in anatomy, a muscle which dilates any part or organ.

di-lāte′, *v.t*; dilated, *pt., pp.*; dilating, *ppr.* [L. *dilatare*, to spread out, extend, make wider; *dis-*, apart, and *latus*, pp. of *ferre*, to bring.]

1. To expand; to distend; to enlarge or extend in all directions; opposed to *contract*; as, air *dilates* the lungs; air is *dilated* by rarefaction.

2. To enlarge upon; to relate at large; to tell copiously or diffusely. [Rare.]

Syn.—Expand, swell, distend, enlarge, amplify, expatiate.

di-lāte′, *v.i.* 1. To widen; to expand; to swell or extend in all directions.

His heart *dilates* and glories in his strength. —Addison.

2. To speak diffusely and copiously; to dwell on in narration; followed by *on* or *upon*; as, an advocate may weaken his argument by *dilating on* trivial circumstances.

di-lāte′, *a.* Expanded; expansive. [Obs.]

di-lāt′ed, *a.* 1. Expanded; distended; enlarged so as to occupy a greater space.

2. In biology, unusually widened or broad, as a part or organ.

di-lāt′ed-ly, *adv.* In a dilated manner.

di-lāt′ẽr, *n.* One who or that which enlarges or expands.

di-lā′tion, *n.* Delay. [Obs.]

di-lā′tion, *n.* The process of dilating; the condition of being dilated; dilatation.

di-lāt′ive, *a.* Causing dilatation; having a tendency to dilate or distend.

dil-ȧ-tom′e-tẽr, *n.* [LL. *dilatatio*, an extension, and L. *metrum*, a measure.] An appliance for measuring the dilatation of matter.

di-lāt′ŏr, *n.* 1. One who or that which widens or expands; specifically, a muscle that dilates.

2. One of a class of instruments used in surgery, such as a tent, bougie, sound, or speculum, to facilitate the examination of a canal or keep apart the lips of a wound or the walls of a constricted passage.

dil′ȧ-tō-ri-ly, *adv.* With delay; tardily.

dil′ȧ-tō-ri-ness, *n.* The quality of being dilatory or late; lateness; slowness in motion; delay in proceeding; tardiness.

dil′ȧ-tō-ry, *a.* [LL. *dilatorius*, tending to delay, from L. *dilator*, a dilatory person, from *dilatus*, pp. of *differre*, to put off, delay.]

1. Literally, drawing out or extending in time; hence, slow; late; tardy; applied to things; as, *dilatory* councils or measures.

2. Given to procrastination; not proceeding with diligence; making delay; slow; late; applied to persons; as, a *dilatory* messenger.

3. In law, intended to make delay; tending to delay; as, a *dilatory* plea, which is designed, or which tends to delay the trial of a cause. —Blackstone.

dil′dō, *n.* A refrain or nonsense-word in old songs, often implying obscenity. [Obs.]

dil′dō, *n.* A cactus, *Cereus Swartzii*, found in the West Indies.

di-lec′tion, *n.* A loving; a preference. [Obs.]

di-lem′mȧ, *n.* [LL. *dilemma*; Gr. *dilēmma*, an argument which presents two or more alternatives; *di-*, two, and *lēmma*, a proposition or assumption, from *lambanein*, to take.]

1. In logic, an argument which presents an antagonist with two or more alternatives, but is equally conclusive against him, whichever alternative he chooses.

2. A difficult or doubtful choice; a state of things in which evils or obstacles present themselves on every side, and it is difficult to determine what course to pursue.

A strong *dilemma* in a desperate case!
To act with infamy, or quit the place. —Swift.

Horns of a dilemma; alternatives which are equally undesirable or dangerous.

dil-et-tănt′, *n.* A dilettante.

dil-et-tăn′te, *n.*; *pl.* **dil-et-tăn′ti.** [It., from ppr. of *dilettare*, to delight; L. *delectare*, to charm, delight.] An admirer or lover of the fine arts; an amateur; one who pursues an art desultorily and for amusement; sometimes applied contemptuously to one who affects a taste for, or a degree of acquaintance with, or skill in, art which he does not possess.

dil-et-tăn′te, *a.* Pertaining to dilettantism; having the characteristics of a dilettante.

dil-et-tăn′te-ish, *a.* Same as *Dilettantish*.

dil-et-tăn′te-ism, *n.* Same as *Dilettantism*.

dil-et-tănt′ish, *a.* Of the nature of or inclined toward dilettantism.

dil-et-tănt′ism, *n.* The pursuits and characteristics of a dilettante; specifically, an aimless, trifling or affected pursuit of art, literature, or science.

dil′i-ġence, *n.* [ME. *diligence*; OFr., *diligence*; L. *diligentia*, carefulness, diligence, from *diligens*, careful, diligent, ppr. of *diligere*, to choose apart, esteem highly, select; *dis-*, apart, and *legere*, to choose.]

1. Steady application to business of any kind; constant effort to accomplish what is undertaken; due attention; industry; assiduity.

Brethren, give *diligence* to make your calling and election sure. —2 Pet. i. 10.

2. Care; heed; heedfulness.

Keep thy heart with all *diligence*.—Prov. iv. 23.

3. In Scots law, (a) the warrant issued by a court for enforcing the attendance of witnesses or the production of writings; (b) the process of law by which persons, lands, or effects are attached on execution, or in security for debt.

Syn.—Industry.—*Industry* has the wider sense of the two, implying an habitual devotion to labor for some valuable end; *diligence* denotes earnest application to some specific object or pursuit. A man may be *diligent* for a time, or in seeking some favorite end, without meriting the title of *industrious*.

dil′i-ġence (*or Fr. pron.* dēl-ē-zhoṅs′), *n.* A kind of stagecoach used especially in France.

dil′i-ġen-cy, *n.* Same as *Diligence*, 1. [Obs.]

dil′i-ġent, *a.* 1. Steady in application to business; constant in effort or exertion to accomplish what is undertaken; assiduous; attentive; industrious; not idle or negligent; applied to persons.

Seest thou a man *diligent* in his business? He shall stand before kings. —Prov. xxii. 29.

2. Steadily applied; prosecuted with care and constant effort; careful; assiduous; as, make *diligent* search.

The judges shall make *diligent* inquisition. —Deut. xix. 18.

Syn.—Active, assiduous, sedulous, laborious, persevering, attentive, industrious, indefatigable, unremitting, untiring, careful.

dil′i-ġent-ly, *adv.* In a diligent manner.

dill, *n.* [ME. *dille*, *dylle*; AS. *dile*, the dill plant.] An annual plant, *Peucedanum graveolens*, of the parsley family, the seeds of which are moderately warming, pungent, and aromatic, and are often used medicinally. The plant is native to the Mediterranean region, but is cultivated extensively in gardens.

dill, *v.t.* To soothe, to allay, as pain. [Obs.]

Dil-lē′ni-ȧ, *n.* [From *Dillen*, a professor of botany at Oxford.] The type genus of the order *Dilleniaceæ*, consisting of lofty forest trees, natives of tropical Asia. They have large leaves and showy white or yellow flowers.

Dil-lē-ni-ā′cē-æ, *n.pl.* A natural order of plants belonging to polypetalous, albuminous exogens, nearly related to the *Ranunculaceæ*, from which it differs in having a persistent calyx and arillate seeds. Seventeen genera and about two hundred species are included in the order. They are trees or shrubs, with alternate leaves, found in the warmer regions of both hemispheres.

dil-lē-ni-ā′ceous, *a.* Of or pertaining to the *Dilleniaceæ*.

dil′ling, *n.* A pet; a child born to an aged father. [Obs.]

dil′lūe, *v.t.* [Prov. Eng.] To sift (tin ore) through a sieve.

dil′ly, *n.* An abbreviated form of *diligence*, a vehicle.

dil′ly, *n.* Same as *Daffodil*.

dil′ly, *n.* A small tree, *Mimusops Sieberi*, of the star-apple family, native to Florida and the West Indies.

dil′ly-dal′ly, *v.i.* [Colloq.] To consume time by trifling.

di-log′iç-ăl, *a.* Conveying a double meaning; ambiguous. [Rare.]

dil′ō-ġy, *n.* [L. *dilogia*; Gr. *dilogia*, repetition; *di-*, twice, and *legein*, to speak.] In rhetoric, (a) repetition, particularly to give emphasis; (b) an expression having (intentionally) more than one meaning.

di-lū′cid, *a.* Clear. [Obs.]

di-lū′ci-dāte, *v.t.* To make clear; to elucidate. [Obs.]

di-lū-ci-dā′tion, *n.* The act of making clear. [Obs.]

di-lū-cid′i-ty, *n.* Clearness. [Obs.]

di-lū′cid-ly, *adv.* Clearly. [Obs.]

di-lū-en′dō, *a., adv.* and *n.* Same as *Diminuendo*.

dil′ū-ent, *a.* [L. *diluens* (*-entis*), ppr. of *diluere*, to dilute.] Diluting; tending to weaken or dilute.

dil′ū-ent, *n.* 1. That which thins or attenuates; that which makes more liquid.

2. In medicine, any substance which thins the blood.

di-lūte′, *v.t.*; diluted, *pt., pp.*; diluting, *ppr.* [L. *dilutus*, pp. of *diluere*, to wash away; *dis-*, off, from, and *luere*, to wash.]

1. To render liquid, or more liquid; to make thin, or more fluid.

2. To weaken, as spirit or an acid, by an admixture of water; to make weak or weaker, by mixture.

di-lūte′, *v.i.* To become weak or thin.

di-lūte′, *a.* Thin; attenuated; reduced in strength, as spirit or color.

di-lūt′ed, *a.* Made liquid; rendered more fluid; weakened; made thin, as liquids.

di-lūt′ed-ly, *adv.* In a diluted form.

di-lūte'ness, *n.* The quality or state of being dilute.

di-lūt'ēr, *n.* One who or that which makes thin, or more liquid.

di-lū'tion, *n.* [L. *dilutus*, pp. of *diluere*, to wash away.]

1. The act of making thin, weak, or more liquid; the state of being diluted.

2. A substance which has been diluted.

di-lū'vi-ăl, *a.* [LL. *diluvialis*, pertaining to a flood, from L. *diluvium*, a flood, deluge, from *diluere*, to wash away.]

1. Pertaining to a flood or deluge, especially to the deluge in Noah's days.

2. Of, pertaining to, or consisting of diluvium.

di-lū'vi-ăl-ist, *n.* One who explains geological phenomena by reference to a general deluge, especially the one in the days of Noah.

di-lū'vi-ăn, *a.* Of the nature of or pertaining to a deluge.

di-lū'vi-ăn-ism, *n.* The theory that a former universal deluge explains all geological phenomena.

di-lū'vi-āte, *v.i.* To run as a flood. [Obs.]

di-lū'vi-um, *n.* [L. *diluvium*, a deluge, from *diluere*, to wash away.] In geology, a deposit of superficial loam, sand, gravel, pebbles, etc., caused by the deluge, or ancient currents of water.

dim, *a.*; *comp.* dimmer; *superl.* dimmest [ME. *dim*, *dym* AS *dim*, *dimm*, dim, dark.]

1. Not seeing clearly; having the vision obscured and indistinct.

My heart is breaking and my eyes are *dim*.
—Tennyson.

2. Not clearly seen; obscure; imperfectly seen or discovered; faint, vague; as, a *dim* prospect; a *dim* recollection

Dim with the mist of years, gray flits the shade of power —Byron.

3. Somewhat dark; dusky; not luminous; as, a *dim* shade.

And storied windows richly dight
Casting a *dim* religious light. —Milton.

4. Dull of apprehension; having obscure conceptions

The understanding is *dim*. —Rogers.

5. Having its luster obscured; sullied; tarnished.

How is the gold become *dim*! —Lam. iv. 1.

Syn.—Obscure, dusky, dark, mysterious, indistinct, ill-defined, indefinite, imperfect, dull, sullied, tarnished.

dim, *v.t.*; dimmed, *pt.*, *pp.*; dimming, *ppr.* [ME. *dimmen*; AS *dimmian*, to make dim.] To render dim; to render less bright; to render less clear or distinct; to becloud; to obscure; to tarnish or sully; to becloud the understanding of; to render dull the mental powers of; as, to *dim* the eye; to *dim* the vision; to *dim* the prospect; to *dim* gold.

dim, *v i* To become dim; as, the light *dims* and dies away.

Di-mas'ti-gȧ, *n.pl* [L., from Gr *di-*, two, and *mastix* (*igos*), a whip.] A division of *Infusoria* having two whiplike cilia.

di-mas'ti-gāte, *a* Of or pertaining to the *Dimastiga*, having two flagella.

dim'ble, *n.* A dingle; a dell. [Obs.]

dime, *n.* [ME. *dyme*, *disme*; OFr *disme*, a tithe, tenth; L. *decimus*, a tenth, from *decem*, ten.] A subsidiary silver coin of the United States, equal to ten cents or one-tenth of a dollar.

dime, *a.* Costing a dime; sold for a dime.

Dime novel; a paper-covered book sold for ten cents, usually very melodramatic as to style.

di-men'sion, *n.* [OFr. *dimension*; L. *dimensio*, a measuring, from *dimensus*, pp. of *dimetiri*, to measure off; *dis-*, off, from, and *metiri*, to measure.]

1. Extension in a single line or direction, as length, breadth, and thickness or depth; as, a line has one *dimension* or length; a superficies has two *dimensions*, length and breadth; and a solid has three *dimensions*, length, breadth, and thickness or depth. The word is generally used in the plural, and denotes the whole space occupied by a body, or its capacity, size, measure; as, the *dimensions* of a room, or of a ship; the *dimensions* of a farm, of a kingdom, etc.

These as a line their long *dimension* drew.
—Milton.

2. Outline; shape. [Obs.]

In *dimension*, and the shape of nature, a gracious person. —Shak.

3. Figuratively, bulk; consequence; importance; as, the question is assuming great *dimensions*.

4. In algebra, a term used in the same sense as degree. Thus, ax^2y^2 and ax^2y^3, are equations of five and six *dimensions* respectively.

5. In physics, a quantity, as the linear unit of mass, length, or time, to which all other units, as those of area, velocity, power, etc., are referred; as, the *dimensions* of density are mass divided by the cube of length.

di-men'sion-ăl, *a.* 1. Having a dimension or dimensions; measurable, used in composition; as, a cube is a three-*dimensional* object.

2. Relating or pertaining to dimension; as, *dimensional* equations.

di-men'sioned, *a.* Having dimensions. [Rare.]

di-men'sion-less, *a.* Without definite measure or extent; boundless.

di-men'sion-lum"bēr, *n.* Lumber cut to definite and precise sizes.

di-men'sion-stōne, *n.* Rough stone which will dress to a specified size; sometimes, the dressed stone.

di-men'sion-wŏrk, *n.* Masonry in which dimension-stones are used.

di-men'si-ty, *n.* [Rare.] Same as *Dimension.*

di-men'sive, *a.* Pertaining to boundaries or outlines.

Dim'e-rȧ, *n.pl.* [LL., from Gr. *dimerēs*, divided into two parts; *di-*, two, and *meros*, a part.]

1. A group of beetles of the order *Coleoptera.*

2. A group of hemipterous insects having two-jointed tarsi, including the aphids.

dim'ēr-ăn, *a.* and *n.* I. *a.* Pertaining to or of the nature of the *Dimera.*

II. *n.* One of the *Dimera.*

dim'ē-rous, *a* 1. Composed of two parts; bipartite

2. In botany, having two members in each whorl or verticil.

3. In entomology, having the tarsi jointed; dimeran.

dim'e-tēr, *a.* and *n.* [Gr *dimetros*, consisting of two feet or measures; *di-*, two, and *metron*, a measure.]

I. *a.* Having two measures.

II. *n.* A verse of two measures.

dī-meth'yl, *n.* Ethane.

dī-meth-yl-an'i-line, *n.* [*Di-*, and *methyl*, and *aniline*.] An oily liquid $C_8H_{11}N$, the base of many coal-tar colors.

dī-met'rig, *a* [*Di-*, two, and Gr. *metron*, a measure.] In crystallography, tetragonal.

dim-i-cā'tion, *n.* A battle or fight; contest. [Obs.]

di-mid'i-āte, *v.t.* [L. *dimidiatus*, pp. of *dimidiare*, to divide into halves, from *dimidium*, a half; *dis-*, apart, from, and *medius*, middle.]

1. To divide into two equal parts.

2. In heraldry, to divide into two parts, showing but one.

di-mid'i-āte, *a.* [L. *dimidiatus*, pp. of *dimidiare*, to halve.]

1. In zoölogy and anatomy, one-sided; specifically, applied to cases of hermaphroditism when the organs on one side are male and on the other, female.

2. In botany and entomology, applied to an organ when half of it is so much smaller than the other as to appear to be missing; as, a *dimidiate* leaf; also, split into two on one side, as the calyptra of some mosses.

Dimidiate Calyptra.

3. In heraldry, halved; reduced by half.

di-mid-i-ā'tion, *n.* The act of halving; the condition of being dimidiated.

di-min'ish, *v.t.*; diminished (-isht), *pt.*, *pp.*, diminishing, *ppr.* [Fr *diminuer*; L *deminuere*, to make smaller, diminish; *de*, from, and *minuere*, to make smaller, from *minus*, small.]

1. To lessen; to make less or smaller, by any means, opposed to *increase* and *augment*; as, to *diminish* the size of a thing by contraction, or by cutting off a part; to *diminish* a number by subtraction; to *diminish* the revenue by limiting commerce, or reducing the customs; to *diminish* strength or safety; to *diminish* the heat of a room. It is particularly applied to bulk and quantity, as *shorten* is to length.

2. To lessen; to impair, to degrade.

I will *diminish* them, that they shall no more rule over the nations. —Ezek. xxix. 15.

3. In music, to take from a note by a sharp, flat, or natural.

Diminished arch; an arch less than a semicircle.

Diminished bar; in joinery, the bar of a sash which is thinnest on its inner edge.

Diminished column; one tapering from top to bottom.

Diminished interval; in music, an interval made less than minor, thus G sharp to F natural is a diminished seventh.

Syn.—Decrease, reduce, abate, curtail, impair, degrade.

di-min'ish, *v.i.* To lessen; to become or appear less.

di-min'ish-ȧ-ble, *a.* Capable of being reduced or diminished.

di-min'ish-ēr, *n.* One who or that which diminishes

di-min'ish-ing-ly, *adv.* In a diminishing manner.

di-min'ish-ing-rule, *n.* A concave rule to measure the swell of a column.

di-min'ish-ing-scāle, *n.* A scale which assists in drawing the spiral of the scroll of an Ionic column.

di-min'ish-ment, *n.* Diminution. [Rare.]

di-min-ū-en'dō, *a.* and *adv.* [It., from *diminuere*, to diminish.] In music, gradually diminishing in volume of sound; decrescendo; also used substantively as a composition so diminishing.

di-min'ū-ent, *a.* Lessening. [Rare.]

dim-i-nū'tăl, *a.* Having diminution. [Obs.]

dim'i-nūte, *a.* Small. [Obs.]

dim'i-nūte-ly, *adv.* Minutely. [Obs.]

dim-i-nū'tion, *n.* [ME. *diminution*; L. *deminutio*, a lessening, diminishing, from *deminuere*, to diminish.]

1. The act of lessening; a making smaller; opposed to *augmentation*; as, the *diminution* of size, of wealth, of power, of safety.

2. The state of becoming or appearing less; opposed to *increase*; as, the *diminution* of the apparent diameter of a receding body.

3. Deprivation of dignity; a lessening of estimation; degradation.

4. In architecture, the contraction of the upper part of a column, by which its diameter is made less than that of the lower part.

5. In music, the imitation of or reply to a subject in notes of half the length or value of those of the subject itself.

6. In law, an omission in the record, or in some point of the proceedings, which is certified in a writ of error on the part of either plaintiff or defendant.

7. In heraldry, the defacing of some particular point in the escutcheon.

di-min-ū-ti'văl, *a.* and *n.* Same as *Diminutive.*

di-min'ū-tive, *a.* [LL. *diminutivus*, from L. *deminutus*, pp. of *deminuere*, to make small.]

1. Small; little; narrow; contracted as, a *diminutive* race of men; a *diminutive* thought.

2. Having the power or tendency to lessen; decrease; abridge.

3. In grammar, expressing or indicating diminution; as, a *diminutive* suffix.

di-min'ū-tive, *n.* 1. In grammar, a word formed from another word, usually an appellative or generic term, to express a little thing of the kind; as, streamlet, a little stream.

2. Anything smaller than the average in size, importance, etc.

di-min'ū-tive-ly, *adv.* In a diminutive manner.

di-min'ū-tive-ness, *n.* Smallness; littleness; want of bulk; want of dignity.

dim'ish, *a.* Same as *Dimmish.*

di-mis'sion (-mish'un), *n.* Leave to depart. [Obs.]

dim'is-sō-ry, *a.* [LL. *dimissorius*, from L. *dimissus*, pp. of *dimittere*, to send away.]

1. Sending away; dismissing to another jurisdiction.

2. Granting leave to depart.

A letter dimissory; one given by a bishop dismissing a person who is removing into another diocese, and recommending him for reception there.

di-mit', *v.t.* [L. *dimittere*, to send away.]

1. To permit to go; specifically, in Freemasonry, to give a dimit.

2. To grant; to farm; to let.

di-mit', *n.* In Freemasonry, a letter from a lodge, permitting a member in good standing to affiliate with another Masonic lodge.

dim'i-ty, *n.* [Gr. *dimitos*, two-threaded, dimity; *dis-*, two, and *mitos*, thread.]

1. A stout cotton fabric with raised stripes or patterns, sometimes printed in colors, used for hangings and upholstering.

2. A light-weight cotton fabric, with fine twills, much used for dresses.

dim'ly, *adv.* [ME. *dimly*, *dimliche*, from AS. *dimlic*, dim.] In a dim or obscure manner; with a faint light; not brightly or clearly; with imperfect sight.

dim'mēr, *a.*, comp. of *dim.*

dim'mest, *a.*, superl. of *dim.*

dim'mish, **dim'my**, *a.* Slightly dim; also written *dimish.*

dim'ness, *n.* [ME. *dimnes*; AS. *dimnes*, from *dim*, dim.]

1. The state or quality of being dim.

2. Want of clear apprehension; stupidity; as, *dimness* of perception.

dī'mọrph, *n.* [L. *dimorphus*; Gr. *dimorphos*, having two forms; *di-*, two, and *morphē*, form.] Either form taken by a dimorphous substance; as, sulphur is a *dimorph.*

dī-mọr'phig, *a.* 1. Dimorphous.

2 Of, relating, or pertaining to dimorphism.

dī-mọr'phism, *n.* [Gr. *di-*, two, and *morphē*, form.]

1. The property of crystallizing in two distinct forms not derivable from one another. Sulphur assumes one form when crystallizing at a high temperature, and another wholly different when becoming solid at the ordinary temperature.

2. In botany, the condition when analogous

organs of plants of the same species appear under two very dissimilar forms; thus in the flowers of the oak, beech, chestnut, and pine, the stamen-bearing ones have no pistils, and the pistil-bearing ones no stamens.

3. In zoölogy, difference of form between members of the same species, as when the females vary according to the seasons, or the males are constantly unlike the females.

dī-mor′phous, *a.* [Gr. *dimorphos*, having two forms; *di-*, two, and *morphē*, form.] Existing in two forms; applied specifically in crystallography to a substance crystallizing under different conditions in two distinct forms.

dim′ple (-pl), *n.* [Origin obscure.] A slight depression or dent, occurring in some soft part of the body, most commonly in the chin or in the cheek, when smiling; by extension, a slight dent or cavity on any surface.

dim′ple, *v.i.*; dimpled, *pt.*, *pp.*; dimpling, *ppr.* To form dimples; to sink into depressions or little inequalities.

And smiling eddies *dimpled* on the main. —Dryden.

dim′ple, *v.t.* To make dimples in; to mark with a dimple or dimples.

dim′ple-ment, *n.* The state of being dimpled. [Rare.]

dim′ply, *a.* Full of dimples or small depressions; as, the *dimply* flood.

Dim-y-ā′ri-ȧ, Dim′y-ȧ, *n.pl.* [L., from Gr. *di-*, two, and *mys*, a muscle.] A general name for those bivalves whose shells are closed by two adductor muscles, distinct and widely removed from each other, as in the common clam. The two muscular attachments are always visible on the inside of the shell.

dim-y-ā′ri-ăn, *a.* and *n.* I. *a.* Of or resembling the *Dimyaria.*

II. *n.* One of the *Dimyaria.*

dim′y-ȧ-ry, *a.* and *n.* Same as *Dimyarian.*

din, *n.* [ME. *dyn*; AS. *dyne*, a loud noise, a rumbling.] Noise; a loud sound; particularly, a rattling, clattering, or rumbling sound, long continued; as, the *din* of arms; the *din* of war.

The guests are met, the feast is set,—
May'st hear the merry *din*. —Coleridge.

din, *v.t.*; dinned, *pt.*, *pp.*; dinning, *ppr.* 1. To strike with continued or confused sound; to stun with noise; to harass with clamor; as, to *din* the ear with cries; to *din* with clamor.

2. To tell repeatedly or persistently; as, he *dinned* his story into my ears.

din, *v.i.* To make a din or noisy clamor.

dī-nän-de-riē′, *n.* [Fr., from *Dinant*, a city in Belgium, noted for its copper ware.]

1. Utensils of copper, originally intended for use in the kitchen, but of quaint and beautiful form, and oftentimes ornamented with coats of arms and other devices.

2. Ornamental brasswork of the Orient.

dī-naph′thyl, *n.* [*Di-* and *naphthyl*ene.] A crystalline substance, $C_{20}H_{14}$, formed from naphthylene.

dī-när′, *n.* [Ar., from L. *denarius*, a silver coin containing originally ten asses, from *decem*, ten.]

1. A medieval gold coin of the Orient; specifically, one issued by the Damascene califs.

2. A small Persian money of account.

din′är-çhy, *n.* [*Di-*, and Gr. *archein*, to rule.] A form of government in which the supreme power is vested in two persons.

din′dle, *n.* [Local, Eng.] A local name for the common and corn sow-thistles, as also for hawkweed.

dīne, *v.i.*; dined, *pt.*, *pp.*; dining, *ppr.* [ME. *dinen*, *dynen*; OFr. *disner*, *disgner*, to dine; origin uncertain, thought to be from L. *de-*, intens., and *cenare*, to dine, from *cena*, dinner.] To take dinner; to eat the principal meal of the day.

To dine with Duke Humphrey; to be dinnerless.

dīne, *v.t.* 1. To give a dinner to; to furnish with the principal meal; to feed; to entertain at a dinner; used especially in the sense of festivities for an honored guest; as, society wined and *dined* the poet; the landlord *dined* a hundred men.

2. To dine upon; as, what will you *dine*? [Obs.]

dīn′ẽr, *n.* One who dines.

dīn′ẽr-out, *n.* One who is often entertained at dinner away from home.

dī-net′iç-ăl, *a.* Whirling around; turning on an axis; rotatory. [Obs.]

ding, *v.t.*; dinged, *pt.*, *pp.*; dinging, *ppr.* [ME. *dingen*, to strike, beat.]

1. To thrust violently; to pound; to punch. [Rare.]

2. To throw away with violence. [Obs.]

3. To sound or urge repeatedly.

To ding in one's ears; to make an impression by frequent repetition.

ding, *v.i.* 1. To strike; to pound. [Obs.]

2. To resound monotonously, as a bell; to toll; to ring; to clang.

3. To repeat vehemently and monotonously; to scold; to bluster.

ding, *n.* A stroke or blow, as of a bell.

ding′dong, *n.* [Imitative origin.] 1. The sound of bells, or any similar sound of continuous strokes.

2. A device in a clock by which the quarter-hours are struck upon bells of variant pitch.

dinġe, *v.t.*; dinged, *pt.*, *pp.*; dingeing, *ppr.* To make dinges or indentations in; to dint; to dent. [Eng.]

dinġe, *v.t.* [Colloq. Eng.] To make dingy.

diñ′ghy, diñ′gey, diñ′gy, dhiñ′gy, *n.* [Bengalese, *dingi*, a boat.] 1. An East Indian boat varying in size in different localities; as, the *dinghies* of Bombay and Calcutta.

2. A ship's small boat, used for ordinary purposes; also, the smallest boat of a ship of war.

3. In some parts of the United States, a flat-bottomed boat; a dory.

din′ġi-ly, *adv.* In a dingy manner.

din′ġi-ness, *n.* A dusky or dark hue.

diñ′gle, *n.* [Etym. uncertain.] A narrow dale or valley between hills; a small secluded valley.

diñ′gle-dañ′gle, *adv.* In a loose or dangling manner.

diñ′gō, *n.* [Native Australian name.] A wild dog of Australia, of a wolf-like appearance and extremely fierce. The ears are short and erect, the tail rather bushy and the hair of a reddish-dun color. It is very destructive to the flocks, and is systematically hunted and killed.

ding′thrift, *n.* A spendthrift. [Obs.]

din′ġy, *a.*; *comp.* dingier; *superl.* dingiest. [AS. *dung*, a heap.] Soiled; sullied; of a dark color; brown; dusky; dun.

Dī-nich′thys, *n.* [Gr. *deinos*, terrible, and *ichthys*, fish.] A genus of large extinct fishes of the Devonian period; their fossil remains, found in Ohio, indicate that they attained a length of twenty feet.

dīn′ing, *n.* The act of eating dinner; used adjectively in composition; as, a *dining*-room, a *dining*-car, etc.

dī-nī″trō-cel′lū-lōse, *n.* [*Di-*, and *nitric*, and *cellulose*.] A substance resembling guncotton, produced by the action of a mixture of sulphuric and nitric acids on cotton; also called *soluble pyroxylin.*

diñk, *a.* [Scot.] Neatly dressed; tidy; trim.

diñk, *v.t.*; dinked, *pt.*, *pp.*; dinking, *ppr.* To dress; to adorn; to deck; followed by *out* or *up.* [Scot.]

diñk′ly, *adv.* In a neat, trim fashion.

din′mŏnt, *n.* A Scotch term applied to a wether which has been once sheared.

din′nȧ. A Scotch form of *do not.*

din′nẽr, *n.* [ME. *diner*, *dyner*; OFr. *disner*, dinner.]

1. The principal meal of the day, eaten either at noon or in the late afternoon or early evening. The word is often used adjectively or in compounds; as, *dinner*-hour, *dinner*-bell, a *dinner*-jacket, etc.

2. An entertainment; a banquet.

din′nẽr-less, *a.* Being without dinner.

din′nẽr-ly, *a.* Pertaining to dinner. [Rare.]

dī-nō-. A combining form from Gr. *deinos*, terrible, mighty, from *deos*, fear, used in scientific words of Greek origin signifying terrible, fearful, mighty, huge.

Dī-noc′e-ras, *n.* [L., from Gr. *deinos*, huge, and *keras*, horn.] A genus of huge extinct mammals, so called from the three pairs of horn-cores forming remarkable protuberances of the skull. Their remains are found in the early Tertiary deposits of North America.

Dī-nor′nis, Deī-nor′nis, *n.* [L., from Gr. *deinos*, huge, terrible, and *ornis*, a bird.] A genus of enormous extinct birds, resembling, but much larger than the ostrich, and found in New Zealand. [See *Moa.*]

Dinornis (pelvic and leg bones and outline of body).

Dī-nor′ni-thēṣ, *n.pl.* The group of enormous extinct birds of which *Dinornis* is the type genus; a general name for the moas.

dī′nō-saur, deī′nō-saur, *n.* One of the *Dinosauria.*

Dī-nō-sau′ri-ȧ, *n.pl.* [L., from Gr. *deinos*, terrible, and *sauros*, a lizard.] An order of extinct Mesozoic reptiles of colossal size and possessing certain bird-like characteristics, on which account they have been variously classified.

dī-nō-sau′ri-ăn, deī-nō-sau′ri-ăn, *a.* and *n.* I. *a.* Pertaining to the *Dinosauria.*

II. *n.* Same as *Dinosaur.*

dī′nō-thēre, *n.* A dinotherium.

Dī-nō-thē′ri-um, *n.* [L., from Gr. *deinos*, terrible, and *thērion*, a wild beast.]

1. A genus of enormous extinct elephant-like mammals, remarkable for a pair of immense lower incisors, turned down or away from the mouth. There are several species from the Miocene of Europe and Asia.

2. [d—] An animal of this genus.

din-ox′id, *n.* An incorrect form of *dioxid.*

din′sŏme, *a.* [Scot.] Full of din; noisy; loud.

dint, *v.t.*; dinted, *pt.*, *pp.*; dinting, *ppr.* To dent; to make a mark or cavity in by a blow or pressure.

dint, *n.* [ME. *dint*, *dynt*; AS. *dynt*, a blow, stroke.]

1. A blow; a stroke.

2. Force; violence; agency; power exerted; as, to win by *dint* of arms, by *dint* of war, by *dint* of argument or importunity.

3. The mark made by a blow; a cavity or impression made by a blow or by pressure on a substance.

His hands had made a *dint*. —Dryden.

dī-nū-mẽr-ā′tion, *n.* Enumeration; a counting. [Obs.]

dī-oc′ē-săn (or dī′ō-cē-săn), *a.* Pertaining to a diocese.

dī-oc′ē-săn, *n.* [ME. *dyocesan*; OFr. *diocesain*, pertaining to a diocese, from LL. *diœcesis*, a diocese.]

1. A bishop; one who has authority over a diocese.

2. One of the people or clergy belonging to a diocese. [Obs.]

dī′ō-cēse, *n.* [ME. *diocise*; OFr. *diocise*; LL. *diœcesis*, a bishop's jurisdiction; L. *diœcesis*, a district, government.] The circuit or extent of a bishop's jurisdiction; an ecclesiastical division of a country, subject to the authority of a bishop.

dī-ō-cē′se-nẽr, *n.* A person belonging to a diocese. [Obs.]

dī-oc-tȧ-hē′drăl, *a.* [*Di-*, and Gr. *oktō*, eight, and *hedra*, a seat, base.] In crystallography, having the form of an octahedral prism with tetrahedral summits.

Dī′ō-don, *n.* [L. *diodon*, from Gr. *di-*, two, and *odous* (*odontos*), tooth.] A Linnean genus of teleostean fishes now giving its name to a family, *Diodontidæ*, of the order *Plectognathi*, so called because their jaws are not divided, but exhibit one piece of bony substance above and another below, so that the creature appears to have only two teeth. They are all natives of warm climates, and live on crustaceans and sea-weeds, for the trituration of which their mouths are admirably adapted. Several of them, especially of the genera *Diodon* and *Tetraodon*, are remarkable for the array of spiny points which they bear on their skin, and for the power they have of inflating the belly, which then gives them the appearance of the bristly husk of a chestnut; also called *porcupine-fish*, *sea-porcupine*, *sea-hedgehog*, and *prickly globe-fish.*

Diodon hystrix.

dī′ō-dont, *a.* and *n.* I. *a.* Having two teeth; of or pertaining to *Diodontidæ.*

II. *n.* One of the *Diodontidæ.*

Dī-ō-don′ti-dæ, *n.pl.* A family of fishes named from its type genus, the *Diodon.*

Dī-œ′ci-ȧ (-ē′shi-ȧ), *n.* [L., from Gr. *di-*, two, and *oikos*, house.] A class of plants having the stamens on one plant and the pistils on another.

dī-œ′cious, dī-œ′ciăn, *a.* [L., from Gr. *di-*, two, and *oikos*, house.]

1. In botany, unisexual, the stamens being on one plant and the pistils on another; opposed to *monœcious.*

Diœcia.—Male and Female Plants of *Vallisneria spiralis.*

2. In zoölogy, sexually distinct; having the germ cell or ovum produced by one individual, the female, and the sperm-cell or spermatozoid, by another, the male; opposed to *monœcious.*

dī-œ′cious-ly, *adv.* In a diœcious manner.

dī-œ′cious-ness, *n.* In biology, the state or quality of having separate sexes.

dī-œ′cism, *n.* Diœciousness.

Di-og′e-nēs-crab, *n.* A hermit-crab, *Cenobita diogenes*, a habitant of the West Indies.

Dī-ō-gen′ic, *a.* Of, pertaining to, or resembling Diogenes, a famous Athenian philosopher of the fourth century before Christ; cynical.

dī′oic, dī-oi′cous, *a.* Same as *Diœcious.*

Dī′ō-mē-dē′ȧ, *n.* [L., from *Diomedes*; Gr. *Diomēdēs*, Diomedes, lit. Zeus-counseled; *Zeus* (*Dios*), Zeus, and *mēdos*, counsel.] The type genus of the albatross family.

Dī′on, *n.* Same as *Dioön.*

Dī-ō-næ′ȧ (-nē′ȧ), *n.* [L., from Gr. *Diōnē*, the mother of Aphrodite, also a name for Aphrodite.] A genus of plants of the order *Droseraceæ*. Only one species is known, *Dionæa muscipula*, or Venus's fly-trap, a native of the sandy savannas of the Carolinas and Florida. It has a rosette of root leaves, from which rises a naked scape bearing a corymb of large white flowers. The bristles on the leaves are remarkably irritable, and when touched by a fly or other insect the lobes of the leaf suddenly close upon and capture the insect.

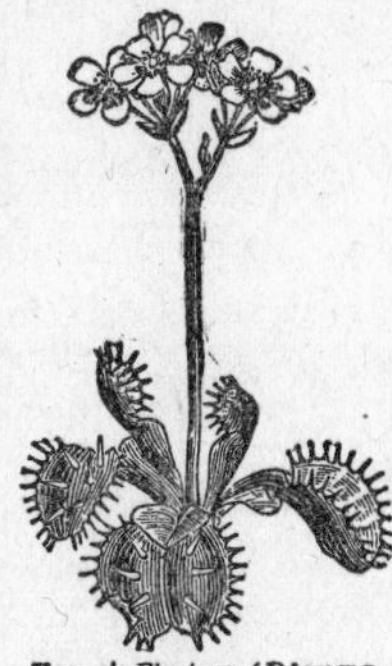

Venus's Fly-trap (*Dionæa muscipula*).

dī′ō-nym, *n.* A two-termed name, particularly in zoölogy.

Dī-ō-nys′i-ȧ, *n.pl.* [L., from Gr. *Dionysia* (supply *hiera*, offerings), the Dionysia, from *Dionysos*.] In classical antiquity, a Greek series of festivals corresponding to the Roman bacchanalia, but marked by competitive dramatic productions as well as by orgiastic revelry.

Dī-ō-nys′i-ac, *a.* Of or pertaining to the Dionysia; Bacchic.

Dī-ō-nys′i-ăn, *a.* [Gr. *Dionysios*, pertaining to Dionysus, from *Dionysos*.]

1. Same as *Dionysiac.*

2. Pertaining to or resembling the Syracusan tyrants, Dionysius the Elder, or the Younger, of fifth century B. C., noted for their cruelty.

3. Of or pertaining to the abbot Dionysius, who lived in the sixth century and introduced the system of reckoning dates from the birth of Christ.

Dionysian period; a period of 532 Julian years, used in computation of the date of Easter.

Dī-ō′on, *n.* [L., from Gr. *di-*, two, and *ōon*, an egg.] A genus of plants of the *Cycadaceæ* family, palm-like in appearance, with short, stout stems and large pinnate leaves with spiny tips. There are only two species, both of them native to tropical Mexico.

Dī-ō-phan′tine, *a.* Relating to or pertaining to Diophantus, the ancient Greek authority on algebra.

Diophantine analysis; in algebra, a method of solution for indeterminate equations by determining a rational number which may be substituted for one of the unknown quantities.

dī-op′side (*or* -sīd), *n.* [Gr. *diopsis*, a view through; *dia*, through, and *opsis*, a view.] A variety of pyroxene (Mg, Ca)SiO_3.

Dī-op′sis, *n.* [L., from Gr. *di-*, two, and *opsis*, a view.] A genus of dipterous insects, family *Muscidæ*, the members of which are remarkable for the immense prolongation of the sides of the head, the head appearing as if it were furnished with two long horns, each having a knob at its apex. All the known species are from the tropical parts of the Old World.

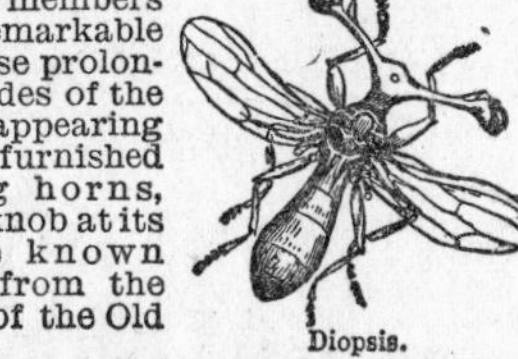

Diopsis.

dī-op′tāse, *n.* A rare ore, a hydrous silicate of copper. It occurs in rich, emerald-green crystals, having the form of six-sided prisms, terminated at each end by a three-sided prism.

dī-op′tēr, *n.* [L. *dioptra*; Gr. *dioptra*, a leveling instrument invented by Hipparchus.]

1. The theodolite as anciently made.

2. The indicator of a graduated circle.

3. An appliance for measuring skull-projections.

4. In optics, a dioptric.

dī-op′trȧ, *n.*, pl. of *dioptron.*

dī-op′trāte, *a.* [*Dia-*, and Gr. *opt-*, from root of *opsesthai*, to see.] In entomology, having transverse divisions or partitions; applied to the eyes, as of certain beetles.

dī-op′tre, *n.* [Obs.] See *Diopter*, 1.

dī-op′tric, dī-op′tric-ăl, *a.* [Gr. *dioptrikos*, pertaining to the use of the diopter.]

1. Affording a medium for the sight; assisting the sight in the view of distant objects; as, a *dioptric* glass.

2. Pertaining to dioptrics, or the science of refracted light.

dī-op′tric, *n.* In optics, the unit equal to one meter divided by the focal distance of a lens; used as a standard of refractive power.

dī-op′trics, *n.* That part of optics which treats of the refraction of light passing through different media, as air, water, glass, etc.

dī-op′tron, *n.*; *pl.* **dī-op′trȧ.** [Gr. *dioptron*, a surgical speculum; *dia*, through, and *opt-*, from *opsesthai*, to see.] A speculum used in surgery.

dī-op′try, *n.* Same as *Dioptric.*

dī-ō-rä′mȧ, *n.* [From Gr. *diorān*, to see through; *dia*, through, and *horān*, to see.]

1. A contrivance for giving a high degree of optical illusion to paintings exhibited in a building prepared for the purpose. A great diversity of scenic effect is produced by means of transparent paintings, through which the light is admitted, varying in intensity and color at different times.

2. A building used for this purpose.

dī-ō-ram′ic, *a.* Pertaining to a diorama.

dī′ō-rism, *n.* [Gr. *diorismos*, division, distinction, from *diorizein*, to divide.] Definition. [Rare.]

dī-ō-ris′tic, *a.* Distinguishing; defining. [Rare.]

dī-ō-ris′tic-ăl-ly, *adv.* In a distinguishing manner. [Rare.]

dī′ō-rīte, *n.* [From Gr. *diorizein*, to divide.] A variety of trap-rock composed of hornblende and triclinic feldspar.

dī-ō-rit′ic, *a.* Relating to or containing diorite.

dī-or-thō′sis, *n.* [L., from Gr. *diorthōsis*, a making straight, correcting, from *diorthoun*, to make straight; *dia*, through, and *orthoun*, to make straight, from *orthos*, straight.]

1. A surgical operation, by which crooked or distorted limbs are restored to their proper shape.

2. A revised edition of a literary work.

dī-or-thot′ic, *a.* Of the nature of or pertaining to diorthosis.

Dī-os-cō′rē-ȧ, *n.* [L., from *Dioscorides*, a Greek physician.] The genus of plants, natural order *Dioscoreaceæ*, which furnish the tropical esculents called yams. They are perennial fleshy-rooted or tuberous diœcious plants, with annual twining stems and loose clusters of small green flowers.

Dī-os-cō-rē-ā′cē-æ, *n.pl.* An order of tropical plants including eight genera and about 160 species; the yam family.

dī-os-cō-rē-ā′ceous, *a.* Of, pertaining to, or resembling the *Dioscoreaceæ.*

dī-os-mō′sis, dī-os′mōse, *n.* [L., from Gr. *dia*, through, and *ōsmos*, a thrusting, from *ōthein*, to thrust, push.] In physical chemistry, transfusion through a membrane having imperceptible pores; osmose.

dī-os-mot′ic, *a.* Of or pertaining to diosmosis; osmotic.

Dī-os′py-ros, *n.* [Gr. *diospyros*, lit. Zeus's wheat, a certain plant; *Dios*, genit. of *Zeus*, Zeus, and *pyros*, wheat.] A large genus of trees and shrubs of the ebony family, found in tropical regions. They are noted for their valuable hard wood and delicious fruit. The persimmon or date-plum, *Diospyros Virginiana*, is the best known species in the United States.

dī-ox′id, dī-ox′ide, *n.* [*Di-*, and *oxide.*] An oxid consisting of one atom of a metal and two atoms of oxygen.

dip, *v.t.*; dipped *or* dipt, *pt.*, *pp.*; dipping, *ppr.* [ME. *dippen*; AS. *dyppan*, *dippan*, to dip, plunge, from *deop*, deep.]

1. To plunge or immerse, for a short time, in water or other liquid substance; to put into a fluid and withdraw.

> The priest shall *dip* his finger in the blood.
> —Lev. iv. 6.

2. To take with a ladle, or other vessel, by immersing it in a fluid; as, to *dip* water from a boiler; often with *out*; as, to *dip out* water.

3. To engage in, with all one's energy or ambition; to plunge into.

4. To engage as a pledge; to mortgage. [Obs.]

5. To moisten; to wet.

6. To baptize by immersion.

7. To lower and raise again, as if in immersion; as, to *dip* a flag in salute.

Dipped candle; a candle made by successive dippings of a wick in melted tallow.

To dip snuff; to take snuff by means of a stick, applying it to the teeth and gums. [Southern U. S.]

dip, *v.i.* 1. To sink; to immerge in a liquid.

2. To enter; to pierce; followed by *in* or *into.*

3. To thrust into something, as the hand or a ladle, and remove part of a liquid or soft substance.

4. To enter slightly; to look cursorily, or here and there; as, to *dip* into a volume of history.

5. In geology, to form an angle with the horizon, as a stratum.

6. To incline downward; as, the magnetic needle *dips.*

dip, *n.* 1. Inclination downward; a sloping; depression.

2. The action of placing in a liquid, for a short space of time.

3. An amount of liquid taken by dipping; the act of dipping or scooping up.

4. The depth to which a paddle-wheel or screw is immersed.

5. In mining, a heading meeting an extremely angular stratum of coal; a dip-head.

6. In geology, the measure of the angle made by strata with the plane of the horizon.

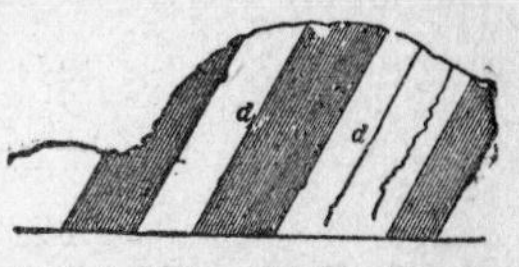

7. Any preparation, as a sauce, a coating, or cleaning liquid, or other fluid, into which something is dipped.

Geological Dip. *d d*, Direction or Angle of Dip.

8. A candle made by dipping. [Colloq.]

Dip or *depression of the horizon*; the angle contained by two straight lines drawn from the observer's eye, the one to a point in the visible horizon, and the other parallel to the horizon, the eye of the observer being supposed to be elevated above the level of the sea. Hence, the greater the elevation of the observer's eye, the greater the *dip of the horizon.* In the figure, C represents the earth's center, E the observer's eye, E A its height above the level of the sea, B and D points in the visible horizon, H E O a horizontal line; the angle B E O or D E H the *dip of the horizon.*

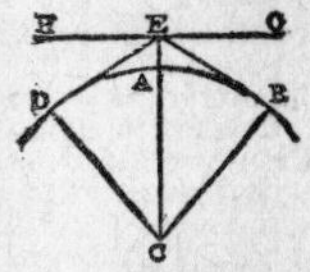

Dip of the Horizon.

Dip of the needle or *magnetic dip*; the angle which a magnetic needle, freely suspended, makes, at a given place, with the horizon; also called *inclination of the needle.*

dī-pas′chăl, *a.* [*Di-*, and Gr. *pascha*, a passover.] Including two passovers.

dip′chick, *n.* Same as *Dabchick.*

dip′-cīr″cle, *n.* A dipping-compass.

dī-pet′ăl-ous, *a.* [*Di-*, and Gr. *petalon*, a leaf.] Having two flower-leaves or petals; two-petaled.

dī′phāse, *a.* [*Di-*, and Gr. *phasis*, an appearance, from *phainein*, to appear.] Of or denoting an electrical circuit made up of two alternating currents, one of which has a maximum value when the other is zero, the phase difference between them being 90°; also written *two-phase.*

dip′-head, *n.* See *Dip*, n. 5.

dī-phē′nyl, *n.* A white crystalline compound, $C_{12}H_{10}$, obtained from the coal-tar oils.

diph-thē′ri-ȧ (*or* dip-), *n.* [Gr. *diphthera*, a prepared skin, leather, from *dephein*, to soften hides, to tan.] An epidemic inflammatory disease of the air-passages, and especially of the throat, characterized by the formation of a false membrane. It frequently proves fatal.

diph-thē′ri-ăl, diph-ther′ic, *a.* Same as *Diphtheritic.*

diph-thē-rit′ic, *a.* Of the nature of, pertaining to, caused, or affected by diphtheria.

diph′thē-roid, *a.* Having the nature of or similar to diphtheria.

diph′thong, *n.* [LL. *diphthongus*; Gr. *diphthongos*, a diphthong; *di-*, two, and *phongos*, voice, sound, from *phthengesthai*, to utter.] A coalition or union of two vowels, pronounced in one syllable. In uttering a *diphthong* both vowels are pronounced; the sound is not simple, but the two sounds are so blended as to be considered as forming one syllable, as in *joy, noise, bound, out.*

Improper diphthong; two or more vowels placed together, only one being sounded; as *ea* in *breath.*

diph′thong, *v.t.* Same as *Diphthongize.* [Rare.]

diph-thon′găl, *a.* Belonging to a diphthong; consisting of two vowel sounds, pronounced in one syllable.

diph-thon′găl-ly, *adv.* In a diphthongal manner.

diph-thon′găl-īze, *v.t.* Same as *Diphthongize.* [Rare.]

diph-thon-gā′tion, *n.* The formation of a diphthong; the changing of a single vowel into a diphthong by adding another vowel.

diph-thong′ic, *a.* Of or pertaining to a diphthong.

diph-thong-i-zā′tion, *n.* Same as *Diphthongation.*

diph′thong-īze, diph′thong-īse, *v.t.* and *v.i.* To change into a diphthong; to pronounce as a diphthong.

diph-y-cēr′căl, diph′y-cērc, *a.* [Gr. *diphyēs*, of a double nature or form, and *kerkos*, a tail.] In ichthyology, having the tail divided symmetrically, as by the spinal column.

diph′y-cēr-cy, *n.* The state of having the tail diphycercal; applied to fishes.

diph-y-gen′ic, *a.* [Gr. *diphyēs*, of a double nature or form, and *genesis*, origin, birth.] In zoölogy, having two forms of embryo.

diph′yl-lous, *a.* [*Di-*, and Gr. *phyllon*, a leaf.] In botany, having two leaves, as a calyx.

diph′y-ō-dont, *a.* Growing in two sets; applied to teeth.

diph′y-ō-dont, *n.* [L. *diphyodons* (*-ontis*); Gr. *diphyēs*, of a double form, and *odous* (*-ontos*), a tooth.] One of that group of mammals which possess two successive sets of teeth, a deciduous or milk set, and a permanent set, as distinguished from the *monophyodonts*, which develop only one set.

diph′y-site, *n.* One who believes in diphysitism.

diph′y-sī-tism, *n.* [*Di-*, and Gr. *physis*, nature.] In theology, the belief that Christ possessed two distinct natures, one human, one divine; opposed to *monophysitism.*

diph-y-zō′oid, *n.* [Gr. *diphyēs*, of a double nature, *zōon*, an animal, an *eidos*, form.] One of the detached reproductive portions of adult members of an order of oceanic *Hydrozoa.* They swim about by means of their calyx.

dī-plā′nãr, *a.* Having or pertaining to two planes.

dī-plā-net′iç, *a.* [*Di-*, and Gr. *planētikos*, disposed to wander, from *planan*, to wander.] In botany, having a period of rest alternating with two active periods.

dī-plā-si-as′mus, *n.* [Gr. *diplasiasmos*, a doubling, from *diplasiazein*, to double, from *diplasios*, double; *di-*, two, and *-plasios*, -fold.]

1. In orthography, the doubling of a letter; as, *petalled* for *petaled.*

2. In rhetoric, the repetition of a word for the purpose of emphasis; as, "Break! break! break! on thy cold, gray stones, O sea!"

dī-plas′iç, *a.* [Gr. *diplasios*, double.] In the ratio of two to one; applied specifically in ancient prosody to a class of feet in which the (accented) arsis has twice the length of the (unaccented) thesis.

dī-plē′gi-à, *n.* [L., from Gr. *di-*, two, and *plēgē*, a stroke.] Paralysis in which similar parts on the two sides of the body are affected.

dī-plei′dō-scōpe, *n.* [Gr. *diploos*, double, *eidos*, appearance, and *skopein*, to see.] An instrument for indicating the passage of the sun or a star over the meridian, by the coincidence of two images of the object, the one formed by single and the other by double reflection.

dī′plex, *a.* See *Duplex.*

dip-lō-. A combining form, from Greek *diploos*, double, signifying two, double, twin, etc.

dip″lō-bac-tē′ri-à, *n.pl.* [*Diplo-*, and L. *bacteria*, bacteria, from Gr. *baktron*, a staff.] Bacteria which are two-celled or exist in pairs.

dip-lō-blas′tiç, *a.* [*Diplo-*, and Gr. *blastos*, a germ.] In embryology, having a two-layered germinal membrane.

dip-lō-çãr′di-aç, *a.* [*Diplo-*, and Gr. *kardia*, heart.] Having the heart double, with the right and left sides distinctly separate, as in birds and mammals.

dip-lō-çoç′çus, *n.*; *pl.* **dip-lō-çoç′cī.** [L., from Gr. *diploos*, double, and *coccus*, a berry.] In biology, a micrococcus, consisting of two united cells; a joined spherule.

dip′lō-ē, *n.* [L., from Gr. *diploē*, f. of *diploos*, double.] The soft, medullary substance or porous part between the plates of the skull.

dip-lō-et′iç, *a.* Same as *Diploic.*

dip-lō-gen′e-sis, *n.* [L., from Gr. *diploos*, double, and *genesis*, origin, generation.] In biology, the abnormal doubling of parts; applied to monstrosities.

dip″lō-ġē-net′iç, *a.* Of or pertaining to diplogenesis.

dip-lō-ġen′iç, *a.* Diplogenetic.

dī-plō′iç, *a.* Of or pertaining to the diploe.

dip′loid, *n.* [Gr *diploos*, double, and *eidos*, form.] In crystallography, a solid, included under twenty-four equal, trapezoidal planes.

dī-plō′mà, *n.* [L. *diploma*; Gr. *diploma*, a letter folded double.] Anciently, a letter or other composition written on paper or parchment and folded; afterward, any letter, literary monument, or public document; now, a letter or writing, usually under seal and signed by competent authority, conferring some power, privilege, or honor, as that given to graduates of colleges on their receiving the usual degrees, to physicians who are licensed to practise their profession, and the like.

dī-plō′mà-cy, *n.* [Fr. *diplomatie*, from L. *diploma*, a diploma.]

1 The science which treats of the intercourse between nations, based on international law, and conducted by their heads directly, or through accredited representatives; the art of managing international negotiations.

2. The practice of conducting such negotiations.

3. A diplomatic body; the whole body of ministers at a court.

4. Dexterity; skill; tact; shrewdness in managing affairs of any kind.

dip′lō-mat, *n.* [Fr. *diplomate*, from L. *diploma*, a diploma.] One who is versed in or makes a business of diplomacy; a diplomatist.

dip′lō-māte, *v.t.* To confer a diploma upon; to invest with authority or privilege by a diploma. [Rare.]

dip-lō-mā′tiăl (-shăl), *a.* Same as *Diplomatic.* [Rare.]

dip-lō-mat′iç, dip-lō-mat′iç-ăl, *a.* 1. Of or pertaining to diplomas or diplomatics.

2. Of or pertaining to, or concerned with diplomacy.

3. Characterized by artful dealings, tact, and cleverness in avoiding blunders; politic in conduct.

Diplomatic corps or *body*; the entire body of ministers or official agents accredited to and resident at a court or capital.

dip-lō-mat′iç-ăl-ly, *adv.* According to the rules of diplomacy; artfully; tactfully.

dip-lō-mat′içs, *n.* The science of diplomas, or of ancient writings, literary and public documents, which has for its object the deciphering of old writings to ascertain their authenticity their dates, signatures, etc.

dī-plō′mà-tişm, *n.* Diplomacy. [Rare.]

dī-plō′mà-tist, *n.* One who is officially employed in diplomatic service; one skilled in diplomacy; a diplomat.

dip-lō-neū′răl, *a.* [*Diplo-*, and Gr. *neuron*, nerve.] In anatomy, having two nerves different in origin.

dī-plō′pi-à, dip′lō-py, *n.* [L., from Gr. *diploos*, double, and *ōps* (*ōpis*), eye.] In pathology, a morbid condition of the eye, in which an object appears double to the patient; double sight.

dī-plop′iç, *a.* Pertaining to, caused by, or suffering with diplopia.

dip-lō-plaç′ū-là, *n.*; *pl.* **dip-lō-plaç′ū-læ.** [L., from Gr. *diploos*, double, and *plax*, a plate.] In embryology, a placula or germ having two layers.

dip′lō-pod, *a.* and *n.* I. *a.* Double-footed; of or pertaining to the *Diplopoda.*

II. *n.* One of the *Diplopoda.*

Di-plop′ō-dà, *n.pl.* [L., from Gr. *diploos*, double, and *pous* (*podos*), foot.] One of the two divisions of the *Myriapoda*, synonymous with *Chilognatha.*

dī-plop′ō-dous, *a.* Diplopod.

Dī-plop′tē-rà, *n.pl.* [L., from Gr. *diploos*, double, and *pteron*, a wing.] A group of aculeate hymenopterous insects, having the upper wings folded longitudinally when at rest, as in the hornet.

dī-plop′tēr-ous, *a.* In entomology, having folded front wings, as the hornet; of or pertaining to the *Diploptera.*

dip′lō-py, *n.* See *Diplopia.*

dip-lō-stem′ō-nous, *a.* [*Diplo-*, and Gr. *stēmōn*, the warp, from *histanai*, to stand.] Having two stamens to every petal.

dip-lō-stem′ō-ny, *n.* Diplostemonous growth or condition.

Dip-neū′mō-nà, *n.pl.* [L., from Gr. *di-*, two, and *pneumōn*, lung.]

1. A division of *Dipnoi*, having paired lungs.

2. A division of holothurian enchinoderms, having two branching gills.

dip-neū′mō-nous, *a.* Having two lungs or respiratory organs; of or pertaining to the *Dipneumona.*

dip-neūs′tăl, *a.* Same as *Dipnoan.*

dip′nō-ăn, *a.* and *n.* I. *a.* Pertaining to or resembling the *Dipnoi.*

II. *n.* One of the *Dipnoi.*

Dip′nō-ī, *n.pl.* [L., from Gr. *di-*, two, double, and *pnein*, to breathe.] An order of fishes, including only the singular mudfishes (*Lepidosiren*), important as exhibiting the transition between fishes and the *Amphibia.*

dip′noid, *a.* and *n.* Same as *Dipnoan.*

dip′ō-dy, *n.* [Gr. *dipodia*, a dipody, from *dipous* (*-podos*), two-footed.] In prosody, a double foot; a pair of like feet composing a measure.

dī-pō′lãr, *a.* Of, pertaining to, or having two poles.

dip′pēr, *n.* [ME. *dippere*, from *dippen*, *dyppen*, AS. *dyppan*, to dip.]

1. One who or that which dips.

2. A vessel used to dip water or other liquid; a ladle.

3. One of certain swimming and diving birds; as, (a) any oscine bird of the family *Cinclidæ*, of which *Cinclus* is the type genus, the water-ouzel being *Cinclus aquaticus*; (b) any aquatic bird which is an active diver, particularly the buffle-duck; also the grebe or the dabchick.

Dipper (*Cinclus aquaticus*).

4. [D—] A name popularly applied in the United States to seven stars in the constellation of Ursa Major.

5. One who dips snuff.

6. [D—] A Dunker.

dip′ping, *n.* The act or process of *dipping* in any sense of the verb *dip.*

dip′ping-çom″pàss, *n.* A combination of a dipping-needle and a vertical graduated indicator in the form of a circle, to measure the angular inclination of the magnetic needle.

dip′ping-nee″dle, *n.* A magnetized needle suspended by its center of gravity for determining the earth's magnetic direction.

dī-priş-mat′iç, *a.* [*Di-*, and Gr. *prisma*, a prism.]

1. Doubly prismatic.

2. Having cleavages parallel to the sides of a four-sided vertical prism, and at the same time, to a horizontal prism.

dī-prō-pãr′gyl, *n.* [*Di-* and *propargyl.*] An isomer of benzene, being a volatile, pungent liquid distilled from certain diallyl compounds.

Dī-prō′tō-don, *n.* [L., from Gr. *di-*, two, *prōtos*, first, and *odous* (*odontos*), tooth.]

1. A genus of extinct gigantic marsupial mammals, characterized by two large upper incisor teeth; it is found in the Pleistocene or recent beds of Australia.

2. [d—] Any animal of this genus.

dī-prō′tō-dont, *a.* Having two front teeth on the lower jaw; of or pertaining to the *Diprotodon.*

Dip-sà-çā′cē-æ, *n.pl.* [L., from Gr. *dipsakos*, the teazel, from *dipsa*, thirst, from *dipsan*, to thirst.] An order of herbs of the Old World, having two cotyledons and flowers with both calyx and corolla. They are nearly allied to the *Compositæ*, but have distinct anthers.

dip-sà-çā′ceous, dip-sā′ceous, *a.* Of, pertaining to, or having the characteristics of the *Dipsacaceæ.*

Dip′sà-çus, *n.* The type genus of the order *Dipsacaceæ.* They are coarse, prickly, biennial herbs. The principal species is *Dipsacus fullonum* or fuller's-teazel, the prickly flower-heads of which are used to raise a nap on woolen cloth.

Fuller's-Teazel (*Dipsacus fullonum*). *a*, Scale of the Receptacle. *b*, Corolla.

dip′sas, *n.* [L., from Gr. *dipsas*, a serpent whose bite was thought to produce thirst, from *dipsios*, thirsty, from *dipsa*, thirst.]

1. A serpent whose bite was believed to produce a mortal thirst.

2. [D—] A genus of tropical American and Asiatic nonvenomous serpents.

dip-set′iç, *a.* Producing thirst.

dip′sey, dip′sy, *n.* [Local U. S.; probably a nautical corruption of *deep-sea.*] A deep-sea fishing-tackle; locally, a sinker.

dip-sō-mā′ni-à, *n.* [L., from Gr. *dipsa*, thirst, and *mania*, madness.] The name given to that condition to which habitual drunkards of a nervous and sanguine temperament are liable to reduce themselves, and in which they manifest an uncontrollable craving for stimulants.

dip-sō-mā′ni-aç, *a.* and *n.* I. *a.* Of the nature of, pertaining to, or affected by dipsomania.

II. *n.* One who suffers with dipsomania; an habitual drunkard.

dip-sō′sis, *n.* [L., from Gr. *dipsa*, thirst.] In medicine, morbid thirst; excessive desire of drinking.

dip′tēr, *n.* One of the *Diptera.*

Dip′te-rà, *n.pl.* [L., from Gr. *di-*, two, and *pteron*, wing.] An order of insects having only two wings, with two halteres or poisers instead of the hinder pair. The common house-fly and the blue-bottle fly are examples. They have six legs, furnished with five-jointed tarsi, two maxillary palpi, two antennæ, three ocelli or simple eyes, and a suctorial proboscis.

Diptera (*Ctenophora festiva*). *a a*, Halteres, Balancers, or Poisers.

dip′tēr-ăl, *a.* [Gr. *dipteros*, having two wings; *di-*, two, and *pteron*, a wing.]

1. Having two wings only; belonging to the order of *Diptera.*

2. In ancient architecture, denoting one of the seven orders of sacred buildings, a temple which had a double row of columns on each of its flanks, as well as in front and rear.

dip′tēr-ăn, *n.* Any insect belonging to the order *Diptera.*

dip-tē-ro-. A combining form from Gr. *dipteros*, two-winged; *di-*, two, and *pteron*, a wing, signifying having two wings.

dip″te-rō-cär-pā′ceous, *a.* Of or pertaining to the order *Dipterocarpeæ*.

Dip″te-rō-cär′pē-æ, *n.pl.* [L., from Gr. *dipteros*, two-winged, and *karpos*, fruit.] An order of East Indian trees, bearing fruit with two long wings. Some species produce wood-oil and some a fragrant resin.

Dip″te-rō-cär′pus, *n.* A genus of East Indian, and chiefly insular trees, the type of the order *Dipterocarpeæ*. The species are enormous trees, abounding in resinous juice, with erect trunks, an ash-colored bark, strong spreading limbs, and oval leathery entire leaves with pinnated veins.

Plan of Dipteral Temple.

dip-tēr-ol′ō-ġy, *n.* [*Diptero-*, and Gr. *logos*, description.] The entomological division treating of dipterous insects.

dip′te-ros, *n.* In architecture, a dipteral temple or portico.

dip′tēr-ous, *a.* Having two wings; belonging or pertaining to the order *Diptera*.

Dip′te-ryx, *n.* [L., from Gr. *di-*, two, and *pteryx*, a wing.] A genus of trees of the bean family, found in tropical South America. They bear a one-seeded pod. Some yield the tonka bean. The wood is hard and durable and is called *camara-wood*.

dip′tōte, *n.* [LL. *diptota*; Gr. *diptōtos*, with a double case-ending; *di-*, two, and *ptōsis*, a falling, a case, from *piptein*, to fall.] In grammar, a noun having but two cases.

dip′tych, dip′ty-chum, *n.* [Gr. *diptycha*, a pair of writing tablets, neut. pl. of *diptychos*, folded together, double-folded; *di-*, two, and *ptychē*, a fold, from *ptyssein*, to fold.]

1. In ancient history, a sort of book or tablet, so called because it generally consisted of two leaves folded, used for writing with the style on wax. The term was applied particularly to a public register of the names of consuls and other magistrates among pagans, and of bishops, martyrs, and others among Christians. The sacred diptych was a double catalogue, in one of which were registered the names of the living, and in the other the names of the dead, which were to be rehearsed in the prayers of the church.

2. In art, two similar pictures or carved panels united by a hinge.

di-pȳre′, *n.* [Gr. *dipyros*, with double lights, twice put in the fire; *di-*, twice, and *pyr* (*pyros*), fire.] A mineral occurring in minute prisms, either single or adhering to each other in fascicular groups. Before the blowpipe, it melts with ebullition or intumescence, and its powder on hot coals phosphoresces with a feeble light.

di-pȳ-rē′nous, *a.* In botany, having two pyrenes or nutlets; said of fruit.

di-pyr′i-dine, *n.* [*Di-* and *pyridine*.] A compound, $C_{10}H_{10}N_2$, obtained from pyridine, of which it is a polymer.

di-rā-di-ā′tion, *n.* [L. *dis-*, apart, and *radiatio*, radiation.] Radiation.

dīre, *a.*; *comp.* direr; *superl.* direst. [L. *dirus*, fearful, awful.] Dreadful; dismal; horrible; terrible; evil in a great degree.

> *Dire* was the tossing, deep the groans. —Milton.

di-rect′, *a.* [ME. *directe*; L. *directus*, straight, upright, pp. of *dirigere*, to lay straight, put in a straight line, direct; *di-* for *dis-*, apart, from, and *regere*, to keep straight, to rule, control.]

1. Straight; right; as, to pass in a *direct* line from one body or place to another. It is opposed to *crooked, winding, oblique*; also to *refracted*; as, a *direct* ray of light.

2. In astronomy, appearing to move forward in the order of the signs, i. e., from west to east; opposed to *retrograde*; as, the motion of a planet is *direct*.

3. In the line of father and son; opposed to *collateral*; as, a descendant in the *direct* line.

4. Leading or tending to an end, as by a straight line or course; not circuitous; as, *direct* means to effect an object; a *direct* course; a *direct* way.

> It was no time by *direct* means to seek her. —Sidney.

5. Plain; express; not ambiguous; as, he said this in *direct* words; he made a *direct* acknowledgment.

> He nowhere says it in *direct* words.—Locke.

Direct discourse; a quotation which gives the exact words of a speaker.

Direct evidence; evidence that is positive, not inferred or circumstantial.

Direct process; in mining, a process whereby metal in a working condition is obtained from the ore, in a single stage.

Direct tax; a tax assessed on real estate, personal property, polls, etc., as distinguished from tariff and excise duties.

di-rect′, *v.t.*; directed, *pt.*, *pp.*; directing, *ppr.* [ME. *directen*, from L. *directus*, pp. of *dirigere*, to direct.]

1. To point or aim in a straight line toward a place or object; as, to *direct* an arrow or a piece of ordnance; to *direct* the eye; to *direct* a course or flight.

2. To point; to show the right road or course to; as, he *directed* me to the left-hand road.

3. To regulate; to guide or lead; to govern; to cause to proceed in a particular manner; as, to *direct* the affairs of a nation.

4. To order; to instruct; to point out a course of proceeding to, with authority; to command.

5. To write a name and address upon; as, he *directed* the letter.

6. In music, to conduct; to lead, as does the leader of a band or chorus.

Syn.—Conduct, guide, dispose, order, contrive, manage, regulate, sway.

di-rect′, *v.i.* To act as a guide, especially as a leader of a band or chorus.

di-rect′, *n.* In music, a character placed at the end of a staff to direct the performer to the first note of the next staff.

di-rect′, *adv.* In a direct manner; directly.

di-rect′=ac″tion, *a.* Acting directly; applied specifically, in mechanics, to those steam-engines and steam-pumps in which connection is made from the piston-rod of the engine direct to the crank or plunger, without working-beams or intervening gear; also written *direct-acting*.

di-rect′ēr, *n.* Same as *Director*.

di-rec′tion, *n.* [L. *directio*, a making straight, the act of directing.]

1. Aim at a certain point; a pointing toward, in a straight line or course; as, the *direction* of good works to a good end.

2. The line in which a body moves or to which its position is referred; course; as, matter cannot alter the *direction* of its own motion; a star appeared in the *direction* of a certain tower.

3. The act of governing; administration; management; guidance; superintendence; as, the *direction* of public affairs; *direction* of domestic concerns; the *direction* of a bank.

4. Order; prescription, either verbal or written; instruction in what manner to proceed; as, the employer gives *directions* to his workmen.

5. The superscription of a letter.

6. A body or board of directors.

7. In law, that part of the bill in which the court is addressed.

Line of direction; (a) in gunnery, the direct line in which a piece is pointed; (b) in mechanics, the line in which a body moves or endeavors to proceed according to the force impressed upon it.

Syn.—Administration, guidance, management, superintendence, oversight, government, control, order, command, instruction.

di-rect′ive, *a.* 1. Having the power of direction; as, a *directive* rule.

2. Informing; instructing; showing the way.

3. Capable of being directed; as, a *directive* arrow. [Obs.]

Directive corpuscle; in biology, the body which detaches from the ovum at maturation.

di-rect′ly, *adv.* 1. In a straight line or course; rectilineally; not in a winding course; as, aim *directly* at the object; gravity tends *directly* to the center of the earth.

2. Immediately; soon; without delay; as, he will be with us *directly*.

3. On the instant that; as soon as; immediately when; a common but incorrect English usage.

> *Directly* he stopped, the coffin was removed by four men. —Dickens.

4. Openly; expressly; without circumlocution or ambiguity; without a train of inferences.

> No man hath been so impious, as *directly* to condemn prayer. —Hooker.

5. Exactly; precisely; just; as, he is *directly* in the way.

6. Without the interposition or intercession of any person or thing; as, I conducted my business *directly* with the owner.

Syn.—Immediately, instantly, instantaneously, forthwith, at once, promptly.—"I will do it *directly*," means, "I will go straightway about it." "I will do it *immediately*," means, "I will do it as the very next thing." "I will do it *instantly* or *instantaneously*," allows not an instant of delay.

di-rect′ness, *n.* The state or quality of being direct; a straight course; nearness of way; straightforwardness; openness.

di-rect′ŏr, *n.* [L. *directus*, pp. of *dirigere*, to direct.]

1. One who directs; one who superintends, governs, or manages; specifically, (a) one of a duly constituted board of managers, as of a corporation; (b) a leader, as of a band or choir.

2. That which directs, specifically, (a) in a medical electric battery, the applier; (b) in surgery, a grooved probe, intended to direct the edge of the knife or scissors.

di-rect′ō-rāte, *n.* 1. A board of directors, considered collectively.

2. The office or authority of a director.

di-rec-tō′ri-ăl, *a.* 1. Capable of directing or commanding; directive.

2. Of or pertaining to a director or a directory; specifically, to the Directory of France.

di-rect′ŏr-ship, *n.* The condition or office of a director.

di-rect′ō-ry, *a.* Containing directions; enjoining; instructing.

di-rect′ō-ry, *n.* [LL. *directorius*, serving to direct, from L. *directus*, pp. of *dirigere*, to direct.]

1. A guide; a rule to direct; especially, a book containing directions for public worship or religious services.

2. A book containing an alphabetical list of the inhabitants of a city, with their places of residence and often much additional information.

3. A board of directors.

4. [D—] The executive power of the French Republic, A. D. 1795–99. It consisted of five persons called directors, and was quashed by Napoleon Bonaparte at the suggestion of Sièyes, and the Consulate established on its ruin.

di-rect′ress, *n.* A woman who directs or manages; a directrix.

di-rect′rix, *n.*; *pl.* **di-rect′ri-cēs** or **di-rect′rix-eṣ.** 1. A woman who governs or directs.

2. In an embrasure or other firing-point, the median line of fire; a term used in gunnery.

3. In mathematics, a line perpendicular to the axis of a conic section, and so placed that the distance from it of any point in the curve is to the distance of the same point from the focus in a constant ratio; also, the name given to any line, whether straight or not, that is required for the description of a curve.

Directrix of a parabola; a line perpendicular to the axis produced, and whose distance from the vertex is equal to the distance of the vertex from the focus. Thus, A B is the directrix of the parabola V E D, of which F is the focus.

Directrix of a Parabola.

dīre′fụl, *a.* Dire; dreadful; terrible; calamitous; as, *direful* fiend; a *direful* misfortune.

dīre′fụl-ly, *adv.* In a dire or dreadful manner.

dīre′fụl-ness, *n.* The state of being direful; calamitousness.

dīre′ly, *adv.* In a dire manner.

di-rempt′, *a.* Separated; parted. [Obs.]

di-rempt′, *v.t.* To separate; to tear apart forcibly. [Obs.]

di-remp′tion, *n.* [L. *diremptio*.] A separation. [Obs.]

dīre′ness, *n.* Terribleness; horror; dismalness.

di-rep′tion, *n.* The act of plundering. [Obs.]

di-rep-ti′tious (-tish′us), *a.* Of the nature of or pertaining to direption. [Obs.]

di-rep-ti′tious-ly, *adv.* In a direptitious manner. [Obs.]

dirġe, *n.* [ME. *dirge*, *dorge*, from L. *dirige*, imper. of *dirigere*, to direct; so called from the first word of a funeral hymn, taken from Vulgate, Psalm v. 8: "*Dirige*, Domine, Deus meus, in conspectu tuo, vitam meam." Direct, O Lord, my God, my life in thy sight.] A song or tune intended to express grief, sorrow, and mourning; as, a funeral *dirge*.

dirġe′fụl, *a.* Moaning; funereal; like a dirge.

dir′i-ġē, *n.* A service for the dead; a dirge. [Obs.]

dir′i-ġent, *a.* and *n.* [L. *dirigens* (*-gentis*), ppr. of *dirigere*, to direct.]

I. *a.* Directing.

II. *n.* In geometry, the line or plane along which another line or plane is supposed to move in the generation of a surface or solid; a directrix.

dir′i-ġi-ble, *a.* Capable of being guided, steered, or controlled; as, a *dirigible* balloon.

dir′i-ment, *a.* [L. *dirimens* (*-mentis*), ppr. of *dirimere*, to separate; *dis-*, from, and *emere*, to take.] In law, nullifying.

Diriment impediment of marriage; in the Roman Catholic church, a sufficient cause for rendering marriage null and void from the very beginning, as close relationship, etc.

dirk, *n.* [Ir. *duirc*, a dirk, poniard.] A kind of dagger or poniard, formerly much used in the Highlands of Scotland and still worn as essential to complete the Highland costume. [See illus. p. 480.]

dirk, *v.t.*; dirked, *pt.*, *pp.*; dirking, *ppr.* To poniard; to stab.

dirk, *a.* [ME. and Scot.] Dark. [Obs.]

dirk, *v.t.* To darken. [Obs.]

dirk′ness, *n.* Darkness. [Obs.]

dirl, *v.i.* [Scot.] To vibrate; to thrill; to tremble.

dirl, *n.* [Scot.] A blow which causes a thrilling sensation or a tremulous sound; also, the sensation or sound itself.

dirt, *n.* [ME. *drit.*]

1. Any foul or filthy substance; excrement; earth; mud; mire; dust; whatever, adhering to anything, renders it foul or unclean.

2. Meanness; sordidness. [Obs.]

3. In placer-mining, earth, sand, and gravel, before the gold has been washed out.

Pay dirt; earth containing enough gold to warrant the cost of mining it.

To eat dirt; to submit humbly to an insult or degradation; to retract one's own words.

To fling dirt at; to slander; to abuse.

Dirk (front and profile).

dirt, *v.t.* To make foul or filthy; to soil; to bedaub; to pollute; to defile. [Rare.]

dirt′=bed, *n.* A bed or layer of mold with the remains of trees and plants, found especially in working the freestone in the oölite formation of Portland. They are evidently the soil in which the cycads, zamias, and conifers of the period grew. The thickest layer is from twelve to eighteen inches thick.

dirt′=eat″ing, *n.* 1. Cachexia Africana, a disorder of the nutritive functions among negroes, and in certain kinds of disturbance of the feminine health, in which there is an irresistible desire to eat dirt.

2. The practice of certain tribes of South America, as the Ottomacs, of using certain kinds of clay for food.

dirt′i-ly, *adv.* 1. In a dirty manner; foully; nastily; filthily.

2. Meanly; sordidly; by low means.

dirt′i-ness, *n.* 1. Filthiness; foulness; nastiness.

2. Meanness; baseness; sordidness.

dirt′y, *a.*; *comp.* dirtier; *superl.* dirtiest. 1. Foul; nasty; filthy; not clean; as, *dirty* hands.

2. Not clean; not pure; turbid; as, *dirty* water.

3. Cloudy; dark; dusky; as, a *dirty* white.

4. Mean; base; low; despicable; groveling; as, a *dirty* fellow; a *dirty* employment.

5. Muddy; rainy; stormy; not pleasant; as, *dirty* weather or roads.

Syn.—Foul, filthy, nasty, unclean, soiled, base.

dirt′y, *v.t.*; dirtied, *pt.*, *pp.*; dirtying, *ppr.* 1. To foul; to make filthy; to soil; as, to *dirty* the clothes or hands.

2. To tarnish; to sully; to scandalize; applied to reputation.

di-rup′tion, *n.* [Obs.] Same as *Disruption.*

dis-, *prefix.* A combining form from L. *dis-*, apart, asunder, from *duo*, two, used with separative force to signify apart, asunder, in different directions, as *dis*tribute, *dis*tend, or with privative or negative force, as *dis*ability, *dis*agree; sometimes written *dif-*, or *di-*, for the sake of euphony, as in *dif*fer.

Dis, *n.* [L.] In Roman mythology, a name sometimes given to Pluto, the ruler of the infernal regions; hence, sometimes to Hades.

dis-ȧ-bil′i-ty, *n.* [*Dis-* priv., and L. *habilitas*, ability.]

1. Want of competent natural or bodily power, strength, or ability; weakness; impotence; as, *disability* arising from infirmity or broken limbs.

2. Want of competent intellectual power or strength of mind; incapacity.

3. Want of competent means or instruments.

4. Want of legal qualifications; incapacity.

Syn.—Weakness, inability, incompetence, impotence, incapacity.

dis-ā′ble, *a.* Unable; incompetent. [Obs.]

dis-ā′ble, *v.t.*; disabled, *pt.*, *pp.*; disabling, *ppr.*

1. To render unable; to deprive of competent natural strength or power; as, a broken leg *disables* a man.

2. To deprive of mental power, as by destroying or weakening the understanding.

3. To deprive of adequate means, instruments, or resources; as, lack of funds *disables* a nation to carry on war.

4. To destroy the strength of; to weaken or impair so as to render incapable of action, service, or resistance; as, a fleet is *disabled* by a storm, or by a battle.

5. To deprive of legal qualifications, or competent power; to incapacitate; to render incapable.

> An attainder of the ancestor corrupts the blood, and *disables* his children to inherit. —Blackstone.

dis-ā′ble-ment, *n.* Weakness; disability; legal impediment.

dis-ȧ-būṣe′, *v.t.*; disabused, *pt.*, *pp.*; disabusing, *ppr.* To free from mistake; to undeceive; to disengage from fallacy or deception; to set right.

> Now sufficiently enlightened to *disabuse* themselves of artifice, hypocrisy, and superstition. —J. Adams.

dis-aç-çom′mō-dāte, *v.t.* To inconvenience; to discommode. [Rare.]

dis-aç-çom-mō-dā′tion, *n.* A state of being unaccommodated; a state of being unprepared. [Rare.]

dis-aç-çord′, *v.i.* To refuse assent. [Obs.]

dis-aç-çord′, *n.* Disagreement; incongruity.

dis-aç-çord′ănt, *a.* Not accordant.

dis-aç-çus′tŏm, *v.t.*; disaccustomed, *pt.*, *pp.*; disaccustoming, *ppr.* To cause to neglect familiar or customary practice; to destroy the force of habit in, by disuse; as, to *disaccustom* oneself to the use of whisky.

dis-ȧ-cid′i-fȳ, *v.t.* To deprive of acid.

dis-aç-knowl′edġe (-nol′ej), *v.t.* To deny; to disown. [Obs.]

dis-aç-quaint′ (-kwānt′), *v.t.* To dissolve acquaintance with. [Obs.]

dis-aç-quaint′ănce, *n.* Neglect or disuse of familiarity, or familiar knowledge of. [Obs.]

dis-aç′ryl, *n.* [*Dis-* and *acr*olein.] An amorphous polymer of acrolein.

dis-ȧ-dorn′, *v.t.* To deprive of ornaments. [Obs.]

dis-ad-vȧnce′, *v.t.* and *v.i.* To check; to halt; to stop. [Obs.]

dis-ad-vȧn′tāġe, *n.* [ME. *disadvauntage*; OFr. *desavantage*; *des-* priv., and *avantage*, advantage.]

1. That which prevents success, or renders it difficult; a state not favorable to successful operation; as, the *disadvantage* of ill health.

2. Loss; injury; hindrance; prejudice to interest, fame, credit, profit, or other good; as, to sell goods at a *disadvantage*.

Syn.—Hurt, injury, detriment, loss, damage.

dis-ad-vȧn′tāġe, *v.t.*; disadvantaged (-tajd), *pt.*, *pp.*; disadvantaging, *ppr.* To injure an interest of; to prejudice; to hinder; to place at a disadvantage.

dis-ad-vȧn′tāġe-ȧ-ble, *a.* Not advantageous. [Obs.]

dis-ad-vȧn-tā′ġeous, *a.* Unfavorable to success or prosperity; inconvenient; not adapted to promote interest, reputation, or other good; as, the situation of an army is *disadvantageous* for attack or defense; we are apt to view characters in the most *disadvantageous* lights.

dis-ad-vȧn-tā′ġeous-ly, *adv.* In a manner not favorable to success, or to interest, profit, or reputation; with loss or inconvenience.

dis-ad-vȧn-tā′ġeous-ness, *n.* Unfavorableness to success; inconvenience; loss.

dis-ad-ven′tūre, *n.* Misfortune. [Obs.]

dis-ad-ven′tūr-ous, *a.* Unprosperous. [Obs.]

dis-af-feçt′, *v.t.*; disaffected, *pt.*, *pp.*; disaffecting, *ppr.* 1. To alienate the affection of; to make less friendly to; to make less faithful to a person, party, or cause, or less zealous to support it; to make discontented or unfriendly; as, an attempt was made to *disaffect* the army.

2. To disdain or dislike; to hold aloof from. [Rare.]

3. To throw into disorder. [Obs.]

dis-af-feçt′ed, *a.* Having the affections alienated; unfriendly.

dis-af-feçt′ed-ly, *adv.* In a disaffected manner.

dis-af-feçt′ed-ness, *n.* The state or quality of being disaffected.

dis-af-feç′tion, *n.* [Fr. *désaffection*; *des-* priv., and *affection.*]

1. Alienation of affection, attachment, or good will.

2. Disorder; bad constitution. [Rare.]

dis-af-feç′tion-āte, *a.* Not well disposed; not friendly. [Rare.]

> A beautiful but *disaffectionate* and disobedient wife. —Hayley.

dis-af-fīrm′, *v.t.*; disaffirmed, *pt.*, *pp.*; disaffirming, *ppr.* 1. To deny; to contradict.

2. In law, to overthrow or annul, as a judicial decision, by a contrary judgment of a superior tribunal.

dis-af-fīrm′ănce, dis-af-fīr-mā′tion, *n.* 1. Denial; negation; disproof; confutation.

2. In law, the overthrow or annulment by the decision of a superior tribunal; as, *disaffirmance* of judgment.

dis-af-for′est, *v.t.* In English law, to reduce from the privileges of a forest to the state of common ground; to strip of forest laws and their oppressive privileges.

dis-ag′grē-gāte, *v.t.*; disaggregated, *pt.*, *pp.*; disaggregating, *ppr.* To separate into component parts, as an aggregate mass.

dis-ag-grē-gā′tion, *n.* The act or operation of separating an aggregate body into its component parts.

dis-ag′i-ō, *n.* The discount on any currency not standard. [See *Agio.*]

dis-ȧ-gree′, *v.i.*; disagreed, *pt.*, *pp.*; disagreeing, *ppr.* 1. To differ; to be not accordant or coincident; to be not the same; to be not exactly similar; as, histories often *disagree.*

2. To differ in opinion; as, the best judges sometimes *disagree.*

3. To be unsuitable; as, medicine sometimes *disagrees* with the patient.

4. To quarrel; to contend.

Syn.—Differ, dissent, quarrel, vary.

dis-ȧ-gree′ȧ-ble, *a.* 1. Contrary; unsuitable; not conformable; not congruous.

2. Unpleasant; offensive to the mind, or to the senses; but expressing less than *disgusting* and *odious.*

dis-ȧ-gree′ȧ-ble-ness, dis-ȧ-gree-ȧ-bil′i-ty, *n.* 1. Unsuitableness; contrariety. [Rare.]

2. Unpleasantness; offensiveness to the mind or to the senses; as, the *disagreeableness* of another's manners; the *disagreeableness* of a taste, sound, or smell.

dis-ȧ-gree′ȧ-bly, *adv.* In a disagreeable manner; unpleasantly; offensively.

dis-ȧ-gree′ănce, *n.* Disagreement. [Obs.]

dis-ȧ-gree′ment, *n.* 1. Difference, either in form or essence; dissimilitude; diversity; as, the *disagreement* of two ideas, of two pictures, of two stories or narrations.

2. Difference of opinion or sentiments.

3. Unsuitableness.

4. A controversy; a contention; a quarrel; a difference.

Syn.—Difference, diversity, unlikeness, discrepancy, variance, dissent, misunderstanding, dissension, division, dispute, discord.

dis-ȧ-grē′ẽr, *n.* One who disagrees.

dis-al-liēġe′, *v.t.* To alienate from allegiance. [Rare.]

dis-al-low′, *v.t.*; disallowed, *pt.*, *pp.*; disallowing, *ppr.* To refuse to permit; not to grant; not to make or suppose lawful; not to authorize; to reject.

dis-al-low′ȧ-ble, *a.* Not allowable; not to be suffered.

dis-al-low′ȧ-ble-ness, *n.* The state of being disallowable.

dis-al-low′ănce, *n.* Disapprobation; refusal to admit or permit; prohibition; rejection.

dis-al-lȳ′, *v.t.*; disallied, *pt.*, *pp.*; disallying, *ppr.* To terminate the alliance of. [Obs.]

dis′ȧ-mis, *n.* In logic, one of the valid moods. [See *Mood.*]

dis-ȧ-nal′ō-găl, *a.* Contrary to analogy; lacking similarity. [Obs.]

dis-an′chŏr, *v.t.* and *v.i.*; disanchored, *pt.*, *pp.*; disanchoring, *ppr.* 1. To force from its anchors, as a ship.

2. To weigh anchor. [Obs.]

dis-an-ġel′iç-ăl, *a.* Not angelical. [Rare.]

dis-an′i-māte, *v.t.*; disanimated, *pt.*, *pp.*; disanimating, *ppr.* 1. To deprive of life. [Rare.]

2. To deprive of spirit or courage; to discourage; to dishearten; to deject.

dis-an-i-mā′tion, *n.* 1. The act of discouraging; depression of spirits.

2. Privation of life. [Rare.]

dis-an-nex′, *v.t.* To disunite. [Obs.]

dis-an-nul′, *v.t.*; disannulled, *pt.*, *pp.*; disannulling, *ppr.* 1. To annul completely; to render absolutely void.

2. To divest of. [Rare.]

dis-an-nul′lẽr, *n.* One who disannuls.

dis-an-nul′ment, *n.* Annulment.

dis-ȧ-noint′, *v.t.*; disanointed, *pt.*, *pp.*; disanointing, *ppr.* To render invalid the consecration of.

dis-ap-par′el, *v.t.*; disappareled *or* disapparelled, *pt.*, *pp.*; disappareling *or* disapparelling, *ppr.* To disrobe; to strip of raiment.

dis-ap-pēar′, *v.i.*; disappeared, *pt.*, *pp.*; disappearing, *ppr.* [OFr. *desaperer*; *des-* priv., and *aperer*, to appear; L. *dis-* priv., and *apparere*, to appear.]

1. To vanish from sight; to recede from view; to go away or out of sight; to cease to appear or to be perceived; to be no longer seen.

dis-ap-pēar′ing=gun, *n.* A heavy cannon used mainly for coast defense, so arranged that the gun is concealed until fired, immediately disappearing and automatically storing up sufficient energy by recoil to bring into firing position again. Most highly perfected in United States.

2. To cease; as, the epidemic has *disappeared.*

dis-ap-pēar′ănce, *n.* The act of disappearing.

dis-ap-pend′en-cy, *n.* A detachment or separation from a connection or union. [Rare.]

dis-ap-pend′ent, *a.* Detached; disconnected. [Rare.]

dis-ap-point′, *v.t.*; disappointed, *pt.*, *pp.*; disappointing, *ppr.* [OFr. *desapointer*, to disappoint; *des-* priv., and *apointer*, to appoint; L. *dis-* priv., *ad*, to, and *punctum*, point.]

1. To defeat of expectation, wish, hope, desire, or intention; to frustrate; to balk; to hinder from the possession or enjoyment of that which was intended, desired, hoped, or

expected; often followed by *of*; as, a bad season *disappoints* the farmer *of* his crops; a defeat *disappoints* an enemy *of* his spoil; the man promised me a visit, but he *disappointed* me.
2. To thwart; to prevent the realization or success of.
Syn.—Frustrate, balk, baffle, delude, foil, defeat.

dis-ap-point′ed, *a.* 1. Thwarted; frustrated; brought to nothing; as, a *disappointed* lover or a *disappointed* hope.
2. Unprepared or poorly prepared. [Obs.]

dis-ap-point′ment, *n.* 1. Defeat or failure of expectation, hope, wish, desire, or intention; miscarriage of design or plan.
2. A state or condition of defeat of one's plans; the feeling resulting from such defeat.

dis-ap-prē′ci-āte (-shi-), *v.t.*; disappreciated, *pt., pp.*; disappreciating, *ppr.* To undervalue; not to esteem.

dis-ap-prē-ci-ā′tion, *n.* The act of undervaluing.

dis-ap-prō-bā′tion, *n.* Disapproval; dislike; the act of the mind which condemns what is distasteful or wrong.

dis-ap′prō-bā-tō-ry, *a.* Containing disapprobation; tending to disapprove.

dis-ap-prō′pri-āte, *a.* In English law, not appropriated, or not having appropriated church property; a *disappropriate* church being one from which the appropriated parsonage, glebe, and tithes are severed.

dis-ap-prō′pri-āte, *v.t.*; disappropriated, *pt., pp.*; disappropriating, *ppr.* 1. To sever or separate, as an appropriation; to withdraw from an appropriate use.
2. To deprive of appropriated property, as a church.

dis-ap-prō-pri-ā′tion, *n.* The act of disappropriating.

dis-ap-pröv′ăl, *n.* Disapprobation; dislike.

dis-ap-pröve′, *v.t.*; disapproved, *pt. pp.*; disapproving, *ppr.* 1. To dislike; to condemn in opinion or judgment; to censure as wrong; as, we often *disapprove* the conduct of others. It is usually followed by *of*; as, to *disapprove of* his behavior.
2. To manifest dislike or disapprobation of; to reject what is proposed for sanction; as, the sentence of the court-martial was *disapproved* by the president.

dis-ap-pröv′ẽr, *n.* A person who disapproves.

dis-ap-pröv′ing-ly, *adv.* With disapprobation.

dis′ărd, *n.* A prattler; a boasting talker. [Obs.]

dis-ärm′, *v.t.*; disarmed, *pt., pp.*; disarming, *ppr.* [ME. *desarmen*; OFr. *desarmer*, to disarm; L. *dis-* priv., and *armare*, to arm.]
1. To deprive of arms; to take the arms or weapons from, usually by force or authority; as, he *disarmed* his foes; the prince gave orders to *disarm* his subjects; with *of* before the thing taken away; as, to *disarm* one *of* his weapons.
2. To deprive of means of attack or defense; as, to *disarm* a venomous serpent.
3. To deprive of force, strength, or means of annoyance; to render harmless; to quell; as, to *disarm* rage or passion.
4. To strip; to divest of anything injurious or threatening; as, piety *disarms* death of its terrors.

dis-ärm′, *v.i.* 1. To lay arms down or aside; to divest oneself of arms.
2. To dismiss or disband troops; to reduce forces to a peace footing.

dis-ärm′ȧ-ment, *n.* The act of disarming; specifically, the reduction of forces from a war to a peace footing.

dis-är′mȧ-tūre, *n.* The act of disarming or disabling, either oneself or another. [Rare.]

dis-ärmed′, *a.* 1. Deprived of arms; stripped of the means of defense or annoyance; rendered harmless; subdued.
2. In heraldry, having no claws, teeth, or beak; applied to animals or birds of prey.

dis-ärm′ẽr, *n.* One who disarms.

dis-ar-rānge′, *v.t.*; disarranged, *pt., pp.*; disarranging, *ppr.* To put out of order; to unsettle or disturb the order or due arrangement of, as the parts of anything.

dis-ar-rānge′ment, *n.* The act of disturbing order or method; the state of being disarranged; disorder.

dis-ar-rāy′, *v.t.*; disarrayed, *pt., pp.*; disarraying, *ppr.* [OFr. *desareer*; *des-* priv., and *areer*, to array.]
1. To undress; to divest of clothes.
2. To throw into disorder; to rout, as troops.

dis-ar-rāy′, *n.* 1. Disorder; confusion; loss or want of array or regular order.
2. Undress; incomplete attire.

dis-ar-rāy′ment, *n.* Disorder; disturbance. [Rare.]

dis-är-tiç′ū-lāte, *v.t.*; disarticulated, *pt., pp.*; disarticulating, *ppr.* To separate, divide, or loosen the joints of.

dis-är-tiç-ū-lā′tion, *n.* The act of sundering joints or articulations; amputation at a joint.

dis-är-tiç′ū-lā-tŏr, *n.* One who disarticulates or sunders.

dis-as-sent′, *v.i.* To dissent. [Obs.]

dis-as-sent′, *n.* Dissent; refusal. [Obs.]

dis-as-sent′ẽr, *n.* One who dissents; a dissenter. [Obs.]

dis-as-si-dū′i-ty, *n.* Want of assiduity or care. [Obs.]

dis-as-sim′i-lāte, *v.t.* In physiology, to subject to the process of disassimilation.

dis-as-sim-i-lā′tion, *n.* Destructive metabolism; catabolism.

dis-as-sim′i-lā-tive, *a.* Of the nature of disassimilation; capable of disassimilation.

dis-as-sō′ci-āte (-shi-āt), *v.t.*; disassociated, *pt., pp.*; disassociating, *ppr.* To disunite; to disconnect, as things associated.

dis-as-sō-ci-ā′tion, *n.* In chemistry, the decomposition of a compound by heat; dissociation.

diṣ-ȧs′tẽr, *n.* [OFr. *desastre*, disaster, misfortune; L. *dis*, from, here in the sense of ill, and *astrum*, from Gr. *astron*, a star.]
1. A blast or stroke of an unfavorable planet. [Obs.]
2. Misfortune; mishap; calamity; any unfortunate event, especially a sudden misfortune; as, we met with many *disasters* on the road.
Syn.—Calamity, mischance, misfortune, mishap.

diṣ-ȧs′tẽr, *v.t.* To blast by the stroke of an unlucky planet; also, to injure; to afflict. [Obs.]

diṣ-ȧs′tẽr-ly, *adv.* Disastrously. [Obs.]

diṣ-ȧs′trous, *a.* 1. Unlucky; unfortunate; calamitous; occasioning loss or injury; as, the day was *disastrous*; the battle proved *disastrous*.
2. Gloomy; dismal; threatening disaster.

> The moon,
> In dim eclipse, *disastrous* twilight sheds.
> —Milton.

diṣ-ȧs′trous-ly, *adv.* Unfortunately; in a disastrous manner.

diṣ-ȧs′trous-ness, *n.* Unfortunateness; calamitousness.

dis-at-tīre′, *v.t.* To disrobe; to undress. [Obs.]

dis-at-tūne′, *v.t.* To put out of tune or harmony.

dis-aug-ment′, *v.t.* To decrease; to diminish. [Rare.]

diṣ-au′thŏr-īze, *v.t.* To deprive of authority or credit.

dis-ȧ-vaunce′, *v.t.* To drive back; to repel. [Obs.]

dis-ȧ-ven′tūre, *n.* A misadventure; a misfortune. [Obs.]

dis-ȧ-vouch′, *v.t.* To retract profession of; to deny; to disown. [Rare.]

dis-ȧ-vow′, *v.t.* [ME. *disavouen*; OFr. *desavouer*, to disavow; *des-* priv., and *avouer*, to avow.]
1. To deny; to disown; to deny to be true, as a fact or charge respecting oneself; to disclaim responsibility for or connection with.
2. To disprove; to refute. [Obs.]

dis-ȧ-vow′ăl, *n.* Denial; disowning; rejection.

> A *disavowal* of fear often proceeds from fear.
> —Richardson.

dis-ȧ-vow′ănce, *n.* Disavowal. [Obs.]

dis-ȧ-vow′ẽr, *n.* One who disavows.

dis-ȧ-vow′ment, *n.* Denial; a disowning.

dis-band′, *v.t.*; disbanded, *pt., pp.*; disbanding, *ppr.* 1. To dismiss from military service; to break up (a band or body of men enlisted); as, to *disband* an army or a regiment.
2. To scatter; to disperse.

dis-band′, *v.i.* [OFr. *desbander*, to loosen, scatter; *des-* priv., and *bander*, to tie.]
1. To retire from military service; to separate; to break up; as, the army, at the close of the war, *disbands*.
2. To separate; to become disconnected, disunited, or dissolved.

> Human society may *disband*. —Tillotson.

dis-bär′, *v.t.*; disbarred, *pt., pp.*; disbarring, *ppr.* In law, to deprive (a lawyer) of the right to appear in court; to expel from the bar.

dis-bärk′, *v.t.* [OFr. *desbarquer*; *des-* priv., and *barque*, a bark.] To land from a ship; to disembark. [Rare.]

dis-bärk′, *v.t.* To peel the bark from. [Rare.]

dis-bär′ment, *n.* The act of disbarring or the state of being disbarred.

dis-bāse′, *v.t.* To debase. [Obs.]

dis-bē-cŏme′, *v.t.* To misbecome. [Obs.]

dis-bē-liēf′, *n.* Refusal of credit or faith; denial of belief; the act of disbelieving.

> Our belief or *disbelief* of a thing does not alter the nature of the thing. —Tillotson.

Syn.—Unbelief.—*Unbelief* is a mere failure to admit; *disbelief* is a positive rejection. One may be an *unbeliever* in Christianity from ignorance or want of inquiry; a *disbeliever* has the arguments before him, and incurs the responsibility of setting them aside.

dis-bē-liēve′, *v.t.*; disbelieved, *pt., pp.*; disbelieving, *ppr.* Not to believe; to hold not to be true or not to exist; to refuse to credit.

dis-bē-liēv′ẽr, *n.* One who refuses belief; one who denies a thing to be true or real; an unbeliever.

dis-bench′, *v.t.* [*Dis-* and *bench*.]
1. To drive from a bench or seat. [Rare.]
2. In English law, to deprive (a bencher) of status and privileges.

dis-bend′, *v.t.* To unbend. [Obs.]

dis-bīnd′, *v.t.* To loosen. [Obs.]

dis-blāme′, *v.t.* To clear from blame. [Obs.]

dis-bod′ied (-bod′id), *a.* Disembodied. [Rare.]

dis-bọrd′, *v.i.* To disembark. [Obs.]

dis-bos-çā′tion, *n.* [*Dis-*, and ME. *boskage*; OFr. *boscage*, a grove.] The clearing of forest land; the act of deforesting.

dis-bow′el, *v.t.* To take out the intestines of; to disembowel. [Rare.]

dis-brȧnch′, *v.t.* 1. To cut off or separate, as the branch of a tree. [Rare.]
2. To deprive of branches. [Rare.]

dis-bud′, *v.t.* To deprive of buds or shoots.

dis-bûr′den, *v.t.* [*Dis-* and *burden*.]
1. To remove a burden from; to unload; to discharge.
2. To cast a burden from; to disencumber; to clear of anything weighty, troublesome or cumbersome; as, to *disburden* oneself of grief or care; to *disburden* of superfluous ornaments.

dis-bûr′den, *v.i.* To ease the mind; to be relieved.

dis-bûr′ġeŏn, *v.t.* To strip of sprouts or buds. [Rare.]

dis-bûrse′, *v.t.*; disbursed, *pt. pp.*; disbursing, *ppr.* [OFr. *disbourser*; *des-*, from, and *bourse*, a purse.] To pay out, as money; to spend or lay out; to expend.

dis-bûrse′ment, *n.* 1. The act of paying out, as money from a public or private chest.
2. The money or sum paid out; as, the annual *disbursements* exceed the income.

dis-bûrs′ẽr, *n.* One who pays out or disburses money.

disç, *n.* Same as *Disk*.

dis-çāge′, *v.t.* To free from a cage. [Rare.]

dis′çăl, *a.* Of, pertaining to, resembling or situated on a disk.

dis-çal′cē-āte, *v.t.* [L. *discalceatus*, unshod; *dis-* priv., and *calceatus*, pp. of *calceare*, to shoe, from *calceus*, a shoe.] To pull off the shoes or sandals from. [Obs.]

dis-çal′cē-ā-ted, *a.* Stripped of shoes; discalced.

dis-çal-cē-ā′tion, *n.* The act of pulling off the shoes or sandals. [Obs.]

dis-çalced′ (-kalst′), *a.* [L. *discalceatus*, unshod; *dis-* priv., and *calceatus*, pp. of *calceare*, to shoe, from *calceus*, a shoe, from *calx* (*calcis*), heel.] Without covering for the feet; barefooted.

dis-çamp′, *v.t.* To break up, or drive from a camp. [Obs.]

dis-çan′dy, *v.i.* To melt; to dissolve. [Obs.]

dis′çant, *n.* Same as *Descant*.

dis-çȧ-pac′i-tāte, *v.t.* To incapacitate. [Rare.]

dis-çärd′, *v.t.*; discarded, *pt., pp.*; discarding, *ppr.* 1. In card-playing, (a) to throw out of the hand, as a card which is useless or superfluous; (b) in some games, as whist, to throw away on a trick, as a card of a suit other than the one led, when one cannot follow suit and does not wish to take the trick with a trump.
2. To dismiss from service or employment, or from society; to cast off; as, to *discard* an old servant; to *discard* an associate.
3. To thrust away; to reject; as, to *discard* prejudices.
Syn.—Discharge, dismiss, reject, displace, abjure.

dis-çärd′, *v.i.* In card-playing, to throw a card or cards out of one's hand.

dis-çärd′, *n.* 1. The act of discarding or the card or cards thrown out.
2. One who or that which is rejected or dismissed. [Rare.]

dis-çär′dūre, *n.* Rejection. [Rare.]

dis-çär′nāte, *a.* Stripped of flesh. [Obs.]

dis-çāse′, *v.t.* To take off a covering from; to strip; to undress. [Obs.]

dis-çēde′, *v.i.* To give up; to surrender; to yield; to depart. [Obs.]

dis-cept′, *v.i.* To discuss; to debate; to dispute. [Obs.]

dis-cep-tā′tion, *n.* Controversy. [Obs.]

dis-cep-tā′tŏr, *n.* One who arbitrates or decides. [Obs.]

diṣ-cẽrn′ (diz-zẽrn′), *v.t.*; discerned, *pt., pp.*; discerning, *ppr.* [ME. *discernen*; OFr. *discerner*; L. *discernere*, to separate, divide, distinguish between; *dis-*, apart, and *cernere*, to separate.]
1. To see distinctly; to separate from surrounding objects; to perceive by the eye; as, he *discerned* the sail at a distance.
2. To distinguish; to see the difference between (two or more things); to discriminate; as, to *discern* the blossom-buds from the leaf-buds of plants.
3. To discover by the intellect; to distinguish; hence, to have knowledge of; to judge.

> So is my lord the king to *discern* good and bad. —2 Sam. xiv. 17.

Syn.—Descry, discriminate, distinguish, penetrate, perceive.

dis-cėrn′ (diz-zẽrn′), *v.i.* 1. To see or understand the difference; to make distinction; as, to *discern* between good and evil, truth and falsehood.

2. To have judicial cognizance. [Obs.]

dis-cėrn′ănce, *n.* Discernment. [Obs.]

dis-cėrn′ẽr (diz-zẽrn′ẽr), *n.* 1. One who discerns, discovers, or distinguishes; an observer.

He was a great observer and *discerner* of men's natures and humors. —Clarendon.

2. That which distinguishes; that which serves as a means of discrimination. [Obs.]

The word of God is quick and powerful, a *discerner* of the thoughts and intents of the heart. —Heb. iv. 12.

dis-cėrn′i-ble (diz-zẽrn′), *a.* Capable of being seen distinctly; discoverable by the eye or the understanding; distinguishable; as, a star is *discernible* by the eye; the identity or difference of ideas is *discernible* by the understanding.

Syn.—Apparent, evident, manifest, palpable, perceptible.

dis-cėrn′i-ble-ness, *n.* The state or quality of being discernible.

dis-cėrn′i-bly, *adv.* In a manner to be discerned, seen, or discovered; visibly.

dis-cėrn′ing (diz-zẽrn′), *a.* Having power to discern; capable of seeing, discriminating, knowing, and judging; sharp-sighted; penetrating; acute; as, a *discerning* man or mind.

dis-cėrn′ing-ly, *adv.* With discernment; acutely; with judgment; skilfully.

dis-cėrn′ment, *n.* 1. The act of discerning.

2. The power or faculty of the mind by which it distinguishes one thing from another; acuteness of judgment; power of perceiving differences of things or ideas, and their relations and tendencies; as, the errors of youth often proceed from the want of *discernment*.

Syn.—Penetration, discrimination.—*Discernment* is accuracy and keenness of mental vision; *penetration* is the power of seeing deeply into a subject in spite of everything that intercepts the view.

dis-cėrp′, *v.t.*; discerped (-sẽrpt), *pt., pp.*; discerping, *ppr.* [L. *discerpere*, to pluck or tear to pieces; *dis-*, asunder, and *carpere*, to pluck.] To separate; to pluck asunder. [Rare.]

This (sedition) divides, yea, and *discerps* a city. —Griffith.

dis-cėrp-i-bil′i-ty, dis-cėrp-ti-bil′i-ty, *n.* Capability or liableness to be torn asunder or disunited. [Obs.]

dis-cėrp′i-ble, dis-cėrp′ti-ble, *a.* Capable of being torn asunder; separable; capable of being disunited by violence.

dis-cėrp′tion, *n.* The act of pulling to pieces or of separating the parts.

dis-cėrp′tive, *a.* Having a tendency to separate or divide.

dis-ces′sion (-sesh′un), *n.* A leaving. [Obs.]

dis-chärġe′, *v.t.*; discharged, *pt., pp.*; discharging, *ppr.* [ME. *dischargen*; OFr. *descharger*, to unload, disburden, discharge; LL. *discargare*, *discarricare*, to unload; L. *dis-*, from, and *carrus*, a wagon, car.]

1. To unload, as a ship; to take out, as a cargo; applied both to the ship and the loading.

2. To free from any load or burden; to throw off or exonerate; as, *discharged* of business.

3. In architecture, to relieve a beam or any other piece of timber too much loaded by an incumbent weight of building, in which case the weight is said to be *discharged*; to distribute or relieve the pressure of.

4. To free of the missile with which anything is charged or loaded; to make the charge of to fly off; to fire off; as, to *discharge* a bow, a catapult, a pistol.

The galleys also did *discharge* their great pieces against the city. —Knolles.

5. To let fly; to shoot; to emit or send out; to give vent to; as, to *discharge* a ball or grape-shot; a pipe *discharges* water; an ulcer *discharges* blood; to *discharge* vengeance; applied also to an electrical jar, battery, etc., charged with electricity, to signify the removing of the charge.

They do *discharge* their shot of courtesy. —Shak.

6. To deliver the amount or value of to the person to whom it is owing; to pay; as, to *discharge* a debt, a bond, a note.

I will *discharge* my bond. —Shak.

7. To satisfy, as a person to whom anything is due; to pay one's debt to; as, he *discharged* his creditors.

8. To free from claim or demand; to give an acquittance or a receipt in full to, as to a debtor; as, the creditor *discharged* his debtor.

9. To free from an obligation, duty, or labor; to relieve; as, to *discharge* a man from further duty or service; to *discharge* a surety.

When he is *discharged* from the labour of uniting two incongruous styles. —Macaulay.

10. To clear from an accusation or crime; to acquit; to absolve; to set free; with *of*; as, to *discharge* a man *of* all blame.

11. To perform or execute, as a duty or office considered as a charge; as, one man *discharges* the office of a sheriff, another that of a priest.

The sun will set before I shall *discharge*
What I must strive to do. —Shak.

12. To divest of an office or employment; to dismiss from service; as, to *discharge* a servant; to *discharge* a jury.

13. To release; to liberate from confinement; as, to *discharge* a prisoner.

14. To clear oneself of, as by explanation; to account for. [Obs.]

dis-chärġe′, *v.i.* 1. To break up.

The cloud, if it were oily or fatty, would not *discharge*. —Bacon.

2. To smear; to blur, as the lines of a drawing not waterproof.

dis-chärġe′, *n.* [OFr. *descharge*, an unloading.]

1. The act of unloading; as, the *discharge* of a ship; the act of taking out; as, the *discharge* of a cargo.

2. The act of freeing of the missile with which anything is loaded; the act of firing off or unloading; as, a *discharge* of firearms.

3. A throwing out; vent; emission; applied to a fluid, a flowing or issuing out, or a throwing out; as, the *discharge* of water from a spring or from a spout; applied also to an electrical jar, battery, etc., to signify the removal of the charge by forming a communication between the positive and the negative surfaces.

4. That which is thrown out; matter emitted; as, a thin serous *discharge*.

5. Dismissal from office or service; the writing which evidences the dismissal; as, the soldier obtained his *discharge*.

6. Release from obligation, debt, or penalty; the writing which is evidence of it; an acquittance; as, the debtor has a *discharge*.

Secure of our *discharge* from penalty. —Milton.

7. Absolution from a crime or accusation; acquittal.

Which word imports an acquittance or *discharge* of a man upon full trial. —South.

8. Ransom; liberation; price paid for deliverance.

Death, who sets all free,
Hath paid his ransom now, and full *discharge*. —Milton.

9. Performance; execution; applied to an office, trust, or duty; as, a good man is faithful in the *discharge* of his duties.

Indefatigable in the *discharge* of business. —Motley.

10. Liberation; release from imprisonment or other confinement.

11. Payment, as of a debt.

My lord of Somerset will keep me here,
Without *discharge*, money, or furniture. —Shak.

12. In architecture, the relief given to a beam or other piece of timber when too much loaded by a superincumbent weight.

13. A substance, such as chlorid of lime or nitric acid, used by calico printers to remove a color from the parts on which the pattern is printed.

Discharge of fluids; the name given to that branch of hydraulics which treats of the issuing of water through apertures in the sides and bottoms of vessels.

Discharge style; a method of calico printing in which a piece of cloth is colored, and from parts of it, forming a pattern, the color is afterward removed by a discharge.

Leyden Jar with Discharger.

dis-chär′ġẽr, *n.* One who or that which discharges; specifically, (a) in electricity, an instrument for discharging a Leyden jar, by making a connection between the two surfaces; (b) in calico printing, a discharge. [See *Discharge*, 13.]

dis-chär′ġing-ärch, *n.* In architecture, an arch formed in the substance of a wall to relieve the part which is below it from the superincumbent weight. Such arches are commonly used over lintels and flat-headed openings.

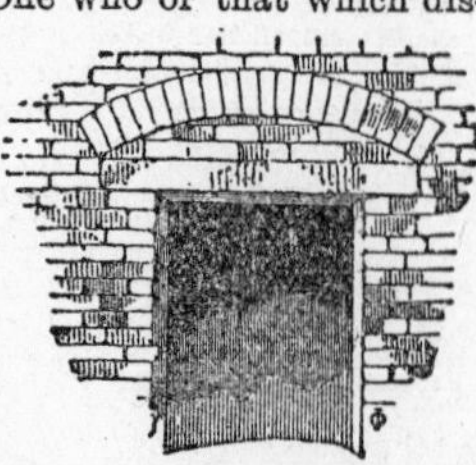
Discharging-arch.

dis-chär′ġing-rod, *n.* In electricity, a discharger.

dis-çhev′ele, *a.* Disheveled. [Obs.]

Dis-çhid′i-ȧ, *n.* [L., from Gr. *dischidēs*, cloven, so named from an obscure process in the conformation of the flower; *di-*, two, and *schizein*, to split.] A genus of *Asclepiadaceæ* found in India, the Indian Archipelago, and Australia. They are herbs or undershrubs, with small white or red flowers. One species, *Dischidia Rafflesiana*, is remarkable for its numerous pitcher-like appendages.

Dischidia Rafflesiana.

dis-chŭrch′, *v.t.*; dischurched, *pt., pp.*; dischurching, *ppr.* 1. To deprive of the rank of a church.

2. To expel (a person) from church-membership.

dis-cīde′, *v.t.* To divide; to cut in pieces. [Obs.]

dis-cif′ẽr-ous, *a.* [L. *discus*, disk, and *ferre*, to bear.] Having disks.

dis-ci-flō′răl, dis-ci-flō′rous, *a.* [L. *discus*, a disk, and *flos* (*floris*), flower.] Of, relating, or pertaining to a number of polypetalous orders of flowers characterized by a conspicuous, expanded disk about the ovary, commonly separate from the calyx.

dis′ci-fọrm, *a.* [L. *discus*, a disk, and *forma*, shape.] Having the form of a disk or circular plate.

Dis-cī′nȧ, *n.* The type genus of *Discinidæ*.

dis-cinct′, *a.* Ungirded. [Obs.]

dis-cind′, *v.t.* To cut in two. [Obs.]

dis-cī′ple, *n.* [ME. *disciple*, *desciple*; OFr. *disciple*; L. *discipulus*, a learner, from *discere*, to learn.]

1. A learner; a scholar; one who receives or professes to receive instruction from another; as, the *disciples* of Plato.

2. A follower; an adherent to the doctrines of another; as, the *disciples* of Christ.

Disciples of Christ; the sect variously called *Christians* or *Campbellites*.

The disciples; the twelve votaries of Christ.

Syn.—Learner, scholar, pupil, follower, adherent.

dis-cī′ple, *v.t.*; discipled, *pt., pp.*; discipling, *ppr.* 1. To teach; to train or bring up.

2. To make disciples of; to convert to doctrines or principles.

This authority he employed in sending missionaries to *disciple* all nations.—Griffin.

3. To punish; to discipline. [Obs.]

dis-cī′ple-ship, *n.* The state of a disciple or follower in doctrines and precepts.

dis-cī′pless, *n.* A female adherent. [Obs.]

dis′ci-plin-ȧ-ble, *a.* 1. Capable of instruction and improvement in learning.

2. Capable of subjection to discipline.

3. Subject or liable to discipline, as the member of a church.

dis′ci-plin-ȧ-ble-ness, *n.* The state or quality of being disciplinable.

dis′ci-plin-ăl, *a.* Pertaining to discipline.

Dis′ci-plin-ănt, *n.* One of a religious order, so called from their practice of scourging themselves, or of other rigid discipline.

dis″ci-plin-ā′ri-ăn, *a.* Pertaining to discipline.

dis″ci-plin-ā′ri-ăn, *n.* 1. One who disciplines; one who makes discipline a hobby; a martinet.

2. [D—] A Puritan or Presbyterian; so called from his rigid adherence to religious discipline.

dis′ci-plin-ā-ry, *a.* Pertaining to discipline; intended for discipline or government; promoting discipline; as, *disciplinary* measures.

dis′ci-pline, *n.* [ME. *discipline*; L. *disciplina*, instruction, training, discipline, from *discipulus*, a learner, from *discere*, to learn.]

1. Education; instruction; the cultivation of the mind and formation of the manners; training.

Wife and children are a kind of *discipline* of humanity. —Bacon.

2. Instruction and government, comprehending the communication of knowledge and the regulation of practice; the training to act in accordance with rules; drill; as, military *discipline*.

Obey the rules and *discipline* of art.—Dryden.

3. Rule of government; method of regulating principles and practice; as, the *discipline* prescribed for the church.

4. Subjection to rule; submissiveness to control.

The most perfect, who have their passions in the best *discipline*. —Rogers.

5. Correction; chastisement; punishment inflicted by way of correction and training; instruction by means of misfortune, suffering, and the like.

A sharp *discipline* of half a century had sufficed to educate us. —Macaulay.

6. In the Roman Catholic church, (a) chastisement or bodily punishment inflicted on a delinquent by himself or another, or that chastisement or external mortification which a penitent inflicts on himself; (b) the scourge so used.

7. Anything taught; branch of knowledge; art. [Obs.]

dis′ci-pline, *v.t.*; disciplined, *pt., pp.*; disciplining, *ppr.* 1. To instruct or educate; to inform the mind of; to prepare by instruction; to train; as, to *discipline* youth for a profession or for future usefulness.

They were with care prepared and *disciplined* for confirmation. —Addison.

2. To accustom to systematic action; to teach rules and practice, and accustom to order and subordination; to drill; as, to *discipline* troops.

His mind imperfectly *disciplined* by nature. —Macaulay.

3. To correct; to chastise; to punish.

Has he *disciplined* Aufidius soundly? —Shak.

4. To execute the laws of a church on, with a view to bring to repentance and reformation of life.

5. To keep in subjection; to regulate; to govern.

Disciplining them (appetites) with fasting. —Scott.

Syn.—To train, form, educate, instruct, drill, regulate, correct, chastise, punish.

dis′ci-plin-ẽr, *n.* One who or that which disciplines.

dis-cip′ū-lăr, *a.* Of or becoming to a disciple.

dis-cis′sion (-sish′un), *n.* [LL. *discissio*, a separation, from *discissus*, pp. of *discindere*, to cut apart; *dis-*, asunder, and *scindere*, to cut.] In surgery, a cutting apart.

dis-clāim′, *v.t.*; disclaimed, *pt., pp.*; disclaiming, *ppr.* [OFr. *disclaimer*; LL. *disclamare*, to renounce; L. *dis-* priv., and *clamare*, to cry out.]

1. To deny or relinquish all claim to; to reject as not belonging to oneself; to renounce; as, he *disclaims* all pretension to military skill.

Here I *disclaim* all my paternal care.—Shak.

2. To deny responsibility for or approval of; to disavow; to disown.

Each *disclaimed* all knowledge of us. —Tennyson.

3. To refuse to acknowledge; to renounce; to reject.

He *disclaims* the authority of Jesus.—Farmer.

4. In law, (a) to deny or disavow, as another's claim; (b) to decline accepting, as an estate, interest, or office.

Syn.—Disown, disavow, deny, reject, renounce.

dis-clāim′, *v.i.* To disavow all part or share.

Nature *disclaims* in thee. —Shak.

dis-clāim′ẽr, *n.* 1. A person who disclaims, disowns, or renounces.

2. In law, an express or implied denial or renunciation of certain things in question.

3. A public disavowal, as of pretensions, etc.

dis-clȧ-mā′tion, *n.* The act of disclaiming; a disavowing; specifically, in Scots law, the act of a vassal disavowing or disclaiming a person as his superior, whether the person so disclaimed be the superior or not.

dis-clāme′, *v.t.* [Obs.] See *Disclaim.*

dis-clan′dẽr, *v.t.* To slander or abuse. [Obs.]

dis-clōak′, *v.t.* To uncloak; to discover. [Obs.]

dis-clōṣe′, *v.t.*; disclosed, *pt., pp.*; disclosing, *ppr.* [ME. *disclosen*; L. *discludere*, to shut up separately, to keep apart; *dis-*, apart, and *claudere*, to close.]

1. To uncover; to open; to remove a cover from, and lay open to the view.

The shells being broken, the stone included in them is *disclosed.* —Woodward.

2. To cause to appear; to lay open to the view; to bring to light; as, events have *disclosed* the designs of the ministry.

3. To reveal by words; to tell; to utter; as, to *disclose* the secret thoughts of the heart.

4. To make known; to show in any manner; as, a blush may *disclose* a secret passion.

5. To open; to hatch. [Obs.]

The ostrich layeth her eggs under sand, where the heat of the sun *discloseth* them.—Bacon.

Syn.—Uncover, unveil, discover, reveal, divulge, tell, utter.

dis-clōṣe′, *n.* An uncovering. [Obs.]

dis-clōṣed′, *a.* 1. Uncovered; exposed to view; made known; revealed; told; uttered.

2. In heraldry, a term applied to tame fowls to denote that the wings are spread open or expanded on each side, but with their points downward.

A Dove Disclosed.

dis-clōṣ′ẽr, *n.* One who or that which discloses.

dis-clō′ṣūre (-zhūr), *n.* The act of disclosing; also, that which is disclosed.

dis-cloud′, *v.t.* To free from clouds or obscurity. [Obs.]

dis-clout′, *v.t.* To free from a clout or covering. [Obs.]

dis-clū′ṣion, *n.* An emission; a throwing out. [Obs.]

dis-cō-. A combining form from L. *discus*, Gr. *diskos*, a quoit, disk, and signifying disk-shaped, relation to, or connection with, a disk.

dis-cōast′, *v.i.* To depart; to quit the coast. [Obs.]

dis-cō-blas′tic, *a.* [*Disco-*, and Gr. *blastos*, a germ.] Having discoidal segmentation of the formative yolk.

dis-cō-blas′tū-lȧ, *n.* The blastula which a discoblastic ovum yields.

dis-cob′ō-lus, *n.*; *pl.* **dis-cob′ō-lī.** [L., from Gr. *diskobolos*, a discus-thrower; *diskos*, a discus, and *ballein*, to throw.]

1. A discus-thrower.

2. [D—] A Greek statue sculptured by Myron about 450 B. C., being the representation of an athlete throwing the discus.

Discobolus throwing the Discus.

dis′cō-cärp, *n.* [*Disco-*, and Gr. *karpos*, fruit.] In botany, (a) a collection of fruit in a hollow receptacle, as in many roseworts; (b) an apothecium.

Dis-cō-ceph′ȧ-lī, *n.pl.* [*Disco-*, and Gr. *kephalē*, head.] A suborder of fishes; the sucking-fishes, of which the remora is the best known example.

dis-cō-ceph′ȧ-lous, *a.* Having a suctorial disk attached to the head; of or pertaining to the *Discocephali.*

dis-cō-dac′tyl, *a.* and *n.* I. *a.* Of or pertaining to the *Discodactylia.*

II. *n.* One of the *Discodactylia.*

Dis″cō-dac-tyl′i-ȧ, *n.pl.* [*Disco-*, and Gr. *daktylos*, finger, toe.] A division of amphibians having terminally dilated toes by which they adhere to plane surfaces; the tree-toads and tree-frogs.

dis-cō-dac′tyl-ous, *a.* Having terminally dilated toes; discodactyl.

dis-cō-gas′trụ-lȧ, *n.* [*Disco-*, and L. *gastrula*, dim. of *gaster*; Gr. *gastēr*, belly.] The gastrula which a discoblastic ovum yields.

dis-cō-hėr′ent, *a.* Lacking coherence. [Rare.]

dis′coid, *n.* [LL. *discoides*; Gr. *diskoeidēs*, disk-shaped; *diskos*, a disk, and *eidos*, form.] Something in the form of a discus or disk; specifically, a univalve shell whose whorls are disposed vertically in the same plane, so as to form a disk, as the *Planorbis.*

dis′coid, dis-coid′ăl, *a.* 1. Having the form of a disk.

2. In conchology, applied to certain univalve shells. [See *Discoid*, n.]

Discoid or *discous flowers*; compound flowers not radiated, but with florets all tubular, as the tansy.

Dis-coi′dē-ȧ, *n.pl.* [L., from Gr. *diskoeidēs*, disk-shaped.] A group of mammals including those with a placenta of disklike shape.

dis′cō-lith, *n.* [*Disco-*, and Gr. *lithos*, a stone.] A calcareous body with an organic structure found imbedded in bathybius.

dis-cŏl′ŏr, *v.t.*; discolored, *pt., pp.*; discoloring, *ppr.* [LL., *discolorare*, to deprive of color.]

1. To alter the natural hue or color of; to change to a different color or shade; to stain; to tinge; as, sea-water *discolors* silver.

Drink water, either pure, or but *discolored* with malt. —Temple.

2. To alter the complexion of; to change the appearance of; to give a false tinge to; as, to *discolor* ideas.

Jealousy with jaundice in her eyes,
Discoloring all she viewed. —Dryden.

dis-cŏl′ŏr-āte, *v.t.* To discolor.

dis-cŏl-ŏr-ā′tion, *n.* The act of altering the color of; the alteration or thing so altered.

dis-cŏl′ŏred, *a.* Altered in color; stained.

dis-cŏl′oūr, dis-cŏl′oūred, etc. The English spelling of *discolor, discolored*, etc.

Dis″cō-mē-dū′sæ, *n.pl.* [*Disco-*, and L. *Medusæ*, a genus of jelly fishes.] An order of hydrozoans including *Discophora*; more strictly, the *Discophora.*

dis″cō-mē-dū′săn, *a.* Of or pertaining to the *Discomedusæ*; also used substantively.

dis-cŏm′fit, *v.t.*; discomfited, *pt., pp.*; discomfiting, *ppr.* [ME. *discomfiten*; OFr. *desconfire*; LL. *disconficere*, to defeat, discomfit; L. *dis-* priv., and *conficere*, to do, achieve; *con-*, intens., and *facere*, to do.]

1. To rout; to defeat; to scatter in fight; to cause to flee; to vanquish.

He, fugitive, declined superior strength, *Discomfited*, pursued. —Philips.

2. To disconcert; to foil; to frustrate the plans of; to throw into perplexity and dejection.

dis-cŏm′fit, *a.* Confused; discomfited. [Obs.]

dis-cŏm′fit, *n.* Confusion; discomfiture. [Obs.]

dis-cŏm′fi-tūre, *n.* 1. Rout; defeat in battle; dispersion; overthrow.

Every man's sword was against his fellow, and there was a very great *discomfiture.* —1 Sam. xiv. 20.

2. Defeat; frustration; disappointment.

After five days' exertion, this man resigns the task in *discomfiture* and despair.—Disraeli.

dis-cŏm′fŏrt, *v.t.*; discomforted, *pt., pp.*; discomforting, *ppr.* [ME. *discomforten*; OFr. *desconforter*, to discomfort; L. *dis-* priv., and LL. *confortare*, to comfort, from L. *con-*, intens., and *fortis*, strong.] To disturb the peace or happiness of; to make uneasy; to pain; to grieve; to sadden; to deject.

Her champion went away *discomforted* as much as discomfited. —Sidney.

dis-cŏm′fŏrt, *n.* Absence or opposite of comfort or pleasure.

What mean you, sir,
To give them this *discomfort?* Look, they weep. —Shak.

Syn.—Uneasiness, disturbance, pain, grief, sorrow, inquietude.

dis-cŏm′fŏrt-ȧ-ble, *a.* Uncomfortable. [Rare or Obs.]

dis-cŏm′fŏrt-ȧ-ble-ness, *n.* Discomfort. [Obs.]

dis-cŏm-mend′, *v.t.*; discommended, *pt., pp.*; discommending, *ppr.* To blame; to censure; to mention with disapprobation.

I do not *discommend* the lofty style in tragedy. —Dryden.

dis-cŏm-mend′ȧ-ble, *a.* Blamable; censurable; deserving disapprobation.

dis-cŏm-mend′ȧ-ble-ness, *n.* Blamableness; the quality of being worthy of disapprobation.

dis-cŏm-men-dā′tion, *n.* Blame; censure; reproach.

dis-cŏm-mend′ẽr, *n.* One who discommends; a dispraiser.

dis-cŏm-mis′sion, *v.t.* To dispossess of a commission.

dis-cŏm′mō-dāte, *v.t.* To inconvenience. [Obs.]

dis-cŏm-mōde′, *v.t.*; discommoded, *pt., pp.*; discommoding, *ppr.* [OFr. *descommoder*; L. *dis-* priv., and *commodare*, to make fit or suitable, from *commodus*, fit, suitable.] To put to inconvenience; to incommode; to molest; to trouble.

dis-cŏm-mō′di-ous, *a.* Inconvenient; troublesome.

dis-cŏm-mō′di-ous-ly, *adv.* In a discommodious manner.

dis-cŏm-mō′di-ous-ness, *n.* Discommodity.

dis-cŏm-mod′i-ty, *n.* Inconvenience; trouble; hurt; disadvantage.

dis-cŏm′mŏn, *v.t.*; discommoned, *pt., pp.*; discommoning, *ppr.* 1. To appropriate, as common land, by separating and inclosing.

2. To deprive of the privileges of a place; specifically, in some English universities, to deprive (a dealer) of the student trade.

dis-cŏm-mū′ni-ty, *n.* A state in which there is an absence of community, as in relationship or characteristics. [Rare.]

dis-cŏm′pȧ-ny, *v.t.* To sever from company or association. [Rare.]

dis-cŏm-plex′ion, *v.t.* To change the complexion or color of. [Obs.]

dis-cŏm-plī′ănce, *n.* Noncompliance.

dis-cŏm-pōṣe′, *v.t.*; discomposed, *pt., pp.*; discomposing, *ppr.* [L. *dis-* priv., and *componere*, to put in order, compose.]

1. To unsettle; to disorder; to disturb; to disarrange; to interfere with; to break up.

Now Betty from her master's bed had flown,
And softly stole to *discompose* her own. —Swift.

2. To disturb peace and quietness in; to

agitate; to ruffle; applied to the temper or mind.

Ill in death it shows,
Your peace of mind by rage to *discompose*.
—Dryden.

3. To displace; to discard; to discharge. [Obs.]

He never put down or *discomposed* counsellor, save only Stanley. —Bacon.

Syn.—To disorder, derange, unsettle, disturb, disconcert, agitate, ruffle, fret, vex.

dis-çŏm-pōşed′, *a.* Unsettled; disordered; ruffled; agitated; disturbed.

dis-çŏm-pōş′ed-ly, *adv.* In a discomposed manner.

dis-çŏm-pōş′ed-ness, *n.* The state or quality of being discomposed.

dis-çom-pō-şi′tion, *n.* Discomposure. [Obs.]

dis-çŏm-pō′şūre, *n.* 1. Disorder; agitation; disturbance; perturbation; as, *discomposure* of mind.

2. Inconsistency; disagreement. [Obs.]

dis-çompt′, *v.t.* [Obs.] See *Discount.*

Dis″çō-mȳ-cē′tēş, *n.pl.* [L., from Gr. *diskos*, a disk, and *mykēs* (pl. *mykētes*), fungus.] An order of small fungi having the openings of the fruit above, with waxlike or fleshy tissue; including *Peziza* and the common morel.

dis″çō-mȳ-cē′tous, *a.* Of or pertaining to the order *Discomycetes.*

dis-çŏn-çērt′, *v.t.*; disconcerted, *pt.*, *pp.*; disconcerting, *ppr.* [L. *dis-* priv., and *concertare*, to contend.]

1. To throw into disorder or confusion; to undo, as a scheme or plan; to defeat; to frustrate; as, the emperor *disconcerted* the plans of his enemy.

2. To unsettle the mind of; to discompose; to disturb the self-possession of; to confuse.

dis-çon′çērt, *n.* Lack of concert or harmony.

dis-çŏn-çēr′tion, *n.* The act of disconcerting; the state of being disconcerted or confused. [Rare.]

dis-çŏn-dū′çive, *a.* Not conducive; tending to hinder or prevent. [Rare.]

dis-çŏn-fọrm′ȧ-ble, *a.* Lacking conformity.

dis-çŏn-fọrm′i-ty, *n.* Want of agreement or conformity; inconsistency.

dis-çŏn-gru′i-ty, *n.* Want of congruity; incongruity; disagreement; inconsistency.

dis-çŏn-neçt′, *v.t.*; disconnected, *pt.*, *pp.*; disconnecting, *ppr.* To separate; to disunite; to dissolve connection in; to interrupt, as an electric current.

To disconnect an engine; in machinery, to remove the connecting-rod.

dis-çŏn-neçt′ed-ly, *adv.* In a disconnected manner.

dis-çŏn-neç′tion, *n.* The act of separating; the state of being disunited; separation; want of union.

Nothing was therefore to be left in all the subordinate members, but weakness, *disconnection*, and confusion. —Burke.

dis-çon′sē-grāte, *v.t.* To desecrate. [Rare.]

dis-çŏn-sent′, *v.i.* To demur; to vary. [Obs.]

dis-çon′sō-lā-çy, *n.* The state or quality of being without consolation. [Obs.]

dis-çon′sō-lănçe, *n.* Disconsolateness. [Obs.]

dis-çon′sō-lāte, *a.* [ME. *disconsolat*; LL. *disconsolātus*, comfortless; L. *dis-* priv., and *consolatus*, pp. of *consolari*, to console.]

1. Destitute of comfort or consolation; sorrowful; hopeless, or not expecting comfort; sad; dejected; melancholy; as, a *disconsolate* widow.

2. Not affording comfort; cheerless; as, the *disconsolate* darkness of a winter's night.

dis-çon′sō-lā-ted, *a.* Disconsolate. [Obs.]

dis-çon′sō-lāte-ly, *adv.* In a disconsolate manner; without comfort.

dis-çon′sō-lāte-ness, *n.* The state of being disconsolate or comfortless.

dis-çon-sō-lā′tion, *n.* Want of comfort; grief; melancholy. [Rare.]

dis-çŏn-tent′, *v.t.*; discontented; *pt.*, *pp.*; discontenting, *ppr.* To cause discontent in; to make dissatisfied with existing conditions.

dis-çŏn-tent′, *a.* Discontented.

dis-çŏn-tent′, *n.* 1. Want of content; uneasiness or inquietude of mind; dissatisfaction at any present state of things; as, discomforts produce *discontent.*

2. One dissatisfied or rebellious. [Rare.]

Changelings and poor *discontents.* —Shak.

dis-çon-ten-tā′tion, *n.* Discontent. [Obs.]

dis-çŏn-tent′ed, *a.* Uneasy in mind; dissatisfied; unquiet; as, *discontented* citizens make bad subjects.

dis-çŏn-tent′ed-ly, *adv.* In a discontented manner or mood.

dis-çŏn-tent′ed-ness, *n.* Uneasiness of mind; inquietude; dissatisfaction.

dis-çŏn-tent′fụl, *a.* Full of discontent.

dis-çŏn-tent′ing, *a.* 1. Discontented. [Obs.]

2. Giving discontent; disappointing.

dis-çŏn-tent′ive, *a.* Pertaining to or causing discontent. [Rare.]

dis-çŏn-tent′ment, *n.* The state of being uneasy in mind; uneasiness; inquietude; discontent.

dis-çŏn-tin′ū-ȧ-ble, *a.* Capable of being discontinued. [Rare.]

dis-çŏn-tin′ū-ănçe, *n.* 1. Want of continuance; cessation; intermission; interruption of continuance.

2. Want of continued connection or cohesion of parts; solution of continuity; want of union; disruption.

3. In law, the interruption or dismissal of a suit by reason of the plaintiff's omission of formalities to keep it pending.

4. In old English law, an interruption or break of a right of entry, consequent upon a wrongful alienation by the tenant in possession, for an estate larger than that to which he was entitled.

dis-çŏn-tin-ū-ā′tion, *n.* Breach or interruption of continuity; disruption of parts; separation of parts which form a connected series.

dis-çŏn-tin′ūe, *v.t.*; discontinued, *pt.*, *pp.*; discontinuing, *ppr.* [L. *dis-* priv., and *continuare*, to continue.]

1. To leave off; to cause to cease, as a practice or habit; to stop; to put an end to; as, to *discontinue* the use of steam as a motive power.

The depredations on our commerce were not to be *discontinued.* —Pickering.

2. To break off; to interrupt.

3. To cease to take or receive; as, to *discontinue* a daily paper.

dis-çŏn-tin′ūe, *v.i.* 1. To cease; to leave the possession, or lose an established or long-enjoyed right.

Thyself shalt *discontinue* from thine heritage. —Jer. xvii. 4.

2. To lose the cohesion of parts; to suffer disruption or separation of substance. [Rare.]

dis-çŏn-tin-ū-ee′, *n.* In law, one of whom something is discontinued.

dis-çŏn-tin′ū-ẽr, *n.* One who discontinues a rule or practice.

dis-çon-ti-nū′i-ty, *n.* Disunion of parts; want of cohesion.

dis-çŏn-tin′ū-ŏr, *n.* A discontinuer; the form of spelling used in law.

dis-çŏn-tin′ū-ous, *a.* 1. Broken off; interrupted.

2. Separated; wide; gaping.

Discontinuous function; in mathematics, one that varies discontinuously, and whose differential coefficient may therefore become infinite.

dis-çŏn-tin′ū-ous-ly, *adv.* In a discontinuous manner.

dis-çŏn-vēn′iençe (-yens), *n.* Incongruity; disagreement. [Obs.]

dis-çŏn-vēn′ient, *a.* Incongruous. [Obs.]

Dis-çoph′ō-rȧ, *n.pl.* [Gr. *diskophoros*, bringing the discus; *diskos*, a disk, and *pherein*, to carry, bring.]

1. A subclass of the *Hydrozoa*, comprising most of the organisms known as sea-jellies, jellyfishes, or sea-nettles.

2. A name sometimes given to the order of annelids, *Hirudinea*, to which the leech belongs.

dis-çoph′ō-rous, *a.* Resembling or pertaining to the *Discophora.*

dis″çō-plȧ-çen′tȧ, *n.* [*Disco-*, and L. *placenta*, a round flat cake, the placenta.] A placenta having a disk-like form.

dis″çō-plȧ-çen′tăl, *a.* Pertaining to a discoplacenta.

dis′çord, *n.* [ME. *discord*; OFr. *descorde*; L. *discordia*; discord; *dis*, from, and *cor* (*cordis*), the heart.]

1. Disagreement; want of concord or harmony; said of persons or things. Applied to persons, difference of opinions; variance; opposition; contention; strife; any disagreement which produces angry passions, contest, disputes, litigation, or war.

All *discord*, harmony not understood.—Pope.

2. In music, disagreement of sounds; dissonance; a union of sounds which is inharmonious, grating, and disagreeable to the ear, or an interval whose extremes do not coalesce.

Arms on armour clashing bray'd
Horrible *discord.* —Milton.

Syn.—Disagreement, discordance, variance, difference, opposition, dissension, contention, strife, rupture, clashing, dissonance.

dis-çord′, *v.i.* To disagree; to jar; to clash; not to suit; not to be coincident. [Obs.]

dis-çord′ȧ-ble, *a.* Discordant. [Rare.]

dis-çord′ănçe, dis-çord′ăn-çy, *n.* [L. *discordans.*] Disagreement; opposition; inconsistency; as, a *discordance* of opinions, or of sounds.

dis-çord′ănt, *a.* [ME. *descordaunt*; L. *discordans* (*-antis*), ppr. of *discordare*, to disagree.]

1. Disagreeing; incongruous; contradictory; being at variance; as, *discordant* opinions; *discordant* rules or principles.

2. Dissonant; not in unison; not harmonious; not accordant; harsh; jarring; as, *discordant* notes or sounds.

3. In geology, lacking parallelism; applied to strata.

dis-çord′ănt-ly, *adv.* Dissonantly; in a discordant manner.

dis-çord′ănt-ness, *n.* The state of being discordant. [Rare.]

dis-çord′fụl, *a.* Quarrelsome; contentious. [Obs.]

dis-çord′ous, *a.* Discordful. [Obs.]

dis-çor′pō-rāte, *a.* Divested of the body or of corporate privileges. [Obs.]

dis-çor-re-spond′ent, *a.* Lacking in correspondence. [Rare.]

dis-çōst′, *v.i.* [Obs.] Same as *Discoast.*

dis-ços′tāte, *a.* [L. *dis-*, apart, and *costa*, rib.] Having leaves with ribs radiating like the spokes of a wheel.

dis-çoun′sel, *v.t.* To dissuade. [Obs.]

dis′çount, *n.* [OFr. *disconter*, to reckon off; LL. *discomputare*, to reckon off, discount; *dis-*, off, from, and *computare*, to reckon, count.]

1. A sum deducted for prompt or advanced payment; an allowance or deduction from a sum due, or from a credit; a certain rate per cent deducted from the credit price of goods sold, on account of prompt payment; or any deduction from the customary price or from a sum due, or to be due, at a future time.

2. In finance, the amount of deduction or the rate per cent of such deduction from the face of negotiable paper purchased for future collection.

3. The act of discounting; as, a note may be deposited at a bank subject to *discount.*

4. In billiards, a handicap by which the player giving odds has deducted from his string an agreed number of counts for every count made by his opponent.

At a discount; below par; opposite of *at a premium*; hence, in low esteem; in disfavor; as, alchemy is now *at a discount.*

Bank discount; see under *Bank*, n.

True discount; that sum which, placed at interest at the given rate of discount for the given time, would amount to the interest on the face value of the discounted paper.

dis′çount (*or* dis-çount′), *v.t.*; discounted, *pt.*, *pp.*; discounting, *ppr.* 1. To deduct a certain sum or rate per cent from (the principal sum); as, a merchant *discounts* five per cent for prompt payment.

2. To lend or advance the amount of, deducting the interest or other rate per cent from the principal at the time of the loan or advance; as, the banks *discount* notes and bills of exchange on good security.

The first rule . . . to *discount* only unexceptionable paper. —Walsh.

3. To avoid the consideration of; to disregard.

His application is to be *discounted*, as here irrelevant. —Hamilton.

4. To estimate (a matter) or take (it) into account beforehand; to enjoy or suffer (anything) by anticipation; to discuss and form conclusions concerning (any event) before it occurs; as, he *discounted* all the pleasure of the journey before setting out.

5. In billiards, to give (an opponent) a discount.

dis′çount, *v.i.* To lend or make a practice of lending money, deducting the interest at the time of the loan; as, the banks *discount* for sixty or ninety days.

dis-çount′ȧ-ble, *a.* Capable of being discounted; as, certain forms are necessary to render notes *discountable* at a bank.

dis-çoun′tē-nănçe, *v.t.*; discountenanced, *pt.*, *pp.*; discountenancing, *ppr.* [*Dis-* and *countenance.*]

1. To abash; to ruffle or discompose the countenance of; to put to shame; to put out of countenance. [Obs.]

How would one look from his majestic brow
Discountenance her despised! —Milton.

2. To discourage; to check; to restrain by censure, arguments, opposition, or cold treatment; as, to *discountenance* drunkenness.

dis-çoun′tē-nănçe, *n.* Disapprobation; whatever tends to check or discourage. [Obs.]

He thought a little *discountenance* on those persons would suppress that spirit. —Clarendon.

dis-çoun′tē-năn-çẽr, *n.* One who discountenances.

dis′çount-ẽr, *n.* One who discounts, as a broker who buys mercantile paper at a discount.

dis-çour′āġe, *v.t.*; discouraged, *pt.*, *pp.*; discouraging, *ppr.* [ME. *discouragen*; OFr. *descoragier*, to discourage; *des-* priv., and *coragier*, to encourage.]

1. To extinguish the courage of; to dishearten; to depress the spirits of; to deject; to deprive of confidence.

Fathers, provoke not your children, lest they be *discouraged.* —Col. iii. 21.

2. To attempt to repress or prevent; to dissuade from; as, to *discourage* an effort.

Syn.—Dishearten, depress, dissuade, dispirit, deter.

dis-çour'āge, *n.* Fear. [Obs.]

dis-çour'āge-à-ble, *a.* Capable of discouragement.

dis-çour'āge-ment, *n.* 1. The act of disheartening, or depriving of courage; the act of deterring or dissuading from an undertaking; the act of depressing confidence.

2. The state of being discouraged; depression of spirit or loss of interest and hope.

3. That which destroys or abates courage; that which depresses confidence or hope; that which deters, or tends to deter, from an undertaking or from the prosecution of anything; as, the revolution was commenced under every possible *discouragement.*

dis-çour'ā-ġēr, *n.* One who or that which discourages.

dis-çour'ā-ġing, *a.* Tending to dishearten, or to depress the courage; as, *discouraging* prospects.

dis-çour'ā-ġing-ly, *adv.* In a manner tending to discourage.

dis-çōure', *v.t.* [Obs.] See *Discover.*

dis-çourse', *n.* [ME. *discourse*; OFr. *discours*; LL. *discursus*, discourse, conversation; L. *discursus*, a running to and fro, from *discursus*, pp. of *discurrere*, to run to and fro; *dis-*, from, in different directions, and *currere*, to run.]

1. Literally, a running about; hence, a shifting of ground and traversing to and fro, as a combatant. [Obs.]

2. The act of the understanding by which it passes from premises to consequences; reason or an act of reason. [Obs.]

3. A running over a subject in speech; hence, a communication of thoughts by words; expression of ideas; mutual intercourse; talk; conversation.

> The vanquished party with the victors joined,
> Nor wanted sweet *discourse*, the banquet of the mind. —Dryden.

4. A written treatise; a formal dissertation; a homily; a sermon; as, the *discourse* of Plutarch on garrulity; of Cicero on old age.

5. Intercourse; dealing; transaction. [Obs.]

dis-çourse', *v.i.*; discoursed, *pt., pp.*; discoursing, *ppr.* 1. To converse; to speak; to hold forth in a formal manner.

2. To tell something; to narrate.

3. To give information on a subject in writing and in a formal manner.

4. To reason; to pass from premises to conclusions. [Obs.]

dis-çourse', *v.t.* 1. To treat of; to talk over. [Obs.]

> Let us *discourse* our fortunes. —Shak.

2. To utter or give forth; as, to *discourse* excellent music.

3. To talk, reason, or confer with. [Obs.]

dis-çours'ēr, *n.* 1. One who discourses; a speaker; a haranguer.

2. The writer of a treatise or dissertation.

dis-çours'ive, *a.* 1. Reasoning; passing from premises to conclusions.

2. Containing dialogue or conversation; interlocutory.

> The epic is interlaced with dialogue or *discoursive* scenes. —Dryden.

3. Talkative; as, a *discoursive* woman. [Rare.]

dis-çours'ive-ness, *n.* The state of being discoursive. [Obs.]

dis-çour'tē-ous, *a.* Impolite; uncivil; rude; uncomplaisant; wanting in good manners; as, a *discourteous* knight.

dis-çour'tē-ous-ly, *adv.* In a rude or uncivil manner; with incivility.

dis-çour'tē-ous-ness, *n.* Discourtesy.

dis-çour'tē-sy, *n.* Incivility; rudeness of behavior or language; ill manners; act of disrespect.

> Be calm in arguing; for fiercenesse makes
> Errour a fault, and truth *discourtesie.*
> —Herbert.

dis-çourt'ship, *n.* Want of respect. [Obs.]

dis'çous, *a.* Discoid.

dis-çov'e-nănt, *v.t.* To dissolve covenant with. [Obs.]

dis-çov'ēr, *v.t.*; discovered, *pt., pp.*; discovering, *ppr.* [ME. *discoveren*; OFr. *descovrir*; LL. *discooperire*, to discover, reveal; L. *dis-* priv., and *cooperire*, to cover.]

1. To uncover. [Obs.]

2. To lay open to view; to disclose; to show; to make visible (something before unseen or concealed).

> Go, draw aside the curtains, and *discover*
> The several caskets to this noble prince.
> —Shak.

3. To reveal; to make known; to find out; to obtain the first knowledge of; as, Columbus *discovered* America.

4. To subject to examination. [Obs.]

Syn.—Invent, manifest, declare, disclose, reveal, divulge, uncover.—We *discover* what existed before but remained unknown; we *invent* by forming combinations which are either entirely new or which attain their end by means unknown before. We *discover* by any means direct or indirect; we *manifest* by unquestionable marks; we *declare* by express words; talents and dispositions *discover* themselves; particular feelings and sentiments *manifest* themselves; facts, opinions, and sentiments are *declared.*

dis-çov'ēr, *v.i.* To uncover; to unmask oneself. [Obs.]

dis-çov''ēr-à-bil'i-ty, *n.* The state or quality of being discoverable.

dis-çov'ēr-à-ble, *a.* Capable of being discovered.

dis-çov'ēr-ēr, *n.* 1. One who discovers; one who first sees or espies; one who finds out or first comes to the knowledge of something.

2. A scout; an explorer. [Obs.]

dis-çov'ēr-ment, *n.* [Obs.] See *Discovery.*

dis-çov'ērt, *a.* [ME. *discovert*; OFr. *descovert*, from LL. *discoopertus*, pp. of *discooperire*, to uncover; L. *dis-* priv., and *cooperire*, to cover.] Not covert; applied specifically in law to unmarried women or widows. [See *Covert.*]

dis-çov'ērt-ūre, *n.* A state of being released from coverture; freedom of a woman from the coverture of a husband.

dis-çov'ēr-y, *n.* 1. The action of disclosing to view or bringing to light; as, by the *discovery* of a plot, the public peace is preserved.

2. Disclosure; a making known; as, a bankrupt is bound to make a full *discovery* of his estate and effects.

3. The action of finding something hidden; as, the *discovery* of lead or silver in the earth.

4. The act of finding out, or coming to the knowledge of; as, the *discovery* of truth; the *discovery* of magnetism.

5. The act of espying; first sight of; as, the *discovery* of America by Columbus.

6. That which is discovered, found out, or revealed; that which is first brought to light, seen, or known; as, wireless telegraphy was an important *discovery.*

7. In dramatic poetry, the unraveling of a plot, or the manner of unfolding the plot or fable of a comedy or tragedy.

8. Exploration. [Obs.]

dis-çrā'dle, *v.i.* To come forth from or as if from a cradle; to emerge. [Obs.]

dis-çred'it, *n.* [LL. *discredere*, to disbelieve; L. *dis-* priv., and *credere*, to believe.]

1. Want of credit or good reputation; some degree of disgrace or reproach; disesteem; applied to persons or things; as, frauds in manufactures bring them into *discredit.*

2. Want of belief, trust, or confidence; disbelief; as, later accounts have brought the story into *discredit.*

Syn.—Disgrace, dishonor, disrepute, ignominy, reproach, scandal.

dis-çred'it, *v.t.*; discredited, *pt., pp.*; discrediting, *ppr.* 1. To disbelieve; to give no credit to; not to credit or believe; as, the report is *discredited.*

2. To deprive of credit or good reputation; to make less reputable or honorable; to bring into disesteem; to bring into some degree of disgrace, or into disrepute.

> He least *discredits* his travels, who returns the same man he went. —Wotton.

3. To deprive of credibility.

dis-çred'it-à-ble, *a.* Tending to injure credit; injurious to reputation; disgraceful; disreputable.

dis-çred'it-à-bly, *adv.* In a discreditable manner.

dis-çred'it-ŏr, *n.* One who discredits.

dis-çreet', *a.* [ME. *discret*; OFr. *discret*, prudent, discreet, from L. *discretus*, pp. of *discernere*, to distinguish, discern; *dis-*, apart, from, and *cernere*, to separate, to see.]

1. Prudent; wise in avoiding errors or evil, and in selecting the best means to accomplish a purpose; circumspect; cautious; wary; not rash.

2. Distinct; distinguishable. [Obs.]

3. Polite; courteous; civil. [Scot.]

dis-çreet'ly, *adv.* In a discreet manner.

dis-çreet'ness, *n.* The quality of being discreet; discretion.

dis-çrep'ānce, *n.* Discrepancy.

dis-çrep'ăn-cy, *n.*; *pl.* **dis-çrep'ăn-cies.** [OFr. *discrepance*; L. *discrepantia*, discordance, disagreement, from *discrepare*, to sound differently.] Difference; disagreement; contrariety; especially of facts or opinions.

> There is no real *discrepancy* between these two genealogies. —Faber.

dis-çrep'ănt, *a.* Different; disagreeing; contrary.

dis-çrep'ănt, *n.* A dissenter. [Obs.]

dis-çrēte', *a.* [L. *discretus*, pp. of *discernere*, to distinguish, separate.]

1. Separate; distinct; disjunct.

> The parts are not *discrete* or dissentany.
> —Milton.

2. Disjunctive; as, I resign my life, but not my honor, is a *discrete* proposition.

3. In music, applied to a movement in which each successive note varies considerably in pitch; opposed to *concrete.*

4. In botany, not coalescing; standing apart.

Discrete proportion; proportion where the ratio of two or more pairs of numbers or quantities is the same, but there is not the same proportion between all the numbers; as, 3:6::8:16, 3 bearing the same proportion to 6 as 8 does to 16. But 3 is not to 6 as 6 to 8. It is thus opposed to *continued* or *continual proportion*; as, 3:6::12:24.

Discrete quantity; a quantity which is not continued and joined together in its parts, as any number, since a number consists of units.

dis-çrēte', *v.t.* To separate; to discontinue. [Obs.]

dis-çrēte'ly, *adv.* In a discrete manner.

dis-çre'tion (-kresh'un), *n.* [ME. *discrecion*; OFr. *discretion*; L. *discretio* (*-onis*), a separation, distinction, from *discretus*, pp. of *discernere*, to discern.]

1. Disjunction; separation. [Obs.]

2. The quality of being discreet; prudence; that discernment which enables a person to judge critically of what is correct and proper, united with caution; nice discernment and judgment, directed by circumspection, and primarily regarding one's own conduct.

> *Discretion* is the victor of the war,
> Valour the pupil. —Massinger.

3. Liberty or power of acting without other control than one's own judgment; as, the management of affairs was left to the *discretion* of the president.

Syn.—Sagacity, circumspection, wariness, prudence, caution.

dis-çre'tion-ā-ry, dis-çre'tion-ăl (-kresh'un-), *a.* Left to discretion; unrestrained except by discretion or judgment; as, *discretionary* powers of an appointing officer.

dis-çre'tion-ā-ri-ly, dis-çre'tion-ăl-ly, *adv.* At discretion; according to discretion.

dis-çrē'tive, *a.* [LL. *discretivus*, serving to distinguish, from L. *discretus*, pp. of *discernere*, to distinguish, discern.] Disjunctive; noting separation or opposition.

Discretive proposition; in logic, a proposition which expresses some distinction, opposition, or variety, by means of *but, though, yet*, etc.; as, travelers change their climate, *but* not their temper.

dis-çrē'tive-ly, *adv.* In a discretive manner.

dis-çrim'i-nà-ble, *a.* That may be discriminated. [Rare or Obs.]

dis-çrim'i-năl, *a.* Making division; separating; specifically, in palmistry, denoting the dividing line between the hand and the arm.

dis-çrim'i-nănt, *n.* In mathematics, the eliminant of the *n* first derived functions of a homogeneous function of *n* variables.

dis-çrim'i-nāte, *a.* Distinguished; having the difference marked.

dis-çrim'i-nāte, *v.t.*; discriminated, *pt., pp.*; discriminating, *ppr.* [L. *discriminatus*, pp. of *discriminare*, to divide, distinguish, from *discrimen*, a division, distinction, interval, from *discernere*, to divide.]

1. To distinguish; to observe the difference between; to select from others.

> When a prisoner first leaves his cell he is unable to *discriminate* colors or recognize faces. —Macaulay.

2. To mark with notes of difference; to distinguish by some note or mark.

> In outward fashion . . . *discriminated* from all the nations of the earth.—Hammond.

dis-çrim'i-nāte, *v.i.* 1. To make a difference or distinction; as, in the application of law, the judge should *discriminate* between degrees of guilt.

2. To observe a difference; to treat differently; as, transportation companies often *discriminate* in favor of the large shipper.

dis-çrim'i-nāte-ly, *adv.* Distinctly; with minute distinction; particularly.

dis-çrim'i-nāte-ness, *n.* Distinctness; marked difference.

dis-çrim'i-nā-ting, *a.* Discriminative.

dis-çrim'i-nā-ting-ly, *adv.* In a discriminating manner.

dis-çrim-i-nā'tion, *n.* 1. The act of distinguishing; the act of making or observing a difference; distinction; as, the *discrimination* between right and wrong.

2. The faculty of distinguishing or discriminating; penetration; judgment; as, a man of nice *discrimination.*

> Their own desire of glory would . . . baffle their *discrimination.* —Milman.

3. The state of being discriminated, distinguished, or set apart.

There is a reverence to be showed them on the account of their *discrimination* from other places. —Stillingfleet.

4. That which discriminates; mark of distinction.

Take heed of abetting any factions, or applying any public *discriminations* in matters of religion. —Gauden.

5. In transportation, the observance of different tariffs for different shippers.

Syn.—Discernment, penetration, clearness, acuteness, acumen, judgment, distinction.

dis-crim'i-nā-tive, *a.* Marked by or observing discrimination; as, a *discriminative* decision; *discriminative* tariffs.

dis-crim'i-nā-tive-ly, *adv.* With discrimination or distinction.

dis-crim'i-nā-tŏr, *n.* One who discriminates.

dis-crim'i-nā-tō-ry, *a.* Discriminative.

dis-crim'i-nous, *a.* Hazardous. [Obs.]

dis-crive', *v.t.* [Obs.] See *Describe.*

dis-crown', *v.t.*; discrowned, *pt., pp.*; discrowning, *ppr.* To deprive of a crown.

dis-cru'ci-āte (-shi-āt), *v.t.* To torment; to torture. [Obs.]

dis-cū'bi-tō-ry, *a.* Leaning; inclining; fitted to a leaning posture. [Obs.]

dis-cul'pāte, *v t.* [L. *dis-* priv., and *culpare*, to blame, from *culpa*, a fault.] To free from blame or fault; to exculpate; to excuse.

dis-cul-pa'tion, *n.* Exculpation.

dis-cul'pa-tō-ry, *a.* Tending to exculpate.

dis-cum'ben-cy, *n.* [L. *discumbens (-entis)*, ppr. of *discumbere*, to lie down; *dis-*, intens., and *cubare*, to lie down, recline.] The act of leaning or reclining at meals, according to the manner of the ancients.

dis-cum'bēr, *v.t.* To unburden; to disencumber. [Obs.]

dis-cūre', *v.t.* To discover; to reveal. [Obs.]

dis-cur'rent, *a.* Not current. [Obs.]

dis-cūr'sion, *n.* [LL. *discursio*, a running different ways, from L. *discursus*, pp. of *discurrere*, to run different ways.]

1. A running or rambling about.

2. Rambling or desultory talk; expatiation.

3. The act of discoursing or reasoning.

dis-cūr'sist, *n.* A disputer. [Obs.]

dis-cūr'sive, *a.* 1. Moving or roving about; desultory.

2. Argumentative; reasoning; proceeding regularly from premises to conclusions.

Whence the soul
Reason receives; and reason is her being,
Discursive or intuitive. —Milton.

dis-cūr'sive-ly, *adv.* In a discursive manner; argumentatively.

dis-cūr'sive-ness, *n.* The state or quality of being discursive.

dis-cūr'sō-ry, *a.* Argumental; rational.

dis-cūr'sus, *n.* [L.] Ratiocination; argumentation; discourse.

dis'cus, *n.*; *pl.* **dis'cus-es** or **dis'ci**. [L. *discus*; Gr. *diskos*, a discus, quoit.]

1. A quoit; a piece of iron, copper, or stone, to be thrown in play, used by the ancients. [See cut under *Discobolus.*]

2. A disk; used specifically in biology.

Discus proligerus; in biology, a cumulus.

dis-cuss', *v.t.*; discussed, *pt., pp.*; discussing, *ppr.* [ME. *discussen*, to examine, scatter, from L. *discussus*, pp. of *discutire*, to strike asunder, shake apart, scatter: *dis-*, apart, and *quatere*, to shake.]

1. To shake or strike asunder; to dissolve; to repel; as, to *discuss* a tumor. [Obs.]

2. To shake off; to put away. [Obs.]

All regard of shame she had *discust.*
—Spenser.

3 To debate; to agitate by argument; to clear of objections and difficulties, with a view to find or illustrate truth; to sift; to examine by disputation; to ventilate; to reason on, for the purpose of separating truth from falsehood.

We might *discuss* the Northern sin,
Which made a selfish war begin.—Tennyson.

4. To speak; to declare; to explain.

Discuss the same in French to him.—Shak.

5. To make an end of, by eating or drinking; to consume; as, to *discuss* a fowl; to *discuss* a bottle of wine. [Colloq.]

6. In law, to proceed against (a principal debtor) before calling upon his surety or sureties.

Syn.—Debate, argue, dispute, controvert.

dis-cuss'ēr, *n.* One who discusses; one who sifts or examines.

dis-cus'sion, *n.* 1. The act or process of discussing, breaking up, or resolving; dispersion, as of a tumor, coagulated matter, and the like.

2. Debate; disquisition; the agitation of a point or subject with a view to elicit truth.

Compatible with a liberty of *discussion* and of individual action never before known.
—Macaulay.

3. In Scots law, a technical term signifying the doing diligence against a principal debtor in a cautionary obligation before proceeding against the cautioners, or against an heir for a debt due by his ancestor in respect of the subject to which he has succeeded before proceeding against the other heirs, etc.

4. In civil law, the act of thorough procedure against a debtor before calling upon his surety or sureties.

dis-cus'sion-ăl, *a.* Of or relating to discussion.

dis-cuss'ive, *a.* Having the power to discuss, resolve, or disperse, as tumors or coagulated matter.

dis-cuss'ive, *n.* A medicine that discusses; a discutient.

dis-cū'tient (-kū'shient), *a.* [L. *discutiens.*] Discussing; dispersing morbid matter.

dis-cū'tient, *n.* A medicine or application which disperses a tumor.

dis-dāin', *v.t.*; disdained, *pt., pp.*; disdaining, *ppr* [ME. *disdainen*; OFr. *desdaignier*, to disdain; L. *dis-* priv., and *dignari*, to deign, deem worthy, from *dignus*, worthy.] To think unworthy; to deem worthless; to consider to be unworthy of notice, care, regard, esteem, or unworthy of one's character; to scorn; to contemn; to reject as unworthy of oneself; as, the man of elevated mind *disdains* a mean action; Goliath *disdained* David.

Whose fathers I would have *disdained* to set with the dogs of my flock. —Job xxx. 1.

dis-dāin', *v.i.* To be filled with scorn, anger, or impatience; to be indignant.

Ajax, deprived of Achilles's armor, *disdains*, rageth and runs mad. —Jonson.

dis-dāin', *n.* 1. Contempt; scorn; a passion excited by the hatred or detestation of what is mean and dishonorable.

2. State of being despised; the state of feeling oneself disgraced; ignominy; disgrace. [Obs.]

The *disdain* and shame whereof hath ever since kept Hector fasting and waking.
—Shak.

3. That which is worthy of disdain. [Obs.]

Most loathsome, filthy, foul, and full of vile *disdain.* —Spenser.

Syn.—Scorn, scornfulness, contempt, arrogance, haughtiness, pride, superciliousness.

dis-dāined', *a.* Disdainful. [Obs.]

dis-dāin'ful, *a.* Full of disdain; expressing disdain; as, a *disdainful* look.

Syn.—Contemptuous, scornful, haughty, indignant.

dis-dāin'ful-ly, *adv.* Contemptuously; with scorn; in a haughty manner.

dis-dāin'ful-ness, *n.* Contempt; contemptuousness; haughty scorn.

dis-dāin'ish-ly, *adv.* Disdainfully. [Obs.]

dis-dāin'ous, *a.* Disdainful. [Obs.]

dis-dāin'ous-ly, *adv.* Disdainfully. [Obs.]

dis-dē'i-fȳ, *v.t.* To reduce from or deprive of deity or of the rank of deity. [Obs.]

dis-deign' (-dān'), *v.t.* To disdain. [Obs.]

dis-di'ă-clast, *n.* [From Gr. *dis-*, twice, and *diaklan*, to break apart; *dia-*, through, and *klan*, to break.] A term applied by Brücke to dark particles forming, by their apposition on the same plane, the doubly-refracting disk, band, or layer of striated muscular tissue.

dis-di-ă-clas'tic, *a.* Doubly refractive.

dis-di-ă-pā'sŏn, *n.* [LL., from Gr. *dis dia pasōn*, lit. twice through all.] In music, a compound concord in the quadruple ratio of 4:1 or 8:2.

dis-ēase', *v.t.*; diseased, *pt., pp.*; diseasing, *ppr.* 1. To interrupt or impair any or all the natural and regular functions of (the several organs of a living body), to afflict with pain or sickness; to make morbid; used chiefly in the past participle; as, a *diseased* body; a *diseased* stomach.

2. To pain; to make uneasy. [Obs.]

dis-ēase', *n.* [ME. *disese*; OFr. *desaise*, disease; *des-* priv., and *aise*, ease; L. *dis-* priv., and *esse*, to be.]

1. Pain; uneasiness; distress. [Obs.]

2. Any morbid state of the body generally, or of any particular organ or part of the body; the cause of pain or uneasiness; distemper; malady; sickness; disorder; any state of a living body in which the natural functions of the organs are interrupted or disturbed, either by defective or preternatural action, without a disruption of parts by violence, which is called a *wound.* The word is also applied to the disorders of other animals, as well as to those of man, and to any derangement of the vegetative functions of plants.

The shafts of *disease* shoot across our path in a variety of courses. —Buckminster.

3. Any disorder, or depraved condition or element, moral, mental, social, political, etc.; as, a political foundation laid in *disease* and corruption.

Basedow's disease; an exophthalmic disease, accompanied by swelling of the thyroid gland; exophthalmic goiter. It derives its name from Dr. Basedow, a German physician.

Syn.—Distemper, ailment, malady, disorder, sickness, illness, indisposition, complaint, infirmity.

dis-ēased', *a.* Affected by disease; sick.

dis-ēas'ed-ness, *n.* The state of being diseased; sickness. [Rare.]

dis-ēase'ful, *a.* 1. Abounding with or producing disease; as, a *diseaseful* climate. [Obs.]

2. Occasioning uneasiness. [Obs.]

dis-ēase'ful-ness, *n.* The state of being diseaseful; sickness. [Rare.]

dis-ēase'ment, *n.* Lack of ease. [Obs.]

dis-edge' (-ej'), *v.t.* To destroy or dull the edge of. [Rare.]

dis-ed'i-fȳ, *v.t.* To misteach. [Obs.]

dis-eld'ēr, *v.t.* To dispossess of an elder or elders. [Obs.]

dī-sel'e-nide, *n.* [*Di-* and *selenide.*] A compound in which the molecule has two atoms of selenium.

dis-em-bärk', *v.t.*; disembarked, *pt., pp.*; disembarking, *ppr.* [OFr. *desembarquer*, to disembark; L. *des-* priv., and *embarquer*, to embark.] To land; to debark; to remove from on board a ship to the land; to put on shore.

dis-em-bärk', *v.i.* To land; to debark; to go ashore.

dis-em-bär-kā'tion, dis-em-bär-cā'tion, *n.* The act of disembarking.

dis-em-bärk'ment, *n.* Disembarkation. [Rare.]

dis-em-bar'răss, *v.t.*; disembarrassed, *pt., pp.*; disembarrassing, *ppr.* [OFr. *desembarasser*; *des-* priv., and *embarrasser*, to embarrass.] To free from embarrassment or perplexity; to clear; to extricate.

dis-em-bar'răss-ment, *n.* The act of extricating from perplexity.

dis-em-bāy', *v.t.* To clear from a bay. [Obs.]

dis-em-bel'lish, *v.t.* To deprive of embellishment.

dis-em-bit'tēr, *v.t.*; disembittered, *pt., pp.*; disembittering, *ppr.* To free from bitterness; to clear from acrimony; to render sweet or pleasant.

dis-em-bod'ied (-bod'id), *a.* Divested of a body; as, *disembodied* spirits or souls.

dis-em-bod'i-ment, *n.* The act of disembodying or the state of being disembodied.

dis-em-bod'y, *v.t.*; disembodied, *pt., pp.*; disembodying, *ppr.* 1. To divest of body; to free from flesh.

2. To discharge from military incorporation; as, the militia was *disembodied.*

dis-em-bōgue' (-em-bōg'), *v.t.*; disembogued, *pt., pp.*; disemboguing, *ppr.* [Sp. *desembocar*; *des-* priv., and *embocar*, to enter by the mouth; L. *dis-* priv., and *in*, in, and *bucca*, cheek.] To pour out or discharge at the mouth, as a stream; to vent; to discharge into the ocean or a lake.

Rolling down, the steep Timavus raves,
And through nine channels *disembogues* his waves. —Addison.

dis-em-bōgue', *v.i.* 1. To flow out at the mouth, as a river; to discharge waters into the ocean or into a lake.

2. To pass out of a gulf or bay; said of a ship or other vessel.

dis-em-bōgue'ment, *n.* Discharge of waters into the ocean or a lake.

dis-em-bos'ŏm (-booz'), *v.t.* To separate from the bosom. [Rare.]

dis-em-bow'el, *v.t.*; disemboweled *or* disembowelled, *pt., pp.*; disemboweling *or* disembowelling, *ppr.* To take out the bowels of; to take or draw from the bowels, as the web of a spider.

dis-em-bow'el-ment, *n.* The act of disemboweling.

dis-em-bow'ēred, *a.* Removed from a bower, or deprived of a bower.

dis-em-bran'gle, *v.t.* To free from litigation. [Obs.]

dis-em-broil', *v.t.*; disembroiled, *pt., pp.*; disembroiling, *ppr.* To disentangle; to free from perplexity; to extricate from confusion.

dī-sē'mic, *a.* [Gr. *disēmos*, having two moræ; *di-*, two, and *sēma*, a mark, mora.] Containing two units of time; equaling two shorts (⏑⏑) or one long (—); applied in ancient prosody to meter.

dis-em-ploy', *v.t.* To deprive of employment. [Obs.]

dis-em-ploy'ment, *n.* The state of being thrown out of employment. [Obs.]

dis-em-pow'ēr, *v.t.* To deprive of authority.

dis-en-ā'ble, *v.t.*; disenabled, *pt., pp.*; disenabling, *ppr.* To deprive of power; to disable. [Obs.]

dis-en-am'ŏr, *v.t.* To rid of the bonds of love. [Obs.]

Don Quixote *disenamored* of Dulcinea del Toboso. —Shelton.

dis-en-chāin', *v.t.* To release from chains. [Obs.]

dis-en-chȧnt′, *v.t.*; disenchanted, *pt.*, *pp.*; disenchanting, *ppr.* [OFr. *desenchanter*; L. *dis-* priv., and *incantare*, to enchant.] To free from enchantment; to deliver from the power of charms or spells; to disillusion.

dis-en-chȧnt′ẽr, *n.* One who or that which disenchants.

dis-en-chȧnt′ment, *n.* The act of disenchanting.

dis-en-chärm′, *v.t.* To disenchant. [Obs.]

dis-en-clōṣe′, *v t.* See *Disinclose.*

dis-en-cour′āge, *v.t.* To discourage. [Obs.]

dis-en-cour′āge-ment, *n.* [Obs.] See *Discouragement.*

dis-en-crēase′, *v.t.* To decrease. [Obs.]

dis-en-crēase′, *n.* Decrease. [Obs.]

dis-en-cum′bẽr, *v.t.*; disencumbered, *pt.*, *pp.*; disencumbering, *ppr.* To free from encumbrance; to deliver from clogs and impediments; to disburden; as, to *disencumber* troops of their baggage.

Ere dim night had *disencumbered* Heaven.
—Milton.

dis-en-cum′brănce, *n.* Freedom or deliverance from encumbrance, or anything burdensome or troublesome.

dis-en-dow′, *v.t.* To take away an endowment of.

dis-en-dow′ment, *n.* The act of disendowing.

dis-en-frȧn′chiṣe, *v.t.* To disfranchise. [Rare.]

dis-en-frȧn′chiṣe-ment, *n.* Disfranchisement. [Rare.]

dis-en-gāġe′, *v.t.*; disengaged, *pt.*, *pp.*; disengaging, *ppr.* [OFr. *desengager*; *des-* priv., and *engager*, to promise, engage.]

1. To release or liberate from a promise or obligation; to set free by dissolving an engagement; as, the men who were enlisted are now *disengaged.*

2. To separate or free from an outward attachment, as a bird from a snare; to free or liberate from innate or chemical union; as, to *disengage* oxygen from water.

3. In fencing, to transpose the position of (the weapons used), so as to bring the advantage in favor of the one making the movement.

Syn.—Separate, liberate, free, loose, extricate, clear, disentangle, detach, withdraw, wean.

dis-en-gāġe′, *v.i.* To withdraw; to free oneself; as, we *disengage* reluctantly from old associations.

dis-en-gā′ġed-ness, *n.* The quality or state of being disengaged.

dis-en-gāġe′ment, *n.* 1. The state of being disengaged; the act of disengaging.

It is easy to render this *disengagement* of caloric and light evident to the senses.
—Lavoisier.

2. Freedom from attention; vacancy; leisure.

3. Tranquillity; graciousness; repose; as, the *disengagement* of one's bearing.

4. The move in fencing by which one disengages his weapon.

dis-en-nō′ble, *v.t.*; disennobled, *pt.*, *pp.*; disennobling, *ppr.* To deprive of title or that which ennobles.

dis-en-rōll′, *v.t.*; disenrolled, *pt.*, *pp.*; disenrolling, *ppr.* To erase from a roll or list; also spelled *disenrol.*

dis-en-san′i-ty, *n.* Lack of sanity. [Obs.]

dis-en-shroud′, *v.t.* To unveil. [Rare.]

dis-en-slāve′, *v.t.* To free, as from slavery. [Rare.]

dis-en-tāil′, *v.t.*; disentailed, *pt.*, *pp.*; disentailing, *ppr.* To cut off the entail of.

dis-en-tañ′gle, *v.t.*; disentangled, *pt.*, *pp.*; disentangling, *ppr.* 1. To unravel; to untwist; to loose, separate, or disconnect from being interwoven or united without order; as, to *disentangle* network; to *disentangle* a skein of yarn.

2. To free; to extricate from perplexity; to disengage from complications, to set free; to separate; as, to *disentangle* oneself from business, from political affairs, or from the cares and temptations of life.

To *disentangle* truth from error. —Stewart.

Syn.—Unravel, untwist, loosen, extricate, disembarrass, disembroil, clear, disengage, separate.

dis-en-tañ′gle-ment, *n.* A disentangling.

dis-en-tẽr′, *v.t.* Same as *Disinter.*

dis-en-thrạll′, *v.t.* To liberate from slavery, bondage, or servitude; to free or rescue from oppression; also spelled *disenthral.*

In straits and in distress
Thou didst me *disenthrall.* —Milton.

dis-en-thrạll′ment, *n.* The state of being disenthralled.

dis-en-thrōne′, *v.t.*; disenthroned, *pt.*, *pp.*; disenthroning, *ppr.* To dethrone; to depose from sovereign authority.

dis-en-tī′tle, *v.t.*; disentitled, *pt.*, *pp.*; disentitling, *ppr.* To deprive of title.

dis-en-tōmb′ (-tōm′), *v.t.* To remove from a tomb.

dis-en-trạil′, *v.t.* To deprive of the entrails or bowels; to disembowel; to draw forth. [Obs.]

dis-en-trȧnce′, *v.t.*; disentranced, *pt.*, *pp.*; disentrancing, *ppr.* To awaken from a trance, or from deep sleep; to arouse from a trance, sleep, or reverie.

dis-en-twīne′, *v.t.* To release from a twisted state.

dī-sep′ăl-ous, *a.* Furnished with two sepals.

dis-ẽrt′, *a.* Eloquent. [Obs.]

dis-es-pouṣe′, *v.t.* To separate after espousal or plighted faith; to divorce.

dis-es-tab′lish, *v.t.*; disestablished, *pt.*, *pp.*; disestablishing, *ppr.* 1. To remove from establishment; to cause to cease to be established; specifically, to withdraw, as a church, from its connection with the state.

2. To unsettle; to break up. [Obs.]

dis-es-tab′lish-ment, *n.* The act of depriving, or the condition of being deprived of the position and privileges of an established body; specifically, the act of withdrawing a church from its connection with the state.

dis-es-teem′, *n.* Want of esteem; slight dislike; disregard.

dis-es-teem′, *v.t.*; disesteemed, *pt.*, *pp.*; disesteeming, *ppr.* [OFr. *desestimer*; *des-* priv., and *estimer*, to esteem.]

1. To dislike in a moderate degree; to consider with disregard, disapprobation, dislike, or slight contempt; to slight.

2. To withdraw esteem from; to cause to be brought into disrepute. [Obs.]

dis-es-teem′ẽr, *n.* One who disesteems.

dis-es-ti-mā′tion, *n.* Disesteem; bad repute.

dis-ex′ẽr-ciṣe, *v.t.* To deprive of exercise. [Obs.]

dis-fāme′, *n.* Disesteem. [Rare.]

dis-fan′cy, *v.t.* To disapprove. [Obs.]

dis-fash′ion (-un), *v.t.* To injure or mar. [Obs.]

dis-fā′vŏr, *n.* [L. *dis-* priv., and *favor*, favor.]

1. Dislike; slight displeasure; discountenance; unfavorable regard; disesteem.

2. A state of unacceptableness; a state in which one is not esteemed or favored, or not patronized, promoted, or befriended; as, to be in *disfavor* at court.

3. An ill or disobliging act; as, no generous man will do a *disfavor* to the meanest of his fellows.

dis-fā′vŏr, *v.t.*; disfavored, *pt.*, *pp.*; disfavoring, *ppr.* 1. To discountenance; to withdraw or withhold from (one) kindness, friendship, or support; to check or oppose by disapprobation.

2. To mar; to deface. [Obs.]

dis-fā′vŏr-ȧ-ble, *a.* Not favorable. [Obs.]

dis-fā′vŏr-ȧ-bly, *adv.* Not favorably. [Obs.]

dis-fā′vŏr-ẽr, *n.* One who disfavors. [Obs.]

dis-fēa′tūre, *v.t.* To deprive of features; to disfigure. [Rare.]

dis-fel′lōw-ship, *v.t.*; disfellowshiped, *pt.*, *pp.*; disfellowshiping, *ppr.* To refuse to associate with; used particularly in reference to church fellowship or communion.

dis-fig-ū-rā′tion, *n.* 1. The act of disfiguring, or marring external form.

2. The state of being disfigured; some degree of deformity.

dis-fig′ūre, *v.t.*; disfigured, *pt.*, *pp.*; disfiguring, *ppr.* [ME. *disfiguren*; OFr. *desfigurer*; L. *dis-* priv., and *figurare*, to fashion, form, from *figura*, figure.] To change to a worse form; to impair, as shape or form; to mar; to injure the beauty, symmetry, or excellence of.

Syn.—Deface, botch, injure, mar.

dis-fig′ūre, *n.* A deformity. [Obs.]

dis-fig′ūre-ment, *n.* 1. Change of external form for the worse; defacement of beauty.

2. Anything that disfigures or defaces.

dis-fig′ūr-ẽr, *n.* One who disfigures.

dis-flesh′, *v.t.* To take off flesh from. [Obs.]

dis-for′est, *v.t.*; disforested, *pt.*, *pp.*; disforesting, *ppr.* 1. Same as *Disafforest.*

2. To clear of timber or forest.

dis-for-es-tā′tion, *n.* The act of disforesting a piece of land.

dis-fọrm′i-ty, *n.* The state of being different or unlike in form. [Obs.]

dis-frȧn′chiṣe, *v.t.*; disfranchised, *pt.*, *pp.*; disfranchising, *ppr.* To deprive of the rights and privileges of a free citizen; to deprive of chartered rights and immunities; to deprive of any franchise, as of the right of voting in elections, etc.

dis-frȧn′chiṣe-ment, *n.* The act of disfranchising, or depriving of the privileges of a free citizen or of some particular immunity.

dis-frī′ăr, *v.t.* To unfrock; to depose from a friarship. [Obs.]

dis-frock′, *v.t.* To unfrock.

dis-fūr′nish, *v.t.*; disfurnished, *pt.*, *pp.*; disfurnishing, *ppr.* To deprive of furniture; to strip of apparatus, habiliments, or equipage.

dis-fūr′nish-ment, *n.* The state of being disfurnished.

dis-fūr′ni-tūre, *v.t.* Disfurnish. [Rare.]

dis-gāġe′, *v.t.* To redeem from pawn. [Obs.]

dis-gal′lănt, *v.t.* To deprive of gallantry. [Obs.]

dis-gär′lănd, *v.t.* To divest of a garland. [Rare.]

Thy locks *disgarland.* —Drummond.

dis-gär′nish, *v.t.* To divest of garniture or ornaments; to degarnish. [Rare.]

dis-gar′ri-sŏn, *v.t.* To deprive of a garrison. [Rare.]

dis-gav′el, *v.t.*; disgaveled *or* disgavelled, *pt.*, *pp.*; disgaveling *or* disgavelling, *ppr.* In English law, to take away the tenure of gavelkind from; said of land.

dis-ġē-ner′ic, *a.* Of different genera than another species; opposite of *congeneric.*

dis-ġest′, *v.t.* Digest. [Obs.]

dis-ġes′tion (-chun), *n.* Digestion. [Obs.]

dis-glō′ri-fȳ, *v.t.* To dishonor; to treat with disrespect. [Rare.]

dis-glō′ry, *n.* Disrespect; dishonor. [Obs.]

dis-gọrġe′, *v.t.*; disgorged, *pt.*, *pp.*; disgorging, *ppr.* [OFr. *desgorger*; *des-*, from, and *gorge*, throat.]

1. To eject or discharge from the stomach, throat, or mouth; to vomit.

2. To throw out with violence; to discharge violently or in great quantities from a confined place; as, volcanoes *disgorge* streams of burning lava, ashes, and stones.

3. To yield up or give back (what had been seized upon as one's own); as, to *disgorge* his ill-gotten gains.

dis-gọrġe′, *v.i.* 1. To vomit.

2. To make restitution.

dis-gọrġe′ment, *n.* The act of disgorging.

dis-gos′pel, *v.i.* To differ from the precepts of the gospel. [Obs.]

dis-grāce′, *n.* [OFr. *disgrace*, disgrace, disfavor; L. *dis-* priv., and *gratia*, favor.]

1. A state of being out of favor; disfavor; disesteem; as, the minister retired from court in *disgrace.*

2. A state of ignominy; dishonor; shame.

3. A cause of shame; as, to turn the back to the enemy is a foul *disgrace*; every vice is a *disgrace.*

4. An act of unkindness. [Obs.]

Syn.—Ignominy, dishonor, shame, infamy, opprobrium, humiliation, blemish.

dis-grāce′, *v.t.*; disgraced, *pt.*, *pp.*; disgracing, *ppr.* 1. To put out of favor; to dismiss in dishonor; as, the officer was *disgraced* for his treachery.

2. To bring to shame; to dishonor; to sink in estimation; as, men often boast of actions which *disgrace* them.

3. To revile; to reproach. [Obs.]

Syn.—Abase, degrade, humiliate, defame, humble, dishonor.

dis-grāce′fụl, *a.* Shameful; reproachful; dishonorable; bringing shame or disgrace; as, cowardice is *disgraceful* to a soldier.

dis-grāce′fụl-ly, *adv.* With disgrace; shamefully; reproachfully; ignominiously; in a disgraceful manner; as, the troops fled *disgracefully.*

dis-grāce′fụl-ness, *n.* Ignominy; shamefulness.

dis-grā′cẽr, *n.* One who disgraces; one who exposes to disgrace; one who brings into disgrace, shame, or contempt.

dis-grā′cious, *a.* Ungracious; unpleasant. [Obs.]

dis-grā′cive, *a.* Disgraceful. [Obs.]

dis-grā-dā′tion, *n.* In Scots law, degradation; deposition; specifically, the stripping of a person of a dignity or degree of honor, and taking away the title, badge, and privileges thereof.

dis-grāde′, dis-grad′ū-āte, *v.t.* To degrade. [Obs.]

dis′grē-gāte, *v.t.* To separate; to disperse. [Obs.]

dis-grē-gā′tion, *n.* Separation; dissociation; specifically, in chemistry, decomposition.

dis-grun′tle, *v.t.* To chagrin; to disappoint; to make sulky; to vex. [Colloq.]

dis-guiṣe′, *v.t.*; disguised, *pt.*, *pp.*; disguising, *ppr.* [ME. *disguisen*; OFr. *desguiser*, to counterfeit, disguise; *des-* priv., and *guise*, manner, fashion.]

1. To conceal by an unusual habit or mask; as, *disguised* for criminal purposes.

2. To hide by a counterfeit appearance; to cloak by a false show, by false language, or an artificial manner; as, to *disguise* anger, sentiments, or intentions.

3. To disfigure; to alter the form of; to cause to exhibit an unusual appearance.

They saw the faces, which too well they knew,
Though then *disguised* in death. —Dryden.

4. To disfigure or deform by liquor; to intoxicate.

Syn.—Mask, dissemble, hide, change, conceal, feign, pretend.

dis-guiṣe′, *n.* 1. That which disguises or makes recognition difficult; any deceptive dress, action, manner, or speech; as, treachery is often concealed under the *disguise* of great candor.

2. The act of disguising or the state of being disguised; as, a detective in *disguise.*

3. A masquerade. [Obs.]

4. Change of manner by drink; intoxication.

dis-guiṣ′ed-ly, *adv.* In disguise. [Rare.]

dis-guiṣ′ed-ness, *n.* The state of being disguised. [Rare.]

dis-guiṣe′ment, *n.* The act of disguising; a disguise. [Rare.]

dis-guiṣ′ēr, *n.* 1. One who conceals another by a disguise; a disfigurer.

Death's a great *disguiser*. —Shak.

2. One who assumes a disguise.

You are a very dexterous *disguiser*.—Swift.

3. A masker. [Obs.]

dis-guiṣ′ing, *n.* 1. The act of giving a false appearance.

2. Theatrical mummery or masking. [Obs.]

dis-gust′, *n.* 1. Disrelish; distaste; aversion to the taste of food or drink; an unpleasant sensation excited in the organs of taste by something disagreeable, and, when extreme, producing loathing or nausea.

2. Dislike; aversion; an unpleasant sensation in the mind, excited by something offensive in the manners, conduct, language, or opinions of others; as, obscenity in language excites *disgust*.

Syn.—Abhorrence, loathing, nausea, aversion, antipathy, dislike, distaste.

dis-gust′, *v.t.*; disgusted, *pt.*, *pp.*; disgusting, *ppr.* [OFr. *desgouster*; L. *dis-* priv., and *gustare*, to taste, from *gustus*, a tasting.]

1. To excite aversion in the stomach of; to offend the taste of.

2. To displease; to offend the mind or moral taste of; with *at* or *with*; as, to be *disgusted at* foppery or *with* vulgar manners.

dis-gust′fụl, *a.* Offensive to the taste; nauseous; exciting aversion in the natural or moral taste.

dis-gust′fụl-ness, *n.* The condition of being disgustful.

dis-gust′ing, *a.* Causing disgust; offensive.

dis-gust′ing-ly, *adv.* In a disgusting manner.

dish, *n.* [ME. *dissh*, *disch*; AS. *disc*, a dish, plate, from L. *discus*, Gr. *diskos*, a discus, disk, a round plate, a trencher.]

1. Any vessel, concave or hollow in form, made of a variety of materials, and used at table for holding food; by extension, in the plural, such vessels as are commonly included in the preparation and consumption of a meal; as, a set of *dishes*; a device for washing *dishes*.

2. The food served in a *dish*; as, a *dish* of berries.

3. Concavity; *dish*-shape; used especially in tire-setting; as, the *dish* of a wagon-wheel.

4. In English mining, a measuring-trough, the inside dimensions of which are 4x6x28 inches.

5. In agriculture, a concavity in land in which water settles.

6. Anciently, a discus.

dish, *v.t.*; dished (disht), *pt.*, *pp.*; dishing, *ppr.* 1. To serve (food) at table by putting in a dish or dishes; often with *up* or *out*; as, to *dish up* the dessert; to *dish out* sherbet.

2. To give a dish or concavity to; said especially in tire-setting.

3. To cheat; to ruin; to play out; as, the hot weather about *dished* me. [Slang.]

Where's Brummell? *Dished*. —Byron.

To dish out; in architecture, to make a gutter in.

dish, *v.i.* To be or become concave like a dish; as, the ground *dished*.

dis-ha-bil′i-tāte, *v.t.* To disqualify. [Rare.]

dis-ha-bïlle′ (dis-a-bēl′), *n.* [Fr. *déshabillé*, undress, a morning-wrapper, from pp. of *déshabiller*, to undress.] Undress; implying looseness or carelessness of attire, or both.

We have a kind of sketch of dress among us, called a *dishabille*. —Guardian.

dis-hab′it, *v.t.* To drive from a habitation. [Obs.]

dis-ha-bit′ū-āte, *v.t.* To make strange or unaccustomed.

dis-hā′ble, *v.t.* 1. To disable. [Obs.]

2. To belittle. [Obs.]

dis-hal′lōw, *v.t.* To desecrate; to render unholy.

dis-här-mō′ni-ous, *a.* Incongruous. [Obs.]

dis-här′mo-ny, *n.* Want of harmony; discord; incongruity. [Obs.]

dis-haunt′, *v.t.* To cease to haunt or frequent. [Obs.]

dish′çlọth, *n.* A cloth used for washing dishes; a dishrag.

dish′çlout, *n.* A dishrag.

dis-heärt′, *v.t.* [Obs.] See *Dishearten*.

dis-heärt′en, *v.t.*; disheartened, *pt.*, *pp.*; disheartening, *ppr.* To discourage; to deprive of courage; to depress the spirits of; to deject; to impress with fear; as, it is weakness to be *disheartened* by small obstacles.

dis-heärt′en-ment, *n.* Lack of courage or spirit; dejection.

dis-heir′ (-âr′), *v.t.* To debar from inheriting. [Obs.]

dis-helm′, *v.t.* To divest of a helmet.

Dishelmed and mute, and motionlessly pale. —Tennyson.

dis-her′i-ṣŏn, *n.* [OFr. *desheritison*, disinheritance; L. *dis-* priv., and *heres* (*heredis*), an heir.] The act of disinheriting, or cutting off from inheritance.

dis-her′it, *v.t.* To disinherit. [Obs.]

dis-her′it-ānce, *n.* Disinheritance. [Obs.]

dis-her′it-ŏr, *n.* One who disinherits or deprives another of an inheritance.

di-shev′el, *v.t.*; disheveled *or* dishevelled, *pt.*, *pp.*; disheveling *or* dishevelling, *ppr.* [ME. *dischevelen*; OFr. *descheveler*, to tear, pull, or disorder the hair, dishevel; L. *dis-*, apart, and *capillus*, hair.] To cause to have a disordered, neglected, or careless appearance; originally said of the hair, but now often said of the clothing; used chiefly in the past participle and adjectively.

di-shev′el, *v.i.* To be in disorder; to be spread out carelessly, as the hair. [Rare.]

di-shev′ele, di-shev′el-y, *a.* Disheveled. [Obs.]

dish′-fāced (-fāst), *a.* 1. Having a round, flat face, shaped like an inverted plate; said of persons.

2. Having the nasal bone higher at the nose than at the depression where it joins the cranial bone; said of dogs.

dish′fụl, *n.* The amount which a dish can hold.

dish′ing, *a.* Concave; having the hollow form of a dish.

dis-hon′est (-on′est), *a.* [ME. *dishonest*; OFr. *deshoneste*, dishonest; L. *dis-* priv., and *honestus*, honest.]

1. Void of honesty; destitute of probity, integrity, or good faith; faithless; fraudulent; knavish; having or exercising a disposition to deceive, cheat, and defraud; as, a *dishonest* man.

2. Proceeding from fraud, or marked by it; fraudulent; knavish; as, a *dishonest* transaction.

3. Disgraced; dishonored. [Obs.]

Dishonest with lopped arms the youth appears. —Dryden.

4. Disgraceful; ignominious. [Obs.]

Inglorious triumphs and *dishonest* scars. —Pope.

5. Unchaste; lewd. [Obs.]

Syn.—Unfaithful, faithless, fraudulent, knavish, perfidious.

dis-hon′est, *v.t.* To bring dishonor or disgrace to. [Obs.]

dis-hon′est-ly (-on′est-ly), *adv.* In a dishonest manner.

dis-hon′es-ty (-on′es-ty), *n.* 1. The quality of being dishonest; want of probity, or integrity in principle; faithlessness; a disposition to cheat or defraud, or to deceive and betray.

2. Violation of trust or of justice; fraud; treachery; any deviation from probity or integrity.

3. Unchastity; incontinence; lewdness. [Obs.]

dis-hon′ŏr, dis-hon′oûr (-on′ūr), *n.* [ME. *deshonour*; OFr. *deshonor*, dishonor, disgrace, from L. *dis-* priv., and *honor*, honor.]

1. Reproach; disgrace; ignominy; shame; whatever constitutes a stain or blemish on the reputation.

It was not meet for us to see the king's *dishonor*. —Ezra iv. 14.

2. In commerce, the failure or refusal of the drawee or acceptor of commercial paper to accept it or to pay it, when presented or due.

Syn.—Ignominy, blemish, opprobrium, disgrace, shame, censure, disrespect.

dis-hon′ŏr, *v.t.*; dishonored, *pt.*, *pp.*; dishonoring, *ppr.* 1. To disgrace; to bring reproach or shame on; to stain the character of; to lessen the reputation of.

2. To treat with indignity.

3. To violate the chastity of; to debauch.

4. To refuse or decline to accept or pay; as, to *dishonor* a bill of exchange.

Syn.—Disgrace, shame, abase, disparage, degrade, seduce, ravish.

dis-hon′ŏr-ȧ-ble, *a.* 1. Shameful; reproachful; base; vile; bringing shame on; staining the character, and lessening reputation; as, every act of meanness and every vice is *dishonorable*.

2. Destitute of honor; as, a *dishonorable* man.

3. In a state of neglect or disesteem. [Rare.]

He that is *dishonorable* in riches, how much more in poverty! —Eccles. x. 31.

dis-hon′ŏr-ȧ-ble-ness, *n.* The quality of being dishonorable.

dis-hon′ŏr-ȧ-bly, *adv.* In a dishonorable manner.

dis-hon′ŏr-ā-ry, *a.* Bringing dishonor on; tending to disgrace; lessening reputation.

dis-hon′ŏr-ēr, *n.* One who dishonors or disgraces; one who treats another with indignity.

dis-hôrn′, *v.t.* To deprive of horns.

dis-hôrse′, *v.t.*; dishorsed, *pt.*, *pp.*; dishorsing, *ppr.* To unhorse.

dis-hôrse′, *v.i.* To dismount.

dis-house′, *v.t.* To dislodge; to take away the house or home of. [Rare.]

dish′rag, *n.* A rag or cloth with which to wash dishes; a dishcloth.

dis-hū′mŏr, *n.* Peevishness; ill humor. [Obs.]

dis-hū′mŏr, *v.t.* To put out of humor; to disgruntle. [Obs.]

dish′wäsh″ēr, *n.* 1. One who or that which washes dishes.

2. A bird, the pied wagtail. [Prov. Eng.]

dish′wạ-tēr, *n.* The water in which dishes have been or are to be washed.

dis-il-lū′ṣion, *n.* The act of freeing from an illusion; the state of being free from illusion; disenchantment.

dis-il-lū′ṣion, *v.t.* To free from that which deludes or is illusory.

dis-il-lū′ṣion-īze, *v.t.* To disillusion.

dis-il-lū′ṣion-ment, *n.* The state of being disillusioned; the act of disillusioning.

dis-im-bit′tēr, *v.t.* To disembitter.

dis-im-pärk′, *v.t.* To free from the barriers of a park; to free from restraints or seclusion. [Rare.]

dis-im-pas′sioned, *a.* Unimpassioned; calm; tranquil.

dis-im-prōve′, *v.t.* To make poorer in quality. [Rare.]

dis-im-prōve′, *v.i.* To deteriorate. [Rare.]

dis-im-prōve′ment, *n.* Reduction from a better to a worse state; as, the *disimprovement* of the earth. [Rare.]

dis-in-cär′cēr-āte, *v.t.* To liberate from prison; to set free from confinement. [Rare.]

dis-in-çli-nā′tion, *n.* Want of inclination; want of propensity, desire, or affection; slight dislike; aversion.

Disappointment gave him a *disinclination* to the fair sex. —Arbuthnot.

Syn.—Unwillingness, dislike, aversion, repugnance.

dis-in-çlīne′, *v.t.*; disinclined, *pt.*, *pp.*; disinclining, *ppr.* To excite dislike or aversion in; to make disaffected; to alienate from; as, his timidity *disinclined* him from such an arduous enterprise.

dis-in-çlōṣe′, *v.t.*; disinclosed, *pt.*, *pp.*; disinclosing, *ppr.* To open (an inclosure); to throw open (what has been inclosed); to dispark.

dis-in-çor′pō-rāte, *v.t.*; disincorporated, *pt.*, *pp.*; disincorporating, *ppr.* 1. To deprive of corporate powers; to disunite (a corporate body or an established society).

2. To detach or separate from a corporation or society.

dis-in-çor′pō-rāte, *a.* Disincorporated; separated from or not included in a body or society. [Obs.]

dis-in-çor-pō-rā′tion, *n.* Deprivation of the rights and privileges of a corporation.

dis-in-çrust′ānt, *n.* That which prevents the formation of crust or scale in boilers.

dis-in-feçt′, *v.t.*; disinfected, *pt.*, *pp.*; disinfecting, *ppr.* To cleanse from infection; to purify; to destroy putrefaction in.

dis-in-feçt′ānt, *a.* and *n.* I. *a.* Disinfecting.

II. *n.* An agent for destroying disease-germs, or arresting fermentation or decay.

dis-in-feç′tion, *n.* Purification from that which infects.

dis-in-feçt′ŏr, *n.* One who or that which disinfects; a disinfecting apparatus.

dis-in-flāme′, *v.t.* To deprive of flame. [Obs.]

dis-in-ġe-nū′i-ty, *n.* Disingenuousness. [Obs.]

dis-in-ġen′ū-ous, *a.* Not ingenuous; not open, frank, and candid; unfair; meanly artful; underhanded.

Persons entirely *disingenuous* who really do not believe the opinions they defend. —Hume.

Syn.—Unfair, uncandid, insincere, hollow, crafty, sly, cunning.

dis-in-ġen′ū-ous-ly, *adv.* In a disingenuous manner.

dis-in-ġen′ū-ous-ness, *n.* Unfairness; want of candor; low craft.

dis-in-hab′it-ed, *a.* Deprived of inhabitants. [Obs.]

dis-in-her′i-ṣŏn (-z′n), *n.* 1. The act of cutting off from hereditary succession; the act of disinheriting.

2. The state of being disinherited.

dis-in-her′it, *v.t.*; disinherited, *pt.*, *pp.*; disinheriting, *ppr.* To cut off from hereditary right; to deprive of an inheritance; to prevent, as an heir, from coming into possession of any property or right which by law or custom would devolve on him in the course of descent; as, a father sometimes *disinherits* his children by will.

dis-in-her′it-ānce, *n.* The act of disinheriting or the state of being disinherited; disherison.

dis-in-hūme′, *v.t.* To disinter. [Rare.]

dis-in-sūre′, *v.t.* To render unsafe; to place in danger. [Obs.]

dis-in′tē-grȧ-ble, *a.* Capable of disintegration.

dis-in′tē-grāte, *v.t.*; disintegrated, *pt.*, *pp.*; disintegrating, *ppr.* [*Dis-* priv., and L. *integratus*, pp. of *integrare*, to renew, repair, from *integer*, whole.] To separate the integrant parts of; to cause to decompose into integrant parts; to reduce to powder.

dis-in′tē-grāte, *v.i.* To fall to pieces; to become reduced to powder; to crumble.

dis-in-tē-grā′tion, *n.* The act of separating the component particles of a substance, as distinguished from decomposition or the separation of its elements; specifically, in geology, the breaking up of rocks by natural causes, as by the action of frost.

dis-in′tē-grāt-ŏr, *n.* One who or that which disintegrates; specifically, in mechanics, a crusher or stamper used for breaking up ore.

dis-in-tẽr′, *v.t.*; disinterred, *pt.*, *pp.*; disinterring, *ppr.* [L. *dis-* priv., and LL. *interrare*, to inter, from L. *in*, in, and *terra*, earth.]

1. To take out of a grave or out of the earth; as, to *disinter* a dead body.

2. To take out, as from a grave; to bring from obscurity into view.

The philosopher may be concealed in a plebeian, which a proper education might have *disinterred*. —Addison.

dis-in′tẽr-ess, *v.t.* To disinterest. [Obs.]

dis-in′tẽr-ess-ment, *n.* Disinterestedness. [Obs.]

dis-in′tẽr-est, *a.* Disinterested. [Obs.]

dis-in′tẽr-est, *n.* 1. What is contrary to the interest or advantage; disadvantage; injury. [Obs.]

2. Indifference to profit; want of regard to private advantage. [Obs.]

dis-in′tẽr-est, *v.t.* To disengage from private interest or personal advantage. [Obs.]

dis-in′tẽr-est-ed, *a.* Having no separate personal interest or private advantage in a question or affair; uninterested; unbiased; free from partiality or unfairness; as, a *disinterested* arbitrator.

Every true patriot is *disinterested*.—Whately.

Syn.—Unbiased, impartial, uninterested, indifferent, generous, unselfish, magnanimous.

dis-in′tẽr-est-ed-ly, *adv.* In a disinterested manner.

dis-in′tẽr-est-ed-ness, *n.* The state or quality of being disinterested.

dis-in′tẽr-est-ing, *a.* Uninteresting. [Obs.]

dis-in-tẽr′ment, *n.* The act of disinterring or taking out of the earth.

dis-in-thrạl′, dis-in-thrạll′, *v.t.* To disenthrall. [Obs.]

dis-in-thrạl′ment, *n.* Disenthralment. [Obs.]

dis-in′tri-cāte, *v.t.* To free of intricacy. [Rare.]

dis-in-ūre′, *v.t.* To deprive of familiarity or custom. [Obs.]

dis-in-va-lid′i-ty, *n.* Want of validity. [Obs.]

dis-in-ves′ti-tūre, *n.* The act of depriving of investiture; the state of being deprived of investiture. [Rare.]

dis-in-vig′ŏr-āte, *v.t.* To weaken; to deprive of force or strength. [Rare.]

dis-in-vīte′, *v.t.* To recall an invitation to. [Obs.]

dis-in-volve′, *v.t.* To uncover; to unfold or unroll; to disentangle. [Rare.]

dis-jec′tion, *n.* The act of overthrowing or dissipating. [Obs.]

dis-join′, *v.t.*; disjoined, *pt.*, *pp.*; disjoining, *ppr.* [L. *disjungere*, to separate; *dis-*, apart, and *jungere*, to join.] To part; to disunite; to separate; to sunder.

dis-join′, *v.i.* To become separated; to part.

dis-joint′, *v.t.*; disjointed, *pt.*, *pp.*; disjointing, *ppr.* 1. To separate a joint of; to separate parts of, united by joints; as, to *disjoint* the limbs; to *disjoint* bones; to *disjoint* a fowl in carving.

2. To put out of joint; to force out of its socket; to dislocate.

3. To break in pieces; to separate the united parts of, as, to *disjoint* an edifice.

4. To break the natural order and relations of; to make incoherent.

dis-joint′, *v.i.* To fall in pieces.

dis-joint′, *a.* Disjointed. [Obs.]

dis-joint′, *n.* A difficult situation. [Obs.]

dis-joint′ed, *a.* Separated at the joints; parted limb from limb; carved; put out of joint; not coherent.

dis-joint′ed-ly, *adv.* In a disjointed manner.

dis-joint′ed-ness, *n.* The state of being disjointed.

dis-joint′ly, *adv.* In a divided state.

dis-jū-di-cā′tion, *n.* Judgment; determination. [Obs.]

dis-junct′, *a.* [L. *disjunctus*, pp. of *disjungere*, to disjoin, separate.]

1. Disjoined; separated.

2. In entomology, a term applied to an insect having the head, thorax, and abdomen separated by a deep incision.

Disjunct tetrachords; in music, tetrachords having such a relation to each other that the lowest interval of the upper is one note above the highest interval of the other.

dis-junc′tion, *n.* 1. The act of disjoining; disunion; separation; a parting; as, the *disjunction* of soul and body.

2. A disjunctive proposition. [Rare.]

dis-junc′tive, *a.* [LL. *disjunctivus*, from L. *disjunctus*, pp. of *disjungere*, to disjoin, separate; *dis-*, apart, and *jungere*, to join.]

1. Separating; disjoining.

2. Incapable of union. [Rare.]

3. In grammar, marking separation or opposition; a term applied to a word or particle which unites sentences or the parts of discourse in construction, but disjoins the sense; as, I love him, *or* I fear him; I neither love him *nor* fear him.

4. In logic, a term applied to a proposition in which the parts are opposed to each other by means of disjunctives; as, it is either day or night; a term applied to a syllogism in which the major proposition is disjunctive; as, the earth moves in a circle or an ellipsis; but it does not move in a circle, therefore it moves in an ellipsis.

5. In music, pertaining to disjunct tetrachords; as, a *disjunctive* interval.

dis-junc′tive, *n.* 1. In grammar, a word that disjoins, as *or*, *nor*, *neither*.

2. In logic, a disjunctive proposition.

dis-junc′tive-ly, *adv.* In a disjunctive manner; separately.

dis-junc′tūre, *n.* Separation.

disk, disc, *n.* [L. *discus*; Gr. *diskos*, a discus, dish, trencher, disk.]

1. A quoit. [See *Discus*.]

2. Anything having a flat surface and circular or nearly so in form; specifically, in mechanics, a thin circular plate; also used attributively; as, a *disk* pulverizer; a *disk* crank.

Disk-bearing Wood-cells.

3. In botany, (a) one of the rings of the woody fiber of certain trees, as conifers, visible in a longitudinal section of the wood; (b) the surface of an organ, as a leaf or petal; opposed to *margin*; (c) the convex center (sometimes the whole head) of composite flowers exclusive of the rays; (d) an expanded receptacle, commonly a nectary, taking a variety of forms; an epigynous *disk* being on the summit of an inferior ovary; an hypogynous *disk* under the ovary; while a perigynous *disk* is formed by fleshy matter on the inner wall of the calyx.

Flower of Common Daisy (*Bellis perennis*). *rr*, Rays. *d*, Disk.

4. In zoölogy, any discoid part; a discus; as, (a) a surface used for locomotion or for attachment, such as creeping- or sucking-*disks*; (b) the area about the mouth of certain of the *Cœlentera*; (c) the set of feathers extending radially from about the eye of an owl; (d) the space in a bivalve shell included between the margin and the umbo.

Epigynous and Hypogynous Disks.—A, Umbelliferous flower: *d*, Disk; *o*, Ovary. B, Flower of the orange family: *d*, Disk; *o*, Ovary.

Arago disk; a disk of non-magnetic metal, which, when rapidly rotated under a free magnetic needle, causes its deflection or rotation.

disk′-ar″mà-tūre, *n.* An armature consisting of thin, flat coils mounted on the periphery of a thin disk. The advantages of this over other forms are freedom from hysteresis and eddy current losses.

disk′-coup″ling (-kup″), *n.* A kind of permanent coupling consisting of two disks keyed on the connected ends of the two shafts. In one of the disks are two recesses, into which two corresponding projections on the other disk are received, and thus the two disks become locked together. This kind of coupling wants rigidity, and must be supported by a journal on each side, but it possesses the double advantage of being easily adjusted and disconnected.

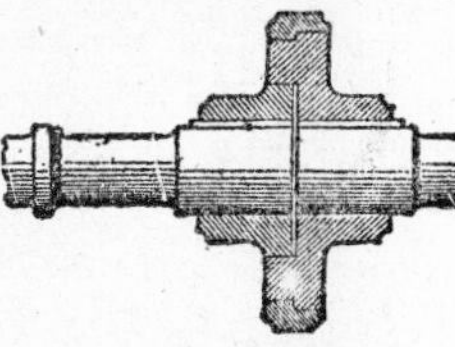

Disk-coupling.

dis-kind′ness, *n.* Unkindness; an ill turn. [Rare.]

disk′less, *a.* Without a disk or disks; said of a star appearing as a point when viewed through a telescope.

dis-lāde′, *v.t.* To unload. [Obs.]

dis-lēal′, *a.* Disloyal. [Obs.]

dis-lēave′, *v.t.* To rid of leaves. [Rare.]

dis-līke′, *n.* 1. Disapprobation; disinclination; displeasure; aversion; a moderate degree of hatred.

You discover not only your *dislike* of another, but of himself. —Addison.

Our likings and *dislikes* are founded rather upon fancy than upon reason.—L'Estrange.

2. Discord; disagreement. [Obs.]

A murmur rose
That showed *dislike* among the Christian peers. —Fairfax.

Syn.—Disapprobation, disinclination, displeasure, disrelish, distaste, aversion, antipathy, repugnance, disgust.

dis-līke′, *v.t.*; disliked (-līkt), *pt.*, *pp.*; disliking, *ppr.* 1. To disapprove of; to regard with some aversion or displeasure; to disrelish; as, we *dislike* proceedings which we deem wrong; we *dislike* persons of evil habits.

2. To displease.

I'll do't; but it *dislikes* me. —Shak.

3. To express disapprobation of. [Obs.]

dis-līke′ful, *a.* Disaffected. [Obs.]

dis-līke′li-hood, *n.* The state of being improbable.

dis-līk′en, *v.t.* To make unlike. [Obs.]

dis-līke′ness, *n.* Unlikeness; want of resemblance; dissimilitude.

dis-līk′ẽr, *n.* One who disapproves or disrelishes.

dis-limb′ (-lim′), *v.t.* To tear the limbs from.

dis-limn′ (-lim′), *v.t.* To destroy the outlines of; to obliterate; to efface; to cause to vanish. [Obs.]

dis-link′, *v.t.* To separate. [Rare.]

dis-live′, *v.t.* To kill. [Obs.]

dis′lō-cāte, *v.t.*; dislocated, *pt.*, *pp.*; dislocating, *ppr.* [LL. *dislocatus*, pp. of *dislocare*, to dislocate; L. *dis-* priv., and *locare*, to place, from *locus*, place.] To displace; to put out of its proper place; particularly, to put out of joint; to disjoint; to move (a bone) from its socket, cavity, or place of articulation.

dis-lō-cā′tion, *n.* 1. The act of moving from its proper place; particularly, the act of removing or forcing a bone from its socket; luxation.

2. The state of being displaced.

3. A joint displaced.

4. In geology, the displacement of parts of rocks, or portions of strata, from the situations which they originally occupied.

dis-lodge′ (-loj′), *v.t.*; dislodged, *pt.*, *pp.*; dislodging, *ppr.* [OFr. *desloger*; *des-* priv., and *loger*, to lodge; L. *dis-* priv., and LL. *lobia*, a gallery, lobby.]

1. To remove or drive from a lodge or place of rest; to drive from the place where a thing naturally rests or inhabits.

The shellfish resident in the depths are never *dislodged* by storms. —Woodward.

2. To drive from any place of hiding or defence, or from any station; as, to *dislodge* the enemy from their quarters, from a hill, or wall.

dis-lodge′, *v.i.* To go from a place of rest. [Rare.]

dis-lodge′, *n.* A lodging apart. [Rare.]

dis-lodg′ment (-loj′), *n.* The act of dislodging.

dis-loign′ (-loin′), *v.t.* To remove. [Obs.]

dis-loy′ăl, *a.* Not true to allegiance; false to any government, movement, principle, or obligation to which one should give support; exhibiting neglect or treachery where support is due; as, a *disloyal* citizen; a *disloyal* disciple; a *disloyal* wife.

Syn.—Faithless, false, treacherous, perfidious, dishonest, inconstant.

dis-loy′ăl-ly, *adv.* In a disloyal manner.

dis-loy′ăl-ty, *n.* Lack of loyalty.

dis-māil′, *v.t.* To remove a coat of mail from.

diṣ′măl, *a.*; *comp.* dismaller; *superl.* dismallest. [ME. *dismal*, *disemal*, *dysmall*, dismal; origin uncertain, perhaps originally signifying a decimal or tithing day, when tithes were to be collected by the feudal lords, from OFr. *disme*, a tithe; L. *decimus*, a tenth, from *decem*, ten.] Having or exhibiting depression, melancholy, or gloom; lacking cheer; presaging ill; characterized by darkness or dolefulness; as, a *dismal* appearance; *dismal* prospects.

The very *dismallest* of all the entertainments which Amelia had in her honeymoon. —Thackeray.

Syn.—Dreary, gloomy, dark, doleful, horrid, dire, direful, frightful, horrible, lamentable, dolorous, calamitous, sorrowful, sad, melancholy, unfortunate, unhappy.

diṣ′măl, *n.* 1. The dismal or tithing day. [Obs.]

2. Satan. [Obs.]

3. [*pl.*] Mourning-garb; weeds. [Obs.]

4. [*pl.*] Mental depression; the blues; dumps; as, in the *dismals*.

5. A peat-swamp or bog; a term used in southern United States.

diṣ′măl-ly, *adv.* In a dismal manner.

diṣ′măl-ness, *n.* The state or quality of being dismal.

dis-man′, *v.t.* 1. To unman. [Obs.]
2. To exterminate or remove the men of; as, to *disman* a province.

dis-man′tle, *v.t.*; dismantled, *pt., pp.*; dismantling, *ppr.* [OFr. *desmanteller*, to take off one's cloak, to raze or beat down the wall of a fortress; L. *dis-* priv., and *mantellum*, a cloak.]
1. To deprive of dress; to strip; to divest. [Obs.]
2. To loose; to throw open. [Rare.]
3. To destroy. [Obs.]
4. To strip or deprive of accessory or essential parts; to remove the furniture, accouterments, or rigging of; as, to *dismantle* a house, ship, cannon, etc.

dis-märch′, *v.i.* To march out or away. [Obs.]

dis-mar′ry, *v.t.* To divorce. [Obs.]

dis-mär′shȧl, *v.t.* To derange or throw into disorder. [Rare.]

dis-mȧsk′, *v.t.* To strip off, as a mask; to uncover; to remove, as that which conceals. [Obs.]

dis-mȧst′, *v.t.*; dismasted, *pt., pp.*; dismasting, *ppr.* To deprive of a mast or masts; to break and carry away the masts from; as, a storm *dismasted* the ship.

dis-mȧst′ment, *n.* The act of dismasting; the state of being dismasted. [Rare.]

dis-maw′, *v.t.* To disgorge. [Rare.]

dis-māy′, *v.t.*; dismayed, *pt., pp.*; dismaying, *ppr.* [ME. *dismayen*, from *dis-* priv., and O.H.G. *magan*, to have power, be strong.]
1. To deprive of that strength or firmness of mind which constitutes courage; to discourage; to dishearten; to sink or depress in spirits or resolution; hence, to affright or terrify.

> Be strong, and of a good courage; be not afraid, neither be thou *dismayed*.—Josh. i. 9.

2. To subdue; to defeat. [Obs.]
3. To disquiet. [Obs.]
Syn.—Terrify, fright, affright, frighten, appal, daunt, dishearten, dispirit, discourage, deject, depress.

dis-māy′, *v.i.* To have or exhibit dismay; to fear.

> *Dismay* not, princes, at this accident. —Shak.

dis-māy′, *n.* 1. Fall or loss of courage; a sinking of the spirits; depression; dejection; a yielding to fear; that loss of firmness which is effected by fear or terror; fear impressed; terror felt.

> And each
> In other's countenance read his own *dismay*. —Milton.

2. Ruin; defeat; destruction. [Obs.]

> Like as a ship, whom cruell tempest drives
> Upon a rocke with horrible *dismay*. —Spenser.

Syn.—Dejection, discouragement, depression, fear, fright, terror.

dis-māy′ed-ness, *n.* A state of being dismayed; dejection of courage; dispiritedness. [Obs.]

dis-māy′fụl, *a.* Dreadful.

disme (dēm), *n.* [Obs.] See *Dime.*

dis-mem′bẽr, *v.t.*; dismembered, *pt., pp.*; dismembering, *ppr.* 1. To divide limb from limb; to separate a member or members from; to tear or cut in pieces; to mutilate; to break in parts; to divide.

> Fowls obscene *dismembered* his remains. —Pope.

2. To take away the membership of; as, to *dismember* one from a church. [Rare.]
Syn.—Disjoint, dislocate, dilacerate, mutilate, divide, sever.

dis-mem′bẽr-ment, *n.* The act of dismembering or state of being dismembered; severance; separation.

dis-met′tled, *a.* Destitute of fire or spirit. [Rare.]

dis-miss′, *v.t.*; dismissed (-mist), *pt., pp.*; dismissing, *ppr.* [L. *dismissus* or *dimissus*, pp. of *dimittere*, to send away; *di-*, from, and *mittere*, to send.]
1. To send away; to give leave of departure; to permit to depart; implying authority in a person to retain or keep.

> With thanks, and pardon to you all,
> I do *dismiss* you to your several countries. —Shak.

2. To discard; to remove from office, service, or employment; as, the master *dismisses* his servant.
3. In law, to remove from a docket; to discontinue; to reject as unworthy of notice or of being granted; as, to *dismiss* a petition or a motion in a court.
Syn.—Discharge, banish, abandon, remove, reject.

dis-miss′, *n.* Discharge; dismission. [Obs.]

dis-miss′ȧl, *n.* Dismission.

dis-mis′sion (-mish′un), *n.* 1. The act of sending away; leave to depart; as, the *dismission* of the grand jury.
2. Removal from office or employment; discharge, implying disgrace; expulsion.
3. In law, removal of a suit in equity; rejection of something as unworthy of notice or of being granted.

dis-miss′ive, *a.* Giving dismission.

dis-mort′gāge (-mor′gāj), *v.t.* To redeem from mortgage. [Obs.]

dis-mount′, *v.i.*; dismounted, *pt., pp.*; dismounting, *ppr.* 1. To alight from a horse; to descend or get off, as a rider from a beast; as, the officer ordered his troops to *dismount*.
2. To descend from an elevation.

dis-mount′, *v.t.* 1. To throw or remove from a horse; to unhorse; as, the soldier *dismounted* his adversary.
2. To throw or bring down from any elevation. [Obs.]
3. In mechanics, to separate the parts of; to dismantle.
4. To throw or remove, as cannon or other artillery from their carriages; to break the carriages or wheels of and render useless.

dis-nat′ū-rȧl-īze, *v.t.* To make alien; to deprive of the privileges of birth.

dis-nā′tūred, *a.* Deprived or destitute of natural feelings; unnatural. [Obs.]

dis-ō-bē′di-ence, *n.* Neglect or refusal to obey; violation of a command or prohibition; the omission of that which is commanded to be done, or the doing of that which is forbidden; breach of duty prescribed by authority.

dis-ō-bē′di-en-cy, *n.* Disobedience. [Obs.]

dis-ō-bē′di-ent, *a.* 1. Neglecting or refusing to obey; omitting to do what is commanded, or doing what is prohibited; refractory; not observant of duty or rules prescribed by authority; as, children *disobedient* to parents; citizens *disobedient* to the laws.

> I was not *disobedient* unto the heavenly vision. —Acts xxvi. 19.

2. Not yielding to exciting force or power; as, nerves *disobedient* to the brain.

dis-ō-bē′di-ent-ly, *adv.* In a disobedient manner.

dis-ō-bēl′sȧnce, *n.* Disobedience. [Obs.]

dis-ō-bēl′sȧnt, *a.* Disobedient.

dis-ō-bey′, *v.t.*; disobeyed, *pt., pp.*; disobeying, *ppr.* To neglect or refuse to obey; to omit or refuse obedience to; to transgress or violate an order or injunction of; to refuse submission to; as, refractory children *disobey* their parents; men *disobey* the laws.

dis-ō-bey′, *v.i.* To refuse obedience; to be neglectful of commands.

dis-ō-bey′ẽr, *n.* One who disobeys.

dis-ob-li-gā′tion, *n.* The state or condition of being without obligation; also, a disobliging act. [Obs.]

dis-ob′li-gā-tō-ry, *a.* Releasing from obligation.

dis-ō-blīge′, *v.t.*; disobliged, *pt., pp.*; disobliging, *ppr.* To do an act which contravenes the will or desires of (another); to offend by an act of unkindness or incivility; to injure in a slight degree.

> My plan has given offense to some gentlemen whom it would not be very safe to *disoblige*. —Addison.

dis-ō-blīge′ment, *n.* The act of disobliging.

dis-ō-blī′gẽr, *n.* One who disobliges.

dis-ō-blī′ging, *a.* Not obliging; not disposed to gratify the wishes of another; not disposed to please; unaccommodating; as, a *disobliging* coachman.

dis-ō-blī′ging-ly, *adv.* In a disobliging manner; offensively.

dis-ō-blī′ging-ness, *n.* Offensiveness; disposition to displease, or want of readiness to please.

dis-oc′ci-dent, *v.t.* 1. To veer from a westerly line. [Obs.]
2. To impair the sense of direction of.

dis-oc-cū-pā′tion, *n.* The state of being without occupation.

di-som′ȧ-tous, *a.* [Gr. *disōmatos*, double-bodied; *di-*, two, and *sōma*, body.] Double-bodied.

dis-ō-pin′iŏn (-yun), *n.* Disbelief. [Obs.]

dis-op′pi-lāte, *v.t.* To open. [Obs.]

dis-orb′, *v.t.* To displace from an orbit, as a star.

dis-ord′, *n.* Disorder. [Obs.]

dis-or-deined′, *a.* Corrupt; pernicious. [Obs.]

dis-or′dẽr, *n.* [OFr. *desordre*, disorder; L. *dis-* priv., and *ordo*, order, arrangement.]
1. Want of order or regular disposition; irregularity; immethodical distribution; confusion; as, the troops were thrown into *disorder*; the papers are in *disorder*.
2. Neglect of rule; irregularity.

> From vulgar bounds with brave *disorder* part,
> And snatch a grace beyond the reach of art. —Pope.

3. Breach of laws; violation of standing rules or enactments; disturbance of the peace of society; as, the city is sometimes troubled with the *disorders* of its citizens.
4. Irregularity, disturbance or interruption of the functions of the animal economy; disease; distemper; sickness; also, some specific disease of the body; as, catarrh is a common *disorder*.
5. Discomposure of the mind; turbulence of passions.

> There is such *disorder* in my wit. —Shak.

Syn.—Irregularity, disarrangement, confusion, tumult, bustle, disturbance, illness, indisposition, sickness, malady, distemper, disease.

dis-or′dẽr, *v.t.*; disordered, *pt., pp.*; disordering, *ppr.* [OFr. *desordrer*; L. *dis-* priv., and *ordinare*, to order, regulate.]
1. To break the order of; to derange; to disturb the regular disposition or arrangement of; to put out of method; to throw into confusion; to confuse; applicable to everything susceptible of order.

> The incursions of the Goths and other barbarous nations *disordered* the affairs of the Roman Empire. —Arbuthnot.

2. To disturb or interrupt the natural functions of, as the animal economy; to produce sickness or indisposition in; to disturb the regular operations of, as reason or judgment; to derange; as, the man's reason is *disordered*.

> A man whose judgment was so much *disordered* by party spirit. —Macaulay.

3. To discompose or disturb, as the mind; to ruffle.

> *Disordered* into a wanton frame.—Barrow.

4. To depose from holy orders. [Obs.]

> Let him be stripped and *disordered*, that the world may behold the inside of a friar. —Dryden.

Syn.—Disarrange, derange, confuse, discompose, disturb, ruffle.

dis-or′dẽred, *a.* 1. Put out of order; deranged; indisposed.
2. Disorderly; irregular; vicious. [Obs.]
Syn.—Confused, deranged, disturbed, diseased.

dis-or′dẽred-ly, *adv.* In a disordered manner.

dis-or′dẽred-ness, *n.* A state of disorder or irregularity; confusion.

dis-or′dẽr-li-ness, *n.* The state of being disorderly.

dis-or′dẽr-ly, *a.* 1. Being without proper order or disposition; confused; immethodical; irregular; as, the books and papers are in a *disorderly* state.

> A crowd,
> Heartless, unarmed, *disorderly*, and loud. —Cowley.

2. Tumultuous; irregular; turbulent; rebellious.

> If we subdue our *disorderly* passions we should live more easily. —Stillingfleet.

3. Lawless; contrary to law; violating or disposed to violate law and good order; violating the restraints of morality; of bad repute; as, *disorderly* people; drunk and *disorderly*.
4. Not regulated according to laws, rules, or ordinances duly enacted; forming a nuisance; disreputable; as, a *disorderly* house.
5. Inclined to break loose from restraint; unruly; as, *disorderly* cattle.
6. Not acting in an orderly or regular way, as the functions of the body.
Syn.—Irregular, immethodical, confused, tumultuous, inordinate, intemperate, unruly, lawless, vicious, loose.

dis-or′dẽr-ly, *adv.* Without order, rule, or method; irregularly; in a disorderly manner.

dis-or′di-nȧnce, *n.* Disarrangement. [Obs.]

dis-or′di-nāte, *a.* Disorderly. [Obs.]

dis-or′di-nāte-ly, *adv.* Inordinately; irregularly; viciously. [Obs.]

dis-or-di-nā′tion, *n.* Disorder. [Obs.]

dis-or″gȧn-i-zā′tion, *n.* 1. The act of disorganizing; the act of destroying organic structure, or connected system; the act of destroying order.
2. The state of being disorganized; as, the *disorganization* of the body, or of government, or of society, or of an army.

dis-or′gȧn-īze, *v.t.*; disorganized, *pt., pp.*; disorganizing, *ppr.* To break or destroy the organic structure or connected system of; to dissolve the regular system or union of parts of; as, to *disorganize* a government or society; to *disorganize* an army.

dis-or′gȧn-īz-ẽr, *n.* One who or that which disorganizes.

dis-ō′ri-ent, dis-ō-ri-en′tāte, *v.t.* To change from an easterly line; to turn from the east, as the altar of a church; also, to confuse as to the east; hence, to confuse mentally.

dis-ōwn′, *v.t.*; disowned, *pt., pp.*; disowning, *ppr.* 1. To deny; not to own; to refuse to acknowledge as belonging to oneself; as, a parent can hardly *disown* his child.
2. To deny; not to allow.

dis-ōwn′ment, *n.* Act of disowning. [Rare.]

dis-ox′i-dāte, *v.t.* To deoxidate. [Rare.]

dis-ox-i-dā′tion, *n.* Deoxidation. [Rare.]

dis-ox′y-gen-āte, *v.t.* To deprive of oxygen. [Rare.]

dis-ox-y-gen-ā'tion, *n.* The act or process of separating oxygen from any substance containing it. [Rare.]

dis-pāce', *v.i.* To range about. [Obs.]

dis-pāir', *v.t.* To separate (a pair or couple). [Rare.]

dis-pand', *v.t.* To display. [Obs.]

dis-pan'sion, *n.* The act of spreading or displaying. [Obs.]

dis-par'ȧ-dīsed (-dīst), *a.* Removed from paradise. [Rare.]

dis-par'āġe, *v.t.*; disparaged, *pt.*, *pp.*; disparaging, *ppr.* [ME. *disparagen*; OFr. *desparager*, to marry one of inferior rank; *des-* priv., and *parage*, rank, condition; L. *dis-* priv., and *par*, equal.]

1. To marry unequally, as to one of inferior condition in life. [Obs.]

2. To match unequally; to injure or dishonor by union with something of inferior excellence, or by a comparison with something of less value or worth. [Rare.]

3. To view or speak of in a slighting manner; to place too slight an estimate on; to undervalue; as, an attempt to *disparage* the dangers of war.

> Appearances which sometimes *disparage* the actions of men sincerely pious. —Atterbury.

Syn.—Depreciate, undervalue, vilify, reproach, detract from, derogate from, decry, degrade.

dis'pȧ-rāġe, *n.* A misalliance.

dis-par'āġe-ment, *n.* 1. Misalliance. [Obs.]

2. A condition of injurious comparison, implying unjustness; the act of making such contrast; dishonor; detraction; often with *to*.

> It ought to be no *disparagement to* a star that it is not the sun. —South.

Syn.—Derogation, detraction, reproach, dishonor, debasement, degradation, disgrace.

dis-par'ā-ġẽr, *n.* One who disparages or dishonors; one who vilifies or disgraces.

dis-par'ā-ġing-ly, *adv.* In a manner to disparage or dishonor.

dis'pȧ-rāte, *a.* [L. *disparatus*, pp. of *disparare*, to separate; *dis-* priv., and *parare*, to make equal, from *par*, equal.] Having a degree of difference; being (a) of different species; (b) characteristic of disparates; totally different.

dis'pȧ-rātes, *n.pl.* Things so unequal or unlike that they cannot be compared with each other.

dis-pȧ-ri'tion (-rish'un), *n.* A disappearing. [Obs.]

dis-par'i-ty, *n.* [Fr. *disparite*; LL. *disparitas*, difference, disparity; L. *dispar*, unequal.] Unlikeness; difference in degree, in age, rank, condition, or excellence; as, a *disparity* of years or of age; *disparity* of condition or circumstances; followed by *of*, *in*, *between*, etc.; as, *disparity of* ages; the *disparity in* their accounts.

dis-pärk', *v.t.*; disparked, *pt.*, *pp.*; disparking, *ppr.* 1. To throw open, as a park; to lay open.

2. To set at large; to release from inclosure or confinement.

dis-pär'kle, *v.t.* and *v.i.* To disperse; to scatter. [Obs.]

dis-pärt', *v.t.* [OFr. *despartir*; L. *dispartire*, to divide, distribute; *dis-*, apart, from, and *partire*, to part, divide, from *pars*, part.]

1. To part asunder; to divide; to separate; to sever; to burst; to rend; as, *disparted* air.

2. In gunnery, (a) in taking aim, to make allowance for the dispart of; (b) to fix, as a piece of ordnance, with a dispart-sight.

dis-pärt', *v.i.* To separate; to open; to cleave.

dis-pärt', *n.* In gunnery, (a) the difference between the semidiameter of the base ring at the breech of a gun, and that of the ring at the swell of the muzzle; (b) a dispart-sight.

dis-pärt'=sight (-sīt), *n.* In gunnery, a piece of metal cast on the muzzle of a piece of ordnance to make the line of sight parallel to the axis of the bore.

dis-pas'sion (-pash'un), *n.* Freedom from passion; an undisturbed state of the mind; apathy.

dis-pas'sion-āte, *a.* 1. Free from passion; calm; composed; impartial; moderate; temperate; unmoved by feelings; as, *dispassionate* men or judges.

2. Not dictated by passion; not proceeding from temper or bias; impartial; as, *dispassionate* proceedings.

dis-pas'sion-āte-ly, *adv.* In a dispassionate manner.

dis-pas'sion-āte-ness, *n.* The state or quality of being dispassionate.

dis-patch', **dis-patch'ẽr** (-pach'), etc. See preferred spellings, *despatch*, *despatcher*, etc.

dis'pȧ-thy, *n.* [Gr. *dyspatheia*, from *dyspathēs*, impatient of suffering, impassive; *dys-*, hard, ill, and *pathos*, feeling.] Want of passion.

dis-pau'pẽr, *v.t.* To deprive of the claim of a pauper to public support, or of the capacity of suing *in forma pauperis*; to reduce back from the state of a pauper.

dis-pau'pẽr-īze, *v.t.* To liberate from a state of pauperism.

dis-peed', *v.t.* To despatch. [Obs.]

dis-pel', *v.t.*; dispelled, *pt.*, *pp.*; dispelling, *ppr.* [L. *dispellere*, to drive away, disperse; *dis-*, apart, away, and *pellere*, to drive.] To scatter by driving or force; to disperse; to dissipate; to banish; as, to *dispel* vapors; to *dispel* darkness or gloom; to *dispel* fears.

Syn.—Disperse, scatter, dissipate, drive away, dismiss.

dis-pence', *v.i.* and *n.* An obsolete variant of *dispense.*

dis-pend', *v.t.* To expend. [Obs.]

dis-pend'ẽr, *n.* One who expends. [Obs.]

dis-pen'sȧ-ble, *a.* 1. That may be dispensed with.

2. Capable of being remitted; pardonable.

3. Capable of being conveyed to another; bestowable.

dis-pen'sȧ-ble-ness, *n.* The capability of being dispensable.

dis-pen'sȧ-ry, *n.*; *pl.* **dis-pen'sȧ-ries**. 1. That part of a building or institution where medicines are dispensed; as, the *dispensary* adjoined the operating-room.

2. A place at which medicines are dispensed to the poor, and medical advice given, payment generally being optional.

dis-pen-sā'tion, *n.* [OFr. *despensation*; L. *dispensatio*, management, charge, from *dispensare*, to weigh out, pay; *dis-*, apart, and *pensare*, freq. of *pendere*, to weigh.]

1. Distribution; the act of dealing out to different persons or places; as, the *dispensation* of water indifferently to all parts of the earth.

2. The dealing of God to his creatures; the distribution of good and evil, natural or moral, in the divine government.

> Neither are God's methods or intentions different in his *dispensations* to each private man. —Rogers.

3. The granting of a license, or the license itself, to do what is forbidden by laws or canons, or to omit something which is commanded; specifically, in the Roman Catholic church, a definite exemption of a person from some ecclesiastical obligation, requirement, or vow.

> A *dispensation* was obtained to enable Dr. Barrow to marry. —Ward.

4. That which is dispensed or bestowed; a system of principles and rites enjoined; as, the Mosaic *dispensation*; the Gospel *dispensation*; the former, including the Levitical law and rites, the latter, the scheme of redemption by Christ.

dis-pen'sȧ-tive, *a.* Granting dispensation.

dis-pen'sȧ-tive-ly, *adv.* By dispensation.

dis'pen-sā-tŏr, *n.* [L.] A dispenser.

dis-pen'sȧ-tō-ry, *a.* Having power to grant dispensations.

dis-pen'sȧ-tō-ry, *n.*; *pl.* **dis-pen'sȧ-tō-ries**. [L. *dispensator*, a steward, treasurer, from *dispensare*, to weigh out, dispense.] A book containing the method of preparing the various kinds of medicines used in pharmacy, or containing directions for the composition of medicines, with the proportions of the ingredients, and the methods of preparing them.

Syn.—Pharmacopœia.—A *pharmacopœia* is a book of standard formulæ, particularly one issued decennially by authority; a *dispensatory* is, rightly, a commentary on the *pharmacopœia.*

dis-pense', *v.t.*; dispensed (-penst), *pt.*, *pp.*; dispensing, *ppr.* [L. *dispensare*, to weigh out, pay out; *dis-*, out, from, and *pensare*, freq. of *pendere*, to weigh.]

1. To deal or divide out in parts or portions; to distribute; as, the steward *dispenses* provisions; the society *dispenses* medicines.

2. To administer; to apply, as laws to particular cases.

> While you *dispense* the laws and guide the state. —Dryden.

3. To atone for; to compensate for; to grant pardon for. [Obs.]

4. To grant dispensation to; to relieve; to excuse; to set free from an obligation; to exempt; as, good management *dispenses* one from many troubles.

dis-pense', *v.i.* 1. To make amends; to counterbalance. [Obs.]

2. To issue dispensation.

To dispense with; (a) to put up with; to connive at; (b) to forego; (c) to omit what is commonly required or performed, as a ceremony; to nullify, as a law; (d) to repudiate, as a promise or one's word. [Obs.]

dis-pense', *n.* 1. Dispensation. [Obs.]

2. Expense; profusion. [Obs.]

dis-pens'ẽr, *n.* One who or that which dispenses.

dis-pēo'ple, *v.t.*; dispeopled, *pt.*, *pp.*; dispeopling, *ppr.* To depopulate; to rid of inhabitants, as by destruction, expulsion, or other means.

dis-pēo'plẽr, *n.* One who depopulates; a depopulator; that which deprives of inhabitants.

dis-pẽrġe', *v.t.* To sprinkle. [Obs.]

di-spẽr'mous, *a.* [*Di-*, and Gr. *sperma*, a seed.] In botany, two-seeded.

dis-pẽr'ple, *v.t.* To disparkle. [Obs.]

dis-pẽr'sȧl, *n.* A scattering or dispersion.

dis-pẽrse', *v.t.*; dispersed, *pt.*, *pp.*; dispersing, *ppr.* [L. *dispersus*, pp. of *dispergere*, to scatter abroad.]

1. To scatter; to drive asunder; to cause to separate in different directions; as, the Jews are *dispersed* among all nations.

2. To distribute.

Syn.—Spread, scatter, dissipate, dispel, disseminate, distribute.

dis-pẽrse', *v.i.* To become scattered; to separate; to go or move into different parts; as, the company *dispersed* at ten o'clock; to vanish, as fog or vapors.

dis-pẽrsed' (-pẽrst'), *a.* Scattered; specifically, in entomology, closely placed, but irregular, as spots.

Dispersed harmony; see under *Harmony.*

dis-pẽrs'ed-ly, *adv.* In a dispersed manner; separately.

dis-pẽrs'ed-ness, *n.* The state of being dispersed or scattered.

dis-pẽrse'ness, *n.* Thinness; a scattered state. [Obs.]

dis-pẽrs'ẽr, *n.* One who disperses; as, the *disperser* of libels.

dis-pẽr'sion, *n.* [LL. *dispersio*, a scattering, dispersion, from *dispersus*, pp. of *dispergere*, to scatter.]

1. The act of scattering or the state of being scattered; as, the Jews, in their *dispersion*, retained their rites and ceremonies.

2. In optics, (a) a phenomenon exhibited by white light passing from one medium into another; the separation of light into different colors, as by a prism; (b) the angle of separation of two selected rays produced by a prism.

3. In medicine and surgery, the removal of inflammation from a part, and restoring it to its natural state.

Dispersion of the optic axes; in crystallography, the phenomenon presented by a crystal in having two axes along which a ray of light can proceed without bifurcation.

The dispersion; the Jews who were scattered during and after the Babylonian captivity; the diaspora.

dis-pẽrs'ive, *a.* Tending to scatter or separate.

Dispersive power; in optics, the ratio of the angle of dispersion to the mean deviation of the two rays from which it is measured.

dis-pẽrs'ive-ly, *adv.* In a dispersive manner; due to dispersion.

dis-pẽrs'ive-ness, *n.* The state or quality of being dispersive.

dis-pẽr'sŏn-ăl-īze, **dis-pẽr'sŏn-āte**, *v.t.* To disguise, destroy, or change the individuality of. [Rare.]

dis-pir'it, *v.t.*; dispirited, *pt.*, *pp.*; dispiriting, *ppr.* 1. To depress the spirits of; to deprive of courage; to discourage; to dishearten; to deject; to cast down.

2. To comprehend thoroughly; to imbibe the spirit of; said of a book. [Obs.]

dis-pir'it-ed-ly, *adv.* Dejectedly.

dis-pir'it-ed-ness, *n.* Want of courage; depression of spirits.

dis-pir'it-ment, *n.* The state of being in a dispirited condition; the act of dispiriting.

dis-pit'ē-ous, *a.* Having no pity; cruel; furious. [Obs.]

dis-pit'ē-ous-ly, *adv.* Cruelly. [Obs.]

dis-plāce', *v.t.*; displaced, *pt.*, *pp.*; displacing, *ppr.* [OFr. *desplacer*, to displace; *des-* priv., and *placer*, to place.]

1. To put out of the usual or proper place; to remove from its place; as, the books in the library are all *displaced.*

2. To remove from any state, condition, office, or dignity; as, to *displace* an officer of the revenue.

3. To take the place of, especially by force.

4. To dislodge; to drive out; to disturb.

dis-plāce'ȧ-ble, *a.* Having the capability of displacement.

dis-plāce'ment, *n.* 1. The act of displacing; the act of removing from the usual or proper place, or from a state, condition, or office.

2. The quantity of water displaced by a body floating at rest, as a ship. Its weight is equal to that of the displacing body.

3. In medical chemistry, the method by which the active principles of organic bodies are extracted from them. The body is first reduced to a powder, and then subjected to the action of a liquid, which dissolves the soluble matter; percolation.

4. In mechanics, the difference, expressed geometrically, between the primary position of a body and its position at a given time.

5. In a machine having a piston, as a steam-pump, the measure of space acted through or the amount of liquid displaced during each piston-stroke.

dis-plā′cen-cy, *n.* [L. *displicentia*, from *displicere*, to displease; *dis-*, and *placere*, to please.] That which displeases or disobliges; displeasure. [Obs.]

dis-plā′cēr, *n.* One who or that which displaces; specifically, an appliance for effecting chemical displacement.

dis-plant′, *v.t.*; displanted, *pt.*, *pp.*; displanting, *ppr.* 1. To pluck up or to remove.

2. To drive away or remove from the usual place of residence; as, to *displant* the people of a country.

3. To deprive of what is fixed or settled; as, to *displant* a city of its citizens.

dis-plan-tā′tion, *n.* The act of displacing.

dis-plat′, *v.t.* To untwist; to uncurl. [Obs.]

dis-plāy′, *v.t.*; displayed, *pt.*, *pp.*; displaying, *ppr.* [ME. *displayen*; L. *dis-*, apart, and *plicare*, to fold.]

1. To unfold; to open; to spread wide; to expand.

> The northern wind his wings did broad *display*. —Spenser.

2. To spread before the view; to show; to exhibit to the eyes or to the mind; to make manifest; to parade.

3. In printing, to make prominent, as a line, paragraph, advertisement, etc., by large or heavy-faced type.

4. To discover; to spy out. [Obs.]

dis-plāy′, *v.i.* 1. To make a show or display.

2. To lay anything open, as in carving or dissection.

> He carves, *displays*, and cuts up to a wonder. —Spectator.

3. To talk without restraint; to make a great show of words.

> *Displayed* so saucily against your highness. —Shak.

dis-plāy′, *n.* 1. An opening or unfolding; an exhibition of anything to the view.

2. Show; exhibition; as, a great *display* of magnificence.

dis-plāyed′, *a.* 1. Unfolded; opened; spread; expanded; manifested.

2. In heraldry, a term used to express the position of any bird of prey when it is erect, with its wings expanded.

3. In printing, set so as to be more noticeable than ordinary matter.

Displayed.

dis-plāy′ēr, *n.* One who or that which displays.

dis′ple (-pl), *v.t.* To discipline; to inflict penitentiary whippings on. [Obs.]

dis-pleas′ănce (-plez′), *n.* Anger; discontent. [Obs.]

dis-pleas′ănt, *a.* Unpleasant. [Obs.]

dis-pleas′ănt-ly, *adv.* Unpleasantly. [Obs.]

dis-pleas′ănt-ness, *n.* Unpleasantness. [Obs.]

dis-plēașe′, *v.t.*; displeased, *pt.*, *pp.*; displeasing, *ppr.* [ME. *displesen*; L. *displicere*, to displease; *dis-* priv., and *placere*, to please.]

1. To offend; to make angry in a slight degree; to fail to please; to be disagreeable to; as, his coarseness *displeased* his friends; stale food *displeases* the taste; a deformity *displeases* the eye.

2. To fail to accomplish; to fall short of satisfying. [Obs.]

Syn.—Offend, anger, vex, disgust, provoke, dissatisfy, pique.

dis-plēașe′, *v.i.* To disgust; to raise aversion.

dis-plēaș′ed-ly, *adv.* In a displeased manner. [Rare.]

dis-plēaș′ed-ness, *n.* Displeasure; uneasiness. [Rare.]

dis-plēaș′ēr, *n.* One who or that which displeases.

dis-plēaș′ing, *a.* Offensive to the eye, to the mind, or to any of the senses; disgusting; disagreeable.

dis-plēaș′ing-ly, *adv.* Disagreeably.

dis-plēaș′ing-ness, *n.* Offensiveness; the quality of giving some degree of disgust.

dis-pleas′ūre (-plez′), *n.* 1. The state of feeling displeased; vexation; dissatisfaction; disapproval of the conduct of another; indignation.

2. An offense; a cause of irritation.

> Now shall I be more blameless than the Philistines, though I do them a *displeasure*. —Judges xv. 3.

3. A state of disgrace or disfavor. [Obs.]

> He went into Poland, being in *displeasure* with the pope for overmuch familiarity. —Peacham.

Syn.—Dissatisfaction, anger, pique, vexation, dislike, indignation, resentment, annoyance.

dis-pleas′ūre, *v.t.* To displease. [Obs.]

dis-plen′ish, *v.t.* To disfurnish; to strip. [Scot. and North Eng.]

dis′pli-cence, dis′pli-cen-cy, *n.* Dislike. [Rare.]

dis-plōde′, *v.t.* To vent, discharge, or burst with a violent sound. [Obs.]

dis-plōde′, *v.i.* To burst; to explode. [Obs.]

dis-plō′șion, *n.* An explosion. [Obs.]

dis-plō′sive, *a.* Explosive. [Obs.]

dis-plūme′, *v.t.*; displumed, *pt.*, *pp.*; displuming, *ppr.* [L. *dis-* priv., and *plumare*, to cover with feathers, from *pluma*, a feather.] To strip or deprive of plumes or feathers; to strip of badges or honors.

dis′pō-line, *n.* An alkaloid, $C_{11}H_{11}N$, an isomer of several other compounds of the quinoline series.

dis-pond′, *n.* Same as *Despond*.

dī-spon′dee, *n.* [L. *dispondeus*; Gr. *dispondeios*, a double spondee; *di-*, two, and *spondeios*, a spondee.] In Greek and Latin prosody, a double spondee, consisting of four long syllables.

dis-pōne′, *v.t.*; disponed, *pt.*, *pp.*; disponing, *ppr.* [ME. *disponen*; OFr. *disponer*, to dispose, from L. *disponere*, to set in different places, distribute, dispose.]

1. To set in order; to arrange. [Obs.]

2. In Scots law, to make over or give to another, as property.

dis-pōne′, *v.i.* To dispose; to decide; to settle. [Obs.]

dis-pō-nee′, *n.* In Scots law, the one to whom anything is made over or deeded.

dis-pō′nent, *a.* Disposing or preparing for what is sought.

dis-pōn′ēr, *n.* In Scots law, the one who makes over or deeds property to another.

dis-pŏnġe′, *v.t.* To ooze; to dribble, as a sponge. [Obs.]

dis-pōpe′, *v.t.*; dispoped, *pt.*, *pp.*; dispoping, *ppr.* To deprive of the power or dignity of a pope.

dī-spōr′ous, *a.* Two-spored.

dis-pōrt′, *n.* Play; sport; pastime; diversion; amusement; merriment.

dis-pōrt′, *v.i.*; disported, *pt.*, *pp.*; disporting, *ppr.* [ME. *disporten*, to bear, support, manage, from L. *deportare*, to carry away, transport; *de*, away, and *portare*, to carry.] To play; to wanton; to move lightly and without restraint; to move in gaiety; as, lambs *disporting* on the mead.

> Where light *disports* in ever-mingling dyes. —Pope.

dis-pōrt′, *v.t.* 1. To divert or amuse; as, he *disports* himself.

2. To remove from a port; to transport; to deport. [Obs.]

dis-pōrt′ment, *n.* The act of disporting; play. [Obs.]

dis-pōș′ȧ-ble (-pōz′ȧ-bl), *a.* Subject to disposal; not previously engaged or employed; free to be used or employed as occasion may require.

dis-pōș′ăl, *n.* 1. The act of disposing; a setting or arranging; as, the *disposal* of the troops in two lines.

2. Regulation, order, or arrangement of things, by right of acknowledged authority or possession; dispensation.

> Tax not divine *disposal*. —Milton.

3. A disposing of; an ordering, arranging, or distributing by gift, riddance, alienation or outlay; as, *disposal* of a daughter in marriage; of time; of money; of refuse.

4. The power or right of bestowing; as, certain offices are at the *disposal* of the president.

dis-pōșe′, *v.t.*; disposed, *pt.*, *pp.*; disposing, *ppr.* [ME. *disposen*; OFr. *disposer*, to dispose, put in order, arrange; L. *disponere*, to arrange, dispose; *dis-*, apart, and *ponere*, to place.]

1. To combine in an orderly manner; to place or distribute; to arrange; as, the general *disposed* his troops in three lines.

2. To regulate; to adjust; to set in right order.

> The knightly forms of combat to *dispose*. —Dryden.

3. To apply to a particular purpose; to give; to place; to bestow; as, you have *disposed* much in works of public piety. [Obs.]

4. To set, place, or turn to a particular end or consequence.

> Endure and conquer; Jove will soon *dispose*
> To future good our past and present woes. —Dryden.

5. To adapt; to form for any purpose.

> Then must thou thee *dispose* another way. —Hubbard's Tale.

To dispose of; to come to a determination concerning; to make a disposal of; specifically, (a) to part with; to alienate; to sell; as, the man has *disposed of* his house; (b) to part with to another; to put into another's hand or power; to bestow; as, the father has *disposed of* his daughter to a man of worth; (c) to give away or transfer by authority; as, to *dispose of* a prize; (d) to use or employ; as, they know not how to *dispose of* their time; (e) to put away; to get rid of; as, the stream supplies more water than can be *disposed of*.

Syn.—Arrange, settle, adjust, regulate, bestow, give.

dis-pōșe′, *v.i.* 1. To bargain; to make terms. [Obs.]

2. To regulate; to determine; to settle.

> Man proposes, God *disposes*.—Old Proverb.

dis-pōșe′, *n.* 1. Disposal; power of disposing; management. [Obs.]

2. Disposition; cast of mind; inclination. [Obs.]

dis-pōșed′, *a.* 1. Inclined; in the humor; as, she was *disposed* to be generous.

2. Characterized by a particular condition of health or disposition; following an adverb; as, well or ill *disposed*.

dis-pōș′ed-ness, *n.* Inclination; disposition; tendency. [Rare.]

dis-pōșe′ment, *n.* Disposal. [Obs.]

dis-pōș′ēr, *n.* One who or that which disposes.

dis-pōș′ing-ly, *adv.* In a manner to dispose, settle, or govern.

dis-poș′it-ed, *a.* Disposed. [Obs.]

dis-pō-și′tion (-zish′un), *n.* [ME. *disposition*; L. *dispositio*, arrangement, from *disponere*, to put in different places, to dispose.]

1. The act of disposing or state of being disposed.

2. The manner in which things, or the parts of a complex body, are placed or arranged; order; method; distribution; arrangement; as, the *disposition* of the trees in an orchard; the *disposition* of the several parts of an edifice, of the parts of a discourse, or of the figures in painting.

3. Natural fitness or tendency; as, a *disposition* in plants to grow in a direction upward; a *disposition* in bodies to putrefaction.

4. Temper or natural constitution of the mind; as, an amiable or an irritable *disposition*.

5. Inclination; propensity; the temper or frame of mind as directed to particular objects; humor; as, the *disposition* of a person to undertake a particular work; the *dispositions* of men toward each other; a *disposition* friendly to any design.

6. Disposal; alienation; distribution; a giving away, or giving over to another; as, he has made *disposition* of his effects; he has satisfied his friends by the judicious *disposition* of his property.

7. In Scots law, a unilateral deed of alienation, by which a right to property, especially heritable, is conveyed.

8. One of the six essentials of architecture. It is the arrangement of the whole design by means of ichnography (plan), orthography (section and elevation), and scenography (perspective view), and differs from distribution, which signifies the particular arrangements of the internal parts of a building.

Syn.—Inclination, tendency.—A man's *disposition* is the prevailing spirit or governing purpose of his mind; his *inclinations* are excited states of desire or appetency; *tendency* is a strong determination or proclivity toward some particular mode of action.

dis-pō-și′tion-ăl, *a.* Pertaining to disposition.

dis-pō-și′tioned, *a.* Having a particular disposition, or bent of mind; used in compounds; as, mean-*dispositioned*.

dis-poș′i-tive, *a.* Of, relating, or pertaining to disposition. [Obs.]

dis-poș′i-tive-ly, *adv.* In a dispositive manner; distributively. [Obs.]

dis-poș′i-tŏr, *n.* 1. A disposer.

2. In astrology, the planet which is lord of the sign where another planet is. [Obs.]

dis-pŏș-sess′, *v.t.*; dispossessed (-zest′), *pt.*, *pp.*; dispossessing, *ppr.* [OFr. *despossesser*, from L. *dis-* priv., and *possessus*, pp. of *possidere*, to possess.] To put out of possession by any means; to deprive of the actual occupancy of a thing, particularly of land or real estate; to disseize; usually followed by *of*, before the thing taken away; as, to *dispossess* a king of his crown.

dis-pŏș-ses′sion (-zesh′un), *n.* 1. The act of putting out of possession.

2. In law, an ousting by legal process.

dis-pŏș-sess′ŏr, *n.* One who or that which dispossesses.

dis-pōst′, *v.t.* To deprive of a post. [Obs.]

dis-pōș′ūre, *n.* 1. Disposal; the power of disposing; management; direction.

2. State; posture; disposition.

dis-prāiș′ȧ-ble, *a.* Blameworthy. [Rare.]

dis-prāișe′, *v.t.*; dispraised, *pt.*, *pp.*; dispraising, *ppr.* [ME. *dispreisen*; OFr. *despreiser*, to dispraise, blame; L. *dis-* priv., and LL. *pretiare*, to prize, praise, from L. *pretium*, price, prize.] To blame; to censure; to mention with disapprobation, or some degree of reproach.

> I *dispraised* him before the wicked.—Shak.

dis-prāișe′, *n.* The state of being dispraised; censure; reproach.

dis-prāiș′ēr, *n.* One who or that which dispraises.

dis-prāiș′ing-ly, *adv.* By way of dispraise; with blame or some degree of reproach.

dis-pread′ (-pred′), *v.t.* To spread in different ways; to extend or flow in different directions.
dis-pread′, *v.i.* To expand or be extended. [Rare.]
dis-pread′ẽr, *n.* A publisher; a divulger. [Rare.]
dis-prej′ū-dice, *v.t.* To remove prejudice from. [Obs.]
dis-prē-pāre′, *v.t.* To make unprepared. [Obs.]
dis-prince′, *v.t.* To rid of princely characteristics. [Rare.]
dis-priş′ŏn, *v.t.* To let loose from prison; to set at liberty. [Obs.]
dis-priv′i-leġe, *v.t.* To deprive of a privilege. [Rare.]
dis-prize′, *v.t.* To lower in value. [Rare.]
dis-prō-fess′, *v.t.* To give up the profession of. [Rare.]
dis-prof′it, *n.* Loss; detriment; damage. [Rare.]
dis-prof′it-ȧ-ble, *a.* Unprofitable. [Obs.]
dis-prọọf′, *n.* Confutation; refutation; a proving to be false or erroneous; as, to offer evidence in *disproof* of a fact, argument, principle, or allegation.
dis-prop′ẽr-ty, *v.t.* To deprive of property; to dispossess. [Rare.]
dis-prō-pōr′tion, *n.* 1. Want of proportion of one thing to another, or between the parts of a thing; want of symmetry; as, the *disproportion* of a man's arms to his body; the *disproportion* of the length of an edifice to its height.
2. Want of suitableness or adequacy; disparity; inequality; unsuitableness; as, the *disproportion* of strength or means to an object.
dis-prō-pōr′tion, *v.t.*; disproportioned, *pt.*, *pp.*; disproportioning, *ppr.* To make unsuitable in form, size, or quantity; to violate symmetry in; to mismatch; to join unfitly.

To shape my legs of an unequal size,
To *disproportion* me in every part.—Shak.

dis-prō-pōr′tion-ȧ-ble, *a.* Disproportional; not in proportion; unsuitable in form, size, or quantity, to something else; inadequate.
dis-prō-pōr′tion-ȧ-ble-ness, *n.* Want of proportion or symmetry; unsuitableness to something else.
dis-prō-pōr′tion-ȧ-bly, *adv.* With want of proportion or symmetry; unsuitably to something else.
dis-prō-pōr′tion-ăl, *a.* Not having due proportion to something else; not having proportion or symmetry of parts; unsuitable in form or quantity; unequal; inadequate; as, studies *disproportional* to the requirements.
dis-prō-pōr-tion-al′i-ty, *n.* The state of being disproportional.
dis-prō-pōr′tion-ăl-ly, *adv.* Unsuitably with respect to form, quantity, or value; unequally.
dis-prō-pōr′tion-āte, *a.* Not proportioned; unsymmetrical; unsuitable to something else, in bulk, form, or value; inadequate; as, in a perfect form of the body, none of the limbs are *disproportionate*; it is wisdom not to undertake a work with *disproportionate* means.
dis-prō-pōr′tion-āte-ly, *adv.* In a disproportionate degree; unsuitably; inadequately.
dis-prō-pōr′tion-āte-ness, *n.* Unsuitableness in form, bulk, or value; inadequacy.
dis-prō′pri-āte, *v.t.* To destroy appropriation in; to withdraw from an appropriate use. [Obs.]
dis-prōv′ȧ-ble (-prọọv′ȧ-bl), *a.* Capable of being disproved or refuted.
dis-prōv′ăl, *n.* The act of disproving; disproof; confutation.
dis-prōve′, *v.t.*; disproved, *pt.*, *pp.*; disproving, *ppr.* [ME. *disproven*; OFr. *desprover*, to refute; *des-* priv., and *prover*, to prove; L. *dis-* priv., and *probare*, to test, prove.]
1. To prove to be false or erroneous; to confute; as, to *disprove* an assertion, a statement, an argument, a proposition.
2. To disallow or disapprove. [Obs.]
3. To prove not to be just or genuine; as, to *disprove* a person's right to an allotment.
dis-prōv′ẽr, *n.* One who disproves or confutes.
dis-prō-vīde′ (-vīd′), *v.t.* To fail to provide. [Obs.]
dis-pun̄ct′, *v.t.* To strike off; to take out. [Obs.]
dis-pun̄ct′, *a.* Ill-mannered; rude; discourteous.
dis-punġe′ (-punj′), *v.t.* To expunge; to erase; also, to discharge, as from a sponge. [Obs.]
dis-punġe′, *v.t.* Same as *Dispone*.
dis-pun′ish-ȧ-ble, *a.* [Prefix *dis-* and *punishable*.] Without penal restraint; not punishable. [Rare.]
dis-pūr′pōse, *v.t.* To turn or divert from a purpose or aim. [Obs.]
dis-pūrse′, *v.t.* To disburse; to expend. [Obs.]
dis-pūr-vey′, *v.t.* To rob, as of provisions.
dis-pūr-vey′ănce, *n.* Want of provisions. [Obs.]
dis′pū-tȧ-ble, *a.* [L. *disputabilis*, disputable, from *disputare*, to dispute.]
1. That may be disputed; liable to be called in question, controverted, or contested; controvertible; of doubtful certainty; as, *disputable* opinions, statements, propositions, arguments, points, cases, questions, etc.
2. Given to controversy; disputatious.
dis′pū-tȧ-ble-ness, *n.* The quality or state of being disputable.
dis-pū-tac′i-ty, *n.* Proneness to dispute. [Obs.]
dis′pū-tănt, *n.* [Fr. *disputant*, from L. *disputans* (*-antis*), ppr. of *disputare*, to dispute.] One who disputes; one who argues in opposition to another; a controvertist; a reasoner in opposition.
dis′pū-tănt, *a.* Disputing; engaged in controversy.
dis-pū-tā′tion, *n.* [L. *disputatio*.]
1. The act of disputing; a reasoning or argumentation in opposition to something, or on opposite sides; controversy in words; verbal contest respecting the truth of some fact, opinion, proposition, or argument.
2. A debate; a rhetorical contest. [Archaic.]
dis-pū-tā′tious (-tā′shus), *a.* Inclined to dispute; apt to cavil or controvert; as, a *disputatious* person or temper.
dis-pū-tā′tious-ly, *adv.* In a disputatious manner.
dis-pū-tā′tious-ness, *n.* Inclination to dispute.
dis-pū′tȧ-tive, *a.* Disposed to dispute; inclined to cavil or to reason in opposition; as, a *disputative* temper.
dis-pūte′, *v.i.*; disputed, *pt.*, *pp.*; disputing, *ppr.* [ME. *disputen*; OFr. *desputer*, from L. *disputare*, to dispute, discuss.]
1. To contend in argument; to reason or argue in opposition; to debate; as, to *dispute* in a certain case.
2. To altercate; to wrangle; as, to *dispute* about trifles.
3. To debate or contest against a rival; as, to *dispute* for a medal. [Archaic.]
Syn.—Argue, discuss, debate, question.
dis-pūte′, *v.t.* 1. To attempt to disprove by arguments or statements; to attempt to prove to be false, unfounded, or erroneous; to controvert; to attempt to overthrow by reasoning; as, to *dispute* assertions or allegations.
2. To contest; to battle for; as, to *dispute* an advance of the enemy; to *dispute* the way.
3. To meet in strife; encounter. [Obs.]
dis-pūte′, *n.* 1. Strife or contest in words, or by arguments; an attempt to prove and maintain one's own opinions or claims, by arguments or statements, in opposition to the opinions, arguments, or claims of another; controversy in words; as, a *dispute* on the situation in Turkey.
2. A quarrel; an ill-natured wrangle; a clash; as, family *disputes*.
Beyond, *past*, or *without dispute*; beyond the possibility of being controverted; indisputably.
To be in dispute; to be unsettled; to be the subject of disputation or controversy.
Syn.—Controversy, quarrel, argument, disagreement, contention.
dis-pūte′less, *a.* Admitting no dispute; incontrovertible.
dis-pūt′ẽr, *n.* One who disputes or who is given to disputes; a controvertist.

Where is the *disputer* of this world?
—1 Cor. i. 20.

dis-pū′ti-şŏn, *n.* Discussion; argumentation. [Obs.]
dis-quăl″i-fi-çā′tion (-kwăl″), *n.* The act of disqualifying; the state of being disqualified; that which disqualifies; that which renders unfit, unsuitable, or inadequate; as, sickness is a *disqualification* for labor or study.
dis-quăl′i-fȳ, *v.t.*; disqualified, *pt.*, *pp.*; disqualifying, *ppr.* 1. To make unfit; to deprive of natural power, or the qualities or properties necessary for any purpose; with *for*; as, indisposition *disqualifies* the body *for* labor.
2. To deprive of legal capacity, power, or right; to disable; as, a conviction of perjury *disqualifies* a man from being a witness.

In spite of the law *disqualifying* hired champions, they were always to be had for money. —Pearson.

dis-quăn′ti-ty (-kwăn′), *v.t.* To diminish. [Obs.]
dis-quī′et (-kwī′), *a.* Unquiet; restless; uneasy. [Rare.]
dis-quī′et, *n.* Want of quiet; uneasiness; restlessness; want of tranquillity in body or mind; disturbance; anxiety.
dis-quī′et, *v.t.*; disquieted, *pt.*, *pp.*; disquieting, *ppr.* To disturb; to deprive of peace, rest, or tranquillity; to make uneasy or restless; to harass the body of; to vex the mind of.

That he may *disquiet* the inhabitants of Babylon. —Jer. i. 34.

Syn.—Excite, disturb, annoy, irritate.
dis-quī′et-ăl, *n.* The act of disquieting. [Obs.]
dis-quī′et-ẽr, *n.* One who disquiets; he or that which makes uneasy.
dis-quī′et-fụl, *a.* Producing inquietude or restlessness. [Rare.]
dis-quī′et-ive, *a.* Tending to disquiet. [Rare.]
dis-quī′et-ly, *adv.* Without quiet or rest; as, he rested *disquietly* that night. [Rare.]
dis-quī′et-ment, *n.* Act of disquieting. [Rare.]
dis-quī′et-ness, *n.* Uneasiness; restlessness; disturbance of peace in body or mind.
dis-quī′et-ous, *a.* Causing uneasiness. [Rare.]
dis-quī′e-tūde, *n.* Want of peace or tranquillity; uneasiness; disturbance; agitation; anxiety.
dis-quip′ȧ-răn-cy, dis-quip′ȧ-rănce (-kwip′), *n.* [LL. *disquiparantia*, from L. *dis-* priv., and *æquiparans*, ppr. of *æquiparare*, to put on a level, compare; *æquus*, equal, level, and *parare*, to make equal, from *par*, equal.] In logic, that relation which exists between two objects mutually implying each other yet not having sameness of relationship, as in the phrase mother and daughter; opposed to *equiparancy*, a state of equality, as in the phrase sister and sister.
dis-qui-şi′tion (-kwi-zish′un), *n.* [L. *disquisitio* (*-onis*), an inquiry, investigation, from *disquisitus*, pp. of *disquirere*, to investigate, inquire; *dis-*, apart, and *quærere*, to seek.] A formal or systematic inquiry into any subject, by arguments, or discussion of the facts and circumstances that may elucidate truth; as, a *disquisition* on government or morals.
dis-qui-şi′tion-ăl, *a.* Of, relating, or pertaining to a disquisition.
dis-qui-şi′tion-ā-ry, *a.* Disquisitional.
dis-quiş′i-tive, *a.* Disquisitorial.
dis-quiş-i-tō′ri-ăl, dis-quiş′i-tō-ry, *a.* Of the nature of a disquisition; critical.
dis-rān̄ge′, *v.t.* To disarrange. [Obs.]
dis-răn̄k′, *v.t.* 1. To degrade from rank. [Obs.]
2. To throw out of rank or into confusion.
dis-rāte′, *v.t.* To lower in rank; to abase.
dis-rāy′, *v.t.* To disarray. [Obs.]
dis-rē′ăl-īze, *v.t.* To make unreal. [Obs.]
dis-rē-gärd′, *n.* Neglect; omission of notice; slight; implying indifference or some degree of contempt; as, to pass one with *disregard*.
dis-rē-gärd′, *v.t.*; disregarded, *pt.*, *pp.*; disregarding, *ppr.* To omit to take notice of; to neglect to observe; to slight as unworthy of regard or notice; as, to *disregard* the wants of the poor.

Studious of good, man *disregarded* fame.
—Blackmore.

dis-rē-gärd′ẽr, *n.* One who neglects.
dis-rē-gärd′fụl, *a.* Neglectful; negligent; heedless.
dis-rē-gärd′fụl-ly, *adv.* Negligently; heedlessly.
dis-rel′ish, *n.* 1. Distaste; dislike of the palate; some degree of disgust; as, a *disrelish* for tobacco.
2. Distaste or dislike, in a figurative sense; dislike of the mind; aversion; antipathy; as, a *disrelish* for exertion.
dis-rel′ish, *v.t.*; disrelished (-rel′isht), *pt.*, *pp.*; disrelishing, *ppr.* 1. To dislike the taste of; as, to *disrelish* a particular kind of food.
2. To make nauseous or disgusting; to infect with a bad taste. [Rare.]

And not *disrelish* thirst
Of nectarous draughts between. —Milton.

3. To dislike; to feel some disgust at; as, to *disrelish* vulgar jests.

Enjoyments lost or *disrelished*. —Pope.

dis-rē-mem′bẽr, *v.t.* To forget; to choose to forget. [Humorous.]

Not to *disremember* the old saying, but let every man skin his own skunks.—Crockett.

dis-rē-pāir′, *n.* A state of being in poor repair or condition.
dis-rep″ū-tȧ-bil′i-ty, *n.* The state of being disreputable.
dis-rep′ū-tȧ-ble, *a.* Not reputable; not in esteem; not honorable; low; mean; disgracing the reputation; tending to impair the good name, and bring into disesteem; as, it is *disreputable* to associate familiarly with the mean, the lewd, and the profane.
dis-rep′ū-tȧ-bly, *adv.* In a disreputable manner.
dis-rep-ū-tā′tion, *n.* Loss or want of reputation or good name; disrepute.
dis-rē-pūte′, *n.* Loss or want of reputation; disesteem; discredit; dishonor.
dis-rē-pūte′, *v.t.* To bring into disreputation. [Obs.]
dis-rē-speçt′, *n.* Want of respect or reverence; incivility; rudeness.
dis-rē-speçt′, *v.t.* To show disrespect to.
dis-rē-speçt-ȧ-bil′i-ty, *n.* Lack of respectability.
dis-rē-speçt′ȧ-ble, *a.* Lacking respectability; in disrepute.
dis-rē-speçt′ẽr, *n.* One who exhibits disrespect.
dis-rē-speçt′fụl, *a.* Wanting in respect; manifesting disesteem or want of respect; discourteous; as, *disrespectful* behavior.
dis-rē-speçt′fụl-ly, *adv.* In a disrespectful manner.
dis-rē-speçt′fụl-ness, *n.* The state or quality of being disrespectful.
dis-rē-speçt′ive, *a.* Disrespectful. [Obs.]

dis-rev′ẽr-ence, *v.t.* To treat with irreverence. [Obs.]

dis-rōbe′, *v.t.*; disrobed, *pt., pp.*; disrobing, *ppr.* 1. To divest of a robe; to divest of garments; to undress.

2. To strip of covering; to divest of any surrounding appendage; as, autumn *disrobes* the fields of verdure.

These two peers were *disrobed* of their glory. —Wotton.

dis-rōb′ẽr, *n.* One who disrobes.

dis-ro͝of′, *v.t.* To unroof. [Rare.]

dis-ro͝ot′, *v.t.*; disrooted, *pt., pp.*; disrooting, *ppr.* 1. To tear up the roots of, or by the roots.

2. To tear from a foundation; to loosen or undermine.

A piece of ground *disrooted* from its situation by subterraneous inundations.—Goldsmith.

dis-rout′, *v.t.* To put to rout.

dis-rud′dẽr, *v.t.* To make rudderless.

dis-rū′li-ly, *adv.* In a disruly manner. [Obs.]

dis-rū′ly, *a.* Unruly. [Obs.]

dis-rupt′, *a.* Rent from; torn asunder; severed by rending or breaking.

dis-rupt′, *v.t.*; disrupted, *pt., pp.*; disrupting, *ppr.* [From L. *disrumptus*, pp. of *disrumpere*, to break or burst apart.] To part forcibly; to break in parts.

dis-rup′tion, *n.* [L. *diruptio*, a tearing to pieces.]

1. The act of rending asunder; the act of bursting and separating; the rupture or fissure so made; as, the *disruption* of an empire; *disruption* of mountains.

2. Ecclesiastically, the rupture which took place in the Established Church of Scotland in 1843, when 474 ministers and professors demitted their charges.

dis-rupt′ive, *a.* Characterized by disruption; resulting in disruption; effected by disruption; as, *disruptive* causes or effects.

dis-rup′tūre, *n.* Disruption. [Rare.]

diss, *n.* [Native Algerian name.] A reedy, Mediterranean grass, *Ampelodesma tenax*, the fiber of which is used for twine, rope, and other articles of utility.

dis-sat-is-fac′tion, *n.* The state of being dissatisfied; discontent; uneasiness proceeding from the want of gratification, or from disappointed wishes and expectations.

The ambitious man is subject to uneasiness and *dissatisfaction.* —Addison.

Syn.—Discontent, discontentment, mortification, disappointment, displeasure, disapprobation, distaste, dislike.

dis-sat-is-fac′tō-ri-ness, *n.* Inability to satisfy or give content; a failing to give content.

dis-sat-is-fac′tō-ry, *a.* Causing dissatisfaction; giving discontent; mortifying; displeasing.

One uniform rule would probably have been as *dissatisfactory* to some of the states, as difficult for the convention. —Hamilton.

dis-sat′is-fȳ, *v.t.*; dissatisfied, *pt., pp.*; dissatisfying, *ppr.* To render discontented; to displease; to excite uneasiness in by frustrating wishes or expectations.

dis-seat′, *v.t.* To remove from a seat. [Rare.]

dis-sect′, *v.t.*; dissected, *pt., pp.*; dissecting, *ppr.* [L. *dissectus*, pp. of *dissecare*, to cut apart, cut up; *dis-*, apart, and *secare*, to cut.]

1. To cut in pieces; to divide, as an animal body, with a cutting instrument, by separating the joints; as, to *dissect* a fowl.

2. To cut in pieces, as an animal or plant, for the purpose of examining the structure and use of its several parts, or to observe morbid affections of its tissues; to anatomize.

Following life in creatures we *dissect*,
We lose it in the moment we detect.—Pope.

3. To divide into its constituent parts for the purpose of examination; to analyze for the purpose of criticism; to describe with minute accuracy.

To *dissect* . . . fabled knights . . . ; or to describe races and games. —Milton.

dis-sect′ed, *a.* Cut in pieces; separated by parting the joints; divided into its constituent parts; specifically, in botany, deeply lobed in many places; incised, as a leaf.

dis-sect′i-ble, *a.* Capable of dissection.

dis-sect′ing, *a.* 1. Of, relating, or pertaining to dissection; as, a *dissecting* scalpel.

2. Causing the disconnection of integral parts; as, a *dissecting* medium.

dis-sec′tion, *n.* [From L. *dissectus*, pp. of *dissecare*, to cut up.]

1. The act of dissecting, or of cutting in pieces an animal or vegetable for the purpose of examining the structure and uses of its parts; anatomy.

2. The act of separating into constituent parts for the purpose of critical examination.

So true and so perfect a *dissection* of human kind is the work of extraordinary diligence. —Granville.

dis-sect′ŏr, *n.* One who dissects; an anatomist.

dis-sēize′, *v.t.*; disseized, *pt., pp.*; disseizing, *ppr.* [OFr. *desseisir*, to dispossess; *des-* priv., and *seisir*, to take possession of.] In law, to dispossess wrongfully; to deprive of actual seizin or possession: followed by *of*; as, to *disseize* a tenant *of* his freehold; also spelled *disseise.*

A man may suppose himself *disseized*, when he is not. —Blackstone.

dis-sēi-zee′, *n.* A person put out of possession of an estate unlawfully; also spelled *disseisee.*

dis-sēiz′in, *n.* [OFr. *disseisin*, from *disseisir*, to disseize.] In law, the act of disseizing; an unlawful dispossessing of a person of his lands, tenements, or incorporeal hereditaments; a deprivation of actual seizin; also spelled *disseisin.*

dis-sēiz′ŏr, *n.* One who puts another out of possession wrongfully; he that dispossesses another; also spelled *disseisor.*

dis-sēiz′ŏr-ess, *n.* A woman who disseizes.

dis-sēl′zūre, *n.* Disseizin.

dis′sel-bo͝om, *n.* [D. *disselboom*, a wagon-pole; *dissel*, an axletree; and *boom*, pole.] A wagon-tongue.

dis-sem′blănce, *n.* Want of resemblance. [Rare.]

dis-sem′ble, *v.t.*; dissembled, *pt., pp.*; dissembling, *ppr.* [OFr. *dessembler*, to be unlike; L. *dissimulare*, to feign to be different, dissemble; *dis-* priv., and *similis*, like.]

1. To hide under a false appearance; to conceal; to disguise; to pretend (that) not to be which really is; as, I will not *dissemble* the truth; I cannot *dissemble* my real sentiments.

2. To feign, as something which is not; to make a false appearance of.

Your son Lucentio
Doth love my daughter, and she loveth him,
Or both *dissemble* deeply their affections.
—Shak.

3. To appear like; to resemble. [Obs.]

4. To disguise. [Obs.]

Syn.—To hide, screen, disguise, cloak, cover, veil, conceal.

dis-sem′ble, *v.i.* To be hypocritical; to assume a false appearance; to conceal the real fact, motives, intention, or sentiments, under some pretense.

He that hateth *dissembleth* with his lips. —Prov. xxvi. 24.

dis-sem′blẽr, *n.* One who dissembles; a hypocrite; one who conceals his opinions or dispositions under a false appearance.

Syn.—Hypocrite, pretender, deceiver.

dis-sem′bling, *a.* Hiding under a false appearance; acting the hypocrite.

dis-sem′bling-ly, *adv.* In a dissembling manner.

dis-sem′i-nāte, *v.t.* and *v.i.*; disseminated, *pt., pp.*; disseminating, *ppr.* [L. *disseminatus*, pp. of *disseminare*, to scatter seed, spread abroad, disseminate; *dis-*, apart, and *seminare*, to sow, from *semen*, seed.]

1. To scatter or sow, as seed. [Rare.]

2. To scatter morally for growth and propagation; to spread abroad, as doctrines, etc.

Preached, and *disseminated*, and taken deep root. —Atterbury.

3. To spread by diffusion or dispersion.

A uniform heat *disseminated* through the body of the earth. —Woodward.

Syn.—Spread, diffuse, propagate, publish, promulgate, circulate, disperse.

dis-sem′i-nā-ted, *a.* In mineralogy, occurring in small scattered portions; scattered; said of one mineral embedded in another.

dis-sem-i-nā′tion, *n.* The act of scattering and propagating, like seed; the act of spreading for growth and permanence; as, the *dissemination* of altruistic doctrines.

dis-sem′i-nā-tive, *a.* Conducive to dissemination.

dis-sem′i-nā-tŏr, *n.* One who disseminates; one who spreads and propagates.

dis-sen′sion, *n.* [ME. *dissencion*; OFr. *dissension*; L. *dissensio*, difference of opinion, disagreement, from *dissensus*, pp. of *dissentire*, to disagree; *dis-*, apart, and *sentire*, to think.] Disagreement in opinion, usually a disagreement which is violent, producing warm debates or angry words; contention in words; strife; discord; quarrel; breach of friendship and union.

Debates, *dissensions*, uproars are thy joy. —Dryden.

Syn.—Contention, discord, dispute, disagreement, strife, quarrel.

dis-sen′sious (-shus), *a.* Disposed to discord; quarrelsome; contentious; dissentious. [Rare.]

dis-sen′sious-ly, *adv.* Dissentiously.

dis-sent′, *v.i*; dissented, *pt., pp.*; dissenting, *ppr.* [ME. *dissenten*; L. *dissentire*, to differ in opinion, disagree.]

1. To disagree in opinion; to differ; to think in a different or contrary manner; with *from*; as, they *dissent from* each other.

2. Ecclesiastically, to differ from an established church in regard to doctrines, rites, or government.

3. To differ; to be of a contrary nature. [Obs.]

dis-sent′, *n.* 1. Difference of opinion; disagreement.

2. Declaration of disagreement in opinion; as, they entered their *dissent* on the journals of the house.

3. Separation from an established church, especially that of England.

4. Contrariety of nature; opposite quality. [Obs.]

dis-sen-tā′nē-ous, *a.* Disagreeable; contrary. [Rare.]

dis′sen-tā-ny, *a.* Dissentaneous; inconsistent. [Obs.]

dis-sen-tā′tion, *n.* Act of dissenting. [Obs.]

dis-sent′ẽr, *n.* 1. One who dissents; one who differs in opinion; one who declares his disagreement.

2. One who separates from the service and worship of any established church. The word is in England applied particularly to those Protestants who separate from or who do not unite with the Church of England.

dis-sent′ẽr-iṣm, *n.* The beliefs or doctrine of dissenters.

dis-sen′ti-āte (-shi-), *v.t.* To disturb; to make dissent in.

dis-sen′tient (-shient), *a.* Disagreeing; declaring dissent.

dis-sen′tient, *n.* One who disagrees and declares his dissent.

dis-sen′tious (-shus), *a.* Disposed to disagreement or discord.

In religion they have a *dissentious* head; in the commonwealth a factious head. —Ascham.

dis-sen′tious-ly, *adv.* In a dissentious manner.

dis-sent′ive, *a.* Dissenting. [Obs.]

dis-sep′i-ment, *n.* [LL. *dissæpimentum*, a partition, from L. *dissæpire*, to hedge in, separate; *dis-*, apart, and *sæpire*, to hedge in, from *sæpes*, or *sepes*, a hedge.]

1. In botany, a partition formed in an ovary by the united sides of cohering carpels, separating the inside into cells.

a a, Dissepiments.

2. In zoölogy, the imperfect horizontal plates which connect the vertical septa in corals, and divide the loculi inclosed between the septa into a series of cells communicating with each other.

dis-sẽrt′, *v.i.* To discourse or dispute. [Obs.]

dis′sẽr-tāte, *v.i.* To deal in dissertation; to write dissertations. [Rare.]

dis-sẽr-tā′tion, *n.* [LL. *dissertatio*, a treatise, discourse, from L. *dissertatus*, pp. of *dissertare*, to discuss; *dis-*, apart, and *serere*, to join.]

1. An elaborate or formal discourse, intended to illustrate a subject.

2. A written essay, treatise, or disquisition; as, Plutarch's *dissertation* on the poets.

Syn.—Disquisition, essay, discourse, treatise.

dis-sẽr-tā′tion-ăl, *a.* Pertaining to a dissertation.

dis-sẽr-tā′tion-ist, *n.* One who writes dissertations.

dis′sẽr-tā-tŏr, *n.* One who writes a dissertation; one who debates.

dis-sẽrt′ly, *adv.* Disertly. [Obs.]

dis-sẽrve′, *v.t.*; disserved, *pt., pp.*; disserving, *ppr.* [OFr. *desservir*, to disserve, injure, from L. *dis-* priv., and *servire*, to serve.] To injure; to hurt; to harm; to do injury or mischief to; as, too much zeal may *disserve* a good cause.

dis-sẽrv′ice, *n.* Injury; harm; mischief, as, violent remedies often do a *disservice.*

dis-sẽrv′ice-ȧ-ble, *a.* Injurious; hurtful.

dis-sẽrv′ice-ȧ-ble-ness, *n.* The quality of being injurious; tendency to harm.

dis-sẽrv′ice-ȧ-bly, *adv.* In a disserviceable manner.

dis-set′tle, *v.t.* To unsettle. [Obs.]

dis-set′tle-ment, *n.* The act of unsettling.

dis-sev′ẽr, *v.t.*; dissevered, *pt., pp.*; dissevering, *ppr.* [ME *disseveren*; OFr. *dessevrer*, to sever, from L. *dis-*, apart, and *separare*, to sever, separate.] To part in two, to divide; to separate; to disunite; as, lightning may *dissever* a branch from the trunk of a tree; jealousy *dissevers* the bonds of friendship; the Reformation *dissevered* Protestants from Roman Catholics.

dis-sev′ẽr, *v.i.* To part company; to separate.

dis-sev′ẽr-ănce, dis-sev′ẽr-ā-tion, *n.* The act of dissevering; separation.

dis-sev′ẽr-ment, *n.* Disseverance.

dis-shad′ōw, *v.t.* To bring forth from shadow, shade, or obscurity. [Obs.]

dis-shēathe′, *v.t.* and *v.i.* To draw from, as a sheath; to unsheathe. [Obs.]

dis-ship′, *v.t.* To remove from a ship. [Obs.]

dis-shiv′ẽr, *v.t.* and *v.i.* To shiver; to break in pieces, to shatter. [Obs.]

dis′si-dence, *n.* [L. *dissidentia*, disagreement, from *dissidens* (*-ntis*), ppr. of *dissidere*, to disagree.] Disagreement; dissent; nonconformity.

Dissidence in Poland is dissent in England. —Latham.

dis′si-dent, *n.* One who dissents from others; one who votes or gives his opinion about any point in opposition to others; specifically, (a) a dissenter; one who separates from an established religion; (b) a Lutheran, Calvinist, or adherent of the Greek church in Poland, who, under the old elective monarchy, was allowed the free exercise of his faith.

dis′si-dent, *a.* Not agreeing; dissenting. [Rare.]

dis′si-dent-ly, *adv.* With dissidence.

dis-sil′i-ence, dis-sil′i-en-cy, *n.* The act of leaping or starting asunder.

dis-sil′i-ent, *a.* [L. *dissiliens*, ppr. of *dissilire*, to leap or burst apart; *dis-*, apart, and *salire*, to leap.] Starting asunder; bursting and opening with an elastic force, as the dry pod or capsule of a plant; as, a *dissilient* pericarp.

dis-si-li′tion (-lish′un), *n.* The act of bursting open; the act of starting or springing apart. [Rare.]

dis-sim′i-lăr, *a.* [L. *dissimilis*, unlike; *dis-* priv., and *similis*, like.] Unlike, either in nature, properties, or external form; not similar; not having the resemblance of; heterogeneous; as, the tempers of men are as *dissimilar* as their features.

dis-sim-i-lar′i-ty, *n.* Unlikeness; want of resemblance; dissimilitude; as, the *dissimilarity* of human faces and forms.

dis-sim′i-lăr-ly, *adv.* In a dissimilar manner.

dis-sim′i-lāte, *v.t.* To make dissimilar. [Rare.]

dis-sim-i-lā′tion, *n.* [From L. *dissimilis*, unlike.] The act of changing similarity to dissimilarity; the process of making unlike; specifically, (a) in biology, disassimilation; (b) in philology, sound-substitution, to rid a word of one of two like contiguous sounds, as in cha*m*ber for German Ka*mm*er.

dis-sim′i-lā-tive, *a.* Of or tending toward dissimilation; specifically, in biology, catabolic.

dis-sim′i-lē, *n.* Same as *Dissimilitude*, 2.

dis-si-mil′i-tūde, *n.* [L. *dissimilitudo*, unlikeness, from *dissimilis*, unlike.]

1. Unlikeness; want of resemblance; as, a *dissimilitude* of form or character.

2. In rhetoric, comparison or illustration by contrasts.

dis-sim′ū-lāte, *v.t.*; dissimulated, *pt., pp.*; dissimulating, *ppr.* To hide by pretense; to simulate the opposite of.

dis-sim′ū-lāte, *v.i.* To feign; to pretend; to dissemble.

dis-sim′ū-lāte, *a.* Feigning; dissembling. [Obs.]

dis-sim-ū-lā′tion, *n.* [ME. *dissimulation*; L. *dissimulatio*, a dissembling, from *dissimulare*, to dissemble; *dis-* priv., and *similis*, like.] The act of dissembling; a hiding under a false appearance; a feigning; false pretension; hypocrisy.

dis-sim′ū-lā-tive, *a.* Characterized by dissimulation.

dis-sim′ū-lā-tŏr, *n.* One who dissimulates.

dis-sim′ūle, *v.t.* To dissemble. [Obs.]

dis-sim′ū-lẽr, *n.* One who dissembles. [Obs.]

dis′si-pȧ-ble, *a.* Liable to be dissipated; that may be scattered or dispersed. [Rare.]

The heat of those plants is very *dissipable*. —Bacon.

dis′si-pāte, *v.t.*; dissipated, *pt., pp.*; dissipating, *ppr.* [L. *dissipatus*, pp. of *dissipare*, to scatter, disperse; *dis-*, apart, and *supare*, to throw.]

1. To scatter; to disperse; to dispel; as, wind *dissipates* fog; the heat of the sun *dissipates* vapor; mirth *dissipates* care and anxiety; the cares of life tend to *dissipate* serious reflections.

2. To expend; to squander; to scatter, as property or physical or mental powers in wasteful extravagance; to waste; to consume; as, a man has *dissipated* his fortune in the pursuit of pleasure.

dis′si-pāte, *v.i.* 1. To scatter; to disperse; to separate into parts and disappear; to waste away; to vanish; as, a fog or cloud gradually *dissipates* before the rays or heat of the sun.

2. To be extravagant or reckless in the gratification of one's senses; to be loose in morals or irregular in conduct.

dis′si-pā-ted, *a.* Loose; irregular; given to extravagance in the expenditure of property; devoted to pleasure and vice; as, a *dissipated* man; a *dissipated* life.

dis-si-pā′tion, *n.* 1. The act of scattering; dispersion; the state of being dispersed; as, the *dissipation* of vapor or heat.

2. Distracted attention; that which diverts and calls off the mind from any subject.

3. A dissolute, irregular course of life; a wandering from object to object in pursuit of pleasure; a course of life usually attended with careless and exorbitant expenditures of money, and indulgence in vices, which impair or ruin both health and fortune.

What! is it proposed, then, to reclaim the spendthrift from his *dissipation* and extravagance, by filling his pockets with money? —P. Henry.

Dissipation of energy; in physics, transformation of energy so as to be nonavailable to man; degradation of energy.

dis′si-pā-tive, *a.* Having or exhibiting a tendency toward dissipation.

Dissipative system; in physics, the theory which accounts for dissipation of energy.

dis″si-pȧ-tiv′i-ty, *n.* In physics, the rate of dissipation of energy divided by two.

dis-sīte′, *a.* Separate; found apart. [Obs.]

dis-slan′dẽr, *v.t.* To slander. [Obs.]

dis-slan′dẽr, *n.* Defamation; slander. [Obs.]

dis-slan′dẽr-ous, *a.* Slanderous. [Obs.]

dis-sō-ciȧ-bil′i-ty (-shiȧ-bil′i-ty), *n.* 1. Lack of sociability; unfriendliness.

2. Capability of dissociation.

dis-sō′ciȧ-ble (-shiȧ-), *a.* [Fr. *dissociable*, unsociable; L. *dissociabilis*, incompatible, from *dissociare*, to separate; *dis-* priv., and *sociare*, to associate, from *socius*, a companion.]

1. Not well associated, assorted, or united; incongruous; not reconcilable with.

2. Capable of being dissociated.

dis-sō′ciăl (-shăl), *a.* 1. Not social; having a tendency to avoid society.

2. Lacking in sympathy and friendship.

dis-sō′ciăl-ize, *v.t.*; dissocialized, *pt., pp.*; dissocializing, *ppr.* To make unsocial; to separate; to disunite.

dis-sō′ci-āte (-shi-āt), *v.t.*; dissociated, *pt., pp.*; dissociating, *ppr.* [L. *dissociatus*, pp. of *dissociare*, to separate from fellowship.]

1. To separate; disconnect; to sever the association of.

2. In chemistry, to decompose; to separate into the component elements, by the action of heat.

dis-sō-ci-ā′tion, *n.* [L. *dissociatio* (*-onis*), a separation, from *dissociare*, to separate.]

1. The act of taking apart or dissociating; a state of disunion; separation.

2. In chemistry, the reduction of a substance to its elements by the action of heat; disassociation.

dis-sō′ci-ā-tive (-shi-ā-), *a.* Tending to or characterized by dissociation.

dis″sō-lū-bil′i-ty, *n.* Capacity of being dissolved.

dis′sō-lū-ble, *a.* [L. *dissolubilis*, from *dissolvere*, to dissolve.]

1. Capable of being dissolved or melted; having its parts separable by heat or moisture; convertible into a fluid.

2. Capable of being disunited or divided into parts.

dis′sō-lū-ble-ness, *n.* The quality of being dissoluble.

dis′sō-lūte, *a.* [L. *dissolutus*, loose, careless, licentious, pp. of *dissolvere*, to loosen; *dis-*, apart, and *solvere*, to loosen.]

1. Loose in behavior and morals; given to vice and dissipation; wanton; lewd; luxurious; debauched; not under the restraints of law; as, a *dissolute* man; *dissolute* company.

2. Vicious; wanton; devoted to pleasure and dissipation; as, a *dissolute* life.

Syn.—Abandoned, profligate, loose, licentious, wanton, vicious.

dis′sō-lūte-ly, *adv.* In a dissolute manner.

dis′sō-lūte-ness, *n.* Looseness of manners and morals; vicious indulgences in pleasure, as in intemperance and debauchery; dissipation; as, *dissoluteness* of life or manners.

dis-sō-lū′tion, *n.* [L. *dissolutio*, a breaking up, dissolution, from *dissolutus*, pp. of *dissolvere*, to dissolve.]

1. The act of liquefying or changing from a solid to a fluid state by heat; a melting; a thawing; as, the *dissolution* of snow and ice, which converts them into water.

2. In chemistry, the reduction of a body into its elements.

3. The separation of the parts of a body by putrefaction, or the analysis of the natural structure of mixed bodies, as of animal or vegetable substances; decomposition.

4. The substance formed by dissolving a body in a menstruum; solution. [Obs.]

5. Death; the separation of the soul and body.

6. Destruction; the separation of the parts which compose a connected system, or body; as, the *dissolution* of the world, or of nature; the *dissolution* of government.

7. The breaking up of an assembly, or the putting an end to its existence.

Dissolution is the civil death of Parliament. —Blackstone.

8. Looseness of manners; dissipation. [Obs.]

9. Retrogression, as opposed to *evolution*. [Rare.]

Dissolution of the blood; in medicine, that state of the blood, as in certain malignant fevers, in which it does not readily coagulate, when drawn from the body.

dis-ṣolv-ȧ-bil′i-ty, *n.* Solubility.

dis-ṣolv′ȧ-ble, *a.* Capable of being dissolved; capable of being melted or converted into a fluid; as, sugar and ice are *dissolvable*; also spelled *dissolvible*.

dis-ṣolv′ȧ-ble-ness, *n.* The state of being dissolvable.

dis-ṣolv′ȧ-tive, *a.* Solvent. [Obs.]

dis-ṣolve′, *v.t.*; dissolved, *pt., pp.*; dissolving, *ppr.* [ME. *dissolven*, from L. *dissolvere*, to loosen; *dis-*, apart, and *solvere*, to loosen.]

1. To convert from a solid or fixed state to a fluid state, by the action of a fluid; to make a solution of; as, to *dissolve* sugar in water.

2. To melt; to soften; to liquefy; as, the sun *dissolves* the snow.

3. To disunite; to break up; to cause to separate into parts; as, to *dissolve* Parliament, friendship, or a partnership.

4. To destroy; to remove the power of; as, to *dissolve* a charm, spell, or enchantment.

5. To make languid; to relax; as, *dissolved* in pleasure.

6. In law, to annul; to rescind; as, to *dissolve* an injunction.

7. To clear; to solve; to remove; to dissipate or to explain; as, to *dissolve* doubts. [Archaic.]

dis-ṣolve′, *v.i.* 1. To be melted; to be converted from a solid to a fluid state.

2. To fade slowly; to vanish by degrees; as, the hills *dissolved* in the darkness.

3. To melt away in weakness; to relax; to lose force; to become soft or languid.

4. To fall asunder; to crumble; to be broken; as, a government may *dissolve* by its own weight.

5. To waste away; to perish; to be decomposed.

dis-ṣolv′ent, *a.* Having power to melt or dissolve; as, the *dissolvent* juices of the stomach.

dis-ṣolv′ent, *n.* 1. Anything which has the power or quality of melting or converting a solid substance into a fluid, or of separating the parts of a fixed body so that they mix with a liquid; a solvent.

2. In medicine, a remedy supposed to be capable of dissolving concretions in the body, such as calculi, tubercles, etc.

dis-ṣolv′ẽr, *n.* One who or that which dissolves, or has the power of dissolving.

dis-ṣolv′ing, *a.* Melting; fading.

Dissolving view; an effect produced by a magic lantern, or sometimes by two lanterns having the same focus, in which, as one view fades from sight, another takes its place so gradually that there is neither a pause nor an abrupt change.

dis-ṣolv′ing-ly, *adv.* In a dissolving manner.

dis′sō-nănce, *n.* [Fr. *dissonance*; LL. *dissonantia*, dissonance, from L. *dissonans*, disagreeing in sound; *dis-*, from, and *sonus*, a sound.]

1. Discord; a mixture or union of harsh, inharmonious sounds, which are grating or unpleasing to the ear; as, the *dissonance* of notes.

2. Disagreement.

dis′sō-năn-cy, *n.* [Obs.] Same as *Dissonance*.

dis′sō-nănt, *a.* 1. Discordant; harsh; jarring; inharmonious; unpleasant to the ear; as, *dissonant* notes or intervals.

2. Disagreeing; incongruous; usually with *from*; as, he advanced propositions very *dissonant from* truth.

dis-spir′it, *v.t.* Same as *Dispirit*.

dis-suāde′ (-swād′), *v.t.*; dissuaded, *pt., pp.*; dissuading, *ppr.* [L. *dissuadere*, to dissuade; *dis-*, away, from, and *suadere*, to persuade, from *suavis*, sweet.]

1. To advise or exhort against; to attempt to draw or divert from a measure by offering reasons or motives; as, the minister *dissuaded* the prince from adopting the measure.

2. To represent as unfit, improper, or dangerous. [Obs.]

War therefore, open or concealed, alike
My voice *dissuades*. —Milton.

dis-suād′ẽr, *n.* He that dissuades; a dehorter.

dis-suā′ṣion (-swā′zhun), *n.* [L. *dissuasio*, an advising to the contrary, dissuasion, from *dissuadere*, to dissuade.]

1. The act of dissuading; the state of being dissuaded; dehortation; as, the *dissuasion* of friends.

2. A dissuasive motive.

dis-suā′sive, *a.* Tending to dissuade or divert from a measure or purpose; dehortatory.

dis-suā′sive, *n.* Reason, argument, or counsel employed to deter one from a measure or purpose.

dis-suā′sive-ly, *adv.* In a dissuasive manner.

dis-suā′sō-ry, *a.* and *n.* Dissuasive.

dis-sun′dẽr, *v.t.* To separate; to rend. [Obs.]

dis-sweet′en, *v.t.* To deprive of sweetness. [Obs.]

dis-syl-lab′iç, *a.* Consisting of two syllables only; as, a *dissyllabic* foot in poetry.

dis-syl-lab″i-fi-çā′tion, *n.* A division into two syllables.

dis-syl-lab′i-fȳ, *v.t.* To divide into two syllables.

dis-syl′lȧ-bīze, *v.t.* Same as *Dissyllabify.*

dis-syl′lȧ-ble (*or* dis′syl-lȧ-ble), *n.* [L. *disyllabus*; Gr. *disyllabos*, of two syllables.] A word consisting of two syllables only, as paper.

dis-sym-met′ri-cȧl, *a.* [*Dis-* priv., and Gr. *symmetros*, symmetric.] Destitute of symmetry.

dis-sym′me-try, *n.* Lack of symmetry.

dis-sym′pȧ-thy, *n.* Disinterest. [Rare.]

dis′tad, *adv.* In anatomy, away from the center; toward the far extremity; toward the distal aspect of the body

dis′tȧff, *n.*; *pl.* **dis′tȧffs** or **dis′tȧves.** [ME. *distaf*, *dystaf*; AS. *distæf*, a distaff.]

1. The staff of a spinning-wheel, to which a bunch of flax or tow is tied, and from which the thread is drawn.

She layeth her hands to the spindle, and her hands hold the *distaff*. —Prov. xxxi. 19.

2. Figuratively, a woman, or the female sex.

His crown usurped, a *distaff* on the throne. —Dryden.

Distaff day or *St. Distaff's day*; January 7th, the day which marked the resumption of spinning after the festivities of Christmas; also called *Rock day.*

Distaff side; a former term for the female side (of the house).

dis-tāin′, *v.t.* [ME. *disteinen*; OFr. *desteindre*, to distain, discolor; *dis-* priv., and *tingere*, to tinge, color.]

1. To stain; to tinge with any different color from the natural or proper one; to discolor; used poetically.

That crown *distained* with gore. —Pope.

2. To blot; to sully; to defile; to tarnish.

She *distained* her honorable blood.—Spenser.

dis′tăl, *a.* In biology, applied to the end of a bone, limb, or organ farthest removed from the point of attachment or insertion, or to the quickly-growing end of the organism of a hydrozoön; situated away from or at the extremity most distant from the center; as, the *distal* aspect of a bone.

dis′tăl-ly, *adv.* In a distal direction.

dis′tănce, *n.* [ME. *distance*; L. *distantia*, distance, remoteness, from *distans* (*-antis*), ppr. of *distare*, to stand apart, to be separate; *dis-*, off, from, and *stare*, to stand.]

1. An interval or space between two objects; the length of the shortest line which intervenes between two things that are separate; as, a great or small *distance.*

2. Remoteness of place; often with *at.*

He waits *at distance* till he hears from Cato. —Addison.

3. Space of time; any indefinite length of time, past or future, intervening between two periods or events; as, the *distance* of an hour, of a year, of an age.

4. Ideal space or separation.

Qualities that affect our senses are, in the things themselves, so united and blended, that there is no *distance* between them. —Locke.

5. Contrariety; opposition.

Banquo was your enemy,
So he is mine, and in such bloody *distance.* —Shak.

6. The remoteness which respect requires; often preceded by *thy, his, her, your, their*; as, keep *your distance*; hence, respect.

'Tis by respect and *distance* that authority is upheld. —Atterbury.

7. The remoteness or reserve which one assumes from being offended, from dislike, etc.; often preceded by *my, our,* etc.; as, I will keep *my distance* from that fellow; hence, reserve; coldness; alienation of heart.

On the part of heaven,
Now alienated, *distance* and distaste. —Milton.

8. Remoteness in succession or relation; as, the *distance* between a descendant and his ancestor.

9. In music, the interval between two notes; as, the *distance* of a fourth or seventh.

10. In horse-racing, a specified length back from the winning-post, at which point is placed the distance-post. If any horse has not reached this distance-post before the first horse in that heat has reached the winning-post, such horse is *distanced*, and disqualified for running again during that race.

This was the horse that ran the whole field out of *distance.* —L'Estrange.

11. Militarily, space between bodies of troops measured from front to rear.

Accessible distances; such distances as may be measured by the application of any lineal measure.

Angular distance; the angle of separation which the directions of two bodies include. Thus, if the spectator's eye be at any point O, and straight lines be drawn from that point to two objects A and B separated from each other, the angle A O B contained by these lines is called the *angular distance* of the two objects.

Angular Distance.

Inaccessible distances; such as cannot be measured by the application of any lineal measure, but by means of angles and trigonometrical rules and formulæ.

Lunar distance; see under *Lunar.*

Mean distance of the planets; in astronomy, a mean between their aphelion and perihelion distances.

Proportional distances of the planets; the distances of the several planets from the sun, compared with the distance of any one of them considered as unity.

Real distances; the absolute distances of those bodies as compared with any terrestrial measure, as miles, leagues, etc.

To keep one's distance; to stand aloof; to accord proper respect to another.

Syn.—Interval, removal, separation, interspace, remoteness, absence, space, length.

dis′tănce, *v.t.*; distanced, *pt., pp.*; distancing, *ppr.* 1. To place at a remote point.

2. In racing, to leave behind in a race; to win the race by a great superiority; more specifically, to overcome in a race by at least the space between the distance- and winning-posts.

3. To leave at a great distance behind; to outdo; to excel greatly.

He *distanced* the most skilful of his contemporaries. —Milner.

4. To cause to appear at a distance; to cause to appear remote. [Rare.]

His peculiar art of *distancing* an object to aggrandize his space. —Miller.

dis′tăn-cy, *n.* Distance. [Obs.]

dis′tănt, *a.* 1. Separate; apart; the intervening space being of any indefinite extent; as, one point may be less than a line or a hair's breadth *distant* from another.

2. Remote, as (a) in place; as, a *distant* object appears under a small angle; (b) in time, past or future; as, a *distant* age or period of the world; (c) in the line of succession or descent, indefinitely; as, a *distant* descendant; a *distant* ancestor; *distant* posterity; (d) in natural connection or consanguinity; as, a *distant* relation; *distant* kindred; a *distant* collateral line; (e) in kind or nature; hence, not allied; not agreeing with or in conformity to; as, practice very *distant* from principles or profession; (f) in view or prospect; hence, not very likely to be realized; slight; faint; as, a *distant* glimpse; a *distant* hope or prospect; (g) in connection; hence, slight; faint; as, a *distant* idea; a *distant* resemblance.

3. Sounding remote, or as if remote; sounding faintly.

The boy's cry came to her from the field,
More and more *distant.* —Tennyson.

4. Indirect; not obvious or plain.

In modest terms and *distant* phrases. —Addison.

5. Not cordial; characterized by haughtiness, coldness, indifference, or disrespect; reserved; shy; as, the manners of a person are *distant.*

He passed me with a *distant* bow. —Goldsmith.

Syn.—Separate, remote, removed, apart, far, slight, faint, indirect, indistinct, shy, cold, haughty, cool.

dis-tan′tiăl (-shăl), *a.* Distant. [Obs.]

dis′tănt-ly, *adv.* Remotely; at a distance; with reserve.

dis-tāste′, *n.* 1. Aversion of the taste; dislike of food or drink; disrelish; disgust, or a slight degree of it.

2. Dislike; uneasiness.

Prosperity is not without many fears and *distastes*, and adversity is not without comfort and hopes. —Bacon.

3. Dislike; displeasure; alienation of affection.

Syn.—Disrelish, disinclination, dislike, displeasure, dissatisfaction, disgust.

dis-tāste′, *v.t.*; distasted, *pt., pp.*; distasting, *ppr.* 1. To disrelish; to dislike; to loathe; as, to *distaste* drugs or poisons.

2. To offend; to disgust. [Obs.]

3. To vex; to displease; to sour. [Obs.]

dis-tāste′, *v.i.* To taste bad. [Obs.]

dis-tāste′fu̇l, *a.* 1. Nauseous; unpleasant or disgusting to the taste.

2. Offensive; displeasing; as, a *distasteful* truth.

3. Malevolent; as, *distasteful* looks.

dis-tāste′fu̇l-ly, *adv.* In a distasteful manner.

dis-tāste′fu̇l-ness, *n.* Disagreeableness; dislike.

dis-tāst′ive, *n.* Something distasteful. [Obs.]

dis-tāst′ive, *a.* Distasteful.

dis-tās′tūre, *n.* Something distasteful. [Obs.]

di-stem′ō-nous, *a.* [*Di-*, and Gr. *stēmōn*, stamen.] Furnished with two stamens.

dis-tem′pẽr, *n.* 1. An undue or unnatural temper or disproportionate mixture of parts.

2. Disease; malady; indisposition; any morbid state of an animal body or of any part of it; its application being commonly restricted to brutes; particularly, some form of catarrh.

3. Weather, when extremely hot or cold. [Obs.]

4. Want of due balance of parts or opposite qualities and principles. [Obs.]

5. Political disorder; tumult.

Syn.—Disorder, disease, sickness, malady, indisposition.

dis-tem′pẽr, *n.* [It. *distemperare*, to dissolve or mix with liquid.] In painting, (a) a preparation of opaque color, ground with size and water; tempera; (b) a kind of painting in which the pigments are mixed with size, and chiefly used for scene-painting and interior decoration.

dis-tem′pẽr, *v.t.*; distempered, *pt., pp.*; distempering, *ppr.* [ME. *distemperen*; OFr. *destemprer*; LL. *distemperare*, to derange, disorder; L. *dis-* priv., and *temperare*, to temper.]

1. To disease; to disorder; to derange the functions of, as the body or mind.

2. To disturb; to ruffle.

3. To deprive of temper or moderation.

4. To make disaffected, ill-humored, or malignant.

5. To make drunk. [Rare.]

dis-tem′pẽr, *v.t.* In painting, to make into distemper. [Rare.]

dis-tem′pẽr-ănce, *n.* Distemperature. [Obs.]

dis-tem′pẽr-āte, *a.* 1. Immoderate. [Obs.]

2. Having distemper. [Obs.]

dis-tem′pẽr-āte-ly, *adv.* In a distemperate manner. [Obs.]

dis-tem′pẽr-ȧ-tūre, *n.* 1. Bad temperature; intemperateness; excess of heat or cold, or of other qualities; a noxious state; as, the *distemperature* of the air or climate. [Obs.]

2. Violent tumult; confusion; disorder.

3. Perturbation of mind.

4. Slight illness; indisposition.

dis-tem′pẽr-ment, *n.* A state of distemperature. [Obs.]

dis-tend′, *v.t.*; distended, *pt., pp.*; distending, *ppr.* [L. *distendere*, to stretch asunder; *dis-*, apart, and *tendere*, to stretch.]

1. To stretch or spread in all directions; to dilate; to enlarge; to expand; to swell; as, to *distend* a bladder; to *distend* the lungs.

2. To lengthen out in one direction; to extend. [Rare.]

dis-tend′, *v.i.* To become inflated or puffed up.

dis-ten-si-bil′i-ty, *n.* The quality or capacity of being distensible. [Rare.]

dis-ten′si-ble, *a.* Capable of being distended or dilated.

dis-ten′sion, *n.* See *Distention.*

dis-ten′sive, *a.* Distensible; capable of distention.

dis-tent′, *a.* Spread; distended. [Obs.]

dis-tent′, *n.* Breadth. [Obs.]

dis-ten′tion, *n.* [L. *distentio*, from *distendere*, to stretch apart, distend.]

1. The act of distending; the act of stretching in breadth or in all directions; the state of being distended; as, the *distention* of the lungs or bowels.

2. Breadth; extent or space occupied by the thing distended.

dis-tẽr′, *v.t.* To banish from a country. [Obs.]

dis-tẽr′mi-nāte, *a.* [L. *disterminatus.*] Separated by bounds. [Obs.]

dis-tẽr-mi-nā′tion, *n.* Separation. [Obs.]

dis′thēne, *n.* [*Di-*, and Gr. *sthenos*, strength.] A mineral, so called by Haüy, because its crystals have the property of being electrified both positively and negatively; cyanite.

dis-thrōne′, *v.t.* To dethrone. [Obs.]

dis-thrōn′ize, *v.t.* To dethrone. [Obs.]

dis′tich, *n.* [L. *distichon*; Gr. *distichon*, a distich, from *distichos*, having two rows; *di-*, two, and *stichos*, a row, rank.] A couplet; a couple of verses, or poetic lines, making complete sense; an epigram of two verses.

dis′tich-ous, **dis′tich**, *a.* Having two rows, or disposed in two rows; specifically, in botany, placed opposite upon the axis, as certain leaves.

dis′tich-ous-ly, *adv.* In a distichous manner.

dis-til′, *v.i.*; distilled, *pt., pp.*; distilling, *ppr.* [ME. *distillen*; OFr. *distiller*; L. *destillare*, to drop, to trickle down; *de-*, down, and *stillare*, to drop, from *stilla*, a drop.]

1. To drop; to fall in drops.

Soft showers *distilled*, and suns grew warm in vain. —Pope.

2. To flow gently, or in a small stream.

The Euphrates *distilleth* out of the mountains of Armenia. —Raleigh.

3. To use a still; to practise distillation.

dis-til′, *v.t.* 1. To let fall in drops; to throw down in drops.

The dew which on the tender grass
The evening had *distilled*. —Drayton.

2. To obtain or extract by the process of distillation; as, to *distil* brandy from wine.

3. To subject to the process of distillation; to rectify; to purify; as, to *distil* molasses; to *distil* water.

4. To dissolve or melt. [Rare.]

Swords by the lightning's subtle force *distilled.* —Addison.

dis-till′ȧ-ble, *a.* That may be distilled; fit for distillation.

dis-till′āte, *n.* The result of distillation.

dis-til-lā′tion, *n.* 1. The act of falling in drops, or the act of pouring or throwing down in drops.

2. An operation by which a volatile liquid may be separated from substances which it holds in solution, or by which two liquids of different volatilities may be separated.

3. The substance extracted by distilling.

4. That which falls in drops. [Rare.]

Dry or *destructive distillation*; chemical decomposition induced by heating a substance, without water, and collecting the distillates.

Fractional distillation; see under *Fractional.*

dis-til′lȧ-tō-ry, *a.* Belonging to distillation; used for distilling; as, *distillatory* vessels.

dis-til′lȧ-tō-ry, *n.* A still or other apparatus for distillation.

dis-till′ẽr, *n.* One who or that which distils.

dis-till′ẽr-y, *n.*; *pl.* **dis-till′ẽr-ieș.** 1. The building and works where distilling is carried on.

2. Distillation. [Rare.]

dis-till′ment, *n.* A distillate. [Obs.]

dis-tinct′, *a.* [ME. *distinct*; OFr. *distinct*, from L. *distinctus*, pp. of *distinguere*, to distinguish.]

1. Having the difference marked; separated by a visible sign. [Obs.]

2. Different; separate; not the same in number or kind; as, he holds two *distinct* offices.

3. Separate in place; not conjunct; as, the regiments had *distinct* encampments.

4. So separated as not to be confounded with any other thing; clear; not confused; as, *distinct* ideas; *distinct* orders.

5. Spotted; variegated. [Obs.]

Distinct with eyes. —Milton.

Syn.—Separate, different, disjoined, disunited, well-marked, clear, plain, obvious.

dis-tinct′, *v.t.* To distinguish. [Obs.]

dis-tinc′tion, *n.* [L. *distinctio*, from *distinguere*, to distinguish.]

1. The act of separating or distinguishing; separation; division.

Standards and gonfalons . . . for *distinction* serve. —Milton.

2. A note or mark of difference; as, the only *distinction* between the two is the color.

3. Distinguishing quality; a separation or disagreement in kind or qualities, by which one thing is known from another; as, a *distinction* between matter and spirit; a *distinction* between the animal and vegetable kingdoms; a *distinction* between good and evil.

If he does really think that there is no *distinction* between virtue and vice, why, sir, when he leaves our houses, let us count our spoons. —Boswell.

4. Difference regarded; regard to distinguishing characteristics or circumstances, as in the phrase, *without distinction*, which denotes promiscuously, indiscriminately, all together, alike.

Maids, women, wives, *without distinction*, fall. —Dryden.

5. The power of distinguishing in what respect two things differ; discrimination; discernment; judgment.

She (Nature) left the eye *distinction*, to cull out
The one from the other. —Beau. and Fl.

6. Eminence; superiority; elevation of rank in society, or elevation of character; honorable estimation; as, men who are eminent for their talents, services, or worth are called men of *distinction.*

7. That which confers or marks eminence or superiority; office, rank, or public favor.

Loaded with literary *distinctions.*—Macaulay.

Syn.—Division, difference, separation, discernment, discrimination, rank, note, eminence.

dis-tinc′tive, *a.* 1. That marks distinction or difference; as, *distinctive* names or titles.

2. Having the power to distinguish and discern. [Obs.]

dis-tinc′tive-ly, *adv.* With distinction; plainly.

dis-tinc′tive-ness, *n.* State of being distinctive; individuality.

dis-tinct′ly, *adv.* 1. Separately; with distinctness; clearly; not confusedly; without the blending of one part or thing with another; as, a proposition *distinctly* understood; a figure *distinctly* defined.

2. Meaningly; with significance. [Obs.]

Syn.—Clearly, explicitly, definitely, precisely, plainly, obviously.

dis-tinct′ness, *n.* 1. The quality or state of being distinct; a separation or difference that prevents confusion of parts or things; as, the *distinctness* of two ideas or of distant objects.

2. Nice discrimination; clearness; precision; as, he stated his arguments with great *distinctness.*

dis-tinc′tūre, *n.* Distinctness. [Rare.]

dis-tin′guish (-gwish), *v.t.*; distinguished, *pt.*, *pp.*; distinguishing, *ppr.* [ME. *distingwen*; L. *distinguere*, to separate, divide, distinguish.]

1. To indicate difference in by some external mark; to set apart as distinct; as, the farmer *distinguishes* his sheep by marking their ears.

2. To perceive or recognize the individuality of; to note (one thing) as differing from another by some mark or quality; to know or ascertain difference in by use of the senses or perceptions; as, to *distinguish* various fruits; to *distinguish* good from evil.

3. To classify or divide by any mark or quality which constitutes difference; to separate by definitions; as, we *distinguish* sounds into high and low, soft and harsh, lively and grave; we *distinguish* causes into direct and indirect, immediate and mediate.

4. To discern critically; to judge.

No more can you *distinguish* of a man
Than of his outward show. —Shak.

5. To separate from others by some mark of honor or preference; as, Homer and Virgil are *distinguished* as poets, Demosthenes and Cicero as orators; to make eminent or known.

dis-tin′guish, *v.i.* 1. To make a distinction; to find or show the difference; as, a judge will *distinguish* between cases apparently similar.

2. To become distinct or distinguishable; to become differentiated. [Obs.]

dis-tin′guish-ȧ-ble, *a.* 1. Capable of being distinguished; that may be separated, known, or made known, by notes of diversity or by any difference; as, a tree at a distance is *distinguishable* from a shrub; a simple idea is not *distinguishable* into different ideas.

2. Worthy of note or special regard.

dis-tin′guish-ȧ-ble-ness, *n.* The state or quality of being distinguishable.

dis-tin′guish-ȧ-bly, *adv.* So as to be distinguished.

dis-tin′guished (-gwisht), *a.* 1. Separated or known by a mark of difference, or by different qualities.

2. Separated from others by superior or extraordinary qualities; hence, eminent; extraordinary; transcendent; noted; famous; celebrated; as, we admire *distinguished* men, *distinguished* talents or virtues, and *distinguished* services.

Syn.—Eminent, conspicuous, celebrated, illustrious.—A man is *eminent* when he stands high as compared with those around him; *conspicuous* when he is so elevated as to be generally seen and observed; *distinguished* when he has something which makes him stand apart from others in the public view; *celebrated* when he is widely spoken of with honor and respect; *illustrious* when a splendor is thrown around him which confers the highest dignity.

dis-tin′guished-ly (-gwisht-), *adv.* In a distinguished manner.

dis-tin′guish-ẽr, *n* 1. One who or that which distinguishes, or that separates one thing from another by marks of diversity.

2. One who discerns accurately the difference of things; a nice or judicious observer.

dis-tin′guish-ing, *a.* Constituting difference, or distinction from everything else; peculiar; as, the *distinguishing* colors of a bird.

Distinguishing pennant; a signaling pennant used to designate a certain ship.

dis-tin′guish-ing-ly, *adv.* With distinction; with some mark of preference.

dis-tin′guish-ment, *n.* Distinction; observation of difference.

dis-tī′tle, *v.t.* To deprive of right.

Dis′tō-mȧ, *n.* [L., from Gr. *distomos*, two-mouthed; *di-*, two, and *stoma*, a mouth.]

1. A genus of trematoid or suctorial parasitical worms or flukes, inhabiting various parts in different animals. *Distoma hepaticum*, or the common liver-fluke, is the best known.

2. [d-] Any worm of this genus.

di-stom′ȧ-tous, *a.* Of or pertaining to the *Distoma.*

dis-tort′, *v.t.*; distorted, *pt.*, *pp.*; distorting *ppr.* [L. *distortus*, pp. of *distorquere*, to twist, to turn different ways, to untwist.]

1. To twist out of natural or regular shape; as, to *distort* the features.

2. To force or put out of the true posture or direction.

Wrath and malice, envy and revenge *distort* the understanding. —Tillotson.

3. To wrest from the true meaning; to pervert; as, to *distort* passages of Scripture, or their meaning.

dis-tort′, *a.* Distorted. [Obs.]

dis-tort′ẽr, *n.* One who or that which distorts.

dis-tor′tion, *n.* [L. *distortio*, from *distorquere*, to turn, twist.]

1. The act of distorting; a twisting out of regular shape; a twisting or writhing motion; as, the *distortions* of the face or body.

2. The state of being twisted out of shape; deviation from natural shape or position; an unnatural direction of parts from whatever cause, as a curved spine, a wry mouth, squinting, etc.; crookedness.

3. A perversion of the true meaning of words.

These absurdities are all framed by a childish *distortion* of my words. —Wren.

dis-tort′ive, *a.* Productive of distortion.

dis-tract′, *a.* Mad; also, separate. [Obs.]

dis-tract′, *v.t.*; distracted *or* distraught [Obs.], *pt.*, *pp.*; distracting, *ppr.* [ME. *distracten*, to distract, from L. *distractus*, pp. of *distrahere*, to draw apart, pull in different directions, distract.]

1. To draw apart; to pull in different directions, and separate; hence, to throw into confusion. Sometimes in a literal sense.

Distract your army, which doth most consist
Of war-mark'd footmen. —Shak.

2. To turn or draw from any object; to divert from any point toward another point, or toward various other objects; as, to *distract* the attention.

If he cannot avoid the eye of the observer, he hopes to *distract* it by a multiplicity of the object. —South.

3. To draw toward different objects; to fill with different considerations; to perplex; to confound; to harass; as, to *distract* the mind with cares; you *distract* me with your clamor.

A thousand external details must be left out as irrelevant and only serving to *distract* and mislead the observer. —Caird.

4. To disorder the reason of; to derange the regular operations of the intellect of; to render insane; most frequently used in the participle *distracted.*

A poor mad soul, . . . poverty hath *distracted* her. —Shak.

dis-tract′ed, *a.* Disordered in intellect.

Syn.—Deranged, perplexed, mad, frantic, crazed.

dis-tract′ed-ly, *adv.* In a distracted manner.

dis-tract′ed-ness, *n.* The state of being perplexed; madness.

dis-tract′ẽr, *n.* One who or that which distracts.

dis-tract′fụl, *a.* Distracting. [Rare.]

dis-tract′i-ble, *a.* That may be distracted.

dis-tract′ile, *a.* In botany, denoting a connective attached to the filament in a horizontal manner, so as to separate the two anther lobes.

dis-tract′ing, *a.* Having inclination or tendency to distract.

dis-trac′tion, *n.* [ME. *distractioun*; L. *distractio*, from *distrahere*, to pull apart.]

1. The act of distracting; a drawing apart; separation. [Obs.]

2. Confusion from multiplicity of objects crowding on the mind and drawing the attention different ways; perplexity; embarrassment.

That ye may attend upon the Lord without *distraction.* —1 Cor vii. 35.

3. Confusion of affairs; tumult; disorder; as, political *distractions.*

Never was known a night of such *distraction.* —Dryden.

4. Madness; a state of disordered reason; frenzy; insanity.

This savors not much of *distraction.*—Shak.

5. Folly in the extreme, or amounting to insanity.

Irreligion is nothing better than *distraction.* —Buckminster.

6. Violent mental excitement; extreme perturbation or agony of mind, as from pain or grief; as, this toothache drives me to *distraction.*

This quiet sail is a noiseless wing
To waft me from *distraction.* —Byron.

7. Diversity of direction; variety of route; in the following passage only:

> While he was yet in Rome,
> His power went out in such *distractions* as
> Beguiled all spies. —Shak.

8. Anything calling the mind away from business, study, care, or the like; anything giving the mind a new and less onerous occupation; a diversion; as, after a spell of hard work I found boating a wholesome *distraction*; the *distractions* of a city are enemies to study.

9. In Greek grammar, a doubling of two long vowels or the use of two vowels pronounced nearly alike, for one; as, κράατος for κρᾶτος.

10. In French law, a diversion of costs from the usual beneficiary to some other person having equitable title to them.

Syn.—Perplexity, embarrassment, disturbance, disorder, dissension, tumult, diversion, derangement, insanity, madness, frenzy, recreation.

dis-trac′tious, *a.* Distractive. [Obs.]

dis-trac′tive, *a.* Causing perplexity; as, *distractive* cares.

dis-trāin′, *v.t.*; distrained, *pt.*, *pp.*; distraining, *ppr.* [ME. *distreynen*, to compel, constrain, from L. *distringere*, to pull asunder, to distract.]

1. To tear asunder; to seize; to confine. [Obs.]

2. In law, to seize for debt; to transfer (a personal chattel) from the possession of a wrongdoer to the possession of the injured party, to satisfy a demand, or compel the performance of a duty; as, to *distrain* goods for rent or for an amercement.

dis-trāin′, *v.i.* To make a seizure of goods to satisfy a claim.

dis-trāin′ȧ-ble, *a.* That is liable to be taken for distress.

dis-trāin′ẽr, dis-trāin′ŏr, *n.* In law, one who seizes goods for debt or service.

dis-trāint′, *n.* In law, a distress.

dis-trāit′ (-trā′), *a.* Preoccupied; pensive; abstracted.

dis-traught′ (-trat′), *a.* [ME. *distrauht*, from L. *distractus*, pp. of *distrahere*, to draw apart.]

1. Torn apart; rent. [Obs.]

2. Bewildered; in a state of perplexity.

dis-traught′ed, *a.* Distraught. [Obs.]

dis-trēam′, *v.i.* To spread or flow over. [Obs.]

> Yet o'er that virtuous blush *distreams* a tear. —Shenstone.

dis-tress′, *n.* [ME. *distresse*; OFr. *destresse*, distress, constraint.]

1. Extreme pain; anguish of body or mind; great unhappiness.

2. A condition of affliction or wretchedness; danger; calamity.

3. Oppression; compulsion. [Obs.]

4. In law, (a) the act of distraining; the taking of any personal chattel from a wrongdoer, to answer a demand or procure satisfaction for a wrong committed; (b) the thing taken by distraining; that which is seized to procure satisfaction.

Abuse of distress; in law, wrongful use of the powers of distress

Syn.—Suffering, pain, agony, misery, calamity, misfortune, adversity.

dis-tress′, *v.t.*; distressed (-trest′), *pt.*, *pp.*; distressing, *ppr.* [ME. *distressen*; OFr. *destresser*, to restrain, constrain, distress, from L. *distringere*, to pull asunder, distract.]

1. To afflict greatly; to afflict with pain or anguish; to harass; to oppress or crush with calamity; to make miserable.

> *Distress* not the Moabites. —Deut. ii. 9.

> We are troubled on every side, yet not *distressed*. —2 Cor. iv. 8.

2. To compel or constrain by pain or suffering.

> Men who can neither be *distressed* nor won into a sacrifice of duty. —Hamilton.

3. In law, to distrain.

Syn.—Pain, grieve, afflict, harass, trouble, perplex.

dis-tress′ed-ness, *n.* A state of being greatly pained.

dis-tress′fụl, *a.* Inflicting or bringing distress; denoting or accompanied by distress; caused by distress; as, *distressful* pains; a *distressful* sight.

dis-tress′fụl-ly, *adv.* In a distressful manner.

dis-tress′ing, *a.* Painful; harassing; annoying.

dis-tress′ing-ly, *adv.* In a distressing manner.

dis-trib′ū-tȧ-ble, *a.* Capable of distribution.

dis-trib′ū-tā-ry, *n.* In the delta of a river, an outgoing branch.

dis-trib′ūte, *v.t.*; distributed, *pt.*, *pp.*; distributing, *ppr.* [L. *distributus*, pp. of *distribuere*, to divide, distribute; *dis-*, apart, and *tribuere*, to give, from *tribus*, tribe.]

1. To divide among two or more; to deal out; to give or bestow in parts or portions; as, Moses *distributed* lands to the tribes of Israel.

> Walk your dim cloister, and *distribute* dole. —Tennyson.

2. To dispense; to administer; as, to *distribute* justice.

3. To divide or separate, as into classes, orders, genera, and species.

4. In printing, (a) to return to their separate compartments (the type used in composed matter or pi); (b) to spread, while being worked, as on a form or roller; said of ink.

5. In logic, to employ in its full extent, as a term.

6. In the postal service, (a) to work, as mail designed for other postal stations; (b) to place, as the various pieces of incoming mail, each in its proper box or drawer.

Syn.—Dispense, deal out, apportion, partition, allot, share, assign.

dis-trib′ūte, *v.i.* To make an allotment, distribution, or division.

dis-trib′ū-tẽr, *n.* One who or that which distributes.

dis-trib′ū-ting-mȧ-chïne″, *n.* An automatic machine for distributing type.

dis-tri-bū′tion, *n.* [L. *distributio*, from *distribuere*, to distribute.]

1. The act of dividing among a number; allotment in parts or portions; as, the *distribution* of an estate among heirs or children.

2. The act of giving in charity; the bestowing in portions.

> Of great riches there is no real use except it be in the *distribution*. —Bacon.

3. Dispensation; administration to numbers; a rendering to individuals; as, the *distribution* of justice.

4. The act of separating into distinct parts or classes; classification; systematic arrangement; as, the *distribution* of plants into genera or species.

5. In logic, the distinguishing of a universal whole into its several kinds or species.

6. In architecture, the dividing and disposing of the several parts of the building according to some plan or to the rules of the art.

7. In rhetoric, a division and enumeration of the several qualities of a subject.

8. In printing, (a) the returning of type to its proper compartment in a case or slide; (b) the spreading of ink, as on a disk or rollers.

9. In steam-engines, the operation by which steam is admitted into and withdrawn from the cylinder at each stroke of the piston.

10. That which is distributed.

> Our charitable *distributions*. —Atterbury.

Geographical distribution; in botany and zoölogy, that branch of the respective sciences which treats of the distribution of plants and animals over the surface of the earth.

Syn.—Apportionment, allotment, partition, arrangement, classification, dispensation, disposal.

dis-tri-bū′tion-ăl, *a.* Relating to distribution.

dis-tri-bū′tion-ist, *n.* One who distributes. [Rare.]

dis-trib′ū-tive, *a.* 1. That distributes; that divides and assigns in portions; that deals to each his proper share; as, *distributive* justice.

2. In logic, that assigns the various species of a general term.

3. Expressing separation or division; as, a *distributive* prefix; specifically, in grammar, an epithet applied to certain words which denote the persons or things that make a number, as taken separately and singly, or separation and division in general.

4. In mathematics, affecting every part as well as the whole; applied to operations.

dis-trib′ū-tive, *n.* In grammar, a word that divides or distributes, as *each* and *every*.

dis-trib′ū-tive-ly, *adv.* In a distributive manner.

dis-trib′ū-tive-ness, *n.* The state or quality of being distributive.

dis-trib′ū-tŏr, *n.* One who or that which distributes; specifically, in printing, (a) a roller to facilitate the distribution of ink; (b) a machine to effect type-distribution.

dis′trict, *n.* [Fr. *district*; LL. *districtus*, in feudal law a territory within which a lord had the right to administer jurisdiction, a district, from L. *districtus*, pp. of *distringere*, to stretch or draw in different directions, to distrain; *dis-*, apart, and *stringere*, to draw.]

1. A limited extent of country; a circuit or territory within which a person may be compelled to legal appearance, or within which power, right, or authority may be exercised, and to which it is restrained; a word applicable to any portion of land or country, or to any part of a city or town, which is defined by law or agreement.

2. A region; a territory within given lines; as, the *district* of the earth which lies between the tropics.

3. A region; a country; a portion of territory without very definite limits; as, the *districts* of Russia covered by forest.

Congressional district; see under *Congressional*.

District attorney; one elected or appointed to represent the people in legal cases within a certain district.

District court; one which has cognizance of certain causes within a district defined by law. [See under *Court*.]

District judge; the judge of a district court.

District school; one held for the pupils of a certain district.

Syn.—Division, quarter, locality, province, tract, region, country.

dis′trict, *a.* Stringent; exacting. [Obs.]

dis′trict, *v.t.*; districted, *pt.*, *pp.*; districting, *ppr.* To divide into districts or limited portions of territory; as, legislatures *district* states for the choice of representatives.

dis-tric′tion, *n.* Sudden display. [Rare.]

dis′trict-ly, *adv.* Stringently. [Obs.]

dis-trin′gas, *n.* [L., lit., that you may distrain, from second pers. sing. pres. subj. of *distringere*, to distrain.] In law, a writ commanding the sheriff to distrain a person for debt or for his appearance at a certain day.

dis-trou′ble (-trub′l), *v.t.* To disturb. [Obs.]

dis-trust′, *v.t.*; distrusted, *pt.*, *pp.*; distrusting, *ppr.* To doubt or suspect the truth, fidelity, firmness, or sincerity of; not to confide in or rely on; as, we may often *distrust* our own firmness.

dis-trust′, *n.* 1. Doubt or suspicion of reality or sincerity; want of confidence, faith, or reliance; doubt; as, *distrust* mars many pleasures.

2. Loss of confidence; discredit.

Syn.—Diffidence, suspicion, doubt, skepticism.

dis-trust′ẽr, *n.* One who distrusts.

dis-trust′fụl, *a.* 1. Apt to distrust; suspicious.

2. Not confident; diffident; as, *distrustful* of ourselves.

dis-trust′fụl-ly, *adv.* In a distrustful manner.

dis-trust′fụl-ness, *n.* The state of being distrustful; want of confidence.

dis-trust′ing-ly, *adv.* Suspiciously; with distrust.

dis-trust′less, *a.* Free from distrust or suspicion.

dis-tūne′, *v.t.* To put out of tune. [Obs.]

dis-tūrb′, *v.t.*; disturbed, *pt.*, *pp.*; disturbing, *ppr.* [ME. *disturben*; L. *disturbare*, to drive asunder, tear in pieces; *dis-*, apart, and *turbare*, to disorder, throw into confusion.]

1. To stir; to move; to discompose; to excite from a state of rest or tranquillity; to disquiet; to excite uneasiness or a slight degree of anger in the mind of; to move the passions of; to ruffle; as, to *disturb* one asleep.

2. To move from any regular course or operation; to interrupt regular order of; to make irregular; as, to *disturb* the motions of the planets in their orbits; to *disturb* a chemical operation.

3. To turn off from any direction; with *from*. [Rare.]

> And *disturb*
> His inmost counsels *from* their destined aim. —Milton.

dis-tūrb′, *n.* Confusion; disorder. [Obs.]

dis-tūrb′ănce, *n.* [ME. *disturbance*; OFr. *destourbance*, from *destourber*; L. *disturbare*, to disturb.]

1. A stirring or excitement; any disquiet or interruption of peace; as, to move without *disturbance*.

2. Interruption of a settled state of things; disorder; tumult; as, the *disturbances* of war.

3. Emotion of the mind; agitation; excitement of passion; perturbation; disorder of thoughts; confusion.

> They can survey a variety of complicated ideas, without fatigue or *disturbance*. —Watts.

4. In law, the hindering or disquieting of a person in the lawful and peaceable enjoyment of his right; the interruption of a right; as, the *disturbance* of a franchise, of common, of ways, of tenure, of patronage. —Blackstone.

dis-tūr-bā′tion, *n.* Disturbance. [Obs.]

dis-tūrb′ẽr, *n.* 1. One who or that which disturbs or disquiets.

2. In law, one that interrupts or incommodes another in the peaceable enjoyment of his right.

dis-tūrn′, *v.t.* To turn aside. [Obs.]

dis′tȳle, *n.* [*Di-*, and Gr. *stylos*, column.] A portico of two columns. It applies rather to a portico with two columns in antis than to the mere two-columned porch.

dis′tȳle, *a.* Pertaining to a two-columned portico.

di-sul′phāte, *n.* [*Di-* and *sulphate*.] In chemistry, (a) a salt containing one equivalent of sulphuric acid and two equivalents of the base; (b) a salt of disulphuric acid.

di-sul′phid, di-sul′phide, *n.* In chemistry, a sulphid containing two atoms of sulphur.

di-sul′phū-ret, *n.* A disulphid.

di-sul-phū′ric, *a.* In chemistry, designating the acid, $H_2S_2O_7$.

Disulphuric acid; an oily liquid used to

dissolve indigo, in the manufacture of artificial alizarin, and to decompose substances not affected by sulphuric acid; also called *pyro-, fuming*, or *Nordhausen sulphuric acid.*

dis-ū′ni-fọrm, *a.* Not uniform.

dis-ūn′iȯn (-yun), *n.* Separation; disjunction, or a state of not being united; as, the *disunion* of the states of the United States.

dis-ūn′iȯn-ist, *n.* An advocate of disunion; specifically, in United States history, one in favor of secession during the Civil War period.

dis-ū-nīte′, *v.t.*; disunited, *pt., pp.*; disuniting, *ppr.* 1. To separate; to disjoin; to part; as, to *disunite* particles of matter.

2. To set at variance; to interrupt the harmony of; as, to *disunite* a delegation.

dis-ū-nīte′, *v.i.* To part; to fall asunder; to become separate; as, parties and churches *disunite.*

dis-ū-nīt′ẽr, *n.* One who or that which disjoins.

dis-ū′ni-ty, *n.* A state of separation.

dis-ūṣ′āġe, *n.* Gradual cessation of use or custom; neglect of use, exercise, or practice; as, the growing *disusage* of the frock coat.

dis-ūse′, *n.* Cessation of use, practice, or exercise; as, the limbs lose their strength by *disuse.*

dis-ūṣe′, *v.t.*; disused, *pt., pp.*; disusing, *ppr.* 1. To cease to use; to neglect or omit to practise.

2. To disaccustom; with *from, in,* or *to*; as, *disused to* toils; *disused from* pain. [Archaic.]

dis-ū′til-īze, *v.t.* To deprive of usefulness.

dis-val-ū-ā′tion, *n.* Disesteem; disreputation. [Obs.]

dis-val′ūe, *v.t.* To undervalue; to disesteem. [Obs.]

dis-val′ūe, *n.* Disesteem; disregard. [Obs.]

dis-van-tā′ġeous (-jus), *a.* Disadvantageous. [Obs.]

dis-vel′ŏp, *v.t.* To develop. [Obs.]

dis-ven′tūre, *n.* [Obs.] Same as *Disadventure.*

dis-vouch′, *v.t.* To discredit; to contradict. [Obs.]

dis-wạrn′, *v.t.* To dissuade from by previous warning. [Obs.]

dis-wär′ren, *v.t.* In old English law, to rid (land) of a privilege as a warren.

dis-wit′ted, *a.* Deprived of wits or understanding. [Obs.]

dis-wŏnt′, *v.t.* To rid or deprive of wonted usage. [Obs.]

dis-wŏrk′măn-ship, *n.* Bad or defective workmanship. [Obs.]

dis-wŏr′ship, *v.t.* To deprive of reverence; to refuse to revere or worship; to dishonor. [Obs.]

dis-wŏr′ship, *n.* A deprivation of worship, reverence, or honor. [Obs.]

dis-wŏrth′, *v.t.* To make worthless; to lower in value. [Obs.]

dis-yōke′, *v.t.*; disyoked, *pt., pp.*; disyoking, *ppr.* To take off the yoke of; to unyoke.

dit, *v.t.* To stop up or close up. [Obs.]

dit, *n.* 1. A word; a sentence; a saying; a decree. [Obs.]

2. A ditty. [Obs.]

dī′tȧ-bärk′, *n.* [Tagalog *dita*, the name of the tree.] The bitter bark of the devil-tree, used for medicinal purposes.

dī-tā′tion, *n.* The act of making rich. [Obs.]

ditch (dich), *v.t.*; ditched (dicht), *pt., pp.*; ditching, *ppr.* 1. To dig a ditch or ditches in; to drain by a ditch.

2. To surround with a ditch.

3. To overturn, or throw in or as in a ditch; said especially of vehicles; as, to *ditch* a car or carriage.

ditch, *v.i.* To dig or make a ditch or ditches, particularly as an occupation.

ditch, *n.*; *pl.* **ditch′eṣ.** [ME. *diche*; AS. *dic*, a ditch, dike.]

1. A trench in the earth made by digging; particularly a trench for draining wet land, or for making a fence to guard inclosures, or for preventing an enemy from approaching a town or fortress. In the latter sense, it is called also a *fosse* or *moat*, and is dug round the rampart or wall between the scarp and counterscarp.

2. Any long, hollow receptacle of water on the earth's surface.

ditch′ẽr, *n.* [ME. *dichere*; AS. *dicere*, a digger, a ditcher, from *dic*, a ditch.]

1. One who digs ditches.

2. A machine for digging ditches or trenches.

ditch′-wa″tẽr, *n.* Bad water, such as is found in a ditch.

dīte, *v.t.* To prepare; to dight; to make ready. [Obs.]

di-ter′e-bēne, *n.* Same as *Colophene.*

dī-tē-trag′ō-năl, *a.* [*Di-*, and Gr. *tetragōnos*, a four-angled figure; *tetra*, four, and *gōnia*, an angle.] In crystallography, denoting a tetragonal prism, having faces eight in number and similar.

dī-tet-rȧ-hē′drăl, *a.* [*Di-*, and Gr. *tetra-*, four, and *hedra*, base.] In crystallography, having the form of a tetrahedral prism with dihedral summits.

dī-thē′căl, dī-thē′cous, *a.* [*Di-*, and Gr. *thēkē*, a case.] In botany, having two loculaments or cavities in the ovary.

dī′thē-iṣm, *n.* [*Di-*, and Gr. *theos*, god.] The doctrine that there are two coequal gods, one good and one evil; dualism.

dī′thē-ist, *n.* One who believes in ditheism; a dualist.

dī-thē-is′tic, dī-thē-is′tic-ăl, *a.* Of or pertaining to ditheism or characterized by it; dualistic.

dith′ẽr, *v.i.* To tremble. [Obs.]

dith′ẽr, *n.* The act of dithering; a trembling. [Obs.]

dī-thi-on′ic, *a.* [*Di-*, and Gr. *theion*, sulphur.] Containing two atoms of sulphur; applied to compounds.

Dithionic acid; an acid, $H_2S_2O_6$, of theoretical importance only.

dith′y-ramb (-ram), *n.* [L. *dithyrambus*; Gr. *dithyrambos*, dithyramb.]

1. In ancient Greek poetry, a hymn originally in honor of Bacchus, afterward of other gods, composed in an elevated style, and sung to the music of the flute.

2. In modern poetry, an ode of an impetuous and irregular character.

dith-y-ram′bic, *a.* Pertaining to a dithyramb.

dith-y-ram′bic, *n.* A dithyramb.

dith-y-ram′bus, *n.* [L.] Same as *Dithyramb.*

dī′tion, *n.* Rule; power; government. [Obs.]

dī′tion-ā-ry, *a.* and *n.* Tributary. [Obs.]

dī′tō-kous (*or* dit′ō-kous), *a.* [Gr. *ditokos*, twin or twice bearing; *di-*, two, and *tokos*, an offspring, from *tiktein*, to bear, bring forth.] In zoölogy, marked by two; specifically applied to (a) the number of eggs in a clutch; (b) the number of young at a birth; (c) the kinds of young, as of certain worms.

dī-tol′yl (*or* dī′tō-lil), *n.* The double radical, $C_{14}H_{14}$, of the hydrocarbon tolyl.

dī′tōne, *n.* [Gr. *ditonon*, a major third; *di-*, two, and *tonos*, tone.] In music, an interval comprehending two major tones. The proportion of the sounds that form the ditone is 4:5, and that of the semiditone, 5:6.

Dī-trē′mȧ-tȧ, *n.pl.* [L., from Gr. *di-*, two, and *trēma*, a hole.]

1. A family of fishes, the *Ditremidæ.*

2. A class of geophilous gasteropods having widely separated male and female orifices.

dī-trē′mȧ-tous, *a.* Of or pertaining to the *Ditremata*; having two genital apertures.

dī-trē′mid, *n.* One of the *Ditremidæ.*

Dī-trē′mi-dæ, *n.pl.* A family of viviparous fishes having an anal and a genital orifice.

dī-tri-chot′ō-mous, *a.* Divided into parts numbering two and three; specifically, in botany, branching twice and three times.

dī-trī′glyph, *n.* [*Di-*, and L. *triglyphus*; Gr. *triglyphos*, three-grooved, a triglyph; *treis*, three,

Ditriglyph.

and *glyphein*, to hollow out.] In architecture, an interval between two columns, admitting two triglyphs in the entablature; used in the Doric order.

dī-trig′ō-năl, *a.* Twice-three-sided, a term used in crystallography.

dī-trō-chē′ăn, *a.* Made up of two trochees.

dī-trō′chee, *n.* [LL. *ditrochæus*; Gr. *ditrochaios*, a double trochee.] In prosody, a double trochee; a foot made up of two trochees.

dit′rō-īte, *n.* [From *Ditro* in Transylvania.] A rock of igneous origin, an elæolite-syenite having sodalite and spinel as constituents.

ditt, *n.* A ditty. [Obs.]

dit-tan′dẽr, *n.* [ME. *ditaundere*, from *ditane*, dittany.] Pepperwort, the popular English name of *Lepidium latifolium*, a cruciferous herb, found in salt marshes.

dit′tȧ-ny, *n.* [ME. *ditane*; L. *dictamnus*; Gr. *diktamnos*, the dittany plant, so called from Mount Dicte in Crete, where it grew in abundance.] The popular name of the plants of the genus *Dictamnus*, a rutaceous herb, found in the Mediterranean region. The *dittany* of the United States is *Cunila Mariana.* The *dittany* of Crete is *Origanum Dictamnus*, and the bastard *dittany* is a species of *Marrubium.*

dit′tāy, *n.* In Scots law, a technical term signifying the matter of charge or ground of indictment against a person accused of a crime; also, the charge itself.

dit′tied (-tid), *a.* Sung; adapted to music; as, sweet-*dittied* verse. [Rare or Poet.]

dit′tō, *n.* [It. *ditto*; L. *dictum*, a saying, from *dicere*, to say.] That which has been said; the aforesaid; the same thing; an abbreviation used to save repetition; being further shortened to *do.*, or in printing to " or in writing to ".

dit′tō, *adv.* As before mentioned; in a like manner; also.

dit′tō-gram, *n.* An unintentional or absent-minded repetition in copying or writing.

dit-tog′rȧ-phy, *n.* [Gr. *dittos, dissos*, double, and *graphein*, to write.] Unmeant repetition in a writing, as by absent-mindedness; also, the part so repeated.

dit-tol′ō-ġy, *n.* A twofold interpretation or reading.

dit′ty, *n.*; *pl.* **dit′tieṣ.** [ME. *dite*; OFr. *dite*, a song, a little poem, a story, from L. *dictatum*, a thing dictated.]

1. A song; a sonnet; a little poem to be sung.

> And to the warbling lute soft *ditties* sing. —Sandys.

2. A saying, especially one frequently repeated. [Obs.]

dit′ty, *v.i.* To sing; to warble a little tune. [Obs.]

dit′ty-bag, *n.* A bag used by sailors in which to stow away sewing-tackle; called also *sailor's housewife.*

dit′ty-box, *n.* A box for the same purpose as a ditty-bag.

dī-ū′rē-ide, *n.* A compound containing two molecules of urea.

dī-ū-rē′sis, *n.* [Gr. *diourein*, to urinate; *dia-*, through, and *ourein*, to urinate, from *ouron*, urine.] Increase in urine-secretion.

dī-ū-ret′ic, *a.* [Gr. *diourētikos*, promoting urine, from *diourein*, to urinate.] Tending to produce or increase the urinary discharge.

dī-ū-ret′ic, *n.* A diuretic medicine.

dī-ū-ret′ic-ăl, *a.* Diuretic. [Obs.]

dī-ū-ret′ic-ăl-ness, *n.* The state of being diuretical.

dī-ū-rē′tin, *n.* A coal-tar compound used in medicine as a diuretic.

Dī-ŭr′nȧ, *n.pl.* [L., from *diurnus*, daily, from *dies*, day.] According to Latreille, a section of lepidopterous insects, corresponding with the Linnean genus *Papilio*, or butterflies.

dī-ŭr′năl, *a.* [ME. *diurnal*; L. *diurnalis*, day by day, from *diurnus*, daily, from *dies*, day.]

1. Relating to a day; pertaining to the daytime; as, *diurnal* heat; *diurnal* hours.

2. Daily; happening every day; performed in a day; as, a *diurnal* task.

3. Performed in twenty-four hours; as, the *diurnal* revolution of the earth.

4. Having some peculiarity or characteristic which appears and disappears with the day; specifically, (a) in medicine, growing more severe in the daytime; as, a *diurnal* fever; (b) in botany, opening by day and closing by night, as the morning-glory and other flowers; (c) in biology, active during the day, as certain birds of prey; also, of or pertaining to the *Diurna.*

Diurnal aberration of the fixed stars; the small periodical change of the position of the stars and other heavenly bodies, arising from the earth's motion of rotation, and hence different in different places.

Diurnal arc; the apparent arc described by heavenly bodies from their rising to their setting, in consequence of the earth's rotation.

Diurnal circle; see under *Circle.*

Diurnal motion of a planet; the number of degrees, minutes, etc., which a planet moves in twenty-four hours.

dī-ŭr′năl, *n.* 1. A day-book; a journal. [Obs.]

2. In zoölogy, (a) a raptorial bird, which flies by day and has lateral eyes; (b) a lepidopterous insect which is active only during the day.

3. A daily newspaper. [Obs.]

4. In the Roman Catholic church, a small book containing the prayers for the various hours of the day.

dī-ŭr′năl-ist, *n.* A journalist. [Obs.]

dī-ŭr′năl-ly, *adv.* Daily; every day.

dī-ŭr′năl-ness, *n.* The quality of being diurnal.

dī-ŭr-nā′tion, *n.* The somnolent state in the daytime, of nocturnal animals, as the bat, in contrast to their activity at night.

dī-ū-tŭr′năl, *a.* [L. *diuturnus*, of long duration, from *diu*, a long time, by day, from *dies*, a day.] Lasting; being of long continuance. [Rare.]

dī-ū-tŭr′ni-ty, *n.* Length of time; long duration. [Rare.]

dī′vä, *n.* [It., from L. *diva*, a goddess, f. of *divus*, a god.] A prima donna.

dī-vȧ-gā′tion, *n.* [L. *divagari*, to wander about.] A going astray; a digression. [Rare.]

dī′vā-lent (*or* div′ȧ-lent), *a.* [*Di-*, and L. *valens* (*-entis*), ppr. of *valere*, to be powerful.] In chemistry, having a valence of two; bivalent.

di-van′, *n.* [Turk. *dīwān*; Per. *dīvān, dīwān*, a council.]

1. An Oriental council of state; specifically, in Turkey, the great council composed of the ministers, judges, and heads of departments.

2. A council-chamber; an audience-chamber; a court.

3. A smoking-room where meals or refreshments are served.
4. A cushioned seat along the wall of a room; a low sofa, usually piled with cushions.
5. A book of poems, especially one containing the works of a single poet.
dī-var′i-cāte, *v.t.*; divaricated, *pt., pp.*; divaricating, *ppr.* [L. *divaricatus*, pp. of *divaricare*, to spread asunder.] To divide into branches; to cause to divide.
dī-var′i-cāte, *v.i.* 1. To branch off; to diverge; to digress; as, to *divaricate* from the dictates of wisdom.
2. In biology, to diverge widely.
dī-var′i-cāte, *a.* 1. In botany, branching off as from a stem or axis, at or almost at a right angle; turning off so as to form an obtuse angle above and an acute angle below.
2. In zoölogy, applied to the divisions of any part that spread out widely.
dī-var′i-cāte-ly, *adv.* In a divaricate manner.
dī-var-i-cā′tion, *n.* [L. *divaricare*, to spread apart.]
1. A forking; a separating into two branches.
2. In biology, a crossing or intersection of fibers at different angles.
3. Ambiguity. [Obs.]
dī-var′i-cā-tŏr, *n.* In zoölogy, a muscle which separates parts, as the one opening the shell of a bivalve.
dive, *v.i.*; dived *or* dove [colloq.], *pt., pp.*; diving, *ppr.* [ME. *diven, dyven*; AS. *dyfan*, to dive.]
1. To descend or plunge into water, headfirst; to thrust the body into water or other liquid; as, to *dive* from a springboard.
2. To plunge from one medium or condition to another; as, to *dive* into the fray; to *dive* into one's pocket.
3. To plunge into any subject, business, or condition, so as to be thoroughly engaged in it; as, to *dive* into art.

> *Dived* in a hoard of tales. —Tennyson.

dive, *v.t.* To explore by diving. [Rare.]
dive, *n.* 1. A descent or plunge headfirst into water; any plunge in imitation of a *dive*; as, a *dive* into a net.
2. A low resort; as, an opium *dive*. [Colloq.]
dīve′dap″pēr, dīve′dop″pēr, *n.* A bird, the dabchick. [Obs.]
dī-vel′, *v.t.* To tear apart; to rend. [Obs.]
dī-vel′lent, *a.* [L. *divellens (-ntis)*, ppr. of *divellere*, to pull asunder.] Drawing asunder; separating. [Rare.]
dī-vel′li-cāte, *v.t.* To pull in pieces. [Obs.]
dīv′ēr, *n.* 1. One who or that which dives; as, a *diver* for pearls.
2. One who goes deeply into a subject, or enters deeply into study.
3. A bird remarkable for its habit of diving. The divers, *Colymbidæ*, are a family of swimming birds, *Natatores*. They prey upon fish, which they pursue under water. The leading species are the great northern diver, the red-throated diver, and the black-throated diver. These birds inhabit the Arctic seas, being especially abundant in the Hebrides, Norway, Sweden, and Russia.

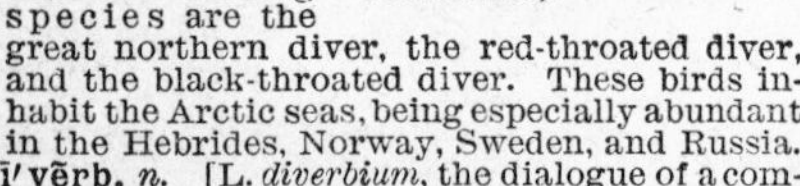
Red-throated Diver (*Colymbus septentrionalis*).

dī′vērb, *n.* [L. *diverbium*, the dialogue of a comedy; *di-, dis-*, apart, and *verbum*, a word.] A proverb in which the clauses are antithetical. [Rare.]

> England is a paradise for women, a hell for horses; Italy a paradise for horses, a hell for women; as the *diverb* goes. —Burton.

dī-vēr′bēr-āte, *v.t.* To penetrate or ring through, as sound. [Obs.]
dī-vēr-bēr-ā′tion, *n.* A sounding through. [Obs.]
dī-vērge′, *v.i.*; diverged, *pt., pp.*; diverging, *ppr.* [Fr. *diverger*; L. *di-, dis-*, apart, and *vergere*, to turn, incline.]
1. To tend from a common point and recede from each other; opposed to *converge*; as, the sides of an angle *diverge* from the apex.
2. To become separated; to tend to draw apart; as, their lives *diverged*.
3. To differ from a typical form; to vary from a normal state, or from the truth.
4. In mathematics, to grow larger without converging to a limit; said of an infinite series.
dī-vērge′ment, *n.* The act of diverging.
dī-vēr′gence, dī-vēr′gen-cy, *n.* 1. The act or state of diverging or receding from each other; a going farther apart; as, the *divergence* of lines; the angle of *divergence*.
2. Deviation or departure from a certain plan or standard; as, *divergence* from truth.
3. Disagreement; conflict; difference; as, there was great *divergence* in the two reports.
dī-vēr′gent, dī-vēr′ging, *a.* 1. Departing or receding from each other, as lines which proceed from the same point; opposed to *convergent*; as, *divergent* lines; *divergent* paths.
2. Disagreeing with or differing from some standard; deviating; variant.
Divergent rays; rays which, proceeding from a point of a visible object, continually depart from each other in proportion as they recede from the object.
Divergent or *diverging series*; in mathematics, a series, the terms of which increase more and more, the further they are continued.
dī-vēr′ging-ly, *adv.* In a diverging manner.
dī′vērs, *a.* [ME. *divers*; OFr. *divers*, different, several, from L. *diversus*, pp. of *divertere*, to turn in different directions.]
1. Different; various. [Obs.]

> Thou shalt not sow thy vineyard with *divers* seeds. —Deut. xxii. 9.

2. Several; sundry; more than one, but not a great number; as, we have *divers* examples of this kind.
dī′vērse (*or* di-vērs′), *a.* [L. *diversus*, pp. of *divertere*, to turn in different directions.]
1. Different; differing.

> Four great beasts came up from the sea, *diverse* one from another. —Dan. vii. 3.

2. Capable of assuming various and different forms; various; multiform.

> Eloquence is a *diverse* thing. —Jonson.

dī-vērse′, *adv.* In different directions.

> And with tendrils creep *diverse*. —Philips.

dī-vērse′, *v.i.* To turn aside. [Obs.]
dī′vērse-ly (*or* di-vērs′ly), *adv.* 1. In different ways; differently; variously; as, a passage of Scripture *diversely* interpreted or understood.
2. In different directions; to different points.

> On life's vast ocean *diversely* we sail.—Pope.

dī-vērse′ness, *n.* The quality of being diverse.
dī-vēr-si-fī-ā-bil′i-ty, *n.* The capacity of being diversifiable.
dī-vēr-si-fī′ā-ble, *a.* Capable of diversification.
dī-vēr″si-fi-cā′tion, *n.* [L. *diversus*, diverse, and *facere*, to make.]
1. The act of changing forms or qualities, or of making various.
2. Variation; variegation; change; as, *diversification* of voice.
dī-vēr′si-fīed, *a.* Distinguished by various forms, or by a variety of objects; as, *diversified* scenery; a *diversified* landscape.
dī-vēr′si-fī-ēr, *n.* One who or that which diversifies.
dī-vēr-si-flō′rous, *a.* [L. *diversiflorus*; *diversus*, different, and *flos* (*floris*), a flower.] Having two or more kinds of flowers.
dī-vēr-si-fō′li-ous, *a.* [L. *diversus*, different, and *folium*, a leaf.] Having leaves which differ in form, color, etc.
dī-vēr′si-fọrm, *a.* [L. *diversus*, different, and *forma*, form.] Of a different form; of various forms.
dī-vēr′si-fȳ, *v.t.*; diversified, *pt., pp.*; diversifying, *ppr.* [Fr. *diversifier*; LL. *diversificare*, to make different; L. *diversus*, different, and *facere*, to make.] To make different or various in form or qualities; to give variety to; to variegate; as, to *diversify* the colors of a robe; to *diversify* a landscape with mountains, plains, trees, and lakes.
dī-vēr-sil′ō-quent, *a.* [L. *diversus*, different, and *loquens (-entis)*, ppr. of *loqui*, to speak.] Speaking in different ways. [Rare.]
dī-vēr′sion, *n.* 1. The act of turning aside from any course; as, the *diversion* of a stream from its usual channel.
2. That which diverts; that which turns or draws the mind from care, business, or study, and thus relaxes and amuses; sport; play; pastime; whatever unbends the mind; as, the *diversions* of youth.
3. In military speech, the act of drawing the attention and force of an enemy from the point where the principal attack is to be made, as by an attack or alarm on one wing of an army, when the other wing or center is intended for the principal attack.
Syn.—Amusement, entertainment, pastime, recreation, sport.
dī-vēr′si-ty, *n.* [ME. *diversite*; L. *diversitas*, difference, from *divertere*, to turn in different directions.]
1. Difference; dissimilitude; unlikeness; as, there is a great *diversity* in human constitutions.
2. Variety; as, a *diversity* of ceremonies in churches.
3. Distinct being, as opposed to *identity*. [Rare.]
4. Variegation.

> Blushing in bright *diversities* of day.—Pope.

dī-vēr-siv′ō-lent, *a.* [L. *diversus*, different, and *volens (-entis)*, ppr. of *velle*, to wish.] Desiring trouble or differences. [Rare.]
dī-vēr′sō-ry, *a.* Tending to divert. [Obs.]
dī-vēr′sō-ry, *n.* [L. *diversorium*, an inn.] An inn by the wayside. [Obs.]
dī-vērt′, *v.t.*; diverted, *pt., pp.*; diverting, *ppr.* [ME. *diverten*; OFr. *divertir*; L. *divertere*, to turn in different directions.]
1. To turn off from any course, direction, or intended application; to turn aside; as, to *divert* a river from its usual channel; to *divert* commerce from its usual course; to *divert* appropriated money to other objects; to *divert* a man from his purpose.
2. To turn the mind from business or study; hence, to please; to amuse; to entertain; to exhilarate; as, children are *diverted* with sports; men are *diverted* with works of wit and humor.
3. To subvert. [Obs.]
dī-vērt′, *v.i.* To turn in another direction; to digress. [Obs.]
dī-vērt′ēr, *n.* One who or that which diverts.
dī-vērt′i-ble, *a.* Capable of diversion.
dī-vēr′ti-cle, *n.* [L. *diverticulum*, a byway, an inn, from *devertere*, to turn away; *de-*, away, from, and *vertere*, to turn.]
1. A turning; a byway. [Obs.]
2. In anatomy, a blind tube; a diverticulum.
dīv-ēr-tiç′ū-lȧ, *n.*, pl. of *diverticulum*.
dīv-ēr-tiç′ū-lăr, *a.* Of or designating a diverticulum.
dīv-ēr-tiç′ū-lā-ted, *a.* 1. Cæcal.
2. Possessing blind processes.
dīv-ēr-tiç′ū-lum, *n.*; *pl.* **dīv-ēr-tiç′ū-lȧ**. [L., from *diverticulum*, a byway.] In anatomy, a blind tube or cæcum branching out of the course of a longer one, either normally or as a malformation.
dï-ver-ti-men′tō, *n.*; *pl.* **dï-ver-ti-men′ti**. [It.] In music, a short pleasant composition, vocal or instrumental, written in a light and familiar style.
dī-vērt′ing, *a.* Pleasing; amusing.
dī-vērt′ing-ly, *adv.* In an amusing manner.
dī-vērt′ing-ness, *n.* The state or quality of being diverting.
dī-vērt′ise, *v.t.* To divert; to please. [Obs.]
dī-vērt′ise-ment, *n.* [Fr. *divertissement*, from *divertir*, to divert.]
1. Diversion. [Rare.]
2. A short ballet or other entertainment between acts or longer pieces.
dī-vērt′ive, *a.* Tending to divert; amusing.
dī-vest′, *v.t.*; divested, *pt., pp.*; divesting, *ppr.* [OFr. *devestir*; L. *devestire*, to undress; *de-*, from, and *vestire*, to dress, clothe, from *vestis*, a garment.]
1. To strip of or as of clothes, arms, or equipage: to strip of anything that surrounds or attends; opposed to *invest*; as, to *divest* one of his glory.

> Like bride and groom
> *Divesting* them for bed. —Shak.

2. To deprive; as to *divest* one of his rights or privileges.
3. In law, to devest.
dī-vest′i-ble, *a.* That can be divested.
dī-vest′i-tūre, *n.* 1. The act of stripping, putting off, or depriving.
2. In law, the act of surrendering one's effects or any part thereof; opposed to *investiture*.
dī-vest′ment, *n.* A divesting. [Rare.]
dī-ves′tūre, *n.* Divestiture. [Obs.]
dīv′et, *n.* A turf; a divot. [Obs.]
dī-vid′ȧ-ble, *a.* 1. That may be divided.
2. Separate; parted.
dī-vid′ănt, *a.* Different; separate.
dī-vīde′, *v.t.*; divided, *pt., pp.*; dividing, *ppr.* [ME. *dividen*; L. *dividere*, to divide.]
1. To part or separate into pieces; as, to *divide* an apple.

> *Divide* the living child in two.—1 Kings iii. 25.

2. To cause to be separate; to keep apart by a partition or by an imaginary line or limit; as, a wall *divides* two houses; the equator *divides* the earth into two hemispheres.
3. To make partition of among a number.
4. To open; to cleave.

> Thou didst *divide* the sea. —Neh. ix. 11.

5. To disunite in opinion or interest; to make discordant.

> There shall be five in one house *divided*, three against two. —Luke xii. 52.

6. To share the profits or dividends of; as, to *divide* a year's accumulations; to *divide* the net earnings among the directors.
7. To embarrass by indecision; to allow to hesitate or fluctuate between different motives or opinions; as, he was *divided* in his allegiance.
8. In music, to vary, as a theme.
9. In mathematics, (a) to cause to undergo the operation of division; (b) to be contained in an equal number of times; as, ten *divides* thirty.
10. In logic, to classify or arrange, as a genus into species.
11. To mark into equal or regular parts; to graduate; as, to *divide* a micrometer.

To divide the house; to cause a vote by division; said of a legislative body, as the House of Commons.

Syn.—Sever, sunder, cleave, deal out, distribute, share.

di-vīde′, *v.i.* 1. To become disunited; to come apart.

2. To be of different opinion; to hold opposite or contrary views; as, families *divide*.

3. To vote by the division of a legislative house into two parts.

> The emperors sat, voted, and *divided* with their equals. —Gibbon.

di-vīde′, *n.* A watershed.

di-vīd′ed, *a.* Formed into divisions; parted; specifically, in botany, denoting a leaf cut into divisions by incisions extending nearly to the midrib.

di-vīd′ed-ly, *adv.* Separately.

div′i-dend, *n.* [L. *dividendus*, that which is to be divided, gerundive of *dividere*, to divide.] A sum of money for division; one of the divisions so made; specifically, (a) the declared profits of a firm or corporation; as, only preferred stock paid a *dividend*; (b) a distributive share or apportionment, as of a firm that has failed.

div′i-dent, *n.* A dividend. [Obs.]

di-vīd′ẽr, *n.* 1. One who or that which divides or separates into parts.

2. A distributer; one who deals out to each his share.

> Who made me a judge or *divider* over you? —Luke xii. 14.

3. One who or that which disunites.

4. [*pl.*] A pair of small compasses, of which the opening is adjusted by means of a screw and nut, used for dividing lines, describing circles, etc.

5. The conical projection at the end of a cutter-bar, separating the swath of a reaper or mower.

di-vīd′ing, *a.* That indicates separation or difference; as, a *dividing* line.

di-vīd′ing-en″gine, *n.* An apparatus for producing the divisions of the scales or limbs of mathematical and philosophical instruments; also called *dividing-machine*, *graduation-engine*.

di-vīd′ing-ly, *adv.* By division.

dĭ′vĭ-dĭ′vĭ, *n.* The native and commercial name of *Cæsalpinia coriaria* and its pods. These are excessively astringent, containing a large proportion of tannic and gallic acid, for which reason they are used by tanners and dyers. The plant is a native of tropical America.

Divi-divi (*Cæsalpinia coriaria*).

di-vid′ū-ăl, *n.* In arithmetic, one of the groups of figures into which the dividend is separated to determine, one by one, the figures of the quotient.

di-vid′ū-ăl, *a.* Divided, shared, or participated in common with others. [Rare.]

di-vid′ū-ăl-ly, *adv.* By dividing. [Obs.]

di-vid′ū-ous, *a.* Divided. [Obs.]

div-i-nā′tion, *n.* [L. *divinatio*, the faculty of foreseeing, from *divinatus*, pp. of *divinare*, to foresee.]

1. The act of divining; the pretended foretelling of future events or discovering things secret or obscure, by the aid of superior beings or by other than human means. In ancient times divination was divided into two kinds, *natural* and *artificial*. *Natural* divination was supposed to be effected by a kind of inspiration or divine afflatus; *artificial* divination was effected by certain rites, experiments, or observations, as by sacrifices, cakes, flour, wine, observation of entrails, flight of birds, lots, verses, omens, position of the stars, etc.

2. Conjectural presage; prediction; an indication of the future; omen; augury.

div′i-nā-tŏr, *n.* A diviner. [Obs.]

di-vin′ȧ-tō-ry, *a.* Professing divination.

di-vīne′, *a.* [ME., *divine*; OFr. *divin*; L. *divinus*, divine, inspired, pertaining to a deity, from *divus*, a deity.]

1. Of, relating to, or characteristic of God, or any god, goddess, or deity; as, a *divine* being; a *divine* nature.

2. Appropriated to God or celebrating his praise; as, *divine* songs; *divine* worship.

3. Godlike; heavenly; excellent in the highest degree; extraordinary; apparently above what is human.

> A *divine* sentence is in the lips of the king. —Prov. xvi. 10.

4. Relating to divinity or theology.

5. Divining; augural. [Obs.]

di-vīne′, *n.* 1. A man skilled in divinity; a theologian; as, a great *divine*.

2. A minister of the gospel; a clergyman.

di-vīne′, *v.t.*; divined, *pt.*, *pp.*; divining, *ppr.* [L. *divinare*, to foresee, divine, from *divinus*, divine, prophetic.]

1. To foreknow; to foretell; to presage.

2. To surmise; to know by intuition; as, I *divined* his meaning in his face.

3. To deify. [Obs.]

di-vīne′, *v.i.* 1. To use or practise divination; to utter presages or prognostications.

2. To have presages or forebodings.

3. To guess or conjecture.

Syn.—Foretell, guess, presage, conjecture, predict, prognosticate, augur.

di-vīne′ly, *adv.* 1. In a divine or godlike manner; in a manner resembling deity.

2. By the agency or influence of God; as, a prophet *divinely* inspired.

3. Excellently; in the supreme degree; as, *divinely* fair; *divinely* brave.

di-vīne′ness, *n.* 1. Divinity; participation in the divine nature; as, the *divineness* of the Scriptures.

2. Excellence in the supreme degree.

di-vīn′ẽr, *n.* 1. One who professes divination; one who pretends to predict events or to reveal occult things by supernatural means.

2. One who guesses; a conjecturer.

di-vīn′ẽr-ess, *n.* A female diviner.

dīv′ing, *n.* The art or act of descending into water to considerable depths, and remaining there for a time.

dīv′ing-bee″tle, *n.* The water-tiger, a beetle of any species of the family *Dytiscidæ*, normally living under water.

dīv′ing-bell, *n.* A contrivance for the purpose of enabling persons to descend and to remain below the surface of water for a length of time, to perform various operations, such as examining the foundations of bridges, blasting rocks, recovering treasure from sunken vessels, etc. The diving-bell is now generally made of cast-iron in the form of an oblong chest (A), open at the bottom, being supplied with fresh air injected into a flexible pipe by means of forcing-pumps (B) placed in the lighters, while the heated air escapes by a cock in the upper part of the bell.

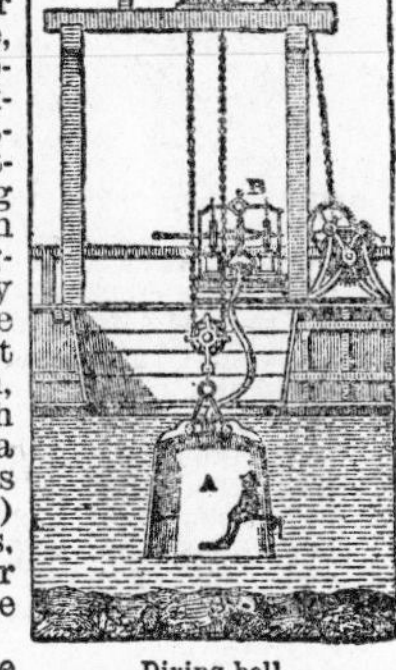
Diving-bell.

dīv′ing-buck, *n.* See *Duykerbok*.

dīv′ing-dress, *n.* Submarine armor.

dīv′ing-spī″dẽr, *n.* *Argyroneta aquatica*, the water-spider, which builds a submarine nest.

dīv′ing-stōne, *n.* A name given to a species of jasper.

di-vīn′ing, *n.* The act of a diviner or augur.

di-vīn′ing-rod, *n.* A rod, commonly of hazel, with forked branches, used by those who pretend to discover water or metals underground.

di-vin′i-ty, *n.*; *pl.* **di-vin′i-ties**. [ME. *divinite*; L. *divinitas*, a divinity, from *divinus*, divine.]

1. The state of being divine; divineness; deity; godhead; divine element; divine nature; as, Christians ascribe *divinity* to one Supreme Being only.

2. God; the Deity; the Supreme Being; with *the*.

3. A celestial being; a being divine or regarded as divine; one of the deities belonging to a polytheistic religion.

4. Something supernatural; supernatural power or virtue.

> They say there is *divinity* in odd numbers. —Shak.

5. The science of divine things; the science which unfolds the character of God, his laws and moral government, the duties of man, and the way of salvation; theology; as, the study of *divinity*; a system of *divinity*.

Divinity circuit binding; a style of bookbinding in which the covers are made to overlap the edges; used chiefly on teachers' Bibles.

div″i-ni-zā′tion, *n.* The act of making divine; deification.

div′i-nīze, *v.t.* To make divine; to treat as divine. [Rare.]

di-vis-i-bil′i-ty, *n.* The quality of being divisible; the property of bodies by which their parts are capable of separation.

di-vis′i-ble, *a.* [LL. *divisibilis*, divisible, from L. *divisus*, pp. of *dividere*, to divide.]

1. Capable of division; that may be separated or disunited; separable.

2. In mathematics, that may be divided, leaving no remainder.

di-vis′i-ble, *n.* That which is divisible.

di-vis′i-ble-ness, *n.* Divisibility.

di-vis′i-bly, *adv.* In a divisible manner.

di-vi′ṣion (-vizh′un), *n.* [ME. *divisioun*; L. *divisio*, a division, separation, from *divisus*, pp. of *dividere*, to divide.]

1. The act of dividing or separating into parts any entire body.

2. The state of being divided.

3. That which divides or separates; that which keeps apart; partition.

4. The part separated from the rest by a partition or a line, real or imaginary; as, the *divisions* of a field.

5. A separate body of men; as, communities and *divisions* of men.

6. A part or distinct portion; as, the *divisions* of a discourse.

7. A part of an army or militia or other organized body of men, as a police force, etc.; a body consisting of a certain number of brigades, usually two, and commanded by a major-general. But the term is often applied to other bodies or portions of an army, as to a brigade, a squadron, or platoon.

8. A part of a fleet, or a select number of ships under a commander, and distinguished by a particular flag or pennant.

9. A territorial military command, including two or more departments; as, the military *division* of the Philippines, consisting of the departments of Luzon, Viscayas, and Mindanao.

10. Disunion; discord; variance; difference.

> There was a *division* among the people. —John vii. 43.

11. Distinction; difference of condition; a line of separation.

> I will put a *division* between my people and thy people. —Ex. viii. 23.

12. The separation of voters in a legislative house.

13. In arithmetic, the dividing of a number or quantity into any parts assigned; or the rule by which is found how many times one number or quantity is contained in another.

14. In biology, a subgroup; subkingdom; series.

15. In logic, the separation of a genus into its constituent parts.

16. In heraldry, markings by horizontal lines, quarterings, or diagonals.

17. In music, a course of notes so connected that they form one series.

Cell division; in biology, the division of a cell into two or more cells, each having its own nucleus, occurring in plant or animal development. [See *Karyokinesis*.]

Long division; in arithmetic, a method of division in which the divisor is multiplied by every figure or term of the quotient, and the product subtracted from the dividend or remaining portion of it; commonly used where the divisor is a number larger than ten.

Short division; a method of division in which the multiplications and subtractions are performed mentally, the quotient being set down directly below on a line under the dividend; used where the divisor is not larger than ten.

Syn.—Compartment, section, portion, detachment, separation, partition, difference, discord, disunion.

di-vi′ṣion-ăl (-vizh′un-ăl), *a.* 1. Pertaining to division; noting or making division; as, a *divisional* line.

2. Belonging to or connected with a division; as, a *divisional* officer.

di-vi′ṣion-ăl-ly, *adv.* In a divisional manner.

di-vi′ṣion-ā-ry, *a.* Divisional.

di-vi′ṣion-ẽr, *n.* One who divides. [Obs.]

di-vī′sive, *a.* [L. *divisus*, pp. of *dividere*, to divide.]

1. Forming division or distribution.

2. Creating division or discord.

di-vī′sive-ly, *a.* So as to cause division, separation, or difference.

di-vī′sive-ness, *n.* A tendency to division or separation.

di-vī′ṣŏr, *n.* [L. *divisor*, a divider.] In arithmetic, the number by which the dividend is divided.

Common divisor; in mathematics, a number or quantity that divides two or more numbers or quantities without a remainder; a common measure.

di-vōrce′, *n.* [OFr. *divorce*; L. *divortium*, a separation, divorce, from *diversus*, pp. of *divertere*, to turn or go different ways.]

1. In law, (a) a legal dissolution of the bonds of matrimony, or the separation of husband and wife by a judicial sentence. This is properly a *divorce*, and called, technically, *divorce a vinculo matrimonii*, "from the bands of matrimony"; (b) the separation of a married woman from the bed and board of her husband, *a mensa et thoro*, "from board and bed."

2. Separation; disunion of things closely united.

3. The sentence or writing by which marriage is dissolved.

di-vōrce′, *v.t.*; divorced (-vorst′), *pt.*, *pp.*; divorcing, *ppr.* 1. To dissolve the marriage contract between; to separate from the condition of husband and wife.

2. To separate or disunite from close connection; to force asunder.

Divorced from my experience. —Tennyson.

3. To take away; to put away.

di-vōrce'ā-ble, *a.* That may or can be divorced.

di-vōr-cée' (-sā'), *n.* A divorced person.

di-vōrce'less, *a.* Destitute of divorce; that cannot be divorced.

di-vōrce'ment, *n.* Divorce; dissolution of the marriage tie.

di-vōr'cēr, *n.* One who or that which divorces or separates.

di-vōr'ci-ble, *a.* Same as *Divorceable.*

di-vōr'cive, *a.* Able to divorce; having the effect of a divorce.

div'ŏt, *n.* [Scot.] A piece of turf, often used for building dikes, etc.

di-vō'tō, *a.* [It., devout, from L. *devotus*, pp. of *devovere*, to vow, devote.] In music, devout, grave, solemn.

di-vul'gāte, *a.* Published. [Obs.]

di-vul'gāte, *v.t.* To divulge. [Rare.]

div'ul-gā-tēr, *n.* One who divulges. [Rare.]

div-ul-gā'tion, *n.* [LL. *divulgatio*, from L. *divulgare*, to make public.] The act of divulging or publishing. [Rare.]

di-vulge', *v.t.*; divulged, *pt.*, *pp.*; divulging, *ppr.* [L. *divulgare*, to make public; *di-*, *dis-*, apart, and *vulgare*, to make public, from *vulgus*, the common people.]

1. To make public; to tell or make known, as something before private or secret; to reveal; to disclose; as, to *divulge* the secret sentiments of a friend; to *divulge* the proceedings of the cabinet.

2. To declare by a public act; to proclaim. [Rare.]

3. To impart; to give; to confer generally. [Rare.]

Syn.—Disclose, reveal, tell, communicate, betray, impart.

di-vulge', *v.i.* To become public; to be made known. [Rare.]

di-vulge'ment, *n.* The act of divulging. [Rare.]

di-vul'gēr, *n.* One who divulges or reveals.

di-vul'sion, *n.* [L. *divulsio*, a pulling or tearing apart, from *divulsus*, pp. of *divellere*, to tear apart.] The act of pulling or plucking away; a rending asunder.

And dire *divulsions* shook the changing world. —Barlow.

di-vul'sive, *a.* Pulling asunder; rending.

di-wan', *n.* Same as *Divan.*

Dix'ie, *n.* [From Mason and *Dixon's* line, the former northern limit of slavery.] A popular name for the southern part of the United States, especially at the time of the Civil War; also called *Dixie's land.*

diz'en (*or* di'zn), *v.t.*; dizened, *pt.*, *pp.*; dizening, *ppr.* [From AS. *dis-* in *disstæf*, distaff.]

1. To furnish with flax for spinning, as a distaff.

2. To dress gaily; to deck; to bedizen.

dizz, *v.t.* To astonish; to puzzle; to make dizzy. [Obs.]

diz'zard, diz'ărd, *n.* A blockhead. [Obs.]

diz'zărd-ly, *adv.* In the manner of a dizzard. [Obs.]

diz'zi-ly, *adv.* In a dizzy manner.

diz'zi-ness, *n.* Giddiness; a whirling in the head; vertigo.

diz'zy, *a.*; *comp.* dizzier; *superl.* dizziest. [ME. *dysy*; AS. *dysig*, stupid, foolish.]

1. Giddy; having a sensation of whirling in the head, with instability or proneness to fall; vertiginous.

2. Causing giddiness; as, a *dizzy* height.

3. Giddy; thoughtless; heedless; as, the *dizzy* multitude.

diz'zy, *v.t.*; dizzied, *pt.*, *pp.*; dizzying, *ppr.* [ME. *desien*; AS. *dysigian*, to be foolish, to confuse, from *dysig*, foolish.] To make giddy; to confuse.

diz'zy, *v.i.* To be foolish; to act in a confused manner. [Obs.]

djer-eed', djer-rīd' (jer-ēd'), *n.* Same as *Jereed, Jerid.*

djinn, djin'nee (jin'), *n.* Same as *Jinn, Jinnee.*

djō'lan (jō'), *n.* [Native E. Ind. name.] The year-bird, or wreathed hornbill, *Buceros plicatus*, inhabiting the Sunda islands and Malakka.

do. A contracted form of *ditto.*

dō, *n.* In solmization, the name of the first of the musical syllables; the tonic of a scale; also, the tone C, as the keynote of the typical scale of the piano keyboard.

dö, *v.t.*; did, *pt.*; doing, *ppr.*; done, *pp.* [This verb, when transitive, is formed in the indicative, present tense, thus: I *do*, thou *doest* or *dost*, he *does*, *doeth*, or *doth*; when auxiliary, the second person is thou *dost.*—ME. *don*, to do, *dyde*, I did; AS. *don*, to do, *dyde*, I did; O.H.G. *tuon*, to do; L. *facere*, to do; Gr. *tithenai*, to put; Sans. *dhā*, to do.]

1. To perform; to execute; to carry into effect; to exert labor or power upon to bring anything to the state desired or to completion; to bring to pass; as, this man *does* his work well; he *does* more in one day than some men will *do* in two days; to *do* good.

Six days shalt thou labor and *do* all thy work. —Ex. xx. 9.

2. To perform for the benefit or injury of another; with *for* or *to*; *for*, when the thing is beneficial; *to*, in either case.

Till I know what God will *do for* me. —1 Sam. xxii. 3.

3. To deliver; to discharge; to convey; as, *do* a message to the king. [Obs.]

4. To perform; to practise; to observe.

We lie and *do* not the truth. —1 John i. 6.

5. To exert; to put forth; as, I will *do* my best.

6. To transact; as, to *do* business with another.

7. To finish; to execute or transact and bring to a conclusion; as, we will *do* the business and adjourn; we *did* the business and dined; I am *done* sorrowing.

8. To perform in an exigency; to have recourse to, as a last effort; to take a step or measure; as, in this crisis we know not what to *do.*

9. To make or cause. [Obs.]

Nothing but death can *do* me to respire. —Spenser.

10. To put; obsolete, save in the phrase *do to death.*

Who should *do* the duke *to death*? —Shak.

11. To answer the purpose of; to serve; as, this salary will *do* me. [Colloq.]

12. To act or deal in reference to (an object), so as to achieve a desired result; to prepare; to arrange; to modify; as, to *do* (dress) one's hair; to *do* (cook) the meat, thoroughly; to *do* (solve) the problem; to *do* (translate) the Iliad into English. In this sense, *do* is the most comprehensive verb in the English language, as it is used to express almost any kind of action and is involved in innumerable idiomatic constructions.

13. To perform, as an act which is the cause of some result, or exhibits intention, emotion, or purpose; to render; to offer; to show. In this sense, *do* before such nouns as *grace*, *reverence*, *favor*, *honor*, etc., takes an indirect objective, as *him*, *her*, etc., and is nearly equal to the English verb-forming prefix *be*, implying action or exertion, the noun to which it is prefixed regulating the mode of action. To *do honor* is thus equivalent to a hypothetical form *behonor*, where *do*, taken in connection with the noun, simply energizes it into a verb.

None so poor to *do* him *reverence.* —Shak.

14. To act or assume the character of; as, to *do* the good Samaritan.

15. To defraud; to cheat; as, they *did* him out of twenty dollars. [Colloq.]

16. To see; to explore; to visit; as, to *do* the town; to *do* the sights. [Colloq.]

17. To inflict serious injury upon; to kill; as, if you say one word I'll *do* you. [Slang.]

18. To outdo, as in fighting; to beat.

To do away with or *to do away*; to remove; to destroy; as, *to do away with* imperfections; *to do away* prejudices.

To do one proud; to make one have a feeling of pride; also, to do exceedingly well; to do one's best; used with a reflexive pronoun; as, the singer *did herself proud.* [Colloq.]

To do over; to do again; to repeat.

To do up; (a) to wash and iron; as, the laundry maid *does up* the waists; (b) to exhaust; as, the work *did* me *up* [Colloq.]; (c) to dress; to arrange; as, she *does up* her hair in the latest fashion; (d) to wrap or tie up in a package; as, *do up* this picture.

To do with; (a) to dispose of; to make use of; to employ; as, we know not what *to do with* our ships; (b) to gain; to effect by influence; as, a smile will *do with* one so innocent; (c) to have concern with; to have business; to get on with; as, we can *do* nothing *with* him.

To have to do with; to have concern with; as, he *has* nothing *to do with* us.

As an auxiliary, *do* is used most commonly in forming negative and interrogative sentences; as, *do* you intend to go? *Does* he wish me to come? He *does* not care.—It is also used to express emphasis; as, she is coquettish, but still I *do* love her.—In the imperative it expresses an urgent request or command; as, *do* come; help me, *do*; *do* make haste.—In the past tense it is sometimes used to convey the idea that what was once true is not true now; as, you once *did* love me.—It is sometimes used as an auxiliary without adding anything to the meaning of the verb to which it is joined.

Expletives their feeble aid *do* join. —Pope.

As a substitute, *do* is used for a verb to save the repetition of it; as, I shall probably come, but if I *do* not, you must not wait; that is, if I *do* not *come*, if I *come* not.

Syn.—Accomplish, achieve, execute, effect, perform.

dö, *v.i.* 1. To act or behave, in any manner, well or ill; to conduct oneself.

They fear not the Lord, neither *do* they after the law and commandment. —2 Kings xvii. 34.

2. To fare; to be in a state with regard to sickness or health; as, how do you *do*, or how *do* you?

3. To succeed; to accomplish a purpose; as, we shall *do* without him.

4. To serve; to fit; to be adapted; to answer the design; with *for*; as, this piece of timber will *do for* the door.

To do by; to act toward; to treat.

To do for; (a) to act or provide for; as, he *does* well *for* his children; (b) to injure; to ruin; to hurt fatally; as, that shot *did for* him. [Colloq.]

To do without; to manage without.

To have done; to have finished.

To have done with; to have no further connection or relation with; to be through with.

Well to do; in good circumstances.

dö, *n.* 1. Act; deed. [Obs.]

2. Bustle; ado. [Rare.]

3. A fraud; a swindle. [Slang, Eng.]

dō'ab, *n.* [Hind. *doab*, a section of land between two rivers; *do*, from Sans. *dva*, two, and *ab*, from Sans. *ap*, water, a river.] A section of land between two rivers directly above their confluence.

dōab, *n.* [Ir. *dob*, plaster, mire.] A kind of dark-colored clay found near bogs in Ireland, and used for plastering purposes.

dö'ā-ble, *a.* Capable of being done.

dö'ạll, *n.* A general servant; a factotum.

dōat, *v.i.* Same as *Dote.*

dob'bēr, *n.* 1. Same as *Dabchick.*

2. A float used in fishing. [Local, U. S.]

dob'bin, *n.* 1. An old work-horse; a common use of the proper name Dobbin.

2. A mixture of gravel and sand. [Prov. Eng.]

dob'by, dob'bie, *n.* [Scot. and Prov. Eng.; variant of *Robert.*]

1. A childish old man; a stupid fellow; a dolt.

2. A sprite, sometimes of a malicious nature.

3. The device that adjusts the harness-frames in a loom; called also *witch.*

dob'chick, *n.* Same as *Dabchick.*

dō'bee, *n.* Same as *Dhobie.*

dō'bhash (-bash), *n.* [Hind.] An interpreter. [India.]

dō'bie, *n.* Adobe. [Colloq.]

dō'blā, *n.* [OSp., f. of *doblo*, double; L. *duplus*, double; *duo*, two, and *plus*, more.] An ancient gold coin of Spain, no longer used. Its value was about $2.47.

dō'ble, *a.* Double. [Obs.]

dō'blēr, *n.* A doubler. [Obs.]

dō'blet, *n.* A doublet. [Obs.]

dob'sŏn, *n.* [Local, U. S.] The larva of one of several neuropterous insects, especially *Corydalus cornutus*, used for bait in fishing; hellgrammite.

dob'ūle, *n.* [L. *dobula.*] A fresh-water fish, *Leuciscus dobula*, allied to the roach, found in European rivers.

dō'cent, *a.* Teaching. [Obs.]

dō'cent, *n.* [L. *docens*, ppr. of *docere*, to teach.] An instructor or tutor in a university, usually considered as a member of the faculty, though not generally receiving a regular salary.

Dō-cē'tæ, *n.pl.* [LL., from Gr. *Dokētai*, from *dokein*, to seem.] In church history, a heretical sect of Christians of the first and second centuries, whose chief tenet was that Christ's body was a mere phantom, or, if real, of celestial origin, and therefore that the incarnation, crucifixion, and resurrection were only appearances or illusions.

Dō-cet'iç, *a.* Pertaining to or resembling the Docetæ; as, *Docetic* doctrine.

Doc'e-tişm, *n.* The doctrines of the Docetæ.

Dō-çē'tist, *n.* One of the Docetæ.

doçh'mi-aç, *a.* and *n.* [Gr. *dochmiakos*, from *dochmios*, aslant.]

I. *a.* In ancient Greek prosody, consisting of, characterized by, or pertaining to dochmii.

II. *n.* A verse or stanza made up of dochmii.

doçh-mī'ā-sis, *n.* The diseased condition of the body caused by the presence of parasites of the genus *Dochmius*; ankylostomiasis.

doçh'mi-us, *n.*; *pl.* **doçh'mi-ī.** [L., from Gr. *dochmios*, across, aslant.] In ancient Greek prosody, a foot of five syllables, the first and fourth being short and the others long.

Doçh'mi-us, *n.* A genus of nematoid worms of the family *Strongylidæ*. It includes several species, one of which, *Dochmius duodenalis*, is an intestinal parasite and produces the disease known as Egyptian chlorosis, which is very common in Egypt and often proves fatal.

doçh'tēr, *n.* Daughter. [Scot.]

doc-i-bil'i-ty, doc'i-ble-ness, *n.* The quality of being docible; teachableness; docility.

doc'i-ble, *a.* [OFr. *docible*; LL. *docibilis*, teachable, from L. *docere*, to teach.] Teachable; docile; tractable; easily taught or managed.

doc'ile, *a.* [L. *docilis*, easily taught, from *docere*, to teach.]

1. Teachable; easily instructed; ready to learn; tractable; easily managed.

2. Tractable; readily worked or easily handled; said of ores.

dō-cil'i-ty, *n.* [L. *docilitas* (*-atis*), aptness for being taught, from *docilis*, easily taught.] Teachableness; readiness to learn; aptness to be taught; as, the *docility* of elephants is remarkable.

doc'i-mȧ-cy, *n.* Same as *Docimasy*.

doc-i-mas'tic, dok-i-mas'tic, *a.* [Gr. *dokimastikos*, from *dokimastēs*, an assayer, examiner, from *dokimazein*, to test, examine.] Proving by experiments; relating to the assaying of ores or metals; as, metallurgy is the *docimastic* art.

doc'i-mȧ-sy, doc'i-mȧ-cy, *n.* [Gr. *dokimasia*, an examination, proving, from *dokimazein*, to examine, from *dokimos*, examined, approved, from *dechesthai*, to receive, approve.]

1. The art or practice of assaying ores or metals; metallurgy.

2. The testing of medicines or the ascertaining of facts in physiology.

3. In ancient Greece, a judicial scrutiny of officers-elect, applicants for citizenship, etc.

doc-i-mol'ō-ġy, *n.* [Gr. *dokimos*, approved, and *logos*, discourse.] A treatise on the assayer's art.

dō'cious, *a.* Docile; tractable. [Colloq., west. U. S.]

doc'i-ty, *n.* [A contracted form of *docility*.] Willingness to be taught; docility.

dock, *n.* [ME. *docke*, *dokke*; AS. *docce*, dock.] The common name of the species of *Rumex*, natural order *Polygonaceæ*, the leaves of which are not hastate. They are perennial herbs, with stout rootstocks, erect stems, very abundant in waste ground and pastures.

dock, *v.t.*; docked (dokt), *pt.*, *pp.*; docking, *ppr.* [ME. *docken*, to cut off or shorten the tail, from *dok*; Ice. *dockr*, a short, stumpy tail.]

1. To cut off, as the end of a thing; to curtail; to cut short; to clip; as, to *dock* the tail of a horse.

2. To cut off a part from; to shorten; to deduct from; as, to *dock* an account; to *dock* wages.

3. To cut off, destroy, or defeat; to bar; as, to *dock* an entail.

dock, *n.* 1. The tail of a beast cut short or clipped; the stump of a tail; the solid part of the tail.

2. A case of leather to cover a horse's dock.

dock, *n.* [M.D. *docke*, a dock; origin uncertain.]

1. The place where a criminal stands in court.

2. A place artificially formed on the side of a harbor or the bank of a river for the reception

Dry Dock.

of ships, the entrance of which is sometimes closed by gates. In the United States, spaces between wharves are also called *docks*. There are two kinds of docks, *dry* or *graving docks* and *wet docks*. The former are used for receiving ships to be inspected and repaired. For this purpose the dock must be so contrived that the water may be admitted or excluded at pleasure, so that a vessel can be floated in, and the water run out with the fall of the tide, or pumped out, the closing of the gates preventing its return. *Wet docks* are basins formed for the purpose of keeping vessels always afloat at the same level, to facilitate loading and unloading.

Floating dock; a structure which serves as a dry dock, being constructed so that it may be sunk to admit a vessel and then raised with it, by pumping out water from tanks or compartments round its sides.

Hydraulic dock; a dock, on the platform of which a vessel may be raised clear of the water by hydraulic presses.

dock, *v.t.* To bring into or place in a dock; as, the ship was *docked* for repairs.

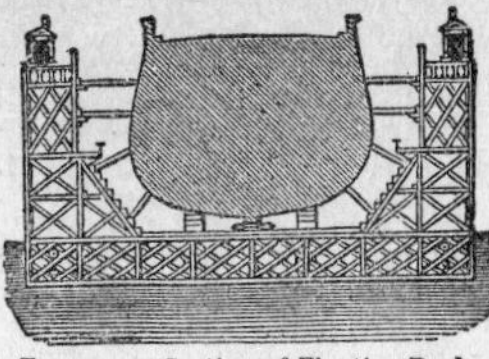

Transverse Section of Floating Dock.

dock'āġe, *n.* Provision for docking a vessel; space granted in a dock; the rental or charge for using a dock.

dock'āġe, *n.* Deduction, as of wages; as, his *dockage*, on account of illness, was ten dollars.

dock'=cress, *n.* In botany, the nipplewort, *Lapsana communis*.

dock'en, dock'ăn, *n.* The dock-plant, of the genus *Rumex*. [Prov. Eng.]

dock'et, *v.t.*; docketed, *pt.*, *pp.*; docketing, *ppr.*

1. To indorse the title and note the contents on the back of (a document); to summarize the contents of; as, to *docket* important letters, etc.

2. In law, to enter in a docket; to make an abstract of, as judgments, etc.

3. To designate with a tag.

dock'et, *n.* [ME. *docket*, lit., a thing cut short, from *docken*, to cut, dock.]

1. A list of the subjects or heads contained in a writing; a digest; a summary; any summarized statement.

2. The calendar of subjects to be considered by an assembly.

3. In law, a record kept by court clerks, containing the roster of parties litigant and minutes of the action taken in each case; a list of causes for trial or hearing.

4. A bill tied to goods, containing some direction, as the name of the owner, or the place to which they are to be sent; a tag.

dock'mack-ie, *n.* A common name for the *Viburnum acerifolium*, a shrub found in the United States and Canada.

dock'yärd, *n.* A yard or magazine in or near a harbor, for containing all kinds of naval stores; a navy-yard.

doc'maç, *n.* An edible kind of catfish, *Bagrus docmac*, inhabiting the Nile.

Doc-ō-glos'sȧ, *n.pl.* [L., from Gr. *dokos*, a wooden beam or bar, a shaft, and *glōssa*, tongue.] In conchology, an order of diœcious gasteropods, having many beam-like teeth in transverse rows on the radula. It includes the limpets.

doç'quet (-ket), *n.* and *v.* [Obs.] Same as *Docket*.

doç'tŏr, *n.* [ME. *doctour*, *doctur*, a doctor of medicine, law, or divinity; OFr. *doctour*; L. *doctor*, a teacher, from *docere*, to teach.]

1. A teacher; a learned man; a man skilled in a profession; a man of erudition.

> Then stood up one in the council, a Pharisee, named Gamaliel, a *doctor* of the law.
> —Acts v. 34.

2. One who has passed all the degrees of a faculty, and is empowered to practise and teach the subjects included in the faculty; as, a *doctor* of divinity, of medicine, or of law; or, according to modern usage, a person who has received the highest degree in a faculty. The degree of *doctor* is often conferred by universities and colleges as an honorary mark of distinction. It is conferred on physicians as a professional degree.

3. A physician; one whose occupation is to cure diseases; a licensed practitioner of medicine or surgery.

4. In England, a licensed practitioner of medicine; the term is applied to surgeons only by courtesy.

5. A term applied to various mechanical contrivances for performing subsidiary operations in machinery.

Doctors' Commons; see under *Commons*.

doç'tŏr, *v.t.*; doctored, *pt.*, *pp.*; doctoring, *ppr.*

1. To prescribe for, or treat, as a physician; to treat medicinally; as, to *doctor* a child; to *doctor* a headache.

2. To repair; to mend; to readjust; as, to *doctor* a watch. [Colloq.]

3. To confer the title or degree of doctor upon. [Rare.]

4. To adulterate; to falsify; to tamper with; to change for the purpose of deception; as, to *doctor* butter; to *doctor* accounts. [Slang.]

doç'tŏr, *v.i.* 1. To practise medicine.

2. To take medicine; to subject oneself to medical treatment. [Colloq.]

doç'tŏr-ăl, *a.* Relating to the degree or profession of a doctor.

doç'tŏr-ăl-ly, *adv.* In the manner of a doctor.

doç'tŏr-āte, *n.* The degree of doctor.

doç'tŏr-āte, *v.t.* To make a doctor of by conferring a degree upon. [Rare.]

doç'tŏr-ess, doç'tress, *n.* A female physician.

doç'tŏr=fish, *n.* A tropical fish of the genus *Acanthurus*, the surgeon-fish; so called from the sharp, lancet-like spines of its tail.

doç'tŏr=gum, *n.* An aromatic resin of South America; usually considered a product of *Rhus Metopium*; also called *hog-gum*.

doç'tŏr-ize, *v.t.* [Rare.] Same as *Doctorate*.

doç'tŏr-ly, *a.* Of, pertaining to, or like a doctor or learned man. [Obs.]

doç'tŏr-ship, *n.* The degree or rank of a doctor.

doç'tress, *n.* See *Doctoress*.

doç'tri-nȧ-ble, *a.* Of, pertaining to, or constituting doctrine. [Obs.]

doç-tri-nâire', *n.* [Fr. *doctrinaire*, from L. *doctrina*, doctrine.]

1. One who theorizes without paying sufficient heed to practical considerations; a visionary and unpractical theorist; a political theorist; an ideologist.

2. The name originally applied to one of a section of French politicians of moderately liberal principles, who occupied a place in the Chambers after the Restoration of 1815, and advocated the adoption of a constitution similar to that of Great Britain.

doç-tri-nâire', *a.* Characteristic of a doctrinaire; theoretical.

doç'tri-năl, *a.* [LL. *doctrinalis*, pertaining to doctrine, from L. *doctrina*, doctrine.]

1. Pertaining to doctrine; containing a doctrine or something taught; as, a *doctrinal* observation; a *doctrinal* proposition.

2. Pertaining to the act or means of teaching; educational; instructive.

> The word of God no otherwise serveth than in the nature of a *doctrinal* instrument.
> —Hooker.

doç'tri-năl, *n.* Something that is a part of doctrine; a tenet.

doç'tri-năl-ly, *adv.* In the form of doctrine or instruction; by way of teaching or positive direction.

doç-tri-nā'ri-ăn, *n.* Same as *Doctrinaire*.

doç-tri-nā'ri-ăn-iṣm, *n.* The theories of doctrinaires; blind adhesion to theory; mere speculation.

doç'trine, *n.* [ME. *doctrine*; L. *doctrina*, teaching, instruction, from *doctor*, a teacher, instructor; from *docere*, to teach.]

1. In a general sense, whatever is taught; hence, a principle or position in any science or department of knowledge; whatever is laid down as true by an instructor or master; as, the *doctrines* of the gospel; the *doctrines* of Plato.

2. The act of teaching; instruction.

> He taught them many things by parables, and said to them in his *doctrine*.—Mark iv. 2.

Monroe Doctrine; the declared policy of the United States that it will regard as an unfriendly act any further acquisition by European powers of territory in the Western hemisphere, and that it will not countenance any interference in the internal affairs of any of the independent states on either the North or the South American continent. This doctrine was first promulgated by President Monroe in a message to Congress, December 2, 1823.

Syn.—Dogma, principle, precept, tenet.—A *doctrine* rests on the authority of the individual by whom it is framed; a *dogma* on the authority of the body by whom it is maintained; a *tenet* rests on its own intrinsic merits.

doç'ū-ment, *n.* [ME. *document*; L. *documentum*, a lesson, example, proof, from *docere*, to teach.]

1. Precept; instruction; direction; authoritative dogma. [Obs.]

2. Written instruction, evidence, or proof; any official or authoritative paper containing instructions or proof, for information and the establishment of facts; as, the president laid before Congress the report of the secretary, accompanied with all the *documents*.

doç'ū-ment, *v.t.* 1. To furnish with documents; to furnish with instructions and proofs, or with papers necessary to establish facts; as, a ship should be *documented* according to the directions of law.

2. To teach; to instruct; to direct. [Obs.]

doç-ū-men'tăl, *a.* Same as *Documentary*.

doç-ū-men'tȧ-ry, *a.* Pertaining to written evidence; consisting in documents; as, *documentary* evidence.

dod, dodd, *v.t.*; dodded, *pt.*, *pp.*; dodding, *ppr.* [ME. *dodden*, to cut off.] To clip or cut off.

dod'därt, *n.* [Local, Eng.] A game resembling hockey; also, the stick with which it is played.

dod'ded, *a.* Hornless, as sheep or cattle. [Scot.]

dod'dẽr, *n.* [ME. *doder*; AS. *dodder*, the plant dodder.] The common name of plants of the genus *Cuscuta*.

Lesser Dodder (*Cuscuta Epithymum*).

They are almost destitute of leaves, parasitical, creeping, and injurious to cultivated crops, especially to hops, flax, etc.

Dodder grass; the quaking-grass, *Briza media.*

dod′dẽr, *v.i.*; doddered, *pt., pp.*; doddering, *ppr.* To tremble, shake, or totter. [Eng., Dial.]

dod′dẽred, *a.* 1. Overgrown with dodder.

2. Infirm with age.

dō-dec-a-. A combining form from L. *dodeca-*; Gr. *dōdeka*, twelve, from *dyo*, two, and *deka*, ten, and signifying twelve, as in *dodecandria.*

dō-dec′ȧ-gon, *n.* [*Dodeca-*, and Gr. *gōnia*, an angle.] A polygon bounded by twelve sides and having twelve angles.

Dō″dec-ȧ-gyn′i-ȧ, *n.pl.* [*Dodeca-*, and Gr. *gynē*, a female.] A term applied by Linnæus to orders of plants having twelve styles or pistils.

dō″dec-ȧ-gyn′i-ăn, dō-de-cag′y-nous, *a.* In botany, having twelve styles.

dō″dec-ȧ-hē′drăl, *a.* Pertaining to a dodecahedron; consisting of twelve equal sides.

dō″dec-ȧ-hē′drŏn, *n.* [*Dodeca-*, and Gr. *hedra*, a seat, base.] A solid having twelve faces; a regular solid bounded by twelve equal and regular pentagons, or having twelve equal bases.

Dō-de-can′dri-ȧ, *n.pl.* [*Dodeca-*, and Gr. *anēr* (*andros*), a male.] A class of plants having twelve stamens, or any number of stamens, from twelve to nineteen inclusive.

Dodecandria (Common Houseleek).

dō-de-can′dri-ăn, dō-de-can′drous, *a.* Pertaining to the *Dodecandria.*

dō′de-cāne, *n.* [Gr. *dōdeka*, twelve.] A hydrocarbon of the paraffin series.

dō′dec-ant, *n.* One of the twelve parts into which the space around a hexagonal crystal is divided by the diametral planes.

dō″dec-ȧ-pet′ăl-ous, *a.* [*Dodeca-*, and Gr. *petalon*, a leaf.] In botany, having twelve petals.

dō′de-cärch, *n.* [*Dodeca-*, and Gr. *archos*, a ruler, from *archein*, to rule.] One of a government consisting of twelve chiefs or kings.

dō′dec-ȧ-stȳle, *a.* and *n.* [*Dodeca-*, and Gr. *stylos*, a column.]

I. *a.* In architecture, characterized by twelve columns in front.

II. *n.* A portico having twelve columns in front.

dō″dec-ȧ-syl-lab′ic, *a.* Containing twelve syllables.

dō″dec-ȧ-syl′lȧ-ble, *n.* [*Dodeca-*, and Gr. *syllabē*, a syllable.] A word made up of twelve syllables.

dō″dec-ȧ-tem′ō-ry, *n.* [Gr. *dōdekatēmorion*, a twelfth part; *dōdeka*, twelve, and *morion*, a part.] A name formerly sometimes given to each of the twelve signs of the zodiac.

dodge (doj), *v.i.*; dodged, *pt., pp.*; dodging, *ppr.* [Origin uncertain.]

1. To start suddenly aside; to shift place by a sudden start.

2. To play tricks; to be evasive; to play fast and loose; to raise expectations and disappoint them; to quibble.

dodge, *v.t.* 1. To evade by a sudden shift of place; to escape by starting aside; as, to *dodge* a blow; to *dodge* a cannon-ball.

2. To evade by tricks.

dodge, *n.* The act of evading by devices or tricks; an ingenious trick; an evasion. [Colloq.]

dodg′ẽr (doj′ẽr), *n.* 1. One who dodges or evades; an artful, crafty fellow.

2. A small, cheap handbill.

3. A cake or loaf made of corn-meal; a corn-dodger.

dodg′ẽr-y, *n.* Trickery; craftiness. [Obs.]

dod′i-pāte, dod′dy-pāte, *n.* [ME. *dodypate*, from *dodden*, to shave, and *pate*, the crown of the head.] A blockhead; a dull fellow; a natural; a dunce.

dod′i-pōll, dod′dy-pōll, *n.* Same as *Dodipate.*

dod′kin, *n.* [D. *doitkin*, dim. of *duit*, a doit.] A little doit; a small coin.

dod′măn, *n.* A fish that casts its shell like the lobster and crab; also called *hodmandod.*

Dodo, from a painting in the Belvedere, Vienna.

dō′dō, *n.* [Port. *doudo*, a dodo, from *doudo*, *doido*, a simpleton, foolish.] An extinct bird, *Didus ineptus*, of the order *Columbæ*, known to have survived in Mauritius until 1681. Its existence was formerly doubted, but in recent years its bones have been found in abundance. It appears to have been about the size of a swan, covered with down instead of feathers, with short, strong legs, and wings too small for flight.

Dō-dō-næ′ăn, Dō-dō-ni′ăn, *a.* [L. *Dodonæus*, from *Dodona*; Gr. *Dōdōnē*, Dodona, a city in Epirus.] Pertaining to the ancient Grecian city Dodona, or to its celebrated sanctuary and oracle of Zeus.

dōe, *n.* A feat. [Obs.]

dōe, *n.* [ME. *doo*; AS. *dā*; L. *dama*, *damma*, the doe.] The female of the deer, the male being called a *buck*; also, the female of the hare or rabbit.

doeg′lic (dēg′), *a.* Pertaining to the doegling.

doeg′ling (dēg′), *n.* [Faroese.] The piked or rorqual whale, *Balænoptera rostrata.*

dō′ẽr, *n.* [ME. *doer*; AS. *dōere*, from *dōn*, to do.]

1. One who does, performs, or executes; an actor; an agent.

2. One who performs what is required; one who observes, keeps, or obeys, in practice.

> The *doers* of the law shall be justified. —Rom. ii. 13.

dōeṣ (duz), *v.*, third person singular of the verb *do*, indicative mode, present tense.

dōe′skin, *n.* 1. The skin of a doe.

2. A compact woolen cloth, for men's garments.

doff, *v.t.*; doffed (doft), *pt., pp.*; doffing, *ppr.* [ME. *doffe*; *do* and *off*; lit., to do off, to doff.]

1. To put or take off, as dress.

> And made us *doff* our easy robes of peace. —Shak.

2. To strip or divest (oneself) of; as, he *doffs* himself.

3. To put or thrust away; to get rid of.

4. To strip off by a machine, as in cotton or wool manufacture.

doff, *v.i.* To take off dress; especially, to remove the hat.

dof′fẽr, *n.* A revolving cylinder, in a carding-machine, which doffs, or strips off, the cotton from the cards; the operator of a *doffer.*

dof′fẽr-rōll, *n.* The roll which delivers the cloth from a mangle.

dog (*or* dŏg), *n.* [ME. *dog*, *dogge*; OFr. *dogue*; M.D. *dogge*; Sw. *dogg*; from AS. *docga*, a dog.]

1. A quadruped, belonging to the genus *Canis*, of many varieties, as the mastiff, hound, spaniel, collie, terrier, etc.

2. A term used for *male*, when applied to several other animals; as, a *dog*-fox; a *dog*-otter; a *dog*-ape. In distinguishing canine sex, it denotes a male animal, as opposed to *bitch.*

3. An andiron or fire*dog*, formerly so named from the figure of a dog's head on the top.

4. A term of reproach or contempt, given to a man; a mean, worthless fellow.

5. The constellation called Sirius or Canicula.

6. An iron hook or bar with a sharp fang, which can be driven into a log of timber to move it in water.

7. An iron used by sawyers to fasten a log of timber in a saw-pit.

8. A gay young man; a buck; as, a gay *dog.* [Colloq.]

A dead dog; a person or thing of no use whatever.

A dog's age; a comparatively long time; as, I have not seen you for *a dog's age.*

A dog's death; a disgraceful death.

A dog's life; a wretched, miserable life.

Dog in the manger; one who will neither enjoy the use of a thing himself nor let any one else enjoy it.

Dog robber; an army officer's body-servant. [Soldiers' slang.]

To give or *throw to the dogs*; to throw away as useless.

To go to the dogs; to be ruined; to go to pieces.

dog, *v.t.*; dogged, *pt., pp.*; dogging, *ppr.* 1. To hunt; to follow insidiously or indefatigably; to follow close; to urge; to worry with importunity.

> I have been pursued, *dogged*, and waylaid. —Pope.

2. To fasten with a dog; as, the log was *dogged* by the movement of a lever.

dō′găl, *a.* Belonging or pertaining to a doge.

dō-gä′nȧ, *n.* [It.] In Italy, a customhouse or customs duty.

dog′-āpe, *n.* The male ape.

dō′gāte, *n.* The office or dignity of a doge.

dog′bāne, *n.* A plant, *Apocynum androsæmifolium*, having a bitter taste and the properties of an emetic.

dog′-bee, *n.* A drone bee; also, a fly troublesome to dogs.

dog′-belt, *n.* A coal-miner's belt, consisting of a leather girdle and chain for drawing small trucks in the lower levels. [Eng.]

dog′ber″ry, *n.* The berry of the dogwood, *Cornus sanguinea.*

dog′ber″ry-tree, *n.* The dogwood.

dog′-bis″cuit (-kit), *n.* A food for dogs prepared in the form of a biscuit or cake and made partly of meat.

dog′bōlt, *n.* A fool; a butt; an old English term of contempt.

dog′-bri″ẽr, *n.* Same as *Dogrose.*

dog′cärt, *n.* A one-horse cart with two transverse seats placed back to back.

dog′-chēap, *a.* Very cheap.

dog′-col″lăr, *n.* 1. A collar for a dog.

2. An ornamental neckband sometimes worn by women.

dog′-dāi″ṣy, *n.* The common field daisy.

dog′-dāyṣ, *n.pl.* A period of the year including about six weeks of the hottest and most sultry days of July and August, at which period the dog-star rises with the sun; often reckoned from July 3 to August 11.

dog′drăw, *n.* The apprehension of an offender against the venison in the forest, when he was found drawing after the deer by the scent of a hound led by the hand.

dōge, *n.* [It. *doge*, from L. *dux* (*ducis*), a leader, from *ducere*, to lead.] The chief magistrate of the old republics of Venice and Genoa.

Doge of Venice.—Vecellio.

dog′-ēared, *a.* Having the corners of the leaves bent back and soiled by careless usage; said of a book.

dōge′āte, *n.* Same as *Dogate.*

dōge′less, *a.* Having no doge.

dog′-fāced (-fāst), *a.* With a face like a dog's.

dog′-fan″ci-ẽr, *n.* A breeder and seller of dogs; one who takes pleasure in the study of dogs and their characteristics; one who is fond of dogs.

dog′-fen″nel, *n.* See *Dog's-fennel.*

dog′fish, *n.* 1. A name given to several small sharks, as the spotted shark or greater *dogfish*, the piked *dogfish*, etc.

Small-spotted Dogfish (*Scyllium canicula*).

2. One of a variety of fishes, as the bowfin, the burbot, the mudminnow, etc.

dog′-fly, *n.* A kind of fly common in woods and bushes and very troublesome to dogs.

dog′-foot″ed, *a.* Having feet like those of a dog.

dog′-fox, *n.* 1. The male of the fox.

2. The name of some small species of *Vulpes* which resemble both the dog and the fox.

dog′ged, *a.* 1. Sullen; sour; morose; surly; severe. [Obs.]

2. Continuously determined; obstinately persistent; pertinacious.

dog′ged-ly, *adv.* Sullenly; gloomily; sourly; morosely; severely; with obstinate resolution.

dog′ged-ness, *n.* 1. Sullenness; moroseness. [Rare.]

2. Continuous determination; obstinate persistence; pertinacity.

dog′gẽr, *n.* A Dutch fishing-vessel, used particularly in the herring fisheries. It is equipped with two masts, and somewhat resembles a ketch.

Dutch Dogger.

dog′gẽr, *n.* [Prov. Eng. *dogger*, a round stone.] A concretion of silica and iron, found in the Jurassic formation in England. It rests upon the alum shale in Yorkshire and is much worked for the iron ore it contains.

dog′gẽr-el, *a.* [ME. *dogerel*, doggerel; origin unknown.] A term applied to a kind of loose, irregular measure in burlesque poetry; as, *doggerel* verse or rime.

dog′gẽr-el, *n.* A loose, irregular kind of poetry; rime trivial in sentiment and poor in execution.

dog′gẽr-măn, *n.* A sailor on a dogger.

dog′get, *n.* [Obs.] Same as *Docket.*

dog′gish, *a.* Like a dog; churlish; growling; snappish; brutal.

dog′gish-ly, *adv.* In a doggish manner.

dog′gish-ness, *n.* The quality of being doggish.
dog′-grȧss, *n.* A coarse, sharp-bearded grass, *Agropyrum caninum.*
dog′-grāte, *n.* A basket-shaped fire-grate supported by firedogs or andirons.
dog′grel, *a.* and *n.* Same as *Doggerel.*
dog′gy, *a.* Relating to dogs; having the smell of dogs.
dog′gy, *n.* A pet term for a dog; a little dog.
dog′-head (-hed), *n.* The hammer of a gun.
dog′-head″ed, *a.* Having a head like that of a dog; as, a *dog-headed* baboon.
dog′-heärt″ed, *a.* Unfeeling; cruel; savage; inhuman; pitiless.
dog′hōle, *n.* A low squalid habitation, fit only for dogs.
dog′-hook, *n.* A wrench or hook used for separating and connecting hose, boring rods, etc.; a kind of iron hook used in handling logs.
dog′-ken″nel, *n.* A hut, house, or shelter for dogs.
dog′-Lat″in, *n.* Barbarous Latin.
dog′-leech, *n.* One who treats the diseases of dogs.
dog′-legged, *a.* In architecture, having a bend and structure suggesting the shape of a dog's leg; said especially of a stairway in which the upper and under flights are built with their handrails and balusters in the same vertical plane.
dog′-let″tēr, *n.* The letter *r*, so called because suggested by the snarl or growl of the dog; the canine letter.
dog′-lī″chen, *n.* The common name of *Peltigera canina*, a plant once supposed to be a specific for hydrophobia.
dog′-louse, *n.* A parasite peculiar to the dog.
dog′mȧ, *n.* [L. *dogma*; Gr. *dogma*, that which one thinks true, an opinion, decree, from *dokein*, to think, seem.]

1. A principle, maxim, or tenet; a settled opinion.

2. A principle or set of principles bearing on and expounding the doctrine of a church or society; the whole system of Christian doctrine.

3. Doctrine adopted through authority, instead of reason or experience; an oracular opinion.

Syn.—Tenet, proposition, precept, opinion.—A *tenet* is an article of faith which is firmly held. *Dogma* has now a somewhat odious sense, from its carrying with it the idea of authority or undue assumption, as in its derivative, *dogmatism.*

dog-mat′iç, dog-mat′iç-ăl, *a.* 1. Pertaining to a dogma, or to settled opinion.

2. Positive; magisterial; asserting or disposed to assert with authority or with overbearing and arrogance.

Syn.—Doctrinal, theological, imperious, dictatorial, authoritative, arrogant, magisterial, self-opinionated, positive.

dog-mat′iç, *n.* 1. One who is positive or self-opinionated in his beliefs.

2. [D—] A member of an ancient sect of physicians founded by Hippocrates, who were guided by general principles; named in contradistinction to *Empirics* and *Methodists.*

dog-mat′iç-ăl-ly, *adv.* Positively; in a magisterial manner; arrogantly.
dog-mat′iç-ăl-ness, *n.* The quality of being dogmatical; positiveness.
dog-mȧ-ti′ciăn (-tish′un), *n.* Same as *Dogmatist.*
dog-mat′içs, *n.* Doctrinal theology; the exposition of the dogmas of the Christian church.
dog′mȧ-tişm, *n.* [LL. *dogmatismus*, from Gr. *dogmatizein*, to lay down a decree, from *dogma*, a decree, dogma.]

1. Positive assertion; arrogance; positiveness in opinion.

2. [D—] The principles of the ancient Dogmatic sect of physicians.

dog′mȧ-tist, *n.* 1. A positive asserter; a magisterial teacher; a bold or arrogant advancer of principles.

2. [D—] One of the Dogmatic school of physicians.

dog′mȧ-tīze, *v.t.*; dogmatized, *pt., pp.*; dogmatizing, *ppr.* To assert positively; to teach with bold and undue confidence; to advance with arrogance.
dog′mȧ-tīze, *v.i.* To deliver opinions in a dogmatic manner.
dog′mȧ-ti-zēr, *n.* One who dogmatizes; a bold asserter; a magisterial teacher.
dog′-nāil, *n.* A strong nail with a projection on one side, used by carpenters and locksmiths.
dog′-pärs″ley, *n.* A malodorous and poisonous herb, *Æthusa Cynapium*, resembling parsley; also called *fool's-parsley.*
dog′-pig, *n.* A sucking pig.
dog′-poi″şŏn, *n.* Same as *Dog-parsley.*
dog′-rāy, *n.* Same as *Dogfish.*
dog′rōşe, *n.* The common European wild rose, *Rosa canina.*
dog′-salm″ŏn (-sam″), *n.* A salmon of the genus *Oncorhynchus*, found on the coasts of Alaska and British Columbia and in Puget Sound.

dog's′-bod″y, *n.* 1. A kind of boat with a square stern.

2. Among seamen, a pease pudding boiled in a cloth.

dog's′-chop, *n.* A name applied to a kind of marigold.
dog's′-ēar, *n.* A corner of a leaf of a book bent over by careless usage.
dog's′-ēar, *v.t.*; dog's-eared, *pt., pp.*; dog's-earing, *ppr.* To bend over in dog's-ears, as the leaves of a book.
dog's′-fen″nel, *n.* A common weed of disagreeable odor; mayweed.
dog's′-grȧss, *n.* Same as *Dog-grass.*
dog′-shärk, *n.* A kind of spotted dogfish, *Scyllium canicula.*
dog′ship, *n.* The quality or character of a dog.
dog′shōre, *n.* One of a number of shores or pieces of timber used to hold a ship in place before launching.
dog′-shōw, *n.* An exhibition of dogs; a bench-show.
dog′sick, *a.* Sick as a dog; very sick. [Colloq.]
dog′skin, *a.* Made of the skin of a dog; as, a pair of *dogskin* gloves.
dog′sleep, *n.* Pretended sleep; light sleep like that of a dog.
dog's′-mēat, *n.* Refuse; offal; meat for dogs.
dog's′-mēr″çū-ry, *n.* A common name for the plant *Mercurialis perennis.*
dog′-stär, *n.* The common name of the brightest star in the firmament, *Sirius* or *Canis Major*, whose rising and setting with the sun gives name to the dog-days.
dog′-stōne, *n.* A name applied to a kind of rough stone used for millstones.
dog's′-tŏngue (-tung), *n.* A plant, *Cynoglossum officinale.*
dog′-tent, *n.* A tent designed for one person; a small tent, in shape and size suggesting a dog-kennel.
dog′-tick, *n.* A tick that infests dogs.
dog′tie, *n.* In architecture, a piece of iron bent at the ends for holding timbers, etc., together.
dog′-tīred, *a.* Tired as a dog after a long chase.
dog′tooth, *n.* 1. A sharp-pointed human tooth standing in the upper jaw between the fore teeth and the grinders, and resembling the pointed teeth of the dog; an eye-tooth; a canine, or canine tooth.

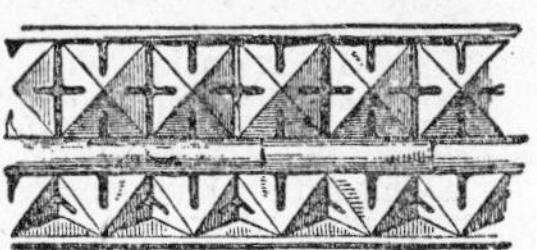
Dogtooth Molding.

2. An ornamental molding in architecture, so called from its resemblance to the teeth of a dog.

3. A tooth-shaped shell.

Dogtooth spar; see under *Spar.*
Dogtooth violet; see under *Violet.*

dog′-town, *n.* A settlement of prairie-dogs.
dog′trick, *n.* A low trick; mean, brutal treatment.
dog′trot, *n.* A gentle, uniform, continuous trot.
dog′vāne, *n.* A vane made of some very light material and set on the weather gunwale of a vessel to indicate the direction of the wind.
dog′watch, *n.* Among seamen, a watch of two hours, designed to change the watches kept by a crew. The first dogwatch is from 4 to 6 P. M., the second from 6 to 8 P. M.
dog′-wēa″ry, *a.* Same as *Dog-tired.*
dog′-whelk, *n.* The popular name of any species of univalve shell of the genus *Nassa.*
dog′wood, *n.* 1. A common name of different species of *Cornus*; the cornel. The flowering *dogwood* is the best known in the United States.

2. The wood obtained from various trees of the genus *Cornus*, much used for manufacturing purposes on account of its hardness.

Striped dogwood; a variety of striped maple.

dog′wood-tree, *n.* Same as *Dogwood*, 1.
dō′gy, *n.* [Local, U. S.] A motherless calf; a term used on the cattle-ranges of the United States.
doi′ly, doy′ley, *n.* [Said to be named after a Mr. *Doily* or *Doyley*, a London draper of the latter half of the seventeenth century.]

1. A species of woolen stuff. [Obs.]

2. A small piece of embroidered, worked, or ornamental table-linen, used under finger-bowls, dessert-dishes, flower vases and the like, or on dessert-plates; a finger-bowl napkin.

dō′ing, *n.*; *pl.* **dō′ings.** Anything done; a transaction; a feat; an action, good or bad; as, the *doings* of a day.
doit, *n.* [D. *duit*, a small coin.]

1. A small Dutch coin, formerly current and worth about half a cent; also, a similar small coin once used in Scotland.

Doit, from British Museum.

2. A trifle; hence, the phrase, I care not a *doit.*

doit′kin, *n.* A doit, or any small coin.
Dō-ket′iç, Dok′e-tişm. Same as *Docetic, Docetism.*
dokh′mȧ, dokh′meh (dok′), *n.* [Per. *dakhma.*] A pit surrounded by a low stone tower with a grated top, on which the Parsees place their dead. The bodies are preyed upon by carnivorous birds until the bones fall into the pit. Also called *tower of silence.*

Dokhma, Malabar Hill, Bombay.

dok-i-mas′tiç, *a.* Same as *Docimastic.*
dō′kō, *n.* [African.] See *Lepidosiren.*
dō-lā′brȧ, *n.*; *pl.* **dō-lā′bræ.** [L., from *dolare*, to hew, chip with an ax.] In Roman antiquity, an ax, hatchet, or mattock used in making intrenchments, etc., and also in slaughtering sacrificial victims.

Pontifical Dolabræ.

dō-lab′ri-fōrm, *a.* [L. *dolabra*, an ax, and *forma*, form.] Having the form of an ax or hatchet. In botany, applied to certain fleshy leaves, which are straight at the front, taper at the base, compressed, dilated, rounded, and thinned away at the upper end at the back. In zoölogy, applied to the foot of certain bivalves.

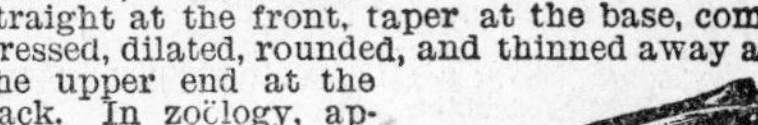
Dolabriform Leaf of *Mesembryanthemum dolabriforme.*

dōl′ce (-che), *a.* [It., from L. *dulcis*, sweet.] In music, sweet; an instruction to sing or play softly and sweetly.
dōl-ce-men′te, *adv.* In music, softly and sweetly.
dōl-ci-ȧ′nō (-che-), **dōl-ci′nä** (-chē′), *n.* [It., from *dolce*; L. *dulcis*, sweet.] A small bassoon.
dol′drumş, *n.pl.* Nautically, the parts of the ocean near the equator where light winds or dead calms prevail, often making navigation impossible for weeks at a time.

To be in the doldrums; to be in a bored or listless state of mind.

dōle, *n.* [ME. *dol*; OFr. *dol*, from L. *dolere*, to grieve.] Grief; sorrow. [Obs.]
dōle, *n.* [ME. *dole, dale*; AS. *dal*, a division, part.]

1. The act of dealing or distributing; as, the power of *dole* and donative. [Obs.]

2. That which is dealt or distributed; a part, share, or portion.

3. That which is given in charity; alms; gratuity.

4. A void space left in tillage. [Prov. Eng.]

5. A boundary; a landmark. [Obs.]

dōle, *v.t.*; doled, *pt., pp.*; doling, *ppr.* To deal; to distribute; commonly with *out*; as, to *dole out* charity.
dōle′-fish, *n.* A fisherman's share of a catch. [Eng.]
dōle′fụl, *a.* [ME. *doleful*, from *dol*; OFr. *dol*, sorrow, from L. *dolere*, to feel pain.]

1. Sorrowful; expressing grief; as, a *doleful* whine; a *doleful* cry.

2. Melancholy; sad; afflicted; as, a *doleful* sire.

3. Dismal; impressing sorrow; gloomy; as, *doleful* shades.

Syn.—Dismal, piteous, rueful, sorrowful, woeful, cheerless, dolorous.

dōle′fụl-ly, *adv.* In a doleful manner; sorrowfully; dismally; sadly.
dōle′fụl-ness, *n.* Sorrow; melancholy; querulousness; gloominess; dismalness.
dō′lent, *a.* Sorrowful. [Obs.]
dol′ēr-īte, *n.* [Gr. *doleros*, deceptive, from *dolos*, deceit.] A variety of trap-rock or greenstone, composed of augite and feldspar, and difficult to distinguish from other varieties of greenstone.
dōle′sŏme, *a.* Gloomy; sorrowful; dismal; doleful.

The *dolesome* passage to the infernal sky.
—Pope.

dōle′sōme-ly, *adv.* In a dismal manner.

dōle′sōme-ness, *n.* The state of being dismal.

dol-i-chō-. A combining form from Greek *dolichos*, long.

dol″i-chō-ceph′ăl-ic, dol″i-chō-ceph′á-lous, *a.* [*Dolicho-*, and Gr. *kephalē*, head.] Having a skull long in proportion to its breadth.

dol″i-chō-ceph′á-lus, *n.* One with the dolichocephalic characteristic.

dol″i-chō-ceph′á-ly, dol″i-chō-ceph′á-lişm, *n.* The state of being dolichocephalic.

dō′li-ō-fọrm, *a.* [L. *dolium*, a large jar, and *forma*, a form.] Like a barrel in form.

Dō-li′ō-lum, *n.* [L. *doliolum*, dim. of *dolium*, a cask, jar.]

1. A genus of oceanic ascidians, allied to the *Salpæ*, and like them exhibiting interesting forms of alternate generation.

2. [d—] Any free-swimming oceanic tunicate of this genus.

dō′-lit″tle, *n.* One who professes much but accomplishes little. [Colloq.]

Dō′li-um, *n.* [L. *dolium*, a large jar.]

1. A genus of univalve mollusks of large size, including the partridge-shell, *Dolium perdix*.

2. [d—] In Roman antiquity, an earthen wine or grain jar.

doll, *n.* [Origin uncertain.] A puppet or toy baby for a child; a small image in the human form for the amusement of little girls.

dol′lăr, *n.* [M.D. *daler*; G. *taler*, *thaler*, a dollar, shortened form of *Jochimstaler*, *Jochimsthaler*, so called from *Joachimsthal*, Joachim's dale, in Bohemia, where the silver from which it was coined was first obtained.]

1. In the United States, the monetary unit or standard of value represented by a silver coin made of 371.25 grains of silver and 41.25 grains of alloy; also, formerly, by a gold coin containing 23.22 grains of gold and 2.58 grains of alloy, which is no longer coined.

2. The English name of a coin, similar to the United States silver *dollar*, current in Mexico, a great part of South America, Singapore, the Philippine islands, etc.

Mexican dollar; the peso of Mexico, a silver coin containing 377.17 grains of pure silver.

Trade dollar; a silver coin formerly made at the United States mints and intended for use in Oriental trade. It contained 378 grains of silver with 42 grains of alloy. It was recalled by act of Congress, March 1, 1887.

dol′lăr-dee, *n.* A species of sunfish, common in the United States; also called *blue sunfish*.

dol′lăr-fish, *n.* Same as *Butterfish*.

dol′lee-wood, *n.* The wood of a tree native to tropical America, *Myristica Surinamensis*.

dol′ly, *n.*; *pl.* **dol′lieş.** 1. In mining, a contrivance for stirring ore in the process of concentration. [Eng.]

2. A tool for shaping the head of a rivet; a snap-head.

3. In pile-driving, a block or extension-piece placed between the ram of the driver and the head of the pile.

4. A device used in washing clothes, consisting of a kind of mop with projecting pegs attached to a handle.

5. A small truck used for moving heavy beams in building.

6. A small locomotive used for hauling construction trains, etc., on narrow-gauge tracks.

dol′ly, *n.* A child's name for a doll.

dol′ly-shop, *n.* A junk-shop. [Eng.]

dol′ly-tub, *n.* In mining, the keeve or tub in which ore is washed and tossed; used especially in Cornwall in the preparation of tin.

dol′măn, *n.* [Turk. *dolama*, a long robe.]

1. A long cassock worn by the Turks.

2. A kind of woman's cloak.

dol′men, *n.* [Fr. *dolmen*; Breton, *dolmen*, from *dol*, a table.] A term properly applied to one large, unhewn stone resting on two or more unhewn stones placed erect in the earth; a cromlech.

Constantine Dolmen, Cornwall.

dol-men′ic, *a.* Pertaining to dolmens.

dol′ō-mīte, *n.* [Named after the French geologist *Dolomieu*.] A granular magnesian carbonate of lime, often forming extensive beds. Much of the common white marble is *dolomite*.

dol-ō-mit′ic, *a.* Pertaining to dolomite; of the nature of dolomite.

dol′ō-mīze, *v.t.*; dolomized, *pt.*, *pp.*; dolomizing, *ppr.* To make into dolomite.

dō′lŏr, *n.* [L. *dolor*, pain, grief.] Pain; grief; lamentation.

Feast of Dolors; a Roman Catholic celebration, held on the Friday after Passion Sunday and also on the third Sunday of September, to commemorate the sorrows of the Virgin Mary.

dol-ŏr-if′ĕr-ous, *a.* [L. *dolor*, pain, and *ferre*, to produce.] Producing pain.

dol-ŏr-if′ic, dol-ŏr-if′ic-ăl, *a.* [L. *dolor*, pain, and *facere*, to make.] Causing or expressing pain or grief.

dō-lō-rō′sō, *a.* and *adv.* [It., from LL. *dolorosus*, painful, mournful.] Pathetic; pathetically; a musical direction.

dol′ŏr-ous, *a.* [ME. *dolerous*; LL. *dolorosus*, painful, mournful.]

1. Sorrowful; doleful; dismal; expressing sorrow or grief; as, a *dolorous* object; a *dolorous* sigh.

2. Painful; giving pain.

dol′ŏr-ous-ly, *adv.* Sorrowfully; in a manner to express pain.

dol′ŏr-ous-ness, *n.* The state or quality of being dolorous.

dol′phin, *n.* [ME. *dolphyn*; L. *delphinus*; Gr. *delphis*, *delphin*, dolphin.]

1. The popular name of several species of *Delphinus*, a genus of cetaceous mammals, characterized by having numerous, similar, nearly conical teeth in both jaws, comprehending the *dolphin* proper, the bottle-nosed *dolphin*, the grampus, etc. The common *dolphin*, *Delphinus delphis*, bears a great resemblance to the porpoise, but has a much longer and sharper snout.

Common Dolphin (*Delphinus delphis*).

2. A name given by poets and others to the coryphene, *Coryphæna hippurus*, a teleostean fish, long celebrated for the swiftness of its swimming, and the brilliant and beautiful colors which it assumes in succession in the act of dying. It is about five feet long.

3. In Greek antiquity, a ponderous mass of lead or iron suspended from the yardarm of a vessel, to be suddenly let down upon an enemy's ship.

4. In nautical language, a spar or buoy, made fast to an anchor, and usually supplied with a ring to enable vessels to ride by it.

5. A mooring-post placed at the entrance of a dock. The name is also sometimes applied to the mooring-post placed along a quay or wharf.

6. In military language, a handle of a gun or mortar made in the form of a *dolphin*.

7. [D—] In astronomy, a constellation, so called from its fancied resemblance to a *dolphin*.

8. In heraldry, a heraldic fish, resembling a *dolphin*, the device of the French dauphins.

dol′phin-et, *n.* A female dolphin.

dol′phin-flow″ĕr, *n.* The larkspur.

dol′phin-flȳ, *n.* A black aphis, *Aphis fabæ*, very destructive to the leaves of bean-crops; the collier-aphis or bean-aphis.

dol′phin-strīk″ĕr, *n.* In nautical language, a spar extending downward from the bowsprit; also called *martingale*.

dōlt, *n.* [ME. *dold*, *dult*, from *dul*; AS. *dol*, dull, stupid.] A heavy, stupid fellow; a blockhead.

dōlt, *v.i.* To waste time foolishly; to behave foolishly. [Obs.]

dōlt′ish, *a.* Dull in intellect; stupid; blockish; as, a *doltish* clown.

dōlt′ish-ly, *adv.* In a doltish manner.

dōlt′ish-ness, *n.* Stupidity.

dō′lus, *n.* [L. *dolus*; Gr. *dolos*, deceit, treachery.] In law, fraud; deceit practised maliciously.

dolv′en, *v.*, past participle of *delve*. [Obs.]

-dom. A suffix from ME. *-dom*; AS. *-dom*, from *dom*, jurisdiction, law, signifying dominion, province, jurisdiction, as in king*dom*, Christen*dom*, or state, condition, quality, as in free*dom*, wis*dom*.

dom, *n.* [Sp. *don*; L. *dominus*, lord, master.]

1. In Portugal and Brazil, a don; as *Dom Pedro*.

2. A title formerly given to the pope and later to dignitaries and the members of certain orders of the Roman Catholic church.

3. In card-playing, the joker or blank card in the game of *dom*-pedro.

dom′á-ble, *a.* [OFr. *domable*; L. *domabilis*, tamable, from *domare*, to tame, subdue.] Capable of being tamed.

dom′á-ble-ness, *n.* The state or quality of being domable.

dom′āge, *n.* Damage. [Obs.]

dom′āge, *n.* Subjugation. [Obs.]

dō-māin′, *n.* [OFr. *domaine*; L. *dominium*, right of ownership, dominion, from *dominus*, lord, master.]

1. Dominion; empire; territory under the government of a sovereign; a commonwealth; as, the vast *domains* of the Russian emperor.

2. Possession; estate; the land about the mansion-house of a lord, and in his immediate occupancy.

3. In law, immediate or absolute ownership of land; permanent or ultimate ownership; demain; demesne.

4. The range, limits, or sphere of any branch of knowledge or field of action; as, the *domain* of art or of politics.

5. In logic, the extension or sphere of a concept or idea.

Eminent domain or *right of eminent domain*; the inherent sovereign power of the state over all the property within its limits, by which it is entitled to appropriate private property to the public use, giving compensation for the same.

Public, *national*, or *state domain*; public lands, whether reserved for sale or grants or for specific uses.

dō′măl, *a.* [L. *domus*, a house.] In astrology, pertaining to a house.

dō-mā′ni-ăl, *a.* [Fr. *domanial*, from L. *dominium*, domain.] Of or pertaining to a domain or landed estate.

Dōm′bŏc, Dōme′book, *n.* [AS., lit., doom-book; *dom*, doom, and *boc*, book.] The book of laws of the Saxons, now lost, compiled under the direction of King Alfred, and containing the local customs of the several provinces of the kingdom.

dōme, *n.* [OFr. *dome*, a dome, cathedral, cupola, from L. *domus*, house.]

1. A building, especially a stately or majestic building; a cathedral or temple. [Poet.]

2. In architecture, a tholus or cupola in the form of an inverted cup; the hemispherical coving of a building. This restriction of the application of the term appears to have arisen from the Italian custom of calling an archiepiscopal church *Il duomo*, and from the circumstance that the chief churches of Italy were at one time almost universally so roofed.

3. Anything shaped like a *dome*; as, (a) a hemispherical arch; (b) the steam-chamber of a locomotive; (c) in chemistry, the upper part of a furnace, resembling a hollow hemisphere or small *dome*.

4. In crystallography, a termination of a prism by two planes meeting above in a horizontal edge, like the roof of a house.

5. The hemispherical part of the roof of an astronomical observatory, placed over the telescope, so contrived that it rotates, thus allowing any portion of the heavens to be viewed through the instrument, which projects through a slit.

dōme, *n.* and *v.* [Obs.] Same as *Doom*.

Dōme′book, *n.* See *Dombōc*.

dōmeş′dāy, *n.* [Obs.] Same as *Doomsday*.

dōmeş′măn, *n.*; *pl.* **dōmeş′men.** Same as *Doomsman*.

dō-mes′tic, *a.* [OFr. *domestique*; L. *domesticus*, pertaining to the house, from *domus*, a house, home.]

1. Belonging to the house or home; pertaining to one's place of residence and to the family; as, *domestic* concerns; *domestic* life; *domestic* duties.

2. Remaining much at home; living in retirement; fond of home and home duties; as, a *domestic* man or woman.

3. Living near the habitations of man; tame; not wild; as, *domestic* animals.

4. Pertaining to a nation considered as a family, or to one's own country; intestine; not foreign; as, *domestic* troubles; *domestic* dissensions.

5. Made in one's own house, nation, or country; as, *domestic* manufactures.

dō-mes′tic, *n.* 1. A household servant.

2. [*pl.*] Home-made cloths of common grades; specifically, cotton cloths.

dō-mes′tic-ăl, *a.* 1. Domestic.

2. Of a homelike nature; local in origin and character. [Rare.]

dō-mes′tic-ăl, *n.* A family. [Obs.]

dō-mes′tic-ăl-ly, *adv.* 1. In relation to domestic affairs.

2. Privately.

dō-mes′ti-cănt, *a.* Forming part of the same family. [Obs.]

dō-mes′ti-cāte, *v.t.*; domesticated, *pt.*, *pp.*; domesticating, *ppr.* [LL. *domesticatus*, pp. of *domesticare*, to tame, to live in a family, from L. *domesticus*, pertaining to a home, domestic, from *domus*, a house.]

1. To make domestic; to accustom to remain much at home; as, to *domesticate* oneself.

2. To make familiar; as, to *domesticate* a foreign word.

3. To accustom to live near the habitations of man; to tame; as, to *domesticate* wild animals.

dō-mes-ti-cā′tion, *n.* 1. The act of withdrawing from public notice and living much at home.

2. The act of taming or reclaiming wild animals or plants.

dō-mes′ti-cā-tŏr, *n.* One who domesticates.

dō-mes-tic′i-ty, *n.* The state of being domestic.

dom'ett, *n.* A baize cloth woven with a cotton warp and a woolen filling.

dō'mey-kite, *n.* [After I. *Domeyko*, a Chilean mineralogist.] A native arsenid of copper, of white or gray color, occurring massive in Chile.

dom'i-căl, *a.* Pertaining to or similar to a dome.

dom'i-cīde, *n.* [L. *domus*, house, home, and *cædere*, to kill.] The breaking up of a family by the removal of children on account of poverty.

> *Domicide*, or the breaking up of the home, is to the poor man what regicide is to the loyal subjects of any king. —F. De L. Booth-Tucker.

dom'i-cile, dom'i-cil, *n.* [L. *domicilium*, a dwelling, home, from *domus*, a house.]

1. An abode or dwelling; a place of permanent residence, either of an individual or family; a residence.

2. In law, the place of a person's legal residence, as determined by the laws of the state or country.

dom'i-cile, *v.t.*; domiciled, *pt., pp.*; domiciling, *ppr.* To establish in a fixed residence.

dom-i-cil'i-ăr, *n.* A domestic; a member of a household.

dom-i-cil'i-ā-ry, *a.* [LL. *domiciliarius*, from L. *domicilium*, a home, abode.] Pertaining to an abode or the residence of a person or family.

Domiciliary visit; a visit to a private dwelling, particularly for the purpose of searching it, under authority.

dom-i-cil'i-āte, *v.t.*; domiciliated, *pt., pp.*; domiciliating, *ppr.* 1. To provide with a domicile; to domicile.

2. To domesticate, to tame. [Obs.]

dom-i-cil-i-ā'tion, *n.* The act of domiciliating or the state of being domiciliated; permanent residence; inhabitancy.

dom'i-çul-tūre, *n.* [L. *domus*, house, home, and *cultura*, care, culture.] Domestic science. [Rare.]

dom'i-fȳ, *v.t.* [L. *domus*, a house, and *facere*, to make.] In astrology, to divide (the heavens) into twelve houses, in order to erect a theme or horoscope. [Obs.]

dom'i-nȧ, *n.*; *pl.* **dom'i-næ.** [L. *domina*, lady, mistress, f. of *dominus*, lord, master.] In old English law, a title given to a lady who held a barony in her own right.

dom'i-nănce, dom'i-năn-cy, *n.* Superiority; authority.

dom'i-nănt, *a.* [L. *dominans* (*-antis*), ppr. of *dominari*, to rule.]

1. Ruling; prevailing; governing; predominant; as, the *dominant* party or faction.

2. Most conspicuous; overshadowing.

Dominant chord; in music, the common chord, based on the dominant or fifth tone of the scale.

Dominant estate or *tenement*; in Scots law, the estate or tenement in favor of which a servitude exists over another estate.

Dominant owner; one who owns a dominant estate or tenement.

Syn.—Controlling, predominant, governing, ruling, prevailing.

dom'i-nănt, *n.* In music, (a) the recitative tone in Gregorian scales; (b) the fifth tone in the modern diatonic scale.

dom'i-nănt-ly, *adv.* In a dominant manner.

dom'i-nāte, *v.t.*; dominated, *pt., pp.*; dominating, *ppr.* [L. *dominatus*, pp. of *dominari*, to rule.]

1. To rule; to govern; to predominate over.

2. To influence most prominently; to have the greatest effect upon; to give specific character or appearance to; to overshadow; as, the mountain *dominated* the entire scene; kindness *dominated* his character.

dom'i-nāte, *v.i.* To predominate; to prevail.

dom-i-nā'tion, *n.* [L. *dominatio*, rule, dominion, despotism, from *dominari*, to rule.]

1. The exercise of power in ruling; dominion; government.

2. Control of the superior over the inferior; mental or spiritual control; prevailing force; as, the *domination* of a strong mind over a weak one.

3. [*pl.*] The fourth order of angelic beings in Dionysius's scheme of the celestial hierarchy.

> Thrones, *dominations*, princedoms, virtues, powers. —Milton.

dom'i-nā-tive, *a.* Governing; imperious.

dom'i-nā-tŏr, *n.* [L. *dominator*, a ruler, from *dominari*, to rule.] A ruler or ruling power; the presiding or predominant power.

dom'i-ne, *n.* [L. *dominus*, master, ruler.]

1. A clergyman; a pastor; specifically, a colloquial title given to pastors of the Dutch Reformed church in the United States.

2. A large fish, *Epinnula magistralis*, found in the West Indies.

dom-i-neer', *v.i.*; domineered, *pt., pp.*; domineering, *ppr.* [L. *dominari*, to rule, to be master, from *dominus*, master, ruler.]

1. To rule with insolence or arbitrary sway.

2. To bluster; to hector; to swell with conscious superiority or haughtiness.

> Go to the feast, revel and *domineer*.—Shak.

dom-i-neer', *v.t.* To govern; to control; to sway; to influence.

dom-i-neer'ing, *a.* Ruling with insolence; blustering; manifesting haughty superiority.

Syn.—Arrogant, overbearing, tyrannical, imperious, haughty, dogmatic, arbitrary.

dom-i-neer'ing-ly, *adv.* In a domineering manner.

dō-min'iç-ăl, *a.* [LL *dominicalis*, pertaining to the Lord's day or Sunday, from L. *dominicus*, pertaining to a lord, from *dominus*, lord, master.]

1. Connected with or denoting Sunday or the Lord's day.

2. Pertaining to Christ as the Lord.

Dominical letter; the letter used in almanacs to indicate Sunday, the first seven letters of the alphabet being used in regular order year after year.

Dominical prayer; the Lord's prayer.

dō-min'iç-ăl, *n.* 1. The Lord's day; Sunday. [Obs.]

2. The Lord's prayer.

3. A cathedral; a church edifice.

4. A dominicale.

dō-min-i-çā'lē, *n.* 1. In the Roman Catholic church, the veil formerly worn at the celebration of communion.

2. A Sunday dress.

Dō-min'i-căn, *n.* and *a.* [Named after *Dominic* de Guzman, the founder.]

I. *n.* A member of an order of monks, formerly known in England as Black Friars. The order is devoted to preaching and studying the sacred sciences. The members are sworn to chastity, obedience to their superiors, and poverty. They are required to abstain from a meat diet and to observe silence.

II. *a.* Belonging or relating to the order of Dominicans or to St. Dominic.

Dominican or Black Friar.

Dominican nuns; an order of nuns founded by St. Dominic.

Dominican tertiaries; the third order of St. Dominic.

dō-min'i-cīde, *n.* [L. *dominus*, master, and *cædere*, to kill.] One who kills his master; the act of killing one's master. [Rare.]

dom'i-nie, *n.* [L. *domine*, vocative of *dominus*, a master.]

1. In Scotland, the usual term for a schoolmaster; a pedagogue.

2. A clergyman. [Scot. and U. S. Colloq.]

dō-min'ion (-yun), *n.* [L. *dominium*, dominion, from *dominus*, master, lord.]

1. Sovereign or supreme authority; the power of governing and controlling; domination; supremacy; sovereignty; independent possession; control.

2. In law, power to direct, control, use, and dispose of at pleasure; right of possession and use without being accountable; as, the private *dominion* of individuals.

3. Territory under a government; region; country; district governed, or within the limits of the authority of a prince or state; that which is governed or controlled; as, the British *dominions*.

4. [D—] Specifically, the Dominion of Canada.

5. Predominance; ascendancy.

6. [*pl.*] An order of angels. [See *Dominations*.]

> Whether they be thrones, or *dominions*, or principalities, or powers. —Col. i. 16.

The Old Dominion; the State of Virginia, formerly known as the Dominion.

Syn.—Authority, government, jurisdiction, territory, region.

dō-min'i-um, *n.* [L., from *dominus*, lord.] In law, ownership; authority; complete title.

dom'i-nō, *n.*; *pl.* **dom'i-nōeş** or **dom'i-nōş.** [L. *dominus*, lord, master.]

1. A long, loose cloak, with a hood removable at pleasure, used as a general disguise at masquerades.

2. A mask or half-mask used at masquerades; formerly worn by ladies when traveling, as a partial disguise for the features.

3. The wearer of a *domino*.

4. A loose garment with a hood, worn by the canons of a cathedral; also, the hood alone.

5. One of the pieces used in the game of dominoes.

dom'i-nōeş, *n.pl.* Any one of a number of games played with a number (usually 28) of small, flat, rectangular pieces of wood, ivory, bone, or celluloid, the pieces being used somewhat as cards are in card games. One side of the piece is blank, the other is divided into two equal spaces or fields, each of which is either blank or marked in the same way as dice, with from 1 to 6 spots.

dom'i-nus, *n.* [L. *dominus*, lord, master.] Lord, sir, or master; a mode of address; a title formerly given to knights, lords of a manor, or clergymen.

Sir Joshua Reynolds in Domino and Mask.—After Thackeray.

dom'i-tȧ-ble, *a.* That can be tamed. [Rare.]

dō'mite, *n.* [Name derived from Puy-de-*Dome*, in Auvergne, France, where it is found.] In mineralogy, a variety of trachyte.

don, *v.t.*; donned, *pt., pp.*; donning, *ppr.* [ME. *don on*; AS. *don on*, lit., to do on.] To put on; to dress oneself with, as an article of clothing; as, *don* your best.

don, *n.* [Sp. *don*, Mr., sir, from L. *dominus*, lord, master.]

1. Mr.; sir; señor; a title and form of address used in Spanish-speaking countries; as, *Don* Alfonso. Formerly applied only to the nobility or higher clergy, now common to all grades of society.

2. A person bearing the title; a gentleman.

3. A personage of importance, or, ironically, one striving to appear important. [Colloq.]

4. In England, a college master or head; also, one of the tutors and fellows at the universities. [Colloq.]

dō'ñȧ (-nyä), *n.* In Spanish, the feminine of *don*; lady; madam; used as a title of respect.

dō'nȧ-ble, *a.* That may be given. [Rare.]

dō'nȧ-cīte, *n.* A petrified shell, of the genus *Donax*. [Obs.]

dō'nȧ-ry, *n.* [L. *donarium*, a sanctuary, offering, from *donum*, a gift.] A thing given to a sacred use. [Rare.]

don'at, *n.* A grammar. [Obs.]

dō'nāte, *v.t.*; donated, *pt., pp.*; donating, *ppr.* [L. *donatus*, pp. of *donare*, to donate, from *donum*, a gift, from *dare*, to give.] To give; to present; to bestow as a gift; to contribute; especially used of contributions of large amounts.

dō-nā'tion, *n.* [L. *donatio* (*-onis*), a giving, from *donatus*, pp. of *donare*, to give.]

1. The act of donating; a granting.

2. That which is given, bestowed, or donated; a gift; a grant; as, a *donation* of a million dollars to a university.

3. In law, the act or contract by which a thing, or the use of it, is transferred to a person or corporation, as a free gift; also, the thing so alienated without valuable consideration.

Donation party; a party assembling at the house of some person to be honored or gratified, in which each participant brings with him some gift; usually the beneficiary is a minister.

Syn.—Grant, benefaction, gratuity, endowment, present, gift.

Don'ȧ-tişm, *n.* The principles embraced by those African schismatics, of the fourth century, who were called Donatists, from Donatus, their leader. They considered theirs as the only true church, and the ordinances administered in other churches as invalid.

Don'ȧ-tist, *n.* An adherent of the schism of Donatus.

Don-ȧ-tist'iç, *a.* Pertaining to Donatism.

don'ȧ-tive, *n.* and *a.* [OFr. *donatif*, from L. *donare*, to give.]

I. *n.* 1. A gift; a gratuity; a present; a dole.

> The Romans were entertained with shows and *donatives*. —Dryden.

2. In the canon law, a benefice given and collated to a person, by the founder or patron, without either presentation, institution, or induction by the ordinary.

II. *a.* Vested or vesting by donation; as, a *donative* advowson. —Blackstone.

dō-nā'tŏr, *n.* [L., from *donare*, to give.] A donor.

don'ȧ-tō-ry, *n.* In Scots law, one to whom escheated property is, under certain circumstances, given by the crown.

dö'-naught (-nat), *n.* A do-nothing.

dō'nax, *n.* 1. A species of grass, *Arundo Donax*, growing to a great height in southern Europe, its stems being used for fishing-rods, walking-canes, etc.

2. [D—] A genus of lamellibranchiate mollusks, of the family *Donacidæ*; the wedge-shells.

don-cel′lȧ, *n.* [Sp., a maiden, damsel.] In zoölogy, a fish, *Platyglossus radiatus*, found in West Indian waters and the gulf of Florida; also, the ladyfish.

dŏne (dun), *pp.* of *do.* 1. Performed; executed; finished.

2. A word by which agreement to a proposal is expressed; as, in laying a wager, an offer being made, the person accepting or agreeing says, *Done*; that is, it is agreed, I agree, I accept.

3. Sufficiently cooked; figuratively, swindled.

4. Exhausted; played out; utterly fatigued; also, sick unto death, or fatally injured.

Done brown; cheated; thoroughly swindled. [Colloq.]

To have done with; to cease to have concern or business with; to withdraw oneself from.

dŏne, *a.* Executed; signed; issued; chiefly used in dating an official document signed by some high official, as a proclamation or important deed; as, *done* at Washington, etc.

dō-nee′, *n.* [OFr. *doné, donné*, pp. of *doner, donner*, from L. *donare*, to give, donate.]

1. The person to whom a gift or a donation is made.

2. The person to whom lands or tenements are given or granted; as, a *donee* in fee tail.

don′et, *n.* Same as *Donat.*

don′gȧ, *n.* [South African.] A very steep bank or deep channel of a river; a ravine, wet or dry.

dō′ni, *n.* A single-masted trading-vessel of light draft, usually about 70 feet long, used on the coast of Ceylon and the southern coast of India.

dō-nif′ẽr-ous, *a.* [L. *donum*, a gift, and *ferre*, to bring, bear.] Bringing gifts. [Rare.]

dŏn′jŏn (dun′jun), *n.* [ME. *dongeon*; OFr. *donjon*; LL. *dominio (-onis)*, a dungeon, from L. *dominio (-onis)*, power, from *dominus*, master, lord.] The inner building, or keep, of an ancient castle, to which the garrison could retreat in case of necessity. It contained the great hall and the prison-cells; whence, the modern dungeon.

Donjon, Castle Headingham.

doñ′key (*or* duñ′), *n.* [Prob. from *dun*; AS. *dun*; W. *dwn*, dusky, and dim. suffix *-key.*]

1. An ass.

2. A stubborn, stupid, or obstinate person.

doñ′key-en″gine, *n.* A small pumping or hoisting engine.

doñ′key-pump, *n.* An independent or auxiliary steam-pump used to wash decks, feed boilers, etc.

don′nȧ, *n.* [It., from L. *domina*, mistress, lady.] A lady; a title of respect given to ladies in Italy and Portugal.

Prima donna; the leading lady of an opera troupe.

don′nism, *n* Self-importance, or distance and loftiness of carriage. [Eng. Slang.]

dō′nŏr, *n.* [L. *donator*, a giver, from *donare*, to give.]

1. One who gives or bestows; one who confers anything gratuitously; a benefactor.

2. One who grants an estate; as, a conditional fee may revert to the *donor*, if the donee has no heirs of his body.

dö′-nöth″ing, *a.* Idle; inactive; lazy; as, a *do-nothing* policy.

dö′-nöth″ing-ism, dö′-nöth″ing-ness, *n.* Idleness; inactivity.

don′ship, *n.* The quality or rank of a don.

dōn′t. A contraction of *do not.* [Colloq.]

don′zel, *n.* A young attendant; a page. [Obs.]

dọọb′-grass, *n.* [Hind. *dūb*; Sans. *dūrvā.*] A perennial, creeping grass, *Cynodon Dactylon*, highly prized in Hindustan as food for cattle, and acclimated in the southern part of the United States.

dọọ′dle, *n.* A trifler; a simple fellow.

dọọ′dle-sack, *n.* [Prov. Eng., from G. *dudelsack*, a bagpipe.] A bagpipe.

dọọk, *n.* [Scot.] A piece of wood inserted in a wall as a support for finishings.

dọọl, *n.* [Obs.] See *Dole.*

dọọ′ly, *n.* [Hind. *dūli*, a litter.] A palanquin or kind of light litter.

dọọm, *v.t.*; doomed, *pt., pp.*; dooming, *ppr.* 1. To judge. [Obs.]

2. To pronounce sentence or judgment on; to condemn to any punishment; to consign by a decree or sentence; as, the criminal is *doomed* to death.

3. To destine; to fix irrevocably the fate or direction of; as, we are *doomed* to suffer for our sins.

4. Formerly, in New England, to assess taxes upon by estimate, when the owner of property made no statement. [Obs.]

dọọm, *n.* [ME. *doome*; AS. *dom*, judgment, sentence, from *don*, to do.]

1. Judgment; judicial sentence.

2. Condemnation; sentence; decree; determination affecting the fate or future state of another; usually a determination to inflict evil, sometimes otherwise.

> Revoke that *doom* of mercy. —Shak.

3. The state to which one is doomed or destined; one's fate, lot, or destiny; as, to suffer misery is the *doom* of sinners.

4. Ruin; destruction.

5. Discrimination. [Obs.]

dọọm′āge, *n.* A penalty or fine for neglect. [Obs.]

dọọm′fụl, *a.* Full of destruction.

dọọm′-pälm (-päm), *n.* The so-called gingerbread-tree of Egypt and Abyssinia, *Hyphæne Thebaica.* Its fruit, which is used for food, has a mealy outer husk or pulp, much like gingerbread in taste.

Doom-palm (*Hyphæne Thebaica*).

dọọmṣ′dāy, *n.* [ME. *domesdai*; AS. *domes dæg*, doomsday or day of doom; *domes*, genit. of *dom*, doom, and *dæg*, day.]

1. The day of the last judgment.

2. A day of sentence or condemnation.

Dọọmṣ′dāy Book, Dōmeṣ′dāy Book. A book compiled by order of William the Conqueror, containing a survey of all the lands in England, together with a list of owners of estates, their possessions, tenants, and the like. It consists of two volumes, a large folio and a quarto.

dọọmṣ′măn, *n.* A judge. [Obs.]

dọọm′stẽr, *n.* One who pronounces judgment; the name formerly given in Scotland to the public executioner.

dọọn, *n.* [Native name.] A tree of Ceylon, *Doona Zeylanica*, which yields varnish, resin, and lumber.

dōọr, *n.* [ME. *dore, dur*; AS. *dor, duru*, pl. *dura*, door; compare O.H.G. *tor, turi*, D. *deur*, G. *thor, thür*, L. *foris*, Gr. *thyra*, door.]

1. An opening for passage into or out of a house or other building, or any room, apartment, or closet; as, he stood by the church *door.*

2. A frame of boards, or any piece of board or plank, that shuts the opening of a house, or closes the entrance into an apartment or any inclosure; usually turning on hinges.

3. Avenue; passage; means of approach or access; as, an unforgiving temper shuts the *door* against reconciliation, or the *door* of reconciliation.

> I am the *door*; by me if any man enter in, he shall be saved. —John x. 9.

False door; see *Blank door* under *Blank.*

In doors; within the house; at home.

Next door to; near to; bordering on.

Out of doors; out of the house; in the open air.

To lie at one's door; in a figurative sense, to be imputable or chargeable to one; as, if the thing is wrong, the fault *lies at my door.*

dōọr′cāse, *n.* The frame which incloses a door.

dōọr′cheek, *n.* The jamb of a door.

Dọọr′gȧ, *n.* See *Durga.*

dōọr′ing, *n.* A doorcase. [Obs.]

dōọr′keep″ẽr, *n.* 1. A porter; one who guards the entrance of a house or apartment; a janitor.

2. In the Roman Catholic church, same as *ostiary.*

dōọr′less, *a.* Having no door.

dōọr′nail, *n.* The nail or knob on which the knocker of a door formerly struck.

As dead as a doornail; dead beyond a doubt.

dōọr′plāte, *n.* A plate for a house-door, bearing the name of the occupant or the number of the house, etc.

dōọr′pōst, *n.* The post or side-piece of a door.

dōọr′sill, *n.* The sill of a door; a threshold.

dōọr′stead (-sted), *n.* The entrance or place of a door.

dōọr′stōne, *n.* The stone at a threshold.

dōọr′stop, *n.* That part of a doorcase against which the door shuts; also, a device to prevent a door from being opened too widely.

dōọr′wāy, *n.* The passage of a door; the entrance into a room or building.

dōọr′weed, *n.* A low weed, *Polygonum aviculare*; also called *knotgrass.*

dōọr′yärd, *n.* A yard adjacent to a house.

dop, dopp, *n.* [D. *dop*; M.D. *dop, doppe*, a shell, husk, cover.] A device for holding a diamond when being cut or polished.

dop, *v.i.* To dip. [Obs.]

dop, *n.* A dip; a courtesy or low bow. [Obs.]

dōpe, *n.* [D. *doop*, sauce, dip, baptism, from *doopen*, to dip, baptize, from *diep*, deep.]

1. Any stupefying compound. [Slang.]

2. Any preparation of a thick, liquid, or pasty character; any greasy compound used as a lubricant, as axle-grease.

3. Any absorbent material, such as cotton-waste, sawdust, etc., used to hold lubricants, etc.

dōpe, *v.t.*; doped (dōpt), *pt., pp.*; doping, *ppr.* To treat with dope.

Dop′pẽr, *n.* [ME. *dopper*; AS. *doppa*, from *doppettan*, to dive, from *deop*, deep.]

1. One of a primitive South African Dutch sect.

2. An Anabaptist; used in contempt.

3. [d—] A diving bird.

dop′plẽr-ite, *n.* [Named after Christian *Doppler*, a German physicist.] A hydrocarbon of a brownish-black color, found in peat-bogs.

doq′uet (dok′et), *n.* A warrant; a docket. [Obs.]

dọr, dọrr, *n.* [AS. *dora*, a bumblebee, beetle, cockchafer.] The black-beetle or hedge-chafer, a species of *Scarabæus*; a common British beetle.

dọr, *n.* A deception, joke, trick, or humbug. [Obs.]

dọr, *v.t.* To humbug; to hoax; to trick. [Obs.]

Dō-rā′dō, *n.* [Sp. *dorado*, pp. of *dorar*; LL. *deaurare*, to gild; L. *de*, down, and *aurare*, to overlay with gold, from *aurum*, gold.]

1. A southern constellation, containing six stars.

2. [d—] A large fish resembling the dolphin.

dọr′bee″tle, *n.* A dor.

Dọr′cās sō-cī′e-ty. [Named after *Dorcas*, mentioned in Acts ix.] An association of ladies for supplying clothes to the poor.

dō-ree′, *n.* A fish. [Same as *Dory.*]

dōre′tree, *n.* A doorpost. [Obs.]

dọr′fly, *n.* The dorbeetle.

dọr′hawk, dọrr′hawk, *n.* The goatsucker of Europe; so called because it lives on dorbeetles.

Dō′ri-ăn, *a.* 1. Of or pertaining to Doris, a district of ancient Greece; relating to or originating with the people of Doris.

2. Pertaining to the Doric race; Doric.

Dō′ri-ăn, *n.* An inhabitant or native of Doris in Greece; one of the Doric race.

Dor′ic, *a.* [L. *Doricus*; Gr. *Dōrikos*, Doric, from *Dōris*, Doris.]

1. In general, pertaining to Doris in Greece, or to the Dorians.

2. In architecture, designating the second Roman order of columns, between the Tuscan and Ionic. The *Doric* order is distinguished for simplicity and strength. It is used in the gates of cities and citadels, on the outside of churches, etc.

Doric mode; in music, the first of the authentic modes of the ancients. Its character is severe, tempered with gravity and joy.

Doric Order.

Dor′ic, *n.* The dialect of the Dorians.

Dor′i-cism, Dō′rism, *n.* A characteristic of the Doric dialect.

Dō′ris, *n.* [LL., from Gr. *doris*, a sacrificial knife.] A genus of gasteropods, having the gills disposed circularly in a posterior rosette; the sea-lemons.

dọr′king, *n.* [Name derived from *Dorking*, England.] One of a breed of large domestic fowls, having five toes on each foot, and especially valued for the table.

dọr′măn-cy, *n.* [OFr. *dormance.*] Quiescence; abeyance; a dormant state.

dor'mănt, *a.* [ME. *dormant*; L. *dormiens (-entis)*, ppr. of *dormire*, to sleep.]

1. Sleeping; at rest; not in action; in abeyance; quiescent; as, *dormant* passions.

2. Being in a sleeping posture; as, the lion *dormant*, in heraldry.

Dormant partner; in commerce, a partner who takes no share in the active business of a company or partnership, but is entitled to a share of the profits, and subject to a share in losses. More generally called *sleeping partner*, or *silent partner*.

Lion Dormant.

Syn.—Sleeping, slumbering, latent, undeveloped, quiescent, inert.

dor'mănt, *n.* A sleeper, or large beam in the roof of a house, forming a base for other timbers.

dor'mẽr, *n.* [OFr. *dormeor*; L. *dormitorium*, a sleeping-room.] A beam; a sleeper.

dor'mẽred, *a.* Having dormers, or dormer-windows.

dor'mẽr-win"dōw, *n.* A window pierced through a sloping roof, and placed in a small gable which rises on the side of the roof.

dor'mice, *n.*, pl. of *dormouse*.

dor'mi-tive, *a.* and *n.* [L. *dormitivus*, from *dormire*, to sleep.]

I. *a.* Producing sleep or tending to produce sleep; soporific.

II. *n.* A medicine which promotes sleep; an opiate.

A Dormer-window.

dor'mi-tō-ry, *n.* [L. *dormitorium*, a sleeping-room, from *dormire*, to sleep.]

1. A room or building to sleep in; a building containing many bedrooms; especially applicable to the sleeping-apartments connected with a boarding-school, college, monastery, or convent.

2. A burial-place. [Obs.]

dor'mouse, *n.*; *pl.* **dor'mice**. [ME. *dormous*, lit., slumber-mouse.] A rodent of the family *Myoxidæ*, found in Europe and Asia and sometimes in Africa. They resemble squirrels, live in trees, and are torpid or dormant during the winter. The common *dormouse*, *Myoxus avellanarius*, is about the size of an ordinary mouse.

Common Dormouse (*Myoxus avellanarius*).

dor'my, *a.* [Scot.] In golf, ahead as many holes as there remain holes to play; said of a player or a side.

dorn, *n.* [G. *dorn*, a thorn.] A fish, the British thornback-ray.

dor'nick, dor'nock, *n.* 1. A coarse damask, formerly used for altar-cloths and ecclesiastical hangings. [Obs.]

2. A pebble, cobblestone, or small piece of rock. [Western U. S.]

dorp, *n.* [D.] A small village. [Rare.]

dorr, *n.* and *v.* Same as *Dor*.

dorr'fly̆, *n.* A species of beetle. [See *Dor*.]

dorr'hawk, *n.* Same as *Dorhawk*.

dor'sȧ, *n.*, pl. of *dorsum*.

dor'sad, *adv.* [L. *dorsum*, the back, and *ad*, to, toward.] In anatomy and zoölogy, toward the back; dorsally; opposed to *ventrad*.

dor'săl, *a.* [Fr. *dorsal*; LL. *dorsalis*, of or pertaining to the back, from L. *dorsum*, the back.]

1. In anatomy and zoölogy, of, pertaining to, or situated on or near the back of an animal or any organ; as, a *dorsal* fin; the *dorsal* aspect of the hand.

2. In botany, pertaining to the under surface of a leaf.

Dorsal vessel; a long blood-vessel lying along the back of an insect, and performing the functions of a heart.

dor'săl, *n.* 1. In anatomy, a dorsal vertebra.

2. In ichthyology, a dorsal fin.

3. The back of the orphrey of a priest's chasuble.

dor'săl-ly, *adv.* On, near, or toward the back; in a dorsal position or direction.

dorse, *n.* [OFr. *dors, dos*; L. *dorsum*, the back.]

1. The back; as, books with rich *dorses*. [Obs.]

2. A piece of silk, damask, or other rich material, used to cover the back of a chair, or hung behind an altar or within the chancel; especially, a rich hanging, covering the back of a chair of state or a throne.

dorse, *n.* [G. *dorsch*, a paddock; L.G. *dorsh*, a codfish.] A young cod, once believed to be a distinct species.

dor'sel, *n.* [OFr. *dorsal*, tapestry, so called because hung at the back; L. *dorsum*, back.]

1. A hanging; a drapery; a dorse.

2. A pannier.

3. A woolen cloth.

dor'sẽr, *n.* Same as *Dorsel*.

dor-si-, dor-sō-. Combining forms from L. *dorsum*, the back, denoting connection with or situation near or on the back, as *dorsi*meson, *dorsi*gerous.

dor'si-branch, *a.* and *n.* Same as *Dorsibranchiate*.

Dor"si-bran-chi-ā'tȧ, *n.pl.* [*Dorsi-*, and L. *branchiæ*, gills.] The second order of the *Annelides*, in which the branchiæ lie along the back. It includes the free marine worms.

dor-si-bran'chi-āte, *a.* and *n.* I. *a.* Having dorsal branchiæ; of or pertaining to the *Dorsibranchiata*.

II. *n.* One of the *Dorsibranchiata*.

dor-si-cum'bent, *a.* [*Dorsi-*, and L. *-cumbens*, ppr. of *-cumbere*, in *incumbere*, to lie down.] Lying upon the back.

dor-sif'ẽr-ous, *a.* [*Dorsi-*, and L. *ferre*, to bear.]

1. Same as *Dorsigerous*.

2. Same as *Dorsiparous*.

dor'si-fixed (-fixt), *a.* [*Dorsi-*, and L. *fixus*, pp. of *figere*, to fix.] Attached dorsally; said of anthers, etc.

dor-sig'ẽr-ous, *a.* [*Dorsi-*, and L. *gerere*, to carry.] In zoölogy, bearing or carrying the young on the back, as certain opossums.

dor-si-mes'ŏn, *n.* [*Dorsi-*, and Gr. *meson*, middle.] The line running lengthwise of the middle of the back. [Rare.]

dor-sip'ȧ-rous, *a.* [*Dorsi-*, and L. *parere*, to produce.]

1. In botany, bearing or producing seeds or fruit on the back; applied to ferns or plants of the capillary kind, without stalks.

2. In zoölogy, hatching the young upon the back, as the Surinam toad.

dor-si-ven'trăl, dor-sō-ven'trăl, *a.* [*Dorsi-*, and L. *venter*, belly.]

1. In zoölogy, pertaining to the back and the abdomen.

2. In botany, having two surfaces, as most leaves; bifacial.

dor'sū-lum, *n.*; *pl.* **dor'sū-lȧ**. [L., dim. of *dorsum*, the back.] The mesonotum of insects, when large and conspicuous, as in bees.

dor'sum, *n.*; *pl.* **dor'sȧ**. [L., the back.]

1. In anatomy, the back; also, the back of any part or organ; as, the *dorsum* of the foot.

2. The ridge of a hill. [Obs.]

dor'tẽr, *n.* A dormitory; also written *dortour*, *dorture*. [Obs.]

dō'ry, *n.*; *pl.* **dō'ries**. [Origin unknown.] A small, flat-bottomed rowboat, especially one used by fishermen at sea.

dō'ry, *n.* [Fr. *dorée*, the dory, lit., gilt, f. of *doré*, pp. of *dorer*; LL. *deaurare*, to gild.]

1. A popular name for the edible fish, *Zeus faber*, found in European seas; the John-dory.

2. A local name in the United States and Canada for the wall-eyed pike, *Stizostedion vitreum*.

Dory (*Zeus faber*).

Dō-ryph'ō-rȧ, *n.* [L., from Gr. *doryphoros*, spear-bearing; *dory*, the stem of a tree, a beam, shaft, and *pherein*, to bear.] A genus of beetles which live on and destroy plants. It includes the potato-bug or Colorado beetle. [See *Beetle*.]

dō-ryph'ō-rus, *n.*; *pl.*, **dō-ryph'ō-ri**. [Gr. *doryphoros*, bearing a spear; *dory*, a shaft, spear, and *pherein*, to bear, carry.] In the fine arts, a spear-bearer; specifically, the figure of a man, nude or nearly nude, holding a spear. This was a favorite subject in ancient sculpture, one of the most noted examples being the *Doryphorus* of Polycletus.

dōs-ȧ-dōs' (dō-zä-dō'), *adv.* [Fr., lit., back to back.] Back to back; used specifically of a figure in a reel or other dance, in which two dancers advance toward each other, pass around each other back to back, and return to their original places.

dōs'āge, *n.* 1. In medicine, the act or practice of giving medicine in regular doses.

2. The process of adding to wines, especially to champagnes, anything which will give a distinctive character.

dōse, *n.* [Gr. *dosis*, a gift, from *didonai*, to give.]

1. The quantity of medicine given or prescribed to be taken at one time.

2. Anything given to be swallowed; especially, anything unpleasant or nauseous that one is obliged to take, either literally or figuratively; as, that was a bitter *dose*.

3. A certain quantity; a portion; as much as one can swallow.

dōse, *v.t.*; dosed (dōst), *pt., pp.*; dosing, *ppr.*

1. To administer in doses; to form into suitable doses.

2. To give doses to; to give physic or medicine to.

3. To give anything nauseous to.

dos'el, *n.* [Obs.] Same as *Dossal*.

dō-sim'e-tẽr, *n.* [Gr. *dosis*, a gift, dose, and *metron*, measure.] A device used to measure small quantities of fluid; a drop-meter.

dō-si-met'ric, *a.* In pharmacy, pertaining to medicines sold in doses or small quantities.

dō-sim'e-try, *n.* The accurate and systematic measurement of a dose.

dō-sol'ō-gy, *n.* [Gr. *dosis*, a dose, and *logos*, description.]

1. The science of dividing medicines into doses.

2. A treatise on dosing.

doss, *n.* A bed; hence, sleep. [Eng. Slang.]

dos'săl, dos'sel, *n.* [OFr. *dossel*; LL. *dorsale*, a canopy, tapestry, from L. *dorsum*, the back.] A rich hanging of silk, damask, cloth of gold, etc., at the back of the altar or the sides of the chancel of a church.

dos'sel, *n.* 1. See *Dossil*.

2. See *Dossal*.

dos'sẽr, *n.* [ME. *dosser*; OFr. *dossier*; LL. *dorserium*, tapestry, a canopy, from L. *dorsum*, the back.]

1. A tapestry, usually richly embroidered, formerly hung on the walls of a hall, and sometimes in the chancel of a church.

2. A pannier or basket.

3. A chair or throne covering; a dorse.

dos'sẽr, *n.* One who sleeps at a doss-house; a vagrant; a tramp. [Eng. Slang.]

doss'-house, *n.* In London, a very cheap kind of lodging-house.

dos-si-ère' (-âr'), *n.* [OFr. *dossiere*, a curtain.] That part of a suit of armor which protected the back, extending from the neck to the waist.

dos'sil, dos'sel, *n.* [ME. *dosil*; LL. *docillus*, a spigot, from L. *ducere*, to lead.]

1. A plug; a spigot.

2. In surgery, a pledget or small piece of lint rolled in the form of a cylinder and used for cleaning a wound or sore.

3. In printing, a roll of cloth for cleaning ink from an engraved plate previous to taking an impression from it.

dōst, *v.*, second person singular, present indicative of *do*.

dot, *n.* [AS. *dott*, a dot, speck, from *dyttan*, to stop up, plug.] A small point or spot made with a pen or other pointed instrument; a speck; especially, one intentionally made as an indication mark, as in printing, to show the pronunciation of a letter or as a part of the letter; as, the *dot* of the letter *i*; in music, a point or speck placed after a note or rest, to indicate that the note or rest is to be maintained half as long again as its regular time.

dot, *n.* [Fr., from L. *dos* (*dotis*), dowry.] A marriage portion brought by a woman to her husband; a dowry.

dot, *v.t.*; dotted, *pt., pp.*; dotting, *ppr.* 1. To mark with a small dot or spot; as, to *dot* an *i*.

2. To mark or diversify with small detached objects; as, a landscape *dotted* with cottages or clumps of trees.

dō'tāge, *n.* [ME. *dotage*, from *doten, dotien*, to dote.]

1. Feebleness or imbecility of understanding or mind, particularly in old age; the childishness of old age; as, a venerable man, now in his *dotage*.

2. A doting, foolish, and excessive fondness.

3. Foolish expressions; drivel.

dō'tăl, *a.* [L. *dotalis*, pertaining to a dowry, from *dos* (*dotis*), a dowry.] Pertaining to a dower or a woman's marriage portion; constituting a dower, or comprised in it.

dō'tănt, *n.* Same as *Dotard*.

dō'tărd, *n.* [ME. *dotard*, from *dotien*, to dote.]

1. A man whose intellect is impaired by age; one in his second childhood.

2. One who is foolishly fond.

3. A decayed tree. [Prov. Eng.]

dō'tărd, *a.* 1. Foolish; doting; imbecile.

2. Decayed, as a tree. [Prov. Eng.]

dō'tărd-ly, *a.* Like a dotard; weak; foolish; imbecile.

dō-tā'tion, *n.* [LL. *dotatio* (*-onis*), an act of endowing, from L. *dotare*, to endow, from *dos* (*dotis*), a dowry.]

1. The act of endowing or bestowing a marriage portion on a woman.

2. Endowment; establishment of funds for support, as of a hospital or eleemosynary corporation. —Blackstone.

dotch'in (doch'), *n.* [Corruption of Chinese *toh*, to take up in the hand, and *ching*, to weigh.] A portable steelyard or balance used in China and Japan.

dōte, *v.i.*; doted, *pt., pp.*; doting, *ppr.* [ME. *dotien, doten*, to dote.]

1. To have the intellect impaired by age, so that the mind wanders or wavers; to be silly or insane.

Time has made you *dote*, and vainly tell
Of arms imagined in your lonely cell.
—Dryden.

2. To be excessively in love; to be unusually fond; usually with *on* or *upon*; as, to *dote on* one's child; to *dote upon* cherries.

3. To decay; to wither, as a tree. [Prov. Eng.]

dōte, *n.* 1. A dowry; a dot. [Obs.]

2. [*pl.*] Natural gifts or endowments. [Obs.]

dōte, *n.* An imbecile; a dotard. [Obs.]

dōt′ed, *a.* 1. Foolish, silly; stupid.

2. Partially decayed, as a tree.

dōte′head (-hed), *n.* One who is given to foolish affections or fancies; a dotard. [Rare.]

dōt′ẽr, *n.* 1. One in his dotage; a person whose understanding is weakened by age.

2. One who is excessively fond; one who dotes; with *on* or *upon*.

dōt′ẽr-y, *n.* The acts, speech, or behavior of a dotard or doter.

dŏth, *v.*, third person singular, present indicative of *do*.

Dō-thid-ē-ā′cē-æ, *n.pl.* [L., from Gr. *dothiēn*, a boil, abscess.] A family of fungi, the spores of which form in asci, having the perithecia immersed in a black or blackish stroma. Some are found on growing plants, others on dead vegetable substances.

doth′i-en, *n.* [Gr. *dothiēn*, a boil, abscess.] In pathology, a boil or abscess.

doth″i-en-en-te-rī′tis, *n.* [Gr. *dothiēn*, a boil, abscess, and *entera*, intestines.] Inflammation of the intestines, characteristic of typhoid fever; also, the fever itself.

dōt′ing, *a.* 1. Excessively fond.

2. Weak-minded from old age.

dōt′ing-ly, *adv.* In a doting manner.

dōt′ish, *a.* Foolishly fond; imbecile; weak.

dot′kin, *n.* Same as *Doitkin*.

dot′ted, *a.* Marked with or made up of dots or small spots; diversified with small detached objects.

dot′tel, *n.* See *Dottle*.

dot′tẽr-el, *n.* [ME. *dotrelle*, a dunce, a foolish person, from *dotien*, to dote, to be foolish.]

1. The popular name of a migratory plover, *Ægialites* or *Eudromias morinellus*, common in Europe and Asia. It derives its name from its apparent stupidity or tameness. Its flesh is considered a great delicacy.

2. A person easily duped or deceived; a gull.

dot′ting-pen, *n.* A drawing-pen which consists of a small wheel with blunt projections, which rotates freely in a handle. It makes a succession of dots on the surface over which it is passed.

dot′tle, dot′tel, *n.* [ME. *dottel*, a plug or tap of a vessel; AS. *dott*, a dot, point, from *dyttan*, to plug, stop up.]

1. A stopper; a bung; a plug.

2. The half-smoked refuse of a tobacco-pipe. [Scot.]

dot′ty, *a.* Wavering; imbecile. [Slang.]

dō′ty, *a.* [Local, U. S.] Decaying or decayed, as rotten timber.

dōu-āne′, *n.* [Fr.] A customhouse in France.

dōu-ā-niēr′, *n.* [Fr.] An officer of the French customs.

dou′ăr, dow′ăr, *n.* [Ar. *daur*, a circle.] A group of Arab tents, arranged in a circle, serving as an inclosure for the horses, etc.

dōu-blé′ (-blā′), *a.* In bookbinding, having the inside of the cover lined with leather.

dŏu′ble (dub′l), *a.* [ME. *double*; OFr. *double*; L. *duplus*, double; *duo*, two, and *plenus*, full, from *plere*, to fill.]

1. Coupled; composed of two mutual or corresponding parts; being in pairs; as, *double* chickens in the same egg; a *double* chin.

2. Twice as much; containing the same quantity or length repeated; twofold.

Take *double* money in your hand.
—Gen. xliii. 12.

3. Combining two in one; as, to hold a *double* office.

4. Deceitful; acting two parts, one openly, the other in secret.

And with a *double* heart do they speak.
—Ps. xii. 2.

5. In botany, having more than the usual number of petals; said of flowers the stamens and pistils of which have been transformed into petals.

6. Of extra weight, size, thickness, strength, etc.; as, a *double* sole; *double* ale.

Double is often used in combination, especially with perfect participles, and denotes two ways, or twice the number or quantity.

Double entry; see under *Bookkeeping*.

Double note; in music, a breve.

Double octave; in music, an interval of two octaves or fifteen notes.

Double play; in baseball, a play by which two men are retired.

Double point; in geometry, the crunode of a curve, or the point where it intersects itself.

Double salt; in chemistry, (a) one in which the hydrogen of an acid has been replaced by different bases or radicals acting as bases; (b) two salts in molecular combination; a compound salt, as alum.

Double standard; see *Bimetallism*.

Double star; in astronomy, two stars, so near each other, either in fact or in appearance, that they cannot be distinguished apart without a telescope.

dŏu′ble (dub′l), *n.* 1. Twice as much; twice the number, sum, value, quantity, or length.

If the thief be found, let him pay *double*.
—Ex. xxii. 7.

2. A turn in running to escape pursuers.

3. A trick; a shift; an artifice to deceive.

4. A counterpart; an exact copy; a duplicate; as, he is my *double*; hence, an apparition; a wraith.

5. A fold, or the place where a thing is folded; a plait.

6. Beer of more than ordinary strength.

A pot of good *double*. —Shak.

7. In music, (a) a variation; (b) a repetition of words or a refrain in singing; (c) an understudy to an actor or singer, prepared to play or sing a part in an emergency; (d) an organ-stop, or separate instrument, which sounds an octave below unison in pitch.

8. In lawn tennis, etc., a game in which two play on a side; opposed to a single, in which there is but one on a side.

9. Same as *Doublet*, 3.

10. In military parlance, a contraction of *double-quick*; as, to advance at the *double*.

dŏu′ble, *adv.* Twice.

I was *double* their age. —Swift.

To see double; to see two images of the same object.

dŏu′ble, *v.t.*; doubled, *pt.*, *pp.*; doubling, *ppr.* [ME. *doublen*; OFr. *doubler*, to double, from L. *duplus*, double.]

1. To fold; as, to *double* the leaf of a book; to *double* down a corner.

2. To increase or extend by adding an equal sum, value, quantity, or length; as, to *double* a sum of money; to *double* the quantity or size of a thing; to *double* the length; to *double* dishonor.

3. To contain twice the sum, quantity, or length of, or twice as much as; as, the enemy *doubles* our army in numbers.

4. To repeat; to add to; as, to *double* blow on blow.

5. To clench, as the hand.

6. In navigation, to sail round or by, as a cape, point, etc., so that the cape or point shall be between the ship and her former situation.

dŏu′ble, *v.i.* 1. To increase to twice the sum, number, value, quantity, or length; to increase or grow to twice as much; as, a sum of money *doubles* by compound interest in a little while.

2. To enlarge a wager to twice the sum laid.

I am resolved to *double* till I win. —Dryden.

3. To turn back or wind in running.

Doubling and turning like a hunted hare.
—Dryden.

4. To play tricks; to use deceit.

5. In printing, to set up the same word or words, unintentionally, a second time.

6. In military parlance, to march at the double-quick; as, to *double* across the parade-ground.

To double upon; in naval tactics, to inclose between two fires.

dŏu′ble-aç″ting, *a.* In mechanics, acting or exerting power in two directions, producing a twofold result.

dŏu′ble-bank, *v.t.* To work or pull, as by means of a rope or oar, with men working in pairs, that is, with two men to each oar or with men on both sides of a rope.

dŏu′ble-banked (dub′l-bankt), *a.* Having two opposite oars managed by rowers on the same bench, or having two men to the same oar.

dŏu′ble-bar″reled, *a.* Having two barrels, as a gun.

dŏu′ble-bāss′, *n.* The largest musical instrument of the viol kind. It has three or four strings and a range of more than three octaves.

dŏu′ble-bas-soon′, *n.* An instrument of the oboe kind, pitched an octave lower than the ordinary bassoon.

dŏu′ble-breast″ed, *a.* Having a row of buttons and buttonholes on each side, as a waistcoat or coat, so that it may be lapped and buttoned on either side.

dŏu′ble-çon′cāve, *a.* Same as *Concavo-concave*.

dŏu′ble-çon′vex, *a.* Same as *Convexo-convex*.

dŏu′ble-dēal″ẽr, *n.* One who is deceitful or tricky; one who says one thing and thinks or intends another; one guilty of duplicity.

dŏu′ble-dēal″ing, *n.* Artifice; duplicity; deceitful practice; the profession of one thing and the practice of another.

dŏu′ble-deck′ẽr, *n.* 1. A vessel having two decks above the water-line.

2. A street-car or other public conveyance having a second floor and seats on top.

3. A freight-car with two floors.

4. A tenement-house having two families to each floor; so called in New York. [Slang.]

dŏu′ble-dȳe, *v.t.* To dye twice over.

dŏu′ble-dȳed, *a.* 1. Twice dyed.

2. Figuratively, thorough; complete; utter; as, a *double-dyed* villain.

dŏu′ble-ēa′gle (-ē′gl), *n.* 1. A gold coin of the United States, worth $20.

2. The representation of an eagle with two heads, as in the national arms of Russia and Austria.

dŏu′ble-edġed (-ejd), *a.* 1. Having two edges.

2. Figuratively, cutting both ways; applied to an argument which makes both for and against the person employing it, or to any statement having a double meaning.

dŏu′ble-end″ẽr, *n.* Anything with its two ends alike, so that it may move or operate in both directions with equal facility.

dŏu′ble-en-ten′dre (dōb′l-ăn-tăn′dr), *n.* [Fr. *double*, double, and *entendre*, to understand.] A word or expression having two meanings, the less obvious of which is usually indelicate or indecent.

dŏu′ble-eȳed (-īd), *a.* Keen of sight; watchful.

dŏu′ble-fāce, *n.* Duplicity.

dŏu′ble-fāced (-fāst), *a.* 1. Having two faces looking in opposite directions, as the Roman god Janus.

2. Having both sides or surfaces equally well finished and designed for use; as, a *double-faced* shawl; a *double-faced* hammer.

3. Deceitful; hypocritical.

dŏu′ble-fīrst, *n.* In Oxford University, a familiar designation for (a) one who after a final or honors examination in the classics and mathematics, gains a place in the first class in each; (b) a university degree taken with first-class honors in the classics and mathematics; as, he took a *double-first* at Oxford.

dŏu′ble-floor, *n.* A floor constructed with binding and bridging joists.

dŏu′ble-hand″ed, *a.* 1. Having two hands.

2. Deceitful. [Obs.]

dŏu′ble-head″ed, *a.* Having two heads; as, a *double-headed* eagle in a coat of arms.

dŏu′ble-head″ẽr, *n.* A railroad train with two locomotives, either drawn by both or having one in front and one behind. [Colloq.]

dŏu′ble-heärt″ed, *a.* Having a false heart; deceitful; treacherous.

dŏu′ble-hung, *a.* Being so suspended as to move up or down with equal ease; said of the two sashes of a window hung with cords and weights.

dŏu′ble-lock, *v.t.* 1. To fasten with two bolts, or secure with double fastenings.

2. To secure by turning a key or shooting a bolt twice, as in some forms of lock.

dŏu′ble-milled, *a.* Twice milled or fulled, as cloth to make it finer.

dŏu′ble-mīnd″ed, *a.* Unsettled; wavering; unstable; undetermined.

dŏu′ble-ness, *n.* 1. The state of being double or doubled.

2. Duplicity; deceit.

dŏu′ble-quick (-kwik), *n.* In military language, the quickest step next to the run, consisting of 165 to 180 steps in the minute; also called *double-time*.

dŏu′ble-quick, *a.* 1. Performed in the time of the double-quick; pertaining to or in conformity with the double-quick; as, *double-quick* step.

2. Very quick or rapid; as, he disappeared in *double-quick* time.

dŏu′ble-quick, *adv.* In double-quick step; as, we were marching *double-quick*.

dŏu′ble-quick, *v.t.* and *v.i.* To march or cause to march in double-quick time.

dŏu′blẽr, *n.* 1. One who or that which doubles.

2. An instrument for augmenting a very small quantity of electricity, so as to render it manifest by sparks or the electrometer.

dŏu′ble-rip″pẽr, *n.* A sled used for coasting down-hill, and composed of two sleds placed one behind the other, united by and supporting a long board used for the seat; a bobsled. [Local, U. S.]

dŏu′ble-shāde, *v.t.* To double the natural darkness of.

dŏu′ble-snīpe, *n.* The greater snipe, *Gallinago major*.

dŏub′let (dub′), *n.* [ME. *dublet*, *dobbelet*; OFr. *doublet*, a double stone, a close-fitting garment, dim. of *double*, double.]

1. A close-fitting garment, covering the body from the neck to a little below the waist. It was introduced from France into England in the fifteenth century, and was worn by both sexes and all ranks until the time of Charles II., when it was superseded by the vest or waistcoat.

2. One of two like things; a duplicate; sometimes, but less correctly, a pair.

3. A word or phrase unintentionally doubled, or set up the second time, by printers.

4. Among lapidaries, a counterfeit gem composed of two pieces of crystal, with a color

1. Doublet, time of Edward IV. 2. Doublet, Portrait of Sir Wm. Russell; 3. Peasecod-bellied Doublet; both time of Elizabeth. 4. Doublet, time of Charles I.

between them, so that they have the same appearance as if the whole substance of the crystal were colored.

5. [*pl.*] A game somewhat like backgammon, played with dice. [Obs.]

6. A simple form of microscope, consisting of a combination of two plano-convex lenses whose focal lengths are in the ratio of three to one, placed with their plane sides toward the object, and the lens of shortest focal length next the object.

7. In philology, a duplicate form of a word; one of two (or more) words originally the same, but different in form, and often slightly different in meaning, as *drag* and *draw*.

dŏu′ble-thread″ed, *a.* 1. Sewing by means of two threads, as a sewing-machine.

2. In mechanics, having two screw-threads or double pitch.

dŏu′ble-time, *n.* A rapid marching step; double-quick.

dŏu′ble-tŏngue, *n.* Duplicity. [Obs.]

dŏu′ble-tŏngue (-tung), *v.i.* In music, to apply the tongue rapidly to the roof of the mouth in playing the flute and certain brass instruments, as the cornet, so as to insure a brilliant execution of a staccato passage.

dŏu′ble-tree, *n.* The bar of a vehicle to which the two singletrees are attached; an equalizing bar.

dŏub′lets, *n.pl.* A throw, or the result of a throw, of dice, by which the faces lying uppermost show the same number of spots on each die; as, to throw *doublets*.

dŏu′ble-vault, *n.* In architecture, one vault built over another, with a space between the convexity of the one and the concavity of the other. It is used to preserve artistic proportions in domes and domical roofs when it is desired to give them the appearance of a dome, both externally and internally.

Double-vaults, dome of San Pietro in Montorio, Rome.

dŏu′bling, *n.* 1. The act of making double; a repetition; that which is or has been doubled.

2. A shift; an artifice; a turning; as, the *doubling* of a fox.

3. The second distillation of spirits.

4. In heraldry, the lining of a mantle or mantling.

5. [*pl.*] In nautical language, (a) the part of a mast between the trestletrees and the cap of the lower spar; (b) the false skin or sheathing secured to a ship's side as a protection against chafing by ice, etc., as on Arctic whalers.

6. A double course of roofing material, as slates or shingles.

7. The act of marching at the double-quick.

dŏub-lo͝on′, *n.* [Fr. *doublon*; Sp. *doblon*, a doubloon, from *doblo*, double; from L. *duplus*, double.] A Spanish and Portuguese gold coin, no longer minted. It was originally a double pistole, and varied in value from five to fourteen dollars.

dŏu′bly, *adv.* In twice the quantity; to twice the degree; as, *doubly* wise or good; to be *doubly* sensible of an obligation.

doubt (dout), *v.i.*; doubted, *pt., pp.*; doubting, *ppr.* [ME. *douten*, *dowten*; OFr. *douter*, to doubt, fear; L. *dubitare*, to doubt, hesitate, from *duo*, two.]

1. To waver or fluctuate in opinion; to hesitate; to be in suspense; to be uncertain respecting the truth or fact; to be undetermined; as, I *doubt* whether it is proper; I *doubt* whether I shall go.

2. To fear; to be apprehensive. [Obs.]

I *doubt* there's deep resentment in his mind.
—Otway.

doubt (dout), *v.t.* 1. To question or hold as questionable; to withhold assent from; to hesitate to believe; as, I *doubt* the truth of the story.

2. To fear; to suspect. [Obs.]

3. To distrust; to withhold confidence from; as, to *doubt* one's ability to execute an office.

doubt (dout), *n.* 1. Uncertainty of mind; suspense; unsettled state of opinion concerning a state or condition of things; question; hesitation.

2. Uncertainty of condition.

Thy life shall hang in *doubt* before thee.
—Deut. xxviii. 66.

3. Suspicion; fear; apprehension. [Obs.]

4. Difficulty urged for solution, or presented for removal; objection.

To every *doubt* your answer is the same.
—Blackmore.

Syn.—Hesitation, mistrust, perplexity, suspense, uncertainty.—*Doubt* belongs to the understanding, and *hesitation* to the will. While there are serious *doubts* in the mind, there must be a painful *hesitation* as to the course to be pursued.

doubt′ȧ-ble, *a.* 1. That may be doubted; questionable.

2. Redoubtable. [Obs.]

doubt′ănce, *n.* Uncertainty. [Obs.]

doubt′ẽr, *n.* One who doubts; one whose opinion is unsettled; one who scruples.

doubt′fụl, *a.* 1. Dubious; not settled in opinion; undetermined; wavering; hesitating; applied to persons; as, we are *doubtful* of a fact, or of the propriety of a measure.

2. Dubious; ambiguous; not clear in meaning; as, a *doubtful* expression.

3. Admitting of doubt; not obvious, clear, or certain; questionable; not decided; as, a *doubtful* case; a *doubtful* proposition; the result of the war is *doubtful*.

4. Of uncertain issue.

Who have sustained one day in *doubtful* fight.
—Milton.

5. Not secure; suspicious; as, we cast a *doubtful* eye.

6. Not certain or defined; as, a *doubtful* hue.

7. Of questionable character; as, he employed *doubtful* agents.

Syn.—Ambiguous, equivocal, dubious, precarious, questionable, uncertain.

doubt′fụl-ly, *adv.* In a doubtful manner; dubiously.

doubt′fụl-ness, *n.* 1. A state of doubt or uncertainty of mind; dubiousness; suspense; instability of opinion.

2. Ambiguity; uncertainty of meaning.

3. Uncertainty of event or issue; uncertainty of condition.

doubt′ing, *a.* Wavering in mind; calling in question; hesitating; as, a *doubting* Thomas.

doubt′ing-ly, *adv.* In a doubting manner; dubiously; without confidence.

doubt′less, *a.* Free from fear; confident.

doubt′less, *adv.* Without doubt or question; unquestionably; undoubtedly.

doubt′less-ly, *adv.* Unquestionably.

doubt′ous, *a.* Doubtful. [Obs.]

doug, *n.* [Fr.] A peculiarly colored monkey of the genus *Semnopithecus*, found in Cochin China.

douce, *a.* [Scot., from ME. *douce*; OFr. *douce*, f. of *doux*, sweet; L. *dulcis*, sweet.]

1. Sweet; gentle; luxurious. [Obs.]

2. In Scotland, sober; sedate; tranquil; undisturbed; serious.

douce′pēre, douze′pēre, *n.* [Fr. *douze pairs*; OFr. *doze pers*, the twelve peers, from *douze* (L. *duodecim*), twelve, and *per*, peer; from L. *par*, equal.] One of the twelve peers of France, renowned in fiction as followers of Charlemagne.

dŏu′cet, *n.* [ME., from OFr. *doucet*, sweet, gentle; from L. *dulcis*, sweet.]

1. A pastry; a custard.

2. A testicle of a deer; written also *dowcet*, *dowset*.

3. A flute.

dōu-cēur′, *n.* [Fr. *douceur*; OFr. *douçor*, sweetness, a gift; L. *dulcis*, sweet.]

1. Sweetness or charm of manner. [Rare.]

2. A gift; a reward; something given for service done or to be done; especially, a bribe; a tip.

dōuçhe, *n.* [Fr., from L. *ductus*, pp. of *ducere*, to lead, bring, conduct.]

1. A jet or stream of water directed with considerable force on to some part of the body, sometimes for medicinal purposes.

2. A syringe.

dōu′cine, *n.* [Fr.] A molding, concave above and convex below, serving as a cyma to a delicate cornice; a cyma recta.

dōuck′ẽr, *n.* A bird that dips or dives in water; a diver; a ducker. [Prov. Eng.]

dōugh (dō), *n.* [ME. *dow*, *dowe*; AS. *dah*, dough.]

1. Paste of bread; a soft mass of flour or meal moistened and kneaded and ready to be baked into bread, cake, etc.

2. Any soft paste-like mass having the consistency of dough, as potter's clay, etc.

To have one's cake dough; see under *Cake*.

dōugh′-bāked (dō′bākt), *a.* Not hardened to perfection; soft; imperfectly baked; figuratively, soft-witted; foolish. [Colloq.]

dōugh′bĩrd, *n.* The curlew of Arctic America, *Numenius borealis*.

dōugh′boy, *n.* 1. A nautical name for a flour-dumpling, boiled in salt water.

2. An infantryman; so called by cavalrymen. [Slang.]

3. In the World War, an American soldier, the term applying to all branches of the service. [Slang.]

dōugh′fāce, *n.* A timid, easily-influenced politician; first used in the United States, to designate politicians of the North who, in antebellum days, were accused of truckling to the slave interests.

dōugh′fāced (dō′fāst), *a.* Easily influenced; pliable.

dōugh′fāce″ism, *n.* The character of a doughface; pliability; uncertainty of purpose.

dōugh′i-ness, *n.* The state of being doughy.

dōugh′-knēad″ed (dō′nēd″ed), *a.* Resembling dough; soft.

dōugh′nut, *n.* A small round cake, made of flour, eggs, and sugar, and boiled in lard.

dough′ti-ly (dou′), *adv.* With doughtiness.

dough′ti-ness, *n.* Valor; bravery.

dōugh′tren (dō′tren), *n.pl.* Daughters. [Obs.]

dough′ty (dou′), *a.* [ME. *doughty*; AS. *dohtig*, *dyhtig*, strong, valiant, from O.H.G. *tugan*, to be strong.] Brave; valiant; eminent; noble; illustrious; as, a *doughty* hero; now seldom used, except in irony or burlesque.

dōugh′y, *a.* Like dough; soft; yielding to pressure; pale; flabby; not thoroughly baked.

dōu-loc′rȧ-cy, dū-loc′rȧ-cy, *n.* [Gr. *doulos*, a slave, and *kratein*, to rule.] A government controlled by slaves.

dōum′-pälm, *n.* See *Doom-palm*.

doup, *n.* [Scot.] The breech or buttocks; the bottom or butt-end.

dōur, *a.* [Scot.] Hard; obstinate; sour; unyielding.

dōu′rȧ, *n.* A species of millet. [See *Durra*.]

dōu-rōu-cōu′li, *n.* [Native name.] A small, large-eyed, nocturnal South American monkey of the genus *Nyctipithecus*; also written *durukuli*.

douse, *v.t.*; doused (doust), *pt., pp.*; dousing, *ppr.* [Etym. uncertain.]

1. To thrust or plunge into water.

2. In seamen's language, to strike or lower in haste; to slacken suddenly; as, *douse* the topsail.

3. To extinguish. [Slang.]

douse, *v.i.* 1. To fall suddenly into water.

2. To prospect for ore, water, etc., by the aid of a dousing-rod.

douse, *n.* A blow; a stroke. [Scot.]

dous′ing-chock, *n.* One of several pieces of timber joined together across the apron and lapped within the inside planking above the upper deck of a vessel.

dous′ing-rod, *n.* A divining-rod used as a means of locating lodes or veins of ore, wells or water, etc.

dout, *v.t.* To put out; to extinguish; to douse. [Obs.]

dout′ẽr, *n.* An extinguisher for candles. [Obs.]

dōuze′pēre, *n.* Same as *Doucepere*.

dōve, *n.* [ME. *dove*, *douve*, a dove; AS. *dufan*, to dive, to dip.]

1. The popular name of several species of *Columba*, a genus of birds of the family *Columbidæ*, most of which are also called pigeons. The different species popularly called *doves* are distinguished by some additional term prefixed; as, the ringdove, the turtledove, etc. The *dove* is regarded in poetry as symbolic of peace, gentleness, and purity; in ecclesiastical art, as a symbol of the Holy Spirit. The mourning-*dove* symbolizes love.

2. A word of endearment for one gentle and pure of mind.

3. A receptacle shaped like a *dove*, used in the middle ages to contain the host.

Soiled dove; a lewd woman. [Slang.]

dŏve′=cŏl″ŏr, *n.* Gray, with a shade of purple or pink.

dŏve′cōte, dŏve′cot, *n.* A small building or box, raised to a considerable height above the ground, in which domestic pigeons breed; a pigeon-house.

dŏve′=eyed (-īd), *a.* Having eyes expressive of tenderness.

dŏve′kie, *n.* 1. The little auk, *Mergulus alle.*

2. The black guillemot.

dŏve′let, *n.* A young or small dove.

dŏve′like, *a.* Having the characteristics of a dove; mild; gentle; pure.

dŏve′=plant, *n.* A beautiful Brazilian orchid bearing a flower resembling a white dove in flight; also called *Holy Ghost plant.*

dŏve′ṣ′=foot, *n.* 1. A small English geranium having a leaf of the shape of a dove's foot.

2. The columbine. [Prov. Eng.]

dŏve′ship, *n.* The quality of being mild, gentle, and pure; the character of a dove; gentleness.

dŏve′tāil, *n.* In carpentry, the manner of fastening boards and timbers together by letting one piece into another in the form of a dove's tail spread, or wedge reversed, so that it cannot be drawn out, except one way. This is the strongest of all fastenings or joints.

1. Common Dovetail. 2. Lap Dovetail.

Dovetail molding; in architecture, a kind of convex molding resembling a series of dovetails.

Dovetail saw; in carpentry, the saw used in cutting dovetails.

dŏve′tāil, *v.t.*; dovetailed, *pt., pp.*; dovetailing, *ppr.* To unite by a tenon in form of a pigeon's tail spread, let into a board or timber; used also in a figurative sense; as, the details of the two plots *dovetail* into each other.

dŏve′=tick, *n.* A minute parasite infesting doves and other birds.

dŏve′wood, *n.* The wood of *Alchornea latifolia*, a tree of the spurge family common in Jamaica.

dŏv′ish, *a.* Like a dove; innocent. [Rare.]

dow, *n.* See *Dhow.*

dow, *v.t.* To endow. [Obs.]

dow′ȧ-ble, *a.* Capable of being endowed; entitled to dower.

dow′ȧ-ġẽr, *n.* [OFr. *douagiere*, from *douage*, a dowry, from *douer*; L. *dotare*, to endow.]

1. A widow; a title particularly given to the widows of princes and persons of rank. Thus, the widow of a king is called *queen dowager*, to distinguish her from the wife of her late husband's successor.

2. In law, a widow endowed or possessed of a jointure.

dow′ȧ-ġẽr-iṣm, *n.* The state of being a dowager.

dow′ăr, *n.* See *Douar.*

dow′cet, *n.* [OFr. *doucet*, sweet, gentle.] A testicle of a deer; a doucet.

dow′di-ly, *adv.* In a dowdy manner.

dow′di-ness, *n.* The state of being dowdy.

dow′dy, *n.*; *pl.* **dow′dieṣ.** [Eng. dial.] A slovenly, ill-dressed, inelegant woman; a slattern.

dow′dy, *a.* Slovenly; ill-dressed; vulgar-looking; applied to women; as, a *dowdy* creature.

dow′dy-ish, *a.* After the manner of a dowdy.

dow′el, *n.* [Fr. *douille*, a socket, the barrel of a pistol, a little pipe, from M.H.G. *tübel*; O.H.G. *tupili*, a tap, plug.]

1. A wooden or metallic pin or peg uniting two adjacent pieces of wood, stone, etc., and keeping them in their proper relative positions.

2. A piece of wood in a wall, either built or driven in, to which other parts may be nailed; a dook.

Barrel-end in three pieces joined by Dowels.

dow′el, *v.t.*; doweled, *pt., pp.*; doweling, *ppr.* To fasten together, as two boards, by pins inserted in the edges; as, a cooper *dowels* pieces for the head of a cask.

dow′el=bit, *n.* A bit used for doweling.

dow′el=joint, *n.* A joint made by doweling.

dow′el=pin, *n.* A dowel.

dow′el=point″ẽr, *n.* An instrument for pointing dowels.

dow′ẽr, *n.* [ME. *dower*, *dowere*; OFr. *doaire*; LL. *dotarium*; L. *dos* (*dotis*), a dower.]

1. In law, that portion of a man's estate which his widow enjoys during her life, after the death of her husband.

2. The property which a woman brings to her husband at marriage; dowry.

3. One's personal gifts or share of natural endowments.

dow′ẽr, *v.t.* To furnish with dower; to portion; to endow.

dow′ẽred, *a.* Furnished with dower or a portion.

dow′ẽr-less, *a.* Destitute of dower; having no portion or fortune.

dow′ẽr-y, *n.* [Obs.] See *Dowry.*

dowf, *a.* and *n.* [Scot.] I. *a.* Dull; hollow; stupid.

II. *n.* One who is stupid.

dow′ie, *a.* Sad; mournful. [Scot.]

dow′itch-ẽr, *n.* [A corruption of G. *deutscher*, a German.] In zoölogy, the red-breasted or gray-backed snipe, *Macrorhamphus griseus.*

dowl, *n.* See *Dowle.*

dow′lăs, *n.* [Name probably from *Doullens*, in France, where the cloth is said to have been first made.] A kind of coarse linen cloth much used in southern Scotland and Yorkshire in the eighteenth century.

dowle, dowl, *n.* [OFr. *douille*, something soft, downy, from L. *ductilis*, ductile.] Fine down; a feather filament.

down, *n.* [ME. *down*, *downe*, down; prob. of Scand. origin; compare Ice. *dunn*, Sw. *dun*, down.]

1. The fine soft covering of fowls under the feathers, particularly on the breasts of water-fowl, as the duck and swan. The eider-duck yields the best kind.

2. The soft hair of the human face when beginning to appear.

> The first *down* begins to shade his face.
> —Dryden.

3. The soft pubescence upon plants and some fruits; the pappus or little crown of certain seeds of plants; a fine feathery or hairy substance by which seeds are conveyed to a distance by the wind, as in the dandelion and thistle.

4. A place, usually with the idea of softness, where one finds rest; anything that soothes or mollifies.

> Thou bosom softness; *down* of all my cares.
> —Southern.

down, *v.t.* To cover, stuff, or line with down.

down, *n.* [ME. *doun*, *down*; AS. *dun*, a hill.]

1. A bank or elevation of sand thrown up by the sea; a dune; a somewhat rounded and grassy hill.

2. A term applied in England to a tract of rolling or hilly land, used mainly for pasturing sheep; generally in the plural; as, Epsom *downs.*

> Seven thousand broad-tailed sheep grazed on his *downs.* —Sandys.

The Downs; a well-known roadstead and rendezvous for shipping in the English channel, near Deal.

down, *prep.* [ME. *down*, *doun*, down, abbrev. form of *adune*, adown; AS. *adun*, *adune*, *of-dune*, from the hill; *a*, *of*, off, from, and *dune*, dat. of *dun*, hill.]

1. Along a descent; from a higher to a lower place; as, to run *down* a hill; to fall *down* a precipice; to go *down* the stairs.

2. Toward the mouth of a river, or toward the place where water is discharged into the ocean or a lake; as, we sail or swim *down* a stream; an excursion *down* the bay.

3. In a direction from a metropolis or center of government or population to the country districts, or from the main terminus of a railroad and the like to its subordinate stations; as, *down* the state; *down* the main line.

Down the country; toward the sea, or toward the part where rivers discharge their waters into the ocean.

down, *adv.* 1. In a descending direction; from a higher to a lower position, degree, or place in a series; from a metropolis to the country districts, or from the main terminus of a railroad to the subordinate stations; as, he is going *down.*

2. On the ground or at the bottom; as, he is *down*; hold him *down.*

3. Figuratively, in a low condition; in humility, dejection, calamity, etc.

4. Below the horizon; as, the sun is *down.*

5. Into disrepute or disgrace; as, a man may sometimes preach *down* error; he may write *down* himself or his character, or run *down* his rival.

6. From a larger to a less bulk; from a greater to a less consistency; as, to boil *down* in decoctions and culinary processes.

7. From former to latter times; from a remoter or higher antiquity to more recent times.

> And lest I should be wearied, madam,
> To cut things short, come *down* to Adam.
> —Prior.

8. At length; extended or prostrate on the ground or on any flat surface; as, to lie *down*; he is lying *down.*

9. An elliptical and sometimes interjectional alternative for *go down*, *come down*, *kneel down*, etc.; as, *down!* dog, *down!*

> *Down*, therefore, and beg mercy of the duke.
> —Shak.

10. Followed by *with*, in energetic commands, a contraction of *take down*, *throw down*, *put down*; as, *down with* the sail; *down with* tyranny.

11. At a lower rate or price; as, goods marked *down.*

12. Actually in the hand; as, to pay cash *down.*

13. On some writing surface; as, to set or write *down.*

Down in the mouth; dispirited; dejected. [Vulgar.]

To be down upon or *come down upon*; (a) to seize with avidity and with rapidity; as, a bird of prey *comes down upon* its victim; (b) to rate one soundly; to make a violent attack upon a person with the tongue; in this sense, colloquial.

To be down at heel; literally, to have the back part of the upper or heel of a shoe or slipper turned down; figuratively, to be slipshod, slovenly, shabbily dressed, or seedy.

Up and down; here and there; in a rambling manner.

Down east; in or into New England. [U. S.]

Down south; in or into the southern states. [U. S.]

down, *a.* 1. Cast or directed downward; downcast; dejected; as, a *down* look.

2. Downright; plain; positive; as, her many *down* denials. [Rare.]

3. Downward; that goes down; as, a *down* train or boat.

down, *n.* 1. A downward fluctuation; a depression; a low state; as, ups and *downs* of fortune.

2. In football, the act of placing the ball down for a scrimmage, (a) if the player having the ball is tackled and the movement of the ball is stopped, or if the player cries "Down"; (b) as soon as a runner attempting to go through is tackled and goes down, being held by an opponent, or whenever a runner having the ball goes out of bounds.

down, *v.t.*; downed, *pt., pp.*; downing, *ppr.* To cause to go down; to knock down; to overthrow; to put down; to subdue; to dishearten; to dispirit; as, to *down* proud hearts; to *down* an opponent at fisticuffs or in argument.

down, *v.i.* To go down; to sink; to be palatable or acceptable.

> Probably it will hardly *down* with anybody at first hearing. —Locke.

down′beăr, *v.t.* To bear down; to depress.

down′ċast, *a.* Cast downward; directed to the ground; as, a *downcast* eye or look; hence, depressed; dejected; as, *downcast* spirits.

down′ċast, *n.* 1. Sadness; melancholy look.

2. In mining, the ventilating shaft down which the air passes in circulating through a mine.

down′ċast-ing, *a.* Casting down; dejecting.

down′ċast-ly, *adv.* In a downcast manner; dejectedly.

down′ċast-ness, *n.* The state of being downcast; sadness.

down′ċōme, *n.* Downfall; ruin.

down′ċōm-ẽr, *n.* The vertical pipe which conducts the waste gases from the top of a close-mouthed blast furnace into the blast main; also called *downtake.*

down′=drăft, down′=drȧught (-drȧft), *n.* A downward current of air, as in a furnace.

down′fạll, *n.* 1. A falling, or body of things falling; as, the *downfall* of a flood.

2. Ruin; destruction; a sudden fall or ruin by violence; complete failure or overthrow; as, the *downfall* of the Roman Empire; the *downfall* of a city.

down′fạll″en, *a.* Fallen; ruined.

down′fạll″ing, *a.* Descending.

down′ġȳved, *a.* Hanging down like the loose links of fetters. [Rare.]

down′hạul, *n.* In seamen's language, a rope made fast to the upper corner of a sail to haul it down.

down′heärt″ed, *a.* Dejected in spirits.

down′hill, *n.* Declivity; descent; slope. [Rare.]

down′hill, *a.* Descending; sloping.

down′hill, *adv.* With a downward tendency; toward the bottom.

down′i-ness, *n.* The state of being downy.

down′looked (-lookt), *a.* Having a downcast countenance; dejected; gloomy; sullen.

down′lȳ″ing, *n.* The time of retiring to rest; time of repose; time of lying-in; as, she's at the *downlying.*

down′pōur, *n.* A copious pouring; specifically, a heavy shower of rain.

down′right (-rīt), *adv.* [ME. *downright*, *dounright*, *dunriht*; *dun*, down, and *rihte*, right, straight.]

1. Right down; straight down; perpendicularly.

2. In plain terms; without ceremony or circumlocution.

> We shall chide *downright.* —Shak.

3. Completely; thoroughly; also, without delay; without stopping short; as, she fell *downright* into a fit.

down′right, *a.* 1. Directly to the point; plain; open; artless; undisguised; as, *downright* madness; *downright* wisdom; *downright* falsehood.

2. Plain; artless; unceremonious; blunt; as, he spoke in his *downright* way.

3. Straight downward; as, a *downright* blow.

down′right-ly, *adv.* Plainly; in plain terms; bluntly.

down′right-ness, *n.* The state or quality of being downright or direct and plain.

down′-shāre, *n.* A breastplow used to cut the turf off downs. [Eng.]

down′sit″ting, *n.* The act of sitting down; repose; a resting.

> Thou knowest my *downsitting* and mine uprising. —Ps. cxxxix. 2.

down′stāirs′, *adv.* Down to a lower floor; beneath; down from the bedroom floor; as, she is now sufficiently recovered to go *downstairs*.

down′stāirs′, *a.* On a lower floor; related to the lower floor; as, a *downstairs* window.

down′steep″y, *a.* Very steep. [Obs.]

down′strēam′, *adv.* In the direction of the current of a stream.

down′strōke, *n.* A stroke made with a downward motion; a downward blow.

down′tāke, *n.* 1. See *Downcomer*.

2. Any pipe, etc., leading downward.

down′thrōw, *n.* 1. In geology and mining, the sinking of a stratum or strata, by which a bed of rock or seam of coal is brought into a lower position than before.

2. The process of throwing down, or the condition of being overthrown.

down′town, *adv.* Toward or in the business section of a city or town; as, I am going *downtown*; he works *downtown*.

down′town, *a.* Situated in the business section of a city; as, a *downtown* street. [Local, U. S.]

down′-tree, *n.* A tree of the West Indies (*Ochroma Lagopus*) whose seeds are incased in a woolly covering.

down′trod″den, down′trod, *a.* Trodden down; trampled down.

> The *downtrodden* vassals of perdition. —Milton.

down′wărd, down′wărds, *adv.* [ME. *dounward, duneward*; AS. *aduneweard*; *adune*, adown, down, and *-weard*, -ward.]

1. From a higher place to a lower; in a descending course, whether directly toward the center of the earth or not; as, to tend *downward*; to move or roll *downward*; to look *downward*; to take root *downward*.

2. In a course or direction from a head, spring, origin, or source; as, water flows *downward* toward the sea; we sailed *downward* on the stream.

3. In a course of lineal descent from an ancestor, considered as a head, or from an earlier to a later period of time; as, to trace successive generations *downward* from Adam or Abraham.

4. In the course of falling or descending from elevation or distinction.

5. In the lower parts; as to the lower extremities.

down′wărd, *a.* 1. Moving or extending from a higher to a lower place, as on a slope or declivity, or in the open air; tending toward the earth or its center; as, a *downward* course; he took his way with *downward* force.

2. Declivitous; bending; as, the *downward* heaven.

3. Descending from a head, origin, or source.

4. Tending to a lower condition or state; depressed; dejected; as, *downward* thoughts.

down′weed, *n.* An old English name for the cudweed, *Filago Germanica*.

down′weigh (-wā), *v.t.* To press or weigh down.

down′y, *a.* 1. Covered with down or nap; as, a *downy* feather; *downy* wings.

2. Covered with pubescence or soft hairs, as a plant.

3. Made of down or soft feathers; as, a *downy* pillow.

4. Soft; calm; soothing; as, *downy* sleep.

5. Resembling down.

6. Knowing; cunning; as, a *downy* cove. [Slang.]

dow′ry, *n.* [ME. *dowrye, dowrie*; OFr. *doaire*; LL. *dotarium*; L. *dos* (*dotis*), a dowry.]

1. The money, goods, or estate which a woman brings to her husband in marriage; the portion given with a wife.

2. The reward paid for a wife.

3. A gift; a fortune given; an endowment. [Rare.]

dowse *v.t.* and *v.i.* See *Douse*.

dowse, dowst, *n.* A blow on the face. [Obs.]

dows′ēr, *n.* A rod for dousing. [Rare.]

dow′ve, *n.* A dove. [Obs.]

dow′y, *a.* Same as *Dowie*.

dox-ō-log′iç-ăl, *a.* Pertaining to doxology; giving praise to God.

dox-ol′ō-ġize, *v.i.* To give glory to God, as in a doxology.

dox-ol′ō-ġy, *n.*; *pl.* **dox-ol′ō-ġies**. [LL. *doxologia*; Gr. *doxologia*, a praising; *doxologos*, giving or uttering praise; *doxa*, praise, opinion, from *dokein*, to think, and *logos*, a word, from *legein*, to speak.] A short form of words giving glory to God, suitable for being sung or chanted.

dox′y, *n.*; *pl.* **dox′ies**. [Old Slang.] A loose woman; a prostitute; the mistress of a rogue or vagabond.

doy-eṅ′ (dwä-yäṅ′), *n.* [Fr.] The senior in any special group, by virtue of length of appointment, age, or length of business or professional career; a dean.

doy′ley, *n.* Same as *Doily*.

dōze, *v.i.*; dozed, *pt.*, *pp.*; dozing, *ppr.* [Origin uncertain.]

1. To slumber; to sleep lightly; to drowse.

> If he happened to *doze* a little, the jolly cobbler waked him. —L'Estrange.

2. To live in a state of drowsiness; to be dull or half asleep; as, to *doze* over a book.

dōze, *v.t.* 1. To pass or spend in drowsiness; as, to *doze* away one's time.

2. To make dull; to stupefy. [Obs.]

dōze, *n.* A light sleep; a slumber.

doz′en (duz′n), *n.* [ME. *dozeyn*; OFr. *dozaine*, a dozen; L. *duodecim*, twelve; *duo*, two, and *decem*, ten.]

1. Twelve things collectively, usually twelve of a like kind; used with or without *of*; as, a *dozen* eggs, or a *dozen of* eggs; ten *dozen* collars.

2. An indefinite number; as, I have a *dozen* things to do.

Baker's dozen; see under *Baker*.

dōz′enth, *a.* Twelfth. [Rare.]

dōz′ēr, *n.* One who dozes.

dōz′i-ness, *n.* Drowsiness; heaviness; inclination to sleep.

dōz′y, *a.* 1. Drowsy; heavy; inclined to sleep; sleepy; sluggish; as, a *dozy* head.

2. Decaying; half rotten; used of wood, trees, fruit, etc.

drab, *n.* [Ir. *drabog*, a slut, slattern, from *drab*, a spot, stain; AS. *drabbe*, dregs, lees.]

1. A strumpet; a prostitute.

2. A slatternly woman.

3. A kind of wooden box, used in salt-works to hold the salt when taken out of the boiling pans.

drab, *n.* [Fr. *drap*, cloth.]

1. A kind of thick, woolen cloth of a yellowish-gray color.

2. A yellowish-gray tint.

3. A quaker moth.

drab, *a.* Of a yellowish-gray color; as, *drab* cloth.

drab, *v.i.*; drabbed, *pt.*, *pp.*; drabbing, *ppr.* To associate with strumpets.

drab′bēr, *n.* One who keeps company with drabs.

drab′bets, *n.* A coarse linen duck of a drab color.

drab′bish, *a.* Having the qualities of a drab; somewhat of the color of drab.

drab′ble, *v.t.*; drabbled, *pt.*, *pp.*; drabbling, *ppr.* [ME. *drabelen, drablen*, to soil, prob. from AS. *drabbe*, dregs.] To draggle; to make dirty by drawing in mud and water; as, to *drabble* a gown.

drab′ble, *v.i.* To fish for barbels with a long line and a rod.

drab′blēr, *n.* A small additional sail, sometimes laced to the bottom of a bonnet on a square sail, in sloops and schooners.

drab′ble-tāil, *n.* An untidy woman; a slattern.

Dră-cæ′nȧ (*or* -kē′nȧ), *n.* [LL. *dracæna*, a female dragon; Gr. *drakaina*, f. of *drakōn*, a serpent, dragon.] A genus of trees, family *Liliaceæ*, found in the tropics, resembling the palms and often attaining large size. The resin called dragon's-blood is obtained from *Dracæna Draco*, one of the largest species.

Dragon's-blood Tree (*Dracæna Draco*).

drā′ganth, *n.* Gum tragacanth.

drachm (dram), *n.* See *Dram* and *Drachma*.

drach′mȧ, drach′me, *n.* [L. *drachma*; Gr. *drachmē*, a drachma, from *drachma*, as much as one can hold in the hand, a handful, from *drassesthai*, to grasp, take by handfuls.]

1. A silver coin among the ancient Greeks, having a different value in different states and at different periods. The average value of the Attic *drachma* was about that of the modern French franc, or 19.3 cents.

2. In modern Greece, a silver coin worth about the same as the ancient *drachma*, though its purchasing power is considerably less.

3. In ancient Greece, a weight of about 70 grains.

4. In modern Greece, a weight of one gram or 15.4 grains.

drȧ-ci′nȧ, drā′cine, *n.* [L. *draco*, dragon.] The red coloring-matter of the resinous substance called dragon's-blood, much used to color varnishes.

Drā′cō, *n.* [L. *draco*; Gr. *drakōn*, a serpent, dragon.]

1. A genus of dragon-lizards, of the family *Agamidæ*.

2. [d—] A luminous exhalation from marshy grounds.

3. The Dragon, a constellation of the northern hemisphere.

Drȧ-cō′ni-ăn, *a.* [L. *Draco* (*-onis*); Gr. *Drakōn*, Draco, from *drakōn*, a dragon.]

1. Relating to or like Draco, the archon, supposed to have been the author of the severe code of laws in effect in Athens about 621 B. C. The punishments inflicted under it were so harsh that it was spoken of as having been written in blood.

2. Severe; rigorous; inexorable; relentless; applied to laws.

Drȧ-con′iç, *a.* 1. Same as *Draconian*.

2. Relating to the constellation Draco.

drȧ-cō′nin, *n.* Same as *Dracina*.

drȧ-con′tiç, *a.* In astronomy, belonging to that space of time in which the moon performs one entire revolution; also written *draconitic*.

Dracontic month; the time which the moon takes in making a revolution from a node back to that node.

Drȧ-cun′cū-lus, *n.* [L., dim. of *draco*, a dragon.]

1. A genus of plants, natural order *Araceæ*, with a long stalk, spotted like a serpent's belly, and pedate leaves. They are natives of southern Europe.

2. [d—] A fish of the genus *Callionymus*; the dragonet.

3. A genus of worms, including *Dracunculus medinensis*, or guinea-worm, found in tropical climates, which insinuates itself under the skin of the legs of man, causing a suppurating sore.

drad, *a.* Terrible; dreaded. [Obs.]

drăff, *n.* [ME. *draf*, refuse, chaff; prob. of Celtic origin.] Refuse; lees; dregs; the wash given to swine; specifically, the refuse of malt which has been brewed or distilled from, given to swine and cattle.

> Still swine eat all the *draff*. —Shak.

drăff′ish, *a.* Worthless.

drăff′y, *a.* Like draff; waste; worthless.

drȧft, draught (drȧft), *n.* [ME. *draught, draht*, a drawing, pulling, pull, stroke, from AS. *dragan*, to draw, drag, pull.]

1. The act of drawing; that which is drawn. In this sense and several of the others, generally spelled *draught*, which is the older form.

> Upon the *draught* of a pond not one fish was left. —Hale.

2. A selection of men or things for a special duty or purpose; specifically, a selection of soldiers from an army or part of an army, or any military post, to serve with some other body or in another place; or of men from various ships to serve in another ship; or of ships from various squadrons to act on a particular expedition; as, these important posts were weakened by heavy *drafts*.

> Several of the States had supplied the deficiency by *drafts* to serve for the year. —Marshall.

3. An order from one man to another directing the payment of money; a bill of exchange.

4. A drawing of lines for a plan; a figure described on paper; delineation; sketch; plan.

5. Depth of water necessary to float a ship.

6. A writing of any kind as first drawn up; a preliminary suggestion or sketch, to be worked up and finished; as, the first *draft* of a set of resolutions.

7. A confined current of air; the drawing or moving of air.

8. The degree of slant given to the furrow of a millstone.

9. A line or border cut on the surface of a stone to guide the stonecutter.

10. A deduction made from the gross weight of merchandise to allow for loss from various causes. [Eng.]

11. The area of the openings through which water is discharged from a turbine-wheel or through a sluice-gate.

12. The act of drinking; also, the quantity of a liquid drunk at one time; as, a *draught* of pure water.

13. The act of depleting, or taking away part; as, a *draft* upon one's health or resources.

14. In mechanics, the quantity of air which passes through a furnace in a given time.

Angle of draft; for vehicles or heavy bodies, the angle which the line of direction of the pulling force makes with the plane over which the body is drawn.

Forced draft; a strong draft in a flue produced by artificial means, as by a blower or the injection of a jet of steam.

Natural draft; a draft produced by the exhaustion of the air in a furnace or chimney by heat.

On draught; drawn direct from the cask, without being bottled; as, ale *on draught*.

dráft, dráught, *a.* 1. Being on draught; drawn direct from the cask as required; as, *draught* beer.

2. Relating to or used for drafting or pulling; as, *draft*-cattle.

dráft, *v.t.*; drafted, *pt.*, *pp.*; drafting, *ppr.* 1. To draw in outline; to delineate.

2. To compose and write; to sketch in writing; as, to *draft* a memorial or a lease.

3. To draw for military or naval service; to select; to detach; to conscript; to draw from any company, collection, or society.

4. In weaving, to draw through the heddles.

5. To draw; to pull. [Rare.]

dráft′=bär, *n.* 1. A singletree.

2. The bar to which the coupling of a railroad-car is attached.

dráft′=cat″tle, *n.pl.* Animals that may be used in drawing loads.

dráft′=en″gine, *n.* A steam-engine used for pumping, etc.

dráft′ėr, *n.* One who drafts.

dráft′=fûr″nāce, *n.* A furnace in which forced draft is used.

dráft′=hook, *n.* One of the iron hooks on the sides of a gun-carriage, to which ropes are attached for moving the gun backward and forward.

dráft′=hôrse, *n.* A horse used for drawing heavy loads.

dráft′i-ness, dráught′i-ness, *n.* The condition of being drafty or abounding in currents of air.

dráft′=net, *n.* A dragnet.

dráft′=ox, *n.* An ox used for drawing loads.

dráfts′măn, dráughts′măn, *n.* 1. One who draws plans or designs.

2. One skilled in the preparation of written instruments.

3. One who drinks drams; a tippler. [Rare.]

4. One of the pieces used in the game of checkers or draughts. In the last two senses, spelled *draughtsman*.

dráfts′măn-ship, dráughts′măn-ship, *n.* The office or work of a draftsman; skill in drawing, especially architectural or mechanical drawing.

dráft′y, dráught′y, *a.* Pertaining to a draft or drafts; exposed to drafts; as, a *drafty* hall.

Great *draughty* rooms. —Yonge.

drag, *v.t.*; dragged, *pt.*, *pp.*; dragging, *ppr.* [ME. *draggen, dragen*; AS. *dragan*, to drag, draw.]

1. To pull; to haul; to draw along the ground by main force; applied particularly to drawing heavy things, with labor, along the ground or other surface; as, to *drag* stone or timber; to *drag* a net in fishing.

2. To break, as land, by drawing a drag or harrow over it; to harrow.

3. To draw along slowly or heavily, as anything burdensome; as, to *drag* a lingering life; to *drag* one foot after another.

4. To search with a hooked instrument, as a river, pond, etc., for drowned persons, etc.

5. Figuratively, to search painfully or carefully.

While I *dragg'd* my brains for such a song. —Tennyson.

To drag an anchor; to draw or trail an anchor along the bottom when loosened, or when the anchor will not hold the ship.

Syn.—Pull, draw, haul.

drag, *v.i.* 1. To hang so low as to trail on the ground; to serve as a hindrance.

2. To fish with a drag; as, they have been *dragging* for fish all day.

3. To be drawn along; to trail; as, the anchor *drags*.

4. To move slowly; to proceed heavily; as, this business *drags*.

drag, *n.* 1. Something to be drawn along the ground, or on the bottom under water, as a weighted net or grapnel; a dragnet.

2. The act of dragging; a heavy motion indicative of some impediment; motion effected with slowness and difficulty; as, a heavy *drag* uphill; he had a *drag* in his walk.

3. A rough, heavy sledge used for dragging heavy loads, as stones, over the ground.

4. A long coach or carriage, generally drawn by four horses; it is uncovered and has seats round the sides; sometimes applied to a mail-coach or tallyho.

5. Whatever is drawn, as a boat in tow; whatever serves to retard a ship's way.

6. An attachment for retarding the rotation of a carriage-wheel; a skid.

7. Figuratively, a person or thing forming an obstacle to one's progress or prosperity; as, his brother has been a great *drag* upon him.

8. A heavy harrow; a brake.

9. The bottom part or section of a founder's molding-box.

10. A stonecutter's instrument used for finishing soft stone which has no grit.

11. In marine engineering, the difference between the speed of a steamship under sail and that of the screw, when the ship outruns the latter; the difference between the propulsive effects of the different floats of a paddle-wheel.

12. The scent or trail left by a fox; also, an artificial scent, as that made by an aniseed bag, used as a substitute for a fox by hunters.

13. A kind of floating anchor, usually of spars and sails, to keep a ship's head to the wind or diminish leeway.

14. The difference between the draft of a vessel forward and that aft.

drag, *n.* A variety of confectionery; a drug. [Obs.]

dra-gan′tin, *n.* A mucilage obtained from gum tragacanth.

drag′bär, *n.* Same as *Drawbar*.

drag′bōlt, *n.* A pin used for coupling.

dra-gée′ (-zhā′), *n.* [Fr. *dragée*, sugarplum.] A sugarplum; in pharmacy, any medicine, as a pill, coated with sugar.

drag′gle, *v.t.*; draggled, *pt.*, *pp.*; draggling, *ppr.* [Freq. of *drag*.] To wet and soil by drawing on the ground, in the mud, or on wet grass; to drabble; to trail.

drag′gle, *v.i.* To be drawn on the ground; to become wet or dirty by being drawn through mud or wet grass.

drag′gle=tāil, *n.* One who allows her clothes to draggle; a slatternly woman.

drag′gle=tāiled, *a.* Slovenly; slatternly; untidy.

drag′=hook, *n.* A hook attached to the back and front of locomotives and railroad-cars for coupling.

drag′=hound, *n.* A hound trained to follow the scent made by a drag.

drag′=hunt, *n.* A hunt in which a drag or artificial scent is used.

drag′link, *n.* In marine engines, a link connecting the crank of the main shaft with that of the inner paddle shaft.

drag′măn, *n.* A fisherman who uses a dragnet.

drag′net, *n.* A weighted net to be drawn on the bottom of a river or pond for taking fish, etc.

drag′ō-măn, *n.*; *pl.* **drag′ō-măns.** [Fr. *dragoman*; ME. *drogman*; OFr. *droguemen*; Ar. *tarjumān*, an interpreter, from *tarjama*, to interpret, explain.] An interpreter; an interpreter and traveler's guide or agent; an interpreter attached to an embassy or a consulate; a term in general use among travelers in the Levant and other parts of the East.

drag′ŏn, *n.* [ME. *dragon, dragun*; OFr. *dragon*, a dragon, a standard; L. *draco* (*-onis*); Gr. *drakōn*, a dragon, a serpent, lit., the seeing one, from *derkesthai*, to see.]

1. In mythology, a fabulous animal, conceived physically as a sort of winged crocodile, with fiery eyes, crested head and enormous claws, spouting fire, and morally as the embodiment of evil, of malicious watchfulness, and oppression.

2. A saurian of the genus *Draco*, distinguished by false ribs extending outward in a nearly straight line, and sustaining an extension of the skin, which forms a kind of wing comparable to that of the squirrel. All the species are small and inoffensive. *Draco volans*, the best type of the genus, is about 10 or 12 inches in length, the tail being extremely long in proportion to the body, which is not above 4 inches. Also called *flying dragon* or *flying lizard*.

Flying Dragon (*Draco volans*).

3. A fierce, violent person, male or female; generally applied to a spiteful, watchful woman.

4. [D—] A constellation of the northern hemisphere.

5. A kind of carrier pigeon; also called *dragoon*.

6. A short carbine, carried in the seventeenth century by the original dragoons, attached by a swivel to the belt; so named from a representation of a dragon's head at the muzzle.

7. The popular name of various araceous plants, as the *green dragon* of the genus *Dracunculus*, so called because the stem is mottled like the skin of a serpent.

8. In Scripture, (a) the devil; (b) a large marine fish or serpent; (c) a venomous land serpent.

9. In heraldry, a winged quadruped borne in shields, crests, and supporters.

Dragon.

Dragon's head and tail; in astronomy, the nodes of the planets, or the two points in which the orbits of the planets intersect the ecliptic.

drag′ŏn, *a.* Suitable for or resembling dragons; pertaining to, performed by, or consisting of dragons; fierce; formidable; as, the duenna kept *dragon* watch over her ward.

drag-ŏ-nāde′, drag-ŏn-nāde′, *n.* [Fr. *dragon*, a dragoon.] One of a series of persecutions of French Protestants in the reign of Louis XIV.; so named from dragoons generally riding at the head of the troops and being remarkable for their ferocity.

drag′ŏn=bēam, *n.* In architecture, a beam or piece of timber bisecting the angle formed by the wall-plate at corners, used to receive and support the foot of the hip-rafter.

drag′ŏn-et, *n.* 1. A little dragon.

2. The popular name of the species of a genus (*Callionymus*) of fishes belonging to the goby family.

drag′ŏn=fish, *n.* Same as *Dragonet*, 2.

drag′ŏn=flȳ, *n.* The popular name of a family of insects, *Libellulidæ*, having large, strongly reticulated wings, a large head with enormous eyes, a long body, and strong, horny mandibles.

drag′ŏn-ish, *a.* Dragon-like.

drag′ŏn-rōot, *n.* An American plant, *Arisæma Dracontium*.

drag′ŏn's=blood (-blud), *n.* The popular name of the inspissated juice of various plants, as *Calamus Draco*, *Dracæna Draco*, *Pterocarpus Draco*, etc. It is of a red color, and is used for coloring varnishes, for tooth-tinctures and powders, for staining marble, etc.

drag′ŏn's=head, *n.* A plant of the genus *Dracocephalum*, closely allied to the common catnip.

drag′ŏn=shell, *n.* A kind of limpet.

drag′ŏn-wŏrt, *n.* A plant belonging to the genus *Artemisia*; also, the snakeweed, *Polygonum Bistorta*.

drag′ŏn=tree, *n.* A tree, *Dracæna Draco*, yielding dragon's-blood.

drag′ŏn=wa̤″tēr, *n.* 1. A medicine used early in the seventeenth century.

2. A plant of the genus *Calla*.

drȧ-gōōn′, *n.* [Fr. *dragon*, a dragoon, a dragon.] Originally, a soldier who served on horseback or on foot, as occasion required; now, a cavalryman. In the British army there are light and heavy *dragoons*, according to the weight of equipment, etc.

drȧ-gōōn′, *v.t.*; dragooned, *pt.*, *pp.*; dragooning, *ppr.* 1. To persecute by abandoning to the rage of soldiers.

2. To enslave or reduce to subjection by soldiers.

3. To harass; to persecute; to compel to submit by violent measures; to force.

The colonies may be influenced to anything, but they can be *dragooned* to nothing. —Price.

drag-ōōn-āde′, *n.* Same as *Dragonade*.

drȧ-gōōn′=bīrd, *n.* The umbrella-bird of South America, *Cephalopterus ornatus*.

drȧ-gōōn′ėr, *n.* A dragoon. [Obs.]

drag′=rōpe, *n.* A rope that drags or serves to drag something; specifically, a stout rope used to drag pieces of artillery.

drag′=sheet, *n.* A contrivance for lessening the drift of vessels in heavy gales of wind, being a sort of floating anchor formed of a square sheet, kept stretched by metallic bars, and having a beam attached to it, which serves as a float to the apparatus.

drāil, *v.t.* To trail; to drag. [Obs.]

drāil, *v.i.* 1. To fish by trolling.

2. To be trailed or dragged.

drāin, *v.t.*; drained, *pt.*, *pp.*; draining; *ppr.* [AS. *drehnian*, to drain, from *dragan*, to draw, drag.]

1. To filter; to cause to pass through some porous substance.

Salt water, *drained* through twenty vessels of earth, hath become fresh. —Bacon.

2. To empty or clear of liquor, by causing the liquor to drop or run off slowly; as, to *drain* a vessel of its contents.

3. To make dry; to exhaust of water or other liquid, by causing it to flow off in channels or through porous substances; as, to *drain* land; to *drain* a swamp or marsh.

4. To empty; to exhaust; to draw off gradually; as, a foreign war *drains* a country of specie.

Syn.—Draw, strain, drip, percolate, drop, exhaust, empty, dry.

drāin, *v.i.* 1. To flow off gradually; as, let the water *drain* off.

2. To be emptied of liquor by flowing or dropping; as, let the vessel stand and *drain*; let the cloth hang and *drain*.

drāin, *n.* 1. A channel through which water or other liquid flows off; particularly, a trench or ditch to convey water from wet land; a water-course; a sewer; a sink.

2. The act of drawing off or draining; as, a *drain* upon one's resources.

3. [*pl.*] The last dregs of anything; as, brewers' *drains*, the leavings of the mash-tub.

4. In surgery, a hollow sound or tube used to draw off pus from a deep-seated abscess or a wound.

Right of drain; in law, the right to drain off water in pipes through the estate of another.

drāin'ȧ-ble, *a.* Capable of being drained.

drāin'āġe, *n.* 1. A draining; a gradual flowing off of any liquid.

2. The waters of a country which pass off by its streams and rivers.

3. The system by which superfluous water is removed from towns, mines, railway beds, etc.; as, the *drainage* is well executed.

4. The art of draining; as, an engineer skilled in *drainage*.

5. The tract or territory drained; as, the *drainage* of the Mississippi.

6. The process of draining off fluids from a wound, etc.

drāin'āġe-tūbe, *n.* In surgery, a tube introduced to secure efficient drainage of a wound, abscess, etc.

drāine, *n.* [Fr.] The missel-thrush.

drāin'ẽr, *n.* 1. One who drains; one who constructs drains.

2. A utensil on which articles are placed to drain; that which takes off superfluous fluids.

drāin'pipe, *n.* A pipe through which surplus water drains.

drāin'tile, *n.* A tile used in making drains.

drāin'trap, *n.* A contrivance to prevent the escape of foul air from drains; a chamber in a drain arranged so that the liquid contents prevent the escape of air or gas, but permit the downward flow of liquids.

Draintraps shown in Sections.

drāke, *n.* [ME. *drake*; Ice. *andriki*; M.D. *endtrick*, a male duck; AS. *ened*, *æned*, a duck, and *-rice*, *-rike*, *-rake*, masc. suffix from Goth. *reiks*, chief, mighty.]

1. The male of the duck kind.

2. The silver shilling of the reign of Queen Elizabeth.

3. A small piece of artillery. [Obs.]

4. A fly used as bait in angling; also called *drake-fly*.

drāke'stōne, *n.* A flat stone that may be so thrown upon the surface of the water as to skim from point to point; also the sport of making such stones skim.

dram, *n.* [ME. *drame*, a dram; OFr. *drame*; L. *drachma*; Gr. *drachmē*, an Attic weight, a drachma.]

1. A unit of weight. In apothecaries' weight, the eighth part of an ounce, or sixty grains. In avoirdupois weight, the sixteenth part of an ounce.

2. A small quantity; as, he has not a *dram* of judgment.

3. As much spirituous liquor as is drunk at once; as, a *dram* of brandy.

4. On the St. Lawrence river, a division of a raft of staves.

dram, *v.i.* To drink drams; to indulge in the use of ardent spirits.

dram, *v.t.* To ply with drink.

drä'mȧ, *n.* [LL. *drama*; Gr. *drama*, a deed, act, drama, tragedy, from *drān*, to do.]

1. A composition in poetry or prose, or both, representing a picture of human life, arranged for action, and having a plot, developed by the words and actions of its characters, which culminates in a final situation or climax of human interest. It is usually designed for production on the stage, with the accessories of costumes, scenery, music, etc. The principal forms of the *drama* are tragedy and comedy; from modifications or combinations of these result the lyric drama or grand opera, melodrama, tragicomedy, opera bouffe or comic opera, farce and burlesque.

2. An acted story, or actual representation of human affairs; a play.

3. Dramatic representation, with all the adjuncts which assist in giving reality and liveliness to the scenes; theatrical entertainment; as, he has a strong taste for the *drama*.

4. A series of actual events possessing dramatic unity and interest; as, the *drama* of his life; the *drama* of war.

5. Dramatic literature collectively, especially that of any particular period or people; as, the Elizabethan *drama*; the Greek *drama*; the modern French *drama*.

The legitimate drama; the standard drama, or serious dramatic compositions, as distinguished from ephemeral productions, as burlesques, farce-comedies, and the like.

The pastoral drama; a form of drama dealing with rustic life.

The romantic drama; the form of drama in which the scenes and dialogue reproduce a historical story or series of events, as the dramas of Shakspere.

The society drama; the form of drama in which a present-day story is told, and the language, dress, and manners of the actors are those of polite modern society.

drȧ-mat'iç, drȧ-mat'iç-ăl, *a.* [LL. *dramaticus*; Gr. *dramatikos*, dramatic, from *drama*, a drama.]

1. Of or pertaining to the drama; represented by action; appropriate to or in the form of a drama; theatrical.

2. Characterized by the force and fidelity appropriate to the drama; as, a *dramatic* description; a *dramatic* picture.

drȧ-mat'iç-ăl-ly, *adv.* By representation; in the manner of the drama; vividly and strikingly.

dram'ȧ-tis pẽr-sō'næ. [L., from LL. *dramatis*, genit. of *drama*, a drama, and L. *personæ*, pl. of *persona*, a character.] Actors representing the characters in a play.

dram'ȧ-tist, *n.* The author of a dramatic composition; a writer of plays; a playwright.

dram'ȧ-ti-zȧ-ble, *a.* Capable of being dramatized.

dram-ȧ-ti-zā'tion, *n.* The act of dramatizing.

dram'ȧ-tize, *v.t.*; dramatized, *pt.*, *pp.*; dramatizing, *ppr.* [Fr. *dramatiser*, from LL. *drama*, a drama.] To compose in the form of the drama; to put into the form of a play; to adapt for representation on the stage; as, to *dramatize* a novel.

dram-ȧ-tŭr'ġiç, *a.* Relating to dramaturgy; theatrical; unreal.

dram-ȧ-tŭr'ġist, *n.* A playwright.

dram'ȧ-tŭr-ġy, *n.* [Fr. *dramaturgie*; Gr. *dramatourgia*, a dramatic composition; *drama*, drama, and *ergon*, work.] The art of composing and arranging a drama and giving it representation; histrionism.

dram'ming, *n.* The habitual drinking of drams.

dram'sell"ẽr, *n.* One who sells liquors by the glass or dram.

dram'shop, *n.* A saloon.

drañk, *v.*, past tense of *drink*.

drañk, *n.* A local term for wild oats or darnel-grass. [Prov. Eng.]

drap' d'é-té' (drä' dā-tā'). A thin, twilled woolen cloth.

drāpe, *v.t*; draped (drāpt), *pt.*, *pp.*; draping, *ppr.* [OFr. *draper*, to make into cloth, from *drap*, cloth; LL. *drappus*, *trapus*, cloth.]

1. To cover or invest with clothing or cloth; to dispose drapery about, for use or ornament.

> Sculpture *draped* from head to foot.
> —Tennyson.

2. To banter; to jeer; to satirize; this sense is derived from painters representing ludicrous or satirical scenes on canvas, etc. [Obs.]

3. To make into cloth. [Obs.]

drāpe, *v.i.* To design or arrange draperies.

drā'pẽr, *n.* One who sells cloths; a dealer in cloths; as, a linen-*draper*; a woolen-*draper*; a *draper* and tailor.

drā'pẽr-ied (-id), *a.* Adorned with drapery.

drā'pẽr-y, *n.*; *pl.* **drā'pẽr-ieṣ.** [ME. *draperie*; OFr. *draperie*, drapery, from *drap*, cloth.]

1. The occupation of a draper; the trade of selling or making cloth.

2. Cloth; stuffs of wool or linen.

3. The clothes or hangings with which any object is draped or hung; specifically, in sculpture and painting, the representation of the clothing or dress of human figures; also, tapestry, hangings, curtains, etc.

drā'pet, *n.* A cloth; a tablecloth; a coverlet. [Obs.]

drap'pie, *n.* A little drop. [Scot.]

dras'tiç, *a.* [Gr. *drastikos*, active, from *drān*, to do, act.]

1. Acting with force; severe; as, the police took *drastic* measures.

2. In medicine, powerful; efficacious; as, a *drastic* cathartic.

dras'tiç, *n.* A medicine which speedily and effectually purges.

dras'ty, *a.* Trashy; filthy. [Obs.]

drat, *v.t.* [Prob. contracted from *'od rot.*] A word expressive of a mild form of oath, similar to *plague take* or *bother*; as, *drat* that cat! [Prov. Eng.]

drȧugh (drȧf), *n.* Same as *Draff*.

drȧught (drȧft), *n.*, *a.*, and *v.* See *Draft.*

drȧught'bōard, *n.* The checkered board on which the game of draughts or checkers is played.

drȧught'house, *n.* A house for the reception of filth or waste matter; a privy. [Obs.]

drȧughts, *n.pl.* The English name of the game of checkers.

drȧughts'măn, *n.* See *Draftsman.*

drȧught'y, *a.* See *Drafty.*

drāve, *v.*, obsolete past tense of *drive.*

Drȧ-vid'i-ăn, *a.* Of or pertaining to Dravida, or Dravira, an old province of India; specifically applied to a family of tongues spoken in southern India and Ceylon, supposed by some to be Turanian, by others to belong to the Aryan class of languages. It includes Tamil, Telugu, Canarese, Malayalam or Malabar, Tulu, etc. Called also *Tamilian.*

drạw, *v.t.*; drew, *pt.*; drawing, *ppr.*; drawn, *pp.* [ME. *drawen*, *drahen*; AS. *dragan*, to draw, drag.]

1. To pull along; to haul; to cause to move forward by force applied in front of the thing moved, or at the fore end, as by a rope or chain.

2. To bring by compulsion; to cause to come; as, to *draw* a prisoner before the court.

3. To pull up or out; to raise from any depth; as, to *draw* water from a well.

4. To suck; as, to *draw* the breasts.

5. To attract; to cause to move or tend toward itself; to allure; as, to *draw* steel with a magnet.

> Like birds the charming serpent *draws.*
> —Tennyson.

6. To cause to slide, as a curtain, either in closing or unclosing; to open and discover, or to close and conceal; as, to *draw* the blinds.

7. To represent by lines drawn on a plane surface; to form (a picture or image); as, to *draw* the picture of a man; hence, to represent in fancy; as, the speaker *drew* a picture of poverty.

8. To derive; to have or receive from some source, cause, or donor; as, to *draw* consolation from divine promises.

9. To deduce; as, to *draw* arguments from facts, or inferences from circumstantial evidence.

10. To bear; to produce; as, a bond or note *draws* interest from its date.

11. To compose; to write in due form; to form in writing; as, to *draw* a bill of exchange; to *draw* a deed or will.

12. To extend; to stretch; as, to *draw* wire; to *draw* a piece of metal by beating.

13. To require for floating; as, a ship *draws* fifteen feet of water.

14. To bend; as, to *draw* the bow.

15. To eviscerate; to pull out the bowels of; as, to *draw* poultry.

16. To unsheathe; as, to *draw* the sword.

17. To let run out; to extract; as, to *draw* wine from a cask; to *draw* blood from a vein.

18. To cause to turn toward itself; to engage; as, a beauty or a popular speaker *draws* the eyes of an assembly, or *draws* their attention.

19. To inhale; to take into the lungs; as, there I first *drew* air; I *draw* the sultry air.

20. To extract; as, to *draw* spirit from grain or juice.

21. To lengthen; to extend in length.

> How long her face is *drawn.* —Shak.

22. To give vent to or utter in a lingering manner; as, to *draw* a deep sigh.

23. To form between two points; to run or extend, as by a marking instrument or by construction of any kind; as, to *draw* a line on paper or a line of circumvallation.

24. To allure; to entice; to lead by persuasion or moral influence; to excite to motion; as, to *draw* a crowd; to *draw* disciples.

25. To lead, as a motive; to induce to move.

> My purposes do *draw* me much about.—Shak.

26. To receive from customers or employers; to earn; to gain; as, the bookkeeper *drew* a hundred dollars a month.

27. To receive or take, as from a fund or store; as, to *draw* money from a bank.

28. To take out of a box or wheel, as tickets in a lottery; to receive or gain by such drawing; as, to *draw* a number in the lottery; to *draw* a prize.

29. In billiards, to cause to recoil after impact; as, to *draw* a ball.

Syn.—Drag, haul, pull, pluck, tug, delineate, derive.—*Draw* expresses the idea of putting a body in motion from behind oneself or toward oneself; to *drag* is to *draw* a thing with violence, or to *draw* that which makes resistance; to *haul* is to *drag* it with still greater violence. We *draw* a cart; we *drag* a body along the ground; we *haul* a vessel to the shore. To *pull* signifies only an effort to *draw* without the idea of motion; horses *pull* very long sometimes before they can *draw* a heavily laden cart. To *pluck* is to *pull* with a sudden twitch, in order to separate; thus, feathers are *plucked* from birds. To *tug* is to *pull* with violence; thus, men *tug* at the oar.

To draw a badger, fox, etc.; to drag or force it from its cover.

To draw a cover; to search it for game.

To draw a game; to bring it to an inconclusive finish.

To draw back; to receive back, as duties on goods for exportation.

To draw in; (a) to contract; to bring to a smaller compass; to pull back; as, *to draw in* the reins; (b) to collect; to bring together; (c) to entice, allure, or inveigle; as, *to draw in* others to support a measure.

To draw off; (a) to draw from or away; also, to withdraw; to abstract; as, *to draw off* the mind from vain amusements; (b) to draw or take from; to cause to flow from; as, *to draw off* wine or cider from a vessel; (c) to extract by distillation.

To draw on; (a) to allure; to entice; to persuade or cause to follow; (b) to occasion; to invite; to bring on; to cause.

To draw over; (a) to raise or cause to come over, as in a still; (b) to persuade or induce to revolt from an opposing party, and to join one's own party; as, some men may be *drawn over* by interest, others by fear.

To draw out; (a) to lengthen; to stretch by force; to extend; (b) to lengthen in time; to protract; to cause to continue; (c) to cause to issue forth; to draw off, as liquor from a cask; (d) to extract, as the spirit of a substance; (e) to call forth; to elicit, by questioning or address; to cause to be declared; to call forth; as, *to draw out* facts from a witness; (f) to detach; to separate from the main body; as, *to draw out* a file or party of men; (g) to range in battle; to array in line.

To draw together; to collect or be collected.

To draw up; (a) to raise; to lift; to elevate; (b) to form in order of battle; to array; (c) to compose in due form, as a writing; to form in writing; as, *to draw up* a deed; *to draw up* a paper.

draw, *v.i.* 1. To pull; to exert strength in drawing; as, a horse or an ox *draws* well.

2. To act as a weight; as, bias of mind may *draw* too much.

3. To shrink; to contract.

4. To move; to advance; as, the day *draws* toward evening.

5. To be filled or inflated with wind, so as to press on and advance a ship in her course; as, the sails *draw*.

6. To unsheathe a sword; as, to *draw* in love's cause; *draw* and defend thyself.

7. To use or practise the art of delineating figures; as, he *draws* with exactness.

8. To collect the matter of an ulcer or abscess; to cause to suppurate; to excite to inflammation, maturation, and discharge; as, a plaster or poultice *draws* well.

9. To make a draft or written demand upon a person for payment of a sum of money; as, he *drew* upon me for fifty pounds.

10. To be susceptible to the action of drawing or pulling; as, the cart *draws* easily.

11. To sink or settle in water; as, great ships *draw* deep.

To draw back; (a) to retire; to move back; to withdraw; (b) to renounce the faith; to apostatize.

To draw by; to come to an end; as, the day *draws by*.

To draw dry foot; in coursing, to trace the marks of the foot of an animal without the scent.

To draw near or *nigh*; to approach; to come near.

To draw off; to retire; to retreat; as, the company *drew off* by degrees.

To draw on; (a) to advance; to approach; as, the day *draws on*; (b) to gain on; to approach in pursuit; as, the ship *drew on* the flying frigate.

To draw up; to form in regular order; to assume a certain order or arrangement; as, the troops *drew up* in front of the palace; the fleet *drew up* in a semicircle.

draw, *n.* 1. The act of drawing.

2. The lot or chance drawn.

3. That part of a movable bridge which is drawn up or aside.

4. A drawn game; the result of a game when neither party gains the advantage; as, the match ended in a *draw*.

5. In card-playing, the act of taking a card or cards from the pack or from another person's hand.

6. The game of poker. [Colloq.]

draw'a-ble, *a.* Capable of being drawn.

draw'back, *n.* 1. Money or an amount paid back; usually, a certain amount of duties or customs dues paid back or remitted to an importer on the exportation of goods previously imported by him, or a certain amount of excise paid back or allowed on the exportation of home manufactures.

2. Any loss of advantage or deduction from profit; hindrance.

draw'bär, *n.* A strong iron bar projecting from the end of a locomotive or railway car for the purpose of receiving the coupling link and pin.

draw'bench, *n.* A machine used in wire-drawing; called also *drawing-bench*.

draw'bōlt, *n.* A coupling-pin.

draw'bōre, *n.* In carpentry, a hole pierced through a tenon, nearer to the shoulder than the holes through the cheeks are to the abutment with which the shoulder is to come into contact, so that a pin when driven into it will draw these parts together.

draw'bōre, *v.t.*; drawbored, *pt.*, *pp.*; drawboring, *ppr.* To make a drawbore in.

draw'boy, *n.* In weaving, a boy who helps a weaver in drawing the heddles to form the pattern of the cloth he is weaving; hence, a mechanical device employed for this purpose.

draw'bridge (-brij), *n.* A bridge which may be raised up, let down, or drawn aside to admit or hinder communication, as before the gate of a town or castle, or over a navigable river. Modern *drawbridges* are generally made to open horizontally. The movable portion is called a bascule, balance, or lifting bridge, a turning, swivel, or swing bridge, or a rolling bridge, in accordance with the mode in which it is made to open.

An Ancient Drawbridge.

draw'can-sir, *n.* A blusterer; a braggart; so called from a bullying character in a play, "The Rehearsal," given in London in the seventeenth century.

draw'can-sir, *a.* Having the characteristics of a braggart; as, a *drawcansir* fellow.

draw'-cut, *n.* A single cut with a knife or other cutting-tool drawn toward the wielder.

draw-ee', *n.* One on whom an order or bill of exchange is drawn; the payer of a bill of exchange.

draw'ẽr, *n.* 1. One who draws, as one who takes water from a well or liquor from a cask.

2. One who or that which draws or attracts, or has the power of attraction.

3. One who draws a bill of exchange, or an order for the payment of money.

4. A draftsman.

5. A box-shaped receptacle which slides in and out of a table, a cabinet, etc., and is used for holding clothes, papers, silverware, etc.; as, a chest of *drawers*.

6. [*pl.*] An undergarment, worn on the legs and lower part of the body by both sexes.

draw'file, *v.t.*; drawfiled, *pt.*, *pp.*; drawfiling, *ppr.* To file smooth by drawing the file sidewise instead of lengthwise.

draw'gear, *n.* 1. A harness especially adapted for draft-horses.

2. The coupling gear of a railway-car.

draw'glōve, *n.* An old game in which words were expressed by the fingers; also used in the plural.

draw'head (-hed), *n.* 1. The flanged head of a drawbar.

2. In spinning, a contrivance in which the slivers are lengthened and receive an additional twist.

draw'ing, *n.* 1. The act of pulling, hauling, or attracting.

2. The art or act of representing the appearance or figures of objects on a plain surface, by means of lines and shades, as with a pencil, crayon, pen, compasses, etc.; delineation.

3. A sketch, plan, figure, or design made with a pen, crayon, chalk, pencil, or the like.

4. The operation by which metals are drawn out or extended into various forms; as, wire-*drawing*.

5. The distribution of prizes and blanks in a lottery.

A drawing of tea; a small quantity of tea to be steeped.

Free-hand drawing; the art or act of drawing without the use of compasses or other auxiliaries, the eye being the only guide; also, a drawing so made.

Geometrical or *mechanical drawing*; the art or act of drawing with the aid of rules, compasses, and other mechanical devices, to insure accuracy; also, a drawing so made.

Out of drawing; incorrectly drawn; out of proportion.

draw'ing-knife (-nīf), *n.* 1. A cutting tool having a handle at each end of the blade, by which it is held in both hands and drawn toward the user.

2. A knife with which an incision is made as a path for a saw to follow; also called *draw-knife*.

draw'ing-pen, *n.* A pen with two blades holding ink, used in ruling lines; called also *ruling-pen*.

draw'ing-room, *n.* 1. A room appropriated for the reception of company; a room in which distinguished personages hold levees, or private persons receive guests.

2. The company assembled in a *drawing-room*.

3. A formal reception at the English court; as, she was presented at the last *drawing-room*.

drawk, *n.* [ME. *drauc*, *drauke*.] Darnel; wild oats.

drawl, *v.t.*; drawled, *pt.*, *pp.*; drawling, *ppr.* [Freq. of *drag*, from AS. *dragan*, to draw, drag.] To utter in a slow, lengthened tone.

drawl, *v.i.* To speak with slow utterance.

drawl, *n.* A lengthened utterance of the voice.

draw'latch (-lach), *n.* A housebreaker; a sneak-thief. [Obs.]

drawl'ẽr, *n.* One who drawls.

drawl'ing-ly, *adv.* With a drawling utterance or manner.

draw'link, *n.* A bar of iron or link for connecting two railroad-cars or an engine and its tender.

draw'loom, *n.* A loom on which figured cloth is woven.

drawn, *v.*, past participle of *draw*.

drawn, *a.* 1. Undecided, each party having equal advantage and neither a victory; as, a *drawn* battle.

2. Having a sword drawn.

3. Eviscerated; as, a *drawn* chicken.

4. In a diffused or melted state; as, *drawn* butter.

At daggers drawn; prepared for a fight; hence, antagonistic; mutually belligerent.

Drawn and quartered; disemboweled and cut into four pieces.

draw'net, *n.* A net with wide meshes, used to catch birds.

drawn'-wŏrk, *n.* A kind of ornamental work in which certain threads of a woven fabric, usually linen, are drawn or cut out, and those remaining are drawn into patterns.

draw'plāte, *n.* A plate of hardened steel or of ruby, having a gradation of conical holes, through which wires are drawn to be reduced and elongated.

draw'-pō''kẽr, *n.* A game at cards. [See *Poker*.]

draw'rod, *n.* A rod connecting two drawbars or drawgears.

draw'spring, *n.* A spring by which a drawbar is connected with a car.

draw'-well, *n.* A deep well, from which water is drawn by a long cord or pole and a bucket.

drāy, *n.* [AS. *dræge*, lit., that which is drawn, from *dragan*, to draw.]

1. A strong cart used for drawing heavy loads.

2. A sled. [Eng.]

drāy, *v.t.*; drayed, *pt.*, *pp.*; draying, *ppr.* To cart; to carry by means of a dray.

drāy, *n.* [Origin obscure.] A squirrel's nest; also written *drey*.

drāy'āge, *n.* 1. The use of a dray; the act of transporting by means of a dray.

2. A sum charged or paid for the use of a dray or drays.

drāy'-cärt, *n.* A dray.

drāy'-horse, *n.* A horse used for drawing a dray.

drāy'măn, *n.*; *pl.* **drāy'men.** A man who drives and attends a dray.

draz'el, *n.* [From Scot. *dratch*, to loiter, delay.] A dirty woman; a slut; a drossel. [Obs.]

dread (dred), *n.* 1. Great fear and continued alarm in anticipation of impending evil or danger; as, *dread* of suffering; *dread* of disaster.

2. An overpowering horror or fright; as, a *dread* of serpents.

3. Awe; fear united with respect.

4. One who or that which is feared or revered.

Let him be your *dread*. —Isa. viii. 13.

5. Doubt. [Obs.]

dread, *a.* 1. Exciting great fear or apprehension; terrible; frightful.

2. Solemn; venerable in the highest degree; as, *dread* sovereign; *dread* majesty.

dread (dred), *v.t.*; dreaded, *pt.*, *pp.*; dreading, *ppr.* [ME. *dreden*, to fear; AS. *on-drædan*, *a-drædan*, to fear, to be afraid of.] To fear in a great degree; to be in fearful apprehension or expectation of; as, to *dread* death or disgrace.

dread, *v.i.* To be in great fear.

dread'a-ble, *a.* Of a nature to inspire dread.

dread'ẽr, *n.* One who fears or lives in fear.

dread'ful, *a.* 1. Inspiring great fear; terrible; formidable; as, a *dreadful* storm; a *dreadful* night.

2. Awful; venerable.

How *dreadful* is this place!—Gen. xxviii. 17.

3. Fearful; full of dread. [Obs.]

Syn.—Terrible, shocking.—*Terrible* is stronger and more vivid than *dreadful*; *shocking* strikes with all its force on the moral feelings. A *dreadful* accident; a *terrible* catastrophe; a *shocking* exhibition of wickedness.

dread′fụl, *n.* A sensational newspaper or periodical; a print chiefly devoted to the narration of stories of criminal life, frightful accidents, etc.; as, he gloated over the penny *dreadfuls.* [Eng.]

dread′fụl-ly, *adv.* Terribly; in a manner to be dreaded.

dread′fụl-ness, *n.* Terribleness; the quality of being dreadful; frightfulness.

dread′ing-ly, *adv.* With dread or misgiving. [Rare.]

dread′less, *a.* 1. Fearless; bold; not intimidated; undaunted; free from fear or terror; intrepid.

2. Secure from dread; free from danger; safe. [Obs.]

dread′less, *adv.* Doubtless; without fear or doubt. [Obs.]

dread′less-ness, *n.* Fearlessness; undauntedness; freedom from fear or terror; boldness.

dread′ly, *a.* Dreadful. [Obs.]

dread′ly, *adv.* With dread. [Obs.]

dread′naught (-nat), *n.* 1. A thick cloth, with a long pile, used for warm clothing, or to keep off rain.

2. A garment made of such cloth.

3. A person who fears nothing.

4. A type of war-ship distinguished by its huge size, and carrying ten 12-inch guns.

drēam, *v.i.*; dreamed *or* dreamt, *pt., pp.*; dreaming, *ppr.* 1. To have ideas or images in the mind when in the state of sleep; with *of* before a noun; as, to *dream of* a battle; to *dream of* an absent friend.

2. To think; to imagine; as, he little *dreamed* of his approaching fate.

3. To think idly.

drēam, *v.t.* To see in a dream.

To dream away; to waste in idle thoughts; as, *to dream away* one's time.

drēam, *n.* [ME. *dreme, dreem*, a dream; AS. *dream*, a joyful sound, joy, gladness; of Teutonic origin; compare D. *droom*, G. *traum*, O.H.G. *troum*, a dream.]

1. The thought, or series of thoughts, of a person in sleep; a series of thoughts not under the command of reason. We apply *dream*, in the singular, to thoughts which occupy the mind of a sleeping person, in which he imagines he has a view of real things or transactions.

2. A vain fancy; a wild conceit; an unfounded suspicion.

3. A thing of beauty; perfection; as, her dress was a *dream.* [Colloq.]

drēam′ẽr, *n.* 1. One who dreams.

2. A fanciful man; a visionary; one who forms or entertains vain schemes; as, a political *dreamer.*

3. A sluggard; a mope.

4. A puff-bird of the genus *Chelidoptera.*

drēam′fụl, *a.* Full of dreams.

drēam′fụl-ly, *adv.* In a dreamy manner.

drēam′i-ly, *adv.* As if in a dream; languidly; in a dreamy manner.

drēam′i-ness, *n.* The condition of being dreamy.

drēam′ing-ly, *adv.* In a dreamy manner.

drēam′land, *n.* A fanciful, pleasant country such as is sometimes seen in a dream; the land of fancies; the region of reverie.

drēam′less, *a.* Free from dreams.

drēam′less-ly, *adv.* In a dreamless manner.

drēam′y, *a.* 1. Full of dreams.

2. Appropriate to or like a dream; as, a *dreamy* eye; a *dreamy* silence.

3. Resembling a dream; faint; visionary; dim.

Syn.—Abstracted, absent-minded, oblivious, preoccupied, visionary.

drēar, *n.* Dread; dismalness. [Obs.]

drēar, *a.* [ME. *drery*; AS. *dreorig*, dismal, dreary.] Dismal; gloomy with solitude.

A *drear* and dying sound. —Milton.

drēar′i-head (-hed), **drēar′i-hood**, *n.* Dreariness; gloominess; affliction. [Obs.]

drēar′i-ly, *adv.* In a dreary manner; dismally; cheerlessly.

drēar′i-ment, *n.* Dreariness. [Obs.]

drēar′i-ness, *n.* 1. Gloominess; dismalness; dreary solitude; lonesomeness.

2. Sorrow; grief; wretchedness. [Obs.]

drēar′ing, *n.* Dreariness. [Obs.]

drēar′i-sŏme, *a.* Exceedingly dreary.

drēar′y, *a.* [ME. *drery, dreri*; AS. *dreorig*, sad, mournful, also bloody, gory, from *dreor*, blood, from *dreosan*, to fall.]

1. Dismal; gloomy; as, a *dreary* waste; *dreary* shades.

2. Sorrowful; distressing. [Obs.]

3. Tiresome; monotonous; as, a *dreary* book.

drec′che (drech′i), *v.t.* 1. To vex; to trouble; to annoy; to torment. [Obs.]

2. To retard; to delay. [Obs.]

drec′che, *v.i.* To delay. [Obs.]

dredġe (drej), *v.t.*; dredged, *pt., pp.*; dredging, *ppr.* [ME. *dragg*, a mixture of different kinds of grain or pulse; OFr. *dragie*, a kind of digestive powder, sweetmeat; LL. *tragemata*; Gr. *tragēmata*, dried fruits, sweetmeats, from *trogein*, to gnaw, nibble, eat.] To sprinkle flour or some powdered substance on; as, to *dredge* roasting beef.

dredġe, *n.* A term applied to oats and barley when sown together.

dredġe, *v.t.* 1. To take or catch with a dredge.

2. To make deeper with a dredging-machine; to widen, as a river, a channel, a harbor, etc., by removing sand, mud, or silt from.

dredġe, *v.i.* To make use of a dredge; as, to *dredge* for oysters.

dredġe, *n.* [OFr. *drege*, an oyster-net; O.D. *draghe*, a dredge, a dragnet, from *dragen*; AS. *dragan*, to drag, draw.]

1. Any appliance used for dragging or bringing up solid substances from under water; a dragnet.

2. A dredging-machine.

3. In mining, ore of second quality; also called *dradge.* [Eng.]

dredġ′ẽr, *n.* 1. One who uses a dredge to catch fish.

2. A machine for dredging.

3. A boat or vessel used in dredging.

dredġ′ẽr, *n.* A box with a perforated lid used for sprinkling flour, etc.; a dredging-box.

dredġ′ẽr-man, *n.* One engaged in dredging.

dredġ′ing, *n.* The act of sprinkling with flour.

dredġ′ing, *n.* 1. The act or process of using a dredge.

2. That which is brought up by a dredge.

dredġ′ing-box, *n.* A box with a perforated lid used for sprinkling flour, etc.

dredġ′ing-mà-chïne″, *n.* An apparatus used to take up mud, etc., from the bottom of rivers, docks, etc.

dree, *v.t.* [ME. *dreen*; AS. *dreogan*, to bear, suffer, endure.] To suffer; to bear. [Scot.]

To dree one's weird, or *a weird*; to abide one's fate. [Scot.]

dree, *v.i.* To be able to do; to endure or continue. [Obs.]

dree, *a.* 1. Great; important. [Obs.]

2. Tedious; tiresome. [Prov. Eng.]

dreg, *n.*, sing. of *dregs.* [Obs.]

dreg′gi-ness, *n.* Fullness of dregs or lees; foulness; feculence.

dreg′gish, *a.* Full of dregs; foul with lees; feculent.

dreg′gy, *a.* Containing dregs or lees; consisting of dregs; foul; muddy; feculent.

dregṣ, *n.pl.* [ME. *dregges*; Ice. *dregg*, dregs, lees.]

1. The sediment of liquors; lees; grounds; feculence; any foreign matter of liquors that subsides to the bottom of a vessel.

2. Waste or worthless matter; dross; sweepings; refuse; hence, what is most vile and despicable; as, the *dregs* of society.

Syn.—Sediment, dross, scum, refuse.—All these terms designate the worthless part of any body; *dregs* is that which is altogether of no value; but the *sediment* may sometimes form a necessary part of the body. The *dregs* and *sediment* separate of themselves, but the *scum* and *dross* are forced out by a process; the former from liquids, and the latter from solid bodies rendered liquid or otherwise. *Dross* is applied to solid bodies in the same sense as *scum*, being that which remains after the purifying. *Refuse* is always said of that which is intentionally separated to be thrown away, and agrees with the former terms only inasmuch as they express what is worthless.

Drei′bŭnd (-bŭnt), *n.* [G. *drei*, three, and *bund*, an alliance, bond.] A triple alliance formed by Germany, Austria-Hungary, and Italy during the last quarter of the nineteenth century.

drein, *v.i.* To drain. [Obs.]

Dreis′se-nȧ, *n.* The type genus of the *Dreissenidæ.*

Dreis-sen′i-dæ, *n.pl.* [L., from Dr. *Dreysen*, of Belgium.] A family of bivalves, having the membranous covering open only for the foot in front of the umbones, and for the siphons at the distal margin; also called *Dreissenacea, Dreisseninæ, Dreissensinæ.*

drench, *v.t.*; drenched, *pt., pp.*; drenching, *ppr.* [ME. *drenchen*, to soak, drench; AS. *drencan*, to give to drink, to drown.]

1. To wet thoroughly; to soak; to fill or cover with water or other liquid; as, garments *drenched* in rain or in the sea; the flood has *drenched* the earth; swords *drenched* in blood.

2. To saturate or gorge with a liquid; as, he *drenched* himself with whisky.

3. To purge violently.

Syn.—Soak, steep, imbrue, saturate, souse, deluge.

drench, *v.i.* To drown. [Obs.]

drench, *n.* [ME. *drench*; AS. *drinc*, a drink.]

1. A draught.

2. A large portion of liquid medicine administered to an animal by pouring or forcing down the throat.

3. Any solution in which a thing is steeped or soaked; as, a *drench* for hides.

drench′ẽr, *n.* 1. One who or that which drenches.

2. One who gives a drench to a beast.

3. A heavy rain-storm. [Colloq.]

dreng, *n.* In old English law, a tenant in capite; usually applied to a rent-paying tenant holding in virtue of some service less honorable than knighthood.

dreñ′gāġe, *n.* In old English law, the tenure by which a dreng held land, or the land itself.

dre-pan-i-. A combining form from Gr. *drepanē*, sickle, and signifying sickle-shaped, or resembling a sickle; as, *drepani*form.

drep′ȧ-ni-fŏrm, *a.* [*Drepani-*, and L. *forma*, form, shape.] Shaped like a sickle; falciform.

dre-pā′ni-um, *n.*; *pl.* **dre-pā′ni-ȧ.** In botany, a sickle-shaped cyme.

drep′ȧ-noid, *a.* Resembling or shaped like a sickle.

Dres′den, *n.* A famous and beautiful variety of chinaware or porcelain first made in the early part of the eighteenth century near Dresden, Saxony; also called *Dresden ware.*

dress, *v.t.*; dressed *or* drest, *pt., pp.*; dressing, *ppr.* [ME. *dressen*, to make straight, direct; OFr. *dresser*, to set up, arrange, from L. *directus*, pp. of *dirigere*, to straighten, arrange.]

1. To make straight; to adjust to a right line, as in the military phrase, *dress* ranks.

2. To adjust; to put in good order; to fasten. [Obs.]

3. To prepare; to put in the condition desired; to make suitable or fit; specifically, (a) to reduce to the proper dimensions, form, and smoothness; as, to *dress* a board or a stone; (b) to make ready for food by cooking or adding suitable ingredients; as, to *dress* a salad; (c) to cultivate; to till; as, to *dress* a garden; (d) to curry; to rub; as, to *dress* a horse; (e) to prepare for the market, for consumption, or manufacture; as, to *dress* a lamb; to *dress* hides; to *dress* hemp; (f) to comb and arrange; as, to *dress* hair; (g) in mining, to sort or separate in preparing for the smelting-furnace; as, to *dress* ore; (h) to break, tame, and train for service; as, to *dress* a horse.

4. To treat with curative remedies; to apply bandages to; as, to *dress* a wound or sore.

5. To put clothes upon; to apparel; as, she *dressed* the child quickly.

To dress up or *out*; to clothe pompously, elegantly, or in one's best apparel.

To dress a ship; to ornament a ship with flags, as on days of rejoicing.

dress, *v.i.* 1. To arrange in a line; as, look to the right, and *dress.*

2. To clothe or apparel oneself; specifically, to dress in suitable, conventional, or elegant attire; as, to *dress* for dinner; she loves to *dress.*

dress, *n.* 1. That which is used as the covering or ornament of the body; clothes; garments; habit; as, she gives all her thought to *dress.*

2. A gown or robe worn by women and children, consisting of a skirt and waist, either made separately or in one garment.

3. Splendid clothes; a habit of ceremony; as, full *dress.*

4. Skill in adjusting dress, or the practice of wearing elegant clothing; as, men of *dress.*

5. The system of furrows which makes the finish of a millstone.

6. In ornithology, plumage.

Full dress; a style of dress which fashion and convention require to be worn on occasions of ceremony or at fashionable entertainments given in the evening.

Syn.—Apparel, raiment, clothing, clothes, vestments, garments, habiliments, accouterments, attire, array, habit.

dress′-cĩr″cle, *n.* A section of a theater usually in the first or lower gallery and comprising the more expensive seats.

dress′-cōat′, *n.* The coat worn by men in full dress; especially, a black coat fitting tightly, and having the skirts cut away over the hips; a swallowtail; a claw-hammer.

dress′ẽr, *n.* [Fr. *dressoir.*] A sideboard; a table or bench on which meat and other things are dressed or prepared for use; also, a cupboard or set of shelves for dishes and cooking-utensils; a bureau.

dress′ẽr, *n.* 1. One who dresses; one who is employed in clothing and adorning another; one who is employed in preparing, trimming, or adjusting anything.

2. An assistant in a hospital, who dresses wounds, etc.

3. In mechanics, a tool for dressing.

4. In type-founding, one employed to dress or finish type.

5. In plumbing, a mallet for bending or straightening lead pipe.

dress′-goods, *n.pl.* Fabrics for women's and children's dresses.

dress′i-ness, *n.* The state of being dressy.

dress′ing, *n.* 1. Raiment; attire.

2. That which is used as an application to a wound or sore.

3. That which is used in preparing land for a crop; manure spread over land. When it remains on the surface, it is called a *top-dressing.*
4. Correction; a flogging or beating. [Slang.]
5. In cookery, the stuffing of fowls, pigs, etc.; the sauce added to meats, salads, etc.
6. A term applied to gum, starch, and other substances used in stiffening or preparing silk, linen, and other materials.
7. [*pl.*] In architecture, the moldings round doors, windows, etc.; the stone frames which surround the wall-openings in brick buildings.
8. The preparation of ore for smelting.

dress'ing-căse, *n.* A box or case fitted with toilet requisites.

dress'ing-fŏr"ceps, *n.* Forceps used in dressing wounds.

dress'ing-gown, *n.* A gown used by a person while dressing or in dishabille.

dress'ing-rooṃ, *n.* A room used in a theater for dressing; a room in a private house in which to make one's toilet, usually connected with a bedroom.

dress'ing-tā"ble, *n.* A toilet-table provided with conveniences for a person when dressing.

dress'măk"ẽr, *n.* A maker of women's gowns or similar garments.

dress'măk"ing, *n.* The occupation, business, or work of making dresses.

dres-soir' (-swär'), *n.* [Fr.] A sideboard; a dresser.

dress'y, *a.* Showy in dress; wearing rich or showy dresses. [Colloq.]

dretch, *v.t.* and *v.i.* [Obs.] See *Drecche.*

dreūl, *v.i.* [Obs.] See *Drool.*

drev'il, *n.* [Obs.] See *Drivel.*

drey, *n.* A squirrel's nest; usually written *dray.*

dreynt, *v.*, obsolete past participle of *drench.*

drib, *v.t.*; dribbed, *pt.*, *pp.*; dribbing, *ppr.* [A dial. variant of ME. *drepen*; AS. *drepan*, to strike.]
1. To chop or cut off; to defalcate.
2. In archery, to shoot at pointblank at short range. [Obs.]

drib, *v.i.* To shoot at a mark at short range. [Obs.]

drib, *n.* A drop [Obs.]

drib'ble, *v.i.*; dribbled, *pt.*, *pp.*; dribbling, *ppr.* [Freq. of *drip*, from ME. *drippen, dryppen*, to drip; AS. *dryppan*, to cause to drop.]
1. To fall in drops or small drops, or in a quick succession of drops; as, water *dribbles* from the eaves.
2. To drivel, as a child or an idiot.
3. To fall weakly and slowly; as, the *dribbling* dart of love. [Obs.]

drib'ble, *v.t.* 1. To throw down in drops or bits.
2. To give by piecemeal; as, to *dribble* out aid.
3. In various games, to propel (a ball) by slight hits or kicks, so as to have it always within reach, as in football, polo, hockey, etc.

drib'ble, *n.* A dropping or dripping; a drizzle.

drib'blẽr, *n.* 1. One who dribbles.
2. A driveler.

drib'let, drib'blet, *n.* A small piece or part; as, money paid in *driblets.*

drid'dle, *v.i.*; driddled, *pt.*, *pp.*; driddling, *ppr.* [Scot.] 1. To waste time and strength to little purpose.
2. To wander about aimlessly.
3. To play unskilfully, as on the violin.

drïe, *v.t.* [Obs.] Same as *Dree.*

dried, *a.* Freed from moisture or sap; as, *dried* fruit.

dri'ẽr, *n.* 1. One who dries, or that which has the quality of drying; that which may expel or absorb moisture; a desiccative.
2. A substance mixed with paint, varnish, or printing ink to make it dry quickly.
3. A mechanical contrivance for expelling moisture; a drying machine.

drift, *n.* [ME. *drift, dryft*, an act of driving, a shower of rain or snow, from AS. *drifan*, to drive.]
1. That which is driven by any kind of force.
2. A heap of any matter driven together; as, a *drift* of snow; a *drift* of sand.
3. A drove or flock, as of cattle, sheep, birds, etc.
4. A driving; a force impelling or urging forward; impulse.
5. Course of anything; tendency; aim; as, the *drift* of reasoning or argument; the *drift* of a discourse.
6. Intention; design; purpose.
7. A shower; a number of things driven at once; as, a *drift* of bullets.
8. In mining, a passage cut between shaft and shaft; a passage within the earth.
9. Nautically, the leeway which a vessel makes when lying to or hove to during a gale.
10. In shipbuilding, the difference between the size of a bolt and the hole into which it is to be driven, or between the circumference of a hoop and the circumference of the mast on which it is to be driven.
11. In architecture, the horizontal force which an arch exerts with a tendency to overset the piers.
12. In geology, a term applied to earth and rocks which have been conveyed by icebergs or glaciers and deposited over a country while submerged.
13. In mechanics, a longish round and slightly tapering piece of steel used for enlarging a hole in a metallic plate; a drift-bolt; a punch.
14. In military language, (a) a tool used in ramming down the composition contained in a rocket or similar firework; (b) a priming iron to clean the vent of a piece of ordnance from burning particles after each discharge. [Eng.]
15. In a galvanometer, that motion of the needle caused by torsion of the suspending filament.
16. In aviation, the resistance of a flying-machine to the air.
Drift of the forest; in English law, a view or examination of the cattle that are in the forest, in order to know whether it be surcharged or not, or whether the beasts be commonable, etc.
Syn.—Tendency, direction, motion, tenor, meaning, purport, object, intention, purpose, scope, aim, result, issue, inference, conclusion, end, course.

drift, *v.i.*; drifted, *pt.*, *pp.*; drifting, *ppr.* 1. To accumulate in heaps by the force of wind; to be driven into heaps; as, snow or sand *drifts.*
2. To float or be driven along by a current of water; as, the ship *drifted* astern; a raft *drifted* ashore.
3. In mining, to make a drift; to search for metals or ores.

drift, *v.t.* 1. To drive into heaps; as, a current of wind *drifts* snow or sand.
2. To cover with or as with a drift or drifts; as, the roads were badly *drifted.*
3. In mining, to make or drive a drift in.

drift, *n.* [D. *drift*, a course, current; compare AS. *drifan*, to drive.] In South Africa, a ford.

drift'āġe, *n.* 1. That which drifts or is drifted.
2. Nautically, the amount of deviation from a ship's course due to leeway.

drift'-an"chŏr, *n.* See *Sea-anchor.*

drift'bōlt, *n.* See *Drift*, n. 14.

drift'-land, *n.* A quitrent or yearly payment formerly made by some tenants to the king or their landlords, for driving their cattle through a manor to fairs or markets. [Obs.]

drift'less, *a.* Without direction; aimless.

drift'-net, *n.* A large net used as a gill-net.

drift'piēce, *n.* In shipbuilding, one of the upright or curved pieces of timber that connect the plank-sheer and the gunwale.

drift'pin, *n.* Same as *Drift*, n. 14.

drift'wāy, *n.* 1. A common way for driving cattle in.
2. Nautically and in mining, drift.

drift'weed, *n.* Seaweed thrown upon the shore by the waves.

drift'wind, *n.* A wind or storm that makes drifts.

drift'wood, *n.* Wood drifted or floated by water; also used figuratively; as, human *driftwood.*

drift'y, *a.* Inclined to drift; full of drifts or heaps, as snow.

drill, *v.t.*; drilled, *pt.*, *pp.*; drilling, *ppr.* [D. *drillen*, to bore, turn round, brandish, train, from M.D. *drille*, a hole.]
1. To pierce with a drill; to perforate by turning a sharp-pointed instrument of a particular form; to bore and make a hole in by turning an instrument.
2. In agriculture, (a) to sow in rows, drills, or channels; as, to *drill* wheat; (b) to sow with seed in drills; as, the field was *drilled*, not sown broadcast.
3. In military wording to teach and train in the use of arms by frequent exercises; hence, to teach by repeated exercise or repetition of acts.
4. To draw on; to entice. [Obs.]
5. To exhaust or waste slowly; as, this accident hath *drilled* away the whole summer. [Obs.]
6. In railroading, to make up, as a train; to switch. [Local, U.S.]

drill, *v.i.* 1. To take part in a military drill.
2. To sow seed with a drill or in drills.

drill, *n.* 1. A pointed instrument used for boring holes, particularly in metals and other hard substances; a boring tool that cuts its way as it revolves; a drilling-machine or drill-press.
2. The act of training soldiers to their duty.
3. In agriculture, a row of seeds deposited in the earth; also, the trench or channel in which the grain or seed is deposited.
4. A machine for sowing seeds in regular rows; as, a turnip-*drill.*
5. *Urosalpinx cinerea*, or an allied marine gasteropod which destroys young oysters by boring into their shells.

drill, *v.t.* and *v.i.* To drain; to trickle.

drill, *n.* A sip; also, a rill. [Obs.]

drill, *n.* A cloth, drilling.

drill, *n.* An ape; a baboon.

drill'-bar"rōw, *n.* An agricultural drill resembling a wheelbarrow.

drill'-bōw, *n.* A small bow, whose string is used for the purpose of rapidly turning a drill.

drill'ẽr, *n.* One who or that which drills.

drill'-har"rōw, *n.* A small drag or harrow for working between drills.

drill'ing, *n.* A kind of coarse linen or cotton cloth.

drill'ing-mȧ-chïne", *n.* A machine for operating a drill; a drill-press.

drill'mas"tẽr, *n.* One who instructs in military drill, gymnastics, or the like.

drill'-plow, drill'-plough (-plow), *n.* A plow which opens a drill for seeds.

drill'-press, *n.* A machine armed with one or more drills for boring holes in metal, and designed as *vertical, horizontal*, or *universal*, in accordance with its mode of working.

drill'stock, *n.* In mechanics, the holder (of which there are many kinds) for receiving the fixed end of a drill.

dri'ly, *adv.* Same as *Dryly.*

drink, *v.i*; drank *or* drunk, *pt.*; drunk *or* drunken, *pp.*; drinking, *ppr.* [ME. *drinken*; AS. *drincan*, to drink.]
1. To swallow something liquid, as for the purpose of quenching thirst; as, the horse stopped to *drink.*
2. To be in the habit of using spirituous liquors to excess; to tipple.

drink, *v.t.* 1. To swallow, as liquids; to receive, as a fluid, into the stomach; to imbibe; as, to *drink* water or wine.
2. To suck in; to absorb; to imbibe.

> And let the purple violets *drink* the stream.
> —Dryden.

3. To take in through the senses, as the ear or eye; to hear; to see; as, to *drink* words or the voice.

> I *drink* delicious poison from thy eye.—Pope.

4. To take in the fumes of; to smoke; as, to *drink* tobacco. [Obs.]
To drink down; to act on by drinking; to reduce or subdue; as, *to drink down* unkindness.
To drink health or *to the health*; to perform a civility, in which a person, on taking a glass or cup, expresses his respect or kind wishes for another.
To drink in; to absorb; to take or receive into any inlet.
To drink off; to drink the whole at a draught; as, *to drink off* a cup of cordial.
To drink up; to drink the whole.

drink, *n.* [ME. *drink, drinke*; AS. *drinc*, a drink, from *drincan*, to drink.]
1. Liquor to be swallowed; any fluid to be taken into the stomach, for quenching thirst, or for medicinal purposes.
2. Intoxicating liquor; booze; as, a victim of *drink.*
3. A draft; as, a *drink* of water.
In drink; drunk; tipsy.

drink'ȧ-ble, *a.* That may be drunk; fit or suitable for drink; potable.

drink'ȧ-ble, *n.* A liquor that may be drunk.

drink'ȧ-ble-ness, *n.* State of being drinkable.

drink'ẽr, *n.* One who drinks, particularly one who practises drinking spirituous liquors to excess; a drunkard; a tippler.

drink'ẽr-moth, *n.* *Odonestis potatoria*, a large British moth, having long, beaklike palpi.

drink'ing, *n.* 1. The act of swallowing liquids, or of absorbing.
2. The practice of drinking to excess.
3. A carousal.

drink'ing-horn, *n.* A horn cup.

drink'less, *a.* Destitute of drink.

drip, *v.i.*; dripped (dript), *pt.*, *pp.*; dripping, *ppr.* [ME. *dryppen*, to drip; AS. *dryppan*, to cause to drop.]
1. To fall in drops; as, water *drips* from eaves.
2. To shed any liquid or moisture in drops; as, a wet garment *drips.*

drip, *v.t.* To let fall in drops.

> The thatch *drips* fast a shower of rain.
> —Swift.

drip, *n.* 1. A falling in drops, or that which falls in drops; as, in building, avoid the *drip* of your neighbor's house.
2. In architecture, a large flat member of the cornice projecting so as to throw off water. [See *Dripstone.*]
Right of drip; in law, an easement or servitude, in virtue of which a person has a right to let his drip fall on another person's property.

drip'ping, *n.* That which falls in drops; the fat which falls from meat in roasting.

Dripstone, Westminster Abbey.

drip'ping-pan, *n.* A pan for receiving the fat which drips from meat in roasting.

drip'ple, *a.* Weak or rare. [Obs.]

drip'stōne, *n.* 1. In architecture, a

projecting molding or cornice over doorways, windows, etc., to throw off the rain. It is also called a *weather-molding*, or more properly *hood-mold*, and *label* when it is turned square. It is of various forms, and when a head is not used as a termination or support, an ornament or simple molding is adopted.

2. A filtering-stone, familiarly so called by seamen.

Dripstone Terminations.
1. St. Cross, Winchester. 2. Chaddesley Corbett, Worcestershire.

drīve, *v.t.*; drove *or* drave, *pt.*; driven, *pp.*; driving, *ppr.* [ME. *driven, drifen*; AS. *drifan*, to drive, compel to go, urge on, etc.]

1. To impel or urge forward by force; to move by physical force; as, we *drive* a nail into wood with a hammer; the wind or steam *drives* a ship on the ocean.

2. To compel or urge forward by other means than absolute physical force, or by means that compel the will; to cause to move forward or onward; to impel to move or act in any way; to force; to constrain; as, to *drive* cattle to market; smoke *drives* company from the room.

Drive thy business; let not thy business *drive* thee. —Franklin.

3. To chase; to hunt.

To *drive* the deer with hound and horn,
Earl Percy took his way. —Chevy Chase.

4. To impel (a team of horses or other animals) to move forward, and to direct the course of; hence, to guide or regulate the course of (the carriage drawn by them); to guide or regulate (a machine); as, to *drive* a team, or to *drive* a carriage drawn by a team; to *drive* an engine.

5. To take on a drive; to convey (a person) in a carriage or other vehicle; as, to *drive* a person to his door.

6. To overrun and devastate. [Obs.]

7. To distress; to straiten; as, desperate men far *driven*.

8. To urge; to press; as, to *drive* an argument.

9. To carry on; to prosecute; to engage in busily; as, to *drive* a trade; to *drive* business.

10. In mining, to dig horizontally.

11. In various games, as baseball, cricket, golf, etc., to impel (the ball) swiftly.

12. In lumbering, to direct the course of (logs) in a stream.

To drive an engine; to run an engine.

To drive away; to force to remove to a distance; to expel; to dispel; to scatter.

To drive feathers or *down*; to place them in a machine which, by a current of air, drives off the lightest to one end, and collects them by themselves.

To drive over or *out*; in typesetting, to space out or carry over, as matter being corrected.

drīve, *v.i.* 1. To be forced along; to be impelled; to be moved by any physical force or agent; as, a ship *drives* before the wind.

The hull *drives* on, though mast and sail be torn. —Byron.

2. To rush and press with violence; as, a storm *drives* against the house.

Fierce Boreas *drove* against his flying sails. —Dryden.

3. To go in a carriage; to travel in a vehicle drawn by horses or other animals; as, he *drove* to Minneapolis.

4. To aim at something; to strive toward a point; to make an effort to obtain a thing; as, we know the end the author is *driving* at.

5. To aim a blow; to strike with force.

At Anxur's shield he *drove*, and at the blow
Both shield and arm to ground together go. —Dryden.

6. To distrain. [Obs.]

To let drive; to throw; to strike.

drīve, *v.*, past tense and past participle of *drive*. [Obs.]

drīve, *n.* 1. The act of driving; an excursion in a carriage, for exercise or pleasure, distinguished from a ride, which is taken on horseback.

2. A road or any place suitable for driving.

3. In forging and type-founding, a matrix formed by a die or punch.

4. Swift or violent motion, or anything resulting therefrom; as, a *drive* of business.

5. A collection of objects to be driven or urged onward, as a pile of logs to be floated down a river.

6. In lumbering, a gang of men who drive logs down a river.

7. The course over which game is driven.

8. An effort put forward for the purpose of making a special sale of a particular line of goods, usually at a reduced price, in order to attract custom; as, a *drive* on shoes, hats, etc.

9. A jest or cutting remark directed at a person. [Colloq.]

10. In such games as cricket, baseball, tennis, etc., the act of striking or impelling the ball with force.

driv′el, *v.i.*; driveled *or* drivelled, *pt.*, *pp.*; driveling *or* drivelling, *ppr.* [ME. *drivelen*, a variant of *dravelen, drabelen*, to drabble, from *dryppen*; AS. *dryppan*, to drip.]

1. To slaver; to let spittle drop or flow from the mouth, like a child, idiot, or dotard.

2. To be weak or foolish; to dote; as, a *driveling* hero; *driveling* love.

driv′el, *n.* 1. Slaver; saliva flowing from the mouth.

2. A driveler; a fool; an idiot. [Obs.]

3. Foolish talk; senseless utterance; twaddle.

4. A servant; hireling. [Obs.]

Syn.—Fatuity, nonsense, trifling, rubbish, babble.

driv′el-ẽr, *n.* A slaverer; a slabberer; an idiot; a fool; also spelled *driveller*.

driv′en, *v.*, past participle of *drive*.

drīv′ẽr, *n.* 1. One who drives; the person or thing that urges or compels anything else to move.

2. The person who drives a carriage; one who conducts a team.

3. One who sets something before him as an aim or object; an aimer.

4. Nautically, (a) a large quadrilateral sail, called also the spanker; (b) the foremost spur in the bulgeways.

5. In machinery, the main wheel by which motion is communicated to a train of wheels.

6. A substance interposed between the driving instrument and the thing driven.

7. In weaving, a piece of wood or other material, upon a spindle, and placed in a box, which impels the shuttle through the opening in the warp.

8. A subordinate official formerly employed in driving for rent in Ireland. [See *Drive*, v.i.]

9. In golf, a wooden-headed club used in delivering the heaviest strokes. The *driver* is employed when the ball lies well.

drīv′ẽr-ant, *n.* *Anomma arcens*, a singular species of ant, a native of West Africa, so named from its driving before it almost every animal that comes in its way.

drīve′wāy, *n.* A road or passage along which a carriage may be driven; a drive.

drīve′-well, *n.* A well made by driving a pointed tube until water is reached; also called *driven well*.

drīv′ing, *a.* Having great force of impulse; as, a *driving* wind or storm.

drīv′ing, *n.* 1. The act of impelling.

2. Tendency. [Rare.]

drīv′ing-ax″le (-ak″sl), *n.* The axle of a driving-wheel.

drīv′ing-belt, *n.* The belt by which machinery is driven by the engine; any belt which conveys motion.

drīv′ing-box, *n.* 1. The journal-box of a driving axle.

2. The seat in a carriage occupied by the driver or coachman.

drīv′ing-nōtes, *n.pl.* In music, syncopated notes; notes which vary the natural accent in a bar.

drīv′ing-rein, *n.* A rein attached to the bit-rings and held by the driver of the vehicle.

drīv′ing-shaft, *n.* The shaft upon which a driving-wheel rests.

drīv′ing-spring, *n.* A spring resting upon the box of a driving-axle of a locomotive, which bears the weight and aids in deadening shocks. [Eng.]

drīv′ing-wheel (-hwēl), *n.* 1. In machinery, a wheel that communicates motion to another or to others.

2. One of the large wheels in a locomotive engine fixed upon the crank-axle or main-shaft; called also *driver*.

driz′zle (driz′zl), *v.i.*; drizzled, *pt.*, *pp.*; drizzling, *ppr.* [AS. *dreosan*, to fall.] To rain in small drops; to fall, as water from the clouds, in very fine particles; as, it *drizzles*; *drizzling* drops; *drizzling* rain; *drizzling* tears.

driz′zle, *v.t.* To shed in small drops or particles.

The air doth *drizzle* dew. —Shak.

driz′zle, *n.* Rain falling in small particles; mist.

driz′zly, *a.* Shedding small rain, or small particles of snow.

Winter's *drizzly* reign. —Dryden.

drock, *n.* [Prov. Eng.] A watercourse.

drof′land, dryf′land, *n.* [Obs.] See *Driftland*.

drō′gẽr, drō′ghẽr (-gẽr), *n.* [Prob. native name.]

1. A small West Indian coasting craft, built for carrying goods, having long, light masts and lateen sails.

2. Any slow-moving coaster.

drog′măn, drog′ō-măn, *n.* See *Dragoman*.

drōgue (drōg), *n.* A buoy attached to the end of a harpoon line.

droil, *v.i.* To work sluggishly or slowly; to plod. [Obs.]

droil, *n.* 1. A mope; a drone; a sluggard; a drudge. [Obs.]

2. Toil; mean work. [Obs.]

droit (*or Fr. pron.* drwä), *n.* [Fr., from OFr. *droit*; LL. *directum*, right, justice, from L. *directus*, right, straight.]

1. In old law, right; title; fee.

2. In finance, duty; custom.

Droit d'aubaine; see under *Aubaine*.

Droits of the Admiralty; in English law, the perquisites formerly attached to the office of admiral of England or lord high admiral, now paid into the exchequer for the benefit of the public service.

droi′tū-răl, *a.* In old English law, relating to a right to property as distinguished from possession.

drōll, *a.*; *comp.* droller; *superl.* drollest. Odd; merry; facetious; comical; as, a *droll* fellow.

Syn.—Laughable, comical.—*Laughable* is generic, denoting anything calculated to excite laughter; *comical* denotes something humorous of the kind exhibited in comedies; *droll* stands lower on the scale, being derived from the French *drôle*, a buffoon or antic, who awakened laughter by queer tricks.

drōll, *n.* [OFr. *drolle, draule*, a good fellow, wag; M.D. *drol*, a merry, humorous fellow, a round lump.]

1. One whose occupation or practice is to raise mirth by odd tricks; a jester; a buffoon.

2. A farce; something exhibited to raise mirth or sport.

drōll, *v.i.* To jest; to play the buffoon. [Rare.]

drōll, *v.t.*; drolled, *pt.*, *pp.*; drolling, *ppr.* 1. To cheat; to influence by trick or jest; to banter; to cajole.

2. To jest. [Rare.]

drōl′ẽr, *n.* A jester; a buffoon. [Obs.]

drōll′ẽr-y, *n.*; *pl.* **drōll′ẽr-ieṣ**. 1. Sportive tricks; buffoonery; comical stories; gestures, manners, or tales adapted to raise mirth.

2. Something inanimate adapted to raise mirth, as a puppet-show; a puppet; a lively, comical sketch. [Obs.]

drōll′ing-ly, *adv.* In a jesting manner.

drōll′ish, *a.* Somewhat droll.

drōll′ist, *n.* A droll. [Rare.]

dro-mæ-, dro-mæ-ō-. Combining forms from Gr. *dromaios*, running at full speed, swift, from *dramein*, to run, signifying swift, running.

drō-mæ-og′nā-thous (-mē-og′nā-thus), *a.* [*Dromæo-*, and Gr. *gnathos*, jaw.] Having the bones of the palate similar anatomically to the ostrich.

drom-ā-thē′ri-um, *n.* [L., from Gr. *dromas*, running, and *thērion*, a wild beast.] A small marsupial found in the American Triassic formations of North Carolina.

drōme, *n.* [Fr., from Gr. *dromas*, running.] A bird, the crab-plover.

drŏm′ē-dā-ry, *n.*; *pl.* **drŏm′ē-dā-rieṣ**. [ME. *dromedarie*; LL. *dromedarius*, a dromedary, from Gr. *dromas*, a running, from *dramein*, to run.]

1. A species of camel, called also the *Arabian camel*, with one hump or protuberance on the back, in distinction from the *Bactrian camel*, which has two humps.

Dromedary (*Camelus dromedarius*).

2. A dromon. [Obs.]

drom′ic, drom′ic-ăl, *a.* [Gr. *dromikos*, good at running, pertaining to a running or race-course, from *dromos*, a running, a race-course.] Of, pertaining to, or characteristic of a dromos.

drom′on, drom′ond, *n.* A large, fast-sailing war-vessel. [Obs.]

drom′os, *n.*; *pl.* **drom′oi**. [Gr. *dromos*, a running, a race-course, from *dramein*, to run.]

1. In Grecian antiquity, a course for racing.

2. In archæology, an avenue, as one leading into a tomb or temple.

drōne, *n.* [ME. *drone, drane*; AS. *dran, drǣn*, a drone; prob. imitative of the sound.]

Drone-bee.

1. The male of the honeybee. It is smaller than the queen bee, but larger than the working bee. The drones make no honey, but after living a few weeks, they are killed or driven from the hive.

2. An idler; a sluggard; one who earns nothing by industry.

drōne, *n.* 1. A humming or low sound; also, the instrument of humming.

2. In music, (a) the largest tube of the bagpipe which emits a continuous deep note; (b) drone-bass.

drōne, *v.i.*; droned, *pt., pp.*; droning, *ppr.* 1. To live in idleness; as, a *droning* king.

2. To give a low, heavy, dull sound; as, the cymbal's *droning* sound.

drōne′-bȧss, *n.* A bass of one or, at most, two notes.

drōne′-bee, *n.* A male honeybee; a drone.

drōne′-fly̆, *n.* *Eristalis tenax*, a fly resembling the drone-bee.

drōne′pīpe, *n.* One of the bass pipes of the bagpipe; the drone.

dron′gō, *n.* [South African.] One of a family of fly-catching birds, with long, forked tails. They inhabit India, the Asiatic islands, and South Africa: also called *drongo-shrike*.

drōn′ish, *a.* Idle; sluggish; lazy; indolent; inactive: slow.

drōn′ish-ly, *adv.* In a dronish manner.

drōn′ish-ness, *n.* State of being dronish.

drōn′kē-lew, *a.* Drunken. [Obs.]

dron′te, *n.* [Fr.] A bird, the dodo.

drōn′y, *a.* Lazy; sluggish; dronelike.

drook, *v.t.* See *Drouk*.

drool, *v.i.*; drooled, *pt., pp.*; drooling, *ppr.* To drivel or drop saliva.

droop, *v.i.*; drooped (drööpt), *pt., pp.*; drooping, *ppr.* [ME. *droupen*; Ice. *drupa*, to droop.]

1. To sink or hang down; to lean downward, as a body that is weak or languishing; to faint; to grow weak; to be dispirited; as, the soldiers *droop* from fatigue; the human body *droops* in old age.

2. To languish from grief or other cause; to fail or sink; to decline; as, the courage or the spirits *droop*.

3. To draw to a close; to proceed downward; as, the day *drooped*.

Syn.—Fade, languish, pine, sink.

droop, *v.t.* To let sink or bend; as, the flowers *drooped* their heads.

droop, *n.* A drooping.

droop′ēr, *n.* One who or that which droops.

droop′ing-ly, *adv.* In a drooping manner.

drop, *n.* [ME. *drope*; AS. *dropa*, a drop; O.H.G. *tropfo*; G. *tropfen*; Sw. *droppe*; Ice. *dropi*, a drop.]

1. A small portion of any fluid in a spherical form, which falls at once, or a globule of any fluid which is pendent, as if about to fall; as, a *drop* of water; a *drop* of blood.

2. A diamond hanging from the ear; an earring; something hanging in the form of a *drop*.

3. A very small quantity of liquor; as, he had not drunk a *drop*.

4. In architecture, (a) a gutta; (b) a pendent ornamentation of any kind.

5. Anything that projects or falls from a higher position; anything used to bring or let down something else; as, (a) a door in a stage or platform; a trap; (b) the part of a gallows which sustains the criminal before execution, and which is suddenly dropped; (c) a drop-curtain; (d) a tube used to convey gas from a fixture to a burner at a lower level; (e) an arrangement for bringing down heavy weights to a vessel's deck; (f) a drop-hammer; (g) the movable cover of a keyhole.

6. The process of falling; an abrupt fall.

7. [*pl.*] Any liquid used as a medicine which is administered in *drops*; also, various kinds of candy; as, laudanum *drops*; lemon *drops*.

8. In nautical language, the depth of the lowest square sail at its center.

9. A decrease in the potential of an electric current.

Drop by drop; drop following drop; little by little.

Drop in the bucket; a very small or inadequate quantity.

Drop serene; total or partial loss of sight; amaurosis.

Prince Rupert's drop; same as *Detonating-bulb*.

To get or ***have the drop on***; to get one's gun or pistol ready to fire sooner than one's adversary; hence, to forestall another or seize an advantage.

drop, *v.t.*; dropped *or* dropt, *pt., pp.*; dropping, *ppr.* [ME. *droppen*; AS. *droppan, dropian*, from *dropa*, a drop.]

1. To pour or let fall in small portions or globules, as a fluid; to distil.

2. To let fall, as any substance; as, to *drop* the anchor; to *drop* a stone.

3. To let go; to dismiss; to lay aside; to quit; to leave; to permit to subside; as, to *drop* an affair.

4. To utter slightly, briefly, or casually; to insert indirectly, incidentally, or by way of digression; as, to *drop* a word of suggestion.

5. To send informally; as, to *drop* a note.

6. To set down and leave; as, the coach *dropped* a passenger at the inn.

7. To bedrop; to speckle; to variegate, as if by sprinkling with drops; as, a coat *dropped* with gold.

8. To lower; as, to *drop* the muzzle of a gun.

drop, *v.i.* 1. To fall in small portions, globules, or drops, as a liquid.

2. To let drops fall; to discharge in drops.

3. To fall; to descend suddenly or abruptly.

4. To die, or to die suddenly; as, we see one friend after another *dropping* around us.

5. To come to an end; to cease; to be neglected and come to nothing; as, the affair *dropped*.

6. To come; with *in* or *into*; as, my old friend *dropped in* a moment.

7. To fall short of a mark. [Rare.]

8. To fall lower; as, the point of the spear *dropped*.

9. To be deep in extent, as a sail.

To drop down; in seamen's language, to sail, row, or move down a river, or toward the sea.

Syn.—Ooze, emanate, distil, percolate, fall, decline, descend, faint, droop.

drop′-bär, *n.* In machinery, any bar having a regular descending motion.

drop′-bot″tŏm, *n.* A bottom in a car or wagon, opening downward to unload earth, coal, etc.

drop′-çall, *n.* A device on an electric switchboard giving a signal by dropping a movable piece.

drop′-cũr″tain (-tin), *n.* In theaters, a curtain lowered between acts to hide the stage.

drop′-fin″gẽrs, *n.pl.* Rods which hold a sheet in place in a printing-press.

drop′-fly̆, *n.* In angling, an artificial fly attached to the line above another at the end.

drop′-fọrġe, *v.t.* To forge (metal) with a drop-press.

drop′-fọr″ġing, *n.* Metal forged by a drop-press.

drop′-glȧss, *n.* A small glass tube used as a dropper.

drop′-ham″mẽr, *n.* A drop-press.

drop′-kick, *n.* In football, a kick made by letting the ball drop from the hands and kicking it the instant it rises from the ground.

drop′let, *n.* A little drop.

drop′-let″tẽr, *n.* A letter to be delivered by the office in which it is mailed.

drop′light (-līt), *n.* A portable stand bearing a gas-burner or electric light, and connected by a tube, wire, etc., with a fixture, usually at a higher level.

drop′mēal, drop′mēle, *adv.* [AS. *dropmælum*; *dropa*, drop, and *mæl*, portion.] By drops. [Obs.]

drop′-net, *n.* 1. A net hanging from a projecting arm to be dropped over a shoal of fish.

2. Lace resembling a net.

drop′pẽr, *n.* 1. One who or that which drops.

2. A glass tube used to deliver a liquid in drops.

3. A harvesting-machine that drops the grain for binding.

4. A dog which suddenly drops or crouches on the ground when it sees game.

5. A drop-fly.

drop′ping, *n.* 1. Falling; the act of falling or letting fall in drops.

2. That which drops; especially, in the plural, dung; manure,

drop′ping-bot″tle, *n.* A bottle arranged to deliver its contents in drops.

drop′ping-ly, *adv.* In drops.

drop′ping-tūbe, *n.* Same as *Dropper*, n. 2.

drop′-press, *n.* A machine for stamping, forging, etc., consisting usually of a heavy weight which drops between perpendicular guides, being raised by hand or by other power.

drop′-scēne, *n.* A scene across the entire stage, used as a curtain.

drop′-shut″tẽr, *n.* A device used in instantaneous photography for obtaining short exposures; originally, a slide which dropped in front of the lens.

drop′si-çăl, *a.* Partaking of the nature of dropsy; diseased with or inclined to dropsy.

drop′si-çăl-ness, *n.* Dropsical condition.

drop′sied (-sid), *a.* Affected with dropsy.

drop′stōne, *n.* A stalactite.

drop′sy, *n.* [ME. *dropsie, dropesie*; OFr. *idropisie*; L. *hydropisis*, from Gr. *hydrops*, dropsy, from *hydōr*, water.]

1. In pathology, an infiltration of the tissues with a watery fluid or the collection of such fluid in any body-cavity.

2. A disease produced in some succulent plants, by excess of water.

dropt, *v.*, past tense and past participle of *drop*.

drop′-tin, *n.* Granulated tin formed by pouring molten tin into water.

drop′wīse, *adv.* In the shape of a drop or drops; by drops. [Rare.]

drop′wŏrm, *n.* The caterpillar of any geometrid; a measuring-worm.

drop′wŏrt, *n.* *Spiræa Filipendula*, a European herb.

Sundew (*Drosera rotundifolia*).

Dros′e-rȧ, *n.* [Gr. *droseros*, dewy, from *drosos*, dew, juice.] A genus of the *Droseraceæ*, glandular hairs on the leaves of which secrete a viscid fluid resembling dew, whence the common name of *sundew*.

Dros-e-rā′cē-æ, *n.pl.* [Gr. *droseros*, dewy, from *drosos*, dew, water, juice, and *-aceæ*.] The sundew family, an order of insectivorous plants of which *Drosera* is the typical genus.

dros-e-rā′ceous, *a.* Of or like the *Droseraceæ*.

drosh′ky, dros′ky, *n.*; *pl.* **drosh′kieṣ, dros′kieṣ**. [G. *droschke*; Russ. *drozhki*, dim. of *drogi*, a carriage.] A light, four-wheeled vehicle used in Russia. The *droshky* proper has no top, and the traveler sits astride a narrow bench which connects the front and rear axles; but the name is now applied to various kinds of vehicles, as to the common cabs plying in the streets of German cities, etc.

Droshky.

drō-som′e-tẽr, *n.* [Gr. *drosos*, dew, and *metron*, a measure.] An instrument for measuring the quantity of dew on a surface in the open air.

dross, *n.* [ME. *drosse*; AS. *dros*, dregs, from *dreosan*, to fall.]

1. The scum or extraneous matter of metals, thrown off in the process of melting; slag; scoria.

2. Rust; crust of metals. [Rare.]

3. Waste matter; refuse; any worthless matter separated from the better part; impure matter.

dros′sel, *n.* A slut; a dirty wench. [Obs.]

dross′i-ness, *n.* The condition of being drossy.

dross′less, *a.* Free from dross.

dross′y, *a.*; *comp.* drossier; *superl.* drossiest. Like dross; pertaining to dross; full of dross; impure; worthless; as, *drossy* gold.

drotch′el, *n.* An idle wench; a sluggard. [Obs.]

droud, *n.* [Scot.] A codfish; also a kind of fish-trap or weir.

drōugh (drö), *v.*, past tense of *draw*. [Obs.]

drought (drout), **drouth**, *n.* [ME. *drought, drowght, drougth, drugthe*; AS. *drugath, drugoth*, dryness; from *dryge*, dry.]

1. Dryness; want of rain or of water; particularly, dryness of the weather, which affects the earth and prevents the growth of plants; aridness; aridity

2. Dryness of the throat and mouth; thirst; want of drink.

3. Insufficiency; want of something necessary.

drought′i-ness, *n.* A state of drought.

drought′y, *a.* 1. Dry; arid; wanting rain.

2. Thirsty; dry; wanting drink.

drouk, *v.t.* [Scot.] To drench.

drou′my, *a.* Troubled; muddy. [Obs.]

drouth, *n.* Same as *Drought*.

drouth′y, *a.* Same as *Droughty*.

drōve, *v.*, past tense of *drive*.

drōve, *n.* [ME. *drove, drof*; AS. *draf*, a drove, from *drifan*, to drive.]

1. A collection of cattle driven; a number of animals, as oxen, sheep, or swine, driven in a body; hence, any collection of irrational animals, moving or driving forward; as, a finny *drove*.

2. A crowd of people in motion.

Where *droves*, as at a city gate, may pass.
—Dryden.

3. A road for driving cattle. [Eng.]

4. A narrow irrigation canal.

drōve, *n.* 1. A chisel used to tool the surface of stone roughly.

2. The grooved surface made by a drove-chisel.

drōve, *v.t.*; droved, *pt., pp.*; droving, *ppr.* [Scot.] To dress, leaving the surface rough, as stone.

drōve′-chis″el, *n.* Same as second *Drove*, n. 1.

drō′ven, *v.*, obsolete past participle of *drive.*

drō′vẽr, *n.* 1. One who drives cattle or sheep to market; a man who makes it his business to purchase cattle and drive them to market.

2. A boat driven by the tide. [Obs.]

drō′vy, *a.* [ME. *drovy, drovi*; AS. *drofi, drof,* turbid, muddy.] Roily; mixed with filthy dregs. [Obs.]

drow, *v.*, past tense of *draw.* [Obs.]

drow, *n.* [Scot.] A tiny elf of a race fabled to dwell in caves and to forge magic metal-work.

drown, *v.t.*; drowned, *pt., pp.*; drowning, *ppr.* [ME. *drownen, druncnen*, to drown, sink; AS. *druncnian*, to become drunk, to drown, sink, from *druncen*, pp. of *drincan*, to drink.]

1. Literally, to overwhelm in water; to extinguish life in, by immersion in water or other fluid; also, to destroy as if by submersion.

2. To overflow; to inundate; as, to *drown* land.

3. To immerse; to plunge and lose; as, to *drown* oneself in sensual pleasure.

4. To overwhelm; to overpower.

My private voice is *drowned* amid the senate.
—Addison.

To drown out; to force out by flooding; as, *to drown out* a ground-hog from his burrow.

Syn.—Sink, immerse, swamp, overwhelm, engulf, deluge, inundate, submerge.

drown, *v i.* To be suffocated in water or other fluid; to perish in water.

drown′āġe, *n.* The act of drowning. [Obs.]

drown′ẽr, *n.* One who or that which drowns.

drowṣe, *v.i.*; drowsed (drouzd), *pt., pp.*; drowsing, *ppr.* [AS. *drusan, drusian*, to sink, become slow or inactive; *dreosan*, to fall.]

1. To sleep imperfectly or unsoundly; to slumber; to be heavy with sleepiness.

2. To look heavy; to be heavy or dull.

drowṣe, *v.t.* To make heavy with sleep; to make dull or stupid.

drowṣe, *n.* A semiconscious condition induced by need of sleep or by the influence of a soporific.

drow′ṣi-head, drow′ṣi-hed, *n.* Same as *Drowsyhead.*

drow′ṣi-ly, *adv.* In a drowsy manner.

drow′ṣi-ness, *n.* The condition of being drowsy.

drow′ṣy, *a.*; *comp.* drowsier; *superl.* drowsiest.

1. Inclined to sleep; sleepy; heavy with sleepiness; lethargic; comatose.

2. Dull; sluggish; stupid.

3. Disposing to sleep; lulling; as, a *drowsy* couch.

drow′ṣy-head (-hed), *n.* Sleepiness. [Rare.]

drowth, *n.* Same as *Drought.*

droyle, *v.i.* [Obs.] Same as *Droil.*

drub, *v.t.* and *v.i.*; drubbed, *pt., pp.*; drubbing, *ppr.* [Ice. and Sw. *drabba*, to beat, hit; Dan. *dræbe*, to slay; AS. *drepan*, to beat.]

I. *v.t.* To beat with a stick; to thrash; to cudgel.

II. *v.i.* To strike lightly with the fingers; to thrum.

drub, *n.* A blow with a stick or cudgel; a thump; a knock.

drub′bẽr, *n.* One who drubs.

drudġe (druj), *v.i.*; drudged, *pt., pp.*; drudging, *ppr.* [ME. *druggen*, to work hard; Ir. *drugaire*, a slave; Scot. *drug*, a rough pull.] To work hard; to labor with toil and fatigue at tedious, servile tasks.

drudġe, *v.t.* 1. To pass irksomely; as, he *drudged* away the time.

2. To subject to drudgery; to impose upon.

drudġe, *n* One who works hard; one who labors without interest at mechanical work.

drudġ′ẽr, *n.* 1. A drudge.

2. A dredging-box.

drudġ′ẽr-y, *n.* Hard labor; toilsome work; ignoble toil; hard work in servile or dull occupations.

drudġ′ing-box, *n.* Same as *Dredging-box.*

drudġ′ing-ly, *adv.* In a drudging manner.

dru̇′ẽr-y, *n.* Same as *Drury.*

drug, *n.* A drudge. [Obs.]

drug, *v.t.*; drugged, *pt., pp.*; drugging, *ppr.* 1. To season with drugs; hence, to make narcotic by means of drugs; as, she *drugged* his food.

2. To give drugs to, especially, narcotic drugs or drugs in too great a quantity; hence, to deaden or make stupid.

3. To tincture with something offensive. [Rare.]

drug, *v.i.* 1. To prescribe or administer drugs or medicines, particularly, to an excessive degree.

2. To use drugs from habit.

drug, *n.* [Fr. *drogue*, a drug, stuff; Sp., Port., and It. *droga*, from D. *droog*, dry, any dried substance, as herbs.]

1. Any substance used in the preparation of medicines or of chemical mixtures employed in the arts; especially, a narcotic.

2. Any unsalable commodity, especially from overproduction.

drug, *n.* Same as *Drag*, n. 13.

drug′gẽr, *n.* A druggist. [Obs.]

drug′get, *n.* [Fr. *droguet*, dim. of *drogue*, stuff, trash.] A coarse woolen cloth, thick and strong, stamped on one side with figures, used as a covering and protection for carpets and for covering tables; by extension, any rug.

drug′gist, *n.* [Fr. *droguiste*, from *drogue*, a drug.]

1. A pharmacist; one skilled in compounding drugs in accordance with prescriptions.

2. One whose business it is to buy and sell drugs.

drug′stẽr, *n.* A druggist. [Obs.]

drụ′id, *n.* [Fr. *druide*, a druid, from L. *druida*, a druid; Ir. *draoi, druidh*, a magician, sorcerer.]

1. A priest or minister of religion among the ancient Celtic nations in Gaul, Britain, and Germany. The *druids* possessed some knowledge of geometry, natural philosophy, etc., superintended the affairs of religion and morality, and performed the office of judges.

2. [D—] A member of an order known as the United Ancient Order of Druids, founded 1781, in London.

drụ′id-ess, *n.* A female druid.

drụ-id′iç, drụ-id′iç-ăl, *a.* Pertaining to the druids.

Druidical circles; in England, certain ancient inclosures formed by rude stones circularly arranged, as at Stonehenge, near Salisbury.

drụ′id-ish, *a.* Pertaining to or like druids.

drụ′id-iṣm, *n.* The system of religion, philosophy, and instruction taught by the druids, or their doctrines, rites, and ceremonies.

drum, *n.* [Ir. *druim*, a ridge, a hill.] A long, narrow hill; a ridge; a ridge-like unstratified moraine.

drum, *n.* [D. *trom*; L.G. *trumme*; D. *trommel, drummel*, a drum; M.H.G. *trumme, trumbe*; O.H.G. *trumba, trumpa*, a trump, trumpet; Dan. *drum*, a boom, a noise. The word is probably of imitative origin.]

1. A martial instrument of music, in the form of a hollow cylinder covered at the ends with vellum, or a hemisphere of metal covered at one end with vellum, which is stretched or slackened by tighteners, and played by striking the end with a drumstick.

2. In machinery, a short cylinder revolving on an axis, generally for the purpose of turning several small wheels, by means of straps passing round its periphery.

3 The tympanum of the ear; the hollow part of the ear, behind the membrane of the tympanum.

4. A quantity packed in the form of a *drum*; as, a *drum* of figs.

5. Sheet-iron in the shape of a *drum*, to receive heat from a stovepipe.

6. In architecture, (a) one of the blocks of which the shaft of a column is composed; (b) an upright wall, either circular or polygonal in construction, supporting a dome or cupola.

7. Formerly, a noisy, crowded, fashionable, social gathering, as for playing cards; a rout; hence, a tea-party; a kettledrum.

8. One of several fishes of the family *Sciænidæ* that make a drumming sound, probably by the use of the bones of the pharynx and the resonance of the air-bladder.

9. In zoölogy, (a) the drum-like apparatus of a cicada, by which it produces its song; (b) the resonant hyoid of the howler monkey.

drum, *v.i.*; drummed, *pt., pp.*; drumming, *ppr.* 1. To beat a drum with sticks; to beat or play a tune on a drum.

2. To beat with the fingers, as with drumsticks; to beat with a rapid succession of strokes; as, to *drum* on the table.

3. To beat, as the heart.

drum, *v.t.* 1. To expel with the accompaniment of the beat of a drum; as, to *drum* a deserter from camp.

2. To perform on a drum; as, to *drum* the rogue's march.

3. To draw together, as by beating a drum; to canvass; as, to *drum* up business.

drum′bēat, *n.* The sound made by beating a drum.

drum′ble, *v.i.* 1. To be slow and inactive. [Obs.]

2. To speak in a mumbling manner. [Obs.]

drum′fish, *n.* See second *Drum*, 8.

drum′head (-hed), *n.* 1. The skin or vellum covering the end of a drum.

2. The head or top part of a capstan.

Drumhead court-martial; a court-martial held in an emergency, usually upon the field, where the drumhead serves as a table for writing.

drum′lin, *n.* Same as first *Drum.*

drum′loid, *n.* An irregular drumlin or glacial ridge.

drum′ly, *a.* [Scot.] Turbid; hence, gloomy.

drum′-mā′jŏr, *n.* 1. The chief or first drummer of a regiment; a teacher of drummers.

2. The leader of a military band on the march.

3. A noisy social company. [Obs.]

drum′mẽr, *n.* 1. One whose office is to beat the drum in military exercises and marching; one who drums.

2. In the United States, one who travels and solicits trade for a wholesale business.

3. One of a certain kind of fish, so called from the noise they make; as, (a) the weakfish; (b) a sculpin of California.

4. *Blatta gigantea*, a large cockroach of tropical America which drums on wood with its head to call the opposite sex.

Drum′mŏnd light. [Named after Thomas *Drummond.*] The calcium light.

drum′stick, *n.* 1. The stick with which a drum is beaten.

2. Anything in the form of a *drumstick*; as, the outer or lower joint of a dressed fowl's leg.

drum′stick-tree, *n.* A tropical tree, *Cassia Fistula*, having legumes resembling drumsticks.

drum′wood, *n.* A small tree of the West Indies (*Turpinia occidentalis*).

druñk, *a.* [Pp. of *drink.*] 1. Intoxicated; inebriated; overwhelmed or overpowered by spirituous liquor; stupefied or inflamed by the action of spirits on the stomach and brain.

2. Drenched or saturated with moisture or liquor.

druñk, *n.* One who is drunk; also, a period of drunkenness; as, the officer arrested four *drunks*; on a *drunk.* [Slang.]

druñk′ărd, *n.* One given to an excessive use of strong liquor; a person who is habitually drunk.

druñk′en, *a.* 1. Intoxicated; inebriated; proceeding from intoxication; done in a state of drunkenness; as, a *drunken* quarrel.

2. Given to drunkenness; as, a *drunken* butler.

3. Saturated with liquor or moisture; drenched.

druñk′en-head, *n.* Drunkenness. [Obs.]

druñk′en-ly, *adv.* In a drunken manner. [Rare.]

druñk′en-ness, *n.* 1. Intoxication; inebriation; the quality or condition of being drunk.

2. Habitual intoxication.

3. Disorder of the faculties, resembling intoxication by liquors; inflammation; frenzy; rage.

Syn.—Intoxication, inebriation.—*Drunkenness* refers more to the habit of excessive drinking; *intoxication* and *inebriation* to specific acts.

druñk′en-ship, druñk′ship, *n.* Intoxication. [Obs.]

Drụ-pā′cē-æ, *n.pl.* [L. *drupa*; Gr. *dryppa*, an overripe, wrinkled olive.] A suborder of *Rosaceæ*, including the plum, cherry, peach, and other similar drupaceous trees.

drụ-pā′ceous, *a.* Of, producing, consisting of, or resembling drupes; as *drupaceous* trees; *drupaceous* fruit.

drụp′ăl, *a.* Drupaceous.

drụpe, *n.* [L. *drupa*, Gr. *dryppa*, an overripe olive, from *drypepēs*, ripened on the tree, *drys*, a tree, and *peptein* to ripen.] A fruit having a fleshy, coriaceous, or fibrous sarcocarp, without valves, inclosing a nut or stone which contains the kernel or seed proper; a stone-fruit, as the plum, cherry, apricot, peach, almond, olive, date, etc.

Drupe.

drụp′el, *n.* A little drupe; called also *drupeole.*

drụpe′let, *n.* A drupel.

drụ′ry, *n.* Love; a lover; a token of love. [Obs.]

drụṣe, *n.* [G.] A geode.

Drụṣe, *n.* [Turk.] One of an independent and warlike tribe of the mountains of Lebanon in Syria, whose religious beliefs are derived from Mohammedan, Christian, and Persian sources.

drụ′ṣy, drụṣed, *a.* Studded with small crystals.

drux′y, drux′ey, *a.* Spotted with decay; having whitish streaks or spots, as trees.

drȳ, *a.*; *comp.* drier; *superl.* driest. [ME. *drye, dryge, drie*; AS. *dryge, drige.*]

1. Destitute of moisture; arid; not moist or damp; lacking the ordinary or average amount of moisture; (a) free from juice, sap, or water; not green; as, *dry* wood; *dry* leaves; (b) without tears; as, *dry* eyes; (c) not giving milk; as, the cow is *dry*; (d) thirsty; craving drink; as, salt makes me *dry*; (e) not rainy; free from rain or mist; as, *dry* weather; (f) in medicine, characterized by absence of moisture; as, *dry* pleurisy; a *dry* blow (i.e., a severe blow which does not cause a wound or bleeding); (g) in mining, not having or not using water; as, *dry* separation.

2. Devoid of interest; barren; jejune; unembellished; plain; as, a *dry* style; a *dry* subject.

3. Devoid of sympathy or cordiality; formal; cold; as, a *dry* reception; a *dry* manner.

4. Severe; sarcastic; cynical; sneering; as, a *dry* retort.

5. Destitute of nonessentials; pithy; expressed slyly and without apparent intention; laconic; shrewdly and quietly witty or sarcastic; as, *dry* wit; a *dry* pun.

6. In art, having a sharp, frigid preciseness of execution; lacking delicacy or softness of contour or coloring; stiff; formal; hard.

7. Having little sugar or sweetness; as, a *dry* wine, in which the sugar of the fruit juice has

become converted into alcohol and carbonic acid gas.

8. In metallurgy, having more oxygen than is desired; said of copper when not thoroughly poled.

9. Controlled by or favoring laws prohibiting the sale of liquors; as, a *dry* district. [Colloq.]

10. Severe; hard; as, a *dry* basting. [Obs.]

Dry battery; a battery for generating electricity with dry chemicals.

Dry dock; a dock from which the water may be shut or pumped out, used for building and repairing ships.

Dry light; a light free from color or shadows; hence, an unbiased observation, judgment, or point of view.

Dry measure; a measure or system of measures used in ascertaining or expressing the volume of articles not liquid.

Dry pile; a dry form of voltaic pile in which the liquid is replaced by a solid hygrometric substance.

Dry plate; a photographic plate having a hard, dry coating sensitive to light, and capable of use while dry.

Syn.—Arid, parched, moistureless, juiceless, barren, sarcastic, dull, tedious, uninteresting.

dry̆, *v.t.*; dried, *pt., pp.*; drying, *ppr.* [ME. *dryen, drygen*; AS. *drygan, drigan*, to dry; from *dryge, drige*, dry.]

1. To make dry; to deprive of moisture; to exsiccate; as, the servant *dries* the plates; the sun *dries* the earth.

2. To take out or remove by evaporation; evaporate; as, to *dry* out the water from a cloth.

3. To arrange or prepare in such a manner as to cause to become dry; to jerk; to desiccate; as, to *dry* beef; to *dry* malt.

dry̆, *v.i.* 1. To grow dry; to lose moisture; to become free of water, moisture or juice; as, paint *dries* in the sun; the roads will soon *dry*.

2. To wither; to shrivel; as, to *dry* to a mummy.

3. To stop flowing; to become evaporated; as, the creek *dries* up.

dry̆′ad, *n.* [L. *dryas* (*-adis*); Gr. *dryas* (*-ados*), a wood-nymph, from *drys*, a tree.] In mythology, a nymph of the woods.

dry̆′=ā″rē-a, *n.* An outside sunken space protecting the foundation of a building from dampness.

dry̆′as, *n.*; *pl.* **dry̆′a-dēs.** A dryad.

dry̆′=as=dust′, *a.* and *n.* I. *a.* Very prosaic or dull.

II. *n.* A dull, unimaginative person.

dry̆′=bēat, *v.t.* To beat with severity. [Obs.]

dry̆′=bōne, *n.* Smithsonite.

dry̆′=bōned, *a.* Having dry bones.

dry̆′=cup″ping, *n.* See *Dry cupping*, under *Cupping*.

dry̆′=dock, *n.* See second *Dock*, n. 2.

dry̆′ēr, *n.* Same as *Drier*.

dry̆′=eyed (-id), *a.* Not having a tear in the eyes.

dry̆′=fat, *n.* A dry-vat. [Obs.]

dry̆′=fist″ed, *a.* Tight-fisted; stingy.

dry̆′foot, *adv.* 1. With the feet dry.

2. By the scent of the foot. [Obs.]

dry̆′=goods, *n.pl.* Textile fabrics and similar wares, in distinction from hardware, groceries, etc.

dry̆′ing, *a.* 1 Adapted to exhaust moisture; as, a *drying* wind or day.

2. Forming a vesicle over the surface and quickly becoming hard.

Drying oil; oil which has the property of drying rapidly when exposed to the atmosphere, hence used in preparing paints and varnishes.

dry̆′ite, *n.* [Gr. *drys*, a tree, oak, and *-ite.*] Petrified wood; fossil wood.

dry̆′ly, *adv.* In a dry manner; also written *drily*.

dry̆′=mul″tūre, *n.* In Scots law, a yearly tax levied upon lands to support a mill.

dry̆′ness, *n.* The state or quality of being dry.

dry̆′=nŭrse, *n.* 1. A nurse who attends and feeds a child without suckling it.

2. One who attends another; especially, one who informs a superior what to do. [Slang.]

dry̆′nŭrse, *v.t.* To perform the duties of a dry-nurse toward.

Dry̆-o-bal′a-nops, *n.* [Gr. *drys*, an oak, *balanos*, an acorn, and *opsis*, appearance.] A genus of resinous evergreen trees which yield camphor-oil and Borneo camphor.

dry̆′=pipe, *n.* In a boiler, a steam-pipe conveying dry steam.

dry̆′=plāte, *a.* Denoting the process of photography in which dry plates or films are used.

dry̆′=point, *n.* 1. A needle used by etchers to incise fine lines in copperplate without employing acid.

2. An engraving made with such a needle, or a print from an engraving so made.

3. The process of making such engravings.

dry̆′=point, *a* Made by means of a dry-point.

dry̆′=rent, *n.* In law, a rent reserved without clause of distress.

dry̆′=rot, *n.* 1. A rapid decay of timber, due to fungi, by which its substance is converted into a dry powder, which issues from minute tubular cavities, resembling the borings of worms.

2. Hidden or unsuspected inward corruption.

Dry-rot Fungus (*Merulius lacrymans*).

dry̆′=rub, *v.t.*; dry-rubbed, *pt., pp.*; dry-rubbing, *ppr.* To rub and cleanse without wetting.

dry̆′=sạlt″ēr, *n.* A dealer in salted or dry meats, pickles, sauces, etc.

dry̆′=sạlt″ēr-y, *n.* The articles kept by a dry-salter; the business of a dry-salter or his warehouse.

dry̆′=shod, *a.* Without wetting the feet.

dry̆′=stōne, *a.* Built of stone without cement or mortar.

dry̆′=stōve, *n.* A hothouse.

dry̆th, *n.* Drought. [Obs.]

dry̆′=vat, *n.* A receptacle intended for dry articles.

dū′ad, *n.* [L. *duo*, two.] A union of two. [Rare.]

dū′ăl, *a.* [L. *dualis*, from *duo*, two.] Expressing the number two; consisting of two; twofold; as, the *dual* number in Greek.

Dual Alliance; the compact between Germany and Austria-Hungary after Italy's withdrawal from the original Triple Alliance in 1914.

dū′a-lin, *n.* A form of dynamite containing saltpeter, sawdust, and nitroglycerin.

dū′ăl-iṣm, *n.* [L. *dualis*, of two, from *duo*, two.]

1. A state in which anything under consideration may be regarded as divisible into, depending upon, or made up of two distinct but related parts; duality; as, the *dualism* of man's nature, considered as corporeal and spiritual.

2. In philosophy, the doctrine that recognizes two radically independent elements as underlying all known phenomena; opposed to *monism*.

3. In theology, the recognition of two radically different principles in operation, one good, the other bad; also, the doctrine that in Christ existed a twofold personality, the divine logos being distinct from the human person.

4. In physiology, the theory that the two hemispheres of the brain act separately and independently.

5. In chemistry, the theory that every definite compound consists of two parts having opposite electrical activity.

dū′ăl-ist, *n.* 1. One who upholds dualism.

2. An incumbent of two offices at once.

dū-ăl-is′tiç, *a.* Consisting of two; belonging to dualism; being dual.

Dualistic theory or *system*; same as *Dualism*, 5.

dū-al′i-ty, *n.* [LL. *dualitas*, from *dualis*, of two; *duo*, two.] The state or quality of being two or dual.

dū′ăn, *n.* [Gael.] One of the divisions of a poem; also, the poem itself.

dū′ăr-çhy, *n.* [Gr. *duo*, two, and *archē*, rule.] Government by two persons. [Rare.]

dub, *v.t.*; dubbed, *pt., pp.*; dubbing, *ppr.* [ME. *dubben*; AS. *dubban*, to strike, beat; OFr. *duber, aduber*, to equip with arms, prepare.]

1. To strike with a sword in conferring knighthood; hence, to invest with the rank of knight.

2. To confer any dignity or appellation upon; to call; to name; to designate.

3. To dress or make smooth; (a) to cut smooth with an adz; as, to *dub* a stick of timber; (b) to strike with teazels in dressing cloth; (c) to rub a dressing into; as, to *dub* leather; (d) to dress with feathers, etc.; as, to *dub* a fishing-fly; (e) to cut or trim the comb and wattles of; as, to *dub* a gamecock for a fight.

To dub out; to bring out (an uneven surface) to a level plane ready for plastering.

dub, *v.i.* To make a quick noise like a drum-beat.

dub, *n.* A blow. [Rare.]

dub, *n.* [Ir. *dob*, mire.] A puddle; a pool. [Prov. Eng.]

dū′bash, *n.* Same as *Dobhash*.

dubb, *n.* *Ursus syriacus*, the Syrian bear.

dub′bēr, *n.* One who or that which dubs.

dub′bēr, *n.* [E. Ind.] A leather vessel or bottle, used in India, to hold ghee, oil, etc.

dub′bing, *n.* 1. The act of conferring knighthood; hence, the giving of any appellation.

2. The act of dressing or making smooth.

3. The material used (a) to dub leather; (b) to dress an artificial fly; (c) to dub out a wall for plastering.

dū-bi′e-ty, *n.*; *pl.* **dū-bi′e-ties.** [L. *dubietas*, from *dubius*, doubtful.] Doubtfulness. [Rare.]

dū-bi-os′i-ty, *n.*; *pl.* **dū-bi-os′i-tieṣ.** A thing doubtful; dubiousness. [Rare.]

dū′bi-ous, *a.* [L. *dubius*, doubting, uncertain, from *duo*, two.]

1. Doubtful; wavering or fluctuating in opinion; not determined; as, the mind is in a *dubious* state.

2. Uncertain; of which the truth is not known; causing doubt; not clear; as, a *dubious* signal.

3. Of uncertain event or issue; as, *dubious* battle.

4. Of doubtful propriety; questionable; causing suspicion; as, *dubious* methods.

dū′bi-ous-ly, *adv.* In a dubious manner.

dū′bi-ous-ness, *n.* Dubious quality or state.

dū′bi-ta-ble, *a.* [L. *dubitabilis*, from *dubitare*, to doubt.] Susceptible of being doubted; doubtful; debatable.

dū′bi-ta-bly, *adv.* Not certainly; questionably. [Rare.]

dū′bi-tăn-cy, *n.* Doubt; uncertainty. [Obs.]

dū′bi-tāte, *v.i.* [L. *dubitatus*, pp. of *dubitare*, to doubt.] To doubt. [Obs.]

dū-bi-tā′tion, *n.* [L. *dubitatio*, from *dubitare*, to doubt.] The act of doubting; doubt; hesitation. [Rare.]

dū′bi-tā-tive, *a.* Tending to doubt. [Rare.]

dū′bi-tā-tive-ly, *adv.* With doubt. [Rare.]

Dū-boi′si-a, *n.* [Named after F. N. A. *Dubois*, a French botanist.]

1. In botany, a genus of the *Solanaceæ*, native to Australia.

2. [d—] Duboisine.

dū-boi′sine, dū-boi′sin, *n.* In medicine, an alkaloid derived from *Duboisia myoporoides*.

dū′căl, *a.* [LL. *ducalis*, from L. *dux, ducis*, leader.] Pertaining to a duke, or to the estate of a duke; as, a *ducal* coronet.

dū′căl-ly, *adv.* After the fashion of a duke.

duç′ăt, *n.* [Fr. *ducat*; LL. *ducatus*, a ducat, duchy, from L. *dux, ducis*, a leader.]

1. Any of various coins of silver or gold formerly current in Europe; especially one coined by a duchy. The gold ducat of Austria is worth $2.287.

2. [*pl.*] Money. [Slang.]

duç-a-tọọn′, *n.* [Fr. *ducaton*; It. *ducatone*, from *ducato*, a ducat.] Formerly, a silver coin of Venice worth about 96 cents.

dū′cēṣ tē′çum. See *Subpœna duces tecum* under *Subpœna*.

duch′ess, *n.* [Fr. *duchesse*, from *duc*, a duke.] The consort or widow of a duke; also, a lady who has the sovereignty of a duchy in her own right.

duch′y, *n.*; *pl.* **duch′ieṣ.** [ME. *duchie, duchee*; OFr. *duchee, duchet*; LL. *ducatus*, the territory of a duke, from L. *dux, ducis*, a leader.] The territory or dominion of a duke; a dukedom.

duck, *n.* [D. *doek*, linen cloth, light canvas; Ice. *dukr*, cloth.]

1. A coarse cloth lighter than canvas, used for small sails, ticking of beds, etc.

2. [*pl.*] Light trousers or other clothing of such cloth.

duck, *n.* [Dan. *dukke*; Sw. *docka*; G. *docke*, a baby, a puppet.] A word of endearment or fondness.

duck, *n.* 1. A web-footed bird of the subfamily *Anatinæ*.

2. The female of this bird, in contradistinction to the male, known as the *drake*.

3. An abrupt jerking of the head or body downward; a plunge into or under water.

To make or *play ducks and drakes*; to skip a stone or other flat object along the surface of the water; hence, to risk one's fortune in such a way as to squander it foolishly.

Bombay duck; same as *Bummalo*.

duck, *v t.*; ducked (dukt), *pt., pp.*; ducking, *ppr.* [ME *duken, douken*; D. *duiken*; M.H.G. *tuchen*, to duck, dive, stoop.]

1. To dip or plunge into or under water; to souse; to wet by or as by immersion.

2. To bow, lower, or nod quickly, after the manner of a duck's head; to bob; as, to *duck* one's head from a blow.

duck, *v.i.* 1. To plunge one's head or body suddenly under a liquid, as water; to dip; to dive, usually for a short time only.

2. To drop the head suddenly; to bow; to cringe.

duck′=ant, *n.* A white Jamaican ant which makes nests in trees.

duck′bill, *n.* An oviparous, burrowing aquatic mammal, with webbed feet and a bill like that of a duck; the *Ornithorhynchus paradoxus*.

duck′=billed, *a.* Having a bill resembling that of a duck.

duck′ēr, *n.* One who or that which ducks.

duck′ēr-y, *n.*; *pl.* **duck′ēr-ieṣ.** A place for raising ducks.

duck′=hawk, *n.* The peregrine falcon.

duck′ing, *n.* The act of plunging or the state of being plunged under water; as, to get a *ducking*.

duck′ing, *n.* The sport of hunting ducks as game.

duck′ing=stọọl, *n.* A stool or chair in which common scolds were formerly tied and plunged into water.

duck′=legged, *a.* Having short legs.

duck′ling, *n.* A young duck.

duck'=mēat, duck's'=mēat, *n.* A plant of the genus *Lemna.* [See *Lemna.*]

Ducking-stool.

duck'=mōle, *n.* Same as *Duckbill.*

duck-oy', *n.* [Obs.] Same as *Decoy.*

duck's'=foot, *n.* The May-apple.

duck'=snipe, *n.* The willet.

duck'weed, *n.* Same as *Duckmeat.*

duct, *n.* [L. *ductus*, a leading, a conducting, from *ducere*, to lead.]

1. Any tube or canal by which a fluid is conducted or conveyed; specifically, (a) in anatomy, a tubular passage which conveys a fluid, as the blood, lymph, chyle, etc., especially the secretion of a gland; (b) in botany, a large tubular canal or cell.

2. Guidance; leading. [Obs.]

duc̦'ti-ble, *a.* Ductile. [Rare.]

duc̦'tile, *a.* [L. *ductilis*, from *ducere*, to lead.]

1. Easily influenced or led; complying; yielding to motives, persuasion, or instruction; as, the *ductile* minds of youth.

2. Capable of being drawn out into wire or thread; as, gold is a *ductile* metal.

duc̦'tile-ly, *adv.* In a ductile manner.

duc̦'tile-ness, *n.* The quality of being ductile.

duc̦-ti-lim'e-tēr, *n.* [L. *ductilis*, ductile, and *metrum*, measure.] An instrument by which the ductility of metals may be accurately determined.

duc̦-til'i-ty, *n.* [L. *ductilis*, from *ducere*, to lead.]

1. The property of solid bodies, particularly metals, which renders them capable of being extended by drawing without breaking.

2. Flexibility; ready compliance.

duc̦'tion, *n.* Guidance. [Obs.]

duct'less, *a.* Without a duct.

duc̦'tŏr, *n.* [L., from *ducere*, to lead.]

1. One who guides. [Obs.]

2. In a printing-press, a roller which conveys ink from a fountain to another roller.

3. In calico-printing, a knife which distributes color on or removes it from a roller.

duc̦'tūre, *n.* Guidance. [Obs.]

dud, *n.* 1. [*pl.*] Articles of clothing, implying poorness or scantiness; belongings. [Colloq.]

2. A rag. [Scot. or Obs.]

dud'dēr, *v.t.* and *v.i.* I. *v.t.* To confuse or stun with noise.

II. *v.i.* To tremble; to quake; to totter.

dud'dēr, *n.* A duffer. [Prov. Eng.]

dud'dēr-y, *n.*; *pl.* **dud'dēr-ieş.** A place for the purchase and sale of old clothes or rags. [Slang.]

dūde, *n.* A youth or man whose chief desire and aim is to be dressed in the height of fashion; a fop; a dandy; an exquisite.

dū-deen', *n.* [Ir.] A tobacco-pipe of clay having a short, straight stem; written also *dudheen.*

dudġ'eŏn (duj'un), *a.* Unpolished; uncultured; coarse. [Obs.]

dudġ'eŏn, *n.* [W. *dygen*, anger, grudge.] Anger; resentment; ill will; discord.

dudġ'eŏn, *n.* [D. *duig*, a stave.]

1. The wood of the root of the box-tree or any mottled wood used for dagger-handles.

2. The handle of a dagger; also, the dagger itself.

dūd'ish, *a.* Resembling or having the character of a dude.

dū'e, *a.* [It.] In music, two.

Due corde; two strings; for a stringed instrument, a direction to use two strings simultaneously in playing a note.

Due volte; two times; twice.

dūe (dū), *a.* [ME. *due*; OFr. *deu*; Fr. *dû*, pp. of *devoir*, to owe; L. *debere*, to owe.]

1. Owed; that ought to be paid or done to another; owed and already matured; as, the note is *due.*

2. Proper; fit; appropriate; suitable; becoming; required by the circumstances; as, the event was celebrated with *due* solemnities.

3. Seasonable; as, he will come in *due* time.

4. Exact; proper; as, musicians keep *due* time.

5. Owing; attributable; followed by *to*; as, his death was *due to* an accident.

6. Required or expected to arrive or to have arrived or to be present, before the time specified; as, two mails are now *due.*

dūe, *adv.* Directly; exactly, as, a *due* east course.

dūe, *n.* 1. That which is owed; that which one should or must pay, do, or perform to another; a toll, fee, or charge.

2. Just title; right. [Obs.]

dūe, *v.t.* To endue. [Obs.]

dūe'bill, *n.* A statement in writing given by a debtor to a creditor acknowledging certain indebtedness, but not specifying any time for payment.

dūe'fụl, *a.* Fit; becoming. [Obs.]

dū'el, *v.t.* and *v.i.* To fight in single combat.

dū'el, *n.* [Fr. *duel*; It. *duello*, from L. *duellum*, old form of *bellum*, war, from *duo*, two.]

1. Single combat; a premeditated combat between two persons with deadly weapons.

2. Any contention or contest between two parties.

dū'el-ēr, dū'el-lēr, *n.* A duelist. [Obs.]

dū'el-ing, dū'el-ling, *a.* and *n.* I. *a.* Pertaining to or employed in a duel.

II. *n.* The act or practice of fighting in single combat.

dū'el-ist, dū'el-list, *n.* One who fights, or maintains the propriety of fighting duels.

dū-el'lō, *n.* [It.] 1. A duel. [Obs.]

2. The practice or rules of dueling. [Obs.]

dụ-e'ñä, *n.* Same as *Duenna.*

dūe'ness, *n.* Fitness; propriety.

dū-en'nȧ, *n.* [Sp. *dueña*, *dona*, from L. *domina*, a mistress, lady.] An elderly woman who is kept to guard a younger; formerly, a governess of the young ladies in a Spanish or Portuguese family.

dū-et', *n.* [It. *duetto*, from L. *duo*, two.] A piece of music composed for two performers, whether vocal or instrumental.

dụ-et-tī'nō, *n.* [It., dim. of *duetto*, a duet.] A short duet of simple arrangement.

dụ-et'tō, *n.* [It.] A duet.

duff, *v.t.* In Australia, to acquire (stock) by stealing and altering the brands; as, to *duff* a cow or a horse. [Slang.]

duff, *n.* [Another form of *dough*, with *gh* sounded as *f.*]

1. A paste or dough made of flour. [Prov. Eng.]

2. A pudding made by boiling flour in a bag.

3. The vegetable matter which covers the ground in a forest, as leaves, twigs, dead logs, etc.

4. Small-sized coal.

duf-fä-där', *n.* [E. Ind.] A petty officer of some kind, as a noncommissioned officer, a boss, foreman, or the like.

duff'=dāy, *n.* On shipboard, the day on which sailors are served with duff, usually Sunday.

duf'fel, *n.* Same as *Duffle.*

duf'fēr, *n.* [From Scot. *duffart*, *doofart*, a dull, stupid fellow.] A person of but little wit or ability; one who plods along seemingly in the performance of important duties, yet lacking grasp and efficiency; a fogy.

duf'fēr, *n.* [Prov. Eng.] A peddler of cheap, flashy articles; also, something worthless.

duf'fil, *n.* [Obs.] Same as *Duffle.*

duf'fing, *n.* The body of a fisherman's artificial fly.

duf'fle, *n.* [D. *duffle*; L.G. *duffel*, a kind of cloth, from *Duffel*, a town near Antwerp.]

1. A kind of coarse woolen cloth, having a thick nap or frieze.

2. The outfit of a sportsman while camping.

dū-fren'īte, *n.* [From *Dufrenoy*, French mineralogist.] A mineral, hydrous iron phosphate, of dark green color.

duf'tēr, *n.* In British India, official papers in a bundle.

dug, *v.*, past tense and past participle of *dig.*

dug, *n.* [From same stem as Sw. *dægga*, Dan. *dægge*, to suckle.] The pap or nipple of an animal that suckles; applied to that of a woman only in contempt.

dū-gong', *n.* [Malay.] A herbivorous, cetaceous animal of the Indian ocean, with a tapering body ending in a crescent-shaped or two-lobed fin; also written *duyong.*

dug'out, *n.* 1. A canoe made by hollowing a log to a shell.

2. A rough structure, primarily an excavation, as in a sidehill; often made by digging vertically into the ground and covering the cavity with a rude framework and sod. *Dugouts* are used for temporary houses, for storage, or commonly as cyclone-cellars. [Middle and Western U. S.] In the World War, used for storage of supplies and for protection against gun-fire, etc.

dug'wāy, *n.* A road made by digging.

dūke, *n.* [ME. *duke*, *duk*, *duc*; OFr. *duc*, *dux*; L. *dux*, a leader, general.]

1. In Great Britain, one of the highest order of nobility; a title of honor or nobility next below the princes and the archbishops; as, the *duke* of Bedford.

2. In some Continental countries, a sovereign prince, without the title of king; as, the *duke* of Parma.

3. A chief; a prince. [Obs.]

4. [*pl.*] Fists. [Slang.]

Coronet of a Duke.

dūke, *v.i.* To act the duke. [Rare.]

dūke'dŏm, *n.* 1. The seigniory or territory of a duke; a duchy.

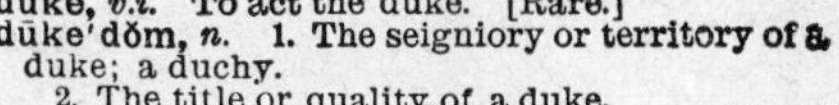

2. The title or quality of a duke.

dūke'ling, *n.*, diminutive of *duke.*

dūke'ship, *n.* The state of being a duke; the person of a duke.

Dụ'khō-bọr (dụ'kō-), *n.* One of the Dukhoboretsi.

Dụ-khō-bō'ret-si (dụ-kō-), *n.pl.* [Russ.] A peculiar religious sect, inhabiting the region of the Caucasus, who deny the divinity of Christ. They have no fixed place or form of worship and no authorized ministry. In the '90's numbers emigrated to Cyprus and Manitoba. In 1903 the Canadian government was obliged to restrain the sect from making fanatical pilgrimages in search of Christ; also written *Dukhobors.*

dul-ç̇ȧ-mä'rȧ, *n.* A plant, the bittersweet.

dul-ç̇ȧ-mä'rin, *n.* [L. *dulcis*, sweet, and *amarus*, bitter.] A glucoside derived from *Solanum Dulcamara*, the bittersweet.

dulce, *v.t.* To sweeten. [Obs.]

dulce, *a.* and *n.* [L. *dulcis*, sweet.]

I. *a.* Sweet; pleasing; gentle. [Obs.]

II. *n.* Any of various sweet articles, as a bonbon, sweet wine, candied fruit, etc.

dulce'ness, *n.* Sweetness; softness. [Obs.]

dul'cet, *a.* [L. *dulcis*, sweet.]

1. Sweet to the taste; luscious.

2. Sweet to the ear; melodious; harmonious; as, *dulcet* sounds; *dulcet* symphonies.

3. Sweet or pleasing to the mind.

dul-ci-an'ȧ, *n.* [LL., from L. *dulcis*, sweet.] In music, a soft, sweet-toned organ-stop.

dul″ci-fi-c̦ā'tion, *n.* The act of sweetening.

dul-cif'lụ-ous, *a.* [LL. *dulcifluus*; *dulcis*, sweet, and *fluere*, to flow.] Flowing sweetly. [Rare.]

dul'ci-fȳ, *v.t.*; dulcified, *pt.*, *pp.*; dulcifying, *ppr.* [Fr. *dulcifier*; LL. *dulcificare*; L. *dulcis*, sweet, and *-ficare*, from *facere*, to make.] To sweeten; to free from acidity, saltness, or acrimony; to mollify.

Dulcified spirits; a compound of alcohol with mineral acids; as, *dulcified spirits* of niter.

dul-cil'ō-quy (-kwi), *n.* Softness in speaking. [Obs.]

dul'ci-mēr, *n.* [OFr. *doulcimer*; It. *dolcemele*, a musical instrument; L. *dulce melos*; *dulce*, neut. of *dulcis*, sweet, and *melos*, from Gr. *melos*, a song, strain.]

Italian Dulcimer.

1. An instrument of music strung with wires which are played upon with padded hammers.

2. In Biblical history, a sort of bagpipe, composed of two pipes connected with a leather sack.

dul'cin, *n.* Same as *Dulcitol.*

dul-cin'ē-ȧ, *n.* A mistress of one's affections; from Don Quixote's *Dulcinea* del Toboso.

dul'ci-ness, *n.* Softness; easiness of temper. [Obs.]

dul-ci'nō (-chē'nō), *n.* Same as *Dolciano.*

dul'ci-tăn, *n.* [*Dulcite* and *-an.*] An alcohol, $C_6H_{12}O_5$, derived from dulcitol by heating.

dul'cīte, *n.* Same as *Dulcitol.*

dul'ci-tōl, *n.* [*Dulcite* and *-ol.*] A saccharine, crystalline isomer of mannite, $C_6H_{14}O_6$, found in various plants; called commercially, when crude, *Madagascar manna.*

dul'ci-tūde, *n.* [L. *dulcitudo*, from *dulcis*, sweet.] Sweetness. [Rare.]

dul'cō-rāte, *v.t.* [LL. *dulcoratus*, pp. of *dulcorare*, to sweeten; L. *dulcis*, sweet.] To sweeten; to make less acrimonious. [Rare.]

dul-c̦ō-rā'tion, *n.* The act of sweetening. [Rare.]

dū'ledge (-lej), *n.* In mechanics, a peg of wood which joins the ends of the six fellies that form the round of the wheel of a gun-carriage.

dū-lī'ȧ, *n.* [LL., from Gr. *douleia*, service, from *doulos*, a slave.] In the Roman Catholic church, an inferior kind of worship or adoration; veneration due to saints and angels; distinguished from *latria.*

dull, *a.*; *comp.* duller; *superl.* dullest. [ME. *dull*, *dul*; AS. *dol*, foolish, stupid.]

1. Stupid; doltish; blockish; slow of understanding; as, a lad of *dull* mind.

2. Heavy; sluggish; without life or spirit; as, a surfeit leaves a man very *dull.*

> Somewhat *duller* than at first,
> I sit (my empty glass reversed).—Tennyson.

3. Slow of motion; sluggish; as, a *dull* stream.

4. Wanting sensibility or keenness in some of the senses; not quick; as, *dull* of hearing; *dull* of seeing.

> You never would hear it; your ears are so *dull.* —Tennyson.

5. Sleepy; drowsy.

6. Sad; melancholy; depressing; dismal.

Fly, fly, profane fogs . . .
With your *dull* influence. —Crashaw.

7. Gross; inanimate; insensible.

8. Not pleasing or delightful; not exhilarating; cheerless.

The *dull*, tame shore. —Procter.

9. Not bright or clear; clouded; tarnished; as, the mirror is *dull*.

10. Not bright; not briskly burning; not vivid; dim; obscure; as, a *dull* fire; a *dull* light.

11. Blunt; obtuse; having a thick edge.

The murderous knife was *dull* and blunt.
—Shak.

12. Cloudy; overcast; not clear; not enlivening; as, *dull* weather.

Syn.—Stupid, stolid, doltish, sluggish, slow, sleepy, drowsy, lifeless, insipid, tiresome, commonplace, uninteresting, prosy, prosaic, turbid, tarnished, blunt, obtuse.

dull, *v.t.*; dulled, *pt.*, *pp.*; dulling, *ppr.* 1. To make dull; to stupefy; to blunt; to render less acute; to damp; to cloy; to pall; to render lifeless; to make less eager.

Those (drugs) she has
Will stupefy and *dull* the sense awhile.
—Shak.

2. To make sad or melancholy.

The people are all *dulled*
With this usurping king. —Beau. and Fl.

3. To make insensible or slow to perceive; as, to *dull* the ears; to *dull* the wits.

4. To make heavy or slow of motion; as, to *dull* industry.

5. To render dim; to sully; to tarnish or cloud; as, the breath *dulls* a mirror.

dull, *v.i.* To become dull, in any sense.

dull, *n.* and *v.i.* [Southern U. S.]

I. *n.* A snare used to catch fish.

II. *v.i.* To use a dull in fishing.

dull'ărd, *n.* A person slow of apprehension.

dull'ărd, *a.* Dull; slow of apprehension.

dull'-brāined, *a.* Stupid.

dull'-browed, *a.* Having a gloomy look.

dull'ẽr, *n.* One who or that which dulls.

dull'-eyed (-īd), *a.* Having a stupid look.

dull'head (-hed), *n.* A dolt; a blockhead.

dull'ish, *a.* Rather dull.

dull'ness, dul'ness, *n.* The state or condition of being dull in any sense.

dull'-sight"ed, *a.* Having imperfect sight.

dull'-wit"ted, *a.* Having a dull intellect.

dul'ly, *adv.* In a dull and lifeless manner.

dū-loc'ră-cy, *n.* See *Doulocracy.*

dulse, *n.* [Gael. *duileasg*; *duille*, a leaf, and *uisge*, water.] A kind of seaweed belonging to the suborder *Ceramiaceæ*, the *Rhodymenia palmata*, used in some parts of Scotland for food.

dul'wil-ly, *n.* [Prov. Eng.] A bird, the ring-plover.

dū'ly, *adv.* [From *due* and *-ly*.] Properly; fitly; in a suitable or becoming manner or time; as, he *duly* attended church.

Dū'mä, Dou'mä, *n.* [Rus.] The lower branch of the Russian parliament, created Aug. 19, 1905, consisting of representatives elected for five years by the people.

dū'măl, *a.* [LL. *dumalis*, from L. *dumus*, a bramble.] Beset with bushes or brambles; bushy.

du-mas'in, *n.* [Named after J. B. *Dumas*, a French chemist.] A colorless volatile oil, $C_6H_{10}O$, formed along with acetone by destructive distillation of acetates.

dumb (dum), *a.* [AS. *dumb*; Ice. *dumbr*, mute; D. *dom*; L.G. *dum*; Dan. *dum*, stupid, dull.]

1. Destitute of the power of speech; not able to make articulate sounds; as, the *dumb* brutes.

2. Mute; silent; not speaking; not accompanied with speech; as, *dumb* with wonder; a *dumb* show.

3. Not bright; as, a *dumb* white. [Rare.]

4. Destitute of some ordinary accompaniment or characteristic; as, a *dumb* barge, without sails; a *dumb* ague, without the usual chills.

5. Without clearness of perception; as, a *dumb* pupil.

Dumb show; pantomime.

To strike dumb; to confound; to astonish; to render silent with astonishment.

dumb, *v.t.* To silence. [Obs.]

dumb'-bell, *n.* A weight used for exercise; usually made in the form of two balls connected by a rigid handle.

Dumb-bell.

dumb'-cāke, *n.* A cake made on St. Mark's eve in silence, by which a maid attempts to learn who is to be her husband.

dumb'-cāne, *n.* A plant, *Dieffenbachia Seguine*, growing in the West Indies, which, upon being chewed, causes swelling of the tongue, and thus produces loss of speech.

dumb'found, *v.t.* See *Dumfound.*

dum'ble-dōre, *n.* [Prov. Eng.] 1. A cockchafer.

2. The common bumblebee.

dumb'ly (dum'ly), *adv.* Mutely; silently.

dumb'ness, *n.* Muteness; silence; incapacity to speak.

dumb'-wāit'ẽr, *n.* 1. A framework with shelves, placed between a kitchen and dining-room, for conveying food, etc. When the kitchen is in the basement, the dumb-waiter is made to rise and fall by means of pulleys and weights.

2. A revolving stand for dishes. [Eng.]

dum'dum-bul"let, *n.* [So called from *Dumdum*, in India, where bullets are made for the English army.] A bullet shaped so that it will expand when it strikes, thus causing so great a shock that the wounded man will be compelled to stop advancing. It is intended to cause a lacerated wound that will either kill or permanently disable, being used against savages, but not countenanced by military authorities.

dū'me-tōse, *a.* Resembling a bush.

dum'found, *v.t.*; dumfounded, *pt.*, *pp.*; dumfounding, *ppr.* To strike dumb; to confuse; also spelled *dumbfound.*

dum'found-ẽr, dumb'found-ẽr, *v.t.* To dumfound. [Rare.]

dum'mȧ-dōr, *n.* Same as *Dumbledore.*

dum'mẽr-ẽr, *n.* One who feigns dumbness. [Obs.]

dum'my, *a.* 1. Mute. [Obs.]

2. Imitative; sham; as, a *dummy* sign.

dum'my, *n.*; *pl.* **dum'mies**. 1. One who is dumb. [Colloq.]

2. An actor who plays a silent part.

3. A dumb-waiter.

4. A locomotive, furnished with condensing engines, and hence without the noise of escaping steam.

5. The name given by firemen to the jets from the mains, or chief water-pipes.

6. A hatter's pressing iron.

7. The fourth or exposed hand when three persons play whist; also, a game at whist when there are only three playing.

8. A general name for a class of objects which are not what their appearance indicates, but do service for real ones; as (a) empty drawers or bottles in a drug store, or sham packages, etc., in other stores, generally made up so as to have the appearance of containing goods; (b) a lay-figure on which clothing, styles of dressing hair, etc., are exhibited; (c) one of various signs appropriate to some line of trade, as a false roll of carpet, a paper ham, a wooden book, etc.; (d) an abridged sample book for canvassing; (e) the preliminary make-up of a book or paper before being printed.

Double dummy; a game at whist with only two players, each having a hand exposed.

dū'mōse, dū'mous, *a.* [L. *dumosus*, bushy, from *dumus*, a bramble.]

1. Having many bushes and brambles.

2. Bushy in form.

dump, *n.* [Dan. *dump*; G. *dumpf*, damp, musty, dull; Sw. *dumpin*, melancholy; D. *dompig*, dull, musty.]

1. A dull, gloomy state of the mind; sadness; melancholy; sorrow; only in the plural.

2. Absence of mind; revery. [Obs.]

3. A tune or air. [Obs.]

dump, *n.* 1. A thump or thud, as of something heavy falling.

2. A place where refuse is deposited; also, the refuse itself; especially, the pile near the mouth of a shaft.

3. A rude leaden counter formerly used by boys in playing certain games. [Eng.]

4. A coin once used in Australia.

5. [*pl.*] Money. [Slang.]

dump, *v.t.*; dumped, *pt.*, *pp.*; dumping, *ppr.* [ME. *dumpen*, to fall down, throw down; Dan. *dumpe*; Sw. *dimpa*, to fall suddenly, to rush.]

1. To empty or to unload in a mass; as, to *dump* a load of gravel.

2. To knock with violence. [Prov. Eng.]

3. To make into a compact bale, as wool. [Australia.]

dump, *v.i.* 1. In printing, to lift type from a stick when set and put it into a galley, form, etc.

2. To get rid of a load by unloading it in a mass.

3. To plunge abruptly downward. [Obs.]

dump'āġe, *n.* The act or privilege of dumping; the material dumped or the fee paid for dumping.

dump'-cärt, *n.* A tipcart.

dump'ish, *a.* Dull; stupid; sad; melancholy.

dump'ish-ly, *adv.* In a moping manner.

dump'ish-ness, *n.* The state of being dumpish.

dum'ple, *v.t.* To crumple. [Rare.]

dump'ling, *n.* 1. A kind of pudding or mass of paste, boiled or baked; usually, a cover of paste inclosing fruit and boiled; as, *apple-dumpling.*

2. A dwarf. [Prov. Eng.]

dump'y, *a.*; *comp.* dumpier; *superl.* dumpiest.

1. Short and thick.

2. Petulant; sulky; dumpish.

dump'y-lev"el, *n.* A spirit-level having a short telescope with a large aperture, and a compass, used for surveying purposes. [Eng.]

dun, *a.* [AS. *dun*, *dunn*, from W. *dwn*, dun, dusky, swarthy.] Of a dark color; of a color partaking of a brown and black; of a dull brown color; swarthy.

Dun crow; the hooded crow.

Dun diver; the merganser.

dun, *v.t.*; dunned, *pt.*, *pp.*; dunning, *ppr.* [ME. *dunnen*; AS. *dynian*, to make a noise, from *dyne*, Ice. *dynr*, *duna*, a noise, thunder.] Literally, to clamor for payment of (a debt); hence, to demand a debt from in a pressing manner; to urge for payment with importunity.

dun, *v.t.* To cure, as fish, in a manner to give a dun color.

dun, *n.* 1. A person who duns for payment.

2. An urgent request or demand for payment in writing; as, he sent his debtor a *dun.*

dun, *n.* [AS. *dun*, a hill.] An eminence or mound; found in place names, as *Dun*dee, or as *don-*, in *Don*egal.

dun'bīrd, *n.* A dun-colored bird; (a) the ruddy duck; (b) the pochard; (c) the female of the scaup-duck.

dunce, *n.* [From *Duns* Scotus, called the "Subtle Doctor," leader of the schoolmen of the thirteenth century, and opposed to the revival of classical learning. His followers were called *Dunsmen*, *Duncemen*, and ultimately simply *Dunses*, *Dunces*. The word came to be applied to any opponent of education, and then to stupid persons in general.] A person of weak intellect; a blockhead; one slow of apprehension.

dunce'dŏm, *n.* The figurative domain of dunces; dunces collectively. [Humorous.]

dun'cẽr-y, *n.* Dullness; stupidity.

dunch, *v.t.* and *v.i.* [Scot. or Prov. Eng.] To jog or push with the elbow.

dun'ci-căl, *a.* Dunce-like.

dun'ci-fȳ, *v.t.* To render stupid. [Rare.]

dun'cish, *a.* Rather dunce-like. [Rare.]

dun'cish-ness, *n.* Stupidity; folly. [Rare.]

dun'dẽr, *n.* [Sp. *redundar*; L. *redundare*, to overflow.] Lees; dregs; especially cane-juice dregs.

The use of *dunder* in the making of rum answers the purpose of yeast in the fermentation of flour. —Edwards.

dun'dẽr-fuñk, *n.* Hardtack soaked in water, mixed with sweetening and fat, and baked; so called by sailors.

dun'dẽr-head (-hed), *n.* A dull-brained fellow.

dun'dẽr-head"ed, *a.* Dull-brained and obstinate.

dun'dẽr-pāte, *n.* Same as *Dunderhead.*

dūne, *n.* [Scot.] An ancient fort with a domed or conical roof.

dūne, *n.* [Fr. *dune*; AS. *dun*, a hill, fortified hill; Gael. *dun*; W. *din*, a hill.] A low hill of drifted or drifting sand, on or near the coast of a sea or large lake.

dun'fish, *n.* Codfish cured by dunning.

dung, *v.t.*; dunged, *pt.*, *pp.*; dunging, *ppr.* [ME. *dungen*; AS. ge-*dyngan*, to manure, dung, from *dunge*, dung, manure.]

1. To cover with dung, as a fertilizer.

2. In calico-printing, to subject (the fabric) to a solution of cow-dung to remove the excess of mordant.

dung, *v.i.* To discharge excrement.

dung, *n.* [ME. *dung*; AS. *dung*, *dyng*; O.H.G. *tunge*; Gr. *dung*, dung; Dan. *dynge*, a heap, mass.] The excrement of animals.

duñ-gȧ-ree', *n.* [Anglo-Ind.] A coarse cotton cloth used for making the clothes of sailors.

dung'-bee"tle, *n.* Any beetle laying its eggs in dung upon which the larvæ feed, as the tumblebug.

dung'-bīrd, *n.* A bird, the jager.

dun'ġeŏn, *n.* [ME. *dungeon*, *dongon*; OFr. *dongeon*, *donjon*; Pr. *donjon*; LL. *domnio*, dungeon, tower, a contr. of *dominio*, domain, possession, from L. *dominus*, lord.] A donjon; hence, a prison or place of confinement; especially, a subterranean chamber or other dark and gloomy place of incarceration; a close prison.

dun'ġeŏn, *v.t.* To confine in a dungeon. [Rare.]

dung'-flȳ, *n.* A dung-eating insect of the genus *Scatophaga.*

dung'fork, *n.* A fork, having four or more tines, used in handling dung.

dung'hill, *n.* 1. A heap of dung.

2. A mean or vile abode or condition.

Dunghill fowl; a mongrel domestic fowl.

dung'mēre, *n.* A manure-pit. [Prov. Eng.]

dung'y, *a.* Full of dung; filthy; vile.

dung'yärd, *n.* A yard where dung is collected.

dun'īte, *n.* [Named from *Dun* Mountain, New Zealand.] An igneous rock consisting chiefly of chrysolite.

dun-i-was'săl, dun-nie-was'săl, *n.* [Scot.] A gentleman of secondary rank, as a cadet of the nobility.

duñ-kȧ-dōō', *n.* [An imitative word.] The bittern. [Local, U. S.]

Duñ'kärd, *n.* A Dunker.

Duñ'kẽr, *n.* [G. *tunker*, a dipper, from *tunken*,

to dip.] A member of a German-American religious sect practising various primitive rites, as the laying on of hands, washing of the feet before the eucharist, the kiss of charity, and triple immersion. Called also *German Baptist*, *Dunkard*, *Dipper*, and *Tunker*.

Seventh-day Dunkers; a sect of Dunkers observing Saturday as their Sabbath.

dun′lin, *n.* [A corruption of *dunling*; *dun*, dark brown, and dim. *-ling*.] A bird, the red-backed sandpiper.

dun′nāge, *n.* Filling, usually of fagots, loose wood, or the like, used about or below a ship's cargo to prevent shifting or damage in transit; by extension, baggage.

dun′nẽr, *n.* One who duns.

dun′nish, *a.* Somewhat dun.

dunn′īte, *n.* A picric acid explosive for projectiles, invented by and named for Major B. W. Dunn.

dun′nŏck, *n.* [Local, Eng.] The hedge-sparrow.

dun′ny, *a.* [Local, Eng.] Deaf; dull of apprehension.

dun′pic″kle, *n.* [Local, Eng.] A bird, the moor-buzzard.

dunt, *n.* [Scot. and Prov. Eng.]

1. The staggers, a sheep-disease.
2. A stroke; a blow.

dunt, *v.t.* [Scot. and Prov. Eng.] To strike, knock, or jolt.

dun′tẽr, *n.* [Scot.] 1. The eider-duck.

2. A porpoise.

dun′tẽr-goose, *n.* Same as *Dunter*, 1.

dū′ō, *n.* [L., two.] A duet.

dū-ō-dec-ă-hē′drăl, dū-ō-dec-ă-hē′drŏn. See *Dodecahedral*, *Dodecahedron*.

dū″ō-dē-cen′ni-ăl, *a.* [L. *duodecim*, twelve.] Made up of twelve years.

dū-ō-dec′i-măl, *a.* [L. *duodecim*, twelve.] Proceeding in computation by twelves.

dū-ō-dec′i-măl, *n.* 1. A member of a duodecimal system.

2. [*pl.*] In arithmetic, a kind of multiplication in which the denominations proceed by twelves.

dū-ō-dec′i-măl-ly, *adv.* By twelves.

dū-ō-dec′im-fid, *a.* [L. *duodecim*, twelve, and *findere*, to cleave.] Divided into twelve parts.

dū-ō-dec′i-mō, *a.* [L. *duodecim*, twelve.] Having or consisting of twelve leaves to a sheet, or of twelve or twenty-four pages to a form; having pages measuring about 4½ by 7½ inches; as, a *duodecimo* size. Usually written *12mo*, or *12°*.

dū-ō-dec′i-mō, *n.* Originally, a book in which a sheet was folded into twelve leaves; hence, a book having pages measuring about 4½ by 7½ inches, without regard to manner of folding.

dū-ō-dec′ū-ple, *a.* [L. *duo*, two, and *decuplus*, tenfold.] Consisting of twelves.

dū-ō-dē′nȧ, *n.*, pl. of *duodenum*.

dū-ō-dē′năl, *a.* Of or relating to the duodenum.

dū″ō-dē-nī′tis, *n.* Inflammation of the duodenum.

dū″ō-dē-not′ō-my, *n.* [*Duodenum*, and *-tomy*, from Gr. *tomē*, a cutting.] A cutting into the duodenum.

dū-ō-dē′num, *n.* [From L. *duodeni*, twelve each, so called because its length is about twelve fingers' breadth.] The first of the small intestines, the twelve-inch intestine.

dū-ō-lit′ẽr-ăl, *a.* [L. *duo*, two, and *litera*, a letter.] Consisting of two letters only; biliteral.

dū′ō-logue (-log), *n.* [L. *duo*; Gr. *dyo*, two, and *logos*, a word, story.] A dialogue for two persons only.

duō′mō (dwō′), *n.* [It.] A cathedral.

dup, *v.t.* [For *do up*.] To open; as, to *dup* a door. [Obs.]

dūp′ȧ-ble, *a.* Susceptible of being duped.

dūpe, *n.* [Fr. *dupe*, a dupe; OFr. *dupe*, *duppe*, the hoopoe, a stupid bird.] A person who is deceived; one easily led astray by his credulity; as, the *dupe* of a party.

dūpe, *v.t.*; duped (dūpt), *pt.*, *pp.*; duping, *ppr.* [Fr. *duper*, to dupe, take in, from *dupe*, one easily taken in.] To deceive; to trick; to mislead by imposing on one's credulity.

dūp′ẽr, *n.* One who dupes.

dūp′ẽr-y, *n.* The act or practice of duping.

dū′pi-ŏn, *n.* [Fr. *doupion*; It. *doppione*, from *doppio*; L. *duplus*, double.] A double cocoon, formed by two silkworms.

dū′ple, *a.* [L. *duplus*, double.] Double.

Duple ratio; that in which the antecedent term is double the consequent, as of 2 to 1.

dū′plex, *a.* [L. *duplex*, double, twofold; *duo*, two, and *plicare*, to fold.]

1. Of two parts; two at a time; in two ways.
2. In electricity, designating multiple telegraphy in which one wire is used to transmit two messages simultaneously. The term *duplex* is generic, comprehending any double use of such a wire with the essential instruments; *diplex* and *contraplex* are specific, the former designating simultaneous transmission of two messages in the same direction, while the latter denotes opposite simultaneous transmission.

dū′plex, *v.t.* and *v.i.* I. *v.t.* To arrange (a wire, system, etc.) for duplex telegraphy.

II. *v.i.* To operate a duplex system.

dū′pli-cāte, *a.* [L. *duplicatus*, from *duplicare*, to double.] Double; twofold.

Duplicate proportion or *ratio*; the proportion or ratio of squares. Thus, in geometrical proportion, the first term to the third is said to be in a *duplicate* ratio of the first to the second, or as its square is to the square of the second. Thus, in 2, 4, 8, 16, the ratio of 2 to 8 is a *duplicate* of that of 2 to 4, or as the square of 2 is to the square of 4.

dū′pli-cāte, *n.* 1. Another corresponding to the first in all essentials or exactly; a second thing of the same kind; a copy; a transcript.

2. In law, one of two or more writings or documents containing the same matter and having equal force and validity; as, a lease made in *duplicate*.

dū′pli-cāte, *v.t.*; duplicated, *pt.*, *pp.*; duplicating, *ppr.* [L. *duplicatus*, pp. of *duplicare*, to double.]

1. To double; to obtain or make a copy, transcript, or duplicate of.
2. In biology, to sever, spontaneously or in due process of development, into two.

dū-pli-cā′tion, *n.* 1. The act of doubling; the state of being folded over or duplicated.

2. In biology, the spontaneous division of one cell into two.
3. In botany, chorisis.
4. A doubling; a fold. [Rare.]
5. Celebration of the eucharist by the same priest twice in one day.

Duplication of the cube; see *Delian problem* under *Delian*.

dū′pli-cā-tive, *a.* 1. Characterized by duplication.

2. In biology, of or formed by duplication.

dū′pli-cā-tūre, *n.* A doubling or folding, as of the peritoneum. [Rare.]

dū″pli-ci-den′tāte, *a.* [L. *duplex*, *duplicis*, double, and *dens*, *dentis*, a tooth.] Having a double set of incisors, two in front and two behind, as in the rabbit.

dū-plic′i-ty, *n.*; *pl.* **dū-plic′i-ties.** [Fr. *duplicité*; LL. *duplicitas* (*-atis*), from L. *duplex* (*-icis*), double.]

1. Doubleness. [Rare.]
2. Doubleness of heart or speech; the act or practice of exhibiting a different or contrary conduct, or uttering different or contrary sentiments, at different times, in relation to the same thing; doubledealing.
3. In law, the pleading of two or more distinct matters in the same count.

dup′pẽr, *n.* Same as second *Dubber*.

dūr, *a.* [G. *dur*, from L. *durus*, hard.] In music, major; as, D *dur*.

dū′rȧ, *n.* [F. of L. *durus*, hard.] In anatomy, the dura mater.

dū-rȧ-bil′i-ty, *n.* [LL. *durabilitas*, from L. *durabilis*, lasting, durable.] The power of lasting or continuing in any given state without perishing; as, the *durability* of oak timber.

dū′rȧ-ble, *a.* [L. *durabilis*, from *durare*, to harden; *durus*, hard.] Having the quality of lasting or continuing long in being, without perishing or wearing out; as, *durable* cloth; *durable* happiness.

Syn.—Enduring, lasting, permanent.—*Durable* respects the texture of bodies and marks their capacity to hold out; *lasting* signifies to remain the last or longest, and is applicable only to that which is supposed of the longest duration. *Permanent* signifies remaining to the end. *Durable* is usually said of material substances, and *lasting* of those which are spiritual; *permanent* applies more to the affairs of men.

dū′rȧ-ble-ness, *n.* Power of lasting; durability.

dū′rȧ-bly, *adv.* In a lasting manner.

dū′răl, *a.* In anatomy, relating to or derived from the dura mater.

dū′rȧ mā′tẽr. [L.] The outer membrane of the brain and spinal cord.

dū-rā′men, *n.* [L., hardness, from *durare*, to harden.] The central layers or heartwood of the trunk or branches of an exogenous tree.

dūr′ănce, *n.* [OFr. *durance*; L. *durans*, ppr. of *durare*, to harden, to last.]

1. Imprisonment; restraint of the person.
2. Continuance; duration. [Obs.]
3. Durable material of any kind, as buff leather. [Obs.]

dūr′ăn-cy, *n.* Continuance; durance. [Obs.]

dūr′ănt, *n.* Same as *Durance*, 3.

dū-ran′te, *prep.* [L., abl. ppr. of *durare*, to harden, last.] During; as, *durante vita*, during life; *durante bene placito*, during pleasure.

dū-rā′tion, *n.* Continuance in time; length of existence; the period during which a thing continues.

dūr′ȧ-tive, *a.* Implying or expressing continuance. [Rare.]

dūr′bär, *n.* [Anglo-Ind.] 1. An audience-room of a governing officer in India.

2. An audience, levee, or state reception held by the viceroy of India or by a native prince; also written *darbar*.

dūre, *a.* Rough; rigorous; irksome. [Obs.]

dūre, *v.i.* and *v.t.* [OFr *durer*; L. *durare*, to harden, last.] To last; to hold on in time or being; to continue; to endure. [Obs.]

dūre′fụl, *a.* Lasting. [Obs.]

dūre′less, *a.* Not lasting; fading. [Obs.]

dū′rēne, *n.* [L. *durus*, hard.] A coal-tar derivative, $C_{10}H_{14}$, of crystalline structure.

dū′ress (*or* dū-res′), *n.* [ME. *duresse*, *duresce*; OFr. *durece*, *duresse*; L. *duritia*, hardness, harshness, from *durus*, hard.]

1. Hardness. [Obs.]
2. Constraint; imprisonment; restraint of liberty.
3. The state of compulsion or necessity in which a person is induced, by the restraint of his liberty or menace of bodily harm, to execute a deed, or do any legal act, or to commit a misdemeanor.

dū-ress′, *v.t.* To place under duress. [Obs.]

dū-ress′ŏr, *n.* In law, one who places another under duress.

Dụr′gȧ, *n.* [Anglo-Ind.] A Hindu divinity; one of the names given to the consort of Siva, other names being *Devi*, *Kali*, *Parvati*, *Bhavani*, *Uma*, etc. She is the Amazon champion and protectress of the gods, and has been compared to the Hera (Juno), and the Pallas or armed Athene of the Greeks. She is generally represented with ten arms; also spelled *Doorga*.

Durga, from Coleman's Hindu Mythology.

Dụr′hăm (dụr′ăm), *n.* One of a breed of cattle, short-horned and noted as beef producers, coming originally from the county of Durham, England. Used also attributively.

dū′ri-ăn, *n.* The fruit of *Durio Zibethinus*; also the tree itself. [See *Durio*.]

dūr′ing, *prep.* [ME. *duringe*, prep., originally ppr. of *dure*, to last, continue; OFr. *durant*; L. *durare*, to harden, to last; *durus*, hard, lasting.] In or throughout the time or existence of; as, he came *during* the day; it continued *during* the whole hour.

Dū′ri-ō, *n.* [From Malay *duryon*, the durian.] A genus of trees of the mallow family. *Durio Zibethinus*, the durian, is the only species, being a large and lofty tree growing in the Malayan archipelago. The large flowers, of a yellow-green color, are produced on the stem or main branches, and are followed by the large fetid fruit, which is of the size of a man's head, and is a favorite food of the natives during the time (May and June) when it is in season.

dū′ri-ty, *n.* [L. *duritas*, hardness, from *durus*, hard.]

1. Hardness; firmness.
2. Hardness of mind; harshness. [Rare.]

Durian (*Durio Zibethinus*).

dūr′măst, *n.* [Origin uncertain; the second part, *-mast*, is from AS. *mæst*, an acorn.] *Quercus sessiliflora*, variety *pubescens*, an oak of Europe; also, its wood.

dūrn, *n.* [Corn. *dorn*, a door-post.] A supporting mine-timber; a sett.

dū′rō, *n.* [Sp.] A Spanish silver coin worth about a dollar.

dū-rom′e-tẽr, *n.* [L. *durus*, hard, and *metrum*, measure.] A drill used to test the relative hardness of steel rails by the depth of hole made when the drill, number of rotations, and drill-pressure are the same.

dū′rous, *a.* Hard. [Obs.]

dur′rȧ, *n.* Indian millet; Guinea corn.

dūrst, *v.*, past tense of *dare*.

dū-rū-kū′li, *n.* See *Douroucouli*.

dū-ryl′ic, *a.* Of, relating to, or derived from, durene.

dū′sack, *n.* [G. *dusak*, from Bohem. *tesak*, a sword.] A kind of rough German cutlas, the blade and hilt being of one piece, used in the sixteenth and seventeenth centuries.

dush, *v.t.* and *v.i.* [Prov. Eng.] I. *v.t.* To shove; to strike hard.

II. *v.i.* To fall hard; to rush.

dusk, *a.* [ME. *dosk, dosc, deosk, deosc,* dark; Sw. *dusk,* raw weather, chilliness.] Tending to darkness; moderately dark; swarthy; shadowy; dusky.

dusk, *n.* 1. A tending to darkness; incipient obscurity; a middle degree between light and darkness; twilight; gloaming; as, the *dusk* of the evening.

2. Tendency to a black color; darkness of color; swarthiness.

dusk, *v.t.* and *v.i.* I. *v.t.* To make dusky. [Rare.]

II. *v.i.* To grow dark. [Rare.]

dusk'en, *v.t.* and *v.i.* Same as *Dusk.*

dusk'i-ly, *adv.* With partial darkness.

dusk'i-ness, *n.* Incipient or partial darkness.

dusk'ish, *a.* Moderately dusky; partially obscure.

dusk'ish-ly, *adv.* Cloudily; darkly.

dusk'ish-ness, *n.* Duskiness.

dusk'y, *a.*; *comp.* duskier; *superl.* duskiest. 1. Partially dark or obscure; not luminous; dimly lighted; as, a *dusky* valley.

2. Tending to blackness in color; partially black; dark-colored; not bright; as, a *dusky* brown.

3. Gloomy; sad. [Rare.]

Dusky duck; Anas obscura, the black duck.

dust, *n.* [AS. *dust*; L.G. *dust*; Ice. *dust,* dust; D. *duist,* meal-dust; Dan. *dyst,* fine meal.]

1. Earth or any other substance so finely powdered and so dry that it may be easily raised and carried by the wind; anything in the form of a fine powder; as, marble *dust.*

2. Figuratively, the commotion and confusion accompanying a struggle, and the consequent obscuration of the true state of matters caused by them.

Great contest follows, and much learned *dust.*
—Cowper.

3. In cookery, a small amount of some powder dusted upon anything; as, just a *dust* of cinnamon.

4. Earth; the earthy portion of an animal body, especially after death; as, *dust* to *dust.*

5. The grave; as, now shall I sleep in the *dust.*

6. Figuratively, a low condition, as, his fame had fallen to the *dust.*

7. Anything worthless; refuse, as ashes and rubbish. [Eng.]

8. Gold-dust; wealth; money; as, he has the *dust.* [Slang.]

9. A small particle or atom; as, not a *dust* is left. [Rare.]

Down with the dust; pay the cash down. [Slang.]

To kick up or *raise a dust;* to create a commotion or disturbance.

To throw dust in one's eyes; to confuse or deceive, as by misleading answers.

dust, *v.t.*; dusted, *pt., pp.*; dusting, *ppr.* 1. To free from dust; to brush, wipe, beat, or sweep away dust from; as, to *dust* a table or a carpet.

2. To sprinkle with dust.

3. To levigate; to make into dust.

To dust one's jacket; to beat one, as if to remove dust; to thrash. [Colloq.]

dust, *v.i.* To get away in a hurry; to run; as, to get up and *dust.* [Slang.]

dust'-brand, *n.* A fungus; smut.

dust'brush, *n.* A brush designed to remove dust from pictures, walls, furniture, etc.

dust'ẽr, *n.* 1. One who dusts.

2. Anything used to remove dust; (a) a dustbrush; a feather *duster*; (b) a sieve; (c) any machine used to take out fine particles, as in milling.

3. A loose, light outer coat or cloak, usually of linen, to protect clothing from dust in traveling.

4. A contrivance used to sift or blow dry poison upon plants to kill insects.

dust'-guärd, *n.* A washer or packing of wood, leather, felt, waste, etc., to keep dust from a bearing, as in a journal-box.

dust'i-ness, *n.* The state of being dusty.

dust'less, *a.* Having no dust.

dust'man, *n.*; *pl.* **dust'men.** 1. One whose employment is to carry away dirt and rubbish.

2. In nursery songs and sayings, the being who causes sleep; from the actions of a sleepy child in rubbing his eyes as if there was dust in them.

dus-tọọr', dus-tọọr'y, *n.* Same as *Dastur,* 2.

dust'pan, *n.* A utensil shaped like a short, broad shovel upon which to sweep dust, etc.

dust'-point, *n.* A kind of country sport. [Obs.]

dust'-shot, *n.* The smallest kind of bird-shot; known also as *mustard-seed.*

dust'-stọrm, *n.* A windstorm accompanied by much dust.

dust'-whirl, *n.* Dust carried about in a whirl of wind.

dust'y, *a.*; *comp.* dustier; *superl.* dustiest. 1. Filled, covered, or sprinkled with dust; clouded with dust.

2. Like dust; of the color of dust; as, a *dusty* white: a *dusty* pollen.

dust'y-mil"lẽr, *n.* 1. A moth-miller.

2. *Primula Auricula,* the auricula, whose leaves appear floury.

3. *Senecio Cineraria,* a grayish foliage-plant.

Dutch (duch), *a.* [ME. *Dutche, Duche*; D. *duitsch,* Dutch; O.H.G. *diutisk,* from *diot, diota,* a people, nation.]

1. Related in any way to the Netherlands, its people, or their language.

2. Pertaining to the Teutonic race in general. Colloquially equivalent to *German.*

Dutch auction; see under *Auction.*

Dutch clinker; a long, narrow, hard, yellowish brick made in the Netherlands.

Dutch cheese; cottage cheese.

Dutch clover; Trifolium repens, white clover.

Dutch courage; courage due to intoxicating liquor; hence, any intoxicating drink.

Dutch door; a door in two parts, one above the other, each acting independently.

Dutch foil, Dutch gold, Dutch leaf; same as *Dutch metal.*

Dutch liquid; ethylene dichlorid, $C_2H_4Cl_2$, made first in Holland by combining chlorin with ethylene.

Dutch metal; one of the most malleable of copper alloys, used in a thin leaf for decorative work, in place of gold.

Dutch oven; an iron pot heated by placing live coals over or around it; also, a tin oven open on the side next the fire and baking by both radiated and reflected heat.

Dutch rush; Equisetum hiemale, the horsetail or scouring-rush.

Dutch, *n.* 1. [*pl.*] The Low German people, especially the people of Holland.

2. [*pl.*] The Germanic or Teutonic race.

3. Any or all of the languages of the Dutch peoples, especially that spoken by the people of Holland.

High Dutch, Low Dutch; see *High* or *Low German* under *German.*

Pennsylvania Dutch; a dialect used in parts of Pennsylvania by descendants of High Germans.

dutch, *v.t.* To treat by placing in hot sand, as a quill, to harden and clean.

Dutch'măn, *n.*; *pl.* **Dutch'men.** 1. A Hollander; hence, colloquially, any Teuton.

2. [d—] A wedge or block of wood used to fill a space made by a poorly constructed joint or by the removal of broken or defective material; also, a shim.

Dutch'măn's-breech"eṣ (-brich"ez), *n.* *Dicentra Cucullaria,* a low perennial whose flowers have two broad spurs like the legs of baggy breeches.

Dutch'măn's-lau"dă-num, *n.* *Passiflora Murucuja,* a plant of Jamaica, or the narcotic prepared from its flowers.

Dutch'măn's-pipe, *n.* *Aristolochia Sipho,* a climber whose calyx resembles a tobacco-pipe. [U. S.]

dū'tē-ous, *a.* 1. Respectful to those who have natural or legal authority to require service or obedience; obedient; dutiful.

2. Subservient; obsequious. [Obs.]

3. Of, relating to, or required by duty. [Rare.]

dū'tē-ous-ly, *adv.* In a duteous manner.

dū'tē-ous-ness, *n.* Quality of being duteous.

dū'ti-ȧ-ble, *a.* Subject to the imposition of duty or customs; as, *dutiable* goods.

dū'tied, *a.* Subjected to duties or customs. [Rare.]

dū'ti-fụl, *a.* 1. Performing the duties or obligations required by law, justice, or propriety; obedient; submissive to natural or legal superiors; as, a *dutiful* son or daughter; a *dutiful* subject.

2. Expressive of respect or a sense of duty; respectful; required by duty; as, *dutiful* attentions.

Syn.—Obedient, compliant, duteous, submissive, docile, respectful, deferential.

dū'ti-fụl-ly, *adv.* In a dutiful manner.

dū'ti-fụl-ness, *n.* Dutiful state or quality.

dū'ty, *n.*; *pl.* **dū'tieṣ.** [ME. *duete, dewtie*; *due, dewe,* due, and *-te, -tie.*]

1. That which a person is bound, by any natural, moral, or legal obligation, to pay, do, or perform; as, one's *duty* to a friend.

2. The natural, moral, or legal obligation to follow a certain line of conduct, or to do a certain thing; the force by which such obligation controls one's will or actions; as, the struggle between *duty* and desire.

3. Obedience; submission; also, anything expressing deference or respect; homage; regards; devoir; as, sends her *duty* in a letter. [Archaic.]

4. Any service, labor, function, or office required of any particular person; also, the state of being occupied with such services; as, the *duties* of the motorman; on *duty.*

5. Tax, toll, impost, or customs; excise; any sum of money required by government to be paid on the importation, exportation, or consumption of goods.

6. The amount of work in foot-pounds done by an engine or motor by the use of a given amount of fuel, current, etc.; as, the *duty* of a steam pumping-engine.

7. Dues; compensation. [Obs.]

Syn.—Obligation, part, business, function, office, province, calling, service.

dū-um'vir, *n.*; *pl.* **dū-um'vi-rī** or **dū-um'virṣ.** [L., from *duo,* two, and *vir,* a man.] One of two Roman officers or magistrates united in the same public functions.

dū-um'vi-răl, *a.* Pertaining to the duumvirs or duumvirate of Rome.

dū-um'vi-rāte, *n.* [L. *duumviratus,* the office of a *duumvir.*] The union of two men in the same office; or the office, dignity, or government of two men thus associated, as in ancient Rome.

dū-um'vi-rī, *n.,* pl. of *duumvir.*

dụ-vet' (dụ-vā'), *n.* [Fr.] A bedquilt of down.

dux, *n.*; *pl.* **dū'cēṣ.** [L.] 1. A leader; applied to the head of a class in certain schools.

2. In a fugue, the principal theme or subject, as distinguished from the answer or comes.

duy̆'kẽr-bok, *n.* [D.] A small antelope, the diving-buck of South Africa which dives through thickets in escaping enemies.

dū-yong', *n.* Same as *Dugong.*

D'-valve (dē'-valv), *n.* A valve used on steam-engines for opening and closing the induction and eduction passages; so called from its section resembling the letter D. The usual form of the D-valve is shown in fig. 1, where it is seen detached, and at *a a,* fig. 2, which represents a section of a steam cylinder and nozles.

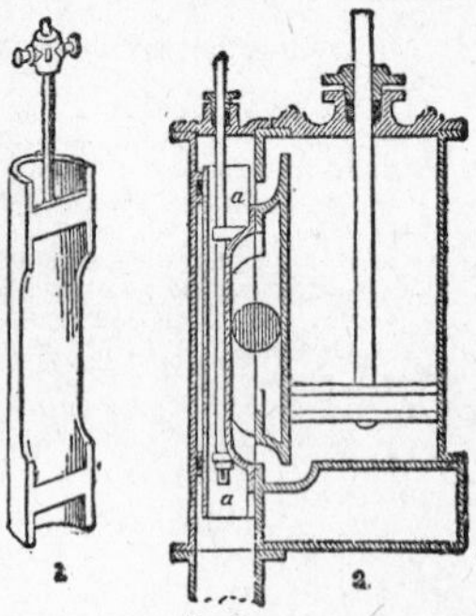

D-valve.
Fig. 1. D-valve detached. Fig. 2. *a, a,* D-valve in place.

dwāle, *n.* [ME. *dwale, dwole*; AS. *dwala, dwola,* error, delusion, heresy.]

1. In heraldry, a sable or black color.

2. The deadly nightshade, *Atropa Belladonna.*

3. A sleeping-potion. [Obs.]

dwälm, dwạum, *n.* [AS. *dwolma,* confusion, a chasm.] A swoon. [Scot.]

dwang, *n.* 1. A strut between the timbers of a floor to strengthen them. [Scot.]

2. A crowbar; a heavy wrench.

dwạrf, *n.* [ME. *dwarf, dwerf*; AS. *dweorg, dweorh,* a dwarf.] An animal or plant which is much below the ordinary size of its species or kind; particularly, an adult person of diminutive stature.

dwạrf, *a.* Below the ordinary size of its species or kind; dwarfed; stunted; diminutive; as, a *dwarf* cedar.

Dwarf elder; the danewort.

Dwarf male; same as *Micrander.*

Dwarf wall; in architecture, any wall lower than a single story of a building.

dwạrf, *v.t.*; dwarfed (dwarft), *pt., pp.*; dwarfing, *ppr.* 1. To hinder from growing to the natural size; to make or keep small; to stunt.

2. To cause to appear small or petty by contrast; as, the mountain *dwarfs* the foothills.

dwạrf, *v.i.* To decrease in dimensions; to become or remain stunted.

dwạrf'ish, *a.* Like a dwarf; below the common stature or size; very small; petty; despicable.

dwạrf'ish-ly, *adv.* Like a dwarf.

dwạrf'ish-ness, *n.* Smallness of stature.

dwạrf'ling, *n.* A very small dwarf.

dwạrf'y, *a.* Dwarfish. [Rare.]

dwell, *v.i.*; dwelt *or* dwelled, *pt., pp.*; dwelling, *ppr.* [ME. *dwellen, dwelien,* to err, linger; AS. *dwellan,* to deceive, hinder, delay; *dwelian,* to err.]

1. To abide as a permanent resident; to inhabit a place for a time; to live in a place; as, he *dwelt* in the valley.

2. To linger or tarry in thought or action; to expatiate; followed by *on* or *upon*; as, he *dwelt upon* her words; to *dwell upon* a note in singing.

3. To continue in any state or condition; as, to *dwell* in harmony.

4. To delay. [Obs.]

Syn.—Continue, stay, reside, rest, sojourn, abide, live, exist.

dwell, *n.* A momentary cessation of motion in some part of a machine, as in a printing-press, when the platen remains stationary a short time in order to produce a better impression.

dwell'ẽr, *n.* An inhabitant; a resident in a place.

dwell'ing, *n.* 1. Habitation; place of residence; abode; especially, a dwelling-house.

2. Continuance; state of life. [Obs.]

Syn.—Abode, domicile, habitation, residence.

dwell'ing-house, *n.* A house in which to live; a residence.

dwell'ing-plāce, *n.* A place of residence; a habitation; an abiding-place.

dwelt, *v.*, past tense and past participle of *dwell.*

dwin'dle, *v.i.*; dwindled, *pt., pp.*; dwindling, *ppr.* [Freq. of ME. *dwinen*; D. *dwijnen*, to languish, waste away; Ice. *dvina*; Sw. *tvina*, to languish, cease.]

1. To diminish; to become less; to shrink; to waste or consume away; as, the body *dwindles* in wasting diseases.

2. To degenerate; to sink; to fall away in excellence or usefulness; as, religious societies may *dwindle* into factious clubs.

Syn.—Decrease, diminish, fall off, decline, lessen, shrink, waste.

dwin'dle, *n.* Progressive decline or degeneration. [Obs.]

dwin'dle-ment, *n.* A decline. [Rare.]

dwine, *v.i.* [ME. *dwinen*; AS. *dwinan*, to dwindle, pine away; Ice. *dvina*; Sw. *tvina*, to languish.] To languish; to become feeble, especially through sickness. [Prov. Eng.]

dȳ'ad, *a.* [LL. *dyas, dyadis*; Gr. *dyas, dyados*, two.]

1. In chemistry, bivalent; having a valence of two.

2. Same as *Dyadic.*

dȳ'ad, *n.* 1. A duad; a pair or couple of units considered as one.

2. In chemistry, a bivalent element, atom, or radical.

3. In morphology, a secondary organic unit derived from an aggregate of monads.

4. In mathematics, the symbolic expression of a certain operation in vector analysis.

dȳ-ad'iç, *a.* 1. Relating to the number two; having two parts or elements; binary.

2. In chemistry, relating to a dyad.

3. In prosody, having two different meters or rhythms.

Dyadic arithmetic; same as *Binary arithmetic* under *Binary.*

Dȳ'ak, *n.* An aboriginal of the island of Borneo; written also *Dayak.*

Dȳ'as, *n.* [LL. *dyas*; Gr. *dyas*, two.] In geology, the Permian formation.

dȳ-as'tẽr, *n.* Same as *Diaster.*

dȳe, *v.t.*; dyed, *pt., pp.*; dyeing, *ppr.* [ME. *dyen, deyen*; AS. *deagian, degian*, to dye, color; *deah, deag*, a dye, color.] To stain; to color; to give a new and permanent color to.

dȳe, *v.i.* 1. To absorb and retain color in dyeing; as, silk *dyes* well.

2. To practise the art of dyeing; as, this man *dyes* for a living.

dȳe, *n.* [AS. *deag, deah*, a dye, color.]

1. A color, tinge, or hue produced by or as by dyeing.

2. A coloring matter used for dyeing; the solution used in dyeing.

dȳe, *n.* [Obs.] Same as *Die*, singular of *Dice.*

dȳe'house, *n.* A building in which dyeing is carried on.

dȳe'house, *n.* A dairy; a house for milk. [Prov. Eng.]

dȳe'ing, *n.* The art or practice of giving new and permanent colors; the art of coloring cloth, etc.

dȳ'ẽr, *n.* One whose occupation is to dye.

dȳ'ẽr's-brōōm, *n.* A plant, *Genista tinctoria.* [See *Genista.*]

dȳ'ẽr's-moss, *n.* Same as *Archil.*

dȳ'ẽr's-weed, *n.* 1. In botany, a plant of the mignonette family, *Reseda luteola*, which yields various colors according to the mordant used.

2. Woad, *Isatis tinctoria*, used in dyeing blue.

3. *Genista tinctoria.* [See *Genista.*]

dȳe'stuff, *n.* Any substance used as coloring matter in dyeing.

dȳe'weed, *n.* Dyer's-broom. [See *Genista.*]

dȳe'wood, *n.* Any wood which yields coloring matter for dyeing.

dȳ'ing, *n.* A passing from life to death; dissolution.

dȳ'ing, *a.* 1. Losing life; expiring; gradually fading away; as, a *dying* child; a *dying* day.

2. Destined to death; mortal; as, *dying* bodies.

3. Related in any way to the phenomenon or the time of death; as, *dying* words, hour, day, request, bed, etc.

dȳ'ing-ly, *adv.* In a dying manner.

dȳ'ing-ness, *n.* The condition of a dying person; hence, an affected languishment.

dȳke, *n.* Same as *Dike.*

dȳ-naç-ti-nom'e-tẽr, *n.* [Gr. *dynamis*, power, *aktis, aktinos*, a ray, and *metron*, a measure.] An instrument for measuring actinic power, and thus for determining the relative quickness of lenses.

dȳ'nȧ-grȧph, *n.* [Gr. *dynamis*, power, and *graphein*, to write.] An instrument carried upon a railway-train which automatically records the speed, condition of track, consumption of fuel, and many other important facts about the line traversed by it.

dȳ'nam, dȳ'name, *n.* [Gr. *dynamis*, power, strength.]

1. A foot-pound as a unit of work.

2. A resultant of all the forces which act on a body.

dȳ-nam'e-tẽr, *n.* [Gr. *dynamis*, power, and *metron*, a measure.] An instrument for determining the magnifying power of telescopes.

dȳ-nȧ-met'riç, dȳ-nȧ-met'riç-ăl, *a.* Pertaining to a dynameter.

dȳ-nam'iç, dȳ-nam'iç-ăl, *a.* [Gr. *dynamikos*, from *dynamis*, power, strength.]

1. Pertaining to strength or power; involving or causing energy, motion, action, or change; causal; motive; effective; efficient.

2. Pertaining to or involving mechanical forces in general.

3. Of or relating to dynamics; involving forces not in equilibrium; relating to motion, considered as the result of force; opposed to *static.*

dȳ-nam'iç, *n.* 1. A motive force; an incentive.

2. Dynamics, the theory or science.

dȳ-nam'iç-ăl-ly, *adv.* In a dynamic way; as regards or according to dynamics.

dȳ-nam'içs, *n.* [Gr. *dynamikē* (supply *technē*, art), f. of *dynamikos*, pertaining to power, from *dynamis*, power.]

1. That branch of mechanics which treats of bodies in motion; called also *kinetics*; opposed to *statics.*

2. The science and mathematical theory of the laws of force, including statics and kinetics.

3. The motive and controlling forces of any kind; also, their mode of action.

4. That part of the science of music which treats of or relates to the quality or power of tones.

dȳ'nȧ-miṣm, *n.* [Gr. *dynamis*, power, strength, and *-ism.*] The doctrine of Leibnitz, that, besides matter, some necessary material force exists which is the prime mover in all physical as well as mental phenomena.

dȳ'nȧ-mist, *n.* One who believes in the theory of dynamism.

dȳ'nȧ-mi-tärd, *n.* One who dynamites through political zeal and frenzy.

dȳ'nȧ-mīte, *v.t.*; dynamited, *pt., pp.*; dynamiting, *ppr.* 1. To destroy by the use of dynamite.

2. To charge or prepare for destruction with dynamite.

dȳ'nȧ-mīte, *n.* [Gr. *dynamis*, power, and *-ite.*] An explosive consisting of an absorbent, as infusorial earth, sawdust, etc., saturated with nitroglycerin.

dȳ'nȧ-mīte-gun, *n.* An air-gun for throwing shells filled with dynamite or other explosives.

dȳ'nȧ-mī-tẽr, *n.* One who makes use of dynamite for the destruction of life and property; especially, a political destructionist.

dȳ'nȧ-mī-ting, *n.* The act of destroying by the use of dynamite, especially to accomplish a political purpose.

dȳ'nȧ-mī-tiṣm, *n.* The work done by dynamiters; also, the doctrine that approves the methods of the dynamiter.

dȳ″nȧ-mi-zā'tion, *n.* 1. In homeopathy, the process of rendering medicines more effective, as by pulverization, solution, or shaking.

2. Increased activity or efficiency.

dȳ'nȧ-mīze, *v.t.*; dynamized, *pt., pp.*; dynamizing, *ppr.* [Gr. *dynamis*, power, and *-ize.*] To increase the strength of (medicines) by certain processes or manipulations, as by shaking, pulverizing, etc.

dȳ-nȧ-mō-. A combining form from Gr. *dynamis*, power, and signifying power, strength, energy; as, *dynamo*graph; *dynamo*geny.

dȳ'nȧ-mō, *n.* [An abbrev. of *dynamo-electric* machine.] A species of mechanism by which a high percentage of mechanical energy may be converted into electrical energy by means of rotating an armature through powerful magnetic fields.

dȳ'nȧ-mō-e-lec'triç, *a.* [*Dynamo-*, and Gr. *ēlektron*, amber.] Of, relating, or pertaining to the two kinds of energy called mechanical and electrical, especially to their dynamic relations, as the conversion or transmutation of the one into the other.

dȳ-nȧ-moġ'e-ny, dȳ″nȧ-mō-ġen'e-sis, *n.* [*Dynamo-*, and Gr. *geneia*, genesis, from *gignesthai*, to become, be born.] The awakening or exciting in the nerve-centers of a higher degree of activity, as by the administration of a nerve tonic.

dȳ-nam'ō-grȧph, *n.* [*Dynamo-*, and Gr. *graphein*, to write.] A dynamometer which has an attachment for automatically registering its measurements, as in the dynagraph; specifically, an instrument, variously constructed, for testing, measuring, comparing, and recording the muscular strength of man or of the lower animals.

dȳ-nȧ-mom'e-tẽr, *n.* [*Dynamo-*, and Gr. *metron*, a measure.] An instrument for measuring force, especially the relative strength of men and other animals.

dȳ″nȧ-mō-met'riç, dȳ″nȧ-mō-met'riç-ăl, *a.* Relating to a dynamometer or to dynamometry.

dȳ-nȧ-mom'e-try, *n.* The act or the process of using a dynamometer.

dȳ'nast, *n.* [L. *dynastes*; Gr. *dynastēs*, a lord, ruler, from *dynasthai*, to be able, strong.]

1. A ruler; a governor; a prince.

2. A government; a dynasty. [Obs.]

dȳ-nas'tȧ, *n.* A tyrannical ruler. [Obs.]

dȳ-nas'tiç, dȳ-nas'tiç-ăl, *a.* [Gr. *dynastikos*, from *dynastēs*, a lord, ruler.] Relating to a dynasty or line of kings.

Dȳ-nas'ti-dæ, *n.pl.* [Gr. *dynastēs*, a lord, ruler.] In entomology, a family of beetles of gigantic size having hornlike processes, of which *Dynastes hercules* of South America is a type and the largest known beetle.

dȳ-nas'ti-dăn, *n.* One of the beetle family *Dynastidæ.*

dȳ'nas-ty, *n.*; *pl.* **dȳ'nas-tieṣ.** [Gr. *dynasteia*, lordship, rule, from *dynastēs*, a lord, ruler; *dynasthai*, to be able, strong.] Government; sovereignty; or rather, a race or succession of kings of the same line or family, who govern a particular country; as, the *dynasty* of Egypt.

dyne, *n.* [Abbrev. of *dynam*, from Gr. *dynamis*, power.] The unit of electrical force, being that force which in one second can impart a velocity of one centimeter per second to a mass of one gram.

dȳ'nō-grȧph, *n.* Same as *Dynamograph.*

dȳ″ō-cæ-tri-ȧ-çon-tȧ-hē'drŏn, *n.* [Gr. *dyo kai triakonta*, thirty-two, and *hedron*, a seat, base.] In geometry, a solid with thirty-two faces.

dȳ-oth'el-iṣm, *n.* [Gr. *dyo*, two, and *thelein*, to will.] The doctrine that the will of Christ was twofold, human and divine.

dȳ-oth'e-lite, *n.* An advocate of dyothelism.

dys-. An inseparable prefix, from Gr. *dys-*, hard, ill, bad, and signifying hard, ill, bad, difficult; as, *dys*genesis, *dys*nomy.

dys-æs-thē'si-ȧ, *n.* [Gr. *dysaisthēsia*, insensibility, from *dysaisthētos*; *dys-*, hard, and *aisthēsthai*, to perceive.] In pathology, numbness; partial insensibility; also spelled *dysesthesia.*

dys-är'thri-ȧ, *n.* [*Dys-*, and Gr. *arthron*, a joint.] Defective articulation in pronouncing.

dys-är-thrō'sis, *n.* [*Dys-*, and Gr. *arthron*, a joint.] Disability or disease of a joint.

dys-çrā'si-ȧ, *n.* [Gr. *dyskrasia*, bad temperament; *dys-*, bad, and *krasis*, a mixture, from *kerannynai*, to mix.] A diseased condition of the system marked by general ill-health and debility; also written *dyscrasy.*

dys-çrā'siç, *a.* Of or characterized by dyscrasia.

dys'çrā-site, *n.* [*Dys-*, and Gr. *krasis*, a mixture.] A lustrous, grayish mineral made up of antimony and silver.

dys-çrā'sy, *n.* Dyscrasia.

dys-en-ter'iç, dys-en-ter'iç-ăl, *a.* 1. Pertaining to dysentery; accompanied with dysentery; proceeding from dysentery.

2. Afflicted with dysentery.

dys'en-ter-y, *n.* [L. *dysenteria*; Gr. *dysenteria*, dysentery; *dys-*, bad, and *enteron*, pl. *entera*, the bowels.] A disease of the large intestine, accompanied by griping and frequent desire to evacuate, the discharges being meager and consisting mainly of mucus mixed with blood.

dys-ġē-nes'iç, *a.* Affected by dysgenesis; relating or pertaining to dysgenesis.

dys-ġen'e-sis, *n.* [*Dys-*, and Gr. *genesis*, birth.] Lack of ability to breed freely; a condition of only partial fertility or infecundity, as in hybrids which do not breed among themselves, but may with the parent stock. The mule is an example.

dys-ġen'iç, *a.* [*Dys-*, and Gr. *genos*, race, family.] Militating against the improvement of the race through breeding. Opposed to *eugenic.*

dys-lex'i-ȧ, *n.* [*Dys-*, and Gr. *lexis*, speech.] Loss of power to grasp the meaning of that which is read.

dys-lō-ġis'tiç, *a.* [*Dys-*, and Gr *logos*, discourse.] Not flattering; disparaging; opposed to *eulogistic.*

dys'lū-ite, *n.* [*Dys-*, and Gr. *lyein*, to loose, dissolve.] A variety of gahnite, or zinc spinel, containing iron and manganese.

dys-men-or-rhē'ȧ (-rē'ȧ), *n.* [*Dys-*, and Gr. *mēn*, a month, and *rhoia*, a flowing.] Difficult menstruation, often accompanied by pain.

dys″me-rō-ġen'e-sis, *n.* [*Dys-*, and Gr. *meros*, part, and *genesis*, birth.] In biology, generation marked by irregularity of constituent parts, differing in function, time of budding, etc.; opposed to *eumerogenesis.*

dys'mẽr-ō-morph, *n.* [*Dys-*, and Gr. *meros*, part, and *morphē*, shape.] In biology, a form resulting from dysmerogenesis.

dys'nō-my, *n.* [Gr. *dysnomia*, lawlessness, a bad constitution; *dys-*, bad, and *nomos*, law.] Bad legislation; the enactment of bad laws.

dys'ō-dile, *n.* [Gr. *dysōdēs*, ill-smelling; *dys-*, bad, and *ozein*, to smell.] A species of coal of a greenish or yellowish-gray color, in masses composed of thin layers.

dys'ō-dont, *n.* [*Dys-*, and Gr. *odous, odontos*, a tooth.] In conchology, monomyarian.

dys-ō'pi-ȧ, dys-op'sy, *n.* [*Dys-*, and Gr. *opsis*, view, sight.] Dimness of sight.

dys-ō-rex'i-ȧ, *n.* [Gr. *dysorexia*, feebleness of appetite; *dys-*, bad, and *orexis*, appetite.] A bad or depraved appetite; a want of appetite.

dys-pep′si-ȧ, *n.* [L. *dyspepsia*; Gr. *dyspepsia*, indigestion, from *dyspeptos*; *dys-*, bad, and *peptos*, from *peptein*, to soften, cook, digest.] Indigestion, especially when chronic; also written *dyspepsy*.

dys-pep′tiç, *n.* A person afflicted with bad digestion.

dys-pep′tiç, *a.* 1. Afflicted with bad digestion; as, a *dyspeptic* person.

2. Pertaining to or having the characteristics of dyspepsia; as, a *dyspeptic* complaint.

3. Taking a morbid view of things; testy; pessimistic; applied to persons or things; as, a *dyspeptic* writer; *dyspeptic* literature.

dys-pep′tiç-ăl, *a.* Afflicted with dyspepsia; tending toward morbidness and pessimism.

dys-pep′tōne, *n.* [*Dys-*, and Gr. *peptein*, to digest.] An albuminoid formed from certain proteid substances, as casein, in the process of gastric digestion.

dys-phā′ġi-ȧ, dys′phā-ġy, *n.* [*Dys-*, and Gr. *phagein*, to eat.] Difficulty or impracticability of deglutition.

dys-phā′şi-ȧ, *n.* [*Dys-*, and Gr. *phasis*, speech.] An affection characterized by impairment of speech, arising from disease of the brain.

dys-phō′ni-ȧ, dys′phō-ny, *n.* [Gr. *dysphonia*; *dys-*, bad, and *phōnē*, voice.] A difficulty of speaking, occasioned by a malformation of the organs of speech.

dys-phō′ri-ȧ, *n.* [Gr. *dysphoria*; *dys-*, hard, and *pherein*, to bear.] Impatience under affliction; general restlessness.

dysp-nœ′ȧ (-nē′ȧ), *n.* [L., from Gr. *dyspnoia*; *dys-*, hard, and *pnein*, to breathe.] Difficulty of breathing.

dysp-nœ′iç (-nē′iç), *a.* Pertaining to dyspnœa; short of breath.

dys-prō′si-um, *n.* One of a group of rare elements discovered by spectrum analysis. [See Table of Elements under *Element*, n. 2.]

dys-te-lē-ol′ō-ġy, *n.* [*Dys-*, and Gr. *telos*, end, purpose, and *-logia*, from *legein*, to speak.] A word formed by Haeckel to express that branch of physiology which treats of the apparent purposelessness observable in living organisms in connection with rudimentary structures.

dys-thym′iç, *a.* [Gr. *dysthymikos*, from *dysthymia*, despondency, despair; *dys-*, bad, and *thymos*, spirit, courage.] Afflicted with chronic melancholy; depressed in spirits.

dys-tō′ci-ȧ, *n.* [Gr. *dystokia*; *dys-*, hard, and *-tokia*, from *tiktein*, to bear.] Childbirth attended by danger; difficult parturition.

dys′tōme, *a.* Dystomic.

dys-tom′iç, dys′tō-mous, *a.* [Gr. *dystomos*; *dys-*, hard, bad, and *tomos*, from *temnein*, to cut.] In mineralogy, cleaving with difficulty.

dys′trō-phy, *n.* [*Dys-*, and Gr. *trophē*, from *trephein*, to nourish.] Abnormal or defective nourishment; unnatural nutrition.

dys-ū′ri-ȧ, dys′ū-ry, *n.* [*Dys-*, and Gr. *ouron*, urine.] Difficulty in discharging the urine, attended with pain and a sensation of heat.

dys-ū′riç, *a.* Relating to or suffering with dysuria.

dzē′ren, dzē′rŏn, *n.* [Mongolian name.] The Chinese antelope, a remarkably swift animal, *Procapra gutturosa*, inhabiting the dry, arid deserts of central Asia, Tibet, China, and southern Siberia.

dzig′ge-tai, *n.* [Mongolian.] The wild ass of Asia, *Equus hemionus*, described in the Book of Job, and thought to be the *hemionos* of Herodotus and Pliny. It is a habitant of the arid steppes of central Asia.

E

E (ē). The second vowel and the fifth letter of the English alphabet. It has the same position in our alphabet as the corresponding sign or character had in the Latin, Greek, and Phenician alphabets, from which ours is derived. It has a long sound, as in *here, mere, me*; a short sound, as in *met, men*, and the sound of *a* open or long, in *prey, vein*. As a final letter it is generally silent. After *c* and *g*, the final *e* serves to indicate that *c* is to be pronounced as *s*, and *g* as *j*. Thus, without the final *e* in *mace* (mās), this word would be pronounced *mac* (mak), and *rage* (rāj) would be pronounced *rag*. The numerous irregularities in the use of *e* are not reducible to rules. In all cases not covered by the regular diacritical marks we have respelled the words.

E, e, *as a symbol*. As a numeral, *E* stands for 250. In the calendar, it is the fifth of the dominical letters. As an abbreviation, it stands for *East*, as in charts: E. N. E., east-northeast; E. S. E., east-southeast; E. by S., east by south.

In music, it stands for the third tone of the diatonic scale, designating the first line in a staff with the G clef.

e-, *prefix*. A Latin prefix usually used instead of *ex-* before consonants, and meaning out, out of, from, without.

ēach, *a.* [ME. *eche, ech, ælc, elc*; AS. *ælc*; *a*, always, and *gelic*, like; G. *jeglich*, each.] Being one of two or more individuals making up an aggregate, considered or treated distinctly from the rest; often followed by *one*; as, *each* person was called upon to speak; *each one* of them believed the statement.

ēach, *pron.* Every one of two or more individuals forming an aggregate, considered individually; each one; as, *each* did his share; *each* of them heard the remark.

Each other; each the other; as, they despise *each other*, that is, *each* despises the *other*.

ēach′where (-hwãr), *adv.* Everywhere. [Obs.]

ead′ish (ed′ish), *n.* Same as *Eddish*.

ēa′gẽr, *a.* [ME. *eger, egre*; OFr. *egre, aigre*; L. *acer, acris*, sharp, keen.]

1. Excited by desire in the pursuit of any object; ardent to pursue, perform, or obtain; keen; vehement; intent; as, the soldiers were *eager* to engage the enemy; men are *eager* in the pursuit of wealth.

2. Sharp; sour; acid. [Obs.]

3. Sharp; keen; biting; severe. [Obs.]

4. Brittle; inflexible; not ductile. [Obs.]

Syn.—Earnest, fervent, zealous, enthusiastic, vehement, intense, fervid.—*Eager* marks an excited state of desire or passion; *earnest* denotes a permanent state of moral sentiment or feeling.

ēa′gẽr, ēa′gre, *n.* [AS. *eagor, egor*, water, sea, in comp. as *eagor-stream, egor-stream*, ocean-stream.] The whole body of spring-tide water moving up a river or estuary in one wave, or in a few successive waves, of great height, and sometimes presenting a formidable surge, as in the Ganges, Severn, and the Bay of Fundy; a bore.

ēa′gẽr-ly, *adv.* In an eager manner; zealously.

ēa′gẽr-ness, *n.* 1. The quality or state of being eager.

2. Tartness; sourness. [Obs.]

Syn.—Fervor, zeal, ardor, impetuosity, enthusiasm, impatience, vehemence.

ēa′gle (ē′gl), *n.* [ME. *egle*; OFr. *egle, aigle*; Pr. *aigla*; Sp. *aguila*; It. *aquila*; L. *aquila*, an eagle; f. of *aquilus*, dark colored, brown.]

Golden Eagle (*Aquila chrysaetus*).

1. Any bird of the family *Falconidæ*, especially of the genera *Aquila* and *Haliaëtus*. The eagle is one of the largest species of birds, has a keen sight, and preys on small animals, fish, etc. On account of the elevation and rapidity of its flight, and of its great strength, it is called the king of birds.

2. A gold coin of the United States, of the value of ten dollars.

3. [E—] The northern constellation Aquila.

4. A military standard of ancient Rome, upon which was borne the figure of an *eagle*; adopted by France under Napoleon.

5. In roulette, a representation of an *eagle* on a spot outside of the numbered spots; called also *eagle-bird*.

6. A lectern, the design of which is an *eagle* with outstretched wings supporting the desk on which the book rests.

Bald eagle; the white-headed earn or sea-eagle of America, *Haliaëtus leucocephalus*, a species of aquatic eagle that feeds not only on fish but on small land animals and various sea-fowl. This is the eagle which is emblazoned as the national emblem on the coat of arms of the United States and is also represented on the coinage.

Golden eagle; a large species having feathers of a reddish-brown color. It is found in both Europe and North America.

Imperial eagle; a European species, *Aquila mogilnik*.

ēa′gle-eyed (-īd), *a.* Sharp-sighted as an eagle.

ēa′gle-gull, *n.* The gull with a black back, *Larus marinus*.

ēa′gle-hawk, *n.* A hawk of the genus *Morphnus*, as the South American *eagle-hawk* or the *Morphnus guianensis*.

ēa′gle-owl, *n.* The great horned owl of Europe, *Bubo maximus*, or the American *Bubo virginianus*.

ēa′gle-rāy, *n.* *Myliobatis aquila*, a large species of ray; any ray of the family *Myliobatidæ*.

ēa′gle-sight″ed, *a.* Having acute sight, as an eagle.

ēa′gless, *n.* A female or hen eagle. [Rare.]

ēa′gle-stōne, *n.* A variety of argillaceous oxid of iron, occurring in hollow nodules varying from the size of a walnut to that of a man's head. To these the ancients gave the name of *eaglestones*, from an idea that the eagle transported them to her nest to facilitate the laying of her eggs.

ēa′glet, *n.* A young eagle or a diminutive eagle.

ēa′gle-vul″tūre, *n.* An eagle-like vulture of western Africa, *Gypohierax angolensis*.

ēa′gle-winged, *a.* Having the wings of an eagle; swift as an eagle.

ēa′gle-wood, *n.* A fragrant wood, used by the Asiatics for burning as incense. [See *Agallochum*.]

ēa′grȧss, *n.* [Obs.] See *Eddish*.

ēa′gre (-gẽr), *n.* Same as *Eager*.

ēal′dŏr-măn, *n.* [Obs.] Same as *Alderman*.

ēale, *n.* Ale. [Obs.]

ēam, *n.* [AS. *eam*, uncle.] Uncle. [Obs.]

ēan, *v.t.* and *v.i.* [AS. *eanian*, to be pregnant.] To yean. [Obs.]

ēan′ling, *n.* A lamb just brought forth. [Obs.]

ēar, *n.* [AS. *ear, eare*; D. *oor*; Sw. *öra*; Dan. *öre*; G. *ohr*; L. *auris*, an ear.]

Parts of the Human Ear: C, Concha. *a*, Helix. *b*, Lobe. *c*, Antihelix. *d*, Antitragus. *e*, Tragus. *f*, Crura of antihelix. *g*, Fossa navicularis. *h*, Fossa innominata. *k*, Auditory opening. *l*, Scala. *m*, Cochlea. *n*, Vestibule. *o*, Semicircular canals. *p*, Incus or anvil. *q*, Stapes. *r*, Malleus or hammer. (*p, q, r*, Ossicles or small bones.) *s*, Membrane of the tympanum or drum.

1. The organ of hearing, contained partly in the substance of the temporal bone, and partly projecting externally behind the joint of the lower jaw. In man and higher animals the ear is composed of the external ear, which is a cartilaginous funnel for collecting the sound-waves and directing them inward; of the drum of the ear, a bony cavity lined by mucous membrane, separated from the external ear by a delicate membrane, and containing a chain of small bones which transmit the vibrations of the latter to the internal ear, in which are the terminal expansions of the auditory nerve. The internal ear consists of a bony cavity, called the vestibule, which communicates with three semicircular canals, and with a bony structure in the form of a spiral shell, called the cochlea.

2. The external *ear* alone; the pinna, auricle, or concha.

3. The sense of hearing; the power of distinguishing sounds and judging of harmony; the power of nice perception of the differences of sound; as, she has a good *ear* for music.

4. A part of any inanimate object resembling an *ear*; a projecting part from the side of anything; a handle; as, the *ears* of a dish, tub, or other receptacle.

5. A favorable hearing; attention; heed; regard.

> Give every man thine *ear*. —Shak.

6. In architecture, a crossette.

7. In ornithology, (a) the feathers which cover the external ear-passage; (b) a corniplume.

All ears; listening with great attention.

By the ears; in a discordant state.

To give ear to; to heed; to pay attention to.

To set by the ears; to make strife between; to cause to quarrel.

Up to the ears, over head and ears; deeply absorbed or engrossed; overwhelmed; as, *over head and ears* in debt.

ēar, *v.t.* To listen to; to hear with deep attention.

ēar, *v.i.* To shoot, as an ear; to form ears, as corn.
ēar, *v.t.* To plow or till. [Obs.]
ēar, *n.* A spike or head of corn or grain; that part of a cereal plant which contains the flowers and seed.
ēar′ȧ-ble, *a.* That can be tilled; arable. [Obs.]
ēar′āche, *n.* Pain in the ear.
ēar′ăl, *a.* Receiving by the ear. [Obs.]
ēar′=bōred, *a.* Having the ear perforated.
ēar′çap, *n.* A cover for the ears against cold.
ēar′ço̤c″kle, *n.* A disease in wheat caused by the presence in the grain of worms belonging to the genus *Vibrio.*
ēar′=conch, *n.* The external ear; the pinna.
ēar′drop, *n.* An ornamental pendant for the ear.
ēar′drum, *n.* In anatomy, the tympanum; also, the tympanic membrane.
ēared, *a.* 1. Having ears; having earlike parts or appendages. In heraldry, animals borne in coat-armor with their ears differing in tincture from that of the body are blazoned *eared* of such a metal or color.
2. In biology, auriculate.
ēar′i-ness, *n.* Same as *Eeriness.*
ēar′ing, *n.* In seamen's language, a small rope attached to the cringle of a sail, by which it is bent or reefed; also, a name for other fastening-lines.
ēar′ing, *n.* A plowing of land. [Obs.]
ēar′ing, *n.* The forming of ears, as in corn.
ẽarl, *n.* [AS. *eorl*, a nobleman of high rank.] A British title of nobility; a nobleman, the third in rank, being next below a marquis, and next above a viscount. The title answers to *count* [*compte*] in France and *graf* in Germany.

Coronet of an Earl.

Earl marshal; an officer in Great Britain, the head of the College of Arms, who determines all rival claims to arms, and grants armorial bearings, through the medium of the king-at-arms, to parties not possessed of hereditary arms. He also makes the formal proclamation of war or peace and has charge of all military ceremonies.
ēar′lap, *n.* The tip of the ear.
ẽarl′dŏm, *n.* [ME. *erldom*; AS. *eorldom*; *eorl*, earl, and *-dom.*] The seigniory, jurisdiction, or dignity of an earl.
ẽarl′dŏr-măn, *n.* [Obs.] See *Alderman.*
ẽarl′duck, *n.* The red-breasted merganser.
ēarleș′=pen″ny, *n.* Money in ratification of a contract; earnest-money. [Obs.]
ēar′less, *a.* Having no ears; hence, not inclined to hear or listen.
ēar′let, *n.* 1. A diminutive ear.
2. An earring.
ẽar′li-ness, *n.* The state of being early; a state of advance or forwardness; a state of being before something else, or at the beginning.
ēar′lock, *n.* [AS. *earlocc*; *eare*, ear, and *-locc*, a lock.] A lock or curl of hair near the ear, worn by men of fashion in the reigns of Elizabeth and James I.; a lovelock.
ẽar′ly, *adv.* [ME. *erly*, *erli*, *erliche*; AS. *ærlice*; *ær*, sooner, and *lic*, like.] Soon; in good season; betimes; as, rise *early.*
ẽar′ly, *a.*; *comp.* earlier; *superl.* earliest. 1. In advance of some usual or necessary date; before the appointed time; in good season; as, *early* fruit; an *early* harvest; an *early* riser.
2. First; in or near the beginning of a period of time or of some course in time; coming among the first of a series of incidents, acts, etc.; as, an *early* stage of existence; one of his *early* writings.
3. Soon to take place; occurring in the near future; as, I shall take an *early* opportunity to inquire into the matter.
Early English architecture; the style of architecture into which the Norman passed, in the twelfth and thirteenth centuries. Its general characteristics, as distinguished from the Norman, are delicacy, refinement, and grace. Its distinctive features are pointed arches and long, narrow, lancet-shaped windows without mullions. Toward the end of the period the windows became grouped in a manner that led to the development of tracery, and so into the decorated style.

Early English Style.—Northwest Transept of Beverley Minster.

ēar′märk, *n.* 1. A mark on the ear of a domestic animal by which it is known.
2. Hence, figuratively, in law, any mark for identification, as a privy mark made by any one on a coin.
3. Any distinguishing mark, natural or other, by which the ownership or relation of anything is known.
ēar′märk, *v.t.*; earmarked (-märkt), *pt.*, *pp.*; earmarking, *ppr.* To place an earmark upon.
ēar=mind′ed, *a.* Tending to learn and remember and think in terms of auditory images. Opposed to *eye-minded.*
ẽarn, ẽrn, ẽrne, *n.* [AS. *earn*, eagle.] An eagle.
ẽarn, *v.t.*; earned, *pt.*, *pp.*; earning, *ppr.* [ME. *ernen*, *ernien*, *earnien*; AS. *earnian*, to earn, merit.]
1. To merit or deserve, as by labor or any performance; to do that which entitles one to (a reward), whether the reward is received or not.
2. To gain by labor, service, or performance; to deserve and receive as compensation; as, to *earn* a dollar a day; to *earn* a good living; to *earn* honors.
Earned run; in baseball, a run made by a player without the aid of errors on the part of the opponents.
Syn.—Merit, deserve, acquire, gain, attain.
ẽarn, *v.i.* To yearn. [Obs.]
ẽarn, *v.i.* To grieve; to sorrow. [Obs.]
ẽarn, *v.i.* [Prov. Eng.] To curdle, as milk.
ẽar′nest, *a.* [ME. *ernest*, *eornest*; AS. *eornest*, *eornost*; D. *ernst*; G. *ernst*, zeal, vigor.]
1. Ardent in the pursuit of an object; eager to obtain; having a longing desire; zealous; importunate; as, *earnest* in prayer; an *earnest* appeal.
2. Intent; fixed.

Their *earnest* eyes were fixed. —Milton.

3. Serious; important.
Syn.—Sincere, eager, urgent, zealous, importunate, fervent, warm.
ẽar′nest, *n.* Seriousness; reality, as opposed to jesting or feigned appearance; as, it may turn from jest to *earnest.*
In earnest; earnestly; with honest intent.
ẽar′nest, *v.t.* To be earnest with; to use in earnest. [Obs.]
ẽar′nest, *n.* [W. *ernes*, an earnest, pledge, from *ern*, a pledge; related to Gael. *earlas*, an earnest.]
1. Anything which gives assurance, pledge, promise, or indication of what is to follow; first-fruits.
2. A part of something delivered beforehand, as a security; specifically, in law, part of the price of the commodity bargained for, paid by the buyer to the seller to prove the validity of the transaction.
Syn.—Pledge.—An *earnest*, like first-fruits, gives assurance that more is coming of the same kind; a *pledge*, like money deposited, affords security and ground of reliance for the future.
ẽar′nest-fu̇l, *a.* Earnest; serious. [Obs.]
ẽar′nest-ly, *adv.* [ME. *ernestly*; AS. *eornostlice*; *eornost*, earnest, and *lice*, like.] In an earnest manner; zealously; eagerly; importunately.
ẽar′nest=mŏn″ey, *n.* Money paid as earnest to bind a bargain or ratify a sale.
ẽar′nest-ness, *n.* The quality or condition of being earnest; eagerness; seriousness; anxiety.
ẽarn′fu̇l, *a.* [A variant of *yearnful.*] Full of anxiety. [Obs.]
ẽarn′ing, *n.* That which is earned; that which is gained or merited by labor, services, or performance; wages; used chiefly in the plural.
ẽarn′ing, *n.* [Prov. Eng.] Rennet.
ēar′pick, *n.* An instrument for cleansing the ear.
ēar′=piẽr″cẽr, *n.* The earwig.
ēar′=piẽr″cing, *a.* Piercing the ear, as a shrill or sharp sound.
ēar′rēach, *n.* Hearing-distance; earshot.
ēar′ring, *n.* An ornament, sometimes provided with a pendant, and frequently set with diamonds, pearls, or other jewels, worn at the ear, by means of a ring passing through the lobe.
ẽarsh, *n.* See *Ersh.*
ēar′=shell, *n.* A shell of the genus *Haliotis*; a sea-ear.
ēar′shot, *n.* Reach of the ear; the distance at which words may be heard.
ēar′shrift, *n.* Auricular confession. [Obs.]
ēar′sōre, *n.* Something offensive to the ear. [Obs.]
ēar′=split″ting, *a.* Loud and harsh to the ear; deafening.
ẽarst, *adv.* [Obs.] See *Erst.*
ẽarth, *n.* [ME. *erthe*, *eorthe*, AS. *eorthe*; D. *aarde*; O.H.G. *erdha*, *erda*; Ice. *jördh*; Dan. *jord*; Goth. *airtha*, the earth.]
1. The planet on which we live, as distinguished from other heavenly bodies, or from the dwelling-place of spirits.
2. The solid matter which composes the globe, as distinguished from air and water; the land.
3. The soft material of which part of the surface of the globe consists; soil, as distinguished from rock; especially soil capable of being cultivated; the ground; as, to fill up a ditch with *earth.*
4. A distinct part of the globe; a country; a region.

This English *earth.* —Shak.

5. The inhabitants of the globe.

The whole *earth* was of one language. —Gen. xi. 1.

6. The hole in which a fox or other burrowing animal hides itself.
7. Things of a worldly nature, as opposed to spiritual or divine things.
8. Dirt; anything mean or contemptible.
9. In chemistry, any one of certain inodorous, dry, and uninflammable substances, the most important of which are lime, baryta, strontia, magnesia, alumina, zirconia, glucina, yttria, and thorina.
10. In electricity, (a) the ground forming part of an electric circuit; (b) the contact of any part of a conductor with the ground; (c) a fault in a telegraphic or other line resulting from accidental contact of the line with the ground.
Bad earth; in electricity, a faulty connection of a line with the earth.
Cologne earth; a variety of lignite or partially fossilized wood, used as a pigment.
Dead earth or *total earth*; in electricity, an earth-connection in which the resistance is very slight.
Earth of alum; a substance obtained by precipitating the earth from alum dissolved in water by adding ammonia or potash; it is used for paints.
Heavy earth; baryta.
To run to earth; in hunting, to pursue an animal to its hole or hiding place.
ẽarth, *v.t.*; earthed (ẽrtht), *pt.*, *pp.*; earthing, *ppr.* 1. To hide or cause to hide in the earth.

The fox is *earthed.* —Dryden.

2. To cover with earth or mold; to bury.

We *earthed* her in the shades. —B. Jonson.

3. In electricity, to connect with the earth.
ẽarth, *v.i.* To retire underground; to burrow.
ẽarth, *n.* A plowing. [Obs.]
ẽarth′=au″gẽr, *n.* An earth-borer.
ẽarth′bag, *n.* In fortification, a bag filled with earth, used to repair defenses.
ẽarth′=ba̤ll, *n.* A species of truffle, *Tuber cibarium.*
ẽarth′=bȧth, *n.* A remedy occasionally used, consisting of a bath of earth.
ẽarth′=bat″tẽr-y, *n.* A voltaic battery having its elements sunk in the earth to receive its moisture.
ẽarth′bōard, *n.* The board of a plow that turns over the earth; the moldboard.
ẽarth′=bōr″ẽr, *n.* A kind of auger for boring holes in the ground, the twisted shank of which revolves inside a cylindrical box, which retains the earth till the tool is withdrawn.
ẽarth′bo̤rn, *a.* 1. Born of the earth; terrigenous; springing originally from the earth.
2. Relating to or arising from earthly considerations.

All *earthborn* cares are wrong.—Goldsmith.

ẽarth′=bound, *a.* Fastened by the pressure of the earth; firmly fixed in the earth.
ẽarth′bred, *a.* Low; abject; groveling.
ẽarth′=chest″nut, *n.* The earthnut.
ẽarth′=clos″et, *n.* A night-stool or similar convenience in which the feces are received in a quantity of earth.
ẽarth′=çrab, *n.* A name given to the mole-cricket.
ẽarth′=çrē-ā″ted, *a.* Formed of earth.
ẽarth′=çur″rent, *n.* An electric current flowing through the earth, caused by a difference of potential.
ẽarth′din, *n.* An earthquake. [Obs.]
ẽarth′drāke, *n.* [AS. *eorth-draca*; *eorthe*, earth, and *draca*, a dragon.] In Anglo-Saxon mythology, a monster possessing qualities analogous to those of the dragon of chivalry.
ẽarth′en, *a.* Made of earth; made of clay or other like substance; as, an *earthen* vessel.
ẽarth′en=heärt″ed, *a.* Having a selfish heart; sordid.
ẽarth′en-wāre, *n.* A vessel or anything made of clay hardened in a fire; often used in a collective sense.
ẽarth′fall, *n.* A landslide.
ẽarth′=flax, *n.* A fine variety of asbestos, the

long, flexible, parallel filaments of which are so delicate as to resemble flax.

ĕarth′=flēa, *n.* The chigoe.

ĕarth′=fly, *n.* Same as *Earth-flea.*

ĕarth′=gall, *n.* 1. Any bitter plant of the gentian family especially, *Erythræa Centaurium*, the lesser centaury.

2. *Veratrum viride*, the American green hellebore.

ĕarth′=hog, *n.* The aardvark; called also *earth-pig.*

ĕarth′=house, *n.* The name generally given throughout Scotland to any one of the underground buildings known as "Picts' houses" or "Picts' dwellings" In its simplest form it consists of a single irregular-shaped chamber, formed of unhewn stones, the side-walls gradually converging toward the top until they can be roofed by stones four or five feet in width, all being covered in by a mound of earth rising slightly above the level of the surrounding district.

ĕarth′=in-duct″ŏr, *n.* In electricity, a contrivance for measuring the strength of a magnetic field as compared with that of the earth, consisting essentially of a rotating coil of wire in which a current is induced, placed in connection with a galvanometer.

ĕarth′i-ness, *n.* The quality of being earthy or of containing earth; grossness.

ĕarth′li-ness, *n.* The quality of being earthly; grossness; worldliness; strong attachment to worldly things.

ĕarth′ling, *n.* An inhabitant of the earth; a mortal.

ĕarth′ly, *a.* 1. Pertaining to the earth or to this world; pertaining to the present state of existence; as, *earthly* objects; *earthly* residence.

2. Belonging to the earth or world; carnal, as opposed to spiritual or heavenly; mean; vile.

3. Made of earth; earthy. [Obs.]

4. Among the things of this earth; possible; conceivable.

What *earthly* benefit can be the result?
—Pope.

Syn.—Worldly, mundane, groveling, carnal, vile, mean, sordid, corrupt.

ĕarth′ly=mīnd″ed, *a.* Having a mind devoted to earthly things.

ĕarth′ly=mīnd″ed-ness, *n.* Grossness; sensuality.

ĕarth′mad, *n.* A kind of worm or grub. [Obs.]

ĕarth′=moss, *n.* Any moss of the genus *Phascum.*

ĕarth′nut, *n.* 1. In botany, the tuber of *Bunium flexuosum* or of *Bunium Bulbocastanum*, two European umbelliferous plants.

2. *Arachis hypogæa*, the peanut.

3. The tuberous root of any one of several species of the genus *Cyperus*, especially *Cyperus rotundus.*

ĕarth′pēa, *n.* A species of pea, *Lathyrus amphicarpos*, a climbing plant.

ĕarth′=pig, *n.* See *Earth-hog.*

ĕarth′=pitch, *n.* A kind of asphalt.

ĕarth′=pul-sā″tion, *n.* A gradual undulating movement of the earth's surface, so slight and of so long a period as not to be commonly observed.

ĕarth′quāke (-kwāk), *n.* A quaking, vibratory, undulating, or other movement of a portion of the earth's crust produced by forces acting from beneath. No part of the earth is entirely free from the influence of earthquakes, but they usually occur in regions where active volcanoes exist; called also *earthshock* and *earthquave.*

ĕarth′=shine, *n.* In astronomy, a faint light visible on the part of the moon not illuminated by the sun, due to the light which the earth reflects on the moon. It is most conspicuous when the illuminated part of the disk is at its smallest, soon after new moon.

ĕarth′=smōke, *n.* *Fumaria officinalis*, the plant fumitory.

ĕarth′stär, *n.* A fungus of the genus *Geaster*, having the outer layer split in such a manner as to resemble a star in shape.

ĕarth′=tā″ble, *n.* In architecture, a course of stones resting immediately upon the foundation; called also *ground-table* or *grass-table.*

ĕarth′=tŏngue (-tung), *n.* Any one of certain club-shaped fungi of the genus *Geoglossum*, found in lawns and grassy pastures.

ĕarth′wărd, ĕarth′wărds, *adv.* Toward the earth.

ĕarth′wolf (-wụlf), *n.* The aardwolf.

ĕarth′wŏrk, *n.* 1. In engineering, any operation in which earth has to be removed or filled in, as in cuttings, embankments, etc.

2. In fortification, any construction for defense or attack, formed largely of earth.

3. Any construction resembling a military *earthwork.*

ĕarth′wŏrm, *n.* 1. Any worm belonging to the family *Lumbricidæ*, especially of the genus *Lumbricus*, of which *Lumbricus terrestris* is the best known species.

2. Figuratively, a mean, sordid wretch.

ĕarth′y, *a.* 1. Of or pertaining to earth; consisting of earth; partaking of the nature of earth; terrene; as, *earthy* matter.

2. Resembling earth or some of the properties of earth; as, an *earthy* taste or smell.

3. Inhabiting the earth; terrestrial. [Rare.]

4. Gross; not refined.

5. In mineralogy, without luster, or dull and roughish to the touch.

ēar′wax, *n.* Cerumen.

ēar′wig, *n.* [AS. *eárwicga*; *eáre*, ear, and *wicga*, beetle, worm.]

1. Any insect belonging to certain genera of the suborder *Euplexoptera*, especially to the genus *Forficula*, of which *Forficula auricularis* is the commonest species. The name was given from the notion that these insects creep into the ear and injure it.

2. In the United States, any small centiped, especially of the genus *Geophilus.*

3. One who gains the ear of another by stealth and whispers insinuations; a prying informer; a whisperer.

ēar′wig, *v.t.*; earwigged, *pt.*, *pp.*; earwigging, *ppr.* To gain the ear of and influence by covert statements or insinuations; to whisper insinuations in the ear of against another; to fill the mind of with prejudice by covert statements.

ēar′wit″ness, *n.* One who is able to give testimony to a fact from his own hearing.

ēar′wŏrm, *n.* Same as *Bollworm.*

ēaṣe, *n.* [ME. *ese*, *eise*; OFr. *aise*, *ayse*, *aize*; It. *agio*, ease.]

1. Rest, contentment, comfort, or relaxation, whether of body or mind; freedom from pain or annoyance of any kind; tranquillity.

2. Facility; freedom from difficulty or great labor.

The mob of gentlemen who wrote with *ease.*
—Pope.

3. Freedom from constraint or formality; unaffectedness; as, *ease* of behavior.

4. Satisfaction; relief; accommodation; entertainment. [Obs.]

At ease; in an undisturbed state; free from pain or anxiety.

Chapel of ease; see under *Chapel.*

Syn.—Rest, comfort, tranquillity, restfulness, satisfaction, facility, readiness, easiness.

ēaṣe, *v.t.*; eased, *pt.*, *pp.*; easing, *ppr.* 1. To free from labor or from anything that pains or annoys the body or mind; to give relief to; often with *of*; as, the medicine *eased* the patient; the traveler was *eased of* his burden.

2. To mitigate; to alleviate; to assuage; to allay; to abate or remove in part, as any burden, pain, grief, anxiety, or disturbance.

3. To relieve or release from tension, weight, pressure, or restraint; to make looser; to move or shift slightly; as, to *ease* a nut or bar in machinery; to *ease* a vessel in a heavy sea by putting the helm hard alee, or by jettisoning part of the cargo

4. To render less difficult; to facilitate.

Ease her! The command given to reduce the speed of a steamer's engine, generally preparatory to the command to "stop her," or "turn astern."

To ease off, to ease away; nautically, to slacken a rope gradually.

To ease the helm; to put the helm a little to midships in order to relieve the rudder and the steering-gear of the strain.

Syn.—Relieve, mitigate, alleviate, quiet, tranquilize, pacify, allay, disburden.

ēaṣe′fụl, *a.* Affording ease; promoting rest; quiet; peaceful.

ēaṣe′fụl-ly, *adv.* With ease or quiet.

ēaṣe′fụl-ness, *n.* The state or quality of being easeful.

ēa′ṣel, *n.* [D. *ezel*; G. *esel*, an ass, a wooden frame, easel.] A stand or frame slightly inclined and having three legs, used to support a canvas, blackboard, etc., for the artist's convenience or merely for display.

ēaṣe′less, *a.* Wanting ease. [Rare.]

ēaṣe′ment, *n.* 1. Convenience; accommodation; that which gives ease, relief, or assistance.

2. In law, any privilege or convenience which one man has in the land of another, without remuneration or profit, as a right of way, access to water, air, etc.

3. Same as *Ease-off.*

ēaṣe′=off, *n.* In carpentry, a curve formed at the junction of two members and taking the place of an angle.

ēaṣ′i-ly, *adv.* 1. In an easy manner; with ease; without much effort; as, this task may be *easily* performed; that event might have been *easily* foreseen.

2. Without pain, anxiety, or disturbance; in tranquillity; as, to pass life well and *easily.*

3. Readily; without reluctance.

4. Smoothly; quietly; gently; without tumult or discord.

5. Without violent shaking or jolting; as, a carriage moves *easily.*

ēaṣ′i-ness, *n.* 1. The state of being easy; the act of imparting ease; comfort; as, the *easiness* of a vehicle; the *easiness* of a seat.

2. Freedom from difficulty; as, the *easiness* of the work.

3. Flexibility; readiness to comply; prompt compliance; a yielding or disposition to yield without opposition or reluctance; as, *easiness* of temper.

4. Freedom from stiffness, constraint, effort, or formality; as, *easiness* of style.

ēast, *n.* [ME. *east*, *æst*, east; AS. *eást*; D. *oost*, *oosten*; O.H.G. *ostan*; G. *ost*, *osten*; Dan. *ost*, *osten*; Ice. *austr*; L. *aurora*, for *ausosa*, dawn, the east; Gr. *ēōs*, *heōs*; Sans. *ushas*, the dawn; from Sans. root *ush*, to burn.]

1. The point of the horizon at which the sun is seen to rise at the equinoxes; opposite to the west; that point of the horizon lying on the right hand when one's face is turned toward the north pole; the point of the compass in a direction at right angles to that of north and south.

2. [E—] The eastern parts of the earth: the regions or countries which lie east of Europe; the Orient. In this indefinite sense, the word is applied to Asia Minor, Syria, Chaldea, Persia, India, China, etc.; as, the riches of the *East*; the diamonds and pearls of the *East*; the kings of the *East.*

3. The eastern part of a country or region; as, a town in the *east* of France.

4. [E—] In the United States, formerly New England, or, in a broader sense, the country between the Alleghany Mountains and the Atlantic Ocean; now, generally, the entire territory to the *east* of the Mississippi river, especially that north of the Ohio river and Maryland.

5. In ecclesiastical usage, that part of a church toward which one is turned when looking at the altar from the nave.

6. [E—] In church history, the church of the Empire of the *East.*

East by north; a point of the compass, one-eighth of a quadrant north of east.

East by south; one-eighth of a quadrant south of east.

ēast, *a.* 1. Toward the rising sun, or toward the point where the sun rises, when in the equinoctial; as, the *east* gate; the *east* border; the *east* side; the *east* wind is a wind that blows from the east.

2. In ecclesiastical usage, situated in the direction of the altar of a church, looking from the nave.

ēast, *adv.* 1. In an easterly direction; eastward; as, to steer *east.*

2. In ecclesiastical usage, in the direction of the altar of a church, looking from the nave.

ēast, *v.i.* To move in the direction of the east; to veer toward the east; to orientate.

ēast′ā-bout, *adv.* In the direction of the east.

ēast′ẽr, *v.i.* In nautical language, to veer or shift to the east, as the wind.

Ēas′tẽr, *n.* [ME. *ester*, *æster*; AS. *eástre*, *eástran*, a paschal feast, originally a festival in honor of the Goddess of Spring, *Eástre*, held in April.]

1. A festival of the Christian church, observed annually in commemoration of the resurrection of Jesus Christ, and occurring on Sunday, the second day after Good Friday; it answers to the Jewish pasch or passover, and most nations still give it that name.

2. The day on which Easter is kept.

Easter day; the day on which the Easter festival is observed.

Easter dues or *offerings*; in the Church of England, certain dues paid to the parochial clergy by the parishioners at Easter as a compensation for personal tithes or the tithe for personal labor.

Easter egg; a painted egg or an artificial egg, ornamented and used at Easter as a gift.

Ēas′tẽr=flow″ẽr, *n.* *Euphorbia* or *Poinsettia pulcherrima*, a Brazilian shrub of the spurge family, the flowers of which are surrounded by large, brilliant bracts.

Ēas′tẽr=gī″ănt, *n.* *Polygonum Bistorta*, the bistort.

ēast′ẽr-ling, *n.* 1. A native of some country eastward of another; an Oriental; formerly, in England, a trader from the Baltic.

2. The name given to an English silver penny coined by Richard II. in the East.

3. The smew.

ēast′ẽr-ling, *a.* Belonging to the money of the Easterlings or Baltic traders.

ēast′ẽr-ly, *a.* 1. Coming from the eastward; as, an *easterly* wind.

2. Situated toward the east; as, the *easterly* side of a lake.

3. Moving or directed eastward; as, an *easterly* current; an *easterly* route.

4. Looking toward the east; as, an *easterly* exposure.

ēast′ẽr-ly, *adv.* On the east; in the direction of east; eastward.

ēast′ẽrn, *a.* 1. Pertaining to the east; Oriental; being or dwelling in the east; as, *eastern* kings; *eastern* countries; *eastern* customs.

2. Situated toward the east or on the east part; as, the *eastern* side of a town or church; the *eastern* gate.

3. Going toward the east, or in the direction of east; as, an *eastern* voyage.

Eastern empire; the Byzantine empire which had its seat at Constantinople. On the death of Theodosius the Great in A.D. 395, it separated from the Western empire, and existed till 1453 when Constantinople fell into the hands of the Turks.

Eastern Question; the term applied to the vexatious problems arising because of the Turks holding Southeastern Europe, and their consequent relations with states adjoining.

ēast′ērn-ēr, *n.* A native or inhabitant of eastern United States. [Colloq.]

ēast′ērn-mōst, *a.* Farthest to the east; most eastern.

Eas′tēr-tīde, *n.* The time of Easter; the week of special religious observances; the fifty days from Easter to Whitsuntide.

East′=In′di-ȧ-man, *n.* A ship engaged in the East India trade.

East In′di-ăn. Pertaining to or belonging to the East Indies.

East In′di-ăn. A native or inhabitant of the East Indies.

ēast′ing, *n.* In surveying and in sailing, the distance eastward from a given meridian; the distance gained by a ship on an easterly course.

ēast′=nọrth-ēast′, *n.* The fourth part of a quadrant, 22° 30′ north of east.

ēast′=sọuth-ēast′, *n.* The fourth part of a quadrant, 22° 30′ south of east.

ēast′wȧrd, ēast′wȧrds, *adv.* Toward the east; in the direction of east from some point or place; as, New Haven lies *eastward* from New York.

ēast′wȧrd, *a.* Having a direction toward the east.

ēa̤s′y, *a.*; *comp.* easier; *superl.* easiest. 1. At ease; (a) quiet; being at rest; free from pain or annoyance; as, the patient has slept well and is *easy*; (b) free from anxiety, care, or peevishness; quiet; tranquil; as, an *easy* mind; (c) comfortable; free from want; affording a comfortable living without toil; as, *easy* circumstances; an *easy* fortune.

2. Not difficult; not heavy or burdensome; giving or requiring no great labor or exertion; presenting no great obstacles; as, an *easy* task

3. Giving no pain or uneasiness; affording comfort; as, an *easy* posture; an *easy* carriage.

4. Gentle; moderate; not imposing or exacting; as, a ship under *easy* sail.

5. Yielding with little or no resistance; complying.

He gained their *easy* hearts. —Dryden.

6. Not constrained; not stiff or formal; as, *easy* manners; an *easy* address.

7. Self-indulgent.

His conscience was large and *easy*. —George Eliot.

8. In commerce, not straitened or restricted as regards money; opposed to *tight*; as, the money-market is *easy*, that is, loans may be easily procured.

9. Sparing; frugal. [Obs.]

Honors are easy; in the game of whist, the honors are equally divided between the opponents; hence, in a dispute between two parties, there is no advantage to either side.

Syn.—Quiet, comfortable, indulgent, facile, lenient, unconstrained, gentle, unconcerned, manageable, not difficult.

ēa̤s′y, *adv.* Easily.

ēa̤s′y=chāir, *n.* A cushioned armchair affording a comfortable seat.

ēa̤s′y=gō″ing, *a.* Inclined to take matters in an easy way; good-natured.

ēat, *v.t.*; ate (*or colloq.* eat, *et*), *pt.*; eaten (*sometimes* eat), *pp.*; eating, *ppr.* [ME. *eten*; AS. *etan*; L.G. *eten*; D. *eten*; Ice. *eta*; Dan. *æde*; O.H.G. *ezan*; L. *edere*; Gr. *edein*, to eat; Sans. root *ad*, to eat.]

1. To masticate and swallow as nourishment; to partake of as food; said especially of solids; as, to *eat* bread.

How fairy Mab the junkets *eat*. —Milton.

2. To corrode; to wear away; to waste; to consume; as, the acid *eats* away the metal.

To eat humble pie; see under *Humble*.

To eat one out of house and home; to reduce one to indigence by supporting others without compensation.

To eat one's head off; to cost more in feeding than one's utility is worth, as a horse, cow, or other animal.

To eat one's heart; to brood over one's sorrows or disappointments.

To eat one's words; to take back what has been uttered; to retract one's assertions.

Syn.—Devour, consume, corrode, wear, gnaw.

ēat, *v.i.* 1. To take food; to feed; to board.

He did *eat* continually at the king's table. —2 Sam. ix. 13.

2. To taste or relish; as, it *eats* like the tenderest beef. [Colloq.]

3. To make way by corrosion; to gnaw; as, a cancer *eats* into the flesh.

To eat up into the wind; nautically, to make good headway to windward.

ēat′ȧ-ble, *a.* and *n.* I. *a.* That may be eaten; fit to be eaten; proper for food; esculent.

II. *n.* Anything that may be eaten; that which is fit for food.

ēat′āge, *n.* Food for horses and cattle from aftermath.

ēat′ēr, *n.* One who eats; that which eats or corrodes; a corrosive.

ēath, *a.* and *adv.* [AS.] I. *a.* Easy. [Obs.]

II. *adv.* Easily. [Obs.]

ēat′ing, *n.* 1. The act of taking food.

2. That which is fit to be eaten; food; as, salmon are good *eating*.

ēat′ing=house, *n.* A house in which food is sold and served; a restaurant.

eau (ō), *n.*; *pl.* **eaux** (ōz). [Fr., water.] Water; a word used with some other words to designate various spirituous waters, particularly perfumes; as, *eau* de Cologne; *eau* de Luce; *eau* de Portugal, etc.

Eau Créole; a highly esteemed liqueur made in Martinique, West Indies, by distilling the flowers of the mammee-apple, *Mammea Americana*, with spirit of wine.

Eau de Cologne; same as *Cologne*.

Eau de Javelle; in chemistry, a mixture of potassium carbonate, bleaching-powder, and water, used as an antiseptic and for bleaching.

Eau de Luce [from *Luce*, who invented it]; a strong solution of ammonia, scented and rendered milky by mastic and oil of amber; used in India as an antidote to the bites of venomous serpents.

eau=de=vie′ (ō-de-vē′), *n.* [Fr., lit., water of life.] The French name for brandy; specifically applied to the coarser and less purified varieties of brandy, the term cognac being applied to the best kinds.

ēave′drop, *n.* [Rare.] See *Eavesdrop*.

ēaveș, *n.pl.* [AS. *efese*, *yfese*, eaves, edge; O.H.G. *obisa*, *opasa*, a porch, hall; G. *oben*; G. dial. *ousch*, a gutter along the eaves.]

1. The edges or lower borders of the roof of a building, which overhang the walls and cast off the water that falls on the roof; figuratively, any projecting rim.

And closing *eaves* of wearied eyes. —Tennyson.

2. Margin; edge. [Obs.]

ēaveș′=bōard, ēaveș′=catch, *n.* An arris-fillet, or a thick board with a feather-edge, nailed across the rafters at the eaves of a roof to raise the course of slates a little; called also *eaves-lath*.

ēaveș′=drip, *n.* An ancient custom or law which forbade the erection of a house so near to the boundary of the estate that the eaves-drop would fall on a neighbor's land.

ēaveș′drop, *n.* The water which falls in drops from the eaves of a house.

ēaveș′drop, *v.i.* To stand under the eaves or near the windows of a house, to listen and learn what is said within doors; hence, to watch for an opportunity of hearing the private conversation of others.

ēaveș′drop″pēr, *n.* One who stands under the eaves, or near a house, to listen to what is said inside; hence, one who tries to overhear.

ēaveș′drop″ping, *n.* The act of an eaves-dropper.

ēaveș′=lath, *n.* See *Eaves-board*.

ēaveș′=swăl″lōw, *n.* 1. A species of swallow that builds a nest of mud under the eaves of houses; the cliff-swallow.

2. The house-martin.

ēaveș′=trọugh (-trŏf), *n.* A trough or gutter hanging immediately below the eaves of a building to catch the eavesdrop and convey it away.

é-bau-ḉhoir′ (ā-bō-shwor′), *n.* [Fr.] 1. A large chisel used by statuaries to rough-hew their work.

2. A great hatchel or beating instrument used by rope-makers.

ebb, *n.* *Emberiza miliaria*, the common bunting. [Obs.]

ebb, *n.* [AS. *ebbe*, *ebba*; D. *eb*, *ebbe*; G. *ebbe*, the falling back of the tide.]

1. The reflux of the tide; the return of tide-water toward the sea; opposed to *flood* or *flow*.

2. A flowing backward or away; decline; decay; a falling from a better to a worse state; as, the *ebb* of life; the *ebb* of prosperity.

ebb, *v.i.*; ebbed, *pt.*, *pp.*; ebbing, *ppr.* 1. To flow back; to return, as the water of a tide toward the ocean; opposed to *flow*.

2. To decay; to decline; to return or fall back from a better to a worse state.

Syn.—Recede, retire, withdraw, decrease, wane, decline, decay.

ebb, *v.t.* To cause to recede. [Obs.]

ebb, *a.* Not deep; shallow. [Obs.]

ebb′=an″ḉhŏr, *n.* The anchor used by a vessel during the ebb-tide.

ebb′=tīde, *n.* The reflux of tide-water; the retiring tide.

Eb-ē-nā′cē-æ, *n.pl.* [From L. *ebenus*, ebony. A natural order of gamopetalous exogens, the ebony family, chiefly inhabiting the tropics, containing six genera and about two hundred and fifty species, which consist entirely of shrubs or trees, some being of large size. *Diospyros* is the largest and most important genus.

eb-ē-nā′ceous, *a.* Pertaining to the *Ebenaceæ*.

Eb-en-ē′zēr, *n.* [Heb., stone of help.]

1. Any memorial of divine aid.

2. Among English dissenters, a chapel or place of worship.

E′bi-ō-niṣm, *n.* Ebionitism.

E′bi-ō-nīte, *n.* [LL. *Ebionitæ*; Gr. *Ebiōnaioi*; Heb. *ebyonīm*, the poor.] One of an early sect of heretics who united the ceremonies of the law with the precepts of the Gospel, observing both the Jewish and Christian Sabbaths. They denied the divinity of Christ and rejected many parts of the New Testament.

E″bi-ō-nit′iḉ, *a.* Of or pertaining to Ebionitism or the Ebionites.

E′bi-ō-nī″tiṣm, *n.* The doctrine or practice of the Ebionites.

eb′lȧ-nin, *n.* Same as *Pyroxanthine*.

Eb′lis, Ib′lees, *n.* [Ar. *Iblis*.] In Mohammedan mythology, an evil spirit or devil, the chief of the fallen angels or wicked jinns.

ē′bōe, *n.* [W. Ind.] A negro from Benin.

ē′bōe=light, *n.* *Erythroxylon brevipes*, a West Indian shrub.

ē′bōe=tọrch″wood, *n.* Same as *Eboe-light*.

ē′bōe=trēe, *n.* *Dipteryx oleifera*, a leguminous tree of Central America, the seeds of which yield a considerable quantity of oil.

eb′ŏn, *a.* and *n.* I. *a.* Consisting of ebony; like ebony in color; dark; black.

II. *n.* Ebony.

eb′ŏn-ist, *n.* A worker in ebony.

eb′ŏn-īte, *n.* A hard black compound obtained by blending caoutchouc or gutta-percha with variable proportions of sulphur. It is extensively used in manufacture.

eb′ŏn-īze, *v.t.*; ebonized, *pt.*, *pp.*; ebonizing, *ppr.* 1. To make black or tawny; to tinge with the color of ebony; as, to *ebonize* the fairest complexion.

2. To make or stain black, as wood, in imitation of ebony.

eb′ŏn-y, *n.*; *pl.* **eb′ŏn-ieș.** [L. *ebenus*; Gr. *ebenos*, from Heb. *eben*, a stone; so called from its hardness and weight.] A hard, heavy, and durable wood, which admits of a fine polish or gloss. The usual color is black, but red and green varieties are also found. The most valuable is the heartwood of *Diospyros Ebenum*, which grows in great abundance in the flat parts of Ceylon, and is of such size that logs of its heartwood, 2 feet in diameter and from 10 to 15 feet long, are easily procured. Other varieties of valuable ebony are obtained from *Diospyros Ebenaster* of the East Indies and *Diospyros melanoxylon* of the Coromandel coast in Hindustan. The green ebony of Jamaica, known also as the West Indian or American ebony, is the wood of the leguminous tree *Brya Ebenus*.

Ebony (*Diospyros Ebenum*).

eb′ŏn-y, *a.* Made of ebony; like ebony; as, an *ebony* walking-stick.

é-bōule′ment (ā-bōl′moṅ), *n.* [Fr., from *ebouler*, to tumble down.]

1. In fortification, the crumbling or falling of the wall of a fortification.

2. In geology, a sudden landslip in a mountainous region; a landslide.

ē-braḉ′tē-āte, *a.* [L. *e-* priv., and *bractea*, a thin plate.] In botany, without a bract or bracts.

ē-braḉ′tē-ō-lāte, *a.* [L. *e-* priv., and *bracteola*, dim. of *bractea*, a thin plate.] In botany, without bractlets.

E-brā′iḱe, *a.* An obsolete form of *Hebraic*.

ē-brī′e-ty, *n.*; *pl.* **ē-brī′e-tieș.** [L. *ebrietas*, from *ebrius*, drunken.] Drunkenness; intoxication by spirituous liquors.

ē-bril′lāde, *n.* [Fr.] A check given to a horse, by a sudden jerk of one rein, when he refuses to turn.

ē-bri-os′i-ty, *n.* [L. *ebriositas*, from *ebrius*, drunken.] Habitual drunkenness.

ē′bri-ous, *a.* Inclined to excessive drinking; given to tippling. [Rare.]

ē-bul′li-āte, *v.i.* [LL. *ebullatus*, pp. of *ebullare*, from L. *ebullire*, to boil up.] To send up bubbles by boiling or as by boiling. [Obs.]

ē-bul′lience (-yens), **ē-bul′lien-cy** (-yen sy), *n.* An overflow by boiling.

ē-bul′lient, *a.* Boiling over; hence, showing much exuberance or exhilaration.

ē-bul′li-ō-sçōpe, *n.* [L. *ebullire*, to boil up, and Gr. *skopein*, to view.] An instrument for determining the boiling-point of a liquid, and from this determining the proportion of alcohol in the mixture, or vice versa.

eb-ul-li′tion (-lish′un), *n.* [L. *ebullition*, from *ebullire*, to boil up.]

1. The condition of any liquid when bubbles are rapidly forming in its mass and rising to the surface. This is primarily due to the application of heat, but may result either from the lowering of pressure beyond the escaping point of dissolved or compressed gas, or from chemical activity; formerly called *bullition*.

2. A state of agitation of a liquid resembling boiling; as, below the falls the water is in a constant state of *ebullition*.

3. A sudden display; a violent outburst, as of temper or passion.

eb′ūr-ine, *n.* [L. *ebur*, ivory, and *-ine*.] An imitation of ivory, being a composition of some cement and the dust of ivory or of bone.

ē-bur-nā′tion, *n.* [L. *eburnus*, of ivory, from *ebur*, ivory.] In pathology, the abnormal ossification or hardening in a cartilage, bone, or any other tissue, making it resemble ivory in hardness and texture.

ē-būr′nē-ăn, *a.* Made of ivory; of or pertaining to ivory.

ē-būr″ni-fi-çā′tion, *n.* [L. *eburnus*, of ivory, and *-ficare*, from *facere*, to make.] The change of a substance into another resembling ivory; eburnation.

eb′ūr-nine, *a.* Relating to ivory.

eç-. A prefix from L. *ec-*, Gr. *ek-*, from *ek* or *ex*, out, out of, from. It is usually used before consonants (as, *ec*lipse, *ec*logue), and in scientific terms is sometimes equivalent to *ecto-* or *exo-*.

ē-çal′cȧ-rāte, *a.* [L. *e-* priv., and *calcar*, a spur.] In biology, destitute of a spur, or calcar.

E-çăr′di-nēş, *n.pl.* [L. *e-* priv., and *cardo* (*-inis*), a hinge.] In zoölogy, an order of hingeless brachiopods, the *Lyopomata*.

ē-çăr′i-nāte, *a.* [L. *e-* priv., and *carina*, a keel.] In zoölogy, keelless.

é-çăr-té′ (ā-kär-tā′), *n.* [Fr., from *écarter*, to discard, set aside.] A two-handed game of cards in which the players may discard, and receive other cards from the deck.

ē-çau′dāte, *a.* [L. *e-* priv., and *cauda*, a tail.]

1. In zoölogy, having no tail; anurous.

2. In botany, having no spur, tail, or tail-like appendage.

Eç-bal′li-um, *n.* [Gr. *ekballein*, to throw out.] A genus of *Cucurbitaceæ*, native to southern Europe and known as the squirting cucumber. [See *Squirting cucumber* under *Cucumber*.]

eç′bȧ-sis, *n.* [L., from Gr. *ekbasis*, a going out, the issue or event of a matter; *ek*, out, and *bainein*, to go.] In rhetoric, a figure in which the orator treats of things according to their events and consequences.

eç-bat′iç, *a.* [From Gr. *ekbainein*, a going out, issue, event; *ek*, out, and *bainein*, to go.] In grammar, denoting a mere result or consequence, as distinguished from *telic*, which denotes intention or purpose. Thus, the Greek phrase, *hina plerōthē*, if rendered "so that it was fulfilled," is *ecbatic*; if rendered "in order that it might be," etc., is *telic*.

eç-blas-tē′sis, *n.* [Gr. *ekblastēsis*, a shooting or budding out; *ek*, out, and *blastanein*, to sprout.] In botany, the unusual phenomenon of buds growing in the axils of any of the parts of a flower.

eç′bō-lē, *n.* [Gr. *ekbolē*, a throwing out; *ek*, out, and *ballein*, to throw.] In rhetoric, a digression in which a person is introduced speaking his own words.

eç-bol′iç, *n.* [Gr. *ekballein*, to throw out.] A medicine, such as ergot, tending to cause contraction of the uterus in pregnancy and the consequent expulsion of the fetus.

eç′bō-line (-lin or -lēn), *n.* [Gr. *ekballein*, to throw out.] An alkaloid constituent of ergot.

eç″çȧ-lē-ō′bi-ŏn, *n.* [Gr. *ekkalein*, to call out, and *bios*, life.] A contrivance for hatching eggs by artificial heat.

Eç′cē Hō′mō. [L.] 1. The words of Pilate, Behold the Man!

2. In painting, a representation of Christ crowned with thorns.

eç-cen′triç, *n.* [LL. *eccentros*, out of the center, eccentric; Gr. *ekkentros*; *ek*, out, and *kentron*, center.]

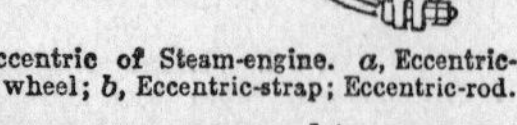

Eccentric of Steam-engine. *a*, Eccentric-wheel; *b*, Eccentric-strap; Eccentric-rod.

1. In ancient astronomy, a great circle with its center remote from the earth, whose circumference was supposed to carry an epicycle, the path of a planet.

2. In modern astronomy, a great circle tangent to an elliptical orbit at the two extremities of its major axis.

3. In mechanics, a device in which a circular journal is mounted upon an axle with its center not coinciding with that of the axle, whereby circular motion is converted into reciprocating linear motion; as, the *eccentric* of a steam-engine.

4. Anyone or anything that acts or operates in an abnormal or unusual manner.

eç-cen′triç, *a.* 1. Deviating or departing from the center.

2. In geometry, not having the same center; a term applied to circles and spheres, in opposition to *concentric*, having a common center.

3. Deviating from stated methods, usual practice, or established forms or laws; irregular; anomalous; departing from the usual course; as, *eccentric* conduct; an *eccentric* genius.

4. Not terminating in the same point or directed by the same principle.

5. In mechanics, relating or pertaining to an eccentric; written also *excentric*.

6. In pathology, having location remote from a nervous center.

7. In forestry, having a trunk wanting in symmetry or regularity of shape; said of a tree.

Eccentric anomaly; the angular distance of a planet from its perihelion as seen from the center of its orbit.

Eccentric chuck; in machinery, a lathe-chuck in which the position of the center of the piece turned may be changed at will.

Eccentric gear; in machinery, (a) the entire apparatus by which an eccentric is utilized; (b) cog-wheels which rotate on eccentric axes.

Syn.—Anomalous, odd, abnormal, singular, strange, unnatural, peculiar.

eç-cen′triç-ăl, *a.* Same as *Eccentric*.

eç-cen′triç-ăl-ly, *adv.* With eccentricity; in an eccentric manner.

eç-cen′triç=hook, *n.* In steam-engineering, a journal-box in the shape of an inverted U opposite the eccentric-strap, furnishing a detachable fastening.

eç-cen-triç′i-ty, *n.*; *pl.* **eç-cen-triç′i-tieş.**

1. Departure or deviation from that which is stated, regular, or usual; as, the *eccentricity* of a man's genius or conduct.

2. In mathematics, the ratio existing between the distance from the center of a conic to its focus and one-half of its transverse axis.

3. In astronomy, the distance of the center of a planet's orbit from the center of the sun; that is, the distance between the center of an ellipse and its focus. Thus, in the ellipse, D E F G, of which A and B are the foci, and C the center, A C or B C is the *eccentricity*.

4. In mechanics, the linear extent of reciprocating motion obtained in an eccentric; the throw.

eç-cen′triç=rod, *n.* The rod attached to the eccentric-strap for transferring the motion of the eccentric.

eç-cen′triç=strap, *n.* The encircling ring clasping the journal of the eccentric, receiving the motion therefrom; called also *eccentric-hoop*.

eç-cen-trom′e-tēr, *n.* [LL. *eccentros*, out of the center, and *metrum*, a measure.] An instrument for determining eccentricity, especially that of a hollow projectile.

eç-ceph-ȧ-lō′sis, *n.* [Gr. *ek*, out, and *kephalē*, head.] In obstetrics, the operation of separating and taking away the brain of a fetus in order to accomplish delivery.

eç-çhon-drō′mȧ, *n.* [Gr. *ek*, out, and *chondros*, cartilage.] A tumor having its origin in normal cartilage.

eç-çhy-mō′mȧ, *n.*; *pl.* **eç-çhy-mō′mȧ-tȧ.** [Gr. *ek*, out, and *chymos*, juice, from *chein*, to pour.] In pathology, a tumorous condition of the cellular tissue beneath the skin; a black-and-blue swelling.

eç-çhy-mō′sis, *n.*; *pl.* **eç-çhy-mō′sēş.** [Gr. *ekchymōsis*, from *ekchymoesthai*, to shed the blood and leave it extravasated under the skin; *ek*, out, and *chymos*, juice, from *chein*, to pour.] In medicine, an appearance of livid spots on the skin, occasioned by extravasated blood resulting from contusion.

eç-çhy-mot′iç, *a.* Relating to ecchymosis.

eç′cle, *n.* Same as *Eckle*, 1.

eç′cle=grass, *n.* In botany, the common butterwort, *Pinguicula vulgaris*.

eç-clē′şi-ȧ, *n.*; *pl.* **eç-clē′şi-æ.** [L. *ecclesia*; Gr. *ekklēsia*, an assembly of the people, from *ekklētos*, summoned; *ekkalein*, to summon, call out.]

1. The political assembly in the ancient Greek states, at which all free citizens could vote.

2. The early Greek and Latin name for the church; a congregation.

eç-clē′şi-ăl, *a.* Relating to the church; ecclesiastic. [Obs.]

eç-clē′şi-ärçh, *n.* [LL. *ecclesiarcha*, from Gr. *ekklēsia*, assembly, and *archos*, a ruler.]

1. A ruler of the church, especially one high in authority.

2. A kind of sexton in the Greek church.

eç-clē′şi-ast, *n.* [LL. *ecclesiastes*; Gr. *ekklēsiastēs*, a member of an assembly, from *ekklēsia*, an assembly.]

1. An executive officer of the church.

2. [E—] The Book of Ecclesiasticus. [Obs.]

3. A citizen taking part in the ecclesia of ancient Athens. [Rare.]

Eç-clē-şi-as′tēş, *n.* [LL., from Gr. *ekklēsiastēs*, a preacher.] A canonical book of the Old Testament.

eç-clē-şi-as′tiç, *n.* A person in orders or one consecrated to the service of the church and the ministry of religion.

eç-clē-şi-as′tiç-ăl, eç-clē-şi-as′tiç, *a.* [Gr. *ekklēsiastikos*, from *ekklēsia*, an assembly or meeting called out, the church; from *ekkalein*, to call forth or convoke; *ek*, out, and *kalein*, to call.] Pertaining or relating to the church; as, *ecclesiastical* discipline or government; *ecclesiastical* affairs, history, or polity; *ecclesiastical* courts.

Ecclesiastical commissioners for England; a body of commissioners appointed by Parliament in 1836 to investigate the affairs of the Church of England and to report their condition.

Ecclesiastical courts; courts whose business it is to consider all cases pertaining to the discipline of the church.

Ecclesiastical law; the law administered by ecclesiastical courts.

Ecclesiastical modes; the particular arrangement and disposition of the notes in the musical scale, as formerly appointed and practised in church service.

Ecclesiastical state; the body of the clergy.

Ecclesiastical States; the territory once subject to the pope of Rome as its temporal ruler.

eç-clē-şi-as′tiç-ăl-ly, *adv.* In an ecclesiastical manner; in accordance with ecclesiastical usage.

eç-clē-şi-as′ti-çişm, *n.* Attachment to ecclesiastical forms and usages.

Eç-clē-şi-as′ti-çus, *n.* [LL. *ecclesiasticus*, of or belonging to the church; Gr. *ekklēsiastikos*, from *ekklēsia*, an assembly.] A book of the Apocrypha.

eç-clē-şi-ol′ȧ-try, *n.* Undue attachment to and veneration for the forms and ceremonies of the church.

eç-clē″şi-ō-log′iç-ăl, *a.* Belonging to ecclesiology.

eç-clē-şi-ol′ō-ġist, *n.* One versed in ecclesiology.

eç-clē-şi-ol′ō-ġy, *n.* [Gr. *ekklēsia*, an assembly, a church, and *-logia*, from *legein*, to speak.]

1. The science of church architecture.

2. The science of church organization and management.

eç-cri-nol′ō-ġy, *n.* [Gr. *ekkrinein*, to separate, and *-logia*, from *legein*, to speak.] The department of physiological science which treats of the secretions of the body.

eç-crit′iç, *n.* [Gr. *ekkritikos*, secretive, from *ekkritos*; from *ek*, out, and *krinein*, to separate.] An eliminative medicine.

eç-cy-ē′sis, *n.* [From Gr. *ekkyein*, to bring forth; *ek*, out, and *kyein*, to be pregnant.] Pregnancy occurring outside the uterus.

eç′dēr-on, *n.* [Gr. *ek*, out, and *deros*, skin.] In histology, the superficial layer of cells upon the skin or upon the mucous membrane.

eç-dēr-on′iç, *a.* Pertaining to the ecderon.

eç′dy-sis, *n.*; *pl.* **eç′dy-sēş.** [Gr. *ekdysis*, from *ekdyein*, to get out of, strip off; *ek*, out, and *dyein*, to put on, enter.] The act of putting off an old outer covering and appearing in a new one, as in the case of a snake, a lobster, or certain insects.

eç′gō-nine, *n.* In chemistry, an alkaloid base, $C_9H_{15}NO_3$, formed by treating cocaine with hydrochloric acid.

é-çhau-guette′ (ā-shō-get′), *n.* [Fr.] A structure devised for the protection of a sentinel, usually a small turret projecting from the wall of a castle.

eçh′e, *a.* and *pron.* Obsolete Middle English form of *each*.

eçh′e-lon, *n.* [Fr., from *échelle*; OFr. *eschelle*; It. *scala*, from L. *scala*, a ladder.]

1. In military tactics, the position of an army in the form of steps, or with one division more advanced than another.

2. In naval encounters, a disposition of the vessels in the form of a wedge.

eçh′e-lon, *v.t.*; echeloned, *pt.*, *pp.*; echeloning, *ppr.* To dispose the forces of in echelon.

eçh′e-lon, *v.i.* To form into and take position in echelon.

E-çhid′nȧ, *n.* [L., from Gr. *echidna*, a viper, an adder.]

1. A genus of ant-eaters, found in Australia. They are monotrematous edentate mammals, nearly allied to the duck-billed animal or *Ornithorhynchus*.

2. [e—] Any animal of this genus.

e-chid'nine, *n.* [L. *echidna*, a viper, and *-ine.*] The virus extracted from the transparent viscous fluid secreted by the glands of poisonous serpents.

ech'i-nāte, ech'i-nā-ted, *a.* [L. *echinatus*, set with prickles, from *echinus*, a hedgehog.] Set with prickles; prickly, like a hedgehog; having sharp points; bristled; as, an *echinated* pericarp.

e-chi'nid, *a.* and *n.* Same as *Echinoid.*

e-chin'i-dăn, *n.* A radiate animal, one of the family *Echinoidea.*

e-chin'i-tăl, *a.* Relating to an echinite.

ech'i-nite, *n.* [Gr. *echinos*, a hedgehog, and *-ite.*] An echinoid in a state of petrifaction.

ech-i-nō-. A combining form from Greek *echinos*, a hedgehog, sea-urchin, and used to signify connection with or relation to a hedgehog or sea-urchin; as, *echino*coccus; *echino*cystis.

E-chi-nō-cac'tus, *n.* [*Echino-*, and Gr. *kaktos*, a cactus.] A genus of cactaceous plants abounding in Mexico and in southwestern United States. They are remarkable for the singular forms of their stems. They have showy flowers and are frequently cultivated.

Variegated-flowered Echinocactus.

e-chi'nō-chrōme, *n.* [*Echino-*, and Gr. *chrōma*, a color.] A pigment obtained from the bodies of certain echinoderms, usually of a brown or brownish color.

e-chi-nō-chrō'mō-ġen, *n.* [*Echino-*, and Gr. *chrōma*, color, and *-genēs*, producing.] In chemistry, any substance containing echinochrome.

e-chi-nō-coc'cus, *n.*; *pl.* **e-chi-nō-coc'cī.** [*Echino-*, and Gr. *kokkos*, a berry.] A parasitic larva, *Tænia echinococcus*, of a tapeworm peculiar to the dog but found in other animals and in man, where it produces fatal tumors in the lungs or liver.

E-chi-nō-cys'tis, *n.* [*Echino-*, and Gr. *kystis*, a bladder.] In botany, a genus of the gourd family, a species of which, *Echinocystis lobata*, grows in the eastern part of the United States.

e-chi'nō-dērm, *n.* [*Echino-*, and Gr. *derma*, skin.] One of the *Echinodermata.*

e-chi-nō-dēr'măl, *a.* Same as *Echinodermatous.*

E-chi-nō-dēr'mȧ-tȧ, *n.pl.* [From Gr. *echinos*, a hedgehog, sea-urchin, and *derma*, skin.] A great division of the animal kingdom, characterized by a somewhat radial structure and often by a spiny exoskeleton. The *Echinus* is the type genus.

e-chi-nō-dēr'mȧ-tous, *a.* Having the characteristics of an echinoderm; echinodermal.

e-chi'noid, *n.* and *a.* I. *n.* One of the *Echinoidea.*

II. *a.* Of or related to the *Echinoidea.*

Ech-i-noi'dē-ȧ, *n.pl.* [Gr. *echinos*, a hedgehog, sea-urchin, and *eidos*, form.] A class of *Echinodermata* including the sea-urchin.

ech-i-nol'ō-ġy, *n.* [*Echino-*, and Gr. *-logia*, from *legein*, to speak.] That branch of zoölogy which treats of the characteristics and classification of echinoderms.

e-chi-nō-pæ'di-um, *n.*; *pl.* **e-chi-nō-pæ'di-ȧ.** [*Echino-*, and Gr. *paidion*, dim. of *pais, paidos*, a child.] A bilateral, ciliated larva of an echinoderm.

E-chi-nō-zō'ȧ, *n.pl.* [*Echino-*, and Gr. *zōon*, pl. *zōa*, an animal.] An old name for *Echinodermata.*

e-chin'ū-lāte, *a.* [L. *echinus*, a hedgehog.] Having a coat or setting of small spines.

e-chin'ū-li-fōrm, *a.* [L. *echinus*, a hedgehog, sea-urchin, and dim. *-ulus*, and *forma*, form.] In the form of small spines.

e-chi'nus, *n.*; *pl.* **e-chi'nī.** [L., from Gr. *echinos*, a hedgehog, sea-urchin.]

1. A hedgehog.

2. A sea-urchin.

3. [E—] A genus of annuloids, constituting the type of the class *Echinodermata.* The body is covered with a test or shell, often beset with movable spines. There are various species, several of them eatable.

Sea-urchin (*Echinus esculentus*).

4. In architecture, an ornament of the form of an egg, alternating with an anchor-shaped or dart-shaped ornament, peculiar to the ovolo molding, whence the molding is sometimes called *echinus.*

Echinus.

Ech-i-ū-roi'dē-ȧ, *n.pl.* [From Gr. *echis, echidos*, an adder, viper, and *oura*, a tail.] A suborder of worms, under *Gephyrea.*

ech'ō, *n.* [L. *echo*; Gr. *ēchō*, a reverberated sound, an echo; *ēchē, ēchos*, a sound, noise; *ēchein*, to sound.]

1. A sound reflected from a solid body and repeated at or near the place of its origin; as, an *echo* from a distant hill.

2. [E—] In classical mythology, a nymph, the daughter of the Air and Earth, who, for love of Narcissus, pined away till nothing remained of her but her voice.

3. In architecture, a vault or arch for redoubling sounds.

4. Repetition with assent; close imitation, either in words or sentiments.

5. In music, the repetition of a melodic phrase, frequently written for the organ on account of the facility with which it can be produced by the stops.

Echo organ; in music, a set of organ-pipes attuned and placed in a resonant box at some distance from the player and which, through sympathetic vibrations, repeat a prominent short passage of the music performed on the organ.

ech'ō, *v.i.*; echoed, *pt., pp.*; echoing, *ppr.* 1. To resound; to reflect sound.

2. To be sounded back; as, *echoing* noise.

ech'ō, *v.t.* 1. To reverberate or send back sound from; to return, as what has been uttered.

> Those peals are *echoed* by the Trojan throng.
> —Dryden.

2. To repeat as assenting to; as, he but *echoes* the sentiments of his master.

ech'ō-ēr, *n.* One who or that which echoes.

ē-chō'ic, *a.* Imitative, as in the formation of words which imitate or repeat natural sounds; as, flap, crunch, spit, pitapat, are *echoic.*

ech'ō-ism, *n.* The act of imitating or the imitation of a natural sound.

ech-ō-lā'li-ȧ, *n.* [Gr. *ēchō*, an echo, and *lalia*, from *lalein*, to babble.] A phase of mental disorder in which a patient, without purpose, repeats words heard or addressed to him.

ech'ō-less, *a.* Giving back no echo; not returning in echo.

ē-chom'e-tēr, *n.* [Gr. *ēchō*, sound, echo, and *metron*, a measure.] An appliance used in the measurement of the duration of sounds.

e-chom'e-try, *n.* 1. The art or act of measuring the duration of sounds.

2. The art of constructing vaults to produce echoes.

ēch-ōn', ēch-ōon', *pron.* Old forms for *each one.* [Obs.]

ech'ō-scōpe, *n.* [Gr. *ēchō*, an echo, sound, and *skopein*, to view.] A kind of stethoscope which intensifies sounds made by tapping on the chest.

ech'ō-stop, *n.* A stop attached to an organ, used by the performer to produce echo-like sounds.

Ec'i-ton, *n.* [Etym. doubtful.] A genus of American ants, often known as *army ants* from their practice of marching in large numbers. They are carnivorous and very destructive.

eck'le, *n.* [Prov. Eng.] 1. An icicle.

2. [*pl.*] The comb of a cock.

é-clāir' (ā-klãr'), *n.* [Fr.] A kind of confection or cake, filled with flavored cream and incrusted with a preparation of chocolate and sugar.

ē-clāir'cisse-ment (*or Fr. pron.* ā-klãr-sis-moṅ'), *n.* [Fr.] Explanation; the clearing up of anything not before understood.

ē-clāir'cīze, *v.t.* [Fr. *eclairir*, to lighten, illuminate.] To make clear: to explain; to clear up (what is not understood or misunderstood); also spelled *eclaircise.* [Rare.]

ec-lamp'si-ȧ, ec-lamp'sy, *n.* [Gr. *eklampsis*, a shining forth, from *eklampein*, to shine forth; *ek*, out, and *lampein*, to shine.]

1. An acute nervous affection attended by convulsions and loss of consciousness, afflicting for the most part pregnant women and small children.

2. An imaginary perception of light flashing in front of the eyes, one of the symptoms or precursors of epilepsy.

ec-lamp'tic, *a.* Caused by or suffering from eclampsia.

ē-clăt' (ē-klä'), *n.* [Fr., from *eclater*, to split, shiver, break forth, shine.]

1. A burst of applause; acclamation; approbation; renown.

2. Splendor; show; pomp.

ec-lec'tic, *a.* [Gr. *eklektikos*, from *eklegein*, to select, pick out; *ek*, out, and *legein*, to choose, pick.] Selecting; choosing; not original nor following any one model or leader, but choosing at will from the doctrines, works, etc., of others.

Eclectic physician: one of the class of physicians who combine practices and medicines selected from all schools of medicine; formerly often used as a synonym for *botanic doctor.*

Eclectic school; same as *Bolognese school* under *Bolognese.*

ec-lec'tic, *n.* One who believes in or practises an eclectic method; especially used in philosophy and medicine.

ec-lec'tic-ăl-ly, *adv.* In accordance with the practices of eclecticism.

ec-lec'ti-cism, *n.* 1. The method or system of an eclectic.

2. The philosophy advanced by Potamon and other Neo-Platonists of Alexandria in the second century, which tried to combine in one system all the truths of all the systems of philosophy.

ec-legm' (-lem'), *n.* [L. *ecligma*; Gr. *ekleigma*, from *ekleichein*, to lick up; *ek*, out, and *leichein*, to lick.] A medicine made by the incorporation of oils with syrups. [Obs.]

ē-clip-sā'rē-ŏn, *n.* An instrument for explaining the phenomena of eclipses.

ē-clipse', *v.t.*; eclipsed (-klipst'), *pt., pp.*; eclipsing, *ppr.* 1. To hide, as a luminous body, in whole or in part, and intercept its rays; as, to *eclipse* the sun or a star.

2. To cloud; to darken; to obscure; as, to *eclipse* the glory of a hero.

ē-clipse', *v.i.* To suffer an eclipse.

ē-clipse', *n.* [L. *eclipsis*; Gr. *ekleipsis*, an eclipse, a failing, from *ekleipein*, to leave out, pass over, fail; *ek*, out, and *leipein*, to leave.]

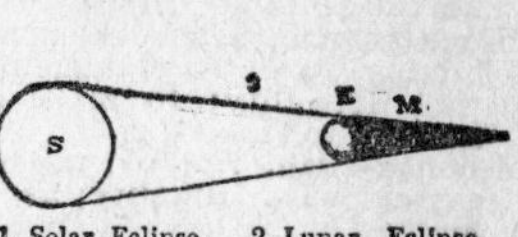
1. Solar Eclipse. 2. Lunar Eclipse. S, Sun. M, Moon. E, Earth. *u*, Umbra, or total eclipse. *p*, Penumbra, or partial eclipse.

1. An interception or obscuration of the light of the sun, moon, or other luminous body. An *eclipse* of the sun is caused by the intervention of the moon, which totally or partially hides the sun's disk; an *eclipse* of the moon is occasioned by the shadow of the earth, which falls on it and obscures it in whole or in part, but does not entirely conceal it.

2. Darkness; obscuration.

> All the posterity of our first parents suffered a perpetual *eclipse* of spiritual life.
> —Raleigh.

Annular eclipse; see under *Annular.*

Cycle of eclipses; see under *Cycle.*

ē-clip'sis, *n.* [L., from Gr. *ekleipsis*, an eclipse, a failing.]

1. Temporary unconsciousness; trance.

2. A cutting out of words from a sentence; ellipsis. [Rare.]

ē-clip'tic, *a.* [L. *eclipticus*; Gr. *ekleiptikos*, pertaining to an eclipse; from *ekleipein*, to leave out, fail.]

1. Pertaining to or described by the ecliptic.

2. Suffering an eclipse.

Lunar ecliptic limit; the greatest angular distance from the moon's node at which an eclipse of the moon may occur, which is 12°.

Solar ecliptic limit; the greatest angular distance from the moon's node at which an eclipse of the sun may occur, which is 17°.

An eclipse of the moon can occur only when it is at the full phase, while an eclipse of the sun can occur only when the moon is at the new phase.

ē-clip'tic, *n.* 1. A great circle of the sphere, supposed to be drawn through the middle of the zodiac, making an angle with the equinoctial of about 23° 27', which is the sun's greatest declination. The ecliptic is the apparent path of the sun, or the path or way among the fixed stars which the earth, in its orbit, appears to describe to an eye placed in the sun.

2. In geography, a great circle on the terrestrial globe, answering to and falling within the plane of the celestial *ecliptic.*

ec'lō-ġite, *n.* [Gr. *eklogos*, picked out, chosen, from *eklegein*, to pick out, choose.] A rock of rare beauty, made up of hornblende, granular garnet, and other minerals.

ec'logue (-log), *n.* [Fr. *eclogue*; L. *ecloga*; Gr. *eklogē*, a selection, especially of poems, from *eklegein*, to pick out, choose; *ek*, out, and *legein*, to choose.] A pastoral poem introducing shepherds conversing with each other; as, the *Eclogues* of Virgil.

ē'coid, *n.* Same as *Œcoid.*

ē-col'ō-ġy, *n.* Same as *Œcology.*

ē-cō-nom'ic (*or* ek-ō-), *a.* [L. *œconomicus*; Gr. *oikonomikos*, pertaining to the management of a household, from *oikonomia*, management of a household or state, the public revenue, from *oikonomos*; *oikos*, house, household, and *nemein*, to distribute, manage.]

1. Relating or pertaining to the household; domestic. [Obs.]

2. Pertaining to the regulation of household concerns. [Obs.]

3. Managing any affairs with frugality; not extravagant; not wasteful; saving; as, a man of *economic* habits.

4. Not characterized by extravagance; regulated by frugality; frugal; as, an *economic* use of money.

5. Relating to the science of economics or the pecuniary and other productive resources of a country; relating to the means of living; as, *economic* questions; *economic* administration.

Economical is commonly used instead of *economic* when meaning saving, frugal, sparing.

ē-cō-nom′iç-ăl (*or* ek-ō-), *a.* Same as *Economic.*

ē-cō-nom′iç-ăl-ly (*or* ek-ō-), *adv.* In an economic manner.

ē-cō-nom′içs (*or* ek-ō-), *n.* [Gr. *ta oikonomika*, the science of household management.]

1. The science of household affairs or of domestic management. [Obs.]

2. The science of the useful application of the wealth or material resources of a country; political economy.

ē-çon″ō-mi-sā′tion, ē-çon′ō-mīşe, etc. See *Economization*, etc.

ē-çon′ō-mist, *n.* 1. One who manages domestic or other concerns with frugality; one who expends money, time, or labor, judiciously and without waste.

2. One who studies or is conversant with political economy.

ē-çon″ō-mi-zā′tion, *n.* The act or practice of economizing or managing frugally or to the best advantage. [Rare.]

ē-çon′ō-mize, *v.i.*; economized, *pt., pp.*; economizing, *ppr.* To manage pecuniary concerns with frugality; to make a prudent use of money; to be saving.

ē-çon′ō-mize, *v.t.* To use with prudence; to expend with frugality; as, to *economize* one's income.

ē-çon′ō-mi-zēr, *n.* 1. One who or that which economizes.

2. In engineering, a contrivance by which waste heat is employed to heat the feed-water.

ē-çon′ō-my, *n.*; *pl.* **ē-çon′ō-mieş.** [L. *œconomia*; Gr *oikonomia*, the management of a household or state, the public revenue, from *oikonomos*, a manager, administrator; *oikos*, house, and *nemein*, to distribute, manage.]

1. The management, regulation, and government of a household; especially, the management of the pecuniary concerns of a household; as, it is not good *economy*.

2. A frugal and judicious use of money, etc.; that management which expends money to advantage and incurs no waste; frugality in the necessary expenditure of money.

3. The disposition or arrangement of any work; the system of rules and regulations which control any work, whether divine or human; specifically, (a) the operations of nature in the generation, nutrition, and preservation of animals and plants; the regular, harmonious system in accordance with which the functions of living animals and plants are performed; as, the animal or vegetable *economy*; (b) the regulation and disposition of the internal affairs of a state or nation, or of any department of government.

Syn.—Frugality, management, thrift, system, arrangement.

é-çor-çhé′ (ā-kor-shā′), *n.* [Fr., lit., flayed, pp. of *écorcher*, to flay.] In the fine arts, a model of a body with the skin completely removed, so as to form a study of the muscular system.

ē-çor′ti-çāte, *a.* [L. *e-* priv., and *corticatus*, from *cortex* (*-icis*), bark, rind.] In botany, without a layer of cortex or cork-like tissue; said specifically of certain lichens.

é-ços-sāişe′ (ā-), *n.* [Fr., f. of *Écossais*, Scotch.]

1. A rustic Scotch dancing-tune; also, the music for such a dance.

2. A kind of alternating hot and cold douche practised in Scotland.

ē-ços′tāte, *a.* [L. *e-* priv., and *costa*, a rib.]

1. In botany, destitute of veins or ribs; said of a leaf.

2. In zoölogy, (a) having no ribs; (b) having no ribs attached; said of a vertebra.

é-çoute′ (ā-), *n.* [Fr., from *écouter*, to listen.] A kind of gallery projecting from the glacis of a fortification, constructed for the protection of troops resisting the advance of an enemy's miners.

eç′phȧ-sis, *n.* [Gr. *ekphasis*, from *ekphanai*, to speak out, *ek*, out, and *phanai*, to speak.] In rhetoric, an explicit declaration.

eç-phō-nē′mȧ, *n.* [Gr. *ekphōnēma*, from *ekphōnein*, to cry out, pronounce; *ek*, out, and *phōnein*, from *phōnē*, voice, sound.] In rhetoric, a sudden and passionate ejaculation.

eç′phō-nēme, *n.* The exclamation point (!).

eç-phō-nē′sis, *n.* An animated or passionate exclamation.

eç′phō-rȧ, *n.* [Gr. *ekphora*, a carrying out, projection in a building, from *ekpherein*; *ek*, out, and *pherein*, to bear.]

1. In architecture, the jutting of stone-work, molding, or any member beyond the surface immediately under it.

2. [E—] In conchology, a genus of gasteropods having a somewhat spindle-shaped shell, of which the red whelk of England, *Ecphora antiquus*, is a type.

eç-phraç′tiç, *a.* [Gr. *ekphraktikos*, from *ekphrassein*, to clear away obstructions, open up; *ek*, out, and *phrassein*, to inclose.] In medicine, tending to remove obstructions by producing attenuation; deobstruent; aperient.

eç-phraç′tiç, *n.* An ecphractic medicine.

eç-phȳ′mȧ, *n.* [Gr. *ekphyma*, from *ekphyesthai*, to grow out.] In medicine, an excrescence; an abnormal growth upon the skin, as a wart or a corn.

é-craşe-meṅt′ (ā-kräz-moṅ′), *n.* [Fr., from *écraser*, to crush, bruise.] A surgical operation performed without cutting, the severing being accomplished by the gradual tightening of a ligature.

é-crȧ-şeur′ (ā-), *n.* [Fr., from *écraser*, to crush, bruise.] In surgery, the instrument used in ecrasement.

é-cre-visse′ (ā-), *n.* [Fr.] A kind of armor made by fastening overlapping scale-like plates upon a ground of leather.

é-cru′ (ā-), *a.* [Fr., unbleached, raw, from L. *crudus*, raw.] In a natural state; unaffected as to color by any artificial process; as, *écru* silk, cotton, etc.

ē-crus-tā′ceous, *a.* [L. *e-* priv., and *crusta*, a crust.] Without a crustaceous covering; said of thallogens.

eç′stȧ-sy, *n.* [LL. *ecstasis*; Gr. *ekstasis*, a being put out of its place, distraction, astonishment, trance, from *ek*, out, and *histanai*, to place.]

1. Primarily, a fixed state; a trance; a state in which the mind is arrested and fixed, or, as is said, lost; a state in which the functions of the senses are suspended by the contemplation of some extraordinary or supernatural object.

> Whether what we call *ecstasy* be not dreaming with our eyes open, I leave to be examined. —Locke.

2. Excessive joy; rapture; a degree of delight that arrests the whole mind; as, the *ecstasy* of love; joy may rise to *ecstasy*.

3. Enthusiasm: excessive elevation and absorption of mind; extreme delight; as, to listen with *ecstasy*.

4. Excessive grief or anxiety. [Obs.]

5. Madness; distraction. [Obs.]

6. In medicine, a species of catalepsy, when the person remembers, after the paroxysm is over, the ideas he had during the attack.

Syn.—Delight, rapture, transport, overjoy.

eç′stȧ-sy, *v.t.*; ecstasied, *pt., pp.*; ecstasying, *ppr.* To fill with rapture or enthusiasm. [Obs.]

eç-stat′iç, eç-stat′iç-ăl, *a.* [Gr. *ekstatikos*, from *ekstasis*, ecstasy.]

1. Arresting the mind; suspending the senses; entrancing.

2. Rapturous; transporting; ravishing; delightful beyond measure; as, *ecstatic* bliss or joy.

3. Tending to external objects. [Obs.]

eç-stat′iç, *n.* A wild enthusiast. [Rare.]

eç-stat′iç-ăl-ly, *adv.* Rapturously; ravishingly.

eçt-, eç-tō-. Combining forms from Greek *ektos*, outside, signifying without, outside, external; as, *ecto*derm; *ecto*zoa.

eç′tad, *adv.* [Gr. *ektos*, outside, and L. *ad*, to.] Outwardly; used in anatomy.

eç′tăl, *a.* [Gr. *ektos*, outside, and *-al*.] Related to the outside; exterior.

eç-tā′si-ȧ, *n.* [Gr. *ektasis*, extension, from *ekteinein*; *ek*, out, and *teinein*, to stretch.] An enlargement, inflation, or swelling of any hollow organ; as, *ectasia* of the veins.

eç′tȧ-sis, *n.* [LL., from Gr. *ektasis*, extension; *ek*, out, and *teinein*, to stretch.] In prosody, the changing of a syllable from short to long.

eç-ten′iç, *a.* [Gr. *ektenēs*, stretched out; *ek*, out, and *teinein*, to stretch.] Hypnotic.

eç-ten′tăl, *a.* [Gr. *ektos*, without, and *entos*, within.] Having mutual relation to the ectoderm and the entoderm of a gastrula.

eç′tēr-on, *n.* Same as *Ecderon*.

eç-teth′moid, *a.* [*Ect-*, and Gr. *ēthmoeidēs*, like a sieve; *ēthmos*, a sieve, and *eidos*, form.] In anatomy, situated outside the ethmoid bone.

eç′thē-sis, *n.* [Gr. *ekthesis*, from *ektithenai*, to put forth, set forth.] The promulgation of a belief by means of a thesis, as the edict of Heraclius forbidding discussion as to the duality of the will of Christ.

eç-thlip′sis, *n.* [LL., from Gr. *ekthlipsis*, a squeezing out, from *ekthlibein*; *ek*, out, and *thlibein*, to squeeze.] In Latin prosody, the elision of the final syllable of a word ending in *m*, when the next word begins with a vowel.

eç-thō-ræ′um, *n.*; *pl.* **eç-thō-ræ′ȧ.** [Gr. *ek*, out, and *thoraion*, from *thoros*, seed.] In zoölogy, the delicate lasso or nettle-thread possessed by the *Cœlenterata* and some other animals, used to sting and poison their prey; written also *ecthoreum*.

eç-thȳ′mȧ, *n.* [Gr. *ekthyma*, from *ekthyein*, to break out, as tumors; *ek*, out, and *thyein*, to rage, boil.] In medicine, an eruption of the skin in which large deep-seated pustules stand upon broad inflamed bases.

eç-tō-. Same as *Ect-*.

eç′tō-blast, *n.* [*Ecto-*, and Gr. *blastos*, a bud, germ.]

1. In biology, the membrane composing the walls of a cell.

2. In embryology, an ectoderm.

eç-tō-broṅ′çhi-um, *n.*; *pl.* **eç-tō-broṅ′çhi-ȧ.** [*Ecto-*, and Gr. *bronchos*, the windpipe, trachea.] In ornithology, a subdivision of the bronchi lying on the side toward the back of the bird.

eç-tō-cär′di-ȧ, *n.* [*Ecto-*, and Gr. *kardia*, heart.] A malformation in which the heart is out of its natural location.

Eç″tō-cär-pā′cē-æ, *n.pl.* [*Ecto-*, and Gr. *karpos*, fruit, and *-aceæ*.] A family of seaweeds of the order *Fucoideæ*. They are olive-colored, articulated, filiform, with sporanges either external, attached to the jointed ramuli, or formed out of some of the interstitial cells.

eç″tō-cär-pā′ceous, *a.* Pertaining to the *Ectocarpaceæ*.

eç-tō-cär′pous, *a.* [*Ecto-*, and Gr. *karpos*, fruit.] In zoölogy, having the sexual organ external to or developed from the ectoderm.

Eç-tō-cär′pus, *n.* [*Ecto-*, and Gr. *karpos*, fruit.] A typical genus of seaweeds of the family *Ectocarpaceæ*.

eç-tō-cœ′liç, *a.* [*Ecto-*, and Gr. *koilion*, a hollow.] Lying outside the cavity of the body; applied to cœlenterates.

eç-tō-çū′nē-i-fọrm, *n.* [*Ecto-*, and L. *cuneus*, a wedge, and *forma*, form.] The outer cuneiform tarsal bone; also used adjectively.

eç′tō-cyst, *n.* [*Ecto-*, and Gr. *kystis*, a bladder.] In zoölogy, the external integumentary layer of the *Polyzoa*.

eç′tō-dērm, *n.* [*Ecto-*, and Gr. *derma*, skin.] In anatomy, an outer layer or membrane, as the epidermal layer of the skin.

> The body (of the *Cœlenterata*) is essentially composed of two layers or membranes, an outer layer or *ectoderm*, and an inner layer or endoderm. —Nicholson.

eç-tō-dēr′măl, eç-tō-dēr′miç, *a.* Belonging or related to the ectoderm.

eç-toġ′e-nous, *a.* [*Ecto-*, and Gr. *-genēs*, producing.] In bacteriology, having the power of developing outside the harboring body.

eç-tō-leç′i-thăl, *a.* [*Ecto-*, and Gr. *lekithos*, yolk.] In embryology, having, at the beginning of segmentation, the nourishing yolk surrounding the vitellus or formative part of the embryo; as, *ectolecithal* segmentation.

eç′tō-mēre, *n.* [*Ecto-*, and Gr. *meros*, part.] In embryology, the mass of transparent cells which eventually move to the surface and form the ectoderm.

eç-tō-par′ȧ-site, *n.* [*Ecto-*, and Gr. *parasitos*, a parasite.] A parasitic animal infesting the outside of animals, as opposed to *endoparasite*, which lives in the body.

eç″tō-par-ȧ-sit′iç, *a.* Pertaining to or resembling an ectoparasite.

eç-tō′pi-ȧ, *n.* [Gr. *ektopios*, *ektopos*, out of place, out of the way; *ek*, out, and *topos*, place.] In pathology, the condition of being out of place; said of an organ; as, *ectopia* of the liver.

eç-top′iç, *a.* Pertaining to ectopia; affected by ectopia.

eç′tō-plaşm, *n.* [*Ecto-*, and Gr. *plasma*, a thing formed, from *plassein*, to form.]

1. In zoölogy, that part of the outer protoplasmic portion of a cell generally distinguished by greater thickness and density than the endosarc; the ectosarc.

2. In botany, the envelope of the protoplasmic mass within a cell.

eç-tō-plas′tiç, *a.* Relating to or made up of ectoplasm.

Eç-tō-proç′tȧ, *n.pl.* [*Ecto-*, and Gr. *prōktos*, the anus, hinder parts.] An order of polyzoans having the anus placed outside the tentacular disk.

eç′tō-py, *n.* See *Ectopia*.

eçt-ọr′găn-işm, *n.* An ectoparasitic organism.

eç′tō-särç, *n.* [*Ecto-*, and Gr. *sarx*, *sarkos*, flesh.] The ectoplasm.

eç-tō-skel′e-tŏn, *n.* Same as *Exoskeleton*.

eç′tō-sōme, *n.* [*Ecto-*, and Gr. *sōma*, body.] The cortex or envelope of a sponge.

eç-tō-sō′măl, *a.* Pertaining to or resembling the ectosome.

eç-tos′tē-ăl, *a.* [*Ecto-*, and Gr. *osteon*, a bone.]

1. Having relation to ectostosis.

2. Having relation to the surface of a bone.

eç-tos-tō′sis, *n.* [*Ecto-*, and Gr. *osteon*, a bone.] A process of ossification carried on in the membranous covering of the cartilage, which is either replaced or surrounded by the newly-made bone.

eç-tō-thē′çȧ, *n.* [*Ecto-*, and Gr. *thēkē*, a case.] The outside layer of the hard covering of certain hydroids.

eç-tō-zō′iç, *a.* [*Ecto-*, and Gr. *zōon*, pl. *zōa*, an animal.] Relating to ectoparasites; epizoic.

ec-tō-zō′on, *n.*; *pl.* **ec-tō-zō′ȧ.** An ectoparasite.

ec-trop′ic, *a.* [Gr. *ektropos*, from *ek*, out, and *trepein*, to turn.] Having the inside abnormally turned outward.

ec-trō′pi-on, ec-trō′pi-um, *n.* [Gr. *ektropion*, from *ektropos*, turning outward.] An eversion or turning inside out; as, *ectropion* of the lips of a wound.

ec-trot′ic, *a.* [Gr. *ektrōtikos*, from *ektrōsis*, abortion, from *ektitrōskein*, to abort; *ek*, out, and *titrōskein*, *trōein*, to wound, injure.] In medicine, preventive; arresting a disease in its inception.

ec-ty-lot′ic, *a.* [Gr. *ek*, out, and *tylos*, a knot, callus.] Having power to remove callosities and excrescences from the skin.

ec-ty-lot′ic, *n.* An ectylotic remedy.

ec′ty-pȧl, *a.* Taken from the original; copied. [Rare.]

ec′tȳpe, *n.* [L. *ectypus*; Gr. *ektypos*, engraved in relief, formed in outline; *ek*, out, and *typos*, a figure, outline.]

1. A reproduction of or very close resemblance to an original; opposed to *prototype*.

2. In architecture, a copy in relief or embossed.

ec-ty-pog′rȧ-phy, *n.* [Gr. *ektypos*, wrought in relief, and *-graphia*, from *graphein*, to write.] A method of etching or engraving by a chemical process that leaves the lines in relief instead of being sunk.

é′cu (ā′kü), *n.* [Fr.] 1. A medieval shield of a mounted soldier.

2. A coin formerly used in European countries.

3. Tracing-paper made from a vegetable substance.

ec-ū-men′ic, œc-ū-men′ic (ek-), *a.* Ecumenical.

ec-ū-men′ic-ăl, œc-ū-men′ic-ăl (ek-), *a.* [LL. *œcumenicus*; Gr. *oikoumenikos*, of or from the whole world; *oikoumenē* (supply *gē*, earth), the inhabited world; f. of ppr. pass. of *oikein*, to dwell, inhabit.] Universal; used specifically in reference to the Christian church.

Ecumenical bishop; the title assumed by the pope of Rome.

Ecumenical council; see under *Council*.

ec′ū-rie, *n.* [Fr.] A stable.

ec′zē-mȧ, *n.* [Gr. *ekzema*, an eruption of the skin, from *ekzein*; *ek*, out, and *zein*, to boil.] A cutaneous disease characterized by inflammation, redness, itching, and the formation of vesicles which exude a watery substance that evaporates and leaves the skin covered with crusts; salt-rheum; tetter.

ec-zem′ȧ-tous, *a.* Relating to or afflicted with eczema.

-ed. A suffix used in many words, chiefly in forming the past tense and past participle of regular verbs, and analogous adjectives formed from nouns; as, walk*ed*; train*ed*; pigment*ed*.

ē-dā′cious, *a.* [L. *edax* (*-acis*), from *edere*, to eat.] Given to eating; characterized by edacity.

ē-dā′cious-ly, *adv.* Greedily.

ē-dā′cious-ness, *n.* The quality of being edacious.

ē-dac′i-ty, *n.* [L. *edacitas*, from *edax*, given to eating; from *edere*, to eat.] Greediness; voracity; ravenousness; rapacity.

Ed′dȧ, *n.* [Ice., great-grandmother. A name given to the book by Bishop Brynjulf Sveinsson, to indicate that it is the mother of all Scandinavian poetry.] A book containing a system of Runic or Scandinavian mythology, with some account of the theology and philosophy of the northern nations of Europe. The first part contains the mythology of the people, and the second specimens of the poetry of the Scalds. It was composed by Snorri Sturluson, judge of Iceland, from 1215 to 1222.

Ed-dā′ic, Ed′dic, *a.* Of or pertaining to the Edda.

ed′dēr, *n.* [AS. *edor*, *eodor*, a hedge.] In husbandry, such flexible wood as is worked into the top of hedge stakes to bind them together. [Obs.]

ed′dēr, *v.t.* To tie or bind (the top of a hedge) with edder. [Obs.]

ed′dish, *n.* [AS. *edisc*, a pasture, a park for game.] The later pasture, or grass that comes after mowing or reaping; written also *eadish*, *edish*.

ed′dōes, ed′dērs, *n.pl.* [W. Ind. and W. African.] The roots of the taro.

ed′dy, *n.*; *pl.* **ed′dies.** [Ice. *idha*, an eddy, whirlpool; Norw. *ida*; Sw. dial. *idha*; Ice. *idh*; AS. *ed-*, backward.] That part of a freely moving body, as of air or water, maintaining a circular whirl relatively small in circumference.

> And smiling *eddies* dimpled on the main.
> —Dryden.

Eddy current; see *Foucault current* under *Current*.

ed′dy, *v.i.*; eddied, *pt.*, *pp.*; eddying, *ppr.* To move circularly or as an eddy.

ed′dy, *v.t.* To cause to move in an eddy. [Rare.]

e′del-weiss (ā′del-vīs *or* ed′el-wīs), *n.* [G., from *edel*, noble, precious, and *weiss*, white.] *Gnaphalium Leontopodium*, a downy composite plant inhabiting the high Alps, having starlike white flowers.

ē-dē′mȧ, œ-dē′mȧ, *n.* [Gr. *oidēma*, a swelling, tumor, from *oidein*, to swell.] Local dropsy.

ē-dem′ȧ-tōse, œ-dem′ȧ-tōse, *a.* Same as *Edematous*.

ē-dem′ȧ-tous, œ-dem′ȧ-tous, *a.* [Gr. *oidēma* (*-atos*), a swelling, from *oidein*, to swell.] Swelling with a serous humor; dropsical.

E′den, *n.* [LL. *Eden*; Heb. and Ch. *'ēden*, pleasure.]

1. In the Bible, the first home of Adam and Eve.

2. A region mentioned in 2 Kings xix. 12 of the Bible, being one of the dependencies of Assyria.

3. Any delightful region.

E-den′ic, *a.* Pertaining to or like Eden.

ē′den-ite, *n.* A variety of amphibole containing aluminium.

E′den-ize, *v.t.*; Edenized, *pt.*, *pp.*; Edenizing, *ppr.* To transform into an Eden.

E′den-ized, *a.* Admitted into paradise.

ē-den′tăl, *a.* and *n.* Same as *Edentate*.

ē-den′tăl-ous, *a.* Edentate.

E-den-tā′tȧ, *n.pl.* [Neut. pl. of L. *edentatus*, pp. of *edentare*, to render toothless; *e*, out, and *dens*, *dentis*, a tooth.] In zoölogy, an order of animals that are destitute of front teeth, as the armadillo and ant-eater.

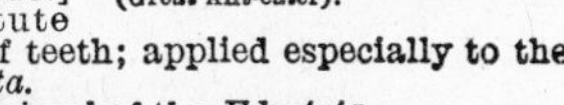

Edentata. 1. Skull and (3) Tooth of *Chlamydophorus truncatus*. 2. Skull of *Myrmecophaga jubata* (Great Ant-eater).

ē-den′tāte, *a.* and *n.* [L. *edentatus*.]

I. *a.* Destitute or deprived of teeth; applied especially to the order *Edentata*.

II. *n.* An animal of the *Edentata*.

ē-den′tā-ted, *a.* Same as *Edentate*.

ē-den-tā′tion, *n.* A depriving of teeth.

ē-den′tū-lous, *a.* Without teeth.

edge (ej), *n.* [ME. *egge*; AS. *ecg*; D. *egge*; G. *eck*, *ecke*; L. *acies*; Gr. *akē*, a point, edge; Sans. *açri*, an edge, corner.]

1. The sharp border or the thin cutting side of an instrument; as, the *edge* of an ax, razor, knife, sword, or scythe.

2. The abrupt border or margin of anything; the brink; as, the *edge* of the table; the *edge* of a book; the *edge* of a precipice.

3. The border or part adjacent to a line of division; the part nearest some limit; the commencement or early part; the beginning; as, the *edge* of a field; the *edge* of evening.

> The new general, unacquainted with his army, and on the *edge* of winter, would not hastily oppose them. —Milton.

4. Sharpness of mind or appetite; keenness; intenseness of desire; fitness for action or operation; as, the *edge* of appetite or hunger.

> Silence and solitude set an *edge* on the genius.
> —Dryden.

5. Keenness; sharpness; acrimony; wounding or irritating power.

> Abate the *edge* of traitors. —Shak.

To set the teeth on edge; to cause a tingling or grating sensation in the teeth.

Syn.—Border, rim, brink, verge, skirt, margin, brim.

edge, *v.t.*; edged, *pt.*, *pp.*; edging, *ppr.* 1. To sharpen.

2. To furnish with an edge, fringe, or border; as, to *edge* a flower-bed with box.

> Their long descending train,
> With rubies *edged*. —Dryden.

3. To sharpen; to exasperate; to embitter.

> By such reasonings the simple were blinded and the malicious *edged*. —Hayward.

4. To incite; to provoke; to instigate; to urge on; to egg. [Rare.]

5. To move sidewise; to move little by little.

> *Edging* by degrees their chairs forwards, they were in a little time got up close to one another. —Locke.

edge, *v.i.* To move sidewise; to move gradually or so as not to attract notice; to advance or retire gradually; as, to *edge* along this way.

> When one has made a bad bet, it's best to *edge* off. —Colman.

To edge away; nautically, to decline gradually from the shore, or from the line of the course.

To edge in; to go in through difficult and narrow passages; as, *to edge in* through a multitude of people in a great crowd.

To edge in with; to draw near to, as a ship in chasing.

To edge down upon an object; to approach it in a slanting direction.

edge′bōne, *n.* Same as *Aitchbone*.

edge′less, *a.* Having no sharp edge; blunt; obtuse; unfit for cutting; as, an *edgeless* sword.

edge′long, *adv.* Edgewise. [Obs.]

edge′-mill, *n.* A mill for crushing and triturating by means of a heavy stone rolled round on its edge upon a hard, level, inclosed floor; used for grinding oil-seeds and for crushing ores.

edge′-mōld″ing, *n.* A molding in which two curved surfaces form an angle where they meet.

edge′-plāne, *n.* A plane for shaping and dressing the edges of boards; also, a tool for trimming and shaping edges of leather.

edge′-plāy, *n.* Swordplay using the edge of the blade.

edg′ēr, *n.* One who or that which edges; specifically, a machine for cutting away superfluous parts of timber, such as slabs from a log.

edge′-rail, *n.* In railroading, (a) a broad, thin track-rail, set with its edge upward; opposed to *flat rail*; (b) a rail placed alongside the main rail at a switch as a guard.

edge′shot, *a.* Dressed on the edges only; said of a board in carpentry.

edge′-tool, *n.* Any tool with a sharp edge for cutting, as a chisel or an ax; also, a tool used for sharpening *edge-tools*; more appropriately, an *edging-tool*.

edge′wīse, edge′wāys, *adv.* With the edge foremost; opposed to *flatwise*.

edg′ing, *n.* 1. That which is added on the border or which forms the edge, as lace, fringe, trimming, added to a garment for ornament.

2. In horticulture, a row of small plants set along the border of a flower-bed; as, an *edging* of box.

3. The act of fitting edges, as in carpentry.

edg′ing-ly, *adv.* Shyly; cautiously; mincingly. [Rare.]

edg′ing-mȧ-chīne″, *n.* A machine for shaping and dressing the edge of anything, as a board, a metal plate, etc.

edg′y, *a.* 1. Irritable; easily offended; said of a person. [Rare.]

2. Showing an edge; sharply defined; angular. [Rare.]

> The outlines of their body are sharpe and *edgy*. —Knight.

ed-i-bil′i-ty, *n.* Fitness for food; the quality of being fit to be eaten.

ed′i-ble, *a.* and *n.* [LL. *edibilis*, from *edere*, to eat.]

I. *a.* That may be eaten with safety and benefit; eatable; esculent.

II. *n.* Anything that may be eaten for food; as, corn is an *edible*; one of the *edibles*.

Edible bird's-nest; see *Bird's-nest*, 3.

Edible crab; any crab that can be used as food, especially the common crab of the Atlantic coast, *Callinectes hastatus*, the blue crab.

Edible frog; *Rana esculenta*, the green frog with dark spots and yellow longitudinal streaks on the back.

Edible snail; any snail that may be eaten, especially those of the genus *Helix*.

ed′i-ble-ness, *n.* Edibility; the quality of being suitable for food.

ē′dict, *n.* [L. *edictum*, from *edicere*, to utter or proclaim; *e-*, out, and *dicere*, to speak.] That which is uttered or proclaimed by authority as a rule of action; an order issued by a sovereign to his subjects, as a rule or law requiring obedience; a proclamation of command or prohibition.

Edict of Nantes; an edict issued by Henry IV. of France, in 1598, giving his Protestant subjects the free exercise of their religion. The revocation of this edict, by Louis XIV., about a century after, led to a cruel persecution, which drove most of the Protestants out of the kingdom.

Syn.—Decree, proclamation, order, manifesto, announcement, law, command.

ē-dic′tăl, *a.* [LL. *edictalis*, from L. *edictum*, an edict.] Having the character of or pertaining to an edict or edicts.

ed′i-fi-cănt, *a.* [L. *ædificans* (*-antis*), ppr. of *ædificare*, to build.] Relating to an edifice or building.

ed″i-fi-cā′tion, *n.* 1. The act of building or the thing built; figuratively, the fact of moral, intellectual, or spiritual growth.

2. Instruction; improvement of the mind in any species of useful knowledge.

ed′i-fi-cā″tō-ry, *a.* [LL. *ædificatorius*, from *ædificator*, a builder.] Having a tendency to build or to improve.

ed′i-fice, *n.* [Fr. *edifice*; L. *ædificium*, a building, from *ædificare*, to build; *ædes*, *ædis*, a building, temple, and *-ficare*, from *facere*, to make.] A structure, especially one of imposing appearance, as a temple, a church, a public building, or a fine massive house.

ed-i-fi′ciăl (-fish′ăl), *a.* Pertaining to an edifice or structure.

ed′i-fī-ēr, *n.* 1. One who improves another by instructing him; especially by moral or spiritual teaching.

2. A builder. [Obs.]

ed′i-fȳ, *v.t.*; edified, *pt.*, *pp.*; edifying, *ppr.* [ME. *edifien*, *edefien*; L. *ædificare*, to build, erect.]
1. In a literal sense, to construct. [Obs.]
2. To teach or persuade. [Obs.]
3. To instruct and improve the mind of, particularly in moral and religious knowledge; as, the sermon greatly *edified* the congregation.

ed′i-fȳ, *v.i.* To be improved or enlightened. [Rare.]

ed′i-fȳ-ing, *a.* Adapted to instruct and improve; as, an *edifying* discourse.

ed′i-fȳ-ing-ly, *adv.* In an edifying manner.

ed′i-fȳ-ing-ness, *n.* The quality of being edifying.

ē′dile, *n.* See *Ædile.*

ē′dile-ship, *n.* See *Ædileship.*

ed′ing-tŏn-ite, *n.* A rare zeolitic mineral which occurs in the cavities of thomsonite near Dumbarton, Scotland; named after Mr. Edington, a Glasgow mineralogist.

ed′it, *v.t.*; edited, *pt*, *pp.*; editing, *ppr.* [L. *editus*, pp. of *edere*, to give out, put forth, publish; *e-*, out, and *dare*, to give.] To superintend the publication of; to prepare, as a book or paper, for the public eye, by writing, correcting, or selecting the matter; to conduct or manage, as a periodical.

ē-di′tion (-dish′un), *n.* [L. *editio* (*-onis*), from *edere*, to put forth, publish.]
1. The publication of any book or writing; as, the first *edition* of a new work.
2. A special issue of a publication; as, Chalmers' *edition* of the Bible.
3. Figuratively, the reproduction of anything; as, the boy is a second *edition* of his father.
Diamond edition; an edition printed in diamond type, the smallest English font in common use
Edition de luxe; a superfine edition, the typography, paper and binding of the best; usually limited in number, and often signed by the author.

ē-di′tion-ẽr, *n.* An editor. [Obs.]

ed′i-tŏr, *n.* [L. *editor*, from *edere*, to put forth, publish.] One who edits; particularly, a person who superintends an edition of a book; the person who superintends, revises, corrects, and prepares a book, newspaper, or magazine for publication.

ed-i-tō′ri-ăl, *a.* Pertaining to an editor; as, *editorial* labors; written by an editor; as, *editorial* items

ed-i-tō′ri-ăl, *n.* An article written by an editor; a leading article in a newspaper or magazine, in accordance with the editorial policy of the publication; often called a *leader.*

ed-i-tō′ri-ăl-ly, *adv.* In the nature of an editorial.

ed′i-tŏr-ship, *n.* The business of an editor; the care and superintendence of a publication.

ed′i-tress, *n.* A female editor.

ē-dit′ū-āte, *v.t.* [LL. *ædituatus*, pp. of *ædituare*, to govern a house or temple.] To defend or govern a house or temple. [Obs.]

E′dŏm-īte, *n.* A descendant of Edom or Esau; an Idumean.

Ed″ri-oph-thal′mȧ, *n.pl.* [Gr. *hedraios*, fixed, and *ophthalmos*, the eye.] One of the two orders of higher crustaceans whose eyes are fixed and attached at the base instead of being borne upon stalks.

Edriophthalma.
1. Fresh-water Shrimp (*Gammarus pulex*); *a*, Single eye. 2. Head of *Cymothoa*; *b*, Cluster of simple eyes.

ed″ri-oph-thal′mous, *a.* Pertaining to the *Edriophthalma.*

Ed″ū-cȧ-bil′i-ȧ, *n.pl.* [From L. *educare*, to educate.] A high order of placental mammals whose cerebrum has the distinctive fissure of Sylvius and is considerably larger than the cerebellum, overlapping it as well as the olfactory lobes. [See *Ineducabilia.*]

ed″ū-cȧ-bil′i-ăn, *a.* Pertaining to the *Educabilia.*

ed″ū-cȧ-bil′i-ăn, *n.* One of the *Educabilia.*

ed″ū-cȧ-bil′i-ty, *n.* Capacity for receiving education or of being instructed.

ed′ū-cȧ-ble, *a.* That may be educated.

ed′ū-çāte, *v.t.*; educated *pt.*, *pp.*; educating, *ppr.* [L. *educatus*, pp. of *educare*, to bring up, rear, or train a child, from *educere*; *e*, out, and *ducere*, to lead, draw, bring.] To bring up, as a child; to instruct; to inform and enlighten the understanding of; to cultivate; to train; as, to *educate* the perception; to *educate* children
Syn.—Instruct, nurture, discipline, train, teach, develop, ground, school, initiate.

ed′ū-çā-ted, *a.* Brought up; instructed; furnished with knowledge or principles; trained; disciplined.

ed-ū-çā′tion, *n.* [L *educatio*, from *educare*, to educate.]
1 Cultivation and training, as of the mind; the acquisition or imparting of knowledge.
2. The complete result of mental training along a certain line; as, law *education.*
3. Animal training; bacterial or similar culture; a cultivated brood.
Syn.—Instruction, teaching, breeding, cultivation, nurture, training, tuition.—*Education* includes the whole course of training, moral, intellectual, and physical. *Instruction* and *teaching* apply to the communication of knowledge, the latter term being the more familiar of the two *Breeding* relates to the manners and outward conduct.

ed-ū-çā′tion-ăl, *a.* Pertaining to education; derived from education; as, *educational* habits.

ed-ū-çā′tion-ist, **ed-ū-çā′tion-ăl-ist**, *n.* A theorist in or a practical exponent of educational matters.

ed′ū-çā-tive, *a.* Relating to educational matters; possessing educational qualities or tendencies; as, an *educative* career.

ed′ū-çā-tŏr, *n.* [L. *educator*, a rearer, foster-father, pedagogue, from *educare*, to educate.] One who educates or trains mentally; a teacher.

ed′ū-çā-tress, *n.* A woman educator.

ē-dūce′, *v.t.*; educed (-dūst′), *pt.*, *pp.*; educing, *ppr.* [L. *educere*; *e-*, out, and *ducere*, to lead, draw.] To bring or draw out; to extract; to produce from a state of occultation.

ē-dū′ci-ble, *a.* That may be educed.

ē′duct, *n.* [L. *eductum*, from *educere*, to lead or draw forth.]
1. A substance separated or drawn from another by decomposition, as by fractional distillation
2. An inference. [Rare.]

ē-duc′tion, *n* [L. *eductio* (*-onis*), from *educere*, to lead or bring forth.] The act of drawing out or bringing into view.

ē-duc′tion-pipe, *n.* The pipe through which exhaust steam passes; an exhaust-pipe.

ē-duc′tion-valve, *n.* A valve for the passage of exhaust fluid or steam; an exhaust-valve.

ē-duc′tive, *a.* Tending to elicit or extract.

ē-duc′tŏr, *n.* One who or that which brings forth, elicits, or extracts.

ē-dul′cō-rănt, *n.* An edulcorant substance.

ē-dul′cō-rănt, *a.* Having a sweetening and purifying tendency; removing acridity.

ē-dul′cō-rāte, *v.t.*; edulcorated, *pt.*, *pp.*; edulcorating, *ppr* [L. *e-*, out, and *dulcoratus*, pp. of *dulcorare*, to sweeten, from *dulcor*, sweetness; *dulcis*, sweet.]
1. In chemistry, to cleanse, as pulverulent substances, by washing away all particles soluble in water
2. To free from acidity or acridity; to soften; to sweeten; to purify.

ē-dul-cō-rā′tion, *n.* 1. Literally, the act of sweetening.
2. In chemistry, the act of freeing pulverulent substances from acids or any soluble impurities, by repeated affusions of water. [Rare.]

ē-dul′cō-rā-tive, *a.* Having the quality of sweetening or purifying by affusion.

ē-dul-cō-rā′tŏr, *n.* One who or that which edulcorates; specifically, a device formerly used as a dropping-bottle.

ē-dū′li-ous, *a.* Edible. [Obs.]

Ed-wärds′i-ȧ, *n.pl.* A typical genus of *Actiniaria*, named after the French naturalist, Henri Milne-Edwards.

ed-wärds′i-id, *n.* One of the *Edwardsia.*

Ed-wärds-ī′i-dæ, *n.pl.* In zoölogy, a division of the *Anthozoa*, of the family *Actiniaria*, of which the *Edwardsia* is the type; the body is divided into eight septa, each of which is reproductive.

ed-wärds′i-oid, *a.* Like or pertaining to the *Edwardsia.*

ed-wite′, *v.t.* [AS *edwitan*, to reproach; *ed-*, back, and *witan*, to blame.] To rebuke; upbraid. [Obs.]

ed-wite′, *n.* Blame; censure. [Obs.]

e′dy, **e′di**, *a.* Prosperous; rich. [Obs.]

ee, *n.*; *pl.* **een.** [Scot.] An eye.

But steal me a blink o' your bonny black *ee.*
—Burns.

-ee. A suffix from OFr. pp. ending *-e* masc., *-ee* f.; L. *-atus* masc., *-ata* f. It is used chiefly in OFr. law terms, or words similarly formed, to indicate the direct or indirect object of an action, the recipient of an action, or one upon whom a right is conferred; as, pay*ee*; assign*ee*; employ*ee*. It is correlative to *-or*, *-er.*

-ee. A dim. suffix, as in goat*ee*, boot*ee*.

eek, **ēke**, *v.*, *adv.*, and *conj.* [Obs.] See *Eke.*

eel, *n.* [ME *el*, *ele*; AS. *æl*; D. *aal*; G. *aal*, an eel.] In zoölogy, the popular name of the *Anguilla*, a genus of soft-finned fishes belonging to the family *Anguillidæ*. The head is smooth; there are ten rays in the membrane of the gills; the eyes are covered with a common skin; the body is cylindrical and slimy. [See *Conger-eel* and *Electric-eel.*]
Salt eel; a whip made of eelskin; hence, in nautical terms, a rope's end.

eel′bas″ket, *n.* A fisherman's pot, basket, or other receptacle for eels.

eel′buck, *n.* A British provincialism for an

Framework with Eelbucks.

eelpot or eel-basket.

eel′fāre, *n.* An English provincialism, indicating, (a) the autumnal passage of young eels upstream toward salt water; or, (b) a brood of eels.

eel′-fork, *n.* A spear for catching eels.

eel′grȧss, *n.* *Zostera marina*, a marine plant.

eel′pot, *n.* 1. A box-like trap for catching eels.
2. The homelyn or spotted ray. [Local, Eng.]

eel′pout, *n.* [AS. *ælepute*; *æl*, eel, and *pute*, pout.]
1. *Zoarces anguillaris*, the lamper-eel.
2. The viviparous blenny; also, the burbot. [Local, Eng.]

eel′-shärk, *n.* An eel-shaped Japanese shark.

eel′skin, *n.* The skin of an eel.

eel′spēar, *n.* A barbed spear for use in spearing eels.

eel′-trap, *n.* A funnel-shaped structure for catching eels; an eelpot.

een, *n.*, pl. of *eye.* [Obs., except in Scotland.]

e′en, *adv.*, contraction of *even.*

e′er (âr *or* ār), *adv.* Ever, a contraction.

-eer. A suffix from Fr. *-ier*; L. *-arius.* It is used in nouns of agent; as, engin*eer*; pamphlet*eer*; cannon*eer*.

ee′rie, *a.* Same as *Eery.*

ee′ri-ly, *adv.* In an eery manner.

ee′ri-ness, *n.* Fear; fright; state of being eery.

ee′ry, *a.* [Scot.] 1. Inspiring fear; awesome.
2. Affected with fear; timid.

eet, *v.*, obsolete past tense of *eat.*

ef′fȧ-ble, *a.* [L. *effabilis*, utterable, from *effari*, to utter, speak out; *ex*, out, and *fari*, to speak.] Utterable; that may be uttered or spoken. [Rare.]

ef-fāce′, *v.t.*; effaced (-fāst′), *pt.*, *pp.*; effacing, *ppr.* [Fr. *effacer*; *es-* (L. *ex*, out), and *face*, face.]
1. To destroy, as a figure, on the surface of anything, whether painted or carved, so as to render it invisible or not distinguishable; to blot out; to erase, strike, or scratch out, so as to destroy or render illegible; as, to *efface* the letters on a monument; to *efface* a writing; to *efface* a name.
2. To remove from the mind; to wear away; as, to *efface* the image of a person in the mind; to *efface* ideas or thoughts; to *efface* gratitude.
Syn.—Erase, obliterate, cancel, expunge, annul, blot out, destroy.

ef-fāce′a-ble, *a.* Capable of effacement.

ef-fāce′ment, *n.* The act or result of effacing.

ef-fȧ-ré′ (-rā′), *a.* [Fr.] In heraldry, denoting an animal represented as rearing on its hind legs, as if it were frightened or enraged; written also *effearé.*

ef-fas′ci-nāte, *v.t.* [L. *effascinatus*, pp. of *effascinare*, to charm; *ex-*, intens., and *fascinare*, to charm.] To charm; to bewitch. [Obs.]

ef-fas-ci-nā′tion, *n.* Fascination.

ef-fect′, *n.* [L. *effectus*, pp. of *efficere*, to bring to pass, accomplish; *ex*, out, and *facere*, to do.]
1. That which is produced by an operating agent or cause; the result or consequence of the application of a cause or of the action of an agent on some subject; consequence; result; as, the *effect* of luxury; of intemperance; of cold, etc.; he spoke with great *effect*; the *effect* of this war was the breaking up of the kingdom.

Effect is the substance produced, or simple idea introduced into any subject, by the exerting of power. —Locke.

2. Power to produce consequences or results; force; validity; importance; account; as, the obligation is void and of no *effect.*

Christ is become of no *effect* unto you.
—Gal. v. 4.

3. Purport; tenor; import or general intent; as, he made the purchase for his friend and immediately wrote him to that *effect.*
4. Completion; perfection.

Not so worthily to be brought to heroical *effect* by fortune or necessity. —Sidney.

5. Reality; not mere appearance; fact; substance.

No other in *effect* than what it seems. —Denham.

6. The impression produced on the mind, as by scenery, a picture, or the like; the general result of all the qualities of a work of art.

The *effect* was heightened by the wild and lonely nature of the place. —Irving.

7. [*pl.*] Goods; movables; personal estate; as, the people escaped from the town with their *effects*.

8. A conclusion, as of a story. [Obs.]

9. In mechanics, the amount of effective work accomplished by a machine during a stated time.

10. In electricity, a phenomenon of a special nature named after its discoverer.

Hall effect; the phenomenon noted as to the effect of the interference of a magnetic field with the onward flow of an electric current.

Peltier effect; a raising or lowering of temperature at the point where two metals of different powers of electric conductibility come together, dependent upon the direction of the current.

Thomson effect; the production or absorption of heat caused by the flow of an electric current from one point of a conductor to another where the temperature is different.

Syn.—Consequence, event, issue, meaning, reality, result.

ef-fect′, *v.t.*; effected, *pt.*, *pp.*; effecting, *ppr.* 1. To produce, as a cause or agent; to cause to be.

2. To bring to pass; as, to *effect* an object or purpose.

Syn.—Accomplish, perform, consummate, achieve, execute.

ef-fect′ẽr, ef-fect′ŏr, *n.* One who effects; that which effects; an agent.

ef-fect′i-ble, *a.* That may be effected. [Rare.]

ef-fec′tion, *n.* Creation; production. [Rare.]

ef-fect′ive, *a.* [LL. *effectivus*, from *effectus*, pp. of *efficere*, to bring to pass.]

1. Having the power to cause or produce; efficacious.

2. Having the power of active operation; able; fit for service; as, an *effective* force.

3. Real; actual; the opposite of *nominal*.

Effective money; coin, as distinguished from paper money.

Syn.—Cogent, influential, forcible, potent, conclusive, convincing.

ef-fect′ive, *n.* 1. That which causes or produces a given effect; a cause.

2. One qualified for efficient or active service, as a soldier or sailor.

ef-fect′ive-ly, *adv.* With effect; powerfully; with real operation.

ef-fect′ive-ness, *n.* The quality of being effective.

ef-fect′less, *a.* Without effect; without advantage; useless.

ef-fect′less-ly, *adv.* In an effectless manner.

ef-fect′ŏr, *n.* See *Effecter*.

ef-fec′tū-ăl, *a.* 1. Producing an effect, or the effect desired or intended; having adequate power or force to produce the effect; as, the *effectual* working of the plan.

2. Veracious; expressive of facts. [Obs.]

Effectual calling; one of the five tenets of Calvinism; the agency of the Holy Ghost, through Christ, in the scheme of salvation.

ef-fec′tū-ăl-ly, *adv.* 1. With effect; efficaciously; in a manner to produce the intended effect; thoroughly; as, the city is *effectually* guarded.

2. Actually. [Obs.]

ef-fec′tū-ăl-ness, *n.* The state or quality of being effectual.

ef-fec′tū-āte, *v.t.*; effectuated, *pt.*, *pp.*; effectuating, *ppr.* 1. To bring to pass; to achieve; to accomplish; to fulfil.

2. To make effectual.

ef-fec-tū-ā′tion, *n.* The act of bringing about or effectuating.

ef-fec′tū-ous, ef-fec′tū-ōse, *a.* Effective. [Obs.]

ef-fec′tū-ous-ly, *adv.* Effectively. [Obs.]

ef-fem′i-nă-cy, *n.*; *pl.* **ef-fem′i-nă-cies.** The quality of being effeminate or womanish; unmanly delicacy; womanish softness, delicacy, or weakness; used reproachfully of men.

ef-fem′i-nāte, *a.* 1. Having the qualities of the female sex; soft or delicate to an unmanly degree; womanish; as, by idleness and luxury he became weak and *effeminate*.

2. Womanlike; tender. [Obs.]

ef-fem′i-nāte, *v.t.*; effeminated, *pt.*, *pp.*; effeminating, *ppr.* [L. *effeminatus*, pp. of *effeminare*, to make womanish; *ex*, out, and *femina*, a woman.] To make womanish; to weaken; as, to *effeminate* children.

ef-fem′i-nāte, *v.i.* To grow womanish or weak; as, in a slothful peace courage will *effeminate*.

ef-fem′i-nāte-ly, *adv.* 1. In a womanish manner.

2. By means of a woman; as, *effeminately* vanquished. [Rare.]

ef-fem′i-nāte-ness, *n.* Unmanlike softness.

ef-fem-i-nā′tion, *n.* The quality of being womanish.

ef-fem′i-nīze, *v.t.* To make womanish. [Obs.]

ef-fen′di, *n.* [Turk. *efendi*, a corruption of modern Gr. *aphentēs*; Gr. *authentēs*, a master, ruler.] In Turkish, a master; subjoined to the names of persons in token of respect, corresponding to *sir* or *monsieur*; also used as part of titles of officers; as, *Reis Effendi*, principal secretary of state.

ef′fẽr-ent, *a.* [L. *efferens* (*-entis*), ppr. of *efferre*, to carry out; *ex*, out, and *ferre*, to bear.]

1. Carrying or conveying away from or outward; the reverse of *afferent*, as certain nerves, blood-vessels, etc.

2. Carried or conveyed away from or outward, as impulses in nerves from the nerve center outward.

ef′fẽr-ent, *n.* An efferent canal, vessel, or nerve; as, that nerve is an *efferent*; the *efferent* of a pond is its drainage channel.

ef-fẽr-vesce′, *v.i.*; effervesced (-vest′), *pt.*, *pp.*; effervescing, *ppr.* [L. *effervescere*, to boil up, foam up; *ex*, out, and *fervescere*, to begin to boil, from *fervere*, to boil.]

1. To be in natural commotion, like liquor when gently boiling; to bubble and hiss, as fermenting liquors or any fluid when some part escapes in a gaseous form; to work, as new wine.

2. To reveal one's emotions by one's appearance or actions; to bubble over; as, to *effervesce* with joy or mirth.

ef-fẽr-ves′cence, ef-fẽr-ves′cen-cy, *n.* That commotion of a fluid which takes place when some part of the mass flies off in a gaseous form, producing innumerable small bubbles; as, the *effervescence* of new wine.

ef-fẽr-ves′cent, *a.* Gently boiling or bubbling, by means of the disengagement of gas; hence, temporarily enthusiastic; as, strive for stability, not *effervescent* emotion.

ef-fẽr-ves′ci-ble, *a.* That has the quality of effervescing; capable of producing effervescence.

ef-fẽr-ves′cive, *a.* Productive of effervescence.

ef′fet, *n.* An eft. [Prov. Eng.]

ef-fēte′, *a.* [L. *effetus*, that has brought forth, exhausted; *ex*, out, and *fetus*, that has brought forth.] Barren; not capable of producing, as an animal, a soil, etc.; hence, exhausted; barren; sterile; inefficient through age, use, or decay; as, the *effete* East.

ef-fi-cā′cious, *a.* [L. *efficax* (*-acis*), from *efficere*, to bring to pass, accomplish.] Producing the effect intended; having power adequate to the purpose intended; as, an *efficacious* remedy for disease.

ef-fi-cā′cious-ly, *adv.* With efficacy.

ef-fi-cā′cious-ness, *n.* Efficacious quality.

ef-fi-cac′i-ty, *n.* [Rare.] Same as *Efficacy*.

ef′fi-cā-cy, *n.* [L. *efficacia*, from *efficere*, to accomplish.] Power to produce effects; production of the effect intended.

ef-fi′cien-cy (-fish′en-), **ef-fi′cience** (-fish′ens), *n.* 1. The condition or quality of being efficient; effective agency or power.

2. The condition of being competent; possession of the necessary knowledge or dexterity to accomplish a task.

3. In mechanics, the ratio of useful effect to the expenditure of energy.

ef-fi′cient (-fish′ent), *a.* Causing effects; causative; active; efficacious; competent.

Syn.—Able, capable, effective, competent.

ef-fi′cient, *n.* 1. The agent or cause which produces or causes to exist.

2. A volunteer in the English army who has a competent knowledge of the duties of the service, and has attended a certain requisite number of drills.

ef-fi′cient-ly, *adv.* In an efficient manner.

ef-fierce′, *v.t.* To make fierce or furious. [Obs.]

ef-fig′i-ăl, *a.* Pertaining to an effigy. [Rare.]

ef-fig′i-āte, *v.t.* [LL. *effigiatus*, pp. of *effigiare*, to form, fashion, from *effigies*, an image, likeness.] To image. [Rare.]

ef-fig-i-ā′tion, *n.* The act of forming in resemblance; also, an effigy. [Rare.]

ef-fig′i-ēs, *n.* [L.] An effigy.

ef-fig′ū-rāte, *a.* [L. *ex*, out, and *figuratus*, pp. of *figurare*, to figure; *figura*, a figure.] In botany, having a well-defined form, as opposed to *effuse*; said of lichens.

ef′fi-gy, *n.*; *pl.* **ef′fi-gies.** [L. *effigies*, *effigia*, a copy, image, likeness, from *effingere*; *ex*, out, and *fingere*, to form, fashion.] The image or likeness of a person; representation; portrait; a figure in sculpture or painting or on coins; especially a stuffed figure representing a person who has incurred hatred, commonly hanged or burned in public.

Effigy on a brass of Wm. Abell, vicar of Coleshill, Warwickshire, 1507.

ef-flag′i-tāte, *v.t.* [L. *efflagitatus*, pp. of *efflagitare*, to demand urgently.] To demand earnestly. [Obs.]

ef-flāte′, *v.t.* [L. *efflatus*, pp. of *efflare*; *ex*, out, and *flare*, to blow.] To fill with breath or air. [Rare.]

ef-flā′tion, *n.* An emanation; a puff; also, the act of breathing forth. [Rare.]

ef-flō-resce′, *v.i.*; effloresced (-rest′), *pt.*, *pp.*; efflorescing, *ppr.* [L. *efflorescere*, to begin to bloom; incept. from *ex*, out, and *florere*, to blossom; *flos*, *floris*, a flower.]

1. In chemistry, to become pulverulent on the surface or throughout by losing the water of crystallization on exposure to air.

2. To become covered with a powdery or crystalline crust, as some kinds of brick, plaster, etc.

3. In botany, to burst into bloom; to flower.

ef-flō-res′cence, *n.* 1. In botany, the process of flowering; the season when a plant shows its blossoms; the condition of being flowery or in flower.

2. In pathology, a redness of the skin; eruptions, as in rash, measles, smallpox, etc.

3. In chemistry, the formation of a powder or crust by efflorescing; also, the powder or crust itself.

ef-flō-res′cen-cy, *n.* The quality or condition of being efflorescent.

ef-flō-res′cent, *a.* [L. *efflorescens* (*-entis*), ppr. of *efflorescere*, to begin to blossom.]

1. Liable to effloresce.

2. Coated with efflorescence.

3. In blossom; blooming.

ef-flow′ẽr, *v.t.* [Fr. *effleurer*, to graze, strip the leaves off; *ef-*, L. *ex*, out, and *fleur*; G. *flur*, plain.] In making leather, to divest (a skin) of its epidermis.

ef′flū-ence, *n.* [L. *effluens* (*-entis*), ppr. of *effluere*, to flow out.] A flowing out; that which flows or issues from any body or substance; emanation; outflow.

ef′flū-en-cy, *n.* Same as *Effluence*.

ef′flū-ent, *a.* Flowing out.

ef′flū-ent, *n.* A stream flowing out from a lake or from another stream.

ef-flū′vi-ȧ-ble, *a.* Of a character to be emitted in the form of an effluvium. [Rare.]

ef-flū′vi-ăl, *a.* Of, like, or containing effluvia.

ef-flū′vi-āte, *v.i.* To emit or throw off effluvium. [Rare.]

ef-flū″vi-og′rȧ-phy, *n.* The action of a silent electric discharge on a photographic plate.

ef-flū′vi-um, *n.*; *pl.* **ef-flū′vi-ȧ.** [L., a flowing out, an outlet, from *effluere*, to flow out; *ex*, out, and *fluere*, to flow.] Something flowing out in a subtle or invisible form; exhalation; emanation; especially applied to noxious or disagreeable exhalations; as, the *effluvia* from diseased bodies or putrefying animal or vegetable substances.

ef′flux, *n.* [L. *effluxus*, from *effluere*, to flow out.]

1. The act of flowing out or issuing in a stream; as, an *efflux* of blood from a wound.

2. That which flows out; emanation.

ef-flux′, *v.i.* To run or flow away. [Obs.]

ef-flux′ion (-fluk′shun), *n.* 1. The act of flowing out.

2. That which flows out; effluvium; emanation.

ef-fō′di-ent, *a.* [L. *effodiens* (*-entis*), ppr. of *effodire*, to dig out, dig up.] Digging; accustomed to dig.

ef-fō-li-ā′tion, *n.* [A variant of *exfoliation*.] The process of losing foliage.

ef-fōrce′, *v.t.* [Fr. *efforcer*; LL. *effortiare*, to force, compel; L. *ex*, out, and *fortis*, strong.] To force; to break through by violence; to ravish. [Obs.]

ef-fōrm′, *v.t.* To fashion; to form. [Obs.]

ef-fŏr-mā′tion, *n.* Formation. [Obs.]

ef′fōrt (*or* ef′fẽrt), *n.* [Fr. *effort*; LL. *effortiare*, to strengthen, compel; L. *ex*, out, and *fortis*, strong.]

1. A straining; a voluntary exertion of strength; endeavor; strenuous exertion to accomplish an object.

2. In mechanics, the effective force in the direction of motion of any body.

Syn.—Attempt, endeavor, trial, essay.

ef′fōrt, *v.t.* To furnish an auxiliary to. [Obs.]

ef′fōrt-less, *a.* Making no effort.

ef-fos′sion, *n.* [L. *effossus*, pp. of *effodire*, to dig out.] The act of digging out of the earth. [Obs.]

ef-frac′tŏr, *n.* One who unlawfully enters a building, as a burglar.

ef-fran′chise, *v.t.* [OFr. *effranchir*, *esfranchir*, to enfranchise; *es-*, L. *ex*, out, and *franchir*, to free.] To invest with franchises or privileges. [Rare.]

ef-frāy′, *v.t.* [Fr. *effrayer*, to frighten.] To frighten. [Obs.]

ef-frāy′ȧ-ble, *a.* Frightful; dreadful. [Obs.]

ef-frē-nā′tion, *n.* [L. *effrenatio* (*-onis*), from *effrenare*, to unbridle; *ex*, out, and *frenare*, to bridle.] Unbridled rashness or license; unruliness. [Obs.]

ef-frŏnt′, *v.t.* To inspire with effrontery. [Obs.]

ef-frŏnt′ẽr-y, *n.* [OFr. *effronterie*, from *effronte*, shameless, L. *effrons* (-*ontis*), putting forth the forehead; barefaced, shameless; *ex*, out, and *frons*, the forehead.] Impudence; assurance; shameless boldness; boldness transgressing the bounds of modesty and decorum; as, *effrontery* is a sure mark of ill-breeding.

ef-frŏn′tū-ous-ly, *adv.* With effrontery. [Obs.]

ef-fulġe′, *v.t.* and *v.i.* [L. *effulgere*, to shine forth; *ex*, out, and *fulgere*, to shine.]

I. *v.t.* To radiate. [Rare.]

II. *v.i.* To send forth a flood of light. [Rare.]

ef-ful′ġence, *n.* A flood of light; great brightness; splendor; as, the *effulgence* of divine glory.

ef-ful′ġent, *a.* Shining; bright; splendid; diffusing a flood of light; as, the *effulgent* sun.

ef-ful′ġent-ly, *adv.* In a splendid manner.

ef-fū-mȧ-bil′i-ty, *n.* The quality of flying off in fumes or vapor. [Obs.]

ef-fūme′, *v.t.* To breathe out. [Obs.]

ef-fund′, *v.t.* To pour out. [Obs.]

ef-fūṣe′, *v.t.*; effused, *pt.*, *pp.*; effusing, *ppr.* [L. *effusus*, pp. of *effundere*, to pour forth; *ex*, out, and *fundere*, to pour.] To pour out as a fluid; to spill; to shed.

ef-fūṣe′, *v.i.* 1. To escape through pores or small apertures.

2. To be poured out; to emanate.

ef-fūse′, *a.* 1. Dissipated; profuse. [Obs.]

2. In botany, spreading loosely; not having a definite figure.

3. In conchology, expanded; applied to shells having the lips separated by a gap or groove.

ef-fūse′, *n.* A pouring out; a loss. [Obs.]

ef-fū′ṣion, *n.* [L. *effusio* (-*onis*), from *effundere*, to pour forth.]

1. The act of pouring out; as, the *effusion* of blood, of words, of grace, etc.

2. That which is poured out; figuratively, an utterance; a trifling piece of verse or prose; as, the *effusions* of a youthful poet.

3. Demonstrative cordiality of manner; eager welcome; overflowing kindness.

4. In pathology, (a) the escape of any fluid out of the vessel containing it into another part; (b) the fluid thus effusing.

5. The escape of gases through minute apertures into a vacuum.

ef-fū′sive, *a.* Pouring out; that pours forth largely.

Effusive rocks; surface volcanic rocks, as distinguished from *intrusive rocks*.

ef-fū′sive-ly, *adv.* In an effusive manner.

ef-fū′sive-ness, *n.* State of being effusive.

ef′reet, *n.* Same as *Afrit*.

eft, *n.* [ME. *efte*, *eefte*, *evete*, *ewt*; with noun of indef. art. *an*, united with it, *newt* is formed.] A small lizard, or newt.

eft, *adv.* [AS. *eft*, *æft*, afterward, again.] Soon after; again. [Obs.]

eft-sọọn′, eft-sọọns′, *adv.* Soon afterward; in a short time. [Rare and Poet.]

ē-gad′, *interj.* A modification of the oath "by God"; formerly used to express surprise, pleasure, etc.

ē′găl, *a.* [Obs.] Same as *Equal*.

ē-gal′i-ty, *n.* [Obs.] Same as *Equality*.

E-ġē′ăn, *a.* Same as *Ægean*.

ē′ġence, *n.* [L. *egens* (-*entis*), ppr. of *egere*, to be in want, need.] Need; state of want. [Rare.]

ē′gẽr, *a.* Sharp; sour. [Obs.]

ē′gẽr, *n.* Same as *Eager*.

E-ġē′ri-ȧ, *n.pl.* See *Ægeria*.

ē-ġẽr′mi-nāte, *v.i.* To germinate. [Obs.]

ē-ġest′, *v.t.*; egested, *pt.*, *pp.*; egesting, *ppr.* [L. *egestus*, pp. of *egerere*, to bear out, discharge.] To cast or throw out; to void, as excrement.

ē-ġes′tȧ, *n.pl.* [Neut. pl. of L. *egestus*, pp. of *egerere*, to throw out, discharge.] Any waste matter thrown out of the body; excreta.

ē-ġes′tion (-jes′chun), *n.* [L. *egestio* (-*onis*), from *egerere*, to bear out, discharge.] The act of voiding excreta; defecation.

ē-ġes′tive, *a.* Excretory; not ingestive.

egg, *v.t.*; egged, *pt.*, *pp.*; egging, *ppr.* [ME. *eggen*, to incite, urge on; Ice. *eggja*, from *egg*, edge.] To arouse to action; to incite; to urge; usually followed by *on*; as, *egged on* by pride.

egg, *v.t.* 1. To throw eggs at.

2. To cover, mix, or treat with eggs.

egg, *n.* [ME. *egge*; Ice. *egg*; AS. *æg*; Sw. *ägg*; Dan. *æg*, an egg.]

1. A body formed in the ovary of the females of birds and many other animals, containing the substance from which a like animal is produced under certain conditions of incubation. In its generic sense, the word *egg* is used synonymously with ovum; when unqualified, the *egg* of the domestic hen is meant.

2. Anything like or considered like the *egg* of a fowl.

3. A certain size of coal.

4. An origin, germ, nucleus, or elementary idea.

Egg and anchor, dart, or *tongue*; any of various forms of molding in which egg-shaped and dart-shaped ornaments alternate.

egg′-ap-pȧ-rā″tus, *n.* In botany, a female organ consisting of three cells at the opening of the embryo-sac in the higher flowering plants, an egg-cell and two coöperating cells.

egg′-ap″ple, *n.* The eggplant.

eg′gȧr, *n.* A moth. [See *Egger*.]

egg′-bird, *n.* Any one of several kinds of sea-birds whose eggs have a commercial value; specifically, the sooty tern.

egg′-cell, *n.* An ovum.

egg′-clēav″āġe, *n.* The segmentation of an egg-cell.

egg′-cup, *n.* A special form of cup for holding soft-boiled eggs.

eg′ġe-ment, *n.* [Obs.] Same as *Eggment*.

eg′gẽr, *n.* One whose business is the collecting of eggs, as of wild fowl, turtles, etc.

eg′gẽr, *n.* [ME. *eggen*, to incite, urge on.] One who incites to action.

eg′gẽr, *n.* [Origin unknown.] A moth of either of the two genera, *Eriogaster* or *Lasiocampa*.

egg′ẽr-y, *n.* A depository for eggs. [Rare.]

egg′-glȧss, *n.* 1. A three-minute sandglass, used for timing the boiling of eggs.

2. An egg-cup made of glass.

egg′-glūe, *n.* A viscid, gluey substance holding the eggs of some animals together and attaching them to the body of the parent.

egg′hot, *n.* A warm drink containing eggs, brandy, ale, and sugar.

egg′lẽr, *n.* An egger; a collector of or dealer in eggs.

egg′ment, *n.* [ME. *eggement*, from *eggen*, to incite, urge on.] Incitement to action; urging.

egg′-mīte, *n.* Any of various mites that destroy the eggs of other insects.

egg′nog, *n.* A cold drink composed of egg, milk, and sugar, usually with the addition of a distilled liquor.

egg′-par″ȧ-sīte, *n.* In zoölogy, a parasitic hymenopter whose eggs are laid in the eggs of other insects.

egg′plant, *n.* A plant allied to the tomato, and bearing a smooth fruit, shaped like an egg, used in cookery; the *Solanum Melongena*.

Eggplant (*Solanum Melongena*).

egg′-shāped (-shāpt), *a.* Shaped like an egg; of such shape that any transverse section is a circle and a longitudinal section an oval.

egg′shell, *n.* 1. The brittle outside covering of an egg; figuratively, anything fragile or easily crushed.

2. In zoölogy, a gasteropod shaped like an egg.

Eggshell china or *porcelain*; an extremely thin variety of porcelain ware. In Europe, it is usually made by coating the interior of a plaster mold with barbotine, which, after firing, can be removed.

egg′-squȧsh (-skwosh), *n.* A squash having ovoid fruit.

egg′-tūbe, *n.* In zoölogy, a tube in which ova develop or by which they are conveyed from an ovary.

egg′-ūr″chin, *n.* Any globular sea-urchin.

ē′ghe (-ge), *n.*; *pl.* **ē′ghen** (-gen). An eye. [Obs.]

ē′gi-lops, *n.* Same as *Ægilops*.

ē′ġis, *n.* Same as *Ægis*.

ē-glan′dū-lăr, *a.* [L. *e-* priv., and *glandula*, dim. of *glans*, *glandis*, an acorn.] Without glands; glandless.

ē-glan′dū-lōse, ē-glan′dū-lous, *a.* Same as *Eglandular*.

eg′lăn-tīne, *n.* [Fr., from OFr. *aiglent*, sweetbrier, hip-tree, from L. *aculeus*, a sting, prickle; *acus*, a point, sting.]

1. The sweetbrier, *Rosa rubiginosa*.

2. The dogrose or wild rose, *Rosa canina*.

eg′len-tere, eg′lăn-tere, *n.* [Obs.] Same as *Eglantine*.

eg′ling, *n.* A two-year-old perch. [Prov. Eng.]

ē-glom′ẽr-āte, *v.t.* [L. *e-*, out, and *glomeratus*, pp. of *glomerare*, to wind up into a ball.] To unwind, as a thread from a ball. [Obs.]

ē′gō, *n.* [L. *ego*, I.] Literally, the "I"; the self that feels, thinks, wills, and acts, as distinguished from its attributes, from the bodily organization, and from every other object of thought; the subject as distinguished from everything objective.

ē′gō-hood, *n.* The state of having self-existence and self-consciousness; personality. [Rare.]

ē-gō′iç-ăl, *a.* Of or characteristic of egoism. [Rare.]

ē′gō-iṣm, *n.* 1. In metaphysics, the opinion of one who thinks everything uncertain except his own existence.

2. A passionate love of self, leading a man to consider everything as connected with his own person and to prefer himself to everything in the world; the theory that makes the happiness of self the highest motive.

3. In ethics, the striving to secure personal pleasure or advantage, as distinguished from *altruism*, or the effort to benefit others. In this meaning, not of necessity unworthy and not the same as def. 2.

ē′gō-ist, *n.* 1. One who is habitually selfish.

2. One who maintains the theory of egoism.

ē-gō-is′tiç, ē-gō-is′tiç-ăl, *a.* 1. Habitually selfish.

2. Self-seeking; relating to self.

3. In metaphysics, involving egoism.

ē-gō-is′tiç-ăl-ly, *adv.* In an egoistic way.

ē-gō′i-ty, *n.* Personality. [Rare.]

ē-goph′ō-ny, *n.* Same as *Ægophony*.

ē′gō-thē-iṣm, *n.* [Gr. *egō*, I, and *theos*, God.] The identification of self with the Deity; self-deification. [Rare.]

ē′gō-tiṣm (or eg′ō-), *n.* [L. *ego*, I, and *-tism*, for *-ism*.] The practice of thinking and speaking much about oneself; vanity and self-conceit as manifested in the too frequent use of "I"; the practice of magnifying one's attainments or importance; also, the habit of mind which causes one to estimate all things by their relation to oneself.

Syn.—Self-conceit, vanity.—*Self-conceit* is an overweening opinion of oneself; *egotism* is the expression of self-conceit in words or actions; *vanity* is inflation of mind arising from the idea of being thought highly of by others.

ē′gō-tist, *n.* [L. *ego*, I, and *-ist*, for *-ist*.] One who talks about himself inordinately; one who magnifies his own achievements and faculties; a person characterized by egotism.

ē-gō-tis′tiç, ē-gō-tis′tiç-ăl, *a.* 1. Showing egotism.

2. Pertaining to egotism.

ē-gō-tis′tiç-ăl-ly, *adv.* In an egotistic manner.

ē′gō-tīze, *v.i.* To convert everything to the glorification of self, whether by act, thought, or conversation. [Rare.]

ē-gran′ū-lōse, *a.* [L. *e-* priv., and *granulum*, dim. of *granum*, a grain.] In botany, without granules.

ē′gre (-gẽr), *a.* and *n.* Same as *Eager*.

ē-grē′ġious (-jus *or* -ji-us), *a.* [L. *egregius*, lit., chosen or separated from the herd, select, choice, eminent; *e*, out, and *grex*, *gregis*, herd.]

1. Eminent; remarkable, extraordinary; distinguished; as, *egregious* exploits.

2. Great; extraordinary, remarkable: enormous; in a bad sense; as, an *egregious* mistake; an *egregious* rascal.

ē-grē′ġious-ly, *adv.* Greatly; enormously; shamefully; as, he is *egregiously* mistaken.

ē-grē′ġious-ness, *n.* State of being egregious.

eg′rē-moine, *n.* [Obs.] Same as *Agrimony*.

ē′gress, *n.* [L. *egressus*, from *egredi*, to go out; *e*, out, and *gradi*, to step, go.]

1. The act of going or issuing out; exit; departure from any inclosed or confined place.

2. A door or way out; an exit; as, a broad *egress*.

3. In astronomy, the apparent passage of a heavenly body out from before or behind the disk of another.

ē′gress, *v.i.* To depart; to pass out. [Rare.]

ē-gres′sion (ē-gresh′un), *n.* [L. *egressio*, from *egredi*, to go out.] The act of going out from any inclosure.

ē-gress′ōr, *n.* One who goes out. [Rare.]

ē′gret, ē-grette′, *n.* [Fr. *aigrette*, a sort of heron, a tuft of feathers.]

1. Any one of those species of herons which have the feathers on the lower part of the back lengthened and the barbs loose, so that this part of the plumage is very soft and flowing.

2. A heron's feather.

3. An aigret.

4. A plumicorn or feathery topknot of some birds.

5. In botany, the flying, feathery, or hairy crown of seeds, as the down of the thistle.

6. In zoölogy, a variety of monkey found in Java.

ē-grett′, *n.* Same as *Egret*.

eg′ri-mō-ny, *n.* Same as *Agrimony*.

eg′ri-mō-ny, *n.* [L. *ægrimonia*, sorrow, anxiety, from *æger*, sick.] Mental distress; acute sorrow. [Obs.]

ē′gri-ot, *n.* [OFr. *agriote*, a sharp or tart cherry.] A kind of sour cherry.

eg′ri-tūde, *n.* [L. *ægritudo*, from *æger*, sick.] Egrimony; also, bodily distress. [Obs.]

e-guăl-men′te (-gwäl-), *adv.* [It., from *equale*, L. *æqualis*, equal.] In music, evenly.

ē-gũr′gi-tāte, *v.t.* [L. *egurgitatus*, pp. of *egurgitare*, to pour out; *e*, out, and *gurgitare*, from *gurges*, a whirlpool.] To emit with a gush, as water from a geyser.

E-ġyp′tiăn (-shăn), *a.* [L. *Ægyptius*; Gr. *Aigyptios*, Egyptian, from *Aigyptos*, Egypt.]

1. Pertaining to Egypt, in Africa.

2. Gipsy. [Obs.]

Egyptian architecture; the style of architecture developed and carried to a high state of perfection by the ancient Egyptians and illustrated by some of the oldest structures in existence in the form of pyramids, temples, and monoliths.

Egyptian cross; the ankh; the tau cross.

Egyptian thorn; in botany, a tree, the *Acacia vera*, which yields gum arabic or gum acacia.

E-gyp'tiăn, *n.* 1. A native of Egypt.

2. The language of modern or ancient Egypt.

3. A real or pretended gipsy.

E'gypt-īze, *v.t.* To cause to become, or to claim (something) to be, Egyptian in character, origin, etc. [Rare.]

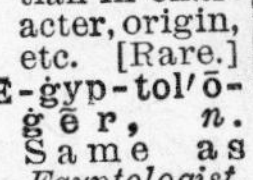

Court of Temple at Edfu.

E-gyp-tol'ō-gẽr, *n.* Same as *Egyptologist*.

E-gyp-tō-log'ic-ăl, *a.* Relating to Egyptology.

E-gyp-tol'ō-gist, *n.* A student of or expert in Egyptology.

Egyptian Columns.—1. From Rhamession, Thebes. 2. Portico of Temple at Dendera. 3. In British Museum.

E-gyp-tol'ō-gy, *n.* [Gr. *Aigyptos*, Egypt, and *-logia*, from *legein*, to speak.] The science which embraces the study of the ancient language, history, etc., of Egypt.

eh, *interj.* An exclamation denoting inquiry or slight surprise.

eh'lite (ā'), *n.* [Named from *Ehl*, in Austria, where it is found, and *-ite*.] A massive, dark-green, hydrous, copper phosphate sometimes containing vanadium.

ei'dẽr, *n.* 1. Same as *Eider-duck*.

2. Same as *Eider-down*.

ei'dẽr-down, *n.* Down or soft feathers of the eider-duck, much used in the manufacture of coverlets, pillows, etc., on account of its warmth and light weight.

ei'dẽr-duck, *n.* [Ice. *æthr*; Sw. *eider*, an eider, eider-duck; Dan. *ederfugl*, eider-fowl.] A large species of sea-duck of the genus *Somateria*, especially *Somateria mollissima*, which is found on both sides of the North Atlantic, its down being much valued from its superior warmth, lightness, and elasticity. Other species are *Somateria dresseri*, the American eider-duck, *Somateria* (*Arctonetta*) *fischeri*, the spectacled eider-duck, and *Somateria spectabilis*, the king eider-duck.

Eider-duck (*Somateria mollissima*).

ei'dẽr-goose, *n.* The eider-duck.

ei'dẽr-yärn, *n.* A knitting-yarn spun from the wool of the merino sheep.

ei'dō-grăph, *n.* [Gr. *eidos*, form, figure, and *graphein*, to write.] An instrument for copying designs, reduced or enlarged in any proportion within certain limits.

ei-dol'ō-clast, *n.* An iconoclast.

ei-dō'lon, *n.*; *pl.* **ei-dō'lă**. [Gr. *eidōlon*, an image, idol.] A likeness, image, or representation; a shade or specter; an apparition.

ei'dō-scōpe, *n.* [Gr. *eidos*, form, shape, and *skopein*, to see.] An instrument on the principle of the kaleidoscope, which produces an infinite variety of geometrical figures by the independent revolution of two perforated metallic disks on their axes.

ei-dou-rā'ni-ŏn, *n.*; *pl.* **ei-dou-rā'ni-ă**. [Gr. *eidos*, form, and *ouranos*, the heavens.] A device for illustrating the motions and phases of heavenly bodies.

eigh (ā), *interj.* An exclamatory expression; aye.

eight (āt), *n.* An ait. [Obs.]

eight (āt), *a.* [ME. *eight*, *eihte*, *ehte*, *auhte*; AS. *eahta*; D. *acht*; O.H.G. *ahto*; L.G. *acht*; Sw. *otta*; Ice. *atta*; Goth. *ahtau*; L. *octo*; Gr. *oktō*; Sans. *ashta*, eight.] One more than seven; as, *eight* men.

eight (āt), *n.* 1. A cardinal number; seven and one; eight units or objects.

2. A symbol representing eight units, as 8 or viii; hence, any curved outline in the shape of the figure 8.

3. A playing-card bearing eight spots.

eight'een (āt'ēn), *a.* [ME. *eightene*, *æhtene*; AS. *eahtatyne*, *eahtatiene*; *eahta*, eight, and *tene*, *tyn*, ten.] Eight and ten, or one more than seventeen; twice nine; as, *eighteen* months.

eight'een, *n.* 1. The sum of ten and eight; eighteen units or objects.

2. A symbol representing eighteen units, as 18 or xviii.

eight-een'mō, *a.* and *n.* [An English reading of *18mo*, which stands for L. *octodecimo*, from *octodecim*, eighteen.]

I. *a.* Of the size of a sheet making eighteen leaves or thirty-six pages; made up of such sheets; as, an *eighteenmo* book.

II. *n.* A size of book in which each sheet is folded into eighteen leaves or thirty-six pages; usually written *18mo*.

eight'eenth, *a.* [AS. *eahtateotha*, eighteenth.]

1. Next in order after the seventeenth.

2. Being one of eighteen equal divisions of anything.

eight'eenth, *n.* 1. The quotient of unity divided by eighteen; an eighteenth part.

2. In music, an interval comprehending two octaves and a fourth.

eight'e-teth-e, *a.* Eighteenth. [Obs.]

eight'foil, *n.* In heraldry, a grass that has eight leaves; called also *double quatrefoil*.

eight'fōld, *a.* Eight times the number or quantity.

eighth (ātth), *a.* [ME. *eightethe*; AS. *eahtotha*, eighth.]

1. Next in order after the seventh.

2. Consisting of one of eight equal parts into which anything is divided.

eighth, *n.* 1. The quotient of unity divided by eight; one of eight equal parts.

2. In music, an octave; an interval consisting of five tones and two semitones.

eighth'ly, *adv.* In the eighth place; for the eighth time.

eighth'-nōte, *n.* In music, a note which is the eighth part of a semibreve or whole note; a quaver.

eighth'-rest, *n.* In music, a rest which is the eighth part of a semibreve rest; a quaver rest.

eight'i-eth, *a.* 1. Next in order after the seventy-ninth.

2. Consisting of one of eighty equal parts into which anything is divided.

eight'i-eth, *n.* The quotient of unity divided by eighty; one of eighty equal parts.

eight'ling, *n.* In crystallography, a compound or twin crystal composed of eight individuals.

eight'scōre, *a.* and *n.* Eight times twenty; a hundred and sixty.

eight'y, *a.* [AS. *eahtatig*; *eahta*, eight, and *-tig*, a form of ten.] Eight times ten; fourscore.

eight'y, *n.* 1. The number containing eight times ten.

2. A symbol representing eighty units, as 80 or lxxx.

eigne (ān *or* ā'ne), *a.* [OFr. *aisné*, *ainsné*; *ains*, before, and *né*, born; L. *ante natus*; *ante*, before, and *natus*, born.]

1. Eldest; an epithet used in law to denote the eldest son. —Blackstone.

2. Unalienable; entailed; belonging to the eldest son. [Obs.]

Bastard eigne; an eldest son born before the marriage of his parents.

ei'kon, *n.*; *pl.* **ei'kō-nēs**. [Gr. *eikōn*, an image, likeness.] A likeness; an effigy; an image; also written *icon*.

ēild, *n.* Eld; age. [Obs.]

eire (ãr), *n.* Air. [Obs.]

ei'rē-närch, *n.* Same as *Irenarch*.

ei-ren'ic, *a.* Same as *Irenic*.

ēi'rie, **ēi'ry**, *n.* See *Aery*.

ei-se-gē'sis, *n*; *pl.* **ei-se-gē'sēs**. [Gr. *eisēgēsis*, a bringing in; from *eisēgeisthai*; *eis*, into, and *hēgeisthai*, to lead, guide.] An improper method of exposition by which the expounder introduces his own ideas into the interpretation; opposed to *exegesis*.

ēi'sel, *n.* [ME. *eisel*; OFr. *aisil*, vinegar.] Vinegar. [Obs.]

ei-sod'i-con, **ei-sod'i-kon**, *n.* See *Isodicon*.

eis-tedd'fōd (is-teth'vōd), *n.* [W., a sitting, session, assembly, from *eistedd*, to sit.] An assembly or session of bards and minstrels held in Wales in ancient times. These meetings were revived by the Tudor sovereigns, and annual meetings for the recitation of prize poems and musical performances are now held under this name.

ēi'thẽr (*or* ī'thẽr), *a.* [ME. *either*, *eyther*, *aither*; AS. *ægther*, contr. of *æghwæther*, either, each; *a-*, ever, *ge-*, and *hwæther*, pron., whether.]

1. One of two taken indifferently; one or the other; as, *either* side may win; give me *either* orange.

2. Each of two; both; as, they lined up on *either* bank of the river.

On *either* side one, and Jesus in the midst. —John xix. 18.

ēi'thẽr, *pron.* 1. One of two; one or the other, taken indifferently; as, *either* of them may succeed.

2. Each of two; the one and other considered separately.

The king of Israel and Jehoshaphat sat *either* of them on his throne. —2 Chron. xviii. 9.

ēi'thẽr, *conj.* 1. A disjunctive conjunction always used as correlative to and preceding *or*. It is placed before the first of two or more alternatives, *or* being placed before the second or succeeding alternatives.

Either he is talking, *or* he is pursuing, *or* he is in a journey, *or* peradventure he sleepeth. —1 Kings xviii. 27.

2. At all; in any case; as, he would not go, and I would not, *either*. He was right; no, he wasn't, *either*. [Colloq.]

3. Or. [Obs.]

Can the fig-tree, my brethren, bear olive berries? *either* a vine, figs? —James iii. 12.

ē-jac'ū-lāte, *v.t.*; ejaculated, *pt.*, *pp.*; ejaculating, *ppr.* [L. *ejaculatus*, pp. of *ejaculari*, to cast out, throw out; *e*, out, and *jaculari*, from *jaculum*, a dart, missile; *jacere*, to throw.]

1. To throw out, to cast forth; to shoot; to dart. [Obs. except in technical usage.]

2. To utter suddenly and briefly, or as an exclamation; as, he *ejaculated* a prayer.

ē-jac'ū-lāte, *v.i.* To utter ejaculations; to make brief and sudden exclamations.

Ejaculating to himself. —Scott.

ē-jac-ū-lā'tion, *n.* 1. The act of throwing or darting out with a sudden force and rapid flight. [Obs. except in technical usage.]

2. The uttering of a sudden exclamation; an exclamatory sentence or word, especially a short, sudden prayer.

3. In physiology, the ejection of the spermatic fluid.

ē-jac'ū-lā-tŏr, *n.* One who or that which ejaculates; specifically, in anatomy, a muscle which effects the emission of the spermatic fluid.

ē-jac'ū-lā-tō-ry, *a.* 1. Suddenly darted out; uttered in short sentences; as, an *ejaculatory* prayer or petition.

2. Sudden; hasty. [Obs.]

3. Casting or throwing out; as, *ejaculatory* seminal vessels.

ē-ject', *v.t.*; ejected, *pt.*, *pp.*; ejecting, *ppr.* [L. *ejectus*, pp. of *ejicere*, to throw out; *e*, out, and *jacere*, to throw.]

1. To throw out; to cast forth; to thrust out; to expel; to dismiss; as, they forcibly *ejected* him.

2. In law, to dispossess; to evict by writ of ejectment; as, to *eject* a tenant.

Syn.—Banish, dismiss, discharge, expel, oust, evict.

ē'ject, *n.* A word first used by W. K. Clifford to express something inferred to be in actual existence, as a mental condition or act of another, but which is not accessible to the consciousness of the person making the inference.

ē-jec'tȧ, *n.pl.* [L., pl. of *ejectum*, neut. of *ejectus*, pp. of *ejicere*, to throw out.] Refuse; matter thrown out, as by a volcano.

ē-jec-tȧ-men'tȧ, *n.pl.* Same as *Ejecta*.

ē-jec'tion, *n.* [L. *ejectio*, from *ejicere*, to throw out; cast out.]

1. The act of casting out; expulsion; dis charge.

2. The discharge of any excrementitious matter; evacuation.

3. Dispossession; the state of being ejected; dismissal.

ē-ject'ive, *a.* 1. Pertaining to ejection or expulsion; expelling.

2. Pertaining to or of the nature of an eject.

ē-ject'ment, *n.* 1. A casting out; a dispossession; an expulsion.

2. In law, a writ or action for the recovery of possession of realty from which the owner has been ejected, and for damages for the unlawful detention of the same.

ē-ject'ŏr, *n.* 1. One who or that which ejects.

2. A device wherein a body of elastic fluid, such as steam or air, under pressure and in

motion, is made the means of driving a liquid such as water or oil.

3. That device in a breech-loading firearm which withdraws the empty shell from the bore of the gun.

ē-ject'ŏr-çon-dens"ẽr, *n.* In a steam-engine, a form of condenser worked by the exhaust-steam from the cylinder.

ę-jï'dō (ā-hē'dō), *n.* [Sp.] In Spanish and Mexican law, a common used by the people of a town or pueblo.

ē'joo, *n.* [Malay.] The fiber of the gomuti.

ej-ū-lā'tion, *n.* [L. *ejulatio*, from *ejulare*, to wail, lament.] Outcry; a wailing; lamentation. [Obs.]

ek-à-bō'ron, *n.* See *Scandium.*

ek"al-ū-min'i-um, *n.* See *Gallium.*

ek-à-sil'i-çon, *n.* See *Germanium.*

ēke, *v.t.*; eked (ēkt), *pt., pp.*; eking, *ppr.* [ME. *eken*; AS. *ecan, ican*; Ice. *auka*; Sw. *öka*; Goth. *aukan*; L. *augere*; Gr. *auxanein*, to increase.]

1. To increase; to enlarge; to lengthen; to protract; to prolong. [Obs.]

2. To add to; to supply deficiencies in; to enlarge by addition; commonly with *out*; as, to *eke* or *eke out* a piece of cloth; to *eke out* a performance.

ēke, *adv.* and *conj.* [AS. *eac*; D. *ook*; G. *auch*; Sw. *och*; Dan. *og*; W. *ac*; L. *ac*, and, also.] Also; likewise, in addition. [Obs.]

ēke, *n.* Something added; an addition. [Rare.]

ek'ē-bẽrg-ite, *n.* [Named after *Ekeberg*, a mineralogist.] A variety of scapolite.

ēke'nāme, *n.* A nickname; an epithet. [Obs.]

ēk'ing, *n.* [From *eke*, to increase.]

1. The act of adding.

2. That which is added; specifically, (a) a piece of wood fitted to make good a deficiency in length, as the end of a knee and the like; (b) the carved work under the lower part of the quarter-piece of a vessel at the aft part of the quarter-gallery.

ek'lō-gīte, *n.* Same as *Eclogite.*

E'lä, *n.* In music, applied originally to the highest note in the scale of Guido; hence, often used by the old dramatists to indicate the extreme of any quality, but especially any extravagant or hyperbolical saying.

ē-lab'ō-rāte, *v.t.*; elaborated, *pt., pp.*; elaborating, *ppr.* [L. *elaboratus*, pp. of *elaborare*, to work out, labor greatly; *e-*, out, and *laborare*, from *labor*, labor, work.]

1. To produce with labor.

They in full joy *elaborate* a sigh. —Young.

2. To improve or refine by successive operations; to work out with great care; to work out fully or perfectly; as, to *elaborate* a work of art.

ē-lab'ō-rāte, *a.* Wrought with labor; finished with great diligence; studied; executed with exactness; as, an *elaborate* discourse; an *elaborate* performance.

Syn.—Labored, perfected, studied, highly wrought.

ē-lab'ō-rāte-ly, *adv.* In an elaborate manner; with nice regard to exactness.

ē-lab'ō-rāte-ness, *n.* The quality of being elaborate or wrought with great labor.

ē-lab-ō-rā'tion, *n.* 1. The act of elaborating; improvement or refinement by successive operations; a developing or bringing to perfection by degrees.

2. In physiology, the several processes by which the appropriate food of animals and plants is transformed or assimilated so as to render it adapted for the purposes of nutrition.

ē-lab'ō-rā-tive, *a.* Serving or tending to elaborate; possessing the power of developing or refining by successive operations, whether of nature or of art; working out with minute attention to details; laboriously bringing to a state of completion or perfection.

Elaborative faculty; in psychology, the intellectual power of discerning relations and of viewing objects by means of or in relations; the understanding as described by the German philosophers; the discursive faculty; thought.

ē-lab'ō-rā-tŏr, *n.* One who or that which elaborates.

ē-lab'ō-rā-tō-ry, *a.* Elaborating.

ē-lab'ō-rā-tō-ry, *n.* A laboratory. [Obs.]

ē-lā'brāte, *a.* [L. *e-* priv., and *labrum*, a lip.] In entomology, destitute of a distinct labrum or lip, as most dipterous insects.

E"læ-ag-nā'cē-æ, *n.pl.* [Gr. *elaiagnos, eleagnos*, a Bœotian marsh-plant; *elaia*, an olive-tree, and *agnos*, equal to *eygos*, a willow-tree, and *-aceæ.*] In botany, the oleaster family, a small order of apetalous exogens, covered with silvery or brown scales, and having alternate or opposite leaves, and small white or yellow flowers. The order includes three genera and twenty-five or thirty species.

ē"læ-ag-nā'ceous, *a.* Pertaining or belonging to the *Elæagnaceæ.*

E-læ-ag'nus, *n.* In botany, the typical genus of the *Elæagnaceæ.*

E-læ'is, *n.* [Gr. *elaion*, olive-oil, oil, from *elaia*, the olive-tree.] In botany, a small genus of palms of Africa and South America. *Elæis Guineensis* is an African species which yields an oil used by the natives in cookery and for anointing the body.

ē-læ-ō-. A combining form from Greek *elaion*, olive-oil, oil, used to signify relation to or connection with oil.

ē-læ'ō-blast, *n.* [*Elæo-*, and Gr. *blastos*, a shoot, germ.] In zoölogy, the urochord of certain of the *Tunicata.*

ē"læ-ō-blas'tiç, *a.* Pertaining to the elæoblast.

E"læ-ō-cär'pus, *n.* [*Elæo-*, and Gr. *karpos*, fruit.] A genus of trees and shrubs of the natural order *Tiliaceæ*, containing fifty species, natives of India and Australia and the neighboring islands. They have simple leaves and racemes of small flowers. The fruit is oblong or globose, with a rough-shelled nut, surrounded by a fleshy pulp, which is used in curries or pickled like olives.

ē-læ'ō-līte, *n.* [*Elæo-*, and Gr. *lithos*, stone.] A coarse, massive variety of nephelin, of a waxy, greasy luster, and presenting various shades of green, gray, and red. The predominance of soda in its composition renders its alteration a frequent source of zeolites, as thomsonite.

ē-læ'ō-līte-sy'e-nīte, *n.* A syenite containing elæolite.

ē-læ-om'e-tẽr, ē-lāi-om'e-tẽr, *n.* [*Elæo-*, and Gr. *metron*, a measure.] A hydrometer for testing the purity of olive- and almond-oils, by determining their densities.

ē-læ-op'tēne, *n.* [*Elæo-*, and Gr. *ptēnos*, winged, fleeting.] The liquid portion of volatile oils, as distinguished from the concrete or crystallizable portion called *stearoptene*; written also *elaopten, oleoptene.*

ē-lā'i-dāte, *n.* [*Elaid*ic and *-ate.*] A salt formed by the union of elaidic acid with a base.

ē-lā-id'iç, *a.* [Gr. *elais (-idos)*, equal to *elaia*, the olive-tree, and *-ic.*] Of or pertaining to oleic acid or elain.

Elaidic acid; $C_{18}H_{34}O_2$, a fatty acid obtained from oleic acid by adding nitrous or hyponitrous acid.

ē-lā'i-din, ē-lā'i-dine, *n.* [Gr. *elais (-idos)*, the olive-tree, and *-in.*] In chemistry, a fatty substance produced by the action of nitric acid upon certain oils, especially castor-oil.

ē-lā'in, ē-lā'ine, *n.* Same as *Olein.*

ē-lāi-od'iç, *a.* [Gr. *elaiōdēs*, oily; *elaion*, olive-oil, oil, and *eidos*, form.] Derived from castor-oil; as, *elaiodic* acid.

ē-lāi-om'e-tẽr, *n.* Same as *Elæometer.*

E'lăm-īte, *n.* One living in or a native of Elam, an ancient kingdom, now Khuzistan.

ē-lamp'ing, *a.* Shining. [Obs.]

é-lăn' (ā-lon'), *n.* [Fr., from *élancer*, to dart, hurl.] Ardor inspired by enthusiasm or passion.

ē-lànce', *v.t.* [Fr. *élancer*; *e-*, L. *e-*, out, and *lancer*, to dart, hurl, from *lance*, a lance.] To throw or shoot; to hurl; to dart. [Rare.]

ē'lănd, *n.* [D. *eland*, an elk.]

1. A large antelope of Africa, *Oreas canna*, the Cape elk. Its flesh, which is dried and used like tongue, is so much prized that the animal has been almost extirpated in Cape Colony, where it once abounded.

2. The moose.

ē-lā'net, *n.* [From Gr. *elaunein*, to drive, set in motion.] A kite belonging to the genus *Elanus.*

ē-lā'ō-līte, *n.* Same as *Elæolite.*

ē-lā-op'ten, *n.* Same as *Elæoptene.*

el'à-phine, *a.* [Gr. *elaphos*, a deer.] Pertaining to the red deer or stag, *Cervus elaphus.*

el'à-phūre, *n.* [Gr. *elaphos*, a deer, and *oura*, a tail.] *Elaphurus davidianus*, a large Chinese deer with peculiar antlers.

E-lap'i-dæ, *n.pl.* A family of venomous serpents typified by the genus *Elaps.*

ē-lap-i-dā'tion, *n.* [L. *elapidatus*; *e-*, out, and *lapidatus*, pp. of *lapidare*, to throw stones; *lapis (-idis)*, a stone.] A clearing away of stones. [Rare.]

el'à-pine, *a.* Pertaining to the *Elapidæ.*

E'laps, *n.* [L. *elops (-idis)*; Gr. *elops*, a sea-fish, serpent.] A genus of venomous snakes, typical of the family *Elapidæ*. Some of the species are called coral-snakes, as *Elaps corallina* of Brazil.

ē-lapse', *v.i.*; elapsed (-lapst'), *pt., pp.*; elapsing, *ppr.* [L. *elapsus*, pp. of *elabi*, to glide away; *e-*, out, and *labi*, to glide, fall.] To slide, slip, or glide away; to pass away silently; used of time; as, two years *elapsed* before he returned.

ē-lap'sion, *n.* The act of elapsing; lapse. [Rare.]

ē-lā'quē-āte (-kwē-), *v.t.* [L. *elaqueatus*, pp. of *elaqueare*, to disentangle; *e-*, out, and *laqueus*, a snare.] To disentangle. [Rare.]

El-à-sip'ō-dà, *n.pl.* Same as *Elasmapoda.*

e-las'mà-pod, *a.* and *n.* I. *a.* Elasmapodous.

II. *n.* One of the *Elasmapoda.*

El-as-map'ō-dà, *n.pl.* [Gr. *elasmos, elasma*, a metal plate, and *pous, podos*, foot.] A group of deep-sea holothurians exhibiting distinct bilateral symmetry, embracing about fifty known species.

el-as-map'ō-dous, *a.* Pertaining to the *Elasmapoda.*

ē-las'mō-braṇch, *a.* and *n.* I. *a.* Pertaining to or characteristic of the *Elasmobranchii.*

II. *n.* A member of the *Elasmobranchii.*

ē-las-mō-braṅ'çhi-ăn, ē-las-mō-braṅ'çhi-āte, *a.* and *n.* Same as *Elasmobranch.*

E-las-mō-braṅ'çhi-ī, *n.pl.* [Gr. *elasmos, elasma*, a metal plate, and *branchia*, gills.] A subclass or order of fishes including the sharks, rays, and the *Chimæra*, having the vertebral column sometimes cartilaginous, and lamelliform gills.

ē-las'mō-saụr, *n.* A reptile of the genus *Elasmosaurus.*

E-las-mō-saụ'rus, *n.* [Gr. *elasmos, elasma*, a metal plate, and *sauros*, a lizard.] A genus of large fossil American reptiles allied to the plesiosaurs.

ē-las'tiç, *a.* [From Gr. *elaunein*, to drive, set in motion.]

1. Springing back; having the power of returning to the form from which a body is bent, extended, pressed, or distorted; having the inherent property of recovering its former figure, after any external force which has altered that figure is removed; rebounding; springy; as, a rubber band is *elastic*; gas is *elastic.*

2. Possessing the power or quality of recovering from depression or exhaustion; capable of resisting depression or exhaustion; capable of sustaining shocks without permanent injury; as, *elastic* spirits.

Elastic cartilage; cartilage in which the matrix is blended with elastic fibers.

Elastic curve; the curve made by a thin elastic rod fixed horizontally at one of its extremities, and weighted at the other.

Elastic fluids; fluids which have the property of expanding in all directions on the removal of external pressure, as gases and vapors.

Elastic limit; in mechanics, the greatest amount of deformation that a body can stand and still resume its original shape when the strain is removed.

Elastic mineral pitch; a brown, massive, elastic variety of bitumen.

Elastic tissue; in anatomy, a variety of connective tissue composed of yellow elastic fibers.

Gum elastic; caoutchouc or india-rubber.

ē-las'tiç, *n.* A woven fabric made partly of india-rubber, and used as a band, garter, suspender, etc.

ē-las'tiç-ăl, *a.* Elastic. [Obs.]

ē-las'tiç-ăl-ly, *adv.* In an elastic manner; by an elastic power; with a spring.

ē-las-tic'i-ty, *n.* 1. The inherent property in bodies by which they recover their former figure or state after the force of external pressure, tension, or distortion has been removed; springiness; as, the *elasticity* of gases.

2. Power to resist or overcome depression or mental strain.

Coefficient of elasticity; the result obtained by dividing a given force or stress exerted upon a body by the resulting strain.

ē-las'tiç-ness, *n.* Elasticity. [Rare.]

ē-las'tin, *n.* In chemistry, a body closely resembling albumen, except that it is free from sulphur, forming the principal substance of the elastic fiber which is the characteristic constituent of certain tissues.

ē-lāte', *a.* [L. *elatus*, pp. of *efferre*, to bring out, to lift up; *ex*, out, and *ferre*, to bear, to bring.]

1. Raised; lifted up. [Rare.]

2. Elated; exalted in spirit or feeling; exultant.

Elate with empty hopes. —Bacon.

Syn.—Exalted, proud, delighted, exultant, jubilant, puffed up, overjoyed.

ē-lāte', *v.t.*; elated, *pt., pp.*; elating, *ppr.* 1. To raise or swell, as the mind or spirits; to elevate with success; to puff up; to make proud.

2. To raise; to exalt. [Rare.]

ē-lāt'ed-ly, *adv.* With elation.

ē-lāt'ed-ness, *n.* The state of being elated.

ē-lāte'ment, *n.* Elation.

ē-lāt'ẽr, ē-lāt'ŏr, *n.* One who or that which elates.

el'à-tẽr, *n.* [Gr. *elatēr*, a driver, hurler, from *elaunein*, to drive, set in motion.]

1. In botany, (a) one of four elastic filaments attached about the middle of one side of the spores in *Equisetaceæ*. They are curled once or twice round the spore, uncoiling elastically when the spore is discharged; (b) an elastic spiral filament which aids in the dispersion of the spores, as in liverworts.

2. In entomology, (a) [E—] a genus of beetles comprising over 100 species, typical of the family *Elateridæ*, the click-beetles; (b) a beetle of the family *Elateridæ*; (c) an elastic bristle at the end of the abdomen of a podurid, by which it leaps.

ē-lat'ẽr-in, ē-lat'ẽr-ine, *n.* [L. *elaterium*, and *-ine.*] The active principle of elaterium. It is a very powerful cathartic.

ē-lat'ẽr-īte, *n.* [Gr. *elatēr*, a driver, and *-ite.*] An elastic mineral resin, of a blackish-brown color, subtranslucent, and occurring in soft flexible masses; called also *elastic bitumen* and *mineral caoutchouc*.

el-ȧ-tē′ri-um, *n.* [L., from Gr. *elatērion*, neut. of *elatērios*, driving away.] A cathartic substance obtained from the fruit of the *Ecballium Elaterium*, or squirting cucumber, which, if gathered a little before it ripens, and the juice gently expressed, deposits a green sediment which is collected and dried.

el″ȧ-tẽr-om′e-tẽr, *n.* [Gr. *elatēr*, a driver, and *metron*, a measure.] An instrument for determining the pressure of a gas; an elatrometer.

el′ȧ-ter-y, *n.* [Gr. *elatērios*, from *elaunein*, to drive, put in motion.] Acting force or elasticity; as, the *elatery* of the air. [Obs.]

Ē-lat-i-nā′cē-æ, *n.pl.* [L. *elatine*; Gr. *elatinē*, a species of toadflax, f. of *elatinos*, from *elatē*, the silver fir.] An order of small polypetalous herbs, the waterwort family, containing only two genera and about twenty species.

ē-lat-i-nā′ceous, *a.* Pertaining to the *Elatinaceæ.*

ē-lā′tion, *n.* [L. *elatio*, from *elatus*, pp. of *efferre*, to carry out, lift up; *ex*, out, and *ferre*, to bear.] Exaltation; an exultant state of mind; pride of prosperity.

Syn.—Enthusiasm, rapture, delight, exultation, transport.

ē-lā′tive, *a.* In grammar, lifted up or raised to the highest degree; absolutely superlative.

el-ȧ-trom′e-tẽr, *n.* [Gr. *elatēr*, a driver, and *metron*, a measure.] An instrument used in determining the degree of rarefaction of the air in the receiver of an air-pump.

ē-lā′yle, *n.* [Gr. *elaion*, olive-oil, oil, and *hylē*, matter.] Same as *Ethylene.*

el′bōw, *n.* [ME. *elbowe*; AS. *elboga*, *elnboga*; *eln*, ell, the forearm, and *boga*, a bow.]

1. The angle made by the bend of the arm at the junction of the upper arm and forearm; the joint which unites the upper arm with the forearm.

2. Any bend resembling the bend of the human *elbow*; specifically, a flexure or angle, especially if not acute, as of a wall, building, or road; a sudden turn or bend, as in a river or the seacoast; a jointed piece of pipe bent or turning at an angle; the raised arm of a chair or sofa.

3. In architecture, one of the upright sides which flank any paneled work.

At one's elbow; near at hand.

Elbow in the hawse; in seamen's language, the twisting of two cables holding a vessel at anchor, caused by her swinging twice the wrong way.

Out at elbows; having holes in the elbows of one's coat; hence, reduced in circumstances; badly off.

To crook the elbow; to drink; to become intoxicated. [Slang.]

Up to the elbows; wholly engaged; very busy.

el′bōw, *v.t.*; elbowed, *pt.*, *pp.*; elbowing, *ppr.* To push with the elbow; as, he *elbowed* his way through; to *elbow* people aside.

el′bōw, *v.i.* 1. To jut into an angle; to project; to bend.

2. To use the elbows so as to jostle; to push one's way; to be rudely self-assertive.

el′bōw-bōard, *n.* The inner sill of a window.

el′bōw-chāir, *n.* A chair with arms to support the elbows; an armchair.

el′bōw=grēase, *n.* A colloquial expression for energetic and continuous hand-labor, as rubbing, scouring, etc.

el′bōw-rōom, *n.* Room to extend the elbows on each side; hence, freedom from confinement; room for motion or action.

el′bōw=scis″sọrs, *n.pl.* Scissors having a bend in the blade or shank.

el-cā′jȧ, *n.* [Ar.] A tree of Arabia, *Trichilia emetica*, the fruit of which is used in the preparation of an itch-ointment.

El-cē′sȧ-īte, *n.* One of a sect of Gnostics which arose among the early Asiatic Christians in the reign of the emperor Trajan. The name is derived from Elcesai, the leader of the sect.

el′chi, el′chee, *n.* [Turk. and Per.] An ambassador or envoy.

eld, *a.* Old. [Obs.]

eld, *n.* [ME. *eld*, *ylde*; AS. *yldu*, *æld*, from *eald*, old.]

1. Old age; decrepitude. [Obs.]

2. Old times; former age. [Obs.]

eld, *v.i.* To become aged. [Obs.]

eld, *v.t.* To make old. [Obs.]

eld′ẽr, *a.* [ME. *elder*, *eldre*; AS. *eldra*, *yldra*, comp. of *eald*, old.]

1. Older; senior; having lived a longer time; born, produced, or formed before something else; as, the *elder* brother.

2. Pertaining to earlier times; earlier; as, in the *elder* days of art.

3. Prior in origin; preceding in the date of a commission; as, an *elder* officer or magistrate; in this sense, we generally use *senior*.

Elder hand; in card-playing, the hand that has by right the priority in leading.

eld′ẽr, *n.* [AS. *ealdor*, an elder, parent, ancestor, chief, from *eald*, old.]

1. One who is older than another or others.

2. An ancestor.

> Carry your head as your *elders* have done before you. —L'Estrange.

3. A person advanced in life and who, on account of his age, experience, and wisdom, is selected for office; as, among the Jews, the seventy men associated with Moses in the government of the people were *elders*; Peter and John called themselves *elders*.

In the earlier churches of New England, the ministers were called *elders* or *teaching elders*, the latter name still being technically applied to clergymen of the Presbyterian church, while laymen charged with executive affairs of that church are known as *ruling elders*. In the Baptist and Methodist denominations, missionaries and itinerant preachers, rather than the settled pastors, are spoken of as *elders*. A Methodist *presiding elder* is an ordained clergyman appointed by the bishop and has supervisory powers over a prescribed district.

el′dẽr, *n.* [ME. *elder*, *eldre*, *ellern*, *eller*; AS. *ellen*, elder.] In botany, the popular name of any shrub or tree of the genus *Sambucus*, bearing large corymbs of white flowers and red or black berries. The common North American elder-bush or elder-tree is *Sambucus Canadensis.*

el′dẽr-ber″ry, *n.* The fruit of the elder, having a sweetish acid taste.

eld′ẽr-ish, *a.* Somewhat old. [Rare.]

eld′ẽr-ly, *a.* Somewhat old; advanced beyond middle age; bordering on old age; as, *elderly* people.

eld′ẽr-ship, *n.* 1. The state of being older; seniority.

2. The office of an elder.

3. A body of elders; a presbytery.

el′dẽr-wŏrt, *n.* A European dwarf elder; called also *danewort.*

eld′est, *a.* [ME. *eldest*, *ealdeste*; AS. *yldesta*, superl. of *eald*, old.] Oldest; most advanced in age; that was born before others; as, the *eldest* son or daughter.

Eldest hand; the first player in cards, or the one to the left of the dealer.

el′ding, *n.* [Ice. *elding*, from *eldr*, fire.] Rubbish; also, fuel. [Prov. Eng.]

El Do-rā′do. [Sp., the golden region.]

1. A fabulous region in the interior of South America, supposed to surpass all others in the richness of its productions, especially gold, gems, etc.

2. Figuratively, any region or source of great abundance.

el′dritch, *a.* [Scot.] Hideous; ghastly; wild; demoniacal; as, an *eldritch* shriek; an *eldritch* laugh.

Ē-lē-at′iç, *a.* and *n.* I. *a.* Pertaining to a certain sect of philosophers, so called from Elea, a town on the western coast of lower Italy.

II. *n.* An Eleatic philosopher.

el-ē-cam-pāne′, *n.* [LL. *inula campana*; L. *inula*; Gr. *helenion*, elecampane; LL. *campana*, from L. *campus*, field.]

1. The popular name of *Inula Helenium*, a plant of a pungent taste, formerly of much repute as a stomachic.

2. A coarse candy, professedly made from the root of the plant.

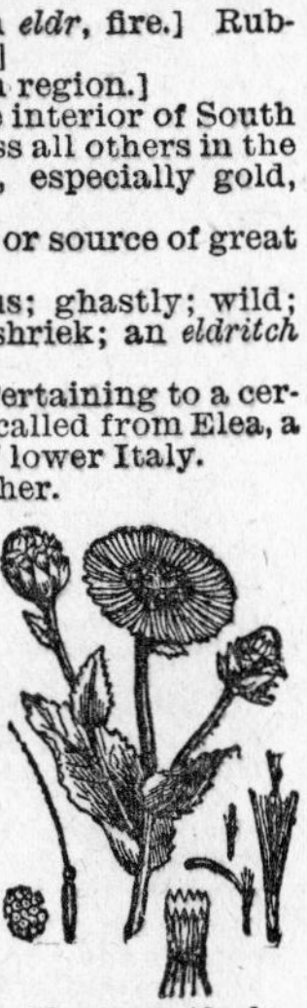

Elecampane (*Inula Helenium*).

ē-leçt′, *v.t.*; elected, *pt.*, *pp.*; electing, *ppr.* [L. *electus*, pp. of *eligere*, to pick out, choose; *e-*, out, and *legere*, to pick, choose, select.]

1. Generally, to pick out; to select from two or more; to determine in favor of.

2. To select or take for an office or employment from among a number; to select or show preference for by vote or designation; as, to *elect* a representative by ballot or viva voce.

3. In theology, to designate, choose, or select as an object of mercy or favor.

Syn.—Choose, select, prefer, adopt, follow.

ē-leçt′, *a.* 1. Chosen; taken by preference from two or more.

2. In theology, chosen as the object of mercy and salvation; predestinated in the divine counsels.

3. Chosen, but not yet inaugurated or invested with office; as, governor or mayor *elect.*

ē-leçt′, *n.* 1. One chosen or set apart.

2. In theology, one chosen or designated by God for salvation; collectively, the saved.

3. Collectively, those chosen or set apart as a peculiar church and people; especially applied to the Israelites.

ē-leçt′ănt, *n.* One having the power of choosing. [Rare.]

ē-leç′tȧ-ry, *n.* [Obs.] Same as *Electuary.*

ē-leç′ti-çişm, *n.* [Rare.] Same as *Eclecticism.*

ē-leç′tion, *n.* [L. *electio*, from *eligere*, to choose, select.]

1. The act of choosing; choice; the act of selecting one or more from others; especially, the act of choosing a person to fill an office or position by any manifestation of preference; hence, a vote upon any public question or matter.

2. Choice; power to choose; free will; liberty to act or not; discrimination; as, it leaves him no *election* in the matter.

3. In theology, divine choice; predetermination of God, by which persons are distinguished as objects of mercy, become subjects of grace, are sanctified, and prepared for heaven.

4. The elect. [Rare.]

5. In law, the choice between two rights or claims mutually inconsistent or alternative.

6. In mathematics, the choice from a group or set of any number that may be taken.

ē-leç-tion-eer′, *v.i.*; electioneered, *pt.*, *pp.*; electioneering, *ppr.* To make interest for a candidate at an election; to use arts for securing the election of a candidate.

ē-leç-tion-eer′ẽr, *n.* One who electioneers.

ē-leçt′ive, *a.* 1. Dependent on choice; bestowed or passing by election; as, an office is *elective.*

2. Pertaining to or consisting in choice or right of choosing; as, *elective* franchise.

3. Exerting the power of choice; as, an *elective* act.

4. Optional; as, an *elective* study in a university.

ē-leçt′ive-ly, *adv.* By choice; with preference.

ē-leçt′ọr, *n.* [L. *elector*, a chooser, from *eligere*, to choose, select.]

1. One who elects, or one who has the right of choice; a person who has, by law or constitution, the right of voting for an officer.

2. Specifically, (a) one of the persons chosen to form the electoral college of the United States, which chooses the President and Vice-President, termed officially a *presidential elector*; (b) in the Holy Roman empire, or Roman-German empire, one of the spiritual or one of the temporal *electors* who, from the twelfth century to the dissolution of the empire in 1806, exercised the right of selecting the emperor.

ē-leçt′ọr-ăl, *a.* Pertaining to choice by election or by electors.

Electoral college; the body of presidential electors of the United States.

ē-leçt-ọr-al′i-ty, *n.* An electorate. [Obs.]

ē-leçt′ọr-āte, *n.* 1. The dignity of an elector in the German empire; also, the territory of such elector.

2. The body of electors or voters in any country.

ē-leçt′ọr-ess, ē-leçt′ress, *n.* The wife or widow of an elector of the Roman-German empire.

ē-leç-tō′ri-ăl, *a.* Electoral. [Rare.]

ē-leçt′ọr-ship, *n.* The office or functions of an elector.

Ē-leç′trȧ, *n.* [L., from Gr. *Elektra*, a feminine proper name.]

1. A bright star in the Pleiades.

2. One of the seven daughters of Atlas and Pleione.

ē-leç′tre, ē-leç′tẽr, *n.* Electrum. [Obs.]

ē-leç-trep′e-tẽr, *n.* [Gr. *ēlektron*, amber, and *trepein*, to turn.] A commutator. [Obs.]

ē-leçt′ress, *n.* See *Electoress.*

ē-leç′triç, *n.* A nonconductor of electricity, in which, therefore, it can be accumulated, as amber, shellac, the resins. [Archaic or Obs.]

ē-leç′triç, ē-leç′triç-ăl, *a.* [L. *electrum*; Gr. *ēlektron*, amber.]

1. Relating or pertaining to electricity; as, an *electrical* convention.

2. Produced by, operated by, or derived from electricity; as, an *electric* shock; an *electric* bell; *electric* power.

3. Conveying, generating, or holding electricity; as, an *electric* wire; an *electric* battery; an *electric* eel.

4. Figuratively, thrilling; bracing; inspiring; electrifying, as, an *electric* orator.

Electric action; a scheme of connections for playing an organ by electrically operating the stops and pedals so that the performer can be at a distance from the organ, using a false keyboard.

Electric adhesion; adhesion caused by the attraction of electrostatic charges of opposite kind.

Electric alarm; an alarm operated or controlled by the making or breaking or the change of resistance of an electric circuit, such as a burglar-alarm, a thermostat, or a fire-alarm.

Electric annunciator; an indicator or one or more drops operated by the making or breaking of an electric current, showing from what location, room, or station a signal has been sent. Usually, an electric bell is sounded at the same time that the annunciator is operated, to call attention to the signal.

Electric apparatus; the instruments, machinery, and appliances used in electrical measurements, in producing and utilizing electric charges and currents, and in the study of electrical phenomena.

Electric atmosphere; see *Electric aura* under *Aura*.

Electric balloon; an electrically driven airship.

Electric battery; see *Cell*, n. 7.

Electric breeze; an air-current caused by a connective discharge of static electricity from a point; also, a discharge from brush terminals used in therapeutics.

Electric brush; a conductor made of a bundle of wires, or finely woven wire mesh or metal plate used for making contact between a fixed circuit and the rotating part of a dynamo-electric machine; e.g., for taking the current off a commutator on a dynamo, or for admitting the current to the commutator of a motor.

Electric burner; a gas-burner fitted with an apparatus for igniting the gas by an electric spark.

Electric candle; see under *Candle*.

Electric cat or *catfish*; a fish found in African waters, capable of giving severe electric shocks to assailants.

Electric cell; see *Cell*, n. 7.

Electric chimes; a chime rung by bells struck by balls oscillating under the influence of electric attraction and repulsion.

Electric clock; see under *Clock*.

Electric column; a voltaic pile.

Electric current; (a) a streaming or flow of electricity along a conductor, usually in a closed circuit and in one direction or in periodically reversed directions. The current manifests itself by producing heat, chemical reactions, light, mechanical forces, and magnetic attraction or repulsion. (b) The rate of flow of the current, commonly called the amount of current. It is equal, for direct currents, to the difference of potential in volts divided by the resistance in ohms, and is measured in amperes, one ampere being equal to one coulomb per second. For alternating currents, the effects of induction must be taken into account.

Electric displacement; the movement of electricity through or in a dielectric subjected to electric stress.

Electric dogfish; a marine fish, the stargazer, occurring along the Atlantic coast of the United States, and said to have electrical properties.

Electric dyeing; a process of dyeing in which the chemical compounds used are decomposed by an electric current.

Electric eel; a South American fish of the genus *Gymnotus*, found in fresh water resembling an eel, and having an organ in its tail capable of giving severe electric shocks.

Electrical energy; the energy possessed by a system because of electric charges resident in, or of currents flowing in the system. The energy of a charged body equals one-half the charge times the potential of the body.

Electrical engineering; the science and art of practically applying electricity in the industries.

Electric expansion; the increase in volume of a body incident to its electrification.

Electric explorer; an apparatus making use of induced currents for locating metallic substances in an unmetallic medium, particularly the human body.

Electric fan; a ventilating or blowing fan, driven by an electric motor.

Electric field; any space in which there is an electric stress.

Electric fish; any fish capable of communicating an electric shock.

Electric fluid; a theoretical fluid, postulated to account for electric phenomena. It is now discredited among scientists.

Electric fog; a fog accompanied by an electric storm.

Electric force; the force of attraction or repulsion exerted by electrically charged bodies.

Electric heat; heat generated in a circuit by current electricity.

Electric indicator; any electrically controlled automatic indicator, as an electric carriage-call, an electric pressure gauge, etc.

Electric jar; a Leyden jar or condenser.

Electric lamp; an apparatus used for lighting in which matter is made luminous by electrical energy.

Electric light; light produced by electrical energy; specifically, the brilliant illuminating light produced by a current flowing through an especially adapted resistance, which is intensely heated, as in the *incandescent light*, in which the luminous resistance is a filament, usually of carbon, inclosed in a bulb of glass from which the air has been exhausted; or as in the *arc light*, in which the light is caused by heating a vapor to incandescence by means of the electric current. In the *arc light*, so called because the source of light is a bow or arc, the current passes between two carbon pencils, volatilizing the carbon and heating it and the air to incandescence.

Electric lock; an electrically controlled lock.

Electric log; a ship's log for which the number of revolutions of a propeller attached to the log is registered by a current flowing in conductors embedded in the tow-line.

Electric machine; a machine for generating electrical charges or currents, usually confined to machines for producing static or frictional electric charges, such as the Holtz and the Wimshurst machines. When the generation of a powerful continuous current of electricity is required, a dynamo, driven by steam or water power is used, thus converting mechanical energy into electrical energy by means of electromagnetic induction.

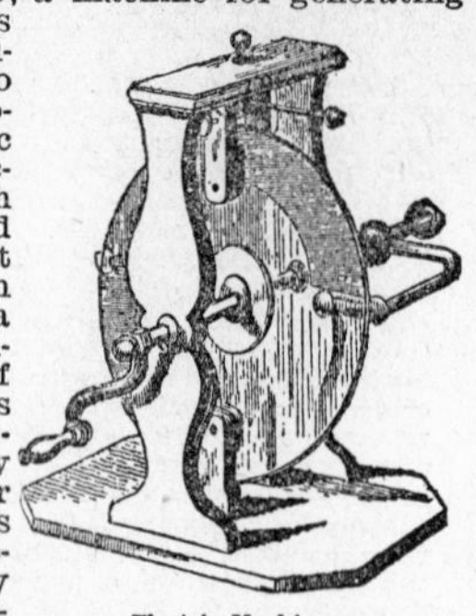
Electric Machine.

Electric main; the principal or trunk conductor or wire of an electric lighting or power circuit. The branches supplying the lamps or motors are led off the main.

Electric meter; an instrument for measuring the current flowing in, the electromotive force applied to, or the power used in a circuit, as an ammeter, a wattmeter.

Electric mortar; a mortar capable of expelling a light ball by the disturbance of the air particles within its bore produced by the disruptive discharge of two oppositely electrified bodies. It has no practical value except as an experimental or lecture apparatus, or as a toy.

Electric motor; a machine very similar to and often identical in construction with a dynamo, to which an electric current is led and by which the electrical energy of the current is converted into mechanical energy. Practically, it is a dynamo reversed in operation and turned by the magnetic effect of the current.

Electric organ; see *Electric action*.

Electric oscillations; alternating currents of very high frequencies. When the amplitude of a series of electric oscillations is constant, continuous or undamped waves result in radiotelegraphy. When the amplitude varies, or is of a decaying nature, damped waves result.

Electric osmose or *osmosis*; the transfer of a substance through a porous wall by an electric current, as the action on various electrodes placed in porous cups in electric batteries, in which the metal particles are transferred through the porous walls and deposited on the cathode.

Electric pen; a pen or pointed style, the point of which is rapidly reciprocated by a small solenoid or similar electric device and is thereby enabled to make fine perforations transferring to another sheet any writing or picture that is to be reproduced or manifolded.

Electric pendulum; a pith-ball suspended by a dry silk thread; used as an electroscope.

Electric pulse; a periodic variation in strength of a current, without any reversal of direction of flow; not an alternation or oscillation.

Electric radiation; the spreading forth of electric energy by wave motion.

Electric railway; a railway on which the rolling stock is moved by electric motors commonly supplied by a current taken off a circuit contiguous and parallel to the line, in which case the circuit is supplied by a dynamo.

Electric ray; a marine fish capable of giving an electric shock; also called *torpedo*.

Electric regulator; an electric engine or machinery governor; an apparatus for controlling the speed or the current generation in electric machines.

Electric sterilization; the destruction of germs by means of an electric current.

Electric strain; a strain due to an electric stress.

Electric stress; force due to the attractions or repulsions of electric charges. If a glass plate be coated on both sides with tin-foil and the two sides be oppositely charged, the glass will be deformed by the electric attraction or force.

Electric tension; the difference of potential; the electromotive force; the voltage; a term loose in its application.

Electric thermometer; a thermometer indicating changes in temperature by the variation of the resistance of a conductor produced by the changes of temperature; also, a thermopile used to indicate differences or variations of temperature.

Electric tower; an elevated structure on which arc lights are mounted.

Electric typewriter; a typewriter, the letters of which are operated by electromagnets.

Electric units; the magnitudes of electrical quantities adopted as standards or units for measurement or reference, as the coulomb, the unit of charge, etc. [See *Unit*.]

Electric varnish; an insulating varnish.

Electric wave; a periodic disturbance of the ether having the character of a wave motion, by means of which electrical energy is transmitted through space.

Electric welding; the process of welding metals, in which the welding heat is produced by an electric current passing through the junction of the pieces to be welded. The heat is localized at the welding points owing to the resistance produced by the gap in the circuit. By means of *electric welding* many metallic substances formerly classed as non-weldable may now be firmly united without seam or break of continuity.

ē-leç′triç-ăl-ly, *adv.* By means of some electrical action or device.

ē-leç′triç-ăl-ness, *n.* The state, condition, or quality of being electrical.

ē-leç-tri′ciăn (trish′ăn), *n.* 1. One versed in the science of electricity; an investigator of the laws governing electricity.

2. One who invents, manufactures, supplies, repairs, or operates electrical apparatus.

ē-leç-tric′i-ty, *n.* [Gr. *ēlektron*, amber. So named because of the production of electricity by friction of amber.]

1. A powerful physical agent which manifests itself mainly by attractions and repulsions, also by luminous and heating effects, by violent shocks, by chemical decomposition, and many other phenomena.

The first knowledge of electric attraction can be traced back to about 600 B. C. The science of electricity had its beginning with Gilbert in the year 1600 A. D. About a century ago, it was believed that electricity was an intangible fluid and that electrification of a body was due to an excess or a deficiency of this fluid. Now, the true nature of electricity is regarded as unknown, but all electrical actions are explained as a transaction in the ether which is postulated to account for the propagation of light, with, however, a partial return toward the fluid or materialistic theory of electricity. For example, when a condenser is charged it can be shown that the dielectric of the condenser is in a strained condition and that the coatings can be removed and handled with impunity. All electricity is classed in one of the two divisions, *static* electricity and *voltaic* electricity.

Static electricity, so called because the charge is at rest, is produced by friction, by pressure, by heating, and by electrostatic induction. This is the form in which electricity was first known.

Voltaic or current electricity involves the transfer of quantities of electricity along the conducting circuit. Currents are produced by chemical decompositions going on in a cell by the movement of a conductor in a magnetic field, by the heating of the junction of two dissimilar metals, and by the inductive action of a varying current in one conducting circuit on another circuit in the neighborhood of the first.

It is found that if a charged pith-ball is attracted by a rod of glass which has been stroked with silk, the pith-ball will be repelled by a rod of black rubber or resin which has been stroked with fur. Originally, this experiment was thought to prove that different kinds of electricity were produced in the glass and the resin by friction. Accordingly, the electricity which resided in the glass was called *vitreous* or *positive*, that in the resin *resinous* or *negative*. For convenience, these terms are retained to indicate the sign of the charge of a body raised to a positive or to a negative potential. [See *Potential*.]

Electric charges of like name repel each other, while those of opposite names attract each other. A positive charge induces a negative charge in a neighboring unelectrified object and therefore attracts that object. Similarly, a negative charge produces a positive induced charge.

2. That branch of physics which treats of the laws and phenomena of *electricity*.

3. In a figurative sense, vitalizing or electrifying energy; the characteristic of being inspiriting.

Animal electricity; see under *Animal*.

Atmospheric electricity; electricity present, induced, or generated in the terrestrial atmosphere or in the clouds. It plays a most important part in meteorological phenomena, probably in the aurora borealis and in hailstorms.

Bound electricity; electricity confined or circumscribed in its motion and action by the attraction of other charged bodies; in contradistinction to *free electricity*. [See *Free electricity*.]

Common electricity; a term sometimes applied

to *frictional* or *statical electricity*. [See *Electricity*, 1.]

Contact theory of electricity, a theory which ascribes the origin of the electromotive force of a galvanic couple, and of frictional electricity, to difference of potential produced by the contact of two dissimilar materials.

Diffusion of electricity; the convection or conduction of electricity, by which electric equilibrium is or tends to be reëstablished.

Distribution of electricity; (a) the quantity of electricity on unit area or in unit volume in various parts of an electrified system, which varies with the shape of the several portions of the system and the proximity of electric charges on other bodies; (b) also, the transmission of electrical energy to the various portions of the conducting circuits for purposes of commercial utilization.

Dynamical electricity; same as voltaic or current electricity. [See *Electricity*, 1.]

Electrostatic units of electricity; see *Unit*.

Excitation of electricity; the production of an electric condition by one of various methods, for example, by rubbing a rod of glass with silk.

Faradaic electricity or *currents*; electrical currents produced by the inductive action of other currents; so called after Faraday, the discoverer of current induction.

Free electricity; the charge on an insulated charged body which is so far removed from the presence of any other charge that it can be considered as existing alone. As every charge is accompanied by another charge of equal quantity and opposite name, none can be absolutely free.

Frictional electricity; statical electricity. [See *Electricity*, 1.]

Galvanic electricity; voltaic electricity. [See *Electricity*, 1.]

Latent electricity; same as *Bound electricity*.

Negative electricity; see *Electricity*, 1.

Organic electricity; electricity developed in living organisms, either animal or vegetable, by processes taking place within the organism and incident to its life.

Positive electricity; see *Electricity*, 1.

Resinous electricity; negative electricity. [See *Electricity*, 1.]

Vitreous electricity; positive electricity. [See *Electricity*, 1.]

ē-leç′triçs, *n.* Electricity as a branch of science.

ē-leç′tri-çūte, *v.t.* See *Electrocute*.

ē-leç-tri-çū′tion, *n.* See *Electrocution*.

ē-leç-trif′ẽr-ous, *a.* That may produce or transmit electricity.

ē-leç′tri-fī-à-ble, *a.* 1. Capable of receiving or being charged with electricity.

2. That may receive and transmit the electric fluid.

ē-leç″tri-fi-çā′tion, *n.* The act of charging with electricity or of making electric; the state of being electrified or of becoming electric. *Electrification* is + (positive) or — (negative) according to the name of the charge, or, more correctly, according to whether its potential is above or below that of the earth. [See *Potential*.]

ē-leç′tri-fȳ, *v.t.*; electrified, *pt.*, *pp.*; electrifying, *ppr.* [*Electric*, and L. *-ficare*, from *facere*, to make.]

1. To charge with electricity; to cause to become influenced by or filled with electricity; as, to *electrify* a storage cell.

2. To effect by the transmission of electricity; to shock by an electric current.

3. Figuratively, to excite suddenly and intensely; to arouse to intense activity; to startle or to surprise, especially by something very inspiriting or intensely interesting; to thrill; as, the despatch reporting the relief of Mafeking *electrified* all England.

ē-leç′trine, *a.* [LL. *electrinus*; Gr. *ēlektrinos*, made of amber or electrum, from *ēlektron*, amber.]

1. Pertaining to or made of amber.

2. Made of electrum. [See *Electrum*.]

ē-leç′trine, *n.* [*Electr*um and *-ine*.] A supposed substance capable of manifesting electric phenomena and held by some scientists to be the prime agent or basis of electricity.

ē-leç′trize, *v.t.*; electrized, *pt.*, *pp.*; electrizing, *ppr.* To electrify; also written *electrise*.

ē-leç′tri-zẽr, *n.* One who or that which electrizes.

ē-leç′trō, *v.t.*; electroed, *pt.*, *pp.*; electroing, *ppr.* [Abbrev. of *electro*type.] To electrotype.

ē-leç′trō, *n.* An electrotype.

ē-leç-trō-. A combining form from Greek *ēlektron*, amber, signifying relating to, operated by, or producing electricity; as, *electro*chronograph; *electro*magnet.

ē-leç″trō-bal-lis′tiç, *a.* Relating to or performed by electroballistics.

ē-leç″trō-bal-lis′tiçs, *n.* The science of measuring the velocity of a projectile between various points of its trajectory by making it cut wire screens placed at those points and forming part of an electric circuit. Cutting the screen breaks the circuit and the instant of break is recorded on a chronograph placed on the circuit, thus fixing the instant of passage through each screen.

ē-leç′trō-bȧth, *n.* The solution used in electroplating or electrotyping.

ē-leç″trō-bī-ō-log′iç-ăl, *a.* Of or pertaining to electrobiology.

ē-leç″trō-bī-ol′ō-ġist, *n.* A person skilled in electrobiology.

ē-leç″trō-bī-ol′ō-ġy, *n.* 1. The branch of biology which treats of electrical manifestations in living organisms, and of the effects of electricity upon them; specifically, the branch of science relating to electric currents generated in living organisms.

2. A branch of animal magnetism or mesmerism in which the persons or animals mesmerized are controlled or alleged to be controlled by the will of the mesmerist operating by some supposed electric connection or means of nerve-control.

ē-leç″trō-bī-os′çō-py, *n.* [*Electro-*, and Gr. *bios*, life, and *skopein*, to view.] Testing the muscles for contractions by passing an electric current through them; done, mainly, to determine whether life is or is not extinct.

ē-leç′trō-bronze, *n.* A coating of bronze given to articles of metal (usually iron) by electrodeposition.

ē-leç′trō-bronze, *v.t.* To make an electrobronze of.

ē-leç″trō-çap-il-lar′i-ty, *n.* That branch of physics which treats of the changes in capillarity which are produced by electric forces.

ē-leç-trō-çap′il-lā-ry, *a.* Of or relating to electrocapillarity.

ē-leç-trō-çau′tẽr-y, *n.* 1. The operation of cauterizing with a platinum wire electrically heated.

2. The wire so used.

ē-leç″trō-çhem′iç-ăl, *a.* Of or pertaining to electrochemistry.

Electrochemical series; a tabulation of the elements, such that each element is electropositive to all placed after it and electronegative to all preceding it.

ē-leç″trō-çhem′is-try, *n.* The science which treats of electricity in relation to chemical processes.

ē-leç″trō-çhron′ō-grȧph, *n.* [*Electro-*, and Gr. *chronos*, time, and *graphein*, to write.] An instrument for accurately recording the instant of any one or more occurrences and the elapsed time between such records. The time records are made by the making or breaking of a current or circuit, with a clock pendulum or other device, and a style making marks on a cylindrical surface revolving at a uniform and known rate.

ē-leç″trō-çhron″ō-grȧph′iç, *a.* Relating to an electrochronograph.

ē-leç-trō-çop′pẽr, *v.t.*; electrocoppered, *pt.*, *pp.*; electrocoppering, *ppr.* To coat with copper by electrodeposition.

ē-leç-trō-çul′tūre, *n.* [*Electro-*, and L. *cultura*, from *colere*, to cultivate.] In plant cultivation, the stimulation of plant growth by electricity, as by sending currents through the soil or by the influence of electric light.

ē-leç′trō-çūte, *v.t.*; electrocuted, *pt.*, *pp.*; electrocuting, *ppr.* [*Electro-* and *execute*.] To put to death or execute by means of an electrical shock or currents. A form more nearly correct, but infrequently used, is *electricute*.

ē-leç-trō-çū′tion, ē-leç-tri-çū′tion, *n.* The act of putting to death by means of an electric current.

ē-leç′trōde, *n.* [*Electro-*, and Gr. *hodos*, path, way.] The path by which electricity passes from or into a conducting medium, as a solution, etc.; specifically, the ends, usually in the form of plates, of the conductors or wires leading from the source of the current and terminating in the medium conveying the current. The positive *electrode* is called the anode, the negative *electrode*, the cathode.

ē-leç″trō-dē-pos′it, *v.t.* To deposit, as a metal, on a surface by means of an electric current; especially, to coat a metallic surface with a metal.

ē-leç″trō-dȳ-nam′iç, ē-leç″trō-dȳ-nam′iç-ăl, *a.* Relating or pertaining to electrodynamics.

ē-leç″trō-dȳ-nam′içs, *n.* [*Electro-*, and Gr. *dynamikos*, powerful, from *dynamis*, power.] The laws of electricity in a state of motion, or the action of electric currents upon each other and upon magnets.

ē-leç″trō-dȳ-nȧ-mom′e-tẽr, *n.* [*Electro-*, and Gr. *dynamis*, power, and *metron*, a measure.] An instrument for measuring electric currents, voltages, or power. It consists of two coils, one movable with respect to the other, with the same or different currents in the coils.

ē-leç″trō-en-grāv′ing, *n.* The process of engraving by means of electricity.

ē-leç″trō-etch′ing, *n.* A method of etching upon metals by electrolytic action.

ē-leç-trō-ġen′iç, *a.* In physiology, of or relating to electrogeny; as, an *electrogenic* state.

ē-leç-troġ′e-ny, ē-leç-trō-ġen′e-sis, *n.* [*Electro-*, and the root of Gr. *gignesthai*, to produce.]

1. In physiology, a tetanic state or condition produced in the muscles of the limbs by the passage of an electric current along the spinal cord or nerves.

2. Origination and growth produced by electricity.

ē-leç″trō-gild′ing, *n.* The process or art of gilding a metallic surface by means of a current.

ē-leç′trō-gilt, *a.* Gilded by means of a current.

ē-leç′trō-gram, *n.* A chart or diagram showing a continuous record of atmospheric electricity.

ē-leç′trō-grȧph, *n.* [*Electro-*, and Gr. *graphein*, to write.]

1. The automatic, continuous tracing of an electromotor used as a record.

2. A device for tracing a design of electro-etching for the printing of textiles, wall-paper, etc.

ē-leç-trog′rȧ-phy, *n.* 1. Galvanography.

2. The reproduction of an engraving by electrodeposition.

ē-leç″trō-kī-net′iç, *a.* Of or relating to electrokinetics.

ē-leç″trō-kī-net′içs, *n.* [*Electro-*, and Gr. *kinētikos*, from *kinein*, to move.] The branch of electric science treating of electricity in motion and the forces producing or controlling it.

ē-leç-trō-liēr′, *n.* [*Electro-* and chandel*ier*.] A fixture for supporting electric lamps.

ē-leç-trō-log′iç, ē-leç-trō-log′iç-ăl, *a.* Of or pertaining to electrology.

ē-leç-trol′ō-ġy, *n.* [*Electro-*, and Gr. *-logia*, from *legein*, to speak.] The branch of physics treating of electricity.

ē-leç″trō-lū″mi-nes′cence, *n.* Luminescence excited by electricity, as the glow of certain gases in a vacuum tube.

ē-leç-trol′y-sis, *n.* [*Electro-*, and Gr. *lysis*, a loosing, from *lyein*, to loose.] The process of chemical decomposition of various substances by the electric current. When an electric current passes through an aqueous solution of ordinary salt, the salt is broken up into its constituents, sodium and chlorin. This process is called *electrolysis* and the constituent parts are known as the ions.

ē-leç′trō-lȳte, *n.* [*Electro-*, and Gr. *lytos*, verbal noun of *lyein*, to loose, dissolve.] A chemical compound which can be decomposed by an electric current.

ē-leç-trō-lyt′iç, ē-leç-trō-lyt′iç-ăl, *a.* Relating or pertaining to electrolysis.

ē-leç-trō-lȳ′zȧ-ble, *a.* Capable of being decomposed by an electric current.

ē-leç-trō-ly-zā′tion, *n.* The act or process of electrolyzing.

ē-leç′trō-lȳze, *v.t.*; electrolyzed, *pt.*, *pp.*; electrolyzing, *ppr.* To decompose by the direct action of an electric current.

ē-leç-trō-mag′net, *n.* A core of magnetizable substance, such as soft iron or nickel, placed within a coil or helix of wire through which an electric current is passing. This magnetizes the core by induction, but the magnetic state thus induced persists during the passage of the current only, and disappears almost wholly with its cessation.

ē-leç″trō-mag-net′iç, *a.* Of, relating to, or produced by magnetism which is excited by an electric current, or by the action between magnets and an electric current.

Electromagnetic engine; an engine in which the motive power is electromagnetic in character, as an electric motor.

Electromagnetic force or *stress*; force between magnets and conductors carrying currents.

Electromagnetic theory of light; a theory which assumes that light consists of periodic electric and magnetic displacements or disturbances in the ether, in which the two kinds of displacements are at right angles to each other and to the direction of propagation of the light ray.

Electromagnetic unit; a unit in electric measurement based on the force with which a unit electric current acts on a magnetic pole of unit strength.

ē-leç-trō-mag′net-ism, ē-leç″trō-mag-net′-içs, *n.* That portion of physics which treats of the various actions and relations between currents and magnets.

ē-leç-trō-met′ăl-lũr-ġy, *n.* 1. The act or process of depositing a metal by electrochemical action on a prepared surface.

2. The separation of metals from their ores or alloys by electrolysis.

ē-leç-trom′e-tẽr, *n.* [*Electro-*, and Gr. *metron*, a measure.] An instrument for measuring differences of potential by the effects of electrostatic force. It consists of at least two conductors, one movable with respect to the other, which can be charged to the difference which is to be measured. From the motion of the movable conductor so produced, or the force necessary to prevent such motion, the difference of potential is inferred. The term is sometimes applied to instruments which merely indicate a difference of potential, properly called *electroscopes*.

Absolute electrometer; one in which the force of electrostatic attraction or repulsion can be compared directly with a weight or some other force which can be expressed in c. g. s. or absolute units.

Balanced or *attracted-disk electrometer*; a balance-electrometer.

Gold-leaf electrometer or *electroscope*; an instrument consisting of two strips of gold-leaf, suspended from the same conducting support. When a charge is brought near, charges of like sign are induced on the two parts, which, therefore, repel one another. The amount of the separation of the leaves so caused measures, roughly, the potential of the inducing charge.

Quadrant electrometer; an electrometer in which the one conductor, usually cylindrical in shape, is divided into four parts, or quadrants, opposite quadrants being connected. The movable portion or needle moves within the quadrants. When the two pairs of quadrants are charged to a difference of potential, and the needle to any fixed potential, the needle will be deflected by electrostatic force. The magnitude of the deflection measures the potential difference of the quadrants.

ē-leç-trō-met′riç, ē-leç-trō-met′riç-ăl, *a.* Of or relating to electrometry; made by an electrometer; as, an *electrometrical* indication.

ē-leç-trom′e-try, *n.* The science or process of measuring electrical quantities by means of an electrometer.

ē-leç-trō-mō′tion, *n.* 1. The passage of an electric current in a dynamic or voltaic circuit.

2. Motion produced by electric power.

ē-leç-trō-mō′tive, *a.* Producing electromotion; of or relating to the motion of electricity or the laws controlling it.

Back electromotive force or *pressure*; the electromotive force in a circuit, opposed in direction to the current. This is caused by the inductive effect of the current, or by the tendency of the products of electrolytic decomposition to reunite.

Electromotive force; the cause of the establishment and maintenance of a difference of potential, and, therefore, of a flow of current, between any two points.

Impressed electromotive force; the electromotive force due to some outside source, as a dynamo or battery, applied to a circuit or branch of the circuit.

ē-leç-trō-mō′tŏr, *n.* 1. Any source of electricity; an apparatus for generating an electric current, as a voltaic cell.

2. A machine or apparatus that transforms electrical into mechanical energy; the opposite of a dynamo-electric generator or dynamo.

ē-leç-trō-mus′çū-lăr, *a.* Relating to the action of electricity on the muscles.

ē-leç′tron, *n.* [Gr. *ēlektron*, amber.]

1. Electrum.

2. The lightest metal known, being a magnesium alloy, which can be cast, pressed, rolled and drawn. Silver white in color, and lends itself to a brilliant polish.

3. The charge of electricity borne by the atom; the atomic charge. Recent experiments seem to show that this charge, the *electron*, can be separated from the atom, and that it is the agent by which electrolysis and the electric discharge in a vacuum are carried on.

ē-leç-trō-neg′ȧ-tive, *a.* 1. In physics and chemistry, possessing the property of being attracted by an electropositive body, or tending to pass to the positive electrode in electrolysis, by the law that opposite electricities attract one another.

2. Acid; negative; nonmetallic; opposed to basic, positive, metallic.

ē-leç-trō-neg′ȧ-tive, *n.* An element which is electronegative.

ē-leç-trō-op′tiç, *a.* Of or pertaining to the interrelations existing between electricity and magnetism and light.

ē-leç-trō-op′tiçs, *n.* [*Electro-*, and Gr. *optikos*, of seeing, from the root *op*, to see.] That branch of physics which treats of the optical phenomena of the electrostatic and electromagnetic fields.

ē-leç-trop′ȧ-thy, *n.* [*Electro-*, and Gr. *pathos*, suffering.] The treatment of disease by electricity; electrotherapeutics.

ē-leç′trō-phōne, *n.* [*Electro-*, and Gr. *phōnē*, sound.] A device for producing sound by means of electric currents.

Ē-leç-trō-phor′i-dæ, *n.pl.* [*Electro-*, and Gr. *pherein*, to bear.] A family of fishes, the electric eels.

ē-leç-troph′ō-rous, *a.* Electriferous.

ē-leç-troph′ō-rus, *n.* [*Electro-*, and Gr. *pherein*, to bear.] An instrument for exciting electricity, small in quantity but of high potential, by induction. It consists of a flat, smooth cake of resin or sulphur in a conducting pan, acted upon by a circular plate of metal with a nonconducting handle. When the resin or sulphur is rubbed with fur it is electrified by friction. If the plate is now put on the resin it will be charged by induction. If the plate is touched and removed it is found to be charged.

Electrophorus.

ē-leç″trō-phys″i-ō-loġ′iç-ăl, *a.* Relating to electrophysiology.

ē-leç″trō-phys-i-ol′ō-ġy, *n.* That branch of biology which treats of electrical phenomena produced by or in living organisms.

ē-leç′trō-plāte, *v.t.*; electroplated, *pt.*, *pp.*; electroplating, *ppr.* To cover with a film or coating by electrolytically depositing a metal on surface to be protected or ornamented.

ē-leç′trō-plāte, *n.* That which has been electroplated.

ē-leç′trō-plā-tēr, *n.* One who electroplates.

ē-leç′trō-plā-ting, *n.* The process or art of plating electrolitically.

ē-leç-trō-poi′on, *n.* [*Electro-*, and Gr. *poiōn*, ppr. of *poiein*, to make.] An electrolyte for electric batteries, made of potassium bichromate, water, and sulphuric acid.

ē-leç-trō-pō′lăr, *a.* Having electric polarity; negatively electrified at one end, or on one surface, and positively at, or on, the other; applied to an electrical conductor.

ē-leç-trō-poş′i-tive, *a.* 1. Having the property of becoming positively electrified by contact or chemical action; tending to the negative pole of a voltaic battery in electrolysis, while the associated body tends to the positive pole; the opposite or correlative of *electronegative*.

2. In chemistry, basic; metallic; positive; opposed to *acid*, *nonmetallic*, and *negative*.

ē-leç-trō-poş′i-tive, *n.* An electropositive element.

ē-leç″trō-punç-tū-rā′tion, ē-leç-trō-punç′-tūre, *n.* The application of currents to the treatment of pathologic growths; galvanopuncture.

ē-leç′trō-sçōpe, *n.* [*Electro-*, and Gr. *skopein*, to view.] An instrument for detecting the presence or the sign of electricity on an object. [See *Electrometer*.]

Condensing electroscope; a kind of electroscope in which greater sensitiveness is obtained by the aid of a condenser.

Gold-leaf Electroscope.

ē-leç-trō-sçop′iç, *a.* Relating to or shown by an electroscope.

ē-leç-trō-stat′iç, *a.* Pertaining to electrostatics; relating to electricity in a state of rest.

Electrostatic measure; measure of static electricity based on the attraction or repulsion of electrically charged objects.

Electrostatic stress; the force exerted near any electrically charged body, on other charges which are in the vicinity of the first.

ē-leç-trō-stat′içs, *n.* [*Electro-*, and Gr. *statikos*, causing to stand, from *histanai*, to stand.] The branch of electrical science which treats of the properties and effects of static or frictional electricity, as distinguished from electricity in motion or current electricity.

ē-leç-trō-stē′rē-ō-tȳpe, *n.* See *Electrotype*.

ē-leç-trō-tech′niç-ăl, *a.* Of or pertaining to electrotechnics.

ē-leç-trō-tech′niçs, *n.* The science which treats of the practical application of electricity in the industrial arts.

ē-leç-trō-tel-ē-graph′iç, *a.* Pertaining to electrotelegraphy; sent by means of electrotelegraphy.

ē-leç″trō-tē-leg′ra-phy, *n.* The science or art of constructing or using the electric telegraph; the sending of messages by means of the electric telegraph.

ē-leç″trō-ther-ȧ-peū′tiçs, *n.* In medicine, the application of electricity in disease; electropathy.

ē-leç-trō-thẽr′măn-cy, *n.* [*Electro-*, and Gr. *thermē*, heat.] That branch of electrical science treating of the effects of electric currents upon the temperature of a conductor or a part of a circuit consisting of two different metals.

ē-leç′trō-tint, *n.* An electro-engraved plate in relief, especially one used for printing in colors.

ē-leç-trō-ton′iç, *a.* 1. In physics, of or pertaining to electric potential.

2. In physiology, of or pertaining to electrotonus.

ē-leç-trot′ō-nīze, *v.t.*; electrotonized, *pt.*, *pp.*; electrotonizing, *ppr.* To produce electrotonus in.

ē-leç-trot′ō-nus, ē-leç″trō-tō-nic′i-ty, *n.* [*Electro-*, and Gr. *tonos*, tension.] In physiology, a modified state of a nerve produced during the passage of an electric current through it.

ē-leç-trot′rō-pişm, *n.* [*Electro-*, and Gr. *tropos*, from *trepein*, to turn.] In biology, the effect produced by electricity on the growth of organisms, particularly that of vegetable organisms.

ē-leç′trō-tȳpe, *n.* [*Electro-*, and Gr. *typos*, figure, image.]

1. A metal facsimile of any surface, as of a die or an engraved plate, made by electric deposition, and used for printing.

2. An impression taken from an electrotype plate.

Electrotype shell; in the process of electrotyping, the thin copper deposit or coating made upon the wax impression of the object to be reproduced.

ē-leç′trō-tȳpe, *v.t.*; electrotyped, *pt.*, *pp.*; electrotyping, *ppr.* To produce an electrotype of; to duplicate by means of an electrotype; as, to *electrotype* a form.

ē-leç′trō-tȳ-pēr, *n.* One who electrotypes.

ē-leç-trō-typ′iç, *a.* Relating to or produced by electrotyping.

ē-leç′trō-tȳ-ping, ē-leç′trō-tȳ-py, *n.* The process or art of producing electrotype plates, or impressions from them. A matrix is made by pouring melted wax into a shallow molding case and impressing the wax plate or cake thus formed with the surface to be duplicated, using a press. The matrix is coated with black lead, then suspended in a bath of copper sulphate acting as an electroplating cell in which a copper plate forms the anode, while the plumbago of the matrix forms the cathode. When the electrodes are connected to the terminals of a source of current, either a battery or dynamo, the copper is deposited on the cathode, forming a thin shell covering the wax impression and preserving all of its outlines. This shell is freed from the wax by melting, is backed with type metal, shaved or trimmed to size and height, and is then ready for the press.

ē-leç-trō-veç′tion, *n.* [*Electro-*, and L. *vectio* (*-onis*), a carrying, from *vehere*, to carry.] The passage of an electrolyzed liquid through a membrane; electrical endosmosis.

ē-leç-trō-vī′tăl, *a.* That is vital and supposed to be of electrical origin or nature.

ē-leç-trō-vī′tăl-işm, *n.* The theory that the functions of living organisms depend upon electricity or kindred phenomena.

ē-leç′trum, *n.* [L., from Gr. *ēlektron*, amber, also, an alloy of gold and silver.]

1. Amber.

2. An amber-colored alloy of gold and silver, used by the ancient Greeks for coins.

ē-leç′tū-ā-ry, *n.*; *pl.* **ē-leç′tū-ā-rieş.** [LL. *electuarium*, *electarium*, from Gr. *ekleikton*, an electuary, from *ekleichein*, to lick up; *ek*, out, and *leichein*, to lick.] A medicine composed of powders or other ingredients, incorporated with some conserve, honey, or syrup.

el-ee-mos′y-nā-ri-ly, *adv.* In an eleemosynary manner.

el-ee-mos′y-nā-ry, *a.* [LL. *eleēmosynarius*, pertaining to alms, one who receives or gives alms, from *eleēmosyna*; Gr. *eleēmosynē*, alms.]

1. Given in charity; given or appropriated to support the poor.

2. Relating to charitable donations; intended for the distribution of alms, or for the use and management of donations.

el-ee-mos′y-nā-ry, *n.*; *pl.* **el-ee-mos′y-nā-rieş.** One who lives on alms.

el′ē-gănce, *n.* 1. The state or quality of being elegant; beauty resulting from perfect propriety or from the absence of anything calculated to produce a disagreeable sensation; refinement; said of manners, language, style, form, architecture, and the like; as, *elegance* of dress.

2. That which pleases by its nicety, symmetry, purity, or beauty.

el′ē-găn-cy, *n.*; *pl.* **el′ē-găn-cieş.** 1. Elegance. [Rare.]

2. That which has or imparts elegance.

el′ē-gănt, *a.* [L. *elegans* (*-antis*), luxurious, choice, fine, from *eligere*, to choose, select.]

1. Polished; polite; refined; graceful; pleasing to good taste; as, *elegant* manners.

2. Polished; pure; rich in expressions; correct in arrangement; as, an *elegant* style or composition.

3. Symmetrical; regular; well-formed in parts, proportions, and distribution; as, an *elegant* structure.

4. Rich; costly and ornamental; as, *elegant* furniture or equipage.

5. Nice; sensible to beauty; discriminating beauty from deformity or imperfection; as, an *elegant* taste.

el′ē-gănt-ly, *adv.* In a manner to please; with elegance; with beauty; with pleasing propriety; as, a composition *elegantly* written.

ē-lē′ġi-ac, *a.* [LL. *elegiacus*; Gr. *elegeiakos*, from *elegeia*, *elegeion*, an elegy.]

1. Belonging to elegy; plaintive; expressing sorrow or lamentation; as, an *elegiac* lay; *elegiac* strains.

2. Used in elegies; as, pentameter verse is *elegiac*.

ē-lē′ġi-ac, *n.* Elegiac verse, consisting of alternate dactylic hexameter and pentameter.

el-ē-ġī'ȧ-ċăl, *a.* Elegiac.

el"ē-ġi-am'bus, *n.*; *pl.* **el"ē-ġi-am'bī.** [Gr. *elegeion*, an elegy, and *iambos*, iambus.] A compound form of versification consisting of seven syllables (two dactyls and one long syllable) and an iambic dimeter.

el"ē-ġi-og'rȧ-phẽr, *n.* [Gr. *elegeiographos*; *elegeion*, an elegy, and *graphein*, to write.] A writer of elegiac verse. [Obs.]

el'ē-ġist, *n.* A writer of elegies.

ē-lē'ġit, *n.* [L., he has chosen; 3rd pers. sing. perf. indic. of *eligere*, to choose, select.]

1. A writ of execution, by which a defendant's goods are appraised and delivered to the plaintiff, and, if not sufficient to satisfy the debt, all his lands are delivered, to be held till the debt is paid by the rents and profits.

2. The title to estate by *elegit*.

el'ē-ġīze, *v.t.*; elegized, *pt.*, *pp.*; elegizing, *ppr.* To bewail, as the loss of a friend, in verse; to write an elegy to.

el'ē-ġy, *n.* [L. *elegia*; Gr. *elegeia*, *elegeion*, from *elegos*, a lament, song of mourning.] A mournful or plaintive poem; a funeral song; a poem; a song or musical composition expressive of sorrow and lamentation.

ē-lē'i-din, *n.* [Gr. *elaia*, olive-oil, oil.]

1. A deposit of pellucid matter in minute granular form, found in the protoplasm of living cells. [See *Hyaline*.]

2. A substance found in various parts of the epidermis, that is intermediate between the tissue-building principle or protoplasm, and ceratin, the builder of such epidermic tissues as hair, horn, and nails.

el'ē-me, *a.* [Turk.] Gathered by hand; hence, of the best quality; said of fruit; as, *eleme* figs.

el'ē-ment, *n.* [L. *elementum*, a first principle, element.]

1. One of the simplest constituent principles, or parts, of which anything consists, or upon which its constitution is based; a fundamental or ultimate part or principle, by the combination or aggregation of which anything is composed; an ingredient; as, the *elements* of earth, water, of animal and vegetable bodies, of a complex mental operation, of sound, etc.; quartz, mica, and feldspar are the *elements* of granite; cells are the *elements* of living bodies.

> Certain minute constituents which, for the present, are the ultimate structural *elements* of the body. —Huxley.

2. In chemistry, one of the eighty-three simple substances which hitherto have resisted resolution by chemical analysis; one of the ultimate, hitherto indecomposable, constituents of any kind of matter.

Elements.	Symbols.	Atomic Weights.
Actinium	Ac	*
Aluminium	Al	26.9
Antimony	Sb	119.3
Argon	A	39.6
Arsenic	As	74.4
Barium	Ba	136.4
Bismuth	Bi	206.9
Boron	B	10.9
Bromine	Br	79.36
Cadmium	Cd	111.6
Cæsium	Cs	132.0
Calcium	Ca	39.8
Carbon	C	11.91
Cerium	Ce	139.0
Chlorin	Cl	35.18
Chromium	Cr	51.7
Cobalt	Co	58.56
Columbium	Cb	93.3
Copper	Cu	63.1
Dysprosium	Dy	*
Erbium	Er	164.8
Europium	Eu	*
Fluorin	F	18.9
Gadolinium	Gd	155.0
Gallium	Ga	69.5
Germanium	Ge	71.9
Glucinum	Gl	9.03
Gold	Au	195.7
Helium	He	4.
Holmium	Ho	*
Hydrogen	H	1.0
Indium	In	113.1
Iodine	I	125.90
Iridium	Ir	191.5
Iron	Fe	55.5
Krypton	Kr	81.2
Lanthanum	La	137.9
Lead	Pb	205.35
Lithium	Li	6.98
Magnesium	Mg	24.18
Manganese	Mn	54.6
Mercury	Hg	198.5
Molybdenum	Mo	95.3
Neodymium	Nd	142.5

Elements—*continued.*

Elements.	Symbols.	Atomic Weights.
Neon	Ne	19.9
Nickel	Ni	58.3
Nitrogen	N	13.93
Osmium	Os	189.6
Oxygen	O	15.88
Palladium	Pd	105.7
Phosphorus	P	30.77
Platinum	Pt	193.3
Polonium	Po	*
Potassium	K	38.86
Praseodymium	Pr	139 4
Radium	Ra	223.3
Rhodium	Rh	102.2
Rubidium	Rb	84.8
Ruthenium	Ru	100.9
Samarium	Sm	148.9
Scandium	Sc	43.8
Selenium	Se	78.6
Silicon	Si	28.2
Silver	Ag	107.12
Sodium	Na	22.88
Strontium	Sr	86.94
Sulphur	S	31.83
Tantalum	Ta	181.6
Tellurium	Te	126.6
Terbium	Tb	158.8
Thallium	Tl	202.6
Thorium	Th	230.8
Thulium	Tm	169.7
Tin	Sn	118.1
Titanium	Ti	47.7
Tungsten	W	182.6
Uranium	U	236.7
Vanadium	V	50.8
Xenon	Xe	127.0
Ytterbium	Yb	171.7
Yttrium	Yt	88.3
Zinc	Zn	64.9
Zirconium	Zr	89.9

*Uncertain; of recent discovery.

There are a number of other supposed elements not sufficiently known to warrant classification, as supposedly new elements are often decomposed into those already known. Radium and polonium are recent discoveries classed among the more important elements, while the existence of krypton, neon, xenon, helium, and a few others discovered in the last decade is of relatively slight importance.

3. [*pl.*] The first or simplest rules or principles of an art or science; rudiments; as, the *elements* of geometry, grammar, etc.

4. In the scholastic philosophy, one of the four constituents of the material world—fire, air, earth, water—which were supposed to be ultimate indecomposable principles. This sense survives in popular usage; whence we say that water is the *element* of fishes, the air of birds, etc.

5. The state or sphere natural to anything or suited to its existence; as, faction is the *element* of a demagogue.

> Our torments also may, in length of time,
> Become our *elements.* —Milton.

6. The air; the sky. [Obs.]

7. A datum or value necessary to be taken into consideration in making a calculation or coming to a conclusion; as, health, character, and qualifications are *elements* necessary to be considered in judging of a person's fitness for a situation; character of strata, length of tunneling, depths of cuttings, etc., in making an estimate for a railway contract.

8. [*pl.*] The bread and wine used in the eucharist.

9. In electricity, a cell. [See *Cell*, 7.]

el'ē-ment, *v.t.* 1. To compound of elements or first principles. [Obs.]

2. To constitute; to make as a first principle. [Obs.]

el-ē-men'tăl, *a.* 1. Pertaining to elements.

2. Produced by some of the four supposed elements; as, *elemental* war.

3. Produced by elements; as, *elemental* strife.

4. Arising from or pertaining to first principles; as, an *elemental* law of our being.

el-ē-men'tăl-işm, *n.* The theory which accounts for the creation of the heathen deities as the personification of the elements or their characteristic powers.

el"ē-men-tal'i-ty, *n.* Composition of principles or ingredients.

el-ē-men'tăl-ly, *adv.* According to elements; literally; as, the words, "Take, eat, this is my body," *elementally* understood.

el-ē-men'tăr, *a.* Elementary. [Obs.]

el-ē-men'tȧ-ri-ness, *n.* The state of being elementary; the simplicity of nature; uncompounded state.

el"ē-men-tăr'i-ty, *n.* Elementariness. [Obs.]

el-ē-men'tȧ-ry, *a.* [L. *elementarius*, pertaining to an element, or rudiment; *elementum*, a first principle, element.]

1. Primary; simple; uncompounded; uncombined; having only one principle or constituent part; as, an *elementary* substance; *elementary* particles into which a body is resolved by decomposition.

2. Initial; rudimental; containing, teaching, or discussing first principles, rules, or rudiments; as, an *elementary* treatise or disquisition.

3. Treating of elements; collecting, digesting, or explaining principles; as, an *elementary* writer.

Syn.—Physical, material, natural, primary, rudimental, simple, inchoate, component, constituent, ultimate.

el"ē-men-tā'tion, *n.* Instruction in primary principles. [Rare.]

el'ē-men-tā"tŏr, *n.* The writer of an elementary treatise or manual. [Rare.]

el-ē-men'toid, *a.* Like an element; having the nature of a simple elementary substance.

el'ē-mi, *n.* [Prob. of Ar. origin.] A resin used in the manufacture of varnishes, plasters, and ointments, and obtained from the bark of the *Canarium* and *Amyris*, genera re ated to the myrrh family.

el'ē-min, *n.* [*Elemi* and *-in*.] Either of two derivatives of various elemis, one crystalline, the other oily.

ē-lench', *n.* [L. *elenchus*; Gr. *elenchos*, from *elenchein*, to cross-examine, for the purpose of refuting, to refute.] A vicious or fallacious argument, which is apt to deceive under the appearance of truth; a sophism.

ē-len'chic, ē-len'chic-ăl, *a.* Pertaining to an elench.

ē-len'chic-ăl-ly, *adv.* By means of an elench. [Obs.]

ē-len'chīze, *v.i.* To dispute. [Rare.]

ē-lench'tic, ē-lench'tic-ăl, *a.* See *Elenchic*, *Elenchical*.

ē-len'chus, *n.* Same as *Elench*.

el'enġe, *a.* [ME. *elenge*; AS. *ellende*, foreign, strange; G. *elend*, miserable.] Troubled; filled with sorrow. [Obs.]

el'enġe-ness, *n.* Misery; loneliness. [Obs.]

E-lē-och'ȧ-ris, *n.* [Gr. *elos*, genit. *eleos*, low ground by rivers, marsh, and *chairein*, to rejoice.] A widely distributed genus of sedge-like plants, comprising about eighty species (of which fully one-fourth are found in North America), commonly known as spike-rushes, because of the appearance of the stalks.

el'ē-phăn-sy, *n.* [L. *elephantia*, from *elephans*, an elephant.] Elephantiasis. [Obs.]

el'ē-phănt, *n.* [L. *elephantus* or *elephas*, *elephantis*; Gr. *elephas*, *elephantos*, an elephant, ivory; perhaps from Heb. *eleph*, an ox.]

1. The popular name of a pachydermatous mammal, with five toes and a long proboscis terminating in a finger-like lobe. The nostrils are also at the end of the proboscis. Its molar teeth are large, and it is especially distinguished by two tusks, which vary in length according to age and variety. Two existing species are *Elephas indicus* and *Elephas africanus.* The former is characterized by a high, concave forehead, and small ears and tusks, the last-named being present in the male only. The tusks and ears are much larger in the African elephant, its forehead is convex, and tusks are grown by both sexes.

Head of African Elephant (*Elephas africanus*).

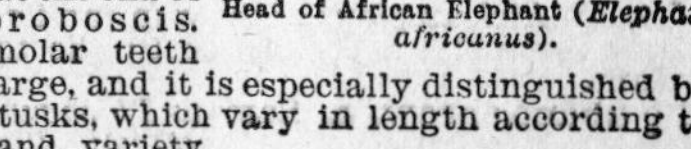

Head of Indian Elephant (*Elephas indicus*).

2. Ivory; the tusk of the elephant. [Obs.]

To see the elephant or *to show the elephant*; to see or show the notable sights of a city, with the implication that they are of a low character.

White elephant; something in one's possession which is costly and unproductive.

el'ē-phănt-ap"ple, *n.* An East Indian tree, *Feronia elephantum*, belonging to the *Rutaceæ*, having an edible fruit like the orange.

el'ē-phănt-bee"tle, *n.* The popular name of the beetles of the genus *Goliathus*, natives of Africa.

el′ē-phănt-bīrd, *n.* A gigantic fossil bird, similar to the ostrich, found in Madagascar; genus *Æpyornis.*

el′ē-phănt=crēep″ēr, *n.* A creeper, *Argyreia speciosa,* allied to the morning-glory, which runs to the tops of the highest trees; it bears large, rose-colored flowers, and is native to both the Indies.

el′ē-phănt=fish, *n.* A fish, *Callorhynchus antarcticus,* with a projection of the snout like a proboscis, belonging to the order *Chimæra.*

el′ē-phănt=gràss, *n.* A plant native to southern Asia and southern Europe, *Typha elephantina,* and considered the congener of the common cattail.

el-ē-phan′ti-ac, *a.* Affected with or characteristic of elephantiasis.

el″ē-phăn-tī′ȧ-sis, *n.* [Gr. *elephantiasis,* a skin disease, from *elephas (-antos),* an elephant.] A disease in which the skin is thick, livid, wrinkled, tuberculate, and in general appearance like an elephant's hide.

el-ē-phan′tid, *n.* One of the *Elephantidæ,* whether living or fossil.

El-ē-phan′ti-dæ, *n.pl.* [L. *elephas (-antis),* an elephant, and *-idæ.*] A family of mammals with proboscides, of which the elephant, *Elephas,* is the type.

El″ē-phăn-tī′næ, *n.pl.* A subfamily of *Elephantidæ,* distinguishing the living species from the mastodons.

el-ē-phan′tine, *a.* [L. *elephantinus,* from *elephas (-antis),* an elephant.]

1. Pertaining to the elephant; huge; resembling an elephant, or perhaps white, like ivory.

2. In antiquity, an appellation given to certain books in which the Romans registered the transactions of the senate, magistrates, emperors, and generals; so called because made of ivory.

3. In geology, the *elephantine* epoch is that in which there was a preponderance of large *Pachydermata.*

Elephantine tortoise; an immense land tortoise of the islands of the Pacific, sometimes weighing five hundred pounds.

el′ē-phănt=leg, *n.* Elephantiasis.

el′ē-phănt=mouse, *n.* A species of jumping or kangaroo mice, one of the African *Insectivora,* with a proboscis-like snout; also called *elephant-shrew.*

el-ē-phan′toid, el″ē-phan-toid′ăl, *a.* [Gr. *elephas (-antos),* an elephant, and *eidos,* form.] Similar to an elephant in appearance or habits.

El-ē-phan′tō-pus, *n.* [Gr. *elephantopous,* ivory-footed; *elephas (-antos),* an elephant, ivory, and *pous,* a foot.] A genus of herb-like plants, native to America and belonging to the aster family. Some South American varieties have medicinal properties.

el-ē-phan′tous, *a.* [L. *elephantiasis,* and *-ous.*] Resembling or of the nature of elephantiasis; leprous; as, an *elephantous* skin disease.

el′ē-phănt=sēal, *n.* A seal, sometimes attaining a length of twenty feet, of the subfamily *Cystophorinæ,* genus *Macrorhinus,* the male of which has a proboscis-like snout; the sea-elephant.

el′ē-phănt′s=ēar, *n.* In botany, a species of the genus *Begonia,* so named because of its great one-sided leaves.

el′ē-phănt′s=foot, *n.* 1. The popular name of the several species of *Elephantopus,* of which it is a translation. These are mostly tropical plants.

2. An African plant of the yam family whose bark resembles a tortoise-shell; the tortoise-plant.

el′ē-phănt=shrew, *n.* Same as *Elephant-mouse.*

el′ē-phănt′s=tusk, *n.* A mollusk, *Dentalium arcuatum,* whose curved tubular shell resembles an elephant's tusk.

El-eū-sin′i-ȧ, *n.pl.* [Gr. *Eleusinia,* neut. pl. of *Eleusinios,* pertaining to *Eleusis (-inos),* Eleusis.] The festival, or series of offerings, originally held at Eleusis, near Athens, Greece, chiefly in honor of Demeter, or Ceres, and her daughter Persephone, the goddesses typical of fruitfulness, plenty, or prosperity.

El-eū-sin′i-ăn, *a.* Relating to Eleusis, Greece, or to the rites celebrated there and at Athens in honor of Demeter; as, *Eleusinian* mysteries or festivals.

el-eū-thē′ri-ăn, *a.* [Gr. *eleutherios,* like a free man, frank, freely giving, from *eleutheros,* free.] Giving freedom; liberating; freely giving; bountiful; applied to Zeus, or Jove, the author of personal and political freedom.

e-leū″thĕr-ō-mā′ni-ȧ, *n.* [Gr. *eleutheros,* free, and *mania,* madness.] A mania for freedom. [Rare.]

e-leū″thĕr-ō-mā′ni-ac, *n.* One whose zeal for freedom has become a mania.

e-leū″thĕr-ō-mā′ni-ac, *a.* Possessed of an unreasonable or maniacal zeal for freedom.

e-leū″thĕr-ō-pet′ăl-ous, *a.* [Gr. *eleutheros,* free, and *petalon,* a leaf.] Having the petals free or noncoherent.

el′ē-vāte, *v.t.;* elevated, *pt., pp.;* elevating, *ppr.* [L. *elevatus,* pp. of *elevare,* to raise, lift up; *e,* out, and *levare,* to make light, lift, from *levis,* light.]

1. To lift or raise from a lower to a higher place; as, to *elevate* a machine or a house.

2. To exalt; to promote; to lift to a higher station.

3. To improve; to refine; to ennoble; as, to *elevate* the standard of morals.

4. To cheer; to animate; to excite; to raise in spirit.

5. To augment or swell; to make louder; as, to *elevate* the voice.

6. To intoxicate slightly or make tipsy. [Colloq.]

Syn.—Raise, hoist, exalt, erect, elate, cheer, animate.

el′ē-vā-ted-ness, *n.* The state of being elevated.

el-ē-vä′ti-ō (-shi-ō), *n.* [L., from *elevare,* to raise, make light.] In music, (a) anciently, rhythmic accent; (b) any composition rendered during the elevation of the host; (c) medievally, the raising of a mode above the common compass.

el-ē-vā′tion, *n.* [L. *elevatio (-onis),* from *elevare,* to raise, make light.]

1. The act of raising from a lower place, rank, or quality, to a higher; as, the *elevation* of ore; *elevation* of character, morals, art, or education.

2. State of being elevated; exaltation; height; dignity.

3. A high or elevated place or locality; high or rising ground; as, an *elevation* on a prairie.

4. In astronomy, the distance of a celestial object above the horizon, or the arc of a vertical circle intercepted between it and the horizon; altitude; as, the *elevation* of a planet.

5. In drawing, a projection of a building or other structure in a vertical plane; as, a front *elevation* of a temple.

6. In dialing, the angle made by the style with the substylar line.

7. In gunnery, the angle between the axis of a gun and the line of sight; the movement of the axis of a gun in a vertical plane.

8. In topography, the height of any land surface above sea-level; altitude.

Angle of elevation; the angle made by an ascending line with a horizontal plane.

Elevation of the host; in Roman Catholic countries, that part of the mass in which the priest raises the host above his head for the people to adore.

el′ē-vā-tŏr, *n.* [LL. *elevator,* one who raises up, a deliverer, from L. *elevare,* to raise up, make light.]

1. One who or that which lifts, raises, or conveys anything.

2. Specifically, (a) a mechanical device of various designs, usually an endless chain or belt, with a series of buckets or scoops, for transferring liquids or grain from lower to higher levels; (b) a platform or cage and its hoisting machinery, used in buildings for transferring persons and goods from and to different floors; the platform or cage itself; (c) a structure designed for elevating, storing, and distributing cereals.

3. In anatomy, a muscle which serves to elevate some organ or part, as the eyelid.

4. In dentistry, an instrument for removing stumps of teeth.

5. In surgery, an instrument for raising the depressed part of a fractured bone.

6. In aeronautics, the plane or planes which, being tilted or dipped, cause the machine to rise or fall at the will of the aviator.

el′ē-vā-tō-ry, *a.* [From LL. *elevator,* one who raises up.] Tending to raise, or having power to elevate; as, *elevatory* tendencies.

ē-lev′en, *a.* [ME. *elleven;* AS. *endleofan,* eleven; *an,* one, and *-lif,* remainder, as in Goth. *twalif,* AS. *twelf,* twelve.] Consisting of ten and one; as, *eleven* dollars.

ē-lev′en, *n.* 1. The sum of ten and one; eleven objects or units.

2. A symbol representing the number, as XI or 11.

3. A team in the games of football or cricket, numbering eleven players.

ē-lev′enth, *a.* 1. The next in order to the tenth; as, the *eleventh* chapter.

2. Relating to one of the eleven equal parts into which a thing may be divided; as, the *eleventh* part of an estate.

3. In music, relating to the interval of a compound fourth.

ē-lev′enth, *n.* 1. The quotient of a unit divided by eleven; as, four is one *eleventh* of forty-four.

2. The interval consisting of an octave and a fourth; a note removed from another by this interval.

elf, *n.; pl.* **elves.** [AS. *ælf, ylf;* Ice. *alfr;* Sw. *alf, elva,* an elf.]

1. A diminutive, wandering spirit; a fairy; a hobgoblin; an imaginary being anciently supposed to inhabit unfrequented places, and in various ways to affect mankind.

2. An evil spirit; a devil; a rogue; a knave.

3. A diminutive person; a dwarf.

4. Pet name for a small, mischievous child.

elf, *v.t.* To entangle (hair) in so intricate a manner, that it cannot be disentangled. This work was formerly ascribed to elves. [Rare.]

elf′=ar″row, *n.* An arrowhead of flint, supposed by rural English folk of long ago to have been shot by an elf; called also *elf-shot, elf-bolt,* and *elf-dart.*

elf′=child, *n.* A child thought to be left by elves in the place of one stolen; a changeling.

elf′=dock, *n.* A root used as a remedy for stomach troubles; the elecampane.

elf′=fire, *n.* The ignis fatuus.

elf′in, *a.* Relating or pertaining to elves.

elf′in, *n.* 1. A little urchin.

2. A butterfly of the genus *Incisalia.*

elf′ish, *a.* Resembling elves.

elf′ish-ly, *adv.* In an elfish manner.

elf′ish-ness, *n.* The quality of resembling an elf.

elf′kin, *n.* A little elf.

elf′land, *n.* The abode of elves or fairies.

elf′lock, *n.* Hair twisted into knots.

elf′=owl, *n.* A small burrowing owl, *Micrathene whitneyi,* of Arizona, California, and Mexico.

El′gin mär′bles. A series of ancient sculptured marbles, named from the Earl of Elgin, who removed them to England, obtaining them from the temple of Minerva and other edifices in Athens. The marbles consist chiefly of matchless statues and casts now deposited in the British Museum.

ē-lic′it, *v.t.;* elicited, *pt., pp.;* eliciting, *ppr.* [L. *elicitus,* pp. of *elicere,* to draw out; *e-,* out, and *lacere,* to entice.]

1. To draw out; to bring to light; to deduce by reason or argument; as, to *elicit* truth by discussion.

2. To strike out; as, to *elicit* sparks of fire by collision.

ē-lic′it, *a.* Brought into act; brought from possibility into real existence. [Obs.]

ē-lic′i-tāte, *v.t.* To elicit. [Obs.]

ē-lic-i-tā′tion, *n.* The act of eliciting; the act of drawing out. [Obs.]

ē-lide′, *v.t.;* elided, *pt., pp.;* eliding, *ppr.* [L. *elidere,* to strike out, to break in pieces.]

1. To break or dash in pieces; to crush. [Obs.]

2. In grammar, to clip or shorten a word, usually to prevent hiatus, as in *th' everlasting hills.*

el″i-ġi-bil′i-ty, *n.* 1. Worthiness or fitness to be chosen; the state or quality of a thing which renders it preferable to another, or desirable.

2. Politically, the capability of being chosen to an office.

el′i-ġi-ble, *a.* [OFr. *eligible,* from L. *eligere,* to choose, select.]

1. Fit to be chosen; worthy of choice; preferable; as, of the two suitors he is the more *eligible.*

2. Suitable; proper; desirable; as, the house stands in an *eligible* situation.

3. Legally qualified to be chosen; as, this man is *eligible* to office.

Syn.—Fit, apt, competent, qualified, expedient, appropriate, becoming.

el′i-ġi-ble-ness, *n.* Fitness to be chosen in preference to another; suitableness; desirableness.

el′i-ġi-bly, *adv.* In a manner to be worthy of choice; suitably.

el′i-māte, *v.t.* [L. *elimatus,* pp. of *elimare,* to file, polish; *e-,* out, and *limare,* from *lima,* a file.] To make smooth. [Obs.]

ē-lim′i-nănt, *n.* [L. *eliminans (-antis),* ppr. of *eliminare,* to turn out of doors, banish.] In mathematics, the result obtained by the elimination of *n* variables between *n* homogeneous equations of any degree; the resultant of two quantics.

ē-lim′i-nāte, *v.t.;* eliminated, *pt., pp.;* eliminating, *ppr.* [L. *eliminatus,* pp. of *eliminare,* to turn out of doors, banish; *e-,* out, and *limen (-inis),* the threshold, door.]

1. To thrust out of doors.

2. To expel; to thrust out; to discharge, or throw off; to set at liberty.

3. In algebra, to cause (a quantity) to disappear from an equation.

4. To leave out of consideration in a process of inductive reasoning.

5. To obtain by deduction. [Recent.]

6. In physiology, to expel from the system; as, the kidneys *eliminate* uric acid.

To eliminate the personal equation; a figurative expression implying the leaving out of all personal matters in the consideration of a question.

ē-lim-i-nā′tion, *n.* 1. The act of expelling or throwing off; the act of discharging or secreting by the pores.

2. In algebra, causing a quantity to disappear from an equation.

3. The act of obtaining by separation from foreign matter.

ē-lim′i-nā-tive, *a.* Carrying on the process of elimination; having capacity to eliminate.

ē-lin′guāte (-gwāt), *v.t.* [L. *elinguatus,* pp. of *elinguare,* to deprive of the tongue.] To remove the tongue from; an ancient mode of punishment. [Obs.]

ē-liñ-guā′tion (-gwā′), *n.* In law, punishment by elinguating.

ē-liñ′guid (-gwid), *a.* Tongue-tied; not having the power of speech. [Obs.]

ē-liq′uȧ-ment (-lik′wȧ-), *n.* A liquid obtained by pressure from fat fish or meat.

el′i-quāte, *v.t.* [L. *eliquatus*, pp. of *eliquare*, to clarify, strain, cause to flow; *e-*, out, and *liquare*, to melt.] In metallurgy, to separate by heat, as an ore from a metal. [Obs. See *Liquate*.]

el-i-quā′tion, *n.* [L. *eliquare*, to melt, clarify, or strain.] In metallurgy, the operation by which a more fusible substance is separated from one that is less so by means of a degree of heat sufficient to melt the one and not the other, as an alloy of copper and lead.

ē-li′sion (-lizh′un), *n.* [L. *elisio*, from *elidere*, to strike off; *e-*, out, and *lædere*, to strike.]

1. In grammar, the cutting off or suppression of a vowel at the end of a word, for the sake of sound or measure, when the next word begins with a vowel, as th' embattled plain; th' empyreal sphere.

2. Division; separation. [Obs.]

ē-li′sŏr, *n.* [OFr. *eliseor*, *eliseur*, a chooser, from *elire*, L. *eligere*, to choose, select.] In law, a sheriff's substitute for returning a jury. In case, on account of their personal interest in the suit, an objection shall lie to the sheriff or the coroners, the venire shall be directed to two clerks of the court, or to two persons of the county, named by the court and sworn, who shall return the jury. —Blackstone.

é-lïte′ (ā-lēt′), *n.* [Fr.] 1. The choicest, most select part, particularly of a body of individuals; the pick; as, the *élite* of the army; the *élite* of society.

2. One selected or chosen. [Obs.]

ē-lix′, *v.t.* [LL. *elixare*, to boil thoroughly; L. *e-*, out, and *lixare*, from *lix*, ashes, lye.] To extract. [Obs.]

ē-lix′āte, *v.t.* To extract by boiling. [Obs.]

el-ix-ā′tion, *n.* 1. The act of boiling or stewing; also, concoction in the stomach; digestion. [Obs.]

2. In pharmacy, the extraction of the virtues of ingredients by boiling or stewing; also, lixiviation. [Obs.]

ē-lix′ĭr, *n.* [OFr. *elixir*; Sp. *elixir*; Port. *elexir*, from Ar. *el iksīr*, the philosopher's stone; *el*, *al*, the, and *iksīr*, philosopher's stone; prob. from Gr. *xēros*, dry.]

1. In medicine, a tincture with more than one base; more properly, a tincture or medicine consisting of a sweetened alcoholic solution of a small quantity of the drug or drugs thus compounded.

2. In alchemy, a liquid or soluble agent thought to exist and sought after, which (a) could transmute baser metals into gold; the philosopher's stone; (b) could prolong life indefinitely.

3. The essence; the refined spirit; the essential principle. [Rare.]

E-liz-ȧ-beth′ăn, *a.* and *n.* I. *a.* Pertaining to Queen Elizabeth or her times, and to a style of architecture then prevalent; especially to the era of general activity and progress in foreign enterprises, in the sciences, religion, art, and above all in literature, which was coeval with her reign; as, the *Elizabethan* architecture; the *Elizabethan* playwrights.

II. *n.* An English contemporary of the Elizabethan era in general, especially an author or statesman.

Elizabethan Window.

elk, *n.* [AS. *elch*; Ice. *elgr*; M.H.G. *elch*; O.H.G. *elaho*, *elho*, elk.] A large deer, several different varieties of which are known. It is characterized by having its upper lip shaped like a proboscis and very massive, palmate antlers; the American moose; the eland.

Elk-horn fern; a fern whose fronds resemble the horns of an elk.

Irish elk; an extinct deer with very large antlers. Its remains are frequently found in the peat-bogs of Ireland.

Order of Elks; see under *Order*.

elk, *n.* [Local, Eng.] 1. In zoölogy, the whistling swan of Europe, *Cygnus ferus*; written also *elke*.

2. In botany, a species of yew from which bows were made.

Elk (*Cervus alces*).

elk′=bärk, *n.* The bark of the *Magnolia glauca*; also, the tree itself.

El-kē′sȧ-īte, *n.* Same as *Elcesaite*.

elk′nut, *n.* The nut of the *Pyrularia oleifera*; also, the shrub bearing the nut.

elk′=tree, *n.* The *Oxydendrum arboreum*, of the heath family; called also *sourwood* and *sorrel-tree*.

elk′wood, *n.* The wood of the *Magnolia Umbrella* of the United States.

ell, *n.* [ME. *elle*, *elne*; AS. *eln*, an ell; D. *el*, *elle*; L. *ulna*, the forearm, elbow, an ell.]

1. A measure, of different lengths in different countries, used chiefly for measuring cloth. The English ell is forty-five inches. The Flemish ell is twenty-seven inches or three-quarters of a yard. This measure is now rarely used.

2. In pipe-fitting, a joining at right angles; as, a stovepipe *ell*.

3. In architecture, an addition to a building giving it the shape of the letter L.

el′lȧ-chick, *n.* [Nesqually Ind. *el-la-chick*.] A large edible fresh-water tortoise found on the Pacific slope of the United States.

el-lag′iç, *a.* [Fr., from *galle*, gall, with the letters transposed.] Related to or derived from nutgalls; bitter and astringent.

Ellagic acid; a weak, insipid acid, $C_{14}H_6O_8$, obtained from gallnuts.

el′lē-bōre, *n.* Obsolete form for *hellebore*.

el-leb′ō-rin, *n.* An acrid resinous substance found in the winter hellebore, *Helleborus hiemalis*.

el′leck, *n.* Provincial English name of the *Trigla cuculus* or cuckoo-fish.

el′lenge, *a.* Same as *Elenge*.

El-lē′ri-ăn, *n.* [Named from Elias *Eller*, the founder of the sect.] One of a German sect of Millenarians, founded in the early part of the eighteenth century; called also *Ronsdorfian* and *Ronsdorfer*.

el-lipse′ (el-lips′), *n.* [L. *ellipsis*; Gr. *elleipsis*, a want, defect, ellipsis, from *elleipein*, to leave in, fall short; *en*, in, and *leipein*, to leave.] A plane figure bounded by a curve such that the sum of the distances from any point in this curve to two points (the foci) within the figure is a constant; an oblique section of a cylinder or of a cone.

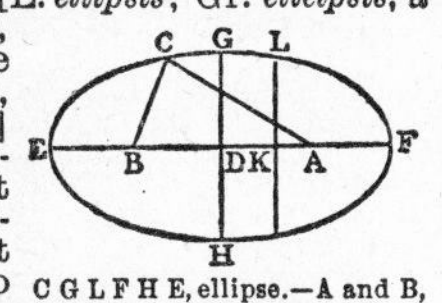

C G L F H E, ellipse.—A and B, the foci; D, the center; D A or D B, the eccentricity; E F, the major or transverse axis; G H, the minor or conjugate axis; L K, an ordinate to the axis; E K and K F, abscissæ.

el-lip′sis, *n.*; *pl.* **el-lip′sēş.** [L. *ellipsis*; Gr. *elleipsis*, a falling short, omission; from *elleipein*; *en*, in, and *leipein*, to leave.]

1. In grammar, defect; omission; a figure of syntax in which there is an omission of a word or words that can be readily supplied; as, the heroic virtues I admire, for, the heroic virtues which I admire.

2. One of the conic sections. [Obs.]

el-lip′sō-graph, *n.* [Gr. *elleipsis*, an ellipse, and *graphein*, to write.] An instrument to describe an ellipse by continued motion; called also *trammel*.

el-lip′soid, *n.* [Gr. *elleipsis*, an ellipse, and *eidos*, form.] In geometry, a solid figure, all plane sections of which are ellipses or circles; a spheroid.

Ellipsoid of revolution; a solid figure generated by the rotation of an ellipse about one of its axes. When the rotation is about the major axis the figure is a prolate spheroid; when about the minor axis, an oblate spheroid.

el-lip-soi′dăl, *a.* Pertaining to an ellipsoid; having the form of an ellipsoid.

el-lip′tiç, el-lip′tiç-ăl, *a.* [Gr. *elleiptikos*, elliptical, defective, from *elleipsis*, a falling short, defect, ellipse.]

1. Pertaining to an ellipse; having the form of an ellipse; as, the planets move in *elliptical* orbits, having the sun in one focus.

2. In grammar or rhetoric, defective; having a part omitted; characterized by ellipsis; as, an *elliptical* phrase.

Elliptic compasses; an instrument devised for describing ellipses.

Elliptic chuck, elliptic function, elliptic integral, elliptic polarization; see under the nouns.

el-lip′tiç-ăl-ly, *adv.* 1. According to the form of an ellipse.

2. Defectively; with a part omitted; as, *elliptically* expressed.

el-lip-tic′i-ty, *n.* Deviation from the form of a circle or sphere; as, the *ellipticity* of the earth is about $\frac{1}{294}$, that being the part of the equatorial diameter by which it exceeds the polar.

el-lip′tiç=lan′cē-ō-lāte, *a.* Having the form of a narrow ellipse with sharp angles at the extremities of the major axis; said of a leaf.

el-lip′tō-grȧph, *n.* Same as *Ellipsograph*.

ell′wänd, el′wänd, *n.* A stick for measuring, having the length of an ell; now out of use.

elm, *n.* [AS. *elm* or *ulm treou*; D. *olm*; G. *ulme*, elm-tree; L. *ulmus*, elm-tree.] Any tree of the genus *Ulmus*, including the lofty and beautiful shade trees in common cultivation. The wood is very tough and resists the action of water for a long time, hence its use for piers, piling, boat-building, etc.

Elm (*Ulmus campestris*).

Winged elm; the American *Ulmus alata*, whose younger branches have bark with corky wing-like expansions. The wood is fine-grained and valuable because of its resistance to splitting; called also *wahoo*.

elm′=bee″tle, *n.* Any beetle that feeds upon the foliage of the elm, as the *Galeruca calmariensis* and the *Galeruca xanthomelæna*.

elm′=bŏr″ẽr, *n.* Any of various beetles whose larvæ damage the elm by boring under the bark and into the wood, especially the *Saperda tridentata*.

elm′=but″tẽr-flȳ, *n.* Any one of several species of butterfly whose larvæ are destructive to the foliage of the elm; specifically, the comma butterfly, *Grapta comma-album*.

elm′en, *a.* Of or belonging to elms. [Obs.]

El′mō's fire, St. El′mō's fire. Same as *Corposant*.

elm′=mŏth, *n.* Any moth the larvæ of which feed upon the foliage of elm-trees, notably the geometer or span-worm, *Eugonia subsignaria*.

elm′=sąw″flȳ, *n.* The *Cimbex americana*, a large sawfly whose larvæ feed upon the foliage of the elm.

elm′y, *a.* Abounding in elms.

el-ō-çā′tion, *n.* [L. *elocare*; *e*, out, and *locare*, to place, hire out.]

1. A removal from the usual place of residence. [Obs.]

2. Departure from the usual mood; an ecstasy. [Obs.]

ē-loç′ū-lăr, *a.* Unicellular; not divided into separate cells.

el-ō-çū′tion, *n.* [L. *elocutio* (*-onis*), from *eloqui*, to speak out, utter.]

1. The art of correct utterance or delivery of words; as, *elocution* tries to use adequate means to convey a thought in all its clearness, force, and beauty.

2. The manner or method of public reading or speaking; as, his *elocution* was poor.

3. The act of speaking; utterance. [Rare.]

4. Eloquence. [Obs.]

el-ō-çū′tion-ā-ry, *a.* Pertaining to elocution or containing it.

el-ō-çū′tion-ist, *n.* One who is versed in elocution or who treats of the subject.

el′ō-çū-tive, *a.* Having the power of eloquent speaking.

ē-lō′dēş, *n.* [Gr. *helōdēs*, marshy.] Marsh-fever; malarial fever accompanied by excessive perspiration.

ē-lō′di-ăn, *n.* [Gr. *helōdēs*, marshy.] A marsh-tortoise; any member of a tribe of tortoises in which the head is retractile.

é-lōge′ (ā-lōzh′), *n.* [Fr., from L. *elogium*, a short observation, an inscription on a tombstone, from Gr. *logos*, discourse.] A panegyric on the dead; a eulogy; usually applied to the memoir upon the decease of a member of the Academy in France.

el′ō-ġist, *n.* A eulogist. [Obs.]

el′ō-ġy, ē-lō′ġi-um, *n.* Praise bestowed on a person or thing; panegyric; an éloge.

El′ō-him, *n.pl.* [Heb.] 1. God; the most frequent Hebrew name for the Creator and divine power.

2. [e—] Deities, false or true.

El′ō-hist, *n.* The author of those parts of the Hexateuch in which *Elohim* is used instead of *Yahveh* as the title of God.

ē-loin′, ē-loign′, *v.t.* [OFr. *eloigner*; LL. *elongare*, to remove, keep aloof; *e*, out, and *longus*, long.]

1. To separate and remove to a distance. [Obs.]

2. To convey to a distance, and withhold from sight, as goods that may be seized. [Obs.]

The sheriff may return that the goods or beasts are *eloined*. —Blackstone.

ē-loin′āte, ē-loign′āte, *v.t.* To remove. [Obs.]

ē-loin′ment, ē-loign′ment, *n.* Removal to a distance; distance.

ē-lŏng′, *v.t.* To put far off; to retard. [Obs.]

ē-lŏn′gāte, *v.t.*; elongated, *pt., pp.*; elongating, *ppr.* [LL. *elongatus*, pp. of *elongare*, to remove, keep aloof, protract; *e-*, out, and *longus*, long.]

1. To lengthen; to extend.

2. To remove farther off. [Obs.]

ē-lŏn′gāte, *v.i.* To recede; particularly, to recede apparently from the sun, as a planet in its orbit.

ē-lŏn′gāte, *a.* Lengthened; extended.

ē-lŏn′gā-tion, *n.* 1. The act of stretching or lengthening; the state of being extended; as, the *elongation* of a wire by stretching.

2. Extension; continuation; lengthening by addition; as, may not the mountains of Westmoreland and Cumberland be considered as *elongations* of these two chains?

3. In astronomy, the angular distance of a planet from the sun; apparent departure of a planet from the sun in its orbit; as, the *elongation* of Venus or Mercury.

4. In surgery, an imperfect luxation, occasioned by the stretching or lengthening of the ligaments; or the extension of a part beyond its natural dimensions.

5. Distance; space which separates one thing from another. [Obs.]

6. Departure; removal; recession. [Obs.]

ē-lōpe′, *v.i.*; eloped (-lōpt′), *pt., pp.*; eloping, *ppr.* [From D. *ontloopen*, to run away; *ont-*, away, and *loopen*, to run.]

1. To run away; to free oneself from legal or natural ties; to escape clandestinely, especially to leave one's home by stealth to marry a lover, or to leave husband or wife to live with a paramour; to run away together; as, opposition forced them to *elope*.

2. To run away clandestinely, as to free oneself from legal or moral restrictions; to abscond.

ē-lōpe′ment, *n.* The act of clandestine departure by eloping.

ē-lōp′ēr, *n.* A person who elopes.

E′lops, *n.* [Gr. *elops*, *ellops*, a kind of sea-fish, a serpent.]

1. A genus of fishes inhabiting the seas of America and the West Indies.

2. [e—] A fabulous serpent. [Obs.] Written also *ellops*.

el′ō-quence (-kwens), *n.* [Fr. *éloquence*, from L. *eloquentia*, from *eloqui*, to speak out.]

1. The expression, in either spoken or written language, of strong emotion, so as to excite corresponding emotions in others; lofty, noble, impassioned, fluent utterance.

2. The quality of being eloquent or arousing emotions; as, the *eloquence* of tears; the *eloquence* of her eyes.

3. Verbal expression; utterance. [Obs.]

el′ō-quent, *a.* 1. Having the power of expressing strong emotions in a vivid and appropriate manner; as, an *eloquent* orator or preacher.

2. Adapted to express strong emotion with fluency and power; as, an *eloquent* address; *eloquent* history; an *eloquent* appeal to a jury.

3. Expressing or manifesting vividly or impressively; as, an *eloquent* pause; an *eloquent* glance.

el′ō-quent-ly, *adv.* With eloquence; in an eloquent manner.

el′rich, *a.* Same as *Eldritch*.

else, *a.* or *pron.* [AS. *elles*, otherwise, in another manner, besides; originally, a genit. sing. from an adj. signifying other, as in *ele-land*, another land.] Other; one or something besides; as, who *else* is coming? What *else* shall I give? Do you expect anything *else*?

else, *adv.* 1. Otherwise; in the other case; if the fact were different; as, thou desirest not sacrifice, *else* would I give it.

2. Besides; except that mentioned; as, nowhere *else*.

el′sen, el′sin, *n.* [Scot. and Prov. Eng.] An awl, especially one used by a shoemaker.

else′where (-hwâr), *adv.* 1. In any other place; as, these trees are not to be found *elsewhere*.

2. In some other place; in other places indefinitely; as, it is reported in town and *elsewhere*.

else′whith″ēr (-hwith″ēr), *adv.* To another or any other place; in another direction; as, he was compelled to go *elsewhither* for it.

else′wīse, *adv.* In some other way. [Rare.]

ē-lū′ci-dāte, *v.t.*; elucidated, *pt., pp.*; elucidating, *ppr.* [LL. *elucidatus*, pp. of *elucidare*, to make light or clear; L. *e-*, out, and *lucidus*, light, clear, from *lux*, light.] To make clear or manifest; to explain; to remove obscurity from and render intelligible; to illustrate; as, an example will *elucidate* the subject.

ē-lū-ci-dā′tion, *n.* The act of explaining or throwing light on any obscure subject; explanation; exposition; illustration; as, one example may serve for an *elucidation* of the subject.

ē-lū′ci-dā-tive, *a.* Making clear; fitted for elucidation.

ē-lū′ci-dā-tŏr, *n.* One who explains; an expositor.

ē-lū′ci-dȧ-tō-ry, *a.* Tending to elucidate. [Rare.]

ē-luc′tāte, *v.i.* [L. *eluctatus*, pp. of *eluctari*, to struggle out.] To escape by struggling; to struggle forth. [Obs.]

ē-luc-tā′tion, *n.* The act of bursting forth; escape from any difficulty. [Obs.]

ē-lū′cū-brāte, *v.i.*, obsolete form of *lucubrate*.

ē-lu-cū-brā′tion, *n.*, obsolete form of *lucubration*.

ē-lūde′, *v.t.*; eluded, *pt., pp.*; eluding, *ppr.* [L. *eludere*, to finish play, parry a blow, frustrate, deceive; *e-*, out, and *ludere*, to play.]

1. To escape; to evade; to avoid by artifice, stratagem, wiles, deceit, or dexterity; as, to *elude* an enemy; to *elude* the sight; to *elude* detection; to *elude* the force of an argument; to *elude* a blow or stroke.

2. To mock by an unexpected escape; as, to *elude* pursuit.

> Me gentle Delia beckons from the plain,
> Then, hid in shades, *eludes* her eager swain.
> —Pope.

3. To escape being seen; to remain unseen or undiscovered; as, to *elude* discovery.

Syn.—Escape, avoid, baffle, shun, evade, parry, fence, mock, frustrate.

ē-lūd′i-ble, *a.* Capable of being avoided or eluded; avoidable.

E′lul, *n.* [Heb., from *alal*, to reap, harvest.] The twelfth month of the civil Jewish year, and the sixth of the ecclesiastical. It corresponds nearly to our September.

ē-lum′bā-ted, *a.* [L. *elumbis*, weakened in the loins; *e-*, out, and *lumbus*, loin.] Weakened in the loins. [Obs.]

ē-lus-cā′tion, *n.* [LL. *eluscare*, to make one-eyed; L. *e-*, out, and *luscus*, one-eyed.] Defective eyesight; purblindness.

ē-lū′sion, *n.* [L. *elusio*, from *eludere*, to parry a blow, deceive.] An escape by artifice or deception; evasion; the act of eluding.

ē-lū′sive, *a.* Practising elusion; using arts to escape; tending to elude.

> *Elusive* of the bridal day, she gives
> Fond hopes to all, and all with hopes deceives.
> —Pope.

ē-lū′sive-ly, *adv.* In an elusive manner.

ē-lū′sive-ness, *n.* The state of being elusive.

ē-lū′sō-ri-ness, *n.* The state of being elusory.

ē-lū′sō-ry, *a.* Tending to elude; tending to deceive; evasive; fraudulent; fallacious; deceitful.

ē-lūte′, *v.t.* [L. *elutus*, pp. of *eluere*, to wash off; *e-*, out, off, and *luere*, to wash.] To cleanse. [Rare.]

ē-lū′tion, *n.* The removal of soluble matter by washing with water, as in refining sugar by washing the calcium sucrate.

ē-lū′tri-āte, *v.t.*; elutriated, *pt., pp.*; elutriating, *ppr.* [L. *elutriatus*, pp. of *elutriare*, to wash out, rack off, from *eluere*, to wash out.] To purify by washing; to cleanse, as a pulverulent substance, by separating foul matter and decanting or straining off the liquid.

ē-lū-tri-ā′tion, *n.* The operation of washing a pulverulent substance by mixing it with water, and pouring off the liquid in which the foul or extraneous substances are floating, while the heavier particles are deposited at the bottom.

ē-lux′āte, *v.t.*; eluxated, *pt., pp.*; eluxating, *ppr.* [L. *e-*, out, and *luxatus*, pp. of *luxare*, to dislocate.] To disjoint; to dislocate. [Rare.]

ē-lux-ā′tion, *n.* The dislocation of a bone; luxation.

el′văn, *a.* [Corn.] In mineralogy, pertaining to a dike-like formation found in Cornwall, England, generally among the granites and running parallel with the tin lodes; as, an *elvan* vein.

el′văn, *a.* Elfin.

el′văn, el′văn-ite, *n.* An elvan vein, or the rock in one; an elvan dike.

el-văn-it′ic, *a.* Of or pertaining to elvan or elvanite.

elve, *n.* An elf. [Obs.]

el′vēr, *n.* [Local, Eng.] A young eel; a young conger- or sea-eel; also written *elvene*.

elves, *n.*, pl. of *elf*.

elv′ish, *a.* Same as *Elfish*.

elv′ish-ly, *adv.* Elfishly.

el′wănd, *n.* See *Ellwand*.

el-y-dor′ic, *a.* [Gr. *elaion*, olive-oil, oil, and *hydōr*, water.] Painted with oil and water, in such a manner as to add the freshness of water-colors to the mellowness of oil painting; as, *elydoric* painting.

E-ly′şiăn, *a.* Pertaining to Elysium or the seat of delight; yielding the highest pleasures; deliciously soothing; exceedingly delightful; as, *Elysian* fields.

E-ly′şium, *n.* [L. *Elysium*; Gr. *Ēlysion* (*pedion*), Elysian plain, the plain of the departed, from *elysis*, a variant of *eleusis*, from *eleusesthai*, fut. of *elthein*, to go or come.]

1. In ancient mythology, a place assigned to happy souls after death; a place in the lower regions, furnished with all picturesque and restful felicitations; the seat of future happiness; the Elysian fields.

2. Figuratively, any delightful place.

el-y-tr-, el-y-tri-, el-y-trō-. Combining forms from Gr. *elytron*, a cover, covering, case, sheath, wing of a beetle, and indicating, (a) in zoölogy, a sheath or protecting integument; (b) in pathology and surgery, an affection of or an operation upon the vagina.

el′y-trȧ, *n.*, pl. of *elytrum*.

el′y-trăl, *a.* Pertaining to elytra.

e-lyt′ri-fọrm, *a.* [*Elytri-*, and L. *forma*, form.] Having the form of an elytrum or wing-sheath.

el′y-trine, *n.* [*Elytrum* and *-ine*.] Chemically, the white compound forming the base of the hard integuments of crustaceans and certain insects; chitin; written also *elytrin*.

el-y-trī′tis, *n.* [*Elytri-*, and *-itis*.] Inflammation of the vagina; vaginitis.

el′y-trō-cēle, *n.* [*Elytr-*, and Gr. *kēlē*, a tumor.] Same as *Colpocele*.

el′y-troid, *a.* [*Elytr-*, and Gr. *eidos*, form.] Similar to a sheath; elytriform; vaginal.

el′y-trō-plas-ty, *n.* [*Elytro-*, and Gr. *plassein*, to form.] Vaginal surgery concerning itself with the restoration of the normal parts; colpoplasty; plastic surgery of the vagina.

el″y-trop-tō′sis, *n.* [*Elytro-*, and Gr. *ptōsis*, a fall.] Falling of the vagina.

el-y-tror′rhȧ-phy, *n.* [*Elytro-*, and Gr. *hraphē*, a seam, suture, from *hraptein*, to sew.] Same as *Colporrhaphy*.

el-y-trot′ō-my, *n.* [*Elytro-*, and Gr. *tomē*, a cutting.] Cutting into or through the walls of the vagina.

el′y-trum, el′y-tron, *n.*; *pl.* **el′y-trȧ.** [Gr. *elytron*, a cover, covering, case, sheath, from *elyein*, to roll round, wrap up.] One of the wing-sheaths or upper crustaceous membranes which form the outer wings or covering in the tribe of beetles.

El′ze-vir, *a.* Relating to the biblical and classical publications of the Elzevir family of Leyden and Amsterdam, who were celebrated for their fine work, from 1583 to 1680; as, *Elzevir* editions.

El′ze-vir, *n.* A small type, with fine uprights and diagonals and heavy tops and bottoms, introduced by the publishers of this name.

em, *n.* [AS. *em*; L. *em*, the name of the letter *M*.]

1. The thirteenth letter in the alphabet; written *M* or *m*.

2. The unit of measure used by printers in the United States, it being the square of the body of a type named from the letter *m*, which was formerly a square type.

'em, *pron.* [A contraction of ME. *hem*, them.] A contraction or elision of *them*; as, we have seen *'em*.

em-. A prefix often used for *en-* before labials.

ē-mac′ēr-āte, *v.t.* [L. *emaceratus*; *e*, out, and *macerare*, to make soft, weaken.] To make lean. [Obs.]

ē-mac-ēr-ā′tion, *n.* A making lean; emaciation. [Obs.]

ē-mā′ci-āte (-shi-āt), *v.i.*; emaciated, *pt., pp.*; emaciating, *ppr.* [L. *emaciatus*, pp. of *emaciare*, to make lean, cause to waste away; *e*, out, and *macere*, to be lean; *macies*, leanness.] To lose flesh gradually; to waste away; to decay in flesh.

ē-mā′ci-āte, *v.t.* To cause to lose flesh gradually; to waste away to leanness; as, sorrow, anxiety, and disease often *emaciate* the most robust bodies.

ē-mā′ci-āte, *a.* Thin; wasted; emaciated. [Poet.]

ē-mā-ci-ā′tion, *n.* The condition of being excessively lean; the act of emaciating.

ē-mag′ū-lāte, *v.t.* To take spots from; to make clean or pure. [Obs.]

ē-mac-ū-lā′tion, *n.* [L. *emaculare*, from *e*, out, and *macula*, a spot.] The act or operation of freeing from spots and making clean or pure. [Obs.]

em-ȧ-jā′guȧ (-gwȧ), *n.* [Sp. Am.] A tropical shrub of both hemispheres, growing abundantly in moist places. It is remarkable for the strength of its fiber, which is used for making ropes and paper. Also written *majagua*, *mahaut*, etc.

em′ȧ-nănt, *a.* [L. *emanans* (*-antis*), ppr. of *emanare*, to flow out, arise; *e*, out, and *manare*, to flow.] Issuing from something else; flowing forth; becoming apparent; applied to mental or spiritual acts.

em′ȧ-nāte, *v.i.*; emanated, *pt., pp.*; emanating, *ppr.* [L. *emanatus*, pp. of *emanare*, to flow out, arise; *e*, out, and *manare*, to flow.]

1. To issue from a source; to flow forth; as, light *emanates* from the sun.

2. To proceed, as from a source or fountain; to take rise; as, the powers of government in republics *emanate* from the people.

em′ȧ-nāte, *a.* Issuing out; emanant. [Rare.]

em-ȧ-nā′tion, *n.* 1. The act of flowing or proceeding from a fountain-head or origin.

2. That which issues, flows, or proceeds from any source, substance, or body; efflux; effluvium; as, light is an *emanation* from the sun;

wisdom, from God; the authority of laws, from the supreme power.

3. The theory that all things have their being, not from the conscious direct action or will of God, but as issuing from the divine essence.

em-ā-nā'tion-ism, *n.* Belief in the theory of emanation.

em'ā-nā-tist, *n.* A believer in the theory of emanation.

em'ā-nā-tive, *a.* Issuing; flowing forth.

em'ā-nā-tive-ly, *adv.* In the manner of an emanation; by means of an emanation.

em'ā-nā-tō-ry, *a.* Of the nature of an emanation; emanative.

ē-man'ci-pāte, *v.t.*; emancipated, *pt.*, *pp.*; emancipating, *ppr.* [L. *emancipatus*, pp. of *emancipare*, *emancupare*, to emancipate; *e*, out, and *mancipare*, to deliver up or make over as property, by means of a formal act called *mancipium*, from *manceps*, a purchaser, contractor; *manus*, hand, and *capere*, to take.]

1. Generally, to set free or to restore to liberty.

2. To set free from servitude or slavery, by the voluntary act of the proprietor; to liberate; to restore from bondage to freedom; as, to *emancipate* a slave.

3. To free from bondage or restraint of any kind; to liberate from subjection, controlling power, or influence; as, to *emancipate* one from prejudices or error.

4. In ancient Rome, to set free, as a son from subjection to his father, giving him the privilege of managing his affairs as if he were of age.

ē-man'ci-pāte, *a.* Set at liberty; emancipated.

ē-man-ci-pā'tion, *n.* The act of setting free from slavery, servitude, subjection, or dependence; deliverance from bondage or controlling influence; liberation; as, the *emancipation* of slaves by their proprietors.

Emancipation proclamation; the proclamation issued by President Lincoln on January 1, 1863, by which the negroes held in slavery in the Confederate states, then in rebellion against the United States, were declared to be thenceforward free. The proclamation was subsequently confirmed by the thirteenth amendment to the Constitution, which finally emancipated all negroes held as slaves throughout the Union.

Syn.—Manumission, deliverance, liberation, freedom, release, enfranchisement.

ē-man-ci-pā'tion-ist, *n.* An advocate of the emancipation of slaves.

ē-man'ci-pā-tōr, *n.* [LL. *emancipator*, from L. *emancipare*, to emancipate.] One who liberates from bondage or restraint.

ē-man'ci-pā-tō-ry, *a.* Relating to emancipation; having the effect of emancipating.

ē-man'ci-pist, *n.* A name given in Australia to a convict who has been set free.

ē-mär'gi-nāte, *v.t.*; emarginated, *pt.*, *pp.*; emarginating, *ppr.* [L. *emarginatus*, pp. of *emarginare*, to deprive of the edge; *e*, out, and *margo* (*-inis*), edge, margin.]

1. To take away or interrupt the margin of.

2. In microscopy, to render more distinct the margin of.

ē-mär'gi-nāte, ē-mär'gi-nā-ted, *a.* 1. In botany, notched in a peculiar manner at the apex; said of a leaf or a petal.

2. In mineralogy, having all the edges of the primitive form truncated, each by one face.

3. In zoölogy, having the margin broken by an obtuse notch on the segment of a circle.

ē-mär'gi-nāte-ly, *adv.* In the form of notches or interrupted margins.

ē-mär-gi-nā'tion, *n.* The state of being emarginate or notched.

Leaf of *Buxus sempervirens* and Flower of *Primula sinensis*, showing Emarginations or Notches.

ē-mas'cū-lāte, *v.t.*; emasculated, *pt.*, *pp.*; emasculating, *ppr.* [L. *emasculatus*, pp. of *emasculare*; *e*, out, and *masculus*, male.]

1. To castrate; to deprive (a male) of certain functions which characterize the sex; to geld; to deprive of virility.

2. To deprive of masculine strength or vigor; to render effeminate; to vitiate by unmanly softness.

> Women *emasculate* a monarch's reign. —Dryden.

3. To take away the stamens of, as a flower.

4. In literature, to deprive of strength or vigor; as, to *emasculate* a manuscript.

ē-mas'cū-lāte, *a.* Unmanned; deprived of vigor.

ē-mas-cū-lā'tion, *n.* 1. The act of depriving a male of the functions which characterize the sex; castration.

2. The act of depriving of vigor or strength; effeminacy; unmanly weakness.

ē-mas'cū-lā-tōr, *n.* Whoever or whatever emasculates.

ē-mas'cū-lā-tō-ry, *a.* Liable to emasculate; tending to render impotent.

em-bāce', *v.t.* [Obs.] See *Embase.*

em-bāle', *v.t.* 1. To make up into a bundle, bale, or package; to pack.

2. To bind; to inclose; as, to *embale* in golden buskins. [Obs.]

em-ball', *v.t.* To encircle or embrace. [Obs.]

em-bälm' (-bäm'), *v.t.*; embalmed, *pt.*, *pp.*; embalming, *ppr.* [OFr. *embaumer*, *embausmer*; LL. *imbalsamare*, from L. *in*, in, and *balsamum*, balsam, balm.]

1. To preserve, as a dead body, by filling with odoriferous and desiccative spices and drugs, to prevent putrefaction.

2. To fill with sweet scent.

3. To preserve with care and affection from loss or decay; as, to *embalm* in one's affections.

Syn.—Conserve, preserve, treasure, store, enshrine, consecrate.

em-bälm'ēr, *n.* One who embalms.

em-bälm'ment, *n.* Act of embalming.

em-bank', *v.t.*; embanked (-bankt'), *pt.*, *pp.*; embanking, *ppr.* To inclose with a bank; to defend by banks, mounds, or dikes.

em-bank'ment, *n.* 1. The act of surrounding or defending with a bank.

2. A mound or bank raised for various purposes, as for protecting against inundations or for the passage of a railroad.

em-bär', *v.t.*; embarred, *pt.*, *pp.*; embarring, *ppr.* [OFr. *embarrer*, *enbarrer*, to bar, bar in.]

1. To shut, close, or fasten with a bar; to make fast.

2. To inclose so as to hinder egress or escape.

> Where fast *embarred* in mighty brazen wall. —Spenser.

3. To stop; to shut from entering; to hinder; to block up.

> He *embarred* all further trade. —Bacon.

em"bär-cā-de'rō, *n.* [Sp. *embarcar*, to embark.] In Spanish America and the Philippines, a wharf.

em-bär-cā'tion, *n.* See *Embarkation.*

em-bärge', *v.t.* To place on a barge. [Poet.]

em-bär'gō, *n.*; *pl.* **em-bär'gōes.** [Sp. *embargo*, from *embargar*, to arrest, seize, from L. *in*, in, on, and *barra*, a bar.] In commerce, a restraint on ships, or prohibition of sailing, either out of port or into port, or both, which prohibition is by public authority, for a limited time; generally, a prohibition of ships to leave a port.

Civil embargo; one laid on the ships of citizens by their own government.

Hostile embargo; one laid on the ships of an enemy.

em-bär'gō, *v.t.*; embargoed, *pt.*, *pp.*; embargoing, *ppr.* [Sp. and Port. *embargar*, to seize, restrain, block up.] To hinder or prevent (ships) from sailing out of port or into port, or both, by some law or edict of sovereign authority, for a limited time; as, our ships were for a time *embargoed* by an act of Congress.

em-bärk', *v.t.*; embarked (-bärkt'), *pt.*, *pp.*; embarking, *ppr.* [Fr. *embarquer*; Sp. *embarcar*; L. *in*, in, and LL. *barca*, a bark.]

1. To put or cause to enter on board a ship or other vessel or boat; as, the general *embarked* his troops.

2. To engage (a person) in any affair; as, this projector *embarked* his friends in the expedition.

em-bärk', *v.i.* 1. To go on board of a ship, boat, or vessel; as, the troops *embarked* for Lisbon.

2. To engage in any business; to undertake; to invest in; as, the young man *embarked* rashly in speculation and was ruined.

em-bär-kā'tion, *n.* 1. The act of putting on board of a ship or other vessel, or the act of going aboard.

2. That which is embarked; as, an *embarkation* of Jesuits.

em-bärk'ment, *n.* [OFr. *embarquement*, from *embarquer*, to embark.] The act of going or putting aboard a vessel.

em-bärque' (-bärk'), *v.t.*, an obsolete form of *embargo.*

em-bar'rȧss, *v.t.*; embarrassed (-rȧst), *pt.*, *pp.*; embarrassing, *ppr.* [Fr. *embarrasser*, to encumber, obstruct; It. *imbarazzare*, to embarrass; *em-*, L. *in*, in, and Pr. *barras*, a bar.]

1. To perplex; to render intricate; to entangle; as, want of order tends to *embarrass* business.

2. To perplex, as the mind or intellectual faculties; to confuse; as, our ideas are sometimes *embarrassed.*

3. To perplex, as with debts or demands, beyond the means of payment; as, a man or his business is *embarrassed* when he cannot meet his pecuniary engagements.

4. To perplex; to confuse; to disconcert; to abash; as, a young man may be too much *embarrassed* to utter a word.

Syn.—Puzzle, perplex, disconcert, hamper.—We are *puzzled* when our faculties are confused by something we do not understand; we are *perplexed* when our feelings as well as judgment are so affected that we know not how to decide or act; we are *embarrassed* when there is some bar or hindrance upon us which impedes our powers of thought, speech, or motion.

em-bar'rȧss, *n.* [Local, U. S.] 1. An obstruction to navigation in a stream, caused by the lodging of driftwood, trunks of trees, etc.

2. Obsolete form of *embarrassment.*

em-bar'rȧss-ment, *n.* 1. Perplexity; intricacy; entanglement.

2. Confusion of mind.

3. Perplexity arising from insolvency, or from temporary inability to discharge debts.

4. Confusion; abashment.

5. The cause or source of perplexity; obstruction.

em-bāse', *v.t.* To lower in value; to vitiate; to deprave; to impair; to degrade; to debase. [Obs.]

em-bāse'ment, *n.* Act of depraving; depravation; deterioration. [Obs.]

em'bȧs-sāde, *n.* An embassy. [Obs.]

em-bas'sȧ-dōr, *n.* Same as *Ambassador.*

em-bas-sȧ-dō'ri-ăl, *a.* Same as *Ambassadorial.*

em-bas'sȧ-dress, *n.* Same as *Ambassadress.*

em'bȧs-sāge, *n.* 1. The business of an embassy or of an ambassador.

2. An official body of ambassadors.

em'bȧs-sy, *n.* [OFr. *embascée*, *ambassée*; LL. *ambasciata*, from *ambasciare*, *ambactiare*, to go on a mission, from L. *ambactus*, a dependent, vassal.]

1. The message or public function of an ambassador; the charge or employment of a public minister, whether ambassador or envoy; as, the king sent an *embassy*, meaning an envoy, minister, or ministers; or, the king sent a person on an *embassy.*

2. A solemn message; as, nineteen centuries ago, the gospel went forth from Jerusalem on an *embassy* of mingled authority and love.

3. Ironically, an errand.

4. The business-office of an ambassador.

em-bas'tȧrd-ize, *v.t.* To render illegitimate. [Obs.]

em-bāthe', *v.t.* To bathe; to imbathe. [Rare.]

em-bat'tle, *v.t.*; embattled, *pt.*, *pp.*; embattling, *ppr.* [ME. *embatailen*, *embatelen*; OFr. *embataillier*, to array for battle; *en-*, L. *in*, in, and *bataille*, battle.] To arrange in order of battle; to array (troops) for battle; also, to furnish with battlements.

em-bat'tle, *v.i.* To be ranged in order of battle. [Obs.]

em-bat'tled (-tld), *a.* 1. Arrayed in order of battle.

2. Furnished with battlements; in heraldry, having the outline resembling a battlement, as an ordinary.

3. Having been the place of battle; as, an *embattled* plain or field.

A Fesse Embattled.

Embattled molding; in architecture, a molding having indentations like those of a battlement.

em-bat'tle-ment, *n.*

1. A parapet with an indented outline.

2. The act of preparing a fortification with battlements.

Embattled Molding.

em-bāy', *v.t.*; embayed; *pt.*, *pp.*; embaying, *ppr.* 1. To inclose in a bay or inlet; to landlock; to inclose between capes or promontories.

2. To bathe; to wash. [Obs.]

em-bāyle', *v.t.*, obsolete form of *embale.*

em-bāy'ment, *n.* An inclosure of a body of water, as in a bay.

em-bēam', *v.t.* To cause to beam. [Rare.]

em-bed', im-bed', *v.t.*; embedded, *pt.*, *pp.*; embedding, *ppr.* To lay as in a bed; to lay in surrounding matter; as, to *embed* a thing in clay or in sand.

em-bed'ment, *n.* Act of embedding; state of being embedded.

em-bel'lish, *v.t.*; embellished (-lisht), *pt.*, *pp.*; embellishing, *ppr.* [ME. *embelisshen*, *embelisen*, from OFr. *embellir*; It. *imbellire*; L. *in*, in, and *bellus*, beautiful, fair.]

1. To adorn; to beautify; to decorate; to make beautiful or elegant by ornaments; as, we *embellish* the person with rich apparel, a garden with shrubs and flowers, and style with metaphors.

2. To make graceful or elegant; as, to *embellish* manners.

Syn.—Beautify, adorn, ornament, illustrate, decorate.

em-bel'lished (-lisht), *a.* Adorned; decorated; beautified; as, an *embellished* edition of a book.

em-bel'lish-ēr, *n.* One who embellishes.

em-bel'lish-ing-ly, *adv.* So as to embellish.

em-bel'lish-ment, *n.* 1. The act of adorning.

2. Ornament; decoration; anything that

adds beauty or elegance; that which renders anything pleasing to the eye or agreeable to the taste, in dress, furniture, manners, or in the fine arts; as, rich dresses are *embellishments* of the person, virtue is an *embellishment* of the mind, and liberal arts are the *embellishments* of society.

em-bench′, *v.t.* To render bench-like, as in making terraces.

em′bẽr, *n.* [ME. *eymbre, eymery*, pl. *emmeres, emeres*; AS. *æmergean*, pl. *æmyrian*; Ice. *eimyrja*, an ember.] A small coal of fire with ashes; the residuum of wood, coal, or other combustibles not extinguished; used chiefly in the plural; as, to stir up the *embers* of a smoldering fire.

em′bẽr, *n.* [ME. *ymber*; AS. *ymbren, ymbryne*, a running around, a circuit; *ymbe*, around, and *ryne*, from *rinnan*, to run.] A regularly occurring event; a cycle.

em′bẽr-dāys, *n.pl.* Three days (Wednesday, Friday, and Saturday) in each of the four seasons, set apart by the Roman Catholic and some other churches as days of fasting and prayer.

em′bẽr-goose, *n.* A web-footed bird of the genus *Urinator*; the great northern diver, *Urinator imber*; the loon.

em′bẽr-ing, *n.* An ember-day. [Obs.]

em′bẽr-week, *n.* Any one of the four weeks in which ember-days occur, viz., the first week after the first Sunday in Lent, the first after Whitsuntide, the first after September 14th, and the first after December 13th.

em-bez′zle, *v.t.*; embezzled, *pt., pp.*; embezzling, *ppr.* [Early modern Eng. *imbezzle, embesyll*, to weaken, filch; OFr. *imbecille*, weak, feeble.]

1. To appropriate fraudulently to one's own use (what is intrusted to his care and management); as, it is not uncommon for men intrusted with public money to *embezzle* it.

2. To waste; to dissipate in extravagance. [Obs.]

When thou hast *embezzled* all thy store.
—Dryden.

Syn.—Appropriate, peculate, misappropriate, misuse, purloin.

em-bez′zle-ment, *n.* 1. The act of fraudulently appropriating to one's own use the money or goods intrusted to one's care and management; as, the *embezzlements* of public money.

2. The thing appropriated.

em-bez′zlẽr, *n.* One who embezzles.

em-bil′lōw, *v.i.* To swell and rise like billows on the sea. [Rare.]

em-bi-ot′ō-coid, *n.* [Gr. *embios*, in life, living, and *tiktein*, to bring forth, and *eidos*, form.] One of a large family of viviparous fishes found on the Californian coast, called surf-fishes.

em-bit′tẽr, *v.t.*; embittered, *pt., pp.*; embittering, *ppr.* 1. To impart a bitter taste to. [Rare.]

2. To render unhappy, as by wrong or disappointment; to fill with distress or anguish.

em-bit′tẽr-ment, *n.* The condition of being embittered; the act of making bitter; that which makes bitter.

em-blanch′, *v.t.* To make white. [Obs.]

em-blāze′, *v.t.*; emblazed, *pt., pp.*; emblazing, *ppr.* 1. To adorn with glittering embellishments.

No weeping orphan saw his father's stores
Our shrines irradiate, or *emblaze* the floors.
—Pope.

2. To blazon; to paint or adorn with figures armorial; to emblazon.

The imperial ensign, streaming to the wind,
With gems and golden luster rich *emblazed*.
—Milton.

3. To set on fire; to start a blaze.

em-blā′zŏn, *v.t.*; emblazoned, *pt., pp.*; emblazoning, *ppr.* 1. To adorn with figures of heraldry or ensigns armorial.

2. To deck in glaring colors; to display pompously.

3. To celebrate in laudatory terms, or by florid speech.

We find Augustus *emblazoned* by the poets.
—Hakewill.

em-blā′zŏn-ẽr, *n.* 1. A blazoner; one who emblazons; a herald.

2. One who publishes and displays with pomp.

em-blā′zŏn-ing, *n.* The act or art of adorning with ensigns armorial.

em-blā′zŏn-ment, *n.* An emblazoning.

em-blā′zŏn-ry, *n.* Pictures on shields; display of figures; the art of an emblazoner.

em′blem, *n.* [L. *emblema (-atis)*, raised ornaments on vessels; Gr. *emblēma*, an insertion, from *emballein*; *en*, in, and *ballein*, to throw, put.]

1. Inlay; inlaid or mosaic work. [Obs.]

2. A picture representing one thing to the eye and another to the understanding; a painted enigma or a figure representing some obvious history, instructing us in some moral truth, as the image of Scævola holding his hand in the fire, with these words, "*Agere et pati fortiter Romanum est*," to do and to suffer with fortitude is Roman.

3. A painting or representation, intended to hold forth some moral or political instruction; an allusive picture; a typical designation; as, a balance is an *emblem* of justice, a crown is the *emblem* of royalty; a scepter, of power or sovereignty.

Syn.—Symbol, type, token, sign, semblance, similitude.

em′blem, *v.t.* To represent by emblems; to symbolize. [Rare.]

em-blem-at′iç, em-blem-at′iç-ăl, *a.* Pertaining to or comprising an emblem; symbolic; typically representative; representing by some allusion or customary connection; as, a crown is *emblematic* of royalty; whiteness is *emblematic* of purity; *emblematic* worship.

em-blem-at′iç-ăl-ly, *adv.* By way or means of emblems; in the manner of emblems; by way of allusive representation.

em-blem-at′i-cize, *v.t.* To transform into an emblem. [Rare.]

em-blem′ȧ-tist, *n.* A writer or inventor of emblems.

em-blem′ȧ-tīze, *v.t.*; emblematized, *pt., pp.*; emblematizing, *ppr.* To represent by an emblem; to emblemize.

em′blē-ment, *n.* [OFr. *emblaement, emblaiement*, crop, harvest, from *emblaer, emblaier*, from LL. *imbladare*, to sow with grain; L. *in*, in, and *bladum*, grain.] In law, any product of land not spontaneous, but requiring the care and labor of the tenant; as, corn, wheat, and potatoes are *emblements*, while grass, wild grapes, apples, etc., are not; usually in the plural.

em′blem-ize, *v.t.*; emblemized, *pt., pp.*; emblemizing, *ppr.* To represent by an emblem.

em′bliç, *n.* [Name in the Moluccas.] The fruit of an East Indian tree, *Phyllanthus emblica*, used, when dried, for dyeing and tanning, under the name *myrobalan*.

em-bloom′, *v.t.*; embloomed, *pt., pp.*; emblooming, *ppr.* To cover or enrich with bloom. [Rare.]

em-blos′sŏm, *v.t.* Same as *Embloom*.

em-bod′i-ẽr, *n.* One who or that which embodies.

em-bod′i-ment, *n.* 1. The act of embodying; the state of being embodied.

2. The organized body that includes; the thing included; as, the *embodiment* of virtue or of courage in a person.

em-bod′y, *v.t.*; embodied, *pt., pp.*; embodying, *ppr.* 1. To form into a body; to make corporeal; to invest with matter; as, to *embody* the soul or spirit; a form *embodied*.

2. To form or collect into a body or united mass; to collect into a whole; to incorporate; to make a part of the body; to concentrate; as, to *embody* troops; to *embody* detached sentiments.

Syn.—Methodize, systematize, codify, incorporate, aggregate, integrate, compact, introduce, enlist, combine, comprehend.

em-bod′y, *v.i.* To unite in a body, mass, or collection; to coalesce.

em-bōgue′ (-bōg′), *v.i.* [Sp. *embocar*, to enter by the mouth; It. *imboccare*, to feed, instruct; L. *in*, in, and *bucca*, the cheek.] To empty or discharge; said of a river at its mouth. [Rare.]

em-bō′guing (-bō′ging), *n.* The mouth of a river or place where its waters are discharged into the sea. [Rare.]

em-boil′, *v.i.* To swell with rage. [Obs.]

em-boil′, *v.t.* To cause to swell with rage; to excite uncontrollable rage in. [Obs.]

em-boî″te′ment (oṅ-bwot′moṅ), *n.* [Fr., a jointing, fitting in, from *emboîter*, to joint, fit in; OFr. *emboister*, to inclose, fasten up; *en*, in, and *boisi*, a box.] In biology, the doctrine that generation proceeds from an original single germ which contains the germs of all future existences incased one within another.

em-bōld′en, *v.t.*; emboldened, *pt., pp.*; emboldening, *ppr.* To give boldness or courage to; to encourage.

em-bōld′en-ẽr, *n.* One who emboldens.

em-bol′iç, *a.* [L. *embolus*; Gr. *embolos*, from *emballein*, to throw, thrust in.]

1. Relating to embolism; intercalary.

2. In medicine, caused by embolism.

3. In biology, entering by growth; as, *embolic* invagination in developing a gastrula.

em′bō-lism, *n.* 1. Intercalation; the insertion of days, months, or years, in an account of time, to produce regularity. The Greeks made use of the lunar year of 354 days, and to adjust it to the solar year of 365, they added a lunar month every second or third year, which additional month they called *embolimos*.

2. Intercalated time.

3. In medicine, the pathological condition arising from an obstruction in a blood-vessel caused by the presence of an embolus.

em-bō-lis′măl, *a.* Pertaining to intercalation; intercalated; inserted.

em″bō-lis-mat′iç, em″bō-lis-mat′iç-ăl, *a.* Embolismic.

em-bō-lis′miç, em-bō-lis′miç-ăl, *a.* Related to embolism; affected by embolism; as, the *embolismic* year.

em′bō-līte, *n.* [Gr. *embolē*, from *emballein*, to throw in, insert, and *-ite*.] A grayish-green mineral containing both chlorid and bromide of silver.

em-bō′li-um, *n.* [Gr. *embolion*, something thrown in.] A part of the margin of the anterior wing in certain *Hemiptera*.

em′bō-lus, *n.* [L., from Gr. *embolos*, anything put in, a wedge, from *emballein*; *en*, in, and *ballein*, to throw, cast.]

1. Something inserted or acting in another; that which thrusts or drives, as a piston.

2. In medicine, any substance carried by the blood and lodging within a blood-vessel so as to obstruct the normal circulation.

em′bō-ly, *n.* [Gr. *embolē*, an insertion.] In embryology, development in a segmentation-sphere by the movement of one of its sides inward to form a gastrula.

em-bon-point′ (oṅ-boṅ-pwaṅ′), *n.* [Fr.] Plumpness of body or person; roundness of form.

em-bor′dẽr, *v.t.* To adorn with a border.

em-bos′ŏm (-buz′), *v.t.*; embosomed, *pt., pp.*; embosoming, *ppr.* To furnish comfort, safety, or protection in one's bosom; hence, to take into one's affections; to befriend; to encourage; to nourish.

em-boss′, *v.t.*; embossed (-bost′), *pt., pp.*; embossing, *ppr.* [ME. *embossen*; OFr. *embosser*, to swell up, rise in bunches; *en*, in, on, and *bosse*, a bunch, protuberance.]

1. To form bosses, knobs, etc., in; to fashion in relief or raised work; to cut or form with prominent figures.

2. To form with bosses; to cover with protuberances.

3. To drive hard in hunting, till a deer foams, or a dog's knees swell. [Obs.]

em-boss′, *v.t.* [Fr. *emboîter*, for *emboister*, from *boîte, boiste*, a box.] To inclose, as in a box; to include; to cover. [Obs.]

em-boss′, *v.t.* [It. *imboscare*, from *bosco*, a wood.] To inclose in a wood; to conceal in a thicket. [Obs.]

em-bossed′ (-bost′), *a.* 1. Formed or covered with bosses or raised figures.

2. Armored and shielded. [Obs.]

3. Enlarged by swelling; puffed out. [Obs.]

em-boss′ẽr, *n.* 1. One who embosses.

2. An instrument, die, or press for embossing.

em-boss′ing, *n.* The formation of ornamental figures in relief; the figures thus formed.

em-boss′ment, *n.* 1. A prominence, like a boss; a jut; also, the act of embossing.

2. Relief; figures in relief; raised work.

em-bot′tle, *v.t.*; embottled, *pt., pp.*; embottling, *ppr.* To put into a bottle; to bottle; to include or confine in a bottle.

em-bou-chūre′ (oṅ-bö-shūr′), *n.* [Fr.] 1. A mouth or aperture, as of a river, cannon, etc.

2. The mouth-hole of a wind-instrument of music; also, the fitting of the lips and tongue in playing a wind-instrument.

em-bōw′, *v.t.* To form like a bow; to arch; to vault. [Obs.]

em-bow′el, *v.t.*; emboweled or embowelled, *pt., pp.*; emboweling or embowelling, *ppr.* 1. To sink or inclose in another substance.

2. To take out the entrails of; to eviscerate; to take out the internal parts of; as, to *embowel* or disembowel minerals from the earth.

em-bow′el-ẽr, *n.* One that takes out the bowels.

em-bow′el-ment, *n.* The act of taking out the bowels; evisceration.

em-bow′ẽr, *v.i.*; embowered, *pt., pp.*; embowering, *ppr.* To lodge or rest in a bower.

em-bow′ẽr, *v.t.* To cover with a bower; to shelter with trees.

em-bōwl′, *v.t.* To make into the shape of a bowl. [Obs.]

em-box′, *v.t.* To shut up in a box; to furnish with a box.

em-boxed′ (-boxt′), *a.* Inclosed, as in a box.

em-boysse′ment, *n.*, old form of *ambushment*.

em-brāce′, *v.t.*; embraced (-brāst′), *pt., pp.*; embracing, *ppr.* [OFr. *embracer*; It. *imbracciare*; LL. *imbrachiare*, to take in the arms, embrace; L. *in*, in, and *brachium*, arm.]

1. To take, clasp, or inclose in the arms; to press to the bosom, in token of affection.

Paul called to him the disciples and *embraced* them. —Acts xx. 1.

2. To seize eagerly; to lay hold on; to receive or take with willingness that which is offered; as, to *embrace* the Christian religion; to *embrace* the opportunity of doing a favor.

3. To comprehend; to include or take in; as, natural philosophy *embraces* many sciences.

4. To comprise; to inclose; to encompass; to contain; to encircle.

Low at his feet a spacious plain is placed,
Between the mountain and the stream *embraced*. —Denham.

5. To find; to take; to accept.

Fleance—must *embrace* the fate
Of that dark hour. —Shak.

6. In biology, to wholly or partly surround,

as the stalk of a leaf around a stem, or the wings of an insect appressed to the body in repose.

Syn.—Clasp, encircle, hug, comprehend, accept, contain, espouse.

em-brāce′, *v.i.* To join in an embrace.

em-brāce′, *n.* Inclosure or clasp with the arms; pressure to the bosom with the arms; conjugal endearment.

em-brāce′, *v.t.* [OFr. *embracer*, *embraser*, to set on fire, incite, instigate; *en*, in, and *braise*, live coals.] To attempt to influence corruptly, as a jury.

em-brāce′ment, *n.* 1. A clasp in the arms; a hug; embrace.

2. Hostile hug; grapple. [Obs.]

3. Comprehension; state of being contained; inclosure. [Obs.]

4. Willing acceptance. [Obs.]

em-brā′cēr, em-brāce′ŏr, *n.* [OFr. *embraceor*, *embraseor*, from *embracer*, *embraser*, to set on fire, incite, instigate.] One who attempts to influence a jury corruptly.

em-brā′cēr, *n.* The person who embraces.

em-brā′cēr-y, *n.* In law, an attempt to influence a jury corruptly to one side, by promises, persuasions, entreaties, money, entertainments, or the like.

em-brā′cive, *a.* Inclined to embrace; having a love for hugging; receptive.

em-brāid′, *v.t.* To upbraid; to put up in braids, as the hair. [Obs.]

em-brail′, *v.t.* To haul up by brails. [Rare.]

em-branch′ment, *n.* Ramification, as in a tree or a river.

em-brañ′gle, im-brañ′gle, *v.t.* To mix up in confusion; to make complicated; to bewilder.

em-brā′sŏr, *n.* Same as first *Embracer*.

em-brā′ṣūre (-zhūr), *n.*, obsolete form of *embrace*.

em-brā′ṣūre (-zhūr), *n.* [Fr., from OFr. *embraser*, to skew, or splay the jambs of a door or window; *en*, in, on, and *braser*, to skew.]

1. An opening in a wall or parapet, through which cannon are pointed and discharged.

2. In architecture, the enlargement of the aperture of a door or window, on the inside of the wall, for giving greater play for the opening of the door or casement, or for admitting more light.

em-brāve′, *v.t.* 1. To embellish; to make showy. [Obs.]

2. To inspire with bravery; to make bold. [Obs.]

em-brawn′, *v.t.* To make muscular; to impart strength to. [Obs.]

em-brēathe′ment, *n.* The act of inspiration in breathing. [Rare.]

em-brew′, *v.t.* Same as *Imbrue*.

em-bright′, *v.t.*, obsolete form of *brighten*.

em-brōad′en, *v.t.* To make broader. [Rare.]

em′brō-cāte, *v.t.*; embrocated, *pt.*, *pp.*; embrocating, *ppr.* [LL. *embrocatus*, pp. of *embrocare*, to foment.] In surgery and medicine, to moisten and rub, as a diseased part of the body, with a liquid substance, as with spirit, oil, etc., by means of a cloth or sponge.

em-brō-cā′tion, *n.* 1. The act of moistening and rubbing a diseased part with a cloth or sponge dipped in some liquid substance, as spirit, oil, etc.

2. The liquid or lotion with which an affected part is rubbed or washed; a kind of liniment.

em-brōgl′iō (-brōl′yō), *n.* Same as *Imbroglio*.

em-broid′, *v.t.* Same as *Embroider*.

em-broid′ēr, *v.t.*; embroidered, *pt.*, *pp.*; embroidering, *ppr.* [OFr. *embroder*; *em-* (L. *in*), in, and *broder*, to broider, from *bord*, LL. *bordus*, a border, margin.]

1. To border with ornamental needlework or figures; to adorn with raised figures of needlework, as cloth, stuffs, or muslin.

2. Figuratively, to attach ornamental additions to; hence, to exaggerate, especially in narrative; as, the story comes out beautifully *embroidered*.

em-broid′ēr-ēr, *n.* One who embroiders.

em-broid′ēr-y, *n.*; *pl.* **em-broid′ēr-ieṣ**. 1. Designs in gold, silver, silk, or other thread, formed by the needle on cloth, stuffs, and muslin; variegated needlework.

2. Any variegation or diversity of figures and colors; as, the natural *embroidery* of meadows; rhetorical *embroidery*.

em-broil′, *v.t.*; embroiled, *pt.*, *pp.*; embroiling, *ppr.* [OFr. *embroillir*, *embrouillir*, to become troubled, confused.]

1. To perplex or entangle; to intermix in confusion.

> The Christian antiquities at Rome are *embroiled* with fable and legend. —Addison.

2. To involve in troubles or perplexities; to disturb or distract by connection with something else; to throw into confusion or commotion; to perplex.

> The royal house *embroiled* in civil war. —Dryden.

em-broil′, *n.* Same as *Embroilment*.

em-broil′ēr, *n.* One who instigates or promotes embroilments.

em-broil′ment, *n.* [OFr. *embrouillement*, from *embrouiller*, to embroil.] A state of contention, perplexity, or confusion; disturbance.

em-bronze′, *v.t.*; embronzed, *pt.*, *pp.*; embronzing, *ppr.* To make a statue or figure of in bronze.

em-broth′el, *v.t.* To inclose in a brothel. [Obs.]

em-brown′, *v.t.*; embrowned, *pt.*, *pp.*; embrowning, *ppr.* 1. To render brown or dark-colored.

2. To make dark, dim, or obscure; to render dusky.

em-brūe′, *v.t.* Same as *Imbrue*.

em-brūte′, *v.t.*; embruted, *pt.*, *pp.*; embruting, *ppr.* To make brute-like.

em-bry-ō-, em-bry-o-ni-. Combining forms from Gr. *embryon*, an embryo, fetus, a thing newly born; used in biology, zoölogy, etc., to indicate connection with or relation to an embryo or fetus; as, *embryo*logy; *embryoni*form.

em′bry-ō, *n.*; *pl.* **em′bry-ōṣ**. [Gr. *embryon*, the embryo, fetus, a thing newly born, neut. of *embryos*, growing in; *en*, in, and *bryein*, to swell, be full.] In biology, the fecundated or fertilized germ of an individual organism; a rudimentary animal in the ovum or a rudimentary plant in the ovule; an organism which, when developed, becomes an individual of its species.

In embryo; a stage in which anything is conceived and planned, but not carried into execution; as, a benevolent enterprise *in embryo*.

em′bry-ō, *a.* Pertaining to or denoting anything in its first rudiments or undeveloped state; as, an *embryo* leaf.

Embryo bud; a bud located at an unusual place on a plant, as under the bark, fitted to develop when normal buds are accidentally destroyed; called also *adventitious bud*.

em-bry-oc′tō-ny, *n.* [*Embryo-*, and Gr. *-ktonia*, from *kteinein*, to kill.] The production of abortion by the destruction of the embryo.

em″bry-ō-ġen′iç, *a.* Relating to embryogeny.

em-bry-oġ′e-ny, em-bry-oġ′ō-ny, *n.* [*Embryo-*, and Gr. *-geneia*, from *-genēs*, producing.] The science treating of the origin, growth, and development of organisms.

em-bry-oġ′rà-phy, *n.* [*Embryo-*, and Gr. *-graphia*, from *graphein*, to write.] A description or treatise upon embryos and their development.

em″bry-ō-loġ′iç, em″bry-ō-loġ′iç-ăl, *a.* Relating to embryology.

em-bry-ol′ō-ġist, *n.* One who is skilled in the science of embryology.

em-bry-ol′ō-ġy, *n.* [*Embryo-*, and Gr. *-logia*, from *legein*, to speak.] A branch of biological science devoted to the investigation of all the phenomena connected with embryonic existence, including its relation to the completely developed adult.

em′bry-ŏn, *n.* and *a.* Same as *Embryo*.

em′bry-ō-năl, em′bry-ous, *a.* Related to an embryo.

em′bry-ō-nāte, em′bry-ō-nā-ted, *a.* Containing an embryo; in the state of an embryo.

em-bry-on′iç, em-bry-ot′iç, *a.* Like an embryo; rudimentary; in the state of an embryo.

Embryonic sac; an embryo-sac.

em″bry-ō-nif′ēr-ous, *a.* [*Embryoni-*, and L. *ferre*, to bear.] Possessed of an embryo.

em-bry-on′i-form, *a.* [*Embryoni-*, and L. *forma*, form.] Shaped like an embryo.

Em-bry-oph′y-tà, *n.pl.* [*Embryo-*, and Gr. *phyton* (pl. *phyta*), a plant.] A subdivision of the vegetable kingdom according to Engler and Prantl, embracing all plants having vascular tissue and produced through embryonic generation.

Embryophyta asiphonogama; one of the two divisions of the *Embryophyta*, coextensive with vascular cryptogams of other botanists.

Embryophyta siphonogama; one of the two divisions of the *Embryophyta*, coextensive with *Phanerogamia* of other botanists.

em″bry-ō-plas′tiç, *a.* [*Embryo-*, and Gr. *plastos*, from *plassein*, to form.] Auxiliary in the formation of an embryo.

em′bry-ō-saç, *n.* [*Embryo-*, and L. *saccus*, a sac.] That cell in the ovule of a phanerogam which contains the embryonal vesicle.

em′bry-ō-sçōpe, *n.* [*Embryo-*, and Gr. *skopein*, to view.] An optical instrument for observing the formation and development of embryos in eggs.

em-bry-ot′e-gà, *n.* [*Embryo-*, and Gr. *tegos*, a roof.] A kind of hard lid or cap covering part of the embryo in some seeds before germination, and pushed off by the growth of the radicle.

em-bry-ot′iç, *a.* See *Embryonic*.

em-bry-ot′ō-my, *n.* [*Embryo-*, and Gr. *tomē*, a cutting.]

1. A cutting or forcible separation of the fetus from the womb.

2. The process and practice of dissecting embryos in the interest of science.

em′bry-ō-troph, *n.* [*Embryo-*, and Gr. *trophē*, nourishment.] The part of the egg furnishing nourishment to the embryo.

em′bry-ous, *a.* Same as *Embryonal*.

em-bulk′, *v.t.* To effect an increase of in bulk. [Rare.]

em-bŭrse′, *v.t.* Same as *Imburse*.

em-bush′, *v.t.*, obsolete form of *ambush*.

em-bush′ment, *n.*, obsolete form of *ambushment*.

em-bus-qué′ (kā′), *n.* [Fr. lit. in ambush or in hiding.] A shirker; a slacker. One who has been mobilized, but has used political influence to secure a billet far removed from the firing line. [Slang.]

em-bus′y (-biz′i), *v.t.* To employ. [Obs.]

ēme, *n.*, old form of *eam*.

e-meer′, *n.* See *Emir*.

ē-mend′, *v.t.*; emended, *pt.*, *pp.*; emending, *ppr.* [L. *emendare*, to correct, amend; *e*, out, and *menda*, *mendum*, a fault, blemish.]

1. To make better; to amend. [Rare.]

2. To change the form of or to revise in order to correct and improve; said of a work.

ē-mend′à-ble, *a.* [L. *emendabilis*, from *emendare*, to correct, amend.] Capable of being emended or corrected.

em′en-dāte-ly, *adv.* Faultlessly.

em-en-dā′tion, *n.* [L. *emendatio*, from *emendare*, to correct, amend.]

1. The act of altering for the better, or correcting what is erroneous or faulty; correction.

2. An alteration for the better; correction of an error or fault; as, the last edition of the book contains many *emendations*.

em′en-dā-tŏr, *n.* One who emends; one who edits critically; a corrector.

ē-mend′à-tō-ry, *a.* Relating to emendation or correction.

ē-mend′ēr, *n.* Same as *Emendator*.

ē-men′di-cāte, *v.t.* and *v.i.* [L. *emendicatus*, pp. of *emendicare*, to obtain by begging.] To beg. [Obs. See *Mendicate*.]

em′ēr-ăld, *n.* [ME. *emeraude*; OFr. *esmeraude*, *esmeralde*; L. *smaragdus*; Gr. *smaragdos*, *maragdos*, a precious stone supposed to be the emerald.]

1. A precious stone of the beryl variety, of a rich green color and highly valued, ranking with the diamond and ruby as one of the most costly gems. [See *Beryl*.]

2. A rich, bright green color, similar to that of the *emerald*.

3. A printing-type, in size between nonpareil and minion.

em′ēr-ăld, *a.* 1. Having the characteristics of an emerald; especially of a typical green.

2. Printed with the emerald type; as, an *emerald* edition.

Emerald copper; a silicate of copper, crystalline and emerald in color; called also *dioptase*.

Emerald green; a vivid light green pigment obtained from aceto-arsenite of copper and used in oil-paints or water-colors; sometimes also used adjectively.

Emerald Isle; a cognomen first applied to Ireland, because of its brilliant verdure, by Dr. William Drennan in his poem "Erin."

Emerald nickel; a green incrustation of carbonate of nickel; zaratite.

Emerald spodumene; an emerald-green variety of spodumene or lithia emerald, found in North Carolina; also called *hiddenite*.

em′ēr-ăld-fish, *n.* A goby, *Gobionellus oceanicus*, found in the West Indies and the Gulf of Mexico, and distinguished by the bright green and blue color at the root of the tongue.

em′ēr-ăld-ine, *n.* A green dyestuff produced by subjecting goods treated with aniline black to some kind of acid before the black color is fully set.

em′ēr-ăld-moth, *n.* A moth, grass-green in color, of the genus *Hipparchus*.

em′ēr-aud, *n.* An emerald. [Obs.]

ē-mērġe′, *v.i.*; emerged, *pt.*, *pp.*; emerging, *ppr.* [L. *emergere*, to rise out, rise up; *e*, out, and *mergere*, to dip, immerse.] To rise out of a fluid or other covering; to come forth from concealment or obscurity; to appear; to come in sight; as, to *emerge* from the sea; the sun *emerges* from the eclipse; the deer *emerged* from the dusk; the people *emerged* from savagery.

ē-mēr′ġence, *n.* [L. *emergens* (-*entis*), ppr. of *emergere*, to rise up, rise out.]

1. The act of rising out of a fluid or coming forth from any concealment.

2. In botany, any one of various outgrowths coming from the tissue beneath the epidermis, as a hair or a prickle.

ē-mēr′ġen-cy, *n.*; *pl.* **ē-mēr′ġen-cieṣ**. A sudden or unexpected occurrence or combination of occurrences demanding prompt action; urgent necessity; as, she could do it in an *emergency*.

Syn.—Exigency, crisis, strait, necessity, urgency.

ē-mēr′ġent, *a.* 1. Rising out of a fluid, or anything that covers or surrounds.

2. Coming suddenly; sudden; casual; unexpected; hence, calling for immediate action or remedy; urgent; pressing; as, an *emergent* occasion.

3. Relating to or prepared for emergencies.

Emergent year; the date from which time is

historically computed; the first year of an epoch; as, the *emergent year* of the United States is 1776; the birth of Christ marks the *emergent year* of Christianity.

ē-mẽr′ġent-ly, *adv.* In an emergent manner; by emergency.

ē-mẽr′ġent-ness, *n.* The condition or quality of being emergent. [Rare.]

em′ẽr-il, *n.* 1. Emery. [Obs.]

2. A diamond used by a glazier.

ē-mer′it-ed, *a.* Honorably retired from public and active service after having served the full term; an obsolete form of *emeritus*

ē-mer′i-tus, *a.* [L., having served one's time as a soldier, from *emereri*, to serve out one's time; *e*, out, and *mereri*, to serve, earn, merit.] Retired from long, active service on account of age or infirmity, but retained on the professional rolls; as, professor *emeritus*.

ē-mer′i-tus, *n.*; *pl.* **ē-mer′i-tī.** One who has been honorably discharged from public service; usually applied to a member of a profession.

em′ẽr-odṣ, em′ẽr-oidṣ, *n.pl.* [OFr. *emmeroide*; L. *hæmorrhois*, a hemorrhoid.] Hemorrhoids; piles. [Rare.]

ē-mẽrsed′ (-mẽrst′), *a.* [L. *emersus*, pp. of *emergere*, to rise up, rise out.] In botany, (a) standing above surrounding water; (b) standing above surrounding leaves. [See *Emerge.*]

ē-mẽr′sion, *n.* [From L. *emergere*, to come forth, rise out; *e*, out, and *mergere*, to dip, merge.]

1. The act of emerging from anything, either literally or figuratively; as, *emersion* from water or from difficulties; opposed to *immersion*.

2. In astronomy, the reappearance of a heavenly body after an eclipse; as, the *emersion* of the moon from the shadow of the earth; also, the time of reappearance; the reappearance of a star which has been hidden by the effulgence of the sun's light.

em′ẽr-y, *n.* [OFr. *emeril*, emery; It. *smeriglio*, from Gr. *smyris*, *smiris*, emery.] A massive variety of corundum, in structure finely granular, its color varying from a deep gray to a bluish or blackish gray, sometimes brownish; used in polishing metals and hard stones.

em′ẽr-y=bag, *n.* A small bag filled with emery and used for cleaning and sharpening needles.

em′ẽr-y=bōard, *n.* Paper-pulp mixed with emery dust and shaped as desired.

em′ẽr-y=cloth, em′ẽr-y=pā″pẽr, *n.* Cloth or paper coated with glue and emery dust and used for polishing and scouring purposes.

em′ẽr-y=wheel, *n.* A polishing and grinding wheel made of emery or covered with emery; called also *buff-wheel* and *glazer*.

em′e-sis, *n.* [Gr. *emesis*, a vomiting, from *emeein*, to vomit.] A vomiting; discharges from the stomach by the mouth.

ē-met′iç, ē-met′iç-ăl, *a.* [L. *emeticus*; Gr. *emetikos*, causing vomiting, from *emeein*, to vomit.] Inducing to vomit; exciting the stomach to discharge its contents by the esophagus and mouth.

ē-met′iç, *n.* A medicine that provokes vomiting.

ē-met′iç-ăl-ly, *adv.* In such a manner as to excite vomiting.

em′e-tine, *n.* [*Emetic* and *-ine.*] A white or yellowish powder, supposed to be an alkaloid, which is obtained from ipecacuanha-root. [See *Emetic.*]

em′e-tō-çà-thär″tiç, *a.* Causing both vomiting and purging simultaneously

em-e-tol′ō-ġy, *n.* [Gr. *emetos*, a vomiting, and *-logia*, from *legein*, to speak.] That branch of medicine which deals with emetics, their nature and effects; the diagnosis and treatment of emesis.

em″e-tō-mọr′phi-à, *n.* Same as *Apomorphine.*

ē′meū, ē′mew, *n.* See *Emu.*

é-meute′ (ā-mėt′), *n.* [Fr.] An insurrection; a seditious uprising.

e. m. f. An abbreviation in physics for electromotive force.

em-fōrth′, *prep* [ME., contr. of *evenforth.*] In accordance with. [Obs.]

em-gal′là, *n* A native name for the South African wart-hog.

em′i-çănt, *a.* [L. *emicans* (*-antis*), ppr. of *emicare*, to break forth, spring out; *e*, out, and *micare*, to sparkle, quiver.] Flashing forth like sparks. [Rare.]

em-i-çā′tion, *n.* A sparkling; a flying off in small particles, as from heated iron or fermenting liquors.

ē-miç′tion, *n.* [L. *e*, out, and *mictio*, from *mingere*, to urinate.] The discharging of urine; urine. [Rare.]

ē-miç′tō-ry, *a.* Promoting a urinary flow; diuretic.

ē-miç′tō-ry, *n.* That which promotes a flow of urine; a diuretic.

em′i-grănt, *a.* [L. *Emigrans* (*-antis*), ppr. of *emigrare*, to emigrate.] Removing, or having removed, from one place or country to another distant place, with a view to reside.

em′i-grănt, *n.* One who removes his habitation or quits one country or region to settle in another.

em′i-grāte, *v.i.*; emigrated, *pt.*, *pp.*; emigrating, *ppr.* [L. *emigratus*, pp. of *emigrare*, to move away, depart from a place; *e*, out, and *migrare*, to move, depart.] To quit one country, state, or region and settle in another; to remove from one country or state to another, for the purpose of residence; as, Germans, Swiss, Irish, and Scotch *emigrate* in great numbers to America; inhabitants of New England *emigrate* to the western states. The word *migrate* lacks the element of permanent settlement, being applied to birds and wandering tribes. [See *Migrate.*]

em′i-grāte, *a.* Roving; migratory. [Obs.]

em-i-grā′tion, *n.* 1. Removal of inhabitants from one country or state to another for the purpose of residence, as from Europe to America, or, in America, from the Atlantic states to the western.

2. Emigrants taken collectively; as, the *emigration* to the United States.

em-i-grā′tion-ăl, *a.* Pertaining to emigration.

em-i-grā′tion-ist, *n.* One who is in favor of or helps emigration.

em′i-grā-tōr, *n.* An emigrant. [Rare.]

é-mï-gré′ (ā-mē-grā′), *n.* [Fr.] A Frenchman who left his country because of the revolution which began in 1789.

em′i-nence, *n.* [L. *eminentia*, from *eminens* (*-entis*), excellent, prominent, ppr. of *eminere*, to stand out, project.]

1. Elevation or height, in a literal sense; but usually, a rising ground, a hill of moderate elevation above the adjacent ground.

> The temple of honor ought to be seated on an *eminence.* —Burke.

2. An elevated situation among men; a place or station above men in general, either in rank, office, or celebrity; as, *eminence* is always exposed to envy.

3. A title of honor given to cardinals and others; as, His *Eminence.*

em′i-nen-cy, *n.* Condition or state of being eminent; eminence.

em′i-nent, *a.* [L. *eminens* (*-entis*), ppr. of *eminere*, to stand out, project.]

1. High; lofty; as, an *eminent* place.

2. Exalted in rank; high in office; dignified; distinguished; as, ambassadors hold *eminent* stations in society.

3. High in public estimation; conspicuous; distinguished above others; remarkable; as, an *eminent* historian or poet.

Right of eminent domain; the right which a government possesses of taking the property of its subjects for necessary public uses, at a fair valuation.

Syn.—Famous, illustrious, celebrated, noted, distinguished.

em′i-nent-ly, *adv.* In a high degree; in a degree to attract observation; in a degree to be conspicuous and distinguished from others; as, to be *eminently* learned or useful.

ē-mïr′, *n.* [Ar. *amīr*, *emīr*, a commander, ruler, prince.] A title of dignity among the Turks and Mohammedans, denoting a prince; a title of Turkish officials of superior rank, such as those at the head of departments of the government service. [See *Ameer.*]

e-mïr′ship, *n.* The office held by an emir.

em-is-sā′ri-um, *n.* See *Emissary*, n.

em′is-sā-ry, *n.* [L. *emissarius*, from *emittere*, to send out; *e*, out, and *mittere*, to send.]

1. A person sent on a mission with authority to act for another; particularly, in a cause or for a purpose which has some ulterior motive.

2. An agent or plotter sent out by any power at war to create a feeling of unrest or dissatisfaction among the enemy; a spy; a scout.

3. A lobbyist employed by firms, corporations, or private interests, for the furtherance of special legislation.

4. An outlet or opening whereby water or other liquid can be conducted from one receptacle to another, or from river to lake

5. In anatomy, an excretory or connecting duct, such as the veins passing from the cranium through apertures in its walls; as, the mastoid *emissary.*

Syn.—Spy, scout.—An *emissary* differs from a *spy*. A *spy* in war is one who enters an enemy's camp or territory to learn the condition of the enemy; an *emissary* may be a secret agent employed not only to detect the schemes of an opposing party, but to influence their councils. A *spy* in war must be concealed, or he suffers death; an *emissary* may in some cases be known as the agent of an adversary, without incurring similar hazard. A *scout* is concerned with military operations only, has an official standing in the service, and, if captured, is dealt with as an honorable prisoner-of-war.

em′is-sā-ry, *a.* 1. Pertaining to one sent forth on a spying or investigating expedition.

2. In anatomy, applying to ducts which emit fluids or serve as connecting canals; as, *emissary* veins.

em′is-sā-ry-ship, *n.* Office or rank of an emissary.

ē-mis′sile, *a.* In zoölogy, capable of protrusion or of emission.

ē-mis′sion (-mish′un), *n.* [L. *emissio*, from *emittere*, to send out.]

1. The act of sending or throwing out; as, the *emission* of light from the sun; the *emission* of odors from plants.

2. The act of sending abroad, or into circulation, notes of a state or of a private corporation; as, the *emission* of bills of credit or treasury notes.

3. That which is sent out or issued at one time; an impression or a number of notes issued by one act of government; as, notes or bills of various *emissions* were in circulation.

Emission theory; Newton's theory relative to light. [See *Corpuscular theory* under *Corpuscular.*]

em-is-si′tious (-sish′us), *a.* [L. *emissitius*, from *emittere*, to send out.] Looking or narrowly examining; prying. [Obs.]

ē-mis′sive, *a.* Giving out, radiating, or emitting.

em-is-siv′i-ty, *n.* Rate at which emission takes place; capacity for emission.

ē-mis′sō-ry, *a.* Having a duct or ducts for emitting; emissive.

ē-mit′, *v.t.*; emitted, *pt.*, *pp.*; emitting, *ppr.* [L. *emittere*, to send out; *e*, out, and *mittere*, to send.]

1. To send forth; to throw or give out; as, fire *emits* heat; the sun and moon *emit* light; animal bodies *emit* perspiration.

2. To let fly; to discharge; to dart or shoot; as, to *emit* an arrow. [Rare.]

3. To issue forth, as an order or decree. [Rare.]

4. To issue, as notes or bills of credit; to print and send into circulation.

ē-mit′tent, *a.* [L. *emittens*, ppr. of *emittere*, to send out.] Sending out or forth.

em-măn-ché′ (-shā′), *a.* [Fr., pp. of *emmancher*, to put a handle on; *en*, in, on, and *manche*, a handle, haft, from L. *manus*, handle.]

1. Possessing a handle similar to that of an ax.

2. In heraldry, having a wedge-shaped design or pile at the side of the field.

em-man′tle, *v.t.* To protect or cover over; to encircle as with a wall for fortifications. [Obs.]

Em-man′ū-el, *n.* 1. A variant of *Immanuel* (God with us), the Hebrew name for Christ.

2. [e—] A popular ointment of the sixteenth century.

em-mär′ble, *v.t.* To work in marble; to decorate with or turn into marble; also written *enmarble.* [Obs.]

em-me-lē′ià (-yà), *n.* [Gr. *emmeleia*, harmony, unison, from *emmelēs*; *en*, in, and *melos*, song.] The Grecian musical term for (a) harmony, (b) a stately dance in drama or tragedy, or (c) the music accompanying the latter.

em-men′à-gogue (-gog), *n.* [Fr. *emmenagogue*; Gr. *emmēna*, menses, neut. pl. of *emmēnos*, monthly, and *agogos*, a leading, drawing forth, from *agein*, to lead.] A substance with medicinal properties designed to assist and promote the menstrual discharges.

em-men-i-op′à-thy, *n.* [Gr. *emmēna*, menses, and *-patheia*, from *pathos*, suffering.] Disordered or faulty menstruation.

em-me-nol′ō-ġy, *n.* [Gr. *emmēna*, monthly, menses, and *-logia*, from *legein*, to speak.] That division or branch of the science of medicine dealing with menstruation, its disorders, and causes.

em′mens-ite, *n.* A picric acid explosive for projectiles, invented by S. H. Emmens, for whom it is named.

em′met, *n.* An ant or pismire.

em-me-trō′pi-à, *n.* [Gr. *emmetros*, in measure, measured; *en*, in, and *metros*, measure, and *ōps*, *ōpos*, eye.] The normal power of optic refraction, whereby light is concentrated to a single point on the retina.

em-me-trop′iç, *a.* Pertaining to the normal refractive condition of the eye.

em-met′rō-py, *n.* Same as *Emmetropia.*

em-mew′, *v.t.* [*Em-* (L. *in*, in), and *mew*, a cage.] To mew; imprison; confine; coop up. [Obs.]

em-möve′, *v.t.* [Obs.] See *Emove.*

em′ō-din, *n.* A crystalline substance, reddish-yellow in color, found especially in rhubarb-root and buckthorn-bark.

em-ol-les′cence, *n.* [L. *emollescens*, softening, ppr. of *emollescere*; *e-*, out, and *mollescere*, freq. of *mollire*, to soften.] In metallurgy, that degree of softness in a fusible body which alters its shape; the first or lowest degree of fusibility.

ē-mol′li-āte, *v.t.*; emolliated, *pt.*, *pp.*; emolliating, *ppr.* [From L. *emollire*, to soften.] To soften; to render effeminate.

ē-mol′lient, *n.* [L. *emolliens* (*-entis*), ppr. of *emollire*, to soften; *e-*, out, and *mollire*, to soften, from *mollis*, soft.] A warm, external application of an oleaginous, starchy, or mucilaginous nature, which allays irritation and alleviates inflammatory soreness, swelling, and pain, and, in the latter case, contributes either to a resolution or to suppuration, according to the stage at which the application is made.

ē-mol′lient, *a.* Softening; making supple; acting as an emollient; as, oatmeal is *emollient*.

em-ol-li′tion (-lish′un), *n.* The act of softening or relaxing.

ē-mol′ū-ment, *n.* [L. *emolumentum*, gain, profit, advantage, from *emolire*, to accomplish, effect; *e*, out, and *molire*, to exert oneself.]

1. The profit arising from office or employment; that which is received as a compensation for services or which is annexed to the possession of office, as salary, fees, and perquisites.

2. Advantage; gain in general; that which promotes the public or private good.

Syn.—Profit, gain, benefit, improvement, service, avail, advantage.

ē-mol-ū-men′tăl, *a.* Producing profit; useful; profitable; advantageous. [Rare.]

ē-mŏng′, ē-mŏngst′, *prep.*, obsolete forms of *among*.

ē-mō′tion, *n.* [From L. *emovere*, to move out, stir up, agitate; *e-*, out, and *movere*, to move.]

1. A moving of the mind or soul; hence, any agitation of mind or excitement of the feelings, whether agreeable or disagreeable; particularly, an excitement of the mind manifesting itself by some sensible effect on the body; affection; desire; also, state of excitement of the physical feelings.

2. In psychology, the faculty of feeling, of reacting to mental impressions involving the sentiments; the sensibility; as, the *emotions* of an individual are equivalent to the sum total of his sentient powers. *Emotions* are principally and primarily applicable to the sensible changes and visible effects which particular passions produce on the frame.

3. Disturbed motion. [Obs.]

Syn.—Agitation, perturbation, commotion, excitement, disturbance, feeling.

ē-mō′tion-ăl, *a.* 1. Pertaining to emotion; characterized by emotion.

2. Arising from or appealing to the emotions; of a nature to move the feelings or passions; moving; touching.

3. Readily receptive to emotions; excitable; easily moved; as, an *emotional* nature.

ē-mō′tion-ăl-ism, *n.* The cultivation of the superficial emotions; the tendency to yield to the emotions or to exalt the emotions; to view matters more from the standpoint of feeling than of reason or morals.

ē-mō′tion-ăl-ist, *n.* 1. One characterized by emotionalism; an excitable or impressionable person.

2. One who practises the art of exciting emotions in others; a sensationalist.

ē-mō-tion-al′i-ty, *n.* The quality or condition of being emotional.

ē-mō′tion-ăl-īze, *v.t.*; emotionalized, *pt., pp.*; emotionalizing, *ppr.* To render emotional; to excite the feelings of; to give an emotional character to. [Rare.]

ē-mō′tion-ăl-ly, *adv.* In an emotional manner.

ē-mō′tioned, *a.* Affected by emotion. [Rare.]

ē-mō′tive, *a.* Attended or characterized by emotion; emotional.

ē-mōve′, *v.t.* To excite; arouse. [Obs.]

em-pæs′tic (-pes′), **em-pes′tic**, **em-pāis′tic**, *a.* [Gr. *empaistikē* (supply *technē*, art), from *empaiein*, to strike in, emboss; *en*, in, and *paiein*, to stamp.] Of, or relating to, or characterized by Grecian inlaid or embossed work.

em-pāir′, *v.t.* To impair. [Obs.]

em-pāle′, *v.t.* Same as *Impale*.

em-pāle′ment, *n.* Same as *Impalement*.

em-pan′el, *n.* [Obs.] See *Impanel*.

em-pan′el, *v.t.* See *Impanel*.

em′pen-nage (or än-pe-näzh), *n.* [Fr.] In aviation, the stabilizing tail of an aeroplane or dirigible balloon.

em-pan′ō-ply, *v.t.*; empanoplied, *pt., pp.*; empanoplying, *ppr.* To invest with a panoply.

em-par′ȧ-dīse, *v.t.* Same as *Imparadise*.

em-pärk′, *v.t.* [Obs.] See *Impark*.

em-pär′lāunce, *n.* [Obs.] See *Imparlance*.

em-pasm′, *n.* [From Gr. *empassein*, to sprinkle in or on; *en*, in, and *passein*, to sprinkle.] A perfumed powder used to conceal the bad scent of the body.

em-pas′sion (-pash′un), *v.t.* [Obs.] See *Impassion*.

em-pas′sion-āte, *a.* Strongly affected. [Obs.]

em-pawn′, *v.t.* [Obs.] See *Impawn*.

em-peach′, *v.t.* [Obs.] See *Impeach*.

em-pēarl′, *v.t.* Same as *Impearl*.

em-pēo′ple, *v.t.* To form into a people or community. [Rare.]

em′pēr-ess, *n.*, an obsolete form of *empress*.

em-per′il, *v.t.* [Obs.] See *Imperil*.

em-per′ish, *v.t.* To destroy. [Obs.]

em′pēr-ŏr, *n.* [ME. *emperour*; OFr. *empereor*; L. *imperator*, a commander-in-chief, ruler, emperor, from *imperare*, to command; *in*, in, and *perare*, to prepare.] A sovereign or supreme monarch of an empire; a title of dignity superior to that of king; as, the *emperor* of Germany or of Austria.

Emperor of Japan; in zoölogy, a fish found in the seas of southern Japan, characterized by preopercular spines, brilliant color, and its excellence as a food-fish, the *Holacanthus imperator*; called also *emperor-fish*.

Purple emperor; in zoölogy, a butterfly of Great Britain, large and beautifully spotted, its larvæ feeding upon the willow and its cocoon hatching in July.

em′pēr-ŏr-fish, *n.* See *Emperor of Japan* under *Emperor*.

em′pēr-ŏr-goose, *n.* A large and handsome goose with transversely barred plumage and white crown, found in Alaskan waters; the *Philacte canagica*.

em′pēr-ŏr-moth, *n.* One of several handsome moths with transparent spots on their wings, as the American cecropia-moth, *Platysamia cecropia*.

em′pēr-ŏr-pen″guin (-gwin), *n.* The largest known penguin; the great king-penguin, *Aptenodytes patagonica*.

em′pē-ry, *n.* Empire. [Obs.]

Em-pe-trā′cē-æ, *n.pl.* A small family of low-growing evergreen shrubs.

em-pe-trā′ceous, *a.* Pertaining to the *Empetraceæ*.

Em′pe-trum, *n.* [Gr. *empetron*, a rock-plant; neut. of *empetros*, growing on the rocks; *en*, in, on, and *petros*, a rock.] A genus of plants growing in mountainous regions. The crowberry is the fruit of the *Empetrum nigrum*.

em′phȧ-sis, *n.* [L., from Gr. *emphasis*, an appearing in, outward appearance, from *emphainein*, to show forth; *en*, in, and *phainein*, to show, from *phasis*, appearance.]

1. In rhetoric, a particular stress of utterance or force of voice given to the words or parts of a discourse whose signification the speaker intends to impress specially upon his audience; or a distinctive utterance of words, specially significant, with a degree and kind of stress suited to convey their meaning in the best manner.

2. In a wider sense, a peculiar impressiveness of expression or weight of thought; as, to dwell on a subject with great *emphasis*.

em′phȧ-size, *v.t.*; emphasized, *pt., pp.*; emphasizing, *ppr.* 1. To utter or pronounce with a particular or more forcible stress of voice; as, to *emphasize* a word.

2. To give force or emphasis to; as, to *emphasize* a thought.

em-phat′ic, em-phat′ic-ăl, *a.* 1. Forcible; impressive; strong; as, an *emphatic* voice, tone, or pronunciation; *emphatic* reasoning.

2. Requiring emphasis; as, an *emphatic* word.

3. Uttered with emphasis; as, we remonstrated in *emphatic* terms.

4. Striking to the eye; as, *emphatic* colors.

Syn.—Earnest, forcible, strong, energetic, impressive, positive, important, consummate.

em-phat′ic-ăl-ly, *adv.* With emphasis; strongly; forcibly; in a striking manner.

em-phat′ic-ăl-ness, *n.* The quality of being emphatic; forcefulness; impressiveness.

em-phren′sy, *v.t.* To madden; to render wild and desperate. [Obs.]

em-phy-sē′mȧ, *n.* [Gr. *emphysēma*, an inflation, from *emphysān*, to inflate, blow in; *en*, in, and *physān*, to blow.] In medicine, an abnormal distention of the body or its members, from air accumulated in natural cavities; as, *emphysema* of the lungs.

em-phy-sem′ȧ-tous, *a.* Pertaining to emphysema; swelled, bloated, but yielding easily to pressure.

em-phy-teū′sis, *n.* [LL., from Gr. *emphyteusis*, lit., an implanting, from *emphyteuein*, to implant, from *emphyein*; *en*, in, and *phyein*, to produce.] Under Roman civil law, a kind of perpetual lease of real estate upon condition of taking care of and paying the taxes upon the estate; ground-rent.

em-phy-teū′tȧ, *n.* A holder of an estate under emphyteutic contract.

em-phy-teū′tic, *a.* Taken on hire, for which rent is to be paid; as, *emphyteutic* lands.

em-pierce′, *v.t.* To pierce into; to penetrate. [Obs.]

em-pight′ (-pīte′), *a.* Fixed; fastened; placed. [Obs.]

em′pīre, *n.* [OFr. *empire*; L. *imperium*, command, sovereignty, dominion, realm, empire, from *imperare*, to command, order; *in*, in, and *parare*, to order.]

1. Supreme power in governing; supreme dominion; sovereignty; imperial power; as, no nation can rightfully claim the *empire* of the ocean.

2. The territory, region, or countries under the jurisdiction and dominion of an emperor. An *empire* is usually a territory of greater extent than a *kingdom*, which may be, and often is, a territory of small extent; as, the Russian *empire*; the German *empire*; the *kingdom* of Italy.

3. Any region, land or water, over which dominion is extended; as, the *empire* of the sea.

em-pir′ic, *n.* [L. *empiricus*; Gr. *empeirikos*, experienced, from *empeiria*, experience; *en*, in, and *peira*, a trial, attempt.]

1. Literally, one who makes experiments; a physician who enters on practice without a regular professional education, and relies on the success of his own experience; a quack; an ignorant pretender to medical skill; a charlatan.

2. [E—] Among the ancient Greeks, (a) a philosopher whose conclusions were founded on experience or experiment alone; (b) one of a medical fraternity who excluded theory and reasoning altogether.

em-pir′ic-ăl, em-pir′ic, *a.* 1. Pertaining to experiments or experience.

2. Versed in experiments; as, an *empiric* alchemist.

3. Known only by experience; derived from experiment; used and applied without science; as, *empirical* skill.

em-pir′ic-ăl-ly, *adv.* By experiment; according to experience; without science; in the manner of quacks.

em-pir′i-cism, *n.* 1. Dependence of a person on his own experience and observation, disregarding theory, reasoning, and science.

2. The practice of medicine without a medical education; hence, quackery; the pretensions of an ignorant man to medical skill.

> Shudder to destroy life, either by the naked knife or by the surer and safer medium of *empiricism*. —Dwight.

3. In philosophy, the theory that experience only is the source of knowledge.

em-pir′i-cist, *n.* One who practises empiricism; an empiric.

em-pi-ris′tic, *a.* Associated with empiricism; growing out of experimental methods; imbued with empiricism.

em-plāce′, *v.t.* To put in position; to place; to determine emplacement of. [Rare.]

em-plāce′ment, *n.* The assigning or appointing of a definite place; fixing upon a locality, place, or ground; specifically, the place assigned to a piece of heavy ordnance.

em-plas′tēr, *n.* and *v.*, an obsolete form of *plaster*.

em-plas′tic, *n.* Any medicine tending to produce constipation.

em-plas′tic, *a.* [Gr. *emplastikos*, stopping the pores, clogging, from *emplassein*, to plaster up, daub over.] Viscous; glutinous; adhesive; fit to be applied as a plaster; as, *emplastic* applications.

em-plas-trā′tion, *n.* 1. The act of grafting. [Obs.]

2. The act of covering with plaster; process of plastering.

3. The act of applying a plaster or a salve.

em-plēad′, *v.t.* [Obs.] See *Implead*.

em-plec′tite, *n.* [Gr. *emplektos*, inwoven, and *-ite*.] In chemistry, a combination of copper and bismuth with sulphur ($CuBiS_2$) of a tin-white luster, which crystallizes in the orthorhombic system.

em-plec′ton, *n.* Same as *Emplectum*.

em-plec′tum, *n.* [L., from Gr. *emplekton*, neut. of *emplektos*, interwoven, from *emplekein*, to inweave; *en*, in, and *plekein*, to weave.] In ancient architecture, a method of constructing walls with squared stones outside, and with rough stones in the interior.

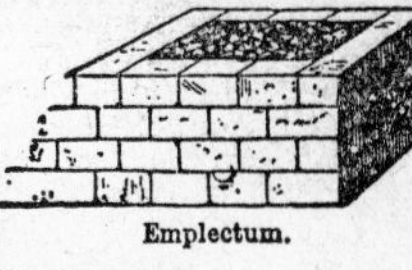
Emplectum.

em-plōre′, *v.t.* [Obs.] See *Implore*.

em-ploy′, *v.t.*; employed, *pt., pp.*; employing, *ppr.* [OFr. *employer*, *emploier*; L. *implicare*, to infold, engage; *in*, in, and *plicare*, to fold.]

1. To occupy the time, attention, and labor of; to keep busy or at work; to use; as, we *employ* our hands in labor; we *employ* our heads or faculties in study or thought; the attention is *employed* when the mind is fixed or occupied upon an object; we *employ* time when we devote it to an object.

2. To use as an instrument or means; as, we *employ* pens in writing, and arithmetic in keeping accounts.

3. To use as materials in forming anything; as, we *employ* timber or bricks in building.

4. To engage in one's service; to use as an agent or substitute in transacting business; to commission and intrust with the management of one's affairs; as, the president *employed* an envoy to negotiate a treaty.

5. To occupy; to use; to apply or devote to an object; to pass in business; as, to *employ* time.

Syn.—Use, hire, occupy, devote, busy, engage, commission.

em-ploy′, *n.* 1. That which engages the mind or occupies the time and labor of a person; business; object of study or industry; employment; as, the *employ* of both body and mind.

2. Occupation, as art, trade, profession; as, he entered his *employ*.

em-ploy'ȧ-ble, *a.* That may be employed; capable of being used; fit or proper for use.

em-ploy-ee', em-ploy-é' (-ā'), *n.* [Fr. *employé*, f. *employée*, one employed, from *employer*, to employ, engage.] One who is employed.

em-ploy'ẽr, *n.* One who employs; one who uses; one who engages or keeps in service.

em-ploy'ment, *n.* 1. The act of employing or using.

2. Occupation; business; that which engages the head or hands; as, agricultural *employments*; mechanical *employments*.

3. Office; public business or trust; agency or service for another or for the public; as, the secretary of the treasury has laborious and responsible *employment*.

Syn.—Business, calling, occupation, engagement, trade, profession, vocation.

em-plūme', *v.t.*; emplumed, *pt.*, *pp.*; empluming, *ppr.* To grace or ornament with plumes.

em-plunġe', *v.t.* To plunge. [Obs.]

em-pō'di-um, *n.*; *pl.* **em-pō'di-ȧ**. [Gr. *en*, in, and *pous*, *podos*, a foot.] In zoölogy, an imperfect claw or hook (called sometimes a *spurious claw*) between the true claws of certain kinds of insects.

em-poi'ṣon, *v.t.* To poison. [Obs.]

em-poi'ṣon, *n.* Poison. [Obs.]

em-poi'ṣon-ment, *n.* The act of poisoning. [Obs.]

em-pō-ret'iç, em-pō-ret'iç-ăl, *a.* [L. *emporeticus*; Gr. *emporeutikos*, mercantile, commercial, from *emporeuesthai*, to trade, traffic.] Relating to a place of trade. [Obs.]

em-pō'ri-um, *n.*; *pl.* **em-pō'ri-umṣ** or **em-pō'ri-ȧ**. [L., from Gr. *emporion*, a trading-place, mart, from *emporia*, trade, commerce, from *emporos*, a traveler; *en*, in, and *poros*, way.]

1. A place for bartering; a town or city of trade; particularly, a city or town of extensive commerce, or in which the commerce of an extensive country centers, or to which sellers and buyers resort from different countries.

2. A shop for the sale of a variety of goods; a bazaar.

3. In physiology, the brain. [Obs.]

em-pov'ẽr-ish, *v.t.* See *Impoverish*.

em-pow'ẽr, *v.t.*; empowered, *pt.*, *pp.*; empowering, *ppr.* 1. To give legal or moral power or authority to; to authorize, either by law, commission, letter of attorney, natural right, or verbal license; as, the Supreme Court is *empowered* to try and decide all cases, civil or criminal.

2. To give physical power or force to; to enable.

Syn.—Authorize, license, commission, delegate, warrant.

em'press, *n.* [ME. *empresse*, *emperesse*; OFr. *empereis*, *empereresse*; L. *imperatrix*, f. of *imperator*, a commander, ruler.]

1. The consort or spouse of an emperor.

2. A woman who governs an empire; a woman invested with imperial power or sovereignty.

Empress cloth; a woolen cloth for women's wear, with a finely corded surface, resembling merino.

Empress dowager; the widow of an emperor.

em-presse'ment (oṅ-pres'moṅ), *n.* [Fr.] Demonstrative earnestness; extreme cordiality.

em-print', *n.* and *v.* [Obs.] See *Imprint*.

em-priṣe', *n.* [ME. *emprise*; OFr. *emprise*, from *emprendre*, to undertake, from L. *in*, in, and *prehendere*, *prendere*, to take, seize.]

1. An undertaking; an enterprise.

2. Adventurousness.

em-priṣe', *v.t.* To undertake. [Obs.]

em-priṣ'ing, *a.* Full of adventure; very daring. [Obs.]

em-priṣ'ŏn, *v.t.* [Obs.] See *Imprison*.

em-pros-thot'ō-nos, *n.* [Gr. *emprosthotonos*, *emprosthen*, forward, in front, and *teinein*, to stretch.] In pathology, a state of the body in which it is drawn forward through muscular spasm; opposed to *opisthotonos*.

empt, *v.t.* To empty. [Dial.]

emp'tē, *v.t.* [Obs.] See *Empty*.

emp'ti-ẽr, *n.* One who or that which empties or exhausts.

emp'ti-ness, *n.* 1. A state of being empty; a state of containing nothing or nothing but air; absence of matter; as, the *emptiness* of a vessel.

2. Void space; vacuity; vacuum.

3. Want of solidity or substance; as, the *emptiness* of light and shade.

4. Unsatisfactoriness; inability to satisfy desire; as, the *emptiness* of earthly things.

5. Want of intellect or knowledge; lack of sense.

emp'tion, *n.* [L. *emptio*, from *emere*, to buy.]

1. The act of buying; a purchasing. [Rare.]

2. That which is bought. [Obs.]

emp'tion-ăl, *a.* Purchasable.

emp'tŏr, *n.* [L., from *emere*, to buy.] In old law, a buyer. [Obs.]

emp'ty, *a.*; *comp.* emptier; *superl.* emptiest. [ME. *empty*, *emti*; AS. *æmtig*, *emtig*, *æmetig*, from *æmta*, *æmetta*, leisure, rest.]

1. Containing nothing or nothing but air; evacuated; void of contents; as, an *empty* chest; *empty* space; an *empty* purse.

2. Void; devoid; destitute.

3. Destitute of force or effect; as, *empty* words.

4. Unsubstantial; unsatisfactory; not able to fill the mind or the desires; as, the pleasures of life are *empty* and unsatisfying.

5. Not supplied; having nothing to carry.

They beat him, and sent him away *empty*.
—Mark xii. 3.

6. Hungry; fasting.

My falcon now is sharp and passing *empty*.
—Shak.

7. Unfurnished with intellect or knowledge; vacant of head; ignorant; as, an *empty* coxcomb.

8. Unfruitful; producing nothing.

Seven *empty* ears blasted with the east wind.
—Gen. xli. 27.

9. Wanting substance; wanting solidity; as, *empty* dreams.

Syn.—Hollow, unfilled, unfurnished, unoccupied, vacant, barren, bare, fruitless, meaningless, vacated, weak, silly, senseless, unsatisfying.

emp'ty, *n.*; *pl.* **emp'tieṣ**. An empty packing-case, crate, barrel, box, etc.; as, returned *empties*.

emp'ty, *v.t.*; emptied, *pt.*, *pp.*; emptying, *ppr.* [ME. *empten*; AS. *æmtian*, from *æmetta*, leisure.]

1. To exhaust; to make void or destitute; to deprive of contents; as, to *empty* a vessel; to *empty* a well or a cistern.

2. To pour out the contents of; as, rivers *empty* themselves into the ocean.

emp'ty, *v.i.* 1. To pour out or discharge its contents; as, the Connecticut river *empties* into the Sound.

2. To become empty.

emp'ty-hand'ed, *a.* Poor; destitute; without resources; having nothing in the hands.

emp'ty-head"ed (-hed"), *a.* Having few ideas.

emp'ty-ing, *n.* 1. The act of making empty.

2. That which is emptied out.

3. [*pl.*] The lees of beer, cider, or yeast, or anything by which bread is leavened. [Colloq.]

emp'ty-sis, *n.* In medicine, a discharge of blood from the mouth, caused by hemorrhage of the lungs; hemoptysis.

em-pugn' (-pūn'), *v.t.* [Obs.] See *Impugn*.

em-pŭr'ple, *v.t.*; empurpled, *pt.*, *pp.*; empurpling, *ppr.* To tinge or dye of a purple color; to discolor with purple.

The deep *empurpled* ran. —Philips.

Em-pū'sȧ, *n.* [From Gr. *empousa*, a hobgoblin.] In botany, a genus of parasitic fungi infesting the bodies and causing the death of insects. *Empusa muscæ* is parasitic upon the common house-fly.

em-pūse', *n.* [Gr. *empousa*, a hobgoblin.] A phantom or specter. [Obs.]

em-puz'zle, *v.t.* To puzzle. [Obs.]

em-py-ē'mȧ, *n.* [Gr. *empyēma*, from *empyein*, to suppurate, from *empyos*; *en*, in, and *pyon*, pus.] A collection of purulent matter in the cavity of the pleura.

em-py-ē'sis, *n.* [Gr. *empyēsis*, suppuration, from *empyein*, to suppurate.] In pathology, an eruption of pustules on the skin.

em-pyr'ē-ăl, *n.* Same as *Empyrean*.

em-pyr'ē-ăl, *a.* [L. *empyrius*, *empyreus*; Gr. *empyrios*, *empyros*, fiery, in fire; *en*, in, and *pyr*, fire.] Formed of pure fire or light; refined beyond aerial substance; pertaining to the highest and purest region of heaven; pure; vital.

Go, soar with Plato to the *empyreal* sphere.
—Pope.

em-py-rē'ăn, *a.* Empyreal.

em-py-rē'ăn, *n.* The highest heaven, where the pure element of fire was supposed by the ancients to exist.

The *empyrean* rung
With hallelujahs. —Milton.

em-py-reu'mȧ, *n.* [Gr. *empyreuma*, from *empyreuein*, to set on fire, kindle, from *empyros*; *en*, in, on, and *pyr*, fire.] In chemistry, burnt smell; the odor of animal or vegetable substances when burned in close vessels or subjected to destructive distillation.

em"py-reu-mat'iç, em"py-reu-mat'iç-ăl, *a.* Pertaining to empyreuma.

Empyreumatic oil; an oil obtained by decomposing organic substances by means of heat.

em-py-reu'mȧ-tīze, *v.t.* To render empyreumatic; to burn. [Rare.]

em-pyr'iç-ăl, *a.* Pertaining to combustion or combustibility.

em-py-rō'sis, *n.* [Gr. *empyrōsis*, from *empyroein*, *empyrenein*, to set on fire.] A general fire; a conflagration. [Obs.]

em'rodṣ, *n.pl.* [Obs.] Same as *Hemorrhoids*.

ē'mū, *n.* [Fr. *émou*, *émeu*, prob. from native name.] The original and popular name of a large cursorial bird, *Dromaius novæ-hollandiæ*, found in Australia. It is about seven feet in length, and stands higher than the cassowary, from which it differs in not having the helmet. Written also *emew*, *emeu*.

Emu (*Dromaius novæ-hollandiæ*).

ē'mū, *n.* An Australian wood used for turners' work.

em'ū-lȧ-ble, *a.* Worthy of emulation. [Rare.]

em'ū-lāte, *v.t.*; emulated, *pt.*, *pp.*; emulating, *ppr.* [L. *æmulatus*, pp. of *æmulari*, to try to equal or excel another, from *æmulus*, trying to equal or excel.] To strive to equal or excel in qualities or actions; to imitate, with a view to equal or to excel; to vie with; to rival.

Thine eye would *emulate* the diamond.—Shak.

em'ū-lāte, *a.* Emulative. [Obs.]

em-ū-lā'tion, *n.* 1. The act of attempting to equal or excel in qualities or actions; rivalry; desire of superiority, attended with effort to attain it; ambition to equal or excel.

2. Contest; contention; strife; competition; rivalry accompanied with a desire of depressing another.

Such factious *emulations* shall arise.—Shak.

Syn.—Competition, rivalry.—*Competition* is the struggle of two or more persons for the same object; *emulation* is an ardent desire for superiority arising from competition, but not implying, of necessity, any improper feeling; *rivalry* is a personal contest, and almost of course gives rise to envy, resentment, or detraction.

em'ū-lā-tive, *a.* Inclined to emulation; disposed to rival; as, an *emulative* student.

em'ū-lā-tive-ly, *adv.* In an emulative manner.

em'ū-lā-tŏr, *n.* [L., from *æmulari*, to try to equal or excel.] One who emulates; a rival; a competitor.

em'ū-lā-tress, *n.* A woman who emulates another. [Rare.]

em'ūle, *v.t.* To emulate. [Obs.]

ē-mulġe', *v.t.* To milk out. [Obs.]

ē-mul'ġent, *a.* [L. *emulgens* (*-entis*), ppr. of *emulgere*, to milk out, drain out; *e-*, out, and *mulgere*, to milk.] In anatomy, milking or draining out; said of the renal arteries, which supply the kidneys with blood; as, the *emulgent* veins return the blood, after the urine is secreted.

ē-mul'ġent, *n.* 1. An emulgent vessel or vein.

2. A remedy which excites the flow of bile.

em'ū-lous, *a.* [L. *æmulus*, trying to equal or excel.]

1. Desirous or eager to imitate, equal, or excel another; desirous of like excellence with another; with *of*; as, *emulous of* another's example or virtues.

2. Rivaling; engaged in competition.

3. Factious; contentious.

em'ū-lous-ly, *adv.* With desire of equaling or excelling another.

em'ū-lous-ness, *n.* The quality of being emulous.

ē-mul'siç, *a.* In chemistry, pertaining to or procured from emulsin; specifically, applied to an acid procured from the albumen of almonds.

ē-mul'si-fȳ, *v.t.*; emulsified, *pt.*, *pp.*; emulsifying, *ppr.* To make or form into an emulsion.

ē-mul'sin, *n.* [L. *emulsus*, pp. of *emulgere*, to milk or drain out.] An albuminous or caseous substance of which the white part both of sweet and bitter almonds chiefly consists.

ē-mul'sion, *n.* [OFr. *emulsion*, from L. *emulgere*, to milk or drain out.]

1. A soft liquid remedy of a color and consistence resembling milk; any milk-like mixture prepared by uniting oil and water, by means of another substance, saccharine or mucilaginous.

2. In photography, an emulsified mixture used in the preparation of dry plates, etc.

ē-mul'sive, *a.* 1. Softening; milk-like.

2. Producing or yielding a milk-like substance; as, *emulsive* acids.

3. Yielding oil when pressed; as, *emulsive* seeds.

ē-munc'tō-ry, *n.* and *a.* [LL. *emunctorium*, a pair of snuffers, from L. *emungere*, to wipe or blow the nose, to cleanse; *e-*, out, and *mungere*, to blow the nose.]

I. *n.* In anatomy, any part of the body which serves to carry off excrementitious matter, as the kidneys, skin, etc.

II. *a.* Performing the function of discharging waste matter; excretory.

em-us-çā'tion, *n.* [L. *emuscare*, to clear from moss; *e-*, out, and *muscus*, moss.] A freeing from moss. [Rare.]

ē'mū=wren (-ren), *n.* An Australian bird, *Stipiturus malachurus*, of the family *Sylviadæ*, so named from the tail-feathers being loose-webbed, and bearing some resemblance to those of the emu.

ē'myd, ē'myde, *n.* A member of the family *Emydidæ.*

E-myd'i-dæ, *n.pl.* [Gr. *emys*, the water-tortoise, and *eidos*, resemblance.] A family of chelonian reptiles, including the fresh-water tortoises or terrapins, and intermediate in form between the turtles and land-tortoises.

en-. A prefix from ME. *en-*, OFr. *en-*, L. *in-*, from preposition *in*, in, into, and used chiefly in words borrowed from the French. Some words are written with either *en-* or *in-*, due to a confusion of *in-* of English origin and *in-* of Latin origin; as, *en*close, *in*close; *en*quire, *in*quire. It is sometimes used to give a causal force to a word; as, *en*feeble, to cause to be feeble; *en*able, to cause to be able. *En-* becomes *em-* before *p*, *b*, and *m*, for the sake of euphony, as in *em*ploy, *em*body, *em*mew.

en-. A prefix derived from Gr. *en-*, from preposition *en*, in, and used chiefly in scientific and technical words; as, *en*cephalon, *en*anthema.

-en. A suffix from AS. *-an*, used to form the plurals of some nouns; as, ox*en*, brethr*en*, e*en* (that is, ey*en*).

-en. A suffix from ME. *-en, -e*, AS. *-an, -ian*, and used in the formation of verbs, as the infinitive suffix in sing*en*, escap*en*, etc.; as the past participle in ris*en*, writt*en*, etc.; and also in forming verbs from adjectives; as, fat, fatt*en*; weak, weak*en*.

-en. A suffix from ME. *-en*, AS. *-en*, and used in the formation of adjectives from nouns of material; as, wood, wood*en*; gold, gold*en*.

-en. A feminine suffix from ME. *-en*, AS. *-en*, and used in such words as vix*en*, from AS. *fyxen*, a female fox.

-en. A suffix from AS. *-en*, used as the termination of the past participle of many strong verbs; as, broke, brok*en*; trod, trodd*en*.

en, *n.* 1. The name given to the fourteenth letter of the English alphabet, *N*, *n*.

2. In printing, a space half as wide as an em; used as a unit of measurement.

en-ā'ble, *v.t.*; enabled, *pt.*, *pp.*; enabling, *ppr.* 1. To make able; to supply with power, physical or moral; to furnish with sufficient power or ability; as, learning and industry *enable* men to investigate the laws of nature.

2. To supply with means; as, wealth *enables* men to live in luxury.

3. To furnish with legal ability or competency; to authorize; as, the law *enables* us to dispose of our property by will.

4. To furnish with competent knowledge or skill, and, in general, with adequate means; to endow.

en-ā'ble-ment, *n.* The act of enabling. [Obs.]

en-aςt', *v.t.*; enacted, *pt.*, *pp.*; enacting, *ppr.* 1. To decree; to establish; to make, as a law; to pass, as a bill, into a law; to perform the last act of a legislature to, as a bill, giving it validity as a law; to give legislative sanction to, as a bill.

2. To act; to perform; to effect.

3. To represent in action; as, to *enact* Hamlet.

en-aςt', *n.* Purpose; determination.

en-aςt'ive, *a.* Having power to enact or establish as a law.

en-aςt'ment, *n.* 1. The passing of a bill into a law; the act of voting, decreeing, and giving validity to a law.

2. A statute; a law enacted; an act; a decree; authoritative prescription.

3. The acting of a part or representation of a character in a play.

en-aςt'ŏr, *n.* 1. One who enacts or passes a law; one who decrees or establishes as a law.

2. One who performs anything.

en-aςt'ō-ry, *a.* Relating to the establishment of a law; especially, conferring new powers or creating new duties not before existing, as opposed to *declaratory.*

en-aς'tūre, *n.* 1. Purpose; effect. [Obs.]

2. Fulfilment. [Obs.]

en-al'i-ō-sạur, *n.* A member of the *Enaliosauria.*

En-al"i-ō-sạu'ri-ȧ, *n.pl.* [Gr. *enalios*, living in the sea; *en*, in, and *hals*, the sea, and *sauros*, a lizard.] A group of fossil marine reptiles of great size, including the ichthyosaurus.

en-al"i-ō-sạu'ri-ăn, *a.* and *n.* I. *a.* Relating to the *Enaliosauria.*

II. *n.* Same as *Enaliosaur.*

e-nal'lȧ-ġē, *n.* [L. *enallage*; Gr. *enallagē*, an interchange, from *enallassein*; *en*, in, and *allassein*, to change, from *allos*, other.] In grammar, a change of words, or a substitution of one gender, number, case, person, tense, mode, or voice, of the same word, for another.

en-am'bușh, *v.t.* To hide in ambush; to place in ambush. [Obs.]

en-am'el, *v.t.*; enameled *or* enamelled, *pt.*, *pp.*; enameling *or* enamelling, *ppr.* [ME. *enamelen*; OFr. *enamailler*, *enameler*; *en-*, in, on, and *esmailler*, to enamel, from *esmail*, enamel.]

1. To paint in enamel; to lay enamel into or upon; to decorate by means of enamel; to give an enamel-like surface to; as, to *enamel* a vase; to *enamel* paper.

2. To color with varied hues. [Rare.]

3. To coat with a cosmetic resembling enamel; as, to *enamel* the face.

en-am'el, *v.i.* To practise the art of enameling or the use of enamel.

en-am'el, *n.* 1. A fusible kind of glass used in the arts to decorate porcelain or metals, either through its own color when fused or as a base for coloring and inlaying. It is usually a mixture of ground glass and oxids. Employed as a glaze or lining for vessels used in chemistry and cookery.

2. That which is enameled; as, this vase is a choice *enamel.*

3. A lacquer or varnish for leather, cardboard, paper, etc., usually applied with the aid of heat.

4. The smooth, hard substance which covers the crown of a tooth, overlying the dentin.

5. A form of cosmetic coating for the skin of the face.

6. Smooth or finished outward appearance; gloss; polish; as, hardships will soon take off his *enamel.*

Enamel paper; a kind of paper with a smooth glazed surface.

en-am'el-ăr, en-am'el-lăr, *a.* Consisting of enamel; resembling enamel; smooth; glossy. [Rare.]

en-am'el=cell, *n.* One of the cells of the enamel of the teeth.

en-am'el-ẽr, en-am'el-lẽr, *n.* One who enamels; one whose occupation is to lay on enamels, or inlay colors.

en-am'el-ing, *n.* The act or art of laying on enamels.

en-am'el-ist, *n.* An enameler.

en-am'el=ọr"găn, *n.* In a developing tooth, the layer of enamel-cells which, with its adjacent tissues, forms a cap over the dentin.

en-am'el=pāint"ing, *n.* Painting done upon a metal or mineral surface in colors and afterward subjected to intense heat for the purpose of fixing it.

en-am'ŏur, en-am'ŏr, *v.t.*; enamoured *or* enamored, *pt.*, *pp.*; enamouring *or* enamoring, *ppr.* [OFr. *enamourer*, *enamorer*; LL. *inamorari*, to be in love; L. *in*, in, and *amor*, love.] To inflame with love; to charm; to captivate; with *of* or *with* before the person or thing; as, to be *enamoured of* a lady; to be *enamoured of* or *with* books or science.

Syn.—Captivate, fascinate, enslave, charm, endear, bewitch, enchain.

en-am'ŏur-ment, *n.* The state of being enamoured.

en-an-thē'mȧ, *n.* [Gr *en*, in, and *anthēma*, an eruption.] In medicine, an eruptive affection of the mucous membrane; distinguished from *exanthema*, an eruption of the skin.

en-an-them'ȧ-tous, *a.* Relating to enanthema.

ē-nan-thyl'iç, *a.* Same as *Œnanthylic.*

e-nan-ti-ō-. A combining form from Gr. *enantios*, opposite, over against; *en*, in, and *antios*, contrary, from *anti*, against.

e-nan"ti-ō-mọr'phiç, *a.* Same as *Enantiomorphous.*

e-nan"ti-ō-mọr'phous, *a.* [*Enantio-*, and Gr. *morphē*, form.] In crystallography, having symmetry but not likeness; related, as the right hand to the left; said of certain hemihedral crystals.

e-nan"ti-ō-path'iç, *a.* In medicine, serving to bring about an opposite pathological condition; palliative.

e-nan-ti-op'ȧ-thy, *n.* [*Enantio-*, and Gr. *-patheia*, from *pathos*, feeling, affection.] An opposite passion or affection; hence, the science which aims to cure an ailment by superinducing one of an opposite kind; allopathy, as opposed to homeopathy.

e-nan-ti-ō'sis, *n.* [Gr. *enantiōsis*, contradiction, opposition, from *enantios*, opposite, contrary; *en*, in, and *antios*, opposite, from *anti*, against.] In rhetoric, a figure of speech by which what is meant to be conveyed in the affirmative is stated in the negative, and vice versa; as, he didn't drink it—oh no! He is a wonderfully good man—oh yes!

en-ärch', *v.t.*, an obsolete form of *inarch.*

en-ärched' (-ärcht'), *a.* In heraldry, combined with or supported by an arch; arched.

Chevron Enarched.

en-är'ġite, *n.* [Gr. *enargēs*, visible, distinct; *en*, in, and *argos*, bright, and *-ite.*] An iron-black or grayish-black mineral, orthorhombic in crystallization, composed chiefly of copper, arsenic, and sulphur, but usually containing a little antimony and zinc, and sometimes silver.

en-ärme', *n.* [OFr., from *enarmer*, to provide with straps.] The strap or gear for fastening a shield to the arm.

en-ärmed', *a.* In heraldry, having arms, that is, horns, hoofs, etc., of a different color from that of the body; armed.

en-ar-rā'tion, *n.* [L. *enarratio*, from *enarrare*, to relate in detail.] Recital; relation; account; exposition. [Obs.]

en-är-thrō'di-ȧ, *n.* Same as *Enarthrosis.*

en-är-thrō'di-ăl, *a.* Pertaining to enarthrosis.

en-är-thrō'sis, *n.* [Gr. *enarthrōsis*, from *enarthros*, jointed; *en*, in, and *arthron*, a joint.] In anatomy, a ball-and-socket joint; that species of articulation which consists in the insertion of the round end of a bone in the cuplike cavity of another, forming a joint movable in every direction.

ē-nas'cent, *a.* [L. *enascens* (*-entis*), ppr. of *enasci*, to spring up, arise; *e*, out, and *nasci*, to be born.] Coming into existence; incipient. [Obs.]

ē-nā-tā'tion, *n.* [From L. *enatatus*, pp. of *enatare*, to swim out; *e*, out, and *natare*, to swim.] A swimming out; escape by swimming. [Obs.]

ē-nāte', *a.* 1. Growing out.

2. Related through the mother.

ē-nā'tion, *n.* [From L. *enatus*, pp. of *enasci*, to spring up.]

1. In botany, an abnormal growth of an organ or of an excrescence upon any part of a plant, as the growth of a flower upon a leaf.

2. In ethnology, maternal relationship.

ē-naun'tẽr, *adv.* [For ME. *in aunter*, peradventure.] Lest that. [Obs.]

ē-nav'i-gāte, *v.t.* [L. *enavigatus*, pp. of *enavigare*, to sail out.] To sail out or over. [Obs.]

en-bat'tled (-tld), *a.* [Obs.] See *Embattled.*

en-bibe', *v.t.* [Obs.] See *Imbibe.*

eǹ bloç (oǹ blok). [Fr.] In block; in a lump; as, the tickets were sold *en bloc.*

en-broude', *v.t.* [Obs.] See *Embroider.*

en-çæ'ni-ȧ (-sē'), *n.pl.* Same as *Encenia.*

en-çāġe', *v.t.*; encaged, *pt.*, *pp.*; encaging, *ppr.* [Fr. *encager*; *en-*, in, and *cage*, a cage.] To shut up or confine in a cage, to coop; also written *incage.*

en-çal'en-dăr, *v.t.*; encalendared, *pt.*, *pp.*; encalendaring, *ppr.* To register in a calendar, as the saints of the Roman Catholic church.

en-çamp', *v.i.*; encamped (-kampt'), *pt.*, *pp.*; encamping, *ppr.* To pitch tents or form huts, as an army; to halt on a march, spread tents, and remain for a night or for a longer time, as an army or company.

en-çamp', *v.t.* To form into a camp; to place in a temporary habitation or quarters.

Bid him *encamp* his soldiers. —Shak.

en-çamp'ment, *n.* 1. The act of pitching tents or forming huts, as an army or traveling company, for temporary lodging or rest.

2. The place where a body of men is encamped; a camp.

en-çan'kẽr, *v.t.* To corrode; to canker. [Obs.]

en-çap'sū-lāte, *v.t.*; encapsulated, *pt.*, *pp.*; encapsulating, *ppr.* To put into a capsule.

en-çap-sū-lā'tion, *n.* The act of surrounding with a capsule.

en-çap'sūle, *v.t.* Same as *Encapsulate.*

en-çär'năl-īze, *v.t.* To make carnal; to carnalize.

en-çär'pi-um, *n.*; *pl.* **en-çär'pi-ȧ.** [Gr. *enkarpios*, containing seed; *en*, in, and *karpos*, fruit.] A sporophore.

en-çär'pus, *n.* [Gr. *enkarpos*, containing fruit; *en*, in, and *karpos*, fruit.] In architecture, a festoon-like ornament, bearing fruit, flowers, leaves, or anything appropriate to the design or purpose of the building in which it is used.

Encarpus, from Palazzo Niccolini, Rome.

en-çāse', *v.t.* Same as *Incase.*

en-çāse'ment, *n.* Same as *Incasement.*

en-çash', *v.t.*; encashed, *pt.*, *pp.*; encashing, *ppr.* In English banking, to cash; to convert into cash, as a note, draft, etc.

en-çash'ment, *n.* The payment in cash of a note, draft, etc.; the act of encashing.

en-çạu'mȧ, *n.* [Gr. *enkauma*, from *enkaiein*, to burn in; *en*, in, and *kaiein*, to burn.] A mark left upon the skin by a burn; also, an ulcerous affection of the cornea, causing the loss of the humors.

en-çạus'tiç, *a.* [L. *encausticus*; Gr. *enkaustikos*, from *enkaustos*, burnt in; from *enkaiein*, to burn in.] Pertaining to the art of painting in heated or burnt wax, or to the art of enameling; burned in.

Encaustic painting; a kind of painting in which, by heating or burning in wax, the colors are rendered permanent in all their original splendor.

Encaustic tile; a tile made of clay and stamped in relief, decorated, glazed, and burned to hardness; much used in the ornamentation of walls and pavements.

en-çaus′tiç, *n.* The art of painting in heated or burned wax or in enamel; encaustic painting.

en-çāve′, *v.t.*; encaved, *pt.*, *pp.*; encaving, *ppr.* To hide in a cave or recess; also written *incave.*

-ence. A suffix from Fr. *-ence*, L. *-entia*; used in the formation of nouns, and signifying action, state, quality, or that which relates to the action or state; as, emerg*ence*, dilig*ence*, excel*lence*.

eṅ-ceinte′ (oṅ-saṅt′), *n.* [Fr., from *enceinte*, pp. of *enceindre*, from L. *incingere*, to gird about, surround.] In fortification, inclosure; the wall or rampart which surrounds a place, sometimes composed of bastions and curtains; the inclosure of a town or of a convent, castle, or cathedral.

eṅ-ceinte′ (oṅ-saṅt′), *a.* Pregnant; with child.

en-çē′ni-ȧ, *n.pl.* [LL. *encænia*; Gr. *enkainia*, neut. pl., a feast of dedication; *en*, in, and *kainos*, new.] Festivals anciently commemorative of the days on which cities were built or churches consecrated; and, in later times, ceremonies renewed at certain periods, as at Oxford, in commemoration of founders and benefactors.

en-cense′, *v.t.* and *v.i.* [Obs.] See *Incense.*

en-ce-phal-, en-ceph-ȧ-lō-. Combining forms from Gr. *enkephalos*, the brain; used in anatomy and medicine to indicate connection with or relation to the brain; as, *encephal*algia, *encephalo*cele.

en-ceph-ȧ-lal′gi-ȧ, *n.* [*Encephal-*, and Gr. *algos*, pain.] A pain in the head; cephalalgia.

en-ce-phal′iç, *a.* Pertaining to the brain.

en-ceph-ȧ-lit′iç, *a.* Pertaining to or afflicted with encephalitis.

en-ceph-ȧ-lī′tis, *n.* [Gr. *enkephalos*, the brain, and *-itis*.] Inflammation of the brain.

en-ceph-ȧ-lō-. See *Encephal-.*

en-ceph′ȧ-lō-cēle, *n.* [*Encephalo-*, and Gr. *kēlē*, a tumor.] Hernia of the brain.

en-ceph′ȧ-lō-cœle (-sēl), *n.* [*Encephalo-*, and Gr. *koilos*, hollow.] The entire cavity within the encephalon.

en-ceph′ȧ-loid, *a.* [*Encephalo-*, and Gr. *eidos*, form.] Resembling brain-tissue.

Encephaloid cancer, a soft, malignant cancer which in form, consistency, and appearance resembles the matter of the brain; medullary cancer.

en-ceph′ȧ-loid, *n.* Soft carcinoma.

en-ceph-ȧ-lol′ō-ġy, *n.* [*Encephalo-*, and Gr. *-logia*, from *legein*, to speak.] The science of the brain.

en-ceph′ȧ-lon, *n.*; *pl.* **en-ceph′ȧ-lȧ.** [Gr. *enkephalos*, the brain, properly an adj., within the head; *en*, in, and *kephalē*, head.] The brain; the contents of the skull, consisting of the cerebrum, cerebellum, medulla oblongata, and membranes.

en-ceph″ȧ-lō-path′i-ȧ, *n.* [*Encephalo-*, and Gr. *pathos*, suffering.] Any disease of the brain.

en-ceph-ȧ-lop′ȧ-thy, *n.* Same as *Encephalopathia.*

en-ceph′ȧ-los, *n.* Same as *Encephalon.*

en-ceph-ȧ-lot′ō-my, *n.* [*Encephalo-*, and Gr. *tomē*, a cutting.] Dissection of the brain.

en-ceph′ȧ-lous, *a.* [Gr. *enkephalos*, within the head; *en*, in, and *kephalē*, head.] Having a head; cephalous; cephalate; opposed to *acephalous*; applied to a subdivision of mollusks.

en-chāfe′, *v.t.* To chafe or fret; to provoke; to enrage; to irritate. [Obs.]

en-chāin′, *v.t.*; enchained, *pt.*, *pp.*; enchaining, *ppr.* [OFr. *enchainer*; Pr. *encadenar*; It. *incatenare*, to enchain; from L. *in*, in, and *catenare*, to chain; *catena*, a chain.]

1. To fasten with a chain; to bind or hold in chains; to hold in bondage.

2. To hold fast; to restrain; to confine; as, to *enchain* the attention.

3. To link together; to connect.

en-chāin′ment, *n.* The act of enchaining or state of being enchained.

en-chāir′, *v.t.*; enchaired, *pt.*, *pp.*; enchairing, *ppr.* To seat in a chair; to install in a dignified position; to make chairman.

en-chan′nel, *v.t.*; enchanneled, *pt.*, *pp.*; enchanneling, *ppr.* To cause to flow in a channel; as, to *enchannel* the stagnant waters of a marsh.

en-chȧnt′, *v.t.*; enchanted, *pt.*, *pp.*; enchanting, *ppr.* [OFr. *enchanter*, *encanter*; Pr. *encantar*; It. *incantare*; L. *incantare*, to bewitch, enchant, to mutter in a magic formula; *in*, in, and *cantare*, to sing.]

1. To practise sorcery or witchcraft on; to subdue by spells or charms; to bewitch.

And now about the caldron sing,
Like elves and fairies in a ring,
Enchanting all that you put in. —Shak.

2. To delight in the highest degree; to charm; to ravish with pleasure; as, the description *enchants* me; we were *enchanted* with the music.

Syn.—Charm, fascinate, bewitch, entrance, captivate, enrapture, ravish.

en-chȧnt′ed, *a.* 1. Charmed; fascinated.

2. Inhabited or possessed by elves, witches, or other imaginary spirits; as, an *enchanted* castle.

en-chȧnt′ēr, *n.* 1. One who enchants; a sorcerer or magician; one who practises enchantment.

2. One who charms or delights.

Enchanter's nightshade; the popular name of plants of the genus *Circæa*, found in damp, shady woods in the northern hemisphere.

en-chȧnt′ing, *a.* Charming; irresistibly attractive; captivating; as, an *enchanting* face; *enchanting* music.

en-chȧnt′ing-ly, *adv.* In a charming manner; delightfully.

en-chȧnt′ment, *n.* 1. The act of producing certain wonderful effects by the invocation or aid of demons or by the agency of certain supposed spirits; the use of magic arts, spells, or charms; incantation.

The magicians of Egypt did so with their *enchantments*. —Ex. vii. 11.

2. Irresistible influence; overpowering influence of delight; that which enchants.

The warmth of fancy—which holds the heart of a reader under the strongest *enchantment*. —Pope.

3. The state of being enchanted.

Syn.—Magic, spell, witchery, fascination, charm, captivation, allurement, incantation, sorcery, necromancy.

en-chȧnt′ress, *n.* 1. A sorceress; a woman who uses magic arts or spells.

2. A woman who fascinates or exercises irresistible influence.

From this *enchantress* all these ills are come. —Dryden.

en-chärġe′, *n.* An injunction; a charge. [Obs.]

en-chärġe′, *v.t.* To give in charge or trust. [Rare.]

en-chāse′, *v.t.*; enchased (-chāst′), *pt.*, *pp.*; enchasing, *ppr.* [Fr. *enchâsser*, to enchase; *en-*, in, and *châsse*, a frame.]

1. To incase or inclose in another body, so as to be held fast, but not concealed; to place in a setting.

2. To adorn by embossed work; to enrich or beautify by some design or figure in low relief, as a watchcase.

3. To adorn by settings, as of jewels; to incrust.

To drink in bowls which glittering gems *enchase*. —Dryden.

en-chās′ēr, *n.* One who enchases.

en-chās′ten (-chās′n), *v.t.* To chasen; to chastise. [Rare.]

en-chē′ṣŏn, en-chēa′ṣŏn, *n.* [ME. *encheson*, *ancheson*, from OFr. *achaison*, from L. *occasio*, occasion, cause, from *incidere*, to happen, chance.] Cause; occasion. [Obs.]

en-chest′, *v.t.* Same as *Inchest.*

eṅ-chi-rid′i-on, *n.* [LL., from Gr. *encheiridion*, a handbook, neut. of *encheiridios*, in the hand; *en*, in, and *cheir*, hand.] A manual; a book to be carried in the hand; especially, a handbook of devotions.

en-chiṣ′el, *v.t.* To cut with a chisel.

Eṅ-chō-dus, *n.* [Gr. *enchos*, a spear, and *odous*, a tooth.] A genus of scomberoid fossil fishes found in the chalk formation; so called from their spear-shaped teeth.

eṅ-chon-drō′mȧ, *n.* [Gr. *en*, in, and *chondros*, a cartilage, and *-oma*.] Same as *Chondroma.*

eṅ-chō′ri-ăl, en-chor′iç, *a.* [LL. *enchorius*; Gr. *enchorios*, in or belonging to the country; *en*, in, and *chōra*, country.] Belonging to or used in a country; native; indigenous; popular; common; demotic; as, an *enchorial* or *enchoric* alphabet.

en-chy-lē′mȧ, *n.* [Gr. *enchein*, to pour in (*en*, in, and root *chy-*, to pour), and *lemma*, a thing received.] A fluid granular substance filling the interstices of the cell-body and the nucleus.

eṅ′chy-mȧ, *n.* [Gr. *enchyma*, an infusion; *en*, in, and *chein*, to pour.] In biology, the formative fluid from which cell-tissue is developed.

eṅ-chym′ȧ-tous, *a.* Distended by infusion; applied to glandular epithelial cells.

en-ciṅç′tūre, *n.* An encircling band or belt; a cincture.

en-ciṅç′tūre, *v.t.*; encinctured, *pt.*, *pp.*; encincturing, *ppr.* To surround with or as with a girdle or belt; to encompass; as, the lake is *encinctured* by a dense forest.

en-cin′dēred, *a.* Burned to cinders.

en-cīr′çle (-kl), *v.t.*; encircled, *pt.*, *pp.*; encircling, *ppr.* 1. To form a circle about; to inclose or surround; said of a circle or ring, or anything in a circular form; as, luminous rings *encircle* Saturn.

Her brows *encircled* with his serpent rod. —Parnell.

2. To encompass; to surround; to environ; as, the army *encircled* the city.

3. To inclose within or as within a ring; hence, to embrace; as, to *encircle* one in the arms.

4. To make the circuit of; to go around.

en-cīr′çlet, *n.* A small circle; a ring. [Obs.]

en-clȧsp′, *v.t.*; enclasped, *pt.*, *pp.*; enclasping, *ppr.* To clasp; to embrace.

en-clāve′ (*or Fr. pron.* oṅ-kläv′), *n.* [Fr., from *enclaver*, to inclose.]

1. A place or country completely surrounded by the possessions of another power, as among the states of the German empire.

2. In heraldry, anything let into something else, especially when the thing so let in is square.

en-clāve′ (*or Fr. pron.* oṅ-kläv′), *v.t.*; enclaved, *pt.*, *pp.*; enclaving, *ppr.* [ME. *enclaven*; OFr. *enclaver*, to inclose, lock in; LL. *inclavare*; L. *in*, and *clavis*, a key.] To surround or inclose (a place or country) with the territories of another power.

en-clāve′ment (*or Fr. pron.* oṅ-kläv′moṅ), *n.* The condition of being isolated, as a country, place, or territory; also, the act of enclaving.

en-clit′iç, en-clit′iç-ăl, *a.* [LL. *encliticus*; Gr. *enklitikos*, enclitic, leaning on, from *enklinein*, to lean toward, incline; *en*, in, and *klinein*, to lean.] Literally, inclined; in grammar, attached; joined to; said of a word or particle which always follows another word and is so closely connected with the preceding word as to seem to be a part of it.

en-clit′iç, *n.* In grammar, a word or particle connected with the preceding word so closely as to almost form part of it; as, *que* (and) in Latin *arma virumque*, arms and the man.

en-clit′iç-ăl-ly, *adv.* In an enclitic manner; by throwing the accent back.

en-clit′içs, *n.* In grammar, the art of inflecting words.

en-clois′tēr, *v.t.*; encloistered, *pt.*, *pp.*; encloistering, *ppr.* [OFr. *enclostrer*, from *en-*, in, and *cloistrer*, to inclose, from *cloistre*, an inclosure.] To shut up, as in a cloister; to cloister; to immure.

en-clōṣe′, *v.t.* Same as *Inclose.*

en-clō′ṣūre (-zhūr), *n.* Same as *Inclosure.*

en-clōthe′, *v.t.*; enclothed, *pt.*, *pp.*; enclothing, *ppr.* To clothe.

en-cloud′, *v.t.*; enclouded, *pt.*, *pp.*; enclouding, *ppr.* To obscure with a cloud or clouds; to darken.

en-cōach′, *v.t.*; encoached, *pt.*, *pp.*; encoaching, *ppr.* To carry in a coach. [Rare.]

en-cof′fin, *v.t.*; encoffined, *pt.*, *pp.*; encoffining, *ppr.* To put in a coffin.

en-cōld′en, *v.t.* To make cold. [Obs.]

en-col′lăr, *v.t.* To surround with a collar. [Rare.]

en-cŏl′ŏr, en-cŏl′oŭr, *v.t.* To give color to. [Rare.]

en-cō-lūre′ (oṅ-kō-lūr′), *n.* [Fr. *encolure*, the neck and shoulders; *en-* (L. *in*, in, on), and *col*, from L. *collum*, the neck.]

1. The neck, or the neck and shoulders, of an animal, especially of a horse.

2. In needlework, an opening in a dress, as at the neck or armhole.

en-cŏm′bēr, *v.t.* [Obs.] Same as *Encumber.*

en-cŏm′bēr-ment, *n.* Molestation; encumberment. [Obs.]

en-cō′mi-ast, *n.* [Gr. *enkōmiastēs*, from *enkōmiazein*, to praise, from *enkōmion*, a hymn in honor of a victor, a song of praise.] One who praises another; a panegyrist; one who utters or writes commendations or encomiums.

en-cō-mi-as′tiç, en-cō-mi-as′tiç-ăl, *a.* Bestowing praise; commending; laudatory; as, an *encomiastic* address.

en-cō-mi-as′tiç-ăl-ly, *adv.* In an encomiastic manner.

en-cō′mi-on, *n.* [Obs.] Same as *Encomium.*

en-cō′mi-um, *n.*; *pl.* **en-cō′mi-umṣ.** [L. *encomium*; Gr. *enkōmion*, a hymn in honor of a victor, a song of praise; neut. of *enkōmios*; *en*, in, and *kōmos*, a revel.] Praise; panegyric; commendation; as, men are quite as willing to receive as to bestow *encomiums*.

Syn.—Eulogy, panegyric, praise, laudation.

en-cŏm′pȧss, *v.t*; encompassed (-pȧst), *pt.*, *pp.*; encompassing, *ppr.* 1. To encircle; to surround; as, a ring *encompasses* the finger.

2. To environ; to inclose; to surround; to shut in; as, a besieging army *encompassed* the city of Jerusalem.

3. To go or sail round; as, Drake *encompassed* the globe.

Syn.—Encircle, inclose, surround, include, environ, invest, hem in, shut up.

en-cŏm′pȧss-ment, *n.* 1. The act of surrounding; the condition of being surrounded.

2. Circumlocution in speaking. [Rare.]

eṅ-çōre′ (oṅ-kōr′), *adv.* [Fr. *encore*; It. *ancora*,

yet, still, again, from L. *in hanc horam*, to this hour.] Again; once more; used by the auditors and spectators of plays and other performances when they call for a repetition of a particular part. This use of the word is unknown to the French, who use the word *bis* (twice) if they wish a part, song, or the like repeated.

eṅ-çōre′ (oṅ-kōr′), *v.t.*; encored, *pt.*, *pp.*; encoring, *ppr.* To call for a repetition of, as a song; to call for the return of, as a singer.

eṅ-çōre′ (oṅ-kōr′), *n.* 1. A call by an audience or spectators for the repetition of some particular part of a performance.

2. The repetition of any particular part of a musical or theatrical performance; as, the orchestra rendered several *encores*.

en-çor′pōre, *v.t.* To incorporate. [Obs.]

en-çou′bert, *n.* [Fr., from Port. *encoberto*, covered, concealed.] An armadillo typical of the family *Dasypodidæ*, especially *Dasypus sexcinctus* of Brazil.

en-çoun′tẽr, *n.* [OFr. *encontre*, a meeting, from *encontrer*, to encounter, meet.]

1. A meeting, particularly a sudden or accidental meeting of two or more persons or bodies.

To shun the *encounter* of the vulgar crowd. —Pope.

2. A meeting in contest; a single combat; a fight; a conflict; a skirmish; a battle; but more generally a fight between a small number of men, or an accidental meeting and fighting of detachments, rather than a set battle or general engagement.

3. In physics, the mutual approach of the rapidly moving molecules of a gaseous body, at the point of their sudden deflection; so called in the kinetic theory of gases.

Syn.—Attack, assault, combat, engagement, meeting, onset.

en-çoun′tẽr, *v.t.*; encountered, *pt.*, *pp.*; encountering, *ppr.* 1. To meet face to face; particularly, to meet suddenly or unexpectedly.

2. To meet in opposition or in a hostile manner; to rush against in conflict; to engage with in battle; as, two armies *encounter* each other.

3. To come upon; to light upon; to meet with; as, to *encounter* obstacles, impediments, etc.

4. To meet and oppose; to resist; to attack and attempt to confute; as, to *encounter* the arguments of opponents.

5. To oppose; to oppugn. [Obs.]

6. To meet in mutual kindness; to express an equal amount of kindly feeling toward. [Rare.]

See, they *encounter* thee with their hearts' thanks. —Shak.

7. To befall; to betide. [Obs.]

en-çoun′tẽr, *v.i.* 1. To meet face to face; to meet unexpectedly.

I will *encounter* with Andronicus. —Shak.

2. To meet in hostile fashion; to come together in combat; to fight; to conflict.

If thou *encounter* with the boar. —Shak.

3. To meet in opposition or debate.

en-çoun′tẽr-ẽr, *n.* 1. One who encounters; an opponent; an antagonist.

2. One who seeks encounters; one who is ready to accost another.

O, these *encounterers*, so glib of tongue. —Shak.

en-çour′āġe, *v.t.*; encouraged, *pt.*, *pp.*; encouraging, *ppr.* [OFr. *encouragier*, *encourager*, to encourage; *en*, in, and *courage*, courage, valor.] To give courage to; to give confidence to; to inspire with courage, spirit, or strength of mind; to embolden; to animate; to incite; to inspirit.

But charge Joshua and *encourage* him. —Deut. iii. 28.

Syn.—Embolden, inspirit, animate, incite, cheer, urge, impel, stimulate, instigate, comfort, promote, advance, forward.

en-çour′āġe-ment, *n.* [OFr. *encoragement*, encouragement, from *encoragier*, *encourager*, to encourage.]

1. The act of giving courage or confidence of success; incitement to action or to practice; incentive; as, the *encouragement* of youth in generous deeds.

2. That which serves to incite, support, promote, or advance, as favor, countenance, rewards, profit; incentive; as, the fine arts find little *encouragement* among a rude people.

en-çour′ā-ġẽr, *n.* One who encourages, incites, or stimulates to action; one who supplies incitements, either by counsel, reward, or means of execution.

The pope is a master of polite learning and a great *encourager* of arts. —Addison.

en-çour′ā-ġing, *a.* 1. Inspiring with hope and confidence; exciting courage.

2. Furnishing ground to hope for success; as, an *encouraging* prospect.

Syn.—Cheering, animating, emboldening.

en-çour′ā-ġing-ly, *adv.* In a manner to give courage, or hope of success.

en-cowl′, *v.t.* To invest with a cowl, as a monk.

en-çrā′dle, *v.t.* To lay in a cradle.

En′çrá-tīte, *n.* [LL. *Encratitæ*; Gr. *enkratitai*, pl. of *enkratitēs*, self-disciplined, being in possession of power; *en*, in, and *kratos*, power.] In early church history, one of a sect that abjured marriage and the use of wine and meat; also called *Continent*.

en-çrēase′, *v.t.* and *v.i.* [Obs.] See *Increase*.

en-çrim′ṣŏn, *v.t.* To cover with a crimson color.

en′çri-năl, en-çrin′iç, *a.* Relating to encrinites; containing encrinites, as certain kinds of limestone.

en-çrin′i-tăl, *a.* Same as *Encrinal*.

en′çri-nīte, *n.* [Gr. *en*, in, and *krinon*, a lily.] A name often applied to the whole order of the *Crinoidea* or stone-lilies, but more specifically restricted to the genera having rounded, smooth stems. The petrified remains of the *encrinites* compose vast strata of marble in northern Europe and North America. In the cut representing the piece of marble, the variety in the figures of the *encrinites* is caused by the different angles at which they occur.

Piece of Marble, showing Encrinites.

Encrinite.—*a a*, Portions of the stem. *b*, Separate joints.

en-çri-nit′iç, en-çri-nit′iç-ăl, *a.* Same as *Encrinal*.

En-çri-noid′ē-ȧ, *n.pl.* Same as *Crinoidea*.

En′çri-nus, *n.* [Gr. *en*, in, and *krinon*, a lily.]

1. A genus of fossil crinoids.

2. [e—] Any encrinite.

en-çrisped′ (-krispt′), *a.* Curled; formed in curls. [Rare.]

en-çrōach′, *v.i.*; encroached (-krōcht′), *pt.*, *pp.*; encroaching, *ppr.* [ME. *encrochen*; OFr. *encrochier*, *encrocher*, *encrocier*, to seize upon, to take; *en*, in, and *croc*, a hook.]

1. To enter on the rights and possessions of another; to intrude; to take possession of what belongs to another by gradual advances into his limits or jurisdiction, and usurping a part of his rights or prerogatives; with *on* or *upon*; as, he *encroaches on* my property; the sea *encroaches on* the land when it wears it away gradually.

2. To advance gradually and by stealth; to approach or take hold unperceived; as, old age *encroaches* upon a man.

Syn.—Infringe, trespass, invade, intrude.

en-çrōach′, *n.* [Obs.] See *Encroachment*.

en-çrōach′ẽr, *n.* One who encroaches; one who lessens or limits an object, as a right or privilege, by narrowing its boundaries.

en-çrōach′ing-ly, *adv.* By way of encroachment.

en-çrōach′ment, *n.* 1. The entering gradually on the rights or possessions of another, and taking possession; unlawful intrusion.

2. That which is taken by encroaching on another.

3. In law, the illegal diminution of another's possessions; the taking of more than is one's right or due.

4. The act of advancing gradually and by stealth; unperceived approach, seizure, or progress; as, the *encroachments* of disease.

en′çrust, *v.t.* See *Incrust*.

en-çrust′ment, *n.* Incrustation.

en-çuī-rassed′ (-kwē-rast′), *a.* In zoölogy, having a covering like a cuirass; cuirassed; loricate.

en-çum′bẽr, *v.t.*; encumbered, *pt.*, *pp.*; encumbering, *ppr.* [ME, *encombren*; OFr. *encombrer*; *en-*, in, and *combrer*, to hinder, from LL. *cumbrus*, a heap, from L. *cumulus*, a hill.]

1. To load; to clog; to impede with burdens; to retard; to weigh down; to obstruct; to embarrass; to perplex; as, to *encumber* with packages; to *encumber* with cares.

2. To load with debts or other financial obligations; as, to *encumber* an estate with mortgages.

en-çum′bẽr-ing-ly, *adv.* In a manner to encumber or impede.

en-çum′bẽr-ment, *n.* The act of encumbering; obstruction. [Rare.]

en-çum′brănce, in-çum′brănce, *n.* [OFr *encombrance*, from *encombrer*, to encumber.]

1. A load; anything that impedes action, or renders it difficult and laborious; a clog; an impediment.

2. In law, a lien or burden on an estate; a legal claim on an estate, for the discharge of which the estate is liable.

3. A family charge; a dependent; particularly, a child or children; as, a widow without *encumbrances*. [Colloq.]

4. Any useless addition or load.

Syn.—Clog, burden, hindrance, impediment, load.

en-çum′brăn-cẽr, in-çum′brăn-cẽr, *n.* One who has an encumbrance or a legal claim on an estate.

en-çũr′tain (-tin), *v.t.* To inclose or drape with curtains or as with curtains.

-en-cy. A noun suffix from L. *-entia*, nearly equivalent to *-ence*, but usually signifying the quality or state; as, effici*ency*, emerg*ency*, conveni*ency*. [See *-ance*.]

en-çyç′liç, en-çyç′li-căl, *a.* [L. *encyclios*; Gr. *enkyklios*, in a circle, general, common: *en*. in, and *kyklos*, a circle.] Circular; sent to many persons or places; intended for many or for a whole order of men; as, the *encyclic* letters of the pope.

en-çyç′liç, en-çyç′li-căl, *n.* A circular letter; especially one from the pope to the bishops of the Roman Catholic church on a topic of general interest.

en-çȳ-clō-pē′di-ȧ, en-çȳ-clō-pæ′di-ȧ, *n.* [Gr. *enkyklopaideia*, for *enkyklios paideia*, instruction in the circle of the arts and sciences; *enkyklios*, in a circle, general, and *paideia*, education, from *paideuein*, to educate, bring up a child, from *pais*, *paidos*, a child.]

1. The circle of sciences; a general system of instruction or knowledge. [Rare.]

2. Specifically, a work in which the various branches of knowledge, or many of them, are discussed separately, and usually in alphabetical order; a cyclopedia; as, the French *Encyclopedia*.

en-çȳ″clō-pē-dī′ȧ-căl, *a.* Same as *Encyclopedic*.

en-çȳ-clō-pē′di-ăn, *a.* Embracing the whole circle of learning. [Rare.]

en-çȳ-clō-pē′diç, en-çȳ-clō-pæ′diç, *a.* Relating to or resembling an encyclopedia; comprehending or treating of a wide range of subjects.

en-çȳ-clō-pē′diç-ăl, en-çȳ-clō-pæ′diç-ăl, *a.* Same as *Encyclopedic*.

en-çȳ-clō-pē′dism, *n.* 1. The art or act of writing or compiling encyclopedias; the possession of broad and varied knowledge; extensive learning.

2. [E—] The doctrines of the French Encyclopedists.

en-çȳ-clō-pē′dist, *n.* 1. The compiler of an encyclopedia or one who assists in such compilation.

2. One whose knowledge comprehends a great variety of subjects.

3. [E—] In French history, one of the collaborators in the great French Encyclopedia, published in the latter half of the eighteenth century. They were the chief exponents of the French skepticism of their period.

en-cyst′, *v.t.*; encysted, *pt.*, *pp.*; encysting, *ppr.* To envelop in a cyst.

en-cys-tā′tion, *n.* See *Encystment*.

en-cyst′ed, *a.* Inclosed in a cyst or vesicle; as, an *encysted* tumor.

en-cyst′ment, *n.* 1. The act or process of encysting or the state of being encysted.

2. In biology, a process undergone by certain of the *Protozoa* and *Infusoria* previous to fission. They coat themselves with a secretion of gelatinous matter, which gradually hardens and incloses the body in a cyst. Sometimes peculiar vesicular bodies become formed in the interior of the cyst, through which they finally burst, and, becoming ruptured at the apex, give exit to the embryos contained in their interior.

end, *n.* [ME. *ende*, *eende*; AS. *ende*; D. *einde*, *eind*; O.H.G. *enti*; G. *ende*; Ice. *endir*, *endi*; Sw. *ände*; Goth. *andeis*; Sans. *anta*, end, limit, border.]

1. The extreme point of a line or of anything that has more length than breadth; the extremity or last part, in general; the close or conclusion; limit; termination; as, the *end* of a house; the *end* of a table; the *end* of a finger; the *end* of a chain or rope.

At the *end* of two months, she returned. —Judges xi. 39.

2. Consequence; issue; result; conclusive event; conclusion.

The *end* of those things is death. —Rom. vi. 21.

3. Close of life; death; decease; destruction; also, the cause of death; a destroyer.

Unblamed through life, lamented in thy *end*. —Pope.

And award
Either of you to be the other's *end*.—Shak.

4. A fragment or broken piece; a scrap; that which is left; as, candle-*ends*

5. The ultimate point or thing at which one aims or directs his views; the object intended to be reached or accomplished by any action or scheme; purpose intended; scope; aim; drift; as, private *ends*; public *ends*.

The *end* of all is an action, not a thought, though it were of the noblest. —Carlyle.

6. In spinning, a loose, untwisted ribbon of cotton or wool; a sliver.

7. In mining, the farthest or last portion of a level driven on the course of the lode.

8. In football, one who plays at either extremity of the rush-line; also, the position played; as, right *end*; left *end*.

An end, for *on end*; upright; erect; as, his hair stands *an end*.

At one's wit's end; in such a position that one does not know what further to do.

End for end; in nautical language, applied to a rope or any article, as a log of timber, a spar, etc., reversed, so that the one end occupies the place that the other did before.

End on; with the bow foremost; said of vessels.

In the end; at the end; finally.

On end; (a) standing erect; upright; as, place the log *on end*; (b) continuously; as, he spoke for two hours *on end*.

The ends of the earth; in Scripture, the remotest parts of the earth or the inhabitants of those parts.

To make both ends meet; to keep one's expenditure within one's income or at least to keep them equal.

To put an end to; to terminate or destroy.

Syn.—Extremity, close, cessation, finish, sequel, termination.—*End* and *extremity* imply the last of those parts which constitute a thing, but the *end* designates that part generally; the *extremity* marks the particular point. *End* may be said of that which bounds anything; but *extremity* of that which extends farthest from us; we may speak of the *ends* of that which is circular in its form or of that which has no specific form, but we speak of the *extremities* of that only which is supposed to project lengthwise. The *end* is opposed to the beginning; the *extremity* to the center or point from which we reckon.

end, *v.t.*; ended, *pt.*, *pp.*; ending, *ppr.* [ME *enden*, *endien*; AS. *endian*; D. *einden*; G. *enden*; Ice. *enda*, to end.]

1. To finish; to close; to conclude; to terminate; as, to *end* a controversy; to *end* a war.

On the seventh day God *ended* his work. —Gen. ii. 2.

2. To destroy; to put to death.

3. To complete or to be at the end of; as, that *ends* my task; the cane is *ended* by a ferrule.

To end up; to set on end, as a cask.

end, *v.i.* 1. To come to the ultimate point; to cease; as, a voyage *ends* with the return of a ship.

2. To terminate; to close; to conclude; as, the discourse *ended* with impressive words.

All's well that *ends* well. —Shak.

Syn.—Terminate, close.—To *end* is indefinite in its meaning and general in its application; *terminate* and *close* are modes of *ending*; to *terminate* is to *end* finally; to *close*, to *end* gradually. Whatever is begun will *end*, and it may *end* in any way; but what *terminates* is that which has been designedly brought to an *end*; a string, a line, a verse, etc., may *end*, but a road is said properly to *terminate*.

end'ȧ-ble, *a.* Capable of being ended; terminable.

end'=all, *n.* Final close. [Rare.]

en-dam'āġe, *v.t.* To bring loss or damage to; to harm; to injure; to prejudice. [Rare.]

The trial hath *endamaged* thee no way. —Milton.

en-dam'āġe-ȧ-ble, *a.* Capable of being injured; damageable. [Obs.]

en-dam'āġe-ment, *n.* Damage; loss; injury [Obs.]

en-dam'ni-fȳ, *v.t.* To injure; to impair; to cause loss to; to damnify. [Rare.]

en-dān'ġẽr, *v.t.*; endangered, *pt.*, *pp.*; endangering, *ppr.* 1. To put in hazard; to bring into danger or peril; to expose to loss or injury; as, we dread anything that *endangers* our life, our peace, or our happiness.

2. To incur the hazard of. [Rare.]

Syn.—Imperil, expose, peril, jeopardize, hazard, risk.

en-dān'ġẽr-ment, *n.* Hazard; danger.

en-därk', *v.t.* To darken. [Obs.]

en-das-pid'ē-ăn, *a.* [Gr. *endon*, within, and *aspis* (*-idos*), a shield.] In ornithology, having the anterior scutellæ lapped around the inner side of the tarsus, but deficient on the outer side.

en-daz'zle, *v.t.* To dazzle. [Obs.]

end'=bulb, *n.* One of the bulbous end-organs of sensory nerves.

en-dēar', *v.t.*; endeared, *pt.*, *pp.*; endearing, *ppr.* 1. To make dear; to make more beloved; to bind by ties of affection and love.

2. To raise the price of. [Rare.]

en-dēar'ed-ly, *adv.* With affection; in an endearing manner; dearly.

en-dēar'ed-ness, *n.* The state of being endeared.

en-dēar'ing, *a.* Making dear or more beloved.

en-dēar'ing-ly, *adv.* In an endearing or affectionate manner.

en-dēar'ment, *n.* 1. The manifestation of love; that which excites or increases tenderness of affection.

Her first *endearments* twining round the soul. —Thomson.

2. The act of endearing; the state of being beloved; tender affection.

en-deav'ŏr, en-deav'oŭr (-dev'), *n.* An effort; an essay; an attempt; an exertion of physical strength or the intellectual powers toward the attainment of an object; as, labor is a continued *endeavor* or a succession of *endeavors*.

To do one's endeavor; to do one's best.

Syn.—Effort, exertion, struggle, trial, essay, attempt.—*Endeavor* is the widest term. An *effort* is a vigorous *endeavor* or taxing of one's powers; an *exertion* is a peculiarly earnest and prolonged *effort*; a *struggle* is a violent and exhausting *effort* of the body.

en-deav'ŏr (-dev'), *v.t.*; endeavored, *pt.*, *pp.*; endeavoring, *ppr.* [Fr. *en*, in, and *devoir*, duty, from the use of these words in such expressions as *se mettre en devoir*, to try to do, to set about; *devoir*, from L. *debere*, to owe, be under obligation.] To attempt to gain; to try to effect; to strive to achieve or attain; to strive after.

It is our duty to *endeavour* the recovery of these beneficial subjects. —Chatham.

en-deav'ŏr (-dev'), *v.i.* To exert physical strength or intellectual power for the accomplishment of an object; to try; to essay; to attempt; as, in a race each man *endeavors* to outstrip his antagonist.

en-deav'ŏr-ẽr, *n.* One who makes an effort or attempt.

en-deav'ŏr-ment, *n.* Endeavor. [Obs.]

en-deg'ȧ-gon, *n.* See *Hendecagon*.

en-de-çag'y-nous, *a.* See *Hendecagynous*.

en'dē-çāne, *n.* See *Hendecane*.

en-deç-ȧ-phyl'lous, *a.* See *Hendecaphyllous*.

en-deiç'tiç, *a.* [Gr. *endeiktikos*, from *endeiknynai*, to point out, give proof; *en*, in, and *deiknynai*, to point out.] Showing; exhibiting; as, an *endeictic* dialogue, in the Platonic philosophy, is one which exhibits a specimen of skill.

en-deix'is, *n.* [Gr. *endeixis*, a pointing out, from *endeiknynai*, to point out.] In medicine, an indication or symptom.

en-dē'mi-ăl, *a.* [Rare.] Same as *Endemic*.

en-dem'iç, en-dem'iç-ăl, *a.* [Gr. *endēmos*, equal to *endēmos*, native, belonging to a people; *en*, in, and *dēmos*, the people.]

1. Peculiar to a people or nation; thus, an *endemic* disease is one to which the inhabitants of a particular country are peculiarly subject, and which, for that reason, may be supposed to proceed from local causes, as bad air or water. The word is also applied to a disease which prevails in a particular season, chiefly or wholly in a particular place.

2. Native; not introduced or naturalized.

en-dem'iç, *n.* A disease of an endemic nature.

en-dem'iç-ăl-ly, *adv.* In an endemic manner.

en-dem-i-ol'ō-ġy, *n.* [Gr. *endēmios*, native, belonging to the people, and *-logia*, from *legein*, to speak.] The branch of medicine treating of endemic diseases; a treatise on endemic diseases.

en-den-i-zā'tion, *n.* The act or ceremony of naturalization. [Rare.]

en-den'ize, *v.t.* Same as *Endenizen*.

en-den'i-zen, *v.t.* [*En-*, and *denizen*, from OFr. *denzein*, one living within.] To naturalize. [Rare.]

end'ẽr, *n.* One who ends or finishes.

en-dẽr-mat'iç, *a.* Same as *Endermic*.

en-dẽr'miç, *a.* [Gr. *en*, in, and *derma*, the skin.] In medicine, applied to the skin or acting through the skin; a term applied to that method of using medicines in which they are rubbed into the skin, especially after the cuticle has been removed, as by a blister.

Endermic method; the method of medical treatment in which the medicine enters the system through the skin.

en-dẽr'miç-ăl-ly, *adv.* In medicine, according to the endermic method.

en'de-ron, *n.* [Gr. *en*, in, and *deros*, the skin.] In anatomy, the dermis or true skin, and the corresponding deep part of the mucous membrane, as distinguished from the epidermis.

en-de-ron'iç, *a.* Pertaining to the enderon.

en-dew', *v.t.* To endue. [Obs.]

end'=flȳ, *n.* A bobfly.

en-dī'ȧ-demed, *a.* Diademed. [Rare.]

en-dī'ȧ-pẽr, *v.t.* To apply a diaper pattern to, by way of embellishment.

en-diçt' (-dīt'), *v.t.* [Obs.] See *Indict*.

en-diçt'ment (-dīt'), *n.* [Obs.] See *Indictment*.

end'ing, *n.* 1. Termination; conclusion.

2. In grammar, the terminating syllable or letter of a word.

en-dīte', *v.t.* [Obs.] See *Indite*.

en-dīte', *n.* [Gr. *endon*, within, and *-ite*.] In zoölogy, an appendage on the inner side of the limbs of some crustaceans.

en'dive, *n.* [Fr. *endive*; Sp. *endibia*; LL. *intiba*, from L. *intibus*, *intybus*, endive.] A plant, *Cichorium Endivia*, natural order *Compositæ*, a native of Asia, but now widely cultivated and used as a salad.

end'less, *a.* 1. Without end; having no end or conclusion; applied to length and to duration; as, an *endless* line; *endless* duration; *endless* bliss.

2. Perpetually recurring; seemingly without end; incessant; continual; as, *endless* praise; *endless* clamor.

3. Profitless. [Obs.]

4. Lacking design or object; aimless.

Endless chain; see under *Chain*.

Endless screw; a screw, the thread of which gears into a wheel with skew teeth, the obliquity corresponding to the angle of pitch of the screw. It is generally used as a means of producing slow motion in the adjustments of machines, rather than for transmitting any great amount of power.

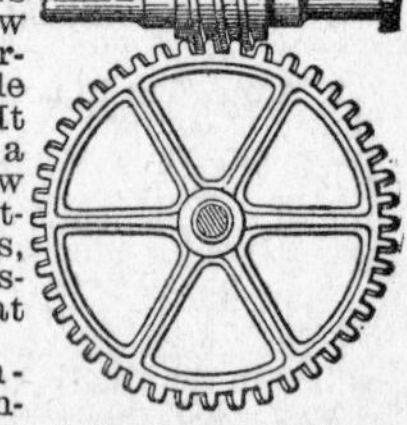
Endless Screw and Wheel.

Syn.—Boundless, unending, interminable, infinite, imperishable, eternal, unceasing, undying, unlimited, continual, uninterrupted.

end'less-ly, *adv.* 1. Without end or termination; as, to extend a line *endlessly*.

2. Incessantly; perpetually; continually.

3. Without purpose; uselessly; aimlessly; as, he is laboring quite *endlessly*

end'less-ness, *n.* 1. Extension without end or limit.

2. Perpetuity; endless duration.

end'long, *adv.* Along; in a line; with the end forward. [Rare.]

end'=man, *n.* Any man at the end of a line or row of men, or at the end of some object; in negro minstrelsy, a comedian who sits at one of the ends of the semicircle of performers.

end'mōst, *a.* Farthest; remotest.

en-dō-, end-. Combining forms from Gr. *endon*, within, and signifying within, inside; as, *endo*cœlar; *endo*cardium.

en'dō-blast, *n.* [*Endo-*, and Gr. *blastos*, a germ.] In biology, same as *nucleus*.

en-dō-blas'tiç, *a.* Pertaining to the endoblast.

en-dō-çär'di-aç, en-dō-çär'di-ăl, *a.* [*Endo-*, and Gr. *kardia*, heart.]

1. Relating to the endocardium.

2. Generated within the heart; situated within the heart.

en"dō-çär-dī'tis, *n.* [*Endo-*, and Gr *kardia*, heart, and *-itis*.] Inflammation of the endocardium.

en-dō-çär'di-um, *n.* A colorless transparent membrane which lines the interior of the heart.

en'dō-çärp, *n.* [*Endo-*, and Gr *karpos*, fruit.] In botany, the inner layer of the pericarp, when its texture differs from the outer layer. It may be hard and stony as in the plum and peach, membranous as in the apple, or fleshy as in the orange. The *endocarp* or stone, the epicarp or outer skin, and the mesocarp or fleshy part are shown in the cut.

Fruit of Common Peach (*Amygdalus Persica*).

en-dō-çhon'drăl, *a.* [*Endo-*, and Gr. *chondros*, cartilage, and *-al*.] Situated or developing within cartilage.

en-dō-çhō'ri-on, *n.* [*Endo-*, and Gr. *chorion*, a membrane, the chorion.] The layer of the allantois, lining the chorion.

en'dō-çhrōme, *n.* [*Endo-*, and Gr. *chrōma*, color.] In botany, the coloring matter, other than green, in plant-cells.

en-dō-cœ'lăr (-sē'), *a.* Situated on the inner wall, or visceral side, of the body-cavity.

en'dō-çōne, *n.* [*Endo-*, and Gr. *kōnos*, a cone.] One of the internal conical sheaths of certain cephalopods.

en-dō-çrā'ni-ăl, *a.* Within the cranium; pertaining to the endocranium.

en-dō-çrā'ni-um, *n.* [*Endo-*, and Gr. *kranion*, the skull.] The inner surface of the cranium.

en-doç'trine, *v.t.* To teach; to indoctrinate. [Obs.]

en'dō-çyst, *n.* [*Endo-*, and Gr. *kystis*, a bladder.] The inner layer of the cell of a polyzoön.

en'dō-dẽrm, *n.* [*Endo-*, and Gr. *derma*, skin.]

The innermost layer of cells in metazoic animals, representing the lining of the enteron.

en-dō-dẽr′măl, en-dō-dẽr′mic̦, *a.* Pertaining to the endoderm.

en-dō-dẽr′mis, *n.* In botany, a layer of cells forming a sheath around a fibrovascular bundle.

en-dog′ȧ-mous, *a.* [*Endo-*, and Gr. *gamos*, marriage.] Pertaining to or indicating marriage of persons of the same tribe or group.

en-dog′ȧ-my, *n.* Marriage within one's own tribe, a custom of some savage peoples; opposed to *exogamy*.

en′dō-ġen, *n.* [*Endo-*, and Gr. *-genēs*, producing.] An endogenous plant.

en-dō-ġen′e-sis, *n.* Same as *Endogeny*.

en″dō-ġē-net′ic̦, *a.* Endogenous.

en-doġ′e-nous, *a.* [*Endo-*, and Gr. *-genēs*, producing.]

1. In botany, increasing by internal growth, without distinction of pith, wood, and bark, as in the date-palm, sugar-cane, etc.

2. Starting from within; growing internally.

Endogenous multiplication; in biology, a method of cell-formation, of both animal and vegetable cells, dependent on progressive multiplication by repeated division of nucleus and protoplasm.

Endogen. 1. Section of the stem of a Palm: *c*, Portion of stem, natural size, showing the ends of the bundles of woody fiber; *e*, Remains of leaf-stalks; *f*, Bundles of woody fiber. 2. Endogenous Leaf, showing its parallel veins. 3. Monocotyledonous Seed, showing its single cotyledon: *a a*, Cotyledon. 4. Germination of Palm: *c*, Cotyledon; *b*, Albumen; *d*, Plumule; *e*, Radicle issuing from a short sheath, endorhiza. 5. Flower of Endogen.

en-doġ′e-nous-ly, *adv.* In biology, in an endogenous manner.

en-doġ′e-ny, *n.* In biology, a growing from within; a multiplication of cells within a cell.

en′dog-nath, *n.* [*Endo-*, and Gr. *gnathos*, a jaw.] In zoölogy, the chief or inner division of the oral apparatus of a crustacean. [See *Maxilla*.]

en-dog′nā-thăl, *a.* In zoölogy, of or relating to the endognath.

en′dō-lymph, *n.* [*Endo-*, and L. *lympha*, water.] In anatomy, the aqueous fluid characteristic of the internal ear.

en″dō-lym-phan′ġi-ăl, *a.* [*Endo-*, and L. *lympha*, water, and Gr. *angeion*, a vessel.] In anatomy, situated or included in a lymphatic vessel.

en″dō-lym-phat′ic̦, *a.* [*Endo-*, and L. *lympha*, water, and *-atic*.] In anatomy, (a) relating to or inclosing endolymph; (b) situated or included in a lymphatic vessel.

en-dōme′, *v.t.* To furnish with a dome.

en-dō-mẽr′sion, *n.* See *Endomersion objective* under *Objective*.

en″dō-mē-tri′tis, *n.* [*Endo-*, and Gr. *mētra*, womb, and *-itis*.] In medicine, an inflammatory condition of the endometrium.

en-dō-mē′tri-um, *n.* [*Endo-*, and Gr. *mētra*, the womb.] In anatomy, the inner lining of the womb.

en′dō-morph, *n.* [*Endo-*, and Gr. *morphē*, form.] In mineralogy, a crystal of one kind inclosed within one of another kind.

en-dō-mor′phic̦, *a.* [*Endo-*, and Gr. *morphē*, form, and *-ic*.] Having been formed within, as one kind of rock within another.

en-dō-mys′i-um, *n.* [*Endo-*, and Gr. *mys*, a muscle.] In anatomy, the tissue connecting muscular fibers.

en-dō-neū′ri-um, *n.* [*Endo-*, and Gr. *neuron*, a nerve.] In anatomy, tissue connecting nerve fibers.

en-dō-par′ȧ-sīte, *n.* [*Endo-*, and Gr. *parasitos*, a parasite.] In zoölogy, any parasite that inhabits the internal organs of animals, as the tapeworm.

en″dō-par-ȧ-sit′ic̦, *a.* Of or relating to endoparasites.

en-dō-path′ic̦, *a.* [*Endo-*, and Gr. *pathos*, suffering.] In medicine, relating to diseases arising from internal causes; autopathic.

en″dō-pe-rid′i-um, *n.*; *pl.* **en″dō-pe-rid′i-ȧ.** [*Endo-*, and *peridium*, from Gr. *peri*, around, and dim. *-idion*.] In botany, the inner of two peridia, as distinguished from *exoperidium*.

en-doph′ȧ-ġy, *n.* [*Endo-*, and Gr. *phagein*, to eat.] In anthropology, cannibalism in which the cannibals find their victims in their own families or in their own tribes.

en-dō-phlœ′um (-flē′), *n.* [*Endo-*, and Gr. *phloios*, bark.] In botany, the part of the bark of a tree that is next to the wood.

en′dō-phragm (-fram), *n.* [*Endo-*, and Gr. *phragma*, a fence.] In zoölogy, a horny partition in the thorax of some *Crustacea*; written also *endophragma*.

en-dō-phrag′măl (-frag′), *a.* In zoölogy, of or relating to the endophragm.

en-doph′yl-lous, *a.* [*Endo-*, and Gr. *phyllon*, a leaf.] Involved in a leaf or sheath.

en′dō-phȳte, *n.* [*Endo-*, and Gr. *phyton*, a plant.] Same as *Entophyte*.

en-dō-phyt′ic̦, *a.* Same as *Entophytic*.

en-doph′y-tous, *a.* [*Endo-*, and Gr. *phyton*, a plant.] In zoölogy, fitted for penetrating and for living within plant-tissues, as some insects and their larvæ.

en′dō-plașm, *n.* [*Endo-*, and Gr. *plasma*, a thing formed, from *plassein*, to form, mold.] In biology, (a) the granular semifluid part of the protoplasm in a vegetable cell, as distinguished from the *ectoplasm*; (b) the endosarc of an animal cell; called also *chyme-mass* and *parenchyma*.

en-dō-plaș′mȧ, *n.* Same as *Endosarc*.

en′dō-plast, *n.* [*Endo-*, and Gr. *plastos*, formed.] In protozoan life, a plasmic collection resembling the nucleus of a histological cell.

En-dō-plas′ti-cȧ, *n.pl.* [*Endo-*, and Gr. *plastos*, from *plassein*, to form.] In zoölogy, a group of *Rhizopoda*, characterized by having a distinct endoplast, as in the amœba.

en-dō-plas′tron, *n.* Same as *Entoplastron*.

en-dō-plas′tūle, *n.* [*Endo-*, and Gr. *plastos*, formed, molded, and dim. *-ule*.] In biology, among the higher *Protozoa* (as the amœbas), that which corresponds to the nucleolus in a metazoic cell.

en-dō-pleū′rȧ, *n.*; *pl.* **en-dō-pleū′ræ.** [*Endo-*, and Gr. *pleura*, rib, side.] In botany, a membrane for the seed of a plant, the innermost when there are three; a tegmen.

en-dō-pleū′rīte, *n.* In zoölogy, among certain crustaceans, a lateral piece on the inside of the thorax attached to the membrane connecting the epimera; a part of the apodeme.

en-dop′ō-dīte, *n.* In zoölogy, the inner or principal branch of an ambulatory appendage of a crustacean.

En-dō-proc̦′tȧ, *n.pl.* Same as *Entoprocta*.

en-dō-proc̦′tous, *a.* Same as *Entoproctous*.

end′=ŏr″găn, *n.* The functional termination of a sensory nerve.

en-dō-rhī′zȧ, *n.*; *pl.* **en-dō-rhī′zæ.** [*Endo-*, and Gr. *rhiza*, a root.]

1. A monocotyledon; an endogenous plant.

2. [E—*pl.*] A name given by Richard in 1808 to the endogens as a class.

Endorhiza.

en′dō-rhi-zăl, *a.* Pertaining to the *Endorhizæ*.

en-dō-rhī′zous, *a.* Endorhizal.

en-dors′ȧ-ble, en-dorșe′, etc. See *Indorsable*, etc.

en-dorșe′, *n.* In heraldry, a pale-like subordinary much narrower than a pale.

en-dor-see′, *n.* See *Indorsee*.

en-dorșe′ment, *n.* See *Indorsement*.

en-dors′ẽr, *n.* See *Indorser*.

en′dō-sărc̦, *n.* [*Endo-*, and Gr. *sarx*, *sarkos*, flesh.] The granular inner layer of one-celled organisms; endoplasma.

en′dō-sc̦ōpe, *n.* [*Endo-*, and Gr. *skopein*, to view.] An instrument used for observing the inner organs of the body, as the rectum, the throat, etc.

en-dos′c̦ō-py, *n.* The art of using the endoscope.

en-dō-sī′phŏn, *n.* [*Endo-*, and Gr. *siphōn*, a tube.] The small inner siphon of a cephalopod cell.

en-dō-skel′e-tăl, *a.* Belonging to or associated with the endoskeleton.

en-dō-skel′e-tŏn, *n.* [*Endo-*, and Gr. *skeleton*, a dry body.] The bone or bone-like interior framework of an animal as distinguished from the outer covering, or *exoskeleton*.

en-dos′mic̦, *a.* Pertaining to endosmose.

en-dos-mom′e-tẽr, *n.* [*Endo-*, and Gr. *ōsmos*, a thrusting, impulsion, and *metron*, a measure.] An instrument to measure the rapidity of endosmotic action.

en-dos-mō-met′ric̦, *a.* Pertaining to measurements of endosmotic action.

en′dos-mōse, *n.* [*Endo-*, and Gr. *ōsmos*, a thrusting, impulsion, from *ōthein*, to push, thrust.] Same as *Endosmosis*.

en-dos-mō′sis, *n.* In physics, the passing of a fluid inward through a porous partition separating it from another fluid of different character; the opposite of *exosmosis*.

en-dos-mos′mic̦, *a.* Same as *Endosmotic*.

en-dos-mot′ic̦, *a.* Relating to endosmosis; endosmic.

Endosmotic equivalent; see *Osmotic equivalent* under *Osmotic*.

en′dō-sōme, *n.* [*Endo-*, and Gr. *sōma*, body.] In zoölogy, the interior part of a sponge.

en′dō-spẽrm, *n.* [*Endo-*, and Gr. *sperma*, seed.] In botany, the albumen contained in the embryonic part of a seed.

en-dō-spẽr′mic̦, *a.* Relating to the endosperm; of the nature of the endosperm.

en′dō-spōre, *n.* [*Endo-*, and Gr. *sporos*, a sowing, seed.] In biology, (a) the very thin inner covering of some spores; (b) spore formed and contained within a single living cell.

en-dō-spōr′ous, *a.* Characterized by endogenous spore-formation, as certain fungi.

en-doss′, *v.t.* [Fr. *endosser*, to put on the back, indorse; *en*, in, and *dos*, back, from L. *dorsum*, back.] To indorse. [Obs.]

en-dos′tē-ȧ, *n.*, pl. of *endosteum*.

en-dos′tē-ăl, *a.* 1. Relating to endostosis.

2. Situated inside the bone.

en-dō-stẽr′nīte, *n.* [*Endo-*, and Gr. *sternon*, the breast, chest, and *-ite*.] One of the parts of the endothorax of crustaceans and insects, originating in the intersternal membrane.

en-dō-stẽr′num, *n.* [*Endo-*, and Gr. *sternon*, the breast, chest.] Same as *Entosternum*.

en-dos′tē-um, *n.*; *pl.* **en-dos′tē-ȧ.** In anatomy, the membrane lining the cavity of a bone.

en-dos′tō-mȧ, *n.* [*Endo-*, and Gr. *stoma*, mouth.]

1. In some crustaceans, a posterior plate which supports the labrum.

2. In pathology, a tumor within a bone.

en′dō-stōme, *n.* [*Endo-*, and Gr. *stoma*, the mouth.]

1. In botany, (a) the opening through the inner integument of an ovule; (b) the inside peristome of a moss.

2. In zoölogy, same as *endostoma*.

en-dos-tō′sis, *n.* [*Endo-*, and Gr. *osteon*, a bone, and *-osis*.]

1. In physiology, the process by which bone is formed within the cartilaginous substance.

2. In pathology, an endostoma or tumor within a bone.

en-dos′trȧ-c̦um, *n.* [*Endo-*, and Gr. *ostrakon*, a shell.] In zoölogy, the inner layer of a crustacean's exoskeleton.

en′dō-stȳle, *n.* [*Endo-*, and Gr. *stylos*, a pillar.] In zoölogy, (a) a peculiar fold of the endoderm projecting into the blood-cavity of an ascidian; (b) in the *Amphioxus*, a fold of the ventral side of the pharynx similar to that in the ascidians.

en-dō-thē′c̦ȧ, *n.*; *pl.* **en-dō-thē′c̦æ** (-sē). [*Endo-*, and Gr. *thēkē*, a case, chest.] The hard substance making up the lining of the visceral chamber of a coral.

en-dō-thē′c̦ăl, *a.* Of or pertaining to endotheca.

en-dō-thē′ci-um, *n.* [*Endo-*, and Gr. *thēkē*, a case, chest.] In botany, (a) a mass of cells in the center of a rudimentary capsule of a moss; (b) in flowering plants, the interior lining of an anther-cell.

en-dō-thē′li-ăl, *a.* Pertaining to endothelium.

en-dō-thē′li-oid, *a.* Having the nature or appearance of endothelium.

en″dō-thē-li-ō′mȧ, *n.* [*Endo-*, and Gr. *thēlē*, nipple, and *ōma*, a tumor.] A tumor originating in or resembling the structure of endothelium.

en-dō-thē′li-um, *n.*; *pl.* **en-dō-thē′li-ȧ.** In anatomy, the delicate lining of the blood-vessels, lymphatics, and all serous cavities.

en-dō-thẽr′mic̦, *a.* [*Endo-*, and Gr. *thermē*, heat, and *-ic*.] Relating to chemical reaction in which heat is absorbed; opposed to *exothermic*.

en-dō-thō′rax, *n.* [*Endo-*, and Gr. *thōrax*, a breastplate, chest.] In zoölogy, the internal processes of the sternal plate in an insect or a crustacean.

en-dow′, *v.t.*; endowed, *pt.*, *pp.*; endowing, *ppr.* [ME. *endowen*; OFr. *endouer*; *en*, in, and *douer*, to endow, from L. *dotare*, to give.]

1. To furnish with a portion of goods or estate, called dower; to settle a dower on, as on a married woman or widow.

2. To settle on as a permanent provision; to furnish with a permanent fund of property; as, to *endow* a church; to *endow* a college with a fund to support a professor.

3. To enrich or furnish with any gift, quality, or faculty; to indue; as, man is *endowed* with reason.

en-dow′ẽr, *v.t.* To endow; to enrich with a portion. [Obs.]

en-dow′ẽr, *n.* One who enriches with a portion.

en-dow′ment, *n.* 1. The act of providing with a dower, fund, or permanent provision for the support of a person.

2. That which is bestowed or settled on; property, fund, or revenue, permanently appropriated to any object; as, the *endowments* of a church, of a hospital, or of a college.

3. That which is given or bestowed on the person or mind; gift of nature; as, natural activity of limbs is an *endowment* of the body.

Syn.—Gift, provision, benefit, benefaction, capacity, attainment, qualification.

En-dō-zō′ȧ, *n.pl.* [*Endo-*, and Gr. *zōon*, pl. *zōa*, an animal.] Same as *Entozoa*.

en-dō-zō′ic̦, *a.* Same as *Entozoic*.

end′=plāte, *n.* In anatomy, a kind of expansion of tissue connecting a muscle with the terminal of a motor nerve.

end′=plāy, *n.* In machinery, space allowed for movement endwise.

en-drudge′ (-druj′), *v.t.* To make a drudge or slave of. [Obs.]

end′=stōne, *n.* One of the jewels in a timepiece against which a pivot abuts.

en-dūe′, *v.t.*; endued, *pt., pp.*; enduing, *ppr.* 1. To invest, as with grace or some spiritual quality; as, to *endue* men's minds with patience.

2. To endow. [Obs.]

en-dūe′, *v.t.* [OFr. *enduire, induire*, to bring in, cover, digest.] To digest; said of birds, especially of hawks. [Obs.]

en-dūe′ment, *n.* Endowment.

en-dūr′ȧ-ble, *a.* That can be borne or suffered.

en-dūr′ȧ-ble-ness, *n.* The state or quality of being endurable.

en-dūr′ȧ-bly, *adv.* In an endurable manner.

en-dūr′ănce, *n.* 1. Continuance; a state of lasting or duration; lastingness.

2. A bearing or suffering; a continuing under pain or distress without resistance, or without sinking or yielding to the pressure; sufferance; patience.

Their fortitude was most admirable in their patience and *endurance* of all evils, of pain, and of death. —Temple.

Syn.—Fortitude, patience, resignation, sufferance.

en-dūr′ănt, *a.* Having ability to endure suffering, pain, disappointment, etc. [Rare.]

en-dūre′, *v.i.*; endured, *pt., pp.*; enduring, *ppr.* [ME. *enduren*; OFr. *endurer*, to bear, last, from L. *indurare*; *in*, in, and *durare*, to harden, to hold out, last; *durus*, hard.]

1. To last; to continue in the same state without perishing; to remain; to abide.

The Lord shall *endure* forever. —Ps. ix. 7.

2. To bear; to brook; to suffer without resistance, or without yielding.

How can I *endure* to see the evil that shall come unto my people? —Esther viii. 6.

en-dūre′, *v.t.* 1. To bear; to sustain; to support without breaking or yielding to force or pressure; as, metals *endure* a certain degree of heat without melting.

Both were of shining steel, and wrought so pure,
As might the strokes of two such arms *endure*.
—Dryden.

2. To bear with patience; to bear without opposition or sinking under the pressure.

Therefore I *endure* all things for the elect's sakes. —2 Tim. ii. 10.

3. To undergo; to sustain.

I wish to die, yet dare not death *endure*.
—Dryden.

4. To harden; to inure. [Obs.]

Syn.—Bear, last, suffer, remain, continue, submit to, sustain, undergo, continue.

en-dūr′ẽr, *n.* 1 One who bears, suffers, or sustains.

2. He who or that which continues long.

en-dūr′ing, *a.* Having capacity for remaining or continuing; durable; not to be destroyed; as, an *enduring* monument; *enduring* remembrance.

en-dūr′ing-ly, *adv.* For a long time; permanently.

en-dūr′ing-ness, *n.* The quality or state of enduring; permanence; lastingness.

end′wīse, end′wāys, *adv.* 1. On the end; erectly; in an upright position.

2. With the end forward.

en′dy-mȧ, *n.* Same as *Ependyma*.

en′dy-mal, *a.* Same as *Ependymal*.

en′dy-sis, *n.*; *pl.* **en′dy-sēs.** [Gr. *endysis*, a putting on, entering into, from *endyein*, to put on, get into.] In biology, the growth of new plumage, hair, or scales; opposite of *ecdysis*.

-ene A suffix from L. *-enus*, used (a) as a termination of adjectives of Latin origin; as, ser*ene*; (b) in chemistry, to denote a hydrocarbon which belongs to the olefine series; as, ethyl*ene*; benz*ene*.

en′ē-çāte, *v.t.* [L. *enecatus*, pp. of *enecare*, to kill off; *e*, out, and *necare*, to kill.] To kill; to destroy. [Obs.]

ē-nē′ci-ȧ (-shi-ȧ), *n.* [Gr. *ēnekēs*, bearing onward, continuous.] In medicine, any protracted fever

E-nē′id, *n.* Same as *Æneid*.

en′e-mȧ (*or* e-nē′mȧ), *n.*; *pl.* **e-nem′ȧ-tȧ.** [Gr. *enema*, an injection, from *enienai*, to send in; *en*, in, and *hienai*, to send.] An injection, introduced into the rectum, as a medicine, or to impart nourishment.

en′e-my, *n.*; *pl.* **en′e-mieṣ.** [ME. *enemy*; OFr. *enemi*; L. *inimicus*, unfriendly, hostile (as substantive, an enemy); *in-* priv., and *amicus*, a friend.]

1. A foe; an adversary.

2. One who hates or dislikes; as, an *enemy* to truth or falsehood.

3. That which harms; something dangerous; as, disease is an *enemy* of the human race.

4. In military affairs, the opposing army or naval force in war.

en′e-my, *a.* Hostile; opposed. [Obs.]

en-ep-i-dẽr′miç, *a.* [Gr. *en*, in, and *epidermis*, the outer skin; *epi*, upon, and *derma*, skin, and *-ic*.] In medicine, applied to or laid on the skin without rubbing; as, *enepidermic* treatment.

en-ẽr-get′iç, *a.* [Gr. *energētikos*, from *energein*, to be in action, from *energēs, energos*, working, active; *en*, in, and *ergon*, work.] Characterized by or exhibiting energy; operating with force, vigor, and effect; forcible; powerful; efficacious; as, an *energetic* man; *energetic* methods.

en-ẽr-get′iç-ăl, *a.* Energetic.

en-ẽr-get′iç-ăl-ly, *adv.* With force and vigor; with energy and effect.

en-ẽr-get′iç-ăl-ness, *n.* The quality or state of being energetic.

en-ẽr-get′içs, *n.* The branch of science which treats of physical forces and their phenomena, excluding all phenomena of vital or mental forces.

en-ẽr′ġiç, *a.* Having or exhibiting energy. [Rare.]

en-ẽr′ġiç-ăl, *a.* Energic.

en′ẽr-ġīze, *v.t.*; energized, *pt., pp.*; energizing, *ppr.* To give strength or force to; to give active vigor to; as, to *energize* the will.

en′ẽr-ġīze, *v.i.* To act energetically; to operate with vigor in producing effect; as, men *energize* first, reflect afterward.

en′ẽr-ġī-zẽr, *n.* Any agent or means of imparting or increasing energy.

en′ẽr-ġī-zing, *a.* Capable of giving energy, force, or vigor.

en-ẽr-gū′men, *n.* [L. *energumenus*; Gr. *energoumenos*, ppr. pass. of *energein*, to effect, work on.] A demoniac; one possessed by the devil.

en′ẽr-ġy, *n.* [LL. *energia*; Gr. *energeia*, action, operation, energy, from *energēs, energos*, active, at work; *en*, in, and *ergon*, work.]

1. Internal or inherent power; the power of operating, whether exerted or not; as, men possessing *energies* sometimes suffer them to lie inactive; danger will rouse the dormant *energies* of our natures into action.

2. Power exerted; vigorous operation; force; vigor; as, God, by his almighty *energy*, called the universe into existence; the administration of the laws requires *energy* in the magistrate.

3. Effectual operation; efficacy; strength or force producing the effect.

4. Strength of expression; force of utterance; life; spirit; emphasis; as, the language of Lord Chatham is remarkable for its *energy*.

5. In physics, the power of doing work; capacity for producing effect upon matter.

The fact that any agent is capable of doing work is usually expressed by the saying that it possesses *energy*, and the quantity of energy it possesses is measured by the amount of work it can do. The energy possessed by a mass in consequence of having been raised from the ground is commonly distinguished as *energy of position* or *potential energy*, and is measured by the product of the force tending to cause motion, into the distance through which the point of application of the force is capable of being displaced in the direction in which the force acts. The energy possessed by a body in consequence of its velocity is commonly distinguished as *energy of motion* or *kinetic energy*; it is measured by half the product of the moving mass into the square of its velocity.
—Atkinson's Ganot's Physics.

Conservation of energy; see under *Conservation*.

Correlation of energy; see under *Correlation*.

Degradation or *dissipation of energy*; see under *Dissipation*.

Energy of rotation; in physics, the energy imparted to a body in giving it rotary motion, measurable by the work it will do in coming to rest.

Syn.—Force, vigor.—With *energy* is connected the idea of activity; with *force* that of capability; with *vigor* that of health.

ē-nẽr′vāte (*or* en′ẽr-vāte), *a.* Weakened; weak; without strength or force.

ē-nẽr′vāte, *v.t.*; enervated, *pt., pp.*; enervating, *ppr.* [L. *enervatus*, pp. of *enervare*, to deprive of nerves or sinews, to weaken; *e*, out, and *nervus*, a nerve, sinew.]

1. To deprive of nerve, force, or strength; to weaken; to render feeble; as, idleness and voluptuous indulgences *enervate* the body.

2. To cut the nerves of; as, to *enervate* a horse.

Syn.—Debilitate, weaken, enfeeble.

en-ẽr-vā′tion, *n.* [LL. *enervatio*, from *enervare*, to weaken.]

1. The act of weakening or reducing strength.

2. The state of being weakened; effeminacy.

ē-nẽr′vā-tive, *a.* Having a tendency to enervate; weakening. [Rare.]

ē-nẽr′vā-tŏr, *n.* That which enervates.

ē-nẽrve′, *v.t.* To weaken; to enervate. [Obs.]

ē-nẽr′vōse, *a.* [L. *e*, without, and *nervosus*, nervous, sinewy.] In botany, without nerves or veins; as, *enervose* leaves.

ē-nẽrv′ous, *a.* Lacking vigor; enervated; nerveless. [Rare.]

en-fāce′, *v.t.*; enfaced (-fāst′), *pt., pp.*; enfacing, *ppr.* To write or print on the face of (a note, check, draft, or other negotiable paper).

en-fam′ine, *v.t.* and *v.i.* To famish. [Obs.]

en-fam′ish, *v.t.* To famish. [Obs.]

en-feçt′, *a.* [Obs.] See *Infect*.

en-fee′ble, *v.t.*; enfeebled, *pt., pp.*; enfeebling, *ppr.* [ME. *enfeblen*; OFr. *enfeblir*, to enfeeble; *en-*, in, and *feble*, feeble.] To deprive of strength; to reduce the strength or force of; to weaken; to debilitate; to enervate.

en-fee′ble-ment, *n.* The act of weakening; enervation.

en-fee′blẽr, *n.* One who or that which enfeebles.

en-fee′blish, *v.t.* To weaken. [Obs.]

en-fel′ŏned, *a.* Fierce; frantic. [Obs.]

en-feoff′ (en-fef′), *v.t.*; enfeoffed (-feft′), *pt., pp.*; enfeoffing, *ppr.* [OFr. *enfeofer, enfeffer*; *en-*, L. *in*, in, and *feffer*, to invest with a fief.]

1. To give a feud to; hence, to invest with a fee; to give (another) any corporeal hereditament in fee simple or fee tail, by livery of seizin. —Blackstone.

2. To surrender or give up. [Obs.]

en-feoff′ment (-fef′), *n.* 1. The act of giving the fee simple of an estate.

2. The instrument or deed by which one is invested with the fee of an estate.

en-fes′tẽr, *v.i.* To gather pus. [Obs.]

en-fet′tẽr, *v.t.*; enfettered, *pt., pp.*; enfettering, *ppr.* To fetter; to bind in fetters.

en-fē′vẽr, *v.t.* To excite fever in. [Rare.]

en-fierce′, *v.t.* To make fierce. [Obs.]

en-fi-lāde′, *n.* [Fr., a suite of rooms, a raking fire, a string, from *enfiler*, to thread, string, rake, from LL. *infilare*, to put on a thread, string; L. *in*, in, and *filum*, a thread.] A line or straight passage; specifically, in fortification, the situation of a place or body of men liable to be raked with shot through the whole extent.

en-fi-lāde′, *v.t.*; enfiladed, *pt., pp.*; enfilading, *ppr.* To sweep with shot lengthwise of a trench or line of troops.

en-filed′, *a.* [OFr. *enfiler*, to thread, string, rake.] In heraldry, piercing some object which is held impaled, as a head, a coronet, etc.

en-fīre′, *v.t.* To inflame; to set on fire. [Obs.]

en-flesh′, *v.t.* To put flesh upon. [Obs.]

en-fleu-rāge′ (oṅ-flē-räzh′), *n.* [Fr.] The manufacture of perfumery from flowers by means of oils or fats.

en-flow′ẽr, *v.t.*; enflowered, *pt., pp.*; enflowering, *ppr.* To decorate with flowers. [Poet.]

en-fōld′, *v.t.* Same as *Infold*.

en-fōld′ment, *n.* Same as *Infoldment*.

en-fonced′ (-fonst′), *a.* [Fr. *enfoncer*, to sink, to drive into.] Deeply sunken.

en-fōrce′, *v.t.*; enforced (-fōrst′), *pt., pp.*; enforcing, *ppr.* [ME. *enforcen*; OFr. *enforcer, enforcier*; LL. *infortiare*, to strengthen.]

1. To give strength to; to strengthen; to invigorate.

2. To make or gain by force; to force; as, to *enforce* a passage.

3. To put into action by violence; to drive.

Stones *enforced* from the old Assyrian slings.
—Shak.

4. To urge with energy; to give force to; to impress on the mind; as, to *enforce* remarks or arguments.

5. To constrain.

6. To cause to take effect; as, to *enforce* the laws.

7. To prove; to evince. [Obs.]

Syn.—Urge, compel, require, exact, exert, strain, execute, drive, constrain.

en-fōrce′, *v.i.* To increase; also, to struggle. [Obs.]

en-fōrce′, *n.* Force; strength; power. [Obs.]

en-fōrce′ȧ-ble, *a.* That may be enforced.

en-fōrced′ (-fōrst′), *a.* Strengthened; gained by force; carried into effect.

en-fōr′ced-ly, *adv.* By violence; not by choice.

en-fōrce′ment, *n.* 1. The act of enforcing; compulsion.

2. That which gives force, energy, or effect; sanction; as, the penalties of law are *enforcements*.

3. A putting into execution; as, the *enforcement* of law.

en-fōr′cẽr, *n.* One who enforces.

en-fōr′ci-ble, *a.* Enforceable.

en-fōr′cive, *a.* Having the quality of enforcing.

en-fōr′cive-ly, *adv.* With compulsion.

en-for′est, *v.t.*; enforested, *pt., pp.*; enforesting, *ppr.* [LL. *inforestare*, to convert into a forest.] To convert or transform into a forest.

en-fōrm′, *v.t.* To inform. [Obs.]

en-foul′dẽred, *a.* Mixed with lightning. [Obs.]

en-frāme′, *v.t.* To furnish with a frame. [Rare.]

en-fran′chīse, *v.t.*; enfranchised, *pt., pp.*; enfranchising, *ppr.* [OFr. *enfranchis-*, stem of *enfranchir*, to set free, enfranchise; *en-*, in, and *franchir*, to set free.]

1. To set free; to liberate from slavery.

2. To make free of a city, corporation, or

state; to admit to the privileges of a freeman; to make a citizen of.

3. To confer the right of suffrage upon.

4. To naturalize; to receive as a denizen; as, to *enfranchise* foreign words.

en-fran′chīse-ment, *n.* 1. Release from slavery or custody.

2. Formerly, the admission of persons to the freedom of a corporation or state; investiture with the privileges of free citizens; the incorporating of a person into any society or body politic; now, the conferring of the right of suffrage upon a person or class of persons.

Enfranchisement of copyhold lands; in old English law, conversion of copyhold tenements into freeholds.

en-fran′chis-ēr, *n.* One who enfranchises.

en-free′, *v.t.* To release from captivity or slavery. [Obs.]

en-free′dŏm, *v.t.* To invest with freedom. [Obs.]

en-freeze′, *v.t.* To freeze. [Obs.]

en-frō′wărd, *v.t.* To render froward. [Obs.]

en-gāge′, *v.t.*; engaged, *pt., pp.*; engaging, *ppr.* [OFr. *engager*; It. *ingaggiare*; LL. *invadiare*, to pledge, engage; *in*, in, and *vadium*, a pledge.]

1. To cause to give a pledge; to bind, as by contract or oath.

2. To enlist; to bring into a party; as, to *engage* men for service; to *engage* friends to aid in a cause.

3. To embark in an affair; as, be not hasty to *engage* yourself in party disputes.

4. To gain; to win and attach; to draw to; as, good nature *engages* every one to its possessor.

5. To unite and bind by contract or promise; as, nations *engage* themselves to each other by treaty.

6. To attract and fix; as, to *engage* the attention.

7. To occupy; to employ assiduously; as, we were *engaged* in conversation.

8. To attack in contest; to encounter; as, the army *engaged* the enemy at ten o'clock.

9. To employ; as, to *engage* a teacher for a child.

10. In mechanics, to interlock with so as to produce motion, as one cogwheel with another.

Syn.—Employ, hire, retain, reserve, attack.

en-gāge′, *v.i.* 1. To encounter; to begin to fight; to attack in conflict; as, the armies *engaged* at Marengo in a general battle.

2. To embark in any business; to take a concern in; to undertake; as, be cautious not to *engage* in controversy.

3. To promise or pledge one's word; to bind oneself; as a friend has *engaged* to supply the necessary funds.

4. In mechanics, to articulate, as the teeth of cogwheels.

5. In fencing, to touch and press the weapon of an adversary to prevent his taking one unawares.

en-gāged′, *a.* 1. Occupied; busy; employed; without leisure.

2. Under pledge, as in betrothal.

3. Busily employed; earnestly occupied; attentively studying.

4. Joined in conflict; as, the *engaged* regiment fought on.

5. In mechanics, geared together; interlocked.

Engaged column; in architecture, any column, a part of which is concealed by the wall immediately behind it, to which it is attached; hence, called also *attached column*.

Engaged Column.

en-gā′ged-ly, *adv.* With earnestness; with attachment.

en-gā′ged-ness, *n.* The state of being seriously and earnestly occupied; zeal; animation.

en-gāge′ment, *n.* 1. The act of engaging in any of its meanings.

2. The state of being engaged; a betrothal.

3. Obligation by agreement or contract.

4. Occupation; employment of the attention.

5. Employment in fighting; the conflict of armies or fleets; battle; a general action.

6. In mechanics, the state of fitting and working together of parts, so that motion of one produces motion of another.

en-gā′gēr, *n.* One who enters into an engagement or contract.

en-gā′ging, *a.* Winning; attractive; tending to draw the attention or the affections; pleasing; as, *engaging* manners or address.

Engaging and disengaging gear or *machinery*; that in which one part is alternately united to or separated from another part, as occasion may require.

en-gā′ging-ly, *adv.* In a manner to win the affections.

en-gā′ging-ness, *n.* The state of being attractive or agreeable.

en-gal′lănt, *v.t.* To make a gallant of. [Obs.]

en-gāol′ (-jāl′), *v.t.* To imprison. [Obs.]

en-gär′boil, *v.t.* To disorder. [Obs.]

en-gär′lănd, *v.t.* To encircle with a garland.

en-gar′ri-sŏn, *v.t.*; engarrisoned, *pt., pp.*; engarrisoning, *ppr.* To furnish with a garrison; to defend or protect by a garrison.

en-gas′tri-muth, *n.* [Gr. *engastrimythos*, a ventriloquist; *en*, in, *gastri*, dat. of *gaster*, belly, and *mythos*, speech.] A ventriloquist. [Obs.]

en-ġen′dēr, *v.t.*; engendered, *pt., pp.*; engendering, *ppr.* [OFr. *engendrer*; Pr. *engendrar*, *engenrar*; It. *ingenerare*; L. *ingenerare*, to beget; *in*, in, and *generare*, from *genus*, birth, race.]

1. To produce by sexual union; to bring into being. [Rare.]

2. To produce; to cause to exist; to cause to bring forth.

en-ġen′dēr, *v.i.* 1. To be caused or produced; to be brought into existence.

2. To meet; to copulate.

en-ġen′dēr-ēr, *n.* One who or the thing that engenders.

en-ġen′drūre, *n.* [OFr. *engendrure*, from *engendrer*, to beget.]

1. The act of begetting. [Obs.]

2. Ancestry; direct lineage. [Obs.]

en-gild′, *v.t.* To gild; to brighten.

en′ġine, *v.t.*; engined, *pt., pp.*; engining, *ppr.* 1. To fit out with an engine.

2. To employ war-engines against. [Obs.]

3. To torture with an engine. [Obs.]

en′ġine, *n.* [OFr. *engin*, *enging*, *engeng*, natural ability, artifice, mechanical contrivance; It. *ingegno*; L. *ingenium*, natural ability, genius; *in*, in, and the root of *gignere*, to produce.]

1. Natural skill; capacity; talent. [Obs.]

2. Any agency or instrumentality used to accomplish a purpose.

3. Any material instrument producing an effect; especially a contrivance for disintegration or destruction, generally large or complicated.

4. A complete and complicated machine designed to effect an elaborate process or to do intricate work.

5. A machine by which applied power effects work; especially a converter of some form of motive energy—commonly heat—into work.

Motive-power engines receive their name, (a) from the motive agent employed; as, air-engine, hydraulic engine, steam-engine, etc.; (b) from the function performed or the art or business with which they have connection; as, elevator-engine, locomotive-engine, switch-engine, etc.; (c) from their principal characteristic of mechanism or construction, or their main attachment; as, automatic engine, double-acting engine, grasshopper-engine, upright engine, oscillating engine, rotary engine, high- or low-pressure engine, etc.

Agricultural engine; a portable engine commonly used to run a threshing-machine or other machinery on a farm.

Binary engine; a steam-engine having two sets of cylinders, the exhaust of one vaporizing a fluid furnishing pressure for the other.

Compressed-air engine; an engine driven by the elastic force of compressed air.

Corliss engine; a steam-engine having an automatic drop cut-off, regulated by a wrist-plate controlling four plug-valves.

Cycloidal engine; a lathe for producing on a plate the intricate curved lines seen on currency, watch-cases, etc.

Diesel engine; an internal combustion oil engine which operates at very high compression pressures particularly suited for marine use. Named from the inventor, Rudolph Diesel.

Electrodynamic or *electromagnetic engine*; a motor driven by electricity.

Pony engine; a small locomotive-engine.

Wild engine; a locomotive-engine out of control.

Wildcat engine; a locomotive-engine having no regular time and running without a train attached.

en′ġine-beăr″ēr, *n.* One of the sleepers holding an engine in place in a steamship.

en′ġine-coun″tēr, *n.* A speed-indicator for a steam-engine.

en′ġine-driv″ēr, *n.* [Eng.] A locomotive engineer.

en-ġi-neer′, *v.t.*; engineered, *pt., pp.*; engineering, *ppr.* 1. To plan and guide, as an undertaking; as, to *engineer* a bill through the senate.

2. To serve as an engineer on; as, to *engineer* a locomotive.

en-ġi-neer′, *n.* [ME. *enginer*; OFr. *engignier*; It. *ingegner*; LL. *ingeniarius*, one who makes or uses an engine, from *ingenium*, an engine, mechanical contrivance.]

1. One educated in or competent to practise any of the various lines of engineering.

2. One who has the care of and operates a steam-engine.

Chief engineer; (a) an assistant to the engineer-in-chief; (b) the head engineer of a number.

Chief of engineers; in the United States army, an officer holding the relative rank of brigadier-general, who is commanding officer of the corps of engineers.

en-ġi-neer′-in-chief, *n.* An officer in the United States navy having the relative rank of commodore, who is head of the Bureau of Steam Navigation.

en-ġi-neer′ing, *n.* The business of an engineer; the science and the art of planning, constructing, and managing structures of various kinds.

Civil engineering; the science relating to the building of railroads, canals, and the various kinds of fixed public works.

Dynamic engineering; art applied to the use and control of power, or to machine-designing.

Heating engineering; the science of producing and distributing heat in buildings.

Hydraulic engineering; the science and art of planning, constructing, and managing waterworks and all utilities employing hydraulic machinery, such as dams, locks, levees, etc.

Marine engineering; the science relating to the construction and operation of marine engines.

Mechanical engineering; the science that relates to the invention, contrivance, and adjustment of all kinds of machinery; the properties of materials; control of engines, motors, etc.

Military engineering; the science of planning and constructing works offensive and defensive in the art of war, such as forts, bridges, roads, observation-stations, etc.

Mining engineering; the science which embraces a knowledge of the various minerals and metals found in the earth and the methods of excavating and utilizing them.

Sanitary engineering; engineering in the interest of public health as affected by liquids and gases connected with draining and sewerage.

Steam engineering; the science relating to the construction and use of steam-engines and related parts, appliances, or machines.

Topographical engineering; a branch of civil engineering for ascertaining and recording the variations of level, contour, etc., of a country, from surveys.

en′ġine-keel″sŏn, *n.* See *Engine-bearer*.

en′ġine-lāthe, *n.* An intricate lathe used chiefly for screw-cutting.

en′ġine-man, *n.* A man who manages the engine, as in steamers and steam-cars; an engineer.

en′ġine-plāne, *n.* In coal-mining, a road for a car drawn by a cable.

en′ġin-ēr, *n.* One who contrives or invents, or who controls an engine. [Obs.]

en′ġine-ry, *n.* 1. The act of managing engines, or artillery.

2. Engines in general; instruments of war.

3. Machinery; any contrivance.

en′ġine-sīzed, *a.* Machine-sized; applied to paper.

en′ġine-tûrn″ing, *n.* The act of using a cycloidal engine, or the design so produced.

Examples of Engine-turning.

en′ġi-nous, *a.* [ME. *enginous*; OFr. *engignos*; L. *ingeniosus*, ingenious, from *ingenium*, natural ability.]

1. Relating to an engine or to mechanical construction. [Obs.]

2. Of an inventive nature; skilful in devising. [Obs.]

en-gird′, *v.t.*; engirt *or* engirded, *pt., pp.*; engirding, *ppr.* To surround; to encircle; to encompass.

en-gir′dle, *v.t.*; engirdled, *pt., pp.*; engirdling, *ppr.* To encompass as with a girdle or belt.

en-girt′, *v.t.* To encircle. [Obs.]

en′gi-scōpe, *n.* See *Engyscope*.

en-glā′ci-ăl (-shi-), *a.* In geology, resting within the flow of a glacier; imbedded in the ice of a glacier; as, *englacial* rocks.

en-glāimed′, *a.* [ME. *engleimen*, to smear, from *gleim*, birdlime, glue.] Furred; clammy. [Obs.]

en′gle (-gl), *n.* A gull; a put; a bubble; a dupe. [Obs.]

en′gle, *v.t.* [Obs.] See *Ingle*.

Eng′lish (iṅ′glish), *a.* [ME. *English*, *Englisch*; AS. *Englisc*, from *Engle*, *Angle*, Engles, Angles, a Low German tribe who settled in Britain and called it *Engla land*.] Belonging to or having the characteristics of England or of the inhabitants of England; relating to the race at present called Anglo-Saxon, or to their language.

English bond; see *Bond*, n. 8.

English breakfast tea; a kind of black tea of superior quality.

English horn; a musical instrument resembling the oboe, called, in Italian, *corno Inglese*.

English purple; see *Paris purple* under *Paris*.

English walnut; see under *Walnut*.

Eng′lish, *n.* 1. The people of England or of the English race, those especially of English descent or origin.

2. The English language, used by the inhabitants of England or the descendants of the Anglo-Saxons.

Regarded in its widest acceptation as embracing both Anglo-Saxon and English proper, English has been divided into five periods:—(1) English of the first period, from 450 (the period when the Teutonic invaders began to make settlements in the country) to 1100. In this stage the language was synthetic, not analytic. The *Beowulf* is the most noted example of the English of this period. (2) English of the second period, from 1100 to 1250, when the influence of the Conquest begins to be perceived to a slight extent in the vocabulary and in a general weakening of the terminations. (3) The third period, from 1250 to 1350, when inanimate objects begin to have no longer gender but to be classed as neuter. The infinitive takes *to* before it, and the present participle ends in *ing*. (4) The fourth period, from 1350 to 1460, when the Midland dialect has become the prevailing one. This period embraces the names of Chaucer and Gower. (5) The fifth period, from 1460 to the present time. This period has been subdivided into two—from 1460 to 1520, characterized by the diffusion of classical literature and the introduction of the printing-press, and from 1520 to the present time, in the course of which the language was to a great extent stereotyped by the works of Shakspere and Milton and the translation of the Bible.

3. The English equivalent of another word in a foreign language; as, *Charles* is the *English* of the German *Karl*.

4. In printing, a size of type (about 14 point) between great primer and pica.

This is ENGLISH.

5. In billiards, the rotary motion of the cue-ball when given other than a straight central stroke.

Eng′lish, *v.t.*; Englished (-lisht), *pt.*, *pp.*; Englishing, *ppr.* 1. To translate into the English language.

2. To cause to become English; to Anglicize.

3. In billiards, to give (the cue-ball) English. [See *English*, n. 5.]

Eng′lish-ȧ-ble, *a.* Translatable into the English language.

Eng′lish-ism, *n.* 1. A quality or peculiarity characteristic of the English language.

2. Anglomania; an Anglicism.

Eng′lish-măn, *n.*; *pl.* **Eng′lish-men.** A native of England; a citizen of England.

Eng′lish-ry, *n.* 1. The state or condition of being an Englishman. [Obs.]

2. Collectively, people of English descent; especially applied to the English in Ireland.

Eng′lish-wom-ăn (-woom-), *n.* A woman of English parentage.

en-gloom′, *v.t.* To make gloomy. [Rare.]

en-glue′, *v.t.*; englued, *pt.*, *pp.*; engluing, *ppr.* To fasten close together; to join firmly with glue.

en-glut′, *v.t.* 1. To swallow. [Obs.]

2. To fill; to glut. [Obs.]

en-gōre′, *v.t.* 1. To pierce; to gore. [Obs.]

2. To cause to become bloody. [Obs.]

en-gorge′, *v.t.*; engorged, *pt.*, *pp.*; engorging, *ppr.* [Fr. *engorger*, from *en-*, in, and *gorge*, the throat.]

1. To swallow; to devour; to gorge; to swallow with greediness or in large quantities.

2. To fill to repletion; to congest.

en-gorge′, *v.i.* To devour greedily; to feed with eagerness or voracity.

en-gorged′, *a.* 1. Swallowed in a greedy manner; taken in with voracity.

2. In medicine, choked with blood or other liquid.

en-gorge′ment, *n.* 1. The act of swallowing greedily; a devouring with voracity; glutting.

2. In medicine, excessive fullness of an organ caused by a flow of blood or pus.

3. In metallurgy, a choking or clogging in the furnace, interfering with reduction.

en-gōuled′, *a.* In heraldry, engoulée.

en-gōu-lée′ (oṅ-gö-lā′), *a.* [Fr. *engouler*, to gobble up, swallow; *en-*, in, and OFr. *goule*, throat.] In heraldry, swallowed in part; held by the jaws of anything; as, a child *engoulée* by a serpent; also used of an ordinary, when its two ends rest in the mouths of any heraldic animal.

A Bend Engoulée.

en-grȧff′, *v.t.* To ingraft. [Obs.]

en-grȧff′ment, *n.* Ingraftment. [Obs.]

en-grȧft′, *v.t.* To ingraft.

en-grȧft′ment, en-grȧf-tā′tion, *n.* Same as *Ingraftment, Ingraftation.*

en-grāil′, *v.t.*; engrailed, *pt.*, *pp.*; engrailing, *ppr.* [Fr. *engrêler*, to engrail.] In heraldry, to variegate; to spot, as with hail; to indent or make ragged at the edges, as if broken with hail; to indent in curved lines.

en-grāiled′, *a.* 1. Variegated; spotted.

2. Having an indented outline.

3. In heraldry, indented in a series of curves with the points outward. It is said of one of the lines of partition, and applies to one of the forms in which bends and other ordinaries are represented.

A Bend Engrailed.

en-grāil′ment, *n.* 1. The ring of dots round the edge of a medal.

2. In heraldry, the indentation made by engrailing.

en-grāin′, *v.t.* Same as *Ingrain.*

en-grap′ple, *v.i.* [Obs.] See *Grapple.*

en-grȧsp′, *v.t.* [Obs.] See *Grasp.*

en-grāve′, *v.t.*; engraved, *pt.*; engraved, engraven, *pp.*; engraving, *ppr.* [OFr. *engraver*, to engrave; *en-*, in, and *graver*, to engrave, impress.]

1. To scratch or scrape.

2. To cut, as metals, stones, or other hard substances, with a chisel or graver; to cut, as figures, letters, or devices, on stone or metal; to mark by incisions.

> Thou shalt *engrave* the two stones with the names of the children of Israel. —Ex. xxviii. 11.

3. To picture or represent by incisions.

4. To imprint; to impress deeply; to infix; as, let the principles of morality be *engraved* on the mind.

en-grāve′, *v.t.* To inter. [Obs.]

en-grāve′ment, *n.* Engraved work; act of engraving. [Rare.]

en-grāv′ẽr, *n.* One who engraves; a cutter of letters, figures, or devices, on stone, metal, or wood; a sculptor; a carver.

en-grāv′ẽr-y, *n.* The work of an engraver. [Rare.]

en-grāv′ing, *n.* 1. In its widest sense, the art of cutting designs, writing, etc., on any hard substance, as stone, metal, wood.

2. Specifically, one of various processes, in which a block or plate is prepared for printing. The oldest of these is wood-*engraving*, now comparatively little used, being almost superseded by various processes, particularly photo-*engraving*, and to some extent by lithography.

3. That which is engraved; an engraved plate.

4. An impression from an engraved plate; a print.

en-gredge′ (-grej′), *v.t.* To depress; to worry. [Obs.]

en-griēve′, *v.t.* To grieve. [Obs.]

en-grōss′, *v.t.*; engrossed (-grōst′), *pt.*, *pp.*; engrossing, *ppr.* [ME. *engrossen*; OFr. *engrossir*, *engroisser*; LL. *ingrossare*, to make large, write large; L. *in*, in, and *grossus*, large.]

1. To make thick or gross; to thicken. [Obs.]

2. To make larger; to increase in bulk. [Obs.]

3. To seize in the gross; to take the whole of; as, worldly cares *engross* the attention of most men.

4. To buy a part or the whole of (any commodity) with a view to controlling its price and making a profit by selling it to those who must buy it; to corner. [Eng.]

5. To write or copy in a large, bold handwriting on paper or parchment; as, to *engross* a legal document.

6. To take or assume in undue quantities or degrees; as, to *engross* power.

Syn.—Absorb, occupy, forestall, monopolize.

en-grōss′ẽr, *n.* 1. A penman whose specialty is engrossing.

2. One who corners a product with a view of raising the price. [Eng.]

en-grōss′ing-hand, *n.* In penmanship, a bold, shaded, round handwriting employed in transcribing important documents.

en-grōss′ment, *n.* 1. The act of engrossing; the act of taking the whole.

2. The appropriation of things in the gross, or in exorbitant quantities; exorbitant acquisition.

3. The state of being wholly absorbed or occupied with something.

en-guärd′, *v.t.* To guard. [Obs.]

en-gulf′, *v.t.*; engulfed (-gulft′), *pt.*, *pp.*; engulfing, *ppr.* [OFr. *engolfer*, to engulf, from L. *in*, in, and LL. *golfus*, *gulfus*, a gulf.] To swallow up or overwhelm completely; to absorb; also written *ingulf.*

en-gulf′ment, *n.* A swallowing up; also written *ingulfment.*

en′gyn, *n.* [Obs.] See *Engine.*

en′gy-scōpe, *n.* [Gr. *engys*, near, and *skopein*, to view.] A kind of reflecting microscope.

en-hā′lō, *v.t.*; enhaloed, *pt.*, *pp.*; enhaloing, *ppr.* To provide with a halo.

en-hȧnce′, *v.t.*; enhanced, *pt.*, *pp.*; enhancing, *ppr.* [OFr. *enhauncer*, *enhancer*; *en-*, in, and *hancer*, to raise, from OFr. *halt*, *haut*, from L. *altus*, high.]

1. To raise; to lift. [Obs.]

2. To raise or advance, as price or value; to increase; to augment; to aggravate; as, war *enhances* prices.

> Experience of want *enhances* the value of plenty. —L'Estrange.

en-hȧnce′, *v.i.* To grow larger; as, a debt *enhances* rapidly by compound interest.

en-hȧnce′ment, *n.* The state or quality of being enhanced; rise; increase; augmentation; as, the *enhancement* of value, price, enjoyment, pleasure, beauty.

en-hȧn′cẽr, *n.* One who or that which enhances.

en-här′bŏr, *v.t.* To find shelter in; to inhabit. [Obs.]

en-härd′en, *v.t.* To harden; to encourage; to make bold. [Obs.]

en-här-mon′iç, en-här-mon′iç-ăl, *a.* [Gr. *enarmonikos*, in accord, in harmony.]

1. In ancient Greek music, denoting such pieces of composition as proceed on very small intervals, or smaller intervals than the diatonic and chromatic.

2. In modern music, (a) having intervals less than a semitone; (b) denoting the use of notes, which, though differently indicated to the eye, as A♯ and B♭, yet have no difference to the ear when sounded upon an instrument, as a pianoforte, having a fixed scale.

en-här-mon′iç-ăl-ly, *adv.* In enharmonic style.

en-heärt′en, *v.t.* To encourage. [Rare.]

en-hedge′ (-hej′), *v.t.* To encircle with or as with a hedge. [Rare.]

en-hort′, *v.t.* [L. *inhortari*, to incite, instigate.] To uplift; to inspire with hope. [Obs.]

en-hun′gẽr, *v.t.* To cause to be hungry. [Rare.]

en-hȳ′drīte, *n.* [Gr. *enydros*, containing water, and *-ite*.] A mineral inclosing water in a small cavity.

en-hȳ′dros, *n.* A chalcedonic enhydrite.

en-hȳ′drous, *a.* [Gr. *enydros*, in water, living in water.] Containing water within; used in relation to some crystals.

ē-nig′mȧ, *n.* [L. *ænigma*; Gr. *ainigma* (-*atos*), a riddle, dark saying, from *ainissesthai*, to speak darkly, speak in riddles, from *ainos*, a tale, story.]

1. A puzzling or mystifying saying, in which some known thing is concealed under obscure language; an obscure question; a riddle.

2. Something seemingly having no explanation; as, his eccentricities were an *enigma.*

ē-nig-mat′iç, ē-nig-mat′iç-ăl, *a.* Relating to or containing a riddle; obscure; darkly expressed; ambiguous.

ē-nig-mat′iç-ăl-ly, *adv.* In an obscure manner.

ē-nig′mȧ-tist, *n.* A maker or dealer in enigmas and riddles.

ē-nig′mȧ-tīze, *v.i.* To utter or form enigmas; to deal in riddles. [Rare.]

ē-nig-mȧ-tog′rȧ-phy, *n.* [Gr. *ainigma* (-*atos*), a riddle, and *-graphia*, from *graphein*, to write.] The art of making riddles.

ē-nig-mȧ-tol′ō-gy, *n.* [Gr. *enigma* (-*atos*), a riddle, and *-logia*, from *legein*, to speak.] The science of solving enigmas.

en-īsled′ (-īld′), *a.* Constituted an island; isolated, as on an island. [Rare.]

en-jāil′, *v.t.*; enjailed, *pt.*, *pp.*; enjailing, *ppr.* To imprison by putting in jail.

en-join′, *v.t.*; enjoined, *pt.*, *pp.*; enjoining, *ppr.* [ME. *enjoinen*, *enjoynen*; OFr. *enjoindre*; L. *injungere*, to join or fasten into, to charge, lay upon; *in*, in, and *jungere*, to join.]

1. To order or direct with urgency; to admonish; to instruct with authority; to command; as, a parent *enjoins* on his children the duty of obedience.

2. In law, to forbid judicially; to stop or prohibit by issuing a legal injunction.

> This is a suit to *enjoin* the defendants from disturbing the plaintiffs. —Kent.

en-join′, *v.t.* [Obs.] See *Join.*

en-join′ẽr, *n.* One who enjoins.

en-join′ment, *n.* Direction; command; authoritative admonition.

en-joy′, *v.t.*; enjoyed, *pt.*, *pp.*; enjoying, *ppr.* [ME. *enjoyen*; OFr. *enjoier*, *enjoer*, to give, receive with joy; *en-*, in, and *joie*, joy.]

1. To feel or perceive with pleasure; to take pleasure or satisfaction in the possession or experience of; as, we *enjoy* the dainties of a feast, the conversation of friends, and our own meditations.

> I could *enjoy* the pangs of death,
> And smile in agony. —Addison.

2. To possess with satisfaction; to take pleasure or delight in the possession of.

> Thou shalt beget sons, but thou shalt not *enjoy* them. —Deut. xxviii. 41.

3. To have, possess, and use with satisfaction; to have, hold, or occupy, as a good or profitable thing, or as something desirable; as, we *enjoy* a free constitution and inestimable privileges.

That the children of Israel may *enjoy* every man the inheritance of his fathers.
—Num. xxxvi. 8.

4. To have sexual intercourse with.

To enjoy oneself; to feel pleasure or satisfaction in one's own mind, or to relish the pleasures of which one partakes; to be happy.

en-joy′, *v.i.* To live in happiness. [Rare.]

en-joy′ȧ-ble, *a.* Capable of being enjoyed.

en-joy′ẽr, *n.* One who enjoys.

en-joy′ment, *n.* 1. Pleasure; satisfaction; agreeable sensations; fruition.

2. Possession with satisfaction; occupancy of anything good or desirable; as, the *enjoyment* of an estate; the *enjoyment* of civil and religious privileges.

Syn.—Fruition, gratification.—*Enjoyment* signifies either the act of *enjoying*, or the pleasure itself derived from that act; *fruition* is employed only for the act of *enjoying*; *gratification* signifies either the act of giving pleasure, or the pleasure received; *enjoyment* is either corporeal or spiritual; as, the *enjoyment* of music, or the *enjoyment* of study; *fruition* is used in speaking of those pleasures which are received, in distinction from those which are had in expectation; *gratification*, which is a species of *enjoyment*, is obtained through the medium of the senses.

en-ken′nel, *v.t.* To place in a kennel. [Obs.]

en-kẽr′chief, *v.t.*; enkerchiefed (-chĕft), *pt., pp.*; enkerchiefing, *ppr.* To cover with or to infold in a kerchief; to bind with a kerchief.

en-kin′dle, *v.t.*; enkindled, *pt., pp.*; enkindling, *ppr.* 1. To kindle; to set on fire; to inflame; as, to *enkindle* sparks into a flame.

2. To excite; to rouse into action; as, to *enkindle* the passions into a flame.

en-lāce′, *v.t.*; enlaced (-lāst′), *pt., pp.*; enlacing, *ppr.* [ME. *enlacen*; OFr. *enlacer*, to interlace, infold; It. *inlacciare*, to ensnare, entangle; from L. *in*, in, and *laqueus*, a noose, snare.] To encircle with lace; to lace; to infold; to entangle.

en-lāce′ment, *n.* The state of being enlaced, or the act of enlacing; an encircling; a surrounding.

en-lärd′, *v.t.* To cover with lard or grease; to baste. [Obs.]

en-lärġe′, *v.t.*; enlarged, *pt., pp.*; enlarging, *ppr.* [ME. *enlargen*; OFr. *enlargier*; *en-*, in, and *large*, large.]

1. To make greater in quantity or dimensions; to extend in limits, breadth, or size; to expand in bulk; as, every one desires to *enlarge* his possessions.

God shall *enlarge* Japhet. —Gen. ix. 27.

2. To dilate; to expand, as with joy or love.

O ye Corinthians, our mouth is open to you, our heart is *enlarged*. —2 Cor. vi. 11.

3. To expand; to make more comprehensive; as, science *enlarges* the mind.

4. To increase in appearance; to magnify to the eye, as by a glass.

5. To set at liberty; to release from confinement or pressure. [Obs.]

To enlarge an order or *rule*; in law, to give additional time for compliance with it.

To enlarge oneself; to speak freely and at length; to be elaborate in speech.

To enlarge the heart; to open and expand in good will; to make free, liberal, and charitable.

en-lärġe′, *v.i.* 1. To grow large or larger; to extend; to dilate; to expand; as, a plant *enlarges* by growth.

2. To be diffuse in speaking or writing; to expatiate; as, I might *enlarge* on this topic.

3. To exaggerate.

4. Nautically, to veer toward the stern or parallel with the course of the vessel; to favor sailing; said of the wind.

en-lärġed′, *a.* Expanded; dilated; swollen.

en-lär′ġed-ly, *adv.* With enlargement.

en-lär′ġed-ness, *n.* The state of being enlarged.

en-lärġe′ment, *n.* 1. Increase of size or bulk, real or apparent; extension of dimensions or limits; augmentation; dilatation; expansion; as, the *enlargement* of a farm by adding land.

2. Expansion or extension, applied to the mind, to knowledge, or to the intellectual powers.

3. Release from confinement, servitude, distress, or straits.

4. Diffusiveness of speech or writing; an expatiating on a particular subject; a wide range of discourse or argument.

en-lär′ġẽr, *n.* One who or that which enlarges, increases, extends, or expands; an amplifier.

en-lär′ġing-ham″mẽr, *n.* A very heavy hammer with a hexagonal, slightly convex, smooth face used by a gold-beater.

en-lāy′, *v.t.* [Obs.] See *Inlay*.

en-lēague′ (-lēg′), *v.t.* To unite, as in a league or confederacy.

en-length′en, *v.t.* To make longer. [Obs.]

en-lev′en, *n.* [Obs.] See *Eleven*.

en-light′ (-līt′), *v.t.* To illuminate; to enlighten. [Obs.]

en-light′en, *v.t.*; enlightened, *pt., pp.*; enlightening, *ppr.* 1. To make light; to shed light on; to supply with light; to illuminate; as, the sun *enlightens* the earth.

His lightnings *enlightened* the world.
—Ps. xcvii. 4.

2. To give light to; to give clearer views to; to illuminate; to instruct; to enable to see or comprehend truth; as, to *enlighten* the mind or understanding.

Syn.—Illuminate, inform, instruct.

en-light′en-ẽr (-līt′n-ẽr), *n.* One who illuminates; one who or that which communicates light to the eye or clear views to the mind.

en-light′en-ment, *n.* Act of enlightening; state of being enlightened or instructed.

en-limn′ (-lim′), *v.t.* To embellish with illumined letters or figures, as a book. [Obs.]

en-liṅk′, *v.t.* To chain together; to connect.

en-list′, *v.t.*; enlisted, *pt., pp.*; enlisting, *ppr.* 1. To enroll; to register; to enter, as a name on a list.

2. To engage in public service by entering the name in a register; as, an officer *enlists* men.

3. To unite firmly to a cause; to employ in advancing some interest; as, to *enlist* persons of all classes in the cause of truth.

4. To gain the favor, interest, or support of; as, to *enlist* one's aid in the support of a measure.

Syn.—Enter, register, enroll, incorporate, embody, interest.

en-list′, *v.i.* 1. To engage in public service by subscribing articles or enrolling one's name.

2. To enter heartily into a cause, as one devoted to its interests.

en-list′ment, *n.* 1. The act of enlisting.

2. The writing by which a man is bound on enlisting.

en-līve′, *v.t.* To animate. [Obs.]

en-līv′en, *v.t.*; enlivened, *pt., pp.*; enlivening, *ppr.* 1. To give action or motion to; to make vigorous or active; to excite; as, fresh fuel *enlivens* a fire.

2. To give spirit or vivacity to; to animate; to make cheerful; as, social mirth and good humor *enliven* company.

Syn.—Cheer, rouse, exhilarate, inspire, invigorate.

en-līv′en-ẽr, *n.* One who or that which enlivens or animates; one who or that which invigorates.

en-lock′, *v.t.* [Obs.] See *Lock*.

en-lū′mine, *v.t.* To illumine; to enlighten. [Obs.]

en-lūte′, *v.t.* [ME. *enluten*; *en-*, and L. *lutum*, mud, clay.] To cover or coat with mud or clay; to lute. [Obs.]

eṅ-mäṅ-çhé′ (oṅ-moṅ-shā′), *a.* [Fr., from *en-* (L. *in*, in), and *manche*, a sleeve.] In heraldry, like a sleeve, or covered with a sleeve.

en-mär′ble, *v.t.* To make hard as marble; to harden. [Obs.]

eṅ masse′ (oṅ mas′). [Fr.] In mass, as a body; all together.

en-mesh′, *v.t.*; enmeshed (-mesht′), *pt., pp.*; enmeshing, *ppr.* To net; to entangle; to entrap.

en-mew′, *v.t.* See *Emmew*.

en-mist′, *v.t.*; enmisted, *pt., pp.*; enmisting, *ppr.* To surround with mist.

en′mi-ty, *n.* [ME. *enmyte*, *enemyte*; OFr. *enemite*, *ennemite*, from L. *inimicus*, an enemy.]

1. The quality of being an enemy; the opposite of friendship; ill-will; hatred; unfriendly disposition; malevolence.

I will put *enmity* between thee and the woman.
—Gen. iii. 15.

2. A state of opposition.

The friendship of the world is *enmity* with God. —James iv. 4.

Syn.—Animosity, hostility.—*Enmity* lies in the heart; it is deep and malignant; *animosity* lies in the passions; it is fierce and vindictive; *hostility* lies in the action; it is mischievous and destructive; *enmity* is altogether personal; *hostility* respects public or private measures.

en-mossed′ (-most′), *a.* Covered with moss.

en-mōve′, *v.t.* [Obs.] See *Emove*.

en-muf′fle, *v.t.* To muffle. [Rare.]

en-mūre′, *v.t.* [Obs.] See *Immure*.

en-nē-ȧ-. A combining form from Gr. *ennea*, nine, signifying nine, as in *ennea*gon.

en″nē-ȧ-çon-tȧ-hē′drăl, *a.* [Gr. *enenēkonta*, ninety, and *hedra*, a seat, base.] Having ninety faces.

en′nē-ad, *n.* [Gr. *enneas* (*-ados*), from *ennea*, nine.] The number nine; a series of nine objects; a division of a work containing nine books.

The Enneads; the works, in six books of nine chapters each, of Plotinus, the philosopher, published by Porphyry, his pupil.

en′nē-ȧ-gon, *n.* [*Ennea-*, and Gr. *gōnia*, an angle.] In geometry, a polygon or plane figure, with nine sides and nine angles.

en-nē-ag′ō-năl, *a.* Pertaining or belonging to an enneagon; having nine sides and nine angles.

en-nē-ag′y-nous, *a.* [*Ennea-*, and Gr. *gynē*, a woman.] In botany, bearing nine pistils, or having nine styles.

en″nē-ȧ-hē′drăl, *a.* [*Ennea-*, and Gr. *hedra*, a seat, base.] Having nine faces.

en″nē-ȧ-hē′dri-ȧ, **en″nē-ȧ-hē′drŏn**, *n.* [*Ennea-*, and Gr. *hedra*, a seat, base.] A figure having nine faces.

En-nē-an′dri-ȧ, *n.* [*Ennea-*, and Gr. *anēr*, *andros*, a man.] In botany, a class of plants having nine stamens; so classified by Linnæus.

Enneandria.—Flower of *Butomus umbellatus*.

en-nē-an′dri-ăn, **en-nē-an′drous**, *a.* [*Ennea-*, and Gr. *anēr*, *andros*, a man.] Having nine stamens.

en″nē-ȧ-pet′ăl-ous, *a.* [*Ennea-*, and Gr. *petalon*, a leaf.] Having nine petals.

en-nē-aph′yl-lous, *a.* With nine leaflets.

en″nē-ȧ-spẽr′mous, *a.* [*Ennea-*, and Gr. *sperma*, a seed.] Nine-seeded.

en-nē-at′iç, **en-nē-at′iç-ăl**, *a.* [Gr. *ennea*, nine.] Occurring every ninth time; every ninth one of a series.

Enneatical day; every ninth day of the course or period of a disease.

Enneatical year; every ninth year of a person's life.

en-new′, *v.t.* To make new. [Obs.]

en-niche′, *v.t.* To put in a niche. [Rare.]

en′nis, **in′nis**, *n.* [Ir. and Gael. *innis*, *inis*, an island, a sheltered valley.] A prefix found frequently in Irish names of places; as, *Ennis*killen, etc.

en-nō′ble, *v.t.*; ennobled, *pt., pp.*; ennobling, *ppr.* [Fr. *ennoblir*; *en-*, in, and *noble*, noble.]

1. To make noble; to raise to nobility; as, to *ennoble* a commoner.

2. To dignify; to exalt; to elevate in degree, qualities, or excellence.

What can *ennoble* sots, or slaves, or cowards?
—Pope.

3. To make famous or illustrious. [Obs.]

en-nō′ble-ment, *n.* 1. The act of ennobling or dignifying, or the state of being ennobled or exalted; advance or elevation to the rank of a noble.

2. That which ennobles or exalts; excellence; nobility; dignity.

en-nō′blẽr, *n.* One who or that which ennobles.

eṅ-nuï′ (oṅ-nwē′), *n.* [Fr., weariness, from L. *in odio*, in hatred, disgust.] Dullness of spirit; languor or uneasiness connected with a feeling of disgust; want of interest in present scenes and surrounding objects.

eṅ-nuy-é′ (oṅ-nwē-yā′), *a.* [Fr., pp. of *ennuyer*, to affect with ennui.] Suffering with ennui; wearied; bored; exhausted emotionally; mentally and emotionally satiated.

eṅ-nuy-é′, *n.* One suffering from ennui.

ē-nōd′ăl, *a.* Having no node or nodes, as a plant.

en-ō-dā′tion, *n.* [L. *enodatio*, from *enodare*, to clear from knots; *e*, out, and *nodus*, a knot.]

1. The act or operation of clearing of knots, or of untying. [Obs.]

2. Solution of a difficulty. [Obs.]

ē-nōde′, *a.* Destitute of knots or joints. [Obs.]

ē-nōde′, *v.t.* To clear of knots; to make clear. [Obs.]

ē-noint′, *v.t.* [Obs.] Same as *Anoint*.

ē-nom′ō-tärçh, *n.* [Gr. *enōmotarchēs*, from *enōmotia*, an enomoty, and *archein*, to rule.] The commander of an enomoty.

ē-nom′ō-ty, *n.* [Gr. *enōmotia*, lit., a sworn band, from *enōmotos*, sworn, bound by oath; from *en*, in, and *omnynai*, to swear.] In ancient Greece, the smallest division of the Spartan army; twenty-five to thirty-six oath-bound soldiers.

En′ō-plȧ, *n.pl.* [Gr. *enoplos*, in armor; *en*, in, and *hopla*, arms.] A suborder of nemertean worms, having a peculiar spinal or plate-like armature in the proboscis.

en′ō-plan, *a.* Of or relating to the *Enopla*.

en′ō-plan, *n.* One of the *Enopla*.

en-op′tō-man-cy, *n.* [Gr. *enoptos*, seen in, and *manteia*, divination.] A kind of divination by the use of a mirror.

ē-nọrm′, *a.* Abnormal; wicked. [Obs.]

ē-nọr′mi-ty, *n.*; *pl.* **ē-nọr′mi-tieş**. [L. *enormitas*, irregularity, unusual size, from *enormis*, out of rule, irregular; *e*, out, and *norma*, rule.]

1. The condition or quality of being beyond the limits of a measure or rule, or of being immoderate, monstrous, or outrageous, especially the quality of being extremely wicked; as, the *enormity* of atrocious crime or of flagrant villainy.

2. The state of being excessively or abnormally large; vastness or immensity; not in a derogatory sense. [Rare.]

ē-nọr′mous, *a.* [L. *enormis*; *e*, out of, and *norma*, rule.]

1. Immense in size; far exceeding the usual measure or rule; gigantic; inordinate; abnormally large

2. Outrageously wicked; heinous; monstrous; atrocious.

Syn.—Immense, excessive, huge, vast.—We speak of a thing as *enormous* when it overpasses its ordinary law of existence, and becomes abnormal in its magnitude. *Immense* and *excessive* are figurative terms used to intensify, and are somewhat indefinite in their degree of strength; *huge* is great only in the superlative degree; *vast* comprehends only a very great or unusual excess.

ē-nor′mous-ly, *adv.* Excessively; beyond measure; as, an opinion *enormously* absurd.

ē-nor′mous-ness, *n.* The state of being enormous or excessive; greatness beyond measure.

en-or′thō-trōpe, *n.* [Gr. *en*, in, and *orthos*, straight, and *trepein*, to turn.] A card on various parts of which are drawn in apparent confusion parts of figures, which form to the eye entire figures when the card is rapidly revolved; used to illustrate the persistence of visual impressions. [See *Thaumatrope*.]

en-os-tō′sis, *n.*; *pl.* **en-os-tō′sēs**. [From Gr. *en*, in, *osteon*, bone, and *-osis*.] A tumor or a morbid bony growth within a bone.

ē-nough′ (-nuf′), *a.* [ME. *enogh*, *enoh*, *enow*; AS. *genoh*, from *geneah*, it suffices.] Satisfying the desire; giving content; adequate to the need; sufficient; usually following its noun.

How many hired servants of my father's have bread *enough* and to spare! —Luke xv. 17.

ē-nough′ (-nuf′), *n.* A sufficiency; a quantity of a thing which satisfies desire or is adequate to the wants; as, we have *enough* of this sort of cloth.

And Esau said, I have *enough*, my brother. —Gen. xxxiii. 9.

ē-nough′, *adv.* 1. Sufficiently; in a quantity or degree that satisfies or is equal to the desires or wants.

Ye have dwelt long *enough* in this mount. —Deut. i. 6.

2. Fully; quite; denoting a slight augmentation of the positive degree; as, he is ready *enough* to embrace the offer.

3. In a tolerable or reasonable degree; expressing rather less than is desired or such a quantity or degree as commands acquiescence rather than full satisfaction; as, the song or the performance is well *enough*.

ē-nough′, *interj.* An exclamation meaning it is enough, or, stop.

ē-nounce′, *v.t.*; enounced (-nounst′), *pt.*, *pp.*; enouncing, *ppr.* [Fr. *énoncer*, from L. *enunciare*, *enuntiare*, to say out, declare; *e*, out, and *nuntiare*, to speak, declare.] To declare; to enunciate; to announce; as, to *enounce* a plan of action.

en-pā′trŏn, *v.t.* To act as a patron toward; to have under one's care. [Obs.]

en-pierce′, *v.t.* [Obs.] See *Impierce*.

en-quēre′ (-kwēr′), *v.i.* [Obs.] See *Inquire*.

en-quīre′, en-quīr′ēr, en-quīr′y. Same as *Inquire*, etc.

en-rāce′, *v.t.* To implant. [Obs.]

en-rāge′, *v.t.*; enraged, *pt.*, *pp.*; enraging, *ppr.* [OFr. *enrager*, to rave, rage; *en-*, in, and *rage*, rage.] To excite rage in; to exasperate; to provoke to fury or madness; to make furious.

Syn.—Anger, inflame, exasperate, infuriate.

en-rāge′ment, *n.* The state of being enraged. [Obs.]

en-rāil′, *v.t.* To furnish with railing. [Obs.]

en-rānge′, *v.t.* 1. To arrange. [Obs.]

2. To range; traverse; travel over. [Obs.]

en-rank′, *v.t.* To place in ranks or order. [Rare.]

en-rapt′, *a.* Carried or borne away with overpowering emotion; thrown into an ecstasy.

en-rap′tūre, *v.t.*; enraptured, *pt.*, *pp.*; enrapturing, *ppr.* To transport with pleasure; to delight greatly.

en-rav′ish, *v.t.* To enrapture. [Rare.]

en-rav′ish-ing-ly, *adv.* So as to throw into ecstasy. [Obs.]

en-rav′ish-ment, *n.* Ecstasy of delight; rapture. [Obs.]

en-reg′is-tēr, *v.t.* To register; to enroll or record. [Obs.]

en-rheum′ (-rūm′), *v.i.* and *v.t.* To receive or to transfer rheum. [Obs.]

en-rich′, *v.t.*; enriched (-richt′), *pt.*, *pp.*; enriching, *ppr.* [ME. *enrichen*; OFr. *enrichier*, *enrichir*; *en-*, in, and *riche*, rich.]

1. To make rich, wealthy, or opulent; to supply with abundant property; as, agriculture, commerce, and manufactures *enrich* a nation.

2. To fertilize; to supply with the nutriment of plants and render productive; as, to *enrich* land by manure.

3. To store; to supply with an abundance of anything desirable; as, to *enrich* the mind with knowledge, science, or useful observations.

4. To supply with anything splendid or ornamental; as, to *enrich* a painting with elegant drapery.

en-rich′ēr, *n.* One who or that which enriches.

en-rich′ment, *n.* Augmentation of wealth; improvement; increase of value or fertility; embellishment.

en-ridge′ (-rij′), *v.t.* To form into ridges. [Obs.]

en-ring′, *v.t.* To encircle; to inclose.

en-rip′en, *v.t.* To ripen; to bring to perfection. [Obs.]

en-rīve′, *v.t.* To rive; to cleave. [Obs.]

en-rōbe′, *v.t.*; enrobed, *pt.*, *pp.*; enrobing, *ppr.* To clothe with a robe; to dress.

en-rock′ment, *n.* A mass of large stones thrown into the water at random to form the base of a pier, breakwater, etc.

en-rōll′, *v.t.*; enrolled, *pt.*, *pp.*; enrolling, *ppr.* [ME. *enrollen*; OFr. *enroller*, from LL. *inrotulare*, to write in a roll; L. *in*, in, and *rotulus*, a wheel.]

1. To write in a roll or register; to enter in a list or catalogue; hence, to engage for some service or as a member of an organization; to enlist; as, they *enrolled* his name; he *enrolled* himself for service.

2. To record; to insert in records, as a decree; to place in writing for a record.

3. To transcribe in a legible hand in the manner prescribed for the use of the executive; said of a measure passed by a legislature, which is to be submitted for the signature of the executive officer

4. To wrap; to involve. [Obs.]

Also written *enrol*.

en-rōll′ēr, *n.* He who enrolls or registers.

en-rōl′ment, en-rōll′ment, *n.* 1. A register; a record; a writing in which anything is recorded.

2 The act of enrolling.

en-root′, *v.t.* To fix by the root; to fix fast; to implant deep.

en-round′, *v.t.* To environ; to inclose. [Obs.]

en route (oṅ röt′). [Fr.] Upon the road; in progress

ens, *n.* *pl.* **en′ti-ȧ** (-shi-ȧ). [L. *ens*, *entis*, a being or thing.]

1. Entity; being; existence; an existing thing or person; hence, anything conceived of as existing.

2. Power; virtue; efficacy; essence. [Obs.]

en-sāfe′, *v.t.* To render safe. [Obs.]

en-sam′ple, *n.* [It. *esempio*; L. *exemplum*.] An example; a pattern or model for imitation. [Obs.]

en-sam′ple, *v.t.* To exemplify; to show by example [Obs.]

en-san′guine (-gwin), *v.t.* To stain or cover with blood; to smear with gore; to make blood-red; as, an *ensanguined* field.

en′sāte, *a.* [L. *ensis*, a sword.] Having sword-shaped leaves.

en-scāle′, *v.t.* To cover with or as with scales. [Rare.]

en-sched′ūle, *v.t.* To insert in a schedule. [Rare.]

en-sconce′, *v.t.*; ensconced, *pt.*, *pp.*; ensconcing, *ppr.* To cover or shelter, as with a sconce or fort; to protect, to secure; to hide.

en-seal′, *v.t.* To seal; to fix a seal on; to confirm. [Obs.]

en-sēam′, in-sēam′, *v.t.* To sew up; to inclose by a seam or juncture of needlework. [Rare.]

en-sēam′, *v.t.* To make foul with or as with grease. [Obs.]

en-sēar′, *v.t.* To sear; to cauterize. [Obs.]

en-sēarch′, *v.i.* and *v.t.* To search. [Obs.]

en-seel′, *v.t.* To seel, as a hawk. [Obs.]

en-seint′, *a.* Enceinte; pregnant. [Obs.]

en-sem′ble (oṅ-som′bl), *n.* [OFr. *ensemble*; LL. *insimul*, at the same time; L. *in*, in, and *simul*, at the same time.]

1. All the parts of anything taken together so that each part is considered only in relation to the whole; the general effect of a whole work of art, as a picture, drama, etc.

2. In music, the union of all the performers in a concerted composition, as in a chorus with orchestral accompaniment.

3. In mathematics, an aggregate manifold, or collection of elements or points connected by a series of relations.

Tout ensemble; the appearance or effect as a whole.

en-sem′ble, *adv.* All together; simultaneously.

en-sē′tē, *n.* [Abyssinian.] The *Musa Ensete*, a plant closely allied to the banana. It produces the largest entire leaf of any known plant, specimens measuring 18 feet by $3\frac{1}{2}$. Only the flower-stalks are edible, the fruit being worthless.

en-shel′tēr, *v.t.* To shelter. [Obs.]

en-shield′, *v.t.* To shield, to cover. [Obs.]

en-shrīne′, *v.t.* To inclose in or as in a shrine or chest; to cherish.

en-shroud′, *v.t.*; enshrouded, *pt.*, *pp.*; enshrouding, *ppr.* To cover, as with a shroud.

en-sif′ēr-ous, *a.* [L. *ensis*, sword, and *ferre*, to bear.] Bearing or carrying a sword. [Obs.]

Ensiform Leaf.

en′si-form, *a.* [L. *ensis*, sword, and *forma*, form.] Having the shape of a sword; as, the *ensiform* or xiphoid cartilage; an *ensiform* leaf.

Ensiform cartilage; in anatomy, the somewhat sword-shaped process at the lower extremity of the sternum; also called *ensiform process* and *xiphisternum*.

en′sign (en′sīn), *n.* [OFr. *ensigne*, *enseigne*, from LL. *insigna*, a standard, badge; L. *insigne*, neut. of *insignis*, distinguished by a mark, remarkable.]

1. The flag or banner of a company of soldiers, an army, or vessel; the colors; a standard.

2. Any signal to assemble or to give notice. Obs.]

3. A badge; a mark of distinction, rank, or office; as, *ensigns* of power or virtue.

4. An officer of the lowest grade in commission in the United States navy.

5. Formerly, the commissioned officer of lowest grade in the infantry of Great Britain; changed to *second lieutenant* in 1871.

en′sign, *v.t.*; ensigned, *pt.*, *pp.*; ensigning, *ppr.* [ME. *ensignen*; OFr. *ensigner*, *enseigner*, from LL. *insignare*, to mark, indicate.]

1. To give some distinguishing mark to; in heraldry, to distinguish (a charge) by placing over it a crown or some other honorable emblem.

2. To point out as by an ensign. [Obs.]

Ensigned.

en′sign-bēar″ēr, *n.* He who carries the ensign.

en′sign-cy, *n.*; *pl.* **en′sīgn-cies**. The rank, office, or commission of an ensign.

en′sign-ship, *n.* Ensigncy.

en′si-lāge, *n.* [Fr. *ensilage*; *en-*, in, and *silo*, from Sp. *silo*, a silo, from L. *sirus*, Gr. *siros*, *seiros*, a pit to keep corn in, an underground pit.] The operation and method of preserving green fodder (clover, millet, etc., especially green cornstalks), by packing it in a silo; also, the fodder thus ensiled.

en′si-lāge, *v.t.*; ensilaged, *pt.*, *pp.*; ensilaging, *ppr.* To convert into ensilage; to put into a silo.

en′sīle, *v.t.*; ensiled, *pt.*, *pp.*; ensiling, *ppr.* [Sp. *ensilar*, to preserve grain in a place underground; *en-*, in, and *silo*, a silo, underground pit.] To make ensilage of; to ensilage.

en-skȳ′, *v.t.* To place among the stars; to render immortal. [Poet.]

en-slāve′, *v.t.*; enslaved, *pt.*, *pp.*; enslaving, *ppr.* To reduce to slavery or bondage; to deprive of liberty and subject to the will of a master; hence, figuratively, to reduce to subjection; as, men are often *enslaved* by their passions.

en-slāv′ed-ness, *n.* State of being enslaved.

en-slāve′ment, *n.* The state of being in slavery; bondage; servitude; also, the act of enslaving.

en-slāv′ēr, *n.* One who reduces to bondage.

en-snāre′, *v.t.*; ensnared, *pt.*, *pp.*; ensnaring, *ppr.* To entrap; to catch in a trap; to insnare.

en-snār′ēr, *n.* One who ensnares; also written *insnarer*.

en-snärl′, *v.t.* To entangle. [Obs.]

en-sō′bēr, *v.t.* To make sober. [Obs.]

en-sor′cel, en-sor′cell, *v.t.* [OFr. *ensorceler*, to bewitch; *en-*, in, and *sorceler*, to bewitch.] To practise the art of a sorcerer upon.

en-soul′, *v.t.* To put a soul into; to convert into a soul. [Rare.]

en-sphēre′, *v.t.*; ensphered, *pt.*, *pp.*; ensphering, *ppr.* 1. To place in or surround with a sphere.

2. To make into a sphere.

en-stamp′, *v.t.* To impress as with a stamp; to impress deeply. [Obs.]

en-stāte′, *v.t.* [Obs.] Same as *Instate*.

en′stȧ-tite, *n.* [Gr. *enstatēs*, an adversary; *en*, in, and *histanai*, to stand, and *-ite*.] In mineralogy, a magnesium silicate of various colors from gray to brown, of orthorhombic crystallization, but occurring also massive and fibrous.

en-stȧ-tit′ic, *a.* Of or like enstatite.

en-stōre′, *v.t.* To restore; to repeat. [Obs.]

en-style′, *v.t.* To style; to name; to call. [Obs.]

en-sū′ȧ-ble, *a.* Following as a consequence.

en-sūe′, *v.t.*; ensued, *pt.*, *pp.*; ensuing, *ppr.* [ME. *ensuen*; OFr. *ensuer*; L. *insequi*, to follow upon; *in*, in, on, and *sequi*, to follow.] To follow; to pursue. [Obs.]

Seek peace, and *ensue* it. —1 Pet. iii. 11.

en-sūe′, *v.i.* 1. To follow as a consequence of premises; as, this result *ensues*.

2. To follow in a train of events or course of time; to succeed; to come after; as, he spoke, and silence *ensued*; the *ensuing* age or years.

en suite (oṅ swēt′). [Fr.] In or forming a connected series, as rooms.

en-sūre′, *v.t.* Same as *Insure*.

en-sūr′ēr, *n.* Same as *Insurer*.

en-swāthe′, *v.t.* To swathe; to inwrap.

en-swāthe′ment, *n.* The act of inwrapping or the condition of being inwrapped.

en-sweep′, *v.t.* To sweep over rapidly. [Rare.]

-ent. A suffix from OFr. *-ent*, L. *-en(t)s*, a ppr. suffix of verbs of 2d, 3d, and 4th conjugations, and used as a suffix of adjectives, and nouns originally adjectives. It signifies action or being, as, ard*ent*, cad*ent*, emerg*ent*.

en-tab′lȧ-tūre, *n.* [OFr. *entablature*, from *entabler*; LL. *intabulare*, to construct a basis; L. *in*, in, on, and *tabulatum*, a flooring, floor.] In architecture, that part of the order of a column which is over the capital, including the architrave, frieze, and cornice; all that part between the capital and the roof.

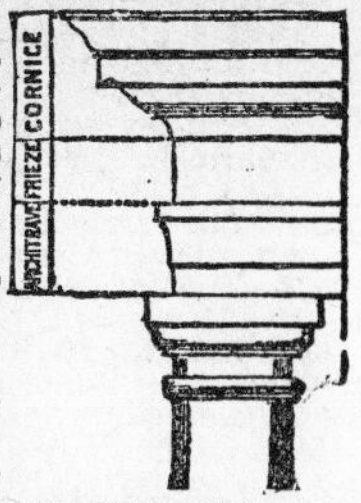

ARCHITRAVE FRIEZE CORNICE

Entablature of Tuscan Column.

en-tā′ble-ment (-bl-), *n.* An entablature. [Obs.]
en-tac′kle, *v.t.* To supply with tackle. [Obs.]
en′tad, *adv.* [Gr. *entos*, within, and L. *-ad*, toward.] In anatomy, in an inward direction; toward the interior of an organ or body; opposed to *ectad*.
en-tāil′, *v.t.*; entailed, *pt.*, *pp.*; entailing, *ppr.* [ME. *entailen*; LL. *intaliare*, to cut into, carve; L. *in*, in, and LL. *taliare*, to cut, carve.]
1. To settle the descent of (lands and tenements) to certain heirs specified, so that neither the donee nor any subsequent possessor can alienate or bequeath; as, to *entail* a manor to A B and to his eldest son or to his heirs by a particular wife.
2. To fix inalienably on a person or thing, or on a person and his descendants; as, the intemperate often *entail* diseases and ruin on their children.
3. To carve, as in ornamental work. [Obs.]
en-tāil′, *n.* 1. In law, (a) the settlement of a landed estate on a particular line or succession of individuals in such a way that none of them can alienate it by his own act; (b) the condition thus produced; (c) an entailed estate.
2. Figuratively, any fixed or settled transmission or inheritance; as, an *entail* of criminal tendencies.
3. Delicately carved ornament; intaglio. [Obs.]
4. Device; pattern; shape. [Obs.]
en-tāil′ment, *n.* The act of entailing; the estate entailed; the state of being limited by entail.
en′tăl, *a.* [Gr. *entos*, within, and *-al*.] In anatomy, of or having reference to the interior of a body or organ, as opposed to *ectal*.
en-tāme′, *v.t.* To tame; to subdue. [Obs.]
en-tan′gle (-gl), *v.t.*; entangled, *pt.*, *pp.*; entangling, *ppr.* 1. To twist or interweave in such a manner as not to be easily separated; as, to *entangle* the hair.
2. To involve in anything complicated and from which it is difficult to extricate oneself; to involve in difficulties; to perplex; to ensnare; as, to be *entangled* in a net.
en-tan′gle-ment, *n.* 1. The state of being entangled.
2. Anything that entangles; a device intended to impede the advance of an attacking force; an obstruction; a snare; a complication.
3. The act of entangling.
en-tan′glẽr, *n.* One who entangles.
en-tȧ′si-ȧ, *n.* Same as *Entasis*, n. 2.
en′tȧ-sis, *n.* [Gr. *entasis*, a stretching, distention, from *enteinein*, to stretch; *en*, in, and *teinein*, to stretch.]
1. In architecture, the almost imperceptible swelling of the shaft of a column.
2. In pathology, the rigidity of tonic spasm, as in tetanus; also, a disease having such symptom.
en-tasse′ment, *n.* [OFr. *entassement*, from *entasser*, to heap up.] A heap; accumulation. [Rare.]
en-tas′tic, *a.* [From Gr. *entasis*, a stretching, from *enteinein*, to stretch.] Relating to or involving entasis.
en-tel′e-chy, *n.* [L. *entelechia*; Gr. *entelecheia*, actuality, from *en telei echein*; *en*, in, *telei*, dat. of *telos*, end, completion, and *echein*, to hold.] In philosophy, that complete realization or full development which is the last stage in the process from potentiality to actuality.
en-tel′lus, *n.* [From Gr. *entellein*, to command, enjoin; *en*, in, and *tellein*, to make to arise.] An East Indian bearded sacred monkey, *Semnopithecus entellus*. It has yellowish fur, a face of a violet tinge, and a long and powerful tail, not prehensile; called also *hanuman*.
en-tend′, *v.t.* To intend. [Obs.]
en-ten′dẽr, *v.t.* To treat with tenderness or kindness; also, to mollify, to soften. [Obs.]
en-tente′ (än-tänt′), *n.* [Fr.] An understanding, esp. between nations.
en-ten′tive, *a.* Attentive. [Obs.]
en′tẽr, *v.t.*; entered, *pt.*, *pp.*; entering, *ppr.* [ME. *entren*; L. *intrare*, to go into, enter, from *intro*, into the inside, within.]
1. To come or go into in any manner whatever; to pass into the inside or interior of; to penetrate; to go inside by way of; as, to *enter* a house; the river *enters* the sea.
2. To advance into, in progress; as, a youth has *entered* his tenth year; to *enter* a new era.
3. To begin (a business, employment, or service); to engage in; to join; to become a member of; as, to *enter* the army; to *enter* college.
4. To admit or introduce; to initiate; as, to *enter* one into a secret. [Obs.]
5. To cause to enter; to put or set in; to insert; as, to *enter* a wedge.
6. To set down in writing, as in a book; to enroll; to inscribe; as, the clerk *entered* the account.
7. To report at the customhouse, as a vessel on arrival in port, by delivering a manifest; as, to *enter* a ship or her cargo.
8. In law, (a) to go in or upon and take possession of, as lands; (b) to place upon the records of a court; as, to *enter* a rule, an appearance, etc.; (c) to file the necessary particulars to secure preëmption rights to (public land); (d) to file in order to obtain copyright protection, as a literary production.
9. To cause the name of to be proposed; to offer for entry; to enroll; as, to *enter* a pupil in school; to *enter* an exhibit or an animal for a prize.
en′tẽr, *v.i.* 1. To go or come in; to make or effect an entry or entrance.
2. Specifically, on the stage, to appear or make an entrance; as, *enter* King Dodo, laughing.
To enter into; (a) to get into the inside or interior of; to penetrate; as, water *enters into* a ship; (b) to engage in; as, *to enter into* business; (c) to be or become initiated in; as, they *entered into* a taste of magnificence; (d) to deal with or treat, as a subject, by discussion, argument, and the like; to make inquiry or scrutiny into; as, *to enter into* the merits of the case; (e) to be an ingredient in; to form a constituent part of; as, lead *enters into* the composition of pewter.
Entering edge; the forward edge of an aeroplane which encounters the air when flying.
To enter on or *upon*; to begin; to commence.
en-tẽr-. See *Entero-*.
en″tẽr-ad-ē-nog′rȧ-phy, *n.* [*Enter-*, and Gr. *adēn*, a gland, and *-graphia*, from *graphein*, to write.] A treatise on intestinal glands.
en″tẽr-ad-ē-nol′ō-ġy, *n.* [*Enter-*, and Gr. *adēn*, a gland, and *-logia*, from *legein*, to speak.] That part of anatomy dealing with intestinal glands.
en-tẽr-al′ġi-ȧ, *n.* [*Enter-*, and Gr. *algos*, pain.] Enteric neuralgia.
en′tẽr-āte, *a.* [Gr. *enteron*, an intestine, and *-ate*.] Having an alimentary canal.
en′tẽr-dēal, *n.* Mutual dealings. [Obs.]
en′tẽr-ẽr, *n.* One who is making a beginning.
en-ter′ic, *a.* [Gr. *enteron*, an intestine, and *-ic*.] Of, belonging to, or affecting the intestines; intestinal; also, enterate.
Enteric fever; typhoid fever.
en-te-rī′tis, *n.* [Gr. *enteron*, an intestine, and *-itis*.] An inflammation of the intestines.
en-tẽr-lāce′, *v.t.* [Obs.] See *Interlace*.
en-tẽr-met′, en-tẽr-mit′, *v.i.* To meddle. [Obs.]
en′tẽr-mew-ẽr, *n.* A hawk gradually changing the color of his feathers, commonly in the second year.
en-tẽr-mīṣe′, *n.* [Fr. *entremise*, from *s'entremettre*, to intermeddle, interpose.] Interposition. [Obs.]
en-tẽr-ō-. A combining form from Gr. *enteron*, an intestine, and used in medicine and anatomy to indicate connection with or relation to the intestines; as, *entero*cœle, *entero*pathy. Before vowels *entero-* becomes *enter-*.
en′tẽr-ō-cēle, *n.* [*Entero-*, and Gr. *kēlē*, tumor.] In surgery, a hernia in any situation, whose contents are intestine.
en″tẽr-ō-chlō′rō-phyl, *n.* [*Entero-*, and Gr. *chlōros*, light green, and *phyllon*, a leaf.] A kind of chlorophyl found in certain invertebrates.
en′tẽr-ō-cœle (-sēl), *n.* [*Entero-*, and Gr. *koilos*, hollow.] A perivisceral body-cavity, especially of an actinozoan.
en-tẽr-og′rȧ-phy, *n.* [*Entero-*, and Gr. *-graphia*, from *graphein*, to write.] A treatise on the intestines.
en″tẽr-ō-hem′ȧ-tin, *n.* [*Entero-*, and Gr. *haima* (*-atos*), blood.] A reddish pigment found in certain invertebrates.
en′tẽr-ō-līte, en′tẽr-ō-lith, *n.* [*Entero-*, and Gr. *lithos*, a stone.] A concretion in the intestines.
en-tẽr-ol′ō-ġy, *n.* [*Entero-*, and Gr. *-logia*, from *legein*, to speak.] A treatise on the internal parts of the body.
en-tẽr-om′phȧ-lus, en-tẽr-om′phȧ-los, *n.*; *pl.* **en-tẽr-om′phȧ-lī.** [*Entero-*, and Gr. *omphalos*, navel.] An umbilical hernia whose contents are intestine.
en′te-ron, *n.*; *pl.* **en′te-rȧ.** [Gr. *enteron*, an intestine.] The digestive space or alimentary canal derived from the primitive endoderm.
en-tẽr-op′ȧ-thy, *n.* [*Entero-*, and Gr. *pathos*, suffering.] Any intestinal disease.
en′tẽr-ō-plas″ty, *n.* [*Entero-*, and Gr. *plastos*, from *plassein*, to form, mold.] A plastic operation for the restoration of an injured intestine.
En″te-rop-neūs′tȧ *n.pl.* [*Entero-*, and Gr. *pnein*, to breathe.] A group or class of animals allied to the tunicates and comprising *Balanoglossus* as the sole genus.
en″tẽr-or-rhā′phi-ȧ, *n.* [*Entero-*, and Gr. *rhaphē*, a seam, suture.] The process of stitching up an injured part of an intestine; spelled also *enterorrhaphy*.
en′tẽr-ō-tōme, *n.* [*Entero-*, and Gr. *tomē*, a cutting.] A special form of scissors for slitting intestines.
en-tẽr-ot′ō-my, *n.* [*Entero-*, and Gr. *tomē*, a cutting.]
1. Intestinal dissection.
2. A cutting into an intestine.
en″tẽr-ō-zō′ăn, en″tẽr-ō-zō′on, *n.* An entozoan; a metazoan.
en-tẽr-pär′lănce, *n.* [Fr. *entre*, between, and *parler*, to speak.] Parley; mutual talk or conversation; conference. [Obs.]
en-tẽr-plēad′, *v.i.* Same as *Interplead*.
en′tẽr-prīṣe, *n.* [Fr., from *entreprendre*, to undertake; *entre*, in or between, and *prendre*, to take; *prise*, a taking.]
1. That which is undertaken or attempted to be performed; a project attempted; particularly, a bold, arduous, or hazardous undertaking, either physical or moral; as, the attack on Stony Point was a bold, but successful, *enterprise*.
2. Ardor in entering upon and carrying forward projects or movements requiring daring and energy.
Syn.—Adventure, undertaking, venture.
en′tẽr-prīṣe, *v.t.* 1. To undertake; to begin and attempt to perform. [Rare.]
2. To entertain. [Obs.]
en′tẽr-prīṣe, *v.i.* To venture. [Obs.]
en′tẽr-prī-ṣẽr, *n.* One who undertakes a scheme, especially a bold or hazardous one. [Rare.]
en′tẽr-prī-ṣing, *a.* Bold or forward to undertake; resolute, active, or prompt to attempt great or untried schemes; as, *enterprising* men often succeed beyond all human probability.
Syn.—Active, bold, daring, adventurous, speculative, dashing, venturesome.
en′tẽr-prī-ṣing-ly, *adv.* In an enterprising manner.
en-tẽr-tāin′, *v.t.*; entertained, *pt.*, *pp.*; entertaining, *ppr.* [Fr. *entretenir*; LL. *intertenere*, to entertain; L. *inter*, among, between, and *tenere*, to hold.]
1. To receive into the house and treat with hospitality; to show hospitality to; as, to *entertain* a guest.
2. To take or receive into one's service; to hire. [Obs.]
3. To engage the attention of, with anything that causes the time to pass pleasantly, as conversation, music, or the like; to divert; to please; to amuse.
4. To receive or admit with a view to consider and decide; to take into consideration; as, to *entertain* a proposal.
5. To keep, hold, or maintain in the mind; to harbor; to cherish; as, to *entertain* charitable sentiments.
6. To experience; to suffer; to undergo; to bear. [Obs.]
7. To cause to pass pleasantly; to while away; as, to *entertain* the irksome hours. [Obs.]
8. To maintain. [Obs.]
9. To engage or encounter in combat. [Obs.]
Syn.—Harbor, maintain, foster, receive, recreate, amuse.
en-tẽr-tāin′, *v.i.* To receive guests; to furnish entertainment.
en-tẽr-tāin′, *n.* Entertainment. [Obs.]
en-tẽr-tāin′ẽr, *n.* One who entertains.
en-tẽr-tāin′ing, *a.* Pleasing; amusing; diverting.
en-tẽr-tāin′ing-ly, *adv.* In an entertaining way.
en-tẽr-tāin′ing-ness, *n.* The quality of entertaining.
en-tẽr-tāin′ment, *n.* [OFr. *entretenement*, from LL. *intertenementum*, from *intertenere*, to entertain.]
1. The act of entertaining; as, the *entertainment* of guests, of an audience, of a proposition.
2. Accommodation for a guest or guests; food, lodging, or other things required by a guest; a hospitable repast; as, to buy *entertainment*.
3. The amusement, pleasure, or instruction derived from conversation, oratory, music, dramatic performances, etc.; the pleasure which the mind receives from anything which holds or arrests the attention.
4. That which serves for amusement; a dramatic or other performance; as, a musical *entertainment*.
5. Reception; admission. [Rare.]
6. The state of being in pay or service. [Obs.]
Syn.—Amusement, diversion, recreation,

reception, admission, accommodation, feast, banquet, repast.

en-tẽr-tāke′, *v.t.* To entertain. [Obs.]

en-tẽr-tis′sūed (-tish′ụd), *a.* Interwoven; having various colors intermixed.

en′thē-ăl, en′thē-ăn, *a.* [L. *entheus*; Gr. *entheos*, inspired; *en*, in, and *theos*, god.] Divinely inspired. [Obs.]

en′thē-ạṣm, *n.* Inspiration. [Obs.]

en-thē-as′tiç, *a.* [Gr. *entheastikos*, from *entheos*, inspired; *en*, in, and *theos*, god.] Marked by entheasm.

en-thē-as′tiç-ăl-ly, *adv.* In an entheastic manner.

en′thē-at, *a.* Entheal. [Obs.]

en-thel-min′thȧ, en-thel-min′thēṣ, *n.pl.* Entozoa; enteric worms.

en-thel-min′thiç, *a.* Of or like enthelmintha.

en-thet′iç, *a.* [Gr. *enthetikos*, fit for planting, from *enthetos*, verbal adj. of *entithenai*; *en*, in, and *tithenai*, to put.] Coming from without; propagated by inoculation; introduced by infection; as, a contagious disease is *enthetic*.

en-thrạll′, en-thrạl′, *v.t.*; enthralled, *pt., pp.*; enthralling, *ppr.* To enslave; to lead or keep in subjection or under some controlling force; as, anarchy *enthralled* his reason.

en-thrạl′ment, en-thrạll′ment, *n.* The act of enthralling; the condition of being enthralled; that which enthralls.

en-thrill′, *v.t.* To pierce. [Obs.]

en-thrōne′, *v.t.*; enthroned, *pt., pp.*; enthroning, *ppr.* 1. To place upon, or as upon a throne; to exalt to the seat of royalty.

> Beneath a sculptured arch he sits *enthroned*.
> —Pope.

2. To enthronize.

en-thrōne′ment, *n.* Act of enthroning; state of being enthroned.

en-thrōn-i-zā′tion, *n.* The act of enthroning or of enthronizing, as a bishop.

en-thrōn′īze, *v.t.*; enthronized, *pt., pp.*; enthronizing, *ppr.* To set upon a throne; to induct, as a bishop, into a vacant see. [Rare.]

en-thūṣe′, *v.t.* and *v.i.*; enthused, *pt., pp.*; enthusing, *ppr.* I. *v.t.* To cause to become enthusiastic. [Colloq.]

II. *v.i.* To grow enthusiastic. [Colloq.]

en-thū′ṣi-aṣm, *n.* [Gr. *enthousiasmos*, inspiration, enthusiasm, from *enthousiazein*, to be inspired, to be possessed by a god, to inspire; from *enthous*, *entheos*, possessed by a god; *en*, in, and *theos*, god.]

1. An ecstasy of mind, as if from inspiration or possession by a spiritual influence; hence, a belief or conceit of being divinely inspired, or of being possessed of a private revelation of the divine. [Archaic.]

2. Strong and pleasurable emotion manifested by expressions of approval or eager interest; ardor or excitement in pursuit of some object, inspiring extravagant hope and confidence of success; predominance of the emotional over the intellectual powers; fervor; as, the *enthusiasm* of an audience.

3. An intense, profound, and eager interest, with a liveliness of imagination and an ardent zeal for an object believed to be worthy; as, the *enthusiasm* of the scientist, the artist, or the inventor.

en-thū′ṣi-ast, *n.* [Gr. *enthousiastēs*, from *enthousiazein*, to be inspired.]

1. One who imagines he has supernatural relations with God, or special communications from him. [Archaic.]

2. One whose imagination is highly excited with the love or in the pursuit of an object; a person of ardent zeal; as, an *enthusiast* in poetry or music.

Syn.—Zealot, devotee, visionary.

en-thū-ṣi-as′tiç, en-thū-ṣi-as′tiç-ăl, *a.* Filled with or characterized by enthusiasm; warm and ardent; zealous.

en-thū-ṣi-as′tiç-ăl-ly, *adv.* With enthusiasm.

en″thy-mē-mat′iç, en″thy-mē-mat′iç-ăl, *a.* Pertaining to or including an enthymeme.

en′thy-mēme, *n.* [L. *enthymema*; Gr. *enthymēma*, a thought, argument, from *enthymeisthai*, to consider, keep in mind; *en*, in, and *thymos*, mind.] In rhetoric, an argument having one premise of the syllogism suppressed; as, we are dependent, therefore we should be humble. Here the major proposition is suppressed. The complete syllogism would be: dependent creatures should be humble; we are dependent creatures; therefore we should be humble.

en-tīce′, *v.t.*; enticed (-tīst′), *pt., pp.*; enticing, *ppr.* [ME. *enticen*, *entisen*; OFr. *enticer*, *enticher*, to excite, entice.] To allure; to lead on by exciting hope or desire; to induce to act wrongly by false promises or persuasions; to seduce; to lead astray; to tempt; to incite.

Syn.—Allure, decoy, seduce, inveigle.

en-tīce′ȧ-ble, *a.* Susceptible of being enticed.

en-tīce′ment, *n.* 1. The act or practice of enticing.

2. Alluring quality; also, means of enticing.

3. The state of being enticed.

en-tī′cẽr, *n.* One who entices.

en-tī′çing, *a.* Alluring; tempting; inviting.

en-tī′çing-ly, *adv.* In an enticing manner.

en-tier′ty, *n.* Entirety. [Obs.]

en′ti-fȳ, *v.t.* [L. *ens*, *entis*, a thing, and *-ficare*, from *facere*, to make.] To consider as, or cause to become an entity. [Rare.]

en-tīre′, *a.* [ME. *entyre*; OFr. *entier*; L. *integer*, whole, untouched, undiminished.]

1. Whole; undivided; unbroken; complete in all its parts; undiminished; full; perfect; not mutilated; having all normal elements; as, not an article was left *entire*; *entire* confidence.

2. In biology, not divided; (a) without branches; (b) without an opening in the edge, as a leaf; (c) of one piece, as a fin; (d) uncastrated, as a horse.

3. In full strength; unalloyed; unqualified; pure; sincere; faithful; unfeigned. [Archaic.]

4. Interior. [Obs.]

en-tīre′, *n.* 1. The whole; also, entireness. [Rare.]

2. Porter; stout; so called as being drawn from the cask at once and not necessitating any mixing. [Eng.]

3. A stallion.

en-tīre′ly, *adv.* Wholly; completely; fully; unreservedly.

en-tīre′ness, *n.* 1. The state of being entire; completeness; totality; entirety.

2. Integrity. [Archaic.]

3. Closeness; intimacy; unity. [Obs.]

en-tīre′ty, *n.*; *pl.* **en-tīre′tiēṣ**. 1. Wholeness; completeness; entireness; as, *entirety* of interest.

2. The whole.

en′ti-tā-tive, *a.* Considered by itself as an entity or independent existence. [Rare.]

en′ti-tā-tive-ly, *adv.* As abstract existence. [Rare.]

en-tī′tle, *v.t.*; entitled, *pt., pp.*; entitling, *ppr.* [ME. *entitlen*; OFr. *entituler*; LL. *intitulare*, to give title or name to; L. *in*, in, and *titulus*, a title.]

1. To give a title to; to give or prefix a name or appellation to; as, to *entitle* a book "Commentaries."

2. To give a claim to; to give a right to demand or receive; as, his labor *entitles* him to his wages.

3. To assign or appropriate as by giving a title. [Obs.]

4. To ascribe. [Obs.]

en-tit′ūle, *v.t.* Same as *Entitle*.

en′ti-ty, *n.*; *pl.* **en′ti-tiēṣ**. [LL. *entitas*, from L. *ens*, *entis*, being, ppr. of *esse*, to be.]

1. Being; essence; existence.

2. A real being, or species of being.

en-tō-. A combining form from Greek *entos*, within, signifying within; as, *ento*cele.

en′tō-blast, *n.* [*Ento-*, and Gr. *blastos*, a shoot, germ.] In biology, (a) the innermost germinal layer; the hypoblast or endoderm; (b) a nucleolus.

en-tō-bran′chi-āte, *a.* [*Ento-*, and Gr. *branchia*, gills.] Having the gills entirely internal.

en-tō-bron′chi-um, *n.*; *pl.* **en-tō-bron′chi-ȧ**. [*Ento-*, and Gr. *bronchos*, the windpipe.] In zoölogy, a ventral branch of a bird's bronchus.

en′tō-cēle, *n.* [*Ento-*, and Gr. *kēlē*, a rupture.] In pathology, displacement of an internal organ.

en″tō-çū-nē′i-fọrm, *n.* [*Ento-*, and L. *cuneus*, a wedge, and *forma*, form.] In anatomy, the innermost of the three tapering or wedge-shaped bones of the tarsus.

en′tō-dẽrm, *n.* The endoderm.

en-tō-dẽr′măl, en-tō-dẽr′miç, *a.* Same as *Endodermal*.

en-tō-gas′triç, *a.* [*Ento-*, and Gr. *gastēr*, *gastros*, stomach.] Of or relating to the inside of the gastric cavity.

Entogastric gemmation or *proliferation*; a process of asexual multiplication seen in certain *Discophora*, in which budding occurs within the gastric cavity.

en-toġ′e-nous, *a.* Same as *Endogenous*.

en-tō-glos′săl, *a.* and *n.* [*Ento-*, and Gr. *glōssa*, the tongue.]

I. *a.* Inside the tongue; said of the glossohyal bone.

II. *n.* The glossohyal bone.

en-toil′, *v.t.* To ensnare; to entangle. [Obs.]

en-tōmb′ (-tōm′), *v.t.*; entombed, *pt., pp.*; entombing, *ppr.* To deposit in a tomb; to bury; to inter.

en-tōmb′ment, *n.* The act of entombing or state of being entombed; burial; sepulture.

en′tō-mēre, *n.* [*Ento-*, and Gr. *meros*, a part.] In embryology, the more granular portion of a mammalian ovum, becoming the inner portion in the process of development.

en-tom′iç, en-tom′iç-ăl, *a.* [Gr. *entomon*, an insect.] Relating to insects; entomological.

en-tō-mō-, en-tom-. Combining forms from Greek *entomon*, an insect, signifying insect; as, *entomo*phagous, *entom*ology.

en-tō-moġ′e-nous, *a.* Having the place of growth in or upon insects; said of certain fungi.

en′tō-moid, *a.* and *n.* [Gr. *entomon*, an insect, and *eidos*, form.]

I. *a.* Like an insect.

II. *n.* A thing, as a leaf, with the appearance of an insect.

en-tom′ō-lin, *n.* Same as *Chitin*.

en-tom′ō-līte, *n.* A fossil considered to be that of an insect.

en″tō-mō-loġ′iç, en″tō-mō-loġ′iç-ăl, *a.* Pertaining to entomology.

en″tō-mō-loġ′iç-ăl-ly, *adv.* According to entomology.

en-tō-mol′ō-ġist, *n.* One who is versed in or studying entomology.

en-tō-mol′ō-ġīze, *v.i.*; entomologized, *pt., pp.*; entomologizing, *ppr.* To collect insects for scientific study; to study entomology.

en-tō-mol′ō-ġy, *n.*; *pl.* **en-tō-mol′ō-ġiēṣ**. [*Entomo-*, and Gr. *-logia*, from *legein*, to speak.]

1. The part of zoölogy which treats of insects.

2. A systematic treatise on insects.

En-tō-moph′ȧ-gȧ, *n.pl.* [*Entomo-*, and Gr. *phagein*, to eat.]

1. A group of hymenopters having larvæ parasitic on other insects.

2. A section of the edentates which includes ant-eaters and pangolins.

3. A tribe of marsupials which are insectivorous, but not exclusively so, including bandicoots and opossums.

en-tō-moph′ȧ-găn, *a.* and *n.* I. *a.* Of or pertaining to the *Entomophaga*.

II. *n.* A member of the *Entomophaga*.

en-tō-moph′ȧ-gous, *a.* Insectivorous; entomophagan.

en-tō-moph′i-lous, *a.* [*Entomo-*, and Gr. *philos*, loving.] Depending chiefly upon insects for fertilization; said of certain flowers.

En″tō-moph-thō′rē-æ, *n.pl.* [*Entomo-*, and Gr. *phthora*, destruction, from *phtheirein*, to destroy.] A group of fungi containing five known genera, commonly parasitic upon and destructive to insects.

en-tō-moph′y-tous, *a.* [*Entomo-*, and Gr. *phyton*, a plant.] Same as *Entomogenous*.

En-tō-mos′trȧ-çȧ, *n.pl.* [*Entom-*, and Gr. *ostrakon*, an earthen vessel, a shell.] A main division of *Crustacea*, including, according to Huxley's system, the *Epizoa*, *Copepoda*, *Pectostraca*, *Branchiopoda*, and *Ostracoda*.

en-tō-mos′trȧ-çăn, *a.* and *n.* I. *a.* Of or pertaining to the *Entomostraca*.

II. *n.* A member of the *Entomostraca*.

en-tō-mos′trȧ-çous, *a.* Entomostracan.

Entomostraca.—1. *Cyclops quadricornis*: *a*, Eye; *c c*, Eggs. 2. *Cypris*: *a*, Eye.

en″tō-mō-tax′y, *n.* [*Entomo-*, and Gr. *taxis*, arrangement.] The art of arranging and preserving entomological specimens.

en-tō-mot′ō-mist, *n.* One who dissects insects.

en-tō-mot′ō-my, *n.* [*Entomo-*, and Gr. *tomē*, a cutting.] Insect dissection; entomological anatomy.

en-ton′iç, *a.* [Gr. *entonos*, stretched, strung, from *enteinein*, to stretch, strain tight; *en*, in, and *teinein*, to stretch.] In pathology, strained; having violent action or abnormal tension.

en-tō-par′ȧ-sīte, *n.* A parasite living within its host; opposed to *ectoparasite*.

en″tō-pe-riph′ẽr-ăl, *a.* [*Ento-*, and Gr. *periphereia*, periphery; *peri*, around, and *pherein*, to bear.] In physiology, arising or developing within the body's periphery.

en′tō-phȳte, *n.* [*Ento-*, and Gr. *phyton*, a plant.] A parasitic plant living within another organism, as a bacterium.

en-tō-phyt′iç, *a.* Of, like, caused by, or characteristic of entophytes.

en′tō-plaṣm, *n.* Same as *Endoplasm*.

en-tō-plas′trŏn, *n.*; *pl.* **en-tō-plas′trȧ**. [*Ento-*, and LL. *plastra*, a thin plate of metal.] The median and anterior piece of the ventral part of the shell of a turtle or tortoise.

En-tō-proç′tȧ, *n.pl.* [*Ento-*, and Gr. *prōktos*, the anus.] A group of polyzoans having the anus close to the mouth and within the tentacles of the lophophore.

en-tō-proç′tous, *a.* Pertaining to or having the characteristics of the *Entoprocta*.

ent-op′tiç, *a.* [*Ent-*, and Gr. *optikos*, pertaining to sight.] Of or relating to the interior of the eye.

ent-op′tiçs, *n.* The science of the internal phenomena of the eye.

ent-ọr′găn-iṣm, *n.* An internal parasite.

en-tọr-ti-lā′tion, *n.* [Fr. *entortiller*, to twist; *en-*, in, *tortiller*, from L. *torquere*, to twist.] A turning into a circle. [Obs.]

en-tō-stẽr′năl, *a.* [*Ento-*, and Gr. *sternon*, the breast, chest.] Pertaining to the entosternum.

en-tō-stẽr′nīte, *n.* A cartilaginous plate developed internally as a support for muscles, as in some crustaceans.

en-tō-stẽr′num, *n.* 1. One or all of the internal processes of an insect's sternum.

2. An entoplastron.

en-tos′thō-blast, *n.* [Gr. *entosthe*, from within, and *blastos*, a bud, germ.] In biology, a granule inside of the nucleolus of a cell.

en-tō-thō′rax, *n.* Same as *Endothorax.*

ent-ot′ic, *a.* [*Ento-*, and Gr. *ous*, *ōtos*, the ear.] Of or relating to the inside of the ear.

eṅ-tōu-rāġe (oṅ-tö-räzh′), *n.* [Fr., from *entourer*, to surround; from *en tour*, around; *en*, in, and *tour*, round.] Surroundings; environment; especially, the persons with whom one usually comes into association.

En-tō-zō′ȧ, *n.pl.* [*Ento-*, and Gr. *zōon* (pl. *zōa*), an animal.] In zoölogy, a general name for those annulose parasitical animals which infest the bodies of other animals. Some are found in the intestines, others in the liver, brain, muscles, and other tissues. They pass through different stages in their development, and at each stage occupy a different tissue and usually a different animal.

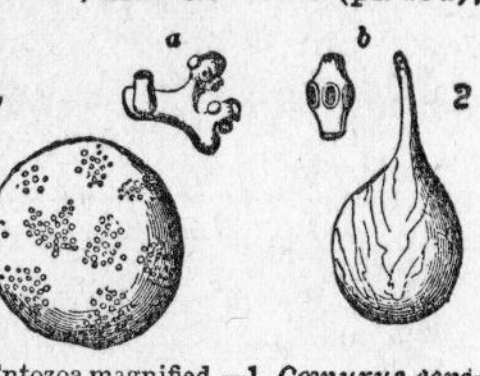

Entozoa magnified.—1 *Cœnurus cerebralis* (producing the staggers in sheep). *a*, Heads (shown on the surface) separately. 2. *Cysticercus cellulosæ* (causing the measles in pigs). *b*, Head.

en-tō-zō′ic, en-tō-zō′ăl, *a.* 1. Composed of or relating to the *Entozoa.*

2. Existing as an entoparasite.

en″tō-zō-ol′ō-ġist, *n.* A student of the *Entozoa.*

en-tō-zō′on, *n.*; *pl.* **en-tō-zō′ȧ.** [*Ento-*, and Gr. *zōon*, an animal.] An intestinal worm; an animal living in some parts of another animal; a member of the *Entozoa.*

eṅ-tr′acte′ (oṅ-trakt′), *n.* [Fr., from *entre*, between, and *acte*, an act.]

1. An intermission between the acts of a play.

2. Music, a ballet, or the like, rendered between the acts of a play.

en′trāil, *n.*; *pl.* **en′trāilṣ.** [ME. *entraile*; OFr. *entraille*; LL. *intralia*, from L. *interaneum*, pl. *interanea*, intestine; *interaneus*, inward, interior, from *inter*, between, among.]

1. An internal part of an animal body; the viscera; used chiefly in the plural.

2. Any internal part; as, the *entrails* of the earth.

en-trāil′, *v.t.* [*En-*, and Fr. *treiller*, to lattice, trellis.] To interweave; to diversify. [Obs.]

en-trāil′, *n.* Entanglement. [Obs.]

en-trāin′, *v.i.* and *v.t.*; entrained, *pt.*, *pp.*; entraining, *ppr.* To go or cause to go aboard a railway train.

en-trāin′, *v.t.* To draw after oneself.

en-tram′mel, *v.t.* To trammel; to entangle. [Obs.]

en′trănce, *n.* [OFr. *entrance*, from *entrant*; L. *entrans* (-*antis*), ppr. of *intrare*, to enter, from *intro*, to the inside, within.]

1. The act of entering into a place; as, the *entrance* of a person into a house or an apartment.

> His own door being shut against his *entrance.* —Shak.

2. The power or liberty of entering; admission.

> Truth is sure to find an *entrance* and a welcome too. —South.

3. The doorway, gateway, passage, or avenue by which a place may be entered; passage into.

> And wisdom at one *entrance* quite shut out. —Milton.

4. Commencement; initiation; beginning.

> This is that which, at first *entrance*, balks and cools them. —Locke.

5. The act of taking possession, as of property or an office; as, the *entrance* of an heir or a disseizor into lands and tenements; magistrates at their *entrance* into office usually take an oath.

6. Acquaintance; knowledge. [Obs.]

7. The act of entering a ship or goods at the customhouse.

8. The bow of a vessel, or form of the forebody under the load water-line; it expresses the figure of that which encounters the sea, and is the opposite of *run.*

Syn.—Ingress, entry, admission, admittance, doorway, gateway.

en-trănce′, *v.t.*; entranced (trănst′), *pt.*, *pp.*; entrancing, *ppr.* 1. To put into a trance; to withdraw the soul from, as the material body, producing thereby a kind of deep sleep or insensibility.

2. To put into an ecstasy; to ravish the soul of, with delight and wonder.

> I stood *entranced*, and had no room for thought. —Dryden.

en-trănce′ment, *n.* A state of trance or ecstasy; the act of putting into a trance.

en′trănt, *n.* and *a.* I. *n.* One who is entering; a beginner; a novice.

II. *a.* Entering; beginning; admitting.

en-trap′, *v.t.*; entrapped (-trapt′), *pt.*, *pp.*; entrapping, *ppr.* [OFr. *entraper*, *entrapper*, to catch in a trap; *en-*, in, and *trape*, a trap.] To catch by artifice; to involve in difficulties or distresses; to entangle; to catch or involve in contradictions; in short, to involve in any difficulties from which an escape is not easy or possible; as, we are *entrapped* by the devices of evil men.

Syn.—Decoy, lure, inveigle, ensnare.

en-trēat′, *v.t.*; entreated, *pt.*, *pp.*; entreating, *ppr.* [ME. *entreten*, to treat, or deal with, to beseech; OFr. *entraiter*, to treat of, entertain; *en-*, in, and *traiter*, to treat.]

1. To ask earnestly; to beseech; to petition or pray with urgency; to supplicate; to solicit pressingly; to importune.

> Isaac *entreated* Jehovah for his wife. —Gen. xxv. 21.

2. To prevail on by prayer or solicitation.

> It were a fruitless attempt to appease a power whom no prayers could *entreat.* —Rogers.

3. To treat in any manner; to use or manage; to deal with; to manifest to others any particular deportment, good or ill. [Obs.]

> I will cause the enemy to *entreat* thee well. —Jer. xv. 11.

4. To entertain; to amuse. [Obs.]

5. To entertain; to receive. [Obs.]

Syn.—Beg, implore, beseech, solicit, importune.

en-trēat′, *v.i.* 1. To make an earnest petition or request.

> The Janizaries *entreated* for them, as valiant men. —Knowles.

2. To offer a treaty. [Obs.]

3. To treat; to discourse. [Obs.]

en-trēat′, *n.* [Obs.] See *Entreaty.*

en-trēat′ȧ-ble, *a.* That may be entreated, or is soon entreated.

en-trēat′ănce, *n.* Entreaty; solicitation. [Obs.]

en-trēat′ẽr, *n.* One who entreats.

en-trēat′fụl, *a.* Of an entreating disposition.

en-trēat′ing-ly, *adv.* In an entreating manner.

en-trēat′ive, *a.* Pleading; characterized by entreaty.

en-trēat′ment, *n.* Entreaty. [Obs.]

en-trēat′y, *n.*; *pl.* **en-trēat′ieṣ.** 1. Urgent prayer; earnest petition; pressing solicitation; supplication.

> The poor useth *entreaties*; but the rich answereth roughly. —Prov. xviii. 23.

2. Treatment; amusement. [Obs.]

Syn.—Solicitation, importunity, supplication, prayer.

eṅ-trée′ (oṅ-trā′), *n.* [Fr.] 1. Literally, a coming in, or entry.

2. Freedom of access; as, the *entrée* of a house.

3. A side-dish; a dish served with a principal dish or between courses; originally, the first small course served.

4. In music, the opening number; especially of a ballet or opera.

eṅ-tre-mets′ (oṅ-tr-mā′), *n.* [Fr. *entre*, between, and *mets*, a dish, mess.]

1. A relish or sweetmeat served with or after the principal dish; a side-dish.

2. A short burlesque. [Obs.]

3. An interlude. [Rare.]

en-trench′, *v.t.* Same as *Intrench.*

eṅ-tre-pot′ (oṅ-tr-pō′), *n.* [Fr., from L. *interpositum*, neut. of *interpositus*, pp. of *interponere*, to place between; *inter*, between, and *ponere*, to place.]

1. A warehouse or magazine for the deposit of goods; a building or place where goods from abroad may be deposited, and afterward withdrawn for exportation without paying a duty.

2. A distributing point for goods, as a seaport or large inland city.

eṅ-tre-prē-neur′ (oṅ-tr-prē-nẽr′), *n.* [Fr., from *entreprendre*, to undertake.] One who organizes and directs industrial enterprises; also, the originator or manager of public entertainments, or of a musical enterprise.

en′tre-sol (*or Fr. pron.* oṅ-tr-sol′), *n.* [Fr. *entre*, between, and *sol*, ground.] A mezzanine, especially a half-story just above the ground floor; any half-story between higher ones.

en-trick′, *v.t.* To trick; to deceive. [Obs.]

en′trō-chăl, *a.* Relating to or made of entrochites; as, *entrochal* marble.

en′trō-chite, *n.* [Gr. *en*, in, and *trochos*, a wheel, and *-ite.*] A wheel-like joint of a fossil crinoid or encrinite; called also *wheelstone.*

en-trō′pi-on, en-trō′pi-um, *n.* Introversion or turning inward of the edge of the eyelid.

en′trō-py, *n.* [Gr. *entropia*, *entropē*, a turning toward; *en*, in, and *trepein*, to turn.] See *Thermodynamic function* under *Thermodynamic.*

en-trust′, *v.t.* Same as *Intrust.*

en′try, *n.*; *pl.* **en′trieṣ.** [ME. *entree*; OFr. *entree*; Pr. *intrada*; LL. *intrata*, entry, entrance, f. pp. of L. *intrare*, to enter, from *intro*, to the inside, within.]

1. The passage by which persons enter a house or other building; a hall; a vestibule; an adit.

2. The act of entering; entrance; ingress; as, the *entry* of a person into a house or city.

3. The act of committing to writing, or of recording in a book; as, make an *entry* of every sale, of every debit and credit.

Entresol or Mezzanine, Regent Circus, London.

4. The exhibition or depositing of a ship's papers at the customhouse, to procure license to land goods; the giving an account of a ship's cargo to the officer of the customs and obtaining his permission to land the goods.

5. The act of entering and taking possession of lands or other estate.

6. The putting upon record of any action, decree, or order in court.

7. The going into or upon the premises of another wrongfully or feloniously.

8. The placing on file of an application for the privilege to buy or to preëmpt public lands.

9. The beginnings; the first portions. [Rare.]

en′try-clẽrk, *n.* In a commercial office, a clerk who makes original entries of sales, debits, and credits, etc.

Writ of entry; in law, a writ issued authorizing the entering and taking possession of lands held in unlawful possession.

en′tryng, *n.* A going in. [Obs.]

en-tūne′, *v.t.* To intone. [Rare.]

en-twīne′, *v.t.*; entwined, *pt.*, *pp.*; entwining, *ppr.* To twine about; to twist round.

en-twīne′, *v.i.* To become twisted.

en-twīne′ment, *n.* A twisting round; union.

en-twist′, *v.t.* To twist or wreathe around.

ē-nū′bi-lāte, *v.t.* [LL. *enubilatus*, pp. of *enubilare*, to free from clouds; L. *e*, out, and *nubila*, pl. of *nubilum*, a cloud, mist.] To clear from mist, clouds, or obscurity. [Obs.]

ē-nū′bi-lous, *a.* Clear from fog, mist, or clouds.

ē-nū′clē-āte, *v.t.*; enucleated, *pt.*, *pp.*; enucleating, *ppr.* [L. *enucleatus*, pp. of *enucleare*, to take out the kernel, to explain; *e*, out, and *nucleus*, a kernel.]

1. To take out the kernel of; hence, to remove from a sac or enveloping membrane without using a knife, as a tumor.

2. To open, as a nucleus; to explain; to clear from obscurity; to make manifest.

ē-nū′clē-āte, *a.* Possessing no nucleus.

ē-nū-clē-ā′tion, *n.* 1. In surgery, the act of removing an inclosed body completely after opening its surrounding envelope.

2. A disentangling; explanation; exposition. [Rare.]

ē-nū′mẽr-āte, *v.t.*; enumerated, *pt.*, *pp.*; enumerating, *ppr.* [L. *enumeratus*, pp. of *enumerare*, to count over, count out; *e*, out, and *numerare*, to count, from *numerus*, a number.] To count; to tell one by one; to reckon or mention, as a number of things each separately; to recount; as, to *enumerate* the stars in a constellation; to *enumerate* particular acts of mercy.

Syn.—Specify, name, number, recount, detail, reckon, compute, calculate, call over.

ē-nū-mẽr-ā′tion, *n.* [L. *numerus*, number.]

1. The act of counting or numbering.

2. An account of a number of things, in which mention is made of every particular article.

3. In rhetoric, a part of a peroration, in which the orator recapitulates the principal points or heads of the discourse or argument.

ē-nū′mẽr-ā-tive, *a.* Counting; reckoning up.

ē-nū′mẽr-ā-tŏr, *n.* One who computes or recounts.

ē-nun′ci-ȧ-ble (-shi-ȧ-bl), *a.* Fit to be uttered; that may be uttered.

ē-nun′ci-āte, *v.t.*; enunciated, *pt.*, *pp.*; enunciating, *ppr.* [L. *enunciatus*, pp. of *enunciare*, properly *enuntiare*, to say out, declare; *e*, out, and *nuntiare*, to announce, from *nuntius*, a messenger.]

1. To utter; to articulate; as, he *enunciates* his words distinctly.

2. To proclaim; to declare; to relate; as, they *enunciated* their principles in their published works.

ē-nun′ci-āte, *v.i.* To utter words or syllables.

ē-nun-ci-ā′tion, *n.* 1. The act of announcing

or stating; that which is announced; declaration; open proclamation; public attestation; as, the *enunciation* of doctrines.

2. The act or manner of enunciating or pronouncing; mode of utterance; articulation; as, his *enunciation* is very distinct.

3. In logic, a proposition, the truth or falsity of which has not yet been asserted.

ē-nun′ci-ā-tive, *a.* Pertaining to enunciation; declarative.

ē-nun′ci-ā-tive-ly, *adv.* Declaratively.

ē-nun′ci-ā-tŏr, *n.* [LL. *enunciator*, properly *enuntiator*, from L. *enuntiare*, to speak out, declare.] One who enunciates or pronounces; one who proclaims or declares.

ē-nun′ci-ā-tō-ry, *a.* Containing utterance or sound; enunciative.

en-ūre′, *v.t.* See *Inure.*

en-ū-rē′sis, *n.* [From Gr. *enourein*, to make water in; *en-*, in, and *ourein*, from *ouron*, urine.] In pathology, incontinence or involuntary discharge of urine.

en-vas′săl, *v.t.* To reduce to vassalage; to make a slave of. [Obs.]

en-vault′, *v.t.* To inclose in a vault; to entomb. [Rare.]

en-vēi′gle, *v.t.* [Obs.] See *Inveigle.*

en-vel′ŏp, *v.t.*; enveloped (-upt), *pt.*, *pp.*; enveloping, *ppr.* [OFr. *envoluper*, *enveloper*; Pr. *envolopar*, to wrap up, envelop.] To cover, as by wrapping or folding; to inwrap; to invest with or as with a covering; to surround entirely; to cover on all sides; as, smoke *envelops* a town.

en′vel-ōpe, en-vel′ŏp (*or Fr. pron.* oṅ′ve-lōp), *n.* 1. A wrapper; any inclosing cover; an integument; especially, the wrapper for a letter or other paper.

2. In fortification, a work of earth in the form of a parapet or of a small rampart with a parapet, raised to cover some weak part of the works.

3. In astronomy, a coma.

4. In geometry, a curve or surface which is tangent to a continuous series of curves or surfaces.

en-vel′ŏped (-upt), *a.* In heraldry, applied to charges around which serpents, or laurels or other plants, are loosely twisted.

Enveloped.

en-vel′ŏp-ment, *n.* 1. The act of enveloping or covering on all sides.

2. That which envelops; a wrapper; an envelop.

en-ven′ime, *v.t.* [Obs.] See *Envenom.*

en-ven′ŏm, *v.t.*; envenomed, *pt.*, *pp.*; envenoming, *ppr.* [ME. *envenimen*; OFr. *envenimer*, from LL. *invenenare*, to poison, envenom; L. *in*, in, and *venenum*, poison, venom.]

1. To poison; to taint or impregnate with venom, or any substance noxious to life; to render dangerous or deadly by poison; as, an *envenomed* arrow; an *envenomed* potion.

2. To taint with bitterness or malice; to embitter.

The *envenomed* tongue of calumny.—Smollett.

en-vēr′meil (-mil), *v.t.* [OFr. *envermeillir*, to make red; *en-*, in, and *vermeil*, vermilion.] To dye red; to give a red color to. [Obs.]

en′vi-ȧ-ble, *a.* [Fr. *enviable*, from *envier*, to envy.] That may excite envy; capable of awakening ardent desire of possession; as, the position is an *enviable* one.

en′vi-ȧ-ble-ness, *n.* The state or quality of being enviable.

en′vi-ȧ-bly, *adv.* In an enviable manner.

en′vi-ẽr, *n.* One who envies.

en′vi-ous, *a.* [ME. *envious*, *envius*; OFr. *envios*; Sp. *envidioso*; It. *invidioso*; from L. *invidiosus*, envious, exciting envy, from *invidia*, envy.]

1. Feeling or harboring envy.

Be not thou *envious* against evil men.
—Prov. xxiv. 1.

2. Tinctured with envy; characterized by envy; as, an *envious* disposition; an *envious* attack.

3. Enviable. [Obs.]

4. Watchful; cautious; jealous. [Obs.]

en′vi-ous-ly, *adv.* In an envious manner; with envy; spitefully.

en′vi-ous-ness, *n.* The quality or state of being envious.

en-vī′rŏn, *v.t.*; environed, *pt.*, *pp.*; environing, *ppr.* [ME. *environen*, *envirounen*; OFr. *environer*, *envirouner*, to surround, from *environ*, around, about.] To surround; to encompass; to encircle; to hem in; to involve; to envelop.

With mountains round about *environed.*
—Spenser.

en-vī′rŏn, *adv.* Around; about. [Obs.]

en-vī′rŏn-ment, *n.* [Fr. *environnement*, from *environner*, to surround.]

1. The act of surrounding; the state of being environed.

2. That which environs; surroundings.

en-vī′rŏns, *n.pl.* The parts or places which surround another place, or lie in its neighborhood; as, the *environs* of a city or town.

en-vis′āge, *v.t.* [Fr. *envisager*, to envisage; *en-*, in, and *visage*, visage.] To look in the face of; to face; to apprehend directly; to perceive by intuition. [Rare.]

en-vis′āge-ment, *n.* The act of envisaging; apprehension.

en-vol′ūme, *v.t.* To form into or incorporate with a volume. [Rare.]

en-vol′upe, *v.t.* [Obs.] See *Envelop.*

en′voy, *n.* [Fr. *envoyé*, a messenger, one sent, pp. of *envoyer*, to send; It. *inviare*, L. *in*, in, on, and *via*, way.]

1. One despatched upon an errand or mission; a messenger; specifically, a person deputed by a ruler or government to negotiate a treaty, or transact other business, with a foreign ruler or government. The word was formerly applied to a public minister sent on a special occasion or for one particular purpose; hence, an *envoy* was distinguished from an *ambassador*, or permanent resident at a foreign court, and was of inferior rank.

2. Formerly, a postscript to a composition, as a poem, to enforce or recommend it.

en′voy-ship, *n.* The office of an envoy.

en′vy, *n.*; *pl.* **en′vies**. [ME. *envy*, *envie*; OFr. *envie*; Sp. *envidia*; L. *invidia*, hatred, ill will, from *invidus*, having hatred or ill will, from *invidere*, to look askance at; *in*, in, upon, and *videre*, to look, see.]

1. Uneasiness, mortification, or discontent at the sight of another's superiority or success, accompanied with some degree of hatred or malignity, and often or usually with a desire or an effort to depreciate the person envied; often followed by *of.*

2. Rivalry; competition. [Obs.]

3. Malice; malignity. [Obs.]

4. Public odium; ill repute. [Obs.]

5. An object of envy; as, he is the *envy* of all who know him.

en′vy, *v.t.*; envied, *pt.*, *pp.*; envying, *ppr.* [ME. *envien*; OFr. *envier*, to envy.]

1. To feel envy toward; to look upon with envy; to hate (another) for excellence or superiority in any way, and to be desirous of acquiring it; as, to *envy* a wealthy man.

2. To feel envy on account of; to look grudgingly upon, as the advantages possessed by another; to regard with a covetous spirit; as, he *envies* your superior knowledge; they *envy* his advancement.

3. To injure; to do harm to. [Obs.]

4. To oppose; to hate. [Obs.]

5. To emulate. [Obs.]

en′vy, *v.i.* 1. To be affected with envy; to have envious feelings; to regard anything with grudge and longing desire; formerly followed by *at.*

2. To show malice. [Obs.]

3. To vie. [Obs.]

en-wall′, *v.t.* Same as *Inwall.*

en-wal′lōw, *v.t.* To wallow. [Obs.]

en-wheel′, *v.t.* See *Inwheel.*

en-wid′en, *v.t.* To make wider. [Obs.]

en-wind′, *v.t.* To coil about. [Rare.]

en-wom′ăn (-wụm′), *v.t.* To endow with the qualities of woman; to make womanish. [Rare.]

en-wōmb′ (-wōm′), *v.t.* 1. To make pregnant. [Obs.]

2. To bury; to hide, as in a womb, pit, or cavern.

en-wrap′ (-rap′), *v.t.* See *Inwrap.*

en-wrap′ment, *n.* See *Inwrapment.*

en-wrēathe′, *v.t.* See *Inwreathe.*

en-zōne′, *v.t.* To encompass; to encircle.

en-zō-ot′iç, *a.* and *n.* [Gr. *en*, in, among, and *zōon*, an animal.]

I. *a.* Pertaining to a disease which prevails either constantly or at periodic intervals, affecting one or more species of animals in a country. It is opposed to *epizoötic*, to which it stands in the same relation as an endemic to an epidemic disease in man.

II. *n.* A disease restricted to the domestic animals of a district.

en′zym, en′zyme, *n.* [Gr. *en*, in, and *zymē*, leaven.]

1. In chemistry, an unorganized agent that induces fermentation, as rennet, pepsin, etc.

2. Leavened bread, as that used by the Greek church in the eucharist.

en-zy-mō′sis, *n.* See *Zymosis.*

en-zy-mot′iç, *a.* [L.Gr. *enzymos*, leavened, fermented; Gr. *en*, in, and *zymē*, leaven.] Relating to the enzyms.

ē-ō-. A combining form from Gr. *ēōs*, dawn, morning, used in paleontology, geology, etc., to indicate connection or relation to an early period of time; as, *Eocene.*

ē-ō′an, *a.* [L. *eous*; Gr. *ēōos*, from *ēōs*, dawn.] Of or pertaining to the dawn; eastern; auroral.

Ē′ō-cēne, *a.* and *n.* [*Eo-*, and Gr. *kainos*, recent.]

I. *a.* Pertaining to or having existed in the first period of the Tertiary era.

II. *n.* In geology, one of the divisions of the Tertiary.

Ē-ō-gæ′ȧ, *n.* [Gr. *ēōs*, dawn, and *gaia*, earth.] In zoögeography, a division comprising the African, South American, Australian, and New Zealand realms.

Ē-ō-gæ′ăn, *a.* Pertaining to *Eogæa.*

Ē-ō-hip′pus, *n.* [*Eo-*, and Gr. *hippos*, horse.] In paleontology, a genus of *Equidæ*, the oldest known member of the horse family. The animals were of small size, had on the fore feet four toes with a rudimentary thumb, and on the hind ones three toes, all the digits terminating in hoofs. It was found in the Lower Eocene of New Mexico.

Ē-ō′li-ăn, *a.* See *Æolian.*

Ē-ol′iç, *a.* See *Æolic.*

ē-ō-li′nȧ, *n.* See *Æolina.*

ē-ol′i-pīle, ē-ol′i-pȳle, *n.* See *Æolipile.*

Ē′ō-lis, *n.* See *Æolis.*

ē-ō-lith′iç, *a.* [*Eo-*, and Gr. *lithos*, stone.] In archæology, pertaining to the early part of the stone age.

ē″ō-lō-trop′iç, *a.* See *Æolotropic.*

ē′ŏn, æ′ŏn, *n.* [LL. *æon*, from Gr. *aiōn*, an age, lifetime.]

1. A period of immense duration; an unlimited space of time; an age; a cycle; eternity.

2. In Platonic philosophy, a virtue, attribute, or perfection existing throughout eternity.

ē-ō′ni-ăn, æ-ō′ni-ăn, *a.* [Gr. *aiōnios*, from *aiōn*, an age, lifetime.] Lasting for eons; everlasting.

ē-on′iç, æ-on′iç, *a.* Eternal; everlasting.

ē′ō-phȳte, *n.* [*Eo-*, and Gr. *phyton*, a plant.] In paleontology, a fossil plant found in Eozoic rocks.

ē-ō-phyt′iç, *a.* Pertaining to eophytes; Eozoic.

Ē′os, *n.* [Gr. *ēōs*, dawn.] In Greek mythology, the goddess of the dawn, corresponding to the Roman Aurora.

ē′ō-sin, *n.* [Gr. *ēōs*, dawn, and *-in.*] An acid dye produced by the action of bromine on fluorescein suspended in glacial acetic acid. It occurs in red or yellowish crystals and is used as a stain in histology.

ē-ō-sin′iç, *a.* Pertaining to eosin.

ē-ō-sin′ō-phil, *a.* [*Eosin*, and Gr. *philos*, loving.] Showing a peculiar affinity for eosin-stain or for acid-stains in general.

ē-os′phō-rīte, *n.* [Gr. *heōsphoros*, morn-bringing; *ēōs*, dawn, and *-phoros*, from *pherein*, to bear, and *-ite.*] A hydrous phosphate of aluminium and manganese, crystallizing in the orthorhombic system.

Ē-ō-zō′iç, *a.* [*Eo-*, and Gr. *zōē*, life.] Of or pertaining to the oldest fossiliferous rocks, such as the Laurentian and Huronian of Canada, from their being supposed to contain the first or earliest traces of life in the stratified systems.

Ē-ō-zō′on, *n.* [*Eo-*, and Gr. *zōon*, an animal.] The name given to a supposed fossil foraminifer, found in the Laurentian rocks of Canada and other regions.

ē-ō-zō′on-ăl, *a.* Pertaining or belonging to the Eozoön.

ep-. See *Epi-.*

Ep″ȧ-çri-dā′cē-æ, *n.pl.* [Gr. *epi*, upon, and *akron*, top.] A natural order of monopetalous exogens, very closely allied to the *Ericaceæ*, but distinguished by the one-celled anthers opening by a chink. They are chiefly natives of Australia.

ep″ȧ-çri-dā′ceous, *a.* Pertaining to the *Epacridaceæ.*

Ep′ȧ-çris, *n.* [Gr. *epi*, upon, and *akron*, top.] A genus of shrubby plants, chiefly natives of Australia, typical of the *Epacridaceæ.*

ē′paçt, *n.* [LL. *epacta*, from Gr. *epaktē*, f. of *epaktos*, brought in, intercalated.] In chronology, a term denoting the moon's age at the commencement of the calendar year, or the number of days by which the last new moon has preceded the beginning of the year.

Annual epact; the eleven days by which the solar exceeds the lunar year in length.

Menstrual or *monthly epact*; the excess of a calendar over a lunar month.

ē-paç′tăl, *a.* [Gr. *epaktos*, brought in, intercalated.] In anatomy, intercalary; additional; supernumerary.

ep-ȧ-gō′ġē, *n.* [LL. *epagoge*; Gr. *epagōgē*, a bringing to or in, from *epagein*; *epi*, to, on, and *agein*, to bring, lead.] In logic and rhetoric, oratorical induction; a figure of speech which consists in demonstrating and proving universal propositions by particulars.

Epacris grandiflora (garden variety).

ep-ȧ-gog′iç, *a.* Pertaining to epagoge.

ē-pā-lē-ā′ceous, *a.* [L. *e* priv., and *palea*, chaff.] In botany, destitute of chaffy scales.

ē-pal′pāte, *a.* In entomology, having no palpi.

ep″an-ȧ-di-plō′sis, *n.* [LL., from Gr. *epanadiplōsis*, a doubling, repetition, from *epanadiploun*; *epi*, upon, and *anadiploun*, to double.] In rhetoric, a figure by which a sentence ends with the same word with which it begins; as "*Rejoice* in the Lord alway; and again I say, *Rejoice*."

ep″an-ȧ-lep′sis, *n.* [Gr. *epanalēpsis*, a repetition, regaining, from *epanalambanein*, to take up again, repeat; *epi*, upon, and *analambanein*, to take up.] In rhetoric, a figure by which the same word or phrase is repeated after other words have intervened.

ep-ȧ-naph′ō-rȧ, *n.* [L., from Gr. *epanaphora*, a reference, repetition, from *epanapherein*; *epi*, upon, and *anapherein*, to bring back.] In rhetoric, a figure of speech which consists in the repetition of a word or phrase at the beginning of successive clauses; anaphora.

ep-ȧ-nas′trō-phē, *n.* [Gr. *epanastrophē*, a return, from *epanastrephein*; *epi*, upon, and *anastrephein*, to turn back.] In rhetoric, a figure by which the speaker makes the end of one clause the beginning of the next; anadiplosis.

ē-pan′ō-dos, *n.* [Gr., a rising up, return, recapitulation; *epi*, upon, and *anodos*, a way up.] In rhetoric, (a) a figure, when a sentence or member is inverted or repeated backward; (b) the return to the principal heads or to the proper subject of a discourse after a digression, or in order to consider the topics separately and more particularly.

ē-pan′ō-dy, *n.* [Gr. *epanodos*, a return.] In botany, the reversion of an irregular flower to one of a regular form.

ep″an-or-thō′sis, *n.* [LL., from Gr. *epanorthōsis*, a correction, from *epi*, upon, and *anorthoun*, to set up again; *ana*, up, and *orthoun*, from *orthos*, straight.] In rhetoric, a figure by which a person corrects or ingeniously revokes what he just before alleged, as being too weakly expressed, in order to add something stronger and more conformable to the passion with which he is agitated; as, Most *brave* act. *Brave*, did I say? Most *heroic* act.

ep-an′thous, *a.* [*Ep-*, and Gr. *anthos*, a flower.] In botany, growing upon flowers, as certain fungi.

ē-pa-pil′lāte, *a.* Destitute of papillæ.

ē-pap′pōse, *a.* [L. *e-* priv., and Gr. *pappos*, down.] In botany, destitute of pappus; said of certain composite flowers.

ep′ärch, *n.* [Gr. *eparchos*, from *epi*, upon, and *archein*, to rule.] In ancient and modern Greece, the governor or prefect of a province or eparchy.

ep′ärch-y, *n.* [Gr. *eparchia*, from *eparchos*, a ruler, commander.]

1. In ancient Greece, a province, prefecture, or territory under the jurisdiction of an eparch or governor; in modern Greece, a subdivision of a nomarchy or province.

2. In the Greek church, a Russian diocese.

ep-är-tē′ri-ăl, *a.* [*Ep-*, and L. *arteria*, an artery.] In anatomy, located above an artery.

ē-pat′kȧ, *n.* [Alaskan.] *Fratercula corniculata*, the horned puffin.

ē-pau̧le′, *n.* [Fr. *épaule*, the shoulder.] In fortification, the shoulder of a bastion or the angle made by the face and flank.

ē-pau̧le′ment, *n.* Same as *Epaulment*.

ep′au̧-let, ep′au̧-lette, *n.* [Fr., dim. of *épaule*, the shoulder.] A shoulder-piece; an ornamental badge worn on the shoulder by officers in the navy and army, and made of various forms and material according to the rank of the wearer. In the United States army it is worn only by general officers. Epaulets were worn in the British army until 1855, when their use was abolished, but they are still worn by all naval officers of and above the rank of lieutenant, and by some civil officers. All officers in the United States navy above the rank of ensign wear epaulets.

ep′au̧-let-ed, ep′au̧-let-ted, *a.* Furnished with epaulets.

é-pau-lière′ (ā-pō-lyãr′), *n.* [Fr., from *épaule*, the shoulder.] In medieval armor, a shoulder-plate, either of one piece or composed of several successive plates. It was fastened by laces or points to the sleeve of the hauberk.

Épaulière.

ē-pau̧l′ment, ē-pau̧le′ment, *n.* [Fr. *épaulement*, from *épaule*, a shoulder, support.] In fortification, formerly a mass of earth raised for the purpose either of protecting a body of troops at one extremity of their line or of forming a wing or shoulder of a battery to prevent the guns from being dismounted by an enfilading fire. The term is now used to designate the whole mass of earth or other material which protects the guns in a battery both in front and on either flank.

ep-ax′ăl, *a.* See *Epaxial*.

ep-ax′i-ăl, *a.* [*Ep-*, and L. *axis*, an axis.] In anatomy, above or on the dorsal side of the skeletal axis; opposed to *hypaxial*.

E-peī′rȧ, *n.* [From Gr. *epi*, upon, and *eiros*, wool.] A genus of spiders typical of the family *Epeiridæ*. *Epeira diadema*, a handsomely marked species, is the common garden spider.

Epaulment.

E-peī′ri-dæ, *n.pl.* A family of spiders of which *Epeira* is the typical genus.

ē-peī″rō-ġē-net′iç, ē-pei-rō-ġen′iç, *a.* [Gr. *ēpeiros*, mainland, and *genesis*, origin, birth.] In geology, relating to or occasioning widespread elevations and depressions in the earth's crust.

ep-eī-roġ′e-ny, *n.* [Gr. *ēpeiros*, mainland, and *-geneia*, production.] In geology, the process by which the great continental elevations and depressions of the earth's crust were formed.

ep-en′ceph-ăl, *n.* Same as *Epencephalon*.

ep-en-cē-phal′iç, *a.* [*Ep-*, and Gr. *enkephalos*, the brain.]

1. Of or pertaining to the epencephalon.

2. Occipital.

ep-en-ceph′ȧ-lon, *n.* [*Ep-*, and Gr. *enkephalos*, the brain.] In anatomy, the afterbrain or hindbrain; the cerebellum and pons taken together.

ep-en′dū-tēş, *n.* Same as *Ependytes*.

ep-en′dy-mȧ, *n.* [Gr. *ependyma*, an upper garment, from *ependyein*; *epi*, upon, and *endyein*, to put on.] In anatomy, the lining membrane of the cerebral ventricles and of the central canal of the spinal cord.

ep-en′dy-mal, *a.* Pertaining to the ependyma; as, *ependymal* tissue.

ep-en′dy-mis, *n.* Ependyma.

ep-en-dy-mī′tis, *n.* In pathology, inflammation of the ependyma.

ep-en′dy-sis, *n.* Same as *Ependytes*, 1.

ep-en′dy-tēş, *n.* [Gr.] 1. In the Greek church, the outer altar-cloth.

2. Formerly, a monk's outer mantle of skins.

ep-ē-net′iç, *a.* [From Gr. *epainetikos*, from *epainein*, to praise; *epi*, upon, and *ainein*, from *ainos*, a tale, praise.] Laudatory; bestowing praise. [Obs.]

ē-pen′thē-sis, *n.* [Gr. *epenthesis*, an insertion, from *epentithesthai*; *epi*, upon, and *entithesthai*, to put in; *en*, in, and *tithesthai*, to put, place.] In grammar, the insertion of a letter or syllable in the middle of a word, as *alituum* for *alitum*.

ep-en-thet′iç, *a.* Inserted in the middle of a word.

é-pergne′ (ā-pãrn′), *n.* [Fr.] An ornamental stand with a large dish and branches for the center of a table.

é-per′lăn (ā-), *n.* [Fr.] The European smelt.

ep-ex-ē-ġē′sis, *n.* [Gr. *epexēgēsis*, a detailed account, from *epexēgeisthai*, to recount in detail; *epi*, upon, and *exēgeisthai*, to lead, point out.] A full explanation or interpretation of something which has gone before; exegesis.

Épergne.

ep-ex-ē-ġet′iç, *a.* Of the nature of an epexegesis; explanatory of something which has gone before; exegetic.

ep-ex-ē-ġet′iç-ăl, *a.* Epexegetic.

ep-ex-ē-ġet′iç-ăl-ly, *adv.* Exegetically.

ē′phăh, ē′phȧ, *n.* [Heb.] A Hebrew dry measure, equivalent to a bath.

Eph′e-drȧ, *n.* [From Gr. *ephedra*, a setting by or at a thing; *epi*, upon, and *hedra*, a seat.] A genus of gnetaceous shrubs embracing about twenty species, found in certain desert regions of Asia and America.

e-phem′e-rȧ, *n.* [Gr. *ephēmeros*, for the day, short-lived; *epi*, upon, and *hēmera*, a day.]

1. A fever of one day's continuance only.

2. [E—] In entomology, a genus of insects in which are included the May-flies or dayflies of the family *Ephemeridæ*.

3. An insect of the genus *Ephemera* and allied genera.

4. Anything having a very short life.

e-phem′ẽr-ăl, *a.* [Gr. *ephēmeros*, for the day, short-lived; *epi*, upon, at, and *hēmera*, day.]

1. Diurnal; beginning and ending in a day; continuing or existing one day only.

2. Short-lived; existing or continuing for a short time only; as, an *ephemeral* insect.

Syn.—Transient, evanescent, fleeting, fugitive, momentary, transitory.

e-phem′ẽr-ăl, *n.* Anything which has but a brief existence, as certain insects, plants, etc.

e-phem-ẽr-al′i-ty, *n.* The state or quality of being ephemeral.

e-phem′ẽr-ăn, *a.* and *n.* Ephemeral.

e-phem′e-riç, *a.* Ephemeral.

e-phem′e-rid, *n.* In entomology, an insect belonging to the family *Ephemeridæ*.

Eph-ē-mer′i-dæ, *n.pl.* A family of pseudoneuropterous insects, which take their name from the short duration of their lives in the perfect state, as the May-fly and dayfly. In the state of larvæ and pupæ they are aquatic and may exist for two or three years. The May-fly is well known to anglers who imitate it for bait.

eph-ē-mer′i-dēş, *n.*, pl. of *ephemeris*.

e-phem-ẽr-id′i-ăn, *a.* Relating to an ephemeris.

eph-ē-mē′ri-ī, *n.*, pl. of *ephemerius*.

e-phem-e-rī′nous, *a.* Relating to the *Ephemeridæ*.

e-phem′e-ris, *n.*; *pl.* **eph-ē-mer′i-dēş.** [L. *ephemeris*; Gr. *ephēmeris*, a diary, calendar, from *ephēmeros*, for the day, daily; *epi*, upon, at, and *hēmera*, day.]

1. A journal or account of daily transactions; a diary. [Obs.]

2. In astronomy, a collection of tables or data showing the daily positions of the planets or heavenly bodies in general; a publication exhibiting the places of the heavenly bodies throughout the year, and giving other information regarding them for the use of the astronomer and navigator, an astronomical almanac.

3. An ephemerid.

e-phem′ẽr-ist, *n.* 1. One who studies the daily motions and positions of the planets.

2. One who keeps an ephemeris. [Rare.]

eph-ē-mē′ri-us, *n.*; *pl.* **eph-ē-mē′ri-ī.** [Gr. *ephēmerios*, of or for the day, serving for the day.] In the Greek church, (a) the priest whose turn it is to officiate; (b) a parish priest; (c) a domestic chaplain; (d) a monastic officer whose duty it is to prepare, elevate, and distribute the loaf used at the ceremony known as the *elevation of the panagia*. [See *Panagia*.]

e-phem′e-rō-morph, *n.* [Gr. *ephēmeros*, of or for a day, short-lived, and *morphē*, form.] One of the lowest forms of life.

e-phem′e-ron, *n.*, *pl.* **e-phem′e-rȧ.** [Gr. *ephēmeron*, a short-lived insect, from *ephēmeros*, for the day.] Anything which lasts or lives but for a day or for a very short time, as an ephemeral insect.

e-phem′ẽr-ous, *a.* Ephemeral.

E-phē′şiăn, *a.* Of or relating to the ancient Ionian city, Ephesus, in Asia Minor, once an important commercial center.

E-phē′şiăn, *n.* 1. A native or resident of Ephesus.

2. A jovial fellow. [Obs.]

eph-i-al′tēş, *n.* [Gr. *ephialtēs*, a nightmare, from *epi*, upon, and *iallein*, to send, throw.] The nightmare.

eph-i-drō′sis, *n.* [Gr. *ephidrōsis*; *epi*, upon, and *hidrōsis*, perspiration, from *hidroein*, to sweat.] In pathology, excessive perspiration.

e-phip′pi-ăl, *a.* Relating to an ephippium; saddle-shaped.

e-phip′pi-um, *n.* [L., from Gr. *ephippion*, saddle-cloth, *epi*, upon, and *hippos*, horse.]

1. In anatomy, the pituitary fossa of the sphenoid bone.

2. In zoölogy, a saddle-shaped receptacle on the back of the *Cladocera*, in which the winter eggs are deposited.

eph′od, *n.* [LL. *ephod*; Heb. *ēphōd*, from *āphād*, to put on.] In Jewish antiquity, a linen vestment, specifically that worn by the high priest.

eph′ŏr, *n.*; *pl.* **eph′ŏrs** or **eph′ō-rī.** [L. *ephorus*; Gr. *ephoros*, an overseer, from *ephoran*; *epi*, upon, and *horan*, to see.] In ancient Sparta, one of five magistrates chosen by the people. They were intended as a check on the regal power.

eph′ŏr-ăl, *a.* Of or relating to an ephor.

eph′ŏr-ăl-ty, *n.* The office or term of office of an ephor.

Eph″thi-ȧ-nū′rȧ, *n.* [Prob. from Gr. *phthinein*, *phthiein*, to dwindle away, wane, and *oura*, a tail.] A genus of small Australian warblers characterized by diminutive tails.

eph′thi-ȧ-nūre, *n.* One of the *Ephthianura*.

Eph′y-drȧ, *n.* [From Gr. *ephydros*, living on the water; *epi*, on, upon, and *hydōr*, water.] A genus of dipterous insects. [See *Brine-fly*.]

é-pī′ (ā-pē′), *n.* [Fr., an ear of corn, spike, cluster.] A light finial to ornament the apex of a roof or to form the termination of a spire.

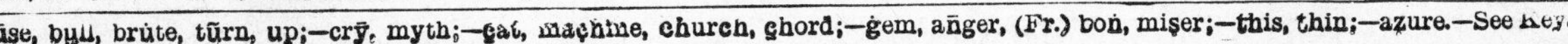

ep-i-. A prefix from Greek *epi-*, from preposition *epi*, signifying on, upon, up to, toward; *epi-* becomes *ep-* before a vowel, and *eph-* before a rough breathing, as in *eph*emeral.

ep′i-blast, *n.* [*Epi-*, and Gr. *blastos*, a bud, shoot.]

1. In embryology, the external or upper layer of the blastoderm; the ectoderm.

2. In botany, a second cotyledon, consisting of a small transverse plate, found on some grasses.

ep″i-blas-tē′mȧ, *n.*; *pl.* **ep″i-blas-tē′mȧ-tȧ.** [*Epi-*, and Gr. *blastēma*, a bud, sprout.] In botany, a superficial outgrowth from any part of a plant.

ep-i-blē′mȧ, *n.* [Gr. *epiblēma*, a cover, patch, from *epiballein*, to throw over; *epi*, upon, and *ballein*, to throw.] In botany, the imperfectly formed epidermis which supplies the place of the true epidermis in submerged plants and on the extremities of growing roots.

e-pib′ō-lē, *n.* 1. In rhetoric, epanaphora.

2. Same as *Epiboly*.

ep-i-bol′ic, *a.* [From Gr. *epiballein*, to throw over, add to; *epi*, upon, and *ballein*, to throw.] Of, pertaining to, or characteristic of epiboly.

e-pib′ō-lişm, *n.* Epiboly.

e-pib′ō-ly, *n.* In embryology, the inclosure of the large yolk-mass of an invertebrate ovum by the overgrowth of cleavage-cells.

ep-i-bran′chi-ăl, *a.* [*Epi-*, and Gr. *branchia*, gills.] Pertaining to the segment above the ceratobranchial bone in a branchial arch.

ep-i-bran′chi-ăl, *n.* An epibranchial bone or cartilage.

ep′ic, *a.* [L. *epicus*; Gr. *epikos*, an epic, from *epos*, a word, that which is related.] Narrated in a grand and impressive style; narrative; heroic; pertaining to or having the characteristics of a kind of poem which narrates a story, real or fictitious, representing, in an elevated style, some signal action or series of actions and events, usually the achievements of some distinguished hero.

ep′ic, *n.* A narrative poem of elevated character, describing generally the exploits of heroes.

ep′ic-ăl, *a.* Same as *Epic*.

ep′ic-ăl-ly, *adv.* In the style of an epic.

ep-i-cā′lyx, *n.*; *pl.* **ep-i-cal′y-cēş.** [*Epi-*, and Gr. *kalyx*, a cup, calyx.] In botany, the outer calyx in plants with two calyces, formed either of sepals or bracts, as in mallow and potentilla.

ep-i-can′thic, *a.* Pertaining to an epicanthis.

ep-i-can′this, *n.*; *pl.* **ep-i-can′thi-dēş.** [*Epi-*, and Gr. *kanthos*, the corner of the eye.] In anatomy, a fold of skin over the inner canthus of the eye.

ep-i-can′thus, *n.*; *pl.* **ep-i-can′thī.** See *Epicanthis*.

ep-i-cär′di-ăl, ep-i-cär′di-ac, *a.* Of or pertaining to the epicardium.

ep-i-cär′di-um, *n.* [*Epi-*, and Gr. *kardia*, heart.] In anatomy, the cardiac layer of the pericardium, united with the substance of the heart and constituting its outer surface.

ep-i-cär′i-dan, *n.* [*Epi-*, and Gr. *karis* (*-idos*), a shrimp.] One of a family of isopodous crustaceans which are parasitic upon shrimps.

ep′i-cärp, *n.* [*Epi-*, and Gr. *karpos*, fruit.] In botany, the outer skin of fruits, the fleshy substance or edible portion being termed the *mesocarp*, and the inner portion the *endocarp*.

ep′i-cēde, ep′i-ced, *n.* A funeral song or discourse. [Rare.]

ep-i-cē′di-ȧ, *n.*, pl. of *epicedium*.

ep-i-cē′di-ăl, *a.* Epicedian.

ep-i-cē′di-ăn, *a.* Elegiac; mournful.

ep-i-cē′di-ăn, *n.* An epicedium.

ep-i-cē′di-um, *n.*; *pl.* **ep-i-cē′di-ȧ.** [LL. *epicedium*; Gr. *epikēdeion*, a dirge, neut. of *epikēdeios*, of or for a funeral; *epi*, on, upon, and *kēdos*, care, sorrow, mourning for one dead.] A funeral song.

ep′i-cēne, *a.* [LL. *epicœnus*; Gr. *epikoinos*, common; *epi*, upon, to, and *koinos*, common.]

1. Common to both sexes; in grammar, designating a noun that has but one form of gender, either the masculine or feminine, to indicate an animal of either sex; as, *bous*, *boos*, for the ox and cow.

2. Sexless.

The literary prigs *epicene*. —J. Wilson.

ep′i-cēne, *n.* In grammar, a noun the gender of which is common.

ep′i-cen-tēr, *n.* [Gr. *epikentros*, on the center-point; *epi*, upon, and *kentron*, center.] In geology, a point on the surface of the earth directly above the focus or point of disturbance of an earthquake.

ep-i-cen′trăl, *a.* In anatomy, situated upon the centrum of a vertebra.

ep-i-cen′trum, *n.*; *pl.* **ep-i-cen′trȧ.** Same as *Epicenter*.

ep″i-ce-ras′tic, *a.* [Gr. *epikerastikos*, tempering the humors, from *epikerannynai*; *epi*, upon, to, and *kerannynai*, to mix.] Lenient; assuaging. [Obs.]

ep′i-chile, *n.* See *Epichilium*.

ep-i-chil′i-um, *n.*; *pl.* **ep-i-chil′i-ȧ.** [Gr. *epicheilēs*; *epi*, upon, and *cheilos*, lip, brim.] In botany, the terminal portion of the lip of an orchid.

ep″i-chi-rē′mȧ, *n.*; *pl.* **ep″i-chi-rē′mȧ-tȧ.** [Gr. *epicheirēma*, from *epicheirein*, to undertake, attempt; *epi*, upon, and *cheir*, the hand.] In logic, a syllogism having the truth of one or both of its premises confirmed by a proposition annexed (called a prosyllogism), so that an abridged compound argument is formed.

ep-i-chor′dăl, *a.* [*Epi-*, and Gr. *chordē*, chord.] In anatomy, situated above or upon the notochord, as certain brain segments.

ep-i-chō′ri-ăl, *a.* [Gr. *epichōrios*, in or of the country; *epi*, in, and *chōra*, country.] Pertaining to the country; rustic; rural. [Rare.]

ep-i-clei′di-um, *n.* See *Epiclidium*.

ep-i-clē′sis, *n.* [Gr. *epiklēsis*, a calling upon, invocation, from *epikalein*; *epi*, upon, and *kalein*, to call.] In the celebration of the eucharist, that part of the prayer of consecration in which is invoked the descent of the Holy Ghost upon the worshipers and the elements.

ep-i-clī′di-um, *n.*; *pl.* **ep-i-clī′di-ȧ.** [From Gr. *epi*, upon, and *kleidion*, dim. of *kleis*, a key.] In ornithology, a distention or separate ossification of the scapular end of the clavicle.

ep-i-clī′năl, *a.* [Gr. *epi*, upon, and *klinē*, a couch, bed, from *klinein*, to recline.] In botany, placed upon the disk or receptacle of a flower.

ep′i-cœle (-sēl), *n.* 1. In anatomy, the epicœlia.

2. In zoölogy, a cavity around the viscera, formed by the invagination of the ectoderm, as in ascidians and perhaps vertebrates.

ep-i-cœ′li-ȧ, *n.*; *pl.* **ep-i-cœ′li-æ.** [From Gr. *epi*, upon, in addition to, and *koilia*, belly, from *koilos*, hollow.] In anatomy, the cavity of the epencephalon, or the upper part of the fourth ventricle.

ep-i-cœ′lous, *a.* Of, pertaining to, or possessing an epicœle.

ep′i-cœne (-sēn), *a.* [Rare.] See *Epicene*.

ep-i-col′ic, *a.* [Gr. *epi*, upon, and *kolon*, the colon.] In anatomy, relating to that part of the abdomen which is over the colon.

ep-i-con′dy-lăr, *a.* Pertaining to or characteristic of the epicondyle.

ep-i-con′dyle, *n.* [From Gr. *epi*, upon, and *kondylos*, a knuckle.] In anatomy, an eminence upon the humeral condyle.

ep-i-con′dy-lus, *n.* See *Epicondyle*.

ep-i-cor′ȧ-coid, *n.* In anatomy, a bone or cartilage of the coracoid in certain animals.

ep-i-cor′ol-line, *a.* [*Epi-*, and L. *corolla*, a little crown or garland.] In botany, inserted upon the corolla.

ep′i-cō-tyl (*or* -kot′il), *n.* [Gr. *epi*, on, upon, and *kotylēdōn*, a cup-shaped hollow.] In botany, the stem of an embryo above the cotyledons; the plumule.

ep-i-cot-y-led′ŏn-ā-ry, *a.* Pertaining to the epicotyl; situated above the cotyledons.

ep-i-crā′ni-ȧ, *n.*, pl. of *epicranium*.

ep-i-crā′ni-ăl, *a.* In anatomy, of or pertaining to the epicranium; situated upon the cranium or skull.

ep-i-crā′ni-um, *n.*; *pl.* **ep-i-crā′ni-ȧ.** [*Epi-*, and Gr. *kranion*, the cranium.]

1. The structures covering the cranium.

2. In zoölogy, the largest dorsal sclerite of an insect's head, reaching from the occiput to the margin of the mouth.

ep-ic′ri-sis, *n.*; *pl.* **ep-ic′ri-sēş.** [Gr. *epikrisis*, determination, from *epikrinein*, to give judgment on, decide; *epi*, upon, and *krinein*, to judge, separate.] A systematic judgment and criticism of a book or paper; a treatise containing such judgment.

Ep-ic-tē′tiăn (-shăn), *a.* Pertaining to Epictetus, a Stoic philosopher in the time of the Roman emperor Domitian.

ep′i-cūre, *n.* 1. [E—] A follower of Epicurus, an Epicurean. [Obs.]

2. One devoted to sensual enjoyments; hence, one who indulges fastidiously in the luxuries of the table.

Ep″i-cū-rē′ăn, *a.* [L. *Epicureus*; Gr. *Epikoureios*, from *Epikouros*, Epicurus.]

1. Pertaining to Epicurus, an ancient Greek philosopher, or to his teachings.

2. [e—] Luxurious; given to luxury or to the pleasures of the table.

Ep″i-cū-rē′ăn, *n.* 1. A follower of Epicurus.

2. [e—] One given to the gratification of the senses, especially to eating and drinking.

Ep″i-cū-rē′ăn-işm, *n.* 1. The doctrines or belief of Epicurus, or attachment to his doctrines.

2. [e—] Gratification of appetite; fondness for luxurious living.

ep′i-cūre-ly, *adv.* Luxuriously.

ep″i-cū-rē′ous, *a.* Epicurean. [Obs.]

ep″i-cū-rişm, *n.* [Fr. *épicurisme*, from L. *Epicurus*, Epicurus.]

1. Luxury; sensual enjoyment; indulgence in gross pleasure; voluptuousness.

2. [E—] The doctrines of Epicurus; Epicureanism.

ep′i-cū-rize, *v.i.*; epicurized, *pt.*, *pp.*; epicurizing, *ppr.* 1. To feed or indulge like an epicure; to feast.

2. To profess the doctrines of Epicurus.

ep′i-cȳ-cle, *n.* [LL. *epicyclus*; Gr. *epikyklos*, an epicycle; *epi*, upon, and *kyklos*, a circle.]

1. In the Ptolemaic system of astronomy, a circle, whose center moves round in the circumference of a greater circle; a small circle whose center, being fixed in the deferent of a planet, is carried along with the deferent, and yet, by its own peculiar motion, carries the body of the planet fastened to it round its proper center.

2. A circle that rolls on the outer or inner circumference of another circle.

ep-i-cyc′lic, *a.* Of or pertaining to an epicycle.

Epicyclic train; in mechanics, any train of gearing, the axes of the wheels of which revolve around a common center. The wheel at one end of such a train, if not those at both ends, is always concentric with the revolving frame.

ep-i-cȳ′cloid, *n.* [Gr. *epikyklos*, an epicycle, and *eidos*, form.] In geometry, a curve generated by a point on the circumference of a circle which rolls upon the convex side of a fixed circle.

ep″i-cȳ-cloid′ăl, *a.* Pertaining to the epicycloid or having its properties.

Epicycloidal wheel; a wheel or ring fixed to a framework, toothed on its inner side, and having in gear with it another toothed wheel of half the diameter of the first, fitted so as to revolve about the center of the latter. It is used for converting circular into alternate motion, or alternate into circular. While the revolution of the smaller wheel is taking place, any point whatever on its circumference will describe a straight line or will pass and repass through a diameter of the circle once during each revolution. In practice, a piston-rod or other reciprocating part may be attached to any point on the circumference of the smaller wheel.

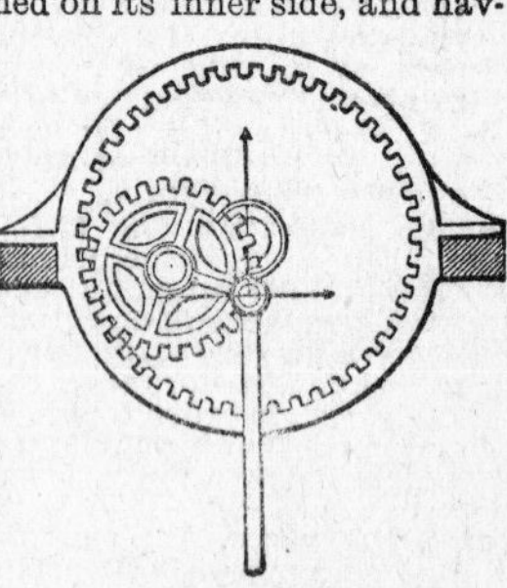

Epicycloidal Wheel.

ep″i-cȳ-ē′māte, *a.* [*Epi-*, and Gr. *kyēma*, an embryo.] In embryology, having the embryo resting upon a large yolk inclosed by the blastodermic vesicle, as certain of the *Ichthyopsida*.

ep-i-deic′tic, *a.* See *Epidictic*.

ep-i-deic′tic-ăl, *a.* See *Epidictical*.

ep-i-dem′ic, *a.* [Gr. *epidēmios*, *epidēmos*, among the people, general; *epi*, upon, and *dēmos*, people.]

1. Common to or affecting a whole people or a great number in a community; prevalent; general; said of any disease of limited duration which seizes a great number of people in a locality at the same time; distinguished from *endemic*.

2. Generally prevailing; affecting great numbers; as, *epidemic* rage; an *epidemic* evil.

ep-i-dem′ic, *n.* 1. A disease temporarily prevalent in a locality; an epidemic disease.

2. Anything that affects great numbers or is generally prevalent; as, an *epidemic* of patriotic ardor; an *epidemic* of terror.

ep-i-dem′ic-ăl, *a.* Epidemic; characteristic of an epidemic.

ep-i-dem′ic-ăl-ly, *adv.* In an epidemic manner.

ep-i-dē-mi-og′rȧ-phy, *n.* [Gr. *epidēmios*, among the people, epidemic, and *-graphia*, from *graphein*, to write.] A treatise on or description of epidemic diseases.

ep-i-dē″mi-ō-log′ic-ăl, *a.* Pertaining to epidemiology.

ep-i-dē″mi-ō-log′ic-ăl-ly, *adv.* In an epidemiological manner.

ep-i-dē-mi-ol′ō-gist, *n.* One who makes a study of epidemiology.

ep-i-dē-mi-ol′ō-gy, *n.* [Gr. *epidēmios*, among the people, epidemic, and *-logia*, from *legein*, to speak.] The science which treats of epidemic diseases.

ep′i-dem-y, *n.* An epidemic. [Obs.]

ep-i-den′drăl, *a.* [*Epi-*, and Gr. *dendron*, a tree.] Growing or existing upon trees, as certain orchidaceous plants.

Ep-i-den′drum, *n.* [From Gr. *epi*, upon, and *dendron*, a tree.] A large genus of tropical American orchids, most of the species of which are epiphytic, growing on trees. The stems are often pseudobulbs, and the leaves are strap-shaped and leathery. The flowers are very handsome, and a large number of the species are in cultivation.

ep′i-dėrm, *n.* The epidermis.

ep-i-dėr′măl, *a.* Epidermic; pertaining to the epidermis; cuticular.

ep″i-dėr-mat′ic, *a.* [Rare.] See *Epidermal*.

ep″i-dėr′mȧ-toid, *a.* [Gr. *epidermatis*, equal

to epidermis, the epidermis, and *eidos*, form.]
1. Epidermal.
2. Resembling or pertaining to the epidermis; written also *epidermoid*.

ep-i-dẽr′mē-ous, *a.* Epidermic. [Rare.]

ep-i-dẽr′mic, *a.* Pertaining to or like the epidermis; covering the skin; epidermal.
Epidermic method; a method of treating diseases by the application of medicinal substances to the skin by friction; called also *iatraliptic method*.

ep-i-dẽr′mic-ăl, *a.* Epidermic.

ep-i-dẽr′mi-dăl, *a.* [Rare.] See *Epidermal*.

ep-i-dẽr′mis, *n.* [LL. *epidermis*; Gr. *epidermis* (*-idos*), the outer skin; *epi*, upon, and *derma*, skin.]
1. In anatomy, the outer layer of the skin; the scarfskin, consisting of a layer of horny cells that protects the true skin; the cuticle.
2. In botany, the outermost layer of cells covering the surfaces of plants.
3. Any external integument; especially, the rind which covers a molluscan shell.

ep-i-dẽr′moid, *a.* See *Epidermatoid*, 2.

ep-i-dẽr′mōse, *a.* and *n.* I. *a.* Epidermal.
II. *n.* Same as *Ceratin*.

ep-i-dẽr′mous, *a.* Epidermal.

ep-i-dic′tic, ep-i-deic′tic, *a.* [L. *epidicticus*, declamatory; Gr. *epideiktikos*, from *epideiknynai*, to display, show, demonstrate; *epi*, upon, and *deiknynai*, to show, point out.] Serving to display, exhibit, or explain; demonstrative; applied by the Greeks to oratory of a rhetorical character.

ep-i-dic′tic-ăl, ep-i-deic′tic-ăl, *a.* See *Epidictic*.

ep-i-did′y-măl, *a.* Relating to the epididymis.

ep-i-did′y-mis, *n.* [Gr. *epididymis*, the epididymis; *epi*, upon, and *didymos*, a testicle.] In anatomy, a small oblong, vermiform, grayish body, lying along the superior margin of the testicle. It is a canal formed by a union of all the seminiferous vessels folded several times upon themselves.

ep-i-did-y-mi′tis, *n.* [Gr. *epididymis*, the epididymis, and *-itis*.] In pathology, inflammation of the epididymis.

ep-i-dī′ō-rīte, *n.* [*Epi-*, and *diorite*.] A variety of diorite containing fibrous hornblende.

ep-i-di-or-thō′sis, *n.* [Gr.] See *Epanorthosis*.

ep-i-dō′sīte (*or* e-pid′), *n.* [Gr. *epidosis*, a giving besides, increase, and *-ite*.] A rock the chief constituent of which is epidote.

ep′i-dōte, *n.* [Fr. *épidote*, from Gr. *epididonai*, to give besides, increase.] A mineral of a green or gray color, vitreous luster, and partial transparency, crystallizing in the monoclinic system, but also occurring fibrous and granular. It is a silicate of aluminium, lime, and oxid of iron or manganese. The epidote group includes epidote proper, zoisite, allanite, and piedmontite.

ep-i-dot′ic, *a.* Pertaining to, resembling, or containing epidote.

Ep-i-gæ′à (-jē′), *n.* [Gr. *epigaios*, upon the earth; *epi*, upon, and *gaia*, poet. form of *gē*, earth.] A genus of shrubs of the heath family. *Epigæa repens*, the trailing arbutus, is the Mayflower of the United States.

ep-i-gæ′ăl, *a.* See *Epigeal*.

ep-i-gæ′ous, *a.* Same as *Epigeous*.

ep-i-gam′ic, *a.* [Gr. *epigamos*, marriageable; *epi*, upon, for, and *gamos*, marriage.] Serving to attract the other sex in the season of propagation; applied to the coloration of birds and animals.

ep-i-gas′trăl, *a.* In anatomy, epigastric.

ep″i-gas-tral′gi-à, *n.* [Gr. *epigastrion*, epigastrium, and *algos*, pain.] In pathology, pain at the epigastrium.

ep-i-gas′tri-ăl, *a.* Epigastric.

ep-i-gas′tric, *a.* [Gr. *epi*, upon, and *gastēr*, *gastros*, stomach, and *-ic*.] Pertaining to the epigastrium; as, an *epigastric* artery or vein.
Epigastric region; the epigastrium, an abdominal region.

ep-i-gas′tri-um, *n.* [Gr. *epigastrion*, neut. of *epigastrios*, over the stomach; *epi*, upon, and *gastēr*, *gastros*, stomach.]
1. In anatomy, the upper and middle part of the abdominal surface; the epigastric region.
2. In entomology, the lower side of the middle segment, and of the posterior segment of the thorax in certain insects.

Ep-i-gē′à, *n.* See *Epigæa*.

ep-i-gē′ăl, *a.* 1. Same as *Epigeous*.
2. In entomology, living near the ground, as insects that dwell on herbage.

ep-i-gē′ăn, *a.* Same as *Epigeous*.

ep′i-gee, *n.* See *Perigee*.

ep′i-gēne, *a.* [*Epi-*, and Gr. *gignesthai*, to produce.]
1. In geology, formed or originating on the surface of the earth; opposed to *hypogene*; as, *epigene* rocks.
2. In crystallography, foreign; unnatural; unusual: said of forms of crystals not natural to the substances in which they are found.

ep-i-gen′e-sis, *n.* [*Epi-*, and Gr. *genesis*, birth, descent.]
1. In biology, the hypothesis that in conception the germ is brought into being and not simply developed by the agency of the parents. In its application to plants, this theory maintains that the embryo does not preëxist in either the ovary or pollen, but is generated by the union of the fecundating principles of the male and female organs.
2. In geology, metamorphism.
3. In pathology, the manifestation of a secondary or auxiliary symptom that does not indicate a change in the character of a disease.

ep-i-gen′e-sist, *n.* One who supports the theory of epigenesis.

ep″i-gē-net′ic, *a.* Of or relating to epigenesis; produced by epigenesis.

ep″i-gē-net′ic-ăl-ly, *adv.* In an epigenetic manner.

e-pig′e-nous, *a.* [From Gr. *epi*, upon, and *gignesthai*, to beget, be born.] In botany, growing upon the surface, especially the upper surface of a part, as many fungi on leaves.

ep-i-gē′ous, *a.* [Gr. *epigaios*, on the earth; *epi*, upon, and *gaia*, poet. form of *gē*, earth.] In botany, growing close to the ground; as, *epigeous* plants.

ep-i-gē′um, *n.* [Obs.] See *Perigee*.

ep′i-glot, *n.* The epiglottis.

ep-i-glot′tic, *a.* Relating to the epiglottis.

ep″i-glot-tid′ē-ăn, *a.* Epiglottic.

ep-i-glot′tis, *n.*; *pl.* **ep-i-glot′ti-dēs**. [Gr. *epiglōttis*; *epi*, upon, and *glōtta*, *glōssa*, the tongue.]
1. In anatomy, a cartilaginous structure behind the tongue, which covers the glottis like a lid during the act of swallowing and thus prevents food and drink from entering the larynx.
2. In zoölogy, (a) the epistoma of a polyzoan; (b) the epipharynx of an insect.

e-pig′nà-thous, *a.* [*Epi-*, and Gr. *gnathos*, the jaw.] In ornithology, hook-billed; having the upper mandible curved downward over the lower, as parrots, gulls, etc.

e-pig′ō-năl, *a.* [*Epi-*, and Gr. *gonē*, seed, generation.] In anatomy, located upon the germgland; as, *epigonal* tissue; an *epigonal* organ.

ep″i-gō-nā′ti-on, *n.* [Gr. *epigonation*; *epi*, upon, to, and *gony*, the knee.] In the Greek church, a lozenge-shaped piece of some stiff material which forms part of the dress of bishops while officiating. It hangs from the girdle on the right side as low as the knee, and is believed to represent the towel with which Christ girded himself at the last supper.

ep′i-gōne, *n.* A descendant; an heir; a successor; especially, an unworthy or inferior one, as in literature.

E-pig′ō-nī, *n.pl.*; *sing.* **E-pig′ō-nus.** [L., from Gr. *epigonos*, born after, from *epi*, upon, after, and *gignesthai*, to be born.] In Greek mythology, the sons or descendants of the princes who fought against Thebes under Adrastus, king of Argos; sometimes applied to inferior successors, as in art or letters.

ep′i-gram, *n.* [L. *epigramma*; Gr. *epigramma*, an inscription, epigram, from *epigraphein*; *epi*, upon, *graphein*, to write.]
1. In Greek literature, a poetical inscription placed upon a tomb or public monument, as upon the face of a temple or public arch.
2. In a restricted sense, a short poem or piece of verse, which has only one subject and finishes by a witty or ingenious turn of thought; in a general sense, an interesting thought represented happily in a few words, whether verse or prose; a pointed or antithetical saying.
3. The style peculiar to an *epigram*.

ep′i-gram-ist, ep′i-gram-mist, *n.* An epigrammatist.

ep″i-gram-mat′ic, *a.* [L. *epigrammaticus*; Gr. *epigrammatikos*, from *epigramma* (*-atos*), an inscription, epigram.]
1. Writing epigrams; dealing in epigrams; as, an *epigrammatic* poet.
2. Suitable to epigrams; belonging to epigrams; like an epigram; concise; pointed; as, *epigrammatic* style or wit.

ep″i-gram-mat′ic-ăl, *a.* Epigrammatic.

ep″i-gram-mat′ic-ăl-ly, *adv.* In an epigrammatic manner or style; tersely and pointedly.

ep-i-gram′mà-tism, *n.* The use of epigrams; epigrammatic style or manner.

ep-i-gram′mà-tist, *n.* One who composes epigrams; one who writes in an epigrammatic style.

ep-i-gram′mà-tīze, *v.t.*; epigrammatized, *pt.*, *pp.*; epigrammatizing, *ppr.* [Gr. *epigrammatizein*, from *epigramma* (*-atos*), an inscription, epigram.] To represent or express by epigrams.

ep-i-gram′mà-ti-zẽr, *n.* An epigrammatist; one who writes in an epigrammatic style.

ep′i-gram-mist, *n.* See *Epigramist*.

ep′i-grȧph, *n.* [Gr. *epigraphē*, an inscription, from *epigraphein*, to write upon.]
1. In architectural antiquity, a terse inscription on a building, tomb, monument, statue, or the like, denoting its use or appropriation.
2. In literature, a citation from some author, or a sentence framed for the purpose, placed at the commencement of a work or at its separate divisions; a motto.

ep-i-graph′ic, ep-i-graph′ic-ăl, *a.* Of, pertaining to, or constituting an epigraph.

ep-i-graph′ics, *n.* The science of inscriptions.

e-pig′rà-phist, *n.* One versed in epigraphy.

e-pig′rà-phy, *n.* The science which inquires into and classifies the knowledge of epigraphs; epigraphics.

e-pig′y-nous, *a.* In botany, growing upon the top of the ovary or seeming to do so, as the corolla and stamens of the cranberry.

Epigynous Stamens of *Philadelphus coronarius.*

ep-i-hȳ′ăl, *a.* and *n.* [*Epi-*, and *hyoid*.]
I. *a.* Pertaining to the stylohyoid ligaments.
II. *n.* One of the stylohyoid ligaments constituting part of the lower or visceral arches.

ep-i-lā′brum, *n.*; *pl.* **ep-i-lā′brà**. [L., from Gr. *epi*, upon, and L. *labrum*, lip.] In entomology, a sclerite running transversely on each side of the labrum of a myriapod.

ep′i-lāte, *v.t.*; epilated, *pt.*, *pp.*; epilating, *ppr.* [L. *e*, *ex*, out of, from, and *pilus*, a hair.] To remove the hair of, as by destroying the root by electricity; to eradicate the hair of.

ep′i-lep-sy, *n.* [Gr. *epilēpsia*, *epilēpsis*, lit., a seizure, epilepsy, from *epilambanein*, to seize upon.] In pathology, a disease of the brain characterized by general muscular agitation, occasioned by clonic spasms, without sensation or consciousness, and commonly recurring at intervals. The attack may be so light as to cause little or no muscular disturbance, though commonly accompanied by violent contractions.

ep-i-lep′tic, *a.* Pertaining to epilepsy; affected with epilepsy; consisting of epilepsy.

ep-i-lep′tic, *n.* One affected with epilepsy.

ep-i-lep′tic-ăl, *a.* Same as *Epileptic*.

ep-i-lep′ti-form, *a.* [Gr. *epilēpsis*, epilepsy, and L. *forma*, form.] Presenting the symptoms of epilepsy.

ep″i-lep-tog′e-nous, *a.* [Gr. *epilēptos*, lit., caught, suffering from epilepsy, and *-genēs*, producing.] Productive of epilepsy.

ep-i-lep′toid, *a.* [Gr. *epilēpsis*, epilepsy, and *eidos*, resemblance.] Of the nature of epilepsy.

ep″i-lō-gā′tion, *n.* An epilogue. [Obs.]

ep-i-log′ic, ep-i-log′ic-ăl, *a.* Of or relating to an epilogue.

e-pil′ō-gism, *n.* [Gr. *epilogismos*, a reckoning over, from *epilogizesthai*, to reckon over; *epi*, upon, over, and *logizesthai*, to consider, reckon, from *logos*, a description, reckoning.] Computation; enumeration. [Obs.]

ep″i-lō-gis′tic, *a.* Pertaining to epilogue; of the nature of an epilogue to.

e-pil′ō-gīze, *v.i.* and *v.t.*; epilogized, *pt.*, *pp.*; epilogizing, *ppr.* To pronounce an epilogue; to add an epilogue to.

ep′i-logue (-log), *n.* [Fr. *épilogue*; L. *epilogus*; Gr. *epilogos*, a conclusion, epilogue, peroration, from *epilegein*, to say in addition, add; *epi*, upon, and *legein*, to say, speak.]
1. In oratory, a conclusion; the closing part of a discourse, in which the principal matters are recapitulated.
2. In the drama, a speech or short poem addressed to the spectators by one of the actors, after the conclusion of the play.

ep′i-lō-guize, *v.t.* and *v.i.* To epilogize.

Ep″i-ma-chī′næ, *n.pl.* [L., from Gr. *epimachos*, assailable, easy to attack; *epi*, on, upon, and *machesthai*, to fight, from *machē*, a battle.] A subfamily of plumed oscine birds, including paradisean birds and birds of allied species.

E-pim′à-chus, *n.* A genus of Australian birds typical of the *Epimachinæ*.

e-pim′à-cus, *n.* [Gr. *epimachos*, equipped for battle.] A heraldic griffin-like monster.

ep″i-man-dib′ū-lăr, *a.* [*Epi-*, and L. *mandibula*, jaw.] On or springing from the lower jaw.

ep″i-man-dib′ū-lăr, *n.* A bone of or springing from the lower jaw.

ep″i-ma-nik′i-on, *n.*; *pl.* **ep″i-ma-nik′i-à**. [Gr. *epi*, upon, and *manikion*, the sleeve, from L. *manica*, the sleeve, from *manus*, the hand.] In the Greek church, a sort of removable sleeve.

e-pim′ē-rà, *n.*, pl. of *epimeron*.

e-pim′ẽr-ăl, *a.* Of or relating to the epimera.

ep′i-mēre, *n.* [*Epi-*, and Gr. *meros*, part, share.] In biology, a transverse axial segment.

e-pim′ē-ron, *n.*; *pl.* **e-pim′ē-rà**. In comparative anatomy, one of the lateral pieces of the dorsal arc of the somite of a crustacean.

ep-i-mys′i-um, *n.* [L., from Gr. *epi*, upon, and *mys*, a muscle.] The inclosing membrane of a muscle.

ep-i-nā′os, *n.* [*Epi-*, and Gr. *naos*, a temple.] In ancient architecture, an opening or space in the rear of the cella; a rear vestibule.

ep-i-nas′tic, *a.* Growing faster on the upper than on the under side, as a plant.

ep′i-nas-ty, *n.* [*Epi-*, and Gr. *nastos*, pressed close, solid, from *nassein*, to press or squeeze close.] In botany, the curvature of a part produced by a growth more rapid on its upper than on its under side, as in the leaves of many plants.

ep-i-neū'răl, *a.* [*Epi-*, and Gr. *neuron*, a nerve.] In anatomy, arising from or attached to a neural arch.

ep-i-neū'răl, *n.* One of the spines of a neural arch.

ep-i-neū'ri-um, *n.* [L., from Gr. *epi*, upon, and *neuron*, a nerve.] In anatomy, the enveloping sheath of a fasciculus of nerves, as distinguished from *perineurium*.

ep-iṅ-glette', *n.* [Fr. *épinglette*, a primer, a priming-wire, a pricker, from OFr. *espingle*; L. *spinula*, dim. of *spina*, a thorn, spine.] In military affairs, a needle or piercer for opening the cartridge of a cannon before priming.

ep-i-ni'ciăn (-nish'ăn), **ep-i-ni'ciăl** (-nish'ăl), *a.* [Gr. *epinikios*, of victory; *epi*, upon, and *nikē*, victory.] Of the nature of a triumphal song; written also *epinikian*.

ep-i-ni'cion, *n.* A song of triumph. [Obs.]

ep-i-nyç'tis, *n.*; *pl.* **ep-i-nyç'ti-dēṣ.** [L., from Gr. *epinyktis*, epinyctis; *epi*, upon, and *nux*, *nuktos*, night.] A pustule appearing in the night.

ē-pi-ọr'nis, *n.* Same as *Æpyornis*.

ep-i-ō'tiç, *a.* [*Epi-*, and Gr. *ous*, *ōtis*, ear.] In anatomy, situated above the ear.

ep-i-ō'tiç, *n.* The outer and upper element of the bone of the internal ear.

ep"i-pe-dom'e-try, *n.* The mensuration of figures standing on the same base. [Obs.]

ep"i-pe-riph'ēr-ăl, *a.* [*Epi-*, and Gr. *periphereia*, a circumference, from *peripherein*, to carry round; *peri*, around, and *pherein*, to bear.] At the periphery, circumference, or external surface of the body; used of sensations produced by contact with the extremities of the nerves

ep-i-pet'ăl-ous, *a.* [*Epi-*, and Gr. *petalon*, a leaf.] Borne upon the petals of a flower.

ē-piph'à-ny, *n.* [ME. *epyphany*, LL. *epiphania*; Gr. *epiphaneia*, an appearance, from *epiphainein*, to show forth, manifest; *epi*, upon, and *phainein*, to show.]

1 An appearance or apparition, especially of a deity or a supernatural being.

2. An ancient Grecian festival commemorating the appearance of a god at some particular place.

3. [E—] The festival celebrated on the sixth day of January, the twelfth day after Christmas, in commemoration of the appearance of Christ to the Magi or philosophers of the East, who came to adore him with presents, or, as others maintain, to commemorate the appearance of the star to the Magi or the manifestation of Christ to the Gentiles. The Greek fathers use the word for the appearance of Christ in the world, the sense in which Paul uses the word. Sometimes called *Twelfth-day*.

ep-i-phar-yn-ġē'ăl, *a.* In anatomy, of, pertaining to, or indicating an epipharynx.

ep-i-phar-yn-ġē'ăl, *n.* A name applied to an epipharyngeal bone or cartilage.

ep-i-phar'ynx, *n.* [*Epi-*, and Gr. *pharynx*, throat.] In entomology, a lobe under the labrum of an insect covering the opening of the gullet.

ep"i-phē-nom'e-non, *n.*; *pl.* **ep"i-phē-nom'e-nà.** [*Epi-*, and Gr. *phainomenon*, a phenomenon, from *phainein*, to appear.]

1. An added or later phenomenon.

2. In pathology, in the course of a disease, a symptom not necessarily produced by the disease.

ep-i-phlœ'ō-dăl (-flē'), **ep"i-phlœ-od'iç** (-flē-), *a.* [*Epi-*, and Gr *phloios*, bark.] In botany, living and growing upon the surface of bark.

ep-i-phlœ'um (-flē'), *n.* [L., from Gr. *epi*, upon, and *phloios*, bark.] In botany, the exterior part of bark.

e-piph'ō-nem, *n.* Epiphonema. [Rare.]

ep"i-phō-nē'mà, *n.* [L., from Gr. *epiphōnēma*, an exclamation; *epi*, upon, and *phōnein*, to speak, from *phōnē*, voice, sound.] In oratory, an exclamatory sentence or striking reflection.

e-piph'ō-rà, *n.* [L., from Gr. *epiphora*, a bringing to or upon, an addition, from *epipherein*, to bring to or upon.]

1 The watery eye; a disease in which the tears, from increased secretion or some disease of the lachrymal passage, accumulate in front of the eye and trickle over the cheek.

2. In rhetoric, the emphatic repetition of a word or phrase at the end of several sentences or stanzas.

ep'i-phragm (-fram), *n.* [L., from Gr. *epiphragma*, a covering, lid, from *epiphrassein*, to block up.]

1. In zoölogy, a kind of lid with a mucous interior lining with which a land-mollusk closes the opening of its shell during seasons of inactivity, as in hibernation or threatened danger.

2. In botany, a thecal covering in some of the lower orders of plants.

ep-i-phyl-lō-spēr'mous, *a.* [*Epi-*, and Gr. *phyllon*, a leaf, and *sperma*, seed.] In botany, bearing the seeds on the back of the leaves, as ferns.

e-piph'yl-lous, *a.* [*Epi-*, and Gr. *phyllon*, a leaf.] In botany, inserted upon the leaf.

Ep-i-phyl'lum, *n.* [L., from Gr. *epi*, upon, and *phyllon*, a leaf.] A Brazilian genus of cactaceous plants having jointed stems and petals united in a tube; cultivated for their showy pink or red flowers.

Part of Epiphyllospermous Frond.

ep-i-phys'i-ăl, *a.* Of or pertaining to an epiphysis; spelled also *epiphyseal*.

e-piph'y-sis, *n.*; *pl.* **e-piph'y-sēṣ.** [L., from Gr. *epiphysis*, an outgrowth, from *epiphyein*, to grow upon.]

1. In anatomy, (a) one of several processes originally distinct, but at last ossified from some distinct center into a single expanse of bone; (b) the pineal gland. [See *Pineal gland* under *Pineal*.]

2. In zoölogy, (a) a hard, minute part of each half of the alveolus of a sea-urchin; (b) a tibial spur of a lepidopter.

e-piph-y-sī'tis, *n.* Inflammation of an epiphysis.

e-piph'y-tăl, *a.* Pertaining to an epiphyte.

ep'i-phȳte, *n.* [L., from Gr. *epi*, upon, and *phyton*, a plant, from *phyein*, to grow.]

1. In botany, a plant which grows on other plants, but does not penetrate their substance nor absorb their juices.

2. In medicine, a vegetable parasite on an animal body; a dermatophyte.

ep-i-phyt'iç, ep-i-phyt'iç-ăl, *a.* Having the nature of an epiphyte.

ep'i-plaşm, *n.* [L., from Gr. *epi*, upon, and *plasma*, anything formed, from *plassein*, to form.] In botany, the residuum of protoplasm in the sporangium of certain fungi; what is left in the spore-case after the spores are formed

ep-i-plas'trŏn, *n.*; *pl* **ep-i-plas'trà.** [*Epi-*, and L. *plastron*, the plastron.] In anatomy, either of the plates of the first pair in the plastron of a turtle.

ep"i-plē-rō'sis, *n.* In pathology, unnatural fullness causing distension, as of the stomach or rectum.

ep-i-pleū'rà, *n.*; *pl.* **ep-i-pleū'ræ.** [L., from Gr. *epi*, upon, and *pleura*, a rib.] In zoölogy, (a) a bony process on the rib of a bird or of a fish; (b) a portion near the inflexed margin of the elytron of a beetle.

ep-i-pleū'răl, *a.* 1. In anatomy, of or relating to an epipleura.

2. Inserted on a pleural element, as on the spine of a vertebra.

ep-i-pleū'răl, *n.* An epipleura.

ep-i-plex'is, *n.* [LL., from Gr. *epiplēxis*, chastisement, blame, from *epiplēssein*, to chastise, blame, lit., to strike at; *epi*, upon, and *plēssein*, to strike.] In rhetoric, a figure by which a person seeks to convince and move by a kind of gentle upbraiding.

e-pip'lō-cē, *n.* [LL., from Gr. *epiplokē*, a plaiting together, from *epiplekein*, to plait together; *epi*, upon, and *plekein*, to plait, twist.] A figure of rhetoric by which one aggravation or striking circumstance is added in due gradation to another; as, he not only spared his enemies, but continued them in employment; not only continued them, but advanced them.

e-pip'lō-cēle, *n.* [Gr. *epiploon*, the caul, and *kēlē*, a tumor.] In medicine, hernia of the epiploön or omentum.

ep-i-plō'iç, *a.* Pertaining to the caul or omentum.

e-pip'lō-on, *n.*; *pl.* **e-pip'lō-à.** [Gr. *epiploon*, the caul.] The caul or great omentum. [See *Omentum*.]

ep-i-pō'di-à, *n.*, pl of *epipodium*.

ep-i-pō'di-ăl, *a.* 1. In anatomy, of or relating to the epipodialia.

2. In zoölogy, of or relating to the epipodium.

ep-i-pō-di-ā'li-à, *n.pl.* [L., from Gr. *epipodios*, upon the feet; *epi*, upon, and *pous*, *podos*, foot.] In anatomy, a term applied to the radius and ulna, the tibia and fibula, taken collectively.

e-pip'ō-dīte, *n.* [*Epi-*, and Gr. *pous*, *podos*, foot.] In comparative anatomy, a process developed upon the basal joint or protopodite of some of the limbs of certain crustacea.

ep-i-pō'di-um, *n.*; *pl.* **ep-i-pō'di-à.** [L., from Gr. *epipodios*, upon the feet; *epi*, upon, and *pous*, *podos*, foot.] In zoölogy, a muscular lobe developed from the lateral and upper surfaces of the foot of some mollusks.

ep-i-pol'iç, *a.* Fluorescent. [Rare.]

e-pip'ō-lişm, *n.* Fluorescence. [Rare.]

e-pip'ō-līzed, *a* Fluorated. [Rare.]

ep-ip-ter'iç, *a.* [*Epi-*, and Gr. *pteron*, a wing.] In anatomy, designating a supernumerary bone rarely found in the human skull at the end of the great wing of the sphenoid.

ep-ip-ter'iç, *n* An epipteric bone.

e-pip'tē-ous, *a.* [*Epi-*, and Gr. *pteron*, a wing.] In botany, a term applied to a fruit or seed which is furnished with a broad margin or wing where it terminates.

ep-ip-ter'y-goid, *a.* and *n.* [*Epi-*, and Gr. *pterygoeidēs*, wing-like, feathery; *pteryx*, wing, and *eidos*, form.]

I. *a.* Lying above the pterygoid bone.

II. *n.* A bone or cartilage in the pterygoid region.

ep-i-pū'biç, *a.* Above the pubis; pertaining to the epipubis.

ep-i-pū'bis, *n.*; *pl.* **ep-i-pū'bēṣ.** [*Epi-*, and L. *pubis*, the pubis.] Bony or cartilaginous matter lying to the front of the pubis.

ep-ir-rhī'zous, ep-i-rhī'zous, *a.* [*Epi-*, and Gr. *rhiza*, root.] In botany, growing on a root.

ē-pis'çō-pà-cy, *n.* [LL. *episcopatus*, the office of a bishop, from *episcopus*, a bishop; Gr. *episkopos*, an overseer, watcher, from *episkopein*, to look upon, examine; *epi*, upon, and *skopein*, to look.]

1. Careful inspection; watch; oversight. [Obs.]

2. Government of the church by bishops; that form of ecclesiastical government in which diocesan bishops are established, as distinct from and superior to priests or presbyters; government of the church by three distinct orders of ministers—deacons, priests, and bishops.

ē-pis'çō-păl, *a.* 1. Belonging to or vested in bishops or prelates; characteristic of or pertaining to a bishop or bishops; as, *episcopal* authority.

2. [E—] Designating as a sect those churches based upon episcopacy, particularly the Anglican church and its branches.

ē-pis-çō-pā'li-ăn, *a.* 1. Episcopal.

2. [E—] Pertaining to the Protestant Episcopal church.

ē-pis-çō-pā'li-ăn, *n.* 1. One who belongs to an episcopal church or adheres to the episcopal form of church government and discipline.

2. [E—] An adherent of the Protestant Episcopal church.

ē-pis-çō-pā'li-ăn-işm, *n.* 1. The system of episcopal government of the church.

2. [E—] The system of government of the Protestant Episcopal church.

ē-pis'çō-păl-ly, *adv.* By episcopal authority; in an episcopal manner.

ē-pis'çō-pănt, *n.* A bishop. [Obs.]

ē-pis-çō-pā'ri-ăn, *a.* Episcopal. [Rare.]

ē-pis'çō-pāte, *n.* [LL. *episcopatus*, the office and dignity of a bishop, from *episcopus*, a bishop.]

1. A bishopric; the office and dignity of a bishop.

2. The order of bishops.

3. The period of incumbency in office of a bishop.

ē-pis'çō-pāte, *v.i.* To act as a bishop; to fill the office of a prelate. [Obs.]

ē-pis'çō-pi-cīde, *n.* [LL. *episcopus*, a bishop, and L. *cædere*, to kill.] The killing of a bishop; also, one who commits such a crime.

ē-pis'çō-pīze, *v.t.*; episcopized, *pt.*, *pp.*; episcopizing, *ppr.* [From LL. *episcopus*, a bishop.]

1. To consecrate as a bishop.

2. To convert to Episcopalianism.

ē-pis'çō-py, *n.* 1. Survey; superintendence.

2. Episcopacy. [Obs.]

ep-i-sep'ăl-ous, *a.* [*Epi-*, and L. *sepalum*, a sepal.] In botany, a term applied to stamens, meaning situated on or adnate to the sepals.

ep-i-skel'e-tăl, *a.* [*Epi-*, and Gr. *skeleton*, a dry body.] Having the origin outside of the internal skeleton; said of muscles.

ep-i-sō'dăl, *a.* See *Episodic*.

ep'i-sōde, *n.* [Gr. *epeisodion*, an addition, episode, neut. of *epeisodios*, following upon the entrance, coming in besides; *epi*, besides, and *eisodos*, an entrance, from *eis*, into, and *hodos*, a way, road.]

1. In rhetoric, a separate incident; an incidental narrative or digression separable from the main subject, but naturally arising from it.

> He does not suffer so much as an ornamental *episode*. —Hallam.

2. An incident or action more or less connected with a complete series of events; as, an *episode* of the war.

3. In music, a variant of the central theme designed to add to the variety, as in a fugue.

ep-i-sod'iç, ep-i-sod'iç-ăl, *a.* Pertaining to an episode; contained in an episode or digression.

ep-i-sod'iç-ăl-ly, *adv.* By way of episode.

ep-i-spā'di-as, *n.* [L., from Gr. *epi*, upon, and *spān*, to draw.] In surgery, a malformation of the penis in which the urethal opening is above, either on the dorsum or glans.

ep-i-spas'tiç, *a.* [Gr. *epispastikos*, drawing to oneself, adapted, from *epispastos*, drawn upon oneself, from *epispān*, to draw upon.] In medicine, attracting the humors to the skin; exciting action in the skin; blistering.

ep-i-spas'tiç, *n.* A blister.

ep'i-spērm, *n.* [*Epi-*, and Gr. *sperma*, a seed.]

In botany, the testa or outer integument of a seed. The figure shows (a) the episperm, (b) the endopleura, and (c) the endosperm.

Section of Seed.

ep-i-spėr'mic, *a.* Of, relating or pertaining to the episperm.

ep'i-spōre, *n.* [*Epi-*, and Gr. *sporos*, seed.] In botany, the outer integument of lichen spores.

ep-i-stax'is, *n.* [L., from Gr. *epistazein*, to bleed at the nose; *epi*, upon, and *stazein*, to fall in drops.] Hemorrhage from the nose.

e-pis-tē-mol'ō-ġy, *n.* [Gr. *epistēmē*, knowledge, and *logos*, discourse.] The theory or science that investigates the basis of knowledge.

ep-i-stėr'năl, *a.* Of, relating or pertaining to the episternum.

ep-i-stėr'nīte, *n.* See *Pleuron.*

ep-i-stėr'num, *n.*; *pl.* **ep-i-stėr'nȧ.** [L., from Gr. *epi*, upon, and *sternon*, breast.]

1. In anatomy, the two bones which form part of the sternum, and are situated upon its superior and lateral part.

2. In comparative anatomy, that portion of a segment of an articulate animal which lies external to the middle inferior pieces or sterna.

ep-i-stil'bīte, *n.* [*Epi-*, and *stilbite*.] A white, translucent mineral of the zeolite group, being a crystalline hydrous silicate of aluminium, sodium, and calcium.

ē-pis'tle (ē-pis'l), *n.* [ME. *epistle*; AS. *epistol*; L. *epistola*, *epistula*; Gr. *epistolē*, a letter, message, from *epistellein*, to send to.]

1. A letter; especially one in a formal, dignified, or studied style, or in ancient or biblical history, as the *epistles* of Pliny or of Paul.

2. [E—] One of a book of extracts, generally from the New Testament, to be read in the communion services of various churches; a lection.

Epistle side; the side to the left of the priest or the right of the audience when the two are face to face.

ē-pis'tle, *v.t.* To write, as a letter. [Obs.]

ē-pis'tlẽr, *n.* 1. A writer of epistles.

2. One who reads the Epistle in a church service; a subdeacon.

ē-pis'tō-lăr, *a.* [LL. *epistolarius*, of or belonging to an epistle, from L. *epistola*, *epistula*, a letter, epistle.] Epistolary.

ē-pis'tō-lā-ry, *a.* 1. Pertaining to epistles or letters; suitable to letters and correspondence; as, an *epistolary* style.

2. Contained in letters; carried on by letters; as, an *epistolary* correspondence.

ē-pis'tō-lā-ry, *n.* A book of Epistles. [See *Epistle*, 2.]

ep-is-tō'lē-ăn, *n.* A letter-writer. [Rare.]

ē-pis'tō-lẽr, *n.* [Obs.] See *Epistler.*

ē-pis'tō-let, *n.* A short epistle or letter.

ep-is-tol'iç, ep-is-tol'iç-ăl, *a.* Epistolary.

ē-pis'tō-līze, *v.i.* To write epistles or letters. [Rare.]

ē-pis'tō-lī-zẽr, *n.* A writer of epistles.

ē-pis″tō-lō-graph'iç, *a.* [Gr. *epistolographikos*, pertaining to or used in writing letters; *epistolē*, a letter, and *graphein*, to write.] Pertaining to the writing of letters.

Epistolographic characters or *alphabet*; the demotic characters of the Egyptians. [See *Demotic*.]

ē-pis-tō-log'rȧ-phy, *n.* [Gr. *epistolē*, a letter, and *graphein*, to write.] The art or practice of writing letters.

ep'i-stōme, ep-i-stō'mȧ, *n.* [L., from Gr. *epi*, upon, and *stoma*, mouth.] In natural history, (a) the space between the antennæ and the cavity of the mouth in crustaceous animals; (b) a valve-like organ which arches over the mouth in the order *Phylactolæmata* of the *Polyzoa*; (c) the clypeus of a dipteral insect.

e-pis'trō-phē, *n.* [LL. *epistrophe*; Gr. *epistrophē*, a turning about, from *epistrephein*, to turn about.]

1. In rhetoric, a figure in which several successive sentences (or clauses) end with the same word or affirmation; as, faith is a good guide, reason is a better guide, truth is the best guide.

2. In botany, the system governing the disposition of granules of chlorophyl grains upon a leaf-surface in diffuse light.

ep-i-strō'phē-ăl, *a.* 1. In botany, relating to epistrophe.

2. In anatomy, relating to the epistropheus.

epi-strō'phē-us, *n.* See *Axis*, 4.

ep-i-stroph'iç, *a.* Of, relating, or pertaining to epistrophe.

e-pis'trō-phīze, *v.t.*; epistrophized, *pt.*, *pp.*; epistrophizing, *ppr.* To excite epistrophe in (a plant).

e-pis'trō-phy, *n.* [Gr. *epistrophē*, a turning about; *epi*, upon, and *strephein*, to turn.] In botany, a return to or toward a normal state from an abnormal.

ep-i-stȳ'lăr, *a.* Of or designating an epistyle.

ep'i-stȳle, *n.* [L. *epistylium*; Gr. *epistylon*, an epistyle; *epi*, upon, and *stylos*, a column.] In ancient architecture, a term used by the Greeks for what is now called the *architrave*, a massive piece of stone or wood laid immediately on the abacus of the capital of a column or pillar.

ep-i-syl'lō-ġism, *n.* [*Epi-*, and Gr. *syllogismos*, syllogism.] A syllogism partly made up of a premise, which was a proposition or conclusion of a syllogism preceding, called the prosyllogism.

ep'i-taph, *n.* [ME. *epitaphe*; OFr. *epitaphe*; L. *epitaphium*, a eulogy; Gr. *epitaphios*, at the tomb, *epitaphios logos*, a funeral oration; *epi*, upon, at, and *taphos*, a tomb, from *thaptein*, to bury.]

1. An inscription on a monument, in honor or memory of the dead.

> A splendid funeral, a towering monument—
> it may be a lying *epitaph*. —Sprague.

2. A eulogy, in prose or verse, composed without any intent to be engraven on a monument, as that on Alexander: "Sufficit huic tumulus, cui non sufficeret orbis."

ep'i-taph-ẽr, *n.* One who writes epitaphs.

ep-i-taph'i-ăl, ep-i-taph'i-ăn, *a.* Of, pertaining to, or of the nature of an epitaph.

ep-i-taph'iç, *a.* and *n.* I. *a.* Epitaphial.

II. *n.* An epitaph. [Obs.]

ep-i-taph'iç, *a.* Of, relating, or pertaining to an epitaph; epitaphial.

ep'i-taph-ist, *n.* An epitapher.

e-pit'ȧ-sis, *n.* [Gr. *epitasis*, a stretching, straining; *epitasis*, from *epiteinein*, to stretch upon or over, to increase.]

1. In the ancient drama, that part which embraces the main action of a play, and leads on to the catastrophe; opposed to *protasis*. The term has also sometimes been applied to that part of an oration which appeals to the passions.

2. In logic, the consequent term of a proposition.

3. In medicine, the paroxysm or period of violence of a fever or a disease.

ep″i-thȧ-lam'iç, *a.* Of, relating, or pertaining to an epithalamium.

ep″i-thȧ-lā'mi-um, *n.*; *pl.* **ep″i-thȧ-lā'mi-ȧ.** [L. *epithalamium*, from Gr. *epithalamios*, nuptial; *epi*, at, and *thalamos*, bridechamber.] A nuptial song or poem, in praise of the bride and bridegroom, and expressing wishes for their prosperity.

ep-i-thal'ȧ-my, *n.* [Obs.] See *Epithalamium.*

ep-i-thal'līne, *a.* [*Epi-*, and Gr. *thallos*, a branch.] In botany, borne on the thallus.

ep-i-thē'çȧ, *n.* [L., from Gr. *epi*, upon, and *thēkē*, a case, sheath.] In zoölogy, a continuous layer surrounding the thecæ in some corals. It is the external indication of tabulæ, and is well seen in the *Tubiporæ* or organ-pipe corals. [See *Tabula*.]

ep-i-thē'ci-um, *n.pl.* [L., from Gr. *epi*, upon, and *thēkē*, a case, sheath.] In botany, the outside of the fruiting disk, as in certain fungi and lichens.

ep-i-thē'li-ăl, *a.* Of, relating, or pertaining to the epithelium; as, *epithelial* cells or scales.

ep-i-thē'li-oid, *a.* Resembling epithelium.

ep-i-thē-li-ō'mȧ, *a.* Any tumor in which the epithelium forms the greater part.

ep-i-thē'li-um, *n.*; *pl.* **ep-i-thē'li-ȧ.** [L., from Gr. *epi*, upon, and *thēlē*, nipple, teat.]

1. In anatomy, a thin and delicate kind of cuticle, like that which covers the nipple; more specifically, the cellular layer which lines the internal cavities and canals of the body, both closed and open, as the mouth, nose, respiratory organs, blood-vessels, etc., and which is analogous to the cuticle of the outer surface. The *epithelium* lining of the blood-vessels is sometimes called *endothelium.*

2. In botany, an epidermis consisting of young thin-sided cells, filled with homogeneous, transparent, colorless sap.

3. In zoölogy, the tough membrane lining the gizzard of a bird.

ep'i-them, *n.* [LL. *epithema*, a poultice; Gr. *epithēma*, anything put on, a cover, lid, from *epitithenai*, to put or lay upon.] In medicine, a term applied to all external applications to the body, excepting only salves and plasters.

ep-i-thē'mȧ, *n.* [L., from Gr. *epithēma*, something put on, a covering, lid.] An outgrowth of hornlike matter on a bird's beak.

e-pith'e-sis, *n.* [L., from Gr. *epithesis*, a laying on, an addition; *epi*, upon, and *tithenai*, to place, put.] See *Paragoge.*

ep'i-thet, *n.* [L. *epitheton*; Gr. *epitheton*, an epithet, from *epitithenai*, to put on; *epi*, on, upon, and *tithenai*, to put.]

1. An adjective expressing some real quality of the thing to which it is applied, or an attributive expressing some quality ascribed to it; as, a *verdant* lawn; a *brilliant* appearance; a *just* man; an *accurate* description.

2. The name of a person or object; an expression; a phrase; a denomination.

Syn.—Title, appellation.—The name *epithet* was formerly extended to nouns which give a title or describe character, but is now confined wholly to adjectives. Some rhetorical writers restrict it still further, considering the term *epithet* as belonging only to a limited class of adjectives, viz., those which add nothing to the sense of their noun, but simply hold forth some quality necessarily implied therein, as the bright sun, the lofty heavens, etc.

ep'i-thet, *v.t.* To describe by epithets. [Rare]

ep-i-thet'iç, ep-i-thet'iç-ăl, *a.* Pertaining to an epithet or epithets; containing or consisting of epithets.

ep'i-thīte, *n.* A vagrant. [Obs.]

ep″i-thū-met'iç, ep″i-thū-met'iç-ăl, *a.* [Gr. *epithymētikos*, desiring, lusting after, from *epithymein*, to set one's heart on, desire eagerly.] Inclined to lust; pertaining to the sexual passion. [Obs.]

ep-i-tith'i-dēş, *n.* [L., from Gr. *epitithenai*, to place upon.] In architecture, the crown or upper moldings of an entablature.

ē-pit'ō-mā-tŏr, *n.* An epitomist. [Rare.]

ē-pit'ō-mē, *n.* [L. *epitome*; Gr. *epitomē*, an abridgment, from *epitemnein*, to cut short, cut upon; *epi*, upon, and *temnein*, to cut.]

1. An abridgment; a brief summary or abstract of any book or writing; a compendium containing the substance or principal matters of a book.

> *Epitomes* are helpful to the memory.
> —Wotton.

2. Figuratively, anything which represents another or others, in a condensed form.

> The Church of St. Mark's itself is an *epitome* of the changes of Venetian architecture.
> —Ruskin.

Syn.—Abridgment, abstract, compend, compendium, summary, synopsis.

ē-pit'ō-mist, *n.* An epitomizer.

ē-pit'ō-mīze, *v.t.*; epitomized, *pt.*, *pp.*; epitomizing, *ppr.* 1. To shorten or abridge, as a writing or discourse; to abstract, in a summary, the principal matters of; to contract into a narrower compass.

> The author they cite and *epitomize*.—Boyle.

2. To diminish, as by cutting off something; to curtail. [Obs.]

> We have *epitomized* many words to the detriment of our tongue. —Addison.

Syn.—Abridge, reduce, abstract, condense, summarize.

ē-pit'ō-mī-zẽr, *n.* One who epitomizes.

ep-i-trich'i-um, *n.* [L., from Gr. *epi*, upon, and *trichion*, dim. of *thrix*, *thrichos*, hair.] An outer epidermal layer lying immediately above that from which the hair grows, the inclosing skin of some animals when in the embryo.

ep'i-trīte, *n.* [LL. *epitritos*; Gr. *epitritos*, one and one-third; *epi*, upon, and *tritos*, a third.] In prosody, a foot consisting of three long syllables and one short one, and denominated first, second, third, or fourth epitrite, according as the short syllable is the first, second, third, or fourth; as, sālūtāntēs, cōncĭtātī, intērcălāns, īncāntārē.

ep-i-troch'lē-ȧ, *n.* [L., from Gr. *epi*, upon, and *trochlia*, a pulley.] In anatomy, the internal condyle of the humerus.

ep-i-troch'lē-ăr, *a.* Pertaining to the epitrochlea.

ep-i-trō'choid, *n.* [*Epi-*, and Gr. *trochos*, a wheel, and *eidos*, form.] In geometry, the curve traced by a point in the plane of a circle which rolls on the convex side of a fixed circle.

e-pit'rō-pē, *n.* [LL., from Gr. *epitropē*, a reference, from *epitrepein*, to turn over; *epi*, upon, and *trepein*, to turn.] In rhetoric, concession; a figure by which one thing is granted, with a view to obtain an advantage; as, I admit all this may be true, but what is this to the purpose? I concede the fact, but it overthrows your own argument.

ep-i-ū'răl, *a.* and *n.* See *Epural.*

e-pix'y-lous, *a.* [*Epi-*, and Gr. *xylon*, wood.] In botany, having growth upon wood, as fungous plants.

ep-i-zeux'is, *n.* [*Epizeuxis*, a joining together, the repetition of a word, from *epizeugnynai*, to fasten or join together.] A figure in rhetoric in which a word is repeated with vehemence; as, you, you, Antony, impelled Cæsar upon the civil war.

Ep-i-zō'ȧ, *n.pl.* [L., from Gr. *epi*, upon, and *zōon*, an animal.]

A term applied to those parasitic animals which live upon the bodies of other animals. The *Epizoa* which infest man may be divided into two groups; (a) those which live upon the surface of the skin, and

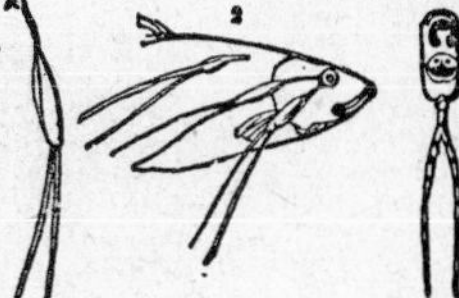

Epizoa.—1. *Lernaeacerna spratti*, and (2) Sprat Infested with it. 3. *Pandarus bicolor.*

(b) those which live in the skin. To the first belong fleas, lice, bugs, ticks, etc.; to the second the itch-insect or *Sarcoptes scabiei*, the folliclemite or *Demodex folliculorum*, etc. The *Epizoa* infesting fish, as the pandarus, which is found on the shark, and the *Lerniacerna spratti*, on the sprat, belong to the inferior crustacea.

ep-i-zō'ăn, *n.* See *Epizoön*.

ep-i-zō'iç, *a.* 1. In zoölogy, parasitic upon other animals, as lice.

2. Pertaining to the *Epizoa*.

ep-i-zō'on, *n.* One of the *Epizoa*.

ep"i-zō-ot'iç, *a.* 1. Pertaining to the *Epizoa*.

2. In geology, containing fossil remains; said of mountains, rocks, formations, and the like. [Obs.]

> *Epizoötic* mountains are of secondary formation. —Kirwan.

3. Prevalent among the lower animals; corresponding to *epidemic* among men.

ep"i-zō-ot'iç, *n.* Any disease of an epidemic character among live stock, especially among horses.

ep-i-zō'ō-ty, *n.* An epizoötic.

ē-pli'ςāte, *a.* [L. *e-* priv., and *plicatus*, pp. of *plicare*, to fold.] In botany, not plicate or folded.

ep'och (*or* ē'pok), *n.* [LL. *epocha*; Gr. *epochē*, a check, cessation, pause, from *epechein*, to hold in, check.]

1. In chronology, a fixed point of time from which succeeding years are numbered; a point from which computation of years begins; any fixed time or period; era; date; as, the exodus from Egypt and the Babylonish captivity are remarkable *epochs* in the history of the Jews.

> The fifteenth century was the unhappy *epoch* of military establishments in time of peace. —Madison.

2. In astronomy, any arbitrary moment of time, as that which marks the date of a given position of a planet.

3. In geology, a minor division of geologic time, used with varying meanings by various geologists.

Syn.—Age, century, cycle, date, era, period, time.

ep'ō-chȧ, *n.*, an archaic form of *epoch*.

ep'ō-chăl, *a.* Relating to an epoch; of the character of an epoch.

ep'ōde, *n.* [OFr. *epode*; L. *epodos*; Gr. *epōdos*, an epode; *epi*, upon, to, and *aeidein*, to sing, from *ōdē*, a song, ode.] In lyric poetry, (a) the third or last part of the ode; that which follows the strophe and antistrophe, the ancient ode being divided into strophe, antistrophe, and epode; (b) a style of lyric poem, after Archilochus, the Greek satirist, characterized by a shorter verse following a longer one.

e-pod'iç, *a.* Pertaining to or resembling an epode.

ē-pol'li-çāte, *a.* [L. *epollicatus*; *e-* priv., and *pollex*, thumb.] In zoölogy, having the thumb or the hind toe lacking.

ep-ō-nyçh'i-um, *n.* [L., from Gr. *epi*, upon, and *onyx*, *onychos*, nail.]

1. The thickened disk of epidermis preceding the formation of a nail on the fingers and toes of a fetal body.

2. The thinned epidermal layer at the sides and base of the nail.

ep'ō-nym, *n.* [Gr. *epōnymos*, given as a name, surnamed; *epi*, upon, and *onyma*, a name.]

1. A surname.

2. A name of a place or people derived from that of a person.

3. A name of a mythical personage called into existence to account for the name of a country or people, as Scota for Scotland.

ep'ō-nyme, *n.* [Obs.] See *Eponym*.

ep-ō-nym'iç, *a.* Eponymous.

e-pon'y-mist, *n.* An eponymous person, as an ancestor.

e-pon'y-mous, *a.* Of or relating to or connected with an eponym.

> Every country, every autonomous town, nay even many a hamlet, thus had its *eponymous* hero. —Cox.

e-pon'y-my, *n.* [Gr. *epōnymia*, a surname.] The use of an eponymist in giving a name to anything.

ep-ō-oph'ō-ron, *n.* See *Parovarium*.

ep-ō-pee', **ep-ō-pœ'iȧ** (-yȧ), *n.* [L. *epopœia*; Gr. *epopoiia*, epic poetry; *epos*, an epic, and *poiein*, to make.]

1. An epic poem.

2. The history, action, or fable which makes the subject of an epic poem.

ep'opt, *n.* [L. *epopta*, Gr. *epoptēs*, one initiated in the mysteries, a spectator.] One to whom secrets have been revealed; an initiate.

ep-op'tiç, *a.* Pertaining to an epopt.

ep-ō-tā'tion, *n.* [L. *epotare*, to quaff, drink out; *e*, out, and *potare*, to drink.] A drinking or drinking out. [Rare.]

é-prōu-vette' (ā-), *n.* [Fr., from *éprouver*, to try, assay; *e-*, from, and *prouver*; L. *probare*, to try.]

1. An instrument for ascertaining the explosive force of gunpowder.

2. An assay-spoon for testing minerals.

ep'sŏm-ite, *n.* Epsom salt, when occurring native. Also called *hair-salt*.

Ep'sŏm sạlt or **sạlts**. Magnesium sulphate, an active cathartic, being especially useful in inflammatory affections. It was so named from its being formerly procured by boiling down the mineral water of *Epsom*, England; it was afterward prepared from sea-water, but is now extracted from certain minerals.

ep'ū-lā-ry, *a.* [L. *epularis*, from *epulum*, a feast.] Pertaining to a feast or banquet.

ep-ū-lā'tion, *n.* A feasting or feast. [Obs.]

e-pū'lis, *n.*; *pl.* **e-pū'li-dēş**. [L., from Gr. *epoulis*, a gumboil; *epi*, upon, and *oulon*, the gum.] A tumor of the alveolar processes of the jaws.

ep'ū-lōse, *a.* Feasting to excess. [Obs.]

ep-ū-lō'sis, *n.* [L., from Gr. *epoulōsis*, a cicatrization; *epi*, upon, and *oulousthai*, to be scarred over, from *oulē*, a wound.] In medicine, the formation of a scar in the process of healing.

ep-ū-los'i-ty, *n.* A feasting to excess. [Obs.]

ep-ū-lot'iç, *a.* and *n.* [Gr. *epoulōtikos*, promoting cicatrization, from *epoulousthai*, to cicatrize.]

I. *a.* Having a healing or cicatrizing power.

II. *n.* A medicament or application which tends to dry, cicatrize, and heal wounds or ulcers.

ē-pū'pil-lāte, *a.* [*E-* priv., and L. *pupilla*, pupil.] Having no pupil; used in entomology when speaking of a color spot without a central dot.

ē-pū'răl, *a.* and *n.* [*Epi-*, and Gr. *oura*, tail.]

I. *a.* Borne dorsally on the tail.

II. *n.* A bone so situated.

ep-ū-rā'tion, *n.* [L. *e-*, intens., and *puratus*, pp. of *purare*, to purify.] The act of purifying.

ē-pūre', *n.* [Fr., a draft, working drawing, from *épurer*, to purify, clarify; L. *e*, out, from, and *purare*, to purify.] In architecture, the plan of a building, or part of a building, traced on a wall or on a horizontal surface, on the same scale as that of the work to be constructed.

ē-py-or'nis, *n.* See *Æpyornis*.

ē-quȧ-bil'i-ty (-kwȧ-), *n.* [L. *æquabilitas*, from *æquabilis*, equable.] The condition or quality of being equable; continued equality, evenness or uniformity; as, the *equability* of the velocity of the blood; the *equability* of the mind.

ē'quȧ-ble, *a.* [L. *æquabilis*, from *æquare*, to make equal, from *æquus*, equal.]

1. Characterized by uniformity, invariableness, or evenness; equal and uniform at all times; uniform in action or intensity; not varying; steady; as, an *equable* temper; an *equable* motion.

> His spirits do not seem to have been high, but they were singularly *equable*.—Macaulay.

2. Even; smooth; having a uniform surface or form; as, an *equable* globe or plain.

Syn.—Uniform, regular, proportionate, even, smooth, easy.

ē'quȧ-ble-ness, *n.* The state of being equable.

ē'quȧ-bly, *adv.* In an equable manner.

ē'quăl (-kwăl), *a.* [ME. *equal*; OFr. *equal*; L. *æqualis*, equal, from *æquus*, plain, even, flat.]

1. The same in magnitude or dimensions, value, qualities, degree, and the like; neither inferior nor superior, greater nor less, better nor worse; as, an *equal* quantity of land; *equal* angles; two commodities of *equal* value; bodies of *equal* hardness or softness; two motions of *equal* velocity.

> All men are created *equal*. —Jefferson.

> Thou therefore also taste, that *equal* lot
> May join us, *equal* joy, as *equal* love.—Milton.

2. Even; uniform; not variable; as, an *equal* mind.

> Ye say, The way of the Lord is not *equal*. —Ezek. xviii. 25.

3. Being in just relation or proportion.

> Commendations *equal* to your merit. —Dryden.

4. Impartial; neutral; not biased.

> *Equal* and unconcerned, I look on all. —Dryden.

5. Of the same interest or concern; of like moment or importance, rank or dignity.

> They who are not disposed to receive them may let them alone or reject them; it is *equal* to me. —Cheyne.

6. Adequate; having competent power, ability, or means; as, we are not *equal* to the undertaking.

> The Scots trusted not their own numbers as *equal* to fight with the English.—Clarendon.

Equal temperament; see under *Temperament*.

Equal voices; in music, an assortment of male or of female voices, not, however, necessarily of like register or compass, though the term should be restricted to voices of similar range.

Syn.—Even, equable, uniform, unvarying, adequate, proportionate, commensurate, fair, just, equitable.—*Equal* is said of degree, quantity, number, and dimensions, as *equal* in years; *even* is said of the surface and position of bodies; a board is made *even* with another board; *like* is said of accidental qualities in things, as *like* in color or in feature; *uniform* is said of things only as to their fitness to correspond; *equable* is used only in the moral acceptation, in which all the others are likewise employed. *Even* and *equable* are applied to the same object in regard to itself; *like* or *alike* is applied to two or more objects in regard to each other; *uniform* is said either of one object in regard to itself or of many objects in regard to each other.

ē'quăl, *n.* 1. A person, thing, or quantity not inferior or superior to another; specifically, one having the same or a similar age, rank, station, office, talents, strength, etc.

> Those who were once his *equals*, envy and defame him. —Addison.

2. The state of being equal; equality. [Obs.]

ē'quăl, *v.t.*; equaled *or* equalled, *pt.*, *pp.*; equaling *or* equalling, *ppr.* 1. To make equal; to make of the same quantity, dimensions, or quality; to cause to be commensurate with or unsurpassed by; to equalize; hence, to regard as equals; to compare.

2. To be equal to; to be adequate to; to be commensurate with.

> On me, whose all not *equals* Edward's moiety. —Shak.

3. To rise to the same state, rank, estimation, or excellence with; to become equal to; as, few commanders *equal* Washington in fame.

> What delights can *equal* those
> That stir the spirit's inner deeps? —Tennyson.

4. To make equivalent to; to recompense fully; to answer in full proportion.

> Who answer'd all her cares, and *equall'd* all her love. —Dryden.

ē"quăl-i-tā'ri-ăn, *n.* One who believes in or maintains certain opinions regarding equality.

ē-quăl'i-ty, *n.*; *pl.* **ē-quăl'i-tieş**. [ME. *egalite*; OFr. *egalite*, *equalite*; L. *æqualitas*, equality, from *æqualis*, equal.]

1. The state of being equal; likeness in magnitude or dimensions, value, qualities, degree, and the like; the state of being neither superior nor inferior, greater nor less, better nor worse; as, the *equality* of men: an *equality* of rights.

> The end of civil society is not to preserve the natural *equality*, for there is none.—Dyer.

2. Evenness; uniformity; sameness in state or continued course; as, an *equality* of temper.

3. Evenness; plainness; uniformity; as, an *equality* of surface.

4. In mathematics, a comparison of two quantities which are in effect equal, though differently expressed or represented; usually denoted by two parallel lines, =; thus $3x+4y=20$.

ē"quăl-i-zā'tion, *n.* The act of equalizing or state of being equalized.

ē'quăl-ize, *v.t.*; equalized, *pt.*, *pp.*; equalizing, *ppr.* 1. To make equal; to cause to be equal in amount or degree as compared; as, to *equalize* accounts; to *equalize* burdens or taxes.

2. To represent as equal; to place on a level with. [Obs.]

3. To be equal to; to equal. [Obs.]

Syn.—Adjust, arrange, balance, neutralize, poise.

ē'quăl-i-zẽr, *n.* 1. One who or that which equalizes.

2. A mechanical device on the plan of the lever to equalize draft, as in a wagon; an evener.

ē'quăl-i-zing-bär, *n.* In mechanics, any lever-like bar used to render strain uniform, as (a) a device to distribute weight equally in a passenger-coach or engine; (b) an equalizer or draft-evener.

ē'quăl-ly, *adv.* In an equal manner or degree.

ē'quăl-ness, *n.* Equality; evenness.

ē-quan'gū-lăr (ē-kwan'gū-lăr), *a.* Equiangular. [Rare.]

ē-quȧ-nim'i-ty, *n.* [L. *æquanimitas*, evenness of mind; *æquus*, even, equal, and *animus*, mind.] Evenness of mind; that calm temper or firmness of mind which is not easily elated or depressed, either by prosperity or adversity.

ē-quan'i-mous, *a.* Possessing equanimity.

ē'quănt, *n.* [L. *æquans* (*-antis*), ppr. of *æquare*, to make equal.] In ancient astronomy, an imaginary circle used for determining the motions of the planets.

ē-quāte', *v.t.*; equated, *pt.*, *pp.*; equating, *ppr.* [L. *æquatus*, ppr. of *æquare*, to make equal.] To render or cause to become equal; to adjust to a standard or average; as, to *equate* distances or losses.

Equating for curves; in railroad engineering, a definite allowance in linear measure for curves.

Equating for grades; in railroad engineering, allowing for ascent at the rate of one mile for each ascent of twenty feet.

ē-quā′tion (-shun *or* -zhun), *n.* [ME *equacion*; L. *æquatio* (*-onis*), an equalizing, from *æquare*, to make equal.]

1. A making equal or an equal division; equality.

Again the golden day resumed its right,
And ruled in just *equation* with the night.
—Rowe.

2. In mathematics, a proposition asserting the equality of two quantities and expressed by the sign = between them; an expression of the same quantity in two dissimilar terms, but of equal value; as, $a+b=c$.

3. In astronomy, the correction or quantity to be added to or subtracted from the mean position of a heavenly body to obtain the true position; more generally, the correction arising from any erroneous supposition whatever.

4. In chemistry, a collection of symbols denoting a reaction has taken place and the rearrangement of the elements concerned; so called because the total weight of the substances remains the same.

Absolute equation; see under *Absolute*.

Equation of the center; in astronomy, the difference between the true and the mean anomaly of a planet.

Equation clock or *watch*; one showing the difference between mean solar and apparent solar time.

Equation of condition; one made up of quantities of which the relation is shown by the entire equation.

Equation of a curve; in mathematics, one giving an expression of the relation of the coördinates of every point in the curve.

Equation of equinoxes; in astronomy, the difference between the mean and apparent places of the equinox.

Equation of payments; an arithmetical rule for the purpose of ascertaining at what time it is equitable that a person should make payment of a whole debt which is due in different parts, payable at different times.

Equation of time; in astronomy, the difference between mean and apparent time, or the reduction of apparent unequal time or motion of the sun or a planet to equable and mean time or motion.

Normal equation; see under *Normal*.

Personal equation; in astronomical observations, a name given to the quantity of time by which a person is in the habit of noting a phenomenon wrongly; it may be called positive or negative, according as he notes it after or before it really takes place.

Theory of equations; that division of algebra dealing with equations containing one unknown quantity.

ē-quā′tion-ăl, *a.* 1. Denoting an equation or the use of equations.

2. In mechanics, differential.

Equational box; a mechanical means for regulating the twist of yarn in spinning-machines, accomplished by the use of (boxed) differential gearing.

-quā′tŏr, *n.* [ME *equator*; LL. *æquator*, the equator, from L. *æquare*, to make equal.]

1. In astronomy, that imaginary great circle in the heavens, the plane of which is perpendicular to the axis of the earth.

2. In geography, that great circle of our globe, every point of which is 90° from the poles, which are also its poles, its axis being also the axis of the earth.

3. Any circle, or line approaching a circle, dividing a spherical body equally and symmetrically.

Magnetic equator; a line on which a dipping-needle carried along it remains horizontal; also called the *aclinic line*.

ē-quȧ-tō′ri-ăl, *a.* Pertaining to the equator; as, *equatorial* climates.

ē-quȧ-tō′ri-ăl, *n.* An astronomical instrument, contrived for the purpose of directing a telescope upon any celestial object of which the right ascension and declination are known, and of keeping the object in view for any length of time, notwithstanding the diurnal motion; called also *equatorial telescope*.

ē-quȧ-tō′ri-ăl-ly, *adv.* So as to have the motion of an equatorial; in a line with the equator.

eq′uer-ry (ek′wer-i), *n.* An equery.

eq′ue-ry (ek′wer-i), *n.*; *pl.* **eq′ue-ries**. [Fr. *ecurie*; OFr. *escuyrie*; LL. *scuria*, a stable, from O.H.G. *sciura*, a shed.]

1. An officer of nobles or princes who has the care and management of their horses. In England, equeries are certain officers of the household of the sovereign, in the department of the master of the horse.

2. A stable or lodge for horses.

ē-ques′tri-ăn, *a.* [L. *equester* (*-tris*), pertaining to a horse or horseman, equestrian, from *eques*, a horseman, from *equus*, a horse.]

1. Pertaining to horses or horsemanship; performed with horses; consisting in or accompanied with performances on horseback; as, *equestrian* feats.

2. In the habit of riding on horseback; fond of or skilled in horsemanship; as, *equestrian* tastes.

3. Representing a person on horseback; as, an *equestrian* statue.

4. Of or pertaining to the Roman equites or knights; as, the *equestrian* order.

ē-ques′tri-ăn, *n.* A rider on horseback.

ē-ques′tri-ăn-iṣm, *n.* The performance of an equestrian; horsemanship.

ē-ques-tri-enne′, *n.* [Spurious French form.] A female rider or performer on horseback.

ē-qui-. A combining form from Latin *æquus*, equal; used in words of Latin origin to signify equal; as, *equi*lateral.

ē-qui-an′gū-lăr, *a.* [*Equi-*, and L. *angulus*, an angle.] In geometry, consisting of or having equal angles.

Equiangular spiral; see under *Spiral*.

Mutually equiangular; a term applied to two figures having similar angles similarly placed.

ē-qui-bal′ănce, *n.* [*Equi-*, and ME. *balance*; OFr. *balance*; L. *bilanx*, a balance.] Equal weight.

ē-qui-bal′ănce, *v.t.* To have equal weight with (something); to counterbalance. [Rare.]

ē-qui-çrū′răl, *a.* [*Equi-*, and L. *crus* (*cruris*), leg.] Having legs of equal length; isosceles; as, an *equicrural* triangle.

ē′qui-çrūre, *a.* Equicrural. [Obs.]

Eq′ui-dæ (ek′wi-dē), *n.pl.* The horse family, the *Solidungula*. [See *Solidungula*.]

ē-qui-dif′fēr-ent, *a.* [*Equi-*, and L. *differens* (*-entis*), ppr. of *differre*, to carry different ways, to be different.] Having equal differences.

ē-qui-dis′tănce, *n.* Equal distance.

ē-qui-dis′tănt, *a.* [*Equi-*, and L. *distans* (*-antis*), ppr. of *distare*, to stand apart, to be distant.] Being at an equal distance from some point or thing.

ē-qui-dis′tănt-ly, *adv.* At the same or an equal distance.

ē″qui-dī-ūr′năl, *a.* [*Equi-*, and L. *diurnus*, daily.] Having the days equal.

ē′qui-fọrm, *a.* [L. *æquiformis*, uniform; *æquus*, equal, and *forma*, shape.] Having the same form.

ē-qui-fọr′mi-ty, *n.* Uniform equality.

ē-qui-lat′ẽr-ăl, *a.* [LL. *æquilateralis*; L. *æquus*, equal, and *latus*, side.] Having all the sides equal; as, an *equilateral* triangle.

Equilateral Triangle

Equilateral bivalve; a shell in which a transverse line, drawn through the apex of the umbo, divides the valve equally and symmetrically.

Equilateral hyperbola; a hyperbola which has the two axes equal to one another, the asymptotes forming a right angle.

Mutually equilateral; a term applied to two figures having equal sides similarly placed.

ē-qui-lat′ẽr-ăl, *n.* A side exactly corresponding to others in length, or a figure of equal sides.

ē-qui-lī′brănt (*or* ē-quil′i-brănt), *n.* [*Equi-*, and L. *librans* (*-antis*), ppr. of *librare*, to poise.] In physics, a force (or forces) keeping or tending to keep another force (or forces) in equilibrium.

ē-qui-lī′brāte, *v.t.*; equilibrated, *pt.*, *pp.*; equilibrating, *ppr.* [*Equi-*, and L. *libratus*, ppr. of *librare*, to poise, weigh out.] To balance equally, as two scales, sides, or ends; to keep even with equal weight on each side.

ē-qui-li-brā′tion, *n.* Equipoise; the act of keeping the balance even, or the state of being equally balanced.

Nature's laws of *equilibration*. —Derham.

ē-qui-lī′brā-tŏr, *n.* Any one of many devices used to maintain or restore equilibrium, as in a flying-machine, etc.

ē-qui-lib′ri-ous, *a.* Equally poised.

ē-qui-lib′ri-ous-ly, *adv.* In equal poise.

ē-qui-lī′brist (*or* e-quil′i-brist), *n.* One who keeps his balance in unnatural positions and hazardous movements; a balancer.

ē-qui-lib′ri-ty, *n.* [L. *æquilibritas* (*-tatis*), from *æquilibris*, evenly balanced; *æquus*, equal, and *libra*, a balance.] The state of being equally balanced; equal balance on both sides; equilibrium. [Rare.]

ē-qui-lib′ri-um, *n.* [L. *æquilibrium*, an even balance, a level, from *æquilibris*, evenly balanced; *æquus*, even, equal, and *libra*, a balance.]

1. In mechanics, equipoise; equality of weight or force; a state of rest produced by the mutual counteraction of two or more forces, as the state of the two ends of a lever or balance when both are charged with equal weight and they maintain an even or level position parallel to the horizon. When two or more forces acting upon a body are so opposed to each other that the body remains at rest, although one of them would move it if acting alone, those forces are said to be in *equilibrium*, that is, equally balanced.

2. A state of just poise or balance in respect to an object, so that it remains firm; as, to preserve the *equilibrium* of the body.

3. Equal balancing of the mind between motives or reasons; a state of indifference or of doubt, when the mind is suspended in indecision between different motives or the different forces of evidence.

4. In the fine arts, (a) the just poise or balance of a figure or other object so that it may appear to stand firmly; (b) the due equipoise of objects, lights, shadows, etc.

5. Equal diffusion or distribution, as of temperature, which all bodies on the earth tend to produce, or equal distribution of magnetism, electricity, etc.

6. Equality of influence or effect; due or just relationship.

Health consists in the *equilibrium* between these two powers. —Arbuthnot.

7. In politics, balance of power.

ē-qui-lib′ri-um-valve, *n.* See *Balance-valve*.

ē′qui-lōbed, *a.* [*Equi-*, and L. *lobus*, lobe.] In botany, having equal lobes or divisions, as a leaf.

ē″qui-mō-men′tăl, *a.* [*Equi-*, and L. *momentum*, moment.] In physics, having the moments of inertia equal.

ē-qui-mul′ti-ple (-pl), *a.* [*Equi-*, and L. *multiplex* (*-plicis*), manifold.] Multiplied by the same number or quantity.

ē-qui-mul′ti-ple, *n.* In mathematics, a product arising from the multiplication of two or more primitive quantities by the same number or quantity. Hence, *equimultiples* of any numbers or quantities are always in the same ratio to each other as the simple numbers or quantities before multiplication. If 6 and 9 are multiplied by 4, the *equimultiples*, 24 and 36, will be to each other as 6 to 9.

ē-quī′năl, *a.* Same as *Equine*.

ē′quīne, *a.* [L. *equinus*, from *equus*, a horse.] Of, pertaining to, or resembling a horse or parts of a horse; denoting the horse kind.

ē-qui-neç′es-sā-ry, *a.* [*Equi-*, and L. *necessarius*, necessary.] Necessary or needful in the same degree. [Rare.]

ē-quin′i-ȧ, *n.* [L., from *equinus*, pertaining to a horse, from *equus*, a horse.] In medicine, a dangerous contagious disorder, originating in the horse, ass, and mule, but communicable to man; glanders in man.

ē-qui-noç′tiăl (-shăl), *a.* [ME *equinoctial*; L. *æquinoctialis*, from *æquinoctium*, the equinox; *æquus*, equal, and *nox*, night.]

1. Pertaining to the equinoxes; designating an equal length of day and night; as, the *equinoctial* line.

2. Pertaining to the regions or climate of the *equinoctial* line or equator; in or near that line; as, *equinoctial* heat; an *equinoctial* sun; *equinoctial* wind.

3. Pertaining to the time when the sun enters the *equinoctial* points; as, an *equinoctial* gale or storm, that is, one which happens at or near the equinox, in any part of the world.

Equinoctial colure; the meridian which passes through the equinoctial points.

Equinoctial dial; a dial whose plane lies parallel to the equinoctial.

Equinoctial flowers; flowers that open and close at regular, stated hours.

Equinoctial line; the celestial equator.

Equinoctial points; the two points wherein the celestial equator and ecliptic intersect each other; the one, being in the first point of Aries, is called the vernal point or equinox; the other, in the first point of Libra, the autumnal point or equinox.

Equinoctial time; time reckoned from a fixed instant common to all the world, that is, the instant when the sun passes the mean vernal equinoctial point.

ē-qui-noç′tiăl, *n.* 1. The equinoctial line.

2. A severe storm or gale which usually occurs at or near the equinox, erroneously supposed to be the result of the sun's crossing the equator.

ē-qui-noç′tiăl-ly, *adv.* In the direction of the equinoctial.

ē′qui-nox, *n.* [ME. *equinoxium*; Fr. *équinoxe*; L. *æquinoctium*, the equinox; *æquus*, equal, and *nox*, night.]

1. The precise time when the sun enters one of the equinoctial points, making the day and night everywhere of equal length. The sun enters the first point of Aries about the 21st of March, and the first point of Libra about the 22d of September. These are called the *vernal* and *autumnal equinoxes*.

2. An equinoctial gale or storm. [Rare.]

ē-qui-nū′mẽr-ănt, *a.* Having or consisting of the same number. [Obs.]

ē-quip′, *v.t.*; equipped (-kwipt′), *pt.*, *pp.*; equipping, *ppr.* [OFr. *equiper*, *esquiper*, to put in order, equip; Ice. *skipa*, to place in order, to arrange.]

1. To dress; to furnish; to array; to accouter; as, to *equip* a person with a suit of clothes.

2. To furnish with arms or a complete suit of arms for military service; to furnish with men, artillery, and munitions of war, as a ship.

3. To prepare for some particular duty or service, whether physically or mentally; to furnish with qualifications; as, a man well *equipped* for the ministry.

Syn.—Accouter, fit out, dress, furnish, adorn.

eq′ui-pāge (ek′wi-pāj), *n.* [OFr. *equipage*, from *equiper*, to equip.]

1. In a general sense, materials with which a person or thing is equipped, furnished, or provided; furniture; garniture; accouterments; habiliments; dress.

> He never saw so many complete gentlemen in his life, and in a neater *equipage*. —Howell.

2. In military language, the furniture of a military man, particularly arms and their appendages; the furniture of an army or body of troops, infantry, or cavalry, including arms, artillery, utensils, provisions, and whatever is necessary for a military expedition.

3. In naval language, the furniture and supplies of an armed ship or the necessary preparations for a voyage, including cordage, spars, provisions, etc.

4. Attendance; retinue; suite; train; especially a carriage of state or of pleasure, including what usually goes with it, as horses, harness, servants, etc.; a showy vehicle and its accompaniments; as, a millionaire's *equipage*.

eq′ui-pāged (ek′wi-pājd), *a.* Furnished with equipage; attended with a splendid retinue.

ē-quip′ȧ-rȧ-ble, *a.* Comparable. [Rare.]

ē-quip′ȧ-rănce, ē-quip′ȧ-răn-cy, *n.* In logic, a state of equality. [See *Disquiparancy*.]

ē-quip′ȧ-rāte, *v.t.* [L. *æquiparatus*, pp. of *æquiparare*, to put on a level, compare; *æquus*, equal, and *parare*, to make ready.]

1. To compare. [Rare.]

2. To reduce to a level; to make or regard as equal. [Rare.]

ē-quip′e-dăl, *a.* [LL. *æquipedus*, equal-footed; L. *æquus*, equal, and *pes*, *pedis*, foot.] In zoölogy, equal-footed; having the pairs of feet equal.

ē-qui-pend′en-cy, *n.* [*Equi-*, and L. *pendere*, to hang.] The act or state of hanging in equipoise or of not being inclined or determined either way; an unbiased condition.

ē-qui-pen′sāte, *v.t.* To weigh, value, or esteem equally. [Obs.]

ē-quip′ment, *n.* [Fr. *équipement*, from *équiper*, to equip.]

1. The act of equipping or fitting out, as for a voyage or expedition.

2. Anything that is used in equipping; furniture; habiliments; warlike apparatus; necessaries for an expedition or for a voyage; as, the *equipments* of a ship or an army.

3 In military art, a name given to certain of the necessaries for officers and soldiers, as horses, horse-appointments, baggage, saddlery, and accouterments; the clothes, arms, etc., of a private soldier.

4. In railroad-engineering, the necessary adjuncts of a railway, as engines, cars, etc.; plant.

ē′qui-poise, *n.* [*Equi-*, and OFr. *pois*, *poise*, poise, from L. *pensum*, weight.]

1. Equality of weight or force; hence, equilibrium; a state in which the two ends or sides of a thing are balanced; as, hold the scales in *equipoise*; figuratively, applied to moral, social, or political interests or forces.

> Our little lives are kept in *equipoise*
> By opposite attractions and desires.
> —Longfellow.

2. Counterpoise; a counterbalancing force.

ē-qui-pol′lence, ē-qui-pol′len-cy, *n.* [ME. *equipolence*; LL. *æquipollens* (*-entis*), having equal power; L. *æquus*, equal, and *pollens*, ppr. of *pollere*, to be strong.]

1. Equality of power or force.

2. In logic, an equivalence between two or more propositions, as when two propositions signify the same thing, though differently expressed.

ē-qui-pol′lent, *a.* [ME. *equipolent*; OFr. *equipolent*; LL. *æquipollens*, having equal power; *æquus*, equal, and *pollens*, ppr. of *pollere*, to be strong.]

1. Having equal power or force; equivalent.

2. In logic, having equivalent signification.

ē-qui-pol′lent-ly, *adv.* With equal power.

ē-qui-pon′dĕr-ănce, ē-qui-pon′dĕr-ăn-cy, *n.* Equality of weight; equipoise.

ē-qui-pon′dĕr-ănt, *a.* Being of the same weight.

ē-qui-pon′dĕr-āte, *v.i.* [*Equi-*, and L. *ponderatus*, pp. of *ponderare*, to weigh.] To be equal in weight; to weigh as much as another thing.

ē-qui-pon′dĕr-āte, *v.t.* To weigh equally in an opposite scale; to counterbalance.

ē-qui-pon′dĕr-ous, *a.* Having the same or equal weight. [Obs.]

ē-qui-pon′di-ous, *a.* Having equal weight on both sides. [Obs.]

ē″qui-pō-ten′tiăl (-shăl), *a.* [*Equi-*, and L. *potentia*, power.] Having the same or equal potential.

Equipotential surface; a surface having equal potential at all points; as, level surfaces on the earth.

ē-qui-rad′i-căl, *a.* [*Equi-*, and Fr. *radical*, radical.] Equally radical. [Rare.]

ē-qui-rō′tăl, *a.* [*Equi-*, and L. *rota*, a wheel.] Having wheels of the same size or diameter, as a machine; of equal rotation. [Rare.]

E″qui-sē-tā′cē-æ, *n.pl.* [L., from *equus*, horse, and *sæta*, a bristle.] A natural order of vascular, cryptogamous plants, with jointed hollow stems; the horsetail family.

ē″qui-sē-tā′ceous, *a.* In botany, pertaining to the natural order *Equisetaceæ*.

ē-qui-set′i-form, *a.* [L. *Equisetum*, and *forma*, form.] Having the shape of *Equisetum* or horsetail; resembling *Equisetum*.

Eq-ui-sē′tum (ek-wi-), *n.* [L., from *equus*, a horse, and *seta*, *sæta*, a bristle.] A genus of plants, the horsetails, being the sole genus of the family *Equisetaceæ*. The cuticle abounds in silicious cells, on which account the stems of some species are used for polishing wood. *Equisetum hiemale*, or the great rough horsetail, is best fitted for that purpose, and is largely imported into England from Holland; called also *Dutch rush* and *scouring-rush*.

Equisetum hiemale.

ē-quis′ō-nănce, *n.* An equal sounding; a name by which the Greeks distinguished the consonances of the octave and double octave.

ē-quis′ō-nănt, *a.* [*Equi-*, and L. *sonans*, ppr. of *sonare*, to sound.] In music, sounding equally, in unison or in octaves.

eq′ui-tȧ-ble (ek′wi-tȧ-bl), *a.* [Fr. *équitable*, from L. *æquitas*, equality, from *æquus*, equal.]

1. Possessing or exhibiting equity; equal in regard to the rights of persons; distributing equal justice; giving each his due; assigning to one or more what law or justice demands; just; impartial; as, an *equitable* judge; an *equitable* decision; an *equitable* distribution of an estate.

2. Pertaining to a court or rule of equity; exercised or determined in a court of equity; as, the *equitable* jurisdiction of a court.

> An *equitable* construction of the law. —Stillingfleet.

Equitable estates; in law, one of the three kinds of property in lands and tenements, the other two being legal property and customary property. An equitable estate is properly one for which a court of equity affords the only remedy; such is the benefit of every trust, express or implied, which is not converted into a legal estate by the statute of uses.

Syn.—Fair, honest, impartial, just, reasonable.

eq′ui-tȧ-ble-ness, *n.* 1. The quality of being just and impartial; as, the *equitableness* of a judge.

2. Equity; the state of doing justice, or distributing to each according to his legal or just claims; as, the *equitableness* of a decision, or distribution of property.

eq′ui-tȧ-bly, *adv.* In an equitable manner; justly; impartially; as, the laws should be *equitably* administered.

eq′ui-tăn-cy, *n.* [L. *equitare*, to ride a horse, from *equus*, a horse.] Horsemanship.

ē″qui-tan-gen′tiăl, *a.* [*Equi-*, and L. *tangens*, ppr. of *tangere*, to touch.] In geometry, a term applied to a curve whose tangent is equal to a constant line.

eq′ui-tănt, *a.* [L. *equitans* (*-antis*), ppr. of *equitare*, to ride, from *eques*, a horseman, from *equus*, a horse.]

1. Mounted or sitting upon a horse; riding on horseback.

2. In botany, a term applied to unexpanded leaves in a leaf-bud that overlap each other entirely and in a parallel manner, without any involution, as in the iris.

eq-ui-tā′tion, *n.* [L. *equitatio* (*-onis*), from *equitatus*, pp. of *equitare*, to ride.] The act of riding on horseback; horsemanship; also, a ride or journey on horseback.

ē-qui-tem-pō-rā′nē-ous, *a.* [*Equi-*, and L. *tempus*, time.] Isochronous; equal in or occupying the same time-lengths.

eq′ui-tēs (ek′wi-), *n.pl.* [L., pl. of *eques*, a horseman, from *equus*, a horse.] An order of Roman citizens, originally forming the cavalry of the army. They held their position by virtue of a certain property qualification, and toward the end of the republic they possessed much influence in the state.

eq′ui-ty (ek′wi-ti), *n.*; *pl.* **eq′ui-ties**. [ME. *equitee*; OFr. *equite*; L. *æquitas* (*-atis*), equality, from *æquus*, equal.]

1. Justice; impartiality; the giving or desiring to give to each man his due.

> With righteousness shall he judge the world, and the people with *equity*.—Ps. xcviii. 9.

2. In law, an equitable claim.

> I consider the wife's *equity* to be too well settled to be shaken. —Kent.

3. In jurisprudence, a term having three leading senses, distinguished as follows: (a) Taken broadly, *equity* means the doing unto all men as we would that they should do unto us. (b) In a narrower sense, *equity* is used in contradistinction to strict law; it expounds and limits the language of the positive laws, and construes them, not according to their strict letter, but rather in their reasonable and benignant spirit. (c) In the sense in which it is to be understood as the substantial justice expounded by English and American courts of equity, it is the system of supplemental law administered in these, founded upon defined rules, recorded precedents, and established principles, the judges, however, liberally expounding and developing them to meet new exigencies. Hence, a *court of equity* or *chancery* is a court which corrects the operation of the literal text of the law, and supplies its defects by reasonable construction, and by rules of proceeding and deciding which are not admissible in a court of law.

> *Equity* is a roguish thing; for law, we have a measure, know what to trust to; *equity* is according to the conscience of him that is chancellor, and, as that is larger or narrower, so is *equity*. —Selden.

Equity of redemption; in law, the advantage, allowed to a mortgager, of a reasonable time to redeem lands mortgaged, when the estate is of greater value than the sum for which it was mortgaged.

Syn.—Justice, fairness, right, impartiality, honesty, uprightness.

ē-quiv′ȧ-lence (-kwiv′), *n.* [LL. *æquivalentia*, from *æquivalens* (*-entis*), ppr. of *æquivalere*, to have equal power; L. *æquus*, equal, and *valere*, to be strong.]

1. The condition of being equivalent; equality of value, signification, or force; as, take the goods and give an *equivalence* in corn.

2. In chemistry, the quality in chemical elements of combining with or displacing one another in certain definite proportions. [See *Valence*.]

Equivalence of force; the doctrine that force of one kind becomes transformed into force of another kind of the same value.

ē-quiv′ȧ-lence, *v.t.* To be equivalent to; to equal; to counterbalance. [Rare.]

ē-quiv′ȧ-len-cy, *n.* Same as *Equivalence*.

ē-quiv′ȧ-lent, *a.* [LL. *æquivalens* (*-entis*), ppr. of *æquivalere*, to have equal power; L. *æquus*, equal, and *valere*, to be strong.]

1. Equal in value, force, power, effect, excellence, or moral worth, import, or meaning; interchangeable; as, circumstantial evidence may be almost *equivalent* to full proof.

2. In geology, contemporaneous in origin; corresponding in position in the scale of rocks; as, the *equivalent* strata of different countries.

3. In geometry, a term applied to surfaces or magnitudes which have equal areas or equal dimensions.

ē-quiv′ȧ-lent, *n.* 1. That which is equal in value, weight, dignity, or force, to something else; as, money damages are no *equivalent* for the loss of a limb.

2. In chemistry, the proportion expressing the weight, or quantity by weight, of any substance which combines with another substance to form a definite compound. There is a law that if a body A unite with other bodies B, C, D, then the quantities B, C, D (the letters being used to denote the combining quantities as well as the bodies) which unite with it, or some simple multiples of these quantities, represent for the most part the proportions in which they unite among themselves. This law is called the *law of equivalents*, and the various quantities A, B, C, D (or a multiple of them) the *equivalents* of each other. Thus, 1 part by weight of hydrogen unites with 8 parts by weight of oxygen to form water, with 35.5 of chlorin to form hydrochloric acid, with 16 of sulphur to form sulphureted hydrogen; these quantities or their multiples are therefore regarded as *equivalents* of each other, 8 parts of oxygen uniting with 35.5 of chlorin to form chlorin monoxid, and 16 of sulphur with 8×2 of oxygen to form sulphurous oxid.

3. In geology, a stratum or series of strata in one district formed contemporaneously with another in a different region.

Mechanical equivalent of heat; in physics, the

amount of mechanical energy which, when transformed into heat, is equivalent to one heat unit. Joule's experiments, the results of which are generally accepted, gave 772 foot-pounds as the energy equivalent to that expended in raising the temperature of one pound of water 1° F.

ē-quiv′ȧ-lent, *v.t.* To be equivalent to; to furnish an equivalent for; to equal. [Rare.]

ē-quiv′ȧ-lent-ly, *adv.* In an equivalent manner.

ē-qui-val′ūe, *v.t.* To put the same or an equal value upon; to rate as equal. [Rare.]

ē′qui-valve, *n.* A bivalve in which the valves are of equal size and form.

ē′qui-valve, ē′qui-valved, *a.* [*Equi-*, and L. *valva*, the leaf of a door.] Having valves equal in size and form, as certain bivalve shells.

ē-qui-val′vū-lăr, *a.* Same as *Equivalve.*

ē-quiv′ō-cȧ-cy, *n.* Equivocalness.

ē-quiv′ō-căl, *a.* [LL. *æquivocus*, of like sound; L. *æquus*, equal, and *vox* (*vocis*), voice.]

1. Being of doubtful signification; capable of being understood in different senses; capable of a double interpretation; ambiguous; as, *equivocal* words, terms, or senses.

> The beauties of Shakspere are not of so dim or *equivocal* a nature as to be visible only to learned eyes. —Jeffrey.

2. Uncertain, as an indication or sign; dubious; unsatisfactory.

> How *equivocal* a test! —Burke.

3. As applied to character, conduct, and the like, generally used in a bad sense, and nearly equivalent to suspicious in the sense of deserving to be suspected; capable of being ascribed to different motives; as, *equivocal* morality; his character is somewhat *equivocal.*

4. Uncertain; proceeding from some unknown cause or not from the usual cause; as, *equivocal* generation.

Equivocal chord; in music, a chord common to two or more keys, and used in transitions from one key to another.

Equivocal generation; the supposed production of animals without the intercourse of the sexes, and of plants without seed.

Syn.—Ambiguous, doubtful, dubious, uncertain, vague, obscure.—An expression is *ambiguous* when different parts of it can be so construed as to bring out a diversity of meanings. It is *equivocal* when, taken as a whole, it expresses a given thought with perfect clearness and propriety, and also another thought with equal propriety and clearness. The former is a mere blunder of language; the latter is usually intended to deceive, though it may occur at times from mere inadvertence.

ē-quiv′ō-căl, *n.* A word or term of doubtful meaning, or capable of different interpretations.

ē-quiv′ō-căl-ly, *adv.* In an equivocal manner; ambiguously.

ē-quiv′ō-căl-ness, *n.* The state of being equivocal; ambiguity; double meaning.

ē-quiv′ō-cāte, *v.i.*; equivocated, *pt., pp.*; equivocating, *ppr.* [LL. *æquivocatus*, pp. of *æquivocari*, to have the same sound, to be called by the same name; L. *æquivocus*, of like sound; *æquus*, equal, and *vox* (*vocis*), voice, sound.] To use words of double meaning or doubtful signification; to express one's opinions equivocally or in terms which admit of different senses; to use ambiguous expressions with a view to mislead or deceive; to prevaricate; to quibble.

Syn.—Prevaricate, quibble, shuffle, evade.

ē-quiv′ō-cāte, *v.t.* To render equivocal. [Rare.]

> He *equivocated* his vow by a mental reservation. —Sir G. Buck.

ē-quiv-ō-cā′tion, *n.* [LL. *æquivocatio* (*-onis*), from *æquivocari*, to have the same sound.]

1. Ambiguity of speech; the use of words or expressions that are susceptible of a double signification, with a view to mislead; prevarication; as, hypocrites are often guilty of *equivocation.*

2. In logic, a fallacy arising from the use or employment of a word of uncertain or doubtful meaning.

Syn.—Evasion, shift, subterfuge, prevarication, quibble.

ē-quiv′ō-cā-tŏr, *n.* One who equivocates.

ē-quiv′ō-cȧ-tō-ry, *a.* Characterized by equivocation.

eq′ui-vōke, eq′ui-vōque (ek′wi-vōk), *n.* [Fr. *équivoque*; L. *æquivocus*, of like sound, ambiguous; *æquus*, equal, and *vox* (*vocis*), voice.]

1. An ambiguous word or phrase; a word or phrase susceptible of various significations; a play upon words.

2. An equivocation.

> I know your *equivokes.* —B. Jonson.

ē-quiv′ō-rous, *a.* [L. *equus*, horse, and *vorare*, to devour.] Feeding or subsisting on horse-flesh; as, *equivorous* Tatars.

ē′quoid, *a.* [L. *equus*, a horse, and Gr. *eidos*, resemblance.] Pertaining to the *Equidæ*; belonging to the horse family; equine.

E′quus (ē′kwus), *n.* [L., a horse.] The typical genus of animals of the order *Equidæ*; the horse is *Equus caballus.*

-er. [ME. *-ere*; AS. *-ere.*] A suffix equivalent to L. *-or*, added to verbs to form nouns of the agent; as, eat*er*, from eat; feed*er*, from feed, etc.

-er. [ME. *-er*, with suffix of declension *-ere*; AS. *-er*, *-or* in adverbs, with suffix of declension, *-a* masc., *-e* f. and neut., added in adjectives.] A suffix used with adjectives to form the comparative degree; as, worthi*er*; cold*er*, etc.

-er. [ME. *-er*, *-ere*; OFr. *-er*, *-ier*; L. *-arius.*] A suffix of Latin origin used to denote a person or an agent; as, offic*er*; jail*er.*

-er. [ME. *-eren*; AS. *erian.*] A suffix used with verbs to give a frequentative or diminutive sense; as, tink*er*, from tink; wav*er*, from wave, etc.

-er. [OFr. *-er*, *-re*, a noun suffix, from inf. suffix *-er*, *-re*, from L. *-āre*, *-ēre*, *-ere*, the active inf. suffix of 1st, 2d, and 3d declensions respectively.] A noun suffix used especially in legal terms; as, attaind*er*; implead*er.*

ē′rȧ, *n.*; *pl.* **ē′rȧș.** [LL. *æra*, an era; earlier use, counters, the items of account, from pl. of L. *æs* (*æris*), brass.]

1. In chronology, a fixed point of time, from which any number of years is reckoned; as, the Christian *era.*

2. A succession of years proceeding from a fixed point or comprehended between two fixed points; as, the *era* of the Seleucides ended with the reign of Antiochus.

3. A time or age distinguished by some remarkable event; a period in which a new order of things prevails; an epoch in general; as, the *era* of Christ's appearance; painting opened the new *era* of culture.

4. In geology, a fixed and definite division of geological time; the highest chronological division of geological history; as, the Paleozoic *era.*

Christian era; see under *Christian.*

Era of contracts or *of kings*; the Seleucidan era, dating from the occupation of Babylon by Seleucus Nicator, 312 B. C., extensively followed in the Levant.

ē-rā′di-āte, *v.i.*; eradiated, *pt., pp.*; eradiating, *ppr.* [L. *e*, from, and *radiatus*, pp. of *radiare*, to radiate, from *radius*, a beam, ray.] To radiate; to shoot out, as rays of light; to beam.

ē-rā-di-ā′tion, *n.* Emission of rays or beams of light; emission of light or splendor.

ē-rad′i-cȧ-ble, *a.* Capable of being eradicated.

ē-rad′i-cāte, *v.t.*; eradicated, *pt., pp.*; eradicating, *ppr.* [L. *eradicatus*, pp. of *eradicare*, to root out; *e*, from, out, and *radix* (*-icis*), root.]

1. To pull up by the roots; to destroy at the roots; to root out; to extirpate; as, to *eradicate* weeds.

2. To destroy thoroughly; to extirpate; as, to *eradicate* errors, false principles, vice, or disease.

Syn.—Extirpate, uproot, exterminate, destroy, annihilate.

ē-rad-i-cā′tion, *n.* [L. *eradicatio* (*-onis*), from *eradicare*, to root out; *e*, out, and *radix*, root.] The act of plucking up by the roots or state of being plucked up by the roots; extirpation; excision; total destruction.

> They affirm the roots of mandrakes give a shriek upon *eradication.* —Sir T. Browne.

ē-rad′i-cā-tive, *a.* Tending to eradicate or extirpate; serving to cure, remove entirely, or destroy thoroughly.

ē-rad′i-cā-tive, *n.* A medicine or course of medical treatment that effects a radical cure.

ē-rad′i-cā-tŏr, *n.* One who or that which eradicates.

ē-rȧ-dic′ū-lōse, *a.* [L. *e-* priv., and *radicula*, dim. of *radix*, root.] In botany, having no rootlets.

Ē-ran′the-mum, *n.* [L., from Gr. *ēr*, spring, and *anthos*, a flower.] A genus of acanthaceous plants, chiefly tropical, some of whose species are occasionally seen in hothouses.

ē-rās′ȧ-ble, *a.* Capable of being erased.

ē-rāse′, *v.t.*; erased (ē-rāst′), *pt., pp.*; erasing, *ppr.* [L. *erasus*, pp. of *eradere*, to scratch out.]

1. To rub or scrape out, as letters or characters written, engraved, or painted; to efface; to blot out; to obliterate; to expunge; as, to *erase* a word or a name.

2. Figuratively, to remove or destroy; to efface, as ideas in the mind or memory.

> All ideas of rectitude and justice are *erased* from his mind. —Burke.

3. To destroy to the foundation; to raze; as, to *erase* a town. [Obs.]

Syn.—Abrade, efface, blot out, obliterate, expunge, cancel, destroy.

A Lion's Head Erased.

ē-rāsed′ (-rāst′), *a.* 1. Rubbed or scratched out; obliterated; effaced.

2. In heraldry, a term applied to anything forcibly torn off, leaving the separated parts jagged and uneven, as distinguished from *couped*, which means cut straight across.

ē-rāse′ment, *n.* The act of erasing; a rubbing out; expunction; obliteration.

ē-rās′ẽr, *n.* One who or that which erases; especially, a sharp instrument, prepared rubber, and the like, used to erase writing, etc.

ē-rā′șion, *n.* [From L. *erasus*, pp. of *eradere*, to erase.] The act of erasing; a rubbing out; obliteration.

E-ras′mi-ăn, *a.* and *n.* I. *a.* Pertaining to the opinions and doctrines of Erasmus, a Dutch scholar of the sixteenth century.

II. *n.* An adherent of Erasmus, especially one who advocates the system of Greek pronunciation which he devised.

Ē-ras′tiăn (-chăn), *n.* 1. A follower of Thomas Erastus, a Swiss physician and theologian of the sixteenth century, who held that holy communion should be open to all, and that the civil jurisdiction of the church should be restricted.

2. In more recent times, one who favors the complete control of the church by the state.

Ē-ras′tiăn-ișm, *n.* The principles of the Erastians.

ē-rā′șūre (-zhūr), *n.* 1. The act of erasing; a scratching out; obliteration; as, *erasure* in a deed without the consent of the party bound by it will make it void.

2. That which has been erased, scratched out, or obliterated; the place where a word or letter has been erased or obliterated; as, the manuscript contained many *erasures.*

3. The act of razing or destroying to the foundation; total destruction; as, the *erasure* of cities. [Obs.]

Er′ȧ-tive, *a.* Pertaining to Erato, one of the Muses.

Er′ȧ-tō, *n.* [L., from Gr. *Eratō*, lit., the Lovely, from *eratos*, beloved, from *eran*, to love.] In classical mythology, one of the Muses. She presided over lyric, especially amatory poetry, and is generally represented with the lyre in the left hand and the plectrum in the right in the act of playing.

Erato, Antique, British Museum.

ẽr′bi-ȧ, *n.* [L., from *erbium.*] In chemistry, the oxid of erbium, a white or pale rose-colored powder soluble in acids only.

ẽr′bi-um, *n.* [L., from *Ytterby*, in Sweden, where gadolinite, the mineral which contains this substance, is found.] A rare metal found along with yttrium, terbium, and a number of other rare elements, in some rare minerals, as euxenite, fergusonite, and gadolinite, in which it exists as a silicate or tantalate.

ẽrd, *n.* [ME. *erd*, *eard*; AS. *eard*, earth, land.] Earth. [Prov. Eng.]

ẽrd′=shrew, *n.* The shrewmouse, *Sorex vulgaris.*

ere (âr), *adv., prep.,* and *conj.* [ME. *ere*, *er*; AS. *ær*, before, sooner.]

I. *adv.* Early; soon; previously; before; formerly. [Obs. or Scot.]

II. *prep.* Before, in respect of time.

> Our fruitful Nile
> Flow'd *ere* the wonted season. —Dryden.

III. *conj.* Before; sooner than.

> *Ere* sails were spread new oceans to explore. —Dryden.

Ere long; soon; before long.

Ere now; formerly; before this time.

ēre, *v.t.* To plow; to ear. [Obs.]

Er′e-bus, *n.* 1. In Greek mythology, the son of Chaos, who married his sister Night and was the father of Light and Day. He was transformed into a river and plunged into Tartarus, because he aided the Titans.

2. Hence, the lower world, particularly that part of it which is the abode of virtuous shades; the subterranean passage to hades.

> The motions of his spirit are dull as night,
> And his affections dark as *Erebus.* —Shak.

Er-ech-thi′tēs, *n.* [L., from Gr. *erechthitēs*, the senecio or groundsel, from *erechthein*, to rend, break.] A small genus of composite plants found in America, Australia, and New Zealand. The fireweed, *Erechthites hieracifolia*, is the only species in the United States.

ē-rect′, *a.* [L. *erectus*, pp. of *erigere*, to set up; out, up, and *regere*, to make straight.]

1. Upright or in a perpendicular posture; he stood *erect.*

2. Directed upward; raised; uplifted.

> His piercing eyes *erect* appear to view
> Superior worlds, and look all nature through. —Pope.

3. Upright and firm; bold; unshaken.
4. Intent; alert; vigilant; as, *erect* attention of mind.
5. In botany, applied to an organ or part of a plant which stands perpendicularly, or nearly so, to its base or stem; as, an *erect* leaf; an *erect* flower; an *erect* ovule.
6. In heraldry, upright in position; elevated vertically, as the heads of serpents, the tips of birds' wings, etc.

Erect stem; in botany, a stem which is without support from twining, or nearly perpendicular.

ē-reçt′, *v.t.*; erected, *pt.*, *pp.*; erecting, *ppr.* 1. To raise and set in an upright or perpendicular position, or nearly so; to set upright; to raise up; as, to *erect* a pole or flagstaff.
2. To raise, as a building; to set up; to build; as, to *erect* a house or a church; to *erect* a fort; to put together the component parts of, as of a locomotive, a printing-press, a dynamo, or other machine.
3. To set up or establish anew; to found; to form; as, to *erect* a kingdom or commonwealth; to *erect* a new system or theory.
4. To raise from a low position; to elevate; to exalt; to lift up.
5. To excite; to animate; to encourage. [Obs.]
6. To set forth, as an assertion, consequence, or conclusion from premises; to propound.
7. To draw upon a base; as, to *erect* a perpendicular.

Syn.—Raise, set up, elevate, build, construct, found, establish, institute.

ē-reçt′, *v.i.* To take an upright position; to rise. [Obs.]

ē-reçt′á-ble, *a.* Capable of being erected; erectile; as, an *erectable* feather.

ē-reçt′ẽr, *n.* One who or that which erects; one who raises or builds.

ē-reçt′ile, *a.* Capable of being erected; susceptible of erection; erectable.

Erectile tissue; in anatomy, a tissue consisting of a network of expansile capillaries that under stimulus become engorged with blood and cause erection of the part.

ē-reç-til′i-ty, *n.* The quality of being erectile or capable of erection.

ē-reç′tion, *n.* [L. *erectio* (*-onis*), from *erectus*, pp. of *erigere*, to erect.]
1. The act of raising and setting perpendicular to the plane of the horizon; a setting upright.
2. The act of raising or building, as an edifice or fortification; as, the *erection* of a wall or of a house; also, the act of putting together component parts, as of a machine.
3. The state of being raised, built, or elevated; as, the church fell immediately after its *erection*.
4. Establishment; settlement; formation; as, the *erection* of a commonwealth or of a new system; the *erection* of a bishopric.
5. Elevation; exaltation of sentiments. [Obs.]
6. The act of rousing excitement; as, the *erection* of the spirits. [Obs.]
7. Anything erected; a building of any kind.
8. In anatomy, the state of a part when it becomes stiff, hard, and swollen by the accumulation of blood in the areolæ of its tissue.

ē-reçt′ive, *a.* Setting upright; raising.

ē-reçt′ly, *adv.* In an erect posture.

ē-reçt′ness, *n.* Uprightness of form; the state of being erect in posture or character.

ē-reç-tō-pā′tent, *a.* [L. *erectus*, erect, and *patens* (*-entis*), open, spreading.]
1. In botany, having a position intermediate between erect and spreading.
2. In entomology, having the primary wings erect and the secondary horizontal.

ē-reç′tŏr, *n.* [L., from *erectus*, pp of *erigere*, to erect.]
1. One who or that which erects or raises.
2. In anatomy, a muscle that causes the erection of any part.
3. In optics, an attachment to a compound microscope, telescope, or other instrument, which causes a second inversion of the image, so that the object viewed is presented in an erect or normal position.

ere′long′ (âr′long′), *adv.* Before long; soon; before much time has passed; usually written as two words, *ere long*.

The world *erelong* a world of tears must weep.
—Milton.

er″e-mȧ-cau′sis, *n.* [L., from Gr. *ērema*, slowly, and *kausis*, a burning, from *kaiein*, to burn.] A term introduced into chemistry by Liebig to express a slow combustion or oxidation; the act of gradual combination of the combustible elements of a body with the oxygen of the air.

e-rē′miç, *a.* [Gr. *eērmos*, desert, from *erēmia*, a desert.] Pertaining to or living in dry, sandy places or deserts; used chiefly in zoölogy.

er′ē-mit-āge, *n.* [Obs.] See *Hermitage*.

er′ē-mite, *n.* [LL. *eremita*; Gr. *erēmitēs*, a hermit, from *erēmia*, a desert; from *erēmos*, desolate, lonely.] A hermit; an anchoret.

er-ē-mit′iç, er-ē-mit′iç-ăl, *a.* [LL. *eremiticus*, like a hermit, from Gr. *erēmitēs*, a hermit.] Pertaining to a hermit; having the nature or character of a hermit; living in solitude or in seclusion from the world.

er′ē-mī-tish, *a.* Eremitic.

er′ē-mit-işm, *n.* The state of a hermit; seclusion from social life.

E-rē-mō-brȳ′ȧ, *n.pl.* [L., from Gr. *erēmos*, desolate, solitary, and *bryon*, a kind of seaweed.] In botany, a group of ferns whose fronds are produced laterally on and articulated with the rootstalk.

e-rē-mō-brȳ′oid, *a.* Pertaining to the *Eremobrya*.

er′ē-nāch, *n.* [Ir. *airchinneach*; LL. *archidiaconus*, an archdeacon of the early Catholic church; Gr. *archos*, a ruler, and *diakonos*, a deacon.] An ecclesiastic of the early Irish church analogous to an archdeacon.

ē-rep-tā′tion, *n.* [L. *erepere*, to creep forth; *e*, out, and *repere*, to creep.] A creeping forth.

ē-rep′tion, *n.* [L. *ereptio* (*-onis*), from *ereptus*, pp. of *eripere*, to snatch or take away by force.] A taking or snatching away by force.

e-reth′iç, *a.* [Gr. *erethein*, to excite.] Pertaining to erethism; excitable; restless; as, an *erethic* temperament.

er′e-thişm, *n.* [Gr. *erethismos*, a stirring up, from *erethizein*, to excite, irritate.] In physiology, excitement or irritation of any organ or tissue, especially of the organs of generation.

er-e-this′tiç, *a.* Relating to erethism.

ere′while′, ere′whiles′ (âr′), *adv.* Some time ago; a little while before, heretofore. [Rare.]

I am as fair now as I was *erewhile*.—Shak.

ẽrf, *n.*; *pl.* **ẽr′ven.** [D.] In Cape Colony, the Dutch name for a piece of garden-ground, usually about one-half an acre in extent.

ẽrg, *n.* [Gr. *ergon*, work.] In physics, the unit of work done by a force which, acting for one second upon a mass of one gram (15.4 grains troy), produces a velocity of a centimeter (.3937 inch) per second.

ẽrg′ăl, *n.* [Gr. *ergon*, work.] In physics, the force function.

Ẽr-gȧ-sil′i-dæ, *n.pl.* [L., from Gr. *ergasia*, work, daily labor.] A family of parasitic crustaceans of the order *Siphonostomata*. The females of the typical genus *Ergasilus* are parasitic upon the gills of fishes, and those of the genus *Nicothoë* upon the gills of lobsters.

ẽr′găt, *v.t.* and *v.i.* [Obs.] See *Ergot*.

ẽrg′mē″tẽr, *n.* [Gr. *ergon*, work, and *metron*, a measure.] In physics, a device for measuring energy in ergs.

ẽr′gō, *adv.* [L., therefore.] Therefore; used in logic to introduce the conclusion of a syllogism.

ẽr-gom′e-tẽr, *n.* [Gr. *ergon*, work, and *metron*, a measure.] In physics, a device or instrument for measuring work; a dynamometer; also called *electro-ergometer*.

ẽr-gō-met′riç, *a.* Pertaining to an ergometer.

ẽr′gon, *n.* Same as *Erg*.

ẽr′got, *n.* [Fr. *ergot*, *argot*, a spur, stub of a branch, disease of cereal grasses. Derivation unknown.]
1. In farriery, a stub, like a piece of soft horn, about the size of a chestnut, situated behind and below the pastern-joint, and commonly hidden under the tuft of the fetlock.
2. In botany, the altered seed of rye and other grasses, caused by the attack of a fungus called *Claviceps purpurea*. The seed is replaced by a dense homogeneous tissue largely charged with an oily fluid. In its perfect state this germinates and produces the *Claviceps*. When the diseased rye of this kind is used for food, it sometimes causes death by a kind of mortification called dry gangrene. *Ergot* is used in obstetric practice to promote the contraction of the uterus.

1. Heads of Ergot (*a a*) produced on a Grass. 2. *Claviceps purpurea* (*b b*) springing from the Ergot.

3. In anatomy, the hippocampus minor of the brain. [Rare.]

ẽr′got, ẽr′gat, *v.t.* and *v.i.* I. *v.t.* To infer; to deduce logically. [Obs.]
II. *v.i.* To draw conclusions. [Obs.]

ẽr′gŏt-ed, *a.* Ergotized.

ẽr-got′iç, *a.* Pertaining to or derived from ergot; as, *ergotic* acid.

ẽr′gō-tine, ẽr′gō-tin, *n.* [Fr. *ergotine*.]
1. In chemistry, the active principle of the ergot of rye. It is obtained as a brown powder having a pungent and bitter taste.
2. An extract of ergot.

ẽr-got′i-nine, *n.* An alkaloid obtained from ergot.

ẽr′gō-tişm, *n.* A logical inference; a conclusion. [Obs.]

ẽr′gŏt-işm, *n.* 1. The spur of rye; ergot.
2. In medicine, the constitutional effects following the prolonged use of ergot or of ergotized rye in food; it occurs in two forms, the convulsive and the gangrenous.

ẽr′gŏt-ized, *a.* Affected with ergot; as, *ergotized* rye; changed into ergot.

ẽrg′=ten, *n.* A unit of work based on the centimeter-gram-second system, and equal to 10^{10} or 10,000,000,000 ergs. One horse-power is about three-quarters of an *erg-ten* per second.

ē′ri, ē′ri-ȧ, *n.* The native name of one of the wild silkworms of Assam, which feeds on the castor-oil bean.

er′i-ach, *n.* Same as *Eric*.

Ē′ri-ăn, *a.* Relating to or designating Lake Erie or its shores.

Erian age; in geology, the Devonian age. [Rare.]

er′iç, *n.* [Ir. *eiric*.] In old Irish law, a pecuniary recompense or blood-fine paid by a murderer to the relatives or family of the murdered person; also written *eriach*, *erick*.

E-rī′çȧ, *n.* [L., from Gr. *ereikē*, *erikē*, heath.] The heaths, a large genus of branched rigid shrubs, natural order *Ericaceæ*, consisting of more than 400 species, chiefly natives of South Africa, a few being found in Europe and Asia.

Erica herbacea.

Er-i-çā′cē-æ, *n.pl.* A natural order of exogens, deriving its name from the genus *Erica*. It also contains *Azalea*, *Rhododendron*, *Kalmia*, *Arbutus*, *Andromeda*, and many other beautiful genera.

er-i-çā′ceous, *a.* [Gr. *ereikē*, *erikē*, the heath.] Pertaining to the natural order of plants *Ericaceæ* or the heath family; resembling heaths; consisting of heaths.

er-i-cē′tăl, *a.* Of or pertaining to the genus *Erica*; composed of heaths.

er-i-cin′e-ous, *a.* Ericaceous.

e-ric′i-nōl, *n.* [L. *erica*, the heath, and *oleum*, oil.] In chemistry, a volatile oil, produced by decomposing ericolin with acid.

e-ri′ci-us, *n.* [L., a hedgehog.] A hedgehog.

e-riç′ō-lin, *n.* [Gr. *ereikē*, *erikē*, the heath.] In chemistry, a bitter yellow glucoside, found in many of the *Ericaceæ*.

E-rid′ȧ-nus, *n.* [L., from Gr. *Ēridanos*, the name of a mythical river.] A winding southern constellation, the River, containing Achernar, a star of the first magnitude.

E-rig′e-ron, *n.* [L., from Gr. *ērigerōn*, the groundsel, lit., early old, so named from its hoary down; *ēri*, early, and *gerōn*, an old man.] A genus of plants, natural order *Compositæ*, nearly related to *Aster*, but having several series of ray-flowers. There are about 100 species, natives of temperate and cold regions. The common fleabane, *Erigeron Philadelphicus*, a native of North America, is used in medicine as a diuretic.

er′i-gi-ble, *a.* Capable of being erected. [Obs.]

E′rin, *n.* [*Erin*, *Eire*, *Iere*, lit., western country.] Ireland.

er-i-nā′ceous, *a.* [L. *erinaceus*, a hedgehog.] Pertaining to the hedgehog family; resembling a hedgehog.

e-rin′ē-um, *n.*; *pl.* **e-rin′ē-ȧ.** [L., from Gr. *erineos*, woolly, from *erion*, wool.] The name given to numerous abnormal growths on the leaves of trees and shrubs, formerly supposed to be due to fungi, but now known to be caused by attacks of mites.

e-rin′gō, *n.* See *Eryngo*.

er′i-nite, *n.* An emerald-green arseniate of copper found in Erin or Ireland.

E-rin′ys, *n.*, *pl.* **E-rin′y-ēş.** [L., from Gr. *Erinys*, an avenging deity.] In Greek mythology, one of the Furies; a goddess of discord; hence, discord in general; written also *Erinnys*.

E″ri-ō-den′drŏn, *n.* [Gr. *erion*, wool, and *dendron*, a tree.] A genus of plants, natural order *Malvaceæ*; the silk-cotton trees. There are eight species, all but one natives of America. They grow from 50 to 100 feet high, and have palmate leaves and red or white flowers. The woolly coat of the seeds is used for stuffing cushions and similar purposes.

Wool-tree (*Eriodendron anfractuosum*).

E-ri-og′ō-num, *n.* [L., from Gr. *erion*, wool, and *gony*, the knee.] A large genus of plants or herbs, natural order *Polygonaceæ*, comprising about 160 species, most of which are found in and are characteristic of western United States. They are chiefly low herbs or woody-based perennials, having small, clustered flowers.

ē-ri-om′e-tẽr, *n.* [Gr. *erion,* wool, and *metron,* a measure.] An optical instrument for measuring small diameters, as of minute particles or fibers, by observing the diameter of the colored rings produced by the diffraction of the light in which the objects are viewed.

E-ris′tȧ-lis, *n.* [L., name first used by Latreille in 1804.] A genus of flies or dipterous insects, typical of the subfamily *Eristalinæ,* with rat-tail larvæ or maggots, feeding in manure or decaying vegetable substances; it includes the drone-flies.

e-ris′tiç, e-ris′tiç-ăl, *a.* [Gr. *eristikos,* given to strife or dispute, from *erizein,* to strive, dispute, from *eris,* strife.] Pertaining to disputes; controversial.

Eristic science; logic.

ẽrke, *a.* Weary; indolent; sick. [Obs.]

ẽrl′=king, *n.* [G. *erl-könig,* elf-king.] The English form of the name given, in German and Scandinavian poetical mythology, to a personified natural power which devises and works mischief, especially to children.

ẽrme, *v.i.* To grieve; to lament. [Obs.]

ẽr′mē-lin, ẽr′mi-lin, *n.* Ermine. [Obs.]

ẽr′mine, *n.* [ME. *ermin;* OFr. *ermin;* M.H.G. *hermelin;* O.H.G. *harmo,* the ermine.]

Ermine (*Putorius erminea*).

1. The stoat, a quadruped of the weasel tribe, *Putorius erminea,* found in temperate regions, but common only in the northern parts of Europe, Asia, and America. In consequence of the change that occurs in the color of its fur at different seasons it is not generally known that the *ermine* and stoat are the same. In winter, in cold countries, the fur changes from a reddish brown to a yellowish white or almost pure white, under which shade the animal is recognized as the *ermine.* In both states the tip of the tail is black. The fur, which is obtained chiefly from Norway, Lapland, Siberia, and the Hudson's Bay territories, is in great demand.

2. The fur of the *ermine,* as prepared for ornamental purposes, by having the black of the tail inserted at regular intervals so that it contrasts with the pure white of the rest of the fur.

3. Figuratively, the office or dignity of a judge, from his state robe being, in England and elsewhere, ornamented or bordered with *ermine.*

> I call upon the judges to interpose the purity of their *ermine,* to save us from this pollution. —Lord Chatham.

4. In heraldry, one of the furs, represented with its peculiar spots black on a white ground; argent, spots sable.

Ermine.

5. In entomology, one of various arctiid moths, as the buff ermine, *Arctia lubricipeda,* or the water-ermine, *Arctia urticæ.*

ẽr′mine, *v.t.;* ermined, *pt., pp.;* ermining, *ppr.* 1. To clothe or adorn with or as with ermine.

2. Hence, to advance to a position of dignity or honor, as to a judgeship.

ẽr-mi-né′ (-nā′), *a.* In heraldry, composed of four ermine spots, as a cross.

ẽr′mined, *a.* Clothed with ermine; adorned with the fur of the ermine.

ẽr′mine=moth, *n.* A moth of the family *Yponomeutidæ,* so called from its beautiful black and white spotted covering, resembling the fur of the ermine.

ẽr′mineş, *n.* In heraldry, a black field marked by white spots, the reverse of *ermine;* sable, spots argent.

Ermines.

ẽr′min-ites, *n.* In heraldry, same as *ermine,* but with a single red hair on each side of the ermine spots.

Erminites.

ẽr′mi-nois, *n.* [Fr., from OFr. *ermin,* ermine.] In heraldry, a fur represented by a gold field with black spots; or, spots sable.

Erminois.

ẽr′mit, *n.* A recluse; a hermit. [Obs.]

ẽrn, ẽrne, *n.* A sea-eagle; also written *earn.*

ẽrn, *v.i.* To mourn; to grieve. [Obs.]

ẽr′nest, *a.* and *n.* Earnest. [Obs.]

ẽr′nest-ful, *a.* Full of earnestness; serious. [Obs.]

ē-rōde′, *v.t.;* eroded, *pt., pp.;* eroding, *ppr.* [L. *erodere,* to gnaw away; *e,* from, off, and *rodere,* to gnaw.]

1. To gnaw into; to eat; to wear away; to canker; often used figuratively.

2. In geology, to wear away or smooth down; used of the action of floods, glaciers, etc., in wearing down the earth's surface.

ē-rōde′, *v.i.* To become worn away.

ē-rōd′ed, *a.* 1. Eaten; corroded; appearing as if gnawed.

2. In botany and zoölogy, having the edge irregularly jagged or denticulated, as a leaf or an insect's wing.

ē-rōd′ent, *a.* and *n.* [L. *erodens* (*-entis*), ppr. of *erodere,* to gnaw.]

I. *a.* Caustic; having a tendency to eat away; said of certain drugs.

II. *n.* A drug which eats away morbid or extraneous growths; a caustic.

E-rō′di-um, *n.* [L., from Gr. *erōdios,* the heron.] A genus of plants, closely allied to *Geranium,* of which there are about 50 species, natives chiefly of the Old World. Some of the common species are known as *heron's-bill* or *stork's-bill.*

er′ō-gāte, *v.t.;* erogated, *pt., pp.;* erogating, *ppr.* To lay out; to give; to bestow upon. [Obs.]

er-ō-gā′tion, *n.* The act of erogating. [Obs.]

e-rog′e-nous, *a.* [Gr. *erōs,* love, and *-genēs,* producing.] Causing erotic sensation; producing or tending to produce sexual desire.

E′ros, *n.* [L., from Gr. *Erōs,* Cupid, the god of love, from *erōs,* love, from *erān,* to love.] The god of love; in mythology, the Greek equivalent of Cupid.

ē-rōse′, *a.* [L. *erosus,* pp. of *erodere,* to gnaw off; *e,* off, and *rodere,* to gnaw.]

1. Uneven; irregular, as if eaten or gnawed away.

2. In botany and zoölogy, having small irregular sinuses in the margin, as if gnawed, as a leaf or an insect's wing.

ē-rōse′ly, *adv.* Irregularly; jaggedly.

ē-rō′şion, *n.* [L. *erosio* (*-onis*), from *erosus,* pp. of *erodere,* to gnaw off.]

1. The act or operation of eating or wearing away; specifically, in medicine, the gradual destruction of the substance of a part by ulceration or by increased action of the absorbents, whether spontaneous or excited by some irritating substance.

2. The state of being eaten or worn away; corrosion; canker.

3. In geology, the wearing away of the earth's surface, as by floods, glaciers, waves, wind, or any natural process.

4. An eroded area or tract.

Erosion theory; in geology, the theory that valleys are due to the wearing influences of water and ice, chiefly in the form of glaciers, as opposed to the theory which regards them as the result of fissures in the earth's crust produced by strains during its upheaval.

ē-rō′sive, *a.* [L. *erosus,* pp. of *erodere,* to gnaw off.] Having the property of eating away or corroding; corrosive.

ē-ros′trāte, *a.* [L. *e-* priv., and *rostratus,* beaked, from *rostrum,* a beak.] In botany, destitute of beak.

er″ō-tē-mat′iç, *a.* [Gr. *erōtēmatikos,* interrogative, from *erōtēma,* a question, from *erōtan,* to ask.] In rhetoric, using questions.

er′ō-tēme, *n.* [LL. *erotema;* Gr. *erōtēma,* a question, from *erōtān,* to ask.] The mark of interrogation (?); a name proposed, but not in common use.

er-ō-tē′sis, *n.* [L., from Gr. *erōtēsis,* a questioning, from *erōtān,* to question.] In rhetoric, a figure of speech by which the speaker implies a strong affirmative, or more frequently a strong negative, under the form of an interrogation, as in the following lines:

> Must we but weep o'er days more blest?
> Must we but blush? Our fathers bled.—Byron.

er-ō-tet′iç, *a.* [Gr. *erōtētikos,* skilled in questioning, from *erōtān,* to question.] Interrogatory.

e-rot′iç, e-rot′iç-ăl, *a.* [Gr. *erōtikos,* from *erōs* (*erōtos*), love.] Pertaining to or prompted by love; treating of love; amorous; tending to excite sexual desire.

> An *erotic* ode is the very last place in which one would expect any talk about heavenly things. —Saturday Review.

e-rot′iç, *n.* An amorous composition or poem.

e-rot′iç-ăl-ly, *adv.* In an erotic manner.

e-rot′i-çişm, *n.* Erotic character, quality, or tendency; as, the *eroticism* of poetry or novels.

e-rō-tō-mā′ni-ȧ, *n.* [L., from Gr. *erōtomania,* raving love; *erōs,* love, and *mania,* madness.]

1. In pathology, melancholy or mental alienation which is the effect of love; love-sickness.

2. Mental alienation characterized by morbid sexual passion.

e-rō-tō-mā′ni-aç, *n.* One who is afflicted with erotomania.

er-pe-tol′ō-ġy, *n.* See *Herpetology.*

ẽrr, *v.i.;* erred, *pt., pp.;* erring, *ppr.* [ME. *erren;* OFr. *errer;* L. *errare,* to wander.]

1. To wander from the right way; to deviate from the true course or purpose; hence, to deviate from the path of duty; to fail morally; to offend occasionally or habitually or through oversight; as, we have *erred* and strayed like lost sheep.

2. To mistake in judgment or opinion; to blunder; to misapprehend; to be mistaken.

3. To wander; to ramble. [Rare.]

ẽr′rȧ-ble, *a.* Having a tendency to err; fallible.

ẽr′rȧ-ble-ness, *n.* Liability to fault or error.

er′rȧ-bund, *a.* [L. *errabundus,* wandering, from *errare,* to wander.] Wandering; erratic. [Rare.]

er′răn-cy, *n.* 1. The state of being in error; a wandering; the condition of containing errors; also, liability to fall into error; fallibility; as, the *errancy* or inerrancy of the Bible.

2. Liability to change one's views frequently.

er′rănd, *n.* [ME. *erende;* AS. *ærende,* an errand, message.]

1. A verbal message; a mandate or order; something to be told or done; a communication to be made to some person at a distance.

2. Any special business to be transacted by a messenger.

3. One's object in going anywhere; a mission; as, she has gone on an *errand* of mercy.

A fool's errand; a foolish or futile enterprise.

er′rănt, *a.* [ME. *erraunt;* OFr. *errant,* a wanderer, a knight errant, from *errans* (*-antis*), ppr. of *errare,* to wander.]

1. Wandering; roving; rambling; applied particularly to knights, who, in the middle ages, wandered about to seek adventures and display their heroism and generosity, being called *knights errant.*

2. In zoölogy, locomotory; unconfined; free; of or pertaining to the *Errantia.*

3. Deviating from the regular course; erring.

4. Itinerant; formerly applicable to judges of assize. [Obs.]

5. Notorious; manifest; arrant. [Obs.]

er′rănt, *n.* A wanderer; a knight errant. [Obs.]

Er-ran′ti-ȧ (-shi-ȧ), *n.pl.* [L., from *errans* (*-antis*), ppr. of *errare,* to wander.] A group or suborder of annelids, commonly known as the sea-centipedes, sea-mice, and nereids. They have their name from the fact that they lead a free existence, and are able to wander about, being thus distinguished from the sedentary group of the same order.

er′rănt-ry, *n.* [From L. *errans* (*-antis*), ppr. of *errare,* to wander.]

1. A wandering; a roving or rambling about.

> After a short space of *errantry* upon the seas, he got safe back to Dunkirk. —Addison.

2. The condition or way of life of a knight errant.

er-rā′tȧ, *n.,* pl. of *erratum.*

er-rat′iç, *a.* [ME. *erratik;* OFr. *erratique;* L. *erraticus,* wandering, from *errare,* to wander.]

1. Wandering; having no certain course; roving about without a fixed destination.

2. Moving; not fixed or stationary; applied to the planets as distinguished from the fixed stars.

3. Irregular; mutable; moving from point to point, as rheumatic pains.

4. Deviating from the proper or usual course in opinion or conduct; eccentric.

Erratic blocks; the name given by geologists to those boulders or fragments of rocks which appear to have been transported from their original sites by ice in the Pleistocene period and carried often to great distances. Such blocks are on the surface or in the most superficial deposits.

Erratic phenomena; the phenomena connected with erratic blocks.

Syn.—Desultory, aberrant, abnormal, flighty, changeful, capricious, unreliable.

er-rat′iç, *n.* 1. A wanderer.

2. One who is peculiar or eccentric; one who is perverse mentally or who deviates from conventional opinions.

3. In geology, a boulder or block which has been conveyed from its original site, probably by ice, and deposited at a distance; an erratic block.

er-rat′iç-ăl-ly, *adv.* Without rule, order, or established method; irregularly.

er-rat′iç-ăl-ness, *n.* The state of being erratic.

er-rā′tion, *n.* A wandering. [Obs.]

er-rā′tum, *n.; pl.* **er-rā′tȧ.** [L. *erratum,* neut. of *erratus,* pp. of *errare,* to wander.] An error or mistake in writing or printing. The list of the *errata* of a book is usually printed at the beginning or end, with references indicating the pages and lines in which they occur.

> A single *erratum* may knock out the brains of a whole passage. —Cowper.

er′rhīne (-rīn), *a.* [Gr. *errhinon,* errhine, from *en-,* in, and *rhis, rhinos,* nose.] Affecting the nose or designed to be snuffed into the nose; occasioning discharges from the nose.

er′rhīne, *n.* A medicine to be snuffed up the nose to promote discharges of mucus.

er-rō′nē-ous, *a.* [L. *erroneus,* wandering about, from *errare,* to wander.]

1. Wandering; roving; unsettled; devious; irregular. [Obs.]

2. Mistaking; misled; deviating, by mistake, from the truth; as, destroy not the *erroneous* with the malicious. [Obs.]

3. Wrong; false; mistaken; not conformable to truth; erring from truth or justice; liable to mislead; as, an *erroneous* opinion; *erroneous* doctrine.

er-rō′nē-ous-ly, *adv.* By mistake; not rightly; falsely.

er-rō′nē-ous-ness, *n.* The state of being erroneous, wrong, or false; deviation from truth or right; as, the *erroneousness* of a judgment or proposition.

er′rŏr, *n.* [ME. *errour, arrore*; OFr. *error*; L. *error*, a wandering or straying about, a mistake, fault, error, from *errare*, to wander.]

1. A wandering or deviation from the truth; a mistake in judgment, by which men assent to or believe what is not true; a mistake as to matter of fact; a misapprehension.

He was guilty of no *error*. —Brougham.

2. A mistake made in writing or other performance; an inaccuracy; an oversight; falsity; as, a clerical *error*; an *error* in a declaration.

3. A wandering; excursion; irregular course. [Obs.]

Driven by the winds and *errors* of the sea. —Dryden.

4. A transgression of law or duty; a mistake in conduct; a fault; a sin; iniquity; transgression.

If it were thine *error* or thy crime,
I care no longer. —Tennyson.

5. In law, a mistake in the proceedings of a court of record either in fact or in law, frequently of such a nature as to entitle the unsuccessful party to have the case reviewed.

6. In astronomy, the difference between the places of any of the heavenly bodies as determined by calculation and by observation.

7. In mathematics, the difference between the approximate result of any operation and the true result; called also *true error*.

8. In baseball, a fault of a player of the side which is in the field, whether a catcher, pitcher, baseman, or fielder, resulting in failure to put out an opposition player, or giving him a base or bases when perfect play would have insured his being put out.

Error of a clock; the difference between the time indicated by a clock and the time which the clock is intended to indicate, whether sidereal or mean time.

Law of error; a law which connects the relative magnitudes of errors with their frequency.

Probable error; see under *Probable*.

Writ of error; an original judicial writ or order, which lies after judgment in an action at law, in a court of record, under which an appellate court may review the proceedings of an inferior court as to questions of law only, apparent in the record, including exceptions noted and filed.

Syn.—Mistake, blunder, fallacy, bull, hallucination, fault, oversight, failure, delusion, sin.

er′rŏr-ful, *a.* Abounding in mistakes; full of errors.

er′rŏr-ist, *n.* One who errs or who encourages error.

ērs, *n.* [Fr. *ers*, from L. *ervum*, the bitter vetch.] The bitter vetch, *Vicia Ervilia*.

Ērse, *n.* [A corruption of *Irish*.] A name given to the language of the descendants of the Gaels or Celts in the Highlands of Scotland, as being of Irish origin. The Highlanders themselves call it *Gaelic*.

Ērse, *a.* Of or belonging to the Celts of Scotland or their language; as, the *Erse* tongue.

ērsh, ēarsh, *n.* [A contr. form of *eddish*, from AS. *edisc*, aftermath.] Stubble of grain.

ērst, *adv.* [ME. *erst*; AS. *ærest*, first.]

1. First; at first; at the beginning.

2. Once; formerly; long ago.

He pensive oft reviews the mighty dead
That *erst* have trod this desolated ground. —Langhorn.

3. Before; till then or now; hitherto.

At erst; at first; for the first time; sometimes it comes to mean at length, at present, especially with *now—now at erst*. [Obs. or Poet.]

ērst′while (-hwīl), *adv.* At one time; formerly.

ērst′while, *a.* Former; as, an *erstwhile* friend.

er-ū-bes′cence, er-ū-bes′cen-cy, *n.* [LL. *erubescentia*, blushing, from L. *erubescens* (*-entis*), ppr. of *erubescere*, to blush; *e*, out, and *rubescere*, to grow red, from *ruber*, red.] A becoming red; redness of the skin or surface of anything; a blushing.

er-ū-bes′cent, *a.* Growing red or reddish; blushing.

er-ū-bes′cīte, *n.* Same as *Bornite*.

e-rū′cȧ, *n.*; *pl.* **e-rū′cæ.** [L. *eruca*, a caterpillar.]

1. An insect in the larval state; a caterpillar.

2. [E—] A genus of plants, natural order *Cruciferæ*, found in the mountains of Europe and central Asia. *Eruca sativa* is the garden-rocket, which when young and tender is used as a salad, especially in continental Europe.

3. [E—] A genus of univalve mollusks.

e-rū′cic, *a.* Pertaining to or derived from plants of the genus *Eruca*; as, *erucic* acid, a crystalline compound obtained from rape-seed, mustard-oil, etc.

e-rū′ci-form, *a.* [L. *eruca*, a caterpillar, and *forma*, form.]

1. In entomology, having the form of a caterpillar, as the larva of the sawfly.

2. In botany, like a caterpillar in shape, as the spores of certain lichens.

ē-ruct′, *v.t.* Same as *Eructate*.

ē-ruc′tāte, *v.t.* [L. *eructare*, to belch or vomit forth; *e*, out, and *ructare*, to belch.] To belch; to cast forth or eject, as wind from the stomach.

Ætna in times past hath *eructated* such huge goblets of fire. —Howell.

er-uc-tā′tion, *n.* [LL. *eructatio* (*-onis*), a belching, from L. *eructare*, to belch.]

1. The act of belching wind from the stomach; a belch.

2. A violent bursting forth or ejection of gaseous or other matter from the earth.

e-rū′di-āte, *v.t.* To teach; to educate. [Obs.]

er′ū-dīte, *a.* [L. *eruditus*, learned, pp. of *erudire*, to instruct; *e*, out, and *rudis*, rude.] Having extensive knowledge; learned; deeply read; characterized by erudition.

er′ū-dīte, *n.* A learned person.

er′ū-dīte-ly, *adv.* With erudition; learnedly.

er′ū-dīte-ness, *n.* The quality of being erudite.

er-ū-di′tion (-dish′un), *n.* [L. *eruditio* (*-onis*), an instructing, from *erudire*, to instruct.] Learning; scholarship; knowledge gained by study or from books and instruction; particularly, learning in literature, history, antiquity, and languages, as distinct from the sciences.

Syn.—Literature, learning, lore, knowledge, instruction, acquirements, attainments, scholarship, cognition.

er′ū-gāte, *a.* [L. *erugatus*, pp. of *erugare*, to clear from wrinkles; *e*, from, and *ruga*, wrinkle.] Freed from wrinkles; smoothed; smooth.

e-rū′gi-nous, *a.* See *Æruginous*.

ē-rupt′, *v.t.* and *v.i.*; erupted, *pt.*, *pp.*; erupting, *ppr.* [L. *eruptus*, pp. of *erumpere*, to break out, burst forth; *e*, out, and *rumpere*, to break.]

I. *v.t.* To throw out suddenly and with great force; to emit violently; to cast out, as lava from a volcano.

II. *v.i.* To burst forth suddenly and violently; to send forth matter, as a geyser or volcano.

ē-rup′tion, *n.* [L. *eruptio* (*-onis*), from *erumpere*, to break out.]

1. The act of breaking or bursting forth from inclosure or confinement; a violent emission of anything, particularly of flames and lava from a volcano.

2. A sudden or violent invasion or display of armed force; sudden excursion.

Incensed at such *eruption* bold. —Milton.

3. In pathology, (a) the breaking out of a cutaneous disease; (b) the exanthema accompanying a disease, as the rash of scarlet fever.

ē-rup′tion-ăl, *a.* Eruptive.

ē-rup′tive, *a.* 1. Bursting forth.

2. Attended with eruption or rash, or producing it; as, an *eruptive* fever.

3. In geology, produced by eruption; as, *eruptive* rocks, such as the igneous or volcanic.

ē-rup′tive, *n.* In geology, any rock or mineral produced by the process of eruption.

-ery. A suffix from Fr. *-erie*, L. *-aria*, used to signify a business, place of business, or place where things are collected, as in groc*ery*, bak*ery*, cann*ery*, fern*ery*, hogg*ery*; also, wares collectively, as in pott*ery*, crock*ery*, etc.

Ē-ryn′gi-um, *n.* [L., from *eryngion*; Gr. *ēryngion*, a sort of thistle.] A genus of perennial herbs, natural order *Umbelliferæ*. There are more than 100 species, found in temperate and subtropical climates. The roots of *Eryngium maritimum*, a European species, were formerly candied as a sweetmeat, and were believed to possess strong aphrodisiac properties. Various other species are highly esteemed for their medicinal and flavoring properties.

ē-ryn′gō, *n.* A plant of the genus *Eryngium*.

er-y-sip′e-lăs, *n.* [OFr. *erysipele*; L. *erysipelas*; Gr. *erysipelas*, erysipelas; *erythros*, red, and *pella*, skin.] An acute infectious disease characterized by diffused inflammation of the skin, accompanied with fever; an eruption of a fiery acrid humor on some part of the body, but chiefly on the face and head; rose; St. Anthony's fire.

er″y-si-pel′ȧ-toid, *a.* [Gr. *erysipelas*, erysipelas, and *eidos*, form.] Resembling erysipelas.

er″y-si-pel′ȧ-tous, *a.* Eruptive; resembling erysipelas or partaking of its nature.

er-y-sip′e-lous, *a.* Same as *Erysipelatous*.

er-y-thē′mȧ, *n.* [L., from Gr. *erythēma*, a redness of the skin, from *erythainein*, *erythrainein*, to redden, blush, from *erythros*, red.] A superficial redness of some portion of the skin, varying in extent and form, as the blush of shame or anger.

er″y-thē-mat′ic, er-y-them′ȧ-tous, *a.* Pertaining to or attended by erythema.

er-y-them′ȧ-toid, *a.* [Gr. *erythēma*, redness of the skin, and *eidos*, form.] Resembling erythema.

e-ryth-r-. See *Erythro-*.

Er-y-thræ′ȧ, *n.* [L., from Gr. *erythraia*, f. of *erythraios*, *erythros*, red.] A genus of annual herbs, natural order *Gentianaceæ*, containing about thirty species, natives of the temperate regions of the northern hemisphere. The species are all extremely bitter. *Erythræa Centaurium*, or centaury, is common in Europe.

er-y-thrē′ăn, er-y-thræ′ăn, *a.* Of a red color.

e-ryth′ric, *a.* [Gr. *erythros*, red.] Pertaining to erythrin.

Erythric acid; an acid obtained from *Roccella tinctoria* and other lichens, which furnish the blue dyestuff called litmus. It possesses the property of forming red coloring-matters in contact with air and ammonia. Called also *erythrin* or *erythrine*.

e-ryth′rin, e-ryth′rine, *n.* 1. See *Erythric acid* under *Erythric*.

2. See *Erythrite*.

Er-y-thrī′nȧ, *n.* [L., from Gr. *erythros*, red.] A genus of tropical leguminous trees, with trifoliate leaves, and clusters of large, usually bright red flowers; commonly known as *coral-trees*.

e-ryth′rism, *n.* [Gr. *erythros*, red.] Excessive or abnormal redness, resulting from a condition of dichromatism; applied to certain birds, as the screech-owl, in the plumage of which there is an excess of red pigment, though their normal color is gray or brown.

e-ryth′rīte, *n.* [Gr. *erythros*, red.]

1. A flesh-colored feldspar, containing 3 per cent of magnesia, found in amygdaloid.

2. A crystalline substance contained in certain lichens, from which it is extracted with milk of lime; called also *erythrol*, etc.

3. A rose-red, hydrous arseniate of cobalt occurring in crystalline forms and also as a pulverulent incrustation; called also *cobalt-bloom* and *erythrin*.

e-ryth-rō-, e-ryth-r-. Combining forms from Greek *erythros*, red.

e-ryth′rō-blast, *n.* [*Erythro-*, and Gr. *blastos*, a bud.] One of the colored cells contained in the red marrow of bones and in other tissues, from which the red corpuscles of the blood are supposed to be developed.

e-ryth-rō-cär′pous, *a.* [*Erythro-*, and Gr. *karpos*, fruit.] Bearing red fruit, as certain lichens.

e-ryth-rō-chrō′ic, *a.* [*Erythro-*, and Gr. *chroa*, color.] Exhibiting excessive or abnormal redness in plumage or hair, as certain birds and mammals.

e-ryth-rō-chrō′ism, *n.* The condition of being erythrochroic.

e-ryth′rō-cyte, *n.* [*Erythro-*, and Gr. *kytos*, cavity.] A red blood-corpuscle.

e-ryth-rō-dex′trine, e-ryth-rō-dex′trin, *n.* [*Erythro-* and *dextrine*.] A variety or modification of dextrine, which is colored red or reddish-brown by iodine.

e-ryth′rō-gen, *n.* [*Erythro-*, and Gr. *-genēs*, producing.] In chemistry, a substance originally colorless but reddened by acids, supposed to be contained in flowers.

e-ryth-rō-gran′ū-lōse, *n.* [*Erythro-*, and LL. *granulum*, dim. of L. *granum*, grain.] A variety of granulose which is colored red by iodine.

er′y-throid, *a.* [Gr. *erythros*, red, and *eidos*, form.] Red or reddish in color.

er′y-thrōl, *n.* See *Erythrite*.

er-y-thrō′lē-ic, *a.* [*Erythro-*, and L. *oleum*, oil.] Of or pertaining to red, oily compounds; red in color and oily in appearance; specifically applied to an acid obtained from archil.

er-y-thrō′lē-in, *n.* A compound contained in litmus. It is soluble in alcohol, ether, and alkalis, giving a purple color.

e-ryth-rō-lit′min, *n.* [*Erythro-*, and L. *litmus*.] A compound contained in litmus. Its color is red, and it dissolves with a blue color in alkalis.

e-ryth″rō-me-lal′gi-ȧ, *n.* [*Erythro-*, and Gr. *melas*, black, and *algos*, pain.] In pathology, an affection of the feet or hands characterized by burning pains and purplish coloration.

Er-y-thrō′ni-um, *n.* [L., from Gr. *erythronion*, a kind of plant, from *erythros*, red.]

1. A genus of liliaceous plants, natives of temperate regions. One species is well known in cultivation under the name of *dogtooth violet*.

2. [e—] A name sometimes given to vanadate of lead. [Rare.]

e-ryth-rō-phlē′ine, *n.* A colorless crystalline alkaloid obtained from sassy-bark.

E-ryth-rō-phlœ′um (-flē′), *n.* [*Erythro-*, and

Gr. *phloios*, bark.] A genus of tropical trees, natural order *Leguminosæ*, containing three species, two found in Africa and the third in Australia. The *Erythrophlœum Guineense* or sassy-bark of Guinea is 100 feet high, and is noted for its poisonous red juice, which is used by the natives as a test of innocence and guilt.

e-ryth′rō-phyl, e-ryth′rō-phyll, *n.* [*Erythro-*, and Gr. *phyllon*, a leaf.] A term applied by Berzelius to the red coloring-matter of fruits and leaves in autumn.

er-y-throph′yl-lin, *n.* Same as *Erythrophyl.*

e-ryth′rō-sçōpe, *n.* [*Erythro-*, and Gr. *skopein*, to view.] An optical device of very simple construction, made by overlapping two plates of glass, one cobalt-blue in color and the other deep yellow, the colors of objects when viewed through it being apparently changed. The plates absorb some rays and transmit others, green foliage appearing red when viewed through these glasses, while the effects of light and shade remain.

e-ryth′rō-sin, *n.* [Gr. *erythros*, red.]

1. A red coloring-matter obtained from fluorescein by the action of iodine.

2. A red compound produced from tyrosin by oxidation.

e-ryth′rō-sis, *n.* [L., from Gr. *erythros*, red.] In pathology, a form of plethora, in which the blood is rich in fibrin and in bright red pigment.

Er-y-throx-yl′ē-æ, *n.pl.* [*Erythro-*, and Gr. *xylon*, wood.] A tribe of the natural order *Linaceæ*, the shrubs or small trees of which have alternate stipulate leaves, small pallid flowers, and drupaceous fruit.

Er-y-throx′y-lon, *n.* The principal genus of the tribe *Erythroxyleæ*, of the flax family. It contains about thirty species, natives chiefly of tropical America. *Erythroxylon Coca*, the most important of the species, yields the coca and cocaine of commerce.

e-ryth′rō-zym, *n.* [*Erythro-*, and Gr. *zymē*, leaven.] A name given to the peculiar fermentative substance of madder, which has the power of effecting the decomposition of rubian.

es-. [ME. *es-*, *as-*; OFr. *es-*, *as-*, from L. *ex-*, from *ex*, out, out of.] A modification of Latin *ex-* found in French and other Romance languages, as in *es*cheat, *es*coffier.

es-. [ME. *es-*; OFr. *es-*; LL. *i-s-*.] An apparent prefix of Romance origin; it was originally an initial *s* used before another consonant with *e* added for the purpose of euphony, as in *es*tray, *es*pecial, *es*tate, *es*carp, which also appear without the initial *e*, as *stray*, *state*, etc.

-es. [ME. *-es*, *-is*; AS. *-es*.] An early form of the possessive or genitive case now written *'s*; as, early form fox*es*, now written fox*'s*.

-es. [ME. *-es*, *-is*; AS. *-as*, the nom. and accus. plural of masc. and neut. nouns having vowel stems.] An early form of the plural suffix *-is*, used after a sibilant, as in ros*es*, church*es*, fox*es*.

-es. [ME. *-es* or *-s*.] The suffix of the third person singular of the present indicative of verbs which end in a vowel, as in go*es*, do*es*, etc.

-es. The nominative singular ending of some Latin nouns and adjectives of the third declension, as cæd*es*, sen*es*.

es″ca-drille′, *n.* [Fr. *escadrille*, small fleet.] An aeroplane unit in the army.

es-çà-lāde′, *n.* [OFr. *escalade*; Sp. *escalada*, an escalade, from *escalar*; LL. *scalare*, to climb, from L. *scala*, a ladder.] An attack made by troops on a fortified place, in which ladders are used to pass or mount its defenses; a mounting by means of ladders.

es-çà-lāde′, *v.t.*; escaladed, *pt.*, *pp.*; escalading, *ppr.* To scale; to mount and pass or enter by means of ladders; as, to *escalade* a wall.

es-çà-lā′tŏr, *n.* [Fr. *escalader*, to scale; *escalier*, a staircase, flight of stairs, from L. *scala*, a ladder.] Moving stairs; a flight of stairs, the steps of which are moved slowly by machinery.

Es-çal-lō′ni-à, *n.* [L., from *Escallon*, a Spanish traveler in South America.] A genus of trees or shrubs, natural order *Saxifragaceæ*, natives of South America. Some are cultivated.

es-çal′lŏp, es-çal′ŏp, *n.* and *v.* Same as *Scallop.*

es-çal-lō-pé′ (-pā′), *a.* In heraldry, same as *escalloped.*

es-çal′lŏped, es-çal′ŏped, *a.* [ME. *scalop*, *skalop*; OFr. *escalope*; M.D. *schelpe*, a shell.]

1. Cut or formed in the figure of a scallop; scalloped.

2. In heraldry, covered, as an escutcheon, with waving curved lines, resembling the outlines of scallop-shells, overlapping each other like slates on a roof.

Escalloped.

es-çam′bi-ō, *n.* [It. *escambio*, *scambio*, exchange.] In English law, a writ formerly granted to merchants to empower them to draw bills of exchange on persons beyond the sea.

es-çāp′à-ble, *a.* That may be escaped; avoidable.

es-çà-pāde′, *n.* [OFr. *escapade*, a prank, trick, from It. *scappata*, a flight, prank, escape.]

1. The fling of a horse or the kicking back of his heels.

2. A freak; a mad prank; a wild adventure.

es-çāpe′, *v.t.*; escaped (-kāpt′), *pt.*, *pp.*; escaping, *ppr.* [ME. *escapen*; OFr. *escaper*, to escape; LL. *ex capa*, out of cape; L. *ex*, out of, and LL. *capa*, cape, cloak.] To flee from and avoid; to get out of the way of; to shun; to be unnoticed by; to obtain security from; to pass without harm; to evade; to elude; as, to *escape* danger; to *escape* attention or notice.

> Be thou as chaste as ice, as pure as snow, thou shalt not *escape* calumny. —Shak.

es-çāpe′, *v.i.* 1. To flee away and be secure from danger; to be free or get free from any danger or injury; to hasten or get away; to be passed or to pass without harm.

> I *escaped* heart-free. —Tennyson.

> *Escape* to the mountain lest thou be consumed. —Gen. xix. 17.

2. To free oneself from custody or restraint; to regain one's liberty.

> Like the caged bird *escaping* suddenly. —Tennyson.

Syn.—Elude, evade, avoid, shun, decamp, flee, depart, abscond, break away.

es-çāpe′, *n.* 1. Flight to shun danger or injury; the act of fleeing from danger or custody.

> I would hasten my *escape* from the windy storm. —Ps. lv. 8.

2. The condition of being passed by without receiving injury when danger threatens; as, every soldier who survives a battle has had such an *escape*.

3. Excuse; subterfuge; evasion. [Obs.]

4. In law, an evasion of legal restraint or of custody without due course of law. *Escapes* are voluntary or involuntary; voluntary, when an officer permits an offender to quit his custody without warrant; and involuntary or negligent, when an arrested person quits the custody of the officer against his will.

5. Sally; flight; irregularity; escapade. [Obs.]

> Rome will despise her for this foul *escape*. —Shak.

6. That which escapes attention; oversight; mistake. [Obs.]

7. In architecture, an apophyge; a scape. [Rare.]

8. In botany, a plant found growing in a wild state in a district or country where originally it was only to be met with in a cultivated state.

9. Leakage or loss of various kinds, as of gas from a main, a current of electricity from a circuit owing to defective insulation, or steam from a valve or pipe.

10. A means of flight; as, a fire-*escape*.

es-çāpe′ment, *n.* [Fr. *échappement*.]

1. The act of escaping; escape. [Rare.]

2. The general contrivance in a timepiece by which the pressure of the wheels (which move always in one direction) and the vibratory motion of the pendulum or balance-wheel are accommodated the one to the other. By this contrivance the wheelwork is made to communicate an impulse to the regulating power (which in a clock is the pendulum and in a watch the balance-wheel), so as to restore to it the small portion of force which it loses in every vibration, in consequence of friction and the resistance of the air. Various kinds of *escapements* have been contrived: such as the crown or verge *escapement*, used in common watches; the anchor or crutch *escapement*, used in common clocks—both these are also termed recoiling *escapements*; the dead-beat *escapement* and the gravity or remontoir *escapement*, used in the finer kind of clocks; the horizontal or cylinder *escapement*, the detached *escapement*, the lever *escapement*, the duplex *escapement*, and the pinwheel *escapement*, all used in the finer classes of watches.

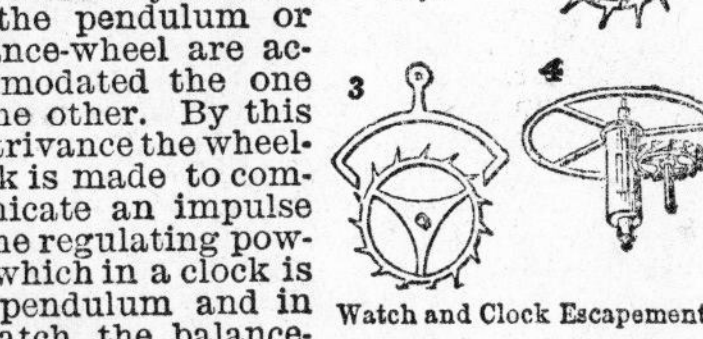

Watch and Clock Escapements.

es-çāpe′-pipe, *n.* In steam-boilers, a pipe used as an outlet for steam that escapes through a safety-valve; also, a pipe for carrying away any waste fluid.

es-çāp′ēr, *n.* One who or that which escapes.

es-çāpe′-valve, *n.* A valve at the end of a steam-cylinder for the escape of condensed steam.

es-çär′bun-çle, *n.* In heraldry, same as *carbuncle*.

es-çär′gà-toire (-twor), *n.* [Fr.] A nursery of snails. [Obs.]

es-çärp′, es-çärpe′, *n.* [Fr. *escarpe*, from *escarper*, to cut steep.] In fortification, that side of the ditch surrounding or in front of a work, and forming the exterior of the rampart; a scarp.

es-çärp′, *v.t.*; escarped (-kärpt′), *pt.*, *pp.*; escarping, *ppr.* In fortification, to slope; to make into a steep slope; to give a steep slope to.

es-çärp′ment, *n.* 1. In fortification, ground cut away nearly vertically about a position in order to prevent an enemy from arriving at the latter.

2. Hence, the precipitous side of any hill or rock; the abrupt face of a high ridge of land; a cliff.

-esce. A suffix from L. *-escere*, used to give an inceptive or inchoative force to verbs, as in convales*ce*.

-escence, -escent. Suffixes from L. *-escens* (*-entis*), ppr. of inceptive ending *-escere*, used to give inceptive force to nouns and adjectives, as in opal*escence*, effer*vescent*.

esch-à-lot′, *n.* Same as *Shallot.*

es′chär, *n.* [Gr. *eschara*, a fireplace, a scab or scar caused by a burn.] In pathology, the crust or scab occasioned on the skin by burns or caustic applications.

es′chär, *n.* See *Eskar.*

Es′çhà-rà, *n.* [L., from Gr. *eschara*, a scar, scab.] A genus of calcareous zoöphytes belonging to the class *Bryozoa* or *Polyzoa.*

es′çhà-rine, *a.* Pertaining to or resembling the genus *Eschara.*

es′çhà-roid, *a.* Same as *Escharine.*

es-çhà-rot′iç, *a.* Caustic; having the power of searing or destroying living tissue or flesh and of forming an eschar.

es-çhà-rot′iç, *n.* [Gr. *escharōtikos*, forming a scar, from *escharoun*, to form a scar, from *eschara*, a scar.] A caustic application; an application which sears or destroys flesh.

es″çhà-tō-log′iç, es″çhà-tō-log′iç-ăl, *a.* Pertaining to eschatology.

es-çhà-tol′ō-gist, *n.* One versed in or a student of eschatology.

es-çhà-tol′ō-gy, *n.* [Gr. *eschatos*, furthest, and *logos*, discourse.] The doctrine of the last or final things, as death, judgment, etc.

es-chaunge′, *n.* Exchange. [Obs.]

es-chēat′, *n.* [ME. *eschete*; OFr. *eschet*, lit., that which falls to one, rent, spoil, from pp. of *escheoir*, to fall to one's share, from LL. *excadere*, to fall upon; L. *ex*, out, and *cadere*, to fall.]

1. In England, the reverting of any land or tenements to the lord of the fee or to the state through failure of heirs. Lands, if freehold, escheat to the king or other lord of the manor; if copyhold, to the lord of the manor. By modern legislation there can be no *escheat* on failure of the whole blood wherever there are persons of the half-blood capable of inheriting.

2. In the United States, the reverting or falling back of real property to the state, as original and ultimate proprietor, in consequence of a failure of persons legally entitled to hold the same.

3. A writ to recover *escheats* from the person in possession.

4. The lands which fall to the lord or state by *escheat*.

5. That which falls to one; a reversion or return.

> To make one great by others' loss is bad *escheat*. —Spenser.

es-chēat′, *v.i.*; escheated, *pt.*, *pp.*; escheating, *ppr.* [OFr. *escheoiter*, to receive an escheat.] To revert or fall back by escheat; to suffer escheat.

es-chēat′, *v.t.* To forfeit.

> The ninepence, with which the little girl was to have been rewarded, being *escheated* to the Kenwigs family. —Dickens.

es-chēat′à-ble, *a.* Liable to escheat.

es-chēat′āge, *n.* The right of succeeding to an escheat.

es-chēat′ŏr, *n.* In England, an officer anciently appointed in every county to look after the escheats of the sovereign and certify them into the treasury.

es′chē-vin, *n.* The elder or warden who was principal of an ancient guild. [Obs.]

es-chew′, *v.t.*; eschewed, *pt.*, *pp.*; eschewing, *ppr.* [ME. *eschewen*; OFr. *eschuer*, to avoid, shun; O.H.G. *sciuhen*, to frighten, shun.]

1. To escape from; to avoid. [Obs.]

> He who obeys, destruction shall *eschew*. —Sandys.

2. To avoid; to shun; to refuse to use; to stand aloof from.

> Let us *eschew* these vulgar fineries of style. —Mathews.

es-chew′ănce, *n.* Avoidance.

es-chew′ēr, *n.* One who eschews.

es-chew′ment, *n.* The act of eschewing. [Rare.]

Esch-schōltz′i-à, *n.* [L., from name of Dr. von

Eschscholtz, a German naturalist.] A small genus of plants, natural order *Papaveraceæ* of western North America, of which the California poppy is the best known species.

es′çhy-nite, *n.* See *Æschynite.*

es-çlan′dre (-dẽr), *n.* [Fr.] Notoriety; disturbance; a disgraceful occurrence or scene.

es-çlā-väġe′ (-väzh′), *n.* [Fr. *esclavage*, slavery.] A necklace worn by ladies in the middle of the eighteenth century; probably so named from the resemblance of its festoons to the chains of a slave.

es-çoch′eŏn (-kuch′un), *n.* An escutcheon. [Obs.]

es-çō-pet′, es-çō-pette′, *n.* [Sp. *escopeta*, a firelock, a gun; It. *schioppetto*, dim. of *schioppo*, a gun, musket.] A short rifle or carbine.

es-çō′ri-ăl, *n.* [Sp.] 1. In western United States, a place where a mine has been exhausted.

2. Same as *Escurial.*

es′çort, *n.* [Fr. *escorte*; It. *scorta*, an escort, guide; L. *ex*, out, and *corrigere*, to set right, correct.]

1. A guard; a body of armed men which attends an officer, or baggage, provisions, or munitions, conveyed by land from place to place, to protect them from an enemy, or, in general, for security; also, a person or persons attending one as a mark of respect, honor, or attention.

2 In a more general sense, protection or safeguard on a journey or excursion; as, to travel under the *escort* of a friend.

es-çort′, *v.t.*; escorted, *pt., pp.*; escorting, *ppr.* [Fr. *escorter*; It. *scortare*, to escort.] To attend and guard on a journey by land; to accompany; as, General Washington was *escorted* by a detachment of dragoons; the guards *escorted* the Duke of Wellington; to *escort* a lady.

Syn.—Accompany, attend, go with, convoy, conduct.

es-çot′, *n.* [Obs.] See *Scot.*

es-çot′, *v.t.* To pay the reckoning for; to support. [Obs.]

es-çouāde′ (-kwäd′), *n.* [Fr.] Same as *Squad.*

es-çout′, *n.* [Obs.] See *Scout.*

es-çribe′, *v.t.*; escribed, *pt., pp.*; escribing, *ppr.* [L. *e*, out, from, and *scribere*, to write.] To draw (a circle) so as to touch one side of a triangle outside of the triangle, and the other two sides produced.

es′çript, *n.* A manuscript. [Obs.]

es-çri-toire′ (-twor′), *n.* [Fr. *écritoire*; OFr. *escriptoire*, a writing-desk, a writing-room; LL. *scriptorium*, a writing-room, from L. *scribere*, to write.] A piece of furniture with conveniences for writing; sometimes a desk or chest of drawers, with an apartment for writing instruments; secretary.

es-çri-tō′ri-ăl, *a.* Pertaining to an escritoire.

es-çrod′, *n.* A young cod. [See *Scrod.*]

es-çroll′, es-çrōl′, *n.* A scroll. [Obs.]

es′çrow, *n.* [OFr. *escroue*, a roll of writings, a bond, scroll.]

1. In law, a deed or other instrument delivered to a third person, to hold till some condition is performed by the grantee, and which is not to take effect till the condition is performed, when it is to be delivered to the grantee. —Blackstone.

2. The conditional execution and deposit of an instrument in such a way.

3. The custody of an instrument so deposited.

es′çū-āġe, *n.* [OFr. *escuage*, from *escu*, a shield.] In feudal law, service of the shield, called also *scutage*; a species of tenure by knight service, by which a tenant was bound to follow his lord to war; afterward exchanged for a pecuniary satisfaction. —Blackstone.

es-çū-de′rō, *n.* [Sp., from LL. *scutarius*, a shield-bearer, from L. *scutum*, a shield.] A shield-bearer; an esquire; hence, an attendant upon a person of rank; a lady's page.

es-çū′dō, *n.*; *pl.* **es-çū′dōs.** [Sp. *escudo*, a shield, a gold coin, from L. *scutum*, a shield.] A Spanish silver coin, the value of which is equivalent to about 50 cents in United States money.

Es-çū-lā′pi-ăn, *a.* and *n.* See *Æsculapian.*

Es-çū-lā′pi-us, *n.* See *Æsculapius.*

es′çū-lent, *a.* [L. *esculentus*, good to eat, from *esca*, food, from *edere*, to eat.] Eatable; fit to be used by man for food; edible; as, *esculent* plants; *esculent* fish.

Esculent swallow; the swallow or swift, *Collocalia esculenta*, whose edible nests are used in soup.

es′çū-lent, *n.* 1. Something that is eatable; that which is or may be safely eaten by man.

2. Specifically, an edible vegetable, as a radish or parsnip.

es-çū′liç, *a.* [L. *æsculus*, the tallest species of oak.] Pertaining to or derived from the horse-chestnut; as, *esculic* acid.

es′çū-lin, æs′çū-lin, *n.* [L. *æsculus*, the winter oak.] A crystalline bitter compound derived from the bark of the horse-chestnut, *Æsculus Hippocastanum*; called also *polychrome.*

Es-çū′ri-ăl, Es-çō′ri-ăl, *n.* [Sp. *escorial*, the place where a mine has been exhausted, from *escoria*; L. *scoria*, dross, rubbish.] A historic palace and mausoleum of the kings of Spain, about 27 miles northwest of Madrid, long regarded as the most superb structure in the kingdom, and one of the most splendid in Europe. It is built in a dry, barren spot, and was erected by Philip II., in honor of St. Lawrence.

es-çutch′eŏn (-kuch′un), *n.* [OFr. *escusson*, an escutcheon, from *escu*, *escut*; L. *scutum*, a shield.]

Escutcheon of Elizabeth, Queen of Henry VII.

1. The shield on which a coat of arms is represented; the shield of a family; the picture of ensigns armorial; the symbol of one's birth and dignity.

2. The panel on a ship's stern where her name is painted.

3. In carpentry, a plate for protecting or ornamenting the keyhole of a door, or to which the handle is attached; a scutcheon.

4. In zoölogy, the depression behind the beak of a bivalve mollusk which corresponds to the lunule or that in front of the beak.

5. A shield-like marking upon the rump of certain mammals, defined by the color or texture of the hair; especially conspicuous in the deer and antelope, and also in some breeds of domestic cattle.

Escutcheon of pretense; in heraldry, the small shield bearing the arms of an heiress placed in the center of her husband's shield, instead of being impaled with his arms.

es-çutch′eŏned (-kuch′und), *a.* Having a coat of arms or ensign.

ē-sçū′tel-lāte, *a.* In entomology, not having an apparent scutellum.

ēşe, *n.* Ease; pleasure. [Obs.]

ēşe′ment, *n.* Easement; relief. [Obs.]

es-em-plas′tiç, *a.* [Gr. *es*, into, *hen*, neut. of *heis*, one, and *plastikos*, skilful in molding, from *plassein*, to mold, form.] Molding, shaping, or fashioning into one. [Rare.]

ē-sep′tāte, *a.* [L. *e-* priv., and *septum*, a partition.] In botany and zoölogy, without partitions or septa.

es′ẽr-ine, *n.* [*Esere*, native African name for the plant, and *-ine.*] A resinous alkaloid obtained from the Calabar bean; used in ophthalmic surgery for its effect in contracting the pupil; called also *physostigmine.*

ē-sex′ū-ăl, *a.* Same as *Asexual.*

es-guärd′, *n.* Escort; guard. [Obs.]

es′kär, es′kẽr, *n.* [Ir. *eiscir*, a ridge.] A term for a late geological formation in the superficial drift, generally consisting of a long linear ridge of sand and gravel, including pieces of considerable size. The materials are derived from the waste of till or boulder-clay, and their arrangement took place probably under water over which icebergs floated, for in Sweden particularly rough erratic blocks are often deposited on the *eskar*. Called in Scotland *kame.*

Es′ki-mō, Es′qui-mau (-ki-mō), *n.*; *pl.* **Es′ki-mōş, Es′qui-maux** (-ki-mō). [Dan. *Eskimo*, from Am. Ind. *Eskimatsic*, *Askimeg*, eaters of raw flesh.] One of a race inhabiting the northern parts of North America and Greenland. They are the most considerable remnant in northern regions of that numerous prehistoric race of European fishers and hunters who were pushed to the verge of the great continents by the successive bands of the Aryan migrations.

Es′ki-mō, *a.* Of or pertaining to the Eskimos.

Eskimo dog; one of a breed of wolf-like dogs extensively spread over the northern regions of America and of eastern Asia. With a team of such dogs attached to his sledge the Eskimo will cover 60 miles a day for several successive days.

es-loin′, es-loyne′, *v.t.* [Fr. *éloigner*; OFr. *esloignier*, to remove.] To remove; to withdraw. [Obs.]

From worldly cares he did himself *esloyne.* —Spenser.

es′nē-cy, *n.* [OFr. *ainsneece*, the right of the firstborn, from LL. *antenatus*, firstborn; L. *ante*, before, and *natus*, pp. of *nasci*, to be born.] In English law, the right of the eldest coparcener, in the case where an estate descends to daughters jointly for want of a male heir, of making the first choice in the division of the inheritance.

ē-sod′iç, *a.* [Gr. *eis*, into, and *hodos*, a way.] In physiology, conducting influences to the spinal marrow; said of certain nerves.

ē-soph′ā-găl, *a.* Same as *Esophageal.*

ē-sō-phaġ′ē-ăl, ē-sō-phaġ′ē-ăn, *a.* In anatomy, pertaining to the esophagus; written also *œsophageal*, *œsophagean.*

ē-soph-ā-got′ō-my, *n.* [Gr. *oisophagos*, gullet, and *tomē*, a cutting.] In surgery, the operation of making an incision into the esophagus for the purpose of removing any foreign substance that obstructs the passage; written also *œsophagotomy.*

ē-soph′ā-gus, *n.* [L. *œsophagus*, from Gr. *oisophagos*, the gullet, lit., the passage for food; *oisein*, fut. inf. of *pherein*, to carry, and *phagein*, to eat.] The gullet; the canal through which food and drink pass to the stomach; written also *œsophagus.*

Ē-sō′pi-ăn, Ē-sop′iç, *a.* See *Æsopian, Æsopic.*

es-ō-ter′iç, es-ō-ter′iç-ăl, *a.* [Gr. *esōterikos*, from *esōteros*, inner, comp. of *esō*, within.]

1. Originally, a term applied to the private instructions and doctrines of Pythagoras, taught only to a select number, and not intelligible to the general body of disciples; hence, designed for and understood only by the initiated; private; opposed to *exoteric* or public.

2. Characterized by secrecy; private; confidential.

es-ō-ter′iç, *n.* 1. A believer in occult science.

2. A treatise on esoterics; esoteric doctrine or philosophy.

es-ō-ter′iç-ăl-ly, *adv.* In an esoteric manner.

es-ō-ter′i-cişm, *n.* 1. Esoteric practices, principles, or beliefs; occultism.

2. The tendency toward or taste for occultism.

es-ō-ter′içs, *n.* Mysterious or secret doctrines; occult science.

es′ō-ter-işm, *n.* Same as *Esotericism.*

es′ō-ter-y, *n.* [Gr. *esōteros*, inner.] Mystery; secrecy; occultism.

E′sox, *n.* [L. *esox*, a pike.] A genus of abdominal fishes of which there are several species, as the common pike, the fox-pike, the garfish, the pickerel, etc.

es-pāce′, *n.* Space. [Obs.]

es′pā-don, *n.* [Sp., a sword; L. *spatha*; Gr. *spathē*, a broadsword.]

1. A long sword of Spanish invention, used by foot-soldiers or for decapitation.

2. The swordfish.

es-pal′iẽr (-yẽr), *n.* [Fr. *espalier*; It. *spalliera*, a support for the shoulders, from *spalla*, the shoulder, from L. *spatula*, a broad piece, a blade.]

1. A latticework of wood, on which to train fruit-trees and ornamental shrubs.

2. A tree or row of trees trained on such a latticework.

es-pal′iẽr, *v.t.*; espaliered, *pt., pp.*; espaliering, *ppr.* To form an espalier of; to protect by an espalier.

es-pär′cet, *n.* [Fr *esparcette*; Sp. *esparceta*, sainfoin, from L. *spargere*, to scatter.] A kind of sainfoin, *Onobrychis sativa.*

es-pär′tō, *n.* [Sp. *esparto*; L. *spartum*; Gr. *sparton*, *spartos*, a kind of broom.] A name given to two or three species of grass, the *Macrochloa* (*Stipa*) *tenacissima*, *Macrochloa arenaria*, and *Lygeum Spartum* of botanists. They are found in the southern provinces of Spain and in North Africa. A large quantity of printing-paper is manufactured from *esparto* or from a mixture of *esparto* and rags, as also are cordage, shoes, matting, baskets, nets, mattresses, sacks, etc.

1. 3. 4. 2. 5.

Esparto Grasses.—1. *Macrochloa tenacissima* 2. Fruit of same. 3. *Lygeum Spartum.* 4. Flowering stem and (5) fruit of same.

es-pau-liere′ (-pō-lyãr′), *n.* [Fr.] Same as *Epauliere.*

es-pe′ciăl (-pesh′ăl), *a.* [ME. *especial*; OFr. *especial*; L. *specialis*, individual, particular, from *species*, kind.]

1. Distinguished in the same class or kind; principal; chief; particular; as, in an *especial* manner or degree.

Abraham, the *especial* friend of God. —Barrow.

2. Special; not general or indefinite; having reference to a particular thing or individual.

es-pe′ciăl-ly (-pesh′ăl-), *adv.* In an especial manner; principally; chiefly; particularly; in an uncommon degree; in reference to one person or thing in particular.

Syn.—Chiefly, mainly, particularly, principally, specially.

es-pe′ciăl-ness, *n.* The state of being especial. [Rare.]

es′pe-rançe, *n.* [Fr.] Hope. [Obs.]

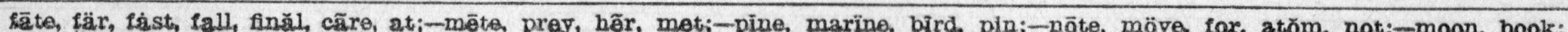

Es-pē-rän′-tō, *n.* An artificial language, designed for universal use, originated by Dr. Zamenhof, Russian. It is based on words common to the principal European languages, the sounds peculiar to any one tongue being eliminated. The spelling is phonetic, and all accents fall on the penult.

es-pī′ăl, *n.* [ME. *espiaile*, from *espien*; OFr. *espier*; O.H.G. *spehon*, to spy.]

1. A spy. [Obs.]

2. The act of espying; observation; discovery.

es-piè-gle-rie′ (es-pyā-gl-rē′), *n.* [Fr.] Frolicsome banter; teasing.

es-pī′ēr, *n.* [ME. *aspiere*, from *espien*, to spy.] One who espies, or watches like a spy.

es′pi-nel, *n.* A kind of ruby. [See *Spinel.*]

es′pi-ō-nāġe (*Fr. pron.* es′pe-on-äzh), *n.* [Fr. *espionnage*, from *espion*; It. *spione*, a spy.] The practice or employment of spies; the practice of watching the words and conduct of others, and trying to make discoveries by or as by means of spies or secret emissaries; the practice of watching others without being suspected, and giving intelligence of discoveries made; excessive surveillance.

es-plȧ-nāde′, *n.* [OFr. *esplanade*, from *esplaner*, to make level, to explain; L. *explanare*, to level, explain.]

1. In fortification, the glacis of the counterscarp, or the sloping of the parapet of the covered way toward the country; the open space between the glacis of a citadel and the first houses of the town.

2. Any open level space near a town, especially a kind of terrace along the seaside, for public walks or drives.

3. A grass-plat.

es-plees′, *n.pl.* [OFr. *esples*; LL. *expleta*, the products of land, from L. *expletus*, pp. of *explere*, to fill up.] In old English law, the products of land, as the hay of meadows, herbage of pasture, corn of arable lands, rents, services, etc.

es-pous′āge, *n.* Espousal. [Obs.]

es-pous′ăl, *a.* Used in or relating to the act of espousing or betrothing.

es-pous′ăl, *n.* [ME. *espousaile*; OFr. *espousailes*; L. *sponsalia*, a betrothal, from *sponsus*, f. *sponsa*, one betrothed, pp. of *spondere*, to betroth.]

1. The act of espousing or betrothing; formal contract or celebration of marriage; frequently used in the plural.

> I remember thee, the kindness of thy youth, the love of thine *espousals*. —Jer. ii. 2.

2. Adoption; protection.

es-pouse′, *v.t.*; espoused, *pt.*, *pp.*; espousing, *ppr.* [ME. *espousen*; OFr. *espouser*; LL. *sponsare*, to betroth; L. *spondere*, to promise solemnly, to betroth.]

1. To give as spouse or in marriage; to betroth; to promise, engage, or bestow in marriage, by contract in writing or by some pledge; to unite intimately or indissolubly; as, the king *espoused* his daughter to a foreign prince.

2. To take in marriage or as a spouse; to marry; to wed.

3. To make oneself a participator in; to become a partisan in; to take to oneself, or make one's own; to embrace; to adopt; as, to *espouse* the quarrel of another; to *espouse* a cause.

es-pouse′, *n.* A spouse. [Obs.]

es-pouse′ment, *n.* The act of espousing; also, the state of being espoused.

es-pous′ēr, *n.* One who espouses; also, one who defends or maintains something, as a cause.

es-pres-sī′vō, *a.* and *adv.* [It.] In music, expressive; with ardent expression; expressively.

es-prin′găl, **es-prin′găld**, *n.* A military engine. [See *Springal.*]

es-prit′ (-prē′), *n.* [Fr.] Spirit; wit.

Esprit de corps; a French phrase frequently used by English writers to signify an attachment to the class or body of which one is a member; the spirit of the body or society; the common spirit or disposition shared by men in association.

es-pȳ′, *v.t.*; espied, *pt.*, *pp.*; espying, *ppr.* [ME. *espyen*, to see at a distance; OFr. *espier*; O.H.G. *spehon*, to spy.]

1. To see at a distance; to have the first sight of, as a thing remote; as, seamen *espy* land as they approach it.

2. To see or discover (something intended to be hid, or in a degree concealed and not very distinct); to discover, as if unexpectedly or unintentionally; as, to *espy* a man in a crowd or a thief in a wood.

3. To inspect narrowly; to examine and make discoveries; to examine and keep watch upon.

> He sends angels to *espy* us in all our ways. —Jer. Taylor.

Syn.—Discern, descry, observe, discover, detect, see, perceive.

es-pȳ′, *v.i.* To look narrowly; to look about; to watch; to spy.

> Stand by the way and *espy*. —Jer. xlviii 19.

es-pȳ′, *n.*; *pl.* **es-pies′**. A spy; a scout; also, espial; espionage. [Obs.]

es-pȳ′ing-ly, *adv.* In a spying manner.

ē-squā′māte, *a.* [L. *e-* priv., and *squama*, scale.] In zoölogy, having no scales.

ē-squam′ū-lōse, *a.* In botany, having no squamulæ or minute scales.

-esque. A suffix from Fr. *-esque*; It. *-esco*; O.H.G. *-isc*, used in adjectives to signify likeness in manner or style, as in grot*esque*, statu*esque*.

Es′qui-mau (-ki-mō), *n.* See *Eskimo.*

es-quire′ (-kwīr′), *n.* [OFr. *esquier*, an esquire, shield-bearer; LL. *scutarius*, a squire, shield-bearer; L. *scutum*, a shield.]

1. Properly, a shield-bearer or armor-bearer; an attendant on a knight.

2. A title of dignity next in degree below a knight. In England, this title is properly given to the younger sons of noblemen, to officers of the king's courts and of the household, to counselors at law, justices of the peace while in commission, sheriffs, gentlemen who have held commissions in the army and navy, etc. It is also usually given to all professional and literary men. In the United States, the title, sometimes shortened to *squire*, is given especially to lawyers and justices of the peace, but in addressing letters, is bestowed on any person at pleasure, and contains no definite description. It is merely an expression of respect, and is commonly abbreviated *Esq.* or *Esqr.*

3. One who attends or escorts a lady or ladies in public.

es-quire′, *v.t.*; esquired, *pt.*, *pp.*; esquiring, *ppr.* To attend; to wait on; a colloquial expression of the eighteenth century, applied when a gentleman attended a lady in public.

es-quisse′ (-kēs′), *n.* [Fr.] In the fine arts, the first sketch of a picture or model of a statue.

-ess. A suffix from ME. *-esse*, *-isse*; L. *-issa*; Gr. *-issa*, added to any masculine to form a feminine noun, as in lion*ess*, author*ess*.

es-sāy′, *v.t.*; essayed, *pt.*, *pp.*; essaying, *ppr.* [ME. *assayen*; OFr. *asaier*, to try, attempt.]

1. To try; to attempt; to endeavor; to exert one's power or faculties upon; to make an effort to perform.

> Then in my madness I *essay'd* the door:
> It gave. —Tennyson.

2. To make experiment of.

3. To test the value and purity of (metals); to assay. [Obs.]

es′sāy, *n.* [ME. *assay*; OFr. *asai*, a trial, attempt, from LL. *exagium*, a trial of weight, from Gr. *exagion*, a weighing.]

1. A trial; attempt; endeavor; an effort made, or exertion of body or mind, for the performance of anything.

> Fruitless our hopes, though pious our *essays*. —Smith.

2. In literature, a composition intended to prove some particular point or illustrate a particular subject, usually shorter and less methodical and finished than a systematic or formal treatise; a short disquisition on a subject of taste, philosophy, or common life; as, an *essay* on the life and writings of Homer; an *essay* on fossils; an *essay* on commerce.

3. A trial or experiment; a test.

> I hope, for my brother's justification, he wrote this but as an *essay* or taste of my virtue. —Shak.

4. An assay or test of the qualities of a metal. [Obs.]

Syn.—Attempt, trial, endeavor, effort, treatise, dissertation, paper, tract.

es-sāy′ēr, *n.* 1. One who essays or attempts to do something; one who makes trial.

2. One who writes essays; an essayist.

es′sāy-ist, *n.* A writer of an essay or of essays.

es′sence, *n.* [Fr. *essence*; L. *essentia*, the being or essence of a thing, from *esse*, to be.]

1. In metaphysics, that which constitutes the particular nature of a being or substance, or of a genus, and which distinguishes it from all others.

> Whatever makes a thing to be what it is, is properly called its *essence*. Self-consciousness, therefore, is the *essence* of the mind, because it is in virtue of self-consciousness that the mind is the mind—that a man is himself. —Ferrier.

2. Existence; the quality of being.

> I could have resigned my very *essence*. —Sidney.

3. A being; particularly, a purely spiritual being; as, heavenly *essences*.

4. Constituent substance; as, the pure *essence* of a spirit.

5. The predominant elements or principles of any plant or drug, extracted, refined, or rectified from grosser matter; or, more strictly, a volatile or essential oil; as, the *essence* of mint; *essence* of coffee.

6. Perfume; odor; scent; the volatile matter constituting perfume.

> Nor let the imprisoned *essences* exhale. —Pope.

7. The distinctive features or characteristics; the most important or fundamental doctrines, facts, ideas, or conclusions; as, the newspaper gave the *essence* of the lecture or the book.

es′sence, *v.t.*; essenced (-senst), *pt.*, *pp.*; essencing, *ppr.* To perfume; to scent.

Es-sēne′, *n.* [LL. *Esseni*; Gr. *Essenoi*, the Essenes.] A member of a peculiar Jewish sect, of the second century, B. C., remarkable for abstinence and general strictness of living.

Es′se-nism, *n.* The teachings and customs of the Essenes.

es-sen′tiăl (-shăl), *a.* [LL. *essentialis*, from L. *essentia*, the essence.]

1. Necessary to the constitution or existence of a thing; pertaining to the essence of an individual, a genus, or a class of objects; as, an *essential* property; an *essential* quality.

> And if each system in gradation roll,
> Alike *essential* to the amazing whole.—Pope.

2. Important in the highest degree; indispensable.

> Judgment is more *essential* to a general than courage. —Denham.

3. Volatile; diffusible; pure; highly rectified; as, *essential* oils.

4. In medicine, idiopathic; not symptomatic; said of a disease.

5. In music, indispensable; said of those tones which constitute a chord and are independent of passing tones.

6. Pertaining to an essence; of the nature of an essence or extract.

Essential character; in natural history, that single quality or property which serves to distinguish one genus, species, etc., from another.

Essential oils; oils which are distilled or expressed from aromatic plants. They dissolve in alcohol, are inflammable, and much used in perfumery.

Syn.—Necessary, requisite, indispensable, vital, leading, inherent, radical.

es-sen′tiăl, *n.* 1. Existence; being. [Obs.]

2. A fundamental or constituent principle; a distinguishing characteristic; as, the *essentials* of religion.

3. A necessary element or factor.

es-sen-ti-al′i-ty (-shi-al′), *n.* The quality of being essential.

es-sen′tiăl-ly, *adv.* 1. By the constitution of nature; in essence; as, minerals and plants are *essentially* different.

2. In an important degree; in effect; fundamentally; as, the two statements differ, but not *essentially*.

es-sen′tiăl-ness, *n.* Same as *Essentiality.*

es-sen′ti-āte, *v.t.*; essentiated, *pt.*, *pp.*; essentiating, *ppr.* To form or constitute the essence or being of. [Obs.]

es-sen′ti-āte, *v.i.* To become of the same essence. [Obs.]

ess′ling, *n.* A young salmon. [Eng.]

es-soin′, **es-soign′**, *n.* [ME. *essoyne*; OFr. *essoine*, an excuse, exemption; *es-*, from, and *soin*, care; L. *exonerare*, to relieve from a burden; *ex*, from, and *onus*, burden.]

1. In old English law, the alleging of an excuse for one who is summoned to appear in court and answer, and who neglects to appear on the day specified.

2. Excuse; exemption. [Obs.]

3. One who is excused for nonappearance in court on the day appointed.

es-soin′, *v.t.* In old English law, to excuse for nonappearance in court.

es-soin′ēr, *n.* In law, one who essoins; an attorney who sufficiently excuses the absence of another.

es′so-nīte, *n.* Cinnamon-stone, a kind of garnet; also written *hessonite*.

es′sō-rănt, *a.* [Fr. *essorant*, ppr. of *essorer*, to soar.] In heraldry, a term applied to a bird standing with its wings half open, as if preparing to take flight.

ēst, *n.* and *adv.* [ME.] East. [Obs.]

-est. A suffix from ME. *-est*, AS. *-est*, used with adjectives to form the superlative.

es-tab′lish, *v.t.*; established (-lisht), *pt.*, *pp.*; establishing, *ppr.* [ME. *establissen*; OFr. *establir*; L. *stabilire*, to make stable, from *stabilis*, stable.]

1. To make steadfast, firm, or stable; to settle on a firm or permanent basis, either to originate and settle, or to settle what is already originated; to set or fix unalterably.

2. To institute and ratify; to enact or decree authoritatively and for permanence; to ordain.

> I will *establish* my covenant with him for an everlasting covenant. —Gen. xvii. 19.

3. To confirm or ratify (what has previously been instituted, settled, or ordained); to fix (what is wavering, doubtful, or weak); to strengthen; to confirm.

So were the churches *established* in the faith. —Acts xvi. 5.

4. To found permanently; to institute or settle; as, to *establish* a colony or an empire.

5. To set up in connection with the state and endow; as, to *establish* a church.

6. To place in a secure or favorable position; to make safe against harm, loss, defeat, and the like; to set up in business; often with reflexive pronoun; as, the father *established* his son as a merchant; the enemy *established themselves* in the citadel.

7. To prove legally; to cause to be recognized as legal and valid; to cause to be accepted; as, to *establish* a marriage; to *establish* a case; to *establish* a theory.

8. To fulfil; to make good; to carry out.

O king, *establish* the decree. —Dan. vi. 8.

9. To settle, as property.

Syn.—Plant, fix, settle, found, demonstrate, organize, confirm, institute, prove, substantiate, constitute.

es-tab′lish-ẽr, *n.* One who establishes, ordains, or confirms.

es-tab′lish-ment, *n.* [OFr. *establissement*, from *establis*, to establish.]

1. The act of establishing.

2. The state of being established; settlement; fixed state; confirmation; ratification of what has been settled or made.

We set up our hopes and *establishment* here. —Wake.

3. Settled regulation; form; ordinance; system of laws; constitution of government.

4. Fixed or stated allowance for subsistence; income; salary.

His excellency might gradually lessen your *establishment*. —Swift.

5. A permanent civil or military force or organization, such as a fixed garrison or a local government; as, the nation has *establishments* to support at home and abroad.

6. That form of doctrine and church government established and endowed by the legislature in any country.

7. The place where a person is settled either for residence or for transacting business; a person's residence and everything connected with it, such as furniture, servants, carriages, grounds, etc.; an institution, whether public or private.

8. The quota or number of men in an army, regiment, etc.; as, a peace *establishment*.

Establishment of the port; the mean interval between the time of high water at any given port and the time of the moon's transit immediately preceding the time of high water at the new or full moon. This interval is influenced by local circumstances and consequently different at different places.

es-tab″lish-men-tā′ri-ăn, *n.* One who supports the doctrine of establishment in religion, or some particular established church.

es-tȧ-çāde′, *n.* [Fr. *estacade*; Sp. *estacada*, a paling, palisade, from *estacar*, to stake in; from *estaca*, a stake.] A palisade; a stockade; a dike set with piles in the sea, a river, or a morass, to check the approach of an enemy.

es-tȧ-fet′, es-tȧ-fette′, *n.* [Fr. *estafette*; It. *staffetta*, a courier, from *staffa*, a stirrup; from O.H.G. *stapho*, *staph*, a step.] A military courier; an express of any kind.

es″tȧ-mi-net′ (-nā′), *n.* [Fr.] A café or coffeehouse where smoking is allowed; a taproom.

es-tan′ci-ȧ, *n.* [Sp.] A mansion; a dwelling; also, landed property, as a cattle-farm; a cattle-ranch; a country estate.

es-tan-ci-e′rō, *n.* [Sp.] The owner or overseer of an estancia; a Spanish-American cattle-raiser.

es-tāte′, *n.* [ME. *estat*; OFr. *estat*; L. *status*, a state, condition, from *stare*, to stand.]

1. Condition or circumstances of any person or thing, state; situation; state of a person as regards external circumstances.

Whose life in low *estate* began.—Tennyson.

2. Rank; quality.

Who hath not heard of the greatness of your *estate*? —Sidney.

3. In law, the interest or quantity of interest an owner has in lands, tenements, or other effects. *Estates* are real or personal. *Real estate* comprises lands, tenements, etc; *personal estate* comprises property of every other description.

4. Fortune; possessions; property in general, especially property left at a man's death; as, his *estate* was of the value of half a million; the trustees proceeded to realize the *estate*.

5. A piece of landed property; a definite portion of land in the ownership of some one; as, there is more wood on his *estate* than on mine.

6. The state; the body politic; the commonwealth; the public; public interest. [Obs.]

7. An order or class of men constituting a part of the state, or represented in the government. In Great Britain the *estates* of the realm are the lords spiritual, the lords temporal, and the commons.

8. A person of high rank. [Obs.]

She is a duchess, a great *estate*. —Latimer.

The fourth estate; the newspaper press; journalists collectively; a humorous designation referring to the public influence wielded by the press.

es-tāte′, *v.t.*; estated, *pt.*, *pp.*; estating, *ppr.*

1. To settle an estate upon; to endow with an estate or other property.

2. To settle as a possession; to bestow. [Rare.]

All the revenue that was old Sir Rowland's will I *estate* upon you. —Shak.

3. To establish. [Obs.]

es-tāte′ly, *a.* Stately. [Obs.]

es-teem′, *v.t.*; esteemed, *pt.*, *pp.*; esteeming, *ppr.* [Fr. *estimer*; L. *æstimare*, to value, consider, estimate.]

1. To set a value on, whether high or low; to estimate; to value.

They that despise me shall be lightly *esteemed*. —1 Sam. ii. 30.

2. To prize; to set a high value on; to regard with reverence, respect, or friendship; as, we *esteem* the industrious, the generous, the brave, the virtuous, and the learned.

3. To consider; to regard; to reckon; to deem; as, I *esteem* it an honor to serve you.

Syn.—Appreciate, prize, regard, respect, revere, value, think, account, deem, consider.

es-teem′, *v.i.* To consider value; to form an estimate; with *of*.

We ourselves *esteem* not *of* that obedience or love or gift. —Milton.

es-teem′, *n.* 1. Estimation; opinion or judgment of merit or demerit; as, this man is worthless in my *esteem*.

2. High value or estimation; great regard; favorable opinion, founded on supposed worth; as, he was held in high *esteem*.

3. Valuation; price. [Obs.]

Syn.—Estimate, estimation, respect, regard, honor, admiration, reverence, veneration.

es-teem′ȧ-ble, *a.* Worthy of esteem; estimable. [Rare.]

es-teem′ẽr, *n.* One who esteems; one who sets a high value on anything.

A proud *esteemer* of his own parts.—Locke.

es′tẽr, *n.* Compound ether. [See under *Ether*.]

es″thē-mȧ-tol′ō-ġy, *n.* See *Æsthematology*.

es-thē′si-ȧ, *n.* See *Æsthesia*.

es-thē-si-om′e-tẽr, *n.* See *Æsthesiometer*.

es-thē′sis, *n.* See *Æsthesis*.

es′thēte, *n.* See *Æsthete*.

es-thet′iç, *a.* and *n.* See *Æsthetic*.

es-thet′iç-ăl, *a.* See *Æsthetical*.

es-thet′iç-ăl-ly, *adv.* See *Æsthetically*.

es-thē-ti′ciăn, *n.* See *Æsthetician*.

es-thet′i-ciṣm, *n.* See *Æstheticism*.

es-thet′iḉs, *n.* See *Æsthetics*.

es-thē-tol′ō-ġy, *n.* [Gr. *aisthētos*, perceptible, and *logos*, description.] The science which treats of the nature, history, and development of the fine arts, as distinguished from the science of the useful arts or technology; the science of the beautiful.

es″thō-phyṣ-i-ol′ō-ġy, *n.* See *Æstho-physiology*.

es-tif′ẽr-ous, æs-tif′ẽr-ous, *a.* [L. *æstus*, heat, and *ferre*, to produce.] Producing heat. [Rare.]

es′ti-mȧ-ble, *a.* [Fr. *estimable*; L. *æstimabilis*, worthy of estimation, from *æstimare*, to estimate, value.]

1. Capable of being estimated or valued; as, *estimable* damage.

2. Valuable; worth a great price. [Rare.]

A pound of man's flesh, taken from a man,
Is not so *estimable*. —Shak.

3. Worthy of esteem or respect; deserving good opinion or regard; as, an *estimable* friend.

es′ti-mȧ-ble, *n.* One who or that which is worthy of regard.

es′ti-mȧ-ble-ness, *n.* The quality of deserving esteem or regard.

es′ti-mȧ-bly, *adv.* In an estimable manner.

es′ti-māte, *v.t.*; estimated, *pt.*, *pp.*; estimating, *ppr.* [L. *æstimatus*, pp. of *æstimare*, to esteem, value.] To form a judgment or opinion regarding the value, size, weight, degree, extent, quantity, etc., of; to rate by judgment, opinion, or a rough calculation; to fix the worth of, to compute; to calculate; to reckon; as, to *estimate* the value of a piece of cloth, the extent of a piece of land, the worth of a friend, the merits or talents of two different men, or profits, loss, and damage.

Syn.—Calculate, value, compute, rate, appraise, measure, reckon, esteem, count, number.—We *esteem* a man for his moral qualities; we *estimate* a person or thing according to our views of real value. The former implies respect and attachment; the latter is a mere exercise of judgment or computation.

es′ti-māte, *n.* A valuing or rating in the mind; an approximate judgment or opinion as to value, degree, extent, quantity, etc.; a value determined by judgment, where exactness is not sought or is not attainable.

Shrewd, keen, practical *estimates* of men and things. —Black.

Syn.—Esteem, estimation.—*Estimate* supposes an exercise of the judgment in determining the amount, value, importance, or magnitude of things, and is especially used of relations that may be expressed numerically; *esteem* is a moral sentiment made up of respect and attachment; it is the result of the mental process of reckoning up the merits or useful qualities of an individual, and is the opinion of an individual arrived at by such process; *estimation*, properly the act of appraising or valuing, is used generally in the sense of *esteem*, though sometimes in that of *estimate*.

es-ti-mā′tion, *n.* [ME. *estymacyon*; L. *æstimatio (-onis)*, a valuation, from *æstimare*, to value, esteem.]

1. The act of estimating.

2. Calculation; computation; an opinion or judgment of the worth, extent, or quantity of anything formed without using precise data; as, an *estimation* of distance, magnitude, or amount; an *estimation* of moral qualities.

3. Esteem; regard; favorable opinion; honor.

I shall have *estimation* among the multitude, and honor with the elders. —Wisdom.

4. Conjecture; supposition; surmise; as, to speak in *estimation*. [Rare.]

5. In chemistry, the act or process of ascertaining by analysis the amount of one or more of the constituents contained in a substance or compound.

Syn.—Supposition, computation, estimate, calculation, appraisement, honor, regard, esteem.

es′ti-mā-tive, *a.* 1. Having the power of estimating, comparing, or judging.

2. Imaginative; contemplative. [Rare.]

3. Pertaining to or based on an estimate. [Rare.]

es′ti-mā-tŏr, *n.* [L. *æstimator*, from *æstimare*, to value, estimate.] One who estimates or appraises.

es′ti-vāġe, *n.* [Fr., from *estiver*; L. *stipare*, to pack.] A mode of stowing or trimming vessels by pressing or screwing the cargo into the vessel by means of capstan machinery; called also *estive*.

es′ti-văl, æs′ti-văl (es′), *a.* [LL. *æstivalis*, from L. *æstivus*, pertaining to summer, from *æstas*, summer.] Pertaining to summer or continuing for the summer.

es′ti-vāte, æs′ti-vāte, *v.i.* [L. *æstivatus*, pp. of *æstivare*, to spend the summer.] To pass the summer.

es-ti-vā′tion, æs-ti-vā′tion, *n.* 1. The act of passing the summer.

On the under story, toward the garden, let it be turned into a grotto, or place of shade or *estivation*. —Bacon.

2. In botany, the disposition of the petals within the bud; prefloration.

3. In zoölogy, the dormancy or more or less permanent condition of sleep of certain animals in summer, as land-snails or mollusks.

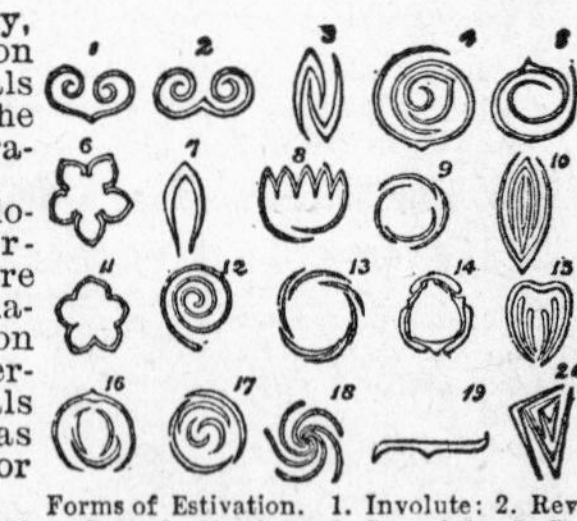

Forms of Estivation. 1. Involute; 2. Revolute; 3. Obvolute; 4. Convolute; 5. Supervolute; 6. Induplicate; 7. Conduplicate; 8. Plaited; 9. Imbricated; 10 and 20. Equitant; 11. Valvate; 12. Circinate, 13. Twisted; 14. Alternative; 15. Vexillary; 16. Cochlear; 17. Quincunx; 18. Contorted; 19. Curvative; 20. Equitant.

es′tive, *n.* See *Estivage*.

es′toç, *n.* [OFr., from G. *stock*, a stock.] A short sword used in medieval wars, worn at the girdle by mounted soldiers; a primitive form of rapier.

es-tō-çāde′, *n.* [Fr., a sword-thrust, from *estoc*, a sword.] A thrust with an estoc or early form of rapier; also, an estoc or thrusting sword.

es-toile′ (-twol′), *n.* [OFr., from L. *stella*, a star.] In heraldry, a star with six, eight or more waved points; distinguished from a mullet, which has only five, and these straight; written also *etoile*.

Estoile.

es-top′, *v.t.*; estopped (-topt′), *pt.*, *pp.*; estopping, *ppr.* [OFr. *estoper*; LL. *stupare*, to stop with tow, cram, from L. *stupa*, oakum, tow.]

1. In law, to impede or bar by one's own act.

A man shall always be *estopped* by his own deed, or not permitted to aver or prove anything in contradiction to what he has once solemnly avowed. —Blackstone.

2. To bar; to stop; to debar.

es-top'pel, *n.* 1. In law, a stop; a plea in bar, grounded on a man's own act or deed, which estops or precludes him from averring anything to the contrary.

2. Stoppage; impediment.

es-tō'vērs, *n.pl.* [OFr. *estover, estovoir,* necessity, need, a substantive use of the inf. *estover, estovoir,* to be necessary.] In law, necessaries or supplies; a reasonable allowance out of lands or goods for the use of a tenant; such as sustenance for the family of a felon during his imprisonment, alimony for a woman divorced, out of her husband's estate, etc.

Common of estovers; see *Common*, n. 2.

es-trāde', *n.* [Fr., from Sp. *estrado*, a drawing-room, from L. *stratum*, a pavement, floor, bed or couch covering, neut. of *stratus*, pp. of *sternere*, to strew.] An elevated part of the floor of a room; an even or level place; a kind of platform.

es-trad'i-ot, *n.* [OFr. *estradiot*; Gr. *stratiōtēs*, a soldier.] An Albanian dragoon or light-horseman, employed in the French and other European armies in the fifteenth and sixteenth centuries. The *estradiots* sometimes fought on foot as well as on horseback, and wore a semi-oriental dress.

An Estradiot, from Boissard.

es-tram'à-çon (-son), *n.* [Fr., from It. *stramazzone*, a cut with a sword.]

1. A sort of two-edged sword used in the middle ages.

2. A slash or pass with a sword.

es-trānge', *v.t.*; estranged, *pt., pp.*; estranging, *ppr.* [OFr. *estranger*, to alienate, from *estrange*, strange; L. *extraneus*, foreign, from *extra*, beyond, without.]

1. To keep at a distance; to withdraw; to cease to frequent and be familiar with; often with the reflexive pronoun.

Had we *estranged* ourselves from them in things indifferent. —Hooker.

2. To alienate; to divert from its original use or possessor; to apply to a purpose foreign to its original or customary one.

They have *estranged* this place and burnt incense in it unto other gods. —Jer. xix. 4.

3. To alienate the affections of; to turn from kindness to indifference or malevolence.

I do not know, to this hour, what it is that has *estranged* him from me. —Pope.

4. To withdraw; to withhold.

We must *estrange* our belief from what is not clearly evidenced. —Glanville.

es-trān'ged-ness, *n.* The state of being estranged.

es-trānge'ment, *n.* The act of estranging or state of being estranged; alienation; a keeping at a distance; removal; voluntary abstraction; as, an *estrangement* of affection.

es-trān'gēr, *n.* One who estranges.

es-tran'gle, *v.t.* To strangle. [Obs.]

es-trà-pāde', *n.* [Fr., from OFr. *strappare*, to pull, break.] The action of a horse, when, to get rid of his rider, he rears, plunges, and kicks furiously. [See fifth *Buck*, 2.]

es-trāy', *v.i.* To stray. [Obs.]

es-trāy', *n.* [Fr. *estraie*, pp. of *estraier*, to stray.] Any domestic animal of value, as a horse, ox, or sheep, which is found wandering or without an owner; a beast supposed to have strayed from the power or inclosure of its owner; a stray.

es'tre (-tēr), *n.* An inward part of a building. [Obs.]

Tho *estres* of the grisly place. —Chaucer.

es-trēat', *n.* [OFr. *estret*, an abstract, extract, from *estraire*; L. *extrahere*, to draw out; *ex*, out, from, and *trahere*, to draw.] In English law, a true copy or duplicate of an original writing, especially of amercements or penalties levied by a court.

es-trēat', *v.t.*; estreated, *pt., pp.*; estreating, *ppr.* In English law, (a) to extract or copy from records of a court of law, as a forfeited recognizance, and return to the court of exchequer for prosecution; (b) to levy (fines) under an estreat.

es-trēpe', *v.i.*; estreped (-trēpt'), *pt., pp.*; estreping, *ppr.* [OFr. *estreper*, to waste, destroy; L. *extirpare*, to uproot; *ex*, from, and *stirps*, root.] In law, to commit waste or destruction, as by depriving trees of their branches, lands of their trees, houses, etc.

es-trēpe'ment, *n.* [OFr. *estrepement*, spoil, waste, from *estreper*, to waste.] In law, spoil; waste; a stripping of land by a tenant, to the prejudice of the owner.

es'trich, es'tridge, *n.* 1. The ostrich. [Obs.]

2. The fine soft down which lies immediately under the feathers of the ostrich; a commercial name.

es'trō, *n.* [L. *œstrus*; Gr. *oistros*, a gadfly.]

1. A gadfly; an œstrus.

2. Irresistible impulse; ardor; inspiration.

es'tū-ānce, *n.* Heat. [Obs.]

es-tū-ā'ri-ăn, *a.* Same as *Estuarine*.

es'tū-ā-rine, *a.* Of or pertaining to an estuary; formed in an estuary.

es'tū-ā-ry, *n.*; *pl.* **es'tū-ā-ries.** [L. *œstuarium*, part of the seacoast over which the tide ebbs and flows, from *œstus*, the tide.]

1. A boiling spring. [Obs.]

2. An arm of the sea; a frith or firth; a narrow passage, or the mouth of a river or lake, where the tide meets the current, or flows and ebbs.

es'tū-ā-ry, *a.* Belonging to or formed in an estuary; as, *estuary* strata.

es'tū-āte, *v.i.* See *Æstuate*.

es-tū-ā'tion, *n.* See *Æstuation*.

es-tù'fà, *n.* [Sp., a stove, a warm room.] An assembly room or council chamber, usually wholly or in part underground, in which heat or fire is steadily maintained, used by the Pueblo Indians as a general meeting-place, and formerly for religious purposes.

es'tūre, *n.* [Obs.] See *Æsture*.

ē-sū'ri-ent, *a.* [L. *esuriens (-entis)*, ppr. of *esurire*, to be hungry.]

1. Inclined to eat; hungry. [Rare.]

2. Greedy, as for riches, honor, or luxury.

ē-sū'ri-ent, *n.* A hungry or greedy person. [Rare.]

es'ū-rine, *a.* Eating; corroding. [Obs.]

es'ū-rine, *n.* In medicine, a substance, acid to the taste, which promotes appetite or causes hunger. [Obs.]

-et. A suffix from ME. *-et*; OFr. *-et*, masc., *-ete*, f., added to nouns to give a diminutive force, as in rivul*et*, latch*et*.

ē-tāag', *n.* The blauwbok.

ē'tà-cism, *n.* [From the Gr. letter η, *ēta*.] The pronunciation of the seventh letter of the Greek alphabet, like *a* in *fate*.

ē'tà-cist, *n.* One who practises or favors etacism.

é-tà-gère' (ā-tà-zhâr'), *n.* [Fr., from *étager*, to elevate by stories or stages, from *étage*, a story.] A piece of domestic furniture supplied with several shelves one above another, as a sideboard, a whatnot, etc.

et'à-mine, *n.* [Fr.] A light woolen dress-goods of a canvas weave; also written *tamin*.

e-tape', *n.* [Fr.] 1. A public warehouse for goods.

2. An allowance of provisions, forage, etc., for troops at temporary stopping-places during a march.

3. In Russia or Siberia, a prison-like building with a stockaded yard, for the temporary confinement and shelter of convicts or exiles in transit under guard.

é-tät'=ma-jor' (ā-tä'ma-zhor'), *n.* [Fr.] The staff of an army or a regiment; the general staff.

et cet'e-rà. [L., and other things; *et*, and, and *cetera*, nom. pl. neut. of *ceterus*, other, another.] And others of the like kind; and so forth; and so on; generally used when a number of individuals of a class have been specified, to indicate that more of the same sort might have been mentioned, but for shortness have been omitted; as, stimulants comprise brandy, rum, whisky, wine, beer, *et cetera*. Written also *etcætera*, *etcetera*, and contracted, *etc.*, *&c.* It is sometimes treated as a noun, forming the plural with *s*.

Come we to full points here, and are *etceteras* nothing? —Shak.

etch, *n.* Same as *Eddish*.

etch, *v.t.*; etched (etcht), *pt., pp.*; etching, *ppr.* [D. *etsen*; G. *ätzen*, to feed, corrode, from M.H.G. *etzen*, to cause to eat.]

1. To produce, as figures or designs, upon a plate of steel, copper, glass, or the like, by means of lines or markings drawn through a coating or varnish covering the plate and corroded or bitten in by some strong acid, which can only affect the plate where the varnish has been removed. The word as used by engravers in recent times generally means simply to draw through the ground or coating with the etching-needle the lines forming the shading. Either the plate or the design may be said to be *etched*.

2. To sketch; to delineate. [Rare.]

3. To subject to the process of etching; to draw upon and corrode with acid; as, to *etch* a metal plate.

etch, *v.i.* To practise etching; to produce etchings.

etch'ēr, *n.* One who etches.

etch'ing, *n.* 1. The act, art, process, or practice of producing designs upon a metal or glass plate by means of lines drawn through a kind of varnish with a pointed instrument and corroded by an acid.

2. The impression taken from an etched plate.

3. Any design carried to completion by means of the etching process, as a pattern on metal, glass, etc.

etch'ing=ground, *n.* The varnish or coating with which plates to be etched are covered.

etch'ing=nee"dle, *n.* An instrument of steel with a fine point, for tracing outlines, etc., in etching.

etch'ing=stitch, *n.* In needlework, a stitch in outline embroidery.

ē-tē-os'tiç, *n.* [Gr. *etos*, a year, and *stichos*, a line, verse.] A chronogrammatical composition. [Rare.]

ē-tēr'mi-nà-ble, *a.* Interminable; without end. [Obs.]

ē-tērn', ē-tērne', *a.* [ME. *eterne*; OFr. *eterne*; L. *æternus*, everlasting, eternal, from *ævum*, an age.] Eternal; perpetual; endless. [Poet.]

ē-tēr'năl, *a.* [ME. *eternal*; OFr. *eternel*; LL. *æternalis*; L. *æternus*, eternal, everlasting, from *ævum*, an age.]

1. Without beginning or end of existence.

To know whether there is any real being, whose duration has been *eternal*.—Locke.

2. Everlasting; endless; immortal; as, *eternal* happiness in a future life; *eternal* fame.

3. Perpetual; ceaseless; continued without intermission.

And fires *eternal* in thy temple shine. —Dryden.

4. Unchangeable; existing at all times without change; as, *eternal* truth.

5. Figuratively, appearing endless; perpetual; unceasing; continued without intermission; frequently implying weariness or disgust; as, *eternal* chatter; *eternal* impecuniosity.

The Eternal City; Rome.

Syn.—Endless, everlasting, boundless, immortal, infinite, interminable, perpetual.—The *eternal* is set above time, the *endless* lies within time; we apply *eternal* to anything sublunary; although *endless* may with propriety be applied to that which is heavenly; that is properly *eternal* which has neither beginning nor end; that is *endless* which has a beginning, but no end; that which is *everlasting* has neither interruption nor cessation; the *endless* may be said of existing things; the *everlasting* naturally extends itself into futurity.

ē-tēr'năl, *n.* 1. [E—] An appellation of God; used with the definite article.

The law whereby the *Eternal* himself doth work. —Hooker.

2. That which is everlasting.

All godlike passion for *eternals* quenched. —Young.

3. Eternity.

Since *eternal* is at hand to swallow time's ambitions. —Young.

ē-tēr'năl-ist, *n.* One who holds the existence of the world or of matter to be from eternity.

ē-tēr'năl-īze, *v.t.*; eternalized, *pt., pp.*; eternalizing, *ppr.* To make eternal; to give endless duration to; to immortalize.

ē-tēr'năl-ly, *adv.* In an eternal manner.

ē-tērne', *a.* See *Etern*.

ē-tēr'ni-fȳ, *v.t.* To make eternal; to immortalize. [Obs.]

ē-tēr'ni-ty, *n.*; *pl.* **ē-tēr'ni-ties.** [ME. *eternite*; OFr. *eternite*; L. *æternitas (-atis)*, eternity, from *æternus*, eternal.]

1. The condition or quality of being eternal; duration or continuance without beginning or end.

2. The whole of time past; endless past time; endless future time; the state or condition which begins at death.

The narrow isthmus 'twixt two boundless seas,
The past, the future, two *eternities*.—Moore.

3. Figuratively, anything which seems endless; as, an *eternity* of suspense; an *eternity* of desert sand.

ē-tēr-ni-zā'tion, *n.* The act of eternizing; the act of rendering immortal or enduringly famous.

ē-tēr'nīze, *v.t.*; eternized, *pt., pp.*; eternizing, *ppr.* [OFr. *eterniser*, from *eterne*; L. *æternus*, eternal.]

1. To make eternal; to make endless.

2. To prolong the existence or duration of indefinitely; to perpetuate; as, to *eternize* woe.

3. To make forever famous; to immortalize; as, to *eternize* a name; to *eternize* exploits.

ē-tē′siăn (-zhăn), *a.* [L. *etesius*; Gr. *etēsios*, lasting a year, yearly, from *etos*, a year.] Recurring every year; blowing at stated times of the year; periodical; especially applied by Greek and Roman writers to the periodical winds in the Mediterranean.

eth′al, *n.* [*Eth*er and *al*cohol.] A substance obtained from spermaceti. It is a solid, fusible at nearly the same point as spermaceti, and on cooling crystallizes in plates. It is susceptible of union with various bases, with which it forms salts or soaps.

eth′āne, *n.* [From *ether*.] A colorless, gaseous compound, C_2H_6, of the paraffin series, forming a constituent of petroleum and illuminating-gas; called also *dimethyl*.

Eth′ă-nim, *n.* [Heb.] The seventh month in the Hebrew year; Tisri.

ēthe, *a.* Easy. [Obs.]

eth′el, *a.* Noble. [Obs.]

eth′el-ing, *n.* See *Atheling*.

eth′ēne, *n.* Same as *Ethylene*.

ē-then′iç, *a.* Pertaining to ethene or ethylene.

eth′ē-nyl, *n.* Same as *Vinyl*.

E-thē-os′tō-mȧ, *n.* [L., from Gr. *ēthein*, to strain, and *stoma*, mouth.] A genus of small fresh-water fishes, commonly called *darters*.

ē-thē-os′tō-moid, *a.* Pertaining to the *Etheostoma*.

ē-thē-os′tō-moid, *n.* One of the *Etheostoma*.

ē′thẽr, *n.* [L. *æther*; Gr. *aithēr*, the upper, purer air, ether, from *aithein*, to kindle, burn.]

1. In astronomy and physics, a hypothetical medium of extreme tenuity and elasticity supposed to be diffused throughout all space (as well as among the molecules of which solid bodies are composed), and to be the medium for the transmission of light and heat.

> There fields of light and liquid *ether* flow.
> —Dryden.

2. In chemistry, a very light, volatile, and inflammable fluid, produced by the replacement of the hydrogen of organic acids by alcohol radicals. Called also *ethyl ether* and *sulphuric ether*. It is lighter than alcohol, of a strong, sweet smell, susceptible of great expansion, and has a pungent taste. A mixture of vapor of ether with atmospheric air is extremely explosive. Its formula is $(C_2H_5)_2O$. It is a solvent of fats and resins, and as an anæsthetic, for which it is chiefly used, it is considered safer than chloroform.

3. The blue heavens; the upper air or sky.

4. In ancient philosophy, a hypothetical element which was supposed to fill the heavens above the moon.

Compound ether; an ethereal salt derived from an oxygenated acid.

ē-thē′rē-ăl, *a.* [L. *ætherius*; Gr. *aitherios*, pertaining to the ether, high in the air, ethereal, from *aithēr*, ether.]

1. Formed of ether; containing or filled with ether; as, *ethereal* space; *ethereal* regions; hence, heavenly; celestial.

> Vast chain of being, which from God began,
> Nature's *ethereal*, human, angel, man.
> —Pope.

2. Existing in the air; looking blue like the sky; as, *ethereal* mountains.

3. In chemistry, of or pertaining to ether; as, *ethereal* salts; *ethereal* liquids.

Ethereal extract; an extract made by means of a menstruum containing ether.

Ethereal oil; a volatile oil.

Ethereal oil of wine; a heavy, yellow liquid consisting of equal volumes of heavy oil of wine and of stronger ether; called also *heavy oil of wine*.

ē-thē′rē-ăl-iṣm, *n.* Ethereality.

ē-thē-rē-al′i-ty, *n.* The state or condition of being ethereal.

ē-thē″rē-ăl-i-zā′tion, *n.* The act or process of etherealizing, or the state of being etherealized.

ē-thē′rē-ăl-ize, *v.t.*; etherealized, *pt.*, *pp.*; etherealizing, *ppr.* 1. To convert into ether; to etherify.

2. To make ethereal; to spiritualize; to purify and refine.

ē-thē′rē-ăl-ly, *adv.* In an ethereal manner.

ē-thē′rē-ăl-ness, *n.* The quality of being ethereal.

ē′thẽr-en″gine, *n.* An engine operated by the vapor of ether.

ē-thē′rē-ous, *a.* Composed of ether; ethereal.

ē″thẽr-i-fi-çā′tion, *n.* The act or process of forming the chemical substance ether.

ē′thẽr-i-form, *a.* Having the form of ether.

ē′thẽr-i-fy, *v.t.*; etherified, *pt.*, *pp.*; etherifying, *ppr.* [L. *æther*, ether, and *facere*, to make.] To change into ether, as alcohol by the action of sulphuric acid.

ē′thẽr-in, *n.* In chemistry, a polymeric form of ethylene which separates in transparent, tasteless crystals from ethereal oil of wine after standing.

ē′thẽr-iṣm, *n.* In medicine, the phenomena resulting from the inhalation of ether as an anæsthetic.

ē″thẽr-i-zā′tion, *n.* 1. In medicine, the act or process of administering ether to a patient.

2. The state or condition of the system when subjected to the influence of ether.

ē′thẽr-ize, *v.t.*; etherized, *pt.*, *pp.*; etherizing, *ppr.* 1. To etherify; to convert into ether.

2. In medicine, to put under the influence of ether; as, to *etherize* a patient.

ē′thẽr-ol, *n.* In chemistry, a pale yellow, oily liquid hydrocarbon, with an aromatic odor, that separates from ethereal oil of wine.

eth′iç, *a.* Ethical.

eth′iç-ăl, *a.* [LL. *ethicus*; Gr. *ēthikos*, ethical, moral, from *ēthos*, character, custom, a man's normal state.] Relating to morals; treating of morality; containing precepts of morality; moral; as, *ethical* discourses or epistles.

> He (Pope) is the great poet of reason, the first of *ethical* authors in verse.—Warton.

Ethical dative; in grammar, the dative of a first or second personal pronoun interjected to imply a degree of interest or sympathetic concern.

eth′iç-ăl-ly, *adv.* According to the doctrines of morality.

eth′i-cist, *n.* A student of or an authority or writer upon ethics.

eth′içs, *n.* [Gr. *ta ēthika*, ethics.]

1. The science which treats of the nature and laws of the actions of intelligent beings, these actions being considered in relation to their moral qualities; the science which treats of the nature and grounds of moral obligation; the science of human duty.

2. The whole of the moral sciences; natural jurisprudence, including moral philosophy, international law, public or political law, civil law, and history, profane, civil, and political.

3. A particular system of principles and rules concerning duty, whether true or false; rules of practice in respect to a single class of human actions; as, social *ethics*; newspaper *ethics*.

eth′ide, *n.* In chemistry, any binary compound of ethyl.

eth′i-dēne, *n.* Ethylidene. [Obs.]

eth′ine, *n.* Acetylene.

eth-i-on′iç, *a.* [*Ethylene*, and Gr. *theion*, sulphur.] Pertaining to a combination of a radical of the ethylene group with a sulphur acid.

Ethionic acid; a dibasic acid (ethylene sulphonic acid), found only in aqueous solution.

E′thi-op, *n.* An Ethiopian.

E-thi-ō′pi-ăn, *n.* [L. *Æthiops*, pl. *Æthiopes*; Gr. *Aithiops*, pl. *Aithiopes*, an inhabitant of Ethiopia, an Ethiopian, lit., burnt face; *aithein*, to burn, and *ōps*, face.]

1. An inhabitant or a native of ancient Ethiopia, which included modern Abyssinia.

2. In a general sense, any African; a negro; a black man.

E-thi-ō′pi-ăn, *a.* 1. Of or pertaining to Ethiopia or to its people.

2. Pertaining to the negro.

E-thi-op′iç, *a.* and *n.* [L. *Æthiopicus*; Gr. *Aithiopikos*, pertaining to the Ethiopians.]

I. *a.* Same as *Ethiopian*.

II. *n.* The language of ancient Ethiopia, of Semitic origin and nearly akin to the Himyaritic of Arabia. It has a Christian literature and is now used only in the services of the Abyssinian church.

ē′thi-ops, *n.* Same as *Æthiops*.

eth-mo-. A combining form from Gr. *ēthmos*, sieve, from *ēthein*, to strain, used in medical and anatomical words to indicate connection with or nearness to the ethmoid bone.

eth′moid, eth-moid′ăl, *a.* Resembling a sieve; pertaining to the ethmoid.

eth′moid, *n.* [Gr. *ēthmos*, a strainer, sieve, from *ēthein*, to strain, and *eidos*, form.] In anatomy, a complicated bone of the cranium at the top of the root of the nose, through which the olfactory nerves pass; also called *ethmoid bone*.

eth-mō-tŭr′bi-năl, *a.* and *n.* [*Ethmo-*, and L. *turbo* (*-inis*), a top.]

I. *a.* Turbinated or scroll-like; pertaining to the ethmoturbinal.

II. *n.* One of the two lateral masses of the ethmoid; the light, spongy bone of which the ethmoid consists for the most part, known as the *superior* and *middle turbinate* bones.

eth-mō-vō′mẽr-ine, *a.* [*Ethmo-*, and L. *vomer*, a plowshare.] Pertaining to the ethmoid and the vomer.

eth′närçh, *n.* [Gr. *ethnarchēs*, from *ethnos*, a nation, people, and *archein*, to rule.] In Greek antiquity, the governor of a province or people; a viceroy.

eth′närçh-y, *n.* The office or authority of an ethnarch; also, the province under his rule.

eth′niç, *n.* A heathen; a pagan.

eth′niç, eth′niç-ăl, *a.* [Fr. *ethnique*; L. *ethnicus*; Gr. *ethnikos*, national, foreign, from *ethnos*, a company, people, nation.]

1. Heathen; pagan; pertaining to the gentiles or nations not converted to Christianity; opposed to *Jewish* and *Christian*.

2. Pertaining to race distinctions and characteristics; racial; ethnological.

eth′niç-ăl-ly, *adv.* In an ethnical manner.

eth′ni-ciṣm, *n.* Heathenism; paganism; idolatry.

eth-noġ′e-ny, *n.* [Gr. *ethnos*, a nation, and *-genēs*, producing.] That branch of ethnology which deals with the origin of the various races or nations.

eth-nog′rȧ-phẽr, *n.* A student of or authority on ethnography.

eth-nō-graph′iç, eth-nō-graph′iç-al, *a.* Pertaining to ethnography.

eth-nō-graph′iç-ăl-ly, *adv.* In accordance with the principles or methods of ethnography.

eth-nog′rȧ-phist, *n.* An ethnographer.

eth-nog′rȧ-phy, *n.* [Gr. *ethnos*, a nation, and *graphein*, to write.] That branch of anthropology which has to do with the classification and description of the various races and nations.

eth-nō-loġ′iç, eth-nō-loġ′iç-ăl, *a.* Relating to ethnology.

eth-nō-loġ′iç-ăl-ly, *adv.* According to the principles and classification of ethnology.

eth-nol′ō-ġist, *n.* One who is a student of or versed in ethnology.

eth-nol′ō-ġy, *n.* [Gr. *ethnos*, a nation, people, and *logos*, a description.] That branch of anthropology which treats of the races and nations, as regards their origin, character, history, customs, and institutions. Ethnography and *ethnology* bear the same relation almost to one another as geology and geography.

eth-ō-loġ′iç, eth-ō-loġ′iç-ăl, *a.* Treating of or pertaining to ethics or morality.

ē-thol′ō-ġist, *n.* One who writes on the subject of manners and morality.

ē-thol′ō-ġy, *n.* [L. *ethologia*; Gr. *ēthologia*, a depicting of character; *ēthos*, custom, character, and *logos*, description, from *legein*, to speak.] A treatise on morality; the science of ethics, especially applied ethics.

eth″ō-pō-et′iç, *a.* [Gr. *ēthos*, character, and *poiein*, to make.] Of the nature of or pertaining to character-making. [Obs.]

ē′thos, *n.* [Gr. *ēthos*, an accustomed place or habitation; hence, habit, custom, character.]

1. The essential principle or dominant characteristic of a people or a community, as expressed in their habits, customs, tastes, etc.

2. In the Greek fine arts, the inherently noble and pure quality of a work, as of a statue or a poem, which produces a high moral impression.

eth′yl, *n.* The monatomic radical (C_2H_5) of ethane and of common alcohol or ether. It is of the paraffin series and has never been obtained in the free state.

eth-yl-am′ine, *n.* A volatile liquid, $C_2H_5.NH_2$, characterized by an ammoniacal odor.

eth′yl-āte, *a.* Same as *Alcoholate*.

eth′yl-ā-ted, *a.* Treated or mixed with ethyl or any of its compounds.

eth′yl-ēne, *n.* A colorless, poisonous gas, C_2H_4, contained in coal-gas and forming one of the constituents of illuminating-gas. It has a suffocating odor and explodes violently when mixed with air.

Ethylene series; in chemistry, a series of hydrocarbons of which ethylene is the type.

e-thyl′iç, *a.* Relating to or derived from ethyl.

e-thyl′i-dēne, *n.* A hydrocarbon radical without symmetry of chemical structure, having two units of combining power. It has the same elements as ethylene.

eth′yl-in, *n.* Any one of the various composite ethers of glycerin and ethyl.

eth″yl-sul-phū′riç, *a.* Containing or relating to ethyl and sulphuric acid.

Ethylsulphuric acid; a thick liquid compound of sulphuric acid and alcohol.

ē′ti-ō-lāte, *v.i.*; etiolated, *pt.*, *pp.*; etiolating, *ppr.* [Fr. *etioler*, to blanch, from OFr. *estioler*, to become slender or puny, from *esteule*; L. *stipula*, a straw.]

1. To become white or whiter; to be whitened by excluding the light of the sun, as plants.

2. In medicine, to become pale or of a sickly color from sickness or from exclusion of light.

ē′ti-ō-lāte, *v.t.* To blanch; to whiten by excluding the sun's rays.

ē′ti-ō-lā-ted, ē′ti-ō-lāte, *a.* Blanched; whitened by excluding the sun's rays.

ē-ti-ō-lā′tion, *n.* 1. In gardening, rendering plants white, crisp, and tender, by excluding light from them; also, the condition of a plant so treated.

2. In medicine, paleness or a sickly color caused by disease or exclusion from light.

ē′ti-ō-lin, *n.* A yellowish coloring-matter in plants grown in dark places; a modified form of chlorophyl.

ē′ti-ō-lize, *v.i.* and *v.t.* Same as *Etiolate*.

ē″ti-ō-loġ′iç-ăl, *a.* Same as *Ætiological*.

ē″ti-ō-loġ′iç-ăl-ly, *adv.* Same as *Ætiologically*.

ē-ti-ol′ō-ġy, *n.* Same as *Ætiology*.

et′i-quette (-ket), *n.* [Fr. *étiquette*, a ticket, label.]

1. The formalities or conventions required by polite society and established by usage; good manners; politeness; proper conduct in social or professional life.

2. A rule or law governing rank and precedence among state functionaries.

3. A label on a specimen in a natural history collection. [Rare.]

et′nȧ, *n.* [L. *Ætna*; Gr. *Aitnē*, a volcano in Sicily.] An apparatus for heating a small quantity of water, the heat being supplied by an alcohol lamp.

Et-nē′ăn, *a.* Pertaining to Etna, a volcanic mountain in Sicily; spelled also *Ætnean*.

é-toile′ (ā-twol′), *n.* 1. Same as *Estoile*.

2. A figure shaped like a star; used in embroidery.

Ē-tō′ni-ăn, *a.* and *n.* I. *a.* Of or pertaining to Eton, England, or the famous Eton College, founded in 1440 by Henry VI.

II. *n.* One who is or has been a student at Eton College.

Ē-trū′ri-ăn, *a.* and *n.* Same as *Etruscan*.

Ē-trus′căn, *a.* [L. *Etruscus*, Etrurian, from *Etruria*, Etruria.] Pertaining to ancient Etruria in central Italy, including modern Tuscany, or to its people, and especially to their civilization, culture, and art.

Ē-trus′căn, *n.* 1. A native or inhabitant of ancient Etruria.

2. The language of the Etruscans, long dead, but remarkable for its total dissimilarity to any known tongue.

et′ten, *n.* A giant or goblin. [Obs.]

et′tēr-pīke, *n.* Same as *Adder-pike*.

et′tle, *v.t.* To expect; to conjecture; to try. [Scot.]

et′tle, *v.i.* [Scot., from Ice. *ætla*, to think, suppose.]

1. To take aim; hence, to aspire; to be ambitious; to direct one's course.

2. To make attempt. [Scot. in all uses.]

et′tle, *n.* Intention; aim. [Scot.]

é-tūde′ (ā-), *n.* [Fr., from L. *studium*, study.] A lesson; an exercise; specifically, in music, a composition, often of musical value and beauty, but primarily intended as an exercise to aid the performer in overcoming some difficulty of technique.

é-tui′ (ā-twē′), *n.* [Fr.] A small case or box, sometimes a chatelaine of ornamental design, for carrying implements for needlework and toilet articles.

et-wee′, *n.* Same as *Etui*.

et′ym, *n.* [Rare.] Same as *Etymon*.

e-tym′ic, *a.* Pertaining to the etymon.

et-y-mol′ō-ġẽr, *n.* An etymologist. [Obs.]

et″y-mō-loġ′iç, et″y-mō-loġ′iç-ăl, *a.* [LL. *etymologicus*; Gr. *etymologikos*, belonging to etymology, from *etymologia*, etymology.] Pertaining to etymology or the derivation of words; according to or by means of etymology.

et″y-mō-loġ′i-cȧ, *n.*, pl. of *etymologicon*.

et″y-mō-loġ′iç-ăl-ly, *adv.* According to etymology.

et″y-mō-loġ′i-con, et″y-mō-loġ′iç-um, *n.*; *pl.* **et″y-mō-loġ′i-cȧ**. [L., from Gr. *etymologikon*, neut. of *etymologikos*, etymological.] A book in which the etymologies of words are traced; a treatise on the derivation of words.

et-y-mol′ō-ġist, *n.* One versed in etymology; one who studies or teaches the origin or history of words.

et-y-mol′ō-ġīze, *v.t.*; etymologized, *pt.*, *pp.*; etymologizing, *ppr.* To trace the derivation of; to give the etymology of or to provide an etymology for.

et-y-mol′ō-ġīze, *v.i.* To search into the origin of words; to trace the history of words from their simple roots.

et-y-mol′ō-ġy, *n.*; *pl.* **et-y-mol′ō-ġieṣ**. [Fr. *étymologie*; L. *etymologia*; Gr. *etymologia*, the true account and analysis of a word; *etymos*, the true literal sense of a word, neut. of *etymos*, true, and *logos*, description, from *legein*, to speak.]

1. That part of philology which explains the origin and derivation of words, with a view to ascertain their radical or primary signification.

2. The history of any word, recording the differences in its spelling, form, or meaning, with the same facts concerning the original or cognate forms of the same word in other languages.

3. In grammar, that division which treats of the various inflections and modifications of words and shows how they are formed from their simple roots.

et′y-mon, *n.* [L. *etymon*; Gr. *etymon*, the true literal sense of a word, etymology, neut. of *etymos*, true.] An original root or primitive word; also, its original signification or root meaning.

ē-typ′iç, ē-typ′iç-ăl, *a.* [L. *e-* priv., and *typus*, a figure, image, from Gr. *typos*, an impression, type, from *typtein*, to beat, strike.] In biology, unconformable to or diverging from the normal type.

eu-. A prefix from the Gr. *eu-*, signifying good, well, as in *eulogy*; opposed to *dys-*, ill or bad.

eū-çāi′rite, *n.* See *Eukairite*.

eū′çȧ-lin, eū′çȧ-lyn, *n.* [From *Eucalyptus*.] In chemistry, a nonfermentable kind of syrupy substance, obtained by the fermentation of melitose, the sugar of eucalyptus.

eū′çȧ-lypt, *n.* Any plant of the genus *Eucalyptus*.

eū-çȧ-lyp′tiç, *a.* Pertaining to the genus *Eucalyptus* or to any of its species.

eū-çȧ-lyp′tol, *n.* A volatile aromatic oil obtained from *Eucalyptus globulus*.

Eū-çȧ-lyp′tus, *n.* [L., from Gr. *eu*, well, and *kalyptein*, to cover, conceal.] An important genus of large, generally glaucous, trees of the order *Myrtaceæ*, native to and abundant in Australia, a few species being also found in the Indian archipelago. Many of the species are valued for their timber or for the gums which they yield.

Flowering Branch of Blue-gum Tree (*Eucalyptus globulus*).

Eū-ceph′ȧ-lȧ, *n.pl.* [L., from Gr. *eu*, well, and *kephalē*, head.] In entomology, a group of long-legged, slender, two-winged insects, the larvæ of which have distinct heads, as craneflies.

eū-ceph′ȧ-lous, *a.* Having a distinct head; specifically, pertaining to the *Eucephala*.

Eū′chȧ-ris, *n.* [L., from Gr. *eucharis*, agreeable; *eu*, well, and *charis*, grace.]

1. In botany, a genus of amaryllidaceous plants found in the mountains of South America, *Eucharis grandiflora*, being widely cultivated for its large white flowers.

2. In entomology, a genus of chalcidians.

eū′chȧ-rist, *n.* [LL. *eucharistia*; Gr. *eucharistia*, thankfulness, gratitude, from *eucharistos*, grateful, thankful; *eu*, well, and *charizesthai*, to show favor to, from *charis*, favor.]

1. The sacrament of the Lord's supper; the solemn act or ceremony of commemorating the death of Christ in the use of bread and wine, as emblems of his flesh and blood; the holy communion; the sacrifice of the mass.

2. Either or both of the elements, bread and wine, which are used in the sacrament.

3. The act of giving solemn thanks. [Obs.]

eū-chȧ-ris′tiç, eū-chȧ-ris′tiç-ăl, *a.* 1. Containing expressions of thanks. [Obs.]

2. Pertaining to the eucharist or sacrament of the Lord's supper.

Eū′chīte, *n.* [L.Gr. *euchitēs*, from Gr. *euchē*, prayer, from *euchesthai*, to pray.] A member of a sect of Christians which arose in Syria, Mesopotamia, and other eastern countries in the fourth century. They were characterized by their rejection of all sacraments, their ascetic lives, and their dependence upon the presence of the Holy Spirit in answer to prayer.

eū-chlō′riç, eū′chlōre, *a.* Of a distinct green color; of or pertaining to euchlorin.

eū-chlō′rin, *n.* [Gr. *eu*, well, and *chlōros*, greenish.] A highly explosive gas, obtained by subjecting potassium chlorate to the action of hydrochloric acid; also written *euchlorine*.

eū-chō-lō′ġi-on, *n.*; *pl.* **eū-chō-lō′ġi-ȧ**. Same as *Euchology*.

eū′chō-logue (-log), *n.* Euchology.

eū-chol′ō-ġy, *n.*; *pl.* **eū-chol′ō-ġieṣ**. [L.Gr. *euchologion*, a prayer-book; Gr. *euchē*, a prayer, and *logos*, a discourse, from *legein*, to speak.] In the Greek church, the formulary of prayers; the ritual in which are prescribed the order of ceremonies, sacraments, and ordinances.

eū′chre (-kẽr), *n.* [Etym. unknown; compare G. *jucks*, a joke.]

1. A game of cards played with the thirty-two highest cards of the pack, or sometimes with twenty-four or twenty-eight, and usually by four persons, each receiving five cards in the deal. The highest trump-card is the knave, the next the knave of corresponding color, these two being called respectively the right bower and the left bower. Sometimes an additional card, called the joker, is used, which card is then the highest of all.

2. The failure of the player or the partners making the trump in this game to score three tricks with one hand.

eū′chre, *v.t.*; euchred, *pt.*, *pp.*; euchring, *ppr.*

1. In the game of euchre, to prevent (the maker of the trump) from taking three tricks.

2. Figuratively, to defeat; to outplay; to get the better of. [Colloq.]

eū-chrō′iç, *a.* [Gr. *euchroos*, well-colored; *eu*, well, and *chroa*, color.] In chemistry, of a good color.

Euchroic acid; a dibasic acid obtained by heating paramide with an alkali.

eū′chrō-īte, *n.* In mineralogy, a hydrous arseniate of copper, transparent, brittle, and of a light emerald-green color.

eū′chrōne, *n.* In chemistry, a dark blue, soluble substance precipitated when zinc is added to a solution of euchroic acid.

eū′chy-my, *n.* [Gr. *euchymia*, goodness of flavor, from *euchymos*, well-flavored; *eu*, well, and *chymos*, juice.] In medicine, a healthy state of the blood and other fluids of the body.

eū′clāse, *n.* [Gr. *eu*, well, and *klasis*, a breaking, from *klān*, to break.] A brittle mineral of the beryl family, consisting of silica, aluminium, and glucinum. It occurs in light green transparent crystals, affording a brilliant diagonal cleavage.

Eū′clid, *n.* A treatise on geometry written in the third century B. C. by Euclid, a Greek mathematician; hence, any treatise or textbook of elementary geometry.

Eū-clid′ē-ăn, Eū-clid′i-ăn, *a.* [L. *Euclides*; Gr. *Eukleidēs*, Euclid.]

1. Pertaining to Euclid or his "Elements of Geometry."

2. Pertaining to Euclid or Eukleides, the Archon Eponymos of Athens for the year 403 B. C., under whom the so-called Ionian alphabet was first used officially. Also spelled *Eukleidean*.

eū′çōne, *a.* [Gr. *eu*, well, and *kōnos*, a cone.] Having crystal cones, as the compound eyes of insects.

Eū-çō-pep′ō-dȧ, *n.pl.* A group of minute entomostracans, including the *Copepoda*.

eū′çrȧ-sy, *n.* [Gr. *eukrasia*, a good mixture or temperature, from *eukratos*, well-tempered; *eu*, well, and *kerannynai*, to mix.] In medicine, such a due or well-proportioned mixture of qualities in bodies as to constitute health or soundness.

eūç′tiç-ăl, *a.* Containing acts of supplication. [Obs.]

eū-dē′mŏn, eū-dæ′mŏn, *n.* [Gr. *eudaimōn*, having a good genius, prosperous; *eu*, well, and *daimōn*, genius, spirit.]

1. A good angel or spirit.

2. In astrology, the eleventh house; so called on account of its signifying favorable happenings.

eū-dē-mon′iç, eū-dē-mon′iç-ăl, *a.* Of or pertaining to eudemonism.

eū-dē-mon′içs, eū-dæ-mon′içs, *n.* Same as *Eudemonism*.

eū-dē′mŏn-ism, eū-dæ′mŏn-ism, *n.* [Gr. *eudaimonizein*, to think or call happy, from *eudaimōn*, prosperous, happy.] The doctrine of happiness, or the system of philosophy which makes human happiness its highest object, declaring that the production of happiness is the foundation of virtue.

eū-dē′mŏn-ist, *n.* An adherent of the doctrine of eudemonism.

eū-dē-mŏn-is′tiç, *a.* Pertaining to eudemonism.

eū-di′ȧ-lyte, *n.* [Gr. *eudialytos*, easy to break up or dissolve; *eu*, well, easy, and *dialytos*, capable of dissolution, from *dialyein*, to dissolve; *dia*, through, and *lyein*, to loosen.] A mineral of a brownish-red color found in Greenland, and containing lime, soda, and iron in combination with zirconium, silicon, tantalum, manganese, and other elements.

eū-di-om′e-tẽr, *n.* [Gr. *eudios*, fine, calm, and *metron*, a measure.] An instrument employed generally in the analysis of gases, for the determination of the nature and proportion of the constituents of any gaseous mixture. It consists of a graduated glass tube, either straight or bent in the shape of the letter U, hermetically sealed at one end and open at the other, arranged for passing an electric spark through the gases held in the closed end by a column of water.

Eudiometer.

eū″di-ō-met′riç, eū″di-ō-met′riç-ăl, *a.* Pertaining to a eudiometer or to eudiometry; performed or ascertained by a eudiometer; as, *eudiometric* experiments or results.

eū-di-om′e-try, *n.* The art or practice of ascertaining the nature and proportions of the constituents of any gaseous mixture by the use of the eudiometer.

eū-di-pleū′răl, *a.* [Gr. *eu*, well, *dis*, two, and *pleura*, side.] In biology, having symmetry in two lateral parts; being right and left, as the two wings of a bird.

Eū′dist, *n.* [Fr. *Eudiste*.] One of a Roman Catholic missionary order founded by Jean Eudes, a French priest, in 1643, the Congregation of Jesus and Mary.

Eū-dox′i-ăn, *n.* One of a sect of heretics of the fourth century who were followers of Eudoxius, bishop of Constantinople, an extreme Arian in his views.

eū-em′ẽr-ism, eū-em′ẽr-ist, etc. Same as *Euhemerism*, *Euhemerist*, etc.

eū′ġē, *interj.* [Gr. *euge*, good!] Well done! well said! an exclamation of applause. [Obs.]

eū-ġen′e-sis, *n.* [L., from Gr. *eu*, well, and *genesis*, origin, birth.] In biology, the state or characteristic of being prolific; fertility; especially, the production of hybrid young.

ū-ġē′ni-ȧ, *n.* [Named in honor of Prince *Eugene* of Savoy.] A genus of dicotyledonous polypetalous plants of the order *Myrtaceæ*. It contains a large number of species, the most important of which is the allspice or pimento. *Eugenia acris* is the wild clove.

eū-ġen′iç, *a.* Of, pertaining to, or derived from cloves.

Eugenic acid; an acid derived from cloves and conferring on them their essential properties.

eū-ġen′iç, *a.* [Gr. *eugenēs*, well born; *eu*, well, and *genos*, race, family.]

1. Of or pertaining to race-culture.

2. Well-born.

eū-ġen′içs, *n.* The science which deals with the improvement and culture of race, especially the human race, through improved conditions in the relation of the sexes.

eū′ġē-nin, *n.* A substance, $C_{10}H_{12}O_2$, which deposits spontaneously from the distilled water of cloves. It crystallizes in small laminæ, which are colorless, transparent, and pearly, but in time become yellow.

eū′ġē-nol, *n.* Same as *Eugenic acid* under *Eugenic*.

eū′ġe-ny, *n.* Nobleness of birth. [Obs.]

eū-ġet′iç, **eū-ġe-tin′iç**, *a.* Of, pertaining to, or derived from eugenic acid or eugenol.

eūgh (ū), *n.* [Obs.] Same as *Yew*.

eūgh′en, *a.* [Obs.] Same as *Yewen*.

Eū-glē′nȧ, *n.* The type-genus of the family *Euglenidæ*.

Eū-glen′i-dæ, *n.pl.* [L., from Gr. *eu*, well, and *glēnē*, the pupil of the eye.] A large family of infusorians with brilliant endoplasm, usually green.

eū-glē′noid, *a.* and *n.* I. *a.* Of, pertaining to, or resembling infusorians of the family *Euglenidæ*.

II. *n.* One of the *Euglenidæ*.

Eū′gū-bine, **Eū-gū′bi-ăn**, *a.* [It. *Eugubbio*; L. *Iguvium*, a city of Umbria.] Of or belonging to ancient Eugubium (now Gubbio), in Italy, or to certain tablets or tables, seven in number, discovered there in 1444.

eū-häṙ-mon′iç, *a.* [Gr. *eu*, well, and *harmonikos*, harmonic.] Producing perfectly concordant sounds, as opposed to sounds produced by tempered instruments.

eū-hē′mēr-iṣm, *n.* [L. *Euhemerus*; Gr. *Euēmeros*, a Greek philosopher of the 4th century B. C.] The doctrine that polytheistic mythology arose exclusively, or in the main, out of the deification of dead heroes; the system of mythological interpretation which reduces the gods to the level of distinguished men, and so regards the myths as founded on real histories.

eū-hem′ēr-ist, *n.* One who believes in euhemerism.

eū-hem-ēr-is′tiç, **eū-hem′ēr-ist**, *a.* Of or pertaining to euhemerism or its advocates.

eū-hem-ēr-is′tiç-ăl-ly, *adv.* After the manner of the euhemerists; rationalistically.

eū-hem′ēr-ize, *v.t.*; euhemerized, *pt.*, *pp.*; euhemerizing, *ppr.* To treat or explain in the manner of the euhemerists; to treat or explain rationalistically; as, to *euhemerize* a myth, or to explain it as being founded on a basis of history.

eū-hem′ēr-īze, *v.i.* To believe in or practise euhemerism; to treat or explain myths euhemeristically.

Eū-i-sop′ō-dȧ, *n.pl.* [L., from Gr. *eu*, well, *isos*, equal, and *pous*, *podos*, foot.] In zoölogy, a group of isopodous crustaceans characterized by seven appendaged thoracic segments.

eū-kāi′rīte, **eū-çāi′rīte**, *n.* [Named by Berzelius on account of its opportune discovery, from Gr. *eukairos*, timely, opportune; *eu*, well, and *kairos*, time, season.] A mineral of a shining lead-gray color and granular structure, consisting chiefly of selenium, copper, and silver.

eū′lȧ-çhon, *n.* Same as *Candle-fish*, 2.

Eū-lē′ri-ăn, *a.* Relating to or invented by the Swiss mathematician Euler (1707-1783).

Eulerian equation; any hydrodynamic equation commonly used, in which the variables are the components of velocity at fixed points in space.

eū-lō′ġi-ȧ, *n.*; *pl.* **eū-lō′ġi-æ**. [LL., from Gr. *eulogia*, praise, blessing, eulogy; *eu*, well, and *legein*, to speak.] In the early church, originally, the eucharist; later, the part of the elements of the eucharist sent to the sick, or from one bishop or church to another, as a symbol of Christian love and fellowship; still later, unconsecrated bread not used in the communion service, but blessed and used as a substitute for the eucharist by those who had the right to commune, but did not, as in the Greek church at the present day. Also called *antidoron* and *eulogy*.

eū-log′iç, **eū-log′iç-ăl**, *a.* Containing praise; commendatory. [Rare.]

eū-log′iç-ăl-ly, *adv.* In a manner to convey praise. [Rare.]

eū′lō-ġist, *n.* One who praises and commends another; one who writes or speaks in commendation of another.

eū-lō-ġis′tiç, **eū-lō-ġis′tiç-ăl**, *a.* Commendatory; full of praise.

eū-lō-ġis′tiç-ăl-ly, *adv.* With high praise.

eū-lō′ġi-um, *n.* Same as *Eulogy*.

eū′lō-ġīze, *v.t.*; eulogized, *pt.*, *pp.*; eulogizing, *ppr.* To praise; to speak or write in commendation of; to extol in speech or writing; to pronounce a eulogy upon.

eū′lō-ġy, *n.*; *pl.* **eū′lō-ġieṣ**. [LL. *eulogia*; Gr. *eulogia*, good or fine language, eulogy, praise; *eu*, good, and *logos*, discourse, from *legein*, to speak.]

1. High commendation or praise of a person or thing; laudation, especially when expressed in formal language.

2. Same as *Eulogia*.

Syn.—Encomium, panegyric, eulogium.—The word *encomium* is applied to both persons and things, and denotes warm praise; *eulogium* and *eulogy* apply only to persons, and are more prolonged and studied; a *panegyric* was originally a set speech in a full assembly of the people, and hence denotes a more formal *eulogy*, couched in terms of warm and continuous praise.

eū′ly-tīte, **eū′ly-tin**, *n.* [Gr. *eulytos*, easy to dissolve; *eu*, well, and *lyein*, to loose, dissolve.] A mineral consisting chiefly of silicate of bismuth, found at Schneeberg, in Saxony.

Eū-men′i-dēṣ, *n.pl.* [L., from Gr. *Eumenidēs*, lit., the gracious ones, from *eumenēs*, well-disposed, gracious; *eu*, well, and *menos*, mind, temper.] In classical mythology, the Furies or Erinyes, so called through fear of offending them.

eū″mēr-ō-ġen′e-sis, *n.* [L., from Gr. *eu*, well, *meros*, part, and *genesis*, birth, descent.] In biology, that particular kind of generation or development by unit parts, as in the tapeworm, in which each part is a repetition of the one preceding; opposed to *dysmerogenesis*.

eū′mēr-ō-mọrph, *n.* [Gr. *eu*, well, *meros*, part, and *morphē*, shape, form.] An organic form produced by eumerogenesis.

Eū-nō′mi-ăn, *a.* and *n.* [LL. *Eunomius*; Gr. *Eunomios*, Eunomius.]

I. *a.* Pertaining to Eunomius or to his teachings.

II. *n.* A disciple of Eunomius, an extreme Arian of the fourth century.

eū′nō-my, *n.* [Gr. *eunomia*, good order, from *eunomos*, well-ordered; *eu*, well, and *nomos*, law.] Equal law, or a well-adjusted constitution of government.

eū′nuçh, *n.* [L. *eunuchus*; Gr. *eunouchos*, a chamberlain, a eunuch; *eunē*, bed, and *echein*, to have, hold.] A male of the human species castrated; specifically, in the Orient, a keeper of the bedchamber or of the harem.

eū′nuçh, **eū′nuçh-āte**, *v.t.* To make a eunuch of; to castrate.

eū′nuçh-iṣm, *n.* The state of being a eunuch.

eū-on′y-min, *n.* In medicine, a bitter substance derived from the *Euonymus Europæus*, or spindle-tree, and used as a tonic, laxative, and expectorant.

Eū-on′y-mus, *n.* [L., from *euonymos*; Gr. *euōnymos*, the spindle-tree, lit., well-named; *eu*, well, and *onoma*, name.]

1. A genus of shrubs or trees, of the order *Celastrineæ*, containing about fifty species, natives of the temperate regions of the northern hemisphere.

2. [e—] The bark of certain species of this genus, used in medicine.

Eū-ọr′ni-thēṣ, *n.pl.* [L., from Gr. *eu*, well, and *ornis* (*ornithos*), a bird.] A group containing all the living kinds of birds except the penguins, the tinamous, and the ratite forms.

eū-oṣ′mīte, *n.* [Gr. *eu*, well, and *osmē*, a smell.] A brownish-yellow fossil resin which derives its name from the strong, spicy odor it emits when heated.

eū′pȧ-thy, *n.* Right feeling. [Obs.]

eū-pat′ō-rine, *n.* An alkaloid obtained from *Eupatorium cannabinum*, or hemp-agrimony. It is a white powder having a peculiar, sharp, bitter taste, insoluble in water, but soluble in ether and alcohol. It combines with sulphuric acid, and the salt crystallizes in silky needles.

Eū-pȧ-tō′ri-um, *n.* [L. *eupatorium*; Gr. *eupatōrion*, agrimony, from Mithridates *Eupator*, king of Pontus, who first used it as a medicine.] An extensive genus of perennial herbs, chiefly natives of America, of the order *Compositæ*. *Eupatorium perfoliatum* of North America, popularly called thoroughwort, crosswort, and boneset, is employed as a substitute for Peruvian bark.

eū′pȧ-tō-ry, *n.* A plant of the genus *Eupatorium*.

eū′pȧ-trid, *a.* and *n.* I. *a.* Of or pertaining to the *Eupatridæ*; noble; high-born.

II. *n.* One of the *Eupatridæ*.

Eū-pat′ri-dæ, *n.pl.* [Gr. *eupatridēs*, of a noble father; *eu*, well, and *patēr*, father.] The hereditary aristocracy of ancient Greece.

eū-pep′si-ȧ, **eū-pep′sy**, *n.* [L., from Gr. *eupeptos*, easy of digestion; *eu*, well, and *peptein*, *pessein*, to digest.] Good digestion.

eū-pep′tiç, *a.* 1. Having good digestion; opposed to *dyspeptic*.

2. Easily digested; said of food.

eū′phē-miṣm, *n.* [Gr. *euphēmismos*, the use of an auspicious word for an inauspicious one, from *euphēmizein*, to use a good or auspicious word for an evil or inauspicious, from *euphēmos*, of good sound or omen; *eu*, good, and *phēmē*, voice, from *phanai*, to speak.]

1. In rhetoric, a figure in which a harsh or indelicate word or expression is softened, or a mild or indirect word or phrase is substituted for a more accurate one, which might be unpleasant, offensive, or embarrassing.

2. A word or phrase used in such a manner; as, "she is at rest" is a *euphemism* for "she is dead."

eū-phē-mis′tiç, **eū-phē-mis′tiç-ăl**, *a.* Pertaining to or containing euphemism.

eū-phē-mis′tiç-ăl-ly, *adv.* In a euphemistic manner.

eū′phē-mīze, *v.t.*; euphemized, *pt.*, *pp.*; euphemizing, *ppr.* [Gr. *euphēmizein*, to use an auspicious for an inauspicious word.] To express by means of a euphemism.

eū′phē-mīze, *v.i.* To speak euphemistically.

eū-phō′nē, *n.* [Gr. *euphōnos*, sweet-voiced, musical; *eu*, good, and *phōnē*, voice.] In organ-building, a stop producing a peculiarly sweet and subdued tone.

eū-phō′ni-ad, *n.* [Gr. *euphōnos*, sweet-voiced.] A musical instrument resembling an orchestrion.

eū-phon′iç, **eū-phon′iç-ăl**, *a.* Agreeable in sound; pleasing to the ear; euphonious.

eū-phon′i-çon, *n.* A musical instrument of sweet tone resembling the upright piano in form.

eū-phō′ni-ous, *a.* Agreeable in sound.

eū-phō′ni-ous-ly, *adv.* With euphony; harmoniously.

eū′phō-niṣm, *n.* An agreeable sound or combination of sounds.

eū-phō′ni-um, *n.* [L., from Gr. *euphōnos*, sweet-voiced, musical.]

1. In music, the lowest instrument of the saxhorn family, having a loud and deep but unsympathetic tone.

2. A musical instrument in which the sounds are produced by the vibrations of glass tubes operated upon by moistened fingers.

eū′phō-nīze, *v.t.* To make euphonic or agreeable in sound.

eū′phō-non, *n.* Same as *Euphonicon*.

eū′phō-nous, *a.* [Rare.] See *Euphonious*.

eū′phō-ny, *n.*; *pl.* **eū′phō-nieṣ**. [LL. *euphonia*; Gr. *euphōnia*, goodness of voice, from *euphōnos*, sweet-voiced, musical; *eu*, well, and *phōnē*, voice.] An agreeable sound; easy, smooth enunciation of sounds; pronunciation which is pleasing to the ear.

Eū-phọr′bi-ȧ, *n.* [L., from Gr. *euphorbion*, an African plant, named from *Euphorbos*, Euphorbus, physician to the king of Mauretania.] A genus of exogenous plants of the order *Euphorbiaceæ*. They are known generally as *spurges*. All abound in a milky acrid juice.

Eū-phọr-bi-ā′cē-æ, *n.pl.* An important order of exogenous plants, consisting of herbs, shrubs, or very large trees, occurring in all regions of the globe except the arctic. They have an acrid milky juice, and some are poisonous, though the roots of others abound in starch.

eū-phọr-bi-ā′ceous, **eū-phọr′bi-ăl**, *a.* Of, relating to, or resembling the *Euphorbiaceæ*.

eū-phọr′bi-um, *n.* [Gr. *euphorbion*, euphorbium, said to be from *Euphorbus*, physician to Juba, king of Mauretania.] The juice of several species of *Euphorbia*, either exuding naturally or from incisions made in the bark. It is a powerful acrid substance, violently purgative and emetic.

eū-phō′ri-ȧ, **eū′phō-ry**, *n.* [L., from Gr. *euphoria*, the power of bearing easily, from *euphoros*, bearing well; *eu*, well, and *pherein*, to bear.] In pathology, (a) ready endurance of pain or affliction; (b) the state of feeling well, especially when not in good health.

eū-phō′tide, *n.* [Fr. *euphotide*, from Gr. *eu*, well, and *phōs*, *phōtos*, light.] In mineralogy, a coarse-grained variety of gabbro, common in the Alps.

Eū-phrā′si-ȧ, *n.* [L., from Gr. *euphrasia*, delight, good cheer, from *euphrainein*, to delight, cheer; *eu*, well, and *phrēn*, mind.] A small genus of herbs, of the order *Scrophulariaceæ*, natives of temperate regions. There are about twelve species.

eū′phrȧ-sy, *n.* The eyebright, *Euphrasia officinalis*.

eū′phrōe, *n.* Same as *Uphroe*.

eū′phū-iṣm, *n.* [From *Euphues*, a fictitious character in John Lyly's works, from Gr. *euphyēs*, shapely, graceful; *eu*, well, and *phyē*, growth, from *phyein*, to grow.] An affectation of excessive elegance and refinement of language, high-flown diction.

eū′phū-ist, *n.* One who affects excessive refinement and elegance of language; applied particularly to a class of writers in the age of Elizabeth, who were noted for their unnatural and high-flown diction.

eū-phū-ist′iç, *a.* Pertaining to the euphuists or to euphuism.

eū′phū-īze, *v.i.* To affect great nicety of expression in speaking or in writing.

eū-pī′on, eū-pī′ōne, *n.* [Gr. *eupiōn*, very fat; *eu*, well, and *piōn*, fat.] In chemistry, a fragrant, colorless, highly volatile, and inflammable liquid, obtained by the destructive distillation of bones, wood, coal, etc.

eū-pit′tōne, *n.* [*Eu-*, and *pitt*acal, and *-one.*] In chemistry, a yellow crystalline substance, resembling aurin and obtained from the oil of wood-tar; also called *eupittonic acid.*

eū-plas′tiç, *a.* and *n.* [Gr. *euplastos*, easy to mold; *eu*, well, and *plassein*, to mold, form.]

I. *a.* Capable of being readily transformed into animal tissue.

II. *n.* A substance thus transformable.

Eū-plec-tel′lȧ, *n.* A genus typical of the *Euplectellidæ*; *Euplectella aspergillum* is the beautiful glass-sponge known as Venus's flower-basket.

Eū-plec-tel′li-dæ, *n.pl.* [L., from Gr. *euplektos*, well-plaited; *eu*, well, and *plektos*, plaited, from *plekein*, to plait.] A family of beautiful silicious sponges having six-rayed spicules; the glass-sponges.

Eū-plex-op′te-rȧ, *n.pl.* [L., from Gr. *eu*, well, *plekein*, to twist, and *pteron*, a wing.] In entomology, a suborder of orthopterous insects, varying from the type of their group, having short anterior wings, under which the posterior ones fold. It includes the *Forficulidæ* or earwigs.

eūp-nœ′ȧ (-nē′ȧ), *n.* [L., from Gr. *eu*, well, and *pnoiē*, breath, from *pnein*, to breathe.] Normal respiration.

eū-pyr′i-on, *n.* [L., from Gr. *eu*, well, and *pyr*, *pyros*, fire.] Any contrivance by which a light may be instantly obtained, as an ordinary match.

Eū-raf′riç, Eū-raf′ri-çăn, *a.* [*Eu*rope and *Africa.*] Designating the close physical relation between the continent of Europe and northern Africa; used in geology, biology, ethnology, physiography, etc.; as, a *Eurafric* type of animal or plant; *Eurafrican* climatic conditions, etc.; also called *Mediterranean.*

Eū-raq′ui-lō (-rak′wi-), *n.* Same as *Euroclydon.*

Eū-rā′siȧ (-shiȧ), *n.* [*Eur*ope and *Asia.*] In geology and physiography, the great landmass made up of Europe and Asia.

Eū-rā′siăn (-shăn), *a.* and *n.* I. *a.* Pertaining to or consisting of both Europe and Asia; combining both European and Asiatic characteristics; as, a *Eurasian* people.

II. *n.* A half-caste or person having one European and one Asiatic parent; originally restricted to one whose father was a European and mother a Hindu; also called *chee-chee.*

Eū-rā-si-at′iç (-shi-), *a.* Same as *Eurasian.*

eū-rē′kȧ, *interj.* [Gr., I have found (it), 1st pers. perf. ind. act. of *heuriskein*, to find, discover.] An expression used upon making a discovery. Literally, I have found (it); attributed to Archimedes, when after long study he suddenly discovered a method by which he might ascertain the amount of alloy in King Hiero's crown.

Eū-rhip-i-dū′rȧ (ū-rip-), *n.pl.* [L., from Gr. *eu*, well, *rhipis*, *rhipidos*, a fan, and *oura*, tail.] A primary group of birds, distinguished by having the tail-feathers arranged like a fan. It includes all living and most extinct birds.

eū-rhip-i-dū′rous, *a.* Having a fan-shaped tail; specifically, of or pertaining to the *Eurhipidura.*

eū′ri-pīze, *v.i.* To fluctuate; to move or be carried hither and thither, as the tide in a strait. [Obs.]

eū-rī′pus, *n.* [L., from Gr. *euripos*, a strait of the sea where the tide is violent; *eu*, well, and *rhipē*, a rushing motion, from *rhipein*, to rush.] A strait; a narrow tract of water where the tide or a current flows and reflows, as that in Greece between Eubœa and Bœotia.

eū′rīte, *n.* [Fr. *eurite*, from Gr. *eurys*, wide.] Feldspathic granite, of which feldspar is the principal ingredient; felsite.

Eū-roç′ly-don, *n.* [Gr. *Euroklydōn*; *Euros*, the east wind, and *klydōn*, a wave, billow, from *klyzein*, to dash against. *Euryklydōn* is another reading for *eurykylon*, a northeast wind, as in the Latin Vulgate *Euro-aquilo*; *Eurus*, the east or southeast wind and *Aquilo*, north wind.] A tempestuous wind which frequently blows from the northeast in the Levant; a levanter; hence, any northeast wind.

Eū-rō-pē′ăn, *a.* Of, pertaining to, or connected with Europe or its inhabitants; native to or derived from Europe.

European plan; a method of hotel-keeping, according to which guests pay a set price per day for lodging and service only, the meals being taken à la carte at the hotel restaurant or wherever the guests may choose. [U. S.]

Eū-rō-pē′ăn, *n.* 1. A native of Europe.

2. One of European descent in any country outside of Europe, as distinguished from the natives of such country.

Eū-rō-pē′ăn-īze, *v.t.*; Europeanized, *pt.*, *pp.*; Europeanizing, *ppr.* To cause to resemble Europeans or to become European in any respect.

Eū-rō-pē′ō-Ā-si-at′iç (-shi-at′iç), *a.* In phytogeography, Eurasian; palearctic; as, *Europeo-Asiatic* flora.

eū-rō′pi-um, *n.* One of a group of elements newly discovered. [See Table of Elements under *Element*, n. 2.]

Eū′rus, *n.* [L., from Gr. *Euros*, the east or east-southeast wind.] The southeast wind.

eū-ry-. A combining form from Gr. *eurys*, broad, used in scientific terms to signify broad, wide, as in *eury*cephalic.

Eū-ry′ȧ-lē, *n.* [*Eury-*, and Gr. *halōs*, a threshing-floor, a round area.]

1. In botany, a genus of water-lilies of India and China, with one species, *Euryale ferox*, the seeds of which are edible.

2. In zoölogy, the type-genus of the *Euryalidæ.*

Eū-ry-al′i-dæ, *n.pl.* A family of brittle-stars or sand-stars, of the order *Ophiuroidea*, having branching rays.

eū″ry-ce-phal′iç, eū-ry-ceph′ȧ-lous, *a.* [*Eury-*, and Gr. *kephalē*, head.] In ethnology, having a broad head.

eū-ryç′ēr-ous, *a.* [*Eury-*, and Gr. *keras*, a horn.] In zoölogy, broad-horned.

eū-ryg′nȧ-thous, *a.* [*Eury-*, and Gr. *gnathos*, the jaw.] In ethnology, characterized by a broad upper jaw.

Eū-ryp-ter′i-dæ, *n.pl.* [*Eury-*, and Gr. *pteron*, wing.] A family of fossil crustaceans of the order *Merostomata*, closely allied to the king-crabs. They range from the upper Silurian to the lower coal-measures, inclusive.

eū-ryp′tēr-oid, *a.* and *n.* I. *a.* Pertaining to or resembling the *Eurypterus.*

II. *n.* Any species of *Eurypterus.*

Eū-ryp′te-rus, *n.* The type-genus of the *Eurypteridæ.*

eū-ryth′my, *n.* [Gr. *eurythmia*, harmony, from *eurythmos*, rhythmical; *eu*, well, and *rhythmos*, rhythm.]

1. In the fine arts, harmony of proportion.

2. In medicine, the regular beating of the pulse.

Eū-sē′bi-ăn, *a.* and *n.* I. *a.* Of or pertaining to Eusebius, a bishop of Constantinople in the fourth century, or to his doctrines, which were Arian.

II. *n.* A follower of Eusebius.

eū-spō-ran′ġi-āte, *a.* [Gr. *eu*, well, *spora*, a seed, and *angeion*, a vessel, receptacle.] Having the spore-cases produced by a group of cells instead of by a single cell, as certain ferns.

Eū-stā′chi-ăn, *a.* 1. Of, pertaining to, or discovered by Eustachius, a famous Italian anatomist and physician of the sixteenth century.

Eustachian catheter; see under *Catheter.*

Eustachian tube; a slender pipe affording a passage for the air from the middle ear to the pharynx.

Eustachian valve; a prolongation of the lining membrane of the inferior vena cava into the right auricle of the fetal heart.

Eū-stā′thi-ăn, *a.* Of or pertaining to Eustathius, an orthodox bishop of Antioch.

Eū-stā′thi-ăn, *n.* 1. One of an orthodox faction in Antioch which in the fourth century supported Eustathius, bishop of Antioch, when an attempt was made to replace him by an Arian.

2. One of a sect of the fourth century who lived an ascetic life, following the example of Eustathius, bishop of Sebaste in Pontus.

Eū-stō′mȧ-tȧ, *n.pl.* [L., from Gr. *eu*, well, and *stoma*, mouth.] A division of *Infusoria*, having a well-developed oral aperture, a body less plastic than that of most infusorians, and not more than two flagella.

eū-stom′ȧ-tous, *a.* Having a well-developed mouth; specifically, resembling the *Eustomata.*

eū′stȳle, *n.* [Gr. *eustylos*, having goodly pillars; *eu*, well, and *stylos*, a column, pillar.] See *Intercolumniation.*

eū′tax-y, *n.* [Gr. *eutaxia*, good arrangement.] Established order. [Rare.]

eū-teç′tiç, *a.* [Gr. *eutēktos*, melting readily; *eu*, well, and *tēkein*, to melt, fuse.] Having the greatest fusibility; said of any given alloy having the lowest melting point attainable; as, a *eutectic* alloy of iron and nickel.

Eū-tēr′pē, *n.* [Gr. *Euterpē*, one of the Muses, from *euterpēs*, delightful, charming; *eu*, well, and *terpein*, to delight, charm.]

1. One of the Muses, considered as presiding over lyric music. She is usually represented as a virgin crowned with flowers, having a flute in her hand or with various musical instruments about her.

2. In botany, a genus of South American palms having slender cylindrical stems, sometimes nearly 100 feet in height, crowned by a tuft of pinnate leaves, the leaflets narrow, regular, and close together. One of the chief species is the *Euterpe edulis* or assai palm of Para, Brazil.

Euterpe, from the Vatican.

Eū-tēr′pē-ăn, *a.* Relating to Euterpe; hence, pertaining to music.

eū-tex′i-ȧ, *n.* [L., from Gr. *eutēxia*, being easily melted; *eu*, well, and *tēkein*, to melt.] The art or process of finding eutectic alloys; the quality of melting readily.

eū-tha-nā′si-ȧ, eū-than′ȧ-sy, *n.* [L., from Gr. *euthanasia*, a painless, happy death; *eu*, well, and *thanatos*, death.]

1. A painless death; a peaceful manner of dying.

> The kindest wish of my friends is *euthanasia.*
> —Arbuthnot.

2. A putting to death by painless means; a means of putting to a painless death.

eū-then′iċs, *n.* 1. The science and art of improving the human race through securing the best of external influences and conditions of environment for the development of the individual physically, mentally and morally, and for maintaining his vigor and his health.

2. The science aiming to secure the conditions most favorable to the growth of plants and animals.

Eū-thy-neū′rȧ, *n.pl.* [L., from Gr. *euthys*, straight, and *neuron*, nerve.] An extensive division of gasteropod mollusks having straight visceral nerve loops.

eū-thy-tat′iç, *a.* [L., from Gr. *euthys*, straight, and *tasis*, a stretching, tension, from *teinein*, to stretch.] In physics, pertaining to or characterized by direct or longitudinal stress.

eū-troph′iç, *a.* and *n.* [Gr. *eutrophos*, nourishing; *eu*, well, and *trephein*, to nourish.]

I. *a.* Pertaining to or aiding nutrition.

II. *n.* Any agent which promotes nutrition.

eū′trō-phy, *n.* [Gr. *eutrophia*, good nurture, from *eutrophos*, nourishing.] In medicine, healthy nutrition.

eū-trop′iç, *a.* [Gr. *eutropos*, easily turning; *eu*, well, and *trepein*, to turn.] Turning with the sun; said of climbing plants, etc.

Eū-tyçh′i-ăn, *a.* and *n.* I. *a.* Of or pertaining to Eutyches or to his religious doctrines.

II. *n.* A follower of Eutyches, a monk of Constantinople in the fifth century, who held that the divine and human natures of Christ, after their union, became so blended together as to constitute but one nature.

eū-tyçh′i-ăn-iṣm, *n.* The doctrine of Eutyches.

eūx-an′thiç, *a.* Pertaining to or derived from euxanthin.

Euxanthic acid; an acid, $C_{21}H_{18}O_{11}$, obtained from euxanthin; also called *purreic acid.*

eūx-an′thin, *n.* [Gr. *eu*, well, and *xanthos*, yellow.] A substance supposed to be derived from the bile or urine of the buffalo, camel, or elephant. It comes from India under the name of *purree* or *Indian yellow*, and is used as a pigment. It forms small yellow crystals, and is the magnesium salt of euxanthic acid.

eūx′e-nīte, *n.* [Gr. *euxenos*, hospitable, friendly; *eu*, well, and *xenos*, a guest, friend.] A brilliant, brownish-black mineral found in Norway. It contains yttrium, columbium, uranium, and some other metals, and crystallizes in the orthorhombic system.

ē-vaç′ū-ănt, *a.* and *n.* [L. *evacuans* (-*antis*), ppr. of *evacuare*, to empty out, evacuate.]

I. *a.* In medicine, emptying; causing evacuations; purgative.

II. *n.* A medicine which causes evacuations or promotes the natural secretions and excretions.

ē-vaç′ū-āte, *v.t.*; evacuated, *pt.*, *pp.*; evacuating, *ppr.* [L. *evacuatus*, pp. of *evacuare*, to empty out, purge; *e*, out, and *vacuare*, to make empty, from *vacuus*, empty.]

1. To make empty; to deprive of anything essential; as, to *evacuate* the Scriptures. [Rare.]

2. To free from contents; to make empty; as, to *evacuate* the stomach.

3. To quit; to withdraw from; as, the enemy *evacuated* the city.

4. To make void; to nullify; as, to *evacuate* a marriage or any contract. [Obs.]

5. To void; to discharge; to eject; as, to *evacuate* excrementitious matter.

ē-vaç-ū-ā′tion, *n.* 1. The act of emptying or clearing of the contents; the act of withdrawing from, as an army or garrison.

2. A discharge by stool or other natural means; a diminution of the fluids of an animal body by cathartics, venesection, or other artificial means.

Evacuation day; the anniversary of the day (Nov. 25, 1783) on which the British troops evacuated the city of New York.

ē-vac′ū-ā-tive, *a.* Tending to evacuate; purgative.

ē-vac′ū-ā-tŏr, *n.* One who or that which evacuates.

ē-vac′ū-ā-tō-ry, *n.* A purgative. [Obs.]

ē-vād′ā-ble, ē-vād′i-ble, *a.* Capable of being evaded.

ē-vāde′, *v.t.*; evaded, *pt., pp.*; evading, *ppr.* [L. *evadere*, to pass beyond, escape; *e*, out, from, and *vadere*, to go.]

1. To avoid by dexterity; to escape cleverly; to avoid or escape by artifice or stratagem; to slip away from; to elude by subterfuge, sophistry, or ingenuity; as, the advocate *evades* an argument or the force of an argument; to *evade* pursuit.

2. To baffle; to foil; as, the mystery *evades* solution.

ē-vāde′, *v.i.* 1. To escape; to slip away; formerly with *from*; as, to *evade from* perils. [Obs.]

2. To attempt to escape; to practise artifice or sophistry for the purpose of eluding; to make use of evasion.

Syn.—Equivocate, prevaricate, avoid, escape, shuffle.—These words designate an artful mode of escaping the scrutiny of an inquirer; we *evade* by artfully turning the subject or calling off the attention of the inquirer; we *equivocate* by the use of equivocal expressions; we *prevaricate* by the use of loose and indefinite expressions; we avoid giving satisfaction by *evading*; we give a false satisfaction by *equivocating*; we give dissatisfaction by *prevaricating*.

ē-vād′i-ble, *a.* Same as *Evadable*.

ev-ȧ-gā′tion, *n.* [L. *evagatio* (*-onis*), from *evagari*, to wander forth; *e*, from, and *vagari*, to wander.] The act of wandering; excursion; a roving or rambling. [Rare.]

ē-vaġ′i-nȧ-ble, *a.* Capable of being evaginated.

ē-vaġ′i-nāte, *v.t.*; evaginated, *pt., pp.*; evaginating, *ppr.* [LL. *evaginatus*, pp. of *evaginare*, to unsheath; L. *e*, from, and *vagina*, a sheath.] To unsheath; to turn inside out.

ē-vaġ′i-nāte, *a.* Evaginated; protruded.

ē-vaġ-i-nā′tion, *n.* 1. The act of unsheathing.

2. That which is unsheathed or protruded, as any protrusible part or organ.

ē′văl, *a.* Relating to time or an age. [Obs.]

ē-val′ū-āte, *v.t.*; evaluated, *pt., pp.*; evaluating, *ppr.* [Fr. *évaluer*, to value; L. *e*, from, and *valere*, to be strong, to be worth.] To determine the value of; to appraise; specifically, in mathematics, to determine the numerical value of.

ē-val-ū-ā′tion, *n.* [Fr.] Valuation; appraisement; the ascertainment of the numerical value of any mathematical expression.

ē-valv′ū-lăr, *a.* [L. *e-* priv., and *valvula*, dim. of *valva*, a valve.] In botany, devoid of valves; as, an *evalvular* pericarp.

ev-ȧ-nesce′, *v.i.*; evanesced (-nest′), *pt., pp.*; evanescing, *ppr.* [L. *evanescere*, to vanish away; *e*, out, and *vanescere*, to vanish.] To disappear; to vanish away; to fade away gradually.

ev-ȧ-nes′cence, *n.* 1. A vanishing; the act of fading away; a gradual departure from sight or possession, either by removal to a distance or by dissipation, as vapor.

2. The state of being liable to vanish and escape possession.

ev-ȧ-nes′cent, *a.* [L. *evanescens* (*-entis*), ppr. of *evanescere*, to vanish away.]

1. Vanishing; fleeting; passing away; liable to dissipation, like vapor, or to become imperceptible; as, the pleasures and joys of life are *evanescent*.

2. Passing beyond the reach of perception; impalpable; imperceptible; unstable.

> The difference between right and wrong, in some petty cases, is almost *evanescent*.
> —Wollaston.

ev-ȧ-nes′cent-ly, *adv.* In an evanescent manner.

ē-van′ġel, *n.* [ME. *evangile*; OFr. *evangile*; LL. *evangelium*, the gospel; New Testament Gr. *euangelion*, good news, the gospel, from Gr. *euangelos*, bringing good news; *eu*, well, and *angelos*, a messenger.]

1. The gospel or any one of the four Gospels.

2. Good tidings.

3. An evangelist. [Rare.]

ē-van-ġē′li-ăn, *a.* Rendering thanks for favors.

ē-van-ġel′iç, *a.* Same as *Evangelical*.

ē-van-ġel′iç-ăl, *a.* [LL. *evangelicus*, from Gr. *euangelikos*, of or for the gospel or glad tidings, from *euangelion*, the gospel, good tidings; *eu*, well, and *angelos*, a messenger.]

1. Contained in the Gospels, or first four books of the New Testament; as, *evangelical* history.

2. According to the gospel or religious truth taught in the New Testament; consonant to the doctrines and precepts of the gospel published by Christ and his apostles; as, *evangelical* righteousness, obedience, or piety.

3. Earnest for the truth taught in the gospel; sound in the doctrines of the gospel; adhering closely to the letter of the gospel; specifically applied to such of the Protestant churches as profess to base their principles on Scripture alone.

Evangelical Alliance; an association of evangelical Christians belonging to various churches and countries, formed in 1845 to concentrate the strength of Protestantism.

Evangelical church; the German United Evangelical church, founded in Prussia in 1817, and the largest of the Protestant churches in Germany.

Evangelical Union; a religious body constituted in Scotland in 1843, its originator being the Rev. James Morison of Kilmarnock.

ē-van-ġel′iç-ăl, *n.* One who maintains evangelical principles.

ē-van-ġel′iç-ăl-işm, *n.* Adherence to evangelical doctrines.

ē-van-ġel′iç-ăl-ly, *adv.* In a manner according to the gospel.

ē-van-ġel′iç-ăl-ness, *n.* The state of being evangelical.

ē-van-ġel′i-çişm, *n.* Evangelicalism.

ē-van-ġe-liç′i-ty, *n.* The quality of being evangelical; evangelicism.

ē-van′ġel-işm, *n.* The promulgation of the gospel; evangelical preaching.

ē-van′ġel-ist, *n.* [ME. *evangeliste*; OFr. *evangeliste*; New Testament Gr. *euangelistēs*, a preacher of the gospel, one of the writers of the Gospels, from *euangelizesthai*, to preach the gospel, from Gr. *eu*, well, and *angelos*, a messenger.]

1. A writer of the history or doctrines, precepts, actions, life, and death of Jesus Christ; as, the four *evangelists*, Matthew, Mark, Luke, and John.

2. A preacher of the gospel of Jesus Christ, especially a traveling preacher; a revivalist; a missionary

ē-van-ġel-is′tȧ-ry, *n.* A selection of passages from the Gospels, as a lesson in divine service; a book containing such passages, used in the Greek and Roman churches.

ē-van-ġel-is′tiç, *a.* Pertaining to an evangelist or to his labors; evangelical.

ē-van″ġel-i-zā′tion, *n.* The act of evangelizing.

ē-van′ġel-īze, *v.t.*; evangelized, *pt., pp.*; evangelizing, *ppr.* [ME *evangelizen*; OFr. *evangeliser*; LL. *evangelizare*; New Testament Gr. *euangelizesthai*, to preach the gospel, from Gr. *eu*, good, and *angelos*, a messenger.] To instruct in the gospel; to preach the gospel to and convert to a belief in the gospel; as, to *evangelize* heathen nations; to *evangelize* the world.

ē-van′ġel-īze, *v.i.* To preach the gospel; to act as an evangelist.

ē-van′ġel-y, *n.* Good tidings; the gospel. [Obs.]

ē-van′ġile, *n.* [Obs.] See *Evangel*.

ē-van′id, *a.* Faint; weak; evanescent; liable to vanish or disappear; as, an *evanid* color or smell. [Obs.]

Ev-ȧ-nī′i-dæ, *n.pl.* [L., from Gr. *euanios*, bearing trouble easily; *eu*, well, and *ania*, trouble.] A family of parasitic insects belonging to the order *Hymenoptera*.

ē-van′ish, *v.i.* [L. *evanescere*, to vanish.] To vanish; to disappear; to escape from sight or perception. [Poet.]

ē-van′ish-ment, *n.* A vanishing; disappearance.

ē-vap′ō-rȧ-ble, *a.* Capable of being evaporated.

ē-vap′ō-rāte, *v.i.*; evaporated, *pt., pp.*; evaporating, *ppr.* [L. *evaporatus*, pp. of *evaporare*, to disperse in vapor; *e*, from, and *vaporare*, to emit vapor, from *vapor*, vapor.]

1. To pass off in vapor, as a fluid; to escape and be dissipated, either in visible vapor or in particles too minute to be visible; to change from a liquid to a gaseous condition.

2. To escape or pass off without effect; to be dissipated; to be wasted; as, arguments *evaporate* in words; the spirit of a writer often *evaporates* in translating.

ē-vap′ō-rāte, *v.t.* 1. To change or convert from a solid or liquid state into a vapor, usually by means of heat; to cause to pass into a gaseous state or condition; to vaporize.

2. To deprive of moisture; to desiccate; as, to *evaporate* apricots, apples, etc.

3. To drive away; to dissipate; as, the laughter *evaporated* his anger. [Rare.]

ē-vap′ō-rāte, *a.* Dispersed in vapors. [Rare.]

ē-vap-ō-rā′tion, *n.* [L. *evaporatio* (*-onis*), evaporation, from *evaporatus*, pp. of *evaporare*, to evaporate.]

1. The act or process of converting or being converted from a solid or liquid state into a vapor or gas.

2. The act or process of concentrating or drying by removing moisture; as, the *evaporation* of fruit.

3. The matter expelled in the process of evaporating; vapor. [Rare.]

ē-vap′ō-rā-tive, *a.* Pertaining to or producing evaporation.

ē-vap′ō-rā-tŏr, *n.* Any appliance used for evaporating, as a shallow pan with slow heat beneath.

ē-vap-ō-rom′e-tẽr, *n.* [L. *evaporare*, to evaporate, and *metron*, a measure.] An instrument for ascertaining the quantity of a fluid evaporated in a given time; an atmometer.

ē-vā′si-ble, *a.* Evadable. [Rare.]

ē-vā′şion, *n.* [L. *evasio* (*-onis*), from *evasus*, pp. of *evadere*, to evade; *e*, from, and *vadere*, to go.] The act of eluding or avoiding, or of escaping, particularly from the pressure of an argument, from an accusation or charge, from an interrogatory, and the like; excuse; subterfuge; equivocation; artifice to elude; shift.

> Thou by *evasions* thy crime uncoverest more.
> —Milton.

Syn.—Sophistry, subterfuge, prevarication, equivocation, artifice.

ē-vā′sive, *a.* 1. Using evasion or artifice to avoid; elusive; shuffling; equivocating; as, he is too *evasive*.

2. Containing evasion; artfully contrived to elude a question, charge, or argument; as, an *evasive* answer; an *evasive* argument or reasoning.

ē-vā′sive-ly, *adv.* In an evasive manner; elusively; in a manner to avoid a direct reply or a charge.

ē-vā′sive-ness, *n.* The quality or state of being evasive.

ēve, *n.* [ME. *even*, *eve*; AS. *æven*, eve.]

1. The decline of the sun; the latter part or close of the day; the beginning of the night; evening; used chiefly in poetry as an equivalent for evening.

> Winter, oft, at *eve* resumes the breeze.
> —Thomson.

2. The evening before a holiday; as, Christmas *eve*.

3. Figuratively, the period just preceding some important event; as, the *eve* of a battle.

ēve′=chŭrr, *n.* The nightjar or goatsucker, *Caprimulgus europæus*. [Prov. Eng.]

ē-vec′tiçs, *n.* [L. *evectus*, pp. of *evehere*, to carry out or away; *e*, out, and *vehere*, to carry.] That branch of medicine which treats of the laws and rules for securing and maintaining a good habit of body.

ē-vec′tion, *n.* [L. *evectio* (*-onis*), a carrying away or out, from *evectus*, pp. of *evehere*, to carry out; *e*, out, from, and *vehere*, to carry.]

1. A carrying out or away; also, a lifting up; exaltation. [Obs.]

2. In astronomy, (a) a periodical inequality in the movements of the moon; (b) the libration of the moon.

ē′ven, *n.* Evening; eve; eventide.

ē′ven, *a.* [ME. *even*, *evin*; AS. *efen*, even, smooth.]

1. Level; smooth; of an equal surface; flat; not rough or waving; as, an *even* tract of land; an *even* country; an *even* surface.

2. Uniform; equal; calm; not easily ruffled or disturbed, elevated or depressed; as, an *even* temper.

3. Level with; parallel to; followed by *with*; as, *even with* the floor.

4. Settled; balanced; owing nothing on either side; having accounts equal; fair; showing no partiality; as, an *even* chance for all; both sides were *even*.

5. Capable of being divided into two equal parts without a remainder; opposed to *odd*; as, 4, 6, 8, 10 are *even* numbers.

6. Whole; having no fractional parts; as, five dollars *even*.

7. In ornithology, having a uniform termination.

8. In entomology, not having a droop or raise at the edge; flat, as the fore wings of some beetles.

9. Chaste; pure; flawless. [Obs.]

10. Clear; plain. [Obs.]

Evenly even; divisible by two and then by two; divisible by four.

Even page; in a book, the left-hand page, always given an even number.

On an even keel; a term applied to the position of the keel of a ship when she draws the same water abaft as forward, or when she is upright or not inclined to either side.

On even ground; on equal terms; without advantage.

To make even; in type-setting, to end a "take" with a full line.

Unevenly even; divisible by two but not by four; opposed to *evenly even*.

Syn.—Equal, level, plain, smooth, uniform.

ē′ven, *v.t.*; evened, *pt., pp.*; evening, *ppr.* [ME. *evenen*, *efnen*; AS. *efnian*, to make even, to compare, from *efen*, adj. even.]

1. To make even or level; to level; to lay smooth.

2. To place in an equal state as to obligation, or in a state in which nothing is due on either side; to balance, as accounts.

3. To liken; to compare; to use as an equal. [Obs.]

4. To end; to set right. [Obs.]

5. To keep up with; to satisfy. [Obs.]

ē'ven, *v.i.* To be equal; followed by *with.* [Obs.]

ē'ven, *adv.* [ME. *even*; AS. *efne*, even, exactly, quite, from *efen*, even, used as an adjective.]

1. To the same or a like degree; at the exact time; so much as; fully; exactly; quite; expressive of surprise, emphasis, concession, or addition to that which might not have been thought probable; as, *even* to the last; not *even* desirable; *even* I; known *even* to the uninitiated.

2. Yet; as much as; as, he could not pass his examination, nor *even* a part of it.

3. In a smooth manner; showing regularity; evenly; as, the soldiers marched *even.*

4. In a plain or exact manner; soon. [Obs.]

ē-vēne', *v.i.* To happen. [Obs.]

ē'ven-ēr, *n.* 1. One who or that which evens.

2. An equalizer in the form of a lever to govern the power applied; commonly applied to a doubletree.

3. In weaving, an appliance to spread the yarn on the beam.

ē'ven-fall, *n.* The first part of the evening; twilight. [Poet.]

ē'ven-hand, *n.* Equality of rank. [Obs.]

ē'ven-hand"ed, *a.* Impartial; equitable; just.

ē'ven-hand"ed-ly, *adv.* In an evenhanded manner.

ē'ven-hand"ed-ness, *n.* The state of being evenhanded.

ē'ven-ing, *n.* [ME. *evening*; AS. *æfnung*, evening, from *æfen*, even, eve.]

1. The latter part and close of the day and the beginning of darkness or night. Strictly speaking, *evening* commences at the setting of the sun and continues during twilight, and *night* commences with total darkness; but, in common usage, *evening* extends to bedtime, whatever that time may be.

2. In some parts of the United States, the afternoon.

3. The decline or latter part of anything; as, the *evening* of power; the *evening* of life.

Evening star; any bright planet seen in the west at the close of day; commonly applied to Venus.

ē'ven-ing-flow"ēr, *n.* In botany, any plant of the genus *Hesperantha*, common to South Africa, characterized by fragrant flowers which open in the evening.

ē'ven-ing-grōs"bēak, *n.* In ornithology, a night-singing bird, *Coccothraustes vespertina*, common in North America.

ē'ven-ing-prim"rōse, *n.* An erect biennial herb, *Œnothera biennis*, having yellow flowers opening in the evening.

ē'ven-ing-tīde, *n.* Evening; eventide.

ē'ven-ly, *adv.* [ME. *evenly, evenliche*; AS. *efenlice*, evenly.]

1. With an even, level, or smooth surface; without roughness, elevations, or depressions; as, things *evenly* spread.

2. Equally; uniformly; in an equipoise; as, *evenly* balanced.

3. In a level position; horizontally.

4. Impartially; without bias from favor or enmity.

ē'ven-mīnd"ed, *a.* Characterized by evenness of temper or equanimity.

ē'ven-ness (ē'vn-ness), *n.* [ME. *evennes*; AS. *efennys*, evenness, equality, from *efen*, even.]

1. The state of being even, level, or smooth; equality; uniformity; regularity.

2. Freedom from extremes; calmness; impartiality; equanimity.

ē'ven-sọng, *n.* 1. A song or hymn to be sung in the evening.

2. In the Anglican and allied churches, a form of worship to be said or sung in the evening; evening prayer.

3. The time of evening service; evening.

ē-vent', *n.* [L. *eventus, eventum*, an event, occurrence, from *evenire*, to happen; *e*, out, and *venire*, to come.]

1. That which comes, arrives, or happens; that which falls out; any incident, good or bad, especially when of considerable importance; as, the course of *events.*

2. The consequence of anything; the issue; conclusion; end; that in which an action, operation, or series of operations terminates; as, the *event* of the Civil War was the preservation of the Union.

3. A contingent, probable, or possible state of affairs; a possible or probable result; as, in that *event* I shall go.

4. Any one of a series of contests or exhibitions; as, the automobile race is the next *event.*

Syn.—Incident, occurrence, issue, result, consequence.

ē-vent', *v.i.* To break forth. [Obs.]

ē-ven'tēr-āte, *v.t.* To rip open; to disembowel. [Obs.]

ē-vent'ful, *a.* Full of events or incidents; producing numerous or great changes; as, an *eventful* period of history; an *eventful* period of life.

Syn.—Important, critical, stirring, notable.

ē'ven-tīde, *n.* Evening. [Poet.]

ē-ven'ti-lāte, *v.t.* 1. To winnow; to fan. [Obs.]

2. To discuss. [Obs.]

ē-ven-ti-lā'tion, *n.* 1. The act of fanning; ventilation. [Obs.]

2. Discussion. [Obs.]

ē-vent'less, *a.* Lacking events or excitement; monotonous; uninteresting.

Ev-en-tog'nȧ-thi, *n.pl.* [L., from Gr. *eu*, well, *entos*, within, and *gnathos*, the jaw.] A large suborder of teleost fishes found in fresh water, including the carps, chubs, etc.

ēv-en-tog'nȧ-thous, *a.* Of or pertaining to the *Eventognathi.*

ē-ven-trā'tion, *n.* [L. *e*, out, from, and *venter* (*-tris*), the belly.] In pathology, (a) evisceration; (b) the escape or protrusion of any considerable part of the viscera through a rupture in the abdominal wall.

ē-ven'tū-ăl, *a.* [L. *eventus*, an event.]

1. Coming or happening as a consequence or result of anything; consequential; final; ultimate; as, *eventual* victory.

2. Contingent upon an ultimate possibility.

ē-ven-tū-al'i-ty, *n.*; *pl.* **ē-ven-tū-al'i-ties.**

1. An event which is a consequence or result; an occurrence which is or may be brought about on account of circumstances.

2. The quality of being contingent or of happening as a consequence.

3. In phrenology, the faculty which takes cognizance of occurrences or events.

ē-ven'tū-ăl-ly, *adv.* In the event or issue.

ē-ven'tū-āte, *v.i.* 1. To come to an end; to close; to terminate.

2. To occur as a result; to happen.

ē-ven-tū-ā'tion, *n.* The act or condition of occurring as a result; the consequence; the termination.

ev'ēr, *adv.* [ME. *ever, evere*; AS. *æfre*, ever.]

1. At any time; at any period or point of time, past or future; as, have you *ever* seen the city of Paris, or shall you *ever* see it?

2. At all times; always; continually; as, *ever* fair.

3. In any degree; any; as, no man is *ever* the richer for injustice.

Ever and anon; at one time and another; now and then.

Ever in one; always; continually. [Obs.]

Ever so; to whatever degree or extent; very; as, *ever so* good.

For ever; eternally; usually written as one word.

For ever and a day; forever, emphatically. [Colloq.]

Or ever; before; as, *or ever* the silver cord be loosed. [Archaic.]

ev'ēr-dūr"ing, *a.* Enduring forever.

ev'ēr-glāde, *n.* A region of low, spongy land, usually flooded with water and covered with tall grass; used especially of the marshes of southern Florida.

ev'ēr-green, *a.* Always green; verdant throughout the year; as, the pine is an *evergreen* tree.

ev'ēr-green, *n.* 1. A plant that retains its verdure through all the seasons, as the conifers, holly, etc.

2. A twig, branch, or entire plant of any evergreen species used for ornamentation; usually in the plural; as, hung with *evergreens.*

3. A variety of woolen cloth resembling cassimere.

ev'ēr-ich, ev'ēr-ilk, *a.* Every. [Obs.]

ev"ēr-ich-ōn', ev"ēr-ich-ōōn', *pron.* Every one. [Obs.]

ev-ēr-lȧst'ing, *a.* 1. Lasting or enduring forever; eternal; immortal.

2. Perpetual; continuing indefinitely or during the present state of things; as, the *everlasting* hills.

3. Incessant; endless; continual; tiresome; as, *everlasting* disputes. [Colloq.]

Everlasting pea; a leguminous perennial plant, *Lathyrus latifolius.*

ev-ēr-lȧst'ing, *adv.* Very; extremely; as, *everlasting* big. [Colloq.]

ev-ēr-lȧst'ing, *n.* 1. Eternity; eternal duration, past and future.

From *everlasting* to *everlasting* thou art God.
—Ps. xc. 2.

2. Any one of various plants, from the permanence of the color and form of their dry flowers, as cudweeds, immortelles, etc.

3. A stout woolen cloth, used for the tops of shoes.

The Everlasting; God.

ev-ēr-lȧst'ing-ly, *adv.* 1. In an everlasting manner.

2. Very; excessively. [Colloq.]

ev-ēr-lȧst'ing-ness, *n.* The state of being everlasting; infinite duration.

ev-ēr-liv'ing, *a.* 1. Living without end; eternal.

2. Continual; incessant; unintermitted.

ev-ēr-mōre', *adv.* Always; eternally; at all times; as, happy *evermore.*

E-vēr'ni-ȧ, *n.* [L., from Gr. *euernēs*, sprouting well; *eu*, well, and *ernos*, a sprout.] A small genus of lichens.

ē-vēr'nic, *a.* Of or derived from lichens of the genus *Evernia.*

ē-vērse', *v.t.* To overthrow or subvert. [Obs.]

ē-vēr'sion, *n.* [L. *eversio* (*-onis*), an overthrowing, from *eversus*, pp. of *evertere*, to overthrow.]

1. An overthrowing; destruction. [Obs.]

2. A turning or rolling backward or inside out.

Eversion of the eyelids; ectropion, a disease in which the eyelids are turned outward, so as to expose the red internal tunic.

ē-vēr'sive, *a.* Designed or tending to evert; subversive. [Obs.]

ē-vērt', *v.t.* [L. *evertere*, to overthrow; *e*, out, from, and *vertere*, to turn.]

1. To overturn; to overthrow; to destroy. [Obs.]

2. To cause to turn inside out.

ē-vēr'tē-brăl, *a.* [L. *e-* priv., and *vertebra*, vertebra.] Not vertebral in origin or character, as the anterior portion of the skull.

E-vēr-tē-brā'tȧ, *n.pl.* Same as *Invertebrata.*

ē-vēr'tē-brāte, *a.* and *n.* Same as *Invertebrate.*

ev'ēr-y, *n.* Ivory. [Obs.]

ev'ēr-y, *a.* [ME. *every, everi*; AS. *æfre ælc.*] All, as of the items or individuals constituting an aggregate, considered separately; each, taken as part of an aggregate; any, as of a class all of whose members have the same attribute or relation.

> *Every* is separative and can be applied only to a whole composed of many individuals. It means each of all, not all in mass. It cannot, therefore, be applied to that which is, in its very nature, inseparable.
> —Richard Grant White.

Every, placed before a collective name, expresses the idea of *all*, and is equivalent to naming each individual of that class. If *not* is used before *every* it does not deny for all individuals the thing predicated, but only for some one or more of the individuals; as, *not every* business man is rich, does not mean that no business man is rich, but that some business men are not rich.

Every often expresses repetition; as, *every* hour a bulletin was issued.

Every bit; in all points; fully; quite; as, that is *every bit* as good.

Every each; every one; also, every other. [Obs.]

Every now and then, every once in a while; frequently; occasionally.

Every other; each alternate; as, *every other* Saturday was a holiday.

ev'ēr-y, *pron.* Each; everyone. [Obs.]

ev'ēr-y-bod"y, *n.* Every person; every one of a body of people; mankind in general, considered collectively.

ev'ēr-y-dāy, *a.* Used or suitable to be used every day; common; usual; as, *everyday* clothes.

ev'ēr-y-one (-wun), *n.* Everybody; usually written as two words.

ev'ēr-y-thing, *n.* 1. Each individual thing; any class of things, considered in relation to the parts of which it is composed; all things, collectively; as, *everything* in human life is interesting.

2. That which is of the greatest value or importance; as, a good reputation is *everything* to a woman.

3. A great deal; as, he thought *everything* of his children. [Colloq.]

ev'ēr-y-when, *adv.* At every point in time. [Rare.]

ev'ēr-y-where (-hwār), *adv.* [ME. *everihwar*, everywhere; *ever, evere*, ever, and *ihwar*, everywhere, from AS. *gehwær*, everywhere.]

1. In every place; in all places.

2. Wherever; as, *everywhere* I roam. [Colloq.]

ev'ēr-y-where"ness, *n.* Omnipresence. [Rare.]

ev'ēr-y-whith"ēr, *adv.* In or to every place or direction. [Rare.]

ēveṣ'drop, *v.i.* Same as *Eavesdrop.*

ēveṣ'drop"pēr, *n.* Same as *Eavesdropper.*

ē-ves'ti-gāte, *v.t.* To investigate. [Obs.]

ev'et, *n.* [AS. *efete*, a newt.]

1. An eft; a newt.

2. The crimson-spotted triton, *Spelerpes ruber.*

ē-vi'brāte, *v.i.* To vibrate. [Obs.]

ē-vict', *v.t.*; evicted, *pt., pp.*; evicting, *ppr.* [L. *evictus*, pp. of *evincere*, to overcome, prevail; *e*, from, and *vincere*, to conquer.]

1. To dispossess by a judicial process or course of legal proceedings; to expel from lands or tenements by law.

2. To take away by sentence of law, as lands.

3. To evince; to prove. [Obs.]

4. To expel by force.

ē-vic'tion, *n.* [LL. *evictio* (*-onis*), from L. *evictus*, pp. of *evincere*, to evict.]

1. The act of evicting, especially by force; the condition of being evicted; ejectment; the recovery of lands or tenements from another's possession, by due course of law.

2. Proof; conclusive evidence. [Obs.]

ev'i-dence, *n.* [ME. *evidence*; OFr. *evidence*, evidence; L. *evidentia*, clearness, from *evidens* (*-entis*), clear, evident; *e*, from, and *videre*, to see.]

1. That which enables the mind to see truth; proof arising from perception by the senses, or

from the testimony of others, or from inductions of reason; as, the senses furnish *evidence* of the existence of matter.

2. In law, the means by which an allegation in a cause is proved true or false.

3. One who supplies *evidence*; a witness; used especially in the phrases *state's evidence*, *king's* or *queen's evidence*.

4. Condition of being evident. [Rare.]

Circumstantial evidence; see under *Circumstantial*.

In evidence; (a) in law, having been accepted by the court as legal and competent proof; (b) plain; visible; conspicuous; as, his nose was very much *in evidence*.

King's or *queen's evidence*; the British equivalent for *state's evidence*.

Moral evidence; evidence sufficient to satisfy the mind, although not susceptible of rigid and incontrovertible demonstration.

State's evidence; (a) the evidence offered by the state in prosecuting criminal cases; (b) a person who gives testimony against accomplices in a crime of which he himself is guilty.

Syn.—Proof, witness, testimony, affirmation, demonstration, certainty.

ev'i-dence, *v.t.*; evidenced (-denst), *pt.*, *pp.*; evidencing, *ppr.* 1. To prove; to make clear.

2. To support by testimony. [Obs.]

ev'i-den-cẽr, *n.* A witness. [Obs.]

ev'i-dent, *a.* [ME. *evident*; OFr. *evident*; L. *evidens* (*-entis*), visible, clear; *e*, out, and *videre*, to see.] Plain; open to be seen; manifest to the senses or to the mind; apparent; as, colors of bodies are *evident* to the eye; the guilt of an offender cannot always be made *evident*.

Syn.—Plain, visible, conspicuous, manifest, indisputable, obvious, clear, palpable, incontrovertible, apparent, discernible.

ev-i-den'tiăl (-shăl), *a.* Of the nature of or affording evidence; proving.

ev-i-den'tiăl-ly, *adv.* In an evidential manner.

ev-i-den'ti-ā-ry (-shi-), *a.* Same as *Evidential*.

ev'i-dent-ly, *adv.* Clearly; obviously; plainly; in a manner to be seen and understood; in a manner to convince the mind; certainly; manifestly.

ev'i-dent-ness, *n.* The state or quality of being evident.

ē-vig'i-lāte, *v.i.* To watch attentively. [Obs.]

ē-vig-i-lā'tion, *n.* A waking or watching. [Obs.]

ē'vil, *a.* [ME. *evel*; AS. *yfel*, evil.]

1. Having bad qualities of a natural kind; mischievous; having qualities which tend to injury, or to produce mischief; as, an *evil* drug.

2. Having bad moral qualities; sinful; bad; wicked; corrupt; perverse; wrong; as, *evil* thoughts; *evil* deeds; *evil* speaking; an *evil* generation.

3. Unfortunate; unhappy; producing sorrow, distress, injury, or calamity; as, *evil* tidings; *evil* arrows; *evil* days.

4. Of ill repute; caused by or considered as being caused by immorality; as, an *evil* name; *evil* fame.

The evil eye; a baleful influence superstitiously ascribed in former times to certain persons, by virtue of which they could injure whatever they cast a hostile or envious look upon.

The evil one; the devil; sometimes personified and written with capitals.

Syn.—Mischievous, pernicious, injurious, hurtful, destructive, noxious, baneful, baleful, wicked, bad, corrupt, perverse, vile, base, wrong, vicious, calamitous.

ē'vil, *n.* [ME. *evel*; AS. *yfel*, evil.]

1. Anything that causes displeasure, injury, pain, or suffering; misfortune; calamity; mischief; injury; the negation or contrary of *good*.

2. Moral depravity; disposition to commit wickedness; malignity; conduct which reveals a depraved disposition.

3. A malady or disease; as, the king's *evil* or scrofula, formerly believed curable by the sovereign's touch.

The social evil; sexual immorality; prostitution.

ē'vil, *adv.* [ME. *evill*; AS. *yfele*, in an evil manner.] Not well; ill; in an evil manner; unfortunately; injuriously; unkindly.

ē'vil-dō"ẽr, *n.* One who does evil.

ē'vil-eyed (ē'vl-īd), *a.* Possessing or believed to possess the evil eye; looking with envy, jealousy, or bad design.

ē'vil-fā"vŏred, *a.* Having a bad countenance or appearance; ill-favored; deformed.

ē'vil-fā"vŏred-ness, *n.* Deformity.

ē'vil-ly, *adv.* In an evil manner.

ē'vil-mind"ed, *a.* Having evil dispositions or intentions; disposed to mischief or sin; malicious; malignant; wicked.

ē'vil-mind"ed-ness, *n.* The state or quality of being evil-minded.

ē'vil-ness, *n.* The state or quality of being evil.

ē-vince', *v.t.*; evinced (-vinst'), *pt.*, *pp.*; evincing, *ppr.* [L. *evincere*, to conquer, overcome; *e*, from, out, and *vincere*, to conquer.]

1. To show in a clear manner; to prove beyond any reasonable doubt; to manifest; to make evident; as, to *evince* a desire; to *evince* stupidity.

2. To conquer. [Obs.]

ē-vince'ment, *n.* The act of evincing.

ē-vin'ci-ble, *a.* Capable of proof; demonstrable.

ē-vin'ci-bly, *adv.* In a manner to evince.

ē-vin'cive, *a.* Tending or having the power to prove.

ē'vi-rāte, *v.t.* To emasculate. [Obs.]

ev-i-rā'tion, *n.* Castration. [Obs.]

ē-vis'cẽr-āte, *v.t.*; eviscerated, *pt.*, *pp.*; eviscerating, *ppr.* [L. *evisceratus*, pp. of *eviscerare*, to deprive of the entrails.] To disembowel; to take out the entrails of.

ē-vis-cẽr-ā'tion, *n.* The act of disemboweling; the state of being disemboweled.

ev'i-tȧ-ble, *a.* [L. *evitabilis*, avoidable, from *evitare*, to shun, avoid.] Capable of being shunned; avoidable. [Rare.]

ev'i-tāte, *v.t.* To shun; to avoid; to escape. [Obs.]

ē-vi-tā'tion, *n.* An avoiding; a shunning. [Obs.]

ē-vīte', *v.t.* To shun; to avoid. [Obs.]

ev-i-tẽr'năl, *a.* Enduring forever; eternal. [Obs.]

ev-i-tẽr'năl-ly, *adv.* Eternally. [Obs.]

ev-i-tẽr'ni-ty, *n.* Eternity. [Obs.]

ē-vit'tāte, *a.* [L. *e-* priv., and *vitta*, a band, fillet.] In botany, having no vittæ, as the fruit of certain plants.

ev'ō-gāte, *v.t.* To evoke; to call forth. [Rare.]

ev-ō-gā'tion, *n.* [L. *evocatio* (*-onis*), a calling out or forth, from *evocatus*, pp. of *evocare*, to call out or forth.]

1. A calling or bringing from concealment; a calling forth.

2. In civil law, the removal of a cause from a lower to a higher court.

ē-vŏ'gȧ-tive, *a.* Tending to evoke; developing.

ev'ō-gā-tŏr, *n.* [L.] One who calls forth. [Rare.]

ē-vōke', *v.t.*; evoked (-vōkt'), *pt.*, *pp.*; evoking, *ppr.* [L. *evocare*, to call forth, summon; *e*, out, from, and *vocare*, to call.]

1. To call forth.

2. To call from one tribunal to another. [Rare.]

ev-ō-lat'iç, ev-ō-lat'iç-ăl, *a.* Apt to fly away. [Obs.]

ev-ō-lā'tion, *n.* The act of flying away. [Obs.]

ev'ō-lūte, *n.* [L. *evolutus*, pp. of *evolvere*, to unroll, unfold; *e*, out, from, and *volvere*, to roll.] In geometry, a curve from which another curve, called the *involute*, may be traced by the end of a thread gradually unwound from it. It thus forms the locus of the centers of curvature of and the envelope of the normals to the involute.

ev"ō-lū-til'i-ty, *n.* In biology, the capability of an organism to exhibit change in structure, size, etc., as a result of nutrition.

ev-ō-lū'tion, *n.* [L. *evolutio* (*-onis*), an unrolling or opening, from *evolutus*, pp. of *evolvere*, to unroll; *e*, out, and *volvere*, to roll.]

1. The act of unfolding or unrolling.

2. A thing or series of things unrolled, unfolded, or evolved; as, the *evolution* of ages.

3. In mathematics; (a) in geometry, the unfolding or opening of a curve, making it describe an involute; (b) in arithmetic and algebra, the extraction of roots; the reverse of *involution*.

4. A turning movement; a change of position, especially in accordance with some definite plan; specifically, (a) in military tactics, the doubling of ranks or files, wheeling, countermarching, or other motion by which the disposition of troops is changed; (b) in naval tactics, the change of form and disposition of a fleet or the movements of a single vessel during maneuvers.

5. In biology, (a) strictly, the theory in which the germ is held to preëxist in the parent, and its parts to be unfolded and expanded, but not formed by the procreative act; (b) the series of regular successive stages through which any individual organism passes, from the time of the fertilization of the ovum to maturity; (c) the theory that all existing organisms have arisen as morphological and physiological modifications of preëxisting forms, that they are all genetically related, and that the change resulting in present differences has been gradual from the simple and less differentiated to the complex and more highly differentiated. An important theory in connection with *evolution* is that characteristics inherited and those acquired through environment, function, etc., are transmitted to the offspring.

6. In metaphysics, the theory which sees in the history of all things, organic and inorganic, a passage from simplicity to complexity, from an undifferentiated to a differentiated condition of the elements. The history of the development of an individual plant or animal, or of society, is an example. The *evolution* theory of the origin of species is that later species have been developed by continuous differentiation of organs and modifications of parts from species simpler and less differentiated, and that thus all organic existences, even man himself, may be traced back to a simple cell.

ev-ō-lū'tion-ăl, *a.* Of the nature of, pertaining to, or due to evolution.

ev-ō-lū'tion-ā-ry, *a.* Pertaining to evolution in any of its meanings; as, the *evolutionary* movements of the ship.

ev-ō-lū'tion-işm, *n.* The theory of biological or metaphysical evolution; belief in that theory.

ev-ō-lū'tion-ist, *n.* 1. One who accepts the theory of evolution.

2. One who is skilful in evolutions, as a military or naval officer.

ē-volve', *v.t.*; evolved, *pt.*, *pp.*; evolving, *ppr.* [L. *evolvere*, to roll out or forth; *e*, out, and *volvere*, to roll.]

1. To unfold; to open and expand; to elaborate.

2. To develop by a natural process from or as if from a germ; to cause to pass from a simple to a complex, or from a more diffused to a more concentrated state.

3. To throw out; to emit; as, to *evolve* gases.

ē-volve', *v.i.* To become open or developed.

ē-volve'ment, *n.* The act of evolving; the state of being evolved.

ē-volv'ent, *n.* [L. *evolvens* (*-entis*), ppr. of *evolvere*, to evolve.] In mathematics, an involute.

ē-vom'it, *v.t.* To vomit. [Obs.]

ev-ō-mi'tion (-mish'un), *n.* The act of vomiting. [Obs.]

ē-vul'gāte, *v.t.* To publish. [Obs.]

ev-ul-gā'tion, *n.* A divulging. [Obs.]

ē-vul'sion, *n.* [L. *evulsio* (*-onis*), from *evulsus*, pp. of *evellere*, to pull or pluck out.] The act of plucking or pulling out by force.

ew (ū), *n.* [Obs.] Same as *Yew*.

ewe (ū), *n.* [ME. *ewe*; AS. *eowu*, a flock of sheep.] A female sheep.

ewe'-neck (ū'nek), *n.* A thin, hollow neck, not arched, as that of some horses.

ewe'-necked (ū'nekt), *a.* Having a ewe-neck.

ew'ẽr, *n.* [ME. *ewer*; OFr. *ewere*, a water-carrier, a water-pitcher, from LL. *aquaria*, a water-pitcher, from L. *aquarius*, for water, from *aqua*, water.] A kind of pitcher with a wide spout, especially one used in the toilet to hold water; any vessel or vase with a spout and handle, especially one of an artistic and decorative nature.

ew'ẽr-y, *n.* [ME. *ewery*, from OFr. *ewere*, a water-pitcher.] Formerly, a room in pretentious houses where linen for the table was kept and water placed in ewers for use in the household; a scullery.

ewt, *n.* A newt. [Obs.]

ex-. A prefix from L. *ex*, and Gr. *ex*, signifying out, out of, from, as in *ex*hale, *ex*alt; sometimes with a privative force, as in *ex*annulate; it often has the force of off or beyond, as in *ex*ceed, *ex*cel; when prefixed to names implying office *ex-* signifies that the person formerly occupied the position, as *ex*-governor, *ex*-president; sometimes *ex-* is merely intensive, as in *ex*acerbate; *ex-* is often written *ef-*, *es-*, or *e-*, for the sake of euphony.

ex-ac'ẽr-bāte (egz-), *v.t.*; exacerbated, *pt.*, *pp.*; exacerbating, *ppr.* [L. *exacerbatus*, pp. of *exacerbare*, to exasperate, make angry; *ex-*, intens., and *acerbus*, bitter, harsh, sour.] To irritate; to exasperate; to inflame; to increase the malignant qualities of; as, to *exacerbate* fever or anger.

ex-ac-ẽr-bā'tion, *n.* [LL. *exacerbatio* (*-onis*), from L. *exacerbatus*, pp. of *exacerbare*, to irritate; *ex-*, intens., and *acerbus*, bitter.]

1. The act of exacerbating or the state of being exacerbated; exasperation; increased violence or malignity.

2. In medicine, an increase in the symptoms of a disease.

ex-ac-ẽr-bes'cence (egz-), *n.* [LL. *exacerbescere*, incept. of L. *exacerbare*, to irritate.] Increase of irritation or violence, particularly the increase of a fever or disease.

ex-ac-ẽr-vā'tion, *n.* The act of heaping up. [Obs.]

ex-ac'i-nāte (egz-), *v.t.* [L. *ex-* priv., and *acinus*, a berry, the seed of a berry.] To deprive of the kernel. [Rare.]

ex-ac-i-nā'tion, *n.* The act of taking out the kernel. [Rare.]

ex-act' (egz-), *a.* [L. *exactus*, precise, accurate, from pp. of *exigere*, to drive out, to measure, determine.]

1. Closely correct or regular, accurate; precise; correctly adjusted; not differing in the least from a standard; true; actual; as, an *exact* representation; the *exact* time; the *exact* amount; that was the *exact* statement.

2. Methodical; careful; not negligent; observing strict method, rule, or order; punctual; as, a man *exact* in business affairs; he is *exact* in keeping an appointment.

3. Characterized by exactness; definite; precisely thought out or stated; as, an *exact* demonstration.

We took as *exact* a survey as we could. —Maundrell.

Syn.—Accurate, correct, careful, methodical, precise, nice.

ex-aċt′, *v.t.*; exacted, *pt.*, *pp.*; exacting, *ppr.* [OFr. *exacter*; LL. *exactare*, freq. of L. *exigere*, to drive out or from, to demand, measure, examine; *ex*, out, from, and *agere*, to drive.] To force or compel to be paid or yielded; to demand or require authoritatively; to demand of right or necessity; to enjoin with pressing urgency; to extort; to wrest; as, to *exact* duty upon goods; to *exact* obedience.

Nature imperiously *exacts* her due. —Browning.

Syn.—Demand, enforce, enjoin, extort.

ex-aċt′, *v.i.* To practise exaction. [Obs.]

ex-aċt′ẽr, *n.* One who exacts; an extortioner.

ex-aċt′ing, *a.* 1. Unreasonably severe in requirements; oppressive; characterized by exaction; as, an *exacting* master; an *exacting* question.

2. Laborious; arduous; requiring strict application; absorbing; as, *exacting* duties; an *exacting* occupation.

ex-aċt′ing-ly, *adv.* In an exacting manner.

ex-aċt′ing-ness, *n.* The quality of being exacting.

ex-aċ′tion, *n.* [L. *exactio (-onis)*, a driving out, expelling, a tax, tribute, from *exactus*, pp. of *exigere*, to drive out, demand, exact.]

1. The act of demanding with authority and compelling to pay or yield; authoritative demand; a levying or drawing from by force; a driving to compliance; as, the *exaction* of tribute or of obedience.

Take away your *exactions* from my people. —Ezek. xlv. 9.

2. That which is exacted; tribute; a fee, reward, or contribution, demanded or levied with severity or injustice.

ex-aċt′i-tūde (egz-), *n.* [Fr. *exactitude*, from L. *exactus*, exact.] The quality of being exact; exactness; accuracy.

ex-aċt′ly, *adv.* In an exact manner; correctly; accurately; precisely; strictly.

ex-aċt′ness, *n.* The quality or condition of being exact; accuracy; precision; nicety; as, to make experiments with *exactness*; *exactness* in business.

ex-aċt′ŏr, *n.* [ME. *exactour*; L. *exactor*, a driver out, expeller, from *exactus*, pp. of *exigere*, to drive out.] One who exacts; one who compels another to pay more than is legal or reasonable; one who is unreasonably severe in his demands; an extortioner; an officer who collects tribute, taxes, or customs.

ex-aċt′ress (egz-), *n.* A female who exacts. [Rare.]

ex-aċ′ū-āte (egz-), *v.t.* To whet or sharpen. [Obs.]

ex-aċ-ū-ā′tion, *n.* The act of whetting or sharpening. [Obs.]

ex-ær′e-sis (egz-er′), *n.* [L., from Gr. *exairesis*, a taking out, from *exairein*, to take out; *ex*, out, and *hairein*, to take.] In old medicine and surgery, the removal from the body of injurious or useless matter.

ex-aġ′ġẽr-āte (egz-), *v.t.*; exaggerated, *pt.*, *pp.*; exaggerating, *ppr.* [L. *exaggeratus*, pp. of *exaggerare*, to heap up, increase, exaggerate; *ex*, out, up, and *aggerare*, to heap up, from *agger*, a heap, mound.]

1. To heap on; to accumulate. [Obs.]

2. To enlarge beyond the truth; to amplify; to represent as greater than truth will warrant; to overstate; as, to *exaggerate* a story.

3. In the fine arts, to heighten extravagantly in effect or design; as, to *exaggerate* particular features in a painting or statue.

Syn.—Amplify, enlarge, heighten, magnify, overstate, stretch.

ex-aġ′ġẽr-āte, *v.i.* To practise exaggeration; to amplify beyond proper bounds in thought or description.

ex-aġ′ġẽr-ā-ted, *a.* Enlarged beyond the truth; unduly increased.

ex-aġ′ġẽr-ā-ted-ly, *adv.* To an exaggerated degree.

ex-aġ′ġẽr-ā-ting-ly, *adv.* In an exaggerating manner.

ex-aġ-ġẽr-ā′tion, *n.* 1. A heaping together; heap; accumulation. [Obs.]

2. The act of exaggerating; amplification; a representation of things beyond the truth; hyperbolical representation.

3. In the fine arts, a representation of things in which their natural features are heightened or magnified.

ex-aġ′ġẽr-ā-tive, *a.* Inclined to exaggerate; characterized by exaggeration.

ex-aġ′ġẽr-ā-tive-ly, *adv.* In an exaggerative manner.

ex-aġ′ġẽr-ā-tŏr, *n.* [LL. *exaggerator*, from L. *exaggerare*, to heap up, increase, enlarge.] One who exaggerates.

ex-aġ′ġẽr-ā-tō-ry, *a.* Containing exaggeration.

ex-aġ′i-tāte (egz-), *v.t.* 1. To shake violently; to agitate. [Obs.]

2. To pursue with invectives or reproaches; to blame. [Obs.]

ex-aġ-i-tā′tion (egz-), *n.* Agitation. [Obs.]

ex-ā′lāte (eks-), *a.* [L. *ex-* priv., and *alatus*, winged, from *ala*, a wing.] In botany, without wings; not alate.

ex-al-bū′mi-nōse (eks-), *a.* Exalbuminous.

ex-al-bū′mi-nous, *a.* [L. *ex-* priv., and *albumen*, albumen, from *albus*, white.] In botany, without albumen; said of seeds.

ex-ạlt′ (egz-), *v.t.*; exalted, *pt.*, *pp.*; exalting, *ppr.* [OFr. *exalter*; L. *exaltare*, to lift up, raise, exalt; *ex*, out, up, and *altus*, high.]

1. To raise high; to elevate.

Exalt thy towery head. —Pope.

2. To elevate in power, wealth, rank, or dignity; to promote; as, to *exalt* one to a high position.

3. To elevate with joy, pride, or confidence; to elate.

4. To elevate in estimation and praise; to magnify; to praise; to extol.

Exalt ye the Lord. —Ps. xcix. 5.

5. To raise or elevate the tone or pitch of, as the voice.

Let Fame *exalt* her voice. —Prior.

6. In alchemy, to purify; to refine; as, to *exalt* the juices or the qualities of bodies. [Obs.]

Syn.—Elevate, heighten, raise, promote, extol, magnify.

ex′ạl-tāte (eks′), *a.* Exalted. [Obs.]

ex-ạl-tā′tion (eks-), *n.* [ME. *exaltacioun*; LL. *exaltatio (-onis)*, an elevation, from L. *exaltare*, to lift up, exalt.]

1. The act of raising high or the state of being raised high; elevation, as to power, office, rank, dignity, or excellence; a state of greatness or dignity; specifically, elevation to the papacy.

2. Mental elevation; a state of mind in which a person possesses noble thoughts and aspirations.

3. In alchemy, the refinement or subtilization of bodies or their qualities and virtues. [Obs.]

4. In astrology, the situation of a planet in the zodiac in which it was supposed its powers were at the highest.

ex-ạlt′ed (egz-), *a.* Raised to a lofty height; elevated; extolled; magnified; refined; dignified; sublime.

ex-ạlt′ed-ly, *adv.* In an exalted manner.

ex-ạlt′ed-ness, *n.* The state of being exalted, elevated, or elated.

ex-ạlt′ẽr, *n.* One who exalts or raises to dignity.

ex-ạlt′ment, *n.* Exaltation. [Obs.]

ex-am′ (egz-), *n.* An examination. [College Slang.]

ex-ā′men, *n.* Examination; disquisition; inquiry. [Obs.]

ex-am′e-tẽr, *n.* A hexameter. [Obs.]

ex-am″i-nȧ-bil′i-ty (egz-), *n.* The quality of being examinable.

ex-am′i-nȧ-ble, *a.* Capable of being examined.

ex-am′i-nănt, *n.* 1. One who is to be examined. [Obs.]

2. An examiner; one who examines.

ex-am′i-nāte, *n.* A person who has been examined.

ex-am-i-nā′tion (egz-), *n.* [L. *examinatio (-onis)*, from *examinare*, to weigh, examine, from *examen*, the tongue of a balance.]

1. The act of examining or the state of being examined; careful search or inquiry, with a view to ascertain the truth or the real state of things; careful and accurate inspection; scrutiny by inquiry or experiment; as, an *examination* of a house or a ship; the *examination* of a theory.

Nothing that is self-evident can be the proper subject of *examination*. —South.

2. In law, a careful inquiry into facts by testimony; an attempt to ascertain truth by inquiries and interrogatories; as, the *examination* of a witness.

3. A process prescribed or assigned for testing qualification, capabilities, knowledge, progress, and the like; as, the *examination* of a candidate for admission to the ministry or bar; the periodical *examination* of a school.

4. Trial or assay by the appropriate methods or tests, as of minerals or chemical compounds.

Examination in chief or *direct examination*; in law, the examination of a witness by the one who has put him on the stand, as distinguished from *cross-examination*, which is made by the opposing side.

Syn.—Inquiry, investigation, search, scrutiny, study, inspection, inquisition.

ex-am-i-nā′tion-ăl, *a.* Pertaining to examination.

ex-am-i-nā′tion-işm, *n.* The practice of relying entirely upon examinations as tests of qualifications, ability, etc.

ex-am-i-nā′tion-pā″pẽr, *n.* A paper on which are written or printed the questions to be answered in a written examination; also, the paper containing the answers to such questions.

ex-am′i-nā-tŏr, *n.* An examiner. [Rare.]

ex-am′ine (egz-), *v.t.*; examined, *pt.*, *pp.*; examining, *ppr.* [ME. *examinen*; OFr. *examiner*; L *examinare*, to weigh, ponder, examine, from *examen*, the tongue of a balance, from *exigere*, to measure, weigh, examine; *ex*, out, and *agere*, to weigh.]

1. To inspect or observe carefully; to look into the state of; to view in all aspects in order to form a correct opinion or judgment; to scrutinize with care; as, to *examine* a ship to know whether she is seaworthy; to *examine* a document.

Examine their counsels and their cares. —Shak.

2. To interrogate; to question; to subject to legal inquiry; as, to *examine* a witness.

3. To inquire into the qualifications, capabilities, knowledge, or progress of, by interrogatories; as, to *examine* a candidate for a degree.

4. To try or assay by appropriate methods or tests; as, to *examine* minerals or chemical compounds.

Syn.—Weigh, investigate, test, scrutinize, criticize, study, discuss, search, try, explore, inspect, observe.

ex-am-i-nee′, *n.* One who is examined or being examined.

ex-am′in-ẽr (egz-), *n.* One who examines, tries, or inspects; one who interrogates; especially, a person appointed to conduct an examination; as, an *examiner* in a university.

ex-am′in-ẽr-ship, *n.* The office of an examiner.

ex-am′in-ing, *a.* Having power to examine; appointed to examine; as, an *examining* committee.

ex′ăm-plā-ry (egz′), *a.* Exemplary. [Obs.]

ex-am′ple (egz-), *n.* [ME. *example*; L. *exemplum*, that which is taken out of a larger quantity, a sample, an example, from *eximere*, to take out; *ex*, out, and *emere*, to buy.]

1. A portion, generally a small quantity of anything, or one of a number of things, exhibited to show the character or quality of the whole; a sample; a specimen.

2. A pattern, in morals or manners, worthy of imitation; a copy or model; one who or that which is proposed or is proper to be imitated.

I have given you an *example*, that ye should do as I have done to you. —John xiii. 15.

3. An instance of something to be avoided; a warning; as, they made an *example* of the thief.

4. An instance serving for illustration of a rule or precept; a particular case or proposition illustrating a general rule, position, or truth; as, the principles of trigonometry and the rules of grammar are illustrated by *examples*.

5. In mathematics, a problem to be solved by a student; as, an *example* in compound interest.

Syn.—Instance, pattern, model, sample, precedent, prototype, standard, specimen, warning.

ex-am′ple, *v.t.* To exemplify; to set an example of. [Obs.]

ex-am′ple-less, *a.* Without example. [Rare.]

ex-am′plẽr, *n.* A pattern; an exemplar. [Obs.]

ex-am′pless, *a.* Having no example; exampleless. [Obs.]

ex-aṅ′gui-ous (eks-aṅ′gwi-us), *a.* [Obs.] See *Exsanguinous*.

ex-aṅ′gū-lous, *a.* [L. *ex-* priv., and *angulus*, a corner.] Having no corners or angles. [Rare.]

ex-an′i-māte (egz-), *a.* [L. *exanimatus*, pp. of *exanimare*, to deprive of life or breath; *ex-* priv., and *anima*, life.] Lifeless; spiritless; disheartened; depressed in spirits. [Rare.]

ex-an′i-māte, *v.t.* To deprive of life; to dishearten; to discourage. [Obs.]

ex-an-i-mā′tion, *n.* [L. *exanimatio (-onis)*, from *exanimare*, to deprive of breath, life, or strength.] Deprivation of life or of spirits. [Rare.]

ex-an′i-mous, *a.* Lifeless; dead. [Obs.]

ex-an′nū-lāte (eks-), *a.* [L. *ex-* priv., and *annulus*, or *anulus*, a ring.] In botany, without a ring; applied to those ferns in which the sporangium is without the elastic ring or annulus.

ex-an′thėm (egz-), *n.* See *Exanthema*.

ex-an-thē′mȧ (eks-), *n.*; *pl.* **ex-an-them′ȧ-tȧ.** [LL., from Gr. *exanthēma*, an efflorescence, eruption, from *exanthein*, to bloom, blossom; *ex*, out, and *anthein*, to flower, from *anthos*, a flower.] In medicine, an eruption upon the skin, especially when accompanied by fever, as in scarlatina, measles, and similar diseases; also applied to the eruptive fever itself.

ex-an-thē-mat′iċ (egz-), *a.* Exanthematous.

ex″an-thē″mȧ-tol′ō-ġy, *n.* [Gr. *exanthēma*, an eruption, and *logos*, description, from *legein*, to speak.] In medicine, the study of the exanthemata.

ex-an-them′ȧ-tous, *a.* In medicine, of the

nature of or characterized by exanthema or eruption; of the nature of an eruptive fever.

ex-an-thē'sis (eks-), *n.* [L., from Gr. *exanthēsis*, efflorescence, eruption, from *exanthein*, to bloom, blossom.] In medicine, a cutaneous eruption; exanthema.

ex-ant'lāte (egz-), *v.t.* To draw out; to exhaust. [Obs.]

ex-ant-lā'tion (eks-), *n.* The act of drawing out; exhaustion. [Obs.]

ex'ā-rāte (eks'), *v.t.* To plow; hence, to mark as if by a plow; to write; to engrave. [Obs.]

ex'ā-rāte, *a.* [L. *exaratus*, pp. of *exarare*, to plow up; *ex*, out, up, and *arare*, to plow.] In entomology, characterized by parallel furrows running lengthwise.

Exarate pupæ; pupæ the limbs of which are free, but closely attached to the body.

ex-ā-rā'tion, *n.* The act of plowing; hence, the act of marking as with a plow, or of writing or engraving. [Obs.]

ex'ärch, *n.* [LL. *exarchus*; Gr. *exarchos*, a beginner, a leader, chief, from *exarchein*, to begin, lead off; *ex*, off, from, and *archein*, to rule.]

1. A prefect or governor under the Byzantine empire.

2. A title assumed for a time by the bishops of the early Eastern church, as superiors over the metropolitans.

3. In the Greek church, a legate of a patriarch, acting as an inspector of the clergy and of ecclesiastical discipline.

ex-är'chāte (egz- *or* eks'är-), *n.* The office, dignity, administration, or province of an exarch.

ex-ā-rē'ō-lāte (eks-), *a.* [L. *ex-* priv., and *areola*, dim. of *area*, area.] In botany, not having areolæ.

ex-ar'il-lāte (eks-), *a.* [L. *ex-* priv., and *arilla*, aril.] In botany, having no aril; as, *exarillate* seeds.

ex-ā-ris'tāte, *a.* [L. *ex-* priv., and *arista*, the awn or beard of grain.] In botany, destitute of an arista, awn, or beard.

ex-är-tē-ri'tis, *n.* [L. *ex*, from, and *arteritis*, from Gr. *arteria*, an artery.] In medicine, an inflamed or morbid condition of the outer coats of an artery.

ex-är-tic'ū-lāte, *v.t.*; exarticulated, *pt.*, *pp.*; exarticulating, *ppr.* [L. *ex-* priv., and *articulatus*, pp. of *articulare*, to divide into joints, from *articulus*, dim. of *artus*, a joint.]

1. To put out of joint; to luxate.

2. In surgery, to amputate at a joint.

ex-är-tic'ū-lāte, *a.* In zoölogy, without articulation; not jointed; composed of a single joint.

ex-är-tic-ū-lā'tion, *n.* 1. Luxation; the dislocation of a joint.

2. The state of being jointless.

3. In surgery, amputation at a joint.

ex-as'pēr-āte (egz-), *v.t.*; exasperated, *pt.*, *pp.*; exasperating, *ppr.* [L. *exasperatus*, pp. of *exasperare*, to irritate; *ex*, out, from, and *asperare*, to roughen, from *asper*, rough.]

1. To anger; to irritate to a high degree; to provoke to rage; to enrage; to excite the anger of, or to inflame to an extreme degree; as, to *exasperate* a person.

2. To aggravate; to inflame; to embitter; to make grievous or more grievous; as, to *exasperate* enmity.

Syn.—Anger, enrage, irritate, inflame, incense, nettle, provoke, chafe.

ex-as'pēr-āte, *a.* 1. Provoked; embittered; inflamed. [Rare.]

2. In botany, covered with short, rigid points; rough.

ex-as'pēr-ā-tēr, *n.* One who exasperates or inflames anger, enmity, or violence.

ex-as-pēr-ā'tion, *n.* [LL. *exasperatio* (*-onis*), from L. *exasperare*, to roughen, irritate.]

1. The act of exasperating or the state of being exasperated; irritation; provocation.

2. Increase of violence or malignity; exacerbation, as of a disease.

Ex-as-pid'ē-æ (eks-), *n.pl.* [L., from Gr. *ex*, from, and *aspis*, *aspidos*, a shield.] A cohort of passerine birds, embracing several South American families, and having exaspidean tarsi.

ex-as-pid'ē-ăn, *a.* In ornithology, having the anterior scutella overlapping the tarsus around the outside, but deficient on the inside.

ex-auc'tōr-āte (egz-), **ex-au'thōr-āte,** *v.t.* To dismiss from service; to deprive of an office or dignity; to degrade. [Obs.]

ex-auc-tōr-ā'tion, ex-au-thōr-ā'tion, *n.* Dismission from service; deprivation; degradation; the removal of a person from an office or dignity. [Obs.]

ex-au'gū-rāte (egz-), *v.t.* [L. *exauguratus*, pp. of *exaugurare*, to profane; *ex*, out, and *augurare*, to consecrate by auguries, from *augur*, an augur.] In Roman antiquity, to change from sacred to secular; to desecrate; to secularize.

ex-au-gū-rā'tion, *n.* In Roman antiquity, the act of exaugurating; secularization.

ex-au'thōr-ize, *v.t.* To deprive of authority. [Obs.]

ex-cal'cā-rāte (eks-), *a.* [L. *ex-* priv., and *calcar*, a spur.] In biology, without calcars; ecalcarate.

ex-cal'cē-āte, *v.t.* To deprive of shoes; to make barefooted. [Obs.]

ex-cal-cē-ā'tion (eks-), *n.* The act of excalceating or depriving of shoes. [Obs.]

ex-cal-fac'tion (eks-), *n.* The act of making warm; calefaction. [Obs.]

ex-cal-fac'tive, *a.* [Obs.] See *Excalfactory.*

ex-cal-fac'tō-ry, *a.* Tending to heat; warming. [Obs.]

ex-camb', ex-cam'bie (eks-), *v.t.* [LL. *excambiare*, to exchange.] In Scots law, to exchange; applied specifically to the exchange of land.

ex-cam'bi-ā-tōr, *n.* One employed to exchange lands; a broker.

ex-cam'bi-um, ex-cam'bi-on, *n.* [LL. *excambium*, an exchange.] In Scots law, exchange; barter; specifically, the contract by which one piece of land is exchanged for another.

ex-can-des'cence, ex-can-des'cen-cy, *n.* [L. *excandescentia*, growing anger, from *excandescere*, to take fire, to burn; *ex*, out, and *candescere*, to begin to burn, incept. of *candere*, to shine, glitter.]

1. A growing hot; a white heat; a glowing heat. [Rare.]

2. Heat of passion; violent anger. [Obs.]

ex-can-des'cent, *a.* White with heat. [Rare.]

ex-can-tā'tion, *n.* Disenchantment by a countercharm. [Obs.]

ex-cär'nāte, *v.t.*; excarnated, *pt.*, *pp.*; excarnating, *ppr.* [LL. *excarnatus*, pp. of *excarnare*, to deprive of flesh; L. *ex-* priv., and *caro* (*carnis*), flesh.] To deprive or clear of flesh.

ex-cär'nāte, *a.* Divested of flesh.

ex-cär-nā'tion, *n.* [L. *ex-* priv., and *caro* (*carnis*), flesh.] The act of divesting of flesh; the state of being divested of flesh; opposed to *incarnation.*

ex-cär'ni-fi-cāte, *v.t.*; excarnificated, *pt.*, *pp.*; excarnificating, *ppr.* [L. *excarnificatus*, pp. of *excarnificare*, to strip of flesh.] To deprive of flesh.

ex-cär"ni-fi-cā'tion, *n.* The act of clearing or depriving of flesh.

ex-cau'dāte, *a.* [L. *ex-* priv., and *cauda*, tail.] In zoölogy, without a tail; tailless.

ex'cā-vāte (eks-), *v.t.*; excavated, *pt.*, *pp.*; excavating, *ppr.* [L. *excavatus*, pp. of *excavare*, to hollow out; *ex*, out, and *cavare*, to make hollow, from *cavus*, hollow.]

1. To hollow out; to make hollow by scooping, digging, or cutting; as, to *excavate* a mound of earth; to *excavate* a watermelon.

2. To remove or uncover, by digging out; as, to *excavate* a cannon from the ruins of a fort.

3. To form by scooping or hollowing out, or by penetrating into any substance and removing the material; as, to *excavate* a canoe from the trunk of a tree; to *excavate* a tunnel.

ex-cā-vā'tion, *n.* 1. The act of making anything hollow, by cutting or scooping out the interior substance or part.

2. A hollow or a cavity formed by removing the interior substance; as, many animals burrow in *excavations* of their own forming.

3. In engineering, (a) an open cutting, as in a railway, in distinction from a tunnel; (b) that which is dug out in excavating.

ex'cā-vā-tōr, *n.* 1. One who or that which excavates.

2. A machine for excavating, as a dredging-machine or digging-machine.

3. A dentist's instrument for excavating a tooth preparatory to filling it.

ex-cāve', *v.t.* To excavate. [Obs.]

ex-cē'cāte (eks-), *v.t.* To make blind. [Obs.]

ex-cē-cā'tion, *n.* The act of making blind. [Obs.]

ex-cēd'ent (eks-), *n.* Excess. [Rare.]

ex-ceed' (eks-), *v.t.*; exceeded, *pt.*, *pp.*; exceeding, *ppr.* [ME. *exceden*; L. *excedere*, to go out, go beyond; *ex*, out, beyond, and *cedere*, to go.]

1. To pass or go beyond; to proceed beyond the given or supposed limit, measure, or quantity of; as, one man *exceeds* another in bulk, stature, or weight; one offender *exceeds* another in villainy.

2. To surpass; to excel.

> To be nameless in worthy deeds *exceeds* an infamous history. —Sir T. Browne.

Syn.—Excel, outdo, surpass, outstrip, outvie, transcend.

ex-ceed', *v.i.* 1. To go too far; to pass the proper bounds; to go over any given limit, number, or measure.

> Forty stripes he may give him, and not *exceed.* —Deut. xxv. 3.

2. To bear the greater proportion; to be more or larger; to predominate.

ex-ceed'ā-ble, *a.* Capable of exceeding. [Obs.]

ex-ceed'ēr, *n.* One who exceeds.

ex-ceed'ing, *a.* Great in extent, quantity, or duration; unusually large.

> Cities were built an *exceeding* space of time before the great flood. —Raleigh.

ex-ceed'ing, *adv.* Exceedingly. [Rare.]

ex-ceed'ing-ly, *adv.* To a very great degree; in a degree beyond what is usual; greatly; very much.

ex-ceed'ing-ness, *n.* Greatness in quantity, extent, or duration. [Obs.]

ex-cel', *v.t.*; excelled, *pt.*, *pp.*; excelling, *ppr.* [OFr. *exceller*; L. *excellere*, to raise, elevate, surpass, excel.]

1. To go beyond or surpass in good qualities or laudable deeds; to outdo.

> *Excelling* others, these were great;
> Thou, greater still, must these *excel.*—Prior.

2. To exceed; to surpass. [Rare.]

ex-cel', *v.i.* To have good qualities, or to perform meritorious actions, in an unusual degree; to be eminent, illustrious, or distinguished; to surpass others.

> It was in description and meditation that Byron *excelled.* —Macaulay.

ex'cel-lence, *n.* [ME. *excellense*; L. *excellentia*, superiority, excellence, from *excellens* (*-entis*), ppr. of *excellere*, to surpass, excel.]

1. The state of possessing good qualities in an unusual or eminent degree; the state of excelling in anything; virtue; superiority.

2. Any valuable quality; anything highly laudable, meritorious, or virtuous in persons, or valuable and esteemed in things.

> Contentment is a moral *excellence.* —Spurgeon.

3. Same as *Excellency*, 2. [Rare.]

Syn.—Eminence, goodness, purity, superiority, worth, perfection, greatness.

ex'cel-len-cy, *n.*; *pl.* **ex'cel-len-cies.** 1. Superiority; dignity; worth; excellence.

2. A title of honor given to governors, ambassadors (as representing, not the affairs alone, but the persons of sovereign princes, to whom the title was formerly applied), ministers, and other high officials; with *your*, *his*, etc.

ex'cel-lent, *a.* 1. Possessing excellence; eminent or distinguished for what is amiable, laudable, or valuable; remarkable for good qualities; of great worth; superior; as, an *excellent* citizen; an *excellent* book; an *excellent* idea; *excellent* fruit.

2. Consummate; complete; in an ill sense. [Obs.]

> Elizabeth was an *excellent* hypocrite. —Hume.

Syn.—Admirable, transcendent, prime, superior, sterling, valuable, worthy, choice.

ex'cel-lent, *adv.* Excellently; exceedingly. [Obs.]

ex'cel-lent-ly, *adv.* 1. In an excellent manner; well in a high degree; in an eminent degree; in a manner to please or command esteem, or to be useful.

2. Exceedingly; superlatively; surpassingly. [Obs.]

ex-cel'si-or (eks-), *a.* [L. *excelsior*, comp. of *excelsus*, lofty, high, pp. of *excellere*, to elevate, excel.] More lofty; more elevated; higher; the motto of the state of New York.

ex-cel'si-or, *n.* A kind of stuffing or packing material for mattresses, sofas, chairs, etc., consisting of fine curled shavings of wood.

ex-cen'trăl, *a.* [L. *ex*, from, and *centrum*, center.] In botany, out of the center.

ex-cen'tric, ex-cen'tric-ăl, etc. See *Eccentric*, etc.

ex-cept' (eks-), *v.t.*; excepted, *pt.*, *pp.*; excepting, *ppr.* [ME. *excepten*; L. *exceptare*, to take out, except; *ex*, out, and *capere*, to take.]

1. To omit from consideration; to exclude; to withhold; to take or leave out, as of any number specified; as, of the thirty persons present, we must *except* two.

2. To object to; to take exception to. [Obs.]

ex-cept', *v.i.* To object; to take exception; usually followed by *to*; sometimes by *against*; as, to *except to* a witness, or *to* his testimony.

ex-cept', *prep.* [ME. *except*, from L. *exceptus*, pp. of *excipere*, to take out, except.] Being excepted or left out; with exception of; excepting.

> I could see nothing *except* the sky.—Swift.

Syn.—Excepting, save, but.

ex-cept', *conj.* Excepting; if it be not that; unless.

> I will not let thee go, *except* thou bless me. —Gen. xxxii. 26.

ex-cept'ănt, *a.* Implying exception. [Rare.]

ex-cept'ing, *prep.* and *conj.* I. *prep.* Except; leaving out; excluding.

II. *conj.* Unless; except.

ex-cep'tion, *n.* [L. *exceptio* (*-onis*), from *exceptus*, pp. of *excipere*, to take out, except.]

1. The act of excepting or excluding, as from a number designated, or from a description; exclusion; as, all voted for the bill, with the *exception* of five.

2. That which is excepted, excluded, or separated from others in a general description: the person or thing specified as distinct or not included; as, almost every general rule has its *exceptions.*

The *exceptions* do not destroy the authority of the rule. —Macaulay.

3. An objection; that which is or may be offered in opposition to a rule, proposition, statement, or allegation; with *to*; sometimes with *against*.

I will answer what *exceptions* he can have *against* our account. —Bentley.

4. Objection with dislike; offense; slight anger or resentment; with *at* or *against*, but more commonly with *to*, and generally used with *take*; as, to *take exception at* a severe remark; to *take exception to* what was said.

5. In law, (a) a denial of anything alleged and considered valid by the other side, either in point of law or in pleading, or a denial of a matter alleged in bar to an action, or a denial of the sufficiency of an answer; (b) a clause by which the grantor of a deed excepts something before granted; (c) a formal objection to a ruling or decision of a judge during a trial, noting a claim of error.

Bill of exceptions; in law, a statement of exceptions or objections on points of law taken to the directions or decisions of a judge presiding at a trial, to be referred for consideration and decision to a superior court, or to a full bench.

Syn.—Objection, exclusion, disapprobation, offense, resentment.

ex-cep′tion-ȧ-ble, *a.* Liable to exception or objection; obnoxious.

ex-cep′tion-ȧ-ble-ness, *n.* The quality of being exceptionable.

ex-cep′tion-ȧ-bly, *adv.* In an exceptionable manner.

ex-cep′tion-ăl, *a.* Relating to or forming an exception; out of the ordinary course; unusual; uncommon; above the average; as, *exceptional* talent.

Syn.—Rare, peculiar, uncommon, irregular, unusual, abnormal.

ex-cep-tion-al′i-ty, *n.* The quality of being exceptional.

ex-cep′tion-ăl-ly, *adv.* In an exceptional manner.

ex-cep′tion-ăl-ness, *n.* Exceptionality.

ex-cep′tion-ẽr, *n.* One who takes exceptions; one who objects. [Obs.]

ex-cep′tion-less, *a.* Without exception; unexceptionable.

ex-cep′tious, *a.* Captious; disposed or apt to cavil, or take exceptions. [Obs.]

ex-cep′tious-ness, *n.* Disposition to cavil. [Obs.]

ex-cept′ive, *a.* 1. Making an exception; forming an exception.

A particular and *exceptive* law. —Milton.

2. Inclined to take exception.

ex-cept′less, *a.* Making no exception; extending to all. [Obs.]

ex-cept′ŏr, *n.* One who takes exceptions or makes objections.

ex-cer′ē-brāte, *v.t.* To remove or beat out the brains of.

ex-cer-ē-brā′tion, *n.* [LL. *excerebratus*, pp. of *excerebrare*, to deprive of brains; L. *ex-* priv., and *cerebrum*, the brain.]

1. The act of removing or beating out the brains.

2. In surgery, the removal of the brain from the head of the fetus to facilitate delivery.

ex-cer′ē-brōse, *a.* [L. *ex-* priv., and *cerebrum*, the brain.] Having no brains. [Rare.]

ex-cẽrn′, *v.t.* [L. *excernere*, to sift out, separate; *ex*, out, and *cernere*, to sift, separate.] To separate and emit through the pores, or through small passages of the body; to excrete. [Rare.]

ex-cẽrn′ent, *a.* In physiology, pertaining to or effecting excretion.

ex-cẽrp′, *v.t.* To excerpt. [Obs.]

ex-cẽrpt′, *v.t.*; excerpted, *pt., pp.*; excerpting, *ppr.* [L. *excerptus*, pp. of *excerpere*, to pick out, choose; *ex*, out, and *carpere*, to pick, pluck.] To pick out; to make an extract of; to cite; to quote.

Out of which we have *excerpted* the following particulars. —Fuller.

ex-cẽrpt′, *n.* An extract from an author or from a writing of any kind.

ex-cẽrp′tȧ, *n.pl.* [L., neut. pl. of *excerptum*, an extract.] Excerpts; passages extracted. [Rare.]

ex-cẽrp′tion, *n.* 1. The act of excerpting or picking out; a gleaning; selection.

2. That which is selected or gleaned. [Rare.]

ex-cẽrp′tive, *a.* Excerpting; choosing.

ex-cẽrp′tŏr, *n.* One who excerpts; a selecter; a culler.

ex-cess′, *n.* [ME. *exces*; L. *excessus*, a departure, a going beyond, from *excessus*, pp. of *excedere*, to go beyond, exceed; *ex*, beyond, and *cedere*, to go.]

1. That which exceeds the ordinary measure or limit; superfluity; superabundance: a going beyond what is necessary or proper; as, an *excess* of provisions; *excess* of bile in the stomach.

2. Undue indulgence of appetite; want of restraint in gratifying the desires; intemperance; overindulgence.

Like one that sees his own *excess*.—Tennyson.

3. The degree or amount by which one thing, number, or quantity is greater than another; overplus; surplus; as, the *excess* of assets over liabilities.

Spherical excess; the excess of the sum of the three angles of a spherical triangle over two right angles, or 180 degrees.

ex-cess′ive, *a.* [LL. *excessivus*, immoderate, from L. *excessus*, pp. of *excedere*, to exceed.] Beyond any given degree, measure, or limit, or beyond the usual measure or proportion; inordinate; abnormal: as, *excessive* bulk; *excessive* labor; *excessive* indulgence.

Dark with *excessive* bright thy skirts appear. —Milton.

Syn.—Extreme, vehement, superfluous, exorbitant, immoderate, inordinate, extravagant, superabundant, undue, abnormal.—Anger or any other feeling may be *extreme* or *vehement* without being of necessity wrong; the occasion may justify it; but to be *excessively* angry, or *excessive* in anything, involves a want of self-command which is blameworthy.

ex-cess′ive-ly, *adv.* In an extreme degree; beyond measure; unduly.

ex-cess′ive-ness, *n.* The state or quality of being excessive; excess.

ex-chănġe′ (eks-), *n.* [ME. *eschange*; LL. *excambium*, exchange, from *excambiare*, to exchange; L. *ex*, out, and *cambiare*, to change.]

1. The act of giving one thing or commodity for another; barter; the act of parting with something in return for an equivalent; traffic by interchange of commodities; mutual substitution; as, an *exchange* of a horse for a cow.

O spare her life and in *exchange* take mine. —Dryden.

2. The act of giving up or resigning one thing or state for another; as, the *exchange* of a crown for a cloister.

3. The act of giving and receiving reciprocally; as, an *exchange* of thoughts; an *exchange* of civilities.

4. The thing given in return for something received, or received in return for what is given.

5. Among journalists, a publication sent in *exchange* for another.

6. In law, a mutual grant of equal interests, the one in consideration of the other. Estates exchanged must be equal in quantity, as fee-simple for fee-simple. —Blackstone.

7. A place where the merchants, brokers, and bankers of a city meet to transact business, at certain hours; often contracted to *'Change*.

8. In commerce, the process of exchanging one debt or credit for another; or the receiving or paying of money in one place, for an equal sum in another, by an order or draft, called a *bill of exchange*. A in London is creditor to B in New York, and C in London owes D in New York a like sum. A in London draws a *bill of exchange* on B in New York; C in London purchases the bill, by which A receives his debt due from B in New York. C transmits the bill to D in New York, who receives the amount from B.

9. A central office of a telephone system, where lines meet and where connection is made between any two instruments.

Arbitration of exchange; see under *Arbitration*.

Bill of exchange; see under *Bill*, and definition 8, above.

Exchange broker; see under *Broker*.

Par of exchange; the established value of the coin or standard value of one country expressed in the coin or standard value of another.

Theory of exchanges; a theory introduced by Prevost, for explaining the equilibrium of temperature of any body. It is founded on the supposition that the quantity of heat which a body diffuses by radiation is equal to the quantity which it receives by radiation from surrounding bodies, and which it absorbs either wholly or in part.

Syn.—Intercourse, commerce, dealing, interchange, reciprocity, reciprocation.

ex-chănġe′, *v.t.*; exchanged, *pt., pp.*; exchanging, *ppr.* 1. In commerce, to part with in return for some equivalent; to transfer for a recompense; to barter; as, the workman *exchanges* his labor for money.

He has something to *exchange* with those abroad. —Locke.

2. To give and receive reciprocally; to give and take; to communicate mutually; to interchange; as, to *exchange* horses, clothes, thoughts, civilities.

Exchange forgiveness with me, noble Hamlet. —Shak.

3. To lay aside, quit, or resign anything, and take something else in place of it; to part with for a substitute; as, to *exchange* a crown for a cowl; to *exchange* a throne for a cell or hermitage; to *exchange* a life of ease for a life of toil.

Syn.—Change, barter, traffic, trade, interchange, swap, commute.

ex-chănġe′, *v.i.* To make an exchange; to pass or to be taken as an equivalent; as, a dollar *exchanges* for one hundred cents.

ex-chănġe-ȧ-bil′i-ty, *n.* The quality or state of being exchangeable.

ex-chănġe′ȧ-ble, *a.* 1. Capable of being exchanged; fit or proper to be exchanged.

2. Ratable by exchange; to be estimated by what may be procured in exchange; as, the *exchangeable* value of goods.

ex-chănġe′ȧ-bly, *adv.* In the way of exchange.

ex-chăn′ġẽr, *n.* One who exchanges; one who practises exchange.

ex-chēat′, *n.* [Obs.] See *Escheat*.

ex-chēat′ŏr, *n.* [Obs.] See *Escheator*.

ex-cheq′uẽr (eks-chek′), *n.* [ME. *escheker*, lit., a chessboard, a court of revenue, treasury; OFr. *escheker*, a chessboard, from *eschecs*, chess.]

1. A state treasury; hence, pecuniary property in general; funds; as, my *exchequer* is very low.

2. [E—] In England, an ancient tribunal and court of record, more fully known as the *Court of Exchequer*, founded chiefly for the collection and care of the royal revenues. The judges consisted originally of the lord treasurer, the chancellor of the exchequer, and three barons. The equitable jurisdiction of the court was afterward abolished, and the chancellor of the exchequer, who belonged to the equity side of the court only, ceased to be one of the judges, these latterly consisting of a chief baron and four (afterward five) puisne barons. In 1875, the court was made a division of the High Court of Justice.

3. In Great Britain and Ireland, that department of the government which controls the public revenue.

Barons of the exchequer; see under *Baron*.

Chancellor of the exchequer; see under *Chancellor*.

Exchequer bills or *bonds*; in England, bills for money, or promissory bills, issued from the exchequer; a species of paper currency emitted under the authority of the government and bearing interest.

ex-cheq′uẽr, *v.t.*; exchequered, *pt., pp.*; exchequering, *ppr.* To institute a process against (any person) in the Court of Exchequer.

ex-cīde′, *v.t.* [L. *excidere*, to cut out; *ex*, out, and *cædere*, to cut.] To remove by cutting; to excise. [Rare.]

ex-cip′i-ent (eks-), *a.* [L. *excipiens (-entis)*, ppr. of *excipere*, to take out, except; *ex*, out, and *capere*, to take.] Exceptive; objecting. [Rare.]

ex-cip′i-ent, *n.* 1. One who excepts. [Rare.]

2. In medicine, any substance combined with an active drug to give the latter an agreeable or convenient form.

ex′ci-ple, ex′ci-pūle, ex-cip′ū-lum (eks-), *n.* [L. *excipulum*, a vessel for receiving liquids, from *excipere*, to take out, receive.] In botany, the part of a thallus which forms a rim or base to the shield of a lichen.

ex-cip′ū-lăr, *a.* Pertaining to the exciple in a lichen.

ex-cip′ū-li-fọrm, *a.* Resembling an exciple.

ex-cir′cle, *n.* [L. *ex*, out, and *circulus*, a circle.] An escribed circle or the radius of such a circle.

ex-cīṣ′ȧ-ble, *a.* Liable or subject to excise; as, whisky is an *excisable* commodity.

ex-cīṣe′ (eks-), *n.* [L. *excisus*, pp. of *excidere*, to cut off; *ex*, off, and *cædere*, to cut.]

1. An inland tax or duty imposed on certain commodities of home production and consumption, as tobacco, spirits, etc.

2. In England, that branch or department of the civil service which is connected with the levying of such duties.

ex-cīṣe′, *v.t.*; excised, *pt., pp.*; excising, *ppr.* 1. To lay or impose a duty on; to levy an excise on.

2. To overcharge; to impose upon. [Prov. Eng.]

ex-cīṣe′, *v.t.* To cut out or off; as, to *excise* the vermiform appendix; to *excise* a tumor.

ex-cīṣe′, *a.* Of, pertaining to, or connected with the excise; as, *excise* acts: *excise* commissioners.

ex-cīṣe′măn, *n.*; *pl.* **ex-cīṣe′men.** An officer who inspects commodities and rates the excise duty on them.

ex-ci′sion (-sizh′un), *n.* [L. *excisio (-onis)*, a destroying, cutting out; *ex*, out, and *cædere*, to cut.]

1. In surgery, a cutting out or off of a part.

2. The act of cutting off; extirpation; destruction.

3. A cutting off from the church; excommunication.

ex-cīt-ȧ-bil′i-ty, *n.* 1. The quality of being capable of excitement; readiness or proneness to be provoked or moved into action; the quality of being easily agitated; nervousness.

2. In physiology, the property of reacting to a stimulus; irritability.

ex-cīt′ȧ-ble, *a.* Susceptible of excitement; capable of being excited; easily stirred up or stimulated; prone to excitement; as, an *excitable* temperament.

ex-cit′ănt, *a.* [L. *excitans (-antis)*, ppr. of *excitare*, to excite.] Tending to excite; exciting.

ex-cit′ănt, *n.* [L. *excitans (-antis)*, ppr. of *excitare*, to excite.] That which produces or may produce increased action in a living organism; specifically, in medicine, an agent or influence which arouses the vital activity of the body or of any of the tissues or organs belonging to it; a stimulant; that which stimulates arterial action.

ex-cit′āte, *v.t.* To excite. [Obs.]

ex-ci-tā′tion, *n.* [LL. *excitatio (-onis)*, from L. *excitare*, to excite.]

1. The act of exciting or putting in motion; the act of rousing or awakening.

2. In medicine, the act of producing excitement; also, the excitement produced.

ex-cit′ȧ-tive, *a.* Having power to excite; tending or serving to excite; excitatory.

ex′ci-tā-tŏr, *n.* [LL. *excitator*, from L. *excitare*, to excite.] In electricity, an instrument employed to discharge a Leyden jar or other electrical apparatus in such a manner as to secure the operator from the force or effect of the shock.

ex-cit′ȧ-tō-ry, *a.* Tending to excite; containing excitement.

ex-cīte′ (eks-), *v.t.*; excited, *pt., pp.*; exciting, *ppr.* [ME. *exciten*; OFr. *exciter*; L. *excitare*, to call out or forth, to stimulate, excite; *ex*, out, and *ciere*, to call, summon.]

1. To rouse; to call into action; to agitate; to stir up to activity; to cause to act, as that which is dormant, sluggish, or inactive; as, to *excite* the spirits; to *excite* a mutiny or insurrection.

2. To stimulate, as an organ of the body; as, to *excite* the liver.

3. In electricity, to induce magnetic properties in.

Syn.—Incite, arouse, stimulate, kindle, agitate, awaken, irritate, stir up, inflame.—When we *excite*, we rouse into action feelings which were less strong; when we *incite*, we urge forward to acts correspondent to the feelings awakened.

ex-cī′ted-ly, *adv.* In an excited manner.

ex-cīte′fụl, *a.* Calculated to excite; full of exciting matter; as, *exciteful* stories or prayers.

ex-cīte′ment, *n.* 1. The act of exciting; the state of being roused into action, or of having increased action; agitation; as, an *excitement* of the people.

2. That which excites or rouses; that which moves, stirs, or induces action; a motive.

3. In medicine, a state of increased activity in the body or in any of its organs or parts.

ex-cīt′ēr, *n.* One who or that which excites.

ex-cīt′ing, *a.* Calling or rousing into action; producing excitement.

Exciting causes; in medicine, causes which tend immediately to produce disease, as distinguished from *predisposing causes*, which during long periods of time prepare the way for it to arise.

ex-cīt′ing-ly, *adv.* In an exciting manner.

ex-cīt′ive, *a.* Tending to excite.

ex-ci-tō-. A combining form from L. *excitare*, to excite, used in medicine and anatomy to signify exciting, as in *excitomotor*.

ex-cī″tō-mō′tŏr, **ex-cī″tō-mō′tō-ry**, *a.* [*Excito-*, and L. *motor*, a mover.] In physiology, exciting motion by reflex action.

ex-cī″tō-nū′tri-ent, *a.* [*Excito-*, and L. *nutriens (-entis)*, ppr. of *nutrire*, to nourish.] In physiology, exciting nutrition by reflex action.

ex-cī″tō-sē-crē′tō-ry, *a.* [*Excito-*, and L. *secretio (-onis)*, a dividing, secretion.] In physiology, exciting secretion in the glands by means of reflex action.

ex-çlāim′ (eks-), *v.t.* and *v.i.*; exclaimed, *pt., pp.*; exclaiming, *ppr.* [L. *exclamare*, to cry out; *ex*, out, and *clamare*, to cry, shout.] To cry out loudly and abruptly; to call out noisily; to protest; to shout; to vociferate.

ex-çlāim′, *n.* Clamor; exclamation. [Obs.]

ex-çlāim′ẽr, *n.* One who cries out or exclaims.

ex-çlȧ-mā′tion, *n.* [OFr. *exclamation*; L. *exclamatio (-onis)*, a calling or crying out, from *exclamare*, to cry out.]

1. Outcry; noisy talk; clamor; vehement vociferation; emphatic utterance; a vehement elevation of voice; a sound, word, or words expressing sudden or strong emotion.

2. In grammar, a word expressing outcry; an interjection; a word expressing some passion, as wonder, fear, or grief.

3. In printing, the exclamation mark (!), used after exclamatory words and sentences.

4. In rhetoric, same as *ecphonesis*.

ex-çlam′ȧ-tive, *a.* Containing exclamation.

ex-çlam′ȧ-tive-ly, *adv.* In an exclamative manner.

ex-çlam′ȧ-tō-ry, *a.* [L. *exclamare*, to cry out, exclaim.] Using exclamation; containing or expressing exclamation; as, an *exclamatory* phrase.

ex-çlam′ȧ-tō-ri-ly, *adv.* In an exclamatory manner.

ex′çlāve (eks′), *n.* [L. *ex*, out, and *clavis*, a key.] A territory politically a part of a country, but geographically separated from it.

ex-çlūde′ (eks-), *v.t.*; excluded, *pt., pp.*; excluding, *ppr.* [ME. *excluden*; L. *excludere*, to shut out; *ex*, out, and *claudere*, to shut.]

1. To hinder from entering; to deny admission to; to shut out; to hinder from participation in or enjoyment of; to except; to reject.

2. To bring forth, extrude, or eject; as, to *exclude* the young.

Excluded middle or *third*; in logic, one of the laws of negation, according to which there is no individual that does not come under a term or its negative, no third state being possible. The formula is "Everything is either A or not-A."

ex-çlū′dẽr, *n.* One who or that which excludes or shuts out.

ex-çlū′ṣion, *n.* [L. *exclusio (-onis)*, from *excludere*, to shut out, exclude.]

1. The act of excluding or shutting out or the state of being excluded; a debarring; non-admission; rejection.

2. In physiology, the act of bringing forth or extruding, as larvæ or an egg.

3. That which is expelled; excretion.

4. In logic, the relation of two classes which lie wholly without each other; thus, animal and mineral stand to each other in a relation of *exclusion*, if it is positive that no mineral is an animal.

Exclusion of the pupil; a disease of the eye in which the iris adheres to the crystalline lens, leaving the center of the eye unaffected and the vision clear; also called *circular* or *annular synechia*.

Method of exclusion; a style of argument advocated by Francis Bacon, which excludes all causes or reasons but one, the assumption then being that that is the correct one.

ex-çlū′ṣion-ā-ry, *a.* Having a tendency to exclude. [Rare.]

ex-çlū′ṣion-ẽr, *n.* An exclusionist.

ex-çlū′ṣion-iṣm, *n.* The principles held by or the practices of an exclusionist.

ex-çlū′ṣion-ist, *n.* One who would preclude another from some privilege; specifically, in English history, one of the political party which sought to debar the heirs of Charles II. from the throne, owing to the fact that they were Roman Catholics.

ex-çlū′sive, *a.* 1. Having the power or effect of excluding from admission or participation; not comprehensive; as, *exclusive* regulations.

2. Of a disposition to exclude or reject; disposed to limit social relations; fastidious; over-particular as to one's associates; as, the family was very *exclusive*.

3. Not taking into the account; not including or comprehending; usually followed by *of*; as, the general had five thousand troops, *exclusive of* artillery and cavalry.

ex-çlū′sive, *n.* 1. One of a very select circle of society.

2. Anything which excludes.

ex-çlū′sive-ly, *adv.* In an exclusive manner; to the exclusion of all others; as, it is his, *exclusively*.

ex-çlū′sive-ness, *n.* The quality or state of being exclusive.

ex-çlū′siv-iṣm, *n.* Exclusiveness; exclusionism.

ex-çlū′siv-ist, *n.* One who favors or practises any form of exclusiveness or exclusion; an exclusionist.

ex-çlū′sō-ry, *a.* [LL. *exclusorius*, from L. *exclusus*, pp. of *excludere*, to shut out, exclude.] Capable of excluding; excluding; serving to exclude.

ex-çoçt′ (eks-), *v.t.* To decoct; to obtain by boiling. [Obs.]

ex-çoç′tion, *n.* The act of excocting. [Obs.]

ex-çoġ′i-tāte, *v.t.*; excogitated, *pt., pp.*; excogitating, *ppr.* [L. *excogitatus*, pp. of *excogitare*, to think out, contrive; *ex*, out, and *cogitare*, to think.] To invent; to devise by thinking; to contrive.

ex-çoġ′i-tāte, *v.i.* To cogitate. [Rare.]

ex-çoġ-i-tā′tion, *n.* Invention; contrivance; the act of devising in the thoughts.

ex-çŏm-mūne′, *v.t.* To exclude; to excommunicate. [Obs.]

ex-çŏm-mū′ni-çȧ-ble, *a.* Liable or deserving to be excommunicated.

ex-çŏm-mū′ni-çănt, *n.* One who has been excommunicated.

ex-çŏm-mū′ni-çāte, *v.t.*; excommunicated, *pt., pp.*; excommunicating, *ppr.* [LL. *excommunicatus*, pp. of *excommunicare*, to expel from communion; L. *ex*, out, and *communicare*, to communicate, from *communis*, common.]

1. To expel from communion; to eject from the communion of the church by an ecclesiastical sentence, and deprive of spiritual advantages; as, to *excommunicate* notorious offenders.

2. To dismiss in disgrace from any association.

3. To interdict; to forbid or prohibit, with excommunication as the penalty of disobedience.

ex-çŏm-mū′ni-çāte, *a.* and *n.* I. *a.* Excommunicated.

II. *n.* One who is excommunicated.

ex-çŏm-mū-ni-çā′tion, *n.* The act of ejecting; specifically, expulsion from the communion of a church, and deprivation of its rights, privileges, and advantages; an ecclesiastical penalty or punishment inflicted on offenders. *Excommunication* is an ecclesiastical interdict of two kinds, the *lesser* and the *greater*; the *lesser excommunication* is a separation or suspension of the offender from partaking of the eucharist; the *greater* is an absolute separation and exclusion of the offender from the church and all its rights and advantages.

ex-çŏm-mū′ni-çā-tŏr, *n.* One who excommunicates.

ex-çŏm-mū′ni-çā-tō-ry, *a.* Of the nature of, pertaining to, or causing excommunication.

ex-çŏm-mūn′iŏn (-yun), *n.* Excommunication. [Obs.]

ex-çō′ri-ȧ-ble, *a.* Capable of being excoriated.

ex-çō′ri-āte, *v.t.*; excoriated, *pt., pp.*; excoriating, *ppr.* [LL. *excoriatus*, pp. of *excoriare*, to strip off the skin; L. *ex*, out, off, and *corium*, the skin.] To flay; to strip or wear off the skin of; to abrade; to gall; to break and remove the cuticle of, in any manner, as by rubbing, beating, or by the action of acrid substances.

ex-çō-ri-ā′tion, *n.* 1. The act of flaying, or the operation of wearing off the skin or cuticle; a galling; abrasion; the state of being galled or stripped of skin.

2. Robbery; spoliation; the act of stripping of possessions. [Obs.]

ex-çor′ti-çāte, *v.t.*; excorticated, *pt., pp.*; excorticating, *ppr.* [LL. *excorticatus*, pp. of *excorticare*, to strip off the bark or rind; L. *ex*, off, and *cortex, corticis*, bark.] To strip off the bark or rind of; to deprive of bark or rind, as a tree.

ex-çor-ti-çā′tion, *n.* The act of stripping off bark.

ex′çrē-ȧ-ble, *a.* Capable of being discharged by spitting. [Obs.]

ex′çrē-āte, *v.t.* To spit out; to discharge from the throat by hawking and spitting. [Obs.]

ex-çrē-ā′tion, *n.* The act of spitting out. [Obs.]

ex′çrē-ment, *n.* [Fr. *excrément*; L. *excrementum*, that which is sifted out, from *excretus*, pp. of *excernere*, to sift out.] Matter excreted and ejected; waste matter discharged from an animal body; specifically, the feces; alvine discharges.

ex′çrē-ment, *n.* [LL. *excrementum*, from L. *excrescere*, to grow out, to rise.] Any natural appendage or outgrowth on the living body, as hair, feathers, etc. [Rare.]

ex-çrē-men′tăl, *a.* Of, pertaining to, or resembling excrement.

ex″çrē-men-ti′tious (-tish′us), **ex″çrē-men-ti′tiăl** (-tish′ăl), *a.* Of the nature of, pertaining to, or consisting of excrement.

ex-çrē-men′tive, *a.* Pertaining to or productive of excrement; as, *excrementive* parts. [Rare.]

ex′çrē-ment-īze, *v.i.* To pass excrement. [Rare.]

ex-çres′cence, *n.* [L. *excrescentia*, excrescences, from *excrescere*, to grow out; *ex*, out, and *crescere*, to grow.]

1. An unnatural protuberance or appendage, as a wart on a body or a knot on a tree; hence, a superfluity.

2. Figuratively, a wild or passionate outbreak. [Obs.]

ex-çres′cen-cy, *n.*; *pl.* **ex-çres′cen-cieṣ**. An excrescence.

ex-çres′cent, *a.* Growing out of something else, in an abnormal manner; superfluous.

Expunge the whole or lop the *excrescent* parts.
—Pope.

Excrescent letter; in philology, a letter which is an addition to the root, as the *b* in *thumb*.

ex-çres-cen′tiăl, *a.* Of, pertaining to, or resembling an excrescence.

ex-çrē′tȧ, *n.pl.* [L., neut. pl. of *excretus*, pp. of *excernere*, to separate.] Matter excreted by the body; specifically, excretory matter contained in urine and sweat.

ex-çrēte′, *v.t.*; excreted, *pt., pp.*; excreting, *ppr.* [L. *excretus*, pp. of *excernere*, to sift out, separate.] To separate and throw off; to discharge; as, to *excrete* urine.

ex′çrē-tin, *n.* An organic crystalline substance, $C_{20}H_{36}O$, contained in human feces when in a healthy condition.

ex-çrē′tion, *n.* [L. *excretus*, pp. of *excernere*, to separate.] The act of excreting; the matter excreted.

ex′çrē-tive, *a.* Having the power of separating and ejecting waste matter from the body.

ex′çrē-tō-ry, *a.* and *n.* [LL. *excretorius*, from L. *excretus*, pp. of *excernere*, to separate.]

I. *a.* Having the quality of excreting or throwing off excrementitious matter.

II. *n.* An excretory organ.

ex-crū′ci-ȧ-ble (-shiȧ-bl), *a.* Liable to torment. [Rare.]

ex-crū′ci-āte (-shi-āt), *v.t.*; excruciated, *pt.*, *pp.*; excruciating, *ppr.* [L. *excruciatus*, pp. of *excruciare*, to torture greatly; *ex-*, intens., and *cruciare*, to torture, from *crux*, *crucis*, a cross.] To torture; to torment; to inflict most severe pain upon; as, to *excruciate* the heart or the body.

ex-crū′ci-ā-ting, *a.* 1. Torturing; tormenting; putting to most severe pain; as, *excruciating* fears or maladies.

2. Excessively elaborate, elegant, or pretentious; as, *excruciating* graciousness. [Colloq.]

ex-crū′ci-ā-ting-ly, *adv.* 1. In an excruciating manner.

2. Extremely; unusually; as, *excruciatingly* polite. [Colloq.]

ex-crū-ci-ā′tion, *n.* The act of torturing or the state of being tortured; extreme pain; vexation. [Obs.]

ex-cū-bā′tion, *n.* [LL. *excubatio (-onis)*, a watching, keeping watch, from L. *excubare*, to lie or sleep out of doors; *ex*, out, and *cubare*, to lie.] The act of watching all night. [Obs.]

ex-cū-bi-tō′ri-um, *n.*; *pl.* **ex-cū-bi-tō′ri-ȧ.** [LL., a post where guards were stationed, from L. *excubare*, to sleep out of doors, to keep watch; *ex*, out, and *cubare*, to lie.] In architecture, a gallery in a church where, in olden times, public watch was kept all night on the eve of some festival, and from which the great shrines were observed. Many of these watching-lofts are very beautiful.

Excubitorium or Watching-loft, St. Albans Cathedral, England.

ex-cul′pȧ-ble, *a.* Capable or worthy of being exculpated.

ex-cul′pāte, *v.t.*; exculpated, *pt.*, *pp.*; exculpating, *ppr.* [L. *ex*, out, and *culpare*, to blame, from *culpa*, fault.] To clear from a charge or imputation of fault or guilt; to excuse; to vindicate; as, we are inclined to *exculpate* ourselves and throw the blame on others.

Syn.—Absolve, exonerate, clear, justify, vindicate.

ex-cul-pā′tion, *n.* The act of vindicating from a charge of fault or crime; excuse.

ex-cul′pȧ-tō-ry, *a.* Able to clear from the charge of fault or guilt; excusing; containing excuse.

ex-cūr′ (eks-), *v.i.* To go to the extreme and beyond proper limits. [Obs.]

ex-cur′rent, *a.* [L. *excurrens (-entis)*, ppr. of *excurrere*, to run out, project.]

1. Running out.

2. In botany, running or extending beyond the edge or point of anything, or to the summit.

3. Giving an exit; affording a passage outward; as, *excurrent* orifices.

ex-cūrse′, *v.t.* To travel or pass through. [Rare.]

ex-cūrse′, *v.i.* [L. *excursus*, pp. of *excurrere*, to run out or forth; *ex*, out, and *currere*, to run.] To make a digression; to make an excursion.

ex-cūr′sion, *n.* [L. *excursio (-onis)*, a running out or forth, from *excursus*, pp. of *excurrere*, to run out; *ex*, out, and *currere*, to run.]

1. Progression beyond fixed limits; as, the *excursions* of the seasons into the extremes of heat and cold.

2. Digression; a wandering from a subject or main design.

3. A jaunt or trip; specifically, a short journey undertaken for a special purpose, as for pleasure, and with the intention of returning soon; as, an *excursion* on the lake or to a convention.

4. A company of people traveling together, as for a pleasure trip; an expedition; as, the *excursion* was late in arriving.

5. In mechanics, reciprocation; stroke.

6. In physics, the average oscillation or vibratory movement of a body, whether real, as that of the tongue of a reed, or apparent, as that of a planet.

ex-cūr′sion-ist, *n.* One who goes on an excursion.

ex-cūr′sive, *a.* Rambling; wandering; deviating; as, an *excursive* fancy or imagination.

ex-cūr′sive-ly, *adv.* In a wandering manner.

ex-cūr′sive-ness, *n.* The act of wandering or passing usual limits.

ex-cūr′sus, *n.* [L. *excursus*, a running forth, a digression, from *excurrere*, to run out.]

1. A digression.

2. A dissertation containing a more full exposition of some important point or topic and appended to a work.

ex-cūr′vāte, ex-cūr′vā-ted, *a.* Same as *Excurved.*

ex-cūrved′, *a.* [L. *ex*, out, and *curvatus*, pp. of *curvare*, to curve, bend.] In zoölogy, curved outward from the center of a part or organ.

ex-cūṣ′ȧ-ble (eks-), *a.* [ME. *excusable*; L. *excusabilis*, from *excusare*, to release from a charge, to excuse.]

1. Deserving to be excused; pardonable; as, the man is *excusable.*

2. Admitting of excuse or justification; as, an *excusable* action.

ex-cūṣ′ȧ-ble-ness, *n.* The state of being excusable; pardonableness; the quality of admitting of excuse.

ex-cūṣ′ȧ-bly, *adv.* Pardonably; in an excusable manner.

ex-cū-ṣā′tion, *n.* Excuse; apology. [Obs.]

ex-cū-ṣā′tŏr, *n.* One who makes or is authorized to make an excuse or carry an apology.

ex-cūṣ′ȧ-tō-ry, *a.* Making excuse; containing excuse or apology; apologetical; as, an *excusatory* plea.

ex-cūṣe′ (eks-), *v.t.*; excused, *pt.*, *pp.*; excusing, *ppr.* [ME. *excusen*; OFr. *excuser*; L. *excusare*, to free from a charge, release, pardon; *ex*, from, and *causa*, a charge.]

1. To pardon; to free from the imputation of fault or blame; to acquit of guilt.

2. To pardon, as a fault; to forgive entirely, or to admit to be little censurable, and to overlook; as, we *excuse* irregular conduct, when extraordinary circumstances appear to justify it.

3. To free from an obligation or duty.

I pray thee have me *excused.*—Luke xiv. 18.

4. To remit; not to exact; as, to *excuse* a forfeiture.

5. To pardon; to admit an apology for.

Excuse some courtly strains. —Pope.

6. To make an excuse or apology for; often used reflexively.

Think you that we *excuse ourselves* to you? —2 Cor. xii. 19.

7. To justify; to vindicate; to furnish or serve as an excuse for; as, ignorance cannot *excuse* his error.

Syn.—Pardon, justify, absolve, exonerate, vindicate, forgive, exculpate, extenuate, exempt.

ex-cūse′, *n.* 1. A plea offered in extenuation of a fault or irregular conduct; apology; as, he has an *excuse* to offer for his neglect of duty; the debtor makes *excuses* for delay of payment.

2. The act of excusing or apologizing.

3. That which excuses; that which extenuates or justifies a fault, or is intended to do so; as, his inability to comply with the request must be his *excuse*; he has no good *excuse.*

ex-cūse′less, *a.* Having no excuse; inexcusable.

ex-cūse′ment, *n.* Excuse. [Obs.]

ex-cūṣ′ẽr, *n.* 1. One who offers excuses or pleads for another.

2. One who excuses or forgives another.

ex-cuss′, *v.t.* [L. *excussus*, pp. of *excutere*, to shake out or off; *ex*, out, and *quatere*, to shake.]

1. To shake off. [Obs.]

2. To seize and detain by law.

3. To discuss; to decipher. [Obs.]

ex-cus′sion, *n.* 1. A seizing by law. [Obs.]

2. The act of excussing; discussion. [Obs.]

ex′ē-at, *n.* [L., lit., let him go, 3rd. pers. sing. pres. subj. act. of *exire*, to go out, depart.]

1. A leave of absence granted a student in English universities.

2. A leave of absence granted by a bishop to a priest who leaves his diocese.

ex′ē-crȧ-ble, *a.* [L. *execrabilis*, from *execrare*, to curse.] Deserving to be cursed; very hateful; detestable; abominable; as, an *execrable* wretch.

ex′ē-crȧ-ble-ness, *n.* The state of being execrable.

ex′ē-crȧ-bly, *adv.* In an execrable manner; hatefully; detestably.

ex′ē-crāte, *v.t.*; execrated, *pt.*, *pp.*; execrating, *ppr.* [L. *execratus*, pp. of *execrare*, to curse; *ex*, out, and *sacrare*, to consecrate, from *sacer*, sacred.] To curse; to denounce evil against or to imprecate evil on; hence, to detest utterly; to abhor; to abominate.

Syn.—Curse, anathematize, denounce, detest, hate.

ex-ē-crā′tion, *n.* 1. The act of cursing; a curse pronounced; imprecation of evil; utter detestation expressed.

Cease, gentle queen, these *execrations.*—Shak.

2. That which is execrated; an object of detestation.

Syn.—Curse, malediction, anathema, imprecation, oath.

ex′ē-crȧ-tive, *a.* and *n.* I. *a.* Cursing; denunciatory.

II. *n.* A word or phrase employed in cursing.

ex′ē-crȧ-tive-ly, *adv.* In an execrative manner.

ex′ē-crȧ-tō-ry, *a.* and *n.* I. *a.* Execrative; abusive.

II. *n.* A formulary of execrations.

ex-ect′, *v.t.* [Obs.] Same as *Exsect.*

ex-ec′tion, *n.* [Obs.] Same as *Exsection.*

ex′ē-cū-tȧ-ble, *a.* Capable of being executed; practicable.

ex-ec′ū-tănt, *n.* [Fr. *exécutant*, ppr. of *exécuter*, to execute.] One who executes or performs; specifically, a musical performer.

ex′ē-cūte, *v.t.*; executed, *pt.*, *pp.*; executing, *ppr.* [ME. *executen*; OFr. *executer*, to execute, from L. *executus* or *exsecutus*, pp. of *exequi*, or *exsequi*, to follow out, pursue; *ex*, out, and *sequi*, to follow.]

1. To follow out or through; to perform; to do; to effect; to carry into complete effect; to complete; to finish; as, we *execute* a purpose, a plan, design, or scheme.

2. To perform; to inflict; as, to *execute* judgment or vengeance.

3. To perform judgment or sentence on; to inflict capital punishment on; to put to death; as, to *execute* a traitor.

4. To kill. [Obs.]

5. To complete, as a legal instrument; to perform what is required to give validity to (a writing), as by signing and sealing; as, to *execute* a deed or lease.

6. To perform; to render, as a musical composition.

Syn.—Do, perform, accomplish, fulfil, effect, realize, achieve, complete, consummate.

ex′ē-cūte, *v.i.* 1. To accomplish the desired result; to produce an effect.

2. To perform a musical composition.

ex′ē-cū-tẽr, *n.* One who performs or carries into effect.

ex-ē-cū′tion, *n.* 1. Performance; the act of completing or accomplishing.

The excellence of the subject contributed much to the happiness of the *execution.* —Dryden.

2. In law, (a) the carrying into effect a sentence or judgment of court; the last act of the law in completing the process by which justice is to be done, by which the possession of land or debt, damages or costs, is obtained, or by which judicial punishment is inflicted; (b) the instrument, warrant, or official order by which an officer is empowered to carry a judgment into effect; (c) the act of signing and sealing a legal instrument, or giving it the forms required to render it a valid act; as, the *execution* of a deed.

3. The last act of the law in the punishment of criminals; capital punishment; death inflicted according to the forms of law.

4. Effect; something done or accomplished; as, every shot did *execution.*

5. Destruction; the pillaging of an enemy's country. [Obs.]

6. In the fine arts, the mode of performing a work of art; the dexterity with which it is accomplished; skill.

ex-ē-cū′tion-ẽr, *n.* 1. One who executes; specifically, one who carries into effect a judgment of death; one who inflicts a capital punishment in pursuance of a legal warrant.

2. The instrument by which anything is performed. [Rare.]

ex-ec′ū-tive (egz-), *a.* [L. *executus*, pp. of *exequi*, to follow out, execute.] Having the quality of executing or performing; as, *executive* power or authority; an *executive* officer. Hence, in government, *executive* is used in distinction from *legislative* and *judicial.* The body that deliberates and enacts laws, is *legislative*; the body that judges, or applies the laws to particular cases, is *judicial*; the body or person who carries the laws into effect, or superintends the enforcement of them, is *executive.*

It is of the nature of war to increase the *executive* at the expense of the legislative authority. —Hamilton.

ex-ec′ū-tive, *n.* The officer, whether king, president, or other chief magistrate, who superintends the execution of the laws; the person who administers the government; executive power or authority in government.

Men most desirous of places in the executive gift, will not expect to be gratified, except by their support of the *executive.*—J. Quincy.

ex-ec′ū-tive-ly, *adv.* In the way of executing or performing.

ex-é-cu-toire′ (egz-ā-kụ-twor′), *n.* In French law, a writ of execution authorizing a creditor to seize and sell a debtor's property to satisfy a debt.

ex-eç'ū-tŏr (egz-), *n.* [ME. *executour*; OFr. *executour*; L. *executor, exsecutor*, a performer, accomplisher, from *exequi, exsequi*, to perform, accomplish.]

1. One who executes; a doer; an executor.

2. The person appointed by a testator to execute his will, or to see it carried into effect.

Executor de son tort or *executor in his own wrong*; one who, without authority, intermeddles with the goods of a deceased person, by which he subjects himself to the trouble of executorship, without the profits or advantages.

ex-eç-ū-tō'ri-ăl, *a.* Pertaining to an executor; executive.

ex-eç'ū-tŏr-ship, *n.* The office of an executor.

ex-eç'ū-tō-ry, *a.* [LL. *exsecutorius*, from L. *exsecutus*, pp. of *exsequi*, to follow out, execute.]

1. Of or pertaining to execution, especially of official duties; executive.

2. In law, to be executed or carried into effect in future; to take effect on a future contingency; as, an *executory* devise or remainder.

ex-eç'ū-trix, ex-eç'ū-tress, *n.* A female executor; a woman appointed by a testator to execute his will.

ex-eç'ū-try, *n.* In Scots law, all of the movable estate of a person deceased, passing to an executor's control.

ex'ē-dent, *a.* [L. *exedens (-entis)*, ppr. of *exedere*, to eat up; *ex*, out, and *edere*, to eat.] Eating; as, an *exedent* cancer.

ex'ē-drȧ, ex'hē-drȧ (eks'), *n.* [L., from Gr. *exedra*; *ex*, out, and *hedra*, a seat.] In ancient architecture, an apartment provided with seats for the purpose either of repose or of conversation. The form of the *exedra* was arbitrary, but it was open to the sun and air, and appended to the portico. The term is also applied to an apse, a recess or large niche in a wall, and sometimes to a porch or chapel projecting from a large building.

ex-ē-ġē'sis (eks-), *n.*; *pl.* **ex-ē-ġē'sēs.** [L., from Gr. *exēgēsis*, an explanation, from *exēgeisthai*, to show the way, to lead, to explain; *ex*, out, and *egēisthai*, to lead, guide, from *agein*, to lead.]

1. The exposition or interpretation of any literary production, but more particularly the exposition or interpretation of Scripture; sometimes applied to the science which lays down the principles of the art of sacred interpretation; more properly called *exegetics* or *hermeneutics*.

2. A discourse intended to explain or illustrate a subject; the name given to one of the exercises prescribed to students of theology in the Scotch universities, and also to students on trial before presbyteries in order to be licensed or ordained.

3. In mathematics, the process for finding the root of an equation. [Obs.]

ex'ē-ġēte, *n.* [Gr. *exēgetēs*, a leader, adviser, from *exēgeisthai*, to lead, explain.] One skilled in exegesis.

ex-ē-ġet'iç, ex-ē-ġet'iç-ăl, *a.* Pertaining to exegesis; explanatory; tending to unfold or illustrate; expository.

Exegetical theology; that branch of theological learning which deals with the interpretation of the Scriptures and the subjects therewith connected.

ex-ē-ġet'iç-ăl-ly, *adv.* By way of explanation.

ex-ē-ġet'içs, *n.* Same as *Exegetical theology* under *Exegetic*.

ex-ē-ġē'tist, *n.* One versed in exegesis; an exegete.

ex-em'bry-ō-nāte (eks-), *a.* [Gr. *ex*, out, and *embryon*, an embryo.] In botany, without an embryo, applied to the spores of cryptogams, which differ in this respect from the seeds of phænogams.

ex-em'plăr (egz-), *n.* [ME. *exemplaire*; LL. *exemplarium*, that which serves as a pattern or model, from L. *exemplum*, a pattern, copy.]

1. A model, original, or pattern, to be copied or imitated; the idea or image of a thing formed in the mind.

2. A copy, especially of a book or writing.

ex-em'plăr, *a.* 1. Of, pertaining to, containing, or constituting an example or examples.

2. Exemplary. [Obs.]

Exemplar proposition; in logic, a proposition which states something to be true of one or more examples of a class, regarded as representative of the entire class.

ex'em-plā-ri-ly, *adv.* 1. In a manner to deserve imitation; in a worthy or excellent manner.

> She is *exemplarily* loyal. —Howell.

2. In a manner that may warn others, by way of terror; in such a manner that others may be cautioned to avoid an evil; in a manner intended to warn others.

> Some he punished *exemplarily* in this world. —Hakewill.

ex'em-plā-ri-ness, *n.* The state or quality of being exemplary.

ex-em-plar'i-ty (eks-), *n.* Exemplariness. [Rare.]

ex'em-plā-ry (eks' or egz-em'plȧ-ry), *a.* 1. Serving for a pattern or model for imitation; worthy of imitation; as, an *exemplary* life.

2. Such as may serve for a warning to others; such as may deter from crimes or vices; as, *exemplary* punishment.

> Tumults repressed by *exemplary* justice, I had obtained all that I designed. —Eikon Basilike.

3. Such as may attract notice and imitation.

4. Illustrating, as the proof of a thing; explanatory. [Obs.]

Syn.—Laudable, praiseworthy, conspicuous, honorable, meritorious, worthy, excellent.

ex'em-plā-ry, *n.* [Obs.] Same as *Exemplar*.

ex-em'pli-fī-ȧ-ble (egz-), *a.* Capable of being exemplified.

ex-em"pli-fi-cā'tion, *n.* [LL. *exemplificatio (-onis)*, from *exemplificare*, to exemplify.]

1. The act of exemplifying; a showing or illustrating by example.

2. That which exemplifies; an illustration or example, as of a theory, principle, etc.

3. In law, a transcript; an attested copy; as, an *exemplification* of a record, deed, or letters patent; an *exemplification* of a contract between persons or corporations.

ex-em'pli-fī-ẽr, *n.* One who exemplifies by following a pattern.

ex-em'pli-fȳ (egz-), *v.t.*; exemplified, *pt.*, *pp.*; exemplifying, *ppr.* [LL. *exemplificare*, to show by example; L. *exemplum*, example, and *facere*, to make.]

1. To show or illustrate by example; as, the life of Jesus *exemplified* his doctrines and precepts.

2. To copy; to transcribe; to take an attested copy of.

3. To prove or show by an attested copy.

ex-empt' (egz-emt'), *v.t.*; exempted, *pt.*, *pp.*; exempting, *ppr.* [ME. *exempten*; L. *eximere*, to take out, deliver, set free; *ex*, out, and *emere*, to take, buy.]

1. To free or permit to be free from any charge, burden, restraint, duty, evil, or requisition to which others are subject; to privilege; to grant immunity from; as, to *exempt* one from military duty.

2. To remove; to set aside or away. [Obs.]

ex-empt', *a.* 1. Free from any service, charge, burden, tax, duty, requisition, or evil of any kind to which others are subject; not subject; not liable to; not coming within the power or sway of; as, to be *exempt* from military duty, or from pain or fear; *exempt* from the jurisdiction of a lord or of a court.

> A nature *exempt* in its colorless purity from the vulgarizing taint of passion. —Caird.

2. Left out, omitted, or excluded; not included.

> His dreadful imprecation hear;
> 'Tis laid on all, not any one *exempt*. —Lee and Dryden.

3. Released; freed; free.

> Who would not wish from wealth to be *exempt?* —Shak.

4. Cut off; removed or remote. [Obs.]

Syn.—Free, irresponsible, unamenable, clear, liberated, privileged, absolved.

ex-empt', *n.* 1. One who is exempted or freed from duty; one not subject to service.

2. In England, one of four officers of the yeomen of the royal guard, styled *corporals* in their commission; an exon.

ex-empt'i-ble, *a.* Capable of being exempted; privileged. [Obs.]

ex-emp'tion (egz-), *n.* [L. *exemptio (-onis)*, a taking out, from *exemptus*, pp. of *eximere*, to take out, exempt.]

1. The act of exempting; the state of being exempt; freedom from any service, charge, burden, tax, evil, or requisition to which others are subject; immunity; privilege; as, *exemption* from feudal servitude.

> The Roman laws gave particular *exemptions* to such as built ships or traded in corn. —Arbuthnot.

2. In the Roman Catholic church, a dispensation occasionally granted by the pope to clergymen, and more rarely to laymen, to exempt them from the authority of their ordinaries.

Syn.—Freedom, immunity, privilege, prerogative.

ex-emp-ti'tious (egz-em-tish'us), *a.* Separable; capable of being exempted. [Rare.]

ex-en'tẽr-āte, *v.t.* [L. *exenteratus*, pp. of *exenterare*; Gr. *exenterizein*, to eviscerate, disembowel; *ex*, out, and *entera*, bowels, vitals.] To take out the bowels or entrails of; to disembowel; to eviscerate. [Rare.]

ex-en-tẽr-ā'tion, *n.* The act of taking out the bowels; evisceration. [Rare.]

ex-ē-quā'tŭr (eks-ē-kwā'), *n.* [L., lit., let him perform or follow it out; third pers. sing. pres. subj. of *exequi, exsequi*, to follow out, perform.]

1. A written recognition of a person in the character of consul or commercial agent, issued by the government, and authorizing him to exercise his powers in the country.

2. An authoritative or official recognition, as of a document or privilege.

3. The right asserted by secular rulers to exclude from their provinces such papal bulls as they may deem unwise and unsafe.

ex-ē'qui-ăl, *a.* [L. *exequialis, exsequialis*, from *exequiæ, exsequiæ*, the following of a corpse, exequies, from *exsequi*, to follow out.] Pertaining to funerals; funereal.

ex-ē'qui-ous, *a.* Pertaining to or belonging to exequies. [Rare.]

ex'ē-quy (eks'ē-kwi), *n.*; *pl.* **ex'ē-quieș.** [L. *exsequiæ, exequiæ*, nom. pl., lit., the following of a corpse beyond the walls, a funeral procession, funeral rites, from *exsequi, exequi*, to follow out, to accompany to the grave.]

1. [*pl.*] Funeral rites; the ceremonies of burial; obsequies.

2. A funeral procession.

3. A funeral hymn. [Rare.]

ex-ẽr'cent (egz-), *a.* Using; practising; following, as a calling or profession. [Obs.]

ex'ẽr-ci-ṣȧ-ble, *a.* Capable of being exercised, used, employed, or exerted.

ex'ẽr-çiṣe (eks'), *n.* [ME. *exercise*; L. *exercitium*, exercise, from *exercere*, to drive out, drill, exercise.]

1. Use; practice; the exertions and movements customary in the performance of business; as, the *exercise* of an art, trade, occupation, or profession.

2. Practice; performance; as, the *exercise* of religion.

3. Use; employment; exertion; as, the *exercise* of the eyes, or of the senses, or of any power of body or mind.

4. Exertion of the body, as conducive to health; action; motion by labor, walking, riding, or other exertion.

> The wise for cure on *exercise* depend. —Dryden.

5. A task; that which is appointed for one to perform for discipline or the attainment of proficiency and skill; as, an *exercise* for the piano; military *exercises*.

6. A performance; specifically, a feature or number on a program; as, the graduating *exercises*.

Exercise bone; a deposit of a hard bony substance in the soft tissues of the body, as a result of continual use.

Syn.—Exertion, use, practice, application, training, employment, drill.

ex'ẽr-çiṣe, *v.t.*; exercised, *pt.*, *pp.*; exercising, *ppr.* 1. To employ actively; to exert; to cause to act in any manner; as, to *exercise* the body or the hands; to *exercise* the mind or judgment.

2. To use; to exert; to perform the duties of; as, to *exercise* authority or an office.

3. To train to use; to discipline; to cause to perform certain acts, as preparatory to service; as, to *exercise* troops; to *exercise* oneself in writing.

4. To give anxiety to; to make uneasy; to cause to think earnestly or anxiously; as, he is greatly *exercised* about his health.

5. To impart; to effect; to exert; as, art *exercises* a good influence.

ex'ẽr-çiṣe, *v.i.* To use action or exertion; as, to *exercise* for health or amusement.

ex'ẽr-çiṣ-ẽr, *n.* One who or that which exercises.

ex'ẽr-ci-ṣi-ble, *a.* [Rare.] See *Exercisable*.

ex-ẽr-ci-tā'tion (egz-), *n.* [ME. *exercitacioun*; L. *exercitatio (-onis)*, exercise, practice, from *exercitare*, freq. of *exercere*, to exercise.]

1. Exercise; practice; use. [Rare.]

2. An act; a performance; specifically, a mental performance done for discipline.

ex-ẽr'ci-tŏr (egz-), *n.* [L. *exercitor*, an exerciser, trainer, from *exercere*, to exercise.] In law, the one entitled to the profits of a ship or trading-vessel, whether the actual owner or some one else, as the charterer or the captain.

ex-ẽrgue' (egz-ẽrg'), *n.* [Fr. *exergue*, lit., that which is out of work, the exergue of a coin; Gr. *ex*, out, and *ergon*, work.] In numismatics, the place on a medal or coin around and without the type or figure, which has generally the date or other particular inscription.

ex-ẽrt' (egz-ẽrt'), *v.t.*; exerted, *pt.*, *pp.*; exerting, *ppr.* [L. *exertare, exsertare*, freq. of *exerere, exserere*, to stretch out, put forth; *ex*, out, and *serere*, to join, fasten together.]

1. To thrust forth; to emit; to push out. [Obs.]

> Before the gems *exert*
> Their feeble heads. —Philips.

2. To put or thrust forth, as strength, force, or ability; to strain; to put in action; to bring into active operation; as, to *exert* the strength of the body or limbs; to *exert* powers or faculties; to *exert* the mind.

3. To put forth; to do or perform.

When the will has *exerted* an act of command on any faculty of the soul. —South.

To exert oneself; to use active efforts; to strive.

ex-ẽr′tion (egz-), *n.* The act of exerting or straining; the act of putting into motion or action; effort; a striving or struggling; as, an *exertion* of the limbs or of the mind; the ship was saved by great *exertions* of the crew.

ex-ẽrt′ive, *a.* Exerting; having power to exert.

ex-ẽrt′ment, *n.* Exertion; the act of exerting.

ex-ē′ṣion (egz-), *n.* The act of eating out or through. [Obs.]

ex-es′tū-āte, *v.i.* To boil; to be agitated. [Obs.]

ex-es-tū-ā′tion, *n.* A boiling; ebullition; agitation caused by heat; effervescence. [Obs.]

ex′ē-unt (eks′). [L., lit., they go out; 3rd pers. pl. pres. ind. of *exire*, to go out.] They go out; a word used in the text of plays or as a stage direction, to indicate the point in the action where two or more actors leave the stage; as, *exeunt* all.

ex-fē-tā′tion, *n.* [L. *ex*, out, and *fœtus*, the fetus.] Fetation in some organ other than the uterus.

ex-flect′, *v.t.* [L. *ex*, out, and *flectere*, to turn, bend.] To cause to turn outward. [Rare.]

ex-fō′di-āte, *v.t.* [L. *ex*, out, and *fodire*, to dig.] To take out by digging.

ex-fō′li-āte, *v.i.* [LL. *exfoliatus*, pp. of *exfoliare*, to strip of leaves.]

1. In surgery, to separate and come off in scales, as pieces of carious bone.

2. In mineralogy, to scale off, as the laminæ of a mineral.

ex-fō′li-āte, *v.t.* To scale; to divest of scales or splinters.

ex-fō-li-ā′tion, *n.* The scaling off or separation of scales or laminæ, as from a rock, a bone, etc.; desquamation.

ex-fō′li-ȧ-tive, *a.* and *n.* I. *a.* Having the power of causing exfoliation.

II. *n.* Anything which produces or hastens exfoliation.

ex-hāl′ȧ-ble (eks-), *a.* That may be exhaled.

ex-hāl′ȧnt, *a.* and *n.* I. *a.* Having the quality of exhaling or evaporating.

II. *n.* Anything which exhales or is exhaled.

ex-hȧ-lā′tion, *n.* 1. The act or process of exhaling or sending forth fluids in the form of steam or vapor; evaporation.

2. That which is exhaled; that which is emitted or which rises in the form of vapor; fumes or steam.

3. In heraldry, a representation of a water-spout, a rain-shower, or some similar atmospheric phenomenon, used as a bearing.

ex-hāle′ (eks-), *v.t.*; exhaled, *pt., pp.*; exhaling, *ppr.* [L. *exhalare*, to breathe out, exhale; *ex*, out, and *halare*, to breathe.]

1. To send out; to emit, as vapor, or as minute particles of a fluid or other substance; as, a rose *exhales* a fragrant odor; the earth *exhales* vapor.

2. To draw out; to cause to be emitted in vapor or minute particles; to evaporate; as, the sun *exhales* the moisture of the earth.

ex-hāle′, *v.i.* To rise or pass off as vapor.

ex-hāle′ment, *n.* Matter exhaled; vapor. [Obs.]

ex-hāl′ence, *n.* The act of exhaling; matter exhaled. [Obs.]

ex-hāl′ent, *a.* and *n.* Same as *Exhalant.*

ex-ha̤ust′ (egz-ast′), *v.t.*; exhausted, *pt., pp.*; exhausting, *ppr.* [LL. *exhaustare*, freq. of L. *exhaurire*, to draw out, drink up; *ex*, out, and *haurire*, to draw, drain.]

1. To draw out or drain off the whole of; to draw out, till nothing of the matter drawn is left; as, to *exhaust* the water in a well; to *exhaust* the contents of a purse.

2. To use or expend the whole of; to consume completely; to cause the loss of; as, to *exhaust* the strength or spirits; to *exhaust* one's patience; to *exhaust* the fertility of the soil.

3. To treat, examine, or discuss exhaustively; to consider thoroughly; as, to *exhaust* a subject or a study.

4. To empty by drawing out the contents; specifically, in chemistry, to remove one or more of the component parts from, by means of solvents.

5. Figuratively, to make weak or worthless; to remove strength or power from; as, he is *exhausted* by his dissipations; the nation was *exhausted* by war.

Syn.—Drain, empty, spend, consume, weary, waste.

ex-ha̤ust′, *a.* Drained; exhausted. [Obs.]

ex-ha̤ust′, *n.* 1. Same as *Exhaust-steam.*

2. Emission; outflow, escape, as of steam from an engine.

3. Impure air escaping from an apartment through a register or pipe provided for that purpose.

ex-ha̤ust′=drȧft, *n.* A draft produced by an exhaust-fan.

ex-ha̤ust′ẽr, *n.* One who or that which exhausts or draws out; specifically, in gas-making, one of several devices which prevent back-pressure on the retorts.

ex-ha̤ust′=fan, *n.* A fan-blower which creates a draft by forming a partial vacuum.

ex-ha̤ust′i-ble, *a.* That may be exhausted, drained off, or completely used up.

ex-ha̤ust′ing, *a.* Causing or tending to cause exhaustion; tiring; fatiguing; as, *exhausting* work.

ex-ha̤us′tion (egz-as′chun), *n.* [L. *exhaustus*, pp. of *exhaurire*, to draw off, exhaust.]

1. The act of drawing out or draining off; the act of emptying completely of the contents.

2. The state of being exhausted or emptied; the state of being deprived of strength or spirits.

3. In mathematics, a method of proving the equality of two magnitudes by showing that if one is supposed either greater or less than the other, there will arise a contradiction.

4. In logic, the method by which a point is proved by showing that any other alternative is impossible, all the elements tending to an opposite conclusion having been brought forth and proved untenable or absurd.

5. In physics, the act or process of exhausting the air of a receiver; also the extent to which the process has been carried.

ex-ha̤ust′ive, *a.* Exhausting or tending to exhaust; specifically, applied to a writing, criticism, etc., which treats of the subject under consideration in a thorough and complete manner.

ex-ha̤ust′ive-ly, *adv.* In an exhaustive manner; thoroughly.

ex-ha̤ust′ive-ness, *n.* The state or quality of being exhaustive.

ex-ha̤ust′less, *a.* Incapable of being exhausted; not to be wholly drawn off or emptied; inexhaustible; as, an *exhaustless* fund or store.

ex-ha̤ust′ment, *n.* Exhaustion. [Obs.]

ex-ha̤ust′=noz″le, *n.* In a steam-engine, the nozle which carries off the exhaust-steam.

ex-ha̤ust′=pipe, *n.* In a steam-engine, the pipe which carries the exhaust-steam.

ex-ha̤ust′=pōrt, *n.* In a steam-engine, the opening through which the exhaust-steam escapes from the cylinder.

ex-ha̤ust′=steam, *n.* Steam which is discharged after performing its work of producing motion in the piston; called also *exhaust.*

ex-ha̤us′tūre, *n.* Exhaustion. [Obs.]

ex-ha̤ust′=valve, *n.* 1. In a steam-engine, the valve which controls the escape of the exhaust-steam from the cylinder.

2. In organ-building, a valve in the bellows for releasing superfluous air rapidly.

ex′hē-drȧ, *n.* Same as *Exedra.*

ex-her′ē-dāte, *v.t.* [L. *exheredatus*, pp. of *exheredare*, to disinherit, from *exheres*, disinherited; *ex-* priv., and *heres*, an heir.] To disinherit. [Rare.]

ex-her-ē-dā′tion, ex-he-red-i-tā′tion, *n.* In Roman law, a disinheriting; a father's excluding a child from inheriting any part of his estate.

ex-hib′it (egz-ib′it), *v.t.*; exhibited, *pt., pp.*; exhibiting, *ppr.* [L. *exhibitus*, pp. of *exhibere*, to hold forth, present; *ex*, out, and *habere*, to hold, have.]

1. To offer or present to view; to present for inspection; to show; as, to *exhibit* paintings or other specimens of art; to *exhibit* papers or documents in court.

2. To show; to display; to manifest publicly; as, to *exhibit* a noble example of bravery or generosity.

3. To present; to offer publicly or officially; as, to *exhibit* a charge of high treason. [Obs.]

4. To administer, as medicines.

5. In law, to submit or present formally, as a document in a case; to file or bring; as, to *exhibit* charges.

ex-hib′it (egz-ib′it), *n.* 1. Any paper produced or presented to a court or to auditors, referees, or arbitrators, as a voucher, or in proof of facts; a voucher or document produced.

2. In law, a deed or writing produced in court, sworn to by a witness, and a certificate of the oath indorsed on it by the examiner or commissioner.

3. Any article or number of articles arranged in a public place for show; a display; as, a live stock *exhibit.*

Syn.—Exhibition, exposition, fair, showing.

ex-hib′it-ẽr (egz-ib′), *n.* One who exhibits; an exhibitor.

ex-hi-bi′tion (eks-i-bish′un), *n.* [LL. *exhibitio* (*-onis*), a handing out, giving up, from L. *exhibere*, to hold forth, present, show.]

1. The act of exhibiting for inspection; a showing or presenting to view; display.

2. The offering, producing, or showing of titles, authorities, or papers of any kind, before a tribunal, in proof of facts.

3. A public show; representation of feats or actions in public; display of literary, artistic, or physical powers in public; any public show; as, a college *exhibition*; an athletic *exhibition.*

4. An allowance for meat and drink; pension; a benefaction settled for the maintenance of scholars in the English universities, not depending on the foundation.

5. In medicine, the act of administering a remedy.

ex-hi-bi′tion-ẽr (eks-i-bish′un-ẽr), *n.* In English universities, one who has a pension or allowance granted for the encouragement of learning.

ex-hib′it-ive (egz-), *a.* Serving for exhibition; representative.

ex-hib′it-ive-ly, *adv.* By representation.

ex-hib′it-ŏr, *n.* One who exhibits; in law, one who presents a petition or a charge.

ex-hib′it-ō-ry, *a.* Exhibiting; showing; displaying.

ex-hil′ȧ-rănt (egz-il′), *a.* and *n.* [L. *exhilarans* (*-antis*), ppr. of *exhilarare*, to gladden.]

I. *a.* Exhilarating.

II. *n.* That which exhilarates.

ex-hil′ȧ-rāte (egz-il′ȧ-rāte), *v.t.*; exhilarated, *pt., pp.*; exhilarating, *ppr.* [L. *exhilaratus*, pp. of *exhilarare*, to gladden, to make merry; *ex*, out, and *hilarare*, to gladden, from *hilaris*, glad.] To make cheerful or merry; to enliven; to make glad or joyous; to gladden; to cheer; as, good news *exhilarates* the mind; good wine *exhilarates* the animal spirits.

ex-hil′ȧ-rāte, *v.i.* To become cheerful or joyous. [Rare.]

ex-hil′ȧ-rā-ting, *a.* Enlivening; giving life and vigor to the spirits; cheering; gladdening.

ex-hil′ȧ-rā-ting-ly, *adv.* In an exhilarating manner.

ex-hil-ȧ-rā′tion, *n.* [LL. *exhilaratio* (*-onis*), a gladdening or enlivening, from L. *exhilaratus*, pp. of *exhilarare*, to gladden.]

1. The act of enlivening the spirits; the act of making glad or cheerful.

2. The state of being enlivened or cheerful.

Exhilaration usually expresses less than *joy* or *mirth*, but it may be used to express either.

ex-hort′ (egz-ort′), *v.t.*; exhorted, *pt., pp.*; exhorting, *ppr.* [ME. *exhorten*; L. *exhortari*, to exhort; *ex*, out, and *hortari*, to urge, incite.] To incite by words or advice; to animate or urge by arguments to a good deed or to any laudable conduct or course of action; hence, to advise; to warn; to caution.

> I *exhort* you to be of good cheer. —Acts xxvii. 22.

ex-hort′, *v.i.* To deliver exhortation; to use words or arguments to incite to good deeds.

> And with many other words did he testify and *exhort.* —Acts ii. 40.

ex-hort′, *n.* Exhortation. [Obs.]

ex-hor-tā′tion (eks-), *n.* [ME. *exhortacion*; OFr. *exhortation*; L. *exhortatio* (*-onis*), an exhorting, from *exhortari*, to exhort.]

1. The act or practice of exhorting; the act of inciting to laudable deeds; incitement to that which is good or commendable.

2. Advice; counsel; admonition.

ex-hor′tȧ-tive (egz-), *a.* Containing exhortation.

ex′hor-tā-tŏr (eks′), *n.* An exhorter; one who exhorts. [Rare.]

ex-hor′tȧ-tō-ry (egz-), *a.* [LL. *exhortatorius*, from L. *exhortari*, to exhort.] Tending to exhort; serving for exhortation; containing exhortation.

ex-hort′ẽr (egz-ort′ẽr), *n.* One who exhorts or encourages.

ex-hū′mā-ted (eks-), *a.* Disinterred. [Obs.]

ex-hū-mā′tion (eks-), *n.* [LL. *exhumatio* (*-onis*), from *exhumare*, to dig up, exhume; L. *ex*, out, and *humus*, the ground.] The act of exhuming; as, the *exhumation* of a corpse.

ex-hūme′ (eks-), *v.t.*; exhumed, *pt., pp.*; exhuming, *ppr.* [LL. *exhumare*, to dig out of the ground; L. *ex*, out, and *humus*, the ground.] To dig out of the earth from its place of burial; to disinter.

ex-ic′cāte (eks-), *v.t.* [Obs.] Same as *Exsiccate.*

ex-ic-cā′tion, *n.* [Obs.] Same as *Exsiccation.*

ex-i-ġeañt′ (egz-i-zhoń′), **ex-i-ġeañte′** (-zhońt′), *a.* [Fr. *exigeant*, masc., *exigeante*, f., exacting, particular, ppr. of *exiger*; L. *exigere*, to exact.] Exacting.

ex′i-ġen-cy, ex′i-ġence (eks′), *n.* [OFr. *exigence*; LL. *exigentia*, necessity, need, from L. *exigens* (*-entis*), ppr. of *exigere*, to drive forth, to exact; *ex*, out, and *agere*, to drive.]

1. The state of being urgent; urgency; imperative need or want; as, the *exigence* of the case; the *exigence* of the times or of business.

2. A pressing necessity; distress; any case which demands immediate action, supply, or remedy; as, in the present *exigency*, no time is to be lost.

3. Command; requirement, as of a writ.

ex-i-ġen′dȧ-ry (eks-), *n.* Same as *Exigenter.*

ex′i-ġent, *a.* [L. *exigens* (*-entis*), ppr. of *exigere*, to drive out, drive forth; *ex*, out, and *agere*, to drive.] Pressing; requiring immediate aid or action.

ex′i-ġent, *n.* 1. An urgent occasion; exigency. [Obs.]

2. In old English law, a writ which lay where

the defendant was not to be found, which required the sheriff to cause the defendant to be proclaimed in five county courts successively before he was declared outlawed.

3. End; extremity. [Obs.]

ex′i-gĕnt-ĕr, *n.* In old English law, an officer in the Court of Common Pleas who made out exigents and proclamations in cases of outlawry.

ex′i-gi-ble (eks′), *a.* Capable of being exacted; demandable; requirable. [Rare.]

ex-i-gū′i-ty, *n.* [L. *exiguitas* (*-atis*), scantiness, smallness, from *exiguus*, scanty, small.] Smallness; slenderness. [Rare.]

ex-ig′ū-ous (egz-), *a.* [L. *exiguus*, scanty, small.] Small; slender; minute; diminutive.

ex-ig′ū-ous-ness, *n.* The state or character of being exiguous. [Rare.]

ex′ile (eks′īl), *n.* [ME. *exil*, *exile*; OFr. *exil*, *essil*; L. *exilium*, *exsilium*, banishment, exile, from *exul*, *exsul*, an exile, one who is banished.]

1. Banishment; the state of being expelled from one's native country or place of residence by authority, and forbidden to return, either for a limited time or for life.

2. An abandonment of one's country or removal to a foreign country for residence, either from choice or necessity.

3. One who is banished or expelled from his country by authority; also, one who abandons his country and resides in another; one who is separated from his country and friends by necessity.

ex′ile (eks′īl), *v.t.*; exiled, *pt.*, *pp.*; exiling, *ppr.* To banish, as a person from his country or from a particular jurisdiction, by authority, with a prohibition of return, either for a limited time or for life; to drive away, expel, or transport from one's country.

To exile oneself; to quit one's country with a view not to return.

ex′ile (eks′il), *a.* Slender; thin; fine. [Obs.]

ex′ile-ment, *n.* Banishment. [Obs.]

ex-il′i-ăn, ex-il′iç (eks-), *a.* [L. *exilium*, exile.]

1. Pertaining to exile or banishment.

2. Specifically, noting the period of the Jewish captivity at Babylon.

ex-i-li′tion (eks-i-lish′un), *n.* A sudden springing or leaping out. [Obs.]

ex-il′i-ty (egz-il′i-ty), *n.* [L. *exilitas*, from *exilis*, small.] Slenderness; fineness; thinness. [Rare.]

ex-im′i-ous, *a.* Excellent. [Obs.]

ex-in′ă-nite (egz-), *v.t.* To make empty; to weaken. [Obs.]

ex-in-ă-ni′tion (-nish′un), *n.* An emptying or evacuation; hence, privation; loss; destitution. [Obs.]

ex-in-dū′si-āte (eks-), *a.* [L. *ex-* priv., and *indusium*, lit., an undergarment; in botany, the indusium.] In botany, not furnished with an indusium; said of ferns.

ex-ist′ (egz-ist′), *v.i.*; existed, *pt.*, *pp.*; existing, *ppr.* [L. *existere*, *exsistere*, to step, or come forth, to stand forth; *ex*, out, and *sistere*, to cause to stand, to set, place, caus. of *stare*, to stand.]

1. To be; to have real existence or being of any kind; as, evils *exist* on every side.

> By whom we *exist* and cease to be.—Milton.

2. To live; to have life or animation; as, men cannot *exist* in water, nor fishes on land.

ex-ist′ence (egz-), *n.* [ME. *existence*; OFr. *existence*; LL. *existentia*, existence, from L. *existere*, *exsistere*, to come forth, to exist.]

1. The state of existing; actual possession or continuance of being; as, the *existence* of the soul; a mere *existence*.

2. Life; sentient being; possession or continuance of real being; as, a struggle for *existence*.

3. Figuratively, a controlling and eternal power of life, which governs the sentient being.

> And fear not lest *existence*, closing your brief account and mine,
> Shall know the like no more.
> —Omar Khayyam.

4. Anything which exists; an entity; an actuality; as, a pin is an *existence*.

5. Reality; truth; actuality. [Obs.]

Syn.—Being, entity, endurance, duration.

ex-ist′en-cy, *n.* Existence. [Rare.]

ex-ist′ent, *a.* Being; having being or existence.

> The eyes and mind are fastened on objects which have no real being, as if they were truly *existent*.
> —Dryden.

ex-is-ten′tiăl (egz-is-ten′shăl), *a.* Having existence. [Obs.]

ex-is-ten′tiăl-ly, *adv.* In an existential manner; actually. [Rare.]

ex-ist′ĕr, *n.* One who or that which exists. [Rare.]

ex-ist′i-ble, *a.* Capable of existing.

ex-is-ti-mā′tion, *n.* Esteem. [Obs.]

ex′it (eks′it). [L., lit., he goes out; 3rd pers. sing. pres. ind. of *exire*, to go out.] Literally, he or she goes out; a direction used in plays, to indicate the time when an actor is to leave the stage.

ex′it, *n.* [L. *exitus*, a going out, from *exitus*, pp. of *exire*, to go out.]

1. The departure of a player from the stage, when he has performed his part.

2. Any departure; the act of quitting the stage of action or of life; death; decease.

3. A way of departure; passage out of a place; as, the building has ten *exits*.

ex-i′tiăl (egz-ish′ăl), **ex-i′tious** (-ish′us), *a.* [L. *exitialis*, destructive, from *exitium*, destruction, ruin.] Destructive to life. [Rare.]

ex li′bris. [L.] From the books of; designating the ownership of; used as an inscription or label in a book.

ex-ō-. A prefix from Greek *exō*, without, signifying without, outside of; used chiefly in scientific words, where it is equivalent to *ecto-* and opposite in meaning to *endo-*, or *ento-*.

ex-ō-cär′di-ăl, ex-ō-cär′di-aç, *a.* [*Exo-*, and Gr. *kardia*, heart.] Located outside the heart.

ex′ō-cärp, *n.* [*Exō-*, and Gr. *karpos*, fruit.] In botany, the external part or layer of a pericarp which has more than one layer.

ex-oç-cip′i-tăl, *a.* [L. *ex*, out, and *occiput*, *occipitis*, the back part of the head, the occiput; *ob*, about, and *caput*, head.] Of or pertaining to the exoccipitals.

ex-oç-cip′i-tăl, *n.* One of the two lateral bones on each side of the basioccipital, separate in the embryo but coössified in the adult of man and other mammals, forming the occipital bone.

ex-ō-chō′ri-on, *n.* [*Exo-*, and Gr. *chorion*, skin, leather.] In zoölogy, the outer coating of the membrane inclosing the egg of an insect.

Ex-ō-cœ′tus, Ex-ō-cē′tus, *n.* [L., from *exocœtus*, a fish that sleeps on the shore; Gr. *exōkoitos*, sleeping out; *exō*, outside, and *koitē*, bed.] A genus of flying-fishes, including the common flying-fishes, and belonging to the family *Exocœtidæ*. The pectoral fins, which are very large, are the principal instruments in its flight, and act as wings in propelling it, or as parachutes or kites in enabling it to sustain itself in the air. It can raise itself from the water and pass through the air to a considerable distance, sometimes as much as 200 yards. The best known species are *Exocœtus volitans*, found in the Atlantic, and *Exocœtus exiliens*, in the Mediterranean.

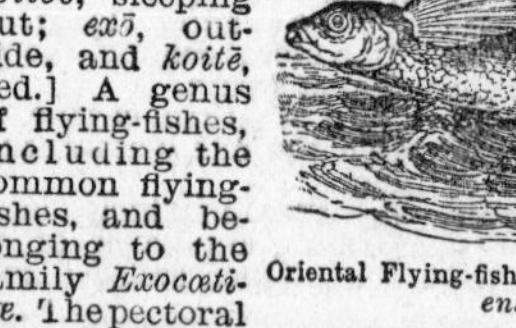

Oriental Flying-fish (*Exocœtus exiliens*).

ex-oç′ū-lāte, *v.t.* To put out or destroy the eyes of. [Rare.]

ex-oç-ū-lā′tion, *n.* [L. *exoculare*, to put out the eyes; *ex*, out, and *oculus*, eye.] The act of putting out or destroying the eyes. [Rare.]

ex′ō-de, *n.* Same as *Exodus*.

ex′ōde (eks′ōd), *n.* [Fr. *exode*; L. *exodium*, a comic interlude, a conclusion, end; Gr. *exodion*, the finale of a tragedy; neut. of *exodios*, belonging to the end or exit; *ex*, out of, from, and *hodos*, way.]

1. In the Greek drama, the tragical conclusion of a play.

2. In the Roman drama, an afterpiece of a farcical or satirical character, sometimes played as an interlude.

ex′ō-dĕrm, *n.* [*Exo-*, and Gr. *derma*, skin.]

1. The outer integument or crust of an insect.

2. In anatomy, the epidermis.

3. In embryology, the ectoderm.

ex-od′iç (eks-), *a.* 1. Pertaining to an exodus.

2. In physiology, same as *efferent*.

ex′ō-dist, *n.* One who makes an exodus or who emigrates. [Rare.]

ex′ō-dus, *n.* [LL. *Exodus*, the Book of Exodus, from Gr. *exodos*, a going out; *ex*, out, and *hodos*, way.]

1. A journeying forth; a going out; an outgoing in great numbers.

2. [E—] The departure from Egypt of the Israelites under the leadership of Moses.

3. [E—] The second book of the Old Testament, believed to have been written by Moses.

ex′ō-dy, *n.* [Obs.] Same as *Exodus*.

ex-of-fi′ciăl (-fish′ăl), *a.* Having the authority of an officer; authoritative. [Rare.]

ex of-fi′ci-ō (-fish′i-ō). [L.] By reason of one's office, but aside from its specified duties; as, the mayor is, *ex officio*, president of the board of aldermen.

ex-ō-gam′iç, *a.* Same as *Exogamous*.

ex-og′ă-mous, *a.* Of, pertaining to, characterized by, or practising exogamy.

ex-og′ă-my, *n.* [*Exo-*, and Gr *gamos*, marriage.] A custom among certain savage tribes which prohibits a man from marrying a woman of his own tribe, and so leads the men frequently to capture their wives from among other tribes.

ex′ō-gen, *n.* [L. *exogenus*; Gr. *exō*, outside, and *-genēs*, producing.] A plant whose stem is formed by successive additions to the outside of the wood. The *exogens* form the larger primary class of plants in the vegetable kingdom. These plants have a pith in the center of their stems not descending into the roots; or they have their woody system separated from the cellular and arranged in concentric zones. They increase by annual additions of new layers to the outside of their wood, formed in the cambium between the wood and the bark, thus differing essentially from *endogens*, whose wood is formed by successive augmentations to the inside. The concentric circles thus annually formed, distinguishable even in the oldest tree, afford a means of computing the age of the tree. All the trees of cold climates and most of those of hot climates are *exogens*

Exogen.

1. Section of a Branch of three years growth. *a*, Medulla or pith. *b*, Medullary sheath. *e e*, Medullary rays. *c c*, Circles of annual growth. *d*, Bark. 2. Netted-veined Leaf (Oak). 3. Dicotyledonous Seed. *a a*, Cotyledons. 4. Germination of Dicotyledonous Seed. *a a*, Seed-leaves or Cotyledons. *o*, Plumula. 5. Exogenous Flower (Crowfoot).

ex″ō-gē-net′iç, *a.* 1. In biology, same as *exogenous*.

2. Due to outside causes or influences; as, an *exogenetic* disease.

ex-og′e-nous (eks-), *a.* 1. Growing by external additions; specifically, in botany, of the nature of or pertaining to the exogens.

2. Produced externally, as many fungi.

3. In anatomy, growing out from another part; applied to processes which are mere outgrowths of a bone, as a vertebra.

ex′ō-lēte (eks′), *a.* Worn; faded; obsolete. [Obs.]

ex-ō-lū′tion, *n.* Relaxation of the nerves. [Obs.]

ex-olve′, *v.t.* To loose. [Obs.]

ex-ō-mol-ō-gē′sis (eks-), *n.* [LL., from Gr. *exomologēsis*, a full confession, from *exomologeisthai*, to confess in full.] A confession in full; a common confession. [Obs.]

ex-om′phă-los, ex-om′phă-lus (egz-), *n.* [L., from Gr. *exomphalos*, having a prominent navel; *ex*, out, and *omphalos*, navel.] In medicine, a navel rupture; umbilical hernia.

ex′ōn (eks′), *n.* In England, a commander of the royal bodyguard; an exempt.

Ex′ōn, *n.* One who is a native or a resident of Exeter, England.

ex-ō-när′thex, *n.* [Modern Gr. *exōnarthēx*; *exō*, outside, and *narthēx*, the narthex.] In architecture, the outer of two narthexes in a Greek church.

ex-ō′nĕr (egz-), *v.t.* [Obs.] See *Exonerate*.

ex-on′ĕr-āte (egz-on′ĕr-āt), *v.t.*; exonerated, *pt.*, *pp.*; exonerating, *ppr.* [L. *exoneratus*, pp. of *exonerare*, to disburden; *ex-* priv., and *onerare*, to load, from *onus*, *oneris*, a load, burden.]

1. To unload; to disburden. [Obs.]

> The vessels *exonerate* themselves into a common duct.
> —Ray.

2. To relieve, as of a charge or blame resting on one; to clear of something that lies upon the character as an imputation; as, to *exonerate* oneself from blame or from the charge of avarice.

3. To relieve, as of an obligation, debt, or duty; to discharge of responsibility or liability; as, a surety *exonerates* himself by producing his man in court.

Syn.—Absolve, clear, justify, acquit, exculpate, relieve.

ex-on-ĕr-ā′tion (egz-), *n.* The act of disburdening or discharging; the act of freeing from a charge or imputation; the state of being exonerated.

ex-on′ĕr-ā-tive, *a.* Freeing from a burden or obligation; tending to absolve.

ex-on′ĕr-ā-tŏr (eks-), *n.* [LL. *exonerator*, from L. *exonerare*, to disburden, exonerate.] One who exonerates.

ex-ō-neū′răl, *a.* [*Exo-*, and Gr. *neuron*, nerve.] Neither included in nor dependent upon the nervous system.

ex-ō-neū′răl-ly, *adv.* In an exoneural manner or situation.

ex-ō-path′iç (eks-), *a.* [*Exo-*, and Gr. *pathos*, suffering.] In pathology, pertaining to or caused by pathogenic factors without the organism; opposed to *endopathic* or *autopathic*.

ex″ō-pē-rid′i-um, *n.*; *pl.* **ex″ō-pē-rid′i-ă.** [L., from Gr. *exō*, outside, and *pēridion*, dim. of *pēra*, a wallet.] In botany, the outer envelop of a fungus having more than one peridium, as in the star-fungus.

ex-oph′ă-ġy (eks-), *n.* [*Exo-*, and Gr. *phagein*,

to eat.] The eating of persons not of the same family or tribe; a custom practised by certain cannibals, where the eating of their kinsmen is forbidden.

ex-oph-thal'mi-a, *n.* [L., from Gr. *exophthalmos*, with prominent eyes; *ex*, out, and *ophthalmos*, eye.] In pathology, a condition in which the eyeball protrudes from the orbit, as the result of disease.

ex-oph-thal'mic, *a.* Of, pertaining to, affected with, or resembling exophthalmia.

Exophthalmic goiter; a disease in which the thyroid gland is swollen, the eyeballs protrude, and the heart palpitates; also called *Graves's* or *Basedow's disease*.

ex-oph-thal'mus, ex-oph-thal'mos, *n.* 1. One who is afflicted with exophthalmia.

2. Same as *Exophthalmia*.

3. [E—] In entomology, a genus of tropical new world curculios.

ex-oph-thal'my, *n.* Same as *Exophthalmia*.

ex-oph'yl-lous, *a.* [*Exo-*, and Gr. *phyllon*, a leaf.] In botany, having a naked plumule or one not sheathed in another leaf.

ex'ō-plasm (eks'), *n.* [*Exo-*, and Gr. *plasma*, anything formed, from *plassein*, to form.] In biology, the outer protoplasm, either of a cell or of a single-celled organism; opposed to *endoplasm*.

ex-op'ō-dite, *n.* [*Exo-*, and Gr. *pous*, *podos*, foot.] In *Crustacea*, the external one of the two main branches of a limb or appendage, opposed to the *endopodite*.

ex-op-ō-dit'ic, *a.* Of or pertaining to the exopodite.

ex-op'tȧ-ble, *a.* [L. *exoptabilis*, desirable, from *exoptare*, to desire.] Worthy of being sought after; desirable. [Obs.]

ex-op'tile (eks-), *n.* [*Exo-*, and Gr. *ptilon*, a feather, down.] In botany, an obsolete synonym of *dicotyledon*.

ex'ō-rȧ-ble (eks'), *a.* [L. *exorabilis*, easily entreated or moved, from *exorare*, to move by entreaty; *ex*, out, and *orare*, to pray.] Susceptible of being moved or persuaded by entreaty.

ex'ō-rāte, *v.t.* To obtain by request. [Obs.]

ex-or'bi-tănce (egz-), **ex-or'bi-tăn-cy**, *n.* [L. *exorbitans* (*-antis*), ppr. of *exorbitare*, to go out of the track; *ex*, out, and *orbita*, track.] A going beyond the rightful or usual limit; hence, enormity; extravagance; a deviation from rule or the ordinary limits of right or propriety; as, the *exorbitances* of desire, of taxes, or of deportment.

ex-or'bi-tănt, *a.* 1. Deviating from the usual course; going beyond the appointed rules or established limits of right or propriety; excessive; extravagant; enormous; as, *exorbitant* appetites and passions; *exorbitant* taxes.

2. Anomalous; not comprehended in a settled rule or method. [Rare.]

ex-or'bi-tănt-ly, *adv.* In an exorbitant manner; excessively.

ex-or'bi-tāte, *v.i.* To go beyond the usual orbit; to deviate from the usual limit. [Obs.]

ex'or-cise (eks'), *v.t.*; exorcised, *pt.*, *pp.*; exorcising, *ppr.* [OFr. *exorciser*; LL. *exorcizare*; New Testament Gr. *exorkizein*, to drive away an evil spirit by adjuration, from Gr. *exorkoun*, to swear a person, administer an oath; *ex*, out, and *horkizein*, *horkoun*, to make one swear, from *horkos*, an oath.]

1. To expel or cast out by conjurations, incantations, or religious or magical ceremonies; as, to *exorcise* evil spirits.

2. To purify or free from unclean spirits by religious or magical ceremonies; as, to *exorcise* a house.

ex'or-cis-ēr, *n.* One who exorcises.

ex'or-cism, *n.* The expulsion of evil spirits from persons or places by certain adjurations and ceremonies; also the solemn ceremony or incantation used for this purpose.

Exorcism was common among the Jews, and still makes a part of the superstitions of some churches; the Greek and Roman Catholic churches using it in the baptism of both infants and adults and in specific cases where individuals are supposed to be possessed by evil spirits. Some Lutheran churches also retain *exorcism* in the administration of baptism.

ex-or-cis'măl, *a.* Of the nature of, pertaining to, or resembling exorcism.

ex'or-cist, *n.* 1. One who exorcises.

2. One of a minor order of both the Greek and Roman Catholic churches, the members of which are supposed to have the power to exorcise evil spirits. They are usually candidates for the priesthood.

3. One who conjures up evil spirits. [Obs.]

ex-or'di-ăl (egz-), *a.* Pertaining to the exordium of a discourse; introductory.

ex-or'di-um, *n.* [L. *exordium*, a beginning, from *exordiri*, to begin, commence.] In oratory, the beginning; the introductory part of a discourse, which prepares the audience for the main subject; the preface.

ex'ō-rhiz, ex-ō-rhi'zȧ (eks-), *n.* [L. *exorhiza*; Gr. *exō*, outside of, and *rhiza*, root.] An exogenous or dicotyledonous plant. [Rare.]

ex-ō-rhi'zăl, ex-ō-rhi'zous (-zus), *a.* Of or pertaining to an exorhiz. [Rare.]

Exorhizal Root.

ex-or-nā'tion (eks-), *n.* Ornament; decoration, embellishment. [Obs.]

ex-or'tive, *a.* [L. *exortivus*, pertaining to the rising of the heavenly bodies, from *exortus*, pp. of *exoriri*, to rise out or forth; *ex*, out, and *oriri*, to rise.] Rising; relating to the east. [Rare.]

ex-os'cū-lāte, (eks-), *v.t.* [L. *exosculatus*, ppr. of *exosculari*, to kiss fondly; *ex-*, intens., and *osculari*, to kiss.] To kiss; especially to kiss again and again. [Obs.]

ex-ō-skel'e-tăl, *a.* Relating to the exoskeleton.

ex-ō-skel'e-tŏn, *n.* [L., from Gr. *exō*, outside, and *skeleton*, a dried body, skeleton.] In zoölogy and anatomy, the hardened covering of an animal, usually composed of a horny, bony, or chitinous substance in the form of plates or scales, as in crustaceans, turtles, and fishes.

ex-os'mic (eks-), *a.* Same as *Exosmotic*.

ex-os-mō'sis, ex'os-mōse, *n.* [L., from Gr. *ex*, out, and *ōsmos*, a thrusting, from *ōthein*, to thrust, push, drive.] The passage of gases, vapors, or liquids, through porous media from within outward, or in the direction of slowest passage.

ex-os-mot'ic, *a.* Relating to exosmosis.

ex'ō-spērm, *n.* Same as *Exospore*.

ex'ō-spōre, *n.* [*Exo-*, and Gr. *spora*, a seed.] The outer covering of a spore; the epispore.

ex-ō-spōr'ous, *a.* [*Exo-*, and Gr. *sporos*, a seed, a sowing.] With the spores naked or growing on the outside.

ex-os'sāte, *v.t.* To remove the bones from; to bone. [Obs.]

ex-os-sā'tion, *n.* The act or process of removing the bones or other similar hard substance from; the state of having such parts removed. [Obs.]

ex-os'sē-ous, *a.* Without bones; boneless. [Obs.]

ex'ō-stōme, *n.* [*Exo-*, and Gr. *stoma*, mouth.] In botany, the aperture through the outer integument of an ovule, which together with the endostome completes the foramen. The figure shows the *exostome* and *endostome* in the ovule of the mallow, *Malva sylvestris*.

Exostome and Endostome.

ex-os-tō'sis, *n.* [L., from Gr. *exō*, outside, and *osteon*, a bone.]

1. Any protuberance of a bone which is not natural; an excrescence or morbid enlargement of a bone.

2. In botany, a knot formed upon the stem or root of a plant.

ex-os-tot'ic, *a.* Of the nature of or pertaining to exostosis.

ex-ō-ter'ic, *a.* and *n.* [LL. *exotericus*; Gr. *exōterikos*, external, from *exō*, outside.]

I. *a.* External; public; popular; intended or suitable to be imparted to the public; hence, capable of being easily or fully understood; opposed to *esoteric* or secret; originally applied to the public lectures of Aristotle. The *exoteric* doctrines of the ancient philosophers were those which were openly professed and taught; the *esoteric* were secret or taught only to a few chosen disciples.

> He has ascribed to Kant the foppery of an *exoteric* and esoteric doctrine.—DeQuincey.

II. *n.* One of the general public and not the select few given esoteric instruction; one receiving exoteric doctrines.

ex-ō-ter'ic-ăl, *a.* Same as *Exoteric*.

ex-ō-ter'ic-ăl-ly, *adv.* In an exoteric manner.

ex-ō-ter'i-cism, *n.* The doctrines and principles promulgated exoterically, or the practice of such doctrines and principles.

ex-ō-ter'ics, *n.* Instruction, especially in philosophy, which is given publicly and is popular in its character; first applied to the public lectures of Aristotle.

ex'ō-ter-y, *n.*; *pl.* **ex'ō-ter-ies**. That which is obvious, common, or exoteric.

ex-ō-thē'cȧ, *n.*; *pl.* **ex-ō-thē'cæ** (-sē). [L., from Gr. *exō*, outside, and *thēkē*, a case.] The calcareous substance covering the outer wall or the visceral chamber of a coral.

ex-ō-thē'cāte, *a.* Having exothecæ, as a coral.

ex-ō-thē'ci-um, *n.* [L., from Gr. *exō*, outside, and *thēkē*, a case.] In botany, the outer covering of an anther.

ex-ō-thēr'mic, *a.* [*Exo-*, and Gr. *thermē*, heat.] Pertaining to a liberation of heat.

Exothermic compound; in chemistry, a compound in the formation of which heat is liberated, and in the reduction of which to its original components heat is absorbed.

ex-ot'ic (egz-), *a.* and *n.* [L. *exoticus*; Gr. *exōtikos*, foreign, alien, from *exō*, outside.]

I. *a.* Foreign; introduced from a foreign country; not native; extraneous; as, an *exotic* plant; an *exotic* term or word.

II. *n.* Anything of foreign origin introduced into a country and not fully acclimated or naturalized, as a plant, a word, or a custom.

ex-ot'ic-ăl, *a.* Same as *Exotic*.

ex-ot'ic-ăl-ness, *n.* The state or quality of being exotic.

ex-ot'i-cism, *n.* 1. The state or quality of being exotic.

2. Anything which is exotic, as a word or phrase.

ex-pal'pāte (eks-), *a.* [L. *ex-* priv., and *palpus*, a feeler, from *palpare*, to stroke, touch softly.] In entomology, not furnished with palpi or feelers.

ex-pand', *v.t.*; expanded, *pt.*, *pp.*; expanding, *ppr.* [L. *expandere*, to spread out, *ex*, out, and *pandere*, to spread, extend.]

1. To open; to spread; as, a flower *expands* its leaves.

2. To dilate; to enlarge in bulk; to distend; to inflate; as, to *expand* the chest by inspiration; heat *expands* all bodies; air is *expanded* by rarefaction.

3. To enlarge in range or scope; to make more comprehensive; to extend; as, to *expand* the sphere of benevolence; to *expand* the heart or affections.

4. In mathematics, to enlarge by performing operations indicated; as, $(a+b)(a-b) = a^2-b^2$.

Syn.—Diffuse, dilate, spread, unfold, swell, enlarge, extend, amplify.

ex-pand', *v.i.* 1. To open; to spread; as, buds *expand* in spring.

2. To dilate; to extend in bulk or surface; as, metals *expand* by heat; a lake *expands* when swelled by rains; hearts *expand* with joy.

3. In zoölogy, to extend over a space, as the distance from tip to tip of the wings of an insect or of a bird.

ex-pand'ēr, *n.* One who or that which expands; in mechanics, a tool for expanding metal, as for enlarging the opening in the end of a tube or for spreading the lead packing at the joining of iron pipes, so as to make gastight joints.

ex-pand'ing, *a.* Becoming larger; increasing in dimensions; as, an *expanding* cloud.

Expanding bit, *expanding drill*; in mechanics, a bit or a drill so made that it expands as it bores or drills, thus increasing the diameter of the aperture as it advances.

Expanding pulley; in mechanics, a pulley made in sections and admitting of variations in its diameter.

ex-panse' (eks-), *n.* [ME. *expans*; L. *expansus*, pp. of *expandere*, to spread out, expand.]

1. A spreading; extent; a wide extent of space or body; as, the *expanse* of heaven.

> The smooth *expanse* of crystal lakes.—Pope.

2. In zoölogy, the distance from tip to tip of outspread wings, as of an insect or bird.

ex-panse', *v.t.* To expand. [Obs.]

ex-pan-si-bil'i-ty, *n.* The capacity of being expanded; capacity of extension in surface or bulk; as, the *expansibility* of air.

ex-pan'si-ble, *a.* Capable of being expanded or spread; capable of being extended, dilated, or diffused.

> Bodies are not *expansible* in proportion to their weight. —Grew.

ex-pan'si-ble-ness, *n.* Expansibility.

ex-pan'si-bly, *adv.* In an expansible manner.

ex-pan'sile, *a.* Capable of expanding or of being dilated.

ex-pan'sion, *n.* [LL. *expansio* (*-onis*), a spreading out, expanding, from L. *expansus*, pp. of *expandere*, to spread out, expand.]

1. The act of expanding or spreading out.

2. The state of being expanded; enlargement; distention; dilatation; the increase of bulk which a body undergoes by the recession of its particles from one another so that it occupies a greater space, its weight remaining still the same. *Expansion* is one of the most general effects of heat, being common to all bodies, whether solid, liquid, or gaseous.

3. Extended surface; extent; space to which anything is enlarged; wide extent; immensity.

> The starred *expansion* of the skies.—Beattie.

4. In commerce, increase of trade or liabilities; an increase of the issues of bank-notes.

5. In mathematics, the development at length of an expression indicated in a contracted form, as $(a+x)^2 = a^2+2ax+x^2$.

6. In a steam-engine, the increase in bulk of steam in a cylinder, when its communication with the boiler is cut off, in which case its pressure on the piston retreating before it is in inverse ratio to the space it fills.

7. In naval architecture, the laying out of the vessel's lines in exact proportions and desired size by enlarging according to mathematical rules the lines of the model or drawing.

ex-pan'sion-cūrb, *n.* A contrivance to counteract expansion and contraction by heat.

ex-pan'sion-cūrve, *n.* In a steam-engine, (a) the hyberbolic curve which indicates theoretically the ratio between the pressure and the volume of expanding gas or vapor in the cylinder; (b) that part of an indicator-diagram which shows the decreasing pressure while expansion is going on in the cylinder.

ex-pan'sion-en''gine, *n.* A steam-engine in which the supply of steam is cut off previous to the stroke being complete, the expansive power of the steam admitted being sufficient to complete the stroke.

ex-pan'sion-gear, *n.* In a steam-engine, the apparatus by which the access of steam to the cylinder is cut off at a given part of the stroke. It is of various forms.

ex-pan'sion-ist, *n.* In civics, one who favors expansion, as of national currency or territory.

ex-pan'sion-joint, *n.* In a steam-engine, (a) a joint for connecting steam-pipes, made with a stuffing-box, so as to allow one of them to slide within the enlarged end of the other when the length increases by expansion; (b) an attachment of a boiler in its framing to allow the former to expand without affecting the latter.

ex-pan'sion-valve, *n.* In a steam-engine, the cut-off valve of an expansion-gear.

ex-pan'sive, *a.* 1. Having the power to expand, to spread, or to dilate; as, the *expansive* force of heat.

2. Having the capacity of being expanded; as, the *expansive* quality of air; the *expansive* atmosphere.

3. Widely extended; comprehensive; broad-minded; as, *expansive* benevolence.

ex-pan'sive-ly, *adv.* In an expansive manner; by means of expansion.

ex-pan'sive-ness, *n.* The state or quality of being expansive.

ex-pan'sure, *n.* Expanse. [Obs.]

ex-pär'tē, *a.* [L., lit., from a part; *ex*, out, from, and *parte*, ablative of *pars*, part.] Relating to only one part or side.

Ex-parte council; a council which assembles at the request of only one of the parties in dispute when a full council is impossible.

Ex-parte evidence; evidence which is brought forward by one side only without notice to the other.

ex-pā'ti-āte (eks-pā'shi-āt), *v.i.*; expatiated, *pt.*, *pp.*; expatiating, *ppr.* [L. *expatiatus*, pp. of *expatiari*, *exspatiari*, to go out of one's course, wander; *ex*, out, and *spatiari*, to walk, roam.]

1. To move at large; to rove without prescribed limits; to wander in space without restraint.

> Bids his free soul *expatiate* in the skies.—Pope.

2. To enlarge in discourse or writing; to be copious in argument or discussion; as, the orator thinks himself at liberty to *expatiate*.

ex-pā'ti-āte, *v.t.* To allow to wander at large; to broaden.

ex-pā-ti-ā'tion, *n.* The act of expatiating.

ex-pā'ti-ā-tŏr, *n.* One who enlarges or amplifies in language.

ex-pā'ti-ȧ-tō-ry (-shi-ȧ-), *a.* Expatiating.

ex-pā'tri-āte, *v.t.*; expatriated, *pt.*, *pp.*; expatriating, *ppr.* [LL. *expatriatus*, pp. of *expatriare*, to banish; L. *ex*, out of, and *patria*, native country, fatherland, from *pater*, father.] To banish; reflexively, *to expatriate oneself*; to withdraw from one's native country; to renounce the rights of citizenship where one was born, and become a citizen of another country.

> Abeillard indulged the romantic wish of *expatriating* himself for ever. —Berington.

ex-pā-tri-ā'tion, *n.* Banishment; specifically, in law, the forsaking of one's own country, with a renunciation of allegiance, and with the view of becoming a permanent resident and citizen in another country.

ex-pect', *v.t.*; expected, *pt.*, *pp.*; expecting, *ppr.* [L. *expectare*, *exspectare*, to look for, await; *ex*, out, and *spectare*, to look.]

1. To wait for. [Obs.]

> The guards,
> By me encamped on yonder hill, *expect*
> Their motion. —Milton.

2. To look for; to have a previous apprehension of, as of something future, whether good or evil; as, we *expect* a visit that has been promised; we *expected* nothing better.

3. To reckon upon; to require; used especially in the sense of intimating that some duty or obligation must be fulfilled; as, I shall *expect* to find that job finished by Saturday; your bill is due and immediate payment is *expected*.

> England *expects* every man to do his duty. —Nelson.

4. To suppose; to believe; to conclude; applied to things past or present as well as future; as, I *expect* I did the damage. [A solecism.]

Syn.—Anticipate, await, forecast, forebode, wait for, rely on, look for, foresee.

ex-pect', *v.i.* To wait; to stay. [Obs.]

ex-pect', *n.* Same as *Expectation*. [Obs.]

ex-pect'ȧ-ble, *a.* To be expected; that may be expected. [Rare.]

ex-pect'ănce, ex-pect'ăn-cy, *n.* [LL. *expectantia*, from L. *expectare*, *exspectare*, to look for, expect.]

1. The act or state of expecting; expectation.

2. Something expected or hoped for.

Estate in expectancy or *expectant estate*; in law, an estate which one will receive at some future time. It may be either a reversion, a remainder, or an executory interest.

Tables of expectancy; tables showing the expected duration of life calculated from any year; for the special use of life-insurance companies.

ex-pect'ănt, *a.* 1. Waiting; looking for; expecting; often followed by *of*.

> *Expectant of* that news that never came. —Tennyson.

2. In medicine, (a) relating to a medicine that waits for the efforts of nature, or (b) to a method of treatment which consists in observing the progress of diseases and removing deranging influences without prescribing active medicines unless absolutely required.

Expectant estate; see *Estate in expectancy* under *Expectance*.

ex-pect'ănt, *n.* [L. *expectans* (*-antis*), ppr. of *expectare*, to expect.] One who expects; one who waits in expectation; one held in dependence by his belief or hope of receiving some good.

ex-pect'ănt-ly, *adv.* In an expectant manner.

ex-pec-tā'tion, *n.* 1. The act of expecting or looking forward to an event as about to happen.

> The same weakness of mind which indulges absurd *expectations*, produces petulance in disappointment. —Irving.

2. The state of being expected or looked for; the state of being awaited.

> Our preparation stands in *expectation*.—Shak.

3. That which is expected; the object of expectation; often used figuratively of the Messiah or promised Saviour.

> Now clear I understand
> Why our great *Expectation* should be called
> The seed of woman. —Milton.

4. Prospect of future good, as of possessions, wealth, and the like; usually in the plural.

> His magnificent *expectations* made him . . . the best match in Europe. —Prescott.

5. In medicine, the method of leaving a disease to the efforts of nature, or of waiting for further development before treating it actively.

6. The value of any prospect of prize or property depending upon the happening of some uncertain event.

Expectation of life; a term applied to the mean or average duration of the life of individuals, after any specified age.

Expectation week; in church calendars, the week ending with Whitsunday, or the day of Pentecost, the period within which the apostles prayed for and expected the descent of the Holy Ghost.

Syn.—Hope.—*Expectation* differs from *hope*, in that the latter originates in desire, and may exist with little or no ground of belief that the desired event will arrive, whereas *expectation* is founded on some reasons which render the event probable. *Hope* looks forward to some good; *expectation* looks forward to good or evil.

ex-pect'ȧ-tive, *a.* [L. *expectare*, *exspectare*, to expect.] Constituting an object of expectation; arousing expectation; anticipatory. [Rare.]

ex-pect'ȧ-tive, *n.* 1. That which is expected.

2. Formerly, in the Roman Catholic church, the right to a benefice when it should become vacant, granted by the pope or the sovereign; also, the person upon whom the right was conferred.

ex-pect'ed-ly, *adv.* In the expected manner; according to expectation.

ex-pect'ẽr, *n.* One who expects; one who waits for something, or for another person.

ex-pect'ing-ly, *adv.* In a state of expectation.

ex-pect'ive, *a.* Expectative. [Rare.]

ex-pect'ŏr, *n.* Same as *Expecter*.

ex-pec'tō-rănt, *a.* and *n.* [L. *expectorans* (*-antis*), ppr. of *expectorare*, to banish from the mind, to expectorate.]

I. *a.* In medicine, pertaining to, causing, or increasing expectoration.

II. *n.* A medicine for causing or increasing expectoration, or discharge of mucus through the mouth.

ex-pec'tō-rāte, *v.t.*; expectorated, *pt.*, *pp.*; expectorating, *ppr.* [L. *expectoratus*, pp. of *expectorare*, to banish from the mind, to expel from the breast; *ex*, out, and *pectus* (*-oris*), breast.] To eject from the trachea or lungs; to discharge, as phlegm or other matter, by coughing, hawking, and spitting.

ex-pec'tō-rāte, *v.i.* To eject from the mouth mucus from the lungs or trachea by hawking, coughing, and spitting.

ex-pec-tō-rā'tion, *n.* 1. The act of discharging phlegm or mucus from the lungs, by coughing, hawking, and spitting.

2. The matter expectorated.

ex-pec'tō-rā-tive, *a.* and *n.* I. *a.* Having the quality of promoting expectoration.

II. *n.* An expectorant.

ex-pēde' (eks-), *v.t.*, obsolete variant of *expedite*.

ex-pē'di-āte, *v.t.* To expedite. [Obs.]

ex-pē'di-en-cy, ex-pē'di-ence, *n.* 1. Fitness or suitableness to effect some desired end or the purpose intended; advisability under the particular circumstances of the case.

2. That which is the most practical or expedient, taking all the circumstances into account.

3. In ethics, the principle of seeking immediate or selfish gain or advantage at the expense of or without consideration of genuine principle; the quality of being utilitarian or self-seeking, regardless of the right.

4. An expedition; adventure. [Obs.]

5. Expedition; haste; despatch. [Obs.]

Syn.—Utility, advantage, interest, fitness, propriety.

ex-pē'di-ent, *a.* [L. *expediens* (*-entis*), ppr. of *expedire*, to bring forward, despatch; *ex*, out, and *pes*, *pedis*, foot.]

1. Tending to promote the object proposed; fit or suitable for the purpose; proper under the circumstances; advantageous; as, many things may be lawful which are not *expedient*.

2. Contributing or tending to contribute to present advantage or self-interest; utilitarian.

3. Quick; expeditious. [Obs.]

ex-pē'di-ent, *n.* 1. That which serves to promote or advance; any means which may be employed to accomplish an end; as, let every *expedient* be employed.

2. A shift; means devised or employed in an exigency.

ex-pē-di-en'tiăl (-shăl), *a.* Prompted by expediency; resulting from expediency or expedients.

ex-pē-di-en'tiăl-ly, *adv.* In an expediential manner, or through expediential means.

ex-pē'di-ent-ly, *adv.* 1. In an expedient manner; suitably; conveniently.

2. Hastily; quickly. [Obs.]

ex-ped'i-ment, *n.* 1. In old English law, the whole of a man's goods. [Obs.]

2. An expedient. [Obs.]

ex-ped'i-tāte, *v.t.*; expeditated, *pt.*, *pp.*; expeditating, *ppr.* [LL. *expeditatus*, pp. of *expeditare*; L. *ex*, from, and *pes*, *pedis*, foot.] In the forest laws of England, to cut out the balls or claws of, as of a dog's forefeet, to prevent it from chasing deer.

ex-ped-i-tā'tion, *n.* The act or process of expeditating, or the state of being expeditated.

ex'pē-dīte (eks'), *v.t.*; expedited, *pt.*, *pp.*; expediting, *ppr.* [L. *expeditus*, pp. of *expedire*, lit., to free one caught by the feet, to hasten, despatch; *ex*, out, and *pes*, *pedis*, foot.]

1. To hasten; to quicken; to accelerate motion or progress of; to facilitate; as, artificial heat may *expedite* the growth of plants.

2. To despatch; to send forth.

Syn.—Hasten, speed, hurry, drive, accelerate, push.

ex'pē-dīte, *a.* 1. Quick; speedy; expeditious; as, *expedite* execution.

2. Easy; clear of impediments; unencumbered; as, to make a way plain and *expedite*.

ex'pē-dīte-ly, *adv.* Readily; hastily; speedily; expeditiously.

ex'pē-dīte-ness, *n.* The state or quality of being expedite. [Rare.]

ex-pē-di'tion (eks-pē-dish'un), *n.* [OFr. *expedition*; L. *expeditio* (*-onis*), a despatching, from *expedire*, to despatch.]

1. Haste; speed, quickness; despatch; as, the mail is conveyed with *expedition*.

2. A voyage or journey taken by a number of persons for a definite purpose; also, the company engaged in such an undertaking and its outfit; as, the *expedition* of Xerxes into Greece; an *expedition* to the north pole; a trading *expedition*.

3. March; progress. [Obs.]

ex-pē-di'tion-ā-ry, *a.* Of, pertaining to, or composing an expedition.

ex-pē-di'tion-ist, ex-pē-di'tion-ẽr, *n.* One who makes an expedition or goes as one of an expedition. [Rare.]

ex-pē-di'tious (eks-pē-dish'us), *a.* 1. Performed quickly; hasty; speedy; as, an *expeditious* march.

2. Nimble; active; swift; acting with celerity; as, an *expeditious* messenger or runner.

Syn.—Quick, speedy, prompt.

ex-pē-di'tious-ly, *adv.* In an expeditious manner; hastily; with celerity or despatch.

ex-pē-di'tious-ness, *n.* The quality of being expeditious; celerity; quickness.

ex-ped'i-tive, *a.* Performing with speed. [Obs.]

ex-pel' (eks-), *v.t.*; expelled, *pt.*, *pp.*; expelling, *ppr.* [ME. *expellen*; OFr. *expeller*; L. *expellere*, to drive or thrust out; *ex*, out, and *pellere*, to thrust, drive.]

1. To drive out; to force to leave; to dismiss forcibly; as, to *expel* a traitor from a country; to *expel* air from the lungs; to *expel* a student

2. To reject; to refuse. [Obs.]
3. To exclude; to keep out or off. [Rare.]
Syn.—Banish, exile, eject, cast out, oust, eradicate.

ex-pel'lȧ-ble, *a.* 1. Capable of being expelled or driven out.

Acid *expellable* by heat. —Kirwan.

2. Subject to expulsion; as, he is not *expellable* from his club on account of his heresy.

ex-pel'lẽr, *n.* One who or that which expels.

ex-pend' (eks-), *v.t.*; expended, *pt.*, *pp.*; expending, *ppr.* [L. *expendere*, to weigh out, pay out; *ex*, out, and *pendere*, to weigh.] To lay out; to disburse; to spend; to pay out; to consume; to use; as, to *expend* money, time, or labor; oil is *expended* in burning.

ex-pend', *v.i.* 1. To be laid out, used, or consumed. [Rare.]
2. To pay out, spend, or disburse money.

ex-pend'i-tŏr, *n.* [LL. *expenditor*, from L. *expendere*, to weigh out: *ex* out, and *pendere*, to weigh.] In old English law, one who was appointed by the commissioners of sewers to pay, disburse, or expend the money collected by taxes for the repair of sewers.

ex-pend'i-ture, *n.* 1. The act of expending; a laying out, as of money; disbursement; as, a corrupt administration is known by extravagant *expenditures* of public money.
2. That which is expended; expense.

The receipts and *expenditures* of this extensive country. —Hamilton.

ex-pense', *n.* [ME. *expense*; OFr. *expense*; LL. *expensa* (supply *pecunia*, money), expense, money spent; L. *expensum*, money spent, neut. of *expensus*, pp. of *expendere*, to expend.]
1. A laying out or expending; the disbursing of money; employment and consumption, as of time or labor; as, the enterprise was accomplished only by a great *expense* of money, time, and labor.
2. That which is expended; specifically, money expended; cost; charge; as, a prudent man limits his *expenses* by his income.
3. Cost, with the idea of loss, damage, or discredit; as, he did this at the *expense* of his character.

Courting popularity at his party's *expense*. —Brougham.

4. Anything which involves or requires great or undue cost; as, sickness is always an *expense*; he was a great *expense* to his father.
Syn.—Price, cost, charge, payment, expenditure, outlay.

ex-pense'fụl, *a.* Costly; expensive. [Obs.]

ex-pense'fụl-ly, *adv.* In a costly manner; with great expense. [Obs.]

ex-pense'fụl-ness, *n.* Same as *Expensiveness.*

ex-pense'less, *a.* Without cost or expense. [Rare.]

ex-pense'-mag'ȧ-zīne, *n.* A small magazine of ammunition prepared for immediate use.

ex-pen'sive, *a.* 1. Costly; requiring much expense; as, an *expensive* dress or equipage; an *expensive* family.
2. Given to expense; free in the use of money; extravagant; lavish; as, an *expensive* woman. [Rare.]
Syn.—Costly, dear, high-priced.

ex-pen'sive-ly, *adv.* With great expense; at great cost or charge.

ex-pen'sive-ness, *n.* Costliness; the quality of incurring or requiring great expenditures of money; extravagance; as, the *expensiveness* of war is not its greatest evil.

ex-pẽr-ġe-fac'tion (eks-), *n.* An awakening or arousing. [Obs.]

ex-pē'ri-ence, *n.* [ME. *experience*; L. *experientia*, a trial, proof, experiment, from *experiens* (-*entis*), ppr. of *experiri*, to try, put to test.]
1. Trial, practice, proof, or test; especially, frequent trial or a series of trials; observation of a fact or of the same fact or events happening under like circumstances; continued and varied observation.

Having broadly laid down the principle that all the materials of our knowledge come from *experience*, Locke goes on to explain his theory more particularly. —Morell.

2. The knowledge gained by trial, or repeated trials, or observation; practical acquaintance with any matter by personal observation or trial of it, by feeling the effects of it, by living through it, and the like; practical wisdom taught by the changes and trials of life.

To most men *experience* is like the stern-lights of a ship, which illumine only the track it has passed. —Coleridge.

3. In philosophy, knowledge acquired through external or internal perceptions, especially by the senses; all that is perceived, understood, and remembered; opposed to *intuition*.
4. Individual or particular instance of trial or observation.

This is what distance does for us, the harsh and bitter features of this or that *experience* are slowly obliterated and memory begins to look on the past. —Black.

5. That feeling which is connected with conversion or regeneration in a spiritual sense.
Experience meeting; a meeting, especially among Methodists, for prayer and the relating of religious experiences.

ex-pē'ri-ence, *v.t.*; experienced, *pt.*, *pp.*; experiencing, *ppr.* 1. To try by use, by suffering, or by enjoyment; to feel; to have trial of; to know by practice or trial; to gain knowledge or skill of, by practice or by a series of observations; as, we all *experience* pain, sorrow, and pleasure; we *experience* good and evil; we often *experience* a change of sentiments and views.
2. To exercise; as, to *experience* oneself for hard work. [Obs.]
To experience religion; to be converted to Christianity; to be conscious of a change of heart. [Local, U. S.]
Syn.—Try, feel, undergo, encounter, endure.

ex-pē'ri-enced (-enst), *a.* Taught by practice or by repeated observations; skilful or wise by means of trials, use, or observation; as, an *experienced* artist; an *experienced* physician.

ex-pē'ri-en-cẽr, *n.* 1. An experimenter. [Obs.]
2. One who experiences.

ex-pē'ri-ent, *a.* Experienced. [Obs.]

ex-pē-ri-en'tiăl (-shăl), *a.* Acquired from or pertaining to experience; empirical.

Necessary truths are derived from our own thoughts; *experiential* truths are derived from our observation of things about us. —Whewell.

ex-pē-ri-en'tiăl-iṣm, *n.* In philosophy, the theory that experience is the origin and test of all knowledge; opposed to *intuitionalism*.

ex-pē-ri-en'tiăl-ist, *n.* and *a.* I. *n.* One who believes in the doctrine of experientialism.
II. *a.* Of the nature of or pertaining to experientialism.

ex-pē-ri-en'tiăl-ly, *adv.* By means of experience; empirically.

ex-per'i-ment (eks-), *n.* [ME. *experiment*; OFr. *experiment*; L. *experimentum*, a trial, test, from *experiri*, to try, test.]
1. A trial; an act or operation designed to discover some unknown truth, principle, or effect, or to establish it when discovered. It differs from *observation*, which is merely the attentive consideration of things, as they exist.

A political *experiment* cannot be made in a laboratory, nor determined in a few hours. —J. Adams.

2. An experience. [Obs.]

ex-per'i-ment, *v.i.*; experimented, *pt.*, *pp.*; experimenting, *ppr.* To make trial; to make an experiment; to operate on a body in such a manner as to discover some unknown fact, or to establish it when known; used with *on*, *upon*, *in*, *by*, and *with*; as, scientists *experiment on* natural bodies for the discovery of their qualities and combinations.

ex-per'i-ment, *v.t.* To try; to know by trial. [Obs.]

ex-per-i-men'tȧ, *n.*, pl. of *experimentum*.

ex-per-i-men'tăl, *a.* [Fr. *experimental*, from L. *experimentum*, an experiment.]
1. Pertaining to, derived from, founded on, or known by experiment; given to or skilled in experiment; as, an *experimental* philosopher; *experimental* knowledge or philosophy.
2. Taught by experience; having personal experience; known by or derived from experience; experienced; as, *experimental* religion.

Admit to the holy communion such only as profess and appear to be regenerated and *experimental* Christians. —H. Humphrey.

Experimental philosophy; philosophy which states nothing as positive truth, but teaches that scientific thought and research will gradually approximate to the truth.
Experimental proposition; in logic, a proposition based on actual experience.
Experimental religion; religion which consists of practical piety and a righteous life, as distinguished from that which is chiefly concerned with doctrines and tenets or manifests itself in outward forms.

ex-per-i-men'tăl-ist, *n.* One who makes experiments.

ex-per-i-men'tăl-īze, *v.i.*; experimentalized, *pt.*, *pp.*; experimentalizing, *ppr.* To practise the experimental process of discovery.

ex-per-i-men'tăl-ly, *adv.* By experiment; by trial; by experience; as, we are all *experimentally* acquainted with pain and pleasure.

ex-per"i-men-tā'ri-ăn, *a.* and *n.* I. *a.* Depending on experiments or actual experience.
II. *n.* One given to experimenting.

ex-per"i-men-tā'tion, *n.* The act, practice, or process of making experiments.

ex-per-i-men'tȧ-tive, *a.* Experimental.

ex-per'i-men-tā-tŏr, *n.* An experimenter. [Obs.]

ex-per'i-men-tẽr, *n.* One who makes experiments; one skilled in experiments.

ex-per'i-men-tist, *n.* One who makes experiments; an experimenter.

ex-per-i-men'tum, *n.*; *pl.* **ex-per-i-men'tȧ.** [L.] An experiment.
Experimentum crucis; (L., lit., a trial of the cross) a test of the most severe and searching character; a decisive experiment.

ex-per-rec'tion, *n.* An awakening from sleep or lethargy; a rousing up. [Obs.]

ex'pẽrt (*or* eks-pẽrt'), *n.* [ME. *expert*; OFr. *expert*; L. *expertus*, skilled, experienced, pp. of *experiri*, to try, test.]
1. A specialist in a particular branch or calling; one who is thoroughly acquainted with all matters, details, methods, uses, and values, and has a complete knowledge of his calling or any special branch of learning through experience.
2. In law, a scientific or skilled specialist in a particular profession or department of science or learning, whose testimony is admitted in court regarding the subject-matter in which he is particularly versed.

ex-pẽrt', *a.* 1. Experienced; taught by use, practice, or experience; hence, skilful; well instructed; having familiar knowledge of; as, an *expert* philosopher.
2. Having a facility of operation or performance from practice; usually followed by *in*; as, *expert in* surgery; *expert in* performance on a musical instrument.
Syn.—Adroit, clever, dexterous, proficient, ready, skilful, adept, versed in, able.

ex-pẽrt', *v.t.* To experience. [Obs.]

ex-pẽrt'ly, *adv.* In a skilful or dexterous manner; adroitly; with readiness and accuracy.

ex-pẽrt'ness, *n.* Skill derived from practice; readiness; dexterity; adroitness; as, *expertness* in musical performance, *expertness* in war or in seamanship; *expertness* in reasoning.

ex-pet'i-ble, *a.* Worthy of being wished for; desirable. [Obs.]

ex'pi-ȧ-ble, *a.* [OFr. *expiable*, from L. *expiare*, to expiate.] Capable of being atoned for or expiated.

ex'pi-āte, *v.t.*; expiated, *pt.*, *pp.*; expiating, *ppr.* [L. *expiatus*, pp. of *expiare*, to make satisfaction or atonement; *ex*, out, and *piare*, to appease, propitiate, from *pius*, devout, pious.]
1. To atone for; to make satisfaction or reparation for; to extinguish the guilt of, as of a crime, by sufferance of penalty or performance of counterbalancing good.

The treasurer obliged himself to *expiate* the injury. —Clarendon.

2. To avert by certain observances. [Rare.]

Frequent showers of stones . . . could . . . be *expiated* only by bringing to Rome Cybele. —T. H. Dyer.

ex'pi-āte, *a.* Finished; ended. [Obs.]

ex-pi-ā'tion, *n.* 1. The act of atoning for a crime; the act of making satisfaction for an offense, by which the guilt is done away and the right or necessity of punishing the crime is canceled; atonement; satisfaction.
2. The means by which atonement for crimes is made.
3. An act by which threatened prodigies were averted. [Obs.]

Upon the birth of such monsters, the Grecians and Romans did use divers sorts of *expiations*. —Hayward.

ex'pi-ȧ-tist, **ex'pi-ȧ-tŏr**, *n.* One who expiates.

ex"pi-ȧ-tō'ri-ous, *a.* [Obs.] Same as *Expiatory*.

ex'pi-ȧ-tō-ry, *a.* Having the power to make atonement or expiation; as, an *expiatory* sacrifice.

ex'pi-lāte, *v.t.* To strip off; to pillage; to plunder; to rob. [Obs.]

ex-pi-lā'tion, *n.* The act of expilating; pillage. [Obs.]

ex'pi-lā-tŏr, *n.* One who strips off; a pillager. [Obs.]

ex-pīr'ȧ-ble, *a.* Capable of expiring or coming to an end.

ex-pīr'ănt, *n.* One who is expiring.

ex-pi-rā'tion, *n.* [L. *expiratio* (-*onis*), *exspiratio* (-*onis*), a breathing out, from *expirare*, to breathe out, expire.]
1. The act of breathing out, or forcing the air from the lungs; opposed to *inspiration*.
2. The last emission of breath; death.
3. The emission of volatile matter from any substance; evaporation; exhalation; as, the *expiration* of warm air from the earth. [Obs.]
4. Cessation; close; end; conclusion; termination of a limited time; as, the *expiration* of a month or year; the *expiration* of a lease; the *expiration* of a contract or agreement.
5. That which is produced by expiring or breathing out; the sound caused by respiration.

ex-pīr'ȧ-tō-ry, *a.* Pertaining to the emission or expiration of breath from the lungs.

ex-pīre', *v.t.*; expired, *pt.*, *pp.*; expiring, *ppr.*

[OFr. *expirer*; L. *expirare, exspirare*, to breathe out, exhale, expire; *ex*, out, and *spirare*, to breathe.]

1. To breathe out; to expel from the lungs; opposed to *inspire*; as, we *expire* air at every breath.

2. To exhale; to emit in minute particles, as a fluid or volatile matter; as, the earth *expires* a damp or warm vapor; the body *expires* fluid matter from the pores; plants *expire* odors. [Rare.]

3. To conclude. [Obs.]

ex-pire′, *v.i.* 1. To emit the breath; opposed to *inspire*.

2. To emit the last breath; to die.

3. To fly out; to be thrown out with force. [Obs.]

The ponderous ball *expires*. —Dryden.

4. To come to an end; to cease; to terminate; to close or conclude, as a given period; as, the lease will *expire* on the first of May; the year *expires* on Monday.

ex-pi-ree′, *n.* A convict who has served his period of punishment. [Rare.]

ex-pir′ing, *a.* 1. Breathing out air from the lungs; emitting fluid or volatile matter; exhaling; breathing the last breath; dying; ending; terminating.

2. Pertaining to or uttered at the time of dying; as, *expiring* words; *expiring* groans.

ex′pi-ry, *n.* Expiration; end.

We had to leave at the *expiry* of the term. —Lamb.

ex-pis′cāte (eks-), *v.t.* [L. *expiscatus*, pp. of *expiscari*, to search out, fish out; *ex*, out, and *piscari*, to fish, from *piscis*, a fish.] To fish out; to discover by artful means or by strict examinations.

Expiscating if the renown'd extreme
They force on us will serve their turns.
—Chapman.

ex-pis-cā′tion, *n.* The act of expiscating or fishing out; the act of getting at the truth of any matter by strict inquiry and examination; as, he discovered the truth by careful *expiscation*.

ex-pis′cā-tŏr, *n.* One who expiscates.

ex-pis′cā-tō-ry, *a.* Suited or designed to expiscate.

ex-plain′, *v.t.*; explained, *pt., pp.*; explaining, *ppr.* [OFr. *explaner*; L. *explanare*, to flatten, spread out; *ex*, out, and *planare*, to make level, from *planus*, level, plain.]

1. To make plain, manifest, or intelligible; to clear of obscurity; to expound; to illustrate by discourse or by notes; as, to *explain* an example; to *explain* the reason a body falls.

2. To make plane; to flatten out; to expand. [Obs.]

To explain away; to get rid of or palliate any statement one may have made, or any act one may have committed, by explanation.

Syn.—Illustrate, elucidate, interpret, expound.—To *explain* is to render intelligible; to *illustrate* and *elucidate* are to give additional clearness; everything requires to be *explained* to one who is ignorant of it; but the best informed will require to have abstruse subjects *illustrated* and obscure subjects *elucidated*.

ex-plain′, *v.i.* To give explanations.

ex-plain′ȧ-ble, *a.* Capable of being cleared of obscurity or of being made plain to the understanding; capable of being interpreted.

ex-plain′ēr, *n.* One who explains; an expositor; an interpreter.

ex-plāit′, *v.t.* To explain. [Obs.]

ex′plȧ-nāte, *a.* In biology, having outward extension in a flat form.

ex-plȧ-nā′tion, *n.* [L. *explanatio (-onis)*, a making plain, an explanation, from *explanare*, to explain; *ex*, out, and *planus*, plain.]

1. The act of explaining, expounding, or interpreting; exposition; illustration; interpretation; the act of clearing from obscurity and making intelligible; as, the *explanation* of a passage in Scripture, or of a contract or treaty.

2. That which makes clear or explains.

3. The sense given a thing by one explaining it; interpretation; meaning.

4. The process of adjusting a misunderstanding by explaining the circumstances; reconciliation.

5. That division of rhetoric devoted to modification of an old conception or to forming a new one, by an intelligent presentation of the object of discourse.

Syn.—Definition, description, exposition, interpretation.

ex-plan′ȧ-tive, *a.* Explanatory.

ex-plan′ȧ-tō-ri-ness, *n.* The quality of being explanatory.

ex-plan′ȧ-tō-ry, *a.* Serving to explain; containing explanation; as, *explanatory* notes.

Syn.—Explicit, express.—That which is *explanatory* is superadded to clear up difficulties or obscurities; that which is *explicit* of itself obviates every difficulty, while that which is *express* requires the language used to be unambiguous.

ex-plāt′, *v.t.* To explain; to exploit. [Obs.]

ex-plē′tion, *n.* Accomplishment; fulfilment. [Obs.]

ex′plē-tive, *a.* [LL. *expletivus*, serving to fill, from L. *expletus*, pp. of *explere*, to fill; *ex*, out, up, and *plere*, to fill.] Filling; added to fill a vacancy, or for emphasis; used especially of words.

ex′plē-tive, *n.* 1. Something which is not necessary, but is added to fill up or to ornament; specifically, in rhetoric and grammar, a word or syllable which is not necessary for the meaning or construction, but is added for rhetorical, rhythmical, or metrical reasons.

2. A profane interjection; an oath; an imprecation; as, he answered with *expletives*.

ex′plē-tive-ly, *adv.* In an expletive manner.

ex′plē-tō-ry, *a.* Serving to fill.

ex′pli-cȧ-ble, *a.* [L. *explicabilis*, from *explicare*, to unfold.] Explainable; capable of being unfolded to the mind or made intelligible; capable of being accounted for.

ex′pli-cȧ-ble-ness, *n.* The state or quality of being explicable.

ex′pli-cāte, *a.* Opened; unfolded; explained.

ex′pli-cāte, *v.t.*; explicated, *pt., pp.*; explicating, *ppr.* [L. *explicatus*, pp. of *explicare*, to unfold, spread out; *ex*, out, and *plicare*, to fold.]

1. To unfold; to expand; to open. [Obs.]

2. To unfold the meaning or sense of; to explain; to clear of difficulties or obscurity; to interpret.

ex′pli-cāte, *v.i.* To give an explanation.

ex-pli-cā′tion, *n.* 1. The act of opening or unfolding.

2. The act of explaining; explanation; exposition; interpretation; as, the *explication* of the parables.

3. The sense given by an expositor or interpreter.

ex′pli-cā-tive, *a.* [From L. *explicatus*, pp. of *explicare*, to unfold, explain.] Serving to unfold or explain; tending to lay open to the understanding.

ex′pli-cā-tŏr, *n.* [L. *explicator*, from *explicare*, to unfold, explain.] One who unfolds or explains; an expounder.

ex′pli-cā-tō-ry, *a.* Explicative.

ex-plic′it (eks-), *a.* [L. *explicitus*, pp. of *explicare*, to unfold, explain; *ex*, out, and *plicare*, to fold.]

1. Plain in language; open to the understanding; clear; not obscure or ambiguous; express, not merely implied.

2. Plain; open; clear; unreserved; having no disguised meaning or reservation; applied to persons; as, he was *explicit* in his terms.

Syn.—Express, definite, plain, positive.

ex′pli-cit. [An abbrev. of L. *explicitus (est liber)*, the book is unfolded or ended; *explicitus*, properly pp. of *explicare*, to unfold, explain.] A word formerly used at the conclusion of books, as *finis* is now used.

ex-plic′it-ly, *adv.* Plainly; expressly; without duplicity; without disguise or reservation of meaning; not by inference or implication; as, he *explicitly* avows his intention.

ex-plic′it-ness, *n.* The quality of being explicit; plainness of language or expression; clearness; direct expression of ideas or intention, without reserve or ambiguity.

ex-plōde′, *v.i.*; exploded, *pt., pp.*; exploding, *ppr.* [L. *explodere*, to drive off by clapping; *ex*, off, and *plaudere*, to clap, applaud.]

1. To be broken into pieces suddenly and with a great noise, by an internal force; as, the boiler *exploded*; the shell *exploded*.

2. To burst out suddenly and violently; to expand suddenly into volumes of gas and flame; as, gunpowder *explodes*.

3. To burst into sudden activity; to break forth; as, to *explode* with laughter or rage; a geyser frequently *explodes*.

ex-plōde′, *v.t.* 1. To decry or reject with noise; to express disapprobation of, with noise or marks of contempt; as, to *explode* a play on the stage. [Obs.]

2. To disprove; to demonstrate the fallacy of; to treat with contempt and drive from notice; to drive into disrepute; to reject; as, astrology is an *exploded* science.

3. To drive out with violence and noise.

The kindled powder *exploded* the ball.
—Blackmore.

4. To detonate; to cause to burst suddenly and with a loud report into flames or gas, or into pieces; as, to *explode* a torpedo.

ex-plōd′ent, *n.* In philology, same as *explosive*.

ex-plōd′ēr, *n.* 1. One who or that which explodes.

2. A hisser; one who rejects with contempt. [Obs.]

ex-ploit′, *n.* [ME. *esploit*; OFr. *esploit*, an exploit, action, deed, from LL. *explicta*, neut. pl., a judicial act, writ, from L. *explicitus*, pp. of *explicare*, to unfold.]

1. A deed or act; achievement; performance; especially, a heroic act; a deed of renown; a great or noble achievement; as, the *exploits* of Alexander, of Cæsar, of Washington.

2. Combat; battle; war. [Obs.]

Syn.—Deed, act, achievement, performance, feat.

ex-ploit′, *v.t.*; exploited, *pt., pp.*; exploiting, *ppr.* [ME. *esploiten*; OFr. *esploiter*, to perform, despatch, from LL. *explectare*, to execute, from *explicta*, a judicial act, writ.]

1. To achieve. [Obs.]

2. To tell broadcast; to recount in detail; as, his victories were *exploited* abroad.

3. To make fully available; to work up; to get value from; to utilize; as, to *exploit* a mine.

4. To derive profit from without regard to rights; to speculate on; to use for one's own benefit; as, to *exploit* one's friends and acquaintances.

ex-ploi′tāge, *n.* Exploitation.

ex-ploi-tā′tion, *n.* The act of exploiting; the act of utilizing or turning to one's own use.

ex-ploi′tēr, *v.t.* An erroneous form of *Exploit*.

ex-ploi′tēr, *n.* One who exploits.

ex-ploi′tūre, *n.* The act of exploiting.

ex-plōr′ȧ-ble, *a.* Capable of being explored.

ex-plō′rāte, *v.t.* To explore. [Obs.]

ex-plō-rā′tion, *n.* [L. *exploratio (-onis)*, from *explorare*, to explore.] The act of exploring; close search; strict or careful examination; specifically, the investigation of an unknown region or country.

ex-plōr′ȧ-tive, *a.* Exploratory.

ex′plō-rā-tŏr, *n.* One who explores; one who searches or examines closely. [Rare.]

ex-plōr′ȧ-tō-ry, *a.* Serving to explore; searching; examining.

ex-plōre′, *v.t.*; explored, *pt., pp.*; exploring, *ppr.* [L. *explorare*, to search out, investigate; *ex*, out, and *plorare*, to cry out, wail.]

1. To hunt for; to seek after; to search carefully for. [Obs.]

2. To investigate or make a thorough search of, either to find some special thing or to make general discoveries; specifically, to travel or range over (a country or region), to ascertain the features, conditions, or state of; as, Stanley *explored* equatorial Africa; to *explore* a wound to find the bullet causing it; to *explore* science.

Syn.—Examine, pry into, search, seek, scrutinize.

ex-plōre′ment, *n.* The act of exploring; search; trial. [Rare.]

ex-plōr′ēr, *n.* One who or that which explores; specifically, (a) one who travels in regions little known, in order to investigate conditions and make geographical discoveries; (b) an instrument for exploring a wound, etc.

ex-plōr′ing, *a.* Engaged in or intended for exploration; as, an *exploring* party.

ex-plō′sion, *n.* [L. *explosio (-onis)*, a driving off by clapping, from *explodere*, to drive off by clapping; *ex*, out, off, and *plaudere*, to clap, applaud.]

1. The act of exploding; a sudden, forcible expansion of a substance, as gunpowder or an elastic fluid, usually accompanied by a loud sound; as, an *explosion* of dynamite; an *explosion* of fire-damp.

2. A sudden bursting or flying to pieces as a result of internal pressure; as, the *explosion* of a boiler.

3. A sudden and violent outburst of emotion; as, an *explosion* of anger.

ex-plō′sive, *a.* Driving or bursting out with violence and noise; liable to explode; causing explosion; as, the *explosive* force of gunpowder.

ex-plō′sive, *n.* [L. *explosus*, pp. of *explodere*, to explode.]

1. Any substance which explodes or causes an explosion; any agent by whose decomposition and combustion gas is so rapidly generated as to be capable of use in blasting or in firearms; as, gunpowder, nitroglycerin, dynamite and guncotton are *explosives*.

2. In philology, a mute or noncontinuous consonant, as *k, t, p*; also called *explodent*.

High explosive; any explosive which acts with greater rapidity and force than gunpowder.

ex-plō′sive-ly, *adv.* In an explosive manner.

ex-pō-li-ā′tion, *n.* A spoiling; a wasting. [Obs.]

ex-pol′ish, *v.t.* To polish carefully. [Obs.]

ex-pōne′, *v.t.* 1. To explain. [Obs.]

2. To represent; to give the characteristics of. [Obs.]

3. To imperil; to expose to danger. [Obs.]

ex-pō′nent, *n.* [L. *exponens (-entis)*, ppr. of *exponere*, to set forth, indicate; *ex*, out, and *ponere*, to place.]

1. One who expounds or explains.

2. In algebra, the number or letter which, placed above a quantity at the right hand, denotes how often that quantity is repeated as a factor to produce the power. Thus, a^2 denotes the second power of a; a^4 denotes the fourth power of a; a^x denotes the xth power of a, or a repeated as a factor x times. A fractional *exponent* or index is used to denote the root of a quantity. Thus, $a^{1/3}$ denotes the cube root of a.

3. One who or that which stands as an index

or representative; as, the leader of a party is the *exponent* of its principles.

Exponent of a ratio; the quotient arising when the antecedent is divided by the consequent; as, 6 is the *exponent of the ratio* of 30 to 5.

ex-pō′nent, *a.* Exemplifying; explicating.

ex-pō-nen′tiăl (-shăl), *a.* Pertaining to exponents.

Exponential curve; a curve whose nature is defined by means of an exponential equation.

Exponential equation; an equation which contains an exponential quantity.

Exponential quantity; in algebra, a quantity whose exponent is unknown or variable.

Exponential series; a series in which exponential equations and quantities are developed.

ex-pōrt′, *v.t.*; exported, *pt.*, *pp.*; exporting, *ppr.* [L. *exportare*, to carry out or away; *ex*, out, and *portare*, to carry.] To carry out or away; specifically, in commerce, to send, as produce or goods, from one country to another, or from one state or jurisdiction to another, either by water or land; as, to *export* cotton goods; to *export* machinery.

ex′pōrt, *n.* 1. The act of exporting; as, to encourage the *export* of cured meat.

2. That which is exported; goods of any kind sent to a foreign country for sale; usually in the plural; as, our *exports* grow larger year by year.

ex-pōrt-ȧ-bil′i-ty, *n.* The state or quality of being exportable.

ex-pōrt′ȧ-ble, *a.* Capable of being exported.

ex-pōr-tā′tion, *n.* [L. *exportatio* (*-onis*), a carrying out, exportation, from *exportare*, to carry out.]

1. The act of exporting; the act of conveying goods and products from one country or state to another in the course of commerce.

2. The act of carrying out.

3. The goods exported.

ex-pōrt′ẽr, *n.* One who exports; one who ships goods, wares, and merchandise of any kind to a foreign country, or who sends them to market in a distant country or state; opposed to *importer*.

ex-pōs′ăl, *n.* Exposure.

ex-pōṣe′, *v.t.*; exposed, *pt.*, *pp.*; exposing, *ppr.* [OFr. *exposer*, from L. *expositus*, pp. of *exponere*, to put or set forth, expose.]

1. To set or cast out; to leave in a place unprotected and uncared for; to abandon; as, among the ancient Greeks, parents *exposed* their children.

2. To make bare; to uncover; to disclose; as, to *expose* one's breast; to *expose* a fraud.

3. To put forward or place in a position to be seen; to exhibit; as, to *expose* goods for sale.

4. To set out to view, as an opinion, set of principles, and the like; to lay open to examination; to promulgate; to interpret; to explain.

> Those who seek truth only freely *expose* their principles to the test. —Locke.

5. To make liable; to subject; to place in the way of something to be avoided; as, vanity *exposes* a person to ridicule; this *exposed* him to danger.

6. To hold up to censure by disclosing the faults of; to divulge the reprehensible practices of; to show the folly or ignorance of; as, to *expose* a hypocrite or a rogue; to *expose* oneself.

7. To submit to the action or influence of; as, to *expose* a photographic plate to the light.

ex-pō-ṣé′ (eks-pō-zā′), *n.* [Fr., pp. of *exposer*, to expose.]

1. An exposure; a disclosure; specifically, a revelation concerning a person or persons, or a condition of affairs, disagreeable or embarrassing to those involved.

2. A formal and detailed setting forth of the facts, causes, and modifying circumstances of any act, series of acts, or condition of affairs; a demonstration.

ex-pōṣed′, *a.* Laid open; laid bare; unsheltered; uncovered; unprotected; made liable to attack; disclosed; especially, not covered with clothing; indecently or insufficiently clothed; also, placed in a position or condition favorable to the contracting of disease or contagious infection; as, an *exposed* position.

Syn.—Liable, subject.

ex-pōṣ′ed-ness, *n.* The state of being exposed, open to attack, or unprotected; as, an *exposedness* to sin or temptation.

ex-pōṣ′ẽr, *n.* One who exposes.

ex-pō-ṣi′tion (-zish′un), *n.* [ME. *expositioun*; OFr. *exposition*; L. *expositio* (*-onis*), a setting forth, narration, from *expositus*, pp. of *exponere*, to set forth, display.]

1. The act of exposing; a laying open or making bare; a setting out to public view.

2. A situation in which a thing is exposed or laid open, or in which it has an unobstructed view; exposure. [Obs.]

3. Explanation; interpretation; a laying open of the sense or meaning; as, the *exposition* of an author, a passage, or an argument.

4. An exhibition or show, as of the products of art and manufacture; as, the Louisiana Purchase *Exposition* of 1904.

5. The act of abandoning to danger; exposure; as, the *exposition* of infants among the ancients. [Rare.]

6. In logic, the making plain of any abstract law by means of a supposition of a concrete example, as the ordinary mode of mathematical demonstration.

ex-poṣ′i-tive, *a.* [L. *expositus*, pp. of *exponere*, to set forth.] Serving to expose or explain; expository; explanatory.

ex-poṣ′i-tŏr, *n.* One who or that which expounds or explains; an interpreter.

ex-poṣ′i-tō-ry, *a.* Serving to explain; tending to illustrate.

ex pōst fac′tō. [L., lit., from what is done afterward; *ex*, from, *post*, afterward, and *facto*, ablative of *factus*, pp. of *facere*, to do.] In law, done after another thing; from a later point of view; retrospectively.

Ex post facto law; a law declaring an act penal or criminal which was innocent when done; or raising the grade of an offense, making it greater than it was when committed; or increasing the punishment after the commission of the offense; or altering the rules of evidence, so as to allow different or less evidence to convict the offender than was required when the offense was committed; such laws are prohibited in the United States by its Constitution.

ex-pos′tū-lāte, *v.i.*; expostulated, *pt.*, *pp.*; expostulating, *ppr.* [L. *expostulatus*, pp. of *expostulare*, to demand vehemently, require; *ex*, out, and *postulare*, to demand.] To reason earnestly with a person on some impropriety of his conduct, representing the wrong he has done or intends, and urging him to desist or to make redress; followed by *with*.

> The emperor's ambassador *expostulated with* the king that he had broken the league with the emperor. —Hayward.

ex-pos′tū-lāte, *v.t.* To discuss; to examine. [Obs.]

ex-pos-tū-lā′tion, *n.* [L. *expostulatio* (*-onis*), from *expostulare*, to expostulate.]

1. The act of expostulating or reasoning with a person in opposition to his conduct; the act of pressing on a person reasons or arguments against the impropriety of his conduct; dissuasion.

> *Expostulations* end well between lovers, but ill between friends. —Spectator.

2. In rhetoric, an address containing *expostulation*.

ex-pos′tū-lā-tŏr, *n.* One who expostulates.

ex-pos′tū-lȧ-tō-ry, *a.* Containing expostulation; as, an *expostulatory* address or debate.

ex-pos′tūre, *n.* Exposure. [Obs.]

ex-pō′ṣūre (-zhŭr), *n.* 1. The act of exposing, laying open, or revealing.

2. The state of being laid open to view, to danger, or to any inconvenience; as, *exposure* to observation; *exposure* to cold or to the air; *exposure* to censure; *exposure* to disease.

3. The situation of a place in regard to points of the compass, or to a free access of air or light; as, a building has a northern or a southern *exposure*.

4. In photography, the act of subjecting a sensitized plate to the action of the light; as, the *exposure* was too short.

5. The act of exposing to danger or abandoning to chance; as, the *exposure* of an infant.

ex-pound′ (eks-), *v.t.*; expounded, *pt.*, *pp.*; expounding, *ppr.* [ME. *expounden*; OFr. *expondre*; L. *exponere*, to put forth, expose, expound; *ex*, out, and *ponere*, to put.]

1. To explain; to lay open the meaning of; to clear of obscurity; to interpret; as, to *expound* a text of Scripture; to *expound* a law.

2. To lay open; to examine; as, to *expound* the pocket. [Obs.]

ex-pound′ẽr, *n.* [ME. *expownere*, from *expounen*, to expound.] One who expounds; an explainer; one who interprets or explains the meaning.

ex-press′, *a.* [ME. *expresse*; L. *expressus*, prominent, distinct, pp. of *exprimere*, to press out, describe.]

1. Given in direct terms; not implied or left to inference; clearly expressed; not ambiguous; plain; as, *express* terms; an *express* covenant or agreement.

2. Copied; closely resembling; bearing an exact representation.

> His face *express*. —Milton.

3. Intended or sent for a particular purpose or on a particular errand; as, to send an *express* messenger.

4. Traveling with special speed; swift; special; as, *express* haste.

ex-press′, *n.* 1. A system of despatching or conveying freight, usually in small pieces, such as trunks, boxes, or parcels, at speed much superior to that of ordinary freight movement, and in special conveyances, under special safeguards and guarantees, at special fixed rates, by a common carrier, usually a company, called an express company; as, perishable goods are usually sent by *express*.

2. Any means of rapid or direct transportation; a railway passenger-train which travels at an unusually high rate of speed and stops only at the most important stations and junctions; as, the Chicago and St. Louis *express*.

3. A messenger or vehicle sent on a particular errand or occasion, as to communicate information of an important event, or to deliver important despatches; also, the message carried.

4. A sporting-rifle firing a light bullet with a large charge of powder, giving great velocity and a low trajectory.

5. A clear or distinct image or representation; an expression. [Obs.]

ex-press′, *v.t.*; expressed, *pt.*, *pp.*; expressing, *ppr.* [ME. *expressen*; L. *expressus*, pp. of *exprimere*, to press or squeeze out.]

1. To press or squeeze out; to force out or cause to flow by pressure; as, to *express* the juice of grapes or of apples.

2. To communicate or set forth to the understanding or notice; to manifest plainly by speech or written language; to show in general; to make known; to exhibit or indicate, as a state of mind or an impression, by a gesture, look, or the countenance; as, his face *expressed* amazement; to *express* religious sentiments; often used reflexively; as, he *expressed himself* freely.

3. To denote; to designate.

> Moses and Aaron took these men, who are *expressed* by their names. —Num. i. 17.

4. To represent or show by imitation or the imitative arts; to form a likeness of, as in painting or sculpture. [Obs.]

> Each skilful artist shall *express* thy form. —Smith.

5. To despatch, forward, or send by express; as, to *express* a package.

ex-press′āġe, *n.* 1. The business of carrying by express.

2. The charges made for carrying by express.

ex-press′i-ble, *a.* 1. Capable of being expressed or squeezed out.

2. Capable of being expressed, uttered, or shown.

ex-press′i-bly, *adv.* In an expressible manner.

ex-pres′sion (eks-presh′un), *n.* [L. *expressio* (*-onis*), a pressing out, an expression, from *expressus*, pp. of *exprimere*, to press out, express.]

1. The act of expressing or forcing out by pressure, as juices and oils from plants; hence, figuratively, the eliciting or extracting anything desired to be kept back; as, a forcible *expression* of truth.

2. The act of uttering, declaring, or representing; utterance; declaration; representation; as, an *expression* of the public will.

3. Representation by words; descriptive power; style, as expository of one's thoughts, feelings, sentiments, ideas, etc.; as, Shakspere's wonderful power of *expression*.

4. That which is expressed or uttered; a phrase or mode of speech; as, an old *expression*; an odd *expression*.

5. In rhetoric, elocution; diction; the peculiar manner of utterance suited to the subject and sentiment.

6. Cast of countenance, as indicative of character; play of features, as expressive of feeling or any emotion; as, she had a sweet *expression*.

7. In music and art, the tangible embodiment of an idea; the natural and lively representation or suggestion of any state or condition; effective execution.

8. In algebra, a symbol or combination of symbols.

ex-pres′sion-ăl, *a.* Of or pertaining to expression; having the power of expression.

ex-pres′sion-less, *a.* Destitute of expression.

ex-press′ive, *a.* 1. Serving to express; serving to utter or represent; followed by *of*; as, he spoke in terms *expressive of* his gratitude.

2. Full of expression; representing clearly and forcibly; significant.

ex-press′ive-ly, *adv.* In an expressive manner.

ex-press′ive-ness, *n.* The quality of being expressive; the power of expression or representation.

ex-press′ly, *adv.* In an express manner; plainly; in direct terms; particularly; especially; as, I wrote for you *expressly*.

ex-press′măn, *n.*; *pl.* **ex-press′men.** One who is employed in any capacity by an express company, especially one who drives a wagon for collecting and delivering express packages; one who makes a business of transporting goods quickly.

ex-press′ness, *n.* The state of being express.

ex-press′-trāin, *n.* A railroad-train designed to carry mail, parcels, or passengers at a high rate of speed, and making but few stops between terminal stations.

ex-pres′sūre, *n.* Expression; utterance; representation; mark; impression. [Obs.]

ex-prīme′, *v.t.* To express. [Obs.]

ex′prō-brāte, *v.t.* [L. *exprobratus*, pp. of *exprobrare*, to reproach, upbraid.] To upbraid; to censure, as reproachful; to blame; to condemn. [Rare.]

ex-prō-brā′tion, *n.* The act of charging or censuring reproachfully; reproachful accusation; the act of upbraiding. [Obs.]

ex-prō′brā-tive, *a.* Upbraiding; expressing reproach. [Obs.]

ex-prō′brā-tō-ry, *a.* Same as *Exprobrative.*

ex-prō-mis′sion (-mish′un), *n.* [L. *expromissus*, pp. of *expromittere*, to promise to pay; *ex*, out, and *promittere*, to promise.] In civil law, the act by which a creditor accepts a new debtor in the place of the old debtor, who is discharged.

ex-prō-mis′sŏr, *n.* In civil law, one who becomes bound for the debt of another by substituting himself as principal debtor in the place of the former obligant.

ex-prō′pri-āte, *v.t.*; expropriated, *pt.*, *pp.*; expropriating, *ppr.* [L. *ex*, out, and *proprius*, one's own.]

1. To disengage from appropriation; to hold no longer as one's own; to give up a claim to exclusive property in.

2. To take for public use by exercising the right of eminent domain.

3. To deprive of proprietary rights; to exclude from rights or property.

ex-prō-pri-ā′tion, *n.* The act or result of expropriating; the giving up of all claim to; the depriving of or excluding from property.

ex-pūgn′ (eks-pūn′), *v.t.* To conquer; to take by assault. [Obs.]

ex-pug′nà-ble, *a.* [L. *expugnabilis*, from *expugnare*, to take by assault.] Capable of being expugned or taken by assault. [Rare.]

ex-pug-nā′tion, *n.* Conquest; the act of taking by assault. [Rare.]

ex-pūgn′ẽr (-pūn′), *n.* One who subdues or conquers.

ex-pulse′, *v.t.* To drive out; to expel. [Obs.]

ex-puls′ẽr, *n.* An expeller. [Obs.]

ex-pul′sion, *n.* [L. *expulsio* (*-onis*), a driving out, expulsion, from *expulsus*, pp. of *expellere*, to drive out.]

1. The act of driving out or expelling; as, the *expulsion* of a student from college.

2. A driving away by violence; forcible ejection.

ex-pul′sive, *a.* Having the power of driving out or away; serving to expel.

ex-punc′tion, *n.* [LL. *expunctio* (*-onis*), from L. *expunctus*, pp. of *expungere*, to prick or blot out, erase, expunge.] The act of expunging or the state of being expunged; the act of blotting out or erasing.

ex-punge′, *v.t.*; expunged, *pt.*, *pp.*; expunging, *ppr.* [L. *expungere*, to prick or blot out, erase, expunge.]

1. To blot out, as with a pen; to rub out; to efface, as words; to obliterate.

2. To efface; to strike out; to wipe out or destroy; to annihilate; as, to *expunge* an offense.

> *Expunge* the whole, or lop the excrescent parts. —Pope.

ex′pūr-gāte (*or* eks-pẽr′gāt), *v.t.*; expurgated, *pt.*, *pp.*; expurgating, *ppr.* [L. *expurgatus*, pp. of *expurgare*, to purge, cleanse; *ex*, out, and *purgare*, to cleanse, purify.] To purge; to cleanse; to purify from anything obnoxious, offensive, or erroneous; specifically, to free, as a book, from parts objectionable; as, an *expurgated* edition of Shakspere.

ex-pūr-gā′tion, *n.* 1. The act of expurgating or the condition of being expurgated; specifically, the removal of anything offensive from an edition of a literary work.

2. In astronomy, the emerging of the sun or moon from the umbra after an eclipse.

ex′pūr-gā-tŏr, *n.* One who expurgates or purifies.

ex-pūr-gȧ-tō′ri-ăl, *a.* Expurgating; expunging; purifying.

ex-pūr-gȧ-tō′ri-ous, *a.* [Obs.] Same as *Expurgatory.*

ex-pūr′gȧ-tō-ry, *a.* Cleansing; purifying; serving to purify from anything erroneous or obnoxious.

Expurgatory index; see *Index Expurgatorius* under *Index.*

ex-pūrge′, *v.t.* To purge away. [Obs.]

ex-quīre′ (eks-kwīr′), *v.t.* To search into or out. [Obs.]

ex′qui-şite (eks′kwi-), *a.* [ME. *exquisite*; L. *exquisitus*, choice, selected, pp. of *exquirere*, to search out; *ex*, out, and *quærere*, to ask.]

1. Choice or elegant in a high degree; fine; dainty; delicately beautiful; as, *exquisite* lace.

2. Of delicate perception or refined nature; discriminating and not easily satisfied; as, she has *exquisite* taste in dress.

3. Giving or characterized by intense emotion; keen; poignant; as, *exquisite* joy or sorrow; an *exquisite* sensibility.

Syn.—Choice, rare, refined, delicate, perfect, matchless, intense, consummate, delicious, nice, exact.

ex′qui-şite, *n.* One who is extremely particular as to dress and ornament; a dandy; a fop; a coxcomb; a dude.

> Such an *exquisite* was but a poor companion for a quiet, plain man like me. —Hook.

ex′qui-şite-ly, *adv.* In an exquisite manner; delicately; accurately; with great perfection; intensely; sensitively; as, to feel pain *exquisitely*; a work *exquisitely* finished.

ex′qui-şite-ness, *n.* The quality of being exquisite; *exquisiteness* of workmanship.

ex-quis′i-tive, *a.* Curious; eager to discover. [Obs.]

ex-quis′i-tive-ly, *adv.* Curiously. [Obs.]

ex-saṅ′gui-nāte (eks-saṅ′gwi-), *v.t.*; exsanguinated, *pt.*, *pp.*; exsanguinating, *ppr.* [L. *exsanguinatus*, bloodless; *ex-* priv., and *sanguinare*, to be bloody, from *sanguis*, blood.] To make bloodless.

ex-saṅ′guine (-gwin), *a.* Bloodless.

ex-saṅ-guin′ē-ous, *a.* Same as *Exsanguinous.*

ex-saṅ-guin′i-ty, *n.* In pathology, lack of sufficient blood; anemia.

ex-saṅ′gui-nous, *a.* [L. *exsanguis*, bloodless.] Deficient in blood; anemic.

ex-saṅ′gui-ous, *a.* [Rare.] Same as *Exsanguinous.*

ex-scind′ (eks-sind′), *v.t.*; exscinded, *pt.*, *pp.*; exscinding, *ppr.* [L. *exscindere*, to cut or tear off; *ex*, out, and *scindere*, to cut, tear.] To cut off.

ex-scrībe′, *v.t.* To copy; to transcribe. [Obs.]

ex′script, *n.* A copy; a transcript. [Obs.]

ex-scrip′tūr-ăl, *a.* Unscriptural.

ex-sculp′tāte, *a.* [L. *exsculptus*, pp. of *exsculpere*, to carve out; *ex*, out, and *sculpere*, to carve.] In entomology, covered with irregular and varying longitudinal depressions, as if carved.

ex-scū′tel-lāte, *a.* Same as *Escutellate.*

ex-sect′, *v.t.* [L. *exsectus*, pp. of *exsecare*, to cut out or away; *ex*, out, and *secare*, to cut.] To cut out.

ex-sec′tion, *n.* [L. *exsectio* (*-onis*), from *exsecare*, to cut out or away.] A cutting out or away; specifically, in surgery, the act of cutting a part out from its surroundings.

ex-sẽrt′ed, ex-sẽrt′, *a.* [L. *exsertus*, pp. of *exserere*, to put out or forth, thrust out; *ex*, out, and *serere*, to join.] Standing out; projecting beyond something else; as, *exsert* stamens; *exserted* organs of an animal.

ex-sẽrt′ile, *a.* Capable of being thrust out or protruded.

ex-sic′cănt, *a.* and *n.* [L. *exsiccans* (*-antis*), ppr. of *exsiccare*, to dry up.]

I. *a.* Drying; evaporating moisture; having the quality of drying.

II. *n.* In medicine, any drug which has drying properties.

ex-sic-cā′tæ, ex-sic-cā′tī, *n.pl.* [L., from *exsiccatus*, pp. of *exsiccare*, to dry up.] In botany, dried specimens of plants, especially those issued in numbered sets for herbariums.

ex-sic′cāte, *v.t.*; exsiccated, *pt.*, *pp.*; exsiccating, *ppr.* [L. *exsiccatus*, pp. of *exsiccare*, to make dry; *ex*, out, and *siccare*, to dry, from *siccus*, dry.] To dry; to exhaust or evaporate the moisture of.

ex-sic-cā′tion, *n.* The act or operation of drying; evaporation of moisture; dryness.

ex-sic′cȧ-tive, *a.* and *n.* I. *a.* Tending to make dry.

II. *n.* Any preparation which has drying properties.

ex′sic-cā-tŏr, *n.* An apparatus which removes moisture; a desiccator; an evaporator; also, in chemistry, an absorbent.

ex-sil′i-en-cy, *n.* [L. *exsiliens* (*-entis*), ppr. of *exsilire*, to spring or leap forth.] A springing forth. [Rare.]

ex-sō-lū′tion, *n.* Relaxation. [Rare.]

ex-spō-li-ā′tion, *n.* [Rare.] Same as *Spoliation.*

ex-spū-i′tion (-ish′un), *n.* [L. *exspuitio* (*-onis*), a spitting out, from *exspuere*, to spit out.] A discharge of saliva by spitting. [Rare.]

ex-spū′tō-ry, *a.* [L. *exsputus*, pp. of *exspuere*, to spit out.] Spit out; ejected, as if by spitting; rejected. [Rare.]

ex-stip′ū-lāte, *a.* [L. *ex-* priv., and *stipula*, a stalk, stem.] In botany, having no stipules.

ex′strō-phy, *n.* [Gr. *ekstrophē*, a dislocation, from *ekstrephein*, to turn aside, overturn; *ek*, out, and *strephein*, to turn.] In pathology, the turning inside out of any organ or part of the body.

ex-suc′cous, *a.* [L. *exsuccus*, from *ex-* priv., and *succus*, juice.] Destitute of juice; dry.

ex-suc′tion, *n.* [L. *exsuctus*, pp. of *exsugere*, to suck out; *ex*, out, and *sugere*, to suck.] The act of sucking out.

ex-sū-dā′tion, *n.* See *Exudation.*

ex-suf′flāte, *v.t.*; exsufflated, *pt.*, *pp.*; exsufflating, *ppr.* [LL. *exsufflatus*, pp. of *exsufflare*, to blow away.] To drive away, as an evil spirit, by blowing; to exorcise.

ex-suf-flā′tion, *n.* 1. A blowing or blast from beneath. [Obs.]

2. A kind of exorcism performed by blowing.

ex-sū′pẽr-ȧ-ble, *a.* Surmountable. [Obs.]

ex-sū′pẽr-ănce, *n.* Excess; superiority. [Obs.]

ex-sū′pẽr-ănt, *a.* Conquering; surpassing. [Obs.]

ex-sū′pẽr-āte, *v.t.* To conquer; to overcome. [Obs.]

ex-sũr′gent, *a.* [L. *exsurgens* (*-entis*), ppr. of *exsurgere*, to rise up.] Rising up.

ex-sus′ci-tāte, *v.t.* To rouse; to excite. [Obs.]

ex-sus-ci-tā′tion, *n.* A stirring up; a rousing. [Obs.]

ex′tȧ-cy, *n.* [Obs.] See *Ecstasy.*

ex′tănce, *n.* Outward existence. [Obs.]

ex′tăn-cy, *n.* [L. *exstantia*, *extantia*, from *exstans* (*-antis*), ppr. of *exstare*, to stand out.]

1. The state of rising above others.

2. A part rising above the rest; a projection. Rare.]

ex′tănt (*or* eks-tant′), *a.* [OFr. *estant*, extant, existing, from L. *extans* (*-antis*), *exstans* (*-antis*), ppr. of *extare*, *exstare*, to stand out or forth; *ex*, out, and *stare*, to stand.]

1. Standing out or above any surface; protruded. [Obs.]

> That part of the teeth which is *extant* above the gums. —Ray.

2. In being; now subsisting; not suppressed, destroyed, or lost; as, a part only of the history of Livy is *extant.*

3. Conspicuous; evident; publicly known. [Obs.]

ex′tȧ-sy, *n.* [Obs.] Same as *Ecstasy.*

ex-tat′ic, *a.* [Obs.] Same as *Ecstatic.*

ex-tem′pō-răl, *a.* Extemporaneous; extemporary. [Obs.]

ex-tem′pō-răl-ly, *adv.* Extemporaneously. [Obs.]

ex-tem-pō-rā′nē-ăn, *a.* [Obs.] Same as *Extemporaneous.*

ex-tem-pō-rā′nē-ous, *a.* [L. *ex*, out, and *tempus* (*-oris*), time.] Composed, performed, or uttered offhand at the time, without previous study or preparation; unpremeditated; provided for the immediate occasion; as, an *extemporaneous* address; an *extemporaneous* production; an *extemporaneous* shelter.

ex-tem-pō-rā′nē-ous-ly, *adv.* In an extemporaneous manner; without previous study.

ex-tem-pō-rā′nē-ous-ness, *n.* The quality of being extemporaneous.

ex-tem′pō-rā-ri-ly, *adv.* Without previous study or preparation.

ex-tem′pō-rā-ry, *a.* [L. *ex*, out, and *temporarius*, temporary, from *tempus*, time.]

1. Composed, performed, or uttered without previous study or preparation.

2. Prepared or secured for immediate use; as, *extemporary* shelter.

ex-tem′pō-rē, *adv.* [L., lit., from the moment; *ex*, from, out of, and *tempore*, ablative of *tempus*, time, a period of time, a moment.] Without previous study or meditation; without preparation; suddenly; as, to write or speak *extempore.*

ex-tem′pō-rē, *a.* Extemporaneous; unpremeditated; unstudied; as, an *extempore* speech.

ex-tem′pō-rē, *n.* Language spoken or written extemporaneously.

ex-tem′pō-ri-ness, *n.* The state of being extemporary. [Obs.]

ex-tem″pō-ri-zā′tion, *n.* The act of extemporizing.

ex-tem′pō-rīze, *v.i.*; extemporized, *pt.*, *pp.*; extemporizing, *ppr.* 1. To speak extempore; to speak without previous study or preparation.

2. To sing or play on an instrument, composing the words or music, or both, as one proceeds; to improvise.

ex-tem′pō-rīze, *v.t.* 1. To make hurriedly or without forethought; to make or provide for a sudden occasion; to prepare in haste with the means within one's reach; as, to *extemporize* a speech, a dinner, or a shelter.

2. To compose on the spur of the moment; as, to *extemporize* a song or an accompaniment.

ex-tem′pō-rī-zẽr, *n.* One who extemporizes.

ex-tend′, *v.t.*; extended, *pt.*, *pp.*; extending, *ppr.* [ME. *extenden*; OFr. *extendre*; L. *extendere*, to stretch out; *ex*, out, and *tendere*, to stretch.]

1. To stretch out in any direction; to carry forward, or continue in length, as a line; to spread in breadth; to expand or dilate in size; as, to *extend* lines in surveying; to *extend* roads, limits, bounds; to *extend* metal plates by hammering.

2. To stretch; to reach forth; as, to *extend* the arm or hand.

3. To spread; to expand; to enlarge; to widen; as, to *extend* the capacities or intellectual powers; to *extend* the sphere of usefulness; to *extend* commerce.

4. To continue; to prolong; as, to *extend* the time of payment; to *extend* a furlough.

5. To communicate; to bestow on; to use or exercise toward; to impart.

> And hath *extended* mercy to me before the king. —Ezra vii. 28.

6. In law, to levy on, as lands under an execution.

7. To put forth the full strength of; used reflexively; as, to *extend oneself*.

8. To place horizontally, at full length; as, *extended* on a couch.

Syn.—Increase, enlarge, lengthen, protract, stretch, amplify.

ex-tend′, *v.i.* To stretch; to reach; to be continued in length or breadth; as, Massachusetts *extends* west to the border of New York; how far will your argument or proposition *extend?*

ex-ten′dănt, *a.* [OFr. *extendant, estendant*, ppr. of *estendre*; L. *extendere*, to extend.]

1. Stretched out.

2. In heraldry, same as *displayed*.

ex-tend′ed-ly, *adv.* In an extended manner.

ex-tend′ẽr, *n.* One who or that which extends or stretches.

ex-tend′i-ble, *a.* 1. Capable of being extended, enlarged, widened, or expanded.

2. In law, capable of being taken by a writ of extent and valued.

ex-tend′less, *a.* Extended indefinitely. [Obs.]

ex-tend′less-ness, *n.* Extension without limit. [Obs.]

ex-tense′, *a.* [L. *extensus*, pp. of *extendere*, to extend.] Extended. [Rare.]

ex-ten-si-bil′i-ty, *n.* The quality or state of being extensible; a capacity for being extended, or of suffering extension; as, the *extensibility* of a fiber or of a plate of metal.

ex-ten′si-ble, *a.* [Fr. *extensible*, from L. *extendere*, to extend.] Capable of being extended or stretched in length or breadth; susceptible of enlargement.

ex-ten′si-ble-ness, *n.* Extensibility.

ex-ten′sile, *a.* Capable of being extended.

ex-ten′sion, *n.* [L. *extensio (-onis)*, a stretching out, extension, from *extendere*, to extend.]

1. The act of extending; a stretching.

2. The state of being extended; enlargement in breadth, or continuation of length.

3. In physics and metaphysics, that property of a body by which it occupies a portion of space.

4. In commerce, a written engagement on the part of a creditor, allowing a debtor further time to pay a debt.

5. In law, a postponement, by agreement of the parties or act of the court, of the time set for any legal procedure.

6. In logic, the extent of the application of a general term; sphere; compass; scope.

7. In anatomy, (a) the extending of any organ or part away from another part; as, the *extension* of the tongue; (b) the straightening of a part, as a limb; (c) the function of any extensor muscle.

8. In surgery, the operation of drawing a broken limb in a direction from the trunk in order to bring the parts in line.

9. An addition; an annex; a part added to extend; as, the *extension* to the house is finished.

ex-ten′sion-ăl, *a.* Having great extent.

ex-ten′sion-ist, *n.* An advocate of extension, as of territory or field of action.

ex-ten′sive, *a.* 1. Wide; large; having great enlargement or extent; as, an *extensive* farm; an *extensive* sphere of operations; *extensive* benevolence.

2. Extensible. [Obs.]

ex-ten′sive-ly, *adv.* Widely; largely; to a great extent; as, a story is *extensively* circulated.

ex-ten′sive-ness, *n.* 1. Wideness; largeness; extent; as, the *extensiveness* of the ocean; the *extensiveness* of a man's charities or benevolence.

2. The capacity of being extended. [Obs.]

ex-ten-som′e-tẽr, *n.* [L. *extensus*, pp. of *extendere*, to extend, and *metrum*, measure.] An apparatus for measuring the minute degrees of expansion or contraction of metal bars when acted upon by a tensile force.

ex-ten′sọr, *n.* [LL. *extensor*, a stretcher, used in the sense of one who stretches a victim on the rack, a torturer, from L. *extensus*, pp. of *extendere*, to stretch out.] In anatomy, a muscle which serves to extend or straighten any part of the body, as an arm or a finger; opposed to *flexor*.

ex-ten′sūre, *n.* Extension; extent. [Rare.]

ex-tent′, *a.* Extended. [Obs.]

ex-tent′, *n.* [ME. *extente*; OFr. *extente*, extent, extension, from L. *extendere*, to extend.]

1. The space or degree to which a thing is extended; hence, compass; bulk; size; as, a great *extent* of country, or of body.

2. Length; as, an *extent* of line.

3. Communication; distribution. [Obs.]

> The *extent* of equal justice. —Shak.

4. In English law, a writ of execution, directed to the sheriff, against the body, lands, and goods, or the lands only, of a debtor; also, the act of the sheriff or officer upon the writ itself.

Syn.—Degree, distance, quantity, space, size.

ex-ten′ū-āte, *v.t.*; extenuated, *pt., pp.*; extenuating, *ppr.* [L. *extenuatus*, pp. of *extenuare*, to make thin, reduce, diminish; *ex*, out, and *tenuare*, to make thin, from *tenuis*, thin.]

1. To make thin, lean, or slender; as, sickness *extenuates* the body. [Obs.]

2. To lessen; to diminish, as a crime or guilt.

> But fortune there *extenuates* the crime. —Dryden.

3. To lessen in representation; to palliate; opposed to *aggravate*.

4. To lessen or diminish in honor; to detract from. [Rare.]

ex-ten′ū-āte, *v.i.* To become thin or thinner; to be attenuated. [Rare.]

ex-ten′ū-āte, *a.* Thin; slender. [Rare.]

ex-ten-ū-ā′tion, *n.* [L. *extenuatio (-onis)*, a thinning, lessening, from *extenuare*, to make thin.]

1. The act of making thin; the process of growing thin or lean; the losing of flesh. [Rare.]

2. The act of making anything less wrong, faulty, or criminal, in fact or in estimation; palliation; as, there is no *extenuation* for such a crime as his.

ex-ten′ū-ā-tọr, *n.* One who extenuates.

ex-ten′ū-ā-tō-ry, *a.* Tending to extenuate.

ex-tē′ri-ọr, *a.* [L., comp. of *exter, exterus*, the outside.]

1. External; outward; applied to the outside or outer surface of a body, and opposed to *interior*; as, the *exterior* surface of a concavo-convex lens.

2. Outwardly manifested; on the outside, with reference to a person; not intrinsic.

3. Foreign; relating to foreign nations; as, the *exterior* relations of a state or kingdom.

4. In botany, placed on the side away from the axis; anterior.

Exterior angle; see *External angles* under *Angle*.

Exterior side; in fortification, the side of an imaginary polygon, upon which the plan of fortification is constructed.

Exterior slope; in fortification, that slope of a work toward the country which is next outward beyond its superior slope.

ex-tē′ri-ọr, *n.* 1. The outward surface; that which is external.

2. Outward or visible deportment; appearance.

ex-tē-ri-or′i-ty, *n.* The character or fact of being exterior; surface; superficies.

ex-tē′ri-ọr-ly, *adv.* Externally.

ex-tẽr′min-ā-ble, *a.* Capable of being exterminated.

ex-tẽr′mi-nāte, *v.t.*; exterminated, *pt., pp.*; exterminating, *ppr.* [L. *exterminatus*, pp. of *exterminare*, lit., to drive beyond the boundaries, to drive out or away, destroy; *ex*, out, and *terminus*, a boundary.]

1. To drive without the limits or borders; to expel. [Rare.]

2. To destroy completely; to root out utterly; to extirpate; as, to *exterminate* weeds, heresy, or a tribe.

3. In algebra, to take away; to cause to disappear; to eliminate; as, to *exterminate* surds or unknown quantities.

Syn.—Uproot, abolish, annihilate, destroy, eradicate, extirpate, overthrow.

ex-tẽr-mi-nā′tion, *n.* [LL. *exterminatio (-onis)*, destruction, from L. *exterminare*, to destroy.]

1. The act of exterminating; total expulsion or destruction; eradication; extirpation; excision; as, the *extermination* of inhabitants or tribes, of error or vice, or of weeds from a field.

2. In algebra, a taking away; elimination, as of unknown quantities.

ex-tẽr′mi-nā-tọr, *n.* [LL. *exterminator*, a destroyer, from L. *exterminare*, to destroy.] One who or that which exterminates.

ex-tẽr′mi-nā-tō-ry, *a.* Serving or tending to exterminate.

ex-tẽr′mine, *v.t.* To exterminate. [Obs.]

ex-tẽrn′, *a.* [L. *externus*, without, from *exter*, outward.] External; outward; visible; not inherent. [Obs.]

ex-tẽrn′, ex-tẽrne′, *n.* 1. A pupil in a college or seminary who lives without its walls.

2. The outer or external part; the exterior. [Obs.]

3. One of a hospital staff who resides outside the institution.

ex-tẽr′năl, *a.* [L. *externus*, outward, external, from *exter*, without.]

1. Outward; exterior; as, the *external* surface of a body; opposed to *internal*.

2. Outward; not intrinsic; not being within; specifically, in metaphysics, forming part of the material or phenomenal world; considered as outside the perceiving mind; as, *external* objects; *external* causes or effects.

3. Superficial; visible; apparent; as, *external* deportment.

4. Foreign; relating to or connected with foreign nations; as, *external* trade or commerce; the *external* relations of a state or kingdom.

5. In zoölogy, on the side farthest removed from the body and the mesial plane; as, the *external* side of a bird's leg.

ex-tẽr′năl, *n.* 1. An outward part; something pertaining to the exterior.

> Adam was then no less glorious in his *externals*; he had a beautiful body, as well as an immortal soul. —South.

2. An outward rite or ceremony; visible form; as, the *externals* of religion.

ex-tẽr′năl-iṣm, *n.* 1. Regard for or devotion to externals; specifically, undue devotion to externals, as of religion.

2. In philosophy, same as *phenomenalism*.

ex-tẽr-năl-is′tiç, *a.* Of or pertaining to externalism.

ex-tẽr-nal′i-ty, *n.* 1. The state of being external; location on the outside.

2. In metaphysics, existence in the world of space or phenomena outside of the perceiving mind.

3. An external; an outward rite, form, or symbol.

4. Undue regard for and devotion to externals; the sacrifice of the spirit to the form.

ex-tẽr″năl-i-zā′tion, *n.* The act of externalizing; the state or condition of being externalized or made real in space and time; embodiment; also written *externalisation*.

ex-tẽr′năl-īze, *v.t.*; externalized, *pt., pp.*; externalizing, *ppr.* To embody in time and space; to give shape and form to; also written *externalise*.

ex-tẽr′năl-ly, *adv.* In an external manner; outwardly; with reference to the outside.

ex-tẽr-nat, *n.* [Fr., a day-school, from *externe*, a day-scholar.] A day-school.

ex-tẽr′nize, *v.t.*; externized, *pt., pp.*; externizing, *ppr.* Same as *Externalize*.

ex-tẽr-nō-mē′di-ăn, ex-tẽr-nō-mē′di-ăl, *a.* [L. *externus*, outward, and *medius*, middle.] In entomology, exterior to the central line or plane.

ex-tẽr-rā′nē-ous, *a.* [LL. *exterraneus*, of another country; L. *ex*, out, and *terra*, country.] Foreign; coming from abroad.

ex-ter-ri-tō′ri-ăl, *a.* [L. *ex*, out, and *territorium*, territory.] Of or pertaining to exterritoriality; exempt from the laws of one's abode; also written *extraterritorial*.

ex-ter-ri-tō-ri-al′i-ty, *n.* In international law, the privilege granted to all diplomatic representatives of foreign powers and their families of being exempt from the laws of the land of their abode and of enjoying, in general, the rights and privileges of their own country; also written *extraterritoriality*.

ex-tẽr′sion, *n.* [L. *extersus*, pp. of *extergere*, to wipe off, to wipe dry; *ex*, out, and *tergere*, to wipe.] The act of wiping or rubbing out.

ex-til′, *v.i.* To drop or distil from. [Obs.]

ex-til-lā′tion, *n.* The act of distilling from, or falling from in drops. [Obs.]

ex-tim′ū-lāte, *v.t.* To stimulate. [Obs.]

ex-tim-ū-lā′tion, *n.* Stimulation. [Obs.]

ex-tinct′, *a.* [L. *extinctus, exstinctus*, pp. of *extinguere, exstinguere*, to put out, destroy.]

1. Extinguished; put out; quenched.

> Her weapons blunted, and *extinct* her fires. —Pope.

2. Being at an end; having no survivor; having ceased; having no force; as, an *extinct* law; the enmity is *extinct*; a family or race is *extinct*.

ex-tinct′, *v.t.* To put out; to destroy. [Obs.]

ex-tinc′tion, *n.* 1. The act of extinguishing or the state of being extinguished, as fire or flame.

2. A putting an end to; a coming to an end; destruction; annihilation; as, the *extinction* of a race; the *extinction* of a feud.

ex′tine (eks′tin), *n.* [From L. *exterus*, outside, and *-ine*.] In botany, the outer coat of the pollen-grain in plants.

ex-tin′guish (-tin′gwish), *v.t.*; extinguished (-gwisht), *pt., pp.*; extinguishing, *ppr.* [L. *extinguere*, to put out, quench; *ex*, out, and *stinguere*, to quench.]

1. To put out; to quench; to suffocate; to destroy; as, to *extinguish* fire or flame.

2. To destroy; to put an end to; as, to *extinguish* love or hatred in the breast; to *extinguish* desire or hope; to *extinguish* a claim or title.

3. To obscure by superior splendor; to eclipse.

4. In law, to put an end to, by union or consolidation.

Syn.—Abolish, destroy, extirpate, eradicate, kill, quench, annihilate.

ex-tin′guish-ȧ-ble, *a.* Capable of being extinguished, quenched, destroyed, or suppressed.

ex-tin′guish-ẽr, *n.* One who or that which extinguishes; especially, a device to be put on a candle or lamp to extinguish it.

ex-tin′guish-ment, *n.* 1. The act of putting out or quenching; extinction; suppression; destruction; as, the *extinguishment* of fire or flame, of discord or jealousy, of love or affection, of a race or tribe.

2. In law, the putting an end to a right or estate by consolidation or union.

ex-tīrp′, *v.t.* To extirpate. [Obs.]

ex-tīr′pȧ-ble, *a.* Capable of being extirpated.

ex-tīr′pāte, *v.t.*; extirpated, *pt.*, *pp.*; extirpating, *ppr.* [L. *extirpatus, exstirpatus*, pp. of *extirpare, exstirpare*, to root out, eradicate; *ex*, out, and *stirps*, the lower part of a tree, the root.] To pull or pluck up by the roots; to root out; to eradicate; to destroy totally; as, to *extirpate* weeds or noxious plants from a field; to *extirpate* a sect.

Syn.—Uproot, exterminate, destroy, eradicate, annihilate, abolish.

ex-tīr-pā′tion, *n.* [L. *extirpatio (-onis), exstirpatio (-onis)*, from *extirpare, exstirpare*, to root out, extirpate.] The act of rooting out; eradication; excision; total destruction; as, the *extirpation* of weeds from land; the *extirpation* of a race of men; the *extirpation* of heresy.

ex′tīr-pā-tive, *a.* Pertaining to or causing extirpation.

ex′tīr-pā-tŏr, *n.* One who roots out; a destroyer.

ex-tīr′pȧ-tō-ry, *a.* Extirpative; eradicative.

ex-tīr′pẽr, *n.* One who extirps or extirpates. [Obs.]

ex-tis′pex, *n.*; *pl.* **ex-tis′pi-cēs**. [L., from *exta*, the nobler entrails, and *specere*, to view.] Same as *Haruspex*.

ex-ti-spi′cious (-spish′us), *a.* Augurial; relating to the inspection of entrails in order to prognosticate. [Obs.]

ex-tog′e-nous, *a.* Same as *Exogenous*.

ex-tōl′ (eks-tōl′), *v.t.*; extolled, *pt.*, *pp.*; extolling, *ppr.* [OFr. *extoller*; L. *extollere*, to raise up, lift up; *ex*, out, up, and *tollere*, to raise.]

1. To raise aloft; to set on high; to elevate. [Obs.]

2. To speak in laudatory terms of; to praise; to eulogize; to magnify; as, to *extol* virtues, noble exploits, and heroism.

> *Extol* him that rideth upon the heavens by his name Jah. —Ps. lxviii. 4.

Syn.—Laud, praise, applaud, commend, magnify, celebrate, glorify.

ex-tōl′lẽr, *n.* One who extols; a praiser or eulogist.

ex-tōl′ment, *n.* [OFr. *extollement*, from *extoller*, to raise.] The act of extolling or the state of being extolled.

ex-tor′sive, *a.* [L. *extortus*, pp. of *extorquere*, to twist or turn out; *ex*, out, and *torquere*, to turn, twist.] Serving to extort; tending to draw from by compulsion.

ex-tor′sive-ly, *adv.* In an extorsive manner; by extortion.

ex-tort′, *v.t.*; extorted, *pt.*, *pp.*; extorting, *ppr.* [L. *extortus*, pp. of *extorquere*, to twist or turn out; *ex*, out, and *torquere*, to twist.]

1. To draw from by force or compulsion; to wrest or wring from by physical force, by menace, duress, violence, authority, or by any illegal means; to exact; as, conquerors *extort* contributions from the vanquished.

2. In law, to obtain by pretense of authority without legal right; as, to *extort* excessive fees.

ex-tort′, *v.i.* To practise extortion.

ex-tort′, *a.* Extortionate. [Obs.]

ex-tort′ẽr, *n.* One who extorts or practises extortion.

ex-tor′tion, *n.* [ME. *extorcioun*; LL. *extorsio (-onis)*, a wrenching away, from L. *extortus*, pp. of *extorquere*, to wrench away.]

1. The act of extorting; the act or practice of wresting anything from a person by force, duress, menaces, authority, or by any undue exercise of power; illegal exaction; illegal compulsion to pay money or to do some other act.

2. In law, the offense of claiming or taking as a fee, under pretense of authority, money or any article of value, where none is due, or before due, or in excess of the amount due.

3. Anything extorted; overcharge.

Syn.—Exaction, oppression, overcharge.

ex-tor′tion-ā-ry, *a.* Pertaining to or implying extortion.

ex-tor′tion-āte, *a.* Oppressive; characterized by extortion.

Syn.—Hard, severe, rigorous, exorbitant, preposterous, monstrous, exacting.

ex-tor′tion-ẽr, ex-tor′tion-ist, *n.* One who practises extortion.

ex-tor′tion-ous, *a.* [Obs.] Same as *Extortionate*.

ex-tor′tious, *a.* Oppressive; violent; unjust. [Obs.]

ex-tor′tious-ly, *adv.* In an extortionate manner. [Obs.]

ex-trȧ-. A prefix from L. *extra*, outside, beyond, signifying outside of, beyond, more than, besides, as in *extra*ordinary.

ex′trȧ (eks′), *a.* Being more than is stipulated or usual; additional; supplementary; as, *extra* compensation; an *extra* edition.

ex′trȧ, *n.* [L. *extra*, adv., more than, outside.]

1. Something in addition to what is due or expected; something over and above the usual course or charge; something beyond what is usual; as, dancing is charged as an *extra*.

2. An edition of a newspaper, issued in addition to the regular editions and at another hour, to convey some special intelligence; as, an *extra* was issued every hour to give the latest news of the president's illness.

ex′trȧ, *adv.* Beyond the usual standard; extraordinarily; unusually; as, you did *extra* well. [Colloq.]

ex′trȧ-ax′il-lā-ry, ex′trȧ-ax′il-lăr, *a.* In botany, growing from above or below the axils; as, an *extra-axillary* bud.

ex-trȧ-brañ′chi-ăl, *a.* [*Extra-*, and Gr. *branchia*, gills.] In anatomy, not located within the branchial arches; said of the cartilages of certain fishes.

ex″trȧ-ca-lic′ū-lăr, *a.* [*Extra-*, and L. *calyx*, the calyx.] Situated outside the calyx of a cœlenterate.

ex″trȧ-ca-non′ic-ăl, *a.* Not included among the canonical writings.

ex-trȧ-cap′sū-lăr, ex-trȧ-cap′sū-lā-ry, *a.* In anatomy, situated outside a capsule; specifically, of or pertaining to the extracapsularium.

ex″trȧ-cap-sū-lā′ri-um, *n.*; *pl.* **ex″trȧ-cap-sū-lā′ri-ȧ**. [L., from *extra*, beyond, and *capsula*, capsule.] In zoölogy, that part of a radiolarian which is situated without the central capsule.

ex-trȧ-cel′lū-lăr, *a.* [*Extra-*, and L. *cella*, a cell.] 1. Placed outside a cell.

2. In physiology, existent, developed, or acting outside organic cells; as, *extracellular* digestion.

ex-tract′, *v.t*; extracted, *pt.*, *pp.*; extracting, *ppr.* [L. *extractus*, pp. of *extrahere*, to draw or drag out; *ex*, out, and *trahere*, to draw.]

1. To draw out; as, to *extract* a tooth.

2. To draw out, as the juices or essence of a substance, by distillation, solution, or other means; as, to *extract* spirit from the juice of cane; to *extract* salts from ashes.

3. Figuratively, to obtain as if by distilling; to draw out; as, to *extract* knowledge from a chance acquaintance; to *extract* pleasure from work.

4. To take out or select a part of; to take a passage or passages from, as a book or writing.

> I have *extracted* out of that pamphlet a few notorious falsehoods. —Swift.

To extract the root; in mathematics, to find the root of a number or quantity.

ex′tract, *n.* 1. That which is extracted or drawn from something.

2. A passage taken from a book or writing; a quotation; an excerpt.

3. Anything drawn from a substance by heat, solution, distillation, or chemical process, as an essence, a tincture, and the like.

4. In old chemistry, a peculiar principle once supposed to form the basis of all vegetable extracts; called also the *extractive principle*.

5. Extraction; descent. [Obs.]

6. In Scots law, a copy, authenticated by the proper officer, of a deed, writing, or other entry, the principal of which either is in a public record, or a transcript of which taken from the the principal has been preserved in a public record.

Compound extract; in pharmacy, an extract containing the essence of more than one drug.

Fluid extract; in pharmacy, a liquid preparation whose volume is equal to a measure of distilled water weighing the same as the amount of drug used.

ex-tract′ȧ-ble, ex-tract′i-ble, *a.* Capable of being extracted.

ex-tract′i-form, *a.* [L. *extractus*, pp. of *extrahere*, to draw out, and *forma*, form.] In chemistry, having the characteristics of an extract.

ex-trac′tion, *n.* [L. *extractus*, pp. of *extrahere*, to draw out, extract.]

1. The act of drawing out; as, the *extraction* of a tooth; the *extraction* of a bullet from the body.

2. Descent; lineage; birth; derivation of persons from a stock or family; as, he is of good *extraction*.

3. That which is extracted; essence.

ex-tract′ive, *a.* 1. Capable of being extracted; serving to extract.

2. Of the nature of an extract; extracted.

ex-tract′ive, *n.* 1. An extract. [Obs.]

2. In chemistry, any one of various substances, such as creatine and xanthin, found in minute quantities in animal tissue.

3. In pharmacy, that portion of an extract which is of doubtful nature and which during evaporation becomes insoluble.

ex-tract′ŏr, *n.* [L., from *extractus*, pp. of *extrahere*, to extract.]

1. One who or that which extracts.

2. An evaporator.

3. In surgery, a forceps for extracting substances from the human body.

4. A cartridge-shell ejector in a firearm.

5. A metal vessel in which bones are treated to extract glue and gelatin.

6. In Scots law, the official who prepares and authenticates extracts.

ex-trȧ-dic′tion-ā-ry, *a.* Consisting not in words, but in realities. [Obs.]

ex-trȧ-dī′tȧ-ble, *a.* 1. Amenable to extradition, as a criminal arrested in a foreign country.

2. Rendering liable to extradition; as, *extraditable* crimes.

ex′trȧ-dīte, *v.t.*; extradited, *pt.*, *pp.*; extraditing, *ppr.* [L. *ex*, out, and *traditus* pp. of *tradere*, to give over.]

1. To surrender or give up, as to another nation or state; as, to *extradite* a criminal.

2. To project (a sensation) to a distance from the body by a psychological process; as, when we shake a locked gate and feel the stability of the ends where the hinges, bolts, and locks are, we *extradite* the sensation to that point.

ex-trȧ-di′tion (-dish′un), *n.* [Fr. *extradition*, from L. *ex*, out, and *traditus*, pp. of *tradere*, to give up, give over.]

1. Delivery from one state or nation to another; specifically, the delivery of fugitives from justice.

2. The projection, by a psychological process, of a sensation to a distance from the body.

Extradition treaty; a treaty between two governments regulating the surrender of fugitives from justice, and prescribing the crimes for which they may be extradited.

ex-trā′dos, *n.* [Fr., from L. *extra*, beyond, and *dorsum*, back.] In architecture, the upper or convex surface of an arch or vault; also, the outer curve of a voussoir.

ex-trā′dosed (-dost), *a.* Having an extrados; said of an arch when the curves of the intrados and extrados are concentric and parallel.

ex-trȧ-dō′tăl, *a.* [*Extra-*, and L. *dos, dotis*, dowry.] In civil law, not belonging to the dowry; said of a married woman's property.

ex-trȧ-flō′răl, *a.* [*Extra-*, and L. *flos, floris*, flower.] In botany, located outside a flower.

ex″trȧ-fō-li-ā′ceous, *a.* [*Extra-*, and L. *folium*, a leaf.] In botany, away from the leaves, or inserted in a different place from them; as, *extrafoliaceous* prickles.

ex″trȧ-fō-rā′nē-ous, *a.* [*Extra-*, and L. *foris*, a door.] Outdoor. [Rare.]

ex-trȧ-gē′nē-ous, *a.* [*Extra-*, and L. *genus*, kind.] Belonging to another kind.

ex″trȧ-jū-di′ciăl (-dish′ăl), *a.* Out of court or out of the proper court; out of the ordinary course of legal procedure.

ex″trȧ-jū-di′ciăl-ly, *adv.* In an extrajudicial manner, in a manner out of the ordinary course of legal proceedings.

ex-trȧ-lim′it-ăl, *a.* [*Extra-*, and L. *limes, limitis*, limit, boundary.] In zoölogy, (a) not found within a specified faunal area; as, an *extralimital* species; (b) lying outside a specified part or surface; as, *extralimital* spots on a bird's wing.

ex-trȧ-lim′it-ā-ry, *a.* [*Extra-*, and L. *limes*, limit.] 1. Being or lying outside the limit or boundary; as, *extralimitary* land.

2. Same as *Extralimital*.

ex-trȧ-log′ic-ăl, *a.* Being outside the domain of logic, when restricted to its syllogistic and subsidiary doctrines without concern as to the truth of reasonings.

ex-trȧ-log′ic-ăl-ly, *adv.* In an extralogical manner.

ex″trȧ-mal-lē′ō-lus, *n.*; *pl.* **ex″trȧ-mal-lē′ō-li**. [*Extra-*, and L. *malleolus*, dim. of *malleus*, a hammer.] In anatomy, the outer malleolus or projection of the ankle, formed by the lower end of the fibula.

ex-trȧ-mis′sion (-mish′un), *n.* A sending out; emission.

ex-trȧ-mun′dāne, *a.* [LL. *extramundanus*, beyond the world; L. *extra*, beyond, and *mundus*, the world.] Beyond the limit of the material world; as, *extramundane* beings.

ex-trȧ-mū′răl, *a.* [LL. *extramuranus*, beyond the walls; L. *extra*, beyond, and *murus*, wall.] Beyond the walls, as of a fortified city or university; hence, beyond the fixed limits of a place; as, *extramural* residents.

ex-trȧ-nē′i-ty, *n.* The quality of being extraneous or foreign. [Rare.]

ex-trā′nē-ous, *a.* [L. *extraneus*, that which is without, external, from *extra*, without, beyond.] Foreign; not belonging or essential to a thing; not intrinsic; as, to separate gold from *extraneous* matter.

ex-trā′nē-ous-ly, *adv.* In an extraneous manner.

ex-trȧ-nū′clē-ăr, *a.* [*Extra-*, and L. *nucleus*, a kernel.] Not included within the nucleus of a cell.

ex″trȧ-oc′ū-lăr, *a.* [*Extra-*, and L. *oculus*, an eye.] In entomology, located outside of the eyes; said of the antennæ of certain insects.

ex″trȧ-of-fi′ciăl (-fish′ăl), *a.* Not within the limits of official duties, rights, etc.

ex-traor′di-nā-ri-ly, *adv.* In an extraordinary, uncommon, or special manner or degree.

ex-traor′di-nā-ri-ness, *n.* The quality of being extraordinary; uncommonness. [Rare.]

ex-traor'di-nā-ry, *a.* [L. *extraordinarius*, out of the common course, rare; *extra*, beyond, and *ordinarius*, ordinary, from *ordo* (*-inis*), a straight line, order.]

1. Beyond or out of the common order or method; not in the usual, customary, or regular course; not ordinary; as, *extraordinary* evils require *extraordinary* remedies.

2. Exceeding the common degree or measure; hence, remarkable; uncommon; rare; wonderful; as, the *extraordinary* talents of Shakspere.

3. Special; particular; for a special purpose or on a particular occasion; as, an *extraordinary* courier or messenger; an ambassador *extraordinary*.

Syn.—Unwonted, uncommon, peculiar, unusual, unprecedented, wonderful, marvelous, prodigious, monstrous, remarkable, preposterous.

ex-traor'di-nā-ry, *n.*; *pl.* **ex-traor'di-nā-ries.** Anything extraordinary or unusual; something exceeding the usual order, kind, or method; especially, in the British army, any allowance to or for troops in addition to gross pay.

ex"trá-pá-rō'chi-ăl, *a.* Not within the limits of a parish.

ex"trá-pá-rō'chi-ăl-ly, *adv.* In an extraparochial manner.

ex-trá-phys'iç-ăl, *a.* Beyond physical laws or processes.

ex"trá-pō-lā'tion, *n.* [Fr.] In mathematics, the calculation, by an empirical law, of the approximate value of a function, when there is no way of ascertaining the exact value; as, the estimation of the population at a future date, from the population in previous years, is an *extrapolation*.

ex"trá-prō-fes'sion-ăl (-fesh'un-ăl), *a.* Not within the ordinary limits of professional duty or business.

ex"trá-prō-vin'ciăl (-shăl), *a.* Not within the same province or jurisdiction.

ex-trá-reg'ū-lăr, *a.* Not comprehended within a rule or rules.

ex"trá-stā-pē'di-ăl, *a.* and *n.* [*Extra-*, and LL. *stapes*, a stirrup, from O.H.G. *stapf*, step.]

I. *a.* In anatomy, situated beyond the stapes; said of part of the axis of the cochlea.

II. *n.* That part of the columella of the ear which is extrastapedial.

ex"trá-ter-ri-tō'ri-ăl, *a.* Same as *Exterritorial*.

ex"trá-ter-ri-tō-ri-al'i-ty, *n.* Same as *Exterritoriality*.

ex-trá-thē'çăl, *a.* [*Extra-*, and L. *theca*, from Gr. *thēkē*, a case.] In biology, not included within a theca.

ex-trá-trop'iç-ăl, *a.* Not within the tropics.

ex-traught' (-trat'), *a.* 1. Extracted. [Obs.]

2. Distracted; frenzied; distraught. [Obs.]

ex"trá-ū'tĕr-ine, *a.* Situated or occurring outside the uterus; applied to pregnancy in which the fetus is outside the uterus.

ex-trav'á-gănce, *n.* [OFr. *extravagance*; L. *extra*, beyond, and *vagari*, to wander.]

1. A wandering beyond a limit; an excursion or sally from the usual way, course, or limit. [Rare.]

2. The state or quality of being extravagant; excess; especially, excess in expenditure of property; prodigality; irregularity; as, *extravagance* of passion, outlay, statement, etc.

3. Any act of excess or such acts in general; a going beyond or wandering from what is reasonable or proper; especially, the expending of money without necessity, wastefully, or beyond due limits; as, this was the least of his *extravagances*.

ex-trav'á-găn-cy, *n.* Extravagance. [Rare.]

ex-trav'á-gănt, *a.* 1. Wandering beyond limits or bounds; roving. [Obs.]

2. Excessive; exceeding due bounds; unreasonable; as, the wishes, demands, desires, and passions of men are often *extravagant*.

3. Prodigal; profuse in expenditure; wasteful; as, an *extravagant* man.

Syn.—Prodigal, lavish, profuse.—The idea of using immoderately is implied in all these words, but *extravagant* is the most general in its meaning and application. The *extravagant* man spends his money without reason; the *prodigal* man spends it in excesses; one may be *extravagant* with a small sum where it exceeds one's means; one can be *prodigal* only with large sums. *Extravagant* and *prodigal* designate habitual as well as particular actions; *lavish* and *profuse* are properly applied to particular actions, the former to denote an expenditure more or less wasteful or superfluous, the latter to denote a full supply without any sort of scant.

ex-trav'á-gănt, *n.* 1. One who is confined to no general rule; an eccentric person. [Rare.]

2. [E— *pl.*] Certain decretal epistles or constitutions of the popes which were published after the Clementines, but not at first arranged and digested with the other parts of the canon law.

ex-trav'á-gănt-ly, *adv.* In an extravagant manner.

ex-trav-á-gan'zá, *n.* [It. *estravaganza*, extravagance.]

1. Anything out of rule, as in music, the drama, etc.; a species of composition noted for its fantastic irregularity and extravagance; a burlesque.

2. An extravagant flight of feeling or language.

ex-trav'á-gāte, *v.i.* To wander beyond due limits. [Obs.]

ex-trav-á-gā'tion, *n.* A wandering beyond limits. [Obs.]

ex-trav'á-sāte, *v.t.* extravasated, *pt.*, *pp.*; extravasating, *ppr.* [*Extra-*, and L. *vas*, a vessel.] To let out of the proper vessels, as blood.

ex-trav'á-sāte, *v.i.* To pass out of the proper vessel, especially by infiltration into the tissues; as, blood *extravasates* around a bruised spot.

ex-trav-á-sā'tion, *n.* 1. The act of extravasating or the state of being extravasated.

2. The fluid which has been extravasated.

3. In geology, the extrusion of volcanic matter.

ex-trá-vas'çū-lăr, *a.* [*Extra-*, and L. *vasculum*, dim. of *vas*, a vessel.] Outside of or not having blood-vessels.

ex-trav'e-nāte, *a.* [*Extra-*, and L. *vena*, vein.] Let out of the veins. [Obs.]

ex-trá-vĕr'sion, *n.* The act of throwing out; the state of being turned or thrown out. [Obs.]

ex-trēat', *n.* Extraction. [Obs.]

ex-trēme', *a.* [OFr. *extreme*; L. *extremus*, last, outermost, superl. of *exter*, outer, outward.]

1. Outermost; farthest; at the utmost point, edge, or border; as, the *extreme* verge or point of a thing.

2. Greatest; utmost in degree; of the best or worst that can exist in reality or in imagination; as, *extreme* pain, grief, or pleasure.

3. Last; beyond which there is none; final; as, an *extreme* remedy.

4. Radical in opinion, especially in political matters; ultra; uncompromising and unyielding; exacting; severe.

5. In music, augmented; increased by a half step.

Extreme and mean ratio; in geometry, the ratio existing between a line and its segments, when the line is so divided that the whole line is to the greater segment as that segment is to the less.

Syn.—Terminal, final, remote, ultimate, utmost, farthest, last, extravagant, immoderate.

ex-trēme', *n.* 1. The utmost point or verge; that part which terminates a body; extremity.

2. The furthest or utmost limit or degree; the extreme point or degree possible or imaginable; a condition, quality, or act very widely removed from the usual; as, the *extremes* of heat and cold; avoid *extremes*.

3. In logic, the predicate or subject of the conclusion; as, in the syllogism, "Man is an animal; Peter is a man, therefore Peter is an animal", the word *animal* is the greater *extreme*, *Peter* the less *extreme*, and *man* the middle term.

4. In mathematics, (a) the first and last terms of a proportion; as, when three magnitudes are proportional, the rectangle contained by the *extremes* is equal to the square of the mean; (b) the largest or the smallest of three or more magnitudes; (c) in a right-angled or quadrantal spherical triangle, any part other than the one assumed to be the mean.

In the extreme; in the highest degree.

To go to extremes; to act or speak in an extreme manner; to use or favor extreme measures.

ex-trēme'less, *a.* Having no extremes; infinite.

ex-trēme'ly, *adv.* In the utmost degree; to the utmost point; to a very great degree; exceedingly; as, it is *extremely* hot or cold.

ex-trēm'ist, *n.* One who goes to extremes in opinions or measures.

ex-trem'i-ty, *n.* [L. *extremitas* (*-atis*), the extremity, end, from *extremus*, furthest, extreme.]

1. The utmost point or side; the verge; the limit or border; as, the *extremities* of a country.

2. In zoölogy, an appendage or limb; an organ of locomotion.

3. The utmost point; the most intense kind; the highest or furthest degree; as, the *extremity* of cruelty.

4. Extreme or utmost distress, straits, or difficulty; as, a city besieged and reduced to *extremity*.

5. [*pl.*] Extreme methods or measures; as, do not force me to *extremities*.

ex'tri-çá-ble, *a.* Capable of being extricated.

ex'tri-çāte, *v.t.*; extricated, *pt.*, *pp.*; extricating, *ppr.* [L. *extricatus*, pp. of *extricare*, to disentangle, extricate; *ex*, out, and *tricæ*, trifles, toys.]

1. To disentangle; hence, to free from difficulties or perplexities; to disembarrass; as, to *extricate* one from troublesome alliances or from debt.

2. To send out; to cause to be emitted or evolved.

Syn.—Disembarrass, disengage, disentangle, liberate, evolve.

ex'tri-çāte, ex'tri-çā-ted, *a.* In entomology, extruded, as the ovipositor of certain insects.

ex-tri-çā'tion, *n.* The act of extricating or freeing from perplexities; disentanglement; the act of sending out or evolving.

ex-trin'siç, ex-trin'siç-ăl, *a.* [L. *extrinsecus*, from without, outer; *exter*, without, and *secus*, otherwise, besides.]

1. External; outward; not contained in or belonging to the essence or nature of a body; not inherent; extraneous; opposed to *intrinsic*.

2. In anatomy, having its origin outside the limits of an organ or limb to which it is partly attached, as certain muscles.

3. In Scots law, irrelevant.

ex-trin-si-çal'i-ty, *n.* The state or quality of being extrinsic.

ex-trin'siç-ăl-ly, *adv.* In an extrinsic manner.

ex-trin'siç-ăl-ness, *n.* Extrinsicality.

ex-trō'i-tive (eks-trō'i-tiv), *a.* [L. *extra*, outside, and *ire*, to go.] Searching out external matters or things. [Rare.]

ex-tror'săl, *a.* Extrorse.

ex-trorse', *a.* [Fr. *extrorse*; L. *extra*, outside, and *versus*, pp. of *vertere*, to turn.]

1. In botany, turned or facing outward or away from the floral axis; said of certain anthers.

2. In zoölogy, turned outward or away from the median line.

Extrorse Anthers of *Tamarix Indica*.

ex-trō-vĕr'sion, *n.* [*Extra-*, and LL. *versio* (*-onis*), a turning, from L. *vertere*, to turn.] In pathology, the state of being turned inside out, as an eyelid or the bladder.

ex-truçt', *v.t.* To build; to construct. [Obs.]

ex-truç'tion, *n.* A building. [Obs.]

ex-truçt'ive, *a.* Forming into a structure. [Obs.]

ex-truçt'ŏr, *n.* A builder. [Obs.]

ex-trụde', *v.t.*; extruded, *pt.*, *pp.*; extruding, *ppr.* [L. *extrudere*, to thrust out or forth; *ex*, out, and *trudere*, to thrust.] To thrust out; to urge, force, or press out; to expel; to drive away or off.

ex-trụ'sion, *n.* [L. *extrusus*, pp. of *extrudere*, to thrust out.] The act of extruding or throwing out; expulsion; especially, the forcing outward of fused rock upon the surface.

ex-trụ'sive, *a.* Resulting from or tending toward extrusion; as, *extrusive* rocks; *extrusive* forces.

ex-tū'bĕr-ănce, ex-tū'bĕr-ăn-cy, *n.* Protuberance. [Obs.]

ex-tū'bĕr-ănt, *a.* Protuberant. [Obs.]

ex-tū'bĕr-āte, *v.i.* To swell; to protrude. [Obs.]

ex-tū-bĕr-ā'tion, *n.* Protuberance. [Obs.]

ex-tū-mes'cence, *n.* [L. *ex*, out, and *tumescere*, incept. of *tumere*, to swell.] A swelling or rising. [Rare.]

ex-tund', *v.t.* To beat or squeeze out. [Obs.]

ex-ū'bĕr-ănce, ex-ū'bĕr-ăn-cy (eks-), *n.* [LL. *exuberantia*, superabundance, from L. *exuberans* (*-antis*), ppr. of *exuberare*, to come forth in abundance.] The state of being exuberant; an abundance; an overflowing quantity; richness; as, an *exuberance* of fertility or fancy.

Syn.—Abundance, copiousness, plenty, plenitude, superabundance, wantonness.

ex-ū'bĕr-ănt, *a.* Distinguished by or revealing great abundance; plenteous; luxuriant; rich; overabundant; superfluous; as, *exuberant* fertility; *exuberant* goodness.

ex-ū'bĕr-ănt-ly, *adv.* In an exuberant manner; in great plenty; to a superfluous degree.

ex-ū'bĕr-āte, *v.i.* [L. *exuberatus*, pp. of *exuberare*, to come forth in abundance; *ex*, out, and *uberare*, to be fruitful, from *uber*, an udder.] To abound; to be in great abundance. [Obs.]

ex-uç'çous, *a.* [Obs.] Same as *Exsuccous*.

ex-ū'dāte, *n.* An exudation.

ex-ū'dāte, *v.t.* and *v.i.* [Obs.] Same as *Exude*.

ex-ū-dā'tion, *n.* 1. The act of exuding or state of being exuded; a discharge of liquid through small openings.

2. That which is exuded.

ex-ūde', *v.t.*; exuded, *pt.*, *pp.*; exuding, *ppr.* [L. *exudare*, *exsudare*, to sweat out, exude; *ex*, out, and *sudare*, to sweat.] To discharge through small openings or pores, as by sweating; to give out slowly, as moisture.

ex-ūde', *v.i.* To flow slowly or ooze from a body through pores or small openings.

ex-ul'cĕr-āte (egz-), *v.t.*; exulcerated, *pt.*, *pp.*; exulcerating, *ppr.* [L. *exulceratus*, pp. of *exulcerare*, to make sore, cause to ulcerate; *ex*, out, and *ulcerare*, to ulcerate, from *ulcus* (*-eris*), a sore, ulcer.]

1. To cause an ulcer or ulcers upon.

2. To afflict; to corrode; to fret or anger.

ex-ul'cĕr-āte, *v.i.* To become ulcerous.

ex-ul'cĕr-āte, *a.* Ulcerated; vexed; enraged. [Obs.]

ex-ul-cĕr-ā'tion, *n.* 1. Suppuration; ulceration.

2. Exacerbation; irritation; vexation.

ex-ul'cĕr-ȧ-tive, ex-ul'cĕr-ȧ-tō-ry, *a.* Having a tendency to form ulcers or become ulcerous.

ex-ult' (egz-), *v.i.*; exulted, *pt.*, *pp*; exulting, *ppr.* [L. *exultare, exsultare*, to leap up, leap for joy, *ex*, out, and *salire*, to leap.] To leap for joy; to rejoice in triumph; to rejoice exceedingly; to be glad above measure; to triumph; as, to *exult* over a fallen adversary.

ex-ult'ănce, ex-ult'ăn-cy, *n.* Exultation. [Obs.]

ex-ult'ănt, *a.* Exulting; rejoicing triumphantly.

ex-ul-tā'tion, *n.* [L. *exultatio* (*-onis*), *exsultatio* (*-onis*), a leaping up, rejoicing, from *exultare, exsultare*, to leap for joy, exult.] The act of exulting; lively joy at success or victory, or at any advantage gained; great gladness; rapturous delight; triumph.

ex-ult'ing-ly, *adv.* In a triumphant manner.

ex-un'dāte (eks-), *v.i.* To overflow. [Obs.]

ex-un-dā'tion, *n.* [L. *exundatio* (*-onis*), from *exundare*, to overflow; *ex*, out, and *undare*, to rise in waves, from *unda*, a wave.] An overflowing abundance. [Obs.]

ex-un'gū-lāte (egz-), *v.t.* To pare off the hoofs or nails of. [Rare.]

ex-ū'pĕr-ȧ-ble, ex-ū'pĕr-ănce, etc. See *Exsuperable*, etc.

ex-us'ti-ble (egz-), *a.* Combustible. [Obs.]

ex-us'tion (egz-), *n.* Combustion. [Obs.]

ex-ū'tō-ry (eks-), *n.* [L. *exutus*, pp. of *exuere*, to draw or strip off.] In medicine, an issue.

ex-ū"vi-ȧ-bil'i-ty (eks-), *n.* State of being exuviable.

ex-ū'vi-ȧ-ble, *a.* Capable of being cast or thrown off in the form of exuviæ.

ex-ū'vi-æ, *n.pl.* [L., that which is stripped or taken off, spoils.]

1. Cast skins, shells, or coverings of animals; any parts of animals which are shed or cast off, as the skins of caterpillars, the shells of lobsters, etc.

2. In geology, the fossil shells and other remains which animals have left in the strata of the earth.

3. Hides or pelts intended for preservation.

ex-ū'vi-ăl, *a.* Of the nature of or pertaining to exuviæ.

ex-ū'vi-āte, *v.i.* and *v.t.*; exuviated, *pt.*, *pp.*; exuviating, *ppr.* I. *v.i.* To molt; to cast some part of the body, as skin, feathers, shell, etc.

II. *v.t.* To shed or cast off, as feathers, a shell, teeth, etc.

ex-ū-vi-ā'tion, *n.* The act of exuviating.

ex'=vō'tō, *n.* [L. *ex voto*, lit., from a vow; *ex*, out of, and *voto*, ablative of *votum*, vow.] In the Roman Catholic church, a votive offering, as a picture or a tablet for a shrine.

-ey. A termination appearing in such words as all*ey*, mon*ey*, donk*ey*, monk*ey*, etc. It is a reduced form of some final syllables in Latin, French, Anglo-Saxon, etc.

ey, *n.* An egg. [Obs.]

ey, *interj.* Eh! what! [Obs.]

e-yā'let, *n.* [Turk., from Ar. *wali, weli*, a governor, lord, master.] Formerly, an administrative province of the Turkish empire; a pashalic; now known as a *vilayet*.

ey̆'ăs (ī'ăs), *n.* [Fr. *niais*, fresh from the nest, from L. *nidus*, nest.] A young hawk just taken from the nest, not able to prey for itself; also, one raised from a fledgling.

ey̆'ăs, *a.* Unfledged. [Obs.]

ey̆'ăs=mus"ket, *n.* A young unfledged male sparrow-hawk; also formerly used as a pet name for a child. [Obs.]

eye (ī), *n.* [ME. *eye, eghe* (pl. *eyen, eghen*); AS. *eage* (pl. *eagan*), eye.]

1. The organ of sight or vision; properly, in vertebrates, the globe or ball movable in the orbit. In all vertebrates, the eye closely resembles that of man, being formed by the combination of two segments from a larger and a smaller sphere. The segment of the lesser sphere forms the anterior part of the eye, and is composed externally of a strong hornlike membrane, called the *cornea*, within which are the aqueous humor and the iris. The iris is a colored muscular membrane, capable of contraction and dilatation, suspended in the aqueous humor, with a hole (the pupil) in the center for the transmission of light. The larger sphere presents three coats, the outermost being the sclerotic, within which is the choroid, and lastly the retina. The last is the sentient coat, and consists of a cuplike expansion of the optic nerve, spread on the black coat or *pigmentum nigrum* covering the inner surface of the choroid. The anterior orifice of the choroid is firmly connected to a thick ring of grayish pulpy substance, forming the point at which the sclerotic and cornea without, and the iris within, are united. This ring is named the *ciliary circle* or *ligament*. Posterior to this is a range of prominent minute bodies, with free extremities, lying over the crystalline lens, varying in number from seventy to eighty. They are trilateral-prismatic in shape, and are known as the *ciliary processes*. The interior sphere is filled with a jelly-like, transparent mass called the *vitreous humor*, immediately in front of which, and just behind the pupil, is the crystalline lens, bearing the same relation to the retina that the lens of a camera does to the sensitive plate.

Eye.

Interior. *a*, Pupil. *b*, Iris. *c*, Cornea. *d*, Crystalline lens. *e*, Vitreous humor. *f*, Retina. *g*, Choroid coat. *h*, Sclerotic coat. *i i*, Central vein of the retina. *k*, Optic nerve. *m*, Ciliary processes. *n*, Ciliary ligament or circle. Exterior. *l*, Supercilium or eyebrow. *o p*, Upper and lower eyelids. *x x*, Cilia or eyelashes. *r*, Caruncula lachrymalis. *s*, Plica semilunaris. The pupil and iris are also shown at *a* and *b* respectively.

2. In a restricted sense, some conspicuous part of the *eye* or part of its surroundings; (a) the pupil; as, the cat's *eyes* contract; (b) the space or fissure between the eyelids; as, to close the *eyes*; (c) the iris; as, her *eyes* are brown; (d) the orbit of the eye; the socket; as, vacant *eyes* in a skull; (e) the skin about the opening of the eye; as, he has a black *eye*.

3. The act of seeing; sight; view; hence, observation; notice; watch; as, I have a man now in my *eye*; generally in the plural.

> Before whose *eyes* Jesus Christ hath been evidently set forth, crucified among you.
> —Gal. iii. 1.

4. The power of seeing; power, range, or delicacy of vision; keenness and accuracy of perception, conjoined with delicacy of appreciation; as, to have the *eye* of an artist; he has an *eye* for color.

5. View of the mind; mental perception; opinion formed by observation or contemplation.

> It hath, in their *eye*, no great affinity with the form of the Church of Rome. —Hooker.

6. Aspect; regard; respect; view; as, the authors have an *eye* to their own advantage.

7. Look; countenance; face; aspect; as, a sober *eye*.

8. Anything resembling or suggesting an *eye* in shape or general appearance; as, (a) the bud or shoot of a plant or tuber; (b) the hole or aperture in a needle to receive the thread; (c) the circular catch of a hook and eye; (d) the loop or ring for fastening the rigging of ships; (e) the center of a target; (f) the spot marking a peacock's tail-feather; (g) in architecture, in general, the center of anything; thus, the *eye* of a volute is the circle at its center from which the spiral lines spring; the *eye* of a dome, the circular aperture at its apex; the *eye* of a pediment, a circular window in its center; (h) a muscular impression on the inner side of a bivalve, to which the adductor muscle is attached; (i) the hole in the upper millstone through which grain passes; (j) an eyebolt; (k) an opening intended to receive a handle, pin, shaft, etc., as in an adz, wheel, crank, anchor, or the socket of a carriage-pole.

9. In nautical language, an opposite direction; as, to sail in the wind's *eye*.

10. A shade of color; a tint; a tinge. [Obs.]

11. Anything of supreme brilliance or beauty, importance or power; as, the sun is the *eye* of day.

> Athens, the *eye* of Greece, mother of arts.
> —Milton.

12. A calcareous deposit found in the walls of the stomach of crustaceans.

All in one's eye; imaginary; not real. [Slang.]

Black eye; (a) an eye having a black iris; (b) an eye whose lids and adjacent parts are discolored, as by a blow; (c) defeat; injury; disfavor; as, the anecdote gave him a *black eye*. [Slang.]

Eyes of a ship, or *the eyes of her*; in nautical language, the foremost part in the bows of a ship.

Half an eye; a hasty or careless glance; imperfect observation.

The mind's eye; intellectual perception or comprehension.

To find favor in the eyes of; to be graciously received and treated by.

To have an eye to; to watch; to take care of.

To have or *keep an eye on*; to watch carefully.

To set or *lay the eyes on*; to see; to have a sight of.

eye, *n.* A brood; as, an *eye* of pheasants.

eye, *v.t.* and *v.i.*; eyed, *pt.*, *pp.*; eying *or* eyeing, *ppr.* I. *v.t.* To fix the eye on; to look on; to view; to observe; particularly, to observe or watch narrowly, or with fixed attention.

II. *v.i.* To appear; to have an appearance. [Obs.]

eye'=an-i-mal'cūle, *n.* A flagellate infusorian, especially one of the family *Euglenidæ*; so called from having a colored spot resembling an eye, and usually green, at one end.

eye'ball, *n.* The ball or globe of the eye.

eye'bär, *n.* In engineering, a bar of steel or iron with an eye at one end or at both.

eye'bēam, *n.* A glance of the eye.

eye'bōlt, *n.* A bar, or bolt of iron, with an eye at one end.

eye'bright (-brīt), *n.* The popular name of *Euphrasia officinalis* of the figwort family; formerly much used as a remedy for diseases of the eye.

eye'brow, *n.* [ME. *egebrew*; AS. *eaganbregh*; *eage*, eye, and *bræw*, brow.] The brow or hairy arch above the eye, or a line resembling it.

eye'cup, *n.* Same as *Eyeglass*, n. 3.

eyed (īd), *a.* [AS. *-eaged, -eged*, from *eage*, eye.] Having eyes; used in composition; as, brown-*eyed*; Argus-*eyed*.

eye'drop, *n.* A tear. [Poet. or Archaic.]

eye'flap, *n.* A blinder on a horse's bridle.

eye'fụl, *a.* Attracting the sight; remarkable. [Obs.]

eye'glance, *n.* A glance of the eye.

eye'glȧss, *n.* 1. A lens of glass or crystal to assist sight by correcting any defect of vision; usually in the plural. *Eyeglasses* resemble spectacles but have no bows, being held in place by a spring.

2. The eyepiece of a telescope, microscope, or similar instrument.

3. In surgery, a glass for the application of a collyrium to the eye.

4. The crystalline lens of the eye. [Obs.]

eye'hōle, *n.* An eyelet; also, a peephole.

eye'lash, *n.* 1. The line of hair that edges the eyelid; usually in the plural.

2. One of the small hairs which grow in a row on the edge of the eyelid.

eye'less, *a.* Wanting eyes; destitute of sight.

eye'let, *n.* [ME. *oylet*; OFr. *oeillet*, dim. of *oeil*, eye, from L. *oculus*, eye.]

1. A small hole or perforation; specifically, a small hole, either worked around with a buttonhole stitch or protected by a metal ring, and used in dressmaking, sailmaking, working in leather, etc.

2. A metal ring used to protect an *eyelet* by being pressed around its edge.

eye-let-eer', *n.* A small, pointed instrument used in making eyelets.

eye'let=hōle, *n.* Same as *Eyelet*.

eye'lid, *n.* The cover of the eye; that portion of movable skin with which an animal covers the eyeball or uncovers it at will.

eye'=mem"ō-ry, *n.* Memory of visual perceptions.

eye=mīnd'ed, *a.* Having the tendency to acquire knowledge through the eye and to conduct mental processes in association with visual images.

ey̆'en, *n.pl.* Eyes. [Obs.]

eye'pïece, *n.* In a telescope or other optical instrument, the lens or combination of lenses through which the image is viewed and by which it is magnified.

Erecting or *terrestrial eyepiece*; an eyepiece, commonly used in spyglasses, which reinverts the image, thus presenting it erect.

Huygenian eyepiece; a negative eyepiece consisting of two lenses flat on one side and convex on the other, the convex sides being turned away from the eye.

Negative eyepiece; an eyepiece in which the rays are focused between the lenses.

Positive eyepiece; an eyepiece in which the rays are focused before they reach the lenses.

ey̆'ẽr, *n.* One who eyes or watches attentively.

eye'rēach, *n.* The range of vision; the distance to which one can see.

eye'=sāint, *n.* One who is very pleasing to the eyes; one who is adored with the eyes. [Obs.]

eye'sälve (-säv), *n.* A medicine or ointment for the eye.

eye'sẽrv"ănt, *n.* A servant who attends to his duty only when watched, or under the eye of his master or employer.

eye'sẽrv"ice, *n.* Service performed only under inspection or the eye of an employer.

eye'shot, *n.* Sight; view; glance of the eye; eyereach.

eye'sight (-sīt), *n.* 1. The sight of the eye; view; observation.

2. The sense of seeing; as, his *eyesight* fails.

eye'sōre, *n.* Something offensive to the eye or sight.

> Mordecai was an *eyesore* to Haman.
> —L'Estrange.

eye'=splice, *n.* Nautically, a sort of eye or circle formed by splicing the end of a rope into itself.

eye'=spot, *n.* 1. One of the rudimentary organs of sight of many of the lower animals, consisting of a few pigment-cells covering the end of a nerve which is sensitive to light.

2. A rudimentary eye in the embryo of higher animals.

3. An ocellus.

4. A spot resembling an eye, as on a peacock's tail.

ēye′-spot″ted, *a.* Marked with spots like eyes.

ēye′stạlk (ī′stạk), *n.* A stem or stalk bearing an eye at the end, as in some crustaceans.

ēye′stōne, *n.* A small, calcareous stone used for taking substances from between the lid and ball of the eye.

ēye′string, *n.* The tendon by which the eye is moved.

ey′et (ā′et), *n.* Same as *Ait.*

ēye′tooth, *n.*; *pl.* **ēye′teeth.** A tooth under the eye; a pointed tooth in the upper jaw next to the grinders; called also a *canine tooth.*

To cut one's eyeteeth or *to have one's eyeteeth cut*; to be old enough to understand things and not to be imposed upon. [Slang.]

ēye′wash, *n.* A medicated water for the eyes.

ēye′wa″t r, *n.* 1. Same as *Eyewash.*

2. The aqueous and vitreous humor of the eye.

ēye′wink, *n.* A wink or motion of the eyelid; a hint or token.

ēye′wink″ēr, *n.* An eyelash. [U. S.]

ēye′wit″ness, *n.* One who sees a thing done; one who has ocular view of anything.

> We were *eyewitnesses* of his majesty.
> —2 Pet. i. 16.

eyght (āt), *n.* Same as *Ait.*

eyle (āl), *v.t.* and *v.i.* To ail. [Obs.]

ey′li-ad, *n.* An amorous look; an ogle. [Obs.]

eyne (īn), *n.*, obsolete plural of *eye.*

ey′ŏt (ā′ŏt), *n.* Same as *Ait.*

ȳ′rà (ī′rà), *n.* [Native South Am. name.] A reddish or chestnut-colored wildcat, *Felis eyra*, ranging from Texas southward into South America. Its body is very long and slender and its legs short, especially the fore legs.

eyre (âr), *n.* [ME. *eyre*; OFr. *erre, oire*, a journey; L. *iter*, a journey.]

1. A journey or circuit.

2. A court of itinerant justices.—Blackstone.

Justices in eyre; formerly, in England, itinerant judges who rode the circuit to hold courts in the different counties.

ey′ren, *n.*, pl. of *egg.* [Obs.]

ēy′rie, ēy′ry (ē′ri), *n.* [Obs.] See *Aery.*

ey′sell, *n.* [Obs.] Same as *Eisel.*

ey′stēr, *n.* An oyster. [Obs.]

F

F (ef). The sixth letter and fourth consonant of the English alphabet; it is taken from the Latin in both form and sound. The Latin *F* is derived from Old Greek digamma (ϝ), so called because it resembled two gammas in form, which had a sound between English *f* and *w*. The Greek digamma came from the Phenician *vav* or *waw*, meaning peg or hook, equivalent in sound to English *w*. *F* historically represents *p, k, v,* and *b*, as Eng. *father*, L. *pater*, Gr. *patēr*.

F is a labiodental articulation, formed by the passage of breath between the lower lip and the upper front teeth. It is classed as a surd spirant, its corresponding sonant spirant being *v*, which is distinguished from *f* by being pronounced with voice instead of breath, as may be perceived by pronouncing *ef, ev.* *F* is a common consonant in English words, both initially, medially, and finally, in the latter two cases being often doubled. As an initial it is very common in conjunction with *l* and *r*, as in *fly, free.* In plurals it often becomes *v*, as in *knife, knives, calf, calves*; compare also *life, live; strife, strive,* etc. Anglo-Saxon *f* has often been changed into *v* in modern English, as in *heaven, leave, carve,* etc., but such a change (as in *vixen*) is rare initially. In *enough, rough, trough,* an *f*-sound now represents a former guttural.

In music, (a) the fourth tone in the scale of C; (b) the key of one flat of which *F* is the keynote; (c) on the pianoforte, the white key to the left of each group of three black keys.

fä, *n.* [It.] In music, (a) the fourth tone or subdominant of the diatonic scale; (b) the tone *F*, so called because in the major scale of C, *F* is the fourth note or *fa.*

fa-bā′ceous (-bā′shus), *a.* [L. *fabaceus*, of or consisting of beans, from *faba*, a bean.] Having the nature of a bean; like a bean.

fa-bel′lȧ, *n.*; *pl.* **fa-bel′læ.** [L., dim of *faba*, a bean.] In anatomy, one of the small bones on the back of the kneejoint or behind the condyle of the femur.

Fā′bi-ăn, *a.* Delaying; dilatory; avoiding battle, in imitation of Quintus Fabius Maximus, a Roman general who conducted military operations against Hannibal by declining to risk a battle in the open field, but harassing the enemy by marches, countermarches, and ambuscades.

Fabian policy; a policy of delays and indirect methods.

Fabian Society; a society of English socialists who propose to win by a long process of political education and by indirect methods.

fā′ble, *n.* [ME. *fable*; OFr. *fable*; L. *fabula*, a narrative, story, from *fari*, to speak.]

1. A feigned story or tale, intended to instruct or amuse; a fictitious narrative intended to enforce some useful truth or precept, in which often are introduced animals and sometimes inanimate objects represented as speakers and actors.

> Jotham's *fable* of the trees is the oldest extant, and as beautiful as any made since.
> —Addison.

2. A story or legend invented and developed by imagination or superstition and at one time quite generally believed, but now known to be imaginary; a myth.

3. An idle story; a vicious or vulgar tale.

> But refuse profane and old wives' *fables.*
> —1 Tim. iv. 7.

4. The plot, or connected series of events, in an epic or dramatic poem.

> The moral is the first business of the poet; this being formed, he contrives such a design or *fable* as may be most suitable to the moral.
> —Dryden.

5. By euphemism, a lie; a falsehood.

Syn.—Allegory, apologue, legend, myth.

fā′ble, *v.i.*; fabled, *pt., pp.*; fabling, *ppr.* [ME. *fablen*; OFr. *fabler*; L. *fabulare*, to speak, converse, from *fabula*, a fable.]

1. To write fiction.

> Vain now the tales which *fabling* poets tell.
> —Prior.

2. To tell falsehoods; as, he *fables* not.

fā′ble, *v.t.* To feign; to invent; to devise and speak of as true or real.

fā′blēr, *n.* A writer of fables or fictions; a dealer in feigned stories; a falsifier.

fa-bli-au′ (-ō′), *n.*; *pl.* **fa-bli-aux′** (-ōz′). [Fr., from OFr. *fabliaus*, from L. *fabella*, dim. of *fabula*, a fable.] In French literature, a metrical tale especially popular in the twelfth and thirteenth centuries.

fab′riç, *n.* [Fr. *fabrique*; L. *fabrica*, a workshop, trade, any product of a trade, fabric, from *faber*, a workman, artisan.]

1. The structure of anything; the manner in which the parts of a thing are united by art and labor; workmanship; texture; as, cloth of a beautiful *fabric.*

2. A material intended for wear or ornament; the production of weaving or the allied arts, as cloth, lace, or hosiery.

3. Any complex construction fabricated or put together; any system composed of connected parts; as, the political *fabric* of our country; that immense *fabric*, the Masonic Temple of Chicago.

4. The act of building; construction. [Rare.]

fab′riç, *v.t.* To frame; to construct. [Obs.]

fab′ri-çănt, *n.* One who fabricates or manufactures.

fab′ri-çāte, *v.t.*; fabricated, *pt., pp.*; fabricating, *ppr.* [L. *fabricatus*, pp. of *fabricari*, to construct, frame, build, from *fabrica*, any skilful production, a fabric.]

1. To frame; to build; to construct; to form, as a whole, by connecting its parts; as, to *fabricate* a bridge or a ship.

2. To form by art and labor; to manufacture; as, to *fabricate* woolens.

3. To invent and form; to forge; to devise falsely; as, to *fabricate* a lie or story.

> Our books were not *fabricated* with an accommodation to prevailing usages. —Paley.

Syn.—Frame, construct, make, manufacture, produce.

fab-ri-çā′tion, *n.* [Fr. *fabrication*; L. *fabricatio* (-*onis*), a making, framing, from *fabricari*, to make.]

1. The act or art of fabricating in any of its senses.

2. That which is fabricated or manufactured, especially a falsehood or forgery; as, the rumors were mere *fabrications.*

Syn.—Fiction, figment, falsehood, fable, invention, untruth.

fab′ri-çā-tŏr, *n.* [L. *fabricator*, a maker, framer, from *fabricari*, to make.] One who constructs or makes; one who invents a fictitious story; a falsifier.

fab′ri-çā-tress, *n.* A woman fabricator.

fab′rile, *a.* [OFr. *fabrile*; L. *fabrilis*, from *faber*, a workman.] Pertaining to a worker in stone, metal, or similar craft, or to his work.

fab′ū-list, *n.* [L. *fabula*, a fable.] One who writes or tells fables.

fab′ū-līze, *v.i.*; fabulized, *pt., pp.*; fabulizing, *ppr.* [L. *fabula*, a fable.] To invent, compose, or relate fables.

fab-ū-los′i-ty, *n.* 1. The quality of being fabulous. [Rare.]

2. A fable. [Obs.]

fab′ū-lous, *a.* [L. *fabulosus*, celebrated in fable, legendary, from *fabula*, a story.]

1. Feigned, as a story; devised; fictitious; as, a *fabulous* story; a *fabulous* description.

2. Beyond the limits of belief; exceedingly great; incredible; enormous; immense; as, a *fabulous* sum.

3. Given to the telling of fables and legends.

Fabulous age; in a nation, the time before the beginning of authentic history; the legendary period.

Syn.—Feigned, fictitious, legendary, mythical.

fab′ū-lous-ly, *adv.* In fable or fiction; in a fabulous manner.

fab′ū-lous-ness, *n.* The quality of being fabulous or feigned.

fab′ūr-den, *n.* [OFr. *faux bourdon.*] In music, the simplest or rudest counterpoint; a drone-bass; a monotonous refrain or burden. [Obs.]

faç, *n.* [Abbrev. of L. *factum simile.*] A large ornamental letter used at the beginning of a chapter or other division of a book by printers of the seventeenth and eighteenth centuries.

fa-çade′, *n.* [It. *facciata*, the front of a building, from *faccia*, L. *facies*, face.] In architecture, an elevation or exterior face of a building, especially the front or most important face; as, the *façade* of St. Mark's; the *façade* of the Pitti palace.

face, *n.* [ME. *face*; OFr. *face*; L. *facies*, the face, visage, appearance.]

1. In a general sense, the surface of a thing, or the side which presents itself to the view of a spectator; as, the *face* of the earth; the *face* of the waters.

> A mist watered the whole *face* of the ground.
> —Gen. ii. 6.

2. The front part of an animal's head, particularly of the human head made up of the forehead, eyes, nose, mouth, cheeks, etc.; the visage.

3. The expression of the *face* as indicative of favor, disfavor, or anger; hence, favor, disfavor, or anger; as, I set my *face* against it.

> Therefore came I forth to meet thee, diligently to seek thy *face*, and I have found thee. —Prov. vii. 15.

4. A plane surface of a solid; one of the sides bounding a solid; as, a cube or die has six *faces*; an octahedron has eight *faces.*

5. Confidence; effrontery; boldness; assurance.

> He has the *face* to charge others with false citations. —Tillotson.

6. Presence; sight; as in the phrases, before the *face*; in the *face*; to the *face*; from the *face.*

> There he stood once more before her *face*
> Claiming her promise. —Tennyson.

7. In entomology, the front of the head lying between the compound eyes.

8. In commerce, the exact sum expressed on a bill, note, etc., exclusive of interest accrued by law or discount.

9. That part of the cog of a geared wheel which extends beyond the working diameter.

10. The edge of any tool which cuts.

11. In mining, especially in coal-mining, the front of a working or the end of a tunnel or excavation.

12. In printing, the surface of the type, which gives the impression; also, the character of the type, its size, and cut.

13. In astrology, one of the thirty-six parts of the zodiac, assigned to one of the planets.

14. In botany, the upper or free surface, as opposed to the *back*.

15. In bookbinding, the front edge of a book, as opposed to the *back*.

Face to face; (a) in a confronting attitude; in the actual presence; as, to have accusers *face to face*; (b) clearly; without the interposition of any other body.

> Now we see through a glass, darkly; but then *face to face*. —1 Cor. xiii. 12.

On the face of it; on the internal evidence; on the showing of a thing itself without necessity of further proof; as, it was a lie *on the face of it*.

To fly in the face of; to dare; to defy.

To make a face; to make a grimace; to distort one's countenance.

Syn.—Countenance, feature, physiognomy, visage.

fāce, *v.t.*; faced (fāst), *pt.*, *pp.*; facing, *ppr.*

1. To meet in front; to oppose with firmness; to resist, or to meet for the purpose of stopping or opposing; as, to *face* an enemy in the field of battle.

> I'll *face*
> This tempest, and deserve the name of king. —Dryden.

2. To stand opposite to; to stand with the face or front toward; as, the colleges in New Haven *face* the public square.

3. To cover with additional superficies; to cover with a layer or strip, usually of another material; as, a fortification *faced* with marble; to *face* a garment with silk.

4. To make flat and smooth, as the surface of marble, a stone, etc.

5. To give a deceptive and more attractive appearance to; as, to *face* tea with coloring matter.

6. To place in a certain position as to its front; as, he *faced* the piano toward the window.

To face down; to oppose boldly or impudently; to contradict.

To face it out; to adhere to anything under all circumstances; to persist steadfastly or impudently.

To face the music; to meet the emergency unflinchingly; to meet the consequences, however unpleasant they may be. [Slang.]

fāce, *v.i.* 1. To carry a false appearance; to play the hypocrite.

2. To turn the face; as, to *face* to the right or left.

fāce′-āche, fāce′-ā″gūe, *n.* In pathology, neuralgia of the face; also called *tic douloureux* and *ague-face*.

fāce′-cärd, *n.* One of the twelve cards of a pack of playing-cards bearing a face; a king, queen, or knave of any suit.

fāce′-cloth, *n.* A cloth laid over the face of a corpse.

fāce′-cŏv″ẽr, *n.* In fortifications, an interior glacis placed in the ditch, to prevent damage from the besiegers' fire.

fāced (fāst), *a.* 1. Having a face; used in composition; as, two-*faced*; sweet-*faced*.

2. Having its upper or outer surface dressed or smoothed; as, a *faced* stone.

3. Having a covering or facing, usually of another material; as, a dress *faced* with silk.

fāce′-guärd, *n.* A mask to protect the face, worn by workers in foundries and laboratories, and by participants in certain games.

fāce′-ham″mẽr, *n.* 1. A hammer with a flat face.

2. A large, heavy hammer used in facing stone.

fāce′-mīte, *n.* A minute mite, *Demodex folliculorum*, parasitic in the hair and sebaceous glands, especially of the nose and ears.

fāce′-mōld, *n.* A pattern used to mark the plank or board, out of which are to be cut ornamental hand-railings, etc.

fāce′-plāte, *n.* 1. A plate used as a standard in testing a plane surface.

2. A plate which shields an object from shock and wear.

3. A disk attached to the revolving spindle of a lathe, to the face of which the piece to be turned is often clamped.

fā′cẽr, *n.* 1. One who faces; one who is impudent or brazen. [Obs.]

> There be no great talkers, nor boasters, nor *facers*. —Latimer.

2. A severe blow in the face; hence, any sudden check that staggers one. [Slang.]

fac′et, fac′ette, *n.* [Fr. *facette*; OFr. *facete*, dim. of *face*, face.]

1. A little face; a small surface; as, the *facets* of a diamond.

2. In architecture, a flat projection between the flutings of a column.

3. In anatomy, a small, circumscribed portion of the surface of a bone.

4. In entomology, an ocellus, or its surface, of an insect's compound eye.

fac′et, *v.t.*; faceted, *pt.*, *pp.*; faceting, *ppr.* To cut facets upon; as, to *facet* a diamond.

fa-cēte′, *a.* Pleasant; bright; facetious; witty. [Obs.]

fac′et-ed, fac′et-ted, *a.* Having facets or cut into facets.

fa-cēte′ly, *adv.* In a facete manner. [Obs.]

fa-cēte′ness, *n.* The quality of being facete. [Obs.]

fa-cē′ti-æ (-shi-ē), *n.pl.* [L., from *facetus*, witty.]

1. Witty or humorous writings or sayings; witticisms.

2. Books which are so coarsely witty or broad as to be objectionable, considered collectively.

fā-cē′tious (-sē′shus), *a.* [L. *facetus*, witty.]

1. Merry; sportive; jocular; sprightly with wit and good humor; as, a *facetious* companion.

2. Witty; full of pleasantry; playful; exciting laughter; as, a *facetious* story; a *facetious* reply.

Syn.—Humorous, witty, jocose, bright, merry.

fā-cē′tious-ly, *adv.* In a facetious manner; merrily; gaily; wittily; with pleasantry.

fā-cē′tious-ness, *n.* The quality of being facetious; sportive humor; pleasantry; the quality of exciting laughter or good humor.

fa-cette′, *n.* See *Facet*.

fāce′-wheel, *n.* Same as *Crown-wheel*.

fā′ciăl (fā′shăl), *a.* [LL. *facialis*, from L. *facies*, face.] Pertaining to the face; as, the *facial* artery, vein, or nerve.

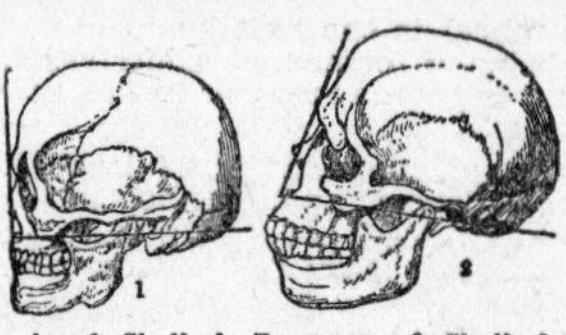

Facial Angle. 1. Skull of a European. 2. Skull of a Negro.

Facial angle; in anatomy, the angle formed by the plane of the face with a certain other plane. The *facial angle* of Camper is contained by a line drawn horizontally from the middle of the external entrance of the ear to the edge of the nostrils, and another from this latter point to the superciliary ridge of the frontal bone.

Facial nerve; the portio dura of the seventh pair of nerves, arising from the upper part of the respiratory tract, supplying the facial muscles, and known as the *nerve of expression*.

fā′ciăl-ly, *adv.* In a facial manner; with reference to the face.

fā′ci-end, *n.* Same as *Operand*.

fā′cient (-shent), *n.* [L. *faciens* (*-entis*), ppr. of *facere*, to do, make.]

1. A doer; one who does anything, good or bad. [Obs.]

2. In mathematics, (a) a variable of a quantic; (b) the multiplier.

fā′ci-ēs (-shi-ēz), *n.* [L.] 1. The face.

2. The general aspect or appearance of anything; specifically, the appearance of an organism before it has been studied deeply; as, the *facies* of a stratum, of fauna, etc.

Facies Hippocratica; the peculiar appearance of the face immediately before death, first described by Hippocrates.

fac′ile, *a.* [Fr. *facile*; L. *facilis*, easy to do, doable, from *facere*, to do, make.]

1. Easy to be done or performed; easy; not difficult; performable or attainable with little labor.

> Order will render the work *facile* and delightful. —Evelyn.

2. Easy to be surmounted or removed; easily conquerable.

> The *facile* gates of hell too slightly barred. —Milton.

3. Easy of access or converse; mild; courteous; not haughty, austere, or distant.

> I mean she should be courteous, *facile*, sweet. —Jonson.

4. Pliant; flexible; easily persuaded to good or bad; yielding; ductile to a fault.

> Since Adam, and his *facile* consort Eve,
> Lost Paradise, deceived by me. —Milton.

5. Ready; skilful; dexterous; quick; as, a *facile* artist; a *facile* pen.

fac′ile-ly, *adv.* In a facile manner; easily. [Rare.]

fac′ile-ness, *n.* The state or quality of being facile. [Rare.]

fā-cil′i-tāte, *v.t.*; facilitated, *pt.*, *pp.*; facilitating, *ppr.* [Fr. *faciliter*, to facilitate, from L. *facilitas* (*-atis*), facility, from *facilis*, easy.] To make easy or less difficult; to free from difficulty or impediment; to lessen the labor of; as, machinery *facilitates* manual labor.

fā-cil-i-tā′tion, *n.* The act of making easy.

fā-cil′i-ty, *n.*; *pl.* **fā-cil′i-tieṣ**. [L. *facilitas* (*-atis*), easiness, from *facilis*, easy.]

1. The quality of being easily done; freedom from difficulty; ease.

> Though *facility* and hope of success might invite some other choice. —Bacon.

2. Ease of performance; readiness proceeding from skill or use; dexterity; as, practice gives a wonderful *facility* in executing works of art.

3. Pliancy; easiness to be persuaded; readiness of compliance, usually in a bad sense, implying a disposition to yield to solicitations to evil.

> It is a great error to take *facility* for good nature. —L'Estrange.

4. Easiness of access; complaisance; condescension; affability.

> He offers himself to the visits of a friend with *facility*. —South.

5. The means by which the performance of anything is rendered easy; convenient opportunity or advantage; aid; help; usually in the plural.

Syn.—Expertness, readiness.—*Facility* supposes a natural or acquired power of despatching a task with lightness and dexterity; *expertness* is *facility* acquired by long-continued practice; *readiness* marks the promptitude with which anything is done.

fā′cing, *n.* 1. A covering in front for ornament, distinction, protection, defense, or other purpose; as, (a) in architecture, the thin covering of polished stone over an inferior stone, or the stratum of plaster or cement on a brick or rough stone wall; (b) in joinery, the woodwork which is fixed round apertures in interiors, to ornament them or to protect the plaster from injury; (c) in engineering, a layer of earth, turf, or stone laid upon the bottom and sloping sides of a canal, railway, reservoir, etc., to protect the exposed surface or to give it a steeper slope than what is natural; (d) the trimmings on the front of a regimental jacket or coat, by which one regiment is usually distinguished from another, used in the plural; that part of the lining of a garment which is in any way exposed to view.

2. In founding, powder applied to the face of a mold which receives the metal, to give a smooth surface to the casting.

3. A mode of adulterating tea by mixing it with coloring-matter and other substances so as to cause it to resemble tea of a better quality and a higher value than the original unfaced tea; also, the materials used in this process of adulteration.

4. The movement of soldiers in turning round to the right, left, etc.

fā′cing-ly, *adv.* In a facing position.

fa-cin′ō-rous, *a.* Atrociously wicked. [Obs.]

fa-cin′ō-rous-ness, *n.* Extreme or atrocious wickedness. [Obs.]

fac′ound, *a.* and *n.* [Obs.] Same as *Facund*.

faç-sim′i-lē, *n.* [L. *factum simile*, made like; *factum*, neut. of *factus*, pp. of *facere*, to make, and *simile*, neut. of *similis*, like.] An exact copy or likeness, as of handwriting.

faç-sim′i-lē, *a.* 1. Exactly reproduced or similar; as, a *facsimile* engraving.

2. Producing or intended to produce facsimiles.

Facsimile telegraph; a telegraphic apparatus which reproduces at the receiving end of the line an autograph copy of the message written at the transmitting end.

faç-sim′i-lē, *v.t.* To make a facsimile of. [Rare.]

fact, *n.* [L. *factum*, that which is done, a deed, fact, neut. of *factus*, pp. of *facere*, to do, act.]

1. Anything done; an act; a deed. [Obs.]

2. Reality; truth; actuality; a true account; as, in *fact*, he never came.

3. Something declared to have happened, or to have existed; the assertion of something as existing or done; a loose use of the word; as, he depends upon his imagination for his *facts*; there are many false *facts* in his report.

4. In law, something that has taken place, either actually or by supposition, distinguished from a purely legal result.

Accessory before or *after the fact*; see *Accessory*, n. 1.

fac′tȧ, *n.*, pl. of *factum*.

fac′tion, *n.* [Fr. *faction*; L. *factio* (*-onis*), a making, doing, company, faction, from *factus*, pp. of *facere*, to do, make.]

1. A number of persons having a common end in view; especially a party within a party seeking to further its own ends, often by unscrupulous methods; used especially of political parties but applied to any society or association of people.

> By a *faction*, I understand a number of citizens, whether amounting to a majority or minority of the whole, who are united and actuated by some common impulse of passion, or of interest, adverse to the rights of other citizens, or to the permanent and aggregate interests of the community. —Madison.

2. Tumult; discord; dissension.

3. In Roman antiquity, one of the different troops or companies of combatants in the games of the circus.

fac'tion-ā-ry, *a.* Factious; zealous; partizan. [Obs.]

fac'tion-ēr, *n.* One of a faction. [Obs.]

fac'tion-ist, *n.* One who promotes faction.

fac'tious (fak'shus), *a.* [L. *factiosus*, lit., fond of doing, powerful, of or for a party or factions, from *factio* (-*onis*), a faction.]

1. Given to faction; addicted to form parties and raise dissensions, in opposition to government; turbulent; prone to clamor against public measures or men; as, no state is free from *factious* citizens.

2. Pertaining to faction; proceeding from faction; as, *factious* tumults; *factious* quarrels.

fac'tious-ly, *adv.* In a factious manner.

fac'tious-ness, *n.* The state or quality of being factious; disposition to clamor and raise opposition.

fac-ti'tious (-tish'us), *a.* [L. *facticius*, artificial, factitious, from *factus*, pp. of *facere*, to do.] Made by art, in distinction from what is produced by nature; artificial; as, *factitious* stones; *factitious* air.

Syn.—Unnatural.—A thing is *unnatural* when it departs in any way from its simple or normal state; it is *factitious* when it is wrought out or wrought up by labor and effort.

fac-ti'tious-ly, *adv.* In a factitious or artificial manner.

fac-ti'tious-ness, *n.* The state or condition of being factitious.

fac'ti-tive, *a.* [L. *factus*, pp. of *facere*, to do.]

1. Causing; causative; effective.

2. In grammar, pertaining to that relation existing between two words, as between an active transitive verb and its object, when the action of the verb produces a new condition in the object.

fac'tive, *a.* Making; having power to make. [Obs.]

fac'tŏr, *n.* [L. *factor*, a doer, maker, performer, from *facere*, to do, make.]

1. One acting for another; an agent; specifically, a commission-merchant.

2. One of several circumstances, influences, elements, or causes which produce a result.

3. In mathematics, one of the two or more numbers, elements, or quantities, which when multiplied together form a given product; as, 7 and 3 are *factors* of 21.

4. A steward, bailiff, agent, or caretaker of an estate. [Scot.]

5. In biology, the latent physical units which when crossed produce the new characters found in the hybrid.

fac'tŏr, *v.t.*; factored, *pt.*, *pp.*; factoring, *ppr.*

1. To manage as an agent; to act as factor for. [Scot.]

2. In mathematics, to resolve into factors.

fac'tŏr-āge, *n.* The allowance given to a factor by his employer, as a compensation for his services; called also a *commission.*

fac'tŏr-ess, *n.* A woman factor.

fac-tō'ri-ăl, *a.* 1. Pertaining to a factory.

2. In mathematics, of or pertaining to factorials.

fac-tō'ri-ăl, *n.* In mathematics, a term proposed by Arbogast for the different cases of the symbol $x^{\frac{n}{a}}$.

fac'tŏr-īze, *v.t.*; factorized, *pt.*, *pp.*; factorizing, *ppr.* In United States law, to garnishee or attach the money or effects of.

fac'tŏr-ship, *n.* 1. A body of factors.

2. The business of a factor.

fac'tō-ry, *n.*; *pl.* **fac'tō-ries**. [Fr. *factorie*, a factory; LL. *factoria*, a treasury, from L. *factor*, a doer, maker.]

1. An establishment for the manufacture of goods, including the necessary buildings and machinery; a manufacturing plant.

2. A house or place where factors reside, to transact business for their employers; as, the English merchants have *factories* in the East Indies, Turkey, Portugal, Hamburg, etc.

3. The body of factors in any place; as, a chaplain to a British *factory.*

Factory cotton; a cloth of unbleached cotton manufactured in the United States.

fac-tō'tum, *n.* [L. *fac totum*, lit., do everything; *fac*, imper. of *facere*, to do, and *totum*, neut. of *totus*, all, the whole.] A person employed to do all kinds of work.

fac'tū-ăl, *a.* Pertaining to or consisting of facts; literal; exact; genuine. [Rare.]

fac'tum, *n.*; *pl.* **fac'tȧ**. [L., neut. of *factus*, pp. of *facere*, to do.]

1. An act; a deed accomplished; a fact.

2. In law, a deed or a grant or claim which has been sealed.

3. In mathematics, a product.

fac'tūre, *n.* [Fr. *facture*; L. *factura*, a making, from *factus*, pp. of *facere*, to do.]

1. The art or manner of making; construction. [Rare.]

2. In commerce, an invoice.

fac'ū-lȧ, *n.*; *pl.* **fac'ū-læ**. [L., dim. of *fax* (*facis*), a torch.] A small shining spot on the sun's surface, brighter than the rest of the photosphere.

fac'ū-lăr, *a.* Of, pertaining to, or resembling a facula.

fac'ul-tā-tive, *a.* [L. *facultas* (-*atis*), faculty, ability.]

1. Importing or conferring a faculty, right, or power; qualifying.

2. Endowing with power or authority but not making its exercise obligatory; rendering optional; contingent.

Facultative parasite; an organism, usually a fungus, which in its normal state is a saprophyte, but which is capable of developing as a parasite.

Facultative saprophyte; an organism, usually a fungus, which in its normal state is a parasite, but which is capable, during part of its development, of growing as a saprophyte.

fac'ul-tā-tive-ly, *adv.* In a facultative manner.

fac'ul-ty, *n.*; *pl.* **fac'ul-ties**. [ME. *faculte*; OFr. *faculte*; L. *facultas* (-*atis*), ability, capability, power, means, from *facul*, *facilis*, easy.]

1. That power of the mind or intellect which enables it to receive, revive, or modify perceptions; as, the *faculty* of seeing, of hearing, of imagining, of remembering.

2. Facility of performance; the peculiar skill derived from practice, or practice aided by nature; habitual skill or ability; dexterity; adroitness; knack; as, one man has a remarkable *faculty* of telling a story.

3. Power; authority. [Rare.]

4. In the Roman Catholic church, a privilege; a right or power granted to a person by favor or indulgence, to do what by law he may not do; specifically, an authorization by a superior bestowing ecclesiastical rights upon a subordinate; often used in the plural.

5. The individuals constituting a scientific profession, or a branch of one, taken collectively; especially, the medical profession.

6. Collectively, the masters and professors of the several departments of a university, or any one of the departments; as, the *faculty* of arts, of theology, of medicine, or of law.

fac'und, *a.* and *n.* I. *a.* Eloquent; fluent. [Obs.]

II. *n.* Eloquence; fluency of speech. [Obs.]

fa-cun'di-ous, *a.* [Obs.] Same as *Facund.*

fa-cun'di-ty, *n.* Eloquence; readiness of speech. [Obs.]

fad, *n.* [Eng. dial.] A whim, hobby, or fancy, adopted and pursued, for a time, with undue zeal; a passing fashion, as in dress, social diversions, etc.; as, her *fad* is collecting old silver; sailor hats are all the *fad* again.

fad'dist, *n.* One who is enthusiastic over a fad or whim.

fad'dle, *v.i.* To trifle; to toy; to play. [Prov. Eng.]

fāde, *a.* [Fr.] 1. Stale; insipid; flat; as, a *fade* conversation.

2. Faded. [Obs.]

fāde, *v.i.*; faded, *pt.*, *pp.*; fading, *ppr.* [ME. *faden*; OFr. *fader*, to become pale or weak, fade, from *fade*, pale, from L. *fatuus*, foolish, silly.]

1. To wither, as a plant; to lose strength, health, or vigor gradually; to decay; to perish gradually.

> The flower ripens in its place,
> Ripens, and *fades*, and falls. —Tennyson.

2. To lose freshness, color, or brightness; to tend from a stronger or brighter color to a more faint shade of the same color, or to lose color entirely; to grow dim or indistinct; to disappear gradually.

> Adieu, adieu! my native shore
> *Fades* o'er the waters blue. —Byron.

Syn.—Fall, fail, decline, sink, droop, dwindle, vanish, change, pale, bleach, etiolate.

fāde, *v.t.* To cause to wither; to wear away; to deprive of freshness or vigor.

> No winter could his laurels *fade.*—Dryden.

fād'ed, *a.* Having become less vivid, as color; withered; decayed; vanished.

fād'ed-ly, *adv.* In a faded manner.

fāde'less, *a.* Unfading.

fāde'less-ly, *adv.* In a fadeless manner.

fā'dēr, *n.* Father. [Obs.]

fadġe (faj), *v.i.* [AS. *fegan*, *gefegan*, to fit, to compact.] To suit; to fit; to come close, as the parts of things united; hence, to have one part consistent with another. [Obs.]

fād'ing, *a.* and *n.* I. *a.* Losing color; becoming less vivid; decaying; declining; withering.

II. *n.* Decay; loss of color, freshness, or vigor.

fad'ing, *n.* An Irish dance and the refrain of a song. [Obs.]

fād'ing-ly, *adv.* In a fading manner.

fād'ing-ness, *n.* Decay; liableness to decay.

fād'me, *n.* A fathom. [Obs.]

fād'y, *a.* Wearing away; losing color or strength. [Rare.]

fæ'căl, *a.* Same as *Fecal.*

fæ'cēs, *n.pl.* Same as *Feces.*

fæc'ū-lȧ, *n.* Same as *Fecula.*

fā'ēr-ie, **fā'ēr-y**, *a.* and *n.* [Obs.] Same as *Fairy.*

faf'fle, *v.i.* To stammer. [Obs.]

fag, *v.i.*; fagged, *pt.*, *pp.*; fagging, *ppr.* [Etym. uncertain, compare LG. *fakk*, wearied; Scot. *faik*, AS. *fægan*, to fail, stop.]

1. To drudge; to labor to weariness.

2. To act as a fag; to do drudgery for another.

3. To become weary; to fail in strength. [Obs.]

Syn.—Work, toil, slave, drudge.

fag, *v.t.* 1. To use or treat as a fag; to require or compel to do drudgery for one's own benefit.

2. To exhaust; to make weary by labor; usually with *out*; as, he is *fagged out* with his hard study.

3. To beat. [Obs.]

fag, *n.* 1. A laborious drudge; a drudge for another; specifically, in certain English public schools, as Eton, Harrow, Winchester, and Rugby, a boy who does menial services for another boy of a higher form or class.

2. Anything which wearies and fatigues; a wearisome task.

fag, *n.* [Etym. uncertain; compare Ice. *flakkia*; O.H.G. *flacken*, to flutter, flag.]

1. A knotty, coarse, or imperfect part in the web of a cloth.

2. The fag-end.

fag'-end', *n.* 1. The end of a web of cloth, generally of coarser materials.

2. The refuse or meaner part of anything; the very end; used in contempt.

3. Among seamen, the untwisted end of a rope.

fag'ging, *n.* Laborious drudgery; the acting as a drudge for another at an English school.

Fag-ō-pȳ'rum, *n.* [L., from *fagus*, the beech-tree, and Gr. *pyros*, wheat.] A small genus of annual plants of the buckwheat family, native to central Asia. Two species, *Fagopyrum esculentum* or common buckwheat, and *Fagopyrum Tataricum* or Indian or Tatarian buckwheat, have been introduced into the United States and are cultivated for food.

fag'ŏt, **fag'gŏt**, *n.* [ME. *fagott*; OFr. *fagot*, a bundle of sticks, prob. from L. *fax*, *facis*, a torch.]

1. A bundle of sticks, twigs, or small branches of trees, used for fuel or for raising batteries, filling ditches, and other purposes in fortification; a fascine.

2. A bundle of pieces of iron for remanufacture, or of steel in bars.

3. A person formerly hired to take the place of another at the muster of a military company or to hide deficiency in its number when it was not full. [Eng.]

4. A term of contempt for a dry, shriveled old woman. [Eng. Slang.]

5. The punishment of burning at the stake, as for heresy.

6. A badge representing a *fagot*, worn on the sleeve in the middle ages by those who had recanted heresy, to show the punishment they had so narrowly escaped.

fag'ŏt, **fag'gŏt**, *v.t.* To tie together; to bind in a bundle; to collect promiscuously.

fag'ŏt-ī''ron (-ī''ŭrn), *n.* Iron manufactured from fagots.

fa-got'tō, *n.* [It., so called from its resemblance to a fagot or bundle of sticks.] A musical wind-instrument with a reed and mouthpiece like the clarinet and resembling the bassoon. The *alto-fagotto* has a range of three octaves, rising from C in the second space of the bass clef. It is so called from its being able to be taken to pieces and made up into a bundle like a small fagot, for convenience of carriage.

Fagotto.

fag'ŏt-vōte, *n.* In Great Britain, a vote procured by the purchase of property under mortgage or otherwise, so as to constitute a nominal qualification without a substantial basis.

fag'ŏt-vōt''ēr, *n.* One who holds or exercises a fagot-vote.

Fā'gus, *n.* [L. *fagus*, the beech-tree.] A genus of trees, the beeches, of the order *Cupuliferæ.* There are about twenty species distributed over the temperate regions of the world. They are trees with close, smooth, ash-gray bark, and simple straight-veined leaves.

fā'hăm (fā'ăm), **fā'ăm**, *n.* [Native African name.] An orchid, *Angræcum fragrans*, having fragrant leaves from which a tea, used in diseases of the stomach and lungs, is made.

fähl'händ (fäl'bänt), *n.* [G. *fahl*, pale, and *band*, a band.] A stratum of rock named from the pale, dull color it has from the disintegration of the sulphids contained in it.

fähl'ērz, **fähl'ōre**, *n.* Same as *Tetrahedrite.*

fäh'lun-ite, *n.* [Named from *Fahlun*, in Sweden.] A hydrous form of iolite.

Fäh'ren-heit, *a.* [Named from its inventor,

Gabriel Daniel *Fahrenheit*, who made the first instrument in Amsterdam about 1720.] Of or conforming to the scale established by the German physicist, Gabriel Daniel Fahrenheit, for the graduation of the thermometer stem. The Fahrenheit thermometer, which is the standard in the United States and Great Britain, places the freezing point of water at 32 degrees above zero and the boiling point of water at 212 degrees above zero.

fâ-i-ence′ (fâ-yäns′), *n.* [Fr. *faïence*; It. *faenza*, from *Faenza* in Romagna, Italy, the original place of its manufacture.] In the fine arts, imitation porcelain; a kind of fine pottery embellished with painted designs; said to have first been made near the close of the thirteenth century.

fāil, *v.i.*; failed, *pt.*, *pp.*; failing, *ppr.* [ME. *failen*; OFr. *faillir*, to fail, miss; L. *fallere*, to deceive, disappoint.]

1. To become deficient; to be insufficient; to cease to be abundant for supply; to be entirely wanting; as, the crops *failed*; our ammunition *failed*.

2. To decline; to sink; to become weaker; as, the invalid *fails* daily.

3. To miss; not to produce the effect; to miscarry; to be frustrated or disappointed; to be unsuccessful; as, the experiment was made with care, but *failed*; the attack *failed*; the enemy *failed*.

4. To be deficient in duty; to omit or neglect; as, he *failed* to fulfil his promise.

5. To become insolvent or bankrupt; to make an assignment; to quit business because of inability to meet one's debts and fulfil one's business obligations.

6. To be extinct; to cease; to be entirely wanting; to be no longer produced. [Obs.]

> Help, Lord, for the godly man ceaseth; for the faithful *fail* from among the children of men. —Ps. xii. 1.

fāil, *v.t.* 1. To desert; to disappoint; to cease or to neglect or omit to afford aid, supply, or strength to; as, fortune never *fails* the brave.

2. To omit; not to perform. [Rare.]

> The inventive God, who never *fails* his part. —Dryden.

3. Not to attain or reach to; to come short of; to fail of. [Obs.]

> Though that seat of earthly bliss be *failed*. —Milton.

4. To deceive; to cheat. [Obs.]

fāil, *n.* 1. Omission; nonperformance.

> He will without *fail* drive out from before you the Canaanites. —Josh. iii. 10.

2. Death. [Obs.]

Without fail; without doubt; certainly; assuredly.

fāil′ānce, *n.* Fault; failure. [Obs.]

fāil′ing, *n.* 1. The act of becoming deficient; imperfection; lapse; fault.

2. The act of becoming insolvent.

Syn.—Fault, foible, weakness.—A *fault* is positive, something definite and marked which impairs excellence; a *failing* is negative, some weakness in a man's character, disposition, or habit; a *foible* is a less important weakness, which we overlook or smile at. A man may have many *failings*, and yet commit but few *faults*; or, his *faults* and *failings* may be few, while his *foibles* are obvious to all.

faille (fāl), *n.* [Fr.] A silk fabric with a very light, untwilled cord and no gloss.

fāil′ūre, *n.* 1. A failing; deficiency; cessation of supply, or total defect; as, the *failure* of springs or streams; *failure* of rain; *failure* of crops.

2. Omission; nonperformance; as, the *failure* of a promise.

3. Decay, or defect from decay; as, the *failure* of memory or of sight.

4. A becoming insolvent or bankrupt; as, there were many *failures* that year.

5. One not successful; usually specifically applied; as, she was an utter *failure* as an actress.

6. A failing; a slight fault. [Obs.]

fāin, *a.* [ME. *fain*, *fayn*, *fæin*; AS. *fægen*, to be glad.]

1. Glad; pleased; rejoiced.

2. Content or willing to accept an alternative when the more desirable thing cannot be attained; followed by an infinitive; as, he was *fain to eat* whatever he could get.

fāin, *adv.* Gladly; with joy or pleasure; with *would*.

> He *would fain* have filled his belly with the husks that the swine did eat.—Luke xv. 16.

fāin, *v.t.* 1. To wish or desire.

2. To make glad.

fāin, *v.i.* To be glad; to rejoice.

fāi′ne-ānce, *n.* Idling; laziness.

fāi-né-ānt′ (fā-nā-oṅ′), *a.* and *n.* [Fr., idle, lazy; *faire*, to do, and *néant*, nothing.]

I. *a.* Lazy; shiftless; useless.

II. *n.* An idler; a sluggard.

fāin′head, *n.* Gladness. [Obs.]

fāint, *a.*; *comp.* fainter; *superl.* faintest. [ME. *faynt*, *feynt*, weak; OFr. *feint*, *faint*, feigned, negligent, sluggish, pp. of *feindre*, *faindre*, to pretend, from L. *fingere*, to touch, handle, feign.]

1. Weak; feeble; languid; exhausted; inclined to swoon; as, *faint* with fatigue, hunger, or thirst.

2. Weak; not bright or vivid; not strong; as, a *faint* color; a *faint* sound; a *faint* recollection.

3. Cowardly; timorous; as, a *faint* heart never wins a fair lady.

4. Feeble; not vigorous; not active; as, a *faint* resistance; a *faint* exertion.

5. Dejected; depressed; dispirited.

> My heart is *faint*. —Lam. i. 22.

Syn.—Weak, languid, fatigued, unenergetic, timid, irresolute, feeble, exhausted, obscure, half-hearted, dim, pale, faded, inconspicuous.

fāint, *n.* 1. The act of fainting or the state of one who faints; swoon; syncope; sudden loss of consciousness, with feeble respiration and heart action.

2. [*pl.*] The impure spirit which comes over first and last in the distillation of whisky, the former being called the *strong*, and the latter, which is much more abundant, the *weak faints*. This crude spirit is much impregnated with fetid essential oil (fusel-oil); it is therefore very unwholesome, and must be purified by rectification.

fāint, *v.i.*; fainted, *pt.*, *pp.*; fainting, *ppr.* [ME. *fainten*, from OFr. *feindre*, to feign, work negligently.]

1. To lose sensation and consciousness; to swoon; sometimes with *away*; as, he *fainted* from loss of blood.

> On hearing the honor intended her, she *fainted away*. —Guardian.

2. To become feeble; to decline or fail in strength and vigor; to be weak.

> If I send them away fasting to their own houses, they will *faint* by the way. —Mark viii. 3.

3. To sink into dejection; to lose courage or spirit.

> Let not your hearts *faint*. —Deut. xx. 3.

4. To decay; to disappear; to vanish; to fade.

> Gilded clouds, while we gaze on them, *faint* before the eye. —Pope.

fāint, *v.t.* To deject; to depress; to weaken. [Obs.]

fāint′-heärt″ed, *a.* Cowardly; timorous; dejected; easily depressed, or yielding to fear.

> Fear not, neither be *faint-hearted*.—Isa. vii. 4.

fāint′-heärt″ed-ly, *adv.* In a cowardly manner.

fāint′-heärt″ed-ness, *n.* Cowardice; timorousness; want of courage.

fāint′ing, *n.* A faint; syncope; a swoon.

fāint′ish, *a.* Slightly faint.

fāint′ish-ness, *n.* A slight degree of faintness.

fāint′ling, *a.* Timorous; feeble-minded. [Obs.]

fāint′ly, *adv.* In a faint manner; feebly; languidly; timorously.

fāint′ness, *n.* The state or quality of being faint; dejection; timorousness; want of strength, brightness, vividness, etc.

fāint′y, *a.* Weak; feeble; languid. [Rare.]

fāir, *a.*; *comp.* fairer; *superl.* fairest. [ME. *fair*, *fayr*; AS. *fæger*, beautiful, pleasant, fair.]

1. Of a light color; not dark or dusky; clear; not discolored; as, a *fair* complexion; *fair* hair.

2. Pleasing to the eye; handsome, beautiful, or comely; as, a *fair* woman; a *fair* landscape.

> Thou art a *fair* woman to look upon. —Gen. xii. 11.

3. Free from stain or blemish; unspotted; untarnished; pure; free from anything which might impair the appearance, quality, or character; as, a *fair* character; a *fair* name; a *fair* copy; *fair* water; a *fair* cloth.

4. Open; frank; honest; hence, equal; just; equitable; impartial; as, his offer is *fair*.

5. Moderately or passably good, but not excellent; free from serious defects; nearly or fully up to the average; as, he gets a *fair* salary; he has a *fair* reputation.

6. Open to attack or access; unobstructed; free from obstacles; distinct; positive; direct; as, a *fair* aim; in *fair* sight; a *fair* view.

7. Honest; honorable; mild; opposed to *insidious* and *compulsory*; as, to accomplish a thing by *fair* means.

8. Frank; civil; pleasing; not harsh; sometimes in a bad sense, flattering; deceitful; as, the treacherous friend spoke *fair* words.

> When *fair* words and good counsel will not prevail on us, we must be frighted into our duty. —L'Estrange.

9. Characterized by favorable conditions; admitting of ample facilities or advantages; as, you are in a *fair* way to promotion; a *fair* subject of ridicule.

10. Comparatively favorable; passably clear or good; specifically, in the United States Weather Bureau, designating a sky which is neither clear nor cloudy, but is from fourtenths to seven-tenths covered with clouds.

11. In sports, according to the rules of the game; specifically, in baseball, said of a ball (a) which is properly delivered to the batsman or, (b) fairly batted; latter called a *fair hit*.

12. A term applied to goods, conditions or institutions sanctioned by labor-unions.

A fair field; an even chance or opportunity.

Fair and square; honest; without deceit; honorable; often used adverbially.

Fair play; a fair chance; impartiality; honorable dealing; justice.

Fair to middling; moderately good or satisfactory; used in commerce to designate a specific grade or quality of a commodity.

The fair sex; women.

Syn.—Honest, equitable, reasonable, open, frank, clear, impartial, candid, beautiful, just, pure.—*Fair* is said of persons or things; *honest* mostly characterizes the person, either as to his conduct or his principle. When *fair* and *honest* are both applied to the external conduct, the former expresses more than the latter; a man may be *honest* without being *fair*; he cannot be *fair* without being *honest*. *Fair* and *equitable* suppose two objects put in collision; *reasonable* is employed abstractedly; what is *fair* and *equitable* is so in relation to all circumstances; what is *reasonable* is so of itself.

fāir, *adv.* [ME. *faire*, *fayre*; AS. *fægere*, *fægre*, beautifully, pleasantly, from *fæger*, fair.]

1. Politely; frankly; civilly; complaisantly.

2. Candidly; honestly; equitably; as, I shall deal *fair* with him.

3. Happily; successfully.

4. On good terms; as, to keep *fair* with the world; to stand *fair* with one's companions.

To bid fair; see under *Bid*.

fāir, *n.* 1. Beauty. [Obs.]

2. A woman; especially, a beautiful woman or a beloved one; a sweetheart. [Obs.]

The fair; women collectively; especially, young and beautiful women.

fāir, *v.t.* [ME. *fayren*, to make beautiful; AS. *fægrian*, to become beautiful, *afægrian*, to make beautiful, from *fæger*, beautiful, fair.]

1. To make fair or beautiful.

> *Fairing* the foul with art's false borrow'd face. —Shak.

2. To adjust; to make regular; to form into correct shape; specifically, in nautical language, to clip regularly, as the timbers of a ship.

fāir, *v.i.* To clear up, applied to the atmosphere in reference to preceding rain; to cease raining. [Scot.]

fāir, *n.* [ME. *feire*, *feyre*; OFr. *feire*; LL. *feria*, a fair, a holiday; L. *feriæ*, nom. pl., feast days, holidays.]

1. A stated market in a particular town or city; a stated meeting of buyers and sellers for trade, either annual or more frequent. Among the most celebrated *fairs* in Europe are those of Frankfort and Leipzig in Germany, of Nizhni Novgorod in Russia; of Lyons and St. Germain in France.

2. An exhibition and sale of articles for some special purpose; a bazaar; a festival; as, a church *fair*.

3. An occasional or periodical joint exhibition of articles or products, more for the sake of inspection than for sale; as, an agricultural *fair*; the world's *fair*.

After the fair or *the day after the fair*; too late. [Colloq.]

fāir′-fāced (-fāst), *a.* 1. Comely; having a fair face.

2. Two-faced; deceitful; hypocritical in professing affection and kindness; treacherous.

fāir′-ground, *n.* The inclosure in which a fair is held. [U. S.]

fāir′-hāired, *a.* Having fair hair.

fāir′hood, *n.* Fairness; beauty. [Obs.]

fāir′ieṣ′-hoṛse, *n.* An Irish name for the ragwort, *Senecio Jacobæus*.

fāir′ieṣ′-tā″ble, *n.* 1. A popular name in the north of Wales for the common mushroom, *Agaricus campestris*, and similar fungi.

2. The pennywort, *Hydrocotyle vulgaris*.

fāir′i-ly, *adv.* In a fairylike manner; in a fashion suggestive of fairies.

fāir′ing, *n.* A present, especially one brought from or given at a fair.

fāir′-lēad″ẽr, *n.* In nautical language, (a) a thimble or cringle to guide a rope; (b) a strip of board with holes in it, for running-rigging to pass through and be kept clear, so as to be easily distinguished at night.

fāir′ly, *adv.* [ME. *fayrely*, from *fair*; AS. *fæger*, fair, beautiful.]

1. Frankly; honestly; justly; equitably; without disguise, fraud, or prevarication; as, the question was *fairly* stated and argued; let us deal *fairly* with all men.

2. Commodiously; conveniently; as, a town *fairly* situated for foreign trade.
3. Softly; gently. [Obs.]
4. Beautifully; handsomely.
5. Completely; evidently; beyond a doubt; as, his antagonist fought till he was *fairly* defeated.
6. Moderately; passably; reasonably; as, the book is *fairly* good.

fāir′=māid, *n.* 1. The dried pilchard. [Prov. Eng.]
2. The porgy or scup. [Local, U. S.]

fāir′=māids′=of=Feb′rū-ā-ry, *n.* A flower, the snowdrop.

fāir′=māids′=of=Frânce′, *n.* One of various flowers, as, (a) *Ranunculus aconitifolius*, the crowfoot; (b) meadow saxifrage; (c) ragged-robin.

fāir′=mīnd″ed, *a.* Just; upright; unprejudiced; impartial.

fāir′=mīnd″ed-ness, *n.* The quality or character of being fair-minded.

fāir′=nā′tūred, *a.* Good-natured; of a pleasant disposition.

fāir′ness, *n.* [ME. *fairnesse*; AS. *fægernes*, from *fæger*, beautiful.] The state, quality, or character of being fair, in any sense of the word.

fāir′=seem″ing, *a.* Appearing fair.

fāir′=spō″ken, *a.* Using fair speech; bland; civil; courteous; plausible.

fāir′wāy, *n.* The port of a river, bay, etc., through which vessels enter or depart.

fāir′=weath″ēr (-weth″), *a.* Existing or capable of existing in pleasant weather only; hence, figuratively, suited only to pleasant, comfortable surroundings; not capable of overcoming hardships or opposition; not willing to make sacrifices; as, a *fair-weather* friend; a *fair-weather* sailor.

fāir′=wōrld, *n.* Prosperity. [Obs.]

fāir′y, *n.*; *pl.* **fāir′ieṣ.** [ME. *fairye, fayry*, enchantment, the fairy folk; OFr. *faerie*, enchantment, from *fae*, a fairy.]
1. An imaginary being or spirit, usually represented as of small and dainty human form, but capable of changing to any form at will, and capable of and inclined to play pranks, either sportively or maliciously, and do good or evil to humans; a fay.
2. An enchantress. [Obs.]
3. Fairyland. [Obs.]
4. Illusion; magic. [Obs.]
5. Fays or fairies collectively. [Obs.]
Fairy of the mine; an imaginary being supposed to inhabit mines, wandering about in the drifts and chambers, always employed in cutting ore, turning the windlass, etc., yet effecting nothing. German folklore tells of two species, one fierce and malevolent, the other gentle.

fāir′y, *a.* Pertaining to or in some manner connected with fairies; coming from fairies; resembling a fairy; fanciful; as, *fairy* creatures; *fairy* money or favors.
Fairy beads; in geology, the small perforated and radiated joints of the fossil *Crinoidea*, sometimes called *St. Cuthbert's beads*, which occur in the shales and limestones of the carboniferous or mountain limestone formation.
Fairy ring or *circle*; a circular area having a growth of fungi which has killed the grass; popularly supposed to be the place of fairies' dances.
Fairy sparks; the phosphoric light from decaying wood, fish, and other substances; believed at one time to be lights prepared for the fairies at their revels.

fāir′y=bĩrd, *n.* A popular name in England for the least tern, *Sterna minuta.*

fāir′y=but″tēr, *n.* A common name in the north of England for certain fungi, as *Tremella albida* and *Exidia glandulosa*; so called because once believed to be made by the fairies in their dairy.

fāir′y=cups, *n.* A fungus, *Peziza coccinea*, which is bright red in color and shaped like a cup.

fāir′y=fin″gērṣ, *n.* The foxglove, *Digitalis purpurea.*

fāir′y-land, *n.* The imaginary land or abode of fairies.

fāir′y-līke, *a.* Of the nature of or resembling a fairy; suited to a fairy; delicate; dainty; as, *fairylike* music.

fāir′y=lōaf, *n.*; *pl.* **fāir′y=lōaveṣ.** A common name in England for a fossil sea-urchin.

fāir′y=mär″tin, *n.* An Australian swallow, *Hirundo ariel.*

fāir′y=shrimp, *n.* The *Chirocephalus diaphanus*, a beautiful species of phyllopodous crustacean, occurring occasionally in fresh-water ponds in Great Britain.

fāir′y=stōne, *n.* An echinite. [Prov. Eng.]

fāith, *n.* [ME. *faith, feith*; OFr. *feid*; L. *fides*, faith, belief, trust, from *fidere*, to trust, confide in.]
1. The assent of the mind to the truth of what is declared by another, resting on his authority and veracity, without other evidence, or on probable evidence of any kind; assent of the mind to a statement or proposition of another, on the ground of the manifest truth of such statement or proposition; firm and earnest belief, on probable evidence of any kind; as, I have strong *faith*, or no *faith*, in the testimony of a witness.
2. The assent of the mind to what is given forth as a revelation of man's relation to God and the infinite; a settled conviction in regard to religion; specifically, in Christian theology, (a) belief in the historic truthfulness of the Scripture narrative and the supernatural origin of its teaching; also called *historical* or *speculative faith*; (b) the assent of the mind to the truth of divine revelation, on the authority of God's testimony, accompanied by a cordial assent of the will or approbation of the heart; an entire confidence or trust in God's character and declarations, and in the character and doctrines of Christ, with an unreserved surrender of the will to his guidance, and dependence on his merits for salvation; also called *evangelical, justifying*, or *saving faith.*
3. The object of belief; a doctrine or system of doctrines believed, whether scientific, political, or religious; especially, a creed; a religious system; specifically, the Christian religion.

> They heard only, that he who persecuted us in times past, now preacheth the *faith* which once he destroyed. —Gal. i. 23.

4. Faithfulness; fidelity; a strict adherence to duty and fulfilment of promises.

> Her failing, while her *faith* to me remains,
> I would conceal. —Milton.

5. Word or honor pledged; promise given; fidelity; as, violated his plighted *faith.*

> For you alone
> I broke my *faith* with injured Palamon.
> —Dryden.

6. Credibility or truth. [Rare.]

> The *faith* of the foregoing narrative.
> —Mitford.

In good faith; in real honesty; with perfect sincerity; as, he fulfilled his engagements *in good faith.*
Punic or *Carthaginian faith*; bad faith; infidelity; perfidy; from the popular Roman belief concerning the people of Carthage.
Syn.—Belief, trust, confidence, credence, fidelity, conviction, creed, tenets, doctrine, opinion.

fāith, *interj.* Verily; by my faith; in truth. [Colloq.]

fāith′=brēach, *n.* Breach of fidelity; disloyalty; perfidy. [Rare.]

fāith′=cūre, *n.* The cure or alleged cure of bodily ills by means of prayer only and belief in its efficacy.

fāith′=cūr″ēr, *n.* One who practises, advocates, or believes in faith-cure.

fāithed (fātht), *a.* Honest; sincere. [Obs.]

fāith′fụl, *a.* 1. Full of faith; believing, strong or firm in one's faith.

> Be thou *faithful* to death, and I will give thee a crown of life. —Rev. ii. 10.

2. Firmly adhering to duty; of true fidelity; loyal; true to allegiance; constant in the performance of duties or services; loyal and firm in fidelity; constant; exact in attending to commands; as, a *faithful* servant; a *faithful* subject; a *faithful* husband or wife.
3. Observant of compact, treaties, contracts, vows, or other engagements; true to one's word; as, a government should be *faithful* to its treaties; individuals, to their word.
4. True; exact; in conformity to the letter and spirit; as, a *faithful* execution of a will; a *faithful* narrative or representation; a *faithful* likeness.
Syn.—True, firm, attached, loyal, accurate, close, consistent, correspondent, exact, equivalent, stanch, incorruptible.

fāith′fụl, *n.* One who is faithful.
The faithful; (a) in the early Christian church, those who had been received into the church as communicants; believers; this meaning is still used by the Roman Catholic and Anglican churches; (b) among Mohammedans, the followers of Mohammed; (c) in politics, the partizans who can be relied on by a party; often used contemptuously by other parties, to indicate that they are unreasoning and prejudiced.

fāith′fụl-ly, *adv.* In a faithful manner; loyally; sincerely; honestly; truthfully.

fāith′fụl-ness, *n.* The quality of being faithful; loyalty, constancy in affection; fidelity.

fāith′=hēal″ēr, *n.* One who heals or is supposed to heal by faith; a faith-curer.

fāith′=hēal″ing, *n.* Faith-cure.

fāith′less, *a.* 1. Without belief in the revealed truths of religion; unbelieving.

> O *faithless* generation. —Matt. xvii. 17.

2. Not adhering to allegiance or duty; disloyal; perfidious; treacherous; as, a *faithless* subject.
3. Not true to the marriage covenant; false; as, a *faithless* husband or wife.
4. Deceptive.

> Yonder *faithless* phantom. —Goldsmith.

fāith′less-ly, *adv.* In a faithless manner.

fāith′less-ness, *n.* The state or quality of being faithless.

fāi′tŏr, fāi′tŏur, *n.* An evil-doer; a scoundrel; a mean fellow. [Obs.]

fāke, *n.* In nautical language, one of the circles or windings of a cable or hawser, as it lies in a coil; a single turn or coil.

fāke, *v.t.*; faked (fākt), *pt., pp.*; faking, *ppr.* [ME. *faken*, to fold, from *vecka*, a fold.] To fold; specifically, in nautical language, to coil in fakes, as a rope, hawser, etc.

fāke, *n.* [Etym. uncertain, perhaps from Hind. *fakir*, a poor man, *fakr*, poverty.]
1. A trick; a swindle; a deception; specifically, in newspaper language, any false news intentionally published as real; as, the interview was pronounced a *fake.*
2. One who fakes; a swindler; a trickster.
3. Anything which is worthless or worn-out, especially in theatrical property; hence, any valueless or spurious article sold by street-venders.
4. Same as second *Faker*, 4.

fāke, *v.t.* 1. To cheat; to deceive. [Slang.]
2. To cover up defects in, usually with intent to deceive; as, to *fake* a dog by coloring its hair.
3. To furnish (something spurious) as though genuine; to palm off something inferior or worthless upon; specifically, (a) in theatrical parlance, to interpolate, as a speech or piece of business, especially in an emergency; also, to play, as an accompaniment, without previous preparation or knowledge; (b) to write and publish, as in a newspaper, without foundation or authority; as, to *fake* an interview; to *fake* a story.
4. To pick or rifle, as a pocket.

fāk′ēr, *n.* One who fakes; specifically, in the life-saving service, one whose duty it is to coil a rope or shot-line in the faking-box.

fāk′ēr, *n.* [Slang.] 1. A pickpocket; a petty thief.
2. A street-vender.
3. One who originates or takes part in a fake of any kind.
4. A hanger-on or dependent of the theatrical profession.

fāk′ing=box, *n.* In the life-saving service, a box in which ropes or shot-lines are coiled in such a way as to prevent tangling or knotting and facilitate uncoiling when needed.

fa-kïr′, *n.* [Ar. *fakir, faquir*, a poor man, from *fakr, faqr*, poverty.]
1. A Mohammedan ascetic or mendicant priest.
2. A Hindu ascetic; a yogi.

fa-kïr′iṣm, *n.* 1. The ascetic and austere practices of the Hindu devotees or fakirs.
2. Religious mendicancy, especially that among the Mohammedans.

fa-la-nā′kȧ, *n.* [Native name.] A viverrine carnivore, *Eupleres goudoti*, native to Madagascar.

fal-çāde′, *n.* [Fr. *falcade*, from L. *falcatus*, bent, from *falx* (*falcis*), a sickle.] The action of a horse when he throws himself on his haunches two or three times, as in very quick curvets.

fal′çāte, *a.* and *n.* [L. *falcatus*, bent, curved, from *falx* (*falcis*), a sickle.]
I. *a.* Hooked; bent like a sickle or scythe; falciform; used specifically in anatomy, zoölogy, and botany to designate organs or parts whose edges are sharp and curved and meet at a point.
II. *n.* A figure shaped like a sickle.

fal′çā-ted, *a.* Falcate; applied specifically to the moon when less than half its disk is illuminated.

fal-çā′tion, *n.* 1. The state of being falcate.
2. That which is falcate.

fal′chiŏn (*or* -shŭn), *n.* [OFr. *fauchon*, from L. *falx* (-*cis*), a sickle.] A broad, short sword, with a slightly curved point; hence, poetically, any sword.

> I've seen the day with my good biting *falchion*
> I would have made them skip: I am old now.
> —Shak.

Fal-cid′i-ăn, *a.* Of or pertaining to Publius Falcidius, who was a Roman tribune in 40 B. C.
Falcidian law; a law, the passage of which was procured by Falcidius, stipulating that at least one-fourth of a decedent's estate should go to the heir.

fal′ci-fọrm, *a.* [L. *falx* (*falcis*), a sickle, and *forma*, form.] In the shape of a sickle; resembling a reaping-hook.

fal′cŏn (fa′kn *or* fal′kn), *n.* [ME. *faucon, faukon*; OFr. *faucon, falcun*; LL. *falco* (-*onis*), a falcon, from L. *falx* (-*cis*), a sickle; so named on account of its curved beak and talons.]
1. In zoölogy, a member of the *Falconinæ*, a

subfamily of the *Falconidæ*, characterized by a short beak, curved from the base, and very long wings. The species most commonly used in falconry are the gerfalcon, *Falco gyrfalco*, and the peregrine falcon, *Falco peregrinus*. The former is regarded as the boldest and most beautiful of its family, and next to the eagle the most formidable, active, and intrepid of birds. The term *falcon* is by sportsmen restricted to the female, the male, which is smaller and less courageous, being called *tercel, tiercel*, or *tercelet*.

Peregrine Falcon (*Falco peregrinus*).

2. A sort of cannon used in former times.

fạl′cŏn-ẽr (fa′kn-ẽr *or* fal′kŏn-ẽr), *n.* [ME. *fauconer*; OFr. *fauconier*; LL. *falconarius*, a falconer, from *falco* (*-onis*), a falcon.] One who breeds and trains hawks for taking game; one who follows the sport of fowling with hawks.

fal′cō-net, *n.* 1. A small sixteenth-century cannon.

2. A little falcon; specifically, a finch-falcon of the genus *Ierax, Hierax*, or *Microhierax*.

3. A shrike of the genus *Falcunculus*.

fạl′cŏn=gen″tle (fa′kn-), **fạl′cŏn=gen″til,** *n.* The female and young of the goshawk, *Astur palumbarius*, of Europe.

Fal-con′i-dæ, *n.pl.* [L., from LL. *falco* (*-onis*), a falcon.] A family of raptorial birds or birds of prey, in which the destructive powers are most perfectly developed. The true falcons are inferior in size to the eagles and vultures, but they are of all birds the most symmetrical in their form, and the most daring in the capture of their prey, being also endowed with wonderful strength and powers of flight. The family includes the different species of eagles, the hawks, and falcons properly so called.

Fal-co-nī′næ, *n.pl.* A subfamily of the *Falconidæ*, comprising the falcons.

fal′cō-nine, *a.* and *n.* I. *a.* Of or pertaining to the family *Falconidæ* and especially the subfamily *Falconinæ*.

II. *n.* One of the *Falconidæ* or *Falconinæ*.

fal′cō-noid, *a.* Pertaining to the *Falconidæ*.

fạl′cŏn-ry (fa′kn-ry *or* fal′kŏn-ry), *n.* [OFr. *faulconnerie*, from LL. *falco* (*-onis*), a falcon.]

1. The art of training hawks to the exercise of hawking.

2. The practice of taking game by means of falcons or hawks.

fal′cō-pẽrn, *n.* A kite-falcon.

fal′cū-lȧ, *n.*; *pl.* **fal′cū-læ.** [L., dim. of *falx* (*falcis*), a sickle.] A compressed, curved claw with a sharp point, as that of a cat.

fal′cū-lāte, *a.* Shaped like a falcula.

fạld′āge, *n.* [LL. *faldagium*, from AS. *fald*, a fold.]

1. In old English law, a right of the lord of a manor to require a tenant to pasture his sheep on the lord's fields, a fold having been provided for them.

2. A fee which a tenant could pay to the lord of a manor in lieu of pasturing his sheep on the lord's fields.

fal-det′tȧ, *n.* [It.] An outer silk wrap worn by the women of Malta, combining a hood and cape.

fạld′fee, *n.* Same as *Faldage*, 2.

fạld′ing, *n.* A kind of coarse cloth. [Obs.]

fạl′dis-tŏr, fạl′dis-tō-ry, *n.* Same as *Faldstool*.

fạld′stool, *n.* [OFr. *faldestoel*; LL. *faldistolium*; O.H.G. *faltstuol*, lit., a folding stool; *faldan*, to fold, and *stuol*, a chair, stool.]

1. A folding stool similar to a camp-stool; especially, a kind of stool placed at the south side of the altar, at which the kings and queens of England kneel at their coronation; a folding stool, provided with a cushion, like a camp-stool, for a person to kneel on during the performance of certain acts of devotion.

Faldstool.

2. A small desk at which, in cathedrals, churches, etc., the litany is enjoined to be sung or said; also called *litany-stool* or *litany-desk*.

Fā-lẽr′ni-ăn, *a.* and *n.* [L. *Falernus*, a mountain in Campania.]

I. *a.* Of, pertaining to, or coming from a district (Falernus ager) in Campania, Italy, famous in ancient times for its excellent wine.

II. *n.* The wine made in ancient times in Falernus ager.

fạlk (fak), *n.* [Scot.] The razor-billed auk, *Alca torda*.

fạll, *v.i.*; fell, *pt.*; falling, *ppr.*; fallen, *pp.* [ME. *fallen*; AS. *feallan*, to fall, from the same root as D. *vallen*; Ice. *falla*, to fall; L. *fallere*, to deceive; Gr. *sphallein*, to cause to fall, to trick.]

1. To descend from a higher to a lower position, either suddenly or gradually, through loss or lack of support; to descend by the power of gravity; to drop down; to sink; to ebb; as, rain *falls* from the clouds; a man *falls* from his horse; ripe fruits *fall* from trees; water *falls* over the dam; the blow *fell* on his head.

> I beheld Satan as lightning *fall* from heaven. —Luke x. 18.

2. To sink; to be lowered; to settle or sink down; as, the mercury in a thermometer rises and *falls* with the increase and diminution of heat; the river *falls* during the dry season; the tide *falls*.

3. To drop from an erect posture; to become prostrate; as, the tree had *fallen*.

> I *fell* at his feet to worship him.—Rev. xix. 10.

4. To disembogue; to pass at the outlet; to flow out of its channel into a pond, lake, or sea, as a river; as, the Mississippi *falls* into the Gulf of Mexico.

5. To die, particularly by violence; to be slain; to come to ruin or destruction.

> A thousand shall *fall* at thy side.—Ps. xci. 7.

6. To pass into a new state of body or mind; to become; as, to *fall* asleep; to *fall* heir to an estate; to *fall* sick; to *fall* into rage or passion; to *fall* in love; to *fall* into temptation.

7. To pass or be transferred by chance, lot, natural classification, distribution, inheritance, or otherwise; as, the estate *fell* to his brother; unhappiness *fell* to her lot; the book *falls* under this classification.

8. To decline in power, wealth, or glory; to sink into weakness; to deteriorate; to decrease in amount, estimation, character, etc.; to be overthrown; to be degraded; to sink into disrepute or disgrace; to be plunged into misery; as, to *fall* from a high station or from a prosperous state; prices *fall*; to *fall* into disuse; to *fall* into bondage, etc.

> Heaven and earth will witness,
> If Rome must *fall*, that we are innocent.
> —Addison.

9. To come to pass; to occur; to befall; as, Christmas *fell* on a Sunday.

10. To come unexpectedly.

> It happened this evening that we *fell* into a pleasing walk. —Addison.

11. To depart from the faith or from rectitude; to sink into vice; to sin; to apostatize; as, Adam *fell* by eating the forbidden fruit.

12. To sink into dejection, discontent, anger, sorrow, or shame; to be downcast or dejected; as, his spirits *fell*; his face *fell* at the news.

> I have observed of late thy looks are *fallen*. —Addison.

13. To be brought forth; to be born; used especially of lambs; as, take care of lambs when they first *fall*.

14. To be dropped or uttered carelessly; as, an unguarded expression *fell* from his lips.

15. To hang; to droop; as, her gown *fell* about her in graceful folds.

To fall afoul of; to assail violently; to attack; also, to collide with, as a ship.

To fall among; to come upon unexpectedly and often against one's wish; as, he *fell among* thieves.

To fall astern; in nautical language, to move or be driven backward; to recede.

To fall away; (a) to lose flesh; to become lean or emaciated; to pine; (b) to decline gradually; to fade; to languish or become faint; (c) to renounce or desert the faith; to apostatize; to sink into wickedness.

To fall back; (a) to recede; to give way; (b) to fail of performing a promise or purpose; not to fulfil.

To fall back upon; to have recourse to some support or expedient, generally one formerly tried.

To fall behind; to be outstripped; to lose ground; to be left behind.

To fall calm; to cease to blow; to become calm.

To fall down; (a) to sink to the ground; (b) to prostrate oneself in worship; (c) in nautical language, to sail toward the mouth of a river; to drift down stream; (d) in slang, to fail; followed by *on*; as, she tried to do the work, but *fell down on* it.

To fall flat; to fail utterly to attract attention, admiration, purchasers, or any desired object; as, his boom *fell flat*; the book *fell flat*.

To fall from; to recede from; to depart; not to adhere to; as, to *fall from* an agreement or engagement.

To fall from grace; to lose standing; to backslide; to sin.

To fall home; (a) in mechanics, to drop or fall into the place intended; (b) in shipbuilding, to curve or incline inward from the perpendicular; said of the top-sides of a ship.

To fall in; (a) to come in; to join; to enter; to take one's place in an organized body of men, as soldiers; as, to *fall in* on the right; (b) to come to an end; to terminate; to lapse; as, an annuity *falls in* when the annuitant dies; (c) to sink; to form a hollow; as, her cheeks *fell in*; (d) to bend or sink inward; as, the cave *fell in*.

To fall into one's hands; to come into one's possession; to pass into one's control.

To fall in with; (a) to meet, often by chance, as a person or a ship; also, to discover or come near, as land; (b) to concur with; to agree with; to comply with; to yield to; as, the measure *falls in with* popular opinion.

To fall off; (a) to withdraw; to separate; to be broken or detached; to apostatize; to withdraw from the faith or from allegiance or duty; as, friends *fall off* in adversity; (b) to perish; to die away; to become disused; as, the custom *fell off*; (c) to drop; as, fruits *fall off* when ripe; (d) to become depreciated; to depart from former excellence; to become less valuable or interesting; to become less; to decline; to decrease; as, the magazine or the review *falls off*; the circulation of the paper is *falling off*; (e) in nautical language, to deviate or depart from the course directed, or to which the head of the ship was before directed; to fall to leeward.

To fall on; (a) to begin immediately and vigorously; (b) to attack; to assail; (c) to come upon, usually with some degree of suddenness and unexpectedness; to drop on; to descend on; as, fear *fell on* them; (d) to come upon; to discover; as, he *fell on* the plan by chance.

To fall on one's feet; to pass successfully through an adventure or predicament; from the ability of a cat to come down on its feet in falling.

To fall out; (a) to quarrel; to begin to contend; to become estranged; (b) to happen; to chance; (c) in nautical language, to lean or curve outward; to fall into the wrong place; opposite of *to fall home*; (d) in military language, to leave or drop out of the ranks.

To fall over; (a) to revolt; to desert from one side to another; (b) to fall beyond; (c) to become overturned.

To fall short; to be deficient; to fail to come up to a standard; as, the crops *fell short*; we all *fall short* in duty.

To fall through; to fail; to come to nothing; as, his plan *fell through*. [Colloq.]

To fall to; (a) to begin hastily and eagerly; as, he *fell to* as soon as his dinner was served; (b) to apply oneself to; to begin with haste, ardor, or vehemence; to rush or hurry to; as, they *fell to* blows; (c) to drop into position; to close.

To fall under; to come under or within the limits of; to become the subject of; to be ranged or reckoned under; as, they *fell under* the jurisdiction of the emperor; these substances *fall under* a different class or order.

To fall upon; (a) to attack; (b) to make trial of; to attempt.

fạll, *v.t.* 1. To let fall; to drop. [Obs.]

> For every tear he *falls*, a Trojan bleeds. —Shak.

2. To sink; to depress; as, to raise or *fall* the voice. [Obs.]

3. To diminish; to lessen or lower; as, to *fall* the price of commodities. [Rare.]

4. To bring forth; as, to *fall* lambs. [Rare.]

5. To fell; to cut down; as, to *fall* a tree. [Obs. or Colloq.]

6. To throw; to unseat, as a rider. [Colloq.]

fạll, *n.* 1. The act of dropping or descending from a higher to a lower place by gravity; descent; as, a *fall* from a horse; the *fall* of a piston; the *fall* of a meteor.

2. The act of dropping or tumbling from an erect posture; as, he was walking on ice and had a *fall*.

3. Death; destruction; overthrow.

4. Downfall; degradation; loss of office; declension of greatness, power, or dominion; ruin; as, the *fall* of the Roman Empire; the *fall* of Adam.

5. The surrender of a place in a state of siege; as, the *fall* of Richmond.

6. Diminution; decrease of price or value;

depreciation; as, the *fall* of stocks; the *fall* of rents.

7. In music and oratory, a sinking of tone; cadence; as, the *fall* of the voice at the close of a sentence.

8. Declivity; the descent of land or a hill; a slope.

9. Descent of water; a cascade; a cataract; a rush of water down a steep place; a waterfall; as, the *falls* of Niagara; the Horseshoe *falls*.

10. The outlet or discharge of a river or current of water into the ocean or into a sea or lake, etc.; as, the *fall* of the Po into the Gulf of Venice.

11. Extent of descent; the distance which anything falls; as, the stream has a *fall* of fifty feet to the mile.

12. That which falls; a falling; as, a *fall* of rain or snow.

13. The act of felling or cutting down; as, the *fall* of timber.

14. Same as *Falling band* under *Falling*.

15. That part of a hoisting-rope to which the power is applied.

16. Autumn, as the time when the leaves fall.

17. In botany, an outer and drooping division of the perianth in plants of the genus *Iris*.

18. In astrology, the part of the zodiac opposite the exaltation of a planet.

19. [*pl.*] Descent of a deck lengthwise from a fair curve, to add to the height of a cabin.

Fall and tackle; a block and tackle.

The fall of man or *the fall*; in theology, the lapse of the human race from a state of innocence into one of innate sinfulness or original sin, owing to the disobedience of Adam and Eve in the Garden of Eden, when they ate the forbidden apple.

The fall of the leaf; autumn; hence, figuratively, the time of decay or of failing power.

To try a fall; to have a bout at wrestling; hence, to make a test of strength or to contend in any manner.

fal-lā′cious, *a.* [L. *fallaciosus*, deceptive, from *fallacia*, deceit, deception, from *fallere*, to deceive.] Deceptive; deceitful; wearing a false appearance; misleading; producing error or mistake; sophistical; of the nature of, pertaining to, or embodying a fallacy.

Syn.—Deceitful, fraudulent, delusive, illusive, sophistical.—The *fallacious* has respect to falsehood in opinion; *deceitful* to that which is externally false. *Fallacious*, as characteristic of the mind, excludes the idea of design; *deceitful* excludes the idea of mistake; *fraudulent* is a gross species of the *deceitful*.

fal-lā′cious-ly, *adv.* In a fallacious manner.

fal-lā′cious-ness, *n.* The character of being fallacious.

fal′lȧ-cy, *n.*; *pl.* **fal′lȧ-cieṣ**. [ME. *fallace*; OFr. *fallace*; L. *fallacia*, deception, from *fallax* (*-acis*), deceitful, from *fallere*, to deceive.]

1. Deceptive or false appearance; deceitfulness; that which misleads; a mistake.

2. In logic, any unsound mode of arguing which appears to carry conviction and to be decisive of the question in hand, when in reality it is not; an argument or proposition, apparently sound, though really fallacious; a fallacious statement or dogma, of which the error is not obvious, and which is therefore calculated to deceive or mislead.

Syn.—Sophistry, illusion, delusion, sophism. —A *fallacy* is an argument which professes to be decisive, but in reality is not; *sophistry* is also false reasoning, but of so specious and subtle a kind as to render it difficult to expose its *fallacy*. Many *fallacies* are obvious, but the evil of *sophistry* lies in its consummate art.

fal′lal′, *a.* and *n.* [Colloq.] I. *a.* Foppish; finical; trifling.

II. *n.* A gaudy trinket; a trifling ornament; often used in the plural.

fal′lax, *n.* A fallacy. [Obs.]

fa̤ll′en, *a.* Dropped; descended; disgraced; degraded; decreased; ruined.

fal′len-cy, *n.* [Obs.] Same as *Fallacy*.

fa̤ll′en-stär, *n.* 1. A common name for species of bluish-green algæ of the group *Nostochineæ*, which grow rapidly on damp ground after a rain.

2. A sea-nettle, *Medusa æquorea*. [Prov. Eng.]

fa̤ll′ẽr, *n.* 1. One who or that which falls, as the parts of certain machines which perform their work by falling.

2. The hen-harrier, *Circus cyaneus*.

fa̤ll′ẽr-wīre, *n.* The horizontal bar in a spinning-mule which lowers the yarn so that it may be wound upon the spindles.

fa̤ll′fish, *n.* A fresh-water cyprinoid fish, *Semotilus bullaris*, found in the eastern part of North America; also called *chub* and *silver chub*.

fal-li-bil′i-ty, *n.* The state or quality of being fallible; liableness to deceive or to be deceived; possibility of error.

fal′li-ble, *a.* [LL. *fallibilis*, liable to err, from L. *fallere*, to deceive.]

1. Liable to fail or mistake; capable of erring or being deceived in judgment; as, all men are *fallible*.

2. Liable to be inaccurate or false; as, judgment and opinions are *fallible*.

fal′li-bly, *adv.* In a fallible manner.

fa̤ll′ing, *a.* Descending; dropping; declining; sinking; decreasing in value or volume.

Falling band; a broad collar of cambric, linen, lace, etc., turning over upon the shoulders, popular in the seventeenth century.

Falling sickness; epilepsy.

Falling star; one of a well-known class of meteors which appear as luminous points shooting or darting through larger or smaller arcs of the sky, and followed by long trains of light. They are observable in the night sky throughout the year; also called *shooting star*.

fa̤ll′ing, *n.* 1. That which falls or drops; that which sinks; an indentation; a hollow; as, risings and *fallings* in the ground.

2. The act of falling.

3. In pathology, displacement; sinking; as, *falling* of the womb.

Fal-lō′pi-ăn, *a.* Of, pertaining to, or discovered by Gabriel Fallopius, or Fallopio, a famous Italian anatomist of the sixteenth century.

Fallopian tubes; a pair of ducts by which the ova are carried from the ovary to the uterus.

fal′lōw, *a.* [ME. *falow*; AS. *fealu*, yellow, yellowish, pale, faded.]

1. Pale red or pale yellow.

2. Unseeded; not tilled; left to rest after a year or more of tillage; as, a *fallow* field; hence, neglected; uncultivated; often used figuratively; as, her mind lay *fallow*.

fal′lōw, *v.t.*; fallowed, *pt.*, *pp.*; fallowing, *ppr.* [ME. *falowen*, *falwen*, to plow, from AS. *fealuwian*, to become yellow, fallow, from *fealu*, fallow.] To plow, harrow, and break without seeding, as land, for the purpose of destroying weeds and insects, and rendering it mellow; as, it is to the interest of the farmer to *fallow* cold, strong, clayey land.

fal′lōw, *v.i.* To fade; to become fallow. [Obs.]

fal′lōw, *n.* [ME. *falow*, plowed land, from AS. *fealu*, yellow, fallow.]

1. Land that has lain a year or more untilled or unseeded; land which has been plowed without being sown.

2. In agriculture, the act or method of plowing or tilling land without sowing it for a season.

Green fallow; in England, land rendered mellow and clean from weeds by means of some green crop, as turnips or potatoes.

fal′lōw-crop, *n.* The crop taken from a green fallow.

fal′lōw-deer, *n.* A European deer, *Cervus dama*, very common in English preserves. It is smaller than the stag, or red deer, and of a brownish bay color. The horns, which are peculiar to the male, are very different from those of the stag; they are not properly branched, but are broader toward the upper part, and divided into processes down the outside.

Fallow-deer (*Cervus dama*).

fal′lōw-finch, *n.* A small European bird, *Saxicola œnanthe*.

fal′lōw-ist, *n.* One who favors the practice of fallowing land. [Rare.]

fal′lōw-ness, *n.* The state of being fallow.

Fallow-finch.

fal′sȧ-ry, *n.* A falsifier. [Obs.]

fa̤lse, *a.* [ME. *fals*, *false*, untrue, false; OFr. *fals*; L. *falsus*, deceptive, pretended, false, pp. of *fallere*, to deceive.]

1. Not true; not comformable to fact; expressing what is contrary to fact or truth; as, a *false* report.

2. Untruthful; mendacious; uttering what is not true; as, a *false* witness.

3. Not well founded; as, a *false* claim.

4. Not faithful or loyal; treacherous; perfidious; inconstant; deceitful; as, a *false* lover; the king's subjects were *false* to him.

5. Counterfeit; not genuine or real; as, a *false* diamond; *false* teeth.

6. Hypocritical; feigned; made or assumed for the purpose of deception; as, *false* tears; *false* modesty.

7. Irregular; not according to standard or usage; contrary to rule; incorrect; as, a *false* measure; a *false* construction of language.

8. Temporary; not permanent; as, a *false* pillar; *false* work in building.

9. In music, out of tune; inharmonious; as, a *false* note.

Syn.—Untrue, erroneous, fallacious, sophistical, spurious, deceptive, fabricated, bogus, counterfeit, mendacious, sham, mock, unfaithful, dishonorable, faithless, incorrect.

fa̤lse, *adv.* Not truly; not honestly; falsely.

To play false or *to play one false*; to act treacherously; to be untrue to one.

fa̤lse, *v.t.* [ME. *falsien*; OFr. *falser*, to make false, falsify, from L. *falsus*, pp. of *fallere*, to deceive.]

1. To mislead by want of truth; to deceive. [Obs.]

2. To defeat; to balk; to evade. [Obs.]

3. To violate by want of veracity. [Obs.]

4. To feign, as a blow; to aim by way of feint. [Obs.]

To false a doom; in Scots law, to protest against a sentence.

fa̤lse, *v.i.* To be false. [Obs.]

fa̤lse′-fāced (-fāst), *a.* Hypocritical.

fa̤lse′-heärt″ed, **fa̤lse′-heärt**, *a.* Having a false heart; treacherous; deceitful; perfidious.

fa̤lse′-heärt″ed-ness, *n.* Perfidiousness; deceit; treachery.

fa̤lse′hood, *n.* [ME. *falshod*, from AS. *fals*, fraud, counterfeit, and *hod*, condition, quality.]

1. Contrariety to fact or truth; not necessarily intentional or immoral; error; falseness; as, the *falsehood* of a report.

2. Want of truth or veracity; a lie; an untrue assertion; mendacity.

3. Want of honesty, treachery; deceitfulness; perfidy.

4. A counterfeit, false appearance; imposture.

Syn.—Untruth, lie, fabrication, fib, falsity, fiction, fallacy, fraud.

fa̤lse′ly, *adv.* 1. In a false manner or a manner contrary to truth and fact; not truly; as, to speak or swear *falsely*, to testify *falsely*.

2. Treacherously; perfidiously.

> Swear unto me that thou wilt not deal *falsely* with me. —Gen. xxi. 23.

3. Erroneously, by mistake; incorrectly; as, he quoted the verse *falsely*.

fa̤lse′ness, *n.* The state or quality of being false; lack of integrity and veracity, either in principle or in act; as, the *falseness* of a man's heart, or his *falseness* to his word.

fa̤ls′ẽr, *n.* A deceiver. [Obs.]

fa̤l-set′tō, *n.*; *pl.* **fa̤l-set′tōṣ**. [It. *falsetto*, dim. of *falso*, false, from L. *falsus*, pp. of *fallere*, to deceive.] The highest register of the voice; a false or artificial voice produced by the tightening of the ligaments of the glottis; also called *throat-* or *head-voice*, in contradistinction to the *chest-voice*, which is the natural one.

fa̤l-set′tō, *a.* 1. Of the quality or having the compass of the falsetto; shrill; high; artificial.

2. Unnatural, constrained, affected, artificial; as, the book is full of *falsetto* pathos and sentiment. [Rare.]

fa̤l′si-fī-ȧ-ble, *a.* [OFr. *falsifiable*, from *falsifier*, to falsify.] Capable of being falsified, counterfeited, or corrupted.

fa̤l″si-fi-cā′tion, *n.* [OFr. *falsification*; LL. *falsificatio* (*-onis*), the act of falsifying, from *falsificare*, to falsify, L. *falsus*, false, and *facere*, to make.]

1. The act of making false; a counterfeiting; the giving to a thing an appearance of something which it is not, as, the *falsification* of weights and measures.

2. Confutation; the act or process of disproving; refutation; as, the *falsification* of a charge.

3. In law, (a) the offense of falsifying a record; (b) in equity, the act of showing an item of a charge to be wrong.

fa̤l′si-fi-cā-tŏr, *n.* A falsifier.

fa̤l′si-fī-ẽr, *n.* 1. One who counterfeits, or gives to a thing a deceptive appearance; specifically, one who makes false coin.

2. A liar.

fa̤l′si-fȳ, *v.t.*; falsified, *pt.*, *pp.*; falsifying, *ppr.* [OFr. *falsifier*; LL. *falsificare*, to make false, corrupt, from L. *falsificus*, that acts falsely, from *falsus*, false, and *facere*, to make.]

1. To represent falsely; to counterfeit; to forge; to make (something) false or in imitation of that which is true; as, to *falsify* coin.

2. To show to be unsound; to disprove; to prove to be false; to cause to turn out false.

3. To violate; to break by falsehood; as, to *falsify* one's faith or word.

4. To baffle; as, to *falsify* a blow.

5. In law, (a) to prove to be false, as a judgment; to avoid or defeat; (b) in equity, to show (an item in a charge) to be wrong.

To falsify a record, to injure a record of a court of justice, as by obliterating or destroying it, or by certifying a copy of a document to be a true one when it is known to be false in a material part.

Syn.—Mistake, misinterpret, misrepresent, belie, betray, garble, pervert, misstate.

fa̤l′si-fȳ, *v.i.* To lie; to tell untruths.

fa̤ls′iṣm, *n.* A clear or self-evident falsity; a statement or assertion, the falsity of which is plainly apparent; opposed to *truism*. [Rare.]

fa̤l′si-ty, *n.* [ME. *falsete*, OFr. *fausete*; LL.

falsitas (-*atis*), falsehood, from L. *falsus*, pp. of *fallere*, to deceive.]

1. Contrariety or nonconformity to truth; the quality of being false.

Probability does not make any alteration, either in the truth or *falsity* of things. —South.

2. Falsehood; a lie; a false assertion.

Syn.—Falsehood, lie, incorrectness, erroneousness, fallaciousness.—*Falsity* denotes the state or quality of being false; a *falsehood* is a false declaration designedly made; a *lie* is a gross, unblushing falsehood.

fal'tẽr, *n.* The act of faltering; hesitation; quavering; unsteadiness.

fal'tẽr, *v.i.*; faltered, *pt.*, *pp.*; faltering, *ppr.* [ME. *falteren*; OFr. *fauter*, to be deficient, from L. *fallere*, to deceive.]

1. To hesitate, fail, or break, in the utterance of words; to speak with a broken or trembling utterance; to stammer; as, he speaks with a *faltering* tongue; he *falters* at the question.

2. To fail, tremble, or waver in exertion; to be unsteady; as, his legs *falter*.

3. To fail in the regular exercise of the mental or moral faculties.

Syn.—Halt, hesitate, hobble, slip, doubt, stammer, stutter, demur, waver, flinch, vacillate.

fal'tẽr, *v.t.* To utter in a hesitating or stammering manner; often with *out*; as, she *faltered out* her request.

fal'tẽr-ing-ly, *adv.* In a faltering manner.

fȧ'lŭns, *n.pl.* [Fr.] In geology, fossiliferous strata in Touraine, France, of the Miocene Tertiary age. They abound with shells, mixed with sand, and also contain the bones of mammals.

fal'we, *a.* and *n.* [Obs.] Same as *Fallow*.

falx, *n.*; *pl.* **fal'cēs**. [L., a sickle.]

1. In anatomy and zoölogy, any part or process which is falcate or falciform; specifically, one of the folds of the dura mater which separate the parts of the brain.

2. In herpetology, a poison-fang of a serpent; generally used in the plural.

3. In entomology, a chelicera.

4. In echinology, a rotula or mouth-part of a sea-urchin.

fam'ble, *v.i.* To stammer. [Obs.]

fam'ble, *n.* A hand. [Obs. Slang.]

fāme, *n.* [ME. *fame*; L. *fama*, fame, reputation, from *fari*, to speak; compare Gr. *phēma*, a voice, rumor, reputation, from *phanai*, to speak.]

1. Public report or rumor. [Obs.]

The *fame* thereof was heard in Pharaoh's house. —Gen. xlv. 16.

2. Report widely diffused, either favorable or unfavorable, but especially the former; celebrity; renown; as, the *fame* of Washington; the *fame* of Solomon; literary *fame*.

Syn.—Report, rumor, notoriety, celebrity, renown, reputation, credit, honor.

fāme, *v.t.* 1. To make famous. [Rare.]

2. To report. [Rare.]

fāmed, *a.* Famous.

fāme'less, *a.* Without renown.

fāme'less-ly, *adv.* In a fameless manner.

fā'mi-cide, *n.* [L. *fama*, reputation, and *cædere*, to kill.] A slanderer; a calumniator. [Rare.]

fȧ-mil'iȧr(-yăr), *a.* [ME. *famylier*; OFr. *familier*; L. *familiaris*, of or pertaining to a household, domestic, from *familia*, household, family.]

1. Pertaining to a family; domestic. [Rare.]

2. Having, characterized by, or arising from close acquaintance or constant companionship; intimate; not distant; as, a *familiar* friend; on *familiar* terms.

3. Having an intimate knowledge; well versed; knowing by frequent use or association; usually followed by *with*; as, he is *familiar with* the classics.

4. Unceremonious; free; unconstrained; easy; affable; as, the emperor conversed with us in the most *familiar* manner.

Be thou *familiar*, but by no means vulgar. —Shak.

5. Well known; well understood by frequent use or acquaintance; as, I hear a *familiar* voice; a *familiar* quotation.

6. Intimate in an unlawful degree.

Familiar spirit; a demon or evil spirit supposed to attend one and come at call.

Syn.—Intimate, free, unceremonious, affable, common, habitual, near, fraternal, frank, conversant.

fȧ-mil'iȧr, *n.* 1. An intimate; a close companion; one long acquainted; one accustomed to another by free, unreserved converse.

All my *familiars* watched for my halting. —Jer. xx. 10.

2. A demon or evil spirit supposed to attend at a call; a familiar spirit.

3. In the Court of Inquisition, a person who assisted in apprehending and imprisoning the accused.

4. In the Roman Catholic church, a member of the household of a pope or bishop, rendering domestic but not menial service.

fȧ-mil-i-ar'i-ty, *n.*; *pl.* **fȧ-mil-i-ar'i-ties**. [ME. *familarite*; OFr. *familiarite*; L. *familiaritas*, intimacy, from *familiaris*, familiar.]

1. The state of being familiar, in any sense of the word; intimacy; close acquaintance; frequency of converse; followed by *with*; as, their *familiarity with* each other; his *familiarity with* German literature.

2. An unusual liberty in act or speech; conduct warranted only by the closest friendship; often in a bad sense; as, I could not countenance his *familiarity*; his *familiarities* show lack of breeding.

fȧ-mil''iȧr-i-zā'tion, *n.* The act or process of making familiar; the state of being familiar.

fȧ-mil'iȧr-ize, *v.t.*, familiarized, *pt.*, *pp.*; familiarizing, *ppr.* 1. To make familiar or intimate; to habituate; to accustom; to make well known by practice or converse; as, to *familiarize* oneself with scenes of distress.

2. To make easy by practice or customary use; as, to *familiarize* the details of a business. [Rare.]

fȧ-mil'iȧr-ly, *adv.* In a familiar manner; unceremoniously; without constraint; without formality.

fȧ-mil'iȧr-ness, *n.* Familiarity. [Rare.]

fȧ-mil'iȧ-ry, *a.* Pertaining to a household or family. [Obs.]

Fam'i-lism, *n.* 1. The tenets of the Familists.

2. [f—] The tendency to live in families; fondness for family life; a social system having the family as its unit.

Fam'i-list, *n.* [L. *familia*, a family.]

1. One of a religious sect called the Family of Love which arose in Holland in 1556. They taught that religion consists wholly in love, independently of any form of truth held and believed.

2. [f—] The head of a family; a family man. [Rare.]

fam'i-lis-tẽr-y, *n.* [Fr. *familistère*, from *familiste*, lit., one of a family, from L. *familia*, a family.] A community of communists living together as one family; also, the building in which they live; a phalanstery; also written *familistère*.

fam-i-lis'tic, fam-i-lis'tic-ăl, *a.* Pertaining to Familists or their doctrines.

fam'i-ly, *n.*; *pl.* **fam'i-lies**. [L. *familia*, the servants in a household, a household, from *famulus*, a servant, from Oscan *famel*, a servant.]

1. The collective body of persons who live in one house, and under one head or manager; a household, including parents, children, and servants, and, as the case may be, lodgers or boarders.

2. A father, mother, and their children, or any group of blood relations.

3. Children, as distinguished from the father and mother; as, they have no *family*.

4. Those who descend from one common progenitor; a tribe or race; kindred; lineage; as, the Israelites were a branch of the *family* of Abraham.

5. Course of descent; genealogy; line of ancestors.

Go and complain thy *family* is young.—Pope.

6. Honorable descent; noble or respectable stock; as, he is a man of *family*.

7. A collection or union of things having common characteristics and so regarded as related; as, a *family* of languages.

The states of Europe were, by the prevailing maxims of its policy, closely united in one *family*. —E. Everett.

8. In scientific classifications, a group of individuals, more comprehensive than a genus and less so than an order, based on fewer or less definite points of resemblance than the former, and more or more definite ones than the latter. In zoölogy a *family* is always of a lower rank than an order, in botany they are sometimes synonymous.

Family man; a man having a wife and children dependent upon him; also, a man of domestic habits or tastes.

Family of curves or *surfaces*; in geometry, a series of curves or surfaces differing from each other only in the value of one of the constants in the equation of one of them.

Family of Love; see *Familist*, 1.

Holy Family; the family of which Jesus was one in his childhood; specifically, the group comprising Joseph, Mary, and the infant Jesus, a frequent subject in painting.

In the family way; pregnant. [Colloq.]

fam'ine, *n.* [ME. *famine*; OFr. *famine*; LL. *famina*, famine, from L. *fames*, hunger.] Scarcity of food; dearth; a general want of provisions; figuratively, a dearth of anything; as, a *famine* of spirituality.

There was a *famine* in the land.—Gen. xxvi. 1.

fam'ine-bread (-bred), *n.* In botany, an arctic lichen, *Umbilicaria arctica*, sometimes used as food by arctic navigators.

fam'ine-fē"vẽr, *n.* Typhus fever.

fam'ish, *v.t.*; famished (-isht), *pt.*, *pp.*; famishing, *ppr.* [ME. *famen*; OFr. *afamer*, to famish, from L. *ad*, to, and *fames*, hunger.]

1. To starve; to kill or destroy with hunger.

2. To exhaust the strength of, by hunger or thirst; to distress with hunger.

The pains of *famished* Tantalus he'll feel. —Dryden.

3. To force or constrain by famine or threatened starvation.

He had *famished* Paris into a surrender. —Burke.

fam'ish, *v.i.* 1. To die of hunger.

2. To suffer extreme hunger or thirst; to be exhausted in strength or to come near perishing for want of food or drink.

You are all resolved rather to die than to *famish*. —Shak.

3. To be distressed with want; to be deprived of anything necessary.

The Lord will not suffer the soul of the righteous to *famish*. —Prov. x. 3.

fam'ish-ment, *n.* The pain of extreme hunger or thirst; extreme want.

fȧ-mos'i-ty, *n.* The quality of being famous; renown. [Obs.]

fā'mous, *a.* [ME. *famous*; Fr. *fameux*; L. *famosus*, famed, famous, from *fama*, fame.] Celebrated in fame or public report; renowned; much talked of; distinguished; in either a good or bad sense, but especially the former. It is usually followed by *for*; as, *famous for* beauty, learning, etc.

Syn.—Renowned, illustrious, celebrated, conspicuous, distinguished, eminent, prominent, noted, notorious.—*Famous* is applied to a person or thing widely spoken of as extraordinary; *renowned*, to those who are named again and again with honor; *illustrious*, to those who have dazzled the world by the splendor of their deeds or their virtues.

fā'moused (-must), *a.* Renowned. [Obs.]

fā'mous-ly, *adv.* 1. In a famous manner; with great renown or celebrity.

2. Unusually or exceeding well; admirably; capitally; as, you did *famously*. [Colloq.]

fā'mous-ness, *n.* Renown; great fame; celebrity. [Rare.]

fam'ū-lăr, *a.* and *n.* [Obs.] Same as *Familiar*.

fam'ū-lāte, *v.i.* To serve. [Obs.]

fam'ū-list, *n.* [L. *famulus*, a servant.] In Oxford university, an inferior member of a college; a servitor.

fam'ū-lus, *n.*; *pl.* **fam'ū-lī**. [L., a servant.] An assistant; specifically, an amanuensis of a scholar or an assistant to a magician.

fan, *n.* [ME. *fan*, *fann*; AS. *fann*, from L. *vannus*, a fan for winnowing grain.]

1. An instrument for producing artificial currents of air by the movement of a broad surface; specifically, (a) a device for cooling the face and person, made of various materials, as feathers, silk, papier-maché, etc., usually mounted on a frame or sticks of ivory, wood, etc., and either permanently expanded, as a palm-leaf *fan*, or capable of being folded and opened at will; (b) any revolving contrivance of vanes or disks used for winnowing grain, blowing a fire, cooling fluids, promoting ventilation, etc.; as, an electric *fan*; (c) a small vane or sail used to keep the large sails of a windmill always in the direction of the wind; (d) an apparatus for regulating or checking, by the resistance of the air to its rapid motion, the velocity of light machinery, as in a musical box; a fly; (e) an apparatus, called also the *fan-governor*, for regulating the throttle-valves of steam-engines.

2. Something in the form of a *fan* when spread, as a peacock's tail, a window, etc.

3. Figuratively, anything that stirs to action, or excites a passion or an emotion, as a *fan* excites a flame; as, her answer was but a *fan* to his anger.

4. A quintain. [Obs.]

5. In geology, a mass of debris brought down through a steep ravine by a stream and deposited in the form of a *fan*, or a flat cone, at the mouth of the ravine or on the plain beneath.

6. An enthusiastic follower or supporter of various sports; as, a baseball *fan*; a prize-fight *fan*. [Slang.]

Fan window; same as *Fanlight*.

fan, *v.t.*; fanned, *pt.*, *pp.*; fanning, *ppr.* 1. To cool and refresh, by moving the air with a fan; to blow the air on with a fan; as, to *fan* oneself; the sultan was *fanned* by his slaves.

2. To ventilate; to blow on; to affect by air put in motion; as, to *fan* a fire.

3. To move as with a fan.

The air, *fanned* with unnumber'd plumes. —Milton.

4. To winnow; to ventilate; to separate chaff

from and drive it away by a current of air; as, to *fan* wheat.

5. Figuratively, to stimulate to action; to excite, as a fan excites a flame; as, her silence *fanned* his disappointment into anger.

fan, *v.i.* 1. To move, as if by a fan.

2. To spread like a fan; often followed by *out*.

fȧ-năl′, *n.* [Fr. *fanal*; It. *fanale*, a signal-light; It. dial. *fano*, a lighthouse; L. *pharus*; Gr. *pharos*, a lighthouse.] A beacon-light; a ship's lantern; a lighthouse, or the illuminating apparatus in it.

fȧ-nat′iç, *a.* and *n.* [L. *fanaticus*, pertaining to a temple, inspired, enthusiastic, from *fanum*, a temple, from *fari*, to speak, consecrate.]

I. *a.* Same as *Fanatical*.

II. *n.* A person affected by excessive enthusiasm, particularly on religious subjects; one who indulges wild and extravagant notions of religion; a religious zealot or bigot.

> *Fanatics* are governed rather by imagination than by judgment. —Stowe.

Syn.—Enthusiast, visionary, crank, bigot, zealot.

fȧ-nat′iç-ăl, *a.* [L. *fanaticus*, pertaining to a temple, inspired.]

1. Wild and extravagant in opinions, particularly in religious opinions; excessively enthusiastic; as, he has always been *fanatical*.

2. Characterized by extravagance or inordinate zeal; as, *fanatical* views.

fȧ-nat′iç-ăl-ly, *adv.* In a fanatical manner; with wild enthusiasm.

fȧ-nat′iç-ăl-ness, *n.* Fanaticism.

fȧ-nat′i-ciṣm, *n.* Excessive enthusiasm; wild and extravagant notions, especially of religion; religious frenzy.

fȧ-nat′i-cize, *v.t.*; fanaticized, *pt.*, *pp.*; fanaticizing, *ppr.* To make fanatical. [Rare.]

fȧ-nat′i-cize, *v.i.* To become fanatical; to play the fanatic. [Rare.]

fan′=blōw″ẽr, *n.* A wheel which rotates and produces a current of air; also called *fan-wheel*.

fan′cied, *a.* Imagined; conceived in the fancy; unreal; as, a *fancied* wrong.

fan′ci-ẽr, *n.* 1. One who fancies or has a liking; also, one who keeps for sale some specific class of objects; used especially in composition; as, a bird-*fancier*.

2. One who is under the influence of his fancy.

> Not reasoners but *fanciers*. —Macaulay.

fan′ci-fụl, *a.* 1. Guided by the imagination rather than by reason and experience; subject to the influence of fancy; whimsical; as, a *fanciful* man forms visionary projects.

2. Dictated by the imagination; full of wild images; chimerical; whimsical; ideal; visionary; odd; unusual; unique; as, a *fanciful* scheme; a *fanciful* costume.

Syn.—Fantastical, visionary, ideal, imaginative, chimerical.—*Fanciful* notions are the product of a heated fancy, without any support in reason or truth; *fantastical* schemes or systems are made up of oddly-assorted fancies, often of the most whimsical kind; *visionary* expectations are those which can never be realized in fact.

fan′ci-fụl-ly, *adv.* In a fanciful manner; whimsically; oddly.

fan′ci-fụl-ness, *n.* The quality of being fanciful.

fan′ci-less, *a.* Destitute of fancy or imagination.

fan′=crick″et, *n.* See *Churrworm*.

fan′cy, *n.* [ME. *fantasy*; OFr. *fantasie*; LL. *phantasia*, an idea, notion, fancy; Gr. *phantasia*, the look or appearance of a thing, from *phantazein*, to make visible, from *phainein*, to come to light.]

1. The faculty by which the mind forms images or representations of things at pleasure; imagination in its lowest form, exercised in an aimless or capricious manner; the power or act of conceiving in the mind strange, impossible, or whimsical combinations of things.

2. The result or product of the exercise of the above faculty; a new and pleasing thought or conception; the happy and poetical embodiment of such conception in words or visible representation; a poetical illustration or ornament, as a simile, metaphor, and the like; an ideal image in a picture; as, Byron's poetry is full of beautiful *fancies*.

3. An opinion or notion formed upon slight evidence or investigation; a speculative belief; an impression; as, a mere *fancy*.

4. Taste; conception; design.

> The little chapel is very neat, and built with a pretty *fancy*. —Addison.

5. Inclination; liking; as, how does this strike your *fancy*?

6. Something that pleases or entertains without real use or value; as, skipping the rope is a pretty *fancy*.

7. A light musical composition, usually instrumental; a fantasy. [Obs.]

The fancy; a slang name for sporting characters, especially prize-fighters; sometimes used to designate any class of people who cultivate a special taste.

Syn.—Caprice, conceit, conception, freak, frolic, humor, ideality, image, imagination, inclination, liking, notion, taste, whim.

fan′cy, *a.* 1. Fine; elegant; ornamental; adapted to please the taste or fancy; as, *fancy* goods or articles.

2. Beyond intrinsic value; extravagant; as, I consider that a *fancy* price.

3. In commerce, extra fine; superfine; as, *fancy* butter.

Fancy goods; ornamental fabrics or choice articles of show and ornament, as ribbons, embroideries, ties, toilet articles, etc.; notions.

Fancy shot; in billiards, a shot of unusual character or one exhibiting unusual skill on the part of the player.

Fancy stocks; among brokers, stocks which, having no determinate value from any fixed probable income, fluctuate in price according to the fancy of speculators.

fan′cy, *v.t.*; fancied, *pt.*, *pp.*; fancying, *ppr.* 1. To form a conception of; to portray in the mind; to imagine.

> He whom I *fancy*, but can ne'er express. —Dryden.

2. To like; to be pleased with, particularly on account of external appearance or manners; as, he *fancied* her the first time they met.

3. To imagine; to believe without proof; as, he *fancied* I had wronged him.

fan′cy, *v.i.* 1. To imagine; to figure to oneself; to believe or suppose without proof.

> If our search has reached no farther than simile and metaphor, we rather *fancy* than know. —Locke.

2. To love. [Obs.]

fan′cy=free, *a.* Free from the power of love.

fan′cy=line, *n.* In nautical language, (a) a line used for overhauling the lee topping-lift of the main or spanker boom; (b) a line rove through a block at the jaws of a gaff, used as a down-haul.

fan′cy-mŏn″gẽr, *n.* One who deals in tricks of imagination.

fan′cy=sick, *a.* Love-sick; having a disordered fancy or imagination.

fan′cy=stōre, *n.* A store where fancy goods are sold.

fan′cy-wŏrk, *n.* Ornamental knitting, crocheting, tatting, embroidery, etc., performed by ladies.

fand, *v.*, obsolete past tense of *find*.

fan-dan′gō, *n.* [Sp., from the African name.]

1. A lively dance, universally practised in Spain and Spanish America. It was originally a dance of the Moors. It is danced by two persons, male and female, who hold castanets or sometimes tambourines.

2. Music in triple time, suitable for such a dance.

3. A ball or dance; hence, any noisy entertainment; a jollification; used especially in those parts of the United States which formerly belonged to Spain. [Colloq.]

fāne, *n.* [L. *fanum*, a sanctuary, a temple, from *fari*, to speak, consecrate.] A temple; a place consecrated to religion; a church; used in poetry.

> From men their cities, and from gods their *fanes*. —Pope.

fāne, *n.* 1. A weathercock; a vane. [Obs.]

2. A flag. [Obs.]

fȧ-ne′gȧ, *n.* [Sp.] The Spanish bushel.

fan′fāre, *n.* [Fr. *fanfare*, a sounding of trumpets; Sp. *fanfarria*, bluster, vaunting, from Ar. *farfār*, talkative.] A flourish of trumpets, as in coming into the lists, etc.

fan′fa-ron, *n.* [Fr. *fanfaron*; Sp. *fanfarron*, a blusterer.] A bully; a hector; a swaggerer; an empty boaster; a vain pretender.

fan-far-on-āde′, *n.* A swaggering; vain boasting; ostentation; bluster.

fan′fish, *n.* A sailfish, *Histiophorus gladius*.

fan′foot, *n.* 1. A name given to a harmless North African lizard, *Ptyodactylus gecko*, much dreaded in Egypt for its reputed venomous properties. It can ascend perpendicular walls, owing to the skin of the under surface of the toes forming at the extremities, as in other geckos, a round disk, whence the name, *fanfoot*. The claws are retractile. It is so much dreaded in Cairo as to be popularly termed *abou-burs*, or father of leprosy.

2. A name given to moths of the genus *Polypogon*.

fang, *v.t.* [ME. *fangen*, *fongen*; AS. *fon*, to take hold of, seize.]

1. To catch; to seize; to lay hold of; to grip; to clutch. [Obs. or Prov. Eng.]

> Destruction *fang* mankind! —Shak.

2. To pour water into, as a pump, in order to restore its power of operation. [Scot.]

3. To receive as a guest. [Obs.]

4. To stand sponsor for. [Prov. Eng.]

fang, *n.* [ME. *feng*, a grasping; AS. *feng*, *fang*, booty, a grasping, a seizure, from *gefangen*, pp. of *fon*, to take, seize.]

Fangs of Serpents.

1. Head of Common Viper (*Pelias berus*); *a*, Poison-fang. 2. Head of Rattlesnake cut open; *a*, Poison-fang; *b*, Poison-bag; *c*, Tube which conveys the poison to the fangs. 3. Fang, showing the slit (*d*) through which the poison is communicated to the wound.

1. The tusk of a boar or other animal by which the prey is seized and held; a pointed tooth, as the poison or venom-tooth of a serpent.

2. A claw or talon.

3. Any shoot or other thing by which hold is taken, as a tang of a tool or a prong of a lock or bolt.

> The protuberant *fangs* of the yucca.—Evelyn.

4. In mining, an air-course.

5. In anatomy, the root of a tooth.

6. A coil of a rope; hence, a noose.

fanged, *a.* Furnished with fangs, tusks, or something long and pointed; as, a *fanged* adder.

> Chariots *fanged* with scythes. —Philips.

fan′gle, *v.t.* To fashion. [Obs.]

fan′gle, *n.* [Prob. dim. of AS. *fang*, *feng*, a taking, a seizure.] A new attempt; a trifling scheme; a silly fancy; a gewgaw.

> A hatred to *fangles* and the French fooleries of his time. —Wood.

fan′gled, *a.* New-made; of recent fashion; used only with *new*; as, a *newfangled* necklace.

fan′gle-ness, *n.* The state of being fangled. [Obs.]

fang′less, *a.* Having no fangs or tusks; toothless; as, a *fangless* lion.

fan′got, *n.* [It. *fangotto*, a bundle.] A quantity of wares, as raw silk, etc., from one hundredweight to two and three-quarters hundredweight.

fan′iŏn, *n.* [OFr. *fanion*; O.H.G. *fano*, a banner.]

1. In military language, a small flag carried with the baggage of a brigade.

2. A small marking-flag for a surveying-station.

fan′līght (-līt), *n.* A window in the form of an open fan.

fan′nel, *n.* [Dim. of O.H.G. *fano*, a banner.] Same as *Fanon*.

fan′nẽr, *n.* One who or that which fans; specifically, a fanning-mill.

fan′=nẽrved, *a.* In botany and zoölogy, having the veins or nerves radiate from a common point, as in a leaf or an insect's wing.

fan′ning=mill, **fan′ning=mȧ-çhīne″**, *n.* A blower for removing chaff, husks, dirt, etc., from grain.

fan′ŏn, *n.* [ME. *fanone*; OFr. *fanon*, a pendant, the lappet of a miter, from LL. *fano*; O.H.G. *fano*, a banner.] In ecclesiastical history, (a) a headdress worn by the pope at solemn pontifical celebrations; (b) a maniple; (c) the white linen cloth in which the laity made their oblations at the altar; (d) one of the strings or lappets of the miter; (e) a banner; specifically, the church banner carried in processions. Also called *fannel*.

fan′=pälm (-päm), *n.* The taliput-tree, *Corypha umbraculifera*, a native of Ceylon and Malabar. It attains the height of sixty or seventy feet. The other species of the genus *Corypha* are also called *fan-palms* from the form of their leaves.

fan′=shell, *n.* A scallop; any bivalve of the *Pectinidæ*.

fan′tāil, *n.* 1. Any bird of the genus *Rhipidura* of Australia; a fan-tailed flycatcher.

2. A variety of domestic pigeon, which spreads its tail in the shape of a fan.

fan′=tāiled, *a.* Having the feathers of the tail arranged in the shape of a fan.

fan′=tan, *n.* [Chinese *fan*, number of times, and *tan*, apportion.]

1. A form of gambling, very popular among the Chinese, in which a pile of coins is covered with a bowl and the players wager as to what the remainder will be when the number of coins is divided by four.

2. A game of cards that may be played by any number of players, the object being to get rid of all the cards dealt; also called *domino whist*.

3. A gambling game played with a layout somewhat resembling that for faro.

fän-tä-ṣī′ȧ, *n.* [It., fancy.] A fanciful air in music, not restricted to the severe laws of composition.

fan′tȧ-ṣied, *a.* Filled with fancies or imaginations; whimsical.

fan′taṣm, *n.* Same as *Phantasm*.

fan′tas-sin, *n.* [Fr., from It. *fantaccino*, a

foot-soldier, from *fante*, a boy, a servant.] A heavily armed foot-soldier.

fan′tast, *n.* One whose manners, speech, or ideas are fantastic.

fan-tas′tiç, *n.* One who is fantastic in any way; a whimsical person.

fan-tas′tiç, fan-tas′tiç-ăl, *a.* [OFr. *fantastique*; LL. *phantasticus*, *fantasticus*, imaginary, from Gr. *phantastikos*, able to present or represent to the mind, from *phantazein*, to make visible.]

1. Fanciful; produced or existing only in imagination; imaginary; not real; chimerical.

2. Having the nature of a phantom.

3. Whimsical; capricious; fanciful; indulging the vagaries of imagination; as, *fantastic* minds; a *fantastic* mistress.

4. Odd in appearance; grotesque; whimsically shaped.

fan-tas-ti-çal′i-ty, *n.* 1. Fantasticalness.

2. Anything which is fantastic.

fan-tas′tiç-ăl-ly, *adv.* In a fantastic manner.

fan-tas′tiç-ăl-ness, *n.* The state of being fantastic; humorousness; whimsicalness; unreasonableness; caprice.

fan-tas′ti-çişm, *n.* Fantasticalness.

fan-tas′tiç-ly, *adv.* Fantastically. [Obs.]

fan-tas′tiç-ness, *n.* Fantasticalness. [Obs.]

fan-tas′ti-cō, *n.* [It.] A fantastic.

fan′tȧ-sy, phan′tȧ-sy, *n.*; *pl.* **fan′tȧ-sieş, phan′tȧ-sieş.** [ME. *fantasye*, *fauntasye*; OFr. *fantasie*; LL. *phantasia*, an idea, notion; Gr. *phantasia*, the look or appearance of a thing.]

1. [Obs.] See *Fancy*.

2. The forming of unreal or grotesque images in the mind; distorted fancy; disordered imagination.

3. An unreal or grotesque image formed in the mind; a chimerical or distorted fancy; a phantasm.

4. A fantastic design, as in architecture, embroidery, etc.

5. In music, same as *fantasia*.

fan′tȧ-sy, *v.t.*; fantasied, *pt.*, *pp.*; fantasying, *ppr.* 1. To conceive fantastically in the mind; to imagine.

2. In music, to compose or perform, as a fantasia.

3. To fancy; to admire; to have a liking for. [Obs.]

fȧn-tōc-cï′nï (fȧn-tō-chē′nē), *n.pl.* [It., pl. of *fantoccio*, a puppet, dwarf, dim. of *fante*, a boy, a servant.]

1. Puppets or marionettes.

2. Dramatic representations in which puppets are substituted in the scene for human performers.

fan′tŏm, *n.* See *Phantom*.

fan′=trȧ″çẽr-y, *n.* In architecture, elaborate geometrical carved work which spreads over the surface of a vault, rising from a capital or corbel and diverging like the folds of a fan.

Fan-tracery vaulting; a very complicated mode of roofing, much used in the perpendicular style, in which the vault is covered by ribs and veins of tracery, of which all the principal lines diverge from a point.

Fan-tracery Vaulting.

fan′=veined, *a.* Same as *Fan-nerved*.

fan′=wheel (-hwēl), *n.* Same as *Fan-blower*.

fap, *a.* Fuddled. [Obs. Slang.]

fȧ-quïr′, *n.* Same as *Fakir*.

fär, *a.*; *comp.* farther *or* further; *superl.* farthest *or* furthest. [ME. *fer*, *ferr*; AS. *feorr*, *feor*, far, distant.]

1. Distant, in space or time; separated by a wide space from the place where one is; remote; as, a *far* country; the *far* future.

> The nations *far* and near contend in choice. —Dryden.

2. Remote from purpose; contrary to design or wishes; as, *far* be it from me to justify cruelty.

3. Remote in affection or obedience; at enmity with; alienated.

> They that are *far* from thee shall perish. —Ps. lxxiii. 27.

4. More distant of two; as, the *far* side of a horse, or the right side; so called because the rider always mounts from the left side.

fär, *adv.*; *comp.* farther *or* further; *superl.* farthest *or* furthest. 1. To a great extent or distance of space; as, the *far*-extended ocean; we are separated *far* from each other.

2. At a distance in time from any point; remotely; as, he pushed his researches very *far* into antiquity.

3. In great part; as, the day is *far* spent.

4. In a great proportion; by many degrees; very much; largely; widely.

> Who can find a virtuous woman? for her price is *far* above rubies. —Prov. xxxi. 10.

As far as; see under *As*.

By far; in a great degree; very much.

Far and away; see under *Away*.

Far and near; over a wide extent; throughout an entire region.

Far and wide; to a great distance; extensively.

Far from; at a great distance; as, *far from* home.

Far off; at a great distance; hence, figuratively, alienated; at enmity; in a state of ignorance and alienation.

Far other; very different.

From far; from a great distance; from a remote place.

In so far as; to the degree that; as, *in so far as* you read fiction, read the best.

fär, *n.* [AS. *fearh*, a pig, a little pig.] The young of swine, or a litter of pigs. [Prov. Eng.]

fär′=ȧ-bout″, *n.* A going out of the way; a wandering; a digression. [Obs.]

far′ad, *n.* [Named from the chemist Michael *Faraday*.] In electricity, the standard unit of electromagnetic capacity; the capacity possessed by a conductor which is capable of holding one coulomb of electricity at one volt potential.

Far-ȧ-dā′iç, *a.* 1. Pertaining to or discovered by Faraday, the English physicist.

2. [f—] Same as *Faradic*.

far-ad′iç, *a.* Of, pertaining to, producing, or caused by induced electric currents obtained from a variety of machines.

far′ȧ-dişm, *n.* The form of electricity produced by an induced current.

far″ȧ-di-zā′tion, *n.* In physiology and medicine, the stimulation or treatment of a nerve with faradic or induced currents of electricity.

far′ȧ-dīze, *v.t.*; faradized, *pt.*, *pp.*; faradizing, *ppr.* To stimulate or treat, as a muscle, nerve, etc., with faradic or induced currents of electricity.

far′ănd, *a.* [ME. *farand*, comely, handsome, from *favoren*, L. *favere*, to favor.]

1. Comely; handsome; pleasing in appearance. [Prov. Eng.]

2. Appearing; seeming; generally used in composition; as, evil-*farand*; auld-*farand*, etc. [Scot.]

far′ănd, *n.* Manners; custom; humor. [Prov. Eng.]

far′ăn-damş, *n.* [Fr. *ferrandine.*] A mixed fabric of silk and wool.

far′ănd-ly, far′ănt-ly, *adv.* In an orderly or decent manner. [Prov. Eng.]

fa-ran′dō-lȧ, fa-ran′dōle, *n.* [Fr.] A rapid dance of Romance origin, in which the dancers form in a circle and whirl around, facing in and out alternately.

fär′=ȧ-wāy″, *a.* 1. Distant; remote.

2. Abstracted; absent-minded; dreamy; pensive; as, a *far-away* look in her eyes.

färce, *v.t.*; farced (färst), *pt.*, *pp.*; farcing, *ppr.* [ME. *farcen*; OFr. *farsir*, *farcir*; L. *farcire*, to stuff, cram.]

1. To stuff; to fill with mingled ingredients or forcemeat. [Obs.]

2. Figuratively, to fill, as a speech or writing, with wit and humor.

> The first principles of religion should not be *farced* with school points and private tenets. —Sanderson.

3. To extend; to swell out; as, the *farced* title. [Obs.]

4. To fatten. [Obs.]

färce, *n.* [Fr. *farce*, stuffing, a farce, from *farcer*, to stuff; L. *farcire*, to stuff, fill in.]

1. Seasoning; stuffing, as that for a fowl; forcemeat.

2. A dramatic composition, written without regularity, and differing from comedy chiefly in the grotesqueness, extravagance, and improbability of its characters and incidents; low comedy.

3. Ridiculous parade; empty pageantry; mere show; as, it was all a solemn *farce*.

4. A ridiculous sham.

färce′ment, *n.* Stuffing or dressing, as of meat; forcemeat. [Obs.]

fär-çeūr′, *n.* A joker; a writer or actor of farces.

fär′ci-çăl, *a.* Belonging to or of the nature of a farce; appropriate for farce; ludicrous; absurd; burlesque.

> They deny the characters to be *farcical*, because they are actually in nature. —Gay.

fär′ci-çăl, *a.* Pertaining to farcy, a disease of horses.

fär-ci-çal′i-ty, *n.* The quality of being farcical or ludicrous; absurdity.

fär′ci-çăl-ly, *adv.* In a farcical manner; ludicrously.

fär′ci-çăl-ness, *n.* Same as *Farcicality*.

fär′ci-līte, *n.* Pudding-stone. [Obs.]

fär′ci-men, *n.* Same as *Farcy*.

fär′cin, *n.* Same as *Farcy*.

fär′cing, *n.* Stuffing; forcemeat.

färc′tāte, *a.* [L. *farctus*, stuffed, pp. of *farcire*, to stuff.] In botany, stuffed; crammed or full; without vacuities; in opposition to *tubular* or *hollow*; as, a *farctate* leaf, stem, or pericarp.

fär′cy, *n.* [LL. *farciminum*, from L. *farcire*, to stuff, cram.] In farriery, a disease of horses; a form of equinia or glanders, attacking the skin and lymphatic glands.

fär′cy=bud, *n.* A swollen gland, as in farcy.

färd, *v.t.* To paint, as the face or cheeks: as, a *farded* fop. [Obs.]

färd, *n.* Paint; especially rouge. [Obs.]

fär′dāge, *n.* [Fr. *fardage*, from *fardeau*, a load; OFr. *fardel*, a load, probably from Ar. *fardah*, a package.] In nautical language, loose wood or other substances, as horns, rattan, coir, etc., stowed among cargo to prevent its motion, or placed below dry cargo to keep it from bilge-water; dunnage.

fär′del, *n.* A bundle or little pack; hence, anything cumbersome, irksome, or inconvenient. [Obs.]

fär′del, *v.t.* To make up in bundles. [Obs.]

fär′ding=bag, *n.* The first stomach of a cow, or other ruminant animal, where green food lies until it is chewed over again; the rumen or paunch.

fāre, *v.i.*; fared, *pt.*, *pp.*; faring, *ppr.* [ME. *faren*; AS. *faran*, to go, to be in a particular condition, from *ferian*, to carry, convey.]

1. To go; to pass; to move forward; to travel.

> So on he *fares*, and to the border comes
> Of Eden. —Milton.

2. To be in any state, good or bad; to be attended with any circumstances or train of events, fortunate or unfortunate.

> Ill *fares* the land, to hastening ills a prey,
> Where wealth accumulates, and men decay. —Goldsmith.

3. To feed; to be entertained with food and drink; as, we *fared* well, until the crops failed.

4. To happen well or ill; with *it* impersonally; as, we shall see how *it* will *fare* with him.

5. To behave. [Obs.]

fāre, *n.* [ME. *fare*; AS. *faru*, a journey, from *faran*, to go.]

1. The price of passage or going; the sum paid or due for conveying a person by land or water; as, the *fare* for crossing a river; the *fare* for conveyance in a cab, railroad-train, street-car, etc.

2. Food; provisions of the table; as, we had delicious *fare*.

> My lord, eat also, though the *fare* is coarse. —Tennyson.

3. Condition; experience; treatment by circumstances; fortune.

> What *fare*? What news abroad? —Shak.

4. The person or persons conveyed in a vehicle; as, he had not driven far when he was stopped by his *fare*.

5. The quantity of fish taken in a fishing-vessel.

6. Ado; bustle; unusual display; entertainment; adventure, etc. [Obs.]

> What amounteth all this *fare*? —Chaucer.

7. A journey. [Obs.]

fāre′=in″di-çā-tŏr, *n.* A device for registering the number of fares paid in a public conveyance, as an omnibus or street-car.

fāre-well′, *interj.* Fare well; may you be or continue to be happy and well; good-by; originally spoken to a person departing, but by custom now spoken both to those who depart and those who remain; sometimes separated by a pronoun; as, *fare you well*. It is sometimes an expression of separation only; as, *farewell* the year; *farewell*, my happy home; that is, I take my leave of you.

fāre-well′, *n.* 1. A wish of happiness or welfare at parting; the parting compliment; adieu.

2. Leave; departure; a final look or thought.

> And takes her *farewell* of the glorious sun. —Shak.

fāre-well′, *a.* Final; parting; valedictory; as, a *farewell* sermon; a *farewell* call.

Farewell rocks; in coal-mining, the millstone-grit; so called because when miners reach it they bid farewell to the prospect of finding coal below it. [Prov. Eng.]

fär′fet, *a.* [Obs.] Same as *Farfetched*.

fär′fetch, *v.t.* To bring from far; to draw conclusions remote from or little justified by the premises; to search out studiously. [Obs.]

> To *farfetch* the name of Tartar from a Hebrew word. —Fuller.

fär′fetch, *n.* A deep-laid stratagem. [Obs.]

fär′fetched (-fecht), *a.* 1. Brought from a distance. [Rare.]

2. Choice; fine; rare. [Obs.]

3. Forced; strained; irrelevant; not obvious; as, *farfetched* figures of speech.

fär′fōrth, *adv.* Far advanced; far.

fa-rī′nȧ (*or* -rī′nȧ), *n.* [L. *farina*, ground corn, from *far*, a sort of grain, spelt.]

1. Meal or flour; specifically, a soft, tasteless, and commonly white flour, obtained by trituration of the seeds of cereal and leguminous plants, and of some roots, as the potato. It consists of gluten, starch, and mucilage.

2. In botany, a name formerly given to the pollen of flowers.

3. In entomology, a fine, mealy powder found on some insects.

4. A granular preparation of white maize, used for puddings, etc.

Fossil farina; a variety of carbonate of lime, in thin white crusts, light as cotton, and easily reducible to powder.

far-i-nā′ceous, *a.* [LL. *farinaceus*, from L. *farina*, meal.]

1. Consisting or made of meal or flour; as, a *farinaceous* diet.

2. Yielding farina or flour; as, *farinaceous* seeds.

3. Like meal; mealy; pertaining to meal; as, a *farinaceous* taste or quality.

far′i-nōse, *a.* [LL. *farinosus*, mealy, from L. *farina*, meal.]

1. Yielding farina.

2. In biology, mealy; covered with a sort of white, scurfy substance, as the leaves of some poplars or the wings of certain insects.

fa-rin′ū-lent, *a.* Same as *Farinose*, 2.

färl, *v.t.* To furl. [Obs.]

fär′leū, *n.* In Scots law, money paid by tenants in lieu of a heriot; often applied to the best chattel, as distinguished from *heriot*, the best beast.

färm, *n.* [ME. *ferme*, rent, revenue; AS. *feorm*, provision, food, a feast, from LL. *firma*, a feast; so called from the fact that the lands were let on condition that the tenant supply the lord with so many nights' entertainment.]

1. The state of land leased on rent reserved; a lease.

> It is great wilfulness in landlords to make any longer *farms* to their tenants. —Spenser.

2. In old English usage, the rent for lands leased, often paid in natural products. [Obs.]

3. A district farmed out for the collection of revenue. [Rare.]

> The province was divided into twelve *farms*. —Burke.

4. A tract of land, under a single control or management and devoted to agricultural purposes of a general or special nature, or to the raising of cattle, etc.; as, a general *farm*; a fruit-*farm*; a stock-*farm*; a dairy-*farm*.

5. The system, process, or act of farming out revenues or taxes, or of farming out parts of a country for the collection of revenue.

färm, *v.t.*; farmed, *pt.*, *pp.*; farming, *ppr.* 1. To lease, as land, at a fixed rent; to let to a tenant on condition of paying rent.

> We are enforced to *farm* our royal realm. —Shak.

2. To take at a certain rent or rate; to take a lease of.

3. To lease or let, as taxes, imposts, or other duties, at a certain sum or rate per cent. It is customary in some eastern countries for the sovereign or government to *farm* or *farm out* the revenues to individuals, who are to collect and pay them to the government at a certain percentage of the amount collected, or for a fixed remuneration.

4. To cultivate or till and plant, as land.

färm, *v.i.* To be a farmer; to engage in agriculture; to cultivate the soil.

färm′ȧ-ble, *a.* Capable of being farmed.

färm′ẽr, *n.* [ME. *fermour*, a steward, bailiff; OFr. *fermier*, a farmer, lessee, bailiff, or overseer of a farm; AS. *feormere*, a purveyor, from *feormian*, to purvey, supply, from *feorm*, food, provisions.]

1. A tenant; a lessee; one who hires and cultivates a farm; a cultivator of leased ground.

2. One who takes taxes, customs, excise, or other duties to collect for a certain rate per cent; as, a *farmer* of the revenues.

3. One who cultivates a farm, whether a tenant or the proprietor; a husbandman; an agriculturist; one who tills the soil.

4. In mining, the lord of the field, or one who farms the lot and cope of the crown. [Eng.]

Farmer's satin; a durable fabric of cotton and wool, having a glossy surface resembling that of satin, and used especially for linings.

färm′ẽr-ess, *n.* A woman who farms, or the wife of a farmer. [Rare.]

färm″ẽr-ette′, *n.* A female farmer.

färm′ẽr-gen-ẽr-ăl, *n.* In France under the old monarchy, a member of a privileged association which farmed certain branches of the revenue, that is, contracted with the government to pay into the treasury a fixed yearly sum, taking upon itself the collection of certain taxes as an equivalent.

färm′ẽr-ship, *n.* The occupation of farming; the skill or management of a farmer.

färm′ẽr-y, *n.* The buildings, yards, etc., necessary for the business of a farm. [Rare.]

färm′house, *n.* A house on a farm; the residence of a farmer.

färm′ing, *a.* Pertaining to farms or agriculture; as, Iowa is a *farming* state; *farming* machinery.

färm′ing, *n.* 1. The business of cultivating land or employing it for the purposes of husbandry; agriculture.

2. The practice of letting or leasing taxes for collection.

3. The business of collecting taxes.

fär′mōst, *a.* Most distant or remote. [Rare.]

färm′stead (-sted), *n.* The buildings on a farm; a country homestead.

färm′yärd, *n.* The yard or inclosure attached to a barn; the inclosure surrounded by the farm buildings.

fär′ness, *n.* Distance; remoteness; the state of being far off.

fä′rō, *n.* [Fr. *pharaon*, so called from the representation of a *Pharaoh*, the name of the ancient kings of Egypt, upon the back of one of the cards.] A gambling game with cards, in which the players bet on the order in which the cards will appear when dealt singly from the top of the pack by means of a device called a faro-box.

fä′rō-bank, *n.* An establishment where the game of faro is played; also, the amount risked in the game by the proprietor.

fä′rō-box, *n.* A metal box from which the cards are dealt in playing faro. It is so contrived that but one card can be removed at a time from a slit at one side, and has a spring which keeps the top card level with the slit.

Fā-rō-ēse′, *a.* Pertaining to the Faroe islands, their inhabitants, or language.

Fā-rō-ēse′, *n. sing.* and *pl.* [Ice. *Færeyskr*, a Faroese, from *Færeyjar*, lit., the sheep islands, the Faroe islands, from *fær*, sheep.]

1. A native or inhabitant, or the natives and inhabitants collectively, of the Faroe islands, which belong to Denmark and lie between the Shetland islands and Iceland.

2. A Scandinavian dialect, which is the language of the Faroe islands.

fär′-off, *a.* Far-away; remote.

> One *far-off* divine event,
> To which the whole creation moves. —Tennyson.

far-rag′i-nous, *a.* [L. *farrago* (-*inis*), mixed fodder for cattle.] Formed of various materials; mixed; jumbled; as, a *farraginous* speech.

far-rā′gō, *n.* [L. *farrago* (-*inis*), mixed fodder for cattle, a mixture, medley, from *far*, *farris*, spelt.] A mass composed of various materials confusedly mixed; a medley.

far′rănd, *a.* and *n.* Same as *Farand*.

fär′-reach″ing, *a.* Having a tendency to exert influence and produce an effect in far-off places or times.

far-rē-ā′tion, *n.* Same as *Confarreation*.

far′ri-ẽr, *n.* [OFr. *ferrier*, a farrier, from L. *ferrarius*, pertaining to iron, a worker with iron, blacksmith, from *ferrum*, iron.]

1. A shoer of horses; a blacksmith.

2. One who combines veterinary surgery with horseshoeing.

far′ri-ẽr, *v.i.* To practise as a farrier. [Obs.]

far′ri-ẽr-y, *n.* 1. The art of horseshoeing or of preventing, curing, or mitigating the diseases of horses and cattle.

2. A farrier's establishment; a blacksmith's shop.

far′rōw, *v.t.* or *v.i.*; farrowed, *pt.*, *pp.*; farrowing, *ppr.* [ME. *fergen*, to bring forth pigs, from AS. *fearh*, a little pig.] To bring forth, as pigs; said only of swine.

far′rōw, *a.* [D. *vaarkoe*, a young cow that has not yet brought forth a calf, a heifer; *var*, *varre*, a bullock; Ice. *farri*, a bullock; AS. *fearr*, a bull.] Not producing young in a particular season or year; applied to cows only. If a cow has had a calf, but fails in a subsequent year, she is said to *be farrow* or to *go farrow*.

far′rōw, *n.* [ME. *faren*, pl., little pigs, from AS. *fearh*, pl. *fearas*, a little pig.] A litter of pigs.

far′ry, *n.* A farrow. [Obs.]

färse, *n.* [LL. *farsa*, from L. *farsus*, *fartus*, pp. of *farcire*, to stuff, fill up.] In some English churches before the Reformation, an explanation or paraphrase in English of the text of the epistle read in Latin.

fär′see″ing, *a.* Seeing or able to see far; hence, having foresight or forethought; prudent; wise.

fär′sight″ed (-sīt″ed), *a.* 1. Able to perceive objects at a distance more clearly than those near-by; hyperopic.

2. Wise; sagacious; farseeing; as, a *farsighted* statesman.

fär′sight″ed-ness, *n.* The state or quality of being farsighted.

fär′thẽr, *a.*, comp. of *far*. [ME. *ferrer*; AS. *fyrre*, more remote, farther.]

1. More far; more remote; more distant; as, on the *farther* side; *farther* India.

2. Reaching to a greater distance; additional; increased; further; as, his *farther* progress was impeded. The word is often confused with *further*. *Farther* is generally preferred in speaking of distance, *further* in the sense of *additional*, as of time, mention, or treatment.

fär′thẽr, *adv.*, comp. of *far*. [ME. *ferrer*; AS. *fyrre*, farther, beyond.]

1. At or to a greater distance; more remotely; beyond; as, let us look *farther*.

2. Additionally; to a greater degree; in this sense, *further* is generally preferred.

> I will disparage her no *farther*, till you are my witnesses. —Shak.

fär′thẽr, *v.t.* To advance; to further. [Rare.]

fär′thẽr-ănce, *n.* [Rare.] Same as *Furtherance*.

fär′thẽr-mōre, *adv.* [Rare.] Same as *Furthermore*.

fär′thẽr-mōst, *a.* Furthermost; furthest.

fär′thest, *a.*, superl. of *far*. Most distant or remote; as, the *farthest* degree.

fär′thest, *adv.*, superl. of *far*. Same as *Furthest*.

fär′thing, *n.* [ME. *ferthing*, *ferthynge*; AS. *feorthing*, lit., a fourthling, the fourth part of a thing, dim. of *feortha*, fourth.]

1. The fourth of a penny; the smallest coin and money of account of Great Britain, equal to half a cent in United States money.

2. A division of land. [Obs.]

> Thirty acres make a *farthing*-land; nine *farthings* a Cornish acre; and four Cornish acres a knight's fee. —Carew.

3. Anything very small; a small quantity.

> No *farthing* of grease. —Chaucer.

fär′thin-gāle, *n.* [OFr. *verdugalle*, *vertugalle*, a farthingale; Sp. *verdugado*, provided with hoops, a farthingale, from *verdugo*, the young shoot of a tree, a rod, hoop, from *verde*, L. *viridis*, green.] A hoop petticoat, or circles of hoops, formed of whalebone, used to extend the petticoat. The hoop, the last remains of the *farthingale*, was used in court-dress up to the reign of George IV., and revived, after a form, in the use of crinoline, in the reign of Queen Victoria. Sometimes written *fardingale*.

Farthingale, time of Queen Elizabeth.

fas′cēs, *n.pl.* [L. *fascis*, pl. *fasces*, a bundle, packet.] In Roman antiquity, an ax tied up with a bundle of rods, and borne before the chief Roman magistrates as a badge of their authority.

fas′cet, *n.* [ME. *faucet*; OFr. *fausset*, a faucet.]

1. Same as *Faucet*.

2. In glass-manufacturing, (a) a wire basket secured to the end of a rod, for carrying the bottle from the mold to the leer; (b) a rod put into the mouth of the bottle for the same purpose.

fas′ci-ȧ (fash′i-), *n.*; *pl.* **fas′ci-æ**. [L., a band, sash, fillet.]

1. A band, sash, or fillet worn by the women of ancient Rome.

2. In architecture, any flat member with a small projection, as the band of an architrave; also, in brick buildings, the jutting of the bricks beyond the windows in the several stories except the highest.

3. In surgery, a bandage, roller, or ligature.

4. In anatomy, the areolar tissue forming layers beneath the skin.

5. In zoölogy, a band or belt of color, usually broad and transverse, on the skin, feathers, scales, etc.

6. In music, the sides of a violin.

fas′ci-ăl (fash′i-), *a.* Pertaining to, consisting of, or composing a fascia.

fas′ci-ăl, *a.* Belonging to the fasces.

fas′ci-āte (fash′i-), *a.* Same as *Fasciated*, 2 and 3.

fas′ci-ā-ted, *a.* [L. *fasciatus*, from *fascia*, a bundle, fillet.]

1. Bound with a fillet, sash, or bandage.

2. In botany, characterized by fasciation.

3. In zoölogy, marked with transverse bands of color.

fas-ci-ā′tion (fash-i-), *n.* [L. *fascia*, a fillet, band.]

1. The act or manner of binding up diseased parts; a bandaging.

2. That which binds; a fascia.

3. In botany, a malformation in plants, in which a stem or branch becomes flattened and widened laterally into the shape of a ribbon. It is quite common and is the normal condition of the cockscomb.

4. The state of being fasciated.

fas′ci-cle, *n.* [L. *fasciculus*, dim. of *fascis*, a bundle.] A bundle; a collection; specifically, (a) in botany, a form of cyme in which the flowers are clustered together in a more or less compact bundle; (b) in anatomy, a fasciculus; (c) a small number of printed sheets bound together; one of the parts of a book published in parts.

fas′ci-cled, *a.* Same as *Fasciculate.*

fas-cic′ū-lăr, *a.* Same as *Fasciculate.*

fas-cic′ū-lăr-ly, *adv.* Same as *Fasciculately.*

fas-cic′ū-lāte, fas-cic′ū-lā-ted, *a.* [L. *fasciculus*, dim. of *fascis*, a bundle.]

1. Growing in clusters or bunches from the same point, as the leaves of the larch; also applied to the stems and roots of plants.

2. In entomology, having hair-like processes; split into long processes.

3. In mineralogy, occurring in crystals resembling fibrous bundles of needles.

Fasciculate Root (*Ranunculus Ficaria*).

fas-cic′ū-lāte-ly, *adv.* In a fasciculate manner.

fas′ci-cūle, *n.* [Fr., from L. *fasciculus*, dim. of *fascis*, a bundle.] In entomology, a tuft of close-set hairs.

fas-cic′ū-lite, *n.* [L. *fasciculus*, a small bundle, and Gr. *lithos*, stone.] A variety of fibrous hornblende, of a fascicular structure.

fas-cic′ū-lus, *n.*; *pl.* **fas-cic′ū-lī.** [L., dim. of *fascis*, a bundle.]

1. Same as *Fascicle.*

2. In anatomy, a bundle, especially of nerve-fibers or muscular fibers.

3. A nosegay.

fas′ci-nāte, *v.t.*; fascinated, *pt., pp.*; fascinating, *ppr.* [L. *fascinatus*, pp. of *fascinare*, to bewitch, charm; Gr. *baskainein*, to bewitch.]

1. To bewitch; to enchant, to operate on by some powerful or irresistible influence; to obtain influence over.

2. To charm; to captivate; to excite and allure through the passions or affections.

Syn.—Charm, enchant, captivate, entrance, attract, enrapture, bewitch, enamour.

fas-ci-nā′tion, *n.* [L. *fascinatio* (*-onis*), an enchanting.]

1. The act of bewitching or enchanting; enchantment; a powerful or irresistible influence on the affections or passions; unseen, inexplicable, or hypnotic influence.

2. The state of being fascinated.

3. A fascinating influence; a charm; a spell.

fas-cine′, *n.* [Fr. *fascine*; OFr. *fascine*; L. *fascina*, a bundle of sticks, a fagot, from *fascis*, a bundle.] In fortification and engineering, a fagot; a bundle of rods or small sticks of wood, bound at both ends and in the middle; used in raising batteries, in filling ditches, in strengthening ramparts, and making parapets; also used in civil engineering in the construction of dams, etc.

Fascines.

fas-cine′=dwell″ĕr, *n.* In archæology, one of those prehistoric people who built and lived in fascine-dwellings.

fas-cine′=dwell″ing, *n.* In archæology, a lake-dwelling of prehistoric times, built upon a foundation of fascines.

fas′ci-nous, *a.* Caused or acting by witchcraft. [Obs.]

fas-ci′ō-lȧ, *n.*; *pl.* **fas-ci′ō-læ.** [L. *fasciola*, dim. of *fascia*, a bandage.]

1. In anatomy, the convolution bordering the brain, known as the fascia dentata.

2. In entomology, a short or narrow fascia.

fas-ci′ō-lăr, *a.* Pertaining to the fasciola of the brain.

fas′ci-ōle, *n.* 1. Same as *Fasciola*, 2.

2. One of the bands of modified spines of some sea-urchins.

fas′cis, *n.*, sing. of *fasces.*

fash, *v.t.* [Scot., from OFr. *fascher*, to anger, displease; L. *fastidire*, to feel disgust at, dislike, from *fastidium*, loathing, dislike.] To vex; to tease.

fash, *v.i.* 1. To take trouble; to be at pains; as, you needna *fash.*

2. To be weary; to account anything a trouble.

> You soon *fash* of a good office.
> —Scotch proverb.

fash, *n.* [Scot.] 1. Trouble; vexation.

2. Care; pains; attention.

3. One who annoys; one who makes trouble.

fash′iŏn, *v.t.*; fashioned, *pt., pp.*; fashioning, *ppr.* 1. To form; to give shape or figure to; to mold.

> Here the loud hammer *fashions* female toys.
> —Gay.

2. To fit; to adapt; to accommodate; with *to.*

> Laws ought to be *fashioned to* the manners and conditions of the people. —Spenser.

3. To make according to rule.

4. To forge or counterfeit. [Obs.]

fash′iŏn, *n.* [ME. *facioun*; OFr. *faceon*, fashion, form, outward appearance, from L. *factio* (*-onis*), a making, from *facere*, to make.]

1. The make or form of anything; the state of anything with regard to its external appearance; shape; style; pattern; form; as, the *fashion* of a hat; the *fashion* of a building; the *fashion* of a ship.

2. The prevailing mode or customary style in dress or other things subject to change; specifically, the mode or style of dress favored by polite society; as, there is nothing so changeable as *fashion*; out of the *fashion.*

3. Social compliance; good form; style; as, a woman of *fashion.*

4. Custom; usage; common practice; as, it is the *fashion* to belong to some fraternal order.

5. Way; style or method of doing a thing; often in composition; as, climbing monkey-*fashion*; after the *fashion* of sailors.

6. People of style; polite society; fashionable people collectively; as, the beauty and *fashion* of the town.

After a fashion; to a certain extent; indifferently or fairly good but not well; as she did her work *after a fashion.*

In fashion; fashionable.

Out of fashion; not in keeping with prevailing modes.

Syn.—Custom, practice, usage, style, manner, mode, way, sort, conventionality.

fash′iŏn-ȧ-ble, *a.* 1. Made according to the prevailing form or mode; as, a *fashionable* dress.

2. Established by custom or use; current; prevailing at a particular time; as, the *fashionable* philosophy; *fashionable* opinions.

3. Observant of the fashion or customary mode; dressing or behaving according to the prevailing fashion; as, a *fashionable* man.

4. Polite; well-bred; polished; conforming to fashion; as, *fashionable* company or society.

5. Capable of being shaped or fashioned. [Obs.]

fash′iŏn-ȧ-ble, *n.* One who conforms to the styles or fashions; usually in the plural; as, it was a gathering of *fashionables.*

fash′iŏn-ȧ-ble-ness, *n.* The state of being fashionable.

fash′iŏn-ȧ-bly, *adv.* In a manner according with fashion, custom, or prevailing practice.

fash′iŏned, *a.* Having a certain form or fashion; used in composition; as, old-*fashioned.*

fash′iŏn-ĕr, *n.* 1. One who fashions or forms anything.

2. A modiste. [Obs.]

fash′iŏn-ist, *n.* An obsequious follower of the modes and fashions. [Rare.]

fash′iŏn-less, *a.* Having no fashion.

fash′iŏn=mŏn″gĕr, *n.* One who studies the fashions; a fop.

fash′iŏn=mŏn″gĕr-ing, *a.* Behaving like a fashion-monger.

fash′iŏn=piēce, *n.* Same as *Fashion-timber.*

fash′iŏn=plāte, *n.* An engraving or picture illustrating current fashions in dress.

fash′iŏn=tim″bĕr, *n.* One of the hindmost timbers which terminate the breadth and give shape to the stern of a wooden ship.

fas′sȧ-ite, *n.* [From *Fassa*, in the Tyrol, where it is found.] A mineral, a variety of pyroxene.

fȧst, *a.*; *comp.* faster; *superl.* fastest. [From AS. *fæst*, fixed, firm, close; the idea of *fast* as swift came from the idea of close, fixed, for what is close easily becomes urgent or pressing.]

1. Swift; moving rapidly; quick in motion; as, a *fast* horse.

2. Speedily accomplished; done quickly; occupying or consuming comparatively little time; as, a *fast* race; *fast* work.

3. More rapid than the standard; too far ahead; used of timepieces and reckoning of time; as, his watch is *fast.*

4. Eager in seeking pleasure; given to extravagant pleasures or frivolity; dissipated; prodigal; dissolute; of low morals; as, he led a *fast* life; a *fast* woman, etc.

Syn.—Rapid, quick, wild, reckless, gay, dissipated, dissolute.

fȧst, *adv.* [ME. *faste*, swiftly, quickly.] Swiftly; rapidly; with quick steps or progression; as, to run *fast*; the ship moves *fast* through the water; the work goes on *fast.*

fȧst, *v.i.*; fasted, *pt., pp.*; fasting, *ppr.* [ME. *fasten, festen*; AS. *fæstan*, to abstain from food, fast.]

1. To abstain from food beyond the usual time; to omit to take the usual meals for a time; as, to *fast* a day or a week.

2. To abstain from food or from certain kinds of food voluntarily, for the mortification of the body or appetite, or as a token of grief, sorrow, repentance, or religious zeal.

> Thou didst *fast* and weep for the child.
> —2 Sam. xii. 21.

fȧst, *n.* [ME. *fast, faste*; AS. *fæsten*, a fast, from *fæstan*, to fast.]

1. A state of fasting; abstinence from food, either total or partial; as, to break one's *fast.*

2. Voluntary abstinence from food, as a religious penance or discipline; either total or partial abstinence from customary food, with a view to mortify the appetite, or to express grief.

3. The time of fasting, whether a day, week, or longer time.

> The *fast* was now already past.
> —Acts xxvii. 9.

To break fast or *to break one's fast*; to take food after a period of fasting; especially, to take the first food of the day after the night's fast; to eat one's breakfast.

fȧst, *a.* [ME. *fast, fest*; AS. *fæst*, fixed, firm.]

1. Firm; immovable.

> Who, by his strength, setteth *fast* the mountains. —Ps. lxv. 6.

2. Fortified; strong against attack; secure.

> Robbers and outlaws lurking in woods and *fast* places. —Spenser.

3. Firmly fixed; closely adhering; as, to make *fast* a rope.

4. Profound; deep; sound; as, a *fast* sleep.

5. Faithful; firm in adherence; as, a *fast* friend.

6. Durable; lasting; not easily faded by light or water; as, these colors are all *fast.*

Fast and loose pulleys; a pair of pulleys placed side by side on a revolving shaft, the one being rigidly fixed to it and the other loose. The shaft is driven by shifting the belt from the loose to the fixed pulley and is stopped by reversing this action.

Hard and fast; (a) absolutely binding; strictly obligatory; unalterable; as, *hard and fast* rules; a *hard and fast* contract; (b) in nautical language, firmly grounded; immovable; as, the ship was *hard and fast.*

To make fast; (a) to fasten; to make secure; to close; as, *to make fast* the door; (b) in nautical language, to belay; as, *to make fast* a rope.

To play fast and loose; to be tricky; to say one thing and mean or do another; from an old game called *fast and loose*, played by gipsies and sharpers.

Syn.—Firm, secure, fixed, constant, steadfast, stable, unyielding, unswerving.

fȧst, *adv.* 1. Firmly; immovably.

> We will bind thee *fast*, and deliver thee into their hand. —Judges xv. 13.

2. Profoundly; deeply; as, she was *fast* asleep.

3. Near; not far or distant; close; as, *fast* by the house; *fast* beside each other.

Fast by or *fast beside*; close or near to.

fȧst, *n.* [ME. *fest*; Ice. *festr*, a rope, cord.]

1. That which fastens or holds; specifically, in nautical language, a rope or chain by which a vessel is moored to a wharf, dock, etc., and named according to the part of the vessel to which it is made fast; as, a breast*fast.*

2. Immovable shore-ice.

fȧst′=dāy, *n.* 1. A day on which fasting is observed; a day appointed either by ecclesiastical or civil authority for religious fasting; specifically, in New England, a day in March or April appointed to be spent in fasting and prayer.

2. In Scotland, a week-day observed as a day of preparation for the communion, but not now associated in any degree with physical fasting.

fȧs′ten (fȧs′n), *v.t.*; fastened, *pt., pp.*; fastening, *ppr.* [ME. *fastnen, fastnien*; AS. *fæstnian*, to fasten, to confirm, from *fæst*, fast, fixed.]

1. To fix firmly; to make fast or close; to secure; to connect by any means, as by nails, cords, bolts, cements, pins, hooks, etc.; as, to *fasten* a dress, a door, or a chain.

2. Figuratively, to join in close union; to join firmly by any means; to cause to cleave together; as, to *fasten* a reputation or a name on one.

3. To settle; to clench; to confirm; as, to *fasten* a bargain.

4. To lay on with strength; to make to tell. [Obs.]

> Could he *fasten* a blow, or make a thrust, when not suffered to approach?—Dryden.

Syn.—Affix, attach, fix, clench, stick, annex, unite.

fȧs′ten (fȧs′n), *v.i.* To fix oneself; to seize and hold on; to clench.

The leech will hardly *fasten* on a fish.—Brown.

fȧs′ten-ẽr, *n.* One who or that which makes fast or firm.

fȧs′ten-ing, *n.* [ME. *fastnyng*, confirmation, a fastness; AS. *fæstenung*, a fastening.] Anything that binds and makes fast, or is intended for that purpose.

fȧst′ẽr, *n.* One who abstains from food.

fȧst′=hand″ed, *a.* Close-handed; covetous; close-fisted; avaricious. [Rare.]

fas′ti, *n.pl.* [L., from *fastus*, legal, lawful; *fastus dies*, a day on which judgment could be pronounced, from *fas*, divine law, from *fari*, to speak.]

1. The Roman calendar, which gave the days for festivals, courts, etc., corresponding to a modern almanac.

2. Records or registers of important events.

fas-tid-i-os′i-ty, *n.* Fastidiousness. [Rare.]

fas-tid′i-ous, *a.* [L. *fastidiosus*, disdainful, scornful, that feels disgust, from *fastidium*, a loathing, disgust, from *fastus*, disdain, haughtiness, contempt.]

1. Disdainful; squeamish; delicate to a fault; difficult to please; rejecting what is common; suited with difficulty; as, a *fastidious* appetite.

2. Disgusting; loathsome [Obs.]

Syn.—Squeamish, hypercritical, overnice, overparticular, punctilious.—*Fastidious* is applied to one whose taste or feelings are offended by trifling defects or errors; *squeamish* to one who is excessively nice on minor points, or else overscrupulous.

fas-tid′i-ous-ly, *adv.* In a fastidious manner.

fas-tid′i-ous-ness, *n.* The quality of being fastidious; squeamishness of mind, taste, or appetite.

fas-tig′i-ȧ, *n.*, pl. of *fastigium.*

fas-tig′i-āte, fas-tig′i-ā-ted, *a.* [L. *fastigatus*, sloping to a point, sloping, from *fastigium*, a slope, roof.]

1. Narrowing toward the summit, as a sloping roof; pointed.

2. In botany, tapering to a narrow point like a pyramid; having parallel and erect branches, as the Lombardy poplar.

3. In zoölogy, tapering gradually to an apex; forming a conical bundle.

fas-tig′i-āte-ly, *adv.* In a fastigiate manner.

fas-tig′i-um, *n.*; *pl.* **fas-tig′i-ȧ.** [L.] 1. The summit, apex, or ridge of a house or pediment.

2. In entomology, the extreme point of the apex of the head, when, as in many insects, it is developed into a prominence resembling a cone.

fȧst′ing=dāy, *n.* A fast-day.

fȧst′ish, *a.* Rather fast; inclined to be dissipated; as, a *fastish* society.

fȧst′ly, *adv.* Quickly; rapidly. [Obs.]

fȧst′ly, *adv.* Firmly; surely. [Obs.]

fȧst′ness, *n.* [ME. *fastnesse*, firmness, certainty, a stronghold; AS. *fæstnes*, firmness, a stronghold, from *fæst*, firm, fast, fixed.]

1. The state of being fast.

2. Strength; security.

The places of *fastness* are laid open.—Davies.

3. A stronghold; a fortress or fort; a place fortified; a castle; as, the enemy retired to their *fastnesses*.

4. Closeness; conciseness of style. [Obs.]

fas-tū-os′i-ty, *n.* The quality of being fastuous or haughty; ostentation. [Obs.]

fas′tū-ous, *a.* Proud; haughty; disdainful. [Obs.]

fas′tū-ous-ly, *adv.* In a fastuous manner. [Obs.]

fas′tū-ous-ness, *n.* Fastuosity. [Obs.]

fat, *a.*; *comp.* fatter; *superl.* fattest. [ME. *fat, fet*; AS. *fæt, fætt*, fat.]

1. Fleshy; plump; corpulent; obese; having an unusual amount of flesh; opposed to *lean*; as, a *fat* man; a *fat* ox.

2. Containing fat, oil, or grease; rich; oily; unctuous; as, *fat* cheese; *fat* bacon.

3. Dull; heavy; stupid; unteachable.

There is little or no sense in the *fat* parts of any creature, hence the ancients said of any dull fellow that he had a *fat* wit.—Johnson.

4. Prosperous; affluent. [Obs.]

These were terrible alarms to persons grown *fat* and wealthy. —South.

5. Rich; producing a large income; as, a *fat* benefice; a *fat* office.

6. Fertile; as, a *fat* soil; nourishing; as, *fat* pasture.

7. In printing, applied to matter having many blank spaces or cuts; hence, applied to work that pays well.

8. In nautical language, broad, as the quarter of a ship.

Syn.—Corpulent, fleshy, brawny, pursy, rich, luxuriant, portly, stout, fertile, unctuous, obese, oleaginous.

fat, *n.* 1. An oily, solid substance deposited in the cells of the adipose or cellular membrane, under the skin and in various other parts of animal bodies, and also in plants. It is of various degrees of consistence, as in tallow, lard, and oil. All *fats* agree in being insoluble in water, and in not containing any nitrogen, which is a common constituent of most other animal matter. The most common and abundant are stearin, palmitin, and olein. Of these, stearin and palmitin are solids at ordinary temperatures and olein is a liquid.

2. The best or richest part; as, to live on the *fat* of the land.

Abel brought of the *fat* of his flock. —Gen. iv. 4.

3. In printing, work containing much blank space, and therefore paying the workman well.

fat, *v.t.*; fatted, *pt.*, *pp.*; fatting, *ppr.* To make fat; to fatten; to make plump and fleshy with abundant food; as, to *fat* fowls or sheep.

fat, *v.i.* To grow fat, plump, and fleshy.

fat, *n.* [ME. *fat, fet*; AS. *fæt*, a vat.]

1. A large tub, cistern, or vessel; a vat.

The *fats* shall overflow with wine and oil. —Joel ii. 24.

2. An old indefinite measure of capacity, differing for different commodities; thus, a *fat* of grain was a quarter or eight bushels.

fā′tăl, *a.* [ME. *fatal*; OFr. *fatal*; L. *fatalis*, pertaining to fate, fatal, from *fatum*, fate.]

1. Proceeding from fate or destiny; necessary; inevitable. [Obs.]

These things are *fatal* and necessary. —Tillotson.

2. Causing death or destruction; deadly; mortal; as, a *fatal* wound; a *fatal* disease.

3. Foreboding death or calamity; ominous.

4. Influencing or determining destiny; fateful.

Our acts our angels are, or good or ill,
Our *fatal* shadows that walk by us still. —Fletcher.

fā′tăl-ism, *n.* [Fr. *fatalisme*, from L. *fatalis*, fatal.]

1. The doctrine that all things are subject to fate, or take place by inevitable necessity.

2. A disposition to accept everything as inevitable and predetermined by fate.

fā′tăl-ist, *n.* One who believes in fatalism; one who maintains that all things happen by inevitable necessity.

fā-tăl-is′tic, *a.* Pertaining to fatalism; implying fatalism; savoring of fatalism.

fȧ-tal′i-ty, *n.* [Fr. *fatalité*; LL. *fatalitas*, fatal necessity, fatality, from L. *fatalis*, fatal.]

1. The state of being fatal; a fixed, unalterable course of things, independent of any controlling cause; an invincible necessity existing in things themselves.

2. Tendency to destruction or danger, or to some critical or hazardous event; mortality.

Seven times nine, or the year sixty-three, is conceived to carry with it the most considerable *fatality*. —Browne.

3. A fatal occurrence; as, it was not possible to avert this *fatality*.

fā′tăl-ly, *adv.* 1. By a decree of fate or destiny; by inevitable necessity or predetermination.

2. Mortally; destructively; in death or ruin; as, the encounter ended *fatally*.

fā′tăl-ness, *n.* The quality of being fatal; necessity; fatality.

fä′tȧ Mor-gä′nȧ. [It., so called because supposed to be the work of a *fata* or fairy called *Morgana*.] A name given to a very striking optical illusion, a kind of mirage, which has been principally remarked in the Strait of Messina, between the coasts of Sicily and Calabria. The images of men, houses, towers, palaces, columns, trees, etc., are occasionally seen from the coast, sometimes in the water, and sometimes in the air, or at the surface of the water.

fat′back, *n.* 1. The striped mullet, *Mugil cephalus* or *albula*. [Local.]

2. The menhaden, *Brevoortia tyrannus*. [Local.]

fat′bird, *n.* 1. The guacharo or oilbird, *Steatornis caripensis*.

2. The pectoral sandpiper, *Actodromas maculata*.

fat′=brāined, *a.* Dull of apprehension.

fāte, *n.* [ME. *fate*, fate; L. *fatum*, a prophetic declaration, oracle, from *fatus*, pp. of *fari*, to speak.]

1. Primarily, a divine decree or a fixed sentence by which the order of things is prescribed; hence, inevitable necessity; destiny depending on a superior cause, and uncontrollable; as, according to the Stoics, every event is determined by *fate*.

Necessity or chance
Approach not me; and what I will is *fate*. —Milton.

2. Event predetermined; lot; destiny; as, it is our *fate* to meet with disappointments.

Tell me what *fates* attend the duke of Suffolk. —Shak.

3. Final event; death; destruction; as, the *fate* of the enterprise was sealed with that first failure.

Yet still he chose the longest way to *fate*. —Dryden.

4. Cause of death. [Rare and Poet.]

With full force his deadly bow he bent,
And feathered *fates* among the mules and sumpters sent. —Dryden.

5. [F—] In Greek and Roman mythology, destiny; usually in the plural, the Destinies or Parcæ; goddesses supposed to preside over the birth and life of men. They were three in number, Clotho, Lachesis, and Atropos.

6. One destined to be a mate; one's future wife or husband; as, he has met his *fate* at last. [Colloq.]

Syn.—Destiny, doom, lot, fortune, death, destruction.

fāt′ed, *a.* 1. Decreed by fate; doomed; destined; as, he was *fated* to meet a violent end.

2. Appointed or regulated by fate.

Her awkward love indeed was oddly *fated*. —Prior.

3. Invested with the power of determining fates. [Obs.]

The *fated* sky
Gives us free scope. —Shak.

4. Exempted by fate. [Obs.]

fāte′fụl, *a.* 1. Bearing fatal power; producing fatal results.

The *fateful* steel. —J. Barlow.

2. Fraught with fate; determining the future; as, a *fateful* letter; a *fateful* undertaking.

fāte′fụl-ly, *adv.* In a fateful manner.

fāte′fụl-ness, *n.* The state or quality of being fateful.

fat′head, *n.* 1. The blackhead or black-headed minnow, *Pimephales promelas*, having a short round head.

2. A labroid fish, the redfish, *Semicossyphus* or *Pimelometopon pulcher*. It abounds on the coast of California.

fat′=head″ed, *a.* Dull; heavy-witted; stupid.

fä′thẽr, *n.* [ME. *fader, fadir*; AS. *fæder*; L. *pater*, father; compare G. *vater*, O.H.G. *fatar*, Gr. *patēr*, Sans. *pitar*, father.]

1. He who begets a child; the nearest male ancestor; a male parent.

The *father* of a fool hath no joy. —Prov. xvii. 21.

2. A lineal male ancestor; especially, the first ancestor; the progenitor of a race or family; as, Adam was the *father* of the human race; Abraham was the *father* of the Israelites.

David slept with his *fathers*.—1 Kings ii. 10.

3. The appellation of an old man, and a term of respect; as, *Father* Abraham.

4. One who feeds and supports, or exercises paternal care over another.

I was a *father* to the poor. —Job xxix. 16.

5. One of the ecclesiastical writers of the early church, as Polycarp, Jerome, etc.; commonly called the *fathers of the church*.

6. A senator in ancient Rome; as, the conscript *fathers*.

7. A title given to the priests of the Roman Catholic and Greek churches; a confessor.

8. Originator; cause; real or apparent source.

Thy wish was *father*, Harry, to that thought. —Shak.

9. One who through marriage or adoption occupies the position of a male parent; a father-in-law; a stepfather. [Colloq.]

10. [F—] The Supreme Being; God; in orthodox Christian phraseology, the first person in the Trinity.

Go, ye, therefore, and teach all nations, baptizing them in the name of the *Father*, and of the Son, and of the Holy Spirit. —Matt. xxviii. 19.

11. One who creates, invents, makes, or composes anything; the author, former, or contriver; a founder, director, or instructor; the first to practise any art; as, Homer is the *father* of epic poetry; Gutenberg is the *father* of printing; the pilgrim *fathers*.

12. The eldest member of any profession or of any body; as, the *father* of the bar; the *father* of the senate.

Adoptive father; one who adopts the child of another, and acknowledges and treats him as his own; a foster-father.

City fathers; the common council or board of aldermen of a city.

Holy Father; in the Roman Catholic church, the pope.

Natural father; the father of an illegitimate child.

Putative father; one who is reputed to be the father; the supposed father of a child.

Spiritual father; a religious teacher or one who

brings about another's conversion; also, a father confessor.

Father confessor; in the Roman Catholic church, a priest to whom confession is made.

Father in God, a title of a bishop.

Father of lies; Satan; the devil.

Father of the Faithful; among Mohammedans, Mahomet, or the sultan of Turkey, who is regarded as his successor; among Christians, Abraham.

To be gathered to one's fathers; to die and be buried.

fä′thẽr, *v.t.*; fathered, *pt., pp.*; fathering, *ppr.* 1. To beget, to become the father of.

> Cowards *father* cowards, and base things sire base. —Shak.

2. To adopt; to take as one's own, as the child of another.

3. To adopt as one's own; to profess or acknowledge oneself to be the author of or responsible for.

> Men of wit
> Often *fathered* what he writ. —Swift.

4. To ascribe or charge to one as his offspring or production; with *on* or *upon*.

> Come, *father* not your lies *upon* me, widow. —Middleton.

5. To furnish or provide with a father.

fä′thẽr-hood, *n.* [ME. *fadirhode*, from AS. *fæder*, father, and *had*, state, condition.] The state of being a father, or the character or authority of a father.

fä′thẽr-in-law″, *n.* 1. The father of one's husband or wife.

2. A stepfather. [Colloq., Eng.]

fä′thẽr-land, *n.* [Imitated from G. *Vaterland*, fatherland.] One's native land; the native land of one's fathers or ancestors.

fä′thẽr-lash″ẽr, *n.* A salt-water fish, *Cottus bubalis*. Its head is large and its spines formidable.

fä′thẽr-less, *a.* [ME. *faderles*; AS. *fæderleas*, fatherless; *fæder*, father, and *-leas*, -less.]

1. Destitute of a living father; as, a *fatherless* child.

2. Without a known author.

fä′thẽr-less-ness, *n.* The state of being without a father.

fä′thẽr-li-ness, *n.* The qualities of a father; parental kindness, care, and tenderness.

fä″thẽr-long′legs, *n.* Same as *Daddy-longlegs*.

fä′thẽr-ly, *a.* [AS. *fæder*, father, and *-lic*, like.]

1. Like a kind father in affection and care; tender; paternal; protecting; careful; as, *fatherly* care or affection.

2. Pertaining to a father.

fä′thẽr-ly, *adv.* In the manner of a father.

> Thus Adam, *fatherly* displeased. —Milton.

fä′thẽr-ship, *n.* The state of being a father.

fath′ŏm, *n.*; *pl.* **fath′ŏms** or **fath′ŏm**. [ME. *fathome*, a measure of length about six feet; AS. *fæthm*, the space reached by the arms extended, a measure of length.]

1. A measure of length, containing six feet, the space to which a man may extend his arms; used chiefly at sea for measuring cables, cordage, and the depth of the sea in sounding by a line and lead.

> The shipmen sounded and found it twenty *fathoms*. —Acts xxvii. 28.

> Full *fathom* five thy father lies;
> Of his bones are coral made. —Shak.

2. Mental depth; intellectual reach or scope; penetration; depth of thought or contrivance; as, a man of *fathom*. [Rare.]

fath′ŏm, *v.t.*; fathomed, *pt., pp.*; fathoming, *ppr.* [ME. *fadomen*, *fadmen*, to embrace, encompass, from AS. *fæthmian*, to clasp, embrace.]

1. To encompass with the arms extended or encircling. [Obs.]

2. To penetrate; to find the bottom or extent of; to sound; to try the depth of.

3. To reach or penetrate with the mind; to master; to comprehend.

> Leave to *fathom* such high points as these. —Dryden.

fath′ŏm-ȧ-ble, *a.* Capable of being fathomed.

fath′ŏm-ẽr, *n.* One who fathoms.

fath′ŏm-less, *a.* 1. Having a depth so great that no bottom can be found, bottomless.

> Seas as *fathomless* as wide. —Cowper.

2. Incapable of being embraced or encompassed with the arms. [Obs.]

3. Incapable of being penetrated by the mind or comprehended.

fȧ-tid′iç, fȧ-tid′iç-ăl, *a.* [L. *fatidicus*, prophesying; *fatum*, fate, and *dicere*, to say, speak.] Having power to foretell future events; prophetic. [Rare.]

> So that the *fatidical* fury spreads wider and wider till at last even Saul must join in it. —Carlyle.

fȧ-tid′iç-ăl-ly, *adv.* In a fatidic manner.

fȧ-tid′i-en-cy, *n.* Divination; augury. [Obs.]

fȧ-tif′ẽr-ous, *a.* [L. *fatifer*, that brings death; *fatum*, fate, and *ferre*, to bring.] Deadly; mortal; destructive. [Rare.]

fat′i-gȧ-ble, *a.* Easily fatigued. [Obs.]

fat′i-gāte, *v.t.* To fatigue; to tire. [Obs.]

fat′i-gāte, *a.* Fatigued; tired. [Obs.]

fat-i-gā′tion, *n.* Fatigue; weariness. [Obs.]

fȧ-tïgue′ (-tēg′), *n.* [Fr. *fatigue*, from *fatiguer*; L. *fatigare*, to weary, fatigue.]

1. Weariness from bodily labor or mental exertion; lassitude or exhaustion of strength.

2. The cause of weariness; labor; toil; as, the *fatigues* of war.

3. The labors of military men, distinct from the use of arms; fatigue-duty; as, a party of men on *fatigue*.

4. In mechanics, the weakening of materials, as metal bars, by repeated or continued vibrations and strains.

Syn.—Lassitude, weariness, exhaustion, languor, enervation.

fȧ-tïgue′, *v.t.*; fatigued, *pt., pp.*; fatiguing, *ppr.* [Fr. *fatiguer*; L. *fatigare*, to weary, tire, fatigue.] To tire; to weary with labor or any bodily or mental exertion; to harass with toil; to exhaust the strength of by severe or long-continued exertion.

fȧ-tïgue′-çall, *n.* A signal summoning soldiers to fatigue-duty; usually a bugle-call or drum-beat.

fȧ-tïgue′-dress, *n.* The uniform worn by soldiers while on fatigue-duty.

fȧ-tïgue′-dū″ty, *n.* That part of a soldier's work which is distinct from the use of arms.

fȧ-tïgue′-pär″ty, *n.* A body of soldiers detailed for fatigue-duty.

fȧ-til′ō-quent (-kwent), *a.* [L. *fatiloquus*, prophesying.] Prophetic; prophesying. [Obs.]

fȧ-til′ō-quist, *n.* A fortune-teller. [Obs.]

Fat′i-mite, Fat′i-mide, *a.* and *n.* [Ar. *Fatimah*, Fatima.]

I. *a.* Descended from Fatima, Mohammed's daughter and only child, and the wife of the Calif Ali.

II. *n.* One of the members of the Arabian dynasty, descendants of Ali and Fatima, which ruled over Egypt, northern Africa, Syria, and Palestine from 909 to 1171 A. D.

fȧ-tis′cence, *n.* [L. *fatiscens* (-*entis*), ppr. of *fatiscere*, to open in chinks, gape.] A gaping or opening; a state of being chinky.

fȧ-tis′cent, *a.* Opening in chinks; gaping.

fat′-kid″neyed (-nid), *a.* Fat; gross; used in contempt. [Rare.]

> Peace, ye *fat-kidneyed* rascal! What a brawling dost thou keep! —Shak.

fat′ling, *n.* A lamb, kid, or other young animal, fattened for slaughter; a fat animal; applied to quadrupeds whose flesh is used for food.

> David sacrificed oxen and *fatlings*. —2 Sam. vi. 13.

fat′ly, *adv.* Grossly; greasily.

fat′nẽr, *n.* [Obs.] Same as *Fattener*.

fat′ness, *n.* [ME. *fatnes*; AS. *fætnes*, *fætness*; *fæt*, fat, and *-nes*, *-ness*.]

1. The quality of being fat, plump, or full-fed; corpulency; fullness of flesh.

> Their eyes stand out with *fatness*. —Ps. lxxiii. 7.

2. Unctuousness; sliminess; applied to earth; hence, richness; fertility; fruitfulness.

> God give thee of the *fatness* of the earth, and plenty of corn and wine.—Gen. xxvii. 28.

3. That which gives fertility.

> The clouds dropped *fatness*. —Philips.

4. Grossness; sensuality. [Obs.]

fat′ten, *v.t.*; fattened, *pt., pp.*; fattening, *ppr.* [AS. *gefætnian*, to fatten.]

1. To make fat; to feed for slaughter; to make fleshy or plump with fat.

2. To make fertile and fruitful; to enrich; as, to *fatten* land; to *fatten* fields with blood.

fat′ten, *v.i.* To grow fat or corpulent; to grow plump, thick, or fleshy; to be pampered.

> And villains *fatten* with the brave man's labor. —Otway.

fat′ten-ẽr, *n.* One who or that which fattens; that which gives fatness, richness, or fertility.

fat′ti-ness, *n.* The state of being fatty; grossness; greasiness.

fat′tish, *a.* Somewhat fat.

fat′ty, *a.* Composed of, containing, or having the qualities of fat; greasy; as, a *fatty* substance.

Fatty acid; any one of the monobasic acids of the paraffin series, formed by the oxidation of the primary alcohols, as formic and acetic acids. The more complex *fatty acids*, as oleic, stearic, and palmitic acids, combine with glycerin to form fat in all oleaginous compounds.

Fatty degeneration; a diseased condition of certain organs in which the protein elements are changed into a granular fatty matter to such a degree as to injure and eventually to destroy the functional efficiency of the organs.

Fatty series; a series of paraffin hydrocarbons derived from methane.

Fatty tissue; see *Adipose tissue* under *Adipose*.

fȧ-tū′i-tous, *a.* [L. *fatuitas*, foolishness.] Stupid; foolish; fatuous.

fȧ-tū′i-ty, *n.* [L. *fatuitas*, foolishness, from *fatuus*, foolish.] Weakness or imbecility of mind; feebleness of intellect; foolishness.

fat′ū-ous, *a.* [L. *fatuus*, foolish.]

1. Feeble in mind; weak; silly; stupid; foolish.

2. Impotent; without force or fire; illusory; like the ignis fatuus.

> Thence *fatuous* fires and meteors take their birth. —Denham.

fat′vȧ, fat′vȧh, *n.* Same as *Fetwa*.

fat′-wit″ted, *a.* Heavy; dull; stupid.

fau′bōurg (fō′), *n.* [Fr., from OFr. *forbourg*, *forsbourg*, lit., out of town, a suburb.] A suburb of French cities; the name is also given to districts now within the city, but which were formerly suburbs without it; as, the *Faubourg* St. Germain of Paris.

fau′çăl, *a.* [L. *fauces*, the throat.] Pertaining to or produced in the fauces; specifically, applied to certain deep, guttural sounds, produced in the fauces and peculiar to the Semitic and some other tongues.

fau′çēs, *n.pl.* [L., the throat, the gullet.]

1. In anatomy, the gullet or windpipe; the posterior part of the mouth, terminated by the pharynx and larynx.

2. In botany, the mouth or opening of the tube of a monopetalous corolla.

3. In conchology, that portion of the cavity of the first chamber of a shell which may be seen by looking through the aperture.

fau′cet, *n.* [ME. *faucet*, *fawcet*; OFr. *fausset*, a faucet, from *faulser*, to make a breach in, to falsify, from L. *falsus*, false, pp. of *fallere*, to deceive.]

1. A spout inserted in a cask, etc., for drawing a liquid, and fitted with a valve which may be opened and closed at will, thus controlling the flow of the liquid.

2. The enlarged end of a pipe, receiving the spigot end of another pipe.

fau′çhärd (fō′), *n.* [OFr. *fauchard*, *faussard*, from *faux*, a scythe, from L. *falx*, a sickle.] A medieval weapon composed of a blade shaped like a scythe, attached to a long handle.

fau′ciăl (-shăl), *a.* In anatomy, relating to the fauces; pharyngeal; faucal.

fau-ci′tis, *n.* [L., from *fauces*, throat.] An inflamed condition of the fauces.

faugh (fa), *interj.* An exclamation of contempt or abhorrence.

faul′çŏn, *n.* [Obs.] Same as *Falcon*.

fauld, *n.* [Scot.] The working-arch or tymp-arch situated above the dam of a blast-furnace.

faule, *n.* A lace collar; a fall. [Obs.]

fault, *n.* [ME. *faut*, *faute*; OFr. *faute*, *faulte*, a lack, fault, from L. *fallere*, to deceive.]

1. Failure; defect; default; absence; lack. [Obs.]

> I could tell to thee, as to one it pleases me, for *fault* of a better, to call my friend. —Shak.

2. A blemish; a flaw; an imperfection.

> As patches set upon a little breach,
> Discredit more in hiding of the *fault*.—Shak.

3. Any error or defect in morals or deportment; an imperfection; any deviation from propriety; a slight offense; a neglect of duty or propriety, resulting from inattention or want of prudence, rather than from design to injure or offend, but liable to censure or objection.

> I do remember my *faults* this day. —Gen. xli. 9.

4. In geology and mining, a break or dislocation of strata. In the coal-fields, *faults* are sometimes beneficial when they serve as natural drains. In the figure, *aa* shows the change of position in the strata occasioned by a *fault*.

Fault.

5. A lost scent; a missing or losing of the trail; said of sporting dogs.

6. In tennis, failure to serve or drive the ball into the proper part of the opponent's court.

7. In electricity, a defect in the efficient operation of a circuit, caused by ground and cross contacts or disconnections.

At fault; (a) in the wrong; worthy of censure; (b) unable to find the scent, as dogs; hence, in trouble or embarrassment, and unable to proceed; puzzled; thrown off the track.

To find fault; to express blame; to complain;

to censure; often followed by *with*; as, *to find fault with* one's friend.

Syn.—Blemish, defect, imperfection, flaw, delinquency, misdeed, failing, omission, foible, misdemeanor, weakness.

fault, *v.i.* To fail; to be wrong; to blunder. [Obs.]

fault, *v.t.*; faulted, *pt.*, *pp.*; faulting, *ppr.* 1. To charge with a fault; to accuse. [Rare.]

2. To lack; to need; to want. [Obs.]

3. In geology, to cause a fault in; as, undulations *faulted* the strata.

fault′-block, *n.* In geology, a body of rock or part of the earth's crust, bounded by faults.

fault′ēr, *n.* An offender; one who commits a fault. [Obs.]

fault′find″ēr, *n.* 1. One who censures or objects; a scold.

2. In electricity, a device for locating faults.

fault′find″ing, *a.* and *n.* I. *a.* Having a disposition to point out faults; complaining.

II. *n.* The act of pointing out faults; the making of frivolous objections; carping criticism.

fault′ful, *a.* Full of faults or sins.

fault′i-ly, *adv.* In a faulty manner.

fault′i-ness, *n.* The state of being faulty.

fault′ing, *n.* In geology, the act or process of producing faults.

fault′less, *a* Without fault; not defective or imperfect; free from blemish; free from vice; perfect; as, a *faultless* poem; a *faultless* life.

Syn.—Perfect, blameless, stainless, correct, spotless.

fault′less-ly, *adv.* In a faultless manner.

fault′less-ness, *n.* Freedom from faults or defects.

fault′y, *a.* [ME. *fauty*, *fawty*; OFr. *fautif*, faulty, from *faute*, fault.]

1. Containing faults, blemishes, or defects; defective; imperfect; as, a *faulty* composition; a *faulty* plan or design; a *faulty* picture.

2. Guilty of a fault or of faults; blamable; worthy of censure.

Syn.—Incomplete, culpable, blameworthy, reprehensible, censurable.

faun, *n.* [ME. *faun*; L. *Faunus*, Faunus, the god of agriculture, from *favere*, to be propitious.] In Roman mythology, one of a kind of demigods or rural deities, differing little from satyrs. The form of the *fauns* was principally human, but with a short goat's tail, pointed ears, and projecting horns; sometimes also with cloven feet.

Rough satyrs danc'd, and *fauns* with cloven heel
From the glad sound would not be absent long.—Milton.

Dancing Faun.—Antique Statue, Florentine Museum.

fau′nȧ, *n.*; *pl.* **fau′næ**. [L. *Fauna*, a Roman goddess, the sister of Faunus.]

1. The animals or animal life of any stated latitude, region, or age; as, the American *fauna*; preglacial *fauna*.

2. A treatise on the animals of any particular region or period.

fau′năl, *a.* Pertaining to fauna.

fau-nā′li-ȧ, *n.pl.* [L., from *Faunus*, Faunus.] In Roman customs, the festivities in honor of Faunus, god of agriculture and shepherds.

fau′nist, *n.* One who classifies and describes faunæ; a naturalist.

fau-nis′tic, fau-nis′tic-ăl, *a.* Pertaining to the classification of faunæ; faunal; determined by faunists.

fau-nō-log′ic-ăl, *a.* Pertaining to faunology.

fau-nol′ō-gy, *n.* [*Fauna*, and Gr. *logos*, a description.] In zoölogy, the scientific study of the geographical distribution of animals; zoögeography.

fau′sen, *n.* A kind of eel. [Obs.]

fausse′brāye (fōs′brā), *n.* [Fr. *fausse-braie*; *fausse*, false, and Scot. *brae*, raised ground, slope.] In fortification, a small mound of earth thrown up about a rampart. [Obs.]

fau-teuil′ (fō-tūl′), *n.* [Fr., from OFr. *faudestueil*; LL. *faldestolium*, *faldistolium*; O.H.G. *faltstuol*, lit., a folding-stool, from *faldan*, to fold, and *stuol*, a chair, seat.]

1. An armchair; an easy-chair.

2. The chair of a president or presiding officer.

3. A seat in the French Academy, referring to the forty seats provided for it by Louis XIV.

fau′tŏr, *n.* A favorer; a patron; one who gives countenance or support. [Obs.]

fau′tress, *n.* A patroness. [Obs.]

fau-vette′ (fō-vet′), *n.* [Fr., from *fauve*, fawn-colored.] A French book-name sometimes applied to any of the soft-billed birds or warblers, such as the nightingale.

faux päs (fō′pä′). [Fr., from *faux*, false, and *pas*, a step.] A false step; a mistake; a slip; especially, an act of a compromising nature; a breach of good manners.

fa-vaġ′i-nous, *a.* Same as *Faveolate*.

fā′vel, *a.* and *n.* [ME. *favell*; O.H.G. *falo*, fallow, yellow.]

I. *a.* Yellow; dun.

II. *n.* A dun horse.

fā′vel, *n.* [ME. *favel*, flattery; OFr. *favele*, a fable, falsehood, flattery, from L. *fabella*, dim. of *fabula*, a story.] Flattery; cajolery; deception accomplished by flattery.

fȧ-vel′lȧ, *n.*; *pl.* **fȧ-vel′læ**. [L., from *favilla*, glowing ashes.] In botany, a cluster of spores resembling a cystocarp, but formed externally and covered by a gelatinous envelope, as in certain florideous algæ.

fav-el-lid′i-um, *n.*; *pl.* **fav-el-lid′i-ȧ**. [L., from *favilla*, glowing ashes, and Gr. *eidos*, form, appearance.] In botany, a favella in the frond of florideous algæ, formed by the development of several contiguous mother-cells.

fȧ-vel′loid, *a.* Resembling a favella.

fȧ-vē′ō-lāte, *a.* [L. *favus*, a honeycomb.] Having cells resembling those of a honeycomb; alveolate.

fȧ-vē′ō-lus, *n.*; *pl.* **fȧ-vē′ō-lī**. [L., from *favus*, a honeycomb.] A small, cellular orifice resembling a honeycomb-cell.

fȧ-vil′lous, *a.* [L. *favilla*, ashes.]

1. Consisting of or pertaining to ashes.

2. Resembling ashes.

fȧ-vis′sȧ, *n.*; *pl.* **fȧ-vis′sæ**. [L.] In Roman antiquity, a crypt; a vault.

fȧ-vō′ni-ăn, *a.* [L. *Favonius*, the west wind, from *favere*, to favor.] Pertaining to the west wind; mild; calm; gentle; propitious.

fā′vŏr, fā′vour, *n.* [ME. *favour*; OFr. *favour*; L. *favor*, good will, favor, from *favere*, to be well disposed, to favor.]

1. Kind regard; kindness; countenance; propitious aspect; friendly disposition; good will.

His dreadful navy, and his lovely mind,
Gave him the fear and *favor* of mankind.
—Waller.

2. Support; defense; vindication; disposition to aid, befriend, support, promote, or justify.

3. A kind act or office; kindness done or granted; benevolence shown by word or deed; any act of grace or good will, as distinguished from acts of justice or remuneration; as, he asked a *favor* of her.

4. Lenity; mildness or mitigation of punishment.

I could not discover the lenity and *favor* of this sentence. —Swift.

5. Leave; good will; a yielding or concession to another; permission.

But, with your *favor*, I will treat it here.
—Dryden.

6. The object of kind regard; the person or thing favored.

All these his wondrous works, but chiefly man,
His chief delight and *favor*. —Milton.

7. A gift or present; something bestowed as an evidence of good will; a token of love; originally, a gift from a woman to a man, as a glove, a knot of ribbon, etc., to be worn as in the days of chivalry; now, specifically applied to the trinkets exchanged in the dance called the *german*, or to the souvenirs of any social entertainment.

8. Features; appearance; countenance. [Rare.]

9. Advantage; convenience afforded for success; as, the enemy approached under *favor* of the night.

10. Partiality; bias; as, without fear or *favor*; kissing goes by *favor*.

11. A letter or written communication; said complimentarily; as, your *favor* of yesterday's date is at hand.

By your favor; with your leave or permission.

Challenge to the favor; in law, the challenge of a juror on account of some supposed partiality, by reason of favor or malice, interest, connection, or acquaintance.

To curry favor; to seek to gain favor by flattery, affected kindnesses, or endearments.

fā′vŏr, *v.t.*; favored, *pt.*, *pp.*; favoring, *ppr.* [ME. *favoren*; OFr. *favorer*, to favor, from L. *favor*, a favor, from *favere*, to be well disposed to, to favor.]

1. To regard with kindness; to support; to aid, or have the disposition to aid; to wish success to; to be propitious to, to countenance; to befriend; to encourage.

The lords *favor* thee not. —1 Sam. xxix. 6.

2. To afford advantages for success; to facilitate; as, the darkness *favored* his approach.

3. To resemble in features; as, the child *favors* his father. [Colloq.]

4. To ease; to spare; as, a man in walking *favors* a lame leg.

5. To extenuate; to palliate; to represent favorably.

He has *favored* her squint admirably.—Swift.

6. In nautical language, to be careful of; as, to *favor* the mast.

fā′vŏr-ȧ-ble, *a.* [ME. *favorabel*; OFr. *favorable*; L. *favorabilis*, favored, in favor, from *favere*, to favor.]

1. Kind; propitious; friendly; affectionate.

Lend *favorable* ear to our requests.—Shak.

2. Conducive to; contributing to; tending to promote; as, conditions *favorable* to population.

3. Convenient; advantageous; affording means to facilitate, or affording facilities; as, *favorable* weather; a *favorable* ground.

4. Beautiful; well-favored. [Obs.]

fā′vŏr-ȧ-ble-ness, *n.* The state or quality of being favorable.

fā′vŏr-ȧ-bly, *adv.* In a favorable manner; kindly; with friendly disposition; with regard or affection; with an inclination to favor; as, to judge or think *favorably* of a measure; to think *favorably* of those we love.

fā′vŏred, *a.* 1. Having a certain appearance; featured; looking; used in composition; as, ill-*favored*; well-*favored*, etc.

2. Adorned with a favor; usually in compounds; as, the white-*favored* horses of the bridal carriage.

fā′vŏred-ly, *adv.* In respect to manners or appearance; used in compounds.

fā′vŏred-ness, *n.* 1. The state of being favored.

2. Appearance; used in compounds.

fā′vŏr-ēr, *n.* One who or that which favors; one who assists or promotes success or prosperity

fā′vŏr-ess, *n.* A woman who favors or gives countenance. [Rare.]

fā′vŏr-ing-ly, *adv.* In a manner which shows favor.

fā′vŏr-ite, *n.* [OFr. *favorit*; It. *favorito*, masc., *favorita*, f., a favorite, from *favorire*, to favor; L. *favor*, a favor.]

1. A person or thing regarded with peculiar favor, preference, and affection; one greatly beloved.

2. One who has gained an influence over a superior by questionable means and for a selfish purpose; as, Acte was Nero's *favorite* until supplanted by Poppæa.

A *favorite* has no friend. —Gray.

3. A ringlet or small curl worn by women of the seventeenth and eighteenth centuries. [Obs.]

4. In sporting language, the competitor considered most likely to win and carrying the lowest odds in the betting; as, the *favorite* does not always win.

fā′vŏr-ite, *a.* Regarded with particular kindness, affection, esteem, or preference; as, a *favorite* walk; a *favorite* author; a *favorite* child; a *favorite* horse.

fā′vŏr-it-ism, *n.* The disposition to favor, aid, and promote the interest of a favorite, or of one person or family, or of one class of men, to the neglect of others having equal claims.

fā′vŏr-less, *a.* 1. Unfavored; not regarded with favor; having no patronage or support.

2. Not favoring; unpropitious. [Obs.]

fȧ-vōse′, *a.* [L. *favus*, a honeycomb.]

1. Honeycombed; like the section of a honeycomb.

2. Pertaining to or affected with the scalp disease called favus.

fav′ō-site, *a.* Of or relating to the fossil genus *Favosites*.

Fav-ō-si′tēs, *n.* [L., from *favus*, a honeycomb.] A genus of fossil corals common to the Silurian, Devonian, and Carboniferous systems, and so called from the regular polygonal arrangement of their pore-cells.

fā′vus, *n.* [L., honeycomb.]

1. Crusted or honeycombed ringworm, a disease chiefly attacking the scalp, characterized by yellowish dry incrustations somewhat resembling a honeycomb. It is produced by a fungous growth.

2. A tile or slab of marble cut into a hexagonal shape, so as to produce a honeycomb pattern in pavements.

fawe, *a.* Pleased; gratified; delighted; fain. [Obs.]

fawk′nēr, *n.* [Obs.] Same as *Falconer*.

fawn, *n.* [ME. *fawn*, *fawne*; OFr. *fan*, *faon*, a fawn, a young deer, from L. *fetus*, pregnant, offspring.]

1. A young deer; a buck or doe of the first year.

2. The young of other animals than the deer. [Obs.]

3. A shade of light yellowish brown, the color of a fawn.

fawn, *a.* Having the color of a fawn.

fawn, *v.i.*; fawned, *pt.*, *pp.*; fawning, *ppr.* [ME. *fawnen*, *faunen*, to be glad, receive with joy, fawn like a dog; AS. *fægenian*, to be glad, fawn, from *fægen*, fain, glad.]

1. To court favor or show attachment, by frisking about one; as, a dog *fawns* on his master.

2. To wheedle; to flatter meanly; to blandish; to court servilely; to cringe and bow to gain favor; as, a *fawning* favorite or minion.

My love, forbear to *fawn* upon their frowns. —Shak.

fawn, *v.i.* [Fr. *faonner.*] To bring forth a fawn.

fawn, *n.* A servile cringe or bow; mean flattery.

fawn'=col"ored, *a.* Having the color of a fawn; of a light brown tinged with yellow.

fawn'ẽr, *n.* One who fawns; one who cringes and flatters meanly.

fawn'ing-ly, *adv.* In a cringing, servile way; with mean flattery.

faxed (faxt), *a.* [AS. *feax*, hair.] Hairy. [Obs.]

fāy, *v.t.*; fayed, *pt.*, *pp.*; faying, *ppr.* [ME. *feyen*; AS. *fegan*, to join.] To fit; to suit; to match; as, to *fay* timbers.

fāy, *v.i.* To lie or fit close together, as two pieces of wood; a term used in shipbuilding.

Faying surface; the face of a thing, as a metal plate, block, or end of a timber, which joins another surface so closely as to leave no interstice.

fāy, *n.* [ME. *fay*; OFr. *fee*, *feie*, *fae*, from L. *fata*, a fairy, *fatum*, fate.] A fairy; an elf.

fāy, *n.* [ME. *fay*, *fey*; OFr. *fei*, faith.] Faith; as, by my *fay*. [Obs.]

fāy, fey, *v.t.* To rid of debris; to clean; to cleanse. [Prov. Eng.]

fāy'ăl-ite, *n.* [Named from the island of Fayal.] A black or dark-colored, sometimes iridescent, mineral, consisting mainly of silicate of iron.

fā-y-ence' (fä-ē-yäns'), *n.* See *Faience.*

fāyleş, *n.* [So called because if a player threw a certain throw of dice he could not carry off his men, and so *fayled* to win the game.] An old game similar to backgammon.

fāy'tŏr, fāy'tour, *n.* [Obs.] Same as *Faitor.*

fāze, *v.t.*; fazed, *pt.*, *pp.*; fazing, *ppr.* To disconcert; to nonplus; to disturb; to hinder; to ruffle; to daunt; also written *phase.* [Colloq. Compare *Feeze.*]

faz'zō-let, *n.* [It. *fazzoletto*, dim. of *fazzolo*, a handkerchief.] A pocket-handkerchief. [Rare.]

fēa'bēr"ry, fēap'bēr"ry, *n.* An English name for the common gooseberry.

fēague (fēg), *v.t.* [Prob. from D. *vegen*, to sweep, strike.] To beat or scourge. [Obs.]

fēak, *n.* [AS. *feax*, hair.] A lock or ringlet of hair. [Obs.]

fēak, *v.t.* In falconry, to wipe the beak of (a hawk) after feeding.

fēak, *v.i.* To be uneasy; to be restless from anxiety; to fidget. [Prov. Eng.]

fē'ăl, *a.* [OFr. *feal*, *feyal*, *fedeil*, from L. *fidelis*, faithful, true, from *fides*, faith.] Faithful; stanch; loyal; as, tenants swore to be *feal* to their lords.

fē'ăl-ty, *n.* [OFr. *fealte*, *feelte*, *feelteit*; L. *fidelitas*, faithfulness, fidelity, from *fidelis*, faithful, trustworthy, from *fides*, faith.]

1. Fidelity to a lord; faithful adherence of a tenant or vassal to the superior of whom he holds his lands; loyalty; as, an oath of *fealty* was required to be taken by all tenants to their landlords.

2. Fidelity to another; loyalty; faithfulness.

fēar, *n.* [ME. *fere*, *feer*, fear; AS. *fær*, fear, terror.]

1 A painful emotion or passion excited by an expectation of evil, or the apprehension of impending danger. It expresses less apprehension than dread, and is accompanied with a desire to avoid or ward off the expected evil.

Fear is the passion of our nature which excites us to provide for our security, on the approach of evil. —Rogers.

2. Anxiety; solicitude; also, the cause or object which excites apprehension.

The principal *fear* was for the holy temple. —2 Mac. xv. 18.

3. In Scripture, reverence for God and his laws, which springs from a just view and love of the divine character.

I will put my *fear* in their hearts. —Jer. xxxii. 40.

4. Reverence; respect; due regard for rightful authority.

Syn.—Apprehension, misgiving, solicitude, timidity, trepidation, anxiety, awe, dismay, consternation, alarm, dread, reverence, veneration.

fēar, *v.t.*; feared, *pt.*, *pp.*; fearing, *ppr.* [ME. *feren*, *færen*, to frighten, to be afraid; AS. *færan*, to terrify.]

1. To feel a painful apprehension of, as some impending evil; to be afraid of; to consider or expect with emotions of alarm or solicitude.

I will *fear* no evil, for thou art with me. —Ps. xxiii. 4.

2. To reverence; to have a reverential awe of; to venerate.

3. To affright; to terrify; to drive away or prevent approach of by fear. [Obs.]

4. To have fear for or be solicitous concerning. [Rare.]

5. To doubt or feel suspicious of. [Obs.]

fēar, *v.i.* 1. To be in apprehension of evil; to be afraid; to feel anxiety on account of some expected evil; often used with a reflexive pronoun; as, I *fear me* it is true.

2. To be uncertain; to doubt.

If you shall see Cordelia,
As *fear* not but you shall. —Shak.

fēar'ẽr, *n.* One who experiences fear.

fēar'fụl, *a.* 1. Affected by fear; feeling pain in expectation of evil; apprehensive or solicitous; afraid.

2. Timid; timorous; wanting courage; fainthearted.

3. Terrible; impressing fear; frightful; dreadful; awful.

It is a *fearful* thing to fall into the hands of the living God. —Heb. x. 31.

Syn.—Apprehensive, solicitous, afraid, timid, timorous, pusillanimous, horrible, distressing, shocking, frightful, dreadful, awful, terrible.

fēar'fụl-ly, *adv.* 1. Timorously; in fear.

In such a night
Did Thisbe *fearfully* o'ertrip the dew.—Shak.

2. Terribly; dreadfully; in a manner to impress astonishment or terror.

fēar'fụl-ness, *n.* 1. Timorousness; timidity.

2. The state of being afraid; awe; dread.

3. The quality which causes alarm or fear; as, the *fearfulness* of the thought startled him.

fēar'less, *a.* Free from fear; bold; courageous; intrepid; undaunted.

fēar'less-ly, *adv.* Without fear; in a bold or courageous manner; intrepidly.

fēar'less-ness, *n.* Freedom from fear; courage; boldness; intrepidity.

fēar'naught (-nat), *n.* 1. A woolen cloth of great thickness; dreadnaught; also, a garment fashioned from such cloth.

2. A person who feels no fear.

fēar'sŏme, *a.* 1. Frightful; that induces fear.

2. Timid; easy to frighten.

fēa-şi-bil'i-ty, *n.* The quality of being capable of execution; practicability.

fēa'şi-ble, *a.* [From OFr. *faisable*, that may be done, from *faire*, to make, do.]

1. That may be done, performed, executed, or effected; practicable; capable of being effected by human means or agency.

2. That may be used or tilled, as land. [Rare.]

fēa'şi-ble-ness, *n.* Feasibility; practicability.

fēa'şi-bly, *adv.* Practicably.

fēast, *n.* [ME. *feeste*, *feste*, *fest*; OFr. *feste*, from L. *festa*, pl. of *festum*, a holiday, festival, feast.]

1. A sumptuous repast or entertainment, of which a number of guests partake; particularly, a rich or splendid public entertainment.

2. A rich or delicious repast or meal; something delicious to the palate.

3. A festival in commemoration of some great event, or in honor of some distinguished personage; an anniversary, periodical, or stated celebration; as, the *feasts* of the Christian church.

4. Something delicious and entertaining to the mind or senses; that which is highly agreeable; as, a *feast* of reason.

Immovable feast; a church festival occurring at a fixed date, as Christmas.

Movable feast; a church festival which occurs on a specific day of the week succeeding a certain day of the month or phase of the moon. Easter is a *movable feast* upon which all other *movable feasts* depend.

Syn.—Entertainment, banquet, treat, refreshment, carousal, wassail, festivity, festival, merrymaking, jollification.

fēast, *v.i.*; feasted, *pt.*, *pp.*; feasting, *ppr.* 1. To eat sumptuously; to dine or sup on rich provisions, particularly in large companies and on public festivals.

2. To be highly gratified or delighted; as, he *feasted* on the music.

fēast, *v.t.* 1. To entertain with sumptuous provisions; to treat at the table magnificently; as, he was *feasted* by the king.

2. To delight; to pamper; to gratify luxuriously.

Whose taste or smell can bless the *feasted* sense. —Dryden.

fēast'=dāy, *n.* A day for feasting; an ecclesiastical festival.

fēast'ẽr, *n.* One who feasts or gives a feast.

fēast'fụl, *a.* Festive; joyful; sumptuous; luxurious.

fēast'fụl-ly, *adv.* Festively; luxuriously.

fēat, *n.* [ME. *feet*, *fete*, *faite*; OFr. *fait*, a deed, fact, from L. *factum*, from *facere*, to make, do.]

1. An act; a deed; an exploit; as, a bold *feat*; *feats* of prowess.

2. An extraordinary act of strength, skill, or cunning; as, *feats* of horsemanship or of dexterity.

Syn.—Act, deed, action, exploit, exercise, execution, movement, attainment, performance, achievement.

fēat, *v.t.* To form; to fashion. [Obs.]

fēat, *a.* [ME. *fete*, short form of *fetis*, from OFr. *fetis*, *faitis*, *faictis*, neat, well-made.] Ready; deft; neat; skilful; ingenious; clever. [Rare.]

Never master had a page so *feat*. —Shak.

fēat'=bod"ied (-id), *a.* Having a lithe, trim body. [Obs.]

fēat'ē-ous, *a.* Neat; dexterous. [Obs.]

fēat'ē-ous-ly, *adv.* Neatly; dexterously. [Obs.]

feath'ẽr (feth'), *v.t.*; feathered, *pt.*, *pp.*; feathering, *ppr.* 1. To dress in feathers; to fit with feathers or to cover with feathers.

2. To cover with foliage in a feathery manner.

3. To tread, as a cock.

4. To enrich; to adorn; to exalt. [Rare.]

The king cared not to *feather* himself.—Bacon.

5. To lighten; to give wings to; to make endurable, as a tedious delay. [Rare.]

6. To join (boards) by inserting the tongue or feather of one in the corresponding groove of another.

7. In rowing, to carry (an oar) forward between strokes in a nearly horizontal position, so that the water runs off in feathery spray, with a view to reducing the resistance and to prevent the oar from striking the water during recovery.

To feather one's nest; to collect wealth, particularly from emoluments derived from agencies for others; a phrase derived from birds which collect feathers for their nests.

To tar and feather a person; to pour heated tar over him and then cover him with feathers. It is a very old method of administering punishment to an obnoxious person or public offender, and is still sometimes practised, especially in rural communities.

feath'ẽr, *v.i.* 1. To become covered with feathers; to produce feathers; often followed by *out.*

2. To assume the appearance of feathers; to be transformed into feathery shapes and figures; to fringe.

Just where the prone edge of the wood began
To *feather* toward the hollow. —Tennyson.

3. To row with a feathering stroke; as, the whole crew *feathers* fairly well.

feath'ẽr, *n.* [ME. *fether*; AS. *fether*, a feather.]

1. One of the epidermal growths which collectively form the covering of birds. It consists of a strong, round, horny stem, hollow at the lower part called the quill, and filled with pith at the upper part called the shaft. On each side of the shaft are the barbs, broad on one side and narrow on the other, consisting of thin laminæ; the barbs and shaft constitute the vane.

2. Kind; nature; species; from the proverbial phrase, birds of a *feather*, that is, of the same species.

I am not of that *feather*, to shake off
My friend when he must need me. —Shak.

3. A slip inserted longitudinally into a shaft or arbor, and projecting so as to fit a groove in the eye of a wheel.

4. A wedge-shaped key placed between two plugs in a hole in a stone, in order to be driven into the hole and thus split the stone.

5. A projection on the edge of a board which fits into a channel on the edge of another board; a tongue.

6. A wing or guide made of part of a *feather* attached to an arrow near its string-end.

7. A tuft of long hair which grows on a horse awry and cannot be made to lie smoothly.

8. The fringe of hair on the back of the legs, on the neck, or on the ears of some breeds of dogs, as the setters.

9. In rowing, the act of feathering; also, the feathery spray of water thrown from the edge of an oar when turned horizontally as it leaves the water.

10. A plume, sometimes dyed or ornamented, to be worn on a hat.

11. Something as light as a *feather*, and so having no weight or consequence.

12. Birds collectively; as, fin, fur, and *feather*.

13. A species of flaw in a precious stone.

14. The feathery spray thrown up by the cutwater of a rapidly moving vessel.

A feather in one's cap; an achievement which gives distinction; something which marks one for favorable notice or honor.

To be in full feather; clothed in one's best attire; figuratively, well supplied with money.

To be in high feather; to be in high or cheerful spirits.

To cut a feather; to render oneself conspicuous.

To show the white feather; to give indications of cowardice; a phrase borrowed from the cockpit, where a white feather in the tail of a cock is considered a token that he is not of the true game breed.

feath'ẽr-al"um, *n.* Same as *Alunogen.*

feath'ẽr-beăr"ẽr, *n.* A name applied to the plume-moths, *Pterophoridæ.*

feath'ẽr-bōne (feth'), *n.* A material made from the quills of poultry feathers, split and pressed into narrow strips. It is used in dress-making as a substitute for whalebone.

feath'ẽr-brāined, *a.* Giddy; silly; unthinking.

feath'ẽr-drīv"ẽr, *n.* One who beats and otherwise prepares feathers to make them light or loose.

feath'ẽred, *a.* 1. Clothed or covered with feathers; as, a bird is a *feathered* animal.

2. Winged; fleet. [Rare.]

> In *feathered* briefness sails are filled. —Shak.

3. Fashioned from or ornamented with feathers; furnished with feathers or feather-like parts; plumose; as, a *feathered* shaft; *feathered* antennæ.

4. Fringed; bordered; margined; bestrewed.

5. In heraldry, applied to an arrow when the shaft and feathers are of different hues.

6. Having the legs, etc., fringed with hair, as certain breeds of dogs.

feath'ẽr-edge (-ej), *n.* An edge like a feather; the thinner edge, as of a board or plank.

feath'ẽr-edged (-ejd), *a.* 1. Having the edges bordered with loops or scallops; said of straw braid, ribbon, etc.

2. Having one thin or beveled edge, as boards, copings, etc.

feath'ẽr-few, *n.* [Prov. Eng.] See *Feverfew.*

feath'ẽr-foil, *n.* The water-violet, *Hottonia palustris*; so called from its peculiar pinnate leaves.

feath'ẽr-grȧss, *n.* A species of grass, *Stipa pennata*, distinguished by its feathered beard.

feath'ẽr-head (-hed), *n.* A frivolous and thoughtless person; a trifler.

feath'ẽr-head"ed, *a.* Gay; heedless; feather-brained.

feath'ẽr-heeled, *a.* Light-footed; frolicsome; capering.

feath'ẽr-i-ness, *n.* The state or quality of being light and feathery.

feath'ẽr-ing, *n.* 1. In architecture, foliation.

2. In rowing, the uniform turning of the blade of an oar to a horizontal position as it is carried forward for the next stroke.

3. A feathery covering; plumage.

feath'ẽr-ing-float, *n.* One of the floats or paddles of a feathering-wheel.

feath'ẽr-ing-screw (-skrö), *n.* A screw propeller whose blades are so arranged that they offer little or no resistance when the ship is moving under sail only.

feath'ẽr-ing-wheel (-hwēl), *n.* A paddle-wheel in which the floats are so arranged as to enter and leave the water edgewise, thus avoiding much resistance.

feath'ẽr-joint, *n.* In joinery, a joint formed by inserting the feather or tongue on one board into the groove made to receive it in another.

feath'ẽr-less, *a.* Destitute of feathers; unfledged.

feath'ẽr-ly, *a.* Resembling feathers. [Obs.]

feath'ẽr-māk"ẽr, *n.* One who prepares plumes and fancy feathers from true and artificial plumage.

feath'ẽr-ōre, *n.* A variety of jamesonite; so called from the peculiar form in which it sometimes occurs.

feath'ẽr-pāt"ed, *a.* Feather-brained.

feath'ẽr-shot, *n.* The name given to copper in the form which it assumes when poured in a molten condition into cold water; also called *feathered-shot.*

feath'ẽr-sprāy, *n.* The spray cast up by the bow of a rapidly moving boat.

feath'ẽr-stär, *n.* See *Comatula.*

feath'ẽr-stitch, *n.* An embroidery-stitch; so called from its fancied resemblance to a feathered quill.

feath'ẽr-top-grȧss, *n.* A European species of grass, bearing a feathery panicle; called also *wood-reed.*

feath'ẽr-veined, *a.* In botany, applied to leaves in which the veins branch from the midrib to the margin like the parts of a feather, as in the oak and chestnut.

feath'ẽr-weight (-wāt), *n.* 1. Weight so exact that the slightest addition, as of a feather, would disturb the balance.

2. In horse-racing, the lightest weight allowed a horse in a handicap race.

3. In athletics, a pugilist or wrestler of the lightest weight generally recognized, belonging to the class next below the light-weights; hence, a person extremely light in weight, or of little importance.

feath'ẽr-wing, *n.* Any plume-moth.

feath'ẽr-y, *a.* 1. Clothed or covered with feathers.

> Or whistle from the lodge, or village cock
> Count the night-watches to his *feathery* dames. —Milton.

2. Resembling feathers; as, *feathery* clouds.

3. In botany, covered with long hairs; plumose.

fēat'ly, *adv.* Neatly; dexterously; adroitly. [Rare.]

fēat'ness, *n.* Dexterity; adroitness; skilfulness.

fēa'tūre, *n.* [ME. *feture, fetour*; OFr. *faiture*, from L. *factura*, a making, formation, from *facere*, to make.]

1. The make, form, or cast of any part of the face; any single lineament; appearance; shape; form.

2. [*pl.*] The countenance, embracing all of the facial parts.

3. The fashion; the shape; the whole turn or cast of the body; the physical frame. [Rare.]

4. The make or form of any part of the surface of a thing, as of a country or landscape.

5. A prominent part; a striking or salient point; as, the *feature* of a treaty.

fēa'tūre, *v.t.*, featured, *pt., pp.*; featuring, *ppr.*

1. To resemble in cast of countenance; to reproduce the features of; to favor; as, children *feature* their parents. [Colloq.]

2. In theatrical parlance, to advertise as an especial attraction; to star.

fēa'tūre, *v.i.* To be advertised as an especial attraction in a show or exhibition; to be a star.

fēa'tūred, *a.* 1. Having a certain shape or figure; formed; fashioned.

2. Having a certain cast of features; possessing features; exhibiting human features.

fēa'tūre-less, *a.* Having no distinct features; formless.

fēa'tūre-ly, *a.* Having good features; handsome. [Rare.]

fēaze, *v.t.*; feazed, *pt., pp.*; feazing, *ppr.* [Scot.] To untwist, as the end of a rope.

fēaze, *v.t.* [Compare Fr. *fesser*, to flog.] To whip with rods; to tease; to worry.

fēaze, *n.* A state of anxiety; fretfulness; vexation. [Colloq.]

fēaz'ings, *n.pl.* A raveled or ragged rope-end.

fē-bric'i-tāte, *v.i.* [L. *febricitatus*, pp. of *febricitare*, from *febris*, a fever.] To be in a fever. [Obs.]

fē-bric'ū-lōse, *a.* [L. *febriculosus*, from *febricula*, a slight fever, dim. of *febris*, a fever.] Affected with slight fever.

feb-ri-fā'cient (-shent), *a.* and *n.* [L. *febris*, a fever, and *faciens* (*-entis*), ppr. of *facere*, to make, do.]

I. *a.* Causing fever.

II. *n.* That which produces fever.

fē-brif'ẽr-ous, *a.* [L. *febris*, a fever, and *ferre*, to bear.] Occasioning fever; productive of fever; as, a *febriferous* climate.

fē-brif'ic, *a.* [L. *febris*, a fever, and *-ficus*, from *facere*, to make.] Producing fever; feverish.

fē-brif'ū-găl, *a.* Having the quality of mitigating or curing fever.

feb'ri-fūge, *n.* [L. *febris*, fever, and *fugare*, to drive away.] Any medicine that mitigates or cures fever.

feb'ri-fūge, *a.* Having the quality of mitigating or subduing fever.

fē'brile (*or* feb'rile), *a.* [Fr. *fébrile*, from L. *febris*, a fever.] Pertaining to fever; indicating fever, or derived from it; as, *febrile* symptoms; *febrile* action.

Fē-brō'ni-ăn, *a.* and *n.* I. *a.* Relating to the ancient doctrine of Febronianism.

II. *n.* An adherent of Febronianism.

Fē-brō'ni-ăn-ism, *n.* [From Justinus *Febronius*, a nom de plume assumed by John Nicholas von Hontheim, archbishop of Trèves, in a work on the claims of the pope.] In Roman Catholic theology, a doctrinal system antagonistic to the admitted claims of the pope, and asserting the independence of national churches, and the rights of bishops to unrestricted action within their own dioceses.

Feb'rụ-ā-ry, *n.* [L. *Februarius* (*mensis*), originally the month of expiation, from *februa*, a Roman festival of purification, pl. of *februum*, a means of purification.] The name of the second month in the year, introduced into the Roman calendar by Numa. In common years, this month contains twenty-eight days; in the bissextile or leap year, twenty-nine days.

feb-rụ-ā'tion, *n.* [L. *februatio* (*-onis*), from *februum*, a means of purification.] Purification; an ancient Roman ceremony or sacrifice. [Obs.]

fē'căl, *a.* [Fr. *fécal*, from L. *fæx, fæcis*, dregs.] Containing or consisting of dregs, lees, sediment, or excrement.

fec'che, *v.t.* [Obs.] See *Fetch.*

fē'cēs, *n.pl.* [L. *fæces*, pl. of *fæx*, dregs, lees.]

1. Dregs; lees; sediment.

2. Excrement; dung.

fē'ciăl (-shăl), *a.* See *Fetial.*

fē'ci-fork, *n.* [L. *fæces*, dregs, and Eng. *fork.*] In zoölogy, the process on which feces are carried by some larval insects.

fē'cit. [Lit., he has made or done it—3rd pers. sing. perf. ind. act. of L. *facere*, to do, make.] A word which is placed on a work of art, along with the name of the maker or designer; as, Stradivarius *fecit*, meaning Stradivarius made it.

feck, *n.* [Scot.] 1. Strength; value; vigor.

2. Space; quantity; number; as, what *feck* of ground? what *feck* o' folk?

3. The greatest part or number; the main part; as, the *feck* of a region.

Maist feck; the greatest part of a thing.

Many feck; a large number.

feck'et, *n.* A waistcoat; an under vest. [Scot.]

> Grim loon! he gat me by the *fecket*,
> An' sair me shook. —Burns.

feck'fụl, *a.* Possessing physical strength; vigorous; sturdy. [Scot.]

feck'fụl-ly, *adv.* Powerfully; manfully; ably. [Scot.]

feck'less, *a.* Spiritless; feeble; weak. [Scot.]

feck'ly, *adv.* For the most part; mostly. [Scot.]

> Wheel-carriages I ha'e but few,
> Three carts, an' twa are *feckly* new.—Burns.

fecks, *interj.* Faith; used as an ejaculation.

fec'ū-lȧ, *n.* [L. *fæcula*, burnt tartar, salt of tartar, dim. of *fæx*, pl. *fæces*, dregs.]

1. Starch; applied to any pulverulent matter obtained from plants by simply breaking down the texture, washing with water, and allowing to settle.

2. The green matter of plants; chlorophyl.

fec'ū-lence, fec'ū-len-cy, *n.* [LL. *fæculentia*, from *fæcula*, dim. of *fæx*, pl. *fæces*, dregs.]

1. Muddiness; foulness; the quality of being foul with extraneous matter or lees.

2. That which is feculent; lees; sediment; dregs; excrement.

fec'ū-lent, *a.* [L. *fæculentus*, abounding in dregs, impure, from *fæx*, pl. *fæces*, dregs.] Foul with extraneous or impure substances; muddy; thick; turbid; abounding with sediment or excrementitious matter.

fec'und, *a.* [L. *fecundus*, fruitful, fertile.]

1. Fruitful in children; prolific.

2. Productive; as, a *fecund* soil.

fec'un-dāte, *v.t.*; fecundated, *pt., pp.*; fecundating, *ppr.* 1. To make fruitful or prolific.

2. In biology, to impregnate; as, the pollen of flowers *fecundates* the stigma.

fec-un-dā'tion, *n.* [L. *fecundatus*, pp. of *fecundare*, to make fertile.] The act of making fruitful or prolific; impregnation.

fe-cun'di-fȳ, *v.t.* [L. *fecundus*, fruitful, and *-ficare*, from *facere*, to make.] To make fruitful; to fecundate. [Rare.]

fe-cun'di-ty, *n.* [L. *fecunditas*, from *fecundus*, fruitful, fertile.]

1. Fruitfulness; the quality of producing fruit; particularly, the quality in female animals of producing young in great numbers.

2. The power of germinating; as, the seeds of some plants retain their *fecundity* for many years.

3. Fertility; the power of bringing forth in abundance; richness of invention.

fed, *v.*, past tense and past participle of *feed.*

fed'ȧ-ry, *n.* See *Federary.*

fed'dăn, *n.* [Ar. *fadan, faddan*, a plow with a yoke of oxen.] A day's plowing for an ox-team, about one and a quarter English acres; a measure of land in Egypt.

fed'ẽr-ăl, *a.* [Fr. *fédéral*, from L. *fœdus* (*-eris*) a league, treaty.]

1. Pertaining to a league or contract; derived from an agreement or covenant between parties, particularly between states or nations.

2. Consisting of a compact between parties, particularly and chiefly between states or nations; founded on alliance by contract or mutual agreement; as, a *federal* government such as that of the United States.

3. Friendly to the Constitution of the United States or that of a similar government; favorable to the preservation of a federation; supporting the inviolability of a federation; specifically, in the Civil War, designating the Union army, the government centered at Washington, and all supporting the cause of the North.

4. Pertaining to or forming part of the United States government; as, a *federal* court; a *federal* judge.

Federal theology; the system of theology founded upon the two covenants, the covenant of works, between God and Adam, and the covenant of grace, between God and Christ. The doctrine was elaborated and promulgated by Cocceius of Leyden, in the seventeenth century. Also called *theology of the covenants.*

Fed'ẽr-ăl, *n.* 1. Same as *Federalist*, 1.

2. During the period of the Civil War and subsequent to it, one of the Northern or Union party; a soldier of the Union armies.

fed'ẽr-ăl-ism, *n.* The principles of a federal government, or of the political party known as Federalists.

fed′ēr-ăl-ist, *n.* 1. An appellation given to friends of the Constitution of the United States at its formation and adoption, and to the political party which favored the administration of President Washington.

2. [f—] One who upholds the principle that a federal government should hold its power from its citizens as an entity, and not from the several states, as opposed to the doctrine of states' rights.

3. One who accepts the principles of federal theology. [See *Federal theology* under *Federal*, a.]

fed′ēr-ăl-īze, *v.t.* and *v.i.*; federalized, *pt.*, *pp.*; federalizing, *ppr* To unite in compact, as different states; to confederate for political purposes.

fed′ēr-ăl-ly, *adv.* In a federal manner; jointly.

fed′ēr-ā-ry, **fed′ā-ry**, *n* [From L. *fœdus* (*-eris*), a league, treaty.] A partner; a confederate; an accomplice. [Obs.]

fed′ēr-āte, *a.* [L. *fœderatus*, pp. of *fœderare*, to league together, from *fœdus* (*-eris*), a league, treaty.] Leagued; united by compact, as sovereignties, states, or nations; joined in federation.

fed′ēr-āte, *v.t.* and *v.i.*; federated, *pt.*, *pp.*; federating, *ppr.* To combine in a league; to unite by a compact; to form into a federation.

fed-ēr-ā′tion, *n.* 1. The act of uniting in a league.

2. A league; a union.

3. A federal government, as that of the United States.

fed′ēr-ā-tive, *a.* Uniting; joining in a league; forming a federation; federal; as, the *federative* capacity of a nation.

fed′i-ty, *n.* [L. *fœditas*, from *fœdus*, foul, vile.] Turpitude; vileness; an act revealing gross depravity. [Obs.]

fee, *n.* [ME. *fee*, *fe*, *feoh*; AS. *feoh*, cattle, money, property; called money because cattle were used as a medium of exchange or barter.]

1. Property; estate; possession; that which forms the foundation of wealth. [Obs.]

2. A reward or compensation for services; recompense, either given voluntarily or established by law and claimed by right; particularly a reward for the performance of professional services; as, physicians' *fees*; a clergyman's *fee*; also, a class of fixed dues for the performance of official acts; as, consular *fees*; notarial *fees*.

3. A sum of money paid for the right to enjoy certain privileges, as to gain entrance to a performance, or to be admitted to membership in a society; as, an entrance *fee*; an initiation *fee*

Retaining fee; a fee paid to a lawyer on engaging him in a particular case.

fee, *n.* [ME. *fe*; OFr *fied*, from LL. *feudum*, property held in fee.]

1. In feudal law, a right to use another's land, in return for services rendered or to be performed; also, the land so used; a fief; hence, in common law, a loan of land or estate in trust, granted by an owner or holder to a grantee, to be held on some condition, as of personal service, and which reverts to the grantor if the grantee fails to comply with the conditions.

2. In English law, a freehold estate of inheritance, with or without the adjunct *simple*, denoting an absolute inheritance descendible to heirs at the pleasure of the proprietor, who is absolute owner of the soil. A *limited fee* is an estate limited or clogged with certain conditions; as, a *qualified* or *base fee*, which ceases with the existence of certain conditions, and a *conditional fee*, which is limited to particular heirs.

3. In the United States, an estate held by a person in his own right, and descendible to the heirs in general, without conditions.

Fee tail; an estate limited to a man and some particular heirs

fee, *v.t.*; feed, *pt.*, *pp*; feeing, *ppr.* 1. To pay a fee to; to reward

2. To engage in one's service by advancing a fee or sum of money to.

3. To hire; to bribe.

fee′ble, *a* [ME. *feble*, *febul*; OFr *feble*, *feuble*, *foible fiebe*, *floibe*, *floible*, from L. *flebilis*, pass., to be wept over, act., weeping, tearful, from *flere*, to weep.]

1. Wanting in bodily strength; weak, as from sickness or old age; debilitated; fragile; infirm.

2. Not full or loud; lacking strength, brightness, or vigor; slow; imperfect; as, a *feeble* voice; a *feeble* light; a *feeble* argument.

Syn.—Wretched, weak, poor, frail, debilitated, dull, forceless, puny, nerveless, enfeebled, enervated, faint, infirm, incomplete, vain, fruitless, scanty, pitiable.

fee′ble, *v.t.* [ME. *feblen*; OFr. *febleier*, *febloier*, to make feeble, from *feble*, feeble.] To weaken; to enfeeble. [Obs.]

fee′ble-mind″ed, *a.* 1. Weak in mind; wanting firmness or constancy; irresolute.

Comfort the *feeble-minded*. —1 Thess. v. 14.

2. Lacking intelligence; idiotic.

fee′ble-mind″ed-ness, *n.* The state of having a feeble mind.

fee′ble-ness, *n.* The state or quality of being feeble in any sense of the word; weakness.

fee′bly, *adv.* Weakly; without strength; as, to move *feebly*.

Thy gentle numbers *feebly* creep.—Dryden.

feed, *v.t.*; fed, *pt.*, *pp.*; feeding, *ppr.* [ME. *feden*; AS *fedan*, to feed, nourish, bring forth, from *foda*, food.]

1 To give food to; to give nourishment for the body, either for immediate consumption or for future use; as, to *feed* an infant; to *feed* domestic animals; flour to *feed* the army for a month.

2. To supply; to furnish with anything of which there is constant consumption, waste, or use; as, streams *feed* lakes; to *feed* fuel into a furnace; to *feed* raw material into a machine.

3. To graze; to cause to be cropped, as herbage by cattle; to give for the purpose of consumption; as, to *feed* turnips; to *feed* meal to poultry.

Once in three years *feed* your mowing lands. —Mortimer.

4. To give food or fodder for fattening; to fatten; to support with food; as, the western prairies *feed* most of the beef consumed by the eastern states.

5. To nourish; to cherish; as, to *feed* hope or expectation.

6. To delight; to supply with something desirable; to entertain; as, to *feed* the eye with the beauties of a landscape.

feed, *v.i.* 1. To take food; to eat; now used principally of animals.

2. To subsist by eating; to prey; as, some birds *feed* on seeds and berries, others on flesh.

3. To pasture; to graze; to place cattle to feed.

4. To grow fat; to take on flesh. [Prov. Eng.]

5. To support or comfort oneself mentally, as by hope.

feed, *n.* 1. That which is eaten by the domestic animals; provender; fodder; pasture.

2. The customary allowance, as of fodder, hay, or grain, given to an animal at one meal; as, to carry on a journey two *feeds* of oats.

3. As much material or other necessary element as is supplied at once to a machine or other contrivance, to make it act or to be operated on; the quantity of water supplied at once to a steam-boiler, and the like; also, any contrivance for giving to a machine a regular and uniform supply of the material to be operated on; as, the *feed* of a turning-lathe. In this mechanical sense, *feed* is used in many self-evident compounds describing the use to which various parts are put.

4. The quantity of water required by a vessel in passing a canal-lock.

Differential feed; a device by which a tool, as a lathe, is made to operate with an even, progressive movement.

feed′-ā″pron (-pŭrn), *n.* An endless carrier upon which raw materials, as cotton, wool, etc., are conveyed to and fed into a machine; called also *feed-cloth*.

feed′-bōard, *n.* The inclined plane or table on a folding-machine or cylinder press, from which the sheets of paper are fed into the machine.

feed′-clọth, *n.* See *Feed-apron*.

feed′-dōor, *n.* 1. The door at the mouth of a furnace through which fuel is fed to the fire.

2. A small sliding door in a grain-chute for regulating the quantity of grain to be fed to stock at a time.

feed′ēr, *n.* 1. One who gives food or supplies nourishment; specifically, one who fattens stock for market.

2. One who furnishes incentives; that which augments either the size or relative value of something else; an encourager.

The *feeder* of my riots. —Shak.

3. A plant or animal in its capacity as a consumer; as, pets become delicate *feeders*; small birds are *feeders* on grain or seeds.

4. A fountain, stream, or channel that supplies a canal, lake, or reservoir with water.

5. A branch railway or short line running into and increasing the business of the main line.

6. In mining, a short cross-vein passing into a lode.

7. A trough or vessel so arranged as to supply food to stock and poultry in proper quantities without waste.

8. In electrical construction, a wire which furnishes the main conductor with additional current at various points, whereby the potential underload is equalized.

9. A mechanical device which supplies material to a machine by introducing the proper quantity, with regular action, into the part designed to receive it.

10. One who feeds a machine, as a printing-press.

11. A contrivance for supplying engine-boilers with water in proper quantities.

12. A servant or dependent supported by his lord. [Obs.]

I will your faithful *feeder* be. —Shak.

feed′-head, *n.* 1. A cistern communicating with a steam-boiler, which it supplies by the gravity of the water, the height being made sufficient to overcome the pressure within the boiler

2. In metal-founding, a preponderance of metal above the mold, the weight of which forces the molten mass to completely fill the mold; also called *riser* and *deadhead*.

feed′-hēat″ēr, *n.* 1. An apparatus which utilizes exhaust-steam to heat the feed-water before it enters the boiler.

2. A kettle or boiler for cooking feed given to stock and poultry in winter,

feed′ing, *n.* 1. The act of eating, or of giving to another to eat; the act of supplying for consumption, as to a machine, fire, stream, or body of water.

2. Feed, or that which furnishes food, particularly for animals; pasture-land; as, there is *feeding* there for a thousand sheep.

feed′ing-ground, *n.* A suitable place to feed animals, or the place where animals habitually feed, either on land or at sea; often used in the plural.

feed′-mō″tion, *n.* The machinery that imparts motion to the parts called the feed in machines; called also *feed-gear*.

feed′-pump, *n.* A steam-pump employed to force water into a boiler.

feed′-rack, *n.* A rack from which cattle and horses are fed hay, grain, etc.

feed′-rod, *n.* A regulator for graduating the speed of a feeding device; called also *feed-regulator*.

feed′-rōll, *n.* The roller that carries into a machine the material to be acted upon; as, the *feed-roll* of a typewriter, about which the paper is secured.

feed′-screw (-skrū), *n.* A long screw forming a part of a lathe, which imparts a uniform feed-motion or advance to the work.

feed′-wạ″tēr, *n.* The water fed into a steam-boiler.

fee′-färm, *n.* A kind of tenure of estates without homage, fealty, or other service, except that mentioned in the feoffment, which is usually the full rent.

fee′-fạw′-fum′, **fee′-fō′-fum′**, *n.* A meaningless expression which, according to the fairy tales, is used by giants and ogres to frighten those in their power; hence, gibberish and farcical display intended to delude the ignorant and unsuspecting.

fee′-fund, *n.* In Scots law, the dues of court out of which the clerks and other officers of the court receive their fees.

Fee-jee′ăn, *a.* and *n.* Same as *Fijian*.

feel, *v.t.*; felt, *pt.*, *pp.*; feeling, *ppr.* [ME. *felen*; AS. *felan*, to feel, perceive.]

1. To perceive or to be made aware of, by the sense of touch; to have sensation excited by contact of (a thing) with the body or limbs.

A hand that pushes thro' the leaf
To find a nest and *feels* a snake.—Tennyson.

2. To have the sense of; to experience; to suffer; to perceive mentally; to have a real and just view of; to appreciate.

Would I had never trod this English earth,
Or *felt* the flatteries that grow upon it.
—Shak.

3. To examine by touching or handling; to determine by means of the sense of touch; hence, to grope after; to make trial of; to seek to discover; to try; to test; to explore.

feel, *v.i.* 1. To have perception by the touch, or by the contact of any substance with the body.

2. To have the sensibility or the passions moved or excited; as, to *feel* for the woes of others.

3. To give tactual perception; to excite tactual sensation; to produce an impression on the nerves of sensation.

Blind men say black *feels* rough, and white *feels* smooth. —Dryden.

4. To have perception mentally; to know for a certainty, from intuition rather than from outside sources; to be persuaded; as, to *feel* hurt; to *feel* grieved; to *feel* assured.

To feel after; to search for; to seek to find; to seek as a person groping in the dark.

To feel for; (a) to seek to find cautiously or secretly; (b) to sympathize with.

feel, *n.* 1. Sense of feeling; perception; sensation; as, a *feel* of spring.

2. The quality of communicating a sensation or impression on being touched; as, some rocks have a greasy *feel*.

feel′ẽr, *n.* 1 One who or that which feels. Specifically, one of the palpi or antennæ of insects, mollusks, and crustaceans.

2. Figuratively, an observation, remark, etc., put forth or thrown out, as if casually, in order to ascertain the views or plans of others.

feel′ing, *a.* 1. Expressive of great sensibility; affecting; tending to excite the passions; as, he spoke with *feeling* eloquence.

2. Possessing great sensibility; easily affected or moved; as, a *feeling* man; a *feeling* heart.

3. Sensibly affected; deep; vivid; as, I had a *feeling* sense of his favors.

feel′ing, *n.* 1. The sense of touch, one of the five senses; the sense by which we perceive external objects which come in contact with the body, and obtain ideas of their tangible qualities. It is by *feeling* we know that a body is hard or soft, hot or cold, wet or dry, rough or smooth. The sense exists in all creatures to some extent, and even some plants show a corresponding sensibility.

2. Mental perception, as distinguished from emotional sensation, whether intuitive or resulting from external causes; consciousness; conviction; as, every one had a *feeling* of the truth of his statement.

3. Faculty or power of perception; sensibility; physical sensation of any kind, except such as is due to any of the four other special senses; as, a *feeling* of hunger; a *feeling* of weariness.

4. Acute emotional endowment; sympathy; tenderness of heart; as, he exhibited no *feeling* during the recital of the whole painful story.

5. Excitement; emotion; passion; as, to display *feeling* in a dispute; to harbor *feeling* against.

6. In the fine arts, the impression or emotion conveyed by the general expression of a work of art, especially as embodying some emotion or conception of the artist.

Syn.—Sensation, sensibility, consciousness, emotion, sense, impression, conviction, sensitiveness, tenderness, opinion, sentiment, agitation, passion.

feel′ing-ly, *adv.* 1. With expression of great sensibility; tenderly; as, to speak *feelingly*.

2. So as to be sensibly felt. [Rare.]

> These are counselors,
> That *feelingly* persuade me what I am.—Shak.

feer, feere, *n.* [ME *feere, fere, ifere,* from AS. *gefera,* a companion, associate, from *feran,* to go, travel.] A mate; a companion, particularly one joined in marriage; hence, a husband or wife. Spelled also *fere* and *fear.* [Obs.]

feeṣe, feeze, *n.* A foot-race; the running start taken before a leap. [Obs.]

feet, *n.,* pl. of *foot.*

feet, *n.* [Obs.] Same as *Feat.*

feet′less, *a.* Destitute of feet; as, *feetless* birds.

feeze, *v.t.*; feezed, *pt., pp.*; feezing, *ppr.* [Scot.] To turn; to twist, as a screw; to tighten by screwing down; as, to *feeze* a violin string.

feeze, fēaze, *v.t.* To beat; to worry; to punish. [Obs.]

feeze, fēaze, *v.i.* To fume; to fret. [Colloq.]

feeze, fēaze, *n.* Irritable excitement. [Colloq.]

feh′me, fehm-ge-rich′te, *n.* See *Vehmgerichte.*

feh′mic, *a.* See *Vehmic.*

feign (fān), *v.t.*; feigned, *pt., pp.*; feigning, *ppr.* [ME. *feinen, feynen, feignen*; OFr. *feindre, faindre*; Pr. *feigner*; It. *fignere,* from L. *fingere,* to touch, handle, shape.]

1. To invent or imagine; to form an idea or conception of.

> There are no such things done as thou sayest, but thou *feignest* them out of thine own heart. —Neh. vi. 8.

2. To make a show of; to pretend; to simulate; to counterfeit; as, to *feign* insanity.

3. To represent falsely; to pretend; to form and relate, as if true.

> The poet
> Did *feign* that Orpheus drew trees, stones, and floods. —Shak.

4. To dissemble; to conceal. [Obs.]

feigned, *a.* Invented; devised; imagined; assumed; simulated; counterfeit.

Feigned issue; in law, a proceeding whereby an action is supposed to be brought by consent of the parties, to determine some disputed right without the formality of pleading, saving thereby both time and expense.

feign′ed-ly, *adv.* In a feigned manner; in pretense; falsely.

feign′ed-ness, *n.* Fiction; pretense; deceit.

feign′ẽr, *n.* One who feigns; an inventor; a deviser of fiction.

feign′ing-ly (fān′), *adv.* In a false [illegible] ous manner; feignedly.

fein, feine, *v.t.* [Obs.] See *Feign.*

feint, *n.* [Fr. *feinte,* a sham, pretense, f. pp. of *feindre,* to feign.] 1. An appearance intended to mislead; a pretense; a stratagem; as, a well-conceived *feint.*

2. A deceptive movement or motion; in boxing, fencing, etc., an appearance of aiming or thrusting at one part when another is intended to be struck; as, to make a *feint* at the head.

feint, *a.* Seeming; simulated; counterfeit. [Obs.]

feint, *v.i.*; feinted, *pt., pp.*; feinting, *ppr.* To make a feint or pretense of attack.

fei-tsui′ (fā-tswē′), *n.* A Chinese name for a valuable variety of jadeite.

fe-lap′ton, *n.* In logic, one of the valid moods.

feld′spär, feld′spath, *n.* [G. *feldspath,* from *feld,* field, and *spath, spat,* spar.] A mineral widely distributed, and usually of a foliated structure, consisting of silica and alumina, with potash, soda, or lime. It is a principal constituent in all igneous and metamorphic rocks, as granite, gneiss, porphyry, greenstone, trachyte, etc. Its hardness is little inferior to that of quartz. There are several varieties. Common *feldspar* or orthoclase is the type of an acid group containing from 7 to 16 per cent of potash. A large percentage of the clays is derived from the decomposition of the feldspars, including kaolin, an important material in the manufacture of pottery and porcelain. Orthoclase or potash *feldspar* is ground and much used for the same purpose.

feld-spath′ic, feld-spath′ōse, *a.* Consisting of, containing, or resembling feldspar.

fēle, *a.* [AS. *fela, feola,* many.] Many. [Obs.]

Fē-li′ciăn (-lish′ăn), *n.* A follower of Felix, an early Spanish theologian, who promulgated the heresy of the Adoptionists.

fē-li-cif′ic, *a.* [L. *felix (-icis),* happy, and *-ficus,* from *facere,* to make.] Causing happiness; giving joy; productive of pleasure.

fē-lic′i-fy, *v.t.* [Obs.] See *Felicitate.*

fē-lic′i-tāte, *a.* Made very happy. [Rare.]

fē-lic′i-tāte, *v.t.*; felicitated, *pt., pp.*; felicitating, *ppr.* [L. *felicitatus,* pp. of *felicitare,* to make happy, from *felix (-icis),* happy.]

1. To make or render happy.

2. To congratulate; to wish joy or pleasure to; as, we *felicitate* our friends on good fortune or an escape from evil.

fē-lic-i-tā′tion, *n.* Expression of joy for another's happiness or good fortune; congratulation.

fē-lic′i-tous, *a.* 1. Distinguished by or producing felicity; as, a *felicitous* occasion.

2. Happy in application or effect; well-chosen; apt and to the point; as, a *felicitous* phrase.

Syn.—Happy, timely, apropos, successful, opportune, joyous.

fē-lic′i-tous-ly, *adv.* In a felicitous manner; happily; suitably.

fē-lic′i-tous-ness, *n.* The state or condition of being felicitous.

fē-lic′i-ty, *n.*; *pl.* **fē-lic′i-tieṣ.** [ME. *felicitee*; OFr. *felicite,* from L. *felicitas,* happiness, from *felix (-icis),* happy.]

1. A state of supreme happiness; perfect content and comfort; bliss.

> And, finally, after this life to attain everlasting joy and *felicity.* —Common Prayer.

2. That which promotes happiness; a source of satisfaction that which yields enjoyment; as, the *felicities* of a quiet life.

> No greater *felicity* can genius attain than that of having purified intellectual pleasure. —Johnson.

3. A skilful or happy faculty; skilfulness; a skilful or happy turn; appropriateness; as, he has a rare *felicity* in applying principles to facts; *felicity* in taking a likeness.

Syn.—Bliss, blessedness, blissfulness, ecstasy, rapture, enjoyment, comfort, appropriateness, blessing, happiness, tact, knack, skill, dexterity.

fē′lid, *n.* Any animal belonging to the cat family, or *Felidæ.*

Fē′li-dæ, *n.pl.* [From L. *felis,* prop. *feles,* a cat, and *-idæ.*] Animals of the cat kind, a family of carnivora in which the predaceous instincts reach their highest development. The incisor teeth are equal; the third tooth behind the large canine in either jaw is narrow and sharp, and these, the carnassial or sectorial teeth, work against each other like scissors in cutting flesh; the claws are sheathed and retractile. This family includes the domestic cat, the wildcat, the lion, tiger, leopard, lynx, jaguar, panther, chetah, ounce, caracal, serval, ocelot, etc.

Felidæ.

Skull and teeth of the tiger. *a,* Canines or tearing teeth. *b,* Incisors or cutting teeth. *c,* True molars or grinding teeth. *d.* Carnassial or sectorial teeth.

fē′line, *a.* [L. *felinus,* from *feles, felis,* a cat.]

1. Catlike; characteristic of the genus *Felis* or family *Felidæ*; typical of the cat kind; as, *feline* habits.

2. Resembling a cat in nature or manner; sly; cruel; treacherous; easy; graceful; as, with *feline* grace; *feline* cunning.

fē′line, *n.* An animal of the family *Felidæ,* especially the domestic cat.

Fē′lis, *n.* [L. *feles* or *felis,* a cat.] The type genus of the family *Felidæ.*

fell, *v.,* past tense of *fall.*

fell, *a.* [ME. *fel, fell*; OFr. *fel,* cruel, furious.]

1. Cruel; barbarous; inhuman; fierce; savage; ravenous; bloody.

> More *fell* than tigers on the Libyan plain. —Pope.

2. Strong and fiery; keen; biting; sharp; clever; active; as, a *fell* cheese; a *fell* body. [Scot.]

fell, *n.* [ME. *fel, fell*; AS. *fel, fell,* a skin, hide; O.H.G. *fel*; Ice. *fjall, fell*; Sw. *fäll*; Norw. *feld,* a skin, hide.] A skin or hide of a beast; a pelt; used chiefly in composition; as, wool*fell.* [Rare.]

fell, *n.* [ME. *fel, fell*; Ice. *fjall, fell*; Dan. *fjæld,* a hill.]

1. A stretch of waste land; a moor.

2. A barren hill or high, rocky ground. In this sense, it has been incorporated into the names of English and Scotch localities, and has but rare use as a separate word.

fell, *n.* [L. *fel,* gall, bitterness.] Anger; melancholy [Obs.]

fell, *n.* In mining, the smaller fragments of ore which wash through the meshes of a sieve or riddle.

fell, *v.t.*; felled, *pt., pp.*; felling, *ppr.* [ME. *fellen*; AS. *fellan, fyllan,* to cause to fall, strike down, caus. of *feallan,* to fall.] To cause to fall; to prostrate; to bring to the ground, either by cutting, as to *fell* trees, or by striking, as to *fell* an ox.

fell, *v.t.* [Compare Gael. *fill,* to fold, Sw. *fall,* a hem.] Literally, to level with the skin; in sewing, to lay flat and sew level with the cloth, as a seam.

fell, *n.* 1. In sewing, a seam uniting two edges which are folded one over the other and sewed together in this position; a French seam.

2. In weaving, the line of termination of a web formed by the last weft-thread driven up by the lay.

fell′ȧ-ble, *a.* Capable of being or fit to be felled.

fel′lăh, *n.*; *pl.* **fel′lăh-een** or **fel′lăhṣ,** or Ar. *pl.* **fel′lăh-ïn.** [Ar. *fellah,* a plowman, peasant, from *falaha,* to cleave the soil, plow.] An Egyptian or Syrian peasant or agricultural laborer. The *fellaheen* are a people of mixed blood, strains of the Arabian and Nubian being infused with the pure Coptic. The name is applied by the Turks to all Egyptians alike, without reference to race or occupation.

fell′ẽr, *n.* 1. One who hews or knocks down; a device for cutting down trees.

2. An attachment by the use of which a sewing-machine is made to fell seams.

fell′fāre, *n.* See *Fieldfare.*

fel′lic, fel-lin′ic, *a.* [L. *fel, fellis,* gall, and *-ic.*] Peculiar to or derived from bile; as, *fellic* acid, one of the biliary acids.

fel-lif′lū-ous, *a.* [L. *fel, fellis,* gall, and *fluere,* to flow.] Flowing with gall.

fel-lin′ic, *a.* See *Fellic.*

fell′mŏn-gẽr, *n.* A dealer in fells or hides.

fell′ness, *n.* Cruelty; fierce barbarity; rage; absolute ruthlessness.

fel′lōe, *n.* See *Felly.*

fel′lŏn, *n.* [Obs.] See *Felon.*

fel′lōw, *n.* [ME. *felow, felaghe,* a companion, partner, from Ice. *felagi,* a partnership, fellowship; *fe,* property, and *lag,* a laying together, fellowship, from *leggja,* to lay.]

1. A person with whom one is habitually in company; a companion: an associate; an accomplice; a comrade; a mate.

> In youth I had twelve *fellows* like myself. —Ascham.

2. An equal; one of the same kind; one equal to or like another; a counterpart; one of a pair or of two things used together and suited to each other.

> And when I am dead, may the better sort say, He's gone, and not left behind him his *fellow.* —Dr. W. Pope.

> Two shoes that were not *fellows.* —Defoe.

3. A term applied in familiarity to any man or boy, and more rarely to a woman; often with the adjective *good*; also, often colloquially used in referring to oneself; as, let a *fellow* have a chance.

> She seemed to be a good sort of *fellow.* —Dickens.

> A *fellow* of infinite jest, of most excellent fancy. —Shak.

4. An appellation of contempt; a man without good breeding or worth; an ignoble man.

Worth makes the man, the want of it the *fellow*. —Pope.

5. A member of a college who holds a fellowship.

6. A member of an incorporated society devoted in most instances to literary, artistic, or scientific pursuits; as, a *fellow* of the Royal Geographical Society.

Fellow is employed in the formation of numerous self-evident compounds, denoting community of nature, station, or employment; as, *fellow*-workman, *fellow*-passenger, *fellow*-citizen, *fellow*-sufferer, *fellow*-mortal, etc.

fel′lōw, *v.t.*; fellowed, *pt., pp.*; fellowing, *ppr.* 1. To suit with; to pair with; to match.

2. To associate with; to accompany. [Obs.]

fel″lōw-com′mŏn-ẽr, *n.* 1. One who has the same right of common.

2. In Cambridge University, England, a student who commons or dines with the fellows.

fel′lōw-craft, *n.* The second degree in Freemasonry; one who has taken this degree.

fel″lōw-feel′, *v.t.* To have a like feeling, as sorrow or joy, with; to feel sympathy with. [Rare.]

fel″lōw-feel′ẽr, *n.* One who shares another's feelings; one who feels sympathy for another. [Rare.]

fel″lōw-feel′ing, *n.* A feeling of fellowship or joint interest; sympathy.

fel′lōw-less, *a.* Having no equal or associate; peerless; unmatched.

fel′lōw-like, *a.* Like an associate or comrade; companionable; on equal terms.

fel′lōw-ly, *a.* Fellowlike; sympathetic. [Rare.]

fel′lōw-ship, *n.* 1. The condition of being an associate; mutual association of persons on equal and friendly terms; communion; companionship; familiar intercourse; intimate familiarity.

Have no *fellowship* with the unfruitful works of darkness. —Eph. v. 11.

Men are made for society and mutual *fellowship*. —Calamy.

2. The state or condition of having a common share; partnership; joint interest; as, *fellowship* in pain.

3. A body of companions or fellows; an association of persons having the same tastes, occupations, or interests; a band; a company.

The great contention of the sea and skies
Parted our *fellowship*. —Shak.

4. In arithmetic, the rule by which profit or loss is divided among those who are to bear it, in proportion to their investments or interests in the transaction; partnership.

5. A sum of money provided by a college or university in the United States, for the assistance of a graduate student in pursuing his study.

6. A position in some colleges in England which entitles the holder to a share in their revenues, the right to apartments in the college, and certain privileges as to commons or meals; most fellowships being confined to graduates of the university to which they belong.

fel′lōw-ship, *v.t.* and *v.i.*; fellowshipped, *pt., pp.*; fellowshipping, *ppr.* I. *v.t.* To associate with as a fellow or member of the same church; to admit to fellowship; specifically, to Christian fellowship; to unite with in doctrine and discipline.

II. *v.i.* To become associated with others.

fel′ly, *adv.* [ME. *felly, felli, fellich,* fiercely, cruelly.] Cruelly; fiercely; barbarously.

fel′ly, fel′lōe, *n.*; *pl.* **fel′lieṣ, fel′lōeṣ.** [ME. *feli, felwe, felow*; AS. *felg, felge,* a felly, felloe, from AS. *fiolan, feolan,* to stick, from the pieces of the rim being put together.]

1. One of the curved pieces of wood which, joined together by dowel-pins, form the circumference or circular rim of a wheel into which the spokes are fitted.

Wheel. *a*, Felly. *b*, Spoke. *c*, Nave.

2. The rim of a wheel.

fē′lō, *n.* [LL. *felo,* a traitor, rebel.] A felon; one guilty of a criminal act.

Felo de se; a suicide.

fē′loid, *a.* [L. *feles, felis,* a cat, and Gr. *eidos,* form.] Of or pertaining to the *Felidæ*; having the characteristics of the cat family.

fel′ŏn, *a.* 1. Malignant; fierce; malicious; proceeding from a depraved heart; traitorous; disloyal.

Vain shows of love to vail his *felon* hate. —Pope.

2. Secured unlawfully or as the result of a crime; stolen; applied specifically to goods.

fel′ŏn, *n.* [ME. *feloun, felon,* from *feloun,* wicked, malignant.] Acute inflammation of the periosteum and adjacent tissue in a toe or finger, usually occurring near the nail; a deep-seated whitlow.

fel′ŏn, *n.* [ME. *felon, feloun*; OFr. *felon, fellon,* a wicked person, traitor, from LL. *fello, felo,* a traitor, rebel.]

1. In law, a person who has committed felony; a criminal.

2. An outlaw; also, a crime. [Obs.]

fel′ŏn-ess, *n.* A woman guilty of felony.

fe-lō′ni-ous, *a.* 1. Malignant; malicious; indicating or proceeding from a depraved heart or evil purpose; villainous; traitorous; perfidious; as, a *felonious* deed.

2. In law, done with the deliberate purpose to commit a crime; as, *felonious* homicide.

fē-lō′ni-ous-ly, *adv.* In a felonious manner; with the deliberate intention of committing a crime.

fē-lō′ni-ous-ness, *n.* The quality of being felonious.

fel′ŏn-ly, *adv.* Feloniously. [Obs.]

fel′ŏ-nous, *a.* Wicked; felonious. [Obs.]

fel′ŏn-ous-ly, *adv.* Feloniously. [Obs.]

fel′ŏn-ry, *n.* A number of felons, considered collectively; a body of convicts, as in a prison or penal colony.

fel′ŏn-wŏrt, *n* A common name of *Solanum Dulcamara,* or bittersweet, given from its use as a cure for whitlow; called also *felonwood.*

fel′ŏn-y, *n.*; *pl.* **fel′ŏn-ieṣ.** [ME. *felony, felonie*; LL. *felonia,* treason, treachery, from *felo* (*-onis*), a traitor, wicked fellow.]

1. An act of wickedness or treachery. [Obs.]

2. In law, (a) under the feudal system, an offense committed by a vassal, the penalty of which was forfeiture of fief; (b) at common law, one of a limited number of crimes the punishment of which is the forfeiture of land or goods or both (cases of particular heinousness sometimes occasioning additional penalty, even death); (c) in modern usage, a grave crime; a high offense.

The present use of *felony* is confused and indefinite. In England, Parliament has by special acts largely modified the signification of the term as established at common law. In the United States, where forfeiture of estate is abolished, *felony* is generally used in distinction from *misdemeanor.*

In many [states] of the United States, felony is defined by statute as including all crimes which are punishable by death or imprisonment in the state prison. . . . Many crimes which were not felonies at common law are made so by statute, being either expressly declared to be so, or such a penalty being attached to them as to bring them within the meaning of the term. —Smith.

To compound a felony; see under *Compound.*

fel′site, *n.* [Fr. *felsite,* from G. *fels,* rock.] A hard compact rock, found amorphous, consisting of common potash feldspar, associated with quartz; called also *felstone.*

fel-sit′iç, *a.* Pertaining to or resembling felsite; containing or composed of felsite.

fel′spär, fel′spath, *n.* Same as *Feldspar.*

fel-spath′iç, *a.* Same as *Feldspathic.*

fel′stōne, *n.* Same as *Felsite.*

felt, *v.,* past tense and past participle of *feel.*

felt, *n.* [ME. *felt*; AS. *felt*; D. *vilt*; G. *filz,* felt.]

1. A cloth or fabric made of wool, or wool and fur or hair, the fibers of which are not woven together, but matted or wrought into a compact substance by rolling and pressure, usually with the aid of sizing, heat, and moisture.

2. Any woven fabric that is partially felted, as by shrinkage or the process of fulling.

3. A strip or piece of *felt*-cloth; also, any article made of *felt,* particularly a hat.

4. A woven or felted material made of asbestos fibers.

5. Skin. [Obs.]

felt, *v.t.*; felted, *pt., pp.*; felting, *ppr.* 1. To mat together, as fibers, so as to form a compact sheet; especially, to make into felt-cloth.

2. To jacket or cover over with felt or some similar material; as, to *felt* a steam-pipe.

felt, *v.i.* To mat; to become closely massed or compacted.

felt′-cloth, *n.* Cloth made of wool united without weaving; felt.

felt′ed, *a.* 1. Matted as in the process of felting; manufactured into felt.

2. In botany, made up of intertwined or matted filaments.

Felted tissue; the tissue occurring in fungi, which consists of separate hyphæ closely intertwined.

felt′ẽr, *v.t.* To clot or mat together like felt. [Obs.]

felt′-grāin, *n.* The grain of wood that runs from the outside of the tree toward the center, crossing the annular rings transversely.

felt′ing, *n.* 1. The process of making felt.

2. The various materials used in the manufacture of felt.

3. Felt-cloth; a general sense used chiefly of a large or indefinite quantity.

4. The splitting or sawing of timber along the felt-grain.

fel′try, *n.* [Obs.] Same as *Felt.*

felt′wŏrt, *n.* A plant, the mullen. [Obs.]

fel′ty, *a.* Felt-like, as in appearance, composition, or feel.

fe-luc′cȧ, *n.* [It. *felucca*; Sp. *feluca*; Ar. *faluka,* from *fulk,* a ship.] A vessel formerly much used in the Mediterranean. It has both oars

Felucca.

and lateen sails, and is characterized by a peculiarity of construction whereby the helm may be applied to the head or stern, as occasion requires.

fel′wŏrt, *n.* A common name for various species of gentian.

fē′māle, *n.* [ME. *femal, femel*; LL. *femella,* dim. of L. *femina,* a woman, one who brings forth.]

1. Among human beings or animals, one of that sex which conceives and brings forth young.

2. In botany, a plant which produces fruit; a plant which bears a pistil and receives the pollen of the male plant, or which has some analogous organ.

fē′māle, *a.* 1. Of or pertaining to the sex which produces young; not male; as, a *female* bee.

2. Pertaining to women; characteristic of a woman; feminine; womanly; tender; delicate; weak.

To the generous decision of a *female* mind we owe the discovery of America.—Belknap.

3. In botany, pertaining to fruit-producing plants; capable of being fertilized; bearing a pistil or some analogous organ; pistillate.

4. Pertaining to or designating any object corresponding in function or quality to another object, or standing in a correlative or contrasting relation to it; as, a *female* die.

Female joint; the socket or faucet-piece of a spigot-and-faucet joint.

Female rime; double rime in which the last syllable is unaccented, as in *motion, ocean*; so called from the French, in which language words having double rime end in a mute, or feminine, *e.*

Female screw; a concave or internal screw into which a corresponding convex or external screw, called the male, works; a screw-nut.

Syn.—Feminine, effeminate, womanly.—*Female* is applicable to the sex and to the essential physiological distinctions from the male; *feminine,* to the mental qualities and finer characteristics of women and to the things appropriate to them; *effeminate* to those qualities which are womanish and in a man unbecoming and weak.

fē′māl-ist, *n.* One devoted to the female sex; a courter of women; a gallant. [Obs.]

fē′māl-ize, *v.t.* To make female or feminine.

feme, femme, *n.* [OFr. *feme, femme,* from L. *femina,* a woman.] A woman.

Feme covert; a married woman who is under the protection and control of her husband.

Feme sole; (a) an unmarried woman; one who has never been married, who is a widow, or who is separated from her husband by divorce; (b) a married woman conducting business or trade or holding property in her own right and responsibility.

fem′ẽr-el, fem′ẽr-ell, *n.* [OFr. *fumeraille,* part of a chimney, from *fumer,* to smoke; L. *fumus,* smoke.] In architecture, a lantern or partially open dome-like structure erected on the roof of a kitchen, hall, etc., to afford ventilation; written also *femeral, fomerell, fumerell.*

fem′i-cīde, *n.* [L. *femina,* a woman, and *-cidium,* from *cædere,* to kill.] The act of killing a woman.

fem′i-năl, *a.* [From L. *femina,* a woman.] Pertaining to a woman; feminine. [Rare.]

fem-i-nal′i-ty, *n.* Female nature; the state or quality of being female; womanliness.

fem′i-nāte, *a.* [L. *feminatus,* from *femina,* a woman.] Feminine. [Obs.]

fem-i-nē′i-ty, *n.* [From L. *femineus,* womanly, from *femina,* a woman.] Feminality; female nature.

fem′i-nine, *a.* [L. *femininus,* from *femina,* a woman.]

1. Of, pertaining to, or characteristic of a woman or women; having the qualities

natural to women; becoming to a woman; as, the *feminine* sex; *feminine* grace.

2. Effeminate; destitute of manly qualities; womanish.

> Ninus was no man of war at all, but altogether *feminine*. —Raleigh.

3. In grammar, belonging to or denoting the female gender, natural or grammatical; applied to words and terminations; as, *mother* is a *feminine* noun, *her* a *feminine* pronoun, *-ess* a *feminine* termination.

Feminine number; a number that is even.

Feminine rime; see *Female rime* under *Female*.

fem′i-nine, *n.* A female; a woman; the female sex. [Obs.]

fem′i-nine-ly, *adv.* In a feminine manner.

fem′i-nine-ness, *n.* The state or quality of being feminine; female nature.

fem′i-nin-iṣm, *n.* Feminineness.

fem-i-nin′i-ty, *n.* [From L. *femininus*, womanly, from *femina*, a woman.]

1. Feminine nature or characteristics; womanliness.

2. Womankind; women, considered collectively.

fem′i-niṣm, *n.* Feminineness. [Obs.]

fē-min′i-ty, *n.* The qualities or nature of the female sex; womanliness; also, effeminacy. [Obs.]

fem″i-ni-zā′tion, *n.* The act of making or becoming feminine or womanish; the condition of being feminized. [Rare.]

fem′i-nize, *v.t.* [L. *femina*, a woman, and *-ize*.] To make feminine; to cause to become womanish. [Rare.]

fem′i-nye, *n.* [From OFr. *feminie*, *femmenie*, from *feme*, a woman.] A body of women; particularly [F—] the race of Amazons or their country. [Obs.]

femme, *n.* [Fr.] A woman.

Femme de chambre; a chambermaid; a lady's maid.

fem′ō-ra̤, *n.*, pl. of *femur*.

fem′ō-ra̤l, *a.* [LL. *femoralis*, from *femur*, the thigh.] Of or pertaining to the thigh or to the thigh-bone, the femur; as, the *femoral* artery; the *femoral* canal.

fem″ō-rō-ça̤u′da̤l, *a.* [L. *femur* (*-oris*), the thigh, and *cauda*, a tail.] Relating to the thigh and the tail, as certain muscles.

fem″ō-rō-tib′i-a̤l, *a.* [L. *femur* (*-oris*), the thigh, and *tibia*, the tibia.] Pertaining to or situated between the femur and the tibia.

fē′mŭr, *n.*; *pl.* **fē′mŭrṣ** or **fem′ō-ra̤.** [L. *femur* (*-oris*), the thigh.]

1. In vertebrate animals, the first bone of the leg or pelvic extremity; the thigh-bone; also, the thigh.

2. In entomology, the third joint of the leg, articulating proximally with the trochanter and distally with the tibia

3. In architecture, the space between the channels in the triglyph of the Doric order.

fen, *n.* [ME. *fen*, *fenne*; AS. *fen*, *fenn*, a marsh, bog, fen.] Low land overflowed, or covered wholly or partially with water, but producing sedge, coarse grasses, or other aquatic plants; boggy land; a moor or marsh; also used adjectively.

> A long canal the muddy *fen* divides. —Addison.

fen′ber″ry, *n.* *Vaccinium Oxycoccus*, the small cranberry.

fen′-boat, *n.* A flat boat suitable for use on fens.

fence, *n.* [ME. *fence*, *fens*, *fense*, a defense, guard, abbrev. of *defense*, *defence*.]

1. A structure erected around or by the side of any open space to prevent passage in or out; especially, a structure inclosing or separating yards, fields, etc. In the United States the term is commonly applied to the various forms constructed of posts carrying boards, rails, pickets, or wire, or to iron structures consisting of vertical or horizontal bars or of open-work. A wall, hedge, or bank, however, may constitute a *fence*; and a ditch is also so considered, in England.

2. A guard; anything to restrain entrance; that which defends from attack, approach, or injury; security; defense.

> A *fence* betwixt us and the victor's wrath. —Addison.

3. The art of self-defense, especially by the sword; fencing; skill in fencing or sword-play; also, ability in argument, especially adroitness in sustaining oneself and baffling an opponent's attacks.

> I bruised my shin th'other day with playing at sword and dagger with a master of *fence*. —Shak.

4. In machinery, tools, etc., a guard, guide, or gauge, to regulate or restrict movement.

5. A person who buys or receives goods that he is aware have been stolen; a place where stolen property is secreted or disposed of.

Ring fence; a fence which encircles a whole estate or some extensive tract of land.

To be on the fence; to have no settled judgment or conviction regarding matters, usually political, or to give no open expression of them.

Worm fence; a kind of rail fence, so called from its crookedness, being made of rails laid to cross at the end, an X-rider being often added; called also *snake* or *serpent fence*, *Virginia rail fence*, and, locally, various other names.

fence, *v.t.*; fenced (fenst), *pt.*, *pp.*; fencing, *ppr.*

1. To inclose with a structure of any kind that prevents ingress or egress; to secure by an inclosure; to erect a fence about.

2. To guard; to fortify; to secure from danger or injury.

> So much of adder's wisdom I have learnt,
> To *fence* my ear against thy sorceries. —Milton.

3. To ward off or parry, as in fencing, argument, or reasoning.

> Reasoning of a very similar character . . . does duty largely as a means of *fencing* off disagreeable conclusions. —Mill.

4. To separate; to divide off; to keep apart; as, to *fence* grainfields from pasture-land.

To fence the tables; in the Church of Scotland, to address intending communicants at the Lord's table with words of counsel and admonition.

fence, *v.i.* 1. To practise the art of fencing; to use a sword or foil for the purpose of learning the art of attack and defense; to fight and defend by giving and avoiding blows or thrusts.

> They *fence* and push, and, pushing, loudly roar. —Dryden.

2. To raise a fence; to guard; figuratively, to parry arguments; to strive by equivocation to baffle an examiner and conceal the information sought.

fence′fụl, *a.* Affording defense; as, a *fenceful* weapon.

fence′less, *a.* 1. Without a fence; unguarded; open; not closed; as, the *fenceless* ocean.

2. Defenseless; having no means of protection.

fence′-liz″ăr̤d, *n.* *Sceloporus undulatus*, the common lizard.

fence′-mŏnth, *n.* In English game-laws, the close-season for deer.

fen′cẽr, *n.* 1. One who fences; one who teaches or practises the art of fencing with sword or foil.

2. A horse good at leaping fences; said generally of a hunter.

fence′-rọọf, *n.* A protective screen or covering. [Obs.]

fence′-time, *n.* Same as *Close-season*.

fen′ci-ble, *a.* and *n.* I. *a.* Capable of being defended or of offering defense; as, a *fencible* castle.

II. *n.* A soldier for defense of the country against invasion, and not liable to serve abroad; as, a regiment of *fencibles*.

fen′cing, *n.* 1. The art of using skilfully a sword or foil in attack or defense.

2. Material with which to build a fence; especially, boards, poles, or the like, as distinguished from posts.

3. That which fences; especially, a protection put round a dangerous piece of machinery; brattishing.

4. The process of erecting a fence.

5. Fences collectively considered, or such fences as may surround the fields on one estate; as, the storm did great damage to *fencing* throughout this section.

6. In debate, skilful discussion, readiness in repartee; the act of parrying questions, as fencers do thrusts.

fen′-crick″et, *n.* Same as *Mole-cricket*.

fend, *v.t.*; fended, *pt.*, *pp.*; fending, *ppr.* [ME. *fenden*, abbrev. of *defenden*, to defend.] To keep off; to prevent from entering; to ward off; to shut out; usually followed by *off*; as, to *fend off* blows.

> With fern beneath to *fend* the bitter cold. —Dryden.

To fend off a boat or *vessel*; to prevent its running against another, or against a wharf, etc., with too much violence.

fend, *v.i.* To act in opposition; to resist; to parry; to shift off.

fend, *n.* [Obs.] See *Fiend*.

fend′ẽr, *n.* One who or that which fends or acts as a defense; specifically, one of various mechanical devices of a protective kind; (a) a screenlike guard against live coals in front of a fireplace; (b) a piece of timber or bundle of rope hung over the side of a vessel to prevent it from being injured by rubbing against another body; (c) a rub-iron for the fore wheels of a vehicle; (d) a mud-guard, as for the wheels of an automobile; (e) the shield of a cultivator, usually of sheet-iron, protecting young plants from dirt worked toward them; (f) the frame suspended in front of a street-car to prevent a person struck from being carried under the wheels.

fend′liche, *a.* Fiendlike; devilish. [Obs.]

fen′-duck, *n.* The shoveler, a species of wild duck found frequently in fens and marshes.

fen′ẽr-āte, *v.t.* [L. *feneratus*, pp. of *fenerare*, to lend on interest, from *fenus*, proceeds, interest.] To put to use, as funds; to lend on interest. [Obs.]

fen-ẽr-ā′tion, *n.* The act of lending on interest; the interest or gain of that which is lent. [Obs.]

fen-es-tel′la̤, *n.* [L., dim. of *fenestra*, a window.] A small opening like a window; particularly, in Roman Catholic churches, the niche on the south side of an altar containing the piscina, and frequently also the credence.

Fenestella with Piscina.

fē-nes′tra̤, *n.*; *pl.* **fē-nes′træ.** [L., a window.]

1. In anatomy, a small orifice; a foramen.

2. In entomology, (a) a hyaline spot, such as is found in the wings of certain butterflies and moths; (b) one of two membrane-covered depressions—supposedly of the nature of simple eyes—near the antennæ of cockroaches.

Fenestra ovalis; in the human ear, an ovoid opening leading to the cavity of the vestibule.

Fenestra rotunda; a smaller opening below the *fenestra ovalis* leading to the cochlea.

fē-nes′tra̤l, *a.* and *n.* [From L. *fenestra*, a window.]

I. *a.* Pertaining to or having the form of a window; relating to a fenestra.

II. *n.* A small window; also, the framed blinds of cloth or canvas that supplied the place of glass previous to the introduction of that material. [Obs.]

fē-nes′trāte, *a.* [L. *fenestratus*, pp. of *fenestrare*, to furnish with windows or openings, from *fenestra*, a window.]

1. Having a network of openings; irregularly perforated; as, *fenestrate* leaves, in which the cellular tissue does not entirely fill the interstices between the veins.

2. Having fenestræ in the wings, as certain *Insecta*.

3. In architecture, same as *fenestrated*.

fē-nes′trā-ted, *a.* 1. Having numerous windows; having walls pierced by windows.

2. Characterized by having fenestræ; fenestrate.

fen-es-trā′tion, *n.* 1. In architecture, a design in which the windows are arranged to form the principal feature; the series or arrangement of windows in a building.

2. In anatomy and entomology, the condition of having fenestræ.

fē-nes′trụle, *n.* [LL *fenestrula*, dim. of *fenestra*, a window.] In zoölogy, one of the spaces inclosed by the intersecting branches of *Polyzoa*.

fen′-fowl, *n.* Any fowl that frequents fens.

fen′ġite, *n.* [L. *phengites*, from Gr. *phengitēs*, from *phengos*, light.] A kind of transparent alabaster or marble, sometimes used as glazing in windows.

fen′-gọọse, *n.* The common European wild gray goose; the graylag.

Fē′ni-ăn, *a.* and *n.* [Named from the *Fiann* or *Fianna*, a name applied to the old militia of Ireland, who were so called from *Finn*, *Fionn*, a hero of Irish tradition.]

I. *a.* Relating to the Fenians.

II. *n.* A member of a secret Irish association, seeking the liberation of Ireland from English rule.

Fē′ni-ăn-iṣm, *n.* The policy of the Fenian Brotherhood.

fenks, *n.* The ultimate refuse of whale-blubber, used as a fertilizer.

fen′land, *n.* Marshy land; applied in particular to a district covered with marshes or fens in the middle and eastern parts of England.

fen′neç, fen′nek, *n.* [Moorish.] An animal of the family *Vulpinæ*, smaller than the fox and having remarkably large ears. It is native to Africa.

fen′nel, *n.* [ME. *fenel*, *fenyl*; AS. *fenol*, *finol*, from L. *feniculum*, *fœniculum*, dim. of *fenum*, *fœnum*, hay.] A plant of the genus *Fœniculum*, cultivated in gardens for the agreeable aromatic flavor of its seeds.

Sweet fennel; a smaller variety than the common fennel. It is used, especially in southern Europe, as a salad herb.

fen′nel-flow″ẽr, *n.* The English name of plants of the genus *Nigella*, given on account of their finely-cut leaves, resembling those of fennel.

fen′nel-wa″tẽr, *n.* A liquor prepared from the seeds of the fennel or from oil extracted from the seeds. It is used in medicine and in the treatment of animals.

fen′nish, *a.* Having numerous fens; fenny; marshy.

fen′ny, *a.* [ME. *fenny*; AS. *fennig, fenneg,* marshy, from *fen, fenn,* marsh, bog.]
1. Boggy; marshy; moorish.
2. Growing in fens; as, *fenny* brake.
3. Inhabiting marshy ground; as, a *fenny* snake.

fen′ōwed, *a.* [AS. *fynig,* musty.] Corrupted; decayed. [Obs.]

fen′-sucked (-sukt), *a.* Drained out of marshes. [Obs.]

fent, *n.* [ME. *fente*; OFr. *fente,* a slit, from *fendre,* L. *findere,* to cleave, split.]
1. An opening left in an article of dress, as in a sleeve or skirt, for convenience in putting on; a placket.
2. A piece of cloth damaged in dyeing or printing.

fen′ū-greek, *n.* [From L. *fenumgræcum, fœnum Græcum,* lit., Greek hay; *fœnum, fenum,* hay, and *Græcum,* neut. of *Græcus,* Greek.] A plant of the genus *Trigonella,* allied to clover, and sometimes cultivated for its seeds, which are used for food and in medicine.

feod (fūd), *n.* Same as *Feud.*

feod′ăl (fūd′ăl), *a.* Same as *Feudal.*

feo-dal′i-ty (fū-), *n.* Feudal tenures; the feudal system. [See *Feudality.*]

feod′ă-ry, *n.* Same as *Feudary.*

feoff (fef), *v.t.*; feoffed, *pt., pp.*; feoffing, *ppr.* [OFr. *feoffer, fiefer,* from *fief,* a fief.] In law, to invest with a fee or feud; to give or grant corporeal hereditament to. [See *Enfeoff.*]

feoff, *n.* See *Fief.*

feof-fee′ (fef-fē′), *n.* [OFr. *feoffe,* pp. of *feoffer,* to invest with a fief.] The beneficiary of a feoffment; one who is invested with a fee or corporeal hereditament.

feof′fẽr, feof′fŏr, *n.* The grantor of a feoffment, in contradistinction to the feoffee or grantee, who receives the feoffment.

feoff′ment (fef′), *n.* [OFr. *feoffement,* from *feoffer,* to invest with a fief.] In law, (a) originally, the grant of a feud or fee; (b) a gift of any corporeal hereditaments to another; (c) the instrument or deed by which corporeal hereditaments are conveyed.

fēr, *adv.* and *a.* [Obs.] See *Far.*

fē-rā′cious, *a.* [L. *ferax (-acis),* from *ferre,* to bear.] Fruitful; producing abundantly. [Rare.]

fē-rac′i-ty, *n.* [L. *feracitas,* from *ferax (-acis),* fruitful.] Fruitfulness. [Rare.]

Fē′ræ (fē′rē), *n.pl.* [L., f. pl. of *ferus,* wild.] An order of mammals, the *Carnivora.*

fē′ræ nā-tū′ræ (fē′rē nā-tū′rē). [L., of a wild nature.] Wild; not tamed or not tamable; applied in law to animals living in a wild state.

fē′răl, *a.* [From L. *ferus,* wild.]
1. A term applied to wild animals descended from tame stocks, or to animals having become wild from a state of domestication, or plants from a state of cultivation; as, *feral* pigs.
2. Wild by nature; untamed; savage; ferine; existing in a state of nature.

fē′răl, *a.* [L. *feralis,* of or belonging to the dead, from *ferre,* to bear, carry, as in a funeral.] Funereal; deadly; destructive; mortal.

Fē-rā′li-ȧ, *n.pl.* [L., neut. pl. of *feralis,* of or pertaining to the dead.] A solemn festival held by the Romans on the 21st of February in honor of the dead.

fer′-de-lance′ (fãr′de-lons′), *n.* [Fr., the iron tip of a lance.] In zoölogy, a venomous snake of Brazil, belonging to the rattlesnake family. It attains a length of from five to seven feet and its bite is generally fatal.

fērd′ness, *n.* [ME. *ferdnes,* from *ferd,* fear, and *-ness.*] The state of being afraid; fearfulness; fright. [Obs.]

fēre, *n.* [Obs.] See *Feer.*

fēre, *n.* Fire. [Obs.]

fēre, *n.* and *v.* Fear. [Obs.]

fēre, *a.* [L. *ferus,* wild.] Fierce; savage. [Obs.]

fer′e-tō-ry, *n.* [L. *feretrum*; Gr. *pheretron,* a bier, litter, from *pherein,* to bear.] A shrine overlaid with precious metals, enamel-work, or carved wood, and usually in the shape of a ridged chest, with a roof-like top, for containing the relics of saints. It is borne in processions.

Feretory.

fēr′fōrth, *adv.* [Obs.] Same as *Farforth.*

fēr′gu-sŏn-ite, *n.* [Named after Robert *Ferguson,* of Scotland.] An ore, of a brownish-black color, consisting of columbic acid and yttria, with some oxid of cerium and zirconia.

fē′ri-ȧ, *n.*; *pl.* **fē′ri-æ.** [LL.] 1. Among the Romans, a holiday upon which labor was suspended, the people visiting the temples of the gods and offering prayers and sacrifices.
2. In the Roman Catholic church, any day of the week, with the exception of Saturday and Sunday, not appointed in the calendar as a feast-day.

fē′ri-ăl, *a.* [LL. *ferialis,* from *feria,* a holiday.] Pertaining to holidays; relating to such days as have no service appointed for them in the church calendar.

fē-ri-ā′tion, *n.* [From L. *feriari,* to keep holiday, from *feriæ,* holidays.] The act of keeping holiday; cessation from work. [Obs.]

fē′rie, *n.* [OFr. *ferie,* from L. *feriæ,* holidays.] A holiday. [Obs.]

fē′ri-ēr, *a.* Fiercer. [Obs.]

fē′rine, *a.* and *n.* [L. *ferinus,* from *ferus,* wild.]
I. *a.* Wild; untamed; savage; never having yielded to domestication.
II. *n.* A wild animal; a savage beast; an animal that man has never tamed.

fē′rine-ly, *adv.* In the manner of wild beasts.

fē′rine-ness, *n.* Wildness; savageness.

Fer-in′gee, Fer-in′ghee, *n.* The name applied among the Hindus to a European, especially to an Englishman in India.

fē′ri-ō, *n.* One of the valid moods. [See *Mood.*]

fē-ri′sŏn, *n.* One of the valid moods. [See *Mood.*]

fer′i-ty, *n.* [L. *feritas,* from *ferus,* wild, savage.] Wildness; savageness; cruelty. [Obs.]

fēr′ly, fär′ly, *a.* and *n.* I. *a.* Wonderful; strange. [Scot.]
II. *n.* A wonder; a strange event or object. [Scot.]

fērm, fērme, *n.* [Obs.] Same as *Farm.*

fēr′mă-cy, *n.* [OFr. *farmacie,* a medicine.] A medicine; a healing draught. [Obs.]

fēr′ment, *n.* [L. *fermentum,* leaven, yeast, from *fervere,* to boil, be agitated.]
1. That which causes fermentation, as yeast, barm, or fermenting beer. [See *Fermentation,* 1.]
2. Intestine motion; heat; tumult; agitation; as, to put the passions in a *ferment*; the people are in a *ferment.*

> Subdue and cool the *ferment* of desire. —Rogers.

3. A gentle boiling; the internal motion of the constituent parts of a fluid. [Rare.]

fēr-ment′, *v.t.*; fermented, *pt., pp.*; fermenting, *ppr.* [L. *fermentare,* from *fermentum,* leaven, yeast, from *fervere,* to boil, be agitated.] To arouse; to stir up; to excite emotion in; to heat; to cause fermentation in.

> While youth *ferments* the blood. —Pope.

fēr-ment′, *v.i.* 1. To work; to effervesce; to be in motion, or to be excited into sensible internal motion, as the constituent particles of an animal or vegetable fluid.
2. Figuratively, to be in agitation; to be excited; to be disturbed, as by violent emotions or passions or great problems.

fēr-ment-ȧ-bil′i-ty, *n.* Capability of being fermented.

fēr-ment′ȧ-ble, *a.* Capable of fermentation; thus, cider, beer of all kinds, wine, and other vegetable liquors are *fermentable.*

fēr-ment′ăl, *a.* Having power to cause fermentation. [Obs.]

Fēr-men-tā′ri-ăn, *n.* An epithet applied in reproach to any member of certain sects of early Christians who used leavened bread in the celebration of the eucharist.

fēr-men-tā′tion, *n.* [LL. *fermentatio,* from L. *fermentare,* to ferment, cause to rise, from *fermentum,* yeast, ferment.]
1. The conversion of an organic substance into new compounds in presence of a ferment, the nature of which determines the kind of *fermentation* produced. It may be checked or altogether prevented by anything which prevents the growth of the fungus, as by keeping away from the liquid the spores or germs from which the fungus springs, by the liquid being either too hot or too cold for its development, by its containing too much sugar, or by the presence of a substance (called an antiseptic) which acts as a poison on the fungus.
2. The state of being in high activity or commotion; agitation; excitement; a state of unrest.

> An age of violent intellectual *fermentation* and of constant action and reaction. —Macaulay.

Acetous fermentation; see under *Acetous.*

Alcoholic or *vinous fermentation*; the change which takes place when a saccharine solution is exposed to the action of any of several fungi known as yeast-plants. The sugar is converted into carbonic acid and alcohol.

Ammoniacal fermentation; the alkaline action which takes place in wine, due to the presence of *Micrococcus ureæ,* transforming the urea into ammonium carbonate.

Lactic fermentation; the chemical change which takes place in milk in the process of becoming sour, when the sugar of the milk is converted into lactic acid.

Putrefactive fermentation; see *Putrefactive.*

Viscous fermentation; a kind of fermentation taking place in saccharine solutions, caused by the presence of certain bacteria.

fēr-ment′ȧ-tive, *a.* Causing or having power to cause fermentation; produced by or consisting in fermentation.

fēr-ment′ȧ-tive-ly, *adv.* In a fermentative manner.

fēr-ment′ȧ-tive-ness, *n.* The state of being fermentative.

fēr′ment-oil, *n.* A volatile oil which is produced when vegetable juices undergo fermentation.

fēr′mēr-ēre, *n.* An officer in charge of the infirmary maintained by an abbey, monastery, or similar religious house. [Obs.]

fēr′me-tūre, *n.* [Fr., from *fermer,* to shut, fasten; L. *firmare,* to make fast.] One of a great variety of more or less complicated devices for closing the bore of a cannon or small-arm which loads at the breech.

fēr′mil-let, *n.* [OFr.] A buckle or clasp. [Obs.]

fērn, *n.* [ME. *ferne*; AS. *fearn*; G. *farn,* a fern.] The popular name of the order of plants called *Filices,* which have their asexual fructification on the back of the fronds or leaves, in one-celled spore-cases or sporangia variously grouped in dots, lines, or masses, and containing but one kind of minute, one-celled, powdery spores. *Ferns* are cryptogamous plants and abound in humid temperate and tropical regions. In size, they vary from the minute species growing epiphytically upon tree-trunks to the giant tree-fern of the tropics. They are very abundant as fossil plants. The earliest known forms occur in Devonian rocks, and their remains contribute largely to the formation of the beds of coal.

Lady-fern (*Athyrium filix-femina*).

Christmas fern; an evergreen fern of North America, *Aspidium acrostichoides.*

Climbing fern; a fern, *Lygodium palmatum,* having climbing fronds, rising from slender, creeping rootstocks. It overruns low shrubs, the fronds sometimes attaining a length of three feet, being the only climbing species native to North America.

Flowering fern; a species, *Osmunda regalis,* common in swamps and wet woods.

Scented fern; a species, *Nephrodium Oreopteris,* whose fronds yield an agreeable odor when crushed.

Sensitive fern; a fern, *Onoclea sensibilis,* growing in wet places, whose fronds exhibit a tendency to roll up when touched.

fērn′ēr-y, *n.* A place for cultivating ferns.

fērn′gāle, *n.* A name for sweet-fern.

fērn′-owl, *n.* 1. The goatsucker. [Prov. Eng.]
2. The short-eared owl, *Asio accipitrinus.*

fērn′-seed, *n.* The seed or spores of fern, formerly supposed to possess wonderful virtues, such as rendering the possessor invisible.

fērn′shaw, *n.* A jungle of ferns; a thicket of bracken; a copse.

fērns′mund, *n.* [Obs.] Same as *Flowering fern.*

fērn′ti-cle, *n.* A freckle. [Prov. Eng.]

fērn′y, *a.* Abounding in or like ferns.

fē-rō′cious, *a.* [L. *ferox (-ocis),* from *ferus,* wild, fierce.] Having or exhibiting ferocity, cruelty, savagery, or the like; as, *ferocious* actions or looks.

Syn.—Fierce, savage, barbarous, untamed, fell, brutal, cruel, sanguinary, bloody.—When these words are applied to human feelings or conduct, *ferocious* describes the disposition; *fierce,* the haste and violence of an act; *barbarous,* the coarseness and brutality by which it was marked; *savage,* the cruel and unfeeling spirit which it showed.

fē-rō′cious-ly, *adv.* Fiercely; with savage cruelty.

fē-rō′cious-ness, *n.* Savage fierceness; cruelty; ferocity.

fē-roc′i-ty, *n.* [L. *ferocitas,* from *ferox (-ocis),* fierce, bold, savage, from *ferus,* wild.] Savage wildness or fierceness; fury; cruelty; as, the *ferocity* of barbarians; *ferocity* of countenance.

fer-ō′hẽr, *n.* A tutelary deity of the ancient Persians; also, a symbol, assuming various forms, found on ancient monuments, supposed to represent the deity in the shape of a sun-god.

Feroher, from Bonomi's, "Nineveh and its Palaces."

-fer-ous. A suffix from L. *-fer,* from *ferre,* to bear, signifying bearing, producing, yielding, as, coni*ferous,* auri*ferous,* chyli*ferous.*

fē'rous, *a.* [L. *ferus*, wild, fierce.] Fierce; wild; untamable. [Rare.]

fer-ran'dine, *n.* [OFr. *ferrandin*, iron-gray, from L. *ferrum*, iron.] A fabric woven partly of silk and used for garments in the 17th century.

Fer-rä'rȧ, *n.* A claymore or broadsword of peculiarly excellent quality, named after a famous swordsmith, Andrea Ferrara.

Fer-rä-rēse', *a.* and *n.* I. *a.* Of or relating to Ferrara, in Italy, or to the art school once located there.

II. *n.* A person native to or residing in Ferrara; collectively, all the inhabitants of Ferrara.

fer'rȧ-ry, *n.* [L. *ferraria*, an iron mine, from *ferrum*, iron.] The iron-worker's art. [Obs.]

fer'rāte, *n.* A salt formed by combining ferric acid with a base.

fẽr're, fẽr'rẽr, *a.* and *adv.* Farther. [Obs.]

fer'rē-ous, *a.* [L. *ferreus*, from *ferrum*, iron.] Partaking of iron; pertaining to iron; like iron; made of iron.

fẽr'rest, *a.* and *adv.* Farthest. [Obs.]

fer'ret, *n.* [ME. *feret, ferette, forette, furette*; OFr. *furet*; LL. *furetus*, a ferret, a dim. of *furo*, a ferret, from L. *fur*, a thief.] An animal of the weasel kind, about fourteen inches in length, of a pale yellow color, with red eyes. It is a native of Africa, but has been introduced into Europe and America. Used in catching rabbits, to drive them out of their holes.

Ferret (*Mustela furo*).

fer'ret, *n.* [It. *fioretto*, a little flower, flower-work upon silk or embroidery, dim. of *fiore*, a flower.] A kind of narrow tape, made of woolen, cotton, or silk, and used as a binding, a lace, or in forming rosettes.

fer'ret, *n.* Among glass-makers, the iron used to try the melted matter, to see if it is fit to work, and to make the rings at the mouths of bottles.

fer'ret, *v.t.*; ferreted, *pt., pp.*; ferreting, *ppr.* To drive out of a lurking-place, as a ferret does the cony; to search for with great care and diligence; generally, with *out*; as, to *ferret out* the conspirators.

fer'ret-ẽr, *n.* One who hunts with a ferret; one who ferrets out secrets.

fer'ret-eye, *n.* A name applied to the spur-winged goose on account of the resemblance of its eye to that of a ferret.

fer-ret'tō, *n.* [It. *ferretto*, dim. of *ferro*, from L. *ferrum*, iron.] Copper calcined with sulphur or white vitriol, used to color glass.

fer-ri-. See *Ferro*.

fer'ri-āge, *n.* The price or fare to be paid at a ferry; conveyance over a river or lake in a boat.

fer'riç, *a.* [From L. *ferrum*, iron.] Pertaining to or extracted from iron; designating compounds into which iron enters in its higher valence.

Ferric acid; an acid of iron, H_2FeO_4, never obtained in the free state. A few salts of this acid are known and are called ferrates.

Ferric oxid; sesquioxid of iron, Fe_2O_3, occurring as hematite, iron-glance, etc.

fer-ri-çal'cite, *n.* [*Ferri-*, and L. *calx, calcis*, lime.] A species of calcareous earth or limestone combined with from seven to fourteen per cent of iron.

fer-ri-çȳ'ȧ-nāte, *n.* Same as *Ferricyanide*.

fer″ri-çȳ-an'iç, *a.* [*Ferri-*, and Gr. *kyanos*, a dark blue substance.] Derived from and having the character of a ferricyanogen.

Ferricyanic acid; an acid, $H_3FeC_6N_6$, obtained by decomposing ferricyanide of lead with sulphuric acid.

fer-ri-çȳ'ȧ-nide, *n.* Any salt of ferricyanic acid.

Potassium ferricyanide; red prussiate of potash, $K_3Fe(CN)_6$, obtained by oxidizing $K_4Fe(CN)_6$ by the action of chlorine.

fer″ri-çȳ-an'ō-ġen, *n.* [*Ferri-*, and Gr. *kyanos*, a dark blue substance.] A sexivalent radical $(Fe(CN)_6)_2$.

fer'ri-ẽr, *n.* A ferryman; a boatman. [Obs.]

fer-rif'ẽr-ous, *a.* [*Ferri-*, and L. *ferre*, to bear.] Producing or yielding iron.

fer'ri-lite, *n.* [*Ferri-*, and Gr. *lithos*, stone.] Rowley rag; a variety of trap containing iron in the state of oxid.

fer-ri-prus'si-āte, *n.* Same as *Ferricyanide*.

fer-ri-prus'siç, *a.* Same as *Ferricyanic*.

fer-rō-, fer-ri-. Combining forms from L. *ferrum*, iron, used in chemistry, geology, etc., to signify iron, as *ferrocyanic, ferrilite*.

fer'rō-bronze, *n.* [*Ferro-*, and *bronze*.] An alloy of iron, copper and zinc; gun-metal.

fer-rō-çal'cite, *n.* [*Ferro-*, and L. *calx, calcis*, lime, and *-ite*.] A kind of limestone which takes on a brown color after exposure, due to the iron contained in it.

fer'rō-chrōme, *n.* [*Ferro-*, and *chrome*.] An alloy of iron, and chromium used in making steel.

fer-rō-çȳ'ȧ-nāte, *n.* A compound of ferrocyanic acid with a base.

fer″rō-çȳ-an'iç, *a.* Containing a compound of cyanogen with iron in its lower valence.

Ferrocyanic acid; an acid, $H_4FeC_6N_6$, obtained by decomposing a ferrocyanide with sulphuric acid. Compare with *Ferricyanic acid*.

fer-rō-çȳ'ȧ-nide, *n.* A salt formed by the union of ferrocyanic acid with a base.

Potassium ferrocyanide, or yellow prussiate of potash, K_4FeCy_6, is obtained by heating scrap-iron in closed iron retorts with potash and animal matter. It serves as the point of departure in the preparation of all the cyanogen compounds, and as a reagent for detecting the presence of iron. It is also used for preparing Prussian blue.

fer″rō-mag-net'iç, *a.* [*Ferro-*, and L. *magneticus*, from *magnes (-etis)*, a magnet.] Paramagnetic, the opposite of diamagnetic; having the effect of iron in a magnetic field.

fer-rō-man'gȧ-nēse, *n.* [*Ferro-*, and Fr. *manganese*, manganese.] A compound of iron and manganese employed in the manufacture of Bessemer steel.

fer-rō-prus'si-āte, *n.* A compound of ferroprussic or ferrocyanic acid with a base; ferrocyanide.

fer-rō-prus'siç, *a.* Same as *Ferrocyanic*.

fer″rō-sō-fer'riç, *a.* [*Ferro-*, and L. *ferrum*, iron.] Pertaining to the black or magnetic oxid of iron, Fe_3O_4, also known as *magnetite* and *lodestone*.

fer'rō-tȳpe, *n.* [*Ferro-*, and Gr. *typos*, impression, image.] A photograph taken on japanned sheet-iron or tin by a collodion process; a tintype.

fer'rous, *a.* [From L. *ferrum*, iron.] Of, relating to, or derived from iron; particularly, having reference to iron combined in its lower valence.

fer-rū'gi-nā-ted, *a.* [From L. *ferruginus*, of the color of iron-rust, from *ferrugo (-inis)*, iron-rust, the color of iron-rust.] Having the color or properties of the rust of iron.

fer-rū-gi-nā'tion, *n.* The act or process of permeating or coloring with iron ore or iron-rust; said of the discoloring of rocks by the presence of iron in solution.

fer-rū-gin'ē-ous, *a.* See *Ferruginous*.

fer-rū'gi-nous, *a.* [L. *ferruginus*, of the color of iron-rust, dusky, from *ferrugo (-inis)*, iron-rust, the color of iron-rust, from *ferrum*, iron.] Partaking of iron; containing particles of iron; having the color of iron oxid; rust-colored.

fer-rū'gō, *n.* [L. *ferrugo*, iron-rust, the color of iron-rust.] A disused botanical term for the disease rust.

fer'rule, fer'ule (fer'ril *or* fer'rụl), *n.* [Formerly *verrel*; OFr. *virole*, an iron ring to put around the end of a staff, from LL. *virola*, a ring, bracelet; L. *viriola*, dim. of *viria*, a bracelet, armlet, from *viere*, to twist, bind around. The spelling of the word was corrupted in imitation of L. *ferrum*, iron.]

1. A ring of metal put round a cane or other thing to strengthen it.

2. A bushing placed in the end of a flue to expand it.

3. The wooden frame fitted about a slate.

fer'ruled (*or* -ild), *a.* Having a ferrule.

fer-rū'mi-nāte, *v.t.* [L. *ferruminatus*, pp. of *ferruminare*, to cement, solder, from *ferrumen*, cement, solder, from *ferrum*, iron.] To unite by solder; to join together; used of metals. [Rare.]

fer-rū-mi-nā'tion, *n.* The soldering or uniting of metals. [Rare.]

fer'ry, *v.t.*; ferried, *pt., pp.*; ferrying, *ppr.* [ME. *ferien*; AS. *ferian*, to carry, convey, especially in a boat, from *faran*, to go.] To carry or transport over a narrow body of water, as a river or strait, in a boat or on a raft.

fer'ry, *v.i.* To pass over water by boat or raft.

fer'ry, *n.*; *pl.* **fer'riçs.** 1. A boat or float in which passengers and goods are conveyed over a river or other narrow body of water; a wherry.

2. The place or passage where boats pass over water to convey passengers or freight.

3. The right or concession of conveying passengers and goods across a river or other narrow body of water, for a reasonable consideration; also, a system for the regular passage of ferry-boats.

fer'ry-boat, *n.* A boat for conveying passengers and goods over streams and other narrow bodies of water.

fer'ry-bridġe (-brij), *n.* 1. A boat to ferry railroad trains across a stream.

2. An adjustable landing-platform for a ferry.

fer'ry-măn, *n.*; *pl.* **fer'ry-men.** One who keeps a ferry or works upon a ferry-boat.

fẽrs, *a.* Fierce; furious. [Obs.]

fẽrth, fẽrthe, *a.* Fourth. [Obs.]

fẽr'tile, *a.* [L. *fertilis*, fruitful, fertile, from *ferre*, to bear.]

1. Fruitful; rich; producing vegetable growth or offspring in abundance; prolific; productive; as, a *fertile* valley; a *fertile* variety of fowls; a country *fertile* in explorers.

2. Productive in mental achievements; inventive; ingenious; active; having abundant resources; as, a *fertile* imagination; a wit *fertile* and keen.

3. Bringing about production; increasing fruitfulness; as, a *fertile* idea; *fertile* rain.

4. Plentiful; produced in large measure; abundant.

5. In botany, (a) having capability of fruit production; (b) having the power of fertilizing.

Syn.—Fruitful, productive, prolific, fecund, rich, luxuriant.—*Fertile* denotes the power of producing, *fruitful* the act.

fẽr'tile-ly, *adv.* Fruitfully.

fẽr'tile-ness, *n.* The state or quality of being fertile; fertility.

fẽr″ti-li-zā'tion, fẽr'ti-līze, fẽr'ti-li-zẽr. Same as *Fertilization*, etc.

fẽr-til'i-tāte, *v.t.* To render fertile; to make productive; to fertilize. [Obs.]

fẽr-til'i-ty, *n.* [L. *fertilitas*, from *fertilis*, fruitful, fertile, from *ferre*, to bear.]

1. Fruitfulness; the quality or state of producing in abundance; productiveness; as, the *fertility* of soil.

2. Richness in intellectual product; abundance of resources; activity in invention; as, the *fertility* of genius, of fancy, or imagination.

fẽr″ti-li-zā'tion, *n.* 1. The act or process of making fertile or productive; also, the state of being fertilized.

2. In biology, the union of a male and female element; impregnation; specifically, in botany, the application of the pollen to the stigma, and its subsequent action upon the ovules, by means of which a perfect seed containing an embryo is produced; fecundation.

Close fertilization; the pollenization of a stigma from the stamens of the same flower; called also *self-fertilization*.

fẽr'ti-līze, *v.t.*; fertilized, *pt., pp.*; fertilizing, *ppr.* 1. To enrich; to make fruitful or productive; as, to *fertilize* the soil.

2. In biology, to impregnate; specifically in botany, to pollenize.

fẽr'ti-li-zẽr, *n.* 1. Any substance rendering land more fertile, as manure or guano.

2. One who applies a fertilizing substance; that which carries or transmits a fertilizing principle, as an insect.

fer'ū-lȧ, *n.*; *pl.* **fer'ū-læ.** [L., the giant fennel, a rod, walking-stick.]

1. A staff or rod; a ferule. [Obs.]

2. A staff of authority; a scepter; applied particularly to the scepter of eastern rulers, as those of the Byzantine empire.

3. [F—] A genus of herbs mostly native to Oriental and Mediterranean countries, a few species however being found on the Pacific coast of America. They are large, coarse plants of the family *Umbelliferæ*, having dissected leaves, yellow umbellate flowers, and thick, resinous roots; certain species yield gums of medicinal value, as asafetida and galbanum.

fer-ū-lā'ceous, *a.* [L. *ferulaceus*, from *ferula*, the giant fennel, a rod, walking-stick.] Pertaining to reeds or canes; having a stalk like a reed; also, resembling the *Ferula*; as, *ferulaceous* plants.

fer'ū-læ, *n.*, pl. of *ferula*.

fer'ū-lăr, *n.* [From L. *ferula*, a rod, walking-stick.] A rod; a ferule. [Obs.]

fer'ule (fer'ril *or* fer'rụl), *n.* [L. *ferula*, a rod, walking-stick, from *ferire*, to strike.] A wooden pallet or stick, used to punish children by striking them on the palm of the hand.

fer'ule, *v.t.* To punish with a ferule.

fer'ule, *n.* See *Ferrule*.

fē-rū'liç, *a.* Of, relating to, or obtained from asafetida.

fẽr'vence, *n.* Fervency. [Obs.]

fẽr'ven-cy, *n.* [L. *fervens (-entis)*, ppr. of *fervere*, to boil, glow, rage.] Heat of mind; ardor; eagerness; animated zeal; warmth of devotion.

fẽr'vent, *a.* 1. Hot; boiling; as, a *fervent* summer; *fervent* blood.

2. Ardent; very warm; earnest; excited; animated; glowing; as, *fervent* zeal; *fervent* piety.

fẽr'vent-ly, *adv.* In a fervent manner.

fẽr'vent-ness, *n.* The state or quality of being fervent; fervency; ardor; zeal.

fẽr-ves'cent, *a.* [L. *fervescens (-entis)*, ppr. of *fervescere*, to begin to boil, glow, incept. of *fervere*, to boil, glow.] Growing hot.

fẽr'vid, *a.* [L. *fervidus*, from *fervere*, to boil, glow.]

1. Very hot; burning; boiling; as, *fervid* heat.

2. Very warm in zeal; vehement; eager; earnest; as, *fervid* zeal.

fẽr-vid'ly, *adv.* Very hotly; with glowing warmth; earnestly; intensely.

fẽr'vid-ness, *n.* The state or quality of being fervid.

fẽr'vŏr, fẽr'voūr, *n.* [L. *fervor*, from *fervere*, to boil, grow hot, glow.]

1. Heat or warmth; as, the *fervor* of a summer's day.

2. Heat of mind; ardor; warm or animated zeal and earnestness; vehemence; passion.

Fes'cen-nine, *a.* Pertaining to Fescennia (Fescennium), an ancient city in Italy, or to the festivals held there, which were characterized by coarse songs and verses; licentious; scurrilous; broad.

Fes'cen-nine, *n.* A coarse, licentious song or poem commonly given at nuptial festivals and other celebrations in Fescennia, Rome, and other ancient Italian cities.

fes'cūe, *n.* [ME. *festue, festu*; OFr. *festu*, from L. *festuca*, a stock, straw.]

1. A small stick or other slender object used to point out letters to children when learning to read.

2. Fescue-grass.

3. The plectrum with which the strings of the harp or lyre were struck. [Obs.]

4. The gnomon or style of a sundial. [Obs.]

fes'cūe, *v.t.* To direct or teach with a fescue; to assist in reading by a fescue. [Obs.]

fes'cūe-grȧss, *n.* The popular name of any species of *Festuca*, a genus of grasses containing several varieties of importance in agriculture.

fesse, fess, *n.* [OFr. *fesse*, a fesse, from L. *fascula*, a band.] In heraldry, a band or girdle comprising the center third part of the escutcheon, and formed by two horizontal lines drawn across the field; one of the nine honorable ordinaries.

Fesse.

fesse'-point, *n.* The exact center of the escutcheon.

fesse'wise, *adv.* In the position of a fesse, or with divisions like those of a fesse; horizontally.

fes'si-tūde, *n.* [From L. *fessus*, weary.] Weariness. [Obs.]

fest, *n.* The fist. [Obs.]

fes'tăl, *a.* [OFr. *festal*, from L. *festum*, a holiday, feast.] Pertaining to a feast or gala-day; joyous; gay; mirthful.

fes'tăl-ly, *adv.* Joyously; mirthfully.

feste, fest, *n.* A feast. [Obs.]

fes'tẽr, *v.i.*; festered, *pt., pp.*; festering, *ppr.* [ME. *festren, feestren*; OFr. *festrir*, to ulcerate, fester, from *festre*, an ulcer.]

1. To suppurate; to ulcerate; to grow virulent; to discharge purulent matter.

2. To become more and more virulent and fixed; to rankle; to grow intense or malignant.

> Passion and unkindness may give a wound that shall bleed and smart; but it is treachery that makes it *fester*. —South.

fes'tẽr, *v.t.* 1. To produce ulceration in; to cause to suppurate.

2. To cause to rankle or become bitter; to cherish.

fes'tẽr, *n.* [ME. *fester, festyr*; OFr. *festre*; It. *fistola*, from L. *fistula*, an ulcer, fistula.]

1. A small inflammatory tumor; a suppurating or ulcerous sore; especially, applied to one situated superficially.

2. The act of festering.

fes'tẽr-ment, *n.* A festering or rankling. [Rare.]

fest'eye, *v.t.* and *v.i.* [ME. *festeyen*; OFr. *festeier*, to feast, from *feste*, a feast.] To dine sumptuously; to feast. [Obs.]

fes'ti-nāte, *a.* [L. *festinatus*, pp. of *festinare*, to hasten, from *festinus*, hasty, quick.] Hasty; hurried. [Obs.]

fes'ti-nāte-ly, *adv.* Hastily. [Obs.]

fes-ti-nā'tion, *n.* [L. *festinatio*, from *festinare*, to make haste.] Haste. [Obs.]

fes-ti'nō, *n.* In logic, one of the valid moods. [See *Mood*.]

fes'ti-văl, *a.* [OFr. *festival*; LL. *festivalis*, from L. *festivus*, festive.] Pertaining to a feast; appropriate to or characteristic of a festival or celebration; joyous; mirthful; as, a *festival* entertainment.

fes'ti-văl, *n.* 1. A time of feasting; an anniversary day of joy, civil or religious.

> The morning trumpets *festival* proclaimed. —Milton.

2. A social gathering, private or public, at which entertainment and refreshments are provided and for which a charge is made, the proceeds being usually devoted to some specified purpose.

fes'tive, *a.* [L. *festivus*, from *festum*, a feast.] Pertaining to or becoming a feast; joyous; gay; mirthful.

> The glad circle round them yield their souls
> To *festive* mirth and wit that knows no gall. —Thomson.

fes'tive-ly, *adv.* In a festive manner.

fes-tiv'i-ty, *n.*; *pl.* **fes-tiv'i-ties.** [L. *festivitas*, from *festum*, a feast.]

1. The mirth of a feast; social joy or exhilaration of spirits at an entertainment; joyfulness; gaiety; merriment.

2. A festival.

fes'tiv-ous, *a.* [L. *festivus*, from *festum*, a feast.] Pertaining to a feast; joyous. [Rare.]

fest'lich, *a.* Festive. [Obs.]

fes-tōon', *n.* [Fr. *feston*, LL. *festo (-onis)*, a garland, prob. from L. *festum*, a festival.]

1. A string or chain of any kind of materials suspended between two points; specifically, a chain or garland of flowers, foliage, drapery, etc., suspended so as to form one or more depending curves.

2. In architecture, a sculptured ornament in imitation of a garland of fruits, leaves, or flowers suspended between two points; an encarpus.

fes-tōon', *v.t.*; festooned, *pt., pp.*; festooning, *ppr.* To form in festoons, or to adorn with festoons.

fes-tōon'y, *a.* Belonging to or resembling festoons; consisting of or decorated with festoons.

Fes-tū'cȧ, *n.* [L., a stalk, strawlike weed.] A genus of grasses containing a great number of species, found in the temperate and colder regions of the world. Among them are found some of the best meadow and pasture grasses, as *Festuca elatior* (the meadow-fescue) and *Festuca ovina* (the sheep's fescue).

fes'tū-cine, *a.* [L. *festuca*, a stalk, strawlike weed and *-ine*.] Straw-colored. [Obs.]

fes'tū-cous, *a.* [L. *festuca*, a straw.] Formed of straw. [Obs.]

fes'tūe, *n.* [ME. *festue*; OFr. *festu*, from L. *festuca*, a straw, strawlike weed.] A straw or slender stalk; also, a pointer. [See *Fescue*.]

fet, *n.* A piece. [Obs.]

fet, *v.t.* [ME. *fetten*; AS. *fetian*, to bring, fetch.] To fetch; to bring to. [Obs.]

fet, *a.* Descended; derived; fetched. [Obs.]

fē'tăl, fœ'tăl, *a.* Pertaining to a fetus; having connection with or characteristic resemblance to a fetus.

fē-tā'tion, fœ-tā'tion, *n.* The development of a fetus; the state of being pregnant; gestation.

fetch, *v.t.*; fetched (fecht), *pt., pp.*; fetching, *ppr.* [ME. *fetchen, fecchen*, from AS. *feccan*, to bring, fetch.]

1. To go and bring, or simply to bring; that is, to bear toward or to the person speaking or sending.

> We will take . . . men . . . to *fetch* victuals for the people. —Judges xx. 10.

2. To derive; to draw, as from a source. [Obs.]

> On, you noblest English,
> Whose blood is *fetched* from fathers of warproof. —Shak.

3. To bring back; to recall; to revive; often used with *to*.

4. To draw; to heave; as, to *fetch* a sigh.

5. To reach; to attain or come to; to arrive at.

> We *fetched* the syren's isle. —Chapman.

6. To bring to a certain state; to draw into a certain place or relation; to cause to come; to make or cause to yield or appear, etc.; as, to *fetch* game; to *fetch* butter by churning.

7. To make or perform; to accomplish or effect; as, to *fetch* a leap or bound; to *fetch* a blow.

8. To bring, on sale or in exchange; to obtain as a price; as, wheat *fetches* only seventy-five cents a bushel; a commodity is worth what it will *fetch*.

9. To attract or charm; to captivate or fascinate. [Colloq.]

To fetch a compass; to go round about; to make a circuitous detour.

To fetch a pump; to start the water by priming the pump.

To fetch headway or *sternway*; to make progress forward or backward; applied to vessels.

To fetch out; to bring or draw out; to cause to appear.

To fetch up; to recover or regain, as time or distance lost; to come even with; to pass or overtake; to cause to stop suddenly; also, to train or educate; to rear.

fetch, *v.i.* To move or turn; to bring oneself; to make headway; to reach or attain.

> We shall *fetch* to windward of the lighthouse this tack. —Falconer.

To fetch and carry; to perform menial services; to become a servile drudge.

To fetch away; to break away and roll to leeward, as articles on shipboard.

To fetch up; to stop suddenly or to arrive at an unexpected destination; as, having lost our way in the dark, we *fetched up* at Dumfries.

fetch, *n.* 1. A stratagem, by which a thing is indirectly brought to pass, or by which one thing seems intended and another is done; a trick; an artifice; as, a *fetch* of wit.

> Straight cast about to overreach
> The unwary conquerer with a *fetch*. —Hudibras.

2. The act of fetching; the act of laying hold upon, or of drawing in to one.

3. The hallucination of seeing as dead a person who is still alive; a wraith; an apparition.

fetch'-can"dle, *n.* A light seen after nightfall, superstitiously believed to foreshadow a person's death; also called *fetch-light*.

fetch'ẽr, *n.* One who fetches.

fetch'ing, *a.* Attractive; pretty; charming. [Slang.]

fēte, *n.* [Obs.] See *Feat*.

fēte, *n.pl.* Feet. [Obs.]

fête (fāt), *v.t.*; fêted, *pt., pp.*; fêting, *ppr.* [Fr. *fêter*, to feast, entertain, from *fête*; OFr. *feste*, L. *festum*, a feast, festival.] To feast; to honor with festivities; to entertain sumptuously.

fête (fāt), *n.* [Fr., from OFr. *feste*, a feast, festival.] A festival, holiday, or celebration of some day.

Fête champêtre (shäṅ-pā'tr); a festival or entertainment held in the open air; a garden-party.

fête'-dāy, *n.* A holiday or birthday; especially, a day celebrated in honor of one's patron saint.

fē'tiăl, fē'ciăl (-shăl), *a.* [L. *fetialis*, pertaining to the fetiales, a college of priests.] In ancient Rome, pertaining to the priests who acted as the guardians of the public faith in the matters of declaring war and concluding peace.

fē'tiăl, *n.* Any one of the fetiales.

fē-ti-ā'lis (-shi-ā'), *n.*; *pl.* **fē-ti-ā'lēs.** One of a Roman college of priests who sanctioned treaties when concluded and demanded satisfaction from the enemy before a formal declaration of war.

fē'tich, etc. See *Fetish*, etc.

fē'ti-ci-dăl, fœ'ti-ci-dăl, *a.* Relating to or used in the practice of feticide.

fē'ti-cide, fœ'ti-cide, *n.* [L. *fetus*, a fetus, and *-cidium*, from *cædere*, to kill.] In medical jurisprudence, the killing of an unborn child; the crime of producing an abortion.

fē'ti-cism, *n.*, an incorrect form of *fetishism*.

fet'id, *a.* [L. *fetidus, fœtidus*, stinking, ill-smelling, from *fetere, fœtere*, to stink.] Having an offensive smell; having a strong or rancid scent.

> Most putrefactions smell either *fetid* or moldy. —Bacon.

fet-id'i-ty, *n.* The condition of being fetid.

fet'id-ness, *n.* The quality of smelling offensively; a fetid quality.

fē-tif'ẽr-ous, *a.* [L. *fetus, fœtus*, a fetus, and *ferre*, to bear.] Producing young, as animals.

fē'tise, fē'tis, *a.* [ME. *fetise, fetis*, from OFr. *faitis, fetis*, neat, well made.] Neat; trim; graceful; pretty. [Obs.]

fē'tise-ly, *adv.* Neatly; adroitly; gracefully; prettily. [Obs.]

fē'tish, fē'tich, *n.* [Fr. *fétiche*; Port. *feitiço*, adj. artificial, n. sorcery, charm, from L. *facticius, factitius*, artificial, from *facere*, to make.]

1 Any object, animate or inanimate, natural or artificial, regarded with a feeling of awe, as having mysterious powers residing in it or as being the representative or habitation of a deity. Among savages, it is usual for each tribe to have a *fetish* in common, but in addition every individual may have one of his own, to which he offers up prayers, and which, if these are not heard, he punishes, throws away, or breaks.

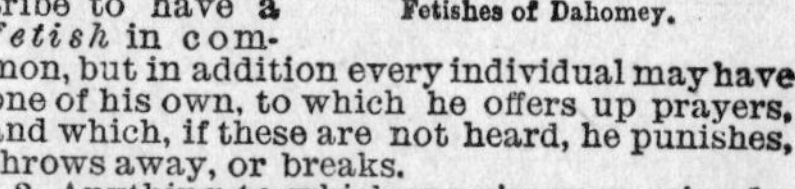

Fetishes of Dahomey.

2. Anything to which one gives excessive devotion or blind adoration.

fē'tish-ism, fē'tich-ism, *n.* 1. The belief in or worship or adoration of fetishes; idolatry.

2. Unreasoning and blind devotion to any object or theory; superstition.

fē'tish-ist, fē'tich-ist, *n.* One who believes in or worships fetishes.

fē-tish-is'tic, fē-tich-is'tic, *a.* Pertaining to or marked by fetishism; abjectly superstitious.

fē'tish-man, *n.* A man credited by savages with supernatural powers; a medicine-man.

fē'tish-snāke, *n.* A large rock-snake of the family *Pythonidæ*, native to Africa.

fet'lock, *n.* [D. *vitlok, vitslok*, the pastern of a horse.]

1. A tuft of hair growing behind the pastern-joint of horses.

2. The part of a horse's leg where the tuft of hair grows behind the pastern-joint; also, the projection of the limb at this joint.

3. A device attached to the leg of a horse in pasture to prevent it from running away or leaping fences. [See *Fetterlock*, 1.]

fē'tŏr, *n.* [L. *fetor, fœtor*, from *fetere*, to stink.] Any strong, offensive smell; stench.

fet'te, *v.t.* [Obs.] See *Fet*.

fet'tẽr, *v.t.*; fettered, *pt., pp.*; fettering, *ppr.* [ME. *feteren*, from AS. *gefeterian*, to fetter.]

1. To put in fetters; to shackle or confine the feet of with a chain.

2. To bind; to enchain; to confine; to restrain motion of; to impose restraints on.

Fetter strong madness in a silken thread. —Shak.

fet′tẽr, *n.* [ME. *feter*; AS. *fetor, feter*, a fetter.]

1. A chain for the feet; a chain by which a person or an animal is confined by the foot, either made fast or fixed, as a prisoner, or impeded in motion and hindered from leaping, as a horse whose fore and hind feet are confined by a chain.

The Philistines bound Samson with *fetters* of brass. —Judges xvi. 21.

2. Anything that confines or restrains from motion; that which destroys liberty and freedom.

Passions too fierce to be in *fetters* bound. —Dryden.

fet′tẽr-bōne, *n.* The great pastern bone of a horse's foot, just below the fetlock-joint.

fet′tẽr-bush, *n.* A shrub of the heath family, found in sandy regions in southern United States. It has thick evergreen leaves and white flowers borne in axillary clusters.

fet′tẽred, *a.* 1. Bound or confined by fetters; enchained.

2. In zoölogy, denoting the feet of animals, when they are stretched backward and appear unfit for walking.

fet′tẽr-ẽr, *n.* One who fetters.

fet′tẽr-less, *a.* Free from restraint; unfettered.

fet′tẽr-lock, *n.* 1. A hopple such as is put on a horse to prevent its escape from pasture.

2. In heraldry, a charge within a shackle or fetter.

Falcon and Fetterlock (Badge of Edward IV).

fet′ti-cus, *n.* A name given to the European corn-salad, *Valerianella olitoria*; called also *lamb's-lettuce* and *white pot-herb.*

fet′tle, *v.t.*; fettled, *pt., pp.*; fettling, *ppr.* 1. To repair; to put in right order; to put the finishing touches to. [Prov. Eng.]

2. To furnish the hearth of (a puddling furnace) with an infusible lining.

fet′tle, *v.i.* To dawdle; to dodder. [Prov. Eng.]

fet′tle, *n.* The state of being prepared or in good condition or order.

In fine fettle; in good spirits; in high feather.

fet′tling, *n.* The infusible lining or coating of oxids of iron used for the protection of puddling furnaces; fixing.

fē′tus, *n.*; *pl.* **fē′tus-eṣ.** [L. *fetus, fœtus*, a bringing forth, bearing, progeny, adj., pregnant, fruitful.] The young of viviparous animals in the womb, and of oviparous animals in the egg, after it is perfectly formed, before which time it is called *embryo.*

fet′wä, fet′wäh, *n.* [Ar. *fatwah*, a judicial decision.] In Turkish law, the written decision of a mufti on some legal point in the interpretation of the Koran.

feū, *n.* [OFr. *feu, fieu*, fief.]

1. In Scots law, a right to the use and enjoyment of lands, houses, or other heritable subjects in perpetuity in consideration of agricultural services or an annual payment in grain or money, called feu-duty, and certain other contingent burdens. This was deemed an ignoble tenure, as distinguished from *ward-holding*, where the service rendered was purely military, and *blanch-holding*, where it was merely nominal.

2. The land or piece of ground so held; a fief.

feū, *v.t.* In Scots law, to give or take in feu.

feū′ăr, *n.* A tenant who has his holdings under a feu.

feūd, *n.* [ME. *fede, feide*; AS. *fæhth*, from *fah*, hostile, guilty, outlawed.]

1. A contention or quarrel; a strife arising from enmity, inveterate hatred, mutual aversion, or similar cause; often, hostility between families or parties in a state; the discord and animosities which prevail among the citizens of a state or city.

Ring out the *feud* of rich and poor,
Ring in redress to all mankind.—Tennyson.

2. In a narrower sense, a war waged by one family or tribe on another to avenge the death of or injury done to one of its members; a combination of the kindred of a murdered or injured person to avenge him upon the offender and all of his blood.

Syn.—Enmity, hostility, animosity, controversy, contention, quarrel, broil, dispute, strife, vendetta.

feūd, *n.* [LL. *feudum, feodum*, a feud, fief, fee; O.H.G. *fihu, fehu*, cattle, property.] A fief; a fee; a right to lands or hereditaments held in trust or on the terms of performing certain conditions; the right which a vassal or tenant has to the lands or other immovable thing of his lord, to use the same and take the profits thereof hereditarily, rendering to his superior such duties and services as belong to the particular tenure which he holds, the property of the soil always remaining in the lord or superior.

feū′dăl, *a.* [LL. *feudalis*, feudal, a vassal, from *feudum*, a feud.]

1. Relating to, based upon, or consisting in feuds, fiefs, or fees.

2. Pertaining to the interrelation of a lord and his vassal.

Feudal system; a form of political organization long in force throughout Europe, under which persons holding lands in feud or fee were bound by an oath of fealty to serve the holder of the fee simple at home or abroad, in all wars and military expeditions, as he should demand of them.

feū′dăl-iṣm, *n.* The feudal system.

Feudalism was really a coöperative association for the mutual defense of the members. — Pollock.

feū′dăl-ist, *n.* A supporter of the feudal system; one versed in feudal law; a feudist.

feū-dal′i-ty, *n.* The state or quality of being feudal; feudal form of constitution.

feū-dăl-i-zā′tion, *n.* The act of reducing to feudal tenure.

feū′dăl-īze, *v.t.*; feudalized, *pt., pp.*; feudalizing, *ppr.* To reduce to a feudal tenure.

feū′dăl-ly, *adv.* After the manner of a feudal holding.

feū′dȧ-ry, *a.* [LL. *feudarius*, from *feudum*, a feud.] Pertaining to or devolving on feudal tenure.

feū′dȧ-ry, *n.* 1. One who has holdings under the feudal system; a feudatory.

2. An ancient officer of the court of wards in England; spelled also *feodary.*

feū′dȧ-tō-ry, feū′dȧ-tā-ry, *n.* [LL. *feudatarius*, from *feudum*, a feud.]

1. A tenant or vassal who holds his lands of a superior on condition of military service; the tenant of a feud or fief.

2. A feud or fief so held.

feū′dȧ-tō-ry, feū′dȧ-tā-ry, *a.* Having possession by feudal tenure.

fēu de joie (fē′de-zhwä′). [Fr., a bonfire, lit., a fire of joy.] A bonfire, or a firing of guns, in token of joy.

feūd′ist, *n.* [Fr. *feudiste*, from LL. *feudum*, a feud.]

1. A writer on feuds; one conversant with feudal law and customs.

2. One holding or letting land under feudal tenure.

Fē-uil-lănts′ (fē-yoṅ′), *n.pl.* A religious order, an offshoot of the Bernardines, founded by Jean de la Barrière; so called from the convent of Feuillans in Languedoc, where it was first established.

fēuille-morte′ (fwēl-), *n.* and *a.* [Fr., lit., dead leaf.]

I. *n.* The color of a faded leaf.

II. *a.* Of a brown color like that of a fallen or faded leaf.

fēu-ille-toṅ′ (fē-ye-toṅ′), *n.* [Fr., from *feuillet*, a leaf, sheet.] A section of a French newspaper, commonly ruled off at the bottom of the page, devoted to criticisms, short stories, or chapters from a serial; the matter which appears in this part.

fēuille′ton-ist (fwēl′ton-ist), *n.* One who contributes to the feuilleton.

fēuille-ton-is′tic, *a.* Ephemeral; shallow; after the style of a feuilleton.

feū′tẽr, *v.t.* [ME. *feutre*; OFr. *feutre, fautre, feltre*, a rest for a lance, felt; LL. *filtrum, feltrum*, felt, a pad for a lance.] To make ready by placing in the rest, as a spear. [Obs.]

feū′tẽr-ẽr, *n.* A dog-keeper. [Obs.]

fē′vẽr, *n.* [ME. *fever, fevere, fevre*; AS. *fefer, fefor*; Pr. *febre*, from L. *febris*, fever.]

1. A disease characterized by an accelerated pulse, with increase of heat, impaired functions, diminished strength, and often with preternatural thirst. *Fevers* are of various kinds, as many diseases of which *fever* is only the leading symptom are designated *fevers*; the principal division of *fevers* is into *remitting fevers*, which subside or abate at intervals; *intermitting fevers*, which intermit or entirely cease at intervals; and *continued* or *continual fevers*, which neither remit nor intermit. *Fevers* receive their names in various ways; from a characteristic symptom or marked pathological condition, from the locality where most prevalent, and from the parts especially involved.

2. Heat; agitation; excitement by anything that strongly affects the passions; as, this quarrel has set my blood in a *fever.*

Duncan is in his grave;
After life's fitful *fever* he sleeps well.—Shak.

Fever and ague; a periodical malarial fever preceded by chills.

fē′vẽr, *v.t.*; fevered, *pt., pp.*; fevering, *ppr.* [AS. *feferian*, from *fefer*, fever.] To put in a fever; to affect with fever, agitation, and passion.

fē′vẽr, *v.i.* To contract a fever. [Rare.]

fē′vẽr-bärk, *n.* *Alstonia* bark, from which a tonic is prepared.

fē′vẽr-blis″tẽr, *n.* A blister or pustular eruption within or in the region of the mouth, produced by fever.

fē′vẽr-bush, *n.* The spicebush or wild allspice, *Lindera Benzoin.*

fē′vẽr-et, *n.* A slight fever. [Obs.]

fē′vẽr-few, *n.* [ME. *fevyrfew, fewerfue*; AS. *feferfuge, feferfugia*; LL. *febrifugia*, a febrifuge; L. *febris*, a fever, and *fugare*, to chase, drive away.] A plant allied to camomile, and so named from supposed febrifuge qualities. The common *feverfew* grows to the height of two or three feet, with compound, radiated, white flowers.

fē′vẽr-fly, *n.* A dipterous insect, *Dilophus febrilis*, said to swarm in the vicinity of cases of fever.

fē′vẽr-hēat, *n.* A temperature which indicates the presence of fever; hence, a passionate or impatient state; a condition marked by stress and excitement.

fē′vẽr-ish, *a.* 1. Having a slight fever; hot; burning; as, the patient is *feverish.*

2. Characteristic of or marking the presence of fever; as, *feverish* symptoms.

3. Uncertain; inconstant; fickle; fluctuating; restless; as, a *feverish* financial condition.

4. Having a morbid eagerness or desire; impatient; ardent; keen; as, a *feverish* thirst; a *feverish* craving for office.

fē′vẽr-ish-ly, *adv.* In a feverish manner.

fē′vẽr-ish-ness, *n.* The state of being feverish; a slight febrile affection.

fē′vẽr-ly, *a.* [Obs.] See *Feverish.*

fē′vẽr-nut, *n.* Same as *Nicker-nut.*

fē′vẽr-ous, *a.* [Rare in all senses; *feverish* is the more common word.]

1. Affected with fever or ague.

2. Having the nature of fever.

3. Having the tendency to produce fever; as, a *feverous* disposition of the year.

fē′vẽr-ous-ly, *adv.* In a feverish manner. [Obs.]

fē′vẽr-root, *n.* A plant of the genus *Triosteum.* It was used by the Indians in the treatment of fevers, and its medicinal qualities are still recognized; called also *feverwort* and *horse-gentian.*

fē′vẽr-sōre, *n.* A vesicle produced upon the body as a result of fever in the system; a fever-blister.

fē′vẽr-trēe, *n.* 1. The blue-gum tree of Australia, considered as such an efficacious agent against fever that it has been extensively planted in malarious districts for the purpose of rendering them more healthful.

2. A small rubiaceous tree or shrub of the southern states, which yields the bitter or Georgia bark used as a febrifuge.

fē′vẽr-twig, *n.* The climbing bittersweet, *Celastrus scandens.*

fē′vẽr-weed, *n.* A plant of the genus *Eryngium*, native to Central America and the West Indies.

fē′vẽr-wŏrt, *n.* See *Feverroot.*

fē′vẽr-y, *a.* Affected with fever. [Obs.]

few, *a.*; *comp.* fewer; *superl.* fewest. [ME. *few, fewe, feawe*; AS. *fea*, pl. *feawe*, few; O.H.G. *fo, fao*; Ice. *far*; Sw. *fa*; Goth. *faus*; L. *paucus*; Gr. *pauros*, small, pl. *fauroi*, few.] Not many; small in numbers; as, a man of *few* words.

few, *n.* or *pron.* 1. Not many; only a limited number; in this sense really an adjective used by ellipsis for a noun, with which the article is omitted; as, *few* cared to listen.

Many be called, but *few* chosen.—Matt. xx. 16.

2. A small number or quantity; a part of the whole; preceded by an article or by a numeral adjective; as, a *few* of many; some *few* members were in attendance.

In few; in a few words; shortly; briefly. [Rare.]

Thus Jupiter *in few* unfolds the charge. —Dryden.

No few; more than a few; many.

Quite a few; a good many; an appreciable or considerable number. In England, the same idea is expressed by the phrase *a good few.*

The few; the minority, as set over against the larger number.

few′el, *n.* and *v.* [Obs.] See *Fuel.*

few′met, *n.* [Obs.] See *Fumet.*

few′ness, *n.* 1. Smallness of number; paucity.

2. Lack of words; brevity. [Obs.]

few′trilṣ, *n.pl.* Small articles; knickknacks. [Prov. Eng.]

fey, *v.t.* [D. *veegen*; G. *fegen*, to sweep.] To cleanse, as a ditch from mud; to clean out. [Obs.]

fey, *n.* Faith. [See *Fay.*]

fey, *a.* Doomed; fated; predestined. [Scot.]

Till *fey* men died awa. —Burns.

feyne, *v.t.* To feign. [Obs.]

feyre, *n.* A fair. [Obs.]

fez, *n.*; *pl.* **fez′zeṣ.** [Turk. *fez*, from *Fez*, the capital of Morocco, where they were made.] A cap or headdress of cloth, fitting closely to the head, with a tassel of silk or wool at the crown, much worn in Moslem countries and as the insignia of the Shriners. The core or central part of a turban consists of a *fez*.

1. Egyptian Fez.
2. Turkish Fez.

fï-ä′ç̄re (-kr), *n.* [Fr.] A French hackney-coach.

fï′ănce, *v.t.* [Fr. *fiancer*, to betroth.] To betroth. [Obs. See *Affiance*.]

fï-äṅ-cé′ (-sā′), *n.*; *f.* **fï-äṅ-cée′** (-sā′). [Fr., masc. and f. pp. of *fiancer*, to betroth.] A betrothed person.

fï′ănts, *n.* [Fr. *fiente*, dung.] The dung of a fox, wolf, badger, or certain other animals.

fï′ăr, *n* [Scot., from *feu*, fee, feud.]

1. The person to whom a property belongs in fee, subject to a life-rent.

2. [*pl.*] The price of grain, as fixed, in the counties of Scotland, by the respective sheriffs and a jury.

fï-ăs′ç̄ō, *n.* [It.] A conspicuous or chagrining failure; a complete frustration; particularly, an utter failure of a play or musical piece, a breakdown.

fï′at, *n.* [L. *fiat*, 3rd pers. sing. pres. subj. of *fieri*, to become, come into existence.]

1. A decree; a command to do something; a decisive or effective command.

2. In English law, a short order or warrant of some judge for making out and allowing certain processes, given by his writing and subscribing the words *fiat ut petitur*, let it be done as is asked.

Fiat in bankruptcy; an order in chancery allowing the institution of proceedings in bankruptcy.

Fiat money; paper currency issued by a government as money, which does not represent coin or bullion, but is made legal tender by law.

fï-aunt′, *n.* [Prob. formed in imitation of L. *fiant*, pl. corresponding to L. *fiat*, sing.] A fiat. [Obs.]

fib, *n.* [Origin unknown.] A lie or falsehood; an untruth told with the purpose of sheltering some one; a white lie.

Ask me no questions, and I'll tell you no *fibs*.
—Goldsmith.

fib, *v.i.*; fibbed, *pt.*, *pp.*; fibbing, *ppr.* To lie; to speak an untruth.

If you have any mark whereby one may know when you *fib* and when you speak truth, you had best tell it me. —Arbuthnot.

fib, *v.t.* To lie to; to speak an untruth to. [Rare.]

fib′bēr, *n.* One who tells lies or fibs.

fī′bēr, **fī′bre**, *n.* [Fr. *fibre*, from L. *fibra*, a fiber, filament.]

1. A thread; a fine, slender body which constitutes a part of plant and animal tissues; the small, slender root of a plant. The *fibers* of animal tissue are elongated cells which combine to form muscle, nerve, and similar structures. In some tissues, as cartilage, the substance between the cells becomes broken up into *fibers* parallel to each other, this structure being independent of the cells.

2. A filament; any thread-like part of a substance, as a filament of spun glass, wool, or hornblende.

3. A filamentous substance; a web of thread-like tissue such as composes living tissue generally; any substance which may be broken up into parts fit to form threads to be woven or spun; as, hemp *fiber*; asbestos *fiber*.

4. That which fundamentally constitutes the strength of a thing; sinew; stuff; character.

Fibers of Corti; minute, rod-like structures contained within the organ of Corti and essential in the transmission of sound to the cochlear nerve.

Vegetable fiber; excessively delicate threads twisted spirally in the interior of a cell or tube. [See *Bast*.]

Vulcanized fiber; paper or other fibrous material treated with a metallic chlorid to render it strong and waterproof.

fī′bēr-cross, *n.* See *Spider-line*.

fī′bēred, **fī′bred**, *a.* Having fibers; composed of fibrous threads.

fī′bēr-fāced (-fāst), *a.* Showing a fiber; applied to paper used in banknotes.

fī′bēr-gun, *n.* An apparatus used for breaking up compact masses of vegetable fiber to be used in manufacturing.

fī′bēr-less, *a.* Having no fibers; not of a fibrous texture.

fī′bēr-stitch, *n.* A stitch employed in the making of pillow-lace.

fī-brā′tion, *n.* A fibrous condition; the formation of a fibrous structure.

fī′bri-form, *a.* [L. *fibra*, a fiber, and *forma*, form.] Of a structure resembling fiber; fibrous.

fī′bril, *n.* [Fr. *fibrille*, dim. of *fibre*; L. *fibra*, fiber.] A small fiber; the branch of a fiber; a very slender thread; a filament; a fibrilla.

fī-bril′lȧ, *n.*; *pl.* **fī-bril′læ.** [A dim. from L. *fibra*, a fiber.] A fiber; especially, a minute fiber.

fī′bril-lăr, **fī′bril-lă-ry**, *a.* Pertaining to fibrils or fibrillæ; of a filamentous structure.

fī′bril-lā-ted, **fī′bril-lāte**, *a.* Furnished with fibrils or fibrillæ.

fī-bril-lā′tion, *n.* The condition of being fibrillar in structure.

fī-bril-lif′ēr-ous, *a.* [*Fibrilla*, a dim. from L. *fibra*, a fiber, and *ferre*, to bear.] Furnished with fibrils.

fī′bril-lōse, *a.* In botany, covered with or composed of fibrils; fibrous; finely marked, as if composed of fibers.

fī′bril-lous, *a.* Pertaining to fibers. [See *Fibrillar*.]

fī′brin, *n.* [L. *fibra*, a fiber, and *-in*.]

1. A peculiar organic compound substance found in animals and vegetables. It is a soft solid, of a greasy appearance, which softens in air, becoming viscid, brown, and semitransparent, but is insoluble in water. *Fibrin* is procured in its most characteristic state from fresh blood by whipping it with a bundle of twigs. It also exists in chyle, and forms the chief part of muscular flesh, and it may be regarded as the most abundant constituent of the soft solids of animals. *Fibrin* is composed of carbon, nitrogen, hydrogen, and oxygen, and is closely allied to albumen and casein. It readily undergoes decomposition, and is a most important element of nutrition.

2. The white fibrous mass remaining after the red corpuscles have been washed from fresh flesh or clotted blood; called also *flesh-fibrin*.

Vegetable fibrin; a vegetable proteid, similar in its properties to animal fibrin, which is present in cereals.

fī-bri-nā′tion, *n.* The condition of containing an excessive proportion of fibrin; as, the *fibrination* of the blood in cases of acute rheumatism.

fī′brine, *a.* [L. *fibra*, a fiber, and *-ine*.] Having the appearance of fibers; fringed. [Rare.]

fī′brin-fēr″ment, *n.* The cause of blood-coagulation.

fī-bri-nō-. A combining form from L. *fibra*, fiber, and *-in*, and used to signify fibrin; as, *fibrino*plastic.

fī-brin′ō-gen, *n.* [*Fibrino-*, and Gr. *-genēs*, producing.] An animal globulin, which is one of the elements which compose fibrin and is concerned in the process of coagulation.

fī-bri-nog′e-nous, *a.* Having properties related to those of fibrinogen; capable of the formation of fibrin.

fī″bri-nō-plas′tiç, *a.* Similar to or possessed of the qualities of fibrinoplastin.

fī″bri-nō-plas′tin, *n.* [*Fibrino-*, and Gr. *plassein*, to form, mold.] A proteid substance in the blood which forms fibrin when combined with fibrinogen and acted upon by the fibrin-ferment; paraglobulin.

fī′bri-nous, *a.* Having or partaking of the nature of fibrin.

fī-brō-. A combining form from L. *fibra*, fiber, used in anatomy, physiology, geology, etc., to signify fibrous matter or structure; as, *fibro*cartilage, *fibro*spongiæ, *fibro*lite.

fī′brō-blast, *n.* [*Fibro-*, and Gr. *blastos*, germ.] Any cell in the structure of connective tissue.

fī-brō-çär′ti-lāge, *n.* [*Fibro-*, and L. *cartilago*, cartilage.] Membraniform cartilage; the substance intermediate between proper cartilage and ligament.

fī-brō-çär-ti-lag′i-nous, *a.* Pertaining to or composed of fibrocartilage.

fī″brō-chon-dros′tē-ăl, *a.* [*Fibro-*, and Gr. *chondros*, gristle, and *osteon*, bone.] Made up of fibrous tissue, cartilage, and bone; said of the human skeleton.

fī′broid, *a.* and *n.* [*Fibro-*, and Gr. *eidos*, form.]

I. *a.* Similar to or containing fiber; assuming a fibrous form; as, a *fibroid* excrescence.

II. *n.* A fibroma; any fibrous tumor.

Fibroid degeneration; a breaking down of normal, healthy tissue into fibroid tissue.

Fibroid phthisis; a kind of phthisis which involves the formation of fibroid tissue in the lungs.

fī′brō-in, *n.* [L. *fibra*, fiber, and *-in*.] The principal chemical constituent of silk, cobwebs, and the horny skeletons of sponges. In the pure state it is white, insoluble in water, ether, or acetic acid, but dissolves in ammoniacal copper solution.

fī′brō-lite, *n.* [*Fibro-*, and Gr. *lithos*, stone.] A mineral of a white or gray color, composed of silica and alumina; same as *sillimanite* and *bucholzite*.

fī-brō′mȧ, *n.*; *pl.* **fī-brō′mȧ-tȧ.** A tumor composed of fibroid tissue.

fī-brō′sis, *n.* [L. *fibra*, a fiber, and *-osis*.] In pathology, the development in any part of a fibrous formation.

Fī-brō-spon′gi-æ, *n.pl.* [*Fibro-*, and L. *spongia*, a sponge.] An order of sponges including various species possessed of a fibrous skeleton; the common commercial sponge belongs to this division.

fī′brous, *a.* 1. Composed or consisting of fibers; as, a *fibrous* body or substance.

2. Of the nature of fibers or filaments; as, *fibrous* roots.

Fibrous fracture; in mineralogy, a cleavage which presents fine threads or slender lines, either straight or curved, parallel, diverging, or stellated, like the rays of a star.

Fibrous Root.

Fibrous tissue; in anatomy, the membrane, (a) that covers the bones and cartilages; (b) that is spread over or that forms a part of certain muscles, constituting the muscular fasciæ; (c) that forms the sheaths in which tendons are included; (d) the outer membrane that envelops the brain and spinal cord; (e) the firm membrane in which the more delicate muscles and the humors of the eye are contained; (f) the outer membrane of the pericardium; and (g) the ligaments and tendons of the joints. The same term is also applied to other parts of the body which present a manifest fibrous structure.

fī′brous-ness, *n.* The condition of being of fibrous structure.

fī-brō-vas′çū-lăr, *a.* [*Fibro-*, and L. *vasculum*, dim. of *vas*, a vessel.] In botany, composed of woody fiber, or of bundles of fiber and vessels.

fib′stēr, *n.* One who fabricates a story; a fibber; a coined word used in a jocular sense.

fib′ū-lȧ, *n.*; *pl.* **fib′ū-læ.** [L. *fibula*, a clasp buckle, pin; so called because the bone, as it appears in man, is like a clasp.]

1. The outer and lesser bone of the leg, much smaller than the tibia.

2. A clasp or buckle such as is found among archæologic remains.

3. An instrument used by surgeons for drawing together the edges of a wound.

fib′ū-lăr, *a.* In anatomy, relating to the fibula; as, the *fibular* artery.

fib-ū-lā′rē, *n.*; *pl.* **fib-ū-lā′ri-ȧ.** [From L. *fibula*, a clasp, pin, brace.] In anatomy, the outer bone of the proximal row of tarsal bones; in man, the largest of the tarsal bones, articulating with the fibula; the heel-bone; called also the *os calcis* or *calcaneum*.

Fibula.—*a*, fibula; *b*, tibia; *c*, femur; *d*, patella or kneecap.

-fiç. A suffix, from L. *-ficus*, from *facere*, to make. It is used in adjectives of Latin origin and signifies making; as, petri*fic*, terri*fic*, calori*fic*.

fīce, **fīse**, *n.* A name given in the South to any small dog of no distinct breed; a cur; a mongrel; also spelled *fyce*, *fiste*, or *phyce*.

fi-ché′ (-shā′), *a.* In heraldry, same as *fitché*.

fiçh′tel-ite, *n.* A mineral resin of greasy feel, white and crystallizable, found in the Fichtelgebirge, Bavaria.

fiçh′ụ, *n.* [Fr., from *ficher*, to drive in, pin up; *fiche*, a hook, pin.] An article of dress worn by women, covering the back and shoulders like a cape and crossing the bosom like a scarf; commonly made of thin material or lace.

fiç′kle, *a.* [ME. *fikel*, *fikil*, *fiykel*, from AS. *ficol*, deceitful, untrustworthy.] Wavering; inconstant; unstable; of a changeable mind; irresolute; not firm in opinion or purpose; capricious.

They know how *fickle* common lovers are.
—Dryden.

Syn.—Wavering, irresolute, fitful, variable changeable, unstable, vacillating, capricious changeful, mutable, inconstant, volatile.

fiç′kle-ness, *n.* A wavering; wavering disposition; inconstancy; changeableness; instability; unsteadiness in opinion or purpose; as, the *fickleness* of lovers.

fiç′kly, *adv.* Without firmness or steadiness. [Rare.]

fī′ç̄ō, *n.* [It., a fig.] An act intended to express scorn; a contemptuous gesture, consisting either of thrusting the thumb into the mouth or between two fingers; called also *fig*, or *fig of Spain*.

fī′çoid, *a.* [L. *ficus*, a fig, and Gr. *eidos*, form.] Like a fig; ficoidal.

fī-çoid′ăl, *a.* Similar to a fig in shape or structure; relating to or characteristic of the order *Ficoideæ*.

Fī-çoi′dē-æ, *n.pl.* [From L. *ficus*, a fig, and Gr. *eidos*, form, and *-eæ*.] An order of dicotyledonous polypetalous herbs, nearly related to the *Cactaceæ*. They are annual or perennial, have thick, fleshy leaves and bright flowers borne in clusters. There are numerous species, all natives of the tropics. The typical genus is *Mesembrianthemum*.

fiç′tile, *a.* [L. *ficti′lis*, from *fingere*, to form, mold, as in clay or wax.] Molded into form by art; manufactured by the potter; capable of being molded into a shape; plastic.

Fictile earth is more fragile than crude earth. —Bacon.

Fictile mosaic; mosaic-work formed of glass and bits of other vitreous material.

fic̦′tile-ness, fic̦-til′i-ty, *n.* The quality of being fictile; plasticity.

fic̦′tion, *n.* [L. *fictio* (*-onis*), from *fingere*, to form, mold, devise.]

1. The act of feigning, inventing, or imagining; as, by the mere *fiction* of the mind.

2. That which is feigned, invented, or imagined; a product of the imagination; an invention; an untruth; as, the story is a *fiction*.

So also was the *fiction* of those golden apples kept by a dragon, taken from the serpent which tempted Eve. —Raleigh.

3. In law, an assumption made of what is not literally true, for the purpose of passing more rapidly over those parts of the subject which are not disputed and arriving at the points really at issue.

4. Fictitious literature. In its widest sense the word comprehends every literary product of the imagination, whether in prose or verse, or in a narrative or dramatic form; but as used commonly it designates especially prose narrative in the form of romances, novels, tales, and the like.

Syn.—Fabrication, falsehood, invention, untruth, figment, story.—*Fiction* is opposed to what is real; it may or may not be intended to deceive; a *fabrication* is a *fiction* wrought up for the purpose of deceiving; a *falsehood* requires less invention, being merely a false statement.

fic̦′tion-ăl, *a.* Relating to or characteristic of fiction; ideal; fictitious; imaginary.

fic̦′tion-ist, *n.* A writer of fiction.

fic̦′tious, *a.* [Obs.] See *Fictitious*.

fic̦-ti′tious (-tish′us), *a.* [L. *fictitius*, *ficticius*, from *fingere*, to form, mold, devise.]

1. Feigned; imaginary; not real.

The human persons are as *fictitious* as the airy ones. —Pope.

2. Counterfeit; false; not genuine; as, *fictitious* fame.

fic̦-ti′tious-ly, *adv.* By fiction; falsely; counterfeitly.

fic̦-ti′tious-ness, *n.* Feigned representation.

fic̦′tive, *a.* Feigned; imaginary; hypothetical; not springing from a real cause.

fic̦′tōr, *n.* [L.] An artist who models statues and reliefs in plastic material, as distinguished from a sculptor who works in marble, bronze, etc.

Fi′cus, *n.* [L., a fig-tree, fig.] A genus of tropical or subtropical trees or shrubs bearing flowers crowded on fleshy receptacles, which in many species, as in the common fig, are edible. The best known species are *Ficus Carica*, the common fig; *Ficus Bengalensis*, the banian; *Ficus elastica* the india-rubber tree; and *Ficus religiosa*, the pipul-tree.

fid, *n.* 1. A small, thick lump. [Prov. Eng.]

2. A square bar of wood or iron, with a shoulder at one end, used to support the topmast, when erected at the head of the lower mast.

3. A pin of hard wood or iron, tapering to a point, used to open the strands of a rope in splicing. [See *Marlinespike*.]

4. A bar of wood or metal used to give support to something.

fi-dal′gō, *n.* A Portuguese title of nobility, answering to *hidalgo* in Spanish.

fid′dle, *n.* [ME. *fidele*, *fydyll*, *fiedele*, *fithele*; AS. *fithele*; O.H.G. *fidula*, a fiddle.]

1. A stringed instrument of music; a violin.

2. Nautically, a contrivance to prevent articles from rolling off the mess-table in bad weather; so called from its resemblance to a *fiddle*, being made of cords passed through wooden bridges and pulled taut.

Scotch fiddle, the itch. [Vulgar.]

To play first fiddle; to assume a leading part in any project or in society. [Colloq.]

To play second fiddle; to take a subordinate place. [Colloq.]

fid′dle, *v.i.*; fiddled, *pt.*, *pp.*; fiddling, *ppr.* 1. To play on a fiddle or violin.

Themistocles said he could not *fiddle*, but he could make a small town a great city. —Bacon.

2. To trifle; to shift the hands often and do nothing; to handle idly; to toy with an article.

fid′dle, *v.t.* To play (a tune) on a fiddle.

To fiddle away; to be busy with insignificant matters; to dally; to trifle; to fritter away.

fid′dle-bee″tle, *n.* A Japanese beetle, *Damaster blaptoides*, having a fiddle-shaped body.

fid′dle-block, *n.* A block used in a ship's rigging, having two sheaves of different sizes, one above the other.

fid′dle-bōw, *n.* A violin-bow.

fid″dle-dē-dee′, *interj.* Nonsense! [Colloq.]

fid′dle-fad″dle, *n.* A trifle; trifling talk.

fid′dle-fad″dle, *a.* Trifling; making a bustle about nothing.

fid′dle-fad″dle, *v.i.* To trifle; to busy oneself with nothing; to talk trifling nonsense.

Ye may as easily
Outrun a cloud, driven by a northern blast,
As *fiddle-faddle* so. —Ford.

fid′dle-fish, *n.* A name given to the angel-fish, from its body being shaped like a fiddle.

fid′dle-head, *n.* The name given to an ornament at the bow of a ship, over the cutwater, when it consists of carved work in the form of a volute or scroll, such as that at the head of a violin.

Fiddle-head.

fid′dlēr, *n.* 1. One who plays on a fiddle or violin.

2. Any fiddler-crab.

3. The common English sandpiper; so called from its peculiar manner of balancing its body. In America, the same species is called *teetertail* or *tip-up*.

Fiddler's fare; food, drink, and money.

fid′dlēr-crab, *n.* Any burrowing crab of the genus *Gelasimus*, having one claw much larger than the other. This it flourishes about as if playing on a fiddle, or as if beckoning; called also *calling-crab*.

fid′dle-shāped (-shāpt), *a.* In botany, a term applied to a leaf having a resemblance to a fiddle, from its deep indentations in either side.

fid′dle-stick, *n.* 1. The bow with which a fiddler plays; a fiddle-bow.

2. An insignificant thing; a mere nothing; a piece of arrant nonsense. Used in the plural as an interjection, meaning fiddle-de-dee! nonsense!

fid′dle-string, *n.* The string of a fiddle, fastened at the ends, and elevated in the middle by a bridge.

Fiddle-shaped Leaf.

fid′dle-wood, *n.* A tree of the genus *Citharexylum*, yielding a heavy, hard building timber.

fī-dē-jus′sion (-jush′un), *n.* [LL. *fidejussio* (*-onis*), from *fidejussus*, pp. of *fidejubere*, *fide jubere*, to be surety or bail, lit., confirm by promise.] Suretyship; the act of being bound as surety for another.

fī-dē-jus′sŏr, *n.* [LL., from *fidejubere*, to be bond or security.] A surety; one bound for another.

fi-del′i-ty, *n.* [L. *fidelitas*, from *fidelis*, faithful, trusty, from *fides*, faith, trust.]

1. Faithfulness; careful and exact observance of duty, or performance of obligations; good faith.

The best security for the *fidelity* of men, is to make interest coincide with duty. —Hamilton.

2. Firm adherence to a person or party with which one is united, or to which one is bound; loyalty; as, the *fidelity* of subjects to their king or government; the *fidelity* of a servant to his master.

3. Honesty; veracity; adherence to truth; absolute conformity to fact; as, the *fidelity* of a witness; the *fidelity* of a portrait.

Syn. — Conscientiousness, trustworthiness, trustiness, fealty, allegiance, constancy, exactness, accuracy, integrity.

Fī′dēs̱, *n.* [L., faith.] In Roman mythology, the goddess of faith.

fidġe (fij), *v.i.* [Scot.] Same as *Fidget*.

fidġ′et, *v.i.*; fidgeted, *pt.*, *pp.*; fidgeting, *ppr.* To shift one way and the other; to move irregularly or in fits and starts; to show impatience or nervousness in the movements of the body.

fidġ′et, *n.* 1. Irregular motion; restlessness.

2. [*pl.*] Restless motions of the body occasioned by nervousness or any bodily or mental discomfort.

fidġ′et-i-ness, *n.* A fidgety condition.

fidġ′et-y, *a.* Restless; uneasy.

Fid′i-ȧ, *n.* [A word coined by Baly, 1863.]

1. A genus of leaf-beetles.

2. [f—] Any beetle of this genus.

fi-dic′i-năl, *a.* [L. *fidicinus*, from *fidicen*, a lutist or lyre-player.] Having reference to stringed musical instruments.

fi-dū′ciăl (-shăl), *a.* [LL. *fiducialis*, from *fiducia*, trust, confidence, from *fidere*, to trust.]

1. Confident; undoubting; firm; as, a *fiducial* reliance on a promise. [Obs.]

2. Same as *Fiduciary*, 2.

3. In physics, that may be used as a standard of comparison by reason of fixity of some characteristic or essential, as the freezing point of water.

Fiducial edge; the thin edge (of a ruler).

fi-dū′ciăl-ly, *adv.* With confidence.

fi-dū′ci-ā-ry (-shi-), *a.* [L. *fiduciarius*, from *fiducia*, trust, a thing held in trust, from *fidere*, to trust.]

1. Confident; steady; undoubting; unwavering; firm; as, to give *fiduciary* assent.

2. Held in trust; committed to trust, especially such as involves the management of funds.

fi-dū′ci-ā-ry, *n.*; *pl.* **fi-dū′ci-ā-ries̱.** 1. One who holds a thing in trust; a trustee.

2. In theology, one who depends for salvation on faith without works; an Antinomian.

fīe, *interj.* An expletive expressing contempt, disapproval, or like sentiments; also written *fy*.

fief, *n.* [OFr. *fief*, *fieu*, from LL. *feudum*, a feud, fief.] An estate held of a superior on condition of military service. [See *Fee* and *Feud*.]

fiēld, *n.* [ME. *feeld*, *feld*, *fild*; AS. *feld*, a field, pasture.]

1. A piece of land inclosed for tillage or pasture; any part of a farm except the garden and appurtenances of the farm buildings; land not covered with wood; a term more strictly applicable to tillage land than to mowing land; a portion of ground designated for a particular purpose; as, a potter's *field*; a football *field*.

2. The ground where a battle is fought; the scene of a military action; a battle; an engagement of forces; hence, open space for action or operation; compass; extent; the sphere of any correlated series of actions; the unrestricted opportunity for action, research, or reflection.

3. A region, considered without reference to its topography, which yields a particular natural formation; as, gold-*fields*; the oil-*fields* of Texas.

4. Any continued extent of surface; specifically, an extensive sheet of ice or snow. [See *Ice-field*.]

5. In art, a surface not covered by the design; a ground; the uncovered surface of a coin or medal.

6. In physics, (a) a space subject to the action of some force exerted so as to act upon every point in that space; (b) those points in an optical instrument visible through the eyepiece.

7. Any district or locality considered as being in the open air or out of doors, as where the outdoor operations of a surveyor, engineer, geologist, and the like are performed; as, the true geologist must study his science in the *field*.

8. In heraldry, the heraldic shield, being a surface of proper tincture upon which are displayed the various bearings with the charges. When the escutcheon is divided by impalements or quarterings, the *field* is the background of each particular division. In a flag, each section is known as a *field*; as, stars on a *field* of blue. [See *Canton*.]

9. In sport, all those taking part in a hunt; in a race, all the competitors against whom a certain one is sent; those upon which bets are laid collectively, as distinguished from the favorite; as, to bet a horse sixty to one against the *field*.

10. In the game of baseball, the ground on which the game is played. The outfield is that part of the ground outside of the diamond and in front of the foul lines; the infield is that part inside of the diamond. The outfield is divided into three sections, called the right-*field*, the center-*field*, and the left-*field*. The players in these sections are known respectively as the right-fielder, the center-fielder, and the left-fielder.

To keep the field; (a) to keep the campaign open; to be in a state to resume active operations; as, at the approach of cold weather, the troops were unable *to keep the field*; (b) to hold one's ground against all odds.

To take the field; to open or enter upon a campaign; said of troops in time of war or of a political candidate; as, *to take the field* for the Democrats.

To bet, back, or *lay against the field*; to back one's own or one's favorite against all competitors.

Uniform field; a magnetic field traversed by the same number of lines of magnetic force per unit of area of cross-section of the field.

fiēld, *v.i.*; fielded, *pt.*, *pp.*; fielding, *ppr.* 1. To go out into the open country for any purpose; as, to *field* for food.

2. In baseball and cricket, to participate in the game as a fielder.

fiēld, *v.t.* In baseball and cricket, to send back from the field, as a batted ball, according to the rules and demands of the game.

fiēld′-ăr-til″lēr-y, *n.* See under *Artillery*.

fiēld′-bas̱′il, *n.* A name sometimes given to basil-thyme, *Calamintha Acinos*.

fiēld′-bat″tēr-y, *n.* A battery of fieldpieces together with the required equipment.

fiēld′-bed, *n.* A bed contrived for carrying into the field; a portable couch or camp bed.

fiēld′-bīrd, *n.* A local name for the golden plover.

fiēld′-book, *n.* A book used in surveying, in which are set down the angles, stations, distances, and similar measurements.

fiēld′-car″riage (-rij), *n.* A gun-carriage upon which a field-gun is transported.
fiēld′-cōl″ōrs, *n.pl.* Small flags for marking out the ground for the squadrons and battalions; also, the flags which mark the position or headquarters of a command while on the march or in camp.
fiēld′-cor″net, *n.* The magistrate of a township in British South Africa.
fiēld′-crick″et, *n.* A large European cricket having a louder, more strident chirp than the house-cricket.
fiēld′-dāy, *n.* A day when troops are drawn out for instruction in field exercises and evolutions; a gala day; a school holiday celebrated by athletic contests.
fiēld′-dog, *n.* A dog belonging to one of the breeds of hunting dogs, as a setter, pointer, or retriever.
fiēld′-drīv″ēr, *n.* In the eastern states, a township officer who takes stray domestic animals to the pound.
fiēld′-duck, *n.* A bird, the little bustard.
fiēld′ed, *a.* Being in the field of battle; encamped.
fiēld′en, *a.* Consisting of open tracts of land. [Obs.]
fiēld′ēr, *n.* 1. In baseball and cricket, a player stationed in the field. [See *Field*, n. 10.]
2 A hunting dog; a field-dog.
fiēld′fāre, *n.* [ME. *feldfare*; AS. *feldefare*; *felde*, a field, and *faran*, to go, travel.] An English name for a bird of the genus *Turdus*, a thrush about ten inches in length, the head ash-colored, the back and greater coverts of the wings of a fine, deep chestnut, and the tail black; called also *fellfare*.

Fieldfare (*Turdus pilaris*).

fiēld′-glȧss, *n.* 1. A compact binocular telescope, varying in size, for use out-of-doors, as on the battlefield, on the race-track, or by tourists on land or sea.
2. The lens in a telescope or microscope nearest to the object-glass; called also the *field-lens*.
3. The form of telescope commonly used on shipboard, having an achromatic lens and from three to six joints.
fiēld′-gun, *n.* A small cannon mounted on a gun-carriage to be used by an army in the field; called also *fieldpiece*.
fiēld′-hos″pi-tăl, *n.* Any building or shelter reserved for the care of the wounded or sick of an army.
fiēld′-ice, *n.* Ice formed into fields such as float in the polar oceans.
fiēld′ing, *n.* In baseball and cricket, the act of playing in the field, or as a fielder.
fiēld′-kāle, *n.* Same as *Charlock*.
fiēld′-lärk, *n.* A name applied to various small birds; (a) the meadow-lark; (b) the tree-pipit or tree-lark; and (c) the English skylark.
fiēld′-lenṣ, *n.* Same as *Field-glass*, 2.
fiēld′-mad″dēr, *n.* The popular name of *Sherardia arvensis*, a European herb, with a prostrate stem spreading from the root, and clusters of small lilac flowers in terminal heads; called also *spurwort*.
fiēld′-mag″nets, *n.pl.* The electromagnets employed to produce the magnetic field of a dynamo-electric machine.
fiēld′-mär″shăl, *n.* The highest rank conferred on general officers in the British and some other European armies.
fiēld′-mär″shăl-ship, *n.* The rank or dignity of a field-marshal.
fiēld′-mär″tin, *n.* The kingbird, *Tyrannus tyrannus* or *carolinensis*; called also *bee-bird* or *bee-martin*.
fiēld′-mouse, *n.* A name given to several species of mice that live in the fields and burrow in banks.
fiēld′-of″fi-cēr, *n.* A military officer above the rank of captain and below that of general, as a major, lieutenant-colonel, or colonel.
Field-officer's court; in the United States army, a court-martial presided over by a field-officer who is amenable only to the garrison and regimental courts.
fiēld′piece, *n.* Same as *Field-gun*.
fiēld′-plŏv″ēr, *n.* 1. The whistling plover.
2. The Bartramian sandpiper or upland plover.
fiēld′-prēach″ēr, *n.* One who preaches in fields and byways.
fiēld′-rọom, *n.* Open space. [Obs.]
fiēld′-sal″ăd, *n.* See *Fetticus*.
fiēld′-shōw, *n.* A field-trial.
fiēld′-span″iel (-yel), *n.* A breed of spaniels trained to hunt; the cockers and springers belong to this breed.
fiēld′-spar″rōw, *n.* 1. A sparrow, *Spizella pusilla*, common in the eastern states.
2. A name for the English hedge-sparrow.
fiēld′-spōrts, *n.pl.* Sports of the field, as shooting and hunting.
fiēld′-stȧff, *n.* A pole carrying a light at one end with which old-pattern field-guns were touched off.
fiēld′-trāin, *n.* A department in the British army which has to do with furnishing supplies of ammunition to the army in the field.
fiēld′-trī″ăl, *n.* A trial and exhibition of dogs in the hunt, as distinguished from an exhibition indoors, or a bench-show.
fiēld′-vōle, *n.* The short-tailed field-mouse.
fiēld′wŏrk, *n.* 1. All the out-of-door operations of a surveyor, engineer, or geologist, as surveying, leveling, making geological observations, collecting specimens, etc.
2. In the army, a temporary work thrown up either by besiegers or besieged, or by an army to strengthen a position.
fiēld′y, *a.* Open, like a field. [Obs.]
fiēnd, *n.* [ME. *feend*, *feond*; AS. *feónd*, an enemy, hater, used of Satan, properly ppr. of *feón*, to hate; L.G. *fiend*, *fijnd*; Ice. *fjande*; Dan. *fjende*, an enemy.]
1. An enemy, in the worst sense; an implacable, malicious, or diabolical foe; the devil; an infernal being.

O woman! woman! when to ill thy mind
Is bent, all hell contains no fouler *fiend*.
—Pope.

2. A person who is wholly engrossed in a particular occupation; one who rides a hobby; a crank; as, a camera *fiend*. [Slang.]
fiēnd′fụl, *a.* Filled with a fiendish spirit, or with diabolical arts.
fiēnd′fụl-ly, *adv.* In a fiendlike manner.
fiēnd′ish, *a.* Like a fiend; malicious; extremely cruel.
fiēnd′ish-ly, *adv.* In a fiendish spirit or manner.
fiēnd′ish-ness, *n.* Maliciousness.
fiēnd′like, *a.* Resembling a fiend; maliciously wicked; diabolical.
fiēnd′ly, *a.* Monstrously malicious; diabolical. [Obs.]
Fi-ē-ras′fēr, *n.* A genus of fishes having eel-like bodies and no ventral fins; most species live parasitically in other marine animals.
fierce, *a.*; *comp.* fiercer; *superl.* fiercest. [ME. *feirce*, *fers*, *fierse*; OFr. *fers*, *fier*, *fer*, from L. *ferus*, wild, savage.]
1. Vehement; violent; furious; rushing; impetuous; as, a *fierce* wind.
2. Savage; ravenous; easily enraged; as, a *fierce* lion.
3. Vehement in rage; eager for mischief; as, a *fierce* tyrant; a monster *fierce* for blood.
4. Violent; outrageous; not to be restrained.

Cursed be their anger, for it was *fierce*.
—Gen. xlix. 7.

5. Passionate; angry; furious.
6. Wild; staring; ferocious; as, a *fierce* countenance.
7. Very eager; ardent; vehement; as, a man *fierce* for his party.
fierce′ly, *adv.* 1. Violently; furiously; with rage; as, both sides fought *fiercely*.
2. With a wild aspect; as, to look *fiercely*.
fierce′ness, *n.* 1. The state or quality of being fierce, in any of its senses.
fierd′ing-cōurt, *n.* [AS. *feorthung*, a fourth part.] An ancient court, so called because four were established within every superior district or hundred. [Obs.]
fī′e-rī fā′ci-as (-shi-as). [L., lit., cause it to be done.] In law, an execution against certain property specified in the writ.
fī′ēr-i-ness, *n.* The quality of being fiery; heat; acrimony; irritability.
fī′ēr-y, *a.* 1. Consisting of fire; like fire; bright; glaring; as, *fiery* billows roll below.
2. Vehement; ardent; very active; impetuous; as, a *fiery* spirit; a *fiery* heart.
3. Passionate; easily provoked; irritable.

You know the *fiery* quality of the duke.—Shak.

4. Unrestrained; fierce; as, a *fiery* steed.
5. Heated by fire.

The sword which is made *fiery*. —Hooker.

A fiery cross; in Scotland, a signal sent in ancient times to call a clan to arms. It consisted of a wooden cross, the extremities of which had been set on fire and then dipped in the blood of a recently slain goat.
Syn.—Parched, feverish, ardent, fervid, impetuous, unrestrained, spirited, vehement, irritable, mettlesome, passionate, fierce.
fī-es′tȧ, *n.* In Spanish-speaking countries and southwestern United States, a feast-day or festival; a holiday celebrated by games, processions, and general merrymaking.
fīfe, *n.* [OFr. *fifre*, a fife; O.H.G. *pfifa*; LL. *pipa*, a pipe, *pipare*, to play on a pipe, from L. *pipire*, *pipare*, to peep, chirp, as a chicken.] A small instrument resembling a flute, but having a shriller tone. It is used in drum corps and bands.
fīfe, *v.i.*; fifed (fīft), *pt.*, *pp.*; fifing, *ppr.* To play on a fife.
fīfe′-mā″jŏr, *n.* A noncommissioned officer in command of the fifers of a battalion.
fīf′ēr, *n.* One who plays on a fife.
fīfe′-rāil, *n.* On a ship, the rail forming the upper fence of the bulwarks on each side of the quarter-deck and poop; also, the rail round the mainmast, and encircling both it and the pumps.
fif′teen, *n.* [ME. *fiftene*; AS. *fiftene*, *fiftyne*; *fif*, five, and *ten*, *tyne*, ten.]
1. The sum of fourteen and one, or of ten and five; a number representing fifteen units or counters.
2. The symbols indicating fifteen units; as, XV; 15.
3. The name of the first point scored on either side in tennis or ping-pong.
fif′teen, *a.* Being five more than ten.
fif′teenth, *a.* 1. The ordinal of fifteen; the fifth after the tenth.
2. Existing as one of fifteen equal portions of anything.
fif′teenth, *n.* 1. A fifteenth part.
2. An ancient tax laid on towns, boroughs, etc., in England, being one-fifteenth part of what each town, etc., had been valued at; or it was a *fifteenth* of each man's personal estate.
3. In music, the double octave; (a) as an interval between two notes; (b) as two such notes played together; (c) either of such notes as related to the other; (d) a stop tuned a double octave above the open diapason.
fifth, *a.* [ME. *fifthe*, *fifte*; AS. *fifta*, from *fif*, five.]
1. The ordinal of five; the next to the fourth.
2. Existing as one of five equal portions of anything.
Fifth Monarchy Men; a fanatical sect in England, who considered Cromwell as commencing the fifth great monarchy of the world, during which Christ should reign on earth a thousand years.
Fifth nerve; in anatomy, the fifth cranial nerve on either side of the head; the trigeminal nerve.
Fifth wheel; a horizontal iron plate, in shape either a circle or a segment of one, placed on the forward axle of a vehicle; upon it the fore part of the body turns freely without tilting.
fifth, *n.* 1. A fifth part; one of five equal divisions of anything; the quotient of one divided by five.
2. In music, (a) the dominant, or fifth note above the keynote; (b) the interval of five diatonic degrees between two notes; (c) a note and its *fifth* sounded in unison.
fifth′ly, *adv.* In the fifth place.
fif′ti-eth, *a.* [ME. *fiftithe*, *fiftugethe*; AS. *fiftigotha*, from *fiftig*, fifty, and *-tha*, *-th*, the ordinal suffix.]
1. The ordinal of fifty; next after the forty-ninth.
2. Existing as one of fifty equal portions of anything.
fif′ti-eth, *n.* The quotient of one divided by fifty; one of fifty equal portions.
fif′ty, *a.* [ME. *fifty*, *fifti*; AS. *fiftig*; *fif*, five, and *-tig*, ten.] Five times ten; as, *fifty* men.
fif′ty, *n.*; *pl.* **fif′tieṣ**. 1. The sum of forty-nine and one; ten fives; half of one hundred.
2. The symbol that represents the number, as L, 50.
fig, *n.* [ME. *fig*, *fyg*; OFr. *figue*, *fige*; Pr. *figa*; It. *fico*, from L. *ficus*, a fig-tree, fig.]
1. The fruit of the fig-tree, *Ficus Carica*, which is a receptacle of the flowers, turbinated and hollow, produced in the axils of the leaves on small round peduncles. This fruit is not of the same nature as the apple, the orange, and other fleshy seed-vessels; but it is a hollow receptacle, containing a great multitude of minute flowers, the ripe carpels of which, erroneously called the seed, are embedded in the pulp. The tree has been cultivated in the Orient for its fruit since the earliest historical times. [See *Ficus*.]

1. Section of fruit of *Ficus Carica*. 2. Female flowers. 3. Male flowers.

2. A trifling amount; the least value; as, not worth a *fig*.
3. A fico or gesture of contempt.
4. A swelling on the frog of a horse's foot.
5. A bit of tobacco; a quid. [Colloq.]
6. A name applied to various trees, of the same or a related genus, which bear fruit resembling the true *fig* in some particular; also, such fruit.
Adam's fig; the fruit of the banana-plant, *Musa sapientium*.
A fig for; a phrase shortened from, "I do not care a fig for," expressing the speaker's contempt for the object or person mentioned.

A fig of Spain; see *Fico*.

Fig Sunday; Palm Sunday or the Sunday next before Easter.

Hottentot fig; a South African plant of the genus *Mesembryanthemum*, which bears a fruit used by the natives for food.

Indian fig; a name given to any one of several cactaceous plants, especially *Opuntia vulgaris* or the prickly-pear; also, the fig-like fruit of such a plant.

Keg fig; an edible fruit, native to Oriental countries, which outwardly resembles a tomato but has a central cavity filled with seeds, like a fig. It is variously called *Chinese fig* or *Japanese persimmon*.

Pharaoh's fig; the sycamore fig, *Ficus Sycomorus*, native to Egypt and Syria. It bears an edible fruit.

Red fig; a large tree, *Ficus pedunculata*, which spreads like the banian and bears a hard red fruit. It is native to tropical America.

Sacred fig; the pipul-tree of India; also called the *sacred bo-tree*.

Wild fig; *Clusia flava*, a tropical American shrub.

fig, *v.t.* 1. To insult with ficos or contemptuous motions of the fingers. [Obs.]

2. To put, as something useless, into one's head. [Obs.]

fig, *n.* [A contr. for *figure*, probably from this contracted form being used in reference to plates in books of fashions.] Dress; employed chiefly in the phrase *in full fig*, in full or official dress; in full equipment. [Slang.]

To be in good fig; to be in good form or condition; as, the horse *was in good fig* for the race. [Slang.]

fig, *v.t.* 1. To dress; as, to *fig* one out. [Slang.]

2. To treat (a horse) in such a way as to make the animal appear lively, as by putting a piece of ginger into the anus.

fig′=ap″ple, *n.* A kind of apple having no core.

fī-gä-rō′, *n.* [From the name of the hero of Beaumarchais's comedies "Le Barbier de Seville" and "Le Mariage de *Figaro*."] A witty, shrewd, and intriguing person.

fig′ȧ-ry, *n.* A frolic. [Obs.]

fig′=cāke, *n.* A preparation of figs and almonds worked up into a hard paste and pressed into cakes.

fig′=dust, *n.* Ground oatmeal, used for feeding cage-birds.

fig′ēat″ẽr, *n.* 1. A beetle, *Allorhina nitida*, particularly destructive to fruit in the South.

2. The European garden-warbler or beccafico.

fig′ent, *a.* Fidgety; unable to keep quiet. [Obs.]

fig′et-ive, *a.* In heraldry, fitché.

fig′=fạun, *n.* A fabulous creature, represented as living in desert places and eating figs.

fig′=gnat (-nat), *n.* An insect of the gnat family, injurious to the fig, into the interior of which it bores.

fig′gum, *n.* Jugglers' tricks generally; the trick of spitting fire.

fīght (fīt), *v.i.*; fought (fọt), *pt.*, *pp.*; fighting, *ppr.* [ME. *fighten*, *fihten*, *fehten*; AS. *feohtan*, to fight.]

1. To strive or contend for victory, in battle or in single combat; to attempt to defeat, subdue, or destroy an enemy, either by blows or weapons; to contend in arms.

> Come and be our captain, that we may *fight* with the children of Ammon.—Judges xi. 6.

2. To contend; to strive; as, to *fight* against jealousy.

To fight against; to act in opposition; to oppose; to strive to conquer or resist.

fīght, *v.t.* 1. To carry on contention with; to maintain a struggle for victory against.

2. To contend with in battle; to war against; as, they *fought* the enemy in two pitched battles.

3. To cause to fight; to control or direct in battle; as, to *fight* cocks; to *fight* one's ship.

To fight shy of; to avoid.

To fight to a finish; to struggle till a decisive result is attained.

Syn.—Contend, strive, dispute, encounter, oppose, combat, struggle, quarrel, battle.

fīght, *n.* [ME. *fight*, *fiht*, *feoht*; AS. *feoht*, a fight, battle, from *feohtan*, to fight.]

1. A battle; an engagement; a contest in arms; a struggle for victory, either between individuals or between armies, ships, or navies.

2. Something to screen the combatants in ships. [Obs.]

> Up with your *fights* and your nettings prepare. —Dryden.

3. Pugnacity; power or inclination to fight; disposition to continue a struggle.

> P. was not, however, yet utterly overcome, and had some *fight* left in him.—Thackeray.

4. A contest or strife of any nature; a struggle; as, a *fight* for supremacy; a *fight* against the plague.

Syn.—Battle, engagement, skirmish, affair, brush, fray, affray, duel, action, strife, struggle, encounter, combat, contest, conflict.

fīght′ẽr, *n.* One that fights; a combatant; a warrior.

fīght′ing, *n.* Contention; strife; quarrel; battle.

> Without were *fightings*, within were fears. —2 Cor. vii. 5.

fīght′ing, *a.* 1. Fitted or trained to fight; qualified to go into battle; skilled in the art of war.

2. Being the scene of a conflict; occupied as a battle-ground.

Fighting chance; a chance of gaining an object or end only by struggle against odds; as, to have a *fighting chance* of recovery.

Fighting crab; same as *Fiddler-crab*.

Fighting sandpiper; the ruff, *Pavoncella* or *Machetes pugnax*, noted for its pugnacity.

fīght′ing=fish, *n.* A small Asiatic fish remarkable for its pugnacious propensities. In Siam, these fishes are kept for fighting, as gamecocks are kept elsewhere.

fīght′ing-ly, *adv.* In a pugnacious manner.

fight′wite, *n.* [AS. *fyhtwite*; *feoht*, fight, and *wite*, a fine.] In old English law, a fine imposed upon a person who disturbed the public peace by indulging in a quarrel.

fig′=lēaf, *n.* The leaf of a fig-tree; also, a thin covering, in allusion to the first covering of Adam and Eve.

> What pitiful *fig-leaves*, what senseless and ridiculous shifts, are these. —South.

fig′=mar″i-gōld, *n.* The popular name for plants of the genus *Mesembryanthemum*.

fig′ment, *n.* [L. *figmentum*, from *fingere*, to make, devise, invent.] An invention; a fiction; something feigned or imagined; as, these assertions are the *figments* of idle brains.

fig′men-tăl, *a.* Having the character of a figment; feigned; unreal; fictitious.

fī′gō, *n.* Same as *Fico*.

fig′peck″ẽr, *n.* The garden-warbler of Europe. [Same as *Figeater*.]

fig′ṡ′=end, *n.* A thing of no consequence; a trifle; a bagatelle.

fig′=shell, *n.* A sea-shell not unlike a fig in shape.

fig′ū-lāte, fig′ū-lā-ted, *a.* [L. *figulatus*, pp. of *figulare*, to form, fashion, from *figulus*, a potter.] Made of potter's clay; molded; shaped. [Rare.]

fig′ū-line, *n.* [L. *figulinus*, contr. *figlinus*, from *figulus*, a potter.] Potter's clay; also, ware made from potter's clay, especially pottery decorated with reliefs of natural objects.

fig″ūr-ȧ-bil′i-ty, *n.* The quality of being capable of a certain fixed or stable form.

fig′ūr-ȧ-ble, *a.* Capable of being brought to a certain fixed form or shape; as, lead is *figurable*, but water is not.

fig′ūr-ăl, *a.* 1. Represented by figure or delineation; as, *figural* resemblances.

2. In music, figurate.

Figural numbers; see *Figurate numbers*.

fig′ū-rănt, *n.*; *f.* **fig-ū-rănte′**. [Fr., masc. and f. ppr. of *figurer*, to figure.]

1. One who dances in the ballet, not singly, but in groups or figures.

2. An accessory character on the stage, who figures in its scenes, but has nothing to say; hence, one who figures in any scene without taking a prominent part.

fig′ūr-āte, *a.* [L. *figuratus*, pp. of *figurare*, to form, shape, from *figura*, a figure.]

1. Of a certain determinate form; resembling anything of a determinate form.

> Plants are all *figurate* and determinate, which inanimate bodies are not. —Bacon.

2. Figurative; not to be taken literally; florid; as, *figurate* eloquence. [Obs.]

3. In music, florid; opposed to *simple*.

Figurate counterpoint; in music, that which is a mixture of discords with concords.

Figurate descant; that in which discords are concerned, though not so much as concords. It may be called the ornament or rhetorical part of music, containing all the varieties of points, figures, syncopes, and diversities of measure.

Figurate numbers; in mathematics, such numbers as do or may represent some geometrical figure, in relation to which they are always considered, as triangular, pyramidal, pentagonal, etc., numbers. They are formed from any arithmetical series in which the first term is unity and the difference a whole number by taking the first term and the sum of the first two, first three, first four, etc., as the successive terms of new series, from which another may be formed in like manner, the numbers in the resulting series being such that points representing them are capable of arrangement in different geometrical figures. In the following examples the two lower lines consist of *figurate numbers*, those in the second line being triangular, and those in the third line square:—

1	2	3	4	5	6	etc.
1	3	6	10	15	21	etc.
1	4	9	16	25	36	etc.

fig′ūr-ā-ted, *a.* Having a determinate form.

fig′ūr-āte-ly, *adv.* In a figurate manner.

fig-ū-rā′tion, *n.* 1. The act of giving figure or determinate form.

2. Determination to a certain form.

3. Mixture of concords and discords in music.

fig′ūr-ȧ-tive, *a.* [L. *figurativus*, figurative, from *figuratus*, pp. of *figurare*, to form, fashion.]

1. Representing something else; representing by resemblance; typical; emblematic.

> This, they will say, was *figurative*, and served by God's appointment. —Hooker.

2. Consisting of or employing a rhetorical figure; not literal or direct; metaphorical.

3. Abounding with figures of speech; expressed in flowery or extravagant language; as, a description highly *figurative*.

4. In music, same as *figurate*.

5. Relating to the representation of the human figure in art, through the mediums of drawing, painting, or sculpture.

fig′ūr-ȧ-tive-ly, *adv.* In a figurative manner.

fig′ūr-ȧ-tive-ness, *n.* State of being figurative.

fig′ūre, *n.* [ME. *figure*, *figoura*; OFr. *figure*; L. *figura*, a form, shape, figure, from *fingere*, to form, shape.]

1. The form of anything, as expressed by the outline or terminating extremities; shape; outline; as, flowers have exquisite *figures*.

2. Shape; form; person; appearance; as, the defeated knight made but a sorry *figure*.

3. Distinguished appearance; eminence; distinction; remarkable character; standing; importance; as, McKinley made a *figure* in congress; to be of some *figure* in the world.

4. Magnificence; splendor; show; as, to live in *figure* and indulgence.

5. Representation of a form either by means of lines on a flat surface or by an image shaped by plastic art; as, the principal *figures* of a picture; the *figure* of a saint above the door.

6. A design or representation wrought in or printed on a surface, as a textile, paper, sheet metal, etc.; a pattern.

7. In logic, the form of a syllogism with respect to the order or disposition of the middle term.

8. In mathematics, a character denoting a number; a digit or the cipher; a diagram; a solid shape; as, a *figure* of a pentagon.

9. A number, either estimated or exact; price; value; as, a conservative *figure*; marked to sell at a low *figure*.

10. In astrology, the horoscope; the diagram of the aspects of the astrological houses.

11. In rhetoric, a mode of speaking or writing in which words are deflected from their ordinary signification; the language of the imagination and passions; as, knowledge is the light of the mind; the soul mounts on the wings of faith. Strictly, the change of a word is a *trope*, and any affection of a sentence, a *figure*; but these terms are often confounded.

12. In grammar, any deviation from the rules of analogy or syntax; an unusual construction.

13. In dancing, the several steps which the dancer makes in order and cadence, considered as they form certain outlines on the floor.

14. A being, object, or event which points to something corresponding to it in the future; a type; a symbol; an emblem.

> The like *figure* whereunto even baptism doth also now save us. —1 Pet. iii. 21.

15. A being of the imagination; a conception of the fancy; a phantasm; an image.

> Where beams of warm imagination play,
> The memory's soft *figures* fade away.—Pope.

16. In music, (a) a short theme or group of chords having a single motive; a harmonic phrase; (b) a numeral written upon the bass staff to represent an unwritten chord.

Figure-of-eight knot; see *Knot*, n.

Figure of speech; a phrase employing words in senses not ordinarily assigned to them. [See *Figure*, n. 11.]

Heroic figure; in art, a figure larger than life-size, while *academy figure* is less than life-size.

Lichtenberg's figures; figures produced on a surface of shellac by rubbing over it the knob of a Leyden jar or other excited electrode. There is left upon the nonconducting surface an electrified path to which a sprinkling of dried powdered sulphur and red lead will cling, forming peculiar figures.

Magnetic figures; the shapes assumed by iron-filings about the poles of a magnetic field.

Terminal figure; a half statue or bust, not placed upon but incorporated with and, as it were, immediately springing out of the square pillar which serves as its pedestal. Formerly, a representation of the Roman god Terminus, who presided over boundaries.

To cut a figure; to attract attention either in admiration or contempt; to make a certain appearance; as, *to cut a* sorry *figure*.

Syn.—Form, mold, shape, outline, condition, appearance, diagram, aspect, likeness, delineation, illustration, pattern, emblem, type, image, metaphor, symbol.

fig′ūre, *v.t.*; figured, *pt.*, *pp.*; figuring, *ppr.* 1. To form or mold into any determinate shape; to make a drawing or image of; as, to *figure* an urn in granite.

2. To cover or adorn with figures or images; to mark with figures; to form figures in by art; to stamp or work with a pattern; to diversify.

3. To represent by a typical or figurative resemblance.

> The matter of the sacraments *figureth* their end. —Hooker.

4. To imagine; to image in the mind; as, we *figure* to ourselves.

5. To prefigure; to foreshow.

6. To form figuratively; to use in a sense not literal; to employ metaphors for.

7. To note by characters; to mark by figures.

> As through a crystal glass the *figured* hours are seen. —Dryden.

8. To perform the several arithmetical operations on; to compute; to cast up; to estimate the result of; as, to *figure* the cost of an article; to *figure* expenses.

To figure out; to solve, as a problem; to compute.

To figure up; to add and find the final amount.

fig′ūre, *v.i.* 1. To make a figure; to be distinguished; as, the envoy *figured* at the court of St. Cloud.

2. To scheme or lay plans; to contrive to secure some result; to calculate; as, he is *figuring* to secure the income. [Colloq.]

3. To use figures; to cipher.

fig′ūre-çȧst″ẽr, *n.* One who casts horoscopes; an astrologer; called also *figure-flinger.*

fig′ūre-çȧst″ing, *n.* The art of making casts of human or animal figures or of anatomical parts of the human figure to serve as illustrations or models.

fig′ūred, *a.* 1. Ornamented with figures; marked with a pattern or design; sprigged; dotted; as, *figured* chintz.

2. Metaphorical; not to be taken literally; figurative. [Obs.]

3. In music, same as *figurate*.

4. In heraldry, bearing a likeness of the human face, as a crescent.

Figured bass; same as *Thorough-bass.*

fig′ūre-fling″ẽr, *n.* Same as *Figure-caster.*

fig′ūre-fling″ing, *n.* The art of casting horoscopes. [Obs.]

fig′ūre-head, *n.* 1. The figure, statue, or bust on the projecting part of the bow of a ship.

2. A person occupying a prominent place who represents others without having authority in his own hands; the ostensible head; as, he is become but the *figurehead* of his party.

Figurehead.

fig′ūre-māk″ẽr, *n.* A modeler; one who practises the most refined part of the art of molding, and casts busts, animals, and other ornaments, as branches, foliage, etc.; a maker of wooden anatomical models for artists.

fig′ūre-stōne, *n.* Agalmatolite or bildstein; a variety of talc-mica, of a gray, green, white, red, or brown color, and so soft as to be easily cut into figures.

fi-gū′ri-ăl, *a.* Shown by figures; diagrammed. [Rare.]

fi-gū-rïne′, *n.* [Fr. *figurine*, dim. of *figure*, a figure.] A small figure or group of small figures molded of clay, baked, and sometimes painted and touched up with gold.

Tanagra figurines; small figures or figurines made by the ancient Greeks as ornaments and as offerings to the gods. They are found in various places throughout Greece, but the first-discovered as well as the finest examples come from Tanagra, whence the name.

fig′ūr-ist, *n.* One who makes use of and interprets figurative language.

fig′wŏrt, *n.* A plant of the genus *Scrophularia*, supposed to be a remedy for scrofula.

Fī-jī′ăn, *a.* Pertaining to the Fiji islands or to the people native to them.

Fī-jī′ăn, *n.* One born in the Fiji islands.

fīke, fȳke, *v.i.* and *v.t.* I. *v.i.* To fidget; to be restless; to be constantly in a state of trivial motion; to be troubled about anything. [Scot.]

II. *v.t.* To vex; to annoy. [Scot.]

fīke, fȳke, *n.* 1. Restlessness or agitation caused by trifling annoyance. [Scot.]

2. Any trifling peculiarity in regard to work which causes unnecessary trouble; teasing exactness of operation. [Scot.]

> You have ower mony *fykes.*—Mrs. Hamilton.

fil, *v.*, past tense of *fall*. [Obs.]

fi-lā′ceous (-shus), *a.* [From L. *filum*, thread, and *-aceous.*] Composed or consisting of threads.

fil′ȧ-cẽr, *n.* [OFr. *filacier, filassier*, from *filace, filasse*, a file, thread on which records of the court were hung, from L. *filum*, a thread.] Formerly, an officer in the English Court of Common Pleas, so called from filing the writs on which he made process. [Obs.]

Fi-lā′gō, *n.* [From L. *filum*, thread.] A genus of slender annual herbs covered with a white cottony substance. [See *Cotton-rose* and *Cudweed.*]

fil′ȧ-ment, *n.* [Fr. *filament*, from L. *filum*, a thread.] A thread; a fiber; specifically, (a) in botany, the thread-like part of the stamen of a plant; (b) one of the soft threads or barbules of a down feather.

fil-ȧ-men′tā-ry, *a.* Formed by a filament or filaments; having the character of a filament.

> In the blennies, the forked hake, the forked beard, and some other fishes, the ventral fins are reduced to *filamentary* feelers. —Owen.

fil″ȧ-men-tif′ẽr-ous, *a.* [Fr. *filament*, filament, and L. *ferre*, to bear.] Producing threads or filamentous growths.

fil-ȧ-men′toid, *a.* [Fr. *filament*, filament, and Gr. *eidos*, form.] Resembling a filament.

fil-ȧ-men′tous, *a.* Like a thread; consisting of fine filaments.

fil-ȧ-men′tūle, *n.* [Fr. *filament*, filament, and dim. *-ule.*] Any small filament, as on the barb of a feather.

fil′an-dẽr, *n.* See *Philander.*

fil′an-dẽrṣ, *n.pl.* [Fr. *filandres*, from L. *filum*, a thread.] A disease in hawks, due to the presence of worms or filaments of coagulated blood; also, small worms wrapped in a thin skin or net, near the reins of a hawk; also called *backworm.*

fi′lăr, *a.* [From L. *filum*, a thread.] Pertaining to a thread; specifically applied to a microscope or other optical instrument, into whose construction one or more threads or wires are introduced.

Fi-lā′ri-ȧ, *n.* [From L. *filum*, a thread.] A genus of nematoid worms, belonging to the class *Scolecida*, including the guinea-worm.

fi-lā′ri-ăl, *a.* Pertaining to or occasioned by *Filaria* and related parasitic worms.

fil-ȧ-rī′ȧ-sis, *n.* A disease characterized by the presence of *Filaria* in the blood.

fi-lar′i-form, *a.* [From L. *filum*, a thread, and *forma*, form.]

1. Like a thread; filamentous.

2. Pertaining to or shaped like *Filaria*, or the guinea-worm.

fi′lāte, *a.* [From L. *filum*, a thread, and *-ate.*] Straight, slender, and unbranched, as the antennæ of certain dipterous insects.

fil′ȧ-tō-ry, *n.* [LL. *filatorium*, a place for spinning, from L. *filare*, to spin, from *filum*, thread.] A machine which forms or spins threads. [Obs.]

fil′ȧ-tūre, *n.* [LL. *filatura*, the art of spinning, a coarse thread, from L. *filare*, to spin; *filum*, thread.]

1. A drawing out into threads; hence, the reeling of silk from cocoons.

2. A reel for drawing off silk from cocoons, or an establishment for reeling.

fil′bẽrt, *n.* [ME. *filberde, fylberde, philliberd*; perhaps named from St. *Philibert*, whose feast came in the nutting season.]

1. The fruit of the cultivated *Corylus Avellana*, or hazel; an egg-shaped nut, containing a kernel, that has a mild, farinaceous, oily taste, which is agreeable to the palate.

2. The shrub or low tree yielding *filberts.*

fil′bẽrt-gall, *n.* A gall thought to resemble a filbert produced on vines by a gallfly, *Cecidomyia.*

filch, *v.t.*; filched (filcht), *pt.*, *pp.*; filching, *ppr.* [ME. *filchen*, to steal; perhaps from *felen*, to hide.] To steal, as something of little value; to pilfer.

> Fain would they *filch* that little food away. —Dryden.

filch, *n.* [Colloq. and Obs.]

1. The act of petty thieving; the thing taken or the person who filches.

2. A staff with a hook in one end used by thieves in snatching small articles.

filch′ẽr, *n.* A thief; one who is guilty of petty theft.

filch′ing-ly, *adv.* By pilfering; in a thievish manner.

fīle, *n.* [OFr. *file*, a file, rank, row; LL. *fila*, a string, series, from L. *filum*, a thread.]

1. A thread, line, wire, or any device by means of which papers are preserved in due order.

2. The whole number of papers strung on a line or wire; a collection of papers arranged according to date or subject for the sake of ready reference; also, a bundle of papers tied together, with the title of each indorsed; as, a *file* of writs; a *file* of newspapers.

3. A roll, list, or catalogue.

> Our present musters grow upon the *file*
> To five and twenty thousand men of choice. —Shak.

4. A straight row; a line; a row of soldiers ranged one behind another, from front to rear; the number of men constituting the depth of the battalion or squadron. Where a battalion is formed in two ranks, a *file* of soldiers means two men.

> So saying, on he led his radiant *files*,
> Dazzling the moon. —Milton.

5. Regular succession of thought or narration; uniform tenor; thread of discourse. [Obs.]

> Let me resume the *file* of my narration. —Wotton.

Flank file; in a body of troops, the outermost file on either side.

Indian file; single file, being the manner in which the American Indians are accustomed to travel.

On file; in orderly preservation; on record.

Rank and file; the lines of soldiers from side to side, and from front to back; all common soldiers under the rank of sergeant; hence, the general body of any party or society as distinguished from the leaders.

Single file; arranged in an unbroken succession, one behind another, as a file of soldiers.

fīle, *v.t.*; filed, *pt.*, *pp.*; filing, *ppr.* 1. To arrange, as papers, documents, manuscripts, etc., conveniently for reference and for preservation, as in a cabinet, box, or holder, arranged to receive them; to classify.

2. To present before a court or legislative body, so that the matter shall go upon the records; as, to *file* a claim.

3. In law, to place among the records of a court; to note on (a paper) the date of its reception in court.

fīle, *v.i.* To march in a file or line, as soldiers, not abreast, but one after another.

To file off; to wheel and march off in file at right angles to the first line of march.

To file with; to hold rank with; to keep pace with, to be equal to.

fīle, *v.t.* [ME. *filen, fylen*, from AS. *afylan*, to make foul, defile.] To soil; to defile; to sully; to pollute. [Obs.]

fīle, *v.t.* 1. To rub, smooth, sharpen, cut away, or polish with a file; as, to *file* a wire or the nails.

2. To smooth; to correct; to polish; to urge toward refinement; to improve; as, association with gentlemen *filed* his manners.

fīle, *n.* [ME. *file, fyle*; AS. *feól*, a file.]

1. A steel instrument used in cutting, polishing, or abrading surfaces or edges of metal, ivory, bone, etc. The cutting surface of a *file* is made in the steel while soft by a chisel which cuts grooves, leaving an evenly ridged surface. *Files* are named either from the nature or number of the cutting-faces, the shape of the tool, or the use to which they are put.

2. Any means used to smooth, polish, or refine, either literally or in a figurative sense.

3. A hard, cunning person; a shrewd person; a deep or artful man, as, a sly old *file.* [Slang.]

> Them two old *files* as was on the bench. —Dickens.

4. A cloth for wiping or washing a floor. [Local, U. S.]

5. In entomology, an organ of an insect covered with transverse grooves by means of which stridulation is produced.

Bastard file; see under *Bastard*, a.

Cabinet file; a fine single-cut file used on hardwood.

Dead file; a finely cut or smooth file, the grade finer than a smooth file.

Second-cut file; a file one grade finer than a bastard, and rougher than a smooth file.

Single-cut file; a file cut with but one series of grooves; a coarse *single-cut file* is called a *float.*

Smooth file; a file which grades between second-cut and dead.

fīle′-blaṅk, *n.* A piece of steel shaped and ground smooth, ready to be cut into a file.

fīle′-clōs″ẽr, *n.* A non-commissioned officer stationed in the rear or on the flank of a company of soldiers to assist in maintaining an exact formation in the ranks.

fīle′-cut″tẽr, *n.* A maker of files.

fīle′-fīr″ing, *n.* Firing by infantry one file at a time or one file following another in rapid succession.

fīle′fish, *n.* A name given to certain fishes from their skin being granulated like a file. They are intermediate between the bony and cartilaginous fishes, and constitute the family *Balistidæ.*

fīle′-lēad″ẽr, *n.* The soldier at the head of a file; the one who leads a file.

file′-märch″ing, *n.* The marching of a line, each file two deep, so that when faced to either the left or right the front and rear rank men are shoulder to shoulder.

fil′e-mot, *n.* [Fr. *feuille-morte*, a dead leaf.] A yellowish brown color; the color of a faded leaf.

fīl′ēr, *n.* One who uses a file in cutting, smoothing, and polishing.

file′-shell, *n.* Any bivalve mollusk of the genus *Pholas*, with a rough shell.

fī-let′ (fē-lā′), *n.* [OFr. *fillet*, a thread, band, from LL. *filetum*, dim. of L. *filum*, a thread.] In decorative art, a line or band forming an outline, or separating ornaments or fields of color. [See *Fillet*.]

fil′iăl (-yăl), *a.* [Fr. *filial*, LL. *filialis*, of a son or daughter, from *filius*, a son, *filia*, a daughter.]

1. Pertaining to a son or daughter; becoming to a child in relation to his parents; as, *filial* love; *filial* duty.

2. Bearing the relation of a child; issuing from as offspring.

> Sprigs of like leaf erect their *filial* heads. —Prior.

fil′iăl-ly, *adv.* In a filial manner.

fil′i-āte, *v.t.*; filiated, *pt.*, *pp.*; filiating, *ppr.* 1. To adopt as a foster-child.

2. In law, to fix paternity upon; hence, to assign as the originator of a hitherto anonymous work.

3. To affiliate.

fil-i-ā′tion, *n.* [Fr. *filiation*; LL. *filiatio* (*-onis*), from *filius*, a son, *filia*, a daughter.]

1. The relation of a son or child to a parent, especially a father; correlative to *paternity*.

2. Adoption.

3. The fixing of a bastard child on some one as its father; affiliation.

4. Descent from a parent, or relationship resembling that of a child; as, the *filiation* of the Romance languages to Latin.

fil′i-beg, *n.* [Gael. *feileadh-beag*, a small kilt; *feileadh*, a kilt, and *beag*, small, little.] A kilt reaching only to the knees, worn in the Highlands of Scotland.

fil′i-bus-tēr, *v.i.*; filibustered, *pt.*, *pp.*; filibustering, *ppr.* 1. To act the part of a filibuster, bucaneer, or free lance.

2. To endeavor to defeat a measure, or to delay legislation, by frivolous questions of order, motions to adjourn, etc., raised by the minority in order to weary the opposite party or to gain time. [Colloq., U. S.]

fil′i-bus-tēr, *n.* [Sp. *filibustero*, from Fr. *flibustier*, *fribustier*, a bucaneer, freebooter; from D. *vrijbuiter*, a freebooter, from *vrij*, free, and *buit*, booty.]

1. A freebooter or soldier of fortune who aids a revolution in a foreign country, in order to enrich himself; first applied to bucaneers in the West Indies who preyed on the Spanish commerce to South America, and later to such adventurers as followed Lopez to Cuba and Walker to Nicaragua in their expeditions of conquest.

2. One who attempts to retard the transaction of business or to check legislation by filibustering.

fil′i-bus-tēr-ism, *n.* The methods, acts, or practices of a filibuster.

fil′i-căl, *a.* Of or resembling the *Filices* or ferns.

Fil′i-cēs, *n.pl.* [L. *filix*, pl. *filices*, fern.] The scientific name of the large group of cryptogamic plants popularly known as ferns.

fi-lic′ic, *a.* [L. *filix* (*-icis*), a fern.] In chemistry, relating to or produced by ferns; as, *filicic* acid.

fil′i-cide, *n.* [From L. *filius*, son, *filia*, daughter, and *-cidium*, from *cædere*, to kill.]

1. The act of murdering one's own child.

2. One who murders his own child.

fi-lic′i-fọrm, *a.* [L. *filix* (*-icis*), a fern, and *forma*, form.] Fern-shaped.

Fil-i-cin′ē-æ, *n.pl.* [From L. *filix* (*-icis*), a fern.] A division of ferns distinguished by having well-developed fronds. The group is subdivided according to the mode of formation of the sporangia.

fil′i-cite, *n.* [L. *filix* (*-icis*), a fern, and *-ite*.] A fossil fern or filicoid plant.

fil′i-çoid, *a.* [L. *filix* (*-icis*), a fern, and Gr. *eidos*, form.] In botany, fernlike; having the form of ferns or like them in manner of propagation.

fil′i-çoid, *n.* A plant resembling a fern.

fil-i-çol′ō-ġy, *n.* [L. *filix* (*-icis*), a fern, and Gr. *-logia*, from *legein*, to speak.] That branch of botany which deals with ferns.

fi-lī′e-ty, *n.* [LL. *filietas*, from L. *filius*, a son.] The relationship sustained by a son to a father; sonship.

> The paternity of A and the *filiety* of B are not two facts, but two modes of expressing the same fact. —J. S. Mill.

fi-lif′ēr-ous, *a.* [L. *filum*, a thread, and *ferre*, to bear.] Producing or bearing threads or threadlike filaments; said of plants and insects.

fil′i-fọrm, *a.* [L. *filum*, a thread, and *forma*, form.] Having the form of a thread or filament; slender and of equal thickness from top to bottom; as, a *filiform* style or peduncle.

fi-lig′ēr-ous, *a.* [L. *filum*, a thread, and *gerere*, to bear.] In zoölogy, flagellate; applied to infusoria and bacteria.

fil′i-grāin, fil′i-grāne, *n.* [Fr. *filigrane*; It. *filigrana*, a filigree, from L. *filum*, a thread, and *granum*, a grain.] Filigree. [Obs.]

fil′i-grāned, *a.* Filigreed. [Obs.]

fil′i-gree, *n.* [Corrupted from *filigrain*.]

1. A kind of ornamental work in gold and silver, wrought delicately in the manner of little threads or grains, or of both intermixed; sculptured work wrought in delicate patterns.

2. Anything which is so fanciful, ornamental, or light in structure as to be perishable or of little use.

> Guarantees, he said, were mere *filigree*, pretty to look at, but too brittle to bear the slightest pressure. —Macaulay.

fil′i-gree, *a.* Pertaining to, resembling, or made of filigree; hence, fanciful; unsubstantial; slight; purely ornamental.

fil′i-greed, *a.* Ornamented with filigree.

fil′i-gree-glȧss, *n.* Glass into which colored threads have been introduced, which, weaving in and out, produce patterns.

fil′i-gree-wọrk, *n.* Work in filigree; also, such architectural and other carvings as are or seem of a character too slight and fragile for the purpose for which they are designed; hence, anything very unsubstantial or fanciful in structure.

> The churches of our ancestors shoot up into spires, towers, pinnacles, and *filigree-work*. —H. Swinburne.

fīl′ing, *n.* A fragment or particle rubbed off by the act of filing; as, iron *filings*.

Fil-i-ō′quē (-kwē), *n.* [L., lit., and from the Son; *filio*, ablative of *filius*, son, and *que*, the enclitic, and.] The clause of the Nicene Creed stating that the Holy Ghost proceeds from the Son as well as from the Father, it being one of the doctrines serving to separate the Greek and Roman churches, the former never accepting it.

fil-i-pen′dū-lȧ, *n.* [L. *filum*, a thread, and *pendulus*, hanging, from *pendere*, to hang.] In botany, the true English dropwort, *Spiræa Filipendula*.

fil-i-pen′dū-lous, *a.* [L. *filum*, thread, and *pendulus*, hanging, from *pendere*, to hang.] Suspended by a thread; in botany, a term applied to tuberous swellings developed in the middle of small, threadlike radicels.

Fil-i-pī′nȧ, *n.* [Sp.] A woman born in the Philippine islands.

Fil-i-pī′nō, *n.* [Sp.] A native of the Philippine islands, especially a mestizo.

fill, *v.t.*; filled, *pt.*, *pp.*; filling, *ppr.* [ME. *fillen*, *fullen*, *fyllen*; AS. *fyllan*, to fill, make full, from *full*, full.]

1. To make full; to cause to be occupied to the full capacity of; to supply with as much as can be contained; to place in or pour into until no more can be held; as, to *fill* a bottle; to *fill* a building with people.

> *Fill* the waterpots with water. And they *filled* them up to the brim. —John ii. 7.

2. To store; to supply with abundance; to occupy the whole of; to pervade; to permeate; to infest.

> Be fruitful, and multiply, and *fill* the waters in the seas. —Gen. i. 22.

3. To satisfy; to content; to supply with a sufficiency; to feed.

4. To supply with an incumbent; as, to *fill* an office or vacancy.

5. To hold; to possess and perform the duties of; to officiate in, as an incumbent; as, a king *fills* a throne; the president *fills* the office of chief magistrate; the speaker of the house *fills* the chair.

6. To round out or complete; to make smooth by the addition of more material; to level; to stop up cracks in; as, to *fill* wood by the application of varnish or a paste.

7. To add material to, to increase the bulk or to lend a finished appearance; to adulterate; to water.

8. In seamanship, to brace, as the yards, so that the wind will act upon the after surface of the sails; also, to press upon and distend by blowing; as, the wind *filled* the sails.

To fill in; (a) to add material sufficient to raise to a given level; as, to *fill in* a ravine; (b) to insert in a blank form; to supply, as missing data; as, to *fill in* particulars.

To fill out; (a) to make full, rounded, or complete; (b) to supply, as data or particulars, on a blank form.

To fill the bill; to be adequate to the need; to meet the requirements; to be what is desired. [Colloq.]

To fill up; to make full; to occupy to the entire capacity of; to complete.

> It pours the bliss that *fills up* all the mind. —Pope.

Syn.—Occupy, pervade, make complete, pack, pour, feed, satisfy, satiate, distend, swell.

fill, *v.i.* 1. To grow or become full; to expand to the full capacity: to be satiated; to swell; as, kernels or pea-pods *fill* well; sails *fill* in a stiff breeze.

2. To pour liquid into a cup or glass for drinking; to give to drink.

> In the cup which she hath filled, *fill* to her double. —Rev. xviii. 6.

To back and fill; see under *Back*, v.i.

To fill away; in nautical language, to brace the yards so that the sails may catch the wind and fill.

To fill up; to grow or become full; as, the channel of the river *fills up* with sand every spring.

fill, *n.* [ME. *fille*, *fulle*, *fylle*; AS. *fyllu*, *fyllo*, fullness, fill.]

1. Fullness; as much as supplies want; as much as gives complete satisfaction; as, eat your *fill*.

2. That which fills; a charge; a load; specifically, in railroad construction, an embankment which fills or crosses a ravine; as, beyond the town lay a *fill* and a draw.

3. Something of no value, as a weed. [Obs.]

fill, *n.* [A dial. form of *thill*.] A shaft; a thill. [Obs.]

> We'll put you i' the *fills*. —Shak.

fil′lȧ-gree, *n.* See *Filigree*.

fill′ēr, *n.* 1. One who or that which fills; especially, a vessel or utensil for conveying a liquid into a bottle, cask, etc.; a funnel.

> They have six diggers to four *fillers*, so as to keep the *fillers* always at work. —Mortimer.

2. That which fills any space; specifically, a composition used to fill the grain of wood before applying paint or varnish.

3. The second grade of tobacco used in the body of cigars, the outside being called the wrapper.

fill′ēr, *n.* A thill-horse. [Prov. Eng.]

fil′let, *n.* [OFr. *fillet*, a thread, band, chine of beef, from LL. *filettum*, dim. of L. *filum*, a thread.]

1. A band; a strip; a ribbon; especially, a little band to tie about the hair of the head.

> A belt her waist, a *fillet* binds her hair.—Pope.

2. A muscle or a piece of meat composed of muscle; especially, the fleshy part of the thigh. The term is applied specifically to the tenderloin of beef, to the fleshy part of a leg of veal or mutton, to the breast of a chicken, and to a thick, boneless slice of fish.

> *Fillet* of a fenny snake,
> In the caldron boil and bake. —Shak.

3. Meat rolled together and tied round.

4. In technology, a term having many applications, viz.: a strip nailed to a wall to support a shelf; a strip for a door to close against; a band of gold-leaf on a picture-frame or elsewhere; a strip of metal rolled to a certain size; the thread of a screw; a ring on the muzzle of a gun, etc.

5. In architecture, a small molding, generally rectangular in section, and having the appearance of a narrow band, used to separate ornaments and moldings; an amulet; a list; a listel; the ridge between the flutes of a column. [See *Filet*.]

6. In heraldry, (a) a barrulet crossing a shield at the height of the lower edge of the chief; (b) a kind of orle or bordure, containing only the third or fourth part of the breadth of the common bordure.

7. In anatomy, a bundle of nerve-fibers; especially, the fibers found at the base of the brain; the lemniscus.

8. The loins of a horse, beginning at the place where the hinder part of the saddle rests.

fil′let, *v.t.*; filleted, *pt.*, *pp.*; filleting, *ppr.* To bind with a fillet or little band.

fil′let-ing, *n.* 1. The material for making fillets.

2. Fillets, collectively.

3. A kind of heavy tape.

fill′-hŏrse, phill′-hŏrse, *n.* The horse which goes in the shafts; a thill-horse.

> Thou hast got more hair on thy chin than Dobbin, my *phill-horse*, has on his tail. —Shak.

fil′li-beg, *n.* See *Filibeg*.

fil′li-bus-tēr, *n.* See *Filibuster*.

fill′ing, *n.* 1. The act of one who fills or supplies.

2. Material used for occupying some vacant space, for completing some structure, stopping up a hole, or the like; as, the *filling* of a tooth, or of a wall.

3. The material employed for filling up the outside pores of certain porous woods used for fine work, such as house-finishing, cabinet-making, etc.

4. The woof in textile fabrics.

fil'lip, *v.t.*; filliped (-lipt), *pt.*, *pp.*; filliping, *ppr.*
1. To strike with the nail of the finger, first bent against the ball of the thumb and let fly from that position suddenly.
2. To snap; to let fly quickly.
3. To urge forward; to incite.

fil'lip, *n.* 1. A jerk of the finger let fly suddenly from the thumb.
2. That which serves to excite, impel, or rouse; something which revives or restores.

fil'li-peen, *n.* Same as *Philopena*.

fil'lis-tẽr, *n.* [Origin unknown.]
1. The rabbet on a sash-bar for holding the glass and putty.
2. A kind of plane used for grooving timber or for cutting rabbets.

fil'ly, *n.*; *pl.* **fil'lieṣ**. [Ice. *fylja*, a filly, from *foli*; AS. *fola*, a foal.]
1. A female colt or foal; a young mare.
2. A lively, bold young woman. [Colloq.]

film, *n.* [ME. *fylme*; AS. *fylmen*, a film, membrane.]
1. A thin skin; a pellicle; a membrane; a delicate coating or outer layer, partially obscuring that which lies beneath; as, a *film* of gelatin; a *film* of lace.
2. A delicate thread, as of a cobweb.
3. In photography, the coating on a sheet of prepared gelatin, which receives and retains the image projected upon it; also, any transparent sheet which has been subjected to a sensitizing coat. The term *film* is applied at any stage during the process and to any length of prepared material, so long as it remains uncut.
4. The flexible strip of prepared celluloid, etc., upon which the successive photographs for the reproduction of a moving picture are taken; also, the similar strip upon which the finished pictures appear, as used in a moving-picture apparatus.
Celluloid film; a transparent celluloid sheet coated with some sensitized material, to be used in a film camera.
Film camera; a photographic camera arranged to carry a reel of film, as distinguished from a *plate camera*, which carries a limited number of sensitized plates.

film, *v.t.*; filmed, *pt.*, *pp.*; filming, *ppr.*
1. To cover with a thin skin or pellicle.
2. To photograph on a film for moving pictures.

film'i-ness, *n.* The state of being filmy.

film'y, *a.* Composed of thin membranes or pellicles.

fil"ō-plū-mā'ceous, *a.* In zoölogy, formed like a filoplume.

fil'ō-plūme, *n.* [L. *filum*, a thread, and *pluma*, a downy feather.] In ornithology, a long, slender, and flexible feather, closely approximating to a hair in form, and consisting of a delicate shaft, either destitute of vanes or carrying a few barbs at the tip.

fī'lōse, *a.* [From L. *filum*, a thread.] In zoölogy, ending in a threadlike process.

fil'ō-selle (*or* fil-ō-sel'), *n.* [Fr.] A sort of silk thread resembling floss; ferret.

fil'tẽr, *n.* [Fr. *filtre*, a filter, from LL. *filtrum*, *feltrum*, felt, fulled wool, this being used for straining liquors.]
1. A strainer; any porous material such as a piece of cloth, paper, stone, or charcoal, through which liquids are passed for defecation. The pores of these substances are sufficiently large to allow the liquids to pass, but not large enough to permit the passage of any substance held in suspension by the liquids.
2. Any vessel or device which contains a substance through which water percolates and is cleansed of impurities.
3. A device for purifying air.

Lelogo's Water Filter.
1, 2, 3, 4. The compartments: *a b*, porous top of 2d compartment; *c d*, filtering top of 3rd compartment; *e*, movable plug.

fil'tẽr, *v.t.*; filtered *pt.*, *pp*; filtering, *ppr.* [Fr. *filtrer*, from LL. *filtrare*, to strain through felt, from *filtrum*, *feltrum*, felt, fulled wool.] To purify or defecate, as water or other liquid, by passing it through a filter, or through any porous substance that retains matter held in suspension in the liquid.

fil'tẽr, *v.i.* To percolate; to pass through a filter; to strain through a purifying medium.

fil'tẽr, *n.* See *Philter*.

fil'tẽr-bed, *n.* A pond or artificial reservoir having a false bottom of sand which acts as a filter.

fil'tẽr-gal"lẽr-y, *n.* An underground tunnel or conduit paralleling a stream, to collect water that is filtered through the sand and gravel which cover the bed of the stream.

fil'tẽr-ing, *n.* The act of passing through a filter; percolation; often used in compounds; as, *filtering*-funnel.

fil'tẽr-pā"pẽr, *n.* A porous, unsized paper used in laboratories for filtering.

filth, *n.* [ME. *filthe*, *felthe*, *fulthe*; AS. *fylthe*, filth, foulness, from *ful*, foul.]
1. Dirt; any foul matter; anything that soils or defiles; waste matter; nastiness.
2. Corruption; pollution; anything that sullies or defiles the moral character.

> Purifying our souls from the dross and *filth* of sensual delights. —Tillotson.

3. A foul condition; squalor.

filth'-diṣ-ēaṣe", *n.* In medicine, any disease supposed to arise from drinking impure water or from unsanitary conditions.

filth'i-ly, *adv.* In a filthy manner; foully; grossly.

filth'i-ness, *n.* 1. The state of being filthy.
2. That which is filthy; foulness; dirtiness; filth; nastiness; corruption; pollution; impurity.

filth'y, *a.* 1. Dirty; foul; unclean; nasty; noisome.
2. Polluted; obscene; morally impure.
3. Low; contemptible; mean.

fil'trāte, *v.t.*; filtrated, *pt.*, *pp.*; filtrating, *ppr.* [LL. *filtratus*, pp. of *filtrare*, to filter.] To filter; to defecate, as a liquid, by straining or percolation; to clarify; to render clear or pure.

fil'trāte, *n.* The liquid which has been passed through a filter.

fil-trā'tion, *n.* The act or process of filtering; the mechanical separation of a liquid from the undissolved particles suspended in it. The filtering substance may consist of any porous matter, as porous earthenware, unsized paper, sand, charcoal, asbestos, etc.

fil-trā'tion plant. The equipment whereby the impurities are removed from a city's or district's water supply, rendering it fit to drink.

fī'lum, *n.*; *pl.* **fī'lȧ**. [L. *filum*, a thread.]
1. In anatomy, a threadlike structure; a minute fiber.
2. In musical notation, the stem or tail attached to a note.
Filum terminale; the slender, gray filament in which the spinal cord terminates.

fim'ble, *n.* [Corrupted from *female*.] Light summer hemp that bears no seed; the male plants of hemp; also called *fimble-hemp*.

fim'bri-ȧ, *n.*; *pl.* **fim'bri-æ**. [LL. *fimbria*, a border, from L. *fimbriæ*, fringe.]
1. One of the filamentous appendages which constitute a fringe; a fringing filum; in the plural, a fringe; a band or row of fringing filaments; specifically, the fringed extremity of a Fallopian tube; also, the fringe of white filaments surrounding a part of the hippocampus major of the brain.
2. In botany, applied to the dentated or fringe-like ring of the operculum of mosses, by the elastic power of which the operculum is displaced.

fim'bri-ăl, *a.* Pertaining to a fimbria.

fim'bri-āte, *a.* [L. *fimbriatus*, fringed, from *fimbria*, a fringe, border.] In botany, fringed; having the margin bordered by filiform processes thicker than hairs.

fim'bri-āte, *v.t.*; fimbriated, *pt.*, *pp.*; fimbriating, *ppr.* To hem; to fringe.

fim'bri-ā-ted, *a.* 1. Fringed; having a fringed border; fimbriate.
2. In heraldry, ornamented with a narrow border or hem of another tincture.

Fimbriate Petals (*Dianthus caryophyllus*).

fim-bri-ā'tion, *n.* The act or process of fimbriating; that which is fimbriated; the condition of being fimbriated; a fringing process; a fringe.

fim-bril'lȧ, *n.*; *pl.* **fim-bril'læ**. [Dim., from L. *fimbra*, a fringe, border.] One of the parts that constitute a minute fringe.

fim-bril'lāte, *a.* Composed of fimbrillæ.

fim-bril-lif'ẽr-ous, *a.* [*Fimbrilla*, dim. from L. *fimbria*, a border, and *ferre*, to bear.] Bordered by fimbrillæ; fimbrillate.

fim-ē-tā'ri-ous, *a.* [L. *fimetum*, dunghill, from *fimus*, dung.] In botany, growing in or on dung.

fin, *v.t.*; finned, *pt.*, *pp.*; finning, *ppr.* To carve or cut up, as a fish; to trim off the fins of (a fish).

fin, *v.i.* To roll on the back and lash the water with the fins; said of a whale when mortally wounded; commonly followed by *out*.

fin, *n.* [ME. *finne*, *fynne*; AS. *finn*, a fin; D. *vinne*; L.G. *finne*; Sw. *finne*, a fin; L. *pinna*, fin, wing.]
1. In fishes, a membrane supported by rays, or little bony or cartilaginous ossicles. The *fins* serve to keep the body upright, and to prevent wavering or vacillation. With the exception of the caudal, the *fins* assist but little in progressive motion, the tail being the principal instrument of swimming.
2. Anything resembling a *fin*; as, (a) a finlike part or attachment; (b) the sharp plate in the colter of a plow; (c) in molding, a thin excrescence on the surface of a casting, caused by the imperfect approximation of two molding-boxes, containing each a portion of the mold, the *fin* being formed by the metal running in between the two parting surfaces; (d) a blade of whalebone; (e) the hand; as, hold up your *fin*; this use is slang.

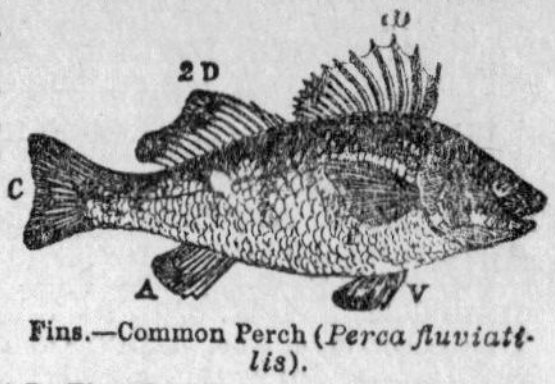

Fins.—Common Perch (*Perca fluviatilis*).
1 D, First Dorsal; 2 D, Second Dorsal; P, Pectoral; V, Ventral; A, Anal; C, Caudal.

3. A finlike organ in marine animals other than fish, as one of the limbs or flippers of a seal.
4. Fish, collectively; as, a sportsman hunting *fin* and feather.
Adipose fin; see under *Adipose*, a.
Paired fins; the pectoral and ventral fins, which correspond to the hands and feet of erect vertebrates.
Unpaired or *vertical fins*; the dorsal, anal, and caudal fins.

fīn'ȧ-ble, *a.* Capable of being refined or clarified; as, *finable* wines.

fīn'ȧ-ble, *a.* Subject to a fine or penalty; as, a *finable* person or offense.

fī'năl, *a.* [ME. *final*; OFr. *final*; L. *finalis*, from *finis*, end.]
1. Pertaining to the end or conclusion; last; ultimate; as, the *final* issue or event of things; *final* hope; *final* salvation.
2. Conclusive; decisive; determinative; as, a *final* judgment.
3. Respecting the end or object to be gained; respecting the purpose or ultimate end in view.

> Thus we necessarily include, in our idea of organization, the notion of an end, a purpose, a design; or, to use another phrase, a *final* cause. —Whewell.

Syn.—Conclusive, ultimate, eventual, last.—*Final* is applied to that which brings with it an end; as, a *final* adjustment. *Conclusive* implies the closing of all future discussion, negotiation, etc.; as, a *conclusive* argument. *Ultimate* has reference to something earlier or preceding; as, a temporary reverse may lead to an *ultimate* triumph.

fī'năl, *n.* 1. That which is the termination; the last.
2. In the Gregorian scale, the note corresponding to the tonic or keynote of the modern scale, being the first tone in the authentic and the fourth from the bottom in the plagal scale.
3. The last and deciding contest or round of a series of athletic events, in which only such players compete as have previously won; as, twelve players qualified for the *finals*.

fi-nä'le, *n.* [It., from L. *finalis*, from *finis*, end.]
1. The last note or end of a piece of music.
2. The last scene or tableau in any act of a play or opera, or that which closes a concert; close; termination.

fī-nal'i-ty, *n.* 1. The state of being final; the state of being settled or finally arranged; completeness.
2. In philosophy, the doctrine that nothing exists or was made except for a determinate end; the doctrine of final causes.

fī'năl-ly, *adv.* 1. At the end or conclusion; ultimately; lastly; as, the cause is expensive, but we shall *finally* recover.
2. Completely; beyond recovery.

> The enemy was *finally* exterminated.—Davies.

fi-nance', *n.* [ME. *finaunce*, a fine, forfeit; OFr. *finance*, wealth, revenue; LL. *financia*, a money payment, money, from *finare*, to pay a fine or tax, from L. *finis*, end.]
1. The system or science of public revenue and expenditure.
2. The management of the funds and resources of a state, society, bank, private corporation, or capitalist.
3. [*pl.*] Revenue; funds in the public treasury or accruing to it; public resources of money; as, *finances* of the king or government were in a low condition; the *finances* were exhausted.
4. [*pl.*] The income or resources of individuals. [Colloq.]

fi-nance', *v.t.* and *v.i.*; financed, *pt.*, *pp.*; financing, *ppr.* I. *v.t.* To have the financial management of; to supply the means for; as, to *finance* an arctic expedition; to *finance* a campaign.
II. *v.i.* To conduct financial operations; to manage finances.

fi-nan'ciăl (-shăl), *a.* Pertaining to finance or public revenue; having to do with money matters; as, *financial* concerns or operations.

fi-nan'ciăl-ist, *n.* A financier.

fi-nan'ciăl-ly, *adv.* In relation to finances or public revenue; in a manner to produce revenue; in respect to funds.

fin-an-cier′, *n.* [Fr., from *finance*, finance.]

1. An officer who receives and manages the public revenues; a treasurer.

2. One who is skilled in financial matters or in the principles or system of public revenue; one who understands money matters; one who is acquainted with the economical management and application of money.

3. In France, previous to the Revolution, a receiver or farmer of the public revenues.

fin-an-cier′, *v.t.* and *v.i.*; financiered, *pt., pp.*; financiering, *ppr.* To negotiate funds for an enterprise, especially by means of an involved system of credit; to act as financier for; to finance.

fin′ȧ-ry, *n.* See *Finery.*

fī′nȧ-tive, *a.* Definitive; final. [Obs.]

fin′back, *n.* A name given to whales of the family *Balænopteridæ*, having a prominent dorsal fin. *Sibbaldius tectirostris* is the common *finback* of the north Atlantic coast, and *Balænoptera velifera* and *Balænoptera davidsoni* are *finbacks* found in the Pacific. Called also *razorback, rorqual, finner*, and *fin-whale.*

finch, *n.* [ME. *finch, fynch*; AS. *finc*, a finch.] The popular name of the small singing birds forming the genus *Fringilla*; a bunting, sparrow, etc. In its widest sense the term is applied to the numerous group constituting the family *Fringillidæ*. It is contained in many compounds, to form the names of various fringilline birds; as, bull*finch*, pine*finch*, gold*finch*, chaf*finch*, mountain-*finch*, etc.

To pull a finch; to cheat one who is ignorant or artless; to swindle. [Obs.]

fin′-chāin, *n.* A heavy chain having rings on the ends or a ring and a hook, used by whalers in lifting the fore part of a whale.

finch′backed (-bakt), *a.* Marked by streaks or blotches of white or a color, as cattle. [Prov. Eng.]

finched, *a.* Same as *Finchbacked.*

finch′-fa̤l″cŏn (-fa̤″kn), *n.* A falcon of the genus *Hierax*, in size no larger than the finch.

fīnd, *v.t.*; found, *pt., pp.*; finding, *ppr.* [ME. *finden*; AS. *findan*, to find.]

1. To come to; to meet with; to discover by sight, touch, taste, or any other sense, whether unexpectedly or by searching; to recover; to obtain; to attain, whether by effort or by chance; to reach; as, water *finds* its level; flowers are *found* in the wood; he *found* the coin he sought; to *find* time to visit; to *find* rest or safety; to *find* one's way.

2. To discover by methodical experiment; to ascertain by trial or study; to learn by experience; to observe; to detect; to invent; as, to *find* the best way to do anything; to *find* the elements in a compound; to *find* a climate healthy; to *find* a person witty; to be *found* in a lie; who first *found* tents for dwellings?

3. In law, to determine after judicial inquiry; to establish, as facts; to come to or arrive at, as a conclusion; as, to *find* a verdict; to *find* damages; to *find* a true bill.

4. To supply; to furnish; to support; as, to *find* provisions for an expedition; wages six dollars a week and everything *found*; he gets ten dollars a week and *finds* himself.

To find fault with; to blame; to censure.

To find in; to supply; to furnish; to provide; as, he *finds* his nephew *in* money, board, and clothes.

To find oneself; to be; to fare in regard to ease or pain, health or sickness; as, how do you *find yourself* this morning?

To find out; (a) to invent; to discover something before unknown; (b) to unriddle; to solve; to discover; to obtain knowledge of what is hidden; as, *to find out* a secret, (c) to understand; to comprehend; (d) to detect; to discover; to bring to light; as, *to find out* a thief or a theft; *to find out* a trick.

Syn.—Meet, confront, ascertain, experience, perceive, discover, furnish, supply, invent, recover, attain, observe, detect, arrive at.

fīnd, *v.i.* 1. To decide a question of fact and present the result to the court; as, the jury *finds* for the defendant.

2. To locate game; as, the pointer *found* quickly.

fīnd, *n.* Any discovery, especially one of value; as, the excavators of Pompeii have made some great *finds*

fīnd′ȧ-ble, *a.* Capable of being found, discovered, or located.

fīnd′ẽr, *n.* 1. That which or one who finds.

2. In astronomy, a small telescope, attached to a larger one, for the purpose of finding an object more readily.

3. A small lens attached to a camera to indicate the extent of the field of view, and locate any desired object.

4. A graduated slide used to locate objects in the field of a microscope.

fin de siè′cle (fan de syā′kl). [Fr., end of the century.] Thoroughly modern; up-to-date; a phrase used to distinguish the period at the close of the nineteenth century.

fīnd′fa̤ult, *n.* A censurer; a faultfinder. [Obs.]

fīnd′fa̤ult″ing, *a.* Faultfinding. [Obs.]

fīnd′ing, *n.* 1. Discovery; the act of discovering; the thing found.

2. In law, the return of a jury to a bill; a verdict.

3. Maintenance; support; expense.

4. [*pl.*] The tools and materials which some workmen have to furnish in their employment; working supplies.

fīnd′ing-list, *n.* A skeleton catalogue of the contents of a library, designed to facilitate the locating of the volumes.

fin′djăn, fin′ġiăn (fin′jăn), *n.* [Ar.] A coffee-cup such as is used in the Levant. It is commonly a footless cup of thin porcelain, supported by an ornamental metal holder, called a zarf. Spelled also *fingan.*

fin′dy, *a.* [AS. *findig, fyndig*, weighty.] Full; heavy; substantial. [Obs.]

> A cold May and a windy,
> Makes the barn fat and *findy.*—Old Proverb.

fīne, *a.*; *comp.* finer; *superl.* finest. [ME. *fin, fyn, fine*; OFr. *fin*, from L. *finitus*, lit., finished, pp. of *finire*, to bound, limit, from *finis*, a limit, bound.]

1. Brought to a finish; perfected; refined, in the sense of being without impurities; in a state of excellence or superiority; elegant; admirable; possessing accomplishments and beauty.

2. Showy; aiming at effect; ornamented, dressed, or decorated to too great an extent; ostentatious.

3. Showing skill or nicety; exhibiting dexterity or artfulness; subtle; delicate; artful.

4. Subtile; thin; tenuous; as, *fine* spirits evaporate rapidly.

5. Made up of minute particles; comminuted; as, *fine* dust.

6. Small; thin; slender; minute; of very small diameter; as, a *fine* thread; *fine* silk; a *fine* hair.

7. Thin; keen; smoothly sharp; as, the *fine* edge of a razor.

8. Made of delicate constituents or materials; not coarse; as, *fine* linen or lace.

9. Composed of a given proportion of pure metal; as, jewelry 14 carats *fine.*

10. Praiseworthy or distinguished in some way; hence, agreeable; pleasurable; pleasant; as, a *fine* visit; a *fine* trip; sometimes used in irony; as, a *fine* piece of work! a *fine* scheme! The word is also colloquially used, like *nice*, to express simply approval or admiration of a thing.

Fine arts; see *Art*, n. 2.

Fine as a fiddle; very fine; high-strung. [Colloq.]

Fine stuff; a lime solution used as a slip-coat to cover previous coats of coarser plaster. Plaster of Paris is sometimes mixed with it when a particularly hard, smooth surface is desired.

To sail fine; in seamen's language, to sail close to the wind.

To train fine; to reduce the body by training to the limit consistent with health; to discipline thoroughly, as the mental powers.

Syn.—Beautiful, attractive, showy, dainty, choice, rare, delicate, excellent, polished, slender, minute, thin, suitable, keen.

fīne, *n.* [ME. *fin, fyn*, end, end of life, payment in settlement; OFr. *fin*, from L. *finis*, a limit, boundary.]

1. End; conclusion; extinction; summing up. [Obs.]

2. A sum of money paid to settle a dispute or claim; especially, a sum paid by way of penalty for an offense; a mulct; an amercement; a pecuniary punishment.

3. In old English law, a conveyance of land, sometimes fictitious; a recorded grant; called also a *fine of lands.*

4. In feudal law, (a) a final agreement between persons concerning lands or rents, prescribing the conditions on which the lands should be held; (b) a sum of money paid to the lord by his tenant, for permission to alienate or transfer his lands to another.

Fine for alienation; under the feudal system, a sum paid by a vassal to his lord on occasion of the transfer, by alienation or succession, of the former's holding.

In fine; to close; in conclusion; at last.

fīne, *v.t.*; fined, *pt., pp.*; fining, *ppr.* 1. To subject to a pecuniary penalty for an offense or breach of law; to set a fine on by judgment of a court; to punish by fine.

2. To end; to bring to a conclusion; to cause to cease. [Obs.]

> Time's office is to *fine* the hate of foes.—Shak.

fīne, *v.i.* [ME. *finen*, to pay a fine; OFr. *finir*, from L. *finire*, to end.]

1. To pay a fine; to pay for a grant, concession, or privilege. [Rare.]

2. To cease; to be ended. [Obs.]

fīne, *v.t.* [ME. *finen*, to refine, purify, from *fin*, fine, pure.]

1. To free from foreign matter; to refine; to clarify; to purify; as, to *fine* wines; to *fine* gold.

2. To change gradually or by imperceptible degrees; to cause to pass by fine gradations from one condition to another.

3. To make less coarse.

fīne, *v.i.* To become pure, slender, or fine in any sense by imperceptible gradation rather than by abrupt change; commonly followed by *down* or *away*; as, liquors *fine down*; awkward puppies *fine down* into well-shaped dogs.

fīne, *adv.* [Scot.] 1. Finely; well; much: as, I ken *fine* what he meant; he would *fine* like to hear it.

2. Cautiously; with precision; as, to fish *fine*; to tread *fine.*

fī′ne, *n.* [It., end.] In music, the word written at the end of a repeated portion or of a composition, to indicate the end; conclusion; finis.

fīne′-ärch, *n.* In glass-making, a small furnace in which to melt the raw materials for glass.

fīne′-cut, *a.* and *n.* I. *a.* Finely chiseled; delicately molded; as, a *fine-cut* profile; cut fine; as, *fine-cut* chewing tobacco.

II. *n.* Tobacco finely shredded for chewing or smoking.

fīne′dra̤w, *v.t.*; finedrew, *pt.*; finedrawing, *ppr.*; finedrawn, *pp.* 1. To sew up, as a rent, with so much nicety that it is not perceived; to close up by drawing in with a needle firm threads in place of broken ones.

2. To draw or spin out, as wire, to a great degree of fineness.

fīne′dra̤w″ẽr, *n.* One who does finedrawing.

fīne′dra̤wn, *a.* Spun out finely; extended or produced to a great or too great a degree.

fi-neer′, *v.i.* To run in debt by having goods made up to order, and then refusing to take them except credit be extended, knowing they are unsuitable for any one else and will otherwise be left upon the dealer's hands. [Rare.]

fi-neer′, *v.t.* To coat over; to veneer. [Obs.]

fīne′less, *a.* Endless; boundless. [Obs.]

fīne′ly, *adv.* In a fine manner; admirably; delicately.

fīne′ness, *n.* 1. The state or quality of being fine in any of the various senses of the word.

2. Clearness; purity; freedom from foreign matter; as, the *fineness* of wine; the *fineness* of gold.

3. The quantity of pure metal contained in alloys, expressed as fractions of 1,000 or in carats.

4. [Obs.] Same as *Finesse.*

fīn′ẽr, *n.* One who refines or purifies.

fīn′ẽr-y, *n.* 1. Fineness; beauty; attraction; charm. [Rare.]

2. Showy articles of dress; gay clothes, jewels, trinkets, and the like.

3. In iron-works, a furnace where cast-iron is converted into malleable iron.

fīne′spun, *a.* Drawn to a fine thread; minute; subtile; unsubstantial.

fi-nesse′, *n.* [Fr. *finesse*, delicacy, nicety, from *fin*, fine.]

1. Artifice; stratagem; subtlety of contrivance to gain a point.

2. In whist-playing, the act of playing with the view of taking the trick with a lower card than may be in the hand of your adversary on the left, while a higher card is in your own hand.

Syn.—Skill, craft, cunning, artifice, deception, maneuver, artfulness, adroitness, subterfuge, machination.

fi-nesse′, *v.i.*; finessed (-nest′), *pt., pp.*; finessing, *ppr.* 1. To use artifice or stratagem.

2. In whist-playing, to use finesse in taking a trick.

fi-nesse′, *v.t.* To practise or perform finesse with; as, to *finesse* the queen.

fīne′still, *v.t.* To distil, as spirit from molasses, treacle, or some preparation of saccharine matter.

fīne′still″ẽr, *n.* One who distils spirit from treacle or molasses.

fīne′top, *n.* The redtop grass. *Agrostis vulgaris.*

fin′ew (-ū), *n.* Moldiness. [Rare.]

fin′ewed, *a.* Moldy; decayed. [Rare.]

fin′fish, *n.* 1. A finback whale.

2. A fin-pike, family *Polypteridae.*

fin′-fish, *n.pl.* Fish having fins by which they balance their bodies or steer their course, as distinguished from shellfish.

fin′foot, *n.*; *pl.* **fin′foots** or **fin′feet.** Any bird of the genus *Heliornis*, allied to the grebes, so called from their feet being lobed.

fin′-foot, *n.*; *pl.* fin′-feet. A swimming-foot or swimmeret of a crustacean.

fin′-foot″ed, *a.* 1. In zoölogy, having palmated feet or feet with toes connected by a membrane; web-footed.

2. In ornithology, having pinnate feet; having a membranous web bordering each toe; pinnatiped.

fin′ġent, *a.* [L. *fingens (-entis)*, ppr. of *fingere*, to form, shape.] Forming; shaping; molding; fashioning. [Rare.]

fin′gẽr, *n.* [ME. *finger*; AS. *finger*, a finger.]

1. One of the five extreme members of the

hand; a digit; also, one of the extremities of the hand, exclusive of the thumb. The word is applied to some other animals, as well as to man.

2. Whatever serves as a *finger*; a part shaped like or which answers the purpose of a *finger*; some device which performs the act of a *finger*.

Fancy, like the *finger* of a clock,
Runs the great circuit, and is still at home.
—Cowper.

3. A fingerbreadth, being a measure a trifle short of an inch, also, the length of the adult middle finger, or about four and one-half inches.

4. In music, ability; skill in playing on a keyed instrument; execution; as, she has a good *finger*.

Fingers all thumbs; fingers which lack skill or dexterity; awkward or stiff fingers.

Mechanical finger; a delicate contrivance used to separate minute particles, for examination, from the mass of matter contained on a microscopic slide.

The finger of God; in Scripture, the power or work of God.

To burn one's fingers; see under *Burn*, v.t.

To have a finger in; to be interested in; to be implicated.

To have a finger in the pie; to have a share in any concern or act; to participate in the doing of anything.

To have at one's finger-ends or *finger-tips*; to be quite familiar with; to be able to make available readily.

fin'gẽr, *v.t.*, fingered, *pt.*, *pp.*; fingering, *ppr.* 1. To handle with the fingers; to touch lightly; to toy with; as, the covetous man delights to *finger* money.

2. To touch or take thievishly; to pilfer.

3. To play on, as a musical instrument; to mark (notes) for the guidance of the fingers in playing.

4. To perform with the fingers; to execute, as delicate manual work.

fin'gẽr, *v.i.* To touch an instrument, etc., with the fingers; to lay the hand on anything lightly, as in playing.

fin'gẽr-al"phȧ-bet, *n.* An alphabet, the letters of which are represented by positions and motions of the hands and fingers; also called the *deaf-and-dumb alphabet*. [See *Dactylology*.]

fin'gẽr-and-tōe', *n.* A popular name given to a disease, due to a fungus, which attacks the roots of cabbages and turnips, rendering them hard and inedible; called also *clubfoot*.

fin'gẽr-bär, *n.* A horizontal bar on a mowing or reaping machine, which carries the knives and the fingers between which they slide.

fin'gẽr-bōard, *n.* The keyboard of a piano or organ; the part of any stringed instrument upon which the strings are pressed by the fingers in order to change the pitch.

fin'gẽr-bōwl, *n.* A bowl or glass to contain water in which the finger-tips are laved at the conclusion of a meal; called also *finger-glass*.

fin'gẽr-breadth (-bredth), *n.* The breadth of a finger, as a measure of length; the fourth part of a palm or hand.

fin'gẽr-cor"ăl, *n.* A variety of coral, *Millepora alcicornis*.

fin'gẽred, *a.* 1. Possessing fingers.

2. In botany, with finger-like leaflets; digitate.

3. In music, (a) touched or played on, as a keyed, stringed, or holed instrument; (b) marked with figures showing what finger is to be used for producing each note; (c) produced by pressing the finger on a particular key, string, or hole, as a note.

fin'gẽr-ẽr, *n.* One who fingers; one who is light-fingered, meddling with or possessing himself of that which does not belong to him; a pilferer.

fin'gẽr-fẽrn, *n.* The common name of a variety of European plants of the fern family, especially spleenwort, *Asplenium Ceterach*.

fin'gẽr-flow"ẽr, *n.* The English foxglove, *Digitalis purpurea*; so called from its slender, tapering raceme of flowers.

fin'gẽr-gráss, *n.* A weed, *Panicum sanguinale*, bearing slender, digitate spikes; called also *crab-grass*.

fin'gẽr-ing, *n.* 1. The act of touching lightly or handling.

2. In music, the order of using the fingers, as on a keyboard; a notation on a piece of music showing the proper finger with which to strike each note.

3. Delicate work made with the fingers.

A shady, fresh, and ripply cove,
Where nested was an arbor, overwove
By many a summer's silent *fingering*.—Keats.

4. A coarse woolen yarn used in knitting stockings. [Eng.]

fin'gẽr-key, *n.* A thumbscrew or key by means of which an electric circuit may be opened and closed; a telegraph-key.

fin'gẽr-ling, *n.* 1. In zoölogy, the young salmon; a parr.

2. Anything no bigger than a finger.

fin'gẽr-märk, *n.* A mark, particularly a stain or smutch, left by a finger or thumb on a surface; an impression of the tip of a finger or thumb, as in wax, which may serve as a signature or mark of identification.

fin'gẽr-nut, *n.* In machinery, a nut having winglike projections which may be readily grasped by the fingers in turning.

fin'gẽr-pōst, *n.* A post set up for the direction of travelers, generally where roads cross or divide, and often with the figure of a hand and pointing finger on a projecting arm.

fin'gẽr-print, *n.* An impression made by a finger or thumb; particularly an impression made by the inside of the first joint of the finger now widely used for identification since its lineation varies with each individual and remains unchanged through life.

fin'gẽr-read"ing, *n.* A system of reading intended for the use of the blind, in which the reader's fingers are passed over letters raised from the surface of the paper so as to be distinguished by the sense of touch.

fin'gẽr-shell, *n.* A marine shell resembling a finger; the piddock.

fin'gẽr-shiēld, *n.* A shield worn on a finger when sewing to protect it from the needle or thread.

fin'gẽr-spŏnge, *n.* A name given to a variety of sponge which branches into finger-shaped lobes; called also *glove-sponge*.

fin'gẽr-stąll, *n.* A shield or cot of rubber, etc., to protect a finger from injury or infection.

fin'gẽr-steel, *n.* A small steel instrument upon which curriers sharpen their knives.

fin'gẽr-tip, *n.* The extremity of a finger; the most sensitive part of the hand.

fin'gi-ăn, *n.* See *Findjan*.

fin'gle-fan'gle, *n.* A trifle. [Colloq.]

fin'gri-gō, *n.*; *pl.* **fin'gri-gōş**. [Jamaica name.] A climbing plant of the genus *Pisonia*, whose fruit is a kind of berry or plum.

fin'i-ăl, *n.* [From L. *finis*, end.] The knot or bunch of foliage, or flower, that forms the upper extremities of pinnacles in Gothic architecture; sometimes, the pinnacle itself.

Finials.—1. Early English Period. 2. Perpendicular Period.

fin'i-căl, *a.* [From the adj. *fine*.] Overnice; spruce; foppish; pretending to great nicety or elegance; over-particular concerning trifles; as, a *finical* fellow.

Syn.—Spruce, foppish, fastidious, affected.—One who is *spruce* is elaborately nice in dress; one who is *finical* shows his affectation in language and manner as well as dress; one who is *foppish* seeks to distinguish himself by the cut of his clothes, the tawdriness of his ornaments, and the ostentation of his manner.

fin-i-cal'i-ty, *n.* 1. The state of being finical.

2. Something finical; finicalness. [Rare.]

fin'i-căl-ly, *adv.* In a finical manner; with extreme nicety.

fin'i-căl-ness, *n.* Extreme nicety in dress or manners; foppishness.

fin'ick-ing, *n.* The quality of being fastidious or of being exacting in trivial matters; fussiness.

fin'ick-ing, fin'ick-y, *a.* Same as *Finikin*.

fi-nif'iç, *a.* [L. *finis*, end, and *-ficus*, from *facere*, to make.] Setting a limit; making finite.

fin'i-fȳ, *v.t.* To make fine; to adorn. [Obs.]

fin'i-kin, *a.* [Compare M.D. *fijnkens*, precisely, exactly, neatly; *fijn*, fine, precise, and dim. *-ken*.]

1. Precise in trifles; idly busy; particular in reference to matters of dress or of the toilet.

2. Dainty; delicate; pretty; fine.

fin'i-kin, *n.* A sort of pigeon, with a crest somewhat resembling the mane of a horse.

fin'ing, *n.* 1. The process of refining or purifying; applied especially to the clarifying of wines, malt liquors, etc.

2. The preparation, generally a solution of isinglass or gelatine or white of egg, used to fine or clarify.

3. The process which cast-iron undergoes before puddling; finery.

4. The act of fixing a penalty.

fin'ing-fōrge, *n.* A refining-furnace.

fin'ing-pot, *n.* A vessel in which metals are refined.

fin'ing-rŏll"ẽr, *n.* A device in a paper-making machine that separates fine pulp from refuse.

fi'nis, *n.* [L.] An end; conclusion; a word placed on the last page of a book to mark its conclusion.

fin'ish, *v.t.*; finished (-isht), *pt.*, *pp.*; finishing, *ppr.* [ME. *finischen*, *finisshen*, from OFr. *finir* (stem of parts *finiss-*), from L. *finire*, to end, from *finis*, end, limit.]

1. To arrive at the end of; to complete; as, to *finish* the day; to *finish* a journey.

2. To bestow the last required labor upon; to perfect; to accomplish; to polish to a high degree, to elaborate carefully; as, to *finish* silver; to *finish* a house.

3. To bring to an end; to end; to put an end to; to disable; to render powerless; to kill; as, to *finish* an opponent. [Colloq.]

Syn.—Close, complete, end, conclude, perfect, terminate, cease, stop.

fin'ish, *v.i.* 1. To come to an end; cease; die.

2. To have done; to desist; to stop.

fin'ish, *n.* 1. That which concludes, terminates, or in any sense completes a thing.

2. The last touch to a work; the last working up of any object of art whereby it is perfected; polish; careful elaboration; as, a dull *finish*; a Roman *finish* on goldwork.

To us who write in a hurry for people who read in a hurry, *finish* would be loss of time. —Caird.

3. The end or completion of any act, movement, or progress, especially of a race or other contest; opposed to *start*, *beginning*, and *commencement*.

4. The woodwork and decorative cabinetwork which finishes the interior of a building; as, a billiard-room in dark oak *finish*.

Hard finish; the last, hard, smooth coat of plaster on a wall.

fin'ished (-isht), *a.* Complete; perfect; polished to the highest degree of excellence; as, a *finished* poem; a *finished* education; a *finished* diplomat.

fin'ish-ẽr, *n.* 1. One who or that which finishes; one who completely performs; one who perfects a piece of work, as the workman who completes an article or operation.

2. That which decides or terminates; that which puts an end to something; as, the rebuke was a *finisher*. [Colloq.]

fin'ish-ing, *n.* Completion; completeness; perfection; last polish; finish.

fin'ish-ing, *a.* Imparting a polish; marking completion; as, a *finishing*-school; a *finishing*-press; a *finishing*-tool.

fi'nite, *a.* [L. *finitus*, pp. of *finire*, to end, limit, bound, from *finis*, end, limit.] Having a limit; limited, bounded; opposed to *infinite*; as, *finite* number; *finite* existence; a *finite* being; *finite* duration.

fi'nite-less, *a.* Infinite; unbounded. [Obs.]

fi'nite-ly, *adv.* Within limits; to a certain degree only.

fi'nite-ness, *n.* The condition of being finite; limitation; confinement within certain boundaries; as, the *finiteness* of our natural powers.

fin'i-tūde, *n.* [From L. *finitus*, pp. of *finire*, to end, limit.] The state of being finite; limitation.

The fullness of the creation, and the *finitude* of the creature. —Chalmers.

Fin'land-ẽr, *n.* A native or inhabitant of Finland; a Finn.

fin'less, *a.* Destitute of fins; as, *finless* fish.

fin'let, *n.* A little fin; part of a divided fin, as in a mackerel.

fin'like, *a.* Resembling a fin; as, a *finlike* oar.

Finn, Fin, *n.* 1. A native of Finland; a Finlander; a member of the Finnic race.

2. [*pl.*] In ethnology, a branch of the Mongolian race, including the Finlanders, Bulgarians, Lapps, Magyars, Permians, Esthonians, Livonians, and various allied tribes of northern Russia and Scandinavia, Siberia, and Hungary.

fin'năn-had"dŏck, fin'năn-had"dle, *n.* Any smoked haddock; originally restricted to haddock cured in peat smoke at Findon (pronounced Fin'an), Scotland; spelled also *findon-haddock*.

finned, *a.* Having broad edges on either side; possessing a fin or fins.

fin'nẽr, *n.* Same as *Finback*.

Finn'iç, *a.* Pertaining to the Finns or the language spoken in Finland; Finnish.

fin'ni-kin, *n.* Same as *Finikin*.

Finn'ish, *a.* and *n.* I. *a.* Pertaining to the Finns or to their language; pertaining to Finland.

II. *n.* The language spoken by the Finns, called by themselves *Suomi*.

fin'ny, *a.* 1. Furnished with fins; as, the *finny* tribes; *finny* prey.

2. Containing, harboring, or abounding in fish; as, the *finny* brook; the *finny* deep.

fi-nō'chi-ō, *n.* [It. *finocchio*, from L. *feniculum*, fennel.] A variety of fennel, *Fœniculum dulce*, or sweet fennel, native to southern Europe.

fi'nōş, *n.pl.* [Sp., pl. of *fino*, fine.] A trade name for wool of the second grade from merino sheep.

fin'pike, *n.* Same as *Bichir*.

fint, *v.*, obsolete form of *findeth*. [See *Find*.]

fin'-tōed, *a.* Same as *Fin-footed*.

fiord, fjord (fyord), *n.* [Dan. and Norw. *fjord*, a frith, bay.] An inlet from the sea; a bay; usually long, narrow, and very irregularly shaped, such as are common on the coast of Norway; a frith.

fi′ō-rin, *n.* A species of creeping bent-grass, *Agrostis vulgaris*, of great value as a meadow-grass.

fi′ō-rite, *n.* [Named from Santa *Fiore*, in Tuscany, where it is found.] In mineralogy, a variety of opal occurring in volcanic rocks and formed by the decomposition of silicious minerals.

flō-ri-tū′rȧ, *n.*; *pl.* **flō-ri-tū′re.** [It., lit., flowering, flourishing.] Musical ornamentation; a musical flourish; commonly used in the plural.

fip′pence, *n.* A contraction of *fivepence.*

Fippenny bit; a fivepence; a colloquial name for a Mexican half real, worth 6¼ cents, or one-sixteenth of a dollar, which was in circulation in the southern states before the Civil War.

fip′ple, *n.* [Perhaps from L. *fibula*, a clasp, pin.] A stopper, as in a wind-instrument of music. [Obs.]

fir, *n.* [ME. *fir, fur, fyrre*; compare Dan. *fyr, fyrr*, and AS. *furh*, in *fuhr-wudu*, fir-wood.]

1. The name of several trees of the genus *Abies*, allied to the pines, from which they differ in their leaves growing singly on the stem, and the scales of the cones being smooth, round, and thin. The *firs* are almost all remarkable for the regularity of their growth, their tapering form, and the great altitude of their stems. Their timber is valuable, being universally used in the construction of buildings and for spars and masts of ships.

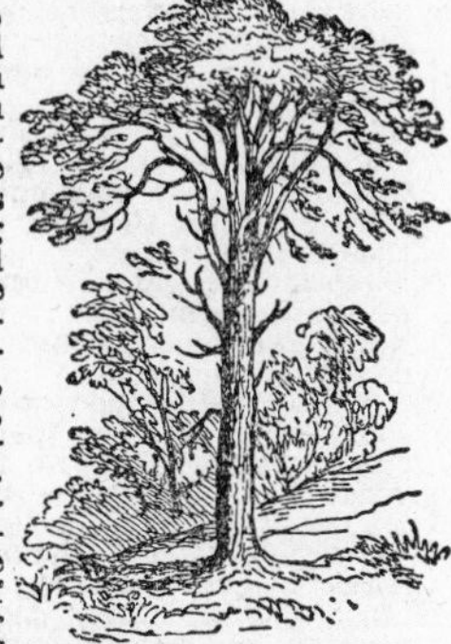

Scotch Fir (*Pinus sylvestris*).

2. A name applied to trees of genera allied to *Abies*, as *Pinus, Picea*, and *Tsuga*.

Among the more widely known species of *firs* are the following: the balsam-fir, *Abies balsamea*; the red fir, *Abies magnifica, Abies nobilis*, or *Abies amabilis*; the white fir, *Abies grandis*; the spruce-fir, *Picea excelsa*; the Scotch fir, *Pinus sylvestris*, and the hemlock-fir, *Tsuga Canadensis*.

fir′-cōne, *n.* The cone-shaped fruit of the fir-tree.

fire, *n.* [ME. *fire, fir, fyre*; AS. *fyr*, fire.]

1. The visible heat and light emanating from any body during the process of its combustion or burning.

2. Any combustible body in a state of ignition, or heated to a redness.

3. Fuel in a state of combustion, as in a stove, grate, or furnace, on a hearth, or on or in the ground; a mass of material lighted and burning for the sake of the warmth it affords, or for the use of its heat in cooking, etc.

> In winter's tedious nights sit by the *fire*
> With good old folks. —Shak.

4. The burning of a house or other building, or of a town, forest, etc.; as, a *fire* in a crowded block; the great *fire* of Chicago; a prairie *fire*.

5. Light; luster; splendor; as, the *fire* of a jewel.

> Stars, hide your *fires!* —Shak.

6. Ardor of passion, whether of love, hate, or anger; violence of passions; consuming violence of temper; as, the *fire* of love.

7. Liveliness of imagination; vigor of fancy; intellectual activity; animation; force of sentiment or expression.

> And warm the critic with a poet's *fire*.—Pope.

8. Torture by burning; hence, trouble; affliction; suffering; severe trial.

9. That which burns and inflames like *fire*; as, the *fire* of the fever burned without ceasing.

10. A spark or a shower of sparks struck out by a blow or friction upon hot iron or from stone.

11. The discharge or firing of firearms; as, to run into the *fire* of a masked battery; a soldier under *fire* for the first time.

Colored fires; the red, blue, green, or yellow flames which result from igniting a mixture of a mineral salt, as barium, copper, or sodium, with an easily combustible substance, as sulphur, niter, or the like.

Fire policy; a policy of insurance against fire.

Greek fire; see under *Greek*.

On fire; ignited; inflamed; burning; hence, eager; ardent; zealous.

Running fire; the discharge of firearms in rapid succession by one line of troops after another; hence, an uninterrupted succession, as of questions, remarks, or interjections.

St. Anthony's fire; a disease, marked by an eruption on the skin or a diffused inflammation, with fever; erysipelas.

St. Elmo's fire; a name given by seamen to a ball of electric light often observed, on dark nights, on the mastheads and yardarms, and along the rigging of a ship at sea.

To set on fire; to kindle; to inflame; to excite violent action in.

To take fire; to become ignited; to begin to burn; hence, to take violent offense; to become enraged; to fly into a passion.

Under fire; on the firing line; exposed to the enemy's fire; hence, in the course of being attacked; as, a politician *under fire*.

fire, *v.t.*; fired, *pt., pp.*; firing, *ppr.* [ME. *firen, fyren, furen*, to set on fire, expose to fire; AS. *fyrian*, to give warmth to.]

1. To set on fire; to kindle; as, to *fire* a house or chimney; to *fire* a pile.

2. To subject to the action of fire; to expose to an intense heat; to burn; as, to *fire* a brick-kiln; to *fire* a piece of china.

3. To inflame; to irritate the passions of; as, to *fire* a man with anger or revenge.

4. To animate; to give life or spirit to; as, to *fire* the genius.

5. To drive by fire. [Rare.]

6. To cause to explode; to discharge; as, to *fire* a rifle or cannon; to *fire* a torpedo.

7. In veterinary surgery, to cauterize.

8. To illuminate strongly; to make to shine as if on fire; to cause to glow; as, the setting sun *fired* the tree-tops.

9. To throw; to hurl; to fling; to turn out; to oust; to eject; as, to *fire* a stone through a window; to *fire* an employee. [Slang.]

10. To provide or supply fuel for; to feed a fire under; as, to *fire* a boiler; coal sufficient to *fire* a furnace during the winter.

To fire out; to eject or dismiss forcibly or peremptorily; to bounce; to expel. [Slang.]

fire, *v.i.* 1. To take fire; to be kindled.

2. To be irritated or inflamed with passion.

3. To discharge artillery or firearms; as, we *fired* on the enemy at daybreak.

4. To become heated, chafed, or inflamed.

To fire up; to become irritated or angry; to fly into a passion.

fire′-ȧ-lärm″, *n.* 1. A signal giving information of the discovery of a fire.

2. An apparatus for instantaneously communicating information of fire, as by telegraphic signal.

fire′-an-nī″hi-lā-tŏr, *n.* Any fire-extinguisher; especially, a device for smothering the flames with carbonic acid gas.

fire′ärm, *n.* Any weapon which expels the charge by the combustion of powder or other explosive, as a pistol, rifle, etc.

fire′-ar″rōw, *n.* A dart furnished with some inflammable substance, formerly used in warfare to start fires within an enemy's lines.

fire′back, *n.* 1. An Asiatic pheasant of the genus *Euplocamus*, having the plumage of its back of a fiery red color; a macartney.

2. The back wall of a fireplace or furnace.

fire′ball, *n.* 1. A grenade; a ball filled with powder or other combustibles, intended to be thrown among enemies, to injure them by its explosion.

2. An electrical phenomenon sometimes occurring in thunder-storms; globe-lightning.

fire′-bal-lo͞on″, *n.* 1. A balloon sent up with fireworks, which are timed to ignite at a certain height.

2. A balloon raised by means of rarefied air, heated by a fire beneath it.

fire′-bär, *n.* A bar in a grate or furnace, on which the burning coals lie.

fire′bāre, *n.* A beacon. [Obs.]

fire′-bas″ket, *n.* A portable grate or brazier in which to carry live coals; a cresset.

fire′-bee″tle, *n.* 1. A South American beetle, *Pyrophorus noctilucus*, which emits a brilliant phosphorescence from two fenestræ on the thorax; called also *cucujo*.

2. A firefly.

fire′-bird, *n.* A common name for the Baltimore oriole, *Icterus galbula*.

fire′-blȧst, *n.* A disease of plants and trees, in which they appear as if burnt by fire.

fire′-blight (-blīt), *n.* Same as *Pear-blight*.

fire′bōard, *n.* A chimney-board used to close a fireplace when not in use.

fire′bōte, *n.* An allowance of fuel to which a tenant of land is entitled.

fire′-box, *n.* In a locomotive, the chamber or box that contains the fire.

fire′brand, *n.* 1. A piece of wood kindled or on fire; a piece of any burning substance.

2. An incendiary; one who inflames factions or causes contention and mischief.

fire′-brick, *n.* A brick that will sustain intense heat without fusion; used for lining furnaces, etc.

fire′-bri-gāde″, *n.* A body of men organized to fight fires in any particular village, city, or district; as, a volunteer *fire-brigade*; a paid *fire-brigade*.

fire′-buck″et, *n.* A bucket to convey water for extinguishing fire.

fire′bug, *n.* An incendiary. [Colloq.]

fire′-clāy, *n.* A kind of clay that will sustain intense heat, used in making fire-bricks.

fire′-cŏm″pȧ-ny, *n.* 1. A company of men equipped with fire-fighting apparatus and organized to extinguish fires.

2. A company which insures property against loss by fire.

fire′crack″ẽr, *n.* A firework consisting of a paper cylinder inclosing powder, through which a fuse is passed, and exploding with a sharp report upon being ignited; used only for the sake of the noise of the explosion.

fire′crest, *n.* A small European bird resembling a wren, having a bright red crest; called also the *fire-crested wren* or *kinglet*.

fire′-cross, *n.* See *Fiery cross* under *Fiery*.

fire′-damp, *n.* Light carbureted hydrogen gas or marsh-gas, CH_4. It is sometimes very abundantly evolved in coal-mines, where it appears to be generated by the decomposition of partially carbonized coal. When it constitutes more than one-thirteenth of the volume of the atmosphere of mines, the whole becomes highly explosive when fire is brought in contact with it.

fire′dog, *n.* An andiron; an iron upright for supporting wood in a fireplace.

fire′drāke, *n.* [ME. *firedrake*; AS. *fyrdraca*; *fyr*, fire, and *draca*, a drake, dragon.]

1. A fiery dragon or serpent. [Obs.]

2. A meteor; an ignis fatuus; hence, a kind of firework which shoots into the sky.

3. One who toils in the glow of a furnace or fire. [Obs.]

fire′-drill, *n.* 1. The drilling of firemen with horses and apparatus for practice; the training of fire-brigades and fire-companies.

2. A drill of the occupants of a building, as of a school or factory, with the object of teaching them the best means of escape in case of fire.

3. A device in use among primitive peoples for producing fire by friction.

fire′-ēat″ẽr, *n.* 1. One who pretends to eat fire.

2. A hot-tempered, excitable, daring person; specifically applied, before the Civil War, to ardent supporters of the southern cause.

fire′-en″gine, *n.* An engine for throwing a continuous stream of water with the object of extinguishing a fire. The common pattern is mounted on wheels, to be drawn by two or three horses, and forces the water out through lines of hose. A chemical *fire-engine* is a large, mounted fire-extinguisher.

fire′-es-cāpe″, *n.* A structure, usually an iron ladder, with a platform at each story, to assist inmates in escaping from the upper part of a burning building.

fire′-ex-tin″guish-ẽr (-gwish-), *n.* A portable apparatus for use in extinguishing small blazes; it throws a stream of water or of water and carbon dioxid.

fire′-fanged, *a.* Dried up as by fire; specifically, applied to manure which has assumed a baked appearance from the heat evolved during decomposition.

fire′fish, *n.* A fish of the genus *Pterois*, having a red body and prominent pectoral and dorsal fins. It is found in East Indian waters.

fire′flāme, *n.* The red European band-fish.

fire′flāre, fire′flāire, *n.* The European sting-ray; also called *fiery-flare*.

fire′flaught (-flạt), *n.* [Scot.] 1. A flash of lightning, especially when unaccompanied by thunder; heat lightning; a gleam.

2. The aurora borealis.

fire′fly, *n.*; *pl.* **fire′flies.** A name indefinitely given to any winged insect which possesses much luminosity. With one exception, the *fireflies* are all coleopterous, and are members of either one of two nearly allied families, the *Elateridæ* and *Lampyridæ*. One of the most brilliant is *Pyrophorus noctilucus* of South America and the West Indies. Called also *glow-worm, cucujid*, etc.

fire′-gild″ing, *n.* A process of gilding with an amalgam of gold and quicksilver, the latter substance afterward being volatilized by heat, leaving a film of gilt.

fire′-gilt, *a.* Gilded by the process of fire-gilding.

fire′-guärd, *n.* A framework of iron wire, to be placed in front of a fireplace.

fire′hook, *n.* A large iron hook for pulling down burning structures, so as to prevent fire from spreading.

fire′-in-sur″ănce (-shụr″), *n.* The system whereby an owner of property is insured against loss by fire.

fire′-ī″rons (-ūrnz), *n.pl.* The irons belonging to a fireplace, as the shovel, tongs, poker, etc.

fire′-lēaves, *n.pl.* A name given in England to plantain-leaves and the leaves of several species of *Scabiosa*, which, if mixed with new hay, are believed to induce fermentation in it.

fīre′less, *a.* Without fire.

fīre′lock, *n.* A flintlock.

fīre′=māin, *n.* A pipe for water, to be resorted to in case of conflagration.

fīre′măn, *n.* 1. A man whose business is to extinguish fires; a member of an organized fire-company or fire-brigade.

2. A man who tends the fires of a steam-engine, either locomotive, marine, or stationary.

3. One whose special duty it is to examine a coal-mine before the workmen enter, to ascertain if fire-damp is present.

fīre′=mär″ble, *n.* Same as *Lumachelle.*

fīre′=mȧs″tēr, *n.* An officer of artillery, who superintended the composition of fireworks. [Obs.]

fīre′=new, *a.* Fresh from the forge; bright.

fīre′=of″fice, *n.* The business-office of a fire-insurance company. [Eng.]

fīre′=ō″păl, *n.* A variety of opal which reflects red and yellow lights.

fīre′=ọr″dē-ăl, *n.* An ancient method of determining the guilt or innocence of an accused person.

fīre′=pan, *n.* 1. A pan for holding or conveying fire.

2. In a flintlock, the receptacle for the priming-powder.

fīre′plāce, *n.* The part of a chimney which opens into an apartment and contains the fire; a hearth; a grate.

Section of Fireplace. 1. Slab. 2. Hearth. 3. Jamb. 4. Fireplace. 5. Mantelpiece. 6. Throat. 7. Gathering. 8. Funnel. 9. Flue. 10. Mantel. 11. Back. 12. Grate. 13. Breast. 14. Damper.

fīre′=plug, *n.* A hydrant through which a fire-engine draws water from a fire-main.

fīre′=pot, *n.* 1. A small earthen pot filled with combustibles, used in medieval warfare.

2. That part of a stove or furnace which contains the fire.

3. A portable soldering-furnace.

4. A crucible.

fīre′prọọf, *a.* That cannot be burned; constructed of incombustible materials; being of a nature to keep out fire; uninflammable; as, *fireproof* construction; *fireproof* paint.

fīre′prọọf″ing, *n.* Incombustible material employed to render a structure or substance fireproof; also, the process of making a thing uninflammable.

fīr′ēr, *n.* One who sets fire to anything; an incendiary.

fīre′=rȧft, *n.* A raft loaded with combustibles, used for setting fire to an enemy's ships by being floated among them when on fire.

fīre′=rōll, *n.* A signal, as the beating of a drum or ringing of a bell, to give warning on shipboard of the outbreak of a fire.

fīre′rọom, *n.* In a ship, the room or space before the furnace or furnaces, where the boilers are managed and the furnaces replenished; in England, called *stokehole.*

fīre′=set, *n.* A set of fire-irons with a holder.

fīre′=set″ting, *n.* A process formerly employed by miners for making an opening into a lode. After being heated, the rock was suddenly cooled by water, which caused it to crack open.

fīre′=ship, *n.* A vessel filled with combustibles and furnished with grappling-irons, to hook and set fire to an enemy's ships.

fīre′sīde, *n.* and *a.* I. *n.* A place near the fire or hearth; home; domestic life or retirement.

II. *a.* Belonging to the fireside or domestic circle; intimate; as, *fireside* friends; *fireside* studies.

fīre′stōne, *n.* 1. A name formerly given to iron pyrites because it strikes fire with steel.

2. A kind of sandstone which bears a high degree of heat; a stone which resists the action of the fire.

fīre′=sûr″fāce, *n.* The part of a steam-boiler that is exposed directly to the heat of the fire.

fīre′=swăb, *n.* A bunch of rope-yarn, secured to the tampion, and immersed in water to wet a gun and clear away any particles of powder which remain after firing.

fīre′tāil, *n.* 1. A common name in England for the redstart; also called *fireflirt* and *redtail.*

2. The ruby-tail, *Chrysis ignita;* the cuckoo-fly.

fīre′=trēe, *n.* 1. A New Zealand tree, *Metrosideros tomentosa,* which bears innumerable red flowers during the winter months.

2. A tree native to Australia, *Nuytsia floribunda,* more commonly called *flame-tree.*

3. A local name for the Queensland tulip-tree.

fīre′wārd, fīre′wārd″en, *n.* An officer who has authority to direct others in the extinguishing of fires.

fīre′=wa″tēr, *n.* The name by which the American Indians called the alcoholic liquor introduced to them by the white settlers; hence, any kind of ardent spirits.

fīre′weed, *n.* A coarse, strong-smelling annual plant, *Erechthites hieracifolia,* which grows abundantly on land that has been burned over.

fīre′wood, *n.* Wood for fuel.

fīre′wŏrk, *n.* 1. A preparation of gunpowder, sulphur, and other inflammable materials, used for making an explosion in the air, on occasions of public rejoicing or for public entertainment. The word is applied also to various combustible preparations used in signaling and in warfare.

2. [*pl.*] An exhibition of pyrotechnics; a display made by the setting off of various kinds of explosive devices.

fīre′wŏrm, *n.* 1. A glowworm.

2. A cranberry-vine worm, the larva of the cranberry leaf-roller.

fīre′=wŏr″ship, *n.* The worship of fire; particularly, worship of the sun as the most glorious visible object in the universe and also the source of light and heat. In the East, the worship of the element of fire was practised by the ancient Persians and is continued by the modern Parsees.

fīre′=wŏr″ship-ēr, *n.* One who worships fire or the sun; a Zoroastrian.

fīr′ing, *n.* 1. The act of discharging firearms.

2. The application of fire or of a cautery.

3. Fuel; firewood or coal.

4. The process of burning or vitrifying bricks, pottery, china, etc., by applying intense heat, as in a kiln.

5. The act of applying fire or of kindling a fire; particularly, the method employed in treating or caring for a fire, the addition of fuel, regulation of dampers, etc.

fīr′ing=ī″ron (-ūrn), *n.* An instrument used by veterinaries in cauterizing.

fīr′ing=pin, *n.* In some breech-loading guns, the pin which discharges the cartridge.

firk, *v.t.* To beat; to whip; to chastise. [Obs.]

firk, *v.i.* [ME. *ferken, firken,* to take off, carry off; AS. *fercian,* to bring or take away.] To spring; to go off or fly out suddenly. [Obs.]

firk, *n.* A freak; a trick; a whim. [Prov. Eng.]

fir′kin, *n.* [D. *vier,* four, and *-ken,* -kin.]

1. In England, a measure of capacity, being the fourth part of a barrel. As the barrels used for various commodities have varied in size, so the *firkins* have varied; the ale and beer *firkin* contains nine imperial gallons.

2. A small wooden vessel or cask of indeterminate size, used for butter, soap, etc.

fir′lot, *n.* [Scot.] A dry measure formerly used in Scotland. The Linlithgow wheat *firlot* was to the imperial bushel as 998 to 1000; the Linlithgow barley *firlot,* as 1456 to 1000.

fi̇rm, *a.*; *comp.* firmer; *superl.* firmest. [ME. *ferme;* OFr. *ferm,* from L. *firmus,* steadfast, strong.]

1. Fixed; closely compressed; compact; hard; solid; as, *firm* flesh; *firm* muscles; a cloth of *firm* texture.

2. Fixed; steady; constant; stable; unshaken; not easily moved; as, a *firm* believer; a *firm* friend; a *firm* adherent.

3. Steady; vigorous; as, to govern with a *firm* hand.

4. Giving evidence of strength and control; as, a *firm* voice; a *firm* grasp.

5. Determined; resolute; stated with distinctness; as, a *firm* refusal.

Syn.—Strong, robust, close-knit, stanch, steadfast, unyielding, tenacious, unfaltering, resolute, rugged, sturdy, steady.

fi̇rm, *n.* [LL. *firma,* a signature, subscription by which a writing was confirmed or rendered valid.] A partnership or association of two or more persons for carrying on a business; a commercial house; a concern; the name, title, or style under which a company transacts business.

fi̇rm, *v.t.*; firmed, *pt., pp.*; firming, *ppr.* [ME. *fermen;* OFr. *fermer,* from L. *firmare,* to make firm, strengthen, from *firmus,* steadfast, strong.]

1. To fix; to settle; to confirm; to establish. [Obs.]

> And Jove has *firmed* it with an awful nod.
> —Dryden.

2. To direct with firmness; to fix steadily upon. [Obs.]

3. To make solid or dense; as, to shovel earth into a hole and *firm* it.

fir′mȧ-ment, *n.* [OFr. *firmament;* L. *firmamentum,* a strengthening, support (LL., the firmament), from *firmare,* to strengthen, from *firmus,* strong, steadfast.]

1. The region of the air; the sky or heavens.

> And God said, Let there be lights in the *firmament.* —Gen. i. 14.

2. Established foundation; basis. [Obs.]

> Custom is the sanction or the *firmament* of the law. —Jer. Taylor.

3. A name given by the early astronomers to the orb of the fixed stars; the word has no place in modern astronomy.

fi̇r-mȧ-men′tăl, *a.* Pertaining to the firmament; celestial; being of the upper regions.

fir′măn, *n.* [Per. *farman,* a mandate, order.] A decree, order, or grant of an Oriental sovereign, as of Turkey, issued for various special purposes, as to insure a traveler protection and assistance; a passport, permit, license, or grant of privileges; written also *firmaun, firmand,* etc.

fi̇rm′ēr=chis″el, *n.* A carpenter's chisel, thin in proportion to its width; it is fastened to its handle by a tang.

fi̇rm′=foot″ed, *a.* 1. Having firm feet; standing firmly; not easily made to stumble or fall.

2. In zoölogy, having an uncloven foot, as the horse.

fi̇rm′i-tūde, *n.* [L. *firmitudo,* from *firmus,* steadfast, strong.] Strength; solidity. [Obs.]

fi̇rm′i-ty, *n.* [L. *firmitas,* from *firmus,* steadfast, strong.] Strength; firmness. [Obs.]

fi̇rm′less, *a.* 1. Detached from substance. [Obs.]

> Does passion still the *firmless* mind control?
> —Pope.

2. Shifting; unstable. [Obs.]

fi̇rm′ly, *adv.* 1. Solidly; compactly; closely; as, particles of matter *firmly* cohering.

2. Steadily; with constancy or fixedness; immovably; steadfastly; as, his resolution is *firmly* fixed.

fi̇rm′ness, *n.* 1. Closeness or denseness of texture or structure; compactness; hardness; solidity; as, the *firmness* of wood, stone, or cloth.

2. Stability; strength; as, the *firmness* of a union or of a federation.

3. Steadfastness; constancy; fixedness; as, the *firmness* of a purpose or resolution; the *firmness* of a man or of his courage; *firmness* of mind or soul.

4. Certainty; soundness; as, the *firmness* of notions or opinions.

Syn.—Constancy, faithfulness, fidelity.—*Firmness* belongs to the will and *constancy* to the affections and principles; the former prevents us from yielding and the latter from fluctuating.

fi̇rmṣ, *n.pl.* The largest rafters of a roof, which carry the heaviest weight. [Obs.]

fi̇rn, *n.* [G. dial. *firn, firne,* a glacier, lit., last year's snow.] The coarsely granular snow which will become ice as it moves downward in a glacier, below the line of perpetual snow.

> The imperfectly consolidated substance, partly snow and partly ice, is known in Switzerland as névé or *firn.* —Huxley.

fir′ringṣ, *n.pl.* In carpentry, same as *Furrings.*

fir′ry, *a.* Of or pertaining to firs; formed of fir; abounding in firs.

> And oft I heard the tender dove
> In *firry* woodlands making moan.—Tennyson.

fīrst, *a.* [ME. *first, fyrst, furst;* AS. *fyrst,* from *fore,* before, and superl. *-st, -est.*]

1. Advanced before or further than any other in progression; foremost in place; preceding all others in numbers or a progressive series; the ordinal of *one;* as, 1 is the *first* number.

2. Preceding all others in the order of time; as, Adam was the *first* man; George Washington was the *first* president.

3. Preceding all others in rank, dignity, or excellence; as, Demosthenes was the *first* orator of Greece.

At first blush; see under *Blush.*

First floor; (a) the ground floor; (b) in England and France, the story immediately above the ground-floor.

First mate; in the merchant service, the officer next to the captain.

First name; the Christian or given name.

First officer; same as *First mate.*

First sergeant; the senior or ranking sergeant of a company.

First watch; on shipboard, the watch from eight P. M. until midnight; also, the men who keep that watch.

First water; the first or highest quality; purest luster; applied to gems and principally to diamonds and pearls; as, a diamond of the *first water.*

Syn.—Aboriginal, earliest, highest, original, primary, primitive, pristine, primordial.

fīrst, *n.* 1. That which precedes all else; the beginning.

> I am Alpha and Omega, the beginning and the end, the *first* and the last.—Rev. xxii. 13.

2. The highest rank, or the one who holds the highest rank in an examination for honors; as, A took a *first* in mathematics.

3. In music, the voice or instrument which performs the leading or highest part in a chorus or orchestra.

4. In baseball, the first base.

At first, at the first; at the beginning, inception, or origin.

fīrst, *adv.* 1. Before anything else in the order of time.

> Adam was *first* formed, then Eve.
> —1 Tim. ii. 13.

2. Before all others in place or progression; as, let the officers enter the gate *first*.

3. Before anything else in order of proceeding or consideration; as, *first*, let us attend to the examination of the witnesses.

4. Before all others in rank; as, he stands or ranks *first* in public estimation.

First and last; altogether; throughout; entirely.

First or last; at one time or another; at the beginning or end.

First aid; more or less skilled emergency aid given by a layman to a sufferer before regular medical or surgical attention can be rendered.

first'born, *a.* and *n.* I. *a.* First brought forth; being the first child; hence, exalted above others; distinguished by particular prerogatives and favors.

II. *n.* The eldest child; the first in the order of birth.

first'-class, *a.* First-rate; of the highest excellence or quality. [Colloq.]

First-class carriage; in Europe, the best equipped railway carriage, for which the highest rate of fare is charged. Inferior to this in appointments, and cheaper, are the second-class and third-class carriages. This system is not in use in the United States. A similar distinction is made on ships between *first-class* and second-class cabins.

First'-day, *n.* The name given to Sunday by the Quakers and some other Christian bodies, from its being the first day of the week.

first'-fruit, *n.* 1. The fruit or produce first matured and collected in any season; generally used in the plural.

2. [*pl.*] The first profits of anything; specifically, (a) in old feudal tenures, one year's profit of the land after the death of a tenant, which was paid to the king; (b) in the Church of England, the income of every spiritual benefice for the first year, paid originally to the crown, but now to a board, which applies the money so obtained to the supplementing of the incomes of small benefices.

3. [*pl.*] The first or earliest effect of anything, in a good or bad sense; as, the *first-fruits* of grace in the heart; the *first-fruits* of vice.

first'-hand, *a.* Obtained direct from the first source, as the producer, maker, etc., and without the intervention of agents or intermediaries.

first'ling, *a.* First produced; as, *firstling* males.

first'ling, *n.* 1. The first produce or offspring; applied to beasts; as, the *firstlings* of cattle.

2. The thing first thought or done.

The very *firstlings* of my heart shall be
The *firstlings* of my hand. —Shak.

first'ly, *adv.* First; in the first place; before anything else; primarily; improperly used in place of *first*.

first'-rate, *a.* and *n.* I. *a.* 1. Of the highest excellence; preeminent; as, a *first-rate* scholar or painter.

2. Being of the largest size; as, a *first-rate* ship.

II. *n.* Anything classified as of the highest rank or excellence; the most powerful of its class; as, this battle-ship is a *first-rate*.

firth, *n.* Same as *Frith*.

fir'-tree, *n.* See *Fir*.

fisc, *n.* [Fr. *fisc*, from L. *fiscus*, a basket of rushes, money-bag, public chest.] The treasury of a prince or state.

fis'cal, *a.* [Fr. *fiscal*; LL. *fiscalis*, from L. *fiscus*, a basket of rushes, the state treasury.] Pertaining to the public treasury or revenue; financial.

fis'cal, *n.* 1. Revenue; the income of a prince or state.

2. A treasurer.

3. In Spain and Portugal, the king's solicitor; answering to an attorney-general.

4. An officer who conducts criminal proceedings on behalf of the state; in Scotland, called a *procurator-fiscal*.

fise'-dog, fice'-dog, *n.* A small dog; a pet. [See *Fice*.]

fi-set'ic, *a.* [From G. *fisetholz*, a kind of fustic, from *fiset*, fustic.] Relating to or derived from fustic; as, *fisetic* acid.

fis'e-tin, *n.* A yellow crystalline dyestuff obtained from the wood of *Rhus cotinus* or young fustic; also called *fisetic acid*.

fish, *n.*; *pl.* **fish'es** or collectively, **fish.** [ME. *fisch, fissh, fisc*; AS. *fisc*, fish.]

1. One of a division of vertebrate animals, breathing by means of gills which are permanent, and having fins. They have a heart with two cavities, cold blood, a naked skin covered only by scales, and an osseous or cartilaginous skeleton, the vertebræ of which are not grouped into regions, as in other vertebrates.

2. One of numerous animals whose life is spent entirely or partially in the water, distinguished from a land-animal, as certain cetaceans, crustaceans, mollusks, echinoderms, or batrachians.

3. [*sing.*] The flesh of fish, used as food.

4. The codfish; so called by way of distinction from other fish along the Massachusetts coast.

5. Pisces, the twelfth sign of the zodiac.

6. Nautically, (a) a purchase used to raise the flukes of an anchor up to the gunwale; a fish-tackle; (b) a long piece of timber used to strengthen a mast when sprung; the term is also used by joiners in a similar sense.

Age of fishes; in geology, the Devonian age.

Neither fish nor flesh; neither the one thing nor yet the other.

To have other fish to fry; to have other affairs engaging one; to have other or more important matters to engross one's attention.

fish, *v.i.*; fished (fisht), *pt.*, *pp.*; fishing, *ppr.* [ME. *fischen, fisshen, fissen*; AS. *fiscian*, to fish.]

1. To attempt to catch fish; to be employed in taking fish, by any means, as by angling or drawing nets.

2. To attempt or seek to obtain by artifice, or indirectly to seek to draw forth; as, to *fish* for compliments.

fish, *v.t.* 1. To search by raking or sweeping; to drag.

2. In seamanship, to strengthen, as a mast or yard, with a piece of timber.

3. To catch; to draw out or up; as, to *fish* up a cask; to *fish* an anchor.

4. To catch or take (fish) by any of the means employed; to take (fish) from any body of water or stream; as, to *fish* nothing but trout; to *fish* the Saguenay.

Fished beam; a beam consisting of two parts joined end to end by a fish-joint.

fish, *n.* A counter, used in various games.

fish'a-ble, *a.* Containing fish; being suitable for fishing, as being accessible and open to fishermen; as, the commissioners have opened the pond and it is now *fishable*.

fish'-ball, *n.* A fish-cake.

fish'-bär, *n.* A bar bolted over the joining of two steel rails. [See *Fish-joint*.]

fish'-beam, *n.* A beam which swells out, usually downward.

fish'-bel"lied, *a.* Shaped like a fish's body; swelling out convexly on the under side; as, a *fish-bellied* rail.

fish'ber-ry, *n.* The poisonous berry of *Anamirta paniculata* (*Cocculus Indicus*), used to stupefy fish and to permit their capture.

fish'-block, *n.* Same as *Fish-tackle*.

fish'bōne-tree, *n.* A small tree of New Zealand, *Panax crassifolium*, of the ginseng family, having deeply incised leaves; hence the name.

fish'-cāke, *n.* A small cake or ball of shredded fish, as codfish, mixed with potato, seasoned, and fried in hot fat; called also *fish-ball*, or *cod-fish-ball*.

fish'-cär, *n.* 1. A submerged cage in which live fish may be kept.

2. A railway-car fitted up with tanks in which living fish may be transported inland for food, or to stock natural waters.

fish'-cärv"ẽr, *n.* An instrument with a broad blade, in shape somewhat resembling a trowel, used to carve and serve fish; called also *fish-slice* and *fish-trowel*.

fish'-cul"tūre, *n.* The hatching and rearing of fish as an industry; the introduction of young fish into localities where their species was not previously found; pisciculture.

fish'-dav"it, *n.* A spar or iron davit with a block and tackle at the end, used in fishing the anchor.

fish'-dāy, *n.* A day when it is forbidden to eat flesh; a fast-day.

fish'-duck, *n.* Any merganser.

fish'ẽr, *n.* 1. One who is employed in catching fish.

2. A carnivorous quadruped of the weasel family; the pekan, *Mustela canadensis*. It is found in northern United States and Canada, where it burrows in the banks of streams and feeds on fish.

fish'ẽr-măn, *n.*; *pl.* **fish'ẽr-men.** 1. One whose occupation is to catch fish.

2. A ship or vessel employed in the business of taking fish, as in the cod and whale fishery.

fish'ẽr-y, *n.*; *pl.* **fish'ẽr-ies.** 1. The business of catching fish or marine products; as, the proceeds of this year's pearl *fishery* in Ceylon.

2. A place where fish are regularly caught, or where other products of the sea or rivers are taken from the water.

3. In law, the right to take fish at any particular place.

Common fishery; the right of taking fish from public waters.

fish'-fall, *n.* The tackle suspended to the fish-davit. [See *Fish-tackle*.]

fish'-flour, *n.* The flesh of fish, dried and powdered, often used in cookery.

fish'ful, *a.* Abounding with fish; as, a *fishful* pond. [Obs.]

fish'-fun"gus, *n.* 1. A red fungus, *Clathrocystis roseopersicina*, seen on salted codfish in warm weather.

2. A fungus, *Saprolegnia ferax*, which causes salmon-disease.

fish'-gärth, *n.* A garth or weir for the taking and retaining of fish; a fish-weir.

fish'gig, *n.* An instrument used for striking fish at sea, consisting of a staff with barbed prongs; spelled also *fizgig* and *fisgig*.

fish'-glūe, *n.* Isinglass, a substance prepared from the walls of the air-bladders of certain fish.

fish'hawk, *n.* The *Pandion haliaëtus*, the osprey, bald buzzard, or fishing-eagle. It feeds principally upon fish which it seizes from the water in its talons.

fish'hook, *n.* 1. A hook for catching fish.

2. The hook on the end of a fish-fall. [See *Fish-tackle*.]

fish'i-fȳ, *v.t.* To change to fish. [Rare.]

fish'i-ness, *n.* The state or quality of being fishy.

fish'ing, *a.* Used or employed in fishery, or by fishermen; as, *fishing*-boat; *fishing*-tackle; *fishing*-village.

fish'ing, *n.* 1. The art or practice of catching fish.

2. A fishery.

fish'ing-banks, *n.pl.* A comparatively shallow area in the sea much frequented by fishermen; specifically, the banks off Newfoundland.

fish'ing-duck, *n.* A fish-duck or merganser.

fish'ing-ēa"gle, *n.* The osprey.

fish'ing-flȳ, *n.* An artificial fly used by anglers in fly-fishing.

fish'ing-hawk, *n.* A fishing-eagle or osprey. [See *Fishhawk*.]

fish'ing-line, *n.* 1. A line used in fishing; a fish-line.

2. Any filamentous tentacle with which a marine animal, as a siphonophoran or a Portuguese man-of-war, reaches out after food.

fish'ing-net, *n.* See *Fish-net*.

fish'ing-smack, *n.* A sloop or similar vessel, manned by fishermen, and employed in sea-fishing, especially for cod along the New England coast and northward.

fish'ing-tūbe, *n.* A glass tube by means of which small particles are lifted from water.

fish'-joint, *n.* A splice consisting of one or more oblong plates, pieces of iron or wood, bolted to one or both sides of two rails or timbers meeting end to end.

fish'-ket"tle, *n.* A kettle of sufficient length to receive a whole fish.

fish'-lad"dẽr, *n.* See *Fishway*.

fish'like, *a.* Resembling fish; suggestive or characteristic of fish; fishy.

fish'-line, *n.* A line to which a hook is attached with which fish are taken.

fish'-louse, *n.* A name for various crustaceans of the order *Siphonostoma* or *Ichthyophthira*, as the genera *Argulus* and *Caligus*, parasitic on fishes.

fish'-maw, *n.* The air-bladder or sound of a fish.

fish'-mēal, *n.* 1. A meal consisting in part, at least, of fish, when flesh is either forbidden or not obtainable.

2. Same as *Fish-flour*.

fish'mŏn"gẽr, *n.* A vender of fish.

fish'-net, *n.* 1. A device, consisting in whole or in part of netting, used in the capture of fish. Nets are widely dissimilar in construction and in manner of using. [See *Dragnet, Seine, Purse-net*, and *Pound-net*.]

2. A curtain fabric of an open weave, similar to the net from which certain fish-nets are made.

fish'-oil, *n.* The oil yielded by the bodies of various marine fishes, as the cod, seal, whale, shark, crocodile, grampus, etc.

fish'-owl, *n.* A large Asiatic or African owl, belonging to the genus *Ketupa* or *Scotopelia*. It has rough feet like the fishhawk, which it also resembles in its manner of capturing fish.

fish'-pēarl, *n.* An artificial pearl of inferior quality, such as is manufactured in Germany.

fish'-plāte, *n.* One of the plates used in the construction of a fish-joint.

fish'-poi"sŏn, *n.* A name given to various berries and leaves which cause sickness, stupor, or even death in fish.

fish'-pot, *n.* A wicker cage or creel for catching lobsters, crabs, shrimps, etc.

fish'-pound, *n.* A fish-weir or pound-net. [Local.]

fish'-sauce, *n.* A sauce served with fish as an appetizing relish.

fish'skin, *n.* 1. The skin of a fish, especially of sharks, rays, etc., used in the arts under the name *shagreen*.

2. In medicine, ichthyosis; in the more severe and advanced stages called *porcupine-disease* or *hystricismus*.

fish'-slice, *n.* Same as *Fish-carver*.

fish'-slide, *n.* A fish-trap set across a current or below a small fall to catch fish in the descent; used principally in the southern states.

fish'-sound, *n.* The air-bladder or air-sac of a fish. *Sounds* are put to various commercial uses, those of the sturgeon being employed in the manufacture of isinglass, and those of the cod being used as food.

fish′=stō″ry, *n.* An extravagant, highly colored, or exaggerated story: a yarn; so called in reference to the propensity attributed to fishermen to exaggerate the size and weight of their catch. [Colloq.]

fish′=tac″kle, *n.* A tackle used for raising an anchor to the gunwale of a ship. To this tackle or fall is attached a large iron hook, called the *fish-hook*.

fish′=tāil, *a.* Shaped like a fish's tail, or resembling it in motion.

Fish-tail burner; a burner from which the blaze issues in the shape of a caudal fin or fish-tail.

Fish-tail propeller; a screw propeller at the stern-post which oscillates after the manner of a fish's tail.

fish′=trap, *n.* A trap used to capture fish. *Fish-traps* are of various shapes, all designed to prevent the fish from finding or passing through the opening by which it entered.

fish′=trow″el, *n.* Same as *Fish-carver*.

fish′wāy, *n.* An arrangement by which fish may ascend a waterfall or dam; also called *fish-ladder*.

fish′=wēir, *n.* Same as *Fish-garth*.

fish′wife, *n.*; *pl.* **fish′wives**. A woman who sells fish.

fish′wom″ăn (-wụm″), *n.* A fishwife.

fish′wood, *n.* The Jamaica dogwood or dogwood-tree, *Piscidia Erythrina*.

fish′y, *a.* 1. Consisting of fish.

2. Inhabited by fish; as, the *fishy* flood.

3. Having the qualities of fish; like fish; as, a *fishy* form; a *fishy* taste or smell.

4. Improbable; overdrawn; extravagant; incredible. [Colloq. See *Fish-story*.]

5. Applied to persons, worn out, as if by dissipation; effete; seedy; probably from the watery or dull appearance of the eyes. [Colloq.]

6. Applied to speculations, equivocal; unsafe; unsound; unreliable; slippery. [Colloq.]

fisk, *v.i.* [ME. *fisken*, to wander about, be in constant motion; Sw. *fjeska*, to fidget.] To run about. [Obs.]

fis′sāte, *a.* Deeply cleft; nearly split; marked by depressions or fissures, as the antennæ of some insects.

fis-si-. A combining form from L. *fissus*, cleft, used in anatomy and biology, to signify cleft; as, *fissi*dactyl, *fissi*gemmation.

fis-si-dac′tyl, fis-si-dac′tyle, *a.* [*Fissi-*, and L. *dactylus*, a finger.] Having the digits divided from one another and free.

Fis′si-dens, *n.* [*Fissi-*, and L. *dens*, *dentis*, a tooth.] A genus of mosses, with stems simple or nearly so, distichous leaves, and sixteen teeth in the peristome cleft to the middle.

fis″si-ġem-mā′tion, *n.* [*Fissi-*, and L. *gemmatus*, pp. of *gemmare*, to put forth buds.] In biology, a method of generation partaking both of gemmation or budding, and fission.

fis′sile, *a.* [L. *fissilis*, cleft, that may be cleft, from *fissus*, pp. of *findere*, to cleave, split.] That may be split, cleft, or divided in the direction of the grain or of natural joints.

This crystal is a pellucid *fissile* stone. —Newton.

fis-si-lin′gual (-gwăl), *a.* [*Fissi-*, and L. *lingua*, tongue.] Having a forked tongue, like a lizard.

Fis-si-lin′gui-ȧ (-gwi-), *n.pl.* [*Fissi-*, and L. *lingua*, tongue.] One of two divisions of the *Lacertilia* or lizards, having the tongue bifid and protrusile. The lizards, the monitors, the genus *Ameiva*, and some fossil genera belong to this section.

fis-sil′i-ty, *n.* [L. *fissilis*, that may be cleft, from *fissus*, pp. of *findere*, to cleave.] The quality of being cleavable.

fis′sion (fish′un), *n.* [L. *fissio* (-onis), from *fissus*, pp. of *findere*, to cleave, split.]

1. A breaking up into parts.

2. In biology, multiplication by means of a process of self-division, consisting of gradual division or cleavage of the body into two parts, each of which then becomes a separate and independent individual, as when a vegetable or animal cell undergoes spontaneous division, the divided parts again subdividing, or when an animalcule or polyp divides into two parts.

fis′sion=fun″ġi, *n.pl.* [L. *fissio*, a cleaving, and *fungus*, a mushroom, fungus.] Bacteria; any vegetable organism of the class *Schizomycetes*.

fis-si-pal′māte, *a.* [*Fissi-*, and L. *palma*, a palm.] Having the toes partially joined by a web; semipalmate.

fis-sip′ȧ-rȧ, *n.pl.* [*Fissi-*, and L. *parere*, to produce.] Animals which propagate by spontaneous cell-division.

fis-sip′ȧ-rism, *n.* A mode of reproduction in certain animals and vegetables, which break spontaneously into minute portions, each having a separate existence and growth.

fis-si-par′i-ty, *n.* Fissiparism.

fis-sip′ȧ-rous, *a.* [*Fissi-*, and L. *parere*, to produce.] In biology, reproducing by spontaneous cell-division.

fis-sip′ȧ-rous-ly, *adv.* By a fissiparous method; by fission or cell-division.

fis-si-pā′tion, *n.* Fissiparous reproduction.

fis′si-ped, *a.* [*Fissi-*, and L. *pes*, *pedis*, a foot.] Having separate toes; relating to the suborder *Fissipedia*.

fis′si-ped, *n.* An animal whose toes are separate or not connected by a membrane. [See *Fissipedia*.]

fis-sip′e-dăl, *a.* Same as *Fissiped*.

Fis-si-pē′di-ȧ, *n.pl.* [*Fissi-*, and L. *pes*, *pedis*, a foot.] A suborder of *Carnivora* having fissiped feet adapted for walking.

fis-si-ros′trăl, *a.* [*Fissi-*, and L. *rostrum*, a beak.] Belonging to the *Fissirostres*; characterized by a deeply-cleft bill, as swallows, goatsuckers, etc.

Fis-si-ros′trēs, *n.pl.* [*Fissi-*, and L. *rostrum*, a beak.] An artificial group of passerine birds distinguished by having the bill very wide, the gape being extended beneath the eyes, culmen short and curved to the top, and feet weak. It includes the swallows, goatsuckers, swifts, martins, etc.

Fissirostres.

fis′sūr-ăl (fish′ūr-) *a.* Relating to a fissure.

fis-sū-rā′tion, *n.* The act of dividing; the state of being divided by fissures.

fis′sūre (fish′ūr), *n.* [L. *fissura*, a cleft, chink, from *findere*, to cleave, split.]

1. A cleft; a narrow chasm made by the parting of any substance; a longitudinal opening; as, the *fissure* of a rock.

2. In surgery, a crack or slit in a bone, either transversely or longitudinally, by means of external force.

3. In anatomy, a deep, narrow sulcus or depression, as that dividing the anterior and middle lobes of the cerebrum on each side.

Fissure of Rolando; a deep fissure separating the frontal lobe of the cerebrum from the parietal lobe.

Fissure of Sylvius; a deep narrow sulcus or depression dividing the anterior and middle lobes of the cerebrum on each side.

fis′sūre, *v.t.*; fissured, *pt.*, *pp.*; fissuring, *ppr.* To cleave; to divide; to crack or fracture.

Fis-sū-rel′lȧ, *n.* [Dim. from L. *fissura*, a cleft, fissure.] A genus of gasteropodous mollusks resembling the limpets in appearance and habits, but differing considerably in structure. The keyhole-limpet belongs to this genus.

fis′sūre=nee″dle, *n.* A spiral needle with which the lips of a wound are sewed together.

fis′sūre=vein, *n.* A vein of ore deposited in a fissure; a true vein.

fist, *n.* [ME. *fist*, *fyst*, *fust*; AS. *fyst*, a fist.]

1. The hand closed; the hand with the fingers doubled into the palm.

2. The talons of a hawk, eagle, etc.

3. In printers' slang, a sign of a hand with index-finger extended (☞), used to call attention to the ensuing matter.

Hand over fist; see *Hand over hand* under *Hand*, n.

fist, *v.t.* 1. To strike with the fist.

2. To grip with the fist. [Rare.]

fist′ic, *a.* A word used colloquially, meaning pugilistic; as, *fistic* exploits; *fistic* heroes.

fist′i-cuffs, *n.pl.* Blows or a combat with the fist; a boxing.

fis′ti-nut, *n.* A pistachio-nut. [Obs.]

fis-tū′cȧ, *n.* [L., a rammer, beetle.] A kind of pile-driver formerly in use.

fis′tū-lȧ, *n.*; *pl.* **fis′tū-læ**. [L., a pipe, cane, ulcer.]

1. A reed; a pipe; a musical wind-instrument. [Obs.]

2. In surgery, a channel excavated between an internal part and the skin-surface, showing no tendency to heal, and generally arising from an abscess.

3. A gold or silver tube through which the communicants of the early church received the holy wine; still used by the pope; a calamus.

Complete fistula; a fistula having both an external and internal outlet; an *incomplete fistula* has but one opening.

Fistula lachrymalis; a fistula of the lachrymal sac, a disorder accompanied with the flowing of tears.

fis′tū-lăr, *a.* Hollow, like a pipe or reed.

Fis-tū-lā′ri-ȧ, *n.* [L. *fistula*, a pipe, cane, ulcer.]

Tobacco-pipe Fish (*Fistularia tabaccaria*).

1. A genus of fishes, characterized by a tube-like snout, with the mouth at the extreme end.

2. [f—] A fish of this genus.

fis-tū-lā′ri-oid, *a.* Relating to or characteristic of the genus *Fistularia*.

fis′tū-lāte, *v.i.* [L. *fistulatus*, pipe-shaped, furnished with a pipe, from *fistula*, a cane, pipe, ulcer.] To become hollow like a pipe or fistula. [Obs.]

fis′tū-lāte, *v.t.* To make hollow like a pipe. [Obs.]

fis′tūle, *n.* [Obs.] Same as *Fistula*.

fis′tū-li-fọrm, *a.* [L. *fistula*, a cane, pipe, ulcer, and *forma*, form.] Being in round, hollow columns, as a mineral.

Stalactite often occurs *fistuliform*.—Phillips.

Fis-tū-lī′nȧ, *n.* [Dim. from L. *fistula*, a cane, pipe, ulcer.] A genus of fungi, allied to *Boletus*, found on old oak, walnut, and chestnut trees, as also on ash and beech; it is much esteemed in some parts of Europe as an article of food.

fis′tū-lōse, *a.* Hollow; like a reed, as the leaves of the onion.

fis′tū-lous, *a.* 1. Having the form or nature of a fistula; as, a *fistulous* ulcer.

2. Hollow, like a pipe or reed.

fit, *n.* [ME. *fit*, *fyt*, *fytt*; AS. *fit*, a struggle, fight.]

1. The invasion, exacerbation, or paroxysm of a disease. The word applies to the return of an ague, after intermission; as, a cold *fit*; to the first attack, or to the return of other diseases; as, a *fit* of the gout or stone; and, in general, to a disease however continued; as, a *fit* of sickness.

2. A sudden and violent attack of disorder, in which the body is often convulsed, and sometimes senseless; as, a *fit* of apoplexy or epilepsy; hysteric *fits*.

3. Any short return after intermission; a turn; a period or interval; as, he moves by *fits* and starts.

By *fits* my swelling grief appears.—Addison.

4. A temporary affection or attack; as, a *fit* of melancholy or of grief; a *fit* of pleasure.

5. A blow; a stroke; thrust. [Obs.]

6. An irregular action; an unusual motion; an impulsive act; a caprice; a humor; as, a child's *fit*.

fit, *a.*; *comp.* fitter; *superl.* fittest. [ME. *fit*, *fitte*, *fytte*, meet, suitable.]

1. Suitable, convenient; meet; becoming; adapted for a certain end or purpose

Is it *fit* to say to a king, Thou art wicked? —Job xxxiv. 18.

2. Qualified; as, men of valor *fit* for war.

No man having put his hand to the plow, and looking back, is *fit* for the kingdom of God. —Luke ix. 62.

3. In good physical condition or excellent trim; especially, prepared by training for athletic sports. [Colloq.]

To see fit; to deem just, suitable, or proper.

Syn.—Proper, appropriate, expedient, congruous, correspondent, apposite, apt, adapted, prepared, competent, adequate, seemly, befitting, conformable.

fit, *v.t.*; fitted, *pt.*, *pp.*; fitting, *ppr.* 1. To adapt; to suit; to make suitable.

2. To accommodate with anything; to make of like proportions, so that one thing may join properly with another; to unite, as corresponding parts; as, to *fit* matched boards; to *fit* garments to the body.

3. To prepare; to put in order for; to furnish with things proper or necessary; as, to *fit* a ship for a long voyage; *fit* yourself for action or defense.

To fit out; to furnish; to equip; to supply with necessaries or means; as, *to fit out* a privateer.

To fit up; to prepare; to furnish with things suitable; to make proper for the reception or use of any person; as, *to fit up* a house for a guest.

fit, *v.i.* 1. To be proper or becoming.

Nor *fits* it to prolong the feast. —Pope.

2. To suit or be suitable; to be adapted; to be adjusted to the form or size required; as, his coat *fits* very well.

fit, *v.*, a form of the past tense and past participle of *fight*, now obsolete or used dialectically.

fit, *n.* The close and easy setting of an article; nice adjustment; adaptation, as of the dress to the body, or parts of machinery to each other.

fit, *n.* A foot; a step. [Scot.]

fit, fitt, *n.* [AS. *fitt*, a song.] A musical strain; a song, or part of a song; a canto. [Rare.]

fitch, *n.*; *pl.* **fitch′es**. The vetch. In the Bible, it is used in two senses; see Isaiah xxviii. 25-27 and Ezekiel iv. 9.

fitch, fitch′et, *n.* [D. *vitsche*, *fisse*, *visse*, a polecat.]

1. In zoölogy, the fitchew.

2. A fitch-brush.

3. The skin of the polecat. It is soft and

warm, but its offensive odor reduces its value.

fitch′-brush, *n.* A fine-pointed brush made from the hair of the fitch or polecat. A similar brush of hog's bristles is likewise called by this name.

fitch′é, fitch′ée (fich′ā), *a.* [Fr. *fiché*, pp. of *ficher*, to fix, drive in.] In heraldry, pointed; terminating in a point, as if sharpened; as, a cross *fitché*.

Cross fitché at the foot.

fitched (ficht), *a.* Same as *Fitché*.

fitch′ẽr, *v.i.*; fitchered, *pt., pp.*; fitchering, *ppr.* In mining, to so operate a drill that it shall stick in the bore-hole or become jammed, as in a wedge.

fitch′et, *n.* Same as *Fitch*, 1.

fitch′ew, *n.* [ME. *fitchew*, *fichew*; OFr. *fissiau*, *fissau*; D. *fisse*, *visse*, *vitsche*.] An English name for the European polecat or foulmart, *Putorius fœtidus*.

fitch′y, *a.* Same as *Fitché*.

fit′fụl, *a.* Irregular; spasmodic; capricious; not sustained but variable; as, a man of *fitful* temper; a *fitful* breeze.

fit′fụl-ly, *adv.* Irregularly; uncertainly; intermittently; as, the moon shone *fitfully* through the clouds.

fit′fụl-ness, *n.* The state of being fitful; uncertainty; capriciousness.

fith′el, *n.* [Obs.] See *Fiddle*.

fit′ly, *adv.* In a fit manner; properly.

fit′ment, *n.* Something adapted to a purpose; equipment; outfit; the state or act of being fitted. [Obs.]

fit′ness, *n.* 1. Suitableness; adaptedness; adaptation; as, the *fitness* of things to their use.

> If *fitness* of parts was what constituted the loveliness of form, the actual employment of them would undoubtedly greatly augment it. —Burke.

2. Propriety; meekness; justness; reasonableness; as, the *fitness* of measures or laws.

3. Preparation; qualification; as, a student's *fitness* for college.

4. Convenience; the state of being fit.

fit′-rod, *n.* In shipbuilding, an iron rod with a hook on one end, which is inserted into the holes made in a vessel's sides, in order to ascertain the required length of the bolts.

fit′tȧ-ble, *a.* Suitable; adaptable. [Rare.]

fit′ted-ness, *n.* The state of being fitted; fitness. [Rare.]

fit′tẽr, *n.* 1. One who makes fit or suitable; one who adapts; one who prepares; specifically, a workman who puts the parts of machinery together, in contradistinction to one who makes the parts.

2. In the tailor's trade, one who shapes and fits a garment to the figure.

3. A coal-broker who sells the coal produced by a particular mine. [Eng.]

The word is frequently combined in compounds indicating the specialized sense in which the term is used; as, steam-*fitter*, gas-*fitter*, dress-*fitter*, coat-*fitter*, etc.

fit′tẽr, *n.* A fragment; a flinder; a rag; a flitter. [Obs.]

fit′ting, *a.* Suitable; fit; appropriate; becoming.

fit′ting, *n.* Anything employed in fitting up permanently; used generally in the plural, in the sense of fixtures, apparatus, equipment; as, school *fittings*; steam *fittings*.

fit′ting-ly, *adv.* Suitably.

fit′ting-ness, *n.* The state of being suitable or appropriate.

Fit-tō′ni-ȧ, *n.* [Named after Sarah and Elizabeth *Fitton*, of England.] In botany, a genus of herbaceous plants of the acanthus family, native to Peru. They are cultivated for the beauty of their gaily colored foliage.

fit′weed, *n.* The name of a plant of the genus *Eryngium*, so called because considered a powerful remedy for hysteria.

fitz (fits), *n.* [OFr. *fiz*, *filz*, *fils*, a son.] A son; more especially applied to the illegitimate offspring of a king, royal prince, or great noble; as, *Fitz*roy, the son of the king; *Fitz*james, the son of James.

five, *a.* [ME. *five*, *fif*; AS. *fif*, five; L.G. *fif*; O.H.G. *finf*; Sw. *fem*; W. *pump*; L. *quinque*; Gr. *pente*; Lith. *penki*; Sans. *pancha*, five.] Four and one added; the half of ten; as, *five* men. It is used in numerous self-explaining compounds in the sense of being of the number of, consisting of, or participated in by *five*.

Five nations; in American history, the Mohawks, Oneidas, Onondagas, Senecas, and Cayugas, otherwise known as the Iroquois Confederacy. With the return of the Tuscaroras, they constituted the league known as the Six Nations, so much involved in the early history of New York State.

five, *n.* 1. The number which consists of four and one; the number of fingers and thumb on one hand.

2. A character symbolizing this number; as, 5 or V.

five′fin″gẽr, *n.* 1. A species of cinquefoil.

2. [*pl.*] A popular name for a starfish.

five′fōld, *a.* and *adv.* In fives; consisting of five in one; five-double; five times repeated.

five′lēaf, *n.* Cinquefoil; fivefinger; five-fingered grass.

five′ling, *n.* A compound crystal composed of five individual parts.

fives, *n.pl.* 1. A kind of play with a ball against the side of a building, resembling tennis; so named because three *fives* or fifteen are counted to the game.

2. The hand, so called from the number of the fingers and thumb; the fist. [Slang.]

fīves, *n.* A corruption of *vives*.

fives′-cōurt, *n.* 1. A place where the game of fives is played.

2. A hall or gymnasium where sparring matches occur. [Slang.]

five′-twen′ty, *a.* and *n.* I. *a.* Relating to the bonds known as five-twenties.

II. *n.* [*pl.*] Bonds issued by the United States government between 1862 and 1865, bearing six per cent interest, to be redeemed at any time after the lapse of five years, and payable in twenty years.

fix, *v.t.*; fixed (fixt), *pt., pp.*; fixing, *ppr.* [Fr. *fixer*, from LL. *fixare*, freq. of L. *figere*, to fix, fasten, drive in.]

1. To make stable; to attach or secure immovably; to establish; to set permanently; to give definiteness or security to; as, the law *fixes* the status of a minor.

2. To make fast; to confine; to fasten; to restrain from free movement or removal; as, to *fix* a tail to a kite; *fix* a thing so that it will not slip.

3. To set or direct steadily; to fasten intently; as, he *fixed* his attention upon the subject; he *fixed* his eyes upon the judge.

4. To transfix; to pierce. [Obs.]

5. In photography, to give permanence to the image on (a plate or film) by removal of the superfluous salts of silver in a bath of hyposulphite of soda.

6. To transform from a fluid state to a solid; to make stable; to render less volatile; to act upon by some agent, as cold, heat, or, in the case of dyes, a mordant. Figuratively, to give definite form or expression to; to give permanence to; as, to *fix* a dream upon canvas; to *fix* a happy fancy.

7. To put in order; to prepare; to adjust; to set or place in the manner desired or most suitable; as, to *fix* clothes or dress; to *fix* the furniture of a room. In this sense *fix* is somewhat general in application and loose in meaning, being colloquially applied to a wide range of acts. It is often called an Americanism.

fix, *v.i.* 1. To rest; to settle or remain permanently; to cease from wandering.

> Your kindness banishes your fear,
> Resolved to *fix* forever here. —Waller.

2. To become firm, so as to resist volatilization; to cease to flow or be fluid; to congeal; to become hard and malleable, as a metallic substance.

To fix on; to settle the opinion or resolution on anything; to determine on; as, the legislature *fixed on* a place for a state prison.

fix, *n.* 1. An embarrassing or difficult position; a dilemma; a trying situation; a plight. [Colloq.]

2. In iron foundries, the material used to line the hearth of a puddling furnace. In England, called *fettling*.

fix′ȧ-ble, *a.* That may be fixed, established, or rendered firm.

fix′āte, *v.t.*; fixated, *pt., pp.*; fixating, *ppr.* [LL. *fixatus*, pp. of *fixare*, freq. of L. *figere*, to fix, fasten.] To fix; to settle and remain in one condition or station.

fix-ā′tion, *n.* 1. The act of fixing.

2. Stability; firmness; steadiness; a state of being established; as, *fixation* in matters of religion.

3. That firm state of a body which resists evaporation or volatilization by heat; as, the *fixation* of gold or other metals.

4. The act or process of ceasing to be fluid and becoming firm; state of being fixed; specifically, in chemistry, that process through which a gaseous body passes on becoming fixed or solid on uniting with a solid body.

5. In microscopy, the process of preparing material for imbedding and sectioning; it results in killing the material in a normal state, also in hardening it against injury by reagents.

fix′ȧ-tive, *n.* 1. Anything which serves to render colors permanent and unfading, as a mordant.

2. A solution sprayed upon charcoal drawings which fixes them and prevents rubbing.

3. In microscopy, (a) any fluid used in fixation of microscopic material; (b) Mayer's albumen for attaching microscopic sections to the slide; it consists of white of egg, 50 c.c.; glycerin, 50 c.c.; salicylate of soda, 1 gram.

fixed (fixt), *a.* Settled; established; firm; fast; stable.

Fixed air; an old name for carbonic acid gas.

Fixed alkalis; potash, soda, and lithia, in contradistinction to ammonia, which is termed volatile alkali.

Fixed ammunition; see *Ammunition*.

Fixed bodies; those which bear a high heat without evaporation or volatilization.

Fixed capital; see *Capital*.

Fixed force; a force inherent in a body itself, as gravitation or cohesive force.

Fixed light; a light emitting steady radiance, not one which sparkles, flashes, or diminishes and increases by turn.

Fixed oils; such as remain in a permanent state, and are not readily volatilized; so called in distinction from *volatile oils*.

Fixed stars; such stars as always retain the same apparent position and distance with respect to each other.

fix′ed-ly, *adv.* Firmly; in a settled or established manner; steadfastly.

fix′ed-ness, *n.* 1. A state of being fixed; stability; firmness; steadfastness; as, *fixedness* of opinion on any subject.

2. The state of a body which resists evaporation or volatilization by heat; as, the *fixedness* of gold.

fix-id′i-ty, *n.* Fixedness. [Obs.]

fix′ing, *n.* 1. The act or process of rendering permanent.

2. That which is fixed or permanent; a fixture.

3. [*pl.*] Furnishings; arrangements; ornaments or accompaniments; anything provided for use; as, household *fixings*. [Colloq.]

fix′i-ty, *n.* Fixedness; unchanging or stable character; coherence of parts; that property of bodies by which they resist dissipation by heat.

fix′tūre, *n.* 1. That which is fixed or attached to something as a permanent appendage; as, the *fixtures* of a pump; the *fixtures* of a farm.

2. Fixedness; firmness; stable state.

3. In law, anything of an accessory character annexed to real property, which, immediately on annexation, becomes part of the realty. No hard and fast rule can be given for the determination of what is and what is not a fixture in law. A thing may be a fixture in certain circumstances and not under others, there being more or less ambiguity in the meaning of the term.

4. A person who has been so long in the same place, as a resident or occupant of a situation, that it is difficult to remove him; as, in former days servants frequently became *fixtures* in families.

fix-ū′ræ, *n.pl.* [Pl. of LL. *fixura*, a fastening.] The filamentous processes on the under surfaces of thalloid plants by means of which they adhere; rhizoids.

fix′ūre, *n.* [LL. *fixura*, a fastening, from L. *figere*, to fasten, fix.] Position; stable pressure; firmness. [Obs.]

fiz′gig, *n.* 1. A fishgig.

2. A gadding flirting girl.

3. A kind of firework, made of damp powder, which gives a hissing or fizzing noise when ignited.

fizz, *v.i.*; fizzed, *pt., pp.*; fizzing, *ppr.* To make a hissing sound. [See *Fizzle*.]

fizz, fiz, *n.* 1. An imitative name given to a hissing or sputtering sound.

2. Anything light and frothy, as champagne or effervescent water, from the sound it makes when uncorked. [Colloq.]

fiz′zle, *n.* [Onomatopoetic; in the first signification probably from the fizzing sound made by a combustible which does not explode instantaneously like gunpowder, but hangs fire.]

1. An ineffectual effort; a failure; an abortive attempt.

2. A restless or excited condition; a state of extreme agitation; stew; ferment; as, to be in a *fizzle* over a delay.

fiz′zle, *v.i.*; fizzled, *pt., pp.*; fizzling, *ppr.* 1. To fizz; to sputter; to produce a sound similar to that made by liquid poured from a small-necked bottle.

2. To come to naught; to result in ignominious failure; to prove a fiasco; to stop short of completion; often followed by *out*. [Colloq.]

fjeld, *n.* A sterile table-land in Scandinavia; also spelled *field*.

fjord (fyord), *n.* Same as *Fiord*.

flab′bẽr-gast, *v.t.*; flabbergasted, *pt., pp.*; flabbergasting, *ppr.* To surprise; to amaze; to daze or render speechless. [Colloq.]

flab″bẽr-gas-tā′tion, *n.* The condition of being flabbergasted; a state of utter confusion or bewilderment. [Colloq.]

flab′bi-ly, *adv.* In a flabby manner.

flab′bi-ness, *n.* A soft, flexible state of a substance, which renders it easily movable and yielding to pressure.

flab′by, *a.*; *comp.* flabbier; *superl.* flabbiest. [A variant of *flappy*, from *flap*, to hang loose.] Soft; yielding to the touch, and easily moved or shaken; easily bent; hanging loose by its own weight; opposed to *muscular* and *firm*; as, *flabby* flesh.

flā′bel, *n.* [L. *flabellum*, a fan, dim. of *flabra*, breezes, from *flare*, to blow.] A fan.

flȧ-bel′lāte, *a.* In biology, having the form of a fan.

flab-el-lā′tion, *n.* In surgery, the act of keeping fractured limbs and the protective dressings cool, as by the use of an electric fan.

flȧ-bel′li-fọrm, *a.* [L. *flabellum*, a little fan, and *forma*, form.] Having the form of a fan; fan-shaped.

flȧ-bel′li-nẽrved, *a.* [L. *flabellum*, a little fan, and *nervus*, nerve.] In botany, having numerous nerves branching in a flabellate manner from a point, as the base of a leaf or petal.

flȧ-bel′lum, *n.*; *pl.* **flȧ-bel′lȧ.** [L., a little fan.]

1. A fan; specifically, an ecclesiastical fan formed of feathers, ivory, metal, or other

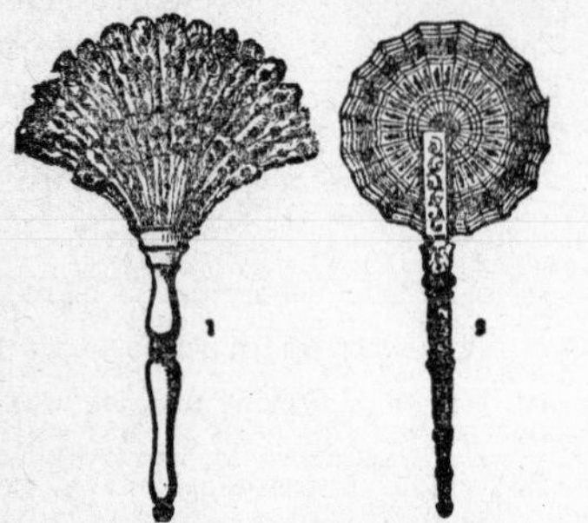

1. Papal Flabellum. 2. Liturgical Flabellum.

material, carried before the pope and certain other dignitaries on state occasions.

2. In zoölogy, a flabellate organ; (a) an epipodite, a part attached to the maxilliped of certain crustaceans; (b) same as *serrula.*

flab′ile, *a.* [L. *flabilis*, airy, from *flare*, to blow.] Liable to be wafted about. [Obs.]

flag′cid, *a.* [L. *flaccidus*, from *flaccus*, flabby.] Soft and weak; limber; lax; drooping; hanging down by its own weight; yielding to pressure for want of firmness and stiffness; as, a *flaccid* muscle; *flaccid* flesh.

flac-cid′i-ty, *n.* [From L. *flaccidus*, flabby, flaccid.]

1. Same as *Flaccidness.*

2. A disease of silkworms caused by the presence of bacteria.

flag′cid-ly, *adv.* In a flaccid manner.

flag′cid-ness, *n.* Laxity; limberness; want of firmness or elasticity.

flache-riē′, *n.* [Fr.] Same as *Flaccidity*, 2.

flack′ẽr, *v.i.* To flutter as a bird. [Prov. Eng.]

flack′et, *n.* [ME. *flaket*, *flaget*, from OFr. *flasquet*, *flachet*, dim. of *flasque*, *flache*, a flask.] A bottle in the form of a barrel.

flȧ-çon′, *n.* [Fr.] A small glass bottle fitted with a screw-top.

Fla-çōur′ti-ȧ, *n.* [Named after Etienne de *Flacourt*, a French traveler.] The type genus of the order *Flacourtiaceæ*, being a genus of small trees or shrubs, having spinose branches and bearing edible fruit. In Asia and Africa, where they are native, various species are cultivated as hedge-plants, or for their fruit, wood, or medicinal properties.

flaff, *v.t.* and *v.i.* To flap; to flutter; to crack, as when blown by the wind. [Scot.]

flag, *n.* [Of D. or Scand. origin; D. *vlag*; Sw. *flagg*; Dan. *flag*, a flag.]

1. An ensign or colors; a standard borne on a staff, displaying a device or a field of a particular color which serves to distinguish one company, party, or nation from another.

Flags are commonly made of bunting, silk, or similar light-weight fabric, rectangular, square, or triangular in shape, attached to a staff or stick along one edge, by an end if of a rectangular shape, and vary in size according to the use to which they are to be put. The designs or letters which distinguish them may be woven, printed, appliqué, painted, or formed by piecing together bits of colored fabrics.

2. The bushy tail of certain hunting-dogs, as of any of the breeds of setters.

3. The tuft of feathers growing around the legs of most falcons and hawks.

4. A bird's wing. [Obs.]

Black flag; see under *Black.*

Flag at half-mast; a flag hoisted some distance below the top of the staff, as a sign of recent death or mourning.

Flag of distress; a flag hoisted reversed, that is, with the canton or union down, as a signal of distress.

Flag of truce; a white flag displayed as an invitation to the enemy to confer, and in the meantime as a notification that the fighting shall cease. It is held in peculiar honor among all civilized peoples, and the violation of its privileges is held to be a nefarious crime.

Red flag; a flag having a plain red field, employed, (a) as a danger-signal; (b) as a challenge; (c) by anarchists, as a symbol of revolution and bloodshed.

Service flag; the flag used in the United States during the World War consisting of a white field with red border and as many blue stars in the field as men from the house or organization displaying the flag enlisted in the service, military or naval, of the United States, a gold star replacing the blue for the men killed in the service.

To dip the flag; to salute by lowering the flag and immediately returning it to place. It is done in token of courtesy, welcome, or respect.

To strike or *lower the flag*; to pull it down as a sign of surrender; figuratively, to capitulate; to signify a desire to make terms.

Yellow flag; the sanitary or quarantine flag. Displayed over a vessel, it indicates the presence of contagion on board; during hostilities, it marks a field-hospital and protects it from the enemy's fire. Over a boat, building, or tent, it may indicate nothing beyond the presence of a quarantine officer.

flag, *n.* [Early modern Eng. *flagge*; ME. *flegge*; Dan. *flæg*, a flag.] A popular name for many endogenous plants with sword-shaped leaves, mostly growing in moist situations; particularly appropriated to plants of the genus *Iris.*

Cooper's flag; the common cattail, or cattail-flag, *Typha latifolia*, used by coopers to render tight the seams of barrels.

flag, *v.i.*; flagged, *pt.*, *pp.*; flagging, *ppr.* 1. To hang loose without stiffness; to bend down, as flexible bodies; to be loose and yielding; as, the *flagging* sails.

2. To grow spiritless or dejected; to droop; to grow languid; as, the spirits *flag.*

3. To grow weak; to lose vigor; as, the strength *flags.*

4. To become dull or languid.

flag, *v.t.* 1. To let fall into feebleness; to suffer to droop; as, to *flag* the wings.

2. To make feeble; to enervate; to exhaust.

flag, *v.t.* 1. To designate by raising a flag over; to hoist a flag over; as, two trading-boats had already been *flagged.*

2. To signal by means of a flag or something used as a flag; to give warning to; to give notice to by waving.

3. In hunting, to decoy, as game, by waving a bright object to which they are attracted, and which they approach out of curiosity.

flag, *n.* [Ice. *flaga*, a slab of stone, lit., a flake.]

1. A flat stone used for paving, or a pavement of flat stones.

2. In geology, evenly stratified sandstone, such as splits naturally into thin layers.

flag, *v.t.* To lay with flat stones; to pave with flags.

flag′=cap″tain (-tin), *n.* The chief of staff commanding under an admiral; a fleet captain.

flag′el-lănt, *n.* [L. *flagellans* (*-antis*), ppr. of *flagellare*, to whip, scourge.] One who whips himself as a means of religious discipline; specifically, [F—] one of a fanatical sect which arose in Italy, A. D. 1260, who maintained that flagellation was of equal virtue with baptism and the other sacraments. They walked in procession, with shoulders bare, and whipped themselves till the blood ran down their bodies.

Flagellant, from Amman's "Habitus (Rom.) Ecclesiæ".

flȧ-gel′lăr, *a.* Pertaining to a flagellum.

Flag-el-lā′tȧ, *n.pl.* [L., neut. pl. of *flagellatus*, pp. of *flagellare*, to whip, scourge.] An order of *Infusoria*, characterized by long cilia like lashes or flagella, either distributed over the body, or grouped, as at the anterior extremity.

flag′el-lāte, *v.t.*; flagellated, *pt.*, *pp.*; flagellating, *ppr.* [L. *flagellatus*, pp. of *flagellare*, to whip, scourge, from *flagellum*, a whip, scourge.] To whip; to scourge; to lash, as with a flagellum.

flag′el-lāte, *a.* 1. Having the form of a flagellum.

2. Pertaining to the *Flagellata.*

flag-el-lā′tion, *n.* A beating or whipping; a flogging; the discipline of the scourge.

flag′el-lā-tõr, *n.* [LL., from *flagellare*, to whip, scourge.] One who punishes or scourges with a lash.

flag-el-lif′ẽr-ous, *a.* [L. *flagellum*, a whip, scourge, and *ferre*, to bear.] In biology, having flagella.

flȧ-gel′li-fọrm, *a.* [L. *flagellum*, a whip, and *forma*, form.]

1. Slender like a whiplash; tapering and pliant.

2. In botany, formed like a flagellum or runner.

flȧ-gel′lū-lȧ, *n.*; *pl.* **flȧ-gel′lū-læ.** [Dim. from L. *flagellum*, a whip.] In biology, a spore having one or more flagella; a monad.

flȧ-gel′lum, *n.*; *pl.* **flȧ-gel′lȧ** or **flȧ-gel′lums.** [L., a whip, scourge.]

1. A whip used for self-punishment; a scourge.

2. In botany, (a) a weak, creeping branch sent out from the bottom of the stem, and giving off at its extremity leaves and roots; a runner; (b) a whiplike extension bearing undeveloped leaves, found in certain of the *Hepaticæ.*

Strawberry Plant (*Fragaria vesca*). *a*, Flagellum.

3. In zoölogy, a lashlike appendage exhibited by many infusorians; an appendage to the legs of some crustacea, having some resemblance to a whip, and used as a locomotory organ; an elongated cilium.

4. In entomology, the distal portion of a jointed antenna, or all of the antenna beyond the basal joint.

flag′eō-let, *n.* [OFr. *flageolet*, dim. of *flageol*, *flajeol*, a pipe, flute, dim. from LL. *flauta*, a flute.] A small wind-instrument of music, played on by means of a mouthpiece inserted in a bulb. The tone produced is similar to that of the piccolo, but is softer in quality, and the range is two octaves. The double *flageolet* consists of two instruments united by one mouthpiece, and producing two-part music.

flag′eō-let=tōnes, *n.* In music, the name given to those harmonic tones on the violin, violoncello, and other stringed instruments, produced by the finger lightly touching the string on the exact part which generates the harmony, and not by pressing the string down to the fingerboard.

flag′gi-ness, *n.* Laxity; limberness; want of tension.

flag′ging, *n.* 1. The act of laying with flagstones.

2. A pavement or sidewalk of flagstones.

flag′ging, *a.* Weak; languid.

flag′ging-ly, *adv.* Weakly; languidly.

flag′gy, *a.* 1. Weak; flexible; limber; not stiff.

2. Weak in taste; insipid; as, a *flaggy* apple.

3. Abounding with the semiaquatic plant, called flag or iris.

4. Like a flag or banner, in any sense, as broad or waving.

flag′i-tāte, *v.t.* To importune; to demand imperiously; to urge imperatively. [Rare.]

flȧ-gi′tious (-jish′us), *a.* [L. *flagitiosus*, from *flagitium*, a shameful or disgraceful act; *flagitare*, to demand, demand fiercely.]

1. Deeply criminal; grossly wicked; villainous; atrocious; scandalous; as, a *flagitious* action or crime.

2. Guilty of enormous crimes; corrupt; wicked; as, a *flagitious* person.

3. Marked or infected with scandalous crimes or vices; as, *flagitious* times.

Syn.—Shameful, corrupt, flagrant, villainous, atrocious, profligate, felonious, abandoned, iniquitous, execrable.

flȧ-gi′tious-ly, *adv.* With extreme wickedness.

flȧ-gi′tious-ness, *n.* Extreme wickedness; villainy.

flag′=lieū-ten″ănt, *n.* An officer who serves under an admiral in a capacity similar to that of an aide-de-camp to a general.

flag′măn, *n.*; *pl.* **flag′men.** 1. A man stationed at a grade crossing to flag trains and warn passers-by of the danger.

2. Formerly, a flag-officer.

flag′=of″fi-cẽr, *n.* A general name applied to any naval officer in command of a fleet, of rank entitling him to display his flag. An admiral carries his flag on the mainmast, a vice-admiral on the foremast, and a rear-admiral on the mizzenmast.

flag′ŏn, *n.* A vessel with a spout and a cover, used for holding and conveying liquors.

flā′grăn-cy, *n.*; *pl.* **flā′grăn-cies.** 1. A burning; great heat; inflammation. [Obs.]

Lust causeth a *flagrancy* in the eyes.—Bacon.

2. Excess; enormity; as, the *flagrancy* of a crime.

flā′grănt, *a.* 1. Glowing; red; flushed; hence, burning; ardent; eager; as, *flagrant* desires. [Obs.]

See Sappho at her toilet's greasy task,
Then issuing *flagrant* to an evening mask.
—Pope.

2. Happening at the present time; now going on.

3. Flaming into notice; glaring; notorious; enormous; as, a *flagrant* crime.

flā′grănt-ly, *adv.* Ardently; notoriously; in a flagrant manner or to a flagrant extent.

flā′grāte, *v.t.* [L. *flagratus*, pp. of *flagrare*, to burn.] To burn. [Obs.]

flȧ-grā′tion, *n.* A burning or conflagration. [Obs.]

flag′=rōōt, *n.* The root of the sweet-flag, *Acorus Calamus*. It has a pungent, aromatic flavor.

flag′=shāre, *n.* The share due to a flag-officer of all prize-money captured by ships under his command.

flag′ship, *n.* The ship which bears the commanding officer of a squadron, and on which his flag is displayed.

flag′staff, *n.* A staff from which a flag flies.

flag′=stā″tion, *n.* A station on a railway-line at which trains do not stop unless flagged.

flag′stōne, *n.* 1. Any fissile sandstone which splits up into flags.

2. A flat stone, such as is used in paving; a flag.

flag′wŏrm, *n.* A worm or grub found among flags and sedge.

flāil, *n.* [ME. *flail*, *flayle*, *flegl*; OFr. *flæl*, *flaiel*; Pr. *flagel*, from L. *flagellum*, a whip, scourge, LL., a flail.]

1. A wooden instrument for threshing or beating grain from the ear by hand, consisting of a staff joined to the swingle or swiple which beats the grain, by a strap, rope, or other device.

2. An ancient military weapon resembling the common *flail*, but having the striking part strengthened with an armor of iron or rows of spikes.

flāil′=stōne, *n.* A stone implement found among paleolithic remains which appears to have formed a part of a flail-shaped weapon. [See *Morning-star*.]

flāil′y, *a.* Resembling a flail in shape or action. [Obs.]

flāin, *v.*, obsolete past participle of *flay*.

flāir, *n.* [ME. *flayre*; OFr. *flair*, odor, from *flairer*, to emit an odor, from L. *flagare*, to emit an odor.]

1. Odor; savor; smell. [Obs.]

2. Keen sense of smell; scent; used literally as a term in hunting, and figuratively, in the sense of discrimination or power of selection.

flāke, *n.* [ME. *flake*, *fleke*, *fleyke*; Ice. *flaki*, a hurdle, a shield of wickerwork for defense.]

1. A light rack or platform, as (a) a scaffold of interwoven hurdles supported from below, used for drying fish, smoked meat, etc.; (b) a staging hung over the side of a vessel for use of a painter or calker.

2. A fence made of slabs; a hurdle. [Prov. Eng.]

flāke, *n.* [ME. *flake*; Norw. *flak*, a slice, a piece torn off; Sw. *flaga*, a flake, flaw.]

1. A thin chip or scale of a substance, commonly one coming off in layers; an indefinite mass; lamina; film; fleck; layer; as, a *flake* of stone, coal, or snow.

2. A collection or small particle of fire or of combustible matter on fire, separated and flying off.

3. A white carnation streaked the whole length of the petals with a color.

4. One turn of a coiled cable; a fake.

flāke, *v.t.*; flaked (flākt), *pt.*, *pp.*; flaking, *ppr.* To form into flakes.

flāke, *v.i.* To break or separate in layers; to peel or scale off.

flāk′ẽr, *n.* 1. A workman who chips flint into flakes.

2. In archæology, an instrument of bone used to shape flint arrowheads.

flāke′=feath″ẽr (-feth″), *n.* A down-feather, very fine and growing in tufts; a plumule.

flāke′=knife (-nīf), *n.* A knife used by Indians made of a chip of flinty stone.

flāke′=stand, *n.* The cooling-tub for the worm of a still.

flāke′=white, *n.* 1. The purest white-lead, in the form of scales or plates, sometimes gray on the surface. After grinding or levigation, it is called body-white.

2. Basic nitrate of bismuth, or pearl-white.

flāk′i-ness, *n.* The state of being flaky.

flāk′y, *a.* 1. Consisting of flakes or locks or small, loose masses.

2. Lying in flakes; consisting of layers or cleaving off in layers.

flam, *n.* 1. A freak or whim; also, a falsehood; a lie; an illusory pretext; deception; delusion.

2. In music, written for the drum, an appoggiatura or grace-note.

flam, *v.t.*; flammed, *pt.*, *pp.*; flamming, *ppr.* To deceive with falsehood; to delude.

flam-bé′ (floṅ-bā′), *a.* [Fr., pp. of *flamber*, to flame, singe.] In ceramics, having an iridescent luster imparted by the action of the kiln-heat on the glaze.

flam′beau (flam′bō), *n.*; *pl.* **flam′beaux (-bōz).** [Fr., from L. *flamma*, a flame.]

1. A flaming torch; formerly one made of thick wicks covered with wax, designed to be carried at night in illuminations, processions, and the like.

2. An ornamental candlestick of large size.

3. A large kettle used for boiling sugar; it is exposed directly to the flames.

flam-boy′ănt, *a.* [Fr., ppr. of *flamber*, to flame.]

1. Bombastic; showy; not evincing good taste; extravagant.

2. A term applied to that style of Gothic architecture in France which was contemporary with the Perpendicular style in Great Britain. Its chief characteristic is a wavy, flame-like tracery in the windows; whence the name.

3. Blazing; flaming.

4. Having a wavy edge, similar to a flame; said of a sword.

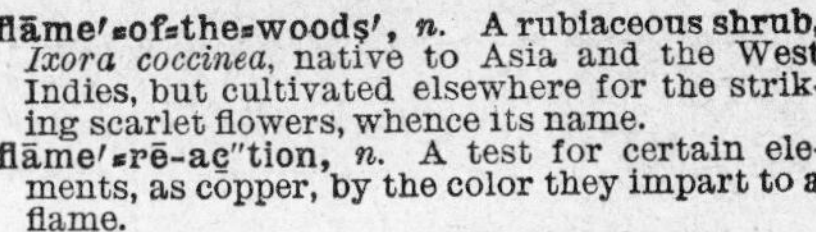

Flamboyant Window, Church of St. Ouen, Rouen.

flāme, *v.i.*; flamed, *pt.*, *pp.*; flaming, *ppr.* [ME. *flamen*, *flamben*, *flaumben*; OFr. *flamber*, *flamer*, from L. *flammare*, to flame, blaze, kindle, inflame, from *flamma* a flame.]

1. To burn; to be on fire; to stream forth, as vapor or a body undergoing combustion.

2. To shine or glow as with a flame; flash; as, her cheeks *flamed*.

3. To break out; to rush forth; to burst forth, as in violence of passion.

flāme, *v.t.* To inflame; to excite. [Obs.]

flāme, *n.* [ME. *flambe*, *flaume*, *flaumbe*; OFr. *flame*, *flambe*, from L. *flamma*, a flame, from *flagrare*, to burn.]

1. A stream of vapor or gas undergoing combustion and giving forth light; a blaze; fire. A candle-flame may be considered as divided into three zones: an inner zone containing chiefly unburned gas, another zone containing partially burned gas, and an outer zone where the gas is completely consumed by combination with the oxygen of the air. The luminosity of flame depends upon the presence of solid matter or of dense gaseous products of combustion.

2. Strong zeal; burning passion; noble enthusiasm; a carrying away of the mind by passion, excitement, or anger.

3. Ardor of inclination; warmth of affection; the passion of love; ardent love.

4. One beloved; as, she was my first *flame*. [Colloq.]

5. In heraldry, fire; being usually represented by the tincture red surrounding or being breathed by the salamander, phenix, and the like.

6. The flash of a school of herrings. [Eng.]

7. The moth, *Anticlea rubidata*. [Eng.]

König's flames; manometric flames.

Oxidizing flame; the tip of the flame issuing from a blowpipe capable of oxidizing metals. It is nonluminous and contains an excess of oxygen at a very high temperature.

Reducing flame; the inner luminous portion of the flame issuing from a blowpipe, which will reduce compounds to the metallic state.

flāme′=bridge, *n.* A partition in a fire-chamber, nearly as high as the bottom of the boiler, leaving but a small space through which all the flame and heated gases must pass to the flues.

flāme′=cell, *n.* A cell in which the excretory canal of any flatworm terminates, and into which project minute cilia having a vibratory movement.

flāme′=chām″bẽr, *n.* A space behind the fire-bridge in a furnace to complete the combustion of the gases given off by the fuel.

flāme′=cŏl″ŏr, *n.* Bright color, as that of flame.

flāme=cŏl″ŏred, *a.* Of the color of flame; of a bright yellow color.

flāme′=en″gine, *n.* A former name for the gas-engine.

flāme′flow″ẽr, *n.* A species of the genus *Kniphofia*, or *Tritoma*, native to South Africa. It is a liliaceous plant, having long, grassy leaves, and a raceme of red flowers which change to yellow. Called also *red-hot poker*.

flāme′less, *a.* Destitute of flame.

flāme′let, *n.* A little flame; a single tongue of flame.

flā′men, *n.* [L.] In ancient Rome, a priest devoted to a particular god. Originally there were three priests so called: the *Flamen Dialis*, consecrated to Jupiter; *Flamen Martialis*, sacred to Mars, and *Flamen Quirinalis*, who superintended the rites of Quirinus or Romulus.

flā′men-ship, *n.* The rank or dignity of a flamen.

flāme′=of=the=woods′, *n.* A rubiaceous shrub, *Ixora coccinea*, native to Asia and the West Indies, but cultivated elsewhere for the striking scarlet flowers, whence its name.

flāme′=rē-ac″tion, *n.* A test for certain elements, as copper, by the color they impart to a flame.

flāme′=tree, *n.* 1. The Australian fire-tree.

2. The *Sterculia acerifolia* of Australia, so called from its brilliant red flowers.

flȧ-min′ē-ous, *a.* [L. *flaminius*, from *flamen*, a priest.] Relating to the person or dignity of a flamen; flaminical.

flām′ing, *a.* 1. Giving forth fire or flames; blazing; illuminating.

2. Brilliant; dazzling; flame-colored; showy red.

3. Passionate; marked by ardency and strong zeal.

flām′ing-ly, *adv.* Most brightly; with great show or vehemence.

flȧ-min′gō, *n.* [Port. *flamingo*, *flamengo*; Sp. *flamenco*; Pr. *flammant*, properly ppr. of *flamar*, to flame, blaze.] One of a genus of tropical birds called *Phœnicopterus*. The beak is naked, toothed, and bent as if broken; the neck and legs are very long; the feet have the three front toes palmated to the end, and the hind one extremely short. When in full plumage, they are almost entirely red.

flȧ-min′gō=plant, *n.* A tropical plant of the arum family, *Anthurium Scherzerianum*, cultivated for the beauty of its brilliant scarlet flowers.

Flȧ-min′i-ăn, *a.* Relating to Caius Flaminius, a Roman censor, or to the public works which were constructed under his censorship.

flȧ-min′i-căl, *a.* Pertaining to a Roman flamen.

flam-mȧ-bil′i-ty, *n.* Inflammability. [Obs.]

flam′mȧ-ble, *a.* Capable of being enkindled into flame. [Obs.]

flam-mā′tion, *n.* The act of setting aflame. [Obs.]

flam′mē-ous, *a.* [L. *flammeus*, from *flamma*, a flame.] Consisting of flame; like flame. [Obs.]

flam-mif′ẽr-ous, *a.* [L. *flammifer*; *flamma*, a flame, and *ferre*, to bear.] Producing flame. [Obs.]

flam-miv′ō-mous, *a.* [L. *flammivomus*; *flamma*, a flame, and *vomere*, to vomit.] Vomiting flames, as a volcano. [Rare.]

flam′mū-lā-ted, *a.* [L. *flammula*, dim. of *flamma*, a flame.] Having a red tinge; ruddy; said of the plumage of birds.

flām′y, *a.* 1. Blazing; burning; as, *flamy* breath.

2. Having the nature of flame; as, *flamy* matter.

3. Having the color of flame.

flaṅ, *n.* [Fr.] An unstamped coin; a blank.

flan, *v.i.*; flanned, *pt.*, *pp.*; flanning, *ppr.* To make flaring, as a dish or the jamb of a window. [Prov. Eng.]

flanch, *n.* [A softened form of flank.]

1. In mechanics, a flange.

2. In heraldry, a flanched bearing.

flanched (flancht), *a.* In heraldry, having a segment of a circle encroaching on each side of a field.

flaṅ-çō-nāde′, *n.* [Fr., from *flanc*, flank, side.] In fencing, a thrust aimed at the side of the opponent.

flȧ-ne-riē′, *n.* [Fr.] That which characterizes a flaneur.

flȧ-nėūr′, *n.* [Fr., a lounger, loiterer, from *flâner*, to lounge.] One who idly saunters without destination or aim; a lounger; a stroller; as, a *flaneur* of the boulevards.

flang, *n.* In mining, a two-pointed pick.

flange, *n.* [A corruption of *flanch*, which is a softened form of *flank*.]

1. A raised or projecting edge, rib, or rim for strength, as in a T-rail; for guidance, as on a rail to keep wheels in place; for connection with some other object, as in some pipes; and for many other uses, as ornament, etc.

2. A band, ring, or plate which forms a ridge or rim when attached to a pipe.

Blank or *blind flange*; a plate used to close an opening, as a cylinder-head or the end of a pipe.

flange, *v.t.* and *v.i.*; flanged, *pt.*, *pp.*; flanging, *ppr.* I. *v.t.* To form a flange on; to provide with a flange.

II. *v.i.* 1. To extend outward; to flare.

2. To be in the form of a flange.

flanged, *a.* Provided with a flange.

flange′=joint, *n.* A joint formed by the union of two flanges, as when two flange-pipes are bolted end to end.

flange′=pipe, *n.* A pipe having a flange at each end to form connections; piping of which each length has such flanges.

flan′gẽr, *n.* 1. One who or that which makes flanges.

2. A device or machine for removing snow from the inside of a rail; used in cleaning railway tracks.

flange′=rail, *n.* A rail provided with an edge or flange on one side to keep the wheel on the track.

flange'-wheel, *n.* Any wheel flanged on one or both edges of the tread to prevent its slipping from the rail.

flank, *n.* [ME. *flank, flawnk,* the flank; OFr. *flanc;* LL. *flancus,* the side, flank; O.H.G. *hlanca, lanka,* loin, flank, side.]

1. The fleshy or muscular part of the side of an animal, between the ribs and the hip.

2. In entomology, the lateral surface of the thorax of an insect.

3. The side of an army, or of any division of an army, as of a brigade, regiment, or battalion; the extreme right or left; thus, to attack in *flank* is to attack on the side.

4. In fortification, that part of a bastion which reaches from the curtain to the face, and defends the opposite face, the *flank,* and the curtain; a line drawn from the extremity of the face toward the inside of the work.

5. In architecture, the side of any building.

6. The straight part of the tooth of a gear-wheel which receives the impulse.

7. That portion of the hide of an animal that covered its *flank.*

8. [*pl.*] In farriery, any wrench or injury in the back of a horse.

Flank en potence; a portion of an army's wing formed at an angle with it for protection.

Flank file; in military tactics, the first row on the right or the last row on the left of a body of soldiers formed for marching or on the march.

Flank march; a march in the general direction of the enemy, with the object of turning his line or attacking on the flank.

Flank movement; a movement of troops to turn the flank of an enemy or to execute a flank attack.

Flank patrols; patrols moving parallel to and in advance of the flanks of an army for the purpose of reconnoitering and observing the movements of the enemy.

Flanks of a frontier; points of eminent importance in a boundary line, such as are fortified against hostile invasion.

flank, *a.* Relating to the side or flank; as, a *flank* steak; a *flank* attack; a *flank* company.

flank, *v.t.;* flanked (flankt), *pt., pp.;* flanking, *ppr.* 1. To form a border of; to be on the side of; as, rocks *flank* the road.

2. To attack the side or flank of, as an army or body of troops; to place (troops) so as to command or attack the flank.

3. To post so as to overlook or command the side of; as, to *flank* a passage.

4. To turn the flank of; to pass round the side of.

flank, *v.i.* 1. To border; to touch.

2. To be posted on the side.

flank'ēr, *n.* 1. A fortification projecting so as to command the side of an assailing body; a body of troops guarding an army's flanks.

2. In driving game, one who beats along the side to keep the quarry within bounds.

flank'ēr, *v.t.* 1. To defend by lateral fortifications or flankers. [Obs.]

2. To attack sidewise. [Obs.]

flan'nel, *a.* Made or consisting of flannel.

flan'nel, *n.* [OFr. *flannelle,* perhaps from *flaine,* a pillow-case, feather-bed.] A soft, nappy, woolen cloth, of loose texture.

Adam's flannel; the common mullen.

Canton or *cotton flannel;* a firm cotton fabric, generally having a long silky nap on one side.

Flannel cake; a kind of griddlecake.

flan'neled, *a.* Covered or wrapped in flannel.

flan'nel-flow''ēr, *n.* 1. The common mullen, *Verbascum Thapsus.*

2. The *Macrosiphonia longiflora,* a tropical vine of the dogbane family, having leaves of a flannel-like texture and long tubular flowers.

flan'nen, *a.* and *n.* [Obs.] See *Flannel.*

flap, *n.* [ME. *flap, flappe,* a stroke, blow, a loose, flexible part of a garment; D. *flap,* a stroke, blow on the ear.]

1. Anything broad and limber that hangs loose or is easily moved; as, the *flap* of a coat.

2. The motion of anything broad and loose, or a stroke with it; as, the *flap* of a bird's wings.

3. A portion of flesh or skin left after an operation intended to cover the end of a bone or to form a new part.

4. [*pl.*] A disease in the lips of horses.

flap, *v.t.;* flapped, *pt., pp.;* flapping, *ppr.* [ME. *flappen,* to flap, slap; D. *flappen,* to flap; prob. imitative in origin.]

1. To beat with a flap.

> Yet let me *flap* this bug with gilded wings. —Pope.

2. To swing or sway; to move with a clapping sound; as, a stiff breeze *flapped* the sails.

flap, *v.i.* 1. To move, as wings, or as something broad or loose.

2. To fall, as the brim of a hat or other broad thing.

flap'drag''ŏn, *n.* 1. A sport formerly practised in England and Holland in which the players snatched in their mouths from burning liquor raisins, plums, etc., and swallowed them without injury.

2. The thing thus caught and eaten.

flap'drag''ŏn, *v.t.* To swallow or devour quickly; to snatch and swallow at a single gulp, as a player at flapdragon.

flap'-eared, *a.* Having broad, loose ears.

flap'jack, *n.* A sort of broad pancake; a batter cake baked on a griddle over the fire and turned in tossing it up, so that it falls upon the pan with a flap.

flap'pēr, *n.* 1. One who or that which flaps.

2. A young bird or waterfowl before it is able to fly, so called from its habit of flapping its wings without rising in the air.

3. A pert, ultra-modern young woman. [Colloq.]

4. A limb used in swimming; a flipper.

flap'pēr-skāte, *n.* A name given in Great Britain to various species of ray.

flap'-tile, *n.* A tile so bent up as to form an angle or a trough.

flap'-valve, *n.* A hinge-valve; a valve that flaps when it closes.

flāre, *v.i.;* flared, *pt., pp.;* flaring, *ppr.* [Compare Norw. *flara,* to blaze, flame, adorn with tinsel; Sw. dial. *flasa,* to burn furiously.]

1. To waver; to flutter; to burn with an unsteady light; as, the candle *flares.*

2. To flutter with splendid show; to be loose and waving, as a showy thing.

> With ribbons pendant *flaring* 'bout her head. —Shak.

3. To glitter with transient luster.

4. To glitter with painful splendor.

> When the sun begins to fling
> His *flaring* beams. —Milton.

5. To be exposed to too much light. [Obs.]

> I cannot stay
> *Flaring* in sunshine all the day. —Prior.

6. To open or spread outward.

To flare up; to become highly excited quickly.

flāre, *v.t.* To cause to flame unsteadily or to burst out in flashes; hence, to display or exhibit ostentatiously.

flāre, *n.* 1. A broad, unsteady light; a glare.

2. A spreading from within outward; a broadening; the part of anything which spreads out or widens.

3. Display; ostentation; pageantry.

4. In photography, a blemish on a developed plate; an optical ghost.

flāre, *n.* A flake or leaf of lard.

flāre'-up, *n.* 1. A sudden shooting up and spreading, as of a flame.

2. A sudden display of anger. [Colloq.]

flār'ing, *a.* 1. Burning with a wavering light; fluttering; glittering; showy.

2. Opening or widening outward; as, a *flaring* fireplace.

flār'ing-ly, *adv.* Flutteringly; showily.

flash, *v.i.;* flashed (flasht), *pt., pp.;* flashing, *ppr.* [ME. *flaskien, vlaskien,* to pour, sprinkle; Sw. dial. *flasa,* to burn furiously.]

1. To break forth, as a sudden flood of light; to burst or open instantly on the sight, as splendor.

2. To burst or break forth with a flood of flame and light; as, the powder *flashed* in the pan.

3. To burst out into any kind of violence.

> Every hour
> He *flashes* into one gross crime or other. —Shak.

4. To break out, as a sudden expression of wit, merriment, or bright thought; to exhibit transient brilliance.

5. To move rapidly; as, the train *flashed* by.

To flash in the pan; in a flintlock gun, to burn the powder in the pan without igniting the charge in the breech of the gun, which fails to go off; hence, to fail conspicuously.

Syn.—Glitter, glisten, gleam.—*Flash* differs from *glitter, glisten,* and *gleam,* in denoting a flood or wide extent of light. The latter words may express the issuing of light from a small object, or from a pencil of rays. A diamond may *glitter* or *glisten,* but it does not *flash.* A star may *gleam,* but it does not *flash.*

flash, *v.t.* 1. To expose suddenly; as, to *flash* a light or a dagger.

2. To send or convey quickly; as, to *flash* a message around the world.

3. To dress in a gaudy style, especially in showy colors, so as to appear flashy.

4. To emit, as something showy, attractive, or startling, as in the eruption of a volcano or a geyser.

5. In glass-making, to fuse (glass) in colors by flashing.

6. In making electric lamps, to treat (filaments) by flashing.

flash, *n.* The slang language of thieves, robbers, etc.

flash, *n.* 1. A sudden burst of light; a flood of light instantaneously appearing and disappearing; as, a *flash* of lightning.

2. A sudden burst, as of wit or merriment; as, a *flash* of wit; a *flash* of joy or mirth.

> His companions recollect no instance of premature wit, no striking sentiment, no *flash* of fancy. —Wirt.

3. A short, transient state or period of time.

> The Persians and Macedonians had it for a *flash.* —Bacon.

4. A body of water driven by violence. [Obs.]

5. A pungent adulterant of liquor.

6. [*pl.*] The febrile periods in a remittent fever. [Prov. Eng.]

flash, *n.* [ME. *flasshe, flasche, flask;* OFr. *flache, flasque, flac,* a pool, estuary.]

1. A little pool. [Prov. Eng.]

2. In engineering, a sluiceway for adding water to a stream in order to help vessels over a shallow place.

flash, *a.* 1. Offensively showy; conspicuous; as, *flash* dress, jewelry, etc.

2. Vulgar; offensively conspicuous, especially in dress; as, a *flash* person.

flash'bōard, *n.* A board placed on the top of a dam in time of low water to increase the depth of water in the dam; a flashing-board; a flush-board.

flash'ēr, *n.* 1. A man of more appearance of wit than reality.

2. A rower. [Obs.]

flash'-house, *n.* A place where thieves, robbers, etc., resort and deposit their plunder.

flash'i-ly, *adv.* With empty show; with a sudden glare; without solidity of wit or thought.

flash'ing, *n.* 1. In architecture, pieces of lead or other metal let into the joints of a wall, so as to lap over the gutters and prevent the plashing of rain on the interior works; any metal or other material inserted in a building to prevent the ingress of rain, as tin or tarred paper in a hip-roof.

2. In making electric lamps, a process of treatment in which the incandescent filament is subjected to a bath of carbon vapor to give it firmness and uniformity of resistance.

3. In glass-making, the process of fusing colors into glass; also, the process of reducing a plastic globe to a disk by whirling.

flash'ing-bōard, *n.* A flashboard.

flash'ing-bot''tle, *n.* A bottle in which electric-lamp filaments are flashed.

flash'ing-point, *n.* The temperature at which a volatile oil gives off vapor that will ignite with a flash when it comes into contact with a flame. The *flashing-point* of illuminating oils is fixed by law in most states and countries, and must be considerably below the temperature at which the illuminant burns with a steady flame.

flash'-light (-līt), *n.* A light which is hidden and recurrent at short intervals; also, a light used in tableaux and photography; commonly produced by burning powdered magnesium.

flash'-wheel, *n.* A paddle-wheel placed in a trough for raising water to a higher level.

flash'y, *a.;* *comp.* flashier; *superl.* flashiest. 1. Showy, but empty; dazzling for a moment, but not solid; as, *flashy* wit.

2. Showy; gay; as, a *flashy* dress.

3. Insipid; vapid; without taste or spirit, as food or drink.

4. Washy; plashy. [Obs.]

flask, *n.* [AS. *flasce, flaxe,* a bottle.]

1. A kind of bottle; as, a *flask* of wine or oil.

2. A vessel for gunpowder.

3. A bed in a gun-carriage.

4. In founding, a frame or box with compartments for holding the sand in which a mold is made.

Erlenmeyer flask; a thin cone-shaped flask with a flat bottom, used in the laboratory.

Florence flask; a thin glass flask with a globular body and a long neck, sometimes with a small flat bottom.

flask'et, *n.* [OFr. *flasquet, flaschet, flachet,* dim. of *flasque,* a flask.]

1. A vessel in which viands are served up. [Obs.]

2. A long, shallow basket. [Obs.]

3. A small flask for holding gunpowder. [Obs.]

flat, *a.;* *comp.* flatter; *superl.* flattest. [ME. *flat;* Ice. *flatr;* Sw. *flat;* O.H.G. *flaz,* flat.]

1. Having an even surface without risings or indentures, usually horizontal or nearly so; as, a *flat* roof; a *flat* rock.

2. Prostrate; lying the whole length on the ground; not elevated or erect; fallen.

> Cease to admire, and beauty's plumes
> Fall *flat.* —Milton.

3. In painting, wanting relief or prominence of the figures.

4. Tasteless; stale; vapid; insipid; dead; as, fruit *flat* to the taste.

5. Dull; unanimated; frigid; without point or spirit; applied to discourses and compositions; as, the sermon was very *flat.*

6. Depressed; spiritless; dejected.

7. Unpleasing; not affording gratification; as,

how *flat* and insipid are all the pleasures of this life!

8. Peremptory; absolute; positive; downright; as, he gave the petitioner a *flat* denial.

Thus repulsed, our final hope
Is *flat* despair. —Milton.

9. Low, as the prices of goods; dull; as, the market is *flat*; stocks are *flat*.

10. In music, (a) designating a tone a half-step lower than natural; as B *flat*, a *flat* third; (b) not up to pitch; out of tune.

Flat arch; in architecture, an arch which does not rise in a curve, but is covered by a stone or a series of stones fitted to support one another and forming a horizontal roof.

Flat cap; in the United States, a paper 14x17 inches, used for writing and for printing.

Flat chasing; the ornamenting of silverware, etc., with a punching-tool.

Flat chisel; a chisel used by a sculptor for smoothing.

Flat rail; a plain, flat bar of iron fastened to a sleeper with spikes, used formerly on railroads.

Flat rope; a rope made by plaiting or by fastening twisted ropes side by side, used in hoisting.

Flat tint; in painting, a uniformly colored background made by one coat of water-color.

Syn.—Dull, tame, insipid, vapid, spiritless, level, horizontal, absolute, even, downright, mawkish, tasteless, lifeless.

flat, *adv.* 1. Even; as, he ran 100 yards in 10 seconds *flat*.

2. In music, not up to the proper pitch.

To fall flat; to utterly fail to accomplish the end in view; to meet with no favor; as, his acting *fell flat*.

flat, *n.* 1. A level or extended plain; in the United States, low ground or meadow that is level; any land of even surface and of some extent.

2. A level ground lying at a small depth under the surface of water; a shoal; a shallow; a strand; a sandbank under water.

3. The broad side of a blade.

4. In music, (a) a character (♭) denoting a tone lower by half an interval than the natural; (b) the tone itself designated by such a character; as, the *flat* of B; (c) on the piano keyboard, the key which is next lower.

5. A boat, broad and flat-bottomed, called a flatboat.

6. A hat made of straw braid, with a low crown and broad brim.

7. A story or loft in a building. [Obs.]

8. One who is easily duped; opposed to one who is *sharp*. [Slang.]

9. In architecture, an apartment for housekeeping occupying a single floor of a building. [Compare *Apartment*.]

10. In mining, any part of a vein of ore lying in a horizontal position.

11. A platform embellished with emblems, wares, decorations, etc., carried on wheels in a public parade; also called a *float*.

flat, *v.t.*; flatted, *pt.*, *pp.*; flatting, *ppr.* 1. To level; to depress; to lay smooth or even; to make broad and smooth; to flatten.

2. To make vapid, tasteless, or dull.

3. To lower, as a musical note; particularly, to lower half an interval.

flat, *v.i.* 1. To grow flat; to fall to an even surface.

2. To become insipid, or dull and unanimated.

3. In music, to depress the voice or the tone of an instrument.

To flat out; to collapse; to disappoint all expectations after an auspicious beginning. [Colloq.]

flat'bill, *n.* In zoölogy, any bird with a flat bill; specifically, the flycatchers, genus *Platyrhynchus*.

flat'bōat, *n.* A broad, boxlike boat with a flat bottom, formerly much used on the western rivers of the United States for transporting all kinds of goods and merchandise.

flat'=bot"tōmed, *a.* Having a flat bottom, as a boat.

flat'=cap, *n.* A cap with a low crown, once much worn in London; hence, a Londoner.

flat'fish, *n.* A name applied in common to those fishes which have the body of a flattened form, swim on the side, and have both eyes on one side, embracing such as the flounder, turbot, halibut, and sole of the family *Pleuronectidæ*.

Flat-caps of the Sixteenth Century.

flat'foot, *n.* In anatomy and medicine, a condition, usually congenital, in which the foot lacks the arched form in the instep.

flat'=foot"ed, *a.* 1. Afflicted with flatfoot.

2. Positive in action or expression; as, he at last came out *flat-footed* for reform. [Slang.]

Flat'head (-hed), *n.* 1. An American Indian of the Salishan or Selish stock, originally dwelling in the valley of the Columbia river; a Chinook Indian.

2. [f—] An Australian fish, the barramunda.

3. [f—] The puff-adder of North America.

flat'head, *c.* Having a head flattened artificially by binding a board upon the forehead in childhood, causing the front part of the head to become flat and to slope backward, as practised by the Flathead Indians.

flat'=head"ed, *a.* Characterized by a flat head; as, a *flat-headed* bolt, nail, or screw.

flat'i"ron (-ūrn), *n.* An iron for smoothing cloth.

flā'tive, *a.* [L. *flatus*, pp. of *flare*, to blow.] Producing wind; flatulent. [Obs.]

flat'ling, *adv.* [Obs.] See *Flatlong*.

flat'long, *adv.* With the flat side downward; not edgewise.

flat'ly, *adv.* 1. Horizontally; without inclination.

2. Evenly; without elevations and depressions.

3. Without spirit; dully; frigidly.

4. Peremptorily; positively; downright.

He *flatly* refused his aid. —Sidney.

flat'ness, *n.* 1. Evenness of surface; levelness; equality of surface.

2. Want of relief or prominence; as, the *flatness* of a figure in sculpture.

3. Deadness; vapidness; insipidity; as, the *flatness* of cider or beer.

4. Dejection; a low state of the spirits; depression; want of life.

5. Dullness; want of point; insipidity; frigidity.

Some of Homer's translators have swelled into fustian, and others sunk into *flatness*. —Pope.

6. Gravity of sound, as opposed to sharpness, acuteness, or shrillness.

flat'ten, *v.t.*; flattened, *pt.*, *pp.*; flattening, *ppr.* 1. To make flat; to reduce to an equal or even surface; to level.

2. To beat down to the ground; to lay flat.

3. To make vapid or insipid; to render stale.

4. To depress; to deject, as the spirits; to dispirit.

5. In music, to depress, as the voice; to render less acute or sharp.

To flatten a sail; in marine language, to extend a sail lengthwise of the vessel, so that its effect is only lateral.

flat'ten, *v.i.* 1. To grow or become even on the surface.

2. To become dead, stale, vapid, or tasteless.

3. To become dull or spiritless.

4. In music, to depress the voice; to render a sound less sharp.

flat'ten-ing=ōv"en, *n.* A heated chamber in which hollow glass cylinders, after being split, are laid upon a plane bed for flattening.

flat'tẽr, *v.t.*; flattered, *pt.*, *pp.*; flattering, *ppr.* [Fr. *flatter*; OFr. *flater*; Pr. *flatar*, to pat, stroke, flatter, perhaps from Ice. *flatr*, flat, as if smoothed by the patting of the hand.]

1. To soothe by praise; to gratify the self-love of by praise or obsequiousness; to please (a person) by applause or favorable notice, by respectful attention, or by anything that exalts him in his own estimation, or confirms his good opinion of himself.

A man that *flattereth* his neighbor spreadeth a net for his feet. —Prov. xxix. 5.

2. To please; to gratify; to encourage by favorable notice; to raise false hopes in by representations not well founded; as, to *flatter* one with a prospect of success; to *flatter* a patient with the expectation of recovery, when his case is desperate.

3. To soothe.

A concert of voices—makes a harmony that *flatters* the ears. —Dryden.

4. To cause to appear better than a strict adherence to truth would warrant; as, to *flatter* a person in a portrait.

flat'tẽr, *a.*, comp. of *flat*.

flat'tẽr, *n.* Any agent or instrument of flattening, as a plane-faced hammer for flattening sheets of metal, or a narrow slit in a steel plate for drawing flat wire, watch-springs, etc.

flat'tẽr-ẽr, *n.* One who flatters.

Syn.—Sycophant, parasite.—The *flatterer* is one who flatters by words; the *sycophant* or *parasite* is therefore always a *flatterer*, and something more, for the *sycophant* adopts every mean artifice by which he can ingratiate himself, and the *parasite* submits to every degradation and servile compliance by which he can obtain his purpose.

flat'tẽr-ing, *a.* Having or exhibiting flattery.

flat'tẽr-ing-ly, *adv.* In a flattering manner; in a manner to flatter.

flat'tẽr-y, *n.*; *pl.* **flat'tẽr-ies**. [ME. *flaterie*, *flaterye*; OFr. *flaterie*, from *flater*, to flatter.] False praise; commendation bestowed for the purpose of gaining favor and influence, or to accomplish some purpose; adulation; obsequiousness.

Simple pride for *flattery* makes demands. —Pope.

Syn.—Adulation, sycophancy, fawning, servility, toadyism, obsequiousness.

flat'test, *a.*, superl. of *flat*.

flat'ting, *n.* 1. A mode of house-painting, in which paint, being mixed with turpentine, leaves the work flat or without gloss.

2. A method of preserving gilding unburnished, by touching it with size.

3. Any process for making flat, as rolling or hammering metal, flattening glass in an oven, etc.

flat'ting=cōat, *n.* In painting, a last coat without gloss.

flat'ting=fũr"nāce, *n.* A flattening-oven.

flat'ting=mill, *n.* A mill with rollers for flattening metals.

flat'tish, *a.* Somewhat flat; approaching to flatness.

flat'top, *n.* In botany, a name given to the ironweed, *Vernonia Noveboracensis*, from its broad, level-topped corymb.

flat'ū-lence, *n.* 1. Windiness in the stomach; gas generated in a weak stomach and intestines by imperfect digestion, occasioning distention, uneasiness, and pain.

2. Airiness; emptiness; vanity.

flat'ū-len-cy, *n.* Flatulence.

flat'ū-lent, *a.* [From L. *flatus*, pp. of *flare*, to blow.]

1. Gaseous; affected with gases generated in the stomach and intestines.

2. Turgid with gas; as, a *flatulent* tumor.

3. Generating or apt to generate gases in the stomach.

4. Empty; vain; big without substance or reality; puffy; as, a *flatulent* writer; *flatulent* vanity.

flat'ū-lent-ly, *adv.* In a manner characterized by flatulence.

flat-ū-os'i-ty, *n.* Flatulence. [Obs.]

flat'ū-ous, *a.* [From L. *flatus*, pp. of *flare*, to blow.] Windy; generating wind. [Obs.]

flā'tus, *n.*; *pl.* **flā'tus-es** or **flā'tus**. [L., a blowing, from *flare*, to blow.]

1. A breath; a puff of wind.

2. Gas generated in the stomach or other cavities of the body; flatulence.

flat'wise, *adv.* With the flat side downward or next to another object; not edgewise.

flat'wŏrm, *n.* Any worm of the *Platyhelminthes*, a group of worms characterized by bodies that are flat or approximately flat.

flaught (flat), *n.* 1. A flutter, as that of a bird; wave; waft. [Scot.]

2. A flight; a flock. [Scot.]

flaught'ẽr, *v.t.* To pare or cut from the ground, as turf. [Scot.]

flaught'ẽr, *v.i.* To flutter; to shine fitfully; to flicker. [Scot.]

Flaun'drish, *a.* Same as *Flemish*.

flaunt, *v.i.*; flaunted, *pt.*, *pp.*; flaunting, *ppr.* [Origin doubtful, compare Sw. dial. *flankt*, from *flanka*, to waver, wave about.] To throw or spread out; to flutter; to display ostentatiously; as, a *flaunting* show.

You *flaunt* about the streets in your new gilt chariot. —Arbuthnot.

One *flaunts* in rags, one flutters in brocades. —Pope.

flaunt, *v.t.* To make a showy and offensive display of; as, to *flaunt* a despised emblem.

flaunt, *n.* Anything displayed for show. [Obs.]

flaunt'ing-ly, *adv.* In a flaunting way.

flä-ū-ti'nō, *n.* [It., dim. of *flauto*, a flute.] In music, (a) a small instrument like a flute; a piccolo; (b) a diminutive accordion.

flau'tist, *n.* Same as *Flutist*.

flä-ū'tō, *n.* Same as *Flute*.

Flauto piccolo; same as *Piccolo*.

Flauto traverso; a modern flute; a flute with the opening for blowing on the side, in contradistinction to the flute with a beak at the end for blowing.

flā-van'i-line, flā-van'i-lin, *n.* [L. *flavus*, yellow, and E. *aniline*.] In chemistry, a crystalline dyestuff, $C_{16}H_{14}N_2$, a product of coal-tar, giving a yellow color to fabrics.

flā-vē'dō, *n.* [From L. *flavus*, yellow.] In botany, a diseased condition of a plant in which the green parts become yellow.

Flā-vē'ri-ȧ, *n.* [From L. *flavus*, yellow.] A genus of tropical American composite plants.

flā-ves'cent, *a.* [From L. *flavus*, yellow, and *-escent*.] Growing yellow.

flā-vig'ō-mous, *a.* [L. *flavicomus*; *flavus*, yellow, and *coma*, hair.] Having yellow hair. [Rare.]

flā′vin, *n.* [L. *flavus*, yellow, and *-in*.] In chemistry, a dyestuff of vegetable origin coloring yellow.

flā′vol, *n.* [L. *flavus*, yellow, and *-ol*.] In chemistry, a yellow substance, $C_{14}H_{10}O_2$, derived from anthracene in crystals.

flā-vō-pūr′pū-rin, *n.* [L. *flavus*, yellow, and *purpura*, purple, and *-in*.] In chemistry, a dye of the coal-tar series, $C_{14}H_8O_3$, coloring red with a tinge of yellow.

flā′vŏr, *n.* [OFr. *flaveur*, odor; LL. *flavor*, from L. *flavus*, yellow.]

1. The quality of a substance which affects the taste in any manner; as, the wine has a fine *flavor* or a disagreeable *flavor*; the fruit has a bad *flavor*.

2. The quality of a substance as affecting the sense of smell; as, the rose has a sweet *flavor*. [Rare.]

3. Intellectual or moral quality; as, the works of some authors have a delicious *flavor* throughout.

Syn.—Taste, savor, relish, smack.

flā′vŏr, *v.t.*; flavored, *pt., pp.*; flavoring, *ppr.* To communicate some quality to, so as to affect the taste or smell; to impart any characteristic quality to.

flā′vŏr-ing, *n.* Any substance used for imparting flavor.

flā′vŏr-less, *a.* Without flavor; tasteless; having no smell or taste.

flā′vŏr-ous, *a.* Pleasant to the taste or smell.

flā′vous, *a.* [L. *flavus*, yellow.] Yellow. [Obs.]

flaw, *n.* [ME. *flawe*, from Sw. *flaga*, a flake, flaw, break; Dan. *flage*, a flake.]

1. A breach; a crack; a defect made by breaking or splitting; a gap or fissure; as, a *flaw* in a scythe, knife, or razor; a *flaw* in a china dish, or in a glass; a *flaw* in a wall.

2. A defect; a fault; any defect made by violence, or occasioned by neglect; as, a *flaw* in reputation; a *flaw* in a will, or in a deed, or in a statute.

3. A sudden burst of wind; a sudden gust or blast of short duration.

4. A sudden burst of noise and disorder; a tumult; uproar. [Obs.]

Syn.—Blemish, defect, imperfection, breach, break, crack, split, rent.

flaw, *v.t.*; flawed, *pt., pp.*; flawing, *ppr.* 1. To break; to crack.

> The brazen caldrons with the frosts are *flawed*. —Dryden.

2. To break; to violate; as, to *flaw* a league. [Obs.]

flaw′less, *a.* Without cracks; without defect.

flawn, *n.* [ME. *flaun*, *flawn*; OFr. *flaon*; LL. *flado* (*-onis*), from O.H.G *flado*, a flat cake, pancake.] A sort of flat custard or pie. [Obs.]

flaw′tẽr, *v.t.* To scrape or pare, as skin. [Obs.]

flaw′y, *a.*; *comp.* flawier; *superl.* flawiest. 1. Full of flaws or cracks; broken; defective; faulty.

2. Subject to sudden gusts of wind.

flax, *n.* [ME. *flax*, *flex*; AS. *fleax*, *flex*, flax.] A plant of the genus *Linum*; specifically, *Linum usitatissimum*, or its fiber. Besides being raised extensively in various European countries, it is an important farm product of the United States, the grain being used extensively in the manufacture of oil, and the fiber in making paper and linen. The name is extended to cover numerous similar plants of other genera.

Flax (*Linum usitatissimum*), with section of seed-vessel.

False flax; in botany, a plant, *Camelina sativa*, of the *Cruciferæ*, resembling flax, with pale yellow flowers.

Mountain flax; in mineralogy, a very fine, silky variety of asbestos.

Native flax; same as *Flax-plant*.

New Zealand flax; same as *Flax-plant*.

flax′-bîrd, *n.* The scarlet tanager; also, any one of various birds feeding upon flaxseeds.

flax′-brāke, *n.* A machine for breaking the dried stems of flax in order to remove them from the fiber.

flax′-cōmb, *n.* A kind of comb with long, sharp steel teeth for removing the woody parts of flax from the fiber; a hatchel.

flax′-cot″tŏn, *n.* A cotton-like form of flax produced by artificial process upon the fiber.

flax′-dress″ẽr, *n.* Any agent or device that prepares flax for the spinner by breaking, scutching, and combing.

flax′en, *a.* Made of flax or resembling flax.

flax′-mill, *n.* A mill for manufacturing flax fabrics.

flax′-plant, *n.* In botany, a plant, *Phormium tenax*, of the lily family, whose leaves yield a strong, coarse fiber used for cordage; called also *flax-bush* and *New Zealand flax*.

flax′-pull″ẽr, *n.* A machine for uprooting and gathering flax.

flax′seed, *n.* The seed of flax.

flax′-stär, *n.* A species of primrose with green flowers.

flax′weed, *n.* *Linaria vulgaris*; common toadflax; butter and eggs.

flax′-wench, *n.* A woman flax-spinner; hence a working-woman.

flax′y, *a.*; *comp.* flaxier; *superl.* flaxiest. Like flax; being of a light color; fair.

flāy, *v.t.*; flayed, *pt., pp.*; flaying, *ppr.* [ME. *flean*, *flan*; AS. *flean*; D. *vlaen*, to flay.] To skin; to strip off the skin of; as, to *flay* an ox.

flāy′ẽr, *n.* One who strips off the skin.

flēa, *n.* [ME. *flee*, *fle*; AS. *fleah*, *flea*, a flea, prob. from *fleon*, to flee.] An insect of the genus *Pulex*, having two eyes and six feet; remarkable for its agility in jumping, and armed with a stiff inflected beak containing a sting which renders its bite painful. *Pulex irritans* is the typical species.

A flea in one's ear; unwelcome intelligence.

flēa′bāne, *n.* A name given to various plants, from their supposed efficacy in driving away fleas. They belong to the genera *Conyza*, *Erigeron*, and *Pulicaria*.

flēa′-bee″tle, *n.* Any one of several species of small beetles characterized by strong hind legs and jumping like a flea, as the *Haltica chalybea*, infesting and injuring grape-vines.

flēa′bīte, *n.* 1. The bite of a flea, or the red spot caused by the bite.

2. A trifling wound or pain, like that of the bite of a flea.

flēa′bit″ten, *a.* 1. Bitten or stung by a flea.

2. Covered with minute spots of a brown color; said of white horses.

flēak, *n.* A lock; a flake. [Obs.]

flēak′ing, *n.* An under layer of reeds in thatching. [Eng.]

flēa′-louse, *n.* A small insect of the *Psyllidæ* family, resembling the plant-louse.

flēam, *n.* [OFr. *flieme*, from LL. *flebotomus*, *phlebotomus*; Gr. *phlebotomon*, a lancet; *phleps*, *phlebos*, a vein, and *temnein*, to cut.] In farriery, a sharp instrument, used for opening veins for letting blood.

flēam′-tooth, *n.* A tooth, as of a saw, having the form of an isosceles triangle, cutting equally on both sides.

flēam′y, *a.* Filled with phlegm. [Obs.]

flēar, *v.t.* and *v.i.* Same as *Fleer*.

flēa′wŏrt, *n.* An herb of the plantain kind, bearing nauseous mucilaginous seeds, employed medicinally.

flèche (flāsh), *n.* [Fr., an arrow.]

1. In military engineering, a simple, two-faced parapet or other fortification, forming a sharp angle in front and open at the rear.

2. In architecture, a spire; restrictedly, a spire over the intersection of the nave with the transepts.

3. In decorative art, a picture or other representation of a spire.

fleck, *n.* [Ice. *flekkr*, Sw. *fläcka*, a spot.]

1. A spot; a colored area; a mark.

2. A lock, as of wool. [Obs.]

fleck, *v.t.*; flecked (flekt), *pt. pp.*; flecking, *ppr.* [ME. *flecken*, *flekken*; Ice. *flekka*, to spot, stain, from *flekkr*, a spot, stain.] To spot; to streak or stripe; to variegate; to dapple.

> Both *flecked* with white, the true Arcadian strain. —Dryden.

fleck′ẽr, *v.t.* To fleck.

fleck′less, *a.* Not flecked; without a stain; hence, clean; innocent; blameless.

flect′ed, *a.* [From L. *flectere*, to bend.] Bent; used in heraldry.

flec′tion, *n.* [L. *flectio* (*-onis*), from *flectere*, to bend.]

1. The act of bending, or state of being bent.

2. In grammar, inflection.

flec′tion-ăl, *a.* Relating to flection.

flec′tŏr, *n.* A flexor.

fled, *v.*, past tense of *flee*.

fledge (flej), *a.* [ME. *flegge*, *fligge*, able to fly, from AS. *fleogan*, to fly.] Feathered; furnished with feathers or wings; able to fly.

fledge, *v.t.*; fledged, *pt., pp.*; fledging, *ppr.* To furnish with feathers or with a soft covering; to supply with the feathers necessary for flight or with a beard or other soft covering.

> The birds were not yet *fledged* enough to shift for themselves. —L'Estrange.

fledge, *v.i.* To become covered with feathers; to become well enough feathered to fly; as, the birds have *fledged* and gone.

fledg′ling, fledge′ling, *n.* A young bird just fledged; figuratively, a young and inexperienced person.

fledg′ling, fledge′ling, *a.* Raw; inexperienced; unskilled; as, a *fledgling* doctor.

fledg′y, *a.* Covered with feathers or down.

flee, *v.i.*; fled, *pt., pp.*; fleeing, *ppr.* [ME. *flee*, *fleen*, *fleon*; AS. *fleon*, to flee.]

1. To run with rapidity, as from danger; to attempt to escape; to hasten from danger or expected evil; as, the enemy *fled* at the first fire.

> Arise, take the young child and his mother, and *flee* into Egypt. —Matt. ii. 13.

2. To depart; to leave; to hasten away.

> Resist the devil, and he will *flee* from you. —James iv. 7.

flee, *v.t.* To avoid; to keep at a distance from.

fleece, *n.* [ME. *fleese*, *flese*, *fleose*; AS. *fleos*, *fles*, fleece.]

1. The coat of wool worn by a sheep or other wool-bearing animal; also, the coat shorn from the animal at one time.

2. Any covering or lining of a fleecy character.

3. In manufacturing, a thin delicate layer of wool or cotton fiber gathered upon a cylinder in a carding-machine and stripped off by a doffing-knife.

Golden fleece; see under *Golden*.

fleece, *v.t.*; fleeced (flēst), *pt., pp.*; fleecing, *ppr.* 1. To shear off, as a covering or growth of wool.

2. To strip of money or property; to take from, by severe exactions, under color of law or justice, or pretext of necessity, or by virtue of authority; as, clients complain that they are sometimes *fleeced* by their lawyers.

3. To spread over as with wool; to make white. [Rare.]

fleeced (flēst), *a.* 1. Furnished with a fleece or with fleeces; as, a sheep is well *fleeced*.

2. Robbed; as, when he left the room he discovered that he had been *fleeced*.

fleece′less, *a.* Having no fleece.

fleece′-lined, *a.* Having the inner surface fleeced, as in underwear.

flee′cẽr, *n.* One who strips or takes by severe exactions or by trickery.

fleece′-wool, *n.* Wool shorn from a living animal, as distinguished from that taken from a dead animal.

flee′cy, *a.*; *comp.* fleecier; *superl.* fleeciest. 1. Covered with wool; woolly; as, a *fleecy* flock.

2. Resembling wool or a fleece; soft; complicated; as, *fleecy* snow; *fleecy* locks; *fleecy* hosiery.

fleen, *n.pl.*, obsolete Middle English for *fleas* and for *flies*, plurals of *flea* and *fly*.

flē′ẽr, *n.* One who flees or runs away.

fleer, *v.i.*; fleered, *pt., pp.*; fleering, *ppr.* [ME. *flerien*, *fliren*; Norw. *flira*, to titter, laugh at nothing.]

1. To deride; to sneer; to mock; to gibe; to make a wry face in contempt, or to grin in scorn; as, to *fleer* and flout.

> Covered with an antic face,
> To *fleer* and scorn at our solemnity.—Shak.

2. To leer; to grin with an air of civility. [Obs.]

fleer, *v.t.* To mock; to flout at.

fleer, *n.* 1. Derision or mockery, expressed by words or looks.

> And mark the *fleers*, the gibes, and notable scorns. —Shak.

2. A grin of civility. [Obs.]

> A sly treacherous *fleer* upon the face of deceivers. —South.

fleer′ẽr, *n.* A mocker; a fawner.

fleer′ing-ly, *adv.* In a fleering manner.

fleet, *n.* [ME. *fleet*; AS. *fleot*, an arm of the sea, estuary, place where ships float.] A creek, inlet, bay, river, or estuary; an arm of the sea; now used only in English place-names; as, North*fleet*, *Fleet* street, *Fleet*ditch.

Fleet marriages; clandestine and often scandalous marriages formerly performed in or near the Fleet Prison, without license or other requisite legal formality, by impecunious and unscrupulous clergymen. They were forbidden by statute in 1753.

The Fleet or *Fleet Prison*; a famous prison in London, long used for debtors, but abolished in 1845; so called from its location near the Fleet ditch, now a covered sewer.

fleet, *n.* [ME. *fleet*, *flete*, *fleot*, a fleet, ship; AS. *fleot*, a ship, from *fleotan*, to float.]

1. A number of ships or vessels in company, whether ships of war or merchant vessels, etc.; as, the United States *fleet* at Santiago; the fishing-*fleet* on the Banks; a *fleet* of clipper-ships; the yachting *fleet*.

2. A number of ships of war organized for combined action in peace or war, and usually under the command of a rear-admiral; as, the Pacific *fleet*; such a *fleet* may be subdivided into separate commands called *squadrons*.

3. A naval armament; a navy.

4. In fishing, a single line of 100 hooks; a bultow.

Fleet captain; in the United States navy, an officer temporarily appointed to act as chief of staff to the admiral commanding a fleet.

fleet, *a.*; *comp.* fleeter; *superl.* fleetest. [Origin uncertain.]

1. Swift of pace; moving or able to move with rapidity; nimble; light and quick in motion, or moving with lightness and celerity; as, a *fleet* horse or dog.

2. Moving with velocity; as, *fleet* winds.

3. Light; superficially fruitful; thin; not penetrating deep, as soil. [Obs.]
4. Skimming the surface. [Obs.]
fleet, *adv.* On the surface; in a superficial manner; as, to plow ground *fleet*. [Obs.]
fleet, *v.i.*; fleeted, *pt.*, *pp.*; fleeting, *ppr.* 1. To fly swiftly; to hasten; to flit, as a light substance.

How all the other passions *fleet* to air!—Shak.

2. To be in a transient state; to change place; as, sailors *fleet* forward and aft.
3. To float. [Obs.]
4. To slip, as a cable on the ridges of a capstan.
5. To gutter, as a candle.
To fleet away; to vanish.
fleet, *v.t.* [ME. *fleten*, to skim, from AS. *flete*, *fliete*, cream, skimmings, from *fleotan*, to float.]
1. To skim the surface of; to pass over rapidly; as, a ship that *fleets* the gulf.
2. To cause to pass lightly, or in mirth and joy; as, to *fleet* the time. [Obs.]
3. In nautical language, to move or cause to move; to cause to change position; as, to *fleet* the crew aft; to *fleet* a cable higher.
4. To skim, as milk. [Prov. Eng.]
fleet'en, *n.* Milk that has been fleeted; skim-milk. [Obs.]
fleet'en-face, *n.* One who has a face of the color of whey or skim-milk; a whey-face; a coward. [Rare.]
fleet'-foot, *a.* Swift of foot; running or able to run with rapidity.
fleet'ing, *a.* Passing rapidly; flying with velocity; not durable; as, the *fleeting* hours or moments; *fleeting* pleasures.
Syn.—Transient, transitory, brief, ephemeral, evanescent, flitting, fugitive, flying, passing, temporary, vanishing.—*Transient* represents a thing as short at the best; *transitory* as liable at any moment to pass away. *Fleeting* goes further, and represents it as in the act of taking its flight.
fleet'ing-ly, *adv.* In a fleeting manner.
fleet'ings, *n.pl.* Buttermilk mixed with boiling whey; also, curdled milk; curds. [Prov. Eng.]
fleet'ly, *adv.* Rapidly; lightly and nimbly; swiftly.
fleet'ness, *n.* Swiftness; rapidity; velocity; celerity; speed; as, the *fleetness* of a horse or deer.
Syn.—Celerity, quickness, rapidity, velocity, swiftness, speed.
Flem'ing, *n.* A native or inhabitant of Flanders; a member of the Flemish race.
Flem'ish, *a.* Pertaining to Flanders, its people, or their language; resembling the Flemings.
Flemish accounts; in nautical language, brief, incomplete accounts.
Flemish beauty; a species of pear.
Flemish bond; see *Bond*, n. 8.
Flemish brick; a hard paving-brick.
Flemish coil; a coil of rope similar to that of a watch-spring.
Flemish eye; in nautical language, an eye made by dividing the strands of a rope at the end and lapping them over each other.
Flemish horse; the outer short footrope on a topsail yardarm.
Flemish pottery; pottery made in the districts formerly included in Flanders.
Flemish school; a school of painting originating in Flanders at the beginning of the fifteenth century, Rubens and Vandyck being among its best-known exponents.
Flem'ish, *n.* 1. The people of Flanders; the Flemings.
2. The language of the Flemish.
flem'ish, *v.t.*; flemished, *pt.*, *pp.*; flemishing, *ppr.* To coil, as a rope, in a Flemish coil.
flench, *v.t.* To flense.
flense, *v.t.*; flensed (flenst), *pt.*, *pp.*; flensing, *ppr.* [Dan. *flense*; Sw. *flänsa*, to slash, cut up.] To cut up, as a whale, to obtain the blubber.
flesh, *n.* [ME. *flesh*, *fleisch*, *flesc*; AS. *flæsc*, flesh.]
1. A compound substance forming a large part of an animal body, consisting of the softer solids, as distinguished from the bones and the fluids; sometimes restricted to the muscular tissue alone, exclusive of the fat, etc.
2. Animal food, in distinction from vegetable.
3. The substance of beasts and birds used as food, as distinguished from fish; as, one may abstain from *flesh*, but eat fish.
4. The body, as distinguished from the soul.

As if this *flesh*, which walls about our life,
Were brass impregnable. —Shak.

5. Man in general; mankind; humanity.

She was fairest of all *flesh* on earth,
Guinevere. —Tennyson.

6. Human nature, in a good or bad sense; human tenderness or feeling; also, carnality; the body as the seat of appetite.

Ye judge after the *flesh*. —John viii. 15.

7. Kindred; stock; family.

He is our brother, and our *flesh*.
—Gen. xxxvii. 27.

8. In botany, the soft, pulpy substance of fruit; also, that part of a root, fruit, etc., which is fit to be eaten.
After the flesh; according to outward appearances; carnally; humanly.
Arm of flesh; the human arm or power, as distinguished from divine power.
Flesh and blood; see under *Blood*.
Flesh broth; broth containing the juices extracted from flesh.
Flesh side; in tanning, the side of a hide that lay next to the flesh.
One flesh; one person; as, husband and wife become *one flesh*.
Proud flesh; see under *Proud*.
flesh, *a.* Consisting of animal substance; applied to food, etc.; as, a *flesh* diet.
flesh, *v.t*; fleshed (flesht), *pt.*, *pp.*; fleshing, *ppr.*
1. To encourage or train by giving flesh to; to initiate; from the practice of training hawks and dogs by feeding them with the first game they take, or other flesh; hence, to introduce or incite to battle; as, to *flesh* a maiden sword.
2. To harden; to accustom; to establish in any practice; as, men *fleshed* in cruelty; women *fleshed* in malice.
3. To glut; to satiate; to feed full with flesh or fleshly pleasures.
4. In tanning leather, to clean of flesh, fat, etc., as hides.
flesh'-brush, *n.* A brush for exciting action in the skin or flesh by friction.
fleshed (flesht), *a.* 1. Initiated; accustomed; glutted.
2. Fat; fleshy.
flesh'ėr, *n.* 1. A kind of two-handled, blunt-edged knife used for scraping the flesh from hides.
2. One who scrapes the flesh from hides.
3. A butcher. [Scot.]
flesh'-flēa, *n.* The chigoe.
flesh'-fly, *n.* An insect that lays its eggs in dead or decaying flesh, as those of the genus *Sarcophaga*.
flesh'hood, *n.* The condition of being an animal or of being a body of flesh.
flesh'i-ness, *n.* The state of being fleshy; abundance of flesh or fat in animals; plumpness; corpulence; grossness.
flesh'ings, *n.pl.* 1. Flesh-colored tight-fitting garments, intended to represent the natural skin; flesh-colored tights.
2. Scrapings removed from hides by the flesher.
flesh'less, *a.* Destitute of flesh; lean.
flesh'li-ness, *n.* Carnal passions and appetites; a fleshly state.
flesh'ling, *n.* A person devoted to carnal things.
flesh'ly, *a.* 1. Pertaining to the flesh; corporeal.
2. Carnal; worldly; lascivious.

Abstain from *fleshly* lusts. —1 Pet. ii. 11.

3. Animal; not vegetable.
flesh'ly, *adv.* Carnally; lasciviously; humanly; after the manner of the fleshly.
flesh'-mēat, *n.* Animal food; the flesh of animals prepared or used for food.
flesh'ment, *n.* Eagerness gained by a successful initiation; the state or the process of being fleshed.
flesh'mŏn"gẽr, *n.* 1. One who deals in flesh.
2. A procurer; a pimp. [Rare.]
flesh'pot, *n.* A vessel in which flesh is cooked; hence, food; in the plural, plenty; as, the *fleshpots* of Egypt.
flesh'quāke (-kwāk), *n.* A trembling of the flesh. [Obs.]
flesh'-tint, *n.* The natural color of flesh; a term used in painting.
flesh'-wŏrm, *n.* 1. The larva of a flesh-fly; a maggot.
2. The trichina or spiral threadworm.
flesh'y, *a.*; *comp.* fleshier; *superl.* fleshiest.
1. Full of flesh; muscular; as, the sole of the foot is *fleshy*.
2. Fat; gross; corpulent; as, a *fleshy* man.
3. Corporeal; pertaining to the bodily nature, as distinguished from the moral.
4. Full of pulp; pulpous; plump, as fruit.
flet, *v.*, obsolete past participle of *fleet*.
fletch, *v.t.* To feather, as an arrow. [Obs.]
fletch, *v.t.* To cut in strips, as fish; to flitch.
fletch'ẽr, *n.* [ME. *fletcher*, *flecchere*; OFr. *flechier*, an arrow-maker, from *fleche*, an arrow.] An arrow-maker; a manufacturer of bows and arrows.

It is commended by our *fletchers* for bows, next unto yew. —Mortimer.

flēte, *v.i.* [Obs.] See *Fleet*.
fleth'ẽr, *v.t.* To flatter. [Scot.]
fle-tif'ẽr-ous, *a.* [LL. *fletifer*; *fletus*, weeping, tears, and *ferre*, to bear.] Producing tears. [Obs.]
fletz, *n.* [G. *flötz*, *fletz*, a layer, stratum; M.H.G. *vletze*, a floor, level.] In geology, a term formerly applied to the secondary strata, because they generally occur in flat or horizontal beds; a stratum or layer; a distinct layer of rock.
fleūr"-de-lis' (-lē'), *n.*; *pl.* **fleūrs"-de-lis'** (flẽr"). [Fr. flower of the lily.]
1. A bearing in heraldry, representing a lily, emblematic of royalty.
2. In botany, the iris.

Fleur-de-lis.

fleū-roṅ', *n.* [Fr., a flower, jewel, from *fleur*, a flower.] In ornamental art, a conventional form of a small flower, usually terminal or apical, but sometimes constituting a member, as the link of a chain.
fleūr'y, *a.* See *Flory*.
flew, *v.*, past tense of *fly*.
flewed, *a.* Having large flews; deep-mouthed; said of dogs.
flews, *n.pl.* [Origin unknown.] The large chop or overhanging lip of a deep-mouthed hound.
flex, *v.t.*; flexed (flext), *pt.*, *pp.*; flexing, *ppr.* [L. *flexus*, pp. of *flectere*, to bend, curve.] To bend; as, a muscle *flexes* the arm.
flex-an'i-mous, *a.* [L. *flexanimus*, from *flexus*, pp. of *flectere*, to bend, and *animus*, mind.] Having power to change the mind. [Rare.]
flex-i-bil'i-ty, *n.* [LL. *flexibilitas*, from L. *flexibilis*, that may be bent or curved.] The quality of being flexible; pliancy; flexibleness; as, the *flexibility* of rays of light, of whalebone, or of an individual.
flex'i-ble, *a.* [L. *flexibilis*, from *flexus*, pp. of *flectere*, to bend, curve.]
1. That may be bent; capable of being turned or forced from a straight line or form without breaking; pliant; yielding to pressure; not stiff; as, a *flexible* rod; a *flexible* plant.
2. Capable of yielding to entreaties, arguments, or other moral force; that may be persuaded to compliance; not invincibly rigid or obstinate; not inexorable; tractable.

Phocion was no ways *flexible* to the will of the people. —Bacon.

3. That may be adapted or accommodated; plastic; as, a *flexible* language.

This was a principle more *flexible* to their purpose. —Rogers.

Syn.—Pliable, pliant, supple.—*Flexible* is used in a natural or moral sense; *pliable* in the familiar sense only; *pliant* in the higher and moral application only; what can be bent in any degree, as a stick, is *flexible*; what can be bent as wax or folded like cloth, is *pliable*. *Supple*, whether in a literal or a figurative sense, denotes an excess of *pliability*; what can be bent backward and forward like an osier twig, is *supple*.
flex'i-ble-ness, *n.* The condition or quality of being flexible.
flex'i-bly, *adv.* In a flexible manner.
flex-i-ços'tāte, *a.* [L. *flexus*, bent, and *costa*, a rib.] In anatomy, having curved ribs. [Rare.]
flex'ile, *a.* [L. *flexilis*, pliant, that may be bent, from *flexus*, pp. of *flectere*, to bend, curve.] Pliant; pliable; easily bent; yielding to power, impulse, or moral force.
flex'iŏn, *n.* [L. *flexio* (*-onis*), from *flexus*, pp. of *flectere*, to bend, curve.] Same as *Flection*.
flex'iŏn-ăl, *a.* Same as *Flectional*.
flex'ŏr, *n.* [LL., from L. *flexus*, pp. of *flectere*, to bend.] In anatomy, a muscle whose function is to bend the part to which it belongs; opposed to *extensor*.
flex'ū-ōse, *a.* Flexuous.
flex'ū-ous, *a.* [L. *flexuosus*, full of turns, tortuous, from *flexus*, pp. of *flectere*, to bend.]
1. Winding; having turns or windings; as, a *flexuous* rivulet.
2. Wavering; not steady; as, a *flexuous* flame.
3. In botany, bending or bent; changing its direction in a curve, from joint to joint, from bud to bud, or from flower to flower; as, a *flexuous* branch.
flex'ū-ous-ly, *adv.* In a flexuous manner.
flex'ū-răl, *a.* Relating to flexure.
flex'ūre, *n.* [L. *flexura*, a winding.]
1. A winding or bending; the form of bending; incurvation; as, the *flexure* of a joint.
2. The act of bending.
3. The part bent; a joint.
4. The bending of the body; obsequious or servile cringing.
5. In astronomy, the slight bending of an instrument due to its own weight, or the correction of errors due to such change.
6. In geology, a bending of strata.
7. The bend of a bird's wing.
8. In mechanics, a strain under which certain plane surfaces are bent or deformed.
9. In geometry, same as *curvature*.
fley, *v.t.* and *v.i.* To frighten; to take fright. [Scot.]
fley, *n.* A fright.
Flib'bẽr-di-ġib"bet, Flib'bẽr-ti-ġib"bet, *n.* 1. The name of a devil. [Obs.]
2. [f—] An imp; one who looks impish.

flib'bẽr-ġib, flib'bẽr-ġib"bẽr, *n.* A smooth, lying sycophant. [Obs.]

flick, *v.t.*; flicked (flikt), *pt., pp.*; flicking, *ppr.* To whip with a quick jerk of a whip; to pick off with or as with a whiplash; as, to *flick* a horse in driving, or to *flick* a fly from a horse; to *flick* the snow off a coat.

flick, *n.* The stroke made in flicking; a flip.

flick, *n.* [Obs.] See *Flitch.*

flick'ẽr, *v.i.*; flickered, *pt., pp.*; flickering, *ppr.* 1. To flutter; to flap the wings without flying; to strike rapidly with the wings.

And *flickering* on her nest made short essays to sing. —Dryden.

2. To waver, fluctuate, or twinkle; as, the light *flickers* at a distance.

flick'ẽr, *n.* The act of flickering; a wavering; a fluctuating gleam, as of a candle; a flutter.

flick'ẽr, *n.* [Imitative, from the bird's note.] A handsome species of woodpecker, *Colaptes auratus*, characterized by golden-colored wings; called also *yellowhammer, highhole, highholder,* and *pigeon-woodpecker.*

flick'ẽr-ing-ly, *adv.* In a flickering manner.

flick'ẽr-mouse, *n.* The bat; the flittermouse.

flidġe (flij), *a.* [Obs.] See *Fledge.*

flidġe, *v.i.* [Obs.] See *Fledge.*

fli'ẽr, *n.* 1. One who flies or flees.

2. A runaway; a fugitive.

3. Any person or thing capable of great speed; as, he drove a team of *fliers.*

4. A part in machinery that moves rapidly; as, the *flier* of a jack; more commonly called *fly.*

5. A straight flight in a stairway.

6. A handbill or dodger for distribution in quantities.

7. A venture in speculative business; as, to take a *flier* in stocks.

flight (flit), *v.t.* To scare; to cause to flee. [Obs.]

flight, *v.i.* To take flight, as game-birds.

flight, *n.* [ME. *flight, flyght, fluht*; AS. *flugon,* from *fleon,* to flee.] The act of fleeing; the act of running away, to escape danger or expected evil; hasty departure.

Pray ye that your *flight* be not in the winter. —Matt. xxiv. 20.

flight, *n.* [ME. *flight, flyght, fluht*; AS. *flyht,* from *fleogan,* to fly.]

1. The act or power of flying; a passing through the air by the help of wings; volitation; as, the *flight* of birds and insects.

2. The manner of flying; as, every bird has its particular *flight*; the *flight* of the eagle is high; the *flight* of the swallow is rapid.

3. Removal from place to place by flying; also, the space passed in flying.

4. A flock or number of beings or things moving from one place to another; as, a *flight* of angels, birds, arrows, or bees.

5. A periodical flying of birds in flocks; as, the spring *flight* of ducks or geese.

6. A mounting; a soaring; lofty elevation and excursion; as, a *flight* of imagination or fancy; a *flight* of ambition.

7. Excursion; wandering; extravagant sally; as, a *flight* of folly.

8. Swift motion in general; rapid movement caused by a propelling force; as, the *flight* of a bullet.

9. The section of a stairway leading from one landing to the next; as, a *flight* of stairs.

10. In the clapper of a bell, the tail or part below the hammer.

11. The glume or husk of oats, etc.

12. The path of an arrow shot from a bow.

To put to flight or *to turn to flight*; to compel to run away; to force to escape.

flight, *a.* In sporting, belonging to a flight or flock; as, *flight* birds, that is, birds belonging to a migratory flock.

flight'ed, *a.* 1. Taking flight; flying. [Obs.]

2. In heraldry, feathered.

flight'ẽr, *n.* In brewing, a horizontal vane which rotates in a cooler to induce a circular current in the wort.

flight'-feath"ẽr (-feth"), *n.* In ornithology, a stiff feather of a bird's wing.

flight'i-ly, *adv.* In a flighty, wild, or imaginative manner.

flight'i-ness, *n.* The state of being flighty; wildness; slight delirium or mental aberration.

flight'-shot, *n.* The distance which an arrow flies.

flight'y, *a.* 1. Fleeting; swift.

The *flighty* purpose never is o'ertook.—Shak.

2. Wild; indulging in sallies of imagination.

3. Disordered in mind; somewhat delirious.

flim'flam, *n.* [A reduplication of *flam.*] A freak; a trick; a bold trick of deception in changing money.

flim'mẽr-ball, *n.* [G. *flimmern,* to glimmer, glitter.] An almost spherical microscopic marine protozoan, covered with delicate swimming organs or cilia.

flim'si-ly, *adv.* In a flimsy manner.

flim'si-ness, *n.* The state or quality of being flimsy; thin, weak texture; weakness; want of substance or solidity.

flim'sy, *a.*; *comp.* flimsier; *superl.* flimsiest. [Perhaps from W. *llymsi,* sluggish, spiritless.]

1. Weak; feeble; slight; vain; without strength or solid substance; as, a *flimsy* pretext; a *flimsy* excuse; *flimsy* objections.

2. Without strength or force of any kind; spiritless.

Proud of a vast extent of *flimsy* lines.—Pope.

3. Thin; of loose texture; as, *flimsy* cloth or stuff.

Syn.—Gauzy, poor, thin, transparent, trifling, trivial, puerile, inane, slight, superficial, weak, shallow, unsubstantial.

flim'sy, *n.* Extremely thin paper, as transfer-paper.

flinch, *v.i.*; flinched, *pt., pp.*; flinching, *ppr.* [A nasalized form of ME. *flecchen,* to flinch, waver.]

1. To shrink; to withdraw from any suffering or undertaking, from fear of pain or danger; to fail of proceeding, or of performing anything; as, never *flinch* from duty; one of the parties *flinched* from the combat.

2. To fail.

3. In croquet, to let the foot slip when holding a ball under it for a stroke.

flinch, *n.* A failure; a shrinking.

flinch'ẽr, *n.* One who flinches or fails.

flinch'ing, *n.* A shrinking or drawing back under pain or difficulty; a flinch.

flinch'ing-ly, *adv.* In a flinching manner.

flin'dẽr, *n.* See *Flinders.*

flin'dẽr-mouse, *n.* A flittermouse; a bat.

flin'dẽrs, *n.pl.* [G. *flinder, flinter,* a small piece of shining metal; D. *flenter,* a broken piece.] Small pieces or splinters; fragments; as, to break into *flinders.*

fling, *v.t.*; flung, *pt., pp.*; flinging, *ppr.* [ME. *flyngen, flengen,* to hurl, rush; Ice. *flengja,* to whip, ride furiously.]

1. To cast, send, or throw from the hand; to hurl; to cast forth with force or suddenness; to throw in an impatient, passionate, indifferent, or contemptuous manner; as, she *flung* her hat aside.

'Tis fate that *flings* the dice; and as she *flings,*
Of kings makes peasants, and of peasants, kings. —Dryden.

2. To send forth; to emit; to scatter.

Every beam new transient colors *flings.* —Pope.

3. To throw to the ground; to prostrate; hence, to baffle; to defeat; as, to *fling* a party in litigation.

To fling about; to scatter in every direction.

To fling away; to reject; to discard; as, *fling away* ambition.

To fling down; (a) to demolish; to ruin; (b) to throw to the ground.

To fling in; to throw in; to make an allowance or deduction, or not to charge in an account; as, in settling accounts, one party *flings in* a small sum, or a few days' work.

To fling in one's face; to upbraid one in person with; to taunt one with.

To fling off; to baffle in the chase; to defeat of prey; to get rid of.

To fling oneself about; to dash here and there in an agitated manner.

To fling open; to throw open; to open suddenly or with violence; as, *to fling open* a door.

To fling out; to utter; to speak; as, *to fling out* hard words against another.

To fling up; to relinquish; to abandon; as, *to fling up* a situation or an office.

fling, *v.i.* 1. To flounce; to wince; to fly into violent and irregular motions; as, the horse began to kick and *fling.*

2. To utter harsh language; to sneer; to upbraid; as, the scold began to flout and *fling.*

3. To rush or spring with violence or haste; to start or rush away in anger.

4. To discharge or let fly a missile.

fling, *n.* 1. A throw; a flounce; a cast from the hand.

2. A gibe; a sneer; a sarcasm; a severe or contemptuous remark.

I, who love to have a *fling*
Both at senate-house and king. —Swift.

3. A kind of lively individual Scotch dance; also called *Highland fling.*

4. Liberty of action; unrestrained indulgence of oneself in pleasure; as, he had his *fling.*

Give me my *fling,* and let me say my say. —Tennyson.

5. A matter of no importance. [Obs.]

England were but a *fling,*
Save for the crooked stick and the gray goose wing. —Old Proverb.

fling'dust, *n.* A streetwalker. [Obs.]

fling'ẽr, *n.* One who flings; one who jeers.

flint, *a.* Made or composed of flint; hard and firm, like flint; as, *flint*-glass; *flint* wheat; *flint* implements.

Flint age; see *Stone age* under *Stone.*

Flint brick; a fire-brick of hard quality made of pulverized flint.

Flint implements; tools and weapons made of flint and other hard stones and employed by men before they worked in metals. They are still in use among savage tribes, and specimens of them are frequently found associated with extinct animals.

Flint wall; a kind of wall built in England; so called because the black surfaces of broken flints are exposed on the face.

flint, *n.* [ME. *flint*; AS. *flint,* flint rock.]

1. In mineralogy, a variety of silica of a yellowish- or bluish-gray, or grayish-black color. Its surface is generally uneven and covered with a rind or crust, either calcareous or argillaceous. It is very hard, strikes fire with steel, and was extensively used in prehistoric times for cutting implements.

2. A piece of *flint* formerly used to strike fire.

3. Anything very hard; as, a heart of *flint.*

Liquor of flints; a solution of flint or silica in potash; potassium silicate.

To skin a flint; to be guilty of or capable of obtaining money in any mean or hard-hearted way. [Colloq.]

flint'-glass, *n.* The purest and most beautiful kind of glass, distinguished by its containing oxid of lead combined with potassium silicate; used in the manufacture of table glassware, lenses, etc.; named from its formerly having been made from flints.

flint'-heärt"ed, *a.* Having a hard, unfeeling heart; cruel.

flint'i-ness, *n.* The quality of being flinty; hardness.

flint'lock, *n.* 1. A kind of gunlock in which the priming charge was ignited by a spark from a flint held between the jaws of the cock or hammer. It succeeded the matchlock, and was superseded by the percussion-lock.

2. An old-fashioned musket equipped with such a lock.

flint'-mill, *n.* 1. An appliance formerly used for lighting miners at their work by striking sparks from flints attached to a rotating wheel.

2. A mill for grinding and sharpening flints.

flint'stōne, *n.* A hard silicious stone; flint.

flint'wāre, *n.* A kind of earthenware in the manufacture of which ground flints are mixed with the clay.

flint'wood, *n.* The common name for the very hard wood of an Australian tree, the mountain-ash, *Eucalyptus pilularis.*

flint'y, *a.*; *comp.* flintier; *superl.* flintiest. 1. Consisting of flint; as, a *flinty* rock.

2. Like flint; very hard; not impressible; as, a *flinty* heart.

3. Cruel; unmerciful; inexorable.

4. Full of flintstones; as, *flinty* ground.

Flinty slate; a silicious rock of two kinds, the common and the Lydian stone, or basanite. The former has a somewhat slaty structure and contains about 75 per cent of silica. The latter is less hard, and is sometimes used as a touchstone for gold and silver.

flip, *n.* [Origin unknown.] A mixed drink composed of ale, beer, cider, etc., sweetened, spiced, and heated generally by the immersion of a hot iron.

flip, *v.t.*; flipped (flipt), *pt., pp.*; flipping, *ppr.* To snap with or as with the finger or thumb; to fillip; as, to *flip* a marble in playing or a penny in tossing up.

To flip up; to toss up a coin to decide a question, usually, as to first choice in a game.

flip, *v.i.* [A form of *flap.*] To make a noise like flapping or clapping; as, the fish *flipped* all over the bottom of the boat.

flip'-dog, *n.* An iron used, when heated, to warm flip.

flīpe, *v.t.* To turn inside out, as a stocking in drawing it off. [Prov. Eng. and Scot.]

flip'flap, *adv.* With a flapping noise.

flip'flap, *n.* A continued flapping noise, as of something broad and flat, as a board.

flip'păn-cy, *n.* The quality of being flippant, presumptuous, trifling in speech or conduct; pertness.

flip'pănt, *a.* [Ice. *fleipa,* to babble, prattle; *fleipr,* babble, tattle.]

1. Of smooth, fluent, and rapid speech; speaking with ease and rapidity; having a voluble tongue; talkative.

2. Pert; petulant; impertinently talkative; disrespectfully smart; light and trifling in quality; shallow.

Away with *flippant* epilogues. —Thomson.

Syn.—Pert, forward, superficial, thoughtless, saucy, malapert.

flip'pănt, *n.* A person given to flippancy. [Rare.]

flip'pănt-ly, *adv.* In a flippant manner.

flip'pănt-ness, *n.* Flippancy.

flip'pẽr, *n.* The paddle of a sea-turtle; the broad fin of a fish; the paddle-like limb of a seal or a whale.

flirt, *v.t.*; flirted, *pt.*, *pp.*; flirting, *ppr.* [AS. *fleardian*, to trifle, *fleard*, a foolish thing.]
1. To throw with a jerk or sudden effort or exertion; as, the boys *flirt* water in each other's faces.
2. To toss or throw; to move suddenly; to handle with short, quick movements; as, to *flirt* a fan.
3. To jeer or scoff at; to flout.

flirt, *v.i.* 1. To jeer or gibe; to throw bantering or sarcastic words; to utter contemptuous language.
2. To run and dart about; to act with giddiness, or from a desire to attract notice; to be unsteady or fluttering; as, the girls *flirt* about the room or the street.
3. To play the coquette; to coquet; to make insincere advances; as, to *flirt* with gentlemen; to *flirt* with a widow; to *flirt* with a foreign power.

flirt, *n.* 1. A sudden jerk; a quick throw or cast; a darting motion.

In unfurling the fan are several little *flirts* and vibrations. —Addison.

2. One who flirts; especially, a girl or woman who plays at courtship; a coquette.

Several young *flirts* about town had a design to cast us out of the fashionable world. —Addison.

flirt, *a.* Pert; wanton. [Obs.]

flir-tā′tion, *n.* 1. A flirting; a quick, sprightly motion.
2. Playing at courtship; coquetry.

flir-tā′tious, *a.* Inclined to flirt; given to flirtation. [Colloq.]

flirt′-gill, *n.* A pert girl; a wanton. [Obs.]

flirt′i-gig, *n.* A flirt or wanton. [Obs.]

flirt′ing-ly, *adv.* In a flirting manner.

flisk, *v.i.* To frisk; to caper. [Obs.]

flisk, *n.* 1. A playful motion; a caper. [Scot.]
2. A whisk-broom or brush. [Prov. Eng.]
3. A large-toothed comb. [Prov. Eng.]

flit, *v.t.* To cause to flit or remove; to remove; to dispossess. [Prov. Eng. and Scot.]

flit, *v.i.*; flitted, *pt.*, *pp.*; flitting, *ppr.* [ME. *flitten*, *flytten*, *flutten*, to move, depart, migrate; Ice. *flytja*; Sw. *flytta*, to remove, carry.]
1. To fly away with a rapid motion; to dart along; to move with celerity through the air; as, a bird *flits* away or *flits* in air; a cloud *flits* along.
2. To flutter; to rove on the wing.
3. To remove; to migrate; to pass rapidly, as a light substance, from one place to another.

It became a received opinion, that the souls of men, departing this life, did *flit* out of one body into some other. —Hooker.

4. To remove from one residence to another. [Prov. Eng. and Scot.]

flit, *a.* Nimble; quick; swift; fleet. [Obs.]

flitch, *n.*; *pl.* **flitch′es**. [ME. *flicche*, *fliche*; AS. *flicce*; Ice. *flikki*, a flitch of bacon.]
1. The side of a hog salted and cured: used chiefly in the phrase, a *flitch* of bacon.
2. One of several planks, timbers, or iron plates fastened together side by side to make a large girder or compound beam.
3. A slab; a piece sawed from the outside of a log.
4. A thin slice smoked or cut for smoking, as of halibut.

flitch, *v.t.*; flitched, *pt.*, *pp.*; flitching, *ppr.* To cut into flitches, as a hog.

flite, flyte, *n.* The act of scolding; a quarrel with angry words. [Scot.]

flite, *v.i.* To brawl. [Prov. Eng. and Scot.]

flit′tēr, *v.t.* and *v.i.* [Rare.] See *Flutter*.

flit′tēr, *v.i.* To scatter in pieces. [Obs.]

flit′tēr, *n.* A rag; a tatter.

flit′tēr-mouse, *n.* A bat; a flindermouse.

flit′tērn, *a.* In tannery, applied to the bark stripped from young oak-trees, as distinguished from that of old trees, which is less valuable than *flittern* bark.

flit′ti-ness, *n.* Unsteadiness; levity; lightness. [Obs.]

flit′ting, *n.* 1. A flying with lightness and celerity; a fluttering.
2. A removal from one habitation to another. [Scot. and Prov. Eng.]

Two *flittings* are as bad as a fire. —Eng. Proverb.

flit′ting-ly, *adv.* In a flitting manner.

flit′ty, *a.* Unstable; fluttering. [Obs.]

flix, *n.* Down; fur; especially, the fur of the hare. [Obs.]

flix, *n.* [Obs.] See *Flux*.

flix′weed, *n.* A plant, *Sisymbrium Sophia*, a species of water-cress growing on walls and waste grounds, formerly used as a remedy in cases of dysentery.

flō, *n.* [ME. *flo*, *flon*; AS. *flan*, an arrow.] An arrow. [Obs.]

flōat, *n.* [ME. *flote*; AS. *flota*, a boat, ship, from *fleotan*, to float.]
1. That which floats or is borne on water.
2. A body or collection of timber, boards, or planks, fastened together and conveyed down a stream; a raft.
3. The cork, quill, etc., used on a fishing line, to support it and to indicate the bite of a fish.
4. The act of flowing; flux; flood. [Obs.]
5. A plasterer's trowel for spreading plaster.
6. A block for polishing marble.
7. An apparatus for tempering steel by a stream of water.
8. A file for smoothing; a shoemaker's tool for smoothing the inside of a shoe.
9. A coal-cart. [Eng.]
10. A hollow metal ball in a self-acting faucet.
11. A vehicle with a large platform, used for display in a parade.
12. A swinging bed in a wagon for hauling heavy material.
13. A life-preserver; anything used to keep upon the surface of the water persons or objects liable to sink.
14. A drag used by farmers for smoothing plowed ground.
15. In mining, fragments of mineral found on the surface.
16. A floating dock or wharf.
17. In zoölogy, an organ or sac which, inflated by air, serves to support an animal in the water.

flōat, *v.i.*; floated, *pt.*, *pp.*; floating, *ppr.* [ME. *flotien*; AS. *flotian*, to float, swim, from *fleotan*, to float.]
1. To be borne or sustained on the surface of a fluid; to swim; to be buoyed up; as, the ship *floats*.
2. To move or be conveyed on water; to swim; as, the raft *floats* down the river.

Three blustering nights, borne by the southern blast,
I *floated*. —Dryden.

3. To be buoyed up and moved or conveyed in an element, as in air.

They stretch their broad plumes and *float* upon the wind. —Pope.

4. To move with a light, irregular course; as, a rumor has *floated* here.

flōat, *v.t.* 1. To cause to rest or swim on a liquid; to cause to be conveyed on water; as, the tide *floated* the ship into the harbor.
2. To flood; to inundate; to overflow; to cover with water.
3. In plastering, to pass over and level the surface of, as plaster on a wall, with a float dipped frequently in water.
4. To support in business; as, to *float* a company or firm.
5. To sell on the market; to secure recognition of; as, to *float* bonds or stocks.
To float up; to solder the ends of (tin cans) inside.

flōat′ȧ-ble, *a.* Capable of being floated.

flōat′āge, *n.* Anything that floats on the water; also, capacity for floating.

flōat-ā′tion, *n.* Same as *Flotation*.

flōat′-bōard, *n.* 1. A board on the rim of an undershot water-wheel, which receives the impulse of the stream by which the wheel is driven.
2. One of the paddles of a steamer's paddle-wheel.

flōat′-ċase, *n.* An air-tight case or drum used in lifting by means of the upward pressure of water.

flōat′-ċop″pēr, *n.* Minute particles of copper carried away by the action of water.

flōat′ēr, *n.* 1. One who floats or swims.
2. An instrument for registering the level of a liquid.
3. In political slang, a voter who is attached to no particular party, especially one whose vote may be purchased.
4. The corpse of a drowned person found floating. [Slang.]

flōat′-grass, *n.* Any species of grass growing in low marshy places, as the meadow-foxtail, *Alopecurus geniculatus*.

flōat′ing, *a.* 1. Lying flat on the surface of the water; borne up and conveyed along by either a liquid or a gas; as, a *floating* leaf.
2. Circulating; passing; not fixed; as, *floating* capital; a *floating* population.
3. Free; disconnected; as, a *floating* rib.
Floating anchor; a drag; a device used at sea to keep a ship's head to the wind or prevent drifting.
Floating battery; in military affairs, a battery mounted upon a float of some kind, as upon a raft or rafts.
Floating board; a plate of cast-iron used in floating up tin cans.
Floating bridge; (a) a bridge consisting of logs or timber with a floor of plank, supported wholly by the water; (b) in military engineering, a kind of double bridge, the upper one projecting beyond the lower one, and capable of being moved forward by pulleys, used for carrying troops over narrow moats in attacking the outworks of a fort; (c) a kind of large steam ferry-boat; (d) a pontoon-bridge; (e) the movable platform of a ferry-dock.
Floating cartilage; a free cartilage in the hollow of a joint.
Floating derrick; a derrick mounted on a flat boat.
Floating dock; see under *Dock*.
Floating harbor; a harbor inclosed by floating breakwaters.
Floating heart; an aquatic plant, *Limnanthemum lacunosum*, whose leaves are heart-shaped.
Floating island; in cookery, a custard with a mass of whipped cream or whipped whites of eggs floating on the top, sometimes colored with jelly.
Floating lever; one of two horizontal brake-levers under the center of a railroad-car body.
Floating light; a light-ship.
Floating pier; a pier that rises and falls with the tide.
Floating ribs; in anatomy, ribs whose ventral ends are free; in man, the last two pairs.
Floating screed; in plastering, a strip of plastering put on to guide the float.
Floating threads; in weaving, threads dropped but picked up again in the course of the web.

flōat′ing, *n.* 1. The act of supporting oneself, or the state of being supported upon the surface of water; flotation.
2. In weaving, a thread of weft which floats, spans, or crosses on the top of several warped threads.
3. In plastering, the spreading of stucco or plastering on the surface of walls; the second coat of three-coat work.
4. In hunting, the method or practice of hunting game by approaching it with a boat at night.
5. In agriculture, the flooding or overflowing of meadow-lands.

flōat′ing-ly, *adv.* By floating or as if by floating; swimmingly.

flōat′-min″ēr-ăl, *n.* Fragments of ore found at a distance from their native bed or vein, as the result of erosion.

flōat′stōne, *n.* 1. Spongiform quartz, a mineral of a spongy texture, of a whitish-gray color, often with a tinge of yellow, frequently containing a nucleus of common flint.
2. In bricklaying, a stone employed in smoothing curved work.

flōat′y, *a.* Buoyant; swimming on the surface; light. [Rare.]

floc′ci, *n.*, pl. of *floccus*.

floc-cil-lā′tion, *n.* [From L. *floccus*, a flock of wool.] In pathology, a picking of the bedclothes by a sick person, as if picking bunches of wool, an alarming symptom in acute disease; also called *carphologia*.

floc-cōse′, *a.* [LL. *floccosus*, full of flocks of wool, from *floccus*, a flock of wool.] In botany, composed of or bearing tufts of woolly or long and soft hairs; woolly.

floc′cū-lăr, *a.* Pertaining to or resembling a flocculus.

floc′cū-lāte, *v.i.*; flocculated, *pt.*, *pp.*; flocculating, *ppr.* [From L. *floccus*, a flock of wool.] To be associated in tufts or bunches; in geology, to gather in accretions, as nodules.

floc′cū-lāte, *a.* In entomology bearing a bunch of stiff and sometimes curly hairs.

floc-cū-lā′tion, *n.* In geology, the act or process of becoming flocculär.

floc′cūle, *n.* [A dim. from L. *floccus*, a flock of wool.]
1. A detached tuft of any shredded fibrous substance.
2. In chemistry, a small aggregation of insoluble matter.

floc′cū-lence, *n.* 1. The state of being in locks or flocks; adhesion in small flakes.
2. A peculiar white, waxy excretion of certain insects, especially of the *Homoptera*.

floc′cū-lent, *a.* 1. Coalescing and adhering in locks or flakes.
2. Abounding in flocculi.
3. Resembling a flock of wool; woolly; fleecy.
4. In chemistry, designating certain precipitates resembling tufts of wool.
5. In entomology, covered with flocculence.

floc′cū-lī, *n.*, pl. of *flocculus*.

floc′cū-lōse, *a.* Flocculent; in botany, floccose.

floc′cū-lus, *n.*; *pl.* **floc′cū-lī**. [Dim. from L. *floccus*, a flock of wool.]
1. In anatomy, a small tuft-like lobe on the under side of the cerebellar hemisphere.
2. A small tuft of dermal appendages, as hair or feathers; as, the *flocculi* on the legs of an insect or on the leaf or stem of a plant.
3. In chemistry, a small aggregation of particles formed in a liquid by agitation.

floc′cus, *n.*; *pl.* **floc′ci**. [L., a flock of wool.]
1. In zoölogy, a tuft on the end of an animal's tail, or the downy plumage of a very young bird.
2. [*pl.*] In botany, the fibrous, wool-like filaments occurring sometimes in connection with sporules of certain fungi.

flock, *n.* [ME. *flock*, *flok*, *floc*; AS. *floc*, *flocc*, a band, company.]

1. A company or collection of the smaller domestic animals, especially of sheep or goats.

2. A company or collection of birds of any kind, and, when applied to birds on the wing, a flight; as, a *flock* of wild geese; a *flock* of ducks; a *flock* of blackbirds.

3. In ecclesiastical use, the people united in one church, under a leader figuratively called a *shepherd* or *pastor*; a congregation considered in its relation to its minister.

flock, *v.i.*; flocked (flokt), *pt.*, *pp.*; flocking, *ppr.* To gather in companies or crowds; as, people *flock* together in seasons of disaster; they *flock* to the playhouse.

Syn.—Herd, congregate, throng, assemble, crowd.

flock, *n.* [OFr. *floc*; L. *floccus*, a flock or lock of wool.]

1. A lock or tuft of wool or hair.

2. Old cloth, rags, wool refuse and remnants cut and shredded for use in upholstery.

3. Finely powdered wool or cloth used when colored for making flock-paper.

4. In chemistry, light masses of flocculent matter suspended in a solution.

flock, *v.t.* To cover with flock; to distribute flock on.

flock′=bed, *n.* A bed filled with flocks or locks of wool, or pieces of cloth cut up fine; a bed stuffed with flock.

> A house well furnish'd shall be thine to keep;
> And for a *flock-bed* I can shear my sheep.
> —Dryden.

flocked (flokt), *a.* Covered with flock; having the nap raised.

flock′ling, *n.* A small or young member of a flock, as a lamb or a kid.

flock′ly, *adv.* In a body or flock. [Obs.]

flock′=pā″pẽr, *n.* A kind of wall-paper covered with flock or having raised figures resembling cloth, made of flock and attached to the paper by size or varnish; also called *velvet-paper*.

flock′y, *a.* Abounding with flocks or locks; woolly.

flōe, *n.* [Dan. *is-flage*; Norw. *is-flak*, dial. *is-flok*, an ice-floe.] A low, fairly level mass of floating ice of indefinite size.

> The whole sea was covered with *floes* varying from a few yards to miles in diameter.
> —Moss.

flōe′=rat, *n.* The ringed seal, *Pagomys fœtidus*.

flog, *v.t.*; flogged, *pt.*, *pp.*; flogging, *ppr.* [Prob. an abbrev. of L. *flagellare*, to whip.]

1. To beat or strike with a rod or whip; to whip; to lash; to chastise with repeated blows; as, to *flog* a schoolboy.

2. In fishing, to lash (the water) with the line.

3. To beat, in the sense of to surpass; to excel. [Colloq.]

> If I don't think good cherry-bounce *flogs* all the foreign trash in the world! —Hook.

To flog a dead horse; to try to revive interest in a stale subject.

flog′gẽr, *n.* 1. One who flogs.

2. A sort of mallet to start the bung of a cask; also called *bung-starter*.

flog′ging, *n.* A whipping for punishment; a chastisement.

flog′ging=chis″el, *n.* A large chisel for removing irregularities from castings.

flog′ging=ham″mẽr, *n.* A machinist's heavy hammer used for driving a flogging-chisel.

flōne, *n.* An arrow. [Obs.]

flong, *v.*, obsolete past tense and past participle of *fling*.

flong, *n.* The matrix used in the papier-maché process of stereotyping, or the paper of which it is composed.

flood (flud), *v.t.*; flooded, *pt.*, *pp.*; flooding, *ppr.*

1. To overflow; to inundate; to deluge; as, to *flood* a meadow; the river rose and *flooded* the surrounding country.

2. Figuratively, to deluge; as, to *flood* the country with cheap literature or with a depreciated currency.

flood, *v.i.* 1. To be spread out; to rise and overflow; as, the Nile *floods* annually.

2. To have menstrual or post-partum hemorrhage.

flood, *n.* [ME. *flood*, *flod*; AS. *flod*, flowing water, a river.]

1. A great flow of water; a body of moving water; particularly, a body of water, as a river, rising, swelling, and overflowing land not usually covered with water; an inundation; a deluge; as, there is an annual *flood* of the Nile.

2. The inflowing of the tide; the semidiurnal swell or rise of water in the ocean; opposed to *ebb*.

3. A great quantity; an inundation; an overflowing abundance; superabundance; as, a *flood* of bank-notes; a *flood* of paper currency.

4. A great body or stream of any fluid or fluid-like substance; as, a *flood* of light; a *flood* of lava.

5. Menstrual discharge when excessive.

The Flood; the Deluge; the great body of water which inundated the earth in the days of Noah.

Syn.—Deluge, inundation, abundance, overflow, submergence, superabundance.

flood′āge, *n.* An overflow. [Rare.]

flood′=an″chŏr, *n.* The anchor that holds a ship during the flood-tide.

flood′ẽr, *n.* One who causes a flood; one who irrigates.

flood′=fence, *n.* A fence constructed to withstand the force of a flood.

flood′gāte, *n.* 1. A gate to be opened for letting water flow through, or to be shut to prevent it.

2. An opening or passage; an avenue for a flood or great body; a great vent; as, to open the *floodgates* to immigration of foreign labor.

flood′ing, *n.* 1. The act of overflowing or inundating; inundation.

2. A morbid discharge of blood from the uterus.

flood′=märk, *n.* The mark or line to which the tide rises; high-water mark.

flood′=plāin, *n.* In geology, the area in a river-valley covered with alluvial deposits.

flood′=tide, *n.* The rising tide; opposed to *ebb-tide*.

flo͝ok, *n.* Same as *Fluke*.

flo͝ok′ăn, *n.* Same as *Flucan*.

flo͝ok′ing, *n.* See *Flucan*.

flo͝ok′y, *a.* Same as *Fluky*.

flo͞or, *v.t.*; floored, *pt.*, *pp.*; flooring, *ppr.* 1. To lay a floor in or upon; to cover with a floor; to furnish with a floor; as, to *floor* a house with pine boards.

2. To strike down or lay level with the floor; to beat; to conquer, as, to *floor* an antagonist.

3. Figuratively to put to silence by some decisive argument, retort, etc.; as, to *floor* an opponent in debate.

4. To finish; to put an end to; as, to *floor* a bottle of wine. [Slang.]

flo͞or, *n.* [ME. *floor*, *flore*, *flor*; AS. *flor*, a floor.]

1. That part of a building or room on which one walks; the bottom or lower part, consisting, in modern houses, of boards, planks, or pavement; as, the *floor* of a house, room, barn, stable, or hall.

2. A platform of boards or planks laid on timbers, as in a bridge; any similar platform.

3. A story in a building; as, the first *floor*; the ground *floor*.

4. The bottom of a vessel on each side of the keelson.

5. In mining, the comparatively level formation on which a deposit lies; also, a flat, or nearly flat, mass of ore.

6. In legislative bodies, the part of the house set apart for members; as, the distinguished visitor was admitted to the *floor*; hence, the right to be heard; as, the gentleman from Illinois has the *floor*.

7. In malting, a quantity of grain spread out upon a floor for steeping; also called *piece*.

flo͞or′āge, *n.* The area included in a floor or floors; as, the building has a *floorage* of ten thousand square feet.

flo͞or′=clo̤th, *n.* 1. A heavy canvas or oilcloth used as a covering for a floor.

2. Any fabric used for covering carpet as a protection.

flo͞or′=cramp, *n.* A device for holding strips of flooring in place until they are nailed.

flo͞or′ẽr, *n.* 1. One who makes or lays floors.

2. One who or that which floors, as a blow which floors a person; hence, figuratively, anything which leads to a person's defeat or which overmasters him, as, in the universities, an examination question which a student cannot answer. [Slang.]

flo͞or′head (-hed), *n.* In shipbuilding, an outer end of the floor-timbers.

flo͞or′ing, *n.* 1. A platform; the bottom of a room or building; pavement; floors collectively.

2. Materials for floors.

flo͞or′less, *a.* Having no floor.

flo͞or′=light (-līt), *n.* Any glazed opening in a floor for the admission of light.

flo͞or′=plan, *n.* 1. In architecture, a drawing showing a horizontal section of a building at the level of a floor.

2. In shipbuilding, a drawing representing a water-line section of a ship, and showing the bottom timbers.

flo͞or′=tim″bẽr, *n.* One of the timbers on which a floor is laid; in shipbuilding, one of the timbers placed immediately across the keel.

flo͞or′wa̤lk″ẽr (-wa̤k″), *n.* A person employed on the floor of a retail shop or store to give information to buyers, supervise the work of employees, and maintain order, prevent or detect thievery, etc.

flop, *v.t.*; flopped (flopt), *pt.*, *pp.*; flopping, *ppr.* [A form of *flap*.]

1. To clap or strike, as the wings, the tail, or the flippers; to flap.

2. To cause to fall or hang down.

3. To turn over suddenly; as, to *flop* a board.

flop, *v.i.* 1. To turn or come down suddenly; to plump down quickly; as, he *flopped* on his knees. [Colloq.]

2. To change associations suddenly; as, to *flop* in politics. [Slang.]

3. To collapse; to break down. [Slang.]

To flop over; (a) to turn over heavily or suddenly; (b) to go over to another side or party. [Slang.]

flop, *n.* A sudden heavy or awkward change of position.

flop′py, *a.* Liable to flop; given to flopping; flabby; as, a *floppy* hat.

flop′wing, *n.* Same as *Lapwing*.

Flō′rȧ, *n.* [L. *Flora*, goddess of flowers; *flos*, *floris*, a flower.]

1. In classic mythology, the goddess of flowers.

2. [f—] The complete series of plants of any particular country, region, or period; as, the *flora* of New England, of the Mississippi valley, or of the Carboniferous age; frequently used in association with *fauna*; as, the *fauna* and *flora* of North America.

3. [f—] In botany, a work systematically describing the species of plants of a country or geological period.

4. One of the small planets or asteroids between the orbits of Mars and Jupiter.

flō′răl, *a.* [L. *floralis*, from *flos*, *floris*, a flower.]

1. Containing the flower; as, a *floral* bud; immediately attending the flower; as, a *floral* leaf.

2. [F—] Pertaining to Flora; as, *Floral* games.

3. Relating to flowers in general; as, *floral* decorations.

Floral envelope; the perianth of a flower.

Flō-rā′li-ȧ, *n.pl.* In Roman mythology, festive ceremonies held in honor of Flora in the spring.

flō′răl-ly, *adv.* In a floral manner.

flō′rȧ-mōur, *n.* [From Fr. *fleur d'amour*, lit., flower of love.] An old name for *Amarantus melancholicus* or love-lies-bleeding. [Obs.]

flō′ran, *n.* Fine-grained tin, either scarcely perceptible in the stone or stamped very small.

Flō′ré-ăl (-rā-), *n.* [Fr., from L. *floreus*, of flowers, from *flos*, *floris*, a flower.] In the calendar of the first French republic, the eighth month of the year. It commenced April 20 and ended May 19.

flō′rē-ā-ted, flō′ri-ā-ted, *a.* [L. *floreus*, of flowers, from *flos*, *floris*, a flower.] Decked or ornamented with flowers, especially with conventionalized flowers; as, *floreated* columns.

flor′en, flor′ein, *n.* [Obs.] See *Florin*.

flor′ence, *n.* [From *Florence*, in Italy.]

1. An ancient gold coin of Edward III., value six shillings sterling.

2. A kind of thin silk cloth.

3. [F—] A kind of red wine produced in Tuscany.

Florence flask; see under *Flask*.

Flor′en-tine, *a.* Pertaining to the city of Florence, Italy, the chief city of Tuscany.

Florentine frame; a heavily carved gilt frame.

Florentine mosaic; a kind of mosaic, often representing natural objects, as leaves and flowers in colors, and laid in a surface of black or white marble.

Flor′en-tīne, *n.* 1. A native or inhabitant of Florence.

2. [f—] A kind of silk cloth of fine texture.

3. [f—] A kind of meat or fruit pie baked in a dish, without under crust. [Obs.]

flō-res′cence, *n.* [L. *florescens* (-*entis*), ppr. of *florescere*, to begin to bloom, incept. of *florere*, to bloom, from *flos*, *floris*, a flower.] In botany, the act or process of putting forth flowers; the expanding of a bud into a flower; inflorescence.

flō-res′cent, *a.* Putting forth flowers; blooming.

flō′ret, *n.* [OFr. *floret*, dim. of *flor*, a flower.]

1. In botany, a little flower; one of the little flowers in a clustered or compact inflorescence, as in the *Compositæ* or in the spikelet of grasses.

2. A kind of silk floss or yarn.

3. A fencing-foil.

Flower of *Arnica montana*. 1. Ray-floret; 2. Disk-floret.

flō-rē′tum, *n.* [From L. *flos*, *floris*, a flower.] A garden set apart for the cultivation and scientific study of flowers.

flō′ri-āge, *n.* [From L. *flos*, *floris*, a flower, and -*age*.] Bloom; blossom. [Obs.]

flō′ri-ā-ted, *a.* See *Floreated*.

flor′i-căn, *n.* Same as *Florikan*.

flō′ri-cōme, *n.* A sponge-spicule with rays ending in a bunch of curved branches.

flō-ric′ō-mous, *a.* [LL. *floricomus*; *flos*, *floris*, a flower, and *coma*, hair of the head.] Resembling a floricome; having flowers on the head.

flō-ri-cul′tūr-ăl, *a.* Relating to floriculture.

flō′ri-cul-tūre, *n.* [L. *flos*, *floris*, a flower, and *cultura*, cultivation.] The cultivation of flowers or of flowering plants.

flō-ri-cul′tūr-ist, *n.* One engaged in floriculture or skilled in the processes of cultivating flowers and flowering plants.

flor'id, *a.* [L. *floridus*, flowery, from *florere*, to bloom, flower.]

1. Flowery; covered or abounding with flowers. [Rare.]

2. Bright in color; flushed with red; of a lively red color; as, a *florid* complexion.

3. Embellished with flowers of rhetoric; enriched to excess with figures; as, a *florid* style; *florid* eloquence.

4. In architecture, highly ornate.

5. In music, flowery in effect; abounding in passages of an ornamental character.

Syn.—Ruddy, rubicund, flowery, ornate.

Flō-rid'ē-æ, *n.pl.* [From L. *floridus*, flowery, from *flos*, *floris*, a flower.] An order of red or purple marine algæ.

flō-rid'ē-ous, *a.* Relating to the *Florideæ*.

Flō-rid'i-ăn, *a.* and *n.* I. *a.* Pertaining to Florida.

II. *n.* A native or inhabitant of Florida.

flō-rid'i-ty, *n.* Freshness or brightness of color; floridness.

flor'id-ly, *adv.* In a florid manner.

flor'id-ness, *n.* 1. Brightness or freshness of color or complexion.

2. Embellishment; brilliant ornamentation; ambitious elegance; applied to style.

flō-rif'ẽr-ous, *a.* [L. *florifer*; *flos*, *floris*, a flower, and *ferre*, to bear.] Producing flowers.

flor"i-fi-cā'tion, *n.* The act, process, or state of flowering.

flō'ri-fọrm, *a.* [L. *flos*, *floris*, a flower, and *forma*, form.] In the form of a flower.

flor'i-kăn, flor'i-ken, *n.* A kind of Indian bustard, *Sypheotides bengalensis*.

flor'i-lege, *n.* [L. *florilegus*, flower-culling; *flos*, *floris*, a flower, and *legere*, to gather.]

1. The culling or gathering of flowers. [Rare.]

2. A treatise on flowers.

flor-i-lē'ġi-um, *n.*; *pl.* **flor-i-lē'ġi-ȧ.** Same as *Florilege*, 2.

flor'in, *n.* [OFr. *florin*, from It. *fiorino*, originally a coin with a lily on it, from *fiore*, a flower.] A name given to different coins of gold or silver, of different values, and to various moneys of account in different countries. The English *florin* is two shillings, or about 50 cents; the Austrian gulden or *florin* of the present day, about the same; the gulden or *florin* of Germany and the guilder or *florin* of Holland, about 40 cents.

flō-ri-pon'di-ō, *n.* [Sp.] A Peruvian plant, *Datura sanguinea*, an infusion from the seeds of which produces stupefaction and delirium.

flō'rist, *n.* [L. *flos*, *floris*, a flower, and *-ist*.]

1. A cultivator of flowers; one skilled in flowers.

2. One who writes a flora, or an account of plants.

3. A dealer in cultivated and cut flowers; one who raises flowers for sale.

flō-ri-sū'ġent, *a.* [L. *flos*, *floris*, a flower, and *sugens* (*-entis*), ppr. of *sugere*, to suck.] Sucking flowers; applied to birds and insects which suck honey from flowers.

flō-rọọn', *n.* [ME. *flouroun*, flowerwork; OFr. *floron*, a flower, jewel, from *flos*, *floris*, a flower.] A border made ornamental by being worked with flowers; a flower-border.

flor'ū-lȧ, *n.pl.* [Dim. of *flora*.] A small flora; an enumeration of the plants of some particular region.

flor'ū-lent, *a.* [L. *florulentus*, flowery.] Flowery; blossoming. [Obs.]

flō'ry, *a.* [Fr. *fleuré*, flowered, from *fleur*; L. *flos*, *floris*, a flower.] In heraldry, bearing flowers, especially at a terminal; written also *fleury*.

flos'cū-lăr, *a.* [From L. *flosculus*, a little flower, dim. of *flos*, *floris*, a flower.] In botany, composed of florets; said of a composite flower; discoid.

flos-cū-lā'ri-ăn, *n.* In zoölogy, one of a typical genus of wheel-animalcules or rotifers, characterized by ciliated tentacles resembling the florets of a composite flower.

flos'cūle, *n.* [L. *flosculus*, a little flower.] In botany, a single flower of a compound or composite flower; a floret.

flos'cū-lous, *a.* Same as *Floscular*.

flos fer'ri. [L., flower of iron.] A mineral, a variety of aragonite, often occurring in veins of sparry iron.

flosh, *n.* [Perhaps from G. *flösse*, a box in which ore is washed.] A trough in which ore is placed for stamping.

floss, *n.* [OFr. *flosche*; It. *floscia*, soft, flabby, from L. *fluxus*, flowing, loose.]

1. A downy or silken substance in the husks and other parts of certain plants, as maize.

2. A fluid glass floating on iron in a puddling-furnace, produced by the vitrification of oxids and earths.

3. Untwisted filaments of the finest silk, used in embroidering; also called *floss-silk*.

floss'-hōle, *n.* In a blast-furnace, an opening for withdrawing slag.

flos"si-fi-cā'tion, *n.* Florification. [Rare.]

floss'-silk, *n.* The portions of raveled silk broken off in the filature of cocoons; floss. It is used chiefly for embroidery.

floss'y, *a.*; *comp.* flossier; *superl.* flossiest. Pertaining to, composed of, or resembling floss; fluffy.

flot, *n.* [Scot.] Scum; floating grease, as in fatty broth.

flō'tȧ, *n.* [Sp., a fleet.] A fleet; especially, a fleet of Spanish ships which formerly sailed every year from Cadiz to Vera Cruz, in Mexico, to transport to Spain the products of Spanish America.

flō'tāge, *n.* Same as *Floatage*.

flō'tănt, *a.* [Fr. *flottant*, ppr. of *flotter*, to float.] In heraldry, represented as flying, swimming, or floating in air or in water; as, a banner *flotant*.

A Banner Flotant.

flō-tā'tion, *n.* The act of floating; also, the science of floating bodies.

Center of flotation; in shipbuilding, the center of a plane of flotation.

Plane or *line of flotation*; the plane or line in which the surface of a fluid at rest cuts a body floating in it.

Surface of flotation; in a ship, the surface included by the extreme planes of flotation in rolling and pitching.

flō'tȧ-tive, *a.* Pertaining to flotation.

flōte, *v.* and *n.*, obsolete form of *float*.

flōte, *v.t.* To skim; to fleet. [Obs.]

flot'ẽr-y, *a.* [Obs.] See *Fluttery*.

flō-til'lȧ, *n.* [Sp. *flotilla*, dim. of *flota*, a fleet.] A little fleet or a fleet of small vessels.

flot'săm, *n.* [*Float* and *-some*.] Goods lost by shipwreck, and floating on the sea; distinguished from *jetsam*.

flot'sŏm, flot'sŏn, *n.* [Obs.] Same as *Flotsam*.

flounce, *v.i.*; flounced (flounst), *pt.*, *pp.*; flouncing, *ppr.* [Sw. dial. *flunsa*, to plunge, dip; Norw. *flunsa*, to hurry, work hurriedly.]

1. To throw the limbs and body one way and the other; to spring, turn, or twist with sudden effort or violence; to struggle, as a horse in mire.

> You neither fume, nor fret, nor *flounce*.
> —Swift.

2. To move with flings or turns; as, to *flounce* out of a room.

flounce, *v.t.* To deck with a flounce; as, to *flounce* a petticoat or frock.

flounce, *n.* 1. A sudden jerking motion of the body.

2. A narrow piece of cloth sewed to a petticoat, frock, or gown, with the lower border loose and spreading.

floun'cing, *n.* Material for making flounces; flounces collectively.

floun'dẽr, *n.* [ME. *flounder*, *flowndur*; Sw. and Norw. *flundra*, a flounder.]

1. A flatfish of the family *Pleuronectidæ*, as the plaice.

2. A tool used in bootmaking to crimp boot-fronts.

floun'dẽr, *v.i.*; floundered, *pt.*, *pp.*; floundering, *ppr.* [A nasalized form of D. *flodderen*, to dangle, splash.] To fling the limbs and body, as in making efforts to move; to struggle as a horse in the mire; to roll, toss, and tumble; figuratively, to grope uncertainly, as for ideas or facts; to make awkward efforts to extricate oneself from difficulty.

Syn.—Roll, blunder, bungle, boggle, wallow, tumble.

floun'dẽr, *n.* A motion as of floundering.

flour, *v.t.*; floured, *pt.*, *pp.*; flouring, *ppr.* 1. To grind and bolt; to convert into flour.

2. To sprinkle with flour.

flour, *n.* [Earlier spelling of *flower*; compare Fr. *fleur de farine*; Sp. *flor de la harina*, lit., flower of meal.] The meal of wheat or any other grain finely ground; especially the fine part separated by sifting or bolting; hence, any substance in a fine or powdered condition.

Flour of powder; gunpowder used in pyrotechny, before it is granulated.

Fossil flour; an earth composed chiefly of the frustules of diatoms; tripoli.

Graham flour; wheat-flour before being sifted or bolted.

Rock flour; fine particles of rock eroded by glacial action.

flour'-bee"tle, *n.* A beetle living in flour and meal.

flour'-dress"ẽr, *n.* A bolter or grader for flour.

flour'-em"ẽr-y, *n.* A powder used for polishing gems, made of corundum or emery.

flour'-gōld, *n.* Gold in minute particles, obtained by washing.

flŏur'ish (flur'), *v.i.*; flourished (-isht), *pt.*, *pp.*; flourishing, *ppr.* [ME. *flourishen*, *flurishen*, *florischen*, from OFr. *florir*, to bloom, blossom; from L. *florescere*, incept. of *florere*, to blossom, flower.]

1. To thrive; to grow luxuriantly; to increase and enlarge, as a healthy growing plant; as, the beech and the maple *flourish* best in a deep, rich, and moist loam.

2. To be prosperous; to increase in wealth or honor; as, the farmers of the west are *flourishing*.

3. To be in a prosperous state; to grow or be augmented; as, agriculture *flourishes*; manufactures *flourish*.

4. To use florid language; to make a display of figures and lofty expressions; to be copious and flowery.

> They dilate and *flourish* long on little incidents.
> —Watts.

5. To make bold strokes in writing; to make large and fanciful lines; as, to *flourish* with the pen.

6. To move or play in bold and irregular figures.

> Impetuous spread
> The stream, and smoking, *flourished* o'er his head.
> —Pope.

7. In music, to play with bold and irregular notes, or without settled form; as, to *flourish* on an organ or violin.

8. To boast; to vaunt; to brag.

Syn.—Prosper, thrive, triumph, brandish, wave.

flŏur'ish, *v.t.* 1. To adorn with flowers or beautiful figures, either natural or artificial; to ornament with anything showy.

2. To spread out; to enlarge into figures.

3. To move in bold or irregular figures; to move in circles or vibrations by way of show or triumph; to brandish; as, to *flourish* a sword.

4. To embellish with the flowers of diction; to adorn with rhetorical figures; to grace with ostentatious eloquence; to set off with a parade of words.

5. To mark with a flourish or irregular stroke; as, to *flourish* a signature or a manuscript.

6. To display ostentatiously; as, to *flourish* one's wealth or authority.

flŏur'ish (flur'), *n.* 1. Beauty; showy splendor.

> The *flourish* of his sober youth. —Crashaw.

2. Ostentatious embellishment; ambitious copiousness or amplification; parade of words and figures; show; as, a *flourish* of rhetoric; a *flourish* of wit.

> He lards with *flourishes* his long harangue.
> —Dryden.

3. Figures formed by bold, irregular lines or fanciful strokes of the pen or graver; as, the *flourishes* about a signature.

4. A brandishing; the waving of a weapon or other thing; as, the *flourish* of a sword.

flŏur'ish-ẽr, *n.* 1. One who flourishes; one who thrives or prospers.

2. One who brandishes.

3. One who adorns with fanciful figures.

flŏur'ish-ing-ly, *adv.* In a flourishing manner.

flour'-mite, *n.* A mite that lives in flour.

flour'-moth, *n.* One of several kinds of moth whose larvæ live in and feed upon flour and meal, especially *Ephestia kühniella*.

flour'y, *a.* Having the character of flour; resembling flour; coated with flour.

flout, *v.t.*; flouted, *pt.*, *pp.*; flouting, *ppr.* [Old D. *fluyten*; D. *fluiten*, to play the flute, jeer.] To mock or insult; to treat with contempt.

> He *flouted* us downright. —Shak.

flout, *v.i.* To mock; to sneer; to behave with contempt.

> Fleer and gibe, and laugh and *flout*.—Swift.

flout, *n.* A mock; an insult; a gibe.

flout'ẽr, *n.* One who flouts and flings; a mocker.

flout'ing-ly, *adv.* With flouting; insultingly; disdainfully.

flōw, *v.i.*; flowed, *pt.*, *pp.*; flowing, *ppr.* [ME. *flowen*; AS. *flowan*, to flow.]

1. To move by the operation of gravity and with a continual change of place among the particles or parts, as a fluid; as, the river *flows* to the south.

2. To proceed; to issue; as, evils *flow* from different sources; wealth *flows* from industry and economy.

3. To abound; to have in abundance.

> In that day the mountains shall drop down new wine, and the hills shall *flow* with milk.
> —Joel iii. 18.

4. To glide along smoothly, without harshness or asperity; as, a *flowing* period; *flowing* numbers.

5. To hang loose and waving; as, a *flowing* mantle; *flowing* locks.

> The imperial purple *flowing* in his train.
> —Hamilton.

6. To rise, as the tide; opposed to *ebb*; as, the tide *flows* twice in twenty-four hours.

7. To have an excessive discharge of blood from the uterus, as in menstruation.

Syn.—Stream, issue, progress, glide, course, career, run, float.

flōw, *v.t.* 1. To cover with water; to overflow; to inundate; as, the low grounds along the river are annually *flowed*.

2. To cover with any liquid, as varnish or glaze; as, a plate *flowed* with collodion.

flōw, *n.* 1. A stream of water or other fluid; a current; as, a *flow* of water; a *flow* of blood.

2. A current of water with a swell or rise; as, the *flow* and ebb of tides.

3. A stream of anything; as, a *flow* of wealth or immigration into the country.

4. Abundance; copiousness; as, a *flow* of spirits.

5. A stream of diction, denoting abundance of words at command and facility of speaking; volubility; as, an unchecked *flow* of language.

6. Free expression or communication of generous feelings and sentiments.

The feast of reason, and the *flow* of soul. —Pope.

7. In mechanics, the volume of liquid which passes through any given passage in a unit of time.

flōw′āge, *n.* 1. The act of flowing; the state of being overflowed.

2. In geology, that variety of structure which indicates that the substance was in a state of flowing just prior to solidification.

flōw′en, *v.*, obsolete past tense plural and past participle of *fly*.

flow′ẽr, *n.* [ME. *flowre, flour, flur*; OFr. *flor, flur, flour*, from L. *flos, floris*, a flower.]

1. In botany, the part of a plant containing the organs of reproduction, either together in a hermaphrodite flower or separate in male and female flowers.

Complete Flower of *Cheiranthus Cheiri* (wallflower). *a*, peduncle; *b*, calyx; *c*, corolla, *d*, stamens; *e*, pistil.

2. In popular language, a blossom or inflorescence, whether it contains essential organs or not; the showy, attractive part of a plant, usually colored or variegated.

3. The early part of life or of adult age; the prime; youthful vigor; youth; as, the *flower* of manhood.

4. The best or finest part of a thing; the most valuable part; as, young men and women are the *flower* of a nation; the *flower* of the family; the *flower* of an army.

5. In rhetoric, an ornament of style; an apt figure.

6. [*pl.*] In old chemistry, a powdery substance; a condensation of a sublimate; as, the *flowers* of sulphur.

7. [*pl.*] The menstrual flow.

Fertile or *female flower*; a flower having pistils only.

Flowers of tan; figures formed on spent tan by a growth of fungus.

Flowers of wine; a mold-like growth on the surface of fermenting wine.

flow′ẽr, *v.i.*; flowered, *pt., pp.*; flowering, *ppr.* [ME. *flouren*; OFr. *flurir*; L. *florere*, to bloom, blossom.]

1. To blossom; to bloom; to expand the petals, as a plant; as, peach-trees *flower* in April, and apple-trees in May.

2. To be in the prime and spring of life; to flourish; to be youthful, fresh, and vigorous.

When *flowered* my youthful spring.—Spenser.

3. To froth; to ferment gently; to mantle, as new beer.

4. To come as cream from the surface. [Obs.]

flow′ẽr, *v.t.* To cover or embellish with figures of flowers; to adorn with imitated flowers, as ribbons, laces, etc.

When the frost *flowers* the whitened window-panes. —Arnold.

flow′ẽr-āge, *n.* The state of flowering; flowers in general; flower-ornamentation.

flow′ẽr-an″i-măl, *n.* Any of the *Anthozoa*, as a sea-anemone; also called *animal-flower*.

flow′ẽr-bed, *n.* A space in a garden devoted to the cultivation of flowers.

flow′ẽr-bee″tle, *n.* One of numerous species of beetles feeding upon flowers, especially those of the genus *Meligethes*.

flow′ẽr-bīrd, *n.* Any bird of the genus *Anthornis*, or honeysuckers

flow′ẽr-bud, *n.* The bud which produces a flower, as distinguished from a leaf-bud.

flow′ẽr-clock, *n.* A contrivance for measuring time by means of flowers that open and shut at certain hours of the day.

flow″ẽr-de-lūce′, *n.* [From Fr. *fleur de lis*, lit., flower of the lily.]

1. In botany, a name for species of the genus *Iris*; fleur-de-lis; blue flag.

2. In heraldry, same as fleur-de-lis.

flow′ẽred, *a.* Covered with flowers; embellished with flowers; as, a *flowered* gown.

flow′ẽr-ẽr, *n.* A plant that bears flowers, as distinguished from one cultivated for its foliage.

flow′ẽr-et, *n.* [ME. *flourette*; OFr. *florete, flurette*; LL. *florettus*, from L. *flos, floris*, a flower.] A small flower; a floret.

flow′ẽr-fence, *n.* See *Barbados-pride*.

flow′ẽr-fụl, *a.* Abounding with flowers. [Rare.]

flow′ẽr-gen″tle, *n.* A popular name for species of amaranth, especially for *Amarantus tricolor*, whose foliage is brilliantly colored in yellow, green, and red.

flow′ẽr-head, *n.* A dense collection of sessile florets upon a disk more or less convex, as in the sunflower, the daisy, and the *Compositæ* generally.

flow′ẽr-i-ness, *n.* 1. The state of being flowery or of abounding with flowers.

2. Floridness, as of speech; abundance of figures.

flow′ẽr-ing, *a.* 1. Blossoming; blooming; expanding the petals, as plants.

2. Adorning with artificial flowers or figures of blossoms.

Flowering fern; the popular name of *Osmunda regalis*, natural order *Osmundaceæ*. It grows in boggy places and wet margins of woods, and derives its name from the upper pinnæ of the fronds being transformed into a handsome panicle covered with sporangia.

Flowering plants; phenogamous plants, or plants having stamens and pistils as reproducing organs.

Flowering rush; a rushlike aquatic plant, *Butomus umbellatus*, found in Europe and Asia. The leaves are two to three feet long, and the flowers handsome.

Flowering Fern (*Osmunda*).

flow′ẽr-ing, *n.* 1. The act or state of bearing blossoms, etc.

2. The act of adorning with flowers.

flow′ẽr-less, *a.* 1. Having no flowers.

2. In botany, having no organs of fructification.

Flowerless plants; plants without flowers that produce seeds; cryptogamous, as distinguished from phenogamous plants.

flow′ẽr-less-ness, *n.* The state or quality of being without flowers.

flow′ẽr-ŏf-an-hour′ (-our′), *n.* The bladder-ketmia, *Hibiscus Trionum*, a handsome cultivated plant, the flower of which opens only in midday.

flow′ẽr-peck″ẽr, *n.* A bird of the family *Dicæidæ* of India and Australia or of the American family *Cærebidæ*, resembling the humming-bird in plumage and habits.

flow′ẽr-piēce, *n.* 1. An ornamental design of cut flowers for a table.

2. In art, a picture of flowers.

flow′ẽr-pot, *n.* A porous earthenware pot with a drainage hole in the bottom, used in propagating and cultivating flowering plants.

flow′ẽr-shōw, *n.* An exhibition of flowers, generally competitive.

flow′ẽr-stạlk, *n.* The stem of a plant that bears the flower or flowers; a pedicel or peduncle.

flow′ẽr-y, *a.* 1. Full of flowers; abounding with blossoms; as, a *flowery* field.

2. Adorned with artifical flowers, or the figures of flowers; as, a *flowery* pattern.

3. Highly embellished with figurative language; florid; as, a *flowery* style.

Flowery kingdom; a name applied to the Chinese empire.

flow′ẽr-y-kir″tled, *a.* Adorned with garlands of flowers. [Rare.]

flōw′ing, *a.* Moving as a fluid; issuing; proceeding; abounding; smooth, as style; streaming; fluent; hanging loosely, as hair or garments.

Flowing battery; a form of electric battery in which the liquid flows through the cell or cells.

Flowing sheets; in nautical language, a phrase noting the position of the sheets when the principal sails are loosened to the wind, so as to receive it into their cavities in a direction more nearly perpendicular than when they are close-hauled, although more obliquely than when the vessel is sailing before the wind.

flōw′ing, *n.* The act of running or moving as a fluid; an issuing; an overflowing; a flux.

flōw′ing-fūr″nāce, *n.* The cupola in which iron is melted in foundries.

flōw′ing-ly, *adv.* In a flowing manner.

flōw′ing-ness, *n.* The quality of being flowing or fluent; fluency. [Rare.]

flōwk, *n.* A flatfish. [See *Fluke*.]

flōwn, *v.*, past participle of *fly*.

flōwn, *a.* Filled; bloated; excited; as, *flown* with wine. [Rare.]

flū′āte, *n.* [*Fluor*, and *-ate*.] In chemistry, a name formerly given to salts formed by fluoric acid combined with a base; as, *fluate* of alumina or of soda; a fluoride. [Obs.]

flū′ā-vil, *n.* [Perhaps from L. *fluere*, to flow.] In chemistry, a yellow, resinous constituent of gutta-percha, $C_{20}H_{32}O$, extracted by alcohol or some similar solvent; called also *fluanil*.

flū′çăn, flook′ăn, *n.* [Corn.] In mining, the clayey material in a lode lying between the vein and its surrounding rocks; similar to *gouge*.

fluc-tif′ẽr-ous, *a.* [L. *fluctus*, a wave, and *ferre*, to bear.] Producing or tending to produce waves.

fluc-tis′ō-nous, *a.* [L. *fluctus*, a wave, and *sonare*, to sound.] Resembling the sound of waves; roaring like the sea.

fluc″tū-ā-bil′i-ty, *n.* The quality of being liable to fluctuate. [Rare.]

fluc′tū-ăn-cy, *n.* Tendency to fluctuation. [Rare.]

fluc′tū-ănt, *a.* Moving like a wave; wavering; unsteady; fluctuating.

fluc′tū-āte, *v.i.*; fluctuated, *pt., pp.*; fluctuating, *ppr.* [L. *fluctuatus*, pp. of *fluctuare*, to waver, rise in waves, from *fluctus*, a flowing, wave, from *fluere*, to flow.]

1. To move as a wave; to roll hither and thither; to waver; as, a *fluctuating* field of air.

2. To float backward and forward, as on waves.

3. To move now in one direction and now in another; to be wavering or unsteady; as, public opinion often *fluctuates*; men often *fluctuate* between different parties and opinions.

4. To be irresolute or undetermined.

5. To rise and fall; to be in an unsettled state; to experience sudden vicissitudes; as, the prices of stocks *fluctuate* with the events of the day.

Syn.—Vacillate, vary, waver, oscillate, hesitate.

fluc′tū-āte, *v.t.* To produce fluctuation in. [Rare.]

fluc-tū-ā′tion, *n.* [L. *fluctuatio* (*-onis*), from *fluctuare*, to waver, rise in waves.]

1. A motion like that of waves; a moving in this and that direction; as, the *fluctuations* of the sea.

2. A wavering; unsteadiness; as, *fluctuations* of opinion.

3. A rising and falling suddenly; as, *fluctuations* of prices or of values.

4. In medicine, the wavelike motion produced when a body containing fluid is held between the fingers or hands.

fluc′tū-ous, *a.* [L. *fluctuosus*, from *fluctus*, a wave.] Abounding in waves; characterized by waves or wavy motions; flowing.

flūe, *n.* [Compare OFr. *flue, fluie*, a flowing, from L. *fluere*, to flow.]

1. A passage for smoke in a chimney, leading from the fireplace to the top of the chimney, or into another passage; as, a chimney with four *flues*.

2. Any tube-like device for the passage of gas, flame, or hot air; as, the *flues* of a steam-boiler.

3. A passage in a wall for the purpose of conducting heat or air from one part of a building to another.

flūe, *n.* [Fr. *flou*, light, weak; G. *flau*, weak.] Light down, such as rises from cotton, etc.; soft fur or hair; also written *flew*.

flūe, *n.* [Corrupted from *fluke*.] In whale-fishing, a kind of fluke or barb fastened to a harpoon.

flūe, *n.* [Morocco.] A money of account of Morocco of the value of one-thirteenth of a cent.

flūe, *v.i.*; flued, *pt., pp.*; fluing, *ppr.* To expand or splay, as the jambs of a window.

flūe′-boil″ẽr, *n.* See *Boiler*.

flūe′-bridġe (-brij), *n.* In a reverberating furnace, a low fire-brick partition between the flue and the hearth.

flūed, *a.* In whaling, supplied with a flue or fluke; as, a *flued* harpoon.

flūe′-ham″mẽr, *n.* A hammer used by a cooper for flaring iron hoops to fit a barrel.

flū-el′len, *n.* [Prob. from W. *fluellen*, a form of *Llewelyn*, a proper name.] The speedwell, *Veronica officinalis*, a plant of the figwort family.

Female fluellen; the toadflax, *Linaria spuria*.

flū′ence, *n.* A flowing. [Obs.]

flū′en-cy, *n.* [Fr. *fluence*; L. *fluentia*, a flowing, fluency, from *fluens* (*-entis*), ppr. of *fluere*, to flow.]

1. The quality of flowing; smoothness; freedom from harshness; as, *fluency* of numbers.

2. Readiness of utterance; facility of words; volubility; as, *fluency* of speech; a speaker of remarkable *fluency*.

3. Affluence; abundance. [Obs.]

flū′ent, *a.* [L. *fluens* (*-entis*), ppr. of *fluere*, to flow.]

1. Liquid; flowing.

2. Having a flowing motion, or the appearance of flowing; changeable.

Motion being a *fluent* thing. —Ray.

3. Ready in the use of words; voluble; copious; having words at command and uttering them with facility and smoothness; as, a *fluent* speaker.

4. Flowing; voluble; smooth; as, *fluent* speech; a *fluent* style.

flū′ent, *n.* 1. A stream; a current of water. [Obs.]

2. In mathematics, a variable quantity, considered as increasing or diminishing; a function; an integral.

flū′ent-ly, *adv.* In a fluent manner.

flū′ent-ness, *n.* The quality of being fluent; fluency.

flūe′-stop, *n.* In organ-building, a stop with a quality of tone like that of the flute.

flūe′wŏrk, *n.* Flue-stops collectively.

flūe′y, *a.* Having the quality of flue or down; flossy.

fluff, *v.t.*; fluffed (fluft), *pt.*, *pp.*; fluffing, *ppr.* To arrange or cover as with fluff or down.

fluff, *v.i.* To spread so as to give a light fluffy appearance.

fluff, *n.* Soft, light substance; down; downy feathers.

fluff′i-ness, *n.* The state of being fluffy.

fluff′y, *a.*; *comp.* fluffier; *superl.* fluffiest. Pertaining to or having the character of fluff; downy.

flü′gel, *n.* [G., a wing.] In music, a name applied to an instrument resembling a harp in shape; hence, a grand piano or a harpsichord.

flü′gel-man, *n.* A fugleman.

flū′id, *a.* [L. *fluidus*, from *fluere*, to flow.] Having the properties of a fluid.

flū′id, *n.* A body whose particles move easily among themselves, and yield to the least force impressed, and which, when that force is removed, recovers its previous state; a form or condition of matter depending upon heat, in which the molecules readily change their relative positions. *Fluids* may exist in two forms, liquid and gaseous. In the former the molecules are more or less coherent, while in the latter they tend to separate indefinitely.

Fluid dram; a liquid measure equal to one-eighth of a fluid ounce or to 3.7 cubic centimeters.

Fluid ounce; a liquid measure equal to one-sixteenth of a pint or to 29.57 cubic centimeters.

Fluids of the body; in physiology, all the liquid substances of the body, such as blood, bile, urine, lymph, chyle, gastric juices, etc., as distinguished from the part left after thorough drying, and constituting more than 65 per cent of the body by weight.

flū′id-ăl, *a.* Fluid.

Fluidal structure; in geology, a kind of structure found in eruptives in which the lines of flow of lava are indicated in the forms of crystallization.

flū-id′i-fȳ, *v.t.*; fluidified, *pt.*, *pp.*; fluidifying, *ppr.* [L. *fluidus*, a fluid, and *-ficare*, from *facere*, to make.] To change to a fluid condition.

flū-id′i-ty, *n.* The quality of being capable of flowing; a liquid or gaseous state; opposed to *solidity*.

flū′id-īze, *v.t.*; fluidized, *pt.*, *pp.*; fluidizing, *ppr.* To change to a fluid condition; to fluidify.

flū′id-ness, *n.* The state of being fluid; fluidity.

flū′i-tănt, *a.* [L. *fluitans* (*-antis*), ppr. of *fluitare*, to float, swim, freq. of *fluere*, to flow.] Supported by the buoyancy of a fluid; floating; carried by buoyant force; specifically, in botany, noting such plants as float upon water.

flū′kăn, *n.* In mining, flucan.

flūke, *n.* [Prob. a form of L.G. *flunk*, *flunke*, a wing, the fluke of an anchor.]

1. The part of an anchor which fastens in the ground.

2. A lobe or branch of a whale's tail.

3. An instrument for cleaning a hole drilled for blasting.

4. A barb on a harpoon.

5. An accidental count in a game of skill; as, he won the game by a *fluke*.

flūke, *n.* 1. A species of flatfish, of the genus *Platessa*, much like the common flounder.

2. A worm that infests the internal organs of animals. Those found in the liver of the sheep produce the disease called rot.

flūke, *v.t.* and *v.i.*; fluked (flūkt), *pt.*, *pp.*; fluking, *ppr.* To score by accident in a game of skill. [Slang.]

flūke′wŏrm, *n.* Same as second *Fluke*, n. 2.

flūke′wŏrt, *n.* The name of a European plant, *Hydrocotyle vulgaris*, once supposed to cause flukes in sheep.

flūk′y, *a.* Furnished with or as if furnished with flukes; making many flukes, as in playing a game.

flūme, *n.* [ME. *flum*, *flom*, a river, stream; OFr. *flum*; L. *flumen*, a river, stream, from *fluere*, to flow.] Literally, a flowing; hence, the passage or channel for the water that drives a mill-wheel, or that is carried along for the purpose of placer-mining.

flū′mi-nous, *a.* [L. *flumen* (*-inis*), a river.] Of or belonging to rivers; abundantly supplied with rivers.

flum′mĕr-y, *n.* [W. *llymru*, *llymrand*, a kind of food made of oatmeal boiled and soured, from *llymus*, of a sharp quality.]

1. A sort of jelly made of flour or meal; pap.

Milk and *flummery* are very fit for children.
—Locke.

2. In cookery of the present day, a sort of blancmange.

3. In the manufacture of wheat-starch, a jelly-like refuse.

flump, *v.t.* and *v.i.*; flumped, *pt.*, *pp.*; flumping, *ppr.* [Imitative word.] To sit down suddenly; to plump down. [Colloq.]

flung, *v.*, past tense and past participle of *fling*.

flunk, *v.i.*; flunked (flunkt), *pt.*, *pp.*; flunking, *ppr.* To fail in a lesson; to shirk; to back out; to fail in meeting a duty. [Colloq.]

flunk, *n.* A failure, especially in a recitation or examination. [Colloq.]

flun′ky, **flun′key**, *n.*; *pl.* **flun′kies**, **flun′keys**. [Perhaps from Fr. *flanquer*, to flank, run along by the side of, be at one's elbow to render assistance.]

1. A liveried servant; a term of contempt.

2. A cad or snob.

3. A young or inexperienced speculator.

flun′ky-dŏm, *n.* Flunkies in general; the domain of flunkies.

flun′ky-ism, **flun′key-ism**, *n.* The characteristic quality of a flunky; the disposition to cringe to superiors; obsequiousness.

flu-o-. A combining form used in chemistry to indicate combination with fluorin or fluorescence; as, *fluo*phosphate, *fluo*cerin.

flū-ō-bō′rāte, *n.* A compound of fluoboric acid with a base.

flū-ō-bō′ric, *a.* Relating to a compound of fluorin and boron.

Fluoboric acid; in chemistry, a syrupy acid, HBF_4.

flū-ō-bō′rid, *n.* [*Fluobor*ic and *-id*.] A salt formed by the union of hydrofluoric and fluoboric acids.

flū-ō-cär′bō-nāte, *n.* A double salt of carbon and fluorin.

flū-ō-cē′rin, *n.* Fluocerite.

flū-ō-cē′rite, *n.* [*Fluor* and *cerium* and *-ite*.] In mineralogy, a cerium fluoride occurring native.

flū-ō-hȳ′dric, *a.* Same as *Hydrofluoric*.

flū-ō-phos′phāte, *n.* A phosphate containing fluorin.

flū′ŏr, *n.* [LL. *fluor*, a flow, flux, from L. *fluere*, to flow.]

1. A fluid state. [Obs.]

2. Menstrual flux. [Obs.]

3. In mineralogy, fluoride of calcium, usually called *fluor-spar*, a mineral of beautiful colors, much used for vases, brooches, etc.

Fluor albus; leucorrhea.

flū-ŏr-an′thēne, *n.* [*Fluor*ene and phen*anthene*.] In chemistry, a coal-tar product, $C_{15}H_{10}$.

flū-ŏr-ā′ted, *a.* In chemistry, having fluorin in combination.

flū′ŏr-ēne, *n.* [*Fluor*escence and *-ene*.] In chemistry, a product of coal-tar, $C_{13}H_{10}$.

flū-ō-resce′, *v.i.*; fluoresced (-rest′), *pt.*, *pp.*; fluorescing, *ppr.* To exhibit fluorescence.

flū-ō-res′cē-in, *n.* [*Fluoresce* and *-in*.] In chemistry, a compound, $C_{20}H_{12}O_5$, remarkable for the brilliant yellowish-green inflorescence of its alkaline compounds.

flū-ō-res′cence, *n.* [*Fluor* and *-escence*.]

1. A property of certain transparent substances on account of which incident rays of light are emitted in colors different from their own and from those of the fluorescent body.

2. The property of glowing without rise of temperature when exposed to rays of light.

3. The light rendered fluorescent.

flū-ō-res′cent, *a.* [*Fluor* and *-escent*.] Producing fluorescence; glowing without giving off heat.

flū-or′ic, *a.* [*Fluor* and *-ic*.] Pertaining to fluorin; obtained from fluorin; containing fluorin.

flū′ŏr-īde, *n.* [*Fluor* and *-ide*.] A compound of fluorin with some other element.

flū′ŏr-in, **flū′ŏr-ine**, *n.* [*Fluor* and *-in*, *-ine*, so called because it occurs in fluor-spar.] A colorless gas, extremely corrosive and possessing great chemical activity, being found in combination, as it does not exist in a free state.

flū′ŏr-īte, *n.* [*Fluor* and *-ite*.] Fluor-spar.

flū-or′ō-fŏrm, *n.* [*Fluor*in and *form*yl.] A fluoric gas, CHF_3, differing from chloroform in having fluorin in place of chlorin.

flū′ŏr-oid, *n.* In crystallography, a tetrahexahedral crystal, as in fluor-spar.

flū-or′ō-scōpe, *n.* [*Fluor*ene and Gr. *skopein*, to view.]

1. An apparatus for illustrating fluorescence.

2. A device for observing the effects of X-rays, consisting mainly of a fluorescent screen and a hood to protect the eyes.

flū-or-ō-scop′ic, *a.* Pertaining to fluoroscopy.

flū-ŏr-os′cō-py, *n.* [*Fluor*ene and Gr. *skopein*, to view.] The science and art of using a fluoroscope; specifically, the observations made in projecting X-rays upon any part of the human body.

flū′ŏr-ous, *a.* Containing fluorin; relating to fluorin.

flū′ŏr-spär, *n.* [LL *fluor*, a flow, flux, and AS. *spær*, in *spærstan*, chalkstone.] In mineralogy, calcium fluorid, CaF_2, a natural formation occurring in masses and in crystalline form, varying much in color, and when pure containing about equal parts of calcium and fluorin.

flū-ō-sil′i-cāte, *n.* [*Fluosilic*ic and *-ate*.]

1. In chemistry, a compound of fluosilicic acid with some base.

2. In mineralogy, a silicate in compound with essential fluorin.

flū″ō-si-lic′ic, *a.* Pertaining to the combination of fluorin and silicon; having fluorin and silicon as constituents.

Fluosilicic acid; an acid containing both silicon and fluorin; formed by the combination of hydrogen and silicon with fluoric acid.

flur′ry, *n.*; *pl.* **flur′ries**. [Sw. *flurig*, disordered, dissolute.]

1. A sudden blast or gust, or a light, temporary breeze; as, a *flurry* of wind.

2. A light snowfall accompanied by wind.

3. Violent agitation; commotion; bustle, hurry.

4. The violent movements in the death agonies of a whale.

flur′ry, *v.t.*; flurried, *pt.*, *pp.*; flurrying, *ppr.* To put in agitation; to excite or alarm.

flŭrt, *n.* and *v.* [Obs.] See *Flirt*.

flush, *v.i.*; flushed (flusht), *pt.*, *pp.*; flushing, *ppr.* [ME. *fluschen*, to fly up suddenly, penetrate.]

1. To flow and spread suddenly; to rush; as, blood *flushes* into the face.

2. To come in haste; to start.

3. To appear suddenly, as redness or a blush.

Flushing and fading like the changeful play
Of colors on a dolphin. —Percival.

4. To become suddenly red; to glow; as, the cheeks *flush*.

flush, *v.t.* 1. To make red suddenly; to cause the blood to rush suddenly into (the face).

Nor *flush* with shame the passing virgin's cheek. —Gay.

2. To elate; to elevate; to excite the spirits of; to animate with joy; as, *flushed* with victory.

3. To cleanse by forcing water through; to flood; as, to *flush* the sewers.

4. To cause to start; as, to *flush* a covey of quail.

To flush up joints; in masonry, to fill in the joints; to make them even with the surface.

flush, *a.*; *comp.* flusher; *superl.* flushest.

1. Fresh; full of vigor; glowing; bright.

2. Affluent; abounding; well furnished; liberal; prodigal.

3. In architecture, even or level in respect to surface.

flush, *n.* 1. A sudden flow of blood to the face; or, more generally, the redness of face which proceeds from such an afflux of blood; as, hectic constitutions are often known by a frequent *flush* in the cheeks.

2. Sudden impulse or excitement; sudden glow; as, a *flush* of joy.

3. Bloom; growth; abundance.

4. A hand of cards of the same suit.

5. A term for a number of ducks.

Bobtail flush: in the game of poker, a hand of four cards of the same suit and one card of an odd suit.

Straight flush; in the game of poker, a flush in sequence.

Royal flush; in the game of poker, a straight flush with ace at the head.

flush, *adv.* In such manner as to be level.

flush′bōard, *n.* Same as *Flashboard*.

flush′-bōlt, *n.* Any bolt the face of whose head is even with the surface.

flush′-box, *n.* 1. A box placed flush with a street or roadbed and used as an entrance to a conduit containing underground wires.

2. An elevated box for flushing a water-closet, with a float for stopping the flow into the box as it fills.

flush′ĕr, *n.* 1. The lesser butcher-bird of Europe, *Lanius collurio*.

2. One who cleans sewers by flushing.

flush′ing, *n.* 1. A glow of red in the face, as in a fever.

2. In England, heavy shoddy-cloth.

3. In weaving, the floating threads which cover the surface of a web.

flush′ing-ly, *adv.* In a flushing manner.

flush′ness, *n.* Freshness; fullness; abundance.

flush′-riv″et-ed, *a.* Having the rivets flush with the surface, as in the hull of an iron ship.

flus′tĕr, *v.t.*; flustered, *pt.*, *pp.*; flustering, *ppr.* [Ice. *flaustra*, to be flustered, *flaustr*, hurry, fluster.] To make hot and rosy, as with drink ing; to heat; to hurry; to agitate; to confuse.

flus′tĕr, *v.i.* To be in a heat or bustle; to be agitated.

flus′tĕr, *n.* Heat; glow; agitation; confusion; disorder.

flus′tĕr-āte, *v.t.*; flusterated, *pt. pp.*: flusterating, *ppr.* To confuse by agitating; to befuddle; to put into a state of absolute indecision, so as to cause irrational action. [Colloq.]

flus-tĕr-ā′tion, *n.* The act of confusing by agitating; also, the state of confusion or inability to make a rational decision. [Colloq.]

flus′trāte, *v.t.* To flusterate.

flus-trā′tion, *n.* Flusteration.

flūte, *n.* [Fr. *flute*, *flûte*; OFr. *fleüte*, *flaüte*, *flahute*; LL. *flauta*, a flute, from L. *flatus*, a blowing, from *flare*, to blow.]

1. A small wind-instrument; a pipe with lateral holes and keys, played by blowing with the mouth and by stopping and opening the holes with the fingers.

2. In architecture, a channel in a column or pillar; a perpendicular furrow or cavity, cut along the shaft of a column or pilaster; so called from its resemblance to a flute; used chiefly in the Ionic order; sometimes in the Composite and Corinthian; rarely in the Doric and Tuscan.

3. A similar channel in a ruffle of muslin or in other material.

4. One of the several shuttles used in weaving different colors into a web.

5. In bakery, a much elongated breakfast roll.

6. In organ-building, a stop with the pipes closed to make tones like those of the flute.

7. A very slender wine-glass about four times as high as it is wide.

Flûte à bec, a flute with mouthpiece at the end resembling a beak, played like a flageolet.

flūte, *v.i.*; fluted, *pt. pp.*; fluting, *ppr.* To play on a flute; to make a flute-like sound.

flūte, *n.* [A corruption of *float.*] A long vessel or boat with flat ribs or floor-timbers, round behind and swelled in the middle.

Armed en flûte; an armed ship, with her guns in part taken out, as when used as a transport.

flūte, *v.t.* 1. To form flutes or channels in; to furnish with a flute or flutes.

2. To sound, as a note or succession of notes, in a clear, flute-like tone.

flūte′=bīrd, *n.* A bird, the Australian piping crow.

flūte′=bit, *n.* In mechanics, a tool for boring hard woods, such as flutes are made of.

flūt′ed, *a.* 1. Channeled; furrowed, as a column.

2. In music, thin; fine; flute-like; as *fluted* notes.

flūte′mouth, *n.* In zoölogy, a fish with a long, tube-shaped mouth; one of the genus *Aulostoma*.

flūt′ēr, *n.* 1. One who plays on the flute.

2. One who makes ornamental grooves or flutings.

flūte′=shrīke, *n.* A butcher-bird of Africa, genus *Laniarius*.

flūte′=stop, *n.* A bank of wooden pipes in an organ, designed to imitate the tones of a flute.

flūt′ing, *n.* 1. Flute-playing.

2. The act of grooving or furrowing; the groove or furrow so made; fluted work.

3. The groove running lengthwise of a screw-cutting tap.

flūt′ing=ī″ron (-ūrn), *n.* A corrugated, die-like iron for fluting or goffering.

flūt′ing=mȧ-ḉhine″, *n.* 1. A machine with grooved cylinders for fluting cloth and thin metal.

2. A fluting-lathe.

flūt′ing=plāne, *n.* In carpentry, a plane for making flutes in wood.

flūt′ing=scis″ṣŏrṣ, *n.* A three-tined appliance for crimping fabrics, operated like a pair of scissors.

flūt′ist, *n.* A performer on the flute.

flut′tēr, *v.i.*; fluttered, *pt., pp.*; fluttering, *ppr.* [ME. *floteren*; AS. *floterian*, *flotorian*, to float about.]

1. To move or flap the wings rapidly, without flying or with short flights; to hover.

> As an eagle stirreth up her nest, *fluttereth* over her young, spreadeth abroad her wings.
> —Deut. xxxii. 11.

2. To move about briskly, irregularly, or with great bustle and show, without consequence.

> No rag, no scrap of all the beau or wit,
> That once so *fluttered*, and that once so writ.
> —Pope.

3. To move with quick vibrations or undulations; as, a *fluttering* fan; a *fluttering* sail.

4. To be in agitation; to move irregularly; to fluctuate; to be in uncertainty.

> How long we *fluttered* on the wings of doubtful success.
> —Howell.

flut′tēr, *v.t.* 1. To drive in disorder.

2. To disorder; to throw into confusion; to fluster.

3. To vibrate or move rapidly to and fro; as, to *flutter* the wings.

flut′tēr, *n.* 1. Quick and irregular motion; vibration; undulation; as, the *flutter* of a fan.

2. Hurry; tumult; agitation of the mind; confusion; disorder; irregularity in position.

flut′tēr-ēr, *n.* One who or that which flutters, as an agitated person or a flutter-wheel.

flut′tēr-ing-ly, *adv.* In a fluttering manner.

flut′tēr=wheel, *n.* A kind of water-wheel of small diameter with radial paddles against which water strikes either in a fall or from a chute, causing rapid rotation with a sound as of fluttering.

flut′tēr-y, *a.* Wavering; swinging; vacillating.

flūt′y, *a.* Soft and clear in tone like a flute.

flū′vi-ăl, *a.* [L. *fluvialis*, from *fluvius*, a river, stream, from *fluere*, to flow.] Belonging to rivers; growing or living in streams or ponds; as, a *fluvial* plant.

flū′vi-ăl-ist, *n.* One who explains phenomena by the operation of existing streams. [Rare.]

flū-vi-at′iç, *a.* [L. *fluviaticus*, from *fluvius*, a river.] Fluvial.

flū′vi-ȧ-tile, *a.* [L. *fluviatilis*, from *fluvius*, a river.] Belonging to rivers; existing in rivers; as, *fluviatile* strata.

flū-viç′ō-line, *a.* [L. *fluvius*, a river, and *colere*, to inhabit.] Fluvial.

flū-vi-ō-. A combining form from L. *fluvius*, a river, used in geology, to indicate relation to a river or stream.

flū″vi-ō-mȧ-rīne′, *a.* [*Fluvio-*, and L. *marinus*, of the sea, from *mare*, the sea.] In geology, pertaining to formations made by the action of both river and sea, as in the deposits found at the mouths of great rivers.

flū″vi-ō-ter-res′tri-ăl, *a.* [*Fluvio-*, and L. *terrestris*, of the earth, from *terra*, the earth.] Relating to the land and its rivers as distinguished from the ocean and its beds; as, *fluvioterrestrial* deposits or fossils.

flux, *n.* [ME. *flux*; OFr. *flux*; L. *fluxus*, a flowing, flow, from *fluere*, to flow.]

1. The act of flowing; the motion or passing of a fluid.

2. The moving or passing of anything in continued succession; as, things in this life are in a continual *flux*.

3. Any flow or issue of matter; specifically, in medicine, an extraordinary issue or evacuation from the bowels or other part; as, the bloody *flux* or dysentery, hepatic *flux*, etc.

4. In hydrography, the flow of the tide; the ebb being called *reflux*.

5. In chemistry and metallurgy, any substance or mixture used to promote the fusion of metals or minerals, as alkalis, borax, tartar, and other saline matter; or, in large operations, limestone or fluor-spar.

6. Fusion; a liquid state from the operation of heat.

7. That which flows or is discharged, as pus or blood.

8. Concourse; confluence. [Obs.]

9. In physics, the rate of flow or output of water, heat, electricity, magnetism, etc.

flux, *a.* Flowing; moving; maintained by a constant succession of parts; inconstant; variable. [Rare.]

flux, *v.t.*; fluxed (fluxt), *pt., pp.*; fluxing, *ppr.* 1. To melt; to fuse; to make fluid.

> One part of mineral alkali will *flux* two of silicious earth with effervescence.—Kirwan.

2. To cause to overflow. [Obs.]

3. In medicine, to produce an excessive flow or discharge from.

4. To clear out or cleanse. [Obs.]

5. To use with a flux in fusing or welding processes.

flux, *v.i.* To rise or to flow. [Rare.]

flux-ā′tion, *n.* A flowing or passing away, and giving place to others.

flux-i-bil′i-ty, *n.* [LL. *fluxibilitas*, from L. *fluxibilis*, capable of flowing, from *fluere*, to flow.] The quality of admitting fusion.

flux′i-ble, *a.* [LL. *fluxibilis*, from L. *fluxus*, pp. of *fluere*, to flow.] Capable of being melted or fused, as a mineral.

flux′i-ble-ness, *n.* Fluxibility.

flux′ile, *a.* [LL. *fluxilis*, fluid, from *fluxus*, pp. of *fluere*, to flow.] Admitting of fusion. [Rare.]

flux-il′i-ty, *n.* The quality of admitting fusion; possibility of being fused or liquefied. [Obs.]

flux′iŏn (fluk′shun), *n.* [L. *fluxio* (-*onis*), a flowing, from *fluere*, to flow.]

1. The act of flowing or act of fusion.

2. The matter that flows.

3. In mathematics, an increment; the infinitely small increase or decrease of the variable; the same as *differential*, particularly when time is the independent variable.

4. In medicine, an unusual flow, as of blood to the brain.

5. A unit of gradual change, as in the hands of a clock.

Method of fluxions; a variation of calculus introduced by Newton. [See *Differential calculus* under *Calculus*.]

flux′iŏn-ăl, *a.* 1. Pertaining to mathematical fluxions.

2. Of the nature of a flux.

flux′iŏn-ā-ry, *a.* 1. Fluxional.

2. In medicine, relating to a fluxion.

flux′iŏn-ist, *n.* One skilled in fluxions.

flux′iŏn=struc″tūre, *n.* See *Fluidal structure* under *Fluidal*.

flux′ive, *a.* Flowing; wanting solidity. [Obs.]

flux′ūre, *n.* A flowing or fluid matter. [Obs.]

flȳ, *a.* Smart as need be; spirited, implying dash or show; wisely sharp. [Slang.]

flȳ, *v.i.*; flew, *pt.*; flying, *ppr.*; flown, *pp.* [ME. *fleyen*, *flien*, *fleen*, *flyen*; AS. *fleogan*, *fliogan*, to fly.]

1. To move through air by the aid of wings, as fowls.

2. To pass or move in air by the force of wind or other impulse; as, clouds and vapors *fly* before the wind.

3. To rise in air, as light substances, by means of a current of air, or by having less specific gravity than air, as smoke.

> Man is born unto trouble, as the sparks *fly* upward.
> —Job v. 7.

4. To move or pass with velocity or celerity, either on land or water; as, he *flew* to the relief of his distressed friend; the ship *flies* upon the main.

5. To pass away; to depart; with the idea of haste, swiftness, or escape; as, the bird has *flown*; swift *fly* the fleeting hours.

6. To part suddenly or with violence; to burst, as a bottle; to spring by an elastic force; as, the door *flies* open.

7. To pass swiftly, as rumor or report.

8. To flee; to run away; to attempt to escape; to escape.

> I'll *fly* from shepherds, flocks, and flowery plains.
> —Pope.

9. To flutter; to vibrate or play, as a flag in the wind.

To fly about; among seamen, to change about; to veer; said of the wind.

To fly around; to move about hastily. [Colloq.]

To fly at; to spring toward; to rush on; to fall on suddenly; as, a dog *flies at* a man.

To fly in the face; to insult; to oppose with violence; to act in direct opposition to.

To fly off; to separate or depart suddenly.

To fly off the handle; to lose one's temper. [Colloq.]

To fly on; to assail suddenly and furiously.

To fly open; to open suddenly or with violence; as, the doors *flew open*.

To fly out; to rush out; also, to burst into a passion; to issue with violence from any direction.

To let fly; to discharge; to throw or drive with violence; as, *to let fly* a shower of darts; in seamanship, to let go suddenly and entirely; as, *to let fly* the sheets.

flȳ, *v.t.* 1. To shun; to avoid; to decline; as, to *fly* the sight of one we hate.

> Sleep *flies* the wretch.
> —Dryden.

2. To cause to float in the air; as to *fly* a kite.

3. To attack by a bird of prey. [Obs.]

To fly a kite; in commercial slang, to raise cash by exchanging checks, or on accommodation notes.

To fly the black flag; the custom of pirates, to show no quarter in an engagement.

flȳ, *n.*; *pl.* **flīeṣ**. [ME. *flye*, *flie*, *flege*, *fleoge*, a fly, from AS. *fleogan*, to fly.]

1. In zoölogy, a winged insect of various species, whose distinguishing characteristics are that the wings are transparent and have no cases or covers. By these marks *flies* are distinguished from beetles, butterflies, grasshoppers, etc. The true flies or *Diptera* have only two wings, the anterior pair. In common language, *fly* is the house-*fly*, of the genus *Musca*.

2. A hook dressed so as to resemble a fly or other insect used by anglers to catch fish.

3. A familiar spirit; a parasite. [Obs.]

> A trifling *fly*, none of your great familiars.
> —Jonson.

4. That which has little or no value.

5. [*pl.* flȳṣ.] A light carriage formed for rapid motion; a hackney-coach; a cab.

flȳ, *n.*; *pl.* **flīeṣ**. [ME. *flye*; AS. *flyge*, from *fleogan*, to fly.]

1. Flight. [Obs.]

2. An arrangement of vanes upon a revolving axis to regulate the motion of clockwork by the impact of the vanes against the air; a fanner; now chiefly used in musical boxes and the striking parts of clock machinery. The same name is also applied to other contrivances for regulating the motion of machinery, as to cross-arms, loaded at the ends with heavy weights, and placed at right angles to the axis of a windlass, jack, or the like, and to a flywheel.

3. In printing, any means for taking printed sheets from a press; specifically, a frame so oscillated as to remove sheets from the form or tapes and deposit them in a pile.

4. In weaving, a shuttle with wheels driven through the shed by a blow or jerk.

5. In knitting machines, a piece for holding the needle in position while passing through a new loop; also called a *latch*.

6. In spinning, one of the arms that revolve round the bobbin in a spinning-frame, and twist the yarn as it is wound on the bobbin.

7. That part of a vane which points and shows which way the wind blows.

8. The extent of an ensign, flag, or pendant from the staff to the end that flutters loose in the wind.

9. In a theater, a gallery running along the side of the stage at a high level, where the ropes for drawing up parts of the scenes, etc., are worked.

10. The protective canvas stretched above a tent nearly parallel to the roof; also, the flap or tent-door.

11. That part of a garment which laps over and conceals the buttons; also, any similar part.

12. Cotton-waste.

13. That part of a piano, organ, or similar instrument which covers the keys when not folded or pushed back.

On the fly; flying; specifically, in baseball, before having touched the ground.

flȳ'-à-gar"iç, *n.* A mushroom, *Agaricus muscarius*, whose narcotic juices are used for poisoning flies; called also *flybane* and *fly-amanita*.

flȳ'à-wāy", *a.* Apt to fly away; fickle; unsatisfied; restive; giddy.

flȳ'à-wāy", *n.* Any person or thing apt to fly away.

flȳ'à-wāy-gràss, *n.* In botany, a grass of the genus *Agrostis*, characterized by the lightness of its panicle, which is blown about to considerable distances.

flȳ'bāne, *n.* Same as *Fly-agaric.*

flȳ'-bit"ten, *a.* Marked by the bite of flies, or as if by the bite of flies.

flȳ'-block, *n.* Among seamen, a shifting pulley-block.

flȳ'blōw, *v.t.*; flyblew, *pt.*; flyblown, *pp.*; flyblowing, *ppr.* To taint with the eggs which produce maggots.

flȳ'blōw, *n.* The egg of a fly laid in flesh and producing corruption by hatching.

flȳ'blōwn, *a.* Tainted with maggots or flyblows; offensive; said of meats and carcasses.

flȳ'-bōard, *n.* In printing, a table or platform for receiving papers from the fly.

flȳ'bōat, *n.* 1. A large, flat-bottomed Dutch vessel.

2. A swift-flying sailboat.

flȳ'-book, *n.* A book or case in which an angler carries his flies.

flȳ'-çap, *n.* A cap once worn by elderly ladies and ornamented with a crescent on each side resembling a wing.

flȳ'-çāse, *n.* In zoölogy, the elytra of a beetle.

flȳ'çatch"ẽr, *n.* 1. One who or that which catches flies.

2. In zoölogy, a name common to very numerous species of birds, forming the family *Muscicapidæ*, and having a bill flatted at the base, almost triangular, notched or hooked at the upper mandible, and beset with bristles; so named because they feed entirely on flies and other winged insects, which they catch as they fly; a name given to the phœbe, the bee-bird, the kingbird, etc.

White-collared Flycatcher (*Muscicapa albicollis*).

flȳ'-çatch"ing, *a.* Fitted for or accustomed to catching flies.

flȳ'-drill, *n.* A drill operated by the momentum of a loaded wheel attached to an axle holding the drill-bit and having a reciprocating motion imparted to it by the winding and unwinding around the axle of a double cord whose ends are fastened to the wheel in opposite parts of its rim.

flȳ'ẽr, *n.* Same as *Flier.*

flȳ'-fish, *v.i.*; fly-fished, *pt.*, *pp.*; fly-fishing, *ppr.* To angle with flies for bait.

flȳ'fish, *n.* *Sebastichthys rhodochloris*, a fish about a foot long, found in the deep off-shore waters of California, characterized by its brilliant colors.

flȳ'-fish"ing, *n.* Angling; the art or practice of angling for fish with flies, natural or artificial, for bait.

flȳ'-flap, *n.* Something to drive away or to kill flies.

flȳ'-gŏv"ẽrn-ŏr, *n.* In machinery, a governor with fans for regulating speed by the retardation of atmospheric resistance, as in a clock, to regulate the rate of striking.

flȳ'-hŏn"ey-suç-kle (-hun"ne-suk-kl), *n.* A plant of the honeysuckle family, *Lonicera ciliata*; from three to five feet in height and bearing honey-colored flowers producing red berries.

flȳ'-hook, *n.* A fishhook fitted with an artificial fly as bait.

flȳ'ing, *a.* Speedy; rapid; swift; as, a *flying* squadron.

Flying army; a body of troops, usually cavalry, equipped for rapid movements for the purpose of annoying the enemy and for protection to the main army.

Flying artillery; see under *Artillery.*

Flying bridge; see under *Bridge.*

Flying buttress; a contrivance for strengthening the nave or central part of a Gothic building, when it rises considerably above the side aisles or wings, consisting of a kind of brace, in a curved form, or half arch, thrown across from the tops of the side aisle buttresses to the wall of the nave, propping it up and preventing it from spreading outward under the pressure of the roof. From its thus passing through the air, over the roof of the side aisles, it has its name of *flying buttress.*

Flying Buttress.

Flying dragon; see *Dragon*, 2.

Flying jib; among sailors, a sail beyond the outer jib.

Flying-jib boom; an addition to the jib-boom to accommodate the flying jib.

Flying kites; light sails for fair weather.

Flying level; in civil engineering, a trial level over the route of an intended canal, road, etc.

Flying lizard; see *Dragon*, 2.

Flying pinion; the pinion of a fly-governor.

Flying sap; in military affairs, hastily constructed earthworks.

Flying shot; a shot at an object in motion, as at a bird on the wing.

Flying start; a start in a race when the contestants are under way at the moment of starting.

Flying torch; in military affairs, a torch displayed at night in an elevated position as a signal.

flȳ'ing-fish, *n.* A name common to those fishes which have the power of sustaining themselves in the air, for a certain length of time, by means of their long pectoral fins.

flȳ'ing-fox, *n.* A large bat with a head like that of a fox.

flȳ'ing-frog, *n.* An East Indian tree-frog, with long toes fully webbed, enabling it to make sustained flights.

flȳ'ing-gũr"nărd, *n.* A species of flying-fish.

flȳ'ing-lē"mũr, *n.* An insectivorous animal of the genus *Galeopithecus*, characterized by having membranes connecting the fore and hind legs and spreading like a parachute when the animal leaps; named from its resemblance to the lemur; called also *colugo.*

flȳ'ing-mà-çhïne", *n.* A machine designed for flying, usually one of three forms; (a) a modification or extension of a kite or cordon of kites; (b) a device similar to the wings of a bird; (c) a dirigible balloon, usually having a small motor.

flȳ'ing-mouse, *n.* A small marsupial animal of Australia; called also the *opossum-mouse.*

flȳ'ing-phȧ-lan"ġẽr, *n.* A marsupial animal of Australia and New Guinea belonging to the family *Phalangistidæ*, having an extension of the skin on the legs and ventral parts which sustains it in leaping.

flȳ'ing-spī"dẽr, *n.* See *Ballooning spider* under *Ballooning.*

flȳ'ing-squid (-skwid), *n.* In zoölogy, a cephalopod of the genus *Ommastrephes*, having broad lateral flippers or fins.

flȳ'ing-squir"rel (-skwir"), *n.* A species of squirrel having an expansive skin on each side, reaching from the fore to the hind legs, by which it is borne up in leaping.

flȳ'-lēaf, *n.* A blank leaf at the beginning or end of a book.

flȳ'-mag"gŏt, *n.* A larva hatched from the egg of a blowfly.

flȳ'man, *n.* A man who attends to the flies in a theater.

flȳ'-net, *n.* 1. A net to protect a horse from flies.

2. A screen for a door or a window to keep flies out of a house.

flȳ'-nut, *n.* A nut with flattened wings to enable it to be turned with the thumb and finger.

flȳ'-ŏr"çhis, *n.* In botany, an orchid whose flowers look like flies, the *Ophrys muscifera.*

flȳ'-pā"pẽr, *n.* Paper smeared with poison or with a sticky substance for the purpose of killing flies.

flȳ'-pow"dẽr, *n.* An imperfect oxid of arsenic, which, mixed with sugar and water, is used to kill flies; any powder poisonous to flies.

flȳ'-press, *n.* A screw-press with a heavy rimmed wheel or fly.

flȳ'-rāil, *n.* That part of a table which turns out to support the leaf.

flȳ'-rod, *n.* A very light and flexible fishing-rod used when fishing with a fly.

flysch, *n.* [Swiss.] In geology, an extensive formation of sandstone stretching from Switzerland east through the northern Alps as far as Vienna, where it is known as *Vienna sandstone.*

flȳ'-sheet, *n.* A small printed sheet of one page, for distribution by hand; a dodger.

flȳ'snap"pẽr, *n.* In ornithology, (a) a handsome fly-catching bird of southwestern United States and Mexico, the plumage of the male being glossy black and that of the female brownish-gray; the *Phainopepla nitens*; (b) a bird belonging to the subfamily *Myiagrinæ.*

flȳ'speck, *n.* A name given to the excrementitious stains of insects, chiefly of the common fly.

flȳ'speck, *v.t.*; flyspecked (-spekt), *pt.*, *pp.*; flyspecking, *ppr.* To make foul with flyspecks; to deposit flyspecks upon.

flȳ'tāil, *n.* A little net for catching minnows. [U. S.]

flyte, *n.* Same as *Flite.*

flȳ'-trap, *n.* 1. In botany, a species of sensitive plant called *Venus's fly-trap*, the *Dionæa muscipula*, a plant that has the power of seizing insects that light on it.

2. A device for entrapping flies.

flȳ'-up-the-çreek', *n.* 1. In ornithology, the popular name of the little green heron, *Butorides virescens*, common along the streams of the United States; called also *shitepoke.*

2. A term of derision for a fickle, whimsical, or capricious person. [Colloq., U. S.]

flȳ'-wheel, *n.* A heavy wheel attached to a machine to render its movements uniform, its inertia tending to resist either sudden acceleration or sudden retardation of movement.

fnēṣe, *v.i.* To snore. [Obs.]

Fō, *n.* [Chinese.] 1. Same as *Foh.*

2. In Chinese carvings, the representation of an animal resembling a dog, believed to guard Buddhist temples.

fōal, *n.* [ME. *fole*, *foile*; AS. *fola*, a foal, colt.] The young of the horse, of either sex; a colt or filly.

Foal teeth; a foal's first teeth.

With foal; pregnant; said of the female of the horse kind.

fōal, *v.t.*; foaled, *pt.*, *pp.*; foaling, *ppr.* To bring forth, as young; said of a mare or a she-ass.

fōal, *v.i.* To bring forth young, as a mare or a she-ass.

fōal'foot, *n.* The coltsfoot, *Tussilago Farfara*, a plant whose leaf bears a resemblance to a colt's foot.

fōam, *n.* [ME. *fome*, *foom*; AS. *fam*, foam.]

1. Froth; spume; the substance which is formed on the surface of a liquid by fermentation or by violent agitation; also, any similar substance; as, the *foam* from a horse's mouth.

2. Figuratively, unreasonable anger; fury.

fōam, *v.i.*; foamed, *pt.*, *pp.*; foaming, *ppr.* [ME. *fomen*; AS. *fæmen*, to foam, from *fam*, foam.]

1. To froth; to gather foam; as, the billows *foam*; a horse *foams* at the mouth when violently heated.

2. To be in a rage; to be violently agitated.

He *foameth* and gnasheth with his teeth.
—Mark ix. 18.

fōam, *v.t.* 1. To throw out with rage or violence; with *out.* [Rare.]

Foaming out their own shame. —Jude 13.

2. To cause to foam.

fōam'-çock, *n.* A cock for relieving a steam-boiler of foam.

fōam'ing-ly, *adv.* Frothily.

fōam'less, *a.* Having no foam.

fōam'y, *a.*; *comp.* foamier; *superl.* foamiest. [ME. *fomy*; AS. *famig*, from *fam*, foam.] Covered with foam; frothy.

Behold how high the *foamy* billows ride.
—Dryden.

fob, *n.* 1. A little pocket for a watch.

2. A fob-chain.

fob, *v.t.*; fobbed, *pt.*, *pp.*; fobbing, *ppr.* [G. *foppen*, to jeer, mock.]

1. To cheat; to trick; to impose on.

2. To abuse; to mistreat. [Obs.]

To fob off; to shift off by an artifice; to put aside; to dismiss by a trick.

fob'-chain, *n.* A ribbon or ribbon-like fabric used as a hanging watch-chain, one end being attached to the watch, the other usually supporting a seal or charm.

fō'çăl, *a.* Belonging to a focus; as, a *focal* point.

Focal distance; (a) in conic sections, the distance of the focus from some fixed point, viz., from the vertex in the parabola, and from the center in the ellipse and hyperbola; (b) in optics, the distance between the center of a lens or mirror and the point into which the rays are collected.

fō"căl-i-zā'tion, *n.* The bringing to a focus; said of light or of any radiant; also, the condition of being focalized.

fō'căl-īze, *v.t.*; focalized, *pt.*, *pp.*; focalizing, *ppr.* To focus.

fō'çī, *n.*, pl. of *focus.*

fō'çil, *n.* [OFr. *focile*; LL. *focile*, lit., a spindle.]

The ulna or tibia, the greater bone of the fore arm or leg; the radius or fibula, the lesser bone of the fore arm or leg; the former called *greater focil*, the latter *lesser focil*. [Obs.]

foc′il-lāte, *v.t.* [L. *focillatus*, pp. of *focillare*, *focillari*, to revive by warmth, cherish, from *focus*, a fireplace.] To furnish with warmth or nourishment. [Obs.]

foc-il-lā′tion, *n.* Comfort; support. [Obs.]

fō-cim′e-tẽr, *n.* [L. *focus*, a fireplace, (modern use) focus, and *metrum*, a measure.] In optics, an instrument for determining focal lengths of lenses.

fō-cim′e-try, *n.* The science of using a focimeter.

fō′çus, *n.*; *pl.* **fō′cī** or **fō′çus-eṣ.** [L. *focus*, a fireplace, hearth, (modern use) a focus.]

1. In optics, a point in which any number of rays of light meet after being reflected or refracted; as, the *focus* of a lens or of a mirror.

2. In geometry and conic sections, a point on the principal axis of the parabola, ellipse, and hyperbola, so placed that a double ordinate to the axis passing through the point is equal to the parameter. The ellipse and hyperbola have each two foci, the parabola one, though in the latter case we may suppose a second focus at an infinite distance. The foci were so called from the fact that rays of light proceeding from one focus and reflected from the curve pass through the other focus.

3. A central point; point of concentration.

Aplanatic focus; see under *Aplanatic*.

Conjugate focus; in optics, one of two focal points, rays from either of which falling upon a lens or a mirror will be focused at the other; the two focal points are *conjugate foci*.

Focus tube; in physics, an X-ray tube for focusing cathode rays.

Principal focus; in optics, the focus for solar rays or for any rays that are parallel.

fō′çus, *v.t.*; focused (-kust) *or* focussed, *pt.*, *pp.*; focusing *or* focussing, *ppr.* 1. To place so as to bring rays to a focus; as, to *focus* a camera for a photographic picture.

2. To bring to a focus, as rays.

3. To direct toward the same object or purpose; to concentrate.

fod′dẽr, *n.* [ME. *fodder*, *foddur*; AS. *fodor*, *foddor*, *foddus*, food, fodder.] Food, especially dry food, for cattle, horses, and sheep, as hay, straw, and various kinds of vegetables.

fod′dẽr, *n.* An old standard of weight; a fother.

fod′dẽr, *v.t.*; foddered, *pt.*, *pp.*; foddering, *ppr.* To feed with dry food or cut grass, etc.; to furnish with hay, straw, oats, etc.

fod′dẽr-ẽr, *n.* One who fodders cattle.

fō′di-ent, *a.* [L. *fodiens* (*-entis*), ppr. of *fodere*, to dig, dig up.]

1. Digging; throwing up with a spade. [Obs.]

2. Adapted for digging or burrowing; of or pertaining to the *Fodientia*.

fō′di-ent, *n.* In zoölogy, a burrower; an animal of the *Fodientia*.

Fō-di-en′ti-ȧ (-shiȧ), *n.pl.* [From L. *fodiens* (*-entis*), ppr. of *fodere*, to dig, dig up.] In zoölogy, a subdivision of edentates characterized by claws fitted for digging and burrowing.

fōe, *n.* [ME. *fo*, *foo*, *fa*; AS. *gefah*, an enemy, foe, *ge-* and *feh*, *fag*, guilty, outlawed.]

1. An enemy; one who entertains personal enmity, hatred, grudge, or malice against another.

> A man's *foes* shall be they of his own household. —Matt. x. 36.

2. An enemy in war; one of a nation at war with another, whether he entertains enmity against the opposing nation or not; an adversary.

> Either three years' famine, or three months to be destroyed before thy *foes*. —1 Chron. xxi. 12.

3. An opponent; an adversary; one who opposes anything in principle; an ill-wisher; as, a *foe* to religion; a *foe* to virtue; a *foe* to the measures of the administration.

4. One who or that which harms or restricts; as, monopoly is a *foe* to low prices.

Syn.—Antagonist, adversary, enemy, opponent.

fōe, *v.t.* To treat as an enemy. [Obs.]

fœhn (fēn), *n.* [G. *föhn*, *fön*, a warm south wind.] In meteorology, a warm and dry wind in the valleys north of the Alps produced by a cyclonic movement passing over the center of Europe; also spelled *föhn*.

fōe′hood, *n.* Enmity. [Obs.]

fōe′măn, *n.*; *pl.* **fōe′men.** An enemy in war.

Fœ-nic′ū-lum (fē-), *n* [L.] In botany, a genus of umbelliferous plants, native to Europe and cultivated for their sweet aromatic foliage; common fennel.

fœ′tăl (fē-), *a.* Same as *Fetal*.

fœ-tā′tion, *n.* Same as *Fetation*.

fœ′ti-cīde, *n.* Same as *Feticide*.

fœ′tŏr, *n.* Same as *Fetor*.

fœ′tus, *n.* Same as *Fetus*.

fog, *n.* [Dan. *fog*, spray, drift; *snee*fog, snow falling thick, a snowstorm; Ice. *fok*, spray, snowdrift.]

1. Watery globules formed and floating in the lower atmosphere in places where moist atmosphere becomes rapidly cooled, as on the margins of rivers, ponds, lakes, etc.

2. A cloud of dust or smoke.

3. Figuratively, a befuddled state of mind.

4. In photography, an imperfection in a developed plate which produces a print with a foggy appearance.

fog, *n.* [ME. *fogge*, grass, W. *ffwg*, dry grass.]

1. Aftergrass; a second growth of grass; long grass that remains in pastures till winter.

2. In Scotland, a general name for *moss*.

fog, *v.t.*; fogged, *pt.*, *pp.*; fogging, *ppr.* 1. To cover or to obscure with fog; to render dark and confused.

2. In photography, to render (a plate or film) imperfect, as by exposure to light.

fog, *v.i.* 1. To befog. [Rare.]

2. In photography, to become foggy, as a negative.

fog, *v.t.* To strip of fog; to feed with fog. [Eng.]

fog, *v.i.* To act the pettifogger. [Obs.]

fog′-ȧ-lärm″, *n.* A device of some kind placed upon a rock, island, lighthouse, buoy, or boat, and operated by the action of the water, by hand, or by some mechanical contrivance, to warn mariners of danger when fog obscures vision.

fog′-bank, *n.* At sea, a mass of fog, sometimes resembling land at a distance, which vanishes as it is approached.

fog′-bell, *n.* A kind of fog-alarm consisting of a bell so hung as to ring by the action of the waves when the sea is rough, or to be rung by hand or by some mechanical means.

fog′-bōw, *n.* In meteorology, a bow or arch resembling in form a rainbow, but usually white or slightly tinted with a single color, produced by the refraction and reflection of light by the globules of fog as the rainbow is produced by drops of rain.

fog′-dog, *n.* A bright spot in a fog-bank, indicating the disappearance of the fog.

fōge, *n.* A smelting-furnace for tin. [Corn.]

fog′-eat″ẽr, *n.* A fog-dog.

fog′fruit, *n.* *Lippia lanceolata*, a creeping, weedy herb along the banks of rivers, bearing a head of small bluish flowers.

fog′gāge, *n.* Rank or coarse grass not mowed or eaten down in summer or autumn.

fog′gẽr, *n.* One who deals in an underhand way; a pettifogger. [Obs.]

fog′gi-ly, *adv.* With fog; darkly.

fog′gi-ness, *n.* The state of being foggy; a state of the air filled with watery globules.

fog′gy, *a.*; *comp.* foggier; *superl.* foggiest. 1. Filled or abounding with fog or watery globules; as, a *foggy* atmosphere; a *foggy* morning.

2. Producing frequent fogs; as, a *foggy* climate.

3. Dull; stupid; clouded in understanding.

fog′-horn, *n.* 1. A kind of horn kept on board of a vessel to sound as a warning signal in foggy weather.

2. A sounding instrument for warning vessels of their proximity to the coast during a fog.

fō′gie (-gi), *n.* Same as *Fogy*.

fog′less, *a.* Having no fog; not foggy; as, a *fogless* climate; a *fogless* morning.

fō′gy, *n.*; *pl.* **fō′gieṣ.** A slow person; one not abreast of the times; usually with *old*; as, an *old fogy*. [Colloq.]

fō′gy-ism, *n.* The condition of being a fogy; the beliefs or practices of a fogy; the characteristics of a fogy.

fōh, *interj.* An exclamation of abhorrence or contempt, the same as *poh* and *fie*.

Fōh (fō), *n.* The Chinese name of Buddha, who founded his religion about A. D. 67; also written *Fo* and *Foh-to*.

Fōh′ism, *n.* The Buddhism of the Chinese.

Fōh′ist (fō′ist), *n.* A believer in Foh or Buddha; an advocate and devotee of Buddhism.

foi′ble, *a.* Weak. [Obs.]

foi′ble, *n.* [Fr. *foible*, *faible*, from OFr. *feble*, feeble, weak.]

1. A particular moral weakness; a failing.

2. The pointed half of a foil or sword-blade; written also *faible*.

Syn.—Peccadillo, failing, fault, weakness, infirmity, frailty, defect, imperfection.

foil, *v.t.*; foiled, *pt.*, *pp.*; foiling, *ppr.* [ME. *foilen*, *foylen*; OFr. *fouler*, to trample upon, subdue; LL. *fullare*, to full cloth by trampling or beating, from L. *fullo*, a fuller.]

1. To frustrate; to defeat; to render vain or nugatory, as an effort or attempt; as, the enemy attempted to pass the river, but was *foiled*.

> And by a mortal man at length am *foiled*. —Dryden.

2. To blunt; to dull.

> When light-winged toys,
> Of feathered Cupid *foil*. —Shak.

3. To defeat; to interrupt, or to render imperceptible; as, to *foil* the scent in a chase.

foil, *v.t.* [Obs.] See *Foul*.

foil, *n.* Defeat; frustration; the failure of an endeavor when on the point of success. [Obs.]

> Death never won a stake with greater toil,
> Nor e'er was fate so near a *foil*. —Dryden.

foil, *n.* 1. A blunt sword, or one that has a button at the end covered with leather; used in fencing.

> Isocrates contended with a *foil* against Demosthenes with a sword. —Mitford.

Fencing Foils.

2. The track or trail of game when pursued.

3. In wrestling, a fall in which a contestant is not fully thrown.

To run a foil; to puzzle; from the habit of certain animals of running back over their track to mislead pursuers.

foil, *n.* [ME. *foile*; OFr. *foil*, *foel*, *feuill*, a leaf, sheet of paper or metal, from L. *folium*, a leaf.]

1. A leaf or thin plate of metal; as, tin-*foil*, etc.

2. Among jewelers, a thin leaf of metal placed under precious stones to increase their brilliancy or to give them a particular color; as, the stone appears to be of the color of the *foil*.

3. Anything of another color, or of different qualities, which serves to adorn, or set off another thing to advantage.

4. A thin coat of tin, with quicksilver, laid on the back of a looking-glass, to cause reflection.

5. In architecture, an ornamentation in the form of a conventional leaf or combination of leaves; as, tre*foil*, quatre*foil*, cinque*foil*.

foil′ȧ-ble, *a.* That may be foiled.

foil′ẽr, *n.* One who frustrates another, and gains an advantage.

foil′ing, *n.* Foil-work in architecture.

foil′ing, *n.* Among hunters, the slight mark of a passing deer on the grass.

foin, *v.t.* and *v.i.* [ME. *foynen*, from OFr. *foine*, a pitchfork, fish-spear.]

1. To thrust with a sword or spear. [Obs.]

2. To prick; to sting. [Obs.]

foin, *n.* A push; a thrust with a sword or spear. [Obs.]

foin′ẽr-y, *n.* The act or practice of thrusting in fencing. [Obs.]

foin′ing-ly, *adv.* In a pushing manner. [Obs.]

foi′sŏn, *n.* [OFr. *foison*, from L. *fusio*, an outpouring, abundance.] Plenty; abundance. [Obs.]

foist, *v.t.*; foisted, *pt.*, *pp.*; foisting, *ppr.* [Old D. *vysten*, D. *veesten*, to fizzle.] To insert or thrust surreptitiously, wrongfully, or without warrant and with intent to deceive; followed by *in*, *into*, or *upon*.

> Lest negligence or partiality might admit or *foist in* abuses and corruption. —Carew.

foist, *n.* A light and fast-sailing ship. [Obs.]

foist, *n.* 1. One who foists or deceives. [Obs.]

2. A foisting; a deception. [Obs.]

foist′ẽr, *n.* One who inserts without authority; a trickster.

foist′ied, *a.* Of a musty or moldy character; fusty. [Obs.]

foist′i-ness, *n.* Fustiness. [Obs.]

foist′y, *a.* [Obs.] See *Fusty*.

Fōk′kẽr, *n.* A type of German aeroplane.

fōld, *v.t.*; folded, *pt.*, *pp.*; folding, *ppr.* [ME. *folden*, *falden*; AS. *fealden*, to fold, wrap up.]

1. To double; to lap or lay in plaits; to lay one part over another part of; as, to *fold* a piece of cloth; to *fold* a letter.

> As a vesture shalt thou *fold* them up. —Heb. i. 12.

2. To double or lay together, as the arms; to lay one over the other, as the hands.

> Conscious of its own impotence, it *folds* its arms in despair. —Collier.

3. To inclose as in folds; to enfold; to embrace.

> We will descend and *fold* him in our arms. —Shak.

4. To wrap in obscurity; to make intricate or perplexed, as words.

> The *folded* meaning of your words' deceit. —Shak.

fōld, *v.i.* To close over another of the same kind; as, the leaves of the door *fold*.

fōld, *n.* [ME. *fold*, *fald*; AS. *fald*, *falod*, a fold, stall.]

1. A pen or inclosure for sheep; a place where a flock of sheep is kept, whether in the field or under shelter.

2. A flock of sheep; hence, figuratively, the whole Christian church; any church.

Other sheep I have, which are not of this *fold*. —John x. 16.

3. A limit. [Obs.]

fōld, *n.* 1. The doubling of any flexible substance, as cloth; complication; a plait; one part turned or bent and laid on another; as, a *fold* of linen.

2. In composition, the same quantity added; times; as, two*fold*, ten*fold*, etc., meaning two times, etc.

fōld, *v.t.* To gather into a fold, as sheep.

fōld, *v.i.* To be gathered into a fold, as sheep. [Rare.]

fōld'āge, *n.* Same as *Faldage.*

fōld'ēr, *n.* 1. One who or that which folds; specifically, a flat, pointed instrument often of bone, used in folding paper by hand.

2. Printed matter in a folded form; specifically, a combined map and time-table issued by railway and steamship companies in a form handy for the pocket.

3. In entomology, a leaf-folder.

fol'de-rol, *n.* 1. Airy, meaningless talk; the voluble utterances of a conceited person.

2. In the plural, gewgaws; frippery. [Colloq.]

fōld'ing, *n.* 1. A fold; a doubling; the act of making a fold.

2. In agriculture, the keeping of sheep in inclosures on arable land.

Folding boat; a jointed boat covered with flexible waterproof material so as to be folded and carried by tourists or fishermen.

Folding chair; a chair with a hinged frame capable of being compactly folded for transportation or for storing.

Folding doors; two doors swinging and meeting in the middle of the doorway.

fōld'less, *a.* Having no fold; without folds.

fōld'-net, *n.* A seine-like net for taking small birds.

fōld'-yärd, *n.* An inclosure for keeping a fold at night.

fō'li-ȧ, *n.*, pl. of *folium.*

fō'li-ȧ, *n.* [Sp., lit., folly, extravagance.] The name of a Spanish dance, or the music for it, a slow triple measure.

fō-li-ā'ceous, *a.* [L. *foliaceus*, leafy, of leaves, from *folium*, a leaf.]

1. In botany, leafy or relating to a leaf or foliage; having leaves intermixed with flowers; as, a *foliaceous* spike.

2. In mineralogy, consisting of leaves or thin laminæ; having the form of a leaf or plate; as, *foliaceous* spar.

3. In zoölogy, resembling a leaf or leaves in shape and manner of growth; as, *foliaceous* corals.

fō'li-āge, *n.* [OFr. *foillage, feuillage*, from *foille, feuille*, a leaf, from L. *folium*, a leaf.]

1. Leaves in general; as, a tree of beautiful *foliage.*

2. A cluster of leaves, flowers, and branches; particularly, the representation of leaves, flowers, and branches, in architecture, intended to ornament and enrich capitals, friezes, pediments, etc.

fō'li-āge, *v.t.* To work or to form into the representation of leaves. [Rare.]

fō'li-āged, *a.* Furnished with foliage.

fō'li-āge-plant, *n.* A plant cultivated exclusively or mainly for the beauty of its foliage, as the coleus, the begonia, and others.

fō'li-āge-tree, *n.* A tree having a profusion of broad leaves which furnish shade, as distinguished from a tree with small or narrow leaves, as the oak, elm, maple, horse-chestnut, etc.

fō'li-ăr, *a.* [From L. *folium*, a leaf.] In botany, having leaves; related to the leaf.

Foliar gap; the spreading or opening in the fibers of a stem which presages the formation of a leaf.

fō'li-āte, *v.t.*; foliated, *pt., pp.*; foliating, *ppr.* [LL. *foliatus*, pp. of *foliare*, to put forth leaves, from L. *folium*, a leaf.]

1. To beat into a leaf or thin plate.

2. To spread over with a thin coat of tin and quicksilver; as, to *foliate* a looking-glass.

fō'li-āte, *a.* [L. *foliatus*, leafy, from *folium*, a leaf.] In botany, leafy; furnished with leaves; as, a *foliate* stalk.

Foliate curve; same as *Folium*, 3.

fō'li-ā-ted, *a.* 1. Beaten, cast, or otherwise made into a thin plate, as a foil.

2. In art, decorated with ornaments resembling leaves in shape.

3. Foiled, as a window; cusped; lobed.

4. Covered with a thin foil or amalgam.

5. Consisting of plates or thin layers; resembling or in the form of a plate; lamellar; as, a *foliated* fracture.

6. In heraldry, having leaves for adornment.

7. In music, having added notes above or below the air.

Foliated tellurium; same as *Nagyagite.*

fō-li-ā'tion, *n.* [From LL. *foliare*, to put forth leaves, from *folium*, a leaf.]

1. The putting forth of leaves in a plant.

2. The manner of disposal of leaves in the bud before they put forth.

3. The act of beating a metal into a thin plate, leaf, or foil.

4. The act or operation of spreading foil over the back of a mirror or looking-glass.

5. In architecture, an enrichment or decoration using foils in different arrangements.

6. In geology, the property of cleavage possessed by some rocks, by which they divide in plates or slabs.

fō'li-ȧ-tūre, *n.* 1. Leafage; foliage. [Obs.]

2. The state of being beaten into foil.

fō'li-ēr, *n.* Goldsmiths' foil. [Rare.]

fō-li-i-. A combining form from L. *folium*, a leaf; used to signify relation to a leaf.

fō-li-ic'ō-lous, *a.* [*Folii-*, and L. *colere*, to inhabit.] Living and growing upon leaves.

fō-li-if'ēr-ous, *a.* [*Folii-*, and L. *ferre*, to bear.] Bearing foliage; having leaf-like appendages.

fō'li-i-form, *a.* [*Folii-*, and L. *forma*, form.] Shaped like a leaf.

fol'i-ly, *adv.* [ME. *foly*, foolish.] In a foolish manner. [Obs.]

fō'li-ō, *n.* [From L. *folio*, in the phrase *in folio*, in a (one) sheet; *in*, in, and *folio*, ablative of *folium*, a leaf.]

1. A sheet of paper suitable for folding once, or folded once; used in naming the various sizes of paper; as, check *folio.*

2. A book of the largest size, formed by once doubling a sheet of paper; also, the size of book so made.

3. A page; in bookkeeping, two pages of a book. In the latter case both are numbered alike.

4. In printing, the page number, even numbers indicating the left, and odd the right page.

5. In law, the unit of measurement of the length of a document by words per leaf, generally 72 words; by enactment of Congress, 100 words; in parliamentary proceedings in England, 90 words.

6. One of the leaves of a manuscript.

7. A stand or case for loose papers.

fō'li-ō, *v.t.*; folioed, *pt., pp.*; folioing, *ppr.* To page consecutively, as a book or manuscript; specifically, in law, to designate the end of every folio in (a volume).

fō'li-ō, *a.* Pertaining to paper folded but once, or to a volume of the largest size; consisting of sheets forming two leaves.

Folio post; a size of paper for writing and for printing, 17x22 inches.

fō'li-ō-branch, fō''li-ō-bran'chi-āte, *a.* [L. *folium*, a leaf, and *branchiæ*, gills.] In zoölogy, having the branchiæ formed in layers like the leaves of a book.

fō'li-ō-lāte, *a.* Of or pertaining to small leaves.

fō'li-ōle, *n.* [A dim. from L. *folium*, a leaf.]

1. A leaflet; one of the single leaves which together constitute a compound leaf.

2. In zoölogy, any small appendage resembling a leaf.

fō''li-ō-lif'ēr-ous, *a.* [*Foliole*, dim. from L. *folium*, a leaf, and L. *ferre*, to bear.] Bearing little leaves, or folioles.

fō-li'ō-lum, *n.*; *pl.* **fō-li'ō-lȧ.** A foliole.

fō'li-ō-mort, *a.* [L. *folium*, a leaf, and *mortuum*, dead.] Of a dark yellow color, or that of a faded leaf; feuillemorte.

fō'li-ōse, *a.* [From L. *folium*, a leaf.] In botany, having a great number of leaves; full of leaves.

fō-li-os'i-ty, *n.* The bulk or voluminousness, as of a folio. [Rare.]

fō'li-ous, *a.* 1. Leafy; thin; unsubstantial.

2. In botany, having leaves; bearing foliage.

fō'li-um, *n.*; *pl.* **fō'li-ȧ.** [L., a leaf.]

1. A thin leaf.

2. A thin plate; a lamina.

3. In geometry, a looped curve, its formula being $x^3+y^3=axy$.

fōlk (fōk), *n.* [ME. *folk, folc*, people.]

1. People in general, or any part of them without distinction; formerly alike in both singular and plural, but now the plural *folks* is most used; as, *folks* will talk; some *folks* say so.

2. The members of one's family; one's relatives; a colloquial use in the plural in the United States; as, the *folks* down home on the farm; his *folks* are Yankees.

3. A race of people; a nation; a community. [Rare.]

Fōl'ke-thing (-ting), *n.* [Dan. *folk*, people, and *thing*, a meeting.] The lower house of the Danish parliament, the upper house being the Landsthing.

fōlk'land (fōk'), *n.* [AS. *folcland*; *folc*, the people, and *land*, land.] In old English law, land distributed among the people by the lord of the manor, and held entirely at his will; distinguished from *book*land or *charter* land, conveyed by deed.

fōlk'lōre, *n.* The traditions, beliefs, and customs current among the folk or common people; the branch of ethnology allied to primitive ethics, treating of the foregoing.

fōlk'mōot, *n.* [From AS. *folcgemot*; *folc*, the people, and *gemot*, a meeting.] In English history, an assembly of the people to consult respecting public affairs; an annual convention of the people, answering, in some measure, to a modern parliament.

fōlk'mōot''ēr, *n.* An attendant and participant in folkmoots. [Obs.]

fōlk'mōte, *n.* Folkmoot.

fōlk'-sǫng, *n.* A song sung and loved by a people and transmitted from generation to generation.

fōlk'-speech, *n.* The speech of the masses as distinguished from that of the educated and cultured class; the vernacular.

fol'li-cle, *n.* [L. *folliculus*, a small bag, husk, pod, dim. of *follis*, a pair of bellows, a wind-bag, money-bag.]

1. In botany, a univalvular pericarp; a seed-vessel opening on one side longitudinally, and having the seeds loose in it.

2. In anatomy, a small sac-like cavity for secretion or excretion; a simple gland; as, a sebaceous *follicle.*

3. In entomology, a larval covering.

Follicle of Columbine (*Aquilegia vulgaris*).

fol-lic'ū-lăr, *a.* Of, relating to, or affecting a follicle or follicles.

fol-lic'ū-lā-ted, *a.* Having follicular seed-vessels; follicular.

fol-lic-ū-lī'tis, *n.* [L. *folliculus*, a small bag, husk, pod, and *-itis*.] In medicine, an affection in which the follicles are inflamed.

fol-lic'ū-lous, *a.* Having or producing follicles.

fol'li-fụl, *a.* Full of folly. [Obs.]

fol'lōw, *v.t.*; followed, *pt., pp.*; following, *ppr.* [ME. *folowen, folwen, folgen*; AS. *folgian*, to follow.]

1. To go after or behind; to walk, ride, or move behind, but in the same direction or in the same track or course.

2. To pursue; to chase, as an enemy or as game.

3. To accompany; to attend on a journey.

And Rebekah arose, and her damsels, and they rode on the camels, and *followed* the man. —Gen. xxiv. 61.

4. To succeed in order of time; to come after; as, a storm is *followed* by a calm.

5. To succeed logically; as, the conclusion *follows* the premises.

6. To pursue with the senses or the affections; as, to *follow* eagerly a speaker's language and action.

7. To take as a guide; to imitate; as, to *follow* the precepts of a teacher; to *follow* the fashion.

8. To use; to practise; to make the chief business; as, to *follow* the trade of a carpenter; to *follow* the profession of law.

To follow suit; in card-playing, to play a card of the suit led; figuratively, to do as some one else does.

To follow the hounds; to hunt with a pack of hounds.

To follow up; to note persistently changes of circumstances in the pursuit of an object; to lose sight of nothing that may affect the issue of an undertaking.

Syn.—Pursue, succeed.—To *follow* denotes simply to go after; to *pursue* denotes to *follow* with earnestness and with a view to attain some definite object; to *succeed* means to come after in some regular series or succession, as day *succeeds* to day.

fol'lōw, *n.* In the game of billiards, a stroke above the center of the cue-ball, causing it to follow the object-ball; the shot so made.

fol'lōw, *v.i.* 1. To come after another; as, you go and I will *follow* later.

2. To be posterior in time; as, *following* ages.

3. To be consequential, as effect to cause; as, from such measures great mischiefs must *follow.*

To follow on; to continue pursuit or endeavor; persevere.

fol'lōw-bōard, *n.* In founding, a smooth board with a plane surface for holding the pattern and the flask while the sand is being packed in.

fol'lōw-ēr, *n.* [ME. *folwere*; AS. *folgere*, from *folgian*, to follow.]

1. One who comes, goes, or moves after another in the same course; one who takes another as his guide in doctrines, opinions, or example; one who receives the opinions and imitates the example of another; an attendant; an adherent; a disciple; an imitator; an associate or dependent; one of the same faction or party; as, the *followers* of Plato; the warrior distributed the plunder among his *followers.*

That ye be not slothful, but *followers* of them who through faith and patience inherit the promises. —Heb. vi. 12.

2. A male sweetheart. [Colloq.]

3. Among law-stationers, the name given to a sheet of parchment added to the first sheet of an indenture or other deed.

4. In machinery, the part of a machine that receives motion from another part.

5. In the steam-engine, the cover of a piston; the cover of a stuffing-box.

Syn.—Adherent, disciple, partizan, henchman.

fol'lōw-ing, *n.* 1. Collectively, one's attendants or followers; those of like opinions and principles of action; as, Lincoln had a large and enthusiastic *following.*

2. An occupation, trade, or profession.

fol'lōw-ing, *a.* Being next after; succeeding; as, the journey was resumed on the *following* day.

fol'lōw-shot, *n.* In billiards, a follow.

fol'ly, *n.*; *pl.* **fol'lies**. [ME. *folye*, *folie*; OFr. *folie*, folly, foolishness, from *fol*, a fool, foolish.]

1. Weakness of intellect; imbecility of mind; want of understanding.

> Here (in newspaper) Fraud and Falsehood labour to deceive,
> And *Folly* aids them both, impatient to believe. —Crabbe.

2. A weak or absurd act; an inconsiderate or thoughtless procedure; weak or light-minded conduct.

> What *folly* 'tis to hazard life for ill.—Shak.

3. Criminal weakness; depravity of mind or actions. [Obs.]

> She turn'd to *folly*, and she was a whore. —Shak.

4. Any structure left incomplete for lack of funds to finish it; usually with the promoter's name to designate it; as, Smith's *folly*.

Syn.—Madness, nonsense, misconduct, imprudence, silliness, foolishness, weakness, absurdity, imbecility, unwisdom.

fol'we, *v.t.* [Obs.] See *Follow.*

Fō'mal-haut, *n.* [Ar. *fom-al-hût*, mouth of a large fish; *fom*, mouth, and *hût*, large fish.] A star of the first magnitude in the constellation *Piscis Australis* or Southern Fish.

fō-ment', *v.t.*; fomented, *pt.*, *pp.*; fomenting, *ppr.* [Fr. *fomenter*; L. *fomentare*, from *fomentum*, a warm application, poultice, from *fovere*, to keep warm.]

1. To apply warm lotions to; to bathe with warm, medicated liquors or with flannel dipped in warm water.

2. To cherish with heat; to encourage growth of. [Obs.]

3. To encourage; to abet; to cherish and promote by incitements; as, to *foment* trouble.

Syn.—Excite, cherish, fan, propagate, encourage, engender, stir up.

fō'ment, *n.* Fomentation. [Obs.]

fō-men-tā'tion, *n.* 1. In medicine, (a) the act of applying warm liquors to a part of the body, by means of flannels dipped in hot water or medicated decoctions, for the purpose of easing pain; (b) the lotion applied or to be applied to a diseased part.

2. Excitation; instigation; encouragement.

fō-ment'ēr, *n.* One who foments; one who encourages or instigates; as, a *fomenter* of sedition.

fō'mēs, *n.*; *pl.* **fō'mi-tēs**. [L. *fomes* (*-itis*), kindling wood, tinder, from *fovere*, to warm, keep warm.] Any substance that by absorbing and holding infectious germs may transport them, as woolen fabrics and other substances.

fon, *n.* [ME. *fon*, *fonne*; Sw. *fane*, a fool.] A fool; an idiot. [Obs.]

fond, *n.* [Fr. *fond*, from L. *fundus*, bottom.] Ground or background; specifically, that upon which lace is worked.

fond, *v.*, obsolete past tense of *find*.

fond, *a.*; *comp.* fonder; *superl.* fondest. [ME. *fond*, contr. of *fonned*, foolish, pp. of *fonnen*, to act like a fool.]

1. Foolish; silly; weak; indiscreet; imprudent.

> Grant I may never prove so *fond*
> To trust man on his oath or bond. —Shak.

2. Foolishly tender and loving; doting; weakly indulgent; as, a *fond* mother or wife.

3. Much pleased; loving ardently; delighted with; as, a child is *fond* of play; a gentleman is *fond* of his sports or of his country-seat.

4. Relishing highly; as, the epicure is *fond* of high-seasoned food.

5. Trifling; valued by folly. [Obs.]

Syn.—Loving, attached, affectionate, foolish, silly, weak, doting, enamored, devoted.

fond, *v.t.* To treat with great indulgence or tenderness; to caress; to coddle. [Obs.]

> The Tyrian hugs and *fonds* thee on her breast. —Dryden.

fond, *v.i.* To be fond; to be in love; to dote. [Obs.]

foṅ-dänt' (-dän'), *n.* [Fr.] A form of confection made by boiling a solution of sugar to the point of crystallization, and placing it in a mold to cool.

foṅ-dänt', *a.* [Fr., ppr. of *fondre*, to found, ground.] In heraldry, bending downward, as an eagle for prey.

fon'dle, *v.t.*; fondled, *pt.*, *pp.*; fondling, *ppr.* To treat with tenderness; to caress; as, a nurse *fondles* a child.

fon'dlēr, *n.* One who fondles.

fond'ling, *n.* The act of caressing or treating with tenderness.

fond'ling, *n.* 1. A person or thing fondled or caressed.

2. A weakling. [Obs.]

fond'ly, *adv.*; *comp.* fondlier; *superl.* fondliest.

1. Foolishly; weakly; imprudently; with indiscreet affection.

> *Fondly* we think we merit honor then,
> When we but praise ourselves in other men. —Pope.

2. With great or extreme affection.

fond'ness, *n.* 1. Foolishness; weakness; want of sense or judgment. [Obs.]

2. Foolish tenderness.

3. Tender passion; warm affection.

> Her *fondness* for a certain earl
> Began when I was but a girl. —Swift.

4. Strong inclination or propensity; strong appetite or relish; as, *fondness* for ardent spirits or for a particular kind of food.

Syn.—Attachment, affection, kindness, desire.

fon'don, *n.* [Sp.] A huge copper-bottomed tub for amalgamating silver ores.

fon-dū', *a.* [Fr.] Denoting a style of printing calico, wall-paper, etc., in which the colors are blended into each other.

fōne, *n.*, obsolete plural of *foe*.

fon'ly, *adv.* [Obs.] See *Foolishly.*

fon'ne, *n.* A fon. [Obs.]

font, *n.* [Fr. *fonte*, a casting, cast of type, from *fondre*, to cast, found.] A complete assortment of printing-types of one size, including a due proportion of all the letters in the alphabet, large and small, points, accents, and whatever else is necessary for printing with that variety of type.

font, *n.* [L. *fons*, *fontis*, a fountain, spring.]

1. A source; a spring; a fountain.

2. A large basin or stone vessel in which water is contained for baptizing children or other persons in the church.

Font with Cover.

font'ăl, *a.* [LL. *fontalis*, from *fons*, *fontis*, a fount, spring.] Pertaining to a font, fountain, source, or origin. [Rare.]

fon-tà-nel', *n.* 1. In medicine, an artificial opening for the discharge of humors from the body.

2. A vacancy between the bones of the infant or fetal cranium, between the frontal and parietal bones, and also between the parietal and occipital, at the two extremities of the sagittal suture.

fon-tà-nelle', *n.* Same as *Fontanel.*

foṅ-täṅge' (-toṅj'), *n.* [Named after the Duchesse de *Fontanges*, who introduced the fashion.] A knot of ribbons formerly worn as a headdress.

fo͞od, *n.* [ME. *foode*, *fode*, from AS. *foda*, food.]

1. In a general sense, whatever is eaten by animals for nourishment, and whatever supplies nutriment to plants; victuals; provisions; nutriment; aliment, as distinguished from that part of the substance eaten which is not digested or absorbed into the circulation.

2. Anything that sustains, nourishes, and augments; fuel; substance; as, flattery is the *food* of vanity; *food* for the flames; *food* for thought.

fo͞od'fụl, *a.* Supplying food; full of food.

fo͞od'less, *a.* Without food; destitute of provisions; barren.

fo͞od'-vac"ū-ōle, *n.* In zoölogy, a space in which a protozoan retains a particle of food during the process of digestion.

fo͞od'y, *a.* Eatable; fit for food. [Rare.]

fo͞od'-yōlk, *n.* In biology, the part of the yolk of an egg that furnishes nourishment for the embryo, as distinguished from the part that produces germination.

fo͞ol, *n.* [Fr. *fouler*, to tread, crush.] A compound of gooseberries scalded and crushed, with cream; commonly called *gooseberry fool.*

fo͞ol, *n.* [ME. *fool*, *fole*, *fol*; OFr. *fol*, a fool, idiot; LL. *follus*, *follis*, foolish, from L. *follis*, a pair of bellows, wind-bag, in allusion to the puffed cheeks of a buffoon.]

1. One who is destitute of reason, or the common powers of understanding; an idiot; an imbecile.

2. A person who is deficient in intellect, but not an idiot; a person who acts absurdly; one who does not exercise his reason; one who pursues a course contrary to the dictates of wisdom.

> Experience keeps a dear school, but *fools* will learn in no other. —Franklin.

3. In Scripture, a wicked or depraved person; one who acts contrary to sound wisdom in his moral deportment.

> The *fool* hath said in his heart, There is no God. —Ps. xiv. 1.

4. A buffoon. [See *Court fool.*]

April fool; see under *April.*

Court fool; a clownish jester formerly kept by princes and noblemen for the amusement of guests and as a butt of ridicule, dressed in a grotesque cap and a garment fringed with little bells.

Feast of fools; a festival held in the middle ages at the time of Christmas holidays, the chief feature of which was the choosing of a bishop, an archbishop, or a pope, usually a boy from the choir, who presided and conducted in a mimicking way the ceremonies usually conducted by the dignitary he impersonated.

Fool's errand; a fruitless errand or adventure; labor performed with no result.

Fool's gold; in mineralogy, iron sulphid; iron pyrites, a hard crystalline mineral with a luster resembling that of gold.

Fool's paradise; an intermediate abode for the spirits of fools and of vain and nonsensical beings; hence, any state of foolish pleasure and imaginary security.

To make a fool of; to deceive by trickery; to subject to ridicule or shame. [Colloq.]

To play the fool; to act in a ridiculous manner.

fo͞ol, *v.i.*; fooled, *pt.*, *pp.*; fooling, *ppr.* [ME. *folen*, *folien*, from OFr. *foler*, *folier*, to be foolish, from *fol*, a fool, idiot.] To trifle; to toy; to spend time in idleness, sport, or mirth.

fo͞ol, *v.t.* 1. To treat with contempt; to disappoint; to defeat; to frustrate; to deceive; to impose on.

2. To infatuate; to make foolish.

3. To cheat; as, to *fool* one out of his money.

To fool away; to spend in trifles, idleness, folly, or without advantage; as, *to fool away* time or money.

Fo͞o'läh, *n.* Same as *Fulah.*

fo͞ol'-bōrn, *a.* Foolish from birth; of foolish origin; as, a *fool-born* jest.

fo͞ol'ēr-y, *n.*; *pl.* **fo͞ol'ēr-ies**. 1. The practice of folly; habitual folly; attention to trifles.

2. An act of folly or weakness; something ridiculous.

fo͞ol'fish, *n.* A name applied to the long-finned filefish, of the genus *Monocanthus*, from its ridiculous manner of swimming with a wriggling motion, its body being sunk and its mouth just on a level with the water.

fo͞ol'hap"py, *a.* Lucky without judgment or contrivance. [Obs.]

fo͞ol'här"di-hood, *n.* The condition characterized by being foolhardy.

fo͞ol'här"di-ly, *adv.* With foolhardiness.

fo͞ol'här"di-ness, *n.* Courage without sense or judgment; mad rashness.

fo͞ol'här"dise, *n.* Foolhardiness. [Obs.]

fo͞ol'här"dy, *a.* [ME. *folhardi*, *folehardi*; OFr. *fol hardi*, foolishly bold; *fol*, foolish, a fool, and *hardi*, pp. of *hardir*, to make bold.] Daring without judgment; madly rash and adventurous; foolishly bold and venturesome.

Syn.—Rash, precipitate, reckless, venturesome, incautious, headlong.

fo͞ol'häs"ty, *a.* Precipitate; making foolish haste. [Obs.]

fo͞ol'i-fȳ, *v.t.* To deceive by trickery. [Obs.]

fo͞ol'ish, *a.* 1. Void of understanding or sound judgment; weak in intellect; applied to general character.

2. Unwise; imprudent; acting without judgment or discretion in particular things.

3. Proceeding from folly or marked with folly; silly; vain; trifling.

> But *foolish* questions avoid. —2 Tim. ii. 23.

4. Ridiculous; despicable.

> A *foolish* figure he must make. —Prior.

5. In Scripture, wicked; sinful; acting without regard to the divine law and glory, or to one's own eternal happiness.

> O *foolish* Galatians. —Gal. iii. 1.

Syn.—Absurd, unwise, silly, simple, shallow, brainless, shallow-brained, incautious, weakminded, imbecile.

fo͞ol'ish-ly, *adv.* 1. Weakly; without understanding or judgment; unwisely; indiscreetly.

2. Wickedly; sinfully.

> I have done very *foolishly*. —2 Sam. xxiv. 10.

fo͞ol'ish-ness, *n.* 1. Folly; want of understanding; the state or quality of being foolish.

2. Absurdity; senselessness.

The preaching of the cross is to them that perish *foolishness*. —1 Cor. i. 18.

fool'-kill"ẽr, *n.* An imaginary being, sometimes humorously alluded to in criticism; as, the *fool-killer* is neglecting his duty. [Colloq.]

fools'cap, *n.* [So called from a fool's head and cap being formerly used as a watermark.] A kind of paper, of small size, usually about 12½ by 16 inches.

fool's'-pärs"ley, *n.* A poisonous plant of the parsley family, *Æthusa Cynapium*.

foot, *n.*; *pl.* **feet**. [ME *foot, fot*; AS. *fot*, a foot; akin to D. *voet*; LG. *foot*; O.H.G. *fuoz*; Dan. *fod*; Sw. *fot*; L. *pes*; Gr. *pous*; Sans. *pad*, a foot, from Sans. root *pad*, to go.]

Skeleton of Human Foot.

a to *b b*, Tarsus. *b b* to *c c*, Metatarsus. *c c* to *d*, Phalanges. 1. Os calcis, calcaneum, or heel-bone. 2. Astragalus. 3. Scaphoid bone. 4. Entocuneiform bone. 5. Mesocuneiform bone. 6. Ectocuneiform bone. 7. Cuboid bone. 8 to 12. Metatarsal bones. 13. First row of phalanges. 14. Last row of phalanges.

1. In animal bodies, the lower extremity of the leg; the part of the leg which treads the earth in standing or walking, and by which the animal is sustained and enabled to step.

2. That which bears some resemblance to an animal's *foot* in shape or office; the lower end of anything that supports a body; as, the *foot* of a table.

3. The lower part; the base; as, the *foot* of a column, of a mountain, or of a tree.

4. Plan of establishment; fundamental principles; as, our constitution may hereafter be placed on a better *foot*. [Rare.]

5. In military language, soldiers who march and fight on *foot*; infantry, as distinguished from cavalry.

6. A linear measure consisting of twelve inches; supposed to be taken from the length of a man's foot; one-third of a yard; 30.48 centimeters.

7. In poetry, a certain number of syllables, constituting part of a verse, as the iambus, the dactyl, and the spondee.

8. The part of a stocking or boot which receives the *foot*.

Foot and mouth disease; a contagious disease, *Aphthæ epizoöticæ*, affecting the lower animals, particularly cattle, characterized by lameness, loss of appetite, fever, and eruptions about the feet and in the mouth; it may be transmitted to man through the use of milk from an affected cow.

Foot of the fine; formerly in law, the last part of an acknowledgment of a title of transfer of land.

On foot; (a) walking; (b) in good condition, as having recovered from a sick-bed; (c) planned and in course of prosecution; as, a movement is *on foot*.

Square foot; a square each of whose sides is one foot in length.

To cover the feet; in Scripture, to relieve oneself of excrement; as, Saul went in *to cover his feet*.

To keep the foot; to maintain uprightness of character.

To put the best foot foremost; to make the best possible showing.

To put one on his feet; to assist by material aid one who has failed in business, so that he may continue.

To put one's foot in it; to make an egregious blunder; to spoil plans; to get oneself into trouble by word or deed. [Slang.]

To put the foot down; to be promptly decisive and determined.

To set on foot; to inaugurate, as a plan of benevolence or reform.

Under foot; down; helpless; at the mercy of some one or some agency of oppression.

foot, *v.i.*; footed, *pt.*, *pp.*; footing, *ppr.* 1. To dance; to tread to measure or music; to skip.

2. To walk; opposed to *ride* or *fly*; commonly followed by *it*.

If you are for a merry jaunt, I'll try, for once, who can *foot it* farthest. —Dryden.

foot, *v.t.* 1. To kick; to strike with the foot; to spurn.

2. To settle; to begin to fix. [Obs.]

3. To tread; as, to *foot* the green.

4. To add the numbers in a column, and set the sum at the foot; as, to *foot* an account.

5. To seize and hold with the foot. [Obs.]

6. To add or make a foot; as, to *foot* a stocking or boot.

To foot a bill; to pay the full amount of it in cash [Colloq.]

foot'āge, *n.* In mining, the measure of work when paid for by the foot.

foot'-är-til"lẽr-y, *n.* Artillerymen serving on foot.

foot'ball, *n.* 1. A large, inflated ball, or more commonly, a thin inflated ball of india-rubber, cased in heavy leather, to be used in games.

2. A game played with a *football* by two parties of eleven players each, the essential of the game being the forcing of the ball past a certain line or goal.

3. Figuratively, one subject to many vicissitudes.

foot'-bank, *n.* In fortification, an elevated path for foot-soldiers inside a parapet.

foot'bàth, *n.* The bathing of the feet, or the vessel, etc., used in bathing them.

foot'bōard, *n.* 1. Any board used for resting or bracing the feet, as for the driver of a carriage or a locomotive, or for the passengers on a street-car.

2. The board or panel at the foot of a bedstead.

3. A lever for the foot in operating a machine.

foot'boy, *n.* A menial; an attendant in livery.

foot'breadth (-bredth), *n.* The breadth of the foot.

foot'bridge (-brij), *n.* A bridge for pedestrians.

foot'-can"dle, *n.* In photometry, the unit of illumination produced by a specified candle at a distance of one foot; the candle itself.

foot'cloth, *n.* 1. A cloth or housing for a horse.

2. A kind of cloth for a carpet; a rug.

foot'ed, *a.* 1. Shaped in the foot; as, *footed* like a goat.

2. Having a footing; holding a position.

foot'fall, *n.* A footstep.

foot'fight (-fit), *n.* A conflict by persons on foot, in opposition to a fight on horseback.

foot'-gēar, *n.* Covering worn on the feet, as shoes, stockings, etc.

foot'glōve, *n.* A kind of clothing for the foot. [Obs.]

foot'-guärds, *n.pl.* Guards of infantry; in England, a part of the king's troops, chosen from different regiments.

foot'halt, *n.* A disease incident to sheep, and said to proceed from a worm which enters between the hoofs.

foot'-ham"mẽr, *n.* A kind of trip-hammer worked by the foot.

foot'hill, *n.* A hill jutting out from the foot of a mountain or of a higher hill.

foot'hōld, *n.* That which sustains the feet firmly and prevents them from slipping or moving; that on which one may tread or rest securely.

foot'hook, *n.* Same as *Futtock*.

foot'hot, *adv.* Immediately; in extreme haste; used in hunting.

foot'ing, *n.* 1. The act of putting a foot to anything; that which is added as a foot.

2. The act of adding up a column of figures; the amount of such a column.

3. Ground for the foot; that which sustains; firm foundation to stand on; established place; permanent settlement; foothold.

In ascents, every step gained is a *footing* and help to the next. —Holder.

4. Basis; foundation.

Taking things on the *footing* of this life only. —Blair.

5. Tread; step; walk.

Hark! I hear the *footing* of a man.—Shak.

6. Dance; rhythmical tread.

And these fresh nymphs encounter every one In country *footing*. —Shak.

7. Road; track. [Rare.]

Like *footings* up and down impossible to be traced. —Bacon.

8. Relative condition; reciprocal state.

Lived on a *footing* of equality with nobles. —Macaulay.

9. The plain edge of cotton lace without figures.

10. The finer detached fragments of whale-blubber, not wholly deprived of oil.

11. In architecture, a spreading course at the base or foundation of a wall.

To pay one's footing; to pay money, usually to be spent on drink, on first doing anything, as on entering upon a trade or on entering a new place to prosecute one's trade.

foot'ing-bēam, *n.* In architecture, a beam that ties the parts of the roof.

foot'-ī"ron (-ūrn), *n.* 1. A step for the foot in entering a carriage.

2. A shackle for the foot of a prisoner.

foot'-jaw, *n.* In zoölogy, in crustaceans, a limb transformed into a jawlike organ.

foot'-kēy, *n.* In music, a pedal of an organ which performs the office of a key.

foot'less, *a.* Having no feet.

foot'-lev"el, *n.* A kind of level used in gunnery, with a vertical graduated scale for giving a gun the proper angle of elevation.

foot'lick"ẽr, *n.* A mean flatterer; a sycophant; a fawner.

foot'light (-lit), *n.* One of a series of lights placed along the front of the stage of a theater near the floor, with a reflector to throw the light back upon the actors.

Before the footlights; exposed to public view, as an actor on the stage; appearing on the stage.

To smell of the footlights; to obtrude stagy manners and conversation.

foot'ling, *n.* 1. Diminutive of foot; a little foot.

2. An object no larger than a foot.

foot'ling, *a.* In obstetrics, presenting the feet first.

foot'măn, *n.*; *pl.* **foot'men**. 1. A soldier who marches and fights on foot.

2. A menial servant; a runner; a manservant in livery.

3. In entomology, a moth, *Lithosia aurelia*, that resembles a *footman* in livery.

foot'măn-ship, *n.* The art or faculty of a runner or of a footman.

foot'-man"tle, *n.* A garment once worn to keep the gown clean in riding. [Obs.]

foot'märk, *n.* A track; mark of a foot.

foot'nōte, *n.* An explanatory note or reference printed at the foot of a page in a book.

foot'pace, *n.* 1. A slow step, as in walking.

2. In a flight of stairs, a stair broader than the rest.

3. In church architecture, a kind of platform on which the celebrant stands throughout the service of mass.

foot'pad, *n.* A highwayman or robber on foot.

foot'-pāge, *n.* [Obs.] See *Page*.

foot'-pas"sen-gẽr, *n.* One who passes on foot, as over a bridge.

foot'pàth, *n.* A narrow path or way for foot-passengers only.

foot'-pāve"ment, *n.* A paved walk, as distinguished from a paved driveway.

foot'plāte, *n.* Same as *Footboard*.

foot'-plow, *n.* A kind of swing-plow.

foot'-pō"et, *n.* A poet of inferior attainments or of servile practices.

foot'-pōst, *n.* A post or messenger that travels on foot.

foot'-pound, *n.* In mechanics, the energy required to lift a pound avoirdupois one foot against the force of gravity; a gravital unit of work.

foot'-pound"ăl, *n.* In mechanics, a force which acting upon a mass of one pound avoirdupois for one second gives it an increase of velocity of one foot per second; an absolute unit of work.

foot'-press, *n.* In mechanics, a press operated by a treadle, as for stamping, compacting, embossing, etc.

foot'print, *n.* An impression or mark of a foot made in some soft material by depression or upon hard material by matter deposited by a footstep; as, *footprints* of birds in mud.

foot'-rāce, *n.* An athletic contest in speed on foot.

foot'-rāil, *n.* 1. In railroading, a rail broad-flanged at the base.

2. Any rail or rail-like structure for supporting the feet, as under a seat or at the foot of a counter.

foot'rōpe, *n.* Among sailors, the rope stretching along a yard, upon which men stand when reefing or furling; formerly called a *horse*; also, that part of the bolt-rope to which the lower edge of a sail is sewed.

foot'-rot, *n.* An ulcer in the feet of sheep and cattle.

foot'-rūle, *n.* A rule or measure twelve inches long and usually subdivided to eighths of an inch or less.

foots, *n.pl.* Lees; settlings at the bottom of a cask or barrel, as of molasses, oil, etc.

foot'-screw, *n.* A leveling screw.

foot'-sē-crē"tion, *n.* In zoölogy, the sclerobasic corallum of *Antipathidæ*; accretions from without, as distinguished from *tissue-secretions*.

foot'-sōl"diẽr (-jẽr), *n.* An infantryman.

foot'sōre, *a.* Tired and worn with traveling on foot.

foot'stalk (-stak), *n.* 1. In botany, the stem of a flower or a leaf.

2. In zoölogy, any stem-like appendage of an animal, resembling the stalk of a flower or leaf, as of a crinoid.

foot'stall, *n.* 1. A woman's stirrup.

2. In architecture, the base of a column.

foot'step, *n.* 1. A track; the mark or impression of the foot.

2. A footfall or the tread of a foot; as, to hear approaching *footsteps*.

3. In the plural, a course of conduct; as, to follow in the *footsteps* of another.

4. In mechanics, (a) that upon which a vertical shaft rotates, as that of a millstone; (b) in a hand printing-press, an inclined board on the floor for bracing the foot in pulling the lever.

foot'-stick, *n.* In printing, a rigid piece of furniture placed at the foot of a form between the chase and the type for equalizing the pressure in locking up.

foot′stōne, *n.* A stone placed at the foot of a grave, to denote the position of the body in the grave; opposed to *headstone.*

foot′stool, *n.* A stool for the feet; that which supports the feet of one when sitting.

To make enemies a footstool; to reduce them to entire subjection.

foot′=stōve, *n.* A small iron box holding live coals, once used in carriages, churches, etc., for keeping the feet warm.

foot′=tŏn, *n.* A force required to raise a ton a foot against the force of gravity, equivalent to 2,240 foot-pounds.

foot′=tū″bẽr-çle, *n.* One of the lateral appendages of worms, resembling a tubercle.

foot′=valve, *n.* A valve at the bottom of a cavity or cylinder opening upward; specifically, the valve in a steam-engine opening between the condenser and the air-pump.

foot′=vīse, *n.* In mechanics, a vise operated by a treadle.

foot′wāl″ing, *n.* The inside lining of the hull of a ship, extending to the lower deck.

foot′=wall, *n.* In mining, the rock upon which a vein of ore rests.

foot′=wäsh″ing, *n.* An ancient duty of hospitality requiring the host to wash the feet of his guests, and still observed as an ordinance by some Christian churches.

foot′wāy, *n.* A way or path for pedestrians only.

foot′wōrn, *a.* 1. Worn by continual stepping upon with the feet; as, a *footworn* pavement.

2. Tired and sore in the feet, as after a long journey on foot; footsore.

foot′y, *a.* 1. Of such a nature as to deposit lees or foots.

2. Low; good-for-nothing.

foo′zle, *v.i.*; foozled, *pt., pp.*; foozling, *ppr.* To mismanage; to bungle; specifically, in golf, to play awkwardly or unskilfully; to make a bungling stroke.

foo′zle, *n.* 1. A slow, awkward person; a bore; a fogy. [Slang.]

2. The act of foozling; in golf, an awkward or bungling stroke.

fop, *n.* [ME. *fop, foppe*, a fool; G. *fopper*, a jeerer, scoffer.]

1. A vain man, of weak understanding and much ostentation.

2. One whose ambition is to gain admiration by showy dress and an affectation of fashion; a coxcomb; a dandy; a dude.

fop′doo″dle, *n.* An insignificant fellow. [Rare.]

fop′ling, *n.* A petty fop.

fop′pẽr-y, *n.* 1. Affectation of show or importance; showy folly; dandyism; as, the *foppery* of dress or of manners.

2. Folly; impertinence.

> Let not the sound of shallow *foppery* enter
> My sober house. —Shak.

3. Foolish vanity; vain or idle practice; idle affectation.

fop′pish, *a.* 1. Vain of dress; making an ostentatious display of gay clothing; dressing in the extreme of fashion; dandified.

2. Vain; trifling; affected in manners.

fop′pish-ly, *adv.* In a foppish manner.

fop′pish-ness, *n.* Vanity and extravagance in dress; showy vanity; dandyism.

for-. A prefix from AS. *for-*, attached to verbs, usually with a negative or privative force; it also has an intensive, alterative, or pejorative force; as, *for*bid, *for*weary, *for*swear.

for, *prep.* [ME. *for*; AS. *for, fore*, before, for, on account of, through; D. *voor*; Ice. *fyrir*, before; Sw. *för*, before, for; Goth. *faúr*; L. *pro*, before; Gr. *pro*, Sans. *pra*, before, away. The radical idea is that of going before, beyond, in place of.]

1. In the place of; as a substitute or equivalent; as, to exchange one thing *for* another; two apples *for* five cents.

> And Joseph gave them bread in exchange *for* horses, and *for* flocks, and *for* the cattle of the herds. —Gen. xlvii. 17.

2. To the advantage of; on behalf of; with reference to the needs of; as, he fought *for* his country; it is good *for* the stomach.

3. In favor of; as, to be *for* good government or *for* reform.

4. Specially appropriate or adapted to; as, the eye is *for* sight, the nose *for* smell; stores *for* the winter.

5. In the direction of; toward; as, he is bound *for* Japan.

6. With reference or in regard to; as, that is sufficient *for* the present; as *for* me, I am content.

7. In expectation of; in quest of; as expecting or seeking; as, wait *for* the next train; to write *for* money or *for* fame.

8. In honor of or in compliment to; as, the plant was named *for* its discoverer.

9. To the extent or amount of; as, his bond is good *for* ten thousand dollars.

10. Notwithstanding; in spite of; as, it is true *for* all that.

11. In quest of; with the view of reaching; as, to search *for* a criminal.

12. Because of; on account of; by reason of; as, *for* this reason I cannot go; to howl *for* pain.

13. Instead of; on behalf of; as, the attorney did his best *for* his client.

14. Expressing inclination, tendency, or bent; as, a love *for* art; a taste *for* drink.

15. As an offset to; as, to give blow *for* blow; tit *for* tat.

16. With a view to the use and benefit of; as, to provide *for* a family.

17. Because of; with regard to; as, to fear *for* one's safety.

18. In the character of; as, to take one *for* a miser.

19. By the want of; as, to suffer *for* money; to be cramped *for* space.

20. During the continuance of; as, to be appointed *for* life.

21. In proportion or with reference to; as, the boy is tall *for* his age.

22. With the purpose of being, becoming, or doing something; as, to run *for* governor; a mill *for* sawing lumber.

23. In order; with the purpose; a redundant use of the word, formerly common; as, I came *for* to see you. [Obs. or Vulgar.]

For all that; in spite of all that has been said or done.

For ever; see *Forever.*

For good; once for all.

For me; as far as I am concerned.

For short; by way of abbreviation; as, they call him Tim *for short.*

For the life of me, or *for my life*; if my life were at stake. [Colloq.]

For to; see *For*, 23.

O for; would that I might have; as, *O for* the wings of a dove.

for, *conj.* [Abbrev. of conjunctional phrases, as AS. *for tham*, for this, because, since; *for thy*, for this, therefore; *for thwæm*, wherefore, etc.]

1. Because; followed by an explanation or reason for what precedes; as, we shall win, *for* fortune is with us.

2. Since; for the reason that; because of the fact that.

For why; because; for; for what reason. [Colloq.]

for, *n.* One who is in favor of something, as a legislative measure or proposition; also, what may be said on the affirmative side; opposed to *against*; as, the *fors* and the *againsts* were evenly matched.

for′āge, *n.* [ME. *forage*; OFr. *fourage*, forage, pillage, from *forrer*, to forage, from *forre, fuerre*, fodder, from L.G. *voder*, food, fodder.]

1. Food of any kind for horses and cattle, as grass, pasture, hay, corn, and oats.

2. The act of providing forage; a search for provisions; as, the troops subsisted by *forage.*

> Col. Mawhood completed his *forage* unmolested. —Marshall.

for′āge, *v.i.*; foraged, *pt., pp.*; foraging, *ppr.* 1. To collect food, as for troops during a campaign, or for horses and cattle, by wandering about and feeding or stripping the country.

2. To wander far; to rove. [Obs.]

3. To ravage; to feed on spoil. [Obs.]

Foraging ant; one of several species of tropical ants characterized by their habit of marching in great armies in quest of food.

Foraging party; a party of soldiers sent into the surrounding country to collect provisions for campaigning troops; hence, any party in search of food in an emergency.

for′āge, *v.t.* 1. To strip of provisions for troops, horses, etc.; as, the army *foraged* the country round about.

2. To supply with food or fodder; as, to *forage* horses.

3. To obtain by forage; as, we *foraged* a midday meal.

for′āge=cap, *n.* A small undress cap worn by soldiers.

for′āge=mäs″tẽr, *n.* The officer of an army, etc., who has charge of foraging and of supplies obtained by foraging.

for′ā-gẽr, *n.* One who forages.

for′ā-ging, *n.* The act of procuring forage.

for′ā-lite, *n.* [L. *forare*, to bore, and Gr. *lithos*, stone.] In geology, a tube-like marking in sandstone, etc., resembling the burrow of a worm.

fō-rā′men, *n.*; *pl.* **fō-ram′i-nȧ**. [L., a hole, from *forare*, to bore.]

1. In anatomy, a hole, opening, or short passage, as a hole in a bone through which a nerve passes.

Foramen.

2. In botany, the orifice of the coats of the ovule; an opening of any kind.

Condylar foramen; a perforation anterior to each condyle of the occipital bone.

Foramen of Monro; in anatomy, the opening between the lateral ventricles of the brain and the third ventricle, admitting the choroid plexus.

Foramen of Winslow; in anatomy, an opening connecting the anterior and posterior cavities of the peritoneum.

fō-ram′i-nā-ted, *a.* Having little holes, supplied with foramina.

for-ȧ-min′i-fẽr, *n.* In zoölogy, one of the *Foraminifera.*

Fō-ram-i-nif′e-rȧ, *n.pl.* [L. *foramen* (*-inis*), a hole, and *ferre*, to bear.] An order of *Rhizopoda*, belonging to the subkingdom *Protozoa*, furnished with a shell or test, simple or complex, usually perforated by pores (foramina), whence the name. Owing to the resemblance of their convoluted chambered shells to those of the nautilus, they were at first reckoned among the most highly organized mollusks. In reality, they are among the simplest of the *Protozoa.*

Foraminifera.
1. Planorbulina Ugeriana. 2. Triloculina tricarinata. 3. Globigerina bulloides. 4. Rotalia beccarii. 5. Nonionina turgida.

fō-ram-i-nif′ẽr-ous, *a.* 1. Composed of or pertaining to *Foraminifera.*

2. Foraminated.

fō-ram′i-nous, *a.* [LL. *foraminosus*, full of holes, from *foramen* (*-inis*), a hole.] Full of holes; perforated in many places; porous. [Rare.]

fō-ram′i-nūle, *n.* [Dim. from L. *foramen* (*-inis*), a hole.]

1. A small foramen.

2. The ostiolum or orifice through which the spores of certain fungi are discharged.

for-ȧ-min′ū-lōse, *a.* Perforated with very small holes.

for-ȧ-min′ū-lous, *a.* Foraminulose.

for-aṣ-much′, *conj.* In consideration that; because that; in view of the fact that; with *as.*

> *Forasmuch* then *as* we are the offspring of God. —Acts xvii. 29.

for′āy, *n.* [A form of *forage.*]

1. A sudden or irregular excursion in border warfare, especially one with a view to plunder.

2. The act of foraging.

for′āy, *v.t.*; forayed, *pt., pp.*; foraying, *ppr.* To ravage; to plunder.

for′āy-ẽr, *n.* One who engages in forays.

for-bade′, *v.*, past tense of *forbid.*

for-bāthe′, *v.t.* To bathe. [Obs.]

for-beār′, *v.i.*; forbore, *pt.*; forbearing, *ppr.*; forborne, *pp.* [ME. *forberen*; AS. *forberan*, to abstain from, bear, endure; *for-*, and *beran*, to bear.]

1. To stop; to cease; to refrain from proceeding; as, *forbear* to repeat these reproachful words.

2. To pause; to delay; as, *forbear* awhile.

3. To abstain; to refrain; to hold oneself from motion or entering on an affair.

> Shall I go against Ramoth-gilead to battle, or shall I *forbear?* —1 Kings xxii. 6.

4. To refuse; to decline.

> Whether they will hear, or whether they will *forbear.* —Ezek. ii. 7.

5. To be patient; to restrain oneself from action or violence; as, bear and *forbear.*

Syn.—Abstain, refrain, pause, spare, desist, stay, leave off.

for-beār′, *v.t.* 1. To avoid voluntarily; to decline.

> *Forbear* his presence. —Shak.

2. To abstain from; to omit; to avoid doing or using.

> *Forbear* your food a little while. —Shak.

3. To spare; to treat with indulgence and patience.

> *Forbearing* one another in love.—Eph. iv. 2.

for-beār′, *n.* Same as *Forebear.*

for-beār′ance, *n.* 1. The act of avoiding, shunning, or omitting; the cessation or intermission of an act commenced, or a withholding from beginning an act; as, the *forbearance* of sin is followed by satisfaction of mind.

2. Command of temper; restraint of passions.

> Have a continent *forbearance*, till the speed of his rage goes slower. —Shak.

3. The exercise of patience; long-suffering; indulgence toward those who injure one; lenity; delay of resentment or punishment.

> Or despisest thou the riches of his goodness and *forbearance* and long-suffering? —Rom. ii. 4.

for-beār′ant, *a.* Having a forbearing disposition. [Rare.]

for-beār′ẽr, *n.* One who forbears.

for-beār′ing, *a.* Patient; long-suffering.

fọr-beãr′ing-ly, *adv.* In a forbearing, patient manner.

fọr-bid′, *v.t.*; forbade, *pt.*; forbidding, *ppr.*; forbidden, forbid, *pp.* [ME. *forbeden*; AS. *forbeodan*, to forbid, prohibit; *for-*, and *beodan*, to command.]

1. To prohibit; to interdict; to command to forbear or not to do; as, to *forbid* smoking; to *forbid* the banns of marriage.

2. To command not to enter; to warn expressly against entering; with a person as indirect object; as, I have *forbidden* him my house or presence.

3. To oppose; to prohibit; to hinder; to obstruct; as an impassable river *forbids* the approach of the army.

> A blaze of glory that *forbids* the sight. —Dryden.

4. To challenge. [Obs.]

Syn.—Interdict, oppose, prohibit, preclude, debar, restrain.

fọr-bid′, *v.i.* To utter a prohibition; to stand in the way; as, I would go, but my health *forbids.*

fọr-bid′dănce, *n.* Prohibition; a command or edict against a thing. [Rare.]

fọr-bid′den, *a.* 1. Prohibited; interdicted; as, the *forbidden* fruit.

2. Hindered; obstructed.

Forbidden fruit; (a) the fruit of the tree of knowledge of good and evil; (b) figuratively, any unlawful indulgence; illicit love; (c) in botany, one of several species of *Citrus*, including *Citrus decumana* and *Citrus Paradisi.*

fọr-bid′den-ly, *adv.* In a forbidden manner.

fọr-bid′den-ness, *n.* The state of being prohibited. [Obs.]

fọr-bid′dẽr, *n.* One who or that which forbids.

fọr-bid′ding, *a.* Repelling approach; repulsive; raising abhorrence, aversion, or dislike; disagreeable; as, a *forbidding* aspect; a *forbidding* formality; a *forbidding* air.

Syn.—Repulsive, deterrent, prohibitory, offensive, disagreeable, odious.

fọr-bid′ding-ly, *adv.* In a forbidding manner.

fọr-bid′ding-ness, *n.* The state or quality of being forbidding; repulsiveness; offense; disagreeableness.

fọr-black′, *a.* [*For-*, intens., and *black.*] Extremely black. [Obs.]

fọr-bō′den, *v.*, obsolete past participle of *forbid.*

fọr-bōre′, *v.*, past tense of *forbear.*

fọr-bōrne′, *v.*, past participle of *forbear.*

fọr-brụ̈iṣe′, *v.t.* To bruise very much. [Obs.]

fọr-bȳ′, *adv.* and *prep.* 1. Very near; close by. [Obs.]

2. Beyond; besides; over and above. [Scot.]

fọr-ċärve′, *v.t.* To cut through completely. [Obs.]

fōrce, *n.* [Ice. *fors*; Dan. *fos*, a waterfall.] A waterfall; so called from its violence or power. [Prov. Eng.]

fōrce, *v.t.* [A corruption of *farce.*] To fill by stuffing.

fōrce, *v.t.* [OFr. *forcer*, to clip, shear, from *forces*, shears.] To cut off with shears. [Obs.]

fōrce, *v.t.*; forced (fōrst), *pt.*, *pp.*; forcing, *ppr.* [OFr. *forcier*; LL. *forciare*, *fortiare*, from L. *fortis*, strong, powerful.]

1. To compel; to constrain to do or to forbear, by the exertion of power; as, masters *forced* their slaves to labor.

2. To overpower by strength; to compel to yield; to ravish; to violate by force.

> I should have *forced* thee soon with other arms. —Milton.

3. To impel; to press; to drive; to draw or push by main strength; as, to *force* along a wagon or a ship; to *force* away a man's arms; water *forces* its way through a narrow channel; a man may be *forced* out of his possessions.

4. To exert to the utmost.

> *Forcing* my strength, and gathering to the shore. —Dryden.

5. To compel by strength of evidence; as, to *force* conviction on the mind; to *force* one to acknowledge the truth of a proposition.

6. To obtain by force; to take by violence; to assault and take; to storm; as, to *force* a passage; to *force* a town or fort.

7. To overstrain; to distort; as, a *forced* conceit.

8. To cause to produce ripe fruit prematurely, as a tree; to cause to ripen prematurely, as fruit; to cause to develop unnaturally; hence, figuratively, to attempt to produce intellectual results at a premature age; as, we should not *force* the mental faculties of a child.

9. To man; to strengthen by soldiers; to garrison. [Obs.]

10. In card games, to compel (a person) to play a trump, or to disclose the strength of his hand.

Syn.—Coerce, compel, drive, make, necessitate.

fōrce, *v.i.* To endeavor; to strive; to use violence; to have force; to be of importance. [Obs.]

fōrce, *n.* [ME. *force*, *fors*; OFr. *force*; LL. *forcia*, *fortia*, force, strength, from L. *fortis*, strong.]

1. Strength, physical or mental; active power; vigor; might; as, by the *force* of the muscles we raise a weight or resist an assault; the *force* of the mind or will.

2. Momentum; the quantity of energy or power exerted by a moving body; as, the *force* of a cannon ball.

3. Violence; power exerted against will or consent; compulsory power; coercion; as, *force* alone can keep what *force* has obtained.

4. Moral power to convince the mind; as, there is great *force* in the argument.

5. Validity; power to bind or hold; as, if the conditions of a covenant are not fulfilled, the contract is of no *force*; a will is of *force* after the testator is dead.

6. Strength or power for war; armament; troops; an army or navy; as, a military or naval *force*; sometimes in the plural; as, military *forces*; hence, a body of men prepared for action in other ways; as, a police *force.*

7. Internal power; as, the *force* of habit.

8. In law, any unlawful violence to person or property.

9. In physics, that which is the source of all the active phenomena occurring in the material world, and of which motion, gravitation, heat, light, electricity, magnetism, cohesion, chemical affinity, etc., are believed to be exhibitions; that which produces or tends to produce change; energy; as, the conservation of *force.*

10. Any one of the various modes or conditions under which *force* exhibits itself, as motion, heat, light, etc.; as, the correlation of *forces.*

Animal force; the force exerted by the muscles of an animal.

Arm of a force; see under *Arm.*

By force and arms; in law, by force; violently.

Moral force; the power of acting on the reason in judging and determining.

Of force; necessarily.

Physical force; the force of material bodies.

Unit of force; the single force in terms of which the amount of any other force is ascertained, and which is generally some known weight, as a pound.

Vital force; in physiology, that force which in a living body keeps or tends to keep all its organs in normal condition; life.

Syn.—Strength, power, might, energy.—*Strength* looks rather to power as an inward capability or energy; as, the *strength* of timber, bodily *strength*, etc.; while *force* looks more to the outward; as, the *force* of momentum, *force* of circumstance, *force* of habit, etc. We do, indeed, speak of *strength* of will and *force* of will; but even here the former may lean toward the internal tenacity of purpose, and the latter toward the outward expression of it in action.

fōrced (fōrst), *a.* 1. Effected by an unusual application of strength or effort; as, a *forced* march.

2. Affected; overstrained; unnatural; as, a *forced* style.

Forced draft; see under *Draft.*

Forced vibration; any vibration which differs in rate from the natural or normal because of the action of some outside force.

fōr′ced-ly, *adv.* In a forced manner; violently; constrainedly; unnaturally. [Rare.]

fōr′ced-ness, *n.* The state of being forced.

fōrce′fụl, *a.* 1. Impelled by violence; driven with force; acting with power.

> Against the steed he threw
> His *forceful* spear. —Dryden.

2. Possessing force; forcible; as, a *forceful* argument or speech.

fōrce′fụl-ly, *adv.* In a forceful manner.

fōrce′less, *a.* Having little or no force; feeble; impotent.

fōrce′mēat, *n.* [Corruption of *farce meat*, from Fr. *farcir*, to stuff.] Meat chopped fine and highly seasoned, either served up alone or used as a stuffing.

fōrce′ment, *n.* A forcing. [Obs.]

fọr′ceps, *n.* [L., a pair of tongs, pincers, from *formus*, hot, and *capere*, to take.]

1. A general name for a two-bladed instrument on the principle of pincers or tongs, used for seizing and holding, and for extracting objects which it would be impracticable thus to treat with the fingers; used by watchmakers and jewelers, dentists, surgeons, etc.

2. The caudal appendages of certain insects, named from their resemblance to a dentist's forceps.

3. Any part or process of an animal body resembling a forceps.

fōrce′-pump, *n.* A pump which delivers the water under pressure, so as to eject it forcibly or to a great elevation, in contradistinction to a *lift-pump*, in which the water is lifted and simply runs out of the spout.

fōr′cẽr, *n.* 1. One who or that which forces, drives, or constrains.

2. The solid piston of a pump; the instrument by which water is driven up a pump under pressure.

3. In mining, a small pump worked by hand, used in sinking small pits. [Corn.]

fōr′ci-ble, *a.* 1. Powerful; strong; mighty.

2. Violent; impetuous; driving forward with force; as, a *forcible* stream.

3. Acting with force; impressive; as, *forcible* words or arguments.

4. Done by force; brought about by force; as, a *forcible* abdication or abduction.

Forcible detainer; a violent withholding of the lands or goods of another from his possession.

Forcible entry; an actual, violent entry into houses or lands without lawful authority.

Syn.—Irresistible, cogent, mighty, potent, powerful, strong, effective.

fōr′ci-ble-fee″ble, *a.* Apparently vigorous but really feeble; applied to intellectual powers; as, a *forcible-feeble* style.

fōr′ci-ble-ness, *n.* The condition or quality of being forcible.

fōr′ci-bly, *adv.* 1. In a forcible manner.

2. Strongly; powerfully; with power or energy; impressively.

> The gospel offers such considerations as are fit to work very *forcibly* on our hopes and fears. —Tillotson.

fōr′cing, *n.* The attainment of an end by some process of abnormal development; in gardening, the art of securing premature vegetation and blooming by means of artificial heat; in wine-making, the fining of wine by artificial methods.

fōr′cing-en″ġine, *n.* Same as *Fire-engine.*

fōr′cing-house, *n.* In horticulture, a hothouse for forcing plants.

fōr′cing-mȧ-ċhine″, *n.* A machine for attaching or detaching very tight metal fittings, as car-wheels, cranks, etc.

fōr′cing-pit, *n.* A pit of wood or masonry, sunk in the earth, for containing fermenting materials to produce bottom-heat in forcing plants.

fōr′cing-pump, *n.* Same as *Force-pump.*

fọr′ci-pȧl, *a.* Of the nature of forceps.

fọr′ci-pāte, *a.* [From L. *forceps* (*-ipis*), a pair of pincers.] Formed like a pair of forceps; as, a *forcipate* mouth.

fọr′ci-pā-ted, *a.* Forcipate.

fọr-ci-pā′tion, *n.* 1. A pinching with pincers; torture by means of forceps.

2. In zoölogy, the state or condition of being shaped like forceps; bifurcation.

fọr-cip′ū-lāte, *a.* [A dim. from *forcipate*, from L. *forceps* (*-ipis*), a pair of pincers.] In zoölogy, relating to an order of echinoderms characterized by small pincer-like dermal appendages.

fōr′cite, *n.* An explosive substance containing nitroglycerin.

fọr-cut′, *v.t.* To cut through. [Obs.]

fōrd, *n.* [ME. *ford*; AS. *ford*, a ford.]

1. A place in a river or other body of water where it may be passed or crossed by man or beast on foot or by wading.

2. A stream to be crossed.

> Permit my ghost to pass the Stygian *ford.* —Dryden.

fōrd, *v.t.*; forded, *pt.*, *pp.*; fording, *ppr.* To pass or cross, as a river or other body of water, by treading or walking on the bottom; to pass through by wading; to wade through.

fōrd′ȧ-ble, *a.* That may be waded or passed through on foot, as water.

fōrd′ȧ-ble-ness, *n.* The state of being fordable.

fōrd′less, *a.* Too deep to be forded; having no ford.

fọr-dō′, *v.t.*; fordid, *pt.*; fordoing, *ppr.*; foredone, *pp.* [ME. *fordon*; AS. *fordon*, to destroy, ruin; *for-* priv., and *don*, to do.]

1. To destroy; to undo; to ruin. [Poet.]

2. To exhaust or overcome, as by fatigue.

> The heavy plowman snores,
> All with weary task *fordone.* —Shak.

fọr-drīve′, *v.t.* To drive hither and thither. [Obs.]

fọr-druñk′en, *a.* [AS. *fordruncen*; *for-*, intens., and *druncen*, drunk.] Very drunk. [Obs.]

fọr-drȳ′, *a.* Exceedingly dry. [Obs.]

fọr-dwīne′, *v.i.* [AS. *fordwinan*; *for-*, away, and *dwinan*, to pine.] To waste away. [Obs.]

fōre-. A prefix from AS. *fore-*, *for-*, equivalent to *before*, in time or place.

fōre, *n.* [AS. *fore*, before.] The front part; hence, the foremast of a ship; as, she flew the royal standard at her *fore.*

At the fore; in nautical language, at the top of the foremast; said of an unfurled flag, etc.

To the fore; to the foremost part; ahead; at hand; as, he at once came *to the fore.*

fōre, *adv.* 1. In the part that precedes or goes first; in front; before, in place; toward the bow of a ship; forward.

2. Before, in time; at the first; in the beginning. [Obs.]

fōre, *prep.* Before; in presence of; obsolete except as an abbreviation of *before*; as, *'fore* God, I am telling the truth.

fōre, *interj.* In the game of golf, a word of warning spoken or shouted by a player to any one who may be in the way of a contemplated stroke.

fōre, *a.* [The prefix *fore-* written separately.]

1. Advanced; being in advance of something in motion or progression; as, the *fore* end of a chain carried in measuring land; the *fore* oxen or horses in a team.

2. Advanced in time; coming in advance of something; coming first; anterior; preceding; prior; as, the *fore* part of the last century; the *fore* part of the day, week, or year.

3. Advanced in order or series; antecedent; as, the *fore* part of a writing or bill.

4. Being in front or toward the face; opposed to *back* or *behind*; as, the *fore* part of a garment.

5. At or near the front; as, the *fore* part of a ship or of a coach.

Fore boot; in a stagecoach, a compartment under the driver's footboard, for stowing baggage.

Fore bow; the front part or pommel of a saddle.

Fore sight; in gunnery, that sight of a gun which is nearest to the muzzle, as distinguished from the *rear sight*.

fōre-ad-mon'ish, *v.t.* To admonish beforehand or before the act or event.

fōre-ad-vīṣe', *v.t.* To advise or counsel before the time of action, or before the event; to preadmonish.

fōre-al-lege', *v.t.* To allege or cite before.

fōre'=and=ȧft', *a.* Extending lengthwise of a ship.

Fore-and-aft sail; a sail whose middle position is in a line with the length of the ship, so that it points in this position to stem and stern.

fōre'=and=ȧft', *n.* 1. A vessel rigged with fore-and-aft sails.

2. A kind of cap having a vizor before and behind.

fōre-ap-point', *v.t.* To set, order, or appoint beforehand.

fōre-ap-point'ment, *n.* Previous appointment; preordination.

fōre-ärm', *v.t.*; forearmed, *pt.*, *pp.*; forearming, *ppr.* To arm or prepare for attack or resistance before the time of need.

fōre'ärm, *n.* In anatomy, that part of the arm between the elbow and the wrist.

fōre-ärmed', *a.* Armed beforehand; as, forewarned, *forearmed*.

fōre'bāy, *n.* A deep receptacle at the end of a mill-race, from which the water is admitted to the wheel.

fōre'bēam, *n.* In weaving, the beam on which the web is wound; the breastbeam.

fōre-bēar', **for-bēar'**, *n.* One of those at the head of a line of descent; a forefather; an ancestor; usually in the plural; as, the courtly manners of our *forebears*.

fōre'bē-liēf, *n.* Previous belief.

fōre-bōde', *v.t.*; foreboded, *pt.*, *pp.*; foreboding, *ppr.* [AS. *forebodian*; *fore-*, before, and *bodian*, to announce, declare.]

1. To foretell; to prognosticate.

2. To foresee; to be prescient of; to feel a secret premonition of; as, my heart *forebodes* a sad reverse.

fōre-bōde', *v.i.* To prophesy.

Syn.—Augur, betoken, portend, foretell, presage, prognosticate, prophesy.

fōre-bōde', *n.* Foresight; augury. [Obs.]

fōre-bōde'ment, *n.* The act of foreboding.

fōre-bōd'ẽr, *n.* One who forebodes; a prognosticator.

fōre-bōd'ing, *n.* Ominous prognostication.

fōre-bōd'ing-ly, *adv.* In a foreboding or threatening manner.

fōre'bod"y, *n.*; *pl.* **fōre'bod"ies**. That part of a ship forward of the midship section.

fōre'brāce, *n.* A rope attached to the fore yard-arm, to regulate the position of the foresail.

fōre'brāin, *n.* In anatomy, the foremost segment of the brain; the prosencephalon.

fōre-bȳ', *adv.* and *prep.* See *Forby*.

fōre'=cab"in, *n.* The cabin in the fore part of a ship with accommodations generally inferior to those of the after-cabin or saloon.

fōre'=car"riage (-rij), *n.* The part of a four-wheeled vehicle including the fore wheels and parts immediately related.

fōre-ċȧst', *v.t.*; forecast, *pt.*, *pp.*; forecasting, *ppr.* 1. To foresee; to provide against.

It is wisdom to *forecast* consequences. —L'Estrange.

2. To scheme; to plan before execution.

He shall *forecast* his devices against the strongholds. —Dan. xi. 24.

3. To calculate beforehand.

The time so well *forecast*. —Dryden.

fōre-ċȧst', *v.i.* To form a scheme previously; to contrive something beforehand.

If it happen as I did *forecast*. —Milton.

fōre'ċȧst, *n.* Previous contrivance; foresight; premeditation; as, a man of little *forecast*.

fōre-ċȧst'ẽr, *n.* One who foresees or contrives beforehand.

fōre'ċȧs-tle (-kȧs-l; *sailors' pron.* fōk'sl), *n.* That part of the upper deck of a vessel forward of the foremast, or forward of the after part of the fore channels; in merchant vessels, a section of the forward part of the vessel, under the deck, where the sailors live.

fōre-chō'ṣen, *a.* Preelected; chosen beforehand.

fōre'cit"ed, *a.* Cited or quoted before or above.

fōre-clōṣe', *v.t.*; foreclosed, *pt.*, *pp.*; foreclosing, *ppr.* 1. To shut out; to preclude; to stop; to prevent.

The embargo with Spain *foreclosed* this trade. —Carew.

2. In law, to enforce, as a mortgage.

To foreclose a mortgager; in law, to cut a mortgager off from his equity of redemption, or the power of redeeming the mortgaged premises, by a judgment of court.

To foreclose a mortgage; to enforce the terms of a mortgage by shutting the mortgager out from the right to redeem the property.

fōre-clō'ṣūre, *n.* 1. Prevention.

2. The act of foreclosing, or depriving a mortgager of the right of redeeming a mortgaged estate.

Strict foreclosure; in law, a proceeding by which mortgaged property passes directly into the possession of the mortgagee.

fōre-ċon-ċeive', *v.t.* To preconceive; to conceive beforehand.

fōre'=ċourse, *n.* In square-rigged ships, the foresail.

fōre-dāte', *v.t.* To antedate.

fōre'deck, *n.* The fore part of a deck, or of a ship.

fōre-deem', *v.t.* and *v.i.* To deem in advance; to foretell.

fōre-dē-ṣign' (-zīn'), *v.t.* To plan beforehand; to forecast.

fōre-dē-tẽr'mine, *v.t.* To decree beforehand.

fōre-dis-pōṣe', *v.t.* To dispose or bestow beforehand. [Rare.]

fōre-dọọm', *v.t.* To doom beforehand; to predestinate.

Thou art *foredoomed* to view the Stygian state. —Dryden.

fōre'dọọm, *n.* Previous doom or sentence.

fōre'=dōor, *n.* The front door. [Obs. or Colloq.]

fōre'=eld"ẽr, *n.* An ancestor. [Prov. Eng. and Scot.]

fōre'fä"thẽr, *n.* An ancestor; one who precedes another in the line of genealogy in any degree, but usually in a remote degree.

Forefathers' day; December 21, the anniversary of the landing of the Pilgrim Fathers on the shores of North America at Plymouth, Massachusetts, on December 21, 1620, celebrated generally throughout the United States by the descendants of the Pilgrim Fathers.

fōre-feel', *v.t.*; forefelt, *pt.*, *pp.*; forefeeling, *ppr.* To feel beforehand.

fōre-feel'ing, *n.* Presentiment.

fōre-fence', *n.* Defense in front.

fōre-fend', *v.t.* See *Forfend*.

fōre'fin"gẽr, *n.* The finger next to the thumb; the index.

fōre-flōw', *v.t.* To flow before. [Obs.]

fōre'foot, *n.* 1. One of the anterior feet of a quadruped or multiped; also written as two words.

2. In a ship, a piece of timber which terminates the keel at the fore end, connecting it with the lower end of the stem.

fōre'frŏnt, *n.* The foremost part or place; as, the *forefront* of a building; the *forefront* of the battle.

fōre'gang"ẽr, *n.* [ME. *foreganger*, a foregoer, forerunner, from AS. *foregangan*, equal to *foregan*, to forego; *fore-*, before, and *gan*, to go.]

1. A predecessor.

2. In whaling, a short piece of rope grafted to the shank of a harpoon, to which the line is attached when the harpoon is used.

fōre-gath'ẽr, *v.i.* Same as *Forgather*.

fōre'gift, *n.* In English law, a premium paid by a tenant upon taking his lease.

fōre'gīrth, *n.* A girth or strap for the forepart, as of a horse; a martingale.

fōre-gō', *v.t.*; forewent, *pt.*; foregoing, *ppr.*; foregone, *pp.* [ME. *forgan*; AS. *forgan*, *foregan*, to go before; *fore-*, before, and *gan*, *gangan*, to go.]

1. To forbear to possess or enjoy; voluntarily to avoid the enjoyment of good; as, let us *forego* the pleasures of sense. Also written *forgo*, the better spelling etymologically but now rarely used.

2. To give up; to renounce; to resign.

3. To quit; to leave.

Stay at the third cup, or *forego* the place. —G. Herbert.

4. To go before; to precede.

A lovely light *forewent* the morn. —Edwin Arnold.

fōre-gō'ẽr, *n.* [ME. *forgœre*, from *forgan*, to go before.]

1. An ancestor; a progenitor.

2. One who goes before another.

3. One who foregoes.

fōre-gō'ing, *a.* Preceding; going before, in time or place; antecedent; as, a *foregoing* period of time; a *foregoing* clause in a writing.

fōre-gọne', *a.* 1. That has gone before; past; preceding.

2. Predetermined; made up beforehand; as, a *foregone* conclusion.

fōre'ground, *n.* The part of the field or expanse of a picture which seems to lie before the figures, or is nearest the eye of the observer; opposed to *background*.

fōre-guess' (-ges'), *v.t.* To conjecture.

fōre'gut, *n.* The embryonic tube corresponding to the pharynx, esophagus, stomach, and duodenum.

fōre'ham"mẽr, *n.* In blacksmithing, the sledge wielded by the striker.

fōre'hand, *n.* 1. The part of a horse which is before the rider.

2. The chief part. [Obs.]

fōre'hand, *a.* Done sooner than is regular.

And so extenuate the *forehand* sin. —Shak.

fōre'hand"ed, *a.* 1. Early; timely; seasonable; as, a *forehanded* care.

2. In good circumstances as to property; free from debt and possessed of means; as, a *forehanded* farmer.

3. Formed in the foreparts.

A substantial, true-bred beast, bravely *forehanded*. —Dryden.

fore'head (for'ed *or* fōr'hed), *n.* [ME. *forhed*, *forehed*, *foreheaved*; AS. *forehedfod*, the front part of the head; *for*, *foran*, before, and *hedfod*, head.]

1. The part of the face which extends from the usual line of hair on the top of the head to the eyes; the brow.

2. Impudence; confidence; assurance; audacity; as, to speak with brazen *forehead*.

fōre-hēar', *v.t.* To be informed of beforehand.

fōre'hearth, *n.* In metallurgy, that part of the hearth of a blast-furnace beneath the tymparch.

fōre-hew', *v.t.* To hew or cut in front.

fōre'hōld, *n.* The hold in the forward part of a ship.

fōre-hōld'ing, *n.* Prediction; ominous foreboding; superstitious prognostication. [Obs.]

fōre'hook, *n.* In ships, a breasthook; a piece of timber placed across the stem, to unite the bows and strengthen the fore part of the ship.

for'eign (-in), *a.* [ME. *forein*, *foreyn*; OFr. *forain*, *forein*, from LL. *foraneus*, outside, exterior, from L. *foras*, out of doors. The *g* is a modern insertion, on the analogy of *reign*.]

1. Belonging to another nation or country; alien; not of the country in which one resides; extraneous; as, the *foreign* population of the United States; a *foreign* minister; *foreign* politics; *foreign* habits and manners.

2. Produced in a distant country or jurisdiction; coming from another country; as, *foreign* goods; goods of *foreign* manufacture.

3. Remote; not belonging; not connected; as, the sentiments you express are *foreign* to your heart.

4. Irrelevant; not pertaining; not to the purpose; as, the observation is *foreign* to the subject.

5. Excluded; not admitted; held at a distance. [Rare.]

Foreign attachment; see under *Attachment*.

Foreign bill of exchange; a bill drawn by a person in one country on his correspondent or agent in another, as distinguished from an *inland bill* which is drawn by one person on another in the same jurisdiction or country.

Foreign body; in medicine, a substance found in a part of the body where it does not belong.

Foreign office; a department of the British government having jurisdiction over all of Great Britain's foreign interests, corresponding to the department of state in the United States.

Syn.—Alien, exotic, extraneous, extrinsic, outside, strange.

for'eign=built (-bilt), *a.* Built in a foreign country.

for'eign-ẽr, *n.* A person born in or owing allegiance to a foreign country; an alien.

Joy is such a *foreigner*,
So mere a stranger to my thoughts. —Denham.

for'eign-ism, *n.* 1. The state of being foreign.

2. Any foreign custom, characteristic, or peculiarity, as of dress, speech, language, etc.

for'eign-ness, *n.* The condition of being foreign; irrelevancy; remoteness; want of relation; as, the *foreignness* of a subject from the main business.

for'ein (-in), *a.* [Obs.] See *Foreign.*

fōre-judġe' (-juj'), *v.t.*; forejudged, *pt., pp.*; forejudging, *ppr.* [ME. *forjugen*; OFr. *forjuger, forsjugier*, to confiscate, judge unjustly; LL. *forisjudicare*, to take away by judicial sentence, deprive; L. *foris*, outside, and *judicare*, to judge.] In old law, to expel from a court for malpractice or nonappearance; also spelled *forjudge.*

fōre-judġe', *v.t.* To judge beforehand or before hearing the facts and proofs; to prejudge.

fōre-judġ'ēr, *n.* In old English law, a judgment by which a man is deprived or put out of the thing in question; a judgment of expulsion or banishment.

fōre-judġ'ment, *n.* A judgment formed before a hearing.

fōre-knōw' (-nō'), *v.t.*; foreknew, *pt.*; foreknowing, *ppr.*; foreknown, *pp.* To have previous knowledge of; to foresee.

Who would the miseries of man *foreknow*?
—Dryden.

fōre-knōw'ȧ-ble, *a.* That may be foreknown.

fōre-knōw'ēr, *n.* One who foreknows.

fōre-knōw'ing-ly, *adv.* With foreknowledge.

fōre-knowl'edġe (-nol'ej), *n.* Knowledge of a thing before it happens; prescience.

If I foreknew,
Foreknowledge had no influence on their fault.
—Milton.

for'el, *n.* [ME. *forel*; OFr. *forel*, a case, sheath, dim. of *forre, fuerre*; LL. *fodrus*, from Goth. *fodr*, a sheath.] A kind of parchment for the cover of books; also written *forrel, forril.*

for'el, *v.t.* To cover or bind with forel. [Rare.]

fōre'land, *n.* 1. A promontory or cape; a point of land extending into the sea some distance from the line of the shore; a headland; as, the North and South *Foreland* in Kent, England.

2. In fortification, a piece of ground between the wall of a place and the moat.

3. In hydraulic engineering, the land lying between an embankment and the water-line.

fōre-lāy', *v.t.* 1. To lie in wait for; to entrap by ambush; also written *forlay.*

2. To contrive beforehand.

fōre-lēad'ēr, *n.* One who leads others by his example.

fōre-lend', *v.t.* To lend or give beforehand. [Obs.]

fōre-let', *v.t.* [Obs.] See *Forlet.*

fōre-lie', *v.i.* To lie in front. [Obs.]

fōre-lift', *v.t.* To lift up in front.

fōre'lock, *n.* 1. The lock of hair that grows from the forepart of the head, especially of a horse.

2. In mechanics, a split pin for holding a bolt in place; a linchpin; a key.

To take time by the forelock; to be prompt and vigilant in taking advantage of an opportunity; to start in good time.

fōre'lock, *v.t.* To fasten with a forelock.

fōre'lock-bōlt, *n.* A bolt in which a forelock is used.

fōre'lock-hook, *n.* In rope-making, a device for twisting and uniting the strands of a rope.

fōre-look', *v.i.* To look beforehand or forward.

fōre'loop"ēr, *n.* In South Africa, one who leads a span of bullocks by means of a rope attached to the horns of the foremost pair; also called *leader, leader-boy.*

fōre'măn, *n.* 1. The first or chief man; the chief man of a jury, who acts as their spokesman.

2. The chief workman in a shop or works of any kind, who arranges and superintends the work of the rest; a superintendent of work; an overseer.

fōre'măn-ship, *n.* The office or position of a foreman.

fōre'mȧst, *n.* The mast of a ship or other vessel which is placed nearest the bow, and carries the forerigging.

fōre-meant' (-ment'), *a.* Intended beforehand.

fōre'men-tioned, *a.* Mentioned before; recited or written in a former part of the same writing or discourse.

fōre'milk, *n.* In physiology, the first milk secreted by a mother, just before or just after giving birth to offspring.

fōre'mōst, *a.* [ME. *formest, firmest*; AS. *formest, fyrmest*, foremost, from *forma*, first, a superl. of *for, fore*, fore, before.]

1. First in place or time; most advanced; as, the *foremost* troops of an army.

2. First in dignity; as, he held the *foremost* rank.

fōre'mōst, *adv.* In the first place; as, to put one's best foot *foremost.*

fōre'mōst-ly, *adv.* Foremost. [Obs.]

fōre'mŏth"ēr, *n.* A female ancestor.

fōre'nāme, *n.* The name that precedes the family name; a given name; a prenomen, as John in the full name John Smith.

fōre'nāmed, *a.* 1. Named or nominated before.

2. Mentioned before in the same writing or discourse.

fōre-nenst', fōr-nenst', *prep.* Opposite to; over against. [Scot. and Prov. Eng.]

fōre'night (-nīt), *n.* The forepart of the night. [Scot.]

fōre'noon, *n.* The former part of the day, from the morning to midday or noon; the first part of the business day.

fōre'nō"tice, *n.* Notice or information of an event before it happens.

fō-ren'săl, *a.* Forensic.

fō-ren'sic, *a.* [From L. *forensis*, public, from *forum*, the market-place.]

1. Belonging to courts of law; used in courts or legal proceedings; as, a *forensic* term; *forensic* eloquence or disputes.

2. Pertaining to or fitted for legal or public argumentation.

Forensic medicine; the science concerned in the relations between medicine and law; medical jurisprudence.

fō-ren'sic, *n.* In certain American colleges, as Harvard, an argumentative contest, either oral or written; a debate.

fō-ren'sic-ăl, *a.* Same as *Forensic.*

fōre-or-dāin', *v.t.*; foreordained, *pt., pp.*; foreordaining, *ppr.* To ordain or appoint beforehand; to preordain; to predestinate; to predetermine.

fōre-or'di-nāte, *v.t.* To ordain beforehand. [Rare.]

fōre-or-di-nā'tion, *n.* Previous ordination or appointment; predetermination; predestination.

fōre'pärt, *n.* The part first in time or in place; as, the *forepart* of a day, a train, or a discourse; generally written as two words.

fōre'pȧst, *a.* Past before a certain time; as, *forepast* sins. [Obs.]

fōre'pēak, *n.* In a ship, the forward sharp-angled part of the forehold.

fōre'-piēce, *n.* The dress-guard on the front part of a lady's saddle.

fōre'-plāne, *n.* In carpentry, a kind of short jointer used to follow the jack-plane in dressing lumber.

fōre-pŏs-sessed' (-zest'), *a.* Holding formerly in possession; also, preoccupied; prepossessed; preëngaged. [Obs.]

fōre'pōst, *n.* An outpost.

fōre-prize', *v.t.* To prize or rate beforehand. [Rare.]

fōre-prom'ised (-ist), *a.* Promised beforehand; preëngaged.

fōre'quōt-ed, *a.* Cited before; quoted in a foregoing part of the work.

fōre-ran', *v.*, past tense of *forerun.*

fōre'rank, *n.* The first rank; the front.

fōre-rēach', *v.t.*; forereached, *pt., pp.*; forereaching, *ppr.* In navigation, to gain or advance upon in progression or motion; to overhaul and pass.

fōre-rēach', *v.i.* In navigation, to glide ahead, especially when in stays; to gain ground in tacking; used with *on.*

fōre-rēad', *v.t.* To signify by tokens beforehand; to predestine. [Obs.]

fōre-rē-cit'ed, *a.* Named or recited before.

fōre-rē-mem'bēred, *a.* Called to mind previously.

fōre'-rent, *n.* In Scotland, rent payable in advance.

fōre'right (-rīt), *a.* Favorable, as a wind. [Obs.]

fōre'right, *adv.* Straight forward; onward. [Obs.]

fōre-run', *v.t.*; foreran, *pt.*; forerunning, *ppr.*; forerun, *pp.* 1. To advance before; to come before as an earnest of something to follow; to introduce as a harbinger; to herald.

Heaviness *foreruns* the good event.—Shak.

2. To precede; to have the start of.

fōre-run'nēr, *n.* 1. A messenger sent before to give notice of the approach of others; a harbinger; a herald.

My elder brothers, my *forerunners* came.
—Dryden.

2. An ancestor or predecessor. [Obs.]

3. A prognostic; a sign foreshowing something to follow; as, certain pains in the head, back, and limbs are the *forerunners* of a fever.

4. In navigation, a piece of bunting or some other material attached to a log-line to note the time for inverting the log-glass.

fōre'said (-sed), *a.* Spoken before; aforesaid.

fōre'sāil, *n.* The principal sail set on the foremast.

fōre-sāy', *v.t.* To predict; to foretell.

fōre-sāy'ing, *n.* A prediction.

fōre-see', *v.t.*; foresaw, *pt.*; foreseeing, *ppr.*; foreseen, *pp.* To see beforehand; to see or know (an event) before it happens; to have prescience of; to foreknow.

A prudent man *foreseeth* the evil.
—Prov. xxii. 3.

fōre-see', *v.i.* To exercise foresight.

fōre-seer', *n.* One who foresees or foreknows.

fōre-sēize', *v.t.* To seize beforehand.

fōre-shad'ōw, *v.t.*; foreshadowed, *pt., pp.*; foreshadowing, *ppr.* To shadow, indicate, or typify beforehand.

fōre-shad'ōw-ing, *n.* The act of indicating beforehand; anticipation.

fōre'-sheet, *n.* 1. In nautical language, the rope or tackle which keeps the clue of the foresail in place when the sail is set.

2. [*pl.*] In a boat, the space in the bow forward of the foremost thwart.

fōre-shew', *v.t.* Same as *Foreshow.*

fōre'ship, *n.* The fore part of a ship; the bow.

fōre'shōre, *n.* The part of a shore adjacent to and sloping toward the sea; especially a part lying between an embankment or a sea-wall and the sea.

fōre-short'en, *v.t.*; foreshortened, *pt., pp.*; foreshortening, *ppr.* 1. In painting, to represent (figures) as they appear to the eye when seen obliquely; to represent in accordance with the laws of perspective.

2. Figuratively, to affect the perception of (an object), as by a change from normal position.

Foreshortened (after figure by Raphael).

fōre-short'en-ing, *n.* The representation or appearance of objects when viewed obliquely.

fōre'shot, *n.* The first running in the distillation of low wines; it is a milky liquid containing much fusel-oil.

fōre-shōw', *v.t.*; foreshowed, *pt.*; foreshowing, *ppr.*; foreshown, *pp.* To show beforehand; to prognosticate.

Next, like Aurora, Spenser rose,
Whose purple blush the day *foreshows.*
—Denham.

fōre-shōw'ēr, *n.* One who predicts.

fōre'side, *n.* The front side.

fōre'sight (-sīt), *n.* 1. Prescience; foreknowledge; prognostication; the act of foreseeing.

2. Provident care; prudence in guarding against evil.

fōre-sight'ed, *a.* Prudent in guarding against evil; provident for the future.

fōre-sight'ful, *a.* Prescient; provident. [Rare.]

fōre-sig'ni-fy, *v.t.* To signify beforehand; to betoken previously; to foreshow; to typify.

fōre'skin, *n.* The fold of skin that covers the penis; the prepuce.

fōre'skirt, *n.* The loose and pendulous part of a coat or skirt in front.

fōre-slack', *v.t.* [Obs.] See *Forslack.*

fōre'sleeve, *n.* The part of a sleeve covering the forearm.

fōre-slōw', *v.t.* and *v.i.* To delay; hinder; impede. [Obs.]

fōre-spēak', *v.t.* and *v.i.* To foresay; to foretell. [Obs.]

fōre-spēak'ing, *n.* A prediction; also, a preface. [Obs.]

fōre'speech, *n.* A preface. [Obs.]

fōre-spent', *a.* Same as *Forspent.*

fōre'spent, *a.* Spent beforehand; irrecoverable. [Obs.]

fōre-spŭr'rēr, *n.* One who spurs or rides before.

for'est, *n.* [ME. *forest*; OFr. *forest*; LL. *forestis, foresta, forestum*, a forest, ground reserved for the chase, from L. *foris, foras*, out of doors, abroad.]

1. An extensive wood, or a large tract of land covered with trees; a wood of native growth, or a tract of woodland which has never been cultivated; as, the Black *Forest* in Germany.

2. In English law, a certain territory of woody grounds and pastures, privileged for wild beasts and fowls of forest, chase, and warren to rest and abide in, under the protection of the king for his pleasure.

3. A designation still retained in Great Britain for some large tracts of land formerly but not now covered with trees; as, the *Forest* of Dean.

We have many *forests* in England without a stick of timber upon them. —Wedgwood.

for'est, *a.* Relating to or existing in a forest; as, *forest* trees; *forest* gloom.

Forest laws; in England, laws for governing and regulating forests, especially those in which game was preserved. These laws are now practically obsolete.

for'est, *v.t.*; forested *pt., pp.*; foresting, *ppr.* To cover with trees or wood; to afforest.

fōre'stăff, *n.* Same as *Cross-staff*, 2.

for'est-āġe, *n.* An ancient service paid by foresters to the king; also, the tribute paid to foresters.

for'est-ăl, *a.* Belonging to or associated with a forest; as, *forestal* privileges.

fōre-stall′, *v.t.*; forestalled, *pt.*, *pp.*; forestalling, *ppr.* [ME. *forstallen*, to stop, obstruct, from AS. *foresteal*, *foresteall*, prop. a placing oneself before another.]

1. To anticipate; to take beforehand.

> Why need a man *forestall* his date of grief,
> And run to meet what he would most avoid?
> —Milton.

2. To hinder by preoccupation or prevention.

> I will not *forestall* your judgment of the rest.
> —Pope.

3. To buy or bargain for corn, or provisions of any kind, before they arrive at (the market) with intent to sell them at higher prices. This was formerly a penal offense.

4. To deprive by something prior. [Obs.]

5. To interfere with, as travel on a public highway.

To forestall the market; to interfere in any way with trade so as to cause prices to rise or fall unnaturally, as by buying and holding marketable produce in order to create a scarcity on the market; to do any act in restraint of free competitive trade.

fōre-stall′ẽr, *n.* One who forestalls; a person who purchases provisions, etc., before they come to market, with a view to raise the price.

fōre′stāy, *n.* In ships, a rope or wire cable running from the top of the foremast toward the head of the bowsprit, as a support for the mast.

for′est-ẽr, *n.* 1. An officer appointed to watch a forest, preserve the game, and institute suits for trespasses.

2. An inhabitant of a forest.

3. A forest-tree. [Rare.]

4. In entomology, any one of several species of moths whose larvæ are injurious to forest plants; specifically, the eight-spotted *forester*, *Alypia octomaculata*, whose caterpillars are destructive to the grapevine.

5. In zoölogy, the large gray kangaroo, *Macropus giganteus*, of Australia.

Ancient Order of Foresters; a fraternal society founded in England in 1745, and having an American branch established in the United States in 1832; also, a similar American society of large membership, existing as a distinct organization.

Catholic Order of Foresters; a fraternal organization, for mutual insurance, etc., of members of the Roman Catholic church.

for′est-fly, *n.* In entomology, any one of several flies which annoy horses and men in woodlands; originally, a blood-sucking horsefly, *Hippobosca equina*.

fōre′stick, *n.* The front stick of a wood fire.

for′est-oak, *n.* The commercial name for the timber of trees of the genus *Casuarina*, belonging to Australia.

for′est-ry, *n.* The art of cultivating forests and of promoting the growth of forests; the occupation of a forester.

fōre′swăt, *a.* Same as *Forswat*.

fōre′-tac″kle, *n.* The tackle on the foremast.

fōre′tāste, *n.* A taste beforehand; anticipation; as, the pleasures of piety are a *foretaste* of heaven.

fōre-tāste′, *v.t.*; foretasted, *pt.*, *pp.*; foretasting, *ppr.* 1. To taste before possession; to have previous enjoyment or experience of; to anticipate.

2. To taste before another.

fōre-tāst′ẽr, *n.* One who tastes beforehand, or before another.

fōre-tēach′, *v.t.* To teach beforehand. [Obs.]

fōre-tell′, *v.t.*; foretold, *pt.*, *pp.*; foretelling, *ppr.* 1. To predict; to tell before an event happens; to prophesy.

2. To foretoken; to foreshow.

Syn.—Predict, prophesy, prognosticate.—*Foretell* is the most general in its sense and familiar in its application. One *predicts* by a supernatural power, real or supposed, and *prophesies* by means of inspiration. *Prognostication* is an act of the understanding.

fōre-tell′, *v.i.* To utter prediction or prophecy.

> All the prophets have likewise *foretold* of these days. —Acts iii. 24.

fōre-tell′ẽr, *n.* One who foretells, predicts, or prophesies.

fōre-thiṅk′, *v.t.* 1. To think beforehand; to anticipate in the mind. [Rare.]

> The soul of every man
> Perpetually does *forethink* thy fall.—Shak.

2. To contrive beforehand. [Rare.]

fōre-thiṅk′, *v.i.* To contrive beforehand.

fōre′thought (-that), *n.* 1. A thinking beforehand; anticipation; prescience; premeditation.

2. Provident care; foresight; precaution.

fōre′thought, *a.* Previously thought; premeditated; aforethought.

fōre′thought-fųl, *a.* Having forethought. [Rare.]

fōre′time, *n.* Time previous to the present; hence, past time.

fōre-tō′ken, *v.t.*; foretokened, *pt.*, *pp.*; foretokening, *ppr.* To foreshow; to foreshadow; to prognosticate.

> Whilst strange prodigious signs *foretoken* blood. —Daniel.

fōre-tō′ken, *n.* A prognostic; a previous sign.

fōre′tooth, *n.*; *pl.* **fōre′teeth.** One of the teeth in the forepart of the mouth; an incisor.

fōre′top, *n.* 1. The hair on the forepart of the head.

2. Formerly, that part of the hair or a headdress that lay in front; sometimes, an erect tuft of hair.

3. In a ship, the platform erected at the head of the foremast; also, the foremast-top.

fōre-top-gal′lănt, *a.* In nautical language, designating the parts of a ship next above the topmast.

fōre-top′măn, *n.*; *pl.* **fōre-top′men.** In ships of war, a sailor detailed for duty in the foretop.

fōre-top′mȧst, *n.* The mast erected at the head of the foremast, and at the head of which stands the foretopgallantmast.

fōre-top′sail (-sl), *n.* In ships, the sail next above the foresail.

fọr-ev′ẽr, *adv.* [Prep. *for*, and adv. *ever*.]

1. Throughout eternity; endlessly; for ever.

2. To the end of time or close of life; at all times; during a period having no limit; unceasingly.

3. Constantly; at all times.

Syn.—Perpetually, continually, always, unceasingly, everlastingly, eternally, endlessly.

Forever and a day, *forever and ever*, *forever and forever*; emphatic forms meaning for all eternity.

fọr-ev′ẽr-mōre, *adv.* Always; through time without end.

fōre-vouched′ (-voucht′), *a.* Affirmed before; formerly told. [Rare.]

fōre′wąrd, *n.* The van; the front. [Obs.]

fōre-wąrn′, *v.t.*; forewarned, *pt.*, *pp.*; forewarning, *ppr.* To admonish beforehand; to inform previously; to give previous notice to; to warn in advance.

fōre-wāste′, *v.t.* Same as *Forwaste*.

fōre-wend′, *v.t.* To go before. [Obs.]

fōre′wind, *n.* A wind that drives a ship forward.

fōre-wish′, *v.t.* To wish beforehand.

fōre′wit, *n.* 1. One who leads, or wishes to lead, in matters of knowledge or fashion. [Obs.]

2. Prudence; judgment; foresight; motherwit.

fōre′wit, **fōre′wīte**, *v.t.* [ME. *forwiten*; AS. *forewitan*, to foreknow; *fore-*, before, and *witan*, to know.] To know beforehand. [Obs.]

fōre′wom″ăn (-woom″), *n.*; *pl.* **fōre′wom″en** (-wim″). A woman who is chief; the head woman in a workshop, department of a store, etc.

fōre′wŏrd, *n.* [G. *vorwort*, a preface; *vor*, fore, and *wort*, word.] An introduction or prefatory note in a literary work.

fōre′wŏrld, *n.* The world before the flood.

fōre-wōrn′, *a.* Worn out; wasted or obliterated by time or use. [Rare.]

fōre′yärd, *n.* 1. The lowest yard on the foremast of a square-rigged ship.

2. A yard in front of a house; a front yard. [Rare.]

for′fạl-tūre, *n.* Forfeiture; attainder. [Obs.]

fọr′feit (-fit), *n.* [ME. *forfet*; OFr. *forfait*; LL. *forisfactum*, a transgression, fault, penalty, neut. pp. of *forisfacere*, to transgress, forfeit, lit., to act beyond; L. *foris*, out of doors, beyond, and *facere*, to do.]

1. A fault; an injury; a crime. [Obs.]

2. That which is forfeited or lost, or the right to which is alienated by a crime, offense, neglect of duty, or breach of contract; hence, a fine; a mulct; a penalty; as, he who murders pays the *forfeit* of his life.

3. Something deposited and redeemable by a jocular fine; as, to play the game of *forfeits*.

4. One whose life is forfeited. [Obs.]

Syn.—Fine, penalty, damages, amercement, mulct, loss.

fọr′feit, *a.* Forfeited; lost or alienated for an offense or crime; liable to penal seizure.

> My bond to the Jew is *forfeit*. —Shak.

fọr′feit, *v.t.*; forfeited, *pt.*, *pp.*; forfeiting, *ppr.* [ME. *forfeten*; OFr. *forfait*, pp. of *forfaire*, from LL. *forisfacere*, to transgress, forfeit; L. *foris*, out of doors, beyond, and *facere*, to do.] To lose or render confiscable, by some fault, offense, or crime; to lose or alienate the right to possess, by some neglect or crime; as, to *forfeit* an estate; to *forfeit* the good will of friends.

fọr′feit, *v.i.* To be guilty of a transgression; to fail in keeping an obligation. [Obs.]

fọr′feit-ȧ-ble, *a.* Liable to be forfeited; subject to forfeiture.

fọr′feit-ẽr, *n.* One who forfeits; one who incurs a penalty, as by forfeiting his bond.

fọr′fei-tūre, *n.* 1. The act of forfeiting; the losing of some right, privilege, estate, honor, office, or property, by an offense, crime, breach of condition, or other act.

2. That which is forfeited; a penalty; a forfeit; a fine or mulct.

Syn.—Fine, penalty, damage, confiscation, sequestration, amercement.

fọr-fend′, *v.t.*; forfended, *pt.*, *pp.*; forfending, *ppr.* [ME. *forfenden*; *for-*, and *fenden*, to fend, keep off.] To fend off; to avert; to forbid; also written *forefend*.

> Heavens *forfend*! I would not kill thy soul. —Shak.

fọr-fēr′ed, *a.* Greatly alarmed; in excessive fear. [Obs.]

fọr′fēte, *v.i.* [Obs.] See *Forfeit*.

fọr′fex, *n.*; *pl.* **fọr′fi-cēṣ.** [L., a pair of shears.] A pair of scissors.

fọr′fi-cāte, *a.* [L. *forfex* (*-icis*), a pair of shears.] Having a deep fork, as the tail of a swallow.

fọr-fic′i-fọrm, *a.* [L. *forfex* (*-icis*), a pair of shears, and *forma*, form.] In zoölogy, having the form of a pair of scissors.

Fọr-fic′ū-lȧ, *n.* [L., dim. of *forfex* (*-icis*), a pair of shears.] A genus of insects characterized by forked tails, as the earwigs.

fọr-fic′ū-lāte, *a.* Forficiform.

fọr-gath′ẽr, *v.i.* [Scot.] To meet; to convene for friendly intercourse; as, Dickens and Carlyle *forgathered* with Emerson; also spelled *foregather*.

fọr-gāve′, *v.*, past tense of *forgive*.

fōrge, *n.* [ME. *forge*; OFr. *forge*, from L. *fabrica*, a workshop, fabric, from *faber*, a workman, artisan.]

1. A furnace in which iron or other metal is heated to be hammered into form; as, a blacksmith's *forge*, consisting essentially of a bellows and fireplace.

Artillery Traveling Forge.

2. A place where anything is made or shaped; a workshop.

3. The act of beating or working iron or steel; the manufacture of metallic bodies. [Obs.]

> In the greater bodies the *forge* was easy. —Bacon.

4. A sort of furnace with a cupola for producing metal directly from its ore; a bloomery.

5. A blacksmith's workshop; a smithy.

American forge; a forge for the direct production of iron by subjecting finely-crushed ore to a continuous heat.

Catalan forge; a forge for making iron directly from its ore, formerly much used in Catalonia, whence its name.

Portable forge; a small and convenient blacksmith's forge mounted upon wheels for transportation from place to place; used in military operations, especially by the artillery and cavalry.

fōrge, *v.t.*; forged, *pt.*, *pp.*; forging, *ppr.* [ME. *forgen*; OFr. *forgier*, *forger*; from L. *fabricari*, *fabricare*, to make, construct, from *fabrica*, a workshop, from *faber*, a workman, artisan.]

1. To form by heating and hammering; to beat into any particular shape, as a metal.

2. To make by any means; to invent.

> Names that the schools *forged*, and put into the mouths of scholars. —Locke.

3. To make falsely; to falsify; to counterfeit; to make in the likeness of something else, with intent to deceive; as, to *forge* coin; to *forge* a check or a receipt.

fōrge, *v.t.* To force or drive ahead; to impel forward; usually with *off*, *on*, *over*, etc.; as, to *forge* a vessel *over* a sand-bar.

fōrge, *v.i.* 1. To advance slowly, as if overcoming resistance; used with *ahead*; as, the train *forged ahead* through the drifted snow.

2. To commit forgery.

3. To overreach and click the shoes together; said of a horse.

fōrge′ȧ-ble, *a.* Capable of being forged.

fōrge′-cin″dẽr, *n.* The hardened residue from a forge or blast-furnace.

fōrge′man, *n.* The chief worker at a blacksmith's forge, as distinguished from the striker or hammerman.

fōr′gẽr, *n.* 1. One who makes or forms at a forge.

2. One who counterfeits; a falsifier.

fōrge′-rōll, *n.* One of a system of rolls used in making bars of metal.

fōr′gẽr-y, *n.* 1. The act of forging or working metal into shape. [Obs.]

2. The act of forging, fabricating, or producing falsely; especially, the crime of fraudulently making, counterfeiting, or altering any writing, record, instrument, register, note, and the like, to the prejudice of the right of another; the making of a thing in imitation of another thing, as a literary production, work of art, natural object, and the like, with a view to deceive, mislead, or defraud; as, the *forgery* of a bond or of coin.

3. That which is forged, fabricated, falsely or fraudulently devised, or counterfeited.

The writings going under the name of Aristobulus were a *forgery* of the second century. —Waterland.

fōrge′-scāle, *n.* The coating of iron oxid formed on the surface of highly heated iron.

fọr-get′, *v.t.*; forgot, *pt.*; forgetting, *ppr.*; forgotten, forgot, *pp.* [ME. *forgeten, forgiten*; AS. *forgitan, forgietan*, to forget; *for-* priv., and *gitan, gietan*, to get.]

1. To lose the remembrance of; to let go from the memory.

Bless the Lord, O my soul, and *forget* not all his benefits. —Ps. ciii. 2.

2. To slight; to neglect.

Can a woman *forget* her sucking child? —Isa. xlix. 15.

To forget oneself; to say or do something, through lack of self-control, that is not consistent with one's dignity or reputation, as to become angry and abusive upon slight provocation.

Syn.—Pretermit, unlearn, overlook, disregard.

fọr-get′ȧ-ble, fọr-get′tȧ-ble, *a.* That may be forgotten; liable to escape the memory.

fọr-get′ȧ-ble-ness, fọr-get′tȧ-ble-ness, *n.* The quality of being forgetable.

fọr-get′fụl, *a.* 1. Apt to forget; easily losing the remembrance of.

Bear with me, good boy, I am much *forgetful.* —Shak.

2. Heedless; careless; neglectful; inattentive.

Be not *forgetful* to entertain strangers. —Heb. xiii. 2.

3. Causing to forget; inducing oblivion; oblivious; as, *forgetful* drugs.

fọr-get′fụl-ly, *adv.* In a forgetful manner.

fọr-get′fụl-ness, *n.* 1. The quality of being apt to let anything slip from the mind.

2. Loss of remembrance or recollection; a ceasing to remember; oblivion.

A sweet *forgetfulness* of human care.—Pope.

3. Neglect; negligence; careless omission; inattention; as, *forgetfulness* of duty.

fōr′ge-tive, *a.* That may forge or produce; inventive. [Obs.]

fọr-get′-me-not, *n.* A small European plant, *Myosotis palustris*, bearing a beautiful blue flower and extensively considered the emblem of fidelity. It is naturalized in some parts of the United States.

The sweet *forget-me-nots*
That grow for happy lovers. —Tennyson.

Forget-me-not (*Myosotis palustris*).

fōrge′-trāin, *n.* A complete set of forge-rolls.

fọr-get′tȧ-ble, *a.* See *Forgetable.*

fọr-get′tȧ-ble-ness, *n.* See *Forgetableness.*

fọr-get′tẽr, *n.* One who forgets; a heedless person.

fọr-get′ting-ly, *adv.* By forgetting or forgetfulness.

fōrg′ing, *n.* 1. The act of beating into shape.

2. The act of counterfeiting.

3. The thing forged; a piece of forged work in metal; a general name for pieces of hammered iron or steel.

fọr-giv′ȧ-ble, *a.* That may be forgiven; pardonable.

fọr-give′, *v.t.*; forgave, *pt.*; forgiving, *ppr.*; forgiven, *pp.* [ME. *forgiven, forgifen*, to give up, forgive, remit; AS. *forgiefan, forgifan*; *for-*, away, and *giefan, gifan*, to give.]

1. To pardon; to remit, as an offense or debt; to overlook (an offense) and treat (the offender) as not guilty.

Forgive us our debts. —Lord's Prayer.

2. To remit, as a debt, fine, or penalty.

3. To grant free pardon to; to cease to blame. This verb may have as its object the person *forgiven* or the injury *forgiven*, or both; as, I *forgive* you; I *forgive* the injury; *forgive* us our sins.

Syn.—Pardon, absolve, remit, cancel, release.

fọr-give′ness, *n.* 1. The act of forgiving; the pardon of an offender, by which he is considered and treated as not guilty.

2. The pardon or remission of an offense or crime; as, the *forgiveness* of sin or of injuries.

3. Disposition to pardon; willingness to forgive.

And mild *forgiveness* intercede
To stop the coming blow. —Dryden.

Syn.—Pardon.—In modern usage, *forgive* points to inward feeling, and supposes alienated friendship; when we ask *forgiveness*, we primarily seek the removal of anger. *Pardon* looks more to outward things or consequences, and is often applied to trifling matters, as when we beg *pardon* for interrupting. The magistrate grants a *pardon*, and not *forgiveness*.

fọr-giv′ẽr, *n.* One who pardons or remits.

fọr-giv′ing, *a.* Disposed to forgive; inclined to overlook offenses; mild; merciful; compassionate; as, a *forgiving* temper.

fọr-giv′ing-ly, *adv.* In a forgiving manner.

fọr-giv′ing-ness, *n.* The state of being forgiving.

fọr-gō′, *v.t.* See *Forego.*

fọr-got′, *v.*, past tense of *forget.*

fọr-got′ten, *v.*, past participle of *forget.*

fọr-hāil′, *v.t.* [*For-*, and ME. *halen, halien*, to draw.] To harass or distress. [Obs.]

fọr-hend′, *v.t.* To apprehend. [Obs.]

fo-rin′se-cal, *a.* [L. *forinsecus*, from without, on the outside.] Foreign; alien. [Obs.]

fō″ris-fa-mil′i-āte, *v.i.*; forisfamiliated, *pt.*, *pp.*; forisfamiliating, *ppr.* In law, to renounce a legal title to a further share of paternal inheritance; to put oneself out of the family.

fō″ris-fa-mil′i-āte, *v.t.* [LL. *forisfamiliatus*, pp. of *forisfamiliare*, to emancipate; *foris*, outside, and *familia*, family.] To put out of family; in law, to emancipate or free from parental authority; to put (a son) in possession of property in his father's lifetime, either at his own request or with his consent, and thus discharge him from the family.

fō″ris-fa-mil-i-ā′tion, *n.* The act of forisfamiliating; the state of being forisfamiliated.

fọr-judge′ (-juj′), *v.t.* See *Forejudge.*

fọrk, *n.* [ME. *fork, forke*; AS. *forc*, from L. *furca*, a fork.]

1. An instrument consisting of a handle with a shank of metal divided into two or more tines or prongs, used for lifting or pitching anything; as, to eat with a knife and *fork*; to pitch hay with a *fork.*

2. Anything resembling a *fork* in shape, or employed for a purpose similar to that for which a *fork* is employed.

3. One of the parts into which anything is bifurcated or divided; a prong; a point; a barb; as, the *fork* of a tree or of a river; a *fork* of lightning.

4. An instrument of steel with two prongs, which when set in vibration produces a musical sound, varying in pitch according to the thickness of the metal, the length of the prongs, or their width apart; a tuning-fork.

5. A piece of steel fitting into the socket or chuck of a lathe, used for carrying round the piece to be turned; also called *fork-chuck.*

6. A gibbet (*furca* being in Latin the name of a kind of gibbet). [Obs.]

7. The bifurcated part of the human frame; the legs; as, he is somewhat long in the *fork.*

fọrk, *v.i.*; forked (fọrkt), *pt.*, *pp.*; forking, *ppr.*

1. To shoot into blades, as corn.

2. To divide into two; as, a road *forks.*

fọrk, *v.t.* 1. To raise or pitch with a fork, as hay.

2. To dig and break (ground) with a fork.

3. In mining, to pump (water) from a shaft or mine.

To fork over; to hand over money at once. [Slang.]

fọrk′-bēam, *n.* In shipbuilding, a short beam for the support of the deck, as at a hatchway.

fọrk′bēard, *n.* In zoölogy, a fish having ventral fins near the head, giving the appearance of a furcate beard.

fọrk′-chuck, *n.* An attachment to a turning-lathe, so called from that part which screws on the mandrel having on the outer side a square hole in which forked pieces of iron of different sizes, according to the strength required, are placed when in use.

fọrked (fọrkt *or* fọrk′ed), *a.* 1. Opening into two or more parts, points, or shoots; as, a *forked* tongue; *forked* lightning.

2. Having two or more meanings; equivocal; as, *forked* advice.

fọrk′ed-ly, *adv.* In a forked form.

fọrk′ed-ness, *n.* The quality of being forked or opening into two or more parts.

fọr-kẽrve′, *v.t.* Same as *Forcarve.*

fọrk′-head (-hed), *n.* 1. In machinery, the fork at the end of a rod forming part of a knuckle-joint.

2. The barbed head of an arrow.

fọrk′i-ness, *n.* The quality of being furcate.

fọrk′less, *a.* Having no fork; not bifurcated.

fọrk′tāil, *n.* 1. A salmon in its fourth year's growth. [Prov. Eng.]

2. One of several sparrows with deeply forked tails.

3. The kite; from its forked tail.

fọrk′-tāiled, *a.* Having the tail forked, as in the swallow; scissor-tailed.

Fork-tailed flycatcher; one of the American tyrant flycatchers, especially *Milvulus tyrannus.*

Fork-tailed kite; the swallow-tailed kite, *Elanoides forficatus.*

Fork-tailed shrike; a drongo; a shrike of the family *Dicruridæ*, as *Dicrurus forficatus.*

fọrk′y, *a.* Forked; furcated; opening into two or more parts, shoots, or points; as, a *forky* tongue.

fọr′laft, *a.* Left off entirely. [Obs.]

fōr-lä′nȧ, *n.* [It.] A piece of spirited Venetian dance-music; also, the dance itself.

fọr-lāy′, *v.t.* Same as *Forelay*, 1.

fọr-lēave′, *v.t.* To leave; to forsake. [Obs.]

fọr-lend′, *v.t.* To relinquish; to give up altogether. [Obs.]

fọr-lēse′, *v.t.* [AS. *forleósan*; *for-*, intens., and *leósan*, to lose.] To lose entirely. [Obs.]

fọr-let′, *v.t.* [AS. *forlætan*; *for-*, away, and *lætan*, to let.] To give over; to neglect; to abandon. [Obs.]

fọr-lie′, *v.i.* To lie before or in front. [Obs.]

fọr-lie′, *v.t.* To suffocate by lying upon, as a child in bed. [Prov. Eng.]

fọr-lōre′, *v.t.* 1. To forsake; to desert. [Obs.]

Thus fell the trees, with noise the deserts roar;
The beasts their caves, the birds their nests *forlore.* —Fairfax.

2. To deprive. [Obs.]

fọr-lọrn′, *a.* [ME. *forlorn, forloren*; AS. *forloren*, pp. of *forleósan*, to lose; *for-*, intens., and *leósan*, to lose.]

1. Deserted; destitute; stripped or deprived; forsaken; lost; helpless; wretched; solitary.

For here *forlorn* and lost I tread.—Goldsmith.

2. Deprived; bereft; destitute.

He went like one that hath been stunned,
And is of sense *forlorn.* —Coleridge.

Forlorn hope; (a) an advanced body of troops; a body of skirmishers; a vanguard; (b) a detachment of men appointed to lead in an assault, to storm a counterscarp, enter a breach, or perform other service attended with uncommon peril. The phrase is derived from Dutch *verloren hoop*, lit., a lost troop.

fọr-lọrn′, *n.* 1. A lost, forsaken, solitary person.

2. A forlorn hope; an advanced body of troops; a vanguard.

Our *forlorn* of horse marched within a mile of where the enemy was drawn up. —Cromwell.

Syn.—Comfortless, helpless, depressed, miserable, wretched, friendless, woebegone, disconsolate, pitiable, abject, destitute, lost, abandoned, forsaken, solitary, hopeless.

fọr-lọrn′ly, *adv.* In a forlorn manner.

fọr-lọrn′ness, *n.* Destitution; misery; a forsaken or wretched condition.

fọr-lȳe′, *v.t.* [Obs.] Same as *Forlie.*

-fọrm. A suffix from L. *-formis*, -like, from *forma*, form, shape. It is used in words of Latin origin or words similarly formed; as, cunei*form*, ovi*form*, ensi*form.*

fọrm, *n.* [ME. *forme, fourme*; OFr. *forme, fourme*, from L. *forma*, shape, figure, image.]

1. The shape or external appearance of a body; the figure, as defined by lines and angles; the manner of being peculiar to a body; the particular disposition of matter in each body or figure, which distinguishes its appearance from that of every other body or figure; as, a globular *form*; a circular *form*; a graceful *form.*

The *form* of his visage was changed. —Dan. iii. 19.

2. Particular arrangement of the several parts or of details; as, a *form* of democracy, of language, of carbon, of Christian worship.

3. A stated method, practice, or procedure; ritual; as, a *form* of marriage; a *form* of law.

4. Manner; system; constitutional structure; as, a republican *form* of government or a siliceous *form* of rock.

5. Anatomical structure; as, the *form* of a mammal or of a marsupial.

6. External appearance; empty show.

Having a *form* of godliness. —2 Tim. iii. 5.

7. Beauty; elegance; splendor; dignity.

He hath no *form* nor comeliness.—Isa. liii. 2.

8. Model; draft; pattern.

Hold fast the *form* of sound words. —2 Tim. i. 13.

9. Regularity; method; order; perfection of shape; as, this is a rough draft to be reduced to *form.*

10. Likeness; image; exact representation.

He took on him the *form* of a servant. —Phil. ii. 7.

11. A long seat or bench; hence, in English schools, a class or grade of pupils; as, he belongs to the fourth *form*.

12. The seat or bed of a hare.

13. A mold; something to give shape, or on which things are fashioned.

14. In printing, an assemblage of types, composed and arranged in order, disposed into pages or columns, and inclosed and locked in a chase for stereotyping or printing; also, a plate or plates arranged and locked in a chase for printing.

15. In the fine arts, the outline of an object.

16. In grammar, the particular structure of a word as constituting a part of speech; as, the adverbial *form* or the participial *form*.

17. In crystallography, the total configuration of planes included under the same symbol. In a *closed form* the planes inclose a space; in an *open form* the planes do not inclose a space.

18. A blank, as of a lease, deed, affidavit, etc.; also, such a blank, properly filled out, to serve as a specimen or sample.

Essential form or *substantial form*; in metaphysics, that mode of existence which constitutes a thing what it is, and without which it could not exist. Thus water and light have each a particular *form* of existence, and the parts of water being decomposed it ceases to be water.

Good form; good condition; as, the team was in *good form* as shown by its excellent play; also, observance of the rules of propriety in conduct, speech, or writing; good style; beauty in works of art; opposed to *bad form*.

fọrm, *v.t.*; formed, *pt.*, *pp.*; forming, *ppr.* [ME. *formen*, *fourmen*, from L. *formare*, to shape, fashion, mold, from *forma*, form, shape.]

1. To make, shape, mold, or fashion; to construct from existing matter; to modify; to arrange; to combine; to devise; to plan; to scheme; as, to *form* an image of clay; to *form* troops into line; to *form* a plan; to *form* a trust.

2. To make up; to constitute; to cause to assume a certain shape; as, these men *form* the company; this substance *forms* the chief ingredient; the smoke *formed* a tree-like mass.

3. To make by derivation or by affixes or prefixes; as, to *form* a noun by adding *ness* to an adjective.

4. To produce by chemical change; as, to *form* lead oxid from the plates of a storage battery.

fọrm, *v.i.* 1. To take a form or shape; as, clouds *form* in the sky.

2. To go to or crouch in a form, as a hare.

fọrm'ȧ-ble, *a.* Capable of being formed.

fọrm'ăl, *a.* [L. *formalis*, from *forma*, form, shape.]

1. According to form; according to established mode; regular; methodical; pertaining to a form or model.

2. Strictly ceremonious; precise; exact to affectation; as, a man *formal* in his dress, his gait, or his deportment.

3. Done in due form, or with solemnity; not incidental, sudden, or irregular; as, he gave his *formal* consent to the treaty.

4. Regular; methodical; as, the *formal* stars.

5. Having the form or appearance without the substance or essence; external; as, *formal* duty; *formal* worship.

6. Depending on customary forms; conventional.

> Still in constraint your suffering sex remains,
> Or bound in *formal* or in real chains.—Pope.

7. Having the power of making a thing what it is; constituent; essential.

> Of letters the material part is breath and voice; the *formal* is constituted by the motions and figure of the organs of speech. —Holder.

8. Retaining its proper and essential characteristic; regular; normal. [Obs.]

> To make of him a *formal* man again.—Shak.

Formal cause; see under *Cause*.

Syn.—Precise, ceremonious, exact, stiff, methodical.—A man is *precise* who reduces things to an exact rule or standard; *formal*, who shapes things by some set form or pattern; *ceremonious*, when he lays much stress on the conventional laws of social intercourse.

fọr-mal'dē-hȳde, *n.* [*Formic* and *aldehyde*.] In chemistry, formic or methyl aldehyde, CH_2O, obtained when a current of air, charged with the vapor of methyl alcohol, is directed on an incandescent spiral of platinum wire. It is extensively used as a disinfectant in cases of infectious disease. *Formaldehyde* is found in the market as a 40 per cent solution of the gas in water or wood alcohol, under the trade names of *formalin* and *formol*.

fọr'mȧ-lin, *n.* See *Formaldehyde*.

fọrm'ăl-ịsm, *n.* The quality of being formal, especially in matters of religion; outside and ceremonial religion.

fọrm'ăl-ist, *n.* 1. One who punctiliously observes forms or practises external ceremonies.

2. One who rests in external religious forms or observes the forms of worship without possessing the life and spirit of religion.

fọr-mal'i-ty, *n.* 1. The practice or observance of forms; conventionality.

2. Ceremony; mere conformity to customary modes.

> Nor was his attendance on divine offices a matter of *formality* and custom, but of conscience. —Atterbury.

3. Established order; rule of proceeding; mode; method; as, the *formalities* of judicial process; *formalities* of law.

4. Order; decorum to be observed; customary mode of behavior.

5. Customary mode of behavior or dress; ceremonial. [Rare.]

6. External appearance.

7. Essence; the quality which constitutes a thing what it is.

> The *formality* of the vow lies in the promise made to God. —Stillingfleet.

8. In philosophy, the manner in which a thing is conceived; a manner in an object importing a relation to the understanding by which it may be distinguished from another object; as, animality and rationality are *formalities*.

Syn.—Ceremony, parade, affectation, stateliness, punctiliousness, etiquette.

fọrm'ăl-ize, *v.t.*; formalized, *pt.*, *pp.*; formalizing, *ppr.* 1. To model. [Obs.]

2. To bring to a formal state.

fọrm'ăl-ize, *v.i.* To affect formality. [Obs.]

fọrm'ăl-ly, *adv.* In accordance with forms, rites, or ceremonies; conventionally.

fọr'māte, *n.* [*Formic* and *-ate*.] A salt composed of formic acid combined with any base.

fọr-mā'tion, *n.* [L. *formatio* (*-onis*), from *formare*, to form, shape.]

1. The act of forming or making; the act of creating or causing to exist; more generally, the operation of bringing things together, or of shaping and giving form; as, the *formation* of the earth; the *formation* of a state or constitution.

2. Generation; production; as, the *formation* of ideas.

3. The manner in which a thing is formed; as, examine the peculiar *formation* of the heart; also, the thing formed; as, the heart is a wonderful *formation*.

4. In geology, any series of rocks referred to a common origin or period, whether they consist of the same or different materials. Geological strata are divided into certain groups of one era of deposition, sometimes of very dissimilar mineralogical character, but inclosing the same fossil species; as, the Carboniferous, Oölitic, Cretaceous, Silurian, Laurentian, etc., *formations*.

5. An arrangement of troops, as in a square, column, etc.

fọrm'ȧ-tive, *a.* [From L. *formatus*, pp. of *formare*, to form, shape.]

1. Giving form; having the power of giving form; plastic; as, the *formative* arts.

> The meanest plant cannot be raised without seeds by any *formative* power residing in the soil. —Bentley.

2. In grammar, serving to form; derivative; inflectional; as, a termination merely *formative*.

3. Relating to formation or development; as, the *formative* period of youth; the *formative* stage of a nation's history.

fọrm'ȧ-tive, *n.* In grammar, that which serves merely to give form, and is no part of the radical.

fọr'me, *a.* [Obs.] See *Former*.

fọrmed, *a.* 1. In astronomy, arranged in groups or constellations; said of stars.

2. In heraldry, seated; crouched, as a hare in its form.

3. In biology, possessing the power of development; organized for formation.

Formed material; in biology, the nongerminal material of a cell.

fọr'me-don, *n.* [OFr., from L. *forma doni*, form of the gift.] In English law, formerly, a writ of right, which lay for him who had right to lands or tenements by virtue of an entail.

fọr'mel, **fọr'mell**, *n.* [ME. *formel*, *formele*; OFr. *forme*, a female of the falcon or hawk.] In zoölogy, the female of the falcon family. [Obs.]

fọr-mēne', *n.* In chemistry, an obsolete name for methane or marsh-gas.

fọrm'ẽr, *n.* 1. One who forms; a maker; an author; a creator.

2. A mechanical device for shaping an article of manufacture; a pattern.

fọr'mẽr, *a.* [ME. *forme*; AS. *forma*, first; from *for*, *fore*, before, and superl. suffix *-ma*. The comp. suffix *-er* was added on the mistaken supposition that *formest*, foremost, was not a double superlative.]

1. Before in time; preceding another or something else in order of time; antecedent; prior; opposed to *latter*.

> The *former* and the latter rain. —Jer. v. 24.

2. Past; especially, ancient; long past.

> Inquire, I pray thee, of the *former* age. —Job viii. 8.

3. Near the beginning; preceding; as, the *former* part of a discourse or argument.

4. Preceding or going before in a series; earlier; as, my *former* letters.

Syn.—Preceding, prior, previous, foregoing, anterior, antecedent.

fọr-me-ret' (-rā), *n.* [Fr.] In architecture, the rib which in ribbed vaulting lies next to and in a plane parallel with the wall.

fọr'mẽr-ly, *adv.* In time past, either in time immediately preceding or at any indefinite distance; of old; heretofore; as, nations *formerly* made slaves of prisoners taken in war.

Syn.—Previously.—*Formerly* means before the present time; *previously*, before some particular event.

fọrm'fụl, *a.* Ready to form; creative; imaginative. [Rare.]

fọrm'=gē'nus, *n.* In biology, a genus composed of similar form-species.

fọr'miç, *a.* [L. *formica*, an ant.] Pertaining to ants; as, *formic* acid.

Formic acid; a fatty acid originally obtained from a fluid emitted by red ants when irritated, but now produced by artificial processes; symbol HCO_2H.

Formic ethers; ethers obtained by the substitution of alcoholic radicals for the replaceable hydrogen of formic acid.

For'mi-cȧ, *n.* [L. *formica*, an ant.] The typical genus of a large family of hymenopterous insects; the ants.

fọr'mi-căn, *a.* Pertaining to the ant; resembling an ant.

fọr'mi-çănt, *a.* Crawling like an ant; in medicine, a term applied to the pulse when extremely small, scarcely perceptible, unequal, and communicating a sensation like that of the motion of an ant perceived through a thin texture.

fọr-mi-çā'ri-ăn, *a.* 1. Pertaining to ants; formicine.

2. Pertaining to ant-birds; formicarioid.

fọr-mi-çā'ri-oid, *a.* Having the characters of the ant-birds, *Formicarioideæ*.

fọr-mi-çā'ri-um, *n.* Same as *Formicary*.

fọr'mi-çȧ-ry, *n.* [LL. *formicarium*, an ant-hill, from L. *formica*, an ant.] The nest or burrow of a community of ants, often consisting of a mound or a pyramid of granular earth with various subterranean passages and apartments; an ant-hill.

fọr'mi-çāte, *a.* [L. *formica*, an ant, and *-ate*.] Pertaining to or resembling an ant or ants.

fọr-mi-çā'tion, *n.* A sensation of the body resembling that made by the creeping of ants on the skin.

fọr'mi-cid, *a.* and *n.* I. *a.* Resembling or belonging to ants.

II. *n.* An ant or ant-like insect.

fọr'mi-cine, *a.* [L. *formica*, an ant, and *-ine*.] Ant-like.

fọr"mi-dȧ-bil'i-ty, *n.* The quality of being formidable.

fọr'mi-dȧ-ble, *a.* [L. *formidabilis*, from *formidare*, to fear, dread.] Exciting fear or apprehension; impressing with dread; adapted to excite fear and deter from approach, encounter, or undertaking.

> They seemed to fear the *formidable* sight. —Dryden.

Syn.—Dreadful, terrible, shocking.—The *formidable* acts neither suddenly nor violently; the *dreadful* may act violently, but not suddenly; the *terrible* and *shocking* act both suddenly and violently, but the former acts both on the senses and the imagination, the latter on the moral feelings.

fọr'mi-dȧ-ble-ness, *n.* The quality of being formidable, or adapted to excite dread.

fọr'mi-dȧ-bly, *adv.* In a formidable manner.

fọr-mid'ō-lōse, *a.* [L. *formidolosus*, from *formidare*, to fear, dread.] Filled with dread; greatly afraid. [Obs.]

fọrm'ing=mȧ-çhine", *n.* Any piece of machinery employed to give definite shape to a body, as in tinsmithing, hat-making, rope-making, etc.

fọrm'less, *a.* Shapeless; without a determinate form; wanting regularity of shape.

fọrm'less-ly, *adv.* In a formless manner.

fọrm'less-ness, *n.* The quality of lacking form.

fọr'mōl, *n.* See *Formaldehyde*.

fọrm'=spē"cies, *n.* A species based upon a single phase of development until a complete cycle furnishes means of correct classification.

fọr'mū-lȧ, *n.*; *pl.* **fọr'mū-læ** or **fọr'mū-lȧs**. [L., a small pattern, rule, mold, dim. of *forma*, form, shape.]

1. A prescribed form; a rule or model.

2. In medicine, a prescription.

3. In church affairs, a confession of faith.

4. In mathematics, a general expression for resolving certain cases or problems.

5. In chemistry, a term applied to the symbols representing the different substances.

Empirical formula; in chemistry, a formula showing all the constituents of a compound without regard to the manner of union, as H_2O.

Graphic formula or *rational formula*; in chemistry, a formula showing the elements or compounds which unite in a formation, as $CaO+CO_2$; called also *structural formula*.

Molecular formula; in chemistry, a kind of graphic formula showing the molecular structure.

fọr′mū-lăr, *a.* Pertaining to a formula.

fọr″mū-là-ris′tiç, *a.* Of a formularizing nature or character.

fọr″mū-lăr-i-zā′tion, *n.* The act of reducing to a formula; anything reduced to a formula.

fọr′mū-lăr-ize, *v.t.*; formularized, *pt.*, *pp.*; formularizing, *ppr.* To express by means of a formula; to reduce to a formula.

fọr′mū-lā-ry, *n.* [Fr. *formulaire*, from L. *formula*, an established mode of procedure, rule, principle.]

1. A book containing stated and prescribed forms, as of oaths, declarations, prayers, and the like; a book of precedents.

2. A prescribed form; a formula.

fọr′mū-lā-ry, *a.* Stated; prescribed; ritual.

fọr′mū-lāte, *v.t.*; formulated, *pt.*, *pp.*; formulating, *ppr.* To reduce to a state of precision; to express in a formula; to state in precise form.

fọr-mū-lā′tion, *n.* The process, act, or result of formulating.

fọr′mūle, *n.* [Fr.] A set or prescribed model; a formula. [Obs.]

fọr″mū-li-zā′tion, *n.* Formulation.

fọr′mū-līze, *v.t.*; formulized, *pt.*, *pp.*; formulizing, *ppr.* Same as *Formulate.*

fọr′myl, *n.* [*Form*ic and *-yl*.] In chemistry, the hypothetical radical HCO.

fọrn-çast′, *v.t.* [Obs.] See *Forecast.*

fọr′ni-căl, *a.* [L. *fornix (-icis)*, an arch, vault.] Pertaining to the fornix.

fọr′ni-çāte, *a.* [L. *fornicatus*, from *fornix (-icis)*, an arch, vault.]

1. Arched; vaulted like an oven or furnace.

2. In botany, arching over, as a leaf or petal.

fọr′ni-çāte, *v.i.*; fornicated, *pt.*, *pp.*; fornicating, *ppr.* [LL. *fornicatus*, pp. of *fornicari*, to fornicate, from L. *fornix (-icis)*, a vault, brothel in an underground vault.] To have illicit sexual intercourse; said of unmarried persons.

fọr-ni-çā′tion, *n.* [LL. *fornicatio (-onis)*, from *fornicari*, to fornicate, from *fornix (-icis)*, a vault, a brothel in an underground vault.]

1. The incontinence or lewdness of unmarried persons, male or female.

> *Fornication* (is) the act of incontinency in single persons; if either party be married, it is adultery. —Wharton.

2. In Scripture, it may mean (a) adultery; (b) incest; (c) idolatry; a forsaking of the true God, and worshiping of idols.

fọr-ni-çā′tion, *n.* [L. *fornicatio (-onis)*, from *fornicatus*, arched, from *fornix (-icis)*, a vault, arch.] The forming of a vault or arch; an arching.

fọr′ni-çā-tẽr, *n.* One who commits fornication.

fọr′ni-çā-tress, *n.* A woman who commits fornication.

fọr′nix, *n.*; *pl.* **fọr′ni-çēs̤.** [L., an arch, vault.]

1. In conchology, the excavated part under the umbo; also, the upper or convex shell in the oyster.

2. In botany, a small elongation on the tube or throat of the corolla.

3. In anatomy, a triangular lamina of white substance extending into each lateral ventricle of the brain, and terminating in two processes which arch downward to the base of the brain.

fọr-ōld′, *a.* Of very great age. [Obs.]

fọr-pȧss′, *v.i.* To go by; to pass unnoticed. [Obs.]

fọr-pīne′, *v.i.* To pine or waste away. [Obs.]

fọr-rāy′, *v.t.* To ravage. [Obs.]

fọr-rāy′, *n.* The act of ravaging. [Obs.]

fọr′rel, fọr′ril, fọr′rill, *n.* [Obs.] See *Forel.*

fọr-sāke′, *v.t.*; forsook, *pt.*; forsaking, *ppr.*; forsaken, *pp.* [ME. *forsaken*; AS. *forsacan*, to give up, refuse, forsake; *for-*, and *sacan*, to contend, strive.]

1. To quit or leave entirely; to desert; to abandon; to depart from; as, friends and flatterers *forsake* us in adversity.

2. To abandon; to renounce; to reject.

> Cease from anger, and *forsake* wrath. —Ps. xxxvii. 8.

Syn.—Abandon, desert, leave, quit, relinquish, fail, renounce, give up.

fọr-sāk′ẽr, *n.* One who forsakes or deserts.

fọr-sāy′, *v.t.* [AS. *forsecgan*, to accuse.] To forbid; to renounce. [Obs.]

fọr-shāpe′, *v.t.* [AS. *forscapan*, to transform.] To put out of shape. [Obs.]

fọr-slack′, *v.t.* To delay. [Obs.]

fọr-slōw′, *v.t.* and *v.i.* To defer; to postpone; to be slow; to lag. [Obs.]

fọr-slōwth′, *v.t.* [AS. *forslawian*, to be slow or unwilling.] To suffer loss of, by sloth or neglect. [Obs.]

fọr-slug′, *v.t.* To suffer loss of, through sluggishness. [Obs.]

fọr-sook′, *v.*, past tense of *forsake.*

fọr-sooth′, *adv.* [ME. *forsoothe, forsothe*; AS. *forsoth*; *for*, prep., and *soth*, sooth, truth.] In truth; in fact; certainly; very well; usually employed ironically.

> A fit man, *forsooth*, to govern a realm! —Hayward.

fọr-spēak′, *v.t.* To bewitch; to harm by too much praise. [Prov. Eng. and Scot.]

fọr-spent′, *a.* Tired out. [Obs.]

fọr-stall′, *v.t.* [Obs.] See *Forestall.*

fọrs′tẽr, *n.* A forester. [Obs.]

fọr-straught′ (-strat′), *a.* Very much perplexed. [Obs.]

fọr-swāt′, *a.* Exhausted by heat and perspiration. [Obs.]

fọr-swēar′, *v.t.*; forswore, *pt.*; forswearing, *ppr.*; forsworn, *pp.* [ME. *forsweren, forswerien*; AS. *forswerian*, to swear falsely; *for-*, and *swerian*, to swear.]

1. To reject or renounce upon oath.

> Like innocence, and as serenely bold
> As truth, how loudly he *forswears* thy gold!
> —Dryden.

2. To deny upon oath.

To forswear oneself; to swear falsely; to perjure oneself.

Syn.—Renounce, abjure.

fọr-swēar′, *v.i.* To swear falsely; to commit perjury.

Syn.—Perjure.

fọr-swēar′ẽr, *n.* One who forswears.

fọr-swŏnk′, *a.* [AS. *forswincan*, to overwork.] Overlabored. [Obs.]

fọr-swōre′, *v.*, past tense of *forswear.*

fọr-swōrn′, *v.*, past participle of *forswear.*

fọr-swōrn′ness, *n.* The state of being forsworn.

For-syth′i-ȧ, *n.* [Named after William *Forsyth*, a British botanist.] In botany, a genus of ornamental shrubs of China and Japan, with golden-yellow bell-shaped flowers.

fōrt, *n.* [OFr. *fort*; LL. *fortis*, a fort, stronghold, from L. *fortis*, strong, powerful.]

1. A fortified place; usually, a small fortified place; a place surrounded with a ditch, rampart, and parapet, or with palisades, stockades, or other means of defense; also, any building or place fortified for security against an enemy; a fortification.

2. A frontier trading-post for barter with the Indians, often fortified though later not; as, *Fort* Dearborn; *Fort* Pierre. [U. S.]

3. Same as *Forte.*

fōrt′ȧ-lĭçe, *n.* [OFr. *fortelesse, fortelesce*; LL. *fortalitia, fortalitium*, a small fort, from L. *fortis*, strong, powerful.] A small outwork of a fortification.

fōr′te, *adv.* [It., strong, loud.] Loudly; with force; used in music.

fōrte, *n.* [Fr. *fort*, a fort, strong point.] The strong point; that art or department in which one excels.

fōrt′ed, *a.* Furnished with forts; guarded by forts. [Rare.]

fōr′te-pĭ-ä′nō, *a.* and *n.* [It.] I. *a.* In music, loud, then soft, with strong and decided accent; sforzando.

II. *n.* A piano; a pianoforte.

fōrth, *adv.* [ME. *forth*; AS. *forth*, forth, forward; from *fore*, for, fore, and *-th*.]

1. Forward; onward in time; in advance; forward in place or order; as, one, two, three, and so *forth.*

2. Out; abroad, noting progression or advance from a state of confinement; as, the plants in spring put *forth* leaves.

3. Out; away; beyond the boundary of a place.

4. Thoroughly; from beginning to end. [Obs.]

fōrth, *prep.* Out of. [Rare.]

> From *forth* the streets of Pomfret.—Shak.

fōrth, *n.* [ME., a ford.] A way. [Obs.]

fōrth′çŏm-ing, *a.* Ready to appear; making appearance.

fōrth′gō-ing, *n.* A going forth or utterance; a proceeding from.

fōrth′gō-ing, *a.* Going forth.

fọr-think′, *v.t.* To repent of. [Obs.]

fōrth′pụt″ting, *n.* 1. Production.

2. A forward disposition; presumption.

fōrth′pụt″ting, *a.* Productive; also, forward; insistent; bold.

fōrth′right, *adv.* Straight forward; in a straight direction. [Obs.]

fōrth′right, *n.* A straight path. [Obs.]

fōrth′right, *a.* [AS. *forthriht*; *forth*, forth, and *riht*, right.] Direct; open; frank; said of conduct. [Rare.]

fōrth′right-ness, *n.* Directness; openness; honesty. [Rare.]

fōrth′wȧrd, *adv.* Forward. [Obs.]

fōrth-with′, *adv.* 1. Immediately; without delay; directly.

2. In law, as soon as the thing required may reasonably be done, commonly within twenty-four hours.

fọr-thȳ′, *adv.* [AS. *for thy*; *for*, prep., and *thy*, instrumental of *thæt*, that.] Therefore. [Obs.]

fọr′ti-eth, *a.* [ME. *fowertuthe, fuwertithe*; AS. *feowertigotha*; *feowertig*, forty, and ordinal suffix, *-tha*, *-th*.]

1. Noting the number next after thirty-ninth.

2. Constituting one of the equal parts, forty in number, into which anything is or may be divided.

fọr′ti-eth, *n.* The quotient of anything divided by forty.

fọr′ti-fī-ȧ-ble, *a.* That may be fortified.

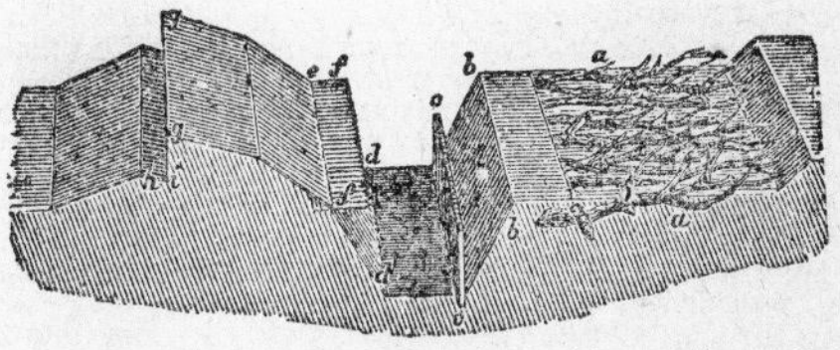

Section of Fortified Work (interior on the left; exterior on the right): *a a*, Abattis; *b b*, The counterscarp; *c c*, The palisade; *d d*, Scarp; *f f*, Fraise; *f e g g*, The parapet; *h*, Banquette; *i g*, The breastheight.

fọr″ti-fi-çā′tion, *n.* 1. The act of fortifying.

2. The art or science of fortifying places to defend them against an enemy, by means of moats, ramparts, parapets, and other bulwarks.

3. The works erected to defend a place from attack; a fortified place; a fort; a castle.

4. Additional strength; a strengthening in any way.

fọr″ti-fi-çā′tion-ag″āte, *n.* That variety of agate exhibiting lines and angles resembling those in a fortification.

fọr′ti-fī-ẽr, *n.* One who or that which fortifies.

fọr′ti-fȳ, *v.t.*; fortified, *pt.*, *pp.*; fortifying, *ppr.* [Fr. *fortifier*; LL. *fortificare*, to strengthen, fortify; from L. *fortis*, strong, and *facere*, to make.]

1. To provide with works of defense; to strengthen and secure by forts, batteries, and fortifications; as, to *fortify* a city.

2. To confirm; to add strength and firmness to; to give the power of resistance to.

3. To add to the strength of; as, to *fortify* wine by the addition of alcohol.

fọr′ti-fȳ, *v.i.* To raise works of defense.

fōr′ti-lāge, *n.* [A form of *fortalice.*] A little fort; a blockhouse. [Obs.]

fōrt′in, *n.* [Fr.] A little fort; a field fort; a sconce. [Obs.]

fọr-tis′si-mō, *adv.* [It.] In music, with the utmost strength or loudness.

fọr-ti′tion (-tish′un), *n.* A trusting to chance. [Rare.]

fọr′ti-tūde, *n.* [L. *fortitudo*, from *fortis*, strong, powerful.]

1. That strength or firmness of mind or soul which enables a person to encounter danger with coolness and courage, or to bear pain or adversity without murmuring, depression, or despondency; patient courage.

2. Physical strength; firmness; power of resisting attack.

3. In astrology, any accidental strengthening of the effect of a planet.

fọr-ti-tū′di-nous, *a.* Having courage and fortitude. [Rare.]

fōrt′let, *n.* A little fort. [Rare.]

fōrt′night (-nit *or* -nīt), *n.* [ME. *fourtenight, fourten night*, fourteen nights. Our ancestors reckoned time by nights and winters.] The space of fourteen days; two weeks.

fōrt′night-ly, *adv.* Once in a fortnight; at intervals of a fortnight.

fọr-tread′ (-tred′), *v.t.* To crush by treading upon. [Obs.]

fọr′tress, *n.* [ME. *fortresse*; OFr. *forteresce, fotelesce*; LL. *fortalitia*, a small fort, from L. *fortis*, strong, powerful.]

1. Any fortified place; a fort; a castle; a stronghold; a place of defense or security; as, the English have a strong *fortress* on the rock of Gibraltar.

2. Defense; safety; security.

> The Lord is my rock and my *fortress*. —Ps. xviii. 2.

Syn.—Fortification, castle, citadel.—A *fortress* is constructed for military purposes only, and is permanently garrisoned; a *fortification* is built to defend harbors, cities, etc.; a *castle* is an antique *fortress* used as a palatial dwelling; a *citadel* is the stronghold of a *fortress* or city.

fọr′tress, *v.t.*; fortressed (-trest), *pt.*, *pp.*;

fortressing, *ppr.* To furnish with fortresses; to guard; to fortify.

fọr-tū′it-ism, *n.* The doctrine or belief that the happenings from natural causes are fortuitous and not designed. [Rare.]

fọr-tū′i-tous, *a.* [L. *fortuitus*, casual, accidental, from *fors, fortis*, a chance, luck.] Accidental; casual; happening by chance; coming or occurring unexpectedly or without any known cause.

fọr-tū′i-tous-ly, *adv.* Accidentally; casually; by chance.

fọr-tū′i-tous-ness, *n.* The quality of being accidental; accident; chance.

fọr-tū′i-ty, *n.* [From L. *fortuitus*, casual, accidental.] Accident.

fọr′tū-nāte, *a.* 1. Coming by good luck or favorable chance; bringing some unexpected good; as, a *fortunate* event; a *fortunate* concurrence of circumstances; a *fortunate* ticket in a lottery.

2. Lucky; successful; receiving some unforeseen or unexpected good, or some good which was not dependent on one's own skill or efforts; as, a *fortunate* competitor for a prize, an office, or an honor.

Syn.—Lucky, fortuitous, prosperous, successful.—*Fortunate* and *lucky* are both applied to that which happens without the control of man; the former more according to the ordinary course of things; the latter something sudden and singular; hence we speak of a man as *fortunate* in his business and the ordinary concerns of life, but *lucky* in games of chance. *Fortuitous* is employed generally in matters of chance, while *prosperous* and *successful* seem to exclude the idea of what is *fortuitous*, although *prosperity* and *success* are both greatly aided by good *fortune*. *Fortunate* is employed for single circumstances; *prosperous* only for a train of circumstances.

fọr′tū-nāte-ly, *adv.* Luckily; successfully; happily; by good fortune, or favorable chance or issue.

fọr′tū-nāte-ness, *n.* Good luck; success; happiness.

fọr′tūne, *n.* [ME. *fortune*; OFr. *fortune*; L. *fortuna*, chance, hap, fate, fortune.]

1. Chance; accident; luck; the arrival of something in a sudden or unexpected manner; also, a fictitious power regarded as bestowing good or ill or controlling one's lot.

> Though *fortune's* malice overthrow my state.
> —Shak.

2. The good or ill that befalls man; success, good or bad; event.

> Our equal crimes shall equal *fortune* give.
> —Dryden.

3. The chance of life; means of living; wealth.

> His father dying, he was driven to London to seek his *fortune*. —Swift.

4. Estate; possessions; as, a gentleman of small or of large *fortune*.

5. The portion of a man or woman; generally, of a woman.

6. Futurity; future state or events; destiny; as, the young are anxious to have their *fortunes* told.

> You, who men's *fortunes* in their faces read.
> —Cowley.

7. One in possession of or heir to considerable wealth; particularly, a marriageable person of wealth; as, she is a great *fortune*. [Colloq.]

8. In astrology, a fortunate planet.

Syn.—Fate, luck, accident, chance, lot, destiny, wealth, possessions.

fọr′tūne, *v.t.* 1. To make fortunate or to tell the fortunes of. [Obs.]

2. To endow with a fortune. [Rare.]

fọr′tūne, *v.i.* To befall; to fall out; to happen; to come casually to pass. [Obs.]

fọr′tūne-book, *n.* A book to be consulted to discover future events.

fọr′tūne-hunt″ẽr, *n.* One seeking wealth by marriage.

fọr′tūne-less, *a.* Luckless; also, destitute of a fortune or portion.

fọr′tūne-tell″ẽr, *n.* One who practises forecasting the future of others.

fọr′tūn-īze, *v.t.* To regulate the fortune of. [Obs.]

fọr′ty, *n.*; *pl.* **fọr′ties.** [ME. *forti, fourty, feowerti*; AS. *feówertig*, forty; *feówer*, four, and *-tig*, ten.]

1. A cardinal number; four times ten, expressed symbolically by 40 or XL.

2. In lawn tennis, the third point scored.

Like forty; a colloquial expression signifying in high degree; as, it rained *like forty*.

The roaring forties; among mariners, the winds prevailing on the Atlantic ocean about the fortieth degree of latitude both north and south and in the Indian and South Pacific oceans.

fọr′ty, *a.* Denoting twice twenty units.

fọr′ty-fīve, *n.* A game at cards in which a game is won by scoring forty-five points.

fọr′ty-knot, *n.* A procumbent, herbaceous tropical plant of the amaranth family, characterized by its many nodes, opposite leaves, and sessile axillary flowers.

fọr′ty-nin′ẽr, *n.* An emigrant to California about or soon after 1849, in search of gold; an Argonaut.

fō′rum, *n.*; *pl.* **fō′rums** or **fō′rȧ.** [L., a market-place, public place.]

1. In Rome, a public place, where causes were judicially tried, and orations delivered to the people; also, a market-place.

2. A tribunal; a court; any assembly empowered to hear and decide causes.

fọr-wāke′, *v.t.* To tire as by loss of sleep. [Obs.]

fọr-wän′dẽr, *v.i.* To wander away; to rove wildly. [Obs.]

fọr′wărd, *v.t.*; forwarded, *pt., pp.*; forwarding, *ppr.* 1. To advance; to help onward; to promote; to accelerate; to quicken; to hasten; as, to *forward* the growth of a plant.

2. To send forward; to send toward the place of destination; to transmit; as, to *forward* a letter or despatches.

3. In bookbinding, to prepare (a book) for the finisher.

fọr′wărd, *a.* 1. Near or at the fore part; in advance of something else; as, the *forward* gun in a ship, or the *forward* ship in a fleet; the *forward* horse in a team.

2. Ready; prompt; strongly inclined.

> Only they would that we should remember the poor; the same which I also was *forward* to do. —Gal. ii. 10.

3. Ardent; eager; earnest; violent.

> Or lead the *forward* youth to noble war.
> —Prior.

4. Bold; confident; less reserved or modest than is proper; as, the boy is too *forward* for his years.

5. Advanced beyond the usual degree; advanced for the season; as, we have a *forward* spring.

6. Quick; hasty; too ready; as, be not *forward* to speak in public.

fọr′wărd, fọr′wărds, *adv.* [ME. *forwarde, forwardes*; AS. *foreweard*, forward; *fore*, fore, before, and *-weard*, -ward. The *s* was originally a genit. ending.] Toward a part or place before or in front; onward; progressively; opposed to *backward*.

fọr′wărd-ẽr, *n.* 1. One who promotes or advances in progress.

2. One who sends forward or transmits goods; a forwarding merchant.

3. In bookbinding, one who does the plain covering of a sewed book and prepares it for the finisher.

fọr′wărd-ing, *n.* 1. The act or employment of transmitting or sending forward merchandise and other property for others.

2. In bookbinding, the operation of plain-covering a sewed book, and preparing it for the finisher.

fọr′wărd-ly, *adv.* Eagerly; hastily; quickly; in a forward manner.

fọr′wărd-ness, *n.* The quality or state of being forward in any of its senses.

fọr-wāste′, *v.t.* To waste; to desolate entirely. [Obs.]

fọr-wēa′ry, *v.t.* To dispirit; to make very weary. [Obs.]

fọr-weep′, *v.i.* To weep much. [Obs.]

fọr-wēte′, *v.t.* [Obs.] See *Forewit*.

fọr-whȳ′, *conj.* Because. [Obs.]

fọr-wōrn′, *a.* Very greatly fatigued; exhausted. [Obs.]

fọr-wot′, *v.*, obsolete past tense of *forewit*.

fọr-wrap′ (-rap′), *v.t.* To wrap securely, so as to conceal. [Obs.]

fọr-yete′, *v.t.* [Obs.] See *Forget*.

fọr-yet′en, *v.*, obsolete past participle of *forget*.

fọr-yield′, *v.t.* To recompense; to give back. [Obs.]

fọr-zän′dō (fort-sän′dō), *adv.* [It., ppr. of *forzare*, to force.] With force; a direction in music.

fọr-zä′tō (fort-sä′tō), *adv.* Forzando.

foss, *n.* [Fr. *fosse*; L. *fossa*, a ditch, trench, f. pp. of *fodere*, to dig.]

1. A ditch, trench, or canal; specifically, the moat around the rampart of a castle.

2. In anatomy, a fossa.

fos′sȧ, *n.*; *pl.* **fos′sæ.** [L., a ditch, trench.] In anatomy, (a) a kind of cavity in a bone with a large aperture; (b) an oval depression in a soft part, as that presented by the septum of the right auricle of the heart.

fos′sāge, *n.* In old English law, a duty which the inhabitants of a walled town had to pay for keeping the moat or ditch clean.

fos′sak, *n.* A trout of English tide-waters, a variety of *Salmo fario*.

Fos-sā′ri-ăn, *n.* [LL. *Fossarii*, pl., from L. *fossa*, a ditch, trench.]

1. In ecclesiastical history, a sect of dissenters practising their peculiar worship in ditches and caves in the fifteenth century.

2. [f—] One of the clergy of the fourth century who dug graves.

fosse, *n.* Same as *Foss*.

fos′set, *n.* [Obs.] See *Faucet*.

fos-sette′, *n.* [Fr., dim. of *fosse*, a ditch, trench.]

1. A little hollow; a dimple.

2. In medicine, a small ulcer of the transparent cornea, the center of which is deep.

fos′sick, *v.i.*; fossicked (-sikt), *pt., pp.*; fossicking, *ppr.* [Prov. Eng. *fossick*, a troublesome fellow.]

1. To be troublesome. [Prov. Eng.]

2. In gold-digging, to undermine another's digging; to search for waste gold in relinquished workings, washing places, etc.; hence, to search for any object by which to make gain; as, to *fossick* for clients. [Australia.]

fos′sick-ẽr, *n.* One who works over the waste of gold fields. [Australia.]

fos′sil, *a.* [Fr. *fossile*; L. *fossilis*, dug out, dug up, from *fodere*, to dig up.]

1. Dug out of the earth; as, *fossil* coal; *fossil* salt.

2. Pertaining to or resembling fossils; changed into stone; petrified; as, *fossil* shells, bones, or wood.

3. Indicating, characteristic of, or suggesting that which is out of date; worn out; stagnant through age.

Fossil copal; Highgate resin; a resinous substance found in perforating the bed of blue clay at Highgate, near London, a true vegetable gum or resin partly changed by remaining in the earth.

Fossil cork, fossil flax, fossil paper, fossil wood; each a variety of the finer kinds of asbestos or amianthus, named from their resemblance to cork, flax, etc.

Fossil farina; a soft granular form of lime carbonate resembling meal; rock-meal; bergmehl.

Fossil ore; fossiliferous ore; specifically, red iron ore or hematite.

Fossil screw; the fossil cast of a univalve mollusk shaped like a uniformly tapering screw.

fos′sil, *n.* 1. Literally, anything dug out of the earth. [Obs.]

2. In geology, one of the various petrified forms of plants and animals which occur in the strata that compose the surface of our globe. Most of these fossil species, many of the genera, and some of the families, are extinct.

3. One who or that which is out of date; specifically, a person who has not advanced as have those about him.

fos-sil-if′ẽr-ous, *a.* [L. *fossilis*, dug out, fossil, and *ferre*, to bear.] Bearing or containing fossils; as, a *fossiliferous* rock or formation.

fos-sil″i-fi-cā′tion, *n.* The act or the process of becoming fossilized; a fossilized object.

fos′sil-ism, *n.* The orderly study of fossils; the condition of being a fossil; fossilology; fossilogy.

fos′sil-ist, *n.* One versed in the science of fossils.

fos″sil-i-zā′tion, *n.* The act or process of converting into a fossil; the state of being fossilized.

fos′sil-īze, *v.t.*; fossilized, *pt., pp.*; fossilizing, *ppr.* 1. To convert into a fossil; as, to *fossilize* bones or wood.

2. To render permanently antiquated; to cause to be out of harmony with present time and circumstances; to render insensible to new influences; as, age has a tendency to *fossilize* men's minds and ideas.

fos′sil-īze, *v.i.* To become or be changed into a fossil; to become rigid or fixed beyond the influence of progressive forces.

fos′sil-īzed, *a.* Changed to a fossil; fixed in views and opinions; antiquated.

fos-sil′ō-ġy, fos-sil-ol′ō-ġy, *n.* Same as *Fossilism*.

fos′sŏr, *n.*; *pl.* **fos-sō′rēs.** [L., from *fodere*, to dig.] A gravedigger. [See *Fossarian*, 2.]

Fos-sō′rēs, *n.pl.* [L., diggers.]

1. An extensive division of hymenopterous insects belonging to the division *Aculeata*, or those furnished with a sting in the females. To this division belong the garden-wasps, the smooth wasps, the sand-wasps, etc.

2. That group of quadrupeds which contains the burrowing-moles.

Fos-sō′ri-ȧ, *n.pl.* A division of insects substantially the same as the *Fossores*.

fos-sō′ri-ăl, *a.* 1. Digging; adapted for digging.

2. Of or pertaining to the *Fossores* or *Fossoria*.

fos-sō′ri-ăl, *n.* [LL. *fossorius*, from L. *fossor*, a digger.] An animal which digs into the earth for a retreat or lodge, and whose locomotive extremities are adapted for that purpose.

fos-sō′ri-ous, *a.* [LL. *fossorius*, from L. *fossor*, a digger.] Fossorial.

foss′rōad, *n.* A fossway.

fos′sū-lȧ, *n.*; *pl.* **fos′sū-læ.** A diminutive of *fossa*; a small ditch or depression.

fos′sū-lāte, *a.* [L. *fossula*, dim. of *fossa*, ditch, trench, and *-ate*.] Having trenches or depressions like trenches.

fos′sūle, *n.* Same as *Fossula.*

foss′wāy, *n.* One of the ancient roads built by the Romans in England, having a foss on each side; spelled also *fosseway.*

fos′tẽr, *v.t.*; fostered, *pt., pp.*; fostering, *ppr.* [ME. *foster*, from AS. *fostor*, *foster*, nourishment, rearing, from *foda*, food.]

1. To feed; to nourish; to support; to bring up.

Some say that ravens *foster* forlorn children. —Shak.

2. To cherish; to forward; to promote the growth of; to encourage; to sustain and promote; as, to *foster* passion or genius.

Syn.—Cherish, harbor, indulge.—To *foster* in the mind is to keep with care and positive endeavors; to *cherish* in the mind is to hold dear or set a value upon; to *harbor* is to allow room in the mind, and is generally taken in the worst sense, for giving admission to that which ought to be excluded; to *indulge* in the mind is to give the whole mind to, to make the chief source of pleasure.

fos′tẽr, *v.i.* To be nourished or trained up together. [Obs.]

fos′tẽr, *n.* A forester. [Obs.]

fos′tẽr-āge, *n.* The charge of nursing and rearing the child of another.

fos′tẽr-bābe, *n.* An infant foster-child.

fos′tẽr-brŏth″ẽr, *n.* A male nursed at the same breast or fed by the same nurse as another, but not the offspring of the same parents.

fos′tẽr-chīld, *n.* A child nursed by a woman not the mother, or bred by a man not the father.

fos′tẽr-dam, *n.* A nurse; one that performs the office of a mother by giving food to a child.

fos′tẽr-daugh″tẽr (-da″tẽr), *n.* A female adopted and nourished as one's own daughter.

fos′tẽr-ēarth, *n.* Earth by which a plant is nourished, though not its native soil.

fos′tẽr-ẽr, *n.* A nurse; one that feeds and nourishes in the place of parents.

fos′tẽr-fä″thẽr, *n.* One who takes the place of a father in bringing up and educating a child.

fos′tẽr-land, *n.* 1. The land or country which one adopts as a home.

2. In law, land set apart for the maintenance of a charity.

fos′tẽr-ling, *n.* A foster-child.

fos′tẽr-ment, *n.* Food; nourishment. [Obs.]

fos′tẽr-mŏth″ẽr, *n.* A nurse; a woman who nurses and cares for the child of another.

fos′tẽr-pâr″ent, *n.* A foster-father or a foster-mother.

fos′tẽr-sis″tẽr, *n.* A female, not a sister, reared with another by the same foster-parent or foster-parents.

fos′tẽr-sŏn, *n.* A male adopted and nourished as one's own son.

fos′tress, *n.* A female who feeds and cherishes; a nurse.

foth′ẽr, *n.* [AS. *fother*, *fothur*, a load, wagon-load.] An old unit of weight of about 2,400 pounds, used in weighing lead, lime, etc.; a two-horse load.

foth′ẽr, *v.t.*; fothered, *pt., pp.*; fothering, *ppr.* [Prob. from Ice. *fodhra*, to line or fur, from *fodhr*, a lining.] To endeavor to stop, as a leak in the bottom of a ship while afloat, by letting down a sail under her bottom by its corners, and putting chopped yarn, oakum, wool, cotton, etc., between it and the ship's sides.

fō′tive, *a* [From L. *fotus*, pp. of *fovere*, to warm.] Nourishing by warmth. [Obs.]

fot′măl, *n.* [Origin unknown.] A commercial term for seventy pounds of lead.

Fōu-cault′ (-kol′) **cur′rent.** See under *Current*, n.

fōu-gāde′, *n.* [Fr., from *fouge*; It. *foga*, fury, passion, from L. *fuga*, flight.] In the art of war, a little mine charged with powder and covered with stones or earth; sometimes dug outside of the works to defend them and sometimes beneath to destroy them by explosion.

fōu-gasse′, *n.* Same as *Fougade.*

fought (fọt), *v.*, past tense of *fight.*

fought′en, *v.*, obsolete past participle of *fight.*

foul, *a.*; *comp.* fouler; *superl.* foulest. [ME. *foul*, *ful*; AS. *fūl*, foul, rotten.]

1. Covered with or containing extraneous matter which is injurious, noxious, or offensive; filthy; dirty; not clean; as, a *foul* cloth; *foul* hands; a *foul* chimney

My face is *foul* with weeping. —Job xvi. 16.

2. Turbid; thick; muddy; as, *foul* water; a *foul* stream.

3. Impure; polluted; as, a *foul* mouth; scurrilous; obscene or profane; as, *foul* words.

4. Cloudy and stormy; rainy or tempestuous; as, *foul* weather.

5. Defiling; as, a *foul* disease.

6. Wicked; detestable; abominable; as, a *foul* deed; a *foul* spirit.

Babylon, the hold of every *foul* spirit. —Rev. xviii. 2.

7. Unfair; not honest; not lawful or according to established rules or customs; as, *foul* play.

8. Hateful; ugly; loathsome. [Obs.]

Hast thou forgot
The *foul* witch Sycorax? —Shak.

9. Disgraceful; shameful; as, a *foul* defeat.

Who first seduced them to that *foul* revolt? —Milton.

10. In printing, (a) having many errors, as a proof; (b) having the type mixed or wrongly distributed, as a case.

11. Among seamen, (a) entangled; hindered, as a rope; (b) covered with weeds or barnacles; as, the ship's bottom is *foul*; (c) not fair; contrary; as, a *foul* wind; (d) not favorable or safe for anchorage; dangerous; as, a *foul* road or bay.

Foul anchor; see under *Anchor.*

Foul ball; in baseball, a batted ball that first strikes the ground outside the foul-lines and does not roll or bound inside before reaching first or third base, or having struck the ground within the foul-lines rolls or bounds outside before reaching first or third base.

Foul-ball lines; in baseball, lines drawn from the home plate through first and third bases to the limits of the field.

Foul berth; in navigation, an anchorage in which a ship is likely to foul another ship.

Foul bill of health; among seamen, a certificate to the effect that a ship hails from a port where contagious disease prevails or that contagion prevails among its crew.

Foul copy; the first draft of a manuscript, containing emendations, corrections, erasures, etc., as distinguished from *fair copy.*

Foul strike; in baseball, a strike by the batsman when any part of his person is upon ground outside the lines of his position.

To fall foul; to come to loggerheads; to disagree; to quarrel.

To make foul water; in navigation, to sail in water so shallow that the keel of the ship stirs the mud at the bottom and renders the water foul.

Syn.—Defiled, dirty, disgusting, impure, low, loathsome, noisome, noxious, offensive, nasty, polluted, filthy, unclean, contaminated, coarse, obscene, vulgar.

foul, *v.t.*; fouled, *pt., pp.*; fouling, *ppr.* [ME. *foulen*, *fulen*; AS. *fylan*, to make foul, from *ful*, foul.]

1. To make filthy; to defile; to daub; to dirty; to bemire; to soil; as, to *foul* the clothes; to *foul* the face or hands.

2. To incrust or cover with dirt or other impediment; as, to *foul* the bore of a gun with burnt powder or the hull of a ship with barnacles.

3. To get into the way; to entangle; to impede; as, a ship *fouls* another ship.

4. In games, to commit an act against, as the established rules.

foul, *v.i.* 1. To become fouled; to be entangled; as, the vessels *fouled* in starting.

2. In games, to make a foul or foul play.

foul, *n.* 1. An interference; an act of fouling.

2. In games, an act, usually wilful, in violation of the rules.

3. In baseball, a ball so batted as to be foul.

fōu-lärd′, *n.* [Fr.] A kind of silk material originally brought from India; also, a silk handkerchief or cravat.

foul′-brọọd, *n.* A contagious bacterial disease affecting the larvæ of bees and giving rise to a foul odor.

foul′dẽr, *v.i.* To emit great heat. [Obs.]

foul′ly, *adv.* Filthily; nastily; hatefully; scandalously; disgracefully; shamefully; unfairly; dishonestly.

foul′märt, *n.* [ME. *fulmart*, *fulmard*; AS. *ful*, foul, and *mearth*, *meard*, a marten.] The stinking marten, *Putorius vulgaris*; the polecat of Europe; written also *foumart.*

foul′-mouthed, *a.* Using language scurrilous, opprobrious, obscene, or profane; commonly using bad language.

So *foul-mouthed* a witness never appeared in any cause. —Addison.

foul′ness, *n.* The quality of being foul or filthy; filthiness; defilement.

foul′-spō″ken, *a.* Slanderous; making use of foul language.

fou′märt, *n.* Same as *Foulmart.*

found, *v.*, past tense and past participle of *find.*

found, *v.t.*; founded, *pt., pp.*; founding, *ppr.* [ME. *founden*; OFr. *fonder*; L. *fundare*, to lay the bottom or foundation of a thing, from *fundus*, bottom.]

1. To lay the basis of; to fix, set, or place, as on something solid for support; to ground; to base; to establish on a basis literal or figurative; to fix firmly.

Power, *founded* on contract, can descend only to him who has right by that contract. —Locke.

2. To take the first steps or measures in erecting or building up; to begin to raise; to begin to form or lay the basis of; to originate; as, to *found* a college or library.

Confusion in the Table Round
Which good King Arthur *founded.* —Tennyson.

Syn.—Establish, institute, fix, set, build, set up, base, endow, rest, ground, plant, root.

found, *v.i.* To rest or rely; followed by *on* or *upon*; as, I *found upon* the evidence of my senses.

found, *v.t.* [Fr. *fondre*, to melt, to cast, from L. *fundo*, *fusum*, to pour out.] To cast; to form by melting a metal and pouring it into a mold.

found, *n.* A file having a thin body used in making combs.

foun-dā′tion, *n.* [ME. *foundacioun*, *fundacioun*; OFr. *fondation*; LL. *fundatio*, from L. *fundare*, to lay the bottom or foundation of a thing.]

1. The act of founding, fixing, establishing, or beginning to build.

2. The solid ground on which the walls of a building rest; also, that part of the building or wall which is under the surface of the ground; hence, the basis or groundwork of anything; that on which anything stands and by which it is supported.

Behold, I lay in Zion for a *foundation*, a stone a precious corner-stone.—Isa. xxviii. 16.

3. A donation or legacy appropriated to support an institution, and constituting a permanent fund, usually for a charitable purpose; a fund invested for a benevolent purpose; endowment.

He had an opportunity of going to school on a *foundation.* —Swift.

4. That which is founded or established by an endowment; an endowed institution or charity.

5. In millinery, dressmaking, fancywork, etc., the stiffening or first portion upon which the rest is formed or to which it is attached.

6. In bee-culture, wax inserted in a section as a start for a comb.

Syn.—Institution, establishment, footing, base, basis, origin, ground, groundwork, rudiments, substratum, underlying principle.

foun-dā′tion-course, *n.* Same as *Base-course.*

foun-dā′tion-ẽr, *n.* One who derives support from the funds or foundation of a college or great school. [Eng.]

foun-dā′tion-less, *a.* Having no foundation.

foun-dā′tion-mus″lin, *n.* A loosely woven gummed fabric used for stiffening in the manufacture of garments.

foun-dā′tion-schọọl, *n.* In England, a school established by endowment.

foun-dā′tion-stōne, *n.* Any one of the great stones constituting the foundation of a building; specifically, the corner-stone.

found′ẽr, *n.* [ME. *founder*, *fondoure*; OFr. *fondeor*, *fondour*; Pr. *fundator*, a founder, from L. *fundare*, to found.] One who or that which founds; a builder; an establisher; an originator.

Founder's shares; in law, shares issued to the promoters of a corporation or public company.

found′ẽr, *n.* [OFr. *fondeur*, from LL. *fundator*, from L. *fundere*, to pour, found.] A caster; one who casts metals in various forms; as, a *founder* of cannon, bells, hardware, printing-types, etc.

Founder's dust; same as *Facing*, 2.

Founder's sand; a fine sand used in molding.

foun′dẽr, *n.* In veterinary surgery, a lameness occasioned by inflammation within the hoof of a horse.

foun′dẽr, *v.i.*; foundered, *pt., pp.*; foundering, *ppr.* [ME. *foundren*, to founder, cast down; OFr. *fondrer*, to fall in, sink, from *fond*, L. *fundus*, bottom.]

1. In seamen's language, to fill or be filled with water, and sink, as a ship.

2. To fail; to miscarry.

3. To trip; to fall, as a lame horse.

foun′dẽr, *v.t.* 1. To cause internal inflammation and great soreness in the feet of (a horse), so as to disable or lame.

2. To cause to fill with water and sink, as a ship.

foun′dẽr-ous, *a.* Liable to sink from beneath; ruinous; as, a *founderous* road.

found′ẽr-shaft, *n.* The first shaft of a mine.

found′ẽr-y, *n.* Same as *Foundry.*

found′ing, *n.* The art of casting or forming of melted metal any article, according to a given design or pattern.

found′ling, *n.* [ME. *foundling*, *fundeling*, from *funden*, pp. of *finden*, to find, and dim. *-ling.*] A deserted or exposed infant; a child found without a parent or owner.

found′ling-hos″pi-tăl, *n.* A hospital for the care of foundlings.

found′ress, *n.* A female founder; a woman who founds or establishes or who endows with a fund.

found'ry, *n.*; *pl.* **found'ries.** 1. A building occupied, fitted, and furnished for casting metals.

2. Metal-casting. [Obs.]

found'ry-i"ron (-ŭrn), *n.* Iron containing the proper amount of carbon to render it fit for castings.

found'ry-lā"dle, *n.* A pot-shaped iron vessel for receiving molten metal from the furnace and transferring it to the molds.

found'ry-proof, *n.* In stereotyping, the last proof previous to making a plate.

fount, *n.* In printing, a font, as of type.

fount, *n.* [L. *fons, fontis*, a fountain.] A fountain; a source of supply, as a spring.

foun'tain (-tin), *n.* [ME. *fountayne, fontayn*; OFr. *funtaine, fontaine*; LL. *fontana*, from L. *fons, fontis*, a fountain.]

1. A spring or source of water which is natural; the head or source of a river.

2. An artificial spout, jet, or shower of water, formed either by the pressure of a head or by means of compressed air; also, the basin or architectural structure erected for receiving and supplying water for any useful or ornamental purpose.

Ornamental Fountain.—Villa Borghese, Rome.

3. Origin; first principle or cause; the source of anything.

4. In heraldry, a circle called a roundel, divided into six spaces by waved lines across the shield, and tinctured argent and azure.

Fountain.

5. One of various reservoirs or supply-chambers from which something is drawn; as, (a) the barrel of a *fountain*-pen; (b) the reserve-bulb of a *fountain*-inkstand; (c) the cylinder holding the oil in various styles of lamps; (d) the container used to hold aerated waters in transit; by extension, the entire apparatus used in drawing aerated drinks; a soda-*fountain*.

Hero's fountain; a pneumatic apparatus in which the elastic force of a confined body of air, increased by hydraulic pressure and reacting upon the surface of water in a closed reservoir, produces a jet which may rise above that surface to a height equal to the effective height of the pressing column.

Fountain of youth; a fabled fountain whose waters were reputed to have the power of restoring youth to the aged.

Hero's Fountain.

foun'tain-head (-tin-hed), *n.* Primary source; original; first principle; the source of a stream.

foun'tain-less, *a.* Having no fountain; wanting a spring.

For barren desert, *fountainless* and dry.
—Milton.

foun'tain-pump, *n.* A force-pump throwing a jet or spray.

foun'tain-shell, *n.* In zoölogy, the conch of the West Indies, *Strombus gigas*.

foun'tain-tree, *n.* 1. A popular name of the Indian cedar, *Cedrus Deodara*, from the large quantity of turpentine which it yields.

2. A popular name for a Brazilian tree, *Cæsalpinia pluviosa*, the young twigs of which yield, when shaken, a clear drinkable fluid.

fount'ful, *a.* Full of springs.

fōur, *a.* [ME. *four, fowr, feower*; AS. *feower*, four.] Twice two; denoting the sum of two and two or three and one.

fōur, *n.* 1. A cardinal number, one more than three, and represented by the symbols 4 and IV.

2. A four-horse team; usually in the phrase, a coach and *four*.

3. A boat having a crew of four rowers; collectively, the crew.

4. A domino, card, etc., having four spots.

5. [*pl.*] In poker, four cards of one denomination.

fōurb, fōurbe, *n.* [Fr. *fourbe*.] A tricky fellow; a cheat. [Obs.]

fōur-ché' (-shā'), *a.* [Fr. *fourché*, from L. *furca*, a fork.] In heraldry, having the ends forked and the forks abruptly terminated, as in a cross.

Cross Fourché.

fōur-chette', *n.* [Fr., dim. of *fourche*, a fork.]

1. In anatomy, the thin posterior commissure by which the labia majora of the pudendum unite.

2. In surgery, an instrument used to raise and support the tongue during the operation of dividing the frenum.

3. In glove-making, the piece between the two fingers to which the front and back portions are sewed.

fōur'-cor"nẽred, *a.* Having four corners.

fōur'-flush, *v.i.*; four-flushed (-flusht), *pt., pp.*; four-flushing, *ppr.* In poker, to draw to fill a bobtail flush; to bet after failing to fill; hence, to bluff; to make a pretense of competency when incompetent. [Slang.]

fōur'-flush, *n.* A bobtail flush; also, an incompetent person posing as competent; a bluff. [Slang.]

fōur'fōld, *a.* [ME. *fourfold, fourfald*; AS. *feowerfeald*; *feower*, four, and *-feald*, -fold.] Quadruple; four times told.

fōur'foot"ed, *a.* Quadruped; having four feet, as the horse and the ox.

fōur-gon', *n.* [Fr.] A tumbril; a baggage-wagon.

fōur'hand"ed, *a.* 1. Having four hands or hand-like extremities.

2. Requiring or adapted to four hands, as a game of cards or a piece of music for the piano or organ.

Fōu'ri-ẽr-ism, *n.* The system of Charles Fourier (1772-1837), a Frenchman, who recommended the reorganization of society into small communities living in common.

Fōu'ri-ẽr-ist, *n.* An adherent of or believer in Fourierism.

Fōu'ri-ẽr-ite, *n.* A Fourierist.

fōur'-in-hand, *n.* 1. A vehicle having one driver for a team of four horses; the team so driven; also used adjectively.

2. A kind of necktie commonly so knotted that the ends hang vertically.

fōur'ling, *n.* 1. A quadruplet; one of four born at a time.

2. In mineralogy, a four-parted crystal.

fōur-neau' (-nō'), *n.*; *pl.* **fōur-neaux'** (-nōz'). [Fr., a stove, chamber of a mine.] In military mining, a powder-chamber.

fōur'-o'clock", *n.* 1. In botany, an ornamental plant with flowers of various colors which open about four o'clock in the afternoon and close in the morning, cultivated for ornament; *Mirabilis jalapa*; also called *marvel-of-Peru*.

2. In zoölogy, a name given to the Australian honey-eater or friar-bird.

fōur'pence, *n.* An English silver coin worth about eight cents of United States money.

fōur'pence-half'pen-ny (-hā'pen-i), *n.* The name of a Spanish silver coin once current in the United States, of the value of the sixteenth part of a dollar; called also *fippenny bit*. [Obs.]

fōur'-pōst"ẽr, *n.* A large bed having four posts or pillars for the curtains.

fōur'-pound"ẽr, *n.* A cannon the bore of which takes a four-pound ball.

four"ra"gere' (fo͞o"rä"zhãr') *n.* [Fr.] A decoration granted an entire body of troops for bravery in action. It is a braided cord of a designated color, worn around the shoulder seam of the left sleeve of the coat by every member of the unit so decorated.

fōur'scōre, *a.* Four times twenty; eighty.

fōur'scōre, *n.* [ME. *fourscore*; *four*, and *score*.] The number eighty.

fōur'sōme, *a.* Consisting of four. [Obs. or Scot.]

fōur'sōme, *n.* In golf, a match with two on each side.

fōur'squāre (-skwãr), *a.* Having four sides and four angles equal; quadrangular.

fōur'teen, *a.* [ME. *fourtene, feowertene*; AS. *feówertyne*, fourteen; *feówer*, four, and *teon*, pl. *-tyne*, ten.] Four and ten; twice seven; represented by the symbols 14 and XIV.

fōur'teenth, *a.* The ordinal of fourteen; the fourth after the tenth; one of fourteen equal parts of the whole of anything.

fōurth, *a.* [AS. *feórtha, feówrtha*; *feówer*, four, and *-tha, -th*, the ordinal suffix.]

1. The ordinal of four; the next after the third.

2. Describing one of four equal parts of a thing or number.

fōurth, *n.* 1. One of four equal parts into which a whole is divided; the quotient of a unit divided by four; a quarter.

2. In music, an interval composed of two tones and a semitone.

The Fourth; in the United States, a popular abbreviation of the fourth of July; Independence day.

fōurth'ly, *adv.* In the fourth place.

fōur'-way, *a.* Pertaining to four ways; denoting four passages.

Four-way cock; a kind of automatic valve used for passing steam alternately to the upper and lower ends of the cylinder and to the condenser, in a steam-engine, and for other purposes. It is shown in sections in the figure; *a* is the communication with the steam-pipe, *b* the passage to the upper end of the cylinder, *c* to the condenser, and *d* to the lower end of the cylinder. When the center is turned a quarter of a revolution the action is reversed, and the steam, instead of entering the cylinder at the lower end by *d*, will enter at the upper end through *b*.

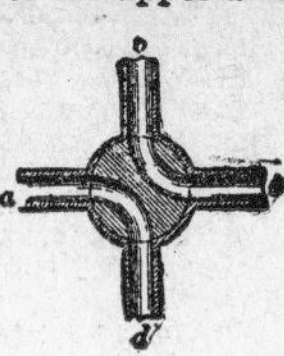

Four-way Cock.

fōur'-wheeled, *a.* Having or running on four wheels.

fōur'-wheel"ẽr, *n.* A four-wheeled vehicle; specifically, in London, a four-wheeled cab.

fōus'sȧ, *n.* [Native name.] A catlike, carnivorous animal of Madagascar, *Cryptoprocta ferox*.

fōu'tẽr, *n.* [Fr. *foutre*, from L. *futuere*, to have sexual intercourse with.] A despicable fellow. [Prov. Eng. and Scot.]

fōu'trȧ, *n.* A fig; a scoff. [Obs.]

fōu'ty, *a.* Despicable; mean; base. [Prov. Eng. and Scot.]

fō'vē-ȧ, *n.*; *pl.* **fō'vē-æ.** [L.] A pit or shallow depression.

fō'vē-āte, *a.* [L. *fovea*, a pit, and *-ate*.] In botany, pitted; having depressions.

fō-vē'ō-lȧ, *n.*; *pl.* **fō-vē'ō-læ.** [Dim. of L. *fovea*, a pit.] A diminutive pit; a fovea.

fō'vē-ō-lāte, *a.* In botany, marked by minute depressions or pits.

fō'vē-ō-lā-ted, *a.* Foveolate.

fō-vil'lȧ, *n.*; *pl.* **fō-vil'læ.** [A dim. from L. *fovere*, to warm, cherish.] In botany, the minute powder or semifluid matter contained in the interior of the pollen-grain, which is the immediate agent in fertilization.

fowl, *n.* [ME. *fowl, fowel, fugel*; AS. *fugel, fugol*, a fowl; D. *vogel*; Ice. *fugl, fogl*, a fowl, bird; perhaps from root, to fly.] Any bird; particularly, any large edible bird, as the hen, duck, or turkey; restrictedly, the domestic cock and hen, sometimes called *barnyard* and *barndoor fowls*. This is now the usual meaning of the word, *bird* being the general term for a feathered biped. *Fowl* is generally unchanged in the plural when used in a collective or generic sense.

fowl, *v.i.*; fowled, *pt., pp.*; fowling, *ppr.* To catch or kill wild birds, either for sport or for food; as, to hunt, fish, and *fowl*.

fowl'ẽr, *n.* A sportsman who pursues wild fowl, or takes or kills them for food; one who engages in fowling.

fow'lẽr-ite, *n.* A zinkiferous variety of rhodonite; named after Dr. Samuel Fowler of New Jersey.

Fow'lẽr's sō-lū'tion. See under *Solution*.

fowl'ing, *n.* The practice of catching or shooting fowls or birds.

fowl'ing-piēce, *n.* A light shotgun for shooting birds.

fox, *n.* [AS. *fox*, a fox.]

1. A carnivorous animal, *Canis vulpes*, with a straight tail and erect ears. It burrows in the earth, is remarkable for its cunning, and preys on rabbits, poultry, wild birds, etc. The red *fox* of Europe, the red, gray, and cross *foxes* of North America, and the white or blue *fox* of the arctic regions are well-known species. The black or silver-gray *fox*, a variety of the red *fox* of North America, produces very valuable fur. The gray *fox* of the United States, found south of Pennsylvania, is sufficiently different to have been placed in another genus, *Urocyon*, to which the coast *fox* of California also belongs. In the English Bible, the word *fox* sometimes refers to the jackal. *Reynard* is an appellation often applied to the *fox* in fable and poetry.

Common Fox (*Canis vulpes*).

2. The foxfish.

3. A sly, cunning fellow; as, that *fox*, Herod Agrippa.

4. In seamen's language, a small strand of rope, made by twisting several rope-yarns together; used for seizings or mats.

5. [F—] One of a tribe of Indians. [See *Foxes*.]

Arctic fox; one of the most notable of the true foxes. It is of a dark or bluish-gray color.

but turns white in winter; also called the *isatis*, and *white* or *blue fox*.

Fox and geese; a game played with pins or checkers on a chessboard or cross-shaped board; also, one of several games resembling tag, played by boys.

fox, *v.t.*; foxed (foxt), *pt.*, *pp.*; foxing, *ppr.* To intoxicate; to stupefy. [Obs.]

fox, *v.t.* To make sour; as, to *fox* beer, in the process of fermentation.

fox, *n.* A sword. [Obs.]

fox, *v.i.* 1. To turn sour; applied to beer when it sours in fermenting.

2. To become discolored by damp, rust, etc., as timber or paper.

fox, *v.i.* 1. To hunt the fox.

2. To act with cunning like a fox; to dissimulate.

fox, *v.t.* In shoemaking, (a) to ornament the upper of (a shoe) with fancy leather; (b) to furnish with a new upper.

fox′=bat, *n.* A bat of the family *Pteropodidæ*, including some of the largest of the bat tribe, one species, the *Pteropus edulis*, or kalong, attaining a length of from four to five feet from the tip of one wing to the tip of the other. It inhabits Australia, Java, Sumatra, Borneo, etc., as well as the continents of Asia and Africa. It has its name from its foxlike face.

fox′=bōlt, *n.* A bolt having one end split to receive a fox-wedge, which, when the bolt is driven in, secures it.

fox′=brush, *n.* The tail of a fox.

fox′=cāse, *n.* The skin of a fox. [Rare.]

fox′=eärth, *n.* A hole in the earth to which a fox resorts to hide itself.

foxed (foxt), *a.* Discolored or stained; literally, with marks resembling the color of a fox; marked with yellowish-brown or rusty spots; often said of paper that has become spotted owing to some fault in the manufacture.

Fox′eṣ, *n.pl.* A tribe of North American Indians, formerly located with the Sacs in the vicinity of Green Bay, Wis.; the Outagamies.

fox′=ē′vil, *n.* Same as *Alopecia*.

fox′fish, *n.* 1. The fox-shark.

2. The gemmous dragonet, so called from its being covered with spots like gems.

fox′glōve, *n.* [AS. *foxes glōfa*, fox's glove.] A common European flowering plant, *Digitalis purpurea*. Its flowers are campanulate, and somewhat resemble the finger of a glove. It is one of the most stately and beautiful of the European herbaceous plants, and is used in medicine as a sedative, narcotic, and diuretic in diseases of the heart and dropsy.

Bring orchis, bring the *foxglove* spire.—Tennyson.

Foxglove (*Digitalis purpurea*).

fox′=grāpe, *n.* A name given to several North American varieties of grape, as *Vitis Labrusca* and *Vitis cordifolia*, from their musky or foxy perfume.

fox′hound, *n.* A hound for chasing foxes; a variety of hound in which are combined fleetness, strength, fine scent, and staying qualities. It is supposed to be of a mixed breed, between the staghound and the greyhound. It is commonly of a white color with patches of black and tan.

Foxhound.

fox′=hunt, *n.* The chase or hunting of a fox.

fox′=hunt″ēr, *n.* One who hunts foxes; or, a horse used in fox-hunting.

fox′=hunt″ing, *n.* The practice or sport of hunting foxes.

fox′=hunt″ing, *a.* Pertaining to or fond of hunting foxes; as, a *fox-hunting* parson.

fox′i-ness, *n.* 1. The condition of being foxy; craft; cunning; shrewdness.

2. The quality of having a musky or foxy smell, as some grapes.

fox′i-ness, *n.* 1. The state of being foxed, as paper or timber.

2. Harsh or sour in taste, as beer.

fox′ish, *a.* Foxlike. [Rare.]

fox′like, *a.* Resembling a fox in qualities; cunning; foxy.

fox′=shärk, *n.* The thresher-shark or sea-fox, *Alopias vulpes*.

fox′ship, *n.* The character or qualities of a fox; cunning; foxiness.

fox′=sleep, *n.* A feigned sleep.

fox′=spar″rōw, *n.* A large sparrow of North America; so called from its rusty-red or fox-like color.

fox′=squir″rel (-skwir″), *n.* The largest tree-squirrel of eastern North America. It is about twelve inches long, and varies in color from black to shades of red, rusty-brown and gray; also called *cat-squirrel*.

fox′tāil, *n.* 1. The tail of a fox; also called *fox-brush*.

2. In metallurgy, the cinder, more or less of a cylindrical form and hollow in the center, obtained in the last stage of the charcoal-finery process.

3. Same as *Foxtail-grass*.

Foxtail wedging; in joinery, a method of wedging performed by sticking into the point of a wooden bolt a thin wedge of hard wood, which, when the bolt reaches the bottom of the hole, splits, expands, and secures it.

fox′tāil=gràss, *n.* The common name given to the grasses of the genera *Alopecurus* and *Setaria* because of the close cylindrical panicle in which the spikelets of flowers are arranged. Of the fourteen species known, one of the commonest, *Alopecurus pratensis*, is an abundant natural grass in meadows and pastures, and is an excellent fodder plant.

fox′=ter′ri-ēr, *n.* One of the different kinds of terriers trained or used to unearth foxes; a close-haired dog, either smooth or rough-coated, generally white, or white with spots of black and tan, commonly kept in the United States as a housedog or watchdog.

fox′=trot, *n.* A short-stepped pace, as of a horse, in slackening speed from a trot to a walk.

fox′=wedġe (-wej), *n.* In carpentry, etc., a wedge used to expand the split end of a fox-bolt, to fasten it in a hole or mortise. [See *Foxtail wedging*.]

fox′=wolf (-wulf), *n.* A South American canine quadruped, one of several which resemble both foxes and wolves.

fox′y, *a.* 1. Pertaining to foxes; resembling a fox in appearance or character; suggestive of a fox or of cunning; wily; tricky.

Modred's narrow *foxy* face. —Tennyson.

2. A term applied to grapes which have the coarse flavor of the fox-grape.

3. Of the color of the red fox; rufous; reddish; applied to paintings when the shadows and lower tones have too much of a yellowish, reddish-brown color.

fox′y, *a.* 1. Discolored; stained; applied in dyeing to colors which take on an undesirable reddish shade.

2. Sour, as beer.

foy, *n.* [OFr. *foy*, *foi*, faith.] Faith; fealty. [Obs.]

foy, *n.* A feast given by one who is about to leave a place, or has just returned from a journey. [Obs.]

foy-er′ (fwo-yā′), *n.* [Fr., hearth, fireside, lobby, from LL. *focarius*, from L. *focus*, a hearth, fireplace.]

1. A public room or lobby near the entrance of a theater or opera-house.

2. In a furnace, the part which holds the molten metal.

foy′ṣōn, *n.* [Obs.] See *Foison*.

fō′zi-ness, *n.* The state or quality of being fozy. [Scot.]

fō′zy, *a.* Spongy; lacking substance; soft and puffy. [Scot.]

frä, *n.* [It.] Brother; a monk's or friar's title; as, *Fra* Augustine.

frä, *adv.* and *prep.* From; fro. [Scot.]

frab, *v.i.* and *v.t.* To nag; to plague; to scold; to worry. [Prov. Eng.]

frab′bit, *a.* Peevish; cross.

frā′cās, *n.* [Fr., a crash, disturbance, tumult, from *fracasser*; It. *frassare*, to break in pieces, destroy; *fra*, within, amidst, and *cassare*, from L. *quassare*, intens. of *quatere*, to shake.] A noisy quarrel; a disturbance; a brawl; an uproar.

frāche, *n.* [Perhaps from Fr. *fraiche*, f. of *frais*, fresh.] In glass-making, an iron pan in which glass vessels newly formed are placed, to be put into the lower oven over the furnace.

fraçt′ed, *a.* [L. *fractus*, pp. of *frangere*, to break.] In heraldry, having a part displaced as if broken; as, a chevron *fracted*.

Chevron Fracted.

frac′tion, *n.* [L. *fractio* (-*onis*), a breaking, from *frangere*, to break.]

1. The act of breaking or state of being broken, especially by violence. [Rare.]

2. Specifically, in ecclesiastical affairs, the rite of breaking the bread in the celebration of the eucharist.

3. A small portion; a fragment; as, a *fraction* of time.

4. In arithmetic and algebra, one or more aliquot parts of a unit or whole number; any division of a whole number or unit, as $\frac{2}{5}$, two fifths, $\frac{1}{4}$, one fourth, which are called *vulgar fractions*. In these, the figure above the line is called the *numerator*, and the figure below the line the *denominator*. In *decimal fractions*, the denominator is 10, 100, 1000, etc. They are commonly expressed by writing the numerator only with a point before it, by which it is separated from whole numbers; thus .5, which denotes five tenths, $\frac{5}{10}$, or half of a unit; .25, that is, $\frac{25}{100}$, or a fourth part of a unit.

Complex fraction; a fraction which has a fraction in either its numerator or denominator, or in each of them.

Compound fraction; a fraction of a fraction.

Improper fraction; a fraction whose numerator is not less than the denominator, as $\frac{5}{5}$, $\frac{8}{5}$.

Proper fraction; a fraction whose numerator is less than the denominator.

Simple fraction; a fraction which expresses one or more of the equal parts into which the unit is divided, without reference to any other fraction.

frac′tion-ăl, *a.* 1. Of or pertaining to fractions; constituting a fraction; as, *fractional* currency; *fractional* numbers.

2. Fragmentary; small; inconsiderable; as, a *fractional* part of the audience.

Fractional crystallization; in chemistry, the separation of different substances by successive solutions and crystallizations.

Fractional currency; see under *Currency*.

Fractional distillation; a method of distillation for separating two liquids which have different boiling-points.

frac′tion-ăl-ly, *adv.* In a fractional manner; by a fraction.

frac′tion-āte, *v.t.*; fractionated, *pt.*, *pp.*; fractionating, *ppr.* To separate chemically by successive operations, as by distillation.

frac′tious, *a.* Apt to break out into a passion; apt to quarrel; cross; snappish; unruly; as, a *fractious* man or horse.

Syn.—Perverse, cross, irritable, petulant, pettish, waspish, snappish, peevish.

frac′tious-ly, *adv.* Passionately; snappishly.

frac′tious-ness, *n.* A cross or snappish temper; the quality of being fractious.

frac′tūr-ăl, *a.* Pertaining to a fracture.

frac′tūre, *n.* [OFr. *fracture*; L. *fractura*, a breaking, a breach, cleft, from *frangere*, to break.]

1. A rupture of a solid body; the act or result of breaking; especially, a break caused by violence.

2. In surgery, the breaking of a bone. A *fracture* is *simple* or *compound*; simple when the bone only is divided; compound when the bone is broken, with a laceration of the integuments. A fracture is termed *transverse*, *longitudinal*, or *oblique*, according to its direction in regard to the axis of the bone.

3. In mineralogy, the manner in which a mineral breaks, and by which its texture is displayed; the broken surface; as, a compact *fracture*; a fibrous *fracture*; foliated, striated, or conchoidal *fracture*, etc.

frac′tūre, *v.t.*; fractured, *pt.*, *pp.*; fracturing, *ppr.* To break; to burst asunder; to separate the continuous parts of; as, to *fracture* the skull; to *fracture* a bone.

frac′tūre, *v.i.* To undergo fracture; to break; as, this stone *fractures* easily.

fræn′ū-lum, *n.* See *Frenulum*.

fræ′num, *n.* See *Frenum*.

Frā-gā′ri-ȧ, *n.* [L. *fraga*, pl., strawberries.] The strawberry genus, a genus of perennial herbs with creeping stolons, natural order *Rosaceæ*. Only a few species are known. The fruit consists of numerous small, hard achenes sunk in the surface of a large fleshy receptacle. [See *Strawberry*.]

fraġ′ile, *a.* [L. *fragilis*, easily broken, frail, from *frangere*, to break.]

1. Brittle; easily broken; frail; delicate.

The stalk of ivy is tough, and not *fragile*. —Bacon.

2. Weak; liable to fail; easily destroyed; as, *fragile* arms.

Syn.—Brittle, frail, frangible, weak.

fraġ′ile-ly, *adv.* In a fragile manner.

frȧ-ġil′i-ty, *n.* [L. *fragilitas*, from *fragilis*, easily broken, frail.]

1. The condition or quality of being fragile; brittleness; easiness to be broken.

2. Weakness; liability to fail; frailness.

frag′ment, *n.* [L. *fragmentum*, a fragment, remnant, from *frangere*, to break.]

1. A part broken off; a piece separated from anything by breaking.

Gather up the *fragments* that remain. —John vi. 12.

2. A part separated from the rest; a small detached portion; an imperfect part; as, *fragments* of ancient writings.

The *fragments* of the golden day.—Tennyson.

frag-men′tăl, *a.* and *n.* I. *a.* Consisting of fragments; fragmentary.

II. *n.* In geology, a fragmentary rock.

frag′men-tā-ri-ly, *adv.* In a fragmentary manner.

frag′men-tā-ri-ness, *n.* The state of being in fragments; lack of connection.

frag'men-tā-ry, *a.* Composed of fragments; disconnected; incomplete; broken up.

Fragmentary rocks; in geology, rocks formed of fragments of other rocks, as tufas, agglomerates, conglomerates, and breccias.

frag'ment-ed, *a.* Broken into pieces; existing in fragments.

frā'gŏr, *n.* A strong, sweet odor. [Obs.]

frā'gŏr, *n.* [L. *fragor*, a breaking, crashing, from *frangere*, to break.] A loud, harsh sound; a crash. [Rare.]

frā'grānce, *n.* [L. *fragrantia*, from *fragrans* (*-antis*), fragrant, ppr. of *fragrare*, to emit an odor.] Sweetness of smell; that quality of bodies which affects the olfactory nerves with an agreeable sensation; pleasing scent; grateful odor; the state of being fragrant.

Eve separate he spies,
Veiled in a cloud of *fragrance*. —Milton.

frā'grăn-cy, *n.* Fragrance.

frā'grănt, *a.* [L. *fragrans* (*-antis*), ppr. of *fragrare*, to emit an odor.] Sweet of smell; odorous; having an agreeable odor.

Fragrant the fertile earth
After soft showers. —Milton.

Syn.—Odorous, scented, perfumed, balmy, sweet-smelling, aromatic, sweet-scented, odoriferous, spicy.

frā'grănt-ly, *adv.* With sweet scent.

frāight (frāt), *a.* Fraught. [Obs.]

frāil, *a.*; *comp.* frailer; *superl.* frailest. [ME. *freyl*, *freel*; OFr. *frele*, from L. *fragilis*, easily broken, brittle.]

1. Weak; infirm; liable to fail and decay; subject to casualties; easily destroyed; perishable; not firm or durable.

That I may know how *frail* I am.
—Ps. xxxix. 4.

2. Weak in mind or resolution; liable to error or deception; specifically, of unstable virtue; as, woman fair but *frail*.

Man is *frail* and prone to evil. —Taylor.

Syn.—Delicate, weak, fragile, frangible.

frāil, *n.* [ME. *fraiel*, *frayle*; OFr. *fraiel*, from LL. *frælum*, a basket.]

1. A flexible basket made of rushes, used in packing dried fruits, as dates, figs, and raisins.

2. A rush used for weaving baskets.

3. The variable quantity of raisins contained in a *frail*; it may be 32, 56, or 75 pounds.

frāil'ly, *adv.* Weakly; infirmly.

frāil'ness, *n.* Weakness; infirmity.

frāil'ty, *n.*; *pl.* **frāil'ties**. 1. Weakness of resolution; infirmity; liableness to be deceived or seduced.

God knows our *frailty*, and pities our weakness. —Locke.

2. A foible or infirmity resulting from some weakness; a fault.

No further seek his merits to disclose,
Or draw his *frailties* from their dread abode.
—Gray.

3. Frailness; infirmity of body.

Syn.—Frailness, infirmity, failing, foible, imperfection.

frāi'schēur (frā'shēr), *n.* [Fr.] Freshness; coolness. [Obs.]

frāiṣe, *n.* [Fr. *fraise*, originally, a ruff.]

1. In fortification, a defense consisting of pointed stakes driven into the ramparts, in a horizontal or inclined position.

2. In mechanics, a grooved tool used by masons for enlarging drill-holes.

frāiṣe, **froiṣe**, *n.* [Prov. Eng.] A pancake with bacon in it. [Obs.]

frāiṣe, *v.t.*; fraised, *pt.*, *pp.*; fraising, *ppr.* 1. In stone-working, to enlarge (a drill-hole) with a fraise.

2. In military affairs, to protect with a fraise.

frak'en, *n.* A freckle. [Obs.]

frām'ā-ble, *a.* Capable of being framed.

fram-bœ'si-ȧ, *n.* [Fr. *framboise*, a raspberry.] In medicine, the yaws, a skin disease, prevalent mostly in the tropics, and characterized by excrescences resembling raspberries.

frāme, *v.t.*; framed, *pt.*, *pp.*; framing, *ppr.* [ME. *framen*, to construct, build; AS. *fremman*, *fremian*, to advance, promote, execute, from *fram*, strong, valiant.]

1. To construct by fitting and uniting together the several parts; to fabricate by orderly construction and union of various parts; as, to *frame* a house or other building.

2. To make; to compose; to contrive; to plan; to devise; in a bad sense, to invent or fabricate, as something false.

For thou art *framed* of the firm truth of valour. —Shak.

3. To fit, as for a specific end; to regulate; to adjust; to shape; to conform; as, to *frame* our lives according to the rules of the gospel.

Framed to make woman false. —Shak.

4. To execute; to perform. [Obs.]

5. To support. [Obs.]

6. To surround or provide with a frame, as a picture.

Syn.—Adjust, compose, contrive, fabricate, fit, form, invent, plan.

frāme, *v.i.* 1. To shape; to arrange. [Obs.]

2. To contrive. [Obs.]

3. To wash out ore with the aid of a frame.

frāme, *n.* [ME. *frame*, a fabric, structure, advantage, benefit, from AS. *fremu*, *freme*, profit, advantage.]

1. Anything composed of parts fitted and united; fabric; structure; specifically, bodily structure; make or build of a person; physical constitution; skeleton; as, a person of robust *frame*.

This goodly *frame*, the earth, seems to me a sterile promontory. —Shak.

2. The main timbers of a structure fitted and joined together for the purpose of supporting and strengthening the whole; framework; as, the *frame* of a house, barn, bridge, or ship.

3. Any kind of case or structure made for admitting, inclosing, or supporting things; as, the *frame* of a window, door, picture, or looking-glass.

4. Among printers, a stand to support the cases in which the types are contained.

5. Among founders, a kind of ledge inclosing a board, which being filled with wet sand, serves as a mold for castings.

6. A sort of loom on which linen, silk, etc., is stretched for quilting or embroidering, or on which lace, stockings, and the like are made.

7. Form; scheme; structure; constitution; system; as, a *frame* of government.

8. The act of planning or contriving; contrivance; invention.

9. Particular state, as of the mind; mental constitution; natural temper or disposition; as, an unhappy *frame* of mind.

10. Shape; form; proportion. [Rare.]

Put your discourse into some *frame*.—Shak.

11. In bowling, a division of a game constituting one inning, the game usually consisting of ten *frames*.

frā'mē-ȧ, *n.*; *pl.* **frā'mē-æ**. [L., from Old G.] A long lance or spear used by the early Franks.

frāme'=bridge (-brij), *n.* A bridge built of timbers framed together.

frāme'=lev"el, *n.* A mason's level.

frām'ēr, *n.* One who frames; a maker; a contriver.

frāme'=saw, *n.* A thin saw made rigid for working purposes by being stretched in a frame.

frāme'wŏrk, *n.* 1. A structure or fabric for inclosing or supporting anything; a frame; a skeleton; as, the *framework* of a building.

2. Structure; constitution; adjusted arrangement; system.

All the *framework* of the land.—Tennyson.

3. Work done in a frame.

frām'ing, *n.* 1. The act or style of constructing a frame.

2. A frame, framework, or system of frames.

3. In metallurgy, the process of grading slimes; also called *ragging*.

frām'ing=chis"el, *n.* In carpentry, a heavy chisel used for making mortises.

fram'pel, **fram'pōld**, *a.* [W. *ffromfol*, passionate.] Unruly; peevish; cross; vexatious. [Obs.]

fraṅc, *n.* [Fr., from the device *Francorum rex*, king of the French, on the coin when first struck by King John in 1360.]

1. The name given to two ancient coins in France, one of gold and the other of silver. The value of the gold *franc* was about $2.50, while the silver *franc* was valued at one-third of the gold one.

2. A French silver coin and money of account which, since 1795, has formed the unit of the French monetary system, and has also been adopted as the unit of currency by Switzerland and Belgium. It is worth about 19.3 cents, and is divided into 100 centimes.

fran'chīṣe (*or* -chiz), *n.* [ME. *franchise*; OFr. *franchise*, freedom, liberty, from *franc*, free.]

1. Property; liberty; freedom; hence, a right or privilege, constitutional or statutory, belonging to the people; especially, the right to vote.

2. In law, a particular privilege or right granted by a government or municipal corporation to an individual, or to a number of persons; as, a street-railway *franchise*.

3. The district or jurisdiction to which a particular privilege extends; the limits of an immunity.

4. An asylum or sanctuary, where persons are secure from arrest; as, monasteries in Spain were *franchises* for criminals.

5. Frankness; generosity. [Obs.]

Corporate franchise; the right to be and act as a corporation.

Elective franchise; the right of suffrage.

fran'chīṣe, *v.t.*; franchised, *pt.*, *pp.*; franchising *ppr.* [ME. *franchisen*, *fraunchisen*, from OFr. *franchir*, to render free, from *franc*, free.] To enfranchise; to give liberty to.

fran'chīṣe-ment, *n.* [OFr. *franchisement*, from *franchir*, to render free.] Release from burden or restriction; freedom; enfranchisement.

Fran'ciç, *a.* Pertaining to the Franks. [Rare.]

fran-cis'çȧ, *n.* [LL., f. of *Franciscus*, Frankish.] A battle-ax used by the ancient Franks, having the head long, curved, and narrow, and set at an obtuse angle to the pole.

Fran-cis'căn, *a.* and *n.* [LL. *Franciscus*, a Franciscan, from *Franciscus*, Francis.]

I. *a.* Pertaining to the Roman Catholic order of St. Francis, or the Franciscans.

II. *n.* In the Roman Catholic church, one of an order of mendicant friars; also called *Minorites* and *Gray Friars*. The order was founded in Italy, in 1210, by St. Francis of Assisi, and its members devote themselves to missions, preaching, nursing, etc. Their garb is of coarse gray or brown cloth, with cowl, girdle, and sandals. The head of the order is a general residing at Rome.

Franciscan or Gray Friar.

Fran'çō-. A combining form from LL. *Francus*, a Frank, and signifying French; as, *Franco*-Chinese.

fraṅ'çō-lin, *n.* [Fr. *Francolin*, a francolin, prob. dim. of Port. *frango*, a chicken.] A bird, genus *Francolinus*, closely allied to the partridges. The common species, *Francolinus vulgaris*, found in India, has a very loud whistle and its flesh is highly esteemed.

fraṅ'çō-līte, *n.* A variety of apatite occurring in Devonshire, England, in a mine called Wheal *Franco*, whence its name.

franc=ti"reur' (frän tē-rūr') *n.*; *pl.* **francs'=ti"reur'** (fran tē-rūr'). [*Fr. franc*, free and *tireur*, shooter.] A French soldier who carried on a guerrilla warfare during the Franco-Prussian war.

fran'gent, *a.* [L. *frangens* (*-entis*), ppr. of *frangere*, to break.] Causing fractures.

fran-gi-bil'i-ty, *n.* The state of being frangible.

fran'gi-ble, *a.* [OFr. *frangible*, from L. *frangere*, to break.] Capable of being broken; breakable; easily broken.

fran'gi-pāne, *n.* [Named after the Italian Marquis *Frangipani*, the inventor.]

1. A species of pastry containing cream, almonds, and sugar.

2. A kind of perfume. [See *Frangipani*.]

fran'gi-pa-ni, **fran'gi-pan-ni**, *n.* A perfume prepared from or imitating the odor of the flower of a West Indian tree, *Plumiera rubra*, or red jasmine.

fraṅ'gū-lȧ, *n.* [Prob. from L. *frangere*, to break; from the brittleness of the stems.] The bark of the alder-buckthorn, *Rhamnus Frangula*, used as a purgative.

fraṅ-gū'liç, **fraṅ-gū-lin'iç**, *a.* Pertaining to frangula.

Frangulic acid; a compound obtained from frangulin.

fraṅ'gū-lin, *n.* [*Frangula* and *-in*.] In chemistry, a yellow coloring-matter contained in the bark of the alder-buckthorn and other species of *Rhamnus*.

fran'iŏn, *n.* A paramour, or a boon companion. [Obs.]

fraṅk, *n.* [From OFr. *franc*, a pigsty, from *franc*, free, privileged.] A pigpen. [Obs.]

fraṅk, *v.t.* To shut up in a sty or frank; hence, to fatten. [Obs.]

fraṅk, *n.* The heron. [Prov. Eng.]

fraṅk, *a.*; *comp.* franker; *superl.* frankest. [Fr. *franc*, frank, free, from LL. *francus*, free, at liberty.]

1. Open; ingenuous; candid; free in uttering real sentiments; not reserved; using no disguise; as, *frank* disposition; *frank* talk.

2. Liberal; generous; not niggardly. [Obs.]

3. Free; without conditions.

Thy *frank* election make. —Shak.

4. Licentious; unrestrained. [Obs.]

5. In law, not restrained in action.

Syn.—Artless, candid, honest, ingenuous, plain, open, unreserved, sincere, undisguised.

fraṅk, *v.t.*; franked (fraṅkt), *pt.*, *pp.*; franking, *ppr.* 1. To send or cause to be sent by public conveyance free of expense; to exempt from charge for postage, etc.; as, to *frank* a letter, a telegram, or express package.

2. In carpentry, to form the joint of, as the joint of a window-sash where the crosspieces of the frame intersect each other, by cutting

froth′i-ly, *adv.* In a frothy manner.
froth′i-ness, *n.* The state of being frothy; emptiness; senseless matter.
froth′ing, *n.* Rant; empty declamation.
froth′-in″sect, *n.* A froghopper.
froth′less, *a.* Free from froth.
froth′-spit, *n.* A kind of white froth on the leaves of plants; cuckoo-spit.
froth′y, *a.*; *comp.* frothier; *superl.* frothiest. 1. Full of foam or froth, or consisting of froth or light bubbles; foamy; spumous.
2. Soft; not firm or solid.
3. Vain; light; empty; unsubstantial; as, a vain, *frothy* speaker; a *frothy* harangue.
frou′frou, *n.* [Fr.] Swish; rustling, as of a silk skirt or dress.
frounce, *n.* 1. A fold. [Obs.]
2. A disease in hawks in which spittle gathers as a fringe about the bill.
3. A mass of pimples on the palate of a horse; the disease so characterized.
frounce, *v.t.*; frounced (frounst), *pt.*, *pp.*; frouncing, *ppr.* [ME. *frouncen*; OFr. *froncer*, *fronser*, to fold, gather, wrinkle.] To fold; to curl; to frizzle the hair of; to furnish with fringe, frills, or the like. [Archaic.]
frounce, *v.i.* To frown. [Obs.]
frounce′less, *a.* Having no plait or wrinkle.
frou′zy, *a.* See *Frowzy.*
frow, *n.* [D. *vrouwe*; G. *frau*, a woman, wife, lady.]
1. A colloquial term for a woman, particularly a wife; also, a Dutch or German dame.
2. An idle, dirty woman; a lazy slattern. [Prov. Eng.]
frōw, *n.* [Of unknown origin.] A kind of cleaving-knife having the blade and handle at right angles; also written *froe*, *frower.*
frōw, *a.* Fragile; crisp; brittle; easily broken. [Prov. Eng.]
frō′wărd, *a.* [ME. *froward*; AS. *framweard*; *fram*, away, from, and *-weard*, -ward.] Not willing to yield or comply with what is required or is reasonable; perverse; unyielding; ungovernable; refractory; disobedient; peevish; as, a *froward* child.

> They are a very *froward* generation, children in whom is no faith. —Deut. xxxii. 20.

Syn.—Perverse, untoward, wayward, unyielding, ungovernable, refractory, disobedient, petulant, cross, peevish.
frō′wărd-ly, *adv.* Perversely.
frō′wărd-ness, *n.* Perverseness; disobedience.
frōw′ēr, *n.* A tool; a frow.
frow′ey, *a.* See *Frowy.*
frown, *v.i.*; frowned, *pt.*, *pp.*; frowning, *ppr.* [ME. *frownen*, *frounen*; Fr. *froigner*, in *se refroigner*, to knit the brow.]
1. To express displeasure by contracting the brow and looking grim or surly; to look stern.

> Heroes in animated marble *frown.* —Pope.

2. To manifest displeasure in any manner; to lower; to look threatening; as, the clouds seemed to *frown.*
frown, *v.t.* To repel by expressing displeasure; to rebuke; as, *frown* the impudent fellow into silence.
frown, *n.* 1. A wrinkled look, particularly expressing dislike; a sour, severe, or stern look, expressive of displeasure.

> His front yet threatens and his *frowns* command. —Prior.

2. Any expression of displeasure; as, the *frowns* of Providence; the *frowns* of fortune.
frown′ing-ly, *adv.* Sternly; with a look of displeasure.
frown′y, *a.* Scowling; having a frowning look.
frow′y, *a.* 1. Musty; rancid; rank. [Obs. or Prov.]
2. Easy to work, as wood.
frow′zy, *a.* 1. Dirty; in a state of disorder; offensive to the eye; slovenly; slatternly; as, *frowzy* dress and hair.
2. Fetid; musty; rank.
3. Peevish; froward. [Prov. Eng.]
frōze, *v.*, past tense of *freeze.*
frō′zen, *a.* 1. Congealed by cold.
2. Cold; frosty; chill; subject to severe frost; as, the *frozen* climates of the north.
3. Chill or cold in affection; void of sympathy; wanting in feeling or interest; lacking natural heat or vigor; unsympathetic.

> Where *frozen* chastity retires,
> Love finds an altar for forbidden fires.
> —Pope.

frō′zen-ness, *n.* A state of being frozen.
frub′ish, *v.t.* To furbish. [Obs.]
fruc′ted, *a.* [L. *fructus*, fruit.] In heraldry, bearing fruit, as trees.
fruc-tes′cence, *n.* [L. *fructus*, fruit, and *-escence.*] The time when the fruit of a plant arrives at maturity; also, the act of bearing fruit.
fruc′ti-cist, *n.* [L. *fructus*, fruit, and (-c) *-ist.*] One who classes plants in botany by means of their fruit.
fruc-tic′ū-lōse, *a.* Bearing fruit in abundance.
Fruc′ti-dor, *n.* [Fr., from L. *fructus*, fruit.] In the calendar of the first French republic, the last month, from August 18 to September 16. [See *Vendémiaire.*]
fruc-tif′ēr-ous, *a.* [L. *fructifer*; *fructus*, fruit, and *ferre*, to bear.] Bearing or producing fruit.
fruc″ti-fi-cā′tion, *n.* [From L. *fructificare*, to bear fruit; *fructus*, fruit, and *-ficare*, from *facere*, to make.]
1. The act of fructifying or rendering productive of fruit; fecundation.
2. In botany, (a) the organs which are concerned in the production of the fruit of a plant, of which the essential are the stamens and pistil; (b) the process by which these parts produce fruit.
fruc′ti-fȳ, *v.t.*; fructified, *pt.*, *pp.*; fructifying, *ppr.* [Fr. *fructifier*; L. *fructificare*; *fructus*, fruit, and *-ficare*, from *facere*, to make.] To make fruitful; to render productive; to fertilize; as, to *fructify* the earth.
fruc′ti-fȳ, *v.i.* To bear fruit.
fruc-tip′ă-rous (-rus), *a.* [L. *fructus*, fruit, and *parere*, to produce.] Denoting a plant affected by the monstrosity of producing several fruits instead of the one which it normally bears.
fruc′tōse, *n.* In chemistry, levulose.
fruc′tū-ă-ry, *n.*; *pl.* **fruc′tū-ă-ries.** [L. *fructuarius*, of or pertaining to fruit, from *fructus*, fruit.] One who enjoys the produce or profits of anything.
fruc-tū-ā′tion, *n.* [L. *fructus*, fruit, and *-ation.*] Produce; fruit. [Rare.]
fruc′tū-ous, *a.* [ME. *fructuous*, from L. *fructuosus*, abounding in fruit, from *fructus*, fruit.] Fruitful; fertile. [Obs.]
fruc′tū-ous-ly, *adv.* Fruitfully; fertilely.
fruc′tū-ous-ness, *n.* Fruitfulness; fertility.
fruc′tūre, *n.* [L. *fructus*, fruit, and *-ure.*] Use; fruition; enjoyment. [Obs.]
frū′găl, *a.* [OFr. *frugal*, from L. *frugalis*, economical, temperate, pertaining to produce; *frux*, pl. *fruges*, the fruits of the earth.]
1. Economical in the use or appropriation of money, goods, or provisions of any kind; saving unnecessary expense, either of money or of anything else which is to be used or consumed; sparing; not profuse, prodigal, or lavish.
2. Denoting economy; indicating the necessity or desire to save; as, a *frugal* meal.
frū-gal′i-ty, *n.*; *pl.* **frū-gal′i-ties.** [Fr. *frugalité*; L. *frugalitas*, from *frugalis*, economical, thrifty.]
1. The state or quality of being frugal; prudent economy; good husbandry or housewifery; a sparing use or appropriation of money or commodities.

> Without *frugality* none can become rich, and with it few would be poor. —Johnson.

2. A prudent and sparing use or appropriation of anything; as, *frugality* of praise.
frū′găl-ly, *adv.* With economy; with good management; in a saving manner.
frū′găl-ness, *n.* Same as *Frugality.*
frū-ġif′ēr-ous, *a.* [L. *frugifer*; *frux*, pl. *fruges*, the fruits of the earth, and *ferre*, to bear.] Producing fruit or grain; fructifying.
Frū-ġiv′ō-ră, *n.pl.* [From L. *frux*, *frugis*, fruit, and *vorare*, to devour.] A division of the bat family comprehending those eating fruit.
frū-ġiv′ō-rous (-rus), *a.* Feeding on fruits rather than on grain.
fruit, *n.* [ME. *fruit*, *frut*; OFr. *fruit*, from L. *fructus*, enjoyment, means of enjoyment, fruit, produce, profit.]
1. In a general sense, whatever vegetable products the earth yields to supply the necessities or enjoyments of man and the lower animals, as corn, grass, cotton, flax, grapes, and all cultivated plants. In this comprehensive sense the word is generally used in the plural.
2. In a more limited sense, the reproductive product of a tree or other plant; the seed of plants or the part that contains the seeds, as wheat, rye, oats, apples, quinces, pears, cherries, acorns, melons, etc.
3. In a still more limited sense, the edible succulent products of certain plants generally covering and including their seeds, as the apple, orange, peach, pear, lemon, cherry, grape, berries, etc.; such products collectively.
4. In botany, the seed of a plant or the mature ovary, composed essentially of two parts, the pericarp and the seed.
5. The produce of animals; offspring; young; as, the *fruit* of the womb, of the loins, of the body.
6. That which is produced; effect, result, or consequence, whether advantageous or disadvantageous.

> We wish to see you reap the *fruit* of your virtue. —Milton.

> The *fruits* of this education became visible. —Macaulay.

Aggregate fruit; see *Aggregate*, a. 2.
Collective fruit; see under *Collective.*
Compound fruits; such as consist of several ovaries. Fruits, scientifically speaking, are either simple or multiple, that is, the produce of one flower or of several flowers united together.
Small fruits; strawberries, currants, blackberries, and the like.
Spurious fruit; in botany, any kind of inflorescence which grows up with the fruit and forms one body with it, as a pine-cone.
fruit, *v.t.*; fruited, *pt.*, *pp.*; fruiting, *ppr.* To develop fruit-bearing qualities in; as, to *fruit* a new apple.
fruit, *v.i.* To produce fruit; to bear.
fruit′āġe, *n.* [OFr. *fruitage*, from *fruit*, fruit, and *-age.*]
1. Fruit collectively; various fruits; fruitery.

> With *fruitage* golden-rinded. —Tennyson.

2. Mental product, the result of experience, study, or development.

> But let me save
> This noble *fruitage* of my mind. —Baillie.

fruit′-bat, *n.* A bat of the division *Frugivora.*
fruit′-bud, *n.* The bud that incloses a fructiferous germ.
fruit′-cake, *n.* A rich cake having a large proportion of raisins, citron, etc.
fruit′-crow, *n.* A South American bird of the genus *Chasmorhynchus*, subsisting upon fruit; also, any allied bird.
fruit′-dot, *n.* The small cluster of sporangia in ferns.
fruit′-dri″ēr, *n.* An evaporator for fruits and vegetables.
fruit′ēr, *n.* A vessel for carrying fruit to market.
fruit′ēr-ēr, *n.* One who buys and sells fruits.
fruit′ēr-y, *n.*; *pl.* **fruit′ēr-ies.** 1. Fruit taken collectively.
2. A repository for fruit.
fruit′es-tere (tār), *n.* A female fruit-dealer. [Obs.]
fruit′-flȳ, *n.* A small fly of the genus *Drosophila.* Its larvæ attack decaying fruit.
fruit′ful, *a.* 1. Very productive; producing fruit in abundance; prolific; as, *fruitful* soil; a *fruitful* tree; a *fruitful* season.
2. Bearing children; not barren.

> Be *fruitful*, and multiply. —Gen. i. 28.

3. Producing or presenting in abundance; productive; as, *fruitful* in expedients or in crimes.

> *Fruitful* of further thought and deed.
> —Tennyson.

Syn.—Prolific, fertile, rich, plenteous, abundant, plentiful.
fruit′ful-ly, *adv.* In a fruitful manner.
fruit′ful-ness, *n.* The quality of being fruitful.
fruit′ing, *a.* Bearing fruit; pertaining to fruit.
fruit′ing, *n.* The bearing of fruit.
frū-i′tion, *n.* [OFr. *fruition*; L. *fruitio*, enjoyment, from *fruire*, to use, enjoy.] Use, accompanied with pleasure, corporeal or intellectual; enjoyment; the pleasure derived from use or possession.
frū′i-tive, *a.* Enjoying. [Obs.]
fruit′-jăr, *n.* A large-mouthed, metal-capped, air-tight, glass jar or bottle for preserving fruit for domestic uses.
fruit′less, *a.* 1. Not bearing fruit; barren; destitute of fruit, increase, or offspring; as, a *fruitless* plant; a *fruitless* union.
2. Productive of no advantage or good effect; vain; idle; useless; unprofitable; as, a *fruitless* attempt; a *fruitless* controversy.
fruit′less-ly, *adv.* Without any valuable effect; idly; vainly; unprofitably.
fruit′less-ness, *n.* The quality of being vain or unprofitable.
fruit′-pig″eon, *n.* The name given to the pigeons of the genus *Carpophaga*, birds of very brilliant plumage, occurring in India, Australia, etc.
fruit′-sug″ăr (-shug″ēr), *n.* Fructose.
fruit′-tree, *n.* A tree bearing edible fruit; applied usually to trees under cultivation.
fruit′-wŏrm, *n.* One of numerous larvæ injurious to fruit.
fruit′y, *a.* 1. Resembling fruit.
2. Fruitful. [Rare.]
frū-men-tā′ceous, *a.* Of, belonging to, or made of a cereal or cereals.
frū-men-tā′ri-ous, *a.* Pertaining to wheat or grain. [Rare.]
frū-men-tā′tion, *n.* [L. *frumentatio*, from *frumentari*, to provide grain or corn, from *frumentum*, corn.] In Roman antiquity, a largess of grain bestowed on the people, to quiet them when uneasy or turbulent.
frū′men-ty, *n.* [ME. *frumenty*, *frumentee*; OFr. *frumentee*, from L. *frumentum*, corn.]
1. A dish made of boiled milk, hulled wheat, and spices or seasoning.
2. A wheat mash used in brewing.
3. Grain or cereals. [Obs.]

frump, *v.t.* To insult; to flout; to mock. [Obs.]

frump, *n.* 1. A joke, jeer, or flout. [Obs.]

2. A dowdyish, ill-dressed woman; a slouch; especially if old or cross.

frump′ẽr, *n.* A mocker. [Obs.]

frump′ish, *a.* 1. Sneering; gossiping.

2. Poorly dressed; out of fashion.

frush, *v.t.* [ME. *frushen*, from OFr. *fruisser*, *froisser*, to bruise, crush.] To bruise; to crush. [Obs.]

frush, *a.* Brittle; easily broken, said of wood. [Obs.]

frush, *n.* Clatter; uproar; noise. [Obs.]

frush, *n.* [ME. *frosh*; G. *frosh*, a frog.]

1. The part of a horse's foot known as the frog.

2. A disease of a horse's hoof; thrush.

frus′trȧ-ble, *a.* That may be frustrated or defeated.

frus-trā′nē-ous, *a.* Vain; useless; unprofitable. [Obs.]

frus′trāte, *v.t.*; frustrated, *pt.*, *pp.*; frustrating, *ppr.* [L. *frustratus*, pp. of *frustrare*, *frustrari*, to disappoint, deceive, trick, from *frustra*, in vain.]

1. To defeat; to disappoint; to balk; to bring to nothing; to baffle; to foil; as, to *frustrate* a scheme; to *frustrate* the purpose of a person.

2. To make null; to nullify; to render of no effect; as, to *frustrate* a conveyance or deed.

frus′trāte, *a.* Vain; ineffectual; useless; unprofitable; null; void; of no effect.

frus′trāte-ly, *adv.* Uselessly; in vain. [Obs.]

frus-trā′tion, *n.* [L. *frustratio*, from *frustrare*, *frustrari*, to disappoint, deceive.] The act of frustrating; disappointment; defeat; as, the *frustration* of one's attempt or design.

frus′trȧ-tive, *a.* Tending to defeat; fallacious. [Obs.]

frus′trȧ-tō-ry, *a.* That makes void; that vacates or renders null; as, a *frustratory* appeal. [Obs.]

frus′tūle, *n.* [LL. *frustulum*, dim. of *frustum*, a piece, bit.] A name given to each of the cells into which the *Diatomaceæ*, an order of seaweeds, divide.

frus′tū-lōse, *a.* Made up of frustules.

frus′tum, *n.*; *pl.* **frus′tums** or **frus′tȧ**. [L. *frustum*, a bit, a part.]

1. A piece or part remaining, as the broken shaft of a column.

2. In geometry, the part of a solid next the base, left by cutting off the top portion by a plane parallel to the base; or the part of any solid between two planes which may be either parallel or inclined to each other. In the figure, the dotted line *c* shows the portion of the cone cut off to form the frustum *f*.

Frustum.

frụ-tes′cent, *a.* [From L. *fruticescens* (*-entis*), ppr. of *fruticescere*, to put forth shoots, become shrubby, from *frutex* (*-icis*), a shrub.] In botany, from herbaceous becoming shrubby; as, a *frutescent* stem.

frụ′tex, *n.* [L.] In botany, a shrub; a plant having a woody, durable stem, but less than a tree.

frụ′ti-căl, *a.* Shrubby. [Obs.]

frụ′ti-cănt, *a.* [L. *fruticans* (*-antis*), ppr. of *fruticare*, to put forth shoots, become bushy.] Full of shoots. [Obs.]

frụ′ti-cōse, **frụ′ti-cous**, *a.* [L. *fruticosus*, from *frutex* (*-icis*), a bush, shrub.] Shrublike; branching like a shrub; as, a *fruticose* stem.

frụ-tic′ū-lōse, *a.* [A dim. from L. *frutex* (*-icis*), a shrub.] Pertaining to or branching like a small shrub.

frȳ, *v.t.*; fried, *pt.*, *pp.*; frying, *ppr.* [ME. *fryen*, *frien*; OFr. *frire*; Pr. *frir*, *frigir*; It. *frigere*; L. *frigere*, to roast, fry; Gr. *phrygein*, to parch; Sans. *bhrajj*, to roast.] To dress with fat by heating or roasting in a pan over a fire; to cook and prepare for eating in a frying-pan; as, to *fry* meat or vegetables.

frȳ, *v.i.* 1. To be heated and agitated, as meat in a frying-pan or a doughnut in boiling lard; to suffer the action of fire or extreme heat.

2. To ferment, as in the stomach, or, figuratively, in the mind. [Obs.]

3. To be agitated. [Obs.]

frȳ, *n.*; *pl.* **frieṣ**. [ME. *fry*, seed, offspring; Ice. *frjo*, *fræ*; Sw. *frö*; Goth. *fraiw*, seed.]

1. A swarm or crowd, especially of little fishes; a swarm of any small animals, or of young people; a great number of small or insignificant objects.

> The *fry* of children young. —Spenser.

2. The young of the salmon at a certain stage of their progress.

frȳ, *n.* 1. Something prepared by frying; as, an oyster *fry*.

2. Mental worry or agitation; as, in a continual *fry*.

frȳ′ing, *n.* The act of preparing by heating with fat.

frȳ′ing-pan, *n.* A pan with a long handle, used for frying meat and vegetables.

fů, fọọ, *n.* In China, a minor division of a province.

fụ′, *a.* Full; drunk. [Scot.]

fū′āge, *n.* Fumage.

fū′ăr, *n.* See *Feuar*.

fub, *v.t.*; fubbed, *pt.*, *pp.*; fubbing, *ppr.* To snub; also, to cheat.

fub, fubṣ, *n.* [Prov. Eng.] A plump young person. [Obs.]

fub′bẽr-y, *n.* Dishonesty; trickery. [Obs.]

fub′by, fub′ṣy, *a.* Plump; chubby.

Fū-çā′cē-æ, *n.pl.* A natural order of dark-colored algæ, consisting of olive-colored inarticulate seaweeds, distinguished from the other algæ by their organs of reproduction, which consist of archegonia and antheridia, contained in common chambers or conceptacles, united in club-shaped receptacles at the ends or margins of the fronds.

fū-çā′ceous, *a.* Of or belonging to the *Fucaceæ*.

fū′çāte, fū′çā-ted, *a.* Painted; disguised with paint; also, disguised with false show.

fu̇chs, *n.* [G., a fox.] In German universities, a student of the first year; a freshman.

Fu̇ch′si-ȧ (*or* fū′shi-ȧ), *n.* [Named after the discoverer Leonard *Fuchs*, a German botanist.]

1. A genus of beautiful flowering shrubs, natives of South America, Mexico, and New Zealand, natural order *Onagraceæ*, characterized by having a funnel-shaped colored deciduous four-parted calyx; four petals set in the mouth of the calyx-tube and alternating with its segments; eight exserted stamens, and a long style with a capitate stigma. These plants are amongst the most common decorative greenhouse plants.

2. [f—] Any plant of this genus.

Fu̇ch′si-ăn, *a.* Of or pertaining to L. Fuchs (1833——), a German authority on mathematics.

Fuchsian function; a function of one value, unaltered by the transformations of a Fuchsian group.

Fuchsian group; see under *Group*.

fu̇ch′sin, fu̇ch′sine, *n.* [*Fuchs*ia and *-in*, *-ine*.] In chemistry, a red dye, $C_{20}H_{19}N_3$, occurring in commerce under the names aniline red, magenta, rosaniline, etc. It is prepared by heating a mixture of dry arsenic acid and aniline to 140° for six or eight hours.

fū-ciph′ȧ-gous, *a.* Fucivorous.

fū-civ′ō-rous, *a.* [L. *fucus*, seaweed, and *vorare*, to eat.] A term applied to animals that subsist on seaweed.

fū′çoid, *a.* [L. *fucus*, seaweed, and *eidos*, form.]

1. In botany, belonging to or resembling the *Fucaceæ*.

2. In geology, having fucoids; marked by traces of fucoids, as certain sandstones.

Also written *fucoidal*, *fucous*.

fū′çoid, *n.* In botany, (a) a plant of the *Fucaceæ*; (b) any plant resembling a seaweed.

fū-çoid′ăl, *a.* Fucoid.

fū′çous, *a.* Fucoid.

fū′çus, *n.* [L., a rock-lichen used as a red dye, paint, from Gr. *phykos*, seaweed, rouge.]

1. A paint; a dye; also, false show. [Obs.]

2. [F—] In botany, a name formerly applied to almost all the solid algæ, but now confined to a genus of the family *Fucaceæ*, comprising those seaweeds which have a flat or compressed forked frond.

3. [*pl.* fū′ci.] Any plant of this genus.

fū′çus, *v.t.* To paint; to rouge. [Obs.]

fū′çū-sol, *n.* [L. *fucus*, seaweed, and *oleum*, oil.] A compound, $C_5H_4O_2$, obtained from seaweed.

fud, *n.* [W. *ffwtog*, a scut, a short tail.] The scut or tail of the hare, cony, etc. [Scot.]

fud, *n.* [From *fud*, a hare's or rabbit's tail.] Woolen waste; the refuse of the new wool taken out in the scribbling process, which is mixed with the mungo for use.

fud′dẽr, *n.* A variant of *fother*, a weight.

fud′dle, *v.t.*; fuddled, *pt.*, *pp.*; fuddling, *ppr.* To make drunk; to intoxicate.

fud′dle, *v.i.* To drink to excess.

fud′dle, *n.* Liquor; strong drink. [Obs.]

fud′dlẽr, *n.* A drunkard.

fudġe (fuj), *v.t.*; fudged, *pt.*, *pp.*; fudging, *ppr.*

1. To poke or prod with a stick. [Prov. Eng.]

2. To make up; to fabricate.

3. To bungle; to botch.

fudġe, *v.i.* To work unskilfully or at a disadvantage.

fudġe, *n.* [Prov. Fr. *fuche*, *feuche*; L.G. *futsh*, exclam., begone.]

1. A made-up story; stuff; nonsense; an exclamation of contempt.

2. A kind of candy, commonly homemade, and having a base of chocolate, with nuts, etc.

fudġe′-wheel, *n.* A tool used in shoemaking to ornament sole-edges.

Fū-ē′ġi-ăn, *a.* Of or relating to Tierra del Fuego.

Fū-ē′ġi-ăn, *n.* A native or inhabitant of Tierra del Fuego.

fū′el, *n.* [ME. *fuel*, *fuelle*; OFr. *fouail*, *fuail*, from LL. *focalium*, pl. *focalia*, brushwood for fuel, from L. *focus*, fireplace.]

1. Any matter which serves to increase the intensity of fire; that which feeds fire; combustible matter, as wood, coal, peat, etc.

2. Figuratively, anything that serves to feed or increase flame, heat, or excitement.

Pressed fuel; any matter too fine for burning while in a powdered state, compressed in blocks as an aid to combustion; called also *artificial fuel*.

fū′el, *v.t.* 1. To feed with combustible matter. [Obs.]

2. To store with fuel or firing. [Obs.]

fū′el-ē-çon′ō-mi-zēr, *n.* An attachment to an engine-furnace by which waste heat is utilized in warming water entering the boiler.

fū′el-ẽr, fū′el-lẽr, *n.* One who or that which supplies fuel. [Obs.]

fū′el-feed″ẽr, *n.* A device in a furnace or firebox to supply fuel to a fire as it may be required.

fū′el-gas, *n.* Gas used for fuel, as distinguished from gas used as an illuminant.

fụ-e′rō, *n.* [Sp., from L. *forum*, a market-place, court.] A Spanish term having such significations as a code of law, a charter of privileges, a custom having the force of law, a declaration by a magistrate, the seat or jurisdiction of a tribunal.

Fuero Juzgo; a code of Spanish law, said to be the most ancient in Europe.

fuff, *n.* [Imitative.] 1. A puff or puff-like noise; also, a spitting, as of a cat. [Scot.]

2. Anger; a fume.

fuff, *v.t.* and *v.i.*; fuffed (fuft), *pt.*, *pp.*; fuffing, *ppr.* To puff. [Scot.]

fuf′fle, *v.t.*; fuffled, *pt.*, *pp.*; fuffling, *ppr.* To dishevel; to disarrange; to muss; to ruffle.

fuff′y, *a.* Light; puffy.

fū-gā′cious, *a.* [L. *fugax* (*-acis*), from *fugere*, to flee.]

1. Transitory; flying or fleeing away; volatile.

2. In biology, denoting a part that is soon shed; not permanent, as the corolla of a plant.

fū-gā′cious-ness, *n.* Fugacity.

fū-gac′i-ty, *n.* [LL. *fugacitas*, from L. *fugax* (*-acis*), apt to flee, from *fugere*, to flee.]

1. Volatility; the quality of flying away; as, the *fugacity* of spirits.

2. Uncertainty; instability.

fū′gȧ-cy, *n.* The act of flying. [Obs.]

fū′găl, *a.* In music, of, relating to, or after the style of a fugue.

fū-gä′rä, *n.* [It.] An organ-stop giving a tone like a stringed instrument.

fū-gā′tion, *n.* [OFr. *fugation*, from L. *fugare*, to cause to flee, chase.] A hunt; a chase. [Obs.]

fugh (fū), *interj.* An exclamation expressing abhorrence; spelled also *faugh*, *foh*.

fū-ghet′tō, *n.*; *pl.* **fū-ghet′ti** (-get′). A short fugal composition.

fū-gi-tā′tion, *n.* [L. *fugitatus*, pp. of *fugitare*, freq. of *fugere*, to flee.] In Scots law, the act of a criminal absconding from justice.

fū′ġi-tive, *a.* [Fr. *fugitif*; L. *fugitivus*, from *fugere*, to flee; Gr. *pheugein*, to flee.]

1. Volatile; apt to flee away; readily wafted by the wind.

> The more tender and *fugitive* parts, the leaves. —Woodward.

2. Staying or lasting but a short time; fleeting; not fixed or durable; readily escaping; as, a *fugitive* idea.

3. Fleeing or running from danger or pursuit, duty or service.

> I cannot praise a *fugitive* and cloistered virtue unexercised and unbreathed.—Milton.

> Can a *fugitive* daughter enjoy herself while her parents are in tears? —Richardson.

4. Wandering; vagabond. [Obs.]

5. Of passing interest, as a literary composition.

Fugitive slave law; in United States history, an act of Congress of 1793 or another of 1850, providing for the return of runaway slaves from any state to that in which they were owned. The latter especially aroused much opposition in free states and contributed to hasten the Civil War of 1861-65. Both were nullified by the emancipation of all slaves in the United States January 1, 1863.

fū′ġi-tive, *n.* 1. One who flees from his station or duty; a deserter; one who flees from danger.

2. One who has fled or deserted and taken refuge under another power, or one who has fled from punishment.

> The homage of rebellious *fugitives*.—Dryden.

3. Anything hard to be caught or detained.

> Or catch that airy *fugitive* called wit. —Harte.

fū′ġi-tive-ly, *adv.* In a fugitive manner.

fū′ġi-tive-ness, *n.* The state or quality of being fugitive; volatility; fugacity; an aptness to fly away.

fū′gle-man, *n.*; *pl.* **fū′gle-men**. [G. *flügelmann*, a file-leader; *flügel*, a wing, file, and *mann*, a man.]

1. A soldier specially expert and well drilled, who takes his place in front of a military

company, as an example or model to the others in their exercises; a file-leader.

2. One who takes the initiative in any movement, and sets an example for others to follow.

fūgue (fūg), *n.* [Fr.] In music, a polyphonic composition constructed on one or more short subjects or themes, which are harmonized according to the laws of counterpoint, and introduced from time to time with various contrapuntal devices, the interest in these frequently heard themes being sustained by diminishing the interval of time at which they follow each other, and monotony being avoided by the occasional use of episodes or passages open to free treatment.

fūgued (fūgd), *a.* In the manner of a fugue.

fū'guist (-gist), *n.* A musician who composes fugues or performs them extemporaneously.

-ful. A suffix from AS. *-ful*, *-full*, and signifying, full of, having; as, boast*ful*, beauti*ful*, care*ful*.

Fū'lăh, *n.* One of a dominant tribe of uncertain ethnic affinities, in western Soudan, of dark color and Mohammedan faith; written also *Foolah, Fulbe, Fellatah, Foulah.*

Fū'lăh, *a.* Of or pertaining to the Fulahs.

Fụl'be, *n.* See *Fulah.*

ful'ci-ble, *a.* [From L. *fulcire*, to prop.] That may be propped up. [Obs.]

ful'ci-ment, *n.* [L. *fulcimentum*, from *fulcire*, to prop.] A prop; a fulcrum; that on which a balance or lever rests. [Obs.]

ful'crȧ, *n.*, pl. of *fulcrum.*

ful-crā'ceous, *a.* Of or relating to the fulcrum of a plant.

ful'crāte, *a.* [From L. *fulcrum*, a prop, *ful-crum*, and *-ate.*]

1. In botany, descending to the earth, as a branch or stem.

2. Furnished with a fulcrum or fulcrums.

ful'crum, *v.t.* [L. *fulcrum*, the post or foot of a couch; a bed-post, from *fulcire*, to prop, support.] To supply with or employ as a fulcrum.

ful'crum, *n.*; *pl.* **ful'crums, ful'crȧ.** [L., a prop, support, from *fulcire* to prop, support.]

1. A prop or support.

2. In mechanics, that by which a lever is sustained; the point about which the lever turns in lifting a body. In the figure L is the lever, by depressing which over F, the fulcrum, the stone is raised.

Fulcrum.

3. In botany, the part of a plant which serves to support or defend it, or to facilitate some necessary secretion, as a stipule, a bract, a tendril, a gland, etc.

4. In zoölogy, (a) one of a number of spines lying anteriorly on the dorsal, anal, or caudal fin of certain ganoids; (b) the elytrine of the ligula of a hymenopter.

fụl-fil', fụl-fill', *v.t.*; fulfilled, *pt., pp.*; fulfilling, *ppr.* [ME. *fulfillen, fulfyllen*; AS. *fullfyllan*; *full*, full, and *fyllan*, to fill.]

1. To fill to the full; to fill entirely. [Obs.]

2. To accomplish or carry into effect, as a prophecy, promise, intention, design, desire, prayer, requirement, legal demand, terms of a bargain or covenant, and the like; to perform; to complete by performance; to comply with the injunctions, requirements, or demands of.

> Here nature seems *fulfilled* in all her ends.
> —Milton.

> He will *fulfil* the desire of them that fear him.
> —Ps. cxlv. 19.

3. To complete, as an agreed-on period of service, or as a term of life; as, to *fulfil* a hundred years, that is, to live a hundred years.

> Give me my wife, for my days are *fulfilled.*
> —Gen. xxix. 21.

Syn.—Accomplish, realize.—To *fulfil* is literally to fill quite full, that is, to bring about *full* to the wishes of a person; to *accomplish* is to bring to perfection, but without reference to the wishes of any one; to *realize* is to make *real*, namely, whatever has been aimed at.

fụl-fil'ẽr, *n.* One who fulfils or accomplishes.

fụl-fil'ment, fụl-fill'ment, *n.* 1. Accomplishment; completion; as, the *fulfilment* of prophecy.

2. Execution; performance; as, the *fulfilment* of a promise.

ful'ġen-cy, *n.* [L. *fulgens (-entis)*, ppr. of *fulgere*, to flash, gleam, shine.] Brightness; splendor; glitter.

ful'ġent, *a.* Shining; dazzling; exquisitely bright.

ful'ġent-ly, *adv.* Dazzlingly; glitteringly.

ful'ġid, *a.* [L. *fulgidus*, from *fulgere*, to shine, gleam.] Shining; glittering; dazzling. [Obs.]

ful-ġid'i-ty, *n.* Splendor.

ful'gôr, *n.* [L. *fulgor*, lightning, a flash, from *fulgere*, to shine, flash.] Splendor; dazzling brightness. [Rare.]

ful'gū-rănt, *a.* [L. *fulgurans (-antis)*, ppr. of *fulgurare*, to lighten.] Lightening. [Obs.]

ful-gū-rā'tȧ, *n.* [L. *fulguratus*, pp. of *fulgurare*, to flash.] A tube or other appliance used in making an observation of the spectrum of the vapor arising from a liquid through which has been passed a current of electricity.

ful'gū-rāte, *v.i.*; fulgurated, *pt., pp.*; fulgurating, *ppr.* [L. *fulguratus*, pp. of *fulgurare*, to flash.] To flash as lightning.

ful'gū-rā-ting, *a.* [L. *fulguratus*, ppr. of *fulgurare*, to lighten.] Darting; flashing; applied in medicine to pains.

ful-gū-rā'tion, *n.* [L. *fulguratio*, from *fulgurare*, to lighten.]

1. Lightning; the act of lightening. [Rare.]

2. The sudden brightening of a fused globule of gold or silver, when the last film of the oxid of lead or copper leaves its surface.

ful'gū-rīte, *n.* [L. *fulgur*, lightning, and *-ite.*] Any rocky substance that has been fused or vitrified by lightning; more strictly, a vitrified tube in sand formed by lightning penetrating the solid ground, and fusing a portion of the materials through which it passes.

ful'gū-rous, *a.* [L. *fulgur*, lightning, and *-ous.*] Emitting lightning; fulgurant; flashing.

ful'gū-ry, *n.* [L. *fulgur*, lightning.] Lightning. [Obs.]

fụl'hăm (fụl'ăm), *n.* See *Fullam.*

fū-lig'i-nōse, *a.* Fuliginous. [Rare.]

fū-lig-i-nos'i-ty, *n.* Sootiness; fuliginous matter; smokiness; gloom.

fū-lig'i-nous, *a.* [L. *fuliginosus*, from *fuligo (-inis)*, soot.] Relating to soot or smoke; sooty; smoky; gloomy; dusky; specifically, of a sooty opaque brown; as, the *fuliginous* tern.

fū-lig'i-nous-ly, *adv.* In a fuliginous manner.

Fū-lig-ū-li'næ, *n.pl.* [From L. *fulica*, a coot.] A subfamily of the *Anatidæ*; the sea-ducks, including the canvasbacks, scoters, eiders, scaups, etc.

fụll, *a.*, *comp.* fuller; *superl.* fullest. [ME. *ful*, *full*; AS. *ful*, *full*, full.]

1. Ha ing within its limits all that it can or should contain; having no space or place vacant or unoccupied; replete; filled; not vacant; as, a *full* bowl; the list is *full*; the bases were *full.*

2. Complete; entire; adequate; sufficient; not defective or partial; without abatement; whole; as, a *full* year; a *full* description; a *full* meal; a *full* supply; a *full* course of instruction; *full* value or measure; *full* age; *full* control; a *full* stop.

3. Abundant; plenteous; copious; ample in dimensions or quantity; as, a *full* body; a *full* face; a *full* voice; the *full* moon, having the whole earthward surface illuminated.

4. Abounding with or in; having a large quantity or abundance; completely occupied by or busied with; with *of*; as, a room *full of* people; *full of* care; *full of* the idea; *full of* work; *full of* expedients.

5. Sated; satiated; satisfied, as if filled with food or with liquor; hence, drunk; intoxicated; as, he ate his fill and was *full*; *full* as a lord.

6. Pregnant or heavy with young or with spawn.

7. High; said of the tide.

8. In poker, comprising a pair and three of a kind; as, a *full* hand or a *full* house.

Full and by; sailing close-hauled, having all the sails full, and lying as near the wind as possible.

Full brothers or *sisters*; children of the same father and the same mother.

Full cousin; the son or daughter of an aunt or uncle.

Full cry; see *In full cry* under *Cry.*

Full dress; see under *Dress.*

Full moon; the moon with its whole disk illuminated, as when opposite to the sun; also, the time when the moon is in this position.

Full swing; unrestrained liberty. [Slang.]

fụll, *n.* 1. Complete measure; utmost extent; highest state or degree; as, this instrument answers to the *full*; fed to the *full.*

> The swan's down feather,
> That stands upon the swell at *full* of tide.
> —Shak.

2. That period in the revolution of the moon when it presents to the spectator its whole face illuminated, as it always does when in opposition to the sun.

Written in full; written without contractions; written in words, not in figures.

fụll, *adv.* 1. Quite; to the same degree; without abatement or diminution; equally.

> The pawn I proffer shall be *full* as good.
> —Dryden.

2. Fully; completely; altogether.

> I am now *full* resolved. —Shak.

3. Exactly.

> *Full* in the center of the sacred wood.
> —Addison.

4. Directly; straight; as, he looked him *full* in the face; he came *full* upon such a one.

5. To satiety.

> I have supped *full* with horrors. —Shak.

Full is placed, especially in poetry, before adjectives and adverbs to heighten or strengthen their signification; as, *full* sad.

> With his cruel bow he laid *full* low
> The harmless albatross. —Coleridge.

Full is prefixed to other words, chiefly participles, to express utmost extent or degree; as, *full*-blown, *full*-grown, etc.

fụll, *v.i.* To become full, as the moon.

fụll, *v.t.* and *v.i.*; fulled, *pt., pp.*; fulling, *ppr.* [ME. *fullen*, from AS. *fullere*, a fuller.] To thicken, as cloth in a mill.

fụll, *v.t.* and *v.i.* In dressmaking, to pucker.

fụll'āge, *n.* The price paid for fulling cloth.

fụl'lăm, fụl'hăm (-ăm), *n.* 1. An old cant word for false dice, named from Fulham, a suburb of London, the most notorious resort for blacklegs in all England.

2. Hence, any sham or make-believe.

fụll'back, *n.* In football, the player or the position back of the rush-line, farthest from the opponents' goal.

fụll'bind"ing, *n.* A bookbinding in which the whole of the sides and back is of leather.

fụll'=blood (-blud), *n.* A person or animal of the purest breed.

fụll'=blood"ed, *a.* 1. Amply supplied with blood.

2. Of unmixed breed on both sides; thoroughbred.

fụll'=blọomed, *a.* Having perfection of bloom.

fụll'=blōwn, *a.* 1. Fully expanded, as a blossom.

2. Fully distended with wind.

fụll'=bot"tŏmed, *a.* 1. Having a large bottom, as a wig.

2. In shipbuilding, having great capacity in the hull.

fụll'=bound, *a.* In bookbinding, having a cover made entirely of leather, in distinction from a *cloth-* or *half-bound* book.

fụll=butt', *adv.* With opposition direct, sudden, and violent, as in a head-on collision. [Colloq.]

fụll'ẽr, *n.* [ME. *fuller, fullere*, from AS. *fullere*, a fuller; L. *fullo*, a fuller.] One whose occupation is to full cloth.

Fuller's earth; a kind of earth composed of clay and silicious material, either natural or artificial, used by fullers for taking grease out of cloth.

fụll'ẽr, *n.* A blacksmith's tool, used like a swage, for making a groove in or spreading iron.

fụll'ẽr, *v.t.*; fullered, *pt., pp.*; fullering, *ppr.* To stamp a groove or channel in, as with a fuller or swage.

fụll'ẽr's=hẽrb, *n.* *Saponaria officinalis*, formerly used for taking stains out of cloth.

fụll'ẽr's=tēa"zel, fụll'ẽr's=this"tle (-this's'l), **fụll'ẽr's=weed,** *n.* The dried flower-head of the common teazel, *Dipsacus fullonum.*

fụll'ẽr-y, *n.*; *pl.* **fụll'ẽr-ies.** The place or the works where the fulling of cloth is carried on.

fụll'=fāced (-fāst), *a.* 1. Possessed of a full, well-rounded face; said of a person.

2. In portraiture, with the face presented fronting; turned toward neither the right nor the left.

3. In printing, designating a face of type having a full, bold face.

☞**This is full-faced type.**

fụll'=fọrmed, *a.* Having full form; well rounded out and matured.

fụll'=grōwn, *a.* Grown to full size; matured.

fụll'=heärt"ed, *a.* Full of courage or confidence.

fụll'=hot, *a.* Heated to the limit.

fụll'ing, *n.* The processes by which cloth is fulled.

fụll'ing=mill, *n.* A mill for fulling cloth by means of pestles or stampers which beat and press it to a close or compact state and cleanse it.

fụll'=manned, *a.* Having a complement of men.

fụll'märt, *n.* Same as *Foulmart.*

fụll'ness, fụl'ness, *n.* The state of being full in any sense of the word.

ful-lon'i-căl, *a.* [L. *fullonicus*, from *fullo (-onis)*, a fuller.] Relating to a fuller or to his art.

fụll'=ọrbed, *a.* Having an entire circular face exposed and illuminated; as, the *full-orbed* moon.

fụll'=sāiled, *a.* 1. With every sail fully set.

2. In complete readiness; having no hindrance.

fụll'=winged, *a.* 1. Having complete wings, or large, strong wings.

2. Ready for flight; eager. [Rare.]

fụl'ly, *adv.* Completely; entirely; without lack or defect; in a manner to give satisfaction; to the extent desired; as, to be *fully* persuaded of the truth of a proposition.

Fully committed; in law, committed to prison for trial, in distinction from being previously detained for examination.

Syn.—Completely, unreservedly, amply, entirely, wholly, sufficiently, perfectly, plentifully.

ful′măr, *n.* [From ME. *fulmar, fulmare,* short forms of *fulmart,* a polecat.] A sea-fowl, the *Procellaria glacialis* of Linnæus, which, like the other petrels, possesses the singular faculty of spouting from its bill a quantity of pure oil against its adversary. It is an inhabitant of northern, especially polar, regions, and feeds on the flesh and blubber of dead whales and seals, or other offal. It is valued for its down, feathers, and oil.

Fulmar (*Procellaria glacialis*).

ful′mi-nănt, *a.* [L. *fulminans (-antis),* ppr. of *fulminare,* to lighten.] Thundering. [Rare.]

ful′mi-nāte, *v.i.*; fulminated, *pt., pp.*; fulminating, *ppr.* [L. *fulminatus,* pp. of *fulminare,* to lighten, strike with lightning, from *fulmen (-inis),* lightning, a thunderbolt.]

1. To thunder; to make a loud, sudden noise, or a sudden, sharp crack; to detonate.

2. To issue ecclesiastical censures, as if with the force of a thunderbolt.

ful′mi-nāte, *v.t.* 1. To cause to explode.

2. To utter or send out, as a denunciation or censure; especially, as menaces or censures sent out by ecclesiastical authority.

ful′mi-nāte, *n.* In chemistry, a compound of fulminic acid with a base; as, *fulminates* of mercury, of silver, or of gold, which detonate or explode by percussion, friction, or heat.

ful′mi-nā-ting, *a.* 1. Thundering; crackling; exploding; detonating.

2. Hurling papal denunciations, menaces, or censures.

Fulminating oil; a name given to nitroglycerin on account of its oiliness.

Fulminating powder; see *Detonating powder* under *Detonating.*

ful-mi-nā′tion, *n.* [L. *fulminatio (-onis),* from *fulminare,* to lighten, strike with lightning.]

1. A thundering.

2. Denunciation by censure or threats, as by papal authority.

3. The explosion of certain chemical preparations; detonation.

ful′mi-nȧ-tō-ry, *a.* Thundering; striking terror.

ful′mine, *v.i.*; fulmined, *pt., pp.*; fulmining, *ppr.* To thunder; to issue an edict, bull, or the like, with or as with authority.

ful′mine, *v.t.* To shoot; to dart like lightning; to proclaim with emphasis.

ful-min′ē-ous, *a.* [L. *fulmineus,* from *fulmen,* lightning, a thunderbolt.] Of the nature of thunder or lightning; like thunder.

ful-min′iç, *a.* Relating to a fulminate or to fulminates.

Fulminic acid; in chemistry, an explosive acid composed of cyanogen and oxygen; $CH_2(NO_2)CN$.

ful-mi-nū′riç, *a.* Containing fulminic and cyanuric acids and designating the compound of these two.

Fulminuric acid; an acid known by its salts, isomeric with cyanuric acid, $H_3C_3N_3O_3$.

ful′ness, *n.* Same as *Fullness.*

ful-sam′iç, *a.* Same as *Fulsome.*

ful′sŏme, *a.* [ME. *fulsum, fulsom,* full, fat, plump *ful,* full, and *-sum, -som, -some.*] Rank; gross; disgusting; nauseous; as, *fulsome* flattery, compliment, or praise. Obsolete in the sense of foul, unclean, lustful.

Syn.—Excessive, gross, loathsome, nauseous, sickening, fawning, offensive.

ful′sŏme-ly, *adv.* Rankly; nauseously.

ful′sŏme-ness, *n.* Nauseousness; offensive grossness.

ful′vid, *a.* Fulvous. [Rare.]

ful′vous, *a.* [L. *fulvus,* deep yellow, tawny.] Tawny; dull yellow, with a mixture of gray and brown.

ful′wȧ, *n.* [Native name.] The butter-tree of India, *Bassia butyracea,* and its oil or butter.

fum, *v.i.* [Imitative.] To play upon a fiddle. [Obs.]

fū-mā′ceous, *a.* [L. *fumus,* smoke, and *-aceous.*] Smoky; hence, pertaining to smoke or smoking; addicted to smoking tobacco.

fū-mä′dō, *n.*; *pl.* **fū-mä′dōeş.** [Sp. *fumado,* pp. of *fumar,* to smoke.] A smoked fish, especially a pilchard.

fū′māġe, *n.* Hearth-money.

fū′mȧ-rāte, *n.* A salt of fumaric acid.

Fū-mā′ri-ȧ, *n.* [From L. *fumus,* smoke.] A genus of plants of the fumitory family, natives of the Old World. *Fumaria officinalis,* the common fumitory, has been naturalized in almost every civilized country.

fū-mȧ-ri-ā′ceous, *a.* Belonging to the *Fumaria.*

fū-mar′iç, *a.* [*Fumar*ia and *-ic.*] Pertaining to or obtained from fumitory.

Fumaric acid; a monobasic acid, a product of the action of heat on malic acid. It exists ready-formed in several plants, as in common fumitory. It forms fine, soft, micaceous scales, soluble in water and alcohol.

fū′mȧ-rin, fū′mȧ-rïne, *n.* [*Fumar*ia and *-in, -ine.*] A base obtained from *Fumaria officinalis.* It crystallizes in irregular six-sided prisms.

fū′mȧ-rōle, *n.* [It. *fumaruolo,* a fumarole, from LL. *fumariolum,* dim. of *fumarium,* a chimney.] A hole from which smoke issues in a sulphur-mine or volcano.

fū′mȧ-tō-ry, *n.* [Obs.] Same as *Fumitory.*

fum′ble, *v.i.*; fumbled, *pt., pp.*; fumbling, *ppr.* [Akin to D. *fommelen*; L.G. *fommeln, fummeln*; Ice. *falma,* to fumble, grope.]

1. To feel or grope about; to make awkward attempts.

2. To grope about in perplexity; to seek awkwardly; as, to *fumble* for an excuse.

3. To handle much; to play childishly; to turn over and over.

> I saw him *fumble* with the sheets, and play with flowers. —Shak.

fum′ble, *v.t.* 1. To manage awkwardly; to crowd or tumble together.

2. In baseball, to handle (the ball) clumsily, making a misplay; in football, to drop (the ball) after the play starts.

fum′blēr, *n.* One who fumbles, gropes, or manages awkwardly.

fum′bling-ly, *adv.* In a fumbling manner.

fūme, *n.* [ME. *fume*; OFr. *fum,* from L. *fumus,* smoke, steam.]

1. Smoke. [Rare.]

2. Smoky or vaporous exhalation from anything, especially if possessing narcotic or other marked properties; volatile matter arising from anything; exhalation; generally in the plural; as, the *fumes* of tobacco; the *fumes* of burning sulphur; the *fumes* of wine.

3. Any mental agitation regarded as clouding or affecting the understanding; angry mood; passion.

4. Anything like *fume* or vapor in being unsubstantial or fleeting, as an idle conceit, vain imagination, and the like.

5. The incense of praise; excessive flattery. [Obs.]

fūme, *v.i.*; fumed, *pt., pp.*; fuming, *ppr.* [Fr. *fumer,* from L. *fumare,* to smoke, from *fumus,* smoke, steam.]

1. To smoke; to throw off smoke, as in combustion.

> Where the golden altar *fumed.* —Milton.

2. To yield vapor or invisible exhalations.

3. To pass off in vapors.

4. To be in a rage; to be hot with anger.

5. To be stupefied or dulled.

fūme, *v.t.* 1. To smoke; to dry in smoke; to fill with fumes.

2. To perfume. [Obs.]

3. To disperse or drive away in vapors; as, the heat will *fume* away most of the scent.

4. To flatter excessively.

fūme′less, *a.* Free from fumes.

fūm′ēr, *n.* 1. A person giving to fuming.

2. A perfumer. [Obs.]

fū′mēr-ell, *n.* See *Femerel.*

fū′met, few′met, *n.* [Fr. *fumées,* from L. *fimus,* dung.] The dung of deer and kindred animals.

fū′me-tere (-tär), *n.* [Obs.] See *Fumitory.*

fū-mette′, *n.* [Fr. *fumet,* odor, fumes of meat, from L. *fumus,* smoke, steam.]

1. The odor from cooking meats.

2. The scent of game kept too long.

fū′mid, *a.* [L. *fumidus,* from *fumus,* smoke, steam.] Smoky; vaporous.

fū-mid′i-ty, fū′mid-ness, *n.* Smokiness.

fū-mif′ēr-ous, *a.* [L. *fumifer*; *fumus,* smoke, and *ferre,* to bear.] Producing smoke.

fū-mif′ū-ġist, *n.* [L. *fumus,* smoke, and *fugare,* to drive away.] One who or that which drives away smoke or fumes.

fū′mi-fȳ, *v.t.* [Obs.] See *Fumigate.*

fū′mi-gănt, *a.* Fuming. [Rare.]

fū′mi-gāte, *v.t.*; fumigated, *pt., pp.*; fumigating, *ppr.* [L. *fumigatus,* pp. of *fumigare,* to smoke, fumigate, from *fumus,* smoke.]

1. To smoke; to perfume.

2. To apply smoke to; to expose to smoke or gas, as in chemistry or in medicine, by inhaling it, or in cleansing infected apartments, clothing, etc.

fū-mi-gā′tion, *n.* 1. The act of smoking or applying smoke or gas, as in disinfecting apparel or apartments; disinfection.

2. Vapors raised by fumigating.

fū′mi-gā-tŏr, *n.* A device for disinfecting by fumigation; also, one using such a device.

fū′mi-gȧ-tō-ry, *a.* Having the quality of cleansing by smoke or gas.

fūm′i-ly, *adv.* Smokily; by means of fumes.

fūm′ing, *a.* Smoking; emitting vapors; raging; fretting.

Cadet's fuming liquid; in chemistry, an inflammable liquid having an intensely disagreeable odor. It is both colorless and poisonous, containing arsenic. [See *Alkarsin.*]

Fuming liquor of Libavius; tin chlorid, $SnCl_4$, named from Andreas Libavius (1588-1616), a colorless compound fuming when exposed to the atmosphere, and upon the addition of water, forming a semisolid substance called *butter of tin.*

Fuming sulphuric acid; see *Disulphuric acid* under *Disulphuric.*

fūm′ing-ly, *adv.* Angrily; in a rage.

fūm′ish, *a.* Smoky; hot; choleric. [Rare.]

fūm′ish-ness, *n.* The quality or state of being fumish.

fū′mi-tēr, *n.* [Obs.] See *Fumitory.*

fū′mi-tō-ry, *n.* [ME. *fumeter, fumetere, fumytere*; OFr. *fume-terre,* from LL. *fumus terræ,* lit., smoke of the earth; so called from its smell.] Any plant of the genus *Fumaria.* The leaves of the *Fumaria officinalis,* or common fumitory, are of a bitter taste, and were formerly used in disorders of the skin.

Climbing fumitory; the *Adlumia cirrhosa,* a climbing plant; also called *mountain-fringe.*

fū′mi-tō-ry, *n.* [From L. *fumatus,* pp. of *fumare,* to smoke.] A smoking-room. [Rare.]

fum′mel, *n.* The offspring of a horse and an ass. [Prov. Eng. See *Hinny* and *Mule.*]

fū′mōse, *a.* Same as *Fumous.*

fū-mos′i-ty, *n.*; *pl.* **fū-mos′i-tieş.** 1. The quality of giving off fumes.

2. [*pl.*] The fumes from a drunken person; eructations. [Obs.]

fūm′ous, *a.* [L. *fumosus,* smoky, from *fumus,* smoke.]

1. Creating smoke; smoky.

2. Producing fumes; filled with vapor.

fūm′y, *a.* Producing fumes; full of vapor.

fun, *n.* [Prob. of Celt. origin; Gael. *fonn*; Ir. *fonn,* delight, pleasure.] Sport; merriment.

To make fun of; to make the object of ridicule.

fū-nam′bū-lāte, *v.i.* [From L. *funis,* a rope, and *ambulatus,* pp. of *ambulare,* to walk.] To walk on a rope; to dance on a rope. [Rare.]

fū-nam-bū-lā′tion, *n.* Dancing or walking on a rope. [Rare.]

fū-nam′bū-lȧ-tō-ry, *a.* Performing like a ropedancer; pertaining to ropedancing. [Rare.]

fū-nam′bū-list, *n.* [L. *funambulus,* a rope-walker.] A ropewalker or dancer.

fū-nam′bū-lō, fū-nam′bū-lus, *n.* [Obs.] See *Funambulist.*

Fū-nā′ri-ȧ, *n.* [LL., f. of *funarius,* of or belonging to a rope, from *funis,* a rope.] A genus of mosses of the family *Bryaceæ* or true mosses.

fuņç′tion, *n.* 1. In a general sense, the doing, executing, or performing of anything; discharge; performance; as, the *function* of a calling or office.

2. Office or employment, or any duty or business belonging to a particular station or character, or required in that station or character; occupation, employment, business, or office in general; as, the *functions* of a chancellor, judge, or bishop; the *functions* of a parent or guardian.

3. The specific office or action which any organ or system of organs is fitted to perform in the animal or vegetable economy; as, the *function* of the heart, of leaves, etc.; the specific office of anything belonging to a living being, as the body as a whole, the mind of man, or any faculty of the mind.

4. A public ceremony; specifically, an elaborate religious ceremonial; in colloquial usage, any social event, when marked by elaborateness and lavishness of display.

5. In mathematics, a quantity so connected with another that no change can be made in the latter without producing a corresponding change in the former, in which case the dependent quantity is said to be a *function* of the other; thus, the circumference of a circle is a *function* of the diameter; the area of a triangle is a *function* of any two of the sides and the angle they contain. In order to indicate in a general way that one quantity y is a *function* of another x the notation $y=f(x)$, or something similar is adopted; thus, if u be the area of a triangle, x and y two of the sides, and θ the contained angle, we should write $u=\phi(x, y, \theta)$.

Algebraic function; a function whose value may be derived by algebraic processes, or that is expressed by the unknown quantity in an algebraic equation.

Animal functions; those which relate to the external world, as the senses, voluntary motions, etc.

Arbitrary function; see under *Arbitrary.*

Calculus of functions; see under *Calculus.*

Carnot's function; in thermodynamics, a function expressing the ratio of the heat expended to the work it does; the reciprocal of absolute temperature.

Circular functions or *inverse trigonometrical functions*; functions expressing the value of an angle or arc as dependent upon the value of any trigonometrical function, as sine, tangent, etc.

Continuous function; a quantity whose real values are not affected by the values of its variables between certain given limits.

Discontinuous function; see under *Discontinuous*.

Elliptic function; a function which returns to the same value when its variable changes; a doubly periodic function; the inverse of an elliptic integral.

Explicit function; a quantity whose value is expressed directly in terms of the variable; as, in $x=2y^2$, x is an *explicit function* of y.

Implicit function; a quantity whose relation to a variable is not directly expressed, but implied in an equation.

Natural or *vegetative functions*; functions less instantly necessary to life, as digestion, absorption, assimilation, expulsion, etc.

One-valued function; a quantity whose value never varies with that of the variable or variables.

The equivalence of functions; a communistic term implying that no man's labor ought to be remunerated at a higher rate than that of any other man, whatever be the difference of capacity or production.

Transcendental function; a quantity whose relation to a variable cannot be determined by algebraic processes; as $y=7^x$.

Trigonometrical function; any function of an arc of a circle or of its angle expressed by a line related thereto; as, in a circle, a line drawn from one extremity of an arc perpendicularly to a radius drawn to its other extremity (radius being unity) is a function of that arc and of the angle it subtends, and is called its sine; other principal functions are cosine, tangent, and cotangent.

Vital functions; functions immediately necessary to life, as those of the brain, heart, lungs, etc.

fun̄c′tion, *v.i.*; functioned, *pt.*, *pp.*; functioning, *ppr.* To perform a function; to have some use; to act.

fun̄c′tion-ăl, *a.* 1. Pertaining to functions or to a function or office.

2. In physiology, relating to a special function or to the bodily functions as a whole.

Functional disease; in medicine, any derangement of an organ interfering with the discharge of its function, as distinguished from an affection of the organ itself.

fun̄c′tion-ăl-ize, *v.t.* To give a function to. [Rare.]

fun̄c′tion-ăl-ly, *adv.* By means of the functions.

fun̄c′tion-ā-ry, *n.*; *pl.* **fun̄c′tion-ā-ries.** [Fr. *fonctionnaire*, from L. *functio* (*-onis*), function.] One who holds an office or trust; as, a public *functionary*; secular *functionaries*.

fun̄c′tion-āte, *v.i.*; functionated, *pt.*, *pp.*; functionating, *ppr.* To function.

fun̄c′tion-less, *a.* Having no function.

fund, *n.* [OFr. *fond*, bottom, ground, stock, capital, from L. *fundus*, bottom, land, estate.]

1. A sum of money, or stock convertible into money, held available for the demands of an individual, company, or corporation engaged in business, or for a similar purpose.

2. Specifically, (a) the capital or assets of a business, corporation, or trust; (b) a permanent capital invested to secure an income; an endowment; a foundation; (c) a collection of money or an appropriation to be devoted to some specific use; as, the *fund* to educate the poor.

3. Money lent to government, constituting a national debt; or the stock of a national debt; used in the plural; as, government *funds* were never so high before.

4. [*pl.*] Money; cash; as, he is out of *funds.* [Colloq.]

5. Abundance; ample stock or store; as, a *fund* of knowledge.

Public funds; (a) government money immediately available; (b) in England, that part of the national debt in annuities redeemable by the government at pleasure.

fund, *v.t.*; funded, *pt.*, *pp.*; funding, *ppr.* 1. To provide and appropriate a fund or permanent revenue for the payment of the interest of; to make permanent provision of resources for discharging the annual interest of; as, to *fund* bills or government notes; to *fund* a national debt.

2. To store. [Obs.]

fund′ȧ-ble, *a.* Convertible into a fund or bonds.

fun′dȧ-ment, *n.* [L. *fundamentum*, from *fundare*, to lay the bottom, foundation, from *fundus*, the bottom.]

1. A basal principle; an element; as, the *fundament* of analytics is the conception of position.

2. The seat; the buttocks; sometimes, the anus.

3 Foundation. [Obs.]

fun-dȧ-men′tăl, *a.* Pertaining to the foundation or basis; serving for the foundation; essential; important; basal; primary; as, a *fundamental* truth or principle; a *fundamental* law.

Fundamental bass; that part, in musical harmony, which sustains the chord; in the natural position of the chord, the lowest part.

Fundamental chord; in music, a chord having its lowest tone for a root.

Fundamental colors; primary colors.

Fundamental tissue; the tissue of plants, unmodified or only slightly modified.

Fundamental tones; tones producing harmonic chords.

Syn.—Primary, important, indispensable, essential.

fun-dȧ-men′tăl, *n.* A leading or primary principle, rule, law, or article, which serves as the groundwork of a system; essential part; as, the *fundamentals* of the Christian faith.

2. In music, the keynote of a chord.

3. In acoustics, a note compared with its overtones.

fun-dȧ-men′tăl-ly, *adv.* Primarily; originally; essentially; at the foundation; as, all power is *fundamentally* in the citizens of a state.

fund′ed, *a.* 1. Converted into a permanent loan, or into a loan or bonds payable on demand or at some specified time.

2. Invested, especially in public funds.

fund′ẽr, *n.* One favoring a sinking-fund; one who funds or wishes to fund a public debt; specifically, at the close of the Civil War, a citizen of Virginia in favor of funding all and not repudiating any part of the debt of the state.

fund′hōld″ẽr, *n.* One who has an investment in public funds.

fun′di, *n.* [Native name.] A millet-like grain, *Paspalum exile*, grown in Africa.

fun′di-fọrm, *a.* [L. *funda*, sling, and *forma*, form.] In anatomy, like a sling in form.

fund′ing, *n.* 1. Providing funds for the payment of a debt.

2. Making an investment in government funds.

Funding system; a scheme of finance or revenue by which provision is made for paying annual interest on a public debt.

fund′less, *a.* Destitute of funds.

fun′dus, *n.* [L.] 1. The bottom, rear, or depths of anything.

2. In anatomy, the part of a hollow organ at a distance from the entrance; the base or bottom.

fū-nē′bri-ăl, fū-nē′bri-ous, *a.* [L. *funebris*, from *funus*, *funeris*, a funeral.] Pertaining to funerals. [Obs.]

fū′nẽr-ăl, *n.* [ME. *funeral*; OFr. *funeral*, *funerail*, from LL. *funeralia*, neut. pl. of *funeralis*, pertaining to a burial, from L. *funus* (*-eris*), a funeral procession, burial.]

1. Burial; the ceremony of burying, or otherwise formally disposing of a dead human body; the solemnization of interment or cremation; obsequies.

2. The procession of persons attending the burial of the dead. [Colloq.]

3. A discourse or sermon given at a funeral; often used in the plural. [Obs.]

fū′nẽr-ăl, *a.* Pertaining to burial; used at the interment of the dead; as, *funeral* ceremonies; *funeral* feast; *funeral* oration.

Funeral pile; a heap of combustible matter arranged to consume a dead body by burning, as a funeral rite; a pyre.

fū′nẽr-ā-ry, *a.* Of or relating to a funeral or to the interment or cremation of a human body.

fū′nẽr-āte, *v.t.* [L. *funeratus*, pp. of *funerare*, to bury with funeral rites.] To hold a funeral for. [Obs.]

fū-nẽr-ā′tion, *n.* Solemnization of a funeral. [Obs.]

fū-nē′rē-ăl, *a.* Suiting a funeral; pertaining to burial; by association, dismal; mournful; gloomy.

fū-nē′rē-ăl-ly, *adv.* Dismally; mournfully.

fū-nest′, *a.* [L. *funestus*, from *funus*, a funeral, death, dead body.] Doleful; mournful; lamentable. [Rare.]

fun̄-gā′ceous, *a.* Of, relating to, or characteristic of a fungus or fungi.

fun̄′găl, *a.* Having reference to fungi.

fun̄′gāte, *n.* A compound of fungic acid and a base.

fuṅġe, *n.* [From L. *fungus*, a mushroom, a dolt.] A fool; a blockhead; a thickwitted person.

Fun′ġi, *n.pl.* [L. *fungus*, a mushroom.] In botany, a large natural order of acotyledonous or cryptogamous plants, 5,000 being known, varying greatly in size, form, color, and consistence. In the upper cut P refers to the *pileus* or cap, S to the *stipes* or stem, V to the *volva* or wrapper, H the *hymenium* or gills, A the *annulus* or ring, C the *cortina* or curtain, M the *mycelium* or spawn. Under the name fungus botanists comprehend various races of mushrooms, toadstools, and similar plants, microscopic plants growing upon other plants, and substances which are known as molds, mildew, smut, rust, brand, dry-rot, etc. Berkeley divides fungi into two sections, the first having the spores naked, and comprising agarics, boleti, puffballs, rust, smut, and mildew; the second comprising the morels, truffles, certain molds, etc., in which the spores are in sacs (asci).

Common Mushroom (*Agaricus campestris*)—illustrative of parts of Fungi and terms employed.

1. *Agaricus comatus* (tall cylindrical agaric). 2. *Boletus edulis* (edible boletus). 3. *Morchella esculenta* (roundheaded morel).

Fun′ġi-ȧ, *n.* [From L. *fungus*, a mushroom.] A genus of corals resembling a mushroom in form. They are flat and circular or elliptical, and some of them are eighteen inches in diameter.

fun′ġi-ăn, *a.* and *n.* I. *a.* Of or pertaining to the *Fungiidæ*, a family of corals of which *Fungia* is the type genus.

II. *n.* A fungian coral.

fun′ġi-ble, *n.* [LL. *fungibilis*, from *fungi*, to perform, execute.]

1. In the civil law, a thing of such a nature that it may be replaced by another of equal quantity and quality.

2. In Scots law, a movable which may be estimated by weight, number, or measure, as grain or money.

fun′ġiç, *a.* Pertaining to or obtained from fungi.

Fungic acid; an acid contained in the juice of most fungi. It is said to be a mixture of citric, malic, and phosphoric acid.

fun′ġi-ci-dăl, *a.* Of or pertaining to fungicides.

fun′ġi-cide, *n.* [L. *fungus*, fungus, and *-cida*, from *cædere*, to kill.] A germicide.

fun-ġiç′ō-lous, *a.* [L. *fungus*, fungus, and *colere*, to inhabit.] Existing in fungi or on fungi.

fun′ġi-fọrm, *a.* [L. *fungus*, a mushroom, and *forma*, form.] Having a termination similar to the head of a fungus or mushroom; specifically, in anatomy, denoting those papillæ of the tongue having a head convex in shape.

fun-ġil′li-fọrm, *a.* [A dim. from L. *fungus*, fungus, and *forma*, form.] Fungiform.

fun′ġin, *n.* [*Fungus* and *-in*.] Fungus-cellulose.

fun′ġite, *n.* [*Fungus* and *-ite*.] A fungian fossil coral.

fun-ġiv′o-rous, *a.* [L. *fungus*, a mushroom, and *vorare*, to devour.] Feeding on fungi.

fun̄′goid, *a.* [L. *fungus*, a fungus, and Gr. *eidos*, form.] Having the appearance or character of a fungus.

fun̄-gol′ō-ġist, *n.* A mycologist.

fun̄-gol′ō-ġy̆, *n.* [L. *fungus*, a mushroom, and *-logia*, from *legein*, to speak.] The science of fungi; mycology.

fun̄-gos′i-ty, *n.* 1. Fungous quality.

2. Proud flesh; a fungoid excrescence.

fun̄′gous, *a.* [ME. *fungous*; It. *fungoso*, from L. *fungosus*, full of holes, spongy, from *fungus*, a mushroom, fungus.]

1. Like fungus or a mushroom; spongy; soft.

2. Growing suddenly; not substantial or durable.

3. Accompanied by fungoid growths.

fun̄′gus, *n.*; *pl.* **fun′ġi** or **fun̄′gus-eṣ.** 1. Any plant of the *Fungi*.

2. A spongy excrescence in animal bodies, as proud flesh formed in wounds.

fun̄′gus-cel′lū-lōse, *n.* The cellulose of fungi.

fū′niç, *a.* Funicular.

fū′ni-çle, *n.* [L. *funiculus*, dim. of *funis*, a cord, rope.]

1. In botany, (a) a small cord; a small ligature; a fiber; a small stalk that connects the seed and the placenta; the stalk that supports the ovule; (b) a pedicel joining the peridiolum to the peridium in certain fungi.

2. A funiculus.

Funicles.

fū-niç′ū-lăr, *a.* [L. *funiculus*, dim. of *funis*, a cord.] Of, due to, consisting of, or resembling a cord, funicle, or funiculus.

Funicular action; in mechanics, the force exerted by a cord upon the supports to which its ends are attached, when moved transversely, as is a bowstring.

Funicular curve; see *Catenary*.

Funicular machine; any of various contrivances intended to illustrate some mechanical principle, and consisting mainly in an arrangement of cords and suspended weights.

Funicular polygon; in statics, the figure assumed by a string supported at its extremities and acted on by several pressures.

fū-niç′ū-lāte, *a.* [L. *funiculus*, a small rope, cord, dim. of *funis*, a rope, cord.]

1. Having or developing funicles.

2. In zoölogy, forming a slender ridge.

fū′ni-çūle, *n.* A funiculus; a funicle.

fū-niç′ū-lus, *n.*; *pl.* **fū-niç′ū-li.** [L., a small cord, dim. of *funis*, a cord, rope.]

1. A fiber; a small cord.

2. In anatomy, (a) the umbilical cord; (b) a

bundle of nerve fibers having a sheath of neurilemma.

3. In zoölogy, (a) a cord or ligament which connects the embryo and the amnion of some myriapods; (b) the chief tendon of an insect's abdomen; (c) a section of the antenna of an insect between the club and the pedicel.

4. In botany, a funicle.

5. Formerly, in physics, a form of ether assumed to explain certain phenomena due to atmospheric elasticity.

6. In Teutonic land-law, a measuring-cord.

fū-nil'i-fọrm, *a.* [From L. *funis*, a rope, and *forma*, form.] In botany, formed of tough, flexible, cord-like fibers, as the roots of some endogens.

fū'nis, *n.* [L., a rope, cord.] A cord; in physiology, the navel-string.

fuṅk, *n.* [ME. *funke*, a spark; OFr. *funkier*, to smoke.]

1. Punk; also, a spark.

2. A smoky, disagreeable smell.

fuṅk, *n.* [Dan. *funk*, a blow.] A kick; ill temper; anger. [Scot.]

fuṅk, *n.* Cowardly fear or panic; cowering terror; as, he was in a blue *funk*. [Slang.]

fuṅk, *v.i.* and *v.t.* To emit or stifle with a strong, smoky, or offensive smell.

fuṅk, *v.i.* and *v.t.* To flinch or shrink; to cause to back out.

fuṅk, *v.i.* and *v.t.* To kick; to grow angry.

fuṅk, *v.i.* To sparkle.

Fuṅ'ki-ȧ, *n.* [Named after Heinrich Christian *Funck*, a botanist of Germany.] A genus of the *Liliaceæ*, the day-lilies or plantain-lilies of China and Japan, bearing blue or white fragrant blossoms.

fun'nel, *n.* [ME. *funelle*, *fonel*, from OFr. *enfonille*, from L. *infundibulum*, a funnel, hopper of a mill, from *infundere*, to pour in; *in*, in, and *fundere*, to pour.]

1. A device for conveying fluids into small openings, consisting of a kind of inverted hollow cone with a pipe at the apex.

2. A passage for a fluid; the shaft or hollow channel of a chimney, through which smoke ascends; especially, the smokestack of a locomotive or steamship.

3. A metal ring on a masthead to which the rigging is fitted.

4. In zoölogy, an infundibulum, as of a squid.

fun'nel-box, *n.* A device used in the separation of crushed ores in the wet process.

fun'nel-fọrm, *a.* Having the form of a funnel, as certain monopetalous corollas.

Funnelform Corolla.

fun'ny, *a.*; *comp.* funnier; *superl.* funniest. Comical; droll; causing laughter; also, colloquially, queer; curious; odd; as, a *funny* way to act.

Syn.—Laughable, humorous, facetious, ludicrous, ridiculous.

fun'ny, *n.*; *pl.* **fun'nieṣ**. A narrow racing-boat, used with a pair of sculls.

fun'ny-bōne, *n.* The crazy-bone; the point at the elbow where the ulnar nerve is only slightly protected and hence sensitive to even a light blow.

fũr, *n.* [ME. *furre*, *forre*, *for*, fur, a pelt, from OFr. *forre*, *fuerre*, a case, sheath; It. *fodero*; Goth. *fodr*, a sheath.]

1. The short, fine, soft hair of certain animals, growing thick on the skin, and distinguished from the hair, which is longer and coarser.

2. The skins of certain wild animals with the fur; peltry; as, a cargo of *furs*.

3. [*pl.*] A muff and boa, or other articles of clothing made principally of *fur*; garments of *fur*.

4. Any furlike material found in nature, as (a) a coat of morbid matter collected on the tongue in persons affected with fever; (b) the coat or crust formed on the interior of vessels by matter deposited by hard water; (c) the down or fuzz on a peach.

5. Collectively, animals yielding fur.

6. In heraldry, one of three tinctures. *Furs* are borne on the shield and charges, and consist either of one color alone or of more colors than one. The *furs* of two colors are ermine, ermines, erminois, pean, vair, vairé, vairy cuppa, and erminites.

fũr, *a.* Pertaining to or made of fur.

fũr, *v.t.*; furred, *pt.*, *pp.*; furring, *ppr.* 1. To line, face, or cover with fur; as, a *furred* robe.

2. To cover with morbid matter, as the tongue.

3. In carpentry, to nail small strips of board on, as joists, rafters, etc., in order to make a level surface for lathing, boarding, etc.

fū-rā'cious, *a.* [L. *furax* (*-acis*), from *furari*, to steal, from *fur*, a thief.] Inclined to steal; thievish. [Obs.]

fū-rac'i-ty, *n.* Thievishness. [Obs.]

fũr'be-lōw, *n.* [Fr. dial. *farbala*; Sp., Port., It., *falbala*, a furbelow.] A piece of stuff plaited or puckered, on a gown or petticoat; a flounce; the plaited border of a petticoat or gown.

Furbelows (time of William and Mary).

fũr'be-lōw, *v.t.*; furbelowed, *pt.*, *pp.*; furbelowing, *ppr.* To put a furbelow on; to furnish with ornamental frills and flounces.

fũr'bish, *v.t.*; furbished, *pt.*, *pp.*; furbishing, *ppr.* [ME. *fourbischen*, *forbischen*, from OFr. *forbir*, *fourbir*; O.H.G. *furpan*, to clean, polish.] To rub or scour to brightness; to polish; to burnish; as, to *furbish* a sword.

fũr'bish-ȧ-ble, *a.* That may be furbished.

fũr'bish-ẽr, *n.* One who polishes or makes bright by rubbing; one who cleans.

fũr'cāte, **fũr'cā-ted**, *a.* [LL. *furcatus*, from L. *furca*, a fork.] Branching like the prongs of a fork; forked.

fũr-cā'tion, *n.* A forking; a branching like the tines of a fork.

fũr-cel'lāte, *a.* [Dim. from L. *furca*, a fork, and *-ate*.] Somewhat furcate.

fũr-cif'ẽr-ous, *a.* [L. *furcifer*, yoke-bearer, scoundrel; *furca*, a fork, an instrument of punishment in the form of a fork, and *ferre*, to bear.]

1. Villainous. [Rare.]

2. In entomology, bearing a yoke-like or forked process.

Fũr-crœ'ȧ, *n.* [Named after A. F. de *Fourcroy*, a French chemist.] A genus of *Amaryllidaceæ*, fibrous plants native to warm regions of America.

fũr'cū-lȧ, *n.*; *pl.* **fũr'cū-læ**. A small fork or forked process; the wishbone; the furculum.

fũr'cū-lăr, *a.* Having the form of a fork; furcated.

fũr'cū-lum, *n.*; *pl.* **fũr'cū-lȧ**. [A dim. from *furca*, a fork.] The anatomical name of the wishbone in birds.

fũr'dle, *v.t.*; furdled, *pt. pp.*; furdling, *ppr.* [OFr. *fardel*, dim. of *fard*, a bundle.] To draw up into a bundle. [Obs.]

fũr'fũr, *n.* [L.] Dandruff; scurf; scales like bran.

fũr-fū-rā'ceous, *a.* [L. *furfuraceus*, from *furfur*, bran, scales on the skin.] Scaly; branny; scurfy; like bran.

fũr'fū-răn, *n.* [From L. *furfur*, bran.] A colorless, oily, chemical compound, C_4H_4O.

fũr-fū-rā'tion, *n.* [From L. *furfur*, bran, scales on the skin.] The shedding of the scales of the cuticle; desquamation.

fũr'fū-rin, *n.* A white crystalline compound, $C_{15}H_{12}O_3N_2$, obtained from furfurol.

fũr'fū-rol, *n.* [L. *furfur*, bran, and *oleum*, oil.] An oily liquid of pleasant odor, $C_5H_4O_2$, formed from the distillation of bran, sugar, etc., with sulphuric acid.

fũr'fū-rous, *a.* [L. *furfurosus*, from *furfur*, bran.] Of or of the nature of bran; furfuraceous.

fū'ri-ăl, *a.* [L. *furialis*, furious, belonging to the Furies, from *furia*, rage, madness.] Furious; vehement; harassing. [Obs.]

fū'ri-bund, *a.* [L. *furibundus*, furious, from *furere*, to be mad.] Abounding in fury; raging wildly; frenzied. [Rare.]

fū-ri-bun'dăl, *a.* Filled with rage. [Obs.]

fū'ril, *a.* [*Furfurol* and *benzil*.] A product of the oxidation of furoin, symbol $C_{10}H_6O_4$.

fū-ril'iç, *a.* Of the character of furil; derived from furil.

fū"ri-ō'sä-men'te, *adv.* [It.] In music, with great agitation; furiously.

fū-ri-ō'sō, *a.* and *n.* [It., furious.] I. *a.* In music, furious.

II. *n.* A furious person.

fū'ri-ous, *a.* [ME. *furious*, from L. *furiosus*, full of madness, raging, from *furia*, madness, rage, from *furere*, to be mad.]

1. Rushing with impetuosity; moving with violence; as, a *furious* stream; a *furious* wind or storm.

2. Raging; violent; transported with passion; as, a *furious* animal.

fū'ri-ous-ly, *adv.* In a furious manner.

fū'ri-ous-ness, *n.* The state or quality of being furious.

fũrl, *v.t.*; furled, *pt.*, *pp.*; furling, *ppr.* [Contr. from *furdle*, *fardle*, from OFr. *fardeler*, to bundle, from *fardel*, a bundle; Sp. *fardo*; Ar. *fardah*, a package.] To draw up; to wrap or roll (a sail) close to the yard, stay, or mast, and fasten it by a gasket or cord; to wrap by rolling; as, to *furl* a flag about the staff.

fũr'lŏng, *n.* [ME. *furlong*, furlong; AS. *furlang*, a measure, lit., the length of a furrow; *furh*, a furrow, and *lang*, long.] A measure of length; the eighth part of a mile; forty rods, poles, or perches; two hundred and twenty yards; six hundred and sixty feet.

fũr'lough (-lō), *n.* [D. *verlof*, from Dan. *forlov*, leave, permission, leave of absence; *for*, for-, and *-lov*, Ice. *lov*, leave.] Leave of absence; specifically, in the United States army, the grant of temporary absence allowed an enlisted man; distinguished from *leave of absence* granted an officer.

fũr'lough, *v.t.*; furloughed, *pt.*, *pp.*; furloughing, *ppr.* To furnish with a furlough; to grant leave of absence to.

fũr'men-ty, **fũr'mi-ty**, *n.* Same as *Frumenty*.

fũr'năce, *n.* [ME. *furnasse*, *fournes*; OFr. *fornais*, *fornaz*; It. *fornace*, from L. *fornax* (*-acis*), a furnace, kiln, from *fornus*, *furnus*, an oven.]

1. A place where intense heat may be made and maintained for smelting ores, melting metals, consuming combustible substances, heating air, baking pottery, etc. Furnaces generally belong to one of three kinds, the *air*, the *blast*, or the *reverberatory*. The *air-furnace* receives its draft from the open air at normal pressure. The *blast-furnace* is supplied with air under high artificial pressure. The *reverberatory furnace* is so constructed as to throw the flame down upon the material to be heated or fused.

2. A place of punishment by cruel bondage and privation; any place, time, or occasion of severe torture; great trial; as, the *furnace* of affliction.

Furnace bridge; a low partition standing vertically in the fire chamber of a furnace for the purpose of deflecting the flame.

Furnace cadmium; a substance accumulating in the chimney of a furnace when smelting zinc-bearing ores.

Furnace hoist; a lift or elevator which carries material to the mouth of a blast furnace.

fũr'năce, *v.t.*; furnaced (-năst), *pt.*, *pp.*; furnacing, *ppr.* To treat by a process in which a furnace is used.

fũr'ni-ment, *n.* [OFr. *fourniment*, from *fournir*, to furnish, supply.] Furniture. [Obs.]

fũr'nish, *v.t.*; furnished (-nisht), *pt.*, *pp.*; furnishing, *ppr.* [ME. *furnysshen*, from OFr. *furnir*, *fournir*, to furnish; O.H.G. *frumjan*, to perform, provide, from *fruma*, gain, utility.]

1. To supply with anything wanted or necessary; as, to *furnish* a family with provisions; to *furnish* arms for defense.

2. To fit up; to supply with the proper goods, vessels, or ornamental appendages; as, to *furnish* a house or a room.

Syn.—Supply, provide, equip, afford, yield, bestow, purvey, give.

fũr'nish, *n.* Specimen; sample. [Obs.]

fũr'nish-ẽr, *n.* One who supplies or fits out.

fũr'nish-ingṣ, *n.pl.* Fixtures or supplies; especially, household furniture and decorations.

fũr'ni-tūre, *n.* [Fr. *fourniture*, from *fournir*, to furnish.]

1. Goods, utensils, and other articles necessary or convenient for housekeeping; whatever is added to the interior of a house or apartment, for use or convenience; chattels; movables; effects.

2. The necessary appendages in various employments or arts; as, the *furniture* of a barber's shop, or of an office.

3. In printing, the pieces placed around a page or form of type preparatory to locking it up.

4. In organ-making, a kind of stop producing a mixture of tones.

fũr'ni-tūre-bug, *n.* Same as *Lepisma*.

fū'rō-in, *n.* [From *furfurol*.] A volatile, crystalline compound, $C_{10}H_8O_4$.

fū'rọr, *n.* [L.] Fury; overpowering enthusiasm.

fū-rō're, *n.* Same as *Furor*.

fũr'ri-ẽr, *n.* [From OFr. *fourreur*, from *fourrer*, to fur.] A dealer in furs; one who makes or sells fur garments.

fũr'ri-ẽr-y, *n.* 1. Furs in general.

2. The occupation of dealing in manufactured furs.

fũr'ring, *n.* 1. Collectively, furs; also, fur trimming.

2. Any fur-like deposit, as the furry scale sometimes found in steam-boilers or the furry roughness of the tongue in certain diseases.

3. In carpentry, (a) the nailing of thin strips of board in order to level a surface for lathing, boarding, etc.; (b) [*pl.*] the strips thus laid on.

fũr'rōw, *n.* [ME. *forowe*, *furwe*; AS. *furh*, a furrow; O.H.G. *furuh*; Dan. *fure*; Sw. *fara*; Ice. *for*, a drain.]

1. A trench in the earth made by a plow.

2. A long, narrow trench or channel in wood or metal; a groove.

3. A hollow made by wrinkles in the face.

To draw a straight furrow; to live a blameless life; to avoid evil.

fũr'rōw, *v.t.*; furrowed, *pt.*, *pp.*; furrowing, *ppr.* [AS. *furan*, from *furh*, a furrow.]

1. To cut a furrow in; to make furrows in; to plow.

2. To cut; to make channels in, literally or figuratively; as, to *furrow* the deep.

3. To make wrinkles in; as, sorrow *furrows* the brow.

fur'rōw-weed, *n.* A weed springing up from the sod overturned by a plow.

fur'ry, *a.* 1. Covered with fur; dressed in fur.
2. Consisting of fur or skins; as, *furry* spoils.
3. Fur-like.

fur'-sēal, *n.* One of several species of seals of the genera *Callorhinus* and *Arctocephalus* of the northern oceans, having fine and soft fur which is a valuable article of commerce; called also *sea-bear.* [See under *Seal.*]

fur'thēr, *a.*, comp. of *far.* 1. More remote; more distant or advanced; as, the *further* end of the field. The word *farther* is generally preferred when speaking of distance in space.
2. Additional; extending beyond; especially in time, mention, or treatment; as, *further* remarks are unnecessary; we have a *further* reason for our opinion.

What *further* need have we for witnesses? —Matt. xxvi. 65.

fur'thēr, *adv.*, comp. of *far.* [ME. *further, forther*; AS. *furthor, furthur,* forward, comp. of *fore,* before.]
1. At or to a greater distance; more remotely; beyond; as, seek *further* for innocence.
2. In addition; to a greater extent; besides; moreover; as, I say *further* that the evidence is conclusive.

fur'thēr, *v.t.*; furthered, *pt., pp.*; furthering, *ppr.* To help forward; to promote; to cause to advance; to forward; hence, to help or assist.

fur'thēr-ănce, *n.* A helping forward; promotion; advancement.

I know that I shall abide and continue with you all, for your *furtherance* and joy of faith. —Phil. i. 25.

fur'thēr-ēr, *n.* One who helps to advance; a promoter.

fur'thēr-mōre, *adv.* Moreover; besides; in addition to what has been said.

fur'thēr-mōst, *a.* Most remote.

fur'thēr-sōme, *a.* Having the quality of helpfulness. [Rare.]

fur'thest, *a.*, superl. of *far.* Most distant, either in time or in place.

fur'thest, *adv.*, superl. of *far.* At the greatest distance.

fur'tive, *a.* [OFr. *furtif,* from L. *furtivus,* stolen, concealed, hidden, from *furtum,* theft, robbery, from *furari,* to steal; *fur,* a thief.] Stolen; obtained by theft; stealthy.

fur'tive-ly, *adv.* Stealthily.

fū'run-cle, *n.* [L. *furunculus,* a thief, pilferer, a boil, dim. of *fur,* a thief.] A superficial, inflammatory tumor, deep red, hard, circumscribed, acutely-tender to the touch, suppurating with a central core; commonly called a *boil.*

fū-run'cū-lăr, *a.* [L. *furunculus,* a furuncle, and *-ar.*] Relating to boils.

fū-run'cū-loid, *a.* [L. *furunculus,* a furuncle, and Gr. *eidos,* form.] Resembling a boil.

fū-run-cū-lō'sis, *n.* [L. *furunculus,* a furuncle, boil, and *-osis.*] The state of being afflicted with boils.

fū'ry, *n.*; *pl.* **fū'ries**. [ME. *furie, furye,* from Fr. *furie,* from L. *furia,* madness, rage, fury.]
1. A violent rushing; impetuous motion; as, the *fury* of the winds.
2. Rage; a storm of anger; madness; turbulence.

I do oppose my patience to his *fury.*—Shak.

3. [F—*pl.*] In classical mythology, the daughters of Earth or of Night, represented with wings, having serpents twined in their hair and blood dripping from their eyes.
4. Any means of vengeance; nemesis.

fū'ry, *n.* A thief. [Obs.]

furze, *n.* [ME. *firs, fyrs*; AS. *fyrs,* furze.] Gorse; whin; a thorny evergreen shrub with beautiful yellow flowers, a common plant of the plains and hills of Great Britain; the *Ulex Europæus* of botanists.

furze'chat, *n.* The whinchat, *Pratincola rubetra,* a turdoid bird frequenting furze or gorse.

furze'ling, *n.* *Melizophilus provincialis,* a small bird found in southern England.

furz'en, *a.* Furzy. [Obs.]

furz'y, *a.* Overgrown with furze; full of gorse.

fū-ṣain' (fū-zaṅ'), *n.* [Fr., the spindle-tree, the charcoal made from it.] A drawing-crayon made of small willow branches reduced to charcoal; also, the drawing made with such crayon.

fū'sa-rōle, *n.* [Fr. *fusarolle*; It. *fusaruolo,* from *fuso,* L. *fusus,* a spindle, shaft of a column.] In architecture, a molding generally placed under the echinus or quarter-round of columns in the Doric, Ionic, and Corinthian orders.

fus-cā'tion, *n.* A darkening; obscurity. [Rare.]

fus-ces'cent, *a.* [L. *fuscus,* dark, dusky, and *-escent.*] Dark brown.

fus'cin, fus'cine, *n.* [L. *fuscus,* dark, dusky, and *-in, ine.*] In chemistry, a brownish matter obtained from empyreumatic animal oil. It is insoluble in water, but may be dissolved by alcohol.

fus'cous, *a.* [L. *fuscus,* dark.] Brown; of a dark color.

fūṣe, *v.t.*; fused, *pt., pp.*; fusing, *ppr.* [L. *fusus,* pp. of *fundere,* to pour out, shed.]
1. To melt; to liquefy by heat; to render fluid; to dissolve.
2. To unite into a mass; to bring together in an aggregation; to conglomerate; as, America *fuses* the characteristics of various races into one.
3. In optics, to blend by bringing the eyes into visual line.

fūṣe, *v.i.* 1. To be melted; to be reduced from a solid to a fluid state by heat.
2. To become united into a mass; to be brought together in an aggregation.
3. In optics, to bring the eyes into visual line.

fūṣe, *n.* A tube filled with combustible matter; a slowly burning ribbon, cord, or the like used in blasting or in discharging a shell; also written *fusee.*

Bickford or *common fuse*; a small tubular fuse made of linen, containing a composition that burns slowly.

Chemical fuse; a fuse in which the materials ignite by contact.

Electric fuse; a fuse made to be ignited by an electric spark.

fūṣe, *n.* The track of a buck; also written *fusee.* [Obs.]

fū-ṣeau' (-zō'), *n.* [Fr., a spindle.] A spindle-shaped object of any kind; specifically, the hilt of a sword.

fū-ṣee', fū-zee', *n.* [OFr. *fusee,* a spindle full of thread, fusee, from LL. *fusata,* from *fusare,* to use a spindle, from L. *fusus,* a spindle.]

Barrel and Fusee of a Watch.

1. The cone or conical part of a watch or clock, round which is wound the chain or cord.
2. A splint for a horse's leg.
3. A figure the shape of a spindle. [Obs.]

fū-ṣee', fū-zee', *n.* [A corruption of Fr. *fusil,* a steel for striking fire, a musket.]
1. A small musket; a fusil.
2. The fuse used in firing a blast.
3. A kind of match used as a cigar lighter.

fū-ṣee', *n.* The track of a buck; a fuse. [Obs.]

fūṣe'-hōle, *n.* A hole for the insertion of the fuse in a shell.

fū'sel-āge, *n.* An elongated body, now usually enclosed, part of the essential structure of an aeroplane.

fū'ṣel-oil, *n.* [G. *fusel,* spirits of an inferior quality.] In chemistry, oil of potato-spirit; crude amyl alcohol; a colorless oily spirit, of a strong and nauseous odor and taste, which produces stupefying effects.

fūṣe'-plug, *n.* The plug that holds the fuse and that fills the fuse-hole when the shell is charged.

fū-ṣi-bil'i-ty, *n.* The quality of being fusible, or of being convertible from a solid to a liquid state by heat.

fū'ṣi-ble, *a.* [ME. *fusible*; OFr. *fusible,* from L. *fundere,* to pour.] Capable of being changed into a liquid state by heat.

Fusible metal; an alloy, usually of lead, tin, and bismuth, compounded in such definite proportions as to melt at a given temperature.

Fusible plug; a plug of fusible metal in the plate of a boiler, so placed that it will melt at a temperature too high for safety and allow the steam to escape freely; also, a plug that melts by heat of electrical resistance to guard against excess of current; also, a plug in a system of water-pipes, for fire-protection of buildings.

fū'si-form, *a.* [L. *fusus,* a spindle, and *forma,* form.] Shaped like a spindle; thick, tapering at each end.

fū'ṣil, *a.* [L. *fusilis,* liquid, molten, from *fundere,* to pour.]
1. Capable of being melted or rendered fluid by heat. [Obs.]
2. Running; flowing, as a liquid. [Obs.]

fū'ṣil, *n.* [Fr. *fusil,* a steel for striking fire, a musket; It. *focile, fucile*; LL. *focile,* a steel for striking fire, from L. *focus,* a fireplace.] A light musket or firelock resembling a carbine, and which might be slung over the shoulder by a belt. [Obs.]

Fusil for projecting Grenades.

fū'ṣil, *n.* [From L. *fusus,* a spindle.] A bearing in heraldry of a rhomboidal figure, named from its shape, which resembles that of a spindle.

Fusil.

fū'ṣile, *a.* [Obs.] See *Fusible.*

fū-ṣil-eer', fū-ṣil-iēr', *n.* [Fr. *fusilier,* from *fusil,* a musket.]
1. Formerly, a soldier armed with a fusil.
2. [F—] A designation applied to certain infantry regiments of the British army; as, the Scots *Fusiliers.*

fū-sil-lāde', *n.* [Fr. *fusillade,* from *fusiller,* to shoot, from *fusil,* a musket.] A simultaneous discharge of musketry; as, a general *fusillade.*

fū-sil-lāde', *v.t.*; fusilladed, *pt., pp.*; fusillading, *ppr.* To attack and fight by fusillades.

fūṣ'ing-point, *n.* The temperature at which a substance passes from the solid to the liquid condition; as, the *fusing-point* of ice is 32° Fahr.

fū'ṣion, *n.* [L. *fusio,* from *fundere,* to pour out, melt.]
1. The act or operation of melting or rendering fluid by heat, without the aid of a solvent; as, the *fusion* of ice or of metals.
2. The state of being melted or dissolved by heat; a state of fluidity or flowing in consequence of heat; as, metals in *fusion.*
3. The state of being blended or brought into union, as if by melting.
4. The bringing together of differing political factions; as, the *fusion* of the two parties was satisfactorily effected.
5. In biology, the union of parts usually separated.
6. In optics, the act of bringing the eyes in visual line so that the rays emanating from a single point fall on corresponding localities in each eye and are conveyed to a single visual center, producing the impression of one. [See *Verticalize, Horizontalize.*]

Watery fusion; the liquefaction of a crystal in its water of crystallization through the agency of heat.

fū'ṣion-iṣm, *n.* In politics, the advocacy and support of coalition of parties for the purposes of election.

fū'soid, *a.* Same as *Fusiform.*

fū'sōme, *a.* Handsome; neat; notable. [Prov. Eng.]

fuss, *n.* [Prob. from ME. *fus, fous,* eager, anxious; AS. *fus,* ready, eager.]
1. A tumult; a bustle; unnecessary activity about trivial matters.
2. A fussy person. [Rare.]
Syn.—Stir, excitement, tumult, worry, ado, bustle, flurry, fidget.

fuss, *v.i.*; fussed (fust), *pt., pp.*; fussing, *ppr.* To make much ado about trifles; to make a bustle; as, she *fusses* continually.

fuss, *v.t.* To disturb or confuse with trifling matters; to make uncomfortable.

fuss'ball, *n.* Same as *Fuzzball.*

fuss'i-ly, *adv.* With much ado.

fuss'i-ness, *n.* The quality of making much of trivial matters.

fuss'ŏck, *n.* A large, fleshy woman. [Prov. Eng.]

fuss'y, *a.*; *comp.* fussier; *superl.* fussiest. Making a fuss; worrying; annoyingly and needlessly active over trivial matters.

fust, *v.i.* To become moldy or fusty. [Obs.]

fust, *n.* [OFr. *fusté,* fusty, tasting of the cask, from *fuste,* a cask.] A strong, musty smell.

fust, *n.* [OFr. *fust, fuist,* a stick, shaft, tree, from L. *fustis,* a knobbed stick, club.] In architecture, the shaft of a column from the astragal to the capital.

fus-tȧ-nelle', fus-tȧ-nel'lȧ, *n.* [LL. *fustanella,* from *fustianum,* a fustian.] A kind of short white petticoat worn by the men of modern Greece since the revolution.

fus'tee, fus'tie, *n.* [W. Ind.] The offspring of a white person and an octoroon.

fus'tēr-ic, *n.* The coloring-matter of the shrub fustet.

fus'tet, *n.* [Fr. *fustet*; LL. *fustetus,* a tree, from L. *fustis,* a stick.] The wood of the *Rhus Cotinus* or Venice sumac; also, the tree itself.

fus'tiăn (-chăn), *n.* [ME. *fustian*; OFr. *fustaine,* from LL. *fustianum, fustanum,* fustian, from Ar. *Fustat,* the name of a suburb of Cairo, Egypt, from which the stuff came.]
1. A kind of coarse twilled cotton stuff, as corduroy, velveteen, etc.
2. An inflated style of writing; a kind of writing in which high-sounding words are used, above the dignity of the thoughts or subject; a swelling style; bombast.

Fustian is thoughts and words ill sorted. —Dryden.

fus'tiăn, *a.* 1. Made of fustian.
2. In style, swelling above the dignity of the thoughts or subject; too pompous; ridiculously tumid; bombastic.

fus'tiăn-ist, *n.* One who writes bombast.

fus'tic, *n.* [Fr. *fustoc*; Sp. *fustoc,* fustic, fustet, from LL. *fustis,* a tree, L. *fustis,* a stick.] The wood of the *Maclura tinctoria* or Don, or *Morus tinctoria,* a tree growing in the West Indies, and used in dyeing yellow. This is the old *fustic* of the English dyers; their young *fustic* is fustet.

fus'ti-gāte, *v.t.*; fustigated, *pt., pp.*; fustigating, *ppr.* [L. *fustigatus,* pp. of *fustigare,* to beat with a stick, from *fustis,* a stick.] To punish with a stick or club.

fus-ti-gā'tion, *n.* [L. *fustigatio*, from *fustigare*, to beat with a cudgel, from *fustis*, a stick or club.] Punishment by beating with a stick or club, inflicted on freemen in ancient Rome.

fus-ti-lā'ri-ăn, *n.* A scamp; a scoundrel. [Obs.]

fust'i-lug, fust'i-lugs, *n.* [Prov. Eng.] A gross, fat, unwieldy person. [Obs.]

fus'tin, *n.* A yellow dyestuff from young fustic.

fust'i-ness, *n.* A fusty state or quality; an ill smell from moldiness, or moldiness itself.

fust'y, *a.*; *comp.* fustier; *superl.* fustiest. 1. Moldy; musty; ill-smelling; rank; rancid.

2. Melancholy; listless. [Obs.]

fū'sūre (-zhūr), *n.* [L. *fusura*, from *fundere*, to pour, melt.] A smelting. [Rare.]

futch'ell, *n.* [Origin unknown.] In a vehicle, a support or holder for the hinder end of the tongue.

fū'thork, fū'thorc, *n.* The Runic alphabet. This word contains in order the first six letters of the Runic alphabet, *f, u, th, o, r, c* (=*k*), and spells the name of that alphabet, *futhork.*

fū'tile, *a* [Fr. *futile*, from L. *futilis*, that easily pours out, from the root of *fundere*, to pour.]

1. Talkative; loquacious; tattling. [Obs.]

2. Trifling; of no weight or importance; answering no valuable purpose; worthless; of no effect.

Syn.—Bootless, unavailing, useless, vain, idle.

fū'tile-ly, *adv.* In a futile manner.

fū-til'i-ty, *n.* [L. *futilitas*, emptiness, vanity, from *futilis*, that easily pours out.]

1. Talkativeness; loquaciousness; loquacity. [Obs.]

2. The quality of producing no valuable effect, or of coming to nothing; as, the *futility* of measures or schemes.

fū'til-ous, *a.* Worthless; trifling. [Obs.]

fut'tŏck, *n.* [Perhaps a corruption of *foot-hook.*] One of the middle timbers between the floor and the upper timbers of a ship, or the timbers raised over the keel which form the breadth of the ship; one of the crooked timbers forming the compound rib in the hull of a vessel.

fut'tŏck-hoop, *n.* A band around a mast for holding the futtock-shrouds.

fut'tŏck-plāte, *n.* One of the iron plates which serve to hold the deadeyes of the topmast-rigging and of the futtock-shrouds.

fut'tŏck-shrouds, *n. pl.* Short, stout iron shrouds connecting the futtock-plates with the mast below.

fū'tūr-ȧ-ble, *a.* That may occur in the future. [Rare.]

fū'tūre, *a.* [ME. *future*; OFr. *futur*, from L. *futurus*, about to be, fut. part. of *esse*, to be.]

1. That is to be or come hereafter; that will exist at any time after the present, indefinitely; as, the next moment is *future* to the present.

2. In grammar, denoting that modification of a verb which expresses a *future* act or event.

Syn.—Forthcoming, coming, advenient, oncoming.

fū'tūre, *n.* 1. Time to come; a time subsequent to the present; as, the *future* shall be as the present; in *future*; for the *future.*

2. Prospect or outlook; possibilities to come; as, he has a wonderful *future* in prospect.

3. In grammar, the name of a tense expressing future time.

To deal in futures; an expression of brokers, meaning to buy or sell on future values.

fū'tūre-less, *a.* Without hope of any better fortune in the future; unfortunate.

fū'tūre-ly, *adv.* In time to come. [Obs.]

fū'tūr-ist, *n.* 1. One who trusts to the future for prosperity; who looks anxiously and expectantly to the future; who takes an optimistic outlook on events. [Rare.]

2. In theology, one who holds that the fulfilment of certain prophecies of the Apocalypse are yet to be realized.

3. One belonging to a new school in literature, music and art which stands for originality even at the sacrifice of tradition.

fū-tū-ri'tiăl (-rish'ăl), *a.* Relating to future events. [Rare.]

fū-tū-ri'tion (-rish'un), *n.* The state of being to come or to exist hereafter. [Rare.]

fū-tū'ri-ty, *n.*; *pl.* **fū-tū'ri-ties.** 1. Future time; time to come.

2. Event to come.

3. The state of being yet to come or to come hereafter.

fūze, *n.* A variant of *fuse*, a tube for firing a blast.

fū-zee', *n.* See *Fusee*, 1.

fū-zee', *n.* See *Fusee*, 2.

fuzz, *v.t.* To fuddle by making drunk. [Obs.]

fuzz, *v.i.* To fly off in minute particles.

fuzz, *n.* Fine, light particles; loose, volatile matter.

fuzz'ball, *n.* A kind of fungus or mushroom, *Lycoperdon*, which, when pressed, bursts and scatters a fine dust; called also *puffball* and *devil's snuffbox.*

fuz'zle, *v.t.* To intoxicate. [Obs.]

fuzz'y, *a.* [Of Prov. Eng. origin.]

1. Light and spongy; loosely woven or braided.

2. Having a covering of fuzz; as, a peach is *fuzzy.*

-fy. A suffix from ME. *-fyen, -fien*; OFr. *-fier*; L. *-ficare*, from *facere*, to make, do. It appears in verbs of Latin origin or modern formation on the Latin model and signifies to make; as, digni*fy*, glori*fy*, lique*fy.*

fȳ, *interj.* Same as *Fie.*

fȳce, *n.* Same as *Fice.*

fȳke, *n.* [D. *fuik*, a bow-net.] A long bag-net used as a fish-trap; called also *fyke-net.*

fȳke, *v.i.* and *v.t.* See *Fike.*

fȳke, *n.* See *Fike.*

fyl'fot, *n.* [Prob. from AS. *fytherfote, fierfete, feowerfete*, four-footed.] A heraldic and religious symbol used as a secret emblem and also as an ornament, by peoples of widely separated origin and locality; called also *gammadion* and *swastika.*

Fylfots. 1. From embroidery on miter of Thomas à Becket. 2. From a brass in Lewknor Church, Oxfordshire.

fyrd, *n.* [AS. *fyrd, fierd, ferd*, an army, expedition.] In Anglo-Saxon history, the national military force, embracing all males qualified to bear arms.

fyr'dung, *n.* [From AS. *fyrd*, an army, expedition.] In Anglo-Saxon history, the national army, or fyrd, under arms and prepared for war.

G

G (jē). The seventh letter and fifth consonant of the English alphabet. It is derived through the French from the Latin *G*, a modification of the Old Latin *C*, which had the same power as *G*, as in *Caius*, pronounced *Gaius*. The Latin *G* or *C* is from the Greek, Γ, *gamma*, which is from the Assyrian *gimel* or *gomal*, meaning camel (so called from its resemblance to the neck of a camel). *G* has two sounds in English: one in words of Anglo-Saxon and Germanic origin, which is hard before *a, o, u*, as in *gate, god*, and, when initial, before *e, i, l*, and *r*; the other in words of Romance origin, which is soft and has a palatal sound like *j*, as in *gem, gin.*

G, g, *as a symbol.* As a numeral *G* was anciently used to denote 400, and with a dash over it, thus, Ḡ, it denoted 400,000. In music, *G* is the fifth tone of the natural scale of C major; called *sol* by the Italians and French.

G clef; the treble clef.

G sharp; the tone one half-interval above G, written G♯.

G string; in musical instruments, the fourth or lowest string of the violin, the third of the violoncello, guitar, and viola, and the first of the bass viol. In physics, the rate of acceleration due to gravity (about 32.16 feet per second).

gab, *n.* [ME. *gabbe*, from *gabben*, to talk idly, to gab; compare Sw. *gabb*, Ice. *gabb*, mockery.] Talkativeness, as in the phrase, the gift of *gab*; loquaciousness; hence, chatter, senseless talk. [Colloq.]

gab, *n.* [Dan. *gab*; Sw. *gap*, the mouth; so called because the *gab* is open to receive whatever is placed within it.] The hook on the eccentric rod of a steam-engine, which engages the rock-shaft pin.

gab, *v.i.*; gabbed, *pt., pp.*; gabbing, *ppr.* [ME. *gabben*, to talk idly, to jest, from Ice. *gabba*, to mock, make game of one.]

1. To talk idly; to prate. [Colloq.]

2. To jest; to lie. [Obs.]

gab, *v.i.* To project like a tooth or tusk; as, to *gab* from the mouth. [Obs.]

gab, *v.t.* To tell falsely. [Obs.]

gab'ăr-āge, *n.* A coarse kind of cloth used for packing goods. [Obs.]

gab-ăr-dīne', gab-ẽr-dīne', *n.* [Sp. *gabardina*, a coarse frock.] A coarse frock or loose upper garment worn by the Jews in the middle ages; a mean dress.

gab'bẽr, *n.* [ME. *gabbere*, a liar, deceiver, from *gabben*; Ice. *gabba*, to mock, make game of.]

1. A liar. [Obs.]

2. One who prates or talks idly.

gab'ble, *v.i.*; gabbled, *pt., pp.*; gabbling, *ppr.* [Freq. of *gab*, to talk idly.]

1. To prate; to talk fast, or to talk without meaning.

Such a rout, and such a rabble,
Run to hear Jack Pudding *gabble.* —Swift.

2. To utter inarticulate sounds with rapidity; as, *gabbling* fowls.

gab'ble, *n.* 1. Loud or rapid talk without meaning.

2. Inarticulate sounds rapidly uttered, as of fowls.

gab'blẽr, *n.* A prater; a noisy talker; one who utters inarticulate sounds.

gab'bling, *n.* Rapid, indistinct utterance; babble.

gab'brō, *n.* [It.] In mineralogy, a composite stone, granitic in nature, used for building purposes.

gā'bel, *n.* [Fr. *gabelle*; LL. *gabella, gabulum*, a tax, tribute, prob. from Ar. *kabāla*, a tax.] A tax, duty, or excise; especially, a former French tax on salt.

gā'bel-ẽr, *n.* A collector of the gabel or of taxes. [Rare.]

gā'bel-man, *n.* A tax-collector; a gabeler. [Rare.]

gab-ẽr-dīne', *n.* Same as *Gabardine.*

gab'ẽr-lun-yie, gab'ẽr-lun-zie, *n.* A beggar's wallet or bag; a beggar. [Scot.]

gā'bi-ăn, *n.* A mineral oil found at Gabian, in the department of Hérault, France.

ga-bil'lȧ, *n.* A finger or parcel of tobacco in Cuba, consisting of about thirty-six to forty leaves. The bales are usually made up of eighty hands, each of four gabillas.

gā'bi-ŏn, *n.* [OFr. *gabion*; It. *gabbione*, agabion, a large cage, from *gabbia*, a cage, coop, from L. *cavea*, a hollow place, a cave, a cage.]

1. In fortification, a hollow cylinder of wickerwork, resembling a basket but having no bottom, filled with earth and serving to shelter men from an enemy's fire.

2. In hydraulic engineering, any open framework to receive stones or other filling, and used to form a foundation for harbor and river improvements, as piers and jetties.

Part of Trench with Gabions and Fascines.

gā''bi-ŏn-āde', *n.* [Fr. *gabionnade*, from It. *gabbionata*, an intrenchment of gabions, from *gabbione*, a gabion.]

1. In military engineering, a traverse protected by gabions or a work formed chiefly of gabions.

2. In hydraulic engineering, any structure composed of gabions, as a dam sunk in a stream to control the current.

gā'bi-ŏn-āge, *n.* An arrangement of gabions as a part of a fortification.

gā'bi-ŏned, *a.* Protected by or made of gabions.

gā'ble, *n.* [OFr. *gable*; LL. *gabulum, gabalum*, a gable, the front of a building, from O.H.G. *gabala, gabal*, a fork.]

Wooden Gable of the Sixteenth Century.

1. The triangular end of a structure from the eaves to the top.

2. The end wall of a building; the gable-end.

gā′ble=end, *n.* The end of a building which is surmounted by a gable.

gā′ble=ro͝of, *n.* In architecture, a ridged roof with a gable at its end or ends.

gā′blet, *n.* A small ornamented gable or canopy formed over a niche or buttress.

gā′ble=wạll, *n.* The wall on which a gable rests.

gā′ble=win″dōw, *n.* In architecture, a window in a gable or a window gable-shaped at the top.

gab′lock, *n.* [ME. *gaveloc*; AS. *gafeluc*, a spear, a javelin.] The metal spur of a fighting-cock.

Gā′bri-el-īte, *n.* In ecclesiastical history, one of a sect of Anabaptists in Pomerania, so called from its founder, Gabriel Scherling.

gā′by, *n.*; *pl.* **gā′bieṣ**. [Ice. *gapi*, a rash person, from *gapa*, to gape.] A silly, foolish person; a simpleton; a lout. [Prov. Eng.]

gad, *n.* [ME. *gad*, *gadde*; AS. *gad*, a goad.]

1. A sharp-pointed rod or pricking instrument; a goad; the point of a spear or arrowhead.

2. Anything that goads; as, the *gad* of poverty.

3. A wedge-shaped bar or ingot of metal.

4. In mining, a metal-pointed punch to break up ore or stone.

5. An instrument of punishment, as a stick or rod. [Colloq.]

Under the gad; under compulsion.

Upon the gad; upon sudden impulse. [Obs.]

gad, *v.i.*; gadded, *pt.*, *pp.*; gadding, *ppr.* To walk about; to rove or ramble idly, or without any fixed purpose; to straggle in growth; to roam abroad for diversion; as, the *gadding* vine; a *gadding* woman.

gad, *v.t.* To get out by the use of gads, as ore.

gad′ȧ-bout, *n.* One who walks about idly, especially from curiosity or for gossip. [Colloq.]

gad′bee, *n.* The gadfly.

gad′bụsh, *n.* In botany, the West Indian mistletoe.

gad′dẽr, *n.* 1. One who gads.

2. In mining, a traveling machine which drills the holes for the gads.

gad′ding, *n.* The act of roving about idly.

gad′ding=cär, *n.* In mining, the car which carries a gadder.

gad′ding-ly, *adv.* In a gadding manner; rovingly.

gad′dish, *a.* Inclined to gad.

gad′dish-ness, *n.* The quality of being gaddish.

gāde, *n.* [LL. *gadus*, the codfish; Gr. *gados*, a certain fish.] In zoölogy, (a) any fish allied to the family *Gadidæ*, including the cod, hake, rockling, and haddock; (b) in Scotland, the ged or pike.

gad′flȳ, *n.*; *pl.* **gad′flīeṣ**. 1. An insect which goads or stings cattle, as a breeze or horsefly.

2. A botfly.

3. Figuratively, an annoying gadabout or busybody.

The *gadflies* of journalism.—N. Y. Tribune.

Gad′hel-iç (-el-), *n.* [Gael. *Gaidhealach*, *Gaelach*, from *Gaidheal*, a Gael.] Generally speaking, a branch of the Celtic language (including the Manx and Gaelic), as distinguished from the Cymric branch. Ireland was its first home.

Gad′hel-iç (-el-), *a.* Pertaining to the branch of the Celtic race which occupied Ireland, Scotland, and the Isle of Man, as distinguished from the Cymric branch.

gad′iç, *a.* Same as *Gadinic.*

Gad′i-dæ, *n.pl.* [LL. *gadus*, the cod, from Gr. *gados*, a certain fish.] A family of fishes whose rounded fins are without spines, the cod (*Gadus*) being the type.

Gadidæ.
Common Codfish (*Gadus morrhua* or *Morrhua vulgaris*). *v*, Ventral Fins, pointed and placed near the pectoral. *p*, Pectoral fin.

gad-in′iç, *a.* Pertaining to or derived from the codfish; as, *gadinic* acid.

gad′i-nin, *n.* [LL. *gadus*, cod.] A poisonous substance obtained from putrescent fish, particularly codfish.

Gad-i-tā′ni-ăn, *a.* [L. *Gaditanus*, from *Gades*, Cadiz, Spain.] Pertaining to the city of Cadiz (ancient Gades), Spain.

gad′ling, *n.* 1. A small gad or spike on armor. [Obs.]

2. One who gads about; a vagabond. [Obs.]

gad′=nāil, *n.* A large nail. [Prov. Eng.]

gā′doid, *a.* and *n.* [LL. *gadus*, the cod, and Gr. *eidos*, form.]

I. *a.* Pertaining to the *Gadidæ*.

II. *n.* A fish of the family *Gadidæ*.

gad-ō-lin′i-ȧ, *n.* [Named after Johan *Gadolin*, a Finnish chemist.] In chemistry, an oxid of gadolinium.

gad-ō-lin′iç, *a.* Pertaining to gadolinium.

gad′ō-lin-īte, *n.* A mineral usually found in shapeless masses of a blackish color, and having the appearance of vitreous lava.

gad-ō-lin′i-um, *n.* A metallic element found in gadolinite.

gadṣ′man, *n.*; *pl.* **gadṣ′men**. One who uses a gad; a driver of cattle.

gad′=steel, *n.* A Flemish steel manufactured in the shape of wedges or gads.

gad′ū-in, *n.* [LL. *gadus*, a codfish.] In chemistry, a yellow amorphous compound found in cod-liver oil.

Gā′dus, *n.* [L., from Gr. *gados*, a fish.] The typical genus of the family *Gadidæ*; it includes the common cod, the haddock, whiting, hake, ling, etc.

gad′wạll, *n.* [E. *gad*, to walk about, and *wall*.] A common name of the gray duck, *Anas strepera*, abundant in the northern hemisphere and nearly as large as the mallard.

gad-zooks′, *interj.* An exclamation corrupted from *God's hooks* (the nails of the cross); an old form of oath.

But the money, *gadzooks*, must be paid in an hour. —Prior.

Gāel, *n.* [Gael. *Gaidheal*, contr. to *Gael*, a Gael.] A Scottish Highlander or Celt.

Gāel′iç, *a.* [Gael. *Gaidhealach*, Gaelic, from *Gaidheal*, a Gael.] Pertaining to the Gaels; as, the *Gaelic* language.

Gāel′iç, *n.* The language of the Celts in the Highlands of Scotland.

gaff, *n.* [ME. *gaffe*; OFr. *gaffe*, an iron hook; Ir. *gafa*, *gaf*, a hook, *gabhal*, a fork, spear, from *gabh*, to take, receive.]

1. A sort of large iron hook fixed on a handle, used to assist in landing large fish, as salmon, when they have been brought near the side by the rod-fisher. The hook is driven into the body of the fish, generally by an assistant, and the fish is then lifted from the water.

2. A metal spur fastened to the tarsus of a fighting-cock; called also *gaffle*.

Cutter.—*a*, Gaff; *b*, Gaff-topsail.

3. In nautical language, a spar for extending the upper edge of fore-and-aft sails which are not set on stays, as the mainsail of a sloop or the spanker of a ship. At the lower or fore end it has a kind of fork called the *jaw* (the prongs are the *cheeks*), which embraces the mast; the outer end is called the *peak*.

gaff, *v.t.*; gaffed (gaft), *pt.*, *pp.*; gaffing, *ppr.* To strike or secure with a gaff; as, to *gaff* a salmon.

gaf′fẽr, *n.* [E. dial., prob. contr. of *grandfather*.]

1. A term of familiarity or contempt, applied mostly to old men, especially rustics; as, he is an old *gaffer*; *Gaffer* Brown.

2. The overseer of a gang of longshoremen or navvies. [Prov. Eng.]

gaf′fle, *n.* [D. *gaffel*, a fork, pitchfork; AS. *geafl*, a fork.]

1. Same as *Gaff*, 2.

2. A steel lever to bend crossbows.

gaff′=top′sāil (-sl), *n.* 1. A light triangular or quadrilateral sail set above a gaff (as the gaff extending the head of a cutter's mainsail), and having its foot extended by it.

2. In zoölogy, a sea-catfish, *Ælurichthys marinus*, having a high and pointed fin on the back.

gag, *v.t.*; gagged, *pt.*, *pp.*; gagging, *ppr.* [ME. *gaggen*, to gag; compare W. *cegiaw*, to choke, from *ceg*, a choking.]

1. To stop the mouth by stuffing something into it; hence, to silence by authority or violence.

The time was not yet come when eloquence was to be *gagged* and reason to be hoodwinked. —Macaulay.

2. To pry or keep open by means of a gag.

Mouths *gagged* to such a wideness. —Fortescue.

3. To cause to heave with nausea.

4. In stage slang, to introduce interpolations into; as, to *gag* a part.

gag, *v.i.* 1. To heave with nausea; to retch.

2. To interpolate gags in acting. [Slang.]

gag, *n.* 1. Something thrust into the mouth and throat to hinder speaking.

2. A device for holding open the mouth in surgical operations.

3. Figuratively, any restraint upon freedom of speech or writing.

4. A choking mouthful. [Rare.]

5. Anything added by an actor to his written part on his own authority, as a local or personal allusion. [Slang.]

6. A serranoid food-fish, *Nycteroperca microlepis*, of the Florida coast.

7. A joke, especially a practical joke; a hoax.

gag′āte, *n.* Agate. [Obs.]

gāge, *n.* A measure; a standard. [See *Gauge.*]

gāge, *v.t.* and *v.i.* To measure. [See *Gauge.*]

gāge, *n.* [ME. *gage*; OFr. *gage*, a gage, pledge, pawn, from LL. *vadium*; Goth. *wadi*, a surety, pledge, bail.]

1. A pledge or pawn; a movable chattel laid down or given as a security for the performance of some act to be done by the person depositing the thing, and which is to be forfeited by nonperformance.

The sheriff is commanded to attach him by taking *gage*: that is, certain of his goods, which he shall forfeit if he doth not appear. —Blackstone.

2. The act of pledging or the state of being pledged; security; pawn.

I was fain to borrow these spurs; I have left my gown in *gage* for them. —B. Jonson.

3. Anything thrown down as a token of challenge to combat. Formerly it was customary for the challenger to cast on the ground a glove, a cap, a gauntlet, or the like, which was taken up by the accepter of the challenge.

There I throw my *gage*. —Shak.

gāge, *v.t.*; gaged, *pt.*, *pp.*; gaging, *ppr.* 1. To pledge; to pawn; to give or deposit as a pledge or security; to wage or wager. [Rare.]

Against the which, a moiety competent
Was *gaged* by our king. —Shak.

2. To bind by pledge, caution, or security; to engage.

gāge, *n.* [Named after Sir William *Gage*, about 1725.] A name applied originally to the plum known as *greengage*, now to several other varieties of plum; as, the blue *gage*, the golden *gage*, the transparent *gage*, etc.

Gā′ġē-ȧ, *n.* [L., from name of the botanist, Sir Thomas *Gage*.] A genus of small plants of the lily family, found in central Asia and Europe.

gag′gẽr, *n.* 1. One who gags.

2. In molding, a lifter consisting of a light T-shaped piece of iron; also, an iron used to hold in position the core of a mold or to keep the sand of a mold from breaking apart.

gag′gle, *v.i.*; gaggled, *pt.*, *pp.*; gaggling, *ppr.* [Onomatopoetic; compare D. *gaggelen*, to cackle; Ice. *gagl*, a wild goose.] To make a noise like a goose.

gag′gle, *n.* A flock of geese; hence, a chattering company.

A *gaggle* of geese . . . a *gaggle* of women. —Strutt.

gag′=lạw, *n.* Any law or regulation for the purpose of obstructing or preventing freedom of speech or discussion.

gag′=rein, *n.* A rein intended to draw the bit into the corners of a horse's mouth.

gag′ro͞ot, *n.* A powerful emetic, *Lobelia inflata*; commonly called *Indian tobacco.*

gag′to͞oth, *n.*; *pl.* **gag′teeth.** A tooth which protrudes. [Obs.]

gag′=to͞othed, *a.* Having a gagtooth or gagteeth.

gähn′īte (gän′), *n.* [Named after J. Gottlieb *Gahn*, a Swedish chemist.] In mineralogy, a varicolored mineral compound of zinc and alumina; called also *automolite.*

gā′iac (-yak), *n.* The French name of *guaiac*, sometimes used in English; also applied to other hard woods besides lignum-vitæ, as to that of the *Diptera odorata*, or tonka-bean tree of Guiana.

gā-id′iç, *a.* [Gr. *gaia*, earth.] Relating to the acid found in the peanut and applied to an acid isomeric with it, called *gaidic* acid.

gāi′e-ty, **gāy′e-ty**, *n.*; *pl.* **gāi′e-tieṣ.** [OFr. *gaiete*, gaiety, from *gai*; O.H.G. *gahi*, gay.]

1. The condition of being gay; mirth; action induced by or inducing merriment; a pleasure; often in the plural; as, the *gaieties* of winter.

2. Finery; showiness of dress.

Syn.—Animation, vivacity, liveliness, sprightliness, airiness, buoyancy.

Gaik′wär, **Gaek′wär** (gīk′), *n.* [Mahrati, a cowherd.] The title held by the native ruler of the state of Baroda in western India, now subject to Great Britain.

gāil′lȧrd, *a.* See *Galliard.*

Gāil-lär′di-ȧ, *n.* [Named after M. *Gaillard*, a French botanist.] A genus of plants of the composite order, originally found in the southwestern part of the United States.

gāil-liärde′ (gāl-yärd′), *n.* A dance. [See *Galliard.*]

gāi′ly, **gāy′ly**, *adv.* [ME. *gaily*, *gaili*, from *gay*; OFr. *gai*; O.H.G. *gahi*, gay.]

1. Splendidly; with finery or showiness; as, to be dressed *gaily*.

2. Joyfully; merrily; in a gay manner.

Wights, who travel that way daily,
Jog on by his example *gaily*. —Swift.

gāin, *a.* [ME. *gayn*, *gein*, from Ice. *gegn*, advantageous, convenient, straight.] Suitable; convenient; straight; direct; near; contiguous; easy; tolerable; handy; dexterous; honest; respectable; profitable; cheap. [Obs. or Prov. Eng.]

gāin, *v.t.*; gained, *pt.*, *pp.*; gaining, *ppr.* [ME. *gainen*, *gaynen*, to profit, be of use, from Ice. *gagna*, help, profit.]

1. To obtain by industry or the employment of capital; to get, as profit or advantage; as, to *gain* a good living; money *gains* six per cent.

What is a man profited, if he shall *gain* the whole world, and lose his own soul? —Matt. xvi. 26.

2. To win; to obtain by superiority or success; as, to *gain* a battle or a victory; to *gain* a prize; to *gain* a cause in law.

3. To obtain; to acquire; to procure; to receive; as, to *gain* favor; to *gain* reputation.

4. To obtain an increase of; as, to *gain* time; to *gain* ten pounds in weight.

5. To draw into any interest or party; to win to one's side; to conciliate.

To gratify the queen and *gain* the court. —Dryden.

6. To reach; to attain; to arrive at; as, to *gain* the top of a mountain; to *gain* a good harbor.

Gained day; the day which a traveler gains in circumnavigating the globe from west to east.

To gain ground; to advance in any undertaking; to prevail; to acquire strength or extent; to increase.

To gain over; to draw to another party or interest; to win over.

To gain the wind; among sailors, to arrive on the windward side of another ship.

Syn.—Win, get, acquire, obtain, earn, conquer, master, procure, attain, reach, achieve, realize.—*Gain* implies only that we get something by exertion; *win*, that we do it in competition with others.

gāin, *v.i.* 1. To have advantage or profit; to grow rich; to advance in interest or happiness; to recover from sickness or to acquire strength.

Thou hast greedily *gained* of thy neighbors by extortion. —Ezek. xxii. 12.

2. To encroach; to advance; to come forward by degrees; to advance nearer; with *on*; as, the ocean or river *gains on* the land; a fleet horse *gains on* his competitor.

3. To get ground; to prevail or have the advantage; to obtain influence; with *on* or *upon*.

My good behavior had so far *gained on* the emperor, that I began to conceive hopes of liberty. —Swift.

gāin, *n.* [ME. *gain*, *gein*; Ice. *gagn*, gain, profit.]

1. Profit; interest; something obtained as an advantage; opposed to *loss*.

But what things were *gain* to me, those I counted loss for Christ. —Philip. iii. 7.

2. The taking of profit or the pursuit or amassment of riches; accession; accumulation; increase; acquisition; as, a clear *gain*; a *gain* in speed or weight.

gāin, *n.* [W. *gan*, a mortise, from *ganu*, to hold, contain.] In carpentry, a beveling shoulder; a lapping of timbers, or the cut that is made for receiving a timber; a mortise.

gāin, *v.t.* In carpentry, to cut gains in or to fit into gains or grooves; to mortise.

gain-. [ME. *gain-*; AS. *gegn-*.] A prefix signifying back, again, against; as, *gain*say, *gain*strive.

gāin′á-ble, *a.* That may be obtained, reached, or accomplished.

gāin′āge, *n.* [ME. *gainage*; OFr. *gaignage*, from *gaagnier* to cultivate.] In feudal laws, the horses, oxen, wagons, and implements for carrying on tillage; also, the land itself, or the profit made by cultivation; also called *wainage*.

gāin′ēr, *n.* One who gains or obtains profit, interest, or advantage.

gāin′fụl, *a.* Producing profit or advantage; profitable; advantageous; advancing interest or happiness; productive of money; adding to the wealth or estate; lucrative.

gāin′fụl-ly, *adv.* With increase of wealth; profitably, advantageously.

gāin′fụl-ness, *n.* Profitableness.

gāin′giv-ing, *n.* A misgiving; a giving against or away. [Obs.]

It is but foolery, but it is such a kind of *gain-giving* as would, perhaps, trouble a woman. —Shak.

gāin′ing=mȧ-ċhïne″, *n.* A machine having a rotating saw, used for cutting gains, grooves, or mortises.

gāin′ing=twist, *n.* In rifled arms, a twist or spiral inclination of the grooves, which increases rapidly toward the muzzle.

gāin′less, *a.* Not producing gain; unprofitable; not bringing advantage.

gāin′less-ness, *n.* Unprofitableness; want of advantage.

gāin′ly, *adv.* Handily; readily; dexterously; conveniently. [Obs.]

gāin′ly, *a.* [ME. *gaynly*, straight, ready.] Handsome; well-formed and active; as, a *gainly* youth. [Rare, except in its negative form, *ungainly*.]

gāin′pāin, *n.* [Fr. *gagne-pain*, lit., bread-gainer; *gagner*, to gain, and *pain*, from L. *panis*, bread.] A name given in the middle ages to the sword of a hired soldier. [Obs.]

gāin-sāy′, *v.t.*; gainsaid, *pt.*, *pp.*; gainsaying, *ppr.* [ME. *geinseyen*; *gain-*, against, and *seyen*, to say.] To contradict; to oppose in words; to deny or declare not to be true; to controvert; to dispute; applied to persons or to propositions, declarations, or facts; as, there is no *gainsaying* him; his cleverness cannot be *gainsaid*.

gāin-sāy′ēr, *n.* One who contradicts or denies what is alleged; an opposer.

gāin-sāy′ing, *n.* Contradiction; opposition, especially in speech.

gāin′sŏme, *a.* 1. Gainful; bringing gain. [Rare.]

2. Prepossessing; comely; well-formed. [Obs.]

gainst (genst), *prep.*, an abbreviated form of *against*. It is used only in poetry, and generally with an apostrophe, *'gainst*.

gāin′stand, *v.t.* To withstand; to oppose; to resist. [Obs.]

And seek ye to *gainstand* the faith in God? —Bailey.

gāin′strīve, *v.i.* and *v.t.* I. *v.i.* To make resistance. [Obs.]

II. *v.t.* To withstand; to oppose. [Obs.]

The Fates *gainstrive* us not. —Grimoald.

gāir′fowl, *n.* See *Garefowl*.

gāir′ish, gāir′ish-ly, gāir′ish-ness. See *Garish*, etc.

gāit, *n.* [Ice. *gata*, a walk, way, path.]

1. A going; a walk; a march; a way. [Scot.]

2. Manner of walking or stepping; carriage of the body in walking; pace; applied to both men and animals; as, he strode along at a rapid *gait*; a horse of awkward *gait*.

Part huge of bulk,
Wallowing unwieldy, enormous in their *gait*. —Milton.

gāit′ed, *a.* In compound words, having a particular gait or manner of walking, as slow-*gaited*, heavy-*gaited*.

gāi′tēr, *n.* [Fr. *guêtre*; OFr. *guestre*, gaiter.]

1. A protection for the shoe and ankle, or for the whole lower leg, usually made of cloth or leather; a spatterdash.

2. A kind of shoe, consisting chiefly of cloth, and covering the ankles; also, a shoe of similar form, with or without cloth, generally with elastic sides.

gāi′tēr, *v.t.*; gaitered, *pt.*, *pp.*; gaitering, *ppr.* To dress with gaiters.

gāi′tēr, *n.* The English name for the dogwood-tree; called also *gaiter-tree*, *gatten-tree*, and *gattridge*. [Obs.]

gāi′tēr=tree, *n.* The dogwood-tree, *Cornus sanguinea*, and various allied species; called also *gatter-tree*, *gatten-tree*, and *gatteridge*. [Obs.]

gä′lȧ, *n.* [Fr. *gala*, festivity, show, from It. *gala*, finery, ornament.] Festivity; festive show.

The river is a perpetual *gala*, and boasts each month a new ornament. —Emerson.

ga-laçt-. See *Galacto-*.

ga-laç′tȧ-gogue (-gog), *n.* [*Galact-*, and Gr. *agōgos*, leading, from *agein*, to lead.] In medicine, a preparation that promotes the secretion of milk in the breast.

Ga-laç′ti-ȧ, *n.* [L., from Gr. *gala* (*-aktos*), milk.]

1. A genus of twining or prostrate leguminous herbs, found chiefly in eastern and southern United States. The flowers are purple and borne in racemes. The common species are called *milk-pea*.

2. [g—] An abnormal secretion of milk, the flow being either deficient or overabundant.

ga-laç′tiç, *a.* [Gr. *galaktikos*, milky, from *gala* (*-aktos*), milk.]

1. Of or belonging to milk; obtained from milk; lactic.

2. In astronomy, a term first applied by Sir John Herschel to that great circle of the heavens to which the course of the Milky Way apparently most nearly conforms.

Galactic poles; the two opposite points of the heavens, situated at 90° from the galactic circle.

ga-laç′tine, *n.* [Gr. *gala* (*-aktos*), milk, and *-ine*.]

1. A milky substance obtained from the sap of the cow-tree of South America.

2. Same as *Lactose*.

3. An amorphous substance, $C_6H_{10}O_5$, obtained from the seeds of leguminous plants.

ga-laç-to-, ga-laçt-. Combining forms from Gr. *gala* (*-aktos*), milk, signifying milk, milky, or containing milk, as *galacto*cele, *galacto*dendron.

ga-laç′tō-cēle, *n.* [*Galacto-*, and Gr. *kēlē*, a tumor.] A tumor of the breast caused by an obstruction of the lacteal glands.

Ga-laç-tō-den′drŏn, *n.* [*Galacto-*, and Gr. *dendron*, tree.] A generic name given by some authors to the cow-tree of South America, now generally referred to the genus *Brosimum*, *Galactodendron* being used as the specific name.

ga-laç″tō-den-sim′e-tēr, *n.* [*Galacto-*, and L. *densus*, dense, and *metrum*, a measure.] Same as *Galactometer*.

ga-laç′toid, *a.* [Gr. *gala* (*-aktos*), milk, and *eidos*, resemblance.] Resembling milk.

gal-aç-tom′e-tēr, *n.* [*Galacto-*, and Gr. *metron*, a measure.] An instrument for ascertaining the quality of milk by its specific gravity; a lactometer.

gal-aç-toph′ȧ-ġist, *n.* [*Galacto-*, and Gr. *phagein*, to eat.] One who drinks or feeds on milk.

gal-aç-toph′ȧ-gous, *a.* Feeding on milk.

gal-aç-toph′ō-rous, *a.* [Gr. *galaktophoros*, giving milk; *gala* (*-aktos*), milk, and *pherein*, to bear.] Producing milk; conveying milk; lactiferous; as, *galactophorous* ducts.

ga-laç″tō-poi-et′iç, *a.* and *n.* [*Galacto-*, and Gr. *poiein*, to make.]

I. *a.* Tending to increase the flow of milk; causing the secretion of milk.

II. *n.* Any substance which tends to increase the secretion and flow of milk.

ga-laç-tor-rhē′ȧ, *n.* [*Galacto-*, and Gr. *rhoē*, a flow, from *rhein*, to flow.] The condition marked by a continued and persistent flow of milk from the breast.

ga-laç′tōse, *n.* [Gr. *gala* (*-aktos*), milk, and *-ose*.] A crystalline sugar obtained by the action of dilute acids on milk-sugar.

gal-aç-tō′sis, *n.* [Gr. *galaktōsis*, a changing into milk, from *gala* (*-aktos*), milk.] The process of secreting or producing milk.

gal-aç-tū′ri-ȧ, *n.* [Gr. *gala* (*-aktos*), milk, and *ouron*, urine.] Same as *Chyluria*.

gā′lȧ=dāy, *n.* A day of festivity; a holiday with rejoicings.

gā′lȧ=dress, *n.* A holiday dress; a person's gayest dress.

ga-lāġe′, *n.* [Obs.] See *Galosh*.

Ga-lā′gō, *n.* 1. The native name of a genus of quadrumanous mammals, found in Africa. The species, which are nocturnal in their habits, have long hind legs, great eyes, and large membranous ears. The great galago, *Galago crassicaudatus*, is as large as a rabbit. They live in trees, and are sought after as food.

2. [g—; *pl.* ga-lā′gōṣ.] A species or individual of the genus *Galago*.

ga-lan̄′găl, ga-lan̄′gȧ, *n.* [ME. *galingale*; OFr. *galingal*; LL. *galanga*; Ar. *khalanjān*, Chinese *Ko-liang-kiang*, lit., mild ginger, galangal; *Ko*, a prefecture in the province of Canton, China, and *liang*, mild, and *kiang*, ginger.]

1. A dried rhizome brought from China and used in medicine, being an aromatic stimulant of the nature of ginger. The drug is mostly produced by *Alpinia officinarum*, a flag-like plant with stems about four feet high. The rhizome of *Kæmpferia Galanga* is known as the *greater galangal*.

2. A sedge, *Cyperus longus*, growing in the south of England. Its aromatic roots have slightly medicinal properties.

Ga-lan′thus, *n.* [Gr. *gala*, milk, and *anthos*, a flower.] A small genus of *Amaryllidaceæ*, represented by the well-known snowdrop, *Galanthus nivalis*, and native to middle and southern Europe. They are herbaceous plants with bulbous roots, narrow leaves, and drooping white bell-shaped flowers.

gal′an-tine, *n.* [OFr. *galentine*; LL. *galatina*, jelly, from L. *gelatus*, pp. of *gelare*, to congeal.] A dish of veal, chicken, or other white meat, freed from bones, tied up, boiled, and served cold in its own jelly.

ga-lan′ty=shōw, *n.* See *Gallanty-show*.

gȧ-lȧ-pä′gō, *n.* [Sp., a tortoise.] In military operations, a covering or defense of large wooden shields so placed that the edges overlap, forming a defense similar to the Roman testudo.

gal′ȧ-pee=tree, *n.* A small tree of the West Indies, *Sciadophyllum Brownei*, not branched, but bearing a crown of large digitate leaves.

gal-ȧ-tē′ȧ, *n.* [L., from Gr. *Galateia*, a sea-nymph.] A striped cotton fabric, largely used in making sailor-suits and outing-garments for children.

Ga-lā′tiăn (-shăn), *a.* Pertaining to Galatia, or the Galatians.

Ga-lā′tiăn, *n.* [L. *Galatia*; Gr. *Galatia*, Galatia.]

1. A native or inhabitant of Galatia in Asia Minor.

2. [*pl.*] The shortened title of the Epistle to the Galatians.

Gā′lax, *n.* [Gr. *gala*, milk; so named from its white flower.] A genus of plants, natural order *Diapensiaceæ*. The sole species, *Galax aphylla*, a native of Virginia and North Carolina, is a smooth perennial herb with a creeping rhizome and evergreen leaves.

Gal′ax-y, *n.* [OFr. *galaxie*; L. *galaxias*; Gr.

galaxias, the Milky Way, from *gala* (*-aktos*), milk.]

1. The Milky Way; the long, white, luminous track, which seems to encompass the heavens like a girdle, occasioned by a multitude of stars at so vast a distance as to be distinguishable apart only by the most powerful lenses.

2. [g-] An assemblage of splendid, illustrious, or beautiful persons or things.

gal′bȧ, *n.* [A corruption of *calaba*.] A tree of the West Indies, *Calophyllum calaba*, yielding an oil and a balsam.

gal′bȧ-num, gal′băn, *n.* [L. *galbanum*; Gr. *chalbanē*; Heb. *khelb′nāh*, *chhĕlbenah*, galbanum, from *kheleb*, fatness.] A fetid gum resin procured from certain species of umbelliferous plants, genus *Ferula*. It consists of the tears of gum resin which exude from the stem and the bases of the leaves. It is used as a stimulating expectorant, and in the manufacture of varnish.

galbe, *n.* [Fr., a graceful outline, sweep, curve; OFr. *galbe*, a garb, comeliness.] In art, the contour of the curved surface of a body; specifically, the contour of a vase or urn, a column, a Doric capital, etc.

gal′bū-lus, *n.*; *pl.* **gal′bū-lī**. [L., the nut of the cypress-tree.] In botany, a cone or strobile, the scales of which are fleshy and combined into a uniform mass, as the fruit of the juniper.

Galbulus (fruit of *Juniperus communis*).

gāle, *n.* [ME. *gale*, a wind, breeze; prob. of Scand. origin; compare Dan. *gal*, mad; Ice. *gol*, *gola*, a breeze.]

1. A vehement wind traveling more rapidly than a breeze, but not so violent as a tempest; particularly, a storm at sea; as, it blew a *gale*; the ship ran into a *gale*. The word is often qualified; as, a hard or strong *gale*, a violent *gale*. A current of wind somewhat less violent is denominated a stiff *gale*. A less vehement wind is called a fresh *gale*, which is a wind not too strong for a ship to carry single-reefed topsails, when closehauled. When the wind is not so violent but that a ship will carry her topgallantsails, it is called a topgallant *gale*.

2. A state of noisy excitement, whether of passion or hilarity. [Colloq.]

gāle, *n.* A song or speech. [Obs.]

gāle, *v.i.* To sing; to cry; to croak. [Obs.]

gāle, *n.* [ME. *gawl*; AS. *gagel*, a myrtle-bush.] A plant, *Myrica Gale*, growing in Europe, Asia, and America in marshy places, and exhaling a pleasant aromatic odor; also called *sweet-gale*.

gāle, *n.* [ME. *gavel*; AS *gafol*, tribute, tax.]

1. A periodical payment of rent, duty, interest, or custom; an instalment of money. [Eng.]

2. In English law, the right of a free miner to work land for coal or iron in certain districts, as in the Forest of Dean.

gā′lē-ȧ, *n.*; *pl.* **gā′lē-æ**. [L., a helmet.]

1. In botany, the upper lip of a ringent corolla, or any similar helmet-like process.

2. In zoölogy, the outer terminal process of the second articulation of the maxillæ in certain species of insects.

3. In surgery, (a) a bandage for the head; (b) an infant's caul; (c) a muscle which covers the vertex of the skull like a cap; the galea capitis.

4. In pathology, a headache which affects the entire head.

5. [G—] In paleontology, a genus of sea-hedge-hogs or echini, found fossil only; they are distinguished by an oval base, from which the shell rises in a vaulted, helmet-like form.

gal′ē-as, *n.* [Obs.] See *Galleass*.

gā′lē-āte, gā′lē-ā-ted, *a.* [L. *galeatus*, pp. of *galeare*, to cover with a helmet, from *galea*, a helmet.]

1. Covered with or wearing a helmet; capped by a helmet-shaped part.

2. In botany, having a flower like a helmet; helmet-shaped, as the monk's-hood and various other aconites.

gāle′=dāy, *n.* Rent-day. [Eng.]

gȧ-lee′, *n.* A miner who holds a gale in crown lands. [Eng.]

Ga-lē′gȧ, *n.* [Gr. *gala*, milk, and *agein*, to lead, induce.] A genus of smooth, erect, perennial leguminous herbs, mostly natives of the Mediterranean region.

Gā′lē-ī, *n.pl.* [Gr. *galeos*, a kind of shark with marks like a weasel, from *galeē*, a weasel.] A suborder of marine animals including the sharks.

gā′lē-id, *a.* Pertaining to the *Galeidæ*.

gā′lē-id, *n.* A shark belonging to the *Galeidæ*.

Gā-lē′i-dæ, *n.pl.* [*Galeus* and *-idæ*.] A family of small sharks including the dogfishes and topes.

gȧ-lē′i-fọrm, *a.* [L. *galea*, a helmet, and *forma*, form.] Resembling a galea or helmet in form; resembling the *Galeidæ*.

gȧ-lē′nȧ, *n.* [L. *galena*, lead ore, the dross of melted lead; Gr. *galēnē*, lit., the stillness of the sea, calm, anything that produces tranquillity; hence, an antidote to poison.]

1. In medicine, theriaca; a preparation supposed to antidote the ill effects of poison. [Obs.]

2. In mineralogy, native lead sulphid, an ore from which the lead of commerce, and often silver, are obtained. The variety carrying silver is called *argentiferous galena*.

False galena; see *Blende*.

gȧ-len′iç, gȧ-len′iç-ăl, *a.* Pertaining to or containing galena.

Gȧ-len′iç, Gȧ-len′iç-ăl, *a.* [L. *Galenus*; Gr. *Galenos*, Galen, a physician and medical writer, born at Pergamum, 130 A. D.] Relating to Galen or his principles and method of treating diseases; as, the *Galenic* remedies consist of preparation of herbs and roots by infusion, decoction, etc.

Gā′len-iṣm, *n.* The doctrines of Galen.

Gā′len-ist, *n.* A follower of Galen in the preparation of medicine and mode of treating diseases.

These *Galenists* were what we should call herb-doctors to-day. —O. W. Holmes.

gȧ-lē′nīte, *n.* Same as *Galena*, 2.

gā′lē-oid, *a.* Weasel-like; applied specifically to certain arachnids and to sharks of the family *Galeidæ*.

Gā″lē-ō-pi-thē′ǥus, *n.* [L., from Gr. *galeē*, a weasel, and *pithēkos*, an ape.] The flying-lemur, a genus of mammals which have been referred to the bats and to the lemurs, but more properly to the *Insectivora*, of so peculiar a structure as to constitute a family, *Galeopithecidæ*, of themselves. These animals have the bones of the arm and leg, but not those of the digits, excessively elongated, and supporting extensive lateral folds of skin serviceable as a parachute, but not as organs of flight. The species are restricted to the islands of the Indian Archipelago.

Galeopithecus volans.

Gā-lē-op′sis, *n.* [L., from Gr. *galiopsis*, a nettle; *galeē*, a weasel, and *opsis*, appearance.] In botany, a genus of labiate herbs, natives of Great Britain. *Galeopsis Tetrahit* is the common hemp-nettle of the United States.

gȧ-lē′rȧ, *n.* [L. *galera*, or *galerum*, a cap, helmet.]

1. In zoölogy, a weasel-like animal, the taira.

2. [G—] The genus of which the taira is the type.

gal-ẽr-iç′ū-lāte, *a.* [L. *galericulum*, dim. of *galerum*, a helmet-like covering for the head, cap, from *galea*, a helmet.] Covered with a small galea.

gal′ẽr-īte, *n.* [L. *galeritus*, one wearing a cap, from *galerus*, *galerum*, a hat or cap.] A name given to a fossil echinus of the chalk formation, from its having some resemblance to a hat.

Galerites albogalerus.
1. Depressed form. 2. Normal form.

gȧ-lette′, *n.* [Fr.] A thin cake; a buttered roll; a bannock.

Gȧ-lē′us, *n.* The typical genus of the family *Galeidæ*.

gāle′wọ̈rt, *n.* In botany, same as *gale*.

Gȧ-li′ciăn (-lish′un), *a.* Pertaining to Galicia in Spain, or to Galicia, a province of Austria.

Gȧ-li′ciăn, *n.* A native or inhabitant of Galicia in Spain or Galicia in Austria.

Gal-i-lē′ăn, *a.* Pertaining or belonging to Galileo, the great Italian astronomer and philosopher (1564-1642); as, the *Galilean* telescope; *Galilean* law.

Galilean telescope; a telescope having a concave eyepiece, like an opera-glass.

Gal-i-lē′ăn, *a.* [L. *Galilæus*; Gr. *Galilaios*, of or pertaining to Galilee, from *Galilaia*, Galilee; Heb. *Galil*, Galilee, lit., a circle.] Relating to Galilee, a Roman province in the north of Palestine, or to the Sea of Galilee.

Last came, and last did go,
The pilot of the *Galilean* lake. —Milton.

Gal-i-lē′ăn, *n.* 1. A native or inhabitant of the province of Galilee.

2. In Jewish history, one of a class among the Jews, during the reign of Augustus, who resisted the payment of tribute to Rome.

3. A Christian; a name used in contempt by Mohammedans and the ancient Jews.

gal′i-lee, *n.* [OFr. *galilee*, from L. *Galilæa*; Gr. *Galilaia*, Galilee, Heb. *Galil*, Galilee, lit., a circle.] A portico or chapel annexed to a church, formerly used for various purposes. In it public penitents were stationed, dead bodies deposited previously to their interment, and religious processions formed; and it was only in the *galilee* that in certain religious houses the female relatives of the monks were allowed to converse with them. The name is said to have been suggested by the passage in Mark: "He goeth before you into Galilee: there shall ye see him."

gal-i-mā′tiȧs (-shȧ), *n.* [Fr., nonsense, gibberish.] Confused speech; jargon; nonsense; a medley of confused or nonsensical things.

She ran into absurdities and a *galimatias* scarce credible. —Fielding.

gal-i-mē′tȧ=wood, *n.* [*Galimeta*, a native name.] The wood of the white bully-tree, *Dipholis salicifolia*, of the West Indies.

gal′in-gāle, *n.* Same as *Galangal*, 2.

gal-iōn-ǥee′, *n.* [Turk. *qalyonji*, a man-of-war's-man, a sailor in the navy, from *qalyon*, a man-of-war.] A Turkish man-of-war's-man.

All that a careless eye could see
In him was some young *Galiongee*.—Byron.

gal′i-ŏt, gal′li-ŏt, *n.* [OFr. *galiote*; LL. *galeota*, dim. of *galea*, a galley.]

1. A small galley or sort of brigantine, built for chase. It was moved both by sails and by oars, having one mast and sixteen or twenty seats for rowers.

2. A Dutch or Flemish vessel for cargoes, with very rounded ribs and flattish bottom,

Dutch Galiot.

with a mizzenmast placed near the stern, carrying a square mainsail and maintopsail, a forestay to the mainmast (there being no foremast), with forestaysail and jibs.

Gal-i-pē′ȧ, *n.* [From native name.] A genus of trees belonging to the order *Rutaceæ*, found in tropical America. One of the species, *Galipea cusparia*, yields angostura-bark.

gal′i-pot, *n.* [Fr.] A white resin or resinous juice, which flows from the pine-tree, especially *Pinus maritima*. After being refined it is called *yellow*, *white*, or *Burgundy pitch*.

Gā′li-um, *n.* [L. *galion*; Gr. *galion*, galium, used in curdling milk, from *gala*, milk.] An extensive genus of plants belonging to the family *Rubiaceæ*. They have erect square stems, leaves in whorls, and small flowers, usually white. The roots of several species produce a dyestuff.

gąll, *v.t.*; galled, *pt.*, *pp.*; galling, *ppr.* [ME. *gallen*; OFr. *galler*, to fret, chafe, from *galle*, a fretting, itching of the skin.]

1. To fret and wear away by friction; to excoriate; to hurt or break, as the skin, by rubbing; as, a saddle *galls* the back of a horse, or a collar his breast.

Tyrant, I well deserve thy *galling* chain. —Pope.

2. To tease; to fret; to vex; to chagrin; as, to be *galled* by sarcasm.

3. To injure; to harass; to annoy; as, the troops were *galled* by the shot of the enemy.

gąll, *v.i.* To fret; to be teased. [Obs.]

gąll, *v.t.* In dyeing, to impregnate with a decoction of gall-nuts.

gąll, *n.* [OFr. *galle*; L. *galla*, a gallnut.]

Aleppo Gall and the Gallfly (*Cynips gallæ tinctoriæ*).
1. Gall split to show the cell in which the larva exists. 2. Exterior of the gall showing the opening by which the perfect insect escapes.

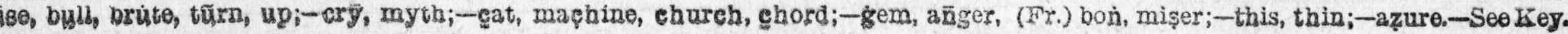

1. A vegetable excrescence produced by the deposit of the egg of an insect in the bark or leaves of a plant. The *galls* of commerce are produced by a species of *Cynips* depositing its eggs in the tender shoots of the *Quercus infectoria*, a species of oak, abundant in Asia Minor, Syria, Persia, etc. When the maggot is hatched it produces a morbid excrescence of the surrounding parts. *Galls* are inodorous, and have a nauseously bitter and astringent taste. When good, they are of a black or deep olive color. They are also termed *nutgalls* or *gallnuts*, and are known in commerce by the names of *white*, *green*, and *blue*. The two latter kinds are the best. The chief products of *galls* are tannin and gallic acid, very extensively used in dyeing and in the manufacture of ink. They are the most powerful of all the vegetable astringents, and are frequently used in medicine. They are chiefly imported from Aleppo, Tripoli, and Smyrna.

2. A form of gallnut produced, though of inferior quality, on the other species of oak, and likewise on plants and trees of different kinds; as, berry-*galls*; apple-*galls*, etc. These *galls* are of various forms and sizes.

3. An excrescence on quadrupeds and birds caused by the bite of ticks and other parasites.

gall, *n.* [ME. *galle*; AS. *gealla*, gall, bile.]

1. In physiology, a bitter, slightly alkaline, yellowish-green fluid, secreted in the glandular substance of the liver, and stored in the gall-bladder beneath it; bile.

2. Anything bitter; bitterness of mind; rancor; malignity.

His daintiest food, his richest wines were all
Turn'd by remorse to bitterness and *gall*.
—Crabbe.

3. The gall-bladder.

4. A preparation of ox-gall, used in painting.

5. Impudence; cheek; brazen assurance. [Slang.]

6. The scum of molten glass.

gall, *n.* [ME. *galle*; AS. *gealla*, a gall on a horse; prob. from L. *galla*, a gallnut.]

1. An abrasion of the skin, caused by rubbing; a sore; an excoriation.

2. A spot of low-lying, barren land. [Southern U. S.]

3. In stone-cutting, a hollow resulting from a change in the direction of the cut.

gal′lănt, *a.* [OFr. *galant*, gay, brave, ppr. of *galer*, to rejoice, make merry from *gale*, show, mirth, festivity.]

1. Gay; well-dressed; showy; splendid; magnificent; now rare except in regard to dress.

The gay, the wise, the *gallant*, and the grave.
—Waller.

2. Brave; high-spirited; courageous; heroic; magnanimous; of a noble bearing; as, a *gallant* soldier; a *gallant* foe.

3. [*Also* gal-lant′.] Showing polite attention to ladies; courteous; chivalrous; courtly; inclined to courtship.

Syn.—Brave, courageous, intrepid, courteous, heroic, fearless, chivalrous, valiant, bold, splendid, showy, gay.—*Courageous* is generic, denoting an inward spirit which rises above fear; *brave* is more outward, marking a spirit which *braves* or defies danger; *gallant* rises still higher, denoting bravery on extraordinary occasions in a spirit of adventure.

gal′lănt, *n.* 1. A gay, sprightly man; a courtly or fashionable man.

2. [*Also* gal-lant′.] A man who is polite and attentive to ladies; a ladies' man.

3. A wooer; a lover; a suitor; also, a seducer; a rake; a libertine.

gal-lant′, *v.t.*; gallanted, *pt.*, *pp.*; gallanting, *ppr.* 1. To attend or wait on, as a lady.

2. To handle with grace or in a modish manner; as, to *gallant* a fan. [Obs.]

gal′lănt-ly, *adv.* 1. In a gallant manner; gaily; showily; as, to be *gallantly* attired.

2. Bravely; heroically; as, to fight *gallantly*.

3. [*Also* gal-lant′ly.] After the manner of a gallant or wooer.

gal′lănt-ness, *n.* The state or quality of being gallant. [Rare.]

gal′lănt-ry, *n.*; *pl.* **gal′lănt-ries**. [OFr. *galanterie*, from *galant*, gallant.]

1. Splendor of appearance; show; magnificence. [Rare.]

2. Bravery; courageousness; heroism; intrepidity; as, the troops entered the fort with great *gallantry*.

3. Courteous attention and deference shown to a weaker party or one in need of succor or assistance, especially a woman.

4. Much courteous attention paid women, either honestly or with evil intent.

5. Gallants collectively; as, all the beauty and *gallantry* of the town.

gal′lănt-y-shōw, *n.* Shadowgraphs in miniature; Chinese shadows.

gall′=ap″ple, *n.* A gallnut; especially, the nut or gall of the gall-oak, *Quercus infectoria*.

gal′lāte, *n.* In chemistry, a salt formed by gallic acid combined with a base.

gal′lȧ-tin, *n.* Oil of coal-tar; dead-oil.

gal′lȧ-tūre, *n.* The chalaza of an egg, which keeps the yolk in position. [Obs.]

gall′=blad″dẽr, *n.* A membranous sac, shaped like a pear, on the under side of the liver, which secretes the gall.

gall′=cyst, *n.* The gall-bladder.

gall′=duct, *n.* A tube or duct by which bile is conveyed, as the cystic duct or the hepatic duct.

gal′lē-ass, *n.* [OFr. *galeace*; It. *galeazza*, from *galea*; LL. *galea*, a galley.] A three-masted galley, with guns on each side, used in the Mediterranean during the sixteenth century.

galled, *a.* Excoriated; denuded; as, a *galled* back; a *galled* tract of land.

Gal-lē′găn, *n.* [Sp. *Gallego*, a native of Galicia, in Spain; L. *Gallæcus*, pl. *Gallæci*, a people in Hispania.] A Galician or the Galician language.

gal′lē-in, *n.* [Pyro*gall*ol and phthal*ein*.] In chemistry, a dye from coal-tar used in dyeing a blue shade, the mordant being iron or alumina.

gal′lē-ŏn, *n.* [Sp. *galeon*; LL. *galea*, a galley.] A large ship, often of three or four decks, used chiefly by the Spaniards and Venetians of the fifteenth and sixteenth centuries, both for commercial and for warlike purposes.

gal′lē-ŏt, *n.* Same as *Galiot*.

gall′ẽr, *n.* Anything that galls, or a tantalizing person.

gal′lẽr-ied, *a.* Arranged in galleries; having galleries.

gal′lẽr-y, *n.*; *pl.* **gal′lẽr-ies**. [OFr. *galerie*, *gallerie*, a long portico, a gallery, prob. from *galerie*, a rejoicing, from *galer*, to rejoice.]

1. An elevated floor in a large building, such as a church or theater, for the accommodation of a part of the audience. It is commonly supported by columns or brackets and furnished with seats, and often extends around three sides of the building. Metaphorically, the term is also used to mean the people occupying such a place, or the promiscuous portion of the audience; as, the applause of the *galleries*; playing to the *gallery*.

2. A passageway having one side open, which may be either a sort of porch, or a kind of room, and used for a promenade or veranda.

3. A hall, hallway, or corridor in a private residence, often used to display paintings, statuary, or the like.

4. A building or a room set apart for the public display of pictures, statuary, or curios; a museum; hence, a collection of such works; as, an art *gallery*.

5. An arcade or passageway in a wall.

6. A passage underground; (a) in military engineering, a means of communication between parts of a fortification; (b) in mining, a heading or working drift; (c) in zoölogy, the burrow or other excavation of an animal.

7. In shipbuilding, a sort of balcony projecting from the after-part of the hull of a ship, called the *stern* or *quarter gallery*.

8. In golf, the spectators of a game who accompany the players over the course.

9. A public resort equipped for practice with firearms; as, a shooting-*gallery*.

10. An ornamental walk or apartment in a garden, formed by trees. [Obs.]

Gallery picture; a picture of a size that prevents it from being exhibited except in a gallery.

Gallery road; a road projecting from a hill, like a gallery.

gal′let, *n.* A chip of stone cut off by a chisel.

gal′let, *v.t.*; galleted, *pt.*, *pp.*; galleting, *ppr.* To fill the interstices of, as a wall, with chips of stone.

gal′let-ing, *n.* The act of filling interstices with chips of stone; also, the material so used.

gal′le-tȳle, *n.* A small glazed earthenware tile. [Obs.]

gal′ley, *n.*; *pl.* **gal′leys**, formerly **gal′lies**. [ME. *galeye*, *galay*; OFr. *galee*; LL. *galea*, a galley.]

1. Nautically, (a) a low, flat-built vessel with one or more rows (banks) of oars supposed to have been first used by the Corinthians; (b) a low, flat-built vessel with one deck, navigated with sails and oars, formerly common in the Mediterranean, one hundred to two hundred feet in length, having two masts and lateen sails, as in the illustration; (c) a barge of state; specifically, a light, open boat, used on the river Thames by customhouse officers, press-gangs, and for pleasure; (d) a clinker-built boat for ship's use from twenty-eight to thirty-six feet long, used for fast rowing; (e) the cookhouse on board ship which is on deck, or in a forward part of the vessel.

Galley.

2. In printing, an oblong tray which receives matter from the composing-stick or machine. It is usually of brass, or wood brass-lined, with flanges on three sides.

gal′ley=bird, *n.* The woodpecker.

gal′ley=proof, *n.* A proof taken from a galley of type.

gal′ley=rack, *n.* A rack holding a number of galleys at an angle.

gal′ley=slāve, *n.* 1. A person, generally a convict, obliged to row in a galley.

2. In printer's slang, a compositor.

gal′ley=wŏrk, *n.* Pottery collectively; coarse pottery.

gal′ley-wŏrm, *n.* Same as *Gallyworm*.

gall′fly, *n.*; *pl.* **gall′flies**. An insect, as those of the genus *Cynips*, which punctures the leaves or other parts of various trees or plants, producing excrescences known as galls.

gall′=gnat (-nat), *n.* One of several small dipterous insects causing galls upon plants.

Gal′lī, *n.*, pl. of *Gallus*.

gal-li-am′bic, *a.* Pertaining to the galliambus as a form of versification.

gal-li-am′bus, *n.*; *pl.* **gal-li-am′bī**. [L. *galliambus*, a song of the Galli, or priests of Cybele, from *Gallus*, a priest of Cybele, and *iambus*, Gr. *iambos*, an iambic.] A kind of verse consisting of two iambic dimeters catalectic, the last wanting the final syllable.

Gal′li-ăn, *a.* Pertaining to Gaul or France; Gallic. [Rare.]

gal′liărd (-yărd), *a.* Gay; brisk; active. [Obs.]

gal′liărd, *n.* [ME. *gaylard*; OFr. *gaillard*, gay, lively, brisk, from Sp. *gallarda*, pleasant, gay, lively, a lively dance.] A brisk, gay man; also, a lively dance, or the music for it. [Obs.]

gal′liărd-ise, *n.* [Fr.] Merriment; excessive gaiety. [Obs.]

gal′liărd-ness, *n.* Gaiety. [Obs.]

gal′li-ass, *n.* See *Galleass*.

Gal′lic, *a.* [L. *Gallicus*, pertaining to Gaul or the Gauls, from *Gallia*, Gaul.] Pertaining to Gaul or France.

gal′lic, *a.* [L. *galla*, the gallnut.] Belonging to galls or oak-apples; derived from galls.

Gallic acid; a substance, $C_7H_6O_5$, crystallizing in white, silky needles and having various methods of preparation, the most common being by boiling tannin with dilute sulphuric acid. It is used in photography and to a limited extent in medicine.

Gal′li-căn, *a.* [L. *Gallicus*, from *Gallia*, Gaul.] Pertaining to Gaul or France; as, the *Gallican* church or clergy.

Gal′li-căn, *n.* A follower of Gallicanism.

Gal′li-căn-ism, *n.* A movement in the Roman Catholic church in the latter part of the seventeenth century to limit the authority of the pope in France and to strengthen that of the national church; the opposite of *ultramontanism*.

Gal′li-cism, *n.* [Fr. *Gallicisme*, from L. *Gallia*, Gaul.] A mode of speech peculiar to the French nation; an idiomatic manner of using words in the French language.

Gal′li-cize, *v.t.*; Gallicized, *pt.*, *pp.*; Gallicizing, *ppr.* To render conformable to the French idiom or language.

gal′lied (-lid), *a.* Bothered; flurried; a nautical term.

gal′li-form, *a.* [L. *gallus*, a cock, and *forma*, form.] Resembling a cock in structure.

gal-li-gas′kins, *n.pl.* [A corruption of OFr. *garguesques*, Greekish, from It. *Grechesco*, Grecian, from *Greco*; L. *Græcus*, Greek.]

1. Large open breeches; wide hose.

2. Leather gaiters worn by sportsmen.

gal-li-mā′tiȧs (-shȧ), *n.* [Obs.] See *Galimatias*.

gal-li-mau′fry, *n.*; *pl.* **gal-li-mau′fries**. A hash; a medley; a hodgepodge. [Obs.]

gal′lin, *n.* A crystalline substance, $C_{20}H_{14}O_7$, used instead of logwood as a dye.

Gal-li-nā′cē-æ, *n.pl.* [L., from *gallinaceus*, pertaining to poultry, from *gallina*, a hen, from *gallus*, a cock.] An order of birds including the domestic fowls; the *Gallinæ*.

gal-li-nā′ceous, *a.* [L. *gallinaceus*, pertaining to poultry.] Designating that order of birds called *Gallinæ*.

Gal-lī′næ, *n.pl.* [L., from *gallina*, a hen, from *gallus*, a cock.] An order of birds established by Linnæus; the same as the old order *Rasores*, to the exclusion of the pigeons.

gall′ing, *a.* Irritating; vexatious.

gall′ing-ly, *adv.* Irritatingly.

gal′li-nip-pẽr, *n.* [Etym. doubtful.] A large mosquito.

gall′=in″sect, *n.* Any hymenopterous insect of the tribe *Gallicola* of which the type is the *Cynips*; loosely, any insect producing galls.

gal′li-nūle, *n.* [L. *gallinula*, dim. of *gallina*, a hen.] Any bird of the genus *Gallinula*, the typical genus of the subfamily *Gallinulinæ*. *Gallinula galeata* is the red-billed mud-hen of

Florida. The term often comprehends birds of an allied genus, as *Ionornis martinica*, the purple *gallinule*.

gal′li-ŏt, *n.* [Obs.] See *Galiot.*

gal′li-pot, *n.* [Corruption of Old Dutch *gleypot*, a gallipot; *gleye*, potter's clay, and *pot*, pot.] A small pot or vessel, painted and glazed, used by druggists and apothecaries for containing medicines.

gal′li-um, *n.* [L., from *Gallia*, Gaul.] A metallic element discovered by Lecoq de Boisbaudran in zinc-blende, its existence having been predicted by Mendelejeff by means of his periodic law. *Gallium* is prepared by dissolving the blende in sulphuric acid, precipitating the metals in solution, heating the filtered product with zinc, redissolving and reheating until the *gallium* is concentrated. It is a hard, silver-white metal melting at 86° Fahr.

gal′li-vant, *v.i.* To gad about with or after one of the opposite sex; to flirt; also, to fuss; to bustle. [Colloq.]

gal′li-vat, *n.* [E. Ind.] A small armed vessel used on the Malabar coast.

gal-liv′ō-rous, *a.* In entomology, gall-devouring; said of the larvæ of gall-insects.

gal′li-wăsp, *n.* [*Galli*, a native West Indian name.] A harmless lizard about twelve inches long, supposed by the natives of the West Indies to be poisonous.

gal′līze, *v.t.*; gallized, *pt., pp.*; gallizing, *ppr.* In wine-making, to add, as water and sugar to (unfermented grape juice), thereby bringing it both to the required vinous acidity and the required sweetness, and improving the yield in quality as well as in quantity; named after Dr. L. Gall of Treves, the originator of the process.

gall′nut, *n.* An excrescence of the gall-oak; a gall.

gall′=oak, *n.* The oak, *Quercus infectoria*, from which the galls or gallnuts of commerce are obtained.

Gal-lō-mā′ni-ȧ, *n.* [L. *Gallus*, a Gaul, Frenchman, and *mania*, madness.] Excessive admiration for everything of French origin.

Gal-lō-mā′ni-ac, *n.* One addicted to Gallomania.

gal′lŏn, *n.* [ME. *galon, galun*; OFr. *galon*; LL. *galo (-onis), galona*, a gallon.]

1. An English land measure, now obsolete, supposed to be as much in extent as a gallon of grain would sow.

2. A measure of capacity for liquid or dry substances, generally the former, containing four quarts or eight pints. The United States standard gallon contains 231 cubic inches, or 8.3389 pounds avoirdupois of distilled water at its maximum density with the barometer standing at thirty inches. This is the same as the old English wine gallon. The old English corn gallon contains 268.6 cubic inches and the old ale gallon 282 cubic inches, being the same as the present beer gallon, used to some extent in the United States. The English imperial gallon now in use contains 277.274 cubic inches.

gal-lo͞on′, *n.* [Sp. *galon*, from *gala*, finery, ornament.]

1. A kind of close lace made of gold or silver, or of silk only. [Obs.]

2. A modern fabric similar to the above, usually in the form of a plain braid.

gal-lo͞oned′, *a.* Furnished or adorned with galloon.

gal′lŏp, *v.i.*; galloped (-lupt), *pt., pp.*; galloping, *ppr.* [ME. *galopen*; OFr. *galoper*, to gallop.]

1. To move or run with leaps or bounds, as a horse; to run or move with speed.

2. To ride with a galloping pace; as, we *galloped* toward the enemy.

3. To move very fast; to run over; to read or examine with haste; as, to *gallop* through a book.

gal′lŏp, *v.t.* To impel to the gait known as a gallop; as, to *gallop* a horse.

gal′lŏp, *n.* [OFr. *galop*, from *galoper*, to gallop.] The motion or pace of a quadruped, particularly a horse, when running at full speed, in which he moves by springs, bounds, or leaps, the fore feet being lifted very nearly together, and while these are in the air, and just upon the point of touching the ground, he lifts both his hind legs almost at once.

gal-lō-päde′, *n.* [Fr. *galopade*, from *galoper*, to gallop.]

1. A kind of dance, and also a kind of music appropriate to the dance.

2. In the manège, a sidelong or curveting kind of gallop.

gal-lō-päde′, *v.i.*; gallopaded, *pt., pp.*; gallopading, *ppr.* 1. To advance with a prancing, sidelong movement, as on a horse.

2. To dance the gallopade.

gal′lŏp-ẽr, *n.* 1. One who or that which gallops.

2. In ordnance, (a) a carriage on which small guns were carried, having shafts so it might be drawn without limbers; (b) a galloper-gun.

gal′lŏp-ẽr=gun, *n.* A light gun carried on a galloper. [Eng.]

gal′lō-pin, *n.* [Fr.] A servant for the kitchen; a scullion. [Obs.]

gal′lŏp-ing, *n.* The act of riding or moving at a gallop.

gal′lŏp-ing, *a.* Rapid in effect; as, *galloping* consumption.

gal-lō-tan nic, *a.* In chemistry, pertaining to or derived from the tannin of nutgalls.

Gallotannic acid; tannic acid obtained from nutgalls.

gal′lōu-ber″ry, *n.* [Prob. a corruption of *curlewberry.*] A plant, the crowberry.

gal′lōu-bīrd, *n.* *Numenius borealis*, the Eskimo curlew.

gal′lōw, *v.t.* To scare; to frighten.

gal-lō-wāy, *n.* 1. A small, hardy horse (now virtually extinct), formerly bred at *Galloway*, Scotland; called also *garran* and *garron*.

2. [G—] One of a breed of black and white cattle, originally coming from *Galloway*, Scotland.

gal′lōw-glȧss, gal′lō=glȧss, *n.* [Ir. *galloglach*, a servant, a heavy-armed soldier; *gall*, a stranger, foreigner, and *oglach*, a youth, servant.] In ancient Ireland, a soldier or feudary bearing heavy arms.

gal′lōws, *n.*; *pl.* **gal′lōws** or **gal′lōws-es.** [ME. *gallows*; AS. *galga*, a gallows, gibbet.]

1. An instrument or apparatus on which criminals are executed by hanging, usually constructed of two posts with a crossbeam from which the criminal is hanged by a rope passing round his neck.

2. A wretch who deserves the gallows. [Rare.]

3. [*pl.*] Suspenders for men's use; colloquially called *galluses*.

4. In printing, a rest for the raised tympan of a hand-press.

5. Two or more hills of cornstalks interlaced and used as a center for a shock of corn.

6. Anything resembling a *gallows*, particularly any gallows-like appliance used in mechanics.

7. Nautically, same as *gallows-bitts*.

gal′lōws, *a.* Fine; dashing; reckless. [Slang.]

gal′lōws, *adv.* To the extreme; very. [Slang.]

gal′lōws=bīrd, *n.* One who merits hanging or has been hanged.

gal′lōws=bitts, *n.pl.* Nautically, a strong frame erected amidships on the deck to hold spare spars; also called *gallows, gallows-frame.*

Gallows-bitts.

gal′lōws=frāme, *n.* 1. The frame of a gallows.

2. Nautically, same as *gallows-bitts*.

3. A support erected at the mouth of a mining-shaft for the hoisting-apparatus. [Eng.]

4. A supporting-frame for the beam of a beam-engine.

gal′lōws=free, *a.* Free from danger of the gallows.

gal′lōws=tree, *n.* The tree of execution; the gallows.

gall′=sick-ness, *n.* A remitting bilious fever common in the Netherlands.

gall′sōme, gal′sōme, *a.* Containing gall; malignant. [Obs.]

gall′stōne, *n.* A biliary concretion, consisting of cholesterin and coloring-matter forming in the gall-bladder.

Gal′lus, *n.*; *pl.* **Gal′lī.** [L., from Gr. *Gallos*, a priest of Cybele.] A priest who had charge of the wild rites attendant upon the worship of Cybele; so named from the river *Gallus*, in Phrygia, whose waters were supposed to produce madness.

Gal′lus, *n.* [L. *gallus*, cock.] A genus of the family *Phasianidæ*, including the domestic hen and similar fowls.

gal′lus-es, *n.*, pl. of *gallows*, in sense of definition 3. [Colloq.]

gall′wăsp, *n.* Same as *Gallfly.*

gal′ly, *v.t.* To gallow. [Obs.]

gal′ly, *n.* A type-galley. [Obs.]

gall′y, *a.* Like gall; bitter as gall.

gal-ly-gas′kins, gal-ly-gas′coynes, *n.pl.* Same as *Galligaskins.*

gal′ly-wŏrm, *n.* One of various worms of *Myriapoda*, having many legs; a chilognath; spelled also *galleyworm.*

ga-loche′, *n* Same as *Galosh.*

ga-lo͞ot′, *n.* One awkward or roughly uncouth in manner; a humorous, affectionate, or contemptuous designation. [Slang.]

gal′ŏp, *n.* [Fr.] 1. A lively round dance in 2/4 time, now often forming part of a set of quadrilles.

2. The music for this dance.

ga-lōre′, *adv.* In plenty; abundantly.

ga-lōre′, *a.* [Ir. *go leor*, enough; *go*, to, and *leor*, sufficient, enough.] Plentiful; in abundance; following the noun; as, money *galore.*

ga-losh′, ga-loche′, *n.* [ME. *galoche*; OFr. *galoche*; LL. *calopedia*, a clog or wooden shoe, from Gr. *kalopodion*, dim. of *kalopous*, a shoemaker's last; *kalon*, wood, and *pous* (*podos*), foot.]

1. A patten, clog, or wooden shoe. [Obs.]

2. An overshoe worn in rain or snow; an arctic.

3. A high gaiter; a legging extending from the uppers to a point above the ankle.

galp, galpe, *v.i.* To gape or yawn. [Obs.]

gal′sōme, *a.* Gallsome. [Obs.]

gȧlt, *n.* [Norw. *gald*, hard ground.]

1. A stiff, blue marl, of the Chalk formation. [Prov. Eng.]

2. In geology, a division of the Upper Cretaceous marking definitely its lower boundary.

gal-van′iç, *a.* 1. Pertaining to galvanism; containing or exhibiting it; producing or using electrical currents.

2. In demonstrative anatomy, resulting from subjection to an electric current; as, the *galvanic* movement of a cadaver.

Galvanic battery; a kind of electric battery in which each cell is made of two elements (as zinc and copper) placed in a liquid (as a solution of chromic acid), whereby a current is produced when the metals are brought into contact externally; also called *voltaic battery.*

Simple Galvanic Battery.

gal′văn-ism, *n.* [It. *galvanismo*, so called from the first investigator in the field, Luigi *Galvani*, professor of anatomy at Bologna in the latter part of the eighteenth century.]

1. Electric currents or electricity arising from chemical action, more particularly from that accompanying the decomposition of metals; a term not in modern scientific use.

2. The branch of physics treating of this form of electricity.

3. In medicine, treatment by electricity generated from a galvanic cell or battery.

gal′vȧ-nist, *n.* One learned in galvanism.

gal″vȧ-ni-zā′tion, *n.* 1. Electroplating.

2. Use of a voltaic current to affect the body, as in medicine.

gal′vȧ-nīze, *v.t.*; galvanized, *pt., pp.*; galvanizing, *ppr.* 1. To make use of electricity to affect (the body), as in electrical treatment for disease.

2. To endow with false or fictitious animation or vitality.

3. To electroplate.

Galvanized iron; (a) iron coated with zinc by galvanic deposition; (b) iron, usually in sheets, coated after cleaning by immersion in melted zinc.

gal′vȧ-nī-zẽr, *n.* One who or that which galvanizes.

gal-van-o-. A combining form from the proper name *Galvani*, the discoverer of galvanism, signifying galvanic, or relating to galvanism.

gal″văn-ō-çaus′tiç, *a.* [*Galvano-*, and Gr. *kaiein*, to burn.] Pertaining to galvanic heat employed as a caustic, particularly in electrotherapeutics.

gal″văn-ō-çau′tẽr-y, *n.* [*Galvano-*, and Gr. *kautēr*, a burner.] Cauterizing with an instrument heated by a galvanic current.

gal-vȧ-nog′ly-phy, *n.* [*Galvano-*, and Gr. *glyphein*, to engrave.] A process of making an electroplate for printing by the use of a zinc plate and etching.

gal-van′ō-grȧph, *n.* [*Galvano-*, and Gr. *graphein*, to write.] A plate made by the galvanographic process; an impression printed from such a plate.

gal″văn-ō-graph′iç, *a.* Pertaining to or produced by galvanography.

gal-vȧ-nog′rȧ-phy, *n.* [*Galvano-*, and Gr. *graphein*, to write.]

1. Same as *Electrotyping.*

2. A method of producing plates for copperplate engraving by the galvanoplastic process without etching.

gal-vȧ-nol′ō-gist, *n.* One who describes the phenomena of galvanism.

gal-vȧ-nol′ō-gy, *n.* [*Galvano-*, and Gr. *logos*, a description, from *legein*, to speak.] A treatise on galvanism or a description of its phenomena.

gal″văn-ō-mag-net′iç, *a.* Same as *Electromagnetic.*

gal-vȧ-nom′e-tẽr, *n.* [*Galvano-*, and Gr. *metron*, a measure.] An instrument for detecting the existence and determining the strength and direction of an electric current. It depends upon the force exerted between a magnetic needle and a wire carrying a current which tends to set the needle at right angles to the direction of the current.

Differential galvanometer; see under *Differential*, a.

Sine galvanometer, cosine galvanometer, tangent galvanometer; a galvanometer in which the sine, cosine, or tangent of the angular deviation of the magnetic needle is proportional to the strength of the current measured.

gal″văn-ō-met′rịç, *a.* Relating to, employing, or measured by a galvanometer.

gal-vȧ-nom′e-try, *n.* The art of or method employed in measuring the force of electric currents.

gal″văn-ō-plas′tịç, *a.* [*Galvano-*, and Gr. *plastos*, formed, molded, from *plassein*, to form, mold.] Pertaining to the electrotypic process, or to any of its products.

gal-van′ō-plas-ty, *n.* Same as *Electrotyping.*

gal″văn-ō-punç′ture, *n.* Same as *Electropuncturation.*

gal-van′ō-scōpe, *n.* [*Galvano-*, and Gr. *skopein*, to view.] An instrument used to ascertain the presence and the direction of weak electric currents.

gal″văn-ō-sçop′ịç, *a.* Relating to or discovered by a galvanoscope.

gal-vȧ-nos′çō-py, *n.* [*Galvano-*, and Gr. *skopein*, to view.] The employment of galvanic electricity in physiology.

gal″văn-ō-thẽr-mom′e-tẽr, *n.* A device employed in ascertaining the amount of heat which an electric current generates while passing through various conducting mediums.

gal-vȧ-not′ō-nus, *n.* [*Galvano-*, and Gr. *tonos*, tone.] Same as *Electrotonus.*

gal-vȧ-not′rō-pịsm, *n.* [*Galvano-*, and Gr. *trepein*, to turn.] In botany, the disposition exhibited by growing plants to turn in certain directions when acted upon by an electric current, as to bend toward the positive electrode.

gal′we, gal′weș, *n.* The hangman's gallows. [Obs.]

gam, *n.* 1. A herd of whales.

2. The exchange of calls and social intercourse which passes between the men on whalers and fishing-smacks when they meet at sea and are at leisure.

gam, *v.i.*; gammed, *pt., pp.*; gamming, *ppr.* [Etym. uncertain; prob. from *jam.*]

1. To herd together, as whales.

2. To exchange calls and friendly greetings with the crew of a ship at sea.

gam, *v.t.* To call upon, chat with, and otherwise communicate with, as the officers and crew of another vessel.

gä′mȧ=grȧss, *n.* [From *Gama*, a cluster of islands in the Maldive group.] A tall, stout, and exceedingly productive grass, grown in the southern states, Mexico, and Cuba, being sown for grazing grass.

ga-mash′eș, *n.pl.* [OFr. *gamaches*, from *gambe*, leg.] Short spatterdashes similar to gaiters; high boots or protective leggings, worn when riding horseback. [Obs.]

gamb, gambe, *n.* [OFr. *gambe*, the leg; LL. *gamba*, a leg, the hoof; prob. of Celtic origin, compare W., Ir., and Gael. *cam*, crooked.] A term in heraldry used to express the whole fore leg of a lion or other beast. If couped or erased near the middle joint it is then only a paw; also written *jambe.*

gam′bȧ, *n.* An abbreviation for *viol da gamba.*

gam-bāde′, gam-bā′dō, *n.* [It. *gamba*, the leg.]

1. A gaiter or legging worn to protect the ankle and leg when riding horseback or walking.

2. [*pl.*] Leather boots fastened to a saddle in place of stirrups, protecting the horseman's legs from mud. [Eng.]

gambe, *n.* Same as *Gamb.*

gam-beer′, *v.t.*; gambeered, *pt., pp.*; gambeering, *ppr.* [Compare Fr. *gambier*, an iron hook.] To take, as fish, particularly mackerel, with a gaff-hook as they swim alongside of a vessel.

gam′be-son, gam′bi-son, *n.* [ME. *gambeson*; OFr. *gambeson*; LL. *gambeso* (-*onis*), *gambasium*, a gambeson, from O.H.G. *wamba*, belly, stomach.] A quilted tunic, stuffed with wool, fitting the body, and worn under the armor. [Obs.]

Quilted Gambeson of the fifteenth century.

gam′bet, *n.* [Fr. *gambette*, a gambet, dim. of OFr. *gambe*, leg.] A name applied to various species of birds of the genus *Totanus*, especially to the large sandpiper *Totanus calidris.*

gam′biẽr, gam′bïr, *n.* [Malayan.] The juice of *Uncaria Gambier*, a shrub growing in the Malayan peninsula. It has medicinal qualities, but is better known as a tannin and dyestuff. Called also *Terra Japonica* and *pale catechu.*

gam′bi-son, *n.* See *Gambeson.*

gam′bist, *n.* The member of an orchestra who plays the viol da gamba.

gam′bit, *n.* [Fr. *gambit*, a gambit, from It. *gambetto*, a tripping up of one's legs, from *gamba*, leg.] One of the openings in chess in which a pawn or piece is exposed for the purpose of placing another piece in an offensive position.

gam′ble, *v.i.*; gambled, *pt., pp.*, gambling, *ppr.* [Freq. of ME. *gamen, gamenen*; AS. *gamenian*, to play, game.] To play or game for money or other stake.

gam′ble, *v.t.* To lose by betting; to waste; to squander; followed by *away.*

> Bankrupts or sots who have *gambled* or slept *away* their estates. —Ames.

gam′ble, *n.* An act which depends upon chance; a risk; an uncertain venture. [Colloq.]

gam′blẽr, *n.* One who games or plays for money or other stake.

Gambier Plant (*Uncaria Gambier*).

gam-bōge′, *n.* [From *Camboja, Cambodia*, a French protectorate in India.] A concrete vegetable juice, or inspissated sap, produced by several species of trees native to southeastern Asia. It is of a dense, compact texture, and of a beautiful red-dish-yellow. It is used chiefly as a pigment, giving a clear yellow color, shading into brown. Taken internally, it is a strong and harsh cathartic and emetic.

Gamboge Plant (*Garcinia Hanburyi*).

gam-bō′gi-ăn, gam-bō′gịç, *a.* Pertaining to gamboge.

gam′bŏl, *v.i.*; gamboled *or* gambolled, *pt., pp.*; gamboling *or* gambolling, *ppr.* To dance and skip about in sport; to frisk; to leap; to start up; to frolic, as children and young animals at play.

gam′bŏl, *n.* [Fr. *gambade*, a gambol, from It. *gambata*, a kick, from *gamba*, the leg.] A skipping or leaping about in frolic; a skip; a hop; a leap; a sportive prank.

gam′brel, *n.* [From It. *gamba*, the leg.]

1. The hind leg of a horse.

2. A stick crooked like a horse's leg, used by butchers.

Gambrel roof; a roof having an obtuse angle which gives the lower part a steep pitch.

gam′brel, *v.t.*; gambreled *or* gambrelled, *pt., pp.*; gambreling *or* gambrelling, *ppr.* [OFr. *gambe*, the leg.]

1. To hang up by a gambrel thrust through the legs, as butchers hang carcasses.

2. To build with a double slope in the roof.

gam-broon′, *n.* [Etym. doubtful; prob. from *Gombroon*, a Persian seaport from which a large export trade was carried on.] A light-weight twilled fabric of linen or of cotton and worsted mixed, used for lining garments and for summer clothing.

gam′de-bọọ, *n.* [Native African name.] A small tree, *Celtis Kraussiana*, native to South Africa, yielding a tough timber; called also *stinkwood*, from its peculiarly offensive odor.

gāme, *n.* [ME. *game*; AS. *gamen*, a game, sport.]

1. Any contrivance, arrangement, or contest intended to furnish sport, recreation, or amusement, or to test skill or strength, or simply to try chance; as, a *game* of chess; the *game* of cricket; the *game* of baseball.

2. The score or number of points to be won by a player or a side to finish a match; the stake for which the *game* is played; as, the reds win the *game*; ten points is the *game.*

3. The art or method of playing at any sport; as, he plays a rapid *game* of tennis.

4. In certain card *games*, a point accredited to the player whose hand counts up the highest score.

5. [*pl.*] In classic antiquity, diversions or contests, as in wrestling, running, throwing the discus, chariot-racing, and in numerous tests of skill, strength, or endurance, usually instituted in honor of some event, and exhibited for the amusement of the people; as, the Nemean *games*; the Olympian *games.*

6. Amusement; pastime; jest; that to which earnest consideration is not given; as, what is a serious matter to one, is simply *game* to another; they made *game* of his rustic ways.

7. Scheme pursued; measures planned; project, especially where the injury or discomfiture of another is planned.

> This seems to be the present *game* of that crown. —Temple.

8. Amorous sport; gallantry. [Obs.]

> Set them down
> For sluttish spoils of opportunity
> And daughters of the *game.* —Shak.

9. Animals which are pursued or killed in the chase, or in the sports of the field, either for the use of man or for pastime; as, the northern forests are rich in *game.*

10. The flesh of wild birds or animals served as food; as, savages live almost wholly upon *game.*

11. An object of pursuit or desire; a person sought, especially one who is a fugitive from justice.

Confidence game; see under *Confidence.*

Round game; a card game in which any number of players may participate.

The game is up; (a) the plan has failed, or the plot been discovered; (b) in hunting, the game has been started from cover.

Syn.—Sport, recreation, pastime, amusement, frolic, diversion, play.

gāme, *a.* 1. Having an undaunted spirit; unwilling to admit defeat; full of pluck.

2. Pertaining to such animals and birds as are hunted either for the use of man or for the sport of the hunt.

3. Consisting of or pertaining to the flesh of game; as, the *game* course; a *game* set.

To be game; (a) to reveal a determined, plucky spirit; (b) to be the winner in a game.

To die game; to maintain reserve and not exhibit emotion when at the point of death; to keep one's nerve to the last; to die unconquered in spirit.

gāme, *v.i.*; gamed, *pt., pp.*; gaming, *ppr.* [ME. *gamen*; AS. *gamenian*, to play, game.]

1. To play at any sport or diversion.

2. To play for a stake or prize; to use cards, dice, or other instruments, according to certain rules, with a view to win the bet waged upon the issue of the contest.

3. To be happy; to rejoice; to receive pleasure. [Obs.]

gāme, *a.* Crooked; lame; hurt; as, a *game* ankle. [Slang.]

gāme′=bag, *n.* A hunter's bag for carrying small game; also, the day's kill.

gāme′=bīrd, *n.* A bird which is hunted for the sake of the sport or for the food or feathers which it furnishes.

gāme′çock, *n.* A cock bred or used to fight

gāme′=egg, *n.* The egg of the game-fowl.

gāme′=fowl, *n.* Any one of several breeds of domestic fowls, the males of which may be trained to fight one another with courage and endurance.

gāme′fụl, *a.* Full of game or games.

gāme′keep″ẽr, *n.* One who has the care of game; one who is employed to look after animals kept for sport.

gāme′=lạw, *n.* A law enacted with regard to the preservation of game-animals of all kinds

gāme′less, *a.* Destitute of game.

gāme′ly, *adv.* In a game or courageous manner.

gāme′ness, *n.* The quality of being game or having an unyielding spirit; courage; pluckiness.

> There was no doubt about his *gameness.* —Hughes.

gāme′=prē-ṣẽrve″, *n.* An area of wooded land in which game abounds and in which it is protected from hunters.

gāme′=prē-ṣẽrv″ẽr, *n.* A landowner or lessee of game, who strictly preserves it for his own sport or profit. The term is generally applied to those who preserve so strictly that the game becomes a nuisance to others.

gāme′sŏme, *a.* Gay; sportive; playful; frolicsome

gāme′sŏme-ly, *adv.* Merrily; playfully.

gāme′sŏme-ness, *n.* Sportiveness; merriment.

gāme′stẽr, *n.* 1. A person addicted to gaming; one accustomed to play for money or other stake; a gambler; one skilled in games.

2. A merry, frolicsome person. [Obs.]

3. A prostitute. [Obs.]

gam″e-tan′gi-um, gam′e-tange, *n.* [L., from Gr. *gametē*, a wife, and *angeion*, a vessel.] The organ or cell from which gametes emerge.

ga-mēte′, *n.* [Gr. *gametē*, a wife, from *gamein*, to marry, from *gamos*, marriage.] A protoplasmic sexual cell which coalesces with another to form a zygote or new individual.

gam′e-tō-phȳte, *n.* [Gr. *gametē*, a wife, and *phyton*, a plant.] That stage in the development of a thallophytic plant in which the sexual organs are produced.

gam′ịç, *a.* [Gr. *gamikos*, pertaining to marriage, from *gamos*, marriage.] Relating to or derived from sexual unions; sexual; capable of being developed only through sexual union.

gam′in, *n.* [Fr.] A street urchin or street arab; a neglected boy who frequents the streets and public places of a city.

gām′ing, *n.* The act or art of playing any game for a prize or stake; gambling.

gam′mȧ, *n.* [L. *gamma*; Gr. *gamma.*]

1. The third letter of the Greek alphabet (Γ, γ), corresponding to the English *g*.

2. A common European noctuid moth, *Plusia gamma*, having on the wing a silvery spot resembling in shape the Greek γ.

3. Same as *Gamut*.

gam-mā′di-on, *n.*; *pl.* **gam-mā′di-ȧ**. [L.Gr. *gammadion*, from Gr. *gamma*, gamma.] A Greek capital gamma, or, in the plural, a cross of four capital gammas, used as a decoration on ancient church vestments. [See *Fylfot*.]

gam′mȧ-moth, *n.* Same as *Gamma*, 2.

gam′mȧ-rid, *n.* One of the *Gammaridæ*.

Gam-mar′i-dæ, *n.pl.* [L. *gammarus*, *cammarus*; Gr. *kammaros*, a kind of lobster, and *-idæ*.] A family of amphipodous crustaceans, typified by the genus *Gammarus*, of which the fresh-water shrimp is a species.

gam′mȧ-roid, *a.* Pertaining to or having the characteristics of the *Gammaridæ*.

gam-mar′ō-līte, *n.* [L. *gammarus*, *cammarus*, a kind of lobster, and Gr. *lithos*, stone.] A fossil crawfish or other crustacean like a species of *Gammarus*.

Gam′mȧ-rus, *n.* A genus typical of the family *Gammaridæ*.

gam-mā′ti-ŏn, *n.* Same as *Gammadion*.

gam′mẽr, *n.* [Dial. contr. of *grandmother*.] An old woman; correlative of *gaffer*, an old man.

gam′mŏn, *n.* [OFr. *gambon*, from *gambe*, leg.] The buttock or thigh of a hog, pickled and smoked or dried; a smoked ham.

gam′mŏn, *v.t.*; gammoned, *pt.*, *pp.*; gammoning, *ppr.* To make into bacon; to pickle and dry in smoke.

gam′mŏn, *v.t.* In seamen's language, to fasten (a bowsprit) to the stem of a ship, as by iron bands or several turns of a rope.

gam′mŏn, *n.* [ME. *gammen*; AS. *gamen*, game, joy.]

1. In the game of backgammon, a victory for a player when he has thrown off all his men before his opponent has thrown off one.

2. An imposition or hoax; a deceitful trick; humbug. [Colloq.]

gam′mŏn, *v.t.* 1. In the game of backgammon, to secure a gammon over.

2. To impose on by improbable stories; to humbug; to hoax; to delude. [Colloq.]

gam′mŏn, *v.i.* To play a part; to pretend. [Colloq.]

gam′mŏn-ing, *n.* Imposition; the act of hoaxing.

gam′mŏn-ing, *n.* In seamen's language, the iron bands or the lashing by which the bowsprit of a vessel is secured to the stem.

gam′mŏn-ing-hōle, *n.* A hole in the knee of the head of a vessel through which the gammoning may be passed.

gam′mŏn-plāte, *n.* An iron plate on the stem of a vessel to which the gammon-shackles are fastened.

gam′mŏn-shac″kles, *n.pl.* In shipbuilding, shackles for securing the gammoning.

gam-o-. A combining form from Gr. *gamos*, marriage, used to signify marriage, married, united; as, *gamo*gastrous.

gam-ō-gas′trous, *a.* [*Gamo-*, and Gr. *gastēr*, belly, womb.] In botany, having the ovaries united; said of a compound pistil in which the styles and stigmas are free.

gam-ō-ġen′e-sis, *n.* [*Gamo-*, and Gr. *genesis*, generation.] In biology, sexual reproduction or generation; opposed to *agamogenesis*.

gam″ō-ġē-net′iç, *a.* Pertaining to gamogenesis; produced by gamogenesis.

gam″ō-ġē-net′iç-ăl-ly, *adv.* In a gamogenetic manner.

gam-ō-mor′phism, *n.* [*Gamo-*, and Gr. *morphē*, form.] That stage of development of organized beings in which the spermatic and germinal elements are formed, matured, and generated, in preparation for an act of fecundation, as the commencement of a new genetic cycle.

gam-ō-pet′ăl-ous, *a.* [*Gamo-*, and Gr. *petalon*, a leaf.] In botany, having the petals united into one piece by their edges; monopetalous.

ga-moph′yl-lous, *a.* [*Gamo-*, and Gr *phyllon*, a leaf.] In botany, having a single perianth-whorl with coherent leaves; symphyllous; opposed to *apophyllous*.

gam-ō-sep′ăl-ous, *a.* [*Gamo-*, and E. *sepal*.] In botany, having the sepals partially or entirely united; monosepalous.

gamp, *n.* A large umbrella; said to be so called from Mrs. Gamp of Dickens's novel "Martin Chuzzlewit." [Colloq.]

gam′ut, *n.* [LL. *gamma ut*; *gamma*, the gamut, from Gr. *gamma*, the third letter of the Gr. alphabet, and *ut*, from L. *ut*, that, used as a musical note.]

1. In music, (a) a scale on which notes in music are written or printed, consisting of lines and spaces, which are named after the first seven letters of the alphabet; (b) the first or gravest note in Guido's scale of music; (c) a major or minor scale.

2. Figuratively, the entire range or extent of anything.

gām′y, *a.* 1. Having the flavor of game; having the flavor of game kept uncooked till it is slightly tainted; as, the venison was in fine *gamy* condition.

2. Plucky; spirited; affording sport; as, a *gamy* salmon.

gän, *v.i.* To yawn. [Obs.]

gan, *v.*, obsolete past tense of *gin*, to begin.

gan, *n.* The mouth. [Obs.]

gȧnch, gąunch, *v.t.* [Fr. *gancher*, from *gancio*, a hook.] To drop from a high place on sharp stakes or hooks, as the Turks did malefactors by way of punishment.

gȧnch, gąunch, *n.* The process of torturing by ganching.

gan′dẽr, *n.* [ME. *gandre*; AS. *gandra*, the gander.] The male of the goose.

gan′dẽr, *v.i.* To walk leisurely or aimlessly; to saunter. [Colloq.]

gan′dẽr-pär″ty, *n.* A friendly party composed entirely of men; a stag-party. [Slang.]

gāne, *v.i.* [Obs.] Same as first *gan*.

Ga-nē′sȧ, *n.* In Hindu mythology, the god of prudence, represented as a man with an elephant's head

gang, *v.i.* [AS. *gangan*, *gongan*, to go.] To go; to walk. [Scot. and Prov. Eng.]

gang, *n.* [ME. *gang*, a going, a course; AS. *gang*, a going, way.]

1. A going; the act of walking. [Obs.]

2. A number going in company; hence, a company or a number of persons associated for a particular purpose; a number of workmen or laborers under the supervision of one person; a squad; as, a *gang* of hod-carriers; a *gang* of stokers; a *gang* of thieves.

3. A combination or set of tools or machines of one kind, so arranged as to operate together; as, a *gang* of plows or saws.

4. As much as one goes for or carries at once. [Scot.]

5. The field or pasture in which animals graze. [Scot.]

6. In mining, see *gangue*.

Round gang; a gang of saws for sawing a round log.

gaṅ′gȧ, *n.* [Sp.] 1. *Pterocles alchata*, a sand-grouse.

2. A species of South American hawk of the genus *Ibycter*.

gang′bōard, *n.* Same as *Gangplank*.

gang′-cȧsk, *n.* A small cask used for bringing water aboard ships in boats.

gang′-cul″ti-vā-tŏr, *n.* A cultivator having a number of shares which are operated in a gang.

gang′-dāy, *n.* [AS. *gangdagas*, gang-days; *gang*, a going, and *dæg* (pl. *dagas*), day.] In England, a day of perambulation of parishes; a rogation-day.

gang′-drill, *n.* A machine for drilling, having several drills which are operated together.

gange, *v.t.*; ganged, *pt.*, *pp.*; ganging, *ppr.* To affix (a fishhook) to the ganging of a line.

gang′ẽr, *n.* 1. In England, one who conducts or superintends a gang, as the foreman of a gang of laborers or plate-layers on a railway.

2. In seamen's language, a chain having one end attached to an anchor and the other to the hawser.

Gan-ġet′iç, *a.* Of or pertaining to the river Ganges; as, the *Gangetic* crocodile.

gang′-flow″ẽr, *n.* A name given to the milk-wort, *Polygala vulgaris*, because of its blooming in gang-week.

Gan′ġiç, *a.* Gangetic. [Rare.]

gan′ġing, *n.* 1. That part of a fishing-line to which the hook is attached, and usually of different material from that of the line proper; called also *ganging-line*.

2. The act or manner of fastening a fishhook to the ganging of a line.

gan′ġing-line, *n.* See *Ganging*, 1.

gan′ġiŏn (-jun), *n.* [Etym. uncertain.] A short line fastened to a trawl.

gaṅ′gli-aç, *a.* Ganglial.

gaṅ′gli-ăl, *a.* Relating to a ganglion; ganglionic.

gaṅ′gli-ăr, *a.* Ganglial.

gaṅ′gli-āte, gaṅ′gli-ā-ted, *a.* Provided with ganglia; as, a *gangliated* lymphatic.

gaṅ′gli-fọrm, gaṅ′gli-ō-fọrm, *a.* [Gr. *ganglion*, a tumor, and L. *forma*, form.] Having the shape of a ganglion.

gaṅ-gli-ī′tis, *n.* See *Ganglionitis*.

gaṅ′gling, *a.* [Freq. of *gang*; AS. *gang*, a going, from *gangan*, to go.] Awkward; ungraceful; loose-jointed. [Colloq.]

gaṅ′gli-ŏn, *n.*; *pl.* **gaṅ′gli-ȧ** or **gaṅ′gli-ŏnṣ**. [LL. *ganglion*, from Gr. *ganglion*, a tumor.]

1. In anatomy, (a) a well-defined collection of nerve-cells and fibers forming a subsidiary nerve-center; (b) a node on a lymphatic; a lymphatic gland.

Ganglion.
Part of the nervous system of the larva of *Calosoma sycophanta*. *a*, *a*, Ganglia.

2. In pathology, an encysted tumor situated somewhere on a tendon, and formed by the elevation of the sheath of the tendon, and the effusion of a viscid fluid into it.

3. In botany, the mycelium of certain *Fungi*.

gaṅ′gli-ŏn-ā-ry, *a.* Composed of ganglia.

gaṅ′gli-ŏn-cell, *n.* In anatomy, the large nerve-cell characteristic of the ganglia; similar cells are found in other parts of the nervous system.

gaṅ-gli-on′iç, *a.* Pertaining to or of the nature of a ganglion; as, the *ganglionic* columns of the spinal cord.

gaṅ-gli-on′i-çȧ, *n.pl.* In medicine, a class of medicinal agents which affect the sensibility or muscular motion of parts supplied by the ganglionic or sympathetic system of nerves.

gaṅ-gli-ō-nī′tis, *n.* In pathology, inflammation of a nervous or lymphatic ganglion.

gaṅ′gli-ŏn-less, *a.* Without ganglia; said of a nerve.

gaṅ′gli-ous, *a.* Pertaining to or having the shape of a ganglion; gangliform.

gang′mas″tẽr, *n.* A master or employer of a gang or body of workers; one who hires a band of persons to perform some specified task.

gang′plaṅk, *n.* A board or plank forming a temporary bridge for passengers between a vessel and the pier; called also *gangboard*.

gang′-plow, *n.* A plow having several shares set in the same frame, and operating together.

gang′-press, *n.* A press which operates upon several objects at the same time.

gang′-punch, *n.* An arrangement of several punches in a single stock.

gaṅ′grel, *n.* [From ME. *gangen*, AS. *gangan*, to go, walk.]

1. A tall clumsy fellow.

2. A vagrant. [Prov. Eng. and Scot.]

3. A child just beginning to walk. [Scot.]

gaṅ′grel, *a.* Vagrant; vagabond.

gaṅ′grē-nāte, *v.t.* To produce gangrene in; to gangrene.

gaṅ′grēne, *n.* [OFr. *gangrene*; L. *gangræna*; Gr. *gangraina*, an eating sore, gangrene, from *grainein*, to gnaw, eat.]

1. In pathology, the first stage of mortification of living flesh.

2. In botany, a disease ending in putrid decay.

gaṅ′grēne, *v.t.*; gangrened, *pt.*, *pp.*; gangrening, *ppr.* To mortify; to produce gangrene in.

gaṅ′grēne, *v.i.* To become mortified.

gaṅ-grē-nes′cent, *a.* Becoming gangrenous; tending to mortification.

gaṅ′grē-nous, *a.* Mortified; indicating mortification of living flesh.

gang′-saw, *n.* A machine consisting of several saws set in the same frame, and acting simultaneously.

gang′-tide, *n.* Same as *Gang-week*.

gangue, gang, *n.* [Fr. *gangue*; G. *gang*, a metallic vein, a passage, from AS. *gang*, a going, way.]

1. In mining, the mineral matters in which metallic ores are embedded.

2. In smelting, the superfluous earthy matter of a smelting-furnace.

gang′wāy, *n.* 1. A passage; a temporary passageway to a building while in the course of erection; a way or avenue into or out of any inclosed place.

2. An opening in the bulwarks of a ship by which persons come on board or disembark; also, the temporary bridge affording means of passage from the ship to the shore, or vice versa.

3. The part of a vessel on the spar-deck, forming a passage along each side, from the quarter-deck to the forecastle; more properly termed the *waist*.

4. In the British House of Commons, a narrow passage running across the house, and dividing the seats on each side into two parts.

To bring to the gangway; in seamen's language, to punish (a seaman) by seizing him up and flogging him.

gang′wāy-lad″dẽr, *n.* A ladder leading down to the water from a ship's gangway.

gang′-week, *n.* Rogation-week, when the bounds of parishes were formerly surveyed.

gan′il, *n.* [Fr.] A name given in England to a variety of brittle limestone.

gan′is-tẽr, gan′nis-tẽr, *n.* [G. dial. *ganster*; M.H.G. *ganster*, a spark.] A close-grained, hard sandstone or grit found under certain coal-beds in the lower coal-measures of England. It is used for macadamizing roads, and also for lining iron furnaces and Bessemer converters.

gan′jȧh, *n.* [Hind. *gania*, *ganjha*, the hemp-plant.] The name for the hemp-plant in the north of India; specifically, the dried plant which has flowered, and from which the resin has not been removed; it is smoked like tobacco.

gan′nen, *n.* In the north of England, a sloping gangway in a coal-mine down which coal is carried in tubs or cars running on tracks.

gan′net, *n.* [ME. *gant*; AS. *ganot*, *ganet*, a sea-fowl.] The solan-goose, *Sula bassana*, of the pelican family. It is about three feet long. The old birds are taken in great numbers for their feathers. [See illus. p. 704.]

Gan-ō-ceph′ȧ-lȧ, *n.pl.* [Gr *ganos*, brightness, and *kephalē*, head.] A group of fossil labyrinthodont amphibians, with polished horny or ganoid plates covering the head.

gan-ō-ceph′ȧ-lous, *a.* Having the characteristic features of the *Ganocephala.*

gā′noid, *a.* [Gr. *ganos,* brightness, and *eidos,* appearance.]

1. Pertaining to the *Ganoidei.*

2. Having an appearance resembling that of enamel; specifically, applied to those scales or plates of fishes which are composed of an inferior layer of true bone, covered by a superior layer of polished enamel.

Gannet or Solan Goose (*Sula bassana*).

gā′noid, *n.* One of the *Ganoidei.*

gȧ-noid′ăl, *a.* Same as *Ganoid.*

gȧ-noid′ē-ăn, *a.* and *n.* Same as *Ganoid.*

Gȧ-noi′dē-ī, *n.pl.* [Gr. *ganos,* brightness, and *eidos,* appearance.] A large subclass of fishes characterized by angular rhomboidal, polygonal, or circular scales, composed of horny or bony plates. The bony pike and sturgeon are examples. The subclass contains many genera, of which the majority are extinct.

Scales of different fossil genera of Ganoids. 1. Lepidosteus; 2. Cheiracanthus; 3. Palæoniscus; 4. Cephalaspis; 5. Dipterus; 6. Acipenser.

gȧ-noid′i-ăn, *a.* and *n.* Same as *Ganoid.*

gā′nō-in, *n.* [Gr. *ganos,* brightness.] The peculiar bony tissue which gives the enamel-like luster and transparency to the plates of ganoid fishes and of some labyrinthodonts. It is simply dense homogeneous bone.

gȧ-nom′ȧ-lite, *n.* [Gr. *ganōma,* brightness, and *lithos,* stone.] A silicate of lead and manganese occurring either massive or in tetragonal crystals.

gan-ō-wan′i-ăn, *a.* [N.Am. Ind.] Relating to a marriage custom common to certain American Indians, in which a man sought a wife from another tribe, and descent was usually in the female line.

gȧnt′let, gȧunt′let, *n.* [Sw. *gatlopp,* a running down a lane; *gata,* street or lane, and *lopp,* a course or run.]

1. An obsolete military punishment and a torture of savages, in which the culprit was partly stripped and compelled to run between two files of men armed with clubs or switches, with which he was struck in passing.

2. Hence, a series of disagreeable incidents.

To run the gantlet; to undergo the punishment of the gantlet; hence, to run or pass through a course of severe treatment, criticism, or opposition.

Winthrop *ran the gantlet* of daily slights from his neighbors. —Palfrey.

gȧnt′lette, *n.* A glove. [See *Gauntlet.*]

gant′line, *n.* See *Girtline.*

gant′lōpe, *n.,* an obsolete form of *gantlet.*

gan′try, gan′tree, *n.* Same as *Gauntree.*

gan′zȧ, *n.* [Sp. *gansa,* goose.] A kind of wild goose, by a flock of which a virtuoso was fabled to be carried to the lunar world.

gāol, *n.* A jail.

gāol′ẽr, *n.* A jailer.

gap, *n.* [ME. *gap, gappe;* Ice. *gap,* a gap, opening, from *gapa,* to yawn, gape.] An opening in anything made by breaking or parting; as, a *gap* in a fence; a passage; an opening for entrance or exit; a vacant space; a breach; a hiatus; a defect or flaw; a vacuity; a narrow passage in a mountain; a chasm.

From the *gaps* and chasms. —Tennyson.

A third can fill the *gap* with laughing.—Swift.

It would make a great *gap* in your own honor. —Shak.

To stand in the gap; to expose oneself for the protection of something; to make defense against any assailing danger.

To stop a gap; to secure a weak point; to repair a defect; to supply a temporary expedient.

gap, *v.t.;* gapped (gapt), *pt., pp.;* gapping, *ppr.*

1. To indent or notch, as the edge of a knife.

2. To breach; to open a passage through.

gāpe, *v.i.;* gaped, *pt., pp.;* gaping, *ppr.* [ME. *gapen,* from Ice. *gapa,* to yawn, gape.]

1. To open the mouth wide, as, (a) indicative of sleepiness, drowsiness, dullness, or indifference, as in yawning; (b) in eager desire for food; as, the young birds were *gaping;* (c) indicative of wonder, surprise, astonishment, or the like; as, the crowd stood *gaping;* (d) expressing earnest desire or expectation; (e) evincing a desire to injure or devour.

They have *gaped* upon me with their mouth. —Job xvi. 10.

2. To open as a gap; to show a fissure or chasm.

May that ground *gape* and swallow me alive. —Shak.

Syn.—Yawn, oscitate, stare, gaze.

gāpe, *n.* 1. The act of gaping; a yawn.

2. In zoölogy, the width of the mouth when opened, as of birds, fishes, etc.

The gapes; (a) a fit of yawning or gaping; (b) a disease of young poultry attended with much gaping, due to the presence of a nematoid worm, *Syngamus trachealis,* in the windpipe.

gāp′ẽr, *n.* 1. One who gapes.

2. In zoölogy, (a) a bivalve mollusk, as *Mya truncata;* (b) a broadbill, as *Cymbirhynchus macrorhynchus,* the blue-billed *gaper* of the East Indies; (c) a serranoid fish, *Serranus cabrilla.*

gāpe′seed, *n.* Any object of wonder or astonishment. [Colloq.]

gāpes′ing, *n.* The act of gazing about. [Prov. Eng.]

gāpe′wŏrm, *n.* A worm that causes the gapes in birds, as *Syngamus trachealis.*

gāp′ing-ly, *adv.* In a gaping manner.

gāp′ing-stock, *n.* One who or that which is an object of open-mouthed wonder or astonishment.

gap′=lāthe, *n.* A lathe which has a gap in its bed so that its swing may be increased; called also *break-lathe.*

gap′=tooth̤ed, *a.* Having interstices between the teeth.

gär, *n.* [ME. *gar,* from AS. *gar,* a spear.] The garfish; any one of several species of fishes of the genera *Belone* and *Tylosurus,* as *Belone vulgaris,* the common garfish; also, a ganoid fish of the genus *Lepidosteus,* found in the fresh waters of America; a garpike.

gär, *v.t.* To cause; to make; to compel. [Scot.]

gȧ-räge′ (-räzh′), *n.* [Fr.] A station, repository, storage room or repair shop for automobiles.

gar′ănce, *n.* [Fr.] *Rubia tinctorum,* the madder.

ga-răn-ceux′ (-sē′), *n.* [Fr., from *garance,* madder.] A product obtained by treating the waste madder of the dyehouses, which still contains a certain quantity of alizarin and other coloring matters, with sulphuric acid, to remove lime, magnesia, etc.

gar′ăn-cin, gar′ăn-cine, *n.* [Fr. *garance;* LL. *garantia,* madder.] The product obtained by treating pulverized madder, previously exhausted with water, with concentrated sulphuric acid.

ga-ran′găn, *n.* [E. Ind.] *Herpestes javanicus,* a species of mongoose or ichneumon.

gär-ȧ-pä′tȧ, gär-rȧ-pä′tȧ, *n.* [Sp. Am.]

1. Any species of tick of the family *Ixodidæ.*

2. *Melophagus ovinus,* the sheep-tick.

gar-ȧ-vance′, *n.* [Sp. *garbanzo,* from Basque, *garbantzua,* the chick-pea; *garau,* grain, and *antzua,* dry.] The chick-pea, *Cicer arietinum.*

gärb, *n.* [OFr. *garbe,* gracefulness, from O.H.G. *garawi, garaur,* preparation, dress, from *garawen,* to prepare, dress.]

1. Clothes; dress, especially an official or other distinguishing dress; fashion or mode of dress; costume; as, the *garb* of a clergyman or judge.

In the *garb* of a barefooted Carmelite. —Longfellow.

2. Outward appearance; mien; fashion; looks; mode of doing anything. [Obs.]

Syn.—Dress, apparel, clothing, costume, attire, raiment.

gärb, gärbe, *n.* [OFr. *garbe,* from O.H.G. *garba,* a sheaf of grain.] A sheaf or bundle, as of grain; in heraldry, a sheaf of any kind of grain, but specifically, a sheaf of wheat; when other than wheat, the kind must be expressed.

gärb, *v.t.;* garbed, *pt., pp.;* garbing, *ppr.* To clothe; to dress.

gär′bāge, *n.* [ME. *garbage,* the entrails of fowls; etym. obscure; compare OFr. *garber,* to make fine; *grabeller,* to examine precisely.] The bowels of an animal; offal; the refuse animal or vegetable matter of a kitchen; refuse generally; hence, anything worthless or offensive, as immoral or obscene writings.

gär′bāge, *v.t.* To disembowel; to eviscerate. [Obs.]

gärbed, *a.* Dressed; habited.

gär′bel, *n.* [Etym. obscure.] The plank next the keel of a ship. [See *Garboard-plank.*]

gär′bel, *n.* [Obs.] See *Garble.*

gär′bel, *v.t.* [Obs.] See *Garble.*

gär′ble, *v.t.;* garbled, *pt., pp.;* garbling, *ppr.* [OFr. *grabeller,* to examine closely, from Sp. *garbillar,* to sift, from *garbillo,* a coarse sieve, from Ar. *ghirbāl,* a sieve.]

1. To sift or bolt; to separate the fine or valuable parts of from the coarse and useless parts, or from dross or dirt; as, to *garble* spices. [Obs.]

2. To pick out such parts of as may serve a purpose; to mutilate; to falsify; as, to *garble* a quotation.

Syn.—Misrepresent, misquote, mutilate, falsify, pervert.

gär′ble, *n.* 1. Anything that has been sifted or from which the coarse parts have been removed. [Obs.]

2. [*pl.*] Impurities separated from goods, as spices, drugs, etc.; trash; garblings.

gär′blẽr, *n.* 1. One who garbles, sifts, or separates.

2. One who picks out, culls, or selects, to serve a purpose; as, a *garbler* of a statement.

gär′bling, *n.* 1. The act of garbling or perverting.

2. [*pl.*] Same as *Garble,* n. 2.

gär′bōard, *n.* [Etym. uncertain.] See *Garboard-plank.*

gär′bōard=plank, *n.* The plank fastened next the keel on the outside of a ship's bottom.

gär′bōard=strāke, *n.* The first range or strake of planks laid on a ship's bottom next the keel; called also *ground-strake.*

gär′boil, *n.* Tumult; uproar. [Obs.]

gär-bū′sȧ, *n.* Same as *Gorbuscha.*

Gär-cin′i-ȧ, *n.* [From Dr. Laurent *Garcin,* a French botanist.] A genus of trees of the gamboge family, found in the tropical regions of Asia and Africa. *Garcinia Mangostana* is the mangosteen-tree.

gär-çon′, *n.* [Fr.] A boy; especially, a serving boy or waiter.

gärd, *n.* A garden. [Obs.]

gärd, *v.* and *n.* [Obs.] See *Guard.*

gär′dănt, guär′dănt, *a.* [Fr. *gardant,* ppr. of *garder,* to look, regard.] In heraldry, having the full face turned toward the spectator; said of an animal passant, rampant, etc., used as a bearing.

Lion gardant.

gärde′=brāce, gärde′=brās, *n.* [Fr. *garde-bras,* arm-guard; *garder,* to guard, and *bras,* arm.] A piece of armor fastened to the elbow-plates, and covering the elbow and upper part of the arm; used in the fifteenth century.

Garde-brace.

gär′den, *n.* [OFr. *gardin, jardin;* O.H.G. *garto,* genit. *gartin,* a yard, garden.]

1. A piece of ground appropriated to the cultivation of herbs, plants, fruits, flowers, or vegetables. A plot devoted to the raising of culinary herbs and roots for domestic use is called a *kitchen-garden;* that to flowers and shrubs, a *flower-garden;* and that to fruits, a *fruit-garden.* But these uses are sometimes blended.

2. A rich, well-cultivated spot or tract of country; a delightful spot.

I am arrived for fruitful Lombardy,
The pleasant *garden* of great Italy. —Shak.

gär′den, *a.* Pertaining to or produced in a garden; as, *garden* implements; *garden* plants.

gär′den, *v.i.;* gardened, *pt., pp.;* gardening, *ppr.* To lay out or to cultivate a garden; to work in a garden.

gär′den, *v.t.* To cultivate as a garden.

gär′den=boo″tle, *n.* A caraboid beetle.

gär′den=dọr″mouse, *n.* The lerot, *Eliomys nitela.*

gär′den=en″gine, *n.* See *Garden-pump.*

gär′den-ẽr, *n.* [ME. *gardiner;* OFr. *jardinier;* O.H.G. *gartinari,* one who cares for a garden, from *garto,* genit. *gartin,* a garden.] One who tends or cultivates a garden; a horticulturist.

gär′den-ẽr=bīrd, *n.* The New Guinea bower-bird, *Amblyornis inornata.*

gär′den-ẽr′s=gär″tẽrs, *n.* *Phalaris arundinacea,* ribbon-grass.

gär-den-esque′ (-esk′), *a.* In horticulture, a term applied to the free symmetrical style of laying out a garden, in which the form of the beds may be varied from formal geometrical outlines.

gär′den=flēa, *n.* A flea-beetle.

gär′den=gāte, *n.* The pansy.

gär′den=glȧss, *n.* 1. A globe of dark-colored glass, generally about $1\frac{1}{2}$ feet in diameter, in which, when placed on a pedestal, the surrounding objects are reflected; much used as an ornament of gardens in Germany.

2. A bell-glass used for covering plants.

gär′den=house, *n.* 1. A summer-house in a garden.

2. In southern United States, a privy.

gär′den=hus″bănd-ry, *n.* The raising of garden produce for market.

Gär-dē′ni-ȧ, *n.* [Named after Dr. Alexander *Garden,* an American botanist.] A genus of trees and shrubs of the madder family, natives of tropical Asia and Africa and of the Cape of Good Hope. *Gardenia florida* and *Gardenia* *radicans* are well known in cultivation as Cape Jasmin.

gär-den'iç, *a.* Pertaining to the genus *Gardenia*; as, *gardenic* acid.

gär'den-ing, *n.* The act of laying out and cultivating gardens; horticulture.

gär'den-less, *a.* Destitute of a garden.

gär'den-mōld, *n.* Mold or rich mellow earth suitable for a garden.

gär'den-pär"ty, *n.* A party held on a lawn or in a garden adjoining a private residence.

gär'den-plot, *n.* A plot of ground appropriated to or suitable for a garden.

gär'den-pump, *n.* A portable pump used for watering gardens; a garden-engine.

gär'den-ship, *n.* Horticulture. [Obs.]

gär'den-snail, *n.* A European species of snail, *Helix aspersa.*

gär'den-spī"dẽr, *n.* The common name of the spider, *Epeira diadema*, from its being found in great numbers in gardens; called also *diadem-spider.*

gär'den-stand, *n.* A stand or frame on which flower-pots are placed.

gär'den-stuff, *n.* Plants growing in a garden; vegetables for the table.

gär'den-sweep, *n.* A curving carriage-drive through a garden.

gär'den-truck, *n.* See *Garden-stuff.*

gärde'-nuque' (-nŭk'), *n.* [Fr. from *garder*, to guard, and *nuque*, the back of the neck.] In armor, that part of a helmet which protects the back of the neck.

gär'den-wär"blẽr, *n.* See *Beccafico.*

gär'den-wāre, *n.* The produce of gardens. [Obs.]

gär'dŏn, *n.* [Fr. and Sp.] A fish of the roach kind, *Leuciscus idus.*

gär'dy-loo, *n.* [Scot., from Fr. *gare l'eau*, beware of the water.] A cry formerly used in Edinburgh, to warn passers-by to beware of slops thrown from a window.

gāre, *n.* Coarse wool growing on the legs of sheep. [Prov. Eng.]

gāre'fowl, *n.* [Ice. *geirfugl.*] The great auk, *Alca impennis*; also, the razorbill.

gär'fish, *n.* [ME. *garfysshe*; AS. *gar*, a spear, and *fisc*, fish.] A fish with a long, narrow, beak-like snout; specifically, (a) *Belone vulgaris*, the common *garfish* of Europe; (b) any one of several species of fishes of the genus *Tylosurus*, especially *Tylosurus marinus*, the common American *garfish*; (c) any garpike of the genus *Lepidosteus.*

Common Garfish (*Belone vulgaris*).

gär'gȧ-līze, *v.t.* To gargle. [Obs.]

gär'gȧ-net, *n.* [Obs.] See *Carcanet.*

gär'gȧ-ney, *n.* [A book-name; *gar*, uncertain meaning, and *ganey*, from AS. *ganet*, a fen, a duck.] A species of duck, the summer teal, *Anas querquedula*, inhabiting Europe and the southern part of Asia; called also *cricket-teal* and *pied widgeon.*

Gär-gan'tū-ăn, *a.* Pertaining to or resembling Gargantua, the hero in the satire of Rabelais, who was inconceivably enormous; hence, incredibly great; enormous; prodigious.

gär'gȧ-rism, *n.* [LL. *gargarisma*, from Gr. *gargarizein*, to gargle.] In medicine, a gargle.

gär'gȧ-rize, *v.t.* [OFr. *gargarizer*; L. *gargarizare*; Gr. *gargarizein*, to gargle.] To wash or rinse, as the mouth, with any medicated liquor; to gargle. [Obs.]

gär'get, *n.* [ME. *gargat*; OFr. *gargate*, the throat, dim. of OFr. *gorge*, the throat, from L. *gurges*, a whirlpool.]

1. The throat. [Obs.]

2. A distemper in cattle, consisting in a swelling of the throat and the neighboring parts.

3. A disease in the udders of cows arising from inflammation of the lymphatic glands.

4. A distemper in hogs, accompanied with staggering and loss of appetite.

5. The poke or pokeweed, *Phytolacca decandra*, which has emetic and cathartic properties, and has been employed in medicine.

gär'gil, *n.* A distemper in geese, which affects the head, and often proves fatal.

gär'gle, *v.t.*; gargled, *pt., pp.*; **gargling,** *ppr.* [OFr. *gargouiller*, to gargle, from *gargouille*, the throat, from O.H.G. *gurgula*; L. *gurgulio*, the throat, windpipe.]

1. To wash or rinse, as the throat or mouth, with a liquid preparation, which is kept from descending into the stomach by a gentle expiration of air.

2. To warble. [Rare.]

gär'gle, *n.* Any liquid preparation for washing or rinsing the mouth and throat.

gär'gle, gär'gol, *n.* See *Garget*, 4.

gär-gou-lette', *n.* See *Gurglet.*

gär'goyle, *n.* [ME. *gargyle*; OFr. *gargoille*, the throat, from L. *gurgulio* (*-onis*), the throat.] In medieval architecture, a quaintly-formed head of a man or animal, employed as a decorative spout for the rainwater from a roof.

gar-i-bal'di, *n.* 1. A kind of jacket worn by ladies, supposed to resemble the colored shirt which formed a prominent part of the dress of the Italian patriot, Garibaldi, and his soldiers.

Gargoyle.

2. *Hypsypops rubicundus*, a pomacentrid fish of California, of a red or orange color.

Gar-i-bal'di-ăn, *a.* Pertaining to Giuseppe Garibaldi (1807-82), who strove to bring about the unity and independence of Italy.

Gar-i-bal'di-ăn, *n.* A follower of Garibaldi or an advocate of his policy.

gãr'ish, gāir'ish, *a.* [ME. *gauren*; OFr. *garer*, to observe, keep watch, from O.H.G. *waron*, to take heed, guard, from *warjan*, to guard.]

1. Gaudy; showy; dazzling; staring; attracting or seeking attraction; flashy; ostentatious.

> The *garish* blaze of day. —Byron.

2. Extravagantly gay; flighty.

gãr'ish-ly, gāir'ish-ly, *adv.* In a garish, showy, or dazzling manner; gaudily.

gãr'ish-ness, gāir'ish-ness, *n.* The state or quality of being garish.

gär'lănd, *n.* [OFr. *garlande*, a garland; compare O.H.G. *wiara*, an ornament of refined gold, a crown.]

1. A wreath or chaplet made of branches, flowers, feathers, and sometimes of precious stones, to be worn on the head like a crown.

2. The top; the principal thing, or thing most prized.

3. A royal crown; a diadem. [Obs.]

4. A collection of short printed pieces, especially of poems or ballads; an anthology.

5. In seamen's language, a name given to a band, collar, or grommet of ropes, used for various purposes; as, (a) a large rope, strap, or grommet lashed to a spar when hoisting it on board; (b) a collar of ropes wound round the head of a mast to keep the shrouds from chafing; (c) a large rope-grommet for retaining shot in its proper place on deck. The name is also given to a band of iron or stone, used in land batteries for a like purpose; (d) a wreath made of hoops ornamented with ribbons, hoisted to a stay or mast on the wedding-day of one of a ship's company.

6. A sort of bag of network, having the mouth extended by a hoop, used by sailors instead of a locker or cupboard to hold provisions.

7. In mining, a curb set in the wall of a shaft, to carry away any water running down its sides.

8. In architecture, a band of ornamental work round the top of a tower.

gär'lănd, *v.t.*; garlanded, *pt., pp.*; garlanding, *ppr.* To deck with a garland.

gär'lănd-flow"ẽr, *n.* 1. Any one of several Asiatic species of the genus *Hedychium*, of the ginger family, bearing flowers of great fragrance and beauty.

2. Any one of several plants, as *Daphne Cneorum.*

gär'lănd-less, *a.* Having no garlands.

gär'lănd-ry, *n.* Anything made into garlands.

gär'liç, *n.* [ME. *garlek, garlec*; AS. *garleác*, garlic, so named from its spearlike leaves; *gar*, a spear, and *leác*, a leek.]

1. A hardy onion-like plant, *Allium sativum*, having a bulbous root, a very strong smell, and an acrid, pungent taste. Each root is composed of several lesser bulbs, called *cloves of garlic*, inclosed in a common membranous coat, and easily separable. It is indigenous to southern Europe, where, as a condiment, it has been used from the earliest period.

2. A jig or farce popular at the beginning of the seventeenth century.

gär'lick-y, *a.* Like or containing garlic.

gär'liç-mus"tărd, *n.* A cruciferous plant, *Sisymbrium Alliaria*, having a garlicky odor.

gär'liç-peãr, *n.* Either of two trees growing in tropical America, *Cratæva gynandra* or *Cratæva Tapia.*

gär'liç-shrub, *n.* 1. A climbing shrub of the West Indies and Guiana, *Adenocalymna alliacea*, having a garlicky odor.

2. Any plant of the genus *Petiveria*, belonging to the pokeweed family, especially *Petiveria alliacea.*

gär'liç-wŏrt, *n.* *Alliaria officinalis*, the hedge-garlic.

gär'ment, *n.* [ME. *garment*; OFr. *garnement*, from *garnir*, to garnish, adorn.] Any article of clothing, as a coat, gown, etc.

> It was only a seamless *garment* which the spirit wore. —Dr. Caird.

gär'ment-less, *a.* Destitute of a garment.

gär'men-tūre, *n.* Dress; clothes; garments. [Rare.]

gär'nẽr, *n.* [ME. *garner*; OFr. *grenier*; L. *granaria*, neut. pl., a granary, from *granum*, grain.] A granary; a building or place where grain is stored for preservation; hence, a store of anything, as of wisdom, thought, etc.

gär'nẽr, *v.t.*; garnered, *pt., pp.*; garnering, *ppr.* To store in or as in a granary; to treasure; often followed by *up.*

gär'nẽr, *v.i.* To accumulate; to become stored up. [Rare.]

gär'net, *n.* [ME. *garnet*; OFr. *grenat*; LL. *granatus*, a garnet, so called from its resemblance to the seeds of a pomegranate, from *granatus*, having seeds, from L. *granum*, a grain, seed.] In mineralogy, an isometric transparent or translucent brittle mineral, with dodecahedral cleavage, sometimes with twin crystals, having an octahedral composition face. It occurs also massive and lamellar, and has a vitreous to resinous luster. Its color is red, brown, yellow, white, or black, with a white streak. There are three leading varieties; (a) alumina garnet, in which the sesquioxid is mainly alumina; (b) iron garnet, in which it is chiefly sesquioxid of iron; (c) chrome garnet, in which it is principally sesquioxid of chrome. Under these are ranked grossularite, pyrope, almandite, spessartite, andradite, bredbergite, and ouvarovite. These, with typical garnet, constitute Dana's garnet group of minerals.

gär'net, *n.* [Origin obscure.] In nautical parlance, (a) a sort of tackle fixed to the mainstay, and used to hoist in and out the cargo; (b) a clue-garnet; (c) a tackle run through a hole in the spar-deck of a war-ship, to assist in handling the guns on the gun-deck.

gär'net-ber"ry, *n.* *Ribes rubrum*, the common red currant.

gär'net-blende, *n.* Zinc-blende; a sulphid of zinc.

gär'net-hinge, *n.* A species of hinge resembling the letter T laid horizontally; thus, ⊢.

gär-net-if'ẽr-ous, *a.* [LL. *granatus*, the garnet, and L. *ferre*, to bear, bring.] In geology, containing garnets, as a rock-matrix.

gär'ni-ẽr-ite, *n.* [From *Garnier*, a French geologist.] In mineralogy, an amorphous hydrous silicate of nickel and magnesium, of an apple-green color. It is an important ore of nickel.

gär'nish, *v.t.*; garnished (-nisht), *pt., pp.*; garnishing, *ppr.* [ME. *garnischen*; OFr. *garnisant*, ppr. of *garnir*, to defend, warn; compare AS. *wearnian*, to take care, warn; of Germanic origin.]

1. To adorn; to decorate with appendages; to set off.

> All within with flowers was *garnished.* —Spenser.

2. To fit with fetters; a cant term.

3. To furnish; to supply.

4. In law, to warn; to give notice. [See *Garnishee.*]

5. In cookery, to ornament, as a dish, with something laid round it.

> No man lards salt pork with orange-peel,
> Or *garnishes* his lamb with spitchcock'd eel. —King.

gär'nish, *n.* 1. Ornament; something added for embellishment; decoration; dress; array.

> Matter and figure they produce;
> For *garnish* this, and that for use. —Prior.

2. In cookery, something placed round a dish as an embellishment.

3. Fetters. [Cant.]

4. A fee, as to a servant; specifically, money formerly paid by a prisoner on his going to prison, as a fee to fellow-prisoners.

gär'nish-bōlt, *n.* A bolt having a chamfered or faceted head.

gär'nished (-nisht), *a.* In heraldry, (a) provided with an ornament; ornamented, as a bearing; (b) armed; said of a human limb.

gär-nish-ee', *n.* In law, a person who has received notice not to pay any money owed to, or deliver any property belonging to, a third party, who is indebted to the party giving the notice.

gär-nish-ee', *v.t.*; garnisheed, *pt., pp.*; garnisheeing, *ppr.* In law, (a) to serve garnishment upon (a person who owes money to, or holds property belonging to, the garnisher's debtor); (b) to restrain (money due to, or property belonging to, the garnisher's debtor) from being paid or delivered.

gär'nish-ẽr, *n.* 1. One who garnishes or decorates.

2. In law, one who serves garnishment upon another.

gär'nish-ment, *n.* 1. Ornament or embellishment.

2. In law, (a) warning not to pay money or deliver property to a defendant, but to appear and answer the plaintiff's suit; (b) legal notice to the agent or attorney of an absconding debtor for him to appear in court or give information.

3. A fee. [See *Garnish*, n. 4.]

gär'ni-sŏn, *n.* A garrison. [Obs.]

gär′ni-tūre, *n.* [Fr. *garniture*, furniture, supply, from *garnir*, to furnish.] Ornamental appendages; embellishment; furniture; dress.

ga-rọọ′kuh (-ku), *n.* [East Indian.] A vessel used on the Persian gulf for fishing purposes. It varies from 50 to 100 feet in length, has a short keel and a long, overhanging prow and stern.

ga-rọọn′=shell, *n.* See *Goroon-shell.*

gā′rous, *a.* [L. *garum*, pickle.] Pertaining to or resembling garum; resembling pickle made of fish.

gär′pike, *n.* 1. The common garfish, *Belone vulgaris.*

2. Any fish of the genus *Lepidosteus* or family *Lepidosteidæ*; a gar.

gär′pipe, *n.* A garpike.

gar′ran, *n.* [Ir. and Gael. *garran*, *gearran*, a work-horse.] A small horse; a Highland horse; a hack; a jade; a galloway; written also *garron.* [Scot.]

gar′ret, *n.* [ME. *garett*; OFr. *garite*, a watch-tower, a lookout, from *garir*, to watch, preserve, from Goth. *warjan*; O.H.G. *werian*, to defend, protect.]

1. That part of a house which is on the upper floor, immediately under the roof.

2. A turret or battlement; a watchtower. [Obs.]

gar′ret, *v.t.* See *Gallet.*

gar′ret-ed, *a.* Protected by or provided with garrets or turrets. [Obs.]

gar-ret-eer′, *n.* An inhabitant of a garret; hence, a poor author.

gar′ret-ing, gar′ret-ting, *n.* See *Galleting.*

gar′ret=mas″tēr, *n.* In England, a maker of household furniture on his own account who sells his goods to the furniture-dealers.

gar′ri-sŏn, *n.* [ME. *garnison*; OFr. *garnison*, provision, supplies for defense, from *garnir*, to provide, supply.]

1. A body of troops stationed in a fort or fortified town, to defend it against an enemy, or to keep the inhabitants in subjection.

2. A fort, castle, or fortified town, furnished with troops to defend it.

gar′ri-sŏn, *v.t.*; garrisoned, *pt.*, *pp.*; garrisoning, *ppr.*

1. To place troops in, as in a fortress for defense; to furnish with soldiers; as, to *garrison* a fort or town.

2. To secure or defend by fortresses manned with troops; as, to *garrison* a conquered territory.

Gar-ri-sō′ni-ăn, *n.* In United States history, a believer in and follower of William Lloyd Garrison (1804–79), a distinguished and persistent abolitionist.

Gar-ri-sō′ni-ăn, *a.* Pertaining to William Lloyd Garrison.

gar′rŏn, *n.* See *Garran.*

gar′rŏt, *n.* [Fr., from *garrotter*, to tie fast.]

1. In surgery, an instrument for compression of an artery by twisting a circular bandage about the part; a tourniquet.

2. An arrow for a crossbow having a square head; a quarrel.

gar′rŏt, *n.* A black and white sea-duck of the genus *Clangula*, having a large white spot near each eye. It is found over a large expanse of the northern hemisphere; called also *goldeneye.*

gar-rōte′, ga-rōte′, *n.* [Sp. *garrote*, a cudgel, a strangling by means of an iron collar, from *garra*, a claw, talon, from Breton *gar*, the shank of the leg.]

1. A mode of punishment in Spain, by strangulation, the victim being placed on a stool with a post behind, to which is affixed an iron collar with a screw; this collar is made to clasp the neck of the criminal, and is drawn tighter by means of the screw, until life becomes extinct.

2. The instrument by means of which this punishment is inflicted; hence, strangulation by any means.

gar-rōte′, ga-rōte′, *v.t.*; garroted, *pt.*, *pp.*; garroting, *ppr.* To strangle by means of the garrote; hence, to seize by the throat for the purpose of strangling and robbing.

gar-rōte′, ga-rōte′, *v.i.* To cheat in card-playing by concealing certain cards at the back of the neck; a mode of cheating practised among card-sharpers.

gar-rŏt′ēr, ga-rŏt′ēr, *n.* One who commits the act of garroting.

Gar-rū-lī′næ, *n.pl.* [L. *garrulus*, chattering, and *-inæ.*] A subfamily of birds of the family *Corvidæ*, including the jays.

gar′rū-line, *a.* Pertaining to the *Garrulinæ.*

gar-rū′li-ty, *n.* [L. *garrulitas*, from *garrulus*, garrulous, from *garrire*, to chatter, talk.] The quality of being garrulous; talkativeness; loquacity.

gar′rū-lous, *a.* [L. *garrulus*, chattering, prattling, from *garrire*, to chatter, prattle.] Inclined or given to much talking, especially of a trivial character; loquacious; talkative; prating.

Syn.—Talkative, loquacious.—A *garrulous* person indulges in long, prosy talk, with frequent repetitions and lengthened details; *talkative* implies simply a great desire to talk, and *loquacious* a great flow of words at command.

gar′rū-lous-ly, *adv.* In a garrulous or talkative manner; chatteringly.

gar′rū-lous-ness, *n.* Talkativeness.

Gar′rū-lus, *n.* A genus typical of *Garrulinæ.*

gar-rū′pȧ, *n.* [Sp. Am. name; prob. from Portuguese *garupa*, a crupper.] Any one of several species of fishes, especially of the genus *Sebastichthys*, found on the coast of California; a rockfish.

Gar′ry-ȧ, *n.* [Named after Mr. *Garry*, of the Hudson Bay Company, who facilitated Douglas's botanical researches in northwestern America.] A genus of opposite-leaved evergreen shrubs of the dogwood family, natives of southwestern United States and of the West Indies. *Garrya elliptica* is cultivated in England for ornament.

gär′tēr, *n.* [ME. *garter*; OFr. *gartier*, a garter, from *garret*, the small of the leg behind the knee, from Breton, *gar*, *garr*, the shank of the leg.]

1. A string or band by which a stocking is held in place upon the leg.

2. In heraldry, a bendlet.

3. [*pl.*] In a circus, the tapes that are held up for a performer to leap over.

4. The badge of the most illustrious order of British Knighthood, called the *Order of the Garter*; hence, membership in the order; also, [G—] the order itself; always used with *the*; as, a knight of *the Garter.*

Garter king-at-arms; the principal king-at-arms in England, by whom arms are granted and confirmed under the authority of the earl marshal; often abbreviated to *Garter.*

Insignia of the Garter. 1. The Star. 2. The lesser George. 3. The Collar. 4. The George. 5. The Garter.

Order of the Garter; the highest order of British Knighthood, instituted at Windsor by Edward III., in 1348. The order consists of the sovereign and twenty-five companions, of whom the Prince of Wales is always one. Recent statutes have provided for the admission of foreign sovereigns and princes. Until the reign of Edward VI., the title of the order was the "Order of St. George."

gär′tēr, *v.t.*; gartered, *pt.*, *pp.*; gartering, *ppr.*

1. To bind with a garter.

2. To invest with the garter as the badge of the Order of the Garter.

gär′tēr=fish, *n.* A fish of the genus *Lepidopus*; the scabbard-fish.

gär′tēr=snāke, *n.* A harmless American snake of the genus *Eutænia*, of which *Eutænia sirtalis* and *Eutænia saurita* are the best known species. They are marked by long yellow stripes.

gärth, *n.* [ME. *garth*; Ice. *gardhr*, a yard, court, garden.]

1. A dam or weir for catching fish.

2. A close; a yard; a croft; a garden. [Rare.]

gärth, *n.* A hoop or band. [Prov. Eng.]

gärth′man, *n.*; *pl.* **gärth′men.** The proprietor of an open weir for taking fish.

ga-rū′bȧ, *n.* [Sp. Am.] A Brazilian parrakeet, *Conurus luteus*, of a yellow color.

gā′rum, *n.* [L. *garum*, *garon*; Gr. *garon.*] A fish-sauce much prized by the ancients, made of small fish preserved in a certain kind of pickle; also, a pickle made of the gills or blood of the tunny.

gär′vie, *n.* [Scot., from Gael. *garbhag*, a sprat, from *garbh*, thick, coarse.] A sprat; called also *garvie-herring.*

gär′vock, *n.* A garvie.

gas, *v.t.*; gassed (gast), *pt.*, *pp.*; gassing, *ppr.*

1. To free (lace, net, etc.) from loose filaments, by passing the material between two rollers, and exposing it to the action of a large number of minute jets of gas.

2. To impose upon by boastful, empty talk. [Slang.]

gas, *v.i.* To talk nonsense. [Slang.]

gas, *n.* [A word invented by the Belgian chemist, Van Helmont (1577-1644).]

1. One of the three recognized conditions of matter; an aeriform substance possessing the condition of perfect fluid elasticity, and presenting under a constant pressure a uniform rate of expansion for equal increments of temperature, but on reaching its maximum density behaving like a vapor. All gases can be condensed into liquids by cold and pressure. Some of the elements, as oxygen, hydrogen, nitrogen, chlorin, and probably fluorin, are gases at ordinary temperature. Gases are formed by the dry distillation of animal and vegetable substances, which yield carbon dioxid, carbon monoxid, ammonia, nitrogen, hydrogen, sulphur dioxid, hydrogen sulphid, and hydrocarbons. Ordinarily, gas is invisible.

2. In popular language, a mixture of gases used for lighting and heating. It is a form of carbureted hydrogen.

3. In coal-mining, a mixture of fire-damp with air.

4. A gaslight; as, to light the *gas.* [Colloq.]

5. Laughing-gas. [Colloq.]

6. Idle talk; empty boasting. [Colloq.]

Air gas; air forced through a mixture of hydrocarbons.

Mustard gas; fumes from a composition first used by the Germans in the World War as a filling for shells. Its effects are blinding, irritating and fatal if inhaled.

Natural gas; gas which issues from wells bored deep into the ground in western Pennsylvania, Ohio, Indiana, etc., used extensively for heating and lighting.

Olefiant gas; ethylene.

gas-ȧ-liēr′, *n.* See *Gaselier.*

gas′=bag, *n.* 1. A bag for holding gas.

2. A bag used for closing a gas-main when repairs are being made.

3. A loquacious individual. [Colloq.]

gas′=bat″tēr-y, *n.* In electricity, a form of voltaic battery in which hydrogen and oxygen or other gases are the elements consumed.

gas′=bleach″ing, *n.* The process of bleaching by the use of sulphur dioxid.

gas′=bŭrn″ēr, *n.* That part of a gas lamp or bracket from which the gas is burned, and which serves to regulate the emission of gas.

gas′=check, *n.* A device behind the charge-chamber of a breech-loading gun, designed to prevent the escape of gas at the breech.

gas′=cōal, *n.* Any coal from which illuminating gas is made.

gas′=cŏm″pȧ-ny, *n.* A company formed to supply gas to a community, generally at a certain rate per 1,000 feet.

gas′=cŏm-press″ŏr, *n.* A kind of pump for compressing coal-gas into portable reservoirs.

Gas′cŏn, *n.* [Fr.] 1. A native of Gascony, in France.

2. [g—] A boaster; a vainglorious individual.

Gas′cŏn, *a.* Pertaining to Gascony.

gas-cŏn-āde′, *n.* [Fr., from *Gascon*, an inhabitant of Gascony, the people of which were noted for boasting.] A boast or boasting; a vaunt; a bravado; a bragging.

gas-cŏn-āde′, *v.i.*; gasconaded, *pt.*, *pp.*; gasconading, *ppr.* To boast; to brag; to vaunt.

gas-cŏn-ad′ēr, *n.* A great boaster.

gas′=cŏn-dens″ēr, *n.* A part of the apparatus used in the manufacture of illuminating gas, consisting of a series of convoluted pipes surrounded by water, in passing through which the gas is freed from the tar it brings with it from the retort.

gas′coynes, *n.pl.* Same as *Galligaskins.*

gas-ē′i-ty, *n.* The state of being gaseous.

gas-e-liēr′, *n.* A chandelier from which gas is burned.

gas′=en″gine, *n.* Any motor which is actuated by the explosive force generated by the compression and subsequent ignition of gaseous compounds. Commonly, coal-gas and air are employed, but various hydrocarbons have also been made use of.

gas′ē-ous, *a.* 1. In the form of gas or an aeriform fluid; of the nature of gas.

2. Figuratively, wanting substance or solidity; flimsy.

> Unconnected, *gaseous* information.
> —Stephen.

gas′ē-ous-ness, *n.* The state or quality of being gaseous.

gas′=field, *n.* A district from which natural gas is obtained.

gas′=fit″tēr, *n.* A workman who lays the pipes and puts up fixtures for gas.

gas′=fix″tūre, *n.* A more or less ornamental device attached to the wall or ceiling, and supplied with one or more burners connecting with a delivery gas-pipe; a gaselier.

gas′=gāuge, *n.* An instrument for ascertaining the pressure of gas, generally consisting of a bent graduated tube containing water or mercury, open at one end, and with the other screwed into the vessel containing the gas.

gas′=gen″ēr-ā-tŏr, *n.* An apparatus used to generate gas.

gas′=glōbe, *n.* A hollow globe used as a shade for a gaslight.

gas′=gŏv″ērn-ŏr, *n.* Any device for the regulation of the flow of gas.

gas′=gun, *n.* A pipe in which gas is exploded in signaling.

gash, *v.t.*; gashed (gasht), *pt.*, *pp.*; gashing, *ppr.* To make a gash, or long, deep incision in; applied chiefly to incisions in flesh.

gash, *n.* [ME. *garse*, a gash, incision; from *garsen*; OFr. *garser*, to gash, scarify, from Gr. *charassein*, to furrow, scratch.] A deep and long cut; an incision considerably long and deep, particularly in flesh.

gash, *a.* [Perhaps an abbrev. from L. *sagax*, sagacious, wise.]

1. Sharp; shrewd; sagacious; having the appearance of sagacity joined with that of self-importance. [Scot.]

2. Trim; well-dressed. [Scot.]

gash, *v.i.* To gossip; to converse; to chatter. [Scot.]

gash, *a.* Ghastly. [Scot.]

gash′ful, *a.* Full of gashes; hideous. [Obs.]

gas′-hōld″ẽr, *n.* A vessel for storing gas after purification; a gasometer.

gash′-vein, *n.* In mining, a vein that does not extend beyond the stratum in which it occurs.

gas″i-fi-cā′tion, *n.* The act or process of converting into gas.

gas′i-form, *a.* [*Gas*, and L. *forma*, form.] Gaseous; aeriform.

gas′i-fy̆, *v.t.*; gasified, *pt.*, *pp.*; gasifying, *ppr.* [*Gas*, and L. *facere*, to make.] To convert into gas or an aeriform fluid, as by the application of heat, or other chemical process.

gas′-in″di-cā-tŏr, *n.* An instrument for indicating the pressure of gas in a pipe, or for showing the presence of fire-damp in a mine.

gas′-jet, *n.* 1. A spout of flame issuing from a gas-burner.

2. A gas-burner.

gas′ket, *n.* [Fr. *garcette*, a gasket, a cat-o'-nine-tails, from Sp. *garceta*, a gasket.]

1. In seamen's language, a cord by which sails when furled are bound close to the yards, booms, masts, or gaffs; called also *casket*.

2. In machinery, a strip of leather, tow, plaited hemp, or similar material, used for packing a piston, as of the steam-engine and its pumps.

gas′king, *n.* Packing of hemp or similar material.

gas′kins, *n.pl.* 1. Gasking.

2. Galligaskins. [Obs.]

gas′light (-līt), *n.* Light produced by the combustion of coal-gas; also, a gas-jet.

gas′-lime, *n.* Lime used as a filter or purifier for illuminating gas.

gas′-liq″uor (-lik″ŭr), *n.* An ammoniacal liquor extracted from coal in the distillation of gas.

gas′-mȧ-chīne″, *n.* An apparatus which carburizes air in the manufacture of illuminating gas.

gas′-māin, *n.* One of the principal pipes which convey the gas from the gas-works to the places where it is to be consumed.

gas′-mask, *n.* A mask worn in the trenches in the World War as a protection against poisonous fumes.

gas′-me″tẽr, *n.* An apparatus through which gas is made to pass, in order to ascertain the number of cubic feet consumed in a given time at a given place.

gas′-mō″tŏr, *n.* A gas-engine.

gas-o-. A combining form from *gas*.

gas′ō-ġēne, *n.* Same as *Gazogene*.

gas′ō-lēne, gas′ō-line, *n.* [*Gas*, and L. *oleum*, oil, and *-ine*.] A volatile hydrocarbonaceous liquid commonly obtained from the distillation of petroleum. It is used in vapor-stoves and for carbonizing air or gas in gas-machines.

gas-ō-liẽr′, *n.* See *Gaselier*.

gas-om′e-tẽr, *n.* [*Gaso-*, and Gr. *metron*, measure.]

1. In chemistry, (a) an instrument or apparatus intended to measure, collect, preserve, or mix different gases; (b) an instrument for measuring the quantity of gas employed in any chemical experiment.

2. A reservoir or storehouse for gas, especially for the ordinary illuminating gas produced in gas-works, which supplies the various pipes employed in lighting streets and houses. It is usually a cylinder closed at one end and having the other end immersed in water, in which it rises or falls according to the amount of gas entering or leaving it.

gas-ō-met′riç, *a.* Of or pertaining to gasometry or the measurement of gases.

Gasometric analysis; in chemistry, the process of separating and estimating the relative proportions of the constituents of a gaseous body. This is effected by the action of absorbents, as on gas contained in a eudiometer, or by exploding the gas with oxygen and observing the volumes before and after explosion.

gas-ō-met′riç-ăl, *a.* Gasometric.

gas-om′e-try, *n.* The science, art, or practice of measuring gases; that department of chemical science which treats of the nature and properties of gases.

gas′ō-sçōpe, *n.* [*Gaso-*, and Gr. *skopein*, to view.] An instrument for indicating the presence of gas in buildings, mines, or other places.

gȧsp, *v.i.*; gasped (gȧspt), *pt.*, *pp.*; gasping, *ppr.* [ME. *gaspen*, *gayspen*, from Ice. *geispa*, to yawn.]

1. To open the mouth wide in catching the breath or in laborious respiration; to respire convulsively; to pant violently.

2. To pant with eagerness; to pant vehemently.

gȧsp, *v.t.* To emit or utter with gaspings or pantings; with *away*, *forth*, *out*, etc.

And with short sobs he *gasps away* his breath. —Dryden.

gȧsp, *n.* The act of opening the mouth to catch the breath; labored respiration.

The last gasp; the last breath of a dying person; hence, the last extremity.

gas′pẽr-eau (-ō), *n.* The French Canadian name of the alewife, a fish of the herring family.

gas′pẽr-gŏu, *n.* [Local U. S., compare Fr. *gasparot*, a sort of herring.] The name of a fresh-water fish known also as the *drum*.

gȧsp′ing, *n.* Convulsive labor in breathing.

gȧsp′ing-ly, *adv.* With a gasp or with gasps.

gas′-pipe, *n.* A pipe for the conveyance of gas.

gas′-plant, *n.* A plant, *Dictamnus Fraxinella*, which emits an inflammable vapor.

gas′-rānġe, *n.* A range or cooking-stove adapted to the use of gas as a fuel.

gas′-reg′ū-lā-tŏr, *n.* A gas-governor.

gas′-rē-tort″, *n.* A chamber in which carbonaceous matter is distilled to produce illuminating-gas.

gas′-sand, *n.* Sandstone which yields natural gas.

Gas-sē′ri-ăn, *a.* Of or relating to the German physician Gasserius, the discoverer of the ganglion which bears his name.

Gasserian ganglion; a ganglion at the root of the fifth cranial nerve; often called by mistake *Casserian ganglion*.

gas′sing, *n.* 1. The process of singeing off loose fibers from cotton, lace, etc., by the flame from minute gas-jets.

2. Boasting; empty or pretentious talking. [Slang.]

gas-sŏul′, *n.* The native name for a mineral soap exported in considerable quantities from Morocco.

gas′-stōve, *n.* A stove which burns gas as fuel.

gas′sy, *a.* 1. Gaseous; full of gas; characteristic of gas; as, a *gassy* flame.

2. Inflated; vaporing; given to boastful talk. [Slang.]

gȧst, *v.t.* To frighten; to terrify. [Obs.]

gȧst, *n.* A ghost. [Obs.]

gas′-tank, *n.* A gasometer; a gas-holder.

gas′-tär, *n.* Coal-tar.

gas-tẽr-ō-, gas-tr-, gas-trō-. Combining forms from Gr. *gastēr*, stomach, signifying the stomach, belly, or womb.

Gas″tẽr-ō-lī-chē′nēs, *n.pl.* [L., from Gr. *gastēr*, stomach, and *leichēn*, lichen.] A group of lichens which produce spores in the same way as the *Gasteromycetes*. It consists of two genera and three species.

Gas″tẽr-ō-my̆-cē′tēs, *n.pl.* [L., from Gr. *gastēr*, stomach, and *mykēs* (*-etos*), mushroom.] An order of fungi represented by the common puffball.

gas″tẽr-ō-my̆-cē′tous, *a.* Pertaining to the *Gasteromycetes*.

gas′tẽr-ō-pod, gas′trō-pod, *n.* One of the *Gasteropoda*.

Gas-tẽr-op′ō-dȧ, Gas-trop′ō-dȧ, *n.pl.* [L., from Gr. *gastēr*, stomach, and *pous* (*podos*), foot.] A class of mollusks variously limited but usually distinguished by having a distinct head and a muscular, disklike foot on the ventral part of the body, for the purpose of locomotion; hence the name. It includes the snails and slugs.

gas-tẽr-op′ō-dous, gas-trop′ō-dous, *a.* Having the characteristics of a gasteropod.

gas″tẽr-ō-thē′çȧ, gas-trō-thē′çȧ, *n.* [L., from Gr. *gastēr*, stomach, and *thēkē*, a case.] In entomology, the abdominal case of a pupa.

Gas-tẽr-ot′ri-chȧ, *n.pl.* Same as *Gastrotricha*.

gas″tẽr-ō-zō′oid, gas-trō-zō′oid, *n.* [*Gastero*, or *gastro-*, and Gr. *zōon*, an animal, and *eidos*, form.] A zoöid supplied with feeding and digestive apparatus.

gȧst′ful, *a.* [Obs.] Same as *Ghastful*.

gas′tight (-tīt), *a.* Capable of containing or of excluding gas; as, a *gastight* flask; a *gastight* stopper.

gȧst′ly, *a.* [Obs.] See *Ghastly*.

gȧst′ness, *n.* [Obs.] See *Ghastness*.

Gas-tor′nis, *n.* [From the name of *Gaston* Planté, the discoverer, and Gr. *ornis*, a bird.] A genus of fossil ostrich-like birds found in the Paris basin.

gas-tr-. A combining form; see *gastero-*.

gas-træ′ȧ, *n.* [L., from Gr. *gastēr*, the stomach.] A hypothetical animal form supposed by Haeckel to have been the ancestor from which all metazoans have descended. It is regarded as similar to the gastrula stage of the metazoan embryo.

gas-træ′um, *n.* [L., from Gr. *gastēr*, the stomach.] In ornithology, the entire ventral side of a bird, as distinguished from the upper side or *notæum*.

gas′trăl, *a.* Belonging to the stomach; intestinal.

gas-tral′ġi-ȧ, *n.* [L., from Gr. *gastēr*, the stomach, and *algos*, pain.] Gastric neuralgia; pain in the stomach or abdomen; belly-ache.

gas′-trap, *n.* A contrivance to prevent the escape of gas from a sewer.

gas-trec′tō-my, *n.* [Gr. *gastēr*, the stomach, and *ektomē*, a cutting out, from *ektemnein*, to cut out; *ek*, out, and *temnein*, to cut.] In surgery, the cutting away of a part of the stomach.

gas-trel-çō′sis, *n.* [L., from Gr. *gastēr*, stomach, and *helkōsis*, ulceration, from *helkoun*, to ulcerate, from *helkos*, an ulcer.] Gastric ulceration.

gas′triç, *a.* [L. *gaster*; Gr. *gastēr*, stomach.] Pertaining to the stomach; abdominal.

Gastric digestion; that part of the digestive process carried on in the stomach.

Gastric fever; any fever accompanied by acute disorder of the stomach; severe dyspepsia with fever; enteric fever.

Gastric juice; the digestive liquid secreted by the glands of the stomach. It contains pepsin etc., and is acid from the presence of hydrochloric acid.

gas-tril′ō-quist (-kwist), *n.* A ventriloquist. [Rare.]

gas-tril′ō-quous (-kwus), *a.* Ventriloquous. [Rare.]

gas-tril′ō-quy (-kwi), *n.* Ventriloquism. [Rare.]

gas-trī′tis, *n.* Gastric inflammation.

gas-trō-. A combining form from Gr. *gastēr*, stomach.

gas′trō-çēle, *n.* [*Gastro-*, and Gr. *kēle*, a tumor.] Gastric hernia.

gas-troç-nē′mi-us, *n.* [L., from Gr. *gastēr*, stomach, and *knēmē*, leg.] The great muscle in the back part of the leg below the knee; the protuberant part of the calf of the leg.

gas-trō-çol′iç, *a.* [*Gastro-*, and Gr. *kōlon*, the colon.] Belonging to both stomach and colon.

gas′trō-disç, *n.* [*Gastro-*, and Gr. *diskos*, a disk.] In embryology, an intestinal germ-disk of a mammal.

gas″trō-dū-ō-dē′năl, *a.* [*Gastro-*, and L. *duodenum*, the duodenum, from *duodeni*, twelve each.] Belonging to both stomach and duodenum; as, the *gastroduodenal* artery.

gas″trō-dū″ō-dē-nī′tis, *n.* Inflammation of both the duodenum and stomach.

gas-trō-dyn′i-ȧ, *n.* [L., from Gr. *gastēr*, stomach, and *odynē*, pain.] Literally, stomach-pain; gastralgia.

gas″trō-el″y-trot′ō-my, *n.* [*Gastro-*, and Gr. *elytron*, sheath, and *tomē*, a cutting.] A surgical operation for removing a fetus by cutting through the abdomen and the anterior part of the vagina, without injuring the peritoneum; used in place of the more dangerous Cæsarean operation.

gas″trō-en-ter′iç, *a.* [*Gastro-*, and Gr. *entera*, intestines.] Pertaining to both stomach and intestines.

gas″trō-en″te-rī′tis, *n.* [*Gastro-*, and Gr. *entera*, intestines.] Inflammation of the mucous membrane of the stomach and bowels.

gas″trō-ep″i-plō′iç, *a.* [*Gastro-*, and Gr. *epiploōn*, the caul.] Belonging to the stomach and epiploön or great omentum.

gas″trō-hē-pat′iç, *a.* [*Gastro-*, and Gr. *hēpar* (*hepatos*), the liver.] Pertaining to both stomach and liver.

gas″trō-hys″tẽr-ot′ō-my, *n.* [*Gastro-*, and Gr. *hystera*, the womb, and *tomē*, a cutting.] In obstetrics, the Cæsarean operation.

gas′troid, *a.* Resembling the stomach; applied to organs of animals and plants.

gas″trō-in-tes′ti-năl, *a.* Gastroenteric.

gas′trō-lith, *n.* [*Gastro-*, and Gr. *lithos*, a stone.] A gastric calculus; a bezoar; specifically, a discoidal concretion occurring in the stomach of certain crustaceans; called also *crab's eye*.

Gas-trō-lō′bi-um, *n.* [*Gastro-*, and Gr. *lobos*, a pod.] A genus of leguminous Australian shrubs with bright yellow flowers and inflated pods; called *poison-plants* by the settlers because often fatal to cattle eating them.

gas-trol′ō-ġy, *n.* [*Gastro-*, and Gr. *logos*, discourse.] A treatise upon or the science of the stomach; also, gastronomy.

gas″trō-ma-lā′ci-ȧ, *n.* [L., from Gr. *gastēr*, stomach, and *malakia*, softness, from *malakos*, soft.] Softening of the walls of the stomach, occurring usually after death.

gas′trō-man-cy, *n.* [Fr. *gastromantie*, from Gr. *gastēr*, stomach, and *manteia*, divination.] Divination by ventriloquial sounds; also, divination by transparent bellied vessels within which images were reputed to appear by magic.

gas-trō-my̆′çēs, *n.* [L., from Gr. *gastēr*, stomach, and *mykēs*, a fungus.] Bacterial growths in the stomach.

gas′trō-myth, *n.* A ventriloquist. [Obs.]

gas-tron′ō-mẽr, gas′trō-nōme, *n.* [Fr. *gastronome*, from Gr. *gaster*, stomach, and *nomos*, rule, law.] One who loves good living; an epicure; a judge of the art of cookery.

gas-trō-nom′iç, gas-trō-nom′iç-ăl, *a.* Pertaining to gastronomy.

gas-tron′ō-mist, *n.* A gastronomer.

gas-tron′ō-my, *n.* [Fr. *gastronomie,* from Gr. *gastēr,* stomach, and *nemein,* to regulate, from *nomos,* rule, law.] The art or science of making ready and serving dainty, luscious, and tempting foods; epicurism.

gas-trop′ȧ-thy, *n.* Disease of the stomach.

gas-trō-phren′iç, *a.* [*Gastro-,* and Gr. *phrēn,* the diaphragm.] Pertaining to the stomach and diaphragm.

gas″trō-pneū-mat′iç, *a.* Same as *Gastropneumonic.*

gas″trō-pneū-mon′iç (-nū-mon′ik), *a.* [*Gastro-,* and Gr. *pneumōn,* the lungs.] Belonging to both stomach and lungs.

gas′trō-pod, Gas-trop′ō-dȧ, etc. See *Gasteropod, Gasteropoda,* etc.

gas′trō-pōre, *n.* [*Gastro-,* and Gr. *poros,* a pore, a passage.] The pore or orifice of a nutritive polypite.

gas-tror′rhȧ-phy, *n.* [*Gastro-,* and Gr. *rhaphē,* a seam, from *rhaptein,* to sew.] Suture of wounds of the abdomen or of the stomach.

gas′trō-sçōpe, *n.* [*Gastro-* and Gr. *skopein,* to view.] A device for illuminating and examining the interior of the stomach.

gas-trō-sçop′iç, *a.* Pertaining to gastroscopy.

gas-tros′çō-py, *n.* The inspection of the interior of the stomach.

gas-trō-splen′iç, *a.* [*Gastro-,* and Gr. *splēn,* the spleen.] Belonging to both stomach and spleen.

gas′trō-stēġe, *n.* [*Gastro-,* and Gr. *stegos,* the roof.] One of the ventral scales or scutes of a snake.

gas-tros′tō-my, *n.* [*Gastro-,* and Gr. *stoma,* mouth.] An operation by which an artificial opening is made in the stomach for the introduction of food in cases of obstruction of the gullet.

gas-trō-thē′çȧ, *n.* Same as *Gasterotheca.*

gas-trot′ō-my, *n.* [*Gastro-,* and Gr. *tomē,* a cutting.] The operation of cutting into or opening the stomach.

Gas-trot′ri-çhȧ, *n.pl.* [Gr. *gastēr,* stomach, and *thrix, trichos,* hair.] A group of worms characterized by ventral cilia.

gas-trot′rō-çhȧ, *n.*; *pl.* **gas-trot′rō-çhæ.** [Gr. *gastēr,* stomach, and *trochos,* a wheel.] A larval form of annelid, having radiated ventral cilia.

gas-trō-vas′çū-lăr, *a.* [*Gastro-,* and L. *vasculum,* a small vessel.] Performing the double function of digestion and circulation; as, the *gastrovascular* canals of the *Cœlenterata.*

gas-trox′i-ȧ, gas-trox-yn′sis, *n.* [*Gastro-,* and Gr. *oxynein,* to make acid.] Abnormal acidity of the gastric juices, as in certain forms of nervous dyspepsia.

gas-trō-zō′oid, *n.* Same as *Gasterozooid.*

gas′trū-lȧ, *n.* [L., dim. of *gaster*; Gr. *gastēr,* stomach.] In embryology, a form assumed by the embryo of the *Metazoa.* It consists essentially of a cuplike body whose walls have two layers, inclosing an archenteron or digestive cavity having an orifice or blastopore.

gas′trū-lăr, *a.* Relating to a gastrula or to gastrulation.

gas-trū-lā′tion, *n.* The process of forming a gastrula; invagination.

Gas-trū′rȧ, *n.pl.* [L., from Gr. *gastēr,* stomach, and *oura,* tail.] The *Stomatopoda.*

gas-trū′rous, *a.* Of or like the *Gastrura.*

gas′=wäsh″ẽr, *n.* A device used to remove ammonia from illuminating gas.

gas′=well, *n.* A boring in the ground from which natural gas issues.

gas′=wŏrks, *n.* An establishment in which illuminating gas is manufactured; a gas-plant.

gat, *v.,* obsolete past tense of *get.*

gatch, *n.* [Per. *gach,* plaster.] Plaster, as used in Persian gatch-work.

gatch′=deç-ō-rā′tion, *n.* In Persian art, decoration molded in plaster.

gatch′=wŏrk, *n.* Work in molded plaster or gatch.

gāte, *n.* [ME. *gate, gat*; AS. *geat,* a gate, door.]

1. A movable frame or barrier, usually of openwork, used to close a passageway into an inclosure; generally distinguished from a *door,* which is usually solid and part of a house, but extended to massive doors, as those giving entrance into a walled city, a castle, a factory, etc.; also, the frame which stops the passage of water through a dam, lock, etc.

2. A passageway into an inclosure; a gateway; an opening, as in a wall or fence, that is or may be closed by a movable barrier; especially, the entrance into a walled city or a large edifice; as, her husband is known at the *gates.*

3. Figuratively, any comparatively narrow natural passageway; as, the Golden *Gate,* the entrance to the harbor of San Francisco.

4. In Scripture, means of access; hence, power; dominion; as, the *gates* of Hell.

5. In founding, (a) a channel or passageway for molten metal; (b) the strip of waste metal left in the pouring-hole.

6. An aperture in the tumblers of a lock for the passage of the stub.

7. A frame in which a saw is extended to prevent buckling or bending.

To break gates; in English universities, to enter the collegiate grounds after the regular hour.

gāte, *v.t.*; gated, *pt., pp.*; gating, *ppr.* 1. To furnish with a gate.

2. In English universities, to punish by restrictions on liberty of passage beyond the gates.

gāte, *n.* Manner; way; course; gait; progress. [Obs. or Scot.]

gāte′=chām″bẽr, *n.* A recess, as in a wall, for the reception of a gate when opened.

gāte′=hook, *n.* The hook or part upon which a gate is hung; also, a hook which fastens a gate.

gāte′house, *n.* A house at a gate, as a porter's lodge. In medieval times, the *gatehouse* was often quite imposing, especially if marking the entrance to a city, and sometimes was made strong for defense.

Gatehouse at Sens, Villeneuve-sur-Yonne.

gāte′less, *a.* Having no gate.

gāte′măn, *n.*; *pl.* **gāte′men.** A man in charge of a gate; a gatetender.

gāte′=mŏn″ey, *n.* Money received for admission at the entrance to an athletic contest, races, or other public exhibition.

gāte pōst, *n.* The post to which a gate is hinged, or the one against which it closes.

gāte′=tend″ẽr, *n.* One intrusted with the duty of opening and closing a gate, as at a railroad crossing.

gāte′=valve, *n.* A valve with a sliding gate for closing and opening a pipe.

gāte′=vein, *n.* The portal vein; the great abdominal vein.

gāte′way, *n.* A way or opening which is or may be closed by a gate; also, any structure surrounding such an opening; hence, any means of entrance.

gāte′wīse, *adv.* After the fashion of a gate.

Gä′thȧ, *n.* [Sans., hymn, psalm.] Any one of five groups of metrical compositions in the Zend-Avesta of the Parsees, attributed to Zoroaster.

gath′ẽr, *v.t.*; gathered, *pt., pp.*; gathering, *ppr.* [ME. *gaderen, gadren*; AS. *gaderian, gædrian,* to gather, from *geador, gader,* together.]

1. To bring together; to collect into one place or into one aggregate body; to assemble; to congregate; as, to *gather* an army.

2. To select and take; to cull; to pluck; to separate from others less desired and bring together; to get in, as a harvest; to reap and bring into barns or stores; as, he *gathered* his crop of wheat.

3. To draw together into smaller space; to contract; to make puckers or small folds in, as cloth along a thread run through it; to pucker; to plait.

4. To deduce by inference; to collect or learn by observation or reasoning; as, from what I hear I *gather* that he was present.

5. To gain; to accumulate; to acquire; as, the snowball *gathered* weight by rolling.

6. To take in; as, to *gather* the slack of a sail.

7. In masonry, to narrow suddenly, as a fireplace to meet the dimensions of a flue.

8. In bookbinding, to collect and arrange the parts of (a book, etc.) in regular order for binding.

To gather breath; to take breath; to pause to reflect.

To gather oneself together; to collect one's powers for a strong effort.

To gather way; to start; to begin to move; to acquire motion, as a ship under sail or steam.

gath′ẽr, *v.i.* 1. To collect; to unite; to accumulate; as, the clouds *gather* in the west.

2. To increase; to grow larger by accretion of like matter; as, the snowball *gathered* as it went.

3. To assemble; as, the people *gather* fast.

4. To reach the stage of suppuration, as a boil.

Syn.—Collect, accumulate, amass, assemble, aggregate, group, congregate, suppurate.

gath′ẽr, *n.* 1. A plait or fold in cloth made fast by a thread run through it.

2. The forward inclination of the journals on a carriage-axle, designed to prevent the wheels from running unevenly.

3. The lower face of the masonry in a fireplace where it narrows to the flue.

gath′ẽr-ȧ-ble, *a.* That may be gathered. [Rare.]

gath′ẽr-ẽr, *n.* 1. One who gathers or collects anything; as, a *gatherer* of grain; a news-*gatherer.*

2. One who gets in a crop; as, a hay-*gatherer.*

3. A sewing-machine attachment to make gathers in cloth.

gath′ẽr-ing, *n.* 1. The act of collecting or assembling; the act of making a collection, as of money, or of making gathers, as in cloth; the act of collecting and arranging the parts of a book, etc., for binding.

2. Anything gathered together; (a) a crowd; an assemblage; (b) a collection, as of money; (c) a suppurating tumor; an abscess.

gath′ẽr-ing=bōard, *n.* The table on which the sheets of a book are gathered in bookbinding.

gath′ẽr-ing=çōal, *n.* A large piece of coal kept smoldering during the night, in order to start a fire in the morning. [Scot.]

gath′ẽr-ing=hoop, *n.* A hoop used by coopers for drawing the ends of barrel-staves together.

gath′ẽr-ing=pal″let, *n.* A pallet or lever controlling the operation of the striking mechanism of a clock.

gath′ẽr-ing=pēat, *n.* 1. A peat serving as a gathering-coal. [Scot.]

2. A fiery peat formerly sent about as a warning signal by the Scottish borderers. [Obs.]

Gat′ling gun. See under *Gun.*

gat′ten=tree, gat′tẽr=tree, *n.* Same as *Gaitertree.*

gat′=tōthed, *a.* [Etymology and meaning doubtful.] Goat-toothed; lustful; or possibly gap-toothed, having open spaces between the teeth. [Obs.]

gaub, *n.* [Hind. *gāb.*] A variety of persimmontree of the East Indies, or its astringent fruit.

gauçhe (gōsh), *a.* [Fr., from O.H.G. *welc, welch,* soft, languid.]

1. Left-handed; hence, crooked; clumsy; awkward.

2. In mathematics, skew; (a) of double curvature; not in a single plane; twisted; (b) deviating from perfect symmetry by the regular reversal of certain parts.

gauçhe-rie′ (gōsh-rē′), *n.* [Fr.] Boorish behavior; awkwardness; a clumsy action.

Gau′chō, *n.* [Sp. Am.] A Spanish-American native of the pampas of South America.

gau′cie, gau′cy, *n.* [Origin obscure.] Plump; lusty; jolly; also written *gausie, gawsy.* [Scot.]

gaud, *n.* [ME. *gaude, gawde,* a jewel, ornament, from L. *gaudium,* gladness, joy.]

1. A worthless or trifling ornament; a trinket; a bauble; as, the *gauds* and vanities of a sumptuous aristocracy.

2. A jest; trick; sport; fraud. [Obs.]

3. One of the beads in a rosary.

gaud, *v.i.* and *v.t.* I. *v.i.* To exult; to rejoice. [Obs.]

II. *v.t.* To deck gaily; to paint; to adorn with gauds. [Rare.]

gaud′=dāy, *n.* A festival; a holiday.

gaud′ẽr-y, *n.* Showy or trifling finery. [Rare.]

gaud′ful, *a.* Joyful; showy.

gaud′i-ly, *adv.* In a gaudy manner; showily.

gaud′i-ness, *n.* The quality or condition of being gaudy.

gaud′ish, *a.* Gaudy. [Rare.]

gaud′less, *a.* Unadorned by gauds. [Rare.]

gaud′y, *a.*; *comp.* gaudier; *superl.* gaudiest. [L. *gaudium,* gladness, joy, from *gaudere,* to rejoice.]

1. Showy; outwardly splendid; gay.

> A goldfinch there I saw, with *gaudy* pride
> Of painted plumes. —Dryden.

2. Ostentatiously fine; gay beyond the simplicity of nature or good taste; vulgarly splendid; flashy.

> Costly thy habit as thy purse can buy,
> But not expressed in fancy; rich, not *gaudy.*
> —Shak.

Syn.—Tawdry, fine, meretricious, bespangled, glittering, showy, gay, garish.

gaud′y, *n.*; *pl.* **gaud′ies.** [ME. *gaudee,* a bead; LL. *gaudium,* the bead on a rosary, from L. *gaudium,* gladness.]

1. One of the beads in the rosary marking the five joys of the Virgin Mary.

2. One of the tapers burnt on an altar in a chapel, etc., in commemoration of the five joyful mysteries of the Virgin.

3. A holiday or festival; a gaud-day; a slang term used in the English universities.

gauf′fẽr, *v.t.* Same as *Goffer.*

gauf′fẽr-ing, *n.* Goffering.

gauf′fre (gō′fẽr), *n.* [Fr., from OFr. *goffre,* a honeycomb, so called from the gopher's honeycombing the earth.] The French name for *gopher,* first used by Cuvier.

gauġe, gāġe, *n.* [OFr. *gauge,* a gauge, a gauging-rod, from LL. *gaugia,* the standard measure of a cask.]

1. A standard of measure; an instrument to determine the dimensions or capacity of anything; a standard of any kind; a measure; means of estimating; as, a steam-*gauge*; a wind-*gauge*; to take the *gauge* of a man's capacity.

2. In railroad construction, the width or distance between the rails; also, the distance between the opposite wheels of a car. The *standard gauge* on American railroads is 4 feet 8½ inches; *broad gauge* is greater and *narrow gauge* less than this width.

3. In nautical language, (a) the depth to which a vessel sinks in the water; (b) the position of a ship with reference to another vessel and to the wind; when to the windward, she is said to have the *weather-gauge*, when to the leeward, the *lee-gauge*.

4. In building, the length of a slate or tile below the lap.

5. In plastering, (a) the quantity of plaster of Paris used with common plaster to accelerate its setting; (b) the composition of plaster of Paris and other materials, used in finishing plastered ceilings, for moldings, etc.

6. In type-founding, a piece of hard wood or polished steel, variously notched, used to adjust the dimensions, slopes, etc., of the various sorts of letters.

7. In joinery, a simple instrument made to strike a line parallel to the straight side of a board, etc.

8. In the air-pump, an instrument of various forms, which points out the degree of exhaustion in the receiver. The siphon-*gauge* is most generally used for this purpose.

9. The diameter of the bore of a shotgun.

Gauge enters into many compounds, as rain-*gauge*, steam-*gauge*, etc., which will be found defined in their regular vocabulary order.

Differential gauge; a gauge employed for testing the slight difference of diameter required in parts which are to be fitted into one another.

External gauge; a male or plug gauge.

Internal gauge; a female or collar gauge.

Joiner's gauge; see definition 7, above.

Printer's gauge; a measure of the length of a page, or a graduated strip of wood, metal, or cardboard for determining the number of lines of any given kind of type in a given space.

Standard gauge; (a) a size that is recognized as standard; (b) a gauge for determining whether tools, etc., are of recognized standard size; (c) see definition 2, above.

gāuge, gāge, *v.t.*; gauged, gaged, *pt., pp.*; gauging, gaging, *ppr.* 1. To measure or to ascertain the contents of; to ascertain the capacity of, as a pipe, puncheon, hogshead, barrel, tierce, keg, vat, etc.

> No eye like his to value horse or cow,
> Or *gauge* the contents of a stack or mow.
> —Lowell.

2. To measure in respect to proportion, capability, or power, or in respect to character or behavior; to take cognizance of the capacity, capability, or power of; to appraise; to estimate; as, I *gauged* his character very accurately.

> You shall not *gauge* me
> By what we do to-night. —Shak.

3. In dressmaking, to gather with thread into equidistant puckers, as cloth or dress-goods.

gāuge'ȧ-ble, gāge'ȧ-ble, *a.* Capable of being gauged or measured.

gāuge'-bär, *n.* An adjustable gauge used in sawing lumber to regulate the depth of the kerf.

gāuge'-block, *n.* In marble-cutting, an iron block used to adjust the saws.

gāuge'-box, *n.* 1. A box in which shingles are piled, measured, and divided into bundles.

2. In manufactures, any box designed to contain or exactly measure a fixed quantity of a material.

gāuge'-cock, *n.* A stopcock which indicates the height of the water in a boiler.

gāuge'-cŏn-cus"sion (-kush"un), *n.* The striking of the flanges of railroad car-wheels against the rails.

gāuged, *a.* 1. Adjusted, fitted, or measured with precision.

2. In dressmaking, gathered; puckered; as, a *gauged* skirt.

gāuge'-dōor, *n.* In coal-mining, a trap in an airway to regulate ventilation.

gāuge'-glȧss, *n.* A vertical tube of strong glass to show the level and condition of the water in a steam-boiler.

gāuge'-knīfe (-nīf), *n.* A knife the size and depth of whose cut is regulated by a gauge.

gāuge'-lad"dẽr, *n.* A horsing-block, used in excavating to lift and support heavy planks designed to form a passageway for wheelbarrows.

gāuge'-lāthe, *n.* A wood-turning lathe with edges shaped to a pattern and with a depth of cut regulated by a stop or gauge.

gāuge'-pin, *n.* A pin attached to the platen of a small printing-press, to keep the sheet to be printed in proper position.

gāuge'-plāy, *n.* The difference between the track-gauge of a railroad and the gauge of its car-wheel flanges, usually from one-quarter to three-quarters of an inch.

gāuge'-point, *n.* In gauging, the diameter of a cylinder that is one inch in height, and has a capacity equal to a unit of a given measure.

gāu'gẽr, gā'gẽr, *n.* 1. One who gauges; specifically, one whose business is to ascertain the contents of casks, vats, etc.

2. An exciseman; an officer of the internal revenue service.

gāuge'-rod, *n.* An instrument used in measuring the contents of casks or vessels; a gauger's measuring staff; also called *gauging-rod*.

gāu'gẽr-ship, *n.* The office or occupation of a gauger.

gāuge'-saw, *n.* A saw furnished with an adjustable gauge-bar to regulate the depth of the kerf.

gāuge'-stuff, *n.* In plastering, a compound containing plaster of Paris or gypsum, used in making cornices, moldings, etc.; also called *gauged stuff*.

gāuge'-wheel (-hwēl), *n.* A wheel on the forward beam-end of a plow, to regulate the depth of the furrow.

gāu'ging, gā'ging, *n.* 1. The art or method of measuring the capacity or contents of a hollow vessel, as a cask, a vat, etc.; the occupation of a gauger.

2. In dressmaking, the process of gathering or puckering a fabric.

Gaul, *n.* [OFr. *Gaule*; L. *Gallus*; Gr. *Gallos*, a Gaul.]

1. An inhabitant of ancient Gaul.

2. In modern use, a Frenchman.

gau'lin, *n.* An egret or white heron; so called by the Jamaica negroes.

Gaul'ish, *a.* Pertaining to ancient France or Gaul. [Rare.]

Gault, *n.* Same as *Galt*.

Gaul-thē'ri-ȧ, *n.* A genus of shrubs of the heath family, of which the wintergreen, *Gaultheria procumbens*, is typical, with evergreen leaves and red edible berries, found in North America, the Andes, Australasia, the mountains of India, and Japan; named after Dr. Gaultier, a Canadian physician.

gaum, *v.t.* [Prov. Eng., from AS. *gyman, giman*, to care for, heed.] To understand.

gaum, *v.t.* To daub or smear. [Prov. Eng.]

gäunt, *a.* [ME. *gawnt, gawnte*, lean, slender; prob. from Norw. *gand*, a thin pointed stick, a tall thin man.] Vacant; hollow; empty, as an animal after long fasting; hence, lean; meager; thin; slender.

gäunt'let, gänt'let, *n.* [OFr. *gantelet*, dim. of *gant*, a glove, from D. *want*, a mitten; Old Sw. *wante*, a glove.]

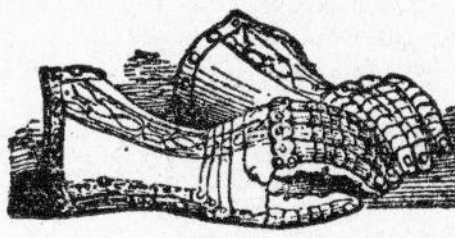

1. A glove; specifically, in medieval armor, the defensive covering of the hand and wrist.

Gauntlets.

2. A long, stout glove, for use in riding, driving, etc.

3. In surgery, a form of bandage for the hand.

4. A mitt.

To throw down the gauntlet; to challenge.

To take up the gauntlet; to accept a challenge.

gäunt'let-ed, *a.* Wearing a gauntlet.

gäunt'ly, *adv.* Leanly; meagerly.

gaun'tree, gaun'try, *n.* [Prov. Eng. *gaun*, a tub, cask, and *tree*, a wooden support.]

1. A frame to support barrels horizontally, usually used in cellars.

2. In engineering, a scaffolding on which a crane or some other machine runs.

gaur, gour, *n.* [Native E. Ind. name, from Sans. *gaura*, a wild ox.] An East Indian variety of wild cattle, similar to the domesticated gayal.

gaur, gāre, gaure, *v.i.* To gape; to stare; to gaze with open mouth. [Obs.]

gauss, *n.* A name proposed for various magnetic units, in honor of the German mathematician, Karl F. Gauss.

Gauss'i-ăn, *a.* Named after or discovered by Karl F. Gauss; as, *Gaussian* logarithms; *Gaussian* function.

gauze, *n.* [Fr. *gaze*, gauze, prob. from *Gaza*, in Palestine, where it was first manufactured.] A very thin, slight, transparent stuff, usually of silk or linen; also applied to other material of similar open texture; as, wire *gauze*.

gauze, *a.* Of or like gauze; gauzy; as, *gauze* underclothing.

gauze'-tree, *n.* The lace-bark tree, *Lagetta lintearia*, of the West Indies.

gauz'i-ness, *n.* The quality of being gauzy.

gauz'y, *a.* Like gauze; thin as gauze.

ga-väge' (-väzh'), *n.* [Fr., from *gaver*, to gorge fowls with food in order to fatten them, from *gave*, the crop or craw of a bird.]

1. Forced feeding of poultry through a tube, for the purpose of fattening them for market.

2. In medicine, a similar method of giving nourishment to a patient.

gāve, *v.*, past tense of *give*.

gav'el, *v.t.*; gaveled, *pt., pp.*; gaveling, *ppr.* To distribute equally, according to the tenure of gavelkind.

gav'el, *n.* [ME. *gavel*; AS. *gafol*, tribute, tax.] In old English law, tribute; toll; customs. [Obs.]

gav'el, *n.* [OFr. *gavelle*, a sheaf of corn.] A small unbound parcel of wheat, rye, or other grain, laid together by reapers. [Rare.]

gav'el, *n.* A gable. [Prov. Eng.]

gav'el, *n.* [Origin obscure.] The mallet used by the presiding officer of a legislative body or public assembly for rapping to attract attention or secure order.

gav'el-et, *n.* [From ME. *gavel*; AS. *gafol*, tribute, tax.] A special writ used in the county of Kent, England, for the forfeiture of property on account of the withholding of rent or services.

gav'el-kind, *n.* [Ir. *gabhail-cine*; *gabhail*, a taking, tenure, and *cine*, family, tribe, race.] In old English law, a tenure by which land descended from the father to all his sons in equal portions, and the land of a brother dying without issue descended equally to his brothers. This species of tenure prevailed in England before the Norman conquest in many parts of the kingdom, perhaps in the whole realm, but particularly in Kent, where it still exists.

gav'e-lock, gav'e-loche, *n.* [ME. *gavelock*; AS. *gafeluc*, a spear or javelin.]

1. A dart; a spear. [Obs.]

2. An iron lever; a crowbar. [Scot.]

gā'vẽr-ick, *n.* The red gurnard. [Prov. Eng.]

Gā'vi-æ, *n.pl.* [L. *gavia*, a sea-mew.] The group of birds of which gulls are the type.

gā'vi-ăl, *n.* [Hind. *ghariyāl*, a crocodile.] A large Indian crocodile, *Gavialis gangeticus*, having a long slender snout with a knob on the upper jaw; found chiefly in the Ganges and called by the natives *nakoo*.

Head of Gavial or Gangetic Crocodile (*Gavialis gangeticus*).

Gā-vi-al'i-dæ, *n.pl.* The family of crocodiles of which the gavial is the type, distinguished by a long, narrow, knobbed snout, and feet completely webbed.

gȧ-vot', gȧ-votte', *n.* [Fr. *gavotte*; OFr. *gavote*, a dance of the *Gavots*, or people of *Gap*, a town in the department of Hautes-Alpes, France, where the dance originated.]

1. A sort of French dance.

2. The music to which the dance was performed. *Gavots* are a favorite movement in concertos, sonatas, etc.

> Who might be heard in his apartment of nights playing tremulous old *gavottes* and minuets on a wheezy old fiddle.
> —Thackeray.

gaw, *n.* 1. A mark on the skin left by pressure or a grip. [Scot.]

2. A little ditch or trench. [Scot.]

gaw'by, *n.* [Obs.] See *Gaby*.

gawk, *n.* [ME. *gowke*, a cuckoo, a fool; Ice. *gaukr*, a cuckoo.]

1. A cuckoo. [Scot.]

2. A fool; a simpleton; a booby.

gawk, *v.i.*; gawked, *pt., pp.*; gawking, *ppr.* To act like a gawk. [Colloq.]

gawk'y, *n.* An awkward, ungainly, or stupid fellow.

gawk'y, *a.* Foolish; awkward; clumsy; clownish; ungainly; uncouth.

gawn, *n.* [Local, Eng.] A small tub or lading vessel.

gāy, *a.* [ME. *gay*; OFr. *gai*; O.H.G. *gahi*, quick, sudden, rash, lively.]

1. Merry; airy; jovial; sportive; frolicsome. It denotes more life and animation than *cheerful*.

> Belinda smiled, and all the world was *gay*.
> —Pope.

2. Fine; showy; as, a *gay* dress.

3. Inflamed or merry with liquor; intoxicated; dissipated. [Colloq.]

Syn.—Merry, lively, blithe, sprightly, sportive, hilarious.

gay̆'ăl (gī'ăl), *n.* [Native E. Ind. name.] A species of ox, *Bos frontalis*, found wild in the mountains of northern Burmah and Assam, and long domesticated in these countries and in the eastern parts of Bengal.

Gā-yȧ-trī', *n.* [Sans.] The great Sanskrit hymn which all Brahmans have used in their daily prayers for thirty centuries or more.

gāy'bine, *n.* A name of several showy twining plants of the genus *Ipomœa*.

gāy'di-ang, *n.* [Native Anamese.] A vessel of Anam with curved decks, somewhat resembling a Chinese junk, and carrying two or three masts and large triangular sails.

Gaydiang of Anam.

gāy'e-ty, *n.* See *Gaiety.*

gāy'=feath"ẽr (-feth"), *n.* The button snakeroot, *Liatris spicata.*

Gāy"lus-sā'ci-ȧ, *n.* [Named after *Gay-Lussac*, the French scientist.] An important genus of ericaceous shrubs, the leaves of some of which drop off in the fall, while others are evergreens. They have clusters of white or pale green flowers, and black or blue edible fruit, commonly known as huckleberries. They are found in the eastern sections of both North and South America. The common or black huckleberry is the fruit of *Gaylussacia resinosa.*

gāy'lus-site, *n.* [Named after the French chemist, *Gay-Lussac.*] A white, brittle, glassy sodium-calcium carbonate, found in Peru and in Nevada.

gāy'ly, *adv.* See *Gaily.*

gāy'ness, *n.* Gaiety; finery. [Rare.]

gāy'sōme, *a.* Full of gaiety.

gāy'=yoū, *n.* [Anglo-Ind.] A narrow, flat-bottomed, Anamese fishing-boat. It has an outrigger and either two or three masts, and is provided with a movable roof amidships.

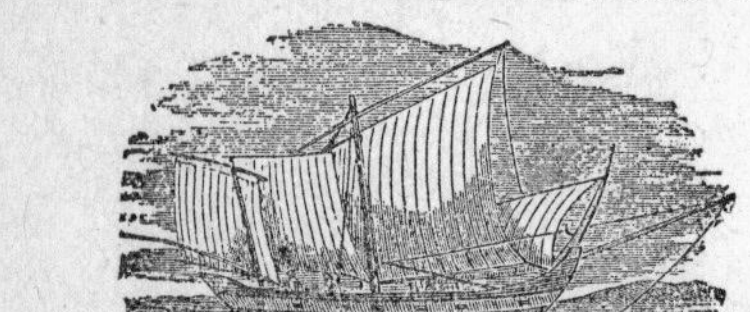

Gay-you of Anam.

Gȧ-zā'ni-ȧ, *n.* An important class of herbs of the aster family, appreciated for their large and showy orange and yellow blossoms, which expand only in bright sunshine. They are native to South Africa and are named after Theodorus Gaza, a medieval Greek scholar of Italy.

gāze, *v.i.*; gazed, *pt.*, *pp.*; gazing, *ppr.* [ME. *gasen*, from Sw. dial. *gasa*, to gaze, stare.] To fix the eyes and look steadily and earnestly; to look with eagerness or curiosity, as in admiration, astonishment, or study.

> Ye men of Galilee, why stand ye *gazing* up into heaven? —Acts i. 11.

Syn.—Gape, stare.—To *gaze* is to look with fixed and prolonged attention, awakened by excited interest or elevated emotion; to *gape* is to look fixedly with feelings of ignorant wonder; to *stare* is to look with the fixedness of insolence or of idiocy.

gāze, *v.t.* To look at intently. [Rare.]

> And *gazed* awhile the ample sky. —Milton.

gāze, *n.* 1. A fixed look; a look of eagerness, wonder, or admiration; a continued look of attention.

> With secret *gaze*
> Or open admiration him behold. —Milton.

2. The object gazed on; that which causes one to gaze. [Poet.]

> Made of my enemies the scorn and *gaze.* —Milton.

At gaze; (a) in stag-hunting, in the position assumed by a stag when becoming aware that the dogs are in chase; in the attitude of gazing; (b) in heraldry, having the head turned so as to look out from the shield; chiefly used in reference to the figures of a buck, hart, hind, or stag.

Stag at Gaze.

gȧ-zē'bō, gȧ-zee'bō, *n.* [Humorously formed from *gaze*, and L. *-ebo*, a fut. ind. 1st pers. sing. ending of a second conjugation verb, meaning lit., I shall gaze.] A summer-house affording a fine prospect. [Colloq.]

gāze'fụl, *a.* Looking with a gaze; looking intently. [Rare.]

gāze'hound, *n.* A hound that pursues by sight rather than by scent.

gȧ-zel', gȧ-zelle', *n.* [OFr. *gazel*, *gazelle*; Ar. *ghazal*, *ghazel*, a gazel.] A small, swift, graceful antelope, celebrated for the luster and soft expression of its eyes; especially applicable to *Gazella dorcas* of North Africa.

gaz'el, ghaz'ăl, *n.* 1. A piece of music with a frequent refrain.

2. A form of Persian verse.

Ga-zel'lȧ, *n.* The type genus of gazels, sometimes called *Dorcas.*

Gazels (*Gazella dorcas*).

Gaz-el-lī'næ, *n.pl.* A group of antelopes of which the gazel is the type.

gāze'ment, *n.* The act of gazing; view. [Obs.]

gāz'ẽr, *n.* One who gazes.

ga-zet', *n.* [It.] A copper coin equal to about one and a half cents in value, formerly issued by the Venetian republic.

ga-zette', *n.* [It. *gazzetta*, a gazette, newspaper, prob. from *gazzetta*, a gazet or small coin, the price paid for the paper; also thought to be from *gazzetta*, a magpie, and to mean a chatterer or tattler.]

1. A newspaper; a printed sheet of paper containing an account of current transactions and events which are deemed important and interesting; often used as the specific name for a newspaper or periodical.

2. One of the official newspapers of Great Britain, containing among other things the authorized announcements of appointments and promotions in the public service and of public honors awarded. The *London Gazette* is published on Tuesdays and Fridays. A similar official newspaper is published also in Edinburgh and Dublin, and all three contain a list of those who have become bankrupt since last publication; hence, the phrases, *to appear in the gazette, to have one's name in the gazette*, signify to become bankrupt.

ga-zette', *v.t.*; gazetted, *pt.*, *pp.*; gazetting, *ppr.* To publish in a gazette; hence, to formally announce, as an appointment to the public service.

gaz-et-teer', *n.* [It. *gazzettiere*, a writer of news, from *gazzetta*, a gazette.]

1. A writer of news, or an officer appointed to publish news by authority.

2. A gazette; a newspaper. [Obs.]

3. A book containing descriptions of natural and political divisions, countries, cities, towns, rivers, mountains, etc., in a portion of the world or in the whole world, alphabetically arranged; a geographical dictionary.

gāz'ing-stock, *n.* A person or thing gazed at; an object of curiosity or contempt.

gaz'ō-ġēne, *n.* An apparatus used for manufacturing aerated water on a small scale for domestic use, by the combination of an alkali and an acid; also written *gasogene*, *gasogen.*

ga-zon', *n.* [Fr., from O.H.G. *waso*, turf, sod.] In fortification, turf used to line parapets and the faces of earthworks.

ġē-ȧ-deph'ȧ-gous, *a.* [Gr. *gē*, the earth, and *adēphagos*, voracious, from *adēn*, enough, and *phagein*, to eat.] Pertaining to a tribe of predaceous beetles living upon the ground, as the carabids.

ġē'ăl, *a.* Pertaining to the earth; terrestrial.

ġēal, *v.i.* To congeal. [Obs.]

ġēan, *n.* [Fr. *guigne*; OFr. *guisne*; LL. *guindolum*, a kind of cherry; prob. of Slavic origin.] The wild cherry of Europe, *Prunus avium.* Its wood is much used for tobacco-pipes.

ġē-an-ti-clī'năl, *n.* [Gr. *gē*, earth, and *anti*, against, and *klinein*, to slope.] In geology, an extensive upward curvature of the earth's surface; opposed to *geosynclinal.*

ġēar, *n.* [ME. *gere*, *ger*; AS. *gearwe*, preparation, dress, ornament, from *gearu*, ready, brisk, prompt.]

1. Whatever is prepared for use or wear; manufactured stuff or material; hence, habit; dress; ornaments; as, head-*gear*; foot-*gear.*

> Array thyself in thy most gorgeous *gear.* —Spenser.

2. Any special equipment or appurtenances for a specific use or purpose; as, hunting-*gear.*

3. In machinery, in a general sense, the appliances or furnishings connected with the acting portions of any piece of mechanism; as, expansion-*gear*; valve-*gear*; specifically, (a) toothed wheels collectively; (b) the connection of toothed wheels with each other; gearing.

4. The harness or furniture of beasts of draft; tackle; trappings.

5. The condition of fitness of parts; a state of preparation; as, this is out of *gear*, or in *gear.*

6. Property; goods; belongings. [Scot.]

7. Business matters; affairs. [Obs.]

> Here's a goodly *gear.* —Shak.

8. Warlike accouterments. [Scot.]

9. Any worthless thing; junk; rubbish. [Rare.]

10. In nautical language, a general name for the ropes, blocks, etc., belonging to any particular sail or spar; as, the mainsail-*gear*; the foretopmast-*gear.*

To throw into gear; to set ready to start; to put into motion, as machinery.

To throw out of gear; to put out of running order; to put out of motion, as by turning a lever to throw off the belt or other operating connection.

ġēar, *v.t.*; geared, *pt.*, *pp.*; gearing, *ppr.* To put into gear; to harness; to dress; to prepare for operation; to furnish with gear; to engage, as parts of machinery.

ġēar, *v.i.* In machinery, to be in gear or in operating order; to engage with the connecting parts.

ġēar'=cut"tẽr, *n.* A manufacturer of toothed wheels for transmitting motion in machinery; a machine for cutting such wheels.

ġēar'ing, *n.* 1. Harness; dress; gear.

2. In machinery, the parts collectively by which motion communicated to one portion of a machine is transmitted to another; a train of toothed wheels for transmitting motion. There are two chief sorts of gearing, namely, spur-*gearing* and beveled-*gearing.* In the former the teeth are arranged round either the concave or convex surface of a cylindrical wheel in the direction of radii from the center of the wheel, and are of equal depth throughout. In beveled-*gearing* the teeth are placed upon the exterior periphery of a conical wheel in a direction converging to the apex of the cone, and the depth of the tooth gradually diminishes from the base.

Spur-gearing.

ġēar'ing=chāin, *n.* An endless chain transmitting motion from one toothed wheel to another.

ġēar'=wheel, *n.* Any wheel having teeth or cogs which act upon the teeth of another wheel to impart or transmit motion.

ġēa'ṣon, *a.* Rare; uncommon; wonderful. [Obs.]

Ġē-as'tẽr, *n.* [Gr. *gē*, earth, and *astēr*, star.] A genus of gasteromycetous fungi taking the form of stars and lying close to the ground; hence, the name, signifying *earth-star.*

ġēat, *n.* [AS. *geotan*, to pour.]

1. In founding, the hole through which metal is poured into a mold.

2. In type-founding, a lip or spout in the casting-ladle.

ġē-cär-cin'i-ăn, *n.* [Gr. *gē*, earth, and *karkinos*, a crab.] In zoölogy, any member of the genus *Gecarcinus*; a land-crab.

Gec'cō, *n.* A genus of lizards; the geckos or wall-lizards.

geck, *n.* 1. A dupe; a gull. [Rare.]

2. A jibe or taunt; derision; scorn. [Rare.]

geck, *v.t.* To cheat, trick, or gull. [Rare.]

geck, *v.i.* To express scorn, derision, or contempt. [Rare.]

geck'ō, *n.*; *pl.* **geck'ōṣ** or **geck'ōes.** [An imitative word.]

1. A name common to a family of saurian reptiles; a wall-lizard.

Wall-gecko (*Gecco fascicularis*).

2. [G—] Same as *Gecco.*

ged, gedd, *n.* [Ice. *gedda*, a pike, from *gaddr*, *gaddo*, a goad, spike.] A fish, the pike. [Scot.]

ġee, *v.i.*; geed, *pt.*, *pp.*; geeing, *ppr.* 1. To agree; to suit; to fit. [Colloq.]

2. To go or turn to the side away from the driver, that is, to the right in America, to the left in England; used by teamsters, generally in the imperative, addressed to the animals they are driving.

ġee, *v.t.* To cause to move to the off side, as a team of oxen.

ġee'hō, *v.i.* Same as *Gee.*

geer, *n.* and *v.*, obsolete spelling of *gear.*

geese, *n.*, pl. of *goose.*

geest, *n.* [L.G. *geest*, sandy, dry, from Old Friesic *gast*, *gest*, dry, barren.] Alluvial matter on the surface of land, not of recent origin. [Obs.]

Gē-ez', Gīz, *n.* [Ethiopic.] The ancient language of Ethiopia or Abyssinia, long superseded by Amharic, except for literary purposes; also, the people using the language.

gee'zẽr, *n.* A term of disrespect, usually applied to an elderly person. [Slang.]

Ġe-hen'nȧ, *n.* [LL. *Gehenna*; Gr. *Geenna*, *Gaienna*; Heb. *ge-hinnom*, the valley of Hinnom, in which was Tophet, where the Israelites sometimes sacrificed their children to Moloch (2 Kings xxiii. 10). On this account the place was afterward regarded as a place of abomination and became the receptacle for the refuse of the city, perpetual fires being kept up in order to prevent pestilential effluvia.] A term used in the New Testament as equivalent to hell, place of fire or torment and punishment, and rendered by the translators *hell, hell-fire*, and *hell of fire*.

The pleasant valley of Hinnom, Tophet thence
And black *Gehenna* called, the type of hell.
—Milton.

gē'iç, *a.* [Gr. *gē*, the earth.] In chemistry, pertaining to or obtained from the earth or decayed vegetation; as, *geic* acid.

gei'gēr-tree, *n.* A small tree of the borage family found in the West Indies and valued for its dark-colored hard wood.

gē'in, *n.* [Gr. *gēinos*, earthy, from *gē*, the earth.] Humin; humic acid.

gei-shä', *n.* [Japan.] A dancing girl of Japan.

Geis'slēr tūbe. [Named after the maker, Heinrich *Geissler*.] In electricity, a tube in which a rarefied gas is hermetically sealed. When electricity is discharged through the tube between electrodes, the gas glows with fluorescence.

gei-tō-nog'ȧ-my, *n.* [Gr. *geitōn*, a neighbor, and *gamos* marriage.] In botany, fecundation of a pistil by pollen from a neighboring flower of the same plant.

ġel'ȧ-ble, *a.* [L. *gelare*, to freeze.] Capable of being converted into jelly, or of being congealed.

ġel'ȧ-dȧ, *n.* [Native name.] A baboon, *Theropithecus gelada*, found in Abyssinia, notable for the heavy mane of the adult male.

Ġe-lā'si-ăn, *a.* Pertaining to or composed by Gelasius, pope from A. D. 492 to 496, who composed some of the prayers in the Roman liturgy.

ġe-las'tiç, *a.* and *n.* I. *a.* Provoking laughter; risible. [Rare.]

II. *n.* Something provoking laughter. [Rare.]

ġel-a-ti-, ġe-lat-i-ni-. Combining forms from *gelatin*.

ġe-lat"i-fi-çā'tion, *n.* The act of turning to gelatin.

ġel-ȧ-tig'e-nous, *a.* [*Gelati-*, and Gr. *-genēs*, producing.] Having the quality of producing gelatin.

ġel'ȧ-tin, ġel'ȧ-tine, *n.* [Fr. *gélatine*, from L. *gelatus*, pp. of *gelare*, to freeze.] A firm, transparent, viscous substance, having no taste or smell, obtained by boiling connective tissue of animals, such as hoofs and horns. It dissolves in hot water and becomes a jelly when cooled. It forms the principal constituent of size, glue, isinglass, etc., and is used in some forms of food of a low nutritive value. Animals fed exclusively on it die with the symptoms of starvation, as it cannot yield albumen, fibrin, or casein.

Blasting gelatin; an explosive made of nine parts by weight of nitroglycerin and one of collodion-cotton.

Gelatin dynamite; blasting gelatin mixed with a dope, decreasing its cost and explosive power.

Gelatin emulsion; an emulsion of a salt of silver in gelatin for use in photography.

Gelatin paper; paper prepared with a coating of gelatin for photographic use.

Gelatin picture; one printed on gelatin paper.

Gelatin process; (a) a copying process by which any matter written or drawn in aniline ink may be transferred to many copies by the use of a gelatin surface kept moist by glycerin, etc. The original when pressed face down on the moist pad leaves a stain in the gelatin and a paper pressed upon that stain receives a copy of the original; the gelatin pad is called a hectograph. (b) In photoengraving, a process depending on the variation in solubility caused by the action of light on gelatin containing a bichromate. A print or negative made on such gelatin is treated with water so as to be swelled or washed away in the portions least affected, and from the resulting film a cast is made, as in one process, or the gelatin used for direct printing, as in another process.

ġe-lat'i-nāte, *v.i.*; gelatinated, *pt.*, *pp.*; gelatinating, *ppr.* To be converted into gelatin or into a substance like jelly.

ġe-lat'i-nāte, *v.t.* To convert into gelatin or into a substance resembling jelly.

ġe-lat-i-nā'tion, *n.* The act or process of converting or being turned into gelatin or into a substance like jelly.

ġe-lat-i-ni-. See *Gelati-*.

ġel"ȧ-tin-if'ēr-ous, *a.* [*Gelatini-*, and L. *ferre*, to produce.] Producing gelatin; capable of being gelatinized.

ġel-ȧ-tin'i-form, *a.* [*Gelatini-*, and L. *forma*, form.] Having the form of gelatin.

ġe-lat"i-ni-zā'tion, *n.* Gelatination.

ġe-lat'i-nize, *v.t.* and *v.i.*; gelatinized, *pt.*, *pp.*; gelatinizing, *ppr.* To gelatinate.

ġe-lat'i-noid, *a.* and *n.* [*Gelatin*, and Gr. *eidos*, resemblance.]

I. *a.* Like jelly in substance.

II. *n.* A substance resembling gelatin.

ġe-lat'i-nous, *a.* Like jelly; of the character of gelatin; viscous.

ġe-lat'i-nous-ly, *adv.* In a gelatinous manner.

ġē-lā'tion, *n.* [L. *gelatio (-onis)*, a freezing, from *gelare*, to freeze.] The passage of a gas or liquid into a solid state, as by cooling; solidification.

geld, gelt, *n.* [AS. *geld, gild*, tribute, payment, from *geldan, gieldan*, to pay, yield.] Money; tribute; compensation; obsolete except in composition, as in Dane*geld*, or Dane*gelt*, a tax imposed by the Danes; were*geld*, compensation for the life of a man, etc.

geld, *v.t.*; gelded *or* gelt, *pt.*, *pp.*; gelding, *ppr.* [ME. *gelden, gilden*, from Ice. *gelda*, to castrate.]

1. To castrate; to emasculate.

2. To deprive of any essential part. [Rare.]

3. To deprive of anything immodest or exceptionable; to expurgate, as a book. [Obs.]

geld'ȧ-ble, *a.* Capable of being gelded.

geld'ȧ-ble, *a.* Liable to taxes. [Obs.]

geld'ēr, *n.* One who castrates animals.

gel'dēr-rōṣe, *n.* See *Guelder-rose*.

geld'ing, *n.* [ME. *gelding*, a eunuch, a castrated horse, from Ice. *geldingr*, a eunuch, from *geldr*, barren.]

1. A castrated horse or other animal.

2. A castrated man. [Obs.]

ġel'id, *a.* [L. *gelidus*, cool, cold, from *gelu*, frost, cold, from *gelare*, to freeze.] Cold; very cold.

ġē-lid'i-ty, *n.* The state of being gelid.

ġel'id-ly, *adv.* Coldly.

ġel'id-ness, *n.* Coldness.

ġel'ly, *n.* Jelly. [Obs.]

ġē-los'cō-py, *n.* [Gr. *gelōs*, laughter, and *skopein*, to view.] The use of laughter as a means of divination of character.

ġē'lōse, *n.* [*Gelatin* and *-ose*.] In chemistry, a gelatin-like carbohydrate, $C_6H_{10}O_5$, found in Chinese and Ceylon moss.

ġel-sē'miç, ġel-sē-min'iç, *a.* In chemistry, pertaining to gelsemium.

ġel'se-min, ġel'se-mine, *n.* A very bitter, solid alkaloid derived from *Gelsemium sempervirens*, the yellow jasmin.

Ġel-sē'mi-um, *n.* [It. *gelsomino*, jasmin.]

1. In botany, a genus of evergreen climbing shrubs, having showy, large, fragrant yellow flowers. *Gelsemium sempervirens* is the common yellow jasmin of the southern states.

2. [g—] In medicine, a preparation of the root of the yellow jasmin.

gelt, *n.* [Obs.] See *Geld*.

gelt, *n.* A castrated animal; a gelding. [Obs.]

gelt, *n.* Tinsel; gilding. [Obs.]

ġem, *n.* [ME. *gemme*; OFr. *gemme*, a precious stone; It. *gemma*, a precious stone, a bud, from L. *gemma*, a swelling, a bud, a precious stone.]

1. In botany, a bud. [Obs.]

2. A precious stone of any kind, as the diamond, ruby, topaz, emerald, etc., particularly when cut, polished, and set ready for wearing; a jewel.

3. Anything rare or perfect that may be compared to a precious stone; specifically, anything small and beautiful, rare, perfect, brilliant, or finely wrought; as, a *gem* of art; a *gem* of a sonnet; a *gem* of eloquence.

4. A moth of the family *Geometridæ*.

5. In England, a name given to type intermediate in size between diamond and brilliant.

ġem, *v.t.*; gemmed, *pt.*, *pp.*; gemming, *ppr.*

1. To adorn with or as with gems; to bespangle; to bedeck; as, to *gem* a crown; a field *gemmed* with daisies.

A coppice *gemmed* with green and red.
—Tennyson.

2. To bud. [Rare.]

Ge-mä'rȧ, *n.* [Heb. *gemara*, supplement, complement; also thought to mean doctrine, from *gemar*, to learn.] The second division of the Talmud, being a commentary on the preceding part, the Mishnah. Many Jewish writers make it synonymous with the *Talmud*.

Ge-mar'iç, *a.* Pertaining to the Gemara.

Ge-mä'rist, *n.* A teacher or believer in the Gemara.

gē-mä'tri-ȧ, *n.* [Heb.] A method of interpretation of the Hebrew scriptures based upon the numerical value of the letters in the words.

ġem'el, *a.* In heraldry, paired.

ġem'el, *n.* [ME. *gemel*; OFr. *gemel*, a twin, from L. *gemellus*, dim. of *geminus*, a twin.]

1. A twin, or one of twins. [Rare.]

2. In heraldry, either of a pair of bars-gemel.

Gemel.

ġem'el-hinge, *n.* In locksmithing, a hinge composed of a hook and eye.

ġem-el-lip'ȧ-rous, *a.* [L. *gemellus*, twin, and *parere*, to produce.] Producing twins. [Rare.]

ġem'el-ring, *n.* A ring composed of two or more separable rings.

ġem'el-win"dōw, *n.* A window which has two bays.

ġem'i-năl, *n.* A pair. [Obs.]

ġem'i-nāte, *a.* Twin; in couples or pairs; double; binate.

ġem'i-nāte, *v.t.* [L. *geminatus*, pp. of *geminare*, to double, from *geminus*, twin.] To double. [Rare.]

ġem-i-nā'tion, *n.* [L. *geminatio (-onis)*, a doubling, from *geminare*, to double.] A doubling; duplication; repetition. [Rare.]

Ġem'i-nī, *n.pl.* [L., twins.]

1. In astronomy, a constellation or sign of the zodiac, containing the two bright stars Castor and Pollux.

2. A quaint form of oath or expletive, now often corrupted into *jiminy*.

O *Gemini*! I'd sooner cut my tongue out.
—Sheridan.

ġem"i-ni-flō'rous, *a.* [L. *geminus*, double, and *flos (floris)*, a flower.] In botany, having flowers in pairs.

ġem'i-nous, *a.* Geminate.

ġem'mȧ, *n.*; *pl.* **ġem'mæ.** [L., a swelling, bud, gem.]

1. In botany, (a) a leaf-bud; (b) a mass of propagative cells in certain mosses and liverworts.

2. In zoölogy, a budlike outgrowth which becomes entirely or partially separated from the parent body as an independent creature, as in certain of the *Protozoa*.

3. [G—] A genus of small bivalve mollusks.

ġem-mā'ceous, *a.* Of, pertaining to, or resembling leaf-buds.

ġem'mȧ-ry, *n.* [ME. *gemmarye*, a gem-engraver; LL. *gemmarius*, a gem-engraver, jeweler, from L. *gemma*, a gem.]

1. A case for gems; a jewel-house; also, gems collectively; also written *gemmery*.

2. A gem-engraver. [Obs.]

3. Scientific knowledge of gems. [Rare.]

ġem'mȧ-ry, *a.* Pertaining to gems.

ġem'māte, *a.* [L. *gemmatus*, pp. of *gemmare*, to put forth buds.] Having or reproducing by means of buds.

ġem'māte, *v.i.*; gemmated, *pt.*, *pp.*; gemmating, *ppr.* In biology, to put forth buds; to reproduce by budding.

ġem'mā-ted, *a.* 1. Furnished with buds.

2. Having gems or jewels.

ġem-mā'tion, *n.* [L. *gemmatus*, pp. of *gemmare*, to put forth buds.]

1. In botany, the act of budding; the state, form, or construction of the bud of plants.

2. In zoölogy, the process of reproduction by gemmæ; budding.

ġem'mē-ous, *a.* [L. *gemmeus*, pertaining to gems, from *gemma*, a gem.] Pertaining to gems; of the nature of gems.

ġem-mif'ē-ous, *a.* Producing buds; in biology, multiplying by gemmæ.

ġem"mi-fi-çā'tion, *n.* [L. *gemma*, a bud, gem, and *facere*, to make.] In biology, the formation of a bud or gemma.

ġem-mi-flō'rāte, *a.* [L. *gemma*, a bud, gem, and *flos (floris)*, a flower.] Having bud-shaped flowers.

ġem'mi-form, *a.* Budlike.

ġem'mi-ness, *n.* Spruceness; smartness.

ġem-mip'ȧ-ȧ, ġem-mip'ȧ-ræ, *n.pl.* [L., from *gemma*, a bud, gem, and *parere*, to produce.] Animals which grow by budding, as the fresh-water polyp, etc.

ġem-mi-par'i-ty, *n.* Propagation by budding; the state or quality of being gemmiparous.

ġem-mip'ȧ-rous, *a.* [L. *gemma*, a bud, and *parere*, to bear.] Producing buds; reproducing by buds on the body, which mature and fall off into independent animals, as some polyps.

ġem'moid, *a.* [L. *gemma*, a bud, and Gr. *eidos*, resemblance.] Like a bud or a gemma.

ġem-mos'i-ty, *n.* The quality of abounding with gems or resembling a gem. [Obs.]

ġem-mū-lā'tion, *n.* Same as *Gemmation*.

ġem'mūle, *n.* [LL. *gemmula*, dim. of L. *gemma*, a bud.]

1. In botany, a little bud; the plumule; a spore; an ovule.

2. In zoölogy, a little bud; a small gemma; in sponges, a germinal mass of spores; in certain cœlenterates, the ciliated embryo.

ġem-mū-lif'ēr-ous, *a.* [LL. *gemmula*, a little bud, and L. *ferre*, to bear.] Bearing gemmules.

ġem'my, *a.* 1. Bright; glittering; full of gems.

2. Neat; spruce; smart; also written *jemmy*. [Colloq. Eng.]

ge-mōt', ge-mōte', *n.* [AS. *gemot*, an assembly.] A meeting; used chiefly in compounds; as, shire-*gemot*, the county court; witena*gemot*, an assembly of the wise, etc.

gemṣ, *n.* [D.] The chamois.

gemṣ'bok, *n.* [D., from *gems*, the chamois, and *bok*, a buck.] In zoölogy, the male of the *Oryx capensis* of South Africa, an antelope with long and nearly straight horns ending in sharp points; called also *kokama*.

gemṣ'horn, *n.* [G., from *gems*, the chamois, and *horn*, horn.] An organ-stop whose horn-like tones are due to tapering metal pipes.

ge-mŭl', *n.* A small deer of South America, *Cariacus chilensis*, having simple forked horns.

-gen. A suffix from L. *-genus*; Gr. *-genēs*, born, producing, from *gignesthai*, L. *gignere*, to be born, become, and signifying born, produced.

or producing, as in exo*gen*, hydro*gen*, oxy*gen*.

ġe'nȧ, *n.* [L., the cheek.] In zoölogy, the region between the eye and the mouth, generally extended over the zygomatic arch; the triangular area which lies between the eye of trilobites and the free margin of the head.

ġe-nappe', *n.* [From *Genappe*, in Belgium, where it was originally manufactured.] A worsted yarn whose smoothness enables it to be conveniently combined with silk, and so well adapted for braids, fringes, etc.

ġen-därme' (*or Fr. pron.* zhän-därm'), *n.*; *pl.* **ġen'därmeṣ'** or Fr. **gens d'armes.** [Fr., from pl. *gens d'armes*, men-at-arms, from L. *gens* (*-ntis*), a people, nation; *de*, of, from, and *arma*, arms.]

1. A member of a troop of cavalry; a man-at-arms. [Obs.]

2. In France, one of the armed and uniformed national police.

ġen-därm'ẽr-ie, *n.* [Fr.] The French national police collectively, or a similar force; spelled also *gendarmery*.

ġen'dẽr, *n.* [ME. *gendyr*; OFr. *gendre*, kind, gender, from L. *genus* (*generis*), race, kind, stock.]

1. Kind; sort. [Obs.]

2. Sex, male or female. [Colloq.]

3. In grammar, one of those classes or categories into which words are divided according to the sex, natural or metaphorical, of the beings or things they denote; a class of words marked by similarity in termination, the termination having attached to it a distinction in sex, as seen in the termination in nouns, adjectives, etc.

4. A formal distinction in words founded on differences of sexual character.

Common gender; the gender-name assigned to nouns, pronouns, etc., that may be either masculine or feminine, as the word *parent*.

ġen'dẽr, *v.t.*; gendered, *pt.*, *pp.*; gendering, *ppr.* To beget; to engender.

ġen'dẽr, *v.i.* To copulate; to breed. [Obs.]

ġen'dẽr-less, *a.* Without gender.

ġen"ē-ȧ-ġen'e-sis, *n.* [Gr. *genea*, race, stock, and *genesis*, generation.] Alternation of generation.

ġen"ē-ȧ-loġ'iç, ġen"ē-ȧ-loġ'iç-ăl, *a.* Pertaining to genealogy.

Genealogical tree; the genealogy of a family shown in the form of a tree, with roots, stems, and branches.

ġen"ē-ȧ-loġ'iç-ăl-ly, *adv.* In a genealogical manner.

ġen-ē-al'ō-ġist, *n.* One who traces descents of persons or families; a writer upon genealogy.

ġen-ē-al'ō-ġize, *v.i.*, genealogized, *pt.*, *pp.*; genealogizing, *ppr.* To trace or relate genealogy.

ġen-ē-al'ō-ġy, *n.*; *pl.* **ġen-ē-al'ō-ġieṣ.** [ME. *genealogie*; OFr *genealogie*; LL. *genealogia*; Gr. *genealogia*, the tracing of one's descent, genealogy; *genea*, race, stock, and *logos*, a discourse, from *legein*, to speak.]

1. An account or history of the descent of a person or family from an ancestor; enumeration of ancestors and their children in the natural order of succession.

2. Pedigree; lineage; regular descent of a person or family from a progenitor.

3. Genealogical investigation.

ġen'ē-ärçh, *n.* [Gr. *genearchēs*, from *genea*, race, family, and *archein*, to rule.] The head of a tribe, clan, or family.

ġe-nēat' (*or* gen-āt'), *n.* [AS., a companion.] A vassal; one holding land for rent or service.

ġé-né-pï' (zhā-nā-pē'), *n.* [Fr.] A sweet absinthe made from two species of Alpine wormwood.

ġen'e-rȧ, *n.*, pl. of *genus*.

ġen"ẽr-ȧ-bil'i-ty, *n.* Capability of being generated.

ġen'ẽr-ȧ-ble, *a.* [L. *generabilis*, from *generare*, to generate.] Capable of being begotten or generated.

ġen'ẽr-ăl, *a.* [ME. *general*; OFr. *general*, general, common; L. *generalis*, of or belonging to a kind, race, class, general, common, from *genus* (*generis*), kind, class.]

1. Relating to all of a genus, class, or order; including all of a kind; as, a *general* law of the animal kingdom applies to all animals alike.

2. Comprehending many species or individuals; not special or particular; as, it is not logical to draw a *general* conclusion from a particular fact.

3. Lax in signification; not restrained or limited to a particular import; not specific; not directed to a single object; as, a loose and *general* expression.

4. Public; common; relating to or comprehending the whole community; common to many or the greatest number; as, a *general* opinion; a *general* custom; a *general* practitioner.

5. Having a relation to all; common to the whole; as, Adam, our *general* sire.

6. Extensive, though not universal; not limited in scope; used of authority conferred, etc.; as, a *general* officer; a *general* power of attorney.

This word affixed to another word is common in names expressive of rank or office. See such words as *Adjutant-general, Attorney-general.*

General agent; one empowered by his principal to act in all matters of a certain kind or in all matters in general.

General dealer; a dealer in many kinds of goods, especially all kinds of articles for the household or for daily use.

General epistle; one written to the entire church; a canonical or catholic epistle.

General guides: two sergeants, one upon each flank of a battalion, whose duties relate to the accuracy of marching.

General issue; an issue taken by a simple denial of an entire charge, or of its substance, as distinguished from a *special issue* raised by denial of a particular part of the allegation.

General officer; a military officer whose rank is superior to that of colonel; an officer who commands an army, division, or brigade.

General orders; those issued from military headquarters to and relating to the entire command.

General practitioner; a physician who does not specialize in any particular branch of medicine or surgery.

General term; a term which is the sign of a general idea.

General verdict; the verdict in a general issue finding simply for the defendant or for the plaintiff.

General warrant; a warrant directed against no particular individual, but suspected persons generally; now illegal.

Syn.—Common, universal.—*Common* denotes that a thing is often met with; *general* is stronger, denoting that it pertains to a majority of the individuals which compose a genus or whole; *universal*, that it pertains to *all* without exception.

ġen'ẽr-ăl, *n.* 1. The whole; the total; that which comprehends all or the chief part; a general notion or term; opposed to *particular*.

> In particulars our knowledge begins, and so spreads itself by degrees to *generals*.—Locke.

2. The commander of an army or of a division or brigade; a general-in-chief, lieutenant-general, major-general, or brigadier-general; a general officer. In the United States, the full rank of *general* has been held, under temporary laws, only by *Generals* Washington, Grant, Sherman, and Sheridan. In European armies the rank is the highest except that of marshal or field-marshal.

3. The head or chief of organizations more or less military in character; the chief of an order of monks, or of all the houses or congregations established under the same rule; as, the *general* of the Jesuits, or of the Dominicans; the *general* of the Salvation Army.

4. A special form of drum-beat for a general assembly of troops, or for preparation to march.

5. The public; the vulgar. [Obs.]

In general; in the main; for the most part.

ġen-e-rā'li-ȧ, *n.pl.* [L., neut. pl. of *generalis*, general.] Things in general; general principles or terms.

ġen"ẽr-ăl-is'si-mō, *n.* [It., superl. of *generale*, general.] The chief commander of an army or military force; a supreme commander; a commander-in-chief of several armies.

ġen-ẽr-al'i-ty, *n.*; *pl.* **ġen-ẽr-al'i-tieṣ.** [Fr. *généralité*; LL. *generalitas* (*-atis*), from L. *generalis*, general.]

1. The quality or state of being general.

2. The main body; the bulk; the greatest part; as, the *generality* of a nation, or of mankind.

3. An idea or expression of a general, indefinite, and vague nature; a general statement or principle; as, that string of glittering *generalities* proves nothing.

> Let us descend from *generalities* to particulars. —Landor.

ġen'ẽr-ăl-ī-zȧ-ble, *a.* Capable of being stated in general terms, or of being comprehended in a general rule.

ġen"ẽr-ăl-i-zā'tion, *n.* 1. The act or process of extending from particulars to generals; the act of making general, or of comprehending under a common name several objects or phenomena agreeing in essential particulars which the general name serves to indicate.

2. Induction; a general conclusion drawn from specific cases.

> *Generalizations* are apt to be as dangerous as they are tempting. —Lowell.

ġen'ẽr-ăl-īze, *v.t.*; generalized, *pt.*, *pp.*; generalizing, *ppr.* [Fr. *généraliser*, from L. *generalis*, general.]

1. To render general; to bring, as a particular fact or series of facts, into relation with a wider circle of facts.

> Copernicus *generalized* the celestial motions by merely referring them to the moon's motion. Newton *generalized* them still more, by referring this last to the motion of a stone through the air. —Nicholson.

2. To deduce, as a general principle, from the consideration of many particulars.

> A mere conclusion *generalized* from a great multitude of facts. —Coleridge.

3. To apply generally; to make of wider application; as, to *generalize* a rule.

ġen'ẽr-ăl-īze, *v.i.* 1. To combine objects into classes; to employ oneself in generalization.

2. To form inductions; to reason inductively.

ġen'ẽr-ăl-īzed, *a.* In biology, primitive; undifferentiated; synthetic; exhibiting a general type of form or function; not specialized; as, a *generalized* type or structure.

ġen'ẽr-ăl-ī-zẽr, *n.* One who generalizes.

ġen'ẽr-ăl-ly, *adv.* 1. In general; commonly; extensively, though not universally; most frequently, but not without exceptions; as, men are *generally* more disposed to censure than to praise.

2. In the main; without detail; in the whole taken together.

> *Generally* speaking, they live very quietly. —Addison.

3. In a body; collectively. [Rare.]

> Therefore I counsel that all Israel be *generally* gathered unto thee. —2 Sam. xvii. 11.

Syn.—Usually, ordinarily, commonly, mainly, principally, chiefly.

ġen'ẽr-ăl-ness, *n.* General quality; commonness.

ġen'ẽr-ăl-ship, *n.* 1. Military skill in a commander, exhibited in the judicious management of troops or the operations of war.

2. Judicious tactics; leadership; as, the clever *generalship* of a political leader.

3. The office, rank, or person of a general.

> Your *generalship* puts me in mind of Prince Eugene. —Goldsmith.

ġen'ẽr-ăl-ty, *n.* A generality. [Obs.]

ġen'ẽr-ănt, *n.* [OFr. *generant*, from L. *generans* (*-antis*), ppr. of *generare*, to beget.]

1. The power that generates; the power or principle that produces; a generator.

2. In mathematics, same as *generatrix*.

ġen'ẽr-āte, *v.t.*; generated, *pt.*, *pp.*; generating, *ppr.* [L. *generatus*, pp. of *generare*, to beget, produce, from *genus* (*-eris*), race, kind.]

1. To beget; to procreate; to propagate; to engender; as, every animal *generates* his own species.

2. To produce; to cause to be; to bring into existence; to form; to originate; as, the dynamo *generates* an electric current; kindness *generates* affection.

3. To form by motion; to give rise to; as, a line *generates* a surface.

ġen-ẽr-ā'tion, *n.* [L. *generatio* (*-onis*), from *generatus*, pp. of *generare*, to beget.]

1. The act of begetting; reproduction; procreation, as of animals.

2. Production; formation; creation; as, the *generation* of sounds.

3. A single succession in natural descent, as the children of the same parents; the people of the same period or living at the same time; as, the third or fourth *generation*; a *generation* of workers.

4. The average length of life of mankind; the period from any point in the life of the parent to the corresponding point in the life of the child; an age.

5. In mathematics, the bringing into being of a geometrical magnitude by the motion of a point, line, plane, or figure; genesis.

6. In biology, the process by which reproduction is accomplished.

7. A family; a race; a class; any allied group of persons.

Alternate generation; the manner of reproduction of certain organisms, both animals and plants, as mosses, plant-lice, etc., in which the offspring differs in appearance from the progenitor, and in which more than one generation must pass before a descendant will appear of the same type as any given progenitor. Several successive propagations may occur without sexual union, but before the cycle is complete, individuals of one generation develop sexual organs and reproduce sexually.

Spontaneous generation; the supposed creation of living matter from inorganic matter; abiogenesis. The phenomena on which the idea was based are now known to be caused by bacteria, etc.

ġen-ẽr-ā'tion-iṣm, *n.* Traducianism.

ġen'ẽr-ā-tive, *a.* 1. Having the power of generating, producing, or originating.

2. Prolific. [Rare.]

ġen'ẽr-ā-tŏr, *n.* [L. *generator*, from *generare*, to beget, produce.]

1. He who or that which begets, causes, or produces.

2. In music, the principal sound or sounds by which others are produced; the fundamental tone of a series of harmonics or of a chord.

3. A dynamo; any device for transforming heat or mechanical energy into electromotive force.

4. Any device for producing a gas or vapor, as an oxygen-retort, a steam-boiler, etc.

5. In chemistry, a substance from which a compound of greater complexity is made.

6. In mathematics, a generatrix.

ġen′ẽr-ā-trix, *n.* [L., f. of *generator*, a producer, generator, from *generare*, to produce, generate.]

1. A line, point, surface, or figure which generates a mathematical magnitude by its motion.

2. A dynamo.

3. A mother.

ġē-ner′iç, *a.* [L. *genus* (*-eris*), race, kind.]

1. Pertaining to a genus or kind; comprehending the genus, as distinct from species, or from another genus; as, a *generic* name.

2. General in application; comprehending large classes; having a large scope.

ġē-ner′iç-ăl, *a.* Same as *Generic.* [Rare.]

ġē-ner′iç-ăl-ly, *adv.* With regard to genus; as, an animal *generically* distinct from another.

ġē-ner′iç-ăl-ness, *n.* The quality of being generic.

ġē-ner″i-fi-çā′tion, *n.* [L. *genus* (*-eris*), kind, and *facere*, to make.] Generalization. [Rare.]

ġen-ẽr-os′i-ty, *n.*; *pl.* **ġen-ẽr-os′i-tieṣ**. [Fr. *générosité*; L. *generositas*, nobility, excellence, goodness, from *generosus*, of good and noble birth, noble, from *genus*, race, kind.]

1. The quality of being generous; liberality in principle; a disposition to give liberally or to bestow favors.

2. Liberality in act; bounty; munificence.

3. Nobility of birth. [Obs.]

ġen′ẽr-ous, *a.* [OFr. *generous*, generous; L. *generosus*, of good and noble birth, excellent, generous, from *genus* (*-eris*), race, kind.]

1. Of honorable birth or origin. [Obs.]

2. Noble; honorable; magnanimous; as, a *generous* foe; a *generous* critic.

3. Liberal; bountiful; munificent; free to give; as, a *generous* friend; a *generous* father; a *generous* gift.

4. Strong; full of spirit; as, *generous* wine.

5. Full; overflowing; abundant; as, a *generous* cup.

6. Sprightly; courageous; thoroughbred; as, a *generous* steed. [Rare.]

Syn.—Beneficent, bounteous, clever, free, liberal, munificent.

ġen′ẽr-ous-ly, *adv.* In a generous manner; honorably; not meanly; nobly; magnanimously; liberally; munificently.

ġen′ẽr-ous-ness, *n.* 1. The quality of being generous; magnanimity; nobleness of mind.

2. Liberality; munificence; generosity.

ġen′e-sēṣ, *n.*, pl. of *genesis.*

ġen-e-si′ă-çăl, *a.* Relating to the book of Genesis. [Rare.]

ġe-nē′si-ăl, *a.* Of or pertaining to generation.

ġe-nē-si-ol′ō-ġy, *n.* [Gr. *genesis*, origin, generation, and *logos*, description, from *legein*, to speak.] Systematic knowledge relating to generation.

ġen′e-sis, *n.* [L. *genesis*; Gr. *genesis*, birth, origin, from *gignesthai*, to become, to be born.]

1. The act of producing or giving origin to; generation; origination.

2. [G—] The first book of the Old Testament, containing the history of the creation, of the fall of man, of the deluge, and of the first patriarchs. In the original Hebrew, this book has no title; the present title was prefixed to it by those who translated it into Greek.

3. In geometry, the formation of a line, plane, or solid, by the motion of a point, line, or surface.

4. An account of the origin of anything.

Ġen-e-sit′iç, *a.* Pertaining to Genesis; recorded in the book of Genesis. [Rare.]

ġen′et, *n.* A small-sized, well-proportioned Spanish horse; a jennet.

ġen′et, *n.* [OFr. *genette*; Sp. *gineta*; Ar. *jarneit*, a genet.]

1. An animal, *Genetta vulgaris*, allied to the civet, and resembling the polecat in appearance.

2. The fur of *Genetta vulgaris*, or any imitation, as that made from catskin.

ġē-neth′li-aç, *n.* [Gr. *genethliakos*, belonging to a birthday, from *genethlios*, belonging to one's birth, natal, from *genethlē*, birth, origin, from *gignesthai*, to be born.]

1. A birthday poem.

2. One who is versed in genethlialogy.

ġē-neth′li-aç, *a.* Pertaining to nativities, as calculated by astrologers; showing the positions of the stars at the birth of any person.

ġe-neth-lī′aç-ăl, *a.* Genethliac.

ġē-neth′li-açs, *n.* The science of calculating nativities, or predicting the future events of life from the stars which preside at a person's birth.

ġē-neth-li-al′ō-ġy, *n.* Genethliacs; astrology.

ġē-neth-li-at′iç, *n.* A genethliac.

ġē-net′iç, ġē-net′iç-ăl, *a.* [Gr. *genētikos*, having the power of producing generation, from *genesis*, generation.] Of or pertaining to the genesis of anything; pertaining to origin or development; as, a *genetical* definition.

ġē-net′iç-ăl-ly, *adv.* In accordance with the laws of natural production.

ġen′e-ting, *n.* Same as *Jenneting.*

Ġē-nē′vȧ, *n.* The principal city of Switzerland, a favorite place for international assemblages.

Geneva arbitration; the arbitration of the claims of the United States against Great Britain for damages done by privateers built in Great Britain to prey upon United States ships during the Civil War. The arbitrators met in Geneva in 1872 and awarded damages to the amount of $15,500,000, which was paid and distributed among those who had suffered losses.

Geneva Bible; the English translation of the Bible published in Geneva in 1560, being the first English Bible printed in Roman type, divided into verses, and without the Apocrypha.

Geneva Convention; an agreement signed by the continental powers of Europe at Geneva in 1864 and by Great Britain in 1865, providing for the neutrality of ambulances and hospitals in time of war, and for the protection and immunity from capture of those engaged in succoring the sick and wounded.

Geneva cross; a red Greek cross on a white ground, the emblem adopted by the Geneva Convention as a means of protection, in time of war, for persons serving with ambulances and hospitals. It is displayed on flags and armlets.

ġē-nē′vȧ, *n.* [Fr. *genièvre*, juniper-berry, from L. *juniperus*, the juniper-tree.] A spirit distilled from grain or malt, with the addition of juniper-berries; Holland gin; gin.

Ġē-nē′văn, *n.* 1. A resident of Geneva.

2. A believer in Genevanism.

Ġē-nē′văn, *a.* Pertaining to Geneva; Genevese.

Ġē-nē′văn-iṣm, *n.* [So called from the residence of Calvin in Geneva.] Calvinism.

Ġen-e-vēṣe′, *a.* and *n.* I. *a.* Pertaining to Geneva in Switzerland; Genevan.

II. *n.* One born or residing in Geneva.

ġen-e-vrette′, *n.* [Fr. *genévrier*, the juniper, from *genièvre*, L. *juniperus*, the juniper-tree.] A European wine made of wild fruits and flavored with juniper-berries.

ġēn′iăl, *a.* [L. *genialis*, pertaining to generation or birth, nuptial, from *genius*, the guardian deity or genius of a person.]

1. Contributing to propagation or production; generative; relating to marriage; nuptial. [Rare.]

2. Enlivening; contributing to life and cheerfulness; supporting life; as, *genial* showers.

3. Native; natural. [Obs.]

4. Characterized by kindly warmth of disposition and manners, such as promotes cheerfulness on the part of others; cordial; kindly; sympathetically cheerful; as, a fine *genial* nature.

> The celebrated drinking ode of this *genial* archdeacon. —Warton.

5. Relating to or exhibiting genius. [Rare.]

> Men of genius have often attached the highest value to their less *genial* works.—Hare.

Genial gods; in mythology, the gods presiding over generation.

Syn.—Warm, cordial, pleasant, cheering, merry, hearty, revivifying, restorative, inspiriting.

ġē′ni-ăl, *a.* [Gr. *geneion*, chin.] In anatomy, of or relating to the anterior part of the lower jaw; as, a *genial* tubercle.

ġē-ni-al′i-ty, *n.* Gaiety; cheerfulness.

ġēn′iăl-ly, *adv.* In a genial manner; cheerfully; cordially.

> The splendid sun *genially* warmeth the fertile earth. —Harris.

ġēn′iăl-ness, *n.* The quality of being genial.

ġē-nī′ăn, *a.* Pertaining to the chin; genial.

ġē-niç′ū-lāte, *v.t.* To form joints or knots in; to bend like a knee-joint.

ġē-niç′ū-lāte, ġē-niç′ū-lā-ted, *a.* [L. *geniculatus*, having knee-joints, jointed, from *geniculum*, dim. of *genu*, knee.] Kneed; knee-jointed; having joints like the knee, a little bent; as, a *geniculate* stem or peduncle.

ġē-niç-ū-lā′tion, *n.* 1. Knottiness; the state of having knots or joints like a knee.

2. Genuflection; kneeling. [Obs.]

3. In anatomy, a geniculate formation.

ġē′nie, *n.* [OFr. *genie*; L. *genius*, a guardian deity, genius.]

1. Genius; disposition; turn of mind.

2. A genius; a demon; a jinnee.

ġē′ni-ī, *n.* Latin plural of *genius.*

ġē′ni-ō, *n.* [It., from L. *genius*, a genius.] A man of a particular turn of mind. [Rare.]

ġē″ni-ō-hȳ′oid, *a.* [Gr. *geneion*, chin, and *hyoeidēs*, hyoid.] In anatomy, connected with the chin and hyoid bone.

Ġen′i-pȧ, *n.* [L., from native W. Ind. name.] A genus of tropical trees of the family *Rubiaceæ.*

ġen′i-pap, *n.* The fruit of the genip-tree.

ġen′ip-tree, *n.* 1. A tree of the genus *Genipa.*

2. A West Indian name for *Melicocca bijuga* and *Hypelate paniculata* of Jamaica.

ġen-i-sä′rō, *n.* [Native name.] A Nicaraguan tree, *Pithecolobium Saman*, the pods of which are used as food for cattle.

Ġē-nis′tȧ, *n.* [L. *genista*, *genesta*, the broom corn.] A large genus of leguminous plants of which the woadwaxen or dyer's-greenweed, *Genista tinctoria*, is probably the best known. It was formerly much used in dyeing, yielding a green color.

Dyer's-greenweed (*Genista tinctoria*).

ġen′i-tăl, *a.* [ME. *genital*; OFr. *genital*; L. *genitalis*, pertaining to generation or birth, from *genitus*, pp. of *gignere*, to beget.] Pertaining to the act or organs of generation.

Genital cord; in embryology, a structure in the fetus of the human species and of most mammals, formed by the union of the ducts, and giving rise to the genital passages in both male and female.

ġen-i-tā′li-ȧ, *n.pl.* [L., neut. pl. of *genitalis*, genital.] The genitals.

ġen′i-tălṣ, *n.pl.* The parts which are the immediate instruments of generation; the sexual organs.

ġen′i-ting, *n.* Same as *Jenneting.*

ġen-i-tī′văl, *a.* Having genitive form; relating to the genitive case in grammar.

ġen′i-tive, *a.* [L. *genitivus*, *genetivus*, pertaining to birth or generation; in grammar, the genitive case, from *genitus*, pp. of *gignere*, to beget, produce.] Pertaining to a case of nouns in Latin and Greek grammar corresponding to the possessive case in English and indicating source or possession.

ġen′i-tive, *n.* The genitive case.

Genitive absolute; in Greek grammar, a construction corresponding to the ablative absolute in Latin. [See *Ablative absolute* under *Ablative.*]

ġen-i-tō-. A combining form from L. *genitus*, pp. of *gignere*, to beget, signifying relation to the genital organs.

ġen″i-tō-çrū′răl, *a.* [*Genito-*, and L. *crus*, *cruris*, the leg.] Connected with the thigh, and the external genital organs; as, the *genitocrural* nerve.

ġen′i-tŏr, *n.* [L., from *genitus*, pp. of *gignere*, to beget.]

1. One who engenders; a father; a sire.

2. [*pl.*] The genital organs. [Obs.]

ġen″i-tō-ū′ri-nā-ry, *a.* [*Genito-*, and L. *urina*, urine.] Same as *Urogenital.*

ġen′i-tūre, *n.* [OFr. *geniture*; L. *genitura*, a begetting, birth, from *genitus*, pp. of *gignere*, to beget.] Generation; procreation; birth.

ġēn′ius, *n.*; *pl.* **ġēn′ius-eṣ** *or* **ġē′ni-ī**. [L. *genius*, the guardian deity or spirit of a person, spirit, natural ability, genius, from *gignere* to produce.]

1. A tutelary deity; the ruling and protecting power of men, places, or things; a good or evil spirit supposed to be attached to a person and influence his actions. In this sense the plural is *genii.*

> Still had she gazed; but midst the tide
> Two angel forms were seen to glide,
> The *genii* of the stream. —Gray.

2. The peculiar structure of mind which is given by nature to an individual; a particular natural talent or aptitude of mind which fits a man in an eminent degree for a particular study or course of life; as, a *genius* for history, for poetry, or painting.

> A *genius* for friendship. —Scott.

3. Intellectual endowment of the highest kind; uncommon powers of intellect, particularly the power of invention or of producing original combinations; as, Homer was a man of *genius.*

> The true *genius* is a mind of large general powers, accidentally determined to some particular direction. —Johnson.

4. A man endowed with uncommon vigor of mind; a man of superior intellectual faculties; as, Shakspere was a rare *genius.*

5. The distinguishing character, bent, or tendency, as of a nation, a religion, a political constitution, or the like; peculiar character; peculiar constitution; pervading spirit or influence from associations or otherwise; as, the

genius of the times; the *genius* of a language; the *genius* of Christianity or of the Semitic races.

Syn.—Talent, wisdom, faculty, aptitude, ability, parts, ingenuity, capacity, cleverness.—*Genius* implies peculiar gifts of nature impelling the mind to certain favorite kinds of mental effort, and producing new combinations of ideas. *Talent* supposes general strength of intellect, with a peculiar aptitude for being molded and directed to specific employments, and valuable ends and purposes.

ġen′ō-blast, *n.* [Gr. *genos*, sex, and *blastos*, germ.] The nucleus of a fertilized ovum, considered as bisexual.

Ġen-ō-ēse′, *n. sing.* and *pl.* One born or resident in Genoa, Italy; the people of Genoa, collectively; also called *Genovese.*

Ġen-ō-ēse′, *a.* Pertaining to Genoa, a city of northwestern Italy

ġē-nöuil-lère′ (zhē-nö-lyãr′), *n.* [Fr., from *génou*; L *genu*, knee.]

1 In ancient armor, a metal covering for the knee.

2. In fortification the part of a parapet lying below the sill of an embrasure

Genouillères.

-ge-nous. A suffix from L *-genus*, producing, born, from *gignere*, to beget, used as a termination of adjectives formed from nouns in *-gen*. to signify producing, as in endo*genous*, nitro*genous*; also added to words to signify born or native, as in indi*genous*, monti*genous*

Ġen-ō-vēse′, *a.* and *n.* Same as *Genoese.*

ġen′re (zhon′r), *n.* [Fr., kind, genus, from L. *genus, generis*, kind.]

1. A style in painting which depicts ordinary life, domestic scenes, etc.

2. Genus; kind; form; style. [Rare.]

ġenṣ, *n.*; *pl.* **ġen′tēṣ.** [L., a clan or family, from Old L. *genere*, to beget, produce.]

1. In Roman history, a family or clan bearing a common name and having a common ancestry.

2. Among primitive peoples, a group whose members have a common descent.

ġent, *a.* Elegant; pretty; gentle; polished; refined. [Obs.]

ġent, *n.* A colloquial and somewhat vulgar abbreviation for *gentleman.*

> The thing named "pants" in certain documents,
> A word not made for gentlemen, but *gents.*
> —Holmes.

ġen-teel′, *a.* [Fr. *gentil*, noble, from L. *gentilis*, of the same clan or race; from *gens, gentis*, race.]

1. Polite; well-bred; refined in manners or behavior; having the manners of well-bred people; as, *genteel* company; *genteel* guests.

2. Easy and graceful; becoming well-bred persons; as, *genteel* manners or behavior; a *genteel* address.

3. Free from anything low or vulgar; dealing with the habits or manners of well-bred society; not partaking of farce or buffoonery; as, *genteel* comedy.

4. Sufficient to maintain a person in a comfortable position in life; furnishing a competence; as, a *genteel* income.

Syn.—Polite, well-bred, well-mannered, well-behaved, refined, polished, elegant, mannerly.

ġen-teel′ish, *a.* More or less genteel.

ġen-teel′ly, *adv.* In a genteel manner.

ġen-teel′ness, *n.* The quality of being genteel.

ġen′tēṣ, *n.*, pl of *gens.*

ġen′tiăn (-shăn), *n.* [ME. *gencyan*; OFr. *gentiane*; L. *gentiana*, gentian, said to be named from *Gentius*, an Illyrian king who was the first to discover its properties.] A plant of the genus *Gentiana*, having opposite leaves and a corolla with four or five lobes. The roots of some varieties are used as tonics in medicine, as that of the yellow gentian, *Gentiana lutea*, a native of Switzerland.

Gentian Plant (*Gentiana lutea*).

Ġen-ti-an′ȧ (-shi-an′ȧ), *n.* A genus of plants typical of the order *Gentianaceæ.*

Ġen″ti-an-ā′cē-æ (-shi-an-ā′sē-ē), *n.pl.* A large order of monopetalous exogens, consisting for the most part of herbaceous plants, with opposite leaves, and yellow, red, blue, or white flowers. The typical genus is *Gentiana*. All are characterized by their bitter principle, which is employed in medicine.

ġen-tiăn-ā′ceous, *a.* Pertaining to the *Gentianaceæ.*

ġen-tiăn-el′lȧ, *n.* [L., from dim. of *gentiana*, gentian.]

1. A kind of blue color.

2. A species of dwarfed gentian, *Gentiana acaulis*, native to the Alps.

ġen-ti-an′iç (-shi-), *a.* Pertaining to the gentian.

ġen′tiăn-in, *n.* A bitter substance derived from the yellow gentian, *Gentiana lutea.*

ġen′tiăn-ōse, *n.* A substance resembling sugar, derived from the gentian.

ġen′tiăn-wŏrt, *n.* Any plant of the order *Gentianaceæ.*

ġen′til, *a.* Gentle. [Obs.]

ġen′tīle, *n.* [L. *gentilis*, belonging to the same race, stock, or family, from *gens, gentis*, race, stock, from *gignere*, to beget, produce.]

1. In Scripture, a pagan; a worshiper of false gods; any person not a Jew or a Christian; a heathen. In the United States, among the Mormons a person outside of their church; commonly written with a capital.

2. In grammar, a noun or adjective derived from the name of a country or place and designating its inhabitants; as, the words *American, Englishman, Spanish* are *gentiles.*

ġen′tīle, *a.* 1. Pertaining to a heathen or non-Jewish nation; pertaining to persons who are not Mormons.

2. In grammar, denoting race or country; as, a *gentile* noun.

ġen-ti-lesse′, *n.* Complaisance; courtesy. [Obs.]

ġen′tīl-ish, *a.* Heathenish; pagan. [Obs.]

ġen′til-iṣm, *n.* 1. Heathenism; paganism.

2. Clannishness.

3. The state of being a gentile.

ġen-ti-li′tious, ġen-ti-li′tiăl (-lish′us, -lish′ăl), *a.* [L. *gentilitius*, pertaining to a clan or gens, from *gentilis*, of or belonging to the same clan or gens, from *gens, gentis*, a clan or gens.]

1. Peculiar to a people; national.

2. Hereditary; entailed on a family.

ġen-til′i-ty, *n.* [ME. *gentylete*; OFr. *gentilite*, gentle birth, from L. *gentilitas (-atis)*, relationship in the same gens, from *gens, gentis*, a gens, clan, tribe.]

1. The quality of being genteel; politeness of manners; easy, graceful behavior; the manners of well-bred people; genteelness.

2. Good extraction; dignity of birth. [Rare.]

3. Gentry. [Rare.]

4. Paganism; heathenism. [Obs.]

ġen′til-ize, *v.i.* To live like a heathen; also, to play the gentleman. [Obs.]

ġen′til-ize, *v.t.* To cause to be gentle or genteel; to render gentlemanly. [Rare.]

ġen′til-ly, *adv.* [Obs.] See *Gently.*

ġen″ti-ō-piç′rin, *n.* [*Gentian*, and Gr. *pikros*, bitter.] A bitter substance derived from gentian-root; also spelled *gentiopikrin.*

ġen′ti-sin, *n.* Gentianin.

ġen′tle, *a.*; *comp.* gentler; *superl.* gentlest. [ME. *gentel*; OFr. *gentil*, of noble or good birth, from L. *gentilis*, of or belonging to the same class or gens, from *gens, gentis*, race, family.]

1. Well-born; of a good family or respectable birth, though not noble.

2. Mild; meek; bland; not rough, harsh, or severe; as, a *gentle* nature, temper, or voice.

3. Tame; peaceable; not wild, turbulent, or refractory; as, a *gentle* horse or beast.

4. Soothing; pacific; easy; soft; not violent or abrupt; as, a *gentle* breeze; a *gentle* slope.

The gentle sex; women collectively; opposed to *the sterner sex.*

Syn.—Tame, mild, meek, placid, pacific, quiet, soft, peaceful, moderate, kind, indulgent.—*Gentle* describes the natural disposition; *tame*, that which is subdued by training; *mild* implies a temper which is, by nature, not easily provoked; *meek*, a spirit which has been schooled to mildness by discipline or suffering.

ġen′tle, *n.* 1. A gentleman. [Obs. or Poet.]

2. A maggot or larva of the flesh-fly, used in fishing.

3. A falcon trained for sport.

ġen′tle, *v.t.* 1. To make gentle; to raise from a vulgar condition. [Obs.]

2. To render docile or kind; to soften; to subdue; as, to *gentle* a colt.

ġen′tle-fōlk (-fōk), *n.* Persons of good breeding and family, a collective noun; now usually in the plural, *gentlefolks.*

ġen′tle-heärt″ed, *a.* Having a gentle disposition.

ġen′tle-măn, *n.* [ME. *gentilman, gentylman*, a nobleman, gentleman.]

1. A man of good breeding, kindness, courtesy, and honor; a man having worthy ideals and refinement of thought and action.

2. Any man of ordinary respectability and good behavior, regardless of occupation, family, or the like; in the plural, the ordinary courteous form of address to a company of men.

3. In England, a man of good family or good social position; every man above the rank of yeomen, including noblemen; in a more limited sense, a man who without a title bears a coat of arms, or whose ancestors have been freemen; in this sense *gentlemen* hold a middle rank between the nobility and yeomanry.

4. In a loose sense, every man whose education, occupation, or income raises him above menial service or an ordinary trade.

> In its more elevated signification the word *gentleman* has in every age signified the conduct, character, habits, and outward appearance, in whomsoever found, which, according to the ideas of that age, belonged, or were expected to belong, to persons born and educated in a high social position.
> —Bain.

5. A personal attendant; a valet; as, a gentleman's *gentleman.* [Colloq.]

The old gentleman; the devil. [Colloq.]

ġen′tle-măn-at-ärmṣ′, *n.* In England, one of a band of forty gentlemen, with six officers, whose office it is to attend the king on state occasions.

ġen′tle-măn-hood, *n.* The condition or character of a gentleman.

ġen′tle-măn-like, *a.* Gentlemanly.

ġen′tle-măn-li-ness, *n.* The state or quality of being gentlemanly.

ġen′tle-măn-ly, *a.* Pertaining to, like, or becoming a gentleman; polite; courteous; as, *gentlemanly* manners; a *gentlemanly* officer.

ġen′tle-măn-ship, *n.* The character of a gentleman.

ġen′tle-ness, *n.* The quality of being gentle; mildness; tenderness; softness; ease.

ġen′tle-ship, *n.* The deportment of a gentleman. [Obs.]

ġent′lesse, *n.* Gentilesse. [Obs.]

ġen′tle-wom″ăn (-woom″), *n.* 1. A woman of good family or of good breeding; a woman above the vulgar; a lady.

2. A woman who attends upon a person of high rank.

ġen′tly, *adv.* 1. In a gentle manner; mildly; tenderly; gradually.

2. After the manner of the gentle of birth; as, *gently* bred.

Ġen-tọọ′, *n.* [Port. *gentio*, a heathen, a gentile.] A language of Hindustan; a Hindu. [Obs.]

ġen′try, *n.* [ME. *gentry, gentrie*, noble or high birth, from OFr. *genterise, gentilise*, rank, nobility.]

1. People of refinement, means, and leisure, or of good birth; especially, in England, the class between the nobility and the yeomanry.

2. Any class of society, in an ironical sense; as, the sporting *gentry.*

3. Civility; complaisance; courtesy. [Obs.]

4. Birth; condition; rank by birth. [Obs.]

ġen′ty, *a.* Neat; trim; slender. [Scot.]

ġē′nū, *n.*; *pl.* **ġen′ū-ȧ.** [L., the knee.] In anatomy, primarily the knee or kneejoint; hence, any body with a knee-like angle; as, the *genu* of the callosum or of the optic tract.

ġen-ū-fleçt′, *v.i.*; genuflected, *pt., pp.*; genuflecting, *ppr.* [L. *genu*, the knee, and *flectere*, to bend.] To make a genuflection.

ġen-ū-fleç′tion, *n.* [LL. *genuflexio (-onis)*, from L. *genu*, the knee, and *flectere*, to bend.] The act of bending the knee, as in worshiping, courtesying, etc.; also spelled *genuflexion.*

ġen′ū-ine, *a.* [L. *genuinus*, innate, natural, from *gignere*, to beget.] Belonging to, derived from, or descended from the original source or stock; not spurious, counterfeit, or false; authentic; typical; pure; as, a *genuine* heir; a *genuine* woman; a *genuine* text.

2. In zoölogy, conformable to type; as, the *genuine* whales.

Syn.—Natural, real, true, unalloyed, unadulterated, unaffected, veritable, authentic.

ġen′ū-ine-ly, *adv.* In a genuine manner.

ġen′ū-ine-ness, *n.* The quality of being genuine.

ġē′nus, *n.*; *pl.* **ġen′e-rȧ.** [L. *genus*, birth, origin, descent, race, from *gen*, the root of *gignere*, to beget; Gr. *gignesthai*, to become.]

1. In biology, a group of species agreeing with one another in the broad features of their organization but differing in detail, such differences being relatively constant and the species composing the group infertile with one another. In the classification of animals and plants the genus ranks next above the species, which constitutes the basic unit, and next below the family, which is a group of genera.

2. In logic, a class of like objects or ideas, having several subordinate species; a class of greater extent than a species.

Subaltern genus; in logic, a genus which may become a species of some higher division or classification.

Summum genus; in logic, a genus which is the highest; that is, which cannot become a species in a higher genus.

ġē′nys, *n.* See *Gonys.*

geo-. A combining form from Gr. *gē*, the earth, and signifying earth, soil, ground, as in *geology, geography*, etc.

ġē-ō-bot′ȧ-ny, *n.* Geographical botany.

ġē-ō-cen′triç, ġē-ō-cen′triç-ăl, *a.* [*Geo-*, and Gr. *kentron*, center.] Pertaining to the earth as a center; considering the earth, or the center of the earth, as the point from which a heavenly body is seen or measured, or as a center of cosmic forces or development; as, the *geocentric* position of a planet; a *geocentric* system of cosmogony.

ġē-oc′rō-nīte, *n.* [*Geo-*, and Gr. *Kronos*, Saturn, the alchemistic name of lead.] A crystalline mineral containing lead, antimony, sulphur, and arsenic.

ġē-o-cyc′liç, *a.* [*Geo-*, and Gr. *kyklos*, a circle.]

1. Of or relating to the movements of the earth; as, a *geocyclic* diagram.

2. Moving round the earth in regular periods.

ġē′ōde, *n.* [Gr. *gaiōdēs*, *geōdēs*, earthlike; *gē*, earth, and *eidos*, form.]

1. A hollow, rounded nodule of rock, the cavity of which is lined with crystals or filled with either solids or liquids.

2. The cavity of a hollow rock nodule or a similar cavity in bedded rock.

ġē-ō-des′iç, ġē-ō-des′iç-ăl, *a.* Geodetic.

ġē-ō-des′iç, *n.* A geodetic line.

ġē-od′e-sist, *n.* A person skilled in geodesy.

ġē-od′e-sy, *n.* [Gr. *geōdaisia*, the art of mensuration; *gē*, the earth, and *daiein*, to divide.] That part of practical geometry which has for its object the determination of the magnitude and figure either of the whole earth or of any given portion of its surface, especially of a large portion.

ġē-ō-det′iç, ġē-ō-det′i-çăl, *a.* Pertaining to geodesy; determined or produced by geodetic processes; geodesic; as, a *geodetic* survey; *geodetic* instruments.

Geodetic line or *curve*; the shortest line upon any surface, as of the earth, connecting two points.

ġē-ō-det′içs, *n.* Geodesy.

ġē-ō-dif′e-rous, *a.* Bearing or having geodes; as, a *geodiferous* stratum.

ġē′ō-duck, *n.* [Am. Ind.] A large clam, *Glycymeris generosa*, of the California coast.

ġē-ō-gen′iç, *a.* Of or pertaining to geogeny.

ġē-oġ′e-nous, *a.* [*Geo-*, and Gr. *-genēs*, produced.] Living in or on the soil, as certain fungi.

ġē-oġ′e-ny, *n.* The study of the origin or genesis of the earth and its formation; also called *geogony*.

ġē-og-nō′sis, *n.* Geognosy. [Rare.]

ġē′og-nost, *n.* [*Geo-*, and Gr. *gnōstes*, one who knows.] A person proficient in geognosy.

ġē-og-nos′tiç, ġē-og-nos′tiç-ăl, *a.* Relating to geognosy; geological. [Rare.]

ġē-og′nō-sy, *n.* [*Geo-*, and Gr. *gnōsis*, knowledge, from *gignōskein*, to know.] The systematic study of the materials composing the earth and of their structural relations; geognosis· geology.

ġē-ō-gon′iç, ġē-ō-gon′iç-ăl, *a.* See *Geogenic*.

ġē-og′o-ny, *n.* See *Geogeny*.

ġē-og′rȧ-phẽr, *n.* One who is versed in geography, or one who compiles a treatise on the subject.

ġē-ō-graph′iç-ăl, ġē-ō-graph′iç, *a.* [LL. *geographicus*; Gr. *geographikos*, of or for geography, from *geōgraphia*, geography.] Relating to geography.

Geographical distribution; see under *Distribution*.

Geographical mile; see under *Mile*.

Geographical variation; a variation of species or variety coincident with or due to variation in geographical location.

ġē-ō-graph′iç-ăl-ly, *adv.* In a geographical manner.

ġē-og′rȧ-phy, *n*; *pl.* **ġē-og′rȧ-phieş.** [L. *geographia*; Gr. *geographia*, geography; *gē*, the earth, and *graphein*, to write.]

1. Systematized knowledge regarding the earth's surface as it exists, its physical features and phenomena, the living creatures upon it, especially man, and the political divisions of mankind. From astronomy, it borrows the knowledge of the earth's relations to the sun as a planet, its motions, form, magnitude, and the resulting physical phenomena (astronomical geography). From applied mathematics, as geodesy and topography, it derives a systematic delineation of the surface (mathematical geography). Physics and geology as used by physiography outline the surface, formation and materials, the natural divisions, the climates, the animal and plant life, with its distribution, and the general physical phenomena (physical geography). From anthropology, especially the divisions of history and ethnology, it gains the knowledge of the political divisions and the races of men, with their social customs and political organizations (political geography).

2. A treatise or text-book treating upon such knowledge.

ġē′oid, *n.* [Gr. *geoidēs*, *geōdēs*, earthlike; *gē*, the earth, and *eidos*, form, resemblance.] A spheroidal figure considered as being coincident with the earth at the mean ocean-level; the earth as it would be if all parts above mean ocean-level were removed and all lower parts were filled.

ġē-ō-ī′sō-thẽrm, *n.* [*Geo-*, and Gr. *isos*, equal, and *thermē*, heat.] An isogeotherm; a line of equal temperatures below the earth's surface.

ġē-ol′ȧ-try, *n.* [*Geo-*, and Gr. *latreia*, worship.] Worship of things terrestrial or of the earth itself.

ġē-ol′o-ġẽr, ġē-ō-lō′ġi-ăn, *n.* A geologist. [Rare.]

ġē-ō-loġ′iç, ġē-ō-loġ′iç-ăl, *a.* Relating to geology.

ġē-ō-loġ′iç-ăl-ly, *adv.* From a geological viewpoint; according to geological laws.

ġē-ol′ō-ġist, *n.* One versed in the science of geology.

ġē-ol′ō-ġize, *v.i.*; geologized, *pt.*, *pp.*; geologizing, *ppr.* To study geology; to make geological investigations.

ġē-ol′ō-ġy, *n.*; *pl.* **ġē-ol′ō-ġieş.** [*Geo-*, and Gr. *logos*, a description, from *legein*, to speak.]

1. The science which deals with the structure of the crust of the globe and of the substances which compose it; or the science of the minerals or aggregate substances which compose the earth, the relations which the several constituent masses bear to each other, their formation, structure, position, and history. It also investigates the successive changes that have taken place in the organic and inorganic kingdoms and inquires into the causes of these changes and the influence which they have exerted in modifying the surface and external structure of our planet.

2. A geological treatise, especially a text-book.

ġē-om′ȧ-lişm, *n.* [*Geo-*, and Gr. *homalos*, even, level.] In biology, a tendency toward equal lateral development because of gravitation.

ġē′ō-man-cẽr, *n.* One who foretells or divines by geomancy.

ġē′ō-man-cy, *n.* [ME. *geomancie*; OFr. *geomancie*; LL. *geomantia*; Gr. *gē*, the earth, and *manteia*, divination.] A kind of divination by figures or lines, formed by dots or points, originally on the earth and afterward on paper.

ġē-ō-man′tiç, ġē-ō-man′tiç-ăl, *a.* Pertaining to geomancy.

ġē-om′e-tẽr, *n.* [L. *geometres*; Gr. *geōmetrēs*, a mathematician, geometer, *gē*, the earth, and *metron*, a measure.]

1. One skilled in geometry.

2. In zoölogy, any moth of the *Geometridæ*.

ġē-om′e-trăl, *a.* Pertaining to geometry. [Obs.]

ġē-ō-met′riç, ġē-ō-met′riç-ăl, *a.* [L. *geometricus*; Gr. *geōmetrikos*, belonging to geometry, from *geōmetria*, geometry.]

1. Pertaining to geometry; according to the rules or principles of geometry; done by geometry.

2. Having as a boundary a succession of straight lines; characterized by or made up of straight lines and angles; as, a *geometric* style; *geometrical* markings of a butterfly's wing.

Geometrical construction; the representation of a proposition by geometrical lines.

Geometrical lathe; see *Cycloidal engine* under *Engine*.

Geometrical pace; five feet in measure.

Geometrical plane; the horizontal projective plane in perspective drawing.

Geometrical progression; see under *Progression*.

Geometrical proportion; see under *Proportion*.

Geometrical radius; the distance from the center of a cogwheel to the pitch-line.

Geometrical ratio; see under *Ratio*.

Geometrical spider; a spider spinning a web more or less circular and intersected by radial lines, as the ordinary garden-spider.

Geometrical stairs; those stairs of which the steps are supported only at one end by being built into the wall.

Geometric curves or *geometric lines*; those in which the relation between the abscissas and ordinates is expressed by a finite algebraic equation.

Geometric decorated style; in architecture, applied to the earlier period of decorated Gothic, in which the tracery and other ornamentation consist entirely of distinct geometrical forms, the principle of verticality and unity by a subordination of parts being fully developed.

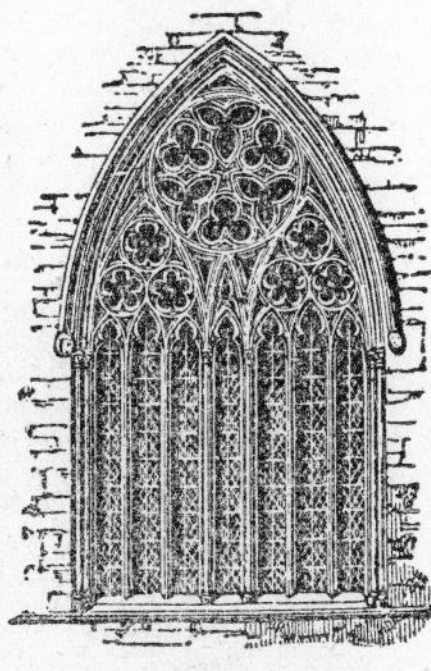

Geometric Decorated Style, as shown in Window.

ġē-ō-met′riç-ăl-ly, *adv.* In a geometrical way; according to geometry.

ġē-om-e-trī′ciăn, (-trish′ăn), *n.* One skilled in geometry; a geometer.

ġē-om′e-trid, *n.* Any moth of the family *Geometridæ*.

ġē-om′e-trid, *a.* Of or relating to the *Geometridæ*.

Gē-ō-met′ri-dæ, *n.pl.* [L., from Gr. *geōmetrēs*, earth-measurer, and *eidos*, resemblance.] A family comprising the moths whose larval forms are known as measuring-worms.

ġē-ō-met′ri-fọrm, *a.* Having the form of a geometrid.

ġē-om′e-trize, *v.i.*; geometrized, *pt.*, *pp.*; geometrizing, *ppr.* To act according to the laws of geometry; to perform geometrically.

ġē-om′e-try, *n.*; *pl.* **ġē-om′e-trieş.** [ME. *geometrie*, *gemetrie*; OFr. *geometrie*; L. *geometria*; Gr. *geōmetria*, the measurement of land, geometry; *gē*, the earth, land, and *metria*, measurement, from *metrein*, to measure.]

1. The science of magnitude in general; the science which treats of the properties of definite portions of space; that science which treats of the properties of lines, angles, surfaces, and solids; that branch of mathematics which treats of the properties and relations of magnitudes.

2. A text-book or other treatise on this science.

Analytical geometry; geometry in which position is represented algebraically, analytical methods of reasoning being used.

Descriptive geometry; see under *Descriptive*.

Elementary or *Euclidean geometry*; that branch of the science based upon the methods and axioms of Euclid, the Alexandrian geometer, and dealing only with the properties of the cone and conic sections, the sphere, the cylinder, solids having plane faces, planes, and straight lines.

Higher or *non-Euclidean geometry*; that branch of the science which uses methods other than those of Euclid and assumes his axiom concerning parallel lines not to be true, holding that such lines diverge toward infinity (*hyperbolic geometry*), or converge toward infinity (*elliptic geometry*).

ġē′ō-mọr-phy, *n.* The study of the form of the earth.

ġē-on′ō-my, *n.* [*Geo-*, and Gr. *nomos*, law.] The science comprehending the physical laws which concern the earth.

ġē-oph′ȧ-ġişm, *n.* [*Geo-*, and Gr. *phagein*, to eat.] The practice of eating clay, chalk, or other earth.

ġē-oph′ȧ-ġist, *n.* An earth-eater.

ġē-oph′ȧ-gous, *a.* Earth-eating.

Gē-oph′i-lȧ, *n.pl.* [L., from Gr. *gē*, earth, and *philos*, loving, from *philein*, to love.] In zoölogy, the division of gasteropods to which slugs and land-snails belong.

ġē-ō-pon′iç, ġē-ō-pon′iç-ăl, *a.* [Gr. *geōponikos*, pertaining to agriculture, from *geōponia*, agriculture, from *geōponos*, a tiller of the earth; *gē*, earth, and *ponos*, work, from *penesthai*, to work, toil.] Pertaining to tillage of the earth, or agriculture.

ġē-ō-pon′içs, *n.* Agriculture. [Obs.]

ġē-ō-rȧ′mȧ, *n.* [*Geo-*, and Gr. *horama*, a view, from *horan*, to see.] A large hollow globe or spherical chamber, lined with cloth on which is depicted a general view of the geography of the earth's surface so as to be seen by a spectator from the interior.

ġeọr′die, *n.* [Nickname for *George*.]

1. The miner's safety-lamp invented by George Stephenson. [Prov. Eng.]

2. In England, a coal-miner, or a collier sailing on the English coast.

3. A guinea bearing an image of St. George. [Prov. Eng. and Scot.]

Geọrġe, *n.* [Fr. *George*; LL. *Georgius*, from Gr. *geōrgos*, a husbandman, farmer; *gē*, the earth, and *ergon*, work.]

1. A figure of St. George on horseback, worn by knights of the Garter as a pendent talisman.

2. [g—] A brown loaf. [Obs.]

The George of the Order of the Garter.

Geọrġe′-nō″ble, *n.* A gold coin of the time of Henry VIII., of the value of 6*s.* 8*d.* sterling.

Geọr′ġi-a bärk. In botany, the bark of a tree, *Pinckneya pubens*, allied to the cinchona; called also *fever-bark* and *Florida quinine*.

Geọr′ġi-ăn, *a.* Relating, (a) to the state of Georgia; (b) to Georgia in Asia; (c) to the four Georges in the history of Great Britain.

Geọr′ġi-ăn, *n.* One born or residing in Georgia.

geọr′ġiç, *n.* [L. *georgicum* (supply *carmen*, song),

a meal song.] A rural poem; a poetical composition on the subject of husbandry, containing rules for cultivating lands; as, the *Georgics* of Virgil.

ġeor'ġiç, ġeor'ġiç-ăl, *a.* [L. *georgicus*; Gr. *geōrgikos*, agricultural, from *geōrgos*, a husbandman, farmer; *gē*, earth, and *ergon*, work.] Relating to rural affairs.

Geor'ġi-um Si'dus. [L.] The name first given, in honor of George III., to the planet Uranus.

ġē-os'çō-py, *n.* [*Geo-*, and Gr. *skopein*, to view.] Knowledge of the earth, ground, or soil, obtained by inspection.

ġē"ō-sē-len'iç, *a.* [*Geo-*, and Gr. *selēnē*, the moon.] Of, relating to, or due to the earth and moon as a system; as, *geoselenic* variations.

ġē-ō-stat'iç, *a.* [*Geo-*, and Gr. *statikos*, causing to stand, from *histanai*, to stand.] In civil engineering, suited to bear or designating the pressure exerted by earth; applied to a form of arch adapted to bear pressure such as that exerted by earth, and called a *geostatic arch*.

ġē-ō-stat'içs, *n.* The science of rigid bodies in a state of rest.

ġē"ō-syn-çli'năl, *n.* [*Geo-*, and Gr. *synklinein*, to incline or lean together; *syn*, together, and *klinein*, to incline, bend.] In geology, a synclinal flexure of considerable extent in the earth's crust.

ġē"ō-teç-ton'iç, *a.* [*Geo-*, and Gr. *tektōn*, a builder.] Pertaining to the earth's structure; especially, to the arrangement of the different parts and materials.

ġē-ō-thẽr'miç, *a.* [*Geo-*, and Gr. *thermos*, heat.] Relating to the internal heat of the earth.

ġē"ō-thẽr-mom'e-tẽr, *n.* [*Geo-*, and Gr. *thermos*, heat, and *metron*, a measure.] A form of thermometer used to measure temperatures beneath the earth's surface.

ġē-ot'iç, *a.* Belonging to earth; terrestrial. [Obs.]

ġē-ō-trop'iç, *a.* [*Geo-*, and Gr. *tropos*, a turning, from *trepein*, to turn.] Growing downward; of or marked by geotropism.

ġē-ot'rō-pişm, *n.* A developmental power or tendency, due to gravitation, by which certain plant-organs grow downward or turn toward the earth.

Gē-phyr'ē-ȧ, *n.pl.* [L., from Gr. *gephyra*, a mound of earth, a dam, a bridge.] A class of worms comprising the spoonworms, *Sipunculidæ*, and their allies.

ġē-phyr'ē-ăn, *n.* A member of *Gephyrea*.

ġē-phyr'ē-ăn, *a.* Of or relating to *Gephyrea*.

ġē-phyr'ē-oid, *a.* Like a gephyrean; gephyrean.

ġē-poun', *n.* [Fr. *jupon*, from *jupe*, skirt.] See *Jupon*.

ġē'rah, *n.* [Heb., lit., a bean.] The twentieth part of a shekel; (a) a weight of 13 grains; (b) a coin of silver of that weight.

Gē-rā-ni-ā'cē-æ, *n. pl.* [L., from *geranium*; Gr. *geranion*, geranium, lit., crane's bill, from *geranos*, a crane.] An order of plants, generally herbaceous, the distinguishing character of which is the growth of fruit composed of five cases, connected with as many flat styles, consolidated round a long conical beak. These plants are usually astringent and odoriferous. The order includes the genera *Geranium*, *Pelargonium*, *Oxalis*, *Impatiens*, and about sixteen others, embracing in all about 1,000 species.

ġē-rā-ni-ā'ceous, *a.* Of or relating to *Geraniaceæ*.

ġē-rā'ni-ēne, ġē-rā'ni-in, ġer'ȧ-nine, *n.* The terpene derived from *Geranium maculatum*, crane's-bill, having the odor of mulberries.

ġē-rā'ni-um, *n.* [L., from Gr. *geranion*, geranium, from *geranos*, a crane.]

1. Any of various plants of the genus *Pelargonium* (formerly classed under genus *Geranium*), commonly cultivated in gardens, as rose *geranium*, etc.; usually of South African origin.

2. Any plant of the genus *Geranium*.

3. [G—] A genus of plants of the *Geraniaceæ*, natives of temperate regions throughout the world. They have usually palmately divided leaves and regular flowers, with ten stamens and five carpels, each tipped by a long glabrous awn (the persistent style). The flowers are usually blue or red, and are often handsome.

ġē'rănt, *n.* [Fr. *gerant*, a manager, from pp. of *gerer*; L. *gerere*, to carry on, perform.] One who manages any business for a company or association; the business manager of a company.

Gē-rär'di-ȧ, *n.* [Named after John *Gerard*, an English herbalist of the 16th century.] A genus of the *Scrophulariaceæ* consisting mostly of root-parasites, with flowers rose-colored, purple, or yellow.

ġer-ȧ-tol'ō-gous, *a.* Of or relating to geratology.

ġer-ȧ-tol'ō-ġy, *n.* [Gr. *gēras* (*geratos*), old age, and *logos*, discourse, from *legein*, to speak.] The systematic study of degeneration, decadence, and dissolution, as of a group of organisms.

ġẽrbe, *n.* [Fr., a sheaf.]

1. In heraldry, a garb or sheaf.

2. In pyrotechnics, a sheaf-like firework.

ġẽr'bil, ġẽr'bill, ġẽr-bille', *n.* [Fr. *gerbille*.] A mouse-like burrowing rodent, having a long tail and long hind limbs, enabling it to leap like a jerboa.

ġẽr-bō', ġẽr-bō'ȧ, *n.* See *Jerboa*.

ġēre, *n.* Gear. [Obs.]

ge-re'fä, *n.* In Anglo-Saxon history, a reeve, bailiff, or sheriff. [Obs.]

ġē-ren'dum, *n.*; *pl.* **ġē-ren'dȧ.** [L., neut. of *gerendus*, gerundive of *gerere*, to do, act.] A thing to be done or carried through.

ġē'rent, *a.* [L. *gerens* (*-entis*), ppr. of *gerere*, to do, act, perform.] Carrying on; managing. [Obs.]

ġẽr'fa̤l"çon (-fa̤"kn), *n.* [ME. *gerfaucon*; OFr. *gerfaucon*; LL. *gerofalco*, *gyrofalco*, a gerfalcon, so named from its circling flight; L. *gyrus*, a circle, and *falco* (*-onis*), a falcon; also thought to be from LL. *hierofalco*, sacred falcon; Gr. *hieros*, sacred, and L. *falco* (*-onis*), falcon.] A large falcon of northern countries; as, the white or Iceland *gerfalcon*, *Falco islandus*.

ġẽr'ful, *a.* [ME. *gerful*, *gereful*, from L. *gyrus*, a circle.] Changeable in mind; variable; giddy.

ġẽr'lănd, ġẽr'lŏnd, *n.* Garland. [Obs.]

ġẽr'ling, *n.* [Prob. for *yearling*.] A salmon on its second return from the sea. Compare *grilse*. [Prov. Eng.]

ġẽrm, *n.* [Fr. *germe*, from L. *germen*, a sprig, offshoot, sprout, bud, germ, embryo.]

1. In biology, the primitive, rudimentary, or embryonic form of an organism; that which is in an undeveloped state; the specific portion of matter from which a new individual is to be developed.

2. A spore; a microbe; any microörganism, especially one causing disease; as, the *germs* of consumption.

3. Origin; first principle; rudiment; vital source; as, the *germ* of human freedom.

Germ theory; (a) the theory that zymotic diseases, with many others, are due to the presence of germs, chiefly spores of cryptogamic plants, as bacteria, ready to become developed and multiply under favorable conditions, and by so doing to set up fermentation, putrefaction, or other morbid action in the bodies on or in which they are parasitic; (b) the theory that the origin or generation of living beings can take place only through the agency of preëxisting living matter or germs.

ġẽr-māine', *a.* [Obs.] See *Germane*.

ġẽr'măn, *a.* [ME. *germayn*, *german*; OFr. *germain*; L. *germanus*, children of the same parents, one closely related.]

1. Sprung from the same parents or grandparents; hence, closely related.

> Brother *german* denotes one who is brother by both the father's and mother's side; cousins *german*, children of brothers or sisters. —Bouvier.

2. Germane; relevant; pertinent. [Obs.]

Gẽr'măn, *a.* [L. *Germanus*.] Of or relating to Germany, to the Germans, or to the language, customs, etc., of the Germans.

German paste; a kind of bird-food.

German silver; an alloy of copper, zinc, and nickel, in various proportions, the higher grades having more nickel. It is of a silvery color, and is used as a base for plated ware, etc.

German text; a style of type-face.

𝔗𝔥𝔦𝔰 𝔱𝔶𝔭𝔢 𝔦𝔰 𝔊𝔢𝔯𝔪𝔞𝔫 𝔗𝔢𝔵𝔱.

German tinder; a dried fungus used as a combustible. [See *Amadou*.]

Gẽr'măn, *n.* 1. A citizen or native of Germany; a person of German stock.

2. The language of the Germans. [See *High German* and *Low German*.]

3. [g—] A series of round dances with many variations, or the party at which such dances are performed; the cotillion.

High German; the language and dialects of the higher and more southern districts of Germany. It is divided into three periods: Old High German, from the eighth to the twelfth century; Middle High German, to the fifteenth century, and Modern High German. The Old High German embraces the Alemannic, Frankish, and other subdialects. The Middle High German is the language of the minnesingers, of the national heroic legends, and of the lay of the Nibelungen. Modern German is properly the dialect of Saxony, which Luther rendered classic by his translation of the Bible.

Low German; the language spoken by the dwellers in the northern and flatter parts of Germany, including, in philology, in addition, Dutch, Flemish, Friesic, Old Saxon, and Anglo-Saxon. The ancient Gothic or Mœsogothic is also generally classed with the Low-German tongues.

ġẽr-man'dẽr, *n.* [ME. *germawnder*; OFr. *germandree*; L. *chamædrys*; Gr. *chamaidrys*, germander; *chamai*, on the ground, and *drys*, a tree.] The popular name of several plants of the genus *Teucrium*; as, the water-*germander*, *Teucrium Scordium*.

ġẽr-māne', *a.* [L. *germanus*, akin.] Closely akin; nearly related; closely connected; relevant; pertinent; appropriate; as, a question *germane* to the case in hand.

Gẽr-man'iç, *n.* The Teutonic language.

Gẽr-man'iç, *a.* 1. German.

2. Teutonic.

Gẽr'măn-işm, *n.* 1. An idiom of the German language; an expression derived from or like the German.

2. A German mode of thought or action.

ġẽr-mā'ni-um, *n.* [L., from *Germania*, Germany.] An element discovered by Winkler at Freiberg, Germany, in 1885. It has a fusing-point of 900° C.; an atomic weight of 72.3; a valence of 4, and a specific gravity of about 5.5. It is a metal similar to tin in appearance.

Gẽr'măn-ize, *v.t.*; Germanized, *pt., pp.*; Germanizing, *ppr.* To cause to become German in character, manners, methods, language, or the like.

Gẽr'măn-ize, *v.i.* To be influenced by or conformed to German methods, thought, etc.

ġẽr-mā'ri-um, *n.* [L., from *germen*, a germ, and *-arium*.] The ovary of a platyhelminth.

ġẽrm'-cell, *n.* A fertile cell from which an individual may be developed; a germ as a single cell.

ġẽr'men, *n.* [L., a sprout, germ, offshoot.] A germ; an ovary.

ġẽrm'-gland, *n.* The primitive gland which develops into a testis or an ovary; a gonad.

ġẽr-mi-cī'dăl, *a.* Of, relating to, or acting as a germicide.

ġẽr'mi-cīde, *n.* [L. *germen*, a germ, and *cædere*, to kill.] A substance or agent having the power of killing germs, especially bacteria and microörganisms causing diseases.

ġẽr'mi-çul-tūre, *n.* [L. *germen*, a germ, and *cultura*, culture.] The act or method of securing the growth and development of bacteria and other microörganisms artificially; also, the germs thus obtained.

ġẽr'mi-năl, *a.* [L. *germen*, a germ.] Pertaining to, composing, or like a germ; germinative.

Germinal disk; in embryology, the disk exhibiting the first appearance of an embryo in an egg.

Germinal layer; a layer of cells in the embryo, as the ectoderm, endoderm, etc.

Germinal spot; the nucleolus of an animal germ-cell or ovum.

Germinal vesicle; the nucleus of an ovum.

Gẽr'mi-năl, *n.* [Fr., from L. *germen*, germ.] The name given to the seventh month of the revolutionary calendar of France, corresponding to the period from March 21 to April 19.

ġẽr'mi-nănt, *a.* [L. *germinans* (*-antis*), ppr. of *germinare*, to sprout forth, bud.] Sprouting; germinating.

ġẽr'mi-nāte, *v.i.*; germinated, *pt., pp.*; germinating, *ppr.* [L. *germinatus*, pp. of *germinare*, to sprout, bud, from *germen*, a sprout, bud.] To sprout; to bud; to begin to vegetate, as a plant or its seed; to start development, as an ovum.

ġẽr'mi-nāte, *v.t.* To cause to sprout. [Rare.]

ġẽr-mi-nā'tion, *n.* [ME. *germinacion*; L. *germinatio* (*-onis*), a sprouting forth, budding, from *germinare*, to sprout, bud, from *germen*, a sprout, bud, germ.] The act of sprouting; the beginning of vegetation, as in a seed; the first act of growth by an embryo plant or animal.

Seeds Germinating. (In center a plant which has newly appeared above ground.)

ġẽr'mi-nā-tive, *a.* Of, causing, or capable of germination.

ġẽr-mi-par'i-ty, *n.* [L. *germen*, a germ, and *parere*, to produce, bring forth.] Propagation by the aid of germs.

ġẽrm'less, *a.* Free from or devoid of germs.

ġẽr'mō-gen, *n.* [L. *germen*, a germ, and Gr. *-genēs*, producing.] A protoplasmic mass with many nuclei, without cellular structure, and the source from which ova are derived.

ġẽr'mŏn, *n.* [Fr.] A fish of the mackerel family.

ġẽrm'-plas"mȧ, *n.* That part of the protoplasm of a germ-cell which is supposed to be transmitted from generation to generation, and, because of its special complexity of chemical and molecular structure, is thought to be the physical source of the phenomena of heredity.

ġẽrm'-pōre, *n.* A pore or opening in the cell wall of a spore or other germ serving as a place of exit for the germ-tube.

ġẽrm'-tūbe, *n.* A tubular outgrowth from a spore at the time of germination.

ġẽrm'ūle, *n.* An incipient germ.

ġẽrn, *v.i.* To grin. [Scot.]

ġẽr'nẽr, *n.* A garner. [Obs.]

ġer-ō-çom′iç-ăl, *a.* Pertaining to gerocomy. [Rare.]

ġē-roç′ō-my, ġer-ō-çō′mi-ȧ, *n.* [Gr. *gerōn*, an old man, and *komein*, to care for.] That part of hygiene which regards the regimen of old age. [Rare.]

ge-ron′tēs, *n.pl.* [Gr. *gerontes*, pl. of *gerōn*, an old man.] Supreme magistrates of Sparta. There were twenty-eight or, according to some, thirty-two, of these magistrates. They could not be elevated to the dignity before their sixtieth year.

ge-ron′tiç, *a.* [Gr. *gerōn*, an old man.] Relating to senility; decadent; senile.

ger-on-toç′rȧ-çy, *n.* [Gr. *gerōn*, an old man, and *kratos*, power.] A government controlled by old men. [Rare.]

ġer-ō-pig′i-ȧ, *n.* [Port.] A Portuguese mixture of brandy, unfermented grape juice, logwood, etc., sweetened, and used to adulterate port wines or other liquors.

-ger-ous. A combining form from L. *gerere*, to bear; used to signify producing, bearing; as, corni*gerous*.

ge-röu′si-ȧ, *n.* Same as *Gerusia*.

ger′ry-man-dēr, *n.* [A word of political formation; prob. from the name of Elbridge *Gerry*, a former governor of Massachusetts and the accredited originator of the method.] An arbitary, unnatural, and unfair arrangement of voting districts, intended to favor one political party or candidate.

ger′ry-man-dēr, *v.t.* 1. To arrange the districts of, by a gerrymander.

2. To distort, misstate, or arrange incorrectly, as facts, arguments, etc., so as to secure a result in accordance with a predetermined theory or conclusion. [Rare.]

ġer′und, *n.* [L. *gerundium*, from *gerere*, to do or carry out.]

1. In Latin, a verbal noun used only in oblique cases of the singular with the force of a present active infinitive, and governing the same cases as its verb.

2. In Anglo-Saxon, a dative form of the infinitive with *to* before it; as, *Ic eom to nimanne*, I am to take (or be taken).

3. In English, a participial noun or infinitive in *-ing*.

ġē-run′di-ăl, *a.* Of or resembling a gerundive.

ġē-run′dive, *n.* [L. *gerundivus*, from *gerere*, to do, act.] In Latin, the future participle passive, used as an adjective.

ġē-run′dive-ly, *adv.* As a gerund or gerundive.

ge-rū′si-ȧ, ge-röu′si-ȧ, *n.* [L. *gerusia*; Gr. *gerousia*, from *gerōn*, an old man.] The senate of Sparta and other Dorian states, embracing all the powers of a state.

ger-vä′ō, *n.* [Native Brazilian name.] A small tropical American shrub, *Stachytarpheta Jamaicensis*, of the *Verbenaceæ*, the leaves of which are sold in Austria under the name of Brazilian tea.

ger′y, *a.* Variable; fickle. [Obs.]

ges′ling, *n.*, obsolete spelling of *gosling*.

Ges′ne-rȧ, *n.* The type genus of the *Gesneraceæ*, mostly natives of Brazil, having tuberous rhizomes, opposite leaves, and usually red or orange blossoms.

Ges-ne-rā′cē-æ, *n.pl.* [L., from the name of Conrad von *Gesner*, a naturalist and scholar of Zurich (1516–65).] An order of monopetalous exogens, mostly tropical or subtropical, comprising nearly a thousand species. The best known genera are *Gloxinia*, *Gesnera*, *Æschynanthus*, and *Achimenes*.

ġes-nēr-ā′ceous, *a.* Of or pertaining to the *Gesneraceæ*.

gesse, *v.t.* and *v.i.* To guess. [Obs.]

ġes′sō, *n.* [It., plaster, chalk, from L. *gypsum*, plaster.] In fine arts, a kind of plaster used to prepare a surface for painting; hence, any similar preparation; also, a surface thus prepared.

Gesso duro; a fine, durable quality of gesso used for statuettes, bas-reliefs, etc. Hence, such a bas-relief, usually mounted in a showy frame and tinted to resemble terra-cotta.

ġest, *n.* 1. A deed, action, or achievement. [Obs.]

2. Show; representation. [Obs.]

3. Deportment; bearing; gesture. [Obs.]

4. A romance; a tale. [Obs.]

gest, *n.* A guest. [Obs.]

ġest, *n.* [OFr. *giste*, abode, lodgings.]

1. A stage, a rest; a stop. [Obs.]

2. A journal of the stages in the journeys of English kings. [Obs.]

ġes′tȧnt, *a.* [L. *gestans (-antis)*, ppr. of *gestare*, to bear or carry about, freq. of *gerere*, to bear, carry.] Pregnant; laden; burdened.

ġes-tā′tion, *n.* [L. *gestatio (-onis)*, a bearing, carrying, from *gestare*, to bear or carry about, freq. of *gerere*, to bear, carry.]

1. The act of carrying young in the womb from conception to delivery; pregnancy.

2. The act of wearing, as clothes. [Obs.]

3. Exercise in which one is borne or carried. [Obs.]

ġes′tȧ-tō-ry, *a.* 1. Pertaining to gestation.

2. Wearable. [Obs.]

ġes′tiç, *a.* 1. Pertaining to deeds; legendary. [Obs.]

2. Relating to bodily motion, especially dancing. [Rare.]

ġes-tiç′ū-lăr, *a.* Gesticulatory.

ġes-tiç′ū-lāte, *v.i.*; gesticulated, *pt.*, *pp.*; gesticulating, *ppr.* [L. *gesticulatus*, pp. of *gesticulari*, to make mimic gestures, from *gesticulus*, dim. of *gestus*, a gesture, from *gestus*, pp. of *gerere*, to bear, carry, do.] To make gestures or motions, as in speaking; to use postures.

ġes-tiç′ū-lāte, *v.t.* To represent by gesture; to act. [Rare.]

ġes-tiç-ū-lā′tion, *n.* [L. *gesticulatio (-onis)*, from *gesticulatus*, pp. of *gesticulari*, to gesticulate.]

1. The act of making gestures to express passion or enforce sentiments.

2. A gesture; a motion of the body or limbs in speaking, or in representing action or passion, and enforcing arguments and sentiments.

3. Antic tricks or motions.

ġes-tiç′ū-lā-tōr, *n.* One who gesticulates.

ġes-tiç′ū-lȧ-tō-ry, *a.* Of or pertaining to gesticulation; representing by gestures.

ġes′tōur, *n.* One who narrates gests or adventures; a story-teller. [Obs.]

ġes′tūr-ăl, *a.* Pertaining to gesture.

ġes′tūre, *n.* [LL. *gestura*, a mode of action, from L. *gestus*, pp. of *gerere*, to bear, carry.]

1. A motion of the body or limbs expressive of sentiment or passion; any action or posture intended to express an idea or a passion, or to enforce an argument, opinion, etc.

2. Movement of the body or limbs; carriage. [Obs.]

ġes′tūre, *v.t.*; gestured, *pt.*, *pp.*; gesturing, *ppr.* To accompany or enforce with gesture or action.

ġes′tūre, *v.i.* To gesticulate; to make gestures.

ġes′tūre-less, *a.* Free from gestures.

ġes′tūre-ment, *n.* The act of making gestures. [Obs.]

get, *n.* 1. Breed; offspring; as, the *get* of a stallion.

2. A child; used contemptuously. [Scot.]

ġet, *n.* The mineral, jet. [Obs.]

get, *n.* Fashion; custom; contrivance; scheme. [Obs.]

get, *v.t.*; got (Obs. gat), *pt.*; got *or* gotten, *pp.*; getting, *ppr.* [ME. *geten*; AS. *gitan*, *gytan*, to take, obtain, *agitan*, to get.]

1. To procure; to obtain; to gain; to receive; to acquire or obtain possession of, by almost any means; to earn; to come by; as, to *get* favor by kindness; to *get* wealth by industry and economy; to *get* land by purchase; to *get* a reward for one's labor.

2. Hence, with *have*, (a) to possess; to have; as, she *has got* blue eyes; (b) to be compelled or obliged; as, he *has got* to do it.

3. To beget; to procreate; to generate.

4. To acquire mental possession of; to commit to memory; to learn; as, he has *got* his recitation.

5. To prevail on; to induce; to persuade; as, to *get* him to go.

6. To procure or cause to be or occur; as, to *get* everything in readiness

> Those things I bid you do; *get* them dispatch'd. —Shak.

7. To carry; to betake; used reflexively.

> *Get* thee out from this land.—Gen. xxxi. 13.

To get by heart; to memorize; to commit to memory.

To get up; to prepare; to arrange; to organize; to construct; as, *to get up* a story; *to get up* an agitation.

get, *v.i.* 1. To make acquisition, to gain.

2. To arrive at any place or state, to become; followed by some modifying word; as, to *get* away; to *get* home; to *get* shaved; to *get* ahead.

Syn.—Obtain, procure, acquire, secure, gain, win.

get′ȧ-ble, get′tȧ-ble, *a.* Capable of being got; obtainable.

get′en, *v.*, obsolete past participle of *get*.

geth, *v.*, obsolete form of *goeth*.

get′=pen″ny, *n.* That which gains money. [Colloq.]

get′tȧ-ble, *a.* See *Getable*.

get′tēr, *n.* 1. One who gets, gains, or acquires.

2. One who begets or procreates.

get′tēr=up, *n.* One who arranges, makes, or contrives anything.

get′ting, *n.* 1. The act of obtaining; acquisition.

2. Gain; profit.

get′=up, *n.* General make-up. [Colloq.]

Gē′um, *n.* [L., the herb-bennet, avens; prob. from Gr. *genein*, to taste.] A genus of hardy herbaceous perennials of the natural order *Rosaceæ*, natives of the northern parts of the globe. The flowers have long, persistent, plumose styles.

gew′gąw, *n.* [Corruption of ME. *givegove*, a gewgaw, trifle, from AS. *gifu*, a gift, from *gifan*, to give.] A showy trifle; a pretty thing of little worth; a toy; a bauble; a splendid plaything.

gew′gąw, *a.* Showy without value.

gey, *adv* [Scot.] Considerably; rather.

gey′sēr, *n.* [Ice. *geysir*, from *geysa*, to gush, from *gjosa*, gush.] A spring which ejects hot water or mud, frequently to a considerable height in the air. Geysers are found in Iceland, New Zealand, and in the Yellowstone region of the United States.

Geyser, Yellowstone National Park.

gey′sēr-iç, *a.* Pertaining to or resembling a geyser.

gey′sēr-ite, *n.* A variety of florite or siliceous sinter, which again is a variety of opal. It is applied to the concretionary deposits around the Icelandic geysers.

ghar′ry (gar′i), *n.* [Hind. *gari*.] A name given in India to any wheeled vehicle.

ghȧst (gȧst), *v.t.* To frighten [Obs.]

ghȧst′ful, *a.* Dreary; dismal; fearful. [Obs.]

ghȧst′ful-ly, *adv.* Frightfully. [Obs.]

ghȧst′li-ness, *n.* The state or quality of being ghastly.

ghȧst′ly, *a.*; *comp.* ghastlier; *superl.* ghastliest. [ME. *gastly*; AS. *gæstlic*, terrible, from *gæstan*, to frighten, terrify.]

1. Like a ghost in appearance; deathlike; pale; dismal; as, a *ghastly* face; *ghastly* smiles.

2. Horrible; shocking; dreadful; as, a *ghastly* wound.

Syn.—Deathlike, ghostlike, lurid, cadaverous, pale, pallid, spectral.

ghȧst′ly, *adv.* In a ghastly manner.

ghȧst′ness, *n.* Ghastliness. [Obs.]

ghąt, ghąut (gąt), *n.* [Hind. *ghat*.]

1. In India, a pass through a mountain; hence, also, a range or chain of mountains.

Ghoosla Ghat, Benares.

2. In India, a landing-place or stairway to a river, generally having at the summit a temple, pagoda, bathing-house, or place of rest and recreation.

ghä-wä′zee, ghä-wä′zï, *n. sing.* and *pl.* [Ar.] Female dancers of low caste in Egypt.

ghaz′el (gaz′), *n.* [Ar.] Same as *Gazel*.

ghä′zï (gä′), *n.* [Ar.] A title of honor assumed by or conferred on those Mohammedans who have distinguished themselves in battle against infidels.

Ghē′bēr, Ghē′bre (gē′bēr), *n.* [Per. *ghebr*.] See *Gueber*.

ghee (gē), *n.* [Hind. *ghi*, from Sans. *ghrita*, butter or fat.] In the East Indies, butter clarified by boiling, and thus converted into a kind of oil.

gher′kin, *n.* [D. *agurkje*; Bohem. *okurka*, a cucumber.]

1. A small cucumber used for pickling.

2. In zoölogy, a sea-gherkin.

ghetch′ọọ (gech′ö), *n.* [E. Ind.] An aquatic plant of India, the tubers of which are edible.

Ghet′tō (get′ō), *n.*; *pl.* Ghet′tï or Ghet′tōş. [It.] The quarter occupied by the poorer class of Jews in any large city; formerly, a section of Italian towns especially set apart for Jews.

Ghib′el-line (gib′), *n.* [It. *Ghibellino*, for G. *Waiblingen*, an estate in the part of Franconia included under Württemberg, which belonged to the house of Hohenstaufen, to which the then reigning Emperor Conrad belonged; said to have been the rallying-cry of the emperor's party at the battle of Weinsberg.] One of a faction in Italy, in the thirteenth century, which favored the German emperors, and opposed the Guelfs, or adherents of the popes.

ghōle (gōl), *n.* See *Ghoul.*

ghost (gōst), *n.* [ME. *gost, goost, gast*; AS. *gast*, breath, spirit.]

1. Spirit; the soul of man; as, to give up the *ghost.*

2. The soul of a deceased person; the soul or spirit separate from the body; an apparition; a phantom.

3. A shadow; a trace; a glimmering; as, the *ghost* of a hope.

4. In optics, a faint secondary image or illumination, as in a telescope, usually due to reflection from the surface of a lens.

Holy Ghost; the Holy Spirit; the third person in the Trinity.

ghōst, *v.t.* To appear to in the form of a ghost. [Obs.]

ghōst, *v.i.* To expire. [Obs.]

ghōst′=dånce, *n.* A North American Indian religious dance, at which the dancers believe ghosts appear.

ghōst′fish, *n.* A pallid variety of *Cryptacanthodes maculatus*, the wrymouth.

ghōst′less, *a.* Without life or spirit. [Rare.]

ghōst′like, *a.* Like a ghost.

ghōst′li-ness, *n.* The state or quality of being ghostly.

ghōst′ly, *a.* [ME. *gostly*; AS. *gastlic*, of a spirit, spiritual, from *gast*, a specter, breath, spirit.]

1. Spiritual; relating to the soul; not carnal or secular.

2. Spectral; supernatural; weird.

ghōst′ly, *adv.* Spectrally; weirdly; spiritually; mystically. [Obs.]

ghōst′=mọth, *n.* A nocturnal lepidopterous insect, *Epialus humuli*, so called from the male being of a white color, and from its habit of hovering with a pendulum-like motion in the twilight over one spot (often in churchyards), where the female, which has gray posterior wings and red-spotted anterior wings, is concealed.

ghōst-ol′ō-ġy, *n.* [*Ghost*, and Gr. *-logia*, from *legein*, to speak.] The science of supernatural things. [Humorous.]

ghōst′=plant, *n.* *Amarantus albus*, the tumbleweed.

ghōst′=wŏrd, *n.* A word which has no real existence or meaning, being a false form due to a blunder in spelling, pronunciation, printing, or the like.

ghōul (gōl), *n.* [Ar. *ghūl*, a demon of the mountains.] An imaginary evil being among eastern nations, which is supposed to prey upon human bodies; a grave-robber.

ghōul′ish, *a.* Demoniac; fiendish; like a ghoul.

ghur′ry, ghur′rie (gur′), *n.*; *pl.* **ghur′rieṣ.** [Sans. *ghaṭi*, a water-clock.]

1. In India, (a) a form of clepsydra; (b) the gong of such an instrument; (c) any kind of clock.

2. (a) Among Hindus, the 60th part of a day; 24 minutes; (b) among Anglo-Indians, 60 minutes.

ghyll (gil), *n.* [Ice. *gil*, a ravine.] A gill; a ravine.

ġiăl-lō-lī′nō, *n.* [It. *giallorino*, yellowish, from *giallo*, yellow.] A pigment known as Naples yellow.

ġī′ănt, *n.* [ME. *giaunt*; OFr. *geant*; L. *gigas* (*-antis*); Gr. *gigas* (*-antos*), a giant; *gē*, earth, and *genēs*, born.]

1. A man of size much above the ordinary stature of men; a man of extraordinary size or bulk.

2. A person of extraordinary powers or genius, bodily or intellectual; as, the judge is a *giant* in his profession.

3. Any object of very great size.

ġī′ănt, *a.* Like a giant; extraordinary in size or strength; as, *giant* brothers; a *giant* son.

ġī′ănt=cell, *n.* See *Osteoclast.*

ġī′ănt=clam, *n.* A huge bivalve shell of the family *Tridacnidæ.*

ġī′ănt-ess, *n.* A female giant.

ġī′ănt-ish, *a.* Like a giant; exceptionally large.

ġī′ănt-īze, *v.i.* To play the giant.

ġī′ănt=ket″tle, *n.* A huge pothole, as found on the coast of Norway.

ġī′ănt-ly, *a.* Giant-like. [Obs.]

ġī′ănt=pow″dẽr, *n.* A form of dynamite.

ġī′ănt-ry, *n.* The race of giants. [Rare.]

ġī′ănt-ship, *n.* The state, quality, or character of being a giant.

ġiaour (jour), *n.* [Turk. *gawur, jawr*; Per. *gāwr*, an infidel.] A name given by Turks to disbelievers in Mohammedanism, and especially to Christians.

ġiär-dī-net′tō, *n.*; *pl.* **ġiär-dī-net′tī.** [It., dim. of *giardino*, garden.] A piece of jewelry decorated with imitations of flowers in precious stones.

ġib, *n.* [Prov. Eng.] A piece of iron employed to clasp together the pieces of wood or iron of a framing which is to be keyed.

Gib and key; the fixed wedge and the driving wedge for tightening the strap which holds the brasses at the end of a connecting rod in steam machinery.

ġib, *v.t.*; gibbed, *pt., pp.*; gibbing, *ppr.* To secure or fasten with a gib or gibs.

ġib, *n.* [OFr. *gibbe*, a sort of arm, a billhook, hoe.]

1. A hooked stick. [Prov. Eng.]

2. The projecting arm of a crane; a gibbet or jib. [Prov. Eng.]

gib, *n.* [Obs.] See *Gib-cat.*

gib, *v.i.* To act like a cat. [Obs.]

gib, *v.t.* [Local, U. S.]

1. To remove the viscera from; to disembowel.

2. To castrate. [Obs.]

ġib, *v.i.* [OFr. *gibber*, to struggle; prob. from Sw. dial. *gippa*, to jerk.] To balk.

ġib-bär′tas, *n.* [Compare L. *gibber*, humpbacked.] A finback or Jupiter whale.

ġib′bẽr, *n.* A horse that balks.

gib′bẽr, *v.i.* [Ice. *gabba*, to mock.] To speak rapidly and inarticulately.

gib′bẽr-ish, *n.* Rapid and inarticulate talk; unintelligible language; unmeaning words.

gib′bẽr-ish, *a.* Unmeaning; unintelligible; incoherent.

gib′bet, *n.* [ME. *gibet*; OFr. *gibet*, a gibbet, prob. from *gibet*, a large stick.]

1. A gallows; the apparatus, consisting of a post of wood with a projecting arm, from which notorious malefactors were hanged in chains and allowed to remain as a warning.

2. The projecting beam of a crane which sustains the pulleys and the weight of goods; a jib.

ġib′bet, *v.t.*; gibbeted *or* gibbetted, *pt., pp.*; gibbeting *or* gibbetting, *ppr.* 1. To hang and expose on a gibbet or gallows; to hang upon anything resembling a gibbet.

2. To expose to ridicule, scorn, infamy, or the like.

ġib′biēr, *n.* [Fr., from OFr. *gibier*, game, fowl.] [Obs.] See *Gibier.*

gib′bŏn, *n.* [Fr.] A name common to apes of the genus *Hylobates*, but more particularly restricted to *Hylobates lar*, which inhabits the islands of the Indian Archipelago. It is distinguished from other quadrumanous animals by the slenderness of its form, by its rudimentary tail, and by the extraordinary length of its arms, which, when the animal is standing, reach nearly to the ankles, and which enable it to swing itself from tree to tree with wonderful agility.

ġib′=bọọm, *n.* See *Jib-boom.*

gib′bōse, *a.* See *Gibbous*

gib-bos′ĭ-ty, *n.* The quality or state of being gibbous; protuberance; convexity.

gib′bous (-bus), *a.* [L. *gibbosus*, humped or hunched, from *gibbus* or *gibba*, a hump.]

1. Swelling; protuberant; convex, as the moon is when more than half and less than full, the enlightened part being then convex on both margins.

2. Hunched; humpbacked; crookbacked.

gib′bous-ly, *adv.* In a gibbous or protuberant form.

gib′bous-ness, *n.* The state or quality of being gibbous; protuberance; a round prominence; convexity.

gibbs′ite, *n.* [Named after George *Gibbs*, an American mineralogist.] A hydrate of aluminium, a whitish mineral, found in Massachusetts in irregular stalactitic masses, presenting an aggregation of elongated tuberous branches, parallel and united. Its structure is fibrous, the fibers radiating from an axis.

gib′=cat, *n.* A castrated tomcat. [Obs.]

ġibe, jibe, *v.i.*; gibed *or* jibed, *pt., pp.*; gibing *or* jibing, *ppr.* [Scand. origin; compare Sw. dial. *gipa*, to talk foolishly; Ice. *geipa*, to talk nonsense.] To cast reproaches and sneering expressions; to rail; to utter taunting, sarcastic words; to flout; to fleer; to scoff.

ġibe, jibe, *v.t.* To reproach with contemptuous words; to deride; to scoff at.

ġibe, jibe, *n.* An expression of sarcastic scorn; a scoff; a railing.

Mark the fleers, the *gibes*, and notable scorns. —Shak.

gib′el, *n.* [G. *gibel, giebel*, a kind of carp, from O.H.G. *gebal*, the head.] The Prussian carp, *Carassius vulgaris* or *gibelio.*

ġīb′ẽr, jīb′ẽr, *n.* One who utters gibes.

gib′fish, *n.* A male salmon. [Prov. Eng.]

ġib′ing-ly, jib′ing-ly, *adv.* In a gibing manner; scornfully.

gib′let, *a.* Made of giblets; as, a *giblet* pie.

gib′let, *n.* [ME. *gibelet*; OFr. *gibelet*, the entrails of fowls.]

1. An internal edible part of a fowl, such as the heart, liver, or gizzard, which has been removed before cooking, and is often served separately in a sauce or pie; chiefly used in the plural.

2. [*pl.*] Rags; tatters. [Rare.]

Gi-bral′tär, *n.* Rock-candy; called also *Gibraltar rock*, in allusion to the Rock of Gibraltar, a fort belonging to Great Britain at the entrance of the Mediterranean.

ġib′ståff, *n.* [OFr. *gibbe*, a sort of arm.]

1. A staff to gauge water or to push a boat.

2. Formerly, a staff used in fighting beasts on the stage.

gid, *n.* [From *giddy*, dizzy.] A disease of sheep; the staggers.

gid′di-ly, *adv.* In a giddy manner; flightily.

gid′di-ness, *n.* The state, quality, or character of being giddy.

Syn.—Flightiness, inconstancy, unsteadiness, levity, thoughtlessness, volatility, fickleness.

gid′dy, *a.*; *comp.* giddier; *superl.* giddiest. [ME. *gidi*, foolish; compare AS. *giddian*, to sing, be merry, from *gid*, a song.]

1. Having in the head a swimming sensation; having lost the power of preserving the balance of the body, and therefore wavering and inclined to fall; dizzy; reeling.

Like music which makes *giddy* the dim brain. —Shelley.

2. Causing giddiness or vertigo; rendering dizzy; as, a *giddy* height.

3. Suggestive of giddiness; rotatory; whirling; running round with celerity.

The *giddy* motion of the whirling mill.—Pope.

4. Inconstant; changeable; fickle; unsteady; wild; heedless.

gid′dy, *v.i.* To turn quickly; to reel.

gid′dy, *v.t.* To make dizzy or unsteady.

gid′dy-head (-hed), *n.* A person without thought or judgment.

gid′dy=head″ed, *a.* Having a giddy head; heedless; unsteady.

gid′dy=pāced (-pāst), *a.* Moving irregularly; reeling; flighty. [Rare.]

gid′dy-pāte, *n.* A giddyhead.

gid′dy=pāt″ed, *a.* Giddy-headed.

gie, *v.t.* To guide. [Obs. See *Guy.*]

ġiē, *v.t.* To give. [Scot.]

ġiēr′=ēa″gle, *n.* [D. *gier*, a vulture.] An eagle or bird of the eagle kind, mentioned in Leviticus xi. 18, supposed to be *Neophron percnopterus*, the Egyptian vulture.

giē′seck-ite, *n.* [Named after Chas. *Gieseck*, an actor and mineralogist.] A variety of pinite. It is a green or brownish mineral, occurring in Greenland in compact feldspar, and in New York in a pyroxene rock.

gif, *conj.* If. [Obs.]

ġif′gaff, *n.* Give and take; tit for tat; mutual obligation.

ġif′fy, *n.* See *Jiffy.*

gift, *n.* [ME. *gift*, a gift, from AS. *gift*, generally in pl. *gifta*, a marriage, nuptials, from *gifan*, to give.]

1. The act, right, or power of giving or conferring; as, the office is in the *gift* of the mayor.

2. That which is given or bestowed; anything, proprietorship of which is voluntarily transferred by one person to another without compensation; a donation; a present.

3. A natural quality or endowment regarded as conferred; power; faculty; as, the *gift* of wit.

4. A bribe; anything given with a corrupt motive.

5. In law, a voluntary transfer of property without compensation or any consideration.

Syn.—Donation, present, benefaction, gratuity, boon.

gift, *v.t.*; gifted, *pt., pp.*; gifting, *ppr.* 1. To confer as a gift; to give. [Obs.]

2. To endow with a gift or with any power or faculty.

gift′ed, *a.* Endowed by nature with any power or faculty; furnished with any particular talent; largely endowed with intellect.

Some divinely *gifted* man. —Tennyson.

gift′ed-ness, *n.* The state of being gifted.

gift′=rōpe, *n.* In seamen's language, a rope attached to a boat for towing it.

gig, *v.t.* To engender. [Obs.]

gig, *v.i.* To fish with a gig or fishgig.

gig, *v.t.* To spear (a fish) with a gig.

gig, *n.* [Etym. uncertain; compare Ice. *gigja*, a fiddle, from *geiga*, to vibrate.]

1. A top or whirligig; any little thing that is whirled round in play.

2. A light carriage, with one pair of wheels, drawn by one horse; a chaise.

3. In nautical parlance, (a) a long narrow rowing-boat, very lightly built, adapted for racing; (b) a ship's boat, intended to be fast, and usually furnished with sails; (c) a boat devoted to the use of the commanding officer.

4. A machine consisting of rotary cylinders covered with wire teeth, for teazeling woolen cloth.

gig, *n.* A wanton silly girl; a giglet.

gig, *n.* A fiddle. [Obs.]

gig, *n.* A dart or harpoon; a fishgig.

ġi-gant-. See *Giganto-.*

ġi-gan-tē′ăn, *a.* [L. *giganteus*; Gr. *giganteios*,

from *gigas* (*-antos*), a giant.] Like a giant; mighty.

ġi-gan-tesque′ (-tesk′), *a.* Befitting a giant; characteristic of a giant.

ġi-gan′tiç, *a.* [L. *gigas* (*-antis*), a giant.]

1. Of extraordinary size; very large; huge; like a giant.

2. Suitable for or characteristic of a giant; immense; very great; as, *gigantic* deeds; *gigantic* wickedness.

A towering specter of *gigantic* mold.—Pope.

Syn.—Colossal, enormous, immense, huge, vast, ponderous.

ġi-gan′tiç-ăl, *a.* Gigantic. [Obs.]

ġi-gan′tiç-ăl-ly, *adv.* In a gigantic manner.

ġi-gan′ti-cīde, *n.* [L. *gigas* (*-antis*), a giant, and *cadere*, to kill.] The act of slaying or murdering a giant.

ġi-gan′ti-cīde, *n.* A giant-killer.

ġi-gan′tine, *a.* Gigantic; befitting a giant. [Rare.]

ġi-gan′tişm, *n.* In biology, excessive growth; enormous stature.

ġi-gan-to-, A combining form from Gr. *gigas* (*gigantos*), a giant, signifying large, gigantic.

ġi-gan′tō-lite, *n.* [*Giganto-*, and Gr. *lithos*, a stone.] A variety of pinite, crystallized in six- or twelve-sided prisms from the gneissose granite of Finland. It is altered iolite.

ġi-gan-tō-log′iç-ăl, *a.* Pertaining to gigantology.

ġi-gan-tol′ō-ġy, *n.* [*Giganto-*, and Gr. *logos*, a description.] An account or description of giants.

ġi-gan-tom′ȧ-çhy, *n.* [LL. *gigantomachia*; Gr. *gigantomachia*, the battle of the giants; *gigas* (*-antos*), a giant, and *machē*, a battle.] In classic mythology, a war of giants; specifically, the fabulous war of the giants against heaven.

ġiġe, *n.* See *Guige.*

ġi-ge-lï′rȧ, *n.* [It.] A xylophone.

ġi-ġē′ri-um, *n.*; *pl.* **ġi-ġē′ri-ȧ.** [L. *gigeria*, neut. pl., the cooked entrails of poultry.] The gizzard of a bird.

gig′get, *n.* [Obs.] See *Gigot.*

gig′ging=mȧ-çhïne″, *n.* A machine for dressing woolen cloth by subjecting it to the action of teazels, the fine hooks of which draw the loose fibers to the surface.

gig′gle, *n.* A kind of laugh, with short catches of the voice or breath.

gig′gle, *v.i.*; giggled, *pt.*, *pp.*; giggling, *ppr.* [From ME. *gagelen*, to gaggle, or make a noise like a goose; prob. of imitative origin.] To laugh with short catches of the breath or voice; to laugh in a silly or affected manner.

gig′glẽr, *n.* One who giggles or titters.

gig′gly, *a.* Given to giggling.

gig′gŏt, *n.* [Obs.] See *Gigot.*

gig′let, gig′lot, *n.* A wanton; a lascivious girl.

gig′=mȧ-çhïne″, *n.* A gigging-machine.

gig′ŏt, *n.* [Fr., from OFr. *gigot*, a leg of mutton, dim. of *gigue*, a fiddle.]

1. A leg of mutton.

2. A small piece of flesh. [Obs.]

ġïgue (zhĕg), *n.* [Fr.] See *Jig.*

Gï′lȧ mon′stẽr (hē′lȧ). [From *Gila*, a river in Arizona.] A large lizard, *Heloderma suspectum*, found in Arizona, New Mexico, etc. With the exception of *Heloderma horridum*, it is the only lizard known to be venomous.

gil′back-ẽr, *n.* *Tachysaurus parkeri*, a siluroid fish found on the northern coast of South America.

Gil′bẽrt-ine, *n.* One of a religious order founded in England about 1148, so named from Gilbert, lord of Sempringham, in Lincolnshire.

Gil′bẽrt-ine, *a.* Belonging to the monastic order founded by Gilbert.

gild, *v.t.*; gilded *or* gilt, *pt.*, *pp.*; gilding, *ppr.* [ME. *gilden*; AS. *gyldan*, to overlay with gold, from *gold*, gold.]

1. To overlay with gold, either in leaf or powder, or in amalgam with quicksilver; to overspread with a thin covering of gold; to cause to appear like gold.

No more the rising sun shall *gild* the morn. —Pope.

2. To illuminate; to brighten; to render bright.

Gild the calm evening of your day. —Trumbull.

3. To give a fair and agreeable external appearance to; recommend to favor and reception by superficial decoration; as, to *gild* flattery or falsehood.

gild, guild, *n.* [ME. *gilde*; AS. *gild, gield, geld*, tribute, a payment, a society or company.]

1. An association or corporation of persons belonging to the same class or engaged in similar pursuits, formed for mutual aid and protection, known in England for many centuries.

2. A gildhall. [Obs.]

gild, *n.* A tax. [Obs. See *Geld.*]

gild′āle, *n.* A drinking-bout in which each person pays an equal share. [Obs.]

gild′ẽr, *n.* One who gilds; one whose occupation is to overlay with gold.

gild′ẽr, *n.* See *Guilder.*

gild′hall, guild′hall, *n.* The hall where a gild or corporation usually assembles; a town or corporation hall; specifically [G—], the corporation hall and seat of several of the courts of the city of London.

gild′ing, *n.* 1. The art or practice of overlaying with gold-leaf, or with a thin coating of gold.

2. Gold, in leaf, powder, or liquid, applied to any surface.

3. That which is laid on in overlaying with gold; hence, any superficial coating employed to give a better appearance to a thing than is natural to it.

gild′ing=met″ăl, *n.* A kind of sheet brass from which cartridge-shells are made.

gīle, *n.* Guile. [Obs.]

ġi-let′ (zhē-lā′), *n.* [Fr., a waistcoat.] A waistcoat or vest; especially, the front of a bodice of a woman's dress resembling a man's vest.

Gil′i-ȧ, *n.* [Named after Philip *Gil*, a Spanish botanist.] A large genus of plants of the phlox family, natives of western United States. Several of the species are cultivated for their beautiful flowers.

gill, *n.* [ME. *gile, gylle*; Dan. *gjælle*, a gill.]

1. The organ of respiration in aquatic vertebrates.

Fishes perform respiration under water by the *gills.* —Ray.

2. The flap that hangs below the beak of a fowl or bird.

3. The flesh on the lower part of the cheeks, or under the chin.

4. The thin plates on the under side of a mushroom.

5. In dressing or spinning flax, a kind of hackle or comb with fine long teeth, used in evenly bunching the fibers.

ġill, *n.* [ME. *gille, gylle*; OFr. *gille*, a sort of measure for wine.] A measure of capacity containing the fourth part of a pint.

ġill, *n.* 1. A plant, ground-ivy, of the genus *Glechoma.*

2. Malt liquor medicated with ground-ivy.

ġill, *n.* A female; a sweetheart; a sportive or wanton girl, from *Gillian*, a woman's name.

Each Jack with his *Gill.* —B. Jonson.

gill, *n.* [Prov. Eng.] In England, a pair of wheels and a frame on which timber is conveyed.

gill, *n.* [ME. *gille, gylle*, from Ice. *gil*, a deep, narrow glen.] A woody glen; a place between steep banks, with a rivulet flowing through it; a brook. [Prov. Eng.]

gill, *n.* A leech; also spelled *gell.* [Scot.]

ġill′=āle, *n.* Malt liquor flavored with ground-ivy.

gill′=ärch, *n.* A branchial arch.

gil-lȧ-rōō′, *n.* [Ir. *giolla ruadh*; *giolla*, boy, and *ruadh*, red.] A variety of the European trout found in Irish waters, characterized by having an exceptionally strong and large stomach.

gill′=bär, *n.* Same as *Gill-arch.*

gill′=çleft, *n.* A branchial cleft.

gill′=cōmb (-kōm), *n.* The gill of a mollusk resembling a comb; a ctenidium.

gill′=cŏv″ẽr, *n.* The operculum.

gill′=flap, *n.* A membrane attached to the posterior edge of the gill-lid, immediately closing the gill-opening.

gill′=flïrt, *n.* A sportive or wanton girl; a thoughtless, giddy girl.

gill′=frāme, *n.* In spinning, a device for elongating and leveling the flax; a spreader.

gill′=head, *n.* Same as *Gill-frame.*

ġill′house, *n.* A place where the liquor gill is sold.

gil′li-ăn, *n.* A girl; in particular, a gill. [Obs.]

gil′lie, gil′ly, *n.* [Scot., from Gael. *gille*, a boy, lad, page.] A boy; a page or menial; in the Scotch highlands, a male servant, particularly a gamekeeper.

gill′=lid, *n.* The covering of the gills.

gill′=net, *n.* A net so constructed that when suspended in the water fishes are caught by putting the heads through the meshes and are held by the gills when they attempt to escape.

gill′=ō″pen-ing, *n.* The aperture of a fish or other animal by which water is admitted to the gills.

gill′=plūme, *n.* Same as *Gill-comb.*

gill′=rāk″ẽr, gill′=rāke, *n.* One of the horny processes within the branchial arch of a fish that protect the gill cavities from injurious substances.

gill′=slit, *n.* Same as *Gill-opening.*

gil′ly-flow″ẽr, *n.* [ME. *gyllofer, gyllofre, gilofre*; OFr. *clou de girofle*, lit., clove of gillyflower; LL. *caryophyllum*; Gr. *karyophyllon*, the clove-tree, lit., nut-leaf, from *karyon*, nut, and *phyllon*, leaf.]

1. Any one of several cruciferous plants, especially of the genus *Matthiola*, embracing the common stock or stock-gillyflower, and the genus *Cheiranthus*, including the wallflower.

2. A name also applied to various plants of other families, as the feathered gillyflower of the pink family.

gil′ŏur, *n.* A deceiver; a beguiler. [Obs.]

gilse, *n.* [W. *gleisiad*, from *glas*, blue.] See *Grilse.*

gilt, *n.* A young female pig. [Prov. Eng.]

gilt, *a.* Overlaid with gold-leaf or a thin coating of gold; illuminated; adorned; gold-colored.

gilt, *n.* 1. Gold or an imitation of gold laid on the surface of a thing; gilding.

2. Money. [Rare.]

gilt′=edġe (-ej), *a.* See *Gilt-edged.*

gilt′=edġed, *a.* 1. Having the edge covered with gold-leaf, as in the case of gift-books, etc.

2. Of superlative quality; first-class; as, *gilt-edged* negotiable paper. [Colloq.]

gilt′head, *n.* 1. A spinous-finned marine fish of the genus *Sparus* or *Chrysophrys*, found in the Mediterranean and prized as food; so named from a golden-yellow space over the eyes; sometimes known as the *giltpoll.*

2. The *Crenilabrus melops* of English waters; the sea-partridge.

gilt′if, *a.* Guilty. [Obs.]

gilt′tāil, *n.* A worm or larva with a yellow tail.

ġim, *a.* Neat; spruce; natty. [Obs.]

ġim′băl, *n.* [OFr. *gemelle*, twin, from L. *gemellus*, dim. of *geminus*, twin, double.]

1. A device allowing a suspended body to incline freely in any direction, commonly consisting of a ring pivoted so as to turn on a horizontal diameter and having the object pivoted in the ring on a diameter at right angles to the other. Used on shipboard to keep compasses, lamps, chronometers, etc., level when the vessel rolls.

2. Joined work whose parts move within each other, as a bridle-bit or interlocked rings. [Obs.]

3. A gemel-ring; hence, any quaint contrivance. [Obs.]

ġim′băl=joint, *n.* A form of universal joint on the plan of a gimbal.

ġim′băl=ring, *n.* The metal support in the center of an upper millstone.

ġim′blet, *n.* A gimlet. [Obs.]

ġim′çrack, *n.* 1. A trivial device or mechanism; a toy; a trinket; a pretty but worthless ornament.

2. A young fop; a neat, pert boy. [Obs.]

ġim′let, *v.t.* To turn, as a gimlet; to use a gimlet upon; to form by the use of a gimlet.

ġim′let, *n.* [ME. *gymlet*; OFr. *gimbelet, guimbelet*, a gimlet; of Teutonic origin; compare O.D. *wimpel*, a bore, from *wemelen*, to bore.] A small, spirally grooved instrument with a pointed screw at the end, for boring holes in wood by turning.

ġim′let=eye (-ī), *n.* 1. A squint-eye.

2. A piercing eye; a keen look.

ġim′măl, *n.* A gimbal. [Obs.]

ġim′mẽr, *n.* A hinge; a gimbal; a gimcrack. [Obs.]

ġim′mẽr, *n.* A gossip; a friend. [Scot.]

ġim′mẽr, *n.* A yearling ewe. [North Eng. and Scot.]

gimp, *a.* Spruce; trim; jimp. [Obs.]

gimp, *v.t.* To jag; to indent.

gimp, *n.* [Fr. *guimpe*; OFr. *guimpe, guimple*, a nun's wimple, a wimple, veil, from O.H.G. *wimpal*, a wimple, veil.]

1. A flat trimming or edging usually of cord in an open pattern stiffened by wire; used for decorating gowns, furniture, etc.

2. A heavy thread used in the edges of the figures in certain lace.

3. A fish-line strengthened with a fine wire.

gimp′=nāil, *n.* An upholsterer's nail used in attaching gimp.

ġin, *n.* [Abbrev. of *geneva*; ME. *gynypre*, juniper.] A distilled alcoholic liquor flavored with oil of juniper; hence, alcoholic liquors collectively, as a term of reprobation.

ġin, *n.* [ME. *gin, ginne*, ingenuity, contrivance, a machine, engine, abbrev. of *engin, engyn*, an engine.]

1. A machine or device by which a mechanical power is employed in aid of human strength; especially, (a) a tripod with pulleys and windlass, used in place of a crane for lifting heavy weights; (b) a machine for driving piles; (c) a cotton-gin; (d) an instrument of torture; (e) a form of windmill-pump; (f) in English coal-mines, a whim or vertical winch.

Gin for raising heavy Weights.

2. A trap; a snare.

ġin, *v.t.*; ginned, *pt.*, *pp.*; ginning, *ppr.* 1. To clear (cotton) of seeds by the use of a gin.

2. To ensnare by or as by a gin. [Obs.]

gin, *prep.* Against (a time specified); by; as, *gin* the morn. [Scot.]

gin, *conj.* If; against; suppose; as, *gin* a body meet a body. [Scot.]

gin, *v.t.* and *v.i.* To begin. [Obs.]

gin, *n.* [Australian.] A female native; an old woman.

ġin'-block, *n.* A single-wheeled tackle-block.

ġin'-fizz', *n.* A mixed drink composed of gin, lemon-juice, and carbonated water, with or without sugar.

ging, *n.* A gang. [Obs.]

ġin'găl, *n.* Same as *Jingal.*

ġin'ġe-ley, *n.* Same as *Gingili.*

ġin'ġẽr, *n.* [ME. *ginger, gynger*; OFr. *gengibre, gingimbre*; L. *zingiber*; Gr. *zingiberis*, ginger; of Eastern origin.]

1. The plant or the root of *Zingiber officinale*, grown extensively in the East and West Indies. The dried roots are used in cookery and in medicine.

2. Pungency; snap; vitality; energy; nerve.

Egyptian ginger; *Colocasia esculenta*, the plant or its rootstock.

Ginger ale, beer, cordial, pop, etc.; beverages flavored with ginger.

Mango ginger; *Curcuma Amada*, the plant or its rootstock.

Ginger-plant (*Zingiber officinale*).

ġin'ġẽr-bread (-bred), *n.* A raised cake usually sweetened with molasses and flavored with ginger.

ġin'ġẽr-bread-plum, *n.* The drupe of the gingerbread-tree.

ġin'ġẽr-bread-tree, *n.* 1. The doom-palm.

2. *Parinarium macrophyllum*, an African tree bearing the drupe known as the gingerbread-plum.

ġin'ġẽr-bread-wŏrk, *n.* Excessive, trivial, or tawdry ornamental work on buildings, furniture, etc., especially in cut or carved designs.

ġin'ġẽr-grass, *n.* 1. *Andropogon Schœnanthus*, an East Indian grass from which an aromatic oil is derived.

2. *Panicum glutinosum*, a coarse, strong grass of the West Indies.

ġin'ġẽr-ly, *adv.* Cautiously; fastidiously.

ġin'ġẽr-ness, *n.* Cautious or fastidious quality.

ġin'ġẽr-snap, *n.* A thin, flat cake, usually round and brittle, flavored with ginger.

ging'hăm (-ăm), *n.* [Fr. *guingan*, from *Guingamp*, a town in Brittany where this fabric is made; also thought to be from Javanese *ginggang*, perishable.] A cotton dress-goods, usually woven in stripes or checks from yarns dyed before weaving.

ġin'ġi-li, *n.* [E. Ind.] The seed or plant of *Sesamum Indicum*. [See *Benne.*]

ġin'ġing, *n.* The lining of a mine-shaft. [Eng.]

ġin'ġi-văl, *a.* [L. *gingivæ*, the gums.] Pertaining to the gums.

ġin-ġi-vī'tis, *n.* [L. *gingivæ*, the gums, and *-itis.*] An inflamed condition of the gums.

ging'kō, *n.* [Japan. *ginko, gingko*, from Chinese *yin-hing*, the silver apricot; *yin*, silver, and *hing*, apricot.]

1. A Japanese tree, *Gingko biloba*, cultivated for its ornamental foliage; called also *naidenhair-tree.*

2. [G—] A genus of the *Coniferæ* allied to the yews, native to Japan and China.

ġiñ'gle, *n.* and *v.* Jingle. [Obs.]

Gin-gly-mō'dī, *n.pl.* [Gr. *ginglymos*, a hinge, and *eidos*, form.] An order of fishes of the *Ganoidei.*

ġiñ'gly-moid, **ġiñ'gly-fọrm**, *a.* Of or like a ginglymus.

ġin-gly-mos'tō-moid, *a.* [Gr. *ginglymos*, a hinge, *stoma*, mouth, and *eidos*, form.] Of or like the *Ginglymostomidæ*, a family of sharks in which the lip-folds seem to hinge together.

ġiñ'gly-mus, *n.*; *pl.* **ġiñ'gly-mī**. [Gr. *ginglymos*, a hinge-joint.] In anatomy, a hingelike joint; that species of articulation in which each bone partly receives, and is partly received by, the other, so as to admit only of flexion and extension, as the elbow joint.

ġin'house, *n.* A house where cotton is ginned.

ġiñk'gō, *n.* Same as *Gingko*, 1.

ġinn, *n.* See *Jinn.*

ġin'net, *n.* [Obs.] See *Jennet.*

ġin'ning, *n.* Beginning. [Obs.]

ġin'ny-car"riaġe (-rij), *n.* [*Ginny*, prob. variant of *Jenny*, a personal name, from Fr. *Jeanne*, f. of *Jean*, John.] A small car on English railroads, to carry materials for construction.

ġin'seng, *n.* [Chinese, *jintsan.*] In botany, a plant of the genus *Aralia*, the root of which is in great demand among the Chinese as a medicine. *Aralia quinquefolia*, a native of the United States, is shipped in considerable quantities to China. It is closely allied to *Aralia ginseng*, the Chinese variety. The root is jointed, fleshy, and tapering, and, when dry, of a yellowish-white color, with a mucilaginous sweetness in the taste, somewhat resembling that of licorice, accompanied with a slight bitterness. *Aralia trifolia*, a low variety, is known as *dwarf ginseng.*

American Ginseng (*Aralia quinquefolia*).

ġin'shop, *n.* A saloon.

ġiō-cō'sō, *a.* [It., from L. *jocosus*, playful.] Sportive; playful; a term used in music.

ġip, *v.t.*; gipped (jipt), *pt., pp.*; gipping, *ppr.* To gib; to eviscerate, as fish.

ġip, *n.* See *Gyp.*

ġi-pon', **ġi-pōun'**, *n.* See *Jupon.*

ġip'sẽr, **ġip'sīre**, *n.* A scrip; a wallet. [Obs.]

Ġip'sy, *n.*; *pl.* **Ġip'sieṣ**. [ME. *Gipsen, Gypcien*; thought to be a corruption of *Egipcien*, Egyptian.]

1. One of a peculiar vagabond race found in every country of Europe, as well as in parts of Asia, Africa, and America, living as nomadic tinkers, horse-dealers, basket-makers, fortune-tellers, etc. Their skin is of a tawny color; eyes large, black, and brilliant; hair long, coal-black, and often ringleted; mouth well shaped; teeth of dazzling whiteness; and their frame light, but lithe and agile. Ethnologists generally regard the Gipsies as descendants of some obscure Hindu tribe.

2. The language of the *Gipsies.* Their language, which they call *Romany chiv* or *chib* or *Romanes*, is a Hindu dialect closely allied to Sanskrit, but much corrupted by admixture with the tongues of the peoples among whom they have sojourned. Thus, in the vocabulary of the Anglo-Scottish Gipsies there are Greek, Slavonic, Rumanian, Magyar, German, and French ingredients, evidencing that they have sojourned in the countries where these languages are spoken.

3. [g—] A person resembling a *Gipsy* in any way, as one with dark hair or eyes; one who is roguish, artful, cunning, tricky, vagabond, or the like; generally a word of reproach.

4. [g—] A gipsy-winch.

ġip'sy, *a.* Of, like, or characteristic of a Gipsy.

Gipsy hat; a hat for a woman or child, generally broad-brimmed and of straw.

ġip'sy, *v.i.*; gipsied, *pt., pp.*; gipsying, *ppr.* To act like a Gipsy; to rove about; to picnic; to camp out.

ġip'sy-hẽrb, *n.* The gipsywort.

ġip'sy-ism, *n.* Any or all of the conditions or characteristics of gipsy life, as cajolery, trickery, thievishness, roving habits, etc.

ġip'sy-mọth, *n.* *Ocneria* or *Hypogymna dispar*, a moth, the sexes of which differ much in appearance, the male being blackish-brown and the female grayish-white. It is very injurious to trees and foliage.

ġip'sy-winch, *n.* A small windlass or winch having a ratchet and pawl, thus being suited for a direct rotary motion or for the reciprocating motion of a lever.

ġip'sy-wŏrt, *n.* Any plant of the genus *Lycopus*, family *Labiatæ*. Common *gipsywort* or water-hoarhound, *Lycopus Europæus*, yields a black dye said to be used by Gipsies to render their skin darker, hence the name.

ġi-raffe', *n.* [Fr. *giraffe*; Sp. Port. *girafa*, from Ar. *zarāf, zarāfa*, a giraffe.]

1. The camelopard, an African ruminant, whose fore legs are much longer than the hinder ones. It is the tallest of animals, being sometimes twenty feet from the hoofs to the top of the head. This is mainly due to the extraordinary length of the neck, in which the seven vertebræ are extremely elongated. It has two bony excrescences on its head resembling horns. Its height is admirably suited to its habit of feeding upon the leaves of trees, and in this the animal is further aided by its tongue, which is both prehensile and protrusile. It rarely attempts to pick up food from the ground. Its color is usually light fawn marked with darker spots. *Giraffa camelopardalis* is the only species extant.

Giraffe (*Giraffa Camelopardalis*).

2. [G—] In astronomy, a constellation, Camelopardalis.

3. An eighteenth century spinet.

4. A special type of car used on inclines in mining, one end being higher than the other.

ġir'ăn-dōle, *n.* [Fr. *girandole*; It. *girandola*, a chandelier, a fire-wheel, from *girare*, L. *gyrare*, to turn, from *gyrus*, a circle.]

1. A chandelier; a kind of branched candlestick.

2. A firework rotating while burning; also, any jet performing a rotation.

3. A number of mines connecting to protect a fortification.

4. A piece of jewelry formed of a pendant or pendants.

ġir'ȧ-sol, **ġir'ȧ-sōle**, *n.* [Fr. *girasol*, from It. *girasole*, the fire-opal, a sunflower; *girare*, to turn, and *sole*, sun; L. *gyrare*, to turn, and *sol, solis*, sun.] The fire-opal.

gird, *n.* 1. A twinge or pang; a sudden spasm which resembles the stroke of a rod, or the pressure of a band. [Obs.]

2. A gibe.

gird, *v.t.* [ME. *girden, gerden*, to strike, thrust, smite, from *gerd*; AS. *gyrd*, a rod.]

1. To strike. [Obs.]

2. To taunt; to gibe.

gird, *v.i.* To gibe; to sneer; to break a scornful jest; to utter severe sarcasm.

gird, *v.t.*; girt *or* girded, *pt., pp.*; girding, *ppr.* [ME. *girden, gerden*; AS. *gyrdan*, to bind.]

1. To bind by surrounding with any flexible substance, as with a cord, bandage, or cloth.

2. To make fast by binding; to put on; usually with *on*; as, to *gird on* a sword.

3. To surround; to encircle; to inclose.

4. To clothe; to dress; to furnish; to equip.

Girded with snaky wiles. —Milton.

To gird up; to surround closely with a girdle; to strengthen.

Girt up; equipped; ready.

gird'ẽr, *n.* One who gibes or girds.

gird'ẽr, *n.* One who or that which girds, binds, or surrounds; specifically, a main beam, of either wood or iron, resting upon a wall or pier at each end, employed for supporting a superstructure or a superincumbent weight, as a floor, the upper wall of a house when the lower part is sustained by pillars, the roadway of a bridge, and the like.

Bowstring girder; see under *Bowstring.*

Half-lattice girder; a girder formed by two horizontal beams joined by bars set diagonally without crossing.

Lattice girder; a girder consisting of two horizontal beams united by diagonal crossing bars, somewhat resembling wooden latticework.

Sandwich girder; a girder made of a plate of iron having a wooden beam bolted to it on both sides.

gird'ing, *n.* A girdle.

gir'dle, *n.* [ME. *girdel, gerdel*; AS. *gyrdel*, a girdle, from *gyrdan*, to gird.]

1. A band or belt; something drawn round a person, and tied or buckled; as, a *girdle* of fine linen; a leathern *girdle.*

2. The zodiac; the equator.

3. In a brilliant-cut diamond, the line of greatest periphery, being that held by the setting.

4. A thin stratum of rock in mining.

5. The annular bony structure in vertebrates to which a limb is attached, as the pelvic *girdle*, formed by the bones of the hips, and the thoracic *girdle*, formed by the clavicles and scapulæ.

6. A seaweed of genus *Laminaria.*

gir'dle, *v.t.*; girdled, *pt., pp.*; girdling, *ppr.*

1. To bind with a belt or sash; to gird.

2. To inclose; to environ; to shut in.

3. To make a circular incision in, as through the bark of a tree.

gir'dle-bōne, *n.* The sphenethmoid.

gir'dlẽr, *n.* 1. One who girdles; a maker of girdles.

2. A beetle that girdles the twig in which it has laid its eggs; the larva thus has decaying wood for food; as, a twig-*girdler*, genus *Oncideres.*

gir'dle-stead (-sted), *n.* The part of the body where the girdle is worn. [Obs.]

gir'dle-wheel, *n.* A wheel for spinning.

ġire, *n.* A circle, or circular motion. [Obs. See *Gyre.*]

gir'kin, *n.* [Obs.] See *Gherkin.*

girl, *n.* [ME. *girle, gerle*, a young person, either girl or boy, most frequently a girl, from L.G. *gör*, masc., a boy, *göre*, f., a girl.]

1. A female child; hence, any young unmarried woman.

2. A maidservant. [Colloq.]

3. A sweetheart. [Colloq.]

4. A child. [Obs.]

5. A roebuck less than two years old. [Obs.]

girl'hood, *n.* The time or state of being a girl.

girl'ish, *a.* 1. Relating to girlhood or to a girl; as, *girlish* hours.

2. Resembling or characteristic of girls; artless; as, *girlish* manners.

girl'ish-ly, *adv.* In the manner of a girl.

gïrl'ish-ness, *n.* Levity; the manners of a girl.

gïr'lond, *n.* [Obs.] See *Garland.*

gïrn, *v.i.*, obsolete corruption of *grin.*

gïrn, *n.* A snarl; a grin; a yawn. [Obs.]

Gi-ron'dist, *n.* [Fr. *Girondiste*, from *Gironde*, a political party of France.] One of a celebrated political party during the French Revolution.

Gi-ron'dist, *a.* Relating to the Girondists.

gïr'rŏck, *n.* A species of garfish.

gïrt, *v.*, past tense and past participle of *gird.*

gïrt, *v.t.* To gird; to surround.

gïrt, *a.* Moored by two cables to two anchors placed on opposite sides, to prevent a vessel from swinging.

gïrth, *n.* [ME. *girth, gerth*; Ice. *gjördh*, a girdle, girth.]

1. That which encircles; a girdle; a belt; a band; specifically, a strap or cinch used in fastening a saddle or load, as upon a horse or mule.

2. The measure of anything cylindrical or resembling a cylinder in form; specifically, the waist measure of a person; as, a man of ample height and *girth.*

3. A circular bandage.

4. Any boundary which incloses; a perimeter; as, a field having a *girth* of hedge.

5. A timber used in car-construction, as a brace to strengthen the frame.

6. The strap, usually of leather, passing about the pulley in a hand-press, which conveys motion to the carriage.

gïrth, *v.t.* To bind with a girth; to gird.

gïrt'line, *n.* A rope used in the process of rigging a ship, to lift the rigging up to the masthead.

gis-ärm', *n.* [Obs.] See *Guisarme.*

ġīse, *v.t.* To feed; to pasture. [Obs.]

ġīse, *n.* [Obs.] Same as *Guise.*

ġis'el, *n.* A pledge. [Obs.]

ġis'lẽr, *n.* [Etym. uncertain.] The salmon fish-louse.

ġis-mon'dine, ġis-mon'dite, *n.* [Named after C. G. *Gismondi*, an Italian mineralogist.] A mineral silicate of calcium and aluminium found near Rome.

ġist, *n.* [OFr. *gist*, abode, lodgings, the point at issue, from 3rd pers. sing. pres. ind. act. of *gesir*, to lie, from L. *jacere*, to lie.] The main point of a question; the point on which an action rests; the essence of a matter.

ġist, *n.* [OFr. *giste*, lodging, abode, from *gesir*, to lie; L. *jacere*, to lie.] A place where one sleeps, lodges, or reposes. [Obs.]

git, *v.* To get; a form obsolete except in dialect.

ġit, *n.* See *Geat.*

ġīte, *n.* A gown. [Obs.]

gith, *n.* [ME. *gith*; AS. *gith*, the cockle; L. *gith*, the Roman coriander.]

1. The fennel-flower.

2. Corn-cockle.

git'tẽrn, *n.* [ME. *giterne*; OFr. *guiterne*; from L. *cithara*, the guitar, cithara.] A guitar-like musical instrument; a cithern.

git'tẽrn, *v.i.* To play on a gittern.

git'tith, *n.* [Heb.] A word occurring frequently in the titles to the Psalms, held by some to signify a sort of musical instrument invented at Gath, by others that the Psalms with this title were set to music.

ġiust, *n.* A joust. [Obs.]

ġius-tȧ-men'te, *adv.* [It.] In music, accurately; strictly; exactly.

ġius'tō, *a.* [It., just, equal, from L. *justus*, just, fair.] In music, in just, equal, correct, or steady time.

give, *v.t.*; gave, *pt.*; given, *pp.*; giving, *ppr.* [ME. *given, geven*, from AS. *gifan, giefan*, to give.]

1. To surrender into the power of another; to convey to another; to bestow; usually implying the action expressed is done freely and without compensation. But the word is used in a great variety of senses, the connection of which with the fundamental meaning is usually obvious.

2. To communicate; as, to *give* an opinion; to *give* counsel or advice.

> *Give* us then your mind at large:
> How say you, war or not? —Tennyson.

3. To utter; to pronounce; as, to *give* the word of command.

> So you must be the first that *gives* this sentence. —Shak.

4. To expose.

> *Give* to the wanton winds their flowing hair. —Dryden.

5. To grant; to permit.

> It is *given* me once again to behold my friend. —Rowe.

6. To admit; to allow by way of supposition; as, let A B be *given* equal to C D.

7. To enable; as, I was *given* to understand; I was *given* to know.

8. To addict; often with *up*; as, he *gave* himself *up* to the study of the ancient classics; the past participle being frequent in this sense; as, *given* to prayer.

> They who *gave* themselves to warlike action and enterprises, went immediately to the temple of Odin. —Temple.

9. To excite; as, to *give* offense or umbrage.

10. To emit; to utter; as, to *give* a shout.

> Bitter notes my harp would *give.*—Tennyson.

11. To reckon or consider.

> The crown and comfort of my life, your favor,
> I do *give* lost. —Shak.

12. To pledge; as, I *give* you my word of honor.

13. To propose, as a toast; as, to *give* the army and navy.

14. To represent.

> Too modest are you,
> More cruel to your good report than grateful
> To us that *give* you truly. —Shak.

15. To ascribe.

> The fault thou *gavest* him. —Shak.

16. To yield, as a result or product.

> The number of men being divided by the number of ships *gives* four hundred and twenty-four men a-piece. —Arbuthnot.

Give me (so and so); a common phrase expressive of predilection for a thing, equivalent to,(so and so) is the thing for me.

> *Give me* the good old times. —Lytton.

Give you good even, good morrow; phrases common in Shakspere, meaning I wish you a good evening or a good morning.

To give birth to; to bear; to bring forth, as a child; to be the origin of.

To give forth; to publish; to tell; to report publicly.

To give ground; to retire under the pressure of an advancing enemy; to yield.

To give the hand; to yield preëminence, as being subordinate or inferior.

To give in; (a) to allow by way of abatement or deduction from a claim; to yield what may be justly demanded; (b) to declare; to make known; to tender; as, *to give in* one's adhesion to a party.

To give it to one; to rate, scold, or beat one severely.

To give one the lie; to charge with falsehood.

To give line, to give head, to give the reins; all figurative expressions meaning to give full liberty to—the first derived from angling, the other two from horsemanship.

To give over; (a) to leave; to quit; to cease; to abandon; as, *to give over* a pursuit; (b) to despair of recovery; to believe to be lost or past recovery.

To give out; (a) to utter publicly; to report; to proclaim; to publish; (b) to issue; to send forth; (c) to represent; to represent as being; to declare or pretend to be; (d) to send out; to emit; to distribute; as, a substance *gives out* steam or odors.

To give place; to retire to make room for another or for something else.

To give tongue; to bark; said of dogs.

To give up; (a) to resign; to quit; to yield as hopeless; as, *to give up* a cause; (b) to surrender; to relinquish; to cede; as, *to give up* a fortress to an enemy; (c) to deliver; to make public; to show up.

To give way; (a) to yield; to withdraw; to make room for; as, inferiors should *give way* to superiors; (b) to fail; to yield to force; to break or fall; to break down; as, the ice *gave way*, and the horses were drowned; the scaffolding *gave way*; (c) nautically, in the imperative, an order to a boat's crew to row after ceasing, or to increase their exertions.

Syn.—Confer, grant.—*Give* is generic and includes the other two; *grant* and *confer* include accessory ideas; *confer* adds the idea of condescension or of allowing that which might be withheld; *grant* implies ceremony or the giving to an inferior, and presupposes a request.

give, *v.i.* 1. To yield, as to pressure; as, the earth *gives* under the feet.

> Only a sweet and virtuous soul,
> Like seasoned timber, never *gives.* —Herbert.

2. To soften; to begin to melt; to grow moist and soft; to thaw; hence, to relent.

> Some things are harder when they come from the fire, and afterwards *give* again and grow soft. —Bacon.

3. To move; to recede.

> Now back he *gives*, then rushes on amain. —Daniel.

4. To weep; to shed tears. [Obs.]

> Whose eyes do never *give*
> But through lust and laughter. —Shak.

5. To have a misgiving. [Obs.]

> My mind *gives* ye're reserved
> To rob poor market women. —Webster.

6. To lead; to open; to afford entrance or view.

> A well-worn pathway courted us
> To one green wicket in a privet hedge;
> This yielding *gave* into a grassy walk. —Tennyson.

To give in; to go back; to give way; to yield; to confess oneself beaten; to confess oneself inferior to another.

To give in to; to yield assent; to adopt.

To give off; to cease; to forbear. [Rare.]

To give on; to rush; to fall on. [Obs.]

To give out; to cease from exertion; to yield; to become exhausted.

To give upon; to front; to look into; as, a gateway *giving upon* a lane.

give, *n.* Capacity to give way; quality of yielding; spring; elasticity.

give'=and=tāke', *a.* Pertaining to the equalization of differences by concessions or handicaps, as in various contests.

give'=and=tāke', *n.* 1. An exchange or interchange of jesting, wit, or repartee.

2. Equalization by giving and taking, as a concession or handicap.

giv'en, *a.* 1. Inclined; addicted; as, *given* to drinking.

2. Known; stated; specified; as, a *given* date.

3. Assumed as a premise; granted.

Given name; all of a person's name except the surname. [Colloq.]

giv'ẽr, *n.* One who gives; a donor; a bestower; a grantor; one who imparts or distributes.

ġīveṣ, *n.pl.* See *Gyve.*

giv'ing, *n.* 1. The act of conferring.

2. A gift. [Obs.]

3. Yielding. [Rare.]

Giving in; collapse.

Giving out; utterance; proclamation.

giz'zärd, *n.* [ME. *giser*; OFr. *gezier, jugier*, the gizzard, from L. *gigeria*, neut. pl., the cooked entrails of poultry.]

1. A muscular division of the stomach in birds, being an elongated sac just below the liver.

2. In entomology, the first muscular stomach designed for crushing food, often having the walls armed with plates or teeth of chitin.

3. A peculiar stomach paved with calcareous plates in the family of mollusks called *Bullidæ*, being strong enough to crush small shellfish.

To fret the gizzard; to harass or vex oneself; to be vexed. [Vulgar.]

To stick in one's gizzard; to be distasteful. [Vulgar.]

giz'zärd=shad, *n.* Any fish of the family *Dorosomidæ*, feeding on mud and resembling the common herring.

giz'zärd=trout, *n.* Same as *Gillaroo.*

glȧ-bel'lȧ, *n.*, pl. of *glabellum.*

glȧ-bel'lȧ, *n.*; *pl.* **glȧ-bel'læ.** A glabellum.

glȧ-bel'lär, *a.* Relating to the glabellum.

glȧ-bel'lum, *n.* [L. *glabellus*, hairless, from *glaber*, smooth, bald.]

1. In human anatomy, the surface between the superciliary ridges.

2. In comparative anatomy, the frontal portion of a trilobite.

glā'brāte, *a.* [L. *glabratus*, pp. of *glabrare*, lit., to make smooth, to deprive of hair, from *glaber*, smooth.] Almost or quite glabrous; growing smooth from age.

glā'brē-āte, glā'bri-āte, *v.t.* To cause to become smooth or hairless. [Obs.]

glab'ri-ty, *n.* Smoothness; baldness. [Obs.]

glā'brous, *a.* [L. *glaber*, smooth, bald.] Smooth; having no hair or pubescence on the surface.

gla-cé' (-sā'), *a.* [Fr., iced, glazed, pp. of *glacer*, to turn into ice, freeze, from *glace*, L. *glacies*, ice.] Having the surface glazed or glossy; glossed; iced; rarely, frozen; as, *glacé* fruit; *glacé* silk.

glā'ciăl (-shăl), *a.* [L. *glacialis*, icy, frozen, full of ice, from *glacies*, ice.] Of or like ice; (a) in geology, of, from, or due to masses of ice, especially in the form of glaciers; (b) in chemistry, having the crystalline appearance of ice at laboratory temperature; as, *glacial* acetic acid.

Glacial epoch or *period*; the time during which a considerable part of the northern hemisphere, including the mountain peaks, was covered with ice; during the *glacial period*, the climate of the polar regions extended over the whole of the present temperate zone, according to many geologists.

Glacial theory; see *Glacier theory* under *Glacier.*

glā'ciăl-ist, *n.* 1. A geologist who holds that the drift phenomena are due to glaciers.

2. One having expert knowledge of glaciers and their formation.

glā'ciăl-ly, *adv.* By glacial action.

glā'ci-āte (-shi-āt), *v.i.*; glaciated, *pt., pp.*; glaciating, *ppr.* [L. *glaciatus*, pp. of *glaciare*, to turn into ice, freeze.] To turn to ice.

glā′ci-āte, *v.t.* 1. To cover with ice; to transform into ice.

2. To leave glacial traces on, as on rocks or drift.

glā-ci-ā′tion, *n.* 1. The act of freezing; ice formed.

2. The appearance or indication of glacial action.

glā′cieṛ (-shēr), *n.* [Fr. *glacier*, from *glace*, L. *glacies*, ice.] A river of ice slowly descending

Glacier of Zermatt, Switzerland.

a mountain side, commonly commencing as a frozen mass of snow formed above the line of perpetual congelation, and consolidated partly by pressure and partly by the freezing of water infiltered into it from its surface.

Glacier theory; (a) the theory attributing important geological changes, as the erosion of valleys, the denudation of large portions of the earth's surface, the transportation and deposition of drift or boulder-clay, the accumulation of moraines, etc., to the action of glaciers; (b) the name given to any theory accounting for the downward motion of glaciers.

gla-cière′ (-siâr′), *n.* [Fr., from *glace*, L. *glacies*, ice.] In geology, the term applied to certain caverns in alpine districts which, although not connected with any glacial system, are filled with ice.

glā′cieṛ-milk, *n.* Water the color of milk, due to sediment. It flows from the bed or base of glaciers.

glā′cieṛ-tā″ble, *n.* A rock supported by a column of ice, the surrounding ice, originally as

Glacier-table.

high as the supporting pedestal, having melted away.

gla-ci-o-. A combining form from L. *glacies*, ice, signifying ice or glacier.

glā″ci-ō-ā′quē-ous (glā″shi-ō-ā′kwē-us), *a.* [*Glacio-*, and L. *aqua*, water.] Pertaining to or caused by the combined action of ice and water.

glā″ci-ō-log′ic-ăl, *a.* Pertaining to glaciology.

glā-ci-ol′ō-ġist, *n.* See *Glacialist.*

glā-ci-ol′ō-ġy, *n.* [*Glacio-*, and Gr. *-logia*, from *legein*, to speak.] The science of the formation of glaciers and icebergs and their action.

glā″ci-ō-nā′tănt, *a.* [*Glacio-*, and L. *natans* (*-antis*), ppr. of *natare*, to swim.] Pertaining to floating ice or caused by it.

glā′cious, *a.* [OFr. *glacieux*, from L. *glacies*, ice.] Like ice; icy. [Obs.]

glā′cis, *n.* [Fr., from OFr. *glacis*, icy, slippery, from L. *glacies*, ice.] A gentle slope or sloping bank; especially, (a) in fortification, a sloping bank so raised as to bring the enemy advancing over it into the most direct line of fire from the fort; that mass of earth which serves as a parapet to the covered way, having an easy slope or declivity toward the champaign or field; (b) in geology, an easy slope, like that of shingle piled on the shore by the action of the tides and waves, less steep than a talus.

glack, *n.* A defile; a narrow opening in a mountain. [Scot.]

gla-çūre′ (-sür′), *n.* [Fr., from *glacer*, L. *glaciare*, to freeze.] A thin glazed coating given to fine earthenware.

glad, *a.*; *comp.* gladder; *superl.* gladdest. [ME. *glad*, *gled*; AS. *glæd*, bright, cheerful, shining, glad.]

1. Pleased; cheerful; gratified; feeling pleasure, joy, or satisfaction; followed by *at*, *of*, or an infinitive.

> He that is *glad at* calamities shall not be unpunished. —Prov. xvii. 5.
>
> He, *glad of* her attention. —Milton.
>
> *Glad to* behold your eyes. —Shak.

2. Expressive of or indicating pleasure or satisfaction; cheerful; joyful; as, a *glad* countenance.

3. Causing or affording pleasure, joy, or satisfaction; gladdening; joyful.

> The *glad* tidings of the kingdom of God. —Luke viii. 1.

4. Wearing a gay or bright appearance; cheerful; bright; showy; gay.

> *Glad* evening and *glad* morn. —Milton.

Syn.—Delighted, gratified, pleased, happy, cheerful, joyous, pleasing.—*Delighted* expresses a much higher degree of pleasure than *glad*; *gratified* always refers to a pleasure conferred by some human agent, and the feeling is modified by the consideration that we owe it in part to another.

glad, *v.t.*; gladded, *pt.*, *pp.*; gladding, *ppr.* To make glad; to gladden; to exhilarate.

> Each drinks the juice that *glads* the heart of man. --Pope.

glad, *v.i.* To be glad; to rejoice. [Obs.]

glad′den, *v.t.*; gladdened, *pt.*, *pp.*; gladdening, *ppr.* [ME *gladen*; AS. *gladian*, to make glad, from *glæd*, glad.] To make glad; to cheer; to please; to exhilarate.

Syn.—Please, gratify, rejoice, animate, delight.

glad′den, *v.i.* To become glad; to rejoice.

glad′den, *n.* [ME. *gladene*, *gladine*; AS. *glædene*, a kind of plant; compare L. *gladiolus*, the sword-lily.] A name given to one of several species of plants of the iris family, especially *Iris fœtidissima*, from the sword-like shape of the leaves.

glad′dēr, *a.*, comp. of *glad.*

glad′dēr, *n.* One who gladdens or gives joy. [Obs.]

glad′dest, *a.*, superl. of *glad.*

glad′dŏn, *n.* See *Gladden.*

glāde, *n.* [Prob. of Scand. origin; compare W. *golead*, a lighting, illumination, from *goleu*, light, clear, AS. *glæd*, bright.]

1. An opening or passage through a wood; an open space in a wood or forest.

2. An opening in the ice of rivers or lakes, or a place left unfrozen; also, a smooth sheet of ice. [Local, U. S.]

3. An everglade. [Local, U. S.]

glāde, *n.* The common buzzard, *Buteo vulgaris.* [Prov. Eng.]

glad′en, *n.* [Obs.] See *Gladden.*

glāde′-net, *n.* A kind of net used for catching birds in the openings of forests.

glad′eȳe, *n.* The yellowhammer, *Emberiza citrinella.*

glad′fụl, *a.* Full of gladness. [Obs.]

glad′fụl-ness, *n.* Joy; gladness. [Obs.]

glad′i-āte, *a.* [L. *gladius*, a sword.] Sword-shaped, as the legume of a plant.

Gladiators, variously Armed.

glad′i-ā-tŏr, *n.* [L., from *gladius*, a sword.]

1. In Roman antiquity, one of a class of men whose profession was to fight in public for the entertainment of the people. They were armed with deadly weapons and usually fought in pairs.

2. A combatant in general; a prize-fighter; also, a disputant.

glad″i-ȧ-tō′ri-ăl, *a.* Pertaining to gladiators or to their combats.

glad″i-ȧ-tō′ri-ăn, *a.* Gladiatorial.

glad′i-ā-tŏr-iṣm, *n.* The act or practice of gladiators; prize-fighting.

glad′i-ā-tŏr-ship, *n.* The conduct, state, or occupation of a gladiator.

glad′i-ȧ-tō-ry, *a.* [L. *gladiatorius*, from *gladiator*, a gladiator.] Relating to gladiators. [Rare.]

glad′i-ȧ-tūre, *n.* Sword-play; fencing. [Obs.]

glad′i-ōle, *n.* [L. *gladiolus*, a dagger, a sword-lily.] A plant of the genus *Gladiolus.*

glȧ-dī′ō-lus, *n.*; *pl.* **glȧ-dī′ō-lī** or **glȧ-dī′ō-lus-eṣ.** [L. *gladiolus*, the sword-lily, a small sword, dim. of *gladius*, a sword.]

1. [G—] An extensive genus of beautiful bulbous-rooted plants, of the natural order *Iridaceæ*, found sparingly in the warmer parts of Europe and in North Africa, but abundantly in South Africa. They have long sword-shaped leaves.

2. A plant of the genus *Gladiolus.*

3. In anatomy, the middle or second piece of the sternum; the mesosternum.

glā′di-us, *n.*; *pl.* **glā′di-ī.** [L., a sword.] In zoölogy, the horny endoskeleton or pen of a two-gilled cuttlefish.

glad′ly, *adv.* [ME. *gladly*, *gladliche*; AS. *glædlice*, gladly, from *glæd*, glad.] With pleasure; joyfully; cheerfully

> The common people heard him *gladly.* —Mark xii. 37.

glad′ness, *n.* [ME. *gladnesse*; AS. *glædnes*, gladness, from *glæd*, glad.] Joy or a moderate degree of joy and exhilaration; pleasure; cheerfulness; the state of being glad.

Gladness is rarely or never equivalent to *mirth*, *merriment*, *gaiety*, and *triumph*, and it usually expresses less than *delight.* It sometimes expresses great joy.

glad′ship, *n.* A state of gladness. [Obs.]

glad′sŏme, *a.* 1. Pleased; joyful; cheerful.

2. Causing joy, pleasure, or cheerfulness; having the appearance of gaiety; pleasing.

glad′sŏme-ly, *adv.* In a gladsome manner.

glad′sŏme-ness, *n.* The state of being gladsome.

Glad′stōne, *n.* [Named after William Ewart *Gladstone.*]

1 A roomy four-wheeled pleasure-carriage with two inside seats, calash top, and seats for driver and footman.

2. A kind of traveling-bag made of leather; called also *Gladstone bag.*

glad′win, **glad′wyn**, *n.* [Obs.] See *Gladden.*

Glag-ō-lit′iç, *a.* [Old Bulg. and Russ. *glagol'*, a word.] Of or pertaining to Glagol, an ancient Slavic alphabet, principally used in several Roman Catholic dioceses of Istria and Dalmatia in the psalms, liturgies, and offices of the church.

glāik, *n.* 1. A deception; a delusion; a trick.

2. A transient gleam or glance.

glāir, *n.* [ME. *glayre*, *gleire*; OFr. *glaire*, the white of an egg, from L. *clarus*, clear.]

1. The white of an egg used as a varnish to preserve paintings, and as a size in gilding.

2. Any viscous, transparent substance, resembling the white of an egg.

3. A kind of halberd.

glāir, *v.t.*; glaired, *pt.*, *pp.*; glairing, *ppr.* To smear with the white of an egg.

glāir′ē-ous, *a.* Glairy.

glāir′in, *n.* A substance resembling glair gathering on certain mineral waters.

glāir′y, *a.* Like glair, or partaking of its qualities.

glāive, *n.* See *Glave.*

glā′mȧ, *n.* [L., from Gr. *glamē*, a humor in the eyes.] A secretion of gummy matter on the eyelids.

glam′ber″ry, *n.*; *pl.* **glam′ber″rieṣ.** A plant, *Byrsonima lucida*, valued for its fruit. It grows in southern Florida and the West Indies.

glam′oụr, *n.* [Scot. *glamour*, *glamer*, prob. from Ice. *glamyr*, *glamr*, the moon, a legendary ghost or spirit.]

1. Witchery; enchantment; a supposed charm on the eyes, making things seem different from what they really are; witchcraft; spell; magic.

> It had much of *glamour* might
> To make a lady seem a knight. —Scott.

2. A haze that does not totally obscure objects, but causes them to be seen in an abnormal aspect.

3. Anything that obscures or deceives vision, physical or mental; fascination.

> To her soul
> All the desert's *glamour* stole. —Whittier.

glam′oū-rie, *n.* [Scot.] Same as *Glamour.*

glănce, *n.* [Of Scand. origin; compare Old Sw. *glans*, splendor, from Old Dan. *glinte*, to shine.]

1. A sudden shoot of light or brilliancy.

2. A shooting or darting of sight; a rapid or

momentary view or directing of the eye; a snatch of sight; as, a sudden *glance*; a *glance* of the eye.

3. A sudden deflection of a moving body by contact with another body; as, the *glance* of a ball from the ground.

4. A fleeting thought.

5. A name given in mineralogy to various lustrous ores; it is the English equivalent of the German *glanz*.

Glance coal; anthracite coal.

Glance copper; native copper sulphid.

Syn.—Glimpse, look, expression.

glȧnce, *v.i.*; glanced (glȧnst), *pt., pp.*; glancing, *ppr.* 1. To shoot or dart a ray of light or splendor.

2. To fly off in an oblique direction; to dart aside; as, the arrow struck the shield and *glanced*; a *glancing* ball or shot.

3. To look with a sudden, rapid directing of the eye; to snatch a momentary or hasty view; as, he *glanced* rapidly over the document.

Then sit again, and sigh, and *glance*.
—Suckling.

4. To hint; to cast a word or reflection; as, to *glance* at a different subject.

5. To appear and disappear rapidly, as a star; to twinkle.

glȧnce, *v.t.* 1. To shoot or dart suddenly or obliquely; to cast for a moment; as, to *glance* the eye.

2. To touch briefly; to suggest; to hint.

glȧn′cing, *a.* Shooting; darting; flying off obliquely; as, *glancing* beams; *glancing* shots.

glȧn′cing-ly, *adv.* In a glancing manner.

gland, *n.* [Fr. *glande*, f. a gland, *gland*, masc. an acorn, from L. *glans, glandis*, an acorn.]

1. In anatomy, an organ which secretes some fluid from the blood, as the parotid *gland*, the liver, the kidneys, etc.; also, a similar body not secretory, as the vascular or ductless *glands*, which include the spleen, thymus, and thyroid *glands*, whose use is not certainly known, and certain portions of the brain, as the pineal and pituitary *glands*, etc.

2. Same as *Glans*.

3. In botany, a secretory duct or vessel; also, any wart-like swelling on the surface of plants.

4. In steam-engines, the cover of a stuffing-box; called also a *follower*.

5. In machinery, a contrivance consisting of a crosspiece or clutch, for engaging or disengaging machinery moved by belts or bands.

glan-dā′ceous, *a.* [L. *glans, glandis*, an acorn.] Yellowish-brown; of the color of an acorn.

glan′dāge, *n.* A feeding upon acorns. [Obs.]

glan-dā′ri-ous, *a.* Acorn-like in shape; glandiform.

glan′dẽr, *v.t.*; glandered, *pt., pp.*; glandering, *ppr.* To affect with glanders.

glan′dẽr-ous, *a.* Having the symptoms of glanders; diseased with glanders.

glan′dẽrs, *n.* [Fr. *glande*, a gland, from L. *glans, glandis*, an acorn.] A dangerous, contagious disease of the mucous membrane of the nostrils of horses, attended with an increased and vitiated secretion and discharge of mucus, and enlargement and induration of the glands of the lower jaw. Man and other animals are liable to be infected by the disease.

glan′dēs, *n.*, pl. of *glans*.

glan-dif′ẽr-ous, *a.* [L. *glandifer*, acorn-bearing; *glans, glandis*, an acorn, and *ferre*, to bear.] Bearing acorns, or other similar nuts.

gland′i-fọrm, *a.* [L. *glans, glandis*, an acorn, and *forma*, form.]

1. In the shape of or resembling a gland.

2. Acorn-like in shape; glandarious.

glan′dū-lăr, *a.* Containing glands; consisting of glands; pertaining to glands.

glan-dū-lā′tion, *n.* In botany, the situation and structure of the secretory vessels in plants.

glan′dūle, *n.* [L. *glandula*, a kernel, gland, dim. of *glans, glandis*, an acorn.] A small gland or secreting vessel.

glan-dū-lif′ẽr-ous, *a.* [L. *glandula*, a gland, and *ferre*, to bear.] Bearing glands.

glan′dū-lōse, *a.* Glandular.

glan-dū-los′i-ty, *n.* 1. A collection of glands. [Rare.]

2. The quality of being glandulous.

3. A glandular body. [Rare.]

glan′dū-lous, *a.* [L. *glandulosus*, containing kernels or glands, from *glandula*, a gland, kernel, dim. of *glans, glandis*, an acorn.] Of, containing, consisting of, or like glands; glandular.

glans, *n.*; *pl.* **glan′dēs.** [L., an acorn.]

1. In botany, a one-celled, compound inferior fruit, with a dry pericarp, as the acorn.

2. In medicine, (a) bronchocele; goiter; (b) a pessary; a suppository.

3. The rounded body forming the end of the penis or clitoris.

glāre, *v.i.*; glared, *pt., pp.*; glaring, *ppr.* [ME. *glaren*, to shine brightly; L.G. *glaren*, to shine brightly, glow, from the same root as AS. *glær*, amber.]

1. To shine with a clear, bright, dazzling light; as, the electric lights *glare* all night.

2. To look with fierce, piercing eyes; to stare.

3. To shine with excessive luster; to be ostentatiously splendid.

She *glares* in balls, front boxes, and the ring.
—Pope.

glāre, *v.t.* To give forth, as a dazzling light.

Every eye *glared* lightning. —Milton.

Syn.—Glisten, scintillate, glitter, glister, gleam, sparkle, coruscate, glimmer, flicker.

glāre, *n.* 1. A bright, dazzling light; clear, brilliant luster or splendor, that distresses the eyes.

2. A fierce, piercing look; a stare.

3. An icy condition; a very smooth surface; usual only in the phrase, a *glare* of ice.

glāre, *a.* Having a very smooth, slippery, or glassy surface; said of ice.

I have seen ponies which had to be knocked down and pulled across *glare* ice on their sides. —T. Roosevelt.

glār′e-ous, *a.* Glaireous.

glār′i-ness, *n.* The quality of being glary.

glār′ing, *a.* 1. Shining with dazzling luster; excessively bright; gaudy; as, *glaring* hues.

2. Notorious; obvious; open and bold; easily noticed; said of errors and offenses; as, a *glaring* mistake.

3. Having a hostile, penetrating gaze; as, a *glaring* eye.

glār′ing-ly, *adv.* In a glaring manner.

glār′y, *a.* 1. Glaring; having a dazzling luster.

2. Covered with glare ice; icy.

glȧss, *n.* [ME. *glas, gles*; AS. *glæs*, glass.]

1. A substance formed by the fusion of silica with two or more metallic oxids. A mixture of fine sand, with soda or potash and lime, or lead oxid, is used for the ordinary kinds. The nature of *glass* depends upon the quality and proportion of ingredients, but it is usually hard, brittle, and transparent or translucent. When heated, it may be rendered so flexible and ductile that it may be blown, rolled, molded, or otherwise shaped into any desired form, and it can be given almost any color by suitable metallic oxids or fusible pigments. *Crown glass* is a lime glass without lead; *flint* or *crystal glass* is a lead glass; *blown glass* is prepared by blowing; *plate glass* is cast and rolled; *spun glass* is drawn out into filaments while ductile; *tempered* or *toughened glass* is hardened by immersion in a hot bath of resin, wax, oil, or other liquid of high boiling-point.

2. In chemistry, any substance brought by fusion to the state of a hard, brittle, transparent mass, whose fracture is conchoidal.

3. Something made of *glass*; (a) a drinking-vessel; as, a beer-*glass*; (b) a mirror; as, a looking-*glass*; (c) an optical instrument composed partly of *glass*; a lens; a telescope; in the plural, spectacles; (d) an instrument for indicating atmospheric or other changes, in the composition of which *glass* is used; a barometer or thermometer; as, a storm-*glass*; (e) a vessel to measure time by the running of sand; as, an hour-*glass*; (f) a pane of *glass* for a window.

4. The quantity of liquid held by a glass drinking-vessel; as, half a *glass*; also, the liquid itself; liquor; as, he is fond of the *glass*.

Claude Lorrain glass; see under *Mirror*.

Cut glass; flint glass shaped or ornamented by cutting or grinding with polishing-wheels, usually in such fashion as to secure prismatic effects.

Ground glass; any glass that has been treated by grinding, etc., so as to destroy its transparency.

Liquid or *soluble glass*; the silicate of potassium or sodium, soluble in water and used to fireproof cloth and as a hardening ingredient of artificial stone; called also *water glass*.

glȧss, *v.t.*; glassed (glȧst), *pt., pp.*; glassing, *ppr.* 1. To mirror; to reflect; as, her face was *glassed* in the pool. [Rare.]

2. To case in or cover with glass; to glaze. [Rare.]

3. To render glassy, as a surface.

glȧss, *a.* Made of glass; vitreous; as, a *glass* bottle.

glȧss′-blōw″ẽr, *n.* One whose business is to blow and fashion glass.

glȧss′-blōw″ing, *n.* A mode of manufacturing glassware and window-glass by taking a mass of viscid glass from the melting-pot on the end of the blowing-tube and then inflating the mass by blowing through the tube, repeatedly heating, if necessary, at the furnace, and subjecting it to various manipulations.

glȧss′-çloth, *n.* 1. A kind of woven fabric containing glass filaments.

2. A variety of absorbent linen cloth used to wipe glassware or china.

glȧss′-çōach, *n.* In England, a coach superior to a hackney-coach, hired for any short period; so called because originally only private carriages had glass windows.

glȧss′-çrab, *n.* A crab of the genus *Scyllarus* or of the genus *Palinurus* in the larval state, being thin as paper, flat, and transparent.

glȧss′-çut″ting, *n.* 1. The art of cutting sheet-glass into panes or other forms.

2. The art of grinding and polishing glassware to produce cut glass.

glȧss′en, *a.* Glassy; glazed. [Obs.]

glȧss′eȳe, *n.* 1. The wall-eyed pike, *Stizostedion vitreum*.

2. In Jamaica, a species of thrush, *Turdus jamaicensis*, so called from the bluish white, pellucid, glass-like iris of its eye.

glȧss′-fāced (-fāst), *a.* Having a face that reflects another's like a mirror; as, a *glass-faced* flatterer.

glȧss′fụl, *n.* The quantity contained by a glass.

glȧss′-gạll, *n.* Sandiver; the scum from the top of fused glass.

glȧss′house, *n.* 1. A factory or salesroom for glass.

2. A house built mainly of glass, or having much glass in walls or roof, as a hothouse, a photographer's room for exposures, etc.

glȧss′i-ly, *adv.* In a glassy manner; so as to resemble glass.

glȧss′i-ness, *n.* The quality of being glassy.

Glȧss′īte, *n.* In church history, one of a sect founded in Scotland by John Glass (1695–1773), whose chief tenet was that faith is simply assent to Christ's teaching. The English and American members are called *Sandemanians*, after Robert Sandeman, a son-in-law of Glass, who founded branches in England and America.

glȧss′-māk″ing, *n.* The art or process of making glass.

glȧss′-met″ăl, *n.* The material of glass in fusion.

glȧss′-pā″pẽr, *n.* A polishing paper made by strewing finely pounded glass on a sheet of paper besmeared with a coat of thin glue.

glȧss′-pot, *n.* A vessel used for melting glass.

glȧss′-rōpe, *n.* A species of silicious sponge, *Hyalonema sieboldi*, found in Japan. It consists of a cup-shaped sponge-body, supported by a rope of long twisted silicious fibers sunk in the mud of the sea-bottom.

glȧss′-snāil, *n.* In zoölogy, a snail of the genus *Vitrina*, having a translucent shell.

glȧss′-snāke, *n.* A species of lizard resembling a snake, and having a brittle tail, as (a) the joint-snake, *Ophiosaurus ventralis*, of southern North America; (b) *Pseudopus gracilis* or *Pseudopus pallasi*, of Asia and Europe.

glȧss′-spōnge, *n.* A sponge with a silicious or vitreous framework resembling spun glass.

glȧss′wāre, *n.* Articles or utensils of glass.

glȧss′weed, *n.* The glasswort.

glȧss′wŏrk, *n.* 1. The manufacture of glassware, window-glass, etc.

2. Glassware; anything made of glass.

glȧss′-wŏrks, *n.* The shop or factory where glass is made.

glȧss′wŏrt, *n.* Any plant of the genus *Salicornia*, marine herbs, which yield by burning a vast quantity of ashes containing soda, formerly much employed in making glass.

glȧss′y, *a.* 1. Made of glass; vitreous.

2. Resembling glass in its properties, as in smoothness, brittleness, or transparency; as, a *glassy* stream.

3. Unintelligent; fixed; lifeless; as, a *glassy* eye.

In one long, *glassy*, spectral stare,
The enlarging eye is fastened there.
—Whittier.

Syn.—Vitreous, smooth, polished, glabrous, brittle, transparent, crystalline, pellucid, limpid, glossy, silken.

glau′bẽr-īte, *n.* [Named after Johann Rudolf *Glauber*, a German alchemist.] A slightly soluble mineral consisting of sulphate of soda and sulphate of lime, found chiefly in rock-salt.

Glau′bẽr's sạlt. Sulphate of soda, a well-known cathartic, found in many mineral waters.

glau-ces′cent, *a.* [L. *glaucus*; Gr. *glaukos*, gleaming, bluish-green.] Having a slight sea-green luster.

glau′çiç, *a.* Of or derived from a plant of the genus *Glaucium*; as, *glaucic* (fumaric) acid.

glau′cin, *n.* In chemistry, a crystalline alkaloid extracted from plants of the genus *Glaucium*.

glau′cine, *a.* Glaucescent.

Glau′ci-um, *n.* [Gr. *glaukion*, the juice of a plant, prob. the horned poppy, from *glaukos*, bluish-green, gray.] A genus of the *Papaveraceæ*, including the yellow horn-poppy.

glau′çō-dot, *n.* [Gr. *glaukos*, bluish-green, and *dotos*, giving, verbal adj. of *didonai*, to give.] A grayish tin-white mineral composed of arsenic, cobalt, iron, and sulphur.

glau-çō′mȧ, *n.* [L., from Gr. *glaukōma*, glaucoma, from *glaukos*, a bluish-green.] A disease in the eye, in which the crystalline humor becomes of a bluish or greenish color, and its transparency is diminished, finally causing blindness if not properly cared for.

glau-cō′ma-tous, *a.* Having the nature of glaucoma.

glau′cŏn-īte, *n.* [Gr. *glaukos*, bluish-green.] A granular silicate of potassium and iron, which gives the greenish color to greensand.

glau′cō-phāne, *n.* [Gr. *glaukos*, bluish-green, and *phanos*, bright, from *phanein*, to appear.] A dark bluish mineral, containing seven per cent of soda, and belonging to the hornblende family.

glau-cō′sis, *n.* In medicine, same as *glaucoma.*

glau′cous, *a.* [L. *glaucus*; Gr. *glaukos*, gleaming, bluish-green.]

1. Of a sea-green color; of a dull green, passing into grayish-blue.

2. In botany, covered with a fine bloom, as that of a cabbage-leaf.

glaum, *v.i.* To grope; to reach out gropingly. [Scot.]

Glaux, *n.* [L. *glaux*; Gr. *glaux*, the milk-vetch (also an owl), from *glaukos*, gleaming.] In botany, a genus of seaside plants, with a single species, *Glaux maritima*, the sea-milkwort or black saltwort.

glāve, glāive, *n.* 1. A lance or spear. [Obs.]

2. A sword; a broadsword. [Rare.]

3. A weapon resembling the halberd; also called *Welsh glave.*

With bills and *glaves* from prison was I led.
—Churchyard.

glav′ẽr, *v.i.* To flatter; to wheedle; to chatter. [Obs.]

glav′ẽr-ẽr, *n.* A flatterer. [Obs.]

glāy′mōre, *n.* Same as *Claymore.*

glāze, *v.t.*; glazed, *pt., pp.*; glazing, *ppr.* [ME. *glasen*, to furnish with glass, cause to shine, from *glas*; AS. *glæs*, glass.]

1. To furnish with glass; as, to *glaze* a house.

2. To incrust with a vitreous substance or glaze; to cover with anything smooth and shining; to render the exterior of, smooth, bright, and showy; as, to *glaze* pottery, cloth, etc.

3. To place a thin, semitransparent pigment upon, to alter the tone, as upon a color or a painting.

glāze, *v.i.* To become glassy; to become covered with a film.

A light on Marmion's visage spread
And fired his *glazing* eye. —Scott.

glāze, *n.* 1. The vitreous coating or glazing of porcelain and fine pottery.

2. Anything that glazes; a bright polish or glazed appearance on any surface.

3. A thin layer of transparent color spread over an oil-painted surface.

glāz′en, *a.* Resembling glass.

glāz′ẽr, *n.* 1. One who glazes; specifically, one who glazes pottery; one who imparts a smooth and glass-like finish to paper.

2. Any device used for glazing, as the roller used for calendering cloth or paper or the wooden wheel used by cutlers for polishing their wares.

glā′ziẽr, *n.* 1. One whose business is to set window-glass.

2. One who glazes pottery.

glāz′ing, *n.* 1. The act or art of setting glass.

2. The art of incrusting with a vitreous substance; also, the glass itself.

3. The vitreous substance with which pottery is incrusted.

4. In painting, transparent or semitransparent colors passed thinly over other colors, to modify the effect.

5. The glass of windows; as, the *glazing* of a house.

glāz′y, *a.* Showing a glaze.

glēad, *n.* A gleed; a coal. [Obs.]

glēam, *v.i.* [Etym. doubtful.] In falconry, to vent refuse matter, as a hawk.

glēam, *n.* [ME. *gleem*, *glem*; AS. *glæm*, splendor, brightness.]

1. A shoot of light; a flash; a beam; a ray; a small stream of light; as, a *gleam* of dawning light; metaphorically, a *gleam* of hope.

2. Brightness; splendor.

In the clear azure *gleam* the flocks are seen.
—Pope.

glēam, *v.i.*; gleamed, *pt., pp.*; gleaming, *ppr.* 1. To shoot, or dart, as rays of light; as, at the dawn light *gleams* in the east.

2. To shine; to cast light; as, windows *gleam* in the sun.

3. To shine out suddenly and intermittingly; to glimmer; as, fireflies *gleam* by night.

Syn.—Glimmer, glitter.—To *gleam* denotes a faint but distinct emission of light; to *glimmer* describes an indistinct and unsteady light; to *glitter*, a brightness that is intense, but varying.

glēam, *v.t.* To shoot or flash out, as light from the eyes.

glēam′y, *a.* Darting beams of light; gleaming.

glēan, *v.t.*; gleaned, *pt., pp.*; gleaning, *ppr.* [ME. *glenen*; OFr. *glener*; LL. *glenare*, to glean.]

1. To gather after reapers, as grain, straw, etc.

2. To take the leavings from; as, to *glean* a wheat-field.

3. To gather in small amounts or from places widely scattered; to get by searching here and there; as, to *glean* a few phrases from an author.

glēan, *v.i.* 1. To gather stalks or ears of grain left by reapers.

2. To obtain anything piecemeal; to make a collection bit by bit.

glēan, *n.* 1. A collection made by gleaning; especially, a handful of grain tied with a band. [Rare.]

The *gleans* of yellow thyme distend his thighs.
—Dryden.

2. A group; a bunch; as, a *glean* of 25 herrings. [Prov. Eng.]

glēan, *n.* The afterbirth of a domestic animal, as a cow. [Obs.]

glēan′ẽr, *n.* One who gleans.

glēan′ing, *n.* 1. The act of gathering after reapers.

2. That which is collected by gleaning.

glē′bȧ, *n.*; *pl.* **glē′bæ.** [L. *gleba*, *glæba*, a clod.] The tissue inclosed by the peridium of gasteromycetous fungi, containing the spores.

glēbe, *n.* [OFr. *glebe*, a glebe, land belonging to a parsonage, from L. *gleba*, *glæba*, clod, lump of earth.]

1. Turf; soil; ground. [Rare.]

Till the glad summons of a genial ray
Unbinds the *glebe.* —Garth.

2. In England, the land belonging to a parish church or ecclesiastical benefice.

glēbe′less, *a.* Without glebe.

glē-bos′i-ty, *n.* A glebous condition.

glēb′ous, glēb′y, *a.* [L. *glebosus*, full of clods, from *gleba*, a clod.] Turfy; cloddy.

glēde, *n.* [ME. *glede*; AS. *glida*, a kite, lit., a glider, from *glidan*, to glide.] The common kite of Europe, *Milvus ictinus.*

glēde, *n.* [Obs.] Same as *Gleed.*

gledġe, *v.i.* To look at anything askance; to squint.

gledġe, *n.* A sly or cunning glance. [Scot.]

Glē-ditsch′i-ȧ (-dich′), *n.* [Named after J. G. *Gleditsch*, a botanist of Leipzig.] A genus of plants of the order *Leguminosæ. Gleditschia triacanthos*, the honey-locust, is a large tree, a native of the United States, where it is commonly cultivated for hedges and for ornamental purposes. The stem and branches are covered with hard prickles; the leaves are abruptly once or twice pinnate, and the inconspicuous greenish flowers are borne in small spikes. They are succeeded by long, thin, flat, curved, and often twisted pods, each containing numerous seeds.

Honey-locust (*Gleditschia triacanthos*).

glee, *n.* [ME. *glee*, *gle*; AS. *gleow*, *gleo*, joy, mirth.]

1. Merriment; mirth; gaiety; exhilaration.

2. In music, a vocal composition in three or more parts, usually without instrumental accompaniment.

3. Music or minstrelsy generally. [Obs.]

glee′-club, *n.* In music, a company of singers organized for the purpose of singing glees and the like.

glee′-craft, *n.* Study or knowledge of music. [Obs.]

gleed, *n.* A glowing coal. [Obs.]

glee′ful, *a.* Merry; gay; joyous.

gleek, *n.* 1. A scoff; a trick. [Obs.]

2. An alluring look. [Obs.]

gleek, *n.* 1. A card game for three. [Obs.]

2. Three of a kind of anything. [Obs.]

gleek, *v.i.* To make sport; to gibe; to sneer; to spend time idly. [Obs.]

glee′măn, *n.*; *pl.* **glee′men.** A singer; formerly a wandering minstrel.

gleen, *v.i.* To shine; to glisten. [Obs.]

glee′sōme, *a.* Merry; joyous.

gleet, *n.* [ME. *glette*; OFr. *glete*, mucus, a flux.] A mucous discharge, especially from the urethra; a thin ichor running from a sore.

gleet, *v.i.* 1. To flow in a thin, limpid humor; to ooze.

2. To flow slowly, as water.

gleet′y, *a.* Ichorous; thin; limpid.

gleg, *a.* [Ice. *glöggr*, sharp, clever.] Keen; acute; alert. [Scot.]

gleire, gleyre (glãr), *n.* Glair. [Obs.]

glen, *n.* [Gael. and Ir. *gleann*, *gleanu*, a valley, glen.] A valley; a dale; a depression or space between two hills.

glen-gar′ry, *n.* [From *Glengarry*, a valley in Scotland.] A Scotch cap of wool, either woven in one piece or made up of cloth, and creased from front to back along the top.

Glen-liv′et, Glen-liv′ăt, *n.* A Scotch whisky, named from the district of its origin, a valley in Banffshire, Scotland.

glē-nō-hū′mẽr-ăl, *a.* [Gr. *glēnoeidēs*, like a ball and socket; *glēnē*, a socket, and *eidos*, form, and L. *humerus*, shoulder.] Joining the humerus to the glenoid fossa of the scapula.

glē′noid, *a.* [Gr. *glēnoeidēs*, like a ball-and-socket joint; *glēnē*, a socket, and *eidos*, form.]

1. Like a socket; cupped and shallow.

2. Formed with a socket-like cavity; as, the *glenoid* border of a scapula.

glē-noid′ăl, *a.* Same as *Glenoid.*

glent, *n.* and *v.* Same as *Glint.*

gleū-com′e-tẽr, *n.* [Gr. *gleukos*, must, and *metron*, a measure.] Same as *Glucometer.*

glew, *n.* Glue. [Obs.]

gley (glī), *v.i.* [ME. *gleyen*, to shine, glance, squint, from Ice. *glja*, to glitter.]

1. To squint; to gledge. [Scot.]

2. To shine; to glance. [Obs.]

gley, *adv.* Obliquely. [Scot.]

glī′ȧ-cell, *n.* [Gr. *glia*, glue.] A cell of neuroglia having many branches.

glī′ȧ-din, *n.* [Gr. *glia*, glue.] A peculiar substance obtained from gluten, slightly transparent, brittle, straw-yellow color, having a slight smell similar to that of honeycomb.

glib, *a.* [D. *glibberen*, freq. of *glippen*, to slide; *glibberig*, glib, slippery.]

1. Smooth; slippery; as, ice is *glib.*

2. Smooth; voluble; as, a *glib* tongue.

glib, *n.* [Ir. *glib*; Gael. *glib*, a lock of hair.] A thick, curled head of hair, hanging down over the eyes; also, a man wearing such hair. [Rare.]

glib, *v.t.* To castrate. [Obs.]

glib, *v.t.* To render glib; as, to *glib* the tongue with liquor. [Rare.]

glib′bẽr-y, *a.* Slippery; fickle; also, voluble. [Obs.]

glib′ly, *adv.* Smoothly; volubly.

glib′ness, *n.* The state or quality of being glib.

glid′dẽr, glid′dẽr-y, *a.* [Prov. Eng., from AS. *glidan*, to glide, slide.] Giving uncertain foothold; slippery. [Prov. Eng.]

glīde, *v.i.*; glided, *pt., pp.*; gliding, *ppr.* [ME. *gliden*; AS. *glidan*, to slip, slide, glide.]

1. To flow gently; to move silently and smoothly; to pass along without apparent effort; to move or pass rapidly and with apparent ease; as, a river *glides* along; the boat *glides* over the lake.

2. In music and phonetics, to pass from tone to tone easily or with a glide; to slur.

Gliding angle; the angle to the horizontal taken by a flying-machine when descending and not propelled by the motor.

Gliding plane; in crystallography, the direction in which a movement of the molecules of a crystal may take place under pressure without fracture.

glīde, *n.* 1. The act or manner of moving smoothly, swiftly, and without labor or obstruction.

2. In music, an even carriage of the voice from tone to tone without a break; a slur.

3. In phonetics, a sound of the voice made in a transition from consonant to vowel or from vowel to consonant, or in the pronunciation of a diphthong or diphthongal consonant.

4. A sliding movement of the foot in waltzing; also, the kind of waltz having this smooth, sliding step.

glīd′ẽr, *n.* 1. One who or that which glides.

2. A flying-machine used for gliding or "sliding down" the air, not fitted with a motor.

glīd′ing-ly, *adv.* In a gliding manner.

gliff, *n.* [Scot.] 1. Fear; sudden fright.

2. A short period of time; a moment.

glīke, *n.* A sneer; a scoff; a flout. [Obs.]

glim, *n.* 1. A light or a candle. [Slang.]

2. An eye; as, he has lost a *glim.* [Slang.]

3. Brightness; sheen. [Obs.]

glim′mẽr, *v.i.*; glimmered, *pt., pp.*; glimmering, *ppr.* [ME. *glimeren*, from *glim*; AS. *gleomu*, brightness.] To emit feeble or scattered rays of light; to shine faintly; to give a feeble light; as, the morning *glimmers* in the east.

glim′mẽr, *n.* 1. A faint light; feeble, scattered rays of light; gleam; sheen; shimmer; as, the fading *glimmer* of a lamp; the *glimmer* of pearls.

2. A momentary knowledge; a glimpse.

3. Mica.

Syn.—Gleam, glow, twinkle, flicker.

glim′mẽr-ing, *n.* 1. A faint beaming of light.

2. A faint idea; an inkling; a glimpse.

glimpse, *n.* 1. A transitory view; a hasty look; a momentary observation.

2. A transient luster; a flash of light.

3. An inkling; a glimmer; a trace.

glimpse, *v.i.* and *v.t.*; glimpsed (glimst), *pt.,*

pp.; glimpsing, *ppr.* [ME. *glimsen*, from *glim*; AS. *gleomu*, brightness.]

I. *v.i.* To appear by glimpses; to look or see momentarily.

II. *v.t.* To catch a glimpse of; to see in short periods; to have a quick view of.

glint, *v.i.*; glinted, *pt.*, *pp.*; glinting, *ppr.* [ME. *glenten*, to shine, gleam; Old Dan. *glinte*, to shine.]

1. To glitter; to gleam; to peep forth; to glance.

2. To glance away, as a sword from armor. [Rare.]

glint, *v.t.* To reflect; as, their armor *glinted* back the light.

glint, *n.* 1. A gleam or flash of light.

2. A glimpse. [Scot.]

gli-ō′mȧ, *n.*; *pl.* gli-ō′mȧ-tȧ. [Gr. *glia*, glue, and *-oma*.] In pathology, a tumor composed of neuroglia.

gli-om′ȧ-tous, *a.* Pertaining to or of the nature of a glioma or gliomata.

glī″ō-sär-cō′mȧ, *n.*; *pl.* glī″ō-sär-cō′mȧ-tȧ. In pathology, a tumor composed of gliomatous and sarcomatous tissue.

Glī′rēṣ, *n.pl.* [L. *glis*, *gliris*, a dormouse.] In zoölogy, an order of mammals practically synonymous with *Rodentia*; the rodents.

glī′rine, *a.* Of, pertaining to, or like the *Glires*; resembling a dormouse.

glisk, *n.* A gleam; a glimpse. [Scot.]

glis-sāde′, *n.* [Fr. *glissade*, from *glisser*, to slide, glide, from O.D. *glitsen*, to slide.]

1. The act of sliding down an incline.

2. In dancing, a sliding step to right or left.

3. In aviation, a wing-slip to the side, and down.

glis-san′dō, *n.* [Formed as if It. ppr., equivalent to Fr. *glissant*, ppr. of *glisser*, to slide.]

1. The effect produced by drawing the fingers rapidly across piano keys without striking them separately.

2. In violin-playing, a quick slur.

glis-sette′, *n.* [Fr., from *glisser*, to slide.] In geometry, the locus of a point rigidly connected with two other points which slip continuously upon one or two fixed curves.

glist, *n.* Glimmer; mica.

glis′ten (glis′n), *v.i.*; glistened, *pt.*, *pp.*; glistening, *ppr.* [ME. *glistnen*; AS. *glisnian*, to glisten, shine.] To shine as if smooth and by reflection of light; to sparkle or scintillate; to gleam with soft, twinkling, or shimmering light.

Syn.—Gleam, shine, glitter, scintillate, sparkle.

glis′tẽr, *v.i.* [ME. *glisteren*, from same root as AS. *glisnian*, to shine, glitter.] To shine; to be bright; to sparkle; to be brilliant; to glitter. [Obs.]

> All that *glisters* is not gold. —Shak.

glis′tẽr, *n.* Glitter; luster. [Obs.]

glis′tẽr-ing-ly, *adv.* With shining luster.

glit′tẽr, *v.i.*; glittered, *pt.*, *pp.*; glittering, *ppr.* [ME. *gliteren*, O.H.G. *glizzan*, to shine, glitter, from the same root as AS. *glitenian*, *glitinian*, OS. *glitan*, to shine, glitter.]

1. To shine; to sparkle with light; to gleam; to be splendid; as, a *glittering* sword.

2. To be showy, specious, or striking, and hence, attractive; as, the *glittering* scenes of a court.

glit′tẽr, *n.* Brightness; brilliancy; splendor; luster; as, the *glitter* of arms; the *glitter* of dress.

glit′tẽr-ănd, *a.* Sparkling. [Obs.]

glit′tẽr-ing-ly, *adv.* In a glittering manner; with sparkling luster.

glōam, *v.i.* 1. To be sullen. [Obs.]

2. To grow dark; to get dusky.

glōam, *n.* The gloaming. [Rare.]

glōam′ing, *n.* [AS. *glomung*, twilight.]

1. Twilight; the dusk of approaching night; hence, a closing period; as, the *gloaming* of life.

2. Sullenness; melancholy. [Obs.]

glōar, *v.i.* To glare. [Obs.]

glōat, *v.i.*; gloated, *pt.*, *pp.*; gloating, *ppr.* [Ice. *glotta*, to smile scornfully, to grin.] To look steadfastly; to gaze earnestly or with eagerness; especially, to look with pleasure at something gratifying to evil desires or morbid passions; as, to *gloat* over a victim; to *gloat* upon an enemy's downfall.

> And then, having drunk, she *gloated* over it, and tasted, and smelt of the cup of this hellish wine. —Hawthorne.

glō′bărd, *n.* A glowworm. [Obs.]

glō′bāte, **glō′bā-ted**, *a.* [L. *globatus*, pp. of *globare*, to make into a ball, from *globus*, a ball, sphere.] Having the form of a globe; spherical; spheroidal.

glōbe, *n.* [OFr. *globe*; L. *globus*, a ball, sphere.]

1. A spherical solid body; a ball; a sphere; a body whose surface is in every part equidistant from the center.

2. The earth; with the definite article.

3. A sphere of metal, paper, etc., on the convex surface of which is drawn a map or representation of the earth or of the heavens. When it represents the earth it is called a *terrestrial globe*; when it represents the constellations in the heavens, it is called a *celestial globe*.

4. Anything of a globular or spherical shape; as, a lamp-*globe*.

5. A body of soldiers formed into a circle. [Obs.]

Globe valve; a valve having a body of globular form; also, a ball valve.

glōbe, *v.i* and *v.t.* To take or cause to take the form of a globe.

glōbe′=am″ȧ-ranth, *n.* A plant of the genus *Gomphrena*, bearing beautiful globular heads of purple and white flowers.

glōbe′=an″i-măl, **glōbe′=an-i-mal″cūle**, *n.* A minute globular plant of the genus *Volvox*.

glōbe′=cock, *n.* A ball-cock.

glōbe′=dāi″ṣy, *n.* A plant, *Globularia vulgaris*.

glōbe′=fish, *n.* A fish of the genus *Diodon* or *Tetrodon*, having the power of inflating its body into a globular form. [See *Diodon* and *Balloon-fish*.]

glōbe′flow″ẽr, *n.* A plant of the genus *Trollius*, bearing handsome globular flowers.

Japan globeflower; see *Corchorus*.

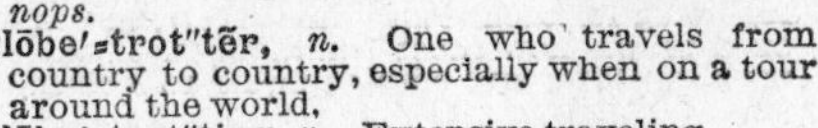

Globeflower (*Trollius Europæus*).

glōbe′=run″nẽr, *n.* One who performs with a large ball by standing on it while moving it about with his feet.

glōbe′=shāped (-shāpt), *a.* Shaped like a globe.

glōbe′=sight (-sīt), *n.* A sight for a rifle, consisting of a small globe set on a pin above the muzzle.

glōbe′=slāt″ẽr, *n.* A crustacean of the genus *Sphæroma*, which rolls itself into globular form.

glōbe′=this″tle (-this″sl), *n.* A plant of the genus *Echinops*.

glōbe′=trot″tẽr, *n.* One who travels from country to country, especially when on a tour around the world.

glōbe′=trot″ting, *n.* Extensive traveling.

glōbe′=tūbe, *n.* An unusually wide-angled photographic lens.

glo-bi-, **glo-bo-**. Combining forms from L. *globus*, a ball, sphere.

glō-bif′ẽr-ous, *a.* [*Globi-*, and L. *ferre*, to bear.] Having a globular terminal.

Glō-big-e-rī′nȧ, *n.* [*Globi-*, and L. *gerere*, to carry.] A genus of minute, pelagic foraminifers having globose calcareous shells which form the chief part of the so-called *globigerina-ooze*, or soft, chalky mud found in the depths of the ocean.

glō″bō-cū′mū-lus, *n.* [*Globo-*, and L. *cumulus*, a heap, pile.] A cumulus cloud of spherical shape.

glō′boid, *n.* and *a.* [L. *globus*, a globe, and Gr. *eidos*, form.]

I. *n.* A spheroidal mass of calcium-magnesium phosphate found in aleurone.

II. *a.* Spheroidal; globular.

glō-bōse′, *a.* [L. *globosus*, round as a ball, from *globus*, a ball.] Rounded; almost spherical; globular.

glō-bōse′ly, *adv.* In a globose way.

glō-bos′i-ty, *n.* [LL. *globositas*, from L. *globosus*, round as a ball, from *globus*, a ball.] The quality of being globose.

glō′bous, *a.* [OFr. *globeux*; L. *globosus*, round as a ball, from *globus*, a ball.] Spherical.

glob′ū-lăr, *a.* [L. *globulus*, dim. of *globus*, a ball.] Round; spherical; having the form of a ball or sphere; as, *globular* atoms.

Globular chart; see under *Chart*.

Globular sailing; sailing on the shortest course between two points, which is on the arc of the great circle passing through them.

glob-ū-lā′ri-ȧ, *n.* [L. *globulus*, dim. of *globus*, a ball.] A genus of plants which grow in the temperate and warm parts of Europe, including the *globe-daisy*.

glob-ū-lar′i-ty, *n.* The quality of being globular; sphericity.

glob′ū-lăr-ly, *adv.* In a spherical form.

glob′ū-lăr-ness, *n.* The quality of being globular.

glob′ūle, *n.* [Fr. *globule*; L. *globulus*, a little ball, dim. of *globus*, a ball.]

1. A little globe; a small particle of matter of a spherical form.

> Hailstones have opaque *globules* of snow in their center. —Newton.

2. A minute spherical structure, such as a corpuscle, coccus, spore, etc.

3. A very small pellet or pill, as those used by homeopathic physicians.

glob′ū-let, *n.* A small globule.

glob-ū-lim′e-tẽr, *n.* [L. *globulus*, dim. of *globus*, a ball, and *metrum*, a measure.] A device for determining the number of red blood-corpuscles in the blood.

glob′ū-lin, **glob′ū-line**, *n.* [*Globule* and *-in*, *-ine*.] Any one of various substances closely allied to albumin, but insoluble in water.

glob′ū-lite, *n.* A spherical mineral form without crystalline structure.

glob′ū-lōse, *a.* Globulous.

glob′ū-lous, *a.* [L. *globulus*, dim. of *globus*, a ball.] Rounded; globular; having the form of a small sphere; spheroidal.

glob′ū-lous-ness, *n.* The state of being globulous.

glōb′y, *a.* Round; orbicular; globelike.

glō-chid′i-āte, *a.* [Gr. *glōchis*, a projecting point.] Having a barbed tip, as a hair or bristle.

glō-chid′i-um, *n.*; *pl.* glō-chid′i-ȧ. [Gr. *glōches*, pl., the beard of corn.]

1. In zoölogy, the larva of any of certain mussels hatched in the gills of the parent.

2. In botany, a hairy appendage of certain heterosporous ferns.

glō′chis, *n.*; *pl.* glō′chi-nēṣ. [Gr. *glōchis*, *glōchin*, a projecting point, an arrow-point.] A glochidiate point, bristle, spine, etc.

glōde, *v.*, obsolete past tense of *glide*.

glōme, **glōmbe**, *v.*, obsolete forms of *gloom*.

glōme, *n.* [L. *glomus*, a ball.]

1. In botany, a soredium.

2. One of the prominences at the rear of the frog of a horse's foot.

3. A spool of thread.

glom′ẽr-āte, *v.t.*; glomerated, *pt.*, *pp.*; glomerating, *ppr.* [L. *glomeratus*, pp. of *glomerare*, to wind or make into a ball, from *glomus*, a ball or clue of yarn.] To gather or wind into a ball; to collect into a spherical form or mass, as threads.

glom′ẽr-āte, *a.* Growing, collected, or arranged in a mass, as glands, flowers, etc.; conglomerate.

glom-ẽr-ā′tion, *n.* [L. *glomeratio (-onis)*, from *glomeratus*, pp. of *glomerare*, to form into a ball, from *glomus*, a ball.] Conglomeration.

glom′ẽr-ous, *a.* [L. *glomerosus*.] Gathered or formed into a ball or round mass.

glom′ẽr-ūle, *n.* [L. *glomus (-eris)*, a ball, and *-ule*.]

1. In botany, (a) a dense, globular, cymose cluster of flowers; (b) a mass of adhesive spores in various lichens.

2. In anatomy, a glomerulus.

glō-mer′ū-lus, *n.*; *pl.* glō-mer′ū-lī. [A dim. from L. *glomus (-eris)*, a ball.] In anatomy, a convoluted tuft of capillaries, as in the Malpighian bodies of the kidney.

glom′ẽr-y, *n.* Grammar; a medieval form of the word, found in the records of Cambridge University, England; as, a master in *glomery*.

glom-ū-lif′ẽr-ous, *a.* [L. *glomus*, a ball, and *ferre*, to bear.] In biology, having powdery masses on the surface, as certain lichens; having clusters of excrescences.

glon′ō-in, *n.* [*Gl*ycerin, and oxygen, and *n*itrogen, and *-in*.] Nitroglycerin for medical use.

glo͝om, *n.* [AS. *glōm*, twilight, from *glowan*, to glow.]

1. Obscurity; partial or total darkness; thick shade; as, the *gloom* of a forest; the *gloom* of midnight.

2. Depression or heaviness of mind; melancholy; aspect of sorrow; as, the mind is sunk in *gloom*; a *gloom* overspreads the face.

3. Darkness of prospect or aspect; a depressing state of affairs.

4. A dusky or gloomy place.

5. An oven for drying gunpowder.

Syn.—Darkness, duskiness, obscurity, sadness, depression, dejection, heaviness.

glo͝om, *v.i.* and *v.t.*; gloomed, *pt.*, *pp.*; glooming, *ppr.* I. *v.i.* To appear gloomy; to feel or cause gloom; to be or become dusky, obscure, or gloomy; to glimmer.

II. *v.t.* To obscure; to darken; to make dismal; to fill with gloom.

glo͝om′i-ly, *adv.* With gloom; in a gloomy manner.

glo͝om′i-ness, *n.* The state or condition of being gloomy.

glo͝om′ing, *n.* Duskiness; gloaming. [Rare.]

glo͝omth, *n.* Gloominess. [Rare.]

glo͝om′y, *a.* 1. Obscure; imperfectly illuminated; dark; dismal; as, the *gloomy* cells of a convent; the *gloomy* shades of night.

2. Wearing the aspect of sorrow; melancholy; depressed; causing gloom; as, a *gloomy* countenance; *gloomy* news.

Syn.—Clouded, dark, depressing, dim, dismal, dull.

glop′pen, *v.t.* [ME. *glopnen*; Ice. *glupna*, to look downcast.] To terrify; to frighten. [Prov. Eng.]

glop′pen, *v.i.* To be terrified or frightened. [Prov. Eng.]

glōre, *v.i.* To glare. [Obs.]

glō′ri-ȧ, *n.* [L., glory.]

1. In ecclesiastical usage, (a) the first word of the doxologies sung at the end of each psalm in the Roman Catholic and certain Protestant

churches; hence, the doxology itself; any doxology; (b) specifically, *Gloria* in excelsis Deo; a portion of the mass so commencing or the musical setting of the same.

2. In ecclesiastical art, a glory.

glō-ri-ā′tion, *n.* Boast; a triumphing. [Obs.]

glō″ri-fi-cā′tion, *n.* [LL. *glorificatio (-onis)*, from *glorificare*, to glorify; L. *gloria*, glory, and *facere*, to make.]

1. The act of giving glory, or of ascribing honors to.

2. That which glorifies or is used in glorifying; a doxology.

3. Exaltation to honor and dignity; elevation to glory.

4. A jollification. [Colloq.]

glō′ri-fȳ, *v.t.*; glorified, *pt., pp.*; glorifying, *ppr.* [ME. *glorifien*; OFr. *glorifier*; LL. *glorificare*, to glorify; L. *gloria*, glory, and *facere*, to make.]

1. To praise; to magnify and honor in worship; to ascribe honor to, in thought or words.

2. To make glorious; to exalt to glory, or to celestial happiness.

3. To cause to become finer or better; to improve; to adorn; as, to *glorify* poverty to the common people.

glō′ri-ōle, *n.* [L. *gloriola*, dim. of *gloria*, glory.] A halo; a nimbus. [Rare.]

Glō-ri-ō′sȧ, *n.* [F. of L. *gloriosus*, glorious.] In botany, a small genus of climbers of the lily family bearing handsome flowers.

glō-ri-ō′sēr, *n.* A braggart. [Obs.]

glō-ri-ō′sō, *n.* [It.] A braggart. [Obs.]

glō′ri-ous, *a.* [ME. *glorious*; OFr. *glorios*; L. *gloriosus*, full of glory, famous, glorious, renowned, boastful.]

1. Illustrious; of exalted excellence and splendor; resplendent in majesty; noble; renowned; celebrated; illustrious; very honorable.

2. Boastful; haughty; ostentatious. [Obs.]

3. Gleeful; hilarious; exhilarating; hence, intoxicated, as with liquor. [Colloq.]

glō′ri-ous-ly, *adv.* In a glorious way.

glō′ri-ous-ness, *n.* The state or quality of being glorious.

glō′ry, *n.* [ME. *glory*; OFr. *glorie*; L. *gloria*, glory, fame, honor, pride, boasting.]

1. Brightness; luster; splendor; magnificence; as, the *glory* of the sun.

2. Honor; praise; fame; renown; celebrity.

3. Pride; boastfulness; arrogance; desire for praise. [Obs.]

4. The divine presence or its manifestation; felicity of heaven; celestial bliss.

5. In painting, a combination of the nimbus and aureola, that is, of the luminous halo encircling the head of holy persons, and that encompassing the whole person; frequently confounded with *nimbus*.

Old Glory; the United States flag; the Stars and Stripes.

Syn.—Brightness, radiance, effulgence, honor, fame, celebrity, renown.

glō′ry, *v.i.*; gloried, *pt., pp.*; glorying, *ppr.* [ME. *glorien*; OFr. *glorier*; L. *gloriari*, to glory, boast, from *gloria*, glory, vaunting.]

1. To exult with joy; to rejoice; with *in*.

2. To boast; to be proud of; with *in*; as, to *glory in* one's strength.

Syn.—Boast, vaunt.—To *glory* is more particularly the act of the mind, the indulgence of the internal sentiment; to *boast* denotes rather the expression of the sentiment. To *glory* is applied only to matters of moment; *boast* is rather suitable to trifling points. To *vaunt* is properly to proclaim praises aloud, and is taken either in an indifferent or bad sense.

glō′ry-hōle, *n.* 1. An opening into a furnace, showing the light within.

2. A place in which to hide valuables; by contrast, a place for kitchen utensils.

glō′ry-pēa, *n.* Either of two plants of the genus *Clianthus*, of Australia and New Zealand.

glō′ry-tree, *n.* A showy, flowering shrub of the tropics, belonging to the genus *Clerodendron*.

glōṣe, *n.* and *v.* Same as *Gloze*.

glōṣ′ẽr, *n.* Same as *Glosser*.

gloss, *n.* [Ice. *glossi*, a blaze, from *gloa*, to glow.]

1. Brightness or luster of a body proceeding from a smooth surface; as, the *gloss* of silk.

2. A specious appearance or representation; external show that may mislead opinion.

gloss, *v.t.*; glossed (glost), *pt., pp.*; glossing, *ppr.*

1. To give a superficial luster to; to make smooth and shining; as, to *gloss* cloth or silk.

2. To give a specious appearance to; to render specious and plausible; to palliate by specious representation; commonly used with *over*; as, to *gloss over* the facts.

gloss, *v.i.* [ME. *glosen*; LL. *glossare*, to explain, gloss, from *glossa*, a gloss, from Gr. *glōssa*, the tongue.]

1. To comment; to write or make explanatory remarks.

2. To make sly remarks; to insinuate.

gloss, *v.t.* To explain; to render clear and evident by comments; to illustrate.

gloss, *n.* [ME. *glose*; LL. *glossa*; L. *glossarium*, a foreign or antiquated difficult word requiring explanation, from Gr. *glōssa*, the tongue, language, an archaic or foreign difficult word requiring explanation.]

1. A word out of the common and needing elucidation.

2. An interpretation or explanatory note.

3. A false or misleading explanation; a specious statement.

glos′sȧ, *n.*; *pl.* **glos′sæ.** [Gr. *glōssa*, the tongue.] The tongue; specifically, the distal appendage of the lingua of an insect.

glos′săl, *a.* Pertaining to the tongue.

glos-san′thrax, *n.* [Gr. *glōssa*, the tongue, and *anthrax*, a carbuncle.] A diseased condition of horses and cattle in which carbuncles affect the mouth and tongue.

glos-sā′ri-ăl, *a.* Containing explanation.

glos-sā′ri-ăl-ly, *adv.* After the style of a glossary.

glos′sȧ-rist, *n.* A writer of glosses or comments.

glos-sā′ri-um, *n.* [Gr. *glōssa*, the tongue.] The labrum or tongue of certain insects, as that of the mosquito.

glos′sȧ-ry, *n.*; *pl.* **glos′sȧ-rieṣ.** [LL. *glossarium*, a vocabulary of foreign or antiquated words, from *glossa*, from Gr. *glōssa*, the tongue, word, a foreign or difficult word.] A dictionary or vocabulary explaining words which are obscure, antiquated, local, or foreign; a vocabulary giving the words of a book, author, dialect, science, or art; a number of glosses or marginal notes collectively.

Glos-sā′tȧ, *n.pl.* [Gr. *glōssa*, tongue.] The *Lepidoptera*.

glos′sāte, *a.* [Gr. *glōssa*, tongue, and *-ate*.] Provided with a glossa or tongue; in entomology, haustellate; specifically, belonging to the *Lepidoptera*.

glos-sā′tōr, *n.* [LL. *glossator*, from *glossare*, to gloss, from *glossa*, a gloss, from Gr. *glōssa*, the tongue.] A writer of comments; a commentator. [Rare.]

gloss′ẽr, *n.* A writer of glosses; a commentator.

gloss′ẽr, *n.* A polisher; one who gives a luster.

Glos′siç, *n.* [Gr. *glōssa*, the tongue, a tongue, language, and *-ic*.] A phonetic system of spelling using for each sound, invariably, the letter or digraph now most commonly used in the usual spelling and employing no new characters.

gloss′i-ly, *adv.* In a glossy manner.

gloss′i-ness, *n.* The state or quality of being glossy.

gloss′ist, *n.* A writer of comments. [Obs.]

glos-sit′iç, *a.* Of or attacked by glossitis.

glos-sī′tis, *n.* [Gr. *glōssa*, the tongue, and *-itis*.] Inflammation of the tongue.

gloss′ly, *adv.* Like gloss. [Obs.]

glos-so-. A combining form from Gr. *glōssa*, the tongue, a word, language.

glos″sō-ep-i-glot′tiç, *a.* [*Glosso-*, and Gr. *epiglōttis*, the epiglottis.] Belonging to both tongue and epiglottis.

glos′sō-grȧph, *n.* A device to register the movements of the tongue in speaking.

glos-sog′rȧ-phẽr, *n.* [Gr. *glossographos*, one writing or interpreting glosses; *glōssa*, the tongue, a gloss, and *graphein*, to write.] A writer of a glossary; a commentator.

glos-sō-graph′iç-ăl, *a.* Belonging to glossography.

glos-sog′rȧ-phy, *n.* 1. The writing of glossaries.

2. A treatise on the tongue.

glos-sō-hȳ′ăl, *a.* and *n.* [*Glosso-*, and Gr. *hyoeidēs*, shaped like the letter upsilon (Υ), hyoid; Υ, upsilon, and *eidos*, form.]

I. *a.* Belonging to both the hyoid bone and the tongue.

II. *n.* The glossohyal cartilage or bone situated anteriorly to the basihyal, as in fishes, birds, etc.

glos-sō-lā′li-ȧ, glos-sol′ȧ-ly, *n.* [*Glosso-*, and Gr. *lalia*, chat, gossip, from *lalein*, to chatter, talk.] The gift of tongues; ability to speak a foreign language, when in a condition other than normal, such power being absent when the subject is not in hypnosis.

glos-sō-log′iç-ăl, *a.* Pertaining to glossology.

glos-sol′ō-ġist, *n.* 1. A glossarist.

2. A philologist.

glos-sol′ō-ġy, *n.* [*Glosso-*, and Gr. *-logia*, from *legein*, to speak.]

1. The definition and explanation of terms.

2. Linguistics.

glos-soph′ȧ-ġine, *a.* Taking in food by the tongue, as certain bats, ant-eaters, and the like.

glos″sō-phar-yn-ġē′ăl, *a.* and *n.* [*Glosso-*, and Gr. *pharynx*, the pharynx.]

I. *a.* In anatomy, belonging both to the tongue and the pharynx.

II. *n.* A glossopharyngeal nerve.

glos-soph′ō-rous, *a.* [*Glosso-*, and Gr. *-phoros*, from *pherein*, to bear.] Provided with a tongue.

glos-sō-plē′ġi-ȧ, *n.* [*Glosso-*, and Gr. *plēgē*, a stroke, from *plēssein*, to strike.] In pathology, paralysis of the tongue.

glos-sō-pō′di-um, *n.* [*Glosso-*, and Gr. *pous*, *podos*, foot.] In botany, the base of the leaf of the quillwort, *Isoetes*.

gloss′y, *a.*; *comp.* glossier; *superl.* glossiest. 1. Smooth and shining; reflecting luster from a smooth surface; highly polished; as, *glossy* silk.

2. Smooth; plausible; beguiling.

glost′-ōv″en, *n.* A kiln for glazing pottery.

glot′tăl, *a.* Of or made by the glottis.

glot′tiç, *a.* Of or belonging to the tongue; glottal.

glot-tid′ē-ăn, *a.* Glottic.

glot′tis, *n.*; *pl.* **glot′ti-dēṣ.** [Gr. *glōttis*, the mouth of the windpipe, the glottis, from Attic Gr. *glōtta*, the tongue.] The narrow opening at the upper part of the trachea or windpipe, which, by its dilatation and contraction, contributes to the modulation of the voice.

glot-tō-gon′iç, *a.* [Attic Gr. *glōtta*, the tongue, language, and *gonos*, birth, product.] Dealing with the origin of language.

glot-tō-log′iç-ăl, *a.* Glossological.

glot-tol′ō-ġist, *n.* A glossologist.

glot-tol′ō-ġy, *n.* Glossology.

glout, *v.i.* To pout; to look sullen. [Obs.]

glout, *v.t.* To view attentively. [Obs.]

glōve, *n.* [ME. *glove*, *glofe*; AS. *glof*, a glove.]

1. A cover for the hand, with a separate sheath for each finger; distinguished from a mitten, which has but one sheath for the four fingers.

2. A boxing-glove.

To be hand and glove; to be on friendly terms; to be intimate.

To handle without gloves; to treat roughly.

glōve, *v.t.*; gloved, *pt., pp.*; gloving, *ppr.* To cover with or as with a glove.

glōve′-but″tōn-ẽr, *n.* A hook used to button gloves.

glōve′-fīght (-fīt), *n.* A boxing contest in which the pugilists wear boxing gloves.

glōve′-mŏn″ey, *n.* A gratuity given to servants ostensibly to buy them gloves; hence, formerly in England, extraordinary rewards given to officers of courts, etc.; also, money given by a sheriff of a county in which no offenders were left for execution, to the clerk of assize and the judges' officers.

glōv′ẽr, *n.* One whose occupation is to make or sell gloves.

Glover's stitch; a peculiar stitch employed in sewing up a wound.

glōve′-sil″vẽr, *n.* Same as *Glove-money*.

glōw, *v.i.*; glowed, *pt., pp.*; glowing, *ppr.* [ME. *glowen*; AS. *glowan*, to glow, to be bright, to glitter.]

1. To shine with intense heat, especially without flame; to exhibit incandescence.

2. To feel great heat of body; to be hot, as the skin; to have a burning sensation.

> Did not his temples *glow*
> In the same sultry winds and scorching heats?
> —Addison.

3. To exhibit a strong, bright color; to be bright or red, as with heat, animation, or with blushes, etc.

4. To feel the heat of passion; to be ardent; to be animated, as by intense love, zeal, anger, etc.; as, the heart *glows* with love or zeal.

5. To burn with intense heat; to rage, as passion.

> With pride it mounts, and with revenge it *glows*. —Dryden.

glōw, *v.t.* To make hot; to make to flush. [Obs.]

glōw, *n.* 1. Shining heat or white heat.

2. Brightness of color; redness; as, the *glow* of health in the cheeks.

3. Vehemence; ardor; animation.

> A *glow* of pleasure follows the solution of a puzzling question. —H. Spencer.

glōw′bărd, *n.* [Obs.] See *Glowbird*.

glōw′bīrd, *n.* The glowworm. [Obs.]

glow′ẽr, glour, *v.i.*; glowered, *pt., pp.*; glowering, *ppr.* To look intensely or watchfully; to scowl; to stare angrily.

glow′ẽr, glour, *n.* A scowl; a menacing stare.

glōw′flȳ, *n.* A firefly.

glōw′ing-ly, *adv.* In a glowing manner; with great brightness; with ardent zeal or passion.

glōw′lamp, *n.* An incandescent electric lamp.

glōw′wŏrm, *n.* An insect of the genus *Lampyris* of the order *Coleoptera*, as *Lampyris noctiluca*, the name being applicable strictly only to the female, which is without wings, somewhat resembles a caterpillar, and emits a shining green light from the extremity of the abdomen. The male is winged, and flies about in the evening, when he is attracted by the light of the female. The name is also given to *Lampyris splendidula* and other species of the same genus.

Glowworm (*Lampyris noctiluca*).
1. Male. 2. Female, upper side. 3. Female, under side, showing the three posterior segments (*a*) from which the light proceeds.

Glox-in'i-ȧ, *n.* [Named after *Gloxin*, a German physician.]

1. A genus of plants of the natural order *Gesneraceæ*, having large bell-shaped flowers. They are natives of tropical America.

Gloxinias.

2. [g—] A plant of the genus *Gloxinia*.

glōze, *v.i.*; glozed, *pt.*, *pp.*; glozing, *ppr.* [ME. *glosen*; AS. *glesan*; LL. *glossare*, to explain, gloss, from *glossa*, an explanation, gloss, from Gr. *glōssa*, the tongue, a gloss.] To flatter; to wheedle; to fawn; to talk smoothly.

So *glozed* the tempter, and his proem tuned. —Milton.

glōze, *v.t.* To gloss over; to put a fair face upon; to extenuate.

glōze, *n.* [ME. *glose*, a gloss, an explanation, flattery; LL. *glossa*, an obsolete or foreign word requiring explanation, a gloss, from Gr. *glōssa*, the tongue, language.]

1. Flattery; adulation.

2. Specious show; gloss. [Obs.]

glōz'ẽr, *n.* A flatterer. [Obs.]

glū'cic, *a.* [Gr. *glykys*, sweet.] Of or pertaining to or obtained from sugar.

Glucic acid; $C_{12}H_{18}O_9$, an acid produced by the action of alkalis or acids on sugar. It is a colorless, amorphous substance, is very soluble in water, attracts rapidly the moisture of the air, and its solution has a decidedly sour taste. All its neutral salts are soluble.

glū-cī'nȧ, *n.* [Gr. *glykys*, sweet.] BeO, the only oxid of the metal glucinum or beryllium. Pure *glucina* is white, tasteless, without odor, and quite insoluble in water, but soluble in the liquid fixed alkalis.

glū-cin'ic, *a.* Of or containing glucinum.

glū-cī'num, *n.* [Gr. *glykys*, sweet.] A white metal, of specific gravity 2.1; it belongs to the group of the alkaline earths, and is prepared from beryl; hence the name of *beryllium* which is often applied to it.

glū'cō-ġen, *n.* See *Glycogen.*

glū-cō-ġen'e-sis, *n.* See *Glycogenesis.*

glū-cō-hē'mi-ȧ, glū-cō-hæ'mi-ȧ, *n.* [Gr. *glykys*, sweet, and *haima*, blood.] Abnormal amount of glucose in the blood.

glū-com'e-tẽr, *n.* [Gr. *glykys*, sweet, and *metron*, a measure.] An instrument for ascertaining the amount of sugar contained in must.

glū-con'ic, *a.* Of or obtained from glucose; maltonic.

Gluconic acid; an acid, $C_6H_{12}O_7$, derived from glucose by oxidation.

glū'cōse, *n.* [Gr. *glykys*, sweet.]

1. $C_6H_{12}O_6$, a variety of sugar less sweet than cane-sugar, produced from cane-sugar, dextrine, starch, cellulose, etc., by the action of acids, certain ferments, and other reagents, and by processes going on in living plants.

2. In chemistry, any one of a class of carbohydrates having the composition $C_6H_{12}O_6$, and of which ordinary glucose is the type.

3. A syrup obtained in the preparation of grape-sugar by the action of sulphuric acid on starch.

glū-cos'ic, *a.* Pertaining to or yielding glucose.

glū'cō-side, *n.* [*Glucose* and *-ide.*] A compound which occurs naturally in plants from which it is extracted by water or by alcohol. It cannot be melted without decomposition, and is resolved by boiling with dilute acids into a saccharine substance, as glucose, and another substance which has generally neutral properties. It is mostly a solid and crystalline substance. It gives a red color when heated to 70° with a dilute solution of gall and a little concentrated sulphuric acid. The most important glucosides are amygdalin, myronic acid, and salicin.

glū-cō-sū'ri-ȧ, *n.* [Gr. *glykys*, sweet, and *ouron*, urine.] In pathology, a form of diabetes, characterized by the presence of glucose in the urine.

glūe, *n.* [ME. *glue*; OFr. *glu*; LL. *glus*, *glutis*, glue; L. *gluten*; Gr. *glia*, glue.] A viscous substance made of the chippings of hides, horns, and hoofs, which are washed in limewater, boiled, skimmed, strained, evaporated, cooled in molds, cut into slices, and dried upon nets. It is used as a cement for uniting pieces of wood or other substances. The name is also given to any sticky or viscous substance.

Liquid glue; glue kept in a liquid state by treatment with an acid.

Marine glue; glue made of equal parts of shellac and caoutchouc dissolved in separate portions of naphtha, and then mixed. It is used in shipbuilding.

glūe, *v.t.*; glued, *pt.*, *pp.*; gluing, *ppr.* To join with glue or a viscous substance; to fasten, as with glue; to join closely.

Congealed blood that *glues* my lips. —Shak.

glūe, *v.i.* To become firmly or closely united, fixed, or attached.

glūe'pot, *n.* A utensil consisting of two pots, one within the other, for dissolving glue. The outer pot is filled with water, the boiling of which causes the glue in the inner one to melt.

glū'ẽr, *n.* One who or that which cements with glue.

glū'ey, *a.* Viscous; glutinous.

glū'ey-ness, *n.* The quality of being gluey.

glū'ish, *a.* Having the nature of glue.

glum, *n.* Sullenness; gloominess; a frown. [Obs.]

glum, *a.* [Scot. *gloum*, a frown.] Frowning; sullen; gloomily silent; moody.

glum, *v.i.* To look sullen; to be sour of countenance. [Rare.]

glū-mā'ceous, *a.* Having glumes; consisting of glumes; glume-like.

glū'măl, *a.* Glumaceous.

glūme, *n.* [L. *gluma*, a hull or husk, from *glubere*, to bark, cast off the shell.] In botany, the imbricate scale-like bract inserted on the axis of the spikelet in grains and grasses.

glū-mel'lȧ, *n.* Same as *Glumelle.*

glū'melle, *n.* [Dim. from L. *gluma*, husk, hull.] In botany, the inner small glume or chaff of a grass. [Rare.]

glū-mif'ẽr-ous, *a.* [L. *gluma*, a husk, hull, and *ferre*, to bear.] Bearing a glume or glumes.

glum'ly, *adv.* In a glum manner; moodily.

glum'my, *a.* Dark; gloomy; dismal. [Obs.]

glum'ness, *n.* Sullenness; gloominess.

glump, *v.i.* [A form of *glum.*] To sulk or appear sullen. [Colloq.]

glump'y, *a.* Glum; grumpy; sulky. [Colloq.]

glunch, *n.* A look implying dislike, disdain, anger, or displeasure. [Scot.]

glunch, *a.* Sour; frowning. [Scot.]

glut, *v.i.*; glutted, *pt.*, *pp.*; glutting, *ppr.* [ME. *gloten*, *glotten*; OFr. *glotir*, *gloutir*; L. *glutire*, *gluttire*, to devour, gulp down.] To eat like a glutton. [Rare.]

glut, *v.t.* To cloy; to fill beyond sufficiency; to feast or delight to satiety; to gorge; as, to *glut* the appetite.

His faithful heart, a bloody sacrifice,
Torn from his breast, to *glut* the tyrant's eyes. —Dryden.

To glut the market; to oversupply the market, as with a commodity, so as to decrease profits or sales.

Syn.—Gorge, fill, stuff, cram, satiate, cloy, surfeit.

glut, *n.* [ME. *glut*; OFr. *glut*, *glot*, a glutton, from *glotir*, *gloutir*; L. *glutire*, *gluttire*, to swallow.]

1. That which is swallowed. [Obs.]

2. Plenty even to loathing; more than enough; superabundance.

3. Anything that fills or obstructs the passage, as (a) a wooden wedge serving to prevent a cleft from closing in splitting wood; (b) a piece of wood inserted beneath a thing to be raised in order to prevent its recoil when freshening the nip of a lever; (c) a brickbat which fills up a course.

4. A piece of canvas sewed into the center of a sail near the head, with an eyelet-hole in its middle for the bunt-jigger or becket to go through.

5. The broad-nosed eel, *Anguilla latirostris.*

6. The offal of fish.

Syn.—Surplus, redundancy, superfluity, overstock.

glū-tȧ-con'ic, *a.* [*Glut*aric and *aco*nitic, and *-ic.*] In chemistry, related to gluten and aconitin.

glū-tæ'us, glū-tē'us, *n.* [Gr *gloutos*, the rump.] One of the three muscles of the hip which form the muscular part of the buttocks in man and other mammals.

glū-tam'ic, *a.* [*Glut*en and *-amic.*] Pertaining to gluten and amidogen.

Glutamic acid; an acid derived from certain albuminous seeds; amido-glutaric acid.

glū-tar'ic, *a.* [*Glut*amic and tart*aric.*] Pertaining to gluten and tartaric acid.

Glutaric acid; a white, crystalline compound, $C_5H_8O_4$, known also as *normal pyrotartaric acid.*

glū'tȧ-zin, glū'tȧ-zine, *n.* A crystalline compound derived from pyridine.

glū'tē-ăl, *a.* Of or connected with the glutæus; pertaining to the buttocks; as, the *gluteal* artery; *gluteal* muscles.

glū'ten, *n.* [L., glue.] A tough elastic substance of a grayish color which becomes brown and brittle by drying, found in the flour of wheat and other grain. It contributes much to the nutritive quality of flour and gives tenacity to its paste. Among its constituents are vegetable fibrin, casein, gliadin, and certain oils.

glū'ten-bread (-bred), *n.* Bread made from grain which has a high percentage of gluten, or from which the gluten has not been removed by bolting.

glū-tē'us, *n.* See *Glutæus.*

glū'tin, *n.* Same as *Gliadin.*

glū'ti-nāte, *v.t.* [L. *glutinatus*, pp. of *glutinare*, to glue.] To unite with glue.

glū-ti-nā'tion, *n.* The act of uniting with glue.

glū'ti-nā-tive, *a.* Tenacious.

glū-ti-nos'i-ty, *n.* Viscousness.

glū'ti-nous, *a.* [L. *glutinosus*, from *gluten* (*-inis*), glue.]

1. Viscous; viscid; tenacious; having the quality of glue; resembling glue; as, starch is *glutinous.*

2. In botany, besmeared with a sticky moisture; as, a *glutinous* leaf.

glū'ti-nous-ness, *n.* The quality of being glutinous; viscosity; tenacity.

glū-ti'tion (-tish'un), *n.* Deglutition. [Rare.]

glut'tŏn, *n.* [ME. *gloton*, *glutun*; OFr. *gloton*, *glouton*; L. *gluto*, *glutto*, a glutton, from *glutire*, *gluttire*, to devour.]

1. One who indulges to excess in eating; a gormandizer.

2. One who indulges in anything to excess.

Gluttons in murder, wanton to destroy. —Granville.

3. The popular name of the wolverene, *Gulo luscus*, intermediate between the bear and the weasel, resembling the former in general structure and the latter in dentition. The fur is valuable, that from Siberia being preferred from its being of a glossy black.

glut'tŏn, *a.* Greedy.

glut'tŏn, *v.t.* and *v.i.* To gormandize. [Obs.]

glut'tŏn-ish, *a.* Gluttonous.

glut'tŏn-ize, *v.i.*; gluttonized, *pt.*, *pp.*; gluttonizing, *ppr.* To eat to excess; to eat voraciously; to indulge the appetite to excess. [Rare.]

glut'tŏn-ous, *a.* [OFr. *glotonos*, from *gloton*, a glutton.] Given to excessive eating; greedy; voracious; grasping.

glut'tŏn-ous-ly, *adv.* In a gluttonous manner.

glut'tŏn-ous-ness, *n.* Gluttony; voracity; the condition of a glutton.

glut'tŏn-y, *n.* [ME. *glotonie*; OFr. *glotonie*, from *gloton*, a glutton.] Excess in eating; extravagant indulgence of the appetite for food; luxury of the table; voracity of appetite.

glyc'ẽr-āte, *n.* [*Glycer*in and *-ate.*] A glycerite.

glyc-ẽr'ic, *a.* [*Glycer*in and *-ic.*] Pertaining to or derived from glycerin.

Glyceric acid; an acid derived from glycerin by the action of nitric acid.

glyc'ẽr-ide, *n.* [*Glycer*in and *-ide.*] A compound ether of the triatomic alcohol glycerin.

glyc'ẽr-in, glyc'ẽr-ine, *n.* [Gr. *glykeros*, sweet, and *-in*, *-ine.*] A transparent, colorless, sweet liquid, $C_3H_5(OH)_3$, that forms the basis of fats; in chemistry, it is *glycerol*, a triatomic alcohol.

glyc'ẽr-ite, *n.* [*Glycer*in and *-ite.*] In medicine, any preparation having glycerol or glycerin as a solvent.

glyc'ẽr-ol, glyc'ẽr-ōle, *n.* 1. In chemistry, same as *glycerin.*

2. Same as *Glycerite.*

glyc'ẽr-yl, *n.* [*Glycer*in and *-yl.*] The hypothetical triatomic radical of glycerin; also called *propenyl.*

glyc'id, glyc'ide, *n.* A compound obtained from certain derivatives of glycerin.

gly-cid'ic, *a.* Pertaining to glycid.

glȳ'cin, *n.* Same as *Glycocoll.*

glȳ-cō-chō'lāte, *n.* [*Glycochol*ic and *-ate.*] A salt formed by the union of glycocholic acid with a base.

glȳ-cō-chol'ic, *a.* [Gr. *glykys*, sweet, and *cholē*, gall.] Derived from gall; as, *glycocholic* acid.

Glycocholic acid; an acid found in ox-gall, in combination with alkalis.

glȳ'cō-cin, *n.* Same as *Glycocoll.*

glȳ'cō-coll, *n.* [Gr. *glykys*, sweet, and *kolla*, glue.] An acid derived from gelatin, glycocholic acid, and other compounds by the action of hydrochloric acid; chemically known as *amido-acetic acid*, and also called *glycin*, *glycocin*, and *gelatin sugar.*

glȳ'cō-ġen, *n.* [Gr. *glykys*, sweet, and *-genēs*, producing.] A white compound found in certain animal tissues, especially in the liver; also called *animal starch.*

glȳ-cō-ġen'e-sis, *n.* In pathology, the formation of glucose in animal tissue.

glȳ-cō-ġen'ic, *a.* Relating to glycogen.

glȳ-coġ'e-ny, *n.* Glycogenesis.

glȳ-cō-hē'mi-ȧ, glȳ-cō-hæ'mi-ȧ, *n.* Same as *Glucohemia.*

glȳ'col, *n.* [*Glyc*erin and alcoh*ol.*] The type of a class of artificial compounds intermediate in their properties and chemical relations between alcohol and glycerin; a diatomic acid, alcohol being a monatomic and glycerin a triatomic. It is liquid, inodorous, of a sweetish taste, and insoluble in water and alcohol.

glȳ-col'ic, *a.* Of or related to glycol.

Glycolic acid; an acid derived from unripe grapes, as a crystalline or syrupy substance, or artificially prepared from glycol.

glȳ'cō-lid, glȳ'cōl-lide, *n.* [*Glycol*ic and *-id.*] A substance derived from glycolic acid as an amorphous powder by treatment with dry heat.

gly̆-c̦ō-lū′ril, *n.* [*Glycol*yl and *uric.*] Acetylene urea, obtained variously, as by the reaction of urea and oxalic aldehyde with hydrochloric acid.

gly̆′c̦ō-lyl, *n.* [*Glycol*ic and *-yl.*] The hypothetical compound, CO.CH_2, considered to be the essential radical of glycolic acid and many other compounds.

Gly̆-c̦ō′ni-ăn, *a.* Same as *Glyconic.*

Gly̆-c̦on′ic̦, *a.* [LL. *Glyconius*; Gr. *Glykōneios*, from *Glycōn*, the inventor of this meter.] Pertaining to a verse or meter, consisting of four feet, one dactyl and three trochees.

Gly̆-c̦on′ic̦, *n.* A Glyconic verse.

gly̆′c̦ō-nin, *n.* An ointment made by emulsifying glycerin with yolk of egg.

gly̆′c̦ōse, *n.* See *Glucose.*

gly̆′c̦ō-sin, gly̆′c̦ō-sine, *n.* [*Glycol* (*-s-*) and *-ine.*] A crystalline compound prepared by treating oxalic aldehyde with ammonia.

gly̆-c̦ō-sū′ri-ȧ, *n.* Same as *Glucosuria.*

Glyc-yr-rhī′zȧ (-rī′), *n.* [Gr. *glykyrrhiza*, licorice, from *glykys*, sweet, and *rhiza*, root.]

1. A genus of plants with sweet roots including the licorice plant, *Glycyrrhiza glabra*, which yields the licorice-root of commerce.

2. [g—] Any plant of the genus; in medicine, licorice-root.

glyc-yr-rhī′zin (-rī′), *n.* A peculiar saccharine matter obtained from the root of *Glycyrrhiza glabra*; licorice.

glyn, glynn, *n.* [W. *glyn*, a glen.] A glen; used in Celtic place-names.

gly̆-ox′ăl, *n.* [*Glycol* and *oxalic.*] Oxalic aldehyde, obtained by slowly oxidizing glycol or acetic aldehyde.

gly̆-ox-al′ic̦, *a.* Pertaining to or derived from glyoxal.

gly̆-ox′ȧ-lin, *n.* [*Glyoxal* and *-in.*] A compound derived from glyoxal by the action of ammonia or a cold solution; hence, any compound of a series similarly constituted.

gly̆-ox′im, gly̆-ox′ime, *n.* [*Glyoxal* and *-oxim.*] A compound derived from glyoxal by treatment with hydroxylamin; hence, any compound of similar structure.

glyph (glif), *n.* [Gr. *glyphē*, a carving, from *glyphein*, to carve, cut.]

1. In sculpture and architecture, a notch, groove, channel, or cavity, intended as an ornament, and usually perpendicular.

2. An incised design; a glyphic.

glyph′ic̦, *n.* [Gr. *glyphikos*, from *glyphē*, a carving.] A hieroglyphic; a picture or figure implying a word.

glyph′ic̦, *a.* Pertaining to grooved or sunken designs.

glyph′ō-grȧph, *n.* A plate or print prepared by glyphography.

glyph-ō-grȧph′ic̦, *a.* Of or pertaining to glyphography.

gly-phog′rȧ-phy, *n.* [Gr. *glyphē*, a carving, and *graphein*, to write.] A method of reproducing drawings, in which a copper plate, prepared as for etching, is electroplated on the incised lines, forming a design in relief from which prints may be made as from an ordinary electrotype.

glyp′tic̦, *a.* [L.Gr. *glyptikos*, from Gr. *glyptos*, fit for carving, carved, from *glyphein*, to carve.]

1. Pertaining to carving, sculpture, or glyptics.

2. In mineralogy, figured.

glyp′tic̦s, *n.* The art of engraving figures on precious stones.

glyp′tō-don, *n.* [Gr. *glyptos*, carved, and *odous*, *odontos*, a tooth.] An extinct quadruped of the armadillo family, of the size of an ox and having a carapace composed of a single solid piece.

Glyptodon (*Glyptodon clavipes*).

glyp′tō-dont, *n.* Any one of the *Glyptodontidæ*, a fossil family of gigantic armadillos.

glyp′tō-grȧph, *n.* [Gr. *glyptos*, carved, and *graphein*, to write.] A carving on a precious stone or other small object.

glyp-tō-grȧph′ic̦, *a.* Pertaining to glyptography.

glyp-tog′rȧ-phy, *n.* A description of the art of engraving on precious stones, etc.; also, the art itself; knowledge concerning glyptographs.

glyp-tō-thē′c̦ȧ, *n.*; *pl.* **glyp-tō-thē′c̦æ.** [Gr. *glyptos*, carved, *glypton*, a carved image, and *thēkē*, a case, repository.] A building or room for the preservation of works of sculpture.

glys′tēr, *n.* Same as *Clyster.*

Gmel′in-ȧ (mel′), *n.* [Named after Prof. S. G. *Gmelin*, of St. Petersburg.] An Asiatic genus of plants belonging to the order *Verbenaceæ*. All the species form shrubs or trees, of which the latter are valued for their timber.

gmel′in-ite, *n.* [Named after Christian G. *Gmelin*, of Tübingen.] In mineralogy, hydrolite or ledererite, a mineral of a white passing into a flesh-red color, occurring in secondary flat six-sided prisms, terminated at both extremities by truncated six-sided prisms; it is a hydrated silicate of alumina, lime, and soda.

gnȧ-phal′i-oid (nā-), *a.* In botany, resembling the genus *Gnaphalium.*

Gnā-phā′li-um (nā-), *n.* [Gr. *gnaphalion*, a downy plant used in stuffing cushions.] A very extensive genus of beautiful and curious plants of the order *Compositæ*, known by the popular names of *cudweed* and *everlasting.*

gnär, gnärr (när), *v.i.* To growl; to murmur; to snarl.

> A thousand wants
> *Gnarr* at the heels of men. —Tennyson.

gnär, gnärr (när), *n.* [ME. *knarre, gnarre*, a knot.] A knot; specifically, a hard knot on a tree; hence, a tough, thickset person. [Rare.]

gnärl (närl), *v.i.*; gnarled, *pt.*, *pp.*; gnarling, *ppr.* [D. *knorren*; G. *gnarren*; L.G. *knurren, gnurren*, to snarl, growl.] To growl; to murmur; to snarl.

gnärl, *n.* [A dim. from *gnar.*] A protuberance on the outside of a tree; a knot; a snag.

> *Gnarls* without and knots within.—Landor.

gnärled, *a.* Knotty; full of knots; as, the *gnarled* oak.

gnärl′y, *a.* Knotty; full of knots; gnarled.

gnash (nash), *v.t.*; gnashed (nasht), *pt.*, *pp.*; gnashing, *ppr.* [ME. *gnasten*, to gnash the teeth; Ice. *gnesta*, to crack; Dan. *knaske*, to crush with the teeth.] To grind together, as the teeth, in anger or pain.

gnash, *v.i.* To grind the teeth together, as in rage or pain.

> There they him laid
> *Gnashing* for anguish, and despite, and shame.
> —Milton.

gnash′ing, *n.* A grinding or grating together of the teeth in rage or anguish.

> There shall be weeping and *gnashing* of teeth.
> —Matt. viii. 12.

gnash′ing-ly, *adv.* With gnashing.

gnat (nat), *n.* [ME. *gnat*; AS. *gnæt*, a gnat.]

1. A name applied to several insects of the genus *Culex*, which includes the mosquito, *Culex pipiens*. The proboscis or sting of the female is a tube containing four spiculæ of exquisite fineness, dentated or edged; these are the modified mandibles and maxillæ. The males are destitute of stings, and are further distinguished by their plumelike antennæ.

2. A name applied to various other dipterous insects; a midge; as, a gall-*gnat*; a buffalo-*gnat*, etc.

gnat′c̦atch″ēr (nat′), *n.* A small bird of the genus *Polioptila*, related to the kinglets.

gnat′=flow″ēr (nat′), *n.* Same as *Bee-orchis.*

gnat′=hawk (nat′), *n.* In zoölogy, the goatsucker.

gnath′ic̦ (nath′), *a.* [Gr. *gnathos*, a jaw, and *-ic.*] In anatomy, pertaining to the jaw.

gnā-thid′i-um (nā-), *n.*; *pl.* **gnā-thid′i-ȧ.** [Gr. *gnathos*, a jaw, and dim. *-idion.*] In ornithology, either prong of the naked portion of the lower mandible.

gnā′thiṣm (nā′), *n.* [Gr. *gnathos*, a jaw, and *-ism.*] The classification of skulls according to measurements of the jaw.

gnath′ite (nath′), *n.* [Gr. *gnathos*, a jaw, and *-ite.*] In zoölogy, any appendage of the mouth of an articulate.

gna-tho-. A combining form from Gr. *gnathos*, jaw, used in zoölogy, anatomy, etc., to signify jaw; as, *Gnatho*stoma, *Gnatho*poda.

gnā-thon′ic̦, gnā-thon′ic̦-ăl (nā-), *a.* [L. *Gnatho*, the name of a parasite in the *Eunuchus* of Terence.] Flattering; deceitful. [Obs.]

gnath′ō-pod (nath′), *n.* 1. An animal belonging to the *Gnathopoda.*

2. Same as *Gnathopodite.*

gnath′ō-pod, *a.* [*Gnatho-*, and Gr. *pous, podos*, a foot.] Having jaw-feet.

Gnā-thop′ō-dȧ (nā-), *n.* [*Gnatho-*, and Gr. *pous, podos*, a foot.] In zoölogy, a division of invertebrates embracing all animals with jaw-feet, or appendages performing the functions of locomotion and mastication, as crustaceans.

gnā-thop′ō-dite (nā-), *n.* [*Gnatho-*, and Gr. *pous, podos*, a foot.] In zoölogy, one of those limbs which, in crustaceans, have been modified into accessory organs of mastication.

gnā-thop′ō-dous (nā-), *a.* Having jaw-feet; pertaining to a gnathopod.

gnā-thos′te-ġite (nā-), *n.* [*Gnatho-*, and Gr. *stegos*, a roof, and *-ite.*] In zoölogy, an expanded maxilliped, occurring on each side of the mouth of a crustacean, which serves as a cover for the other mouth-parts.

Gnā-thos′tō-mȧ (nā-), *n.* [*Gnatho-*, and Gr. *stoma* (*-atos*), a mouth.] A genus of nematoid entozoa, first discovered by Owen in the stomach of the tiger.

Gnath-ō-stō′mȧ-tȧ (nath-), *n.pl.* A division of the *Crustacea* having functional jaws.

Gnā-thos′tō-mī (nā-), *n.pl.* A class of vertebrates with functional jaws, including all except the hags, lampreys, and lancelets.

gnath-ō-thē′c̦ȧ (nath-), *n.*; *pl.* **gnath-ō-thē′c̦æ.** [*Gnatho-*, and Gr. *thēkē*, a case, box.] In ornithology, the horny sheath of the gnathidium.

gnat′ling (nat′), *n.* A little gnat.

gnat′snap″pēr (nat′), *n.* A bird that eats gnats.

gnat′=strāin″ēr (nat′), *n.* One who attaches too much importance to little things.

> Ye blind guides, who *strain* at a *gnat* and swallow a camel. —Matt. xxiii. 24.

gnat′wŏrm (nat′), *n.* The larva of a gnat; a wiggler.

gnaw (na), *v.t.*; gnawed, *pt.*, *pp.*; gnawing, *ppr.* [ME. *gnawen, gnagen*; AS. *gnagan*, to gnaw.]

1. To bite off by little and little; to bite or scrape at, or off with the fore teeth; to wear away by biting; as, the rats *gnaw* a board or plank; a worm *gnaws* the wood of a tree or the plank of a ship.

2. To bite in agony or rage; as, to *gnaw* a pen in anger.

3. To waste; to fret; to corrode.

gnaw, *v.i.* To use the teeth in biting.

gnaw′ēr, *n.* 1. One who or that which gnaws or corrodes.

2. In zoölogy, any rodent.

gneiss (nīs), *n.* [G.] In mineralogy, a species of aggregated rock composed of quartz, feldspar, and mica, of a structure more or less slaty. It often contains hornblende, in place of mica, when it takes the name of *syenitic gneiss*. The only difference between this rock and granite consists in the foliation of *gneiss.*

gneis′sic̦, *a.* Of, like, or composed of gneiss.

gneis′soid, *a.* Having some of the characteristics of gneiss.

gneis′sōse, *a.* Having the general structure of gneiss.

Gnē-tā′cē-æ (nē-), *n.pl.* [From *gnemon* or *gnemo*, the native name in the island of Ternate, and *-aceæ.*] An order of gymnogenous plants, popularly called joint-firs, and consisting of small trees or shrubs, with flowers arranged in catkins or heads. The seeds of some of them are eaten.

gnē-tā′ceous (nē-), *a.* Belonging to the *Gnetaceæ.*

gnew, *v.*, obsolete past tense of *gnaw.*

gnide (nīd), *v.t.* [ME. *gniden*; AS. *gnidan*, to rub, break in pieces.] To break in pieces; to comminute; to rub. [Obs.]

gnoff, gnof (nof), *n.* [Etym. doubtful.] A miser. [Obs.]

gnōme (nōm), *n.* [Fr. *gnome*, from Gr. *gnōmē*, thought, intelligence; so called from the belief that *gnomes* could give information as to secret treasures in the earth.]

1. An imaginary being, supposed in fable to inhabit the inner parts of the earth and to be the guardian of mines, quarries, etc.

2. A small, misshapen person; a dwarf.

3. In zoölogy, the gnome-owl; also, any one of several humming-birds.

gnōme, *n.* [LL. *gnome*, a sentence, maxim; Gr. *gnōmē*, thought, judgment, intelligence, from *gignōskein*, to know.] A brief reflection or maxim; an aphorism.

gnōme′=owl, *n.* A small owl, *Glaucidium gnoma*; called also *pygmy owl.*

gnom′ic̦, gnom′ic̦-ăl (nom′), *a.* [Gr. *gnōmikos*, from *gnōmē*, intelligence, a maxim.] Sententious; uttering or containing maxims or striking detached thoughts; as, *gnomic* poetry, like the book of Proverbs.

Gnomic poets; a group of Greek poets of the fifth century B. C., whose writings consist of precepts for and reflections upon human life and conduct.

gnō-mō-loġ′ic̦, gnō-mō-loġ′ic̦-ăl (nō-), *a.* Pertaining to gnomology.

gnō-mol′ō-gy, *n.* [Gr. *gnōmologia*, a speaking in maxims, a collection of maxims; *gnōmē*, intelligence, a maxim, and *legein*, to speak.] A collection of maxims, grave sentences, or reflections. [Rare.]

gnō′mon (nō′), *n.* [Gr. *gnōmōn*, one who knows or examines, the index of a sundial, a carpenter's rule, from *gignōskein*, to know.]

1. The metal triangle or pin on a sundial, which, by its shadow, shows the time of day.

2. In astronomy, a style or column erected perpendicular to the horizon, for making astronomical observations. Its principal use was to find the altitude of the sun by measuring the length of its shadow.

3. In geometry, the space included between the two lines formed by two similar parallelograms, of which the smaller is inscribed within the larger, so as to have one angle in each common to both.

4. In an arithmetical series, one of the terms by which polygonal numbers are found.

Gnomon of a globe; the index of the hour circle.

gnō-mon′ic̦, gnō-mon′ic̦-ăl, *a.* Relating to dialing or the art of making gnomons.

Gnomonic projection; a representation of one of the hemispheres of the earth on a flat surface, the pole being the center of that surface, and the point of sight being taken at the center of the sphere.

gnō-mon′iç-ăl-ly, *adv.* According to the principles of the gnomonic projection.

gnō-mon′içs, *n.* [Gr. *gnōmonikē* (supply *technē*, art), the art of dialing; *gnōmonikē*, f. of *gnōmonikos*, pertaining to a gnomon or dial.] The art or science of dialing, or of constructing dials to show the hour of the day by the shadow of a gnomon.

gnō-mon-ol′ō-ġy, *n.* [Gr. *gnōmōn*, a gnomon, and *-logia*, from *legein*, to speak.] A treatise on dialing.

gnō′sis, *n.* [Gr. *gnōsis*, knowledge, from *gignōskein*, to know.] Superior wisdom; knowledge of mysteries or spiritual truth.

Gnos′tiç (nos′), *a.* [L. *gnosticus*; Gr. *gnōstikos*, knowing, sagacious, from *gignōskein*, to know.]

1. Of or relating to Gnosticism or its followers; as, the *Gnostic* doctrine.

2. [g—] Shrewd; knowing; wise. [Rare.]

Gnos′tiç, *n.* One of a class of rationalists in the early history of the Christian church; also, any follower of the doctrines of Gnosticism.

gnos′tiç-ăl-ly, *adv.* 1. Knowingly. [Colloq.]

2. In the manner or according to the doctrines of the Gnostics.

Gnos′ti-çism, *n.* An eclectic system of philosophy and religion which flourished during the first six centuries of the present era. It sought to mediate between Christianity and paganism, and taught that knowledge, more than philosophy or faith, was the means of salvation. According to their doctrine all existences, both spiritual and material, originated in the Deity by successive emanations. These they termed eons, and Christ was conceived to be a higher eon only. The system combined the main features of orientalism, Platonism, dualism, and Christianity.

gnū (nū), **gnoo**, *n.* [Hottentot *gnu* or *nju.*] A large kind of antelopine animal of Africa, with heavy mane and bushy tail and with horns and head somewhat resembling those of the bison or buffalo. It is about four feet in height. The common *gnu* is the *Catoblepas gnu.*

Gnu (*Catoblepas gnu*).

gō, *v.i.*; went, *pt.*; gone, *pp.*; going, *ppr.* [ME. *go*, *gon*, *gan*; AS. *gan*, to go.]

1. To move; to pass; to proceed; to be in motion from any cause or in any manner, as by the action of the limbs, by a conveyance, or as a machine; used sometimes literally and sometimes figuratively.

Clocks will *go* as they are set. —Otway.

2. To walk; to move on the feet or step by step; also, to walk step by step or leisurely, as distinguished from running or hastening; as, the child begins to *go* alone when a year old.

You know that love
Will creep in service where it cannot *go*.
—Shak.

3. To depart; to move from a place; opposed to *come*; as, the mail *goes* and comes every day.

I will let you *go* that ye may sacrifice.
—Ex. viii. 28.

4. To be passed on from one to another; to have currency or use; to pass; to circulate; also, to be reckoned; to be esteemed.

And so the jest *goes* round. —Dryden.

The money . . . should *go* according to its true value. —Locke.

5. To proceed or happen in a given manner; to fare; to be carried on; to have course; to come to an issue or result; to succeed; to turn out.

How *goes* the night, boy? —Shak.

I think, as the world *goes*, he was a good sort of man enough. —Arbuthnot.

6. To apply; to be applicable; as, the argument *goes* to this point only.

7. To apply oneself; to set oneself; to undertake.

Seeing himself confronted by so many, like a resolute orator he *went* not to denial.
—Sidney.

8. To have recourse; as, to *go* to law.

9. To be about to do; as, I was *going* to say; I am *going* to begin harvest. [In this usage it may be regarded as an auxiliary verb.]

10. To be guided or regulated; to proceed by some principle or rule; as, we are to *go* by the rules of law or according to the precepts of Scripture.

We are to *go* by another measure. —Sprat.

11. To be with young; to be pregnant; to gestate; as, the females of different animals *go*, some a longer, some a shorter time.

12. To be alienated in payment or exchange; to be sold; to be disposed of; as, if our exports are of less value than our imports, our money must *go* to pay the balance; this article *went* for a trifling sum.

13. To be loosed or released; to be freed from restraint; as, let me *go*; let *go* the hand.

14. To proceed; to extend; to reach; to lead; as, the line *goes* from one end to the other; this road *goes* to St. Louis.

15. To have effect; to extend in effect, meaning, or purport; to avail; to be of force or value; as, money *goes* further now than it did during the war.

His amorous expressions *go* no further than virtue may allow. —Dryden.

16. To proceed or tend toward a result, consequence, or product; to contribute; to conduce; to concur; to be an ingredient; frequently with *to*, *into*, *toward*, and the like.

Against right reason all your counsels *go*.
—Dryden.

17. To be lost or ruined; to perish; to sink or die.

Sweeter far is death than life to me that long to *go*. —Tennyson.

18. To have animation and unflagging interest; as, the drama *goes* well.

19. To become; as, she has *gone* mad; I will *go* bail; he will *go* loser.

To go a-begging; to be undesirable; not in demand.

To go about; (a) to take first steps, as in an enterprise; (b) to retrace steps, as to turn the head of a ship.

To go abroad; (a) to go away from home, as out of one's house or to a foreign country; (b) to forsake obscurity and seek publicity.

To go by; to pass near or beyond; to omit.

To go by the board; to fall overboard; to be passed over; to be lost in the confusion.

To go down; to descend; to sink or founder; to fail.

To go far; to have much weight, influence, value.

To go for; to go in search of; to represent; to pass for; to advocate; to assail personally or otherwise.

To go forth; to issue or emanate; to become public.

To go hard with; to cause much pain or embarrassment.

To go in for; to enter or undertake anything with a view to final results; as, *to go in for* golf, money, honors, politics, etc.

To go off; to leave; to depart; to explode or be discharged; to come to pass; to die.

To go on; to proceed; to advance or continue; to be put on or fitted over.

To go on all fours; to agree point for point; to correspond in every particular.

To go one better; to surpass by one point or grade, as in a contest or rivalry of any kind.

To go out; to go forth; to be extinguished.

To go over; to cross or traverse; to read, peruse, examine, or study; to review; to transcend; to surpass; to be postponed.

To go over to the majority; to join the dead; to die.

To go through; to sustain to the end; to endure, suffer, or bear; to accomplish or perform thoroughly; to exhaust; to rob.

To go to the devil; to go to destruction; to fail in business; to fall into vicious habits.

To go under; to be known by or to pass by (a name, title, etc.); to be overwhelmed or defeated; to perish; to fail in business.

To go up; to rise or ascend; to increase in value; to fail or dissolve.

To go with; to accompany; to suit or harmonize with; to agree or coincide with.

To go without; to manage without.

To go without saying; to be taken as certain.

To go wrong; to stray or wander; to fall from virtue; to be contrary.

gō, *v.t.* 1. To take or partake; to contribute or furnish; as, to *go* expenses; he *went* security for his brother.

2. To stake or bet; as, I'll *go* you a dollar. [Colloq.]

To go halves; to share equally with another.

To go it; to behave wildly or recklessly. [Slang.]

To go it blind; to act without knowledge; to plunge ahead.

gō, *n.* 1. A happening; as, this is a nice *go*.

2. A fad; a custom; a habit; style; as, shirtwaists are all the *go*. [Colloq.]

3. Vitality; spirit; energy; as, there's plenty of *go* to him. [Colloq.]

4. A success; a lucky stroke; good business. [Colloq.]

5. Excitement; noise. [Colloq.]

6. In cribbage, a stage in the game at which a player cannot play any card which will not increase the aggregate amount above thirty-one.

7. A glass of liquor. [Eng. Slang.]

From the word go; from the very beginning.

Great go; *little go*; respectively, the final and preliminary examinations for degrees at Cambridge University, England.

No go; of no avail; of no use; a failure. [Slang.]

On the go; busy; moving about; unsettled. [Colloq.]

gō′ȧ, *n.* [Native name.] 1. An antelope, *Procapra picticauda*, native to Tibet.

2. The marsh-crocodile.

gōad, *n.* [ME. *gode*, *god*, *gad*; AS. *gad*; Ice. *gaddr*, a goad, sting.] A pointed implement for pricking a beast of burden to greater activity; hence, an impelling force.

gōad, *v.t.*; goaded, *pt.*, *pp.*; goading, *ppr.* To drive with a goad; to prick, spur, stimulate; to rouse or incite; as, *goaded* by passion; a people *goaded* by oppression.

That temptation that doth *goad* us on.—Shak.

gōaf, *n.*; *pl.* **gōaveṣ**. 1. In mining, a section from which the mineral has been almost entirely worked; also, the refuse left from the workings.

2. A grain-stack in the straw. [Prov. Eng.]

To work the goaf; to take away the mineral props from a section in a mine.

gō′=ȧ-head′ (-hed′), *a.* Progressive; energetic; live.

gōal, *n.* [OFr. *gaule*, *waule*, a pole, rod; Old Friesic *walu*; Goth. *walus*, a staff, stick.]

1. The point set to bound a race and to which contestants run; the mark.

Part curb their fiery steeds, or shun the *goal*
With rapid wheels. —Milton.

2. The end or final purpose; the end to which a design tends, or which a person aims to reach or accomplish.

Each individual seeks a several *goal*.—Pope.

3. In football, one of the lines which limit the halves of the gridiron, or field, together with the goal-posts and the crosspiece between them; the goal-line.

gōal′keep″ẽr, *n.* In football and some other games, a player whose duty is to prevent the ball from passing through the goal.

gōal′=pōst, *n.* In football, one of the upright posts supporting the crosspiece at the goal.

gō-an′nȧ, *n.* The Australian name of an iguana.

Gō′ȧ pow′dẽr. [From *Goa*, a city of the Malabar Islands, to which it is shipped from Portugal, and Eng. *powder*.] A bitter powder obtained from a Brazilian tree, *Andira araroba*, and used in medicine.

gōar′ish, *a.* Patched; mean. [Obs.]

gōat, *n.* [ME. *gote*, *goot*, *gat*; AS. *gat*, a goat.] A horned ruminant quadruped of the genus *Capra*. The horns are hollow, erect, turned backward, annular on the surface, and scabrous. The male is generally bearded under the chin. *Goats* are nearly of the size of sheep, but stronger, less timid, and more agile. They frequent rocks and mountains, and subsist on scanty, coarse food. Their milk is sweet, nourishing, and medicinal, and their flesh furnishes food. *Goats* are of almost interminable variety, and it is not certainly known from which the domestic goat, *Capra hircus*, is descended. They are found in all parts of the world, and many varieties are valued for their hair or wool, as the *Cashmere goat*, the *Angora goat*, etc. *Haplocerus montanus*, the Rocky Mountain goat, is a species of antelope.

Cashmere Goat.

gōat′=an″tē-lōpe, *n.* An antelope of the genus *Nemorhedus*, much like a goat in general appearance.

gōat-ee′, *n.* A beard so trimmed that a part of it hangs down from the lower lip or chin, like the beard of a goat.

gōat′=ēye, *n.* See *Ægilops*, 1.

gōat′=fig, *n.* The wild fig.

gōat′fish, *n.* 1. The filefish of Europe.

2. *Upeneus maculatus*, a mulloid fish of the West Indies.

gōat′hẽrd, *n.* One whose occupation is to tend goats.

gōat′ish, *a.* Resembling a goat in any quality; hence, wanton; lustful.

gōat′ish-ly, *adv.* In a goatish manner; lustfully.

gōat′ish-ness, *n.* The quality of being goatish.

gōat′=mär″jō-răm, *n.* Goat's-beard.

gōat′milk″ẽr, *n.* See *Goatsucker.*

gōat′=mọth, *n.* *Cossus ligniperda,* a large moth of a dark color which feeds on the wood of willows.

gōat′=owl, *n.* The goatsucker.

gōat's′=bāne, *n.* *Aconitum Lycoctonum,* the plant wolf's-bane.

gōat's′=bēard, *n.* 1. *Tragopogon pratensis,* a composite plant of Europe.

2. *Spiræa Aruncus,* which has its spikes of flowers arranged in a long panicle.

3. *Astilbe decandra,* known as the *false goat's-beard.*

4. Any one of various fungi of the genus *Clavaria.*

gōat's′=foot, *n.* A plant, *Oxalis caprina,* cultivated in greenhouses. It bears flesh-colored flowers.

gōat's′=họrn, *n.* *Astragalus Ægiceras,* a leguminous plant of southern Europe.

gōat′skin, *n.* The skin of a goat, dressed, especially one sewed into the shape of a bottle.

gōat's′=rūe, *n.* A plant, *Galega officinalis.*

gōat's′=thọrn, *n.* Any one of various leguminous plants of the Levant, as *Astragalus Tragacanthus* or *Astragalus Poterium.*

gōat′stōne, *n.* A bezoar from a goat.

gōat′suck″ẽr, *n.* A name common to the various species of birds of the genus *Caprimulgus,* given originally from the erroneous idea that they suck goats. The European *goatsucker, Caprimulgus europæus,* feeds upon nocturnal insects, as moths, gnats, beetles, etc., which it catches on the wing, flying with its mouth open; called also *goatmilker.*

Goatsucker (*Caprimulgus europæus*).

gōats′=whēat (-hwēt), *n.* Any plant of the genus *Tragopyrum.*

gōat′weed, *n.* 1. *Ægopodium Podagraria,* the goutweed.

2. Either of two West Indian plants of the figwort family, *Capraria biflora* or *Stemodia durantifolia.*

gōaveṣ, *n.,* pl. of *goaf.*

gob, *n.* [Abbrev. of *gobbet.*]

1. A little mass or collection; a lump; a mouthful. [Colloq.]

2. In coal-mining, refuse. [See *Goaf.*]

gob, *n.* The mouth. [Prov. Eng.]

gob, *n.* [Abbrev. of Chinese *gobshite.*] A sailor of the United States Navy, the term being self-applied; a bluejacket. First used on the American Naval Asiatic Station.

go-bang′, *n.* [Japan. *goban,* a checker-board.] A game played on a checker-board with colored counters, the object being to place five counters in a row in any direction.

gobbe, *n.* [Name in Surinam.] A tropical leguminous plant, *Voandzeia subterranea,* the pods of which are matured beneath the ground. It much resembles the common peanut.

gob′bet, *n.* [ME. *gobette, gobet;* OFr. *gobet, goubet,* dim. of *gob,* a gulp, from *gober,* to gulp, devour.]

1. A small piece; a mouthful; a lump. [Obs.]

2. A block of stone.

gob′bet, *v.t.* To swallow in masses or mouthfuls. [Obs.]

gob′bet-ly, *adv.* In pieces. [Obs.]

gob′bing, gob′bin, *n.* In mining, the refuse thrown back into the excavations remaining after the removal of the coal.

gob′ble, *v.t.;* gobbled, *pt., pp.;* gobbling, *ppr.* [Freq. from OFr. *gober,* to swallow greedily.]

1. To swallow in large pieces; to swallow hastily; often followed by *up* or *down.*

2. To seize greedily; to acquire graspingly; with *up;* as, he *gobbled up* all the low-priced stock. [Slang.]

3. To sound in the throat, as the note made by a turkey-cock.

gob′ble, *v.i.* To make a noise in the throat, as a turkey-cock.

gob′ble, *n.* 1. The noise made by a turkey-cock.

2. In the game of golf, a rapid, straight putt into the hole, such that, had the ball not gone in, it would have gone some distance beyond.

gob′ble=cock, *n.* See second *Gobbler.*

gob′blẽr, *n.* One who gobbles or swallows in haste; a greedy eater; a gormandizer.

gob′blẽr, *n.* A turkey-cock.

gob′e-lin (*or Fr. pron.* gō-be-laṅ′), *a.* Pertaining to the Gobelins, a French factory, or to the tapestry manufactured there.

gob′e-lin, *n.* A superior kind of tapestry made at the Gobelins in France.

gōbe-mouche′, *n.* [Fr.] A simpleton; a silly, credulous individual.

gob′et, *n.* [Obs.] See *Gobbet.*

gō′=bē-tween″, *n.* One who acts as an intermediary between two parties, as an agent or mediator; usually in a bad sense.

gō′bi-oid, *a.* and *n.* [L. *gobius;* Gr. *kōbios,* the gudgeon, and *eidos,* form.]

I. *a.* Pertaining to or resembling a goby.

II. *n.* A goby; a fish of the genus *Gobius.*

Gō′bi-us, *n.* [L. *gobius;* Gr. *kōbios,* a kind of fish, the gudgeon.] A genus of fishes having the ventral fins fastened together in a funnel-shaped disk.

gob′let, *n.* [OFr. *gobelet, goblet,* dim. of *gobel,* a goblet, from LL. *cupellus,* a cup, dim. of L. *cupa,* a tub, cask.] A kind of cup or drinking-vessel without a handle.

gob′let=cell, *n.* In anatomy, a beaker-shaped cell found on mucous membranes.

gob′lin, *n.* [ME. *gobelyn;* OFr. *gobelin;* LL. *gobelinus, cobalus;* Gr. *kobalos,* a rogue, sprite.] An evil or mischievous spirit or sprite; an elf; a phantom; a malicious fairy.

gob′line, *n.* Nautically, a rope leading from the martingale inward; a back-rope.

gob′lin-ize, *v.t.;* goblinized, *pt., pp.;* goblinizing, *ppr.* To change into a goblin; to render grotesque or mischievous after the fashion of a goblin.

gob′ō-nā-ted, *a.* In heraldry, same as *Componé.*

gob′ō-né (-nā), **gō-bō′ny,** *a.* Same as *Componé.*

gob′stick, *n.* In angling, a device for taking the hook out of a fish's gullet.

gō′by, *n.;* *pl.* **gō′bieṣ.** [L. *gobio, gobius,* a gudgeon.] A fish of the genus *Gobius.*

gō′=bȳ, *n.* A passing without recognition; hence, a slight; a cut; as, to give one the *go-by.*

gō′gärt, *n.* 1. A small framework with casters or rollers, without a bottom, in which children learn to walk without danger of falling.

He (Plato) seems to have thought that the use of letters had operated on the human mind as the use of the *gocart* in learning to walk.
—Macaulay.

Gocart.

2. A light two-wheeled cart.

3. A small wagon or cart used as a plaything for a child.

4. A small folding four-wheeled chair or carriage for a young child to ride in.

god, *a.* and *n.* Good. [Obs.]

god, *n.* [ME. *god, godd;* AS. *god,* god; akin to L.G. *god;* M.H.G. *got;* Ice. *godh;* Sw. *gud;* Dan. *gud;* Goth. *guth,* god. The word is common to Teut. tongues, but not identified outside of them. It was generally in plural, and neut. It was applied to heathen deities and later, when the Teutonic peoples were converted to Christianity, the word was elevated to the Christian sense. There is no connection between *god* and *good* in form, nor was the conception of goodness prominent in the heathen conception of a deity.]

1. [G—] In monotheism, the Supreme Being, having always existed and ever to exist, the Author and Ruler of the universe.

2. In various polytheistic religions, a being, or one of a number of beings, to be worshiped or feared by reason of superior intelligence or supernatural powers; a deity.

3. Figuratively, that which is first in worship, devotion, or admiration; an all-absorbing passion, pursuit, or hobby; something idolized.

Thou *god* of our idolatry, the Press.
—Cowper.

4. An idol.

5. A spectator or auditor in the gallery of a theater. [Slang.]

God's acre; see under *Acre.*

God's day; Sunday.

God's footstool; the earth.

Household gods; (a) in Roman mythology, the gods presiding over the household; (b) those things treasured from association with home life.

The house of God; a house dedicated to the worship of God; a holy temple; a church.

god, *v.t.* To deify. [Obs.]

god′child, *n.* One for whom a person becomes sponsor at baptism and promises to see educated as a Christian.

God′dam, *n.* [So called from the oath common to Englishmen.] An Englishman; a name given contemptuously by the French.

god′daugh″tẽr (-da″), *n.* A female godchild.

god′dess, *n.* 1. A female deity.

2. A charming woman.

god′det, god′et, *n.* [OFr. *godet, goudet,* a tankard.] A tankard. [Obs.]

gōde, *a.* and *n.* Good. [Obs.]

Gō-dē′ti-ȧ (-shi-ȧ), *n.* [Named after M. *Godet,* of Switzerland.] A genus of plants of the evening primrose family, comprising about twenty species, growing in western America. They have gorgeous purple or pink flowers.

gō′=dev″il, *n.* 1. A weight dropped into an oil-well boring to set off a cartridge and thereby start the flow.

2. A kind of flexible plug with scraping branches attached, used for cleaning the pipes of a pipe-line, being driven along by the flowing oil.

3. A kind of rude sled. [Local, U. S.]

god′fä″thẽr, *n.* [ME. *godfader;* AS. *godfæder;* *god,* God, and *fæder,* father.]

1. One who gives a name to any person or thing.

These earthly *godfathers* of heaven's lights.
—Shak.

2. An old jocular name for a juryman.

3. One of the sponsors who take vows upon themselves when they bring an infant to be baptized.

god′fä″thẽr, *v.t.* To act as godfather to; to take under one's fostering care.

God′=fēar″ing, *a.* Reverential; religious.

God′=fọr-säk″en, *a.* 1. Depraved; hopelessly bad.

2. Dreary; desolate; wretched.

god′head (-hed), *n.* 1. The divine nature; deity; divinity; godship.

2. [G—] The Supreme Being, especially as comprehending all his attributes.

3. A divinity; a god or goddess.

The nymphs or native *godheads* yet unknown.
—Dryden.

god′hood, *n.* Godship.

god′less, *a.* 1. Having no reverence for God; impious; ungodly; irreligious; wicked.

2. [G—] Forsaken by God. [Rare.]

3. Atheistical; having no belief in the existence of God.

god′less-ly, *adv.* In a godless manner.

god′less-ness, *n.* The state of being impious or irreligious.

god′like, *a.* Resembling a god or God; having divinity; characterized by divine being or existence; hence, superior.

god′like-ness, *n.* The state of being godlike.

god′li-ly, *adv.* In the manner of a god.

god′li-ness, *n.* Piety; the state or quality of being godly.

god′ling, *n.* A little deity; a diminutive god.

god′ly, *a.* 1. Pious; reverencing God and his character and laws.

2. Pious; conformed to God's law; as, a *godly* life.

3. Of, pertaining to, or characteristic of a god or deity.

god′ly, *adv.* Piously; righteously.

All that will live *godly* in Christ Jesus shall suffer persecution.
—2 Tim. iii. 12.

god′ly-head (-hed), *n.* Goodness. [Obs.]

god′mŏth″ẽr, *n.* A woman who becomes sponsor for a child in baptism.

gō-down′, *n.* In India, China, Japan, etc., a corruption of the Malay word *godong,* a warehouse.

gō-drọọn′, *n.* [Fr. *godron,* a ruffle or plait.] A decorative design of various forms, usually oval or nearly so, employed in embellishing silverware, needlework, etc. Also written *gadroon.*

god′send, *n.* Something sent by God; an unexpected acquisition or piece of good fortune.

god′ship, *n.* Deity; divinity; the rank or character of a god.

O'er hills and dales their *godships* came.
—Prior.

god′smith, *n.* A maker of idols.

god′sŏn, *n.* [ME. *godson, godsone;* AS. *godsunu;* *god,* God, and *sunu,* son.] A male godchild.

God′speed, *n.* Good speed, that is, success; a prosperous journeying; a wish in behalf of another.

God's′pen″ny, *n.* An earnest-penny; money for the poor.

god′=tree, *n.* A tree venerated by the natives in the West Indies, the *Eriodendron anfractuosum.*

God′wärd, *adv.* Toward God.

god′win, *n.* See *Godwit.*

God-win′i-ȧ, *n.* [Named after Chas. *Godwin.*] A genus of plants of the order *Araceæ,* found in tropical America.

god′wit, *n.* [Prob. from AS. *god,* good, and *wiht,* a creature, wight.] A name common to a genus of birds, the *Limosa,* having long legs and long, flexible bills, and resembling curlews. Also called *godwin.*

gō′el, *a.* [AS. *geolu,* yellow.] Yellow. [Obs.]

gō-e-länd′ (-loṅ′), *n.* [Fr.] A white tern, *Gygis candida,* found in the tropics.

gō-e-min′ (-maṅ′), *n.* [From Fr. *goëmon,* seaweed.] A chemical compound found in seaweed, particularly in Irish moss.

gō'en, *v.*, obsolete past participle of *go.*

gō'ēr, *n.* 1. One who or that which goes; a runner or walker; one having a gait, good or bad; as, that horse is a good *goer*; a safe *goer.*

2. A foot. [Obs.]

goe'thite (gü'tīte), *n.* [Named after the poet *Goethe.*] A hydrous oxid of iron.

gō'e-ty, *n* [Gr. *goēteia*, witchcraft, jugglery, from *goēteuein*, to bewitch, from *goēs*, a wizard, sorcerer.] Invocation of evil spirits. [Obs.]

goff, *n.* [OFr. *goffe*, dull, blockish.] A foolish clown. [Obs.]

goff, *n.* Golf. [Obs.]

gof'fēr, *v.t.*; goffered, *pt.*, *pp.*; goffering, *ppr.* 1. To crimp, flute, or plait, as lace, etc.

2. To raise in ornamental relief; as, to *goffer* starched linen.

Godwinia gigas. 1. The plant in leaf. 2. The flower and root. 3. The flower.

goff'ish, *a.* Foolish; stupid. [Obs.]

gog, *n.* [W. *gog*, activity, rapidity.] Haste; ardent desire to go. [Obs.]

gog'gle, *v.i.*; goggled, *pt.*, *pp.*; goggling, *ppr.* [ME. *gogelen*, to look asquint, freq. from Ir. and Gael. *gog*, a nod, a slight motion.] To strain or roll the eyes; to stare.

And wink and *goggle* like an owl. —Butler.

gog'gle, *a.* Full or rolling, as the eyes; staring.

gog'gle, *n.* 1. A strained or affected rolling of the eye.

2. [*pl.*] A kind of spectacles, with plain or colored glasses, worn to protect the eyes, to remedy squinting, etc.

3. [*pl.*] Spectacles. [Slang.]

gog'gled (-gld), *a.* Prominent; staring, as the eye.

gog'gle-eye, *n.* 1. A rolling, squinting, or staring eye.

2. One of several species of fresh-water fishes found in the Great Lakes and in the waters of the Mississippi valley; so named from their prominent eyes.

3. Strabismus; squinting.

gog'gle-eyed (-īd), *a.* Having prominent, distorted, or rolling eyes.

gog'glēr, *n.* The big-eyed scad, a carangoid fish, widely distributed in tropical seas, and also found on the coast of New England; also called *goggle-eyed jack.*

gog'let, *n.* A kind of jar or decanter made of porous material for keeping water cool.

gō'ing, *n.* 1. The act of moving in any manner or of walking; departure.

2. Pregnancy; the period of gestation. [Obs.]

3. Procedure; way; course of life; behavior; deportment; used chiefly in the plural.

His eyes are upon the ways of man, and he seeth all his *goings.* —Job xxxiv. 21.

4. Condition of roads, etc., for walking or driving; as, the *going* is good.

gō'ing-bar"rel, *n.* The cylinder containing the mainspring of a timepiece and carrying a toothed wheel for driving the train of wheels.

gō'ings-on, *n.pl.* Actions; proceedings; usually applied to reprehensible actions, conduct, or behavior. [Colloq.]

gō'ing-wheel (hwēl), *n.* An arrangement for keeping the works of a clock going while it is being wound up.

goi'tēr, goi'tre, *n.* [Fr. *goitre*, from L. *guttur*, throat.] Enlargement of the thyroid gland; also called *bronchocele, tracheocele*, and *Derbyshire neck.*

goi'tēred, goi'tred, *a.* Affected with goiter.

goi'trous, *a.* [Fr. *goitreux*, from L. *gutturosus*, having a tumor on the throat, from *guttur*, throat.] Pertaining to goiter; of the nature of or affected with bronchocele.

gol'ā-dēr, gol'dēr, *n.* An East Indian name for one who has charge of a storehouse.

gōld, *n.* [ME. *gold, goold, guld*; AS. *gold*, gold.] 1. A precious metal of a bright yellow color, and the most ductile and malleable of all the metals. It is one of the heaviest of the metals, and not being injured by exposure to the air, it is well fitted to be used as coin. It may be beaten into leaves so thin that one grain in weight will cover 56 square inches. It is soluble in nitro-hydrochloric acid or *aqua regia.* Its specific gravity is 19.3.

2. Money; wealth; riches.

3. That which is valuable or much prized; as, a heart of *gold.*

4. A bright yellow color, like that of the metal; as, a flower edged with *gold.*

5. In archery, the exact center of the target, so called because marked with *gold*, or of a gold color; hence, a center shot.

6. An alloy or imitation of the metal.

Dead gold; gold in an unburnished state.

Etruscan gold; gold treated with nitric acid, giving it a satiny appearance; called also *Roman* or *colored gold.*

Fool's gold; see under *Fool.*

German gold; gold-powder of an inferior quality prepared from refuse gold-leaf.

Gold lace; lace ornamented with or made of gilt thread.

Gold plate; utensils of gold.

Gold standard; in finance, a standard adopted in the United States and other countries making gold 900 fine the basic metal of the coinage.

Green gold; an alloy of gold and silver, as distinguished from red gold.

Jeweler's gold; a three-to-one alloy of gold and copper.

Mosaic gold; (a) an alloy of tin, zinc, and copper used for cheap jewelry, picture-frames, etc.; (b) tin sulphid.

Old gold; (a) fragments of gold of all kinds collected for refining; (b) a metal finish of a dull yellow luster, resembling gold in color.

Red gold; an alloy of gold and copper.

Rolled gold; a thin plate of gold joined with a plate of inferior metal by rolling.

White gold; an alloy of gold and silver, about one part of gold to five of silver.

gōld, *a.* Made of gold, as, a *gold* ring.

gōld'-bēat"en, *a.* Gilded. [Obs.]

gōld'-bēat"ēr, *n.* One whose occupation is to beat or foliate gold for gilding.

Gold-beater's skin; the outer layer of the cæcum of an ox, which gold-beaters lay between the leaves of the metal while beating it, making the membrane very thin and fit to be applied to wounds and sores.

gōld'-bēat"ing, *n.* The art or process of reducing gold to extremely thin leaves by beating with a hammer.

gōld'-bee"tle, *n.* 1. The popular name of several species of beetles of the genus *Chrysomela*, order *Chrysomelidæ*, characterized by their brilliancy of color.

2. A beetle of the family *Cassididæ*, of a brilliant color.

gōld'-bound, *a.* Encompassed with gold.

gōld'crest, *n.* In zoölogy, a name applied to various kinglets or golden-crested birds of the genus *Regulus.*

gōld'cup, *n.* In botany, a buttercup, as the cuckoobud.

gōld'-cūre, *n.* A mode of treatment for drunkenness, morphine, opium, or tobacco habits, in which a secret fluid commonly supposed to contain gold is given hypodermically.

gōld'-dig"gings, *n.pl.* A gold-field devoted to placer-mining.

gōld'-dust, *n.* 1. Gold in very fine particles.

2. A plant, *Alyssum saxatile*, having golden-yellow flowers; madwort.

gōld'en, *a.* [ME. *golden, gulden, gylden*; AS. *gylden*, from *gold*, gold.]

1. Made of gold; consisting of gold.

2. Of the color or luster of gold; yellow; bright; shining; splendid; as, the *golden* sun; *golden* fruit.

3. Excellent; most valuable; very precious; as, the *golden* rule.

4. Happy; marked by the happiness and prosperity of mankind; as, the *golden* age.

Golden age; (a) that early mythological period in the history of almost all races, fabled to have been one of primeval innocence and happy enjoyments; (b) in Roman literature, the period from 31 B. C. to 14 A. D., being the time during which the finest classics were written; hence, in any nation, the time of the highest perfection in literature and kindred arts.

Golden balls; the three gilt balls placed in front of a pawnbroker's place of business. The golden balls form the Lombardy arms, and were assumed by the Lombards who settled in London as bankers and money-lenders.

Golden fleece; (a) in classic mythology, the fleece of gold taken from the ram that bore Phryxus through the air to Colchis, and in quest of which Jason undertook the Argonautic expedition; (b) in heraldry, an order of knighthood dating back to 1429, the time of its institution by Philip the Good, Duke of Burgundy.

Golden grease; bribe money. [Slang.]

Golden number; a number once written in gold in calendars, indicating the year of the lunar cycle.

Golden pippin; a variety of apple, named from its color.

Golden rose; a rose made of gold, which receives the blessing of the pope on the fourth Sunday of Lent, afterward being presented as a high honor to some worthy member of the church.

Golden rule; (a) in arithmetic, the rule of three or rule of proportion; (b) in morals, the rule of doing to others as you would be done by.

Golden samphire; a seashore herb of the aster family.

Golden saxifrage; a low herb of the genus *Chrysosplenium*, order *Saxifragaceæ*, annual or perennial, with alternate or opposite crenate leaves and inconspicuous greenish axillary and terminal flowers.

gōld'en-chāin, *n.* A yellow-flowering shrub of the bean family, *Cytisus Laburnum.*

gōld'en-club, *n.* A spiked, flowering aquatic plant, *Orontium aquaticum.*

gōld'en-eȳe, *n.* A species of sea-duck, particularly *Glaucionetta clangula.*

gōld'en-ly, *adv.* Splendidly; delightfully.

gōld'en-pērt, *n.* A yellow-flowering herb of the figwort family, *Gratiola aurea.*

gōld'en-rod, *n.* The popular name of plants of the genus *Solidago*, of the order *Compositæ.* The species have rod-like stems and bright yellow flowers.

False goldenrod; a plant of the genus *Brachychæta*, closely allied to the genus *Solidago.*

West India goldenrod; a herb of the genus *Neurolæna*, similar to *Solidago.*

White goldenrod; a white-flowered variety of *Solidago.*

gōld'en-rod-tree, *n.* *Bosea Yervamora*, a shrub, a native of the Canary Islands.

gōld'en-wing, *n.* In zoölogy, the yellowhammer.

gōld'-fērn, *n.* A fern characterized by a frond sprinkled with powder of a waxy-yellow color.

gōld'-fē"vēr, *n.* A mania for digging or otherwise searching for gold; as, the *gold-fever* of '49 in California or of '99 in Alaska.

gōld'-fiēld, *n.* A district or region where gold is found.

gōld'finch, *n.* 1. In zoölogy, *Carduelis elegans*, a common European bird, so named from the yellow markings on its wings. Its brilliant plumage, soft and pleasant song, and docility make it a favorite cage-bird.

2. Any of the small American finches of the genus *Spinus.*

3. Any bird resembling the finch in form, color, or habits.

gōld'fin"ny, *n.* The wrasse; sometimes called *goldsinny.*

gōld'fish, *n.* 1. A fish of the genus *Cyprinus*, of the size of a minnow, so named from its bright color. These fishes were first bred by the Chinese and kept for ornament, and are now common in all countries.

2. A California red or orange-colored fish, the garibaldi.

gōld'flow"ēr, *n.* A composite plant, *Helichrysum Stœchas*, characterized by dry yellow scales.

gōld'-foil, *n.* A thin sheet of gold, thicker than gold-leaf, used by dentists and others.

gōld'ham'mēr, *n.* A bird, the yellowhammer.

gōld'ie, *n.* 1. The English goldfinch.

2. The yellowhammer.

gōld'i-locks, gōld'y-locks, *n.* 1. Any of certain plants of the genus *Chrysocoma*, so called from the yellow flowers which grow in tufts at the ends of the stems.

2. The goldflower.

gōld'in, gōld'ing, *n.* 1. A variety of apple, golden in color.

2. A flower of the genus *Chrysanthemum* that is golden in color.

gōld'-knobs, *n.pl.* A name for the common buttercup, named from the appearance of the unopened flower.

gōld'-leaf, *n.* The finest leaf made of gold, thinner than gold-foil.

gōld'-mine, *n.* 1. A mine from which gold is obtained by sinking a shaft into the earth, distinguished from *gold-diggings*, where gold is washed from the earth.

2. Colloquially, an investment paying large returns.

gōld'-mōle, *n.* A small South African animal resembling the mole, characterized by its lustrous fur in varying colors.

gōld'ney, gōld'ny, *n.* [Perhaps contr. of *goldeneye.*] A fish, the gilthead or golden wrasse.

gōld'-nōte, *n.* A bank-note payable in gold coin.

gōld'-of-pleas'ūre (-ple'zhūr), *n.* A cruciferous annual European plant, *Camelina sativa*, frequently found in flax-fields; false flax.

gōld'-paint, *n.* Paint for bronzing.

gōld'-pow"dēr, *n.* A fine powder made from gold-leaf.

gōld'seed, *n.* The plant dog's-tail grass.

gōld'-shell, *n.* 1. A bivalve, *Anomia ephippium*, found on rocky coasts.

2. In painting, a shell holding gold-paint.

gōld'-size, *n.* 1. A glue used as an adhesive for gold-leaf.

2. A mixture of chrome and varnish used in gold-printing and for other purposes.

gōld'smith, *n.* 1. An artisan who manufactures vessels and ornaments of gold.

2. A banker; from goldsmiths having formerly acted as bankers. [Obs.]

gōld'smith-bee"tle, *n.* *Cotalpa lanigera*, a large golden-yellow American beetle.

gōld'-stick, *n.* A title given to colonels of the British Life Guards and to captains of the gentlemen-at-arms, from the gilt rods which they bear when attending the sovereign on state occasions. [Eng.]

gōld'-stōne, *n.* Closely-spangled aventurin.

gōld'tāil, *n.* A moth of the genus *Porthesia*, distinguished by an anal tuft of yellow.

gōld'=thread (-thred), *n.* 1. A thread formed of flattened gold laid over a thread of silk by twisting it with a wheel and bobbins; also, the same as *gold-wire*.

2. In the United States, a ranunculaceous evergreen plant. *Coptis trifolia*, so named for its yellow roots.

gōld'tit, *n.* The yellow-headed titmouse.

gōld'=tool''ing, *n.* In bookbinding, the application of gold-leaf for ornamentation.

gōld'=wäsh''ēr, *n.* 1. One who washes away the refuse from gold or from gold ore, as in a cradle.

2. The instrument employed in washing the refuse from gold or from gold ore.

gōld'=wire, *n.* Silver superficially covered with gold and drawn to a wire of the requisite fineness; called also *gold-thread*.

gōld'y-locks, *n.* Same as *Goldilocks*.

gō'let, *n.* [ME. form of *gullet*.] The throat or gullet. [Obs.]

gō'let, *n.* A Californian trout, *Salvelinus malma*.

golf, *v.i.*; golfed (golft), *pt., pp.*; golfing, *ppr.* To play the game of golf.

golf, *n.* [From D. *kolf*, a club to strike balls with.] A game played with clubs resembling hockey-sticks, and gutta-percha balls, over grounds or links where a series of small round holes are cut in the turf at distances of from 100 to 200 yards from each other, according to the nature of the ground, so as to form a circuit or round. The object of the game is, starting from the first hole, to drive the ball into the next hole with as few strokes as possible, and so on with all the holes in succession, the player driving his ball into all the holes with the fewest strokes being said to win the game.

golf'=club, *n.* 1 A club used in the game of golf. These are of different uses, for which they are respectively designed; thus, one is the *driver*, another the *putter*, a third the *spoon*, a fourth the *cleek*, etc.

2. An association formed for practising golf-playing

golf'ēr, *n.* One who plays golf.

Gol'gō-thȧ, *n.* [Gr. *Golgotha*; Heb. *Gulgoleth*, a skull, the place of a skull.]

1. Calvary

2. [g—] A charnel-house. [Obs.]

gōl'iärd-ēr-y (-yärd-), *n.* [From the *Goliards*, a kind of monkish rhapsodists.] A satirical kind of poetry of the middle ages.

gō-lī'ȧth=bee''tle, *n.* [From *Goliath*, the Philistine giant.] Any beetle of the genus *Goliathus*, natives of Africa and South America, remarkable for their large size. *Goliathus giganteus* is the typical species.

goll, *n.* A hand; a paw; a claw. [Obs.]

gō-lōe'=shōe, *n.* See *Galosh*.

gō-lōre', *n.* [Obs.] See *Galore*.

gō-losh', *n.* Same as *Galosh*.

Gō'mär-ist, Gō'mär-ite, *n.* In church history, a believer in the creed taught by Francis Gomarus (1563–1641), a Calvinist in Holland who opposed the Arminian theology.

gom-been'ism, *n.* [Ir.] The practice of the poor of depending upon loans of money at high rates of interest, as in parts of Ireland.

gom-been'=man, *n.* [Ir.] A money-lender charging a high rate of interest.

gom'bō, *n* See *Gumbo*.

gōme, *n.* [AS. *guma*, a man.] A man. [Obs.]

gōme, *n.* [Prov. Eng.] Black axle-grease; gorm.

gō'mēr, *n.* See third *Homer*.

gō'mēr, *n.* In gunnery, the cone-like narrowing of the bore at the breech, in mortars, named from the inventor, Gomer, and first used in the wars of Napoleon.

gom'ēr-el, *n.* [Scot.] A blockhead.

gom'me-line, *n.* Same as *Dextrine*.

gom-phī'ȧ-sis, *n.* [Gr *gomphiasis*, toothache, from *gomphios*, a grinder-tooth, molar.] Looseness of the teeth, especially the molars.

gom'phō-dont, *a.* [Gr. *gomphos*, a nail, bolt, and *odous*, *odontos*, a tooth.] In zoölogy, having teeth in sockets.

gom-phō'sis, *n.* [Gr. *gomphōsis*, a bolting together, from *gomphos*, a bolt, nail.] The immovable articulation of the teeth with the jawbone, like a nail in a board.

Gom-phrē'nȧ, *n.* A genus of tropical plants of the amaranth family, of which the globe amaranth or bachelor's-button is a type.

gō-mụ'ti, gō-mụ'tō, *n.* [Malay.] The sago-palm, *Arenga saccharifera*, or the fiber obtained from it, which is very valuable on account of its power of resisting decay when wet.

gon-. See *Gono-*.

gon, *v.* [ME. form of *go*.] Infinitive and past participle of *go*. [Obs.]

gon'ad, *n.* [From Gr. *gonē*, seed, generation.] In biology, generative tissue which eventually becomes a testis or ovary; a germ-gland.

gon'ȧ-duct, *n.* [Contr. of *gonad-duct*.] An oviduct or seminal duct.

gō'nȧ-kie, *n.* [African.] In botany, a tree of the genus *Acacia*, used for timber.

gō-nan-gī'um, *n.*; *pl.* gō-nan-gī'ȧ or gō-nan-gī'ums. In zoölogy, a receptacle furnishing protection to sexual buds in certain hydroids.

Gomuti Palm (*Arenga saccharifera*).

gon-ȧ-poph'y-sis, *n.*; *pl.* gon-ȧ-poph'y-sēs. [Gr. *gonos*, generation, and *apophysis*, an outgrowth, process.] In entomology, one of the parts making up the external genitals.

gon'dō-lȧ, *n.* [It., dim. of *gond*, a gondola, from Gr. *kondy*, a drinking-vessel, said to be a Per. word, so called from the shape.]

1. A flat-bottomed boat, very long and narrow, used at Venice in Italy on the canals. A gondola of middle size is about 30 feet long and 4 broad, terminating at each end in a sharp point or peak rising to the height of 5 feet. Toward the center there is a curtained chamber for the passengers.

Gondola.

2. A kind of flat-car for carrying coal, ore, etc. [U. S.]

3. A freight boat, large, having a flat bottom, and usually of light build. [U. S.]

4. An elongated car carried underneath dirigible balloons.

5. In art, a vessel carved from some semi-precious stone, as agate, etc.

gon'dō-let, *n.* [It. *gondoletta*, dim. of *gondola*, a gondola.] A small gondola.

gon-dō-liēr', *n.* [It. *gondoliere*, from *gondola*, a gondola.] A man who rows a gondola.

gone, *v.*, past participle of *go*.

gone'ness, *n.* A condition of exhaustion or weakness, as resulting from lack of food; faintness. [Colloq.]

gon'ēr, *n.* A person or thing that has reached a stage beyond recovery or recall; as, he is a *goner*. [Colloq.]

gon'fȧ-lon, *n.* [ME. *gonfanon*, *gonfanoun*; OFr. *gonfanon* (Fr. *gonfalon*); LL. *gonfano*, *guntfano*, a banner; O.H.G. *gundfano*, a battle-standard; *gund*, *gunt*, a battle, and *fano*, a banner.] An ensign or standard; especially an ensign having two or three streamers or tails, fixed on a frame made to turn like a ship's vane, or, as in the case of the papal *gonfalon*, suspended from a pole; originally, a banderole.

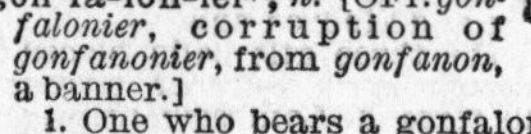

Gonfalon.

gon''fȧ-lon-iēr', *n.* [OFr. *gonfalonier*, corruption of *gonfanonier*, from *gonfanon*, a banner.]

1. One who bears a gonfalon; a chief standard-bearer.

2. A chief magistrate of a medieval republican city of Italy.

gon'fȧ-non, *n.* [Obs.] See *Gonfalon*.

gong, *n.* [AS. *gang*, a going, passage, privy.] A privy or jakes. [Obs.]

gong, *n.* [Malay *agong*, *gong*, a gong.]

1. A Chinese instrument made of an alloy of copper and tin, in form like a round flat dish with a rim. It is struck by a kind of drumstick, the head of which is covered with leather. Used for making loud sonorous signals.

2. A stationary bell, similar in shape to that described above, used for sounding alarms, etc. and operated mechanically.

gong'=met''ạl, *n.* The metal of which gongs are made; an alloy consisting of about seventy-eight parts of copper and twenty-two of tin.

gon-gon'hȧ, *n.* [Braz.] *Ilex Gongonha*, a Brazilian species of holly, from the leaves of which a variety of maté or Paraguay tea is prepared.

Gon-gō-resque' (-resk'), *a.* Pertaining to the Spanish poet Gongora, or resembling his style.

Gon'gō-rism, *n.* An affected style which characterized the writings of the Spanish poet, Gongora y Argote (1561-1627).

gon'gy-lus, *n.* [Gr. *gongylos*, round.] In botany, (a) a name given to a spore of certain fungi; (b) a round, hard, deciduous body connected with the reproduction of certain seaweeds.

gō'ni-ȧ-tīte, *n.* [Gr. *gōnia*, a corner, angle, and *lithos*, stone.] Any species of an extinct genus of fossil shells, belonging to the dibranchiate cephalopodous mollusks and family of ammonites.

gō'nid, *n.* Same as *Gonidium*.

gon-i-dan'gi-um, *n.*; *pl.* gon-i-dan'gi-ȧ. [Gr. *gonē*, generation, seed, and *angeion*, a vessel, receptacle.] In botany, a sporangium in which gonidia are formed.

gō-nid'i-ȧ, *n.*, pl. of *gonidium*.

gō-nid'i-ăl, *a.* Of, relating to, producing, or containing gonidia; as, the *gonidial* grooves of certain anthozoans.

gō-nid'ic, *a.* Gonidial.

gon-i-dim'i-um, *n.*; *pl.* gon-i-dim'i-ȧ. [*Gonidium* and *gonimium*.] In botany, a cell found in some lichens, of a size between a gonimium and a gonidium.

gō-nid-i-og'e-nous, *a.* Producing or capable of producing gonidia.

gō-nid'i-ō-phōre, *n.* In botany, a conidiophore.

gō-nid'i-ōse, *a.* Furnished with gonidia.

gō-nid'i-um, *n.*; *pl.* gō-nid'i-ȧ. [Dim. from Gr. *gonē*, seed, generation.]

1. A reproductive, green, spherical cell in the thallus of lichens, immediately below the surface.

2. In bryology, a cell containing granules.

3. In algology, a conidium or reproductive cell.

gō-nim'ic, *a.* Pertaining to or containing gonimia.

gō-nim'i-um, *n.*; *pl.* gō-nim'i-ȧ. [Gr. *gonimos*, productive, fruitful, from *gignesthai*, to produce.] In botany, a gonidium of a bluish-green color found in some lichens.

gon'i-mous, *a.* Gonimic.

gō-ni-om'e-tēr, *n.* [Gr. *gōnia*, an angle, corner, and *metron*, a measure.] An instrument for measuring solid angles, or the inclination of planes, particularly the angles formed by the faces of crystals.

Contact goniometer; a goniometer with two arms that move about the fixed center of a graduated semicircle. When the crystal faces are in contact with the arms, a pointer indicates the angle.

Reflecting goniometer; a goniometer for measuring the angles of crystals by reflection.

gō''ni-ō-met'ric, gō''ni-ō-met'ric-ăl, *a.* Pertaining to a goniometer or to goniometry.

gō-ni-om'e-try, *n.* [Gr. *gōnia*, an angle, and *metrein*, to measure.] The art of measuring angles; trigonometry.

gō'ni-on, *n.*; *pl.* gō'ni-ȧ. [Gr. *gōnia*, an angle, corner.] In craniometry, the outer side of the angle of the lower jaw.

gō''ni-ō-thē'cȧ, *n.*; *pl* gō''ni-ō-thē'cæ (-sē). [Gr. *gōnia*, angle, and *thēkē*, a case, box.] In botany, same as *macrosporangium*.

gō-ni-ot'rō-pous, *a.* [Gr. *gōnia*, angle, and *tropē*, a turning, from *trepein*, to turn.] In botany, having four corners, with two of the angles lateral, one posterior, and one anterior.

gō-nī'tis, *n.* [Gr. *gony*, knee, and *-itis*.] In pathology, an inflammatory condition of the knee-joint.

gon-o-, gon-. Combining forms from Gr. *gonos*, generation, seed, from *gignesthai*, to produce; used in biology, zoölogy, botany, etc., to signify generative, sexual; as, *gono*coccus, *gono*phore, *gono*poietic.

gon'ō-blast, *n.* [*Gono-*, and Gr. *blastos*, a germ, shoot.] In biology, a germ-cell; a reproductive cell.

gon-ō-blas'tid, *n.* In zoölogy, a gonophore.

gon''ō-blas-tid'i-um, *n.*; *pl.* gon''ō-blas-tid'i-ȧ. [*Gono-*, and Gr. *blastos*, a germ, shoot, and dim. *-idion*.] In zoölogy, a blastostyle.

gon-ō-cā'lyx, *n.*; *pl.* gon-ō-cal'y-cēs. [*Gono-*. and Gr. *kalyx*, a cup.] In zoölogy, the swimming-bell of a gonophore.

gon'ō-chēme, *n.* [*Gono-*, and Gr. *ochēma*, a vehicle.] In zoölogy, a gonophore.

gon-ō-chō'rism, *n.* [*Gono-*, and *chōrismos*, separation, from *chōrizein*, to separate.] In biology, differentiation of the sexes; the development or acquisition of sex distinctions.

gon-ō-coc'cus, *n.* [*Gono-*, and Gr. *kokkos*, grain, seed.] In medicine, the specific micrococcus of gonorrhea.

gon'ō-duct, *n.* Same as *Gonaduct*.

gō-nœ'ci-um (*or* -shi-um), *n.* [*Gon-*, and Gr. *oikia*, a house.] In zoölogy, a procreative zoöid of a polyzoan.

gon'of, gon'oph, *n.* [Perhaps from Heb. *ganābh*, thief.] A thief or pickpocket. [Eng. Slang.]

gon'ō-phōre, *n.* [*Gono-*, and Gr. *-phoros*, from *pherein*, to bear.]

1. In zoölogy, one of the generative buds or receptacles of the reproductive elements in the hydrozoans or zoöphytes.

2. In botany, an elongated receptacle, lifting the stamens and carpels above the perianth.

3. Any duct or organ which holds or conveys

generative cells, as an oviduct or a seminal vesicle.

gon″ō-poi-et′iç, *a.* [*Gono-*, and Gr. *poiētikos*, productive, from *poiein*, to do, make.] In biology, producing generative bodies; genital; as, a *gonopoietic* organ, producing spermatozoa.

gon-or-rhē′ȧ, gon-or-rhœ′ȧ, *n.* [LL. *gonorrhœa*; Gr. *gonorrhoia*; *gonos*, seed, semen, and *rhoia*, from *rhein*, to flow.] In medicine, a specific contagious inflammation of the male urethra or the female vagina, characterized by pain, burning urination, a profuse muco-purulent discharge, and a protracted course; clap. It is due to the microörganism known as the gonococcus.

gon-or-rhē′ăl, gon-or-rhœ′ăl, *a.* In medicine, pertaining to gonorrhea.

gon′ō-sōme, *n.* [*Gono-*, and Gr. *sōma*, body.] In zoölogy, the generative zoöids of a hydrozoan, collectively.

gon-ō-thē′çȧ, *n.*; *pl.* **gon-ō-thē′cæ** (-sē). Same as *Gonangium.*

gon′ō-tōme, *n.* [*Gono-*, and Gr. *tomē*, a cutting, segment.] A segment of a somite in which the reproductive organs develop.

gon-ō-zō′oid, *n.* [*Gono-*, and Gr. *zōoeidēs*, like an animal.] In zoölogy, a reproductive zoöid; a gonophore.

gō′ny, *n.*; *pl.* **gō′nieṣ.** 1. A stupid person; a dunce; a booby. [Slang.]

2. In zoölogy, one of several large pelagic birds; especially, the black-footed albatross, the young of the short-tailed albatross, and the giant fulmar.

-gony. [L. *-gonia*; Gr. *-gonia*, from *gignesthai*, to become.] A suffix used with nouns of Greek origin to signify generation, production, descent; as, theo*gony*.

gō-nyd′ē-ăl *a.* In zoölogy, of or pertaining to the gonys.

gō′nys, *n.* [Gr. *genys*, chin.] The keel or lower outline of a bird's beak as far as the point where the rami branch.

gon-y-thē′çȧ, *n.*; *pl.* **gon-y-thē′cæ** (-sē). [Gr. *gony*, knee, and *thēkē*, a box, case.] The socket in the femur of an insect, with which the tibia articulates.

gọọ′bẽr, *n.* The peanut, *Arachis hypogæa.* [Southern U. S.]

good, *a.*; *comp.* better; *superl.* best. [ME. *good*, *god*; AS. *god*, good; originally, fit, suitable.]

1. Valid; legally firm; not weak or defective; sound; not fallacious; genuine; not counterfeit; acceptable; having strength adequate to its support; as, a *good* title; a *good* deed; a *good* claim; a *good* argument; *good* money.

2. Complete, or sufficiently perfect, in its kind; having the physical qualities best adapted to its design and use; opposed to *bad*, *imperfect, corrupted, impaired*; as, *good* timber; *good* cloth; a *good* soil; a *good* color.

3. Having the qualities which the moral law requires; virtuous; pious; religious; applied to persons or actions; opposed to *bad, vicious, wicked, evil*; as, a *good* woman; a *good* act.

4. Proper; fit; convenient; seasonable; desirable; as, it was a *good* time to commence operations; he arrived in *good* time.

5. Full; complete; as, a *good* third of the people; *good* measure.

6. Useful; valuable; serviceable; suitable; having qualities of a tendency to produce a *good* effect; adequate; competent; often followed by *for*; as, *good* medicine, or medicine *good for* a cold; shoes *good for* a year's wear; security *good for* a debt.

7. Ready; dexterous; clever; often followed by *at*; as, *good at* flattering; *good at* tennis; a *good* mechanic.

8. Kind; benevolent; affectionate; humane; merciful; well-disposed; often followed by *to* or *toward*; as, a *good* father; *good* will; she is *good to* the poor.

9. Agreeable; pleasant; social; genial; as, a *good* time; a *good* fellow.

10. Honorable; fair; unblemished; unimpeached; as, a man of *good* fame or report; a *good* name.

11. Great or considerable; not small nor very great; as, a *good* while ago; a *good* distance; a *good* deal of leisure; a *good* share.

12. Real; serious; not feigned.

Love not in *good* earnest. —Shak.

Good afternoon, good day, good evening, good morning, good morrow, good night, etc.; salutatory expressions meaning "I hope you will have a prosperous, pleasant, or enjoyable afternoon, day, evening, morning, etc."

Good cheap; a good bargain; used adjectively, fairly cheap.

Good consideration; valuable consideration; also, the ties of blood or of love and affection, regarded as consideration for a benefit for which a valuable equivalent is not given.

Good folk or *good people*; fairies; pixies. [Prov. Eng. and Scot.]

Good Friday; the last Friday in Lent, the Friday before Easter Sunday, observed as a fast-day in various churches, in memory of the crucifixion of Christ.

Good humor; a cheerful temper; a disposition not easily vexed; a good-tempered manner.

Good nature; a nature or disposition characterized by kindness and good humor.

Good speed; good luck; success; reasonable quickness.

Good Templar; a member of the Society of Good Templars, an association organized for the purpose of promoting temperance.

Good turn; a kind act or favor.

In good time; (a) at the right time; promptly; (b) in correct or proper time; (c) in creditable time.

To be as good as one's word; to act according to promise.

To hold good; to remain in force; to remain valid; as, the contract *holds good* for a year.

To make good; (a) to carry out, as an offer, etc.; to fulfil; (b) to maintain; (c) to supply, as a deficiency or defect; (d) to manage to accomplish; (e) in theatrical slang, to perform acceptably; to fulfil promises.

To think good, to see good; to be satisfied with; to approve; to consider advisable.

Syn.—Right, complete, virtuous, sound, benevolent, propitious, serviceable, sufficient, competent, valid, real, considerable, reputable, true, just.

good, *n.* 1. That which has or is considered to have desirable qualities, or contributes to diminish or remove pain, or to increase happiness or prosperity; that which is or may be made serviceable, beneficial, advantageous, excellent, or the like; a good quality, state, or thing; opposed to *evil* or *misery*; as, the medicine will do neither *good* nor harm; the police system is a distinct *good* to the city.

2. Welfare; prosperity; benefit; advantage; advancement of interest or happiness; opposed to *harm*; as, he labored for the *good* of the state.

3. A valuable possession or piece of property; almost always in the plural, and equivalent to wares, merchandise, movables, chattels, and personal property in general. In England, *goods* is used of commodities in transit, or freight, especially in compounds; as, a *goods*-train.

All thy *goods* are confiscate to the state. —Shak.

4. In philosophy, anything having such qualities as to satisfy a need, and hence having a value; anything considered as a worthy object of choice or effort; as, the chief *good*.

For good, for good and all; to close the whole business; for the last time; finally.

Green goods; counterfeit paper money. [Slang.]

Syn.—Boon, benefit, advantage, weal, gain, blessing, virtue, prosperity, profit, interest, welfare.

good, *adv.* Well; right. [Obs.]

good, *v.t.* 1. To make good. [Obs.]

2. To manure. [Prov. Eng. and Scot.]

good′=breed″ing, *n.* Polite manners formed by a good education; a polite education.

good″=bȳ′, good″=bȳe′, *interj.* [Contraction of *God be with ye.*] Farewell; adieu.

good″=bȳ′, good″=bȳe′, *n.* and *a.* I. *n.* A farewell; as, to say *good-bys.*

II. *a.* Farewell; parting; as, a *good-by* caress.

good′=con-di′tioned (-dish″und), *a.* Being in a good state; having good qualities or favorable symptoms.

good′=den, *interj.* [Contraction of *good even, good e'en.*] Good evening. [Obs.]

Goo-dē′ni-ȧ, *n.* [Named after Samuel *Goodenough*, Bishop of Exeter.] A genus of the *Goodeniaceæ.*

Good-ē-ni-ā′cē-æ, *n.pl.* An order of shrubs or herbs allied to the *Lobelia* family, and chiefly Australian.

good-ē-ni-ā′ceous, *a.* Of or like the *Goodeniaceæ.*

good″=fel′lōw-ship, *n.* Merry society.

good′=fọr=nŏth″ing, *a.* and *n.* I. *a.* Useless; of no value or account; shiftless.

II. *n.* A worthless fellow.

good″=hū′mōred, *a.* Being of a cheerful temper.

good″=hū′mōred-ly, *adv.* In a cheerful way.

good′ing, *n.* A manner of asking alms, wishing good to the donor in return; formerly practised in England on St. Thomas's day.

good′ish, *a.* Fairly good; also, considerable; as, a *goodish* distance; *goodish* behavior.

good′=King=Hen′ry, *n.* In botany, a herb, *Chenopodium Bonus-Henricus*, introduced into the United States from Europe, and frequently used as a pot-herb; also called *allgood* and *good-King-Harry.*

good′less, *a.* Without goods; destitute.

good′lich, *a.* [ME.] Goodly. [Obs.]

good′li-head (-hed), *n.* Goodliness. [Obs.]

good′li-ness, *n.* Beauty of appearance; comeliness; grace.

good′=look″ing, *a.* Handsome.

good′ly, *adv.* Finely; well. [Obs.]

good′ly, *a.* 1. Pleasing; agreeable.

2. Graceful; handsome; fine.

3. Stout; large; considerable.

Syn.—Pleasant, desirable, excellent, fair, comely, considerable.

good′ly-head (-hed), **good′ly-hood,** *n.* Goodliness. [Obs.]

good′man, *n.*; *pl.* **good′men.** 1. A familiar appellation of civility, equivalent to *Master* or *Mr.*; sometimes used ironically. [Obs.]

2. A husband; the master of a family. [Obs.]

good′=nā″tūred, *a.* Naturally mild in temper; not easily provoked; amiable.

Syn.—Good-tempered, kind, obliging.—*Good-natured* denotes a disposition to please and be pleased; *good-tempered*, a spirit which is not easily ruffled by provocation or other disturbing influences; *kind*, a disposition to make others happy by supplying their wants and granting their requests.

good′=nā″tūred-ly, *adv.* With good nature.

good′ness, *n.* 1. The state of being good; the physical qualities which constitute value, excellence, or perfection; as, the *goodness* of timber.

2. Kindness; favor shown; an act of benevolence, compassion, or mercy.

good′now, *interj.* An exclamation of wonder or surprise.

goodṣ, *n.pl.* See *Good*, n. 3.

goodṣ′=en′gine, *n.* A freight-engine. [Eng.]

good′ship, *n.* Favor; grace. [Obs.]

goodṣ′=shed, *n.* A freight-warehouse. [Eng.]

goodṣ′=trāin, *n.* A freight-train. [Eng.]

goodṣ′=wag″ŏn, *n.* A freight-car. [Eng.]

good″=tem′pẽred, *a.* Not easily angered; equanimous.

good′wife, *n.*; *pl.* **good′wīveṣ.** The mistress of a family.

good′=will′, *n.* 1. Benevolence; friendly disposition; usually two words.

2. In law, the commercial advantage possessed by any business, due to its established popularity, reputation, patronage, advertising, location, etc., over and beyond its mere stock or capital; friendly feeling or influence, exerted with the view of transferring the custom of any shop or trade to a successor; the right and title to take up a trade or business connection, purchased of an outgoing tenant or occupier.

good′y, *n.*; *pl.* **good′ieṣ.** 1. A term of civil address to old women of humble circumstances; as, *Goody* Dobson.

2. A bonbon; a sweetmeat; usually in the plural.

3. In zoölogy, a fish, *Liostomus xanthurus.*

4. A person of good intentions but lacking force.

good′y, good′y=good′y, *a.* Affected with mawkish morality; excessively squeamish in morals.

good′yēar, good′yēarṣ, *n.* Goujeers; used as an oath. [Obs.]

good′y-ship, *n.* The state or quality of a goody.

gọọ′gul, *n.* 1. Any of various species of myrrh-trees which yield fragrant gums.

2. Gum; bdellium.

gọọm′pāin, gọọm′pā-nȧ, *n.* [E. Ind.] In botany, *Odina Wodier*, a timber-tree of East India; also its wood or its gum.

gọọnch, *n.* [Anglo-Ind.] The seeds of *Abrus precatorius*, the Indian licorice.

gọọr, *n.* [Anglo-Ind.] 1. Jaggery.

2. The dziggetai.

gọọ′răl, *n.* Same as *Goral.*

gọọ′rọọ, *n.* Same as *Guru.*

gọọṣ′an-dẽr, *n.* [*Goose* and *gander.*] A merganser.

gọọse, *v.t.* To hiss at; to condemn by hissing. [Slang.]

gọọse, *n.*; *pl.* **geese.** [ME. *goos, gos*; AS. *gos*, a goose.]

1. A web-footed fowl of the *Anserinæ*; by extension, any fowl more or less resembling the true *goose*, as the gannet, called the solan-*goose.*

2. The female as distinguished from the male *goose* or *gander.*

3. A silly, stupid person, from the popular notion as to the stupidity of the *goose*; a simpleton.

4. A tailor's smoothing-iron, so called from the resemblance of its handle to the neck of a *goose.*

5. A game of chance played by two or more persons with two dice on a card divided into small compartments. At every fourth or fifth compartment in succession a goose was depicted on the card, and, if the throw of the dice carried the counter of the player on a goose, he might move forward double the actual number thrown.

6. A player or piece in any of the games of fox and geese.

A wild goose chase; see under *Chase.*

The goose hangs high; perhaps originally *honks high*, that is, cries high, as in fair weather; hence, prospects are good. [Slang.]

goose'=bär"nȧ-cle, *n.* *Lepas anatifera*, a pedunculated barnacle from which the goose was fabled to have originated.

goose'bēak, *n.* A dolphin.

goose'ber"ry, *n.*; *pl.* **goose'ber"ries.** [OFr. *groselle, groiselle*; Gael. *groiseid*, a gooseberry; W. *grws*, from M.H.G. *krus*; D. *kroes*, crisp, crisped.]

1. The fruit of a shrub, and the shrub itself, *Ribes Grossularia*.

2. A foolish person; a goosecap. [Obs.]

Barbados gooseberry; *Pereskia aculeata*, a prickly climber bearing edible berries.

goose'bīrd, *n.* The Hudsonian godwit.

goose'cap, *n.* A fool. [Obs.]

goose'=corn, *n.* *Juncus squarrosus*, a rush.

goose'=egg, *n.* 1. An egg of a goose.

2. A cipher, as in a score. [Slang.]

goose'=fēast, *n.* Michaelmas. [Eng.]

goose'fish, *n.* The angler.

goose'=flesh, *n.* A condition of the skin marked by prominences about the hair-follicles, due to cold, fright, etc.

goose'foot, *n.* Any species of *Chenopodium*; pigweed.

goose'=grȧss, *n.* 1. *Galium Aparine*, cleavers.

2. *Potentilla Anserina*, silverweed.

3. *Polygonum aviculare*, doorweed.

4. *Bromus mollis*, soft chess.

5. *Poa annua*, spear-grass.

goose'=hērd, *n.* One who attends to geese.

goose'=mus"sel, *n.* A goose-barnacle.

goose'neck, *n.* 1. Nautically, (a) a swivel of iron fitted to the end of a yard or boom for various purposes; (b) a davit.

2. In machinery, a pipe shaped like the letter S.

3. A hose-nozle with a swivel-joint.

goose'=quill, *n.* A quill, or the pen made from a quill, of a goose.

goos'ēr-y, *n.* 1. A place for geese.

2. Silliness or stupidity like that of the goose.

goose'=skin, *n.* 1. A goose's skin.

2. Goose-flesh.

goose'=step, *n.* The act of marking time by raising the feet alternately without making progress.

goose'=tan"sy, *n.* In England, the silverweed; also called *goose-grass*.

goose'tŏngue (-tung), *n.* *Achillea Ptarmica*, sneezewort.

goose'wing, *n.* 1. One of the clues or lower corners of a ship's mainsail or foresail, when the middle part is furled or tied up.

2. The fore- or the mainsail of a schooner or other two-masted fore-and-aft vessel, because when running before the wind these sails are set on opposite sides.

goose'winged, *a.* 1. Having a goosewing.

2. Relating to a fore-and-aft-rigged vessel, with mainsail set on one side and foresail on the other.

goos'ey, goos'ey=gan'dēr, *n.* 1. A goose.

2. A stupid person; a blockhead.

goos'ish, *a.* Stupid; like a goose. [Obs.]

gōost, *n.* A ghost. [Obs.]

gōot, *n.* A goat. [Obs.]

gō'=out, *n.* An opening in a sea-wall or dike through which water from the lowlands behind it is allowed to escape when the tide is out.

gō'phēr, *n.* [Fr. *gaufre*, gopher, waffle, honeycomb.]

1. The name given by the French settlers in the valley of the Mississippi, as well as in Canada, to many burrowing animals of different genera, which honeycomb the earth; as, (a) a little quadruped of the genus *Geomys*, as *Geomys bursarius*, having large cheek-pouches extending from the mouth to the shoulders, incisors protruding beyond the lips, and broad, mole-like forefeet; (b) any of several American burrowing squirrels, as *Spermophilus franklini*, the gray *gopher*; *Spermophilus tridecemlineatus*, the ordinary striped *gopher*.

2. A species of burrowing land-tortoise of the Carolina pine-barrens. [Local, U. S.]

3. The gopher-snake.

4. A plow. [Local, U. S.]

5. A waffle. [Local, Eng.]

gō'phēr, *v.i.* To burrow; especially, to mine at random or on a small scale.

gō'phēr=drift, *n.* Same as *Gopher-hole*, 2.

gō'phēr=hōle, *n.* 1. The entrance to a gopher's burrow.

2. A prospector's mining drift dug at haphazard.

gō'phēr=snāke, *n.* *Spilotes couperi*, a burrowing snake.

gō'phēr=wood, *n.* [Heb. *gōpher*, an unknown kind of wood.]

1. The unknown kind of wood used in the building of Noah's ark.

2. *Cladrastis tinctoria*, the yellowwood of southern United States.

gō'pū-rȧ, *n.* [E. Ind.] In the architecture of the East Indies, either the gateway of a temple or the pyramidal tower above it, sometimes ornamented in the most beautiful and intricate manner.

gō-rac'cō, *n.* [E. Ind.] An aromatic tobacco-paste used in western India.

gō'rȧl, *n.* [E. Ind.] A goat-antelope of the Himalayas.

gō'rȧ-my, gou'rȧ-mi, *n.* [Javanese.] A fish of the genus *Osphromenus*, a native of China and the Eastern Archipelago, but introduced on account of the excellence of its flesh into the West Indies, where it has multiplied rapidly. It is one of the few fishes which build nests, which it does by interweaving the stems and leaves of aquatic plants.

gor'bel"lied, *a.* Large-bellied. [Obs.]

gor'bel"ly, *n.* [AS. *gor*, dirt, dung, and *belly*.] A large belly; a person having a big belly.

gor'bū-schȧ, *n.* [Russ.] A Pacific coast salmon.

gorce, *n.* [Norm. Fr. *gorse*; OFr. *gorge*; L. *gurges*, a whirlpool, stream.] A pool of water to keep fish in; a weir.

gor'cock, *n.* [From *gorse*, furze or heath.] The moor-cock, red grouse, or red game.

gor'crōw, *n.* [AS. *gor*, dung, dirt, and *crawe*, a crow.] The carrion-crow. [Prov. Eng.]

gord, *n.* A kind of loaded dice. [Obs.]

Gor-di-ā'cē-ȧ, *n.* The *Gordiidæ*.

Gor'di-ăn, *a.* Of or relating to Gordius, a king of Phrygia, or to the intricate knot tied by him; inextricable; difficult.

Gordian knot; a knot tied by Gordius in the cord which bound the pole of his chariot to the yoke, which was so very intricate that there was no finding where it began or ended. An oracle declared that he who should untie this knot would be master of Asia. Alexander, fearing that his inability to untie it might prove an ill augury, cut it asunder with his sword. Hence the term *Gordian knot* is applied to any inextricable difficulty, and *to cut the Gordian knot* is to remove a difficulty by bold or unusual measures.

gor'di-ăn, *n.* A hairworm.

Gor-dī'i-dæ, *n.pl.* [*Gordius* and *-idæ*.] The hairworms, an order of annuloid animals with a body so long and thin as to resemble horse-hair. In their early stages they inhabit the bodies of several insects, which they leave when developed.

Gor'di-us, *n.* [L. *Gordius* (supply *nodus*, a knot), Gordian knot; so called from the knots into which these worms twist their bodies.]

1. A genus of the *Gordiidæ*.

2. [g—; *pl.* gor'di-i.] A hairworm of this genus.

Gor-dō'ni-ȧ, *n.* [Named after James *Gordon*, a nurseryman of London.]

1. A genus of evergreen shrubs including the loblolly-bay and the mountain-bay.

2. [g—] A shrub of this genus.

gōre, *n.* [ME. *gore*, mud, filth; AS. *gor*, dung, dirt.]

1. Blood that is shed or drawn from the body; thick or clotted blood; blood that after effusion becomes inspissated.

2. Dirt; mud. [Prov. Eng.]

gōre, *n.* [ME. *gore, gare*; AS. *gara*, an angular point of land, from *gar*, a spear.]

1. A wedge-shaped or triangular piece of cloth sewed into a garment, a sail, etc., to widen it in any part.

2. A tapering or triangular piece of land.

3. In heraldry, a charge consisting of two curved lines, one from the sinister chief point, the other from the base middle point, meeting in an acute angle in the middle of the fesse point.

gōre, *v.t.*; gored, *pt., pp.*; goring, *ppr.* 1. To stab; to pierce; to penetrate with a pointed instrument, as a spear or the point of a horn.

2. To cut in a triangular form; to piece with a gore.

3. To dig; to hollow out. [Obs.]

gōre'bill, *n.* The garfish. [Local, Eng.]

gor'flȳ, *n.*; *pl.* **gor'flies.** [AS. *gor*, dung, and *fly*.] A dung-fly. [Eng.]

gorġe, *n.* [ME. *gorge*; OFr. *gorge*, throat, gullet; LL. *gorgia*, a throat, narrow pass; L. *gurges*, a whirlpool, stream.]

1. The throat; the gullet.

2. In architecture, the narrowest part of the Tuscan and Doric capitals, between the astragal, above the shaft of the column, and the annulets; also, a cavetto or hollow molding.

3. A narrow passage or entrance; as, (a) a narrow passage between hills or mountains; (b) the entrance into a bastion or other outwork.

4. A groove in a pulley. [Rare.]

5. A channel underneath a coping.

6. That which is gorged, as by a hawk; the act of gorging.

7. An obstruction or jam filling a channel or narrow way; as, an ice-*gorge*.

8. A sensation of constriction in the muscles of the throat, due to disgust, anger, or the like; as, his *gorge* rose.

9. A gorge-hook.

gorġe, *v.t.*; gorged, *pt., pp.*; gorging, *ppr.* [ME. *gorgen*; OFr. *gorger*, to devour greedily, from *gorge*, a throat, gullet.]

1. To swallow; especially, to swallow with greediness, or in large mouthfuls or quantities.

2. To glut; to fill the throat or stomach of; to satiate.

gorġe, *v.i.* To feed with greediness.

gorġed, *a.* 1. Having a gorge or throat.

2. In heraldry, bearing a crown or the like about the neck.

3. Overfed; sated.

gorġe'=fish"ing, *n.* Trolling and allowing the fish to gorge the hook.

gorġe'=hook, *n.* 1. A fishhook having two barbs leaded together, used with a minnow.

2. A prehistoric form of fishing implement made of a slender rod of bone, stone, etc., sharpened at each end and attached to a line at its middle.

gorġe'let, *n.* [OFr. *gorgelette*, dim. of *gorge*, a throat.] In ornithology, a gorget.

gor'ġeous (-jus), *a.* [OFr. *gorgias, gourgias*, gay, gaudy; *gorgias*, ruff for the neck, from *gorge*, throat.] Showy; resplendent; splendid; glittering with gay colors; inclined to gorgeousness.

Syn.—Showy, magnificent, superb, splendid, brilliant.

gor'ġeous-ly, *adv.* With showy magnificence.

gor'ġeous-ness, *n.* Gorgeous quality or state.

gor-ġē-rette', *n.* [OFr., from *gorge*, throat.] A piece of armor made to protect the neck.

gor'ġet, *n.* [OFr. *gorgette*, from *gorge*, the throat.]

1. A piece of armor for defending the throat or neck; a kind of breastplate.

Plate Gorget.

2. A pendent metallic ornament, worn by officers of some armies when on duty.

3. A ruff or wimple worn by women. [Obs.]

4. In surgery, a cutting instrument used in lithotomy; also, a concave or cannulated conductor, called a *blunt gorget*.

5. In ornithology, a throat-patch, as in many humming-birds, marked by a difference in texture or color of the feathers.

gor'ġet=hum"mēr, *n.* Any humming-bird, as the rubythroat, genus *Trochilus*.

Gor'gŏn, *n.* [L. *Gorgo* (*-onis*); Gr. *Gorgō* (*-onos*), from *gorgos*, terrible, fierce.]

1. A fabled monster, of terrific aspect, the sight of which turned the beholder to stone. The poets represent the *Gorgons* as three sisters, Stheno, Euryale, and Medusa, of whom Perseus slew Medusa. Her head set on the shield of Pallas is also sometimes called a *gorgon*.

2. [g—] Anything very ugly or horrid.

3. [g—] The brindled gnu.

gor'gŏn, *a.* Like a Gorgon; very ugly or terrific; as, a *gorgon* face.

Gor-gō-nā'cē-ȧ, *n.pl.* Same as *Gorgoniaceæ*.

gor-gō'nē-ăn, gor-gō'ni-ăn, *a.* [Gr. *gorgoneios*, from *Gorgō* (*-onos*), Gorgon.]

1. Like a Gorgon; pertaining to gorgons.

2. Relating to the *Gorgoniaceæ*.

gor-gō-nē'iŏn (-yŏn), *n.*; *pl.* **gor-gō-nē'iȧ.** In architectural sculpture, a mask carved in imitation of the Gorgon's or Medusa's head.

gor-gŏn-esque' (-esk'), *a.* Repulsive; gorgonean.

Gor-gō'ni-ȧ, *n.* [L., coral which hardens in the air.]

1. A genus of flexible coral-zoöphytes, growing in the form of shrubs, twigs, and reticulate fronds. The species are often bright-colored, and among them is the sea-fan of the West Indies.

2. [g—] Any gorgonian having slender branches.

Gor-gō-ni-ā'cē-æ, *n.pl.* [*Gorgonia* and *-aceæ*.] An order of *Alcyonaria*, including the sea-shrubs, fan-corals, and the red coral of commerce. In all the organism consists of a composite structure made up of numerous polyps supported by a central branched axis or coral formed by secretions from the bases of the polyps. [See illustration under *Alcyonaria*.]

gor-gō'ni-ăn, *a.* See *Gorgonean*.

gor-gō'ni-ăn, *n.* One of the *Gorgoniaceæ*.

gor'gŏn-īze, *v.t.* To petrify, as if by a Gorgon; to turn to stone. [Rare.]

gor'gŏn's=head, *n.* A basket-fish.

gor'hen, *n.* The female of the gorcock.

gō-ril'lȧ, *n.* [The Phenician navigator, Hanno, found the name in use in W. Africa in the fifth century B. C. as the native name of a wild creature found there.] A large species of ape found in Africa, remarkable for its strength, and for its

Gorilla (*Troglodytes gorilla*).

being the nearest approach to man among the lower animals.

gōr′ing, *a.* Cut gradually sloping, so as to be broader at the clue than at the earing, as a sail.

gōr′ing, gōr′ing-cloth, *n.* 1. That part of the skirt of a sail where it gradually widens toward the bottom or foot.

2. A gore.

gorm, *n.* Axle-grease. [Prov. Eng.]

gorm, *v.t.* To gaum; to smear. [Prov. Eng.]

gor′mȧ, *n.* Same as *Gormaw.*

gor′mănd, gŏur′mănd, *n.* [Fr. *gourmand*, a glutton.]

1. A greedy or ravenous eater; a glutton.

2. A gourmet; an epicure.

gor′mănd, gŏur′mănd, *a.* Gluttonous; voracious.

gor′mănd-ẽr, gŏur′mănd-ẽr, *n.* A gormand. [Obs.]

gor′mănd-ism, gŏur′mănd-ism, *n.* Gluttony.

gor′mănd-īze, gŏur′mănd-īze, *v.i.* and *v.t.*; gormandized, *pt., pp.*; gormandizing, *ppr.* To eat greedily; to swallow voraciously.

gor′mănd-īz-ẽr, gŏur′mănd-īz-ẽr, *n.* A greedy, voracious eater; a gormand.

gor′maw, *n.* A cormorant.

gō-rōōn′-shell, *n.* A triton or trumpet-shell.

gorse, *n.* [ME. *gorst*; AS. *gorst*, gorse, furze.] Furze or whin, a thick, prickly shrub.

gorse′-bīrd, *n.* A European linnet.

gorse′chat, *n.* The whinchat.

gorse′duck, *n.* The corncrake.

gorse′hatch, *n.* The whinchat.

gōr′y, *a.* 1. Covered with congealed or clotted blood; as, *gory* locks.

2. Bloody; murderous.

gōr′y-dew, *n.* Blood-like, gelatinous patches found on damp stones, and consisting of *Palmella cruenta*, an alga.

gos′hawk, *n.* [ME. *goshawk, goshauk*; AS. *goshafoc*; *gos*, goose, and *hafoc*, a hawk.] A raptorial bird of the hawk kind, belonging to the genus *Astur.* The general color of the plumage is a deep brown, the breast and belly white.

gos′hẽrd, *n.* Same as *Goose-herd.*

gos′let, *n.* [AS. *gos*, goose, and dim. *-let.*] Any of several species of small geese found in India, Africa, and Australia and belonging to the genus *Nettapus.*

gos′ling, *n.* [AS. *gos*, a goose, and dim. *-ling.*]

1. A young goose; a goose not full grown.

2. A catkin.

gos′pel, *n.* [ME. *gospel, godspell*; AS. *gōdspel, gŏdspell*, originally good spell, good story, good news; intended to translate Gr. *euangelion*, good tidings, but later by shortening the *o* it became *gŏdspel*; *gŏd*, God, and *spel*, story, history.]

1. Good news; glad tidings; especially, a proclamation of Christ, salvation, or the kingdom of heaven.

2. [G—] A narrative of the birth, life, actions, and doctrines of Jesus Christ; specifically, one of the four records ascribed to Matthew, Mark, Luke, and John, forming part of the New Testament.

3. A portion of one of the four *Gospels*, to be read in a religious service.

4. Any general doctrine; any system or principle exercising strong influence over one; that which chiefly influences one's conduct; that which one regards or affirms to be true.

gos′pel, *a.* Of or accordant with the gospel; as, *gospel* righteousness.

gos′pel, *v.t.* To instruct in the gospel. [Obs.]

gos′pel-ẽr, gos′pel-lẽr, *n.* 1. An evangelist; a writer of a gospel.

2. A follower of Wyclif, the first Englishman who attempted a reformation of religion; hence, an evangelizing Protestant; a Puritan.

3. One who reads the gospel at the altar.

gos′pel-gos″sip, *n.* One who is overzealous in lecturing on religious subjects. [Obs.]

gos′pel-īze, *v.t.* 1. To form according to the gospel. [Obs.]

2. To instruct in the gospel; to evangelize. [Obs.]

goss, *n.* Gorse. [Obs.]

gos′sȧ-mẽr, *n.* [ME. *gossomer, gossummer*, lit., goose-summer; *gos*, goose, and *somer*, summer; so called from its downy appearance; or perhaps from *gaze à Marie*, gauze of Mary, in allusion to the legend that it was the remnant of the Virgin Mary's winding-sheet, left behind when she was taken up into heaven.]

1. A fine, filmy substance, like cobwebs, floating in the air in calm, clear weather, especially in autumn. It is seen in stubble-fields and on low bushes, and is formed by various species of spider.

2. Any thin fabric, especially a fine gauze.

3. A thin waterproof garment.

gos′sȧ-mẽr-spī″dẽr, *n.* See *Ballooning spider* under *Ballooning.*

gos′sȧ-mẽr-y, *a.* Like gossamer; flimsy; unsubstantial.

gos′săn, *n.* [Corn.] Reddish rock in the upper portions of a vein of metal, the color being due to oxidized pyrites.

gos-săn-if′ẽr-ous, *a.* Including or yielding gossan.

gos′sat, *n.* [Local, Eng.] The whistler or three-bearded rockling, a small British sea-fish.

gos′sib, *n.* A gossip. [Obs.]

gos′sip, *n.* [ME. *gossyp, gossib, godsib*; AS. *godsibb*, a sponsor, lit., God-relative; *god*, God, and *sib*, related.]

1. A sponsor; one who answers for a child in baptism. [Obs.]

2. A companion; a friend. [Obs.]

3. One who runs from house to house, tattling and telling news; an idle tattler.

4. Mere tattle; idle talk.

gos′sip, *v.i.*; gossiped (-sipt), *pt., pp.*; gossiping, *ppr.* 1. To prate; to chat; to talk much.

2. To be a companion. [Obs.]

3. To run about and tattle; to tell idle tales.

gos′sip, *v.t.* To be sponsor for. [Obs.]

gos′sip-ẽr, *n.* A gossip.

gos′sip-red, *n.* [ME. *gossiprede, godsibrede*, spiritual relationship; *gossip, godsib*, a sponsor, and *-rede*, from AS. *-rǣden*, condition.]

1. The mutual relation between sponsors and the person for whom they are sponsors. [Obs.]

2. Gossip.

gos′sip-ry, *n.* Gossipred.

gos′sip-y, *a.* Of, full of, or fond of gossip; chatty.

gos-sōōn′, *n.* [A corruption of Fr. *garçon*, a boy, attendant.] A boy; a servant. [Irish.]

gos′sy-pine, *a.* [L. *gossypion* and *-ine.*] Cottony; like cotton.

Gos-syp′i-um, *n.* [L. *gossypion, gossipion*, the cotton-tree.] A genus of the *Malvaceæ*, whose seeds are covered with the fibers that form the cotton of commerce.

got, *v.*, past tense and past participle of *get.*

gōte, *n.* [O.D. *gote*, a ditch, channel.] A gutter; a slough. [Scot. or Prov. Eng.]

gō′tẽr, *n.* A gutter. [Obs.]

Goth, *n.* [LL. *Gothus*, pl. *Gothi*, the Goths.]

1. One of an ancient Teutonic tribe or nation which inhabited the shores of the Baltic. Many great hordes of them migrating southward in the second century dispossessed the Romans of Dacia, and occupied the coast of the Black Sea from the Don to the Danube. There they divided into two sections, Visigoths (Western Goths) to the west of the Dnieper, and Ostrogoths (Eastern Goths) to the east, and under these names overran and assisted in destroying the Roman Empire.

2. One rude or uncivilized; a barbarian; a rude, ignorant person; one defective in taste.

Gō′thăm-ist, *n.* A wiseacre; a person deficient in wisdom; so called from Gotham, in Nottinghamshire, England, noted for some amusing blunders.

Gō′thăm-īte, *n.* A term jocularly applied to an inhabitant of New York city.

Goth′ic, *a.* [LL. *Gothicus*, from *Gothus*, pl. *Gothi*, the Goths.]

1. Pertaining to the Goths; as, *Gothic* customs; *Gothic* barbarity.

2. Denoting the various styles of pointed architecture prevalent in western Europe from the middle of the twelfth century to the revival of classic architecture in the sixteenth. The chief characteristics of Gothic architecture are the predominance of the pointed arch; the prolongation of vertical lines; the absence of the column and entablature of classic architecture, of square edges and rectangular surfaces, and the substitution of clustered shafts, contrasted surfaces, and members multiplied in rich variety.

Goth′ic, *n.* 1. The language of the Goths, especially of those who migrated to Mœsia in the fourth century, who were called *Mœsogoths.*

2. [g—] A style of type without serifs.

☞ **THIS LINE IS SET IN GOTHIC.**

3. The Gothic style of architecture.

Goth′i-cism, *n.* 1. Rudeness of manners; barbarity.

2. A Gothic idiom.

3. Conformity to the Gothic style of building.

Goth′i-cīze, *v.t.* To make Gothic; to bring back to barbarism. [Rare.]

gō′thīte (gē′tīt), *n.* Same as *Gœthite.*

got′ten, *v.*, past participle of *get.*

gouache (gwäsh), *n.* [Fr., water-colors.]

1. A style of water-color painting with opaque pigments; also, the paint itself.

2. A picture so painted.

gŏu′bẽr, *n.* See *Goober.*

goud, *n.* Woad. [Obs.]

gŏu-drŏn′, *n.* [Fr., tar.] A bundle of sticks soaked in pitch, oil, or the like, and used either for lighting up ditches, etc., or for setting fire to an enemy's works.

gouge, *n.* [ME. *gowge*; OFr. *gouge*; LL. *guvia, gubia*, a kind of chisel.]

1. A chisel whose cutting edge is curved, used to cut holes, channels, or grooves in wood or stone, or to cut out forms from paper, leather, etc.

2. A tool used by bookbinders, which forms a curve in gilding.

3. A soft deposit between a vein of ore and its wall.

4. The act of gouging; also, the groove gouged out.

5. A fraud; a cheat; an impostor. [Slang.]

6. A gouge-shell.

gouge, *v.t.*; gouged (goujd), *pt., pp.*; gouging, *ppr.* 1. To scoop out with or as with a gouge.

2. To force out (the eye of a person) with the thumb or finger.

3. To cheat; to overreach. [Slang.]

gouge′-bit, *n.* A boring-bit having a curved cutting edge.

gou′gẽr, *n.* One who or that which gouges, as certain insects.

gouge′shell, *n.* A marine shell having a sharp edge.

gŏu′jeers, gŏu′jēres, *n.* [Fr. *gouge*, a prostitute.] Infectious sexual disease. [Obs.]

gŏu′jon, *n.* [Fr., a gudgeon.] A fish, the mudcat.

gou′lănd, *n.* A gowan. [Obs.]

gou′lash (gū), *n.* [Hung.] A Hungarian meat stew, richly seasoned.

gou′pen, *n.* [Ice. *gaupn*, a handful.]

1. The hollow of one hand, or of two held together; a handful; a grasp. [Scot.]

2. A small quantity of meal given to the servant in a mill as a perquisite. [Scot.]

gour, *n.* A gaur or wild ox of India.

gour, *n.* [Turk. *giaur*, an infidel, a form of *ghebr*, a fire-worshiper.]

1. A giaour; an infidel.

2. A wild horse; an onager; a koulan.

Gou′rȧ, *n.* [From native name.]

1. A genus of large crested pigeons of New Guinea and adjacent islands.

2. [g—] One of this genus.

gŏu′rȧ-mi, *n.* [Javanese.] A fish, the goramy.

gōurd, *n.* [ME. *gourd, gourde*; OFr. *gourde*, contr. of *gouhourde, cougourde*, from L. *cucurbita*, a gourd.]

1. Any plant or fruit of the *Cucurbitaceæ*, including melons, squashes, pumpkins, etc., especially the fruit of the plant *Lagenaria vulgaris*, the bottle-gourd, of many varieties. The rind is tough, and when dried, is often used for dippers, bottles, etc.

Flower and fruit of *Cucurbita Melopepo.*

2. The shell of a *gourd* or any vessel of similar shape.

3. [*pl.*] False dice. [Obs.]

Bitter gourd; the colocynth.

gōurde, gōurd, *n.* [Fr. *gourd*, f. *gourde*, from L. *gurdus*, slow, dull.] A silver dollar. [West Indies.]

gōurd′i-ness, *n.* In farriery, a gourdy condition.

gōurd′-tree, *n.* Same as *Calabash-tree.*

gōurd′wŏrm, *n.* A parasitic worm; specifically, the liver-fluke.

gōurd′y, *a.* Having swelled legs; said of a horse.

gŏur′mănd, *n.* See *Gormand.*

gŏur-met′ (-mā′), *n.* [Fr.] An epicure; a judge of choice foods.

gour′net, *n.* A gurnard.

gousty, *a.* Dreary; gusty. [Scot.]

gout, *n.* [ME. *goute, gowte*; OFr. *goute, goutte*, a drop, gout; L. *gutta*, a drop; so called from the disease being considered a defluxion.]

1. In medicine, a chronic disease occurring by paroxysms, consisting essentially in a perfectly specific and peculiar topical inflammation, having its regular seat in the largest joint of the great toe.

2. A clot or coagulation; as, *gouts* of blood.

3. A diseased condition of grain due to the gout-fly.

gŏut (gō), *n.* [Fr., from L. *gustus*, taste.] Taste; relish.

gout′-fly, *n.* A small fly, *Chlorops tæniopus*, the larva of which does much injury to grain, producing gout or swelling of the joints.

gout′i-ly, *adv.* In a gouty manner.

gout′i-ness, *n.* The state of being subject to the gout; gouty affections collectively.

gout′-stone, *n.* A concretion chiefly composed of urate of soda, occurring abnormally in the joints, and elsewhere, as the result of gout.

gout′weed, gout′wŏrt, *n.* *Ægopodium Podagraria*, a plant of the *Umbelliferæ*, formerly believed to be a specific for gout; called also *acheweed, herb-gerard, goat's-foot*, and *bishop-weed.*

gout′y, *a.* 1. Diseased with the gout, or subject to the gout; as, a *gouty* person; a *gouty* joint.

2. Pertaining to the gout; as, *gouty* matter.

3. Figuratively, having a protuberance or swelling.

4. Boggy. [Obs.]

Gouty concretion; a gout-stone.

Gouty-stem tree; the Australian name for *Sterculia rupestris*, a tree with a bulging trunk.

gout′y-gall, *n.* An excrescence upon the ster

of the raspberry, caused by the larva of the insect *Agrilus ruficollis*.

gōve, *n.* A haymow; a hayrick. [Prov. Eng.]

gŏv′ẽrn (guv′ẽrn), *v.t.*; governed, *pt.*, *pp.*; governing, *ppr.* [ME. *governen*, *guvernen*; OFr. *guverner*; L. *gubernare*; Gr. *kybernān*, to steer or pilot a ship, direct, command.]

1. To direct and control, as the actions or conduct of men, either by established laws or by arbitrary will; to regulate by authority.

2. To regulate; to influence; to direct; to control; to restrain; as, to *govern* one's temper; to *govern* an engine.

3. In grammar, to require to be in a particular case; as, a verb transitive *governs* a word in the accusative case; or to require (a particular case); as, a verb *governs* the accusative case.

gŏv′ẽrn, *v.i.* To exercise authority; to administer laws.

Syn.—Rule, direct, control, moderate, guide, sway, supervise, manage, command, conduct.

gŏv″ẽrn-ȧ-bil′i-ty, *n.* Governableness.

gŏv′ẽrn-ȧ-ble, *a.* Controllable; manageable; obedient; submissive to law or rule.

gŏv′ẽrn-ȧ-ble-ness, *n.* The quality of being controllable.

gŏv′ẽrn-ăil, *n.* A helm or rudder; also, government; also written *governal*. [Obs.]

gŏv′ẽrn-ănce, *n.* [ME. *governance*, *governaunce*; OFr. *governance*, *gouvernance*; LL. *gubernantia*, from L. *gubernare*, to govern, pilot.] Government; exercise of authority; direction; control; management.

gŏv′ẽrn-ȧnte, *n.* [Fr. *gouvernante*.] A governess.

gŏv′ẽrn-ess, *n.* A tutoress; an instructress; a woman who has the care of instructing and directing children.

gŏv′ẽrn-ment, *n.* [Fr. *gouvernement*, from *gouverner*; L. *gubernare*, to govern.]

1. Direction; regulation; control; restraint; the exercise of authority; the administration of public affairs, according to laws and usages, or by arbitrary edicts; as, parental *government*.

2. The system of polity in a state; that form of fundamental rules and principles by which a nation or state is governed; as, a republican *government*.

3. An empire, kingdom, or state; any territory over which the right of sovereignty is extended.

4. The right of governing or administering the laws; as, the king of England vested the *government* of Ireland in the lord lieutenant.

5. The persons or council which administer the laws of a kingdom or state; executive power.

6. In grammar, the influence of a word in regard to construction, as when established usage requires that one word shall cause another to be in a particular case or mode.

gŏv-ẽrn-men′tăl, *a.* Pertaining to government; made by government.

gŏv′ẽrn-ŏr, *n.* [OFr. *governeor*, *gouvernour*; L. *gubernator*, a pilot, steersman, governor, from *gubernare*, to pilot, steer, direct.]

1. One who governs, rules, or directs; one invested with supreme authority to administer or enforce the laws; the supreme executive magistrate of a state, community, corporation, or post.

2. A tutor. [Archaic.]

3. A pilot; one who steers a ship.

4. In mechanics, a piece of mechanism by which the speed of a steam-engine, turbine, water-wheel, or other motor is regulated; more broadly, any regulating device, as one for equalizing the motion of mills and machinery. The common form of governor is shown in the illustration, the centrifugal balls A and B being rotated from the engine and geared with a toggle D E C and F G C pivoted at C and also attached pivotally to the grooved slide M, controlling the lever N O, pivoted at P, which lever in turn regulates the admission of steam into the cylinder.

Governor of a Steam-engine.

gŏv′ẽrn-ŏr=gen′ẽr-ăl, *n.* A governor who has under him subordinate or deputy governors; a viceroy; as, the *governor-general* of India.

gŏv′ẽrn-ŏr-ship, *n.* The office of a governor.

gow′ăn, *n.* [Scot., from Gael. *gugan*, bud, flower, daisy.]

1. The common daisy.

2. Granite rock in a soft or fragile condition.

gow′ăn-y, *a.* Decked with gowans. [Scot.]

gowd, *n.* Money; gold. [Scot.]

gowd′en, *a.* Golden. [Scot.]

gow′die, gow′dy, *n.* A yellow creature, as (a) the dragonet; (b) a gurnard; (c) a goldfinch. [Scot.]

gowd′nook, *n.* The saury-pike, a coast fish. [Scot.]

gowk, *v.t.* To make a fool of. [Obs.]

gowk, *n.* [Scot.] 1. The cuckoo.

2. A silly person.

gowl, *v.i.* [ME. *goulen*, *gowlen*; Ice. *gaula*, to low, bellow.] To howl. [Obs.]

gown, *n.* [ME. *goune*, from W. *gwn*, a gown, loose robe.]

1. A long, generally loose, upper garment; specifically, (a) a woman's outer garment; a dress; (b) a man's dressing-gown; (c) the official dress worn by members of certain peaceful professions, as divinity, medicine, law, as well as by civil magistrates, university professors and students, and the like; hence, the emblem of civil power or place, as opposed to the sword.

2. Garb; dress. [Rare.]

gowned, *a.* Dressed in a gown.

gowns′măn, gown′măn, *n.* 1. One whose professional habit is a gown, as a divine or lawyer, and particularly a member of an English university.

2. A civilian.

gow′pen, gow′pin, *n.* Same as *Goupen*.

goz′zărd, *n.* A gooseherd; a booby. [Prov. Eng.]

Gräaf′i-ăn, *a.* Pertaining to or described by Regnier de *Graaf*, a Dutch scientist.

Graafian follicle, or *vesicle*; a small follicle or sac in the ovary of a mammal in which an ovum matures.

grāal, *n.* A cup. [See *Grail*.]

grab, *n.* [Anglo-Ind.] A vessel used on the Malabar coast, having two or three masts.

grab, *v.t.* and *v.i.*; grabbed, *pt.*, *pp.*; grabbing, *ppr.* [Sw. *grabba*, to grasp.] To seize; to gripe.

grab, *n.* 1. A sudden grasp or seizure; hence, an unlawful or questionable appropriation; as, a salary *grab* by a legislature.

2. An implement for seizing an object to lift it; as, a *grab* to withdraw tools from a drilled hole.

grab′=bag, *n.* A bag in which unseen articles are placed to be grabbed by one who has paid a fee.

grab′bẽr, *n.* One who or that which grabs.

grab′ble, *v.i.* [Freq. of *grab*.]

1. To grope; to feel with the hands.

2. To lie prostrate on the belly; to sprawl.

grab′=gāme, *n.* A swindle or theft in which property is grabbed or taken away; a grab. [Colloq.]

grāce, *n.* [OFr. *grace*, *grasce*; L. *gratia*, favor, esteem, kindness, from *gratus*, pleasing, agreeable.]

1. That element in manner, deportment, movement, carriage, form, or language which renders it appropriate, harmonious, and agreeable; suitableness; elegance with appropriate dignity; beauty of figure, manner, etc.; as, she danced with much *grace*.

Grace was in her steps. —Milton.

2. Natural or acquired excellence; any quality that recommends the possessor to the liking or favor of others; embellishment.

A *grace* beyond the reach of art. —Pope.

3. Affectation of elegance; assumption of refinement; as, he laughed at her airs and *graces*.

4. [G—*pl.*] In mythology, the three goddesses in whose gift were grace, loveliness, and favor, worshiped in Greece under the name of *Charites*, called *Gratiæ* by the Romans. They were generally known as Aglaia, Thalia, and Euphrosyne.

5. In music, a grace-note, as an appoggiatura, shake, etc.

6. Favor; good-will; friendship; kindness; disposition to oblige another; graciousness; as, in one's good *graces*.

7. In a theological sense, (a) the free unmerited love and favor of God; (b) divine influence or the influence of the Spirit in renewing the heart and restraining from sin; (c) a state of reconciliation to God; (d) virtuous or religious affection or disposition, as faith, meekness, humility, patience, etc., proceeding from divine influence; (e) spiritual instruction, improvement, and edification.

My *grace* is sufficient for thee.—2 Cor. xii. 9.

8. A short prayer before or after meat; a blessing asked, or thanks rendered.

9. Clemency; mercy; forbearance; as, give no *grace* to the conquered.

10. A dispensation, privilege, or pardon, granted not of right but by favor; also, in English law, a general and free pardon by act of Parliament; called also *act of grace*.

11. In English universities, an act, vote, or decree, of the government of the institution.

12. [G—] A title or term of respect used in addressing or in speaking of a duke, duchess, or an archbishop, and formerly applied to the sovereign of England; as, his *Grace*, the Duke of Wellington.

13. [*pl.*] A game designed to promote or display *grace* of motion. It consists in passing a small hoop from one person to another by means of two short sticks.

14. Lot; fortune; condition. [Obs.]

15. [*pl.*] Thanks. [Obs.]

Day of grace; in theology, the time of probation when sinners may obtain forgiveness.

Days of grace; see under *Day*.

Good graces; favor; friendship.

With a bad grace; ungracefully; ungraciously; as, the apology came *with a bad grace*.

With a good grace; graciously; gracefully; especially when the air of graciousness is believed to be rather forced; as, he made reparation *with a good grace*.

grāce, *v.t.*; graced (grāst), *pt.*, *pp.*; gracing, *ppr.* 1. To adorn; to decorate; to embellish and dignify; to lend or add grace to.

Graced with wreaths of victory. —Shak.

2. To dignify or raise by an act of favor; to honor.

3. To supply with heavenly grace.

4. In music, to add grace-notes, cadenzas, etc., to; as, to *grace* a melody.

grāce′=cup, *n.* 1. A vessel used to drink a health or toast from after grace.

2. The health drunk after grace

grāced (grāst), *a.* Endowed with grace; graceful; beautiful.

grāce′ful, *a.* Full of or displaying grace or beauty in form or action; elegant; neat; handsome; becoming; well-chosen.

grāce′ful-ly, *adv.* In a graceful manner; elegantly, with a natural ease and propriety; as, to walk or speak *gracefully*.

grāce′ful-ness, *n.* Elegance of manner or deportment; beauty with dignity in manner, motion, or countenance.

grāce′=hoop, *n.* The hoop used in playing graces. [See *Grace*, n. 13.]

grāce′less, *a.* Void of grace or excellence; wanting in propriety; without divine grace; corrupt; depraved.

grāce′less-ly, *adv.* Without grace.

grāce′less-ness, *n.* The condition or quality of being graceless.

grāce′=nōte, *n.* In music, a note added by way of embellishment; an appoggiatura.

grāce′=strōke, *n.* A finishing touch or stroke; a coup-de-grace.

grac′ile, *a.* Slender. [Obs.]

grac′i-lent, *a.* Gracile. [Obs.]

grȧ-cil′i-ty, *n.* The state of being gracile; slenderness; smallness. [Rare.]

grā-ci-ō′sō, *n.* [Sp.] 1. A favorite.

2. In Spanish comedy, a clown.

grā′cious, *a.* [OFr. *gracios*; L. *gratiosus*, in favor, popular, kind, from *gratia*, favor, grace.]

1. Full of grace; beneficent; kind; merciful; benignant; characterized by grace; disposed to exercise kindness or favor.

And the Lord was *gracious* unto them. —2 Kings xiii. 23.

2. Endowed with grace; graceful; attractive; elegant; comely; beautiful.

No face so *gracious* is as mine. —Shak.

3. Characterized by or possessing divine grace; virtuous; good.

Gracious in the eyes of God. —Jer. Taylor.

Syn.—Benignant, kind, merciful, mild, compassionate, tender.

grā′cious-ly, *adv.* 1. In a gracious or friendly manner, courteously

His testimony he *graciously* confirmed. —Dryden.

2. Fortunately; favorably.

grā′cious-ness, *n.* The condition or quality of being gracious.

grac′kle, *n.* [L. *graculus*, the jackdaw; so called from its note.]

1. A bird of the genus *Gracula*; a mina.

2. A passerine bird of America of the family *Icteridæ*; as, the purple *grackle*, *Quiscalus quiscula*, the crow-blackbird; the rusty *grackle*, *Scolecophagus carolinus*; the boat-tailed *grackle*, *Quiscalus major*.

grā′dāte, *v.t.*; gradated, *pt.*, *pp.*; gradating, *ppr.* [L. *gradatus*, arranged in steps or grades, from *gradus*, a step, grade.] To arrange or blend by insensible degrees, as colors.

grā′dāte, *v.i.* To effect gradation.

grȧ-dā′tion, *n.* [OFr. *gradation*; L. *gradatio* (*-onis*), that which goes up or down by steps, a climax, from *gradatus*, having steps or grades, from *gradus*, a step, grade.]

1. A moving or progressing by degrees; a regular advance or progression from step to step; a step or degree in any order, series, or sequence; arrangement in order according to size, quality, rank, degree of advancement, etc.; sequence.

2. In art, the just arrangement or subordination of the parts of any work, so as to produce the best effect; as, the *gradation* of color and light in painting, to express depth and relief,

to define distances, and to show the state of the atmosphere.

3. In logic, a regular advancement from step to step, as in an argument.

4. In music, an ascending or descending, by a regular succession of chords.

5. In rhetoric, an ascending or descending in terms, as toward a climax.

6. In philology, ablaut.

grā-dā′tion, *v.t.* To form by gradations. [Rare.]

grā-dā′tion-ăl, *a.* According to gradation.

grad′ȧ-tō-ry, *a.* 1. Proceeding step by step.

2. In zoölogy, fitted for walking; suitable for a forward movement.

grad′ȧ-tō-ry, *n.* [L. *gradatus*, having steps or grades, from *gradus*, a step.] Steps from the cloisters into the church.

grad′dăn, *n.* Parched grain of any kind; also, meal ground by hand. [Scot.]

grāde, *n.* [Fr. *grade*; L. *gradus*, a step, degree, rank, from *gradi*, to step, walk.]

1. A degree, rank, or step in any order, series, or quality; as, a military officer of first *grade*; second *grade* wheat, etc.

2. A degree of ascent or descent in a road or railway, marked or slight; a gradient; a portion of a road, either level or inclined.

3. A class or order of animals produced by crossbreeding, as of a common breed with a pure-blooded animal, so as to improve the stock.

At grade; at the same level, as when two roads cross *at grade*.

Down grade; the descent in a graded roadbed; figuratively, a downward course in character or fortune.

Grade crossing; see under *Crossing*.

Up grade; the ascent in a graded roadbed; figuratively, an upward course in character or fortune.

grāde, *v.t.*; graded, *pt., pp.*; grading, *ppr.* 1. To arrange in degrees, ranks, or steps, according to order, series, or quality.

2. To reduce (land, roads, roadbeds of railways, and the like) to such levels or degrees of inclination as prepare them for being used.

3. To improve the blood of, as by crossbreeding; to improve the quality of, as by bringing wheat to grade.

grāde′ly, *a.* Decent; orderly. [Prov. Eng.]

grāde′ly, *adv.* Decently; orderly. [Prov. Eng.]

grād′ẽr, *n.* One who grades, or a device to assist in grading.

grā′di-ent, *a.* [L. *gradiens (-entis)*, ppr. of *gradi*, to step, walk.]

1. Moving by steps; walking; also, adapted for walking or stepping; as, a *gradient* animal.

2. Rising or descending by regular degrees of inclination; as, the *gradient* line of a railroad.

grā′di-ent, *n.* 1. The degree of ascent or descent in a road, railway, etc.

2. A part of a road inclined to a horizontal.

3. The rate of variation, or the curve representing it; also, the portion over which it exists; as, a barometric *gradient*.

grā′di-ent-pōst, *n.* 1. A post or stake beside a railway indicating by figures the rise or fall in grade.

2. In construction-work, a stake marking the level to be maintained; the surface mark.

grā′din, grȧ-dïne′, *n.* [Fr., from L. *gradus*, a step, pace.] One of a series of seats, steps, etc., which rise one after another.

grȧ-dïne′, *n.* [Fr.] A sculptor's chisel, having a toothed edge.

grād′ing, *n.* The act or method of bringing to a grade, as in building a roadway.

grȧ-dï′nō, *n.* [It., from L. *gradus*, a grade.] A raised shelf or step, as at the back of an altar; a gradin; a superaltar.

grȧ′dō, *n.* A degree in a scale of music.

grad′ū-ăl, *a.* Proceeding by steps or degrees; advancing step by step; passing from one step to another; regular and slow; as, a *gradual* increase of knowledge; a *gradual* increase of light in the morning is favorable to the eyes.

Syn.—Slow, continuous, unintermittent, gradational, regular, step by step, progressive.

grad′ū-ăl, *n.* [LL. *graduale, gradalis*, a book containing hymns and prayers which were originally sung on the steps of a pulpit, from L. *gradus*, a step.]

1. An order of steps. [Obs.]

2. A grail; an ancient book of hymns and prayers, so called because some of the anthems were chanted on the steps (*gradus*) of the pulpit; also, a book containing the musical portions of a mass.

Gradual Psalm; one of the fifteen psalms (Ps. cxx to cxxxiv inclusive) sung on the steps of the altar at Jerusalem.

grad-ū-al′i-ty, *n.* Regular progression. [Obs.]

grad′ū-ăl-ly, *adv.* 1. By degrees; step by step; regularly; slowly.

2. In degree. [Obs.]

Human reason doth not only *gradually*, but specifically differ from the fantastic reason of brutes. —Grew.

grad′ū-ăl-ness, *n.* The state or quality of being gradual.

grad′ū-āte, *v.t.*; graduated, *pt., pp.*; graduating, *ppr.* [LL. *graduatus*, pp. of *graduare*, to honor with a degree, to graduate, from L. *gradus*, a step, degree.]

1. To honor with a degree or diploma, in a college or university; to confer a degree on; as, to *graduate* a master of arts.

2. To divide any space into small, regular intervals; to mark with degrees; as, to *graduate* a rule.

3. In chemistry, to bring (fluids) to a certain degree of consistency.

4. To modify by degrees; to conform to a degree; to temper; to prepare.

grad′ū-āte, *v.i.* 1. To receive a degree from a college or university.

2. To pass by degrees; to change gradually; as, stone which *graduates* into gneiss.

3. In zoölogy, to taper, as the tail of a bird.

grad′ū-āte, *n.* 1. One who has received a degree in a college or university, or from some professional incorporated society.

2. In a laboratory, a vessel having graduated marking, used for measuring liquids, etc.

grad′ū-āte, *a.* Graduated.

grad′ū-ā-ted, *a.* 1. Honored with a degree or diploma from some learned society or college.

2. Marked with degrees or regular intervals; tempered.

3. In zoölogy, tapered; said of the tail of a bird where the outer feathers are gradually shortened.

Graduated glass, tube, etc.; a glass, tube, etc., with marks on the exterior to indicate the amount of the contents at a certain level.

grad′ū-āte-ship, *n.* The state of a graduate.

grad-ū-ā′tion, *n.* [LL. *graduatio (-onis)*, the act of conferring a degree, from *graduare*, to confer a degree, from L. *gradus*, a step, a degree.]

1. Regular progression by succession of degrees.

2. Improvement; exaltation of qualities.

3. The act of conferring or receiving academical degrees.

4. A division of any space into small regular intervals; as, the *graduation* of a barometer or thermometer.

5. The process of bringing a liquid to a certain consistence by evaporation.

grad′ū-ā-tŏr, *n.* An instrument for dividing any line, right or curve, into small, regular intervals; specifically, (a) a dividing machine; (b) in chemistry, a device for the reduction of a liquid by spreading it out upon a surface.

grā′dus, *n.* [From L. *gradus ad Parnassum*, steps to Parnassus, a name for a book on prosody or poetry.]

1. A dictionary of versification, intended as an aid in composing Greek and Latin poetry.

2. In music, graded exercises, each succeeding one more difficult than its predecessor.

grā′dy, *a.* [L. *gradatus*, furnished with steps, from *gradus*, a step.] In heraldry, arranged in or starting from steps; embattled, as an embattled edge.

A Bend Grady.

grȧf, *n.* [G.] In Germany, a title of nobility signifying rank equal to that of an English earl or a French count.

graff, *n.* [ME. *grafe, greive*, a steward, reeve, from Ice. *greifi*, a steward.] A reeve; a steward.

graff, *n.* [ME. *graf*; AS. *græf*, a ditch, grave, from *grafan*, to dig.] A ditch or moat; a grave. [Scot.]

graff, *v.* and *n.*, obsolete form of *graft*.

graff′āge, *n.* The slope of a moat or ditch nearest the parapet.

graf′fẽr, *n.* In law, a notary or scrivener.

grȧf-fï′tï, *n.pl.* [It., pl. of *graffito*, a scribbling, from *graffiare*, to scratch, scribble, from LL. *graphiare*, to write, from L. *graphium*; Gr. *grapheion*, a style for writing, from *graphein*, to write.] Inscriptions and pictorial representations found on rocks or on the walls of ancient ruins.

grȧft, *n.* [ME. *graffe, gryffe*; OFr. *greffe*; LL. *graphiolum*, a small shoot or scion, from L. *graphium*; Gr. *grapheion*, a style for writing, a pencil, from *graphein*, to write.]

1. A small shoot or scion of a tree inserted in another tree, as the stock which is to support and nourish it. These unite and become one tree, but the graft determines the kind of fruit; a part of a tree growing from an inserted shoot; hence, that which is amalgamated with a foreign stock, as one race with another.

2. In surgery, a piece of living tissue joined to any part or member of a person or animal to supply a deficiency caused by surgical or accidental excision; the portion of foreign tissue so implanted; the surgical operation, autoplasty, by which such a physical repair is effected.

grȧft, *n.* The act of any one, especially an official or public employee, by which he procures money surreptitiously by virtue of his office or position; also, the surreptitious gain thus procured. [Recent Slang.]

> It is for the moralist to draw the line. *Graft* means exactly what you choose to make it. A salary for a sinecure is *graft*. A wide-open expense account is *graft*. Anything and everything that pertains to money or perquisites not accounted for by the stern value-received rule is *graft*, cutting out, of course, the speculative money and money obtained by taking business risks of one kind or another. —W. Norton in Saturday Evening Post, Aug. 22, 1903.

grȧft, *v.t.*; grafted, *pt., pp.*; grafting, *ppr.* 1. To insert, as a scion or shoot or a small cutting from a tree, into another tree; to propagate by insertion or inoculation; to join, as two things in close union; to join to another so as to receive support from it; to insert in a body to which it did not originally belong.

2. In surgery, to operate upon by autoplasty.

To graft by approach; in horticulture, to inarch.

grȧft, *v.i.* 1. To practise the insertion of scions from one tree, or kind of tree, into another.

2. To use public office for private gain, especially in a surreptitious or illegal manner.

grȧft′ẽr, *n.* 1. One who inserts scions into or on foreign stocks, or propagates fruit by ingrafting.

2. A surgeon who performs the operation of autoplasty.

3 A dishonest official; a public officer who grafts; a swindler. [Slang.]

4. An instrument used in grafting trees, etc.

5. The tree from which a scion for grafting is cut.

grȧft′ing, *n.* 1. The art or act of inserting a shoot or scion taken from one tree into the

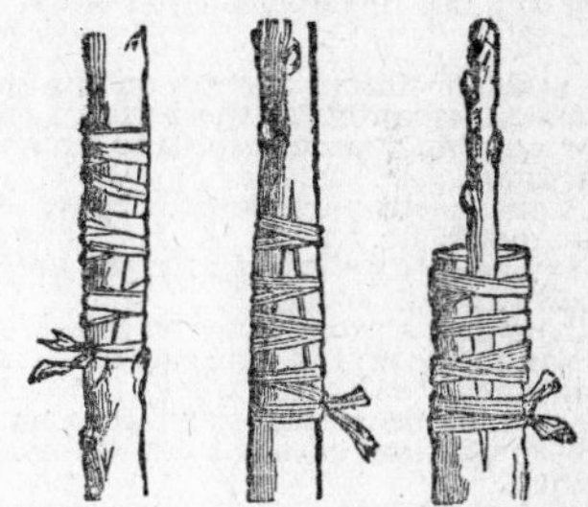

Splice-grafting. Saddle-grafting. Cleft-grafting.

stem or some other part of another, in such a manner that they unite and produce fruit of the kind belonging to the tree from which the scion was taken. The methods of grafting are of great variety, as *splice-grafting, saddle-grafting, cleft-grafting*, etc.

2. The act of obtaining money surreptitiously or illegally, as by a public official who uses his position for the purpose.

3. In carpentry, the joining of two pieces of wood end to end; scarfing.

4. In nautical parlance, the manner of weaving over with fine lines, as a block-strap, ringbolt, etc.

5. In surgery, the performance of the operation of autoplasty.

grȧft′ing-scis″sŏrs, *n.pl.* In surgery, scissors used in autoplasty or skin-grafting.

grȧft′ing-tool, *n.* 1. Any implement used in grafting.

2. A kind of short curved spade used in excavating.

grȧft′ing-wax, *n.* A composition used in grafting to exclude the air and to preserve a new joint, usually made of beeswax, resin, tallow, etc.

Grā′hăm (-ăm), *a.* Relating to the American vegetarian, Sylvester Graham, or to his teachings.

Graham bread; bread made of unbolted wheat-flour.

Graham flour; see under *Flour*.

Grā′hăm-ite, *n.* A believer in the dietetic system of Sylvester Graham; a vegetarian.

grāil, *n.* [OFr. *grael, greel*; LL. *graduale, gradalis*, a service-book, a book of prayers and hymns to be used upon the church steps, from L. *gradus*, a step.] A book of offices in the Roman Catholic church; a gradual. [Rare.]

grāil, *n.* [OFr. *graal, greal*; LL. *gradalis, gradale*, a flat dish, a shallow vessel, prob. corruption of *cratella*, dim. of L. *crater*, a bowl.] A bowl or chalice; specifically, the *Holy Grail*.

Holy Grail; a legendary holy vessel, supposed to have been of emerald, from which our Saviour ate the paschal lamb at the last supper, or, according to other legends, from which he dispensed the wine. It is said to have been taken to England and lost, after which it became the great object of research or quest to knights-errant of all nations, none being considered qualified to discover it but a knight perfectly chaste in thought and act. The stories and poems of Arthur and the Knights of the Round Table are founded on the idea of the quest of the *Holy Grail.*

grāil, *n.* [OFr. *graile, graille,* fine, small, from L. *gracilis,* slender.]

1. Small particles, as the beads or air-bubbles on freshly-drawn liquor.
2. Fine gravel; sand.
3. One of the smaller feathers on a hawk.

grāil, grāille, *n.* A half-round file, single cut, used in making combs.

grāin, *n.* An old form of *groan.* [Scot.]

grāin, *n.* [OFr. *grain, grein;* L. *granum,* a grain, seed, a small kernel.]

1. A minute particle; any small, hard mass; as, a *grain* of sand or gravel.
2. A single seed or hard seed of a plant, particularly of those kinds whose seeds are used for food of man or beast. *Grain,* without a definitive, signifies the edibles of the grass family, such as wheat, rye, barley, oats, and maize; as, a field of waving *grain;* a dealer in *grains; grains* of wheat.
3. A small weight, or the smallest weight ordinarily used, being the twentieth part of a scruple in apothecaries' weight and the twenty-fourth of a pennyweight troy; the unit of the English system of weights.
4. A reddish dye or tincture; sometimes used by the poets to designate Tyrian purple.

All in a robe of darkest *grain.* —Milton.

5. The state of the grit of any body regarded as composed of particles; as, marble, sandstone, or sugar of a fine *grain.*
6. The body or substance of wood as modified by the fibers.

Hard box, and linden of a softer *grain.* —Dryden.

7. A rough or fibrous texture on the outside of the skin of animals; the form of the surface of anything, with respect to smoothness or roughness.
8. A constituent particle of a body, as of a stone, a metal, etc.
9. In stone-cutting, a cut at right angles to the rock's natural break.
10. In botany, a prominence on the back of a leaf, as in the dock; the hair-side of leather, or the markings peculiar to it.
11. Anything proverbially small; a very small particle or portion; as, a *grain* of wit or of common sense.

Neglect not to make use of any *grain* of grace. —Hammond.

12. [*pl.*] The residuum of *grain* and similar material left in the mash-tub after brewing; also called *draff.*

Against the grain; against the direction of the fiber; hence, unwillingly; reluctantly; against the inclination.

A grain of allowance; a small allowance or indulgence; a small portion to be remitted; something above or below just weight.

Grains of paradise; sweet-scented seeds from the African plant *Amomum Melegueta,* used in compounding certain liquors and medicines.

In grain; of a lasting color; set; innate; real.

To dye in grain; to dye in the raw material, as wool or silk before it is manufactured.

grāin, *n.* [Ice. *grein,* the branch of a tree, an arm, point, difference.]

1. A branch or subordinate part of a plant; a stem. [Obs.]
2. In founding, a piece of metal used by molders to keep the core in place.
3. [*pl.*] An iron instrument with four or more barbed points, and a line attached to it, used at sea for striking and taking dolphins and other fish.
4. [*pl.*] A place at which two streams unite; the fork of a river. [Prov. Eng. and Scot.]

grāin, *v.t.;* grained, *pt., pp.;* graining, *ppr.* 1. To form into grains, as powder, sugar, and the like.

2. To paint so as to give the appearance of the grains or fibers of various woods.
3. In making leather, (a) to cause the grain of the leather to rise; (b) to produce artificial markings upon, resembling those of a natural leather; (c) to remove the hair from; (d) to soak in a softening liquid, as bate.
4. To produce a dull surface upon; as, to *grain* a stone in lithography.
5. To clear of grain, as the wort in brewing.

grāin, *v.i.* 1. To yield fruit. [Obs.]

2. To granulate; to become granular.

grāin'age, *n.* 1. An impost on grain.

2. A five-per-cent duty on salt brought to London by aliens. [Obs.]
3. A mangy tumor on a horse's leg.

grāin'-bind"ẽr, *n.* The device on a harvester which binds grain into bundles.

grāine, *n.* [Fr.] Silkworm eggs.

grāin'ẽr, *n.* One who or that which grains, as (a) one who paints in imitation of the grain of wood, etc.; (b) a tool used to produce such an imitation; (c) a knife to remove hair from hides; (d) bate.

grāin'ing, *n.* A fish, the dace.

grāin'ing, *n.* 1. The fork of a stick or tree. [Prov. Eng.]

2. The use of grains in spearing fish.

grāin'ing, *n.* 1. The process of forming a grain or grains; the resulting substance or appearance, as (a) painting in imitation of a grain; (b) indentation; milling, as on a coin; (c) causing a grain on the surface of leather, paper, lithographic stone, etc.; (d) granulation.

2. The process of removing the grain, as from wort.

grāin'ing=bōard, *n.* A board used in graining leather, as in impressing a certain pattern upon it.

grāin'=leath"ẽr (-leth"), *n.* Dressed leather blackened or colored on the grain side.

grāin'=moth, *n.* A minute moth of which two species are known, *Tinea granella* and *Gelechia cerealella,* whose larvæ are destructive to grain in granaries.

grāin'=tin, *n.* The purest kind of tin.

grāin'=wee"vil, *n.* Any weevil destructive to grain in storage; especially *Sitophilus granarius.*

grāin'=wŏrm, *n.* A grain-moth's larva.

grāin'y, *a.* Full of grains; granular.

grāip, *n.* A dungfork. [Scot.]

grāip, *v.t.* To grope; to feel. [Scot.]

grāith, *n.* Gear; outfit; equipment. [Scot.]

grāith, *v.t.* To prepare. [Obs.]

gra'kle, *n.* Same as *Grackle.*

Gral'læ, Gral-là-tō'rēş, *n.pl.* [L. *grallæ,* stilts, from *gradi,* to go, walk.] Orders of birds in the systems of Linnæus and Vigors, characterized by very long legs, and by the nakedness of the lower part of the tibia, adapting them for wading in water without wetting their feathers. They have also generally long necks and long bills. The orders include the cranes, herons, storks, plovers, snipes, rails, coots, etc. Most modern naturalists have, however, made other classifications, and both terms are obsolescent.

Grallatores. *a,* Head and Foot of Bittern. *b,* Do. of Crane. *c,* Do. of Stork.

gral-là-tō'ri-ăl, gral'là-tō-ry, *a.* Relating to the *Grallatores.*

gral'liç, *a.* [L. *grallæ,* stilts, crutches.] Stilted; relating to the *Grallæ.* [Rare.]

gral'line, *a.* Grallic; grallatorial.

gral'lino, *n.* A bird of the *Grallæ.*

gral'lōçh, gral'lŏck, *v.t.* To eviscerate, as a deer.

gral'lōçh, *n.* The entrails of a deer.

gram, *a.* Angry. [Obs.]

-gram. A suffix from Gr. *gramma,* anything written or drawn, a writing, from *graphein,* to write or draw, added to words of Greek origin or words similarly formed, to signify that which is written or drawn; as, dia*gram,* tele*gram.*

gram, gramme, *n.* [Fr. *gramme,* from LL. *gramma,* the weight of two oboli, a small weight, from Gr. *gramma,* that which is written or drawn, a letter, writing, from *graphein,* to write, draw.] The unit of mass in the metric system. It is, theoretically, the mass of a cubic centimeter of water at 4°C. (the point of maximum density); practically it is one-thousandth of a standard platinum kilogram in Paris, or 15.432 troy grains.

Gram equivalent; the mass of an element to which one gram of hydrogen is chemically equivalent.

gram, *n.* [Port. *grão,* from L. *granum,* a grain.] The chick-pea, *Cicer arietinum,* used extensively in India as fodder for horses and cattle.

grä'mà=grass, *n.* Any of various species of low grasses of the genus *Bouteloua,* as *Bouteloua oligostachya,* the mesquit-grass or buffalo-grass of Texas, New Mexico, and other western sections.

gram'ȧ-ry, *n.* [ME. *gramary, gramery,* learning, erudition, magic, *gramere,* grammar.] Learning; hence, magic; wizardry. [Obs.]

grȧ-mash'es, *n.pl.* See *Gamashes.*

gram'=cen'ti-mē-tẽr, *n.* In physics, a unit of mechanical work; the work done when a weight of one gram is raised through the height of one centimeter against the force of gravity.

gram'=dē-gree", *n.* The small calory. [See *Calory.*]

grāme, *n.* Anger; grief; misery. [Obs.]

grȧ-mẽr'cy, *interj.* [OFr. *grant merci, grand merci,* lit., great thanks.] Great thanks; formerly used to express thankfulness with surprise.

Gram-i-nā'cē-æ, *n.pl.* The *Gramineæ.*

gram-i-nā'ceous, *a.* Gramineous.

Grȧ-min'ē-æ, *n.pl.* [L. *gramineus,* of or pertaining to grass, from *gramen* (*-inis*), grass.] A very important group of *Glumaceæ,* the grasses, distributed throughout the globe and comprising about 300 genera and 3500 species.

grȧ-min'ē-ăl, *a.* Gramineous.

grȧ-min'ē-ous, *a.* [L. *gramineus,* from *gramen* (*-inis*), grass.] Grassy; like or pertaining to grass, or to the *Gramineæ.*

gram"i-ni-fō'li-ous, *a.* [L. *gramen* (*-inis*), grass, and *folium,* a leaf.] Bearing grasslike leaves.

gram-i-niv'ō-rous, *a.* [L. *gramen* (*-inis*), grass, and *vorare,* to devour.] Feeding or subsisting on grass, as cattle.

gram-i-nol'ō-ġy, *n.* [L. *gramen* (*-inis*), grass, and Gr. *-logia,* from *legein,* to speak.] Agrostology; science concerning the grasses.

gram'mȧ-logue (-log), *n.* [Gr. *gramma,* a letter, and *logos,* a word.] In shorthand, a word expressed by a single character, usually the principal consonant, as |, representing *d* for *do.*

gram'măr, *n.* [ME. *grammere;* OFr. *gramaire,* grammar; L. *grammatica* (supply *ars,* art); Gr. *grammatikē* (supply *technē,* art), grammar, learning, from *gramma,* something written, a letter, from *graphein,* to write.]

1. The art of speaking or writing a language with propriety or correctness, according to established usage.
2. A system of general principles and of particular rules for speaking or writing a language; a digested compilation of customary forms of speech in a nation; also, a book containing such principles and rules.
3. Speech or writing in accordance with the rules of grammar; propriety of speech.
4. The study or exposition of the principles which underlie the use of language in general; philology.
5. An outline of the principles of any subject; as, a *grammar* of logic.

Comparative grammar; the study which regards the resemblances and differences of various languages, classifying them in accordance with their affinities.

gram'măr, *v.i.* To discourse according to the rules of grammar. [Obs.]

gram'măr, *v.t.* To teach. [Obs.]

gram-mā'ri-ăn, *n.* [Fr. *grammairien,* from *grammaire,* grammar.]

1. One versed in grammar or the construction of languages; a philologist.
2. One who teaches or writes upon grammar.

gram-mā'ri-ăn-işm, *n.* The strict observance of grammatical rules and forms; pedantry. [Rare.]

gram'măr-less, *a.* Devoid of grammar.

gram'mātes, *n.pl.* Elements or rudiments of any subject. [Obs.]

gram-mat'iç, *a.* [L. *grammaticus;* Gr. *grammatikos,* versed in letters or grammar, as noun, a grammarian, from *gramma,* a letter, something written, from *graphein,* to write.] Belonging to or relating to grammar; dealing with the structure of language; as, a *grammatic* principle.

gram-mat'iç-ăl, *a.* 1. According to the rules of grammar; possessing principles of grammar; as, a *grammatical* construction.

2. Relating to grammar; as, a *grammatical* rule.

gram-mat'iç-ăl-ly, *adv.* According to the principles and rules of grammar; as, to write *grammatically.*

gram-mat'iç-ăl-ness, *n.* Quality of being grammatical, or according to the rules of grammar.

gram-mat'i-ças-tẽr, *n.* [LL. *grammaticaster,* a scribe, notary, from L. *grammaticus,* a grammarian, and *-aster.*] A pretender to a knowledge of grammar; a pedant.

gram-mat-i-çā'tion, *n.* A grammatical requirement. [Obs.]

gram-mat'i-çişm, *n.* A principle or rule of grammar.

gram-mat'i-çīze, *v.t.* and *v.i.;* grammaticized, *pt., pp.;* grammaticizing, *ppr.* To render grammatical; also, to show one's knowledge or skill in language.

gram'mȧ-tist, *n.* A grammarian. [Rare.]

gramme, *n.* See *Gram.*

gram'ō-phōne, *n.* [Gr. *gramma,* a letter, and *phōnē,* a sound.] A device invented by E. Berliner to record, retain, and reproduce sounds. It differs from a phonograph, in having a circular disk upon which tracings are made by a recording style, and from which sounds are reproduced by another kind of style attached to the diaphragm of any one of various types of reproducers.

gram'pus, *n.* [Sp. *grand pez;* It. *gran pesce,* lit.

great fish, a grampus, from L. *grandis*, great, and *piscis*, a fish.]

1. Any delphinoid cetacean of the genus *Orca* or the genus *Grampus*. *Orca gladiator* has powerful teeth in both jaws and preys upon other cetaceans, seals, fish, etc. *Grampus griseus*, also known as the *cowfish*, is a toothed cetacean of the north Atlantic whose oil has commercial value.

2. A hellgrammite.

3. The whip-tailed scorpion.

4. The tongs for handling blooms of wrought iron. [U. S.]

grȧ-nāde′, grȧ-nä′dō, *n.* See *Grenade.*

gran-ȧ-dil′lȧ, *n.* [Sp. *granadilla*, or *grandilla*, dim. of *granada*, a pomegranate, from L. *granatus*, containing seeds, from *granum*, a seed.] A plant; the fruit of the *Passiflora quadrangularis*, which is sometimes as large as a child's head and is much esteemed in tropical countries as a pleasant dessert fruit.

gran-ȧ-dil′lȧ-tree, *n.* *Brya Ebenus*, a tree of the *Leguminosæ* whose wood is the greenish-brown false ebony

gran-ȧ-dil′lō, *n.* [Sp.] The granadilla-tree.

gran′ȧ-ry, *n.* [L. *granarium*, a granary, from *grana*, pl., grain.]

1. A storehouse or repository for grain after it is threshed; a cornhouse.

2. Figuratively, a country producing grain in abundance.

gran′ȧ-tīte, *n.* Same as *Staurolite.*

grand, *a.* [OFr. *grand*; L. *grandis*, great, large, grand.]

1. Imposing in magnitude; magnificent in character, size, or proportions; majestic because of great size or inspiring qualities; as, a *grand* torrent; the *grand* cañon of the Colorado; a *grand* cathedral.

2. Exalted in character or expression; lofty in power, beauty, or inspiration; impressive; dignified; noble; as, a *grand* achievement; a *grand* conception; a *grand* epic.

3. Great in ability, dignity, or personal character; preëminent in high and noble qualities; deserving of reverence; as, a *grand* monarch; a *grand* life.

4. First in importance; chief; principal; greatest in size, rank, dignity, or power; as, the *grand* chapter of a lodge; the *grand* stand.

5. Inclusive of all particulars; full; complete; broadly comprehensive; as, a *grand* survey; the *grand* total.

6. Being one degree more remote in ascent or descent of kinship; as, *grand*son; *grand*nephew; *grand*mother, etc.

Grand Army of the Republic; an organization of men who were enlisted in the Union army or navy in the Civil War of 1861-65 and who received honorable discharge; referred to as the *G. A. R.*

Grand cordon; (a) a ribbon or cordon used to indicate high position in certain orders; also, (b) a person of that degree.

Grand cross; (a) the highest degree or rank in certain lodges and orders of knighthood, as in the Order of the Bath; (b) a member of that rank.

Grand days; St. John the Baptist's day, All Saints', Candlemas, and Ascension, English holidays observed in the courts and inns of law and chancery; *dies non juridici*.

Grand duchess; (a) a grand duke's wife or widow; (b) a female sovereign of a grand duchy; (c) a daughter of the czar of Russia.

Grand duke; (a) a sovereign lower in rank than a king; (b) a brother of the czar of Russia; (c) the eagle-owl or great horned owl of Europe.

Grand master; the chief or head of certain orders, as of the Templars and Hospitalers, also, of the Good Templars and certain other orders.

Grand relief; high relief; alto-rilievo.

Grand stand; the chief observation stand at any public gathering, as a parade, a ball-game, a race-track, etc.

Syn.—Magnificent, dignified, elevated, exalted, great, illustrious, lofty, majestic, superb, pompous.—*Grand* is applied to that which expands the mind by a sense of vastness and majesty, *magnificent* is applied to anything which is imposing from its splendor; *sublime* describes that which is awful and elevating.

gran′dam, *n.* [Fr. *grande dame.*] A grandmother; an old woman.

grand′äunt, *n.* The sister of a grandparent.

grand′child, *n.* A son's or daughter's child; a child in the second degree of descent.

grand′daugh″tẽr (-da̤″tẽr), *n.* The daughter of a son or daughter.

gran-dee′, *n.* [Sp. and Port. *grande*, a nobleman, from *grande*, great.]

1. A nobleman; a man of elevated rank or station; in Spain, a nobleman of the first rank, who had formerly special privileges.

2. Any man of high social position, as a nobleman.

gran-dee′ship, *n.* The rank or estate of a grandee.

gran′deūr, (or -jur), *n.* [Fr. *grandeur*, from L. *grandis*, grand.] Greatness; that quality or combination of qualities in an object which elevates or expands the mind and excites pleasurable emotions in him who views or contemplates it; the quality of being grand; splendor; magnificence; stateliness; as, the *grandeur* of a large and well-proportioned edifice, of an extensive range of lofty mountains, of a large cataract, of a pyramid, etc.

gran-dev′i-ty, *n.* Great age. [Obs.]

gran-dē′vous, *a.* Of great age. [Obs.]

grand′fä″thẽr, *n.* A father's or mother's father; the next degree above the father or mother in lineal ascent.

grand′fä″thẽr-lŏng′legs, *n.* See *Daddy-long-legs.*

grand′fä″thẽr-ly, *a.* Having the characteristics, appearance, or actions of a grandfather.

grand′-guärd, *n.* A shoulder and breast protection worn on the left side by knights in tournaments.

gran-dif′iç, *a.* [LL. *grandificus*, from L. *grandis*, great, and *facere*, to make.] Making great.

gran-dil′ō-quence (-kwens), *n.* Lofty speaking; lofty expressions.

gran-dil′ō-quent, *a.* [L. *grandis*, grand, and *loquens* (*-entis*), ppr. of *loqui*, to speak.] Pompous; bombastic.

gran-dil′ō-quous (-kwus), *a.* [L. *grandiloquus*, from *grandis*, grand, lofty, and *loqui*, to speak.] Speaking in a lofty style.

gran′di-nous, *a.* [L. *grandinosus*, full of hail, from *grando* (*-inis*), hail.] Consisting of hail. [Rare.]

gran′di-ōse, *a.* [Fr. *grandiose*; It. *grandioso*; L. *grandis*, great, grand.]

1. Imposing; magnificent; splendid.

2. Flaunting; showy; vaunting; pompous.

gran-di-os′i-ty, *n.* [Fr. *grandiosité*; It. *grandiosità*, from *grandioso*, great, grand, from L. *grandis*, grand.] The grandiose quality; pomposity.

gran-di-ō′sō, *adv.* [It.] In music, grandly; broadly.

grand′i-ty, *n.* Greatness; magnificence. [Obs.]

grand′ly, *adv.* In a grand or lofty manner.

grand′mäm-mä″, grand′mä, *n.* A grandmother

grand′mŏth″ẽr, *n.* The mother of one's father or mother.

grand′mŏth″ẽr-ly, *a.* Resembling a grandmother in age, appearance, or manners; kind.

grand-neph′ew, *n.* The grandson of a brother or sister.

grand′ness, *n.* Grandeur; greatness with beauty; magnificence.

grand′niece (-nēs), *n.* The granddaughter of a brother or sister.

grand′pä-pä″, grand′pä, *n.* A grandfather.

grand′pâr″ent, *n.* A grandfather or a grandmother.

grănd′pèrе (groṅ′pâr), *n.* [Fr., grandfather.] A former style of cotillion.

grand′sīre, *n.* 1. A grandfather.

2. A male ancestor of one's parent.

grand′sŏn, *n.* The son of a son or daughter.

grand′un″cle, *n.* An uncle of one's parent.

grāne, *v.* and *n.*, variant of *groan.* [Scot.]

grānge, *n.* [OFr. *grange*; LL. *granea*, a barn, grange, from L. *granum*, grain, corn.]

1. A farm, with the dwelling-house, stables, barns, etc.; particularly, a house or farm at a distance from other houses or villages; the dwelling of a gentleman-farmer.

2. A combination, society, or lodge of farmers for the purpose of promoting the interests of agriculture and for doing away with middlemen or agents intervening between the producer and the consumer. Granges originated in the western United States in 1867. Officially named *Patrons of Husbandry.*

3. The farming establishment and granary of a religious house or of a feudal lord, where, in addition to their own crops, the grain paid as rent and tithes was stored. [Obs.]

4. A granary. [Obs.]

grān′ġẽr, *n.* [OFr. *grangier*, a farmer, from *grange*, a grange.]

1. A member of a farmers' grange.

2. Any farmer; usually derisive. [Colloq., U. S.]

3. A bailiff or steward of a farm. [Obs.]

4. In stocks, any one of the great railroad corporations in the western part of the United States.

grān′ġẽr-ism, *n.* [Named after Rev. James *Granger*, the author of a "Biographical History of England," published 1769, which was illustrated by this method.] The practice of using illustrations taken from a number of books to illustrate a work.

grān′ġẽr-ism, *n.* The principles of the Patrons of Husbandry, or grangers.

grān′ġẽr-īte, *n.* One who adds to a book extra illustrations, maps, or the like taken from other books or independently collected.

grān′ġẽr-īze, *v.i.*; grangerized, *pt., pp.*; grangerizing, *ppr.* To practise grangerism.

grȧ-nif′ẽr-ous, *a.* [L. *granifer*, grain-bearing, *granum*, grain, and *ferre*, to bear.] Bearing seeds like grain.

gran′i-fọrm, *a.* [L. *granum*, grain, and *forma*, form.] Formed like grains.

grȧ-nil′lȧ, grȧ-nil′lō, *n.* [Sp., dim. of *grana*, a grain, cochineal, from L. *granum*, a grain.] Cochineal in small grains.

gran′ite, *n.* [It. *granito*, granite, lit., grained, pp. of *granire*, to reduce to grains, from *grano*, L. *granum*, a seed, grain.] In geology, an unstratified rock, composed of quartz, feldspar, and mica, or at least of two of these minerals, confusedly crystallized together, varying greatly in texture and color; as, gray *granite*, brown *granite*, etc.

Graphic granite; a species of granite called pegmatite, containing no mica and having the crystals of quartz so arranged that the face of a section of it resembles a tablet covered with Oriental inscriptions.

Porphyritic granite; granite in which distinct crystals of feldspar appear embedded in a matrix of finely crystalline structure.

Syenitic granite; granite containing hornblende, the chief constituent of syenite; called also *hornblende granite.*

gran′ite-wāre, *n.* 1. Ironware covered with an enamel proof against fire and acids, the enamel having granite tints.

2. A strong pottery of fine quality, which is very like ironstone china.

3. A pottery mottled to imitate granite.

gra-nit-i-. A combining form from It. *granito*, granite; signifying granite.

grȧ-nit′iç, grȧ-nit′iç-ăl, *a.* 1. Pertaining to granite; like granite; having the nature of granite; as, *granitic* texture.

2. Consisting of granite; as, *granitic* mountains.

gran-i-tiç′ō-line, *a.* [*Graniti-*, and L. *colere*, to inhabit.] In lichenology, clinging to granite.

grȧ-nit″i-fi-cā′tion, *n.* [*Graniti-*, and L. *facere*, to make.] The art or process of being formed into granite.

grȧ-nit′i-fọrm, *a.* [*Graniti-*, and L. *forma*, form.] Resembling granite in structure or shape.

gran′i-tīte, *n.* Granite in which biotite occurs with little or no muscovite.

gran′i-toid, *a.* Resembling granite.

grȧ-niv′ō-rous, *a.* [L. *granum*, grain, and *vorare*, to devour.] Feeding or subsisting on grain; as, *granivorous* birds.

gran′nam, *n.* A grandam. [Obs.]

gran′ny, *n.* 1. A grandmother.

2. Any old woman. [Colloq.]

gran′ny's-knot, gran′ny-knot (-not), *n.* Among sailors, a knot tied in such a way that it is both insecure and when jammed difficult to untie.

grä′nō, *n.* [It., lit., a grain, from L. *granum*, a grain.] A bronze Maltese coin, worth a little less than one-fifth of a cent, now no longer in use.

grȧnt, *v.t.*; granted, *pt., pp.*; granting, *ppr.* [ME. *granten*, *graunten*; OFr. *granter*, *graanter*, *craanter*, to promise, assure, yield; LL. *creantare*, to promise, yield, from L. *credens* (*-entis*), ppr. of *credere*, to believe.]

1. To admit as true; to allow; to yield; to concede; as, we take that for *granted* which is supposed to be true.

2. To give; to bestow or confer on without compensation, particularly in answer to prayer or request.

> God *granted* him that which he requested
> —1 Chron. iv. 10.

3. To transfer (the title of a thing) to another, for a good or valuable consideration; to convey by deed or writing; as, the legislature has *granted* all the new land.

grȧnt, *v.i.* To consent. [Obs.]

grȧnt, *n.* [OFr. *grant*, *graant*, a promise, assurance, grant, from *granter*, *graanter*, to promise, assure, grant.]

1. The act of granting; a bestowing or conferring.

2. The thing granted or bestowed; a gift; a boon; the thing conveyed by deed or patent.

3. In law, (a) a conveyance in writing of such things as cannot pass or be transferred by word only, as land, rents, reversions, tithes, etc.; (b) the instrument of such conveyance.

> A *grant* is an executed contract.—Z. Swift.

4. That which is granted or conceded; concession; admission of something as true.

> This *grant* destroys all you have urg'd before.
> —Dryden.

5. A vessel used in the process of brewing.

Syn.—Present, gift, boon, allowance, stipend.

grȧnt′ȧ-ble, *a.* That may be granted or conveyed.

grȧn-tee′, *n.* The person to whom a conveyance is made.

grȧnt′ẽr, *n.* One who grants.

grȧnt′ŏr, *n.* In law, the person who grants; one who conveys land, rents, etc.

gran′ū-lăr, *a.* [LL. *granulum*, dim. of L. *granum*, a grain.]
1. Consisting of grains; as, a *granular* substance.
2. Resembling grains; as, a stone of *granular* appearance.
Granular limestone; a limestone or marble having a crystalline, granular texture.

gran′ū-lăr-ly, *adv.* In a granular form.

gran′ū-lā-ry, *n.* Granular

gran′ū-lāte, *v.t.*; granulated, *pt.*, *pp.*; granulating, *ppr.* [L. *granum*, a grain.]
1. To form into grains or small masses; as, to *granulate* powder or sugar.
2. To raise in small asperities; to make rough on the surface.

gran′ū-lāte, *v.i.* To collect or be formed into grains; as, cane-juice *granulates* into sugar; melted metals *granulate* when poured into water.

gran′ū-lāte, gran′ū-lā-ted, *a.* Having numerous small elevations, like shagreen; consisting of grains; having the form of grains; granular.
Granulated steel; a kind of steel resulting from a process in which pig-iron is granulated to furnish the basis of the steel.

gran-ū-lā′tion, *n.* 1. The act of forming into grains; as, the *granulation* of powder or sugar.
2. The state of being crystallized or formed into grains.
3. In pathology, (a) tissue-formation in the natural repair of wounds; (b) [*pl.*] small, grainlike protuberances which form on the surface of ulcers and in suppurating sores, and which serve to fill up the cavity and unite the sides; (c) one of the elevations in a granulated surface.

gran′ūle, *n.* [LL. *granulum*, dim. of L. *granum*, a grain.] A minute grain; a particle.

gran-ū-lif′ẽr-ous, *a.* [LL. *granulum*, a little grain, and L. *ferre*, to bear.] Made up of granulations.

gra-nū′li-fọrm, *a.* [LL. *granulum*, a small grain, and L. *forma*, form.] In mining, having a granular texture.

gran′ū-līte, *n.* A whitish stone composed of feldspar and quartz.

gran-ū-lō′mȧ, *n.* [LL. *granulum*, a small grain, and Gr. *-ōma*, tumor.] In pathology, a diseased growth the tissue of which resembles granulations.

gran′ū-lōse, *a.* Same as *Granular*.

gran′ū-lōse, *n.* In chemistry, the principal part of starch as distinguished from *cellulose*, the other part. *Granulose* is turned into sugar by certain ferments, and turns blue when subjected to iodine.

gran′ū-lous, *a.* Full of granules; granular.

grāpe, *n.* [OFr. *grape*, *grappe*, a bunch or cluster of grapes, from O.H.G. *chrapho*, a hook, clasp.]
1. Properly, a cluster of the fruit of the vine, but commonly a single berry of the vine; the fruit from which wine is made by expression and fermentation.
2. The cascabel or knob at the butt of a cannon.
3. [*pl.*] In farriery, a mangy tumor on the leg of a horse.
4. Grapeshot.
Chicken grape; a small species of wild grape, *Vitis cordifolia*.
Native grape; an evergreen climbing plant of Australia bearing grapes, *Vitis hypoglauca*.
Sour grapes; things despised because they are beyond one's reach. The phrase is borrowed from Æsop's fable of the fox and the grapes.
Summer grape; a grape, *Vitis æstivalis*, that grows wild in the eastern part of North America.

grāpe′=bōr″ẽr, *n.* Same as *Vine-borer*.

grāpe′=cūr-cū″li-ō, *n.* A small black weevil whose larva is destructive to the fruit of the grape.

grāpe′=cūre, *n.* The steady and exclusive use of grapes as a cure for disease.

grāpe′=dis-ēase″, *n.* A consumptive disease of cattle.

grāpe′=fẽrn, *n.* A thick, fleshy fern, belonging to the genus *Botrychium*.

grāpe′flow″ẽr, *n.* *Muscari racemosum*, a garden plant with grapelike clusters of dark blue flowers which have an odor like that of starch; also called *grape-hyacinth*.

grāpe′fruit, *n.* A small variety of the shaddock.

grāpe′=fun″gus, *n.* A mildew that forms on grapevines.

grāpe′=hop″pẽr, *n.* *Erythroneura vitis*, attacking grape leaves.

grāpe′=hȳ″ȧ-cinth, *n.* See *Grapeflower*.

grāpe′less, *a.* Wanting the strength and flavor of the grape.

grāpe′=mọth, *n.* Any moth, as *Eudemis botrana*, the larva of which subsists upon the interior of grapes.

grāp′ẽr-y, *n.*; *pl.* **grāp′ẽr-ies**. A building or inclosure used for the rearing of grapes.

grāpe′shot, *n.* A missile discharged from a cannon intermediate between case-shot and solid shot, having much of the destructive spread of the former with somewhat of the range and penetrative force of the latter. A round of *grapeshot* consists of three tiers of cast-iron balls arranged, generally three in a tier, between four parallel iron disks connected together by a central wrought-iron pin.

Grapeshot.

grāpe′stōne, *n.* A seed of the grape.

grāpe′=sụ″găr (-shụ″găr), *n.* See *Dextrose*.

grāpe′vīne, *n.* The vine which yields the grape.

grāpe′=wọ̈rm, *n.* The larva of the grape-moth.

-graph. A suffix from Gr. *graphē*, a writing or drawing, from *graphein*, to write or draw, used in words of Greek origin or those similarly formed to signify that which writes, draws, or describes, or that which is written or drawn, as tele*graph*, auto*graph*.

graph, *n.* [Gr. *graphē*, a writing, a representation, from *graphein*, to write, draw, represent by lines.] In chemistry, and sometimes in algebra and logic, a diagram representing any system of relationship by means of a number of spots and lines.

graph′iç, graph′iç-ăl, *a.* [L. *graphicus*; Gr. *graphikos*, lit., belonging to painting or drawing, picturesque, writing, from *graphē*, a drawing, a writing, from *graphein*, to represent by means of lines, write.]
1. Pertaining to the art of writing, delineating, or describing.
2. Written; drawn; inscribed; well or plainly delineated.
3. Described with vivid and clear language; vividly or forcibly described; as, a *graphic* description.
4. Having the power or faculty of describing things impressively or clearly; as, a *graphic* writer.
5. Indicating by diagrams or drawings to scale, instead of by mathematical calculations.
Graphic algebra; a branch of algebra in which the relations of quantities are expressed by means of curves and straight lines.
Graphical method; any method involving the use of the relations between the parts of a diagram to indicate the relations between or among objects.
Graphical statics; a method of determining the strength of structures by diagrammatic measurements made to scale.
Graphic arts; arts such as drawing, painting, and engraving, which involve the use of lines or strokes to set forth a concept.
Graphic formula; see under *Formula*.
Graphic tellurium; sylvanite.
Syn.—Picturesque, illustrative, descriptive, pictorial, forcible, vivid.

graph′iç-ăl-ly, *adv.* In a graphic manner.

graph′iç-ăl-ness, *n.* The condition or quality of being graphic.

graph′iç-ness, *n.* Graphicalness.

graph′iċs, *n.* The art or science of drawing; especially of mechanical drawing.

graph-i-ol′ō-ġy, *n.* [Gr. *grapheion*, a style, pencil, and *-logia*, from *legein*, to speak.] The art of writing or delineating; a treatise on that art.

graph′īte, *n.* [Gr. *graphē*, a writing, from *graphein*, to write, draw, and *-ite*.] One of the forms under which carbon occurs in nature; also known as *plumbago* and *blacklead*. It has an iron-gray color, metallic luster, granular texture, and is soft and unctuous to the touch. It is used chiefly in the manufacture of pencils, crucibles, and portable furnaces, for burnishing iron to protect it from rust and for counteracting friction between the rubbing surfaces of wood or metal in machinery.

gra-phit′iç, *a.* Relating to, containing, or derived from graphite.
Graphitic acid; same as *Mellitic acid*.
Graphitic carbon; carbon found in iron or steel which is considered to be graphite.

graph′i-toid, graph-i-toid′ăl, *a.* [Gr. *graphē*, a writing, and *eidos*, form.] Resembling graphite or plumbago.

graph-o-. A combining form from Gr. *graphē*, a writing, drawing, from *graphein*, to write, draw, used in words of Greek origin to signify writing, drawing, or for writing or drawing.

graph′ō-līte, *n.* [*Grapho-*, and Gr. *lithos*, a stone.] A species of slate suitable for writing on.

gra-phol′ō-ġy, *n.* [*Grapho-*, and Gr. *-logia*, from *legein*, to speak.] The science of handwriting as indicative of the writer's character.

graph-om′e-tẽr, *n.* [*Grapho-*, and Gr. *metron*, a measure.] A surveyor's instrument for measuring angles.

graph-ō-met′riç, graph-ō-met′riç-ăl, *a.* Pertaining to or ascertained by a graphometer.

graph′ō-phōne, *n.* [*Grapho-*, and Gr. *phōnē*, sound.] An instrument for recording and reproducing sounds; a form of phonograph.

graph-ō-phon′iç, *a.* Relating to the graphophone.

graph′ō-sçōpe, *n.* [*Grapho-*, and Gr. *skopein*, to view.] An optical apparatus for magnifying and giving fine effects to engravings, photographs, etc.

graph′ō-tȳpe, *n.* [*Grapho-*, and Gr. *typos*, an impression.] A process of making blocks for surface-printing. Drawings are made on blocks of chalk with a silicious ink. When dried, the soft parts are brushed away, and the drawing remains in relief. Stereotypes are then taken from the block. In a later form of the process the chalk block is superseded by a zinc plate covered with finely-powdered French chalk, brought to a hard and firm texture by enormous pressure.

-gra-phy. A suffix from L. *-graphia*; Gr. *-graphia*, writing or drawing, from *graphein*, to represent by means of lines, to write, draw, used in compound words of Gr. origin to signify a writing, drawing, description, discourse, science, as bio*graphy*, geo*graphy*.

grap′nel, *n.* [ME. *grapenel*, *grapinel*; OFr. *grapin*, *grappin*, a grapnel, dim. of *grappe*, a hook.]
1. A small anchor, fitted with four or five flukes or claws, used to hold boats or small vessels.
2. A grappling-iron, used to seize and hold one ship to another in engagements preparatory to boarding.
3. Any device for grasping or holding.

Grapnel.

grap′ple, *n.* [OFr. *grappil*, the grapple on a ship, dim. of *grappe*, a cluster of grapes, from O.H.G. *chrapho*, a hook.]
1. A seizing; close hug in contest; the wrestler's hold.
2. A hook or iron instrument by which one ship fastens on another.
3. Any device for seizing or grasping, as a pair of tongs for lifting blocks of ice.

grap′ple, *v.t.*; grappled, *pt.*, *pp.*; grappling, *ppr.* To seize; to lay fast hold on, either with the hands or with mechanical devices; as, to *grapple* an assailant.

grap′ple, *v.i.* To seize; to contend in close fight, as wrestlers; to clinch; often used figuratively; as, to *grapple* with a problem.

grap′ple-ment, *n.* A grappling. [Obs.]

grap′ple=plant, *n.* *Harpagophytum*, or *Uncaria procumbens*, a South African plant of the natural order *Pedaliaceæ*. Its seed-vessel is provided with claw-like appendages.

grap′ple=shot, *n.* A shot provided with hinged flukes, and attached to a cable. It is used in the life-saving service.

grap′pling, *n.* 1. The act of seizing or laying fast hold on.
2. That by which anything is seized and held.
3. A grapple; a struggle.

grap′pling=ī″ron (-ūrn), *n.* An instrument consisting of several iron claws for grappling and holding fast.

grap′pling=toṅgs, *n.pl.* Oyster-tongs.

grap′soid, *a.* and *n.* [Gr. *grapsaios*, a crab, and *eidos*, resemblance.]
I. *a.* Relating to the family *Grapsidæ*.
II. *n.* A crab of the family *Grapsidæ*.

grap′tō-līte, *n.* [Gr. *graptos*, marked, written, and *lithos*, a stone.] A fossil hydrozoön of the genus *Graptolites*, found in the Silurian rocks.

Block of Stone containing Graptolites.

grap-tō-lit′iç, *a.* Of, belonging to, produced by, or containing graptolites.

grāp′y, *a.* Pertaining to, composed of, or resembling grapes.

grä′sō, *n.* [Etym. unknown.] In zoölogy, the finback whale, *Eschrichtius robustus*.

gråsp, *v.t.*; grasped, *pt.*, *pp.*; grasping, *ppr.* [ME. *graspen*, *grapen*, *grapien*, from AS. *grapian*, to grasp, from *grap*, the grasp of the hand.]
1. To seize and hold by clasping or embracing with the fingers or arms.
2. To seize by the intellect; to comprehend; as, to *grasp* the question.
Syn.—Capture, catch, clutch, comprehend, seize.

gråsp, *v.i.* To seize or grip firmly; to attempt to seize.
To grasp at; to catch at; to try to seize.

gråsp, *n.* 1. The grip or seizure of the hand; also, a seizure by embrace or infolding in the arms.
2. Possession; hold.
3. Reach of the arm; figuratively, the power of seizing; as, Bonaparte seemed to think he had the Russian empire within his *grasp*.
4. The part of a thing to be held or grasped; as, the *grasp* of a sword or of a fishing-rod.

gråsp′ȧ-ble, *a.* That may be grasped.

gråsp′ẽr, *n.* One who grasps or seizes; one who catches at; one who holds.

gråsp′ing, *a.* 1. Seizing; embracing; holding.
2. Greedy; miserly; avaricious.

grȧsp′ing-ly, *adv.* 1. In an eager, grasping manner.

2. Greedily; avariciously.

grȧsp′ing-ness, *n.* The state or quality of being grasping.

grȧsp′less, *a.* Lacking the power of grasping; as, a *graspless* hand.

grȧss, *n.* [ME. *gras, gres*; AS. *græs*, grass, herbage.]

1. In common usage, herbage; the plants which constitute the food of cattle and other beasts.

2. In botany, a plant having simple leaves, a stem generally jointed and tubular or with a cork-like interior, a husky calyx, called glume, and the seed single, including wheat, rye, oats, barley, etc., and excluding clover and some other plants which are commonly called by the name of *grass*.

3. Figuratively, an emblem of the brevity of life; as, his days are as *grass*.

4. In mining, the surface at the mine. [Eng.]

5. In the United States, the season of spring-ing *grass*; spring.

Bahama grass; same as *Bermuda-grass*.

Black-seed grass; a tropical grass, *Sporobolus Indicus*, found in southern United States.

Dog's-tail grass; a European grass, *Cynosurus cristatus*, valuable for its straw.

Grass of Parnassus; a plant of the genus *Parnassia* of the saxifrage family.

Hungarian grass; same as *Bengal-grass*.

Italian rye-grass; *Lolium Italicum*, cultivated for hay and pasture.

To bring to grass; in mining, to bring to the surface of the ground at the mouth of a shaft; said of ore hoisted from a mine.

To go to grass; (a) to go to pasture; said of a horse worn out by work; (b) an expression of contempt and impatience when used imperatively; (c) in prize-fighting, to be disabled temporarily. [Slang.]

To let the grass grow under one's feet; to waste time and opportunity; to procrastinate; to be slow.

grȧss, *v.t.*; grassed (grȧst), *pt.*, *pp.*; grassing, *ppr.* 1. To furnish with grass; as, to *grass* a lawn; to *grass* cattle.

2. To spread out upon grass, as linen for bleaching.

3. To bring to the ground by angling or shooting; as, to *grass* a fish or a bird.

4. In archery, to lose; as, the last arrow was *grassed*.

grȧss, *v.i.* To produce grass; to be clothed with grass. [Rare.]

grȧs-sā′tion, *n.* [L. *grassatio (-onis)*, a rioting, from *grassatus*, pp. of *grassari*, to wander about.] A restless wandering about, especially with evil intent; activity. [Rare.]

grȧss′-bȧss, *n.* A fish, the calico bass; the crappie.

grȧss′-bīrd, *n.* A sandpiper.

grȧss′chat, *n.* A bird, the whinchat.

grȧss′-clọth, *n.* A cloth made out of tough grass fibers.

Grass-cloth plant; a plant of the nettle family furnishing fiber for making grass-cloth.

grȧss′-em-broid′ẽr-y, *n.* A fabric made by American Indians out of dried grasses.

grȧss′-finch, *n.* A kind of sparrow, *Poöcætes gramineus*.

grȧss′-fish″ing, *n.* A method of fishing in which the hook is concealed under a spreading bright covering and agitated so as to attract the fish.

grȧss′-green, *a.* 1. Of the bright, fresh green color of grass.

2. Green with grass.

grȧss′-grōwn, *a.* Overgrown with grass.

grȧss′hop″pẽr, *n.* [ME. *grashopper*; AS. *græshoppa, gærshoppa*, a grasshopper; *græs*, grass, and *hoppa*, a hopper, from *hoppian*, to hop, leap.]

1. A saltatorial orthopterous insect, family *Gryllidæ*, characterized by very long and slender legs, the thighs of the hinder legs being large and adapted to leaping, by large and delicate wings, and by the wing-covers extending far beyond the extremity of the abdomen. Grasshoppers form an extensive group of insects, and are distinguished by the power which they possess of leaping to a considerable distance, and by the stridulous or chirping noise the males produce by rubbing their wing-covers together. They are nearly allied to the locust tribe.

2. The connecting-lever in a pianoforte communicating motion from the key to the hammer.

grȧss′hop″pẽr-en″ġine, *n.* A steam-engine having a walking-beam with the fulcrum at one end and the piston-rod at the other, its form suggesting a huge grasshopper.

grȧss′hop″pẽr-lärk, grȧss′hop″pẽr-wär″blẽr, *n.* A small song-bird of Europe, particularly *Locustella nævia*.

grȧss′i-ness, *n.* The state of abounding with grass; a grassy state.

grȧss′-lamb, *n.* A lamb that follows its dam to pasture.

grȧss′-land, *n.* Land kept for perennial pasturage.

grȧss′less, *a.* Destitute of grass.

grȧss′-mọth, *n.* A moth, found in grass, of the genus *Crambus*.

grȧss′nut, *n.* The edible root of a sedge, *Cyperus repens*.

grȧss′-oil, *n.* An essential oil made in the East, extracted from odorous grasses.

grȧss′-owl, *n.* A bird, *Strix capensis*, of South Africa.

grȧss′-pȧr′rȧ-keet, *n.* A variety of Australian parrot, belonging to the genus *Euphemia*.

grȧss′-pick′ẽr-el, *n.* The small western pickerel. [U. S.]

grȧss′plot, grȧss′plat, *n.* A plot or level spot covered with grass.

grȧss′-plŏv′ẽr, *n.* In ornithology, the plover found in uplands.

grȧss′pol-y, *n.* A plant, a species of *Lythrum* or willowwort.

grȧss′-pōr″ġy, *n.* A fish of the genus *Calamus*, found in the eelgrass of southern Florida.

grȧss′-quit, *n.* Any of the finches of the genus *Euetheia*, found in the American tropics and the West Indies.

grȧss′-snāke, *n.* In zoölogy, any of several species of the group *Colubrina*, venomous or nonvenomous, including the European ringed snake and the green snake of northern United States.

grȧss′-snīpe, *n.* The pectoral sandpiper, *Tringa maculata*.

grȧss′-spī″dẽr, *n.* A spider, *Agalena nævia*, which spins a flat web among grass-stems.

grȧss′-spŏnġe, *n.* A coarse, flat sponge found off the coast of Florida and in the West Indian islands; called also the *honeycomb-sponge*.

grȧss′-tree, *n.* An Australian plant of the genus *Xanthorrhœa*; also called *blackboy-tree*.

grȧss′-vetch, *n.* A plant, *Lathyrus Nissolia*, so called from its grasslike leaves.

grȧss′-wid″ōw, *n.* 1. An unmarried woman who is a mother. [Obs.]

2. A woman living apart or temporarily separated from her husband. [Colloq.]

grȧss′-wid″ōw-ẽr, *n.* A man living apart or temporarily separated from his wife. [Colloq.]

grȧss′-wrack (-rak), *n.* A plant, *Zostera marina*; eelgrass or sea-wrack, found on the seacoast.

grȧss′y, *a.* 1. Covered with grass; abounding with grass; as, *grassy* fields; *grassy* foreground.

2. Resembling grass; green.

grāte, *n.* [ME. *grate*, a trellis, lattice; LL. *grata, crata*; L. *cratis*, a hurdle, a kind of basket.]

1. A work or frame composed of parallel or crossbars, with interstices; a kind of latticework, such as is used in the windows of prisons and cloisters; a grating.

2. An instrument or frame of iron bars in which coal or other fuel is burned; as, an open *grate*.

3. In metallurgy, a sieve for screening ores.

Grate surface; in steam-boilers, the area of a grate available for fuel.

grāte, *a.* Tending to gratify; agreeable. [Obs.]

grāte, *v.t.*; grated, *pt.*, *pp.*; grating, *ppr.* [ME. *graten*; OFr. *grater*; LL. *gratare*, to scrape, scratch, from O.H.G. *chrazzon*, to scrape, scratch.]

1. To rub, as a body with a rough surface against another body; to rub, as one thing against another so as to produce a harsh sound; as, to *grate* the teeth.

2. To wear away in small particles, by rubbing with anything rough or indented; as, to *grate* a nutmeg.

3. To offend; to fret; to vex; to irritate; to mortify; as, harsh words *grate* the heart.

grāte, *v.t.* To furnish with grates; to make fast with crossbars; as, to *grate* a transom or window.

grāte, *v.i.* 1. To rub hard, so as to offend; to offend by oppression or importunity; as, to *grate* upon the ear.

2. To make a harsh sound by the friction of rough bodies.

grāt′ed, *a.* 1. Rubbed harshly; worn off by rubbing; ground to a powder or pulp; as, *grated* horseradish.

2. Protected by a grate; furnished with grates; as, a *grated* aperture.

grāte′ful, *a.* [L. *gratus*, pleasing, agreeable, and *-ful*.]

1. Having a due sense of benefits; kindly disposed toward one from whom a favor has been received; willing to acknowledge and repay benefits; as, a *grateful* heart.

2. Agreeable; pleasing; acceptable; gratifying; pleasing to the taste; delicious; affording pleasure; as, food or drink *grateful* to the appetite; a *grateful* shower of rain.

Syn.—Thankful, agreeable, pleasant, refreshing.

grāte′ful-ly, *adv.* In a grateful, pleasing, or agreeable manner; with gratitude or thankfulness.

grāte′ful-ness, *n.* The state or quality of being grateful; gratitude.

grāt′ẽr, *n.* 1. An instrument or utensil with a rough, indented surface, for rubbing off small particles of a body; as, a *grater* for nutmegs.

2. In bookbinding, an implement for treating the backs of sewed and pasted books.

grā′ti-āte (-shi-), *v.t.* To favor; to prefer. [Obs.]

grȧ-tiç′ū-lāte, *v.t.*; graticulated, *pt.*, *pp.*; graticulating, *ppr.* To divide into squares, giving the appearance of grating.

grȧ-tiç-ū-lā′tion, *n.* The division of a design or draught into squares, for the purpose of reducing to smaller, or enlarging to greater dimensions.

grat′i-cūle, *n.* [Fr. *graticule, craticule*, from L. *craticula*, dim. of *cratis*, a hurdle, wickerwork.] A graticulated design, draught, or plan.

grat″i-fi-cā′tion, *n.* [L. *gratificatio (-onis)*, from *gratificare, gratificari*, to gratify, please.]

1. The act of pleasing, either the mind, the taste, or the appetite; as, the *gratification* of a desire for excitement.

2. That which affords pleasure; satisfaction; delight; as, an accustomed *gratification*.

3. Reward; recompense.

Syn.—Enjoyment, satisfaction, comfort, happiness.

grat′i-fīed, *a.* Pleased; indulged according to desire; as, a *gratified* spectator.

grat′i-fī-ẽr, *n.* One who gratifies or pleases.

grat′i-fȳ, *v.t.*; gratified, *pt.*, *pp.*; gratifying, *ppr.* [Fr. *gratifier*; L. *gratificare, gratificari*, to oblige, please, favor; *gratus*, pleasing, agreeable, and *facere*, to make.]

1. To please; to give pleasure to; to indulge; as, to *gratify* the taste, the appetite, the senses, the desires, the mind; also, to delight; to please; to humor; to soothe; to satisfy; to indulge to satisfaction; as, to *gratify* a child.

2. To requite; to recompense. [Rare.]

Syn.—Indulge, humor, satisfy, please, satiate.—*Gratify* has reference simply to the pleasure communicated; to *indulge* a person implies that something is conceded which he could not claim, and which had better, perhaps, have been spared; to *humor* is to adapt oneself to the varying moods and perhaps caprices of others.

grat′i-fȳ-ing, *a.* Giving pleasure; affording satisfaction; as, a *gratifying* spectacle.

grat′i-fȳ-ing-ly, *adv.* In a gratifying manner.

grāt′ing, *a.* Fretting; irritating; harsh; as, *grating* sounds or a *grating* reflection.

grāt′ing, *n.* 1. A harsh sound or rubbing.

2. A partition of bars, or latticework of wood or iron; as, the *grating* of a prison or convent.

3. An open cover for the hatches of a ship, resembling latticework; the movable floor of a boat.

4. In optics, same as *diffraction grating* under *Diffraction*.

5. In bookbinding, the act of smoothing the back of a sewed and pasted book.

grāt′ing-ly, *adv.* In a grating manner; harshly; offensively.

Grȧ-tī′ō-lȧ, *n.* In botany, a genus of plants of the figwort family, several species of which are native to the United States. The best-known species, *Gratiola officinalis*, hedge-hyssop, is used in medicine.

grȧ-tī′ō-lin, *n.* [L. *gratia*, grace, favor, and *-olin*.] In chemistry, a compound derived from *Gratiola officinalis*, hedge-hyssop.

grā′tis, *adv.* [L., from *gratia*, favor, kindness.] For nothing; freely; without recompense; as, to give a thing *gratis*.

grat′i-tūde, *n.* [Fr. *gratitude*; LL. *gratitudo*, thankfulness, gratitude, from L. *gratus*, pleasing, thankful.] A warm and friendly feeling excited by a favor or benefit received; a sentiment of kindness or good-will to a benefactor, and a disposition to make a suitable return of benefits or services, or, when no return can be made, a desire to see the benefactor prosperous and happy; thankfulness; gratefulness.

grȧ-tū′i-tous, *a.* [L. *gratuitus*, done without pay or profit, free, from *gratia*, favor, kindness.]

1. Free; voluntary; not required by justice; granted without compensation, claim, or merit.

2. Not required, called for, or warranted by the circumstances; made or done without sufficient cause or reason; asserted or taken without proof; as, a *gratuitous* affirmation; a *gratuitous* insult.

grȧ-tū′i-tous-ly, *adv.* In a gratuitous manner; without an equivalent or compensation; without sufficient cause or reason.

grȧ-tū′i-ty, *n.*; *pl.* **grȧ-tū′i-ties.** [OFr. *gratuite*; LL. *gratuitas*, a free gift, from L. *gratuitus*, free, freely done.]

1. A free gift; a present; a donation; that which is given without a compensation or equivalent.

2. Something given in return for service or a favor; an acknowledgment.

grat′ū-lānt, *a.* [L. *gratulans (-antis)*, ppr. of *gratulari*, to wish one joy.] Congratulatory. [Rare.]

grat′ū-lāte, *v.t.* To congratulate. [Rare.]

grat′ū-lāte, *v.i.* To express gratification. [Obs.]

grat′ū-lāte, *a.* Causing gratification. [Obs.]

grat-ū-lā′tion, *n.* Congratulation.

grat′ū-là-tō-ry, *a.* Congratulatory.

grau′wăck-ē (grou′väk-ē), *n.* [G.] See *Graywacke.*

grà-vā′men, *n.* [LL., lit., a burden, trouble, from L. *gravare*, to weigh down, from *gravis*, heavy.] In law, the grievance complained of; the substantial cause of the action.

-grave. A suffix signifying a nobleman, as an earl or a count; hence, a ruler, as, a land*grave.*

grāve, *v.t.*; graved, *pt.*; graving, *ppr.*; graved or graven, *pp.* [ME. *graven*; AS. *grafan*, to dig, bury, carve.]

1. To carve or cut (letters or figures) on, as on stone or other hard substance, with a chisel or edged tool; to engrave.

2. To carve; to form or shape by cutting with a chisel; as, to *grave* an image.

3. To clean, as a ship's bottom, by scraping or burning and paying it over with pitch.

4. To put into a grave; to entomb. [Rare.]

5. Figuratively, to make a deep and lasting impression on; as, *grave* it on the tablets of thy memory.

grāve, *v.i.* To carve; to write or delineate on hard substances; to practise engraving.

grāve, *a.*; *comp.* graver; *superl.* gravest. [L. *gravis*, heavy, weighty.]

1. Solemn; sober; serious; opposed to *gay, light*, or *jovial*; as, a man of *grave* deportment; a *grave* and reverend senator.

2. Plain; not gay; not showy or tawdry; as, a *grave* suit of clothes.

3. Important; momentous; having a serious and interesting import; as, the *grave* affairs of life.

4. In acoustics, of low pitch; opposed to *acute*; in music, slow in movement and solemn in character.

Syn.—Sober, serious, solemn, important, sedate, thoughtful, weighty.—*Sober* supposes the absence of all exhilaration of spirits; *serious* implies considerateness or reflection; *grave* denotes a state of mind, appearance, etc., which results from the pressure of weighty interests; *solemn* is applied to a case in which gravity is carried to its highest point.

grāve, *n.* [ME. *grave, grafe*; AS. *græf, graf*, a trench, a grave, from *grafan*, to dig.]

1. A pit or place excavated for the burial of a dead body; a place for a corpse to be deposited; a tomb; a sepulcher.

2. Figuratively, death; destruction; a place or cause of extinction or loss; as, Russia was the *grave* of Napoleon's army; gambling is the *grave* of his fortune.

3. In the Bible, the abode of the dead; Sheol; Hades.

Syn.—Tomb, sepulcher.—*Grave* has reference to the hollow made in the earth; *tomb* refers to the rising that is made above it; *sepulcher* suggests the use for which it is employed.

grāve′clōtheṣ, *n.pl.* The clothes or dress in which the dead are interred.

grāve′dig″gẽr, *n.* 1. One whose occupation is to dig graves.

2. Same as *Burying-beetle.*

3. In Jamaica, an insect of the genus *Sphex*, which digs holes in the clay, in which it deposits its egg, with a store of disabled caterpillars and spiders, as food for the grub when hatched.

grav′el, *n.* [OFr. *gravele, gravelle*, gravel, from *grave*, gravel, sand.]

1. Small stones, fragments of stone, or very small pebbles, larger than the particles of sand, but often intermixed with them.

2. In medicine, a disease produced by small, calculous concretions in the kidneys and bladder.

Gravel powder; a large-grained gunpowder.

grav′el, *v.t.*; graveled *or* gravelled, *pt., pp.*; graveling *or* gravelling, *ppr.* 1. To cover with gravel; as, to *gravel* a walk.

2. To stick in the sand, as a ship; to run aground.

3. To puzzle; to stop; to embarrass.

4. To hurt the foot of, as a horse, by gravel lodged under the shoe.

grāve′less, *a.* Without a grave; unburied.

grav′el-ing, *n.* 1. The act of covering with gravel.

2. A covering of gravel.

3. A young salmon.

grav′el-li-ness, grav′el-i-ness, *n.* A gravelly condition.

grav′el-ly, grav′el-y, *a.* Abounding with gravel; consisting of gravel; as, a *gravelly* soil or land.

grav′el-ro͝ot, *n.* In botany, (a) *Eupatorium purpureum*, the joepye-weed; (b) *Collinsonia Canadensis*, the horse-balm. Also called *stone-root.*

grav′el-stōne, *n.* A calculus; a pebble.

grāve′ly, *adv.* In a grave, solemn manner.

grāv′en, *v.*, past participle of *grave.*

Graven image; an image carved or shaped artificially and adored as an object of worship; an idol.

grāve′ness, *n.* Seriousness; solemnity; sobriety; the quality of being grave.

grā′ven-stein, *n.* [Named after *Gravenstein*, in Schleswig.] An excellent variety of apple, streaked with red and orange.

grà-vē′ō-lence, *n.* A rank smell. [Rare.]

grà-vē′ō-lent, *a.* [L. *graveolens (-entis)*, strong-smelling; *gravis*, heavy, and *olens (-entis)*, ppr. of *olere*, to smell.] Of a rank odor. [Rare.]

grāv′ẽr, *n.* [ME. *graver, grafer*; AS. *græfere*, a graver, carver, from *grafan*, to dig, grave, carve.]

1. One who carves or engraves; one whose occupation is to cut letters or figures in stone, etc.; a sculptor.

Graver, and mode in which it is held.

2. An engraving-tool; an instrument for graving.

grāv′ẽr-y, *n.* Engraving.

grāveṣ, grēaveṣ, *n.pl.* The residue of fatty tissues left after rendering; called also *cracklings.*

grāve′stōne, *n.* A tombstone.

grāve′yärd, *n.* A yard or inclosure for the interment of the dead; a cemetery.

grav′ic, *a.* Relating to gravitation. [Rare.]

grav′id, *a.* [L. *gravidus*, pregnant, from *gravis*, heavy.] Pregnant; being with child.

grav′i-dā-ted, *a.* Made pregnant; big. [Obs.]

grav-i-dā′tion, *n.* Pregnancy. [Obs.]

grà-vid′i-ty, *n.* Pregnancy. [Obs.]

grav′i-grāde, *a.* [L. *gravis*, heavy, and *gradi*, to walk.] Heavy-footed; of slow movement.

grav′i-grāde, *n.* An animal that walks heavily.

grà-vim′e-tẽr, *n.* [L. *gravis*, heavy, and *metrum*, a measure.] An instrument for ascertaining the specific gravity of bodies, solid or liquid.

grav-i-met′riç, *a.* Relating to weight measurement.

Gravimetric analysis; in chemistry, a kind of analysis distinguished from *volumetric analysis*; a determination of composition by weight.

grav-i-met′riç-ăl-ly, *adv.* In a gravimetric manner.

grāv′ing, *n.* 1. Cleaning a ship's bottom.

2. Carving or cutting, as in sculpturing.

Graving dock; see *Dock*, n. 2.

grāv′ing-piēce, *n.* In shipbuilding, a new piece of wood inserted to repair a damage.

grav′i-tāte, *v.i.*; gravitated, *pt., pp.*; gravitating, *ppr.* [L. *gravitas (-atis)*, heaviness, from *gravis*, heavy.]

1. To be attracted according to the law of gravitation; as, all bodies *gravitate* toward all other bodies.

2. Hence, to have a strong tendency toward a place or condition; as, incapacity *gravitates* toward paternalism.

grav-i-tā′tion, *n.* 1. The act or effect of gravitating.

2. A force in virtue of which every particle of matter tends to approach every other particle in the universe. Newton's *law of gravitation* is that every body or portion of matter attracts and is attracted directly as its quantity of matter, and inversely as the square of its distance from the attracting body.

3. Figuratively, an intellectual or spiritual attraction or tendency toward some condition, activity, or personality.

Attraction of gravitation; that force existing between bodies in the mass, and acting at sensible distances. It is thus distinguished from chemical and cohesive attractions, which unite the particles of bodies together, and act at insensible distances or distances too small to be measured.

grav-i-tā′tion-ăl, *a.* Of, due to, or relating to gravitation; as, *gravitational* impulses.

grav′i-tā-tive, *a.* Inclined to gravitate; due to or yielding to gravitation.

grav′i-ty, *n.* [L. *gravitas (-atis)*, weight, heaviness, from *gravis*, heavy.]

1. Weight; the accelerating force upon any falling mass produced by the earth's attraction; the property of weight as distinguished from mass; heaviness; as, the *gravity* of a stone.

2. In physics, terrestrial gravitation; the force which draws everything toward the center of mass of the earth.

3. Seriousness; sobriety of manners; solemnity of deportment or character.

4. Seriousness; great significance; as, the *gravity* of the situation demands action.

5. In music, lowness of pitch in a tone.

Center of gravity; see under *Center.*

Gravity cell; see under *Cell.*

Specific gravity; the ratio between the weight of a body and the weight of an equal volume of the recognized standard.

grā′vy, *n.* 1. The juices of meat brought out in the process of cooking, often mixed with flour, etc., to form a dressing.

2. A dressing for various kinds of meats and other dishes.

grāy, grey, *a.* [ME. *gray, grey*; AS. *græg*, gray.]

1. Having the color of a mixture of black and white; of the color of wood-ashes or of dark hair turning white.

2. Hoary; having gray hairs; gray-headed.

3. Old; mature; as, *gray* experience.

Gray antimony; stibnite.

Gray cobalt; smaltite.

Gray copper; tetrahedrite.

Gray Friar; a Franciscan.

Gray matter; the matter of a grayish color forming the interior part of the nerve-tissues in the cerebrospinal system of nerves, especially that in the brain.

Gray snapper; a fish, the mangrove-snapper.

Gray snipe; the dowitcher.

Gray whale; a whale of the genus *Rachianectes*, formerly common along the California coast.

grāy, grey, *n.* 1. A gray color; a dull or neutral tint; a mixture of black and white.

2. Anything of a gray color, as (a) a badger; (b) a gray duck; (c) a gray horse; (d) a species of salmon; (e) the gray whale; (f) a gray uniform, etc.

3. The twilight of the morning or evening; as, the *gray* of the morning.

grāy, grey, *v.t.*; grayed, *pt., pp.*; graying, *ppr.* To render gray, as the surface of glass by removing the polish; specifically, to print (a photograph) with a ground glass over the negative.

grāy, *v.i.* To become gray; to age.

grāy′back, *n.* Anything having a gray back, as (a) the gray snipe; (b) the gray whale; (c) the red-headed duck; (d) the black-headed duck; (e) an Irish fish, the dab; (f) a body-louse; (g) the red-breasted sandpiper.

grāy′bēard, *n.* 1. A man with a gray beard; an old man.

2. A stoneware drinking-jug brought into use in the sixteenth century, which had a bearded face of Cardinal Bellarmine in relief on the front part of the neck.

3. A large earthen jar or bottle. [Scot.]

grāy′-buck, *n.* The chikara.

grāy′fly, *n.* The trumpet-fly.

grāy′hound, *n.* [AS. *grighund.*] See *Greyhound.*

grāy′ish, *a.* Somewhat gray.

grāy′lag, *n.* [ME. *gray*; AS. *græg*, gray, and W. *llag*, slack, loose, slow, sluggish.] The common wild goose, *Anser ferus*, of Europe, which is thought to be the original of the domestic goose.

grāy′ling, *n.* 1. Any fish of the genus *Thymallus.* The species are voracious, about 16 or 18 inches in length, found in clear, rapid streams in the north of Europe, and valued as food.

Grayling (*Thymallus vulgaris*).

2. A gray butterfly, *Hipparchia semele*, of Great Britain.

grāy′ness, *n.* The quality of being gray.

grāy′pāte, *n.* A goldfinch in the period before the crimson head-feathers appear.

grāy′stōne, grey′stōne, *n.* A grayish or greenish compact rock composed of feldspar and augite and allied to basalt.

grāy′wacke, grey′wacke, *n.* [G. *grauwacke*; *grau*, gray, and *wacke*, stone.] A conglomerate or gritrock consisting of rounded pebbles and sand firmly united. [Rare.]

grāy′weth″ẽr, *n.* One of many stones found in England scattered over the surface of the ground and bearing a resemblance to a gray sheep; called also *druid-stone, Saracen stone*, and *Sarsen stone.*

grāze, *v.t.*; grazed, *pt., pp.*; grazing, *ppr.* [ME. *grasen, gresen*; AS. *grasian*, to graze, from *græs*, grass.]

1. To feed or supply with grass; to furnish pasture for; as, the farmer *grazes* large herds of cattle.

2. To feed on; to eat from the ground, as growing herbage.

> The lambs with wolves shall *graze* the verdant mead. —Pope.

3. To tend while grazing, as cattle; as, Jacob *grazed* Laban's sheep.

grāze, *v.i.* 1. To eat grass; to feed on growing herbage; as, cattle *graze* on the meadows.

2. To supply grass; as, the ground will not *graze* well.

3. To move on devouring, as spreading fire.

grāze, *v.t.* [Prob. a use of *graze*, to feed.] To touch lightly in passing; to brush lightly against; to barely touch while in motion.

grāze, *v.i.* To touch or brush against a person or thing in passing.

grāze, *n.* The act of grazing. [Colloq.]

grāz′ẽr, *n.* An animal that grazes or feeds on growing herbage.

grā′ziẽr, *n.* One who pastures cattle and rears them for market.

grāz′ing, *n.* 1. The process of eating growing grass.

2. A pasture.

grä-zi-ō′sō (grät-sē-), *adv.* [It.] In music, gracefully, smoothly, and elegantly.

grēase, *n.* [ME. *grese, grece*; OFr. *gresse, graisse*, grease, fat, from LL. *grassus*, L. *crassus*, fat, thick.]

1. Animal fat in a soft state; oily or unctuous matter of any kind, as tallow, lard; especially, the fatty matter of land animals, as distinguished from the oily matter of marine animals.

2. A diseased condition of the legs of a horse.

grēase, *v.t.*; greased, *pt., pp.*; greasing, *ppr.* 1. To smear, anoint, or daub, with grease or fat.

2. To bribe; to corrupt with presents.

3. To cheat. [Obs.]

4. To transmit to or to affect with the disease of horses called grease.

5. To cause to run smoothly, as if greased.

To grease one's palm; to give one a bribe.

grēase′-mọth, *n.* A moth, *Aglossa pinguinalis*, which in a larval state eats greasy cloth.

grēas′ẽr, *n.* 1. One who or that which greases.

2. A name given in contempt in southwestern United States to a Mexican or other Spanish-American. [Colloq.]

grēas′i-ly, *adv.* 1. In a greasy manner.

2. Grossly; indecently. [Obs.]

grēas′i-ness, *n.* The state of being greasy; oiliness; unctuousness.

grēase′wood, *n.* A shrub of the spinach family, very abundant in the alkaline districts of western United States.

grēas′y, *a.*; *comp.* greasier; *superl.* greasiest. 1. Oily; fat; unctuous.

2. Smeared or defiled with grease.

3. Like grease or oil; smooth; as, a fossil that has a *greasy* feel.

4. Fat of body; bulky; gross; indelicate; indecent. [Obs.]

5. Affected with the horse-disease known as grease.

6. In nautical language, foggy; misty; said of the atmosphere.

grēat, *a.*; *comp.* greater; *superl.* greatest. [AS. *great*, great, large.]

1. Large in bulk or dimensions; of extended length or breadth; of large number; as, a *great* multitude.

2. Expressing a large, extensive, or unusual degree of anything; as, *great* wealth.

3. Long continued; as, a *great* while.

4. Pregnant; teeming; as, *great* with young.

5. Possessing large or strong powers of mind; as, a *great* genius.

6. Distinguished by rank, office, or power; as, a *great* nobleman.

7. Worthy of earnest consideration; as, a *great* plea.

8. Denoting consanguinity one degree more remote, in the ascending or descending line; as, *great*-grandfather, the father of a grandfather; *great*-grandson, the son of a grandson, etc.

9. Vast; sublime; dignified; noble; as, a *great* soul; a *great* scene.

10. Swelling; proud; arrogant; as, he was not disheartened by *great* words. [Rare.]

11. Chief; principal; most important; as, the *great* toe; the *Great* Mogul.

Great Basin; the chief continental basin of North America, lying in the United States west of the Rocky Mountains.

Great Bear; see *Bear*, n. 3.

Great Bible; a large Bible prepared under Coverdale in 1539.

Great charter; see *Magna Charta* under *Charta*.

Great circle of a sphere; a circle whose plane passes through the center of the sphere.

Great-circle sailing; the navigation of a ship on a great circle of the globe, that is, on the shortest arc between two points.

Great organ; a part of a grand organ, the largest and most powerful, played by a keyboard of its own and forming in many respects an instrument by itself.

The Great Lakes; the chain of large, freshwater lakes or inland seas lying between the United States and Canada.

The Great Powers; the five principal countries of Europe: Austria-Hungary, England, France, Germany, and Russia; Italy is sometimes included as the sixth *Great Power*.

The Great sea; the Mediterranean.

The great seal; the chief seal of a government.

The Great Spirit; the name given by the North-American Indians to their deity.

Great White Way: Broadway from about 42d to 60th Streets, the theatre section of New York City. So called because of its brilliant illumination.

Syn.—Big, wide, excellent, immense, bulky, majestic, grand, eminent, noble, powerful.

grēat, *n.* 1. The whole; the gross; the lump or mass; as, a shipbuilder contracts to build a ship by the *great*.

2. [*pl.*] Final examinations for degrees at Oxford University; at Cambridge called *great go*.

The great; the distinguished; the powerful; the rich.

grēat′-bel″lied, *a.* Pregnant; teeming.

grēat′cōat, *n.* An overcoat; a surtout.

grēat′en, *v.t.* To enlarge; to magnify.

grēat′en, *v.i.* To increase; to become large. [Rare.]

grēat′-grand′chīld, *n.* The child of a grandson or granddaughter.

grēat′-grand′daugh″tẽr (-da″), *n.* A daughter of a grandson or granddaughter.

grēat′-grand′fä″thẽr, *n.* The father of a grandfather or grandmother.

grēat′-grand′mọth″ẽr, *n.* The mother of a grandfather or grandmother.

grēat′-grand′sọn, *n.* The son of a grandson.

grēat′-heärt″ed, *a.* High-minded; generous; courageous.

grēat′-heärt″ed-ness, *n.* High-mindedness; generosity; courage.

grēat′ly, *adv.* 1. In a great degree; much.

I will *greatly* multiply thy sorrow.—Gen. iii. 16.

2. Nobly; illustriously.

grēat′ness, *n.* [ME. *gretnesse*; AS. *greátnes*, from *greát*, great.]

1. The state or quality of being great; largeness of bulk, dimensions, number, or quantity.

2. Breadth of mind; nobility; worth.

3. Arrogance; swelling pride. [Obs.]

Syn.—Bulk, size, breadth, nobility, dignity.

grēave, *n.* A grove. [Obs.]

grēave, *v.t.* To clean the bottom of (a ship); to grave.

grēaves, *n.pl.* [ME. *greves, grayvez*; OFr. *greves*, greaves, pl. of *greve*, the shin.]

1. Armor for the legs.

2. Boots; buskins. [Prov. Eng.]

grēaves, *n.pl.* Cracklings. [See *Graves*.]

grēbe, *n.* [Fr. *grèbe*, from Breton *krib*, a comb.] A name common to numerous species of web-footed birds with short wings and very expert at diving. They constitute the genus *Podiceps* and have many popular names in local use. The horned *grebe*, *Podiceps cornutus*, is common in the northern hemisphere.

Horned Grebe (*Podiceps cornutus*).

Grē′ciăn (-shăn), *a.* Pertaining to Greece.

Grecian architecture; the architecture which flourished in Greece from about 500 B. C. till the time of the Roman conquest. From the most simple and crude forms it finally developed into characteristic orders under the names Doric, Ionic, and Corinthian, to which may perhaps be added the Caryatic, the Doric being the most distinctive.

Temple of Jupiter at Olympia—Doric order.

Grecian bend; an affected carriage of the body in vogue among women about 1870, in which the lower part of the trunk was projected backward and the upper part forward.

Grecian fire; see *Greek fire* under *Greek*.

Grē′ciăn, *n.* [OFr. *Grecien*, from L. *Græcia*, Greece.]

1. A native of Greece.

2. A Jew who understood Greek; so called in Acts vi. 1.

3. One well versed in the Greek language.

Grē′cism, *n.* An idiom of the Greek language.

Grē′cize, *v.t.*; Grecized, *pt., pp.*; Grecizing, *ppr.* 1. To render Grecian; to cause to take Greek character.

2. To translate into Greek.

Grē′cize, Grē′ciăn-ize, *v.i.* To speak the Greek language; to imitate the Greeks.

Grē″cō-Rō′măn, *a.* Characterized by being partly Greek and partly Roman; pertaining to both Greece and Rome; as, *Greco-Roman* art.

greçque (grek), *n.* [Fr., fretwork, f. of *Grec*, Greek.]

1. An ornamental fret of Greek origin.

2. A strainer placed in a coffeepot to retain the grounds.

gree, *n.* 1. Good-will; favor; satisfaction. [Obs.]

2. A reward or prize. [Obs.]

gree, *n.* A step or stair; rank; degree. [Obs.]

gree, *v.i.* To agree. [Obs.]

greece, *n.* [Obs.] See *Greese*.

greed, *n.* [ME. *grede*; AS. *grǣd*, greed, hunger.] Greediness.

greed, *n.* [AS. *grǣde*, grass.] In botany, the duckweed; also, any species of the genus *Potamogeton*.

greed′i-ly, *adv.* In a greedy manner; voraciously; also, eagerly.

greed′i-ness, *n.* 1. Keenness of appetite for food or drink; ravenousness; voracity.

Fox in stealth, wolf in *greediness*. —Shak.

2. Ardent desire.

Syn.—Avidity, eagerness, rapacity, voracity, piggishness, gluttony.

greed′y, *a.*; *comp.* greedier; *superl.* greediest. [ME. *gredy, gredi*; AS. *grǣdig*, greedy, from *grǣd*, hunger, greed.]

1. Having a keen appetite for food or drink; ravenous; voracious; very hungry; as, a lion that is *greedy* of his prey.

2. Having a keen desire for anything; eager to obtain; as, *greedy* of gain.

Syn.—Gluttonous, voracious, hungry, desirous, avaricious, piggish, insatiable.

greed′y-gut, *n.* A glutton; a devourer; a belly-god. [Vulgar.]

gree′gree, *n.* [Native name.] Same as *Grigri*.

Greek, *a.* [L. *Græcus*; Gr. *Graikos*, a Greek.] Pertaining to Greece or the Greeks; Grecian; Hellenic.

Greek calends; see under *Calends*.

Greek church; the Eastern church; the part of Christendom which withdrew from the Roman or Western church during the ninth century. It is the national church of Russia, Greece, Rumania, Bulgaria, etc.

Greek cross; see illustration under *Cross*.

Greek empire; see *Byzantine empire* under *Byzantine*.

Greek fire; a combustible composition which burns under water, the constituents of which are supposed to be asphalt, niter, and sulphur.

Greek-letter fraternity; see under *Fraternity*.

Greek rose; the flower campion.

Greek, *n.* 1. A native of Greece, ancient or modern.

2. The language of Greece.

3. Anything unintelligible; as, it is *Greek* to me. [Colloq.]

4. An adventurer. [Slang.]

Greek′ess, *n.* A female Greek. [Rare.]

Greek′ish, *a.* Peculiar to Greece; somewhat Greek.

Greek′ling, *n.* A little Greek or one of small account.

green, *a.* [ME. *grene*; AS. *grene*, green, from *growan*, to grow.]

1. Of the color of foliage and plants when growing; verdant.

2. New; fresh; recent; as, a *green* wound.

3. Fresh; flourishing; undecayed; as, *green* old age.

4. Containing its natural juices; not dry; not seasoned; as, *green* wood; *green* timber; *green* hides.

5. Unripe; immature; not arrived at perfection; as, *green* fruit.

6. Immature in age; young; inexperienced; raw; as, *green* in age or judgment.

7. Pale; sickly; wan; of a pale greenish color.

8. Characterized by the presence of verdure; as, a *green* Christmas.

Green blight; a parasitical affection of plants.

Green corn; immature ears of corn, considered a table delicacy.

Green crab; the common edible crab, *Carcinas mœnas*, of Europe.

Green crop; a crop of green vegetables, as distinguished from a crop of grain, hay, etc.

Green diallage; a green variety of pyroxene; smaragdite.

Green earth; a species of mineral earth, used as a pigment; terre verte.

Green ebony; see *Ebony*.

Green fire; a composition of sulphur, potassium chlorate, and salts of barium, which on burning gives a greenish flame.

Green goods; see under *Good*, n.

Green hand; a raw and inexperienced person. [Colloq.]

Green iron ore; dufrenite, a ferric phosphate.

Green lead ore; lead chlorophosphate; pyromorphite.

Green linnet; a greenfinch.

Green looper; in zoölogy, a geometrid larva.

Green manure; a fresh crop plowed up and turned over to nourish the soil.

Green marble; serpentine.

Green mineral; malachite; a pigment of carbonate of copper.

Green monkey; a long-tailed West African monkey, *Cercopithecus callitrichus*.

Green sea; a sea or large wave shipped by a vessel in a gale.

Green smalt; see *Cobalt green* under *Cobalt*.

Green vitriol; ferrous sulphate.

Green ware; pottery before it is baked.

Green woodpecker; the yaffle, *Gecinus viridis*.

green, *n.* 1. The color of foliage or growing

plants; a color composed of blue and yellow rays, which, mixed in different proportions, exhibit a variety of shades; as, apple-*green*, meadow-*green*, leek-*green*, etc.

2. A grassy plain or plat; a piece of ground covered with verdant herbage; as, a village *green*.

O'er the smooth enameled *green*. —Milton.

3. [*pl.*] Fresh leaves or branches of trees or other plants; wreaths; as, Christmas *greens*.

The fragrant *greens* I seek, my brows to bind. —Dryden.

4. [*pl.*] The leaves and stems of young plants used in cookery or dressed for food; as, a dish of *greens*.

5. A pigment of green color.

6. A piece of level ground on which games are played; as, a golf-*green*; a bowling-*green*.

Alkali green; an emerald-green pigment obtained from an aniline dye in the form of an alkaline salt.

Berlin green; see under *Berlin*.

Brilliant green; a dyestuff derived from coal-tar; also called *benzal green*.

Brunswick green; a form of oxychlorid of copper; a light-green powder used as a pigment.

Copper green; a pigment derived from salts of copper.

Emerald green; see under *Emerald*.

Guignet's green; a green coloring-matter used and compounded by the French artist Guignet, whence its name; it is derived from hydrate of chromium and is used in calico-printing.

Malachite green; a hydrated copper carbonate used as a pigment.

Methyl green; a coal-tar dyestuff for cotton, wool, and silk, occurring in commerce as a double zinc salt.

Mineral green; see under *Mineral*.

Mountain green; a natural malachite green; green earth.

Paris green; a highly poisonous powder used as a pigment in many manufactures and as an insecticide; it is a compound of acetate and arsenite of copper; also called *French green*, *emerald green*, *Schweinfurt green*, *Vienna green*, and *mitis green*.

Saxony green; see *Cobalt green* under *Cobalt*.

Scheele's green; a green coloring matter consisting of copper arsenite; also called *Swedish green*.

Vienna green; Paris green.

green, *v.t.*; greened, *pt.*, *pp.*; greening, *ppr.* To make green.

green, *v.i.* To become green; to grow green.

green′back, *n.* 1. A popular name for a legal-tender note of the United States; so called from the back of the note being of a green color. The term is sometimes loosely used to include the notes issued by the national banks. *Greenbacks* were first issued by the government in 1862 in order to meet the exigencies of the Rebellion and to relieve the business of the country.

2. An animal with a green back, as (a) a frog; (b) a garfish; (c) a humming-bird of the genus *Papnolites*; (d) the golden plover.

Green′back″ẽr, *n.* A member of the so-called Greenback party in the United States, which originated in 1874 and demanded that greenbacks constitute the only form of the national currency.

green′bīrd, *n.* A greenfinch.

green′bōne, *n.* 1. The garfish, *Belone vulgaris*, from the color of its bones when boiled.

2. The viviparous blenny, or eelpout, *Zoarces viviparus*.

green′brī″ẽr, *n.* In botany, any species of *Smilax*, a prickly, vinelike climbing shrub, common in the United States.

green′-broom, *n.* A plant, *Genista tinctoria*, used in dyeing green. [See *Genista*.]

green′cloth, *n.* In England, formerly, a board or court of justice held in the counting-house of the king's household, with power to correct offenders and keep the peace within the precincts of the court.

green′-drag″ŏn, *n.* Dragonroot, *Arisæma Dracontium*, akin to jack-in-the-pulpit.

green′ẽr-y, *n.* Green plants; verdure.

green′-eyed (-īd), *a.* 1. Having green eyes.

2. Of a morbid sight; seeing all things discolored or distorted.

The green-eyed monster; jealousy.

green′finch, *n.* 1. The European finch; also called *green grosbeak*, *green linnet*, *greenbird*, etc.

2. The olive-green Texas sparrow.

green′fish, *n.* 1. A pollack or coalfish.

2. The bluefish; the horse-mackerel.

green′fly̆, *n.* 1. A louse or aphid that infests plants.

2. A green flesh-fly, *Musca chloris*.

green′gāge, *n.* A large, rounded, greenish variety of plum.

green′gill, *n.* 1. An oyster whose gills have been colored green by feeding upon *Confervæ*.

2. The green condition thus caused.

green″grō′cẽr, *n.* A retailer of vegetables in their fresh or green state.

green′head (-hed), *n.* 1. A species of striped bass.

2. The mallard.

3. The golden plover.

4. Greenness; immaturity. [Obs.]

green′heärt, *n.* In botany, (a) the *Nectandra Rodiæi*, natural order *Lauraceæ*, a native of Guiana, the bark of which yields bebeerin, an alkaloid of great value in intermittents; it is a large forest tree, 80 or 90 feet high, and its timber is highly valued because of its hardness and durability; (b) the *Colubrina ferruginosa*, allied to the buckthorn, the wood having a twisted grain.

green′hood, *n.* A state of greenness.

green′horn, *n.* A raw youth; a person inexperienced and readily imposed upon.

green′house, *n.* A house, the roof and one or more sides of which consist of glazed frames, for the purpose of cultivating exotic plants, the temperature being kept up by means of artificial heat.

green′ing, *n.* 1. The process or act of growing green.

2. Any of certain varieties of apples of a green color when ripe; as, the Rhode Island *greening*.

green′ish, *a.* Somewhat green; having a tinge of green; as, a *greenish*-yellow.

green′ish-ness, *n.* The quality of being greenish.

Green′lănd-ẽr, *n.* One born or residing in Greenland.

green′-slā″vẽr, *n.* An edible seaweed, *Ulva Lactuca*; also called *sea-lettuce*.

green′-leek, *n.* A parrakeet of the genus *Polytelis*, the scarlet-breasted parrot of Australia.

green′let, *n.* 1. Any green-colored vireo; there are several species peculiar to America; as, the red-eyed *greenlet*, *Vireo olivaceus*.

2. Any similar small green songster.

green′ling, *n.* The greenfish.

green′ly, *a.* Green. [Obs.]

green′ly, *adv.* With a green color; newly; unskilfully.

green′ness, *n.* The state or quality of being green.

green′ŏck-īte, *n.* [Named after Lord *Greenock*, its discoverer.] A mineral sulphid of cadmium, crystalline and of an orange-yellow color.

green′room, *n.* 1. A retiring-room for actors in a theater.

2. A room where new or green cloth, pottery, etc., is received.

greens, *n.pl.* See *Green*, n. 4.

green′sand, *n.* A term applied to beds of sand or sandstone, belonging to the Cretaceous period; so called because green earth or glauconite is ordinarily scattered throughout them.

green′sauce, *n.* The field-sorrel; also, sour sorrel mixed with sugar and vinegar.

green′shank, *n.* A sandpiper of the genus *Totanus*.

green′sick″ness, *n.* Chlorosis; an anemic disease of young women.

green′snake, *n.* A bright green snake of the genus *Cyclophis*.

green′-stall, *n.* A stall on which green vegetables are exposed for sale.

green′stōne, *n.* Any stone having an eruptive origin and a green color, as diorite, melaphyre, and the like. The term is now becoming obsolete.

green′swărd, *n.* Turf green with grass.

greenth, *n.* Verdure; a green condition. [Rare.]

green′weed, *n.* See *Genista*.

green′wing, *n.* A teal with green wings.

green′withe, *n.* A climbing orchid of the genus *Vanilla*.

green′wood, *a.* Pertaining to a greenwood; as, a *greenwood* shade.

green′wood, *n.* 1. A wood when green, as in summer.

2. Wood made green by a certain fungus.

green′y, *a.* Green; greenish.

green′y, *n.* 1. The greenfinch.

2. A greenhorn; a booby; a freshman. [Colloq.]

greese, *n.* A flight of steps; a step; a degree. [Obs.]

greet, *v.t.*; greeted, *pt.*, *pp.*; greeting, *ppr.* [ME. *greten*; AS. *gretan*, to greet.]

1. To address; to accost; to hail; to salute either in meeting or by a message or messenger.

2. To congratulate. [Obs.]

greet, *v.i.* To meet and salute.

greet, *v.i.* To weep. [Scot. or Obs.]

greet, *n.* Salutation; greeting. [Obs.]

greet, *n.* Weeping. [Obs.]

greet, *a.* Great. [Obs.]

greet′ẽr, *n.* One who greets.

greet′ing, *n.* [ME. *gretinge*; AS. *greting*, from *gretan*, to greet.] Salutation at meeting or in a message; welcome; compliment.

greet′ing, *n.* Weeping. [Scot.]

greeve, *n.* [ME. *gryve*, *grayve*; Ice. *greifi*, a steward.] A reeve; a steward; a bailiff.

greeze, *n.* A greese; a step. [Obs.]

gref′fi-ẽr, *n.* [Fr., from OFr. *greffier*, a scribe; LL. *graphiarius*, a notary, from L. *graphiarius*, pertaining to a style for writing, from *graphium*, a style.] A registrar or recorder. [Obs.]

grē′găl, *a.* [L. *grex*, *gregis*, a flock.] Pertaining to a flock. [Rare.]

grē-gā′ri-ăn, *a.* 1. Belonging to the herd; common. [Obs.]

2. Gregarious; living in flocks.

Greg-ȧ-rī′nȧ, *n.* 1. The typical genus of the *Gregarinidæ*.

2. [g—; *pl.* greg-ȧ-rī′næ.] A gregarine.

greg′ȧ-rine, *n.* One of the *Gregarinidæ*.

greg′ȧ-rine, *a.* Of or relating to the *Gregarinidæ*.

Greg-ȧ-rin′i-dæ, *n.pl.* [L. *gregarius*, gregarious, from *grex*, *gregis*, a flock.] A class of parasitic animal organisms comprising the lowest forms of the *Protozoa*, found inhabiting the intestines of various animals, especially the cockroach and earthworm.

grē-gā′ri-ous, *a.* [L. *gregarius*, belonging to a flock, from *grex*, *gregis*, a flock, herd.] Having the habit of assembling or living in a flock or herd; not habitually solitary or living alone.

grē-gā′ri-ous-ly, *adv.* In a flock or herd.

grē-gā′ri-ous-ness, *n.* Disposition to associate.

grege, *n.* [Fr., from It. *greggia* (supply *seta*, silk), raw silk, f. of *greggio*, raw, rough.] A trade-name of raw silk.

greg′ō, **greg′gō**, *n.* In the Levant, a short cloak with a hood. [Obs.]

Grē-gō′ri-ăn, *a.* Belonging to, established, or produced by Gregory.

Gregorian calendar; the calendar established by Pope Gregory XIII. in 1582, in which years divisible by 4 have 366 days, except when terminating a century, as 2100, 2200, etc., when they have only 365, except when divisible by 400, as 2000, 2400, etc.; the ordinary calendar of Christendom except Greece and Russia.

Gregorian chant; one of a series of choral melodies introduced into the service of the Catholic church by Pope Gregory I. about the end of the sixth century; hence, any melody in the same style; canto fermo.

Gregorian telescope; the first and most common form of the reflecting telescope, invented by James Gregory (1638-75), professor of mathematics in the university of St. Andrews.

Gregorian year; a year according to the Gregorian calendar.

greil′lāde, *n.* [Etym. unknown.] The coarse iron-ore as used in a Catalan forge.

grei′sen, *n.* [G. *greissen*, to cleave, split.] A granitic rock composed chiefly of mica and quartz, in which the feldspar is replaced by fluorspar, tourmalin, tin oxid, rutile, and the like.

grēit, *v.i.* To weep or greet. [Scot.]

gre-lōt′ (grā-lō′), *n.* [Fr.] A small bell; usually a small globular sleigh-bell containing a metallic ball.

grē′mi-ăl, *a.* [LL. *gremialis*, from L. *gremium*, the bosom or lap.] Belonging to the lap or bosom. [Rare.]

grē′mi-ăl, *n.* 1. A confidant. [Obs.]

2. A lap-cloth worn by a bishop at mass or ordination as a protection to his vestments.

grē-nāde′, *n.* [OFr. *grenade*, a ball of wildfire, from Sp. *granada*, lit., something containing grains or seeds, a grenade, from L. *granatus*, grained, having seeds, from *granum*, a grain, seed.] A hollow ball or shell of iron or other metal, or of annealed glass, which was filled with powder, fired by means of a fuse, and thrown by hand among enemies; also, a glass bottle filled with fluid and gas to be used as a fire-extinguisher.

Rampart grenade; a grenade used by soldiers defending a rampart, for throwing or rolling down upon besiegers.

gren-ȧ-diēr′, *n.* [Fr., from Sp. *granadero*, from *granada*, a grenade.]

1. Originally, one who threw grenades. Only soldiers of long service and acknowledged bravery were selected for this duty. When hand-grenades went out of general use, the name was still retained for the company, the members of which were of great height and were distinguished by a particular dress, as for instance the high bearskin cap. In the British and French

Grenadier of 1745, blowing his fuse to light a grenade.

armies the grenadier company was the first of each battalion.

2. A bird of brilliant plumage, red above, black below, called also *grenadier grosbeak, Pyromelana oryx*, inhabiting the Cape Colony, and about the size of a sparrow.

3. The rattail, a deep-sea fish of the genus *Macrurus*, with body and tail narrowed to a sharp point.

gren'ȧ-din, *n.* [Fr. *grenade*, a pomegranate.] A dyestuff containing crude magenta or fuchsin.

gren-ȧ-dīne', *n.* [Fr. *grenadine*, grenadine, dim. of *grenade*, a pomegranate.] A gauzy silk or silk and woolen fabric, for ladies' dresses, shawls, etc.

grē-nā'dō, *n.* A grenade. [Obs.]

grēne, *a.* and *n.* Green. [Obs.]

grès (grā), *n.* [Fr.] Grit; sandstone; stoneware.

Grès cérame, grès de Flandres; a kind of German stoneware of the Rhine cities.

gres-so'ri-al, gres-so'ri-ous, *a.* [L. *gressus*, pp. of *gradi*, to walk.] Suitable or suited for walking; in ornithology, a term applied to birds which have three toes forward (two of which are connected) and one behind.

Gret, grēte, *a.* Great. (Obs.)

Gretna Green. A village in Dumfries County, Scotland, just across the English border, famous for its runaway marriages of English couples.

Gretna Green marriage. A runaway marriage.

greve, *n.* A grove; a bush. [Obs.]

grēve, *n.* A grave; a ditch. [Obs.]

grew (grụ), *v.*, past tense of *grow*.

grew'sōme (grụ'sum), *a.* See *Gruesome*.

grew'sōme-ness, *n.* See *Gruesomeness*.

grey, *a.* Gray.

grey'hound, *n.* [ME. *greyhound, grayhund*; AS. *grighund*, a greyhound.]

1. A tall fleet dog kept for the chase, remarkable for the keenness of its sight, the symmetrical strength and beauty of its form, and its great fleetness.

Greyhound (*Canis graius*).

2. A speedy ocean-steamer.

grey'lag, *n.* Same as *Graylag*.

grib'ble, *n.* [Origin unknown; compare Prov. Eng. *grib*, to bite.] *Limnoria terebrans*, a small salt-water crustacean destructive to submerged wood, as piling, etc.

grice, *n.* A little pig; a grise. [Obs.]

grice, *n.* A flight of steps; a greese. [Obs.]

grid, *n.* 1. A grating, gridiron, or other structure with parallel bars.

2. In electricity, a zinc plate more or less resembling a gridiron in a primary battery, or a lead plate with holes, corrugations, or other means of support for the active matter of a secondary, or storage battery.

3. In radiotelegraphy, the helix of fine wire in the vacuum tube to control the amount of electronic flow.

grid'dle, *n.* [ME. *gridel, gridele*; W. *gredyll*, a griddle, a grate, from LL. *graticula*, a gridiron, from L. *craticula*, dim. of *cratis*, a hurdle, a wicker crate.]

1. A pan, broad and shallow, for frying cakes.
2. A griddle-cake. [Local, U. S.]
3. A miner's wire-bottomed sieve.
4. A stove-lid in the form of a grid.

grid'dle-çāke, *n.* A cake baked from a thin batter on a griddle.

gride, *n.* A discordant grating or scraping sound.

gride, *v.t.* and *v.i.*; grided, *pt., pp.*; griding, *ppr.* To grate, or to cut with a grating sound; to cut; to penetrate or pierce harshly; as, the *griding* sword.

grid'e-lin, *n.* [Fr. *gris de lin*, flax-gray; *gris*, gray, *de*, of, and *lin*, flax; L. *de*, of, and *linum*, flax.] A color mixed of white and red, or a gray violet; spelled also *gredaline, grizelin*.

grid'ī"ron (-ī"ŭrn), *n.* [ME. *grydyrne, gredirne*, a gridiron, a griddle.]

1. A grated utensil for broiling flesh over coals, or by means of a hot flame.

2. A frame for supporting ships during repairs, etc.

3. A football field; so-called because of a supposed resemblance of the markings to a gridiron.

Gridiron pendulum; a kind of compensation pendulum, consisting of parallel bars of different metals, so arranged that the length of the pendulum remains unaltered by changes of temperature.

Gridiron valve; a form of slide-valve in which parts arranged somewhat like a gridiron have an equal number of parts similarly arranged in the seat.

grief, *n.* [OFr. *grief*, sorrow, grief, as adj. heavy, grievous, from L. *gravis*, weighty, sad, grievous.]

1. The pain of mind produced by loss, misfortune, injury, or evils of any kind; sorrow; regret; as, we experience *grief* when we lose a friend.

2. Cause of sorrow; that which afflicts.

3. Physical suffering or disease. [Rare.]

To come to grief; to suffer calamity or failure.

Syn.—Sorrow, sadness.—*Sorrow* is generic; *grief* is sorrow for some definite cause, one which commenced, at least, in the past; *sadness* is applied to a permanent mood of the mind.

grief'fụl, *a.* Full of grief or sorrow.

grief'less, *a.* Without grief.

grie'gō, *n.* Same as *Grego*.

griev-ȧ-ble, *a.* Lamentable. [Obs.]

griev'ănce, *n.* [ME. *grevaunce, grevance*; OFr. *grevance*, an injury, grievance, from *grevant*, ppr. of *grever*, to grieve, afflict.]

1. That which causes grief or uneasiness; that which burdens, oppresses, or injures, implying a sense of wrong done, or a continued injury.

2. Grief.

griev'ăn-cēr, *n.* One who is the cause of a grievance. [Obs.]

grieve, *n.* Same as *Greeve*.

grieve, *v.t.*; grieved, *pt., pp.*; grieving, *ppr.* [ME. *greven*; OFr. *grever*; L. *gravare*, to burden, oppress, grieve, from *gravis*, heavy, grievous.]

1. To give pain of mind to; to afflict; to wound the feelings of.

2. To lament. [Rare.]

Syn.—Afflict, hurt, pain, wound.

grieve, *v.i.* To feel pain of mind or heart; to be in pain on account of an evil; to sorrow; to mourn; followed by *at* or *for*; as, to *grieve for* a dead friend; to *grieve at* the calamity which befell him.

griev'ēr, *n.* He who or that which grieves.

griev'ing-ly, *adv.* In a grieving manner.

griev'ous, *a.* [ME. *grevous*; OFr. *grevos*; LL. *gravosus*; L. *gravis*, heavy, burdensome, grievous.]

1. Heavy; oppressive; hard to be borne; burdensome; as, a *grievous* load of taxes.

2. Causing grief or sorrow.

The thing was very *grievous* in Abraham's sight, because of his son. —Gen. xxi. 11.

3. Atrocious.

4. Expressing great grief; as, a *grievous* complaint.

griev'ous-ly, *adv.* In a grievous manner.

griev'ous-ness, *n.* 1. Oppressiveness; whatever gives pain or distress; as, the *grievousness* of a burden.

2. Greatness; enormity; atrociousness; as, the *grievousness* of sin or offenses.

griff, *n.* [G. *griff*, a grasp, grip.]

1. Grasp. [Obs.]

2. A device in a Jacquard loom to shift the warp-threads.

griff, *n.* Same as *Griffin*.

griff, *n.* A rocky chasm. [Prov. Eng.]

griff, griffe, *n.* [Compare Sp. *grifo*, a griffin, *grifos*, frizzled hair.]

1. A mulatto woman.

2. The child of a mulatto woman by a negro man. [Local, U. S.]

3. A person of negro and Indian blood.

griffe, *n.* [OFr. *griffe*, a claw, nail, talon, from *griffer*, to gripe, grasp, seize, from O.H.G. *grifan*, to grip.] A claw-like ornament at the base of medieval columns.

griffe, *n.* The deposit in new wine soon after bottling.

grif'fin, *n.* [ME. *griffyn*; OFr. *grifon*; LL. *griffus, gryphus*, a griffin, a vulture; L. *gryps*; Gr. *gryps*, a griffin, so called from its hooked beak, from *grypos*, hooked, curved.]

1. In mythology, an imaginary animal said to be generated between the lion and the eagle. The fore part is represented as an eagle and the lower part as a lion. This animal was supposed to watch over mines of gold and hidden treasures, and was consecrated to the sun. The figure of the griffin is seen on ancient medals and is still borne in coat-armor. It is also an ornament of Greek architecture.

Griffin (in heraldry).

2. A species of vulture, *Gyps fulvus*, found in the mountainous parts of Europe, North Africa, and Turkey.

3. A close watcher or guard, as of a person; specifically, a chaperon or duenna.

4. A newcomer; also, a race-horse making its first race. [Anglo-Ind.]

grif'fin-āge, *n.* In India, the condition of being a griffin or greenhorn.

grif'fin-işm, *n.* 1. Griffinage; hence, lack of experience.

2. Griffin-like vigilance.

grig, *n.* [Compare Sw. *kräk*, a little creature that crawls, from *kräka*, to creep.]

1. A cricket; a grasshopper.

2. The sand-eel; a small eel of lively and incessant motion.

As merry as a grig; a saying supposed generally to have reference to the mirth and cheerfulness ascribed to the grasshopper, but by Mr. Nares shown to be a corruption for *as merry as a Greek*, the Greeks being proverbially spoken of by the Romans as fond of good living and free potations.

grig, *n.* [W. *grug*, heath.] Heath.

grig'net, *n.* [Compare OFr. *perdrix grignette*, the ordinary partridge.] One of various African birds of the genus *Parisoma*.

gri'grī, *n.* An African fetish; a charm.

gril, *a.* Severe; cruel; causing terror. [Obs.]

grill, *v.t.*; grilled, *pt., pp.*; grilling, *ppr.* [Fr. *griller*, to broil on a gridiron, from *gril*, a gridiron, a grill.]

1. To broil.

2. To torment, as if by broiling.

3. To stamp with a figure of bars and spaces.

grill, *v.i.* To be broiling; figuratively, to fret; to be greatly disturbed.

grill, *n.* [Fr. *gril*; OFr. *greil*, a gridiron, *graille*, a grate, grating, from L. *craticula*, a gridiron, dim. of *cratis*, wicker work, a hurdle.]

1. A gridiron.

2. Anything broiled on a gridiron.

3. A grill-room.

gril-lāde', *n.* [Fr., from *griller*, to grill.] Broiled meat, or something broiled; also, the act of grilling.

gril'lāge, *n.* [Fr., wirework, grating, a frame, from *gril*, a gridiron.] A name given to the sleepers and cross-beams on which some erections are carried up, as piers on marshy soils.

grill'-room, *n.* A restaurant or eating-room where grilling is done.

grille, *n.* [Fr., from OFr. *graille*, a grating.] A lattice or openwork or grating; a piece of grated work, as (a) a metal screen to inclose or protect any particular spot, locality, shrine, tomb, or sacred ornament; (b) a gate of metal inclosing or protecting the entrance to a religious house or sacred building; (c) a small screen of iron bars inserted in the door of a monastic or conventual building, in order to allow the inmates to converse with visitors, or to answer inquiries without opening the door; the wicket of a monastery.

Grilles.

grilled, *a.* Broiled; tormented.

gril'ly, *v.t.* To harass. [Obs.]

grilse, *n.* A young salmon about the time it first returns from the sea to the river. [Scot.]

grim, *a.*; *comp.* grimmer; *superl.* grimmest. [ME. *grim, grym*; AS. *grim*, fierce, savage.]

1. Fierce; ferocious; impressing terror; frightful; horrible; as, a *grim* look; a *grim* face; *grim* war.

2. Ugly; ill-looking; sour; crabbed; peevish; surly.

Syn.—Fierce, ferocious, terrible, hideous, ugly, ghastly, sullen, stern.

gri-māce', *n.* [Fr., from OFr. *grimace*, a wry face, an ugly look, from *grime*, irritated, vexed; of Teut. origin.]

1. A distortion of the countenance, from habit, affectation, or insolence.

2. An air of affectation; hypocrisy.

gri-māce', *v.i.*; grimaced (-māst'), *pt., pp.*; grimacing, *ppr.* To distort the features; to make grimaces.

gri-māced' (-māst'), *a.* Distorted; having a crabbed look.

gri-mal'kin, *n.* [Originally *graymalkin*, from ME. *gray*, AS. *græg*, gray, and ME. *Mal*, Moll, short for Mary.] A name for an old cat.

grime, *n.* [ME. *grim*, prob. of Scand. origin, compare Dan. *grime*, a streak, stripe, Sw. dial. *grima*, smut on the face.] Foul matter; dirt; sullying blackness.

grime, *v.t.*; grimed, *pt., pp.*; griming, *ppr.* To sully or soil deeply; to befoul, as with grime.

grim'i-ly, *adv.* In a grimy manner.

grim'i-ness, *n.* The condition of being grimy; dirtiness.

grim'ly, *a.* Having a hideous or stern look. [Rare.]

grim'ly, *adv.* [ME. *grimly, grymly*; AS. *grimlice*, in a grim manner, from *grim*, grim.]

1. Fiercely; ferociously; with a look of fury or ferocity.

2. Sourly; sullenly.

grimme, *n.* [Etym. unknown.] An antelope, *Cephalophus rufilatus*, of West Africa.

Grimm's lạw. In philology, a law discovered

by Jacob L. Grimm, the great German philologist, formulating certain changes which the mute consonants undergo in corresponding words in the most important branches of the Aryan family of languages. According to this law, stated briefly, the labials *p, b, f* in Greek, Latin, or Sanskrit, become *f, p, b* in Gothic (with which English and the other Low German languages agree), and *b* (*v*), *f, p* in Old High German; the dentals *t, d, th* in Greek, etc., become *th, t, d* in Gothic, and *d, z, t* in Old High German, and the gutturals *k, g, ch* in Greek, etc., become *h* (not quite regularly), *k, g* in Gothic, and *g, ch, k* in Old High German; as Sans. *pitri*, Gr. *patēr*, L. *pater*, Goth. *fadrein*, O.H.G. *vatar*, all=Eng. *father*; Sans. *tvam*, Gr. *tu*, L. *tu*, Goth. *thu*, O.H.G. *du*, all=Eng. *thou*; Sans. *jānu* (for *gānu*), Gr. *gonu*, L. *genu*, Goth. *kniu*, O.H.G. *chniu, chneo*, all=Eng. *knee*, etc.

grim′ness, *n.* Fierceness of look; sternness; crabbedness.

grim′sir, *n.* A stern, overbearing man. [Obs.]

grim′=the=col′liēr (-yẽr), *n.* [So called from its smutty involucre.] In botany, the orange hawkweed of Europe, *Hieracium aurantiacum*, now found in northeastern United States; called also *king-devil*.

grim′y, *a.* Full of grime; foul.

grin, *v.i.*; grinned, *pt., pp.*; grinning, *ppr.* [ME. *grinnen*; AS. *grennian*, to show the teeth, snarl, grin.]

1. To snarl and show the teeth, as a dog.

2. To set the teeth together and open the lips; to show the teeth, as in laughter, scorn, or pain.

grin, *v.t.* To express by grinning.

Grinned horrible a ghastly smile.—Milton.

grin, *n.* The act of closing the teeth and showing them, or of withdrawing the lips and showing the teeth; a broad smile; a forced, meaningless, or sarcastic smile.

grin, *n.* A snare or trap. [Obs.]

grind, *v.t.*; ground, *pt., pp.*; grinding, *ppr.* [ME. *grinden*; AS. *grindan*, to grind.]

1. To break and reduce to fine particles or powder by friction; to comminute by attrition; to triturate; as, to *grind* corn or coffee.

2. To sharpen, wear down, or make smooth by rubbing or friction; to wear off the substance of and reduce to a sharp edge by the friction of a stone; as, to *grind* an ax or scythe; to *grind* a lens.

3. To grate; as, to *grind* one's teeth.

4. To operate, as by turning a crank; as, to *grind* a hand-organ.

5. To oppress by severe exactions; to afflict cruelly; to harass; as, to *grind* the faces of the poor.

6. To satirize; to make a jest of. [Slang.]

An ax to grind; an object or end of one's own to gain or promote; a phrase first used by Benjamin Franklin. [Colloq.]

grind, *v.i.* 1. To perform the operation of grinding; to move or operate a mill.

2. To be moved or rubbed together, as in the operation of grinding; to grate; as, the *grinding* jaws.

3. To be ground or pulverized by friction; as, corn will not *grind* well before it is dry.

4. To be polished and made smooth by friction; as, glass *grinds* smooth.

5. To be sharpened by grinding; as, steel *grinds* to a fine edge.

6. To perform laborious and unpleasant service; to drudge; to study hard. [Slang.]

grind, *n.* 1. The act of pulverizing, polishing, or sharpening by grinding; also, the sound produced by the act; as, the *grind* of an engine.

2. Incessant toil; distasteful labor or study; as, the eternal *grind*. [Colloq.]

3. A plodding student. [Slang.]

4. A satire or satirist. [Slang.]

Grin-dē′li-ȧ, *n.* [Named after H. *Grindel*, a Russian botanist.]

1. In botany, a genus of herbaceous or shrublike plants of the aster family, characterized by foliage covered with a viscid or gummy secretion, whence sometimes called *gum-plants*.

2. [g—] In medicine, a remedy for asthma and bronchitis, derived from the dried leaves and stems of some species of *Grindelia*.

grind′ẽr, *n.* [ME. *gryndere*, a miller, from AS. *grindan*, to grind.]

1. One who grinds or moves a mill.

2. The instrument of grinding, as a grindstone.

3. A tooth that grinds or chews food; a double-tooth; a jaw-tooth; a molar; hence, a tooth in general.

4. An Australian thrush, *Seisura inquieta*; also called *restless flycatcher* or *dishwasher*.

5. A bird which makes a noise resembling the sound made in grinding scissors, as the nightjar, *Caprimulgus europæus*, which is also called *scissor-grinder*. [Prov. Eng.]

Grinder's asthma; a lung disease caused by inhalation of particles thrown from the grinder's wheel.

grind′ẽr-y, *n.* 1. A place where grinding is done, as of knives, edge-tools, etc.

2. Materials used by shoemakers and other workers in leather. [Eng.]

grind′ing, *a.* and *n.* I. *a.* Tending to oppress; as, *grinding* taxation.

II. *n.* The act of one who grinds; the action of a grinder; a crushing or grating sound.

grind′ing=bed, *n.* A kind of planing-machine for grinding stone slabs, consisting of a moving frame on which the stone lies and passes under a rotating cutting-tool.

grind′ing=bench, *n.* In glass-making, a level stone surface, coated with plaster of Paris, on which a plate of glass is laid to be ground or polished.

grind′ing-ly, *adv.* In a grinding manner; oppressively; harshly.

grin′dle, *n.* In zoölogy, the bowfin or mudfish, *Amia calva*; also called *dogfish*, *Johnny Grindle*, and, humorously, *John A. Grindle*.

grin′dle-stōne, *n.* [Obs.] See *Grindstone*.

grind′let, *n.* [Etym. doubtful.] A small ditch or drain.

grin′dle-tāil, *n.* A dog with a curling tail.

grind′stōne, *n.* [ME. *grindston*, from AS. *grindan*, to grind, and *stan*, a stone.]

1. A flat, circular stone, mounted on a spindle and turned by a winch-handle, a treadle, etc., used for grinding or for sharpening tools.

2. A millstone. [Obs.]

To hold one's nose to the grindstone; to keep one at hard, steady labor; to be unremitting in requirements from a person.

grind′=whāle (-hwāl), *n.* See *Bottlenose*, 1.

grin′gō, *n.* [Sp., gibberish.] Among Spanish-Americans, a contemptuous name for an Englishman or one of English speech.

Grin-nel′li-ȧ, *n.* [Named after Henry *Grinnell*, a New York merchant.] In botany, a genus of beautiful seaweeds, of which the *Grinnellia Americana* of the Atlantic coast of the United States is the only species. Its membranaceous fronds are rosy-red.

grin′nẽr, *n.* One who grins.

grin′ning-ly, *adv.* In a grinning manner.

grint, *n.* Grit. [Prov. Eng.]

grin′te, *v.*, obsolete past tense of *grin*.

grint′ing, *n.* Grinding. [Obs.]

gri-otte′, *n.* [Fr.] A spotted marble of the Pyrenees, with veins varying from dark red to deep green.

grip, *n.* [ME. *grip*; AS. *gripe*, a grasp, a firm hold, from *gripan*, to seize, gripe.]

1. A grasp; a holding fast; a firm grasp; the act of grasping.

2. A mode of grasping the hand, peculiar to a secret society, order, fraternity, etc., and intended as a means of recognition, inquiry, or secret communication between members; as, a Masonic *grip*.

3. A device on a cable-railway car for clutching the cable that draws it; also, a car equipped with such a device; a grip-car; as, to ride on a *grip*.

4. A gripsack; a satchel; a valise.

5. Courage; hope; ability to hold or direct; influence; standing; as, he lost his *grip*. [Colloq.]

6. A handle; a part to be gripped; as, the *grip* of a sword, a pistol, etc.

grip, *v.t.*; gripped, *pt., pp.*; gripping, *ppr.* To grasp firmly; to lay hold of; to grasp; to gripe; to seize and hold fast by force of any kind; as, to *grip* a cable.

grip, *v.i.* To take hold; to hold fast; as, the anchor *grips*.

grip, *n.* [ME. *grip, grippe*; AS. *greót, greóp*, a ditch, channel.] A small ditch or furrow.

grip, *v.t.* To trench; to drain.

grip, *n.* A griffin. [Obs.]

grip, *n.* Same as *Grippe*.

grip′=cär, *n.* In a cable system of railroad, the car to which the grip and its means of manipulation are attached.

grīpe, *n.* A griffin; a vulture. [Obs.]

grīpe, *n.* 1. Grasp; seizure; fast hold with the hand or paw, or with the arms; close embrace.

2. Oppression; cruel exactions.

3. Affliction; pinching distress; as, the *gripe* of poverty.

4. [*pl.*] Intestinal pains; cramps; crampcolic.

5. In nautical language, the forefoot, or piece of timber which terminates the keel at the fore end; in the plural, an assemblage of ropes, deadeyes, and hooks, fastened to ringbolts in the deck, to secure the boats.

grīpe, *v.t.*; griped, *pt., pp.*; griping, *ppr.* [ME. *gripen*; AS. *gripan*, to grasp, seize.]

1. To seize; to grasp; to catch with the hand and clasp closely with the fingers; to hold fast; to hold with the fingers closely pressed; to seize and hold fast in the arms; to embrace closely; to press; to compress.

2. To give pain to, as if by pressure or contraction; as, to *gripe* the bowels.

3. To pinch; to straiten; to distress; as, they are *griped* by poverty.

grīpe, *v.i.* 1. To seize or clutch something; to get money by hard bargains or mean exactions.

2. To feel griping pains.

3. To tend to come up to the wind, as a ship.

grīpe′fụl, *a.* Disposed to gripe; eager to extort.

grīpe′=pen″ny, *n.* A miser; a niggard.

grīp′ẽr, *n.* One who gripes; an oppressor; an extortioner.

grīp′ing-ly, *adv.* In a griping manner.

grip′man, *n.* One who operates a grip; specifically, one who controls the levers of the grip-car of a cable-train.

grippe, **grip**, *n.* [Fr., lit., a seizure, from *gripper*, to take hold of, seize.] In medicine, influenza or epidemic catarrh.

grip′pẽr, *n.* 1. One who or that which grips.

2. In printing, a clutch or clasp which catches a sheet of paper and holds it till printed; a nipper.

3. In the railway mail service, a device which automatically catches a hanging mail-bag while the car is in motion and deposits it in the mail-car.

4. A clutch which holds an arc-lamp carbon.

5. The claw or grapple of a submarine dredge.

6. In Ireland, a bailiff.

grip′ping-ness, *n.* Avarice; covetousness.

grip′ping=rŏllṣ, *n.pl.* In machinery, rotating rolls for guiding rough material to the cutting-machine, as in planing, grooving, sawing, etc.

grip′ping=wheel (-hwēl), *n.* A wheel that grips the center rail on an inclined railroad.

grip′ple, *n.* A grasp; a grip; a gripe. [Obs.]

grip′ple, *a.* Covetous; grasping; greedy. [Rare.]

grip′ple-ness, *n.* The condition of being gripple or grasping. [Rare.]

grip′sack, *n.* A traveling-bag; a hand-bag; a valise; a grip.

Grï′quȧ (grē′kwȧ), *n.* One of a South African half-caste race, springing from Boer fathers and native mothers, and inhabiting Griqualand.

grï-ṣaille′, *n.* [Fr., from *gris*, gray.]

1. In art, a style of painting in gray monochrome, resembling bas-relief; also, a painting of this style.

2. A kind of fancy dress-goods made in France.

gris′am″bẽr (*or* grē-sam′), *n.* [A transposed form.] Ambergris.

grïse, **gris**, *a.* and *n.* [OFr. *gris*; O.H.G. *gris*, gray.]

I. *a.* Gray.

II. *n.* Gray fur or hair.

grïse, *n.* [Obs.] See *Greese*.

grïse, **gris**, *n.* A young pig; a little pig. [Prov. Eng.]

gris′ē-ous, *a.* [LL. *griseus*, from O.H.G. *gris*, gray.] Of a light mottled color; gray.

gri-ṣette′, *n.* [Fr., from *gris*, gray; *grisettes* were so called because they formerly wore gowns made of this cloth.]

1. A gray woolen fabric much worn by women of the lower classes in France.

2. In France, a shopgirl or working-girl; applied frequently to a girl of loose manners or habits.

gris′kin, *n.* A hog's spine. [Prov. Eng.]

griṣ′led (-ld), *a.* [Obs.] See *Grizzled*.

griṣ′li-ness, *n.* The quality or state of being grisly or horrible.

griṣ′ly, *a.*; *comp.* grislier; *superl.* grisliest. [ME. *grisly*; AS. *angrislic, ongrislic*, horrible, terrible.] Frightful; horrible; terrible; as, *grisly* locks; a *grisly* countenance; a *grisly* face; a *grisly* specter.

grï′sŏn, *n.* [Fr. *grison*, a graybeard, a donkey, from *gris*, gray.] A South American animal of the glutton kind, a little larger than a weasel; also, a gluttonous monkey of South America.

Grï′ṣŏns, *n.pl.* [Fr.] The inhabitants of the easternmost Swiss Alps.

grist, *n.* [ME. *grist, gryst*; AS. *grist*, a grist, lit., a grinding, from *grindan*, to grind.]

1. That which is ground; grain to be ground; grain carried to a mill to be ground separately for its owner; also, the amount ground at one time; the grain carried to a mill.

Get *grist* to the mill to have plenty in store.
—Tusser.

2. Supply; provision.

3. Profit; gain; used in the phrase, it brings *grist* to the mill. [Colloq.]

4. In rope-making, a certain size of rope regulated by the number of the strands.

All is grist that comes to his mill; he will turn to account anything that comes along. [Colloq.]

To bring grist to the mill; to bring material or matter for one's profit or that one can use to advantage.

gris′tle (gris′l), *n.* [ME. *gristel, grystyl*; AS. *gristle*, cartilage, from *grist*, a grinding; so called on account of the difficulty of masticating it.] Cartilage; a smooth, solid, elastic substance in animal bodies. [See *Cartilage*.]

gris′tly, *a.* Like or consisting of gristle; cartilaginous; as, the *gristly* rays of fins.

grist′mill, *n.* A mill for grinding grain; specifically, a mill to which the grain of many customers is brought to be ground separately.

grit, *n.* [ME. *greet, gret*; AS. *greót*, sand, dust.]
1. The coarse part of meal.
2. [*pl.*] Oats, wheat, or corn, hulled or coarsely ground.

grit, *n.* 1. Sand or gravel; rough, hard particles.
2. A hard sandstone; stone composed of particles of sand agglutinated; any silicious rock.
3. Firmness; pluck; high, determined spirit; indomitable courage; invincible will; resolution.
4. [G—] In Canadian politics, a Liberal; opposed to *Tory*, a Conservative.

grit, *v.t.*; gritted, *pt.*, *pp.*; gritting, *ppr.* To grate; to grind; to rub together; as, to *grit* the teeth.

grit, *v.i.* To grind; to emit a grating sound, like that of sand under the feet.

grith, *n.* Agreement. [Obs.]

grit′rock, grit′stōne, *n.* Any silicious rock.

grit′ti-ness, *n.* The quality of containing or consisting of grit, sand, or small, hard, rough particles of stone; the quality of being gritty.

grit′ty, *a.* 1. Containing sand or grit; consisting of grit; full of hard particles; sandy.
2. Plucky; spirited; courageous. [Colloq.]

griv′et, *n.* [Fr., prob. from *gris*, gray, and *vert*, green.] A small African monkey, *Cercopithecus griseo-viridis*, the upper parts of which are of a greenish color and the lower white.

grize, *n.* [Obs.] See *Greese*.

griz′e-lin, *n.* See *Gridelin*.

griz′zle, *n.* and *a.* [ME. *grisel, grisell*, an old man, from OFr. *gris*; O.H.G. *gris*, gray.]
I. *n.* Gray; a gray color; a mixture of white and black.
II. *a.* Gray; grizzled. [Obs.]

griz′zle, *v.i.*; grizzled, *pt.*, *pp.*; grizzling, *ppr.* To grow grizzly; to grow gray, as from worry. [Rare.]

griz′zled, *a.* Gray; of a mixed color.

griz′zly, *a.* Somewhat gray; grayish.
Grizzly bear; see *Bear*.

griz′zly, *n.*; *pl.* **griz′zlieṣ.** 1. The grizzly bear.
2. A grating used in hydraulic mining for throwing out the large stones swept down by the current.

grōan, *v.i.*; groaned, *pt.*, *pp.*; groaning, *ppr.* [ME. *gronen*; AS. *granian*, to lament, murmur, groan.]
1. To breathe with a deep, murmuring sound; to utter a mournful voice, as in pain or sorrow; to utter a deep, low-toned, moaning sound; often used in a figurative sense; as, a nation *groans* under the weight of taxes.
2. To long or strive earnestly, and as if with groans.

> I'm sure the gallows *groans* for you.—Swift.

grōan, *v.t.* To silence or put down by groans; as, the speaker was *groaned* down.

grōan, *n.* A deep, mournful sound, uttered in pain, sorrow, or anguish; frequently, a deep, murmuring sound uttered in disapprobation or derision; opposed to *cheer*.

> *Groans* of roaring wind and rain. —Shak.

Syn.—Moan, whine, growl, grumble.

grōan′ēr, *n.* One who groans.

grōan′ful, *a.* Sad; inducing groans.

grōat, *n.* [ME. *grote, groote*; L.G. *grote*, O.D. *groot*, a large coin, lit., great.]
1. An old English silver coin equivalent to fourpence.
2. Any small or trifling sum.

grōats, *n.pl.* [ME. *grotes, groten*; AS. *gratan*, groats.] Oats or wheat without the hulls; fragments of wheat somewhat larger than grits.

grō′bi-ăn, *n.* [G., from *grob*, coarse, rude.] A person of rude, uncouth or clownish manners; a boor. [Rare.]

grō′cēr, *n.* [ME. *grocere*, a corruption of *grosser*, a grocer, a wholesale dealer; OFr. *grossier*, LL. *grossarius*, a wholesale dealer, from *grossus*, great, gross.] A trader who deals in tea, sugar, spices, coffee, fruits, etc.
Grocers' itch; a cutaneous disease produced in grocers and persons working in sugar-refineries by the irritation of sugar.

grō′cēr-y, *n.*; *pl.* **grō′cēr-ieṣ.** [OFr. *grosserie*, from LL. *grossarius*, a wholesale dealer.]
1. The commodities sold by grocers; in the United States always in the plural.
2. A grocer's store.

grog, *n.* [Named after Old *Grog*, the nickname given to Admiral Vernon, who introduced the drink about 1745. He was so called because he wore grogram breeches.] A mixture of spirit and water not sweetened; hence, any kind of strong drink.

grog′-blos″sŏm, *n.* An eruption or redness on the face or nose resulting from the excessive use of intoxicants. [Slang.]

grog′gēr-y, *n.*; *pl.* **grog′gēr-ieṣ.** A drinking-saloon of disreputable character; a grogshop.

grog′gi-ness, *n.* 1. The condition of being groggy.
2. In farriery, a tenderness or stiffness in the foot of a horse or weakness in the fore legs, which causes him to move in a hobbling, staggering manner; often produced by much movement on hard ground.

grog′gy, *a.* 1. Overcome with grog, so as to stagger or stumble; tipsy. [Slang.]
2. Acting or moving like a man overcome with grog; stupefied and staggering from blows and exhaustion; said of a pugilist.
3. In farriery, moving in an uneasy, hobbling manner, owing to tenderness of the feet; said specifically of a horse that bears wholly on its heels.

grog′răm, *n.* [OFr. *gros-grain*; *gros*, coarse, gross, and *grain*, grain.] Formerly, a kind of coarse stuff made of silk and mohair; also, a kind of strong coarse silk.

grog′shop, *n.* See *Groggery*.

groin, *n.* The snout of a swine. [Prov. Eng.]

groin, *v.i.* To groan or grunt; to grumble. [Obs.]

groin, *n.* [Ice. *grein*, the branch of a tree, a branch, arm, difference.]
1. In anatomy, the depressed part of the body between the abdomen and the thigh.
2. In architecture, the angular curve made by the intersection of simple vaults crossing each other at any angle. Most of the vaulted ceilings of the middle ages were characterized by *groins*.
3. A wooden breakwater or frame of woodwork constructed across a beach between low and high water to retain sand or mud thrown up by the tide. [Eng.]

a a, Groins.

groin, *v.t.*; groined, *pt.*, *pp.*; groining, *ppr.* In architecture, to form into groins; to ornament or furnish with groins.

groined, *a.* Having an angular curve formed by the intersection of two arches; as, a *groined* arch; a *groined* ceiling or roof.

Groined Roof.

Grō-lier′ (-lyā′), *n.* A binding which takes its name from Jean Grolier de Servier (1479–1565), a noted French bibliophile.
Grolier design or *scroll*; a geometrical decorative style in bookbinding in which gold lines are intermingled with leaves and sprays. Such a style was used by Grolier.

grom′et, *n.* [Fr. *gourmette*, a curb, a curb-chain, from *gourmer*, to curb.] A ring formed of a strand of rope laid round and spliced, used for various purposes, as for fastening the upper edge of a sail to a stay; also, a metallic eyelet, as for a mail-bag.

Gromet for a Sail.

grom′et-wăd, *n.* In ordnance, a wad made of rope, rammed down between the ball and the charge.

grom′met, *n.* See *Gromet*.

grom′well, *n.* [ME. *gromil*; OFr. *gremil*, prob. from L. *granum*, grain, and *milium*, millet.] In botany, the plant *Lithospermum officinale*, of the borage family. Its seeds were formerly supposed to be efficacious in the cure of gravel.
False gromwell; any boraginaceous plant of the genus *Onosmodium*.

grond, *v.*, obsolete past tense of *grind*.

gronte, *v.*, obsolete past tense of *groan*.

grọọm, *n.* [ME. *grom, grome*, a boy, a servant; compare Ice. *gromr*, a man, a servant; etym. doubtful, prob. from AS. *guma*, a man.]
1. A boy or young man; a waiter; a servant; especially, a man or boy who has the charge of horses; one who takes care of horses or the stable.
2. In England, one of several officers of the royal household; as, the *groom* of the chamber; *groom* of the stole.

grọọm, *n.* A man newly married or about to be married; a bridegroom.

grọọm, *v.t.*; groomed, *pt.*, *pp.*; grooming, *ppr.* To tend or care for, as a horse; to curry (a horse).

grọọm′ēr, *n.* One who grooms; that with which one grooms; especially, a device used for cleaning horses, which works mechanically.

grọọm′-pōr″tēr, *n.* In England, formerly an officer of the royal household whose business was to see the king's lodging furnished with tables, chairs, stools, and firing, also to provide cards, dice, etc., and to decide disputes arising at cards and other games.

grọọmṣ′măn, *n.*; *pl.* **grọọmṣ′men.** One who acts as attendant on a bridegroom at his marriage.

grọọp′ēr, *n.* See *Grouper*.

grọọve, *n.* [ME. *grofe*, a pit; D. *groeve, groef*, a channel, groove, from *graven*; Goth. *graban*, to dig.]
1. A furrow or long hollow such as is cut by a tool; a rut or furrow, such as is formed in the ground or in a rock by the action of water; a channel, usually an elongated narrow channel, formed by any agency; specifically, a channel in the edge of a matched board to receive the tongue.
2. The natural course or fixed routine of one's life or events; a rut.
3. In mining, a shaft or pit sunk into the earth. [Prov. Eng.]

grọọve, *v.t.*; grooved, *pt.*, *pp.*; grooving, *ppr.* To cut a groove or channel in; to furrow.

grọọv′ēr, *n.* 1. One who or that which cuts a groove.
2. A miner. [Prov. Eng.]

grọọv′ing, *n.* The act or process of cutting or forming a groove; a groove or system of grooves.

grōpe, *v.i.*; groped, *pt.*, *pp.*; groping, *ppr.* [ME. *gropen, gropien*; AS. *grapian*, to grasp, handle, from *grap*, a grip, or grasp, from *gripan*, to seize, grasp.]
1. To search or seek to find something in the dark, or as a blind person, by feeling about with the hands; to feel one's way, as with the hands.

> We *grope* for the wall like the blind.
> —Isa. lix. 10.

2. To use the hands; to handle. [Obs.]

grōpe, *v.t.* 1. To search out by feeling in the dark; as, we *groped* our way at midnight.
2. To test; to sound. [Obs.]

grōp′ēr, *n.* One who gropes; one who feels his way in the dark, or searches by feeling.

grōp′ing-ly, *adv.* In a groping manner.

grōs (grō). [Fr.] A fabric, usually of silk, of strong texture; as, *gros* de Naples; *gros* de Tours, etc.

grōs′bēak, *n.* A bird having a large thick bill. The name is usually applied to fringilloid birds. The common grosbeak of Europe is *Coccothraustes vulgaris*, which is also known as the *hawfinch*. *Ligurinus chloris* is the green grosbeak. Notable American species are, the blue grosbeak, *Guiraca cœrulea*; the rose-breasted grosbeak, *Habia ludoviciana*, and the black-headed grosbeak, *Habia melanocephala*. Written also *grossbeak*.

Green Grosbeak (*Ligurinus chloris*).

grosch′en, *n.* [G.] A small silver coin worth about two cents, formerly current in Germany.

grōs′grāin (grō′), *n.* [Fr.] A stout corded silk, regarded as very durable.

grōss, *a.* [OFr. *gros*, masc., *grosse*, f., big, thick, from LL. *grossus*, thick, big.]
1. Thick; bulky; particularly applied to animals; fat; corpulent; large; great; as, a *gross* body. Formerly used of size in general.
2. Coarse; rough; not fine or delicate; as, *gross* sculpture; *gross* features.
3. Coarse, in a figurative sense; rough; vulgar; indelicate; obscene; impure; sensual; applying either to persons or things.

> The terms which are delicate in one age become *gross* in the next. —Macaulay.

4. Great; palpable; enormous; shameful; flagrant; as, a *gross* mistake; *gross* injustice.
5. Thick; dense; not attenuated; not refined or pure; as, a *gross* medium; *gross* air; *gross* elements.
6. Not easily roused or excited; not sensitive in perception or feeling; stupid; dull.

> Tell her of things that no *gross* ear can hear.
> —Milton.

7. Whole; entire; total; as, the *gross* sum, or *gross* amount, as opposed to a sum or amount consisting of separate or specified parts, or to a sum or amount from which a deduction has been made.
Gross weight; the weight of merchandise or goods, with the dust and dross, the bag, cask, chest, etc., in which they are contained. After an allowance of tare and tret is deducted, the remainder is denominated *net weight*.

grōss, *n.* 1. The main body; the chief part; the bulk; the mass; as, the *gross* of the people.

> For see the Saxon *gross* begins to move.
> —Dryden.

2. Literally, the gross or great hundred; the number of twelve dozen; twelve times twelve;

as, a *gross* of bottles. It never has the plural form; as, five *gross* or ten *gross*.

Advowson in gross; in law, an advowson separated from the property of a manor, and annexed to the person of its owner.

A great gross; twelve gross or 144 dozen.

Common in gross; see under *Common*.

In the gross, in gross; in the bulk, or the undivided whole; all parts taken together.

Villain in gross; in feudal law, a villain or servant who did not belong to the land, but immediately to the person of the lord, and was transferable by deed, like chattels, from one owner to another.

grŏss′bēak, *n.* Same as *Grosbeak*.

grŏss′-head″ed (-hed″), *a.* Having a thick skull; stupid.

grŏss″i-fi-cā′tion, *n.* [LL. *grossus*, thick, big, and L. *facere*, to make.] The act of making gross; the state of being or becoming gross; specifically, in botany, the enlargement of an ovary upon being fertilized.

grŏss′ly, *adv.* In a gross manner.

grŏss′ness, *n.* The state or quality of being gross.

gros-sū-lā′ceous, *a.* [OFr. *groselle*, a gooseberry.] In botany, relating to the gooseberry or currant.

gros′sū-lăr, *a.* [OFr. *groselle, groiselle*, a gooseberry.] Pertaining to or resembling a gooseberry; as, *grossular* garnet.

gros′sū-lăr, *n.* A species of garnet of a green color; called also *grossularite*.

Gros″sū-lā-ri′ē-æ, *n.* [OFr. *groselle, groiselle*, a gooseberry, a currant; prob. from M.H.G. *krus*, curling, crisp.] A tribe of the order *Saxifragaceæ*, including the gooseberry and currant of gardens, and consisting of only one genus, *Ribes*; now known as *Ribesieæ*.

gros′sū-lăr-īte, *n.* An aluminium garnet; grossular.

gros′sū-lin, *n.* In chemistry, a pectin-like compound found in fruits, especially in the gooseberry.

grŏt, grōte, *n.*, variants of *groat*.

grot, *n.* [Obs.] See *Grotto*.

grō-tesque′ (-tesk′), *a.* [Fr. *grotesque*; It. *grottesco*, odd, extravagant, from *grotta*, a grotto.]

1. Resembling the figures found in grottos; wildly formed; whimsical; extravagant; of irregular forms and proportions; ludicrous; antic; as, *grotesque* paintings; *grotesque* designs.

2. Resembling artificial grottowork, decorated with rockwork, shells, etc. [Obs.]

grō-tesque′, *n.* A grotesque figure, as found in ancient grottoes; any whimsical representation, as in an ornament or a style of writing or printing.

grō-tesque′ly, *adv.* In a fantastical manner.

grō-tesque′ness, *n.* The state of being grotesque.

grō-tes′quēr-y (-kēr-), *n.* The act of indulging in grotesque whims or antics; grotesque conduct; a grotesque action; an embodiment or expression of grotesqueness.

Grō′ti-ăn (-shi-), *a.* Pertaining to the Dutch scholar and statesman, Hugo Grotius (1583–1645). He was the founder of the modern science of international law.

Grotian theory; in theology, a theory of atonement founded upon the basic principle of government; i.e., that the Almighty was constrained by his almighty judgeship not to allow sin to go unatoned, offense without punishment being subversive of all governmental rule; hence, the solemn lesson of Christ's sufferings and death.

grot′tō, *n.*; *pl.* **grot′tōes, grot′tōs.** [It. *grotta*, a grotto, cave, from LL. *grupta*; L. *crypta*; Gr. *kryptē*, a hidden, underground passage, a crypt, from *kryptos*, hidden, from *kryptein*, to hide.]

1. A small cave; a subterranean cavern; a

Grotto of Melidhoni in Crete.

natural cave or rent in the earth, usually of great natural beauty or unusual appearance.

2. An artificial, ornamented cave designed for coolness and refreshment.

grot′tō-wŏrk, *n.* Artificial work in imitation of a natural grotto.

grouch, *n.* One who is sulky or morose; also, the condition of being sulky. [Slang.]

grouch′y, *a.* Morose; sulky; doggedly sullen. [Slang.]

ground, *n.* [ME. *ground*; AS. *grund*, bottom, foundation, soil.]

1. The surface of the earth; the outer crust of the globe; hence, the surface of a floor or pavement, as supposed to be resting upon the earth.

> There was not a man to till the *ground*.
> —Gen. ii. 5.

2. Region; territory; country; land; as, Egyptian *ground*; British *ground*; heavenly *ground*.

3. Land; estate; possession; hence, the place assigned to one in certain games, as baseball, football, etc.

> Thy next design is on thy neighbor's *grounds*.
> —Dryden.

4. That on which anything may stand or rest, or be raised or transacted; that from which anything may rise or originate; foundation of knowledge, belief, or conviction; originating force, agency, or agent; support; ultimate or first principle; generally in a figurative sense.

> To the solid *ground*
> Of nature trusts the Mind that builds for aye.
> —Wordsworth.

5. In the fine arts, (a) in painting, the surface on which a figure or object is represented; that surface or substance which retains the original color, and to which the other colors are applied to make the representation; as, crimson on a white *ground*; (b) in sculpture, the flat surface from which the figures rise; said of a work in relief.

6. In manufactures, the principal color, to which others are considered as ornamental; that portion of manufactured articles, as tapestry, carpeting, etc., of a uniform color, on which the figures are, as it were, drawn or projected.

7. A foil or background that sets off anything.

> Like bright metal on a sullen *ground*.—Shak.

8. [*pl.*] Sediment at the bottom of liquors; dregs; lees; feces; as, coffee-*grounds*; the *grounds* of strong beer.

9. In etching, a composition spread over the surface of the plate to be etched, to prevent the acid from eating into the plate, except where an opening is made with the point of the etching-needle.

10. In music, (a) a composition in which the base, consisting of a few bars of independent notes, is continually repeated to a continually varying melody; (b) the plain song; the tune on which descants are raised.

11. Formerly, the pit of a play-house.

12. In mining, the stratum in which the lode is found.

13. In joinery, one of the pieces of wood fixed to walls and partitions, with their surfaces flush with the plaster, to which the facings or finishings are attached.

14. In electricity, a connection with the earth, as from a wire conveying a current, so as to make the earth a part of the circuit.

Happy hunting-grounds; the place of happiness after death, as conceived by the Indians of North America; the Indian's heaven.

On slippery ground; in a precarious situation; in a position exposed to sudden disaster.

The dark and bloody ground; see under *Dark*.

To be on the ground; (a) to be vigilant in watching one's own interests; (b) to be punctual in keeping an engagement.

To break ground; see under *Break*.

To fall to the ground; to fail; as, the undertaking *fell to the ground*.

To gain ground; see under *Gain*.

To give ground; see under *Give*.

To lose ground; to fall back; to fail to keep up to the required pace; to become less efficient; to lose standing, as in society or in financial matters.

To stand one's ground; to maintain position; to refuse to yield to opposition; to exhibit a courageous disposition.

To take the ground; (a) to assume a position; as, the Declaration of Independence *takes the ground* that all men are born equal, etc.; (b) in navigation, to be stranded, as a vessel.

ground, *v.i.*; grounded, *pt., pp.*; grounding, *ppr.* To run aground; to strike the bottom and remain fixed; as, the ship *grounded*.

ground, *v.t.* [ME. *grounden*; AS. *gryndan, agryndan*, to descend, or set, from *grund*, base, foundation.]

1. To lay or set on the ground.

2. To found; to fix or set, as on a foundation, cause, reason, or principle; as, arguments *grounded* on reason; faith *grounded* on scriptural evidence.

3. To settle in first principles; to fix firmly.

> Being rooted and *grounded* in love.
> —Eph. iii. 17.

4. In electricity, to connect with the earth; as, to *ground* a wire.

5. Among sailors, to cause to run upon the ground; as, to *ground* a ship.

6. In art, to form a ground for; as, to *ground* a canvas by painting a background.

ground, *a.* 1. Being upon a level with the ground; as, a *ground* room.

2. Fundamental; lying at the bottom.

Ground air; the air mingled with the constituents of the ground.

Ground bass; in music, fundamental bass, running through an entire movement regardless of variation in the melody.

Ground cock; a cock having a plug, as of glass or brass, which is ground into its place to secure a tight fit.

Ground floor; a floor about on a level with the ground.

Ground form; in grammar, basic form, as the stem word.

Ground joint; a joint made close-fitting by grinding together its two parts, usually by placing between them oil and some kind of fine grit, as pulverized emery.

Ground tier; the lowest tier of boxes in a theater; (b) in general, any row or tier nearest the ground, as of stone in a building.

ground, *v.*, past tense and past participle of *grind*.

ground′āge, *n.* A tax paid by a ship for the ground or space it occupies while in port.

ground′-an″gling, *n.* Fishing without a float, with a weight placed a few inches from the hook.

ground′-an″nū-ăl, *n.* In Scots law, a perpetual leasehold at a fixed annual ground-rent.

ground′-ash, *n.* In botany, (a) a slender ash-tree or sapling; (b) the goutweed.

ground′-bail″iff, *n.* In mining, an inspector of mines.

ground′-bāit, *n.* 1. In angling, bait scattered on the water and sinking to the bottom to allure fish to a locality.

2. A fish, the groundling.

ground′-bee″tle, *n.* In zoölogy, any one of many carabid beetles living on the ground and hiding under stones.

ground′ber″ry, *n.*; *pl.* **ground′ber″ries,** *n.* In botany, the plant or the globular red berry of the plant *Gaultheria procumbens* or wintergreen.

ground′-cher″ry, *n.*; *pl.* **ground′-cher″ries.** In botany, (a) a herbaceous plant of the nightshade family and of the genus *Physalis*, characterized by a bladder-like calyx, in the cavity of which the fruit is borne, as *Physalis viscosa*; (b) a European shrub of the rose family and of the subgenus *Cerasus*, bearing a small and very sour fruit.

ground′-cir″cuit (-kit), *n.* The connection of an electrical circuit with the earth.

ground′-cis″tus, *n.* *Rhodothamnus Chamæcistus*, a small shrub of Switzerland.

ground′-cŏn-nec″tion, *n.* A ground-circuit.

ground′-cuck″oo, *n.* See *Chaparral-cock*.

ground′-dōve, *n.* Any pigeon closely inhabiting the ground; as, (a) a bird of the genus *Geopelia* or *Geotrygon*; (b) *Columbigallina passerina*, a dwarfish bird common in the southern states of the United States.

ground′ed-ly, *adv.* In a grounded manner; so as to be firmly fixed.

ground′en, *v.*, obsolete past participle of *grind*.

ground′ēr, *n.* A ball keeping close to or frequently hitting the ground, as in baseball.

ground′-finch, *n.* A bird of the genus *Pipilo*.

ground′-fish, *n.* A fish keeping to the bottom of the water, as the cod.

ground′-fūrze, *n.* *Ononis arvensis*, a thorny shrub infesting cultivated land in many parts of Europe; called also *rest-harrow*.

ground′-game, *n.* Running game, as rabbits, distinguished from flying game.

ground′-grū, *n.* Ground-ice.

ground′-hem″lock, *n.* *Taxus baccata*, a creeping variety of the common yew.

ground′-hog, *n.* 1. The popular name of the American rodent, *Arctomys monax*, the woodchuck.

2. A name applied to the *Orycteropus capensis*, a South African ant-eater.

Ground-hog day; see *Woodchuck day* under *Woodchuck*.

ground′-ice, *n.* Ice formed at the bottom of a river, or other body of water, before it begins to appear on the surface.

ground′ing, *n.* 1. The act or process of founding or establishing; instruction in elementary principles.

2. A design-background.

3. A finishing of oil and alumina used as an application for wall-paper.

4. A process in which boiled oil is applied to porcelain ware before it is enameled; ground-laying.

5. In marble-working, the smoothing of marble by the use of emery.

ground′-i″vy, *n.* *Nepeta Glechoma* or *Glechoma hederacea*, a plant common to Europe and growing in some parts of the United States.

ground′-joist, *n.* A joist of a basement or ground-floor.

ground′⸗lärk, *n.* A bird, the pipit of Europe.

ground′⸗lau″rel, *n.* See *Trailing arbutus* under *Arbutus.*

ground′⸗lāy″ing, *n.* See *Grounding,* 4.

ground′less, *a.* Without ground or foundation; baseless; unfounded; as, *groundless* fears.

ground′less-ly, *adv.* In a groundless manner.

ground′less-ness, *n.* The state or quality of being groundless.

ground′⸗līne, *n.* In geometry and perspective, the line of intersection of the horizontal and vertical planes of projection.

ground′ling, *n.* 1. That which inhabits the ground, as an animal.

2. A popular name for two fishes that keep at the bottom of the water; (a) the spined loach, *Cobitis tænia;* (b) the black goby, *Gobius niger;* the former common in fresh water, the latter on the coast.

3. A spectator who stood in the pit of the theater, which was literally on the ground, having neither floor nor benches. [Obs.]

ground′⸗liv″ēr-wŏrt, *n.* A lichen, *Peltigera canina.*

ground′⸗liz″ărd, *n.* 1. A skink, *Oligosoma laterale.*

2. A lizard, *Ameiva dorsalis,* very common in Jamaica, frequenting the roadsides and open pastures.

ground′ly, *adv.* Upon principles; solidly; not superficially. [Obs.]

ground′⸗mäll, *n.* Duty paid for the right of having a corpse interred in a churchyard. [Scot.]

ground′⸗măss, *n.* The compact part of a rock containing a dissemination of crystals throughout its mass.

ground′⸗mōld, *n.* In engineering, a mold or frame by means of which the surface of the ground is wrought to any particular form, as in terracing or embanking.

ground′⸗nest, *n.* A nest on the ground.

ground′⸗niche, *n.* In architecture, a niche whose base or seat is on a level with the ground-floor.

ground′nut, *n.* 1. The peanut.

2. The earthnut, *Bunium flexuosum.*

3. A climbing plant, *Apios tuberosa.*

ground′⸗par″rā-keet, *n.* An Australian parrakeet of terrestrial habits.

ground′⸗par″rŏt, *n.* The kakapo.

ground′⸗pēa, *n.* The peanut.

ground′⸗pēarl, *n.* An insect of the West Indies having a shelly covering. These shells are strung together by the natives, after the fashion of pearls.

ground′⸗pig, *n.* The aardvark of Africa; also, a rodent found in Africa, of the genus *Aulacodus.*

ground′⸗pig″eŏn, *n.* A pigeon of the subfamily *Gourinæ.*

ground′⸗pīne, *n.* 1. A labiate plant, *Ajuga Chamæpitys,* having an odor resembling pine.

2. One of several species of the genus *Lycopodium.*

ground′⸗plan, *n.* In architecture, the representation of the divisions of a building on the same level with the surface of the ground.

ground′⸗plāne, *n.* The horizontal plane of projection in perspective drawing.

ground′⸗plāte, *n.* 1. In architecture, one of the outermost pieces of framing placed on or near the ground; a groundsill.

2. A bed-plate used in soft ground to support sleepers or ties.

3. A plate of metal sunk in the ground to ground an electric current; any means similarly used.

ground′⸗plot, *n.* 1. The ground on which a building is placed.

2. Same as *Ground-plan.*

ground′⸗plum, *n.* A leguminous plant, *Astragalus caryocarpus,* found in the Mississippi valley.

ground′⸗rat, *n.* Another name for the ground-pig.

ground′⸗rent, *n.* Rent paid for the privilege of building on another man's land.

ground′⸗rōom, *n.* A room on the ground-floor of a building; a lower floor.

ground′⸗rōpe, *n.* The rope along the bottom of a trawl-net.

ground′⸗sēa, *n.* The West Indian name for the swell called rollers, or in Jamaica the North sea, occurring in a calm and with no other indication of a previous gale.

ground′sel, *n.* [ME. *grundeswilie;* AS. *grundeswelge, gundeswilge,* lit., pus-swallower, groundsel; *gund,* pus, and *swelgan,* to swallow; so called from its being good for running eyes.] *Senecio vulgaris,* a common annual weed belonging to the order *Compositæ.* It is emollient, and has a slightly acrid taste.

ground′sel-tree, *n.* A shrub of the aster family having a dusty appearance.

ground′sill, ground′sel, *n.* The timber of a building which lies next to the ground; the ground plate; the sill.

ground′⸗slōth, *n.* See *Megatherium.*

ground′⸗snāke, *n.* In zoölogy, (a) a worm-snake; (b) a colubroid snake of Australia.

ground′⸗squir″rel (-skwir″), *n.* A burrowing rodent, as the chipmunk, gopher, etc.

ground′⸗stär″ling, *n.* An American meadow-lark.

ground′⸗sub″stănce, *n.* In anatomy, the matrix in which certain cells and tissues are embedded.

ground′⸗swell, *n.* A wide, sweeping, swell of the sea, caused by a storm, but making itself felt long after the wind has gone down.

ground′⸗tā″ble, *n.* Same as *Earth-table.*

ground′⸗tac″kle, *n.* A general term for the anchors, cables, etc., of a ship.

ground′⸗thrush, *n.* An ant-thrush.

ground′⸗tim″bērs, *n.pl.* In shipbuilding, the structural timbers attached to the keel of a vessel.

ground′⸗tit, *n.* The ground-wren.

ground′wāys, *n.pl.* The foundations in a ship-building yard, on which keel-blocks are laid.

ground′⸗wēave, *n.* The weave that forms the ground for figured cloth, etc.

ground′⸗wheel (-hwēl), *n.* The wheel of a harvester, drill, or other machine which, by revolving upon the ground, moves the mechanism.

ground′⸗wren (-ren), *n.* A small California bird; also called *ground-tit.*

ground′wŏrk, *n.* The work which forms the foundation of anything; the fundamental part, principle, or motive.

grōup, *n.* [Fr. *groupe;* It. *gruppo,* a knot, lump, group; of Germanic origin; compare G. *kropf,* a bunch, a crop.]

1. Generally, a cluster, crowd, or throng; an assemblage either of persons or things; a number collected without any regular form or arrangement; as, a *group* of men or of trees; a *group* of isles.

2. A collection of individuals having some mutual relation or resemblance; as, a *group* of rocks in a geological system. In geology the term is used in many senses, and in biology a *group* may include a number of genera or of species or even of orders.

3. In music, (a) a series of notes sung to the same syllable; (b) a division of an orchestra comprising similar instruments; as, the strings are a *group.*

4. In painting and sculpture, an assemblage of two or more figures of men, beasts, or other things which have some relation to each other and to the design as a whole.

Fuchsian group; a group of linear transformations, $t=\frac{az+b}{cz+d}$, in which z is an imaginary variable and t an imaginary function of this variable.

Laramie group; a series of strata of the Cretaceous and Eocene Tertiary developed chiefly in the *Laramie* Mountains.

Syn.—Assemblage, assembly, cluster, collection, clump, bunch, crowd, audience, congregation, meeting, crew, gang, knot, company, throng.

grōup, *v.t.;* grouped, *pt., pp.;* grouping, *ppr.* [Fr. *grouper.*] To form into a group; to bring or place together in a cluster or knot; to form an assemblage of, usually for harmonious effect.

grōup′ēr, *n.* Any of various food-fishes, especially, (a) a bass-like fish of the genus *Epinephelus* or *Mycteroperca;* (b) the California rock-fish; (c) the triple-tail; (d) the hamlet.

grōup′ing, *n.* The act or result of arranging in a group; specifically, the art of composing or combining the objects of a picture or piece of sculpture.

grouse, *n.* [OFr. *griesche,* gray, as a noun, the gray partridge, from *gris;* O.H.G. *gris,* gray.] A gallinaceous bird of the subfamily *Tetraoninæ,* widely distributed over Europe, Asia, and North America, varying in color, but usually with mottled plumage; as, the ruffed grouse, the partridge or pheasant of the United States, the prairie-hen, the red grouse of England, and the ptarmigan.

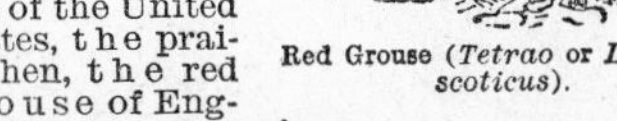

Red Grouse (*Tetrao* or *Lagopus scoticus*).

grouse, *v.i.;* groused, *pt., pp.;* grousing, *ppr.* To hunt or shoot grouse.

grous′ēr, *n.* [Etym. unknown.] A pole or pile, usually pointed and shod with iron, to be driven into the ground as an anchor for a dredging-boat or the like.

grout, *n.* [ME. *grout, growte;* AS. *grut,* coarse meal, grout.]

1. Coarse meal; groats or porridge of groats.

2. A kind of wild apple.

3. A thin, coarse mortar with crushed stone or gravel, used for pouring into the joints of masonry and brickwork; also used for walls, walks, floors, etc., when made with a cement; a kind of concrete.

4. A kind of thick ale. [Prov. Eng.]

5. [*pl.*] Lees; grounds; dregs.

grout, *v.t.;* grouted, *pt., pp.;* grouting, *ppr.* To place grout in; to make with grout; to use as grout; as, to *grout* a foundation or a walk; to *grout* mortar into crevices.

grout′head (-hed), *n.* A blockhead. [Obs.]

grout′noll, *n.* A grouthead; a blockhead. [Obs.]

grout′y, *a.* 1. Turbid; dreggy.

2. Cross; sulky; surly. [Colloq.]

grōve, *n.* [ME. *grove;* AS. *graf,* a grove, a small forest.]

1. A cluster of trees shading an avenue or walk; an assemblage of growing trees of no great extent; a small wood.

2. Something resembling a wood or trees in a wood.

grov′el, *v.i.;* groveled *or* grovelled, *pt., pp.;* groveling *or* grovelling, *ppr.* [From ME. *groveling,* on the face, prostrate, from *grof,* on the face, from Ice. *grufa,* to crouch, grovel.]

1. To creep on the earth, or with the face to the ground; to lie prone, or move with the body prostrate on the earth; to act in a prostrate posture.

2. To be low or mean; as, *groveling* thoughts.

grov′el-ēr, grov′el-lēr, *n.* One who grovels; an abject wretch.

grov′el-ing, grov′el-ling, *a.* Mean; debased; low.

grōv′y, *a.* Pertaining to a grove; frequenting groves; like a grove; abounding in groves.

grōw, *v.i.;* grew, *pt.;* growing, *ppr.;* grown, *pp.* [ME. *growen;* AS. *growan,* to grow, sprout.]

1. To become enlarged in bulk or stature, by a natural and organic process, as animal and vegetable bodies; to vegetate, as plants, or to be augmented by the gradual assimilation of new matter, as animals.

2. To be produced by vegetation; as, wheat *grows* in most parts of the world.

3. To increase; to be augmented; to wax; as, a body *grows* larger by inflation or distention.

4. To advance; to improve; to make progress; as, to *grow* in grace, in knowledge, or in reputation.

5. To come by degrees; to become; to reach any state; as, he *grows* more skilful or more prudent.

6. To root; to become fastened; as, to *grow* to the ground.

7. On a ship, to have a certain position or direction; as, the cables *grow* to port.

To grow out of; to issue from, as plants from the soil or as a branch from the main stem.

To grow up; to arrive at manhood; to advance to full stature or maturity.

To grow upon; to have an increasing effect upon one's mind or feelings; as, the beauty of the scene *grew upon* me as I gazed.

Syn.—Increase, enlarge, wax, augment, swell, vegetate.

grōw, *v.t.* To cause to grow; to raise, cultivate, or produce; as, to *grow* fruit, cereals, etc.

grōw′ăn, *n.* [Corn. *grow,* gravel, sand.] Disintegrated granite.

grōw′ēr, *n.* One who raises or grows; as, a *grower* of vines; also, that which increases or grows; as, this tree is a fine *grower.*

growl, *v.i.;* growled, *pt., pp.;* growling, *ppr.* [ME. *growlen,* to growl; prob. imitative; compare D. *grollen,* to grumble; G. *grollen,* to be angry; OFr. *grouiller,* to rumble.]

1. To utter an angry, grumbling sound; to make a deep, rumbling, guttural sound, as an angry bear.

2. To speak in a grumbling, surly, ill-tempered tone; to complain; to grumble; as, he *growled* about the price.

growl, *v.t.* To express by growling or with a growl; as, he *growled* a reply; to *growl* defiance.

growl, *n.* The low, menacing sound uttered by an angry animal; a deep, rumbling noise; grumbling.

growl′ēr, *n.* 1. One who or that which growls.

2. A fish; (a) the large-mouthed black bass; (b) the grunt.

3. In London, a four-wheeled cab drawn by one horse. [Colloq.]

4. A vessel, as a pitcher or pail, taken by a customer to a saloon for beer. [Slang.]

To rush the growler; to fetch beer in a vessel from a saloon for the use of a party elsewhere. [Slang.]

growl′ing-ly, *adv.* In a growling manner.

grōwn, *v.,* past participle of *grow.*

grōwth, *n.* 1. The gradual increase of animal and vegetable bodies; the process of springing from a germ, seed, or root, and proceeding to full size, by gradual organic development.

2. Increase by development or accretion, as in number, extent, frequency, or power; advancement; progress; augmentation; as, the *growth* of a crystal; the *growth* of population.

3. Anything growing or grown; product;

produce; as, a *growth* of grain; a fine *growth* of hair.

grōwth′fụl, *a.* Able to grow. [Rare.]

groyne, *n.* A groin; a grunt. [Obs.]

grō′zing-ī″ron (-ũrn), *n.* 1. Formerly a kind of glass-cutter having a steel point.

2. A tool for finishing the solder-joints of lead pipe.

grub, *v.i.*; grubbed, *pt., pp.*; grubbing, *ppr.* [ME. *grubben*, to dig; prob. of Germanic origin; compare O.H.G. *grubilon*, to grub, dig; AS. *grafan*, to dig.]

1. To dig; to be occupied in digging, usually for roots, and implying difficult labor.

2. To drudge; to slave; to search or study closely.

3. To eat; to take a meal. [Slang.]

grub, *v.t.* To dig out or up; to root out by digging; as, to *grub* up stumps.

grub, *n.* 1. A larva of a beetle, moth, or other insect; also called *grubworm*.

2. A mean, sordid, or grasping person.

3. Food; victuals; something to eat. [Slang.]

grub′-ax, *n.* A mattock; called also *grub-hoe, grubbing-hoe.*

grub′bẽr, *n.* 1. One who grubs.

2. An instrument for digging up roots.

3. One who eats; a feeder. [Slang.]

grub′ble, *v.i.* To feel in the dark, or as a blind man; to grope. [Rare.]

grub′by, *a.* 1. Filthy; dirty; unclean, as if from grubbing.

2. Having many grubs.

grub′by, *n.* A fish of the genus *Cottus*; a sculpin.

grub′-hook, *n.* An implement in the form of a hook drawn by horses and controlled by handles, used for upturning stones, roots, etc.

grub′-sa̤w, *n.* A rough saw for sawing stone.

grub′stāke, *n.* Equipment supplied to a mining prospector in consideration for receiving a share of whatever may be found by him. [Slang.]

Grub′-street, *n.* 1. Originally the name of a street near Moorfields in London (now called Milton street), much inhabited by men engaged in the production of low-class fugitive literature; whence any mean production is called *Grub-street.*

2. Mean or needy authors collectively.

grub′wŏrm, *n.* A grub.

gruche, grucche, *v.i.* [Obs.] See *Grudge.*

grudġe, *v.t.*; grudged, *pt., pp.*; grudging, *ppr.* [ME. *gruggen*; OFr. *groucier, grouchier*, to murmur, complain, grudge; prob. of Scand. origin; compare Ice. *krytja*, to murmur.]

1. To be discontented at; to look upon with envy; to envy (one) the possession of; as, t *grudge* some one a pleasure.

2. To give unwillingly; to begrudge; to permit or grant reluctantly; as, to *grudge* a contribution.

3. To feel or entertain in a malevolent or discontented spirit. [Obs.]

grudġe, *v.i.* 1. To murmur; to grumble; to repine; to complain; to be unwilling or reluctant.

Grudge not one against another.—James v. 9.

2. To feel compunction; to grieve. [Obs.]

grudġe, *n.* 1. Sullen malice or malevolence; spite; ill-will; a cherished dislike; as, an old *grudge.*

2. Unwillingness; reluctance.

3. Remorse of conscience. [Obs.]

Syn.—Animosity, enmity, ill will, rancor, hatred, pique.

grudġe′fụl, *a.* Grudging. [Obs.]

grudġ′ẽr, *n.* One who grudges.

grudġ′ing-ly, *adv.* Unwillingly; with reluctance; in a grudging manner.

grudġ′ing-ness, *n.* The state or quality of grudging.

grudġ′inġs, *n.pl.* Coarse meal; grouts. [Obs.]

grụ′el, *n.* [ME. *gruel, gruwel*; OFr. *gruel*, coarse meal; LL. *grutellum*, dim. of *grutum*, meal; of Germanic origin, compare O.H.G. *gruzzi*, groats.] A decoction of corn-meal or oatmeal boiled in water or milk to a thick paste.

grụ′el-ly, *a.* Resembling gruel.

grụ-e′sō, *n.* [Sp., bulky, large.] In California, mercury ore of the best quality and largest lumps.

grụe′sŏme, grew′sŏme, *a.* [D. *grue*, to shudder, and *-some.*] Causing repulsion or loathing; exciting abhorrence; hideous; horrible; frightful; ugly.

grụe′sŏme-ness, grew′sŏme-ness, *n.* The quality of being gruesome.

gruff, *a.*; *comp.* gruffer; *superl.* gruffest. [D. *grof*, coarse, heavy.] Of a rough or stern manner, voice, or countenance; sour; surly; severe; rugged; harsh.

gruff′ly, *adv.* In a gruff manner.

gruff′ness, *n.* The state or quality of being gruff.

grụ′grụ, *n.* [Prob. native name.]

1. The grub of the large coleopterous insect, *Calandra palmarum.* It lives in South America in the stems of palm-trees and also in the sugar-cane, and is regarded as delicate eating by the natives.

2. A name given in the West Indies to *Astrocaryum vulgare* and *Acrocomia sclerocarpa*, two species of tropical American palms.

grum, *a.* [ME. *grom, gram*; AS. *grom, gram*, angry, wrathful.]

1. Morose; severe of countenance; sour; surly.

2. Low; deep in the throat; guttural; rumbling; as, a *grum* voice.

grum′ble, *v.i.*; grumbled, *pt., pp.*; grumbling, *ppr.* [M.D. *grommelen*, to murmur, mutter, grunt.]

1. To murmur with discontent; to utter a low muttering complaint.

2. To rumble; to growl; to make a harsh and heavy sound.

grum′ble, *v.t.* To utter grumblingly.

grum′ble, *n.* 1. The act of grumbling; a grumbling complaint.

2. A peevish mood; usually in the plural.

grum′blẽr, *n.* 1. One who grumbles or murmurs.

2. A fish. [See *Grunt.*]

grum′bling-ly, *adv.* With grumbling.

grụme, *n.* [OFr. *grume*, a knot, clot, from L. *grumus*, a little heap.] A thick, viscid fluid; a clot, as of blood.

grum′ly, *adv.* In a grum manner.

grụ′mōse, *a.* Same as *Grumous*, 2.

grụ′mous, *a.* 1. Resembling or containing grume; thick; clotted; as, *grumous* blood.

2. In botany, formed of coarse grains, as some clustered tubercular roots.

grụ′mous-ness, *n.* The state of being grumous.

grump′i-ly, *adv.* In a grumpy, surly, or gruff manner.

grump′y, *a.* Surly; dissatisfied; gruff.

grun′del, *n.* In zoölogy, a fish, the groundling.

grun′dy, *n.* In metallurgy, a kind of granular pig-iron used in a process of making steel.

grunt, *v.i.*; grunted, *pt., pp.*; grunting, *ppr.* [ME. *grunten, gronten*, to grunt, groan; prob. of imitative origin, compare AS. *grunian*, L. *grunnire*, to grunt.] To utter a short groan, or a deep guttural sound like that of a hog.

grunt, *n.* 1. A deep guttural sound, as of a hog.

2. Any fish of the genera *Hæmulon* or *Orthopristis*; also called *grumbler, grunter*, and *pigfish*, from the grunting sound it makes when hooked.

grunt′ẽr, *n.* 1. One that grunts; (a) a fish, as the grunt, the gurnard, and others; (b) a hog.

2. An iron rod bent like a hook, used by ironfounders.

grunt′ing-ly, *adv.* In a grunting manner.

grun′tle, *v.i.* To grunt; to sulk. [Rare.]

grunt′ling, *n.* A young hog.

grụp′pō, *n.* [It.] In music, a group; a turn.

Grụ′si-ăn, *a.* [Russ. *Gruziya*, Georgia.] Georgian; relating to Caucasian Georgia.

grutch, *n.* and *v.* [Obs.] See *Grudge.*

Grụ-yère′ (-yãr′), *n.* [From *Gruyère*, a town in Switzerland.] A kind of French and Swiss cheese; Schweitzerkäse.

grȳ, *n.* [L. *gry*, a small trifle; Gr. *gry*, a grunt, a morsel.]

1. A measure equal to one-tenth of a line.

2. Anything very small, or of little value. [Rare.]

grȳde, *v.i.* To gride. [Obs.]

gryf′ŏn, *n.* A griffin. [Obs.]

Gryl′li-dæ, *n.pl.* [L. *gryllus*, a cricket, and *-idæ.*] A family of insects belonging to the order *Orthoptera*; the crickets.

Gryl′lus, *n.* The typical genus of the *Gryllidæ.*

grȳpe, *v.t.* To gripe. [Obs.]

grȳpe, *n.* A griffin. [Obs.]

Grȳ-phæ′ȧ, *n.* [LL. *gryphus*; L. *gryps*; Gr. *gryps*, a griffin.] A genus of fossil lamellibranchiate bivalves, closely allied to the oyster and very abundant in the secondary strata of Europe.

gryph′ite, *n.* Crowstone, a fossil shell of *Gryphæa.*

gryph′ŏn, *n.* A griffin. [Obs.]

grȳ-pō′sis, *n.* [Gr. *grypōsis*, a hooking, curving, from *grypos*, hooked, bent.] Abnormal inward growth or curvature of the nails.

grȳs′bok, *n.* [D. *grijsbok*; *grijs*, gray, and *bok*, buck.] A South African antelope, *Neotragus melanotis*, about 20 inches high and 3 feet long, of a warm chestnut color flecked with white.

guä-chä′rō (gwä-), *n.* [Sp. *guácharo*, sickly, moaning; so named from its cry.] A nocturnal bird of South America, of the genus *Steatornis.* It feeds on grain and fruits and its oil is used by the natives as butter.

guä′cō, *n.* [S. Am.] 1. A tropical South American plant, *Mikania Guaco*, the juice of which is used as an antidote to snake-bites.

2. A Central American plant, *Aristolochia anguicida*, the roots of which are used for the same purpose.

guai′ăc (gwī′), *n.* Guaiacum.

guai′ăc, *a.* Relating to guaiacum.

guai′ȧ-cŏl, *n.* Same as *Guiacol.*

Guai′ȧ-cum, *n.* [Sp. *guayaco*, from native S. Am. name.]

1 A genus of plants of the order *Zygophyllaceæ. Guaiacum officinale*, popularly called *lignum-vitæ*, is a native of the warmer parts of America. It is an ornamental tree with pretty blue flowers and pinnate leaves; the wood is very hard, ponderous, and resinous.

2. [g—] The resin of guaiacum, greenish-brown, with a balsamic fragrance, and used in medicine as a stimulant in chronic rheumatism and other diseases.

Guaiacum officinale.

guän (gwän), *n.* A South American gallinaceous bird, of the *Penelopinæ*, allied to the curassows.

guä′nȧ, *n.* A fabric made from the bark of the West Indian tree *Lagetta lintearia*, or lacebark.

guä′nȧ, *n.* An iguana.

guä-nä′cō, *n.* [Native S. Am.] The *Auchenia huanaco*, a species of the genus of domestic Andean ruminant mammals to which the llama belongs.

guä-nif′ẽr-ous, *a.* [Sp. *guano*, guano, and L. *ferre*, to bear.] Yielding guano.

guä′nin, *n.* A peculiar substance contained in guano, closely resembling xanthic oxid. It is also found in the liver and pancreas of mammals, and has been found in the scales of some fishes, as the bleak.

guä′nō, *n.* [Sp., from Peruv. *huanu*, dung.]

1. A substance containing ammonia and phosphates, found on some parts of the South American and African coasts which are frequented by sea-birds, and composed chiefly of their excrement; used as a manure.

2. One of various nitrogenous commercial fertilizers.

guä′rȧ, *n.* [Braz.] 1. The scarlet ibis.

2. The maned dog, *Canis jubatus*, of South America.

guä-rä′nȧ, *n.* [Braz.] A preparation made in South America by pounding the seeds of a climbing shrub, *Paullinia sorbilis*, into a kind of paste, and afterward hardening it in the sun. It is employed medicinally and forms the essential constituent of a most refreshing beverage; called also *guarana-bread.*

guä-rä′nin, guä-rä′nine, *n.* Caffein derived from guarana.

guar-ăn-tee′ (gar-), *n.* [OFr. *guarantie, garantie*, from *guarantir, garantir*, to warrant.]

1. The party to whom a guaranty is given; correlative to *guarantor.*

2. A guaranty.

3. A guarantor; a loose and incorrect use of the term.

guar-ăn-tee′, *v.t.*; guaranteed, *pt., pp.*; guaranteeing, *ppr.* 1. To make oneself liable for (the debt, default, or miscarriage of another); to undertake or engage that another person shall perform (what he has stipulated); to obligate oneself to secure the performance of; to warrant; to make sure; as, to *guarantee* the payment of a debt.

2. To indemnify; to save harmless.

Syn.—Answer for, secure, warrant, guard, insure, obligate.

guar′ăn-tọr, *n.* One who engages to see that the stipulations of another are performed; also, one who engages to secure another in any right or possession.

guar′ăn-ty, *v.t.*; guarantied, *pt., pp.*; guarantying, *ppr.* To guarantee. *Guarantee* is the spelling for the verb preferred by lawyers.

guar′ăn-ty, *n.*; *pl.* **guar′ăn-tieṣ.** [OFr. *garantie*, a guaranty, warranty, from *garant, guarant, warant*, a warrant, supporter, from O.H.G. *warjan*, to protect.]

1. A collateral engagement, for a consideration, to answer for the debt, default, or miscarriage of another who is primarily liable; a pledge; security.

2. A fact or thing which warrants.

3. The act of warranting or securing.

guä-rä′pō, *n.* [Sp.] A beverage made by the fermentation of sugar-cane juice.

guärd, *v.t.*; guarded, *pt., pp.*; guarding, *ppr.* [OFr. *garder*, to keep, from M.H.G. *warten*, to watch.]

1. To secure against injury, loss, or attack; to protect; to defend; to keep in safety; as, to *guard* a city by walls and forts.

2. To watch to prevent from committing violence, or from escaping.

3. To provide or secure against objections or attacks; as, to *guard* one's words.

4. To adorn with laces, borders, or bindings, especially as a protection for the edges.

5. To furnish with a guard or guards, as a book, plate, or leaf in bookbinding.

6. To gird. [Obs.]

guärd, *v.i.* To watch by way of caution or defense; to be cautious; to be in a state of defense or security; as, one *guards* against errors.

guärd, *n.* [ME. *garde*; OFr. *garde*, a guardian, warden, from M.H.G. *warten*, to watch.]

1. A state of caution or vigilance; the act of

observing what passes in order to prevent surprise or attack; preservation or security against injury, loss, or attack; defense; care; attention; watch; heed; as, to keep *guard*; to lose *guard*; to be on *guard*.

2. One who or that which protects or keeps in safety; one who or that which secures against danger, attack, loss, or injury; one who keeps watch over, as (a) a man or body of men occupied in preserving a person or place from attack or injury, or in preventing an escape; (b) mental endowment or attitude that keeps off evil; as, modesty is the *guard* of innocence; (c) in fencing or boxing, a posture of defense; the arms or weapon in such a posture; as, to beat down one's *guard*; (d) in England, an official in charge of a railway-train, having duties similar to those of a conductor in the United States; (e) in the United States, an official in charge of gates, platforms, etc., of an elevated railway; (f) in football, either of two players next in position to right or left of the center rush.

3. Any device or appliance intended to guard against loss, injury, or detriment of any kind, as (a) a fender of any kind; (b) a guard-rail; (c) a guard-ring; (d) a watch-chain or cord; (e) the part of the hilt of a sword which protects the hand; (f) any device on a firearm to prevent accidental discharge; (g) any pad or device to protect the body or any part of it in various games; as, a shin-*guard*; a nose-*guard*; (h) in bookbinding, a strip or slip placed between the leaves at the back to make it as thick as the front, as when plates, maps, etc., are to be inserted, or in scrapbooks and the like.

Corporal's guard; see under *Corporal*.

Guard of honor; a guard especially selected to escort an eminent person; as, the *guard of honor* to a distinguished public guest.

Leg-and-foot guard; (a) a device to prevent a horse from interfering; (b) a device to prevent the right leg of an artillery driver from being bruised by the carriage-pole.

National guard; see under *National*.

Off one's guard; not vigilant; unprepared.

On one's guard; ready to meet attack; cautious; alert.

To mount guard; in military operations, (a) to muster, inspect, and place a detail of soldiers upon guard; as, we *mounted guard* every day at nine o'clock; (b) to go on guard.

To run the guard; to pass over the line of guards without being detected or arrested, as a spy or a soldier of the camp without a pass.

guärd'ȧ-ble, *a.* That may be guarded.

guärd'āġe, *n.* Wardship. [Obs.]

guärd'ănt, *a.* Acting as guardian. [Obs.]

guärd'ănt, *n.* A guardian. [Obs.]

guärd'=cell, *n.* In botany, either of the two concave cells surrounding a stoma, as in a fern.

guärd'ed, *a.* 1. Defended; protected; accompanied by a guard; provided with means of defense; as, the house is *guarded* on every side.

2. Cautious, circumspect; as, he was *guarded* in his expressions.

3. In card-playing, accompanied by a lower card of the same suit in the same hand; said of the next to the highest card out.

guärd'ed-ly, *adv.* In a guarded manner.

guärd'ed-ness, *n.* Caution; circumspection.

guärd'en-āġe, *n.* Guardianship. [Obs.]

guärd'ẽr, *n.* One who guards.

guärd'fish, *n.* The garfish. [Prov. Eng.]

guärd'fụl, *a.* Wary; cautious. [Obs.]

guärd'fụl-ly, *adv.* Cautiously. [Obs.]

guärd'house, *n.* The building used by a military guard, and as a place where soldiers are confined for breaches of the regulations; hence, any lockup.

guärd'i-ăn, *n.* [OFr. *gardien*, from *garder*, to guard, watch.]

1. A warden; one who guards, preserves, or secures; one to whom anything is committed for preservation from injury.

2. In law, one who is chosen or appointed to take charge of the estate and education of an orphan who is a minor, or of any person who is not of sufficient discretion to manage his own affairs.

Guardian ad litem; a person appointed by a court to conduct a suit for one under legal incapacity.

Guardians of the poor; in England and Ireland, persons elected to manage the poor-law system within a parish or other district.

guärd'i-ăn, *a.* Protecting; performing the office of a protector; as, a *guardian* angel; *guardian* care.

Feast of the Guardian Angels; in the Roman Catholic church, a festival celebrated on October 2.

Guardian angel; (a) the angel, according to some creeds, that watches over and guards each human being; hence, (b) any one who protects or defends another.

Guardian spirit; a spirit believed to guard the welfare of a person, family, people, or place.

guärd'i-ăn-āġe, *n.* Guardianship. [Obs.]

guärd'i-ănce, *n.* Guardianship. [Obs.]

guärd'i-ăn=cell, *n.* A guard-cell.

guärd'i-ăn-ess, *n.* A female guardian. [Obs.]

guärd'i-ăn-less, *a.* Without a guardian.

guärd'i-ăn-ship, *n.* The office of a guardian; care; watch; protection.

guärd'less, *a.* Without a guard or defense.

guärd'=lock, *n.* A lock to keep the tide from a dock or basin.

guärd'=mount"ing, *n.* The military ceremony of going on guard or of stationing guards.

guärd'=rāil, *n.* 1. A supplemental rail to prevent derailment of trains, as at switches, curves, bridges, etc.

2. A safety-rail or hand-rail on shipboard.

guärd'=ring, *n.* A ring which prevents the loss of another ring from one's finger; a keeper.

guärd'rọom, *n.* 1. The room which a military guard occupies while on duty.

2. A place for the temporary confinement of military prisoners.

guärds, *n.pl.* In European armies, a body of infantry or cavalry of picked men and generally regarded as the élite of the troops composing an army, from its being their special duty to guard the person of their sovereign, etc.

guärd'ship, *n.* Care; protection. [Obs.]

guärdṣ'măn, *n.*; *pl.* **guärdṣ'men.** 1. One who guards or keeps ward; a watchman.

2. [G—] In England, an officer or private in the Guards.

guä-ri'bȧ (gwä-), *n.* [Sp.Am.] A howling monkey.

guar'ish (gar'), *v.t.* To heal. [Obs.]

guä'sȧ (gwä'), *n.* [Sp.] The jewfish.

guä'vȧ (gwä'), *n.* [Braz. *guayaba*.] One of various species of the genus *Psidium*, especially *Psidium Guayava*, a tree of tropical America. Two varieties of the fruit are well known: the pear-shaped or white *guava*, and the apple-shaped or red *guava*, from the pulp of which is made a delicious jelly.

guayule, (gwä-yōō'lā), *n.* The *Parthenium argentatum*, a plant of Mex. and So. Tex., the product of which is used as a substitute for India rubber.

gub, *n.* [From *gob*, a lump.] 1. A tooth or projection on a wheel; especially, on a sprocket-wheel. 2. A lump. [Obs.]

gū-bẽr-naç'ū-lum, *n.*; *pl.* **gū-bẽr-naç'ū-lȧ.** [L., a rudder, from *gubernare*, to steer.]

1. In anatomy, the conical-shaped cord attached above the lower end of the epididymis, passing below to the bottom of the scrotum, and governing the descent of the testes.

2. In biology, the posterior flagellum in certain infusorians, used for steering.

gū'bẽr-nănce, *n.* Government. [Obs.]

gū'bẽr-nāte, *v.t.* To govern. [Obs.]

gū-bẽr-nā'tion, *n.* Government; rule; direction. [Obs.]

gū'bẽr-nā-tive, *a.* Governing. [Obs.]

gū"bẽr-nȧ-tō'ri-ăl, *a.* [L. *gubernator*, a helmsman, governor, from *gubernare*, to steer.] Pertaining to a governor or his office.

gud'ġeon (guj'ŏn), *n.* [ME. *gojon*; OFr. *goujon*; L. *gobio* (*-onis*); Gr. *kōbios*, a kind of fish, a gudgeon]. 1. A small fresh-water fish, *Gobio fluviatilis*, very easily caught. It is commonly used for bait.

2. One who is easily cheated or ensnared.

3. That which may be gained without ability or merit.

gud'ġeŏn, *n.* [OFr. *goujon*, *gojon*, the pivot of a pulley.]

1. In machinery, that part of a horizontal shaft or axle which turns in the collar; formerly the portion revolving in immediate contact with the bearings; now applied only when that part is separate from and independent of the body of the shaft.

a, Wooden Shaft. *b*, Gudgeon.

2. In shipbuilding, (a) an eye or clamp fastened to the sternpost on which the rudder is hung; (b) one of the notches in the carrick-bitts for receiving the metal bushes in which the spindle of a windlass traverses.

3. A pin of metal used to unite two blocks, as of stone.

gud'ġeŏn, *v.t.* To ensnare; to cheat; to impose upon.

gūe, *n.* A rogue; a vagabond; a sharper. [Obs.]

Guē'bẽr (gē'), **Ghē'bẽr**, *n.* [Per. *gabr*, a fire-worshiper, an infidel.] The name given by the Mohammedans to one belonging to the Persian fire-worshipers; a Zoroastrian.

guel'dẽr=rōṣe (gel'), **gel'dẽr=rōṣe**, *n.* [Named from its supposed source, *Gelderland*.] The snowball-tree, *Viburnum Opulus*, especially the cultivated form of that species.

Guelf, Guelph (gwelf), *n.* [It. *Guelfo*, for G. *Welf*, a personal name, from O.H.G. *welf*, a whelp.] A member of a medieval political party favoring the family of the Welfs (*Guelfs*) in their contest against the Hohenstaufen emperors. From the pope also opposing the emperors, the name was used for the papal party in Italy opposed to the Ghibellines. From the Welfs have descended the present royal family of England.

Guelf'iç, Guelph'iç, *a.* Of or belonging to the Guelfs.

guep'ärd (gwep'), **guep'ärde**, *n.* [Fr.] The chetah.

guẽr'dŏn (gẽr'), *n.* [ME. *guerdon*; OFr. *guerdon*; LL. *widerdonum* (a half translation by L. *donum*, a gift), from O.H.G. *widarlon*, a reward; *widar*, again, against, and *lōn*, a reward.] A reward; a requital; a recompense.

guẽr'dŏn, *v.t.* To reward; to give a guerdon to.

guẽr'dŏn-ȧ-ble, *a.* [OFr. *guerrdonnable*, from *guerdonner*, to reward.] Worthy of reward.

guẽr'dŏn-less, *a.* Without reward.

guē-rē'zȧ (gē-), *n.* [Abyssinian.] *Colobus guereza*, a large, black-and-white monkey of Abyssinia having long soft hair and a bushy tail.

gue-ril'lȧ, *n.* See *Guerrilla*.

guẽr'ite (*or Fr. pron.* gā-rēt'), *n.* [Fr.] In fortification, a small projecting tower or box of wood at the salient angles of works, on the top of the revetment, to hold a sentry.

guer-ril'lȧ (ge-ril'), **gue-ril'lȧ**, *n.* [Sp., skirmishing warfare, dim. of *guerra*, war.]

1. An irregular mode of carrying on war, by the constant attacks of independent bands; in this sense commonly used attributively; as, *guerrilla* warfare.

2. One who carries on war in an irregular manner; a member of an independent band engaged in predatory and irregular attacks upon an enemy.

guess (ges), *v.t.*; guessed (gest), *pt., pp.*; guessing, *ppr.* [ME. *gessen*, to guess; compare Sw. *gissa*; Dan. *gizze* or *giette*, to guess; Ice. *gizka*, to guess, *geta*, to get, to guess; AS. *gitan*, to get.]

1. To conjecture; to form an opinion concerning without certain principles or means of knowledge; to judge of at random.

2. To judge or form an opinion of from reasons that render a thing probable, but fall short of sufficient evidence; as, from slight circumstances or occasional expressions, one may *guess* an author's meaning.

3. To conjecture rightly; to solve by a correct conjecture; as, to *guess* a riddle.

4. To think; to suppose; to imagine.

Not altogether; better far, I *guess*,
That we do make our entrance several ways.
—Shak.

Syn.—Think, reckon, suppose, conjecture, estimate, surmise.

guess (ges), *v.i.* To conjecture; to judge at random; as, we do not know which road to take, but must *guess* at it.

guess, *n.* Conjecture; a judgment without any certain evidence or grounds; a surmise.

guess'ȧ-ble, *a.* Susceptible of being guessed.

guess'ẽr, *n.* One who guesses; one who judges or gives an opinion without certain means of knowing.

guess'ing-ly, *adv.* By way of conjecture.

guess'ive, *a.* Conjectural. [Obs.]

guess'=rōpe, *n.* A guess-warp.

guess'=wạrp, *n.* A rope serving to warp a vessel toward a distant object to which the rope is made fast; also, a rope used to secure a boat to a vessel.

guess'wŏrk, *n.* Haphazard or conjectural opinion, action, or results; a guess; conjecture.

guest, *v.i.* and *v.t.* To be or entertain a guest. [Obs.]

guest (gest), *n.* [ME. *gest*, *geest*; AS. *gæst*, *gest*, a guest.]

1. A visitor or friend entertained in the house or at the table of another, whether by invitation or otherwise, and either gratuitously or for pay; specifically, in law, any person received for entertainment at an inn, tavern, or hotel upon the customary terms or without special limiting contract.

2. In zoölogy, an inquiline; a parasite.

3. A stranger. [Obs.]

guest'=chām"bẽr, *n.* An apartment appropriated to the entertainment of guests.

guest'=fly̆, *n.* An insect living in a gall made by another insect.

guest'=house, *n.* An inn. [Obs.]

guest'=mọth, *n.* A moth whose larva lives upon the products or within the domicile of another insect.

guest'=rōpe, *n.* A guess-warp.

guest'wiṣe, *adv.* In the manner of a guest.

gūeu-lette' (gū-let'), *n.* [Fr.] The rear door of an annealing-arch.

guē'vï (gwā'), *n.* [S. African.] A duykerbok or pygmy antelope of the genus *Cephalophus*.

guf'fạw, *v.i.* To utter a guffaw.

guf'fạw, *n.* A loud boisterous laugh.

guf'fẽr, *n.* The eelpout or blenny.

gū-gal', *n.* [Hind.] The sweet-scented resin of various trees of India, used as incense.

gug'gle, *v.t.* and *v.i.* I. *v.t.* To gargle. [Prov. Eng.]

II. *v.i.* To gurgle. [Colloq.]

gug′glet, *n.* Same as *Goglet.*

gŭhr (*or G. pron.* gu̇r), *n.* [G., from *gähren, gären,* to ferment.] A loose, earthy deposit from water found in the cavities or clefts of rocks, mostly white, but sometimes red or yellow, from a mixture of clay or ocher.

guī′ac (gwī′), *n.* Same as *Guaiacum.*

guī′ă-col, *n.* A liquid derived from gum guaiacum by distillation, and also found in wood-tar.

guī′ă-cum, *n.* Same as *Guaiacum.*

guib (gwib), **guī′bȧ,** *n.* *Tragelaphus scriptus,* the West African harnessed antelope, so called from having bars of white on its sides.

Guī′cō-wär (gī′), *n.* Same as *Gaikwar.*

guīd′ȧ-ble (gīd′), *a.* That may be guided.

guīd′āge, *n.* The reward given to a guide for services; also, guidance. [Obs.]

guīd′ănce, *n.* The act of guiding; direction; government; a leading.

guīde (gīd), *v.t.* [ME. *guiden, gyden;* prob. of Teut. origin; compare Goth. *witan,* to watch over, AS. *witan,* to know.]

1. To lead or direct in a way; to conduct in a course or path; as, to *guide* a traveler.

2. To give direction to; to regulate, direct, and manage; to control; to influence; to train; as, to *guide* a child in its studies.

guīde, *n.* [ME. *guide;* OFr. *guis,* a guide.]

1. A person who leads or directs another in his way or course; one who goes before or accompanies to point out the way; especially, one whose business is to conduct strangers; a conductor; a leader.

2. A guidebook.

3. One who or that which directs one in his conduct or course of action; as, experience is one of the best *guides.*

4. In military formations, a soldier whose position regulates the alinements, pivots, etc.

5. Any device for controlling or indicating the correct motion or action of anything; (a) a sewing-machine attachment to regulate the position of the seam; (b) a metallic ring on a fishing-rod through which the line passes; (c) a movable strip of metal used by compositors to indicate the place in the copy for setting; (d) in surgery, a director; (e) in a water-wheel, a plate or partition to direct the current against the buckets.

guīde′=bär, *n.* One of two parallel bars by which the free end of a piston is made to move in a straight line.

guīde′=block, *n.* One of two blocks attached to the crosshead of an engine, which slide between and are guided by the guide-bars.

guīde′bōard, *n.* A board bearing a sign to direct travelers.

guīde′book, *n.* A book containing information concerning places, routes, etc., for the use of tourists.

guīde′less, *a.* Having no guide.

guīde′=pīle, *n.* A pile marking a point to which work is directed.

guīde′pōst, *n.* A signpost for directing travelers.

guīde′=pul″ley, *n.* A pulley which tightens, changes the direction of, or otherwise serves as a guide to a belt.

guīd′ẽr, *n.* One who guides; a guide.

guīde′=rāil, *n.* A guard-rail.

guīd′ẽr-ess, *n.* A female guide. [Obs.]

guid′guid (gwid′gwid), *n.* [Imitative.] A rock-wren whose cry resembles the yelping of a puppy; hence, called also *barking-bird.*

guī′dŏn (gī′), *n.* [Fr., from *guider,* to guide.] A small flag, pointed, rounded, or notched, used as a guiding flag or signal for military bodies or at sea; also, the officer who bears it.

guīge, gīge (gēj), *n.* The strap of a shield. [Obs.]

guild (gild), *n.* See first *Gild,* n.

guild, *n.* A geld; a tax. [Obs.]

guil′dẽr (gil′), *n.* [D. and G. *gulden;* M.H.G. *guldin,* a florin, from *guldin,* golden, from *golt,* gold.] A silver coin of Holland worth about forty cents; formerly, a Dutch gold coin; called also *gulden* and *florin.*

guild′hall, *n.* See *Gildhall.*

guīle (gīl), *n.* [OFr. *guile, gil,* guile; of Teut. origin; compare AS. *wil,* a trick.]

1. Craft; cunning; artifice; duplicity; deceit.

2. A wile; a trick.

guīle, *v.t.* To disguise; to beguile. [Obs.]

guīle, *n.* [Fr. *guiller,* to ferment.]

1. Wort for beer or vinegar.

2. A guilfat; a wort-tub.

3. The amount made at a single brewing.

guīle′ful, *a.* Full of or characterized by guile.

guīle′ful-ly, *adv.* In a guileful manner.

guīle′ful-ness, *n.* Deceitfulness; secret treachery.

guīle′less, *a.* Free from guile or deceit; artless.

guīle′less-ly, *adv.* In a guileless manner.

guīle′less-ness, *n.* Freedom from guile.

guīl′ẽr, *n.* One who beguiles. [Obs.]

guil′fat (gil′), *n.* A vat for fermenting liquors.

guil-le-met′ (*Fr. pron.* gē-lyā-mā′), *n.* A quotation-mark. [Rare.]

guil′le-mot (gil′), *n.* [Fr., from Bret. *gwelan,* a gull, and OFr. *moette,* a sea-mew.] A water-fowl of the genus *Uria,* found in the northern hemisphere.

Common Guillemot (*Uria troile*).

guil′le-vat, *n.* A guilfat.

guil-lōche′, *n.* [Fr. *guillocher,* to decorate with guilloches, said to be named from *Guillot,* the inventor of a machine for tracing them.] An ornament in the form of two or more bands twisting over each other in a continued series; an ornament of curved lines intersecting or entwined.

guil-lōche′, *v.t.* To decorate with a guilloche.

guil′lō-tīne, *n.* [Fr., from the name of Dr. J. I. *Guillotin,* who opposed the slow and cruel methods of execution in use during the French Revolution, and advocated the substitution of a more humane method.]

1. A machine for beheading persons by the fall of a weighted blade with an oblique edge, sliding between upright guides.

2. One of various cutting-machines having an oblique-edged blade.

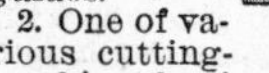

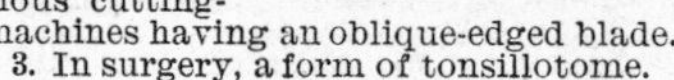

Guillotine as Used in Paris.

3. In surgery, a form of tonsillotome.

guil-lō-tīne′, *v.t.;* guillotined, *pt., pp.;* guillotining, *ppr.* To behead with the guillotine.

guills, *n.* [Dial. variant of *gold.*] The corn-marigold.

guilt (gilt), *n.* [ME. *gilt;* AS. *gylt,* a fault, offense, from *gildan,* to pay, requite.]

1. Criminality; that state of a moral agent which results from his commission of a crime or offense by act, consent or neglect, knowing it to be a crime or violation of law.

2. Criminality, in a political or civil view; exposure to forfeiture or other penalty.

> A ship incurs *guilt* by the violation of a blockade. —Kent.

3. A fault; a crime. [Obs.]

guilt′i-ly, *adv.* In a guilty manner.

guilt′i-ness, *n.* The state of being guilty; guilt.

guilt′less, *a.* 1. Free from guilt or offense; innocent.

2. Without knowledge or experience; ignorant.

> Heifers *guiltless* of the yoke. —Pope.

guilt′less-ly, *adv.* Without guilt; innocently.

guilt′less-ness, *n.* Innocence; freedom from guilt.

guilt′=sick, *a.* Sick with or of guilt.

guilt′y, *a.* [ME. *gilty;* AS. *gyltig,* guilty, from *gylt,* guilt.]

1. Having committed a crime or offense, or having violated a law by an overt act or by neglect, and by that act or neglect being liable to punishment; not innocent; culpable; often followed by *of;* as, to be *guilty of* theft or arson.

2. Wicked; corrupt; sinful; as, a *guilty* world.

3. Liable; deserving; with *of.* [Obs.]

guilt′y-līke, *adv.* Guiltily. [Obs.]

guim′bärd (gim′), *n.* The jews'-harp. [Obs.]

guimpe, *n.* [Fr.] A chemisette to be worn with a décolleté dress.

guin′ēa (gin′ē), *n.* 1. Formerly, a gold coin of Great Britain, made originally (1663) of gold from Guinea, and last issued in 1813. It was valued at 21 shillings, or about $5.11.

2. [G—] A country on the western coast of Africa.

3. A guinea-fowl. [Colloq.]

Guinea current; the Atlantic Ocean current which sets toward Guinea.

Guin′ēa=cloth, *n.* Any cloth made for export to the West African coast.

guin′ēa=corn, *n.* Indian millet, *Sorghum vulgare.*

guin′ēa=drop″pẽr, *n.* One who cheats by dropping guineas. [Obs.]

guin′ēa=edge, *n.* A serrated edge to a book-cover, resembling the edge of a guinea.

guin′ēa=fowl, *n.* A gallinaceous fowl of Africa, of which there are several species, the commonest being the *Numida meleagris.* It is as large as the common domestic hen, and has a kind of colored fleshy horn on each side of the head. Its color is a dark gray, beautifully variegated with small, white spots. It is now domesticated everywhere.

Guinea-fowl (*Numida meleagris*).

guin′ēa=grāins, *n.pl.* Grains of paradise.

guin′ēa=grȧss, *n.* A species of African grass, *Panicum jumentorum,* cultivated in southern United States and used as fodder.

guin′ēa=hen, *n.* 1. A guinea-fowl.

2. A common fritillary, *Fritillaria Meleagris,* whose flowers have spotted petals, in effect like the marks on a guinea-fowl.

Guin′ēa-măn, *n.* A vessel engaged in trade with the coast of Guinea.

guin′ēa=pig, *n.* [Prob. corruption of *Guiana pig.*]

1. In zoölogy, a small rodent mammal of the genus *Cavia,* a native of Brazil. It is the domesticated form of the restless cavy, *Cavia aperea.*

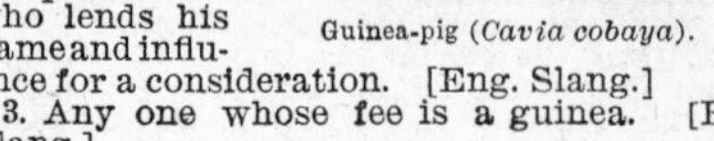

Guinea-pig (*Cavia cobaya*).

2. A nominal director of a corporation who lends his name and influence for a consideration. [Eng. Slang.]

3. Any one whose fee is a guinea. [Eng. Slang.]

guin′ēa=plum, *n.* A West African tree, *Parinarium excelsum,* attaining the height of sixty feet, with long leaves and large terminal bunches of flowers succeeded by a fruit about the size of a plum.

guin′ēa=wŏrm, *n.* A species of parasitic threadworm, *Filaria medinensis,* very common in hot countries, and often causing intense pain by forming abscesses beneath the skin.

guī-pūre′ (gē-), *n.* [Fr.] 1. An imitation of an antique lace.

2. A kind of gimp.

3. Lace without a mesh, but with a distinct pattern held in place by connecting bars.

gūir′lănd, *n.* A garland. [Obs.]

guī-sarme′, gis-ärm′, *n.* A weapon similar to the poleax, having a cutting edge and a point for thrusting.

guīse, *v.i.* To act as a mummer. [Rare.]

guīse, *v.t.* To dress.

guīse, *n.* [OFr. *guise,* way, manner, guise, from O.H.G. *wisa,* way, manner.]

1. External appearance; aspect; dress; garb; as, he appeared in the *guise* of a shepherd.

2. Manner; mien; behavior.

3. Custom; mode; practice; way.

guīs′ẽr, *n.* A person in disguise; a mummer who goes about at Christmas.

gui-tär′ (gi-), *n.* [Fr. *guitare,* from L. *cithara,* Gr. *kithara,* a lyre or lute.] A stringed instrument of music, shaped somewhat like a violin, but played by plucking the strings with the fingers; it usually has three strings of gut and three of silk covered with fine silver wire.

1. French Guitar of 17th Century. 2. Modern Guitar.

gui-tär′ist, *n.* One who plays upon a guitar.

guit′guit (gwit′gwit), *n.* A passerine bird of tropical America, so called from its note.

gū′lȧ, *n.;* *pl.* **gū′læ.** [L. *gula,* the throat.]

1. The gullet; the throat; (a) in ornithology, the part of the throat next to the chin; (b) in entomology, a plate supporting the submentum.

2. In architecture, the ogee or cyma reversa. [See *Cyma.*]

gū-lan′chȧ, *n.* [E.Ind.] *Tinospora cordifolia,* an East Indian climber whose bitter root is used as a tonic and alterative.

gū′lăr, *a.* [L. *gula,* the throat.] Pertaining to the throat.

gū′laund, *n.* [Ice. *gulönd; gulr,* yellow, and *önd,* a duck.] A merganser.

gulch, *n.* [ME. *gulchen,* to swallow greedily, from Norw. *gulka,* to disgorge.] A glutton; a swallowing or devouring. [Obs.]

gulch, *n.* A deep and narrow ravine, as the channel of a former torrent.

gulch, *n.* A sudden fall. [Prov. Eng.]

gulch, *v.t.* To swallow greedily. [Obs.]

guld, *n.* [ME.] Gold. [Obs.]

gul′den, *n.* [G., from *gülden*, golden.]

1. Any of several gold coins once current in Germany and the Netherlands.

2. A silver florin of Austria, worth about forty-eight cents.

3. A guilder.

gūle, *v.t.* To color or tincture red. [Obs.]

gūle, *v.i.* To grin; to sneer; to boast. [Prov. Eng.]

gūle, *n.* The gullet; hence, gluttony [Obs.]

gūleṣ, *n.* [ME. *goules*; OFr. *gueules*, gules, the tincture red, originally pl. of *goule, gole*, the mouth, from L. *gula*, the throat.] In heraldry, red, as a tincture. It is represented in an engraved escutcheon by vertical lines close together.

Gules.

gulf, *n.* [OFr. *golfe, goulfe*, a gulf; L.G. *kolphos*; Gr. *kolpos*, a fold, the bosom, a bay, or gulf.]

1. A tract of water extending from the ocean or a sea into an indentation of the coast-line of a country; a large bay; as, the *Gulf* of Mexico.

2. An abyss; a deep place in the earth; a chasm; as, the *gulf* of Avernus.

3. A whirlpool; an absorbing eddy.

4. A great interval, space, or degree of separation; as, there is a *gulf* between us.

5. In Cambridge University, the bottom of the pass-list for degrees, in which are placed those students who barely pass their examinations.

6. An ore-deposit in a lode.

Gulf Stream; a stream or current of warm water, which flows from the Gulf of Mexico through the channel between Cuba and America, past the Bermudas, touching the great bank of Newfoundland, and thence sweeps on toward Europe, part going north, and part returning southerly to the tropics.

gulf, *v.t.*; gulfed, *pt., pp.*; gulfing, *ppr.* 1. To absorb completely; to swallow up; to engulf.

2. At Cambridge University, to place in the gulf, or at the bottom of a pass-list.

gulf′weed, *n.* A coarse seaweed, *Sargassum bacciferum*, which has grapelike air-vessels by which it is buoyed up on the surface of the water.

Gulfweed (*Sargassum bacciferum*).

gulf′y, *a.* Full of whirlpools or gulfs; as, a *gulfy* sea.

gul′gul, *n.* [Native E. Ind. name.] A cement made of pounded seashells mixed with oil, which hardens like stone, and is put over a ship's bottom in India, so that worms cannot penetrate even when the copper is off.

gū-lin′ū-lȧ, *n.* [A dim. from L. *gula*, the throat.] In zoölogy, the stage of development of an actinozoan at which the gullet is formed.

gū-lin′ū-lăr, *a.* Of or relating to a gulinula.

gū′list, *n.* A glutton. [Obs.]

gull, *v.t.*; gulled, *pt., pp.*; gulling, *ppr* To dupe by taking advantage of inexperience or credulity; to swindle; to mislead by deception; to defraud.

gull, *n.* [ME. *goll*, an unfledged bird, from Ice. *golr*, yellow.]

1. An unfledged bird; a gosling. [Prov. Eng.]

2. A person easily cheated or misled.

3. A fraud; a cheat; a deception; a trick.

gull, *n.* [Corn. *gullan*, a gull.]

1. A web-footed, long-winged sea-fowl of or closely allied to the genus *Larus*. In the larger species, the upper mandible is bent downward at the point.

2. Any of various similar sea-birds, as the gannet, tern, or skua.

Lesser Black-backed Gull (*Larus fuscus*).

gull, *n.* A gully. [Obs.]

gull, *v.t.* To gulp; to swallow. [Obs.]

gull′āge, *n.* The act of gulling or state of being gulled.

gull′=billed, *a.* Having a bill like that of a gull.

gull′=catch″ẽr, *n.* A swindler; an impostor.

gull′ẽr, *n.* A cheat; an impostor.

gull′ẽr-y, *n.* Cheat. [Obs.]

gull′ẽr-y, *n.* The breeding-place of gulls.

gul′let, *n.* [ME. *golet*; OFr. *goulet*, the throat, a narrow passage, dim. of *gole, goule*; L. *gula*, the throat.]

1. The passage in the neck of an animal by which food and drink are taken into the stomach; the esophagus.

2. Anything resembling the food-passage, either in shape or functions, as, (a) a channel for water; (b) a preparatory cut or channel in excavations of sufficient width to admit the passage of a temporary track for dump-cars; (c) a peculiar concave cut in the teeth of some saw-blades; (d) a gore in a skirt.

gul′let, *v.t.* 1. To cut gullets in (a saw); to gum.

2. To construct, as a railroad, in a succession of steps upon which different gangs are employed.

gul-li-bil′i-ty, *n.* Unsuspecting credulity.

gul′li-ble, *a.* Easily gulled.

gull′ish, *a.* Foolish; stupid. [Obs.]

gull′ish-ness, *n.* Foolishness; stupidity. [Obs.]

gull′=tēaṣ″ẽr, *n.* In zoölogy, a bird that annoys gulls, as a jager or tern.

gul′ly, *n.*; *pl.* **gul′lieṣ.** [Fr. *goulet*, a narrow entrance, from OFr. *goulet*, the throat, gullet.]

1. A channel or hollow worn in the earth by a current of water.

2. A kind of grooved rail. [Eng.]

gul′ly, *n.* A small knife. [Obs.]

gul′ly, *v.t.*; gullied, *pt., pp.*; gullying, *ppr.* To wear a hollow channel in (the earth).

gul′ly, *v.i.* To run with noise. [Obs.]

gul′ly=gut, *n.* A glutton. [Obs.]

gul′ly-hōle, *n.* A manhole; an opening into a drain.

gū-los′i-ty, *n.* Greediness; voracity. [Obs.]

gulp, *v.t.*; gulped, *pt., pp.*; gulping, *ppr.* [D. *gulpen*, to swallow eagerly.] To swallow eagerly or in large draughts.

To gulp up; to disgorge.

gulp, *n.* 1. A swallow, as much as is swallowed at once.

2. A disgorging. [Rare.]

gulph, *n.* A gulf. [Obs.]

gum, *v.t.*; gummed, *pt., pp.*; gumming, *ppr.*

1. To smear with gum.

2. To unite by a viscous substance.

gum, *v.t.* To clean out and make larger the spaces between the teeth of; as, to *gum* a worn saw.

gum, *v.i.* 1. To become like gum; as, drying-oil *gums* when exposed to air.

2. To become obstructed or choked up with a gummy or sticky substance; as, a spindle *gums* up.

3. To hunt for gum. [Local, U. S.]

gum, *n.* [ME. *gumme, goome*, a gum, from AS. *goma*, the palate.] The hard, fleshy substance of the jaws which invests the teeth.

gum, *n.* [ME. *gumme, gomme*; OFr. *gomme*; L. *gummi*; Gr. *kommi*, gum.]

1. A juice which exudes from trees either spontaneously or after incisions are made, and thickens on the surface, or is obtained from their seeds or roots. *Gum* is more or less soluble in water, but is insoluble in alcohol, ether, and oils.

2. A gum-tree.

3. A part of a hollow log put to any of various uses. Gum-trees which become hollow when large are put to various uses, as beehives, well-curbs, etc.; hence, any hollow log or common device or utensil made of a hollow log is denominated a *gum*.

4. [*pl.*] Overshoes or rubbers. [Local, U. S.]

5. Any one of various preparations having a base of resin or other tenacious substance, prepared for continuous chewing by the addition of sweet; chewing-gum.

Acaroid gum or *gum acaroides*; a gum exuded by certain species of *Xanthorrhœa*.

Alsace gum; same as *Dextrine*.

Gum anime or *animi*; see *Anime*, n.

Gum arabic or *gum acacia*; a gum usually derived from *Acacia Arabica* and *Acacia vera*. The East Indian variety is from *Feronia elephantum*.

Gum butea; a gum derived from *Butea frondosa*, used in medicine and the arts.

Gum dragon; gum tragacanth.

Gum elastic; same as *Caoutchouc*.

Gum elemi; see *Elemi*.

Gum juniper; see *Sandarac*.

Gum ladanum; the gum or resin of the *Cistus ladaniferus*.

Gum Arabic Plant (*Acacia Seyal*).

Gum resin; any one of certain inspissated saps; a juice of plants, consisting of resin and various other gummy substances. The gum resins do not flow naturally from plants, but are mostly extracted by incision, in the form of white, yellow, or red emulsive fluids, which dry and consolidate. The most important species are olibanum, galbanum, scammony, gamboge, euphorbium, asafetida, aloes, myrrh, and ammoniac.

Gum sandarac; see *Sandarac*.

Gum senegal; a gum resembling gum arabic, brought from the country of the river Senegal, in Africa.

Gum tragacanth; see *Tragacanth*.

gum′=an″i-măl, *n.* The galago of Senegal, a lemur which feeds upon gums.

gum′bō, *n.* [Prob. of Indian or negro origin.]

1. A kind of soup containing okra.

2. A dish made of young okra pods stewed with salt, pepper, and butter.

3. Okra or its young mucilaginous capsules or pods.

4. Prairiemud; a term used in western United States.

5. An illiterate dialect of creole Louisiana and Cuba.

gum′boil, *n.* A boil on the gum.

gum′bō=lim″bō, *n.* *Bursera gummifera*, the West India or Jamaica birch-tree. The bark yields cachibou, a resin similar to elemi-gum.

gum′=buck″et, *n.* In sailors' slang, a tobacco pipe.

gum′=cis″tus, *n.* A European species of rock-rose, *Cistus ladaniferus*, yielding a dark-colored, brittle resin.

gum′=dig″gẽr, *n.* One who digs up the fossil gum or resin from which varnish is made.

gum′=drop, *n.* A form of candy usually made of gum arabic, with sugar, flavoring, etc.; also made of glucose, gelatine, and the like when of inferior quality.

gum′mȧ, *n.* [L. *gummi*, gum.] A syphilitic tumor.

gum′mȧ-tous, *a.* Like or relating to a gumma.

gum′mẽr, *n.* A device for increasing the distance between the teeth of a worn saw.

gum-mif′ẽr-ous, *a.* [L. *gummi*, gum, and *ferre*, to bear.] Producing gum.

gum′mi-ness, *n.* The state or quality of being gummy; viscousness.

gum′mite, *n.* An orange-yellow, gum-like mineral consisting of a complex compound containing uranium, lead, silicon, and oxygen.

gum-mō′sis, *n.* The transformation of vegetable tissues into gum, as in the formation of cherry-gum.

gum-mos′i-ty, *n.* The nature of gum; gumminess; a viscous or adhesive quality.

gum′mous, *a.* [L. *gummosus*, gummy, from *gummi*, gum.] Of the nature or quality of gum; viscous; adhesive.

gum′my, *a.* 1. Consisting of gum; of the nature of gum; viscous; adhesive; productive of gum; covered with gum or viscous matter.

2. Gummatous.

3. Puffy; swollen. [Slang.]

gump, *n.* [Ice. *gumpr*, the rump.] A foolish person; a dolt. [Colloq.]

gum′=plant, *n.* Any of several species of *Grindelia*, the young plants of which are coated with a viscous substance.

gum′=pot, *n.* A vessel in which gums are melted in varnish-making.

gump′tion, *n.* [AS. *gyman*, to understand, heed.]

1. Capacity; shrewdness; address. [Colloq.]

2. The supposed lost medium of the old masters, to which some ascribe their unapproachable excellence; the art of preparing colors.

3. Magilp.

gum′=rash, *n.* A mild papular eruption to which many children are subject soon after birth.

gum′=stick, *n.* A small piece of some hard substance, as of ivory or coral, which a child bites on in teething.

gum′suck″ẽr, *n.* A native white of Australia; so called on account of the gum-sucking habit of the children.

gum′top=tree, *n.* *Eucalyptus Sieberiana*, the Tasmanian and Australian ironbark-tree.

gum′=tree, *n.* 1. The black-gum, of the genus *Nyssa*, one of the largest trees of the southern states. Most of the large trees become hollow, and hence *gum-tree* is the term to denote a hollow tree, in many of the southern states.

2. *Liquidambar Styraciflua*, the sweet-gum; a large tree of the witch-hazel family, native in the Atlantic states.

3. Any species of the genus *Eucalyptus*, a native of Australia.

gum′=wạ″tẽr, *n.* An aqueous solution of a gum, as of gum arabic.

gum′=wood, *n.* Wood of any of the so-called gum-trees, usually of the genus *Eucalyptus*.

gun, *n.* [ME. *gunne, gonne*, a gun; etym. unknown; compare W. *gwn*, Ir. and Gael. *gunna*, a gun, OFr. *mangonnel*, a machine for throwing stones.]

1. Any device by means of which a projectile may be thrown through a tube; (a) a tube of metal, fixed in a stock or mounted on a carriage, from which projectiles are fired by the discharge of an explosive, usually gunpowder; (b) a cannon, as distinguished from *small arms* and *mortars*; (c) colloquially, a revolver or pistol.

2. The report or discharge of a gun; as, a salute of ten *guns*.

3. One who bears a gun in a hunting party. [Colloq.]

4. A kind of jug. [Prov. Eng.]

5. A gauge to establish the width of the plate in rolling plate glass.

Armstrong gun; a cannon of wrought-iron having a rifled inner tube of steel and commonly breech-loading; invented about 1855 by Sir William Armstrong.

Dahlgren gun; a cast-iron smooth-bore cannon invented by Lieut. J. A. Dahlgren, afterward rear-admiral of the United States navy.

Gatling gun; a machine gun having a number of barrels arranged cylindrically which are rotated and fired by means of a crank; invented by Dr. R. J. Gatling, an American, and first used in the Civil War.

Great gun; (a) a cannon; (b) colloquially, a person of reputation for superiority; called also *big gun*; (c) [*pl.*] a tempest; as, to blow *great guns*; (d) [*pl.*] an interjection expressing surprise.

Krupp gun; a breech-loading steel cannon made by the Krupps of Germany.

Machine-gun: a gun of one or more barrels using fixed ammunition and provided with mechanism for continuous loading and firing. It may be operated by man power or by the force of recoil.

Mauser gun; a rifle with a magazine in the stock carrying five cartridges; a gun of great efficiency in military service, having a range of over 2,000 yards, with a high muzzle velocity.

Quaker gun; an imitation cannon.

Rapid-fire gun; a gun of an inch or more in caliber, into which ammunition is loaded at the breech by hand. Rapid fire is attained by the perfection of the breech-loading mechanism, and by great proficiency in drill.

Wire gun; a gun made by wrapping a central tube with wire.

gun, *v.i.*; gunned, *pt.*, *pp.*; gunning, *ppr.* To shoot; to hunt for game with a gun.

gụ'nȧ, *n.* [Sans. *guna*, quality.] The modification produced by prefixing *ă* to certain Sanskrit vowels when accented.

gū'när-ghy, *n.* Same as *Gynarchy.*

gun'bōat, *n.* 1. A light-draft war-ship armed with heavy guns.

2. In Pennsylvania coal-mines, a small self-dumping coal-car.

gun'=car"riage (-rij), *n.* The carriage or structure on which a gun is mounted, moved, and fired.

gun'cot"tŏn, *n.* A substance produced by treating cotton or other forms of cellulose with a mixture of nitric and sulphuric acids. It explodes by percussion, especially when under pressure.

gun'=deck, *n.* The deck carrying a ship's guns.

gun'de-let, *n.* A gondola. [Obs.]

gun'=fīre, *n.* The time of firing regular signal guns.

gun'flint, *n.* A piece of flint for the lock of a flintlock musket or pistol.

gun'jȧh, *n.* Same as *Ganjah.*

gun'lock, *n.* The firing mechanism of a gun.

gun'man, *n.* A desperado, armed and prepared to take life, either for personal revenge or hire.

gun'=met"ăl, *n.* A copper alloy formerly used for small cannon; also, a kind of iron.

gun'nāge, *n.* The number of guns in a ship of war. [Rare.]

gun'nel, *n.* A gunwale.

gun'nẽr, *n.* 1. One skilled in the use of guns; a cannoneer; one who operates a gun.

2. In the navy, a warrant-officer having charge of all the ordnance of a vessel.

3. A person who uses firearms, especially in hunting.

4. The loon.

5. The sea-bream.

Gunner's daughter; a gun to which offenders on shipboard were tied for flogging.

gun'nẽr-y, *n.* The science of artillery; the art of managing cannon.

gun'nieṣ, *n.* Width; a measure of width equal to a yard; a space in a mine where ore has been removed; also spelled *gunniss.*

gun'ning, *n.* The act of hunting or shooting game with a gun.

gun'nung, *n.* *Eucalyptus robusta*, a gum-tree of Australia.

gun'ny, *n.*; *pl.* **gun'nieṣ.** [Bengali *gona* or *goni*, a gunny-bag.] A strong, coarse sackcloth made from jute and sunn-hemp. It is much

gun'ny=bag, *n.* A bag made of gunny.

gun'ny=clọth, *n.* Gunny.

gū-noc'rȧ-cy, *n.* See *Gynecocracy.*

gun'=pōrt, *n.* A porthole for the muzzle of a gun.

gun'pow"dẽr, *n.* An explosive mixture of saltpeter, sulphur, and charcoal, reduced to fine powder, then granulated and dried, largely employed in the discharge of projectiles from guns, as well as in blasting.

Gunpowder plot; in English history, a plot to blow up the Houses of Parliament by gunpowder on Nov. 5, 1605, and destroy King (James I.), lords, and commons.

Gunpowder tea; a fine species of green tea, being a carefully picked hyson, the leaves of which are rolled and rounded, so as to have a granular appearance.

gun'rēach, *n.* Gunshot; the distance a gun will carry.

gun'rọọm, *n.* An apartment on the after-portion of the lower gun-deck of a war-ship, occupied by the junior officers.

gun'shot, *n.* 1. The reach or range of a gun; the distance to which shot can be thrown so as to be effective; the length of the pointblank range of a cannon-shot.

2. The act of firing a gun; the discharge of a gun; a shot.

gun'shot, *a.* Made by the shot of a gun; as, a *gunshot* wound.

gun=shȳ, *a.* Terrorized at sight or report of a gun.

gun'smith, *n.* A maker of small arms; one who makes or repairs small firearms.

gun'smith"ẽr-y, *n.* The business of a gunsmith; the art of making small firearms.

gun'stẽr, *n.* One who uses a gun; a gunner. [Rare.]

gun'stick, *n.* A rammer or ramrod; a stick or rod to ram down the charge of a musket, etc.

gun'stock, *n.* The stock or wood in which the barrel of a gun is fixed.

gun'stōne, *n.* A shot for a cannon, round stones having been originally used for the purpose.

gun'=tag"kle, *n.* The blocks and pulleys affixed to the sides of a gun-carriage and the side of a ship, by means of which a gun is run up to or drawn back from the porthole.

Ship-gun with Gun-tackle.

Gun'tẽr's chāin. [Named after its inventor, Edmund *Gunter.*] See *Chain*, 5.

Gun'tẽr's line. In logarithms, (a) a line on Gunter's scale, used for performing the multiplication and division of numbers mechanically by the dividers; called also *line of lines* and *line of numbers*; (b) a sliding scale corresponding to logarithms for performing these operations by inspection without dividers; called also *Gunter's sliding rule.*

Gun'tẽr's quad'rănt (kwod'). A quadrant made of wood, brass, or other substance, being a kind of stereographic projection on the plane of the equator, the eye being supposed in one of the poles. It is used to find the hour of the day, the sun's azimuth, etc., as also to take the altitude of an object in degrees.

Gun'tẽr's scāle. A large plane scale having various lines upon it, both natural and logarithmic, of great use in solving mechanically by means of a slider problems in navigation and surveying.

gun'wāle, gun'nel, *n.* The upper edge of a ship's side; the uppermost wale of a ship, or that piece of timber which reaches on either side from the quarter-deck to the forecastle, being the uppermost bend which finishes the upper works of the hull; a piece of timber around the top side of a boat, and having rowlocks for the oars.

gūrge, *n.* A whirlpool. [Obs.]

gūrge, *v.t.* To swallow. [Obs.]

gūr'ġeonṣ, *n.pl.* [Obs.] Same as *Grudgings.*

gūr-gi-tā'tion, *n.* [L. *gurgitare*, to flood, from *gurges (-itis)*, a whirlpool.] The movement of a liquid in a boiling or surging state.

gūr'gle, *v.i.*; gurgled, *pt.*, *pp.*; gurgling, *ppr.* [L. *gurgulio*, the throat, from *gurges*, a whirlpool.] To flow with a purling sound; to run or flow in a broken, irregular, noisy current, as water from a bottle.

gūr'gle, *n.* The act of gurgling; the sound made by a liquid flowing from the narrow mouth of a vessel, or through any narrow opening; the sound made when air is forced through a liquid.

gūr'glet, *n.* A very porous earthen vessel for cooling water by evaporation.

gūr'gling-ly, *adv.* In a gurgling manner.

gūr'goyle, *n.* A gargoyle. [Obs.]

gūr'jun, *n.* [E. Ind.] 1. A liquid balsam obtained from East Indian trees of genus *Dipterocarpus*, used in medicine, paints, and varnishes.

2. *Dipterocarpus alatus*, a very large timber-tree of the Philippines and the East Indies.

Gūr'kha, *n.* One of the dominant race of Nepal, India, and noted as being fine soldiers in the Anglo-Indian army. They are of Hindu religion and Indo-European speech.

gūrl, *n.* A girl. [Obs.]

gūr'let, *n.* [Etym. unknown.] In masonry, a pickax having a cutting edge and a sharp point.

gūr'my, *n.*; *pl.* **gūr'mieṣ.** [Etym. unknown.] A level or a working in a mine.

gūr'nărd, *n.* [ME. *gurnard*; OFr. *gournauld*, a gurnard, from *grongner*; L. *grunnire*, to grunt.]

1. A sea-fish of several species, of the genus *Trigla*, having an angular head covered with bony plates, and seven rays in the membranes of the gills. *Trigla gurnardus* is the gray gurnard, common on the British coast; the red gurnard is *Trigla cuculus.*

2. A flying-fish of the genus *Dactylopterus*; the flying-gurnard.

3. The gemmous dragonet, known as the *yellow gurnard.*

Gray Gurnard (*Trigla gurnardus*).

gūr'net, *n.* A gurnard.

gur'rȧh, *n.* [E. Ind.] A kind of plain, coarse India muslin.

gur'ry, *n.* [Etym. obscure.]

1. Fish-offal.

2. The refuse matter of a dissecting-room. [Local, U. S.]

3. The commercial name for a certain grade of menhaden-oil.

4. Feces. [Obs.]

gur'ry, *n.* [Hind. *garhī*, a small fort.] In India a small native fort.

gūrt, *n.* [Etym. obscure.] In mining, a channel for water; a gutter.

gūrts, *n.pl.* Groats. [Obs.]

gụ'rụ, *n.* [Hind., from Sans. *guru*, heavy, weighty, honored.] A Hindu spiritual guide.

gụ'rụ=nut, *n.* A cola-nut.

gush, *v.i.*; gushed, *pt.*, *pp.*; gushing, *ppr.* [ME. *guschen*, to gush; O.D. *guysen*, to flow out with a gurgling sound; compare Ice. *gusa*, to gush.]

1. To issue with violence and rapidity, as a fluid; to flow copiously; to rush forth, as a fluid from confinement; as, blood *gushes* from a vein in venesection.

2. To act with a sudden and rapid impulse; to be extravagantly and effusively sentimental.

gush, *v.t.* To emit in copious effusion; as, to *gush* out a stream of blood.

gush, *n.* 1. A sudden and violent issue of a fluid or the like from an inclosed place; an emission of or as of a liquid in a large quantity and with force; the fluid, etc., thus emitted; as, a *gush* of melody.

2. Extravagant or effusive affectation of sentiment.

gush'ẽr, *n.* 1. One who gushes. [Colloq.]

2. Anything sending forth a copious stream of liquid, as a geyser or an oil-well.

gush'ing, *a.* 1. Rushing forth with violence, as a fluid; flowing copiously; as, *gushing* waters.

2. Emitting copiously; as, *gushing* eyes.

3. Extravagantly sentimental; demonstratively emotional; unreserved. [Colloq.]

gush'ing-ly, *adv.* In a gushing manner.

gus'set, *n.* [OFr. *gousset*, the armhole, a piece of chain-mail used to cover the space between two joints of armor, dim. of *gousse*, a husk, pod.]

1. A small triangular piece of cloth inserted in a garment for the purpose of strengthening or enlarging some part.

2. Anything like such a piece of cloth in shape or function, as (a) a small piece of chain-mail, afterward of plate, placed at the juncture of the armor beneath the arms; (b) an angular piece of iron inserted in a boiler, tank, etc., where it changes from a cylindrical to a square form, etc., as in the junction of the barrel and fire-box of a locomotive.

3. In heraldry, a mark of abatement; a gore.

gust, *n.* [Ice. *gustr*, a gust, blast, from *gjōsa*, to gush, break out.]

1. A sudden squall; a violent blast of wind; a sudden rushing of the wind, of short duration.

2. A sudden violent burst of passion.

gust, *n.* [L. *gustus*, a taste.]

1. Taste; tasting, or the sense of tasting; the pleasure of tasting; relish; gusto.

2. Pleasure; gratification of any kind, especially that which is sensuous.

3. Turn of fancy; intellectual taste.

gust, *v.t.* To taste; to have a relish for. [Obs.]

gust'ȧ-ble, *a.* 1. That may be tasted; tastable. [Obs.]

2. Pleasant to the taste. [Obs.]

gus-tā'tion, *n.* [L. *gustatio (-onis)*, from *gustare*, to taste.] The act of tasting.

gust'ȧ-tō-ry, *a.* Pertaining to gust or taste; as, the *gustatory* qualities of food.

gust'fụl, *a.* Gusty; attended with gusts; squally.

gust'fụl, *a.* Tasteful; well-tasted. [Obs.]

gust'fụl-ness, *n.* Relish. [Obs.]

gust'less, *a.* Tasteless. [Obs.]

gus'tō, *n.* [It. and Sp., from L. *gustus*, taste.] Relish; appreciative taste or enjoyment; zest.

gụs-tō'sō, *a.* and *adv.* [It., from *gusto*, L. *gustus*, taste.] In music, with taste; tastefully.

gust'y, *a.* Subject to sudden blasts of wind; stormy; tempestuous.

Syn.—Blustering, squally, stormy, tempestuous, windy.

gut, *n.* [ME. *gut*, *gotte*; AS. *gut*, the intestine, from *geōtan*, to pour out, flow.]

1. The intestinal canal of an animal; an intestine; as, the large *gut*; the small *gut*; the blind *gut* or cæcum; in the plural, the whole mass

formed by the natural convolutions of the intestines in the abdomen.

2. [*pl.*] The stomach and digestive apparatus generally. [Vulgar.]

3. Any preparation of the intestines of an animal used for various purposes, as for the strings of a violin, etc.; catgut.

4. The fiber taken from a silkworm when about to make its cocoon and drawn into a strong cord.

5. In geography, a narrow passage; a strait; a narrow channel of water.

gut, *v.t.*; gutted, *pt.*, *pp.*; gutting, *ppr.* 1. To take out the bowels of; to eviscerate.

2. To plunder; to take out or ruin the contents of; as, the mob *gutted* the house.

gut′tȧ, *n.*; *pl.* **gut′tæ.** [L., a drop.]

1. A drop; used in pharmacy.

2. In architecture, a pendent, droplike decoration, cylindrical or like the frustum of a cone, used to embellish the lower surface of the mutules or the triglyphs of the Doric frieze.

Guttæ.

3. In zoölogy, a small, droplike marking.

Gutta serena; in old medicine, same as *amaurosis*.

gut′tȧ, *n.* In chemistry, a white substance obtained from gutta-percha.

gut′tȧ-pēr′chȧ, *n.* [Malay *gatah*, *guttah*, gum, and *percha*, *pertja*, the tree from which it is obtained.] A substance resembling caoutchouc, but stronger, more soluble, and less elastic, obtained as a milky juice, which hardens on being exposed to the air; the sap of a tree of the genus *Isonandra*, natural order *Sapotaceæ*, native in the Malayan Archipelago. It is insoluble in water, soluble with difficulty in ether and other caoutchouc solvents, but very readily in oil of turpentine and naphtha. It is used for insulation, in cements, etc.

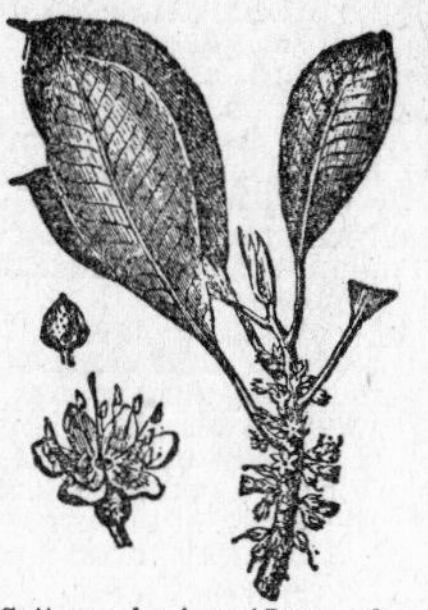

Gutta-percha tree (*Isonandra Gutta*).

gut′tāte, *a.* [L. *guttatus*, from *gutta*, a drop.] Spotted, as if sprinkled with drops of color.

gut′tā-ted, *a.* Besprinkled with drops.

gut′tȧ-trap, *n.* The juice of *Artocarpus incisa*, or breadfruit-tree, from which birdlime is made.

gut′té (-tā), **gut′ty**, *a.* [OFr. *gouté*; L. *guttatus*, spotted, from *gutta*, a drop.] In heraldry, a term implying sprinkled with liquid drops.

gut′tēr, *n.* [ME. *gotere*; OFr. *gutiere*, a channel to receive the drippings from the roof, a gutter, from L. *gutta*, a drop.]

1. A channel for conveying off water at the eaves of a roof; an eaves-trough.

2. A channel or passage for water at the side of a road, street, etc.; a channel worn in the earth by water.

3. In general, any groove, as one of the depressions on the wings of certain beetles, a groove in cabinetwork, etc.

4. In Australia, the bottom of the channel of a river of the Tertiary period, containing deposits of gold.

5. In printing, a grooved piece of furniture used to separate pages in a form.

6. [*pl.*] Mud; mire; dirt. [Scot.]

gut′tēr, *v.t.*; guttered, *pt.*, *pp.*; guttering, *ppr.* 1. To cut or form into narrow channels or grooves, as by the flow of a liquid.

2. To provide with gutters.

3. To carry off, as by a gutter.

gut′tēr, *v.i.* 1. To be hollowed or channeled.

2. To run in drops or hollows, as a candle.

gut′tēr-mem″bēr, *n.* In architecture, a member formed by the decorative treatment of the outer face of a gutter.

gut′tēr-snipe, *n.* 1. A neglected, destitute boy that frequents the streets; a street arab. [Slang.]

2. In printing, a term applied to a small bill for advertising purposes, formerly used by pasting to a curbstone, whence the name.

3. A contemptuous name for one who gathers junk from gutters.

4. In zoölogy, a local name for Wilson's snipe, *Gallinago wilsoni.*

5. A curbstone broker. [Slang.]

gut′tēr-spout, *n.* A pipe which carries off the water from an eaves-trough.

gut′ti-fēr, *n.* [L. *gutta*, drop, and *ferre*, to bear.] In botany, a plant that exudes gum or resin.

Gut-tif′e-ræ, *n.pl.* [L. *gutta*, a drop, and *ferre*, to bear.] A small order of exogenous trees and shrubs, natives of humid and hot places in tropical regions, generally acrid, and yielding a yellow gum resin; the trees which yield gamboge belong to this order.

gut-tif′ēr-ăl, *a.* Of or pertaining to the *Guttiferæ*; gum-bearing.

gut-tif′ēr-ous, *a.* Yielding gum or resinous substances.

gut′ti-fọrm, *a.* [L. *gutta*, a drop, and *forma*, form.] In the shape of a drop.

gut′tle, *v.t.* To swallow; to gobble. [Obs.]

gut′tle, *v.i.* To swallow greedily. [Obs.]

gut′tlēr, *n.* A greedy eater; a glutton. [Obs.]

gut′tū-lȧ, *n.*; *pl.* **gut′tū-læ.** [L., dim. of *gutta*, a drop.] A small drop or speck of color.

gut′tū-lāte, *a.* Marked with small spots or drops.

gut′tū-lous, *a.* In the form of small drops. [Obs.]

gut′tur-ăl, *a.* [L. *guttur*, the throat.] Of or pertaining to the throat; formed in the throat; as, a *guttural* sound.

gut′tur-ăl, *n.* A sound produced in the throat; a letter pronounced in the throat.

gut′tur-ăl-iṣm, *n.* A guttural manner of speaking.

gut-tur-al′i-ty, *n.* The quality of being guttural.

gut′tur-ăl-īze, *v.t.*; gutturalized, *pt.*, *pp.*; gutturalizing, *ppr.* To utter gutturally.

gut′tur-ăl-ly, *adv.* In a guttural manner.

gut′tur-ăl-ness, *n.* The quality of being guttural.

gut′tur-ine, *a.* Pertaining to the throat. [Obs.]

gut′tur-ize, *v.t.* [L. *guttur*, the throat.] To utter in a guttural manner. [Rare.]

gut′ty, *a.* See *Gutté.*

gut′wŏrt, *n.* A plant, *Globularia Alypum*, used as a purgative.

guy̆ (gī), *n.* [OFr. *guye*, *guie*, a guide, a crane, from *guier*, to guide.] A rope or other appliance used to steady anything, as a flagstaff, a telegraph-pole, a hoisting-frame, a balloon, a tight-rope, etc.

guy̆ (gī), *n.* 1. A fright; a dowdy; a person of odd or eccentric looks, manner, or garb; so named from the effigy of Guy Fawkes which used to be burned annually on the 5th of November, in England.

2. In recent slang, a term loosely and flippantly applied to any stranger.

guy̆, *v.t.*; guyed, *pt.*, *pp.*; guying, *ppr.* [Fr. *guier*, to guide.] To steady, stay, or direct by means of a guy.

guy̆, *v.t.* To chaff; to banter; to hold up to ridicule. [Colloq.]

guy̆le, *v.t.* To beguile. [Obs.]

gūze, *n.* [OFr. *gueules*, gules.] In heraldry, a roundlet of sanguine tint, representing an eyeball.

guz′zle, *v.i.*; guzzled, *pt.*, *pp.*; guzzling, *ppr.* [OFr. *gouziller*, only in comp. *desgouziller*, to gulp down, guzzle.] To swallow liquor greedily; to drink much; to drink frequently.

guz′zle, *v.t.* To swallow greedily and often; to swallow with immoderate gust.

Syn.—Drink, quaff, swig, swill.

guz′zle, *n.* An insatiable thing or person; also, a debauch; a drinking-bout.

guz′zlēr, *n.* One who guzzles; an immoderate drinker.

gwyn′i-ad, gwin′i-ad, *n.* [W. *gwyniad*, the fish called whiting, a whitening, from *gwyn*, white.] A fish of the whitefish kind, *Coregonus pennanti*, found plentifully in some of the Welsh lakes and in many lakes on the continent of Europe. It is gregarious, and may be taken in great numbers at a draft; also called *fresh-water herring*, *schelly*, and *powan.*

gy̆′ăl, gy̆′ăll, *n.* Same as *Gayal.*

Gy̆-ăs-çū′tus, *n.* 1. A genus of buprestid beetles.

2. [g—] An imaginary animal of gigantic size; a name said to have been invented by a showman.

ġyb (jib), **ġy̆be**, *n.* A jib. [Obs.]

ġy̆be, *n.* A gibe. [Obs.]

ġy̆be, *v.t.* and *v.i.* To jibe. [Obs.]

gy̆e, *v.t.* To guide. [Obs.]

gy̆le, *n.* [Obs.] See *Guile.*

gym-kä′nȧ (*or* jim-), *n.* [Anglo-Ind., origin doubtful.] A celebration of sports or games of some kind; as, a bicycle *gymkana.*

ġymn-. See *Gymno-.*

gym′năl, gym′năll, *n.* Same as *Gimbal.*

ġym-nan′thous, *a.* [*Gymn-*, and Gr. *anthos*, flower.] In botany, without a perianth; achlamydeous.

ġym-nā′ṣi-ärçh, *n.* [L. *gymnasiarchus*; Gr. *gymnasiarchos*; *gymnasion*, gymnasium, and *archein*, to rule.] In ancient Greece, one of the officials annually appointed to manage the gymnasia.

ġym-nā′ṣi-um, *n.*; *pl.* **ġym-nā′ṣi-ȧ, ġym-nā′ṣi-umṣ.** [L. *gymnasium*; Gr. *gymnasion*, the place where exercises were practised, from *gymnazein*, to train naked, or lightly clad; *gymnos*, naked, stripped.]

1. A place where athletic exercises are performed.

2. A school for the higher branches of literature and science; especially used in connection with German classical schools preparatory to the universities.

3. In Grecian antiquity, an institution common to the towns, which at first was simply an open place for athletic exercises, but to which were added baths, porticos, and chambers, often adorned with works of art, and forming a place for lectures and the schools of philosophers.

ġym′nast, *n.* [Gr. *gymnastēs*, a trainer of athletes, from *gymnazein*, to train in athletic exercises.] One who teaches, learns, or is skilled in gymnastic exercises.

ġym-nas′tiç, ġym-nas′tiç-ăl, *a.* [L. *gymnasticus*; Gr. *gymnastikos*, from *gymnazein*, to train in athletic exercises.]

1. Pertaining to athletic exercises of the body, intended for health, defense, or diversion.

2. Figuratively, relating to mental exercises.

3. Athletic. [Rare.]

ġym-nas′tiç, *n.* 1. A gymnast. [Obs.]

2. Athletic exercise; athletics.

ġym-nas′tiç-ăl-ly, *adv.* In a gymnastic manner.

ġym-nas′tiçs, *n.* The art of performing athletic exercises; athletic exercises; feats of skill or address, mental or bodily.

ġym′niç, ġym′niç-ăl, *a.* Gymnastic; athletic. [Obs.]

ġym′niç, *n.* Athletic exercise. [Obs.]

ġym′nite, *n.* [Gr. *gymnos*, bare, naked, and *-ite*; so called from Bare Hills in Maryland, where it is found.] A whitish amorphous mineral; hydrous silicate of magnesia.

ġym-no-, ġymn-. Combining forms from Gr. *gymnos*, naked, used in botany, zoölogy, etc., to signify naked, bare, stripped, destitute of, as in *gymno*carpous, *gymno*cyte.

Ġym-nō-blas′tē-ȧ, *n.pl.* [*Gymno-*, and Gr. *blastos*, a germ.] In zoölogy, a suborder of hydroid polyps with naked buds.

ġym-nō-blas′tiç, *a.* Of or characteristic of the *Gymnoblastea.*

ġym-nō-çär′pous, *a.* [*Gymno-*, and Gr. *karpos*, fruit.] In botany, having a naked fruit.

ġym-nō-cid′i-um, *n.*; *pl.* **ġym-nō-cid′i-ȧ.** [Gr. *gymnos*, naked, and dim. *-idion.*] In botany, the swelling occasionally found at the base of the spore-case in urn-mosses.

Ġym-noc′lā-dus, *n.* [*Gymno-*, and Gr. *klados*, a branch.] In botany, a genus of leguminous trees having but one species, *Gymnocladus Canadensis*, the Kentucky coffee-tree. The wood is hard, compact, and of a fine rose color; the seeds were once used as a substitute for coffee.

Ġym-nō-çō′pȧ, *n.pl.* [*Gymno-*, and Gr. *kōpē*, an oar.] In zoölogy, a group of *Annelida* whose cephalic appendages only are provided with movable chitinous spines.

ġym-noc′y-tȧ, *n.* [*Gymno*, -and Gr. *kytos*, a hollow.] In biology, a nucleated cell having no cell-wall.

ġym′nō-cy̆te, *n.* See *Gymnocyta.*

ġym-nō-cy̆′tōde, *n.* [*Gymno-*, and Gr. *kytos*, a hollow, and *eidos*, form.] A nonnucleated cytode with no cell-wall.

ġym′nō-dont, *n.* [*Gymn-*, and Gr. *odous*, *odontos*, a tooth.] In zoölogy, one of a group of fishes, including the spinous globe-fishes, in which the projecting beak is covered with numerous dental lamellæ, developed from a subjacent pulp.

ġym′nō-ġen, *n.* [*Gymno-*, and Gr. *-genēs*, producing.] In botany, a gymnosperm.

ġym′nō-ġēne, *n.* [*Gymno-*, and *genys*, chin.] A hawk of the genus *Polyboroides*, found in Africa.

ġym-noġ′e-nous, *a.* [*Gymno-*, and Gr. *-genēs*, producing.]

1. In zoölogy, hatched naked, as certain birds; gymnopædic; psilopædic.

2. In botany, with naked seeds; gymnospermous.

Ġym-nō-glos′sȧ, *n.pl.* [*Gymno-*, and Gr. *glōssa*, the tongue.] A division of free-swimming modified gasteropods in which the radula and jaws are wanting.

Ġym-nō-gram′mē, *n.* [*Gymno-*, and Gr. *grammē*, a mark, line.] An extensive genus of ferns embracing between 80 and 90 species, natives of warm regions. The under surface of the fronds of many of the species is coated with a yellow or silvery powder, by reason of which they are known as *gold-* or *silver-ferns.*

ġym-noġ′y-nous, *a.* [*Gymno-*, and Gr. *gynē*, a female.] In botany, having a naked ovary.

Ġym-nō-læ′mȧ-tȧ, *n.pl.* [*Gymno-*, and Gr. *laimos*, the throat.] In zoölogy, an order of the *Polyzoa*, in which the mouth is devoid of the valvular structure known as the epistome.

Ġym-nō-nō′ti, *n.pl.* [*Gymno-*, and Gr. *nōton*, the back.] A suborder of fishes without dorsal or ventral fins, as the electric eel, *Gymnotus electricus.*

ġym-nō-pæd′iç, *a.* [*Gymno-*, and Gr. *pais*, *paidos*, boy, child.] In zoölogy, psilopædic; gymnogenous; hatched naked.

Ġym-nō-phi′ō-nȧ, *n.pl.* [*Gymn-*, and Gr. *ophis*, a serpent.] An order of tailless amphibians with a long serpent-like body. The limbs are either wanting or rudimentary.

Gym-noph-thal′mȧ-tȧ, *n.pl.* [*Gymn-*, and Gr. *ophthalmos*, the eye.] A tribe of *Medusæ* (the naked-eyed medusæ) having a disk-shaped body, circulating vessels running to the margin, and the eye-specks either uncovered or wanting.

ġym′nō-plast, *n.* [*Gymno-*, and Gr. *plastos*, formed, from *plassein*, to form.] In biology, a naked cell or mass of protoplasm, as a leucocyte.

ġym-nō-rhī′năl, *a.* [*Gymno-*, and Gr. *rhis*, *rhinos*, the nose.] In ornithology, having nostrils without feathers.

Gym-nō-sō′mȧ-tȧ, *n.pl.* [*Gymno-*, and Gr. *sōma*, *sōmatos*, the body.] In zoölogy, an order of pteropods in which the body is not protected by a shell.

ġym-nos′ō-phist, *n.* [L. *gymnosophistæ*; Gr. *gymnosophistai*, the naked philosophers of India; *gymnos*, naked, and *sophistēs*, a philosopher.] One of a sect of ancient Hindu philosophers who lived solitarily in the woods, wore little or no clothing, ate no flesh, renounced all bodily pleasures, and addicted themselves to mystical contemplation.

ġym-nos′ō-phy, *n.* The doctrines of the gymnosophists.

ġym′nō-spērm, *n.* [*Gymno-*, and Gr. *sperma*, a seed.] In botany, a plant that bears naked seeds, as the conifers.

Gym-nō-spēr′mæ, *n.pl.* In botany, a subdivision of exogens having naked ovules, embracing the *Cycadaceæ*, *Coniferæ*, and *Gnetaceæ*.

ġym-nō-spēr′măl, *a.* Relating to gymnosperms.

ġym-nō-spēr′mous, *a.* Of, pertaining to, or resembling the gymnosperms; having naked seeds, or seeds not inclosed in a capsule or other vessel.

ġym′nō-spōre, *n.* [*Gymno-*, and Gr. *sporos*, a sowing, seed.] In biology, a naked spore.

ġym-nos′pō-rous, *a.* In botany, having naked spores.

ġym-nos′tō-mous, *a.* [*Gymno-*, and Gr. *stoma*, a mouth.] In botany, without a peristome, as the mouths of capsules in certain mosses.

Gym-not′ō-cȧ, *n.pl.* [*Gymno-*, and Gr. *tokos*, offspring, from *tiktein*, *tekein*, to bring forth.] The *Gymnoblastea*.

Gym-nō′tus, *n.* [Gr. *gymnos*, naked, bare, and *nōton*, the back.]

1. A genus of South American fresh-water fishes including the electric eel, *Gymnotus electricus*.

2. [g—] A fish of this genus.

ġyn-. A combining form from Gr. *gynē*, a woman, denoting woman, female.

gyn, *v.t.* and *v.i.* To begin. [Obs.]

ġyn-æ-cē′um, ġyn-æ-cī′um, *n.* [L. *gynæceum*; Gr. *gynaikeion*, the women's apartment, from *gynaikeios*, of or belonging to women, from *gynē*, a woman.]

1. The women's quarters in a Greek or Roman house, which were usually the remotest part of a building, lying beyond an interior court.

2. A sort of manufactory in ancient Rome for making clothes and furniture for the emperor's family.

3. In botany, a gynœcium.

ġy-næ′ciăn, *a.* See *Gynecian*.

ġy-nan′dēr, *n.* In botany, a plant of the Linnean class *Gynandria*.

Gy-nan′dri-ȧ, *n.pl.* In the Linnean system of botany, a class of plants whose stamens and pistil are consolidated into a single body.

ġy-nan′dri-ăn, *a.* Relating to the *Gynandria*.

ġy-nan′drō-mọrph, *n.* An animal characterized by having one side male and the other side female.

Gynandria.

a, Face of Stigma; *b*, Anther; *c c*, Abortive Stamina; *l*, Lip; *p p*, Petals; *s s*, Sepals.

ġy-nan-drō-mọr′phiṣm, *n.* [Gr. *gynē*, a female, and *anēr*, *andros*, a man, male, and *morphē*, form, and *-ism*.] In entomology, the condition of having one side male and the other female.

ġy-nan-drō-mọr′phous, *a.* Characterized by gynandromorphism.

ġy-nan′drō-phōre, *n.* [Gr. *gynē*, a female, *anēr*, *andros*, a male, and *pherein*, to bear.] A gynophore bearing stamens as well as pistil, as certain capers.

ġy-nan′thō-rous, *a.* [*Gyn-*, and Gr. *antheros*, flowering, from *anthos*, a flower.] Having the stamens converted into pistils, as in certain flowers.

ġyn′ār-çhy, *n.* [*Gyn-*, and Gr. *archē*, a government, from *archein*, to rule.] Government by a woman or women.

ġyn-e-, ġyn-e-co-. Combining forms from Gr. *gynē*, *gynaikos*, a woman, signifying a woman, or female.

ġyn-ē-cē′um, *n.* Same as *Gynæceum*.

ġy-nē′ciăn, *a.* [Gr. *gynē*, a woman.] Pertaining to women.

ġy-nē′ciç, ġy-næ′ciç, *a.* [Gr. *gynaikikos*, from *gynē*, a woman.] Pertaining to or characteristic of the female sex; female; in medicine and surgery, noting diseases peculiar to females.

ġyn-e-co-. See *Gyne-*.

ġyn-ē-çoç′rȧ-çy, ġyn-æ-çoç′rȧ-çy, *n.* [Gr. *gynaikokratia*, government by women; *gynē*, a woman, and *kratos*, power, from *kratein*, to rule.] Government by a woman or women.

ġyn″ē-çō-loġ′iç-ăl, ġyn″æ-çō-loġ′iç-ăl, *a.* Pertaining to gynecology.

ġyn-ē-çol′ō-ġist, ġyn-æ-çol′ō-ġist, *n.* One skilled in gynecology.

ġyn-ē-çol′ō-ġy, ġyn-æ-çol′ō-ġy, *n.* [*Gyneco-*, and Gr. *-logia*, from *legein*, to speak.] A treatise on or the doctrine of the nature and diseases of women.

ġyn-ē′çō-mas-ty, ġyn-æ′çō-mas-ty, *n.* [*Gyneco-*, and Gr. *mastos*, the breast.] Abnormal development of the breasts in a male.

ġyn″ē-çō-nī′tis, ġyn″æ-çō-nī′tis, *n.* [Gr. *gynaikōnitis*, a gynæceum.] A place or apartment reserved for women; a gynæceum.

ġyn″ē-çō-path′iç, ġyn″æ-çō-path′iç, *a.* Relating to diseases prevalent among women.

ġyn-ē-çop′ȧ-thy, ġyn-æ-çop′ȧ-thy, *n.* [*Gyneco-*, and Gr. *pathos*, suffering.] Any disease to which women only are subject.

ġyn-ē-oç′rȧ-çy, ġyn-æ-oç′rȧ-çy, *n.* Same as *Gynecocracy*.

ġyn-ē-ol′ȧ-try, ġyn-æ-ol′ȧ-try, *n.* [Gr. *gynē*, a woman, and *latreia*, worship.] Excessive fondness for or adoration of women.

ġyn-ē-phō′bi-ȧ, ġyn-æ-phō′bi-ȧ, *n.* [*Gynē-*, and Gr. *phobos*, fear.] Dislike or hatred of women; aversion to women.

ġyn-o-. A combining form from Gr. *gynē*, a woman, used in botany, to signify pistil or ovary; as, *gyno*base, *gyno*phore.

ġyn′ō-bāse, *n.* [*Gyno-*, and Gr. *basis*, base.] An enlargement of the base or receptacle of a flower, supporting the gynœcium.

ġyn-ō-bā′siç, *a.* Characteristic of or pertaining to a gynobase.

ġy-noç′rȧ-çy, *n.* Gynecocracy.

ġyn″ō-dī-œ′cious (-ē′shus), *a.* [*Gyno-*, and Gr. *di-*, two, and *oikos*, a house.] Noting a plant bearing both pistillate and perfect flowers on different individuals.

ġy-nœ′ci-um, *n.* [*Gyno-*, and Gr. *oikos*, house.] The pistils of a flower, taken as a whole.

ġyn″ō-mō-nœ′cious, ġyn″ō-mō-nē′cious, *a.* [*Gyno-*, and Gr. *monos*, alone, single, and *oikos*, a house.] Having flowers of the female and perfect forms growing on the same plant, but none of the male.

ġyn′ō-phōre, *n.* [*Gyno-*, and Gr. *-phoros*, from *pherein*, to bear.]

1. In botany, the pedicel on which stands the ovary in certain flowers, as in the passion-flower.

2. In zoölogy, a female gonophore of a hydrozoan.

Pistil of *Dictamnus Fraxinella*, with Gynophore in center.

ġyn-ō-stē′ġi-um, *n.*; *pl.* **ġyn-ō-stē′ġi-ȧ.** [*Gyno-*, and Gr. *stegē*, a roof.] In botany, a covering of any kind of the gynœcium; a perianth.

ġyn-ō-stē′mi-um, *n.*; *pl.* **ġyn-ō-stē′mi-ȧ.** [Gr. *gynē*, woman, and *stemon*, warp.] In botany, the column formed by the combining of the stamens and style in orchids.

-ġy-nous. A suffix from L. *-gynus*; Gr. *-gynos*, from *gynē*, a woman, signifying a woman, or female; employed especially in botanical terms to denote the possession of female organs, as the pistils and ovaries; as, andro*gynous*, mono*gynous*.

ġyp, *n.* [Prob. from Gr. *gyps*, a vulture.]

1. A cant term for an undergraduate's servant at Cambridge University, England, as *scout* is used at Oxford.

2. A swindler. [Slang.]

ġyp′sē-ous, *a.* [L. *gypseus*, from *gypsum*, gypsum.] Of the nature of gypsum; partaking of the qualities of gypsum; resembling gypsum; containing gypsum.

ġyp-sif′ēr-ous, *a.* [L. *gypsum*, gypsum, and *ferre*, to bear.] Containing gypsum.

ġyp′sine, *a.* Gypseous. [Rare.]

ġyp-sog′rȧ-phy, *n.* [Gr. *gypsos*, gypsum, and *graphein*, to write, draw.] Writing or drawing on gypsum, or the art of engraving on gypsum.

ġyp′sō-plast, *n.* [Gr. *gypsos*, chalk, gypsum, and *plassein*, to mold.] A cast made of plaster of Paris.

ġyp′sum, *n.* [L. *gypsum*; Gr. *gypsos*, chalk, gypsum.] Sulphate of lime, containing twenty-one per cent of water. It often occurs in transparent crystals, or crystalline masses, easily splitting into plates, and is then called *selenite*. When white, fine-grained, and translucent, it constitutes *alabaster*. Burned to drive off the water, and ground up, it forms *plaster of Paris*.

Ġyp′sy, ġyp′sy-iṣm, etc. See *Gipsy*, etc.

ġȳ′răl, *a.* [L. *gyrus*, a circle.]

1. Whirling; moving in a circular form.

2. In anatomy, pertaining to the convolutions of the brain.

ġȳ′rāte, *a.* 1. Winding or going round as in a circle; revolving in a spiral course.

2. In botany, coiled in a circle; circinate.

3. In anatomy, having convolutions.

ġȳ′rāte, *v.i.*; gyrated, *pt.*, *pp.*; gyrating, *ppr.* [L. *gyratus*, pp. of *gyrare*, to turn, whirl, from *gyrus*; Gr. *gyros*, a circle.] To revolve round a central point, as a tornado; to move spirally.

ġy-rā′tion, *n.* [LL. *gyratio* (*-onis*), from L. *gyratus*, pp. of *gyrare*, to turn, from *gyrus*, a circle.]

1. A turning or whirling round; a circular motion; the act of revolving about a fixed center; rotation about an axis.

2. In zoölogy, a whorl on a spiral univalve shell.

Center of gyration; see under *Center*.

Radius of gyration; the distance between the axis of a rotating body and its center of gyration.

Syn.—Circular motion, revolution, rotation.

ġȳ′rȧ-tō-ry, *a.* Moving in a circle.

ġȳre, *n.* [L. *gyrus*; Gr. *gyros*, a circle.] A circular motion; a circle described by a moving body; a turn.

ġȳre, *v.t.* and *v.i.* To turn round. [Obs.]

ġȳred, *a.* Falling in rings. [Obs.]

Ġyr-en-ceph′ȧ-lȧ, *n.pl.* [Gr. *gyros*, a circle, and *enkephalos*, the brain.] One of four subclasses of mammalians which have convoluted cerebra.

ġyr-en-ceph′ȧ-lāte, *a.* Gyrencephalous.

ġyr-en-ceph′ȧ-lous, *a.* Of or pertaining to the *Gyrencephala*.

ġyr′fạl-çon, *n.* See *Gerfalcon*.

ġȳ′ri, *n.*, pl. of *gyrus*.

ġyr′lănd, *n.* and *v.*, an obsolete form of *garland*.

ġȳ-ro-. A combining form from Gr. *gyros*, a circle, used in botany, zoölogy, mathematics, etc., to signify round, circular.

ġy-rog′ō-nīte, *n.* [*Gyro-*, and Gr. *gonos*, offspring, seed.] A petrified spiral seed-vessel of plants of the genus *Chara*, found in fresh-water deposits.

ġy-roid′ăl, *a.* [Gr. *gyroeidēs*, like a circle; *gyros*, a circle, and *eidos*, form.] Spiral in arrangement or action, as (a) in crystallography, having certain planes arranged spirally, so that they incline all to the right or all to the left of a vertical line; (b) in optics, turning the plane of polarization circularly or spirally to the right or left.

ġyr′ō-man-çy, *n.* [*Gyro-*, and Gr. *manteia*, divination.] A kind of divination performed by walking round in a circle or ring.

ġȳ′rŏn-ny, ġī′rŏn-ny, *a.* [Fr. *gironne*, from *giron*, a gyron.] In heraldry, said of a field that is divided into triangular parts or gyrons of two different tinctures.

Gyronny of eight, gules and argent.

ġȳ′rō-piġ″eŏn, *n.* An object which, on being thrown up into the air from a spring-trap, resembles a pigeon in flight. It is used as a mark in shooting-matches.

ġȳ′rō-plāne, *n.* A flying-machine with rotating wings.

ġȳ′rō-sçōpe, *n.* [*Gyro-*, and Gr. *skopein*, to view.] An apparatus consisting of a rotating disk mounted by very accurately fitted pivots in a ring or rings, also rotating in different ways, for illustrating various properties of rotation and the composition of rotations. By means of this instrument the rotation of the earth on its axis can be ocularly demonstrated.

ġȳ-rō-sçop′iç, *a.* Pertaining to the gyroscope or resembling its motion.

ġy-rōse′, *a.* In botany, turned round like a crook; bent to and fro; marked with wavy lines.

Gyroscope of simple form.

ġȳ′rō-stat, *n.* [*Gyro-*, and Gr. *statikos*, stationary, from *histanai*, to stand.] A modification of the gyroscope, serving to illustrate the dynamics of rotating rigid bodies. It consists essentially of a fly-wheel with a massive rim, fixed on the middle of an axis which can rotate on fine steel pivots inside a rigid case.

ġȳ-rō-stat′iç, *a.* Pertaining to the gyrostat or to the principle it illustrates.

ġȳ-rō-stat′iċs, *n.* The theory of the gyrostat; the principles which govern the rotation of bodies.

ġȳ′rus, *n.*; *pl.* **ġȳ′rī.** [L., from Gr. *gyros*, a circle, ring.] In anatomy, a convolution, as of the brain.

ġȳve, *n.* [Of Celtic origin; compare W. *gefyn*, a fetter, Ir. *geimheal*, chains, fetters.] A shackle, usually for the legs; a fetter; chiefly in the plural.

ġȳve, *v.t.*; gyved, *pt.*, *pp.*; gyving, *ppr.* To fetter; to shackle; to chain.

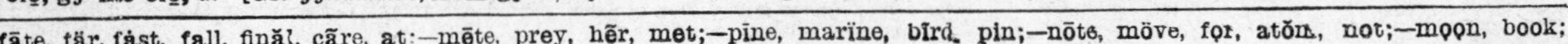

H

H (āch). The eighth letter and sixth consonant of the English alphabet. The written character comes into the English through the Greek and Latin from the Phenician, where it had the same position in order as in the English. Its form is from the Latin and this from the Greek H, which was used as a rough breathing, but later came to represent the long vowel η, and the (ʽ) was used to represent the rough breathing. When the F sign or digamma was dropped it became the seventh letter. In the Phenician the sound is that of a rough guttural aspirate. The Latin and Greek used it as an open breathing before a vowel. In Anglo-Saxon it appears as strongly guttural, and in many words formerly spelled with *h* alone, *g* was added to strengthen it, as in *niht, night*, though the combination is now often silent. The *h* frequently occurs at the beginning of a syllable before *l, n*, and *r*, as *hlaf*, loaf; *hlud*, loud; *hnecca*, neck; *hrim*, rime. In many words coming from the French *h* is silent, as in *honor, hour*. Etymologically *h* is most closely related to *c*, as in Eng. *horn*, L. *cornu*, Gr. *keras*; Eng. *heart*, L. *cors, cordis*, Gr. *kardia*. It is used with certain consonants to form digraphs representing sounds not in the English alphabet, as *th, ph, sh*. In some words, principally from foreign languages, *h* following consonants, as *c* and *g*, indicates that those consonants have a hard sound before *e, i*, and *y*, as in *chemistry, chiropodist, chyme*. The name *aitch* is from French *ache*.

H, h, *as a symbol*. In music, *H* is the German equivalent for B natural, B being with them our B flat; in orchestral music it stands for *horns*.

As a numeral in Latin, *H* denotes 200, and with a dash over it, $\bar{H}$, 200,000.

As an abbreviation in Latin, *H* stands for *homo, hæres, hora*, etc., and in chemistry, for *hydrogen*.

hä, *interj.* **1.** An exclamation denoting surprise, joy, grief, suspicion, wonder, or other sudden emotion. With the first or long sound of *a*, it is used as a question, and is equivalent to "What do you say?" When repeated, *ha, ha*, it is an expression of laughter, or sometimes it is equivalent to "Well! it is so."

2. A sound uttered involuntarily and denoting hesitation, embarrassment, etc., and corresponding to the interjection *er*.

hä, *n.* **1.** An expression of surprise, joy, grief, suspicion, wonder, or other sudden emotion.

2. An expression of hesitancy or embarrassment in speech.

hä, *v.i.* To express hesitation or embarrassment by the interjection *ha*; as, to hum and *ha*.

ha, *v.*, a contracted form of *have*. [Colloq. or Dial.]

ha, *n.* A hall. [Scot.]

häaf, *n.* A deep-sea fishing-ground for cod, ling, and tusk. Also written *haaf, haf*. [Shetland.]

häaf′-boat, *n.* A boat used in haaf-fishing. [Shetland.]

häaf′-fish″ing, *n.* The deep-sea fishing for cod, ling, and tusk. [Shetland.]

häak, *n.* Same as *Hake*.

häar, *n.* A fog or mist; a driving east wind, accompanied by mist. [Scot.]

hā′bē-ăs çor′pus. [L., have the body.] A writ (more fully entitled *habeas corpus ad subjiciendum*, have thou the body to answer) directed to a person detaining another, and commanding him to produce the body of the prisoner to do, submit to, and receive whatsoever the court or judge issuing the writ shall decree. It is applicable in all cases in which a person in custody claims to be illegally detained or wrongfully refused bail, or wishes to be removed from one court to another.

Hab-ē-nā′ri-ȧ, *n.* An extensive genus of terrestrial tuberous-rooted orchids, widely distributed through the temperate and tropical regions of both hemispheres. Of the 400 species, eighteen are found in the northeastern part of the United States.

hā-ben′dum, *n.*; *pl.* **hā-ben′dȧ.** [L., gerund of *habere*, to have.] The second part of a deed or conveyance, following the premises or first part, or that part which determines the extent of the estate or interest conveyed or granted; so called because it begins with the words "to have and to hold," in the old Latin form *habendum et tenendum*.

hab′ẽr-dash, *v.i.* To deal in small wares or in a petty fashion. [Rare.]

hab′ẽr-dash-ẽr, *n.* [Ice. *hapurtask, hafrtask*, a haversack, trumpery; *hafr*, oats, and *task*, pocket.]

1. A dealer in men's furnishings.

2. A dealer in small wares, as thread, needles, buttons, etc.

3. A hatter. [Obs.]

hab′ẽr-dash-ẽr-y, *n.* **1.** The goods and wares sold by a haberdasher.

2. A haberdasher's shop.

hab′ẽr-dine, *n.* [OFr. *habordean*, prob. a corruption of *Aberdeen*, in Scotland, where they were prepared.] Codfish; salted and dried codfish.

hȧ-bẽr′ġē-ŏn, *n.* [OFr. *haubergeon*, dim. of *hauberc*, a coat of mail.] A coat of mail or armor to defend the neck and breast, formed of little iron rings united, and descending from the neck to the middle of the body; a short hauberk.

hab′i-lā-tō-ry, *a.* [Fr. *habiller*, to clothe.] Pertaining to clothes or habiliments; wearing clothes.

hab′ile, *a.* [OFr. *habile*; L. *habilis*, suitable, fit, from *habere*, to have, hold.] Fit; proper. [Obs.]

hȧ-bil′i-ment, *n.* [Fr. *habillement*, from *habiller*, to clothe, from *habile*, fit, suitable.] A garment; clothing; usually in the plural, *habiliments*, denoting dress in general.

hȧ-bil′i-ment-ed, *a.* Clothed; furnished with habiliments.

hȧ-bil′i-tāte, *v.t.*; habilitated, *pt., pp.*; habilitating, *ppr.* [LL. *habilitatus*, pp. of *habilitare*, to make suitable, to qualify, from L. *habilis*, suitable, fit.]

1. To qualify. [Obs.]

2. To furnish with equipment, as for working a mine. [Western U. S.]

hȧ-bil′i-tāte, *v.i.* To become qualified, as for an office or position; specifically, to qualify for teaching in a German university.

hȧ-bil′i-tāte, *a.* Qualified or entitled. [Obs.]

hȧ-bil-i-tā′tion, *n.* 1. Qualification. [Obs.]

2. The furnishing of equipment for the development of mining property. [Western U. S.]

hȧ-bil′i-tā-tŏr, *n.* One who habilitates; specifically, one who furnishes the equipment for developing mining property.

hȧ-bil′i-ty, *n.* [Obs.] Same as *Ability*.

hab′it, *n.* [ME. *habit*; OFr. *habit*; L. *habitus*, condition, appearance, dress, from *habere*, to have, hold.]

1. Garb; dress; clothes; specifically, the costume commonly worn or appropriate for a particular time, use, or vocation; as, a clerical *habit*.

> There are, among the statues, several of Venus, in different *habits*. —Addison.

2. The dress worn by a woman when riding on horseback.

3. A customary or characteristic state, condition, or mode of being; specifically, (a) a usual or characteristic physical state or condition; as, a costive or lax *habit* of body; (b) in biology, the general form, appearance, or the conformity of plants or animals of the same kind in structure and growth; as, the ivy has a twining *habit*.

4. A usual or characteristic mode of action, or tendency toward such a mode, especially when so established by repetition as to be unconscious, involuntary, or spontaneous; custom; usage; practice; as, idleness engenders bad *habits*.

> The force of education is so great, that we may mold the minds and manners of the young into what shape we please, and give the impressions of such *habits* as shall ever afterward remain. —Atterbury.

Syn.—Custom, practice, tendency, garb, costume.—*Habit* is an internal principle which leads us to do easily, naturally, and with growing certainty, what we do often; *custom* is external, being the frequent repetition of the same act.

hab′it, *v.t.*; habited, *pt., pp.*; habiting, *ppr.*

1. To dress; to clothe; to array.

> They *habited* themselves like rural deities. —Dryden.

2. To inhabit. [Obs.]

hab′it, *v.i.* To dwell; to reside. [Obs.]

hab-it-ȧ-bil′i-ty, *n.* Habitableness.

hab′it-ȧ-ble, *a.* [OFr. *habitable*; L. *habitabilis*, from *habitare*, to dwell.] Capable of being inhabited or dwelt in; capable of sustaining human beings; as, the *habitable* world; some climates are scarcely *habitable*.

hab′it-ȧ-ble-ness, *n.* The state of being habitable.

hab′it-ȧ-bly, *adv.* In a habitable manner.

hab′it-ȧ-çle, *n.* 1. A dwelling; a habitation. [Obs.]

2. An alcove; a niche for a statue. [Obs.]

hȧ-bĭ-tan′ (ȧ-bē-toṅ), *n.* [Fr.] Same as *Habitant*, 2.

hab′it-ănce, *n.* Dwelling; abode; residence. [Obs.]

hab′it-ăn-cy, *n.* Inhabitance.

hab′it-ănt, *n.* [Fr. *habitant*; L. *habitans (-antis)*, ppr. of *habitare*, to dwell.]

1. An inhabitant; a dweller; a resident; one who has a permanent abode in a place.

2. [*Fr. pron.* ȧ-bē-toṅ.] A Canadian of French extraction, especially a farmer or peasant of the province of Quebec; also written *habitan*.

> You cannot marry any of the *habitants*. —Gilbert Parker.

hab′i-tat, *n.* [L.] Habitation; the natural abode or locality of an animal, plant, etc.

hab-i-tā′tion, *n.* [L. *habitatio*, from *habitare*, to dwell, freq. of *habere*, to have, hold.]

1. The act of inhabiting; the state of being inhabited.

2. Place of abode; a settled dwelling; a house or other place in which man or any animal dwells; as, stars may be the *habitations* of numerous races of beings.

> The Lord blesseth the *habitation* of the just. —Prov. iii. 33.

Syn.—Dwelling, abode, house, occupancy.

hab′i-tā-tŏr, *n.* [L.] A dweller; an inhabitant.

hȧ-bit′ū-ăl, *a.* [LL. *habitualis*, pertaining to habit or dress, from L. *habitus*, condition, habit, appearance.]

1. Formed or acquired by habit, frequent use, or custom.

> Art is properly an *habitual* knowledge of certain rules and maxims. —South.

2. Customary; according to habit; as, the *habitual* practice of sin; the *habitual* exercise of holy affections.

> It is the distinguishing mark of *habitual* piety to be grateful for the most common blessings. —Buckminster.

3. Formed by repeated impressions; rendered permanent by continued causes; as, a *habitual* color of the skin.

Syn.—Regular, ordinary, perpetual, customary, usual, familiar, accustomed, wonted.

hȧ-bit′ū-ăl-ly, *adv.* In a habitual manner; customarily; by frequent practice or use; as, *habitually* profane; *habitually* kind and benevolent.

hȧ-bit′ū-ăl-ness, *n.* The state or quality of being habitual.

hȧ-bit′ū-āte, *v.t.*; habituated, *pt., pp.*; habituating, *ppr.* [LL. *habituatus*, pp. of *habituare*, to bring into a condition or habit of the body, from L. *habitus*, habit.]

1. To accustom; to make familiar by frequent use or practice; as, men *habituate* themselves to the taste of tobacco.

2. To settle as an inhabitant. [Obs.]

hȧ-bit′ū-āte, *a.* Inveterate by custom; formed by habit; usual; habitual. [Rare.]

hȧ-bit-ū-ā′tion, *n.* The act of habituating or the state of being habituated.

hab′i-tūde, *n.* [Fr. *habitude*; L. *habitudo*, condition, habit.]

1. Relation; respect; state with regard to something else. [Rare.]

2. Frequent intercourse; familiarity. [Obs.]

> To write well, one must have frequent *habitudes* with the best company. —Dryden.

3. Customary manner or mode of life; repetition of the same acts; custom; habit; as, the *habitudes* of fowls or insects.

hȧ-bi-tū-é′ (*or Fr. pron.* ȧ-bē-tü-ā′), *n.* [Fr., properly pp. of *habituer*, to accustom.] A habitual frequenter of any place, especially one of amusement; as, a club *habitué*.

hab′i-tūre, *n.* Habitude. [Obs.]

hab′i-tus, *n.* [L.] 1. In natural history, superficial appearance without regard to structure; facies, as of a plant, animal, or mineral.

2. In medicine, constitutional disposition or tendency.

hā′ble, *a.* [Obs.] Same as *Able*.

hab′nab, *adv.* [*Hap ne hap*, let it happen or not.] At random; by chance; without order or rule; also written *hab or nab*. [Obs.]

hab-rō-mā′ni-ȧ, *n.* [Gr. *habros*, graceful, pleasing, pretty, and *mania*, madness.] In pathology, a form of insanity in which the delusions are pleasing.

hab′rō-nēme, *a.* [Gr. *habros*, delicate, and *nēma*, thread.] In mineralogy, having the form of fine threads.

hach′ūre, *n.* Same as *Hatching*.

hach′ūre, *v.t.*; hachured, *pt., pp.*; hachuring, *ppr.* To cover with hatchings.

hȧ-ci-en′dȧ, *n.* [Sp.] A landed estate, usually the homestead of the owner and devoted to stock-raising, agriculture, manufacturing, mining, etc.; also called *fazenda*. [Sp. Am.]

hack, *n.* [A form of *hatch*.]

1. A grated frame; specifically, (a) a hatch; a wicker or grated door; (b) a rack from which cattle are fed; (c) a rack on which fish, bacon, cheese, etc., are dried; (d) a set of wooden bars in the tailrace of a mill; (e) a place for drying bricks before they are burned; hence, a row of green bricks laid out to dry.

2. In falconry, the tray from which a young hawk is fed; hence, figuratively, the partial liberty allowed young hawks.

hack, *n.* 1. A notch; a cut; specifically, one made in a tree in blazing a path through a forest.

2. A blunt instrument for notching trees in order to release the sap.

3. A pickax; a mattock; a hack-iron. [Prov. Eng.]

4. Hesitating or faltering speech.

5. A dry, broken cough. [Colloq.]

6. In football, a kick on the shin; also, a bruise caused by such a kick.

hack, *n.* [Abbrev. of *hackney*.]

1. A horse kept for hire; a horse much used in draft, or in hard service; a worn-out horse.

2. A coach or other carriage kept for hire; a hackney-coach.

3. A drudge, especially a literary drudge; a writer employed in the drudgery and details of bookmaking.

The last survivor of the genuine race of Grub Street *hacks*. —Macaulay.

4. A procuress; a prostitute. [Obs.]

hack, *a.* Hackneyed; much used; hired; mercenary; as, a *hack* writer.

hack, *v.t.*; hacked, *pt.*, *pp.*; hacking, *ppr.* [ME. *hacken*, *hakken*; AS. to *haccian*, to hew, cut.]

1. To cut or chop irregularly, in a bungling or aimless manner; to mangle with repeated strokes; to notch; as, to *hack* a desk.

2. To utter with stops or catches; to mangle or murder, as language.

3. To dress, as a stone, with a hack-hammer.

4. In football, to kick (another player), especially on the shin.

5. To notch (a tree) in order to release the sap.

6. To chap, as the hands or lips. [Prov. Eng.]

7. To break up, as clods of earth. [Prov. Eng.]

hack, *v.i.* 1. To chop or cut in a clumsy or unskilful way; to make a hack or hacks.

2. To cough faintly and abruptly; as, the *hacking* cough of a consumptive.

3. To stutter; to hesitate in speaking; to stammer. [Prov. Eng.]

4. To drudge; to toil slavishly; to work laboriously.

hack, *v.t.* 1. To arrange (green bricks) in rows for drying.

2. In falconry, to allow (a hawk) partial liberty.

hack, *v.t.* To let out for hire, as a horse or carriage.

hack, *v.i.* 1. To be exposed or offered to common use for hire; to turn prostitute.

2. To drudge, as a literary hack.

3. To ride at the ordinary pace of a horse.

hack′ȧ-mōre, *n.* [Compare Sp. *jaquima*, headstall of a halter.] A halter, the nose-piece of which may be so tightened as to serve as a headpiece. [Western U. S.]

hack′ber″ry, *n.* 1. A North American tree, *Celtis occidentalis*, resembling the elm, bearing sweet edible fruits as large as bird-cherries, which ripen in autumn.

2. A hagberry; a bird-cherry.

hack′bōlt, *n.* The hagden.

hack′but, **hack′buss**, *n.* Same as *Harquebus*.

hack′ee, *n.* [So called from the noise it makes.] The chipmunk; the ground-squirrel; also, the chickaree.

hack′ẽr, *n.* One who or that which hacks; specifically, a tool for notching trees to release the sap.

hack′ẽr-y, *n.* [Anglo-Ind., from Hind. *chhakra*, a cart.] A cart drawn by oxen.

hack′i-ȧ, *n.* A tree of British Guiana, *Ixora triflorum*, which grows to a height of from thirty to sixty feet and is very valuable, owing to the great hardness of the wood.

Hackery or Bullock-cart.

hac′kle, *v.t.*; hackled, *pt.*, *pp.*; hackling, *ppr.* 1. To separate, as the coarse part of flax or hemp from the fine, by drawing through the teeth of a hackle or hatchel.

2. To tear asunder.

hac′kle, *n.* [D. *hekel*; G. *hechel*, a comb for flax and hemp.]

1. A hatchel, heckle, or comb for dressing flax.

2. Raw silk; any flimsy substance unspun.

3. A long pointed feather on the neck of a fowl, or any similar feather.

4. A fly for angling made of feathers or silk.

hac′kle, *v.t.* To hack unevenly or roughly; to mangle; to haggle.

hac′kly, *a.* 1. Rough; broken, as if hacked.

2. In mineralogy, having fine, short, and sharp points on the surface; as, a *hackly* fracture.

hack′măn, *n.*; *pl.* **hack′men**. The driver of a hack.

hack′mȧ-tack, *n.* [Am. Ind.] The American larch, *Larix Americana*, a very large tree, much prized for timber; also called *hackmetack* and *tamarack*.

hack′ney (-ni), *n.* [ME. *hakeney*, *haknay*; OFr. *haquenee*, *hacquenet*; O.D. *hackeneye*, a horse, hackney.]

1. A pad; a nag; a pony.

2. A horse kept for hire; a horse much used.

3. A coach or other carriage kept for hire; a hack.

4. A hireling; a drudge. [Obs.]

5. A prostitute. [Obs.]

hack′ney, *a.* Let out for hire; in common use; much used; trite; as, a *hackney* author or remark.

hack′ney, *v.t.*; hackneyed, *pt.*, *pp.*; hackneying, *ppr.* 1. To exhaust by heavy work, as a horse; to make trite.

2. To carry in a hackney-coach.

hack′ney-cōach, *n.* Same as *Hackney*, n. 3.

hack′ney-cōach″măn, *n.* A man who drives a hackney-coach.

hack′ney-măn, *n.*; *pl.* **hack′ney-men**. A man who lets horses and carriages for hire.

hack′stẽr, *n.* A bully; a ruffian or assassin. [Obs.]

hac′que-tŏn (-ke-), *n.* Same as *Acton*.

had, *v.*, past tense and past participle of *have*.

had′dẽr, *n.* Heather. [Obs.]

had′die, *n.* A haddock. [Scot.]

had′dō, *n.* [Am. Ind.] The gorbuscha or hump-backed salmon.

had′dŏck, *n.* [ME. *hadok*, *haddok*, origin unknown.]

1. A sea-fish, *Melanogrammus æglefinus*, of the cod family. It is smaller than the cod, which it much resembles, has a long body, the upper part of a dusky brown color, and the belly of a silvery hue; the lateral line is black; it has a spot on each side of the body just behind the head.

Haddock.

2. In New Zealand, (a) a fish of the genus *Merlucius*; (b) a fish of the *Gadidæ*.

3. The rosefish or Norway *haddock*.

4. The opah or Jerusalem *haddock*.

hāde, *n.* [A contr. of *heald*, a slope.]

1. The descent of a hill.

2. In mining, (a) the steep descent of a shaft; (b) the slope of the fracture line between two portions of faulted or dislocated strata; the inclination or deviation of a vein from a vertical direction.

hāde, *v.i.* In mining, to deviate from a perpendicular line of descent; to slope; said of a vein.

Hā′dēs, *n.* [Gr. *Haidēs*, Hades; *a* priv., and *idein*, to see.] The abode of the dead; the place or state of departed souls; the world of spirits; Sheol.

Had′ith, *n.* [Ar. *hadith*, a saying, legend.] A legend; a tradition; the appendix to the Koran containing traditions relating to Mohammed.

hadj, *n.* [Ar. *hajj*, a pilgrimage, from *hajja*, to set out, go on a pilgrimage.] The pilgrimage to Mecca performed by Mohammedans.

hadj′ī, **haj′ji**, *n.* [Ar. *hājjī*, a form of *hājj*, a pilgrim, from *hajja*, to go on a pilgrimage.] A Mohammedan who has performed his pilgrimage to Mecca; also used as a title of honor.

had′rōme, *n.* [Gr. *hadros*, thick.] In botany, the xylem of a vascular cryptogam.

Had-rō-sau′rus, *n.* [Gr. *hadros*, thick, and *sauros*, lizard.] A Cretaceous genus of extinct dinosaurian reptiles of higher organization than living reptiles generally, resembling the crocodiles and the iguanodons.

hadst, *v.*, second person singular of *had*, past tense of *have*.

hae, *v.t.* To have. [Scot.]

hæç-cē′i-ty (hek-), *n.* [LL. *hæcceitas*, thisness, from L. *hæc*, f. of *hic*, this.] Literally, the quality of being *this*; thisness; the relation of individuality conceived by the schoolmen as a positive attribute or essence.

Hæck′el-ism, *n.* The theories of Ernst Hæckel, German scientist; more particularly his theory that the life-history of the species is recapitulated in the development of the individual.

hæm-, **hæm-a-to-**, **hæm-o-**. Combining forms from Gr. *haima*, *haimatos*, blood, used in botany, zoölogy, medicine, etc., to signify any relation to blood; as, *Hæmato*crya, *Hæmato*therma; words from Gr. *haima* are also spelled *hem-*, *hemato-*, etc.

hæm′ȧ-chrōme (hem′), *n.* See *Hemachrome*.

Hæ-man′thus, *n.* [*Hæm-*, and Gr. *anthos*, a flower.] The bloodflower, a genus of South African bulbous plants of the order *Amaryllidaceæ*, so called from the fine red color of the corolla and involucre of some species.

hæ-mat′i-num, **hē-mat′i-non**, *n.* [L., from Gr. *haimatinos*, of blood, bloody, from *haima* (*-atos*), blood.] A red glass known to the ancients and used for mosaics, ornamental vases, etc. It contains no tin and no coloring matter except cupric oxid.

Hæm-ȧ-toç′ry-ȧ (hem-), *n.pl.* [*Hæmato-*, and Gr. *kryos*, cold.] In zoölogy, a division of vertebrates comprising all cold-blooded species, as amphibians, reptiles, and fishes, as distinguished from the *Hæmatotherma*.

Hæm-ȧ-tō-phi-li′nȧ, *n.pl.* [*Hæmato-*, and Gr. *philos*, loving.] The *Desmodontes* or bloodsucking vampire bats.

Hæm″ȧ-tō-thẽr′mȧ, *n.pl.* [*Hæmato-*, and Gr. *thermos*, warm.] In zoölogy, a division of vertebrates, comprising all warm-blooded species, as birds and mammals, as distinguished from the *Hæmatocrya*.

Hæm-ȧ-tox′y-lon, *n.* [*Hæmato-*, and Gr. *xylon*, wood.] A genus of the *Leguminosæ*, having but one species, *Hæmatoxylon Campechianum*, the logwood-tree of Central America, from which the logwood of commerce is obtained.

Hæm″ȧ-tō-zō′ȧ, *n.pl.* [*Hæmato-*, and Gr. *zōon* (pl. *zōa*), an animal.] In zoölogy, *Entozoa* parasitic in the blood, as certain nematodes and trematodes.

Hæm″ō-dō-rā′cē-æ, *n.pl.* [Gr. *haima*, blood, *dōron*, a gift and *-aceæ*.] In botany, an order of monocotyledons, consisting of perennials having fibrous roots and sword-shaped leaves with woolly hairs on stems and flowers. The name refers to the red color yielded by the roots of certain species, as *Sanguinaris Canadensis*, the redroot of eastern United States.

hæm″ō-dō-rā′ceous, *a.* Of or like the *Hæmodoraceæ*.

häf, *v.*, obsolete past tense of *heave*.

haf′fle, *v.i.*; haffled, *pt.*, *pp.*; haffling, *ppr.* To speak unintelligibly; to prevaricate. [Prov. Eng.]

Hä′fiz, *n.* [Ar.] A Mohammedan who can recite the Koran from memory; used as a title of honor.

hȧft, *n.* [ME. *haft*, *heft*; AS. *hæft*, a handle, from the same root as *haffan*, to hold.]

1. A handle; used chiefly for the part of a knife, sword, or dagger by which it is held; a hilt.

2. A place of abode. [Scot.]

hȧft, *v.t.* To set in a haft; to furnish with a handle.

hȧft′ẽr, *n.* A caviler; a wrangler; a debater.

hag, *n.* [ME. *hagge*, *hegge*, a witch, hag; AS. *hægtes*, *hægtesse*, a witch, hag.]

1. An ugly old woman.

2. A witch; a sorceress; a fury; a she-monster.

3. A cartilaginous vertebrate of the *Marsipobranchii*, *Myxine glutinosa*, parasitic on other fishes. It is about five or six inches long, and resembles a small eel. It is allied to the lamprey. Also called *hagfish*.

4. A phosphorescent appearance on horses' manes or men's hair. [Prov. Eng.]

5. A shearwater.

hag, *v.t.* To harass; to torment; to weary. [Obs.]

hag, *n.* [Prov. Eng. or Scot. in all senses.]

1. A cutting blow; a hack.

2. Branches cut for firewood; also, a quantity of wood cut, or to be cut, by one man.

3. A portion of woodland divided for cutting.

4. A quagmire; boggy ground.

Hag, tag, and rag; a rabble; rag, tag, and bobtail.

hag′ber″ry, *n.* The bird-cherry. [Scot.]

hag′bọrn, *a.* Born of a hag or witch.

hag′but, *n.* A harquebus.

hag′den, **hag′dŏn**, *n.* [Origin doubtful.] *Puffinus major*, the greater shearwater, or an allied species of the genus *Puffinus*; called also *haglet*, *hag*, and *hagdown*.

hag-gä′dah, *n.*; *pl.* **hag-gä′doth**. [Heb. *haggadah*, from *hagad*, to tell, relate.] The free rabbinical interpretation or illustration of Scripture; also, a parable, legend, or saying from the Talmud; also written *hagadah*.

hag-gad′iç, *a.* Of or pertaining to the haggadah.

hag′gȧrd, *a.* [Corruption of *hagged*.] Having eyes sunk in their orbits; gaunt; having the look of one desperate, wild, careworn, or wasted by hunger, pain, or terror.

hag′gȧrd, *a.* [OFr. *hagard*, wild, strange, unsociable, lit., of the wood, from M.H.G. *hag*, a hedge, wood.] Wild or intractable; disposed to break away; wanton; said of falcons, etc.; as, a *haggard* hawk.

hag′gȧrd, *n.* 1. An untrained or refractory hawk; hence, anything wild and intractable.

2. A hag. [Obs.]

hag′gȧrd, *n.* [AS. *haga*, hay, and *geard*, yard.] A stackyard. [Eng.]

hag′gȧrd-ly, *adv.* In a haggard, ugly, or careworn manner.

hag′ged, *a.* [From *hag*, an old woman.] Lean; ugly; like a hag.

hag′gis, hag′gess, *n.* [Scot. *hag*, to chop, cut.]

1. A Scotch dish, commonly made of the heart, lungs, and liver of a sheep, minced with suet, onions, oatmeal, salt, and pepper, and boiled in a bag, usually the stomach of a sheep.

2. A sheep's head and pluck minced. [Scot.]

hag′gish, *a.* Resembling a hag; ugly; horrid.

hag′gish-ly, *adv.* In a haggish manner.

hag′gle, *v.t.*; haggled, *pt., pp.*; haggling, *ppr.* [A freq. of *hack*, to chop, cut.] To cut into small pieces; to notch or cut in an unskilful manner; to make rough by cutting; to mangle; to hack roughly; as, a boy *haggles* a stick of wood.

hag′gle, *v.i.* To be difficult in bargaining; to hesitate and cavil; to bargain in a tedious way.

hag′gle, *n.* A hesitation; a difficulty; a haggling.

hag′glẽr, *n.* 1. One who haggles.

2. In London, one who buys up vegetables from the producer to sell to the retail dealers; a huckster.

hā′ġi-ăr-ehy, *n.* A hagiocracy. [Obs.]

hā-ġi-oc′rȧ-cy, *n.* [Gr. *hagios*, sacred, and *-kratia*, from *kratein*, to rule.] A hierarchy; sacerdotal government.

Hā-ġi-og′rȧ-phȧ, *n.pl.* [LL., from Gr. *hagiographa*, neut. pl. of *hagiographos*; *hagios*, sacred, and *graphein*, to write.] The Jewish division of the Old Testament known as the *Ketubim* or *writings*, including Ruth, Chronicles, Ezra, Nehemiah, Esther, Job, Psalms, Proverbs, Ecclesiastes, Song of Solomon, Lamentations, and Daniel; all of the Old Testament not classed as the Law or the Prophets.

hā-ġi-og′rȧ-phăl, *a.* Pertaining to the Hagiographa.

hā-ġi-og′rȧ-phẽr, *n.* 1. Any writer of the Hagiographa.

2. One who writes the lives of saints.

hā-ġi-og′rȧ-phy, *n.* [Gr. *hagios*, sacred, and *-graphia*, from *graphein*, to write.] Sacred literature; hagiology.

hā-ġi-ol′ȧ-try, *n.* [Gr. *hagios* sacred (L.Gr., a saint), and *latreia*, worship.] Saint-worship; invocation of saints.

hā-ġi-ol′ō-ġist, *n.* One who writes the lives of saints.

hā-ġi-ol′ō-ġy, *n.* [Gr. *hagios*, sacred (L.Gr., a saint), and *-logia*, from *legein*, to speak.]

1. Literature dealing with the lives and legends of the saints; a list of saints.

2. The sacred writings of any people; a treatise on such writings.

hā′ġi-ō-scōpe, *n.* [Gr. *hagios*, sacred, and *skopein*, to view.] In medieval church architecture, an opening in a wall, etc., to afford a view of the high altar from a chapel or side aisle; also called a *squint*.

hag′-rid″den, *a.* Subject to nightmare, as if ridden by a witch or hag.

hag′seed, *n.* The descendant of a hag.

hag′ship, *n.* The state or title of a hag or witch.

hag′ṣ′-tōōth, *n.* Among sailors, a part of a matting, pointing, etc., which is interwoven with the rest in an erroneous and irregular manner.

hag′-tā″pẽr, *n.* *Verbascum Thapsus*, mullen.

hah, *interj.* A variant spelling of *ha*.

hȧ-hä′, *n.* A fence or bank sunk between slopes, or a ditch not seen till approached closely; also written *haw-haw*.

Häh-ne-mann′i-ăn, *a.* Of or relating to Samuel C. F. Hahnemann, the German physician who founded homeopathy.

Häh′ne-mănn-iṣm, *n.* Hahnemannian homeopathy.

hai′ding-ẽr-īte, *n.* [Named after Wilhelm von *Haidinger*, an Austrian mineralogist.] A mineral arseniate of calcium, which is white and transparent, with a vitreous luster and white streak.

Hai′dụk (hī′), *n.* [Hung. *hajduk*, pl. of *hajdu*, lit., a drover.] One of a class of mercenary Magyar foot-soldiers in Hungary who sold their services to the best bidder, but who displayed great bravery. The name has also been given to macers in the Hungarian courts, halberdiers of Hungarian magnates, and lackeys and other attendants in German courts. Spelled also *Hayduk, Haiduck, Heyduc*, etc.

haik, *n.* A tramp. [Scot.]

haik, *n.* [Ar. *haik*, from *haka*, to weave.] A large piece of woolen or cotton cloth worn by the Arabs over the tunic but under the burnoose.

hāil, *n.* [ME. *hayle, hagel*; AS. *hægel, hagol*, hail.] Moisture precipitated from the atmosphere in the form of ice. The concretions of ice are usually more or less spherical, constituting hailstones, but sometimes consist of plates or laminæ, or of agglomerated masses.

hāil, *v.i.*; hailed, *pt., pp.*; hailing, *ppr.* To pour down masses of ice or frozen vapors.

hāil, *v.t.* To pour down in the manner of hail.

Forms of Hailstones.

Fig. 1. *a*, Hailstone which fell at Bonn in 1822: diameter 1⅓ inch, weight 300 grains. *b, c*, Sections of differently shaped hailstones which fell on the same occasion, showing the radiating nucleus and concentric layers. Fig. 2. *a*, Section of hailstone with minute pyramids on its surface. *b, c, d, e*, Fragments of the same when burst asunder.

hāil, *v.t.* [ME. *hailen, heylen*, to salute, greet, from *hail, heil*, a salutation.]

1. To call; to call to, as a person at a distance, in order to attract attention.

2. To address; to salute; to welcome.

hāil, *v.i.* To call; to extend greeting.

To hail from; to come or claim to come from; as, the ship *hails from* Havana.

hāil, *a.* [ME. *heil, heyl*; Ice. *heill*, whole, sound, healthy.] Hale; whole; healthy; sound. [Scot.]

hāil, *interj.* Be whole; be happy; a term of salutation; as, *Hail*, Columbia!

hāil, *n.* A call; a salutation.

hāil′-fel″lōw, *n.* A close or pleasant companion; a congenial acquaintance.

hāilse, *v.t.* [ME. *hailsen*; Ice. *heilsa*, to greet.] To salute. [Obs.]

hāil′shot, *n.pl.* Small shot which scatter like hail; grapeshot.

hāil′sōme, *a.* Wholesome. [Scot.]

hāil′stōne, *n.* A frozen raindrop; a particle or pellet of hail.

hāil′stọrm, *n.* A precipitation of hail.

hāil′y, *a.* Of or accompanied by hail.

hāin, *v.t.* To fence off for meadow. [Prov. Eng.]

hāin't. A contraction of *has not* or *have not*. [Colloq.]

hāir, *n.* [ME. *here, heer, her*; AS. *hær*, a hair.]

1. One of the small filaments issuing from the skins of most mammals and covering a part or the whole of the body. Each filament contains a tube or hollow within, occupied by a pulp or pith, which is intended for its nutrition and extends only to that part which is in a state of growth.

A B C D

Hairs of Various Animals Magnified. A, Indian bat. B, Mouse. C, Sable. D, Human.

2. The collection or mass of filaments growing from the skin of an animal and forming an integument or covering; such filaments in the mass; as, the *hair* of the head; the *hair* of a horse; a cartload of *hair*; the two *hairs* are of very different values. When the filaments are very fine and short they are called in the aggregate *fur*. Very stiff and strong hairs, such as those on the back of a swine, are called *bristles*. Wool also is a kind of hair.

3. In botany, an external filamentous prolongation composed of one or more transparent delicate cells proceeding from the epidermis and covered with the cuticle; a species of down or pubescence.

4. Anything very small or fine, or a very small distance.

> If the scale turn
> But in the estimation of a *hair*,
> Thou diest. —Shak.

5. Any fine capillary or hairlike outgrowth on animals other than haired mammals; a filament; as, the *hairs* of a caterpillar.

6. In mechanics, the spring in a hair-trigger gun or pistol.

A hair of the dog that bit one; the same thing that caused a malady or trouble employed as a means of cure, as liquor drunk in the morning after a debauch.

Not to turn a hair; to remain unaffected by unwonted exercise or excitement.

To a hair; to a nicety.

To split hairs; to argue points of no importance; to bargain about trifles.

hāir′bell, *n.* See *Harebell*.

hāir′bîrd, *n.* Same as *Chip-bird*.

hāir′-brack″et, *n.* In ship-carpentry, a molding extending aft from the figurehead or intersecting it at the back.

a, Hair-bracket.

hāir′brāined, *a.* See *Harebrained*.

hāir′breadth, hāir′ṣ′breadth (-bredth), *n.* The diameter or breadth of a hair; a very small distance; sometimes, specifically, the 48th part of an inch.

> Every one could sling stones at an *hairbreadth* and not miss. —Jud. xx. 16.

hāir′breadth, *a.* Exceedingly narrow; as, a *hairbreadth* escape.

hāir′-brown, *a.* Of a clear red-brown color.

hāir′brush, *n.* A brush for dressing the hair.

hāir′-cell, *n.* In anatomy, one of the cells with hairlike projections in the sensitory epithelium of the internal ear.

hāir′clọth, *n.* Stuff or cloth made of hair, or in part with hair. In military affairs, pieces of this cloth have been used for covering the powder in wagons, or on batteries, or for covering charged bombs, etc.

hāir′-cŏm″păss-eṣ, *n.pl.* A pair of compasses provided with a very precise screw adjustment.

hāir′-di-vī″dẽrṣ, *n.pl.* Same as *Hair-compasses*.

hāir′dress″ẽr, *n.* One who makes a business of cutting and dressing the hair; a barber.

hāired, *a.* Having hair; used in compounds; as, white-*haired*.

hāir′en, *a.* [AS. *hæren*, from *hær*, hair.] Having much hair. [Obs.]

hāir′-glōve, *n.* A horsehair glove used for rubbing the skin.

hāir′-grȧss, *n.* In botany, one of several species of slender-stemmed and slender-leaved grasses.

hāir′-hung, *a.* Hanging by a hair.

hāir′i-ness, *n.* The state of abounding or being covered with hair.

hāir′-lāce, *n.* A net for confining the hair of the head.

hāir′less, *a.* Destitute of hair; bald; as, *hairless* scalps.

hāir′-līne, *n.* A line made of hair; a fine line in writing or drawing.

hāir′-mọss, *n.* A moss with hairy calyptra, belonging to the genus *Polytrichum*.

hāir′-mọth, *n.* In zoölogy, any moth that feeds on fabrics made of hair, as the *Tineola biseliella*.

hāir′pin, *n.* A pin used in dressing the hair; formerly called *hairneedle*.

hāir′-plāte, *n.* The iron plate at the back of the hearth of a bloomery fire.

hāir′-pow″dẽr, *n.* Any white powder used to give natural hair or wigs a white or gray appearance.

hāir′-sạlt, *n.* [A translation of G. *haar-salz*. So called by Werner.] A variety of native Epsom salt; also, a compound of the sulphates of magnesia and iron.

hāir′-sēal, *n.* In zoölogy, an eared non-fur-producing seal; a sea-lion.

hāir′-sēat″ing, *n.* A haircloth used by upholsterers.

hāir′-shîrt, *n.* A shirt made of or lined with harsh hair, worn as a penance.

hāir′-sieve, *n.* A strainer with a bottom of haircloth.

hāir′-snāke, *n.* In zoölogy, a long, hairlike worm of the genus *Gordius*, which lives in water and is popularly but erroneously supposed to have been originally a horsehair.

hāir′-spāce, *n.* The thinnest piece of metal used in spacing type.

hāir′split″tẽr, *n.* One who makes trivial distinctions; a quibbler.

hāir′split″ting, *a.* Making very minute distinctions in reasoning.

hāir′split″ting, *n.* The act or practice of making minute distinctions in reasoning.

hāir′spring, *n.* In mechanics and in horology, a slender coiled spring; the smallest spring in a watch or clock, which governs the motion of the balance-wheel.

hāir′-stōne, *n.* Same as *Sagenite*.

hāir′strēak, *n.* A small butterfly of the genus *Thecla*, recognizable by hairlike appendages to its rear wings.

hāir′-strōke, *n.* A hair-line, straight or curved.

hāir′tāil, *n.* A slender-tailed fish of the genus *Trichiurus*, found in warm seas; called also *bladefish*.

hāir′-trig″gẽr, *n.* A gun or pistol trigger so nicely adjusted that it can be sprung with very slight pressure; a secondary trigger with which the trigger that discharges the weapon is worked.

hāir′-wŏrm, *n.* Same as *Hair-snake*.

hāir′y, *a.* 1. Overgrown with hair; covered with hair; abounding with hair.

> Esau, my brother, is a *hairy* man. —Gen. xxvii. 11.

2. Consisting of hair.

3. Resembling hair; of the nature of hair.

hāir′y-bāit, *n.* A sea-worm, *Nephthys cæca*; the lurg-worm.

hāir′y-crown, *n.* The *Mergus serrator*, or red-breasted merganser. [Local, U. S.]

hāir′y-head (-hed), *n.* The *Lophodytes cucullatus*, or hooded merganser. [Local, U. S.]

Hāi′ti-ăn, *a.* and *n.* I. *a.* Pertaining to Haiti. II. *n.* A native of Haiti.

hä'jē, *n.* [Ar. *hayya*, a snake.] The African cobra or asp.

hāke, *n.* [Norw. *hakefisk*, lit., a hookfish.]

1. A sea-fish of the cod family, *Merlucius vulgaris*, or common European *hake*, in shape somewhat resembling the pike. It is often salted and dried, but is not very much esteemed as food.

Hake (*Merlucius vulgaris*).

2. An American gadoid fish, the silver *hake* or whiting, *Merlucius bilinearis*.

3. One of several American fishes of the genus *Phycis*; also called *squirrel-hake* and *codling*.

hāke, *n.* A drying-frame, or feeding-frame. [Prov. Eng.]

hāke, *v.i.* To sneak; to go about idly. [Prov. Eng.]

Hā'kē-ȧ, *n.* [Named after Baron *Hake*, a German scientist.] A genus of plants found in Australia, and including many species, several being cultivated, as the native pear, *Hakea acicularis lissosperma*, and the twine-bush, *Hakea flexilis*.

hä-kïm', *n.* [Ar., from *hakama*, to govern.]

1. In Mohammedan countries, a title for a governor or ruler.

2. A physician or a wise man.

hak'kȧ, *n.* [Chinese.] In southern China, an immigrant from northern China, against whom there is much prejudice among the natives.

hak'ŏt, *n.* [A dim. of *hake*.] A fish, the pike. [Dial.]

hä'kū, *n.* [New Zealand.] An amber-fish of New Zealand, *Seriola lalandi*.

hȧ-lä'ḉhăh, *n.*; *pl.* **hȧ-lä'ḉhōth**. [Heb. *halakhah*, the rule by which to go, from *halakh*, to go.] A Jewish oral or traditional law deduced from the Mosaic law.

hā-lā'tion, *n.* In photography, an appearance like a halo of light around the edges of dark objects.

hal'bẽrd, *n.* [OFr. *halebarde*; M.H.G. *helmbarte*, a halberd, an ax with which to split a helmet; *helm*, handle, helve, and *barte*, an ax.]

1. An ancient military weapon, consisting of a pole or shaft of wood, with a head armed with a steel point, with a cross-piece of steel, flat and pointed at both ends, or with a cutting edge at one end, and a bent point at the other.

2. In farriery, an extension on the front of a horseshoe to relieve the foot in lameness.

Halberds.

1. Halberd (time of Henry VIII.); 2. Same with fleur-de-lis (Henry VII.); 3. Double-axed Halberd (Charles I.); 4. Halberd (Charles II.); 5. Same (William III.).

Halberd weed; a plant with leaves in the form of a halberd, found in the West Indies, *Neurolæna lobata*.

hal-bẽrd-iēr', *n.* [OFr. *halebardier*, from *halebarde*, a halberd.] One who is armed with a halberd.

hal'bẽrd-shāped, *a.* Having the shape of a halberd.

hal'cy-ŏn, *n.* [L. *halcyon*, *alcyon*; Gr. *alkyōn*, a kingfisher.] The name given to the kingfisher in poetry and old prose. The bird was believed to lay her eggs on rocks near the sea, during the calm weather about the winter solstice.

hal'cy-ŏn, *a.* Calm; quiet; peaceful; undisturbed; happy.

Halcyon days; seven days before and as many after the winter solstice, when the weather is calm; hence, days of peace and tranquillity.

hal-cy-ō'ni-ăn, *a.* Halcyon; calm. [Obs.]

hal-cy-on'iḉ, *a.* Same as *Alcyonic*.

hal'cy-ō-nine, *a.* Of or pertaining to the kingfishers of the genus *Halcyon*.

hal'cy-ō-noid, *a.* See *Alcyonoid*.

Hal'dăn-īte, *n.* In ecclesiastical history, a follower of the brothers James Alexander and Robert Haldane, who founded an independent evangelical movement in Scotland early in the nineteenth century.

hāle, *a.* [ME. *heil*, *heyl*; Ice. *heill*, whole, healthy.] Sound; entire; healthy; robust; not impaired; as, a *hale* body.

hāle, *n.* Welfare. [Obs.]

hāle, *v.t.*; haled, *pt.*, *pp.*; haling, *ppr.* [ME. *halen*, *halien*; AS. *holian*, *geholian*, to acquire, get.]

1. To pull or draw with force; to drag.

2. To vex; to worry; also, to procure by importunity. [Prov. Eng.]

hāle, *v.i.* To press onward; to go or come by drawing or pushing.

hal'e-cine, *a.* Relating to the shad.

hā'lẽr, *n.* One who hales.

Hā-lē'si-ȧ, *n.* [Named after Stephen *Hales*, a botanist.] A genus of low trees of the storax family, *Styricaceæ* of southern United States, Japan, and China, bearing clusters of white bell-shaped flowers which appear before the leaves.

hälf (häf), *n.*; *pl.* **hälveș** (hävz). [ME. *half*; AS. *healf*, *half*, half.]

1. One part of a thing which is divided into two equal parts, either in fact or in contemplation; a moiety; as, *half* a pound; *half* a tract of land; *half* an orange; *half* the miseries or pleasures of life. It is applied to quantity, number, length, and everything susceptible of division. In practice, *of* is usually omitted after *half*; as, *half* a pound; *half* a mile; *half* the number.

2. A term of school. [Colloq. Eng.]

3. In football, a half-back.

hälf, *a.* 1. Consisting of a moiety or having half a value; as, a *half* dollar; a *half* fare.

2. Consisting of some indefinite portion approximating a half; partial; as, *half* knowledge; *half* sight.

Better half; see under *Better*.

Half pay; the reduced pay of a retired military or naval man.

hälf, *v.t.* To divide into halves. [Obs.]

hälf, *adv.* In part, or in an equal part or degree.

Half loth and *half* consenting. —Dryden.

hal'fȧ, **hal'fȧ-grȧss**, *n.* Same as *Alfa*.

hälf'-and-hälf', *n.* 1. A mixture of two malt liquors, usually ale and porter, or beer and porter, in about equal parts.

2. A mixture of various liquids in equal proportion.

hälf'-āpe, *n.* A lemur.

hälf'-back, *n.* In football, one of the two positions back of the main or rush line, between the quarter-back and full-back. The players occupying the positions are termed *right half-back* and *left half-back*.

hälf'bāked (-bākt), *a.* Not properly baked; raw; inexperienced; stupid. [Colloq.]

hälf'bēak, *n.* A kind of sea-pike of the genus *Hemirhamphus*; so called from a protuberant upper jaw.

hälf'bill, *n.* 1. In zoölogy, a halfbeak.

2. A bird of the genus *Hemignathus* of the Sandwich Islands.

hälf'-bind"ing, *n.* A style of bookbinding in which only the back and corners are covered with leather.

hälf'-blood (-blud), *n.* Relation between persons born of the same father or of the same mother, but not of both; as, a brother or sister of the *half-blood*.

hälf'-blood"ed, *a.* 1. Mean; degenerate.

2. Proceeding from a male and female, each of full blood, but of different breeds; as, a *half-blooded* sheep.

hälf'-blo͞om, *n.* A half-made bloom; a mass of puddled iron before squeezing.

hälf'-bōard, *n.* In seamanship, a maneuver of a sailing vessel to the windward by luffing up into the wind.

hälf'-bōard"ẽr, *n.* A boarder in part only; particularly a school pupil who lives at home but takes a midday meal at school.

hälf'-bo͞ot, *n.* An ankle-boot.

hälf'-bound, *a.* In bookbinding, having only the back and corners bound in leather.

hälf'-box, *n.* In mechanics, a journal-box that is open at one side.

hälf'-bred, *a.* 1. Half-blooded; not thoroughbred.

2. Ill-mannered; not well trained.

hälf'-breed, *a.* Half-blooded.

hälf'-breed, *n.* A person who has parents of different races; in particular, the offspring of an American Indian and a white person.

hälf'-bril"liănt, *a.* Shaped like a single-cut brilliant.

hälf'-brŏth"ẽr, *n.* A brother by one parent, but not by both.

hälf'-ḉap, *n.* A cap not wholly put off, or faintly moved.

hälf'-ḉȧste, *n.* In India, one born of a Hindu parent on the one side and a European on the other.

hälf'-ḉlammed, **hälf'-ḉlemmed**, *a.* Half-starved. [Obs.]

hälf'ḉock, *v.t.*; halfcocked, *pt.*, *pp.*; halfcocking, *ppr.* To place (the hammer of a gun) at the first notch.

To go off halfcocked; (a) to be set off too soon; (b) to do anything hastily and incompletely without being ready. [Colloq.]

hälf'ḉock, *n.* The position of a gun's hammer when placed at the first notch.

hälf'-ḉōurt, *n.* In tennis, half of the court lengthwise.

hälf'-cracked (-krakt), *a.* Half-witted; unsound in mind. [Colloq.]

hälf'-crown, *n.* A common English silver coin worth two shillings and sixpence, or about 61 cents; in circulation since the reign of Edward VI.

hälf'-deck, *n.* 1. A boat-shell of the genus *Crepidula*.

2. The deck immediately under the spar-deck and next the mainmast.

hälf'-decked (-dekt), *a.* Decked over in part.

hälf'-dol"lär, *n.* A silver coin of the United States with an accepted value of fifty cents.

hälf'-dŏz'enth, *a.* Sixth.

hälf'en, *a.* Not having half its proper quantities. [Obs.]

hälf'en-dēal, *adv.* By the half. [Obs.]

hälf'ẽr, *n.* 1. One who shares.

2. A male fallow-deer gelded.

hälf'-fāced (-fāst), *a.* Showing only part of the face.

hälf'-fif"teen, *n.* In tennis, one stroke given at the beginning of the second and at every alternate subsequent game of the set.

hälf'-fish, *n.* A salmon five years old. [Prov. Eng.]

hälf'-hatched (-hacht), *a.* Imperfectly hatched; as, *half-hatched* eggs.

hälf'-hēard, *a.* Imperfectly heard; not heard to the end.

And leave *half-heard* the melancholy tale. —Pope.

hälf'-heärt"ed, *a.* 1. Wanting in spirit or heart; unkind.

2. Lacking in courage or zeal.

hälf'-heärt"ed-ly, *adv.* Indifferently; without enthusiasm.

hälf'-heärt"ed-ness, *n.* Want of enthusiasm; lack of earnestness.

hälf'-hitch, *n.* A hitch made by an overhand knot.

hälf'-hol"i-dāy, *n.* A half of a day given up for recreation.

hälf'-hōșe, *n.pl.* Socks; short stockings.

hälf'-hour'ly (-our'), *a.* Happening or done every half-hour.

hälf'-length, *a.* and *n.* I. *a.* Of half the full or ordinary length, as a portrait.

II. *n.* A portrait showing only the bust or upper half of the body.

hälf'-mȧst, *n.* A point below the top of the mast.

At half-mast; lowered in sign of mourning; said of a flag.

hälf'-mo͞on, *n.* 1. The moon at the quarters, when half its disk appears illuminated.

2. Anything in the shape of a half-moon.

3. In fortification, an outwork composed of two faces, forming a salient angle, whose gorge is in the form of a crescent or half-moon; a ravelin.

4. A fish, *Cæsiosoma californica*; called also *medialuna*.

hälf'-mourn"ing, *n.* 1. Mourning dress in which gray, lavender, and like subdued shades, are used in place of all black.

2. A common butterfly, *Papilio galatea*, having yellow wings with black and white spots.

hälf'ness, *n.* The condition of being a half or of not being whole. [Rare.]

hälf'-nōte, *n.* In music, a minim, being half a semibreve.

hälf'pāce, *n.* See *Footpace*, 2 and 3.

hälf'pen-ny (*or* hā'), *n.*; *pl.* **hälf'pence** (*or* hā'), **hälf'pen-nieș** (*or* hā'). A British copper coin of the value of half a penny; also, the value of half a penny.

hälf'pen-ny (*or* hā'), *a.* Of the price or value of half a penny; as, a *halfpenny* loaf. [Eng.]

hälf'-pike, *n.* A pike having a short shaft.

hälf'-pōrt, *n.* In seamanship, one half of a portlid, for closing portholes.

hälf'-rāy, *n.* In geometry, half a ray; a ray extending from a center in one direction.

hälf'-read (-red), *a.* Superficially informed by reading.

hälf'-round, *n.* A semicircular molding.

hälf'-sēaș-ō'vẽr, *a.* Half-drunk; tipsy. [Slang.]

hälf'-shift, *n.* In playing the violin, a move of the hand a little way upward on the neck of the instrument, to reach a high note.

hälf'-sight"ed, *a.* Seeing imperfectly; having weak discernment.

hälf'-sis"tẽr, *n.* A sister by one parent, but not by both.

hälf'-sov"ẽr-eign (-ăn), *n.* A British gold coin in common use, worth half a pound sterling, or about $2.43.

hälf'-strāined, *a.* Half-bred; imperfect. [Rare.]

hälf'-swōrd (-sōrd), *n.* Half the length of a sword; close fight.

hälf'-tim"bẽr, *n.* In shipbuilding, one of the timbers in the cant-bodies, which are answerable to the lower futtocks in the square body.

hälf'-tim"bẽred, *a.* Denoting a style of decorative housebuilding, in which the foundations and principal supports are of stout timber, and all the interstices of the front of the building are filled in with plaster.

hälf'-tint, *n.* Same as *Demitint*.

hälf′-tōne, *a.* Of, relating to, or designating a process of illustration, using relief-plates prepared by chemically etching a plate subjected to a complicated process of manufacture. The surface of a *half-tone* plate, with the exception of the blacks, presents an arrangement of dots from the screen interposed between the camera and the object reproduced.

hälf′-tōne, *n.* 1. A plate made by the half-tone method; a picture from such a plate.

2. A middle tint or medium light in an engraving or picture.

hälf′-tōngue (-tung), *n.* In law, a jury half of one nationality and half of another.

hälf′ wāy′, *adv.* At the middle point; at half the distance; partially.

hälf′wāy, *a.* Equidistant from the extremes; having a center location; midway.

Halfway covenant; a custom in New England Congregational churches in the middle of the seventeenth century of allowing to moral persons, under certain conditions, all church privileges except admittance to communion.

Halfway house; a stopping-place at a point halfway on a journey; an inn or public house midway between two points.

hälf′-wit, *n.* A foolish person; a dolt; a blockhead.

hälf′-wit″ted, *a.* Weak in intellect; silly; foolish.

hälf′-yēar′ly, *a.* Happening twice in a year; semiannual.

hälf′-yēar′ly, *adv.* Twice in a year; semiannually.

hal-i-, hal-o-. Combining forms from Gr. *hals*, *halos*, the sea, used in zoölogy, entomology, etc., to signify sea, salt; as, *Hali*chondriidæ, *hali*ography.

hal′i-but (hol′), **hol′i-but**, *n.* [ME. *haly*, holy, and *butte*, a flounder, plaice, lit., holy flounder; so called because eaten particularly on holidays.] A large, important food-fish of the genus *Hippoglossus* and family *Pleuronectidæ*, common in the northern seas.

Halibut (*Hippoglossus vulgaris*).

Hal″i-chon-drī′i-dæ, *n.pl.* [*Hali-*, and Gr. *chondros*, cartilage.] An order of sponges having a skeleton of spicule-bundles or cemented scattered spicules.

hal′i-çōre, *n.* See *Dugong*.

hal′i-dŏm, hal′i-dōme, *n.* [ME. *halidom*, *haligdom*; AS. *haligdom*, holiness, a sanctuary, sacred relic; *halig*, holy, and *-dom*, -dom.]

1. Adjuration by what is holy; that which is holy; a sanctuary. [Obs.]

2. Lands held of a church or religious foundation. [Obs.]

hal-i-eū′tiçs, *n.* [L. *halieutica*; Gr. *halieutika*, pl. of *halieutikos*, pertaining to fishing, from *halieuein*, to fish.] The study of or a treatise on fish or the art of fishing.

hal′i-măss, *n.* Hallowmas. [Obs.]

hā-li-og′rȧ-phēr, *n.* One who treats of the sea.

hā-li-og′rȧ-phy, *n.* [*Hali-*, and Gr. *-graphia*, from *graphein*, to write.] The science treating of the sea; a treatise on the sea.

Hā-li-ō′tis, *n.* [*Hali-*, and Gr. *ous*, *ōtos*, the ear.] A genus of gasteropodous mollusks, both fossil and recent, commonly called *sea-ears* or *ear-shells*, obtaining its name from the excessive amplitude of its aperture, and the flatness and smallness of its spire, whence it has been likened to an ear.

hā′li-ō-toid, *a.* Relating to or like the genus *Haliotis*; shaped like an ear.

Hal-i-sau′ri-ȧ, *n.pl.* See *Enaliosauria*.

hā′lite, *n.* [Gr. *hals*, *halos*, salt, and *-ite*.] Salt found native; rock-salt.

ha-lit′ū-ous, *a.* [L. *halitus*, breath.]

1. Like breath; vaporous.

2. In pathology, slightly moist.

hal′i-tus, *n.* [L., from *halare*, to breathe.] Vapor; breath.

halk (hak), *n.* [ME. *halke*, from AS. *healc*, *healoc*, a hollow.] A corner; a nook. [Obs.]

hall, *n.* [ME. *halle*, *haule*; AS. *heall*, *heal*, lit., a cover, shelter, from the root of *helan*, to conceal.]

1. Any room or building of large size used for public purposes; as, the town *hall*; an entertainment at the *hall*.

2. In medieval times, the room of a castle or other large house, in which the family lived; the dining- or living-room distinguished from a sleeping-room called a bower.

3. The first room entered on going into a building; any way or passage in a house or building.

4. In England, (a) a manor or chief mansion house; (b) a building used as the headquarters of a gild or trade association; as, Fishmongers' *Hall*; a building used for trade purposes; as, the market *hall*; (c) one of the colleges at certain universities; (d) the dining-room of a college; (e) dinner-service in a college *hall*.

Syn.—Entrance, vestibule, passage, house, manor, building.

hall′āge, *n.* A fee paid for goods sold in a hall. [Eng.]

hal′lē-çret, *n.* See *Allecret*.

hal′lel, *n.* [Heb., praise.] In Hebrew, a number of the Psalms, usually those from cxiii to cxviii, inclusive.

hal-lē-lū′iȧh, hal-lē-lū′jȧh (-yȧ), *interj.* [LL. *hallelujah*, *alleluiah*; Heb. *halelujāh*, praise ye Jehovah; *halelu*, praise ye, and *Jāh*, a short form of *Jehovah*.] Praise ye Jehovah; give praise to God; a word used in songs of praise, or a term of rejoicing in solemn ascriptions of thanksgiving to God.

hal″lē-lū-iat′iç (-yat′), *a.* [LL. *hallelujaticus* (supply *psalmus*, a psalm), from *hallelujah*, halleluiah.] Pertaining to halleluiahs.

hal′liărd, *n.* Same as *Halyard*.

hal′li-dōme, *n.* Same as *Halidom*.

hal′li-ēr, *n.* [From ME. *halen*, to haul.] A kind of net for catching birds.

hall′-märk, *n.* [So called from Goldsmiths' Hall in London, the seat of the Goldsmiths' Company, by whom stamping is regulated.]

1. In Great Britain, an official stamp of an assay office, on articles of gold or silver, guaranteeing their quality.

2. Figuratively, any evidence of sterling quality or true worth; as, courtesy is the *hall-mark* of a gentleman.

hall′mōte, *n.* [ME., from *halle*, hall, and *mote*, from AS. *gemot*, a meeting.] A court-leet; a court-baron; spelled also *halmote* and *halmot*. [Obs.]

hal-lō′, *interj.* [AS. *eā la*, *eála*, ah lo!] An exclamation used as a salutation or to invite attention. Of the many forms of such expressions *hello* and *hullo* are most common for ordinary greetings and to call the attention of persons near by, also as a telephone call; *halloo* is suited for calling to persons at a distance, and is the usual call to dogs in hunting. Spelled and pronounced variously, as *halloa*, *hilloa*, *holloa*, *hulloa*, *hallow*, *hillo*, *hollo*, etc.

hal-lo͞o′, *interj.* An exclamation used as a call to a person at a distance, and especially as a hunting cry.

hal-lo͞o′, *n.* A shout or call, as to one at a distance.

hal-lo͞o′, *v.t.*; hallooed, *pt.*, *pp.*; hallooing, *ppr.*

1. To call or shout to; to encourage with shouts.

2. To call out; to shout; as, to *halloo* one's message.

hal-lo͞o′, *v.i.* To cry out; to exclaim with a loud voice; to call any one by name or by the word *halloo*.

hal′lōw, *v.t.*; hallowed, *pt.*, *pp.*; hallowing, *ppr.* [ME. *halowen*, *halwen*, *halgien*; AS. *halgian*, to make holy, from *halig*, holy.] To make holy; to consecrate; to reverence; to honor as sacred.

Hal-lōw-ē′en′, Hal-lōw-ēve′, *n.* The evening preceding Allhallows or All-Saints' day; October 31, on which date various pranks are played by the young.

hal′lōw-măs, hal′lōw-măss, *n.* The feast of All-Saints.

hal-loy′şite, *n.* [Named after Dr. d'*Halloy*, a Belgian geologist.] A soft, white, claylike mineral silicate of aluminium.

hall-stat′ti-ăn, *a.* [So called from *Hallstatt*, a town in Austria, where many relics of this period are found.] Relating to the earliest period of the iron age, at which began the change from the use of bronze to that of iron.

hal′lū-çăl, *a.* [L. *hallex*, *allex*, the great toe.] Of or relating to the great toe.

hal-lū′ci-nāte, *v.t.* To impress with a hallucination.

hal-lū′ci-nāte, *v.i.* [L. *hallucinatus*, *allucinatus*, pp. of *hallucinari*, *allucinari*, to wander in mind, rave.] To blunder; to make mistakes.

hal-lū-ci-nā′tion, *n.* [L. *hallucinatio* (*-onis*), *allucinatio* (*-onis*), from *hallucinari*, *allucinari*, to wander in mind, rave.]

1. In psychology, a morbid condition of the brain or nerves, in which perception of objects or sensations takes place when no impression has been made on the organs of the special sense; the object or sensation thus erroneously perceived.

2. A mistaken impression or idea; delusion; error.

hal-lū′ci-nā-tōr, *n.* [LL., from L. *hallucinari*, to wander in mind.] One who makes mistakes because he is the victim of hallucinations.

hal-lū′ci-nā-tō-ry, *a.* Partaking of hallucination or likely to cause it.

hal′lux, *n.*; *pl.* **hal′lū-çēş**. [L. *hallex*, *allex*, the great toe.] The first digit or great toe of the foot.

hălm, haulm (ham), *n.* [ME. *halm*; AS. *healm*, the stalk or stem of grass or grain, stubble.] The stalk of any of the grains, and of pease, beans, etc.; straw.

hal′mȧ, *n.* [Gr. *halma*, from *hallesthai*, to leap.] In the old Greek athletic contests, the long jump made with weights in the hands.

hal′mȧ-lille, *n.* [E. Ind.] A hardwood tree, *Berrya amomilla*, closely allied to the linden or lime-tree of Europe. It is a native of Ceylon, the Philippines, and Australia.

hā′lō, *n.*; *pl.* **hā′lōş**. [L. *halos*, genit. and acc. *halo*; Gr. *halōs*, genit. and acc. *halō*, a threshing-floor on which oxen trod in a circular path, the round disk of the sun or moon, a halo around them, from *halein*, to grind.]

1. A luminous ring or circle, either white or colored, appearing round the sun or moon. Sometimes one only appears, and sometimes several concentric circles.

2. A circular or elliptical representation of radiant light about the heads of saints, in works of art; a nimbus; a glory.

3. Figuratively, a glory or radiance given by imagination to any object or idea; as, a *halo* of romance.

4. In anatomy, an areola.

5. [*pl.* hā-lō′nēş.] In ornithology, one of the colored concentric rings in a developing egg-yolk.

hā′lō, *v.t.*; haloed (-lōd), *pt.*, *pp.*; haloing, *ppr.* To surround or encircle with or as with a halo.

hā′lō, *v.i.* To form a halo. [Rare.]

hal-o-. See *Hali-*.

hal′ō-ġen, *n.* [Gr. *hals*, *halos*, salt, and *-genēs*, producing.] A substance which, by combination with a metal, forms a compound of a saline nature, as chlorin, iodine, bromine, and fluorin, to which cyanogen may be added as a compound halogen.

hȧ-loġ′e-nous, *a.* Having the nature of a halogen.

hā′loid, *a.* [Gr. *hals*, *halos*, salt, and *eidos*, form.] Resembling salt; relating to halogens.

Haloid salt; a salt formed by the union of a halogen and a basic element or radical.

hā′loid, *n.* A haloid salt.

hal′ō-man-cy, *n.* [*Halo-*, and Gr. *manteia*, divination.] Divination by the use of salt.

hā-lō′nēş, *n.*, pl. of *halo*, 5.

hȧ-loph′i-lous, *a.* [*Halo-*, and Gr. *philos*, loving.] Salt-loving, as plants native to salty soils.

hal′ō-phȳte, *n.* [*Halo-*, and Gr. *phyton*, a plant.] The saltwort, which grows in salt-impregnated soils, and by combustion yields barilla.

Hal-ō-rā′ġē-æ, *n.pl.* [*Halo-*, and Gr. *rhax*, *rhagos*, a berry.] An order of dicotyledons containing a few genera of perennial (rarely annual) terrestrial or aquatic herbs, mostly obscure weeds, natives of ponds or moist places.

hal-ō-sau′ri-ăn, *n.* [*Halo-*, and Gr. *sauros*, a lizard.] An extinct marine lizard.

hā′lō-sçōpe, *n.* [Gr. *halōs*, a halo, and *skopein*, to view.] A device used to investigate or illustrate the phenomena of halos.

hal-ō-tri′çhite, *n.* [*Halo-*, and Gr. *thrix*, *trichos*, a hair.] A hydrous sulphate of iron and aluminium found in silky fibrous masses or crystals. Its color is yellowish-white.

hȧ-lox′y-lin, *n.* [*Halo-*, and Gr. *xylon*, wood.] An explosive composed of charcoal, niter, and yellow prussiate of potash.

hălp, *v.*, obsolete past tense of *help*.

hal′pāce, *n.* See *Hautepace*. [Obs.]

hălse, hăls, *n.* [ME. *hals*; AS. *heals*, the neck.]

1. The neck or throat. [Obs.]

2. A hawse. [Obs.]

hălse, *v.t.* [AS. *healsian*, to embrace, from *heals*, the neck.]

1. To embrace about the neck; to greet. [Obs.]

2. To urge; to entreat. [Obs.]

hălse, *v.t.* [Ice *halsa*, to clew up a sail, from *hals*, the neck, front sheet of a sail.] To haul; to raise. [Obs.]

hal′sen-ing, *a.* Sounding harshly in the throat. [Obs.]

hăls′ēr (hăs′), *n.* A hawser. [Obs.]

hălt, *v.*, obsolete third person singular present tense of *hold*.

hălt, *v.i.*; halted, *pt.*, *pp.*; halting, *ppr.* To stop in walking; to cease to advance; to stop on a march, as a body of troops.

hălt, *v.t.* To stop; to cause to cease marching.

hălt, *n.* [OFr. *halte*, from M.H.G. *halten*, to hold.] A stopping; a stop in marching.

hălt, *v.i.* [ME. *halten*; AS. *healtian*, to limp, halt, from *healt*, halt, lame.]

1. To limp; to be lame.

2. To be faulty or lame in versification or thought; as, a *halting* sonnet; a *halting* simile.

And Sidney's verse *halts* ill on Roman feet.
—Pope.

3. To hesitate; to stand in doubt whether to proceed or what to do.

Syn.—Limp, falter, stammer, demur, hesitate.

hălt, *a.* Lame; not able to walk without limping.

hălt, *n.* 1. Lameness; a limp.

2. A sheep disease.

hălt′ēr, *n.* One who halts or limps.

hal′tēr, *n.* [ME. *halter*, *helter*, *helfter*; AS. *hælfter*, *healfter*, a halter.]

1. A rope or strap and headstall for leading or confining a horse or other animal.

2. A rope for hanging criminals condemned to death.

hal'tĕr, *v.t.*; haltered, *pt.*, *pp.*; haltering, *ppr.* To put a halter on; to fasten with a halter.

hal'tĕr, *n.*; *pl.* hal-tē'rēs. A poiser or balancer of a dipterous insect; an aborted wing.

hal'tĕr-sack, *n.* A knave fit for the gallows. [Obs.]

halt'ing-ly, *adv.* In a halting way.

hal'vans, *n.pl.* In mining, ore of poor quality.

hälve (häv), *v.t.*; halved, *pt.*, *pp.*; halving, *ppr.* [ME. *halven*, *halfen*, from *half*, a half.]

1. To divide into two equal parts.

2. To be a half or like a half of. [Rare.]

3. To join, as timbers, by lapping or letting into each other. The upper figure represents the simple lap-joint, and the lower one the common halving.

Halving (in joinery).

hälve, *n.* Half. [Obs.]

hälved (hävd), *a.* 1. In botany, dimidiate; having or seeming to have one-half wanting.

2. In golf, said of a hole when each side or player takes the same number of strokes to make it. A *halved* match is a drawn game.

hälves, *n.*, pl. of *half*.

häl'we, *n.* A saint. [Obs.]

hal'yärd, *n.* One of the ropes or tackles for hoisting or lowering yards, sails, gaffs, etc.

Hal-y-si'tēs, *n.* [Gr. *halysis*, a chain.] A genus of Paleozoic corals, commonly known as the *chain-corals*.

ham, *n.* [AS. *ham*, house, village.] A home, estate, village, or town; a common element in English place-names, as Bucking*ham*, Notting*ham*, Dur*ham*, etc. *Hamlet* is a diminutive.

ham, *n.* [ME. *hamme*, *homme*; AS. *hamm*, the ham.]

1. The inner or hind part of the knee; the inner angle of the joint which unites the thigh and the leg of an animal.

2. The thigh of an animal, particularly the thigh of a hog salted and dried in smoke.

3. [*pl.*] The buttocks. [Colloq.]

ham-ȧ-crat'ic, *a.* [Gr. *hama*, together, at the same time, and *kratein*, to rule.] Of, or exhibiting a rule characterized by unity or harmony of action. [Rare.]

ham'ȧ-dry̆-ăd, *n.* [Gr. *hamadryas*, pl. *hamadryades*; *hama*, together with, and *drys*, a tree.]

1. In Greek mythology, a wood-nymph, supposed to live and die with the tree to which she was attached.

2. A dog-faced ape or baboon, *Cynocephalus hamadryas*, with long mane and whiskers, a native of Abyssinia.

3. A snake of the genus *Ophiophagus*, large and venomous, resembling a cobra.

hȧ-mä'dry-ăs, *n.* The hamadryad or dog-faced ape.

ham'ăl, *n.* [Ar. *hammāl*, a porter, from *hamala*, to carry, bear.] In the Orient, a carrier.

Ham"ȧ-mē-lid'ē-æ, *n.pl.* [*Hamamelis* (-*id*), and -*eæ*.] An order of dicotyledons, the witch-hazels. They consist of small trees or shrubs, with alternate, stipulate, feather-veined leaves, and small axillary unisexual flowers; called also *Hamamelidaceæ*.

Ham-ȧ-mē'lis, *n.* [Gr. *hamamēlis*, a kind of medlar or service-tree; *hama*, at the same time, and *mēlon*, an apple, any tree-fruit.]

1. The typical genus of the *Hamamelideæ*.

2. An astringent fluid extract prepared from *Hamamelis Virginiana*, witch-hazel.

ham'ärch-y, *n.* [Gr. *hama*, together with, at the same time, and *archein*, to rule.] Government in which many heterogeneous elements are organized into a political unit.

ham-är-thri'tis, *n.* [Gr. *hamarthritis*, gout in all the joints at once; *hama*, at the same time, and *arthritis*, gout.] In medicine, gout in all the joints.

hȧ-mär-ti-al'ō-gy̆, *n.* [Gr. *hamartia*, error, sin, and -*logia*, from *legein*, to speak.] That part of anthropology or moral theology which deals with sin; a treatise or discussion concerning sin.

hā'māte, *a.* [L. *hamatus*, furnished with a hook, hooked, from *hamus*, a hook.] Hooked; uncinate; curved into a hook.

hā'mā-ted, *a.* Hooked or set with hooks. [Rare.]

hȧ-mā'tum, *n.* [L. *hamatus*, hooked.] The unciform bone of the carpus.

ham'-bee"tle, *n.* *Corynetes rufipes*, a beetle, the larva of which attacks cured hams.

ham'ble, *v.t.* [ME. *hamelen*; AS. *hamelian*, to mutilate.]

1. To hamstring. [Obs.]

2. To render (dogs) unfit for hunting by cutting out the balls of the feet. [Obs.]

Ham'bŭrg, *n.* 1. A small-sized variety of the common domestic fowl, having blue legs and a rose-colored comb.

2. A fine variety of black grape, usually chosen for hothouse growth.

Hamburg lake; a cochineal pigment of a purplish color inclining to crimson.

hāme, *n.* [D. *haam*, a hame.] A curved bar of metal or wood to which the trace of a draft-harness is attached, and which lies on the collar or has a pad to rest upon the neck of the horse. One is used on each side.

hāme, *n.* Home. [Scot.]

hāme, *n.* Halm. [Obs.]

ham'el, *v.t.* To hamble. [Obs.]

hāmo'suck-en, *n.* [Scot., from AS. *hamsocn*, an attack on a man's house; *ham*, home, and *socn*, a seeking.] In Scots law, the offense of feloniously beating or assaulting a person in his own house or dwelling-place; also written *homesocken*, *hamesecken*, etc.

ham'fat"tĕr, *n.* An actor of low grade and small abilities; a term used in contempt.

hā'mi, *n.*, pl. of *hamus*.

hā'mi-fọrm, *a.* [L. *hamus*, a hook, and *forma*, form.] Hamate; shaped like a hook.

Ham-il-tō'ni-ȧ, *n.* [Named after F. Buchanan, the author of some works relating to India, who in late life took the name of *Hamilton*.] A genus of East Indian plants of the order *Rubiaceæ*. The species are shrubs with fragrant flowers which have a funnel-shaped corolla.

Ham-il-tō'ni-ăn, *a.* Of, relating to, or characteristic of any person named *Hamilton* or of their methods or ideas, as (a) Sir William Hamilton (1788–1856), a logician and philosopher, of Scotland; (b) Sir William Rowan Hamilton (1805–1865), a mathematician, of Ireland; (c) James Hamilton (1769–1831), teacher of languages in England and America; (d) Alexander Hamilton (1757–1804), first Secretary of the Treasury of the United States, statesman and lawyer.

ham-i-nū'rȧ, *n.* [S. Am.] A large South American food-fish.

ham-i-ros'trāte, *a.* [L. *hamus*, a hook, and *rostratus*, beaked, from *rostrum*, a beak.] Hook-beaked; with a beak like a hook.

hā'mīte, *n.* [L. *hamus*, hook, and -*ite*.] The fossil of an extinct genus of cephalopods; so named from the shell being hooked or bent on itself, instead of being spiral. They are peculiar to the Chalk formation.

Ham'īte, *n.* 1. Any person supposed to be descended from Ham, one of Noah's sons, or belonging to a race speaking a Hamitic tongue.

2. A negro; popularly considered a descendant of Ham.

Ham-it'ic, *a.* Of or relating to Ham, or the Hamites.

Hamitic languages, or *stock*; a class of African tongues, comprising the ancient hieroglyphic language, Coptic, the Ethiopian or Abyssinian, the Libyan or Berber, and the Hottentot groups. There are certain resemblances to the Semitic languages.

ham'let, *n.* *Epinephelus striatus*, a bass-like food-fish, commonly called the *Nassau grouper*; found from Florida to the southern West Indies.

ham'let, *n.* [ME. *hamlet*, *hamelet*; OFr. *hamelet*, dim. of *hamel*, a village, a dim. of Germanic origin; compare AS. *ham*, a home.] A small village; a little cluster of houses in the country; especially, in England, one which has no church.

ham'lin-īte, *n.* [Named after A. C. *Hamlin*, an American geologist.] A colorless, crystalline phosphate of aluminium and glucinum.

ham'mĕr, *v.t.*; hammered, *pt.*, *pp.*; hammering, *ppr.* 1. To beat with a hammer; to pound; as, to *hammer* iron or steel.

2. To form or forge with a hammer; to shape by beating.

3. To work in the mind; to contrive by intellectual labor; to excogitate; usually with *out*; as, to *hammer out* a scheme.

ham'mĕr, *v.i.* 1. To work; to be very busy; to labor in contrivance.

> Whereon this month I have been *hammering*.
> —Shak.

2. To strike anything repeatedly, as with a hammer.

3. To be working or in agitation; to keep up an excited state of feeling.

ham'mĕr, *n.* [ME. *hamer*, *homer*; AS. *hamor*, *homer*, a hammer.]

1. An instrument for driving nails, beating metals, and the like. It consists usually of a solid metal head fixed crosswise to a handle.

2. Anything resembling the common hammer in shape or action; (a) the striker of a clock or gong; (b) one of the small padded mallets by which the strings of a piano are struck; (c) that part in the lock of a gun, rifle, etc., which when the trigger is pulled falls with a smart blow, and causes the explosion of the detonating substance; (d) in anatomy, the malleus; (e) in zoölogy, the head of a hammerhead; (f) in sports, a ball of metal at the end of a long handle, used for throwing; (g) a mallet used by auctioneers.

To bring to the hammer; to sell by auction, from the auctioneer using a small hammer or mallet to knock down the goods to the highest bidder.

ham'mĕr-ȧ-ble, *a.* Malleable; capable of being shaped by a hammer.

ham'mĕr-beam, *n.* A short beam attached to the foot of a principal rafter in a roof, in the place of the tie-beam. In the figure, the inner end of the hammer-beam, A, receives the weight of the upper portion of the roof, which is balanced by the pressure of the principal at its outer end.

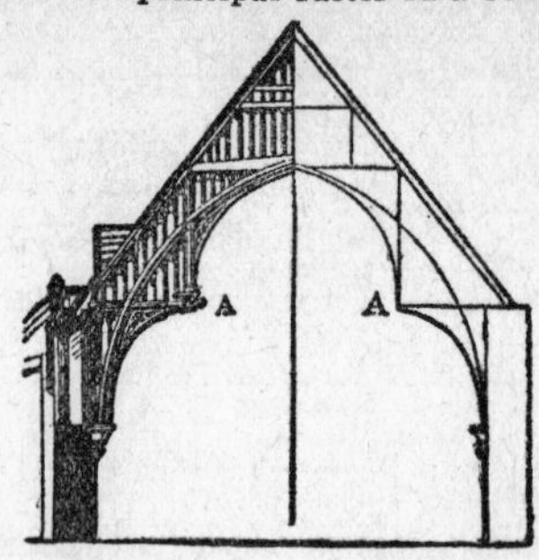

Hammer-beam Roof, Westminster Hall.

ham'mĕr-catch"ĕr, *n.* A pad in a piano against which the hammer returns after striking the string.

ham'mĕr-cloth, *n.* [So called from the practice of carrying a hammer, nails, etc., in a pocket hid by this cloth.] The cloth which covers the driver's seat in some kinds of carriages.

ham'mĕr-dressed (-drest), *a.* Dressed or prepared with a hammer; especially applied to a building-stone which has been dressed with a pointed hammer or pick.

ham'mĕr-ĕr, *n.* 1. One who works with a hammer.

2. The Costa Rican bell-bird, *Chasmorhynchus tricarunculatus*.

ham'mĕr-fish, *n.* The hammerhead.

ham'mĕr-härd"en, *v.t.* To make (a metal) hard by hammering it while cold.

ham'mĕr-head, *n.* 1. A shark, *Sphyrna zygæna*, having a head which resembles a double-headed hammer.

2. The stone-roller, *Hypentelium nigricans*.

3. *Hypsignathus monstrosus*, a fruit-bat of Africa.

ham'mĕr-ing, *n.* A series of ornamental dents in metal-work made with a hammer.

ham'mĕr-kop, *n.* [S. African.] *Scopus umbretta*, the umber.

ham'mĕr-măn, *n.*; *pl.* **ham'mĕr-men.** One who works with a hammer, as a blacksmith, a silversmith, etc.

ham'mĕr-oys"tĕr, *n.* A hammer-shell.

ham'mĕr-shell, *n.* A pearl-oyster of the genus *Malleus*, the shell of which is shaped like a hammer.

ham'mĕr-wŏrt, *n.* The plant pellitory, *Parietaria officinalis*.

ham-mō-chry̆'sos, *n.* [L., from Gr. *hammochrysos*; *hammos*, *ammos*, sand, and *chrysos*, gold.] A variety of sandstone having particles of gold color interspersed in it.

ham'mŏck, *n.* [Sp. *hamaca*, a hammock; of W. Ind. origin.]

1. A kind of hanging bed, consisting of a piece of cloth, usually canvas, or netting, about 6 feet long and 3 feet wide, gathered at the ends and suspended by cords and hooks. It very commonly forms a bed on board of ships.

Sailor's Hammock.

2. In entomology, a hammock-like case or covering of certain caterpillars.

ham'mŏck, *n.* A hummock.

hā'mōse, **hā'mous**, *a.* [L. *hamus*, a hook.] In botany, hamate.

ham'pĕr, *n.* 1. A fetter or some instrument that shackles.

2. Things which, though necessary to the equipment of a ship, are in the way in time of service.

ham'pĕr, *v.t.*; hampered, *pt.*, *pp.*; hampering, *ppr.* [Prob. same as *hamble*, *hamel*, from AS. *hamelian*, to mutilate.]

1. To shackle; to entangle; hence, to impede in motion or progress, or to render progress difficult; to embarrass.

> They *hamper* and entangle our souls.
> —Tillotson.

2. To derange or put out of working order, as a piece of mechanism. [Rare.]

ham'pĕr, *v.t.* To put into a hamper.

ham′pẽr, *n.* [ME. *hamper*, contr. of *hanaper*, from LL. *hanaperium*, a basket or vessel to keep cups in.] A kind of rude basket or wicker-work receptacle, generally of considerable size, and chiefly used as a case in which to put goods.

ham′shag″kle, *v.t.* [*Ham* and *shackle.*] To restrain, as a horse or other animal, by using a short shackle of rope or the like to draw the head down and fasten it to a fore leg; hence, to curb; to restrain; to embarrass.

ham′stẽr, *n.* [G. *hamster*, a hamster; O.H.G. *hamastro*, weevil.] Any rodent of the genus *Cricetus* of the rat family, resembling true rats in dentition, but differing in having a short hairy tail as well as cheek-pouches in which to carry grain, pease, acorns, etc., to the winter burrow. The common *hamster* of northern Europe and Asia, *Cricetus vulgaris* or *frumentarius*, is the size of the water-rat, but browner.

Hamster (*Cricetus vulgaris* or *frumentarius*).

ham′string, *n.* 1. In human anatomy, a tendon of a thigh muscle at either side of the popliteal space or ham.

2. Popularly, the tendon above and behind the hock of a quadruped's hind leg.

ham′string, *v.t.*; hamstrung *or* hamstringed, *pt., pp.*; hamstringing, *ppr.* 1. To cut the hamstring or hamstrings of, so as to lame or disable.

2. To cut the tendons of (a whale's fluke).

ham′ū-lăr, *a.* [L. *hamulus*, dim. of *hamus*, a hook.] Like a hook; curved; hamulate.

ham′ū-lāte, *a.* Having or resembling a small hook or hooks.

ham′ūle, *n.* A hamulus.

ham′ū-lōse, ham′ū-lous, *a.* Hamulate.

ham′ū-lus, *n.*; *pl.* **ham′ū-lī.** [L., dim. of *hamus*, a hook.]

1. In entomology, one of a series of small hooks on the front edge of the lower wings of some of the *Hymenoptera*.

2. In ornithology, a barbicel.

3. In anatomy, a hamular process of a bone.

4. In botany, in the genus *Uncinia*, a kind of hooked bristle or awn in the flowers.

hā′mus, *n.*; *pl.* **hā′mī.** [L., a hook.] A hooklet or hook-shaped projection from the front wing of certain lepidopterous insects.

han, *v.*, infinitive and present indicative plural of *have.* [Obs.]

han′ap, *n.* [OFr. *hanap, hanep*, a drinking-cup; O.H.G. *hnapf*, a cup, bowl, basin.] A goblet, usually of silver or gold. [Obs.]

han′ȧ-pẽr, *n.* [ME. *hanypere*; OFr. *hanapier*, *hanaper*; LL. *hanaperium*, a basket or vessel for keeping cups in.]

1. A kind of hamper used in early days by the kings of England for holding and carrying with them their money as they journeyed from place to place.

Hanaper used for keeping the Records.

2. [H—] An office of the English Court of Chancery, so called because all writs regarding the public were once kept in a *hanaper*, those concerning the crown being in a little sack or bag.

3. A hamper; a hanap. [Obs.]

hance, *v.t.* To lift; to enhance. [Obs.]

hance, hanch, *n.* [ME. *hanche, haunche*; OFr. *hanche, anche, hance*, from O.H.G. *ancha, encha*, the leg, lit., joint or bend.]

1. In architecture, formerly, (a) the lower part, above the springing, of three and four centered arches; (b) a small arch by which a straight lintel is sometimes united to its jamb or impost; written also *hanse.*

2. [*pl.*] In a ship, falls of the fife-rails placed on balusters on the poop and quarter-deck down to the gangway.

han′chi-nol, *n.* [Mex.] *Heimia salicifolia*, a shrub of the order *Lythraceæ*, used as a sudorific, diuretic, and in venereal disorders.

hand, *v.t.*; handed, *pt., pp.*; handing, *ppr.* 1. To give or transmit with the nand; as, *hand* me a book.

2. To lead, guide, or help with the hand; to conduct; as, to *hand* an invalid into a chair.

3. In nautical language, to furl; to wrap a sail close to a yard or mast and fasten it with gaskets.

4. To manage; as, I *hand* my oar. [Obs.]

5. To seize; to lay hands on. [Obs.]

6. To join hands as in making a pledge. [Obs.]

To hand down; (a) to transmit in succession, as from father to son, or from predecessor to successor; as, fables are *handed down* from age to age; (b) to give to a subordinate; as, the supreme court *handed down* its opinion to the lower court.

To hand over; to give possession of; to resign; as, he *handed over* the office to his successor.

To hand round or *around*; to circulate; to spread; to deal out; to pass from hand to hand; as, *to hand round* a bit of news or gossip; *to hand round* refreshments.

hand, *v.i.* To go hand in hand; to coöperate. [Obs.]

hand, *n.* [ME. *hand, hond*; AS. *hand, hond*, a hand, from same root as Goth. *hinthan*, to take, seize.]

1. In man, the extremity of the arm, consisting of the palm and fingers, connected with the arm at the wrist; the part with which we hold and use any instrument. The human *hand* is composed of twenty-seven bones; namely, the eight bones of the carpus or wrist, the five bones of the metacarpus forming the palm, and the fourteen bones or phalanges of the fingers. Of these phalanges the thumb has but two, all the other digits having three each.

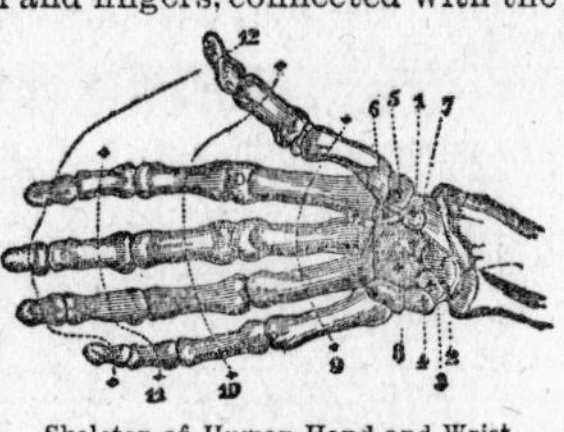

Skeleton of Human Hand and Wrist.

1. Scaphoid bone. 2. Semilunar bone. 3. Cuneiform bone. 4. Pisiform bone. 5. Os trapezium. 6. Os trapezoides. 7. Os magnum. 8. Unciform bone. 9. Metacarpal bones of thumb and fingers. 10. First row of phalanges of thumb and fingers. 11. Second row of phalanges of fingers. 12. Third row of phalanges of thumb and fingers.

2. A member of certain of the lower animals resembling in use or structure the human *hand*, as one of the four extremities of an ape; one of the fore paws of a squirrel; in falconry, the foot of a hawk; in the manège, the forefoot of a horse.

3. A measure of four inches; a palm; applied chiefly to horses; as, a horse 14 *hands* high.

4. Side; part; direction, either right or left; as, on the one *hand* or the other; this is admitted on all *hands*, that is, on all sides or by all parties.

5. Performance; handiwork; workmanship; that is, the effect for the cause, the *hand* being the instrument of action.

> Arborets and flowers
> Imborder'd on each bank, the *hand* of Eve.
> —Milton.

6. Power of performance; skill.

> A friend of mine has a very fine *hand* on the violin. —Addison.

7. Manner of acting or performance; mode of procedure.

> So may she, by a moderate *hand*, from time to time reap the like. —Bacon.

8. Agency; part in performing or executing; as, punish every man who had a *hand* in the mischief.

> The word of the Lord, which he spake by the *hand* of his servant Ahijah the prophet.
> —1 Kings xiv. 18.

9. Possession; power; as, the estate is in the *hands* of the owner.

> Sacraments serve as the moral instruments of God, . . . the use whereof is in our *hands*, the effect in his. —Hooker.

10. In card-playing, (a) the cards held by a single player; (b) one of the players, the *elder hand* being the player sitting next after the dealer in the order in which the cards are dealt; (c) a game at cards; (d) a single round at a game, in which all the cards dealt at one time are played.

> The odd trick at the conclusion of a *hand.*
> —Dickens.

11. As much as may be held in the *hand*; specifically, (a) five of any article of sale; as, five oranges or five herrings make a *hand*; (b) with tobacco-growers, a bundle or head of tobacco leaves tied together, without being stripped from the stem.

12. That which performs the office of the *hand* or of a finger in pointing; as, the *hands* of a clock.

13. The representation of a *hand* with the index finger pointing (☞), as on a guideboard or as a type-character.

14. A person; so used by itself mostly as applied to persons employed on board ship or in manufactories, but more widely in such phrases as, a good *hand* at a speech; a poor *hand* at an explanation, in which there is a reference to some special faculty or ability ascribed or denied to a person, and in one or two other phrases, such as, a cool *hand*, a person not easily abashed or deprived of his self-possession; an old *hand*, a person of long experience, an astute fellow.

15. Style of penmanship; as, a good *hand*; a bad *hand*; a fine *hand.*

16. Terms; conditions; rate; price. [Obs.]

17. In theatrical parlance, applause.

Hand is used in many compounds, with force of made for or used by the hand; as, *hand*-basket, *hand*-gear, *hand*saw; also, with the meaning, given or accomplished by the hand; as, *hand*-shaking, *hand*-work, *hand*made, etc.

At hand; near; either present and within reach, or not far distant, in space or time.

At the hand of; from; as, mercy *at the hand of* the victor.

By hand; by the use of the hand or hands, in contradistinction to the use of machinery; as, these clothes were made *by hand.*

From hand to hand; from one to another.

Hand in hand; in union; conjointly; unitedly.

Hand over hand; *hand over fist*; by passing the hands alternately one before or above another; as, to climb *hand over hand*; hence, easily and rapidly; as, making money *hand over fist.*

Hand running; one after another; as, three victories *hand running.*

Hands off; keep off; forbear.

Hand to hand; in close union; close fight.

Heavy hand; severity or oppression.

In hand; (a) present payment; cash received; as, receiving *in hand* one year's rent; (b) in process of execution; as, I have a great work *in hand*; (c) under control; as, the enterprise is well *in hand.*

Laying on of hands; a ceremony used in consecrating to office, in healing, and in blessing.

Light hand; gentleness; moderation.

Note of hand; a promissory note.

Off hand; without delay, hesitation, or difficulty; without previous preparation; dexterously.

On hand; (a) in present possession; as, a stock of goods *on hand*; (b) present; as, he was *on hand* promptly.

Out of hand; at once; directly; promptly.

Slack hand; idleness; carelessness; sloth.

Strict hand; severe discipline; rigorous government.

To bear a hand; see under *Bear.*

To be hand and glove with or *hand in glove with*; to be intimate and familiar with, as a friend or colaborer.

To bring up by hand; to nurture with food other than mother's milk, as a baby, a calf, etc.

To change hands; to change owners.

To come to hand; to be accepted or received, as a message.

To get one's hand in; to get used to a new occupation, so as to become more skilful.

To get or *have the upper hand*; to obtain an advantage over; to surpass; as, *to get the upper hand* of an adversary.

To his, her, my, one's, etc., *hand*; in readiness; already prepared; ready; as, the task lies *to my hand.*

To lay hands on; (a) to assault or seize; (b) to consecrate by the laying on of hands.

To lend a hand; to give assistance.

To lift hands against; to rebel.

To live from hand to mouth; to obtain food, etc., as want requires without making previous provision; to be improvident, prodigal, and continously bankrupt.

To put forth one's hand against; to kill.

To stand one in hand; to be becoming or needful; to concern or behoove; as, *it stands one in hand* to use caution in dangerous places.

To wash one's hands of; to disclaim all responsibility for; to withdraw from participation in; as, *to wash one's hands of* the whole matter.

Under the hand of; under the signature and seal of.

hand′=bag, *n.* A bag or pouch carried in the hand; any form of satchel or valise carried in the hand.

hand′ball, *n.* 1. A game in which one player strikes a ball against a wall with the hand and an opposing player endeavors to return it to the wall on the rebound, until one fails to make a proper return.

2. The ball used in the game of *handball.*

3. A rubber bulb perforated and used in spraying.

hand′bar″rōw, *n.* 1. A barrow carried with the hands; a litter.

2. A wheelbarrow.

3. A sort of frame used in carrying military supplies.

hand′=bell, *n.* A small bell to be rung by hand instead of by a bell-rope.

hand′bill, *n.* A dodger; a small printed sheet of paper bearing an announcement, etc., to be given out by hand.

hand′bill, *n.* A kind of pruning knife or hook; a billhook.

hand′book, *n.* 1. A book for the hand; a

manual; applied frequently to a guidebook for travelers.

2. In recent sporting parlance, a term applied to a book of bets on horse-races, made by a bookmaker with more or less secrecy, in order to evade antibetting laws, the better receiving no written evidence of his bet.

hand′breadth (-bredth), *n.* A space equal to the breadth of the hand; a palm.

hand′=cär, *n.* A light car used on railways by inspectors or workmen for transportation and for carrying tools, etc., operated by means of a crank or a lever with gearing.

hand′cloth, *n.* A handkerchief.

hand′craft, *n.* See *Handicraft.*

hand′crafts-măn, *n.* See *Handicraftsman.*

hand′cuff, *n.* [AS. *handcops*; *hand*, hand, and *cosp*, *cops*, a fetter.] A shackle for the hand, in the form of a divided ring, to be placed and locked upon the wrist; a manacle. *Handcuffs* are usually in pairs, connected by a short chain.

hand′cuff, *v.t.*; handcuffed, *pt.*, *pp.*; handcuffing, *ppr.* To manacle; to restrain with handcuffs.

hand′=di-rect″ŏr, *n.* A guide for the hand and arm when learning to play on a piano.

hand′=drop, *n.* In pathology, a paralyzed condition of the extensor muscles of the hand, the result of blood-poisoning; called also *wrist-drop.*

hand′ed, *a.* 1. Provided with hands.

2. Having the hands joined. [Rare.]

3. Having a hand or hands possessed of any peculiar property; as, hundred-*handed*; hard-*handed*; right-*handed*; single-*handed*; two-*handed.*

hand′ẽr, *n.* One who hands or transmits; one who conveys.

hand′fäst, *n.* 1. Hold; custody; power of confining or keeping. [Obs.]

2. A pledge or contract; a betrothal. [Obs.]

hand′fäst, *a.* 1. Fast by contract; betrothed by joining hands. [Rare.]

2. Close-fisted. [Rare.]

3. Steadfast. [Rare.]

hand′fäst, *v.t.* [ME. *handfasten*, *handfesten*; Ice. *handfesta*, to conclude a bargain by shaking hands, betroth; *hönd*, hand, and *festa*, to fasten, pledge.] To pledge; to betroth by joining hands, in order to legalize or authorize cohabitation before marriage. [Obs.]

hand′fish, *n.* See *Angler*, 2.

hand′flow″ẽr=tree, *n.* *Cheirostemon platanoides*, a large Mexican and Central American tree of the cola-nut family. The stamens of its flowers are flesh-colored and spread out like the fingers of a hand.

hand′ful, *n.*; *pl.* **hand′fuls.** 1. As much as the hand will grasp or contain.

2. A small quantity or number; as, a *handful* of men.

3. As much as can be done; full employment.

4. A hand; a unit of length equal to four inches. [Obs.]

hand′=gal″lŏp, *n.* A slow and easy gallop, in which the hand presses the bridle to check higher speed.

hand′=gēar, *n.* An arrangement for operating a power-machine by hand; also, the starting-gear of a steam-engine.

hand′=glȧss, *n.* 1. In gardening, a portable glass used for placing over, protecting, and forwarding plants.

2. A small mirror that may be held conveniently in the hand.

3. A lens with a handle for use in reading.

4. A sandglass used to measure the log on shipboard.

hand′=hōle, *n.* A hole through which the hand may be inserted, as in a boiler.

hand′=hōle=plāte′, *n.* An iron covering for a hand-hole.

hand′i-cap, *v.t.*; handicapped (-kapt), *pt.*, *pp.*; handicapping, *ppr.* 1. To encumber with impediments or disadvantages.

2. To place at a disadvantage, by granting an allowance of time, weight, distance, etc., to a competitor supposed to be inferior, as in a race.

3. To lessen the efficiency of; to detract from; to weaken; as, excessive egotism *handicaps* a man.

hand′i-cap, *n.* 1. A restriction or hindrance in a contest imposed upon a superior competitor to offset the supposed inferiority of an opponent, or an allowance of time, distance, or the like given to the inferior contestant.

2. A drawback; an inconvenience.

3. A contest in which some of the participants are handicapped; as, the Brooklyn *handicap.*

4. A kind of game with cards. [Obs.]

hand′i-cap-pẽr, *n.* One who fixes handicaps.

hand′i-craft, *n.* [ME. *handcraft*; AS. *handcræft*, a manual occupation; *hand*, hand, and *cræft*, strength, power, skill. The form of the word was influenced by *handiwork.*]

1. Manual occupation; work performed by the hand; a mechanical trade.

2. A handicraftsman. [Rare.]

hand′i-crȧfts-măn, *n.* A man skilled or employed in manual occupation; a mechanic.

hand′i-ly, *adv.* 1. With dexterity or skill; dexterously; adroitly.

2. With ease or convenience.

hand′i-ness, *n.* The ease of performance derived from practice; dexterity; adroitness.

hand′ī″ron (-ūrn), *n.* Same as *Andiron.*

hand′i-wŏrk, *n.* [ME. *handiwerk*, *handewerc*; AS. *handgeweorc*, work of the hand; *hand*, hand, and *geweorc*, *weorc*, work.]

1. Work done by the hands; hence, work performed by any kind of effort; doing; performance; as, a sample of one's *handiwork.*

2. That which is made or done with the hands; the result of work or doing; hence, a creation; as, this misery is your *handiwork.*

hand′jär (han′), *n.* [Ar. *khanjar*, a dagger.] A broad-bladed one edged sword used throughout Asia Minor.

hand′kẽr-chẽr (hang′), *n.* Handkerchief. [Obs.]

hand′kẽr-chief (-chif), *n.* [*Hand* and *kerchief.*]

1. A piece of cloth, usually linen, cotton, or silk, plain or figured, and generally square, carried about the person for the purpose of wiping the face, hands, nose, etc.; a pocket-handkerchief.

2. A piece of cloth sometimes worn about the neck, and preferably called a *neckerchief* or *neckcloth.* [Colloq.]

hand′=lan″guāge (-gwāj), *n.* Language expressed by the use of the hands; dactylology; sign-language.

hand′=lāthe, *n.* 1. A small lathe operated by hand-power.

2. A lathe in which the tool is applied by hand instead of automatically.

han′dle, *v.t.*; handled, *pt.*, *pp.*; handling, *ppr.* [ME. *handlen*; AS. *handlian*, to handle, feel, from *hand*, hand.]

1. To touch; to feel with the hand; to use or hold with the hand.

> *Handle* me, and see; for a spirit hath not flesh and bones. —Luke xxiv. 39.

2. To manage; to use; to wield; to manipulate; as, to *handle* a rifle or an oar; to *handle* a ship.

3. To treat; to discourse on; to discuss; to use or manage in writing or speaking; as, the lecturer *handled* his subject with much skill.

4. To treat; to use well or ill; to deal with; as, they *handled* the prisoner roughly.

5. To deal in; to trade in; to buy or sell; as, to *handle* groceries; to *handle* stocks and bonds.

6. To exercise with the hands; to make used to the hands; to train; as, to *handle* a spirited horse.

7. To equip with a handle.

han′dle, *v.i.* To use the hands; to feel with the hands; to work or act by means of the hands.

han′dle, *n.* [ME. *handel*, *handyl*; AS. *handle*, a handle, from *handlian*, to handle, feel.]

1. That part of a vessel or instrument which is held in the hand when used, as the haft of a sword, the bail of a kettle, etc.

2. That of which use is made; the instrument of effecting a purpose.

To give a handle; to furnish or supply an occasion, opportunity, or means.

han′dle-ȧ-ble, *a.* Capable of being handled.

hand′less, *a.* Without a hand or hands.

han′dling, *n.* [ME. *handlinge*, *hondlunge*; AS. *handlung*, from *handlian*, to handle, feel.]

1. Manipulation; touch; a touching or using with the hand.

2. The act of equipping with handles.

hand′māde, *a.* Manufactured by the hand, and not by a machine; as, *handmade* paper.

hand′māid, *n.* A maid that waits at hand; a female servant or attendant.

hand′māid″en, *n.* A handmaid.

hand′māid=moth, *n.* *Datana ministra*, a moth of the family *Bombycidæ.*

hand′mill, *n.* A mill for grinding grain, pepper, coffee, etc., moved by the hand, as distinguished from one driven by steam, water, etc.

Handmills.

hand′saw, *n.* A saw to be used with the hand.

hand′screw (-skrū), *n.* An engine for raising heavy timbers or weights; a jack.

hand′sel, han′sel, *n.* [ME. *hansel*, *hanselle*; AS. *handselen*; *hand*, hand, and *selen*, *sylen*, a giving, from *sellen*, *syllan*, to give.]

1. A gift; a New-Year's gift; an earnest, or earnest-penny; a sale, gift, or delivery, which is regarded as the first of a series; the first money received in the morning for the sale of goods; the first money that a merchant receives in a store newly opened; the first present sent to a young woman on her wedding-day, etc.

2. Payment; price; reward. [Obs.]

Handsel Monday; the first Monday of the new year, when it was formerly usual in Scotland for servants, children, and others to ask or receive presents or handsel.

hand′sel, han′sel, *v.t.*; handseled *or* handselled, *pt.*, *pp.*; handseling *or* handselling, *ppr.* To give a handsel to; to use or do for the first time.

hand′sōme, *a.*; *comp.* handsomer; *superl.* handsomest. [ME. *handsom*, *handsum*, easy to handle or use; AS. *hand*, hand, and *-sum*, -some.]

1. Dexterous; handy; ready; convenient. [Obs.]

2. Possessing a form agreeable to the eye or to correct taste; endowed with a certain share of beauty along with dignity; having symmetry of parts; well formed; as, a *handsome* woman or man; she has a *handsome* person or face; a *handsome* building.

3. Graceful in manner; marked with propriety and ease; becoming; appropriate; as, a *handsome* style or composition.

> Easiness and *handsome* address in writing is hardest to be attained by persons bred in a meaner way. —Felton.

4. Ample; large; as, a *handsome* fortune.

> He at last accumulated a *handsome* sum of money. —Knox.

5. Characterized by or expressive of liberality or generosity; as, a *handsome* present; a *handsome* action.

hand′sōme, *v.t.* To render handsome. [Obs.]

hand′sōme-ly, *adv.* 1. In a handsome manner.

> When the kind nymph, changing her faultless shape,
> Becomes unhandsome, *handsomely* to 'scape. —Waller.

2. Nautically, steadily and carefully; leisurely; as, to lower *handsomely.*

hand′sōme-ness, *n.* 1. The condition or quality of being handsome.

2. Favor; approval.

hand′spīke, *n.* A bar, commonly of wood, used with the hand as a lever for various purposes, as in raising weights, heaving about a windlass, etc.

hand′spring, *n.* A somersault or turn in which the hands meet the ground.

hand′stäff, *n.*; *pl.* **hand′stāves.** 1. A javelin.

2. The part of a flail grasped by the hand.

hand′=stamp, *n.* A stamp to be used by hand; specifically, a rubber stamp used with a separate pad, distinguished from a self-inker.

hand′strōke, *n.* A blow or stroke given by the hand. [Obs.]

hand′=tight (-tīt), *a.* Nautically, tight as may be made by the hand; moderately tight.

hand′=tim″bẽr, *n.* Underwood. [Obs.]

hand′=tree, *n.* Same as *Handflower-tree.*

hand′=vīse, *n.* A small portable vise that may be held in the hand while it is used.

hand′=wāled, *a.* Waled or picked out with the hand; carefully selected. [Scot.]

hand′=wea″pŏn (-we″pŏn), *n.* A weapon to be wielded by the hand.

hand′wheel, *n.* A small fly-wheel, having usually a handle inserted in the rim of it, to serve the purpose of a crank in a machine which is worked by hand.

hand′while, *n.* A short interval. [Obs.]

hand′=winged, *a.* Having hands developed into something resembling wings; cheiropterous; said of bats.

hand′=wŏrk, *n.* Work done by the hands; specifically, in the arts, such work as may be or usually is done by machinery, when done by hand.

hand′=wŏrked, hand′=wrought (-wẽrkt, -rąt), *a.* Made with the hands.

hand′wŏrm, *n.* A species of *Acarus.*

hand′wrīte (-rīt), *v.t.* and *v.i.* To write. [Rare.]

hand′wrīt″ing, *n.* 1. The cast or form of writing peculiar to each hand or person; chirography.

2. That which is written by hand; manuscript.

> Blotting out the *handwriting* of ordinances. —Col. ii. 14.

hand′y, *a.*; *comp.* handier; *superl.* handiest.

1. Performed by the hand. [Obs.]

2. Performing with skill and readiness; skilled to use the hands with ease in performance; dexterous; ready; adroit; skilful.

> Them with *handy* care she drest.—Dryden.

3. Ready to the hand; near; suited to the use of the hand; convenient; as, my books are very *handy.*

Syn.—Near, convenient, useful, helpful, ready, ingenious.

hand′y=dan′dy, *n.* A play among children in which something is shaken between two hands, and then a guess is made in which hand it is retained.

hand′y-fight (-fīt), *n.* A boxing-match. [Obs.]

hand′y-grīpe, *n.* Seizure by the hand. [Obs.]

hand′y-strōke, *n.* A blow inflicted by the hand.

hand′y-wŏrk, *n.* Same as *Handiwork.*

hang, *v.t.*; hung *or* hanged, *pt.*, *pp.* (the latter is obsolete except in sense 2); hanging, *ppr.* [In modern Eng. two verbs have been confused; ME. *hangen*, v.t., *hongien*, v.i.; AS. *hangian*, v.i., from *hon*, v.t., to hang, suspend.]

1. To suspend; to fasten to some elevated

point without support from below; often used with *up*; as, to *hang* a coat on a hook; to *hang up* a sign.

2. To put to death by suspending by the neck.

Was *hung* by martial law. —Southey.

3. To fasten in a manner which will allow of free motion upon the point or points of suspension, said of a door, a gate, and the like.

4. To cover, furnish, or decorate by anything suspended, as pictures, trophies, drapery, and the like; as, to *hang* an apartment with curtains or with pictures.

Hung be the heavens with black. —Shak.

5. To cause or suffer to assume a drooping attitude; as, to *hang* the head.

6. To cause to remain or continue undecided or inoperative; as, to *hang* a jury; to be *hung* in doubt.

7. To adjust, as a bladed instrument, so that the whole is in suitable working order; as, to *hang* a scythe.

To hang, draw, and quarter; to hang the body (of a criminal) upon a gibbet, then disembowel it and cut it into pieces; a form of punishment once practised in England.

To hang in effigy; to hang a stuffed figure or effigy (of a person) to express a sentiment of odium incurred.

To hang out the red flag; (a) to present a challenge to fight; (b) to give a warning of danger; (c) to announce the sentiment of anarchy.

To hang up; (a) to put in a state of suspense; to place out of reach; as, *to hang up* a bill or measure in a legislative body; (b) to pawn. [Slang.]

hang, *v.i.* 1. To be suspended; to be sustained wholly or partly by something above; to dangle; to depend; to be supported with free motion on the point or points of suspension; as, his coat was *hanging* on a peg; the door *hangs* well; to *hang* on the neck of a person.

Hang not on my garments. —Shak.

2. To bend forward or downward; to lean or incline.

His neck obliquely o'er his shoulder *hung*. —Pope.

3. To be supported by something raised above the ground; as, a *hanging* garden on the top of a house.

4. Figuratively, to be attached to or connected with in various ways; as, (a) to have origin; to proceed; to arise.

Where curt speech and soft persuasion *hung*. —Prior.

(b) To cling to or remain with one, as habits.

I felt the prejudices of my education . . . still *hanging* about me. —Junius.

(c) To have a basis of certain grounds or considerations; as, this question *hangs* on a single point.

5. To hover; to impend; as, many dangers *hang* over the country.

Sundry blessings *hang* about his throne. —Shak.

6. To be delayed; to be kept back.

Her accents *hung*. —Dryden.

7. To linger; to lounge; to loiter.

I *hung* with grooms and porters on the bridge. —Tennyson.

8. To incline; to have a steep declivity; as, *hanging* grounds.

9. To be put to death by suspension from the neck.

The goose hangs high; see under *Goose*.

To hang around; to haunt persistently; to loaf around; to idle.

To hang back; to hold off; to falter.

To hang by the eyelids; to hold on by a very slender tenure; to be in a precarious condition.

To hang fire; in a firearm, to fail to explode promptly; hence, to fail, as an enterprise, of consummation in the time anticipated; to come to a standstill.

To hang in doubt; to be in suspense or doubt.

To hang in the balance; to be doubtful; to be undecided.

To hang off; same as *To hang back*.

To hang on; to retain hold; to hold fast; to refuse to give up.

To hang on the lips or *words of*; to be charmed or entranced by the eloquence, as of a speaker or actor.

To hang out; (a) to continue unyieldingly, as in a course of conduct or thought; (b) colloquially, to locate, as in a profession; as, the doctor *hangs out* at 79 Gold street.

To hang over; to project; to threaten.

To hang to; to hold to; to take a firm hold upon.

To hang together; (a) to be strongly attached one to another; to agree in sentiment and action; (b) to be coherent or consistent; as, the parts of this story do not *hang together*.

hang, *n.* 1. A slope or declivity; amount of slope or declivity; as, the *hang* of a road.

2. The manner or style of hanging; as, the *hang* of drapery.

3. Nautically, same as *rake*.

4. In shipbuilding, the concavity of planking having the lower edge curving in to the ship's frame; opposed to *sny*.

5. Familiarity coming from practice or intuition; knack of using or doing; as, to get the *hang* of one's work.

6. Underlying thought; main thread; drift; as, the *hang* of a speech.

7. In provincial English, (a) a close clump of weeds; (b) a fruit-crop.

han'gär, *n.* A carriage shed; a shed for housing aeroplanes.

hang'bird, *n.* Any bird that builds a hanging nest; specifically, an oriole; an icterine bird, best represented by the Baltimore oriole, *Icterus galbula*; called also *hanging-bird* and *hangnest*.

hang'by, *n.*; *pl.* **hang'bies**. A subservient fellow; a bore. [Obs.]

hang'dog, *n.* A low, mean, and depraved person.

hang'dog, *a.* Having the appearance of a dog expecting punishment for doing wrong; mean; despicable; degraded.

hang'ẽr, *n.* 1. One who hangs or causes to be hanged.

2. That which hangs or is suspended; specifically, (a) a short broadsword, incurvated at the point, which was suspended from the girdle; (b) a hanging or sloping wood or grove.

3. That from which anything is hung or suspended, as (a) the girdle or belt from which the sword was suspended at the side; (b) in machinery, a part that suspends a journal-box in which shafting, etc., runs; called also *hanging-bracket*.

Hanger or Hanging-bracket.

hang'ẽr-on', *n.*; *pl.* **hang'ẽrs-on'**. One who besets another importunately in soliciting favors; an unwelcome dependent.

hang'ing, *n.* 1. The act of suspending or the state of being suspended.

2. Execution by the gallows.

3. Anything that hangs, as a window-curtain, a portière, or a chandelier.

4. [*pl.*] The drapings of the walls of a room.

hang'ing, *a.* 1. Suspended; having attachment above and being loose below.

2. Fitted for attaching by suspension; as, a *hanging*-hook or a *hanging*-ring.

Hanging garden; a garden elevated by artificial means, as by pillars, masonry, or terraces; as, the *hanging gardens* of ancient Babylon.

Hanging indention; see under *Indention*.

Hanging side or *hanging wall*; in mining, the overhanging side of an ore-vein beneath which miners work.

Hanging sleeves; (a) loose flowing sleeves, as of a lady's dress; (b) loose bands of goods similar to the dress attached at the shoulders and hanging down the back.

hang'ing-bird, *n.* Same as *Hangbird*.

hang'ing-but"tress, *n.* In architecture, a buttress not standing solid on a foundation, but supported on a corbel; used chiefly as a feature in decoration.

hang'ing-com"pass, *n.* A compass so suspended as to provide for its observation from beneath.

hang'ing-moss, *n.* 1. Any one of several species of lichen of the genus *Usnea* growing upon rocks and trees; called also *tree-moss* and *tree-hair*.

2. The long black moss of southern United States, *Tillandsia usneoides*; called also *long-beard*.

hang'ing-pōst, *n.* A post of a gate or door to which the hinges are fastened.

hang'ing-rāil, *n.* The strip on a hanging-post to which the hinges are attached.

hang'ing-stile, *n.* In architecture, the stile in a door-frame or window-frame holding the hangings, such as hinges, pulleys, etc.

hang'măn, *n.* One who hangs another; a public executioner; also, a term of reproach.

Hanging-buttress.

hang'măn-ship, *n.* The office of a hangman; skill in the performance of official duty as a public executioner.

hang'nāil, *n.* [A corruption of *agnail*, from AS. *angnægle*; *ange*, vexation, trouble, and *nægel*, a nail.] A small piece or sliver of skin which hangs from the root of a finger-nail.

hang'nest, *n.* A hangbird.

hang'wŏrm, *n.* Same as *Dropworm*.

hank, *n.* [Ice. *hönk*, a hank, coil, skein; *hankî*, the hasp of a chest.]

1. Two or more skeins of thread or silk tied together.

2. In ships, rings of wood, etc., fixed on stays, to confine the sails when hoisted.

3. A rope or withe for fastening a gate. [Prov. Eng.]

4. A string, tie, clasp, or chain for fastening and holding.

hank, *v.t.*; hanked, *pt.*, *pp.*; hanking, *ppr.* 1. To form into hanks.

2. To fasten with or as if with a rope. [Prov. Eng.]

han'kẽr, *v.i.*; hankered, *pt.*, *pp.*; hankering, *ppr.* [D. *hunkeren*, to long for, hanker.]

1. To long for with a keen appetite and uneasiness; as, to *hanker for* fruit or *after* fruit.

2. To have a vehement desire for (something) accompanied with uneasiness; it is followed by *after* or *for*; as, to *hanker after* the diversions of the town.

han'kẽr-ing, *n.* A keen appetite that causes uneasiness till it is gratified; vehement desire to possess or enjoy.

han'kẽr-ing-ly, *adv.* Longingly.

han'key-pan'key, *n.* See *Hanky-panky*.

han'kle, *v.t.* To twist. [Obs.]

hanks'ite, *n.* In mineralogy, a sulphate and carbonate of sodium, occurring in hexagonal crystals, found in California; named from H. G. Hanks, a mineralogist of California.

han'ky-pan'ky, *n.* The meaningless professional talk of a juggler or magician; hence, jugglery or legerdemain.

Han-ō-vē'ri-ăn, *a.* 1. Relating to Hanover, or to the natives and citizens of Hanover.

2. Pertaining to the English royal house of Hanover.

Han-ō-vē'ri-ăn, *n.* 1. One of the house of Hanover; also, in English history, an adherent of the house of Hanover.

2. An inhabitant of Hanover.

han'särd, *n.* The official record of the debates of the British Parliament; so named after the first publisher, Luke Hansard; also applied to the official record of the Canadian Parliament.

Han'särd, *n.* A merchant or citizen of one of the Hanse towns.

hanse, *n.* [OFr. *hanse*; M.H.G. *hanse*, an association of merchants; O.H.G. *hansa*, a band of men.]

1. A society, league, or confederation.

2. [H—] The Hanseatic league; also used adjectively.

Hanse town; any one of the towns embraced in the Hanseatic league.

hanse, *n.* See *Hance*.

han-sē-at'ic, *a.* 1. Relating to a hanse, league, or confederation.

2. [H—] Pertaining to the confederation of the Hanse towns.

Hanseatic league; an association of certain cities of Europe for the promotion of commerce, formed originally of German towns in the twelfth century and lasting nearly four hundred years, at one time including eighty-five municipalities. The *Hanseatic league* no longer exists, but its remnants, Lübeck, Hamburg, and Bremen are called free cities, and are frequently referred to as Hanse towns.

han'sel, *n.* and *v.t.* Same as *Handsel*.

han'sel-ines, *n.pl.* A sort of breeches. [Obs.]

han'sŏm, han'sŏm-cab, *n.* [Named after *Hansom*, its inventor.] A low-hung hackney carriage with two wheels, seating two persons and having an elevated seat behind for the driver.

ha-num', *n.* [Turk. *khanum*, lady.] A Turkish title of respect for a lady, especially a lady of rank, equivalent to English *Mrs.* or *madam*.

han'u-man, *n.* [Sans., lit., having a jaw, from *hanu*, jaw.]

1. In zoölogy, a sacred monkey of India, *Semnopithecus entellus*; written also *hoonoomaun*.

2. [H—] In Hindu mythology, a god or idol having the characteristics of a monkey.

hap, *n.* [ME. *hap*, *hæp*, *happe*; Ice. *happ*, chance, luck.]

1. That which comes suddenly or unexpectedly; chance; fortune; accident; casual event.

Cursed be good *haps*, and cursed be they that build
Their hopes on *haps*. —Sidney.

2. Fate; fortune; luck.

hap, *v.i.* [ME. *happen*, from *hap*, *happe*; Ice. *happ*, chance, luck.] To happen; to befall; to come by chance. [Obs.]

hap, *v.t.* [ME. *happen*, to wrap, cover.] To wrap; to clothe; to cover. [Prov. Eng. and Scot.]

hap'ā-lōte, *n.* [Gr. *hapalos*, soft, and *ous*, *ōtos*, ear.] A jumping-mouse of Australia about the size of a rat and characterized by long, tapering ears and a tufted tail.

hā'pen-ny, *n.* A halfpenny. [Eng.]

hap'haz"ärd, *a.* Accidental; as, a *haphazard* meeting.

hap'haz"ärd, *n.* Chance; accident.

We take our principles at *haphazard*, on trust. —Locke.

haph-tä'ráh, *n.* [Heb.] In Jewish synagogues, the lesson read from the Prophets on every Sabbath and festival of the year, after the reading of the *parashah* or lesson from the law.

hap'less, *a.* Unlucky; unfortunate; luckless; unhappy; as, *hapless* youth; *hapless* maid.

hap'less-ly, *adv.* In a hapless or unlucky manner.

hap'lite, *n.* A mixture of quartz and orthoclase akin to felsite but of crystalline-granular structure, occurring in dikes.

hap-lo-. A combining form from Gr. *haploos*, single, simple. It is used in botany, zoölogy, surgery, etc., to signify onefold, single; as, *haplo*petalous, *haplo*dont.

Hap'lō-don, *n.* A genus of rodents; the sewellels.

hap'lō-dont, *a.* [*Haplo-*, and *odous*, *odontos*, a tooth.] In zoölogy, (a) having simple-crowned teeth; (b) relating to the *Haplodontidæ*.

hap'lō-dont, *n.* An animal with simple-crowned teeth; one of the *Haplodontidæ*.

Hap-lō-don'ti-dæ, *n.pl.* A family of rodents related to the beavers; the sewellels, *Haplodon*, constitute the sole genus.

hap-log'rȧ-phy, *n.* [*Haplo-*, and Gr. *-graphia*, from *graphein*, to write.] The inadvertent omission of a letter or letters or of a word in copying manuscript, as the writing of *hapily* for *happily*, etc.; also, a writing containing such omission.

Hȧ-plō'mī, *n.pl.* [*Haplo-*, and Gr. *ōmos*, shoulder.] A division of fishes including the pikes.

hap-lō-pet'ăl-ous, *a.* [*Haplo-*, and Gr. *petalon*, a leaf, petal.] In botany, having the petals in a single whorl.

hap-lō-stem'ō-nous, *a.* [*Haplo-*, and Gr. *stēmōn* (*-onos*), a thread.] In botany, having the stamens in one whorl; written also *aplostemonous*.

hap'ly, *adv.* 1. By hap, luck, accident, or chance; perchance; perhaps.

2. By accident; casually.

hā'p'ŏrth (-pērth), *n.* A halfpenny-worth; hence, a small quantity. [Colloq., Eng.]

hap'pen, *v.i.*; happened, *pt.*, *pp.*; happening, *ppr.* [ME. *happenen*, *hapnen*, a form of *happen*, from *happe*; Ice. *happ*, chance, luck.]

1. To occur or befall by chance; to come unexpectedly; to fall out; to chance; as, such things will *happen*.

2. To come to pass in the natural order of things; as, death *happens* to all of us.

To happen in; to arrive in a casual manner.

To happen on; to meet with; to find incidentally.

hap'pi-ly, *adv.* 1. In a happy manner or condition; in happy circumstances; as, they lived *happily* ever after.

2. By good fortune; luckily; as, we are *happily* met.

3. With address or dexterity; gracefully; felicitously; successfully; aptly; as, his allusions were most *happily* made.

4. Haply. [Rare.]

Syn.—Fortunately, contentedly, successfully, felicitously.

hap'pi-ness, *n.* 1. The agreeable sensation which springs from the enjoyment of good; that state of a being in which his desires are gratified by the enjoyment of pleasure without pain; felicity; blessedness; satisfaction.

2. Good luck; good fortune.

3. Fortuitous elegance; unstudied grace, particularly in writing or speaking.

For there's a *happiness*, as well as care. —Pope.

Syn.—Felicity, blessedness, bliss, aptness.

hap'py, *v.t.* To make happy. [Obs.]

hap'py, *a.*; *comp.* happier; *superl.* happiest. [ME. *happy*, from *hap*, *happe*; Ice. *happ*, good luck, chance, hap.]

1. Lucky; fortunate; successful.

Chemists have been more *happy* in finding experiments than the causes of them.—Boyle.

2. Being in the enjoyment of agreeable sensations from the possession of good; enjoying pleasure from the gratification of appetites or desires; blessed; satisfied.

He found himself *happiest* in communicating happiness to others. —Wirt.

3. Prosperous; having secure possession of good.

Happy is that people whose God is Jehovah. —Ps. cxliv. 15.

4. Supplying pleasure; furnishing enjoyment; agreeable; as, a *happy* occasion; a *happy* disposition.

5. Dexterous; ready; able; apt.

One gentleman is *happy* at a reply, another excels in a rejoinder. —Swift.

6. Harmonious; living in concord; enjoying the pleasures of friendship; as, a *happy* household.

7. Propitious; favorable; as, *happy* omens.

8. Intoxicated to the point of merriment. [Slang.]

Happy family; (a) a collection of animals of different propensities and habits, living together harmoniously; (b) ironically, an association of people of antagonistic views and feelings, as a political organization made up of different factions, each seeking to get the better of its antagonist.

Syn.—Lucky, fortunate, felicitous, successful, delighted, joyous, merry, blithesome, prosperous, glad, blissful.

hap'py-gō-luck'y, *a.* and *adv.* I. *a.* Shiftless; trusting to luck or chance; as, a *happy-go-lucky* character.

II. *adv.* Anyhow; just as may happen; at will.

hȧ-pū'kȧ, *n.* [New Zealand.] A large food-fish of New Zealand.

haque'but (hak'), *n.* See *Harquebus*.

hä'rä-ki'ri, *n.* [Japan., from *hara*, belly, and *kiri*, cutting, cut.]

1. Suicide by disembowelment, formerly practised by officials in Japan in accordance with a code of honor; also erroneously written *hari-kiri*, *hari-kari*.

2. Suicide; self-destruction; as, to commit political *hara-kiri*.

hȧ-rangue' (-rang'), *n.* [OFr. *harangue*, a public address, from O.H.G. *hring*, a ring, ring of people, arena.]

1. A speech addressed to a large assembly; an oration; a public address, especially one designed to excite action or to allay excitement in a multitude of hearers.

2. A declamation; a noisy, pompous, or irregular address; a tirade.

Syn.—Speech, oration, declamation, address, tirade.—*Speech* is generic; an *oration* is an elaborate and prepared speech; a *harangue* is a vehement appeal to the passions or a noisy, disputatious address.

hȧ-rangue', *v.i.*; harangued, *pt.*, *pp.*; haranguing, *ppr.* To make a public address or speech; as, he *harangued* without success.

hȧ-rangue', *v.t.* To address by a harangue; to speak to in an impassioned and forcible manner; as, to *harangue* a political club.

hȧ-rangue'fụl, *a.* Like a harangue.

hȧ-rang'uẽr (-ẽr), *n.* A fiery orator; one who addresses an assembly with vehemence or passion; a noisy declaimer.

hä'rä-nut, *n.* The stone-fruit of a plant native to India, *Terminalia citrina*.

har'ăss, *v.t.*; harassed (-ăst), *pt.*, *pp.*; harassing, *ppr.* [OFr. *harasser*, to tire out, vex.]

1. To weary; to fatigue to excess; to tire with bodily labor; as, to *harass* an army by a long march.

2. To weary with importunity, care, or perplexity; to tease; to perplex.

Nature oppressed and *harassed* out with care. —Addison.

3. To lay waste or desolate; to raid, as an enemy's country.

4. To scrape, as in dressing skins.

Syn.—Tire, worry, perplex, annoy, irritate.

har'ăss, *n.* 1. Waste; disturbance; devastation. [Obs.]

2. Worry; annoyance. [Rare.]

har'ăss-ẽr, *n.* One who harasses or teases; a spoiler.

har'ăss-ment, *n.* The act of harassing, or the condition of being harassed.

här'bin-ġẽr, *v.t.*; harbingered, *pt.*, *pp.*; harbingering, *ppr.* To act as a harbinger for; to announce; to precede; to presage; to foretell; as, the early flowers *harbinger* spring.

här'bin-ġẽr, *n.* [ME. *herbergeour*; OFr. *herbergeor*, one who provides a lodging, from *herbergier*, to provide a lodging.]

1. A forerunner; a precursor; one who or that which precedes and gives notice of the arrival of some person or thing.

2. One who provides or secures lodging for another; specifically, a royal officer who rode ahead of a traveling court to secure accommodations.

här'bin-ġẽr-ŏf-spring, *n.* A herb of the parsley family, *Erigenia bulbosa*, characterized by blooming very early and by the appearance of its flowers with white petals and brownish anthers, giving rise to its common name, *pepper-and-salt*.

här'bŏr, *v.t.*; harbored, *pt.*, *pp.*; harboring, *ppr.* 1. To shelter; to secure; to secrete; as, to *harbor* a thief.

2. To entertain; to permit to lodge, rest, or reside; as, to *harbor* malice or revenge.

här'bŏr, *v.i.* 1. To lodge or abide for a time; to receive entertainment.

This night let's *harbor* here in York.—Shak.

2. To take shelter.

här'bŏr, här'bŏur, *n.* [ME. *harbor*, *harber*, *herber*, *herberwe*, *herberge*; Ice. *herbergi*, originally, a shelter for soldiers; *herr*, an army, and *bjarga*, to save, help.]

1. A lodging; a place of entertainment and rest.

For *harbor* at a thousand doors they knocked. —Dryden.

2. A port or haven for ships; a bay or inlet of a sea or large lake in which ships can moor and be sheltered from wind and wave; any navigable water where ships can ride in safety.

3. An asylum; a shelter; a place of safety from storms or danger.

4. In glass-works, a box for holding mixed materials before they are fused.

5. A hiding-place of deer; a covert. [Obs.]

Close harbor; a harbor with gates at the entrance; a harbor that may be opened or closed at will.

Floating harbor; see under *Floating*.

Open harbor; a roadstead; an unsheltered harbor.

här'bŏr-āġe, här'bŏur-āġe, *n.* Shelter; entertainment; lodging.

här'bŏr-dūeṣ, *n.pl.* Certain charges to which a ship or its cargo is subjected for the use of a harbor, moorings, etc.

här'bŏr-ẽr, här'bŏur-ẽr, *n.* One who entertains or shelters.

här'bŏr-gas"ket, *n.* One of a series of broad but short and well-blacked gaskets, placed at equal distances on the yard of a ship, for showing off a well-furled sail in port.

här'bŏr-less, här'bŏur-less, *a.* Without a harbor; destitute of shelter or a lodging.

här'bŏr-log, *n.* That part of the logbook which belongs to the period during which a ship is in port.

här'bŏr-mas"tẽr, *n.* An officer who has charge of the mooring of ships, and executes the regulations respecting harbors.

här'bŏr-ōugh (-ō), *n.* An inn; a lodging; a shelter. [Obs.]

här'bŏr-ous, här'bŏur-ous, *a.* Hospitable; affording shelter. [Obs.]

här'bŏr-rēach, *n.* The reach or stretch of a winding river which leads direct to a harbor.

här'bŏr-sēal, *n.* The common seal, *Phoca vitulina*.

här'bŏr-wätch, *n.* An anchor-watch.

här'brōugh, här'brōw, *n.* [Obs.] See *Harborough*.

härd, *a.*; *comp.* harder; *superl.* hardest. [ME. *hard*; AS. *heard*, hard, firm, brave.]

1. Firm; solid; compact; not easily penetrated or separated into parts; not yielding to pressure; applied to material bodies, and opposed to *soft*; as, *hard* wood; *hard* flesh; a *hard* apple.

2. Difficult to the understanding; not easy to the intellect.

In which are some things *hard* to be understood. —2 Pet. iii. 16.

3. Difficult of accomplishment; not easy to be done or executed; laborious; arduous; as, a *hard* task; a disease *hard* to cure.

4. Difficult to endure; oppressive; severe; cruel; distressing; painful; as, a *hard* lot; a *hard* blow.

5. Unfeeling; not easily moved by pity; not susceptible of kindness, mercy, or other tender affections; harsh; severe; obdurate; exacting; as, a *hard* heart; a *hard* landlord.

6. Difficult to withstand or overcome; powerful.

A power which will always be too *hard* for them. —Addison.

7. Rough; acid; sour, as liquors; as, the cider is *hard*.

8. Harsh; stiff; conventional; constrained; unnatural.

Figures *harder* than the marble itself. —Dryden.

9. In phonetics, applied (a) to the consonants *f*, *k*, *p*, *s*, *t*, and the sound of *th* in *thin*, which are all capable of being pronounced without any voice sound, as distinguished from the consonants *v*, *g* (as in *get*), *b*, *z*, *d*, and the sound of *th* in *thine*, which are incapable of being so pronounced; (b) to the sound of *c* as in *corn* and *g* as in *get*, as distinguished from the sounds of the same letters in *city*, *gin*, etc.

10. In painting, harsh; having the lights and shades too strongly marked and too close to each other.

11. Zealous; industrious; persevering; as, a *hard* worker; a *hard* student.

12. Coarse; unpalatable or scanty; as, *hard* fare.

13. Impregnated with lime so as to be incapable of dissolving soap; said of water.

14. Reprobate; bad; as, a *hard* citizen. [Colloq.]

Hard cash; actual cash; money in hand, as distinguished from any equivalent, as personal property, debts to be collected, etc.

Hard clam; see first *Clam*, n.

Hard coal; anthracite coal.

Hard money; coin, as distinguished from paper money.

In hard condition; in good muscular condition; said of prize-fighters, athletes, race-horses, etc.

Syn.—Solid, firm, arduous, difficult, harsh, severe, oppressive.

härd, *adv.* 1. Close; near.

My soul followeth *hard* after thee.—Ps. lxiii. 8.

2. With pressure; with urgency; vehemently; vigorously; energetically; as, to work *hard* for a living; to run *hard*; to hold *hard*; to blow *hard*.

And prayed so *hard* for mercy from the prince. —Dryden.

3. With difficulty; as, the vehicle moves *hard*.
4. Uneasily; vexatiously.
5. Closely; so as to raise difficulties.

The question is *hard* set. —Browne.

6. Securely; tightly; firmly; fast.

Hard by; near at hand; in close proximity.

Hard up; short of money or of anything needful; in straitened circumstances. [Colloq.]

Hard is often used by seamen to add emphasis to other words of command, and to indicate that the order is to be executed with energy or despatch. When the order is one for turning the helm, as in *hard alee, hard aweather! hard aport! hard up!* etc., the meaning is that the helm is to be turned as much as possible in the proper direction.

härd, *v.t.* To harden. [Obs.]

härd, *n.* 1. The hard part of anything; that which is hard, as the shell of a nut.
2. A hard roadway or path; a paved way. [Prov. Eng.]
3. [*pl.*] A mixture of alum and salt used by bakers to whiten bread.
4. A ford across a river or a causeway over a swamp.

härd′bāke, *n.* A kind of sweetmeat of boiled brown sugar or treacle with blanched almonds, and flavored with the juice of lemons, oranges, or the like.

härd′bēam, *n.* See *Hornbeam*.

härd′bill, *n.* A grosbeak.

härd′en, *v.t.*; hardened, *pt., pp.*; hardening, *ppr.* [ME. *hardnen, hardenen*, to make hard.]
1. To make hard or more hard; to make firm or compact; to indurate; as, to *harden* iron or steel; to *harden* clay.
2. To inure; to render firm; to strengthen; to toughen; as, to *harden* one to a climate or to labor.
3. To confirm in wickedness, opposition, effrontery, obstinacy, or enmity.

Harden not your heart. —Ps. xcv. 8.

härd′en, *v.i.* 1. To become hard or more hard; to acquire solidity or more compactness; as, mortar *hardens* by drying.
2. To become inured; to become unfeeling.

Här-den-bẽr′gi-ȧ, *n.* [From Countess *Hardenberg*, sister of Baron von Hügel, a German traveler.] A genus of leguminous herbs or woody climbing plants, natives of Australia. *Hardenbergia monophylla* is sometimes cultivated in greenhouses.

härd′ened, *a.* Made hard, or more hard or compact; made unfeeling; made obstinate; confirmed in error or vice.

Syn.—Callous, obdurate, insensible, unfeeling.

härd′en-ẽr, *n.* One who or that which makes hard or more firm and compact; specifically, one who brings tools up to the required temper.

Här-dē′ri-ăn, *a.* [Named after J. J. *Harder*, a Swiss anatomist.] Designating a gland of the nictitating membrane in the orbit of the eye in some animals.

härd′=fā″vōred, *a.* Having coarse features; harsh of countenance.

härd′=fā″vōred-ness, *n.* Coarseness of features.

härd′=fēa″tūred, *a.* Having coarse features.

härd′fērn, *n.* Any fern of the genus *Lomaria*, especially *Lomaria Spicant*.

härd′=fist″ed, *a.* 1. Having hard or strong hands, as a laborer.
2. Close-fisted; covetous.

härd′=fought (-fot), *a.* Vigorously contested; as, a *hard-fought* battle.

härd′=grȧss, *n.* The name of any one of various grasses of several genera, as *Rottbœllia, Ægilops*, and *Schlerochloa*.

härd′hack, *n.* In botany, *Spiræa tomentosa*, a plant of the rose family, common in pastures and low grounds, and celebrated for its astringent properties.

härd′=hand″ed, *a.* Having hard hands, as a laborer.

härd′head (-hed), *n.* 1. Clash or collision of heads in contest. [Obs.]
2. An old copper coin of Scotland.
3. In botany, *Centaurea nigra*, the knapweed.
4. In zoölogy, one of several animals; (a) the gray whale of California; (b) the menhaden; (c) the gray gurnard, *Trigla gurnardus*; (d) the ruddy duck.
5. A round boulder found among gravel.
6. A kind of coarse sponge.
7. An alloy left after refining tin.

härd′=head″ed, *a.* Shrewd; intelligent or clear-headed and firm.

härd′=head″ed-ness, *n.* Good judgment.

härd′=heärt″ed, *a.* Cruel; pitiless; unfeeling; inhuman; inexorable.

härd′=heärt″ed-ly, *adv.* In a hard-hearted or cruel manner.

härd′=heärt″ed-ness, *n.* Want of feeling or tenderness; cruelty; inhumanity.

här′di-head (-hed), *n.* [Obs.] See *Hardihood*.

här′di-hood, *n.* Boldness, united with firmness and constancy of mind; bravery; intrepidity; also, effrontery.

It is the society of numbers which gives *hardihood* to iniquity. —Buckminster.

Syn.—Audacity, courage, impudence, resolution, boldness, fearlessness, effrontery.

här′di-ly, *adv.* 1. In a hardy manner; with hardiness.
2. Certainly; surely. [Obs.]

här′di-ment, *n.* [OFr. *hardiment*, from *hardi*, hardy.] Hardihood. [Obs.]

här′di-ness, *n.* 1. Boldness; firm courage; intrepidity; assurance; bravery.
2. Capacity for physical endurance.
3. Hardship; fatigue. [Obs.]

härd′ish, *a.* Rather hard.

härd′=lā″bōred, *a.* Wrought with severe labor; elaborate; studied; as, a *hard-labored* poem.

härd′ly, *adv.* 1. With difficulty; with great labor.

Recovering *hardly* what he lost before. —Dryden.

2. Scarcely; barely; almost not; not quite or wholly; not probably.

Hardly shall you find any one so bad, but he desires the credit of being thought good. —South.

3. Severely; unfavorably; as, to think *hardly* of public men.
4. Rigorously; oppressively; as, the prisoners were *hardly* used or treated.

Syn.—Barely, merely, scarcely, severely.

härd′mouth, *n.* A fish found in the Columbia river, having a remarkably shaped jaw set in a bony plate with a straight edge like a chisel; also called *chisel-mouth*.

härd′=mouthed, *a.* Not sensitive to the bit; not easily governed; as, a *hard-mouthed* horse.

härd′ness, *n.* [ME. *hardnesse*; AS. *heardnes*, from *heard*, hard.]
1. Firmness; close union of component parts; compactness; solidity; the quality of bodies which resists impression or the separation of their particles; opposed to *softness*.
2. The state of being hard in any sense; as, *hardness* of comprehension, of an undertaking, or of the times.
3. Obduracy; impenitence; a confirmed state of wickedness; as, *hardness* of heart.
4. In mineralogy, the quality of bodies which enables them to resist abrasion of their surfaces, the diamond being the hardest body known.
5. The quality imparted to water by reason of holding mineral matter in solution.

härd′pan, *n.* 1. A hard layer of earth beneath the soil, composed mainly of clay, and impervious to water; hence, any solid basis.
2. The lowest level; lowest foundation; as, prices have reached *hardpan*. [Colloq.]

härd′=pēar, *n.* In botany, a small tree of South Africa, the hardwood of which is used to make musical instruments.

härds, *n.pl.* [ME. *hardes, herdes*, from AS. pl. *heordan*, hards.] The refuse or coarse part of flax; tow.

härd′=shell, *a.* 1. In zoölogy, covered with a hard shell; as, a *hard-shell* clam.
2. Fixed; immovable as to belief or practice; uncompromising. [Colloq.]

härd′ship, *n.* 1. Toil; fatigue; severe labor or want; whatever oppresses the body; suffering; adversity; affliction; as, to suffer the *hardships* of poverty.
2. Injury; oppression; injustice; hard treatment.

Syn.—Trial, burden, privation, affliction, injury.

härd′spun, *a.* Tightly twisted.

härd′tack, *n.* Large, coarse, hard biscuit furnished to soldiers or sailors; sea-biscuit.

härd′tāil, *n.* A fish, *Caranx chrysos* or yellow mackerel.

härd′=vis″āged, *a.* Having coarse features; of a harsh countenance.

härd′wāre, *n.* A general name for all wares made of iron or other metal, as pots, kettles, saws, knives, etc.

härd′wāre-măn, *n.* A maker or seller of hardware.

härd′wood, *n.* Wood of a solid texture, such as oak, ash, or hickory.

härd′wood, *a.* Made of hardwood; containing trees furnishing hardwood; as, *hardwood* furniture; a *hardwood* forest.

härd′wood=tree, *n.* A rubiaceous shrub or small tree, *Ixora ferrea*, of the West Indies, valued for its wood.

här′dy, *a.*; *comp.* hardier; *superl.* hardiest. [ME. *hardy, hardi*; OFr. *hardi*, hardy, bold, daring, pp. of *hardir*, to make bold; O.H.G. *harti, herti*, hardy.]
1. Bold; brave; stout; daring; resolute.
2. Strong; firm; compact.

An unwholesome blast may shake in pieces his *hardy* fabric. —South.

3. Confident; full of assurance; impudent; audacious.
4. Inured to fatigue or exposure; as, a *hardy* soldier; a *hardy* plant.

Syn.—Inured, robust, strong, stout-hearted, vigorous, resistant, enduring.

här′dy, *n.* In blacksmithing, a chisel-like tool with a square shank set into a hole of the anvil and used for cutting off pieces from iron rods, etc.

här′dy=hōle, *n.* The hole in an anvil in which a hardy is set.

hāre, *v.t.* To excite, tease, or worry; to harry. [Obs.]

European Hare (*Lepus timidus*).

hāre, *n.* [ME. *hare*; AS. *hara*, a hare.]
1. The common name of the rodent quadrupeds of the genus *Lepus*, with long ears, a short tail, soft hair, a divided upper lip, long hind legs, and hairy soles. The species are numerous and found in most countries, especially those of the northern hemisphere. All closely resemble the common *hare* of Europe, *Lepus timidus*. Some species whiten with the approach of winter, including the American varying hare, *Lepus americanus*.
2. [H—] In astronomy, a constellation situated directly under Orion.

Belgian hare; a species of hare bred for its fur, which is used in the manufacture of hats, and for its flesh as food.

Chief hare, little chief hare; see *Pika*.

First catch your hare; a direction occurring in a well-known cookery-book and used as an aphorism to the effect that, before disposing of a thing, you ought to make sure of the possession of it. In reality the saying arose from a misprint, *catch* being an error for *case*, in the sense of to skin. Properly therefore the direction is, first *case* (skin) your hare, etc.

Hare and hounds; a field-sport in which one or two of a party represent hares and the rest hounds, in imitation of the sport of hare-hunting with hounds. The hare or hares set out from the starting-place, scattering bit of white paper as they go, the hounds following after an interval and endeavoring to catch them before they reach a point previously determined upon.

Mad as a March hare; crazy; eccentric; wild as a hare at breeding-time.

hāre′bell, *n.* [ME. *harebelle*; *hare*, a hare, and *belle*, bell.] A plant of the genus *Campanula*, with campaniform or bell-shaped flowers; the bluebell.

Harebell (*Campanula rotundifolia*).

hāre′brāin, *n.* A wild, careless, foolish person.

hāre′brāined, hāre′brāin, *a.* Wild; giddy; volatile; heedless.

hāre′foot, *n.* 1. A foot resembling that of a hare, slender and extending forward.
2. Figuratively, a swift-footed person.
3. A grouse or ptarmigan.
4. Same as *Hare's-foot*, 1.

hāre′=heärt″ed, *a.* Timorous; easily frightened.

hāre′hound, *n.* A hound used to catch hares.

hāre′=kan-gȧ-rōō″, *n.* A small kangaroo found in Australia, much like a hare in size and habits.

har′eld, *n.* In zoölogy, the *Harelda glacialis*, or long-tailed duck, valued for its down.

hāre′lip, *n.* An upper lip congenitally malformed by a vertical fissure, causing it to resemble a hare's lip.

hāre′lipped (-lipt), *a.* Having a harelip.

hār′em, *n.* [Turk. *harem*; Ar. *haram*, anything forbidden, a sacred place or thing, from *harama*, to forbid, prohibit.]
1. The division allotted to women in the larger dwelling-houses of Mohammedans.
2. The women, especially the wives and concubines, constituting the household of a Mohammedan.
3. A place regarded as sacred among Mohammedans; specifically, either of the two cities Mecca and Medina, from which infidels are excluded. [Rare.]

hȧ-ren′gi-fōrm, *a.* Shaped like a herring.

hãre's'-bāne, *n.* In botany, a species of *Aconitum*, of the crowfoot family; wolf's-bane.

hãre's'-ēar, *n.* A plant of the parsley family, genus *Bupleurum*, having a leaf resembling the ear of a hare.

hãre's'-foot, *n.* 1. A species of red clover, *Trifolium arvense*; also called *harefoot, rabbit-foot clover*, and *stone-clover*.

2. A malvaceous tree of tropical America valued for its wood, which on account of its lightness is used in building boats, rafts, etc.; named from the appearance of the cotton protruding when the boll ripens.

Hare's-foot fern; a fern native in the Madeira and Canary Islands, characterized by its hairy rootstocks.

hãre's'-let"tuce, *n.* The common sow-thistle, *Sonchus oleraceus*; also called *hare-thistle*.

hãre's'-pärs"ley, *n.* An umbelliferous European plant, *Anthriscus sylvestris*.

hãre's'-tāil, *n.* A grass of the sedge family.

Hare's-tail grass; a grass characterized by a perianth of white cottony fibers resembling a hare's tail.

här'fang, *n.* [Sw. *harfang*, lit., hare-catcher; *hare*, hare, and *fanga*, to catch, seize.] A large arctic owl, white with blackish spots; named from its devouring hares.

hä-ri-ä'li-grȧss, *n.* The East Indian name of Bermuda-grass.

har'i-cōt (-kō), *n.* [Fr.] 1. A kind of ragout of meat and vegetables.

2. The kidney-bean or French bean.

har'i-ẽr, *n.* See *Harrier*.

hä'ri-kä'ri, *n.* See *Hara-kiri*.

har"i-ō-lā'tion, *n.* [L. *hariolatio (-onis)*, from *hariolari*, to foretell, from *hariolus*, a soothsayer.] Prognostication; soothsaying. [Obs.]

hãr'ish, *a.* Like a hare.

härk, *v.i.* [Contr. of *hearken*.] To listen; to lend the ear. This word is rarely used, except in the imperative mode, *hark*, meaning listen, hear.

härk, *v.t.* To listen to; to hear.

Hark away! Hark forward! cries used in hunting to urge hounds forward.

Hark back! a hunter's cry to recall the hounds when on the wrong trail.

To hark back; to call back to the original point, as dogs in the chase; hence, to return to a point previously passed, as in a discourse.

härk'en, heärk'en, *v.i.*; harkened, hearkened, *pt., pp.*; harkening, hearkening, *ppr.* [ME. *harkenen, herknen*; AS. *hercnian, hyrcnian, heorcnian*, to hark, listen, a derivative with formative *-c, -k*, from *hyran, hiéran*, to hear.] To listen; to lend the ear; to attend to what is uttered, as to words of advice or admonition.

Dear mother Ida, *harken* ere I die.—Tennyson.

The furies *hearken*, and their snakes uncurl. —Dryden.

härk'en, heärk'en, *v.t.* 1. To hear by listening. [Rare.]

2. To give close attention to. [Rare.]

To harken out; to seek out; to hunt for. [Obs.]

härk'en-ẽr, heärk'en-ẽr, *n.* One who harkens; a listener.

härl, haurl, *v.t.* 1. To drag along with force. [Obs.]

2. To roughcast, as a wall, with lime. [Scot.]

3. To entangle. [Prov. Eng.]

4. To slit the hind leg of (an animal carcass), for the purpose of suspension. [Prov. Eng.]

härl, *n.* [ME. *harlen*, to drag, pull.]

1. The act of dragging. [Scot.]

2. Any substance made up of filaments, as the combings of flax, hair, etc.

3. Property dishonestly obtained.

4. A feather-barb from a peacock's tail used in dressing a hook for fly-fishing.

Här'lech, *n.* [Named after *Harlech*, in Wales.] In geology, the name applied to a group of rocks of the Lower Silurian; also called *Harlech grits*.

Här'lē-ăn, *a.* Relating to Robert Harley, Earl of Oxford, and Edward Harley, his son; as, the *Harleian* collection in the British Museum, which consists of several thousand manuscripts.

här'le-quin (-kin *or* -kwin), *a.* 1. Like a harlequin in character and action; clownish.

2. Characterized by variety in color; fantastic in appearance.

Harlequin bat; an Indian chiropter, *Scotophilus ornatus*, remarkable for its coloring, pale-tawny brown variegated with white spots.

Harlequin beetle; a longicorn coleopter, *Acrocinus longimanus*, resembling a harlequin in the colors of the elytra, which are gray, red, and black.

Harlequin cabbage-bug; same as *Cabbage-bug*.

Harlequin caterpillar; the moth *Euchætes egle* in the larval state, characterized by tufts of white, black, and orange.

Harlequin duck; an arctic ash-colored duck, the male fantastically spotted with white, with eyelids and flanks red.

Harlequin moth; a geometrid moth, *Eufitchia ribearia*, the larva of which feeds on the leaves of the currant and gooseberry; called also *currant-moth, magpie-moth*, and *harlequin*.

Harlequin opal; in mineralogy, an opal characterized by a play of varied colors on a red or reddish ground; one of the precious or noble opals.

Harlequin snake; a venomous snake, *Elaps fulvius*, of southern United States, ringed with red and black.

här'le-quin (-kin *or* -kwin), *n.* [OFr. *harlequin*, a harlequin, from *hierlekin, hellequin*, a demon, Satan.]

1. In French and Italian comedy and modern pantomime, a clownish character, in a costume fantastically formed and ornamented with various colors, bearing in his hand a wand, and playing amusing tricks upon the other actors.

2. Any one who exhibits the characteristics of a stage *harlequin*; a buffoon; a clownish fellow.

3. The harlequin opal.

här'le-quin, *v.t.* and *v.i.*; harlequined, *pt., pp.*; harlequining, *ppr.* I. *v.t.* To remove as if by a harlequin's trick; to conjure away.

II. *v.i.* To play the droll; to make sport by playing ludicrous tricks.

här"le-quin-āde', *n.* [Fr., from OFr. *harlequin*, a harlequin.]

1. A kind of pantomime, or that part of a pantomime which follows the transformation scene, enacted principally by the harlequin and the clown.

2. Buffoonery, or that which resembles the buffoonery of a harlequin; fantastic play.

här'le-quin-ẽr-y (-kin-), *n.* Harlequinade; pantomime.

här'le-quin-flow"ẽr, *n.* In botany, any one of the variegated species of *Sparaxis*, an iridaceous cultivated plant from South Africa.

här'lock, *n.* A plant mentioned by Shakspere, not identified, but probably the burdock.

här'lŏt, *n.* [ME. *harlot, herlot*; OFr. *harlot, herlot, arlot*, a vagabond.]

1. A woman who prostitutes her body for hire; a prostitute; a common woman.

2. A manservant; a churl. [Obs.]

3. A base person; a rogue; a cheat. [Obs.]

här'lŏt, *a.* Wanton; lewd; low; base.

här'lŏt, *v.i.* To practise lewdness.

här'lŏt-īze, *v.i.* To play the harlot.

här'lŏt-ry, *n.*; *pl.* **här'lŏt-ries.** 1. The trade or practice of prostitution; habitual or customary lewdness.

2. Ribaldry; obscenity; profligacy.

3. A woman of ill-fame. [Obs.]

4. False show; meretriciousness. [Obs.]

härm, *n.* [ME. *harm, herm*; AS. *hearm*, grief, injury; Ice. *harmr*, grief; Dan. *harme*; Sw. *harm*, anger, grief; Russ. *srame*, shame; Sans. *çrama*, toil, fatigue.]

1. Physical or material injury; hurt; damage; detriment; misfortune.

2. The thing causing loss, damage, or injury.

3. Moral wrong; evil; mischief; wickedness.

härm, *v.t.*; harmed, *pt., pp.*; harming, *ppr.* [ME. *harmen, hermen, harmien*; AS. *hearmian*, to hurt, injure, from *hearm*, grief, injury.] To hurt; to injure; to damage; to inflict harm upon.

här'mȧ-lȧ, *n.* See *Harmel*.

här'mȧ-līne, här'mȧ-lin, *n.* [*Harmala* and *-in, -ine*.] In chemistry, a compound, bitter yellow salt, $C_{13}H_{14}N_2O$, found in the coverings of harmel seeds.

här-mat'tăn, *n.* [Ar.] An intensely hot dry wind accompanied by clouds of dust, blowing at intervals from the interior of Africa toward the west coast during the first three months of the year.

här'mel, *n.* [Ar. *harmal*.] A herb found in Africa and Asia, *Peganum Harmala*, possessing a very strong odor, the husks yielding the harmala red of commerce, and the seeds a vermifuge and disinfectant.

härm'fụl, *a.* Hurtful; injurious; noxious; detrimental; mischievous.

härm'fụl-ly, *adv.* In a harmful manner.

härm'fụl-ness, *n.* The state of being harmful.

här'min, här'mine, *n.* In chemistry, a white alkaloid, $C_{13}H_{12}N_2O$, crystalline in form, obtained from harmaline or from harmel seeds.

härm'less, *a.* 1. Destitute of power, tendency, or inclination to harm or injure; not hurtful; innocuous; as, *harmless* games; *harmless* drink.

2. Unhurt; undamaged; uninjured.

3. Free from loss or liability; as, to save one *harmless*.

Syn.—Innocent, inoffensive, unoffending, innoxious, innocuous.

härm'less-ly, *adv.* In a harmless manner.

härm'less-ness, *n.* The state of being harmless.

här-mō'ni-ȧ, *n.* [Gr. *harmonia*, harmony.] In anatomy, a suture with articulating parts having regular or nearly regular surfaces; as, the *harmonia* of the palatal bones; called also *harmony*.

här-mon'iç, här-mon'iç-ăl, *a.* [L. *harmonicus*; Gr. *harmonikos*, harmonic, from *harmonia*, harmony.]

1. Concordant; musical; consonant; as, *harmonic* sounds.

2. In music, relating to harmony; harmonious; especially, pertaining to the accessory sounds which accompany the predominant and apparently simple tone of any string, pipe, or other sonorous body.

3. In mathematics, having relations or properties bearing some resemblance to those of musical consonances; said of numbers, terms of certain ratios, proportions, and the like.

4. In anatomy, of or relating to a harmonia.

Harmonic interval; in music, the distance between two notes of a chord or between two consonant notes.

Harmonical mean; in arithmetic and algebra, a term used to express certain relations of numbers and quantities analogous to consonances in music.

Harmonic motion; the motion of a point at the foot of a perpendicular dropped from a point moving uniformly in the circumference of a circle, to a fixed diameter of the circle. Sometimes called *simple harmonic motion*, as distinguished from the combination of more than one harmonic motion.

Harmonic progression; see under *Progression*.

Harmonic proportion; see under *Proportion*.

Harmonic triad; in music, the common chord; the chord of a note with its third and fifth.

Harmonic Triad.

här-mon'iç, *n.* 1. In music, an overtone; a tone made in sympathetic response to another tone whose rate of vibration bears some simple ratio to the rate of the *harmonic*.

2. A note produced on a stringed instrument, as a guitar, by stopping a string lightly.

3. In mathematics, any one of several classes of functions.

här-mon'i-çȧ, *n.* A musical instrument; specifically, (a) a set of glasses or goblets partially filled with liquid and played by contact of the fingers; (b) a number of pieces of wood, glass, or metal, of varying sizes, played with a mallet or mallets; a xylophone; (c) a small reed instrument played by inspiration and expiration of the breath; a mouth-organ.

Harmonica.

här-mon'iç-ăl-ly, *adv.* 1. In a harmonic manner; musically; harmoniously; suitably.

2. In mathematics, in harmonic relation or progression.

här-mon'i-çŏn, *n.*; *pl.* **här-mon'i-çȧ.** [Gr. *harmonikon*, neut. of *harmonikos*, musical, from *harmonia*, harmony.]

1. A mechanical musical instrument imitating an orchestra; an orchestrion.

2. In acoustics, an apparatus in which a flame of hydrogen burning in a glass tube produces musical sounds; a singing-flame.

här-mon'içs, *n.* The doctrine or science of musical sounds.

här-mō'ni-ous, *a.* [L. *harmonia*, harmony.]

1. Adapted to each other; having the parts proportioned to each other; symmetrical.

God hath made the intellectual world *harmonious* and beautiful without us. —Locke.

2. Concordant; consonant; symphonious; musical; as, *harmonious* sounds are agreeable to the ear.

3. Agreeing; living in peace and friendship; as, a *harmonious* family or society.

Syn.—Congruous, accordant, proportioned, melodious, musical, dulcet, tuneful, agreeable.

här-mō'ni-ous-ly, *adv.* In a harmonious manner.

här-mō'ni-ous-ness, *n.* The state of being in harmony.

här-mon'i-phon, *n.* [Gr. *harmonia*, harmony, and *phōnē*, sound.] A musical wind-instrument consisting of a series of free reeds inserted in a tube like a clarinet and played by means of keys like those of an organ.

här'mō-nist, *n.* 1. In music, one skilled in the principles of harmony; a writer of harmony; a musical composer.

2. One who shows the agreement or harmony between corresponding passages of different writers or authors on the same subject.

3. [H—] One of a sect of Protestants from Württemberg, who settled in America in 1803 at Harmony, Pennsylvania. They hold their property in common, and consider marriage a civil contract. Also called *Economite* and *Rappist*.

Här'mō-nīte, *n.* See *Harmonist*, 3.

här-mō'ni-um, *n.* [Gr. *harmonion*, neut. of *harmonios*, harmonious, from *harmonia*, harmony.] A reed-organ supplied with air by foot-power; the usual term in England and France for all reed-organs.

här″mō-ni-zā′tion, *n.* The act of harmonizing or state of being harmonized.

här′mō-nīze, *v.i.*; harmonized, *pt.*, *pp.*; harmonizing, *ppr.* 1. To agree in action, adaptation, or effect; to agree in sense or purport; as, the arguments *harmonize*; the facts stated by different witnesses *harmonize*.

2. To be in peace and friendship, as individuals or families.

3. In music, to form a concord; to agree in sounds or musical effect; as, the tones *harmonize*.

här′mō-nīze, *v.t.* 1. To adjust in fit proportions; to cause to agree; to show the harmony or agreement of; to reconcile.

2. To make musical; to combine according to the laws of counterpoint; to set accompanying parts to, as an air or melody.

här′mō-nī-zēr, *n.* One who harmonizes.

här-mō-nom′e-tēr, *n.* [Gr. *harmonia*, harmony, and *metron*, a measure.] An instrument or monochord for measuring the harmonic relations of sounds, consisting of a single string stretched over movable bridges.

här′mō-ny, *n.*; *pl.* **här′mō-nieș.** [L. *harmonia*; Gr. *harmonia*, a fitting together, agreement, from *harmos*, a fitting, joining.]

1. The just adaptation of parts to each other in any system or combination of things intended to form a connected whole; as, the *harmony* of the universe.

2. Concord or agreement in views, sentiments, or manners, interests, etc.; good correspondence; peace and friendship; as, the citizens live in *harmony*.

3. A literary work which brings together parallel passages of historians respecting the same events and shows their agreement or consistency.

4. In music, (a) just proportion of sound; consonance; musical concord; the accordance of two or more sounds; that union of different sounds which pleases the ear, or a succession of such sounds called chords; (b) the science which treats of such sounds.

5. In anatomy, same as *Harmonia.*

Close harmony; harmony in which the notes composing the chords are separated by the least possible intervals.

Dispersed harmony; harmony in which the tones of the various parts are at wide intervals from each other.

Harmony of the spheres; same as *Music of the spheres* under *Music.*

Syn.—Accordance, agreement, amity, concord, congruity, unison, melody.

här′mōst, *n.* [Gr. *harmostēs*, a governor, from *harmozein*, to set in order, arrange.] In ancient Greece, a Spartan governor, regulator, or prefect.

här′mō-tōme, *n.* [Gr. *harmos*, a joint, and *tomē*, a cutting.] In mineralogy, a hydrous silicate of the zeolite group; called also *cross-stone* from the form of its crystals.

härn, *a.* and *n.* [Scot.] I. *a.* Composed of a coarse kind of linen.

II. *n.* Very coarse linen.

här′ness, *n.* [ME. *harneis*, *harneys*; OFr. *harnas*, *harnois*, armor; Arm. *harnez*, armor, old iron, from *houarn*, iron.]

1. The early name for the armor and weapons of a soldier; restrictedly and, in modern poetical usage, a suit of armor.

2. The equipment of any animal, except those bearing a yoke, as the ox, by which it is fitted for draft and direction, consisting in modern form of a bridle and reins used in guiding, and a collar, traces, etc., used in drawing.

3. Figuratively, an equipment of one at labor; a confining cause or causes; as, always in the *harness.*

4. The apparatus in a loom by which the sets of warp threads are shifted alternately to form the shed. It consists of the heddles and their means of support and motion. Called also *mounting.*

To die in harness; see under *Die.*

här′ness, *v.t.*; harnessed (-nest), *pt.*, *pp.*; harnessing, *ppr.* 1. To dress in armor; to equip with armor for war, as a horseman.

> *Harnessed* in rugged steel. —Rowe.

2. To equip for draft; to put a harness on.

> *Harness* the horses. —Jer. xlvi. 4.

3. To equip or furnish for defense.

här′ness-cask, *n.* Among seamen, a cask lashed to the deck of a vessel, in which is kept the salt meat for daily use; called also *harness-tub.*

här′nessed, *a.* Having marks as if equipped with harness; said of animals.

Harnessed antelope; a guib.

Harnessed moth; same as *Tiger-moth.*

här′ness-ēr, *n.* One who harnesses.

här′ness-māk″ēr, *n.* One whose occupation is the making of harness.

här′ness-shaft, *n.* A device which guides the heddles in a loom.

härnș, *n.pl.* Brains. [Scot.]

härp, *n.* [ME. *harpe*; AS. *hearpe*, a harp.]

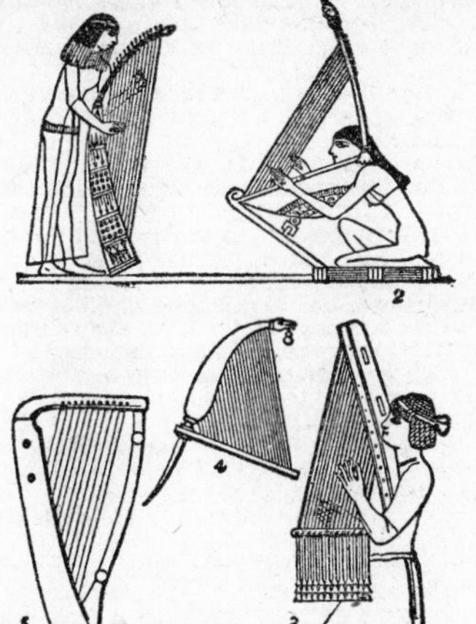

Ancient Harps.
1, 2. Egyptian. 3. Assyrian. 4. Persian. 5. Anglo-Saxon.

1. In music, a stringed instrument of a triangular figure, held upright, and played with the fingers.

2. [H—] In astronomy, a constellation; called also *Lyra* or *the Lyre.*

3. A sieve; especially, a coarse grain-sieve with wires parallel, bearing some resemblance to a harp. [Scot.]

4. A seal. [See *Harp-seal.*]

Æolian harp; see under *Æolian.*

härp, *v.i.*; harped (härpt), *pt.*, *pp.*; harping, *ppr.* 1. To play on the harp.

2. To dwell on a subject tediously or vexatiously, in speaking or writing.

> He seems
> Proud and disdainful, *harping* on what I am—
> Not what he knew I was. —Shak.

3. To touch, as a passion; to affect.

To harp on one string; to dwell tiresomely on one subject or one branch of a subject.

härp, *v.t.* 1. To play, as a tune, upon a harp; to give expression to by art; to sound forth.

> Thou'st *harped* my fear aright. —Shak.

2. To separate, as grain, by means of a harp. [Scot.]

Här′pȧ, *n.* [LL. *harpa*, a harp.]

1. The typical genus of the *Harpidæ.*

2. [h—] A harp-shell of the genus *Harpa*, typical of the *Harpidæ.*

härp′ēr, *n.* 1. A player on the harp.

2. One of several old coins of Ireland with the image of a harp on the reverse side.

3. A name of the harp-seal.

Här′pi-dæ, *n.pl.* A family of gasteropods with longitudinally ribbed shells, suggesting the strings of a harp.

härp′ing, *a.* Pertaining to the harp; as, *harping* symphonies.

härp′ing, *n.* 1. A continual dwelling on.

> Making infinite merriment by *harpings* upon old themes. —Irving.

2. A playing on the harp.

3. [*pl.*] In ships, the fore parts of the wales which encompass the bow of a ship and are fastened to the stem; used to strengthen the ship in the place where she sustains the greatest shock in plunging into the sea. Also written *harpins.*

härp′ing-ī″ron (-ūrn), *n.* A harpoon.

härp′ingș, härp′inș, *n.pl.* See *Harping*, n. 3.

härp′ist, *n.* A harper.

här-poon′, *n.* [D. *harpoen*; Fr. *harpon*, a grappling-iron, harpoon, from *harper*, to gripe, clutch, from *harpe*, a claw, hook; prob. from L. *harpago (-onis)*; Gr. *harpagē*, a hook, from *harpazein*, to seize.] A spear or javelin, used to strike and kill whales or any large fishes or sea-animals. It consists of a long shank with a broad, flat, triangular head, sharpened at both edges. It is thrown from the hand or fired from a gun.

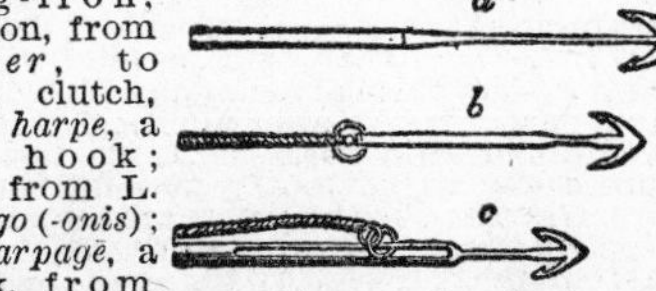

a, Hand-harpoon. *b*, *c*, Gun-harpoons.

här-poon′, *v.t.*; harpooned (-poond), *pt.*, *pp.*; harpooning, *ppr.* To strike, catch, or kill with a harpoon.

här-poon′eer, *n.* Same as *Harpooner.*

här-poon′ēr, *n.* One who casts or directs the harpoon, as at a whale.

här-poon′-fork, *n.* A hayfork consisting of an iron shank having a rope attached to one end, and to the other one or two tines with barbs which close when the tines are driven into the hay.

här-poon′-gun, *n.* A gun or small cannon, usually mounted on the bow of a whaling-boat, for firing a harpoon into a whale.

Harpoon-gun.

härp′ress, *n.* A female harper. [Rare.]

härp′-seal, *n.* In zoölogy, a seal, *Phoca grœnlandica*, of the arctic regions, having on the body a harp-shaped marking; called also *saddler* and *saddleback.*

härp′-shell, *n.* A beautiful shell of the genus *Harpa*, found in tropical seas.

härp′si-chon, *n.* A harpsichord. [Obs.]

härp′si-chord, *n.* [OFr. *harpe-chorde*; *harpe*, harp, and *chorde*, chord.] An old musical instrument with strings of wire, played by the fingers by means of keys operating upon quill-points which plucked the strings, making a light tinkling sound. In form it resembled the modern grand piano, of which it was the precursor.

här′pū-lȧ, *n.* [E. Ind.] An East Indian tree of the genus *Harpullia.*

Här-pul′li-ȧ, *n.* A genus of trees found in the tropical parts of Asia, Africa, and Australia, of the family *Sapindaceæ*, embracing six species, some of which are highly valued for their wood, which admits of a high polish.

här′py, *n.*; *pl.* **här′pieș.** [OFr. *harpie*, *harpye*; L. *harpyia*, pl. *harpyiæ*; Gr. *harpyiai*, pl., the harpies, lit., the snatchers, from *harpazein*, to seize, snatch.]

Harpy, from an antique gem.

1. In antiquity, a fabulous winged monster, ravenous and filthy, having the face of a woman and the body of a vulture, with feet and fingers armed with sharp claws. The harpies were three in number, Aëllo, Ocypete, and Celeno, and they were sent by Juno to plunder the table of Phineus.

2. The harpy-eagle.

3. The *Circus æruginosus*, or marsh-harrier, a British species of hawk, allied to the buzzards.

4. The harpy-bat.

5. Any rapacious or ravenous animal or person; an extortioner; a plunderer.

här′py-bat, *n.* Any fruit-bat of the genus *Harpyia* of the *Pteropodidæ*, with nostrils tubular and protuberant.

här′py-ēa″gle, *n.* A raptorial bird, *Thrasaetus harpyia*, of Mexico and South America, celebrated for the enormous development of its legs and beak, and for the strength and power it evinces in mastering its prey.

här′py-flȳ, *n.* The common house-fly.

här′quē-bus, är′quē-bus (-kē-), *n.* [Fr. *harquebuse*, *arquebuse*, from OFr. *hacquebuche*, *hacquebute*, from D. *haakbus*, a gun with a hook; *haak*, a hook, and *bus*, a box, barrel of a gun.] A hand-gun; a species of firearm resembling a musket. It was fired from a forked rest and sometimes cocked by a wheel, and carried a ball that weighed nearly two ounces. A larger kind, used in fortresses, carried a ball of three and one-half ounces.

här″quē-bus-āde′, *n.* 1. A distilled water applied to a bruise or wound; so called because it was originally used in gunshot wounds.

2. A volley from harquebuses.

här″quē-bus-iēr′, *n.* A soldier armed with a harquebus.

har′rāge, *v.t.* To harry; to harass. [Obs.]

har-rā-teen′, har-ă-teen′, *n.* A kind of coarse cloth made of wool.

har′ri-dăn, *n.* [Prob. corruption of OFr. *haridelle*, a worn-out horse, jade, from *aride*, dry, withered.] A hag; an odious old woman; a vixen; a trollop.

har′ri-ēr, *n.* [From *hare* and *-ier.*] A kind of hound for hunting hares, having an acute sense of smell; originally spelled *harier.*

har′ri-ēr, *n.* [From *harry*, v.]

1. Any person or thing that harries.

2. A hawk of the genus *Circus*, allied to the buzzards, as the marsh-harrier, *Circus æruginosus*, also called the *moor-buzzard* and *harpy*; also, the hen-harrier, *Circus cyaneus*, which is destructive to poultry.

har′rōw, *n.* [ME. *harow, harowe, harwe;* AS. *hearge*, a harrow.]

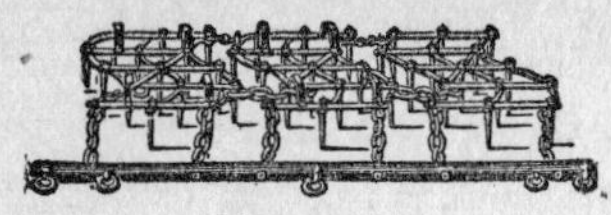

Harrow.

1. An agricultural implement, usually consisting of a frame of wood or metal set with iron teeth. It is drawn over plowed land to level it and break the clods, and to cover seed when sown.

2. Something causing distress, such as might be inflicted by a *harrow*; usually in the phrase *under the harrow* of poverty, etc.

har′rōw, *v.t.*; harrowed, *pt.*, *pp.*; harrowing, *ppr.* 1. To draw a harrow over for the purpose of breaking clods and leveling the surface, or for covering seed sown; to break or tear with a harrow; as, to *harrow* land.

2. To tear; to lacerate; to torment.

har′rōw, *v.t.* To agitate; to harry; to pillage. [Obs.]

har′rōw, *interj.* [ME. *harrow, haro;* OFr. *haro, harou, harau*, an exclamation, a call for help; O. Sax. *herod*, here, hither, from *her*, here.] Help! halloo! an exclamation of sudden distress, surprise, etc.; formerly used by heralds.

har′rōw-ẽr, *n.* One who harrows.

har′rōw-ẽr, *n.* One who or that which harrows or ravages, as a harrier-hawk.

har′ry, *v.t.*; harried, *pt.*, *pp.*; harrying, *ppr.* [ME. *haryen, herien, harwen, herwen, hergien;* AS. *hergian*, to ravage, lay waste, from *here*, an army.]

1. To strip; to pillage; to plunder.

2. To harass; to agitate; to tease; to worry.

har′ry, *v.i.* To make a predatory incursion. [Obs.]

härsh, *a.*; *comp.* harsher; *superl.* harshest. [ME. *harsk;* O.Sw. *harsk*, rank, rusty.]

1. Rough to the touch, to the taste, to the eye, or to the ear; grating; discordant; disagreeable; unpleasant; jarring; as, a *harsh* cloth; *harsh* fruit; a *harsh* contrast of color; a *harsh* voice.

2. Austere; crabbed; morose; peevish; rude; abusive; rigorous; severe; as, *harsh* words; a *harsh* reflection.

Syn.—Austere, rough, stern, morose, rigorous, hard, exacting, severe, acrimonious, sarcastic, cutting, keen, cruel, bitter, ungracious, uncivil, churlish, brutal, ill-tempered.

härsh′ly, *adv.* In a harsh manner.

härsh′ness, *n.* The quality of being harsh in any of its senses.

Syn.—Acrimony, tartness, asperity, acerbity, cruelty, churlishness, roughness, sternness, rudeness.

härs′let, *n.* Same as *Haslet.*

härt, *n.* [ME. *hart, hert, heort;* AS. *heort, heorot*, a hart, stag.] A stag or male red deer when he has passed his fifth year, and the surroyal or crown-antler is formed.

Hart of ten; a hart with ten tines or branches on his horns.

här′tạl, här′tąll, *n.* [Hind. *hartāl.*] The Indian name of orpiment.

härt′beest, härte′beest, *n.* [S. African D. *hartebeest; harte*, a hart, and *beest*, beast.] A species of the antelope, the *Alcelaphus caama*, the most common of the large antelopes inhabiting the plains of South Africa.

härt′ber″ry, *n.* A kind of European whortleberry, *Vaccinium Myrtillus.*

härt′en, *v.t.* To hearten. [Obs.]

härt′in, *n.* [Ober*hart* and *-in.*] A fossil resin found massive, but crystallizing from rock-oil in needles belonging to the trimetric system. It is found with hartite in lignite at Oberhart, Austria.

härt′īte, *n.* [Ober*hart* and *-ite;* so called because found in *Oberhart*, Austria.] A fossil resin resembling hartin.

härt′s′=clō″vẽr, *n.* The yellow sweet clover, *Melilotus officinalis.*

härts′họrn, *n.* 1. The antler of the hart or stag, *Cervus elaphus*, formerly much used as a source of ammonia.

2. Ammonia; spirit of hartshorn; any volatile salt of ammonia.

Hartshorn shavings; originally, shavings from the antlers of harts, now usually cut from the bones of calves to make a kind of jelly.

Salt of hartshorn; an impure carbonate of ammonia.

Spirits of hartshorn; an aqueous solution of ammonia.

härts′họrn=plan″tāin, *n.* *Plantago Coronopus*, a European species of plantain with pinnate leaves.

härt′s′=thọrn, *n.* Same as *Buckthorn.*

härt′s′=tọngue (-tung), *n.* 1. A common British fern, *Scolopendrium vulgare.*

2. A West Indian fern, *Polypodium Phyllitidis.*

härt′s′=trē″foil, *n.* Hart's-clover.

härt′s′=truf″fles, *n.pl.* Lycoperdon-nuts.

härt′wọrt, *n.* Any of certain umbelliferous plants of the genera *Seseli, Tordylium*, and *Bupleurum.*

hãr′um=sçãr′um, *a.* [Formerly *harem-scarem*, a riming compound of *hare* and *scare*, used in allusion to the timidity of the hare.] Wild; precipitate; giddy; rash. [Colloq.]

hãr′um=sçãr′um, *n.* A rash, giddy person.

ha-rus′pex, *n.*; *pl.* **ha-rus′pi-cēs.** [L., lit., an inspector of entrails.] A priest in ancient Rome whose business was to inspect the entrails of victims killed in sacrifice, and by them to foretell future events or declare the will of the deity; written also *aruspex* and *haruspice.*

ha-rus-pi-çā′tion, *n.* Haruspicy.

ha-rus′pice, *n.* A haruspex.

ha-rus′pi-cy, *n.* Divination by a haruspex.

här′vest, *n.* [ME. *harvest, hervest, herfest, harvest*, autumn; AS. *hærfest*, autumn.]

1. The season of gathering a crop of any kind, especially the time of reaping and gathering wheat, corn, and other grain.

2. That which is harvested or ready for harvesting; a crop or crops, as of grain, hay, fruit, ice, etc.

3. The product of labor; reward; fruit or fruits; effects; consequences; results of any conditions or operations; as, the year's *harvest* of books; a *harvest* of woe.

4. The act of harvesting.

här′vest, *v.t.*; harvested, *pt.*, *pp.*; harvesting, *ppr.* To reap or gather, as grain or other crops; often used figuratively; as, he *harvested* his crop of wild oats.

här′vest=ap″ple, *n.* An early autumn apple.

här′vest=bells, *n.* A beautiful gentian of Europe, *Gentiana Pneumonanthe*, blossoming in harvest.

här′vest=bug, *n.* A harvest-tick; a harvest-fly.

här′vest-ẽr, *n.* One who or that which harvests; specifically, (a) a laborer in harvest; a harvestman; (b) a machine used to harvest crops, as grains, beans, potatoes, etc.; a reaper.

här′vest=fiēld, *n.* A field from which a harvest is gathered; a field in which harvesters are at work.

här′vest=fish, *n.* Either of two scombroid fishes of the Atlantic coast of the United States; (a) *Stromateus triacanthus*, or the dollar-fish, (b) *Stromateus paru*, found numerously in harvest-time.

här′vest=fly, *n.* A cicada, as *Cicada tibicen*, commonly called *locust.*

här′vest=gọọse, *n.* The wild gray goose.

här′vest=hōme, *n.* 1. The time of harvest.

2. The song sung by reapers at the feast made when harvest is done, or the feast itself.

3. A religious service held at the time of harvest, as in English churches.

här′vest-less, *a.* Without crops; devoid of harvest.

här′vest=lọrd, *n.* The head reaper at harvest.

här′vest=louse, *n.* The harvest-tick.

här′vest-măn, *n.* 1. A laborer in harvest.

2. A long-legged spider of the family *Phalangidæ*, in which the head and abdomen are united in one piece; called also *shepherd-spider* and *daddy-longlegs.*

här′vest=mīte, *n.* A harvest-tick.

här′vest=mọnth, *n.* In England, September, as being the month for harvesting grain; a month in which a crop is harvested.

här′vest=mọọn, *n.* The moon near the full, about the time of the autumnal equinox, when it rises nearly at the same hour for several days; so named because this is, in England, the period of harvest.

här′vest=mouse, *n.* *Mus minutus*, a very small European species of field-mouse, which builds its nest on the stems of wheat or other plants.

här′vest=queen (-kwēn), *n.* An image representing Ceres, formerly carried about on the last day of harvest.

här′vest-ry, *n.* The act or result of harvesting.

här′vest=spī″dẽr, *n.* See *Harvestman*, 2.

här′vest=tick, *n.* Any of various mites, numerous and annoying in harvest-time. They are usually red, immature forms of the genera *Trombidium* or *Tetranychus*, which fasten themselves to the skin and cause irritation.

här′vey, *v.t.* To harveyize, as steel.

här′vey-īze, *v.t.*; harveyized, *pt.*, *pp.*; harveyizing, *ppr.* [Named after H. A. *Harvey*, the inventor of the process.] To subject (steel) to a process by which the surface is rendered extremely hard; to furnish (a war-ship) with armor-plates made of harveyized steel.

här′vey-īzed, *a.* Hardened by the process invented by H. A. Harvey (1824-1893); applied to steel, armor-plates, and war-ships.

has, *v.*, third person singular present tense of *have.*

haș′ărd, *n.* Hazard. [Obs.]

haș′=been, *n.* A custom, idea, thing, or person antiquated or out of date. [Colloq.]

hāșe, *v.t.* To haze. [Obs.]

hash, *v.t.*; hashed (hasht), *pt.*, *pp.*; hashing, *ppr.* [Fr. *hacher*, to chop, mince.] To chop into small pieces; to mince and mix.

hash, *n.* [OFr. *hachis*, minced meat, from *hacher*, to mince, chop, from G. *hacken*, to hack, cut.]

1. A form of minced food, prepared from materials previously cooked, as meat, potatoes, bread-crumbs, etc., and recooked by stewing or frying.

2. Any mixture and second preparation of old matter; a repetition.

3. A sloven; a country clown; a stupid fellow.

4. Grub; food. [Slang.]

To settle one's hash; to squelch one; to cause one to be silent or inactive.

hash′ish, hash′eesh, *n.* [Ar. *hashish*, hay, herbage, a kind of intoxicating drink.]

1. A narcotic and intoxicating preparation of the plant called Indian hemp, *Cannabis sativa;* it is either smoked or drunk as an infusion, and has been used in Oriental countries for many centuries. [See *Bhang.*]

2. The tender parts of the Indian hemp with their resinous exudations.

hask, *n.* [W. *hesg*, sedge, rushes.] A case made of rushes or flags. [Obs.]

has′let, *n.* The heart, liver, lungs, etc., of a hog or other animal. [Obs.]

hȧsp, *n.* [ME. *hasp;* AS. *hæpse*, a hasp, bolt.]

1. A clasp that passes over a staple to be fastened by a padlock, hook, pin, etc.; also, a metal book-clasp.

2. A spindle to wind thread or silk on.

3. A quantity of yarn, the fourth part of a spindle.

4. A scarifier used on grass-land.

hȧsp, *v.t.*; hasped (haspt), *pt.*, *pp.*; hasping, *ppr.* [ME. *haspen;* AS. *hæpsian*, from *hæpse*, a hasp, bolt.] To shut or fasten with a hasp.

has′sock, *n.* [ME. *hassok*, a coarse grass; AS. *hassuc*, a place where coarse grass grows.]

1. A tussock; a tuft of sedge or coarse grass, often made into footrests. [Prov. Eng.]

2. A besom; anything bushy; a large round turf used as a seat. [Scot.]

3. A thick mat on which persons kneel in church; a padded cushion or footstool.

hast, *v.*, second person singular present tense of *have.*

has′tāte, has′tā-ted, *a.* [L. *hasta*, a spear.] Spear-shaped; resembling the head of a halberd; triangular, hollowed at the base and on the sides, with the angles spreading; as, a *hastate* leaf.

Hastate Leaf (*Atriplex hastata*).

hāste, *n.* [ME. *haste*, haste; AS. *hæst, hǣst*, violence.]

1. Celerity of motion; speed; swiftness; despatch; expedition; applied only to voluntary beings, as men and other animals.

2. Sudden excitement of passion; needless or unwise quickness; precipitance; vehemence.

I said in my *haste*, All men are liars.
—Ps. cxvi. 11.

3. The state of being urged or pressed by business; as, I am in great *haste.*

Syn.—Hurry, speed, despatch, nimbleness, rapidity.—*Haste* denotes quickness of action and a strong desire for getting on; *hurry* includes a confusion and want of collected thought not implied in *haste; speed* denotes the actual progress which is made; *despatch*, the promptitude and rapidity with which things are done.

To make haste; to act or go quickly; to hasten.

hāste, *v.t.* and *v.i.* To hurry; to hasten. [Rare.]

I'll *haste* the writer. —Shak.

hās′ten (hās′n), *v.t.*; hastened, *pt.*, *pp.*; hastening, *ppr.* [An extended form of *haste*, v.] To press; to drive or urge forward; to push on; to precipitate; to accelerate; to expedite; to hurry; as, to *hasten* one's coming.

Syn.—Accelerate, quicken, expedite, hurry.

hās′ten, *v.i.* To move with celerity; to be rapid in motion; to be speedy or quick; to hurry; as, to *hasten* to a conclusion.

hās′ten-ẽr, *n.* 1. One who hastens or urges forward.

2. A haster.

hās′tẽr, *n.* [OFr. *hastier, haster*, a spit, the rack on which a spit turns, from *haste*, a spit.] A metal stand for keeping the heat of the fire to the joint while cooking.

hās′tif, *a.* Hasty. [Obs.]

hās′tif-ly, *adv.* Hastily. [Obs.]

has-ti-fō′li-ous, *a.* [L. *hasta*, a spear, and *folium*, a leaf.] In botany, having hastate leaves.

has′tile, *a.* [L. *hastile*, the shaft of a spear, from *hasta*, a spear.] Hastate.

hās′ti-ly, *adv.* With haste; precipitately.

hās′ti-ness, *n.* The state of being hasty; rashness; precipitation.

hās′ting, *n.* [Ppr. of *haste*, v.] An early fruit or vegetable; specifically, in the plural, pease.

Hās′tings Sand. In geology, the middle group

of the Wealden formation in England, occurring around Hastings, in Sussex.

hās′tive, *a.* Forward; early, as fruit. [Obs.]

hās′ty, *a.*; *comp.* hastier; *superl.* hastiest. [ME. *hasty*, from *haste*, haste.]

1. Quick; speedy; expeditious; moving or acting with haste; opposed to *slow*.

2. Eager; precipitate; rash; opposed to *deliberate*.

3. Irritable; easily excited to wrath; passionate.

4. Early ripe; forward; as, *hasty* fruit. [Obs.]

5. Requiring or characterized by quick action; as, a *hasty* departure.

Hasty pudding; in the United States, mush; corn-meal mush; in England, mush made of oatmeal or flour.

hat, *a.* Hot. [Obs.]

hat, *v.*, obsolete present singular of *hight*.

hat, *n.* [ME. *hat*; AS. *hæt* (pl. *hættas*), a hat.]

1. A covering for the head; a headdress, usually with a crown and brim, made of any of various materials, as felt, silk, wool, straw, etc., and worn by either sex to protect the head from the weather, or for ornament.

2. The dignity of a cardinal; from the broad-brimmed scarlet hat which forms part of a cardinal's dress.

3. In tanning, a layer of bark covering hides when soaking in the tan-vat.

4. In smelting, a detainer for gases in the tunnel-head of a furnace.

5. In soap-making, a depression in the bottom of a copper, in which impurities settle and from which they may be drawn off.

Forms of Hats in 16th, 17th, and 18th centuries.

1, 2. Time of Henry VIII. 3. Time of Mary. 4. Time of Elizabeth. 5, 6. Time of James and Charles I. 7, 8. Time of Commonwealth. 9, 10. Time of William III. 11-16. Eighteenth century.

Gainsborough hat; a lady's hat with a wide brim, such as those seen in paintings by Gainsborough.

To hang up one's hat; to make oneself at home; to take up one's residence in another's house.

To pass round the hat; to ask for money in the shape of charity, subscription, etc.

hāt′ȧ-ble, *a.* That may be hated; odious.

hat′band, *n.* A band of ribbon round the crown of a hat; specifically, a mourning-band of crape.

hat′-block, *n.* A block or mold on which a hat is shaped and ironed.

hat′-bod″y, *n.* The unfinished body of a hat.

hat′box, *n.* A box for a hat, as a leather case or a small trunk.

hatch, *v.t.*; hatched, *pt.*, *pp.*; hatching, *ppr.* [ME. *hacchen*, *hecchen*, to hatch; compare G. *hecken*, Dan. *hekke*, to hatch.]

1. To produce (young) from eggs by incubation, or by artificial heat; to bring to life from an egg or eggs.

2. To contrive or plot; to form by meditation, and bring into being; to originate and produce; as, to *hatch* mischief.

hatch, *v.i.* 1. To produce young; as, eggs *hatch*.

2. To emerge from the egg, as an insect, fish, bird, etc.

hatch, *v.t.* [OFr. *hacher*, to hack; M.H.G. *hacken*, to cut, chop.]

1. To cross with lines, in drawing and engraving.

2. To stain; to steep. [Obs.]

3. To engrave; to chase. [Obs.]

hatch, *v.t.* To close or cover with or as with a hatch.

hatch, *n.* [ME. *hatche*, *hacche*, *hetche*, *hek*, *hec*, a half-door, wicket (pl. *hacches*, the hatches of a ship); AS. *hæc*, a gate.]

1. An opening in a deck, floor, roof, etc., affording a passage for persons or goods; a hatchway; also, a door or grate covering such an opening; a trap-door.

2. An opening into a mine. [Rare.]

3. A half-door, or door with an opening over it.

4. A fish-garth.

5. A box-trap. [Prov. Eng.]

6. A bedstead. [Scot.]

To be under hatches; to be below deck; hence, to be under confinement or adversity.

hatch, *n.* A hatching; a hachure.

hatch, *n.* 1. The act of hatching; that which is hatched.

2. As many chickens, etc., as are produced at one hatching or incubation.

3. The number of eggs put under a fowl or into an incubator for one hatching.

hatch′-bär, *n.* The bar for securing a hatch.

hatch′-bōat, *n.* A fishing-boat with a well for holding fish.

hatch′el, *n.* [ME. *hechele*, *hekele*, a comb for cleaning flax or hemp; compare D. *hekel*, G. *hechel*, a hatchel.] An instrument made of long iron teeth set in a board, for cleansing flax or hemp from the tow or coarse part.

hatch′el, *v.t.*; hatcheled *or* hatchelled, *pt.*, *pp.*; hatcheling *or* hatchelling, *ppr.* 1. To draw (flax or hemp) through the teeth of a hatchel, for separating the coarse part and broken pieces of the stalk from the fine, fibrous parts.

2. To worry; to tease; to heckle. [Scot.]

hatch′el-ẽr, *n.* One who uses a hatchel.

hatch′ẽr, *n.* One who or that which hatches; specifically, an incubator.

hatch′ẽr-y, *n.* A place for the hatching of eggs, especially fish-eggs.

hatch′et, *n.* [ME. *hachet*; OFr. *hachette*, dim. of *hache*, an ax, from G. *hacke*, an ax, from *hacken*, to cut.] A small ax with a short handle, to be used with one hand.

To bury the hatchet; see under *Bury*.

To take up the hatchet; to make war.

hatch′et-fāce, *n.* A sharp, pointed face.

hatch′et-fāced (-fāst), *a.* Having a hatchet-face.

hatch′et-tin, hatch′et-tine, *n.* [Named after Charles *Hatchett*, an English chemist.] A yellowish, semitransparent mineral found in Scotland and Wales. It belongs to the paraffin group of minerals; also written *hatchettite*.

hatch′et-vetch, *n.* *Securigera Emerus*, a plant bearing thin-edged legumes.

hatch′ing, *n.* 1. A method of producing the effect of shading in drawing, engraving, etc., by the use of parallel or intersecting lines.

2. A line or system of lines for such purpose.

hatch′ment, *n.* [Corrupted from *achievement*, which was also spelled *atchievement*, from Fr. *achever*, to finish.]

1. An armorial escutcheon of a dead person. [See *Achievement*.]

2. Any distinctive mark of dignity.

hatch′ūre, *n.* [Fr. *hacher*, to hack.] In engraving, etc., a hatching.

hatch′wāy, *n.* A doorway or opening for passage in a floor, roof, deck, etc.; a hatch.

hāte, *v.t.*; hated, *pt.*, *pp.*; hating, *ppr.* [ME. *haten*, *hatien*; AS. *hatian*, *hatigian*, to hate.]

1. To dislike greatly; to have a great or extreme aversion to; to detest; to have strong ill-will toward.

2. In Scripture, to love less than another.

> If any man come to me, and *hate* not father and mother, etc. —Luke xiv. 26.

Syn.—Abhor, detest, loathe, abominate.

hāte, *n.* [ME. *hate*, *hete*; AS. *hete*, hate.] Great dislike or aversion; hatred.

hāte′fụl, *a.* 1. Odious; exciting great dislike, aversion, or disgust.

2. Malignant; malevolent; as, *hateful* eyes.

Syn.—Execrable, abominable, hateful, detestable.

hāte′fụl-ly, *adv.* In a hateful manner.

hāte′fụl-ness, *n.* The quality of being hateful.

hāt′ẽr, *n.* One who hates.

hath, *v.*, third person singular present tense of *have*.

hat′-hon″ŏr (-on″), *n.* Regard shown for a man or woman by taking off the hat.

hat′less, *a.* Without a hat.

hat′-mŏn″ey, *n.* See *Primage*.

hat′-pièce, *n.* A metal protection formerly worn under a hat, to turn a blow.

hat′rack, *n.* A rack or stand fitted for holding hats, etc.

hā′tred, *n.* [ME. *hatred*, *hatreden*; *hate*, hate, and *-red*, *-reden*, from AS. *-ræden*, signifying state or condition.] Great dislike or aversion; hate; enmity; malevolence; intense ill-will.

Syn.—Antipathy, abhorrence, aversion, detestation, dislike, hostility.

hat′stand, *n.* A hatrack intended to stand on its own base.

hat′te, *v.t.* and *v.i.* [Obs.] Same as *Hight*.

hat′tẽr, *v.t.* To harass. [Obs.]

hat′tẽr, *n.* 1. A maker or seller of hats.

2. In Australia, a miner who has no partner.

Mad as a hatter; extremely angry; quite or nearly insane. [Colloq.]

Hat-tē′ri-ȧ, *n.* 1. A genus of reptiles of New Zealand, comprising certain peculiar lizards.

2. [h—] A member of the genus.

hat′ting, *n.* 1. The business of hat-making.

2. The materials from which hats are made.

hat′ti-sher-īf′, *n.* [Turk. *khattisherif*; *khatt*, a writing, command, and *sherif*, noble.] An irrevocable order issued by the sultan of Turkey and countersigned by him.

hat′tree, *n.* A hatstand.

hạu-bẽr′ġeŏn, *n.* A short hauberk or coat of chain-mail.

hạu′bẽrk, *n.* [ME. *hauberk*, *hawberk*; OFr. *hauberc*, *halberc*, from O.H.G. *halsberc*, *halsberge*, a protection for the neck, gorget; *hals*, the neck, and *bergan*, to protect, to save.] In medieval armor, a coat of mail sometimes without sleeves, formed of steel rings interwoven.

hau′ẽr-ite, *n.* [Named after F. von *Hauer*, an Austrian geologist.] A reddish-brown or brownish-black isometric metallic mineral of an adamantine luster, generally crystallizing in octahedrons, though sometimes in globular clusters.

hạugh, *n.* Low-lying flat ground, properly on the border of a river, and such as is sometimes overflowed. [Prov. Eng. and Scot.]

hạught, *a.* [A corruption of OFr. *haut*, *hault*, high, from L. *altus*, high, lofty; the *gh* was probably introduced on the analogy of *high*.] High; elevated; hence, proud; insolent. [Obs.]

hạugh′ti-ly, *adv.* Proudly; arrogantly; with contempt or disdain; as, to speak or behave *haughtily*.

hạugh′ti-ness, *n.* The quality of being haughty; arrogance.

Syn.—Arrogance, disdain, pride, presumption, contemptuousness.—*Haughtiness* denotes the expression of conscious and proud superiority; *arrogance* is a disposition to claim for oneself more than is justly due, and to enforce it to the utmost; *disdain* is the exact reverse of condescension toward inferiors, since it expresses and desires others to feel how far below ourselves we consider them.

hạugh′ty, *a.*; *comp.* haughtier; *superl.* haughtiest. [ME. *hautein*; OFr. *hautain*, haughty, proud, from *haut*, high; the *gh* was probably inserted after the analogy of *naughty*.]

1. Proud and disdainful; having a high opinion of oneself, with some contempt for others; lofty and arrogant; supercilious.

2. Proceeding from excessive pride or pride mingled with contempt; manifesting pride and disdain; as, a *haughty* air or walk; a *haughty* tone.

3. Lofty; bold. [Obs.]

hạul, *v.t.*; hauled, *pt.*, *pp.*; hauling, *ppr.* [ME. *haulen*, *halen*, *halien*; AS. *geholian*, to acquire, get.]

1. To pull or draw with force; to drag; as, to *haul* a boat on shore.

2. To transport, convey, or move by drawing; as, to *haul* wood to one's house.

To haul over the coals; to reprove; to reprimand.

To haul the wind; to turn the head of a ship nearer to the point from which the wind blows.

hạul, *v.i.* 1. In seamen's language, to alter the course of a ship; to change the direction of sailing.

2. To alter; to shift; to veer, as the wind.

3. To pull or drag with force.

To haul off; to alter a ship's course in order to get farther off from any object.

hạul, *n.* 1. A pulling with force; a violent pull.

2. A draft of a net; as, to catch a hundred fish at a *haul*; also, a place for hauling a seine.

3. That which is gained, as by hauling a net; as, a *haul* of fish.

4. Any acquisition of value; a find. [Colloq.]

5. In railroading, the distance over which something is hauled; as, a long or a short *haul*.

6. In rope-making, a bundle of three or four hundred parallel yarns ready for tarring.

hạul′āġe, *n.* The act or operation of hauling; the force used in hauling; also, hauling-charges.

hạul′ẽr, *n.* 1. One who hauls.

2. A contrivance for catching fish consisting of a number of hooks pulled through the water by a line.

hạulm, *n.* Same as *Halm*.

hạulm, *n.* A part of a harness. [Obs. See *Hame*.]

hạulse, *n.* A hawse. [Obs. See *Halse*.]

hạult, *a.* [OFr. *hault*, *halt*, from L. *altus*, high, lofty.] Haughty. [Obs.]

hạul′yärd, *n.* A halyard.

hạum, *n.* [Obs.] Same as *Halm*.

häunce, *v.t.* To enhance. [Obs. See *Hance*.]

häunch, *n.* [ME. *haunche*, *hanche*; OFr. *hanche*, *hance*, *anche*, the haunch; O.H.G. *ancha*, *encha*, the leg, lit., the joint or bend.]

1. The hip; that part of the body of man and of quadrupeds which lies between the last ribs and the thigh; as, a *haunch* of venison; the horse fell back on his *haunches*.

2. The rear; the hind part. [Obs.]

3. In architecture, the middle part between the vertex or crown and the springing of an arch; sometimes used to include the spandrel or part of it; the flank.

häunch′-bōne, *n.* The innominate bone.

häunched (häncht), *a.* Having haunches.

häunt (*or* hạnt), *v.t.*; haunted, *pt.*, *pp.*; haunting, *ppr.* [ME. *haunten*, *hanten*; OFr. *hanter*, to frequent, resort to.]

1. To frequent; to resort to much or often, or to be much about; to visit customarily.

2. To come to frequently; to trouble with frequent visits.

Thoughts which perpetually *haunt* and disquiet mankind. —Atterbury.

3. To frequent or inhabit, as a ghost or spirit; to appear in or about, as a specter; to be in the habit of visiting, as an apparition.

4. To practise; to pursue. [Obs.]

häunt, *v.i.* To be much about; to be present often; to return from the dead.

häunt, *n.* 1. A place to which one frequently resorts; as, taverns are often the *haunts* of tipplers; a den is the *haunt* of wild beasts.

2. The habit of resorting to a place. [Obs.]

3. Custom; practice. [Obs.]

4. A ghost. [Local, U. S.]

häunt'ed, *a.* Frequently visited or resorted to by apparitions or the shades of the dead.

häunt'ẽr, *n.* One who frequents a particular place, or is often about it.

hau'ri-ent, *a.* [L. *hauriens* (*-entis*), ppr. of *haurire*, to draw or drink in.] In heraldry, placed palewise or upright, as if putting the head above water to draw or suck in the air; said of a fish as a bearing.

A Salmon Haurient.

hau'sen, *n.* [G. *hausen*, a kind of sturgeon.] *Acipenser huso*, a large Russian sturgeon.

haus'männ-īte, *n.* [Named after J. F. L. *Hausmann*, a German mineralogist.] One of the ores of manganese, having a brownish-black color. It crystallizes in the tetragonal system.

hausse, *n.* [Fr., from *hausser*, to lift, raise.] In gunnery, a breech-sight for a cannon, vertically adjustable.

hausse'-çol (hōs'), *n.* [Fr., from *hausser*, to raise, and *col*, neck.] A gorget of plate.

Haus-tel-lā'tȧ, *n.pl.* [L. *haustus*, pp. of *haurire*, to draw in, breathe, swallow.] A very extensive division of insects in which the mouth is furnished with a haustellum or proboscis adapted for suction. It includes the homopterous, heteropterous, lepidopterous, and dipterous insects. The figures show the form and structure of the haustellum in one of the hawk-moths, *Sphingidæ*. Fig. 1 shows the head of the moth with the proboscis extended; figs. 2 and 3 are sections of the proboscis showing its structure, the one (2) viewed from above, the other (3) from beneath.

Haustellum of the Hawk-moth.

haus'tel-lāte, *a.* Provided with a haustellum or sucker, as certain insects.

haus'tel-lāte, *n.* One of the *Haustellata*.

haus-tel'lous, *a.* Haustellate.

haus-tel'lum, *n.*; *pl.* **haus-tel'lȧ.** The suctorial organ of certain insects, otherwise called the proboscis or antlia.

haus-tō'ri-um, *n.*; *pl.* **haus-tō'ri-ȧ.** [LL., a well, from L. *haustor*, a drawer, from *haurire*, to draw in, breathe in.] In botany, the sucker at the extremity of the parasitic root of such a plant as dodder.

haut, *a.* Haughty. [Obs.]

haut'boy (hō'boi), *n.* [OFr. *hautbois*, *haultbois*, lit., high wood; *haut*, high, and *bois*, wood.]

Hautboy.

1. The oboe, a wind-instrument.

2. In botany, a variety of strawberry, *Fragaria elatior*.

haut'boy-ist, *n.* An oboist.

hau'tein, hau'tāin (hō'), *a.* [OFr. *hautein*, haughty, from *haut*, high.] Haughty; high. [Obs.]

hau e'pāce, *n.* [Fr. *haut*, high, and *pas*, a step.] A raised floor in a bay-window. [Obs.]

hau-teūr', *n.* [Fr., from *haut*, high, proud.] Pride; haughtiness; haughty manner or spirit.

haut"gōut' (hō"gö'), *n.* [Fr.] High relish or taste; high seasoning.

haut"päs' (hō"pä'), *n.* [Obs.] See *Hautepace*.

hä'uyne (-win), *n.* A mineral, named from the French mineralogist, Haüy, occurring in grains or small masses, and also in groups of minute, shining crystals Its color is blue, of various shades. It is found imbedded in volcanic rocks, basalt, phonolite, etc. It is a silicate of aluminium and sodium with sulphate of lime; written also *haüynite*.

Hȧ-van'ȧ, *n.* A cigar made from tobacco grown in Cuba, and so called after the capital of that island.

Hav-ăn-ēṣe', *a.* Of or pertaining to Havana, Cuba.

Hav-ăn-ēṣe', *n. sing.* and *pl.* A native or resident of Havana, Cuba, or the people of Havana.

have, *v.t.*; had, *pt.*, *pp.*; having, *ppr.* [ME. *haven*, *habben*; AS. *habban*, to have, hold.]

1. To possess; to hold in possession or power; to possess as a quality, part, appurtenance, relationship, or as a thing contained, controlled, or having any connection; to own; to control; to contain; to comprise; to hold; as, to *have* strength; to *have* a hand, a handle, a brother, a title or index, a right to act or to be, a privilege to speak, etc.; to *have* a farm, a patent, a fault, a plan, authority, etc. The idea of possession is frequently obscured or lost in special uses; as, (a) to *have* a cigar, a smoke, a walk, a rest, a headache, a talk, an encounter, etc., that is, to enjoy, to feel, to participate in, to experience in any way; (b) he *has* neither Latin, French, nor Italian; you *have* me, *have* you not? that is, to understand, to know.

2. To hold in possession by gaining, accepting, receiving, or obtaining in any manner; to possess by acquirement; as, will you *have* this apple? He *has* good wages; to *have* a child, as a father or mother, that is, to beget, to bring forth; the hound *has* the hare; he *has* his opponent, that is, holds him in his power; to *have* a message from home; to *have* one's wish, that is, to receive or obtain.

Break thy mind to me in broken English; wilt thou *have* me? —Shak.

3. To possess in such a way as to have a duty, obligation, or necessity toward; to be urged by necessity or obligation; to be under necessity or impelled by duty; as, I *have* to visit twenty patients every day; we *have* to strive with heavy prejudices.

4. To hold; to hold in opinion; to regard; to maintain; as, to *have* in honor or contempt; to *have* an idea; she will *have* it that she is right.

5. To possess or gain by causing to be; to procure or make to be; to cause, permit, require, or determine; as, he *has* a box made; I *had* the message sent. Hence, in archaic use, to cause to go, or to be brought; as, *have* him away; *have* him here.

Have is used as an auxiliary verb to form certain compound tenses, as the perfect and pluperfect of both transitive and intransitive verbs, the past participle of which completes the tense either alone or with some other auxiliary. In such cases the word *have* no doubt originally had its proper meaning as a transitive verb, and was so used at first only with other transitive verbs, as denoting possession of anything in the condition indicated by the past participle of the latter verb; thus, I *have* received a letter, means, literally, I possess a letter received. The construction was afterward extended to cases in which the possessor of the object and the performer of the action are not necessarily the same, as in I *have* written a letter, and to intransitive verbs. In idiomatic phrases expressing choice, *had* is used in the sense of *would*; as, *I had as good*, it would be as well for me; *I had better*, it would be better for me; *I had best*, it would be best for me; *I had as lief* or *lieve*, I would as willingly; *I had rather* or *liefer*, I should prefer. The form now preferred is, I *would* rather, etc.

To have a care; to take care; to be on guard, or to guard.

To have a person out; to meet him in a duel.

To have it out; to say one's mind fully and come to an understanding.

To have it out of a person; to punish him; to retaliate on him; to take him to task.

have'less, *a.* Having little or nothing. [Obs.]

hav'e-lock, *n.* [Named after Gen. Henry *Havelock*.] A white cloth cover used over a soldier's cap to keep the sunshine from head and neck.

hā'ven, *v.t.* To provide a haven for; to shelter.

hā'ven, *n.* [ME. *haven*, *havene*; AS. *hæfen*, *hæfene*, a haven, harbor.]

1. A harbor; a port; a bay, recess, or inlet of the sea, or the mouth of a river which affords good anchorage and a safe station for ships.

2. A shelter; an asylum; a place of safety.

hā'ven-āġe, *n.* Harbor-dues.

hā'ven-ẽr, *n.* A harbor-master.

hav'ẽr, *n.* One who has or possesses; a possessor.

hā'vẽr, *v.i.* [North Eng. and Scot.] To talk in a silly or incoherent way.

hav'ẽr, *n.* [ME. *haver*; Old L.G. *haboro*, oats.] Oats. [Local, north of England.]

hav'ẽr-bread (-bred), **hav'ẽr-çāke,** *n.* Bread or cake of oats.

hav'ẽr-el, *n.* One who havers. [Scot.]

hav'ẽr-grȧss, *n.* Wild oats.

hā'vẽrṣ, *n.* Manners; behavior. [Scot.]

hav'ẽr-sack, *n.* [Fr. *haversac*; G. *habersack*, lit., a sack of oats; *haber*, *hafer*, oats, and *sack*, a sack.]

1. A soldier's knapsack.

2. A gunner's leather bag used for conveying ammunition to a piece.

3. An oat-sack; a sack for oats or oatmeal. [Prov. Eng.]

Hȧ-vẽr'siăn, *a.* Of, relating to, or described by Clopton Havers, a physician and anatomist of England in the seventeenth century.

Haversian canal; one of a network of minute canals which traverse the solid substance of bones, and proceed from the central cavity, conveying the nutrient vessels to all parts.

hav'il-där, *n.* [Hind. *hawaldar*; *hawala*, charge, custody, care, and *-dar*, having, possessing.] The highest noncommissioned officer in the native armies of India and Ceylon; a sepoy sergeant.

hav'ing, *n.* That which is had or possessed; goods; property; possession.

Our content is our best *having*. —Shak.

hā'vingṣ, *n.pl.* Carriage; behavior in general; good manners; propriety of behavior. [Scot.]

hav'lŏr, *n.* Conduct, behavior. [Obs.]

hav'ŏç, hav'ock, *n.* [ME. *havok*, *havek*, havoc, used in the phrase, to cry havoc, lit., to cry the hawk, a cry of encouragement to a hawk when loosed upon its prey, from AS. *hafoc*, *hafuc*, a hawk; also thought to have originated from the cruel and destructive nature of the hawk.] General destruction or waste; widespread devastation and carnage.

hav'ŏç, *v.t.* To waste; to destroy; to lay waste.

hav'ŏç, *interj.* Originally, a cry of excitement in hunting; afterward, a war-cry and the signal for indiscriminate slaughter.

Cry *havoc!* and let slip the dogs of war. —Shak.

haw, *v.i.* To look. [Prov. Eng.]

haw, *v.t.*; hawed, *pt.*, *pp.*; hawing, *ppr.* To guide to the left, as a horse in driving.

haw, *v.i.* To turn to the left, as a horse in driving.

To haw and gee; to waver or vacillate; to order or direct to move in various directions with groundless changes of purpose.

haw, *v.i.* To stop in speaking with a haw, or to speak with interruption and hesitation; as, to hem and *haw*.

haw, *interj.* A syllable used in hesitating utterances; spelled variously, as *er*, *ur*, *uh*, *huh*, *ah*, *aw*, etc.

haw, *n.* A hesitation or intermission of speech.

haw, *n.* [ME. *hawe*, a haw-berry, a thing of no value; AS. *hagan*, pl. haws.]

1. A berry or seed of the hawthorn.

2. *Viburnum prunifolium*, the black haw, or its fruit.

3. A berry. [Obs.]

4. A thing of trifling value. [Obs.]

haw, *n.* 1. A spot or fleck in the eye; especially, a diseased condition of the third eyelid in horses, usually known as the *haws*.

2. The third eyelid or nictitating membrane, a vestigial organ in mammals, but functional in birds and reptiles.

haw, *n.* [ME. *hawe*; AS. *haga*, an inclosure, a yard, or small field.]

1. A hedge. [Obs.]

2. A small piece of land adjoining a house; a yard; an inclosed piece of land.

3. A dale; a haugh. [Obs.]

Hȧ-wai'iăn (-yăn), *n.* [*Hawaii*, native name.] A native or citizen of Hawaii; also, the language of the natives.

Hȧ-wai'iăn, *a.* Of or relating to the people of the Hawaiian group of islands, or to their language.

haw'finch, *n.* The European grosbeak.

haw-haw', *n.* [Duplication of ME. *hawe*; AS. *haga*, an inclosure.] A ha-ha, or sunk fence.

haw'-haw', *v.i.* To guffaw; to laugh in a coarse or boisterous way.

haw'-haw', *n.* A guffaw; a boisterous laugh.

hawk, *n.* [ME. *hauk*; AS. *hafoc*, *hafuc*, a hawk.] A bird of prey of diurnal habits, and not feeding upon carrion, as distinguished from owls and vultures. The term is applied to almost all members of the *Falconidæ*, including the eagle, buzzard, falcon, kite, etc.; also restricted to designate a section of that family, including the genera *Accipiter* and *Astur*, characterized by having a crooked beak, furnished with a cere at the base, a cloven tongue, the head thickly set with feathers, and wings which reach no farther along the tail than two-thirds of its length. Most of these birds are rapacious, feeding on birds or small animals. Hawks were formerly trained for sport or catching small birds. They were reckoned among the ignoble birds of prey.

hawk, *v.i.*; hawked, *pt.*, *pp.*; hawking, *ppr.* 1 To catch, or attempt to catch (birds), by means of hawks trained for the purpose, and let loose on the prey; to practise falconry.

2. To fly at; to attack on the wing.

hawk, *n.* An effort to force up phlegm from the throat, accompanied with noise.

hawk, *v.i.* [Imitative; compare Dan. *harke*, W. *hochi*, to hawk.] To make an audible effort to force up phlegm, etc., from the throat.

hạwk, *v.t.* To raise, as phlegm, from the throat, by an audible effort.

hạwk, *v.t.* [D. *heuker*, a retailer.] To sell or offer for sale by outcry in a street or other public place; to sell or try to sell, as goods, by offering them at people's doors; to convey through town or country for sale; to peddle.

hạwk, *n.* A small quadrangular board with a handle underneath, used by plasterers to hold the plaster.

hạwk′bill, *n.* *Eretmochelys imbricata*, the tortoise that is the chief source of tortoise-shell.

hạwk′bit, *n.* 1. Any plant of the genus *Hieracium*; a hawkweed.

2. A plant of the genus *Leontodon*, as *Leontodon autumnalis*, or fall dandelion.

hạwked, *a.* Curving, like a hawk's bill. [Obs.]

hạwk′ẽr, *n.* [D. *heuker*, a retailer.] One who offers goods for sale by outcry in the street; a peddler.

hạwk′ẽr, *n.* [AS. *hafecere*, from *hafoc*, *hafuc*, a hawk.] A falconer.

hạwk′ey, *n.* A variant spelling of *hockey*.

Hạwk′eȳe, *n.* [Said to be from the name of an Indian chief.] One born in or a resident of Iowa, nicknamed the "Hawkeye State." [Colloq., U. S.]

hạwk′eȳed (-īd), *a.* Having a keen eye.

hạwk′=flȳ, *n.* A hornet-fly.

hạwk′=moth, *n.* A very large moth of the *Sphingidæ* or sphinxes. The name is given because of its hovering motion when feeding, to which is also due the name, humming-bird hawk-moth, *Macroglossa stellatarum*. The death's-head hawk-moth, *Acherontia atropos*, has a marking closely resembling a skull on the upper side of the thorax. All species have a long proboscis to draw the nectar from flowers and the larvæ are usually naked green caterpillars with a caudal spine.

Privet Hawk-moth (*Sphinx ligustri*).

hạwk′=owl, *n.* 1. *Surnia ulula*, a day-owl of North America, Asia, and Europe. It resembles a hawk in appearance and habits.

2. Any of various other owls, as the snowy owl, the short-eared owl, etc.

hạwk's′=bēard, *n.* A plant of the genus *Crepis* of the *Compositæ*.

hạwk's′=bill, *n.* 1. A hawkbill.

2. A checking device in the striking movement of clockwork.

hạwk′weed, *n.* 1. A plant of the genus *Hieracium*.

2. A plant, *Senecio hieracifolius*.

hạwm, *n.* See *Halm*.

hạwm, *v.i.* To idle; to lounge. [Prov. Eng.]

hä′wok, *n.* [N. Am. Indian.] In numismatics, the perforated, disk-shaped, clam-shell money of the aborigines of southern California.

hạwṣe, *n.* [Ice. *hals*, the neck, part of the forecastle or bow of a ship.] Nautically, (a) that part of a ship's bow in which are the hawse-holes for the cable; (b) the situation of a ship moored with anchors from each bow; (c) the distance between a ship s head and the anchors by which she rides.

Athwart hawse; see under *Athwart*.

Foul hawse; the situation when the cables cross each other or are twisted together.

hạwṣe′=bag, *n.* A bag of oakum used to plug hawse-holes in a head sea.

hạwṣe′=block, *n.* A block used to plug a hawse-hole; called also *hawse-plug*.

hạwṣe′=bōl″stẽr, *n.* A bolster or block of iron or ironed wood placed under a hawse-hole to prevent chafing by the cable.

hạwṣe′=box, *n.* The hawse-hole. [Obs.]

hạwṣe′=buck″lẽr, *n.* An iron plate or hinged shutter for covering the exterior opening of a hawse-hole.

hạwṣe′=hōle, *n.* A cylindrical hole in the bow of a ship, through which a cable passes.

To come in through the hawse-holes; to begin sea service in the lowest grade.

hạwṣe′=hook, *n.* A breast-hook which crosses the hawse-timber above the upper deck.

hạwṣe′=piēce, *n.* One of the foremost timbers of a ship, through which the hawse-hole is cut.

hạwṣe′=pipe, *n.* An iron pipe fitted into the hawse-hole to prevent the wood from being abraded.

hạwṣe′=plug, *n.* A plug used for stopping the hawse-holes; a hawse-block.

hạwṣ′ẽr, *n.* [OFr. *haulseree*, from *haulser*, *hausser*, to raise, lift; LL. *altiare*, to raise, from L. *altus*, high.] A large rope, in size between a cable and a towline.

hạwṣ′ẽr=laid, *a.* Made of three small ropes laid up into one.

hạwṣe′=tim″bẽr, *n.* An upright in the bow through which a hawse-hole is cut.

hạwṣe′=wood, *n.* A general name for the hawse-timbers.

hạwṣ′ing=i″ron (-ī″ũrn), *n.* A calking-iron or chisel.

hạwṣ′ing=mal″let, *n.* A beetle or mallet used in calking.

hạw′thorn, *n.* [ME. *hawethorn*; AS. *hægthorn*, the hawthorn; *haga*, a hedge, haw, and *thorn*, thorn.] A thorny shrub or small tree, *Cratægus Oxyacantha*, bearing the haw; much used in hedges.

hạw′thorn=grōs″bēak, *n.* A bird, the hawfinch.

hāy, *n.* [ME. *hay*, *hey*; AS. *hig*, hay, cut grass, also, growing grass.] Grass cut and dried for fodder; grass prepared for preservation.

Between hay and grass; between seasons; too late for something and too early for something else. [Colloq., U. S.]

Hay tea; a decoction used in cattle-feed.

Neither hay nor grass; not exactly this or that; a hodgepodge.

Tame hay; hay, the grass for which is grown from timothy, clover, etc., distinguished from that cut from wild grass.

To make hay while the sun shines; to make the best use of time and opportunity.

Wild hay; hay made of native grass.

hāy, *n.* [ME. *haye*, *heye*; AS. *hege*, a hedge, fence, from *haga*, a hedge.]

1. A hedge. [Obs.]

2. A net which incloses the haunt of an animal.

3. A round dance.

hāy, *v.i.*; hayed, *pt.*, *pp.*; haying, *ppr.* To cut or put up grass for hay.

hāy, *v.i.* To lay snares for rabbits. [Obs.]

hāy, *n.* In fencing, a home thrust.

hāy′=ba-cil″lus, *n.* A non-pathogenic bacillus present in hay infusions.

hāy′bird, *n.* In ornithology, (a) the blackcap; (b) the American jacksnipe.

hāy′bōte, *n.* [ME. *haye*, hedge, and *boote*, a fine; AS. *hege*, hedge, and *bot*, a fine, reparation.] In old English law, an allowance of wood to a tenant for repairing hedges or fences; hedge-bote.

hāy′=çap, *n.* Any covering placed over a haycock to shield it from rain.

hāy′çock, *n.* A conical pile or heap of hay in the field.

hāy′=çōld, *n.* Hay-fever.

hāy′=cut″tẽr, *n.* A machine for chopping hay for convenience in feeding cattle.

hāy′=fē″vẽr, *n.* In medicine, a catarrhal affection of the mucous membrane of the eyes and nose, attributed to the irritation caused by the pollen of various grasses and plants; called also *hay-asthma*.

hāy′fiēld, *n.* A field in which grass is grown for hay, or a field on which hay is cured and stored.

hāy′fork, *n.* Any fork used in handling hay; specifically, a device for holding a part of a load of hay to be put in a stack or mow.

hāy′=hook, *n.* 1. A hook used for pulling hay from a mow or stack by hand.

2. In heraldry, a hook used as a bearing, sometimes finished with an animal's head.

hāy′ing, *n.* Haymaking; the getting in of hay.

hāy′=knife (-nīf), *n.* A kind of large knife used in cutting hay out of a stack or mow.

hāy′=lōad″ẽr, *n.* An implement by which hay is taken from the swath and delivered on the wagon.

hāy′loft, *n.* The upper part of a building used for hay.

hāy′māk″ẽr, *n.* 1. One who cuts and dries grass for fodder.

2. A device for curing hay by means of hot air.

3. A kind of dance; called also *haymakers' jig*.

hāy′māk″ing, *n.* The work of cutting grass and curing it for fodder.

hāy′=mär″ket, *n.* A place for the sale of hay.

hāy′mow, *n.* A mow or mass of hay laid up in a barn for preservation.

hāy′=press, *n.* A machine for compressing hay into bales.

hāy′rack, *n.* 1. A sort of frame, set on a wagon-body, for hauling hay, straw, etc.

2. An open framework at which stock may feed.

hāy′rāke, *n.* A rake for hay.

hāy′rick, *n.* A pile of hay; usually, a long pile for preservation in the open air.

hāy′seed, *n.* One who is not familiar with city life. [Slang.]

hāy′stack, *n.* A stack or large pile of hay in the open air, laid up for preservation.

hāy′stạlk (-stạk), *n.* A stalk of hay.

hāy′=ted″dẽr, *n.* A machine for scattering hay so as to expose it to the sun and air. It consists of a pair of wheels supporting a reel carrying bars set with curved tines pointing outward. The reel is rotated by a pinion connected with a spur-wheel in the hub of one of the wheels.

Hay-tedder.

hāy′thorn, *n.* Hawthorn.

Hāy′ti-ăn, *a.* and *n.* See *Haitian*.

hāy′wärd, *n.* [ME. *heyward*; AS. *hæigweard*; *haga*, a haw, hedge, and *weard*, keeper.]

1. A person formerly appointed to guard the hedges, and hence to keep cattle from doing them injury. [Eng.]

2. A pound-master; so called in New England.

haz′ärd, *n.* [ME. *hazard*, a game of chance; OFr. *hazard*, a game of dice, adventure; Sp. *azar*, an unforeseen disaster, an accident, an unfortunate card or throw at dice, from Ar. *al-zār*, the die; *al*, the, and *zār*, a die, from Per. *zār*, die.]

1. A game at dice.

2. Danger; risk; peril.

3. A chance; an accident; a casualty.

> But life is a *hazard* at the best. —Byron.

4. The stake in gaming. [Obs.]

5. A stroke in billiards. [Eng.]

6. In fire-insurance, a risk of more than ordinary liability to burn; with a qualifying word; as, special *hazard*.

7. In golf, a general term for any natural impediment to the play.

To run the hazard; to risk; to take the chance.

Syn.—Chance, risk, venture, danger.

haz′ärd, *v.t.*; hazarded, *pt.*, *pp.*; hazarding, *ppr.*

1. To expose to chance; to put in danger of loss or injury; to venture; to risk; as, to *hazard* life to save a friend.

2. To venture to incur or bring on; as, to *hazard* the loss of reputation.

Syn.—Risk, venture.—One *hazards* and *risks* under the fear of an evil; one *ventures* with the hope of a good.

haz′ärd, *v.i.* To try the chance; to run the risk or danger.

haz′ärd-ȧ-ble, *a.* 1. Liable to hazard or chance; hazardous; risky.

2. Of a nature or value not barring from hazard.

haz′ärd-ẽr, *n.* 1. One who ventures or puts at stake.

2. One who plays at hazard. [Obs.]

haz′ärd-īze, *n.* A hazardous venture; hazard. [Obs.]

haz′ärd-ous, *a.* Dangerous; that exposes to peril or danger of loss or evil; as, a *hazardous* attempt or experiment.

haz′ärd-ous-ly, *adv.* In a hazardous manner.

haz′ärd-ous-ness, *n.* The state of being attended with danger.

haz′ärd-ry, *n.* Rashness; temerity; also, gaming at hazard. [Obs.]

haz′ärd=tā″ble, *n.* A table on which hazard is played; any gaming-table.

hāze, *n.* [Origin uncertain; compare Ice. *höss*, gray, AS. *hasu*, *heasu*, gray, Arm. *aëzen*, *ézen*, a warm vapor.]

1. Vapor which renders the air thick and less transparent, but not as damp as in foggy weather.

2. Figuratively, lack of perspicacity.

hāze, *v.t.*; hazed, *pt.*, *pp.*; hazing, *ppr.* [OFr. *haser*, to irritate, vex, annoy.]

1. To urge, drive, harass, especially with labor.

2. To subject to humiliating maltreatment; to make the victim of mock discipline; as, sophomores *haze* freshmen.

hāze, *v.i.* To be hazy or thick with haze.

hā′zel, *n.* [ME. *hasel*, *hesil*; AS. *hæsel*, the hazel.] One of various shrubs or small trees of the genus *Corylus* of an ancient type. *Corylus Americana*, the common *hazel* of America, produces the common hazelnut.

hā′zel, *a.* Pertaining to the hazel or like it; of a light brown color like the hazelnut.

hā′zel=çrot″tles, *n.* *Sticta pulmonacea*, a lichen yielding a dye for woolen goods.

hā′zel=ēarth, *n.* A kind of red loam; soil adapted to the nurture of hazel-trees.

hāze′less, *a.* Devoid of haze.

hā′zel=grouse, *n.* *Bonasa betulina*, the European ruffed grouse.

hā′zel=hen, *n.* The hazel-grouse.

hā′zel-ly, *a.* Of the color of the hazelnut; of a light brown. [Rare.]

hā′zel-nut, *n.* [ME. *haselnote*; AS. *hæselhnutu*; *hæsel*, hazel, and *hnutu*, nut.] The nut or fruit of the hazel.

hā′zel=tree, *n.* 1. The common hazel.

2. *Guevina Avellana*, a proteaceous evergreen tree of Chile, the tough and elastic wood of which is used in building boats.

hā′zel-wŏrt, *n.* In botany, the asarabacca, *Asarum Europæum*.

hā′zẽr, *n.* One who hazes.

hā′zi-ness, *n.* The state of being hazy.

hā′zle, *v.t.* To make dry. [Obs.]

hā′zle, *a.* and *n.* Same as *Hazel*.

hā′zy, *a.* 1. Thick with haze; foggy; misty.

> A tender *hazy* brightness. —Wordsworth.

2. Figuratively, dim; obscure; not clear; as, to have *hazy* notions about anything.

Syn.—Foggy, nebulous, misty, filmy, gauzy, cloudy, murky.

hē, *pron.*; *nom.* he; *poss.* his; *obj.* him; *nom. pl.* they; *poss. pl.* their *or* theirs; *obj. pl.* them. [ME. *he*; AS. *he*.]

1. The masculine singular pronoun of the third person; the man or male being or object previously mentioned.

Thy desire shall be to thy husband, and *he* shall rule over thee. —Gen. iii. 16.

2. An individual described by a following relative clause or by an equivalent of a relative clause; the person indefinitely.

He that walketh with wise men shall be wise. —Prov. xiii. 20.

3. Any person of the male sex; man; used as a noun.

Such mortal drugs I have; but Mantua's law
Is death to any *he* that utters them.—Shak.

He is often prefixed to the names of animals to designate the male kind; as, a *he*-goat; a *he*-bear.

head (hed), *n.* [ME. *hed*, *heved*; AS. *heáfod*, the head.]

1. The upper or anterior part of the body of an animal, containing the brain, the organs of sight, of smell, taste, and hearing, and in man, part of the organs of speech.

2. Understanding; the mental faculties; will or resolution; inclination; mind; as, a good *head*; a cool *head*.

3. A person; an individual; one of a number of persons or animals; as, the tax was raised by a certain rate per *head*; one hundred *head* of cattle. *Head* in this sense is both singular and plural.

4. A chief; a principal person; a leader; a commander; one who has the first rank or place, and to whom others are subordinate; as, the *head* of an army; the *head* of a sect or party.

5. That which gives a striking appearance to the *head*, as the hair, a headdress, antlers of a deer, etc.; as, a beautiful *head* of hair.

6. A part of a thing regarded as in some degree resembling in position or otherwise the human *head*; (a) the top, especially when larger than the rest of the thing; as, the *head* of a spear; the *head* of a cabbage; the *head* of a nail; the *head* of a mast; (b) the main point or part; the most prominent feature; (c) the fore part; hence, the most conspicuous position; as, the *head* of a ship (which includes the bows on both sides); the *head* of a parade; the *head* of a class; (d) the upper part, as of a bed or bedstead, of a street, etc.; (e) in botany, the top of a plant; the part on which the seed grows; a capitulum; (f) that which rises on the top, as the froth on a pot of beer or other effervescing liquor; (g) the maturated part of an ulcer or boil; (h) the principal source of a stream; as, the *head* of the Nile; (i) the part most remote from the mouth or opening into the sea; as, the *head* of a bay, gulf, or creek; (j) a headland; a promontory; (k) that which closes the end of a barrel or the like; a bundle of flax about two feet long and weighing a few pounds; (l) the obverse of a coin or medal; (m) that part of a hammer with which an object is struck; (n) the capital of a column.

7. The vertical height or available fall of water from a dam, reservoir, etc.

8. A topic of discourse; a division of a subject discoursed on; a branch; a title in a printed book.

9. A crisis; a pitch; a height; a degree of strength or force.

10. Power; armed force.

A buck of the first head; a male deer five years old, having grown its first set of antlers.

By the head; see under *By*.

Head and shoulders; (a) by force; violently; as, to drag one *head and shoulders*; (b) by very much; emphatically; as, *head and shoulders* above competitors.

Head foremost; see *Headforemost*.

Head over heels; heels over head; topsy-turvy.

Neither head nor tail; a phrase denoting uncertainty; not reducible to certainty.

Over the head of; above or beyond the comprehension of.

To be out of one's head; bewildered or temporarily insane.

To lose one's head; to lose presence of mind.

Syn.—Top, crown, chief, leader, ruler, mind, source, section, division, topic, gathering, culmination, crisis, leadership, guide, commander, acme, summit.

head, *a.* 1. Chief; principal; as, *head* waiter.

2. In navigation, directly opposing; as, *head* winds.

head (hed), *v.t.*; headed, *pt.*, *pp.*; heading, *ppr.* 1. To lead; to direct; to act as leader to; as, to *head* an army; to *head* an expedition.

2. To behead; to decapitate. [Obs.]

3. To form a head to; to fit or furnish with a head; as, to *head* a nail.

4. To cut off the head of; to lop; as, to *head* trees.

5. To go in front of; to get in front of in order to stop; as, to *head* a drove of cattle.

6. To set on the head of; as, to *head* a cask.

To head off; to get ahead of; intercept; thwart.

To head up; to inclose with a heading, as a barrel.

head, *v.i.* 1. To originate; to spring; to have its source, as a river.

A broad river, that *heads* in the great Blue Ridge. —Adair.

2. To be directed; as, how does the ship *head?*

3. To form a head; as, the cabbages *head* early.

head'āche, *n.* [ME. *hedake*, *heavedeche*; AS. *heáfodece*; *heáfod*, head, and *ece*, ache.]

1. Pain in the head.

2. An English name for the corn-poppy, *Papaver Rhœas*; called also *head-wark*.

head'āche-tree, *n.* *Premna integrifolia*, a shrub of the vervain family found in Madagascar and the East Indies. Its leaves are used by the natives as a remedy for headache.

head'āche-weed, *n.* A shrub, *Hedyosmum nutans*, belonging to the *Chloranthaceæ* found in Jamaica.

head'āch-y, *a.* Afflicted with a headache; subject to headaches.

He awoke *headachy* and feverish. —Farrar.

head'-and-head', *adv.* In nautical language, head on; head to head.

head'band, *n.* 1. A fillet; a band for the head.

2. In bookbinding, the band at each end of the inner back of a book.

3. In printing, an engraved decorative band at the top of a page or at the head of a chapter in a book.

head'band, *v.t.* To put a headband on (the inner back of a book).

head'-bāy, *n.* The space in a canal directly above the lock.

head'-bet"ō-ny, *n.* *Pedicularis Canadensis*, the wood-betony or lousewort.

head'-block, *n.* 1. In a sawmill, the movable crosspiece of a carriage on which the log rests; a device which supports the log and conveys it to the saw.

2. A piece of wood placed beneath the upper ring of the fifth wheel of a carriage or other conveyance.

head'bōard, *n.* A board forming the head, as of a bedstead.

head'bŏr"ough, **head'bŏr"rōw**, *n.* [ME. *heedborow*, *hedborowe*, lit., head-pledge; *heed*, from AS. *heáfod*, the head, and *borow*, from AS. *borh*, a pledge, security.]

1. In England, formerly, the chief of a frankpledge, tithing, or decennary, consisting of ten families; called, in some countries, *borsholder*, and sometimes *tithingman*. —Blackstone.

2. In England, a petty constable.

head'-cāse, *n.* In entomology, the integument covering the head of a pupa.

head'-chāir, *n.* A chair with a high back provided with some device for supporting the head.

head'cheese, *n.* In cookery, portions of the head and feet of swine chopped up fine, seasoned, and, after being boiled, pressed into the form of a cheese.

head'-chute, *n.* A canvas tube reaching from the head of a ship to the water, through which refuse matter is carried overboard.

head'-clŏth, *n.* 1. A turban-like covering for the head.

2. A bed-curtain behind the head of a bed.

head'-cōal, *n.* In England, the upper part of a thick seam of coal worked in separate lifts.

head'-crack"ẽr, *n.* See *Head-spade*.

head'dress, *n.* A covering or ornament for the head; also, any manner of arranging the hair with or without a covering.

Lady's Headdress, 14th century.

head'ed, *a.* Furnished with a head; having a top; used in composition as an adjective; as, clear-*headed*; long-*headed*; thick-*headed*, etc.

head'ẽr, *n.* 1. One who or that which heads nails, pins, etc.; a machine for such a purpose.

2. One who leads a mob or party.

3. In building, (a) a brick or stone laid with its shorter face or head in the surface of the wall; (b) a timber placed between two trimmers, which supports the heads of the tailpieces; (c) a heavy stone extending through the thickness of a wall.

4. A reaping-machine for cutting off only the tops of the grain.

5. In fishing industries, one who removes the heads from fish.

6. A dive or plunge headforemost, as while bathing or cycling.

7. In the manufacture of needles, one who turns all the needles in one direction.

8. One who has charge of a whaleboat.

head'fȧst, *n.* A rope at the head of a ship to fasten it to a wharf or other fixed object.

head-first', *adv.* With the head foremost.

head'fish, *n.* A sunfish of the genus *Mola*.

head-fōre'mōst, *adv.* Headfirst.

head'-frāme, *n.* In mining, the frame over the shaft which supports the head-gear.

head'-gāte, *n.* 1. The up-stream gate of a canal-lock.

2. Any sluice of a race.

head'-gear, *n.* 1. Covering or ornament for the head; headdress; head-harness.

2. The gear of a head-frame over the mouth of an excavation.

3. All the parts of a harness connected with the head.

4. In nautical language, the running-gear of the sails set forward of the foremast.

head'-hār"ness, *n.* In football, a protective covering for the head, usually made of leather.

head'-house, *n.* In mining, the structure inclosing the head-frame which serves to protect it from the weather.

head'-hunt"ẽr, *n.* A savage who indulges in the practice of head-hunting.

head'-hunt"ing, *n.* A savage practice carried on by certain uncivilized tribes, as the Dyaks of Borneo, which consists in making incursions in order to procure human heads as trophies.

head'i-ly, *adv.* In a heady or rash manner; rashly; hastily.

head'i-ness, *n.* The condition or quality of being heady.

head'ing, *n.* 1. The act or process of providing with a head.

2. That which stands at the head; title; as, the *heading* of a paper.

3. Material for the heads of casks, puncheons, barrels, etc.

4. In masonry, the end of a brick or stone presented outward.

5. In mining, (a) a driftway or passage excavated in the line of an intended tunnel, forming a gullet in which the men work; (b) the place where the work of driving a horizontal passage is being done; (c) the mass of gravel above the head of a sluice in a placer.

6. In sewing, the upper edge of a ruffle which appears above the line of stitching.

7. In fireworks, the special device of a rocket when used as a signal.

8. A heading-course.

9. A head-mold.

10. Homespun cloth; a term used in southern United States.

11. A preparation of equal parts of alum and green vitriol used in brewing.

head'ing-chis"el, *n.* A chisel used in cutting away the head of a mortise.

head'ing-cir"clẽr, *n.* A machine used for making heads for barrels, casks, etc.

head'ing-cōurse, *n.* In architecture, a course which consists entirely of headers, or of stones or bricks laid lengthwise across the thickness of the wall.

head'ing-joint, *n.* 1. In architecture, a joint of two or more boards at right angles to the fibers.

2. In masonry, a joint between two voussoirs in the same course.

head'ing-knife (-nīf), *n.* 1. A knife with which fishermen cut off the heads of fish.

2. A cooper's knife for chamfering the heads of barrels, casks, etc.

3. A saddler's knife for making holes in leather that are too large to be punched.

4. A knife used by a currier in scraping leather.

head'ing-mȧ-chine", *n.* 1. A machine by which pins are headed.

2. A reaping-machine which cuts off the heads of the grain.

3. A press for shaping the heads of cartridges.

4. A machine for making heads for casks, barrels, etc.

head'ing-tool, *n.* A tool with which the rod of metal that is used in shaping the heads of nails, bolts, etc., is held.

head'-kid"ney, *n.* In anatomy, the anterior of the three segments of the mesonephros opening into the cloaca. It is the first part of the urogenital system to be differentiated in the vertebrate embryo; the pronephros.

head'-knee (-nē), *n.* In shipbuilding, a piece of molded knee-timber situated beneath the head-rails, and fayed edgewise to the cutwater and stem, for steadying the cutwater.

head'-knot (-not), *n.* A knot of ribbons, etc., worn as part of a headdress.

head'lănd, *n.* [ME. *hevedlond*; AS. *heáfod*, head, and *land*, land.] 1. A cape; a promontory; a point of land projecting from the shore into the sea or other expanse of water.

2. A ridge or strip of unplowed land at the ends of furrows or near a fence.

head'ledge (-lej), *n.* In shipbuilding, a thwartship piece used in framing the hatchways or ladderways.

head'less, *a.* [ME. *heedless*, *hevedles*; AS. *heáfodleás*; *heáfod*, head, and *-leás*, -less.]

1. Having no head; beheaded; as, a *headless* body, neck, or carcass.
2. Destitute of a chief or leader.
3. Destitute of understanding or prudence; rash; obstinate. [Obs.]

head'light (-līt), *n.* 1. A light with a reflector, placed in front of a locomotive, a street-railway car, etc., to light the track during darkness.
2. A white light carried at the masthead of a steamer when under way at night; a masthead-light.

head'līne, *n.* 1. In printing, a line of type set at the head of a page in a paper, book, etc.
2. Among seamen, a headrope.

head'⸗līn"ing, *n.* The fabric sometimes used in ceiling the top of a passenger-car.

head'long, *adv.* 1. With the head foremost; as, to fall *headlong.*
2. Rashly; precipitately; without deliberation.

He hurries *headlong* to his fate. —Dryden.

3. Hastily; without delay or respite.

head'long, *a.* 1. Steep; precipitous.
2. Rash; precipitate; as, *headlong* folly.

head'⸗lugged, *a.* Lugged or dragged by the head. [Obs.]

head'man, *n.*; *pl.* **head'men.** A chief; a leader.

head'⸗märk, *n.* The natural characteristics of each individual of a species.

head'⸗mas"tēr, *n.* The principal master of a school or seminary.

head'⸗mōld, *n.* In architecture, a molding projecting over the head of a window or door.

head'⸗mōld"ing, *n.* A head-mold.

head'mōld⸗shot, *n.* An old name for an abnormal condition of a child in which the sutures of the skull, usually the coronal sutures, have their edges shot over each other.

head'⸗mon"ey, *n.* 1. A capitation-tax; a tax per capita.
2. A reward or bounty per head for the capture of prisoners or outlaws.

head'mōst, *a.* Most advanced; most forward; first in a line or order of progression; as, the *headmost* ship in a fleet.

head'⸗net"ting, *n.* An ornamental netting used in merchant ships instead of the fayed planking of the head-rails.

head'nōte, *n.* 1. A note placed at the top of a chapter or page.
2. In law, a brief statement placed at the top of a report of a case showing the ruling of the court upon the principles involved therein; a syllabus.

head'pan, *n.* The brainpan. [Obs.]

head'⸗pen"ny, *n.* A poll-tax; generally used in the plural, *head-pence.*

head'piēce, *n.* 1. Armor for the head; a helmet; a morion.
2. The head; especially, the head as the seat of the understanding. [Colloq.]
3. An ornamental engraving placed at the top of a page or chapter.

head'⸗plāte, *n.* 1. A plate covering the breast of the cheeks of a gun-carriage.
2. The piece that strengthens the cantle of a saddle.
3. A strip of metal which covers the joints of the top of a landau.

head'⸗pump, *n.* A small pump placed at the bow of a vessel, with the lower end communicating with the sea, used chiefly for washing decks.

head'quar"tērs (-kwar"), *n.pl.* and *sing.* 1. The quarters or place of residence of the commander-in-chief of an army.
2. The residence of any chief, or the place from which orders are issued.
3. The place where one chiefly resides; one's place of business. [Colloq.]

head'rāce, *n.* A strong current of water; the channel in which water is led to a water-wheel.

head'⸗rāil, *n.* In shipbuilding, one of the elliptical rails at the head of a ship.

head'⸗rēach, *v.i* Among seamen, to shoot ahead, as a vessel when brought to the wind and about to be put on the other tack.

head'⸗ring, *n.* A ring worn in the hair by the men of the Kafirs after marriage.

head'rọọm, *n.* In architecture, the clear space below a girder, arch, etc.

head'rōpe, *n.* Among seamen, that part of a boltrope which terminates any sail on the upper edge, and to which it is sewed.

head'sāil, *n.* Any one of those sails of a vessel set forward of the foremast.

head'shāke, *n.* A significant shake of the head.

head'⸗sheet, *n.* Among seamen, any one of the sheets of the headsails.

head'⸗shiēld, *n.* In herpetology a plate on the top of the head of a lizard or snake.

head'ship, *n.* The state or position of being a head or chief; authority; dignity; rule; government.

head'⸗sill, *n.* In sawing, one of the two crosspieces on which the end of the log rests.

head'⸗sil"vēr, *n.* See *Head-penny.*

head'⸗skin, *n.* A tough substance protecting the case of the sperm-whale, capable of resisting the blow of a harpoon.

heads'măn, *n.*; *pl.* **heads'men.** 1. One who cuts off heads; an executioner.
2. In a colliery, one who removes the coal from the workings to the horseway.

head'⸗spāde, *n.* A long-handled implement used by whalers for cutting into the head of a whale; a head-cracker.

head'spring, *n.* Fountain; source; origin.

head'stạll, *n.* That part of the bridle which encompasses the head.

head'⸗stā"tion, *n.* In Australia, the dwelling-house, offices, etc., on a station or farm.

head'⸗stick, *n.* 1. Among seamen, a short, round stick with a hole at each end, through which the headrope of some triangular sails is thrust before it is sewed on.
2. In printing, a piece of furniture placed at the head of a form between the type and the chase.

head'stock, *n.* In machinery, (a) the framing used to support the gudgeons of a wheel; (b) the frame which supports the revolving spindle in a lathe; (c) the member forming the under frame of a railway-car.

head'stōne, *n.* 1. The principal stone in a foundation; the chief or corner stone.
2. The stone at the head of a grave.

head'⸗stọọl, *n.* A form of pillow once used as a rest for the neck and to protect the hair from being disturbed. Such an appliance is still in use among the Japanese and other Oriental people.

head'strong, *a.* 1. Not easily restrained; obstinate; ungovernable; bent on pursuing one's own course.

Now let the *headstrong* boy my will control. —Dryden.

2. Directed by ungovernable will, or proceeding from obstinacy; as, a *headstrong* course.

Syn.—Obstinate, intractable, heady, unruly, stubborn, ungovernable.

head'strong"ness, *n.* Obstinacy. [Rare.]

head'⸗swōrd (-sōrd), *n.* A Cornish mining term for water running through an adit-level.

head'⸗tim"bēr, *n.* In shipbuilding, one of the upright pieces of timber inserted between the upper knee and the curved rail, to support the frame of the head-rails.

head'tīre, *n.* Dress or attire for the head.

head'⸗tōne, *n.* In singing, a tone produced as if in the cavities of the head.

head'⸗valve, *n.* The delivery-valve in a condensing steam-engine.

head'⸗voice, *n.* In singing, that use of the voice which produces head-tones.

head'wărd, head'wărds, *adv.* Toward the head.

head'wạ"tēr, *n.* The upper part of a river, near its source, or one of the streams that contribute their waters to form a larger stream.

head'wāy, *n.* 1. The forward motion of a ship; hence, any kind of progress or advancement.
2. In architecture, headroom.

head'⸗wōrd, *n.* The title-word of a paragraph.

head'wōrk, *n.* 1. Mental or intellectual labor.
2. In architecture, the heads and other ornaments on the keystones of arches.

head'y, *a.* 1. Rash; hasty; precipitate; disposed to rush forward in an enterprise without thought or deliberation; hurried on by will or passion; ungovernable.

All the talent required, is to be *heady,* to be violent on one side or the other.—Temple.

2. Apt to affect the head; inflaming; intoxicating; strong.
3. Violent; impetuous. [Rare.]
4. In recent use, self-possessed or calm; as, a *heady* ball-player. [Colloq.]

head'⸗yärd, *n.* Among seamen, one of the yards of a ship's foremast.

hēal, *v.t.* [ME. *helen, hilen*; AS. *helan,* to cover, conceal.] To cover, as a roof with slates, tin, etc. [Prov. Eng.]

hēal, *v.t.*; healed, *pt., pp.*; healing, *ppr.* [ME. *helen*; AS. *hǣlan,* to heal, make whole, from *hāl,* whole.]
1. To cure of a disease or wound, and restore to soundness, or to that state of body in which the natural functions are regularly performed; as, to *heal* the sick.

Speak, and my servant shall be *healed.* —Matt. viii. 8.

2. To subdue; to remove; to remedy.

I will *heal* their backsliding. —Hos. xiv. 4.

3. To restore to purity; to cleanse; to purify.

Thy gifts may scarce now *heal* my heart. —W. Morris.

4. To remove, as differences or dissension; as, to *heal* a breach.

Syn.—Cure, remedy, restore.

hēal, *v.i.* To grow sound; to return to a sound state; as, the limb *heals,* or the wound *heals;* sometimes with *up* or *over*; as, it will *heal up,* or *over.*

hēal, *n.* Health. [Obs.]

hēal'ȧ-ble, *a.* Capable of being healed.

hēal'ạll, *n.* In botany, *Brunella vulgaris,* a plant formerly supposed to possess healing properties. The name is also applied to the horse-balm, *Collinsonia Canadensis.*

hēald, *n.* Same as *Heddle.*

hēal'ēr, *n.* One who or that which heals.

hēal'fụl, *a.* Tending to heal; healing. [Obs.]

hēal'ing, *a.* Tending to cure; mild; mollifying; curative; as, a *healing* medicine; *healing* words; *healing* influence.

hēal'ing, *n.* The act or process by which a cure is effected.

hēal'ing⸗hērb, *n.* The comfrey, *Symphytum officinale.*

hēal'ing-ly, *adv.* In a healing manner; so as to cure.

health (helth), *n.* [ME. *helth*; AS. *hǣlth,* health, from *hāl,* whole.]
1. That state of a living organism in which the parts are sound, well organized and disposed, and in which all the organs perform their natural functions without pain or disease; soundness of body.

Health is something different from strength; it is universal good condition.—Munger.

2. Moral or intellectual soundness; natural vigor of the faculties.
3. Power to heal, restore, or purify.

The tongue of the wise is *health.*—Prov. xii. 18.

4. A toast wishing health and happiness to another; as, to drink one's *health.*

Come, love and *health* to all. —Shak.

Board of health; an official board appointed by the government of a country, state, city, or town to promote or regulate public sanitary conditions and in general to look after the public health.

Health officer; an officer whose duty it is to enforce the sanitary rules and regulations of any place, particularly a seaport, a quarantine officer.

health'fụl, *a.* 1. Full of or in the enjoyment of health; free from disease; characterized by or resulting from health; healthy; as, a *healthful* body; a *healthful* plant; a *healthful* condition.
2. Serving to promote health; wholesome; salubrious; salutary; as, a *healthful* air or climate; a *healthful* diet,
3. Well-disposed; favorable. [Rare.]

health'fụl-ly, *adv.* In health; wholesomely.

health'fụl-ness, *n.* The state of being healthful or healthy.

health'i-ly, *adv.* In a healthy manner or condition.

health'i-ness, *n.* The state of being healthy; soundness; freedom from disease; as, the *healthiness* of an animal or plant.

health'less, *a.* 1. Infirm; sickly; unhealthy.
2. Not conducive to health. [Rare.]

health'less-ness, *n.* The state of being healthless.

health'⸗lift, *n.* Any of various weight-lifting machines for exercising the muscles of the body.

health'sōme, *a.* Wholesome. [Rare.]

health'sōme-ness, *n.* Wholesomeness. [Obs.]

health'wărd, *a.* and *adv.* Toward health.

health'y, *a.* 1. Being in a sound state; enjoying health; hale; sound; characteristic of health; as, a *healthy* body; a *healthy* color.
2. Conducive to health; wholesome; salubrious; as, a *healthy* exercise; a *healthy* climate.

Syn.—Salubrious, salutary, sound, wholesome, well, hale, robust, vigorous.

hēam, *n.* [Compare AS. cild*hamma,* womb; O.D. *hamme,* the afterbirth.] The afterbirth of an animal.

hēap, *n.* [ME. *heep, heap*; AS. *hēap,* a crowd, or multitude of people, a pile.]
1. A pile or mass; a collection of things laid in a body, so as to form an elevation; as, a *heap* of earth or stones.

Huge *heaps* of slain around the body rise. —Dryden.

2. A crowd; a throng; said of persons. [Colloq.]
3. A large quantity; a great many.

I have noticed a *heap* of things in my life. —R. L. Stevenson.

hēap, *v.t.*; heaped (hēpt), *pt., pp.*; heaping, *ppr.* [ME. *hepen*; AS. *hēapian,* to heap, pile together, from *hēap,* a crowd, multitude.]
1. To throw or lay in a heap; to pile: to accumulate; to amass; as, to *heap* stones; frequently followed by *up* or *on*; as, to *heap up* treasures; to *heap on* coal.
2. To round or form into a heap, as in measuring; to fill to overflowing; as, to *heap* a barrel with potatoes.

Syn.—Pile, accumulate, amass.—To *heap* is an indefinite action; it may be performed with or without order; to *pile* is a definite action done with design and order; to *accumulate* is properly to bring or add heap to heap, which is a gradual and unfinished act; to *amass* is to form into a mass, which is a single complete act.

hēap′ẽr, *n.* One who heaps, piles, or amasses.

hēap′y, *a.* Lying in heaps.

hēar, *v.t.*; heard, *pt.*, *pp.*; hearing, *ppr.* [ME. *heren, heeren*; AS. *hiéran*, to hear.]

1. To perceive by the ear; to receive an impression of through the auditory organs; as, to *hear* sound; to *hear* a voice; to *hear* words.

O friends! I *hear* the tread of nimble feet.
—Milton.

2. To give audience to; to heed; to listen to; as, to *hear* a lesson; the case was *heard* before a full bench.

3. To learn or understand by harkening; to harken to understandingly.

My son, *hear* the instruction of thy father.
—Prov. i. 8.

4. To pay regard to; to answer with favor; to accede to the wishes of.

The Lord hath *heard* my supplication.
—Ps. vi. 9.

5. To be a hearer of; to attend the ministrations of; as, what minister did you *hear?* [Colloq.]

To hear a bird sing; see under *Bird*.

To hear of; to regard with favor the idea of; always used negatively; as, he would not *hear of* such a thing.

To hear say; to hear a person say; to learn by general report. [Colloq.]

To hear tell of; to hear what is said about. [Colloq.]

hēar, *v.i.* 1. To enjoy the sense or faculty of perceiving sound; as, he is deaf, he cannot *hear*.

2. To listen; to harken; to attend; as, he *hears with* solicitude.

3. To be told; to receive by report; as, so I *hear*.

Hear, hear! an exclamatory form of applause used to call approbatory attention to what a speaker is saying.

To hear ill; to be blamed. [Obs.]

To hear well; to be praised. [Obs.]

hẽard, *v.*, past tense and past participle of *hear*.

hēar′ẽr, *n.* One who hears; one who attends or listens to what is orally delivered by another; an auditor; one of an audience.

hēar′ing, *n.* 1. The act of perceiving sound; perception of sound; the faculty or sense by which sound is perceived; one of the five external senses.

Yet in these ears, till *hearing* dies,
One set slow bell will seem to toll.
—Tennyson.

2. Audience; attention to what is delivered; opportunity to be heard; as, I waited on him but could not obtain a *hearing*.

3. A judicial investigation of a suit, as before a court, for the sake of adjudication; attention to the facts, testimony, and arguments in a cause between parties with a view to a just decision.

His last offenses to us
Shall have judicious *hearing*. —Shak.

4. Reach of the ear; extent within which sound may be heard; as, he was not within *hearing*.

Hard of hearing; partly deaf.

Hearing in presence; in the Scotch Court of Session, a formal hearing of counsel before a full bench.

heärk′en, *v.i.* and *v.t.* See *Harken*.

heärk′en-ẽr, *n.* See *Harkener*.

hēar′săl, *n.* Rehearsal. [Obs.]

hēar′sāy, *n.* Report; rumor; fame; common talk; as, the account we have depends on *hearsay*; also used adjectively; as, *hearsay* evidence.

Hearsay evidence; any evidence not based upon the personal knowledge of the witness but known to him only through other persons. Such evidence is accepted only as to such matters as genealogies, reputation, statements contrary to interest, dying declarations, etc.

hẽarse, *n.* A hind in its second year. [Prov. Eng.]

hẽarse, *n.* [ME. *herse, herce*, a frame to hold lights in a church service or at a funeral, the funeral pageant, the bier, the corpse; OFr. *herce*, a harrow, a grated portcullis; L. *hirpex* (*-icis*), a harrow.]

1. A temporary monument erected at a grave. [Obs.]

2. A canopy in a church under which the bier rested during a funeral service. [Obs.]

3. A bier. [Obs.]

4. A carriage for conveying the dead to the grave.

5. In heraldry, a charge resembling a portcullis or a harrow.

hẽarse, *v.t.* To inclose in a hearse. [Obs.]

hẽarse′çlọth, *n.* A pall; a cloth to cover a coffin placed upon a bier.

hẽarse′līke, *a.* Suitable to a funeral.

heärt, *n.* [ME. *hart, herte*; AS. *heorte*, heart.]

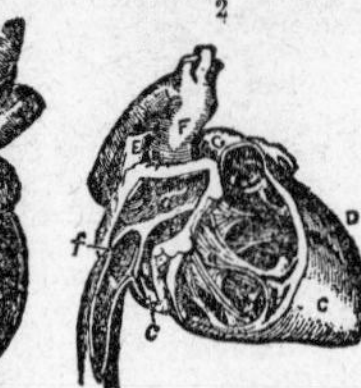

Human Heart.

Fig. 1. Exterior. A, Right auricle. B, Left auricle. C, Right ventricle. D, Left ventricle. E, Vena cava superior. F, Aorta. G, Pulmonary artery. H, Brachiocephalic trunk. I, Left primitive carotid artery. K, Left subclavian artery. L, Left coronary artery.

Fig. 2. Section, right side. C, D, E, F, G, as in fig. 1. *a*, Cavity of right auricle. *b*, Inferior vena cava. *c*, Coronary valve. *d*, Entrance of the auriculo-ventricular opening. *e*, Valve of the pulmonary artery. *f*, Fossa ovalis.

1. A muscular organ which is the propelling agent of the blood in the animal body, situated in the thorax of vertebrate animals. From this organ the primary arteries arise, and in it the main veins terminate. By its alternate dilatation and contraction the circulation is carried on, the blood being received from the veins, and returned through the arteries. In man, quadrupeds, and birds the heart consists of four chambers, reptiles and amphibians have a three-chambered heart, while fishes have two chambers only. The heart of an insect or a spider is a long tube divided into compartments; that of mollusks is two or three-chambered.

2. The human heart regarded as the seat of the mental faculties or capacities; hence, (a) the seat of the affections and passions, either singly or combined, as of love, joy, grief, enmity, courage, pleasure, etc., especially of the more admirable feelings or emotions; as, a good *heart*; a selfish *heart*; sometimes used of the moral side of human nature in contradistinction to the intellectual; as, he was all head and no *heart*; (b) the seat of the will or inclination; disposition of mind; mental tendency; (c) conscience, or sense of good or ill; the seat of moral life and character.

The life of man is in his *heart*. —Bushnell.

3. The inner part of anything; the part nearest the middle or center; as, the *heart* of a country, kingdom, or empire; the *heart* of a town; the *heart* of a tree.

4. The chief part; the vital or most essential part; the vigorous or efficacious part; the core.

5. An appellation of kindness, encouragement, or endearment.

Cheerly, my *hearts*. —Shak.

6. Strength; power of producing; vigor; fertility; as, to keep the land in *heart*. [Rare.]

7. That which has the shape or form of a *heart*; especially, a roundish or oval figure or object having an obtuse point at one end and a corresponding indentation or depression at the other, regarded as representing the figure of a *heart*.

8. One of a suit of playing cards marked with the figure of a *heart*.

9. Courage; spirit; as, to keep up one's *heart*.

10. Secret meaning; real intention.

And then show you the *heart* of my message.
—Shak.

11. [*pl.*] In card-playing, a game the object of which is to take in as few *hearts*, in play, as possible. The player who has the fewest *hearts* at the end of the game is the winner.

12. Among seamen, a wooden block shaped like a *heart* through which the lanyards of the stays are rove.

After one's own heart; in accordance with one's desires or ideas; as, a man *after my own heart*.

At heart; in real character or disposition; at bottom; substantially; really; as, he is good *at heart*.

By heart; thoroughly; as, to learn *by heart*.

Feast of the Sacred Heart; in the Roman Catholic church, a feast celebrated on the Friday after the octave of Corpus Christi.

For one's heart; for one's life; if one's life were at stake; as, I could not *for my heart* refuse his request.

Heart and hand; with enthusiasm; entirely; as, we are with you *heart and hand*.

Heart and soul; with intense earnestness; wholly.

Heart of oak; figuratively, a brave or intrepid person.

Immaculate Heart or *Heart of Mary*; in the Roman Catholic church, the heart of the Virgin Mary, to which reverence is paid.

Sacred Heart; in the Roman Catholic church, the heart of Christ, to which adoration is paid.

Smoker's heart; an abnormal state of the heart arising from the inordinate use of tobacco; called also *tobacco-heart*.

To break the heart of; see under *Break*.

To find in one's heart; to be willing or disposed.

To have at heart; to have an earnest desire for.

To have in the heart; to purpose; to have design or intention.

To have the heart in the mouth; to be badly scared or excited.

To lose heart; to become discouraged.

To lose one's heart; to fall in love.

To set the heart at rest; to make oneself quiet; to be tranquil or easy in mind.

To set the heart upon; to fix the desires on; to be very desirous of obtaining or keeping.

To take heart of grace; to take courage.

To take to heart, to lay to heart; to be much affected by; to have concern for; to grieve about.

To wear one's heart upon one's sleeve; to expose one's disposition, feelings, or intentions to every one.

With all one's heart; completely; intensely; earnestly; thoroughly; fully.

Syn.—Core, nucleus, kernel, interior, center, character, disposition, courage, hardihood, nature, life, feeling, benevolence.

heärt, *v.t.* To encourage. [Obs.]

heärt, *v.i.* To form a close, compact head, as a plant; especially, to have the central part of the head close and compact.

heärt′āçhe, *n.* Sorrow; anguish of mind.

heärt′-bēat, *n.* A pulsation of the heart; hence, in a figurative sense, a thought or an emotion.

heärt′-bīrd, *n.* A sportsman's name for the turnstone, *Strepsilas interpres*.

heärt′-block, *n.* Among seamen, a deadeye formerly used in setting up the stays of the masts.

heärt′-bond, *n.* In masonry, a kind of bond in which two stones forming the width of a wall have one stone of the same width placed over them.

heärt′breāk, *n.* Overwhelming sorrow or grief.

heärt′breāk″ẽr, *n.* 1. One who or that which breaks hearts.

2. A lady's curl; a lovelock. [Humorous.]

heärt′breāk″ing, *a.* Causing great grief or sorrow.

heärt′brō″ken, *a.* Deeply afflicted or grieved.

heärt′bũrn, *n.* An uneasy, burning sensation in the stomach; cardialgia.

heärt′bũrned, *a.* Suffering from heartburn.

heärt′bũrn″ing, *a.* Causing discontent.

heärt′bũrn″ing, *n.* 1. Heartburn.

2. Discontent; secret enmity; jealousy.

heärt′-cam, *n.* In machinery, a wheel or double cam having the form of a heart, the two sides of which may be symmetrical or otherwise, according as the motion is required to be the same in each half-revolution or different. It is used for converting a uniform circular motion into a reciprocating alternating motion. Called also *heart-wheel*.

Heart-cam.

heärt′-clot, *n.* A clot of blood in the cavity of the heart

heärt′-clō″vẽr, *n.* Same as *Heart-trefoil*.

heärt′-coç″kle, *n.* See *Heart-shell*.

heärt′dēar, *a.* Sincerely beloved. [Rare.]

heärt′deep, *a.* Rooted in the heart.

heärt′-dis-ēase″, *n.* Any morbid condition of the heart, either functional or organic.

heärt′-ēat″ing, *a.* Preying on the heart; as, *heart-eating* troubles.

heärt′ed, *a.* 1. Having a heart; chiefly used in composition and in a figurative sense; as, hard-*hearted*, faint-*hearted*, stout-*hearted*, etc.

2. Taken to heart; laid up or seated in the heart. [Obs.]

3. Composed of hearts. [Obs.]

4. Having the shape of a heart; cordate. [Rare.]

heärt′ed-ness, *n.* Earnestness; zeal. [Rare.]

heärt′en, *v.t.* 1. To encourage; to incite or stimulate the courage of.

Hearten those that fight. —Shak.

2. To restore fertility or strength to; as, to *hearten* land. [Rare.]

heärt′en-ẽr, *n.* One who or that which heartens.

heärt′felt, *a.* Deeply felt; sincere; as, *heartfelt* joy or grief.

heärt′-free, *a.* Having the heart or affections disengaged; heart-whole.

heärth, *n.* [ME. *harth, herth*; AS. *heorth*, hearth, fireplace.]

1. A pavement or floor, usually of brick or stone beneath an opening in a chimney, on which a fire is made; the brick, stone, or tiled floor of a fireplace.

Fires unrak'd and *hearths* unswept.—Shak.

2. Figuratively, the house itself, as the abode of comfort to its inmates and of hospitality to strangers; the home.

3. In metallurgy, (a) the floor of a reverberatory furnace on which the ore is heated; (b)

the lowest part in a blast-furnace, through which the melted metal passes into the crucible; (c) a bloomery.

4. The cooking apparatus on board a ship.

5. In soldering, a pan containing live charcoal, in which the tools are heated.

6. In the manufacture of glass, the *hearth* or table of a furnace for the flattening out of cylinder glass.

hearth'=cin"der, *n.* Slag formed in a furnace in which iron is refined.

hearth'=crick"et, *n.* The common house-cricket.

heart'=heav"i-ness (-hev"), *n.* Depression of spirits.

heart'=heav"y, *a.* Sad-hearted; depressed in spirits.

hearth'=ends, *n.pl.* Masses of refuse from a furnace in which lead is smelted.

hearth'=mon"ey, *n.* Hearth-tax.

hearth'=plate, *n.* A plate of cast-iron forming the sole of a refiner's furnace.

hearth'=rug, *n.* A rug placed in front of a hearth or fireplace.

hearth'stone, *n.* 1. Stone forming the hearth; hence, the fireside.

2. A soft stone used to clean and whiten floors, door-steps, etc.

hearth'=tax, *n.* Formerly, a tax imposed in England on every hearth in houses paying the church and poor rates; called also *hearth-money, hearth-penny.*

heart'i-ly, *adv.* 1. From the heart; with all the heart; with sincerity.

I *heartily* forgive them. —Shak.

2. With zeal; actively; vigorously; gladly; cordially; as, he *heartily* assisted the prince.

Syn.—Vigorously, cordially, earnestly, ardently, sincerely, gladly, eagerly.

heart'i-ness, *n.* The quality or state of being hearty.

heart'=leaf, *n.* See *Heart-trefoil.*

heart'less, *a.* 1. Without a heart.

2. Destitute of feeling or affection; cruel; as, he treated her in the most *heartless* manner.

3. Destitute of courage; spiritless; faint-hearted.

Heartless they fought, and quitted soon their ground. —Dryden.

heart'less-ly, *adv.* In a heartless manner.

heart'less-ness, *n.* The quality or state of being heartless.

heart'let, *n.* A little heart.

heart'ling, *n.* A little heart; used in a minced oath. [Obs.]

heart'=net, *n.* The net or pound of a heart-seine.

heart'=of=the=earth' (-ẽrth'), *n.* See *Heal-all.*

heart'pea, *n.* Same as *Heartseed.*

heart'quake (-kwāk), *n.* Trembling of the heart; terror; fear.

heart'rend"ing, *a.* Breaking the heart; overpowering with anguish; deeply afflictive; very distressing.

heart'=rob"bing, *a.* 1. Depriving of heart or thought; ecstatic.

2. Stealing the heart or affections; winning.

heart's'=ease, hearts'ease, *n.* 1. Ease of heart; tranquillity of mind.

2. A name given to any one of various plants of the genus *Viola,* particularly *Viola tricolor,* the pansy.

3. *Polygonum Persicaria,* the lady's-thumb.

Heart's-ease (garden variety).

heart'seed, *n.* Any one of various plants of the genus *Cardiospermum,* with black seeds, having heartshaped white scars indicating their point of attachment. *Cardiospermum Halicacabum,* the commonest species, is found in all tropical countries.

heart'=seine, *n.* A weir or fish-trap having a heartshaped pound, which is capable of taking fish under any condition of the tide. [Local, U.S.]

heart'=shake, *n.* A defect in timber characterized by cracks extending outward from the heart.

heart'shaped (-shāpt), *a.* Shaped like a heart; having the form of a heart; cordate.

heart'=shell, *n.* A mollusk, *Isocardia cor,* having a shell shaped like a heart.

heart'sick, *a.* 1. Sick at heart; deeply afflicted or depressed.

2. Indicating or expressive of sickness of heart; as, *heartsick* groans.

heart'sick"en-ing, *a.* Tending to make the heart sick or depressed.

heart'sick"ness, *n.* Sadness of heart; depression of spirits.

heart'=sink"ing, *n.* Despondency; discouragement.

heart'some, *a.* 1. Inspiring with heart or courage; exhilarating.

2. Merry; cheerful; lively.

heart'=spoon, *n.* The depression in the breast-bone; also, the breast-bone. [Obs.]

heart'=steel, *n.* Same as *Heart-shell.*

heart'=stir"ring, *a.* Exhilarating; inspiring.

heart'strick"en, *a.* Appalled; dismayed.

heart'string, *n.* A supposed nerve or tendon that braces and sustains the heart; hence, in the plural, strongest affections; most ardent feelings; usually in the plural; as, to touch one's *heartstrings.*

heart'struck, *a.* 1. Stricken to the heart; shocked; appalled.

2. Ineradicable.

heart'swell"ing, *a.* Rankling in the heart; causing the heart to swell.

heart'=tre"foil, *n.* *Medicago maculata,* the spotted medic, a leguminous plant having a heart-shaped spot on each foliole; called also *heart-clover* and *heart-leaf.*

heart'=wheel (-hwel), *n.* See *Heart-cam.*

heart'=whole (-hōl), *a.* 1. Not in love; not deeply affected by the passion of love.

2. Having unbroken spirits or good courage.

3. Sincere.

heart'wood, *n.* The central part of the trunk of an exogenous tree; the duramen.

heart'=wound"ed, *a.* Wounded in the feelings; deeply affected with some passion.

heart'y, *a.*; *comp.* heartier; *superl.* heartiest. 1. Proceeding from the heart; sincere; heartfelt; cordial; zealous; as, a *hearty* invitation; a *hearty* reception.

2. Sound; strong; exhibiting health; healthy; as, a *hearty* man.

3. Supplying strength; affording nourishment; adapted for plenty of nourishment; as, a *hearty* breakfast; a *hearty* eater.

Syn.—Cordial, sincere, warm, healthy, zealous, eager, vigorous.—*Hearty* implies honesty and simplicity of feelings and manners; *cordial* refers to the warmth and liveliness with which the feelings are expressed; *sincere* implies that this expression corresponds to the real sentiments of the heart.

heart'y, *n.*; *pl.* **heart'ies.** Good fellow; comrade; a form of address much used by seamen; as, pull away, my *hearties.*

heart'=yarn, *n.* A soft yarn in the center of a rope.

heart'y=hale, *a.* Good for the heart. [Obs.]

heat, *n.* [ME. *heete, hete*; AS. *hætu,* heat, from *hat,* hot.]

1. A condition of matter believed to consist in a certain motion or vibration of the ultimate molecules of which bodies are composed; it is a condition or exhibition of energy, of which motion, light, gravity, electricity, etc., are other exhibitions under different conditions. It is the cause of fluidity and evaporation. It expands all bodies, but the expansions are different in different substances. In general, solids expand least by heat; liquids expand more and more rapidly, and air and gases expand most and most rapidly of all. Heat is always manifested through matter, and although unequally diffused among bodies it is always tending to an equilibrium. It may be communicated to surrounding bodies either by contact or conduction or by radiation, the ether being the medium of communication. Its influence at different distances from the place or point whence it emanates is inversely as the squares of those distances.

2. The sensation produced by *heat* when present in excess; the sensation experienced when the body is subjected to *heat* from any source.

3. A concentration of *heat*; the greatest accumulation of *heat,* or the time of such accumulation; high temperature as compared with low; as, the *heat* of the tropics; the *heat* of the body in fever; the *heat* of the day.

4. Indication of high temperature, as the condition or color of the body or part of the body; redness; high color; flush.

It has raised animosities in their hearts, and *heats* in their faces. —Addison.

5. Exposure to *heat*; a heating, as of a piece of metal in a forge, or a melting, as of a mass of ore in a furnace; as, the iron was given three *heats.*

6. A violent action unintermitted; a single effort; specifically, one of the divisions of a race; as, he ran five *heats.*

Many causes are required for refreshment betwixt the *heats.* —Dryden.

7 Utmost violence; rage; vehemence; as, the *heat* of battle.

8. Agitation of mind; inflammation or excitement; exasperation; as, the *heat* of passion.

Ardor; fervency; animation in thought or discourse.

With all the strength and *heat* of eloquence. —Addison.

10. Fermentation.

11. Sexual desire in an animal, especially in the female.

Atomic heat; in chemistry, the result obtained by multiplying the specific heat of an element by its atomic weight. The *atomic heat* of the elements in a solid state is nearly a constant quantity, the mean value being 6.4.

Black heat; the degree to which a metal is heated when its color remains unchanged.

Black-red heat; the degree of heat in a metal when it begins to be luminous by daylight.

Dynamical theory of heat; the theory of heat which assumes it to be a peculiar form of molecular energy, and not a peculiar kind of matter.

Red heat; the degree to which a metal or other substance is heated when it radiates a red light.

Specific heat; the number of units of heat required to raise a unit of mass of a substance through one degree of temperature.

The heat of the day; that part of the day when the temperature is highest.

White heat; the degree to which a metal is heated when it radiates a white light.

Syn.—Warmth, ardor, passion, excitement, fever, intensity.

heat, *v.t.*; heated, *pt., pp.*; heating, *ppr.* [ME. *heten*; AS. *hætan,* to make hot, from *hat,* hot.]

1. To make hot; to communicate heat to, or cause to become warm; as, to *heat* an oven or a furnace; to *heat* iron.

2. To make feverish; to excite; as, to *heat* the blood.

3. To warm with passion or desire; to rouse into action; to animate.

A noble emulation *heats* your breast. —Dryden.

heat, *v.i.* 1. To grow warm or hot; as, the iron or the water *heats* slowly.

2. To grow warm or hot by fermentation or chemical action; as, green hay *heats* in a mow.

heat'=ap"o-plex-y, *n.* Sunstroke.

heat'=en"gine, *n.* An engine in which heat is transformed into mechanical work.

heat'er, *n.* 1. One who or that which heats.

2. Any device used for heating, as a furnace, radiator, etc.

heat'er=plate, *n.* A contrivance in a lamp exposed to cold air, which conducts the heat of the flame down to the vessel containing the oil, thus keeping the latter from freezing.

heath, *n.* [ME. *hethe, heeth*; AS. *hæth,* the heath plant, a heath.]

1. Any plant of the genus *Erica,* the species of which are widely distributed throughout Europe and South Africa. *Erica,* or *Calluna, vulgaris* is used in Great Britain for brooms, thatch, beds for the poor, and for heating ovens. Its leaves are small, and continue green all the year.

2. A place overgrown with *heath*; any desert tract of land overgrown with shrubs.

Their stately growth, though bare,
Stands on the blasted *heath.* —Milton.

3. One of several butterflies; as, *Erinephila tithonus,* the large *heath.*

heath'=bell, *n.* The flower of either of two species of heath, *Erica Tetralix* and *Erica cinerea.*

heath'ber"ry, *n.* Same as *Crowberry.*

heath'=bird, *n.* The heath-hen or heath-grouse.

heath'clad, *a.* Clothed or crowned with heath.

heath'=cock, *n.* See *Blackcock.*

heath'=corn, *n.* The buckwheat, *Polygonum Fagopyrum.*

heath'cup, *n.* *Artanema fimbriatum,* a plant found in the East Indies and Australia. It is cultivated for its large blue flowers.

heath'=cy"press, *n.* *Lycopodium alpinum,* a species of club-moss found in Europe; so called from its resembling a miniature cypress-tree.

hea'then, *n.*; *pl.* **hea'thens** or, collectively, **hea'then.** [ME. *hethen*; AS. *hæthen,* a heathen, from *hæth,* a heath, a wild and desolate country.]

1. One who worships idols or does not acknowledge the true God; a pagan; an idolater; one who is not a Christian, Jew, or Mohammedan.

2. A rude, illiterate, barbarous, or irreligious person.

Syn.—Gentile, pagan, idolater.

hea'then, *a.* 1. Gentile; pagan; as, a *heathen* author.

2. Heathenish; irreligious.

hea'then-dom, *n.* [ME. *hæthendom*; AS. *hæthendom*; *hæthen,* heathen, and *-dom,* -dom.]

1. That part of the world where heathenism prevails.

2. The condition of a heathen; heathenism.

hea'then-esse, *n.* Heathenness. [Obs.]

hea'then-ish, *a.* 1. Pertaining to, belonging to, or characteristic of the heathen; as, *heathenish* customs.

2. Irreligious; uncivilized; cruel; barbarous.

hea'then-ish-ly, *adv.* In a heathenish manner.

hea'then-ish-ness, *n.* The quality or state of being heathenish.

hea'then-ism, *n.* 1. The rites, beliefs, or system

of religion of a heathen nation; paganism; idolatry.

2. Rudeness; barbarism; ignorance; heathenish manners, morals, and customs.

hēa′then-ize, *v.t.*; heathenized, *pt.*, *pp.*; heathenizing, *ppr.* To render heathen or heathenish.

hēa′then-ness, *n.* The state of being heathen.

hēa′then-ry, *n.* 1. Heathendom.

2. Heathenism; the character of the heathen.

heath′ẽr (heth′), *n.* [From *heath*, an open country, and *-er.*]

1. Heath; especially, *Calluna vulgaris*, the common *heather.*

2. A kind of tweed having the color of *heather.*

heath′ẽr-bell, *n.* Same as *Heath-bell.*

heath′ẽr-claw, *n.* Same as *Dewclaw.*

heath′ẽr-grass, *n.* *Triodia decumbens*, a species of grass growing on cold, wet ground.

heath′ẽr-y, *a.* Heathy; abounding in heather.

hēath′ẽr-y, *n.* A place where heaths grow; a house in which valuable heaths are cultivated.

hēath′-grass, *n.* Same as *Heather-grass.*

hēath′-grouse, *n.* A European species of grouse, *Tetrao tetrix*; called also *heath-game, heath-fowl, moor-fowl*, and *black-grouse.*

hēath′-hen, *n.* The female of the heath-bird.

hēath′-pēa, *n.* *Lathyrus macrorhizus*, a leguminous European plant the tubers of which are eaten as a vegetable.

hēath′-pēat, *n.* Peat taken from land abounding in heather.

hēath′-pōult, hēath′-pout, *n.* The young of the heath-bird.

hēath′-thros″tle (-thros″l), *n.* The ring-ouzel. [Local, Eng.]

hēath′wort, *n.* Any plant of the heath family; chiefly used in the plural.

hēath′y, *a.* Full of heath; abounding with heath; as, *heathy* land.

hēat′ing, *a.* Tending to impart heat; promoting warmth or heat; exciting action; stimulating; as, *heating* medicines or applications.

hēat′ing-back, *n.* A chamber at the back of a forge in which the air for the blast is subjected to the action of heat.

hēat′ing-ly, *adv.* In a heating manner; so as to make or become hot or heated.

hēat′ing-sũr″face, *n.* In steam-boilers, the aggregate surface of the boiler exposed to the action of the fire; called also *fire-surface.*

hēat′ing-tūbe, *n.* In a steam-boiler, a water-tube exposed to the flame.

hēat′less, *a.* Destitute of heat; cold.

hēat′-spot, *n.* 1. A freckle.

2. A spot on the body at which the sensation of heat can be produced.

hēat′-ū″nit, *n.* The unit quantity of heat; the amount of heat required to raise the temperature of a unit mass of water one degree; a calory.

heaume (hōm), *n.* In medieval armor, a helmet which rested on the shoulders and was usually worn over an inner defense. [Obs.]

hē-au-tō-mor′phism, *n.* [Gr. *heauton*, of himself, of oneself, and *morphē*, form.] Same as *Automorphism.*

hēave, *v.t.*; heaved *or* hove, *pt.*, *pp.*; heaving, *ppr.* [ME. *heven*; AS. *hebban*, to heave.]

1. To lift; to raise; to move upward; to hoist.

> Rise, rise, and *heave* thy rosy head
> From thy coral-paven bed. —Milton.

2. To throw; to cast; to send; used chiefly by seamen; as, to *heave* the log.

3. To lift or raise with great effort or exertion; as, to *heave* a large piece of machinery.

4. To raise or force from the breast; as, to *heave* a sigh or groan.

5. Among seamen, to force out of or into a position, as by means of a windlass; as, to *heave* a vessel ahead.

6. To cause to swell, as the breast.

Heave away! a call or order for sailors to commence or continue heaving.

To heave aback; to put (a ship) in such a position that the wind will act on the forward surface of the sails.

To heave about; to put (a ship) about on the other tack.

To heave a cable short; to haul in so much of the cable that the ship is nearly over the anchor.

To heave a ship ahead; to bring a ship forward when not under sail, by means of hawsers, cables, etc.

To heave a ship astern; to bring a ship backward by means of cables, etc.

To heave a ship down; to careen her by means of tackles from the masthead to the shore, for the purpose of cleaning or repairing the bottom.

To heave a ship to; to bring a ship's head to the wind, and stop her motion.

To heave a strain; to heave taut.

To heave in; to haul in (the cable).

To heave in stays; to put a ship about in tacking.

To heave taut; to turn a capstan, etc., till the cable becomes strained.

To heave the lead; among seamen, to sound with a lead.

To heave the log; to throw the log into the water; also, to determine the rate of sailing by means of the log.

hēave, *v.i.* 1. To be thrown or raised up; to rise; to bulge out.

> So high as *heaved* the tumid hills. —Milton.

2. To rise and fall with alternate motions, as the waves of the sea, the lungs in heavy, difficult, or painful breathing, the earth during an earthquake, etc.; to swell; to dilate; to become distended.

> The *heaving* plain of ocean. —Byron.

3. To pant, as after severe labor or exertion; to labor; to struggle.

> He *heaves* for breath. —Dryden.

4. To make an effort to vomit; to retch.

Heave ho! a cry uttered by sailors when hoisting the anchor.

Heave out! an order or call for sailors to leave their bunks.

To heave in sight; to appear; to come within sight, as a ship at sea.

To heave up; to vomit. [Low.]

hēave, *n.* 1. An upward motion; swell or distention, as of the waves of the sea, of the lungs in heavy, difficult, or painful breathing, of the earth during an earthquake, etc.

> None could guess whether the next *heave* of the earthquake would settle or swallow them. —Dryden.

2. An effort to lift something; a raising.

> But after many strains and *heaves*,
> He got upon the saddle eaves. —Hudibras.

3. In geology, the horizontal dislocation occurring when a lode is intersected by another lode which throws the regular lode either to the right or to the left.

heav′en (hev′), *n.* [ME. *heven*; AS. *heofen, heofan, hefon*, heaven.]

1. The region or expanse which surrounds the earth, and which appears above and around us, like an immense arch or vault, in which are seen the sun, moon, and stars; the firmament; the sky.

2. Among Christians, the part of space in which the omnipresent Jehovah is supposed to afford more sensible manifestations of his glory; the habitation of God and the residence of angels and blessed spirits.

3. The Supreme Power; God; as, prophets sent by *heaven.*

> I have sinned against *heaven.*—Luke xv. 21.

4. Supreme felicity; great happiness; a state of bliss; a sublime or exalted condition; as, a *heaven* on earth.

5. [*pl.*] The celestial powers collectively; as, the *heavens* are propitious.

heav′en, *v.t.* To render happy, as if placed in heaven; to make fit for heaven; to beatify in the highest degree. [Rare.]

heav′en-ize, *v.t.* To render like heaven. [Rare.]

heav′en-li-ness, *n.* Supreme excellence; the quality or condition of being heavenly.

heav′en-ly, *a.* 1. Pertaining to heaven; celestial; as, *heavenly* regions; *heavenly* bliss.

2. Resembling heaven; supremely excellent; as, a *heavenly* lyre; a *heavenly* temper.

3. Inhabiting heaven; as, a *heavenly* race; the *heavenly* throng.

heav′en-ly, *adv.* 1. In a manner resembling that of heaven.

2. By the influence or agency of heaven; as, a *heavenly*-guided soul.

heav′en-ly-mind″ed, *a.* Having the affections placed on heaven and on spiritual things; devout.

heav′en-ly-mind″ed-ness, *n.* The state of having the affections and thoughts placed on heavenly things and spiritual objects.

heav′en-wărd, *adv.* Toward heaven.

hēave′-of″fẽr-ing, *n.* Among the Jews, an offering or oblation made to God; so called because it was to be heaved or elevated. [See *Wave-offering.*]

hēav′ẽr, *n.* 1. One who or that which heaves or lifts.

2. In navigation, a staff or bar used as a lever.

hēaves, *n.pl.* An asthmatic disease of horses, characterized by difficult and laborious respiration.

heav′i-ly (hev′), *adv.* 1. In a heavy manner; with great weight; as, to bear *heavily* on a thing; to be *heavily* loaded.

2. With great weight of grief; grievously; afflictively; oppressively; with difficulty; as, to be *heavily* afflicted.

3. Slowly and laboriously; with difficulty; as, to move *heavily.*

> That they drave them *heavily.*—Ex. xiv. 25.

heav′i-ness, *n.* [ME. *hevinesse*; AS. *hefignes*, from *hefig*, heavy.] The quality of being heavy; dejection; sluggishness; oppression; weight; as, the *heaviness* of a body; the *heaviness* of a sorrow; *heaviness* of heart.

hēav′ing, *n.* A rising or swell; a panting.

hēav′ing-līne, *n.* In navigation, a small line having a lead weight at one end, used to catch the hawser on landing.

heav′i-sŏme, *a.* Dull; dark; drowsy. [Prov. Eng.]

hēav′y, *a.* Afflicted with heaves; as, a *heavy* horse.

heav′y (hev′), *a.*; *comp.* heavier; *superl.* heaviest. [ME. *hevy*; AS. *hefig*, heavy, from *hebban*, to heave, lift.]

1. Weighty; ponderous; having great weight; tending strongly to the center of attraction; opposed to *light*; as, a *heavy* stone; a *heavy* load.

2. Sad; sorrowful; dejected; depressed in mind; as, a *heavy* spirit.

3. Grievous; afflictive; depressing to the spirits; as, *heavy* news; a *heavy* calamity.

4. Burdensome; oppressive; as, *heavy* taxes.

5. Wanting life and animation; dull; as, *heavy* eyes.

6. Wanting spirit or animation; destitute of sentiment; dull; as, a *heavy* writer; a *heavy* style.

7. Slow; sluggish; as, a *heavy* gait.

8. Burdensome; tedious; as, *heavy* hours.

9. Moist; deep; soft; miry; as, *heavy* land; a *heavy* road.

10. Difficult; laborious; as, a *heavy* draft.

11. Gravid; pregnant. [Rare.]

12. Large in extent, quality, or effects; as, a *heavy* venture; *heavy* wines; a *heavy* failure.

Heavy artillery; guns of large caliber and long range; also, the gunners who man them; distinguished from *light artillery* and *siege artillery.*

Heavy cavalry; troops mounted on heavy horses and bearing heavy equipment.

Heavy fire; protracted cannonade or rapid rifle-fire.

Heavy metal; in ordnance, large guns or their projectiles.

Heavy metals; see under *Metal.*

Heavy sea; the condition of a body of water when its surface is broken into large waves; also, a high or large wave; as, to ship a *heavy sea*; the ship labored in a *heavy sea.*

Syn.—Dull, burdensome, weighty, ponderous, massive, drowsy.—*Heavy* and *dull* are employed as epithets both for persons and things; *heavy* characterizes the corporeal state of a person; *dull* qualifies the spirits or the understanding of the subject. *Heavy* is the natural property of some bodies; *burdensome* is incidental to some. That which is *weighty* exceeds the ordinary weight of other things; *ponderous* expresses even more than *weighty*, for it includes also the idea of bulk.

heav′y, *v.t.* To make heavy. [Obs.]

heav′y, *adv.* With great weight; heavily. [Rare.]

heav′y-ärmed, *a.* Bearing heavy arms; said of troops under arms.

heav′y-hand″ed, *a.* 1. Lacking dexterity.

2. Ruling with oppression.

heav′y-head″ed, *a.* Thick-headed; dull of apprehension.

heav′y-heärt″ed, *a.* Sorrowful; in low spirits.

heav′y-spär, *n.* Sulphate of barium.

heb′dō-mad, *n.* [L. *hebdomas* (*-adis*); Gr. *hebdomas*, a number of seven, a week, from *hebdomos*, seventh, from *hepta*, seven.]

1. A week; a period of seven days. [Rare.]

2. In Gnostic philosophy, the sphere of seven; the seven planets and their indwelling spirits; the dominion of the demiurge.

heb-dom′ȧ-dăl, *a.* Weekly; consisting of seven days, or occurring every seven days.

heb-dom′ȧ-dăl-ly, *adv.* In weekly periods; by the week; from week to week.

heb-dom′ȧ-dā-ry, *a.* and *n.* I. *a.* Same as *Hebdomadal.*

II. *n.* In the Roman Catholic church, a member of a chapter or convent, whose week it is to officiate in the choir, rehearse the anthems and prayers, and perform other services which on extraordinary occasions are performed by the superiors.

heb-dō-mat′ic-ăl, *a.* Weekly. [Obs.]

Hē′bē, *n.* [L., from Gr. *Hēbē*, from *hēbē*, youth.]

1. In Greek mythology, the goddess of youth, daughter of Jupiter and Juno, cupbearer of Olympus, and wife of the deified Hercules, having power to restore the aged to youth and beauty.

2. One of the minor planets, the sixth in the order of discovery.

3. [h—] In zoölogy, the hamadryad, an African ape.

Hebe, Statue by Canova.

heb′en, *n.* Ebony. [Obs.]

heb'e-nŏn, *n.* A corrupt variant of *henbane*; found only once, in "Hamlet."

heb'ē-tāte, *v.t.* [L. *hebetatus*, pp. of *hebetare*, to make blunt or dull, from *hebes (-etis)*, blunt, dull.] To dull; to blunt; to stupefy; as, to *hebetate* the intellectual faculties. [Rare.]

heb'ē-tāte, *a.* 1. Dull; obtuse; stupid.

2. In botany, having a dull and soft point; as, a *hebetate* spine. [Rare.]

heb-ē-tā'tion, *n.* [L. *hebetatio (-onis)*, from *hebetare*, to make blunt or dull.]

1. The act of making blunt, dull, or stupid.

2. The state of being dulled.

heb'ēte, *a.* Dull; stupid. [Obs.]

heb'ē-tūde, *n.* [L. *hebetudo*, from *hebes (-etis)*, blunt, dull.] Dullness; stupidity.

heb-ē-tū'di-nous, *a.* [L. *hebetudo (-inis)*, dullness.] Affected with hebetude; stupid; lethargic.

Hē-brā'iç, *a.* [LL. *Hebraicus*; Gr. *Hebraïkos*, adj. Hebrew, from *Hebraios*, a Hebrew.] Pertaining to the Hebrews; designating the language of the Hebrews.

Hē-brā'iç-ăl-ly, *adv.* After the manner of the Hebrew language or of the Hebrews.

Hē'brā-ișm, *n.* 1. A Hebrew idiom; a peculiar expression or manner of speaking in the Hebrew language.

2. The type of character or thought peculiar to the Hebrews.

Hē'brā-ist, *n.* One versed in the Hebrew language and learning.

Hē-brā-is'tiç, *a.* Pertaining to or resembling the language, the thought, or the customs of the Hebrews.

Hē'brā-ize, *v.t.*; Hebraized, *pt.*, *pp.*; Hebraizing, *ppr.* [Gr. *Hebraïzein*, to speak Hebrew, from *Hebraios*, a Hebrew.] To convert into the Hebrew idiom; to make Hebrew.

Hē'brā-ize, *v.i.* To speak Hebrew or to conform to the Hebrews.

Hē'brew (-brö), *n.* [ME. *Hebrew*; OFr. *hebreu*; LL. *Hebræus*; Gr. *Hebraios*; Aramaic, *'ebrāyā*; Heb. *'ibri*, a Hebrew, from *'Eber*, Heber, the traditional ancestor of the Hebrews.]

1. One of the descendants of Eber or Heber; particularly, a descendant of Jacob, who was a descendant of Eber; an Israelite; a Jew.

2. The language of the Hebrews, a division of the Semitic family of languages.

Hē'brew, *a.* Pertaining to the Hebrews; as, the *Hebrew* language or rites.

Hē'brew-ess, *n.* An Israelitish woman; a Jewess.

Hē-bri'ciăn (-brish'ăn), *n.* One skilled in the Hebrew language; a Hebraist. [Rare.]

Hē-brid'e-ăn, Hē-brid'i-ăn, *a.* and *n.* I. *a.* Pertaining to the islands called Hebrides, west of Scotland.

II. *n.* An inhabitant or native of the Hebrides.

Heç'ă-tē, *n.* [L. *Hecate*; Gr. *Hekatē*, Hecate.] In Greek mythology (as later in Latin), a goddess of a threefold form, identified sometimes with Selene or Luna then with Artemis or Diana, and again with Proserpine; in later times especially regarded as a goddess of the infernal regions.

heç'ă-tomb (-tom), *n.* [L. *hecatombe*; Gr. *hekatombē*, from *hekaton*, a hundred.]

1. In antiquity, a sacrifice of a hundred oxen or beasts of the same kind, and, it is said, at a hundred altars and by a hundred priests.

2. The sacrifice of any great number, as of oxen, at one time; any great slaughter of persons or animals.

heç-ă-tom'pe-don, *n.*; *pl.* **heç-ă-tom'pe-dă.** [Gr. *hekatompedos*, a hundred feet long; *hekaton*, a hundred, and *pous*, *podos*, foot.]

1. An edifice or temple having a length or width of one hundred feet.

2. [H—] The ancient Parthenon at Athens.

heç'dē-cāne, *n.* Same as *Hexadecane.*

heck, *n.* 1. An engine or instrument for catching fish; as. a salmon-*heck*.

2. A rack for holding fodder for cattle. [Prov. Eng. and Scot.]

3. A bend in a stream. [Rare.]

4. A hatch or latch of a door. [Prov. Eng.]

5. A door with the upper half latticed or arranged to swing; called also *heck-door.*

6. In weaving, a device for separating the threads of warp. [Rare.]

heck'ber"ry, *n.*; *pl.* **heck'ber"ries.** In botany, the small bird-cherry of Europe, *Prunus Padus.*

heck'=bōard, *n.* The backboard of a cart.

heck'=box, *n.* In weaving, a box holding a set of warp-bobbins; a jack.

heck'i-măl, heck'i-mel, *n.* The blue titmouse of Europe, *Parus cœruleus.*

heç'kle, *n.* [ME. *hekele*; D. *hekel*, a heckle.]

1. Same as *Hatchel.*

2. A feather in a Highlander's bonnet. [Scot.]

heç'kle, *v.t.*; heckled, *pt.*, *pp.*; heckling, *ppr.* 1. To hatchel, as flax.

2. To ply, as a speaker or candidate for orders, with questions; to badger. [Scot.]

heç'klẽr, *n.* One who heckles.

heç'tāre, *n.* [Fr. *hectare*, from Gr. *hekaton*, a hundred, and L. *area*, area.] A French measure containing a hundred ares or 10,000 square meters or 2.471 acres.

heç'tiç, *n.* [Fr. *hectique*; Gr. *hektikos*, habitual, hectic, from *hexis*, a permanent condition or habit of the body, from *echein*, to have.]

1. In medicine, a remittent fever, with stages of chilliness, heat, and sweat, variously intermixed, usually present in pulmonary consumption; hectic fever; a wasting away.

2. A hectic flush.

heç'tiç, heç'tiç-ăl, *a.* 1. Habitual; pertaining to hectic.

2. Affected with *hectic* fever; consumptive; as, a *hectic* patient.

heç'tiç-ăl-ly, *adv.* In a hectic manner; constitutionally.

heç-to-. A combining form from Gr. *hekaton*, a hundred, used in biology, mathematics, etc., to signify a hundred; as, a *hecto*liter, *hecto*graph.

heç-tō-çot'y-lized, *a.* In malacology, changed into a hectocotylus, as an arm of certain cuttle-fishes.

heç-tō-çot'y-lus, *n.*; *pl.* **heç-tō-çot'y-lī.** [*Hecto-*, and Gr. *kotylē*, a small cup.] In malacology, one of the arms of a male cephalopod that serves as an instrument of copulation; it becomes detached in conveying the sperm-cells and when attached to the female is often mistaken for a parasite.

heç'tō-gram, heç'tō-gramme, *n.* [Fr. *hectogramme*, from Gr. *hekaton*, a hundred, and *gramma*, that which is written, a small weight, from *graphein*, to write.] In the metric system of weights and measures, a weight containing a hundred grams or about three and one-half ounces avoirdupois.

heç'tō-gràph, hek'tō-gràph, *n.* [*Hecto-*, and Gr. *graphein*, to write.] A gelatin pad for receiving and reproducing impressions of written or typewritten matter.

heç'tō-gràph, *v.t.*; hectographed, *pt.*, *pp.*; hectographing, *ppr.* To make copies of with a hectograph.

heç-tō-graph'iç, *a.* Pertaining to the hectograph; as, a *hectographic* copy.

heç'toid, *a.* Having a hectic appearance.

heç'tō-lī-tẽr, heç'tō-lī-tre, *n.* [Fr. *hectolitre*, from Gr. *hekaton*, a hundred, and *litra*, a pound.] A measure of capacity for liquids, containing a hundred liters or about twenty-six and one-half gallons.

heç'tō-mē-tẽr, heç'tō-mē-tre, *n.* [Fr. *hectomètre*, from Gr. *hekaton*, a hundred, and *metron*, a measure.] A measure equal to a hundred meters; equivalent to about 328 feet.

heç'tŏr, *n.* [L. *Hector*; Gr. *Hektōr*, Hector, a brave warrior who fought on the side of the Trojans in the siege of Troy, from *hektōr*, holding fast, from *echein*, to have, hold.]

1. A bully; a blustering, turbulent, noisy fellow.

2. One who teases or vexes.

heç'tŏr, *v.t.*; hectored, *pt.*, *pp.*; hectoring, *ppr.* 1. To threaten; to bully; to treat with insolence.

2. To tease; to vex; to torment by words.

heç'tŏr, *v.i.* To play the bully; to bluster; to be turbulent or insolent.

heç'tŏr-ișm, *n.* The disposition or practice of a hector; a bullying. [Rare.]

heç'tŏr-ly, *a.* Blustering; insolent.

heç'tō-stēre, *n.* [Fr. *hectostère*, from Gr. *hekaton*, a hundred, and *stereos*, solid.] A measure of solids containing 100 cubic meters.

hed'dle, *v.t.*; heddled, *pt.*, *pp.*; heddling, *ppr.* In weaving, to pass (the warp-thread) through the heddle-eye.

hed'dle, *n.* [Scand. origin.] In weaving, the harness for guiding the warp-threads in a loom; two *heddles* are used for plain weaving; generally called *harness* in the United States.

hed'dle=eȳe, *n.* The loop in each heddle through which a warp-thread passes.

hed'en-bẽrg-īte, *n.* [Named after *Hedenberg*, a Swedish chemist, who first analyzed it.] A dark or nearly black cleavable variety of augite, semimetallic in appearance, containing a large proportion of oxid of iron.

Hē-dē-ō'mă, *n.* [Gr. *hēdys*, sweet, and *osmē*, odor.] In botany, a native American genus of labiate plants bearing fragrant flowers, as *Hedeoma pulegioides*, American pennyroyal.

Hed'e-ră, *n.* [L., the ivy.] In botany, a genus of woody vines of the ginseng family embracing the true ivy, *Hedera Helix.*

hed-ẽr-ā'ceous, *a.* [L. *hederaceus*, from *hedera*, ivy.] Pertaining to ivy; like ivy; producing ivy.

hed'ẽr-ăl, *a.* Composed of ivy; relating to ivy.

hē-der'iç, *a.* Relating to or extracted from the ivy.

Hederic acid; an acid of the acetylene group contained in the berry and leaf of the common ivy, *Hedera Helix.*

hed-ẽr-if'ẽr-ous, *a.* [L. *hedera*, ivy, and *ferre*, to bear.] Producing ivy.

hed'ẽr-ine, *n.* [L. *hedera*, ivy, and *-ine.*] In chemistry, a bitter febrifugal alkaloid found in ivy-seeds.

hed'ẽr-ōse, *a.* [L. *hederosus*, full of ivy, from *hedera*, ivy.] Pertaining to or abounding in ivy.

hedġe, *n.* [ME. *hedge*, *hegge*, from AS. *hege*, an inclosure.] A thicket of thorn-bushes or other shrubs or small trees, planted round a field to fence it or in rows to separate plots of cultivated ground.

To breast up a hedge; see under *Breast.*

hedġe, *v.t.*; hedged, *pt.*, *pp.*; hedging, *ppr.* 1. To inclose with a hedge; to fence with a thicket of shrubs or small trees; to separate by a hedge; as, to *hedge* a field or garden.

2. To obstruct with a hedge or as with a hedge.

I will *hedge* up thy way with thorns.
—Hos. ii. 6.

3. To surround for defense; to fortify; often with *in*; as, the seas *hedge in* England; to surround or encompass; to hem in; as, *hedged in* by laws.

4. In betting, to minimize the risk of; as, to *hedge* a bet; that is, after having bet on one side, to bet also on the other side to prevent or lessen a loss.

hedġe, *v.i.* 1. To hide, as in a hedge; to skulk.

2. In betting, to guard against loss by betting both ways.

3. In speaking, to guard against criticism for a statement, by making some counterbalancing statement.

hedġe'=bells, *n.* Hedge-bindweed.

hedġe'=ber"ry, *n.* The hagberry.

hedġe'=bill, hedġ'ing=bill, *n.* A pruning-hook for trimming hedges.

hedġe'=bīnd"weed, *n.* A climbing vine allied to the morning-glory.

hedġe'=bŏrn, *a.* Born under a hedge; hence, of low birth; of mean parentage; rustic; obscure.

hedġe'=găr"liç, *n.* Garlic-mustard.

hedġe'hog, *n.* 1. In zoölogy, (a) a hibernating, insectivorous quadruped of the genus *Erinaceus*, characterized by a covering of prickly spines; (b) one of several other animals resembling the *hedgehog*, including a prickly fish, *Diodon hystrix*, also called the sea-hedgehog.

Hedgehog (*Erinaceus europæus*).

2. In botany, a leguminous plant of the genus *Medicago*, having spinous pods.

3. A kind of dredging-machine, consisting of a series of spades fixed to the periphery of a cylinder and used for loosening mud, silt, etc., so that it may be carried off by the current.

hedġe'hog=çat"ẽr-pil-lăr, *n.* The bristly larvæ of several bombycid moths, which when disturbed roll up like a hedgehog.

hedġe'hog=fish, *n.* The sea-hedgehog, *Diodon hystrix.*

hedġe'hog=gràss, *n.* A grass with burry spikelets, *Cenchrus tribuloides.*

hedġe'hog=pärs"ley, *n.* A European herb, *Caucalis daucoides*, having fruit covered with hooked prickles.

hedġe'hog=rat, *n.* A West Indian rodent, allied to the porcupines, having stiff hair interspersed with spines.

hedġe'hog=this"tle (-this"l), *n.* Any plant belonging to the cactus family; the prickly pear, *Opuntia vulgaris.*

hedġe'=hys"sŏp, *n.* A bitter perennial herb of the genus *Gratiola*, having both emetic and purgative properties.

hedġe'=mush"rọọm, *n.* An edible mushroom, *Agaricus arvensis*; also called *horse-mushroom.*

hedġe'=mus"tărd, *n.* A plant of the genus *Sisymbrium*, formerly much used in medicine.

hedġe'=net"tle, *n.* A nonstinging plant of the genus *Stachys*, of the mint family.

hedġe'pig, *n.* A young hedgehog. [Obs.]

hedġe'=pink, *n.* The soapwort.

hedġe'=priest, *n.* An illiterate clergyman, such as those formerly existing as a vagabond class in England; also, in Ireland formerly, a priest who had been admitted to orders from a hedge-school without theological training.

hedġ'ẽr, *n.* 1. One who makes or trims hedges.

2. One who hedges his bets.

hedġe'rōw, *n.* A row of shrubs or bushes forming a fence or furnishing an ornament.

hedġe'=sçhọọl, *n.* In Ireland, a school formerly held in the open air.

hedġe'=spar"rōw, *n.* In ornithology, *Accentor modularis*, a small warbler frequenting hedges; called also *dunnock* and *hedge-warbler.*

hē-don'iç, *a.* [Gr. *hēdonikos*, from *hēdonē*, pleasure.]

1. Pertaining to pleasure.

2. Of or related to hedonism.

Hedonic sect; a sect of Greek philosophers that placed the highest happiness in pleasure or the gratification of natural desires; called also *Cyrenaic sect.*

hē-don′iċs, *n.* The science of pleasure or positive enjoyment; the department of ethics which treats of the relation of pleasure to duty.

hed′ŏn-iṣm (*or* hē′dō-nizm), *n.* [Gr. *hēdonē*, delight, pleasure, from *hēdesthai*, to take delight, enjoy oneself.]

1. The doctrine held by the Cyrenaics and the noted Greek philosopher, Aristippus, who taught that pleasure was the only conceivable object in life.

2. In ethics, the theory that the final object of duty is to give pleasure.

hed′ŏn-ist (*or* hē′dō-nist), *n.* One who advocates hedonism.

hed-ō-nis′tiċ, *a.* Pertaining to hedonism or hedonists.

hed′y-phāne, *n.* [Gr. *hēdys*, sweet, and *phainesthai*, to shine, appear.] A variety of mimetite.

heed, *v.t.*; heeded, *pt.*, *pp.*; heeding, *ppr.* [ME. *heden*; AS. *hedan*, to heed, take care of.] To mind; to regard with care; to take notice of; to attend to.

heed, *v.i.* To consider; to be careful. [Obs.]

heed, *n.* 1. Care; attention.

With wanton *heed* and giddy cunning. —Milton.

2. Caution; care; watch for danger; notice; circumspection; usually preceded by *take*; as, *take heed* of evil company.

3. Notice; observation; regard; attention; usually with *give*; as, *give heed* to good advice.

heed′ful, *a.* 1. Attentive; observing; giving heed; as, *heedful* of advice.

2. Watchful; cautious; circumspect; wary.

heed′ful-ly, *adv.* Attentively; carefully; cautiously; watchfully.

heed′ful-ness, *n.* Attention; caution; vigilance; circumspection; care to guard against danger or to perform duty.

heed′i-ly, *adv.* Cautiously; vigilantly. [Obs.]

heed′i-ness, *n.* Attention; caution. [Obs.]

heed′less, *a.* Inattentive; careless; negligent of the means of safety; thoughtless; regardless; unobserving; as, *heedless* of danger or surprise.

heed′less-ly, *adv.* Carelessly; negligently; inattentively; without care or circumspection.

heed′less-ness, *n.* Inattention; carelessness; thoughtlessness; negligence.

heed′y, *a.* Heedful. [Obs.]

heel, *v.i.*; heeled, *pt.*, *pp.*; heeling, *ppr.* To incline; to lean, as a ship; as, the ship *heels* aport or astarboard.

heel, *v.t.* 1. To arm, as a fighting-cock, with gaffs.

2. To add a heel to; as, to *heel* a shoe.

3. To dance; to perform, as a dance, with the heels. [Rare.]

4. To cause to careen, as a ship.

5. To equip or supply; used chiefly in past participle; as, well *heeled*. [Slang.]

heel, *n.* [ME. *heel*, *heele*; AS. *hela*, *hæla*, heel.]

1. The hind part of the foot, particularly of man.

2. Figuratively, the whole foot; as, the stag's winged *heel*.

3. The hind part of any foot-covering, as of a shoe.

4. The laminated support under the hind part of a shoe.

5. Something shaped like the human *heel*; a protuberance or knob.

6. The latter part; as, a bill was introduced into the legislature at the *heel* of the session.

7. A spur; as, to give a horse the *heel*.

8. Any part which corresponds to the human *heel* in position, as the after-part of a ship's keel; the lower end of the sternpost to which it is connected; also, the lower end of a mast; the part of a tool next to the handle, etc.

At one's heels; close behind.

Heels over head; in somersault fashion; recklessly; as, down they came, *heels over head*.

Heel of the hand; the marginal part of the palm of the hand next to the wrist and corresponding to the heel of the foot.

Neck and heels; the whole length of the body.

To be out at the heels; to have on stockings that are worn out; hence, to be in bad condition.

To cool the heels; to wait long and tediously; to dance attendance upon a reluctant patron.

To lay by the heels; to fetter; to shackle; to confine.

To show the heels, to show a clean pair of heels; to run from.

To take to one's heels; to flee; to betake oneself to flight.

To tread on one's heels; to follow closely and eagerly.

heel′bąll, *n.* A composition of wax and lamp-black used in taking impressions of inscriptions, engraved plates, etc., and also in polishing the heels and edges of the soles of shoes.

heel′-blank, *n.* A piece of leather shaped to form a lift or layer in the heel of a shoe.

heel′-chāin, *n.* In a ship, the chain that connects the heel of the jibboom with the bowsprit.

heel′-ċut″tẽr, *n.* An instrument or machine for cutting layers or lifts for shoe-heels.

heeled, *a.* Supplied with heels.

heel′ẽr, *n.* 1. A cock that strikes well with his heels.

2. A political worker of low class; one who is subservient to a political boss. [Colloq., U. S.]

heel′-flȳ, *n.* In southwestern United States, a fly, *Hypoderma lineata*, that attacks the heels of cattle.

heel′ing, *n.* The act of careening, as a ship; heel.

heel′ing-er″rŏr, *n.* The variation in an iron ship's compass, due to the vessel's heeling.

heel′less, *a.* Having no heel or heels.

heel′-lift, *n.* A single layer of leather in a shoe-heel; a heel-blank.

heel′-pȧth, *n.* The bank or path on the side of a canal opposite the towpath. [Local, U. S.]

heel′pïēce, *n.* 1. In medieval armor, a protection surrounding the heel.

2. A piece of leather on the heel of a shoe.

3. The thick piece strengthening the heel of a stocking.

4. Figuratively, the end; the conclusion.

heel′plāte, *n.* 1. The plate on the butt of a gunstock.

2. A perforated iron cap or plate on a shoe-heel, to which a skate may be attached.

3. An iron plate attached to a shoe-heel to prevent wear.

heel′pōst, *n.* 1. The post supporting the outer end of a propeller-shaft.

2. The post to which a door or gate is hinged.

3. A quoin-post of a lock-gate.

4. The outer post in a stall of a stable.

heel′-ring, *n.* The ring which holds a scythe-blade to the snath.

heel′tap, *n.* 1. A heel-lift.

2. That which remains in a glass after drinking.

heel′tap, *v.t.*; heeltapped, *pt.*, *pp.*; heeltapping, *ppr.* To add a piece of leather to the heel of (a shoe).

heel′tool, *n.* A tool that has a heel near the cutting end, used by metal-turners.

heer, *n.* [Etym. obscure.] The length of two cuts or leas of linen or woolen thread.

heft, *n.* A handle; a haft. [Obs.]

heft, *n.* [AS. *hefe*, weight.]

1. Heaving; effort. [Obs.]

2. Weight; ponderousness. [Colloq.]

3. The bulk or larger portion of anything. [Colloq.]

heft, *v.t.*; hefted, *pt.*, *pp.*; hefting, *ppr.* 1. To lift; to raise; to heave up.

2. To lift for the purpose of feeling or judging of the weight. [Colloq.]

heft, *n.* [G.] A kind of notebook.

heft′y, *a.*; *comp.* heftier; *superl.* heftiest. Weighty; forceful. [Colloq.]

Hē-ge′li-ăn, *a.* and *n.* I. *a.* Pertaining to Hegelianism.

II. *n.* A follower of Hegel.

Hē-gē′li-ăn-iṣm, Hē′gel-iṣm, *n.* A system of logic and philosophy introduced by Hegel, a German writer.

hē-gē-mon′iċ, hē-gē-mon′iċ-ăl, *a.* [Gr. *hēgemonikos*, pertaining to the leadership, from *hēgemonia*, leadership.] Principal; ruling; predominant.

hē-gem′ō-ny, *n.* [Gr. *hēgemonia*, leadership, chief command, from *hēgemōn*, a leader, from *hēgeisthai*, to lead.] Leadership, authority, or influence; usually applied to the political preponderance of a state or government over its neighbors, as among the states of ancient Greece.

hē-gï′rȧ, *n.* See *Hejira*.

hē-gū′men, *n.* See *Hegumenos*.

hē-gū′me-nē, *n.* [Gr. *hēgoumenē*, f. of *hēgoumenos*, ppr. of *hēgeisthai*, to lead.] In the Greek church, the head of a nunnery, similar to a Western abbess or prioress.

hē-gū′me-ness, *n.* Same as *Hegumene*.

hē-gū′me-nos, *n.* [Gr. *hēgoumenos*, ppr. of *hēgeisthai*, to lead.] In the Greek church, the head of a monastery, corresponding to a Western abbot or prior.

hē-gū′me-ny, *n.* [Gr. *hēgoumenia*, from *hēgoumenos*, hegumenos, properly ppr. of *hēgeisthai*, to lead.] In the Greek church, the office or station of hegumenos.

hei′dųk, *n.* See *Haiduk*.

heif′ẽr (hef′), *n.* [ME. *hayfare*, *heckfere*; AS. *heahfore*, a heifer, from *heah*, high, and *fear*, a bullock.]

1. A young cow.

2. A young female terrapin.

heigh′-hō, *interj.* An exclamation expressing astonishment, joy, disappointment, weariness, etc.

height, hight (hīt), *n.* [ME. *highte*, *hyghte*; AS. *heáthu*, height, a high place.]

1. The condition of being elevated; elevation; altitude; distance above some assumed base or level; as, the *height* of a mountain; the *height* of a mast.

2. That which has elevation; an eminence; a mountain, hill, or precipice; generally in the plural; as, the *heights* of the Andes; Alpine *heights*.

3. Degree of latitude either north or south. [Obs.]

4. Elevation in excellence of any kind, as in power, learning, arts, etc.; eminence of condition, quality, reputation, etc.

By him that raised me to this careful *height*. —Shak.

5. Greatest extent; utmost degree; extreme limit of progress or advancement; as, the *height* of passion; the *height* of a storm.

My grief was at the *height* before thou camest. —Shak.

6. Haughtiness. [Obs.]

height′en, hīght′en, *v.t.*; heightened, *pt.*, *pp.*; heightening, *ppr.* 1. To make higher; to elevate; as, to *heighten* a tower.

2. To increase; to augment; to intensify; to aggravate; as, to *heighten* virtue.

Foreign states have endeavored to *heighten* our confusion. —Addison.

3. To elevate in condition or sentiment; to increase the excellence of; as, to *heighten* one's ambition.

Syn.—Exalt, increase, enhance, intensify, vivify, aggravate, raise, exaggerate, amplify.

height′en, hight′en, *v.i.* To increase; to augment; to become elevated.

Then the captain's color *heightened*. —Tennyson.

height′en-ẽr, hight′en-ẽr, *n.* One who or that which heightens.

hei′min, *n.* [Japan.] In Japan, the plebeians, including traders, laborers, and artisans.

hei′nous (hā′), *a.* [ME. *heinous*; OFr. *haïnos*, odious, hateful, from *haïr*, hate.] Hateful; odious; atrocious; aggravated; as, a *heinous* sin or crime.

How *heinous* had the fact been, how deserving
Contempt and scorn! —Milton.

Syn.—Flagrant, flagitious, atrocious, infamous, nefarious, wicked.—A crime is *heinous* which seriously offends against the laws of men; an offense is *flagrant* which is in direct defiance of established opinions and practice; it is *flagitious* if a gross violation of the moral law, or coupled with any grossness; a crime is *atrocious* which is attended by any aggravating circumstances.

hei′nous-ly, *adv.* In a heinous manner; hatefully; abominably; enormously.

hei′nous-ness, *n.* The condition or quality of being heinous; odiousness; enormity; as, the *heinousness* of a crime.

heir (ãr), *n.* [ME. *heire*, *heyre*; OFr. *heir*; L. *heres*, an heir.]

1. One who succeeds or is to succeed another in the possession of lands, tenements, and hereditaments by descent; one on whom the law casts an estate of inheritance by the death of the ancestor or former possessor; one in whom the title to an estate of inheritance is vested by the operation of law on the death of a former owner; an inheritor.

2. One who inherits anything from an ancestor; one who receives any endowment from an ancestor; as, the son is often *heir* to the disease of the father.

Heir to an honorable name. —Macaulay.

Heir apparent; see under *Apparent*.

Heir at law; one who by the common law succeeds at the death of an ancestor to his lands and tenements.

Heir presumptive; one who, if the ancestor should die immediately, would be his heir, but whose right of inheritance may be defeated by any contingency, as by the birth of a nearer relative.

heir, *v.t.* To inherit; to succeed to.

One only daughter *heired* the royal state. —Dryden.

heir-ăp-pãr′en-cy, *n.* The state or condition of being heir apparent.

heir′dŏm, *n.* The state of being an heir; succession by inheritance.

heir′ess, *n.* A female heir; especially, a female inheriting or who is expected to inherit wealth.

heir′-land, *n.* Land that is inherited.

heir′less, *a.* Destitute of an heir.

heir′lọọm, *n.* [ME. *heire*; OFr. *heir*; L. *heres*, an heir, and AS. *geloma*, tools, utensils.]

1. A personal chattel which by special custom descends to an heir with the inheritance, being such a thing as cannot be separated from the estate without injury to it, as jewels of the crown, charters, deeds, and the like.

2. Any piece of personal property which has belonged to a family for a long time; a family relic.

heir′ship, *n.* The state, character, or privileges of an heir; right of inheriting.

Heirship movables; in Scotland, the best of certain kinds of movables which the heir is entitled to take, besides the heritable estate.

hē-jī′rȧ (*or* **hej′i-**), *n.* [Ar. *hejira*, lit., separation, flight, the era of Mohammed, from *hajara*, to quit, leave.] A flight or departure; especially, the flight of Mohammed from Mecca A. D. 622, afterward adopted as the name of the era from which the Mohammedans reckon their time, beginning July 16, 622.

hē-kis′tō-thėrm, *n.* [Gr. *hēkistos*, least, worst, and *thermē*, heat.] In botany, a plant capable of subsisting with the minimum of heat, as those in frigid climates.

hek′tō-grȧph, *n.* and *v.* See *Hectograph.*

hel′çoid, *a.* [Gr. *helkos*, a wound, an ulcer, and *eidos*, form.] Ulcerous; bearing resemblance to an ulcer.

hel-çol′ō-ġy, *n.* [Gr. *helkos*, a wound, an ulcer, and *-logia*, from *legein*, to speak.] That branch of the science of pathology which treats of ulcers.

hel′çō-plas-ty, *n.* [Gr. *helkos*, a wound, ulcer, and *plassein*, to form, mold.] In surgery, the operation of grafting on an ulcer a piece of skin from another part of the body or from another person, so as to expedite the process of healing.

held, *v.*, past tense and past participle of *hold.*

Hel′e-nȧ, *n.* [L.Gr. *helenē*, a torch, from *Helenē*, Helen, the wife of Menelaus and the cause of the Trojan War.] See *St. Elmo's fire* under *Fire.*

hel′en-flow″ėr, *n.* A plant of the genus *Helenium.*

hel′ē-nin, hel′ē-nine, *n.* A substance, C_6H_8O, derived from *Inula Helenium* or elecampane by the action of alcohol on the fresh root, or by distilling it with water. It crystallizes in white prisms.

He-lē′ni-um, *n.* [Gr. *helenion*, a plant (perhaps elecampane), from *Helenē*, Helen, the wife of Menelaus.] A genus of herbs of the aster family, having radiate heads and truncate branches of the style. They are natives of North and Central America. *Helenium autumnale*, the sneezeweed, is the best known species.

Hel-ē-ooh′ȧ-ris, *n.* [Gr. *helos*, a marsh, and *chairein*, to rejoice.] A widely distributed genus of plants of the sedge family, embracing about ninety species.

hel′grȧm-īte, *n.* See *Hellgrammite.*

he-li-. A combining form from Gr. *hēlios*, the sun. [See *Helio-.*]

hē′li-aç, *a.* Same as *Heliacal.*

hē-lī′ȧ-çăl, *a.* [LL. *heliacus*; Gr. *hēliakos*, of or pertaining to the sun, from *hēlios*, the sun.] In old astronomy, emerging from the light of the sun, or passing into it; applied to those risings and settings of a star which occurred at the same, or nearly the same, time as those of the sun. The *heliacal* rising of a star is when, after being in conjunction with the sun and invisible, it emerges from the light so as to be visible in the morning before sunrising. On the contrary, the *heliacal* setting of a star is when the sun approaches so near as to render the star invisible by its superior splendor.

hē-lī′ȧ-çăl-ly, *adv.* In a heliacal manner.

hē″li-an-thā′ceous, *a.* Relating to *Helianthus.*

hē-li-an′thin, *n.* [*Heli-*, and Gr. *anthos*, a flower.] In chemistry, a coal-tar dye which when applied to wool or silk gives it an orange color; called also *gold orange, methyl orange.*

hē-li-an′thoid, *a.* Pertaining to the *Helianthoidea.*

hē-li-an′thoid, *n.* One of the *Helianthoidea.*

Hē″li-an-thoi′dē-ȧ, *n.pl.* An order of actinozoans; the sea-anemones.

hē″li-an-thoi′dē-ăn, *a.* and *n.* Same as *Helianthoid.*

Hē-li-an′thus, *n.* [*Heli-*, and Gr. *anthos*, a flower.] A genus of plants of the aster family, containing about fifty species, chiefly North American annual or perennial herbs, with rough leaves and large yellow flowers; the sunflowers.

hel′i-çăl, *a.* [L. *helix* (*-icis*), a kind of ivy, from Gr. *helix* (*-ikos*), a spiral, tendril.] Of or pertaining to a helix; having a spiral form; spiral.

hel′i-çăl-ly, *adv.* In a helical manner; spirally.

Hē-li-chrȳ′sum, *n.* [*Heli-*, and Gr. *chrysos*, golden.] A large genus of plants of the aster family, embracing some 270 species, natives of the Old World. The form remains after the flowers have been dried; hence, they are often called "everlasting flowers."

hel-i-ci-. A combining form. [See *Helico-.*]

hē-lic′i-fọrm, *a.* [*Helici-*, and L. *forma*, form, shape.] Having the form of a helix; helical.

hel′i-cin, *n.* A chemical compound, $C_{13}H_{16}O_7$, derived from salicin.

hel′i-cine, *a.* [Gr. *helix* (*-ikos*), a spiral.]

1. Relating to the helix of the ear; as, the *helicine* fossa.

2. Spiral; coiled; as, the *helicine* arteries of the penis.

hel-i-cin′i-ăn, *a.* In zoölogy, helicine.

hel-i-ço-, hel-i-çi-. Combining forms from Gr. *helix* (*-ikos*), a spiral, used in botany, zoölogy, and mathematics to signify a spiral, spiral-shaped, of or pertaining to a spiral; as, *helico*gyrate, *helico*trema.

hel′i-çō-grȧph, *n.* [*Helico-*, and Gr. *graphein*, to write, draw.] An instrument used in flat drawing for describing spiral lines.

hel-i-çō-ġȳ′rāte, *a.* [*Helico-*, and Gr. *gyros*, a ring, circle.] In botany, applied to a plant, or part of a plant, having a ring carried obliquely round it, as in the spore-cases of *Trichomanes.*

hel′i-çoid, *a.* [Gr. *helikoeidēs*, of winding or spiral form; *helix* (*-ikos*), a spiral, and *eidos*, form.]

1. Coiled like a helix; spiral.

2. In zoölogy, pertaining to the *Helicidæ*, a family of gasteropods.

Helicoid cyme; same as *Bostryx.*

Helicoid dichotomy; in botany, a hypothetical branching of stems in which the sympodium is made up of branches which are either all on the right hand or all on the left.

Helicoid parabola; in mathematics, the curve which arises when the axis of the common parabola is bent round into the periphery of a circle, and is a line then passing through the extremities of the ordinates, which converge toward the center of the circle.

Helicoid spore; in botany, a spore that is coiled somewhat in the form of a helix.

hel′i-çoid, *n.* In geometry, a warped surface resembling that of a screw; as, a right *helicoid*, which is a developable surface, each of its generators passing through a fixed helix and being perpendicular to its axis.

hel-i-çoid′ăl, *a.* Same as *Helicoid*, 1.

hel-i-çom′e-try, *n.* [*Helico-*, and Gr. *metron*, a measure.] The art of describing or measuring spiral lines on a plane.

Hel′i-çon, *n.* [Gr. *Helikōn*, Helicon.]

1. A mountain in Bœotia, in Greece, from which flowed two fountains, Aganippe and Hippocrene, sacred to the Muses. The Greeks supposed it to be the residence of Apollo and the Muses.

2. [h—] [Gr. *helikōn*, from *helix* (*-ikos*), a spiral.] In music, (a) a wind-instrument of brass, carried over the shoulder; (b) an ancient acoustical instrument for demonstrating various musical intervals.

hel-i-çō′ni-ȧ, *n.* A butterfly of tropical America, belonging to the genus *Heliconius.*

Hel-i-çō′ni-ăn, *a.* 1. Pertaining to Helicon, a mountain in Greece.

2. [h—] Heliconoid.

hel-i-çō′nine, *a.* Same as *Heliconoid.*

Hel-i-çō′ni-us, *n.* [L. *Heliconius*, of Helicon, from Gr. *Helikōn*, Mt. Helicon.] A genus of tropical American butterflies, typical of the subfamily *Heliconiinæ*, having produced wings and slender legs.

hel-i-çō′noid, *a.* Pertaining to or resembling butterflies of the genus *Heliconius.*

hĕl-ĭ-çŏp′ter, *n.* A flying-machine with propellers so placed that the apparatus has an upward motion mainly, the forward motion coming when the propellers are tilted.

hel″i-çō-trē′mȧ, *n.* [*Helico-*, and Gr. *trēma*, a hole.] In anatomy, the opening at the summit of the cochlea where the two scalæ communicate.

he-li-o-, he-li-. Combining forms from Gr. *hēlios*, the sun, used in botany, zoölogy, and astronomy to signify the sun, of or like the sun, bright, radiant; as, *helio*graph, *helio*centric.

hē″li-ō-cen′triç, *a.* [*Helio-*, and Gr. *kentron*, center.] In astronomy, relating to the sun as a center; appearing as if seen from the sun's center.

Heliocentric place; the place of the ecliptic in which a planet would appear to a spectator if viewed from the center of the sun.

Heliocentric latitude; the inclination of a line drawn between the center of the sun and the center of a planet to the plane of the ecliptic.

Heliocentric longitude; the longitude of a planet as viewed from the sun.

hē″li-ō-cen′triç-ăl, *a.* Same as *Heliocentric.*

hē″li-ō-cen-tric′i-ty, *n.* The condition of being heliocentric.

hē′li-ō-chrōme, *n.* [*Helio-*, and Gr. *chrōma*, color.] A colored photograph.

hē″li-ō-chrō′miç, *a.* Pertaining to heliochromy.

hē″li-ō-chrō′mō-tȳpe, *n.* [*Helio-*, and Gr. *chrōma*, color, and *typos*, an impression.] A photograph which reproduces the colors of the object.

hē′li-ō-chrō-my (*or* **-ok′rō-**), *n.* The art of producing heliochromes.

hē″li-ō-chrȳ′sin, *n.* [*Helio-*, and Gr. *chrysos*, gold, and *-in.*] A coal-tar dyeing substance producing fine orange shades on silk and wool.

hē′li-ŏd, *n.* [Gr. *hēlios*, the sun, and E. *od.*] The supposed odic force of the sun.

hē″li-ō-ē-lec′triç, *a.* Pertaining to electrical phenomena as caused by the sun.

hē″li-ō-en-grāv′ing, *n.* Same as *Heliogravure.*

hē′li-ō-grȧph, *n.* [*Helio-*, and Gr. *graphein*, to write.]

1. An instrument for taking photographs of the sun.

2. A picture taken by heliography; a photograph.

3. In signaling, surveying, etc., an instrument provided with a movable mirror from which rays of light are flashed to a distance.

hē′li-ō-grȧph, *v.t.*; heliographed, *pt.*, *pp.*; heliographing, *ppr.* 1. To transmit, as a signal, by means of a heliograph.

2. To photograph by sunlight.

hē-li-og′rȧ-phėr, *n.* One who practises or is skilled in heliography.

hē-li-ō-graph′iç, *a.* Pertaining to heliography or the heliograph.

hē-li-ō-graph′iç-ăl, *a.* Heliographic.

hē-li-og′rȧ-phy, *n.* [*Helio-*, and Gr. *graphein*, to write.]

1. The practice, method, or operation of signaling by means of the heliograph.

2. Photography.

3. A description of the sun's surface.

hē-li-ō-grȧv′ūre, *n.* [*Helio-*, and Fr. *gravure*, engraving.]

1. Photo-engraving.

2. A print or plate made by the process of photo-engraving.

hē′li-oid, *a.* [Gr. *hēlios*, sun, and *eidos*, form.] Like the sun.

hē-li-ol′ȧ-tėr, *n.* [*Helio-*, and Gr. *latreuin*, to serve, worship.] A worshiper of the sun.

hē-li-ol′ȧ-try, *n.* [*Helio-*, and Gr. *latreia*, worship, from *latreuin*, to serve.] The worship of the sun.

hē′li-ō-līte, *n.* [*Helio-*, and Gr. *lithos*, a stone.] Same as *Sunstone.*

hē-li-ol′ō-ġy, *n.* [*Helio-*, and Gr. *-logia*, from *legein*, to speak.] The science which treats of the sun.

hē-li-om′ē-tėr, *n.* [*Helio-*, and Gr. *metron*, a measure.] An instrument for determining with accuracy the angular distance between two stars. It was originally devised for measuring the sun's diameter.

hē″li-ō-met′riç, *a.* Pertaining to or determined by means of the heliometer; pertaining to measurements of the sun.

hē″li-ō-met′riç-ăl, *a.* Heliometric.

hē″li-ō-met′riç-ăl-ly, *adv.* Through the medium of the heliometer.

hē-li-om′ē-try, *n.* The art or practice of using the heliometer to determine measurements of the sun or angular distances between celestial objects.

hē′li-ō-phag, *n.* In biology, any heliophagous part of an animal, as a pigment-cell.

hē-li-oph′ȧ-gous, *a.* [*Helio-*, and Gr. *phagein*, to eat.] In biology, absorbing the energy of sunlight, as chlorophyl and pigment-cells.

hē-li-oph′i-lous, *a.* [*Helio-*, and Gr. *philos*, loving.] Fond of or attracted by the sun, as certain flowers.

hē-li-ō-phō′biç, *a.* [*Helio-*, and Gr. *phobeisthai*, to fear.] Having an aversion to the sun; shunning the light of the sun.

Hē-li-op′ō-rȧ, *n.* [*Helio-*, and Gr. *pōros*, tufa.]

1. The typical genus of the family *Helioporidæ* or sun-corals.

2. [h—] One of the *Heliopora*; a heliopore.

hē′li-ō-pōre, *n.* Any species of the genus *Heliopora*; a sun-coral.

Hē-li-op′sis, *n.* [*Helio-*, and Gr. *opsis*, likeness.] A genus of plants of the aster family, mostly perennial herbs with prominent yellow flowers and petioled, opposite leaves. The genus embraces seven species, natives of America.

hē′li-ō-sçōpe, *n.* [*Helio-*, and Gr. *skopein*, to view.] A form of telescope fitted for viewing the sun without pain or injury to the eyes, as when made with colored glasses or glasses blackened with smoke, or with mirrors formed simply of surfaces of transparent glass, which reflect but a small portion of light.

hē-li-ō-sçop′iç, *a.* Pertaining to the helioscope.

hē-li-ō′sis, *n.* [Gr. *hēliousthai*, to bask in the sun, from *hēlios*, the sun.]

1. In medicine, (a) treatment of disease by exposure to the sunlight; (b) sunstroke.

2. In botany, the production of burned spots upon leaves by the concentration of the rays of the sun through inequalities of the glass of conservatories, or through drops of water resting on the leaves.

hē-li-ō-spher′iç-ăl, *a.* [*Helio-*, and *sphairikos*, spherical, from *sphaira*, a sphere.] Round, as the sun.

hē′li-ō-stat, *n.* [*Helio-*, and Gr. *statos*, fixed, from *histanai*, to fix, cause to stand.] An instrument consisting of a mirror moved by clockwork so as to reflect the rays of the sun in a fixed direction.

hē-li-oth′id, *a.* Pertaining to or characteristic of the *Heliothidæ.*

hē-li-oth′id, *n.* One of the *Heliothidæ.*

Hē-li-oth′i-dæ, *n.pl.* [Gr. *hēliōtis*, f. of *hēliōtēs*, of the sun, from *hēlios*, the sun.] A family of noctuid moths.

hē′li-ō-trōpe, *n.* [L. *heliotropium*; Gr. *heliotropion*, a sundial, a plant called the heliotrope; *hēlios*, the sun, and *trepein*, to turn.]

1. In old astronomy, an instrument or machine for showing when the sun arrived at the tropics and the equinoctial line.

2. In signaling and surveying, a heliograph.

3. In mineralogy, a subspecies of quartz of a deep green color, peculiarly pleasant to the eye. It is usually variegated with blood-red or yellowish dots, and is more or less translucent; called also *bloodstone*.

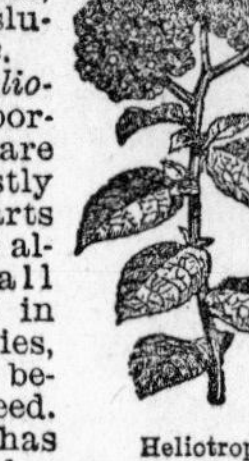
Heliotrope.

4. A plant of the genus *Heliotropium*, belonging to the borage family. The species are herbs or undershrubs, mostly natives of the warmer parts of the world. They have alternate leaves and small flowers usually disposed in scorpioid cymes, one species, *Heliotropium Europæum*, being a common European weed. *Heliotropium Peruvianum* has long been a favorite garden plant on account of the fragrance of its flowers.

5. The color of certain flowers of the *heliotrope*.

False heliotrope; the summer heliotrope.

Summer heliotrope; a small shrub, *Tournefortia heliotropoides*, of the borage family.

Winter heliotrope; *Petasites fragrans*, a European plant of the aster family.

hē′li-ō-trōpe, *a.* Of the bluish-purple or lilac color of some flowers of the heliotrope.

hē′li-ō-trō-pēr, *n.* One who has charge of a heliotrope or heliograph at an observing station.

hē-li-ō-trop′iç, *a.* Pertaining to or characterized by heliotropism.

hē-li-ō-trop′iç-ăl, *a.* Heliotropic.

hē-li-ō-trop′iç-ăl-ly, *adv.* In a heliotropic manner.

hē-li-ot′rō-pişm, *n.* [*Helio-*, and Gr. *tropē*, a turning, from *trepein*, to turn.] Disposition or tendency to turn or incline toward the sun, especially the characteristic tendency of a plant to direct its growth toward the sun or toward light.

Hē-li-ō-trō′pi-um, *n.* A genus of plants of the borage family

hē-li-ot′rō-py (*or* **hē′**), *n.* Same as *Heliotropism.*

hē′li-ō-tȳpe, *n.* [*Helio-*, and Gr. *typos*, an impression.] A picture or impression produced by the process of heliotypy; also, the process of heliotypy itself.

hē′li-ō-tȳpe, *a.* Pertaining to heliotypy.

hē′li-ō-tȳpe, *v.t.*; heliotyped, *pt.*, *pp.*; heliotyping, *ppr.* To produce, as a picture, by a heliotype process.

hē′li-ō-tȳpe, *v.i.* To practise heliotypy.

hē-li-ō-typ′iç, *a.* Heliotype.

hē″li-ō-tȳ-pog′rȧ-phy, *n.* [*Helio-*, and Gr. *typos*, an impression, and *graphein*, to write, draw.] The art or process of producing phototypes; phototypy.

hē′li-ō-tȳ-py, *n.* [*Helio-*, and Gr. *typos*, an impression.] A photographic process by which direct impressions on paper are produced from gelatin plates, by means of a press.

Hē″li-ō-zō′ȧ, *n.pl.* [*Helio-*, and Gr. *zōon*, an animal.] An order of protozoans of spherical form, with radiolarian skeletons; the sun-animalcules.

hē-li-ō-zō′ăn, *n.* One of the *Heliozoa.*

hē-li-ō-zō′ăn, *a.* Pertaining to the *Heliozoa.*

hē-li-ō-zō′iç, *a.* Heliozoan.

hel-i-spher′iç, *a.* [Gr. *helix* (*-ikos*), a spiral, and *sphaira*, a sphere.] Spiral.

hel-i-spher′iç-ăl, *a.* Helispheric.

Helispherical line; see *Loxodromic curve* under *Loxodromic.*

hē′li-um, *n.* [Gr. *hēlios*, the sun.] A hypothetical elementary substance first discovered in the atmosphere of the sun. It has since been found in certain rare minerals.

hē′lix, *n.*; *pl.* **hē′lix-eş** or **hel′i-çēş.** [L. *helix*, a kind of ivy, a spiral; Gr. *helix* (*-ikos*), a spiral, anything of a spiral shape, from *helissein*, to turn round.]

1. A spiral line, as of wire in a coil; a circumvolution; a winding, or something that is spiral; specifically, in geometry, a nonplane curve the tangents of which bear equal inclinations to a fixed right line, such a curve as is described by every point of a screw that is turned round in a fixed nut.

2. In anatomy, the whole circuit or extent of the auricle or external border of the ear. [See illustration of *Ear.*]

3. In architecture, a small volute or twist under the abacus of the Corinthian capital, of which in every perfect capital there are sixteen, two at each angle, and two meeting under the middle of each face of the abacus, branching out of the cauliculi or stalks, which rise from between the leaves.

4. [H—] In zoölogy, a genus of gasteropodous mollusks, the type of the family *Helicidæ*. The common garden-snail, *Helix hortensis*, and the Roman snail, *Helix pomatia*, are examples.

5. In electricity, a coil of wire, as that surrounding an electromagnet.

hĕll, *n.* [ME. *helle*; AS. *hell*, hell, from *helan*, to cover, conceal.]

1. The place of the dead, or of souls after death; the lower regions or the grave; called in Hebrew *Sheol*, and by the Greeks *Hades.*

> Thou wilt not leave my soul in *hell.*
> —Ps. xvi. 10.

2. The place or state of punishment for the wicked after death; the abode of devils.

> Bring with thee airs from heaven, or blasts from *hell.* —Shak.

3. The infernal powers.

> Richard yet lives, *hell's* black intelligencer.
> —Shak.

4. A place or condition regarded as resembling hell; specifically, (a) any mental torment or anguish; (b) a place into which a tailor throws his shreds, or a printer his broken type; (c) in some games, the place to which those who are caught are carried; (d) a gambling-house; (e) a dungeon or prison; now obsolete.

Hel-lȧ-nod′iç, *n.* [Gr. *Hellanodikēs*; *Hellēn* (*-ēnos*), a Greek, and *dikē*, a judgment, decision.] In ancient Greece, a judge of the games, exercises, or combats.

hell′bend-ẽr, *n.* A voracious North American salamander, *Menopoma alleghaniensis*, reputed to be difficult to kill.

hell′=bent, *a.* Resolved or determined to have or do, without regard to consequences; as, he started *hell-bent* after it. [Slang.]

hell′bọrn, *a.* Born of or in hell; hellish in origin or conception; innately vicious.

hell′=box, *n.* In printing, a wastebox for damaged type, rules, etc. [Slang.]

hell′bred, *a.* Produced in hell; atrociously wicked.

hell′brewed (-brụd), *a.* Concocted or prepared in hell.

hell′brọth, *n.* A mixture used in malicious magic; witch-broth.

hell′=çat, *n.* A witch; a hag.

hell′=div″ẽr, *n.* The dabchick.

hell′dọọmed, *a.* Foredoomed to hell.

hel′lē-bōre, *n.* [OFr. *ellebore*; L. *helleborus*, *elleborus*; Gr. *helleboros*, hellebore.]

1. Any plant of the genus *Helleborus.*

2. The powdered root of the white hellebore, *Veratrum album*, used to destroy lice and caterpillars on growing plants.

hel-lē-bō′rē-in, *n.* [*Hellebore* and *-in.*] A crystalline substance, $C_{26}H_{44}O_{15}$, obtained from the root of black hellebore.

hel-leb′ō-rin, *n.* A resin obtained from the root of black hellebore, *Helleborus niger.*

hel-lē-bō′rine, *n.* [L., from Gr. *helleborinē*, a plant like hellebore, from *helleboros*, hellebore.] An orchid of the genus *Epipactis*, or one of the allied genus *Cephalanthera.*

hel′lē-bō-rişm, *n.* [L. *helleborismus*; Gr. *helleborismos*, from *helleborizein*, to dose with hellebore, from *helleboros*, hellebore.] The medicinal use of hellebore, as practised by the ancients.

hel′lē-bō-rīze, *v.t.* [Gr. *helleborizein*, to dose with hellebore, from *helleboros*, hellebore.] To treat with hellebore with the view of bringing one to his senses.

Hel-le′bō-rus, *n.* [L. *helleborus*; Gr. *helleboros*, hellebore.] A genus of plants of the natural order *Ranunculaceæ*, consisting of perennial, low-growing herbs with palmate or pedate leathery leaves, yellowish, greenish, or white flowers having five conspicuous, persistent sepals, eight to ten small, tubular petals, and several many-seeded carpels. *Helleborus Orientalis* is the species which produced the black hellebore of the ancients. *Helleborus niger* is the Christmas rose, the source of black hellebore now used medicinally.

Hel′lēne, *n.* [Gr. *Hellēn* (*-ēnos*), a Greek, as opposed to a Jew, a gentile, from *Hellēn*, the son of Deucalion, the legendary ancestor of the Greeks.] A citizen or native of ancient or modern Greece.

Hel-lē′ni-ăn, *a.* Hellenic.

Hel-len′iç, *a.* [Gr. *Hellēnikos*, from *Hellēn*, a Greek, *Hellēnes*, the Greeks.] Pertaining to the Hellenes, or inhabitants of Greece, or to their art and literature.

Hellenic dialect; the pure Greek tongue in use throughout Greek-speaking countries subsequent to the time of Alexander.

Hel′len-işm, *n.* [Gr. *Hellēnismos*, imitation of the Greeks, from *Hellēnizein*, to speak Greek.]

1. A phrase in the idiom, genius, or construction of the Greek language; a Grecism.

2. The tendency toward intellectual and physical perfection, and the love of the beautiful which characterized the ancient Greeks.

Hel′len-ist, *n.* [Gr. *Hellēnistēs*, an imitator of the Greeks, from *Hellēnizein*, to speak Greek.]

1. A Grecian Jew; a Jew who used the Greek language; any one who adopts the Greek language and Greek usages.

2. One skilled in the Greek language and versed in Greek literature.

Hel-lē-nis′tiç, Hel-lē-nis′tiç-ăl, *a.* Pertaining to the Hellenists; having a mixture of foreign and Greek elements or traits; not truly Hellenic.

Hellenistic dialect; the Greek spoken by the Jews who lived in Egypt and other countries where the Greek language prevailed; called also *Alexandrine dialect.*

Hellenistic period; the time between the Hellenic and Greco-Roman periods, noted for the decadence of Greek art and literature.

Hel-lē-nis′tiç-ăl-ly, *adv.* According to the Hellenistic dialect; in the manner of the Hellenists.

Hel-len-ī-zā′tion, *n.* The act or process of rendering Greek in character; the state of being Hellenized.

Hel′len-ize, *v.i.*; Hellenized, *pt.*, *pp.*; Hellenizing, *ppr.* [Gr. *Hellēnizein*, to imitate the Greeks, to speak Greek, from *Hellēnes*, the Greeks.] To use the Greek language; to conform to Hellenic standards.

Hel′len-īze, *v.t.* To render Greek; to lend a Greek form or character to; to Grecize.

hel-len′ō-tȳpe, *n.* See *Diaphanotype.*

Hel-les-pon′tine, *a.* Pertaining to the strait formerly called Hellespont, now termed the Dardanelles, being the strait between the Ægean Sea and Sea of Marmora.

hell′grăm-mīte, hel′grăm-īte, *n.* The larva of *Corydalus cornutus*, the dobson, a large neuropteral fly. This larva is very attractive to fish, especially trout, and is much used as a bait.

hell′hag, *n.* An old woman of spiteful or malicious tendencies.

hell′hound, *n.* A hound or an agent of hell; a cruel pursuer.

hel′li-ẽr, *n.* A tiler; a slater. [Prov. Eng.]

hell′ish, *a.* Pertaining to hell; like hell in qualities; infernal; malignant; wicked; diabolical.

hell′ish-ly, *adv.* In a hellish or diabolical manner.

hell′ish-ness, *n.* The qualities of hell or of its inhabitants; extreme wickedness, malignity, or impiety.

hell′=kite, *n.* A bird of prey; figuratively, a cruel person.

hel-lō′, *interj.* A colloquial form of *hallo*, used to attract attention and as a preliminary call in telephoning.

hell′wărd, *adv.* Toward hell.

hell′y, *a.* Having the qualities of hell; hellish.

helm, *n.* Same as *Halm.*

helm, *n.* [ME. *helme*; AS. *helma*, a helm, rudder.]

1. The instrument by which a ship is steered, consisting of a rudder, tiller, wheel, etc.; specifically, the wooden or metal bar by which the rudder is shifted.

2. The place or post of direction or management; as, to be at the *helm* of the administration.

3. A helve; a handle. [Obs.]

Helm's alee; see under *Alee.*

Helm amidships; the order to keep the rudder fore and aft of the ship.

Port the helm; the order to put the helm toward the left side of the ship.

Shift the helm; the order to put the helm from port to starboard, or vice versa.

Starboard the helm; the order to put the helm to the right side of the ship.

To ease the helm; to bring the tiller somewhat amidships in order to reduce the strain on the rudder.

To put the helm down; to push the helm down to the lee side in order to put the ship about or to bring her up to the wind.

To right the helm; to put the helm fore and aft of the ship.

Up with the helm; the order to put the helm aweather.

helm, *n.* [ME. *helm*; AS. *helm*, a protection, a helm.]

1. A helmet. [Poet.]

2. A cloud capping a mountain when the sky is clear, indicating a coming storm.

3. An outhouse. [Prov. Eng.]

helm, *v.t.* To steer; to guide; to direct. [Rare.]

helm, *v.t.* [ME. *helmen*; AS. *helmian*, to cover, from *helm*, a covering, a helmet.] To provide with a helmet or helm.

helm′āge, *n.* Guidance. [Rare.]

hel′met, *n.* [OFr. *healmet*, dim. of *heaume*, a helm, from AS. *helm*, a helm, covering.]

Open Helmet.

1. A piece of defensive armor for the head. It was originally made of leather, and afterward strengthened by the addition of bronze and other metals, until finally it was constructed entirely of metal, lined with felt or wadding. In the middle ages, helmets were frequently inlaid with gold, and provided with bars and movable flaps to cover the face in battle, and to be opened at other times. A full barred helmet covered the whole of the head

face, and neck. The military helmet as now worn does not cover or protect the face. The name is also given to a kind of hat worn by police officers, firemen, etc. It is usually made of felt, pith, or similar material.

King. Noble. Knight. Esquire.

2. In heraldry, the part of a coat of arms which bears the crest. Degrees of rank are indicated by changes of form.

3. The upper part of a retort.

4. In botany, same as *galea*.

5. A cloud. [See third *Helm.*]

hel′met-bee″tle, *n.* A beetle of the family *Cassididæ*; so named from its shape.

hel′met-bird, *n.* A touracou.

hel′met-crab, *n.* *Limulus longispinus*, a king-crab.

hel′met-crest, *n.* A crested humming bird of South America, belonging to the genus *Oxypogon*.

hel′met-ed, *a.* Wearing or provided with a helmet.

hel′met-flow″ẽr, *n.* 1. Any variety of monk's-hood.

2. The skullcap.

3. An orchid of South America of the genus *Coryanthes*.

hel′met-shāped (-shāpt), *a.* In botany, having the shape of a helmet; galeate.

hel′met-shell, *n.* The shell of a pectinibranchiate gasteropod of the genus *Cassis*. Most of the species are found on tropical shores, but a few are found on the coast of the Mediterranean. Some of the shells attain a large size. *Cassis rufa*, *Cassis cornuta*, *Cassis tuberosa* and others are the material on which shell-cameos are usually sculptured.

Helmet-shell (*Cassis tuberosa*).

hel′minth, *n.* [Gr. *helmins* (-*inthos*), a worm.] A worm; specifically, a parasitical worm, as the tapeworm or larva infesting the internal parts or intestinal canal of an animal.

hel-minth-, hel-min-tho-. Combining forms from Gr. *helmins* (-*inthos*), a worm, used in botany, zoölogy, and medicine to signify a worm or pertaining to a worm, as *helminth*agogue.

hel-min-thȧ-gog′iç, *a.* [*Helminth*-, and Gr. *agōgos*, leading, driving, from *agein*, to lead, drive.] Efficacious against worms; anthelmintic.

hel-min′thȧ-gogue (-gog), *n.* [*Helminth*-, and Gr. *agōgos*, leading, driving, from *agein*, to lead, drive.] In medicine, a remedy for worms; an anthelmintic; a vermicide; a vermifuge.

Hel-min′thēṣ, *n.pl.* [Gr. *helmins* (-*inthos*), a worm.] A large group of worms, mostly parasitic, including the *Cestoidea*, *Nematoidea*, *Trematoidea*, *Turbellaria*, etc.

hel-min-thī′ȧ-sis, *n.* [Gr. *helminthian*, to suffer from worms, from *helmins* (-*inthos*), a worm.] In medicine, the diseased condition produced by the presence of worms in the body.

hel-min′thiç, *a.* and *n.* [Gr. *helmins* (-*inthos*), a worm.]

I. *a.* Relating to worms; in medicine, expelling worms.

II. *n.* A medicine for expelling worms; a vermicide; a vermifuge; an anthelmintic.

hel-min′thite, *n.* [Gr. *helmins* (-*inthos*), a worm.] A long, sinuous mark or track common on the surface of sandstones, believed to be a fossil worm-trail.

hel-min-tho-. See *Helminth-*.

hel-min′thoid, *a.* [Gr. *helmins* (-*inthos*), a worm, and *eidos*, form.] Wormlike; vermiform.

hel-min-thō-loġ′iç, *a.* Pertaining to helminthology.

hel-min-thō-loġ′iç-ăl, *a.* Helminthologic.

hel-min-thol′ō-ġist, *n.* One who is versed in helminthology.

hel-min-thol′ō-ġy, *n.* [*Helmintho*-, and Gr. -*logia*, from *legein*, to speak.] The science or knowledge of worms, especially parasitic worms.

helm′less, *a.* 1. Destitute of a helmet.

2. Without a helm or steering-apparatus.

helm′-pōrt, *n.* The aperture in the counter of a vessel through which the rudderhead passes.

helmṣ′măn, *n.*; *pl.* **helmṣ′men.** The man at the helm or wheel who steers a ship.

he-lō′bi-ous, *a.* [Gr. *helos*, a marsh, and *bios*, life.] Thriving in marshy ground; palustrine.

hē-loc′e-rous, *a.* [Gr. *hēlos*, a stud, nail, and *keras*, horn.] Having the characteristics of the *Clavicornia*; clavicorn.

hē′lō-dẽrm, *n.* A lizard of the genus *Heloderma*.

Hē-lō-dẽr′mȧ, *n.* [Gr. *hēlos*, a nail, a stud, a wart or knob, and *derma*, skin.] A genus of venomous lizards of Mexico and southern United States. *Heloderma suspectum* is the Gila monster; *Heloderma horridum*, a larger species common to Mexico.

Heloderma horridum.

Hē′lot (*or* hel′ŏt), *n.* [L. *Helotæ*; Gr. *Heilōtes*, pl. of *Heilōs*, a Helot, from *Helos*, a town of Laconia whose inhabitants were enslaved.] A slave in ancient Sparta; by extension, any slave.

hē′lot-iṣm, *n.* Slavery; the condition of the Helots of Sparta.

hē′lot-ry, *n.* Helots collectively; also, slavery.

help, *v.t.*; helped, *pt.*, *pp.*; helping, *ppr.* [ME. *helpen*; AS. *helpan*, to help.]

1. To lend strength or means toward; to aid; to assist; as, to *help* a distressed brother.

2. To lend means of deliverance; to succor; as, *help* us or we perish.

3. To lessen the pain of; to add to the comfort of; to heal; as, the medicine *helped* the patient.

4. To prevent; to hinder; to forbear; to avoid.

> I cannot *help* remarking the resemblance between him and our author. —Pope.

5. To be of assistance to in some way, with an elliptical use of *to go*, *to get*, *to continue*, etc.; as, *help* me out of the carriage; *help* me on my way.

6. To augment; to aggravate. [Rare.]

7. To serve; to apportion; as, shall I *help* you to the meat?

8. To mend. [Prov. Eng.]

Syn.—Assist, aid, succor, relieve.—The idea of communicating to the advantage of another in case of need is common to all these terms. *Help* is the generic term; the rest specific; *help* may be substituted for the others, and in many cases where they would not be applicable. The first three are employed either to produce a positive good or to remove an evil; the two latter only to remove an evil. We *help* a person to prosecute his work, or *help* him out of a difficulty; we *assist* in order to forward a scheme, or we *assist* a person in the time of his embarrassment; we *aid* a good cause, or we *aid* a person to make his escape; we *succor* a person who is in danger; we *relieve* him in time of distress.

To help forward; to advance by assistance.

To help off; to aid in passing; as, *to help off* time.

To help on; to forward; to promote by aid.

To help out; to aid in delivering from difficulty or in completing a design.

To help over; to enable to surmount; as, *to help* one *over* a difficulty.

To help up; to assist to erect posture; to promote financially or socially.

help, *v.i.* 1. To lend aid; to contribute strength or means.

> A generous present *helps* to persuade, as well as an agreeable person. —Garth.

2. To serve or dish out food to one at table.

help, *n.* [ME. *help*; AS. *help*, from *helpan*, to help.]

1. Aid; assistance; strength or means furnished toward promoting an object, or deliverance from difficulty or distress.

2. That which gives assistance; one who or that which contributes to advance a purpose; as, memory is a great *help*.

3. Remedy; relief; succor; as, *help* is at hand.

4. Collectively, all the people employed as workers, as on a farm; sometimes in the singular; as, the *help* are at dinner; the Boston *help* reads Greek.

help′ẽr, *n.* One who helps; an assistant; an auxiliary.

help′fụl, *a.* Rendering aid or assistance; remedial.

help′fụl-ly, *adv.* In a helpful manner.

help′fụl-ness, *n.* Assistance; usefulness.

help′ing, *n.* 1. The act of giving help.

2. A portion of food or drink. [Colloq.]

help′less, *a.* 1. Unable to be of assistance to oneself without outside aid; destitute of the power or means of relieving oneself; as, an infant is *helpless*.

2. Admitting no help; irremediable.

3. Unsupplied; destitute; as, *helpless* of necessities. [Rare.]

help′less-ly, *adv.* In a helpless manner.

help′less-ness, *n.* Want of strength or ability; the condition of being helpless.

help′māte, *n.* An assistant; a coworker; a wife.

help′meet, *n.* A helpmate; wife.

hel′tẽr-skel′tẽr, *adv.* In haste and confusion; in aimless or ineffectual action. [Colloq.]

helve, *n.* [ME. *helve*; AS. *helf*, a handle.]

1. The handle of an ax, adz, or hatchet.

2. A tilt-hammer; also, the handle of a tilt-hammer.

helve, *v.t.*; helved, *pt.*, *pp.*; helving, *ppr.* To furnish with a helve or handle.

Hel-vē′tiăn, *a.* and *n.* I. *a.* Helvetic.

II. *n.* A native of Switzerland; a Swiss.

Hel-vet′iç, *a.* [L. *Helveticus*, from *Helvetii*, the Helvetii.]

1. Pertaining to the Helvetii, the ancient inhabitants of the Alpine country, now named Switzerland.

2. Pertaining to modern Switzerland or its inhabitants.

Helvetic confessions; two Swiss Protestant confessions of faith, the first dated 1536 and the second 1566.

hel′vin, hel′vīte, *n.* [L. *helvus*, light yellow, and -*in*, -*ite*.] A mineral of a yellowish color occurring in regular tetrahedrons, and made up of glucinum, iron, manganese, silica, and sulphur.

hem, *interj.* A sound of an interjectional nature the utterance of which is a sort of half-voluntary cough used to draw attention, to simulate embarrassment, etc.

hem, *n.* [ME. *hem*, AS. *hem*, edge, border, from *ham*, an inclosed field.]

1. The border of a fabric, doubled and sewed to strengthen it and prevent the raveling of the threads.

2. Edge; border.

hem, *v.t.*; hemmed, *pt.*, *pp.*; hemming, *ppr.* 1. To form a hem or border on; to fold and sew down the edge of, as cloth, etc.

2. To border; to edge.

3. To limit; to keep circumscribed; with *in*, *around*, or *about*; as, *hemmed in* by narrow walls.

hem, *v.i.* To make the sound expressed by the word hem; to stammer; as, to *hem* and haw.

hema-, hemato-, hemo-. Combining forms from Gr. *haima* (-*atos*), blood, used in zoölogy, chemistry, and medicine to signify blood, bloody, or of the nature or color of blood; as, *hema*poiesis, *hema*pophysis.

hem′ȧ-çhāte, hæm′ȧ-çhāte, *n.* [*Hema*-, and Gr. *achatēs*, agate.] A form of agate marked by spots of red jasper.

hem′ȧ-çhrōme, hæm′ȧ-çhrōme, *n.* [*Hema*-, and Gr. *chrōma*, color.] Hematin.

hem′ȧ-çīte, *n.* [Gr. *haima*, blood.] A composition of blood and vegetable or mineral materials used in the manufacture of small articles, as buttons.

hem′ȧ-çȳte, hæm′ȧ-çȳte, *n.* [*Hema*-, and Gr. *kytos*, a cavity.] A blood-corpuscle or cell.

hem″ȧ-çȳ-tom′e-tẽr, hæm″ȧ-çȳ-tom′e-tẽr, *n.* [*Hema*-, and Gr. *kytos*, a cavity, and *metron*, a measure.] A device for measuring the number of corpuscles in a definite amount of blood.

hē′mad, hæ′mad, *adv.* [Gr. *haima*, blood, and -*ad*.] To or toward the hemal or ventral part of the body.

hem-ȧ-drom′e-tẽr, hæm-ȧ-drom′e-tẽr, *n.* [*Hema*-, and Gr. *dromos*, a running, and *metron*, a measure.] A device to measure the velocity of arterial blood; spelled also *hemadromometer*.

hem-ȧ-drom′e-try, hæm-ȧ-drom′e-try, *n.* Measurement of blood velocity; spelled also *hemadromometry*.

hem-ȧ-drom′ō-grȧph, hæm-ȧ-drom′ō-grȧph, *n.* [*Hema*-, and Gr. *dromos*, a running, and *graphein*, to write.] A device to record blood velocities.

hem″ȧ-dȳ-nam′ē-tẽr, *n.* A hemadynamometer.

hē″mȧ-dȳ-nam′içs, hæ″mȧ-dȳ-nam′içs, *n.* [*Hema*-, and Gr. *dynamis*, power.] Dynamics as related to the circulation of blood.

hē-mȧ-dȳ-nȧ-mom′ē-tẽr, hæ-mȧ-dȳ-nȧ-mom′ē-tẽr, *n.* [*Hema*-, and Gr. *dynamis*, power, and *metron*, a measure.] An instrument for ascertaining the pressure of the blood in the arteries or veins.

hē′măl, hæ′măl, *a.* [Gr. *haima*, blood.]

1. Pertaining to blood or the circulatory system; vascular.

2. Of or upon the side containing the heart and chief blood-vessels; in vertebrates, ventral; in *Vermes* and *Mollusca*, dorsal; distinguished from *neural*.

3. Like blood; characteristic of blood.

Hemal arch; the arch formed by the projection anteriorly of the ribs and the sternum from the vertebræ.

hem″ȧ-poi-ē′sis, hæm″ȧ-poi-ē′sis, *n.* See *Hematopoiesis*.

hem″ȧ-poi-et′iç, hæm″ȧ-poi-et′iç, *a.* [*Hema*-, and Gr. *poiētikos*, capable of making, from *poiein*, to make.] Blood-producing.

hem-ȧ-poph′y-sis, hæm-ȧ-poph′y-sis, *n.*; *pl.* **hem-ȧ-poph′y-sēṣ, hæm-ȧ-poph′y-sēṣ.** [*Hema*-, and Gr. *apophysis*, an outgrowth, a process; *apo*, from, and *phyein*, to grow.] In anatomy, the element of either half of a hemal arch that is next to the hemal spine; in the thoracic region, a costal cartilage.

hem″ȧ-pō-phys′i-ăl, *a.* Relating to hemapophysis.

hem-ȧ-stat′ic, hæm-ȧ-stat′ic, *a.* [*Hema-*, and Gr. *statikos*, causing to stand, from *histanai*, to stand.]

1. Pertaining to stagnation of the blood.
2. Tending to arrest hemorrhage; styptic.

hem-ȧ-stat′ic, hæm-ȧ-stat′ic, *n.* A styptic medicine.

hem-ȧ-stat′ics, hæm-ȧ-stat′ics, *n.* [*Hema-*, and Gr. *statikos*, causing to stand.] The hydrostatics of the circulatory system.

hem″ȧ-tȧ-chom′ē-tēr, hæm″ȧ-tȧ-chom′ē-tēr, *n.* [*Hema-*, and Gr. *tachos*, swiftness, and *metron*, a measure.] A device to measure the velocity of the flow of blood.

hem-ȧ-tē′in, hem-ȧ-tē′ine, *n.* [Gr. *haima* (*-atos*), blood.] A hematoxylin derivative, $C_{16}H_{12}O_6$, formed by the action of ammonia, and producing dark violet to red-brown crystals.

hem-ȧ-tem′ē-sis, hæm-ȧ-tem′ē-sis, *n.* [*Hema-*, and Gr. *emein*, to vomit.] In medicine, the ejection of blood by vomiting.

hem′ȧ-thērm, hæm′ȧ-thērm, *n.* [*Hema-*, and Gr. *thermē*, heat.] An animal with warm blood.

hem-ȧ-thēr′măl hæm-ȧ-thēr′măl, *a.* Having warm blood; homœothermal.

hem″ȧ-thī-drō′sis, hæm″ȧ-thī-drō′sis, *n.* [*Hema-*, and Gr. *hidrōs*, sweat.] Bloody perspiration; blood-sweating.

hē-mat′ic, hæ-mat′ic, *a.* [Gr. *haimtikos*, of the blood, from *haima* (*-atos*), blood.]

1. Of or relating to the blood.
2. Causing a change in the condition of the blood.

hē-mat′ic, hæ-mat′ic, *n.* A hematic medicine.

hem′ȧ-tin, hæm′ȧ-tin, *n.* [Gr. *haima* (*-atos*), blood, and *-in*.]

1. A coloring-matter derived from hemoglobin by decomposition.
2. Hematoxylin.

hem-ȧ-tin′ic, *a.* Tending to increase the coloring-matter of the blood.

hem-ȧ-tin′ic, *n.* A hematinic medicine.

hem″ȧ-ti-nom′ē-tēr, hæm″ȧ-ti-nom′ē-tēr, *n.* A hemoglobinometer.

hem″ȧ-tin-ō-met′ric, hæm″ȧ-tin-ō-met′ric, *a.* Pertaining to the quantitative determination of hematin or hemoglobin.

hē-mat′i-nŏn, *n.* Same as *Hæmatinum*.

hem′ȧ-tīte, hæm′ȧ-tīte, *n.* [L. *hæmatites*; Gr. *haimatitēs*, lit., blood-like, red iron ore, from *haima* (*-atos*), blood.] Either of two iron ores. Red *hematite*, also called *bloodstone*, *red ocher*, *red* or *specular iron ore*, is a fibrous or crystalline red ferric oxid. Brown *hematite* is a brown or yellow ferric hydroxid; also called *limonite*.

hem-ȧ-tit′ic, hæm-ȧ-tit′ic, *a.* Pertaining to hematite, or resembling it; containing hematite.

hemato-. A combining form from Gr. *haima* (*-atos*), blood. [See *Hema-*.]

hem-ȧ-tō′bic, hæm-ȧ-tō′bic, *a.* Hematobious.

hem-ȧ-tō′bi-ous, hæm-ȧ-tō′bi-ous, *a.* [*Hemato-*, and Gr. *bios*, life.] Living as a parasite in blood.

hem′ȧ-tō-blast, hæm′ȧ-tō-blast, *n.* [*Hemato-*, and Gr. *blastos*, a germ.] A colorless, circular or oval, lenticular disk in the blood, without hemoglobin, and considered as an immature red blood-corpuscle.

hē-mat′ō-cēle, *n.* [*Hemato-*, and Gr. *kēlē*, a tumor.] A tumor filled with blood.

Hem-ȧ-toc′ry-ȧ, *n.pl.* Same as *Hæmatocrya*.

hem″ȧ-tō-crys′tăl-lin, hæm″ȧ-tō-crys′tăl-lin, *n.* [*Hemato-*, and Gr. *krystallos*, ice, crystal, and *-in*.] Hemoglobin.

hem″ȧ-tō-gen′ē-sis, hæm″ȧ-tō-gen′ē-sis, *n.* [*Hemato-*, and Gr. *genesis*, generation.] The formation of blood.

hem″ȧ-tō-gen′ic, hæm″ȧ-tō-gen′ic, *a.* Causing or relating to blood-formation.

hem-ȧ-tog′e-nous, hæm-ȧ-tog′e-nous, *a.* [*Hemato-*, and Gr. *-genēs*, producing.] Arising in the blood; hematogenic.

hem″ȧ-tō-glob′ū-lin, hæm″ȧ-tō-glob′ū-lin, *n.* [*Hemato-*, and L. *globulus*, a globe, and *-in*.] Hemoglobin.

hem′ȧ-toid, hæm′ȧ-toid, *a.* [Gr. *haimatoeidēs*, *haimatōdēs*, blood-like; *haima* (*-atos*), blood, and *eidos*, form.] Blood-like; bloody.

hem-ȧ-toid′in, hæm-ȧ-toid′in, *n.* A crystalline compound often found in extravasated blood. It contains no iron and probably is the same as *bilirubin*.

hem-ȧ-tol′ō-gy, hæm-ȧ-tol′ō-gy, *n.* [*Hemato-*, and Gr. *-logia*, from *legein*, to speak.] The division of medicine dealing with the blood.

hem-ȧ-tō′mȧ, *n.* [Gr. *haima* (*-atos*), blood, and *-ōma*.] A subcutaneous swelling caused by an extravasation of blood.

hem″ȧ-tō-per-i-cär′di-um, *n.* [*Hemato-*, and Gr. *perikardion*, the pericardium.] An effusion of blood into the pericardium.

hem″ȧ-tō-phō′bi-ȧ, *n.* [*Hemato-*, and Gr. *-phobia*, from *phobos*, fear.] An abnormal fear upon seeing blood.

hem″ȧ-tō-plas′tic, hæm″ȧ-tō-plas′tic, *a.* [*Hemato-*, and Gr. *plastikos*, plastic, from *plassein*, to mold.] Forming blood; productive of blood.

hem″ȧ-tō-poi-ē′sis, hæm″ȧ-tō-poi-ē′sis, *n.* [*Hemato-*, and Gr. *poiesis*, a making, from *poiein*, to make.] The making of blood; blood-formation.

hem″ȧ-tō-pọr′phy-rin, hæm″ȧ-tō-pọr′phy-rin, *n.* [*Hemato-*, and Gr. *porphyra*, purple, and *-in*.] A derivative of hematin and corresponding substances in invertebrates, produced by decomposition. It contains no iron.

hem-at′ō-sac, hæm-at′ō-sac, *n.* In some fishes, a vascular cavity opening into the infundibulum.

hem-ȧ-tō′sin, hæm-ȧ-tō′sin, *n.* Hematin.

hem-ȧ-tō′sis, hæm-ȧ-tō′sis, *n.* [Gr. *haimatōsis*, from *haimatoun*, to make bloody.] Blood-formation; sanguification; the transformation of venous blood or chyle into arterial blood.

hem″ȧ-tō-thēr′măl, hæm″ȧ-tō-thēr′măl, *a.* [*Hemato-*, and Gr. *thermos*, warm, from *thermē*, heat.] Having warm blood; homœothermal.

hem″ȧ-tō-thō′rax, *n.* [*Hemato-*, and Gr. *thōrax*, a breastplate.] Hemorrhage into the pleural cavity.

hem-ȧ-tox′y-lin, hæm-ȧ-tox′y-lin, *n.* [*Hemato-*, and Gr. *xylon*, wood, and *-in*.] A derivative of logwood, *Hæmatoxylon Campechianum*, occurring when pure in the form of colorless crystals, $C_{16}H_{14}O_6$. In the presence of alkalis and acids, it gives various shades of red, purple, and blue, and in histological work it forms the reagent used to stain the nucleus.

hem″ȧ-tō-zō′ăn, hem″ȧ-tō-zō′ŏn, *n.* Any of the *Hæmatozoa*.

hem-ȧ-tū′ri-ȧ, *n.* [Gr. *haima* (*-atos*), blood, and *ouron*, urine.] A discharge of bloody urine; called also *hematuresis*.

hem′ble, *n.* A shed for cattle; a stable; a hovel. [Prov. Eng.]

hem-el′y-tron, hem-el′y-trum, *n.* Same as *Hemielytrum*.

hem″ē-rȧ-lō′pi-ȧ, *n.* [Gr. *hēmera*, day, *alaos*, blind, and *ōps*, *ōpos*, the eye.] The peculiarity of vision known as day-sight, which prevents some persons from seeing except by sunlight or an intense artificial light. [See *Nyctalopia*.]

hem-ēr-ō′bi-ăn, *n.* A planipennate insect of the genus *Hemerobius* or related genera.

hē-mer′ō-bid, *a.* Of or pertaining to insects of the genus *Hemerobius* and allied genera.

Hem-ēr-ō′bi-us, *n.* [Gr. *hēmerobios*, living for a day; *hēmera*, a day, and *bios*, life.] A genus of neuropterous insects, the type of the family *Hemerobiidæ*. They are lace-winged flies. Their eggs are placed in a long threadlike pedicel.

Hem″ē-rō-cal′lis, *n.* [Gr. *hēmerokallis*, a yellow lily that blooms but for a day; *hēmera*, day, and *kalos*, beautiful.] A genus of plants of the lily family, natives of Asia and Europe. *Hemerocallis fulva*, the day-lily, is grown in gardens for its beautiful flowers.

hemi-. A prefix from L. *hemi-*, Gr. *hēmi-*, a half; used in many words of Latin and Greek derivation to signify a half, as *hemi*cerebrum, *hemi*cardia.

hem″i-al-bū′min, *n.* See *Hemialbumose*.

hem-i-al′bū-mōse, *n.* The most characteristic and most frequently obtained by-product of proteid digestion. It is the forerunner of hemipeptone; called also *hemialbumin*.

hem-i-an-æs-thē′si-ȧ, *n.* [*Hemi-*, and Gr. *anaisthēsia*, want of perception; *an-* priv., and *aisthanesthai*, to perceive.] In pathology, anæsthesia of one lateral half of the body.

hem-i-an-es-thē′sic, hem-i-an-æs-thē′sic, *a.* Pertaining to or afflicted with hemianæsthesia.

hem″i-ȧ-nō′pi-ȧ, *n.* Hemianopsia.

hem″i-ȧ-nop′si-ȧ, *n.* In pathology, blindness in one half of the visual field. It may be bilateral or unilateral.

hem″i-ȧ-nop′tic, *a.* Pertaining to or afflicted with hemianopsia.

hem-i-at′rō-phy, *n.* In pathology, atrophy confined to one side of the body.

hem′i-branch, *a.* and *n.* I. *a.* Hemibranchiate.
II. *n.* A fish of the order *Hemibranchii*.

hem-i-bran′chi-āte, *a.* Pertaining to the *Hemibranchii*; having the branchial apparatus deficient; half-gilled.

Hem-i-bran′chi-ī, *n.pl.* [*Hemi-*, and Gr. *branchia*, gills.] An order of fishes having deficient branchial arches. It embraces several families and includes the sticklebacks and snipefishes.

hē′mic, hæ′mic, *a.* See *Hemal*, 3.

hem-i-cär′di-ȧ, *n.* [*Hemi-*, and Gr. *kardia*, the heart.] Either half, the right or left, of a four-chambered heart.

hem-i-cär′di-ac, *a.* Of or pertaining to the hemicardia.

hem′i-cärp, *n.* [*Hemi-*, and Gr. *karpos*, fruit.] In botany, one of the halves of a fruit which spontaneously divides into two, as a pea.

hem-i-cer′ē-brăl, *a.* Pertaining to a hemicerebrum.

hem-i-cer′ē-brum, *n.*; *pl.* **hem-i-cer′ē-brȧ**. [*Hemi-*, and L. *cerebrum*, the brain.] In anatomy, the right or left half of the cerebrum.

hem″i-chō-rē′ȧ, *n.* In pathology, a form of chorea in which the convulsive movements are confined to one side of the body.

hem-i-col′lin, *n.* [*Hemi-*, and Gr. *kolla*, glue, and *-in*.] In physiological chemistry, a product obtained in the formation of semiglutin from gelatin; analogous to semiglutin, but partially soluble in alcohol. [See *Semiglutin*.]

hem-i-crā′ni-ȧ, *n.* [L. *hemicrania*; Gr. *hēmikrania*, a pain on one side of the head or face; *hēmi-*, half, and *kranion*, the skull.]

1. Neuralgia of one-half of the head.
2. Imperfect development or absence of the anterior or posterior part of the skull.

hem′i-cy̆-cle, *n.* [L. *hemicyclium*; Gr. *hēmikyklon* or *hēmikyklion*, a semicircle, a semicircular row of seats, from *hēmikyklos* or *hēmikyklios* semicircular; *hēmi-*, half, and *kyklos*, a circle.]

1. A half-circle; a semicircle.
2. A semicircular arena; a semicircular room or division of a room.

hem-i-cyc′lic, *a.* In botany, applied to flowers which have the separate portions of the inflorescence arranged in spirals.

hem-i-dac′tyl, hem-i-dac′tyle, *n.* [*Hemi-*, and Gr. *daktylos*, a finger.] A flat-toed lizard or gecko of the genus *Hemidactylus*.

Hem-i-dac′tyl-us, *n.* A genus of lizards belonging to the gecko family or flat-toed lizards which have an oval disk at the base of the toes.

hem-i-dem-i-sem′i-quā-vēr, *n.* [*Hemi-*, and *demi-*, half, and *semi-*, half, and *quaver*.] In music, the sixty-fourth part of a semibreve.

hem-i-di′tōne, *n.* [*Hemi-*, and Gr. *ditonos*, of two tones; *dis*, twice, and *tonos*, a tone.] In Greek music, the lesser third.

hem-i-dō-mat′ic, *a.* Of or resembling a hemidome.

hem′i-dōme, *n.* In crystallography, a dome parallel to the orthodiagonal, as distinguished from the *clinodome*, in which they are parallel to the clinodiagonal.

hem-i-el′y-trum, hem-i-el′y-tron, *n.*; *pl.* **hem-i-el′y-trȧ**. [*Hemi-*, and Gr. *elytron*, a sheath.] A wing-cover of an insect when it is coriaceous at the base and membranous at the extremity, as in the order *Hemiptera*. In the figure, *a* shows the coriaceous or leathery portion, and *b c* the membranous or transparent portions.

Hemielytrum.

hem″i-en-ce-phal′ic, *a.* Of or pertaining to the hemiencephalon.

hem″i-en-ceph′ȧ-lon, *n.*; *pl.* **hem″i-en-ceph′ȧ-lȧ**. [*Hemi-*, and Gr. *enkephalos*, the brain.] In anatomy, a lateral half of the brain.

hē-mig′ȧ-mous, *a.* [*Hemi-*, and Gr. *gamos*, marriage.] In botany, having one of the two florets in the same spikelet neuter, and the other unisexual, whether male or female; said of grasses.

hem′i-glyph, *n.* [*Hemi-*, and Gr. *glyphē*, a carving.] In architecture, a half-channel at the edge of the triglyph tablet in the Doric entablature.

hē-mig′nȧ-thous, *a.* [*Hemi-*, and Gr. *gnathos*, jaw.] In ornithology, having one mandible of the beak considerably shorter than the other.

hem-i-hē′drăl, *a.* In crystallography, applied to a crystal having only half the number of planes belonging to any particular modification which the law of symmetry requires.

hem-i-hē′drăl-ly, *adv.* In a hemihedral manner.

hem-i-hē′dric, *a.* Hemihedral.

hem-i-hē′drism, *n.* In crystallography, the property or quality of crystallizing in hemihedral forms.

hem-i-hē′dron, *n.* [*Hemi-*, and Gr. *hedra*, a seat, base.] In crystallography, a crystal or other solid with but half the proper number of planes as the tetrahedron.

hem-i-hol-ō-hē′drăl, *a.* [*Hemi-*, and Gr. *holos*, whole, and *hedra*, a seat, base.] In crystallography, applied to hemihedrons in which the entire number of octants contain half the full number of planes.

hem″i-mel-lit′ic, *a.* [*Hemi-*, and Gr. *meli*, honey, and *lithos*, stone.] In chemistry, having half the number of carboxyl radicals contained in mellitic acid.

Hem″i-mē-tab′ō-lȧ, *n.pl.* [*Hemi-*, and Gr. *metabolē*, a change.] In zoölogy, a section of insects which undergo an incomplete metamorphosis. It is divided into three orders, *Hemiptera*, *Heteroptera*, and *Thysanoptera*.

hem-i-met-ȧ-bol′ic, *a.* In zoölogy, of or belonging to insects undergoing only an incomplete metamorphosis.

hem-i-mọr′phic, *a.* [*Hemi-*, and Gr. *morphē*, form.] In crystallography, having the two ends with dissimilar planes.

hem-i-mọr′phism, *n.* The property of being hemimorphic.

hem-i-mor′phīte, *n.* Calamin; so called because the crystals exhibit hemimorphic characteristics.

hē-mī′nȧ, *n.*; *pl.* **hē-mī′næ.** [L., from Gr. *hēmina*, a Sicilian measure, from *hēmi-*, *hēmisys*, half.]

1. In Roman antiquity, a measure containing half a sextary, or about half a pint English wine-measure.

2. In medicine, a measure equal to about ten fluid ounces.

hē-mī′ō-nus, *n.* Same as *Dziggetai.*

hem-i-op′si-ȧ, hem-i-op′sy, *n.* See *Hemianopsia.*

hem-i-or′thō-tȳpe, *a.* See *Monoclinic.*

hem-i-pep′tōne, *n.* [*Hemi-*, and Gr. *peptikos*, pertaining to digestion, from *peptein*, to cook, digest.] An intermediate compound of peptone, formed before peptone is finally produced, by the gastric and pancreatic juices. [See *Peptone.*]

hem-i-plē′gi-ȧ, *n.* [Gr. *hēmiplēx*, *hēmiplēgēs*, stricken on one side; *hēmi-*, half, and *plēssein*, to strike.] Paralysis of one side of the body.

hem-i-pleg′ic, *a.* Of, relating, or pertaining to hemiplegia.

hem′i-pod, *a.* [Gr. *hēmipous* (*-podos*), half-footed; *hēmi-*, half, and *pous*, *podos*, foot.] Of, relating, or pertaining to any bird of the genus *Turnix.*

hem′i-pod, *n.* A hemipod bird.

hem′i-prism, *n.* [*Hemi-*, and Gr. *prisma*, a prism.] In crystallography, a prism in the triclinic system of crystallization including only two parallel planes.

hem-i-pris-mat′ic, *a.* Pertaining to a hemiprism.

hem-i-prō′tē-in, *n.* [*Hemi-*, and *protein.*] In chemistry, a substance supposed to be identical with antialbumid and dyspeptone. It is formed by the heating action of dilute sulphuric acid on albumin.

hē-mip′tēr, *n.* One of the *Hemiptera.*

Hē-mip′te-rȧ, *n.pl.* [*Hemi-*, and Gr. *pteron*, a wing.] An order of four-winged insects having a suctorial proboscis, the outer wings or wing-covers either entirely formed of a substance intermediate between the elytra of beetles and the ordinary membranous wings of most insects, or leathery at the base and transparent toward the tips (hemielytra). The order is subdivided into the suborders, *Heteroptera*, the true bugs; *Homoptera*, plant-lice, cicadas, scale-insects, etc., and the *Parasita*, the true lice.

hē-mip′tēr-ăl, *a.* Hemipterous.

hē-mip′tēr-ăn, *n.* One of the *Hemiptera.*

hē-mip′tēr-ăn, *a.* Relating to the *Hemiptera.*

hē-mip′tēr-ist, *n.* One who makes a collection of or studies the *Hemiptera.*

hē-mip′tēr-ŏn, *n.* A hemipteran.

hē-mip′tēr-ous, *a.* Of or pertaining to the *Hemiptera.*

hem-i-pyr′ȧ-mid, *n.* [*Hemi-*, and Gr. *pyramis* (*-idos*), a pyramid.] In crystallography, a pyramid in the monoclinic system of crystallization, including only four parallel planes.

hem″i-py-ram′i-dăl, *a.* Pertaining to a hemipyramid.

hem′i-sect, *v.t.*; hemisected, *pt.*, *pp.*; hemisecting, *ppr.* [*Hemi-*, and L. *sectus*, pp. of *secare*, to cut.] In anatomy, to bisect; to divide into equal right and left parts, or along the mesial plane.

hem-i-sec′tion, *n.* In anatomy, bisection; division into equal right and left parts, or along the mesial plane; also, one of such divisions.

hem-i-sep′tăl, *a.* Pertaining to a hemiseptum.

hem-i-sep′tum, *n.*; *pl.* **hem-i-sep′tȧ.** [*Hemi-*, and L. *septum*, *sæptum*, a partition.] In anatomy, the lateral half of a partition.

hem′i-sōme, *n.* [*Hemi-*, and Gr. *sōma*, the body.] One half of the body of an animal.

hem′i-spașm, *n.* [*Hemi-*, and Gr. *spasmos*, a spasm.] A spasm affecting only one side of the body.

hem′i-sphēre, *n.* [L. *hemisphærium*; Gr. *hēmisphairon*, a hemisphere; *hēmi-*, half, and *sphaira*, a sphere.]

1. A half-sphere; one-half of a sphere or globe, when divided by a plane passing through its center.

2. Half of the terrestrial sphere; a map or projection of half the terrestrial sphere.

3. In anatomy, either of the two large convoluted masses composing the greater part of the cerebrum.

Magdeburg hemispheres; a device consisting of two hemispherical metal cups fitting closely together so as to form a hollow sphere from which by means of an air-pump the air is exhausted. The instrument was invented by Otto von Guericke at Magdeburg, for the purpose of illustrating by experiment the pressure of the air.

hem-i-spher′ic, *a.* Hemispherical.

hem-i-spher′ic-ăl, *a.* Pertaining to or formed like a hemisphere; as, a *hemispherical* body.

hem-i-sphē′roid, *n.* Half of a spheroid.

hem″i-sphē-roid′ăl, *a.* Having the form of a hemispheroid.

hem-i-spher′ūle, *n.* A half-spherule.

hem′i-stich, *n.* [L. *hemistichium*; Gr. *hēmistichion*, a half line; *hēmi-*, half, and *stichos*, a row, line, verse.] Half a poetic verse, or a verse not completed.

hē-mis′ti-chăl, *a.* Pertaining to or made up of hemistichs; as, a *hemistichal* division of a verse.

hem-i-sym′me-try, *n.* [*Hemi-*, and Gr. *symmetria*, symmetry.] Same as *Hemihedrism.*

hem-i-sys′tō-lē, *n.* [*Hemi-*, and Gr. *systolē*, a drawing together.] A peculiar kind of irregular action of the heart-muscle, in which, with every two beats of the heart, only one beat of the pulse is felt.

hem′i-tōne, *n.* [L. *hemitonium*; Gr. *hēmitonion*, a half tone; *hēmi-*, half, and *tonos*, a tone.] In music, same as *semitone.*

hē-mit′rō-păl, *a.* Same as *Hemitropous.*

hem′i-trōpe, *a.* [*Hemi-*, and Gr. *tropē*, a turning, from *trepein*, to turn.] Half-turned; specifically, in mineralogy, applied to a crystal which has two similar parts or halves, one of which is turned half-round upon the other.

hem′i-trōpe, *n.* 1. Anything hemitropous in structure.

2. In crystallography, a twin crystal.

hem-i-trop′ic, *a.* Hemitropous.

he-mit′rō-pous, *a.* [*Hemi-*, and Gr. *tropē*, a turning, from *trepein*, to turn.]

1. Turned half round; half-inverted.

2. In botany, applied to an ovule in which the axis of the nucleus is more curved than in an anatropous ovule.

Hemitropous Ovule.

hē-mit′rō-py, *n.* In crystallography, twin composition in crystals.

hem′i-tȳpe, *n.* [*Hemi-*, and Gr. *typos*, an impression.] That which is hemitypic, or only partly typical of a given group.

hem-i-typ′ic, *a.* In zoölogy, only partially typical of a given group, because partaking of the characters of some other group.

hem′lock, *n.* [ME. *hemlok*; AS. *hemlic*, *hymelic*, hemlock.]

1. A poisonous plant, *Conium maculatum*, of the parsley family. It is a tall, erect, branching biennial, found throughout Europe and temperate Asia in waste places, on banks, and under walls. The poison administered to Socrates is supposed to have been a decoction of it, though others are of opinion that the potion was obtained from water-hemlock, *Cicuta virosa.* Hemlock is a powerful sedative, and is used medicinally.

Hemlock (*Conium maculatum*).

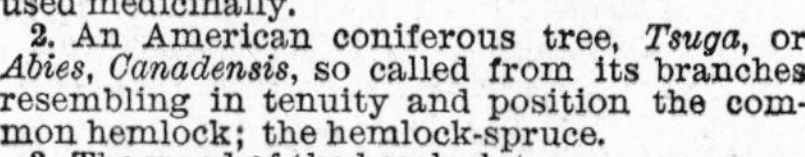

2. An American coniferous tree, *Tsuga*, or *Abies*, *Canadensis*, so called from its branches resembling in tenuity and position the common hemlock; the hemlock-spruce.

3. The wood of the hemlock-tree.

hem′lock-drop″wŏrt, *n.* *Œnanthe fistulosa*, a herb of the parsley family, common in temperate Europe.

hem′lock-pärs″ley, *n.* A plant of the parsley family, belonging to the genus *Conioselinum.* It resembles hemlock, but is not poisonous.

hem′lock-sprūce, *n.* See *Hemlock*, 2.

hem′mel, *n.* Same as *Hemble.*

hem′mēr, *n.* One who or that which hems; specifically, an attachment to a sewing-machine for making a hem.

hem′ming, *n.* 1. The act or process of making a hem.

2. The stitching which secures a hem; a hem or hems collectively.

hem′ming, him′ming, *n.* [ME. *heminge*; AS. *hemming*, a rough shoe.] A shoe or sandal made of rawhide.

hemo-. A combining form from Gr. *haima*, blood. [See *Hema-.*]

hem-ō-chrō′mō-gen, hæm-ō-chrō′mō-gen, *n.* [*Hemo-*, and Gr. *chrōma*, color, and *-gen.*] A substance contained in the blood, and derived from hemoglobin.

hem″ō-chrō-mom′e-tēr, hæm″ō-chrō-mom′e-tēr, *n.* [*Hemo-*, and Gr. *chrōma*, color, and *metron*, a measure.] An apparatus used in determining the quantity of hemoglobin in fluids.

hem-ō-cȳ′ȧ-nin, hæm-ō-cȳ′ȧ-nin, *n.* [*Hemo-*, and Gr. *kyanos*, blue, and *-in.*] A coloring-matter containing copper, found in the blood of certain invertebrates.

hem″ō-cy-tol′y-sis, hæm″ō-cy-tol′y-sis, *n.* [*Hemo-*, and Gr. *kytos*, a hollow vessel, and *lyein*, to loose.] In pathology, dissolution of the blood-corpuscles.

hem-ō-cȳ-tō-tryp′sis, hæm-ō-cȳ-tō-tryp′sis, *n.* [*Hemo-*, and Gr. *kytos*, a hollow vessel, and *tribein*, to rub.] In pathology, a breaking up of the corpuscles of the blood.

hem-ō-drom′e-tēr, hæm-ō-drom′e-tēr, *n.* [*Hemo-*, and Gr. *dromos*, a running, course, and *metron*, a measure.] An instrument to measure the velocity of the arterial flow of blood.

hem-ō-drom′ō-grȧph, hæm-ō-drom′ō-grȧph, *n.* [*Hemo-*, and Gr. *dromos*, a running, a course, and *graphein*, to write.] An instrument which registers automatically the velocity of the blood.

hem″ō-drō-mom′e-tēr, hæm″ō-drō-mom′e-tēr, *n.* See *Hemodrometer.*

hem-ō-gas′tric, *a.* [*Hemo-*, and Gr. *gastēr*, belly.] Relating to the blood and the stomach.

hem-ō-glō′bin, hæm-ō-glō′bin, *n.* [*Hemo-*, and L. *globus*, a ball, and *-in.*] The coloring-matter of the red corpuscles. It is an exceedingly complex body, containing iron; it crystallizes in rhombic flakes or prisms, is composed of hematin and globulin, and has a strong affinity for oxygen.

hem-ō-glō-bi-nē′mi-ȧ, hæm-ō-glō-bi-nē′mi-ȧ, *n.* [*Hemo-*, and L. *globus*, a ball, and Gr. *haima*, blood.] In pathology, a condition in which the hemoglobin is dissolved out of the blood corpuscles and is held in solution in the serum.

hem-ō-glō-bi-nif′ēr-ous, hæm-ō-glō-bi-nif′ēr-ous, *a.* [*Hemo-*, and L. *globus*, a ball, and *ferre*, to bear.] Containing hemoglobin.

hem-ō-glō-bi-nom′e-tēr, hæm-ō-glō-bi-nom′e-tēr, *n.* [*Hemo-*, and L. *globus*, a ball, and *metrum*, a measure.] An instrument for the quantitative estimation of hemoglobin in the blood; a hemochromometer.

hem-ō-glō-bi-nū′ri-ȧ, hæm-ō-glō-bi-nū′ri-ȧ, *n.* [*Hemo-*, and L. *globus*, a ball, and Gr. *ouron*, urine.] In pathology, the presence of hemoglobin in the urine, due either to its solution out of the red corpuscles or to disintegration of the red corpuscles.

hem-ō-glob′ū-lin, hæm-ō-glob′ū-lin, *n.* Same as *Hemoglobin.*

hem′ō-lymph, hæm′ō-lymph, *n.* [*Hemo-*, and L. *lympha*, a spring, pure water.] The nutritive fluid, similar to blood or lymph, of some invertebrates.

hem″ō-lym-phat′ic, hæm″ō-lym-phat′ic, *a.* Pertaining to hemolymph.

hem-ō-lyt′ic, hæm-ō-lyt′ic, *a.* [*Hemo-*, and Gr. *lytikos*, destructive, from *lyein*, to loosen.] Destructive of the blood or of the corpuscles of the blood.

hem-om′e-tēr, hæm-om′e-tēr, *n.* [*Hemo-*, and Gr. *metron*, a measure.] Same as *Hemadynamometer.*

hem-ō-per-i-cär′di-um, hæm-ō-per-i-cär′di-um, *n.* Same as *Hematopericardium.*

hem-ō-phil′i-ȧ, hæm-ō-phil′i-ȧ, *n.* [*Hemo-*, and Gr. *philos*, loving.] In pathology, an abnormal tendency to hemorrhage, usually hereditary.

hem-ō-phil′ic, hæm-ō-phil′ic, *a.* Pertaining to hemophilia; having a tendency to excessive bleeding.

hē-mop′ty-sis, hæ-mop′ty-sis, *n.* [*Hemo-*, and Gr. *ptysis*, a spitting, from *ptyein*, to spit.] The spitting of blood from the larnyx, trachea, bronchi, or lungs.

hem′or-rhāge, hæm′or-rhāge, *n.* [L. *hæmorrhagia*; Gr. *haimorrhagia*, a violent bleeding, from *haimorrhagēs*, bleeding violently; *haima*, blood, and *rhēgnynai*, to break, burst.] A discharge of blood from the blood-vessels.

hem-or-rhag′ic, *a.* Pertaining to a flux of blood; consisting in hemorrhage.

hem-or-rhoid′ăl, *a.* Pertaining to or affected with hemorrhoids; as, *hemorrhoidal* veins; a *hemorrhoidal* flux.

hem′or-rhoidș, *n.pl.* [L. *hæmorrhoidæ*; Gr. *haimorrhoïdes* (supply *phlebes*, veins), veins liable to discharge blood, from *haimorrhoos*, flowing with blood; *haima*, blood, and *rhoos*, a flow, from *rhein*, to flow.] Painful tumors or tubercules, consisting of enlargements of the mucous membrane, formed in the rectum or around the anus, frequently accompanied by bleeding; piles; emerods.

hem′ō-scōpe, hæm′ō-scōpe, *n.* [*Hemo-*, and Gr. *skopein*, to view.] An instrument used in the spectroscopic examination of the blood, by means of which the thickness of the layer of blood can be regulated; also written *hematoscope.*

hem-ō-spas′tic, hæm-ō-spas′tic, *a.* [*Hemo-*, and Gr. *spān*, to draw.] Tending to draw the blood to a part; as, a *hemospastic* agent.

hem-ō-spas′tic, hæm-ō-spas′tic, *n.* That which draws the blood to a part, as a cupping-glass.

hem-ō-stā′si-ȧ, hæm-ō-stā′si-ȧ, *n.* [*Hemo-*, and Gr. *stasis*, a standing, from *histanai*, to stand.] In pathology, hyperemia; also, any method of stopping the flow of blood.

hem-ō-stat′ic, *a.* [*Hemo-*, and Gr. *statikos*, causing to stand, from *histanai*, to cause to stand.] Arresting hemorrhage.

hem-ō-stat′ic, *n.* An agent or remedy that arrests hemorrhage; a styptic.

hem-ō-thō′rax, hæm-ō-thō′rax, *n.* Same as *Hematothorax.*

hemp, *n.* [ME. *hemp*; AS. *henep*, hemp.]

1. A plant of the genus *Cannabis*, of which *Cannabis sativa* is the only known species. It is an annual herbaceous plant, the fiber of which constitutes the hemp of commerce. It is a native of western and central Asia, but has been long naturalized in Brazil and tropical Africa and is now extensively cultivated in many countries.

2. The skin or rind of the plant, prepared for spinning.

3. Any one of various fibers resembling true *hemp*.

Bastard hemp; *Datisca cannabina*, a plant found in western Asia.

Hemp (*Cannabis sativa*).

Bengal and *Bombay hemp*; *Crotalaria juncea*, an East Indian shrub of the bean family; called also *sunn hemp*.

Canada hemp; a species of dogbane, *Apocynum cannabinum*.

Jubbulpore hemp; *Crotalaria tenuifolia*, a plant of the bean family.

Madras hemp; same as *Bengal hemp*.

Manila hemp; the fiber of *Musa textilis*, a musaceous plant.

Sisal hemp; the fiber of species of *Agave*, of Mexico and Yucatan.

Sunn hemp; same as *Bengal hemp*.

Virginian hemp or *water-hemp*; *Acnida cannabina*, a weed of the amaranth family, growing near the coast of eastern United States.

hemp′=ag″ri-mō-ny, *n.* *Eupatorium cannabinum*, a European plant of the aster family, much resembling the American boneset.

hemp′=bụsh, *n.* *Plagianthus pulchellus*, a plant of the mallow family, growing in Australia, and yielding a tough fiber.

hemp′en, *a.* 1. Made of hemp; as, a *hempen* cord.

2. Fibrous. [Rare.]

hemp′=net″tle, *n.* A labiate plant, *Galeopsis Tetrahit*.

hemp′weed, *n.* 1. The hemp-agrimony.

2. Seaweed; kelp. [Scot.]

Climbing hempweed; *Mikania scandens*, an American climbing plant of the aster family.

hemp′y, *a.* Like hemp. [Rare.]

hem-self′, hem-selve′, hem-selv′en, *pron.pl.* Themselves. [Obs.]

hem′stitch, *v.t.*; hemstitched (-sticht), *pt.*, *pp.*; hemstitching, *ppr.* To ornament by hemstitch.

hem′stitch, *n.* The decorative heading of the inner edge of a hem made by drawing out a few threads running parallel to the hem, and fastening the cross threads by successive stitches.

hē′mūṣe, *n.* The roebuck in its third year. [Obs.]

hen, *n.* [ME. *hen*; AS. *henn*, *hænn*, a hen.] The female of any kind of bird; especially, the female of the domestic or barnyard fowl, of which there are numerous varieties. *Hen* is often prefixed or affixed to the names of birds to express the female, as *hen*-sparrow, pea*hen*.

hen′=and=chick′enṣ, *n.* In botany, one of several plants characterized by numerous smaller heads of flowers proceeding from the leaves of the involucre, and surrounding the large central head, as the ground-ivy, garden daisy, etc.

hen′bāne, *n.* In botany, a coarse, erect, biennial herb, *Hyoscyamus niger*, from the seeds and leaves of which a juice is expressed which is used as a medicine. The plant is poisonous, and especially destructive to poultry, hence its name.

hen′bit, *n.* [Middle L.G. *hennebit*.] *Lamium amplexicaule*, a labiate weed, the dead-nettle. The name is also given to *Veronica hederæfolia*, the ivy-leafed speedwell.

Henbane (*Hyoscyamus niger*).

hen′=blind″ness, *n.* Failure of sight in a dim light; nyctalopia; hemeralopia.

hence, *adv.* [ME. *hens*, contr. of *hennes*, this, with adverbial genit. *-es*, from AS. *heonan*, *heona*, hence.]

1. From this place.

Early to-morrow will we rise, and *hence*.
—Shak.

2. From this time; in the future; as, a year *hence*.

3. From this cause or reason, noting a consequence, inference, or deduction.

Hence different passions more or less inflame,
As strong or weak, the organs of the frame.
—Pope.

4. From this source or original.

All other faces borrowed *hence*
Their light and grace. —Suckling.

Hence is used elliptically and imperatively, for *go hence*; *depart hence*; *away*; *be gone*.

Hence with your little ones. —Shak.

Syn.—Consequently, accordingly, therefore, so.

hence, *v.t.* To send away; to despatch. [Obs.]

hence-fōrth′ (*or* hens′), *adv.* [ME. *hensforth*, *hennes forth*; AS. *heonan forth*, henceforth.] From this time forward.

I never from thy side *henceforth* will stray.
—Milton.

hence-fọr′wărd, hence-fọr′wărdṣ, *adv.* From this time forward; henceforth.

hench′boy, *n.* A page; a servant. [Obs.]

hench′man, *n.*; *pl.* **hench′men.** [ME. *hencheman*, *henshman*, a groom, attendant, from AS. *hengest*, *hengst*, a horse, and *man*, a man.]

1. An inferior or assistant engaged in some servile work; especially in politics in the United States, a venal follower of a boss or politician.

2. A servant; a male attendant; a footman; a follower. [Rare.]

hen′=clam, *n.* 1. Same as *Surf-clam*.

2. A clam of the genus *Pachyderma*, found on the western coast of the United States.

hen′cọop, *n.* A coop or pen in which hens are kept.

hend, *v.t.* To seize; to lay hold on. [Obs.]

hend, *a.* 1. Clever; handy. [Obs.]

2. Polite; courteous; gentle. [Obs.]

3. Nigh; near at hand; convenient. [Obs.]

hen-dec-a-. A combining form from Gr. *hendeka*, eleven, from *hen*, neut. of *heis*, one, and *deka*, ten, used in prosody, mathematics, botany, and chemistry to signify eleven; as, *hendeca*hedron, *hendec*androus.

hen-deç-ȧ-çol′iç, *a.* [L.Gr. *hendekakōlos*, of eleven cola; Gr. *hendeka*, eleven, and *kōlon*, a member.] In ancient prosody, consisting of eleven series or cola; as, a *hendecacolic* period.

hen-deç′ȧ-gon, *n.* [*Hendeca-*, and Gr. *gōnia*, an angle.] In geometry, a plane figure of eleven sides and as many angles; written also *endecagon*.

hen-deç-ag′ō-năl, *a.* Pertaining to a hendecagon; written also *endecagonal*.

hen-de-çaġ′y-nous, *a.* [*Hendeca-*, and Gr. *gynē*, a female.] In botany, having eleven pistils.

hen-deç-ȧ-hē′drŏn, *n.* [*Hendeca-*, and Gr. *hedra*, a seat.] In geometry, a solid with eleven plane faces.

hen-de-çan′drous, *a.* [*Hendeca-*, and Gr. *anēr*, *andros*, a man, a male.] In botany, having eleven stamens.

hen′de-çāne, *n.* [Gr. *hendeka*, eleven, and *-ane*.] One of the hydrocarbons of the paraffin series, $C_{11}H_{24}$; also written *endecane*.

hen-deç-ȧ-phyl′lous, *a.* In botany, having eleven folioles; also written *endecaphyllous*.

hen-deç″ȧ-syl-lab′iç, *n.* A line composed of eleven syllables.

hen-deç″ȧ-syl-lab′iç, *a.* Pertaining to a metrical line of eleven syllables.

hen-deç-ȧ-syl′lȧ-ble, *n.* [Gr. *hendekasyllabos*, eleven-syllabled; *hendeka*, eleven, and *syllabē*, a syllable.] A metrical line of eleven syllables.

hen-deç-ȧ-tō′iç, *a.* [Gr. *hendeka*, eleven.] In chemistry, pertaining to or derived from hendecane; undecylic; as, *hendecatoic* acid.

hen-di′ȧ-dys, *n.* [Gr. *hen dia dyoin*, one by two; *hen*, neut. of *heis*, one, and *dia*, through, by, and *dyoin*, genit. dual of *dyo*, two.] In rhetoric, a figure in which two nouns connected by a conjunction are used instead of one noun, or a noun and adjective; or a figure in which the same idea is presented by two words or phrases.

hen′dy, *a.* [Obs.] See *Hend*.

hen′ē-quen (-ken), **hen′nē-quin** (-kin), *n.* Same as *Sisal hemp* under *Hemp*.

hen′fish, *n.* The sea-bream.

heng, *v.*, obsolete past tense of *hang*.

hen′=har″ri-ẽr, *n.* A species of hawk of the genus *Circus*; especially *Circus cyaneus*, so named from its depredations in the poultry-yard.

hen′=hạwk, *n.* Any one of certain species of hawks which make poultry their prey, as *Circus cyaneus*, the hen-harrier.

hen′=heärt″ed, *a.* Having a heart like that of a hen; timid; cowardly; dastardly.

hen′house, *n.*; *pl.* **hen′houṣ-eṣ.** A house in which fowls are sheltered.

hen′huṣ″ṣy, *n.* A man who officiously interferes in women's affairs; a cotquean.

hen′i-quen (-ken), *n.* See *Sisal hemp* under *Hemp*.

hen′=mōld, *n.* A kind of black spongy soil.

hen′nȧ, *n.* [*Hennā*, the Ar. name.]

1. *Lawsonia inermis*, a shrub bearing opposite entire leaves and numerous small white fragrant flowers. It is cultivated extensively in Egypt. The powdered leaves form a large article of export to Persia and the Turkish possessions, where they are used as a dye.

2. A paste made from the leaves of the henna plant, used in the East for staining and dyeing the fingers, nails, hair, etc.

hen′nẽr-y, *n.*; *pl.* **hen′nẽr-ieṣ.** An inclosed place in which fowls are kept.

hen′nes, *adv.* [ME.] Hence. [Obs.]

hen′nin, *n.* [OFr.] A headdress worn by French women in the fifteenth century.

hen-nō-tan′niç, *a.* In chemistry, relating to henna and tannin; derived from henna and tannin.

hen-ō-ġen′e-sis, hē-noġ′e-ny, *n.* [Gr. *heis*, *henos*, one, and *genesis*, origin, birth.] Ontogeny.

Henna Plant (*Lawsonia inermis*).

hen′ō-thē-iṣm, *n.* [Gr. *heis*, *henos*, one, and *theos*, god.] A doctrine of one of the earliest religions, attributing supreme power to one of several divinities in turn.

hen″ō-thē-is′tiç, *a.* Pertaining to henotheism.

hē-not′iç, *a.* [Gr. *henōtikos*, serving to unite, from *henoun*, to unite, from *heis*, *henos*, one.] Reconciling; harmonizing; tending to unite.

hen′peck, *v.t.*; henpecked, *pt.*, *pp.*; henpecking, *ppr.* To subject to or harass by trivial annoyances; to domineer over; said of a wife who thus rules her husband.

hen′=plant, *n.* *Plantago lanceolata*, a species of plantain, the ribwort; also, *Plantago major*, the common plantain.

Hen-ri-et′tȧ=clọth, *n.* A fine light fabric from which women's dresses are very frequently made.

hen′rọọst, *n.* A place where fowls roost at night.

hen′ry, *n.*; *pl.* **hen′ryṣ.** [Named after Joseph *Henry*, an American physicist.] In electricity, the practical unit of electromagnetic or magnetic induction, or the induction in a circuit in which the electromotive force is one volt, the inducing current varying at the rate of one ampere per second.

hen′ṣ′=foot, *n.* An umbelliferous plant, *Caucalis daucoides*, found growing in chalky soils.

hent, *v.t.* To seize; to grasp; to take; to receive. [Obs.]

hen′wāre, *n.* Same as *Badderlocks*.

henx′măn, *n.* A henchman. [Obs.]

hē′=ōak, *n.* *Casuarina stricta*, a somber-looking Australian tree.

hep, *n.* See third *Hip*.

hē′păr, *n.* [Gr. *hēpar*, the liver.]

1. In homeopathy, calcium sulphid.

2. In old chemistry, a term applied to any one of various compounds of sulphur with the metals, having a brown-red or liver color.

hep-at-, hep-a-to-. Combining forms from Gr. *hēpar*, *hēpatos*, the liver, used in medicine, chemistry, etc., to signify the liver or resembling the liver; as, *hepato*cystic, *hepato*pancreas.

hep-ȧ-tal′ġi-ȧ, *n.* [*Hepat-*, and Gr. *algos*, pain.] In pathology, neuralgic pain in the liver.

hē-pat′iç, *a.* [LL. *hepaticus*; Gr. *hēpatikos*, of the liver, from *hēpar*, *hēpatos*, the liver.]

1. Pertaining to the liver; as, *hepatic* pain; *hepatic* artery; *hepatic* disease.

2. Having the color of the liver.

Hepatic air or *gas*; sulphureted hydrogen. [Obs.]

hē-pat′i-çȧ, *n.* [LL. *hepaticus*; Gr. *hēpatikos*, of the liver, from *hēpar* (*hēpatos*), the liver.]

1. In botany, the liverleaf, *Anemone Hepatica*; called also *liverwort*.

2. [H—] A subgenus of *Anemone*, of the natural order *Ranunculaceæ*, having three-lobed radical leaves, and small blue, white, or red flowers.

Hē-pat′i-cæ, *n.pl.* A family of cryptogamous plants comprising five orders; the liverworts.

hē-pat′iç-ăl, *a.* [Rare.] Same as *Hepatic*.

hep′ȧ-tine, *n.* Glycogenic matter.

hep′ȧ-tite, *n.* [L. *hepatites*, an unknown precious stone, the liverstone, from Gr. *hēpar*, *hēpatos*, the liver.] A fetid variety of sulphate of baryta. It sometimes occurs in globular masses, and is either compact or of a foliated structure. By friction or the application of heat, it exhales a fetid odor, like that of sulphureted hydrogen.

hep-ȧ-tī′tis, *n.* [Gr. *hēpar*, *hēpatos*, the liver, and *-itis*.] In pathology, inflammation of the liver.

hep″ȧ-ti-zā′tion, *n.* 1. The act of impregnating with sulphureted hydrogen gas. [Obs.]

2. Conversion into a substance resembling the liver; as, *hepatization* of the lung.

hep′ȧ-tīze, *v.t.*; hepatized, *pt.*, *pp.*; hepatizing, *ppr.* [Gr. *hēpatizein*, to resemble the liver, from *hēpar*, *hēpatos*, the liver.]

1. To impregnate with sulphureted hydrogen gas. [Obs.]

2. To convert into a substance resembling liver; as, *hepatized* lungs.

hepato-. See *Hepat-*.

hē-pat′ō-cēle, *n.* [*Hepato-*, and Gr. *kēlē*, tumor.] In pathology, hernia of the liver.

hep″ȧ-tō-cys′tiç, *a.* [*Hepato-*, and Gr. *kystis*, the bladder.] In anatomy, pertaining to the liver and gall-bladder.

hep″ȧ-tō-gas′triç, *a.* [*Hepato-*, and Gr. *gastēr*, the stomach.] In anatomy, relating to the liver and stomach; as, the *hepatogastric* epiploön.

hep″ȧ-tō-ġen′iç, *a.* [*Hepato-*, and Gr. *-genēs*, producing, and *-ic.*] Proceeding or produced from the liver.

hep-ȧ-toġ′e-nous, *a.* Hepatogenic.

hep-ȧ-tog′rȧ-phy, *n.* [*Hepato-*, and Gr. *graphein*, to write.] A description of the liver.

hep″ȧ-tō-li-thī′ȧ-sis, *n.* [*Hepato-*, and Gr. *lithiasis*, lithiasis, the stone disease, from *lithos*, a stone.] In pathology, a diseased condition characterized by the formation of gallstones in the liver.

hep-ȧ-tol′ō-ġist, *n.* One who studies or is versed in hepatology.

hep-ȧ-tol′ō-ġy, *n.* [*Hepato-*, and Gr. *-logia*, from *legein*, to speak.] The science of the liver; a treatise on the liver.

hep″ȧ-tō-pan′crē-as, *n.* [*Hepato-*, and Gr. *pankreas*, the pancreas; *pas*, *pantos*, all, and *kreas*, flesh.] In zoölogy, a glandular organ of many invertebrates, usually called the liver.

hep″ȧ-tō-pōr′tăl, *a.* [*Hepato-*, and L. *porta*, gate.] In anatomy, relating to the hepatic portal system; portal as distinguished from *reniportal*.

hep″ȧ-tō-rē′năl, *a.* [*Hepato-*, and L. *renalis*, pertaining to the kidneys, from *renes*, the kidneys.] In anatomy, pertaining to the liver and the kidneys; as, the *hepatorenal* ligament.

hep″ȧ-tor-rhē′ȧ, hep″ȧ-tor-rhœ′ȧ, *n.* [*Hepato-*, and Gr. *rhoia*, a flow, from *rhein*, to flow.] A morbid flow of bile.

hep-ȧ-tos′çō-py, *n.* [*Hepato-*, and Gr. *skopein*, to view.] The art or practice of divination by inspecting the livers of animals.

hep-ȧ-tot′ō-my, *n.* [*Hepato-*, and Gr. *tomē*, a cutting, from *temnein*, to cut.] In surgery, incision in the liver.

hep″ȧ-tō-um-bil′iç-ăl, *a.* [*Hepato-*, and L. *umbilicus*, the navel.] Relating to the liver and the umbilicus or navel.

Hē-phæs′ti-ăn (-fes′), *a.* Relating to Hephæstus, the god of fire and metallurgy among the Greeks; hence, relating to metal-working or smithery.

Hē-phæs′tus, *n.* [Gr. *Hēphaistos*.] In Greek mythology, the god of fire and metallurgy, corresponding to the Latin *Vulcan*.

hep′pen, *a.* Neat; fit; comfortable. [Obs.]

hep′pēr, *n.* A young salmon; a parr. [Prov. Eng.]

hepta-, hept-. Combining forms from Gr. *hepta*, seven, used in botany, zoölogy, mathematics, versification, and music to signify seven; as, *hepta*glot, *hepta*gon.

hep′tȧ-çhord, *n.* [Gr. *heptachordos*, seven stringed; *hepta*, seven, and *chordē*, a string, chord.]

1. In ancient music, (a) a system of seven sounds; (b) the interval of the major seventh; (c) an instrument with seven strings.

2. In ancient prosody, a composition sung to the sound of seven chords or tones.

hep-taçh′rō-nous, *a.* [LL. *heptachronus*; Gr. *heptachronos*; *hepta*, seven, and *chronos*, time.] In ancient prosody, heptasemic.

hep-tȧ-çol′iç, *a.* [*Hepta-*, and Gr. *kōlon*, a limb, member.] In ancient prosody, composed of seven cola or series.

hep′tad, *n.* [LL. *heptas* (*-adis*); Gr. *heptas*, the number seven, from *hepta*, seven.]

1. The sum or number of seven.

2. In chemistry, an element having a quantivalence of seven.

hep′tāde, *n.* See *Heptad*.

hep′tȧ-glot, hep′tȧ-glott, *n.* [*Hepta-*, and Gr. *glōtta*, the tongue, language.] A book in seven languages.

hep′tȧ-glot, hep′tȧ-glott, *a.* Written in seven languages.

hep′tȧ-gon, *n.* [Gr. *heptagōnos*, seven-cornered; *hepta*, seven, and *gōnia*, a corner, an angle.]

1. In geometry, a plane figure consisting of seven sides and as many angles.

2. In fortification, a place that has seven bastions for defense.

hep-tag′ō-năl, *a.* Having seven angles or sides.

Heptagonal numbers; in arithmetic, the numbers 1, 7, 18, 34, etc., the differences of which are an arithmetical progression having a common difference of 5, as the progression 1, 6, 11, 16, etc.

Hep-tȧ-ġyn′i-ȧ, *n.* [*Hepta-*, and Gr. *gynē*, a female.] In botany, an order of plants in the Linnean system of classification, having seven styles.

hep-tȧ-ġyn′i-ăn, *a.* Heptagynous.

hep-taġ′yn-ous, *a.* In botany, having seven styles.

hep-tȧ-hē′drăl, *a.* Having seven faces.

hep-tȧ-hē′drŏn, *n.* [*Hepta-*, and Gr. *hedra*, a seat, base.] In geometry, a solid figure with seven faces.

hep-tȧ-hex-ȧ-hē′drăl, *a.* [*Hepta-*, and Gr. *hex*, six, and *hedra*, a seat, base.] Presenting seven ranges of faces one above another, each range containing six faces.

hep-tam′ēr-ide, *n.* [*Hepta-*, and Gr. *meris* (*-idos*), a portion, share, from *meros*, a part.] That which divides into seven parts; that which consists of seven parts.

hep-tam′e-rŏn, *n.* [*Hepta-*, and Gr. *hēmera*, a day.] A book or treatise containing the transactions of seven days; specifically, the Heptameron of the Queen of Navarre (1492–1549), a book of anecdotes declared to have been recited during seven days, in the style of the Decameron of Boccaccio.

hep-tam′ēr-ous, *a.* [*Hepta-*, and Gr. *meros*, a part.] In botany, consisting of seven parts; having its parts in sevens.

hep-tam′e-tēr, *n.* [*Hepta-*, and Gr. *metron*, a measure.] In prosody, a verse consisting of seven feet.

Hep-tan′dri-ȧ, *n.pl.* [*Hepta-*, and Gr. *anēr*, *andros*, a male.] In botany, a class of plants in the Linnean system of classification, having seven stamens.

Heptandria—Flower of Horse-chestnut.

hep-tan′dri-ăn, *a.* Heptandrous.

hep-tan′drous, *a.* Having seven stamens.

hep′tāne, *n.* [Gr. *hepta*, seven, and *-ane*.] In chemistry, a liquid hydrocarbon of the paraffin group, contained in petroleum and also obtained from the resin of *Pinus Sabiniana* by dry distillation.

hep-tan′gū-lăr, *a.* [*Hepta-*, and L. *angulus*, an angle.] Having seven angles.

hep-tȧ-pet′ăl-ous, *a.* [*Hepta-*, and Gr. *petalon*, a leaf.] In botany, having seven petals in the corolla.

hep-taph′ō-ny, *n.* [*Hepta-*, and Gr. *phōnē*, voice, sound.] The union of seven sounds.

hep-taph′yl-lous (*or* -ta-fil′), *a.* [Gr. *heptaphyllos*, seven-leafed; *hepta*, seven, and *phyllon*, a leaf.] In botany, having seven leaves.

hep-tȧ-pod′iç, *a.* In prosody, consisting of or containing seven feet.

hep-tap′ō-dy, *n.* [*Hepta-*, and Gr. *pous*, *podos*, a foot.] In prosody, a verse of seven feet; a heptameter.

hep′tärçh, *n.* See *Heptarchist*.

hep-tär′çhiç, *a.* Pertaining to a sevenfold government; constituting or consisting of a heptarchy.

hep′tärçh-ist, *n.* A ruler of one division of a heptarchy.

hep′tärçh-y, *n.* [*Hepta-*, and Gr. *archē*, a rule, from *archein*, to rule.] A government by seven persons, or a country governed by seven persons. The word is usually applied to England when under the government of seven kings, or divided into seven kingdoms; as, the Saxon *heptarchy*, which comprehended the whole of England when subject to seven independent princes. These petty kingdoms were those of Kent, the South Saxons (Sussex), West Saxons (Wessex), East Saxons (Essex), East Anglia, Mercia, and Northumberland.

hep-tȧ-sē′miç, *a.* [LL. *heptasemos*; Gr. *heptasēmos*; *hepta*, seven, and *sēmeion*, a sign, mark, mora, from *sēma*, a sign.] In ancient prosody, containing seven moræ; heptachronous.

hep-tȧ-sep′ȧ-lous, *a.* In botany, having seven sepals.

hep-tȧ-spēr′mous, *a.* [*Hepta-*, and Gr. *sperma*, a seed.] In botany, having seven seeds.

hep′tȧ-stiçh, *n.* In prosody, same as *heptameter*.

hep-tȧ-syl-lab′iç, *a.* [LL. *heptasyllabus*; Gr. *heptasyllabos*; *hepta*, seven, and *syllabē*, a syllable.] In ancient prosody, composed of seven syllables.

Hep′tȧ-teūçh, *n.* [*Hepta-*, and Gr. *teuchos*, a tool, a book.] The first seven books of the Old Testament.

hep-tȧ-tom′iç, *a.* Same as *Heptavalent*.

hep-tav′ȧ-lent, *a.* [*Hepta-*, and L. *valens* (*-entis*), ppr. of *valere*, to have power, to be strong.] In chemistry, having a valence or combining power of seven.

hep′tēne, *n.* Same as *Heptylene*.

hep′tine (*or* -tēn), *n.* [Gr. *hepta*, seven, and *-ine*.] In chemistry, a hydrocarbon, C_7H_{12}, of the acetylene series.

hep-tō′iç, *a.* [Gr. *hepta*, seven, and *-ic*.] In chemistry, derived from heptane.

hep′tōne, *n.* [Gr. *hepta*, seven, and *-one*.] In chemistry, a hydrocarbon, C_7H_{10}, of the valylene series.

hep′-tree, *n.* The wild dogrose, *Rosa canina*.

hep′tyl, *n.* [*Hept-*, and Gr. *hylē*, matter.] In chemistry, the hypothetical radical, C_7H_{15}, of heptane and its derivatives.

hep′tyl-ēne, *n.* [*Heptyl* and *-ene*.] In chemistry, a hydrocarbon, C_7H_{14}, of the ethylene series. It is a colorless mobile liquid having a peculiar alliaceous odor, and is soluble in alcohol; called also *heptene*.

hep-tyl′iç, *a.* In chemistry, containing or derived from heptyl or heptane.

Heptylic alcohol; a liquid compound, $C_7H_{16}O$, having an agreeable smell.

hēr, *pron.* [ME. *hire*, *here*, *hure*, genit. and dat. sing.; AS. *hire*, genit. and dat. sing. of *heō*, she.]

1. The possessive case of the personal pronoun *she*; as, *her* face; *her* head.

> She gave also unto *her* husband with her, and he did eat. —Gen. iii. 6.

When thus used, *her* is sometimes called an adjective or adjective pronoun agreeing with the following noun. *Her* takes the form *hers* when not followed by the thing possessed.

> And what his fortune wanted, *hers* could mend. —Dryden.

2. The objective case of the personal pronoun *she*.

> Fear attends *her* not. —Shak.

hēr, *pron.* Their. [Obs.]

Hē′rȧ, Hē′rē, *n.* [Gr. *Hēra*; Ionic Gr. *Hērē*, Hera.] In Greek mythology, the supreme goddess of heaven, the wife and sister of Zeus, called *Juno* by the Romans.

Hē-raç′lē-ŏn-ite, *n.* In ecclesiastical history, one of an early sect of heretics belonging to the Gnostics, and followers of Heracleon, who denied that the world was created by the Son of God, and also rejected the authority of the Old Testament.

her′ăld, *n.* [ME. *herald*; OFr. *heralt*; LL. *haraldus*, *heraldus*, a herald; from O.H.G. *hari*, *heri*, an army, and *waltan*, to rule.]

1. In antiquity, an officer whose business was to denounce, to proclaim war, to challenge to battle, to proclaim peace, and to bear messages from the commander of an army.

2. A proclaimer; a publisher; as, the *herald* of another's fame.

3. A forerunner; a precursor; a harbinger.

> It was the lark, the *herald* of the morn.—Shak.

4. In medieval times, an officer whose business was to marshal, order, and conduct royal cavalcades, ceremonies at coronations, royal marriages, installations, creations of dukes and other nobles, embassies, funeral processions, declarations of war, proclamations of peace, etc.; also, to record and blazon the arms of the nobility and gentry, and to regulate abuses therein.

5. *Gonoptera libatrix*, a noctuid moth.

6. *Mergus serrator*, the red-breasted merganser.

Heralds' College; an ancient English royal corporation, first instituted by Richard III. in 1483. The heralds, the earl marshal, and the kings-at-arms are among its members. Its chief business is the granting of armorial bearings or coats of arms, and the tracing and preservation of genealogies. Called also *College of Arms*.

her′ăld, *v.t.*; heralded, *pt.*, *pp.*; heralding, *ppr.* To introduce, as by a herald; to act as herald to; to proclaim; to foretell.

her′ăld-crab, *n.* A crab, *Huenia heraldica*, so called because its carapace presents a fanciful resemblance to the shield and mantle figured by heraldic painters in depicting coat armor.

hē-ral′diç, *a.* Pertaining to heralds or heraldry.

hē-ral′diç-ăl-ly, *adv.* In a heraldic manner; according to the rules of heraldry.

her′ăld-ry, *n.* [OFr. *herauldcrie*, from *heralt*, a herald.] The art or office of a herald; the art, practice, or science of recording genealogies and blazoning arms or ensigns armorial, also of marshaling cavalcades, processions, and other public ceremonies.

her′ăld-ship, *n.* The office of a herald.

her-ȧ-path′ite, *n.* [From Dr. *Herapath*, who discovered it.] A salt obtained by dissolving sulphate of quinine in acetic acid, and then adding an alcoholic solution of iodine. It crystallizes in large tables which have a beautiful green metallic luster and polarize light like tourmalin.

her′ąud, *n.* A herald. [Obs.]

hērb (*or* ērb), *n.* [ME. *herbe*, *erbe*; OFr. *herbe*, *erbe*; L. *herba*, grass, herbage, a herb.]

1. An annual, biennial, or perennial plant in which the stem does not become woody, but dies down to the ground after flowering.

2. (a) A herbaceous plant used for medicinal purposes; (b) herbage.

hēr-bā′ceous, *a.* [L. *herbaceus*.]

1. Of or pertaining to herbs; of the nature of a herb.

2. Herbivorous. [Rare.]

hērb′āġe, *n.* [Fr. *herbage*, from *herbe*, a herb.]

1. Herbs collectively; grass; pasture; green food for beasts.

2. In English law, the liberty or right of pasture in the forest or grounds of another man.
hērb'āged, *a.* Covered with grass.
hērb'ăl, *n.* 1. A book that contains the names and descriptions of plants, or the classes, genera, species, and qualities of vegetables.
2. A hortus siccus or dry garden; a collection of specimens of plants, dried and preserved.
hērb'ăl, *a.* Pertaining to herbs.
hērb'ăl-iṣm, *n.* The knowledge of herbs.
hērb'ăl-ist, *n.* 1. A person skilled in the knowledge of plants; one who makes collections of plants.
2. A dealer in medicinal plants. [Rare.]
hērb'ăr, *n.* A herb. [Obs.]
hēr-bā'ri-ăn, *n.* A herbalist.
hērb'ȧ-rist, *n.* [Obs.] See *Herborist.*
hēr-bā'ri-um, *n.*; *pl.* **hēr-bā'ri-umṣ** or **hēr-bā'ri-ȧ.** [LL., from L. *herba*, a herb.]
1. A collection of dried plants systematically arranged.
2. A book or other contrivance for preserving dried specimens of plants.
hērb'ȧ-rize, *v.t.* See *Herborize.*
hērb'ȧ-ry, *n.*; *pl.* **hērb'ȧ-rieṣ.** A garden of herbs.
hērb'=bāne, *n.* A kind of European broom-rape of the genus *Orobanche*, a parasite on plant-roots.
hērb'=bär'bȧ-rȧ, *n.* An American and European plant, *Barbarea vulgaris*; winter-cress.
hērb'=ben"net, *n.* See *Avens.*
hērb'=cär"pen-tēr, *n.* In botany, the self-heal or heal-all, *Brunella vulgaris*, reputed to heal wounds made by tools; also called *carpenter's-herb.*
hērb'=ċhris'tō-phēr, *n.* Any one of various plants, as baneberry, royal flowering fern, fleabane, meadowsweet, wood-betony, some European vetches, etc.; also called *christopher.*
hērb'=doc"tŏr, *n.* A doctor who uses chiefly herbs or simples as remedies. [Colloq.]
hērb'ēr, *n.* An arbor; a herbary. [Obs.]
hēr'bēr-āġe, *n.* A shelter; harborage. [Obs.]
hēr'bēr-ġeŏur, *n.* A harbinger. [Obs.]
hēr'bērgh, *n.* A harbor. [Obs.]
hēr'bēr-we, *n.* Lodging; shelter. [Obs.]
hēr-bes'cent, *a.* [L. *herbescens (-entis)*, ppr. of *herbescere*, to grow into herbs.] Growing into herbs.
hērb'=ēve, *n.* Herb-ivy.
hērb'=fraṅk"in-cense, *n.* A European umbelliferous plant, the laserwort, *Laserpitium latifolium*, having medicinal properties and an aroma like frankincense.
hērb'=ġēr"ărd, *n.* The goutweed, *Ægopodium Podagraria.*
hērb'=grāce, *n.* Herb-of-grace; rue.
hēr-bic'ō-lous, *a.* [L. *herba*, a herb, and *colere*, to dwell.] Existing on herbaceous plants, as fungi.
hērb'id, *a.* Covered with herbs. [Obs.]
hēr-bif'ēr-ous, *a.* [L. *herba*, a herb, and *ferre*, to bear.] Bearing herbs.
hērb'ist, *n.* One skilled in herbs; a herbalist.
hēr-biv'ō-rȧ, *n.pl.* [L. *herba*, herb, and *vorare*, to devour.] Animals subsisting on herbs or vegetables; the *Ungulata.*
hēr'bi-vōre, *n.* A herbivorous animal.
hēr-biv'ō-rous, *a.* [L. *herba*, a herb, and *vorare*, to devour.]
1. Subsisting on herbaceous plants; opposed to *carnivorous.*
2. Of or pertaining to the *Herbivora.*
hērb'=ī"vy, *n.* In botany, (a) the ground-pine; (b) the hartshorn plantain; (c) the swine's-cress.
hērb'=john', *n.* St.-John's-wort; any tasteless pot-herb.
hērb'less, *a.* Destitute of herbs.
hērb'let, *n.* A small herb.
hērb'=lil"y, *n.* Any tropical American amaryllidaceous plant of the genus *Alstrœmeria.*
hērb'=lōu-ī'ṣȧ, *n.* A South American shrub, *Lippia citriodora*, having lemon-scented flowers and leaves; the lemon-verbena.
hērb'=mär'gȧ-ret, *n.* The daisy; marguerite; bruisewort.
hērb'=mas'tiç, *n.* Either of two medicinal plants; (a) a species of Spanish thyme, *Thymus mastichina*; (b) a germander, *Teucrium Marum*; also called *cat-thyme.*
hērb'=ŏf=grāce', *n.* Any one of three plants: (a) the common rue, *Ruta graveolens*; (b) the hedge-hyssop, *Gratiola officinalis*; (c) the European vervain, *Verbena officinalis.*
hērb'=ŏf=rē-pent'ănce, *n.* Same as *Herb-of-grace.*
hēr'bō-rist, *n.* [Fr. *herboriste*, from *herboriser*, to herborize, from *herbe*, a herb.] A herbalist.
hēr"bō-ri-zā'tion, *n.* [From *herborize.*]
1. The act of seeking plants in the field; botanical research.
2. The figuration of plants in mineral substances.
hēr'bō-rize *v.i.*; herborized, *pt.*, *pp.*; herborizing, *ppr.* [Fr. *herboriser*, from *herbe*, herb.] To search for plants, or to seek new species of plants, with a view to ascertain their characters and to class them.
hēr'bō-rize, *v.t.* To form figures of plants in; to arborize.
hēr'bŏr-ōugh, *n.* Same as *Harborough.*
hēr-bōse', *a.* Same as *Herbous.*
hērb'ous, *a.* [L. *herbosus*, from *herba*, a herb.] Abounding with herbs.
hērb'=rob'ērt, *n.* A kind of geranium.
hērb'=sō-phī'ȧ, *n.* Hedge-mustard.
hērb'=trin'i-ty, *n.* In botany, (a) the pansy, *Viola tricolor*, bearing a tricolored flower; (b) the liverleaf, *Anemone Hepatica*, having a trilobed leaf.
hērb'=twŏ'pence, *n.* Moneywort.
hērb'=wom"ăn, *n.* A woman who sells herbs.
hērb'y, *a.* Having the nature of or pertaining to herbs.
hēr-çog'ȧ-mous, *a.* In botany, characterized by or pertaining to hercogamy; nonautogamous.
hēr-çog'ȧ-my, *n.* [Gr. *herkos*, a fence, wall, and *gamos*, marriage.] Prevention of autogamy in flowers by abnormal structural development, which bars the pollen from the stigmatic chamber.
hēr-çū'lē-ăn, *a.* [L. *Herculeus*, of or pertaining to Hercules, from *Hercules*, Hercules.]
1. Very great, difficult, or dangerous; requiring the strength or courage of Hercules to encounter or accomplish; as, *herculean* labor or task.
2. Having extraordinary strength or size; as, *herculean* limbs.
3. [H—] Pertaining to Hercules, god of strength.
Hēr'çū-lēṣ, *n.* [L., from Gr. *Hēraklēs*, *Hēraklees*, lit., with Hera's glory, Hercules; *Hēra*, Hera, and *kleos*, glory, renown.]
1. A celebrated hero of Greek mythology, the offspring of Zeus and Alcmene, daughter of

Hercules Slaying the Hydra.—From sculpture at Florence.

Electryon, king of Mycenæ. He performed a number of extraordinary feats, which are called the twelve labors of *Hercules*. He is represented as brawny and muscular, with broad shoulders, generally naked, with a lion's skin and a club.
2. A constellation in the northern hemisphere, near Lyra.
Hercules hammer; a kind of drop-hammer.
Hercules powder; a blasting powder or dynamite containing powerful explosives.
Hēr'çū-lēṣ=bee"tle, *n.* A South American lamellicorn beetle, *Dynastes hercules*, the male having two projecting horns, the upper being the longer; the largest true insect known, being about six inches long.
Hēr'çū-lēṣ'ṣ=club, *n.* 1. A West Indian tree of the same genus as the prickly ash.
2. A variety of gourd that grows to a large size.
3. The angelica-tree.
Hēr-cyn'i-ăn, *a.* [L. *Hercynia silva*, Hercynian forest.] Pertaining to an extensive forest in Germany, the remains of which are in Swabia and on the Harz Mountains.
hēr'cy-nīte, *n.* [*Hercyn*ian, and *-ite*, so called from its being found in *Hyrcania silva*, the Roman name of the Bohemian forest.] A vitreous mineral containing alumina and iron; iron spinel.
hērd, *a.* Haired. [Obs.]
hērd, *n.* [ME. *heerde*, *heorde*; AS. *heord*, a herd, flock, a collection of beasts or persons.]
1. A collection or assemblage of animals; a flock; a drove; as, a *herd* of cattle.
2. A company of men or people; a crowd; a rabble; as, a vulgar *herd.*
hērd, *n.* [ME. *herde*, *hirde*, *hurde*; AS. *hirde*, *hierde*, *hyrde*, a herd, a keeper of cattle.] A keeper of live stock; used in composition; as, a shep*herd*; a goat*herd*; a swine*herd.*
hērd, *v.i.*; herded, *pt.*, *pp.*; herding, *ppr.* 1. To unite or associate, as beasts; to feed or run in droves; as, most beasts manifest a disposition to *herd.*
2. To associate; to unite in companies; to become one of a number or party.
3. To act as a herder.
hērd, *v.t.* To form or put into a herd.
hērd'book, *n.* A register containing the pedigrees of choice breeds of cattle.
hērd'ēr, *n.* A herdsman.
hēr'dēr-īte, *n.* [Named from its discoverer, Baron von *Herder.*] A whitish, crystalline fluophosphate of beryllium and calcium; a rare mineral.
hērd'ess, *n.* A shepherdess.
hērd'grōom, *n.* A keeper of a herd. [Obs.]
hēr'diç, *n.* [Named after its inventor, Peter *Herdic* of Pennsylvania.] An American cab having two or four wheels, cranked axle, low-set body, side seats, and back entrance.
hērd'măn, *n.* Same as *Herdsman.*
hērd'ṣ'=grȧss, *n.* A name given to various grasses which are highly esteemed for hay, particularly redtop and timothy.
hērdṣ'măn, *n.*; *pl.* **hērdṣ'men.** A keeper of herds; one employed in tending herds of cattle.
hērdṣ'wom"ăn, *n.* A woman who tends a herd.
hēre, *n.* Hair. [Obs.]
hēre, *pron.* Her or hers; also, their. [Obs.]
hēre, *adv.* [ME. *here*, *heer*, *her*; AS. *hēr*, here.]
1. In this place; in the place where the speaker is; opposed to *there*; as, behold, *here* am I.
2. In the present life or state; as, virtue's reward is *here.*
3. To this place; hither; as, come *here.*
4. At this time or stage; now.
5. At the place or in the situation indicated; as, *here* is a farmhouse and *here* a tree.
Here and there; in one place and another; in a dispersed manner or condition, irregularly.
Here below; in this life; on the earth.
Neither here nor there; not in this place nor in that; irrelevant.
hēre'ȧ-bout, hēre'ȧ-bouts, *adv.* 1. About this place.
2. About this subject. [Obs.]
hēre-ȧft'ēr, *adv.* [ME. *herafter*; AS. *herœfter*; *her*, here, and *œfter*, after.] In time to come; in some future time or state; henceforth; as, *hereafter* you must obey.
hēre-ȧft'ēr, *n.* A future state; life beyond the grave.
hēre-at', *adv.* At this; by reason of this; as, he was offended *hereat.*
hēre'ȧ-wāy", *adv.* In this vicinity; hereabout.
hēre=bē'ing, *n.* Present existence.
hēre-by', *adv.* 1. By this; by virtue of this; as, *hereby* we became acquainted.
2. Near. [Obs.]
hē-red"i-tȧ-bil'i-ty, *n.* Condition of being hereditable.
hē-red'i-tȧ-ble, *a.* [LL. *hereditabilis*, from *hereditare*, to inherit, from L. *hereditas (-atis)*, an inheriting, from *heres*, an heir.]
1. That may be inherited; inheritable.
2. Entitled to inherit.
hē-red'i-tȧ-bly, *adv.* By inheritance; by right of descent.
hēr-e-dit'ȧ-ment, *n.* [LL. *hereditamentum*, property inherited, from *hereditare*, to inherit, from *heres*, an heir.] In law, any species of property that may be inherited; lands, tenements, anything corporeal or incorporeal, real, personal, or mixed, that may descend to an heir.
Corporeal hereditament; property that is visible and tangible.
Incorporeal hereditament; an ideal right, existing in contemplation of law, issuing out of substantial corporeal property, as a right of way, franchise, water-right, rent, etc.
hē"red-i-tā'ri-ăn, *n.* One who believes in the biological doctrine of atavic heredity.
hē-red'i-tā-ri-ly, *adv.* By inheritance; by descent from an ancestor.
hē-red'i-tā-ry, *a.* [L. *hereditarius*, relating to an inheritance, from *hereditas (-atis)*, an inheritance, from *heres (-edis)*, an heir.]
1. Descended from an ancestor; descendible to an heir at law.
2. Capable of being transmitted from a parent to a child; as, *hereditary* pride; *hereditary* bravery; *hereditary* disease.
Syn.—Inherited, ancestral, lineal, patrimonial.
hē-red'i-ty, *n.* [L. *hereditas (-atis)*, heirship, from *heres (-edis)*, an heir.]
1. That which descends by inheritance; hereditary succession; as, the influence of *heredity* made him waver.
2. In biology, (a) same as *atavism*; (b) inheritance as a fact in opposition to environment.
Her'e-fŏrd, *n.* One of a breed of good working and beef-producing cattle originating in Herefordshire, England.
hēre-from', *adv.* From this; from the foregoing; as, *herefrom* we deduce the conclusion.
hēre-in', *adv.* In this; in this circumstance.
hēre-in-ȧft'ēr, *adv.* In the part following.
hēre"in-bē-fōre', *adv.* In the part preceding.
hēre-in-tō', *adv.* Into this.
hēr'e-mit, hēr'e-mite, *n.* A hermit. [Obs.]
hēr-e-mit'iç-ăl, *a.* Eremitical. [Obs.]
hēr'en, *a.* Made of hair. [Obs.]
hēre-of', *adv.* Of this; from this.

hēre-on′, *adv.* On this; hereupon.

hēre-out′, *adv.* Out of this place. [Obs.]

her′e-si-ärch, *n.* [LL. *heresiarcha*; Gr. *hairesiarchēs*, the leader of a school; *hairesis*, a sect or school, and *archein*, to lead.] A leader in heresy; the chief of a sect of heretics.

her-e-si-ärch′y, *n.* Flagrant heresy. [Rare.]

her-e-si-og′rȧ-phēr, *n.* [Gr. *hairesis*, heresy, and *graphein*, to write.] One who writes on heresies.

her-e-si-og′rȧ-phy, *n.* A treatise on heresy.

her″e-si-ol′ō-ġist, *n.* One versed in heresiology.

her″e-si-ol′ō-ġy, *n.* [Gr. *hairesis*, heresy, and *-logia*, from *legein*, to speak.] The study of heresies, or their history.

her′e-sy, *n.*; *pl.* **her′e-sieṣ**. [ME. *heresye*; OFr. *heresie*; L. *hæresis*, a school of thought, either philosophical or religious; Gr. *hairesis*, a taking, selection, school, heresy, from *hairein*, to take.]

1. A doctrine, opinion, or set of opinions or principles at variance with established or generally received principles; an opinion or doctrine tending to create division; an unsound or untenable doctrine of any kind, as in politics, morality, philosophy, etc.

> Duelling, and similar aberrations of honor, a moral *heresy*. —Coleridge.

2. In theology, a doctrine or opinion that is contrary to the fundamental doctrine or creed of any particular church; an error of opinion respecting some fundamental doctrine of religion.

3. In law, an offense against Christianity, consisting in a denial of some of its essential doctrines, publicly avowed, and obstinately maintained.

Syn.—Heterodoxy, false doctrine, schism.

her′e-tiç, *n.* [LL. *hæreticus*, of or belonging to heresy, a heretic, from Gr. *hairētikos*, able to choose, heretical, from *hairein*, to take, (in middle voice) to choose.]

1. One who holds heretical opinions; one who holds to a doctrine or opinion contrary to that which is generally accepted or established.

2. In theology, one who holds to a doctrine or opinion that is contrary to the fundamental doctrine or creed of one's church, or of the church with which one may have been previously connected.

> A man that is an *heretic*, after the first and second admonition, reject. —Titus iii. 10.

Syn.—Schismatic, sectarian.—A *heretic* is one whose errors are doctrinal, and usually of a malignant character, tending to subvert the true faith. A *schismatic* is one who creates a schism or division in the church on points of faith, discipline, practice, etc., usually for the sake of personal aggrandizement. A *sectarian* is one who originates or promotes a sect or distinct organization which separates from the main body of believers.

hē-ret′i-çal, *a.* Containing or pertaining to heresy; contrary to established or generally received opinions or principles; contrary to an established religious faith.

hē-ret′i-çal-ly, *adv.* In a heretical manner; with heresy.

hē-ret′i-çāte, *v.t.* [LL. *hæreticatus*, pp. of *hæreticare*, to make a heretic, charge with heresy, from LL. *hæreticus*, a heretic.] To decide to be heresy; to denounce as heretical. [Rare.]

hē-ret-i-çā′tion, *n.* [LL. *hæreticatio (-onis)*, from *hæreticare*, to charge with heresy, from *hæreticus*, a heretic.] The act of deciding as heretical. [Rare.]

hē-ret-i-fi-çā′tion, *n.* Heretication. [Rare.]

hēre-tō′, *adv.* Hereunto; to this place, time, etc.

her′e-toch, *n.* [Obs.] See *Heretoga*.

hēre-tō-fōre′, *adv.* Up to this time; formerly; hitherto.

her′e-tog, *n.* [Obs.] See *Heretoga*.

her-e-tō′gȧ, *n.* [AS.] In Anglo-Saxon history, the leader or commander of an army, or the commander of the militia in a district.

hēre-un′dēr, *adv.* Under this; in accordance with this.

hēre-un-tō′, *adv.* Unto this or this time; hereto. [Rare.]

hēre-up-on′, *adv.* Upon this; by reason of or following this.

hēre-with′ (*or* -with′), *adv.* With this.

her′i-ot, *n.* [ME. *heriet*; AS. *heregeatu*, military equipment, heriot; *here*, army, and *geatwa*, pl., arms, equipment.] In feudal law, a tribute or fine, as the best beast or other chattel, payable to the lord of the fee on the decease of the owner, landholder, or vassal. Originally the heriot consisted of military furniture, or of horses and arms which went to equip the vassal's successor; in modern use, a customary tribute of goods and chattels to the lord of the fee on the decease of the owner of the land.

Heriot custom; a heriot depending solely on usage.

Heriot service; a heriot due by reservation in a grant or lease of lands.

her′i-ot-ȧ-ble, *a.* Subject to the payment of a heriot.

her′is-sŏn, *n.* [OFr. *herisson*, a hedgehog, a herisson, from L. *ericius*, a hedgehog.] In fortification, a beam or bar armed with iron spikes pointed outward, and turning on a pivot, used to block up a passage.

her″it-ȧ-bil′i-ty, *n.* The state or quality of being heritable.

her′it-ȧ-ble, *a.* [OFr. *heritable*; LL. *hereditabilis*, from L. *hereditas*, inheritance, from *heres (-edis)*, an heir.]

1. Capable of inheriting or taking by descent.

> By the canon law this son shall be legitimate and *heritable*. —Hale.

2. Capable of being inherited; inheritable.

Heritable rights; in Scots law, rights of an heir; all rights in or connected with land.

her′it-ȧ-bly, *adv.* By way of inheritance; so as to be capable of transmission by inheritance; as, to convey a property *heritably*.

her′it-āġe, *n.* [OFr. *heritage*, an inheritance, from *heriter*; LL. *hereditare*, to inherit, from L. *hereditas*, inheritance, from *heres*, an heir.]

1. That which is inherited; an inheritance; specifically, in Scots law, heritable estate; realty.

> While the hollow oak our palace is,
> Our *heritage* the sea. —Cunningham.

2. In Scripture, the people of God, as being claimed by him, and the objects of his special care.

> As being lords over God's *heritage*.
> —1 Pet. v. 3.

her′it-ănce, *n.* Inheritance; heritage. [Rare.]

her′it-ŏr, *n.* [Fr. *heretier*; LL. *heritator*, contr. of *hereditator*, from *hereditare*, to inherit.] In Scots law, a proprietor or landholder in a parish.

hērl, *n.* Same as *Harl*.

hēr′ling, hir′ling, *n.* The young of the sea-trout. [Scot.]

hēr′mæ, *n.*, pl. of *hermes*, 2.

Hēr-mā′iç, *a.* [Gr. *Hermaikos*, of or like Hermes, from *Hermēs*, Hermes.] Relating to Hermes or Mercury.

Hēr-mā′iç-ăl, *a.* Hermaic.

hēr-măn-dăd′ (ĕr-), *n.* [Sp., a brotherhood, from *hermano*, a brother, from L. *germanus*, one closely related, a brother.] In Spanish history, one of the associations formed chiefly for the purpose of resisting the exactions of the nobles. It afterward was recognized as a regular police organization, which has since been superseded by the national gendarmerie

hēr″maph-rō-dē′i-ty, *n.* Hermaphroditism. [Rare.]

hēr-maph′rō-dişm, *n.* Hermaphroditism.

hēr-maph′rō-dīte, *n.* [L. *hermaphroditus*; Gr. *hermaphroditos*, a hermaphrodite, so called from *Hermaphroditos*, Hermaphroditus, in Greek legend the son of *Hermes* and *Aphrodite*, who while bathing became united in one body with the nymph Salmacis.]

1. A bisexual being; a being in which the characteristics of both sexes are either really or apparently combined.

2. In biology, an animal having the parts of generation of both male and female, so that reproduction can take place without the union of two individuals, as certain groups of the inferior worms, mollusks, barnacles, etc.

3. In botany, a flower that contains both the stamen and the pistil, or the male and female organs of generation, within the same floral envelope or on the same receptacle.

hēr-maph′rō-dīte, *a.* Same as *Hermaphroditic*.

Hermaphrodite brig; see under *Brig*.

hēr-maph-rō-dit′iç, *a.* Being of both sexes; characteristic of a hermaphrodite.

hēr-maph-rō-dit′iç-ăl, *a.* Hermaphroditic.

hēr-maph-rō-dit′iç-ăl-ly, *adv.* After the manner of a hermaphrodite.

hēr-maph′rō-dit-işm, *n.* In biology, the state of being a hermaphrodite; the partial or complete development of male and female sexual organs in one individual.

hēr-mē-neū′tiç, *a.* [Gr. *hermēneutikos*, of or for interpreting, from *hermēneutēs*, an interpreter, from *hermēneuein*, to interpret, from *Hermēs*, Hermes.] Explanatory; interpretative; unfolding the signification; as, *hermeneutic* theology, or the art of expounding the Scriptures.

hēr-mē-neū′tiç-ăl-ly, *adv.* According to the acknowledged principles of interpretation.

hēr-mē-neū′tiçs, *n.* The science of interpretation, or of finding the meaning of an author's words and phrases, and of explaining it to others; exegesis; particularly applied to the interpretation of the Scriptures.

hēr-mē-neū′tist, *n.* One versed in hermeneutics.

Hēr′mēṣ, *n.* [Gr. *Hermēs*, Hermes or Mercury, the messenger of the gods.]

1. In mythology, the name given to Mercury by the Greeks.

2. [h—] In Greek antiquity, a statue composed of a head, usually that of the god Hermes, placed on a quadrangular pillar, the height of which corresponded to the stature of the human body. Such statues were placed at the doors of houses, in front of temples, near to tombs, at the corners of streets, on high-roads as sign-posts with distances inscribed upon them, and on the boundaries of lands and states.

3. Hermes Trismegistus, the Egyptian god Thoth, as identified with the Greek Hermes.

Hermes or Mercury.

Hēr-met′iç, *a.* [L. *Hermes*, from Gr. *Hermēs*, Hermes, as the inventor of occult sciences.]

1. Relating to Hermes.

2. [*or* h—] Relating to Hermes Trismegistus, the Egyptian god Thoth, as the fabled originator of science, art, astrology, alchemy, etc.; as, *hermetic* philosophy; hence, alchemic.

> Under the more plausible delusions of the *hermetic* art. —Burke.

3. Designating the system which explains the causes of diseases and the operations of medicine on the principles of the hermetic philosophy, and particularly the system of an alkali and an acid; as, *hermetic* physic or medicine.

4. Perfectly close, so that no gas or spirit can escape or enter; as, a *hermetic* seal.

Hermetic art; alchemy; chemistry.

Hermetic books; (a) books of the Egyptians which treat of astrology; (b) books which treat of universal principles, of the nature and orders of celestial beings, of medicine, and other topics.

hēr-met′iç-ăl, *a.* Hermetic.

hēr-met′iç-ăl-ly, *adv.* 1. In a hermetic manner; chemically; by means of fusion; as, a vessel *hermetically* sealed or closed.

2. In accordance with the Hermetic books.

hēr′mit, *n.* [OFr. *hermite*, *ermite*; LL. *eremita*; Gr. *erēmitēs*, a hermit, from *erēmia*, a solitude, desert-place, from *erēmos*, desolate, solitary.]

1. A person who retires from society and lives in solitude; a recluse; an anchoret; especially, one who spends a life of retirement for the purpose of religious meditation and devotion.

2. A beadsman; one bound to pray for another. [Obs.]

hēr′mit-āġe, *n.* [OFr. *hermitage*, a hermitage, from *hermite*; LL. *eremita*; Gr. *erēmitēs*, a hermit.]

1. The habitation of a hermit; a house or hut in which a hermit dwells.

2. [H—] A kind of French wine produced from vineyards along the River Rhone; so named from a little hill near Tain in the department of Drôme, where a hermitage formerly existed.

hēr′mit-ā-ry, *n.* A cell occupied by a hermit, annexed to an abbey.

hēr′mit-bīrd, *n.* 1. A South American humming-bird of the genus *Phaëthornis*.

2. A South American bird of the genus *Monasa*; a nun-bird.

hēr′mit-çrab, *n.* A decapod crustacean of the family *Paguridæ*. These crabs take possession of and occupy the cast-off univalve shells of various mollusks, carrying this habitation about with them, and changing it for a larger one as they increase in size.

hēr′mit-çrōw, *n.* The chough.

hēr′mit-ess, *n.* A female hermit.

hēr-mit′i-çăl, *a.* Pertaining or suited to a hermit; eremitical.

hēr′mit-thrush′, *n.* A thrush of North America, shy and secluded in habits, but a fine songster.

hēr′mit-wạr′blēr, *n.* A warbler, *Dendrœca occidentalis*, of western United States.

hēr-mō-dac′tyl, *n.* [Gr. *hermodaktylos*, lit., Hermes's finger, a plant; *Hermēs*, Hermes, and *daktylos*, finger.] A bulbous root, supposed to be that of the *Colchicum variegatum*, formerly brought from Turkey and at one time much valued as a cathartic.

Hēr-mō-ġē′nē-ăn, *a.* Pertaining to Hermogenes or the doctrines he taught.

Hēr-mō-ġē′nē-ăn, *n.* One of a sect of ancient heretics, so called from their leader, Hermogenes, who lived near the close of the second century and who held matter to be the fountain of all evil and souls to be formed of corrupt matter.

Hēr-mō-ġē′ni-ăn, *a.* 1. Hermogenean.

2. Pertaining to Hermogenianus, a Roman jurist and writer who lived in the fourth century; as, the Gregorian and *Hermogenian* codes.

Hẽr-mō-ġē′ni-ăn, *n.* Same as *Hermogenean.*

hērn, *n.* A heron.

Hẽr-nan′di-ȧ, *n.* [Named after Dr. *Hernandez*, a Spanish botanist.] A genus of lauraceous East Indian trees containing several species. *Hernandia Sonora*, or jack-in-a-box, is so called from the noise made by the wind whistling through its persistent involucels.

Hernandia Sonora (Jack-in-a-box).

hẽr-nā′ni, *n.* A variously woven fabric used for making dresses for women; a kind of grenadine.

hẽr′nănt-seeds, *n.pl.* The seeds of *Hernandia ovigera*, imported from India for tanning purposes.

hẽr′ni-ȧ, *n.* [L. *hernia*, a rupture, from Gr. *hernos*, a shoot, sprout.] In surgery, a protrusion of a viscus through an abnormal opening in the wall of the containing cavity; used without qualification, the word refers to hernia of the intestines; called also *rupture.*

Strangulated hernia; a hernia which is so tightly constricted at its neck as to interfere with its return, with the circulation of blood, and the passage of feces.

hẽr′ni-ăl, *a.* Pertaining to or connected with hernia.

hẽr′ni-oid, *a.* [L. *hernia*, a rupture, hernia, and Gr. *eidos*, form. Like hernia.

hẽr-ni-ol′ō-ġy, *n.* [L. *hernia*, a rupture, hernia, and Gr. *-logia*, from *legein*, to speak.]

1. That branch of surgery which has reference to ruptures.

2. A treatise on ruptures.

hẽr-ni-ot′ō-my, *n.* [L. *hernia*, hernia, and Gr. *tomē*, a cutting, from *temnein*, to cut.] In surgery, operation for the relief of hernia, by section of the constriction.

hẽr′ni-ous, *a.* Hernial.

hẽrn′shąw, *n.* Same as *Heronshaw.*

hē′rō, *n.*; *pl.* **hē′rōeṣ**. [OFr. *heroe*; L. *heros*; Gr. *hērōs*, a hero.]

1. A man of distinguished valor, intrepidity, or enterprise in danger; a prominent or central personage in any remarkable action or event; a great, illustrious, or extraordinary person.

2. The principal male personage in a poem, play, story, etc., or the person who has the principal share in the transactions related; as Achilles in the Iliad, Ulysses in the Odyssey, and Æneas in the Æneid.

3. In classical mythology, a kind of demigod sprung from the union of a divine with a human being, regarded as mortal but partaking of immortality, and after death placed among the gods.

hē′rō-arch-y, *n.* [Gr. *hērōs*, a hero, and *archē*, rule, from *archein*, to rule.] All dignities of rank, on which human association rests; a government of heroes.

Hē-rō′di-ăn, *n.* [LL. *Herodianus*, from *Herodes*; Gr. *Hērōdēs*, Herod.] One of a sect among the Jews in the time of Christ, who were partizans of Herod.

Hē-rō′di-ăn, *a.* Pertaining to Herod the Great, king of the Jews, or to the family of Herod or its adherents.

hē-rō′di-ăn, *a.* Pertaining to the heron family.

hē-rō′di-ăn, *n.* A bird of the heron family; one of the *Herodiones.*

Hē-rō′di-ī, *n.pl.* Same as *Herodiones.*

Hē-rō-di-ō′nēṣ, *n.pl.* [LL. *herodio (-onis)*; Gr. *herōdios*, a heron.] An order of grallatorial birds, including the herons, storks, ibises, etc.

hē-rō-di-ō′nine, *a.* Pertaining to the *Herodiones.*

hē′rō-ess, *n.* A heroine. [Obs.]

hē-rō′iç, *a.* [L. *heroicus*; Gr. *hērōikos*, pertaining to a hero, from *hērōs*, a hero.]

1. Pertaining to, characteristic of, or becoming a hero; brave; bold; intrepid; noble; renowned; as, a *heroic* deed; a *heroic* soldier; *heroic* enterprises.

2. Characterized by heroes; noted for heroism; as, a *heroic* age; *heroic* settlers.

3. Epic; as, a *heroic* poem.

4. In art, larger than life; said of a statue or of any representation of a human figure larger than life-size.

Heroic age; in Greek history or mythology, the age when the heroes are supposed to have lived, a semimythical period preceding that which is truly historic.

Heroic verse; a verse adapted to heroic or exalted themes; in English poetry, as also in German, the iambic of ten syllables; in French the iambic of twelve; and in classical poetry the hexameter.

Syn.—Brave, courageous, fearless, intrepid, valiant, daring, gallant.

hē-rō′iç-ăl, *a.* [Rare.] Same as *Heroic.*

hē-rō′iç-ăl-ly, *adv.* In a heroic manner; with valor; bravely; courageously; intrepidly; as, the wall was *heroically* defended.

hē-rō′iç-ăl-ness, *n.* The quality of being heroic; heroism. [Rare.]

hē-rō′iç-ly, *adv.* Heroically. [Rare.]

hē-rō′iç-ness, *n.* Heroicalness. [Rare.]

hē″rō-i-çom′iç, *a.* Consisting of the heroic and the ludicrous; denoting high burlesque; as, a *heroicomic* poem.

hē″rō-i-çom′iç-ăl, *a.* Same as *Heroicomic.*

her′ō-ine, *n.* [OFr. *heroine*; L. *heroina*, a female hero, a demigoddess, from Gr. *hērōinē*, a heroine, f. of *hērōinos*, of a hero, from *hērōs*, a hero.]

1. A female hero; a woman of a brave spirit.

2. The principal female character in a poem, play, romance, story, or the like.

her′ō-iṣm, *n.* The qualities of a hero; bravery; courage; intrepidity.

Syn.—Courage, fortitude, bravery, valor, intrepidity, gallantry.—*Courage* is generic, denoting fearlessness of danger; *fortitude* is passive courage, the habit of bearing up nobly under trials, dangers, and sufferings; *bravery* and *valor* are courage in battle or other conflicts with living opponents; *intrepidity* is firm courage, which shrinks not amid the most appalling dangers; *gallantry* is adventurous courage, dashing into the thickest of the fight. *Heroism* may call into exercise all these modifications of courage.

her′ŏn, *n.* [ME. *heroun, heyroun, heiron*; OFr. *hairon*; O.H.G. *heigir*, a heron.] A grallatorial bird of the genus *Ardea*, constituting with the storks and bitterns the family *Ardeidæ*. The species are very numerous, and almost universally spread over the globe. They are distinguished by having a long bill cleft beneath the eyes, a compressed body, long slender legs naked above the tarsal joint, three toes in front, the two outer united by a membrane, and by moderate wings. The common heron of Europe is *Ardea cinerea*; the great blue heron of America is *Ardea herodias.*

Common European Heron (*Ardea cinerea*).

her′ŏn-ẽr, *n.* A hawk trained to hunt the heron. [Obs.]

her′ŏn-ry, *n.*; *pl.* **her′ŏn-rieṣ**. A place where herons breed.

her′ŏn′ṣ-bill, *n.* A plant of the genus *Erodium*, of the natural order *Geraniaceæ*; so named because the long-beaked fruit has been fancied to resemble the head and breast of a heron; called also *stork's-bill.*

her′ŏn-sew (-sū), *n.* A heron. [Prov. Eng.]

her′ŏn-shąw, *n.*, a variant of *heronsew.* [Obs.]

hē-rō-ol′ō-ġist, *n.* [Gr. *hērōologia*, a tale of heroes; *hērōs*, a hero, and *-logia*, from *legein*, to speak.] One who treats of heroes. [Rare.]

hē′rō-ship, *n.* The character or condition of a hero.

hē′rō-wŏr″ship, *n.* The worship of heroes, practised by the nations of antiquity; reverence paid to, or to the memory of, heroes or great men.

hẽr′pēṣ, *n.* [L. *herpes*; Gr. *herpēs*, lit., a creeping, the herpes, from *herpein*, to creep.] In pathology, an acute inflammatory affection of the skin or mucous membrane, characterized by the development of groups of vesicles on an inflamed base.

hẽr-pet′iç, *a.* Pertaining to herpes; resembling herpes or partaking of its nature; as, *herpetic* eruptions.

hẽr-pet′iç-ăl, *a.* Herpetic.

hẽr′pe-tiṣm, *n.* In medicine, a tendency to develop herpes or similar cutaneous diseases.

hẽr′pe-toid, *a.* [Gr. *herpeton*, a reptile, and *eidos*, form.] Resembling a reptile; as, a *herpetoid* bird.

hẽr″pet-ō-loġ′iç, *a.* Pertaining to herpetology.

hẽr″pet-ō-loġ′iç-ăl, *a.* Herpetologic.

hẽr″pet-ō-loġ′iç-ăl-ly, *adv.* From a herpetological standpoint.

hẽr-pē-tol′ō-ġist, *n.* A person versed in herpetology, or the natural history of reptiles.

hẽr-pē-tol′ō-ġy, *n.* [Gr. *herpeton*, a reptile, and *-logia*, from *legein*, to speak.] The study of reptiles; the natural history of reptiles.

hẽr-pē-tot′ō-mist, *n.* One who dissects reptiles; a student of herpetological anatomy.

hẽr-pē-tot′ō-my, *n.* [Gr. *herpeton*, a reptile, and *tomē*, a cutting, from *temnein*, to cut.] The dissection or anatomy of reptiles.

herr, *n.* A form of address in Germany equivalent to English *Mr.*

her′ring, *n.* [ME. *hering*; AS. *hæring*, a herring; prob. from *here*, an army, a post.] A fish of the genus *Clupea*, especially *Clupea harengus*, the common herring of the North Atlantic. Herrings come from high northern latitudes in the spring, and visit the shores of Europe and America in great schools, where they are taken and cured in enormous quantities.

her′ring-bōne, *a.* Like the spine of a herring; specifically, applied to courses of stone laid angularly, so that those in each course are placed obliquely to the right and left alternately.

Herringbone work.

Herringbone stitch; a kind of cross-stitch used in embroidery and woolen work.

her′ring-bōne, *v.t.* and *v.i.* To embroider with a herringbone stitch.

her′ring-buss, *n.* A peculiar boat of ten or fifteen tons, used in England in the herring fishery.

her′ring-gull, *n.* A gull such as *Larus argentatus*, that feeds on herrings.

her′ring-hog, *n.* *Phocœna communis*, the common porpoise.

her′ring-king, *n.* The ribbon-fish; called also *king of the herrings.*

her′ring-pond, *n.* The ocean, particularly the Atlantic Ocean. [Slang.]

Hẽrrn′hut-ẽr, *n.* [G. *Herrnhut*, the village of Herrnhut, where they first settled.] One of a sect established by Nicholas Lewis, count of Zinzendorf, about 1722; a Moravian.

hẽrṣ, *pron.* Belonging to her; of her; used instead of *her* and a noun; as, the book is *hers.*

hẽr′săl, *n.* Rehearsal. [Obs.]

Hẽr′schel, *n.* [Named after Sir William *Herschel*, its discoverer.] Same as *Uranus*, 1.

Hẽr-schē′li-ăn, *a.* Pertaining to Sir William Herschel, the English astronomer, or to Sir John Herschel, his son; as, the *Herschelian* telescope.

hẽr′schel-īte, *n.* [Named after Sir John *Herschel*, the astronomer.] A mineral allied to chabazite.

hẽrse, *n.* [ME. *herse, hers*; OFr. *herce*, a harrow, a portcullis, a triangular candlestick, from L. *hirpex (-icis)*, a harrow.]

1. In fortification, (a) a portcullis in the form of a harrow set with iron spikes; (b) a kind of chevaux-de-frise laid in the way or in breaches, with the points up, to obstruct or incommode the march of an enemy.

2. A carriage for bearing corpses to the grave; a hearse. [Obs.]

3. A framework on which lighted candles were placed at funeral ceremonies in the middle ages. [Obs.]

4. A grating used for any purpose.

Herse, from a manuscript in the Bodleian Library, Oxford.

hẽr-self′, *pron.* An emphasized or reflexive form of the third personal pronoun, feminine, used exactly in the same way as *himself.*

hẽr′ship, *n.* See *Depredation*, 3.

hẽr′sil-lŏn, *n.* [Fr., from *herse*, a portcullis.] In fortification, a plank or beam, set with spikes or nails, to incommode and retard the march of an enemy.

hẽrt, *n.* A hart. [Obs.]

hẽr′te, *n.* A heart. [Obs.]

hẽr′te-ly, *a.* Hearty. [Obs.]

hẽr′te-ly, *adv.* Heartily. [Obs.]

Hẽrtz′i-ăn, *a.* Relating to Heinrich Hertz, a German physicist, or to his discoveries; as, the *Hertzian* waves.

hẽr′y, *v.t.* To regard as holy; to worship. [Obs.]

hẽr′zog (-tsog), *n.* [G.] An Austrian or German duke.

heṣ′i-tăn-cy, *n.* [L. *hæsitantia*, a stammering, from *hæsitans (-antis)*, ppr. of *hæsitare*, to hesitate.] The act of hesitating or doubting; slowness in forming decisions; the action or manner of one who hesitates; indecisive deliberation; doubt; vacillation.

> Some of them reasoned without doubt or *hesitancy.* —Atterbury.

heṣ′i-tănt, *a.* Hesitating; pausing; not ready in deciding or acting; wanting readiness of speech.

> He was a man of no quick utterance, but often *hesitant.* —Baxter.

heṣ′i-tănt-ly, *adv.* With hesitancy or doubt.

heṣ′i-tāte, *v.i.*; hesitated, *pt., pp.*; hesitating, *ppr.* [L. *hæsitatus*, pp. of *hæsitare*, to stick fast, hesitate, intens. of *hærere*, to stick, cleave.]

1. To stop or pause respecting decision or

action; to be doubtful as to fact, principle, or determination; to be in suspense or uncertainty; as, he *hesitated* whether to accept the offer or not.

2. To stammer; to stutter.

Syn.—Doubt, falter, pause, scruple, stammer, stutter.

heș′i-tāte, *v.t.* To be undecided about; to utter or express with hesitation or reluctance; to insinuate hesitatingly. [Rare.]

Just hint a fault, and *hesitate* dislike.—Pope.

heș′i-tā-ting-ly, *adv.* With hesitation or doubt.

heș-i-tā′tion, *n.* [L. *hæsitatio* (*-onis*), from *hæsitare*, to stick fast, hesitate.]

1. The act of hesitating; pause or delay in forming an opinion or commencing action; doubt; suspension of opinion or decision, from uncertainty what is proper to be decided.

2. Stammering; a stopping in speech.

Syn.—Hesitancy, wavering, vacillation, uncertainty, doubt, faltering, suspense.

heș′i-tā-tive, *a.* Showing hesitation.

heș′i-tā-tŏr, *n.* One who hesitates.

heș′i-tā-tō-ry, *a.* Hesitating.

hesp, *n.* A measure of two linen-thread hanks. [Scot.]

Hes′pẽr, *n.* Same as *Hesperus*.

hes-per′e-tin, *n.* A sweetish crystalline compound derived from hesperidin by the action of dilute sulphuric acid.

Hes-pē′ri-ȧ, *n.* A genus of butterflies, the type of the family *Hesperiidæ*.

Hes-pē′ri-ăn, *a.* [L. *hesperius*; Gr. *hesperios*, western, from *Hesperos*, the evening star.] Western; situated in the west. [Poet.]

Hes-pē′ri-ăn, *n.* An inhabitant of a western country. [Poet.]

hes-pē′ri-ăn, *n.* Any butterfly of the family *Hesperiidæ*.

hes-pē′ri-ăn, *a.* Pertaining to the *Hesperiidæ*, a family of lepidopterous insects.

hes′per-id, *n.* A hesperian.

hes′per-id, *a.* Pertaining to the *Hesperiidæ*; hesperian.

hes-per′i-dēne, *n.* A variety of terpene obtained from orange-oil.

Hes-per′i-dēș, *n.pl.* [L., from Gr. *Hesperides*, the Hesperides, from *Hesperos*, Hesperus.] In Greek mythology, (a) the daughters of Hesperus, brother of Atlas, three or seven in number, possessors of the fabulous garden of golden fruit, watched over by an enchanted dragon, at the western extremities of the earth. The apples were stolen by Hercules, who slew the dragon; (b) the garden possessed by the Hesperides.

Hes-pē-rid′i-ăn, *a.* Pertaining to the Hesperides.

hes-per′i-din, *n.* A crystallizable compound, found in the spongy envelope of oranges and lemons. Its nature has not yet been ascertained.

hes-pē-rid′i-um, *n.* [From L. *Hesperides*, the Hesperides; so called in allusion to the golden apples of the Hesperides.] In botany, a fleshy fruit with a separable thick envelope, and divided internally into several separable pulpy cells by membranous dissepiments, as the orange or lemon.

Hes-pē-ri′i-dæ, *n.pl.* [L. *Hesperia*, the west, from *Hesperus*, the evening star.] A family of lepidopterous insects, of which the type is the genus *Hesperia*. These little large-headed butterflies have a peculiar, short, jerking kind of flight, and hence they have received the name of *skippers*. *Hesperia sylvanus* and *Thymele alveolus* are typical examples.

Hes-pē-rọr′nis, *n.* [Gr. *hesperos*, western, and *ornis*, a bird.] A genus of large fossil birds with rudimentary wings. Several species have been found in the Cretaceous deposits of North America.

Hes′pe-rus, *n.* [L., from Gr. *Hesperos*, the evening star.] The evening star, particularly Venus.

Hes′siăn (hesh′ăn), *a.* [L. *Hesse*, *Hessen*, originally a Teut. tribe-name.] Relating to Hesse in Germany or to the Hessians.

Hessian bit; a peculiar kind of jointed bit for bridles.

Hessian boots; long boots originally introduced by the Hessian troops, and worn in England in the beginning of the nineteenth century.

Hessian cloth; a kind of coarse cloth manufactured from hemp, used principally for bagging.

Hessian fly (*Cecidomyia destructor*). *a*, Male (natural size). *b*, Male (magnified). *c*, Pupæ fixed on the joint of the wheat-stalk.

Hessian crucible; see under *Crucible*.

Hessian fly; a small, two-winged fly or midge, *Cecidomyia destructor*, nearly black, very destructive to young wheat; so called from the supposition that it was brought into America by the Hessian troops during the Revolution.

Hes′siăn, *n.* 1. A native or inhabitant of Hesse in Germany.

2. [*pl.*] Hessian boots.

3. [*pl.*] Hessian cloth.

4. In the United States, a hireling or mercenary; a venal person; from the employment of Hessian troops as mercenaries by the British in the Revolutionary War.

Hes′si-ăn, *n.* In mathematics, a symmetric determinant whose elements are the second differential coefficients of a rational integral function of two or more variables.

hess′ite, *n.* A telluride of silver of a lead-gray color, crystallizing in the isometric system.

hes′sō-nite, *n.* A variety of garnet; cinnamon-stone.

hest, *n.* [ME. *hest*, *heste*; AS. *hæs*, a command, from *hatan*, to bid, order, command.] Command; precept; injunction; order. [Rare.]

hes′tẽrn, *a.* Hesternal. [Obs.]

hes-tẽr′năl, *a.* Pertaining to yesterday. [Obs.]

hes-thoġ′e-nous, *a.* [Gr. *esthēs*, dress, and *gonos*, offspring.] In ornithology, ptilopædic.

Hes′y-ċhașm, *n.* [Gr. *hēsychazein*, to be still or quiet.] The doctrine of the Hesychasts.

Hes′y-ċhast, *n.* [Gr. *hēsychastēs*, one who leads a quiet, retired life, a hermit, from *hēsychazein*, to be still or quiet, from *hēsychos*, still, quiet.] One of a sect of mystics who lived during the fourteenth century; a Quietist.

hes-y-ċhas′tiç, *a.* [Gr. *hēsychastikos*, quieting, retired, from *hēsychazein*, to be quiet.] Expressive of mental serenity; conducing to quietude.

hē-tæ′rȧ, hē-tai′rȧ, *n.* [Gr. *hetaira*, f. of *hetairos*, a companion.] In ancient Greece, a courtezan; a concubine; a female paramour.

hē-tæ′ri-ō, *n.* [L., from Gr. *hetaireia* or *hetairia*, society, from *hetairos*, a comrade.] In botany, a collection of distinct indehiscent carpels, as in the strawberry and raspberry.

hē-tæ′rișm, hē-tai′rișm, *n.* [Gr. *hetairismos*, the practice of a hetæra, from *hetairizein*, to be a hetæra, from *hetaira*, a hetæra or concubine.] That condition in primitive states of society when the women of a tribe were held in common; open concubinage; also incorrectly written *hetarism*.

hē-tæ′rist, hē-tai′rist, *n.* [Gr. *hetairistēs*, one who practises hetærism, from *hetærizein*, to be a hetæra.] One who practises hetærism or open concubinage.

het-æ-ris′tiç, het-ai-ris′tiç, *a.* Pertaining to hetærism.

het-æ′rō-līte, *n.* [Gr. *hetairos*, a companion, and *lithos*, a stone.] A mineral allied to hausmannite, supposed to be a zinc-manganese oxid.

hetch′el, *v.t.* and *n.* See *Hatchel*.

heter-. See *Hetero-*.

het′ẽr-ȧ-ċanth, *a.* [*Heter-*, and Gr. *akantha*, spine.] In zoölogy, having asymmetrical dorsal and anal spines.

het-ẽr-aç′my, *n.* [*Heter-*, and Gr. *akmē*, prime, maturity.] In botany, a proterandrous and proterogynous condition or the maturing of the stamens and pistils at different times; opposed to *synacmy*.

het-ẽr-ȧ-den′iç, *a.* [*Heter-*, and Gr. *adēn*, a gland.] Pertaining to or consisting of tissue that is unlike normal glandular tissue, or to glandular tissue occurring in an abnormal place.

het′ẽr-ärċh-y, *n.* The government of an alien. [Obs.]

het″ẽr-ȧ-tom′iç, *a.* [*Heter-*, and Gr. *atomos*, an atom.] Composed of different kinds of atoms.

het″e-rạux-ē′sis (-raks-), *n.* [*Heter-*, and Gr. *auxēsis*, increase.] In botany, unequal or unsymmetrical growth of a part of a plant.

hetero-, heter-. Combining forms from Gr. *heteros*, other, different, used in botany, zoölogy, chemistry, mathematics, etc., to signify other, another, different; as, *hetero*carpus, *hetero*phasia.

het″ẽr-ō-blas′tiç, *a.* [*Hetero-*, and Gr. *blastos*, a bud, germ.] Arising from tissue of a different kind.

het″ẽr-ō-çär′pi-ăn, *a.* Heterocarpous.

het″ẽr-ō-çär′pișm, *n.* [*Hetero-*, and Gr. *karpos*, fruit.] In botany, the property of bearing fruit of two sorts or shapes, as in *Amphicarpæa*.

het″ẽr-ō-çär′pous, *a.* [Gr. *heterokarpos*, bearing different fruit; *heteros*, other, different, and *karpos*, fruit.] In botany, bearing fruit of two sorts or shapes.

het″ẽr-ō-cel′lū-lăr, *a.* Consisting of dissimilar cells.

het″ẽr-ō-ceph′ȧ-lous, *a.* [*Hetero-*, and Gr. *kephalē*, head.] In botany, having some heads of male and some of female flowers, as certain plants of the aster family.

Het-e-roc′e-rȧ, *n.* [*Hetero-*, and Gr. *keras*, horn.] A section of *Lepidoptera* including many families; the moths.

het″ẽr-ō-cẽr′căl, *a.* [*Hetero-*, and Gr. *kerkos*, tail.] In ichthyology, having the vertebral column extending to a point in the upper lobe of the tail, as in the sharks and sturgeons. It is really found in all osseous fishes, but is obscured by the greater size of the inferior tail lobe, which gives the appearance of equality.

het′ẽr-ō-cẽr″cy, *n.* The quality or condition of being heterocercal.

het″ẽr-ō-ċhrō′mous, *a.* [Gr. *heterochrōmos*, of different color; *heteros*, other, different, and *chrōma*, color.] In botany, having the florets of the center or disk different in color from those of the circumference or ray.

het-ẽr-oċh′rō-nișm, *n.* Same as *Heterochrony*.

het″ẽr-ō-ċhrō-nis′tiç, *a.* Same as *Heterochronous*.

het-ẽr-oġh′rō-nous, *a.* Pertaining to heterochrony.

het-ẽr-oċh′rō-ny, *n.* [Gr. *heterochronos*, of different times; *heteros*, other, different, and *chronos*, time.] In biology, a deviation from the true ontogenetic sequence, with reference to the time of formation of organs or parts.

het′ẽr-ō-çlīne, *a.* [*Hetero-*, and Gr. *klinē*, a bed.] Producing two kinds of heads on separate receptacles, as certain plants of the aster family.

het′ẽr-ō-çlī-tăl, *a.* See *Heteroclite*.

het′ẽr-ō-çlīte, *a.* [LL. *heteroclitus*; Gr. *heteroklitos*, irregularly inflected; *heteros*, other, different, and *klinein*, to bend, incline.] Irregular; anomalous; deviating from ordinary forms or rules.

het′ẽr-ō-çlīte, *n.* 1. In grammar, a word which is irregular or anomalous either in declension or conjugation, or which deviates from ordinary forms of inflection in words of a like kind. It is particularly applied to nouns irregular in declension.

2. Any thing or person deviating from common forms.

het-ẽr-ō-çlit′iç, *a.* Heteroclite.

het-ẽr-ō-çlit′iç-ăl, *a.* Heteroclitic.

het-ẽr-og′li-tous, *a.* Heteroclitic. [Obs.]

het′ẽr-ō-cyst, *n.* [*Hetero-*, and Gr. *kystis*, a bag, pouch.] An abnormally large cell found in certain algæ.

het″ẽr-ō-daç′tyl, het″ẽr-ō-daç′tyle, *a.* [*Hetero-*, and Gr. *daktylos*, a finger or toe.] In zoölogy, having the toes irregular, either in regard to number, position, or formation, as in the trogons.

het″ẽr-ō-daç′tyl, het″ẽr-ō-daç′tyle, *n.* A member of the *Heterodactylæ*.

Het″e-rō-daç′ty-læ, *n.pl.* A group of picarian birds having the second toe reversed instead of the fourth; the trogons.

het″ẽr-ō-daç′tyl-ous, *a.* 1. Same as *Heterodactyl*.

2. Pertaining to the *Heterodactylæ*.

het′ẽr-ō-dont, *a.* [*Hetero-*, and Gr. *odous*, *odontos*, a tooth.] Having teeth of different kinds, as canines, incisors, and molars; opposed to *homodont*.

het′ẽr-ō-dont, *n.* Any animal with different kinds of teeth; a heterodont animal.

het′ẽr-ō-dox, *a.* [Gr. *heterodoxos*, of another or different opinion; *heteros*, other, and *doxa* opinion.]

1. In theology, contrary to established or generally received opinions; contrary to some recognized standard of opinion, as the creed of a church or the decrees of councils; not orthodox; heretical.

2. Holding opinions or doctrines at variance with some acknowledged standard; not orthodox; said of persons.

het′ẽr-ō-dox, *n.* An opinion contrary to that which is established or generally received. [Obs.]

het′ẽr-ō-dox-ly, *adv.* In a heterodox manner.

het′ẽr-ō-dox-ness, *n.* The state of being heterodox.

het′ẽr-ō-dox-y, *n.* 1. The quality or condition of being heterodox.

2. A heterodox opinion, belief, or doctrine; a heresy.

het-ẽr-od′rō-mous, *a.* [*Hetero-*, and Gr. *dromos*, a running, from *dramein*, to run.] In botany, running in different directions, as leaves on the stem and branches.

het-ẽr-od′rō-my, *n.* In botany, a change in direction of the spiral sequence of leaves on a stem.

het-ẽr-œ′cious, *a.* [*Heter-*, and Gr. *oikos*, a house.] Pertaining to or characterized by heterœcism.

het-ẽr-œ′çișm, *n.* In botany, a condition characterized by a different state of development occurring in a parasitic organism (especially fungi) as it changes its seat from one body to another. Such a condition is exemplified by the rust of wheat, oats, and other cultivated grasses.

het″e-rœ-çis′măl, *a.* Heterœcious.

het-ẽr-og′ȧ-mous, *a.* [*Hetero-*, and Gr. *gamos*, marriage.] In botany, having two or more sorts of flowers which differ sexually, as in the aster and daisy.

het-ẽr-og′ȧ-my, *n.* 1. In botany, the state or

quality of being heterogamous; mediate or indirect fertilization of plants.

2. In biology, alternation of two kinds of sexual generation, or of a sexual and a parthenogenetic generation.

het-ẽr-ō-gan′gli-āte, *a.* [*Hetero-*, and Gr. *ganglion*, ganglion.] Possessing a nervous system in which the ganglia are scattered and unsymmetrical, as in the *Mollusca*.

het′ẽr-ō-ġene, *a.* Heterogenous. [Obs.]

het″ẽr-ō-ġē′nē-ăl, *a.* Heterogeneous. [Rare.]

het″ẽr-ō-ġe-nē′i-ty, *n.* The state or quality of being heterogeneous; dissimilar nature or constitution; dissimilarity.

het″ẽr-ō-ġē′nē-ous, *a.* [LL. *heterogeneus*; Gr. *heterogenēs*, of different kinds, of different genders; *heteros*, other, different, and *genos*, kind, race, gender.] Differing in kind; unlike in qualities; composed of elements of different kinds; having dissimilar constituents; opposed to *homogeneous*.

Heterogeneous nouns; in grammar, nouns of different genders in the singular and plural numbers; as, *hic locus*, of the masculine gender in the singular, and *hi loci* and *hæc loca*, both masculine and neuter in the plural; *hoc cœlum*, neuter in the singular; *hi cœli*, masculine in the plural.

Heterogeneous quantities; in mathematics, quantities incapable of being compared in respect to magnitude.

Heterogeneous surds; in mathematics, surds which have different radical signs.

het″ẽr-ō-ġē′nē-ous-ly, *adv.* In a heterogeneous manner.

het″ẽr-ō-ġē′nē-ous-ness, *n.* Heterogeneity.

het″ẽr-ō-ġen′e-sis, *n.* [*Hetero-*, and Gr. *genesis*, origin, birth.]

1. In biology, (a) spontaneous generation; abiogenesis; (b) that kind of generation in which the parent, whether plant or animal, produces offspring differing in structure and habit from itself, but in which after one or more generations the original form reappears.

2. Production by a cause different from the effect; heterogeny.

het″ẽr-ō-ġē-net′iç, *a.* Pertaining to heterogenesis.

het-ẽr-oġ′e-nist, *n.* One who believes in the theory of spontaneous generation.

het-ẽr-oġ′e-nous, *a.* Heterogenetic.

het-ẽr-oġ′e-ny, *n.* See *Heterogenesis*, 2.

het-ẽr-og′ō-niṣm, *n.* The quality or state of being heterogonous.

het-ẽr-og′ō-nous, *a.* [*Hetero-*, and Gr. *gonos*, offspring, generation.] In botany, having the individuals of the same species differing in the length of their stamens and pistils; heterostyled.

het-ẽr-og′ō-nous-ly, *adv.* In a heterogonous manner.

het-ẽr-og′ō-ny, *n.* See *Heterogonism*.

het″ẽr-ō-graph′iç, *a.* Pertaining to heterography.

het-ẽr-og′rȧ-phy, *n.* [*Hetero-*, and Gr. *graphein*, to write.] The use of the same letters to represent different sounds in different words or syllables, as *c* in *cell* and *call*; heterogeneous orthography.

het-ẽr-og′y-năl, *a.* Heterogynous.

het-ẽr-og′y-nous, *a.* [*Hetero-*, and Gr. *gynē*, a woman, a female.] In zoölogy, (a) having females of two different kinds, one fertile, the other infertile or neuter, as the ants; (b) having females differing in form and structure from the males.

het-ẽr-oi′dē-ous, *a.* [Gr. *heteroeidēs*, of a different form or kind; *heteros*, other, different, and *eidos*, form.] Diversified in form.

het-ẽr-ol′ō-gous, *a.* [*Hetero-*, and Gr. *logos*, relation, proportion.]

1. Consisting of different elements, or of the same elements in different proportions; opposed to *homologous*.

2. In medicine, differing in structure or form from the normal; as, a *heterologous* tumor, a tumor constituted of a different tissue from that of the part in or on which it is situated.

het-ẽr-ol′ō-ġy, *n.* [*Hetero-*, and Gr. *logos*, relation, proportion.] Abnormality; want or absence of relation or analogy between parts, resulting from their consisting of different elements or of the same elements in different proportions; difference in structure from the type or normal form resulting from morbid action; lack of homology.

het-ẽr-om′ăl-lous, *a.* [*Hetero-*, and Gr. *mallos*, a lock of wool.] In botany, having the leaves or stems turning in different directions, like wool, as certain mosses.

Het-e-rom′e-rȧ, *n.pl.* [Gr. *heteromerēs*, unequal; *heteros*, other, different, and *meros*, part.] A division of coleopterous insects including such as have five joints in the tarsus of the first and second pair of legs, and only four joints in the tarsus of the third pair.

het-e-rom′e-răn, *n.* One of the *Heteromera*.

het-ẽr-om′ẽr-ous, *a.* [Gr. *heteromerēs*, unequal; *heteros*, different, and *meros*, a part.]

1. In chemistry, composed of different elements, though exhibiting similar properties in certain other respects.

2. In botany, having the parts unequal in number.

3. In zoölogy, (a) with the femoral artery abnormally developed, as certain birds; (b) pertaining to the *Heteromera*.

Heteromera.—Churchyard Beetle, *Blaps mortisaga*; *a b*, four anterior feet with five joints; *c*, two posterior feet with four joints.

het″ẽr-ō-mē-tab′ō-lous, *a.* [*Hetero-*, and Gr. *metabolos*, changeable.] Differing in metamorphosis, as certain insects.

het″ẽr-ō-mọr′phiç, *a.* [Gr. *heteromorphos*, of another form; *heteros*, other, different, and *morphē*, form.] Deviating from the standard or normal form; existing under different forms at different stages of development; specifically, in entomology, undergoing complete transformation.

het″ẽr-ō-mọr′phiṣm, *n.* The quality or state of being heteromorphic; deviation from the standard or normal form.

het″ẽr-ō-mọr′phīte, *n.* A variety of jamesonite.

het″ẽr-ō-mọr′phous, *a.* Heteromorphic.

het″ẽr-ō-mọr′phy, *n.* In botany, same as *heteromorphism*.

Het″e-rō-mȳ-ā′ri-ȧ, *n.pl.* [*Hetero-*, and Gr. *mys*, muscle.] A group of mollusks having unequal adductor muscles.

het″e-rō-mȳ-ā′ri-ăn, *a.* Characteristic of the *Heteromyaria*.

het″e-rō-nē-rē′is, *n.* In zoölogy, a dimorphic sexual form of certain nereidians.

het″ẽr-ō-nom′iç, *a.* [*Hetero-*, and Gr. *nomos*, law.] Having unlike polarity; applied to contact of parts of the body in experiments in animal magnetism; opposed to *isonomic*.

het-ẽr-on′ō-mous, *a.* 1. Pertaining or relating to heteronomy; subject to the rule of another.

2. In biology, differing in some way from a common type, in any set of related things.

het-ẽr-on′ō-my, *n.* [*Hetero-*, and Gr. *nomos*, law.]

1. The state of being subject to the law or authority of another; subordination to authority from without; opposed to *autonomy*.

2. In the Kantian philosophy, subjection to the laws or restrictions imposed on us by nature or by our appetites, passions, and desires, and not by reason.

het′ẽr-ō-nym, *n.* [Gr. *heterōnymos*, having a different name; *heteros*, other, different, and *onyma*, name.] A word which has the same spelling as another, but is pronounced differently and has a different meaning, as *sow*, to scatter as seed, and *sow*, a female hog; distinguished from *homonym*.

het″ẽr-ō-nym′iç, *a.* Same as *Heteronymous*.

het-ẽr-on′y-mous, *a.* 1. Having a different name or names.

2. Pertaining to, containing, or of the nature of a heteronym.

3. In optics, said of the two images of an object as seen by the eye under certain conditions.

het-ẽr-on′y-mous-ly, *adv.* In a heteronymous manner.

het-ẽr-on′y-my, *n.* The relation of one or more heteronyms to another or others.

het″ẽr-ō-ou′si-ȧ, *n.* See *Heterousia*.

Het″ẽr-ō-ou′si-ăn, *n.* and *a.* See *Heterousian*.

Het″ẽr-ō-ou′si-ast, *n.* See *Heterousiast*.

het″ẽr-ō-ou′si-ous, *a.* See *Heterousious*.

het″ẽr-ō-path′iç, *a.* [*Hetero-*, and Gr. *pathos*, suffering.] [Rare.] See *Allopathic*.

het-ẽr-op′ȧ-thy, *n.* [Rare.] See *Allopathy*.

het″ẽr-ō-pel′mous, *a.* [*Hetero-*, and Gr. *pelma*, the sole of the foot.] In ornithology, having each of the two flexor tendons so divided that the flexor hallucis supplies the two posterior toes and the flexor perforans the two anterior toes.

Het-e-roph′ȧ-ġī, *n.pl.* [*Hetero-*, and Gr. *phagein*, to eat.] In ornithology, the *Altrices*.

het-e-roph′ȧ-gous, *a.* Requiring to be fed by others, as the young of altricial birds.

het″ẽr-ō-phā′ṣi-ȧ, *n.* [*Hetero-*, and Gr. *phasis*, a saying, from *phanai*, to say, speak.] In pathology, a species of aphasia characterized by the use of words in an improper sense.

het-ẽr-oph′e-miṣm, *n.* 1. Same as *Heterophemy*.

2. An example of heterophemy.

het-ẽr-oph′e-mist, *n.* One who is subject to heterophemy.

het″ẽr-oph-ē-mis′tiç, *a.* Pertaining to heterophemy.

het-ẽr-oph′e-mīze, *v.i.*; heterophemized, *pt.*, *pp.*; heterophemizing, *ppr.* To say one thing when meaning another.

het-ẽr-oph′e-my, *n.* [*Hetero-*, and Gr. *phēmē*, a voice, speech, saying, from *phanai*, to say, speak.] The saying or writing of one thing when another is intended, due to a disordered state of the mental faculty.

het″ẽr-ō-phō′ni-ȧ, *n.* [*Hetero-*, and Gr. *phōnē*, a voice, sound.] In pathology, a broken or cracked voice; an unnatural state of the voice.

het-ẽr-oph′ō-ny, *n.* Heterophonia.

het″ẽr-ō-phō′ri-ȧ, *n.* [*Hetero-*, and Gr. *-phoria*, from *pherein*, to bear.] In pathology, a relation of the visual lines of the two eyes other than that of parallelism.

het″ẽr-ō-phȳ-ad′iç, *a.* [*Hetero-*, and Gr. *phyas*, *phyados*, a shoot, sucker, from *phyesthai*, to grow.] In botany, producing two kinds of stems, one of which bears the fructification, and the other the sterile or vegetative branches, as species of the genus *Equisetum*.

het-ẽr-oph′yl-lous (*or* -ō-fil′lus), *a.* [*Hetero-*, and Gr. *phyllon*, a leaf.]

1. In botany, having two different kinds of leaves on the same stem, as *Potamogeton heterophyllus*, which has broad floating leaves, with narrow leaves submerged in the water.

2. In zoölogy, having different kinds of foliation or volution of the septal margins.

het″ẽr-ō-plā′ṣi-ȧ, *n.* [*Hetero-*, and Gr. *plasis*, a forming, from *plassein*, to form.] In pathology, the presence in a part, of a tissue that does not belong there normally.

het′ẽr-ō-plaṣm, *n.* See *Heteroplasia*.

het″ẽr-ō-plas′tiç, *a.* [*Hetero-*, and Gr. *plastikos*, plastic, from *plassein*, to form.] Pertaining to heteroplasia.

het′ẽr-ō-plas-ty, *n.* 1. Heteroplasia.

2. In surgery, the operation of grafting parts taken from another species.

het′ẽr-ō-pod, *n.* One of the *Heteropoda*.

het′ẽr-ō-pod, *a.* Pertaining to or characteristic of the *Heteropoda*; heteropodous.

Het-e-rop′ō-dȧ, *n.pl.* [Gr. *heteropous*, with uneven feet; *heteros*, other, different, and *pous*, *podos*, a foot.] An order of marine mollusks, the most highly organized of the *Gasteropoda*. In this order the foot is compressed into a vertical muscular lamina, serving for a fin, and the gills, when present, are collected into a mass on the hinder part of the back.

het-ẽr-op′ō-dăn, *n.* A heteropod.

het-ẽr-op′ō-dous, *a.* Same as *Heteropod*.

het″ẽr-ō-pō′lăr, *a.* [*Hetero-*, and Gr. *polos*, pole.]

1. Having polar correspondence to something other than itself.

2. In biology, having unequal or dissimilar poles, as of the primary axis.

het-ẽr-op′tẽr, *n.* One of the *Heteroptera*.

Het-e-rop′te-rȧ, *n.pl.* [*Hetero-*, and Gr. *pteron*, a wing.] A division of hemipterous insects comprising those in which the two pairs of wings are of different consistence, the anterior part being horny or leathery, but generally tipped with membrane. They comprise the land and water bugs.

Heteroptera.—*Tesseratoma Sonerattii*; *a*, scutellum, *bb*, hemelytra.

het-e-rop′te-răn, *n.* A heteropter.

het-e-rop′te-rous, *a.* Having wings differentiated; characteristic of the *Heteroptera*.

het-ẽr-op′tiçs, *n.* [*Hetero-*, and Gr. *optikos*, optic, from *opsesthai*, to see.] False optics.

het″ẽr-op-tō′ton, *n.* [Gr. *heteroptōtos*, differently declined; *heteros*, other, different, and *ptōsis*, a falling, inflection, from *piptein*, to fall.] In grammar and rhetoric, enallage of case; antiptosis.

het-ẽr-os′ciăn (-osh′ăn), *n.* [Gr. *heteroskios*, throwing a shadow, at noon, in opposite directions; *heteros*, other, opposite, and *skia*, a shadow.] One living either north or south of the equator, as contrasted with one living on the other side; so called from the fact that their shadows at noon always fall in opposite directions, the shadow in the northern zones toward the north, and that in the southern toward the south.

het-ẽr-os′ciăn, *a.* Pertaining to any portion of the earth's surface considered relatively to a certain other portion, so situated that the shadows of two objects, one being in the former and the other in the latter, fall in opposite directions.

het′ẽr-ō-sçōpe, *n.* An apparatus to test heteroscopy.

het″ẽr-os′çō-py, *n.* A difference of vision in the two eyes, a very common defect.

het-e-rō′sis, *n.* [Gr. *heterōsis*, alteration; from *heteroioun*, to alter, make different, from *heteros*, other, different.] In grammar and rhetoric, same as *enallage*.

Het″e-rō-sō′mȧ-tȧ, *n.pl.* [*Hetero-*, and Gr. *sōma*, *sōmatos*, body.] A suborder of teleostean fishes, having the body and head not bilaterally symmetrical; the flat-fishes.

het″e-rō-som′ȧ-tous (*or* -sō′mȧ-), *a.* Pertaining to the *Heterosomata*; having a body bilaterally asymmetrical.

het′ẽr-ō-sōme, *n.* One of the *Heterosomata*.

het″ẽr-ō-sō′mous, *a.* Same as *Heterosomatous*.

het″ẽr-ō-spọr′iç, *a.* Heterosporous

het″ẽr-ō-spōr′ous, *a.* [*Hetero-*, and Gr. *sporos*, seed.] In botany, having asexually produced male and female spores.

het″ẽr-ō-stat′iç, *a.* [*Hetero-*, and Gr. *statikos*, causing to stand, from *histanai*, to cause to stand.] In electricity, pertaining to an electrometer or any instrument for measuring potential, in which there is electrification independent of that to be tested.

het-ẽr-os′trō-phē, *n.* Same as *Heterostrophy.*

het″ẽr-ō-stroph′iç, *a.* Pertaining to heterostrophy.

het-ẽr-os′trō-phous, *a.* Heterostrophic.

het-ẽr-os′trō-phy, *n.* [*Hetero-*, and Gr. *strophē*, a turning, from *strephein*, to turn.] The state of being turned in a direction other than the usual one; an opposite turning, as in certain shells.

het′ẽr-ō-stȳled, *a.* [*Hetero-*, and Gr. *stylos*, a pillar.] In botany, heterogonous.

het″ẽr-ō-stȳ′lişm, *n.* The condition of being heterogonous; heterogonism.

het″ẽr-ō-taç′tous, *a.* Pertaining to or characterized by heterotaxis; specifically, (a) in geology, irregular or not uniform in arrangement or stratification; heterogeneous; (b) in botany, having organs deviating in position or arrangement from a normal type.

het″ẽr-ō-tax′iç, *a.* Exhibiting heterotaxis.

het″ẽr-ō-tax′is, *n.* [*Hetero-*, and Gr. *taxis*, arrangement, from *tassein*, to order, arrange.] Arrangement different from that existing in a normal form or type; confused, abnormal, or heterogeneous arrangement or structure.

het′ẽr-ō-tax″y, *n.* See *Heterotaxis.*

het-ẽr-ot′ō-mous, *a.* [*Hetero-*, and Gr. *tomē*, a cutting, from *temnein*, to cut.] In mineralogy, having a different cleavage; applied to a variety of feldspar in which the cleavage differs from common feldspar.

het″ẽr-ō-tō′pi-ȧ, *n.* Heterotopy.

het″ẽr-ō-top′iç, *a.* Same as *Heterotopous.*

het″ẽr-ot′ō-pişm, *n.* Heterotopy.

het-ẽr-ot′ō-pous, *a.* Characterized by heterotopy; misplaced.

het-ẽr-ot′ō-py, *n.* [*Hetero-*, and Gr. *topos*, place.]

1. In pathology, a misplacement of normal tissue, especially a congenital malformation of the brain in which masses of gray matter are found transplanted into the white.

2. In biology, a deviation from the true ontogenetic sequence with reference to the place of organs or parts.

Het-e-rot′ri-chȧ, *n.pl.* [*Hetero-*, and Gr. *thrix*, *trichos*, hair.] In zoölogy, an order of ciliate infusorians, comprising some twenty genera, and containing the largest of the species.

het-e-rot′ri-chous, *a.* Pertaining to the *Heterotricha.*

het-ẽr-ot′rō-păl, *a.* Heterotropous.

het-ẽr-ot′rō-phy, *n.* [*Hetero-*, and Gr. *trophē*, nourishment, from *trephein*, to feed, nourish.] In botany, an irregular method of deriving nutrition; applied especially to certain species of the oak family which have no root-hairs, and are dependent for nutrition upon a fungus, the hyphæ of which surround the roots and perform the functions of root-hairs.

het″ẽr-ō-trop′iç, *a.* Anisotropic; æolotropic.

het-ẽr-ot′rō-pous, *a.* [*Hetero-*, and Gr. *tropos*, a turning, from *trepein*, to turn.] In botany, having the embryo or ovule oblique or transverse to the axis of the seed.

het-ẽr-ou′si-ȧ, **het″ẽr-ō-ou′si-ȧ**, *n.* Different nature or essence.

Het-ẽr-ou′si-ăn, **Het″ẽr-ō-ou′si-ăn**, *n.* [Gr. *heterousios*, of different nature or essence; *heteros*, other, different, and *ousia*, essence, being, from *ousa*, f. of *ōn*, *ontos*, ppr. of *einai*, to be.] In ecclesiastical history, one of a branch of the Arians who affirmed that the Father and Son were unlike in substance.

Het-ẽr-ou′si-ăn, **Het″ẽr-ō-ou′si-ăn**, *a.* 1. Pertaining to the Heterousians or to their belief that the Father and Son are unlike in substance.

2. [h—] Heterousious.

Het-ẽr-ou′si-ast, **Het″ẽr-ō-ou′si-ast**, *n.* A Heterousian.

het-ẽr-ou′si-ous, **het″ẽr-ō-ou′si-ous**, *a.* In theology, having a different nature or essence.

hē′then, *a.* and *n.* Heathen. [Obs.]

hē′thing, *n.* Contempt; mockery. [Obs.]

het′măn, *n.*; *pl.* **het′măns**. [Pol., from G. *hauptmann*, head or chief man; *haupt*, head, and *mann*, man.] The title of the head (general) of the Cossacks. The heir apparent to the throne of Russia is known as the hereditary *hetman.*

het′măn-āte, *n.* The rule of a hetman.

het′măn-ship, *n.* The office or rank of a hetman.

Heū′çhe-rȧ, *n.* [Named after Prof. *Heucher*, a German botanist.] A genus of North American perennial plants of the saxifrage family, having round heart-shaped root-leaves and a prolonged narrow panicle in small clusters of greenish or purplish flowers. The root of *Heuchera Americana* is a powerful astringent, whence it is called alum-root.

heūgh, *n.* 1. A crag; a precipice; a rugged steep; a glen with steep overhanging sides. [Obs.]

2. A coal-mine; a pit. [Obs.]

heūk, *n.* A huke. [Obs.]

heū′lănd-īte, *n.* [Named after H. *Heuland*, an English mineralogist.] A mineral of the zeolite family, occurring in amygdaloid, in pearly, foliated masses, and crystallizing in the monoclinic system. It consists of silica, alumina, and lime.

heū-ret′iç, *n.* [Gr. *heuretikos*, inventive, from *heuriskein*, to invent, discover.] A branch of logic treating of discovery or invention.

heū-ris′tiç, *a.* [Gr. *heuriskein*, to invent, discover.] Serving to discover or invent.

hev′ed, *n.* Head. [Obs.]

hew, *v.t.*; hewed, *pt.*; hewing, *ppr.*; hewed *or* hewn, *pp.* [ME. *hewen*; AS. *heáwan*, to cut, hew.]

1. To cut or fell with an ax or other like instrument; often followed by *down* or *off*; as, to *hew down* a tree; to *hew off* a branch.

2. To form or shape with an edged instrument; often with *out*; as, to *hew out* a sepulcher.

> Rather polishing old works, than *hewing out* new. —Pope.

3. To chop; to cut; to hack; as, to *hew* in pieces.

hew, *n.* Destruction by cutting down. [Obs.]

hew, *n.* Color. [Obs.]

hewe, *n.* A domestic; a retainer. [Obs.]

hewed, *a.* Hued. [Obs.]

hew′ẽr, *n.* One who hews.

hew′hōle, *n.* The green woodpecker.

hewn, *v.*, a past participle of *hew.*

hex-, **hex-ȧ-**. Combining forms from Gr. *hex*, six, used in chemistry, botany, zoölogy, mathematics, etc., to signify six; as, *hexa*dactylous, *hexa*gon.

hex-ȧ-bā′siç, *a.* [*Hexa-*, and Gr. *basis*, a base.] In chemistry, designating an acid having six replaceable atoms of hydrogen.

hex-ȧ-çap′sū-lăr, *a.* [*Hexa-*, and L. *capsula*, a box.] In botany, having six capsules or seed-vessels.

hex′ȧ-cē, *n.* [*Hexa-*, and Gr. *akē*, a point.] A summit of a polyhedron formed by the combination of six faces.

hex′ȧ-çhord, *n.* [*Hexa-*, and Gr. *chordē*, a string, chord.]

1. In Greek music, (a) a diatonic series of six tones; (b) the interval of a major sixth; (c) an instrument having six strings.

2. In music, an interval of four tones and one semitone; a series of six notes.

hex-açh′rō-nous, *a.* [*Hexa-*, and Gr. *chronos*, time.] In prosody, having six moræ; hexasemic.

hex-aç′id, *a.* In chemistry, designating a base having six atoms replaceable by acids.

hex-ȧ-çol′iç, *a.* [*Hexa-*, and Gr. *kōlon*, a member.] In ancient prosody, formed of six cola or series.

hex-ȧ-çor′ăl-line, *a.* [*Hexa-*, and Gr. *korallion*, coral.] Having septa consisting of six parts, as corals.

hex-ȧ-çor′ăl-line, *n.* A hexacoralline coral.

hex′açt, *a.* Hexactinal.

hex-aç′ti-năl, *a.* [*Hex-*, and Gr. *aktis*, *aktinos*, a ray.] In zoölogy, having six rays.

hex-aç-ti-nel′lid, *a.* [*Hex-*, and Gr. *aktis*, *aktinos*, a ray.] In zoölogy, said of certain sponges having silicious six-rayed spicules.

hex-aç-ti-nel′line, *a.* Hexactinellid.

Hex-aç-tin′i-ȧ, *n.pl.* [*Hex-*, and Gr. *aktis*, *aktinos*, a ray.] In zoölogy, the *Anthozoa.*

hex-aç-tin′i-ăn, *a.* In zoölogy, said of certain polyps which have hexamerous septa.

hex′ad, *a.* [LL. *hexas*; Gr. *hexas*, *hexados*, the number six, from *hex*, six.] In chemistry, having a valence of six.

hex′ad, *n.* 1. In chemistry, an element the atoms of which have a valence of six.

2. The number six; a series of six numbers.

hex-ȧ-daç′tyl-işm, *n.* The condition or quality of being hexadactylous.

hex-ȧ-daç′tyl-ous, *a.* [*Hexa-*, and Gr. *daktylos*, a finger or toe.] Having six fingers or toes.

hex′āde, *n.* See *Hexad.*

hex′ȧ-deç-āne, *n.* [*Hexa-*, and Gr. *deka*, ten; so called because each molecule contains 16 atoms of carbon.] A semisolid hydrocarbon, $C_{16}H_{34}$, derived from petroleum; called also *hecdecane.*

hex-ad′iç, *a.* Pertaining to the number six.

hex-ȧ-em′ẽr-on, *n.* [LL. *hexaemeron*, the six days of the creation; L.Gr. *hexaēmeros*, as adj., of or in six days; *hexa*, six, and *hēmera*, day.]

1. A term of six days.

2. The history of the six 'days' work of creation, as contained in the first chapter of Genesis.

hex′ȧ-foil, *a.* Six-foiled or six-lobed.

hex′ȧ-gon, *n.* [L. *hexagonum*; Gr. *hexagōnon*, a hexagon, properly neut. of *hexagōnos*, six-cornered; *hex*, six, and *gōnia*, a corner, an angle.] In geometry, a plane figure of six sides and six angles. If the sides and angles are equal it is a regular hexagon.

hex-ag′ō-năl, *a.* 1. Having six sides and six angles; having the form of a hexagon; six-sided.

2. Formed of hexagons.

hex-ag′ō-năl-ly, *adv.* In the form or after the manner of a hexagon.

hex′ȧ-gram, *n.* [Gr. *hexa*, six, and *gramma*, a line, letter, writing, from *graphein*, to write.]

1. A figure formed of two equilateral triangles which intersect in such a way that their sides are parallel.

2. One of the sixty-four figures made up of six parallel lines, which form the basis of the Chinese Yih-king or Book of Changes.

Hex-ȧ-ġyn′i-ȧ, *n.pl.* [*Hexa-*, and Gr. *gynē*, a female.] In botany, an order of plants in the Linnean system having six styles.

hex-ȧ-ġyn′i-ăn, *a.* In botany, having six styles.

hex-aġ′y-nous, *a.* Hexagynian.

hex-ȧ-hē′drăl, *a.* Having the form of a hexahedron; having six equal superficial sides or faces.

hex-ȧ-hē′drŏn, *n.*; *pl.* **hex-ȧ-hē′drŏns** or **hex-ȧ-hē′drȧ**. [*Hexa-*, and Gr. *hedra*, a seat, base.] A solid body of six sides; especially, a cube or regular hexahedron.

hex″ȧ-kis-oç-tȧ-hē′drŏn, *n.* Same as *Hexoctahedron.*

hex″ȧ-kis-tet-rȧ-hē′drŏn Same as *Hexatetrahedron.*

hex-am′ẽr-ous, *a.* [Gr. *hexamerēs*, of six parts; *hex*, six, and *meros*, a part.] Having six parts; specifically, (a) in botany, having the parts of the flower in sixes; (b) in zoölogy, said of those anthozoans which have the radiating parts or organs arranged in sixes.

hex-am′e-tẽr, *n.* [L. *hexameter*; Gr. *hexametros*, of six measures or feet, hexameter; *hex*, six, and *metron*, a measure.] In prosody, a verse of six feet, the first four of which may be either dactyls or spondees, the fifth normally a dactyl, though sometimes a spondee, and the sixth always a spondee. In this species of vers are composed the Iliad of Homer and the Æneid of Virgil. In English hexameters accent is almost entirely substituted for length, and trochees generally take the place of spondees. The following lines from Longfellow's Evangeline are hexameters:—

> This is the | forest pri | meval. The | murmuring | pines and the | hemlocks
> Bearded with | moss, and with | garments | green, indis | tinct in the | twilight.

hex-am′e-tẽr, *a.* In prosody, composed of six feet; as, a *hexameter* verse.

hex-am′e-trăl, *a.* Hexametric.

hex-ȧ-met′riç, *a.* Consisting of six metrical feet.

hex-ȧ-met′riç-ăl, *a.* Hexametric.

hex-am′e-trist, *n.* One who writes hexameters.

Hex-an′dri-ȧ, *n.pl.* [*Hex-*, and Gr. *anēr*, *andros*, a male.] In the Linnean system of botany, a class of plants having six stamens, which are all of equal or nearly equal length.

hex-an′dri-ăn, *a.* Hexandrous.

hex-an′drous, *a.* Having six stamens.

hex′āne, *n.* [Gr. *hex*, six, and *-ane.*] In chemistry, the sixth member of the paraffin series of hydrocarbons. It is a liquid, boiling at about seventy-one degrees Centigrade, found in various natural oils.

hex-an′gū-lăr, *a.* [*Hex-*, and L. *angulus*, an angle.] Having six angles or corners.

hex-ȧ-pär′tīte, *a.* [*Hexa-*, and L. *partitus*, pp. of *partire*, to divide.] In architecture, applied to a vault divided by its arching into six parts.

Hexandria (*Scilla autumnalis*).

hex-ȧ-pet′ăl-ous, *a.* [*Hexa-*, and Gr. *petalon*, a leaf.] In botany, having six petals or flower-leaves.

hex-aph′yl-lous, *a.* [*Hexa-*, and Gr. *phyllon*, a leaf.] In botany, having six leaves.

Hex′ȧ-plȧ, *n.* [Gr. *ta hexapla*, neut. pl. of *hexaploos*, *hexaplous*, sixfold; *hexa*, six, and *-ploos*, -fold.] A collection of the Holy Scriptures in six versions in parallel columns; particularly, the collection of texts of the Old Testament published by Origen, in the third century.

hex′ȧ-plăr, *a.* Sextuple; containing six columns.

hex′ȧ-pod, *a.* [*Hexa-*, and Gr. *pous*, *podos*, a foot.] Having six feet.

hex′ȧ-pod, *n.* A six-footed animal; one of the *Hexapoda.*

Hex-ap′ō-dȧ, *n.pl.* [*Hexa-*, and Gr. *pous*, *podos*, foot.] The true or six-legged insects.

hex-ap′ō-dăn, *a.* and *n.* Same as *Hexapod.*

hex-ap′ō-dous, *a.* Six-footed; pertaining to the *Hexapoda.*

hex-ap′ō-dy, *n.* [Gr. *hexapous*, having six feet; *hex*, six, and *pous*, *podos*, a foot.] In prosody, a verse or line composed of six feet; a series of six feet.

hex-ap′tẽr-ous, *a.* [*Hexa-*, and Gr. *pteron*, a wing.] In botany, having six parts resembling wings, as a plant.

hex-ȧ-sē′miç, *a.* [LL. *hexasemus*; Gr. *hexasēmos*, containing six moræ; *hex*, six, and *sēmeion*, a sign, mark, mora.] In ancient prosody, composed of or containing six moræ; hexachronous.

hex-ȧ-stem′ō-nous, *a.* [*Hexa-*, and Gr. *stēmōn*, warp, a stamen.] In botany, having six stamens.

hex′ȧ-stich, *n.* [L. *hexastichus*; Gr. *hexastichos*, of six lines or verses; *hex*, six, and *stichos*, a row, line, verse.] A stanza or poem composed of six lines or verses.

hex-as′ti-chon, *n.* A hexastich.

hex-as′ti-chous, *a.* [*Hexa*,- and Gr. *stichos*, a row, line.] In botany, having parts arranged in six vertical rows.

hex′ȧ-stȳ-lăr, *a.* In architecture, having six columns in front.

hex′ȧ-stȳle, *a.* Hexastylar.

hex′ȧ-stȳle, *n.* [L. *hexastylus*; Gr. *hexastylos*, having six columns in front; *hex*, six, and *stylos*, a column.] In architecture, a portico or temple having six columns in front.

Hexastyle—Temple of Jupiter Panhellenius, Ægina.

hex″ȧ-syl-lab′ic, *a.* Consisting of six syllables.

hex-ȧ-tet-rȧ-hē′dron, *n.*; *pl.* **hex-ȧ-tet-rȧ-hē′drȧ.** [*Hexa-*, and Gr. *tetra*, four, and *hedra*, a seat, base.] In crystallography, a hemihedron inclosed by twenty-four scalenes.

Hex′ȧ-teuch, *n.* [*Hexa-*, and Gr. *teuchos*, a tool, implement, book.] The first six books of the Old Testament.

Hex′ȧ-teuch-ăl, *a.* Pertaining to the Hexateuch.

hex-ȧ-tom′ic, *a.* [*Hexa-*, and Gr. *atomos*, an atom.] In chemistry, consisting of six atoms; also applied to atoms that are hexavalent, and to alcohols or other compounds having six replaceable hydrogen atoms.

hex-av′ȧ-lent, *a.* [*Hexa-*, and L. *valens* (*-entis*), ppr. of *valere*, to have power.] In chemistry, having the same combining power as six hydrogen atoms.

hex-ax′ŏn, *a.* [*Hex-*, and Gr. *axōn*, an axle.] Having six axes of growth, as a spicule of a sponge.

hex′dē-cyl, *n.* [*Hex-*, and *decyl*, from L. *decem*, ten.] In chemistry, the radical, $C_{16}H_{33}$, of the hecdecane series.

hex-dē-cyl′ic, *a.* Of, relating to, or derived from hecdecane or its essential radical.

hex-ei′kō-sāne, *n.* In chemistry, a hydrocarbon, $C_{26}H_{54}$, resembling paraffin.

hex′ēne, *n.* See *Hexylene*.

hex-i-col′ō-ġy, *n.* See *Hexiology*.

hex′ine, *n.* [Gr. *hex*, six, and *-ine*.] In chemistry, a volatile compound, C_6H_{10}, of the acetylene series, derived artificially; called also *hexoylene*.

hex″i-ō-loġ′ic-ăl, *a.* Relating to hexiology.

hex-i-ol′ō-ġy, *n.* [Gr. *hexis*, a condition, state, habit, from *echein*, to have, hold, and *-logia*, from *legein*, to speak.] The science which treats of the relation of living beings to their surrounding conditions and influences.

hex-oc-tȧ-hē′drŏn, *n.* [*Hex-*, and Gr. *oktaedron*, an octahedron; *oktō*, eight, and *hedra*, a seat, base.] A solid contained under forty-eight equal triangular faces.

hex-ō′ic, *a.* In chemistry, relating to or obtained from hexane.

hex′ōne, *n.* [Gr. *hex*, six, and *-one*.] In chemistry, one of the hydrocarbons, C_6H_8, of the valylene series, obtained from certain gums and fats by distillation.

hex-tet-rȧ-hē′drŏn, *n.* See *Hexatetrahedron*.

hex′yl, *n.* [Gr. *hex*, six, and *-yl*.] The hypothetical radical, C_6H_{13}, of the hexane series.

hex′yl-ēre, *n.* [*Hex-*, and *-yl*, and ethyl*ene*.] In chemistry, one of the ethylene series of hydrocarbons, C_6H_{12}, obtained by distillation from certain coals, and also produced artificially; called also *hexene*.

hex-yl′ic, *a.* Relating to or obtained from hexyl or hexane.

hey, *interj.* [ME. *hei*, *hey*; compare D. *hei*; Sw. *hej*.] An exclamation used (a) to express surprise or joy; (b) to call attention to; (c) to incite, as dogs; (d) as an interrogative; as, *hey?* what did you say?

hey, *a.* High. [Obs.]

hey′dāy, *interj.* An expression of frolic and exultation and sometimes of wonder.

hey′dāy, *n.* [For *high-day*; ME. *hey*, high, and *day*.] Greatest vigor; high spirits.

hey′dāy-guīse, hey′de-guy, *n.* [Prob. *heyday guise*, heyday fashion.] A kind of dance; a country dance or round. [Obs.]

hey′then, *adv.* Hence. [Obs.]

hī′ȧ-quȧ (-kwȧ), *n.* [Am. Ind.] Money in the form of strings of toothshells, at one time in circulation among the Indians of the northwest coast of America.

hī-ā′tion, *n.* The act of gaping. [Obs.]

hī-ā′tus, *n.*; *pl.* **hī-ā′tus-eş** or **hī-ā′tus.** [L. *hiatus*, pp. of *hiare*, to gape.]

1. An opening; an aperture; a gap; a chasm.

2. In grammar, the concurrence of two vowels in two successive syllables or words.

3. A defect in a manuscript, where some part is lost or effaced; a lacuna.

Hib-bẽr′ti-ȧ, *n.* [Named after George *Hibbert*, an English botanist.] A genus of plants comprising about seventy species, natives of Australia; the rockroses.

hī′bẽr-nā-cle, *n.* [L. *hibernaculum*, a winter residence, pl. *hibernacula*, tents or huts for winter quarters, from *hibernare*, to pass the winter.]

1. That which serves for shelter or protection in winter; winter quarters.

2. In botany, a hibernaculum.

hī-bẽr-nac′ū-lum, *n.*; *pl.* **hī-bẽr-nac′ū-lȧ.**

1. Same as *Hibernacle*, 1.

2. In botany, a bulb or a bud in which the embryo of a future plant is inclosed by a scaly covering and protected from injuries during winter.

3. In zoölogy, (a) a case which serves as a shelter for certain insects during winter; (b) the spurious operculum of a snail.

hī-bẽr′năl, *a.* [L. *hibernalis*, from *hiems*, winter.] Belonging or relating to winter; wintry.

hī′bẽr-nāte, *v.i.*; hibernated, *pt.*, *pp.*; hibernating, *ppr.* [L. *hibernatus*, pp. of *hibernare*, to pass the winter, from *hibernus*, belonging to winter, from *hiems*, winter.] To winter; to pass the season of winter in a torpid condition in close quarters or in seclusion, as certain animals.

hī-bẽr-nā′tion, *n.* The act, state, or time of hibernating.

Hī-bẽr′ni-ăn, *a.* [L. *Hibernia*, Ireland.] Pertaining to Hibernia, now Ireland, or to its people; Irish.

Hī-bẽr′ni-ăn, *n.* A native or an inhabitant of Ireland.

Hī-bẽr′ni-ăn-işm, *n.* Hibernicism.

Hī-bẽr′ni-cişm, *n.* An idiom or mode of speech peculiar to the Irish.

Hī-bẽr′ni-cīze, *v.t.* To render into the language or idiom of the Irish; to make Irish.

hī-bẽr-ni-zā′tion, *n.* Hibernation.

Hī-bẽr′nō-Celt′ic, *n.* The native language of the Irish.

Hī-bẽr′nō-Celt′ic, *a.* Pertaining to the Irish Celts.

Hī-bẽr-nol′ō-ġist, *n.* One who studies Hibernology.

Hī-bẽr-nol′ō-ġy, *n.* [L. *Hibernia*, Ireland, and Gr. *-logia*, from *legein*, to speak.] The study of Irish antiquities and history.

Hī-bis′cus, *n.* [L. *hibiscus* or *hibiscum*; Gr. *hibiskos*, the marshmallow.]

1. In botany, an extensive genus of malvaceous plants chiefly natives of tropical climates, comprising about 150 species, which are remarkable for abounding in mucilage, and for the tenacity of the fiber of their bark. The handsome flowering shrub known in gardens as *Althæa frutex* is a species of *Hibiscus*. *Hibiscus cannabinus* is cultivated in India for its fiber, being known as Indian hemp.

2. [h—] A plant of the genus *Hibiscus*.

hic′ci-us doc′ti-us. A juggler. [Slang.]

hic′cough (-kup), *v.i.* Same as *Hiccup*.

hic′cup, hic′cough (-kup), *n.* [Imitative of the sound.] A spasmodic contraction of the diaphragm causing inspiration, followed by a sudden closure of the glottis; singultus.

hic′cup, *v.i.*; hiccuped (-kupt), *pt.*, *pp.*; hiccuping, *ppr.* To have the hiccups.

hick′-joint, *n.* In masonry, a term applied to a species of pointing in which a portion of mortar is inserted between the courses and joints of a wall, and made correctly smooth or level with the surface.

hick′ō-ry, *n.*; *pl.* **hick′ō-rieş.** [Am. Ind. *pohickory*, the hickory-tree.]

1. A North American tree of the genus *Carya*, belonging to the walnut family. Its wood is heavy, strong, and tenacious. The shagbark, *Carya alba*, yields the hickory-nut of commerce. *Carya olivæformis* yields the pecan-nut.

2. The wood of the hickory-tree.

hick′ō-ry-bŏr″ẽr, *n.* A beetle, the larvæ of which infest the bark of the hickory.

hick′ō-ry-eū-cȧ-lyp′tus, *n.* An Australian tree, *Eucalyptus punctata*, yielding a valuable wood which is used for building and other purposes.

hick′ō-ry-gïr″dlẽr, *n.* An American beetle, *Oncideres cingulatus*, which girdles the branches of the hickory.

hick′ō-ry-head (-hed), *n.* The ruddy duck.

hick′ō-ry-pīne, *n.* *Pinus Balfouriana* of western United States; also, *Pinus pungens* of eastern United States.

hick′ō-ry-shad, *n.* 1. The gizzard-shad.

2. The mattowocca.

Hicks′ite, *n.* One of a sect of Friends or Quakers founded in the United States in 1827 by Elias Hicks, and holding Unitarian doctrines.

hick′up, *n.* and *v.* [Obs.] See *Hiccup*.

hick′wąll, *n.* [Prov. Eng.] 1. A woodpecker, especially *Picus minor*, the little spotted woodpecker.

2. *Parus cœruleus*, the little blue titmouse.

hick′wāy, *n.* See *Hickwall*.

hid, *v.*, past tense and past participle of *hide*.

hid′āġe, *n.* [*Hide*, a quantity of land, and *-age*.] An extraordinary tax formerly paid to the kings of England for every hide of land.

hi-dal′gō, *n.* [Sp., contr. of *hijo de algo*, son of something; *hijo*, son, *de*, of, and *algo*, something.] In Spain, a man belonging to the lower nobility; a gentleman by birth.

hid′den, hid, *v.*, past participle of *hide*.

hid′den, *a.* Concealed; mysterious; unseen; secret.

Hidden fifths or *octaves*; in music, the consecutive fifths or octaves suggested when two voices proceed in similar (not parallel) motion to a fifth or octave.

Syn.—Secret, covert.—*Hidden* may denote either known to no one; as, a *hidden* disease; or intentionally concealed; as, a *hidden* purpose of revenge. *Secret* denotes that the thing is known only to the party or parties concerned; as, a *secret* conspiracy. *Covert* means not open or avowed.

hid′den-ite, *n.* [Named after W. E. *Hidden*.] A variety of spodumene found in North Carolina, and prized as a gem; called also *lithia emerald* from its color and composition.

hid′den-ly, *adv.* In a hidden or secret manner.

hid′den-ness, *n.* The state of being hidden or concealed. [Rare.]

hid′den-veined, *a.* In botany, having concealed veins, as certain leaves; hyphodrome.

hīde, *v.t.*; hid, *pt.*; hiding, *ppr.*; hidden *or* hid, *pp.* [ME. *hiden*, *hyden*; AS. *hydan*, to hide, conceal.]

1. To conceal; to withhold or withdraw from sight; to secrete; to cover up; as, to *hide* a book; to *hide* a wound.

> Till love, victorious o'er alarms,
> *Hid* fears and blushes in his arms. —Scott.

2. To conceal from knowledge; to keep secret; to suppress.

> Tell me now what thou hast done; *hide* it not from me. —Josh. vii. 19.

3. To protect; to keep in safety; to shelter; to remove from danger.

> In the time of trouble he shall *hide* me in his pavilion. —Ps. xxvii. 5.

To hide oneself; to put oneself in a condition to be safe; to secure protection.

> A prudent man foreseeth the evil, and *hideth himself*. —Prov. xxii. 3.

To hide the face; to withdraw support or regard.

> Thou didst *hide thy face*, and I was troubled. —Ps. xxx. 7.

To hide the face from; to overlook; to pardon.

> *Hide thy face from* my sins. —Ps. li. 9.

Syn.—Conceal, secrete, mask, dissemble, protect, disguise, screen, cover.

hīde, *v.t.*; hided, *pt.*, *pp.*; hiding, *ppr.* To beat; to flog. [Colloq.]

hīde, *v.i.* To lie concealed; to keep oneself out of view; to be withdrawn from sight.

> Bred to disguise, in public 'tis you *hide*. —Pope.

hīde, *n.* [LL. *hida*, from AS. *hid*, *higed*, a certain portion of land for the support of one family, from *hiwan*, a family.] In old English law, a certain portion of land, varying in extent from 60 to 100 acres, supposed to be sufficient for the maintenance of one family.

hīde, *n.* [ME. *hide*, *hyde*; AS. *hyd*, a skin, hide.]

1. The skin of an animal, either raw or dressed; generally applied to the undressed skins of the larger domestic animals, as oxen, horses, etc.

2. The human skin; used contemptuously.

hīde′-and-seek′, *n.* A play of children, in which some hide themselves and others seek them.

hīde′bound, *a.* 1. Having the skin sticking so closely to the ribs and back as not to be easily loosened or raised; applied to an animal.

2. Having the bark so close or firm that it impedes the growth; said of a tree.

3. Obstinate; bigoted; narrow-minded; prejudiced.

> To blot or alter what precisely accords not with the *hidebound* humor. —Milton.

4. Niggardly; penurious. [Obs.]

hid′ē-ous, *a.* [ME. *hidyous*, *hidous*; OFr. *hidos*, *hisdos*, from L. *hispidus*, rough, shaggy.]

1. Frightful to the sight; dreadful; shocking to the eye; as, a *hideous* monster; a *hideous* spectacle.

2. Shocking to the ear; exciting terror; as, a *hideous* noise.

3. Detestable; revolting.

Sure, you have some *hideous* matter to deliver. —Shak.

Syn.—Ghastly, grim, grisly, frightful, horrible.—*Hideous* describes natural objects; *ghastly*, more properly that which is supernatural; *grim* is applicable only to the countenance; *grisly* refers to the whole form, but particularly to the color.

hid′ē-ous-ly, *adv.* In a hideous manner.

hid′ē-ous-ness, *n.* The state or quality of being hideous.

hīd′ẽr, *n.* One who hides or conceals.

hīd′ing, *n.* The act of concealing or secreting; concealment.

And there was the *hiding* of his power. —Hab. iii. 4.

hīd′ing, *n.* A flogging. [Colloq.]

hī-drō′sis, *n.* [Gr. *hidrōsis*, perspiration, from *hidroun*, to perspire, sweat, from *idos*, sweat.] In pathology, (a) the formation and excretion of sweat; (b) abnormally profuse sweating; (c) any skin-disease marked by disorder of the sweat-glands.

hī-drot′iç, *a.* In medicine, inducing perspiration; sudorific.

hī-drot′iç, *n.* Any medicine that induces perspiration; a sudorific.

hīe, *v.i.*; hied, *pt.*, *pp.*; hieing *or* hying, *ppr.* [ME. *hien*, *hyen*; AS. *higian*, to hasten, to strive.]

1. To hasten; to go in haste; often with a reflexive pronoun.

The youth, returning, to his mistress *hies*. —Dryden.

hīe, *v.t.* To incite; to urge; to instigate; as, to *hie* on hounds.

hīe, *n.* Haste; diligence. [Obs.]

hī-ē′măl, *a.* [L. *hiemalis*, of winter, from *hiems*, winter.] Belonging to winter.

hī′e-māte, *v.i.* [L. *hiematus*, pp. of *hiemare*, to pass the winter, from *hiems*, winter.] Same as *Hibernate.*

hī-e-mā′tion, *n.* [L. *hiematio* (*-onis*), wintering, from *hiemare*, to pass the winter.] Hibernation.

hī′emṣ, *n.* [L.] Winter.

Hī-e-rā′ci-um, *n.* [Gr. *hierakion*, a plant, the hawkweed, from *hierax* (*-akos*), a hawk.] A large genus of plants, the hawkweeds, belonging to the aster family. There are over 300 species widely distributed throughout the temperate regions of the globe, about 25 being known in North America.

hī-ẽr-ā′cō-sphinx, *n.* [Gr. *hierax* (*-akos*), a hawk, and *sphinx*, a sphinx.] An Egyptian sphinx with the head of a hawk.

hī″e-rȧ-pi′crȧ, *n.* [LL., from Gr. *hiera*, f. of *hieros*, sacred, and *pikra*, f. of *pikros*, sharp, bitter.] A cathartic composed of pulverized aloes and canella-bark.

hī′ẽr-ärch, *n.* [LL. *hierarcha*; Gr. *hierarchēs*, a steward or keeper of sacred things; *hieros*, sacred, and *archos*, a ruler, from *archein*, to rule, lead.] One who rules or has authority in sacred things.

hī′ẽr-ärch-ăl, *a.* Pertaining to a hierarch.

hī-ẽr-ärch′iç, *a.* Pertaining to a hierarchy.

hī-ẽr-ärch′iç-ăl, *a.* Hierarchic.

hī-ẽr-ärch′iç-ăl-ly, *adv.* In a hierarchic manner.

hī′ẽr-ärch-ism, *n.* Hierarchical principles or power; hierarchal character.

The more dominant *hierarchism* of the West. —Milman.

hī′ẽr-ärch-y, *n.*; *pl.* **hī′ẽr-ärch-ieṣ.** [LL. *hierarchia*; Gr. *hierarchia*, the power or rule of a hierarch, from *hierarchēs*, a hierarch.]

1. Dominion, government, or authority in sacred things.

2. The body of persons in whom is confided the government or direction of sacred things, or a body of priests intrusted with a government; a sacred body of rulers.

3. A rank of sacred beings.

I was borne upward till I trod
Among the *hierarchy* of God. —Trench.

4. Rule by sacred persons; a form of government administered by the priesthood or clergy.

5. In science, a series of consecutive classes or groups; as, a *hierarchy* in zoölogy is made up of a kingdom, order, suborder, family, genus, and species.

hī-ẽr-at′iç, *a.* [L. *hieraticus*; Gr. *hieratikos*, of or pertaining to the priest's office, sacerdotal, from *hieros*, sacred.] Consecrated to sacred uses; sacerdotal; pertaining to priests.

hī-ẽr-at′iç-ăl, *a.* hieratic.

hiero-. A combining form from Gr. *hieros*, sacred, holy, used to signify sacred, holy, consecrated, etc.; as, *hierogram*, *hierolatry*

hī-ẽr-oç′rȧ-çy, *n.* [*Hiero-*, and Gr. *kratos*, power, from *kratein*, to rule.] Government by ecclesiastics.

hī′ẽr-ō-dūle, *n.* [*Hiero-*, and Gr. *doulos*, a slave.] In Greek antiquity, a slave dedicated to a divinity; a temple slave.

hī′ẽr-ō-glyph, *n.* [Fr. *hiéroglyphe*; Gr. *hieros*, sacred, and *glyphē*, a carving, from *glyphein*, to hollow out, carve.]

1. The figure of an animal, plant, or other object, intended to convey a meaning or stand for an alphabetical character; a figure implying a word, an idea, or a sound. Hieroglyphs are found sculptured in abundance on Egyptian obelisks, temples, and other monuments, and the term was originally applied to those of Egypt in the belief that they were used only by the priests, but has since been extended to picture-writing in general, as that employed by the Mexicans. The figure shows a cartouche containing the name Kleopatra in hieroglyphs. The objects represented are a knee, K; a lion, L; a reed, E; a noose, O; a mat, P; an eagle, A; a hand, T; a mouth, R; an eagle, A; an egg and semicircle forming a feminine affix.

Egyptian Hieroglyphs.

2. Any character having, or supposed to have, a hidden or mysteriously enigmatical significance.

hī′ẽr-ō-glyph, *v.t.* To represent by hieroglyphs.

hī″ẽr-ō-glyph′iç, *n.* Same as *Hieroglyph.*

hī″ẽr-ō-glyph′iç, *a.* [LL. *hieroglyphicus*; Gr. *hieroglyphikos*, hieroglyphic, from *hieroglyphos*, a carver of hieroglyphs; *hieros*, sacred, and *glyphein*, to carve, hollow out.]

1. Emblematic; expressive of some meaning by characters, pictures, or figures; as, *hieroglyphic* writing; a *hieroglyphic* obelisk.

2. Difficult to decipher; enigmatical.

hī″ẽr-ō-glyph′iç-ăl, *a.* Hieroglyphic.

hī″ẽr-ō-glyph′iç-ăl-ly, *adv.* In a hieroglyphic manner.

hī-ẽr-og′ly-phist, *n.* One versed in hieroglyphics.

hī′ẽr-ō-gram, *n.* [*Hiero-*, and Gr. *gramma*, a writing, from *graphein*, to write.] A writing of a sacred character.

hī″ẽr-ō-gram-mat′iç, hī″ẽr-ō-gram-mat′iç-ăl, *a.* Written in or pertaining to hierograms; relating to sacred writing.

hī″ẽr-ō-gram′mȧ-tist, *n.* A writer of hierograms.

hī-ẽr-og′rȧ-phẽr, *n.* [Gr. *hierographos*, a writer of sacred scripture; *hieros*, sacred, and *graphein*, to write.] A writer of or one versed in hierography.

hī″ẽr-ō-graph′iç, hī″ẽr-ō-graph′iç-ăl, *a.* Pertaining to sacred writing.

hī-ẽr-og′rȧ-phy, *n.* Sacred writing. [Rare.]

hī-ẽr-ol′ȧ-try, *n.* [*Hiero-*, and Gr. *latreia*, worship, from *latreuein*, to worship.] The worship of saints or sacred things. [Rare.]

hī″ẽr-ō-log′iç, hī″ẽr-ō-log′iç-ăl, *a.* Pertaining to hierology.

hī-ẽr-ol′ō-ġist, *n.* One versed in hierology.

hī-ẽr-ol′ō-ġy, *n.* [Gr. *hierologia*, sacred or mystical language; *hieros*, sacred, and *-logia*, from *legein*, to speak.] A discourse on sacred things; particularly, the science which treats of the ancient writings and inscriptions of the Egyptians, or a treatise on that science.

hī′ẽr-ō-man-çy, *n.* [*Hiero-*, and Gr. *manteia*, divination.] Divination by observing the objects offered in sacrifice.

hī″ẽr-ō-mär′tyr, *n.* [Gr. *hieromartys*; *hieros*, sacred, and *martys*, *martyr*, a witness, a martyr.] A priest who suffers martyrdom.

hī″e-rom-nē′mon, *n.* [Gr. *hieromnēmōn*, lit., mindful of sacred things, a representative at the Amphictyonic council, from *hieros*, sacred, and *mnēmōn*, mindful, from *mnāsthai*, to remember.]

1. In Greek antiquity, a sacred recorder; one of the more honorable class of representatives who composed the Amphictyonic council.

2. A minister of religion, as at Byzantium.

hī-ẽr-om′ō-naçh, *n.* [Gr. *hieromonachos*; *hieros*, sacred, and *monachos*, a monk.] In the Greek church, a monk who is also a priest.

hī′ẽr-on, *n.*; *pl.* **hī′ẽr-ȧ.** [Gr. *hieron*, neut. of *hieros*, sacred.] In Greek antiquity, a sacred place; a temple; a chapel.

Hī″ẽr-ō-nym′iç, *a.* Pertaining or belonging to St. Jerome (Hieronymus), a distinguished theologian.

Hī-ẽr-on′y-mīte, *n.* A hermit of the order of St. Jerome (Hieronymus).

hī′ẽr-ō-phant, *n.* [LL. *hierophanta*, *hierophantes*; Gr. *hierophantēs*, a hierophant; *hieros*, sacred, and *phainein*, to show.] In ancient Greece, the priest who expounded the Eleusinian mysteries; hence, one who teaches the mysteries and duties of religion.

hī″ẽr-ō-phan′tiç, *a.* Belonging or relating to hierophants.

hī-ẽr-os′cō-py, *n.* [Gr. *hieroskopia*, divination; *hieros*, sacred, and *skopein*, to view.] Divination by inspection of the entrails of sacrificial victims.

Hī″ẽr-ō-sol′y-mī-tăn, *a.* [LL. *Hierosolymitanus*, of Jerusalem, from L. *Hierosolyma*; Gr. *Hierosolyma*, Jerusalem.] Pertaining to Jerusalem.

hī″ẽr-ō-thē′cȧ, *n.*; *pl.* **hī″ẽr-ō-thē′cæ.** [Gr. *hierothēkē*; *hieros*, sacred, and *thēkē*, a box.] A receptacle in which sacred things are kept.

hī′ẽr-ŭr-ġy, *n.* [Gr. *hierourgia*, religious service, worship.] A holy work or worship. [Obs.]

hī-fȧ-lū′tin, *a.* and *n.* See *Highfalutin.*

hig′gle, *v.i.*; higgled, *pt.*, *pp.*; higgling, *ppr.*

1. To carry provisions about and offer them for sale; to peddle.

2. To chaffer; to haggle; to be tedious and parsimonious in making a bargain.

hig′gle-dy=pig′gle-dy, *adv.* In confusion or disorder; topsy-turvy. [Colloq.]

hig′glẽr, *n.* 1. One who carries about provisions for sale; a peddler.

2. One who is tedious and parsimonious in bargaining; a haggler.

high (hī), *a.*; *comp.* higher; *superl.* highest. [ME. *high*, *heigh*, *heh*; AS. *heáh*.]

1. Having a great extent from base to summit; rising much above the ground or some other object; extending to or situated at an elevation; elevated; lofty; as, a *high* mountain; a *high* tower; a *high* flight; the sun is an hour *high.*

2. Exalted morally or intellectually; exalted in excellence; lofty and chaste in style; as, a man of *high* mind; *high* attainments; *high* art.

The *highest* faculty of the soul. —Baxter.

3. Elevated in rank, condition, office, estimation, etc.; as, a *high* officer; *high* and mighty.

4. Raised above the understanding; difficult to comprehend; abstruse.

They meet to hear, and answer such *high* things. —Shak.

5. Arrogant; boastful; ostentatious; proud; lofty; as, *high* looks.

6. Loud; boisterous; threatening or angry; as, the parties had very *high* words.

7. Possessing some characteristic quality in a marked degree; extreme; intense; strong; forcible; exceeding the common measure or degree; as, a *high* wind; a *high* heat; *high* fare; a *high* color.

8. Dear; of a great price, or greater price than usual.

9. Remote from the equator north or south; as, a *high* latitude.

10. Remote in past time; early in former time; as, *high* antiquity.

11. In music, acute; as, a *high* note; a *high* voice; opposed to *low* or *grave.*

12. In cookery, tending toward putrefaction; somewhat tainted; as, game kept till it is *high.*

A high hand; audacity; oppressiveness; defiance; as, to rule with *a high hand.*

A high time or *a high old time*; a time of much excitement or jollity; a carousal. [Slang.]

High altar; the chief altar in a cathedral or church.

High and dry; completely out of the reach of water; said of a vessel ashore.

High and mighty; haughty; overbearing.

High Church; the name given to the party in the Church of England who supported the high claims to prerogative which were maintained by the Stuarts. The *Low Church* entertained more moderate notions, manifested great enmity to popery, and was inclined to circumscribe the royal prerogatives. The term *High Church*, in the Protestant Episcopal church, is generally applied to those who exalt the authority and jurisdiction of the church, and attach great value to ecclesiastical dignities and ordinances; while the terms *Low-Church party* and *Broad-Church party* are applied to those who hold moderate views in regard to these subjects.

High Commission Court; in England, an ecclesiastical court created and united to the crown by Queen Elizabeth in 1559. It was abolished in 1641.

High court of Parliament; in England, Parliament, which formerly acted as a judicial as well as a legislative body.

High jinks; an old Scotch pastime played in various ways; hence, wild sport; noisy amusement.

High life; the mode of living in aristocratic circles; life among the upper ranks of society.

High living; rich food.

High milling; a method of making flour by grinding and sifting the grain a number of times in succession, instead of subjecting it to a single grinding.

High noon; the time when the sun is in the meridian.

High place; in Scripture, an elevated place where religious rites were performed.

High priest; in Scripture, a chief priest; especially, the head of the Jewish hierarchy.

High seas; that part of the ocean or sea not within the limits of any sovereignty.

High tea; tea at which meats, puddings, etc., are served; a meal that takes the place of a late dinner.

High tide; a tide at its full; high water.

High time; full time; quite time; as, it is *high time* the matter was attended to.

High treason; treason against a kingdom, state, or ruler; the greatest civil offense.

High water; the utmost flow or the highest elevation of the tide; the time when the tide is at its full.

High-water mark; the highest point reached by the tide when full; also used figuratively; as, he has reached the *high-water mark* of success.

High-water shrub; *Iva frutescens*, a plant of the aster family which grows around the borders of salt marshes on the eastern coast of the United States.

High wine; a distilled spirit in which there is a high percentage of alcohol.

On high; at a high elevation; in heaven.

To mount the high horse; to assume a haughty bearing; to stand on one's dignity.

Syn.—Elevated, lofty, tall, eminent, exalted, noble, haughty, proud.

high, *adv.* In a high manner; eminently; powerfully; richly; luxuriously; as, excitement ran *high*; to live *high*; to tower *high*.

High and low; everywhere; in every place; as, he searched *high and low*. [Colloq.]

high, *n.* 1. An elevated place; a superior region.

2. In card-playing, the ace of trumps, or the highest card dealt, drawn, or played.

The Most High; God; the Almighty.

high, *v.i.* To rise to the greatest elevation, as the tide. [Obs.]

high'ball, *n.* A drink consisting of whisky, brandy, or other spirit, diluted with soda-water, ginger ale, or some effervescing mineral water. [Slang.]

high'bind"ẽr, *n.* A ruffian; a bully; a spy; specifically, a member of any one of certain secret societies of the Chinese.

high'-blood"ed (hī'-blud"), *a.* Of high birth; of noble lineage; highborn; as, a *high-blooded* horse.

high'-blōwn, *a.* Inflated, as with pride or conceit.

high'born, *a.* Of noble birth or extraction.

high'-boy, *n.* A chest of drawers furnished with high legs.

high'-bred, *a.* Bred in high life; having a good pedigree; possessed of good manners; having the characteristics of good breeding.

high'-built (hī'-bilt), *a.* Of lofty structure.

High'-church', *a.* Inclined to magnify the authority and jurisdiction of the church; laying great stress on a particular form of ecclesiastical rites and ceremonies; attaching the highest importance to the episcopal office and the apostolic succession, as in the Anglican church and its branches.

High'-church'ism, *n.* The principles of the High-church party.

High'-church'măn, *n.* One who holds High-church principles.

High'-church'măn-ship, *n.* The condition of being a High-churchman.

high'-col"ŏred, *a.* 1. Having a strong, deep, or glaring color.

2. Vivid; strong or forcible in representation; as, a *high-colored* description.

high'-dāy, *n.* [ME. *heigh day*, *hegh dai*; AS. *heáh*, high, and *dæg*, day.] A festival; a feast-day; a holiday.

high'-dāy, *a.* Befitting or appropriate for a holiday.

high'-em-bōwed", *a.* Having lofty arches.

high-fă-lū'tin, *a.* and *n.* I. *a.* Bombastic; high-sounding; pompous; affectedly elevated.

II. *n.* High-flown language; bombast; fustian. [Slang, U. S.]

high'-fed, *a.* Pampered; fed luxuriously.

high'-fin"ished (-isht), *a.* Finished or polished with great care; refined; elaborate.

high'-flā"vŏred, *a.* Having a strong flavor.

high'flī"ẽr, *n.* 1. One who is extravagant in opinions or pretensions.

2. A geometrid moth. *Ypsipetes ruberata* is the ruddy *high-flier*.

high'-flōwn, *a.* 1. Elevated; elated; proud.

2. Turgid; extravagant; inflated; as, a *high-flown* speech.

high'fly"ing, *a.* Extravagant in claims, pretensions, or opinions.

high'-gō, *n.* A drinking-bout; a spree; a frolic. [Slang.]

high'-hand"ed, *a.* Overbearing; oppressive; violent.

high'-heärt"ed, *a.* Full of courage.

high'-heärt"ed-ness, *n.* The quality of being high-hearted.

high'hōe, *n.* In zoölogy, the green woodpecker or yaffle.

high'hōld"ẽr, *n.* The highhole.

high'hōle, *n.* The flicker, *Colaptes auratus*.

high'lănd, *n.* 1. Elevated land; a headland.

2. A mountainous region; used often as a proper name and in the plural; as, the *Highlands* of Scotland.

high'lănd-ẽr, *n.* 1. An inhabitant of highlands.

2. [H—] An inhabitant of the Highlands of Scotland.

high'lănd-ish, *a.* Characterized by high or mountainous land.

High'lănd-man, *n.* A Highlander.

High'lănd-ry, *n.* Highlanders, collectively.

high'-line, high'-lin"ẽr, *n.* The most successful fisherman of a fishing crew. [Slang.]

high'-lōw, *n.* A kind of laced shoe reaching to the ankle.

high'-lōw'-jack', *n.* A game. [See *All-fours*.]

high'ly, *adv.* To a high degree; in a high manner.

high'men, *n.pl.* False dice so loaded as always to turn up high numbers; opposed to *low-men*. [Obs.]

high'-met"tled, *a.* Having high spirit; ardent; full of fire; as, a *high-mettled* steed.

high'-mīnd"ed, *a.* 1. Proud; arrogant. [Obs.]

2. Having honorable pride; magnanimous; opposed to *mean*.

high'-mīnd"ed-ness, *n.* The state or quality of being high-minded.

high'mōst, *a.* Highest. [Obs.]

high'ness, *n.* 1. The condition of being high in any sense.

2. A title of honor given to princes or princesses of royal blood; as, his royal *highness* the Prince of Wales.

high'-pälmed (hī'-pämd), *a.* Having high and full-grown antlers, as a stag of full growth.

high'-pitched, *a.* 1. High-strung; ambitious.

2. In music, toned at a high pitch.

high'-pres"sure (-presh"ur), *a.* Formerly, denoting those steam-engines as a class, worked by steam at a pressure greater than that of the atmosphere. [See *Low-pressure*.]

high'-priēst'hood, *n.* The dignity, position, or office of a high priest.

high'-priēst'ship, *n.* High-priesthood.

high'-prin"ci-pled (-pld), *a.* Having noble principles.

high'-proof, *a.* 1. Highly rectified; very strongly alcoholic; as, *high-proof* spirits.

2. Capable of standing any test.

high'-reach"ing, *a.* 1. Reaching to a great height.

2. Ambitious; aspiring.

high'rōad, *n.* A highway; a main road.

high'-rōll"ẽr, *n.* An individual who lives recklessly; one who leads a fast life. [Slang.]

high'-sound"ing, *a.* Pompous; noisy; ostentatious; as, *high-sounding* words or titles.

high'-spir"it-ed, *a.* Full of spirit or natural fire; easily irritated; irascible; impetuous; courageous.

high'-step"pẽr, *n.* A horse that has a high step or that carries itself proudly; hence, a person with a proud or dignified bearing. [Colloq.]

high'-stŏm"ăched, *a.* Having a lofty spirit; proud; obstinate. [Obs.]

high'-strung, *a.* Strung to a high pitch; spirited; sensitive; as, a *high-strung* woman.

high'-swell"ing, *a.* Swelling greatly; inflated; boastful.

hight (hīt), *n.* See *Height*.

hight, *v.t.* and *v.i.*; hight *or* hot, *pt.*; hight, hote (hōt), *or* hoten (hō'ten), *pp.* [ME. *highten*, *heiten*, *hoten*; AS. *hatan*, to call, name.]

1. To be called; to be named. [Obs.]

2. To command; to impel. [Obs.]

3. To intrust; to commit. [Obs.]

4. To promise. [Obs.]

high'-tā"pẽr, *n.* Same as *Hig-taper*.

hight'en-ẽr, *n.* That which heightens.

highth (hīth), *n.* A variant form of *height*. [Obs.]

high'-tōned, *a.* 1. High in sound or tone.

2. High-principled; honorable.

3. Aristocratic; fashionable. [Colloq.]

high'-top, *n.* The masthead of a ship. [Obs.]

high'ty-tigh'ty, *a.* and *interj.* See *Hoity-toity*.

high'-wa"tẽr, *a.* Of or connected with high tide.

High-water mark; see under *High*.

High-water shrub; see under *High*.

high'wāy, *n.* A road used by the public; a thoroughfare; a main road.

high'wāy-măn, *n.* One who robs on the public road, or lurks in the highway for the purpose of robbing; a highway robber.

high'-wrought (-rat), *a.* 1. Wrought with exquisite art or skill; accurately finished; elaborate.

2. Inflamed to a high degree; as, *high-wrought* passion.

hī'gre (-gẽr), *n.* [Obs.] See *Eager*.

hig'-tā"pẽr, *n.* [AS. *hig*, grass, hay, and *taper*, a taper.] The common mullen, *Verbascum Thapsus*; also called *hag-taper*.

Hij'e-rȧ, Hij'rȧ, *n.* See *Hejira*.

hike, *v.t.* To move carelessly, or with a swing or jerk; to twitch; to hitch; usually with *up*. [Colloq.]

hike, *v.i.* To tramp; to move with effort; to march laboriously, as troops over a difficult road. [Colloq.]

hike, *n.* The act of hiking or tramping; a laborious march. [Colloq.]

hī'lăl, *a.* Same as *Hilar*.

hī'lăr, *a.* 1. In zoölogy and anatomy, pertaining to a hilum, as of the kidney.

2. In botany, pertaining to the hilum or scar produced by the attachment of a seed.

hil'ȧ-rāte, *v.t.* To exhilarate. [Obs.]

hi-lā'ri-ous, *a.* [OFr. *hilarious*, *hilarieux*; L. *hilaris*, *hilarus*; Gr. *hilaros*, cheerful, glad.] Exhilarated and mirthful; exhibiting or characterized by hilarity; jolly; merry; as, *hilarious* with liquor.

hi-lā'ri-ous-ly, *adv.* With hilarity.

hi-lar'i-ty, *n.* [OFr. *hilarite*; L. *hilaritas* (*-atis*), cheerfulness, joyousness, from *hilaris*, cheerful, gay.] Excitement of the animal spirits; mirth; merriment; gaiety, especially when noisy or boisterous; jollity.

Hil'ȧ-ry, *a.* Designating the time on or near about which the festival of St. Hilary (Poitiers, France, fourth century) takes place, which is January 13 in the English calendar and January 14 in the Roman.

Hilary term; in English courts, the sitting from January 11 to Wednesday before Easter; formerly January 11 to January 31; the term before Easter.

Hil'ȧ-ry-mȧs, *n.* The festival of St. Hilary.

hilch, *v.i.* To hobble. [Scot.]

Hil'dē-brand-ine, *a.* Of, relating to, or resembling Hildebrand, who was Pope Gregory VII. (1073-85), celebrated for his vigorous methods of extending and strengthening papal authority.

hil'ding, *a.* Cowardly; base. [Obs.]

hil'ding, *n.* A wretch. [Obs.]

hill, *n.* [ME. *hil*, *hyl*; AS. *hyll*, a hill.]

1. A natural elevation of considerable size on the earth's surface; an eminence generally of a rounded or conical form rising above the common level of the surrounding land. A hill is less than a mountain and larger than a mound or hillock, but no definite limit of size can be assigned, and the term is sometimes applied to what would more properly be called a mountain.

2. A cluster of plants, and the earth raised about them; as, a *hill* of corn or potatoes.

3. A pile; a heap; a hillock; as, a dung*hill*; an ant-*hill*.

hill, *v.t.*; hilled, *pt.*, *pp.*; hilling, *ppr.* 1. To form hills or small elevations of earth around; to form into hills or heaps, as earth; as, to *hill* corn.

2. To heap up; accumulate; as, to *hill* up gold. [Rare.]

hill, *v.i.* To collect or be collected into or on a hill.

hill'-ănt, *n.* Any ant that builds ant-hills, *Formica rufa* being the common species.

hill'ber"ry, *n.* The wintergreen.

hill'bird, *n.* 1. The fieldfare. [Scot.]

2. The Bartramian sandpiper. [Local, U. S.]

hill'ẽr, *n.* A dish used in glazing pottery.

hill'-fōlk (-fōk), *n.pl.* 1. The sect otherwise called *Cameronians*; also, the Covenanters in general. [Scot.]

2. In Scandinavian mythology, a class of beings intermediate between elves and the human race, inhabiting caves and small hills.

hill'i-ness, *n.* The state of being hilly.

hill'ish, *a.* Hilly.

hill'-mi"nȧ, hill'-my̆"nȧ, *n.* [*Hill* and Hind. *mainā*, the mino-bird.] An Asiatic bird of the genus *Gracula*, resembling a starling. It may be trained to repeat words more clearly than a parrot.

hill'ŏck, *n.* [*Hill* and dim. *-ock*.] A small hill.

hill'-pär"tridge, *n.* An Asiatic partridge of the genus *Galloperdix*.

hill'side, *n.* The side or declivity of a hill.

hill'-stär, *n.* A species of humming-bird.

hill'-tit, *n.* An Asiatic songster of the family *Liotrichidæ*.

hill'top, *n.* The top of a hill.

hill'wort, *n.* 1. Wild thyme.

2. A kind of pennyroyal, *Mentha pulegium*.

hill'y, *a.* Abounding with hills; like a hill.

hil'sȧh, hil'sȧ *n.* A fish, *Clupea ilisha*, of the Ganges, highly esteemed for food. It is very oily and bony.

hilt, *n.* [ME. *hilt*; AS. *hilt*, a hilt.]

1. The handle of a sword, dagger, or similar weapon, including the guard. The plural was formerly used with a singular meaning.

2. A sword, foil, rapier, etc. [Obs.]

3. A shield-handle. [Obs.]

hilt'ed, *a.* Having a hilt.

hī'lum, *n.*; *pl.* **hī'lȧ**. [L. *hilum*, a little thing, a trifle.]

1. In botany, the eye of a bean or other seed; the mark or scar produced by the separation of a seed from its placenta.

a, Hilum in common Garden-bean.

2. In anatomy, any depression or fissure forming an inlet or outlet for nerves, bloodvessels, etc.; as, the *hilum* of the kidney. In this sense also written *hilus*.

him, *pron.* [AS. *him*, dat. of *he*, he.]
1. The objective case of *he*.
2. Himself; as, he turned *him* to the fray. [Poet.]
3. Them. [Obs.]

Him-ȧ-lā′yăn (*or* hi-mä′lȧ-yăn), *a.* [Sans. *Himālaya*; *hima*, snow, and *ālaya*, abode.] Of or relating to the Himalayas, the great range of mountains to the north of Hindustan.

hi-mat′i-on, *n.*; *pl.* **hi-mat′i-ȧ.** [Gr.] An ancient Greek mantle, usually of woolen cloth, about ten feet long by five wide. It often formed the sole garment of men and was used with a tunic by both sexes, folded around the body in various ways. It was generally held in place by the left arm.

him′ming, *n.* See second *Hemming*.

himp′ne, *n.* A hymn. [Obs.]

him′rū, *n.* [East Ind.] A cotton fabric peculiarly spun, making it thick and soft and with the feel of wool.

him-self′, *pron.*; *pl.* **them-selveṣ′.** [ME. *himself*; from AS. *him selfum*, dat. sing. of nom. *he self*, himself.]
1. An emphatic or reflexive form of the third personal pronoun masculine. It is generally used along with *he* (or a noun) when a subject, though sometimes alone; as, *he himself*, *the man himself*, did so, or *he* did so *himself*; when in the nominative after the verb *to be* it is used either with or without *he* (or a noun); as, it was *himself* or *he himself*. In the objective it stands alone (as, he hurt *himself*), or with a noun.

With shame remembers, while *himself* was one
Of the same herd, *himself* the same had done.
—Denham.

2. A having command of himself; his true character; possession of his natural temper and disposition, after or in opposition to wandering of mind, irregularity, or devious conduct from derangement, passion, or extraneous influence; as, the man has come to *himself*; let him act *himself*.
By himself; alone; unaccompanied; sequestered; as, he sits or studies *by himself*.

him-selve′, him-selv′en, *pron.* Himself. [Obs.]

Him-yar′iç, *a.* Same as *Himyaritic*.

Him′yăr-īte, *n.* [Named from *Himyar*, king of Yemen.] One of an ancient people of Semitic stock inhabiting Yemen and the surrounding country.

Him-yăr-it′iç, *a.* Of or relating to the Himyarites or to their language.

Him-yăr-it′iç, *n.* The Himyaritic language.

hin, *n.* [LL., from Gr. *hin*, from Heb. *hin*, a measure of liquids.]
1. A Hebrew measure of liquids holding about six quarts.
2. An Egyptian liquid measure of about one pint.

hī′nä-ū-tree, *n.* [Maori.] A tree, *Elæocarpus dentatus*, a New Zealand species of linden bearing an edible fruit.

hind, *n.* [ME. *hind*, *hinde*; AS. *hind*, a hind.]
1. The female of the red deer or stag.
2. A fish, the grouper; any fish of the genus *Epinephelus*.

hind, *n.* [ME. *hine*, *hyne*; AS. *hina*, a domestic servant.]
1. A domestic; a servant. [Obs.]
2. A peasant; a rustic; a countryman; a swain; a boor. [Obsolescent, except in a derogatory sense.]

hīnd, *a.*; *comp.* hinder; *superl.* hindmost *or* hindermost. Pertaining to the part which follows; in opposition to the fore part; situated or belonging in the rear or behind; back; rear; as, the *hind* legs of a dog.

hīnd′ber″ry, *n.* [So named because a favorite food of hinds.] A plant, *Rubus Idæus*, a wild variety of raspberry.

hīnd′-bōw, *n.* The cantle of a saddle.

hīnd′brāin, *n.* In anatomy, (a) the fourth cerebral vesicle or epencephalon of the embryonic medullary tube, and the pons and cerebellum developed from it; (b) the fifth cerebral vesicle or metencephalon and the medulla developed from it; (c) the entire posterior division, including both the fourth and fifth vesicles.

hīnd′ẽr, *a.* [ME. *hindere*, back, from AS. *hinder*, adv., behind.] Hind; posterior; back; rear; as, the *hinder* part of a ship.

hin′dẽr, *v.t.*; hindered, *pt.*, *pp.*; hindering, *ppr.* [ME. *hinderen*, *hindren*; AS. *hindrian*, to hinder, from *hinder*, back, behind.] To retard; to check in progression or motion; to obstruct for a time, or to render slow in motion; to interrupt; to obstruct; to impede or prevent from moving forward by any means; as, cold *hinders* the growth of plants.

hin′dẽr, *v.i.* To interpose obstacles or impediments; as, there is nothing to *hinder*.

Syn.—Prevent, impede, obstruct, oppose, delay, retard, clog, embarrass, check, block, thwart, stop, bar, counteract, encumber, inhibit.—*Hinder*, from *hind* or *behind*, signifies to cause to be behind. *Prevent*, to come before, signifies to *hinder* by coming before, or to cross another by the anticipation of his purpose. *Impede* signifies to come between a person's feet and entangle him in his progress. *Obstruct* signifies to set up something in the way, to block the passage. To *hinder* is said of that rendered impracticable only for the time being, or merely delayed; *prevent* is said of that which is rendered altogether impracticable; *hinder* is an act of the moment and supposes no design; *prevent* is a premeditated act, deliberated upon, and adopted. To *impede* and *obstruct* are a species of *hindering* which is said rather of things than of persons; *hinder* is said of both; mud *impedes*, and trees fallen across a road *obstruct* a march, each *hindering* one's arrival.

hin′dẽr-ănce, *n.*, variant spelling for *hindrance*.

hin′dẽr-ẽr, *n.* One who or that which hinders.

hīnd′ẽr-est, *a.* Hindmost. [Obs.]

hīnd′ẽr-ling, *n.* A hilding. [Obs.]

hīnd′ẽr-mōst, *a.* Hindmost.

hīnd′ẽr-night, *n.* Yesternight; last night. [Scot.]

hīnd′gut, *n.* The rear or posterior portion of the alimentary canal of an embryo, or of an invertebrate.

hīnd′hand, *n.* The hinder part of a horse.

hīnd′head (-hed), *n.* The back part of the head; the occiput.

Hin′dï, *n.* [Per. and Hind., from *Hind*, India.]
1. An Aryan language of northern India.
2. A Hindu.

hīnd′mōst, *a.* Last; in the rear of all others; superlative of *hind*.

He smote the *hindmost* of thee.—Deut. xxv. 18.

Hin′dọọ, etc. Same as *Hindu*, etc.

hin′drănce, *n.* [From ME. *hinderen*, AS. *hindrian*, to hinder.]
1. The act of impeding; the condition of being retarded.
2. Impediment, obstruction; that which hinders.

hīnd′sight, *n.* Knowledge, wisdom, discretion, or tact gained by adverse experience; afterthought; the reverse of *foresight*; as, after an opportunity has passed, one's *hindsight* shows what should have been done. [Humorous.]

Hin′dụ, Hin′dọọ, *n.* [Hind. and Per. *Hindū*, an inhabitant of India, from *Hind*, India.]
1. One of the native race inhabiting Hindustan.
2. An adherent to Hinduism.

Hin′dụ-iṣm, Hin′dọọ-iṣm, *n.* Any of various forms of modified Brahmanism with additions of Buddhistic and other religious and philosophic ideas. It is the religion of about three-fourths of the population of India.

Hin-dụ-stä′nï, Hin-dọọ-stä′nee, *n.* One of the languages of Hindustan, a form of Hindi which grew up in the camps (*urdū*) of the Mohammedan conquerors of India, since the eleventh century. It is the official language and means of general intercourse throughout nearly the whole peninsula. Called also *Urdu*.

hīne, *n.* A hind; a farm servant. [Obs.]

hing, *n.* [Hind.] Asafetida.

hinġe, *n.* [ME. *henge*, from *hangen*, *hongen*; AS. *hangian*, to hang.]
1. A natural or artificial joint or articulation connecting two parts, which permits relative motion; as, a door-*hinge*; the *hinge* of a bivalve shell.
2. That on which anything depends or turns; a pivotal principle, rule, or point; as, this was the real *hinge* on which the question turned.
3. A cardinal point, as east, west, north, or south. [Obs.]
Blank hinge; one which permits motion in either direction.
Cross-garnet, *cross-tailed*, or **T** *hinge*; a hinge having a strap on one side and a butt on the other.

hinġe, *v.t.* 1. To furnish with hinges.
2. To bend like a hinge. [Rare.]

hinġe, *v.i.* To stand, depend, or turn, as on a hinge; as, the question *hinges* on this single point.

hinġe′-joint, *n.* 1. In anatomy, a ginglymus.
2. In mechanics, a joint allowing motion in one plane only.

hinġe′less, *a.* Having no hinge.

hink, *n.* [L.G. *henk*, a hook, handle.] A hook or twibill for reaping.

hin′ni-āte, *v.i.* To hinny; to whinny. [Obs.]

hin′ny, *v.i.* To neigh.

hin′ny, *n.*; *pl.* **hin′nieṣ.** [L. *hinnus*, from Gr. *ginnos*, a hinny.] The issue of a stallion and a she-ass.

hin′ny, *n.* Honey; darling. [Scot. and Prov. Eng.]

hin′oid, *a.* [Gr. *is*, *inos*, a muscle, nerve, strength, vigor, and *eidos*, form.] Having veins which proceed entirely from the midrib of a leaf, and are parallel and undivided, as in the gingerworts.

hint, *v.t.*; hinted, *pt.*, *pp.*; hinting, *ppr.* [ME. *henten*, *hinten*; AS. *gehentan*, *hentan*, to seize, snatch.]
1. To bring to mind by a slight mention or remote allusion; to intimate; to suggest indirectly; as, to *hint* at a past occurrence; to *hint* at difficulty.
2. To seize; a variant of *hent*. [Obs.]

Syn.—Suggest, intimate, insinuate, imply.—*Suggest* is the more general term indicating an indirect or partial expression of one's ideas or desires; *intimate* is used of both slight and broad expressions of desire, especially where doubt exists; as, he *intimated* what he would do, though undecided; *insinuate* usually has a bad sense, as when one suggests evil of another indirectly; *hint* indicates the least open or direct expression of an idea, as where one's manner of speech implies one's desires; *imply* indicates that a certain idea is not expressed but may be inferred from speech or action.

hint, *v.i.* To express one's ideas or wishes by indirect means; to make some reference or allusion that may or may not be apprehended.

hint, *n.* 1. A distant allusion; slight mention; intimation; insinuation; a word or two intended to give notice, or remind one of something without a full declaration or explanation; a suggestion.
2. Occasion; moment. [Obs. or Scot.]

It was my *hint* to speak. —Shak.

hin′tẽr-land, *n.* [G., from *hinter*, back, and *land*, land.] Land extending back from a coast region; used especially of African territory; as, the government that holds the coast owns the *hinterland*.

hint′ing-ly, *adv.* In a hinting manner.

hip, *n.* [ME. *hipe*, *hupe*; AS. *hype*, a hip.]
1. The projecting part of an animal formed by the hip-bone; the haunch; the upper part of the thigh at its junction with the buttocks.
2. In entomology, the coxa.
3. In architecture, (a) the external angle at the junction of two sloping roofs or sides of a roof, whose wall-plates are not parallel; (b) the rafter at such an angle.

AA, Jack-rafters. BC, BC, Hips or Hip-rafters.

4. In engineering, the point of juncture of a sloping end-post and the upper chord of a bridge truss.
To have on the hip; to have the advantage over; a phrase borrowed probably from wrestlers.
To smite hip and thigh; to defeat completely.

hip, *v.t.*; hipped (hipt), *pt.*, *pp.*; hipping, *ppr.*
1. To sprain or dislocate the hip of, as a horse.
2. To throw over the hip, as one's opponent in wrestling.
3. To form with a hip, as a roof.

hip, *n.* [ME. *heepe*, *hepe*; AS. *heópe*, the fruit of the dogrose.] The red berry of the dogrose, *Rosa canina*.

hip, *interj.* A syllable introducing a cheer; usually repeated; as, *hip*, *hip*, *hip*, hurrah!

hip, hyp, *n.* Hypochondria; melancholy; usually in the plural; as, to be in the *hips*; to have the *hips*.

hip′-bōne, *n.* Strictly, the ischium; by extension, the entire innominate bone; also called *haunch-bone*.

hip′-gïr″dle, *n.* 1. The pelvic girdle or arch.
2. A fourteenth-century sword-belt worn diagonally from the right side of the waist to the left hip.

hip′-gout, *n.* Sciatica.

hip′halt, *a.* Lame. [Obs.]

hip′-joint, *n.* The joint of the hip, a ball-and-socket joint, formed by the reception of the globular head of the femur or thigh-bone into the socket or acetabulum of the os innominatum.

Hip-knob.

hip′-knob (-nob), *n.* An ornament placed where the hip-rafters and ridge of a roof meet.

hip′-mōld″ing, *n.* A kind of molding on the rafter that forms the hip of a roof; sometimes used to signify the back of a hip.

hipp-. A combining form. [See *Hippo-*.]

Hip′pȧ, *n.* [Gr. *hippos*, a horse.] A genus of anomurans; the sand-bugs or bait-bugs.

hip-pā′ri-ŏn, *n.* [Gr. *hipparion*, dim. of *hippos*, a horse.] One of an extinct genus of horses found as fossils in the Upper Miocene and Pliocene deposits, distinguished by the fact that each foot possesses a single fully developed toe, bordered by two functionless toes which do not touch the ground. The *hipparion* was about the size of an ass.

Hip-pē-as'trum, *n.* [*Hipp-*, and Gr. *astron*, a star.] A genus of the *Amaryllidaceæ*, consisting of bulbous plants popularly known as knight's-star lilies, usually with scarlet, crimson, or deep orange blossoms.

hipped (hipt), *a.* Having the hip sprained or dislocated.

hipped, *a.* Characterized by melancholy.

hipped, *a.* Built with hips, as a roof.

hip-pi-at'rics, *n.* Hippiatry.

hip-pi-ā'try, *n.* [*Hipp-*, and Gr. *iatreia*, healing, from *iāsthai*, to heal.] The art or practice of a veterinarian.

hip'pish, *a.* Melancholy; hipped.

hippo-, hipp-. Combining forms from Gr. *hippos*, a horse, used in zoölogy, anatomy, mythology, etc., to signify a horse; like or pertaining to a horse; as, *hippo*phagi, *hippo*crepian.

Hip-pō-bos'cȧ, *n.* [*Hippo-*, and Gr. *boskein*, to feed.] A genus of parasitic dipterous insects, including the horse-tick, *Hippobosca equina.*

hip'pō-camp, *n.* Same as *Hippocampus*, 2.

hip-pō-cam'pȧl, *a.* Pertaining to the hippocampus of the brain.

Hip-pō-cam'pus, *n.* [L., a sea-horse, from Gr. *hippokampos*; *hippos*, a horse, and *kampos*, a sea-monster.]

1. A genus of fishes, closely allied to the *Syngnathidæ* or pipe-fishes. The upper parts are like the head and neck of a horse in miniature, whence the name *sea-horse*. When swimming they maintain a vertical position, their general length is from 6 to 10 inches, and they occur in the Mediterranean and Atlantic.

2. [h—] In mythology, a creature, half horse, half dolphin, which drew the car of Neptune; also called *hippocamp*.

Hippocampus heptagonus.

3. [h—] In anatomy, either of two convolutions of the brain, *hippocampus major* being a large white curved body in the inferior cornu of the lateral ventricles of the brain, and *hippocampus minor*, a small eminence of white substance in the posterior cornu.

hip"pō-cen'taur, *n.* [L. *hippocentaurus*; Gr. *hippokentauros*; *hippos*, horse, and *kentauros*, centaur.] A centaur.

hip'pō-cras, *n.* [Fr., from L. *Hippocrates*; Gr. *Hippokratēs*, Hippocrates, a famous physician.] An old medicinal drink composed of wine sweetened and flavored with spices, lemon, rosemary, etc.

Hip-pō-crat'ic, *a.* Of or belonging to Hippocrates, a celebrated physician of Greece, regarded as the father of medicine.

Hippocratic face; the expression which the features assume immediately before death, or in one exhausted by long sickness, great evacuations or excessive hunger; so called from its being vividly described by Hippocrates.

Hip-poc'rȧ-tism, *n.* The doctrines or system of Hippocrates relating to medicine.

Hip'pō-crēne, *n.* [L., from Gr. *hippos*, a horse, and *krēnē*, a fountain.] A spring, fabled to have been produced by a stroke of the hoof of Pegasus, on Mount Helicon in Bœotia, sacred to the Muses, the waters being held to possess the power of giving poetic inspiration.

hip-pō-crē'pi-ăn, *a.* [*Hippo-*, and Gr. *krēpis*, a boot, shoe.] Horseshoe-shaped; a term used of that group of the *Polyzoa* in which the oral tentacles are arranged in a crescentic or horseshoe-like frame.

hip-pō-crē'pi-ăn, *n.* A polyzoan with tentacles arranged in a horseshoe form.

hip-pō-crep'i-form, *a.* [*Hippo-*, and Gr. *krēpis*, a boot, shoe, and L. *forma*, form.] Horseshoe-shaped.

hip'pō-dāme, *n.* A sea-horse. [Obs.]

hip'pō-drōme, *n.* [L. *hippodromos*; Gr. *hippodromos*, a race-course, hippodrome; *hippos*, a horse, and *dromos*, a course, running, from *dramein*, to run.]

1. In ancient Greece, a circus or place in which horse-races and chariot-races were run and horses exercised; sometimes applied to a modern circus, especially that portion comprising feats of horsemanship.

2. A contest, as a race or game, in which the result is fraudulently prearranged. [Slang.]

hip'pō-drōme, *v.i.* To conduct or engage in a contest the result of which has been prearranged.

hip'pō-griff, *n.* [Fr. *hippogriffe*, from Gr. *hippos*, a horse, and *gryps*, a griffin.] A fabulous monster, whose head and forefeet were those of a griffin, but whose hindquarters were those of a horse; a medieval invention; written also *hippogriffin* and *hippogryph*.

hip'poid, *a.* [Gr. *hippos*, a horse, and *eidos*, form, resemblance.] Horselike; having characteristics of a horse.

hip'pō-lith, *n.* [*Hippo-*, and Gr. *lithos*, a stone.] A bezoar found in the alimentary canals of horses.

hip-pol'ō-gy, *n.* [*Hippo-*, and Gr. *-logia*, from *legein*, to speak.] Systematic knowledge concerning the horse.

hip"pō-pȧ-thol'ō-gy, *n.* [*Hippo-*, and Gr. *pathos*, suffering, and *-logia*, from *legein*, to speak.] The science of veterinary medicine; the pathology of the horse.

hip-poph'ȧ-gī, *n.pl.* [Gr. *hippophagos*, horse-eating; *hippos*, horse, and *phagein*, to eat.] Those who feed upon horseflesh.

hip-poph'ȧ-ġism, *n.* Same as *Hippophagy.*

hip-poph'ȧ-gist, *n.* One who feeds on horseflesh.

hip-poph'ȧ-gous, *a.* Eating horseflesh.

hip-poph'ȧ-gy, *n.* The act or practice of feeding on horseflesh.

hip'pō-phīle, *n.* [*Hippo-*, and Gr. *philos*, loving.] A horse-lover.

Hippopotamus (*Hippopotamus amphibius*).

hip-pō-pot'ȧ-mus, *n.* [L. *hippopotamus*; Gr. *hippopotamos*, a river-horse; *hippos*, horse, and *potamos*, river.] A pachydermatous mammal, having a thick and square head, a very large muzzle, small eyes and ears, thick and heavy body, short legs terminated by four toes, a short tail, skin about two inches thick on the back and sides, and no hair, except at the extremity of the tail. The hippopotamus inhabits nearly the whole of Africa, and its flesh is eaten by the natives. It has been found of the length of seventeen feet, and stands about five feet high. It delights in water, living in lakes and rivers, and feeding on water-plants or herbage growing near the water. Also called *river-horse*.

hip-pot'ō-my, *n.* [*Hippo-*, and Gr. *tomē*, a cutting, from *temnein*, to cut.] The anatomy of the horse.

hip-pū'ric, *a.* [Gr. *hippos*, a horse, and *ouron*, urine.] Pertaining to or derived from the urine of a horse.

Hippuric acid; a monobasic acid derived from the urine of horses and cows. It forms colorless, transparent, lustrous prisms.

Hip-pū'ris, *n.* [L., from Gr. *hippouris*, decked with a horsetail, also a plant called the mare's-tail; *hippos*, horse, and *oura*, tail.]

1. A genus of plants of the order *Halorageæ*, the mare's-tails. *Hippuris vulgaris* grows in pools and marshes throughout the temperate and cold regions of the globe. It is a tall plant with whorls of narrow leaves and inconspicuous flowers.

2. [h—] In anatomy, the final division of the spinal marrow, the *cauda equina*, or horse-tail.

hip'pū-rīte, *n.* [Gr. *hippouris*, horsetailed, and *-ite*.] An extinct bivalve mollusk of genus *Hippurites*, occurring in the Chalk formation.

hip'=raft"ẽr, *n.* A timber at the angle of a hip-roof.

hip'=roof, *n.* A roof the ends of which rise immediately from the wall-plates without a gable.

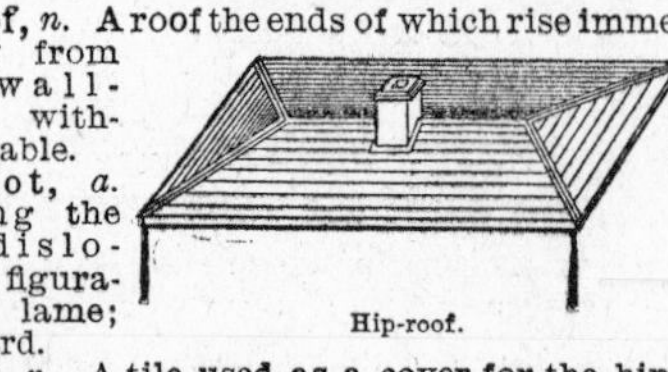

Hip-roof.

hip'shot, *a.* Having the hip dislocated; figuratively, lame; awkward.

hip'=tile, *n.* A tile used as a cover for the hips of roofs.

hip'=tree, *n.* Same as *Dogrose.*

hip'wŏrt, *n.* A plant, *Cotyledon umbilicus*, whose leaf is like a hip-socket.

hīr, *pron.* Her; their. [Obs.]

hīr'cic, *a.* [L. *hircus*, a goat.] Pertaining to or derived from the goat.

hīr'cine, hīr-cī'nous, *a.* [L. *hircinus*, from *hircus*, a goat.] Pertaining to or resembling a goat; smelling like a goat.

hire, *v.t.*; hired, *pt.*, *pp.*; hiring, *ppr.* [ME. *hiren*, *hyren*; AS. *hyrian*, to hire.]

1. To engage the services of; to procure for temporary use for a compensation; to contract to give an equivalent or pay a certain price for the use or services of; as, to *hire* a farm; to *hire* a servant.

2. To grant the temporary use of, or agree to give the services of, for a price, reward, or compensation; to lease; to let; often used with *out*; as, he *hired out* (himself) as a farm-hand; he *hired* his horse to the miller.

Hired girl; a maidservant; a maid of all work.
Hired man; a gardener, stableman, or farm-hand.

hire, *n.* [ME. *hire*, *hyre*; AS. *hyr*, hire, rent, service.]

1. The price or compensation paid or contracted to be given for the temporary use of anything, or paid for personal services; wages; rent; hence, any compensation; a bribe.

2. In law, a bailment in which property is delivered for temporary use for a consideration.

hire'less, *a.* Without hire.

hire'ling, *n.* [ME. *hyrling*; AS. *hyrling*, a hireling; *hyr*, hire, and *-ling*.] One who is hired or who serves for wages; a mercenary.

hire'ling, *a.* Serving for wages; venal; mercenary; employed for money or other compensation.

hīr'ẽr, *n.* One who hires.

hīr'ing, *n.* 1. In law, a species of contract of bailment for a consideration, in which a chattel is delivered to a bailee for his temporary use, for the performance of some labor upon it, or for transportation; the *locatum* of the civil law.

2. A fair at which servants assemble to be hired. [Prov. Eng.]

hīr'mos, hīr'mus, *n.*; *pl.* **hīr'moi, hīr'mī.** [LL. *hirmos*; Gr. *eirmos*, a series, context, from *eirein*, to fasten together, join.] In the Greek church, a stanza or strophe of an ode, used as a model for the rhythm and music of others of the same measure.

hīr-on-delle', *n.* [L. *hirundo*, a swallow.] In heraldry, a swallow as a charge.

hīr'ple, *v.i.* To limp; to hobble; to halt. [Scot.]

hīrst, *n.* [Obs.] See *Hurst.*

hīr-sūte', *a.* [L. *hirsutus*, rough, shaggy, bristly.]

1. Rough with hair; hairy; shaggy; set with bristles.

2. In biology, having a rough or stiff pubescence.

3. Boorish. [Obs.]

hīr-sūte'ness, *n.* Hairiness.

hīr-sū'ti-ēs, *n.* [L. *hirsutus*, hairy.] In entomology, a thick covering of hair; hairiness.

hīr-tel'lous, *a.* [Dim. from L. *hirtus*, hairy, shaggy.] Having a minute rigid pubescence.

hi-rụ'dine, *a.* [L. *hirudo* (*-inis*), a leech.] Relating to leeches.

Hir-ū-din'ē-ȧ, *n.pl.* [L. *hirudo* (*-inis*), a leech.] An order of annelids provided with a suctorial disk at one or both ends; the leeches.

hi-rụ'din-oid, *a.* Like a leech; hirudine.

Hi-rụ'dō, *n.* [L.] A genus of the *Hirudinea*, including the common medical leech, *Hirudo medicinalis.*

hi-run'dine, *a.* [L. *hirundineus*, from *hirundo* (*-inis*), a swallow.] Relating to swallows.

Hi-run'dō, *n.* [L., a swallow.] A genus of passerine birds, including the barn-swallows.

his, *pron.* [AS. *his*, of him, his, genit. masc. and neut. of *he.*]

1. The possessive case of *he*; often used adjectively; as, the book is *his*; it is *his* book.

2. Formerly, the possessive case of *it*; also, erroneously used as a sign of the possessive of any noun considered masculine; as, the man *his* ground, the man's ground.

his'ing-ẽr-īte, *n.* [Named after W. *Hisinger*, a Swedish mineralogist.] A soft, black, iron ore, consisting of silica and iron.

hisn, *pron.* A colloquial form of *his*, imitating *mine* or *thine*, used only absolutely; as, this is mine, that is *hisn*.

His-pan'ic, *a.* [L. *Hispanicus*, from *Hispania*, Spain.] Belonging to Spain or to the Spanish tongue or people.

His-pan'i-cism, *n.* An idiom or mode of speech peculiar to the Spanish tongue.

His-pan'i-cize, *v.t.* To make Spanish in style.

his'pid, *a.* [L. *hispidus*, rough, bristly.] Rough with bristles or minute spines; bristly.

his-pid'ū-lous, *a.* Having small, short bristles.

hiss, *v.i.*; hissed (hist), *pt.*, *pp.*; hissing, *ppr.* [ME. *hissen*, *hyssen*; AS. *hysian*, to hiss; imitative in origin.]

1. To make a sound like that of the letter *s* by driving the breath between the tongue and the upper teeth, especially in contempt or disapprobation.

> The merchants among the people shall *hiss* at thee. —Ezek. xxvii. 36.

2. To emit any similar sound; said of serpents, geese, and other animals, of water thrown on hot metal, of steam rushing through a small orifice, etc.

3. To whizz, as an arrow or other thing in rapid flight.

hiss, *v.t.* 1. To condemn or express disapproval of by hissing; as, the spectators *hissed* him off the stage.

> That of an hour's age doth *hiss* the speaker. —Shak.

2. To utter hissingly; as, he *hissed* his threats.

hiss, *n.* 1. The sound made by propelling the breath between the tongue and upper teeth, as in pronouncing the letter *s*, especially as expressive of disapprobation.

2. Any similar sound, as the noise made by an angry goose, a serpent, escaping steam, water touched by hot metal, etc.

hiss′ing, *n.* 1. A hiss; an expression of scorn or contempt.

2. The occasion or object of scorn and derision.

I will make this city desolate, and an *hissing*. —Jer. xix. 8.

hiss′ing-ly, *adv.* With a hissing sound.

hist, *interj.* A sibilant utterance commanding silence; equivalent to hush! hark! be silent!

his′ti-oid, *a.* [Gr. *histion*, dim. of *histos*, web or tissue, and *eidos*, form.] Resembling normal tissue.

his-ti-ol′ō-ġy, *n.* Same as *Histology*.

histo-. A combining form from Gr. *histos*, web, tissue. It is used in anatomy, medicine, biology, etc., to signify tissue or relation to tissue; as, *histo*logic, *histo*genesis.

his-tō-ċhem′iç-ăl, *a.* Pertaining to histochemistry.

his-tō-ċhem′is-try, *n.* [*Histo-*, and Gr. *chēmeia*, fusion.] That branch of chemistry which treats of the chemical structure of organic tissues and the products of their decomposition.

his-tō-ġen′e-sis, *n.* [*Histo-*, and Gr. *genesis*, generation.] Same as *Histogeny*.

his-tō-ġē-net′iç, *a.* Of or belonging to histogeny.

his-tō-ġen′iç, *a.* Tissue-forming; histogenetic.

his-toġ′e-ny, *n.* [*Histo-*, and Gr. *-genēs*, producing.] The genesis and growth of organic tissues.

his-tog′ra-phẽr, *n.* [*Histo-*, and Gr. *graphein*, to write.] A writer of histography.

his-tō-graph′iç, his-tō-graph′iç-ăl, *a.* Of or belonging to histography.

his-tog′ra-phy, *n.* [*Histo-*, and Gr. *-graphia*, from *graphein*, to write.] A treatise upon organic tissues or histogenetic processes.

his-tō-hem′ȧ-tin, *n.* [*Histo-*, and Gr. *haima* (*-atos*), blood, and *-in*.] One of a series of pigments contained in the tissues of invertebrates.

his′toid, *a.* Like or composed of tissue, especially of connective tissue.

his-tō-loġ′iç, his-tō-loġ′iç-ăl, *a.* Of or belonging to histology; dealing with the microscopic structure of the tissues of organic bodies.

his-tō-loġ′iç-ăl-ly, *adv.* In a histologic manner.

his-tol′ō-ġist, *n.* One who is skilled in histology.

his-tol′ō-ġy, *n.* [*Histo-*, and Gr. *-logia*, from *legein*, to speak.] Microscopic anatomy; that part of biology dealing with the microscopic structure of tissues.

his-tol′y-sis, *n.* [*Histo-*, and Gr. *lysis*, a loosing, from *lyein*, to loose.] The disintegration or dissolution of organic tissue.

his-tō-lyt′iç, *a.* Of or belonging to histolysis.

his-ton′ō-my, *n.* [*Histo-*, and Gr. *nomos*, law.] The laws of the development and arrangement of organic tissue.

his-toph′y-ly, *n.* [*Histo-*, and Gr. *phylē*, a clan, tribe.] In zoölogy, the history of the cells of any phylum or tribe.

his-tō-phys″i-ō-loġ′iç-ăl, *a.* Relating to the physiology of the tissues.

his-tō′ri-ăl, *a.* Historical. [Obs.]

his-tō′ri-ăn, *n.* [OFr. *historien*, from L. *historia*, history.] A writer or compiler of history; one who is skilled in historical study.

his-tō′ri-ā-ted, *a.* Decorated with significant figures of animals, human beings, flowers, and the like, as the manuscripts of the middle ages.

his-tor′iç, his-tor′iç-ăl, *a.* [L. *historicus*; Gr. *historikos*, from *historia*, history.]

1. Containing history or the relation of facts; as, a *historical* poem; *historic* brass.

2. Pertaining to history or historians; as, *historic* care or fidelity.

3. In grammar, used in narration of past actions or facts; as, the *historical* present.

4. Famous in history; as, *historic* scenes.

Historical method; a method of treatment founded upon the study of the historical development of a subject.

Historical painting; a painting dealing with historic events or characters.

Historical sense; that meaning of a passage which is deduced from the circumstances of time, place, etc., under which it was written.

The historic sense; the capacity of grasping and understanding historical facts in all their bearings, and of picturing them in the mind with their concomitant circumstances.

his-tor′iç-ăl-ly, *adv.* In the manner of history; according to history; by way of narration.

his-tor′iç-ăl-ness, *n.* The state of being historical.

his-tō-riç′i-ty, *n.* Historicalness. [Rare.]

his-tor′i-cize, *v.t.* To put on record; to narrate as history. [Rare.]

his′tō-ried (-rid), *a.* Recorded in history; storied.

his-tō′ri-ẽr, *n.* A historian. [Obs.]

his″tō-ri-ette′, *n.* [Fr., dim. of *histoire*; L. *historia*, history.] A brief history; a short story or narrative.

his-tor′i-fȳ, *v.t.* To relate; to record in history; to chronicle. [Rare.]

his-tō-ri-og′rȧ-phẽr, his-tō′ri-ō-grȧph, *n.* [Gr. *historia*, history, and *graphein*, to write.] A historian; a writer of history; particularly, a historian employed or appointed by a government or society; as, the *historiographer* to the king of France.

his-tō-ri-og′rȧ-phẽr-ship, *n.* The position or rank of historiographer.

his-tō-ri-og′rȧ-phy, *n.* The art or employment of a historian; history.

his-tō-ri-ol′ō-ġy, *n.* [Gr. *historia*, history, and *-logia*, from *legein*, to speak.] A discourse on history; the science of history.

his-tō-ri-on′ō-mẽr, *n.* [Gr. *historia*, history, and *nomos*, law.] One familiar with the laws and facts of history.

his′tō-rīze, *v.t.* To chronicle.

his′tō-ry, *n.*; *pl.* **his′tō-rieṣ**. [L. *historia*; Gr. *historia*, a learning by inquiry, knowledge, a narrative, from *histōr* or *istōr*, knowing, learned, a wise man, from the root of *eidenai*, to know.]

1. Narration; the relation of facts or events; a narrative, written or oral; especially, a systematic narrative of events and circumstances relating to man in his social or civic condition; a narration or account of the progress of a nation, an institution, or any phase of human thought or action; an account of any event or series of events. When the narrative deals with the life of an individual, it is a *biography*; if it concerns the life of the narrator, it is an *autobiography*; when dealing with facts within the personal observation or experience of the narrator, it is a *memoir*; when relating to a journey or journeys, it may be termed *travels*. A record of events arranged according to succession in time is a *chronicle*; *annals* are strictly a *chronicle* divided into distinct years, but the word is used poetically for *history*. The divisions of *history* in relation to periods of time have been reckoned three: (a) *ancient history*, which includes the history of the nations of antiquity, and reaches down to the destruction of the Roman Empire, A. D. 476; (b) *medieval history*, which begins with 476 and comes down to the discovery of America in 1492 or to the Reformation; (c) *modern history*, from either of these eras to our own times. *History* often deals with special subjects; as, a *history* of government, of war, of law, of commerce, of art, of the crusades, etc.; when it deals with facts in nature, it is *natural history*.

2. That branch of knowledge which deals with events that have taken place in the world's existence; the study or investigation of the past; as, he is fond of *history*.

3. Fact or facts recorded or accomplished; past events collectively, or such past events as concern any particular period, nation, individual, subject, etc.; as, the supreme event of its *history*; a checkered *history*.

4. A career or past full of events or worthy of narration; as, a woman with a *history*.

5. A play or drama treating of historical events or characters.

his′tō-ry, *v.t.* To record; to relate; to chronicle. [Rare.]

his′tō-ry-piēce, *n.* An artistic pictorial representation of any historical event.

his-tot′ō-my, *n.* [*Histo-*, and Gr. *tomē*, a cutting.] In surgery, the act of dissecting organic tissues.

his-tō-troph′iç, *a.* [*Histo-*, and Gr. *trophē*, nourishment.] Tissue-building; histogenic.

his′tō-zȳme, *n.* [*Histo-*, and Gr. *zymē*, leaven.] One of the soluble animal ferments.

his′tri-ŏn, *n.* [L. *histrio* (*-onis*), a stage-player, from Etruscan *hister*, a buffoon.] A player; an actor. [Obs.]

his-tri-on′iç, his-tri-on′iç-ăl, *a.* 1. Pertaining to a stage-player or to stage-playing; befitting a theater; theatrical; unreal; feigned.

2. Of or pertaining to the muscles of expression; as, *histrionic* spasm.

his-tri-on′iç-ăl-ly, *adv.* In a histrionic manner; theatrically.

his-tri-on′i-ciṣm, *n.* The art of dramatic representation; a theatrical effect.

his-tri-on′içs, *n.pl.* The art of acting; hence, theatrical manners; as, she indulged in *histrionics*.

his′tri-ō-niṣm, *n.* The acts or practice of stage-players; stage-playing; hence, affectation.

his′tri-ō-nize, *v.t.* To act; to portray dramatically.

hit, *v.t.*; hit, *pt.*, *pp.*; hitting, *ppr.* [ME. *hitten*, *hytten*, to hit, meet with; AS. *hittan*, from Ice. *hitta*, to hit upon, meet with.]

1. To strike or touch with some degree of force, especially an object aimed at as a mark; not to miss; to give a blow to, literally or figuratively.

2. To reach or attain to (an object desired); to effect successfully; to light upon; to reproduce successfully; to get hold of or come at; to guess.

Birds learning tunes *hit* the notes right. —Locke.

3. To suit; to be conformable to; to fit; to agree with; as, this *hits* my fancy.

4. In backgammon, to take up, as a man lying single or uncovered, by moving a man of one's own to its point.

To hit off; (a) to determine luckily; as, *to hit off* a secret; (b) to represent or describe by characteristic strokes or hits; as, he *hit off* his manner to perfection. [Obs.]

To hit the pipe; to smoke opium. [Slang.]

hit, *v.i.* 1. To strike; to meet or come in contact; to clash; often followed by *against* or *on*.

If bodies be extension alone, how can they move and *hit* one *against* another?—Locke.

2. To meet or fall on by good luck; to succeed by accident; not to miss.

And oft it *hits*
Where hope is coldest, and despair most shifts. —Shak.

3. To strike or reach the intended point; to succeed; to suit.

And millions miss for one that *hits*.—Swift.

To hit on or *upon*; to light on; to come to or fall on by chance; to meet or find, as by accident.

To hit out; to strike out with the fists.

hit, *n.* 1. A striking against; the collision of one body against another; a stroke or blow.

2. A chance; a casual event; especially, a lucky chance or fortunate event; a successful attempt; as, a lucky *hit*.

3. A striking expression or turn of thought which seems to be peculiarly applicable or to hit the point; as, he made some happy *hits* in his reply.

4. In backgammon, (a) a move which puts an opponent's man for a time out of play and makes him move from the original starting-place; (b) a game won in which the opponent has thrown off one or more of his men.

5. In baseball, a striking of the ball by the batsman; especially, a base-hit.

hit, *pron.* [Obs.] Same as *It*.

hit, *v.*, obsolete third person singular present tense of *hide*; a contraction of *hideth*.

hitch, *v.i.*; hitched (hicht), *pt.*, *pp.*; hitching, *ppr.* [ME. *hitchen*, *hytchen*, *hychen*, prob. from O.D. *hutsen*, to shake, jolt.]

1. To move by jerks or with stops; as, to *hitch* along.

2. To become entangled; to be caught or hooked.

3. To hit the feet together in going, as a horse. [Eng.]

4. To agree or work well together; as, their ideas do not *hitch*. [Colloq.]

hitch, *v.t.* 1. To hook; to catch by a hook; as, to *hitch* a bridle.

2. To fasten by a hitch; as, to *hitch* a horse by a bridle or to *hitch* him to a post.

3. To move with jerks, as a chair.

To hitch up; (a) to harness or attach, as a horse to a vehicle; (b) to raise or lift with a jerk.

hitch, *n.* 1. A catch; an impediment; an obstruction; a break-down; a failure; a stoppage; an obstacle, especially of a casual and temporary nature; as, there is some *hitch* in the proceedings; a *hitch* in one's gait.

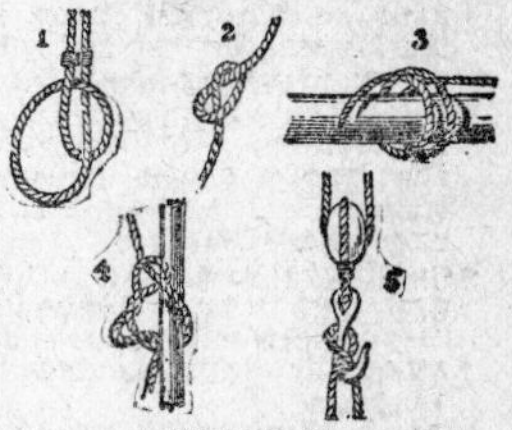

2. The act of catching, as on a hook, etc.

3. A knot or noose in a rope for fastening it to another rope, a hook, a ring or other object; as, a clove-*hitch*; a timber-*hitch*; a rolling *hitch*. etc.

Hitch Knots.
1, 2. Half-hitches. 3. Clove-hitch. 4. Timber-hitch. 5. Blackwall hitch.

4. In mining, a slight dislocation of a vein or bed.

5. A heave or pull-up; as, to give trousers a *hitch*.

6. Temporary assistance; help through a difficulty. [Colloq.]

Blackwall hitch; a hitch in which the rope is put across a hook so as to jam under a strain, yet remain easily detachable when the strain ceases.

hitch′el, *v.t.* To hatchel. [Obs.]

hithe, *n.* [ME. *hithe*, *hythe*; AS. *hyth*, a port, haven.] A port or small haven; obsolete except in compounds, as in Queen*hithe*.

hith′ẽr, *adv.* [AS. *hider*, *higder*, hither.]

1. To this place; used with verbs signifying motion; as, to come *hither*; to bring *hither*.

2. To this point; to this argument or topic; to this end; to this time. [Rare.]

Hither and thither; to this place and that; to and fro.

hith'ẽr, *a.* Nearest; toward the person speaking; as, the *hither* side of a hill; the *hither* end of a house.

On the hither side of; younger than; as, she is *on the hither side of* forty.

hith'ẽr-mōst, *a.* Nearest on this side.

hith'ẽr-tö, *adv.* 1. To this time; till now.

2. To this place; to a prescribed limit. [Obs.]

hith'ẽr-wărd, *adv.* [AS. *hiderweard*; *hider*, hither, and *-weard*, -ward.] This way; toward this place; hither.

hit'tẽr, *n.* One who hits or strikes.

Hit'tite, *n.* [LL. *Hethæus* (pl. *Hethæi*), a Hittite; Heb. *Khittim*, Hittites.] A member of a Hamitic race mentioned in the Old Testament, inhabiting Asia Minor and Syria. Their rock-sculptures and the ruins of their temples are found near Smyrna, in Cappadocia, and as far as Lydia to the west. They seem to have been very powerful and highly civilized.

hīve, *v.t.*; hived, *pt.*, *pp.*; hiving, *ppr.* 1. To collect into a hive; to cause to enter a hive; as, to hive bees.

2. To contain; to receive, as a habitation, or place of deposit; to store.

Where all delicious sweets are *hived*.
—Cleaveland.

hīve, *v.i.* To take shelter or lodgings together; to reside in a collective body, after the manner of bees.

hīve, *n.* [ME. *hive*, *hyve*; AS. *hyfe*, a hive.]

1. A box, chest, basket, or other shelter or cell for the reception and habitation of a swarm of honeybees.

2. A swarm of bees; the bees of a single colony, inhabiting a hive.

3. A busy swarm; any bustling group, company, or organization supposed to resemble a hive of bees; as, the social *hive*; a *hive* of industry.

hīve'=bee, *n.* The ordinary honeybee.

hīve'less, *a.* Having no hive.

hīve'=nest, *n.* A group of nests built together or a large nest built and occupied by several pairs of birds in common, as those of the weaver-birds.

hīv'ẽr, *n.* One who collects bees into a hive.

hīveș, *n.* [Origin obscure.]

1. Croup; laryngitis; rattles.

2. Urticaria or nettle-rash, and certain other affections of the skin.

hīve'=vine, *n.* A trailing evergreen herb, *Mitchella repens*, of the madder family; called also *partridge-berry*.

hizz, *v.i.* To hiss. [Obs.]

hō, *interj.* 1. A call or cry to excite attention or give notice of approach; also, an exclamation of satisfaction.

2. An expression of contempt, wonder, mirth, etc.

3. A call used by teamsters, to stop their teams; usually written *whoa*.

hō, *n.* Stop; moderation; end. [Obs.]

hō-aç̧t'zin, hō-aç̧'zin, *n.* A South American bird, *Opisthocomus cristatus*, somewhat resembling a curassow and about the size of a peacock. It is usually olive-green with a crest of yellow.

hōar, *a.* [ME. *hore*, *hoor*; AS. *har*, hoary, gray-haired.]

1. White; as, *hoar* frost; *hoar* cliffs.

2. Gray; white with age; hoary; as, a matron grave and *hoar*.

3. Of great antiquity; ancient; as, religions *hoar*.

4. Musty; moldy. [Obs.]

hōar, *n.* Hoariness; antiquity. [Rare.]

hōar, *v.i.* 1. To become moldy or musty. [Obs.]

2. To grow white with age. [Rare.]

hōard, *n.* [ME. *hord*; AS. *hord*, hoard, store, treasure.]

1. A store, stock, or quantity of anything accumulated or laid up; a treasure; as, a *hoard* of provisions for winter; a *hoard* of money.

2. A place in which anything is hoarded.

hōard, *v.t.* and *v.i.*; hoarded, *pt.*, *pp.*; hoarding, *ppr.* [ME. *horden*; AS. *hordian*, to hoard, from *hord*, a hoard, treasure.]

I. *v.t.* To collect and lay up; to store secretly; as, to *hoard* silver and gold.

II. *v.i.* To collect and form a hoard; to lay up store; as, she *hoarded* all her life.

hōard'ẽr, *n.* One who lays up a hoard.

hōard'ing, *n.* 1. An inclosure or fence about a building, materials, etc., during the process of construction. [Eng.]

2. A billboard. [Eng.]

3. In medieval fortification, a wooden structure built above or about the walls of a fortress.

hōared, *a.* Moldy; musty. [Obs.]

hōar'frost, *n.* White frost; the white particles formed by the congelation of dew.

hōar'hound, hōre'hound, *n.* [ME. *horhowne*, *horone*, *horehune*; AS. *harhune*, hoarhound; *har*, hoar, white, and *hune*, hoarhound.] Any one of several plants of different genera. The common hoarhound, *Marrubium vulgare*, has a bitter taste, and is used as a tonic, also as a remedy for coughs and colds. It is widely distributed throughout Europe and naturalized in North America.

hōar'i-ness, *n.* The quality or state of being hoary.

White Hoarhound (*Marrubium vulgare*).

hōarse, *a.* [ME. *hoors*, *hors*; AS. *has*, hoarse, rough.]

1. Having a harsh, rough, grating voice, as when affected with a cold.

2. Rough; grating; discordant; raucous, as a voice or other sound; as, the *hoarse* warning of a fog-horn.

Syn.—Harsh, grating, discordant, husky, raucous, rough, gruff.

hōarse'ly, *adv.* In a hoarse manner.

hōars'en, *v.t.* To make harsh or hoarse. [Rare.]

hōarse'ness, *n.* [ME. *hoorsnesse*; AS. *hasnes*, from *has*, hoarse.] Harshness of voice or sound.

hōar'stōne, *n.* [AS. *har stan*, a hoarstone; *har*, hoar, gray, and *stan*, a stone.] A landmark; a stone used to mark the boundary of an estate.

hōar'y, *a.* 1. White or whitish; as, the *hoary* willows.

2. White or gray with age; as, *hoary* hairs; a *hoary* head.

3. Very aged; ancient; as, *hoary* fables.

4. Moldy; mossy. [Obs.]

5. In botany, grayish-white, caused by very short, dense hairs covering the surface.

6. In zoölogy, grayish-white and lustrous.

hōast, *v.i.* To cough. [Prov. Eng. and Scot.]

hō-at'zin, *n.* Same as *Hoactzin*.

hōax, *n.* [A corruption of *hocus*.] Something done for deception or mockery; a trick played off in sport; a practical joke.

hōax, *v.t.* To deceive; to play a trick upon for sport, without malice.

hōax'ẽr, *n.* One who hoaxes.

hō-az'in, *n.* Same as *Hoactzin*.

hob, *n.* [Prob. from the same root as *hump*; compare L.G. *hump*, a hill, stump.]

1. A flat part of a grate at the side, where anything may be placed to be kept warm.

2. The nave of a wheel; the hub.

3. A kind of steel mandrel, used as a cutter in making screw-chasing tools.

4. A hardened steel punch used in making dies.

5. The stick, pin, or peg used as a mark in quoits or hob.

6. A game played with a short stick upon which coins are placed and at which the players pitch stones; the one who knocks the stick over gets all coins falling heads up. [Eng.]

To play hob with; to upset or damage. [Slang.]

hob, *n.* [Originally an abbrev. of *Robin* or *Robert*.]

1. A fairy; an elf; a goblin; a gnome. [Obs.]

2. A clown; an awkward, country fellow. [Obs.]

hob'ȧ-nob', hob'and-nob', *v.i.* To hobnob.

Hobb'ișm, *n.* The principles of Thomas Hobbes, a materialistic English philosopher (1588–1679). He considered an absolute monarchy to be the best form of government, holding that man was naturally incapable of regulating his own morals and religion, and that the state should do it.

Hobb'ist, *n.* A follower of Hobbes.

hob'ble, *v.i.*; hobbled, *pt.*, *pp.*; hobbling, *ppr.* [ME. *hobelen*, *hoblen*, freq. of *hoppen*, to hop.]

1. To walk lamely, bearing chiefly on one leg; to limp; to walk with a hitch or hop, or with crutches.

2. To move roughly or irregularly, as verse, etc.

hob'ble, *v.t.* 1. To perplex. [Obs.]

2. To hopple; to impede the use of the legs of; as, to *hobble* horses with a strap.

hob'ble, *n.* 1. An unequal, halting gait; an encumbered, awkward step; a limp.

2. Difficulty; perplexity.

3. A hopple; a loop of rope or other device to keep an animal from taking a long step; commonly in the plural; as, to put the *hobbles* on a horse.

Hobble skirt; a woman's skirt which is narrow below the knees.

hob'ble-bush, *n.* A kind of low-growing honeysuckle, *Viburnum lantanoides*, with wide-spreading branches which impede progress through them; also called *shinhopple*, *moosewood*, and *American wayfaring-tree*.

hob'ble-dē-hoy', *n.* A stripling; a raw, awkward young man; a youth in the growing stage preceding manhood.

hob'blẽr, *n.* One who or that which hobbles.

hob'blẽr, *n.* [ME. *hobler*, *hobeler*; OFr. *hobeler*, *hobelier*, from *hobi*, *hobin*, a small horse.]

1. One who by his tenure was to maintain a hobby for military service; one who served as a light-armored soldier on horseback. [Obs.]

2. One who tows a vessel either by a rope along a bank, or by the use of a rowboat. [Prov. Eng.]

hob'bling-ly, *adv.* In a hobbling manner; with a limping, interrupted step.

hob'bly, *a.* Uneven; rough, as a path. [Prov. Eng.]

hob'by, *n.*; *pl.* **hob'bieș.** [ME. *hobie*, *hoby*; OFr. *hobe*, from *hober*, to stir, move.] A species of falcon, *Falco subbuteo*, extremely active, and formerly trained for hawking.

hob'by, *n.*; *pl.* **hob'bies.** [ME. *hoby*; OFr. *hobi*, a nag, hobby, from *hober*, to move about.]

1. Any favorite pursuit, topic, or object; that which a person persistently pursues with zeal or delight; as, whist is his *hobby*.

2. A strong, active horse with ambling gait; a nag.

3. A hobbyhorse.

hob'by-hoṛse, *n.* [OFr. *hobi*, a horse, hobby and Eng. *horse*.]

1. A performer in the medieval morris-dance, having a light frame about his waist representing a horse apparently ridden by the performer; also, the contrivance so used.

2. A wooden horse, usually on rockers, on which children may ride; also, a stick, often bearing a wooden horse's head, for children to bestride in play.

3. A hobby; a favorite subject.

4. An early form of bicycle propelled by pushing on the ground with the feet.

hob-by-hoṛs'iç̧-ăl, *a.* Pertaining to or having a hobby; eccentric; full of whims.

hob-by-hoṛs'iç̧-ăl-ly, *adv.* Whimsically.

hob'gob-lin, *n.* [*Hob*, a fairy, and *goblin*.] A fairy; a frightful apparition; an imp; a goblin.

hob'i-lẽr, *n.* In feudal law, a tenant bound to serve as a light horseman; a hobbler.

hō'bit, *n.* [G. *haubitze*, a howitzer.] A small mortar or short gun for throwing bombs. [Obs.]

hob'līke, *a.* Clownish; boorish.

hob'nāil, *n.* 1. A nail with a thick, strong head used in the soles of heavy shoes.

2. A clownish person, in contempt.

hob'nāil, *v.t.*; hobnailed, *pt.*, *pp.*; hobnailing *ppr.* 1. To set with hobnails, as a shoe.

2. To trample roughly, as if with hobnailed boots. [Rare.]

hob'nāiled, *a.* 1. Set with hobnails; rough.

2. Rough; boorish; clumsy, as if wearing hobnailed boots.

Hobnailed liver; a form of cirrhosis of the liver marked by a shrunken condition, with hard knobs, like hobnails, on the surface.

hob'nob, *adv.* [AS. *habban*, to have, and *næbban* for *ne habban*, to not have.]

1. Take or not take; a familiar invitation to reciprocal drinking.

2. Come what will; at random. [Obs.]

hob'nob, *v.i.*; hobnobbed, *pt.*, *pp.*; hobnobbing *ppr.* To drink together or clink glasses in a familiar way; hence, to have familiar associations or relations; as, he *hobnobs* with all sorts of people.

hō'bō, *n.*; *pl.* **hō'bōș** or **hō'bōeș.** A shiftless vagrant workman or laborer; a vagabond; a tramp.

hob'ŏr-nob', *adv.* Same as *Hobnob*.

hō'boy, *n.* [Obs.] Same as *Hautboy*.

hoç̧'ç̧o, *n.* [Native name in Guiana.] The crested curassow, or a bird resembling it, as the hoactzin.

hoche'pot, *n.* Hotchpot. [Obs.]

Hōch'heim-ẽr, *n.* A Rhine wine produced at Hochheim, near Mentz, Germany. Varieties are either red or white, dry or sweet, still or sparkling.

hock, *v.t.* [In allusion to the game of faro, in which the last card in the box is called *hock*; hence, the last chance, the last resort.] To pawn. [Slang.]

hock, *n.* Pawn; as, to put a watch in *hock*; also, prison; as, he is in *hock*. [Slang.]

hock, *n.* [ME. *hok*, *hokke*, *hoc*; AS. *hoc*, mallow.] The hollyhock; also, the mallow. [Obs.]

hock, *n.* Originally, Hochheimer; now, any white Rhine wine.

hock, hough (hok), *n.* [ME. *houg*, *hog*; AS. *hoh*, *ho*, the heel.]

1. The joint between the tibia and the tarsus in the hind leg of a quadruped.

2. In man, the posterior part of the knee-joint; the ham.

hock, *v.t.*; hocked, *pt.*, *pp.*; hocking, *ppr.* To hamstring; to hough; to disable by cutting the tendons of the ham.

hock'ȧ-mōre, *n.* [A corruption of G. *Hochheimer* (supply *wein*, wine), wine made at Hochheim, Germany.] A Rhenish wine; Hochheimer.

hock'dāy, hōke'dāy, *n.* [ME. *hokday*, *hokeday*, a variant of *high-day*; *hok*, a corruption of *high*, *hig*, or *hey*, from AS. *heáh*, high.] High-day; a day of feasting and mirth, formerly held in England the second Tuesday after Easter.

hock'ey, *n.* [Also written *hookey*, from *hook*, in allusion to the curved stick with which the game is played.]

1. A game played with a club curved at the lower end, by two parties or sides, the object of each side being to drive a block or ball into that part of the field marked off as their opponents' goal.

2. A club with which this game is played; also called *hockey-stick, hockey-club*.

hock′ hẽrb, *n*. [AS. *hoc*, mallow.] A plant, the mallow.

hoc′kle, *v.t.*; hockled, *pt.*, *pp.*; hockling, *ppr.* [From *hock* part of the leg.]
1. To hamstring; to hock.
2. To mow. [Prov. Eng.]

hō′çus, *v.t.*; hocused *or* hocussed (-kust), *pt.*, *pp.*; hocusing *or* hocussing, *ppr.* [Abbrev. of *hocus-pocus*.]
1. To cheat; to dupe; to deceive.
2. To drug, as a drink.
3. To make stupid by a drugged drink.

hō′çus, *n*. 1. A tricky person; an impostor; also, a magician; a conjurer.
2. Liquor that has been drugged.

hō′çus-pō′çus, *n*. [A rime invented by jugglers in imitation of Latin.]
1. A juggler. [Obs.]
2. A juggler's trick; a cheat used by conjurers; jugglery.
3. A juggler's riming formula.

hō′çus-pō′çus, *a*. Juggling; deceptive; as, a *hocus-pocus* trick.

hō′çus-pō′çus, *v.t.* To cheat.

hod, *n*. [Fr. *hotte*, a basket for carrying on the back; O.D. *hotte*, a peddler's basket.]
1. A kind of trough for carrying mortar and brick, used in bricklaying; it is fitted with a handle, and borne on the shoulder.
2. A coal-scuttle.
3. In the state of Maine, a tub for carrying and measuring alewives.
4. A pewterer's blowpipe.

hod′-car″ri-ẽr, *n*. A laborer who carries bricks and mortar in a hod.

hod′den-grāy, *n*. Cloth made of wool in its natural state, without being dyed. [Scot.]

hod′dy, *n*. The hooded crow; the dun crow. [Scot.]

hod′dy-dod′dy, *n*. An awkward or foolish person. [Obs.]

hodge′podge, *n*. [A corruption of *hotchpot*, from OFr. *hochepot*, a mingled mass; O.D. *hutspot*, beef or mutton cut into small pieces and boiled together; *hutsen*, to shake, and *pot*, pot.]
1. A mixed mass; a medley of ingredients; a hotchpotch.
2. In law, a hotchpot.

hō′di-ẽrn, *a*. Hodiernal. [Obs.]

hō-di-ẽr′năl, *a*. [L. *hodiernus*, from *hodie*, on this day, contr. of *hoc die*, abl. of *hic dies*; *hic*, this, and *dies*, day.] Of this day; belonging to the present day.

hod′măn, *n*.; *pl.* **hod′men**. A man who carries a hod; a mason's helper; a hod-carrier.

hod′măn-dod, *n*. A snail; a dodman. [Obs.]

hod′ō-grăph, *n*. [Gr. *hodos*, way, and *graphein*, to write.] A curve whose radius vector represents the velocity and direction of motion of a moving point.

hō-dom′e-tẽr, *n*. See *Odometer*.

hoe, *n* [OFr. *houe*, *hoe*, from O.H.G. *houwa*, a hoe, from *houwan*, to hew, cut.] An instrument for cutting up weeds and loosening the earth in fields and gardens, commonly consisting of a thin, flat blade of steel with a long wooden handle set at a convenient angle.

Dutch hoe; a hoe having the cutting blade arranged for use by pushing; called also *scuffle*, *push-hoe*, or *thrust-hoe*.

Horse hoe; a form of cultivator drawn by a horse.

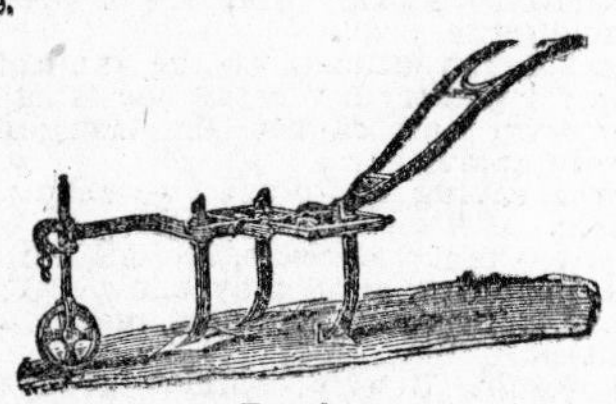

Horse hoe.

hōe, *v.t.*; hoed, *pt.*, *pp.*; hoeing, *ppr.* 1. To cut, dig, scrape, or clean with a hoe; as, to *hoe* the earth in a garden.
2. To clear from weeds, or till the earth about, with a hoe; as, to *hoe* cabbage.

A hard or *a long row to hoe*; a difficult or tiresome task to perform.

To hoe one's own row; to do one's own share; to be independent; to mind one's own business.

hōe, *v.i.* To use a hoe.

hōe′çāke, *n*. A cake made of corn-meal, water, and salt; originally, one baked on the blade of a hoe. [Southern U. S.]

hōo′mŏth″ẽr, *n*. [Orkney name.] The homer or liver-shark.

hō′fụl, *a*. Careful. [Obs.]

hog, *n*. [ME. *hog*, *hoge*, *hogge*, a gelded hog.]
1. A castrated pig. [Obs.]
2. A swine; a boar, sow, or pig; an omnivorous ungulate mammal of the family *Suidæ*. All the varieties of the domestic hog are derived from the wild boar, *Sus scrofa*.
3. By extension, any animal resembling the domestic *hog*, as the peccary.
4. A greedy, gluttonous, or filthy person. [Colloq.]
5. In provincial English, (a) a young sheep, shorn during or just after its first year; (b) a year-old bullock; (c) a young colt.
6. Among seamen, a sort of scrubbing-broom for scraping a ship's bottom under water.
7. In paper-making, an agitator or stirrer in the pulp-vat.

Hog cholera; see under *Cholera*.

To go the whole hog; to go to the limit; to go in for everything. [Slang.]

hog, *v.t.*; hogged, *pt.*, *pp.*; hogging, *ppr.* 1. To scrape (a ship's bottom) under water.
2. To carry on the back. [Local, Eng.]
3. To cut (the hair) short; as, to *hog* a horse's mane.

hog, *v.i.* To bend or droop at both ends, so as to resemble in some degree a hog's back; said of the keel of a ship.

hog′-ap″ple, *n*. The May-apple, *Podophyllum peltatum*.

hog′back, *n*. 1. A convex back like that of a hog.
2. A hogframe.
3. A ridge of sand, gravel, etc., with a sharp crest, rising above the surrounding level; also, the projecting edge of tilted rock-strata, or an abrupt rise in a coal-seam.

hog′-cat″ẽr-pil-lăr, *n*. The larva of *Darapsa myron*, the grapevine sphinx-moth, whose head with the adjoining segments is like a hog's snout.

hog′chāin, *n*. A chain hogframe.

hog′chōk″ẽr, *n*. The American sole, *Achirus lineatus*, so called because worthless as food.

hog′cōte, *n*. A shed or house for swine; a sty.

hog′-deer, *n*. One of various animals, (a) the axis; (b) *Cervus porcinus*, a spotted deer allied to the axis; (c) the babirussa.

hog′-fen″nel, *n*. Sulphurwort.

hog′fish, *n*. Any of various species of fish, (a) the sailor's-choice; (b) the log-perch; (c) the *Lachnolæmus maximus*, a labroid West Indian fish; (d) the *Scorpæna scrofa*, a large, red, European fish.

hog′frāme, *n*. In steam vessels, a fore-and-aft frame, usually above deck, forming, together with the frame of the vessel, a truss to prevent vertical flexure.

hogged, *a*. Having the ends lower than the middle; said of a ship when broken, bent, or sprung, as from stranding.

hog′gẽr, *n*. A footless stocking used by miners.

hog′gẽr-el, *n*. [Eng. dim. of *hog*.] A sheep of the second year.

hog′gẽr-pipe, *n*. The upper pipe of a mining-pump. [Northern Eng.]

hog′gẽr-pump, *n*. The uppermost pump in a mine.

hog′gẽr-y, *n*. 1. A place where hogs are kept.
2. Beastliness; selfishness.

hog′get, *n*. 1. A young boar of the second year.
2. A colt or sheep over one year old. [Eng.]

hog′gish, *a*. Having the qualities of a hog; gluttonous; filthy; mean; selfish.

hog′gish-ly, *adv.* In a hoggish manner.

hog′gish-ness, *n*. The state or quality of being hoggish; voracious greediness in eating; beastly filthiness; mean selfishness.

hog′-gum, *n*. Any of various aromatic resins found in the West Indies.

hōgh (hō), *n*. [Ice. *haugr*, a hill, mound.] A hill; a cliff. [Obs.]

hog′hẽrd, *n*. A keeper of swine.

hog′-in-ăr′mŏr, *n*. The nine-banded armadillo.

hog′-louse, *n*. A wood-louse or sow-bug.

hog′-mēat, *n*. The root of a Jamaican herb, the *Boerhaavia decumbens*, used medicinally.

hog′me-nāy, **hog′mȧ-nāy**, *n*. The day before New Year's day; also, the gifts or entertainment asked or given on that day. [Prov. Eng. and Scot.]

hog′-mol″ly, *n*. 1. The hog-sucker.
2. The log-perch or hogfish.

hog′-mul″let, *n*. The hog-sucker.

hog′nōse-snāke, *n*. The American flathead or puff-adder.

hog′nut, *n*. 1. The pignut or brown hickory-nut.
2. The earthnut, *Bunium flexuosum*.

hō′gō, *n*. [Fr. *haut goût*, high flavor.] Strong flavor or scent. [Obs.]

hog′-pēa″nut, *n*. A vine of the order *Leguminosæ*, *Amphicarpæa monoica*, whose upper flowers are usually sterile while those at the base ripen a single-seeded pod in the ground or on the surface.

hog′pen, *n*. A hogsty.

hog′-plum, *n*. Any of various plants or their fruit, (a) a plant of the genus *Spondias*, of the West Indies, whose plumlike fruit is fed to hogs; (b) a plant of the genus *Ximenia*, of Florida and the West Indies; called also *wild lime* and *mountain-plum*; (c) the Chickasaw plum, *Prunus angustifolia*; (d) the poison-wood, *Rhus Metopium*, of tropical Florida.

hog′-rat, *n*. A Cuban rodent, the hutia.

hog′reeve, *n*. In New England, an officer having the care of stray hogs.

hog′ring, *n*. A ring of metal or a similar device set in a hog's snout to keep it from rooting up the ground.

hog′ring″ẽr, *n*. One who puts rings into the snouts of swine; also, a kind of pincers used for that purpose.

hog′ṣ′-back, *n*. Anything having the shape of the back of a hog; in geology, a hogback.

hog′ṣ′-bāne, *n*. The sowbane or maple-leaved goosefoot.

hog′ṣ′-bēan, *n*. The henbane.

hog′ṣ′-bread (-bred), *n*. Same as *Hog-meat*.

hog′sçōre, *n*. In the game of curling, a line drawn across the rink or course at a point one-sixth of the total distance from each tee.

hog′ṣ′-fen″nel, *n*. Hog-fennel; sulphurwort.

hogṣ′head (-hed), *n*. [ME. *hoggeshed*, *hoggis hed*, *hoggeshede*, a corruption of M.D. *ockshoofd*, *oghshoofd*, lit., oxhead. Perhaps applied to a cask from its having an oxhead branded on it.]
1. An English measure of capacity, containing 63 wine gallons, or about 52½ imperial gallons.
2. In the United States, a cask containing from 100 to 140 wine gallons; as, a *hogshead* of spirits or molasses.
3. A large cask of indefinite contents.

hog′skin, *n*. Tanned leather made of the skins of swine. Also used as an adjective.

hog′-snāke, *n*. A hognose-snake.

hog′stȳ, *n*. A pen or inclosure for hogs.

hog′-suck″ẽr, *n*. A river fish, *Hypentelium nigricans*; also called *hog-molly*, *hog-mullet*.

hog′wăsh, *n*. Swill; the refuse of a kitchen or brewery, or like matter for swine.

hog′weed, *n*. Any of various plants, as the *Ambrosia artemisiæfolia*, ragweed; *Heracleum Sphondylium*, the cow-parsnip; and *Polygonum aviculare*, doorweed or knotgrass.

hog′wŏrt, *n*. An annual plant, *Croton capitatus*, of southeastern United States.

hoiçs, **hoicks**, *v.t.* To cheer on, as hounds, with the cry "hoics!"

hoiçs, **hoicks**, *interj.* A hunting-cry used to encourage dogs.

hoi′den, **hoy′den**, *n*. [O.D. *heyden*, a heathen, gipsy, vagabond.]
1. An awkward, forward girl; a bold girl.
2. A rude, bold fellow. [Obs.]

hoi′den, *a*. Rude; bold; inelegant; rustic.

hoi′den, *v.i.* To romp rudely.

hoi′den-hood, *n*. The state of being a hoiden.

hoi′den-ish, *a*. Having the manners of a hoiden.

hoise, *v.t.* To raise; to hoist. [Obs.]

hoist, *v.t.*; hoisted, *pt.*, *pp.*; hoisting, *ppr.* [A form of *hoise*, with excrescent *t*; from O.D. *hyssen*, to hoise, hoist.] To raise; to lift or bear upward, especially by a mechanical device, as by means of tackle; as, to *hoist* a sail.

hoist, *v.i.* To lift and move the leg backward; used in the imperative by milkers to cows, when they wish them to lift and set back the right leg.

hoist, *n*. 1. In nautical language, the perpendicular height of a flag or sail, as opposed to the *fly*, or breadth from the staff to the outer edge.
2. The operation of hoisting.
3. An apparatus for raising heavy objects; an elevator.

hoist′ȧ-wāy″, *n*. A hoist; an elevator.

hoist′-bridge, *n*. A lift-bridge.

hoist′ẽr, *n*. One who or that which hoists.

hoist′wāy, *n*. An opening through which goods may be hoisted, as in a warehouse; an elevator-shaft.

hoit, *v.i.* To leap; to caper. [Obs.]

hoi′ty-toi′ty, *interj.* Pshaw; an exclamation of surprise or disapprobation with some degree of contempt.

> *Hoity-toity!* what have I to do with dreams?
> —Congreve.

hoi′ty-toi′ty, *a*. Giddy; excitable; easily offended. [Colloq.]

hōke′dāy, *n*. See *Hockday*.

hō′kẽr, *n*. [AS. *hocor*, scorn, mockery.] Censure; abuse; derision. [Obs.]

hō′kẽr-ly, *adv.* Scornfully; abusively. [Obs.]

hō′ky-pō′ky, *n*. 1. Hocus-pocus. [Prov. Eng.]
2. A kind of ice-cream sold by street venders.

hōl, *a*. Whole. [Obs.]

hol-ärc′tiç, *a*. [Gr. *holos*, whole, and *arktikos*, arctic.] Completely arctic; relating to the entire arctic regions.

hol-ăr-thrit′iç, *a*. [Gr. *holos*, whole, and *arthritis*, gout.] Affected with gout in all the joints.

hol-as-pid′e-ăn, *a*. [Gr. *holos*, whole, and *aspis*, (*-idos*), a shield.] In zoölogy, having the posterior sheath of the tarsus entire, as the lark.

hol′çad, *n*. [Gr. *holkas* (*-ados*), a ship that is towed, from *helkein*, to draw.] In ancient Greece, a ship of burden.

hōld, *v.t.*; held, *pt.*; holding, *ppr.*; held (*in law*, holden), *pp.* [ME. *holden*, *halden*; AS. *healdan*, to hold, keep.]
1. To keep fast, as in the hand; to maintain in a certain position, condition, relation, or

place so as to prevent motion, action, or change; to retain; to reserve; to keep; to restrain; to detain; to withhold; as, to *hold* a pen; to *hold* one's head erect; to *hold* a person prisoner; a pail *holds* water; to *hold* a seat vacant; to *hold* one's place in line; to *hold* one's breath; to *hold* a train for orders; to *hold* a foe in check.

2. To have or retain the title or possession of; to own; to occupy; to have; to maintain; to defend; as, to *hold* land; to *hold* an office; he *held* the money; to *hold* the fort.

With what arms
We mean to *hold* what anciently we claim
Of deity or empire. —Milton.

3. To consider; to regard; to think; to judge; to decide; to have in the mind; as, to *hold* one blameless; to *hold* a law to be void; to *hold* an opinion.

4. To carry on; to continue; to pursue; to employ; to sustain; to celebrate; as, to *hold* a conversation; to *hold* a course; to *hold* an argument or debate; to *hold* a feast; to *hold* a council.

5. To retain a legal or moral claim upon; as, to *hold* a security for the payment of a note; to *hold* a man to his promise.

6. To have capacity to receive and contain; as, the cask *holds* thirty gallons; the church *holds* two thousand people.

7. To wager; to bet. [Rare.]

To hold forth; to offer; to propose.

To hold in; to curb; to restrain; to check.

To hold in hand or *in play*; to have control of; to play with.

To hold off; to keep at a distance.

To hold on; to continue; as, *to hold on* a course.

To hold one's own; to keep one's present condition or position; to lose no advantage.

To hold one's peace; to be silent.

To hold out; to offer.

To hold up; (a) to sustain; to lift; (b) to display; to offer as an example; (c) to check; to stop; (d) to stop, as on a highway, with intent to rob.

To hold water; (a) to check a rowboat's headway by holding the oars in the water; (b) to be sound and without leaks; figuratively, to be consistent, as an argument or statement.

hōld, *v.i.* 1. To take or keep a thing in one's grasp; to maintain an attachment; to continue firm; not to give way or break; to adhere; as, he cannot *hold* any longer; the rope will *hold*.

2. To be true or valid; not to fail; to stand; to apply, as a fact or truth; often with *true* or *good*; as, the argument *holds good* in both cases; this *holds true*.

3. To continue unbroken or unsubdued; not to surrender; to stand one's ground; generally followed by *out*; as, the garrison still *held out*.

4. To last; to endure; to continue; often followed by *out* or *on*.

While our obedience *holds*. —Milton.

5. To refrain.

6. To be dependent on another for possessions; to derive right or title; as, petty barons *holding* under greater barons.

7. To stop, stay, or wait; to cease or give over; chiefly in the imperative; as, *hold*, enough!

Hold hard! hold on! hold up! Halt; stop. [Colloq.]

To hold forth; to speak in public; to harangue; to preach; to proclaim.

To hold in; to restrain oneself; as, he could hardly *hold in* from laughing.

To hold off; to remain at a distance.

To hold on; to continue; not to be interrupted; as, the speaker *held on* for an hour.

To hold out; to last; to endure; to continue.

To hold over; (a) to continue in possession, as of an office, after the expiration of some fixed time; (b) to be continued or postponed; as, the matter *holds over*.

To hold to or *with*; to cling or cleave to; to adhere to; to side with; to stand up for.

To hold together; to be joined; not to separate.

To hold up; (a) to cease raining; (b) to maintain one's courage, health, etc.; (c) to continue the same speed.

hōld, *n.* [D. *hol*, a den, cave, hold of a ship.] All that part of a ship's interior below the deck, in which the cargo, ballast, etc., may be stowed.

hōld, *n.* [ME. *hold, hald*; AS. *heald*, hold, protection, from *healdan*, to hold.]

1 The act or holding in any way, physical, mental, or moral; a clutch, grasp, or grip; a seizure; as, his intellectual *hold* is firm; loose your *hold*.

2. Something which may be seized for support; that which supports.

3. Power of keeping; also, authority to seize or keep; claim; custody.

The law hath yet another *hold* on you.—Shak.

4. A prison; a place of confinement.

They laid hands on them, and put them in *hold* unto the next day. —Acts iv. 3.

5. A fortified place; a fort; a castle; a place of security.

6. In music, the character 𝄐, directing the performer to pause on the note or rest over which it is placed; called also a *pause*.

hōld′back, *n.* 1. Check; restraint; hindrance.

2. The iron or strap on the shaft or pole of a vehicle to which a part of the harness is attached, to enable the animal to hold back the vehicle when going downhill; also, the strap connecting this with the harness.

hōld′ẽr, *n.* 1. One who or that which holds; especially, (a) the payee of a note or bill of exchange; (b) a tenant; (c) something by or in which a thing is held; as, a *holder* for a flatiron.

2. A person employed in the hold of a ship.

3. [*pl.*] A dog's sharp teeth or fangs. [Prov. Eng.]

hōld′ẽr-fōrth′, *n.* A haranguer; a preacher.

hōld′fast, *n.* 1. Any of various contrivances for securing and holding things in place, as a long, flat-headed nail, a catch, a hook, etc.

2. Hold; support.

3. A rootlike appendage of a seaweed.

hōld′ing, *n.* 1. The act of keeping or retaining.

2. A tenure; also, that which is held; as, his *holding* is over eighty acres.

3. Hold; influence. [Rare.]

4. The burden or chorus of a song. [Obs.]

5. [*pl.*] Property in general.

hōld′ing-nōte, *n.* In music, a note sustained while other notes are changed.

hōld′-up, *n.* A robbery; from the command given to hold up the hands; also used adjectively; as, a *hold-up* gang.

hōle, *n.* [ME. *hole, hool, hol*; AS. *hol*, a hole, cavern, from *hol*, adj., hollow.]

1. A hollow place or cavity in any solid body, of any shape or dimensions, natural or artificial; a perforation, orifice, aperture, pit, rent, fissure, crevice, or the like.

2. The excavated habitation of certain wild beasts, as the fox, the badger, etc.; hence, a mean habitation; a narrow or dark lodging; a vile place; as, a *hole* of vice; a drinking-*hole*; a miserable *hole* of a dwelling.

3. Figuratively, a perforation; an opening; as, to make a *hole* in a man's argument.

4. A predicament; a scrape; a fix; as, to get into a *hole*. [Colloq.]

5. A level green, or grassy dell or dale. [Local, U. S.]

6. A cove; a narrow channel or small harbor.

7. In golf, a point scored by the player covering the space between two holes in the fewest strokes.

A hole to crawl out of; a means of escape; an excuse.

Hole and corner; underhand; secret.

Toad in the hole; meat baked in batter.

To crawl into one's hole; to give up an argument; to sneak off. [Colloq.]

hōle, *a.* Hollow; empty; hungry. [Prov. Eng.]

hōle, *a.* Whole; hale; healthy. [Obs.]

hōle, *v.i.*; holed, *pt., pp.*; holing, *ppr.* To go into a hole.

hōle, *v.t.* [ME. *holen, holien*; AS. *holian*, to hollow out, dig a hole, from *hol*, hollow.]

1. To cut, dig, or make a hole or holes in; as, to *hole* a post for the insertion of rails or bars.

2. To drive into a hole; as, to *hole* a ball in pool.

3. In mining, (a) to undercut (a coal-seam); (b) to connect, as two workings.

hō′lẽr, *n.* A rogue; a knave; a rake. [Obs.]

hōl-eth′nic, *a.* Of or belonging to a holethnos.

hōl-eth′nos, *n.* [Gr. *holos*, whole, entire, and *ethnos*, nation.] An original race of people undivided into branches.

hōle′wŏrt, *n.* See *Hollowwort*.

hol′i-but, hol′i-but-tẽr, *n.* Same as ***Halibut***.

hol′i-dame, *n.* Same as *Halidom*.

hol′i-dāy, *n.* [ME. *holiday, haliday*; AS. *halig dæg*, lit., holy day; *halig*, holy, and *dæg*, day.]

1. Originally, a religious anniversary; now, a day set apart for exemption from labor or for a formal or informal celebration.

2. Nautically, a spot not covered in the operation of applying tar, paint, or whitewash to a ship.

Bank holiday; in Great Britain, a legal holiday, on which the banks are closed.

Legal holiday; a day appropriated by law to the cessation of ordinary business transactions and given over to celebration or commemoration. In the United States, the holidays most generally observed are January 1, New-Year's day; February 22, the anniversary of Washington's birthday; May 30, Memorial day, in recognition of the nation's dead soldiers and sailors; July 4, the anniversary of the signing of the Declaration of Independence; the fourth Thursday in November, Thanksgiving day; December 25, Christmas day. Arbor day, Labor day, and general election day are also made holidays in some states.

The holidays; any holiday time; specifically, December 25 to January 1, inclusive.

hol′i-dāy, *a.* Pertaining to a festival; gay; adapted for or proper to a special occasion; as, *holiday* manners.

hō′li-ly, *adv.* Piously; with sanctity; in a holy manner; sacredly.

hō′li-ness, *n.* [ME. *holinesse, holynesse, halinesse*; AS. *halignes*, from *halig*, holy.]

1. The state of being holy; purity or integrity of moral character; freedom from sin; sanctity.

2. Sacredness; the state of anything hallowed, or consecrated to God or to his worship.

3. [H—] A title of the pope, and formerly of the Greek emperors.

hōl′ing-ax, *n.* A narrow ax for cutting holes in posts.

hōlk (hōk), *v.t.* To hollow out. [Obs.]

hol′lȧ, *interj.* Same as *Hollo*.

hol′lȧ, *v.i.* Same as *Hollo*.

hol′lănd, *n.* A kind of fine linen originally manufactured in Holland; also, a coarser linen fabric, unbleached or dyed brown, used for covering furniture, carpets, etc.

Hol′lănd-ẽr, *n.* 1. A native of Holland; a Dutchman.

2. [h—] A hard glazed brick; known also as *Dutch clinker*.

Hol′lănd-ish, *a.* Of or relating to Holland; Dutch.

hol′lănds, *n.* Gin made in Holland; Holland gin.

hol′lẽr, *n.* and *v.* Hollo. [Colloq.]

hŏl-lō′, *interj.* and *n.* A word used in hailing to attract attention; hallo; halloo; hello. [Compare *hallo*.]

hŏl-lō′, *v.i.*; holloed, *pt., pp.*; holloing, *ppr.* To call out or exclaim; to halloo; to hail.

hol-lōa′, *interj., n.,* and *v.i.* Same as *Hollo*.

hol′lōw, *n.* [AS. *holg, holh*, a hollow, cavity, hole.] A depression or excavation below the general level or in the substance of anything; an empty space in anything; a cavity, natural or artificial; concavity; a cave or cavern; a den; a hole; a groove; a channel; a canal; as, the *hollow* of the hand; the *hollow* of a tree.

hol′lōw, *v.t.*; hollowed, *pt., pp.*; hollowing, *ppr.* To make hollow, as by digging, cutting, or engraving; to excavate.

hol′lōw, *v.t.* and *v.i.* To hollo.

hol′lōw, *a.* [ME. *holow, holowe, holgh, holg*, hollow, from AS. *holh, holg*, a hollow.]

1. Containing an empty space, natural or artificial, within a solid substance; not solid; as, a *hollow* tree; a *hollow* tile; a *hollow* sphere.

2. Sunk deep in the orbit; depressed; concave; gaunt; as, a *hollow* eye.

3. Deep; low; resembling sound reverberated from a cavity; as, a *hollow* roar.

4. Not sincere or faithful; false; deceitful; not sound; as, a *hollow* heart; a *hollow* friend.

Hollow newel; in architecture, the wellhole or opening in the center of winding stairs.

Hollow square; a body of soldiers drawn up in the form of a square, with an empty space in the middle.

Hollow wall; in architecture, a wall built in two thicknesses, leaving a cavity or cavities between, either for the purpose of preventing moisture from being driven by storms through the brickwork, for ventilating, for preserving a uniform temperature in apartments, or for saving materials.

Hollow wall.

Syn.—Empty, concave, foolish, weak, faithless, insincere, artificial, unsubstantial, void, flimsy, transparent, senseless, vacant, unsound, false.

hol′lōw, *adv.* Utterly; completely; out-and-out; generally with the verbs *beat, carry*, and the like; as, he *beat* him *hollow*.

hol′lōw-brick, *n.* A brick made with perforations through it for the purpose of warming or ventilating, or to prevent moisture from penetrating a wall.

Hollow-bricks.

hol′lōw-heȧrt′′ed, *a.* Insincere; deceitful.

hol′lōw-ly, *adv.* Insincerely; deceitfully.

hol′lōw-ness, *n.* 1. The state of being hollow.

2. Insincerity; deceitfulness; treachery.

3. Completeness; entirety.

hol′lōw-ro͝ot, *n.* A plant, *Adoxa Moschatellina*, of the *Caprifoliaceæ*; the moschatel.

hol′lōw-wâre, *n.* Hollow manufactured articles, especially cooking utensils of cast-iron.

hol′lōw-wŏrt, *n.* *Corydalis cava*, a succulent plant with pink flowers.

hol′lus-chick′′ie, *n.* In Alaska, a male seal that does not breed.

hol′ly, *adv.* Wholly. [Obs.]

hol′ly, *n.* [ME. *holly, holy,* variant of *holin, holyn;* AS. *holen, holegn,* holly.]

1. A plant of the genus *Ilex,* of several species. The common holly grows from 20 to 30 feet high; the stem, by age, becomes large, and is covered with a grayish smooth bark, and set with branches which form a sort of cone. The leaves are oblong-oval, of a lucid green on the upper surface, but pale on the under surface; the edges are indented and waved, with sharp thorns terminating each of the points. The flowers grow in clusters, and are succeeded by roundish berries, which turn to a beautiful red about the last of September. This tree is a beautiful evergreen, and houses and churches at Christmas are often adorned with the leaves and berries, a relic probably of Druidism.

Holly (*Ilex Aquifolium*).

2. The holm-oak, *Quercus Ilex,* an evergreen oak, often called *holly-oak.*

hol′ly-fērn, *n.* A plant, *Aspidium Lonchitis,* an evergreen species of shield-fern.

hol′ly-hock, *n.* [ME. *holihoc, holihocce,* lit., holy hock; AS. *halig,* holy, and *hoc,* mallow; so called because brought from the Holy Land.] A plant of the genus *Althæa,* bearing flowers of various colors.

hol′ly-ōak, *n.* The holm-oak, *Quercus Ilex.*

hol′ly-rōse, *n.* A shrub, *Turnera ulmifolia,* bearing gaudy yellow flowers, native to the West Indies.

hōlm, *n.* [ME. *holme,* a corruption of AS. *holen,* holly.]

1. The holm-oak.

2. The holly.

hōlm, *n.* [AS. *holm,* sea, water, an island.]

1. An islet or river isle.

2. A low flat tract of rich land on the banks of a river.

hol′mi-ȧ, *n.* Holmium oxid.

hol′mi-um, *n.* [Origin unknown.] A substance derived from gadolinite, now placed among the elements.

hōlm′-ōak, *n.* The evergreen oak, *Quercus Ilex.*

hōlm′-thrush, *n.* The missel thrush.

hōlm′-tree, *n.* The holly.

holo-. A combining form from Gr. *holos,* whole. It is used in biology, botany, geology, etc., to signify whole, entire; as, *holo*blast, *holo*cryptic.

hol′ō-blast, *n.* [*Holo-,* and Gr. *blastos,* a germ, shoot.] An ovum whose yolk is entirely germinal.

hol-ō-blas′tiç, *a.* Entirely germinal; said of ova, such as those of mammals, of which the yolk becomes completely segmented.

hol′ō-caust, *n.* [Gr. *holokauston, holokauton,* neut. of *holokaustos, holokautos,* burnt whole; *holos,* whole, and *kaustos* or *kautos,* burnt, from *kaiein,* to burn.]

1. A burnt sacrifice or offering, the whole of which was consumed by fire; a species of sacrifice in use among the Jews and some pagan nations.

2. A great loss of life by fire.

Hol-ō-cen′tri-dæ, *n.pl.* [*Holo-,* and Gr. *kentron,* a point, center.] A family of fishes, the squirrel-fishes.

hol-ō-cen′troid, *a.* Relating to the *Holocentridæ.*

Hol-ō-ceph′ȧ-lī, *n.pl.* [*Holo-,* and Gr. *kephalē,* head.] A suborder of fishes of the order *Elasmobranchii,* characterized by long jaws incased by dental plates and a cartilaginous endoskeleton. Only two genera are known to exist now; the fossil species range from the bottom of the Oölite to the present age.

hol-ō-cryp′tiç, *a.* [*Holo-,* and Gr. *kryptos,* hidden.] Entirely hiding; effectively concealing; specifically, descriptive of a cipher incapable of being read except by one who has the key.

hol-ō-crys′tăl-line, *a.* [*Holo-,* and Gr. *krystallinos,* crystalline, from *krystallos,* ice, crystal.] Entirely crystalline.

hol-ō-gas′trụ-lȧ, *n.* [*Holo-,* and Gr. *gastēr,* the stomach.] A gastrula developed in a holoblastic ovum.

hō-log′nȧ-thous, *a.* [*Holo-,* and Gr. *gnathos,* jaw.] Having the jaw entire, as some land-pulmonates.

hol′ō-grȧph, *a.* [*Holo-,* and Gr. *graphein,* to write.] Wholly written by the person from whom it purports to issue.

hol′ō-grȧph, *n.* [LL. *holographus;* Gr. *holographos,* entirely autograph; *holos,* whole, entire, and *graphein,* to write.] Any writing, as a letter, deed, testament, etc., wholly written by the person from whom it purports to issue.

hol-ō-graph′iç, *a.* Forming or relating to a holograph; holograph.

hol-ō-hē′drăl, *a.* [*Holo-,* and Gr. *hedra,* a seat, base.] In crystallography, completely symmetrical with respect to planes; having all the similar edges or angles similarly replaced with planes.

hol-ō-hē′drism, *n.* The quality of being holohedral.

hol-ō-hē′drŏn, *n.* [*Holo-,* and Gr. *hedra,* a seat, base.] A crystalline form in which the entire number of planes required for complete symmetry are present.

hol-ō-hem-i-hē′drăl, *a.* [*Holo-,* and Gr. *hēmi,* half, and *hedra,* seat, base.] In crystallography, having half the planes required for complete symmetry present in all sectants.

Hol″ō-me-tab′ō-lȧ, *n.pl.* [*Holo-,* and Gr. *metabolē,* change.] The section of the class *Insecta* which undergo a complete metamorphosis.

hol-ō-met-ȧ-bol′iç, *a.* Passing through a complete series of transformations; undergoing entire metamorphosis, as some insects.

hō-lom′e-tēr, *n.* [*Holo-,* and Gr. *metron,* a measure.] A pantometer or measuring instrument for general use. [Obs.]

hol-ō-mor′phiç, *a.* [*Holo-,* and Gr. *morphē,* form.]

1. Having complete symmetry; holohedral.

2. In mathematics, having the characteristics of a complete function, as continuity, uniformity, and a finite value for a finite value of the variable.

hol-ō-phan′ēr-ous, *a.* [*Holo-,* and Gr. *phaneros,* open to sight, visible.] Wholly visible; a term applied to the metamorphosis of insects when complete.

hol-ō-phō′tăl, *a.* Reflecting rays of light in one unbroken mass without appreciable loss; as, a *holophotal* reflector.

hol′ō-phōte, *n.* [*Holo-,* and Gr. *phōs, phōtos,* light.] A form of lamp in which all the light may be used in one direction, as in a lighthouse.

hol″ō-phō-tom′e-tēr, *n.* [*Holo-,* and Gr. *phōs, phōtos,* light, and *metron,* a measure.] A form of photometer devised to estimate the total light emanating from any source.

hō-loph′rȧ-sis, *n.* [*Holo-,* and Gr. *phrasis,* expression.] The use of a single word to convey an entire idea.

hol-ō-phras′tiç, *a.* [*Holo-,* and Gr. *phrastikos,* suited for expressing, from *phrazein,* to speak, indicate.] Equivalent to an entire phrase; said of combinations of syllables in many primitive languages.

hol-ō-phyt′iç, *a.* [*Holo-,* and Gr. *phyton,* a plant.] Taking nutrition in the same manner as an ordinary green plant, as certain infusorians.

hol″ō-plank-ton′iç, *a.* [*Holo-,* and Gr. *planktos,* wandering, from *plazein,* to wander.] Belonging entirely to the pelagic forms of life; passing the entire existence on the surface of water, as certain gasteropods.

hol-op′tiç, *a.* [*Holo-,* and Gr. *optikos,* pertaining to sight, from root *op,* to see.] Having the eyes close together, as certain dipterous insects.

hol-ō-rhī′năl (-rī′), *a.* [*Holo-,* and Gr. *rhis, rhinos,* nose.] Having the nasal bones only slightly divergent or in actual contact.

hol″ō-sē-ri′ceous (-rish′us), *a.* [Gr. *holosērikos,* all of silk; *holos,* whole, and *sērikos,* silken.] Having a complete covering of minute silky hairs.

hol-ō-sid′ēr-īte, *n.* [Gr. *holosidēros,* all of iron; *holos,* whole, and *sidēros,* iron.] A meteorite containing nothing but metallic iron.

hol-ō-sī′phŏn-āte, *a.* [*Holo-,* and Gr. *siphōn,* a tube, pipe.] Having the siphon quite tubular, as a class of cephalopods.

hol″ō-spon-dā′iç, *a.* [Gr. *holospondeios,* all of spondees; *holos,* whole, and *spondeios* (supply *pous,* foot), a spondee.] Having spondees in all six places; said of a kind of hexameter.

hō-los′tē-ăn, *a.* and *n.* I. *a.* Of or belonging to the *Holostei.*

II. *n.* One of the *Holostei.*

Hō-los′tē-ī, *n.pl.* [*Holo-,* and Gr. *osteon,* a bone.] That division of the ganoid fishes in which the skeleton is osseous.

hol-ō-ster′iç, *a.* [*Holo-,* and Gr. *stereos,* solid.] Solid throughout; using no liquid; as, a *holosteric* or aneroid barometer.

Hol-ō-stom′ȧ-tȧ, *n. pl.* [*Holo-,* and Gr. *stoma* (-*atos*), mouth.] A division of gasteropodous mollusks in which the aperture of the shell is rounded or entire.

hō-los′tō-māte, *a.* Holostomatous.

hol-ō-stom′ȧ-tous, *a.* Of or like the *Holostomata;* having the shell mouth rounded or entire.

hol′ō-stōme, *n.* 1. A fish of the *Holostomi.*

2. A gasteropod of the *Holostomata.*

Hō-los′tō-mī, *n.pl.* [*Holo-,* and Gr. *stoma,* mouth.] A division of eel-like fishes in which the bones about the mouth are developed.

hō-los′tō-mous, *a.* 1. Holostomatous.

2. Of or resembling the *Holostomi.*

Hō-los′trȧ-cȧ, *n.pl.* [*Holo-,* and Gr. *ostrakon,* the hard shell of Testacea.] A class of crustaceans having a complete bivalve carapace or shell.

hol″ō-sym-met′riç, *a.* Holohedral.

hol-ō-sym′met-ry, *n.* Holohedrism.

hol-ō-thē′căl, *a.* [*Holo-,* and Gr. *thēkē,* a box, case.] Having the tarsal sheath undivided; booted; said of certain birds.

hol′ō-thūre, *n.* A holothurian.

hol-ō-thū′ri-ăn, *n.* and *a.* I. *n.* A member of the *Holothurioidea.*

II. *a.* Pertaining to the *Holothurioidea.*

Hol-ō-thū-ri-oi′dē-ȧ, *n.pl.* [Gr. *holothourion,* a kind of zoöphyte, and *eidos,* form.] The sea-cucumbers or sea-slugs, an order of echinoderms destitute of the calcareous plates typical of the class, but with a leathery integument open at both ends, and pierced by orifices through which suctorial feet or ambulacra protrude. They abound in the Asiatic seas, the trepang being a member of the family.

Hō-lot′ri-chȧ, *n.pl.* [*Holo-,* and Gr. *thrix, trichos,* hair.] A division of *Infusoria* with cilia upon the entire body.

hol′ōur, *n.* A holer. [Obs.]

hol-ō-zō′iç, *a.* [*Holo-,* and Gr. *zōon,* an animal.] Entirely and characteristically animal; said of the method of nutrition of certain infusorians.

hōlp, hōlp′en, *v.,* past tense and past participle of *help.* [Obs.]

hōl′sŏm, *a.* Wholesome. [Obs.]

Hōl′stein, *n.* [So called because originally from Schleswig-*Holstein* in Prussia.] One of a valuable breed of black-and-white cattle noted for the quantity of milk yielded.

hōl′stēr, *n.* [D. *holster,* a pistol-case, knapsack.] A leather case for a pistol, carried by a horseman at the fore part of his saddle, or worn at the belt.

hōl′stēred, *a.* Having a holster or holsters.

hōlt, *n.* [ME. *holt;* AS. *holt,* a wood, grove.] A wood or woodland; a tree-covered hillside.

hōlt, *n.* A hole, burrow, or place of retreat, as (a) a deep place in a river, frequented by fish; (b) a hollowed-out retreat or lodge, as that of an otter. [Prov. Eng.]

hōlt, *n.* A hold; a grip. [Local, U. S.]

hōlt, *v.,* a contraction of *holdeth.* [Obs.]

hol′we, *a.* Hollow. [Obs.]

hō′ly, *a.;* *comp.* holier; *superl.* holiest. [ME. *holy, holi, halig;* AS. *halig,* holy, sacred.]

1. Hallowed; consecrated or set apart to a sacred use; having a sacred character or associations; as, the *holy* temple; *holy* vessels; *holy* words.

2. Free from sin; pure in heart; immaculate in moral character; perfect in a moral sense; exhibiting holiness; righteous; as, a *holy* man; *holy* zeal.

Holy bread; bread or a piece of bread consecrated for the eucharist; hence, the eulogia.

Holy communion; the sacrament of the eucharist.

Holy Cross day; September 14, celebrated in memory of the apparition of the cross in the heavens to Constantine.

Holy Ghost; the Holy Spirit.

Holy Ghost pear; the avocado.

Holy Ghost plant, the dove-plant.

Holy Land; Palestine.

Holy Office; the Inquisition.

Holy of holies; (a) the innermost apartment of the Jewish tabernacle or temple, where the ark of the covenant was kept, and where no person entered, except the high priest once a year; (b) in an oriental Christian church, the sanctuary or bema. With the Nestorians, this is a space set apart for a cross at the eastern end, which no one ever enters.

Holy One; God.

Holy rood; a crucifix.

Holy Saturday; Saturday before Easter.

Holy Spirit; the divine Spirit; the third person in the Trinity; the Comforter of souls.

Holy Thursday; Ascension day; also, in an incorrect modern usage, the day before Good Friday; Maundy Thursday.

Holy war; any of the crusades.

Holy Week; the week preceding Easter Sunday.

Holy writ; the old and New Testaments.

hō′ly-dāy, *n.* A religious festival; hence, a holiday.

hō′ly-hērb, *n.* A plant, vervain.

hō′ly-stōne, *v.t.* To scrub, as the deck of a vessel, with a sailor's holystone.

hō′ly-stōne, *n.* [So called because used in scrubbing the decks on Sunday.] A soft stone used by seamen for cleaning the decks of ships.

hō′ly-wa″tēr, *n.* Water consecrated by a priest for ritual uses.

hom′ȧ-canth, *a.* [Gr. *homos,* the same, and *akantha,* spine.] Having the dorsal and anal spines symmetrical and depressible backward in the same line.

hom′āge (*or* om′āj), *n.* [OFr. *homage, hommage;* LL. *hominaticum,* a vassal's service, homage, from L. *homo* (-*inis*), a man.]

1. In feudal law, the submission, loyalty, and service which a tenant promised to his lord or superior, when first admitted to the land which he held of him in fee; or rather the act of the tenant in making this submission, on being invested with the fee.

2. Obeisance; respect paid by external action; reverence; reverential affection or worship.

3. The free tenants of a manor assembled for a court-baron.

hom′āġe, *v.t.*; homaged, *pt.*, *pp.*; homaging, *ppr.* [OFr. *hommager*, to pay homage to, from *hommage*, homage.] To pay respect to by external action; to give reverence to; to profess fealty to. [Obs.]

hom′āġe-ȧ-ble, *a.* Subject to homage.

hom′ȧ-ġēr, *n.* One who does homage or holds land of another by homage.

hom″ȧ-lō-gon′ȧ-tous, *a.* [Gr. *homalos*, even, equal, and *gony*, *gonatos*, knee.] In ornithology, possessing an ambiens muscle, as the common fowls.

hom″ȧ-lō-graph′iç, *a.* Homolographic.

hom-ȧ-loid′ăl, *a.* [Gr. *homalos*, even, level, and *eidos*, form.] Flat; resembling a plane; without curvature; said of Euclidean space of any species.

Hom′ȧ-rus, *n.* [Gr. *homarēs*, well-adjusted.] The typical genus of the lobster family.

hō-mat′rō-pine, *n.* [Gr. *homos*, the same, and *atropos*, inflexible.] An alkaloid derived from atropine, which it resembles in properties.

hom-ax-ō′ni-ăl, *a.* [Gr. *homos*, the same, and *axōn*, an axle.] In biology, having equality of axes.

hom-ax-on′iç, *a.* Homaxonial.

hōme, *n.* [ME. *home*, *hoom*, *ham*; AS. *ham*, a home, dwelling.]

1. A dwelling-house; the house or place in which one resides; the seat of domestic life and interests; as, he was not at *home*.

Home is the sacred refuge of our life.—Dryden.

2. One's own country; as, let affairs at *home* be well managed by the administration.

3. The place of constant residence; the seat.

Flandria, by plenty, made the *home* of war. —Prior.

4. The grave; death; a future state.

Man goeth to his long *home*.—Eccles. xii. 5.

5. The place of accustomed location, as of an animal, a plant, etc.; as, the *home* of the seal or of the eucalyptus.

6. The abiding-place of one's affections; as, the *home* is where the heart is.

7. A place provided for the needy and the homeless; as, a *home* for orphans or for veterans.

8. In some games, the place of beginning and ending, as in baseball, cricket, hare and hounds, etc.; the goal.

At home: (a) at one's own house or lodgings; (b) in one's own country; opposed to *abroad*; (c) ready to receive callers.

To be at home on any subject; to be familiar with a subject in every detail.

To make oneself at home; to lay aside conventionalities and conduct oneself as if at one's own home.

hōme, *a.* 1. Pertaining to one's dwelling or country; domestic; as, *home* manufactures.

2. Close; severe; poignant; as, a *home* blow.

Home department; in Great Britain, that department of government relating to the internal affairs of the country, as distinguished from foreign affairs.

Home base; in baseball, the base at which the batsman stands and which a runner must reach in order to score.

Home farm; a farm on which the owner resides, as distinguished from other farms or lands which he may own.

Home lot; in the United States, a lot or portion of a farm on which is located the dwelling with its surrounding buildings, lawns, gardens, etc., as distinguished from the rest of the farm.

Home rule; the principle or form of government by which a state, province, city, or other political division of a country enjoys the control of its own internal affairs; specifically, in British politics, the program of the Irish party advocating a separate parliament for Ireland.

Home run; in baseball, a complete circuit of the bases without stopping.

Home thrust; in dueling with swords, a thrust in a vital part of the body; hence, in controversy, an effective personal attack.

hōme, *adv.* 1. To, at, or toward one's own habitation; as, go *home*; come *home*; bring *home*; carry *home*.

2. Close; closely; to the point; at, to, or toward the intended place; as, the consideration comes *home* to our interest; drive the nail *home*.

To bring home; see under *Bring*.

To come home; see under *Come*.

hōme′bọrn, *a.* 1. Native; natural; domestic; not foreign.

2. Having origin at home; relating to home.

hōme′-bound, *a.* Same as *Homeward-bound*.

hōme′-bred, *a.* 1. Native; natural; as, *home-bred* lusts.

2. Domestic; originating at home; not foreign; hence, plain; rude; artless; uncultivated; not polished by travel.

hōme′-brewed (-bröd), *a.* Brewed or made at home, as opposed to made in a public brewery; as, *home-brewed* ale.

hōme′-cọm″ing, *n.* A coming home or homeward; return from travel or after prolonged absence.

hōme′-driv″en, *a.* Driven to the appropriate place, as by a blow; as, a *home-driven* nail or pile.

hōme′-felt, *a.* Felt in one's own heart; as, *home-felt* pleasures.

hōme′fiēld, *n.* A field near one's home, adjoining the home lot.

hōme′-keep″ing, *a.* Staying at home.

Home-keeping youth have ever homely wits. —Shak.

hōme′less, *a.* Destitute of a home.

hōme′less-ness, *n.* The state of being homeless or without a home.

hōme′līke, *a.* Resembling or like home; comfortable; familiar.

hōme′li-ly, *adv.* In a homely manner; rudely; inelegantly.

hōme′li-ness, *n.* The state or quality of being homely; plainness of features; want of beauty; want of refinement or polish; simplicity; commonplaceness; coarseness; as, the *homeliness* of dress or of sentiments.

hōme′ling, *n.* A person or thing belonging to a home or to a country.

A word treated as a *homeling*. —Trench.

hōme′ly, *a.*; *comp.* homelier; *superl.* homeliest. [ME. *homly*, *hoomly*, domestic, belonging to home, plain, from *home*; AS. *ham*, home.]

1. Pertaining to home or to the household; domestic.

Their *homely* joys, and destiny obscure. —Gray.

2. Of plain features; not handsome; as, a *homely* face.

It is observed by some that there is none so *homely* but loves a looking-glass. —South.

3. Plain; like that which is made for common domestic use; rude; coarse; not fine or elegant; as, a *homely* garment; a *homely* house; *homely* fare.

hōme′ly, *adv.* Plainly; rudely; coarsely; as, *homely* dressed. [Rare.]

hōme′lyn (hōm′lin), *n.* A species of European ray, *Raia maculata*; called also *sand ray* and *spotted ray*.

hōme′māde, *a.* Made at home; being of domestic manufacture; made either in a private family or in one's own country.

hō′mē-ō-path, **hō′mœ-ō-path**, *n.* A homeopathist.

hō″mē-ō-path′iç, **hō″mē-ō-path′iç-ăl**, *a.* Pertaining or belonging to homeopathy.

hō″mē-ō-path′iç-ăl-ly, *adv.* By or in the method of homeopathy.

hō-mē-op′ȧ-thist, *n.* A believer in homeopathy; a homeopathic practitioner.

hō-mē-op′ȧ-thy, *n.* [Gr. *homoiopatheia*, from *homoiopathēs*, having like feelings or affections; *homoios*, like, similar, and *pathos*, feeling, suffering.] The doctrine or theory of curing diseases with very minute doses of medicine which in a healthy person would produce a condition like that of the disease treated.

hōme′-plāte, *n.* In baseball, the base at which the batsman stands and which a runner must reach in order to score.

hōm′ēr, *n.* 1. A pigeon trained to return home.

2. In baseball, a home run.

hō′mēr, *n.* The basking shark; the hoemother, *Cetorhinus maximus*.

hō′mēr, *n.* [Heb. *khōmer*, a homer, a mound, from *khāmar*, to surge up, swell up.] A Hebrew measure containing as a liquid measure ten baths and as a dry measure ten ephahs.

Hō-mer′iç, *a.* [L. *Homericus*; Gr. *Homērikos*, relating to Homer; *Homēros*, Homer.] Pertaining to Homer, the great poet of Greece, or to his poetry; resembling Homer's verse.

Homeric poems; the two great classic epics, the Odyssey and the Iliad.

Homeric verse; hexameter verse; the verse used in the Homeric poems.

hōme′sick, *a.* Depressed in spirits, or grieved at a separation from home.

hōme′sick-ness, *n.* In medicine, nostalgia; grief or depression of spirits, occasioned by a separation from one's home or country.

hōme′-spēak″ing, *n.* Forcible and efficacious speaking.

hōme′spun, *a.* 1. Spun or wrought at home; of domestic manufacture.

2. Plain; coarse; rude; homely; not elegant; as, a *homespu* English proverb; a *homespun* author.

hōme′spun, *n.* 1. Cloth made at home; as, he was dressed in *homespun*.

2. A coarse, unpolished, rustic person. [Obs.]

hōme′stạll, *n.* [Obs.] See *Homestead*.

hōme′stead (-sted), *n.* [AS. *ham*, home, and *stede*, place.]

1. A home; the seat of a family; especially, a dwelling retained as a home by successive generations.

2. The inclosure or ground connected with a home.

3. Native seat; original station, or place of residence of a family.

We can trace them back to a *homestead* on the Rivers Volga and Ural. —Tooke.

Homestead Act; in the United States, an act of Congress passed in 1862 granting land not to exceed 160 acres to any citizen or alien intending to become a citizen upon condition of an occupancy of five years.

Homestead law; in the United States, (a) a law providing for the exemption of a homestead rom seizure and sale for debt; (b) same as *Homestead Act*.

hōme′stead-ēr, *n.* A person who avails himself of the privileges of the Homestead Act. [Local, U. S.]

hōme′-stretch, *n.* The last part of a race, or of the race-track; a straight course ending at the winning-post.

hōme′wȧrd, *a.* Being in the direction of home; as, a *homeward* journey.

hōme′wȧrd, *adv.* Toward home; toward one's habitation, or toward one's native country.

hōme′wȧrd-bound, *a.* Bound or directing the course homeward, or to one's native land; returning homeward; as, the *homeward-bound* fleet.

hom′i-ci-dăl, *a.* Pertaining to homicide; murderous; bloody.

hom′i-cīde, *n.* [OFr. *homicide*; LL. *homicidium*, manslaughter, murder; L. *homo*, man, and *cædere*, to cut, kill.]

1. The killing of one man or human being by another.

2. A person who kills another; a manslayer.

hom′i-fọrm, *a.* Shaped like a man. [Obs.]

hom′i-lēte, *n.* [Gr. *homilētēs*, a companion, hearer, from *homilein*, to be in company, converse.] An expert in homiletics. [Rare.]

hom-i-let′iç, *a.* 1. Pertaining to familiar intercourse; social; conversable; companionable.

2. Pertaining to homiletics.

hom-i-let′içs, *n.* [Gr. *homilētikos*, of or for conversation, affable, from *homilein*, to be in company, converse, from *homilos*, a gathering, company.] The science which teaches the principles of adapting the discourses of the pulpit to the spiritual benefit of the hearers; the art of preparing sermons and of preaching.

hom′i-list, *n.* One who preaches to a congregation; a sermonizer.

hom′i-līte, *n.* In mineralogy, a ferrocalcic borosilicate of a brownish-black color allied to datolite.

hom′i-ly, *n.*; *pl.* **hom′i-lieṣ**. [LL. *homilia*, a sermon, from Gr. *homilia*, intercourse, instruction (L.Gr., a sermon), from *homilos*, an assembly, from *homos*, the same.]

1. A discourse or sermon read or pronounced to an audience; an expository sermon.

2. A serious admonition or exhortation upon a course of conduct; as, to read one a *homily* on his behavior.

Book of homilies; in England, a collection of prepared sermons to be used by the inferior clergy, who were not qualified to write homilies.

hōm′ing, *a.* Returning home; having special facility in finding home; said of animals other than man; as, a *homing* pigeon.

hōm′ing, *n.* The act of going home or of coming home.

hom′i-ny, *n.* [Am. Ind. *auhuminea*, parched corn.] Maize hulled and broken, but coarse, prepared for food by being mixed with water and boiled; hulled corn.

hōm′ish, *a.* Homelike. [Colloq.]

hŏm′mŏck, *n.* Same as *Hummock*.

homo-. A combining form from Gr. *homos*, the same. It is used in chemistry, biology, botany, etc., to signify same, equal; as, *homo*carpous, *homo*dermy.

hō-mō-çăr′pous, *a.* [*Homo-*, and Gr. *karpos*, fruit.] In botany, having similar carpels or fruits, as in the head of a composite flower.

hō-mō-çat-ē-gor′iç, *a.* [*Homo-*, and Gr. *katēgoria*, category.] Being in the same category.

hō-mō-cen′triç, *a.* [*Homo-*, and Gr. *kentron*, a point, center.] Having the same center.

hō-mō-cēr′căl, *a.* [*Homo-*, and Gr. *kerkos*, tail.] In ichthyology, having a caudal fin symmetrically attached and developed; opposed to *heterocercal*.

hō′mō-cēr-cy, *n.* In ichthyology, the condition of being homocercal.

hō-mō-chrō′mous, *a.* [*Homo-*, and Gr. *chrōma*, color.]

1. In botany, like in color; said of the florets in a head.

2. In zoölogy, of uniform color; not spotted or variegated; said of the exoskeleton.

hō-mō-dem′iç, *a.* [*Homo-*, and Gr. *dēmos*, district.] In biology, derived from the same undifferentiated aggregate of cells.

hō-mō-dēr′miç, *a.* In biology, relating to homodermy.

hō′mō-dẽr-my, *n.* [*Homo-*, and Gr. *derma*, skin.] In biology, homology with regard to the germinal layers of the skin.

hom′ō-dŏnt, *a.* [*Homo-*, and Gr. *odous, odontos*, a tooth.] Having a dental armature consisting of similar teeth, as the dolphins; opposite of *heterodont*.

hō-mod′rō-măl, *a.* Homodromous.

hō-mod′rō-mous, *a.* [Gr. *homodromos*, running the same course; *homos*, the same, and *dromos*, a course, race, from *dramein*, to run.]

1. In botany, twining in the same direction, that is, to the right or to the left; said of vines or of the arrangement of buds on a branch.

2. In mechanics, designating a lever of the third class. [See *Lever*.]

hō-mō-dȳ-nam′iç, *a.* Homodynamous.

hō-mō-dȳ′nȧ-mous, *a.* In biology, relating to homodynamy.

hō-mō-dȳ′nȧ-my, *n.* [Gr. *homodynamos*, of like power; *homos*, the same, and *dynamis*, power.] In biology, homology of serial segments.

ho-mœ-o-, ho-me-o-, ho-moi-o-. Combining forms from Gr. *homoios*, like, similar, used in biology, chemistry, botany, etc., to signify like, similar; as, *homœ*omerous, *homœo*morphism.

hō-mœ-om′ẽr-ăl, *a.* [Gr. *homœmeros*, consisting of like parts; *homoios*, like, and *meros*, part.] In ancient prosody, relating to a versification in which occur (a) two similar strophes, or (b) two metrically similar systems of pericope.

hō″mœ-ō-mē′ri-ȧ, *n.* Same as *Homœomery*.

hō″mœ-ō-mer′iç, hō″mē-ō-mer′iç-ăl, *a.* Relating to homœomery.

hō-mœ-om′ẽr-ous, *a.* [*Homœo-*, and Gr. *meros*, part.] Having parts alike; specifically, in lichenology, having a uniform distribution of gonidia and hyphæ over the thallus; written also *homeomerous*.

hō-mœ-om′ẽr-y, *n.* [L., from Gr. *homoiomereia*, the state of being homogeneous; *homos*, like, and *meros*, part.] The doctrine of the likeness of parts to the whole as applied to elementary substances.

hō-mœ-ō-mor′phism, *n.* [Gr. *homoiomorphos*, of like form; *homoios*, like, and *morphē*, form.]

1. In crystallography, likeness of form regardless of chemical composition.

2. Same as *Isomorphism*.

hō′mœ-ō-path, hō-mœ-ō-path′iç, etc. Same as *Homeopath*, etc.

hō″mœ-op-tō′tŏn, *n.* [LL. *homœoptoton*; Gr. *homoioptōtos*, with similar inflection; *homoios*, like, and *ptōsis*, case, inflection.] An old rhetorical figure consisting in the use of the same case endings, inflections, etc., in similar situations, as at the end of phrases.

hō″mœ-ō-tē-leū′tŏn, *n.* [LL., from Gr. *homoioteleuton*, rime, properly neut. of *homoioteleutos*, having a like ending; *homoios*, like, and *teleutē*, ending, from *telein*, to end.] An old rhetorical figure requiring like-sounding words, syllables, or phrases at the close of a series of sentences or lines.

hō-mœ-ō-thẽr′măl, *a.* [*Homœo-*, and Gr. *thermos*, heat.] Preserving a uniform temperature regardless of environment; said of the blood of animals.

hō-mœ-ō-zō′iç, *a.* [*Homœo-*, and Gr. *zōē*, life.] Embracing or marked by similar forms of life; as, *homœozoic* zones.

hō-mō-fō′căl, *a.* Same as *Confocal*.

hō-mog′ȧ-mous, *a.* [Gr. *homogamos*, married together; *homos*, the same, and *gamos*, marriage.] In botany, having all the florets with both male and female organs; bearing the same kind of flowers; said of grasses and composite plants.

hō-mog′ȧ-my, *n.* The state of being homogamous; fertilization in a homogamous plant.

hō-mō-gan′gli-āte, *a.* [*Homo-*, and Gr. *ganglion*, a ganglion.] In zoölogy, characterized by symmetrical arrangement of the ganglia.

hō′mō-ġen, *n.* [Gr. *homogenēs*, of the same race, family, or kind; *homos*, the same, and *genos*, race, family, kind.] In zoölogy, (a) one of a group having its origin in specifically identical parents; (b) an organ having an origin corresponding to that of an organ in a different class; as, the arm of man is a *homogen* of the wing of a bird, and vice versa.

hō′mō-ġēne, *a.* [Obs.] See *Homogeneous*.

hō-mō-ġē′nē-ăl, *a.* Homogeneous.

hō-mō-ġē′nē-ăl-ness, *n.* Homogeneousness.

hō″mō-ġē-nē′i-ty, *n.* The character or quality of being homogeneous.

hō-mō-ġē′nē-ous, *a.* [Gr. *homogenēs*, of the same race, family, or kind; *homos*, the same, and *genos*, race, family, kind.]

1. Of the same character; essentially like; of the same nature.

2. In physics, having the same molecular structure and of uniform density; as, in a *homogeneous* sphere, the mass-center coincides with the mathematical center.

3. In an algebraic equation or expression, having all its unknown terms of the same degree.

Homogeneous strain; in physics, a strain that so affects a body as not to interfere with the relative position of any of its particles; a uniform strain affecting cohesion solely.

hō-mō-ġē′nē-ous-ness, *n.* Sameness of kind or nature.

hō-mō-ġen′e-sis, *n.* [*Homo-*, and Gr. *genesis*, birth.] In biology, the ordinary or regular course of generation, in which the offspring continues to be like the parent. Compare *heterogenesis, xenogenesis, parthenogenesis*, etc.

hō″mō-ġē-net′iç, *a.* 1. Of, relating to, or demoting homogenesis.

2. Of a common origin; characterized by homogeny.

3. In geology, having similar structure, indicating origin through similar agencies.

hō-moġ′e-nous, *a.* [*Homo-*, and Gr. *genos*, race, family, kind.]

1. Derived from the same source.

2. Bearing a resemblance in structure, indicating common origin.

hō-moġ′e-ny, *n.* [Gr. *homogeneia*, community of birth, from *homogenēs*, of the same race or family; *homos*, the same, and *genos*, race, family, kind.]

1. Joint nature. [Obs.]

2. In biology, origin in and descent from a common ancestor, exemplified by certain characteristics of structure; opposed to *homoplasy*.

hō-mog′ō-nous, *a.* [*Homo-*, and Gr. *gonos*, offspring.] In botany, having the stamens and pistils alike in respect to length and location in all the flowers of individuals of the same species.

hō-mog′ō-ny, *n.* In botany, the quality that renders homogonous.

hom′ō-grȧph, *n.* [Gr. *homographos*, of or with the same letters; *homos*, the same, and *graphein*, to write.] In philology, a word of the same spelling as another but derived from a different root and having a different meaning, as *pine*, to languish, and *pine*, a tree.

hō-mō-grȧph′iç, *a.* Relating to homography; specifically, in geometry, noting two figures so related that a point in one has one and but one corresponding point in the other, and vice versa.

hō-mog′rȧ-phy, *n.* 1. In orthography, the method of using a distinctive character to represent each sound.

2. In geometry, the relation that exists between homographic figures.

Hō-moi-ou′si-ăn, *n.* [Gr. *homoiousios*, of like nature or substance; *homoios*, like, and *ousia*, being, from *ousa*, f. of *ōn*, ppr. of *einai*, to be.] One of a sect of Arians, followers of Eusebius, who maintained that the nature of Christ is not the same with, but only similar to, that of the Father, as distinguished from the *Homoousians*, who maintained that he was of the same nature.

Hō-moi-ou′si-ăn, *a.* 1. Relating to the Homoiousians or to their doctrines.

2. [h—] Having a similar nature.

hō-mol′ō-gāte, *v.t.*; homologated, *pt.*, *pp.*; homologating, *ppr.* [LL. *homologatus*, pp. of *homologare*, from Gr. *homologein*, to agree, assent; *homos*, the same, and *legein*, say speak.] To approve of; to assent to; to ratify.

hō-mol-ō-gā′tion, *n.* The act of homologating; approval; ratification; specifically, in Scots law, a technical expression signifying an act by which a person approves of a deed the effect of which approbatory act is to render that deed, though itself defective, binding upon the person by whom it is homologated.

hō-mō-loġ′iç, *a.* 1. In geometry, noting two figures in the same plane one of which may be a projection of the other.

2. Same as *Homologous*.

hō-mō-loġ′iç-ăl, *a.* Pertaining to homology; having a structural affinity.

hō-mō-loġ′iç-ăl-ly, *adv.* In a homological manner or sense.

hō-mol′ō-ġīze, *v.t.* and *v.i.*; homologized, *pt.*, *pp.*; homologizing, *ppr.* I. *v.t.* To render homologous; to prove the existence of homologies in.

II. *v.i.* To correspond; to be homologous.

hō-mol′ō-gon, *n.* Something that agrees with or is a repetition of another.

hō″mō-lō-gou′me-nȧ, *n.pl.* [Gr. *homologoumena*, things granted or conceded, properly neut. pl. of *homologoumenos*, ppr. pass. of *homologein*, to agree, admit; *homos*, the same, and *legein*, to speak.] An epithet applied by Eusebius to the generally acknowledged books of the New Testament, to distinguish them from the *Antilegomena*.

hō-mol′ō-gous, *a.* [Gr. *homologos*, agreeing, assenting; *homos*, the same, and *legein*, to speak.] Having the same relative position, proportion, value, or structure; specifically, (a) in geometry, corresponding in relative position and proportion; as, in similar polygons, the corresponding sides, angles, diagonals, etc., are *homologous*; (b) in algebra, having the same relative proportion or value, as the two antecedents or the two consequents of a proportion; (c) in chemistry, being of the same chemical type or series; differing by a multiple or arithmetical ratio in certain constituents, while the physical qualities are analogous, with small differences, as if corresponding to a series of parallels; as, the species in the several groups of alcohols, fatty acids, and aromatic acids are *homologous* with the others in the same group; (d) in physiology, corresponding in type of structure; having like relations to a fundamental type; thus, the human arm, the foreleg of a horse, the wing of a bird, and the swimming-paddle of a dolphin or whale, being all composed essentially of the same structural elements, are said to be *homologous*, though they are adapted for quite different functions.

hom″ō-lō-grȧph′iç, *a.* [*Homo-*, and Gr. *holos*, whole, and *graphein*, to write.] Maintaining or exhibiting the true proportions of parts; preserving true relations as to size and form.

Homolographic projection; that method of laying down portions of the earth's surface on a map or chart so that the different portions of the surfaces delineated have their due relative size and form.

hom′ō-logue (-log), *n.* [Fr. *homologue*, from Gr. *homologos*, agreeing, assenting.] That which is homologous; that which has the same relative position, proportion, value, or structure; thus, the corresponding sides of similar geometrical figures are *homologues*; an organ agreeing in the plan of its structure with a corresponding organ in a different animal, though differing in function, is a *homologue* of this corresponding organ.

hō-mol′ō-ġy, *n.*; *pl.* **hō-mol′ō-ġieș.** [Gr. *homologia*, agreement, conformity, from *homologos*, agreeing.] The quality of being homologous; correspondence; relation; as, the *homology* of similar polygons; specifically, in biology, that relation between parts which results from their development from corresponding embryonic parts, either in different animals, as in the case of the arm of man, the foreleg of a quadruped, and the wing of a bird, or in the same individual, as in the case of the fore and hind legs in quadrupeds.

General homology; in biology, the general relation or agreement between a part or parts and the basic type.

Serial homology; in biology, homology in a series of parts which are repetitions of a typical form.

Special homology; in biology, the agreement of a part of an animal with a correspondingly situated part of some other animal.

hō-mom′ȧ-lous, *a.* [*Homo-*, and Gr. *homalos*, even, level, equal.] In botany, originating all round a stem, as leaves, and all bending or curving round to one side.

hō-mō-mor′phiç, *a.* 1. In entomology, relating to a series of insects, the *Homomorpha*.

2. Relating to homomorphism; homomorphous.

hō-mō-mor′phism, *n.* [*Homo-*, and Gr. *morphē*, form.] The condition or character of being homomorphous, or of having the same external appearance or form.

hō-mō-mor′phous, *a.* Having the same external appearance or form.

hō-mō-mor′phy, *n.* Homomorphism.

hō-mon′ō-mous, *a.* Relating to homonomy.

hō-mon′ō-my, *n.* [Gr. *homonomos*, under the same laws; *homos*, the same, and *nomos*, law.] Homology; specifically, the homology of parts having a transverse axis.

hom′ō-nym, *n.* [L. *homonymus*; Gr. *homōnymos*, having the same name; *homos*, the same, and *onyma, onoma*, name.] A word which agrees with another in sound, and perhaps in spelling, but differs from it in signification; a word that is the name of more than one object; as, the substantive *bear* and the verb *bear*.

hō-mon′y-mous, *a.* Having the same sound or spelling but different signification; hence, ambiguous; equivocal.

hō-mon′y-mous-ly, *adv.* In a homonymous or equivocal manner.

hō-mon′y-my, *n.* [Gr. *homōnymia*; *homos*, the same, and *onyma*, name.] Sameness of name with a difference of meaning; ambiguity; equivocation.

hō-mō-or′găn, *n.* Same as *Homorgan*.

Hō-mō-ou′si-ăn, *n.* [Gr. *homoousios*, having the same essence; *homos*, the same, and *ousia*, being, substance, from *einai*, to be.] A member of the orthodox party in the church during the great controversy upon the nature of Christ in the fourth century who maintained that the nature of the Father and the Son is the same, in opposition to the *Homoiousians*, who held that their natures were only similar.

hō-mō-ou′si-ăn, *a.* 1. Of the same nature.

2. [H—] Pertaining to the Homoousians or their doctrines.

hom′ō-phōne, *n.* [Gr. *homophōnos*, of the same sound or tone; *homos*, the same, and *phōnē*, voice, sound.]

1. A character representing a sound the same as of another character.

2. Same as *Homonym*.

hom-ō-phon′iç, *a.* Homophonous.

hō-moph′ō-nous, *a.* 1. In music, (a) agreeing

in pitch; (b) designating music or a passage in music in which there is a predominant part; opposed to *polyphonic*.

2. In philology, (a) having the same sound but different sense, as *weigh, way*; (b) representing the same sound by a different character.

hō-moph′ō-ny, *n.* 1. Sameness of sound.

2. In Greek music, music performed in unison; in opposition to *antiphony*.

3. In modern music, simple harmony; in opposition to *polyphony*.

hō-mō-phyl′iç, *a.* [Gr. *homophylia*, sameness of race; *homos*, the same, and *phylē*, race, family.] In biology, of or pertaining to homophyly.

hō-moph′y-ly, *n.* Homology traceable to common ancestry.

hō′mō-plas-my, *n.* [*Homo-*, and Gr. *plasma*, anything formed, from *plassein*, to form, mold.] The condition or quality of being related in characteristics which are not derived from common descent but from similarity of environment.

hom′ō-plast, *n.* [*Homo-*, and Gr. *plastos*, formed, from *plassein*, to form, mold.]

1. In biology, a part agreeing in shape with some other part, but having a distinct nature.

2. Anything having a structure like that of another, but of different origin.

hō-mō-plas′tiç, *a.* Denoting those homologies which arise in consequence of tissues similar in character being subjected to similar influences. Such homologies may arise between groups whose common ancestry is too remote to be credited with the transmission of the characters.

hō′mō-plas-ty, *n.* In biology, the process of forming homologous tissues.

hō-mop′là-sy, *n.* Homology not traceable to common origin; opposed to *homogeny*.

hō-mō-pō′lăr, *a.* [*Homo-*, and Gr. *polos*, a pole.] In promorphology, having equal poles; said of organic forms with a definite number of transverse axes.

hō-mō-pol′iç, *a.* Homopolar.

hō-mop′tēr, *n.* A member of the *Homoptera*.

Hō-mop′te-rà, *n.pl.* [Gr. *homopteros*, of the same plumage; *homos*, the same, and *pteron*, wing.] In zoölogy, a subdivision of hemipterous insects having the wing-covers generally deflexed and of the same consistence throughout, the antennæ mostly short and terminated by a bristle, and the body convex and thick, including the *Aphidæ, Coccidæ, Cicadidæ, Fulgoridæ*, etc.

Homoptera (*Cicada diardi*).

hō-mop′tēr-ăn, *n.* Same as *Homopter*.

hō-mop′tēr-ous, *a.* Of or pertaining to the *Homoptera*.

hō-mor′găn, *n.* In biology, a similarly organized part or system; a homoplastic part.

hō-mo-spōr′ous, *a.* [*Homo-*, and Gr. *sporos*, spore, seed.] In botany, having asexual spores of one kind only.

hō′mō-stȳled, *a.* [*Homo-*, and Gr. *stylos*, pillar.] In botany, denoting species in which the individuals bear styles of the same length and character; opposed to *heterostyled*.

hō-mō-tax′e-ous, *a.* Homotaxial.

hō-mō-tax′i-ăl, *a.* Relating to homotaxis.

hō-mō-tax′iç, *a.* Homotaxial.

hō-mō-tax′is, *n.* [*Homo-*, and Gr. *taxis*, arrangement.] The same arrangement; specifically, in geology, agreement in the arrangement in different localities of strata which occupy the same place or position in the stratified systems, but which may or may not be contemporaneous.

hō′mō-tax-y, *n.* Homotaxis.

hō-mō-thēr′mous, *a.* [*Homo-*, and Gr. *thermē*, heat.] In zoölogy and physiology, having the same degree of bodily temperature.

hō-mot′ō-nous, *a.* [L. *homotonus*; Gr. *homotonos*, of the same tone; *homos*, the same, and *tonos*, tone.] Of the same tone; unvarying in tenor; having equability of beginning, advance, or decline; said of diseases.

hō-mot′rō-păl, *a.* Homotropous.

hō-mot′rō-pous, *a.* [Gr. *homotropos*, having the same turn; *homos*, the same, and *trepein*, to turn.] Turned in the same direction; in botany, said of the radicle of a seed when turned toward the hilum.

hō′mō-tȳ-păl, *a.* Homotypic.

hō′mō-tȳpe, *n.* [*Homo-*, and Gr. *typos*, impression, form, type.] In biology, an organ or part having a structure agreeing with some fundamental form; as, the foot is a *homotype* of the hand.

hō-mō-typ′iç, *a.* Relating to or of the nature of a homotype.

hō-mō-typ′iç-ăl, *a.* Homotypic.

hō′mō-tȳ-py, *n.* In biology, correspondence in structure; said of a part with reference to another part in the same individual, as of segments, limbs, vertebræ, etc.

hō-mun′çū-lus, *n.* [L., dim. of *homo, hominis*, a man.] A little human being; a dwarf or pygmy.

hond, *n.* [Obs.] See *Hand*.

hōne, *v.i.*; honed, *pt., pp.*; honing, *ppr.* [Fr. *hogner*, to mutter, murmur, repine.] To pine; to long. [Prov. Eng. and Southern U. S.]

hōne, *v.t.* To rub and sharpen on or as on a hone; as, to *hone* a razor; to *hone* a knife on one's shoe.

hōne, *n.* [Ice. *hunn*, a knob.] A kind of swelling of the cheek.

hōne, *n.* [ME. *hone, hoone*; AS. *han*, a stone.] A stone of very fine grit, usually of a slaty composition, used in etting fine edges, as of razors, surgical instruments, etc.; an oilstone.

hōne′=slāte, *n.* See *Polishing-slate*.

hon′est (on′), *a.* [ME. *honest, onest*; OFr. *honeste, honneste*; L. *honestus*, full of honor, virtuous, from *honor*, honor.]

1. Frank; sincere; according to truth.

2. Upright; just; fair in dealing.

An *honest* man's the noblest work of God. —Pope.

3. Sincere; proceeding from pure or just principles, or directed to a good object; as, an *honest* inquiry after truth; an *honest* endeavor.

4. Fair; good; unimpeached.

Seek seven men of *honest* report.—Acts vi. 3.

5. Decent; honorable; suitable.

Provide things *honest* in the sight of all men. —Rom. xii. 17.

6. Chaste; faithful.

Wives may be merry, and yet *honest* too. —Shak.

Syn.—Frank, open, truthful, sincere, straightforward, upright, unimpeachable, candid, pure, reliable.

hon′est, *v.t.* To adorn; to grace. [Obs.]

hon-es-tā′tion, *n.* Adornment; grace. [Obs.]

ho-nes′te-tē, ho-nes′te-tee, *n.*, old and obsolete variants of *honesty*.

hon′est-ly (on′), *adv.* In an honest manner; with honesty.

To come honestly by; to come into possession of by honest means; to receive by heredity, as a feature or a proclivity.

hōne′stōne, *n.* Any variety of stone employed for making hones. [See *Novaculite*.]

hon′es-ty (on′), *n.* [OFr. *honeste, honneste, oneste*; L. *honestas*, respectability, character, reputation, from *honestus*, honorable.]

1. The character or quality of being honest; sincerity; honor; virtue; upright conduct; conformity to justice and moral rectitude.

2. In botany, one of several plants, as *Lunaria biennis*, common honesty, and *Lunaria rediviva*, perennial honesty; also called *moonwort* and *satin-flower*.

Syn.—Frankness, integrity, probity, purity, rectitude, sincerity, uprightness.

hōne′wŏrt, *n.* In botany, a plant used as a remedy for hone, a kind of swelling of the cheek.

hŏn′ey, *n.* [ME. *hony, huny, hunig*; AS. *hunig*, honey.]

1. A sweet viscid fluid collected by bees from the flowers of plants and deposited in cells of the comb in hives.

2. Sweetness; lusciousness.

The king hath found,
Matter against him, that forever mars
The *honey* of his language. —Shak.

3. Darling; sweet one; a term of endearment.

hŏn′ey, *a.* Like honey in taste; sweet; luscious.

hŏn′ey=ănt, *n.* A kind of ant, *Myrmecocystus mexicanus*, inhabiting Mexico and southwestern United States and living in communities in subterranean galleries. In summer a certain number of these insects secrete a kind of honey in their abdomens. This is disgorged later and eaten by the others.

hŏn′ey=badġ″ēr, *n.* In zoölogy, the ratel, *Mellivora ratellus*, named from its fondness for honey.

hŏn′ey=bag, *n.* The baglike enlargement in the alimentary canal of a bee in which honey is collected and carried.

hŏn′ey=bälm (-bäm), *n.* In botany, a labiate plant of Europe, having large, handsome flowers.

hŏn′ey=beār, *n.* 1. The kinkajou.

2. The aswail or sloth-bear.

hŏn′ey-bee, *n.* A bee that collects honey; specifically, the hive-bee, *Apis mellifica*.

hŏn′ey-ber-ry, *n.* 1. The berry of *Celtis australis*.

2. The berry of *Melicocca bijuga*.

hŏn′ey-bīrd, *n.* A bird that extracts honey from flowers; specifically, any one of the *Meliphagidæ* or honey-eaters, as *Anthochæra mellivora*, the wattled honey-eater.

hŏn′ey=blọọm, *n.* In botany, the spreading dogbane, *Apocynum androsæmifolium*.

hŏn′ey=bread (-bred), *n.* In botany, a leguminous tree of the Mediterranean region, bearing sweet, fleshy, edible pods.

hŏn′ey=buz″zărd, *n.* A bird, *Pernis apivorus*, of the Old World which feeds on the larvæ of bees; also called *bee-hawk*.

hŏn′ey-çōmb (-kōm), *n.* [AS. *hunigcamb*; *hunig*, honey, and *camb*, comb.]

1. A structure of wax of a firm, close texture, formed by bees into hexagonal cells for repositories of honey and of the eggs which produce their young.

2. A casting of iron or other metal which has cells like a honeycomb.

Honeybird (*Anthochæra mellivora*).

Honeycomb bottom; in navigation, a worm-perforated sea-bottom; called also *hawse-pipe bottom*.

Honeycomb tripe; the mucous membrane of the second stomach of a ruminant, which is divided into small hexagonal cells; called also *honeycomb stomach*.

hŏn′ey-çōmb, *v.t.*; honeycombed (-kōmd), *pt., pp.*; honeycombing, *ppr.* To render like a honeycomb; to fill with openings or holes in the manner of a honeycomb.

hŏn′ey-çōmbed, *a.* Perforated or formed like a honeycomb; specifically, having little flaws or cells, as cast metal when not solid.

hŏn′ey-çōmb=mọth, *n.* A moth which infests beehives, laying its eggs in the honeycomb, which is devoured by the larvæ; a bee-moth.

hŏn′ey-çōmb=spŏnge, *n.* A grass-sponge.

hŏn′ey-dew, *n.* A saccharine substance found on the leaves of trees and other plants in small drops like dew. There are two kinds, one secreted by the plants and the other by insects.

hŏn′ey=ēat″ēr, *n.* 1. Same as *Honeybird*.

2. A honey-bear.

hŏn′eyed (-id), *a.* Covered with or as with honey; hence, sweet; as, *honeyed* words.

hŏn′ey=flow″ēr, *n.* A popular name for the plants of the genus *Melianthus*, natives of the Cape of Good Hope, from the honey contained in the flowers.

hŏn′ey=guīde (-gīd), *n.* A name given to the cuckoos of the African genus *Indicator*, which, by their motions and cries, conduct hunters to hives of wild honey.

hŏn′ey-less, *a.* Destitute of honey.

hŏn′ey=lō″çust, *n.* A North American tree, *Gleditschia triacanthos*, armed with thorns and having wood resembling that of the locust; sometimes called *three-thorned acacia*.

hŏn′ey=lō″tus, *n.* The white sweet clover, *Melilotus alba*.

hŏn′ey-mọọn, *n.* 1. The first month after marriage.

2. The indefinite period usually spent by a newly-married couple in travel and recreation.

3. A period of prosperity and enjoyment [Obs.]

hŏn′ey-mọọn, *v.i.*; honeymooned, *pt., pp.*; honeymooning, *ppr.* To keep one's honeymoon; to take a wedding-trip.

Some decent sort of body to *honeymoon* along with me. —Trollope.

hŏn′ey=mouthed, *a.* Soft or smooth in speech.

hŏn′ey=pod, *n.* In botany, the pod of the algarroba or mesquit, *Prosopis juliflora*; also, the tree.

hŏn′ey-stōne, *n.* Same as *Mellite*.

hŏn′ey-suck-ēr, *n.* Same as *Honeybird*.

hŏn′ey-suç-kle, *n.* [ME. *honysocle*; AS. *hunisuce*; *hunig*, honey, and *sucan*, to suck.]

1. In botany, the name of some species of the genus *Lonicera* of the order *Caprifoliaceæ*, celebrated for the beauty and fragrance of their flowers; the common honeysuckle of the United States is *Lonicera Periclymenum* or the woodbine.

2. The popular name of plants of other families, as the columbine, *Aquilegia Canadensis*. The red clover, *Trifolium pratense*, and the white clover, *Trifolium repens*, are sometimes so called in England on account of the saccharine secretions in their petals.

Honeysuckle (*Lonicera Caprifolium*).

hŏn′ey-suç-kle=ap″ple, *n.* A juicy apple-like fungus growing on the branches of *Rhododendron nudiflorum* or azalea.

hŏn′ey-suc̦-kle-c̦lō″vẽr, *n.* The common white clover, *Trifolium repens.*

hŏn′ey-suc̦-kled, *a.* Covered with honeysuckles.

hŏn′ey-suc̦-kle-tree, *n.* In botany, an Australian tree of the genus *Banksia,* including several species whose flowers yield honey.

hŏn′ey-sug̣″ăr (-shug̣″), *n.* The hard or granulated part of old honey.

hŏn′ey-sweet, *a.* and *n.* I. *a.* Sweet as honey. II. *n.* In botany, *Spiræa ulmaria* or English meadowsweet.

hŏn′ey-tŏngued (-tungd), *a.* Using soft speech.

hŏn′ey-wāre, *n.* Same as *Badderlocks.*

hŏn′ey-wŏrt, *n.* A plant of the genus *Cerinthe,* whose flowers are very attractive to bees.

hong, *n.* [Chinese *hang, hong,* a row, series, a factory.]

1. A Chinese warehouse.

2. Formerly, one of a number of foreign factories in Canton, where each foreign nation had a separate hong; now, any foreign mercantile establishment in China, Japan, etc.

Hong merchant; one of a number of Chinese merchants at Canton who formerly had the sole privilege of trading with foreigners.

hong, *v.,* obsolete form of *hang.*

hŏn′ied, *a.* See *Honeyed.*

hoñk, *v.i.*; honked, *pt., pp.*; honking, *ppr.* [Imitative.] To utter honks; to utter a cry in imitation of that of a wild goose in flight.

hoñk, *n.* The cry uttered by a wild goose.

hoñk′ẽr, *n.* One who or that which honks; specifically, a wild goose.

hon′ŏr, hon′ŏur (on′ẽr), *n.* [ME. *honour, honor, onour, onur*; OFr. *honor, hounor, onor, ounour*; L. *honor, honos,* official dignity, repute, esteem.]

1. The esteem due or paid to worth; high estimation; reverence; veneration.

A prophet is not without *honor,* save in his own country. —Matt. xiii. 57.

2. A testimony or token of esteem; any mark of respect or of high estimation by words or actions; as, military *honors*; civil *honors.*

Their funeral *honors* claimed, and asked their quiet graves. —Dryden.

3. Dignity; exalted rank or place; distinction; dignity of mien; noble appearance.

Godlike erect! with native *honor* clad. —Milton.

4. Reputation; good name; as, his *honor* is unsullied.

5. A nice sense of what is right, just, and true; dignified respect for character, springing from probity, principle, or moral rectitude; scorn of meanness.

6. Any particular virtue much valued, as bravery or integrity in men and chastity in women.

If she have forgot *honor* and virtue.—Shak.

7. One who or that which is a source of glory or esteem; he who or that which confers dignity; glory; boast; as, the chancellor is an *honor* to his profession.

8. Title or privilege of rank or birth; that which gains for a man consideration, as nobility, knighthood, or other titles.

Restore me to my *honors.* —Shak.

9. That which adorns; ornament; decoration.

The sire then shook the *honors* of his head. —Dryden.

10. In English law, a seigniory of several manors held under one baron or lord paramount.

11. In whist, one of the four highest trump cards.

12. A title of address formerly used in addressing or speaking of a person of high rank or office, and still in use with the possessive pronoun when addressing or mentioning certain magistrates, particularly a judge; as, if *his honor* please; may it please *your honor.*

13. [*pl.*] Civilities paid, as at an entertainment.

14. [*pl.*] Academic and university distinction or preëminence; as, he took his degree with *honors* in classics.

Affair of honor; a duel; also, a dispute or quarrel resulting in a duel.

Code of honor; rules specifying the qualities of honorable conduct, especially in respect to settling differences by dueling.

Court of honor; any court convened to decide questions involving a violation of the laws of honor.

Debt of honor; a debt, as a bet, for which no security is required or given except that implied by honorable dealing.

Honor bright! a direct appeal to one's honor. [Colloq.]

Honors of war; (a) magnanimous concessions granted to a vanquished enemy, as of marching out from a camp or intrenchments with all the insignia of military etiquette; (b) formal ceremonies accorded to a soldier at the time of his death and burial; as, he was buried with the *honors of war.*

Laws of honor; rules established for honorable conduct among gentlemen, formerly recognized and rigidly enforced through public opinion.

Maid of honor; (a) a lady of high birth who appears in public with the queen; (b) in the United States, a bride's attendant at the wedding ceremony.

On or *upon one's honor*; words accompanying a declaration as a pledge of one's honor or reputation for the truth of it.

Point of honor; a scruple which, by affecting a person's honor, determines his action on a particular occasion.

To do one honor; to treat one with great consideration; also, to bestow eminence upon one.

To have the honor; to have the opportunity; to be chosen; as, *to have the honor* of introducing a distinguished guest.

Word of honor; a pledge which cannot be violated without reflecting upon the honor of the one pledging.

Syn.—Respect, nobility, dignity, reputation, spirit, self-respect, renown, esteem.

hon′ŏr (on′), *v.t.*; honored, *pt., pp.*; honoring, *ppr.* [L. *honorare,* to honor, respect, decorate, from *honor, honos,* honor, esteem.]

1. To revere; to respect; to treat with deference and submission.

Honor thy father and thy mother.—Ex. xx. 12.

2. To reverence; to manifest the highest veneration for, in words and in actions; to entertain the most exalted thoughts of; to worship; to adore.

That all men should *honor* the Son, even as they *honor* the Father. —John v. 23.

3. To dignify; to raise to distinction or notice; to elevate in rank or station; to exalt.

Thus shall it be done to the man whom the king delighteth to *honor.* —Est. vi. 9.

4. In commerce, to accept and pay when due; as, to *honor* a bill of exchange.

Syn.—Adore, idolize, respect, revere, reverence, venerate, worship, esteem.

hon′ŏr-ȧ-ble (on′), *a.* [L. *honorabilis,* from *honorare,* to honor, esteem.]

1. Worthy of being honored; estimable; holding a distinguished rank in society; illustrious or noble.

Many of them believed; also of *honorable* women which were Greeks . . . not a few. —Acts xvii. 12.

2. Actuated by principles of honor or a scrupulous regard to probity, rectitude, or reputation; as, he is an *honorable* man.

3. Conferring honor, or procured by noble deeds.

Honorable wounds from battle brought. —Dryden.

4. Consistent with honor or reputation; as, it is not *honorable* to oppress the weak or to insult the vanquished.

5. Respected; worthy of respect; regarded with esteem.

Marriage is *honorable* in all. —Heb. xiii. 4.

6. Performed or accompanied with marks of honor or with testimonies of esteem; as, an *honorable* burial.

An *honorable* conduct let him have.—Shak.

7. Proceeding from an upright and laudable cause, or directed to a just and proper end; not base; not reproachful; as, an *honorable* motive.

Is this proceeding just and *honorable*?—Shak.

8. Not to be disgraced.

Let her descend; . . . my chambers are *honorable.* —Shak.

9. Honest; without hypocrisy or deceit; fair; as, his intentions appear to be *honorable.*

10. An epithet of respect or distinction prefixed to a person's name, commonly given in the United States, to one holding or who has held an important public office. In England, this designation is bestowed upon the younger children of earls, and the children of viscounts and barons; also, upon persons enjoying trust and honor, and collectively on the House of Commons, as formerly on the East India Company.

11. Becoming men of rank and character, or suited to support men in a station of dignity; as, an *honorable* salary.

Right honorable; a title given to all peers and peeresses of the United Kingdom; to the eldest sons and all the daughters of peers above the rank of viscount; to all privy-councilors, and to some civic functionaries, as the lord mayors of London and Dublin.

hon′ŏr-ȧ-ble-ness, *n.* 1. The state of being honorable; eminence; distinction.

2. Conformity to the principles of honor, probity, or moral rectitude; fairness.

hon′ŏr-ȧ-bly, *adv.* In an honorable manner; in a manner conferring or consistent with honor.

Syn.—Magnanimously, generously, nobly, worthily, justly, equitably, fairly, reputably.

hon-ō-rā′ri-um, *n.*; *pl.* **hon-ō-rā′ri-ȧ** (on-). [L. *honorarium* (supply *donum,* gift), neut. of *honorarius,* honorary.]

1. A fee paid to a professional man.

2. In England, the fee of a barrister, in allusion to the fact that a barrister cannot enforce payment for services.

hon′ŏr-ā-ry, *n.*; *pl.* **hon′ŏr-ā-ries.** An honorarium.

hon′ŏr-ā-ry, *a.* [L. *honorarius,* relating to or conferring honor, from *honor, honos,* esteem, respect.]

1. Conferring honor, or intended merely to confer honor; as, an *honorary* degree; an *honorary* crown.

2. Possessing a title or place without performing services or receiving a reward; as, an *honorary* member of a society.

hon′ŏr-ẽr, *n.* One who honors.

hon-ŏr-if′ic̦, *a.* Conferring honor; honorary.

hon-ŏr-if′ic̦, *n.* Any expression of mere honor.

hon′ŏr-less, *a.* Destitute of honor; not honored.

hont, honte, *n.* and *v.* Hunt. [Obs.]

hoọ, *interj.* An exclamation having various shades of meaning, indicating joy, surprise, disdain, etc., according to the manner in which it is uttered.

-hood. [ME. *-hode, -hod*; AS. *had,* state, condition, character.] A suffix denoting (a) state, quality, character, condition; as, child*hood,* father*hood,* priest*hood*; (b) collectively, a body or organization; as, brother*hood.* It is equivalent to *-head* in such words as God*head.*

hood, *n.* [ME. *hood, hod*; AS. *hod,* a hood.]

1. One of various kinds of coverings for the head. Hoods are of numerous forms, the simplest being a caplike covering, either tied about the neck or draping the neck and shoulders, sometimes being attached to a cape or jacket.

Hood for Hawk. Monk's Hood.

2. The folding cover of a carriage or other vehicle, designed to protect the occupants from the sun, rain, etc.

3. In falconry, a close covering fitting the head so as to prevent sight of the quarry.

4. Anything that resembles a hood in form or use; as, (a) the upper petal or sepal of certain flowers, as monk's-hood; (b) a low wooden porch leading to the steerage of a ship; (c) the upper part of a galley chimney; (d) the cover of a pump; (e) the covering for a companion hatch, for a mortar, etc; (f) a piece of tarred canvas put on the ends of standing rigging, etc.; (g) in a chemical laboratory, a fixture shaped like an inverted cone or pyramid for catching and guiding noxious gases into a flue.

5. The hooded seal or hoodcap. [Newfoundland.]

6. In shipbuilding, a name given to the foremost and aftermost planks of a ship's bottom, both inside and outside.

hood, *v.t.*; hooded, *pt., pp.*; hooding, *ppr.* 1. To dress in a hood or a cowl; to put a hood on.

The friar *hooded,* and the monarch crowned. —Pope.

2. To cover; to blind.

I'll *hood* my eyes. —Shak.

hood′c̦ap, *n.* A species of seal, *Stemmatopus cristatus,* found in the arctic seas, so called from an appendage on the head which the male inflates when angry or excited.

hood′ed, *a.* 1. Covered with a hood; blinded.

2. In zoölogy, having a head or a marking that is characteristic of a hood.

3. In botany, cucullate; with the apex resembling the toe of a slipper, as in *Cypripedium.*

Hooded crow; see *Crow.*

Hooded gull; a European gull, *Xema ridibundus,* having a black head.

Hooded merganser; a bird of the goose family, characterized by a profuse covering of feathers on the head; the *Lophodytes cucullatus.*

Hooded seal; same as *Hoodcap.*

Hooded snake; any snake with a distensible neck, as the asp, cobra-de-capello, etc.

hood′less, *a.* Having no hood.

hoọd′lum, *n.* [Originally used in California.] A boisterous, mischievous rowdy, a lawless idler. [Colloq.]

hood′măn, *n.* The blindfolded person in the play of blindman's buff.

hood′măn-blind, *n.* A play in which a person blinded is to catch another, and tell his name; blindman's buff.

hood′=mōld, hood′=mōld″ing, *n.* [So called from its shape.] In architecture, the upper and projecting molding of the arch over a Gothic door or window.

a a, Hood-molding.

hoo′doo, *n.* [A variant of *voodoo.*] 1. Anything that brings bad luck; opposite of *mascot.* [Colloq.]

2. A fantastic formation of volcanic rock modified by erosion. [Western U. S.]

hoo′doo, *v.t.* To give or bring bad luck to. [Colloq., U. S.]

hood′wink, *v.t.*; hoodwinked (-winkt), *pt., pp.*; hoodwinking, *ppr.* 1. To blind by covering the eyes.

We will blind and *hoodwink* him. —Shak.

2. To cover; to hide. [Obs.]

For the prize I'll bring thee to,
Shall *hoodwink* this mischance. —Shak.

3. To deceive by external appearances or disguise; to impose on.

hood′wŏrt, *n.* An American plant, *Scutellaria lateriflora*; called also *skullcap* and *madweed.*

hood′y, *n.* The hooded crow; called also *hoodie-crow.* [Scot.]

hoof, *n.* [ME. *hoof, hof*; AS. *hof,* a hoof.]

1. The horny substance that covers or terminates the feet of certain animals, as horses, oxen, sheep, goats, deer, etc.

2. A hoofed animal; a beast.

3. In geometry, an ungula.

On the hoof; alive; unslaughtered; said of beef-cattle.

hoof, *v.t.* To walk, as cattle. [Rare.]

To hoof it; to go afoot; to walk.

hoof′bound, *a.* Having pain in the fore feet, occasioned by the dryness and contraction of the hoof.

hoofed (hōft), *a.* Furnished with hoofs.

hoof′less, *a.* Destitute of hoofs.

hook, *n.* [ME. *hok*; AS. *hoc,* a hook.]

1. A piece of iron or other metal bent into a curve for catching, holding, or sustaining anything; as, a *hook* for catching fish; a tenter-*hook*; a pot-*hook*, etc.

2. A snare; a trap. [Rare.]

3. A curving instrument for cutting grass or grain; a sickle; an instrument for cutting or lopping; as, a grass-*hook.*

4. That part of a hinge which is fixed or inserted in a post.

5. A field sown two years running. [Prov. Eng.]

6. Any hook-shaped termination, as (a) the end of the thigh-bone in cattle; (b) a curved sandy promontory; as, Sandy *Hook*; (c) in music, the flag-like appendage to the stem of a written note.

By hook or crook; see under *Crook.*

Hook and eye; a device for fastening garments, consisting of two small metallic parts, one hooking into the other.

Hook-and-ladder company; a company of firemen equipped with a carriage or truck holding ladders and long poles with hooks for tearing away parts of a building in order to extinguish fire.

On one's own hook; by oneself; independent of any assistance.

To get off the hooks; (a) to die; (b) to get out of working order; to become unhinged, as a gate; hence, to meet with misfortune or disaster. [Slang.]

hook, *v.t.*; hooked (hookt), *pt., pp.*; hooking, *ppr.* 1. To catch with a hook; as, to *hook* a fish.

2. To seize and draw, as with a hook.

3. To fasten with a hook, as a dress.

4. To steal. [Slang.]

5. To toss or gore with the horns; as, he was *hooked* by a steer.

To hook it; to decamp. [Slang.]

To hook on; to fasten by or as by a hook.

hook, *v.i.* 1. To bend; to be curving.

2. To become fastened as by a hook.

3. To be in the habit of tossing with the horns; as, the cow was never known to *hook.*

hook′a, hook′ah, *n.* [Ar. *huqqa,* a pipe for smoking, a casket.] A pipe in which the smoke of tobacco is made to pass through water for the purpose of cooling it; a water-pipe.

Hooka.

hook′=bill, *n.* 1. Any bird with a curved bill.

2. A spent male salmon whose jaws have become hooked.

hook′=billed, *a.* Having a curved beak.

hooked (hookt), *a.* 1. Bent into the form of a hook; curvated; as, the claws of a beast are *hooked.* 2. Furnished with hooks.

hook′ed-ness, *n.* The state of being bent like a hook.

hook′ẽr, *n.* 1. One who or that which hooks; one who uses a hook, as a fisherman.

2. A pilferer. [Slang.]

hook′ẽr, *n.* [D. *hoeker,* from *hoek,* a hook.] A vessel or boat; (a) a Dutch vessel with two masts; (b) an English fishing-boat with one mast; (c) any old dilapidated boat.

Something to set the old *hooker* creaking. —W. C. Russell.

hook′ey, *n.* Same as *Hockey.*

hook′let, *n.* A small hook or hook-shaped process.

hook′=nōsed, *a.* Having a nose curving downward toward the mouth; having an aquiline nose.

hook′um, *n.* [Hind. *hukm,* a command, decree.] In India, an official order.

hook′wŏrm, *n.* The *Necator Americanus,* a human parasite found in the soil of the sandy barrens and pine woods of the So. U. S.

Hookworm disease; a disease produced by the hookworm boring through the skin of the foot, circulating in the blood and finally attaching itself to the mucous membrane, where it sucks the blood and poisons the system with its waste products.

hook′y, *n.* [From *hook it,* to decamp.] A truant; used only in the phrase, *to play hooky*; that is, to absent oneself from school without leave. [Slang.]

hook′y, *a.* Full of hooks; pertaining to hooks.

hool, *n.* Husk; hull. [Obs.]

hoo′lock, *n.* [From native name.] A species of gibbon, *Hylobates hoolock,* found in Assam.

hoo′lee, *n.* [Hind. *holī.*] A festival in honor of Krishna, held by Hindus about the time of the vernal equinox, celebrated by singing, dancing, practical joking, and more or less obscenity.

hoo′li-găn, *n.* A rowdy; a hoodlum; a rioter. [Eng. Slang.]

hoom, *n.* Home. [Obs.]

hoop, *n.* [ME. *hoope, hope*; D. *hoep,* a hoop.]

1. A band of wood or metal used to confine the staves of casks, tubs, etc., or for other similar purposes.

2. A strip of whalebone, steel, etc., used formerly in manufacturing hoop-skirts; in the plural, a hoop-skirt; as, she wears *hoops.*

3. Something resembling a hoop; a ring; anything circular.

4. The quantity of drink in a hooped quart measure up to the first hoop.

5. An old English measure of capacity. [Obs.]

6. The casing around a pair of millstones; also, the band around the rotating millstone.

7. A child's plaything, used for trundling.

hoop, *v.t.*; hooped (hōpt), *pt., pp.*; hooping, *ppr.* 1. To bind or fasten with hoops; as, to *hoop* a barrel or a tub.

2. To clasp; to encircle; to surround.

hoop, *v.i.* Same as *Whoop.*

hoop, *v.t.* Same as *Whoop.*

hoop, *n.* 1. Same as *Whoop.*

2. A bullfinch. [Prov. Eng.]

Hoop Costume, end of 18th century.

hoop, *n.* See *Hoopoe.*

hoop′=ash, *n.* The North American tree, *Fraxinus sambucifolia,* the tough wood of which is used in making hoops.

hoop′ẽr, *n.* One who hoops casks or tubs; a cooper.

hoop′ẽr, *n.* [So called from its cry.] *Cygnus musicus,* the whistling swan of Europe; the whooper.

hoop′ing, *n.* 1. Hoops.

2. The material for making hoops.

3. The hoops or rings around the breech of modern guns of large caliber.

hoop′ing=cough (-kof), *n.* See *Whooping-cough.*

hoop′i″ron (-ũrn), *n.* Iron in thin strips from which hoops are made.

hoop′koop=plant, hoop′coop=plant, *n.* [Origin unknown.] An Asiatic plant of the bean family, *Lespedeza striata,* naturalized in southern United States, where it furnishes food for cattle; called also *bush-clover.*

hoop′le, *n.* [Dim. of *hoop.*] A child's hoop for trundling.

hoop′=lock, *n.* The notched fastening of a wooden hoop.

hoop′ōe, hoop′oo, *n.* [OFr. *huppe, hupe*; L. *upupa,* a hoopoe; prob. imitative of its cry.] A bird of the genus *Upupa,* whose head is adorned with a beautiful crest, which it can erect or depress at pleasure.

hoop′=pet″ti-cōat, *n.* Same as *Hoop-skirt.*

hoop′=pine, *n.* A large coniferous tree of Australia, *Araucaria Cunninghami,* remarkable for its strong fine-grained timber and for its edible fruit; called also *Moreton Bay pine.*

hoop′=pōle, *n.* A small young tree cut for making hoops.

hoop′=skirt, *n.* A kind of skirt stiffened and expanded by means of hoops of cane, whalebone, or steel.

hoop′=snāke, *n.* A snake of southern United States, *Abastor erythrogrammus,* of the family *Colubridæ*; named from an erroneous belief that it moved by taking its tail in its mouth and rolling along like a hoop.

hoop′=tree, *n.* A subtropical shrub or tree of the genus *Melia.*

hōor, *n.* and *v.* [Obs.] See *Hoar.*

hoose, hooze, *n.* A disease of cattle affecting the lungs, caused by the presence on the mucous membrane of minute hair-like worms hatched from eggs found on damp grass.

Hoo′ṣiẽr (-zhẽr), *n.* [Origin obscure.] An inhabitant or a native of the state of Indiana.

Hoo′ṣiẽr (-zhẽr), *a.* Of or belonging to a Hoosier or to the state of Indiana; as, a *Hoosier* poet.

hoot, *v.i.*; hooted, *pt., pp.*; hooting, *ppr.* [ME. *houten, huten*; Sw. *huta ut,* lit., hoot out, from *hut,* begone!]

1. To cry out or shout in contempt.

2. To cry as an owl.

hoot, *v.t.* To drive or pursue with cries or shouts uttered in contempt or derision; to jeer; to mock.

hoot, *n.* 1. A cry or shout in contempt.

2. The cry of an owl.

hoot, *interj.* An exclamation expressing disappointment, surprise, impatience, or incredulity; equivalent to *fie, tut, pshaw,* etc. [Scot.]

hoot′=owl, hoot′ing=owl, *n.* An owl that hoots, as distinguished from a *screech-owl.*

hoove, hoov′en, *n.* [From *heave.*] A disease in cattle consisting in the excessive inflation of the stomach by gas, ordinarily caused by eating too much green food; tympany.

hoov′en, hō′ven, *a.* Affected with hoove; as, *hooven* cattle.

hop, *v.t.*; hopped (hopt), *pt., pp.*; hopping, *ppr.* 1. To leap or skip over; as, to *hop* a fence.

2. To carry or move (a thing) with a hopping motion; as, to *hop* a stick along a floor; to *hop* a tool in cutting teeth in metal.

hop, *v.i.* [ME. *hoppen*; AS. *hoppian,* to hop, leap, dance.]

1. To leap or spring on one foot.

2. To leap; to spring forward by leaps; to skip, as a bird or a toad.

3. To walk lame; to limp; to halt.

4. To dance. [Colloq.]

Hopping mad; enraged beyond one's self-control. [Colloq.]

hop, *n.* 1. A leap on one foot; a leap; a jump; a spring.

2. A dance. [Colloq.]

Hop, step, and jump; the act of taking a leap with one foot, a step, and a jump in succession.

hop, *n.*; *pl.* **hops.** [ME. *hoppe*; M.D. *hoppe,* hop.]

1. In botany, a twining annual of the nettle family, *Humulus Lupulus,* cultivated for its fruit and flowers.

2. [*pl.*] The scale-like floral parts of the hop, used in brewing and in medicine.

hop, *v.t.*; hopped (hopt), *pt., pp.*; hopping, *ppr.* To impregnate with hops.

hop, *v.i.* To pick or gather hops.

hop′=back, *n.* A brewer's sieve.

hop′bine, *n.* The stalk of the hop-plant.

Hop (*Humulus Lupulus*).

hop′=bush, *n.* An Australian sapindaceous shrub whose capsules are used in place of hops.

hop′=clō″vẽr, *n.* The *Trifolium procumbens,* which resembles hops.

hop′=cush″ion, *n.* Same as *Hop-pillow.*

hop′=dog, *n.* A device for removing hop-poles. [Prov. Eng.]

hop′=dri″ẽr, *n.* A heated inclosure in which hops are placed for drying.

hōpe, *n.* 1. An inlet; a small haven or bay; a creek. [Scot.]

2. A sloping plain between ridges of mountains. [Prov. Eng.]

3. A suffix in English place-names, signifying hill or mound; as, Stan*hope,* East*hope.*

hōpe, *n.* [ME. *hope*; AS. *hopa,* hope, expectation, from *hopian,* to hope.]

1. A desire of some good, accompanied with at least a slight expectation of obtaining it, or a belief that it is obtainable.

2. Confidence in a future event; the highest degree of well-founded expectation of good; as, a *hope* founded on God's gracious promises.

3. One who or that which furnishes ground of expectation, or promises desired good; as, the *hope* of a nation is in its youth.

4. An opinion or belief not amounting to certainty, but grounded on substantial evidence;

as, the Christian indulges a *hope* that his sins are pardoned.

Syn.—Expectation, trust, confidence.—*Hope* is that which is welcome; *expectation* is either welcome or unwelcome; *trust* and *confidence* denote dependence on a person or thing to bring about that which is desired.

hōpe, *v.i.*; hoped (hōpt), *pt., pp.*; hoping, *ppr.* [ME. *hopen*; AS. *hopian*, to hope, look for, expect.]

1. To look forward with expectation and desire; to cherish a desire of good, with some expectation of obtaining it, or belief that it is obtainable.

2. To place confidence; to trust with confident expectation of good.

Hope thou in God. —Ps. xlii. 11.

hōpe, *v.t.* 1. To expect with desire; to look forward to with hope.

We *hope* no other from your majesty. —Shak.

2. To entertain hopes of; to anticipate the obtaining or occurrence of.

3. To imagine; to think; as, I *hope* I know what I am saying. [Colloq.]

4. To expect without desire. [Obs.]

hōpe′fụl, *a.* 1. Full of hope; having qualities which give rise to or grounds for hope or expectations of good; full of promise; promising.

2. Full of hope, desire, or confident expectation.

hōpe′fụl-ly, *adv.* In a hopeful manner; with hope or confidence.

hōpe′fụl-ness, *n.* The quality or state of being hopeful; promise of good.

hōpe′ite, hō′pite, *n.* [Named after Prof. Thomas C. *Hope*, of Edinburgh.] A transparent, light-colored mineral, consisting chiefly of oxid of zinc and a large proportion of water, found in the calamin-mines of Altenberg, near Aix-la-Chapelle.

hōpe′less, *a.* 1. Destitute of hope; despairing.

2. Giving no ground of hope; desperate; as, a *hopeless* condition.

Syn.—Desponding, despairing, forlorn, desperate, discouraged, irremediable, irreparable.

hōpe′less-ly, *adv.* Without hope; in a hopeless manner.

hōpe′less-ness, *n.* The state of being hopeless; despair.

hōp′ẽr, *n.* One who hopes.

hop′=fac″tŏr, *n.* One who deals in hops; a salesman of hops.

hop′=flēa, *n.* *Haltica concinna*, an insect which infests hops.

hop′=flȳ, *n.* An aphid, *Phorodon humuli*, destructive to hops.

hop′=frog″flȳ, *n.* A hop-frothfly.

hop′=froth″flȳ, *n.* *Aphrophora interrupta*, an insect infesting hop-vines.

hop′=hornʺbēam, *n.* The American ironwood, *Ostrya Virginica*.

hōp′ing-ly, *adv.* With hope.

Hop-kin′si-ăn, *a.* and *n.* I. *a.* Of or pertaining to Dr. Samuel Hopkins (1721–1803), a Calvinist of New England, or to his doctrines.

II. *n.* An adherent of the theological principles maintained by Dr. Hopkins.

Hop-kin′si-ăn-ism, *n.* In theology, the tenets of Dr. Samuel Hopkins, who held most of the Calvinistic doctrines, even in their extreme form, but rejected the doctrine of imputed sin and imputed righteousness. The basis of the system is that all virtue and true holiness consist in disinterested benevolence, and that all sin is selfishness.

hop′lite, *n.* [Gr. *hoplitēs*, a heavy-armed foot-soldier, from *hoplon*, a tool, weapon.] In Greek antiquity, a heavy-armed soldier.

hop′=med″ick, *n.* See *Hop-trefoil*, 2.

hop′=mil″dew, *n.* The fungus, *Sphærotheca humuli*.

hop′=o′=my=thumb′, *n.* A dwarf; a diminutive person.

hop′pẽr, *n.* 1. One who or that which hops.

2. A wooden trough or shoe through which grain passes into a mill, so named from its moving or shaking; also, a box or frame of boards which receives the grain before it passes into the trough.

3. Any contrivance resembling a grain-hopper in form or use, as (a) a box which receives apples to conduct them into a crushing mill; (b) a box or funnel for supplying fuel to a close furnace, etc.; (c) in glass-making, a hoppet.

4. The trip of a hammer of a double-action piano.

5. A boat having a compartment with a movable bottom, to receive the mud or gravel from a dredging-machine and convey it to deep water, where, upon opening the bottom, the mud or gravel is allowed to fall out; called also *hopper-barge*.

6. [*pl.*] A game in which persons hop or leap on one leg; hopscotch.

7. In zoölogy, (a) a saltatorial insect, as a tree-hopper, cheese-hopper, grass-hopper, etc.; (b) a butterfly, the skipper.

hop′pẽr=boy, *n.* A rake moving in a circle, used in mills to draw the meal over an opening in the floor, through which it falls.

hop′pẽr=clos″et, *n.* A water-closet with a pan above a trap and device for flushing.

hop′pẽr=cock, *n.* The valve which flushes the hopper of a water-closet.

hop′pet, *n.* 1. A hand-basket.

2. In mining, the dish used by miners to measure ore in.

3. An infant in arms. [Prov. Eng.]

4. In glass-making, a conical vessel suspended from the ceiling, containing sand and water for the use of the glass-cutter.

hop′=pick″ẽr, *n.* One who picks hops.

hop′=pil″lōw, *n.* A sack or pillow filled with hops, to act as a soporific.

hop′ping, *n.* The act of one who hops or dances.

hop′ping, *n.* A gathering of hops.

hop′ping=dick, *n.* *Merula leucogenys*, a thrush of Jamaica, much resembling the English blackbird.

hop′ple, *v.t.*; hoppled, *pt., pp.*; hoppling, *ppr.* To fetter by tying the feet together; to trammel; to entangle; to hobble.

hop′ple, *n.* [A form of *hobble*.] A fetter for the legs of horses or other animals, when turned out to graze; used chiefly in the plural.

hop′ple-bush, *n.* A hobblebush.

hop′pō, *n.* [Corruption of Chinese *hupu*, board of revenue.] In China, (a) an overseer of commerce; a collector; (b) a tribunal whose function it is to collect that portion of the public revenue arising from trade and navigation.

hop′=pock″et, *n.* A sack or bag for holding hops.

hop′=pōle, *n.* A pole inserted at the root of the hop-plant for the stem to climb.

hop′py, *a.* Full of hops; having a flavor similar to that of hops.

hop′scotch, *n.* A children's game, in which a stone is driven, by the foot of a person hopping on one foot, from one compartment to another of a figure drawn or scotched on the ground.

hop′=tree, *n.* *Ptelea trifoliata*, a small rutaceous tree of America, the clustered fruit of which is sometimes used as a substitute for hops.

hop′=trē″foil, *n.* 1. *Trifolium procumbens*, a plant of the bean family; called also *hop-clover*.

2. A farmer's name for the plant *Medicago lupulina*, greatly resembling yellow clover, and abundant in waste lands and cultivated fields. It is distinguished from trefoil by its twisted legume. Called also *hop-medick*.

hop′=vīne, *n.* The stalk or plant of the hop.

hop′=yärd, *n.* A field or inclosure where hops are raised.

hō′răl, *a.* [LL. *horalis*, from L. *hora*, hour.] Relating to an hour or to hours.

hō′răl-ly, *adv.* Hourly. [Obs.]

hō-rā′ri-ous, *a.* In botany, enduring only for an hour or two, as the petals of *Cistus*.

hō′rā-ry, *a.* [LL. *horarius*, from L. *hora*, hour.]

1. Pertaining to an hour; noting the hours; as, the *horary* circle.

2. Continuing an hour; occurring once an hour; hourly.

Hō-rā′tiăn, *a.* Relating to or resembling the Latin poet Horace, his poetry, or his style.

hōrde, *n.* [Fr. *horde*, from Turk. *ordū, ordī*, camp.] A tribe, clan, or race of Asiatic or other nomads dwelling in tents or wagons and migrating from place to place to procure pasturage for their cattle or for plunder; hence, a clan; a gang; a migratory crew; a multitude.

hōrde, *v.i.*; horded, *pt., pp.*; hording, *ppr.* To live in hordes; to huddle together like the members of a migratory tribe.

hor-dē-ā′ceous, *a.* [L. *hordeaceus*, from *hordeum*, barley.] Resembling barley; of or pertaining to the genus *Hordeum*.

hor-dē′ic, *a.* [L. *hordeum*, barley.] Of or derived from barley; as, *hordeic* acid, an isomer of lauric acid or identical with it.

hor′dē-in, hor′dē-ine, *n.* [L. *hordeum*, barley, and *-in*.] In chemistry, a modification of starch constituting about fifty-five per cent of barley meal. [Rare.]

hor-dē′ō-lum, *n.* [LL. *hordeolus*, a sty, from L. *hordeum*, barley.] In pathology, a sty; a furuncular inflammation of the connective tissue of the eyelids, near a hair-follicle.

Hor′dē-um, *n.* [L., barley.] A genus of plants of the natural order *Gramineæ*, natives of both hemispheres. *Hordeum sativum* is the cultivated barley.

hōre, *a.* Hoar. [Obs.]

hōre′hound, *n.* Same as *Hoarhound*.

hō-rī′zōn, *n.* [L. *horizon*; Gr. *horizōn* (supply *kyklos*, circle), the bounding circle, horizon, properly ppr. of *horizein*, to bound, limit, from *horos*, boundary, limit.]

1. The line in which the sky and the earth or sea seem to meet; the boundary line of one's vision on the surface of the earth; called the *sensible, visible*, or *apparent horizon*; hence, the limit of one's experience, knowledge, or observation.

2. In astronomy, an imaginary great circle, parallel to the sensible horizon, whose plane passes through the center of the earth, whose poles are the zenith and nadir, and which divides the globe or sphere into two equal parts or hemispheres; called the *celestial, astronomical*, or *rational horizon*.

3. In geology, a well-marked formation which may serve as a starting-point from which to study other formations. Thus, fossils or strata which appear to be of the same age are said to be on the same *horizon*.

Artificial horizon; a contrivance for enabling a person to obtain altitudes of the heavenly bodies when the horizon is obscured by fog, or concealed by intervening land. It consists of a small hollow trough containing quicksilver or any other fluid the surface of which affords a reflected image of a celestial body. By optics it is shown that the angle subtended at the eye by a star and its image in a fluid is double the star's altitude; this angle, after being measured and halved, gives the altitude of the star.

hō-rī′zōn=glȧss, *n.* In astronomy, one of two small speculums on one of the radii of a quadrant or sextant. The one half of the fore-glass is silvered, while the other half is transparent, in order that an object may be seen directly through it; the back-glass is silvered above and below, but in the middle there is a transparent stripe through which the horizon can be seen.

hor-i-zon′tăl, *a.* 1. Parallel to the horizon; on a level; as, a *horizontal* line or surface.

2. Of, relating to, or close to the horizon.

3. Measured or contained in a plane of the horizon; as, *horizontal* distance.

4. Operating or situated in a level plane; as, a *horizontal* drill; a *horizontal* wheel.

Horizontal bar; a smooth, usually round bar, supported horizontally on two upright posts. It is used in gymnastic exercises.

Horizontal line; in perspective, the intersection of the horizontal and perspective planes.

Horizontal plane; a plane parallel to the horizon or not inclined to it; in perspective, a plane parallel to the horizon, passing through the eye and cutting the perspective plane at right angles.

Horizontal projection; a projection made on a plane parallel to the horizon.

Horizontal range of a projectile; the distance at which it falls on or strikes a horizontal plane, whatever be the angle of elevation.

hor″i-zon-tal′i-ty, *n.* The state of being horizontal.

hor-i-zon′tăl-īze, *v.t.*; horizontalized, *pt., pp.*; horizontalizing, *ppr.* To bring (the eyes) into visual line by action of the superior and inferior rectus muscles.

hor-i-zon′tăl-ly, *adv.* In a horizontal direction or position; on a level.

hor-mō-gō′ni-um, *n.*; *pl.* **hor-mō-gō′ni-ȧ.** [Gr. *hormos*, a cord, chain, and *gonos*, offspring.] In some algæ, a chain-like group of reproductive cells.

hor-mog′ō-nous, *a.* Like or provided with a hormogonium.

horn, *v.t.*; horned, *pt., pp.*; horning, *ppr.* 1. To give horns or a horn-like shape to.

2. To hook; to gore; as, the bull *horned* him. [Colloq.]

3. To cuckold. [Obs.]

horn, *n.* [ME. *horn*; AS. *horn*, horn.]

1. A hard projection growing on the heads of certain animals, and particularly on cloven-footed quadrupeds, usually projecting to some length, and terminating in a point. In most ruminants the horns have a core of bone surrounded with a sheath of true horn. They are not branched and are never shed.

2. The antler of a deer, which is composed entirely of bone and is shed annually.

3. A thick and hard form of cuticular substance, as in the scales of reptiles, tortoise-shell, birds' beaks, or the nails, claws, and hoofs of animals, especially the dense fibrous substance composing the sheath of the horns of ruminants.

4. Anything made of horn, or resembling a horn in shape or use; specifically, (a) a wind-instrument of music, originally made of horn; hence, any one of various trumpet-like musical instruments generally made of brass; as, a hunting-*horn*, a French *horn*, etc.; (b) a utensil for holding powder for immediate use, originally made of horn; a powder-flask; (c) a drinking-cup, from having been originally made of horn; a drinking-vessel of any material containing as much as can be swallowed at a draught; a beaker; hence, the contents of such a vessel; (d) a cornucopia; (e) an extremity or point of a crescent-shaped object, as the cusp of the crescent moon, or the extremity of the wing of an army or other body of soldiers when drawn up in crescent form; (f) a branch of a subdivided stream; (g) the feeler of an insect, snail, etc.; (h) a tuft of feathers, as on the head of a horned owl; (i) the horny protuberance surmounting the bill of the hornbill; (j) a horn-like process, as found in flowers of the milkweed family; (k) the beak of an anvil; (l) the Ionic

volute; (m) a projecting corner of an altar; (n) either of two projections on the forward part of a woman's saddle, for supporting the leg; also, the high pommel of a Spanish or half-Spanish saddle, sometimes made of horn; (o) a medieval headdress, or one of its projecting parts, resembling the horn of an ox; (p) in nautical language, one end of a crosstree; (q) a long projection, frequently of silver or other precious metal, worn on the forehead by natives of many Asiatic countries; (r) the imaginary antler on the brow of a cuckold; in this sense obsolete.

5. In Scripture, a symbol of strength, glory, honor, or power.

An *horn* of salvation for us. —Luke i. 69.

Horn of plenty; the cornucopia.

In a horn; not at all; as, he will tell you—*in a horn* (that is, he will not tell you). [Slang.]

To draw, haul, or *pull in one's horns*; to repress one's ardor; to restrain one's pride; in allusion to the habit of the snail withdrawing its feelers when startled. [Colloq.]

To take a horn; to take a glass of liquor. [Colloq.]

hǫrn′bēak, *n.* A garfish.

hǫrn′bēam, *n.* Either of two species of trees of the genus *Carpinus*. *Carpinus Caroliniana*, called also *blue beech, ironwood,* and *water-beech*, is the American hornbeam; its wood is very hard and heavy. The European hornbeam is *Carpinus Betulus*, which is known also as *yoke-elm, hornbeech, hardbeam,* and *horse-beech*.

hǫrn′bill, *n.* Any of various tropical birds of the *Bucerotidæ*, allied to the hoopoes and kingfishers, and noted for the very large size of the bill, and for an extraordinary horny protuberance by which it is surmounted, nearly as large as the bill itself. The rhinoceros-hornbill, *Buceros rhinoceros*, almost the size of a turkey, has a sharp-pointed, slightly curved bill, about ten inches long, and furnished at the base of the upper mandible with an immense appendage in the form of an inverted horn.

Rhinoceros-Hornbill (*Buceros rhinoceros*).

hǫrn′blende, *n.* [G. *hornblende*; *horn*, horn, and *blende*, blende, an ore of zinc, from *blenden*, to blind, dazzle, deceive.] A common mineral; one of the dark green, brown, or black forms of amphibole. It is sometimes in regular distinct crystals, more generally the result of confused crystallization, appearing in masses composed of laminæ, acicular crystals, or fibers, variously aggregated. It enters largely into the composition of several of the trap-rocks, and is an important constituent of several species of gneiss and granite. The name *amphibole* is often used to include all the varieties.

hǫrn′blend-iç, *a.* Containing or resembling hornblende; pertaining to hornblende.

hǫrn′=block, *n.* A horn-plate.

hǫrn′blōw″ẽr, *n.* One who blows a horn.

hǫrn′book, *n.* 1. Formerly, a kind of primer, from which children learned their letters; so called from the transparent horn covering placed over the single page of which it usually consisted, the whole being fixed to a wooden frame with a handle. It generally contained the alphabet in capital and small letters, several rows of monosyllables, and the Lord's Prayer.

2. Any elementary treatise or primer; also, elementary knowledge, as from a hornbook.

H ibook.

hǫrn′bug, *n.* 1. A large flat beetle, *Passalus cornutus*, having the head rmed with a hornlike prominence.

2. A stag-beetle.

hǫrn′=dis-tem″pẽr, *n.* A disease of cattle affecting the internal substance of the horn.

hǫrn′=drum, *n.* A wheel used to raise water.

hǫrned, *a.* Furnished with or having a horn, horns, or hornlike processes; as, the *horned* moon; a *horned* owl.

Horned adder; a hornsman.

Horned bee; *Osmia bicornis*, a species of wild bee having two horns.

Horned dace; a fish of the genus *Semotilus*; the chub.

Horned frog; (a) a toadlike amphibian, *Ceratophrys cornuta*, horned above each eye; (b) a horned toad.

Horned grebe; a grebe, *Podiceps cornutus*, which has two thick feather tufts on the head. [See illustration under *Grebe*.]

Horned horse; the gnu.

Horned lark; the shore-lark.

Horned lizard; the horned toad.

Horned owl; an owl, *Bubo virginianus*, that grows to large size and has a tuft of feathers projecting in a hornlike manner above each ear.

Horned poppy; a horn-poppy.

Horned pout; a bullhead or catfish.

Horned rattler; a rattlesnake, *Crotalus cerastes*, which has two small horns between the eyes.

Horned ray; the sea-devil, *Manta birostris*.

Horned screamer; the kamichi, *Anhima cornuta*.

Horned snake; the cerastes, a viper having two horns between the eyes.

Horned toad; a lizard of the *Iguanidæ*, genus *Phrynosoma*, whose body somewhat resembles that of a toad or frog. The body is rough and the head furnished with horny spines. Several species inhabit the arid plains of southwestern United States and Mexico.

Horned viper; a horned snake.

hǫrn′ed-ness, *n.* The quality of being horned.

hǫrn′el, *n.* A sand-eel. [Scot.]

hǫrn′ẽr, *n.* 1. One who works or deals in horn. [Rare.]

2. One who winds or blows the horn. [Obs.]

3. One who cuckolds or horns. [Obs.]

hǫr′net, *n.* [AS. *hyrnet, hyrnete*, a hornet.] An insect of the genus *Vespa*, much larger and stronger than the wasp, whose sting gives severe pain. Hornets construct nests of leaves or other substances, which resemble coarse gray paper. This is attached to the branches of a tree or placed in a hollow tree. The American hornet is *Vespa maculata*.

To stir up a hornets' nest; to provoke enmity or foster dissensions and strife; to stir up enemies against oneself.

hǫr′net=fly̆, *n.* A fly of large size and fierce disposition that preys on bees and other insects.

hǫrn′fish, *n.* 1. The garfish or sea-needle.

2. The sauger.

3. The pipefish.

hǫrn′=fly̆, *n.* A small fly of the genus *Hæmatobia*, which annoys cattle by clustering about their horns.

hǫrn′foot, *a.* Having a hoof; hoofed.

hǫrn′i-fy̆, *v.t.* 1. To cause to become horny.

2. To cuckold. [Obs.]

hǫrn′ing, *n.* 1. Appearance of the moon when increasing or in the form of a crescent.

2. A charivari; a mock serenade with horns, etc.

Letters of horning; in Scots law, a writ under the king's signet issuing at the instance of a creditor against his debtor, commanding him in the king's name to pay or perform within a certain time under pain of being declared a rebel and put in prison.

hǫrn′ish, *a.* Somewhat like horn; hard; horny.

hǫrn′ist, *n.* One who plays a horn.

hǫr-nī′tō, *n.* [Sp., dim. of *horno*, an oven, kiln.] A fumarole in the form of a small mound, shaped like an oven with a rounded top.

hǫrn′=lead (-led), *n.* Chlorid of lead.

hǫrn′less, *a.* Having no horns.

hǫrn′=mad, *a.* Mad from cuckoldom.

hǫrn′=māk″ẽr, *n.* 1. A maker of cuckolds. [Obs.]

2. One who makes drinking-vessels of horn.

hǫrn′=mẽr″çū-ry, *n.* Calomel.

hǫrn′=mul″let, *n.* The stone-roller. [Local, U. S.]

hǫrn′=ŏf=plen′ty, *n.* 1. A herb, *Fedia Cornucopiæ*, of the valerian family.

2. An ornamental grass of the genus *Cornucopia*.

hǫr′nō-tine, *n.* [L. *hornotinus*, of this year.] In ornithology, a bird in its first year.

hǫrn′owl, *n.* The horned owl.

hǫrn′pike, *n.* The garfish.

hǫrn′pipe, *n.* [ME. *hornpype*, a musical instrument.]

1. A kind of dance for one person, especially popular among sailors.

2. Lively music for or as for such a dance.

3. An early form of pipe having a bell-shaped end of horn, used formerly in England and Wales.

hǫrn′plant, *n.* A kind of seaweed, *Ecklonia buccinalis*.

hǫrn′=plāte, *n.* The pedestal or frame for the axle-box of a car-truck, or a plate in such a frame; an axle-guard.

hǫrn′=pock, *n.* A light form of smallpox or chicken-pox.

hǫrn′=pop″py, *n.* A plant, *Glaucium luteum*, having glaucous leaves and large yellow flowers, frequent on sandy seashores.

hǫrn′pout, *n.* The horned pout.

hǫrn′=pox, *n.* Horn-pock.

hǫrn′=quick″sil-vẽr (-kwik″), *n.* Horn-mercury; calomel.

hǫrn′=sil″vẽr, *n.* Chlorid of silver.

hǫrn′=slāte, *n.* A gray, silicious stone.

hǫrns′măn, *n.* The plumed viper, *Clotho cornuta*; called also *horned adder* and *puff-adder*.

hǫrn′snāke, *n.* The wampum-snake, *Farancia abacura*, of a deep red below, blue-black on the back, and having a row of square red spots along the sides.

hǫrn′stōne, *n.* Chert, a kind of quartz. [Rare.]

hǫrn′tāil, *n.* A hymenopterous insect of the family *Uroceridæ*, characterized by the hornlike abdominal appendage of the male.

hǫrn′=thumb (-thum), *n.* A thimble of horn used to protect the thumb of a cutpurse; hence, a cutpurse.

hǫrn′weed, *n.* The hornplant.

hǫrn′wŏrk, *n.* In fortification, an outwork composed of two demibastions joined by a curtain.

Plan of Parts of Fortification. *a*, Hornwork.

hǫrn′wŏrt, *n.* A floating aquatic herb, *Ceratophyllum demersum*, common in pools and slow streams in most parts of the world.

hǫrn′wrack (-rak), *n.* The sea-mat, a polyzoan.

hǫrn′y, *a.* 1. Hard; callous; resembling horn; as, *horny* hands.

2. Furnished with horns or projections like horns.

3. Corneous; consisting of horn or of a hornlike material.

hǫrn′y=hand″ed, *a.* Having horny palms; having hands calloused by labor.

hǫrn′y-head (-hed), *n.* A fish; the river-chub.

hō-rog′rȧ-phy, *n.* [Gr. *hōrographia*, from *hōrographos*, writing history by seasons or years; *hōra*, hour, and *graphein*, to write.]

1. An account of hours.

2. The art of constructing dials, clocks, or timepieces of any kind.

hor′ō-lōġe, *n.* [OFr. *horologe*; L. *horologium*; Gr. *hōrologion*, an instrument for telling the hour; *hōra*, hour, and *legein*, to tell.]

1. An instrument that indicates the hour of the day; a clock; a timepiece.

2. A servant who announced the hours of the day. [Obs.]

hō-rol′ō-ġẽr, *n.* A maker of or dealer in timepieces; one expert in horology.

hor-ō-loġ′iç-ăl, *a.* Pertaining to a horologe, or to horology.

hor-ō-lō-ġi-og′rȧ-phẽr, *n.* A maker of timepieces or dials.

hor-ō-lō″ġi-ō-graph′iç, *a.* Pertaining to the art of horologiography.

hor-ō-lō″ġi-og′rȧ-phy, *n.* [Gr. *hōrologion*, a horologe, and *graphein*, to write.]

1. An account of instruments that show the hour of the day.

2. The art of constructing timepieces.

hō-rol′ō-ġist, *n.* A horologer.

hō-rol′ō-ġy, *n.* [L. *horologium*; Gr. *hōrologion*, an instrument for telling the hour, horologe.]

1. That branch of science which treats of the principles and construction of machines for measuring and indicating portions of time, as clocks, watches, etc.

2. A timepiece. [Obs.]

hō-rom′e-tẽr, *n.* [Gr. *hōra*, hour, and *metron*, a measure.] A device for measuring time.

hor-ō-met′riç-ăl, *a.* Belonging to horometry.

hō-rom′e-try, *n.* [Gr. *hōra*, hour, and *metron*, a measure.] The art or practice of measuring time by hours and subordinate divisions.

hō-rop′tẽr, *n.* [Gr. *horos*, a boundary, and *optēr*, one who looks, from *optesthai*, to see.] In optics, a straight line drawn through the point where the two optic axes meet, and parallel to that which joins the centers of the two eyes or the two pupils; the sum of all points seen single for any given angular position of a person's two eyes.

hō-rop-ter′iç, *a.* Relating to the horopter.

hor′ō-sçōpe, *n.* [Fr. *horoscope*; Gr. *hōroskopeion*, from *hōroskopos*, one who observes the hour of birth; *hōra*, hour, and *skopein*, to view.]

1. In astrology, a scheme or figure of the twelve houses, or twelve signs of the zodiac, in which is marked the disposition of the heavens at a given time, and by which astrologers formerly told the fortunes of persons, according to the position of the stars at the time of their birth.

2. The part of the ecliptic on the eastern horizon at any given time when a prediction is to be made of a future event.

3. A planisphere invented by John of Padua.

4. A table by which one can tell the length of the days and nights at different places.

hor′ō-sçō-pẽr, *n.* One versed in horoscopy; an astrologer.

hō-ros′çō-pist, *n.* Same as *Horoscoper*.

hō-ros′çō-py, *n.* 1. The art or practice of predicting future events by the observation of the stars and planets.

2. The situation of the planets and stars at the time of a person's birth.

hor-ren′dous, *a.* Fearful; frightful. [Obs.]

hor′rent, *a.* [L. *horrens (-entis)*, ppr. of *horrere*, to bristle.]

1. Bristled; bristling; standing erect, as bristles.

2. Horrible; abhorrent.

hor′ri-ble, *a.* [OFr. *horrible, orible*; L. *horribilis*, terrible, dreadful, from *horrere*, to be terrified, to fear.] Exciting or tending to excite horror; dreadful; terrible; shocking; hideous; as, a *horrible* figure or sight; a *horrible* story.

A dungeon *horrible* on all sides round. —Milton.

Syn.—Fearful, hideous, terrible.

hor′ri-ble-ness, *n.* The state of being horrible; dreadfulness; terribleness; hideousness.

hor′ri-bly, *adv.* In a manner to excite horror; dreadfully; terribly; as, *horribly* mutilated.

hor′rid, *a.* [L. *horridus*, rough, shaggy, bristly, savage, from *horrere*, to bristle.]

1. That does or may excite horror; dreadful; hideous; shocking; as, a *horrid* spectacle.

2. Rough; rugged. [Obs.]

Horrid with fern, and intricate with thorn. —Dryden.

3. Shocking; very offensive; unpleasant; mean.

Syn.—Horrible, awful, abominable, shocking, unpleasant, disagreeable.

hor′rid-ly, *adv.* In a manner to excite horror.

hor′rid-ness, *n.* The state of being horrid.

hor-rif′iç, *a.* [L. *horrificus*; *horrere*, to be afraid, to fear, and *facere*, to make.] Bringing horror.

hor″ri-fi-cā′tion, *n.* The act of horrifying; that which causes horror.

hor′ri-fȳ, *v.t.*; horrified, *pt., pp.*; horrifying, *ppr.* [L. *horrificare*, to make rough or terrible, from *horrificus*, causing terror; *horrere*, to be terrified, fear, and *facere*, to make.] To strike or fill with horror.

I was *horrified* at the notion. —Hook.

hor″rip-i-lā′tion, *n.* [LL. *horripilatio (-onis)*, from *horripilare*, to bristle with hairs; L. *horrere*, to bristle, and *pilus*, hair.] In medicine, a bristling of the hair of the head or body, resulting from disease or terror.

hor-ris′ō-nous, hor-ris′ō-nănt, *a.* [L. *horrisonus*, sounding dreadfully; *horrere*, to be terrible, and *sonus*, a sound.] Having a terrible sound; sounding dreadfully. [Rare.]

hor′rŏr, *n.* [L. *horror*, from *horrere*, to bristle, shake, be terrible.]

1. A rippling or similar movement, as on the surface of water. [Obs.]

2. A shaking, shivering, or shuddering, as in the cold fit which precedes a fever. [Rare.]

3. A painful emotion of fear, dread, and abhorrence; a shuddering with terror and loathing; a feeling inspired by something frightful and shocking.

An *horror* of great darkness fell upon him. —Gen. xv. 12.

4. That which excites fear, loathing, or dread; something happening which causes intense mental aversion or positive suffering; as, the *horrors* of war; a railway *horror*.

And breathes a browner *horror* on the woods. —Pope.

The horrors; delirium tremens; also, the blues. [Colloq.]

hor′rŏr-strick″en, hor′rŏr-struck, *a.* Struck with horror; terrified.

hors de çom-bat′ (or de koṅ-bä′). [Fr., lit., out of the fight.] Out of the combat; disabled; unable to fight.

hors′-d'œuvre′ (or-dēvr′), *n.* [Fr., lit., out of work.] A dish served out of the regular course, usually as a relish.

hörse, *n.* [ME. *hors*; AS. *hors*, a horse.]

1. A quadruped, *Equus caballus*, the most common animal of draft, used throughout the world. There are many varieties, differing in size, color, and adaptability to use. The mane and tail are flowing; hoofs small and rounded; head shapely with erect ears; with callosities on the inner side of the legs. It has, when domesticated, a docile disposition and is one of the most intelligent animals known. The wild horses once common to North America were descendants of domesticated horses run wild, and similar animals are still found in South America.

2. Any animal of the family *Equidæ*, including the asses, the quagga, zebra, etc.

3. The male of the horse as distinguished from the *mare*; restrictedly, a gelding.

4. Cavalry; as a regiment of *horse*.

5. Anything resembling a horse in form, as (a) a wooden frame on which soldiers are made to ride by way of punishment; sometimes called a *timber-mare*; (b) a block used in a gymnasium for vaulting; (c) a clothes-horse; (d) in printing, an apparatus of a desk-like shape, placed on the bank close to the tympan of the press on which the paper to be printed is laid; (e) a support for work; as, a saw*horse*.

Horse.

a, Muzzle. *b*, Gullet. *c*, Crest. *d*, Withers. *e*, Chest. *f*, Loins. *g g*, Girth. *h*, Hip or ilium. *i*, Croup. *k*, Haunch or quarters. *l*, Thigh. *m*, Hock. *n*, Shank or cannon. *o*, Fetlock. *p*, Pastern. *q*, Shoulder-bone or scapula. *r*, Elbow. *s*, Fore thigh or arm. *t*, Knee. *u*, Coronet. *v*, Hoof. *w*, Point of hock. *x*, Hamstring. *z z*, Height.

6. In mining, a hard part of a rock occurring in the middle of a lode, and dividing it into two branches.

7. Nautically, a rope extending from the middle of a yard to its extremity to support the sailors while they loose, reef, or furl the sails; also, a thick rope extended near the mast for hoisting a yard or extending a sail.

8. An aid in an examination or translation; a crib; a pony.

9. A dominant idea; a hobby.

10. In metallurgy, same as *bear*, n. 6.

11. Work charged for before it is executed. [Eng.]

12. In leather-making, a kind of trestle for holding skins while being curried.

13. In a game of dice, a point scored against a player in a series of throws; as, a *horse* on you.

Dark horse; see under *Dark*.

Horned horse; the gnu.

Horse, foot, and dragoons; (a) the entire army; foot-soldiers and cavalry collectively; (b) figuratively and in an adverbial sense; altogether; wholly; without discrimination; as, the opposing factions were routed, *horse, foot, and dragoons*.

Iron horse; a locomotive steam-engine.

To get on one's high horse; to speak or act in an overbearing or haughty manner.

To look a gift horse in the mouth; to receive a gift or favor in a critical or exacting spirit, since the age of a horse is determined by inspecting its teeth.

To put the cart before the horse; see under *Cart*.

To take horse; (a) to set out to ride on horseback; (b) to be covered, as a mare.

Winged horse; Pegasus.

hörse, *v.t.*; horsed, *pt., pp.*; horsing, *ppr.* 1. To provide with a horse; to supply a horse or horses for.

. . . Who *horsed* the coach by which he had traveled so many a time. —Thackeray.

2. To sit astride; to bestride.

Leads are filled, and ridges *horsed*. —Shak.

3. To cover; said of the male.

4. To place on the back of a horse; hence, to take on one's own back.

5. To place (a boy) on the back of another for the purpose of flogging him. [Eng.]

6. To make use of, as a pony or crib in school work. [Slang.]

hörse, *v.i.* 1. To get on horseback.

2. Among workmen, to charge work before it is executed. [Eng.]

3. To be in heat; to rut; said of a mare.

4. Nautically, to calk, using a horse-iron; often with *up*; as, a seam *horsed up* with oakum.

hörse′-ant, *n.* The common ant, *Formica rufa*.

hörse′-är-til′lēr-y, *n.* Artillery arranged for rapid movement, generally accompanying the cavalry, the gunners being also mounted.

hörse′back, *n.* 1. The part of a horse's back on which a person sits in riding.

2. A ridge of earth; sometimes formed by rock-strata, or by a glacial eskar. [See *Hogback*.]

3. A fissure filled with sand or clay in what was once a coal seam.

On horseback; riding or as if riding on a horse's back.

hörse′-bälm (-bäm), *n.* A kind of strong-scented mint, *Collinsonia Canadensis*, with yellowish flowers and large ovate leaves; called also *richweed* and *stoneroot*.

hörse′-bāne, *n.* A plant of the parsley family said to be poisonous to horses.

hörse′-bēan, *n.* A large bean, *Faba vulgaris*, so called from its being fed to horses.

hörse′-beech, *n.* Hurst-beech, *Carpinus Betulus*, the English hornbeam.

hörse′-bōat, *n.* 1. A boat to carry horses.

2. A boat propelled by horse-power.

hörse′-bot, *n.* The botfly.

hörse′-box, *n.* A car or a section of a vessel arranged for the transportation of horses.

hörse′-breāk″ēr, *n.* One who trains horses for use.

hörse′-çāne, *n.* A plant, *Ambrosia trifida*, the great ragweed.

hörse′-çär, *n.* 1. A car drawn by a horse or horses.

2. A car used to transport horses.

hörse′-ças″siȧ (-kash″ĭȧ), *n.* A leguminous plant, *Cassia marginata*, bearing long pods which contain a black cathartic pulp, used in India as a horse medicine.

hörse′-chest″nut (-ches″), *n.* A large nut, the fruit of *Æsculus Hippocastanum*; also, the tree itself.

hörse′-çlọth, *n.* A cloth to cover a horse.

hörse′-çoṅch, *n.* A large spiral seashell, a species of *Triton*.

hörse′-çōurs″ēr, *n.* One who keeps horses to race; also, a dealer in horses. [Obs.]

hörse′-çrab, *n.* The horseshoe crab.

hörse′-çre-vȧl-lé′ (-lā′), *n.* A fish, the cavally; so named in South Carolina to distinguish it from the crevallé; a kind of horse-mackerel.

hörse′-çū″çum-bēr, *n.* A large green cucumber.

hörse′-dev″il, *n.* In botany, a kind of tumbleweed of southeastern United States, *Baptisia lanceolata*, one of the *Leguminosæ*, so named because when in a dried and detached form it is blown about and frightens horses.

hörse′-drench, *n.* 1. A dose of horse medicine.

2. A device for giving medicine to a horse.

hörse′-el″dēr, *n.* Elecampane.

hörse′-em″met, *n.* Same as *Horse-ant*.

hörse′finch, *n.* The chaffinch. [Prov. Eng.]

hörse′fish, *n.* A fish, as (a) the moonfish, *Vomer setipinnis*; (b) the sauger; (c) a sea-horse.

hörse′flesh, *n.* 1. The flesh of a horse.

2. Horses, collectively; as, he has made money in *horseflesh*.

3. The attributes or characteristics of a horse.

4. A term applied to a variety of Bahama mahogany.

Horseflesh ore; bornite, an ore of copper and iron which has a red color when broken.

hörse′flȳ, *n.* Any large fly that bites or stings horses, as (a) a gadfly, breeze, or cleg; (b) a botfly; (c) a horse-tick or forest-fly.

hörse′foot, *n.* 1. In botany, coltsfoot.

2. In zoölogy, the horseshoe crab.

hörse′-ġen″tiăn (-shăn), *n.* Feverwort.

hörse′-gow″ăn, *n.* In botany, the oxeye daisy, *Chrysanthemum Leucanthemum*; also, *Taraxacum officinalis*, and other plants.

hörse′-gram, *n.* In botany, a leguminous tropical plant, *Dolichos biflorus*, the pod of which is used in southern India as food for horses and cattle.

hörse′-guärds, *n.pl.* 1. A guard consisting of a body of cavalry.

2. In England, the cavalry regiments that act as guards of the royal household, government buildings, etc.

3. [H—] The official headquarters at Whitehall, London, of the commander-in-chief of the British army; also, the military authorities of the British army as distinguished from the civil head, the secretary for war.

hörse′hāir, *n.* and *a.* I. *n.* The hair of horses, particularly that of the mane and tail used for stuffing furniture, cushions, and the like; also, a cloth woven of such hair.

II. *a.* Made of horsehair; covered or stuffed with horsehair.

hörse′head (-hed), *n.* 1. One of the moonfishes, *Selene vomer*.

2. A kind of surf-duck; the surf-scoter.

3. A sea-horse.

hörse′hēal, hörse′heel, *n.* Same as *Elecampane*, 1.

hörse′hide, *n.* 1. A horse's hide.

2. Leather made from a horse's hide.

hörse′hide, *a.* Made from the hide of a horse.

hörse′hoof, *n.* Same as *Coltsfoot*.

hörse′-ī″rŏn (-ūrn), *n.* A calking-iron held by one workman and struck by another.

hörse′-jock″ey, *n.* 1. A jockey.

2. One who deals in horses. [Obs.]

hörse′knop (-nop), *n.* In botany, knapweed, *Centaurea nigra*, especially the black flower-head of the plant.

hörse′-lat″i-tūdeș, *n.pl.* A region of calms in the North Atlantic Ocean, where sailing vessels conveying horses from the American colonies to the Bermudas were often forced to jettison some of the animals for lack of water.

hörse′läugh (-läf), *n.* A loud, boisterous laugh.

hörse′-leech, *n.* 1. A large leech which attaches itself to the lips or nostrils of horses and other animals that drink from the water it inhabits.

2. A veterinarian; a farrier.

3. An importunate beggar.

horse′-leech″ẽr-y, *n.* Veterinary practice.

horse′less, *a.* Having no horse; especially, not needing a horse for motive power; as, a *horseless* carriage.

horse′-lit″tẽr, *n.* A kind of wheelless carriage hung on poles borne by and between two horses.

horse′-mack″ẽr-el, *n.* A name given to several very different fishes: (a) the cavally or the jurel; (b) the tunny; (c) in California, the hake; (d) the black candlefish; (e) the bluefish, *Pomatomus saltatrix*; (f) *Trachurus trachurus*, a carangoid fish; (g) the ten-pounder.

horse′măn, *n.*; *pl.* **horse′men.** 1. A rider on horseback; a cavalryman.

2. A man skilled in riding, training, or handling horses.

3. A large variety of carrier-pigeon.

4. An ocypodian Brazilian land-crab.

5. A snipe-like bird of the genus *Totanus*.

6. A fish of the West Indies of the genus *Eques*.

horse′măn-ship, *n.* The act or art of riding horseback; the art of training and managing horses; equestrian skill.

horse′-mȧ-rīne′, *n.* 1. A clumsy lubber; one out of his element, as a horseman would be on board ship.

2. A member of a troop of imaginary seacavalry. [Humorous.]

horse′mint, *n.* In botany, (a) an American species of mint, *Monarda punctata*; (b) a wild mint of Europe, *Mentha sylvestris*.

horse′-mus″sel, *n.* A species of large mussel, *Modiola modiolus*.

horse′nāil, *n.* A horseshoe-nail.

horse′-net″tle, *n.* A rough and prickly American weed, *Solanum Carolinense*.

horse′-pärs″ley, *n.* An umbelliferous herb, *Smyrnium Olusatrum*, once used much as celery is now.

horse′-pis″tŏl, *n.* A bulky firearm such as was once carried in a holster by horsemen; hence, any clumsy or heavy pistol.

horse′plāy, *n.* Rough, coarse play.

horse′pond, *n.* A pond for watering horses.

horse′-pop″py, *n.* An umbelliferous plant of Europe, *Seseli Hippomarathrum*.

horse′-pow″ẽr, *n.* 1. A standard unit of work, indicating the rate at which mechanical work is done. It is the power which will raise 33,000 pounds avoirdupois one foot high in one minute. The real power of the average draft-horse is about three-quarters of a *horse-power*.

2. The power of any engine or motor expressed in such standard units.

3. A device for utilizing the pull or weight of a horse in operating machinery.

Brake horse-power; the effective horse-power as indicated by a friction-brake.

Indicated horse-power; the horse-power, as of a steam-engine, determined by the use of an indicator.

horse′-pûrs″lāne, *n.* A Jamaican plant, *Trianthema monogyna*.

horse′-rāce, *n.* A race by horses; a match of horses in running, trotting, pacing, or steeplechasing.

horse′-rā″cing, *n.* The practice or act of racing with horses.

horse′rad″ish, *n.* A plant of the mustard family, *Cochlearia Armoracia*, having a root of a pungent taste, used as a condiment and in medicine.

horse′rad″ish-tree, *n.* A tree of Africa and the East Indies, *Moringa pterygosperma*, whose root has a pungent flavor resembling that of horseradish.

horse′rāke, *n.* A large rake drawn by a horse.

horse′-rough (-ruf), *n.* An attachment to prevent a horse's shoe from slipping on icy roadways.

horse′-run, *n.* A contrivance used to pull loaded cars, wheelbarrows, etc., up a runway from an excavation, by horse-power.

horse′-sense, *n.* Good, practical common sense; instinctive shrewdness. [Colloq.]

horse′shōe, *n.* 1. A shoe for a horse, consisting of a U-shaped strip of metal made to fit the rim of the hoof, to which it is fastened with nails. The possession of a horseshoe, especially of one found by chance, is superstitiously believed to ward off witchcraft and to bring good luck.

2. Anything shaped like a horseshoe, as a curve in a stream or roadway.

3. The king-crab.

4. A bivalve mollusk, *Lutraria elliptica*.

Horseshoe bat; an Old World bat, having the nose-leaf shaped like a horseshoe; also called *horseshoe nose*.

Horseshoe crab; the king-crab, *Limulus polyphemus*.

Horseshoe head; a disease of infants, in which the sutures of the skull are too open.

Horseshoe magnet; a magnet shaped like a horseshoe, having its poles side by side.

Horseshoe vetch; a plant of the genus *Hippocrepis*, so named from the shape of its seed pods.

horse′shōe″ing, *n.* The act or employment of shoeing horses.

horse′shōe-nāil, *n.* A nail used to fasten a shoe to a horse's hoof. The ordinary form is of wrought iron, thin at the point, with a heavy, wedge-shaped head.

horse′-sponge, *n.* A coarse bath-sponge, *Spongia equina*, of the Mediterranean.

horse′-sting″ẽr, *n.* The dragon-fly.

horse′-sụg″ãr (-shụg″), *n.* The sweetleaf-tree, *Symplocos tinctoria*, of southeastern United States; its sweetish leaves form a fodder for cattle and are also the source of a yellow dye.

horse′tāil, *n.* 1. A plant of the genus *Equisetum*, allied to the ferns. [See *Equisetum*.]

2. A Turkish standard, designating rank.

3. A fossil bivalve; a hippurite.

4. The bundle of nerves into which the spinal cord is separated at the distal extremity; the cauda equina.

horse′tāil-tree, *n.* A leafless tree of Australia, of the genus *Casuarina*, resembling *Equisetum* in some ways.

horse′-this″tle (-sl), *n.* A large, coarse-leaved plant of the genus *Cnicus*.

horse′-tick, *n.* A blood-sucking fly; especially, *Hippobosca equina*, a pupiparous dipterous insect which frequents woodlands; the forest-fly.

horse′-vetch, *n.* Same as *Horseshoe vetch* under *Horseshoe*.

horse′weed, *n.* A troublesome weed, *Erigeron Canadense*.

horse′whip (-hwip), *n.* A whip for driving horses.

horse′whip, *v.t.*; horsewhipped *or* horsewhipt, *pt.*, *pp.*; horsewhipping, *ppr.* To strike with a horsewhip.

horse′wom″ăn (-woom″), *n.*; *pl.* **horse′wom″en** (-wim″). A woman who rides on horseback.

horse′wood, *n.* A West Indian tree, *Calliandra comosa*, having gaudy, deep-red flowers.

horse′wŏrm, *n.* The larva of a botfly.

horse′-wran″glẽr, *n.* A herder in charge of a herd of ponies or horses. [Western U. S.]

hors′i-ness, *n.* 1. The state or quality of being horsy.

2. The characteristics of a horse.

3. Special interest in horses, particularly in horse-racing or horse-breeding.

hors′ly, *a.* Like a horse. [Obs.]

hors′y, hors′ey, *a.* 1. Pertaining to or concerned with horses; as, *horsy* gossip.

2. Interested or engaged in the management of horses; as, a *horsy* company.

3. Characteristic of a horse; as, a *horsy* odor.

hor-tā′tion, *n.* [L. *hortatio* (*-onis*), from *hortari*, to urge strongly, incite, freq. of *hori*, to urge, incite.] The act of exhorting; exhortation. [Rare.]

hor′tȧ-tive, *a.* [L. *hortativus*, from *hortari*, to urge strongly, encourage.] Giving exhortation; advisory.

hor′tȧ-tive, *n.* An exhortation. [Obs.]

hor′tȧ-tō-ry, *a.* [LL. *hortatorius*, from L. *hortator*, an encourager, inciter, from *hortari*, to urge, incite.] Giving exhortation or advice; encouraging; inciting; as, a *hortatory* speech.

hor-ten′siăl (-shăl), *a.* [L. *hortensis*, from *hortus*, a garden.] Fit for a garden. [Obs.]

hor′ti-cul-tŏr, *n.* [L. *hortus*, a garden, and *cultor*, a tiller.] One who cultivates a garden.

hor-ti-cul′tūr-ăl, *a.* Pertaining to the culture of gardens.

hor′ti-cul-tūre, *n.* [L. *hortus*, a garden, and *cultura*, culture, from *colere*, to till.] The cultivation of a garden; the art of cultivating gardens; the cultivation of fruits, flowers, and vegetables.

hor-ti-cul′tūr-ist, *n.* One who is skilled in the art of horticulture; a gardener.

hor′tū-lăn, *a.* [L. *hortulanus*, from *hortus*, a garden.] Belonging to a garden. [Obs.]

hor′tus sic′cus. [L.] Literally, a dry garden; a collection of specimens of plants carefully dried and preserved; a herbarium.

hort′yärd, *n.* An orchard. [Obs.]

hō-san′nȧ, *interj.* and *n.* [Gr. *hōsanna*, from Heb. *hōshī′āh nnā*, lit., save, we pray.] An exclamation of praise to God, or an invocation of blessings or deliverance.

hōse, *n. sing.* and *pl.* [ME. *hose*; AS. *hosa*, hose.] 1. Formerly, a man's garment covering the legs and waist.

2. Covering for the feet and lower legs; stockings; short stockings are called *half-hose* or *socks*.

3. A flexible pipe, made of leather, rubber, rubber-lined cotton, or other impervious material, used for conveying water or other liquids; as, fire-*hose*; mill-*hose*.

hōse′-car″riage (-rij), *n.* A truck or wagon fitted with a reel or rests to carry the hose of a fire-engine; also called *hose-cart*.

hōse′-cŏm″pȧ-ny, *n.* A small body of firemen who man a hose-carriage and handle the hose at fires.

hōse′-coup″ling (-kup″), *n.* A pair of connecting ends by which lengths of hose may be temporarily joined together.

hō′sen, *n.*, obsolete pl. of *hose*.

hō′ṣiẽr (-zhẽr), *n.* One who deals in hose.

hō′ṣiẽr-y, *n.* 1. Stockings in general; socks.

2. The business of a dealer in hose.

hos′pice, *n.* [Fr. *hospice*, from L. *hospitium*, hospitality, an inn, lodging, from *hospes*, a host, guest.] A term applied to a convent or monastery in some of the passes of the Alps, at which entertainment is provided for travelers; any house of entertainment.

hos′pi-tȧ-ble, *a.* [OFr. *hospitable*, from LL. *hospitare*, to receive as a guest, from L. *hospes* (*-itis*), a host, guest.]

1. Receiving and entertaining strangers with kindness and without reward; kind to strangers and guests; disposed to treat guests with generous kindness; as, a *hospitable* man.

2. Proceeding from or indicating hospitality; manifesting generosity; as, a *hospitable* table.

hos′pi-tȧ-ble-ness, *n.* The quality of being hospitable; hospitality.

hos′pi-tȧ-bly, *adv.* With hospitality.

hos′pi-tāge, *n.* Hospitality. [Obs.]

hos′pi-tăl, *n.* [OFr. *hospital*; LL. *hospitale*, a house, inn, from L. *hospitalia*, strangers' apartments, neut. pl. of *hospitalis*, relating to a guest, from *hospes* (*-itis*), a guest, host.]

1. An institution for the reception and treatment of the sick or injured; also, an institution or asylum for the reception of the insane, the aged or infirm, the disabled or paupers, etc.; originally, any place of refuge for the helpless; as, an army *hospital*; a county *hospital*· a detention *hospital*.

2. The building or buildings of such an institution.

3. A place for shelter or entertainment. [Obs.]

Marine hospital; a hospital established at a seaport or port on the Great Lakes for the relief of sick sailors.

hos′pi-tăl, *a.* Hospitable. [Obs.]

Hos′pi-tăl-ẽr, *n.* One of a religious community, of which there were several in the middle ages, whose office it was to relieve the poor, the stranger, and the sick. The most noted of these was the order of military monks, laymen, and knights known as the Knights Hospitalers of the Order of St. John of Jerusalem, called also Knights of St. John and, later, Knights of Malta. Also written *Hospitaller*.

hos′pi-tăl-ism, *n.* The morbid conditions or influences due to the gathering of the sick in improperly managed hospitals.

hos-pi-tal′i-ty, *n.* [L. *hospitalitas*, hospitality, from *hospitalis*, relating to a host or guest, from *hospes*, a host, guest.] The act or practice of receiving and entertaining strangers or guests without reward, or with kind and generous liberality.

hos′pi-tāte, *v.t.* To be hospitable to. [Obs.]

hos′pi-tāte, *v.i.* [L. *hospitatus*, pp. of *hospitari*, to be a guest.] To be treated as a guest. [Obs.]

hos-pi′ti-um (-pish′i-), *n.* [L., an inn.] A hospice; an inn. [Obs.]

hos′pō-där, *n.* [Rumanian.] A title of dignity formerly borne by the vassal princes of Moldavia and Wallachia, and in earlier times by the princes of Lithuania and the kings of Poland; now one of the titles of the czar of Russia.

hōst, *v.t.* To give entertainment to. [Obs.]

hōst, *v.i.* To lodge at an inn. [Obs.]

hōst, *n.* [ME. *host*, *ost*; OFr. *host*, a host, army, from L. *hostis*, a stranger, foreigner, foe.] An army; a great number of men ready for war; hence, any great number or multitude.

hōst, *n.* [ME. *host*, *ost*; OFr. *hoste*; L. *hospes* (*-itis*), a host, guest.]

1. One who receives another as a guest; an innkeeper; a landlord.

2. In biology, an animal or organism in or on whose organs a parasite exists.

3. A guest. [Obs.]

To reckon without one's host; to neglect necessary details or facts; to make a wrong calculation.

hōst, *n.* [ME. *host*, *hoste*; OFr. *hostie*; L. *hostia*, an animal sacrificed, a victim, from *hostire*, to strike.] In the Roman Catholic church, the consecrated wafer representing the body of Christ, or, as Roman Catholics believe, transubstantiated into his own body; the sacramental victim in the eucharist.

hos′tāge, *n.* [ME. *hostage*, *ostage*; OFr. *hostage*, *ostage*; LL. *hostagium*, *hostaticum*, from *obsidaticus*, the condition of a hostage, from L. *obses*, *obsidis*, a hostage, pledge, security.]

1. A person delivered to an enemy or hostile power, as a pledge to secure the performance of the conditions of a treaty or stipulations of any kind, on the performance of which the person is to be released.

2. Anything given as security; a pledge. [Rare.]

hos′tel, *n.* [ME. *hostel*, *ostel*; OFr. *hostel*, *ostel*, from LL. *hospitale*, a large house, an inn, from L. *hospitalis*, of or relating to a guest, from *hospes* (*-itis*), a guest.]

1. An inn.

2. A house or small college in some English and French universities, not included in the

university group proper or in its regular system of government.

hos′tel-ēr, *n.* 1. An innkeeper. [Obs.]

2. A student in a hostel at certain English and French universities.

hos′tel-ry, *n.*; *pl.* **hos′tel-ries**. A hotel; an inn; a lodging-house.

hōst′ess, *n.* 1. A female host; a woman who entertains guests at her house.

3. A woman who keeps an inn.

Hostess House; the place established at army camps and cantonments during the World War by the Young Women's Christian Association where hospitality and help were given to women visitors.

hōst′ess-ship, *n.* The character or business of a hostess.

hos′tie, *n.* The consecrated wafer; an obsolete form of *host*.

hos′tile (*or* -tīl), *a.* [L. *hostilis*, from *hostis*, a foreigner, an enemy.] Of or belonging to an enemy; pertaining to or expressing enmity or opposition; conflicting; antagonistic; inimical; as, *hostile* territory; a *hostile* band.

hos′tile (*or* -tīl), *n.* An enemy; specifically, a North American Indian on the warpath. [Colloq.]

hos′tile-ly (*or* -tīl-), *adv.* In a hostile manner.

hos-til′i-ty, *n.*; *pl.* **hos-til′i-ties**. [LL. *hostilitas* (-*atis*), from L. *hostilis*, of or like an enemy; hostile.]

1. The state or quality of being hostile; enmity; opposition; aggression.

2. A hostile act; in the plural, the attacks of an enemy; hostile actions.

hos′til-īze, *v.t.* To cause to become hostile. [Rare.]

hōst′ing, *n.* A muster; the assembling of an armed body. [Obs.]

hos′tlēr, os′tlēr (-lēr), *n.* [A contr. of *hosteler*.]

1. One who has the care of horses; a groom.

2. One who cleans locomotives.

hōst′ry, *n.* A hostelry; also, a stable. [Obs.]

hot, *a.*; *comp.* hotter; *superl.* hottest. [ME. *hot*, *hote*; AS. *hat*, hot.]

1. Having, feeling, or giving out heat, especially to a greater degree than is expressed by *warm*; opposed to *cold*; as, a *hot* fire.

2. Causing the sensation or effect of heat; pungent; stimulating; acrid; as, *hot* pepper.

3. Ardent in temper; vehement; passionate; fiery.

4. Furious; violent; keen; brisk; as, a *hot* pursuit.

5. Lustful; lewd.

6. Readily absorbent and dry, as a surface for painting.

Hot blast; see under *Blast*.

In hot water; in trouble; in an embarrassing situation.

Syn.—Burning, fiery, glowing, heated, passionate.

hot′bed, *n.* 1. A bed of earth heated artificially, as by fermenting manure, etc., and usually covered with glass, intended for raising early plants or for nourishing exotic plants of warm climates, which will not thrive in cool or temperate air; hence, in a figurative sense, a place which favors rapid growth or development; as, a *hotbed* of sedition.

2. A platform in a rolling-mill used to hold the hot rails, etc., while they cool.

hot′-blood″ed (-blud), *a.* Ardent; excitable; passionate; amatory.

hot′-brāined, *a.* Impetuous; rash; excitable.

hotch, *v.t.* [Scot. and Prov. Eng.]

1. To shake or jolt to cause separation, as peas from beans when mixed; to shake; to jog.

2. To drive, as cattle, etc.

hotch, *v.i.* 1. To fidget; to be agitated or restless.

2. To hobble; to limp; to have a jerky motion.

hotch′pot, *n.* [ME. *hochepot*, *hochepoche*; OFr. *hochepot*, a mingled mass, from O.D. *hutspot*, a mixture of beef or mutton cut in small pieces, and boiled in a pot; *hutsen*, to shake, jolt, and *pot*, a pot.]

1. A mingled mass; a mixture of many ingredients; a hodgepodge.

2. In law, an actual or assumed commixture of property for the purpose of equable division. Thus, a child, taking a share of the estate of an ancestor under any appointment, shall not be entitled to any share in the unappointed part after the death of the ancestor, without bringing his or her share into *hotchpot*, and accounting for the same accordingly. *Collation* is the Scotch term.

hotch′potch, *n.* [A variation of *hotchpot*.]

1. In Scotch cookery, a kind of thick broth made by boiling together various vegetables with lamb, mutton, or beef.

2. A mixture; an indiscriminate jumble or medley; a hotchpot; a hodgepodge.

hot′coc″kles (-klz), *n.* A child's game in which a blindfold player guesses who strikes him or his hand placed behind him.

hōte, *v.t.* and *v.i.* See *Hight*.

hō-tel′, *n.* [Fr. *hôtel*; OFr. *hostel*, from LL. *hospitale*, a large house, an inn, properly neut. of L. *hospitalis*, hospitable, from *hospes* (-*itis*), a stranger.]

1. A house for entertaining strangers or travelers; an inn; especially, an inn of some style and pretensions.

2. In France, (a) a dwelling in a city of a person of rank or wealth; a large town mansion; (b) a public building.

hō′ten, *v.*, obsolete past participle of *hight*.

hot′-flūe, *n.* An apartment heated by stoves or steam-pipes, in which printed calicoes, etc., are dried.

hot′foot, *adv.* Hastily. [Colloq.]

hot′head (-hed), *n.* A person of quick temper.

hot′-head″ed, *a.* Hot-brained; rash; hasty.

hot′house, *n.* 1. A house kept warm to shelter tender plants and shrubs; a place in which the plants of warmer climates may be reared, and native fruits ripened out of their season.

2. Any house or room artificially heated to a high temperature; a drying-room, as for green pottery.

3. A bath-house; also, a brothel. [Obs.]

hot′-liv″ēred, *a.* Irascible; having a violent temper.

hot′ly, *adv.* Ardently; vehemently; violently; lustfully.

hot′-mouthed, *a.* Headstrong; ungovernable.

hot′ness, *n.* The state or quality of being hot; heat; ardor; violence; passion.

hot′press, *v.t.* To apply both heat and mechanical pressure to, as for the purpose of giving a smooth and glossy surface.

hot′-short, *a.* Easily cracked or broken when worked at a red heat, and difficult to weld; as, *hot-short* iron.

hot′-spir″it-ed, *a.* Having a fiery spirit.

hot′spūr, *n.* 1. One who spurs on rashly; a person violent, rash, or impetuous.

2. A kind of pea of early growth. [Obs.]

hot′spūr, hot′spūrred, *a.* Violent; impetuous; rash; headstrong; reckless; hasty. [Obs.]

hot′-tem″pēred, *a.* Having a violent or hasty temper.

Hot′ten-tot, *n.* [D. *Hottentot*, lit., *hot* and *tot*, two syllables much used in their language.] One of a South African race inferior in stature and mental ability to the surrounding tribes. Their skin is yellowish-brown, their hair woolly, and their language noteworthy for its clicks.

Hottentot breadfruit; Kafir bread.

Hottentot cherry; a South African plant, *Cassine Maurocenia*, having a valuable wood.

Hot′ten-tot-ism, *n.* A characteristic of the Hottentots; specifically, a kind of stammering.

Hot′ten-tot's-bread (-bred), *n.* The elephant's-foot or tortoise-plant.

hot′tēr, *v.i.* To move unsteadily; to shiver; to jolt. [Scot.]

hot′-wall, *n.* In gardening, a wall constructed with flues for the conducting of heat for protecting or hastening the growth of fruit-trees.

hot′-well, *n.* The reservoir for the hot water from the condenser of a condensing engine.

hou′dah, *n.* Same as *Howdah*.

hough (hok), *n.* and *v.* Same as *Hock*.

hou′let, *n.* A howlet; an owl. [Obs.]

hōult, *n.* A holt; a wood; a wooded hill. [Obs.]

hound, *n.* [ME. *hound*, *hund*; AS. *hund*, a dog.]

1. A dog, especially of a breed or variety used in the chase, as in hunting the boar, the deer, the fox, the hare, etc., by scent; specifically, when not qualified, a foxhound. The chief varieties called *hounds* are the beagle, bloodhound, foxhound, greyhound, harrier, buckhound, and staghound or deerhound.

Deerhound.

2. A dastard; a low, mean, contemptible wretch.

3. A houndfish.

4. The old-squaw or oldwife, a duck.

5. A horizontal brace or reënforcement in the running-gear of a vehicle.

6. A projection upon each side of a masthead forming a support for the rigging or trestletrees.

hound, *v.t.*; hounded, *pt.*, *pp.*; hounding, *ppr.*

1. To hunt; to chase; to pursue with or as with hounds; to follow the trail of.

2. To set on the chase, as a hound; to urge to pursue.

hound′fish, *n.* 1. A shark of the genus *Galeus* or of allied genera; a dogfish.

2. Any of various other fishes, as (a) the garfish, *Tylosurus acus*; (b) the bluefish, *Pomatomus saltatrix*; (c) the Spanish mackerel, *Scomberomorus maculatus*.

Smooth Houndfish (*Mustelus vulgaris*).

hound′ing, *n.* 1. The hunting of game, especially deer, by or with hounds.

2. Same as *Hound*, 6.

hound's′-tōngue (-tung), *n.* A plant of the genus *Cynoglossum*, a coarse weed having a disagreeable odor and bearing nutlets that cling to the wool of sheep.

hōup, *n.* The hoopoe. [Obs.]

hour (our), *n.* [ME. *houre*, *our*, *oure*, *ure*; OFr. *ure*, *ore*; L. *hora*; Gr. *hōra*, an hour, time, period, season.]

1. A period of time equal to sixty minutes or one twenty-fourth part of a day; formerly, one twelfth of the time from sunrise to sunset or from sunset to sunrise.

2. The time marked or indicated by a chronometer, clock, or watch; the particular time of the day; as, at what *hour* do you go? What *hour* is it?

3. A particular time; a fixed or appointed time; a space of time recurring occasionally; an interval; a season; as, the *hour* of death.

4. [*pl.*] In the Roman Catholic church, certain prayers to be repeated at stated times of the day, as matins and vespers.

5. [H—] One of the female divinities or goddesses of the seasons or *hours* of the day.

6. The distance that may be traveled in an *hour*; as, it is two *hours* from the station.

Canonical hours; see under *Canonical*.

Eight-hour or *ten-hour law*; a law fixing eight or ten hours as the length of a working day for certain classes of labor.

Equinoctial, *sidereal*, or *solar hour*; the twenty-fourth part of a mean solar, a sidereal, or a solar day respectively.

The small hours; the hours indicated by small numerals, as 1, 2, 3, etc., in the early morning.

To keep good hours; to be at home in good season; not to be abroad late or at the usual hours of retiring.

hour′-an″gle, *n.* The angular distance, usually measured to the west, between the meridian of the observer and the meridian of any given point on the celestial sphere.

hour′-cir″cle, *n.* 1. Any great circle of the sphere which passes through the two poles; so called because the hour of the day is ascertained when the circle upon which the sun is for the time being is ascertained.

2. A graduated circle upon an equatorial indicating the hour-angle of the point in the center of its field of view.

hour′glass, *n.* A vessel of glass having two compartments connected by a narrow neck through which a quantity of sand or other substance requires just an hour to run from the upper to the lower part. Similar devices measure any other period of time desired. [See *Egg-glass*.]

hour′-hand, *n.* The hand or pointer which indicates the hour on a clock, watch, etc.

hōu′ri, *n.* [Per. *huri*, a nymph of paradise.] Among the Mohammedans, a nymph of paradise. In the Koran, the *houris* are represented as most beautiful virgins, endowed with unfading youth.

hour′-line (our′), *n.* The line on a sundial on which the shadow of the gnomon falls at any hour.

hour′ly (our′), *a.* Happening or done every hour; occurring hour by hour; frequent; often repeated; continual; as, an *hourly* edition of a newspaper.

hour′ly, *adv.* Every hour; at each succeeding hour; frequently; continually; as, to signal *hourly*.

hour′-plāte, *n.* The plate of a clock or other timepiece on which the hours are marked; the dial.

hous′āge, *n.* A fee for keeping goods in a house. [Obs.]

house, *n.*; *pl.* **hous′es**. [ME. *hous*, *hows*, *hus*; AS. *hus*, a house, prob. from same root as *hydan*, to hide.]

1. A building intended or used as a habitation or shelter for animals of any kind; but especially, a building or edifice for the habitation of man; a dwelling-place; a structure designed to be used by human beings for any purpose; as, a dwelling-*house*; a meeting-*house*; a *house* of entertainment; a school*house*.

2. Any place of abode or lodgment.

The bloody *house* of life. —Shak.

3. A building in which anything is kept or sheltered; a structure for any purpose except human occupation; as, a ware*house*; a slaughter-*house*; a milk-*house*.

4. The members of a family living in the same *house*; a household.

5. A family regarded as consisting of ancestors, descendants, and kindred; a race of

persons from the same stock; a tribe; especially, a noble family or an illustrious race; as, the *house* of Hanover; the *house* of Israel or of Judah.

6. One of the branches of a dual legislature; a body of men assembled in their legislative capacity; as, the *House* of Lords or of Commons; the *House* of Representatives.

7. A quorum of a legislative body; as, the government failed to keep a *house*.

8. The audience or attendance at a place of entertainment; as, there was a good *house*.

9. In commerce, a firm or commercial establishment; as, a wholesale shoe *house*.

10. A square or division on a chessboard.

11. The workhouse. [Colloq., Eng.]

12. The body; the residence of the soul.

This mortal *house* I'll ruin. —Shak.

13. Household affairs; domestic concerns.

14. In astrology, a twelfth part of the heavens as divided by great circles drawn through the north and south points of the horizon, in the same way as meridians pass through the earth's poles. The heavens, visible and invisible, were thus divided into twelve equal parts, six being above the horizon and six below. The first *house* was called the *house* of life; the second, that of fortune or riches; the third, that of brethren; the fourth, that of relations; the fifth, that of children; the sixth, that of health; the seventh, that of marriage; the eighth, that of death or the upper portal; the ninth, that of religion; the tenth, that of dignities; the eleventh, that of friends and benefactors; and the twelfth, that of enemies or of captivity.

House of call; a house where journeymen connected with a particular trade assemble, particularly when out of work, and where the unemployed can be hired by those in search of hands.

House of Commons; see *Commons*, 2.

House of correction; see under *Correction*.

House of God, of the Lord, of worship, of prayer; a church, temple, or other place of worship.

House of ill fame; a bawdy-house.

House of Lords; see under *Lord*.

House of Representatives; see under *Representative*.

Lower house; the lower in rank and the more popular of the two branches of a legislative body, as the House of Representatives in the United States or the House of Commons in England.

Public house; a house of entertainment for the public; in England, a licensed drinking-saloon.

The White House; the official residence of the president of the United States at Washington, D. C.; hence, the presidential office.

To bring down the house; to cause very great applause.

To keep a good house; to provide well for members of the household or for visitors.

To keep house; to keep up an independent home; to manage the affairs of a house.

To keep open house; to entertain freely at all times.

To keep the house; to be obliged to remain in the house, as on account of illness.

Upper house; the higher in rank of the two branches of a legislative body, as the House of Lords in England.

Syn.—Home, residence, abode, dwelling, domicile, habitation.

house, *v.t.*; housed, *pt., pp.*; housing, *ppr.* [ME. *housen, howsen*; AS. *husian*, to house, from *hus*, house.]

1. To cover from the inclemencies of the weather; to place under shelter; to protect by covering; as, to *house* wood; to *house* farming utensils; to *house* cattle.

2. To admit to residence; to harbor.

Palladius wished him to *house* all the Helots. —Sidney.

3. To deposit and cover, as in the grave.

4. To drive to a shelter.

5. In seamen's language, (a) to put or stow in a place of safety or security; as, to *house* a sail; to *house* a topmast; (b) to put up, as an awning, in the form of a ridged roof, so as to throw off water.

house, *v.i.* 1. To take shelter or lodgings; to abide; to reside.

2. To be situated in an astrological house or region of the heavens.

Where Saturn *houses*. —Dryden.

house'-ā"gent, *n.* One who is occupied in looking after the sale, renting, and general care of houses.

house'-bōat, *n.* A covered boat used as a house. Boats constructed to serve as permanent dwellings are especially common in some parts of Asia, as on the Chinese rivers. In England, house-boats consisting of a boat carrying a wooden house are common on the Thames, being used to give their owners and friends an outing on the water in the warmer season.

house'bōte, *n.* [*House*, and ME. *bot, bote*, amends, reward.] In English law, a sufficient allowance of wood given a tenant to repair the house and supply fuel.

House-boat.

house'break"ēr, *n.* One who commits the crime of housebreaking.

house'break"ing, *n.* The breaking or opening and entering of a house with intent to commit a felony or to steal or rob. [See *Burglary*.]

house'build"ēr (-bild"), *n.* One engaged in the business of building houses.

house'-cär, *n.* A closed freight-car; a box-car.

house'-crick"et, *n.* A European cricket, *Acheta domestica*, that infests houses, especially about fireplaces.

house'-dog, *n.* A watch-dog; a dog kept to guard a house.

house'-finch, *n.* The purple finch or burion, *Carpodacus frontalis*, of southwestern United States.

house'-flag, *n.* A flag flown by a merchant ship, indicating the house or firm to which it belongs or is consigned.

house'-fly, *n.* The common fly, *Musca domestica*, found in nearly every country.

house'hōld, *n.* 1. Those who dwell under the same roof and compose a family.

2. An ancestral line; a race or family. [Obs.]

house'hōld, *a.* Belonging to the house and family; domestic; as, *household* furniture; *household* affairs.

Household gods; see under *God*.

Household suffrage or *franchise*; in Great Britain, the right of householders and lodgers to vote for members of Parliament.

Household troops; troops whose special duty it is to attend a sovereign and guard his palaces.

Household word; a name or expression so well known as to be familiar everywhere.

house'hōld"ēr, *n.* The head of a family; one who keeps house with his family; one who owns or rents a house.

Compound householder; see under *Compound*.

house'keep"ēr, *n.* 1. One who occupies a house with his family; a man or woman who maintains a family state in a house; a householder; the head of a family.

2. One who looks after the keeping of a house; especially, a female servant who has the chief care of the family, superintends the other servants, and manages the domestic affairs of the home.

3. One who remains much at home. [Rare.]

4. A house-dog. [Obs.]

house'keep"ing, *a.* Domestic; used in a family; as, *housekeeping* commodities.

house'keep"ing, *n.* 1. The family state in a dwelling; care or management of domestic concerns.

2. Hospitality. [Obs.]

hou'sel, *n.* [ME. *housel*; AS. *husel*, a sacrifice.] The eucharist; the sacred bread; the act of taking or receiving the sacrament. [Rare.]

hou'sel, *v.t.* [ME. *houselen*; AS. *huslian*, from *husel*, a sacrifice.] To give the eucharist to. [Rare.]

house'leek, *n.* A plant of the genus *Sempervivum*, often found in Europe growing on the tops of houses, walls, etc.

house'less, *a.* Destitute of a house or habitation; without shelter; homeless; as, the *houseless* child of want.

house'line, hous'ing, *n.* Among seamen, a small line formed of three strands, used for seizings, etc.

hou'sel-ing, *n.* and *a.* I. *n.* The act of administering the eucharist. [Obs.]

II. *a.* Of or relating to the eucharist. [Rare.]

house'maid, *n.* A female servant employed to keep the rooms and halls of a dwelling in order.

Housemaid's knee; a tumor or swelling on the front of the knee resulting from an enlargement of the bursa; so named because servant-girls whose duty it is to kneel frequently while scrubbing floors, etc., were thought to suffer most from the trouble.

house'-mär"tin, *n.* The house-swallow, *Hirundo urbica*.

house'māte, *n.* One who lives with another in the same house.

house'rōom, *n.* Room or accommodation in a house.

house'-snāke, *n.* The milk-snake.

house'-spar"rōw, *n.* The common European sparrow, *Passer domesticus*.

house'-spi"dēr, *n.* A spider that is found around houses, among the commonest species being *Theridium vulgare* and *Tegenaria domestica*.

house'wärm"ing, *n.* A feast or merrymaking at the time a family enters a new house.

house'wife (*or* huz'wif *or* huz'if), *n.*; *pl.* **house'-wives** (*or* huz'ivz). 1. The mistress of a family; the wife of a householder.

2. A little case or bag for articles used in sewing, carried in the pocket.

Sailor's housewife; a ditty-bag.

house'wife, house'wive, *v.t.* To manage with economy and skill. [Rare.]

house'wife-ly, *a.* Pertaining to the mistress of a family; economical; domestic.

house'wif"ēr-y (*or* huz'if-ri), *n.* The business of the mistress of a family; female management of domestic concerns.

house'wŏrk, *n.* The manual labor pertaining to housekeeping.

house'wright (-rit), *n.* A mechanic who builds houses.

hous'ing, *n.* 1. The act of sheltering or of putting under cover; the state of living in a dwelling.

2. Anything that shelters or covers.

3. In carpentry, the space taken out of one piece to admit the insertion of part of another.

4. In architecture, a niche for a statue.

5. Among seamen, (a) that part of a ship's mast which is concealed beneath the deck; (b) an awning or canopy spread above the deck of a ship when temporarily out of service; (c) a houseline.

6. In machinery, a support or framework to hold something in position, as a journal-box.

hous'ing, *n.* [OFr. *housse*, a short mantle, a cover for a horse.]

1. A cover or cloth over or under a horse's saddle, used originally to keep off dirt, and afterward as an ornamental or military appendage; a saddlecloth; a horse-cloth.

2. [*pl.*] The trappings, accouterments, or caparison of a horse.

3. A cover attached to the collar or hames of a harness.

hous'ling, *n.* and *a.* See *Houseling*.

houss, *n.* A covering; a housing. [Obs.]

Hous-tō'ni-ȧ, *n.* [Named after Dr. William *Houston*, an English botanist.] A genus of low biennial herbs with delicate four-parted blue or white flowers, embracing many species; *Houstonia cærulea* is called *innocence* or *bluet*.

hou'tou, *n.* [From its note.] A beautiful South American bird of the genus *Momotus*; a motmot.

houve, *n.* [ME. *houve, howve*; AS. *hufe*, a covering for the head.] A covering for the head; a hood; a cap. [Obs.]

Hōu'yhnhnm (-inm), *n.* [Prob. coined to represent the whinny of a horse.] One of a race of imaginary beings described by Swift in "Gulliver's Travels" as horses possessing reason, exceptional virtues, and powers of command over the manlike beings called Yahoos.

hōve, *v.*, past tense and past participle of *heave*.

hōve, *v.i.* and *v.t.* To rise; to swell; to cause to rise or swell. [Obs.]

hōve, *v.i.* [Obs.] Same as *Hover*.

hov'el, *n.* [ME. *hovel, hovil*, dim. of AS. *hof*, a house.]

1. An open shed for sheltering cattle or protecting produce, etc., from the weather.

2. A poor cottage; a small mean house.

3. In a porcelain manufactory, a cone-shaped structure of brick around which the ovens or firing-kilns are clustered.

hov'el, *v.t.*; hoveled *or* hovelled, *pt., pp.*; hoveling *or* hovelling, *ppr.* To put in a hovel; to shelter.

hov'el-ēr, hov'el-lēr, *n.* [Prob. so called from their use of *hovels* on the shore for shelter.] One engaged in saving life and property from wrecked vessels; also, a vessel used for coasting. [Prov. Eng.]

hov'el-ing, hov'el-ling, *n.* 1. A mode of preventing chimneys from smoking by carrying up two sides higher than those which are less liable to receive strong currents of air, or leaving apertures on all the sides, so that when the wind blows over the top the smoke may escape below.

2. A chimney so constructed.

hō'ven, *v.*, obsolete past participle of *heave*.

hō'ven, *a.* See *Hooven*.

hov'ēr (*or* hov'), *v.i.*; hovered, *pt., pp.*; hovering, *ppr.* [ME. *hoveren*, freq. of *hoven*, to wait, linger, abide, from AS. *hof*, house.]

1. To hang or remain fluttering in the air or on the wing; to remain, as it were, suspended over a place or object; to remain floating in the air.

Great flights of birds are *hovering* about the bridge. —Addison.

2. To wander about from place to place in a neighborhood; to move to and fro threateningly or watchingly; as, a ship *hovering* on the coast.

3. To be in suspense or expectation; to be in doubt or hesitation; to be irresolute; to waver.

Hovering o'er the paper with her quill.—Shak.

hŏv′ẽr, *v.t.* To shelter by covering with the wings, as a brooding hen.
hŏv′ẽr, *n.* A protection or shelter. [Obs.]
hŏv′ẽr-ẽr, *n.* 1. One who or that which hovers.
2. A shelter-box for young chickens hatched in an incubator.
hŏv′ẽr-ground, *n.* Light ground. [Obs.]
hŏv′ẽr-hawk, *n.* The kestrel.
hŏv′ẽr-ing-ly, *adv.* In a hovering manner.
how, *adv.* [ME. *how, hough, hwu*; AS. *hu*, how.]
1. In what manner; in what way; as, I know not *how* to answer.
2. To what degree, extent, or amount; in what proportion; by what measure or quantity; as, *how* long shall we suffer these indignities? *how* much better is knowledge than gold?
3. For what reason; from what cause.

How now, my love, why is your cheek so pale? —Shak.

4. By what means; as, *how* can this effect be produced?
5. In what state, condition, or plight.

How, and with what reproach, shall I return? —Dryden.

6. At what price; as, *how* is flour selling?
7. By what name or title.
How may be used interrogatively or relatively in any of its senses.
how, *n.* The way or manner of doing or becoming.
how, *n.* 1. Any hollow place; the hold of a ship. [Obs.]
2. A glen; a dell; a plain. [Scot.]
how-adj′i, *n.* [Ar. *khawāja*; Per. *kh'āja*, a merchant, rich gentleman.] A name given to a merchant or traveler in some parts of the East.
how′bē, *adv.* Howbeit. [Obs.]
how-bē′it, *adv.* Be it as it may; nevertheless; notwithstanding; yet; but; however.

Howbeit we must be cast upon a certain island. —Acts xxvii. 26.

how′dah, *n.* [Hind. *haudah*, from Ar. *haudaj*, a litter carried by a camel or elephant.] A seat erected on the back of an elephant for two or more persons to ride in. It is of various forms, and usually covered overhead.

Howdah.

how′die, how′dy, *n.* A midwife. [Scot.]
how′dy, *interj.* A familiar form of greeting; a contraction of *how do ye*, or *how do you* (do). [Southern U. S.]
how′dy-dō′, *n.* A troublesome matter; an embarrassing state of affairs. [Colloq.]
how′el, *n.* [Compare Dan. *hövl*, G. *hobel*, a plane.] A plane with a convex sole, used by coopers for smoothing the insides of barrels and casks.
how′el, *v.t.* To smooth with a howel.
how′ell, *n.* The upper stage in a furnace for firing porcelain.
how-ev′ẽr, *adv.* 1. In whatever manner or degree; as, *however* good or bad it may be.
2. At all events; at least. [Rare.]
how-ev′ẽr, *conj.* Nevertheless; notwithstanding; yet; still; though.
howff, houff, *n.* A haunt; a place of resort. [Scot.]
how′itz, *n.* [Obs.] Same as *Howitzer*.
how′itz-ẽr, *n.* [G. *haubitze*, from Bohem. *haufnice*, a howitzer, originally a sling.] A cannon, differing from ordinary guns in being shorter and lighter in proportion to its bore, and used for throwing shells of case-shot only, with comparatively small charges. A small chamber at the bottom of the bore receives the powder.

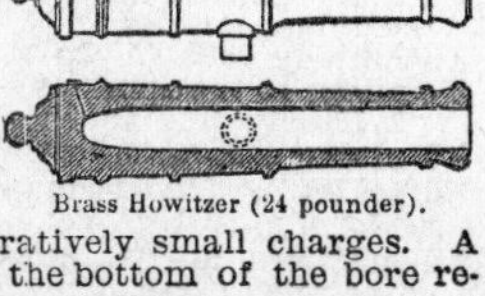

Brass Howitzer (24 pounder).

howk, houk, *v.t.* and *v.i.* To dig; to hollow out by digging; to burrow. [Scot.]
how′kẽr, *n.* Same as *Hooker*.
howl, *v.i.*; howled, *pt., pp.*; howling, *ppr.* [ME. *howlen, houlen*, to howl, an imitative word.]
1. To cry as a dog or wolf; to utter a protracted or mournful cry.
2. To utter a loud, mournful sound, expressive of distress; to wail.

Howl ye, for the day of the Lord is at hand. —Isa. xiii. 6.

3. To make a mournful wailing sound like the wind.
Howling monkey; a howler.
howl, *v.t.*; howled, *pt., pp.*; howling, *ppr.* To utter or speak with outcry.
Howl down; to render a speaker's words inaudible by uttering howls, catcalls, etc.
howl, *n.* 1. The cry of a dog or wolf, or other like sound.
2. The cry of a human being in horror or anguish.
howl′ẽr, *n.* 1. One who howls.
2. A South American monkey of the genus *Mycetes*, noted for its peculiar and very loud cry produced by an enlarged formation of the throat; also called the *howling monkey*.
howl′et, *n.* [Fr. *hulotte*, an owl.] An owlet; called also *houlet*.
howl′ing, *a.* 1. Filled with howls or howling beasts; dreary; as, in the *howling* wilderness and in the great deep.
2. Extravagant; ultra; as, a *howling* dude. [Slang.]
how′lite, *n.* [Named after Henry *How*, a Nova Scotian mineralogist.] In mineralogy, a chalky calcium borosilicate.
howm, *n.* A lowland by a waterside; a holm. [Scot.]
howp, *v.i.* To cry aloud; to whoop. [Obs.]
how′ry, *a.* Dirty; nasty. [Prov. Eng.]
how′sō, *adv.* [Obs.] See *Howsoever*.
how-sō-ev′ẽr, *adv.* 1. In what manner soever; to whatever degree or extent; however.
2. Although; however. [Obs.]
howve, *n.* [Obs.] See *Houve*.
hox, *v.t.* [Obs.] See *Hock*.
hoy, *n.* [Fl. *hui*, a hoy, a lighter.] A small coasting vessel, usually sloop-rigged.
hoy, *interj.* Halloo! Stop! Wait!
hoy, *v.t.* To incite; pursue. [Scot.]
Hoy′ȧ, *n.* [Named after Thomas *Hoy*, an English gardener.] A genus of tropical climbing shrubs of the milkweed family, cultivated for their gaudy flowers.
hoy′den, *n.* Same as *Hoiden*.
hoy′măn, *n.* One who navigates a hoy.
huä′căl (wä′), *n.* [Peruv.] A divinity; a shrine; a tomb.
huä-nä′cō, *n.* Same as *Guanaco*.
hub, *n.* [A form of *hob*.]
1. The center-piece of a wheel; a cylinder through which the axle passes, having peripheral mortises for the convergent spokes; a nave.

Hubs of Wheels.

2. Figuratively, anything in a central or important position.
3. The hilt of a weapon. [Rare.]
4. An obstruction or roughness, as in a road.
5. A block used to scotch wheels.
6. A peg or hob at which quoits are pitched.
7. In plumbing, the double female, a short pipe for coupling ends.
8. A steel punch for impressing devices on coins, dies, etc.
The Hub; a nickname for Boston.
Up to the hub; to a great extent; deeply involved; as, a man is in debt *up to the hub*.
hub′-band, *n.* A metal band to protect a wooden hub.
Hub′bīte, *n.* A resident of the Hub or Boston. [Humorous.]
hub′ble, *n.* 1. A protuberance or projection in a path or road.
2. Confusion; uproar. [Prov. Eng.]
hub′ble-bub″ble, *n.* 1. An East Indian hooka or water-pipe, with bowl made of a cocoanut-shell, so constructed that the tobacco smoke passes through water, making the noise from which it is named.
2. A continuous sound, as of bubbling.

Hubble-bubble.

hub′ble-show, *n.* Confusion or uproar. [Prov. Eng.]
hub′bly, *a.* Filled with hubbles; rough.
hub′bub, *n.* A great noise of many confused voices; a tumult; uproar; riot.
hub′by, *n.* Husband. [Colloq.]
hub′by, *a.* Having hubs and ruts, as a frozen or sun-baked mud-road.
hub′-deep, *a.* Having depth equal to the height of a hub; as, the mire is *hub-deep*.
hüb′nẽr-ite, *n.* [Named after *Hübner*, a German chemist.] In mineralogy, dark-colored manganese tungstate, isomorphous with wolframite.
hub′-plank, *n.* A guard-plank along a bridge-truss, placed at hub height.
Hub′shee, *n.* [Per. *Habshi*, an Abyssinian.]
1. An Abyssinian; an Ethiopian.
2. [h—] A small horse or pony native to the Himalayas.
huç-ȧ-toon′, *n.* A cotton fabric designed especially for the African trade.
hūch, hū′chen, *n.* [G.] In zoölogy, a large salmon found in the Danube; called also *bull-trout*.
huck, *v.i.* To haggle in trading. [Obs.]
huck, *n.* A dialectic form of *hook, husk, hock*, etc.
huck′ȧ-back, *n.* [Prob. originally wares, from L.G. *hukkebak*, pickaback.] A kind of linen with raised figures on it, used for tablecloths and towels; called also *huck*.
huck′ber″ry, *n.* Same as *Hackberry*.
huck′le-buck′le, *n.* A coasting play for children. [Scot.]
huç′kle, *n.* [A dim. from *hook*.]
1. The hip.
2. A bunch or projection resembling the hip.
huç′kle-backed (-bakt), *a.* Having round shoulders; hunchbacked.
huç′kle-ber″ry, *n.* [Corruption of *whortleberry*, from AS. *wyrtil*, a small shrub, and *berie*, berry.]
1. The edible black or dark-blue fruit of various species of the genus *Gaylussacia*.
2. The shrub that bears the huckleberry, *Gaylussacia resinosa*.
huç′kle-bōne, *n.* 1. The hip-bone. [Obs.]
2. The astragalus or upper ankle-bone.
huck′stẽr, huck′stẽr-ẽr, *n.* [ME. *hukster, hucster*; M.D. *heukster*, a huckster, from *hucken*, to stoop, bend; in allusion to the peddler stooping under his pack.]
1. A retailer of small articles, of provisions, nuts, etc.
2. A mean, trickish fellow.
huck′stẽr, *v.i.*; huckstered, *pt., pp.*; huckstering, *ppr.* To deal in small articles or in petty bargains; to higgle.
huck′stẽr-āge, *n.* The business of a huckster; small monetary dealings.
huck′stẽr-ẽr, *n.* See *Huckster*.
huck′stress, *n.* A female peddler.
hud, *n.* The shell or hull of a nut. [Prov. Eng.]
hud′dle, *v.i.*; huddled, *pt., pp.*; huddling, *ppr.* [A freq. from ME. *huden*, from AS. *hydan*, to hide.]
1. To crowd; to press together promiscuously without order or regularity.
2. To perform certain duties in a perfunctory manner, so as to fulfil the conditions of the final oath; said of students at Cambridge University, England.
hud′dle, *v.t.* 1. To throw together in confusion; to crowd together without regard to order; as, to *huddle* people together in a room.
2. To perform hastily, without order or regularity; to produce hurriedly or without due consideration and preparation; often with *up*; as, to *huddle up* work.
3. To put on in haste and disorder; with *on*; as, she *huddled on* her clothes.
4. To still or hush. [Obs.]
hud′dle, *n.* 1. A crowd; a number of persons or things crowded together without order or regularity; tumult; confusion.
2. In shovelboard, a winning throw.
3. An old broken-down person.
hud′dlẽr, *n.* One who huddles or throws things into confusion; a bungler.
hud-dup′, *interj.* A command to a horse, urging him forward. [New Eng.]
hudġe, *n.* An iron hoisting-bucket used in mining.
Hū-di-bras′tiç, *a.* Similar in style to "Hudibras," a satire in mock-heroic style.
Hud-sō′ni-ăn, *a.* Relating to the discoverer Henry Hudson or to the bay or river discovered by him.
hūe, *n.* [ME. *hew, hewe*; AS. *hiw, heow*, form, appearance, color.]
1. Color; shade of color; tint; dye.

Painted in heavenly *hues* above. —Byron.

2. In painting, a compound color in which one of the primaries predominates, as the various grays.
hūe, *n.* [OFr. *hu, hui, heu*, a hunting-cry.] A vociferous cry; clamor; now only used in the phrase, *hue* and cry.
Hue and cry; (a) any great disturbance; (b) in law, pursuit of a felon or offender with loud outcries or clamor to give an alarm. This procedure is taken by a person robbed or otherwise injured, to pursue and get possession of the culprit's person. At common law, a private person who has been robbed, or who knows that a felony has been committed, is bound to raise *hue and cry*, under pain of fine and imprisonment.
hūed, *a.* Having color; as, golden-*hued*.
hūe′less, *a.* Destitute of color.
hū′ẽr, *n.* One whose business is to cry out or give an alarm; specifically, a fisherman stationed on a high point to give notice of the approach of a shoal of fish or of their movements.
huff, *n.* [Compare ME. *hoven*, to puff up, heave.]
1. A restrained puffing or swelling; hence, a sudden exhibition of arrogance, pride, petulance, etc.

2. One swelled with a false opinion of his own value or importance.

Lewd, shallow-brained *huffs* make atheism and contempt of religion the badge of wit. —South.

3. In checkers or chess, the removal of a player's piece from the board after neglect to capture his adversary's piece.

4. A light puffy pie-crust. [Prov. Eng.]

5. A light dry scaly incrustation of the skin. [Prov. Eng.]

huff, *v.t.*; huffed (huft), *pt.*, *pp.*; huffing, *ppr.* 1. To cause to swell up; to distend or puff up.

2. To treat with arrogance; to show an insolent manner toward.

3. In checkers or in chess, to remove from the board, as a forfeited or captured piece.

huff, *v.i.* 1. To swell up; to become distended. [Prov. Eng.]

2. To puff up with anger, conceit, or arrogance; hence, to storm; to rave; to bluster.

A *huffing*, shining, flattering, cringing coward. —Otway.

huff′cap, *n.* A swaggerer; a bully. [Obs.]

huff′cap, *a.* Swaggering; blustering. [Obs.]

huff′ẽr, *n.* A swaggerer; a blusterer; a huff.

huff′i-ness, *n.* The state of being huffy; petulance.

huff′ing-ly, *adv.* In a petulant manner; swaggeringly.

huff′ish, *a.* Arrogant; quick-tempered; petulant.

huff′ish-ly, *adv.* Peevishly; with petty arrogance.

huff′ish-ness, *n.* The state of being huffish; peevishness; arrogance.

huff′y, *a.*; *comp.* huffier; *superl.* huffiest. 1. Swelled; distended; puffed up; as, the bread is *huffy.*

2. Filled with pride, arrogance, or conceit; petulant; swaggering.

hug, *n.* A close embrace; a clasp or gripe.

hug, *v.t.*; hugged, *pt.*, *pp.*; hugging, *ppr.* 1. To press close in an embrace; to grasp firmly with the arms.

2. To cherish in the mind; to hold fast.

We *hug* deformities if they bear our names. —Glanville.

3. In seamen's language, to keep close to; as, to *hug* the land; to *hug* the wind.

To hug oneself; to chuckle with self-congratulation; to be secretly satisfied.

hug, *v.i.* [Prob. of Scand. origin; compare Dan. *sidde paa hug*, to squat on the ground; Ice. *huka*, to sit on one's hams.] To lie close; to crowd together; to huddle; as, to *hug* with swine.

hūge, *a.*; *comp.* huger; *superl.* hugest. [ME. *huge, hoge, hogge, hoghe*, from OFr. *ahoge, ahuge*, great, large, huge.]

1. Having an immense bulk; very large or great: enormous; as, a *huge* mountain; a *huge* ox.

2. Very great in any respect; possessing some one characteristic in a high degree; as, a *huge* space; a *huge* difference.

He took the *hugest* pains to adorn his big person. —Thackeray.

Syn.—Enormous, gigantic, colossal, immense, prodigious.

hūge′ly, *adv.* Very greatly; enormously.

hūge′ness, *n.* The state or condition of being huge.

hug′gẽr, *n.* One who hugs.

hug′gẽr, *v.t.* and *v.i.* To lie in ambush; to conceal. [Obs.]

hug′gẽr-mug″gẽr, *v.t.* and *v.i.* [Prov. E. *hugger*, to lie in ambush, and *mug*, mist.]

I. *v.t.* To hush up; to smother or cover up.

II. *v.i.* To act in a secret way; to consult secretly.

hug′gẽr-mug″gẽr, *a.* 1. Hidden; secret; underhanded.

2. Confused; disordered; slovenly.

hug′gẽr-mug″gẽr, *n.* Concealment; secrecy.

hug′gle, *v.t.* [Freq. of *hug.*] To hug; to cuddle; to snuggle. [Obs.]

Hū′gue-not (-ge-), *n.* [Prob. derived from *Huguenot*, the Christian name of some reformer in France.] One of a band of Protestants who exercised great influence in France in the sixteenth and seventeenth centuries.

Hū′gue-not-ism, *n.* The doctrines, beliefs, or practices of the Huguenots; French protestantism.

hū′gy, *a.* Vast. [Obs.]

hui′ȧ-bird, *n.* [Native name.] In zoölogy, a starling of New Zealand, the *Heteralocha acutirostris*; named from its note.

hui′shẽr, *v.* and *n.* [Obs.] See *Usher*.

hūke, *n.* [OFr. *huque, hucque*; O.D. *huycke*, a cloak, mantle.] A loose outer garment worn in the fifteenth century. [Obs.]

hulch, *n.* [A form of *hunch*.] A hunch. [Obs.]

hulch′y, *a.* Bent; humped. [Obs.]

hulk, *n.* [ME. *hulke*; AS. *hulc*; LL. *hulka, hulca, olca*; Gr. *holkas*, a ship which is towed, a ship of burden.]

1. The body of a ship or decked vessel of any kind; specifically, the body of an old ship or vessel which is laid by as unfit for service.

2. Figuratively, anything bulky or unwieldy, as a large clumsy person.

3. The husk. [Obs.]

The hulks; in England, old or dismasted ships formerly used as prisons.

hulk, *n.* A pen for pigs or for cattle. [Prov. Eng.]

hulk, *v.t.*; hulked, *pt.*, *pp.*; hulking, *ppr.* [Compare Scot. *howk, holk*, to dig, as a pit.]

1. To take out the entrails of; as, to *hulk* a hare. [Rare.]

2. In mining, to remove the loose material lying between the walls of a vein.

hulk, *n.* In mining, the loose material lying between the walls of a vein.

hulk′ing, *a.* Clumsy; awkward; unwieldy. [Colloq.]

hulk′y, *a.* Bulky; unwieldy.

hull, *n.* [ME. *hule, hole, hoole*; AS. *hulu*, hull, husk.]

1. The outer covering of anything, particularly of a nut or of grain.

2. The frame or body of a vessel, exclusive of her masts, yards, sails, and rigging.

Hull down; having the hull (of a ship) concealed by the convexity of the sea.

hull, *v.t.*; hulled, *pt.*, *pp.*; hulling, *ppr.* 1. To strip off or separate the hull or hulls of; as, to *hull* grain.

2. To pierce the hull of with a cannon ball.

hull, *v.i.* To float or drive on the water, like the hull of a ship, without sails. [Obs.]

hul″lȧ-bȧ-lo͝o′, *n.* A loud uproar; a noisy contention; tumult.

hulled, *a.* Stripped of the hulls.

Hulled corn; corn prepared for food by the removal of the hulls; hominy.

hull′ẽr, *n.* One who or that which hulls; specifically, a hulling-machine.

hul-lō′, *interj.* Same as *Hello*.

hull′y, *a.* Having husks or pods; siliquous.

hul′ly, *n.* A wicker eel-trap; a perforated box for keeping crabs, etc., in the water. [Prov. Eng.]

hū′lō-thē-ism, hū′lō-ist, *n.* Same as *Hylotheism, Hylotheist.*

hul′vẽr, *n.* [ME. *hulver, holver, hulfere*, holly; Ice. *hulfr*, dogwood.] Holly, an evergreen shrub or tree.

hum, *v.i.*; hummed, *pt.*, *pp.*; humming, *ppr.* [Of imitative origin.]

1. To utter the sound of bees; to buzz.

2. To make an inarticulate, buzzing sound.

The cloudy messenger turns me his back, And *hums*. —Shak.

3. To make a dull heavy noise like a drone.

Still *humming* on their drowsy course they took. —Pope.

4. To express approval or dissent by an inarticulate murmur.

5. To make a prolonged nasal sound with the mouth closed.

To make things hum; to cause affairs to move in lively fashion. [Colloq.]

hum, *v.t.* To sing in a low voice.

hum, *n.* 1. Any low, inarticulate, monotonous, murmuring, whirring, or buzzing sound, as that made by bees in flight, by a spinning top, or by a crowd of people at a distance; any distant, continuous, confused sound; as, the distant *hum* of the metropolis.

2. A low inarticulate sound uttered by a person as an expression of embarrassment, doubt, pleasure, surprise, or the like; as, *hums* and haws.

3. A strong ale or mixture of ale and spirit. [Obs.]

Venous hum; a hum heard in auscultation of a vein, as in anemia.

hum, *n.* A humbug; a hoax.

hum, *interj.* Ahem! hem! h'm! a sound expressing doubt, deliberation, surprise, pleasure, or the like, according to the intonation.

hū′măn, *a.* [ME. *humain*; OFr. *humain*; L. *humanus*, of or pertaining to man, humane, from *homo (-inis)*, a man.]

1. Of or belonging to man or mankind; having the characteristic qualities or nature of mankind or of a man; consisting of a man or men; as, *human* life; *human* nature; a *human* sacrifice.

2. Of or belonging to man in his distinctive faculties, capacities, or sphere of action, as contrasted with the rest of nature, with the animal, or with the divine; secular; not sacred; as, *human* knowledge; *human* activities; a *human* author.

hū′măn, *n.* A human being. [Colloq.]

hū′măn-āte, *a.* Endued with humanity. [Obs.]

hū-māne′, *a.* [L. *humanus*, from *homo (-inis)*, man.]

1. Having the feelings and dispositions proper to man; having tenderness, compassion, and a disposition to treat others with kindness; particularly in relieving them when in distress or in captivity, when they are helpless or defenseless; kind; benevolent; sympathetic; merciful.

2. Having a tendency to refine or humanize; as, *humane* letters.

3. Human; secular. [Obs.]

hū-māne′ly, *adv.* In a humane manner.

hū-māne′ness, *n.* The quality of being humane.

hū-man′ics, *n.* The science of human nature. [Rare.]

hū-man′i-form, *a.* Anthropomorphic. [Rare.]

hū-man′i-fȳ, *v.t.* To incarnate. [Rare.]

hū′măn-ism, *n.* 1. Humanity; human nature.

2. A mode of thought in which human affairs or interests are of chief importance.

3. The humanities; classical learning; also, the culture due to general classical and literary study.

hū′măn-ist, *n.* 1. A student of the humanities; especially, in the Renaissance, a scholar devoted to the study and diffusion of classical literature and art, particularly that of Greece.

2. One versed in the knowledge of human nature.

hū-măn-is′tic, *a.* Of, belonging to, or characterizing humanism, the humanists, the humanities, or humanity.

hū-man-i-tā′ri-ăn, *n.* 1. In theology, one who denies the divinity of Christ and believes him to be a mere man.

2. One who holds human nature to be capable of perfection without the assistance of grace.

3. One who holds that man's duties are limited to his human relations and surroundings.

4. A philanthropist.

hū-man-i-tā′ri-ăn, *a.* Of, belonging to, or characteristic of humanitarians or humanitarianism; philanthropic.

hū-man-i-tā′ri-ăn-ism, *n.* 1. Humanity; philanthropy.

2. The doctrine that Jesus Christ was possessed of a human nature only.

3. The doctrine that mankind may become perfect without divine aid.

hū-mȧ-ni′tiăn (-nish′ăn), *n.* A humanist. [Obs.]

hū-man′i-ty, *n.*; *pl.* **hū-man′i-ties**. [ME. *humanitye*; OFr. *humanite*; L. *humanitas (-atis)*, human nature, the condition of being a man, from *humanus*, pertaining to man, from *homo (-inis)*, a man.]

1. The quality of being human; the peculiar nature of man, by which he is distinguished from other beings.

2. Mankind collectively; the human race.

Humanity must perforce prey on itself. —Shak.

3. The quality of being humane; the kind feelings, dispositions, and sympathies of man; kindness; benevolence; especially, a disposition to relieve persons in distress, and to treat all created beings with tenderness; opposed to *cruelty*.

4. Mental cultivation; liberal education; instruction in classical and polite literature.

5. Classical and polite literature; a branch of such literature, as philology, grammar, rhetoric, poetry, the study of the ancient classics, and the like. In this sense generally used in the plural with the definite article prefixed, *the humanities*, but in Scotland used in the singular and applied to Latin and Latin literature alone; as, a professor of *humanity*.

hū-măn-i-zā′tion, *n.* The act of humanizing.

hū′măn-īze, *v.t.*; humanized, *pt.*, *pp.*; humanizing, *ppr.* 1. To render humane; to subdue any tendency to cruelty and render susceptible of kind feelings; to soften.

Was it the business of magic to *humanize* our natures? —Addison.

2. To render human; to give a human character or expression to; to invest with the character of humanity.

hū′măn-īze, *v.i.* To grow civilized; to become human.

hū′măn-ī-zẽr, *n.* One who or that which humanizes.

hū′măn-kīnd, *n.* The race of man; mankind; the human species.

hū′măn-ly, *adv.* 1. In a human manner; according to the opinions or knowledge of men.

2. Kindly; humanely. [Obs.]

hū′măn-ness, *n.* A human condition.

hū′māte, *n.* [*Hum*ic and *-ate.*] A salt of humic acid.

hū-mā′tion, *n.* [L. *humatio*, from *humare*, to cover with earth, bury, from *humus*, ground, earth.] Interment. [Rare.]

hum′bird, *n.* The humming-bird.

hum′ble, *a.*; *comp.* humbler; *superl.* humblest. [ME. *humble*; OFr. *humble, humle, humele*; L. *humilis*, low, small, slight, from *humus*, earth, ground.] On or near to the ground; hence, lowly; modest; meek; submissive; inexpensive. In a religious sense, having a low opinion of oneself, and a deep sense of unworthiness in the sight of God.

God resisteth the proud, but giveth grace to the *humble*. —James iv. 6.

To eat humble-pie; to suffer insult or mortification; to abase oneself.

Syn.—Lowly, meek, submissive, unassuming, unobtrusive, unpretending.

hum′ble, *a.* 1. Bruised.

2. Without horns; as, a *humble* cow. [Scot.]

hum′ble, *v.t.*; humbled, *pt., pp.*; humbling, *ppr.* 1. To bring down; to reduce to a low state; as, the power of Rome was *humbled* but not subdued.

2. To mortify or make ashamed; as, one may be *humbled* without having true humility.

3. To make humble or lowly in mind; to abase the pride of; to reduce the arrogance and self-dependence of; to give a low opinion of the moral worth of; in a religious sense, to make meek and submissive to the divine will; often used reflexively.

Syn.—Humiliate, lower, mortify, disgrace, degrade.

hum′ble, *v.t.* [Scot. *hummel, hummle*, having no horns.]

1. To break. [Rare.]

2. To break off the awns of (barley). [Scot.]

3. To break off the horns of.

hum′ble-bee, *n.* [ME. *humbylbee, hombulbe*; compare O.D. *hommel*, a humblebee.] A large bee that draws its food chiefly from clover flowers; a bumblebee.

Humblebee.

hum′ble-head (-hed), *n.* Humility. [Obs.]

hum′ble-ness, *n.* The state of being humble or low; humility; meekness.

hum′ble-plant, *n.* A sensitive plant, *Mimosa pudica*.

hum′blẽr, *n.* He who or that which humbles; one who reduces pride or mortifies.

hum′bleṣ (-blz), *n.pl.* Entrails of a deer; written also *umbles*, originally *numbles*.

hum′blesse, *n.* [OFr. *humblesse*, from *humble*, humble.] Humbleness; humility.

hum′bly, *adv* 1. In a humble manner; with modest submissiveness; with humility.

Hope *humbly* then; with trembling pinions soar;
Wait the great teacher, death, and God adore. —Pope.

2. In a low state or condition; without elevation.

hum′bōldt-ine (-bōlt-), *n.* [*Humboldt*, from Baron von *Humboldt*, a German mineralogist, and *-ine*.] An oxalate of iron occurring in coal.

hum′bug, *n.* [A compound of *hum*, to cheat, hoax, and *bug*, a goblin, specter.]

1. An imposition under fair pretenses; a hoax; also, a person who thus imposes; an impostor; a cheat.

2. A spirit of imposition or deception; trickery; pretense; sham.

3. [*pl.*] A kind of peppermint candy. [Prov. Eng.]

hum′bug, *v.t.*; humbugged, *pt., pp.*; humbugging, *ppr.* To deceive; to impose on.

hum′bug, *v.i.* To practise imposition.

hum′bug″gẽr, *n.* One who humbugs.

hum′bug″gẽr-y, *n.* The practice of imposition.

hum′drum, *a.* Dull; stupid; commonplace.

hum′drum, *n.* 1. A stupid fellow; a bore.

2. Tediousness; monotony.

3. A small three-wheeled cart. [Prov. Eng.]

hū-meçt′, hū-meç′tāte, *v.t.* [L. *humectatus*, pp. of *humectare*, to moisten, wet.] To moisten; to wet; to water. [Obs.]

hū-meç′tănt, *a.* and *n.* I. *a.* Moistening; diluent. [Obs.]

II. *n.* A substance tending to increase the fluidity of the blood. [Obs.]

hū-meç-tā′tion, *n.* 1. The act of moistening, wetting, or watering. [Obs.]

2. In medicine, the softening of drugs for the mortar; the application of moistening remedies.

hū-meç′tive, *a.* Having the power to moisten.

hū′mē-fȳ, *v.t.*; humefied, *pt., pp.*; humefying, *ppr.* [L. *humefacere, umefacere*, to moisten; *humere, umere*, to be moist, and *facere*, to make.] To make moist; to soften with water.

hū′mẽr-ăl, *a.* [L. *humerus*, the shoulder.]

1. Relating to the humerus or upper arm.

2. In entomology, relating to or located near a humerus.

Humeral veil; in the Roman Catholic church, a narrow veil worn round the shoulders at mass by the officiating priest or a subdeacon.

hū″mẽr-ō-ab-dom′i-năl, *a.* Relating to the humerus and the abdomen.

hū″mẽr-ō-rā′di-ăl, *a.* Relating to the humerus and the radius.

hū′me-rus, *n.*; *pl.* **hū′me-rī.** [L. *humerus, umerus*, the shoulder, upper part of the arm.]

1. The bone of the upper arm; also, that part of the arm containing the humerus.

2. The femur of the anterior legs of an insect; the brachium.

3. The subcostal vein of the anterior wings of certain insects of the order *Hymenoptera*.

hum′hum, *n.* [E. Ind.] A kind of plain, coarse Indian cloth, made of cotton.

hū′miç, *a.* [L. *humus*, the earth, soil.] Relating to or derived from humus, or mold; as, *humic* acid.

hū″mi-cū-bā′tion, *n.* [L. *humus*, the ground, and *cubare*, to lie.] The act of lying on the ground; prostration. [Obs.]

hū′mid, *a.* [L. *humidus, umidus*, moist, from *humere, umere*, to be moist.]

1. Moist; damp; containing moisture; as, *humid* air or atmosphere.

2. Somewhat wet or watery; as, *humid* earth.

hū-mid′i-ty, *n.* [ME. *humidytee*; OFr. *humidite*; L. *humiditas* (*-atis*), dampness, moisture, from *humidus*, damp.]

1. Moisture; dampness; a moderate degree of wetness, which is perceptible to the eye or touch, occasioned by the absorption of a fluid or its adherence to the surface of a body.

2. Moisture in the form of visible vapor, or perceptible in the air; specifically, relative humidity, that is, the amount of moisture in the air at a given temperature as compared with the amount necessary to saturate it at the same temperature.

hū-mid′ness, *n.* Humidity.

hū′mid-or, *n.* A box or room for the storage of tobacco, which keeps it moist.

hū′mi-fūse, *a.* [L. *humus*, the ground, and *fusus*, pp. of *fundere*, to pour, spread out.] In botany, procumbent; as, a *humifuse* plant.

hū′mi-fȳ, *v.t.* Same as *Humefy*.

hū-mil′i-ănt, *a.* Humiliating; mortifying.

hū-mil′i-āte, *v.t.*; humiliated, *pt., pp.*; humiliating, *ppr.* [LL. *humiliatus*, pp. of *humiliare*, to humiliate, from L. *humilis*, humble, lowly.] To humble; to reduce to a lower position; to mortify; to subject to shame or disgrace.

hū-mil-i-ā′tion, *n.* The act of humiliating; the state of being humiliated.

hū-mil′i-ty, *n.*; *pl.* **hū-mil′i-tieṣ.** [OFr. *humilite*; L. *humilitas* (*-atis*), lowness, meanness, baseness, from *humilis*, lowly, humble.]

1. Freedom from pride and arrogance; humbleness of mind; a modest estimate of one's own worth; also, self-abasement; penitence for sin.

2. An act of submission.

hū′min, *n.* [*Hum*us and *-in*.] A dark-colored bitter compound derived from humus; also called *humic acid, gein, ulmin*, etc.

hū-mī′rī, *n.* [From native name.] A small Brazilian tree, *Humiria floribunda*, yielding a balsam; called also *umiri*.

hūm′ite, *n.* [Named after Sir Abraham *Hume*.] A variety of chondrodite, a gem of a reddish-brown color and a shining luster, crystallized in octahedrons, much modified by truncation and bevelment.

hum′mel, *a.* See second *Humble*.

hum′mel, *v.t.* To break. [See *Humble*.]

hum′mel-ẽr, *n.* One who or that which hummels; specifically, an instrument or machine for separating the awns of barley from the seed.

hum′mẽr, *n.* 1. One who or that which hums.

2. Same as *Humming-bird*.

3. A person or thing surpassing others; usually, some one of energetic habits or disposition. [Slang.]

hum′ming, *n.* A low, buzzing noise.

hum′ming, *a.* 1. Giving vent to a low, buzzing noise.

2. Having a frothy appearance arising from effervescence; as, *humming* beer.

hum′ming-bird, *n.* The smallest of birds, belonging to the family *Trochilidæ*, of which there are many genera. Most species have a remarkably brilliant plumage and are noted for a humming noise caused by their rapidly vibrating wings while hovering over flowers, the nectar of which they feed upon, as also upon insects. They are found in the Americas as far north as Alaska and as far south as Patagonia.

Tufted-necked Humming-bird (*Ornismya ornata*).

Humming-bird bush; a leguminous shrub of South America, the flowers of which are attractive to humming-birds.

Humming-bird hawk-moth; see *Hawk-moth*.

hum′mŏck, *n.* [A dim. from *hump*.]

1. A hillock; a slight rounded elevation above the surrounding earth.

2. In southern United States a wooded, elevated piece of land.

3. A heap or long ridge of ice.

hum′mŏck-ing, *n.* The forming of hummocks by floating masses of ice pressing against and rising one above another.

hum′mŏck-y, *a.* Full of hummocks.

hum′mum, *n.* A Turkish bath-house.

hū′mŏr, hū′mŏur (*or* ū′), *n.* [OFr. *humor*, from L. *humor*, moisture, from *humere, umere*, to be moist.]

1. Moisture; specifically, the moisture or one of the fluids of animal bodies; as, the vitreous *humor* of the eye.

2. In old medicine, (a) a fluid, of which there were four, on the conditions and proportions of which the bodily and mental health was supposed to depend; (b) animal fluid in a vitiated state; (c) cutaneous eruption.

3. Turn of mind; temper; disposition, or rather, a peculiarity of disposition, often temporary; so called because the temper of mind has been supposed to depend on the fluids of the body.

Examine how your *humor* is inclined. —Roscommon.

4. That mental quality which gives to ideas a ludicrous or fantastic turn, and tends to excite laughter or mirth.

5. Caprice; freak; whim; vagary.

Is my friend all perfection? . . . Has he not *humors* to be endured? —South.

6. A trick; a practice or habit.

I like not the *humor* of lying. —Shak.

Aqueous humor; see under *Aqueous*.

Crystalline humor or *lens*; see *Crystalline lens* under *Crystalline*.

Out of humor; vexed; crusty; crabbed.

Vitreous humor; see under *Vitreous*.

Syn.—Mood, disposition, temper, fancy, caprice, wit, pleasantry.

hū′mŏr (*or* ū′), *v.t.*; humored, *pt., pp.*; humoring, *ppr.* 1. To gratify by yielding to the particular inclination, humor, wish, or desire of; to indulge; to manage by concession or compliance; as, children are sometimes *humored* to their injury; to *humor* the sick, the infirm, and the aged.

2. To adapt oneself to.

Syn.—Gratify, indulge, favor, pamper, please.

hū′mŏr-ăl, *a.* Pertaining to or proceeding from the fluids or humors of the body; as, a *humoral* fever.

Humoral pathology; the old theory of disease that all morbid conditions of the body were traceable to the fluids or humors.

hū′mŏr-ăl-iṣm, *n.* 1. The state of being humoral.

2. Same as *Humorism*, 1.

hū′mŏr-ăl-ist, *n.* One who believes in the theory of humorism.

hū′mŏr-iṣm, *n.* 1. The theory or doctrine that all diseases originate in the humors.

2. The spirit or disposition of a humorist.

hū′mŏr-ist, *n.* 1. One who conducts himself according to his own inclination or bent of mind; one who gratifies his own humor.

2. One who indulges in humor in speaking or writing; one who has a playful fancy or genius.

3. One who has odd conceits; a wag; a droll.

4. A humoralist.

hū-mŏr-is′tiç, *a.* Pertaining to a humorist.

hū′mŏr-ize, *v.i.* To be humorous. [Rare.]

hū′mŏr-less, *a.* Destitute of humor.

hū′mŏr-ous, *a.* [LL. *humorosus*, moist, from L. *humor*, or *umor*, moisture.]

1. Containing humor; full of fanciful images; adapted to excite laughter; jocular; as, a *humorous* essay; a *humorous* story.

2. Having the power to speak or write in the style of humor; fanciful; playful; exciting laughter; as, a *humorous* man or author.

3. Subject to be governed by humor or caprice; irregular; capricious; whimsical.

Rough as a storm, and *humorous* as the wind. —Dryden.

4. Moist; humid. [Obs.]

hū′mŏr-ous-ly, *adv.* 1. Capriciously; whimsically; in conformity with one's humor.

We resolve by halves, rashly and *humorously*. —Calamy.

2. Wittily; pleasantly; jocosely; in a manner to excite mirth or laughter; with a grotesque combination of ideas.

hū′mŏr-ous-ness, *n.* 1. The state or quality of being humorous; oddness of conceit; jocularity.

2. Fickleness; capriciousness.

3. Peevishness; petulance.

hū′mŏr-sōme, *a.* 1. Peevish; petulant; influenced by the humor of the moment.

The commons do not abet *humorsome*, factious arms. —Burke.

2. Odd; humorous; adapted to excite laughter.

hū′mŏr-sōme-ly, *adv.* 1. Peevishly; petulantly.

2. Oddly; humorously.

hump, *n.* [D. *homp*, a hump; L.G. *hump*, a heap, hill.]

1. The protuberance formed by a crooked

back; as, a *hump* produced by curvature of the spine.

2. In zoölogy, the protuberance on the back of an animal; as, the *hump* of a camel.

hump, *v.t.*; humped (humt), *pt.*, *pp.*; humping, *ppr.* 1. To make a hump upon.

2. Reflexively, to crouch or bend (oneself) for a tremendous exertion; as, now *hump* yourself. [Slang.]

hump'back, *n.* 1. A crooked back; a high-shouldered back.

2. A humpbacked person.

3. In zoölogy, (a) a whale of the genus *Megaptera*, having a hump on its back; (b) a species of small salmon of the genus *Oncorhynchus*, of the American Pacific coast.

hump'backed (-bakt), *a.* Having a crooked back.

humped (humt), *a.* Having a crooked back, as a hunchback.

humph, *interj.* An expression of contempt or derision.

hump'=shoul"dẽred, *a.* Having humped shoulders.

hump'y, *a.* Having humps; humped.

hump'y, *n.*; *pl.* **hump'ieṣ**. [Australian.] A hut.

hum'strum, *n.* Music played inartistically; also, an imperfect musical instrument or one out of tune.

hū'mū-lin, *n.* Lupulin; a derivative of hops.

hū'mus, *n.* [L., the earth, the ground, the soil.] A pulverulent brown substance formed by the action of air on solid animal or vegetable matter; vegetable mold.

Hun, *n.* [L. *Hunni*, *Chunni*, *Chuni*, Huns.] A member of an obscure race of wandering and belligerent Asiatic people, who, in the middle of the fifth century, overran Europe and forced the Romans to pay tribute.

hunch, *n.* [A form of *hump*.]

1. A hump; a protuberance; as, the *hunch* of a camel.

2. A lump; a thick piece; as, a *hunch* of bread.

3. A push or jerk with the fist or elbow.

4. An inspiration; an impulse. [Slang.]

hunch, *v.t.*; hunched (huncht), *pt.*, *pp.*; hunching, *ppr.* 1. To push with the elbow; to push or thrust with a sudden jerk; to jog; to jostle.

2. To push out in a protuberance; to crook.

hunch'back, *n.* A humpback.

hunch'backed (-bakt), *a.* Having a humped back.

hun'dred, *n.* [ME. *hundred*, *hunderd*, *hundrith*; AS. *hundred*, *hundræth*, lit., a count or tale of a hundred; *hund*, a hundred, and *-red*, *-ræd*, reckoning.]

1. A collection, body, or sum, consisting of ten times ten individuals or units; the number 100.

2. In England, a division or part of a county supposed by some writers to have originally contained a hundred families, or a hundred warriors, or a hundred manors. The division of hundred was introduced into several of the American colonies and is still retained in the state of Delaware.

hun'dred, *a.* Fivescore; ten times ten; as, a *hundred* men; five *hundred* dollars. Strictly and originally a collective noun, hence always used with a numeral, an article, or a demonstrative; as, ten *hundred* times; a *hundred* men.

hun'dred=çourt, *n.* In England, a court held for the inhabitants of a hundred.

hun'dred-ẽr, *n.* 1. A resident or freeholder of an English hundred.

2. One having the jurisdiction of a hundred.

3. In English law, a man who may be of a jury in any controversy respecting land within the hundred to which he belongs; also written *hundredor*.

hun'dred-fōld, *n.* One hundred times the bulk or measure of anything.

hun'dredth, *n.* One of one hundred equal parts of anything.

hun'dredth, *a.* 1. Being the last in order of one hundred successive things.

2. Consisting of one of one hundred equal parts of anything; the quotient of the division of one tenth by ten; as, the *hundredth* part of an estate.

hun'dred-weight, *n.* 1. In the United States, one hundred pounds.

2. Formerly and still frequently in England, a weight of 112 pounds, or four quarters, each containing 28 pounds; usually denoted by *cwt.*

hung, *v.*, past tense and past participle of *hang*.

Hung beef; the fleshy part of beef slightly salted and hung up to dry; dried beef.

Hun-gā'ri-ăn, *n.* [LL. *Hungaria*, Hungary, from *Hungari*, the Magyars.] A native or inhabitant of Hungary; a Magyar; also, the language of the Hungarians; Magyar.

Hun-gā'ri-ăn, *a.* Of or relating to Hungary, the Hungarians, or the language of Hungary.

hun'gẽr, *n.* [AS. *hunger*, *hungor*, hunger.]

1. An uneasy sensation occasioned by the want of food; a craving for food; the pain or uneasiness of the stomach too long destitute of food.

2. Any strong or eager desire.

> For *hunger* of my gold I die. —Dryden.

3. Famine. [Obs.]

hun'gẽr, *v.i.*; hungered, *pt.*, *pp.*; hungering, *ppr.* [ME. *hungren*, *hongren*; AS. *hyngran*, to hunger, from *hunger*, hunger.]

1. To feel the pain or uneasiness which is occasioned by long abstinence from food; to crave food.

2. To desire with great eagerness; to long for.

> Blessed are they which do *hunger* and thirst after righteousness. —Matt. v. 6.

hun'gẽr, *v.t.* To famish; to starve. [Rare.]

hun'gẽr=bit, **hun'gẽr=bit"ten**, *a.* Pained, pinched, or weakened by hunger. [Obs.]

hun'gẽred, *a.* Hungry [Obs.]

hun'gẽr-ẽr, *n.* One who hungers.

hun'gẽr=flow"ẽr, *n.* The whitlow-grass, *Draba incana*, growing usually in poor soils.

hun'gẽr-ly, *a.* Hungry; wanting food. [Obs.]

hun'gẽr-ly, *adv.* With keen appetite. [Obs.]

hun'gẽr=stärved, *a.* Starved with hunger. [Obs.]

hun'gẽr=strīke, *n.* The refusal of imprisoned militant suffragettes to take food.

hun'gred (-gẽrd), *a.* Hungry; hungered. [Obs.]

hun'gri-ly, *adv.* With keen appetite; voraciously.

hun'gry, *a.* [ME. *hungry*, *hungri*, *hungrig*; AS. *hungrig*, hungry, from *hunger*, hunger.]

1. Having a keen appetite; feeling pain or uneasiness from want of food; having a feeling of hunger.

2. Having eager desire; longing.

3. Lean; emaciated, as if reduced by hunger.

> Cassius has a lean and *hungry* look.—Shak.

4. Not rich or fertile; poor; barren; requiring substances to enrich itself; as, a *hungry* soil.

hunk, *n.* A large piece or slice; a hunch; as, a *hunk* of meat. [Colloq.]

hunk, *n.* [D. *honk*, a post, station, home.] In some children's games, the goal; as, to be on *hunk*. [Local, U. S.]

hunk, *a.* and *adv.* In a secure place; in a satisfactory condition; all right. [Slang.]

Hunk'ẽr, *n.* [Prob. from D. *honk*, a post, station, home, lit., one who stays at home.] In United States politics, formerly a politician of the conservative section of the Democratic party who opposed the Barnburners; hence, a conservative; a fogy; one opposed to progress.

hunk'ẽr, *v.i.* [Prob. from Ice. *hokra*, to crouch, creep.] To squat or crouch with the body resting on the calves of the legs. [Scot.]

hunk'ẽr-iṣm, *n.* Opposition to progress.

hunk'ẽrṣ, *n.pl.* [Nasalized from Ice. *hokra*, *huka*, to sit on one's hams.] The haunches; the hams. [Scot.]

hunks, *n.* [Etym. doubtful.] A covetous, sordid man; a miser; a niggard.

hunk'y, *a.* See third *Hunk*.

hunt, *v.t.*; hunted, *pt.*, *pp.*; hunting, *ppr.* [ME. *hunten*, *honten*; AS. *huntian*, to hunt.]

1. To chase, as wild animals, for the purpose of catching or killing; to search for or follow after, as game; as, to *hunt* a stag or a fox.

2. To search after; to pursue; to follow closely.

3. To use, direct, or manage, as hounds in the chase.

> He *hunts* a pack of dogs. —Addison.

4. To pursue game or wild animals over; especially to pursue foxes over; as, the district was *hunted* by the foxhounds.

5. To search for; to seek; to pursue closely; as, to *hunt* up proof or evidence.

6. To expel or banish by means of pursuing; as, to *hunt* a person from a community.

To hunt down; to pursue and kill or capture; to bear down by persecution or violence; to exterminate.

hunt, *v.i.* 1. To follow the chase; to go out in pursuit of game or wild animals.

2. To seek by close pursuit; to search; with *after* or *for*.

> He *after* honor *hunts*, I *after* love. —Shak.

3. In machinery, to alternate between fast and slow; to run with varying speed, as a stationary engine is sometimes seen to do.

4. In bell-ringing, to shift the place of a bell in its set according to certain rules. When the place of the bell is shifting from first to last, the process is called *hunting-up*; when the place is shifting from last to first, it is called *hunting-down*.

To hunt counter; to trace the scent backward in hunting; to go back on one's steps. [Obs.]

hunt, *n.* 1. The act of chasing wild animals for the purpose of catching them; a pursuit; a chase.

> And, by the happy hollow of a tree,
> Escap'd the *hunt*. —Shak.

2. A pack of hounds. [Obs.]

3. An association of huntsmen; as, the Caledonian *Hunt*.

4. The portion of country hunted with hounds.

5. The game secured in the *hunt*. [Obs.]

6. The act of searching for something; a search; an inquisition.

hunt'=çoun"tẽr, *n.* A dog or hound that runs back on the scent. [Obs.]

hunt'e, *n.* [AS.] A hunter. [Obs.]

hunt'ẽr, *n.* 1. One who pursues wild animals with a view to take them, either for sport or for food.

2. A dog that scents game or is employed in the chase.

3. A horse used in the chase.

4. A person who hunts or goes in search of anything.

5. In zoölogy, a hunting-spider or a spider which hunts for its prey.

6. A cuckoo of Jamaica, *Piaya pluvialis*.

Hunter's screw; a differential screw, named after its inventor, Dr. John Hunter. [See *Differential screw* under *Differential*.]

Hun-tē'ri-ăn, *a.* Pertaining to or named after (a) John Hunter, a famous Scotch surgeon who lived in the eighteenth century; (b) his brother William, a celebrated anatomist.

hunt'ing, *n.* [AS. *huntung*, verbal n. of *huntian*, to hunt.] The act or practice of pursuing wild animals or game; the chase.

hunt'ing=box, *n.* A temporary residence occupied for the purpose of hunting; a hunting-seat.

hunt'ing=cāse, *n.* A watch-case provided with a hinged cover to serve as a protection to the crystal.

hunt'ing=çat, *n.* The chetah.

hunt'ing=çog, *n.* In machinery, an extra cog in one of two geared wheels, serving to change the order of contact of the teeth, so that the same teeth shall not continually meet.

hunt'ing=dog, *n.* 1. A dog trained for hunting.

2. A wild dog of South Africa somewhat resembling a hyena.

hunt'ing=ground, *n.* A district for hunting.

Happy hunting-grounds; the paradise of the North American Indians.

hunt'ing=hōrn, *n.* A horn or bugle used in the chase.

hunt'ing=leop"ărd (-lep"), *n.* The chetah.

hunt'ing=lodġe (-loj), *n.* See *Hunting-box*.

hunt'ing=sēat, *n.* See *Hunting-box*.

hunt'ing=spī"dẽr, *n.* A spider that pursues its prey instead of waiting for it in a web; a hunter.

hunt'ing=wätch, *n.* A hunting-case watch, with a metallic cover on each side.

hunt'ress, *n.* A woman who hunts, or follows the chase.

hunts'măn, *n.*; *pl.* **hunts'men**. 1. One who hunts, or who practises hunting.

2. The man whose office it is to manage the chase and take charge of the hounds.

hunts'măn's=çup, *n.* The sidesaddle-flower or pitcher-plant, *Sarracenia purpurea*.

hunts'măn-ship, *n.* The art or practice of hunting, or the qualifications of a hunter.

hunts'măn's=hōrn, *n.* A plant, *Sarracenia flava*, of southern United States.

hunt's'=up, *n.* A tune formerly played on the horn to arouse huntsmen; hence, any call or sound that awakens.

hū'on=pīne, *n.* [*Huon*, a native name.] A large tree of Tasmania, *Dacrydium Franklinii*, the light yellow wood of which is much used for carving.

Hū'rȧ, *n.* [S. Am. name.] A genus of tropical American plants of the natural order *Euphorbiaceæ*, and differing from all other plants in the order in its many-celled ovary. *Hura crepitans*, the sand-box tree, is remarkable for the loud report with which its seed-vessel bursts, for which reason it is often called the *monkey's dinner-bell*. It is a large branching tree with glossy poplar-like leaves, inconspicuous diœcious flowers, and furrowed roundish fruits of the size of an orange.

Sand-box Tree (*Hura crepitans*).

hūr'den, *n.* A coarse kind of linen. [Obs.]

hūr'dle, *n.* [ME. *hurdel*, *hyrdle*; AS. *hyrdel*, a hurdle.]

1. A frame or structure of twigs, osiers, or sticks; a crate of various forms, according to its uses.

2. In England, formerly a sledge or crate on which criminals were drawn to the place of execution.

3. One of the barriers placed across a racecourse to be leaped by the men or horses contesting in a hurdle-race or steeplechase.

4. A frame of wood or iron used as a gate or fence.

5. A fold for sheep, etc.

hûr'dle, *v.t.*; hurdled, *pt.*, *pp.*; hurdling, *ppr.* 1. To make, hedge, cover, or close with hurdles.

2. To leap over; as, to *hurdle* a gate or fence; to *hurdle* a ditch. [Colloq.]

hûr'dle-măn, *n.*; *pl.* **hûr'dle-men.** A man in charge of the lambs on an Australian sheep-ranch; the keeper of a hurdle or fold.

hûr'dle-rāce, *n.* A race in which the contestants, men or horses, must leap hurdles or other obstacles placed across the race-course; a steeplechase.

hûr'dle-wŏrk, *n.* Work resembling a hurdle.

hûrds, *n.* Same as *Hards.*

hûr'dy-gûr'dy, *n.* [Imitative of the sounds made by the instrument.]

1 A stringed instrument of music, whose sounds are produced by the friction of a wheel and regulated by finger-keys.

2. A hand-organ.

3. A rude impact water-wheel used in California.

hūre, *n.* [OFr.] 1. A cap. [Obs.]

2. In heraldry, the head of an animal.

hûr-kä'rá, *n.* [Hind. *harkara*, a messenger, scout; *har*, every, and *kar*, work.] In India, one who carries messages; a native courier; written also *hurkaru* and *hircarrah.*

hûr'kle, *v.i.* To stoop, crouch, cower, or squat. [Prov. Eng.]

hûrl, *v.t.*, hurled, *pt.*, *pp.*; hurling, *ppr.* [ME. *hurlen*, contr. of *hurtlen*, to dash against, strike forcibly.]

1. To throw with violence; to drive with great force; as, to *hurl* a stone.

> And *hurl* them headlong to their fleet and main. —Pope.

2. To utter with vehemence; as, to *hurl* back an answer to a charge.

hûrl, *v.i.* [A variant of *whirl* in defs. 1 and 5.]

1. To move rapidly; to whirl. [Rare.]
2. To discharge a missile.
3. To throw oneself; to rush. [Obs.]
4. To play the game called hurling.
5. To be wheeled. [Scot.]

hûrl, *n.* 1. The act of throwing with violence.

2. Tumult; riot; commotion. [Obs.]

3. A table used by hat-makers on which they stir and mix materials.

4. Same as *Harl.*

hûrl'bat, *n.* 1. A whirlbat; an old kind of weapon. [Obs.]

2. A bat used in the game of hurling.

hûrl'bōne, *n.* In a horse, a bone near the middle of the buttock; a whirlbone.

hûrl'ẽr, *n.* One who hurls or who plays at hurling.

hûrl'ey, hûrl'y, *n.* 1 Hockey; hurling.

2. A hockey-stick.

hûrl'ing, *n.* 1. A throwing with force; the act of playing at the game called hurling.

2. A ball-game in which opposing sides or parties try to hurl or force a ball through their opponents' goal, or to deposit it at some designated spot at a distance; in Ireland, the game is the same as hockey.

hûrl'wind, *n.* A whirlwind. [Obs.]

hûr'ly-bûr'ly, *n.* [A reduplication of ME. *hurly*, confusion.] Tumult; bustle; confusion.

Hū-rō'ni-ăn, *a.* Pertaining to Lake Huron, one of the Great Lakes; in geology, designating certain rocks on the shores of Lake Huron which are nonfossiliferous and are ascribed to various ages.

hûrr, *v.i.* To make a sound like rolling the letter *r*; to buzz. [Obs.]

hụr-räh', hụr-rä', *interj.* [G. *hurra*; Dan. and Sw. *hurra*, hurrah.] An exclamation expressing applause, joy, or exultation.

hụr-räh', *n.* 1. A word used as a shout of encouragement.

2. Any encouraging shout.

hụr-räh', *v.t.* and *v.i.* I. *v.t.* To encourage with applause; to cheer on.

II. *v.i.* To shout applause; to cheer.

hur'ri-cāne, *n.* [Sp. *huracan*, a hurricane; Caribbean *hurakan*, a hurricane.]

1. A violent storm, distinguished by the vehemence of the wind and its sudden changes; a windstorm of the greatest severity; a tempest.

2. Figuratively, anything suggestive of a tempest; as, a *hurricane* of applause.

Syn.—Gale, storm, cyclone, tornado.

hur'ri-cāne-bīrd, *n.* The frigate-bird.

hur'ri-cāne-deck, *n.* In steamships, (a) a light upper deck; (b) a bridge amidships.

hur-ri-cä'nō, *n.* A hurricane; a waterspout. [Obs.]

hur'ried, *a.* 1. Hastened; impelled to rapid motion or vigorous action.

2. Done hastily; hence, defective; as, *hurried* work.

hur'ried-ly, *adv.* In a hurried manner.

hur'ried-ness, *n.* The state of being hurried.

hur'ri-ẽr, *n.* One who hurries, urges, or impels.

hur'ry, *v.t.*; hurried, *pt.*, *pp.*; hurrying, *ppr.* [ME. *horien*, to hurry; compare Old Sw. *hurra*, to whirl round, M.H.G. *hurren*, to hurry, Ice. *hurr*, a great noise; prob. ultimately of imitative origin.]

1. To hasten; to impel to greater speed; to drive or press forward with more rapidity; to urge to act or proceed with more celerity; as, to *hurry* the workmen or the work.

2. To urge or drive with precipitation and confusion; to flurry.

> And wild amazement *hurries* up and down
> The little number of your doubtful friends.
> —Shak.

Syn.—Hasten, quicken, accelerate, rush, flurry, precipitate.

hur'ry, *v.i.* To move or act with haste; to proceed with celerity or precipitation; as, the business is urgent; let us *hurry.*

hur'ry, *n.* 1. The act of hurrying; the making haste; rapid movement or action.

2. Pressure; urgency; haste; as, we are in a *hurry.*

3. Precipitation that occasions disorder or confusion.

4. Tumult; bustle; commotion.

> Ambition raises a tumult in the soul, and puts it into a violent *hurry* of thought. —Addison.

Syn.—Haste, urgency, bustle, rush.

hur'ry-ing-ly, *adv.* In a hurrying manner.

hur'ry-skur'ry, *adv.* Confusedly; in a bustle.

hûrst, *n.* [ME. *hurst*, *hirst*; AS. *hyrst*, a grove, wood.]

1. A wood or grove; a word found in many names, as in Hazle*hurst.*

2. In milling, the frame of a run of millstones.

3. In mechanics, the ring or collar of a trip-hammer helve bearing the trunnions on which it oscillates.

4. In heraldry, a charge representing a small group of trees

5. A drift or bank of sand near a river. [Scot.]

hûrt, *v.t.*; hurt, *formerly* hurted, *pt.*, *pp.*; hurting, *ppr.* [ME. *hurten*, *hyrten*, *horten*, to knock, hit, hurt; OFr. *hurter*, *heurter*, to push, thrust, hit.]

1. To cause physical pain to; to wound or bruise painfully; as, the body is *hurt* by a severe blow or by tight clothes.

2. To cause injury, loss, or diminution to; to impair in value, quality, usefulness, beauty, or pleasure; to injure; to damage; to harm.

> Virtue may be assailed, but never *hurt.* —Milton.

3. To give mental pain to; to wound the feelings of; to annoy; to grieve.

hûrt, *n.* 1. Anything that gives pain to the body; a wound, a bruise, or the like.

> The pains of sickness and *hurts.* —Locke.

2. Injury; loss; damage; detriment.

> Why should damage grow to the *hurt* of the kings? —Ezra iv. 22.

Syn.—Wound, bruise, injury, harm, damage, loss, detriment, mischief, bane, disadvantage.

hûrt'ẽr, *n.* One who or that which hurts.

hûrt'ẽr, *n.* 1. In fortification, a timber placed at the interior slope as a revetment to prevent injury to the parapet by the wheels of the gun.

2. [*pl.*] In ordnance, pieces of wood or iron at the front of the chassis to prevent the top carriage from running off when in battery.

3. In vehicles, (a) a butting-piece on an axle; (b) a strengthening piece against a shoulder of an axle.

hûrt'ful, *a.* Tending to impair or destroy; injurious; mischievous; occasioning loss or destruction; as, negligence is *hurtful* to property; intemperance is *hurtful* to health.

Syn.—Pernicious, destructive, harmful, baneful, prejudicial, detrimental, disadvantageous, mischievous, injurious, noxious, unwholesome.

hûrt'ful-ly, *adv.* In a hurtful manner.

hûrt'ful-ness, *n.* The state or quality of being hurtful; injuriousness.

hûr'tle, *v.i.*; hurtled, *pt.*, *pp.*; hurtling, *ppr.* [ME. *hurtlen*, *hurtelen*, freq. of *hurlen*, to dash, hurl.] To rush with violence and noise; to move, go, or pass swiftly with a sound produced by such motion; as, a shell *hurtled* through the air.

hûr'tle, *v.t.* 1. To move with violence or impetuosity; to swing or brandish.

2. To push forcibly; to whirl; to hurl.

hûr'tle-ber"ry, *n.* A huckleberry.

hûrt'less, *a.* 1. Harmless; innocent; doing no injury; innoxious; as, *hurtless* blows.

2. Receiving no injury; unharmed.

hûrt'less-ly, *adv.* Without harm.

hûrt'less-ness, *n.* Freedom from any harmful quality. [Rare.]

hus'bănd, *n.* [ME. *husbonde*, *housbonde*; AS. *husbonda*, *husbunda*; *hus*, house, and *bonda*, *bunda*, master, head of a family, married man.]

1. The male head of a household; one who directs the economy of a family. [Obs.]

2. A tiller of the ground; a husbandman. [Obs.]

3. A man joined to a woman by marriage; the correlative of *wife.*

4. The male of a pair of the lower animals; a male animal kept for breeding purposes. [Rare.]

5. Nautically, an agent for the owners of a vessel employed to take the management of it so far as regards the purchasing of stores, seeing that the ship is properly repaired and equipped, attending to the ship's papers, receiving payment of freights, etc.; commonly called *ship's husband.*

6. One who manages well and thriftily; a good and frugal manager; an economist. [Rare.]

hus'bănd, *v.t.*; husbanded, *pt.*, *pp.*; husbanding, *ppr.* 1. To direct and manage with frugality, in expending anything; to use or employ in the manner best suited to produce the greatest effect; to use with economy; as, a man *husbands* his estate, his means, or his time.

> He is conscious how ill he has *husbanded* the great deposit of his Creator. —Rambler.

2. To till; to cultivate with good management. [Rare.]

3. To supply with a husband. [Rare.]

hus'bănd-ȧ-ble, *a.* Manageable with economy. [Rare.]

hus'bănd-āge, *n.* Among seamen, the compensation allowed to a ship's husband.

hus'bănd-hood, *n.* The state of being a husband.

hus'bănd-less, *a.* Destitute of a husband.

hus'bănd-ly, *a.* Frugal; thrifty. [Rare.]

hus'bănd-măn, *n.* 1. A farmer; a cultivator or tiller of the ground; one who labors in tillage.

2. The master of a family. [Obs.]

hus'bănd-ry, *n.* 1. The business of a farmer; agriculture.

2. Frugality; domestic economy; good management; thrift.

hush, *a.* Silent; still; quiet; as, they are *hush* as death.

hush, *v.t.*; hushed (husht), *pt.*, *pp.*; hushing, *ppr.* [ME. *husshen*, *hoschen*; prob. of imitative origin.]

1. To still; to silence; to calm; to make quiet; to repress; as, to *hush* the noisy crowd; the winds were *hushed.*

> My tongue shall *hush* again this storm of war. —Shak.

2. To appease; to allay; to calm, as commotion or agitation.

> Wilt thou, then,
> *Hush* my cares? —Otway.

To hush up; to suppress; to keep concealed.

hush, *v.i.* To be still; to be silent.

hush, *interj.* Be still! be silent! hist!

hush, *n.* Silence; stillness; quiet.

hush'ȧ-by̆, *a.* Tending to lull or soothe.

hush'ȧ-by̆, *interj.* Be still! hush! a word used to lull children to sleep.

hush'ẽr, *n.* An usher. [Obs.]

hush'ing, *n.* In mining, the process of uncovering or washing out minerals by a strong stream of water; flushing.

hush'-mŏn"ey, *n.* A bribe to secure silence; money paid to prevent the disclosure of facts.

husk, *n.* [ME. *husk*, *huske*, related to O.D. *hulsche*, M.H.G. *huldsche*, *hulsche*, a husk.]

1. The external covering of certain fruits or seeds of plants; the rind or hull; specifically, in the United States, the covering of the ears of maize or Indian corn; the shuck. In the parable of the prodigal son, the *husks* were the pods of the carob or St. John's bread.

2. Figuratively, the outer or worthless part of anything; waste; refuse; as, the *husks* of religion.

3. The frame or hurst of a run of millstones.

husk, *v.t.*; husked (huskt), *pt.*, *pp.*; husking, *ppr.* To strip off the external integument or covering of; as, to *husk* corn.

husk, *n.* The greater dogfish, *Scylliorhinus canicula.*

husk, *n.* Huskiness. [Rare.]

husked (huskt), *a.* 1. Stripped of husks.

2. Covered with a husk.

husk'ẽr, *n.* 1. One who husks corn.

2. A husking-pin.
3. A husking-machine.
4. An oyster-opener.

hus'ki-ly, *adv.* Dryly; roughly; hoarsely.

hus'ki-ness, *n.* The state of being dry, rough, or husky; especially, roughness of sound; as, *huskiness* of voice.

husk'ing, *n.* 1. The act of stripping off husks.

2. A husking-bee.

husk'ing-bee, *n.* A gathering of friends or neighbors to assist a farmer in husking corn; usually ending with dancing, feasting, etc.

husk'ing-pin, *n.* A peg or pin used upon the hand to aid in removing the husks from maize.

husk'y, *a.*; *comp.* huskier; *superl.* huskiest. Abounding with, consisting of, or like husks; hence, unprofitable; poor.

hus'ky, *a.* [Prob. a corruption of *husty*, inclined to cough, from AS. *hwōsta*, a cough.] Rough, as sound; harsh; hoarse; as, a *husky* voice.

hus'ky, *n.*; *pl.* **hus'kieṣ.** [Contr. of *Eskimo.*]
1. A term applied to an Eskimo.
2. An Eskimo sledge-dog.
3. An energetic man; used also attributively.

hū'sō, *n.* [O.H.G. *huso*, the huso.] A very large sturgeon, *Acipenser huso*, abounding in the rivers of Russia.

hụṣ-ṣär', *n.* [Hung. *huszár*, the twentieth, from *husz*, twenty, so called because King Matthias I. of Hungary raised a corps of horse-soldiers by ordering every twenty houses to furnish one man.] In European armies, a light cavalryman, usually distinguished by a brilliant and picturesque uniform.

hus'sif, *n.* A housewife; a hussy. [Obs.]

Huss'īte, *n.* A follower of John Huss, the Bohemian reformer, who was burned alive in 1415.

hụṣ'ṣy, *n.* [Contr. from *huswife*, housewife.]
1. A mischievous or pert girl or woman; usually used in disapprobation or reproach.
2. A thrifty woman; a housewife. [Obs.]

hus'tingṣ, *n.pl.* [ME. *husting*; AS. *husting*; Ice. *husthing*, a council called by a king, earl, or guardsman; *hus*, house, and *thing*, an assembly.]
1. A court formerly held in the chief cities of England; especially, a court held within the city of London before the lord mayor, recorder, and sheriffs.
2. In England, the temporary platform on which, previous to the passing of the Ballot Act of 1872, candidates stood when addressing those whom they wished to represent in Parliament; usually constructed close to or in connection with a polling booth.

hus'tle (hus'l), *v.t.*; hustled, *pt.*, *pp.*; hustling, *ppr.* [D. *hutselen*, freq. of *hutsen*, *hotsen*, to shake, jolt.] To shake together in confusion; to push or crowd; to shove roughly; to jostle.

hus'tle, *v.i.* 1. To move with effort and by pushing along; to hurry.
2. To move rapidly and with energy; to be prompt, energetic, and wide-awake. [Colloq., U. S.]

hus'tlẽr, *n.* One who hustles.

hụṣ'wife (huz'if), *n.* 1. A hussy. [Obs.]
2. A housewife. [Obs.]

hụṣ'wife (huz'if), *v.t.* To manage with economy. [Obs.]

hụṣ'wife-ly (-if-), *adv.* Prudently. [Obs.]

hụṣ'wife-ry (-if-), *n.* Housewifery. [Obs.]

hut, *n.* [OFr. *hutte*, *hute*, from O.H.G. *hutta*, a hut, cottage.]
1. A small house, hovel, or cabin; a mean lodge or dwelling; a temporary shelter.
2. The back end of the breech-pin of a musket.

hut, *v.t.* and *v.i.*; hutted, *pt.*, *pp.*; hutting, *ppr.*
I. *v.t.* To place in huts, as troops encamped in winter quarters.
II. *v.i.* To take lodgings in huts.

The troops *hutted* for the winter.—Pickering.

hutch, *n.* [ME. *hucche*, *huche*, *hoche*; OFr. *huche*, a bin, kneading-trough, mill-hopper, from LL. *hutica*, a chest.]
1. A chest, bin, box, coop, or pen in which articles may be kept or animals confined; as, a grain-*hutch*; a rabbit-*hutch*.
2. In mining, a small car in which ore is brought to the surface; also, a trough in which ore is washed.
3. A measure, (a) two Winchester bushels; (b) two hundredweight of iron-pyrites.
4. The casing of a device for bolting flour.
5. The kneading-trough of a baker.

hutch, *v.t.*; hutched, *pt.*, *pp.*; hutching, *ppr.* To hoard, as in a chest.

Hutch-in-sō'ni-ăn, *a.* Pertaining to John Hutchinson, or Mrs. Anne Hutchinson, or to their doctrines.

Hutch-in-sō'ni-ăn, *n.* 1. A believer in the opinions of John Hutchinson, of Yorkshire, England, a philosopher and naturalist of the eighteenth century, who rejected Newton's doctrine of gravitation, and maintained that the Old Testament Scriptures embraced a complete system of natural philosophy as well as of religion.
2. In American history, a believer in the antinomian teachings of Mrs. Anne Hutchinson, who lived in the early years of the settlement of Massachusetts.

hū-tī'ȧ, *n.* [Sp., prob. from native name.] A Cuban rodent of the genus *Capromys*.

Hut-tō'ni-ăn, *a.* In geology, relating to that theory of the earth which was first advanced by Dr. James Hutton (1726–1797), now called the Plutonic theory.

hux'tẽr, *n.* Same as *Huckster*.

Huy-gē'ni-ăn, *a.* Relating to Christian Huygens, a Dutch astronomer and mathematician of the seventeenth century; as, the *Huygenian* eyepiece; written also *Huyghenian*.

huzz, *v.i.* To buzz. [Obs.]

hụz-zä', hụz-zäh', *n.* and *interj.* [G. *hussa*, a form of hurrah.]
I. *n.* A cheer; a hurrah.
II. *interj.* A shout of joy, acclamation, or welcome; hurrah.

hụz-zä', *v.i.* To hurrah.

hụz-zä', *v.t.*; huzzaed, *pt.*, *pp.*; huzzaing, *ppr.* To hurrah for.

He was *huzzaed* into the court. —Addison.

hȳ'ȧ-cine, *n.* A hyacinth. [Obs.]

hȳ'ȧ-cinth, *n.* [L. *hyacinthus*; Gr. *hyakinthos*, the hyacinth.]
1. A plant of the genus *Hyacinthus*, especially the cultivated species, *Hyacinthus orientalis*. It is a native of the Levant and the mountains of Persia. The root is a tunicated bulb; the leaves are broad and green; the scape is erect, bearing numerous often drooping bell-shaped flowers of almost all colors. The hyacinth appears first to have been cultivated as a garden flower by the Dutch about the beginning of the sixteenth century. It was introduced into England about the end of that century, and is now one of the most popular of cultivated bulbous plants.
2. One of several plants of other genera, as (a) *Camassia Fraseri*, the wild hyacinth; (b) *Muscari racemosum*, the grape-hyacinth; (c) *Scilla Peruviana*, the hyacinth of Peru; (d) the California hyacinth, a plant of the genus *Brodiæa*.
3. In mineralogy, a gem formerly thought to be the sapphire; now a variety of zircon of a brownish, orange, or reddish color.

hȳ'ȧ-cinth-bēan, *n.* A climbing plant, *Dolichos Lablab*, of the bean family.

hȳ-ȧ-cin'thi-ăn, *a.* See *Hyacinthine*.

hȳ-ȧ-cin'thine, *a.* [L. *hyacinthinus*; Gr. *hyakinthinos*, from *hyakinthos*, hyacinth.]
1. Made of hyacinth; consisting of hyacinth; resembling hyacinth.
2. Pertaining to or resembling Hyacinthus, a youth fabled to have been a favorite of Apollo; hence, beautiful; very attractive; lovely.

Hȳ-ȧ-cin'thus, *n.* [L.] A genus of bulbous plants of the lily family, including about thirty species, natives of central Europe, Asia, and Africa. *Hyacinthus orientalis* has been long celebrated for the numerous varieties which culture has produced from it.

Hȳ'ȧ-dēṣ, *n.pl.* [L. *Hyades*; Gr. *Hyades*, the ancients derived the word from *hyein*, to rain.] In astronomy, a cluster of stars in Taurus, supposed by the ancients to indicate the approach of rainy weather when they rose with the sun; written also *Hyads*.

Hȳ'adṣ, *n.pl.* See *Hyades*.

hȳ-æ'nȧ, *n.* See *Hyena*.

Hȳ-ȧ'lē-ȧ, *n.* [Gr. *hyaleos*, glassy, from *hyalos*, glass.] A genus of pteropods furnished with lateral finlike organs for swimming.

hȳ-ȧ-les'cence, *n.* The act or process of becoming transparent, as glass; the state of being glassy; glassiness.

hȳ-ȧ-les'cent, *a.* [Gr. *hyalos*, glass, and *-escent*.] Becoming hyaline; manifesting hyalescence.

hȳ'ȧ-lin, *n.* A translucent substance forming the walls of hydatid cysts.

hȳ'ȧ-line, *a.* and *n.* [Gr. *hyalinos*, glassy, from *hyalos*, glass.]
I. *a.* Glassy; resembling glass; consisting of glass; crystalline; transparent; as, a *hyaline* cartilage.
II. *n.* A glassy surface; a transparent body; specifically, (a) the hyaloid membrane; (b) the hyaline cartilage; (c) the fluid portion of the protoplasm of a living cell; hyaloplasm.

hȳ'ȧ-līte, *n.* [Gr. *hyalos*, glass, and *-ite*.] A pellucid variety of opal, looking like colorless gum or resin; called also *Müller's glass*.

hȳ-ȧ-lī'tis, *n.* In pathology, inflammation of the hyaloid membrane of the vitreous humor.

hyalo-. A combining form from Gr. *hyalos*, glass, used in chemistry, geology, etc., to signify, glass, glassy, transparent; as, *hyalo*phane, *hyalo*pterous.

hȳ-al'ō-grȧph, *n.* An instrument for tracing a design on a transparent surface.

hȳ-ȧ-log'rȧ-phy, *n.* [*Hyalo-*, and Gr. *graphein*, to write.] The art of writing or engraving on glass.

hȳ'ȧ-loid, *a.* [*Hyalo-*, and Gr. *eidos*, form.] Of the nature of glass; transparent.

Hyaloid membrane; a membrane investing the whole of the vitreous humor except the front.

Hȳ″ȧ-lō-nē'mȧ, *n.* [*Hyalo-*, and Gr. *nēma*, thread.] The typical genus of the family *Hyalonemidæ*; the glass-sponges.

hȳ-al'ō-phāne, *n.* [*Hyalo-*, and Gr. *phainesthai*, to appear.] A monoclinic mineral occurring as a granular dolomite, or as manganese, lime, etc.

hȳ'ȧ-lō-plaṣm, *n.* [*Hyalo-*, and Gr. *plasma*, anything formed, from *plassein*, to form, mold.] The enchylema of a cell; hyaline.

hȳ-ȧ-lop'tẽr-ous, *a.* [*Hyalo-*, and Gr. *pteron*, a wing.] Having the wings transparent; said of insects.

hȳ-ȧ-lō-sid'ẽr-īte, *n.* [*Hyalo-*, and Gr. *siderītes*, of iron, from *sidēros*, iron.] A ferruginous variety of olivine.

Hȳ″ȧ-lō-spon'ġi-æ, *n.pl.* [*Hyalo-*, and Gr. *spongia*, a sponge.] A family of silicious sponges in which the skeleton is composed of six-rayed spicules becoming ultimately united together. The species are found at great depths of the ocean.

hȳ″ȧ-lō-tē'kīte, *n.* [*Hyalo-*, and Gr. *tēkein*, to melt.] In mineralogy, a white crystalline silicate of lead, barium, and calcium, of a vitreous luster.

hȳ-al'ō-type, *n.* [*Hyalo-*, and Gr. *typos*, impression, figure, image.] A positive photographic picture taken on glass.

hȳ-bẽr'nȧ-cle, *n.* [Obs.] See *Hibernacle*.

hȳ'bẽr-nāte, hȳ-bẽr-nā'tion. [Obs.] See *Hibernate*, *Hibernation*.

Hȳ-blæ'ăn, *a.* Pertaining to the ancient city of Hybla, in Sicily, famous for the honey produced in the neighboring locality.

hyb'ō-dont, *a.* [Gr. *hybos*, humpbacked, and *odous*, *odontos*, tooth.] Pertaining to or resembling a genus, *Hybodus*, of fossil fishes allied to the sharks.

hyb'ō-dont, *n.* A fish of the genus *Hybodus*.

Hyb'ō-dus, *n.* A genus of fossil fishes that prevailed throughout the Oölitic, Triassic, and Cretaceous periods. They are allied to the sharks.

hȳ'brid, *a.* and *n.* [L. *hybrida*, *hibrida*, a mongrel, hybrid.]
I. *a.* Mongrel; produced from the union of two distinct species.
II. *n.* 1. In biology, the offspring of an animal or plant produced by the crossing of different species.
2. Anything of mixed origin, as a word the elements of which belong to different languages.

hȳ'brid-iṣm, *n.* 1. The state of being hybrid.
2. The act of hybridizing.

hȳ'brid-ist, *n.* One who hybridizes.

hȳ-brid'i-ty, *n.* Hybridism; the act of crossing animals or plants.

hȳ'brid-ī-zȧ-ble, *a.* Capable of producing a hybrid by crossing with some other species.

hȳ″brid-ī-zā'tion, *n.* The act of hybridizing or the state of being hybridized.

hȳ'brid-īze, *v.t.*; hybridized, *pt.*, *pp.*; hybridizing, *ppr.* To make hybrid; as, to *hybridize* a plant.

hȳ'brid-īze, *v.i.* To produce hybrids by crossing.

hȳ'brid-ī-zẽr, *n.* One who hybridizes.

hȳ'brid-ous, *a.* Having the characteristics of a hybrid. [Rare.]

hȳd'āġe, *n.* Same as *Hidage*.

hȳ-dan-tō'iç, *a.* Relating to hydantoin.

hȳ-dan'tō-in, *n.* [Gr. *hydōr*, water, and *allantoin*.] In chemistry, a sweetish crystalline compound, $C_3H_4N_2O_2$, obtained from urea.

hȳ'dȧ-tid, hȳ'dȧ-tis, *n.* [Gr. *hydatis* (*-idos*), a drop of water, a water-vesicle, from *hydōr*, *hydatos*, water.]
1. In pathology, a cyst formed by the larva of an intestinal parasite.

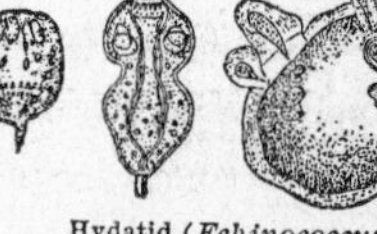
Hydatid (*Echinococcus veterinorum*).

2. In zoölogy, the embryo of a tapeworm living in a cyst containing a pellucid fluid.

Hydatid of Morgagni; in anatomy, one of the small pedunculated growths found beside the head of the epididymis and formed mainly of connective tissue and blood-vessels.

hȳ-dat'i-form, *a.* [Gr. *hydatis* (*-idos*), a water-vesicle, and L. *forma*, form.] Having the form of a hydatid.

hȳ-da-tig'e-nous, *a.* [Gr. *hydatis* (*-idos*), a hydatid, and *-genēs*, producing.] Producing or bearing hydatids.

hȳ'dȧ-toid, *a.* and *n.* [Gr. *hydōr*, *hydatos*, water, and *eidos*, form.]
I. *a.* 1. In anatomy, like water; aqueous.
2. Noting the aqueous humor of the eye.
II. *n.* The aqueous humor of the eye; also, the investing membrane of this humor as distinguished from that investing the vitreous humor.

hydr-. See *Hydro-*.

hȳ'drȧ, *n.* [L. *hydra*; Gr. *hydra*, a water-serpent, from *hydōr* (*-atos*), water.]
1. In Greek mythology, a serpent or monster in the lake or marsh of Lerna, in Peloponnesus, represented as having many heads, one of which being cut off was immediately succeeded by two others, unless the wound was cauterized; hence, a monster of any kind, especially a sea-monster.
2. [H—] In astronomy, an ancient southern constellation having a fancied resemblance to a sea-serpent.
3. [H—] A genus of fresh-water polyps.
4. A poisonous snake of the Indian Ocean.
5. The sexual bud or medusa of a hydroid.
6. A spirit-thermometer having an extended

bulb to render it more sensitive, and which registers automatically.

hȳ-drach'nid, *n.* [*Hydr-*, and Gr. *achnē*, foam.] In zoölogy, a water-mite of the genus *Hydrachna*, parasitic upon mollusks, fishes, and water-insects.

hȳ-drac'id, *n.* [*Hydr-*, and L. *acidus*, sour, sharp.] In chemistry, an acid containing hydrogen and no oxygen; a halogen.

hȳ-drȧ-cryl'ic, *a.* [*Hydr-*, and *acrylic.*] In chemistry, relating to acryl and water; designating an acid differing from acrylic acid by one molecule of water.

Hydracrylic acid; a syrup-like compound, $C_3H_6O_3$, which under heat separates into water and acrylic acid.

hȳ-drac-tin'i-ăn, *n.* [*Hydr-*, and Gr. *aktis* (*-inos*), a ray.] In zoölogy, any marine hydroid of the genus *Hydractinia* or kindred genera, usually found growing upon the shells of mollusks and forming a moss-like coating.

hȳ-dræ'mi-ȧ, *n.* Same as *Hydremia.*

hȳ'drȧ-gogue (-gog), *a.* and *n.* [LL. *hydragogus*; Gr. *hydragōgos*, conducting water, a water-carrier; *hydōr*, water, and *agōgos*, leading, from *agein*, to lead.]

I. *a.* In medicine, causing a watery discharge, as in dropsy.

II. *n.* A medicine that occasions a discharge of watery humors; in general, the stronger cathartics are *hydragogues.*

hȳ'drȧ-head"ed (-hed"), *a.* Having many heads, like the Lernæan monster of Greek mythology; hard to suppress; ever growing in monstrosity; said of evils of all kinds.

hȳ-dram'ide (*or* -id), *n.* [*Hydr-*, and *amide.*] In chemistry, a crystalline substance produced by the action of ammonia on certain aldehydes.

hȳ-dram'ine, *n.* In chemistry, one of a series of organic bases of a viscous nature, produced by the action of ammonia on ethylene oxid.

Hȳ-dran'ġē-ȧ, *n.* [*Hydr-*, and Gr. *angeion*, a vessel.]

1. A genus of shrubs or herbs of the order *Saxifragaceæ*, containing about thirty-three species, natives of Asia and America. The common species, *Hydrangea hortensis*, is a native of China.

2. [h—] A plant of this genus.

hȳ'drănt, *n.* [Gr. *hydrainein*, to irrigate, from *hydōr*, water.]

1. A device with suitable valves and a spout by which water is raised and discharged from a water-main, and so arranged that the discharge-pipe is empty when not in use; specifically, a discharge-pipe in a street, to which fire or other hose may be attached; a fire-plug.

Hydrant.

2. A water-faucet.

hȳ'dranth, *n.* [*Hydr-*, and Gr. *anthos*, a flower.] In zoölogy, a zoöid representing the fundamental structure of the *Hydrozoa*, having proper organs of nutrition.

hȳ-drär'ġil-lite, *n.* [*Hydr-*, and Gr. *argillos*, white clay.] A variety of gibbsite.

hȳ-drär-gō-chlō'rid, *n.* In chemistry, bichlorid of mercury united with some other chlorid. [Obs.]

hȳ-drär'ġy-rāte, hȳ-drär-gyr'ic, *a.* [*Hydrargyrum*, and *-ate.*] Pertaining to or containing mercury.

hȳ-drär-ġy-rī'ȧ-sis, *n.* In pathology, a condition of the body resulting from the use of mercury as a medicine; called also *hydrargyrism.*

hȳ-drär'ġy-rism, *n.* See *Hydrargyriasis.*

hȳ-drär'ġy-rum, *n.* [L. *hydrargyrus*; Gr. *hydrargyros*, quicksilver; *hydōr*, water, and *argyros*, silver.] In chemistry, mercury; quicksilver.

hȳ-drär-thrō'sis, *n.* [*Hydr-*, and Gr. *arthrōsis*, articulation, from *arthron*, joint.] In pathology, the accumulation of a watery deposit in the cavity of a joint, commonly called *white swelling.*

hȳ-dras'tine, *n.* [*Hydr-*, and Gr. *drān*, to run.] A crystalline and nearly tasteless alkaloid derived from the root of a plant, *Hydrastis Canadensis.*

hȳ'drāte, *n.* [Gr. *hydōr*, water, and *-ate.*] In chemistry, a compound of which water is a constituent without alteration of atomic arrangement; in a less restricted sense, any compound containing the molecules of water in combination; as, slaked lime is a *hydrate* of lime.

hȳ'drāte, *v.t.*; hydrated, *pt.*, *pp.*; hydrating, *ppr.* To form into a hydrate; to combine with water.

hȳ'drā-ted, *a.* Formed into a hydrate; as, *hydrated* copper oxid.

hȳ-drā'tion, *n.* The condition of becoming or being a hydrate; the process of hydrating.

hȳ-drau'lic, *a.* [Fr. *hydraulique*; L. *hydraulicus*; Gr. *hydraulikos*, pertaining to a water-organ, from *hydraulis*, *hydraulos*, a water-organ, a water-pipe; *hydōr*, water, and *aulos*, a tube, pipe.] Pertaining to hydraulics, or to fluids in motion; moved by or conveying water.

Hydraulic balance; a regulator for a water-wheel.

Hydraulic cement; a cement having the property of becoming hard under water; a cement made of hydraulic lime.

Hydraulic elevator; an elevator operated by water-power.

Hydraulic lime; a species of lime that hardens in water, used for cementing under water.

Hydraulic main; in gas-works, a pipe containing water through which the gas is passed in the process of purification.

Hydraulic mining; a method of mining by washing the ore out of the bank with a powerful jet of water, as from a hose.

Hydraulic press; a machine in which practical application is made of the well-known principle in hydrostatics, that a pressure exerted on any part of the surface of a liquid is transmitted undiminished to every part of the liquid and in all directions. By this apparatus great power is obtained for compressing objects or drawing or lifting great weights. The press is usually constructed as shown in the accompanying figures.

Hydraulic or Bramah Press.

By means of a small forcing-pump (the handle of which is shown at A in the first figure, the piston at A in the second) water is injected into a strong cast-iron cylinder B, into which is fitted the piston or ram C. The pressure transmitted by the water, acting upon the solid piston C, slowly and powerfully urges upward the table D until the requisite pressure is produced upon the materials placed between the upper and lower tables of the press. The power of this machine increases in proportion to the difference between the diameter of the piston of the forcing-pump and that of the large piston C; thus, if the diameter of the former is 1 inch and that of the latter 1 foot, the area of the cross-section of the latter will be 144 times that of the former, and a pressure of 1 ton upon the former will exert a pressure of 144 tons upon the latter.

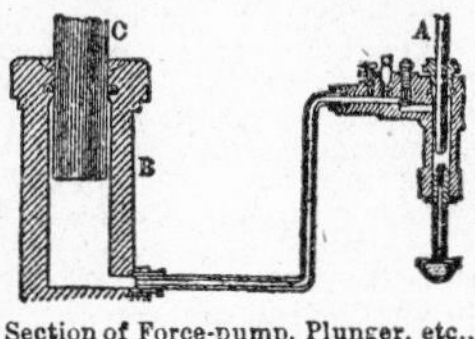

Section of Force-pump, Plunger, etc., of Hydraulic Press.

Hydraulic ram; a machine by which the momentum or weight of falling water can be made available for raising a portion of itself to a considerable height.

Hydraulic valve; an inverted cup which is lowered over the upturned open end of a pipe, the edge of the cup being submerged in water, forming a water-seal and closing the pipe against the passage of air or gases.

hȳ-drau'lic-ăl, *a.* Hydraulic.

hȳ-drau-lic'i-ty, *n.* The property possessed by certain cements, of solidifying under water.

hȳ-drau'li-cŏn, *n.* [Gr. *hydraulikon* (supply *organon*, organ), a hydraulic organ.] An old form of organ in which water was used to regulate the pressure of the air; also called *hydraulic organ.*

hȳ-drau'lics, *n.* That branch of science which treats of the motion of liquids, the laws by which they are regulated, and the effects which they produce; or, as the word is now most commonly used, that department of engineering science which deals with the application of the motion of liquids to machinery and of machinery to the motion of liquids.

hȳ'drȧ-zine, *n.* [*Hydr*ogen and *az*ote and *-ine.*] Any one of a group of colorless gases derived from diamide, H_4N_2.

hȳ-drē'mi-ȧ, *n.* An excess of water in the blood.

hȳ-dren-ceph'ȧ-loid, *a.* Same as *Hydrocephaloid.*

hȳ-dren'tĕr-ō-cēle, *n.* [*Hydr-*, and Gr. *enteron*, intestine, and *kēlē*, a tumor.] A hernial tumor, whose contents are intestinal, with the addition of water.

hȳ'dri-ȧ, *n.*; *pl.* **hȳ'dri-æ.** [L., from Gr. *hydria*, a water-pot, from *hydōr*, water.] A large Greek vase, with three handles and a capacious body.

Hydria.

hȳ'dri-ad, *n.* [Gr. *hydrias* (*-ados*), of or from the water, from *hydōr*, water.] In mythology, a water-nymph.

hȳ'dric, *a.* 1. Relating to or containing hydrogen.

2. Pertaining to water.

hȳ'drid, hī'dride (*or* -drīd), *n.* [*Hydr*ogen and *-id*, *-ide.*] A binary compound of hydrogen and another element.

hȳ'dri-fọrm, *a.* [L. *hydra*, a hydra, and *forma*, form.] Formed like a hydra.

hȳ-drī'ō-dāte. *n.* A salt of hydriodic acid.

hȳ-dri-od'ic, *a.* [*Hydr*ogen and *iod*ine and *-ic.*] Produced by the combination of hydrogen and iodine.

Hydriodic acid; a colorless gas with a suffocating odor, formed by combining hydrogen and iodine.

hydro-, hydr-. Combining forms from Gr. *hydōr*, water; used in chemistry, botany, zoölogy, etc., to signify water; in chemistry, also, to signify hydrogen; as, *hydro*bromic, *hydro*branchiate.

hȳ-drō'ȧ, *n.* [*Hydr-*, and Gr. *ōon*, an egg.] A chronic inflammatory disease of the skin characterized by pustules, vesicles, etc., and intense itching.

hȳ"drō-ā'ĕr-ō-plāne, *n.* An aeroplane constructed for alighting and traveling on, and taking flight from the water.

hȳ"drō-bȧ-rom'e-tĕr, *n.* [*Hydro-*, and Gr. *baros*, weight, pressure, and *metron*, a measure.] A device for measuring the depth of water by its pressure.

Hȳ-drō-bran-chi-ā'tȧ, *n.pl.* [*Hydro-*, and Gr. *branchia*, gills.] A division of gasteropods, containing species which breathe only water.

hȳ-drō-bran'chi-āte, *a.* Pertaining to the *Hydrobranchiata*; breathing water only; breathing through gills.

hȳ-drō-brō'māte, *n.* [*Hydrobromic* and *-ate.*] A salt of hydrobromic acid.

hȳ-drō-brō'mic, *a.* Composed of hydrogen and bromine.

Hydrobromic acid; an acid obtained by bringing phosphorus and bromine together in a little water.

hȳ-drō-cär'bon, *n.* A general term given to compounds of hydrogen and carbon.

hȳ-drō-cär-bō-nā'ceous, *a.* Consisting of or characteristic of hydrocarbon.

hȳ-drō-cär'bŏn-āte. *n.* [*Hydrocarbon* and *-ate.*] Carbureted hydrogen gas, or heavy inflammable air. [Obs.]

hȳ-drō-cär'bū-ret, *n.* [*Hydro*gen and *carburet.*] Carbureted hydrogen gas. [Obs.]

hȳ-drō-cau'lus, *n.*; *pl.* **hȳ-drō-cau'lī.** [*Hydro-*, and Gr. *kaulos*, stem.] The main stem of the cœnosarc of a hydrozoan.

hȳ'drō-cēle, *n.* [Gr. *hydrōkēlē*, hydrocele; *hydōr*, water, and *kēlē*, a tumor.] A collection of serous fluid between the layers of tissue enveloping the testicle or spermatic cord.

hȳ-drō-cel'lū-lōse, *n.* A substance derived from cotton by the action of hydrochloric acid, and produced in the form of a fine powder.

hȳ"drō-cē-phal'ic, *a.* Pertaining to hydrocephalus.

hȳ-drō-ceph'ȧ-loid, *a.* Characteristic of or resembling hydrocephalus.

Hydrocephaloid disease; a condition of coma sometimes developed in children when in a state of exhaustion.

hȳ-drō-ceph'ȧ-lous, *a.* See *Hydrocephaloid.*

hȳ-drō-ceph'ȧ-lus, *n.* [Gr. *hydrokephalon*, water in the head; *hydōr*, water, and *kephalē*, head.] An accumulation of fluid within the cavity of the cranium; dropsy of the brain.

hȳ"drō-cē-ram'ic, *a.* [*Hydro-*, and Gr. *keramikos*, from *keramos*, earthenware.] Allowing liquids to escape through pores; said of certain kinds of pottery which, by evaporation from their surface, cool the liquids they contain.

Hȳ"drō-chȧ-rid'ē-æ, *n.pl.* An order of monocotyledonous floating and creeping plants, inhabiting ditches, rivers, and lakes in various parts of the world; written also *Hydrocharidaceæ.*

Hȳ-droch'ȧ-ris, *n.* [Gr. *hydrocharēs*, delighting in water; *hydōr*, water, and *chairein*, to rejoice.] The typical genus of the *Hydrocharideæ*; the frogbit.

hȳ-drō-chī'non, *n.* Same as *Hydroquinone.*

hȳ-drō-chlō'rāte, *n.* Any salt of hydrochloric acid.

hȳ-drō-chlō'ric, *a.* [*Hydro*gen and *chloric.*] Compounded of chlorin and hydrogen.

Hydrochloric acid; a gaseous compound of hydrogen and chlorin. It is colorless and has a pungent odor and an acid taste. It extinguishes flame, and dissolves very readily in water. The aqueous solution of *hydrochloric acid* has been long known as *muriatic acid.*

hȳ-drō-chlō'rid, *n.* A hydrochlorate.

Hȳ-drō-çor-ăl-lī′næ, *n.pl.* [*Hydro-*, and Gr. *korallion*, coral.] A suborder of the *Hydroidea*, similar to the corals and including the millepores.

hȳ″drō-cō-tär′nine, *n.* An alkaloid derived from opium.

Hȳ-drō-çot′y-lē, *n.* [*Hydro-*, and Gr. *kotylē*, a cavity, cup.] A genus of plants of the order *Umbelliferæ*; the water-pennyworts.

hȳ-drō-cȳ′ȧ-nāte, *n.* Same as *Cyanide*.

hȳ″drō-cȳ-an′iç, *a.* [*Hydro*gen and *cyano*gen and *-ic*.] Composed of hydrogen and cyanogen.

Hydrocyanic acid; a colorless and extremely poisonous liquid compound of hydrogen and cyanogen, derived from various cyanides by the action of hydrochloric acid; also called *prussic acid*.

hȳ-drō-cȳ′ȧ-nīde (*or* -nīd), *n.* Same as *Cyanide*.

hȳ′drō-cyst, *n.* [*Hydro-*, and Gr. *kystis*, a bladder.] In zoölogy, a process, a sort of feeler attached to the cœnosarc of the *Physophoridæ*, an order of oceanic *Hydrozoa*.

Hȳ-drō-dic′ty-on, *n.* [*Hydro-*, and Gr. *diktyon*, a net.] A genus of green-spored algæ, remarkable for beauty and peculiarity of structure; so called because, when full-grown, they resemble a purse composed of a network of threads.

hȳ″drō-dȳ-nam′iç, hȳ″drō-dȳ-nam′iç-ăl, *a.* [*Hydro-*, and Gr. *dynamis*, power, and *-ic*.] Pertaining to or derived from the force or pressure of water or other fluid.

hȳ″drō-dȳ-nam′içs, *n.* That branch of mechanics which treats of fluids, whether in motion or at rest.

hȳ-drō-dȳ-nȧ-mom′e-tẽr, *n.* [*Hydro-*, and Gr. *dynamis*, power, and *metron*, a measure.] A device to measure the speed of a moving fluid by determining the pressure it exerts.

hȳ″drō-ē-lec′triç, *a.* [*Hydro-*, and Gr. *ēlektron*, amber.] Producing electricity by the escape of steam at a high pressure, or pertaining to such action.

Hydro-electric machine; a machine which generates electricity by the friction of steam escaping under high pressure from a series of jets. Positive electricity is collected by directing the steam upon a metal comb communicating with an insulated conductor.

Armstrong's Hydro-electric Machine.

hȳ″drō-ex-tract′ŏr, *n.* [*Hydro-*, and L. *extractus*, pp. of *extrahere*, to draw out.] A centrifugal machine to remove moisture.

hȳ″drō-fer″ri-cȳ-an′iç, *a.* Composed of hydrogen and ferricyanogen.

hȳ″drō-fer″rō-cȳ-an′iç, *a.* Composed of hydrogen, cyanogen, and iron in its lower valence.

hȳ″drō-flū-or′iç, *a.* Consisting of fluorin and hydrogen.

Hydrofluoric acid; a volatile compound, HF, of hydrogen and fluorin, used for etching glass.

hȳ-drō-flū-ō-sil′i-çāte, *n.* Any salt of hydrofluosilicic acid.

hȳ″drō-flū″ō-si-lic′iç, *a.* Composed of fluosilicic and hydrofluoric acids.

hȳ′drō-fūġe, *a.* [*Hydro-*, and L. *fugare*, to put to flight, from *fugere*, to flee.] Shedding or impervious to water.

hȳ″drō-gal-van′iç, *a.* Of, caused by, or belonging to electricity generated by the action of liquids; as, a *hydrogalvanic* current. [Rare.]

hȳ′drō-ġen, *n.* [Gr. *hydōr*, water, and *-genēs*, producing.] An elementary substance existing at ordinary temperatures as a colorless, tasteless, and inodorous gas, the lightest of all known substances. It forms one-ninth of the weight of water and is present in almost all organic compounds.

Bicarbureted hydrogen; ethylene.

Hydrogendioxid or *peroxid*; a colorless, odorless, unstable liquid, H_2O_2, used as an antiseptic and oxidizer.

Hydrogen oxid; water, H_2O.

Hydrogen sulphid; *sulphureted hydrogen*; a strongly odorous gas, H_2S, occurring in some mineral springs and during the decomposition of organic matter containing sulphur, thus forming the odor of rotten eggs.

hȳ′drō-ġen-āte, *v.t.* To hydrogenize.

hȳ″drō-ġen-ā′tion, *n.* The process of hydrogenating or the state of being hydrogenated.

hȳ′drō-ġen-id, *n.* [Rare.] Same as *Hydrid*.

hȳ-drō-ġē′ni-um, *n.* [From *hydrogen*.] Hydrogen considered as a metal; hydrogen in a solid state or as occluded by palladium.

hȳ′drō-ġen-ize, *v.t.*; hydrogenized, *pt.*, *pp.*; hydrogenizing, *ppr.* To combine with hydrogen.

hȳ-drog′e-nous, *a.* 1. Pertaining to or containing hydrogen.

2. Produced by the action of water.

hȳ-drog′nō-sy, *n.* [*Hydro-*, and Gr. *gnōsis*, knowledge.] A description of or treatise upon the world's waters.

hȳ-drog′rȧ-phẽr, *n.* [*Hydro-*, and Gr. *graphein*, to write.]

1. One who makes maps of any division of water, as oceans, seas, lakes, etc.

2. A superintendent of hydrographic surveys.

hȳ-drō-graph′iç, hȳ-drō-graph′iç-ăl, *a.* Of, relating, or pertaining to hydrography.

hȳ-drog′rȧ-phy, *n.* [*Hydro-*, and Gr. *graphein*, to write.]

1. That branch of science which has for its object the measurement and description of the seas, lakes, rivers, and other waters, especially in so far as regards their usefulness for the purposes of navigation and commerce.

2. The state of the earth as regards the distribution of water.

hȳ-drog′ū-ret, *n.* [*Hydro*gen and *-uret*.] A compound of hydrogen with a base.

hȳ′droid, *a.* and *n.* [*Hydra* and *-oid*.]

I. *a.* Of, relating to, or resembling the *Hydroidea*.

II. *n.* One of the *Hydroidea*.

Hȳ-droi′dē-ȧ, *n.pl.* [Gr. *hydroeidēs*, like water; *hydōr*, water, and *eidos*, form.] The typical subclass of *Hydrozoa*. They have an alimentary region provided with an adherent disk and prehensile tentacles. Most of the *Hydroidea* live in societies, each of which constitutes a polypidom so like a seaweed that it is often collected as such.

hȳ″drō-ki-net′iç, *a.* [*Hydro-*, and Gr. *kinētikos*, moving, from *kinein*, to move.] Of or relating to the motion of fluids.

hȳ″drō-ki-net′içs, *n.* The kinetics of fluids.

hȳ-drō-log′iç-ăl, *a.* Pertaining to hydrology.

hȳ-drol′ō-ġist, *n.* One versed in hydrology.

hȳ-drol′ō-ġy, *n.* [*Hydro-*, and Gr. *-logia*, from *legein*, to speak.] The science of water, its properties, phenomena, and laws.

hȳ′drō-lymph, *n.* [*Hydro-*, and L. *lympha*, water.] The watery circulatory fluid serving as blood for certain of the invertebrates, notably the lower.

hȳ-drol′y-sis, *n.* [*Hydro-*, and Gr. *lysis*, loosing, from *lyein*, to loose.] Decomposition of a chemical compound in which the hydrogen and oxygen of water are taken up to form new compounds.

hȳ-drō-lyt′iç, *a.* [*Hydro-*, and Gr. *lyein*, to loose.] Of, relating, or pertaining to hydrolysis; causing decomposition by means of water.

Hydrolytic ferment; a ferment which remains inactive except in the presence of water.

hȳ-drō-mag′nē-site, *n.* [*Hydro-*, *magne*sium, and *-ite*.] A monoclinic, white, brittle mineral of vitreous, silky or almost pearly luster, made up of carbonic acid, magnesia, water, and a trace of silica.

hȳ′drō-man-cy, *n.* [*Hydro-*, and Gr. *manteia*, divination.] A method of divination by means of water.

hȳ-drō-mā′ni-ȧ, *n.* [*Hydro-*, and Gr. *mania*, madness.] In pathology, (a) an unnatural thirst; (b) desire for death by drowning.

hȳ-drō-man′tiç, *a.* Pertaining to divination by water.

hȳ″drō-mē-chan′içs, *n.* [*Hydro-*, and Gr. *mēchanikos*, mechanic, from *mēchanē*, a machine.] The mechanics of water and fluids in general.

Hȳ″drō-mē-dū′sæ, *n.pl.* [*Hydro-*, and Gr. *Medousa*, the Gorgon of classic mythology.] A subclass of hydrozoans comprehending those related to the *Hydra* by reason of reproduction by lateral gemmation.

hȳ′drō-mel, *n.* [L. *hydromel* or *hydromeli*; Gr. *hydromeli*, a kind of mead made of water and honey; *hydōr*, water, and *meli*, honey.] A liquor consisting of honey diluted with water. Before fermentation, it is called simple *hydromel*; after fermentation, it is called vinous *hydromel* or mead.

hȳ″drō-mel-lon′iç, *a.* Pertaining to the hypothetical compound. $C_9H_3N_{13}$. [See *Cyamellone*.]

hȳ-drō-met-ăl-lūr′ġiç-ăl, *a.* Of or pertaining to hydrometallurgy.

hȳ-drō-met-ăl-lūr′ġiç-ăl-ly, *adv.* In a hydrometallurgical manner.

hȳ-drō-met′ăl-lūr-ġy, *n.* [*Hydro-*, and Gr. *metallourgos*, working in metals, a miner; *metallon*, a mine, metal, and *ergon*, work.] The act of assaying or reducing ores by the use of liquid reagents; also, any process utilized for this purpose.

hȳ-drō-met-ȧ-mor′phism, *n.* [*Hydro-*, and Gr. *metamorphōsis*, a transformation, change, metamorphosis.] Metamorphism of rocks by addition and depletion of material in solution in water.

hȳ-drō-mē′tē-ŏr, *n.* [*Hydro-*, and Gr. *meteōron*, a meteor.] Any atmospheric phenomenon dependent for its production upon the vapor of water, as rain, hail, snow, etc.

hȳ-drō-mē″tē-ọr-ō-log′iç-ăl, *a.* Of or pertaining to hydrometeorology.

hȳ-drō-mē″tē-ọr-ol′ō-ġy, *n.* [*Hydro-*, and Gr. *meteōrologia*, meteorology.] The branch of meteorology which concerns itself with water in the atmosphere in the form of rain, clouds, snow, hail, etc.

hȳ-drom′e-tẽr, *n.* [*Hydro-*, and Gr. *metron*, a measure.]

1. In physics, an instrument for determining the specific gravities of substances. Hydrometers are variously constructed. A very common type consists of a graduated stem of uniform diameter and cross-section, a bulb to cause it to float in the fluid, and a weight or counterpoise to cause the stem to stand upright as it floats. On being placed in a liquid it sinks until a certain point on the scale is on a level with the surface of the liquid, and from the reading of the scale at that point the specific gravity of the liquid is ascertained either directly or by a simple calculation.

Hydrometer.

2. An instrument for measuring the flow of water in and its discharge from rivers, conduits, etc.

hȳ-drō-met′riç, hȳ-drō-met′riç-ăl, *a.* 1. Pertaining to a hydrometer or to the determination of the specific gravity, velocity, discharge, etc., of fluids.

2. Made by a hydrometer; as, *hydrometric* observations.

Hydrometric pendulum; an instrument consisting of a hollow ball suspended from the center of a graduated quadrant, and held in a stream to mark by its deflection the velocity of the current.

hȳ-drō-met′rō-grȧph, *n.* [*Hydro-*, and Gr. *metron*, a measure, and *graphein*, to write.] An instrument to determine and record the amount of water discharged in a specific time through any exit.

hȳ-drom′e-try, *n.* [*Hydro-*, and Gr. *metron*, a measure.] The art of finding specific gravities.

hȳ-drō-mī′çȧ, *n.* [*Hydro-*, and L. *mica*, a crumb, grain.] A substance resembling muscovite in composition, but having more water. It is a variety of potash-mica.

hȳ-drō-mō′tŏr, *n.* [*Hydro-*, and L. *motor*, from *movere*, to move.] A motor impelled by the reaction of a jet of water.

hȳ″drō-nē-phrō′sis, *n.* [*Hydro-*, and Gr. *nephros*, a kidney, and *-osis*.] In pathology, a distention of the ureter and the renal pelvis caused by obstruction of the outflow of the urine.

hȳ′drō-path, *n.* One who practises or believes in hydropathy.

hȳ-drō-path′iç, hȳ-drō-path′iç-ăl, *a.* Pertaining to hydropathy.

hȳ-drop′ȧ-thist, *n.* One who advocates or practises hydropathy.

hȳ-drop′ȧ-thy, *n.* [*Hydro-*, and Gr. *pathos*, suffering, disease.] The water-cure, a mode of treating diseases by the copious and frequent use of pure water, both internally and externally. This system is said to increase the cutaneous exhalation to a very large amount, and thus to draw off speedily from the blood certain deleterious matters.

hȳ-drō-per-i-cär′di-um, *n.* [*Hydro-*, and Gr. *perikardion*, the pericardium.] In pathology, cardiac dropsy.

hȳ″drō-per″i-pneū-mō′ni-ȧ (-nū-), *n.* [*Hydro-*, and Gr. *peripneumonia*; *peri*, around, about, and *pneumōn*, the lung.] Inflammation of the lungs complicated with dropsy.

hȳ-drō-per″i-tō-nē′um, *n.* [*Hydro-*, and Gr. *peritonaion*, peritoneum.] In pathology, dropsy of the peritoneal cavity; ascites.

hȳ′drō-phāne, *n.* [*Hydro-*, and Gr. *phanos*, clear.] In mineralogy, a variety of opal made transparent by immersion in water.

hȳ′drō-phid, *n.* [*Hydr-*, and Gr. *ophis*, a snake.] A venomous sea-snake of the family *Hydrophidæ*.

hȳ-drō-phō′bi-ȧ, hȳ′drō-phō-by, *n.* [LL., from Gr. *hydrophobia*, hydrophobia; *hydōr*, water, and *phobos*, fear.]

1. An unnatural dread of water, a symptom of canine madness. This dread of water sometimes causes violent inflammations of the stomach and hysteric fits.

2. A disease produced by the bite of a mad animal, especially of a mad or rabid dog, one of the characteristics of which is an aversion to or inability to swallow liquids. The term is more especially applied to the disease in man, *rabies* being considered preferable as the name of the disease which constitutes madness in animals.

hȳ-drō-phob′iç, *a.* [Gr. *hydrophobikos*, from *hydrophobia*, hydrophobia.] Pertaining to a dread of water or canine madness.

hȳ′drō-phō-by, *n.* Hydrophobia.

hȳ′drō-phoid, *a.* Pertaining to *Hydrophidæ,* a family of sea-snakes.

Hȳ-droph′ō-rȧ, *n.pl.* [Gr. *hydrophoros,* water-bearing; *hydōr,* water, and *pherein,* to bear, carry.] One of the three divisions into which Huxley and other authors divide the *Hydrozoa,* the other two being the *Discophora* and the *Siphonophora.* The members are, in all cases except that of *Hydra,* fixed ramified hydrosomes, on which many hydranths and gonophores are developed.

hȳ′drō-phōre, *n.* [Gr. *hydrophoros,* water-carrying; *hydōr,* water, and *pherein,* to bear.] An instrument for obtaining for examination small quantities of the water of a river, a lake, or an ocean from any specific depth.

Hȳ″drō-phyl-lā′cē-æ, *n.* [*Hydro-,* and Gr. *phyllon,* a leaf, and *-aceæ.*] An order of plants known as waterleaves, including nearly 20 genera and 125 species, the majority of which are American.

hȳ″drō-phyl-lā′ceous, *a.* Of or relating to the *Hydrophyllaceæ.*

hȳ-drō-phyl′li-um, *n.*; *pl.* **hȳ-drō-phyl′li-ȧ** or **hȳ-drō-phyl′li-ums.** [*Hydro-,* and Gr. *phyllon,* a leaf.] In zoölogy, an overlapping appendage or plate which protects the polypites in some oceanic hydrozoans, as the *Siphonophora;* called also *bract.*

Hȳ-drō-phyl′lum, *n.* [*Hydro-,* and Gr. *phyllon,* a leaf.] A genus of American perennial marsh herbs with blue or white flowers, the type of the *Hydrophyllaceæ* or waterleaf family.

hȳ′drō-phȳte, *n.* [*Hydro-,* and Gr. *phyton,* a plant.] An aquatic plant; a plant which lives and grows in water.

hȳ-droph-y-tol′ō-gy, *n.* [*Hydro-,* and Gr. *phyton,* a plant, and *-logia,* from *legein,* to speak.] That branch of botany which relates to water-plants.

hȳ-droph′y-tŏn, *n.*; *pl.* **hȳ-droph′y-tȧ.** [*Hydro-,* and Gr. *phyton,* a plant.] The connective element in a hydroid colony of zoöids.

hȳ-droph′y-tous, *a.* Characteristic of a hydrophyton.

hȳ-drop′ic, *a.* [L. *hydropicus;* Gr. *hydrōpikos,* dropsical, from *hydrōps,* dropsy, from *hydōr,* water.] Containing water; produced by water; dropsical.

hȳ-drop′ic, *n.* 1. A medicine that relieves or cures dropsy.

2. One who is affected with dropsy.

hȳ-drop′ic-ăl, *a.* Hydropic.

hȳ-drop′ic-ăl-ly, *adv.* In a hydropical manner.

hȳ′drō-pi-pẽr, *n.* [*Hydro-,* and L. *piper,* a pepper.] In botany, *Polygonum Hydropiper,* a species of knotweed; water-pepper; smartweed.

hȳ-drō-pneū-mat′ic, *a.* [*Hydro-,* and Gr. *pneumatikos,* of or caused by wind or air, from *pneuma,* wind, air.] Of or pertaining to, or produced by, the action of water and air; involving the combined action of water and air or gas.

hȳ-drō-pol′yp, *n.* [*Hydro-,* and Gr. *polypous,* many-footed, a polyp.] A hydrozoan as distinguished from an actinozoan.

hȳ-drō-prō-pul′sion, *n.* [*Hydro-,* and E. *propulsion.*] Propulsion by means of a hydromotor.

hȳ′drop-sy, *n.* See *Dropsy.*

Hȳ″drop-tē-rid′ē-æ, *n.pl.* [*Hydro-,* and Gr. *pteris (-idos,)* a fern.] A class or group of cryptogams including the families *Marsiliaceæ* and *Salviniaceæ;* the water-ferns; called also *Rhizocarpeæ.*

hȳ′drō-pult, *n.* [*Hydro-,* and L. *catapulta,* a catapult.] A machine for throwing water by hand-power; a garden-pump; written also *hydrapult.*

hȳ″drō-pȳ-ret′ic, *a.* [*Hydro-,* and Gr. *pyretos,* fever.] In pathology, pertaining to fever accompanied with sweating.

hȳ-drō-quī′nōne (-kwī′), *n.* [*Hydro-* and *quinone.*] An isomer of resorcin and pyrocatechin, possessing antipyretic and antiseptic properties.

hȳ-dror′ȧ-chis, hȳ-dror′rhȧ-chis, *n.* [*Hydro-,* and Gr. *rhachis,* spine.] In pathology, an abnormal collection of fluid within the spinal column. The pressure of the fluid tends ultimately to produce atrophy of the cord.

hȳ-drō-rhī′zȧ, *n.*; *pl.* **hȳ-drō-rhī′zæ** or **hȳ-drō-rhī′zȧs.** [*Hydro-,* and Gr. *rhiza,* a root.] In zoölogy, the adherent base or proximal extremity of a hydrozoan.

hȳ-drō-rhī′zăl, *a.* Pertaining to or characteristic of a hydrorhiza.

hȳ-dror-rhē′ȧ, hȳ-dror-rhœ′ȧ, *n.* [Gr. *hydrorroia,* a flowing of water; *hydōr,* water, and *rhoia,* from *rhein,* to flow.] In pathology, a flow of watery liquid.

hȳ′drō-sạlt, *n.* [*Hydro-* and *salt.*] A salt supposed to be formed by a hydracid and a base; rarely, an acid salt.

hȳ-drō-săr′cō-cēle, *n.* [*Hydro-,* and Gr. *sarkokēlē; sarx, sarkos,* flesh, and *kēlē,* a tumor.] In pathology, sarcocele with hydrocele.

hȳ′drō-scōpe, *n.* [Gr. *hydrōskōpion,* a water-clock; *hydōr,* water, and *skopein,* to view.]

1. A kind of water-clock, or instrument used anciently for measuring time, consisting of a cylindrical graduated tube, from which water slowly escaped through an aperture at the bottom, the subsidence of the water marking the lapse of time.

2. An instrument for indicating the humidity of the air; a hygroscope.

3. An instrument invented in 1903 by Cavaliere Pino, an Italian, which makes it possible to examine, at practically any depth, the bed of the sea. It consists of a long tube fitted with various optical instruments at the end. When the hydroscope is fitted to a ship, an image of the water and the things therein beneath the ship can be thrown on a screen on deck, so that a number of people at one time can see what is going on in the water beneath them. The hydroscope, moreover, can be so adjusted that it will reflect not only objects lying beneath it, but those around and above, thus enabling a captain to watch the keel of his ship, or to examine the keel in case of accident, while steaming at full speed.

hȳ-drō-sō′mȧ, *n.*; *pl.* **hȳ-drō-sō′mȧ-tȧ.** [*Hydro-,* and Gr. *soma (-atos),* body.] In zoölogy, the entire organism of a hydrozoan; written also *hydrosome.*

hȳ-drō-sō′măl, *a.* Of or relating to a hydrosoma.

hȳ-drō-som′ȧ-tous, *a.* See *Hydrosomal.*

hȳ′drō-sōme, *n.* Same as *Hydrosoma.*

hȳ′drō-stat, *n.* [Gr. *hydrostatēs,* a hydrostatic balance.]

1. A term applied to any apparatus for preventing the explosion of steam-boilers.

2. An electrical device to detect the presence of water, and thereby prevent leakage, etc.

hȳ-drō-stat′ic, hȳ-drō-stat′ic-ăl, *a.* [Gr. *hydrostatēs,* a hydrostatic balance; *hydōr,* water, and *statos,* standing.] Relating to the science of weighing fluids, or hydrostatics; pertaining to or in accordance with the principles of the equilibrium of fluids.

Hydrostatic balance; see under *Balance.*

Hydrostatic bellows; an apparatus to illustrate the law of the distribution of pressure through liquids; it shows how a great upward pressure may be produced, as in the hydraulic press, and also that the pressure of a fluid upon the bottom of a vessel does not depend upon the quantity of the fluid but upon its altitude. It consists generally of two circular boards, connected with leather fastened closely round their edges, as in an ordinary pair of bellows, and having an upright pipe communicating with the interior. If a certain quantity of water is poured into the bellows, and weights placed upon the upper board, the water will rise in the tube above the level of the water in the bellows to such a height that the pressure caused by the weight of the small quantity of water in the tube is a balance for the water in the bellows and the weights; and it will be seen that the higher the water in the tube the greater the weight that will be sustained.

Hydrostatic Bellows.

Hydrostatic paradox; the principle that any quantity of water however small may be made to balance any weight however great.

Hydrostatic press; see *Hydraulic press* under *Hydraulic.*

hȳ-drō-stat′ic-ăl-ly, *adv.* According to hydrostatics or to hydrostatic principles.

hȳ″drō-stȧ-ti′ciăn (-tish′ăn), *n.* One versed in hydrostatics. [Rare.]

hȳ-drō-stat′ics, *n.* That branch of the science of hydrodynamics which treats of the properties of fluids at rest. It takes into consideration the pressure and equilibrium of nonelastic fluids, the method of determining the specific gravities of substances both solid and liquid, the equilibrium of floating bodies, and the phenomena of capillary attraction.

hȳ-drō-sul′phid, *n.* [*Hydrogen* and *sulphid.*] In chemistry, one of several compounds obtained from hydrogen sulphid, by substituting a base for half of its hydrogen.

hȳ-drō-sul′phīte, *n.* A compound of hydrosulphurous acid and a base.

hȳ-drō-sul′phū-ret, *n.* [*Hydrogen* and *sulphuret.*] A combination of sulphureted hydrogen with an earth, alkali, or metallic oxid.

hȳ-drō-sul′phū-ret-ed, *a.* Combined with sulphureted hydrogen.

hȳ-drō-sul′phŭr-ous, *a.* [*Hydrogen* and *sulphurous.*] Compounded of hydrogen and sulphur.

hȳ-drō-tel′lū-rāte, *n.* [*Hydrogen* and *tellurium* and *-ate.*] A salt formed by the combination of an acid composed of hydrogen and tellurium with a salifiable base.

hȳ-drō-tel-lū′ric, *a.* Of or pertaining to, or obtained from, hydrogen and tellurium.

hȳ-drō-thē′cȧ, *n.* [Gr. *hydrothēkē,* a reservoir for water; *hydōr,* water, and *thēkē,* a case, box.] In zoölogy, a little chitinous cup, in which each polypite of the *Sertularida* and *Campanularida* is protected.

hȳ-drō-ther′ȧ-peū-tics, *n.* [*Hydro-,* and Gr. *therapeutikos,* from *therapeuein,* to attend, serve.] In medicine, treatment by mineral waters and baths.

hȳ-drō-ther′ȧ-py, *n.* See *Hydropathy.*

hȳ-drō-thẽr′măl, *a.* [*Hydro-,* and Gr. *thermos,* hot.] Of or relating to heated water; specifically, applied to the action of heated waters in producing geological changes by dissolving mineral substances and redepositing them when cooled.

hȳ-drō-thō′rax, *n.* [*Hydro-,* and Gr. *thōrax,* the chest.] Dropsy in the chest.

hȳ-drot′ic, *a.* [Gr. *hydrotēs,* moisture, from *hydōr,* water.] Causing a discharge of water.

hȳ-drot′ic, *n.* A medicine that removes water or phlegm.

hȳ-drot′ic-ăl, *a.* Hydrotic.

hȳ′drō-trōpe, *n.* [*Hydro-,* and Gr. *trepein,* to turn.] A pulsometer; an aquometer; a device for raising water by the condensation of steam.

hȳ-drō-trop′ic, *a.* In botany, tending or growing toward moisture, as roots.

hȳ-drot′rō-pism, *n.* In botany, a deflection or inclination due to the persistent influence of moisture.

hȳ′drous, *a.* [Gr. *hydōr,* water, and *-ous.*]

1. Watery.

2. In chemistry, containing hydrogen.

hȳ-drox′id, hȳ-drox′ide, *n.* [*Hydrogen* and *oxid.*] In chemistry, a compound formed by the action of water on an oxid, which may be either basic or acid; as, potassium *hydroxid,* calcium *hydroxid,* etc.

hȳ-drox′yl, *n.* [*Hydrogen* and oxygen and *-yl.*] In chemistry, an unisolated compound radical, of one atom of hydrogen and one of oxygen.

hȳ″drox-yl-am′ine, *n.* [*Hydroxyl* and *amine.*] A nitrogenous unisolated organic base, $NH_2.OH$, which acts powerfully as a reducing agent.

Hȳ-drō-zō′ȧ, *n.pl.* In zoölogy, one of the two divisions of *Cœlenterata,* small aquatic and chiefly marine animals of a great variety of forms but essentially composed of an outer and an inner membrane with a simple vascular stomach-sac.

hȳ-drō-zō′ăl, hȳ-drō-zō′ăn, *a.* Pertaining to the hydrozoa.

hȳ-drō-zō′ăn, *n.* A hydrozoön.

hȳ-drō-zō′on, *n.*; *pl.* **hȳ-drō-zō′ȧ.** [*Hydro-,* and Gr. *zōon,* an animal.] In zoölogy, one of a class of radiated animals forming with the *Actinozoa* the subkingdom *Cœlenterata.* The *Hydrozoa* are divided into four subclasses—*Hydroida, Siphonophora, Discophora,* and *Lucernarida.* The genus *Hydra* may be taken as the type.

hȳ-drū′ri-ȧ, *n.* [*Hydro-,* and Gr. *ouron,* urine.] Excessive discharge of urine of low specific gravity.

Hȳ′drus, *n.* [Gr. *hydros,* a water-serpent.]

1. A genus of water-snakes, now generally called *Hydrophis,* the type of the family *Hydridæ.*

2. A constellation of the southern hemisphere.

hȳ-ē′măl, *a.* See *Hiemal.*

hȳ′ē-māte, *v.i.* See *Hiemate.*

hȳ-e-mā′tion, *n.* See *Hiemation.*

hȳ-ē′nȧ, *n.* [L. *hyæna;* Gr. *hyaina,* a hyena, an animal which has a bristly mane like the hog's, from *hys,* a hog.] In zoölogy, a carnivorous quadruped of the genus *Hyena,* of nocturnal habits and subsisting chiefly upon carrion; characterized by powerful jaws and teeth, four-toed feet with strong blunt claws, long fore legs, shaggy hair, and a cowardly but ferocious disposition akin to that of the wolf. Three living species are known, all of the Old World, and one prehistoric species, the fossils of which are found in caves, the cave hyena.

Striped Hyena (*Hyena striata*).

hȳ-ē′nȧ-dog, *n.* 1. In zoölogy, an animal of Africa, *Lycaon pictus,* bearing some resemblance to a hyena; called also *hunting-dog* and *painted hyena.*

2. Same as *Aardwolf.*

hȳ-en′i-form, *a.* In zoölogy, having the form or characteristics of the hyena or of its family, the *Hyenidæ.*

hȳ-ē′noid, *a.* Like a hyena; hyeniform.

hyet-, hyeto-. Combining forms from Gr. *hyetos,* rain, from *hyein,* to rain, used to signify rain, rainfall, as in *hyetograph, hyetometer.*

hȳ′ē-tăl, *a.* [Gr. *hyetos,* rain, from *hyein,* to

rain.] Of or relating to rain or its distribution with reference to different regions; descriptive of the rainfall of different districts.

hȳ'ē-tō-grȧph, *n.* [*Hyeto-*, and Gr. *graphein*, to write.] A chart showing the average rainfall in the different regions of the earth.

hȳ"ē-tō-graph'iç, hȳ"ē-tō-graph'iç-ăl, *a.* Relating to hyetography.

hȳ-ē-tog'rȧ-phy, *n.* [*Hyeto-*, and Gr. *-graphia*, from *graphein*, to write.] The science of the distribution of rain; a knowledge of the quantities of rain which fall in different localities in a given time.

hȳ-ē-tol'ō-ġy, *n.* [*Hyeto-*, and Gr. *-logia*, from *legein*, to speak.] The branch of meteorology which treats of rain and its attendant phenomena.

hȳ-ē-tom'e-tẽr, *n.* [*Hyeto-*, and Gr. *metron*, a measure.] A rain-gauge; a device that measures the rainfall at a given place.

hȳ"ē-tō-met'rō-grȧph, *n.* [*Hyeto-*, and Gr. *metron*, a measure, and *graphein*, to write.] A hyetometer with an attachment for registering the amount of rainfall for each unit of time.

Hȳ-ġē'iȧ (-yȧ), *n.* [Gr. *Hygieia*, goddess of health, from *hygieia*, health, soundness of body, from *hygiēs*, healthy, sound.]

1. In classical mythology, the goddess of health, daughter of Æsculapius, usually represented as a blooming maid with a bowl in one hand and grasping a serpent with the other.

2. One of the small planets or asteroids between the orbits of Mars and Jupiter, discovered in 1849.

Hȳ-ġē'iăn, *a.* Relating to Hygeia, the goddess of health, or [h—] to health and its preservation.

hȳ'ġiē-ist, hȳ'ġē-ist, *n.* A hygienist.

hȳ'ġi-ēne (*or* -ġēn), *n.* [Fr. *hygiène*, from Gr. *hygiainein*, to be sound, healthy, from *hygiēs*, sound, healthy.] Health; the department of natural science which treats of the preservation of health.

hȳ-ġi-on'iç, *a.* Pertaining to health.

> How small a proportion of them die before the age of maturity in the present state of *hygienic* knowledge. —J. S. Mill.

hȳ-ġi-on'iç-ăl-ly, *adv.* In a hygienic manner; in a manner fitted to preserve health.

hȳ-ġi-en'içs, hȳ'ġi-en-ișm, *n.* The science of health; hygiene; sanitary science.

hȳ'ġi-en-ist, *n.* One versed in hygiene or the science of health.

hȳ-ġi-ol'ō-ġy, *n.* [Gr. *hygieia*, health, and *-logia*, from *legein*, to speak.] The science of or a treatise on the preservation of health.

hȳ'grine, *n.* [Gr. *hygros*, wet, moist, and *-ine*.] In chemistry, an odoriferous and pungent oil extracted from coca-leaves.

hygro-. A combining form from Gr. *hygros*, wet, moist, used in biology, botany, medicine, etc., to signify wet, moisture; as, *hygro*statics, *hygro*plasm.

hȳ'grō-deik, *n.* [*Hygro-*, and Gr. *deiknynai*, to show, point out.] In physics, a hygrometer fitted with thermometers and an index which automatically records the relative humidity.

hȳ'grō-grȧph, *n.* [*Hygro-*, and Gr. *graphein*, to write.] An instrument which registers automatically the variations of the atmospheric moisture.

hȳ-grō'mȧ, *n.*; *pl.* **hȳ-grō'mȧ-tȧ.** [*Hygro-*, and Gr. *-ōma*, a suffix signifying a tumor.] In medicine, a swelling arising from a distended cyst or sac filled with serum.

hȳ-grom'ȧ-tous, *a.* Like or affected by hygroma.

hȳ-grom'e-tẽr, *n.* [*Hygro-*, and Gr. *metron*, a measure.] An instrument for measuring the degree of moisture of the atmosphere, or for ascertaining the relative moisture of the atmosphere under various degrees of temperature.

hȳ-grō-met'riç, hȳ-grō-met'riç-ăl, *a.* 1. Pertaining to hygrometry; made by or according to the hygrometer.

2. Readily absorbing and retaining moisture, as potash.

hȳ-grom'e-try, *n.* The art of measuring the moisture or the relative moisture of the atmosphere.

hȳ-groph'ȧ-nous, *a.* [*Hygro-*, and Gr. *-phanēs*, from *phainein*, to show.] In botany, transparent or watery-like when moist and opaque when dry.

hȳ-groph'i-lous, *a.* [*Hygro-*, and Gr. *philos*, loving.] In biology, fond of moisture; flourishing in damp places, as a snail or a water-lily.

hȳ'grō-plașm, *n.* [*Hygro-*, and Gr. *plasma*, anything formed, molded.] In biology, the fluid element of cell protoplasm, as distinguished from *stereoplasm*.

hȳ'grō-sçōpe, *n.* [*Hygro-*, and Gr. *skopein*, to view.] An instrument for indicating the presence of moisture in the atmosphere without measuring the amount.

hȳ-grō-sçop'iç, hȳ-grō-sçop'iç-ăl, *a.* 1. Pertaining to the hygroscope; perceptible or capable of being detected only by the hygroscope; as, a film of *hygroscopic* moisture covered the glass.

2. Having the property of absorbing or of becoming coated with moisture.

hȳ"grō-sçō-piç'i-ty, *n.* In botany, the property possessed by vegetable tissues of absorbing or discharging moisture and extending or shrinking accordingly.

hȳ-grō-stat'içs, *n.* [*Hygro-*, and Gr. *statikos*, causing to stand, from *histanai*, to cause to stand.] The science of measuring or comparing degrees of moisture.

hȳke, *n.* A loose Arabian garment. [See *Haik*.]

hȳ'læ-ō-sąur, *n.* A fossil lizard of the genus *Hylæosaurus*.

Hȳ-læ-ō-sąu'rus, *n.* [Gr. *hylaios*, of the wood or forest, and *sauros*, a lizard.] A genus of gigantic fossil lizards discovered in the Wealden formation of Tilgate Forest in England. The bony dermal scutes were prolonged along the ridge of the back in a series of enormous spines. One of the species was about twenty-five feet long.

hȳ-lär'çhi-căl, *a.* [Gr. *hylē*, wood, matter, and *archikos*, ruling, from *archein*, to rule.] Presiding over matter. [Rare.]

hȳ'lē, *n.* [Gr. *hylē*, wood, matter.] In philosophy, a term applied to matter in general.

hȳ'leg, *n.* [Ar.] In astrology, the planet which rules at the time of one's nativity; written also *hileg*.

hȳ'li-çișm, *n.* See *Hylism*.

hȳ'li-çist, *n.* [Gr. *hylē*, wood, matter.] A materialist; a believer in the theory of hylism.

Hȳ'li-dæ, *n.pl.* [Gr. *hylē*, wood, forest, matter, and *-idæ*.] A family of amphibian vertebrates, distinguished from the true frogs by having dilated disks or suckers covered with viscid matter at the tips of their toes, which enable them to climb trees; the tree-toads or tree-frogs.

hȳ'lișm, *n.* [Gr. *hylē*, wood, matter.] In metaphysics, a theory which regards matter as the principle of evil; written also *hylicism*.

hylo-, hyl-. Combining forms from Gr. *hylē*, wood, matter, stuff of any kind; used to signify wood, matter, and especially, in philosophy, matter as receiving form or determination from another; as, *hylo*genesis, *hylo*phagous.

hȳ'lō-bāte, *n.* [Gr. *hylobatēs*, one who inhabits or haunts the woods; *hylē*, wood, forest, and *batēs*, one who mounts, from *bainein*, to go.] In zoölogy, an ape of the genus *Hylobates*; the long-armed ape or gibbon.

Hȳ-lob'ȧ-tēș, *n.* A genus of apes including the gibbons.

hȳ-lō'dēș, *n.* [Gr. *hylōdēs*, woody, of the wood; *hylē*, wood, and *eidos*, form.] In zoölogy, a tree-frog, *Hyla pickeringi*, of North America.

hȳ-lō-ġen'e-sis, *n.* [*Hylo-*, and Gr. *genesis*, generation.] The origin of matter.

hȳ'loid, *a.* [Gr. *hylē*, wood, and *eidos*, form.] Pertaining to the *Hylidæ*, a family of tree-toads.

hȳ'loid, *n.* One of the *Hylidæ*.

hȳ'lō-ist, *n.* [Gr. *hylē*, wood, matter, and *-ist*.] One who believes matter to be God.

hȳ-lop'ȧ-thișm, *n.* [*Hylo-*, and Gr. *pathos*, feeling, and *-ism*.] The belief that matter has the faculty of perception and that spirit and matter are retroactive.

hȳ-lop'ȧ-thist, *n.* A believer in hylopathism.

hȳ-loph'ȧ-gous, *a.* [Gr. *hylophagos*, eating wood; *hylē*, wood, and *phagein*, to eat.] Feeding on the young shoots of trees, roots, etc., as certain insects.

hȳ'lō-thē-ișm, *n.* [*Hylo-*, and Gr. *theos*, god, and *-ism*.] The doctrine or belief that matter is God, or that there is no God except matter and the universe.

hȳ'lō-thē-ist, *n.* A believer in hylotheism.

hȳ-lot'ō-mous, *a.* [*Hylo-*, and Gr. *tomos*, cutting, from *temnein*, to cut.] Wood-cutting, as sawflies and certain other insects.

hȳ-lō-zō'iç, *n.* [*Hylo-*, and Gr. *zōē*, life, and *-ic*.] One who holds matter to be animated.

hȳ-lō-zō'iç, *a.* Pertaining to hylozoism.

hȳ-lō-zō'ișm, *n.* [*Hylo-*, and Gr. *zōē*, life, and *-ism*.] The doctrine that matter possesses a species of life, or that matter and life are inseparable.

hȳ-lō-zō'ist, *n.* One who holds that every particle of matter has a species of life or animation inseparable from it.

hȳ'mär, *n.* A wild ass, found in Persia; the onager.

Hȳ'men, *n.* [L., from Gr. *Hymēn* (*-enos*), god of marriage.]

1. In ancient mythology, a fabulous deity, the son of Bacchus and Venus, or of Apollo and Urania, supposed to preside over marriages.

2. [h—] Marriage or the state of marriage.

hȳ'men, *n.* [Gr. *hymēn*, a membrane.]

1. In anatomy, the virginal membrane.

2. In botany, the fine pellicle which incloses a flower in the bud.

Hȳ-men-æ'ȧ, *n.* [F. of L. *Hymenæus*, relating to Hymen, the god of marriage; so called from the leaf being formed of a pair of leaflets.] A genus of trees of the natural order *Leguminosæ*, all natives of tropical America. *Hymenæa Courbaril*, the locust-tree of the West Indies, grows to an enormous size, and lives to a very great age, some of the extant individuals being supposed to be older than the Christian era. The heartwood is very hard and tough, and is hence much valued for wheel-work, particularly for cogs. It is also valuable for posts, rails, and gates. It takes a fine polish, and is so heavy that a cubic foot weighs about 100 lbs. A valuable resin exudes from the trunk.

Hymenæa Courbaril.

hȳ-men-ē'ăl, hȳ-men-ē'ăn, *a.* [L. *Hymenæus*, relating to the god of marriage, from *Hymen*; Gr. *Hymēn*, Hymen.] Pertaining to marriage.

hȳ-men-ē'ăl, hȳ-men-ē'ăn, *n.* A marriage song.

hȳ-mē'ni-ăl, *a.* 1. In botany, of or relating to the hymenium.

2. In anatomy, indicating the hymen.

hȳ-me-niç'ō-lăr, *a.* Existing in the hymenium or on it.

hȳ-me-nif'ẽr-ous, *a.* [Gr. *hymenion*, a membrane, and L. *ferre*, to bear.] Possessing or developing a hymenium.

hȳ-mē'ni-um, *n.*; *pl.* **hȳ-mē'ni-ȧ** or **hȳ-mē'ni-umș.** [Gr. *hymenion*, dim. of *hymēn*, a membrane.] In botany, the fruit-bearing surface of certain fungi, as that of the gills of the mushroom.

hymeno-, hymen-. Combining forms from Gr. *hymēn* (*-enos*), skin, membrane, used in botany, medicine, anatomy, etc., to signify skin, membrane; as, *hymeno*mycetes, *hymenog*eny.

hȳ-men-og'e-ny, *n.* [*Hymeno-*, and Gr. *-genēs*, producing.] The production of artificial membranes by contact of two fluids, as albumen and fat, when the former gives a coating to the globules of the latter.

hȳ'men-oid, *a.* [Gr. *hymēn*, a membrane, and *eidos*, form.] In botany, resembling a hymenium.

hȳ"me-nō-mȳ'çēte, *n.* Any plant belonging to the suborder *Hymenomycetes*.

Hȳ"me-nō-mȳ-çē'tēș, *n.pl.* [*Hymeno-*, and Gr. *mykēs* (pl. *mykētes*), a mushroom.] The highest of the six great divisions of fungi, consisting of those species which are characterized by their reproductive organs, called the hymenium, being naked. This division contains the *Agaricus*, the *Polyporus*, and the jelly-like plants called *Tremella*.

hȳ"me-nō-mȳ-çē'toid, *a.* Having likeness to a hymenomycete.

hȳ"me-nō-mȳ-çē'tous, *a.* Of or relating to the hymenomycetes.

hȳ-men'ō-phōre, *n.* [*Hymeno-*, and Gr. *-phoros*, from *pherein*, to bear.] In botany, that part of a fungus covered by the hymenium.

hȳ-men-oph'ō-rum, *n.* [*Hymeno-*, and Gr. *-phoros*, from *pherein*, to bear.] In botany, the structure which bears the hymenium.

Hȳ"me-nō-phyl'lum, *n.* [*Hymeno-*, and Gr. *phyllon*, a leaf.] Filmy fern, a genus of ferns, including a large number of species with filmy pellucid fronds, found chiefly in hot, damp, tropical forests.

hȳ-men-op'tẽr, *n.* One of the *Hymenoptera*.

Hȳ-men-op'te-rȧ, *n.pl.* [Gr. *hymenopteros*, membrane-winged; *hymēn*, a membrane, and *pteron*, wing.] In entomology, a large order of insects having four membranous wings, and the tail of the female mostly armed with an ovipositor by means of which she perforates the bodies in which she deposits her eggs, or with a sharp needle-like sting with which she kills her enemies or renders them torpid. The order includes the bees, wasps, ants, ichneumon-flies, etc.

Hymenoptera (*Ichneumon grossarius*). *a, a,* Stigmata. *c,* Marginal or radial cell. *x x x,* Submarginal or cubital cells. *d,* Pedunculated abdomen. *o,* Ovipositor of female.

hȳ-men-op'tẽr-ăl, *a.* Hymenopterous.

hȳ-men-op'tẽr-ăn, *n.* Same as *Hymenopter*.

hȳ-men-op'tẽr-ous, *a.* Having the characteristics of the *Hymenoptera*; having membranous wings.

hymn (him), *n.* [AS. *hymen*, *ymen* (pl. *ymnas*); LL. *hymnus*; Gr. *hymnos*, a hymn, festive song, ode.] A song or ode in honor of God or in honor of some deity; a sacred lyric; a song of praise, adoration, or thanksgiving.

And when they had sung an *hymn*, they went out into the Mount of Olives.—Matt. xxvi. 30.

Admonishing one another in psalms and *hymns*. —Col. iii. 16.

hymn, *v.t.*; hymned (himd), *pt.*, *pp.*; hymning (him′ing *or* him′ning), *ppr.* 1. To praise in song; to worship by singing hymns.

2. To sing; to celebrate in song; as, they *hymn* their thanks.

hymn, *v.i.* To sing in praise or adoration.

hym′năl, *n.* A collection of hymns, generally for use in public worship; a hymn-book; a hymnary.

hym′năl, *a.* [LL. *hymnus*, a hymn, and *-al.*] Of or relating to hymns.

hym′nȧ-ry, *n.* A hymn-book.

hymn′-book, *n.* A book containing a collection of hymns.

hym′niç, *a.* Relating to hymns or sacred songs.

hymn′ing, *n.* The singing of hymns.

hym′nist, *n.* One who composes hymns.

hym′nō-dy, *n.* [LL. *hymnodia*; Gr. *hymnōdia*, the singing of a hymn; *hymnos*, a hymn, festive song, and *adein*, to sing.]

1. The art or practice of singing hymns.

2. Hymnology.

hym-nog′rȧ-phẽr, *n.* A writer of hymns, or one who writes on the subject of hymns.

hym-nog′rȧ-phy, *n.* [Gr. *hymnos*, a hymn, and *graphein*, to write.] The art of writing hymns.

hym-nol′ō-ġist, *n.* A composer of hymns; also, one versed in hymnology.

hym-nol′ō-ġy, *n.* [Gr. *hymnologia*, the science of hymns, from *hymnologos*, singing hymns; *hymnos*, a hymn, and *-logia*, from *legein*, to speak.] A collection of hymns; a body of sacred lyrics composed by several authors of a particular period or country; the collection of hymns used by a particular church or sect; hymns collectively; expert knowledge of hymns; a critical essay on hymns.

hymp′ne, *n.* [ME. form of *hymn.*] A hymn. [Obs.]

hynd′reste, *a.* [A form of *hinderest.*] Hindmost. [Obs.]

hyo-, **hy-**. Combining forms from Gr. *hyoeidēs*, shaped like the Gr. letter Y, upsilon, used in anatomy, zoölogy, etc., to indicate relation to the hyoid bone.

hȳ′ō-dont, *n.* In zoölogy, any fish belonging to the family *Hyodontidæ*.

Hȳ-ō-don′ti-dæ, *n.pl.* [*Hyo-*, and Gr. *odous*, *odontos*, a tooth.] A small family of fresh-water fishes, in general character resembling the salmon family.

Hȳ″ō-gȧ-noi′dē-ī, *n.pl.* [*Hyo-*, and Gr. *ganos*, bright, and *eidos*, form.] In zoölogy, a family of ganoid fishes, mostly small and inhabiting fresh water, as the bowfins and garpikes.

hȳ-ō-glos′săl, *a.* [*Hyo-*, and Gr. *glōssa*, tongue.] In anatomy, of or relating to the hyoid arch and the tongue; pertaining to the muscle on either side of the tongue joining it to the hyoid bone.

hȳ-ō-glos′sus, *n.* [*Hyo-*, and Gr. *glōssa*, tongue.] In anatomy, a flat muscle at either side of the base of the tongue by which the tongue is attached to the hyoid bone.

hȳ′oid, *a.* [Gr. *hyoeidēs*, shaped like the letter Y upsilon; Y, upsilon, and *eidos*, form.]

1. Shaped like the Greek letter upsilon (Y, *v*).

2. Denoting a bone which supports the tongue.

Hyoid arch; in anatomy, the branchial arch which joins the tongue on either side to the skull and which includes the hyoid bone.

Hyoid bone; the principal element and central part of the hyoid arch.

hȳ′oid, *n.* The hyoid bone.

hȳ-oid′ē-ăl, **hȳ-oid′ē-ăn**, *a.* Same as *Hyoid*.

hȳ″ō-man-dib′ū-lăr, *a.* [*Hyo-*, and LL. *mandibula*, a jaw.] In anatomy, relating to the hyoid arch and the lower jaw.

hȳ″ō-man-dib′ū-lăr, *n.* In anatomy, the upper part of the hyoid, which in fishes is joined to the skull.

hȳ′ō-men-tăl, *a.* [*Hyo-*, and L. *mentum*, the chin.] In anatomy, of or connected with the hyoid bone and the chin or front part of the lower jaw.

hȳ-ō-plas′trŏn, *n.* [*Hyo-*, and LL. *plastra*, a thin plate of metal.] In zoölogy, one of the second lateral pair of plates in the ventral shield of a turtle; called also *hyosternum*.

hȳ-os′cine, *n.* [*Hyoscyamus* and *-ine.*] In chemistry, an alkaloid isomeric and associated with hyoscyamine and extracted from henbane.

hȳ-os-cȳ′ȧ-mine, *n.* An alkaloid obtained from henbane, *Hyoscyamus niger*, and from the thorn-apple and the nightshade; it is poisonous, being isomeric with atropin, and has a sharp offensive taste.

Hȳ-os-cȳ′ȧ-mus, *n.* [L., from Gr. *hyoskyamos*, henbane, lit., hog-bean; *hys*, *hyos*, hog, and *kyamos*, a bean.]

1. A genus of plants of the nightshade family.

2. [h—] Any plant of this genus; specifically henbane.

hȳ-ō-stẽr′năl, *a.* [*Hyo-*, and Gr. *sternon*, the breast, chest.]

1. In anatomy, relating to the sternum and the hyoid bone.

2. In zoölogy, relating to the hyoplastron of a turtle.

hȳ-ō-stẽr′num, *n.* Same as *Hyoplastron*.

hȳ-ō-styl′iç, *a.* [*Hyo-*, and Gr. *stylos*, a pillar.] Having the jaws hung to the cranium by the hyomandibular part of the hyoid arch, as in fishes, not attached to the skull as in mammals.

hyp, *n.* [A contr. of *hypochondria.*] See *Hip*.

hyp-. See *Hypo-*.

hyp-æs-thē′si-ȧ, *n.* [*Hyp-*, and Gr. *aisthēsis*, sensation, perception.] Impaired susceptibility to sensation.

hȳ-pæ′thrăl, *a.* See *Hypethral*.

hyp-al-ġē′si-ȧ, *n.* [*Hyp-*, and Gr. *algēsis*, sense of pain, from *algein*, to suffer pain, from *algos*, pain.] Hypalgia.

hȳ-pal′ġi-ȧ, *n.* [*Hyp-*, and Gr. *algos*, pain.] Impaired capacity for sensations of pain.

hȳ-pal′lȧ-ġē, *n.* [Gr. *hypallagē*, an exchange, interchange, from *hypallassein*, to interchange; *hypo*, under, and *allassein*, to change.] In grammar, a figure consisting of a mutual change of cases; as, *dare classibus austros*, for *dare classes austris*.

hȳ-pan-i-sog′nȧ-thous, *a.* [*Hyp-*, and Gr. *anisos*, unequal, uneven, and *gnathos*, jaw.] Characterized by teeth on the under jaw narrower than those on the upper jaw.

hȳ-pan′thi-um, *n.* [*Hyp-*, and Gr. *anthos*, flower.] In botany, a fruit or flower having its axis enlarged under the calyx, as the pear or the calycanthus.

hȳ-pan-thō′di-um, *n.*; *pl.* **hȳ-pan-thō′di-ȧ.** [*Hyp-*, and Gr. *anthōdēs*, like flowers, flowery; *anthos*, flower, and *eidos*, form.] In botany, the syconium.

hȳ″pȧ-pō-phyș′i-ăl, *a.* Of or belonging to a hypapophysis.

hȳ-pȧ-poph′y-sis, *n.*; *pl.* **hȳ-pȧ-poph′y-sēș.** [*Hyp-* and Gr. *apophysis*, sprout, process.] In anatomy, a median outgrowth or process on the ventral side of a vertebra.

hȳ-pär-tē′ri-ăl, *a.* [*Hyp-*, and Gr. *artēria*, artery.] Beneath an artery.

hȳ-pas′pist, *n.* [Gr. *hypaspistēs*, a shield-bearer; *hypo*, under, and *aspis*, a shield.] A shield-bearer, especially one of the Macedonian royal guard.

hȳ-pax′i-ăl, *a.* [*Hyp-*, and L. *axis*, an axle, axis.] In anatomy, situated beneath or ventrally from the vertebræ.

hȳ-pẽr-. A prefix from Gr. *hyper* (prep.), over, above, in behalf of, concerning; it usually implies excess or transcendence; (a) in chemistry, it denotes the highest in a series of compounds; as, *hyper*chloric acid; (b) in ancient music, it denotes the modes or scales beginning at the highest point, and also, in respect to intervals, ascending measure; upward; as, *hyper*diapente, *hyper*diapason; (c) it distinguishes certain ecclesiastical modes, as *hyper*dorian, *hyper*phrygian, from those beginning with *hypo-*.

hȳ″pẽr-ȧ-cid′i-ty, *n.* Extreme or excessive acidity.

hȳ-pẽr-æ′mi-ȧ, *n.* Same as *H. peremia*.

hȳ-pẽr-æ′miç, *a.* Same as *Hyperemic*.

hȳ″pẽr-æs-thē′si-ȧ, *n.* [*Hyper-*, and Gr. *aisthēsis*, perception, sensation.] Morbid or excessive sensibility.

hȳ″pẽr-æs-thet′iç, *a.* Same as *Hyperesthetic*.

hȳ″pẽr-al-ġē′si-ȧ, *n.* [*Hyper-*, and Gr. *algēsis*, sense of pain.] Abnormal susceptibility to the influence of pain.

hȳ″pẽr-al-ġē′siç, *a.* Of or relating to hyperalgesia.

hȳ-pẽr-ap-ō-phyș′i-ăl, *a.* Of, relating to, or like a hyperapophysis.

hȳ″pẽr-ȧ-poph′y-sis, *n.*; *pl.* **hȳ″pẽr-ȧ-poph′y-sēș.** [*Hyper-*, and Gr. *apophysis*, a sprout, process.] A process on the dorsal side of a neural spine, locking the vertebra with the one next below.

hȳ-pẽr-as′pist, *n.* [Gr. *hyperaspistēs*, one who holds a shield over, a protector; *hyper*, over, and *aspis*, a shield.] In Greek armies, one who held a shield to protect another; hence, a defender.

hȳ-pẽr-bat′iç, *a.* Transposed; inverted.

hȳ-pẽr′bȧ-ton, *n.*; *pl.* **hȳ-pẽr′bȧ-tȧ.** [L., from Gr. *hyperbatos*, transposed, from *hyperbainein*, to step over; *hyper*, over, and *bainein*, to go.] In rhetoric, inversion; a transposition or change in the usual grammatical order of words or clauses, as "broad is the way" for "the way is broad." It is the principal difference in diction between prose and poetry.

hȳ-pẽr′bō-lȧ, *n.* [Gr. *hyperbolē*, a throwing beyond, excess, as the angle the cutting plane makes with the base, from *hyperballein*, to throw beyond; *hyper*, over, beyond, and *ballein*, to throw.]

1. In geometry, a curve formed by cutting a cone in a direction parallel to its axis, or so that the cutting plane makes a greater angle with the base than the side of the cone makes, and when produced cuts also the opposite cone, or the cone which is the continuation of the former, on the opposite side of the vertex, thus producing another hyperbola, which is called the opposite hyperbola to the former.

2. In general, an algebraic curve the number of whose asymptotes is greater by one than the number of its order.

Hyperbola.

D B E, G A H, opposite hyperbolas; F, *f*, foci; C, center; A B, transverse axis; *a b*, conjugate axis; N C P, a diameter.

hȳ-pẽr′bō-lē, *n.* [Gr. *hyperbolē*, a throwing beyond, excess, from *hyperballein*, to throw beyond or over; *hyper*, over, beyond, and *ballein*, to throw.] In rhetoric, a figure of speech consisting of an exaggeration not intended to deceive but to add force to a statement; a figurative representation of anything as being much greater or less than the reality; as, he was so gaunt, the case of a flageolet was a mansion for him.

hȳ-pẽr-bol′iç, **hȳ-pẽr-bol′iç-ăl**, *a.* 1. Belonging to the hyperbola; having the nature of the hyperbola.

2. Relating to or containing hyperbole; exaggerating or diminishing beyond the fact; exceeding the truth; as, a *hyperbolical* expression.

Hyperbolic functions; functions of the hyperbola corresponding to the trigonometric functions of a circle, as the hyperbolic sine, secant, etc.

Hyperbolic logarithms; the Napierian or natural system of logarithms whose base is 2.7182818.

hȳ-pẽr-bol′iç-ăl-ly, *adv.* 1. In the form of a hyperbola.

2. With exaggeration; in a manner to express more or less than the truth.

hȳ-pẽr-bol′i-form, *a.* [Gr. *hyperbolē*, a hyperbola, and L. *forma*, form.] Having the form of a hyperbola.

hȳ-pẽr′bō-lișm, *n.* The use of hyperbole.

hȳ-pẽr′bō-list, *n.* One who uses hyperbole.

hȳ-pẽr′bō-līze, *v.t.* and *v.i.*; hyperbolized, *pt.*, *pp.*; hyperbolizing, *ppr.* I. *v.t.* To exaggerate.

II. *v.i.* To speak or write with hyperbole.

hȳ-pẽr′bō-loid, *n.* [Gr. *hyperbolē*, a hyperbola, and *eidos*, form.]

1. A quadric surface having one or more of its plane sections hyperbolas; also, a solid having such a surface.

2. A hyperbola of one of the higher orders.

hȳ″pẽr-bō-loi′dăl, *a.* Of or resembling a hyperboloid.

Hȳ-pẽr-bō′rē-ăn, *a.* [LL. *Hyperboreanus*, from *hyperboreus*; Gr. *hyperboreos*, beyond the north wind; *hyper*, over, beyond, and *boreas*, the north wind.]

1. Of or belonging to the Hyperboreans.

2. [h—] Belonging to or inhabiting a region very far north; arctic; also, very cold; frigid.

Hȳ-pẽr-bō′rē-ăn, *n.* 1. In Greek mythology, one of a race favored by the gods, inhabiting a realm beyond the north wind in unending peace, youth, and pleasure.

2. [h—] An inhabitant of the most northern region of the earth.

hȳ-pẽr-cär′bū-ret-ed, *a.* 1. Having the largest proportion of carbon; formerly said of bicarbonates.

2. Having gaseous hydrocarbons in excess; said of water-gas.

hȳ″pẽr-cat-ȧ-lec′tiç, *a.* [Gr. *hyperkatalēktos*; *hyper*, over, beyond, and *katalēktos*, stopping off, incomplete, from *katalēgein*, to cease.] In prosody, having an extra syllable or two beyond the regular measure.

hȳ″pẽr-çȧ-thär′sis, *n.* [Gr. *hyperkatharsis*, excessive purging; *hyper*, over, beyond, and *kathairein*, to purge, purify.] Excessive catharsis.

hȳ-pẽr-ċhlō′riç, *a.* Same as *Perchloric*.

hȳ-pẽr-ċhō′li-ȧ, *n.* [*Hyper-*, and Gr. *cholē*, bile.] The secretion of an excessive quantity of bile.

hȳ″pẽr-ċhrō-mā′si-ȧ, *n.* [*Hyper-*, and Gr. *chrōma*, color.] Abnormal pigmentation of the skin.

hȳ-pẽr-ċhrō′mȧ-tișm, *n.* The state of having abnormally intensified coloration.

hȳ″pẽr-ċhrō-mȧ-tō′sis, *n.* Same as *Hyperchromasia*.

hȳ-pẽr-çor′ȧ-çoid, *n.* [*Hyper-*, and Gr. *korakoeidēs*, shaped like a crow's beak; *korax (-akos)*, crow, and *eidos*, form.] In ichthyology, the scapula.

hȳ-pẽr-ċrit′iç, *n.* [*Hyper-*, and Gr. *kritikos*, a critic; properly an adj., able to discern or decide, from *krinein*, to decide, judge.] One who is critical beyond measure or reason; an over-rigid critic; a captious censor.

hȳ-pẽr-ċrit′iç, *a.* Same as *Hypercritical*.

hȳ-pẽr-ċrit′iç-ăl, *a.* 1. Overcritical; critical beyond reason; captious; as, a *hypercritical* reader.

2. Excessively nice or exact; as, a *hypercritical* statement. [Rare.]

hȳ-pẽr-crit′iç-ăl-ly, *adv.* In a hypercritical manner.

hȳ-pẽr-crit′i-çism, *n.* Excessive rigor of criticism; an exaggerated exercise of the critical faculties.

hȳ-pẽr-crit′i-çīze, *v.t.*; hypercriticized, *pt.*, *pp.*; hypercriticizing, *ppr.* To criticize harshly or with undue severity.

hȳ″pẽr-daç-tyl′i-ȧ, hȳ-pẽr-daç′tyl-y, *n.* Same as *Polydactylism.*

hȳ″pẽr-di-crot′iç, *a.* In physiology, relating to hyperdicrotism.

hȳ-pẽr-di′crō-tism, *n.* [*Hyper-*, and Gr. *dis*, twice, and *krotein*, to knock, beat.] In physiology, an excessive duplication of the beats in the arterial pulse.

hȳ-pẽr-di′crō-tous, *a.* Same as *Hyperdicrotic.*

hȳ″pẽr-dū-li′ȧ, *n.* [*Hyper-*, and Gr. *douleia*, service.] The worship offered by Roman Catholics to the Virgin Mary, so called because higher than that given to other saints (which is known as *dulia*), though inferior to *latria*, the worship due to God alone.

hȳ′pẽr-dū-ly, *n.* [Obs.] See *Hyperdulia.*

hȳ″pẽr-dȳ-nam′i-ȧ, *n.* [Gr. *hyperdynamos*, of higher power; *hyper*, over, above, and *dynamis*, power.] In medicine, excessive functional energy; overexcitement of nervous or muscular action.

hȳ″pẽr-el-lip′tiç, *a.* [*Hyper-*, and Gr. *elleiptikos*, defective, from *elleipein*, to leave in, fall short.] In mathematics, beyond what is elliptic.

hȳ-pẽr-ē′mi-ȧ, *n.* [*Hyper-*, and Gr. *haima*, blood.] An excess of blood in any one part of the body.

hȳ-pẽr-ē′miç, *a.* Affected with hyperemia.

hȳ″pẽr-es-thē′si-ȧ, *n.* Same as *Hyperæsthesia.*

hȳ″pẽr-es-thet′iç, *a.* Abnormally sensitive.

hȳ-pẽr-ġen′e-sis, *n.* [*Hyper-*, and Gr. *genesis*, generation, production.] In medicine, abnormal increase of tissue; overgrowth.

hȳ″pẽr-ġē-ō-met′riç, *a.* Pertaining to hypergeometry.

hȳ″pẽr-ġē-om′e-try, *n.* [*Hyper-*, and Gr. *geōmetria*; *gē*, land, the earth, and *metrein*, to measure.] Geometry which assumes more than three dimensions of space.

Hȳ″pẽr-i-çā′cē-æ, *n.pl.* [*Hypericum* and *-aceæ.*] A natural order of plants of which the genus *Hypericum* is the type.

hȳ″pẽr-i-çā′ceous, *a.* Of or pertaining to the *Hypericaceæ.*

Hȳ-per′i-cum, *n.* [L., from Gr. *hypereikon*, St.-John's-wort; *hypo*, under, and *ereikē*, heath, heather.]

1. A genus of herbaceous plants, usually with dotted leaves and pentamerous yellow flowers. *Hypericum perforatum*, St.-John's-wort, is one of the most common plants of this genus.

2. [h—] Any plant of this genus.

Hypericum calycinum.

hȳ-pẽr-i-dē-ā′tion, *n.* [*Hyper-*, and Gr. *idea*, idea, from *idein*, to see.] Too rapid evolution of ideas; excess of mentality.

hȳ″pẽr-i-nō′sis, *n.* [*Hyper-*, and Gr. *is*, *inos*, strength, fiber.] In medicine, an abnormally fibrinous state of the blood; opposed to *hypinosis.*

Hȳ-pē′ri-ŏn, *n.* In Grecian mythology, the god of the sun, distinguished for his beauty; afterward identified with Apollo.

hȳ″pẽr-ki-nē′si-ȧ, *n.* Same as *Hyperkinesis.*

hȳ″pẽr-ki-nē′sis, *n.* [*Hyper-*, and Gr. *kinēsis*, movement, from *kinein*, to move.] In medicine, abnormal acceleration of muscular movement.

hȳ″pẽr-ki-net′iç, *a.* Related to or resembling hyperkinesis.

hȳ-pẽr-met-ȧ-mor′phō-sis, *n.* [*Hyper-*, and Gr. *metamorphōsis*, a transformation; *meta*, with, over, and *morphē*, form.] In entomology, a kind of metamorphism in which more than the usual number of changes takes place; in some insects the larva itself is more than once completely metamorphosed.

hȳ-pẽr′me-tẽr, *n.* [LL., from Gr. *hypermetros*, going beyond the meter, beyond measure; *hyper*, over, beyond, and *metron*, a measure.]

1. Anything greater than the ordinary standard of measure.

2. In prosody, a verse containing a redundant syllable.

hȳ-pẽr-met′riç, hȳ-pẽr-met′riç-ăl, *a.* Exceeding the common measure; having a redundant syllable.

hȳ-pẽr-met′rōpe, *n.* A person affected with farsightedness.

hȳ″pẽr-me-trō′pi-ȧ, hȳ-pẽr-met′rō-py, *n.* [Gr. *hypermetros*, beyond measure, excessive, and *ōps*, *ōpos*, eye.] A state of imperfect vision resulting from the focusing of parallel rays of light at a point beyond the retina of the eye; called also *longsightedness*, and corrected by the use of convex glasses.

hȳ″pẽr-me-trop′iç, *a.* Pertaining to hypermetropia.

hȳ-pẽrm-nē′si-ȧ, *n.* [*Hyper-*, and Gr. *mnēsis*, remembrance.] Extraordinary power in remembering or recollecting.

hȳ″pẽr-myr″i-ō-rä′mȧ, *n.* [*Hyper-*, and Gr. *myrios*, countless, and *horama*, a view, from *horān*, to see.] A show or panorama exhibiting many objects or scenes.

hȳ′pẽr-niç, *n.* [*Hyper-*, and *Nicaragua* wood.] Nicaragua dyewood, any red dyewood extract.

Hȳ″pẽr-ō-är′ti-ȧ (-shi-ȧ), *n.pl.* [Gr. *hyperōos*, being above, upper, and *artios*, complete, perfect.] In zoölogy, an order of marsipobranchiate lampreys, having many teeth and the nasal aperture in the top of the head and without connection with the mouth.

Hȳ-pẽr-ō′ō-don, *n.* [Gr. *hyperōos*, being above, upper, and *odous*, *odontos*, a tooth.] A genus of whales including the bottlenose whale.

hȳ-pẽr-ō′pi-ȧ, *n.* Same as *Hypermetropia.*

hȳ-pẽr-op′iç, *a.* Pertaining to hyperopia or hypermetropia.

hȳ″pẽr-ō-rex′i-ȧ, *n.* [*Hyper-*, and Gr. *orexis*, desire, appetite, from *oregein*, to reach out, desire.] In medicine, an inordinate craving for food; unsatisfiable appetite; voracity.

hȳ″pẽr-ọr-gan′iç, *a.* [*Hyper-*, and Gr. *organikos*, of or pertaining to organs, from *organon*, an organ.] Outside and beyond the realm of the organic; unclassified and unclassifiable.

hȳ-pẽr-ọr′thō-dox-y, *n.* [*Hyper-*, and Gr. *orthodoxia*, orthodoxy; *orthos*, right, true, and *doxa*, opinion, judgment, from *dokein*, to think.] Orthodoxy indulged to excess.

Hȳ″pẽr-ō-trē′tȧ, Hȳ″pẽr-ō-trē′tī, *n.pl.* [Gr. *hyperōe*, the palate, and *trētos*, perforated.] An order of fishes belonging to the class *Marsipobranchia.*

hȳ-pẽr-ox′id, hȳ-pẽr-ox′ide, *n.* [Obs.] See *Peroxid.*

hȳ-pẽr-ox′y-ġen-ā-ted, hȳ-pẽr-ox′y-ġen-ized, *a.* Containing in combination a supersaturation with oxygen. [Obs.]

hȳ-pẽr-ox-y-mū′ri-āte, *n.* [Obs.] See *Perchlorate.*

hȳ-pẽr-ox-y-mū-ri-at′iç, *a.* [Obs.] See *Perchloric.*

hȳ-pẽr-par′ȧ-sīte, *n.* [*Hyper-*, and Gr. *parasitos*, eating beside, a parasite.] In biology, a parasite of a parasite, as larvæ living in and feeding on other larvæ.

hȳ-pẽr-pep′si-ȧ (*or* -shȧ), *n.* [*Hyper-*, and Gr. *pepsis*, digestion.] In medicine, a kind of indigestion in which an excessive quantity of chlorids is contained in the gastric fluids.

hȳ-pẽr-phā′şi-ȧ (-zhi-), *n.* [*Hyper-*, and Gr. *phasis*, a speaking, from *phanai*, to speak.] In medicine, loss of control of the organs of articulation; uncontrollable utterance.

hȳ-pẽr-phyş′iç-ăl, *a.* [*Hyper-*, and Gr. *physikos*, natural, pertaining to nature, from *physis*, nature.] Supernatural; superior to physical laws.

hȳ-pẽr-plā′şi-ȧ, *n.* [*Hyper-*, and Gr. *plasis*, a forming, from *plassein*, to form, mold.] In pathology, excessive formation of tissue; an increase in the size of a tissue or organ owing to an increase in the number of cells; distinguished from *hypertrophy.*

hȳ-pẽr-plas′iç, *a.* Hyperplastic.

hȳ-pẽr-plas′tiç, *a.* Pertaining to hyperplasia.

hȳ-pẽr-pnœ′ȧ (-nē′), *n.* [*Hyper*, and Gr. *pnoē*, *pnoiē*, breath.] In pathology panting or exaggerated respiration.

hȳ″pẽr-pȳ-rex′i-ȧ, *n.* [*Hyper-*, and Gr. *pyressein*, to be feverish, from *pyretos*, fever.] In pathology, excessively high body-temperature. By some the term is used only when the temperature is above 106° Fahr.

hȳ″pẽr-sär-çō′mȧ, *n.*; *pl.* **hȳ″pẽr-sär-çō′mȧ-tȧ.** [Gr. *hypersarkōma*, overgrown flesh; *hyper*, over, and *sarx*, *sarkos*, flesh.] In pathology, proud or fungous flesh.

hȳ″pẽr-sär-çō′sis, *n.* See *Hypersarcoma.*

hȳ″pẽr-sē-crē′tion, *n.* [*Hyper-*, and L. *secretio* (*-onis*), a dividing, separation.] In pathology, excessive secretion.

hȳ-pẽr-sen′sū-ăl (-shū-), *a.* Supersensual.

hȳ′pẽr-spāce, *n.* [*Hyper-*, and L. *spatium*, space.] An imaginary space regarded as having more than three dimensions.

hȳ′pẽr-stēne, *n.* See *Hypersthene.*

hȳ′pẽr-sthēne, *n.* [*Hyper-*, and Gr. *sthenos*, strength; so called from its difficult frangibility.] An orthorhombic brownish-green, grayish or greenish-black, or pinchbeck brown foliated brittle mineral of nearly pearly luster. Being first found on the coast of Labrador, it was called *Labrador hornblende.*

hȳ-pẽr-sthē′ni-ȧ, *n.* [*Hyper-*, and Gr. *sthenos*, strength.] In pathology, a condition of abnormal excitement of the vital phenomena.

hȳ-pẽr-sthen′iç, *a.* Relating to hypersthenia; overstimulated.

hȳ-pẽr-sthen′iç, *a.* Composed of or containing hypersthene.

hȳ-pẽr-sthē′nīte, *n.* A dark-colored granite-like rock composed of hypersthene and labradorite.

hȳ-pẽr′thē-sis, *n.* [Gr. *hyperthesis*, a passing over, transposition, from *hypertithenai*; *hyper*, over, and *tithenai*, to set, put.]

1. In philology, the removal of a letter from the syllable to which it originally belonged to another syllable immediately preceding or following it; a species of transposition or metathesis; thus, in Greek, *melaina* is used for *melania.*

2. In the Greek church, an additional fast.

hȳ-pẽr-thet′iç-ăl, *a.* [Gr. *hyperthetikos*, superlative; *hyper*, over, and *tithenai*, to place.] Superlative. [Obs.]

hȳ-pẽr-thyr′i-ŏn, *n.* [Gr. *hyperthyrion*; *hyper*, over, and *thyra*, door.] In architecture, that part of the architrave which is over a door or window.

hȳ″pẽr-tri-chō′sis, *n.* [*Hyper-*, and Gr. *thrix*, *trichos*, hair, and *-osis*.] Excessive growth of hair of a part or the whole of the body.

hȳ-pẽr-tri-di-men′sion-ăl, *a.* Having more than three dimensions.

hȳ-pẽr-troph′iç, *a.* Producing or tending to produce hypertrophy; of or pertaining to hypertrophy.

hȳ-pẽr-troph′iç-ăl, *a.* Hypertrophic.

hȳ-pẽr′trō-phous, *a.* Exhibiting hypertrophy.

hȳ-pẽr′trō-phy, *v.t.* and *v.i.*; hypertrophied, *pt.*, *pp.*; hypertrophying, *ppr.* To cause to become hypertrophous; to become hypertrophous.

hȳ-pẽr′trō-phy, *n.* [*Hyper-*, and Gr. *trophē*, nutrition, from *trephein*, to nourish.]

1. An increase in the size of a tissue or organ independent of the general growth of the body; opposed to *atrophy.*

2. In botany, the excessive development of one part of a plant to the detriment of another.

3. Any abnormal growth.

hȳ-pẽr-typ′iç, *a.* Surpassing the type.

hȳ-pẽr-typ′iç-ăl, *a.* Hypertypic.

hȳ-pē′thrăl, hȳ-pæ′thrăl, *a.* [L. *hypæthrus*; Gr. *hypaithros*; *hypo*, under, and *aithēr*, the sky.] Without a roof; open to the sky; applied to a roofless building or an inclosed place.

hȳ′phȧ, *n.*; *pl.* **hȳ′phæ.** [Gr. *hyphē*, a weaving, a web, from *hyphainein*, to weave.] In botany, (a) the mycelium or spawn of certain fungi; (b) the filamentous fleshy watery thallus of certain fungoid plants.

hȳ′phăl, *a.* In botany, relating to or of the nature of a hypha.

hȳ-phē′mi-ȧ, hȳ-phæ′mi-ȧ, *n.* [Gr. *hyphaimos*, suffused with blood, bloodshot; *hypo*, under, and *haima*, blood.]

1. Deficiency of blood.

2. Extravasation of blood.

hȳ′phen, *n.* [LL., from Gr. *hyphen*, a hyphen, lit., under one; *hypo*, under, and *hen*, neut. acc. of *heis*, one.] A mark (- or ₌) made between two words to show that they form a compound word, or are to be connected, as in *five-leaved*, *bold-faced*. It is used to connect the syllables of a divided word, and is placed after the syllable that closes a line, denoting the connection of that syllable, or part of a word, with the first syllable of the next line. It is also used to connect the elements of a syllabified word.

hȳ′phen, *v.t.*; hyphened, *pt.*, *pp.*; hyphening, *ppr.* To join by a hyphen, as two words, so as to form a compound word.

hȳ′phen-āte, *v.t.*; hyphenated, *pt.*, *pp.*; hyphenating, *ppr.* To hyphen.

hȳ-phen-ā′tion, *n.* The act of hyphening or the state of being hyphened.

hȳ-phen′iç, *a.* Of or pertaining to the hyphen.

hȳ-phen-i-zā′tion, *n.* Hyphenation.

hȳ′phen-īze, *v.t.* To hyphen.

hȳ-pher′e-sis, hȳ-phær′e-sis, *n.* [Gr. *hyphairesis*, a taking away, from *hyphairein*, to take away from under; *hypo*, under, and *hairein*, to take.] In philology, the act of removing a letter or syllable from a word.

hȳ′phō-drōme, *a.* [Gr. *hyphē*, a web, and *dromos*, a running.] In botany, said of leaves in which the veins are partially or wholly concealed in the mesophyl.

Hȳ″phō-mȳ-cē′tēs, *n.pl.* [Gr. *hyphē*, a web, and *mykēs*, *mykētos*, a mushroom.] In botany, a division of fungi with naked spores, often septate, and a floccose thallus. It is composed of microscopic plants growing as molds over dead or living organic substances.

hȳ-phō-mȳ-cē′tous, *a.* Pertaining to, relating to, or characteristic of the *Hyphomycetes* or microscopic vegetable molds; as, *hyphomycetous* fungi.

hypi-. See *Hypo-.*

hȳ-pid″i-ō-mor′phiç, *a.* [*Hypi-*, and Gr. *idiomorphos*, of peculiar form; *idios*, peculiar, and *morphē*, form.] In crystallography, idiomorphic in part.

hȳ-pid″i-ō-mor′phiç-ăl-ly, *adv.* In a hypidiomorphic manner.

hyp-i-nō′sis, *n.* [*Hypi-*, and Gr. *is*, *inos*, strength, fiber.] In pathology, a diminished amount of fibrin in the blood; opposed to *hyperinosis*.

hyp-i-not′iç, *a.* Lacking fibrin; characterized by hypinosis.

hypn-. See *Hypno-*.

hyp-nȧ-goġ′iç, *a.* [*Hypn-*, and Gr. *agōgē*, a leading, from *agein*, to lead.] Leading to sleep; hypnotic.

hypno-, hypn-. Combining forms from Gr. *hypnos*, sleep, used to signify sleep or hypnotism; as, *hypno*phobia, *hypno*genesis.

hyp′nō-bāte, *n.* [*Hypno-*, and Gr. *bainein*, to go.] A somnambulist; a sleepwalker. [Rare.]

hyp-nō-bā′ti-ȧ, *n.* Somnambulism.

hyp′nō-cyst, *n.* [*Hypno-*, and Gr. *kystis*, a bladder.] In biology, a dormant encysted protozoan which does not form spores.

hyp-nō-ġen′e-sis, *n.* [*Hypno-*, and Gr. *genesis*, generation, production.] The production of a hypnotic condition.

hyp-nō-ġē-net′iç, *a.* Hypnogenous.

hyp-nō-ġē-net′iç-ăl, *a.* Hypnogenetic.

hyp-nō-ġen′iç, *a.* Same as *Hypnogenous*.

hyp-noġ′e-nous, *a.* [*Hypno-*, and Gr. *-genēs*, producing.] Producing or inducing sleep; inducing hypnotism.

hyp-noġ′e-ny, *n.* Hypnogenesis.

hyp-nō-log′iç-ăl, *a.* Relating to hypnology.

hyp-nol′ō-gist, *n.* One versed in hypnology.

hyp-nol′ō-gy, *n.* [*Hypno-*, and Gr. *-logia*, from *legein*, to speak.] The study or doctrine of the phenomena accompanying sleep; a treatise or discourse on sleep.

hyp′nōne, *n.* [Gr. *hypnos*, sleep, and *-one*.] A compound possessing hypnotic and antiseptic properties, resulting from the action of zinc methyl upon benzoyl chlorid.

hyp-nō-phō′bi-ȧ, *n.* [*Hypno-*, and Gr. *phobos*, fear.] Morbid fear of sleep.

hyp′nō-sçōpe, *n.* [*Hypno-*, and Gr. *skopein*, to view.] An instrument in the form of a small hollow magnet used to determine to what extent a person is susceptible to hypnotic influence.

hyp-nō′sis, *n.* [Gr. *hypnos*, sleep, and *-osis*.]
1. The condition produced by hypnotizing.
2. The production of sleep; also, the gradual approach of sleep.

hyp-nō-spō-rañġe′, *n.* Same as *Hypnosporangium*.

hyp″nō-spō-ran′ġi-um, *n.*; *pl.* **hyp″nō-spō-ran′ġi-ȧ.** [*Hypno-*, and Gr. *spora*, a spore, and *angeion*, a cup.] In botany, a sporangium containing or producing hypnospores

hyp′nō-spōre, *n.* [*Hypno-*, and Gr. *spora*, a spore, generation.] In botany, a resting spore; a spore that requires a period of repose, or quiescence, before germinating.

hyp-not′iç, *a.* [Gr. *hypnōtikos*, tending to sleep, from *hypnos*, sleep.]
1. Having the quality of producing sleep; tending to produce sleep; soporific.
2. Relating to hypnotism; subject to or under the influence of hypnotism.

hyp-not′iç, *n.* 1. A medicine that produces or tends to produce sleep; an opiate; a soporific.
2. One who may be put into a hypnotic condition or who is in that condition.

hyp′nō-tiṣm, *n.* [Gr. *hypnos*, sleep.] An abnormal condition of the mind induced by artificial means, in which the person affected is controlled entirely, in both thought and action, by the will and commands of another; a passive mental condition; a kind of artificial catalepsy; induced somnambulism.

hyp′nō-tist, *n.* One who hypnotizes.

hyp-nō-tis′tiç, *a.* Pertaining to or inducing hypnotism.

hyp-nō-tī′zȧ-ble, *a.* Susceptible to hypnotizing influences; as, a hysterical and *hypnotizable* girl.

hyp″nō-ti-zā′tion, *n.* The act of hypnotizing, or the condition of a hypnotic.

hyp′nō-tīze, *v.t.*; hypnotized, *pt.*, *pp.*; hypnotizing, *ppr.* To put into a hypnotic state; to make hypnotic.

hyp′nō-ti-zēr, *n.* One who induces hypnotism.

hyp′nō-toid, *a.* [*Hypno-*, and Gr. *eidos*, form.] Similar to hypnotism in cause or in effect.

Hyp′num, *n.* [Gr. *hypnon*, moss.] In botany, a very large genus of mosses distributed through all parts of the world, and frequently found in a fossil state.

hypo-, hyp-, hypi-. A prefix from Gr. *hypo* (prefix), from *hypo* (prep.), under; used to signify primarily under, either in space or degree. In chemistry, it is used to indicate a lower place in a series of compounds, or inferior strength; as, *hypo*phosphate, *hypo*bromite. In ancient music, used of modes and scales, it signifies beginning at a lower point, usually a fourth below the authentic, as in *hypo*dorian, *hypo*lydian; used of intervals, it signifies measured downward, as in *hypo*diapente. *Hypo-* is the opposite of *hyper-*.

hy̆′pō, *n.* An abbreviation of hypochondria; low spirits; the blues. [Colloq.]

hy̆′pō, *n.* Among photographers, an abbreviation of sodium hyposulphite.

hy̆-pō-ā′ri-ăn, *a.* In anatomy, relating to a hypoarion.

hy̆-pō-ā′ri-ŏn, *n.*; *pl.* **hy̆-pō-ā′ri-ȧ.** [*Hypo-*, and Gr. *ōarion*, dim. of *ōon*, an egg.] One of a pair of oval-shaped ganglia lying beneath the optic lobes of typical fishes.

hy̆′pō-blast, *n.* [*Hypo-*, and Gr. *blastos*, a germ, shoot.] In biology, the innermost layer of the blastoderm; called also *endoblast*, *entoderm*, *endoderm*, and *hypoderm*; the opposite of *epiblast*.

hy̆-pō-blas′tiç, *a.* Pertaining to a hypoblast; endodermal.

hy̆-pob′ō-lē, *n.* [Gr. *hypobolē*, a throwing under, suggesting, from *hypoballein*, to throw under; *hypo*, under, and *ballein*, to throw.] In rhetoric, a figure in which several things are mentioned that seem to make against the argument, or in favor of the opposite side, each of them being then refuted in order.

hy̆-pō-brañ′çhi-ăl, *a.* [*Hypo-*, and Gr. *branchia*, gills.] Situated under the gills.

hy̆-pō-brañ′çhi-ăl, *n.* A bone or cartilage under the gills of fishes.

hy̆-pō-brō′mite, *n.* [*Hypo-*, and *bromous* and *-ite*.] In chemistry, a compound containing hypobromous acid.

hy̆-pō-brō′mous, *a.* [*Hypo-*, and Gr. *brōmos*, bad-smelling.] In chemistry, designating the acid producing hypobromites, which is a light yellow liquid of strong oxidizing action.

hy̆-pō-bū′li-ȧ, *n.* [*Hypo-*, and Gr. *boulē*, will.] Deficiency of will-power.

hy̆′pō-çärp, hy̆-pō-çär′pi-um, *n.* [*Hypo-*, and Gr. *karpos*, fruit.] In botany, the enlargement of the stem or receptacle beneath the fruit.

hy̆-pō-çär-pō-ġē′ăn, *a.* Same as *Hypogeal*.

hyp′ō-çaust, *n.* [L. *hypocaustum*; Gr. *hypokauston*, a room heated by a furnace below; *hypo*, under, and *kaiein*, to burn.] Among the Greeks and Romans, a subterraneous place containing a furnace to heat baths; in architecture, an arched fire-chamber from which heat is distributed to rooms above, hot-air flues being placed in the walls or beneath the floor.

hy̆″pō-çhlōr-hy̆′dri-ȧ, *n.* [*Hypo-*, and Gr. *chlōros*, green, and *hydōr*, water.] In medicine, a condition resulting from a deficiency of hydrochloric acid in the gastric juice.

hy̆-pō-çhlō′rite, *n.* [*Hypochlorous* and *-ite*.] In chemistry, a salt of hypochlorous acid. Calcium hypochlorite is the chief constituent of bleaching-powder.

hy̆-pō-çhlō′rous, *a.* [*Hypo-*, and Gr. *chlōros*, green.] In chemistry, designating compounds of chlorin having a lower valence than chlorous compounds.

Hypochlorous acid; in chemistry, an acid obtained by passing chlorin gas through water containing calcium carbonate in suspension.

hyp-ō-çhon′drēṣ (-dērz), *n.pl.* See *Hypochondrium*.

hyp-ō-çhon′dri-ȧ, *n.* [LL., from Gr. *hypochondria*, pl. of *hypochondrion*, the soft part of the body below the cartilage and above the navel; *hypo*, under, and *chondros*, cartilage; so called because the morbid condition was supposed to have its seat in this region.]
1. In medicine, a state of mental depression; despondency, usually regarding the patient's own state of health.
2. Low spirits; the blues; a pessimistic attitude of mind.

hyp-ō-çhon′dri-aç, hyp″ō-çhon-drī′ȧ-çăl, *a.* 1. Pertaining to the hypochondrium or the parts of the body so called; as, the *hypochondriac* region.
2. Affected, characterized, or produced by hypochondria

> The *hypochondriac*, melancholy complexion of us islanders. —Berkeley.

3. Producing melancholy or low spirits.

Hypochondriac region; in anatomy, a region on both sides of the abdomen under the cartilages of the false ribs and to the right and left of the epigastrium. Called also *hypochondres* and *hypochondria*.

hyp-ō-çhon′dri-aç, *n.* One affected with hypochondria.

hyp″ō-çhon-drī′ȧ-çăl, *a.* Same as *Hypochondriac*.

hyp″ō-çhon-drī′ȧ-çăl-ly, *adv.* In a hypochondriac manner.

hyp″ō-çhon-drī′ȧ-ciṣm, *n.* Same as *Hypochondria*.

hyp″ō-çhon-drī′ȧ-sis, *n.* Same as *Hypochondria*.

hyp-ō-çhon′dri-aṣm, *n.* Same as *Hypochondria*.

hyp-ō-çhon′dri-um, *n.*; *pl.* **hyp-ō-çhon′dri-ȧ.** [L. *hypochondrium*; Gr. *hypochondrion*; *hypo*, under, and *chondros*, cartilage.] In anatomy, one of the two lateral and superior regions of the abdomen under the cartilages of the false ribs, and to the right and left of the epigastrium. In the plural, also written *hypochondres*.

hyp-ō-çhon′dry, *n.* Same as *Hypochondrium*.

hyp′ō-çist, *n.* [Gr. *hypokistis*, a plant growing on the roots of the cistus; *hypo*, under, and *kistos*, the cistus.] An inspissated juice obtained from a plant, *Cytinus hypocistis*. It is an astringent, useful in diarrhea and hemorrhages.

hyp-ō-çli′di-um, *n.*; *pl.* **hyp-ō-çli′di-ȧ.** [*Hypo-*, and Gr. *kleidion*, a little key, dim. of *kleis*, a key.] A term for the median process at the junction of the clavicles of a bird, as shown in the wishbone of a chicken; also written *hypocleidium*.

hyp″ō-çō-ris′tiç, *a.* [Gr. *hypokoristikos*; *hypo*, under, and *korizesthai*, to caress.] Caressing; hence, designating a diminutive or a short pet name; as, Willie, the *hypocoristic* name of William.

hy̆-pō-çot′yl, *n.* [Abbrev. of *hypocotyledonous*.] In a dicotyledonous embryo, the part just below the cotyledons, constituting the caulicle.

hy̆-pō-çrā-ter′i-fọrm, *a.* [Gr. *hypokratērion*, the stand of a mixing-bowl, and L. *forma*, form.] Tubular below, but suddenly expanding into a flat border at top; salver-shaped.

hy̆″pō-çrā-ter-i-mor′phous, *a.* [Gr. *hypokratērion*, the stand of a mixing-bowl, and *morphē*, form.] With a slender tube below, but suddenly expanding into a broad salver-shaped border, as in the flower of phlox or lilac.

Hypocrateriform Corolla.

hy-poç′ri-sy, *n.* [LL. *hypocrisis*; Gr. *hypokrisis*, a reply, acting a part, feigning, from *hypokrinesthai*, to play a part, pretend; *hypo*, under, and *krinesthai*, to contend, dispute.] Simulation; a feigning to be what one is not; the acting of a false part; a deception as to real character and feeling, especially in regard to morals and religion; a counterfeit of religion; a condition of thought and feeling different from that which appears.

> Beware ye of the leaven of the Pharisees, which is *hypocrisy*. —Luke xii. 1.

Syn.—Deceit, deception, pharisaism, sanctimony, sham.

hyp′ō-çrite, *n.* [Gr. *hypokritēs*, one who answers, plays a part, a pretender, from *hypokrinesthai*, to answer, play a part; *hypo*, under, and *krinesthai*, to dispute, contend.]
1. One who feigns to be what he is not; especially, one who assumes an appearance of piety and virtue, when he is destitute of true religion.

> And the *hypocrite's* hope shall perish. —Job viii. 13.

2. A dissembler; one who assumes a false appearance; a false pretender.

> Fair *hypocrite*, you seek to cheat in vain. —Dryden.

hyp′ō-çrite-ly, *adv.* Deceptively. [Rare.]

hyp-ō-çrit′iç, *a.* Same as *Hypocritical*.

hyp-ō-çrit′iç-ăl, *a.* Proceeding from hypocrisy; having the qualities of a hypocrite; dissembling.

Syn.—Pharisaical, deceptive, sanctimonious, smug, smooth, dissembling, mealy, unctuous, mincing.

hyp-ō-çrit′iç-ăl-ly, *adv.* In a hypocritical manner.

hyp-ō-çrys′tăl-line, *a.* [*Hypo-*, and Gr. *krystallinos*, from *krystallos*, ice, crystal.] Having crystals imbedded in an amorphous groundmass.

hy̆-pō-cy̆′cloid, *n.* [*Hypo-*, and Gr. *kykloeidēs*; *kyklos*, circle, and *eidos*, form.] The line traced by a point in the circumference of a circle rolling on the concave side of the circumference of a stationary circle.

hyp-ō-daç′ty-lum, *n.*; *pl.* **hyp-ō-daç′ty-lȧ.** [*Hypo-*, and Gr. *dactylos*, a finger, a toe.] The under side of the toe of a bird; opposed to *acrodactylum*, the upper side.

hyp′ō-dērm, *n.* Same as *Hypoblast*.

hyp-ō-dēr′mȧ, *n.* [*Hypo-*, and Gr. *derma* (*-atos*), skin.] In botany, (a) the layer of tissue immediately under the epidermis of the stems of plants; (b) the layer of transparent cells beneath the epidermis of leaves; (c) the inside layer in the spore-case of a moss. In zoölogy, the cellular layer which underlies the crustlike covering of arthropods and annelids.

hyp″ō-dēr-mat′iç, *a.* Same as *Hypodermic*.

hyp″ō-dēr-mat′iç-ăl-ly, *adv.* Same as *Hypodermically*.

hyp-ō-dēr′miç, *a.* [*Hypo-*, and Gr. *derma* (*-atos*), skin.] Of or belonging to the tissues immediately under the dermis; subcutaneous; specifically applied to the method of introducing medicines under the skin; as, a *hypodermic* syringe.

hyp-ō-dēr′miç, *n.* 1. A remedy used hypodermically.
2. A hypodermic syringe.
3. A hypodermic injection.

hyp-ō-dēr′miç-ăl-ly, *adv.* In a hypodermic manner.

hyp-ō-dēr′mis, *n.* 1. In annelids, a thick tough layer under the cuticle.

2. In entomology, the soft lining of the abdominal walls of an insect.

3. In embryology, the hypoblast.

hyp-ō-ġæ′ăl, hyp-ō-ġæ′ăn, *a.* See *Hypogeal*, etc.

hyp-ō-ġæ′iç, *a.* [*Hypo-*, and Gr. *gē*, the earth.] Derived from or belonging to the peanut; as, *hypogæic* acid.

hȳ-pō-gas′triç, *a.* Of or relating to the hypogastrium; situated below the stomach.

hyp-ō-gas′tri-um, *n.* [Gr. *hypogastrion*, the lower belly, neut. of *hypogastrios*, abdominal; *hypo*, under, and *gastēr*, belly.] That part of the abdomen below the umbilical region, especially its central part.

hyp-ō-ġē′ăl, hyp-ō-ġæ′ăl, *a.* [LL. *hypogeus*, *hypogæus*; Gr. *hypogaios*, under the earth, underground; *hypo*, under, and *gē*, *gaia*, earth.] In botany, growing under the ground; pertaining to plants living and fructifying beneath the surface of the ground, as a truffle.

hyp-ō-ġē′ăn, hyp-ō-ġæ′ăn, *a.* Same as *Hypogeal*.

hyp′ō-ġēne, *a.* [*Hypo-*, and Gr. *-genēs*, from *gignesthai*, to be born.] In geology, formed beneath the surface of the earth; applied to rocks formed and crystallized at great depths beneath the surface; opposed to *epigene*.

hȳ-poġ′ō-nous, *a.* [*Hypo-*, and Gr. *-genēs*, from *gignesthai*, to be born.]

1. In botany, growing beneath; attached by growth to the under side; opposed to *epigenous*.

2. Hypogeal.

hyp-ō-ġē′ous, *a.* Same as *Hypogeal*.

hyp-ō-ġē′um, *n.* [L., from Gr. *hypogeion*, *hypogaion*, an underground chamber, properly neut. of *hypogeios*, or *hypogaios*, underground; *hypo*, under, and *gē*, or *gaia*, ground, earth.] In architecture, formerly, all the parts of a building which were underground, as the cellar, etc.; a subterranean apartment or passage, as the catacombs or the underground parts of an amphitheater.

hyp-ō-glos′săl, *a.* [*Hypo-*, and Gr. *glōssa*, tongue.] In anatomy, under the tongue; lying or arranged beneath the tongue; specifically applied to the motor nerve and associated parts of the tongue.

hyp-ō-glos′sis, *n.* [Gr. *hypoglōssis*; *hypo*, under, and *glōssa*, the tongue.]

1. In anatomy, the under part of the tongue; in entomology, a part of the second sclerite in coleopters.

2. In pathology, (a) a tumor under the tongue; (b) a pill, etc., to be dissolved beneath the tongue.

Hyp-ō-glos′sus, *n.* A genus of fishes including the halibut.

hyp-ō-glot′tis, *n.* Same as *Hypoglossis*.

hȳ-pog′nȧ-thous, *a.* [*Hypo-*, and Gr. *gnathos*, jaw.] Having the lower jaw or mandible longer than the upper; said of birds.

hyp′ō-ġyn, *n.* A hypogynous plant.

hȳ-poġ′y-nous, *a.* [*Hypo-*, and Gr. *gynē*, a woman, female.] In botany, growing from below the base of the ovary; having all or any of the floral organs situated below the ovary.

hȳ-pō-hȳ′ăl, *a.* [*Hypo-*, and *hy*oid, and *-al*.] In zoölogy, relating to a part of the hyoidean arch in the skeleton of fishes; as, a *hypohyal* bone.

hȳ″pō-ki-net′iç, *a.* [*Hypo-*, and Gr. *kinētikos*, from *kinein*, to move.] In physiology, having an insufficiency of muscular activity.

hȳ-pō-nas′tiç, *a.* Showing the effect of hyponasty.

hȳ′pō-nas-ty, *n.* [*Hypo-*, and Gr. *nastos*, close pressed, solid, from *nassein*, to press or squeeze close.] In botany, a condition characterized by more rapid growth on the lower than on the upper side of an organ, causing it to bend concavely above.

hȳ-pō-nī′trīte, *n.* [*Hyponitr*ous and *-ite*.] In chemistry, any salt produced by combination with a hyponitrous acid.

hȳ-pō-nī′trous, *a.* [*Hypo-*, and *nitro*gen, and *-ous*.] In chemistry, designating chemical derivatives from nitrogen with a lower valence than in nitrous compounds; less than nitrous.

Hyponitrous acid; an acid, HNO, whose salts are produced by reduction from nitrates, the acid itself being too unstable to be isolated and obtainable only in solution.

hyp′ō-nōme, *n.* [Gr. *hyponomē*, an underground passage, properly f. of *hyponomos*, underground; *hypo*, under, and *nemein*, to dwell.] In zoölogy, the pipe or passage in the structure of a cephalopod, used in locomotion by the reactionary force of water ejected.

hȳ″pō-phar-yn′ġē-ăl, *a.* [*Hypo-*, and Gr. *pharynx*, the throat.] In zoölogy, pertaining to the lower part of the pharynx, especially of insects.

hȳ-pō-phar′ynx, *n.* [*Hypo-*, and Gr. *pharynx*, the throat.] In some insects, a part attached to the lower side of the pharynx, sometimes having a long tongue-like extension.

hȳ-pō-phlœ′ō-dăl, *a.* Same as *Hypophlœodic*.

hȳ″pō-phlœ-od′iç, *a.* [*Hypo-*, and Gr. *phloios*, bark.] In lichenology, living under the bark of a plant; also, pertaining to tissues beneath the outer bark.

hȳ-pō-phlœ′ous, *a.* Same as *Hypophlœodic*.

hȳ-pō-phos′phāte, *n.* [*Hypophosph*orous and *-ate*.] In chemistry, a salt produced by the union of hypophosphoric acid with a base.

hȳ-pō-phos′phīte, *n.* [*Hypophosph*orous and *-ite*.] In chemistry, a salt produced by the union of hypophosphorous acid with a base.

hȳ″pō-phos-phor′iç, *a.* [*Hypophosphor*ous and *-ic*.] In chemistry, containing phosphorus with a lower valence than in phosphoric combinations; as, *hypophosphoric* acid.

Hypophosphoric acid; an acid, $P_2H_4O_6$, produced by slow oxidation of phosphorus in contact with water which holds it in solution.

hȳ-pō-phos′phŏr-ous, *a.* [*Hypo-*, and Gr. *phōsphoros*, lit., light bringer; *phōs*, light, and *pherein*, to bear.] In chemistry, designating compounds of phosphorus with less oxygen than that present in phosphorous acid.

Hypophosphorous acid; an acid, H_3PO_2, obtained from phosphorus.

hȳ-poph′y-ġē, *n.* [Gr. *hypophygē*, a refuge, recess; *hypo*, under, and *pheugein*, to flee.] In architecture, a feature of the Doric column consisting of a hollow curve beneath a member, as under a capital; an apophyge.

hȳ-poph′yl-lous, *a.* Same as *Hypogenous*, 1.

hȳ-pō-phys′i-ăl, *a.* [*Hypo-*, and Gr. *physikos*, physical.] In anatomy, relating to the hypophysis.

hȳ-poph′y-sis, *n.*; *pl.* **hȳ-poph′y-sēş.** [Gr. *hypophysis*, an undergrowth, process, from *hypophyein*; *hypo*, under, and *phyein*, to make to grow.]

1. The pituitary body of the brain.

2. In mosses, an enlargement in the pedicel at the base of the capsule.

3. In botany, a layer of cells in the embryo of flowering plants, from which the primary root and rootcap originate.

4. In medicine, an outgrowth.

hȳ-pō′pi-ăl, *a.* Relating to a hypopus.

hȳ-pō-plas′trŏn, *n.* [*Hypo-*, and LL. *plastra*, a thin plate of metal.] The third lateral division in the ventral shell of a turtle.

hȳ-pop′ti-lum, *n.*; *pl.* **hȳ-pop′ti-lȧ.** [*Hypo-*, and Gr. *ptilon*, a feather.] In ornithology, an additional feather springing from a feather; also, the hyporachis or stem of such a supplementary feather; called also *aftershaft*.

hyp′ō-pus (*or* **hī′pō-**), *n.* [*Hypo-*, and Gr. *pous*, *podos*, a foot.] An immature nymph of certain acaridans.

hȳ-pō-pyġ′i-ăl, *a.* Pertaining to the hypopygium.

hȳ-pō-pyġ′i-um, *n.*; *pl.* **hȳ-pō-pyġ′i-ȧ.** [Gr. *hypopygion*, the rump; *hypo*, under, and *pygē*, the buttocks.] In entomology, (a) the clasping-organ at the abdominal extremity of certain male dipterous insects; (b) the last visible ventral segment of the abdomen of an insect.

hȳ-pō′py-um, hȳ-pō′py-on, *n.* [Gr. *hypopyon*, a kind of ulcer, properly neut. of *hypopyos*, tending to suppurate; *hypo*, under, and *pyon*, pus.] An effusion of pus into the anterior chamber of the eye, or that cavity which contains the aqueous humor.

hȳ-pō-rȧ-çhid′i-ăn, *a.* Pertaining to a hyporachis.

hȳ-pō-rā′çhis, *n.*; *pl.* **hȳ-pō-raçh′i-dēş.** [Gr. *hyporrhachis*, the hollow above the hip; *hypo*, under, and *rhachis*, the spine.] In ornithology, (a) the stem of a hypoptilum or aftershaft; also, the hypoptilum or aftershaft itself.

hȳ″pō-rȧ-dī′ō-lus, *n.*; *pl.* **hȳ″pō-rȧ-dī′ō-lī.** [*Hypo-*, and *radiolus*, dim. of L. *radius*, a staff, spoke of a wheel, radius.] A barbule of a hyporadius.

hȳ-pō-rā′di-us, *n.*; *pl.* **hȳ-pō-rā′di-ī.** [*Hypo-*, and L. *radius*, a staff, spoke of a wheel, radius.] In ornithology, a barb of an aftershaft.

hyp′ọr-çhem, *n.* Same as *Hyporcheme*.

hyp-ọr-çhē′mȧ, *n.*; *pl.* **hyp-ọr-çhē′mȧ-tȧ.** See *Hyporcheme*.

hyp″ọr-çhē-mat′iç, *a.* Relating to a hyporcheme.

hyp′ọr-çhēme, hyp′ọr-çhem, *n.* [Gr. *hyporchēma*, from *hyporcheisthai*, to dance, with music; *hypo*, under, and *orcheisthai*, to dance.] In Greek antiquity, a kind of song sung by part of the chorus, accompanied with dancing and dumb show.

hȳ-pō-rhā′çhis, *n.* See *Hyporachis*.

hȳ-pō-scē′ni-um, *n.* [Gr. *hyposkēnion*; *hypo*, under, and *skēnē*, the stage.] A low wall at the front of the proscenium in the ancient Greek theater.

hȳ-pō-skel′e-tăl, *a.* [*Hypo-*, and Gr. *skeleton*, a skeleton, and *-al*.] Developed under the axis of the endoskeleton, as muscles; opposed to *episkeletal*.

hȳ-pō-spā′di-ȧ, *n.* [Gr. *hypospadios*, one having hypospadia; *hypo*, under, and *spān*, to draw.] A malformation of the penis in which the opening of the urethra is along the under side; also called *hypospadias*.

hȳ-pos′tȧ-sis, *n.*; *pl.* **hȳ-pos′tȧ-sēş.** [Gr. *hypostasis*, a supporting, foundation, from *hyphistanai*, to set under, pass, to stand under; *hypo*, under, and *histanai*, to stand, make to stand.]

1. An underlying principle; some fact or supposition which lies at the foundation of a course of reasoning; in theology, substance, entity, or personality, especially of any member of the Trinity.

2. In alchemy, a principle or basic substance; applied to mercury, sulphur, and salt, regarded as the elements of all material bodies.

3. In medicine, any morbid deposit or settling down, as the sediment of urine.

hȳ-pō-stat′iç, hȳ-pō-stat′iç-ăl, *a.* [Gr. *hypostatikos*, belonging to substance, from *hypostatos*, substantially existing, placed under; *hypo*, under, and *histanai*, to stand, cause to stand.]

1. Relating to hypostasis; constitutive.

2. Personal, or distinctly personal; constituting a distinct substance or personality.

3. In medicine, connected with or resulting from pressure or settling from above; as, *hypostatic* congestion.

Hypostatic union; in theology, the union of the two natures or attributes of Christ, the human and the divine.

hȳ-pō-stat′iç-ăl-ly, *adv.* In a hypostatic manner; personally.

hȳ-pos′tȧ-tīze, *v.t.*; hypostatized, *pt.*, *pp.*; hypostatizing, *ppr.* To give distinct personality to; to regard as a separate and distinct reality or individual.

hȳ-pō-stėr′num, *n.*; *pl.* **hȳ-pō-stėr′nȧ.** The hypoplastron.

hȳ-pos′tō-mȧ, *n.*; *pl.* **hȳ-pos′tō-mȧ-tȧ.** [*Hypo* and Gr. *stoma* (*-atos*), the mouth.] In zoölogy, the lower part of the mouth; the proboscis, as of crustaceans and hydrozoans.

hȳ-pō-stom′ȧ-tous, *a.* [*Hypo-*, and Gr. *stoma* (*-atos*), the mouth.] Having the mouth beneath, or on the ventral side, as some infusorians.

hȳ′pō-stōme, *n.* Same as *Hypostoma*.

hȳ-pos′tō-mous, *a.* Same as *Hypostomatous*.

hȳ-pos′trō-phē, *n.* [Gr. *hypostrophē*, a turning about, recurrence, from *hypostrephein*, to turn about; *hypo*, under, and *strephein*, to turn.]

1. In medicine, (a) a recumbent patient's turning of his body; (b) a relapse in disease.

2. In rhetoric, a return to the subject after the interjection of a parenthesis.

hȳ′pō-style, *a.* and *n.* [Gr. *hypostylos*, resting on pillars; *hypo*, under, and *stylos*, a pillar.]

I. *a.* In architecture, supported by columns; having columns beneath.

II. *n.* A structure in which the ceiling is supported by columns; a covered colonnade.

hȳ-pō-sul′phāte, *n.* A compound of hyposulphuric acid and a base.

hȳ-pō-sul′phīte, *n.* A compound of hyposulphurous acid and a base.

hȳ″pō-sul-phū′riç, *a.* [*Hyposulphur*ous and *-ic*.] Pertaining to sulphur less highly oxidized than in its sulphuric compounds.

Hyposulphuric acid; an acid, $H_2S_2O_6$, known only in its salts and in solution with water.

hȳ-pō-sul′phūr-ous, *a.* [*Hypo-*, and L. *sulphurosus*, from *sulphur*, sulphur.] Designating a compound of sulphur with less oxygen than that present in sulphurous acid.

Hyposulphurous acid; an acid, H_2SO_2, obtained by the action of zinc and sulphurous acid, existing as a yellow liquid, having reducing and decolorizing properties.

hȳ-pō-taç′tiç, *a.* Relating to hypotaxis.

hȳ-pō-tär′săl, *a.* Pertaining to or resembling the hypotarsus.

hȳ-pō-tär′sus, *n.*; *pl.* **hȳ-pō-tär′sī.** [*Hypo-*, and Gr. *tarsos*, the flat of the foot.] In ornithology, a process on the back part of the main tarsometatarsal bone; called also *calcaneum*.

hȳ-pō-tax′is, *n.* [Gr. *hypotaxis*, subjection, submission, from *hypotassein*; *hypo*, under, and *tassein*, to arrange.] Subordination of arrangement in grammatical construction; opposed to *parataxis*.

hȳ-pot′e-nūse, hȳ-poth′e-nūse, *n.* [LL. *hypotenusa*; Gr. *hypoteinousa*, lit., subtending, properly f. of ppr. of *hypoteinein*, to subtend, to stretch under; *hypo*, under, and *teinein*, to stretch.] In a right-angled triangle, the side opposite the right angle.

a b, Hypotenuse.

hȳ-pō-thal′lus, *n.*; *pl.* **hȳ-pō-thal′lī.** [*Hypo-*, and Gr. *thallos*, a young shoot or branch.] The mass of delicate filaments upon which the thallus of a crustaceous lichen is developed.

hȳ-poth′eç, *n.* Same as *Hypothecation*, 1.

hȳ-pō-thē′çȧ, *n.* [LL., from Gr. *hypothēkē*, a suggestion, pledge, mortgage, from *hypotithenai*, to put under, pledge.] An ancient form of mortgage.

hȳ-poth′ē-çā-ry, *a.* Relating to hypothecation; founded on pledges.

hȳ-poth′ē-çāte, *v.t.*; hypothecated, *pt.*, *pp.*; hypothecating *ppr.* [LL. *hypothecatus*, pp. of *hypothecare*, to hypothecate, from *hypotheca*; Gr. *hypothēkē*, a pledge, mortgage.]

1. To pledge to a creditor in security for some debt or demand, but without transfer of title or delivery of possession; to mortgage, as ships or other property; to transfer by a bond of bottomry.

2. To put in pawn; to pledge.

hȳ-poth-ē-cā'tion, *n.* 1. A contract lien by which property is pledged without relinquishment of possession on the part of the debtor.

2. The act of putting in pawn.

3. In maritime law, the act of mortgaging a ship; bottomry.

4. In French law, a lien on real estate, etc., for security of a debt, without giving the creditor possession.

5. In American finance, a lien on personal property, as negotiable securities, given as security for a debt by transferring possession to the creditor.

Hypothecation bond; a bottomry bond; a respondentia bond.

hȳ-poth'ē-cā-tŏr, *n.* One who pledges property as security for the repayment of money borrowed.

hȳ-pō-thē'ci-ăl, *a.* Relating to the hypothecium.

hȳ-pō-thē'ci-um, *n.* [*Hypo-*, and Gr. *thēkē*, a case.] In certain fungi, a layer of hyphal tissue beneath the hymenium.

hȳ-poth'ē-năr, *a.* and *n.* [Gr. *hypothenar*; *hypo*, under, and *thenar*, palm.]

I. *a.* Pertaining to the hypothenar.

II. *n.* In anatomy, the fleshy prominence on the palm above the base of the little finger; also called *hypothenar eminence*.

hȳ-poth'ē-nūse, *n.* Same as *Hypotenuse*.

hȳ-pō-thẽr'măl, *a.* [*Hypo-*, and Gr. *thermos*, heat.] Lukewarm; tepid.

hȳ-pō-thẽr'mi-ȧ, *n.* [*Hypo-*, and Gr. *thermos*, heat.] In medicine, subnormal temperature.

hȳ-poth'ē-sis, *n.* [Gr. *hypothesis*, groundwork, foundation, supposition, from *hypotithenai*, to place under; *hypo*, under, and *tithenai*, to place.]

1. A supposition; a proposition or principle which is supposed or taken for granted, in order to draw a conclusion or inference for proof of the point in question; something not proved, but assumed for the purpose of argument.

2. A system or theory imagined or assumed to account for what is not understood.

Nebular hypothesis; see under *Nebular*.

Syn.—Supposition, theory, assumption.—A *hypothesis* is the conclusion of an argument from consequent and antecedent, or a proposition taken for granted to be used as a premise in proving something else. *Supposition* signifies a putting of one's thoughts in the place of reality. A *hypothesis* may be extravagant or absurd; a *supposition* may be false. *Theory* is the fruit of reflection, and serves the purposes of science; practice will be incomplete when the *theory* is false. Hence *theory* is often contrasted with practice, while *hypothesis* is a ground of belief and *supposition* stands for that which is fanciful and unreal. *Assumption* is the act of assuming and denotes a taking to oneself, as an idea which may be untenable. *Hypothesis* is a groundwork upon which to build an argument and is less strong and less practical in application than *theory*.

hȳ-poth'ē-sist, *n.* Same as *Hypothetist*.

hȳ-pō-thet'iç, hȳ-pō-thet'iç-ăl, *a.* Founded on a supposition; conditional; assumed without proof for the purpose of reasoning and deducing proof; conjectural.

hȳ-pō-thet'iç-ăl-ly, *adv.* In a hypothetical manner or relation; by way of supposition; conditionally.

hȳ-poth'ē-tist, *n.* One who defends or seeks to establish a hypothesis.

hȳ"pō-trȧ-chē'li-um, *n.* [L., from Gr. *hypotrachēlion*, the lower part of the neck, the neck of a column; *hypo*, under, and *trachēlos*, the neck.] In architecture, a term applied to the slenderest part of the shaft of a column immediately under the fillet, separating the shaft from the capital; the part which forms the junction of the shaft with its capital.

a, Hypotrachelium.

Hȳ-pot'ri-chȧ, *n.pl.* [*Hypo-*, and Gr. *thrix*, *trichos*, hair.] A division of free-swimming infusorians with cilia on the ventral side only.

hȳ-pō-trō'choid, *n.* [*Hypo-*, and Gr. *trochos*, a wheel, and *eidos*, form.] A curve traced by a point in a circle rolling upon the concave side of the circumference of a fixed circle.

hȳ-pō-typ'iç, hȳ-pō-typ'iç-ăl, *a.* [*Hypo-*, and Gr. *typos*, type.] Not developed to the full type; not quite typical.

hȳ"pō-ty-pō'sis, *n.* [Gr. *hypotypōsis*, an outline, general representation; *hypo*, under, and *typos*, figure, image.]

1. In rhetoric, animated description; word-picturing.

2. In science, a concise outline of a subject.

hȳ-pō-xan'thine, *n.* [Gr. *hypoxanthos*, yellowish-brown, from *hypo*, under, and *xanthos*, yellow, and *-ine*.] A crystalline substance, $C_5H_4N_4O$, present in various organs, particularly in the muscular tissue of animal bodies and also in some plants; it forms compounds with both acids and bases.

hȳ-pō-zō'iç, *a.* [*Hypo-*, and Gr. *zōē*, life.] In geology, designating rocks older than the oldest of those containing evidences of organic life.

hypped (hipt), *a.* See second *Hipped*.

hyp'pish, *a.* Same as *Hippish*.

hyp'pō-griff, *n.* Same as *Hippogriff*.

hypsi-. Same as *Hypso-*.

hyp"si-cē-phal'iç, *a.* [*Hypsi-*, and Gr. *kephalē*, head.] Showing hypsicephaly; high, as a skull.

hyp-si-ceph'ȧ-ly, *n.* High cranial development, having an index over 75.

hyp'si-loid, *a.* [Gr. *hypsiloeidēs*, shaped like upsilon; *v*, upsilon, and *eidos*, form.] Shaped like the Greek letter upsilon (*υ*).

Hyp-sis-tā'ri-ăn, *n.* [Gr. *Hypsistarios*, a worshiper of the Most High God, from *hypsistos*, highest, superl. adj. from *hypsi*, adv., on high, aloft.] One of an Asiatic sect in the fourth century whose religious beliefs were derived from Christian, Jewish, and pagan doctrines.

hypso-, hypsi-. Combining forms from Gr. *hypsi*, on high, used in zoölogy, botany, medicine, etc., to signify possession or connection with something high; as, *hypso*dont, *hypso*phyllum.

hyp'sō-dont, *a.* [*Hypso-*, and Gr. *odous*, *odontos*, tooth.] High-toothed; having teeth with comparatively long crowns and short roots.

hyp-sog'rȧ-phy, *n.* [*Hypso-*, and Gr. *-graphia*, from *graphein*, to write.] That branch of topography relating exclusively to the elevation of land.

hyp-som'e-tẽr, *n.* [*Hypso-*, and Gr. *metron*, a measure.] An instrument for computing altitude through atmospheric pressure as determined from the boiling-point of water.

hyp-sō-met'riç, hyp-sō-met'ri-çăl, *a.* Relating to hypsometry.

hyp-som'e-try, *n.* The science which treats of the measuring of altitudes; also, the art of measuring heights.

hyp'sō-phyl, hyp'sō-phyll, *n.* Any leaf, other than a foliage leaf, borne on a flower-stalk; applied especially to involucral leaves, bracts, and the like.

hyp-soph'yl-lā-ry, hyp-soph'yl-lăr, *a.* Relating to a hypsophyl.

hyp-sō-phyl'lum, *n.*; *pl.* **hyp-sō-phyl'lȧ**. [*Hypso-*, and Gr. *phyllon*, a leaf.] A hypsophyl.

hȳ-pū'răl, *a.* [Gr. *hypo*, under, and *oura*, a tail.] Situated under the tail; specifically, applied to the small bones in fishes, supporting the inferior fin-rays.

hȳ-rā'cē-um, hȳ-rā'ci-um, *n.* [Gr. *hyrax*, the shrewmouse.] A product of South Africa used as a substitute for castoreum and derived from the cony or hyrax.

hȳ-rac'id, *n.* An individual of the *Hyracoidea*.

hȳ-rac'i-fōrm, *a.* Same as *Hyracoid*.

hȳ-rag'ō-dont, *a.* [Gr. *hyrax* (*-akos*), the shrewmouse, and *odous*, *odontos*, tooth.] Having molars resembling those of the genera *Hyrax* and *Rhinoceros*.

hȳ'rȧ-çoid, *a.* Pertaining to or characteristic of the *Hyracoidea*.

Hy-rȧ-çoi'dē-ȧ, *n.* [Gr. *hyrax* (*-akos*), the shrewmouse, and *eidos*, form.] An order of small mammals resembling rabbits, with four toes on each fore foot and three on each hind foot, the *Hyracidæ* being the only family and *Hyrax* the only genus; the hyraxes or rock-rabbits.

hȳ'rax, *n.* [Gr. *hyrax*, the shrewmouse.] One of the *Hyracoidea*, the species being variously known as *cony*, *daman*, *rock-rabbit*, etc.

Hyr-çā'ni-ăn, Hyr'çăn, *a.* Pertaining to Hyrcania, an ancient province southeast of the Caspian (also called *Hyrcanian*) Sea.

hyrse (hĩrs), *n.* [Gr. *hirse*.] Millet.

hyrst, *n.* Same as *Hurst*.

hȳ'sŏn, *n.* [Chinese *hi-tchun*, lit., blooming spring or first crop.] A species of green tea from China.

Hyson skin; the refuse of hyson tea.

Young hyson; an early pick of hyson tea.

hys'sŏp, *n.* [L. *hysopum*, *hyssopum*, *hyssopus*; Gr. *hyssōpos* or *hyssōpon*, an aromatic plant, from Heb. *ēzōph*, an aromatic plant.]

1. A labiate plant, *Hyssopus officinalis*, bearing small clusters of blue flowers; the leaves are aromatic and pungent, and are sometimes used in medicine.

Hyssop (*Hyssopus officinalis*).

2. In Scripture, a plant not fully identified, the twigs of which were used in Mosaic rites for sprinkling.

Wild hyssop; the plant *Verbena hastata*.

hyster-. See *Hystero-*.

hys-tẽr-al'gi-ȧ, *n.* [Gr. *hysteralgēs*; *hystera*, the uterus, and *algos*, pain.] Neuralgic affection of the uterus.

hys-tẽr-an'thous, *a.* [Gr. *hysteros*, later, after, and *anthos*, flower.] In botany, putting forth leaves after the opening of the flowers, as willows and poplars.

hys-tẽr-eç'tō-my, *n.* [*Hyster-*, and Gr. *ektomē*, a cutting out; *ek*, out, and *temnein*, to cut.] In surgery, the removal of the uterus from the body by excision.

hys-te-rē'sis, *n.* [Gr. *hysterēsis*, a coming short, deficiency, from *hysterein*, to be behind, come short, from *hysteros*, later, behind.] In physics, the lagging or retardation of one of two related forces or phenomena on account of some change taking place in the medium through which they act.

hys-tē'ri-ȧ, *n.* [Gr. *hystera*, the uterus, womb.] In medicine, a nervous affection in which the patient loses control of the emotions through loss of will-power, and becomes the victim of imaginary afflictions, often going into a state of convulsion and complete unconsciousness; an ailment suffered by women more frequently than by men; called also *hysterics*.

hys-ter'iç, hys-ter'iç-ăl, *a.* [L. *hystericus*; Gr. *hysterikos*, suffering in the uterus, hysterical, from *hystera*, the uterus, womb.] Apt to lose control of one's emotions; affected by hysteria; excitable.

hys-ter'ics, *n.* Same as *Hysteria*.

hys-te-rī'tis, *n.* See *Metritis*.

hystero-, hyster-. Combining forms from Gr. *hystera*, the uterus, womb, used in medicine, anatomy, etc., to denote any relation to the uterus, or womb, or to hysteria; as, *hysterec*tomy, *hystero*pathy.

hys'tẽr-ō-cēle, *n.* [*Hystero-*, and Gr. *kēlē*, a tumor.] Hernia involving the uterus.

hys"tẽr-ō-dyn'i-ȧ, *n.* [*Hystero-*, and Gr. *odynē*, pain.] Uterine pain.

hys"tẽr-ō-ep'i-lep-sy, *n.* [*Hystero-*, and Gr. *epilēpsis*, a seizure, attack.] In medicine, a form of hysteria accompanied by epileptic convulsions.

hys"tẽr-ō-ep-i-lep'tiç, *a.* Pertaining to or of the nature of hysteroepilepsy.

hys"tẽr-ō-ġen'iç, *a.* [Gr. *hysteros*, later, after, and *-genēs*, producing, from *gignesthai*, to become.] Produced afterward; of later origin; applied to intercellular spaces in plants formed in older tissues.

hys"tẽr-ō-ġen'iç, *a.* Causing hysterical phenomena; producing hysteria.

hys-tẽr-oġ'e-ny, *n.* [*Hystero-*, and Gr. *-genēs*, producing.] The induction of hysteria or hysterical phenomena.

hys'tẽr-oid, *a.* [*Hystero-*, and Gr. *eidos*, form.] Resembling hysteria; as, a *hysteroid* disease.

hys-tẽr-ol'ō-ġy, *n.* Same as *Hysteron-proteron*, 1.

hys"te-ron-prot'e-ron, *n.* [Gr. *hysteron*, neut. of *hysteros*, latter, following, and *proteron*, neut. of *proteros*, former.]

1. A figure in which the word that should follow comes first; as, *valet atque vivit*, he is well and lives.

2. In logic, a form of fallacy which arises from an inversion of terms in the minor premise; as, the good are happy; this man is happy, therefore he is good.

hys-tẽr-op'ȧ-thy, *n.* [*Hystero-*, and Gr. *pathos*, suffering.] Any disease or disorder of the uterus.

Hys-tẽr-oph'y-tȧ, *n.pl.* Same as *Fungi*.

hys-tẽr-oph'y-tăl, *a.* Pertaining to a hysterophyte or to the *Hysterophyta*.

hys-tẽr'ō-phyte, *n.* [*Hystero-*, and Gr. *phyton*, a plant.] In botany, a plant which springs from and lives upon organic matter; a plant of the order *Hysterophyta*; a fungus or any similar growth.

hys-te-rop-tō'sis, *n.* [*Hystero-*, and Gr. *ptōsis*, a falling.] Falling or inversion of the uterus.

hys-tẽr-ot'ō-my, *n.* [*Hystero-*, and Gr. *tomē*, a cutting.] In surgery, incision of the uterus.

hys-tri-ci'ȧ-sis, *n.* Same as *Hystricismus*.

hys'tri-cine, *a.* [L. *hystrix* (*-icis*), a porcupine, and *-ine*.] Pertaining to or resembling a porcupine.

hys-tri-cis'mus, hys'tri-cism, *n.* [L. *hystrix* (*-icis*), a porcupine, and *-ismus*.] In pathology, a disease characterized by spinelike processes of the epidermis; a form of ichthyosis.

hys"tri-cō-mor'phiç, *a.* [L. *hystrix*; Gr. *hystrix* (*-ichos*), a porcupine, and *morphē*, form.] Relating to the *Hystricomorpha*, a series of rodents, including the porcupines; histricine.

Hys'trix, *n.* [L. *hystrix*; Gr. *hystrix*, a porcupine.] A genus of rodents distinguished by having quill-like spines growing among the hairs on certain parts of the body; it includes the old-world porcupines.

hȳthe, *n.* Same as *Hithe*.

I

I (ī). The ninth letter and third vowel of the English alphabet. It comes through the Latin and Greek, from the Phenician, and probably originated in the Egyptian alphabet. In the Phenician the value of *i* was that of the consonant *y*, rather than a vowel. It became a vowel in the Greek, and continued through the Latin, having the sound of Italian *i*, as in *machine*, or long *e*, as in *mete*. The *i* sounds are made by less opening of the mouth than the *e* sounds, the tongue being brought back to the palate and striking the teeth next the cheek plate. In English *i* has two principal sounds; the short sound, as in *pit*, *pin*, *fin*, which is one of the oldest sounds of Indo-European speech, and the long sound, as in *pine*, *fine*, *wine*, which is really a diphthong sound. It has also three other sounds, the sound of neutral vowel *e*, as in *first*, *dirk*; the French sound, as in *intrigue*, *machine*, and the consonant sound when it precedes a vowel, as in *million*, *opinion*. *I* enters into several digraphs with *a* and *e*, as in *fail*, *field*, *seize*. It forms a proper diphthong with *o*, as in *oil*, *join*, *coin*. No genuine English word ends with *i*, this sound when occurring at the end of a word being expressed by *y*; it is written however in foreign words introduced into English, as *alkali*. *I* and *j* were formerly regarded as one character, and in many English dictionaries words beginning with these letters were classed together till comparatively recent times. *I* was first dotted in the fourteenth century.

I, i, *as a symbol*. In Roman notation, *I* represents the number 1, II standing for 2, and III for 3.

In chemistry, *I* stands for *iodine*.

In logic, *I* is the particular affirmative proposition.

In mathematics, *I* is the square root of minus one, $\sqrt{-1}$, and in quaternions, it represents a vector. In dental formulæ, in zoölogy, *I* is an abbreviation for *incisor*.

I, *pron.*; *poss.* my *or* mine; *obj.* me; *nom. pl.* we; *poss. pl.* our *or* ours; *obj. pl.* us. [ME. *i*, *ich*, *ic*; AS. *ic*, I.] The nominative case of the pronoun of the first person; the word by which a speaker or writer denotes himself.

I, *n.* 1. The pronoun *I*.

2. In metaphysics, the conscious, thinking subject; the ego.

i-. [ME. *i-*, *y-*; AS. *ge-*, OS. *gi*.] A prefix, originally thought to have had an indefinite or generalizing force, found very commonly in Middle English verbs, adverbs, adjectives, nouns, and pronouns; also written *y-*.

ī-am-ȧ-tol′ō-ġy, *n.* [Gr. *iama*, remedy, and *-logia*, from *legein*, to speak.] In medicine, the science which treats of remedies; materia medica.

ī′amb (-am), *n.* An iambus. [Rare.]

ī-am′biç, *a.* [LL. *iambicus*; Gr. *iambikos*, iambic, from *iambos*, an iambus.]

1. Of or pertaining to the iambus; as, *iambic* meter.

2. Composed of iambics; as, an *iambic* verse.

ī-am′biç, *n.* In prosody, (a) an iambus, (b) a verse consisting of iambic feet, that is, a verse of short and long, or unaccented and accented syllables alternately. According to Aristotle, the iambic meter was first employed in satirical poems; hence the term *iambic* is used as equivalent to a satirical poem or satire.

ī-am′biç-ăl, *a.* Iambic. [Rare.]

ī-am′biç-ăl-ly, *adv.* In the manner of an iambic.

ī-am′bize, *v.t.* [Gr. *iambizein*, to assail in iambics, from *iambos*, an iambus.] To satirize in iambic verse. [Rare.]

ī-am′bus, *n.*; *pl.* **ī-am′bī.** [L. *iambus*; Gr. *iambos*, an iambus, an iambic verse, from *iaptein*, to drive, assail, lampoon.] In prosody, a foot consisting of a short or unaccented syllable followed by a long or accented.

I-an′thi-nȧ, *n.*; *pl.* **I-an′thi-næ.** [Gr. *ianthinos*, violet-colored; *ion*, violet, and *anthos*, a flower.]

1. A genus of oceanic gasteropodous mollusks; the violet-snails. They are found in the open sea in the warmer parts of the world. The foot of the animal has a float composed of numerous air-vesicles, which serves as a raft and as a place of attachment for the eggs. When irritated it pours out a violet secretion, which serves for its concealment, like the ink of the cuttlefish.

Shell of Violet-snail (*Ianthina communis*).

2. [i—] A violet-snail of the genus *Ianthina*.

-iasis. A suffix from L. *-iasis*, from Gr. *-iasis*, denoting condition or state, used especially in medicine to indicate a morbid condition; as, hypochondr*iasis*, phthir*iasis*.

ī-ā-trȧ-lip′tiç, *a.* [Gr. *iatraleiptēs*, a surgeon who anoints; *iatros*, a physician, and *aleiptēs*, an anointer, from *aleiphein*, to anoint.] Curing by ointments and friction.

Iatraliptic method; see *Epidermic method* under *Epidermic*.

-iatria, -iatry. A suffix from Gr. *iatreia*, healing, medical treatment, denoting medical treatment, or method of treatment; as, in psych*iatry*, hipp*iatry*.

ī-at′riç, *a.* [Gr. *iatrikos*, from *iatros*, a physician, from *iāsthai*, to cure, heal.] Relating to medicine or physicians.

ī-at′riç-ăl, *a.* Iatric.

iatro-. A combining form from Gr. *iatros*, a physician, from *iāsthai*, to heal, cure, used in medical terms to signify a physician, or medicine; as, *iatro*logy, *iatro*physical.

ī-ā-trō-ċhem′iç-ăl, *a.* Of or relating to iatrochemistry.

ī-ā-trō-ċhem′ist, *n.* A physician who practises iatrochemistry.

ī-ā-trō-ċhem′is-try, *n.* [*Iatro-*, and LL. *chimia*, chemistry, from Gr. *chēmeia*, *chymeia*, an infusion, from *chein*, to pour.] The science of the application of chemistry to medicine; used especially in connection with the theories and doctrines of a medical school in the Netherlands in the seventeenth century, which held chemical action to be the sole essential to the due operation of the vital functions.

ī-ȧ-trol′ō-ġy, *n.* [*Iatro-*, and Gr. *-logia*, from *legein*, to speak.] The science of medicine; a treatise on medicine or physicians.

ī-ā-trō-math-ē-mat′iç-ăl, *a.* See *Iatrophysical*.

ī-ā-trō-math″ē-mȧ-ti′ciăn (-tish′ăn), *n.* [*Iatro-*, and Gr. *mathēmatikos*, a mathematician.] One of the iatrophysical school of physicians.

ī-ā-trō-mē-ċhan′iç-ăl, *a.* Iatrophysical.

ī-ā-trō-phys′iç-ăl, *a.* Designating a school of physicians in Italy in the seventeenth century. They sought to explain the functions of the body and the application of remedies by statical and hydraulic laws, and were eager students of anatomy, since it was only by accurate knowledge of all the parts that they could apply their mathematical and dynamical principles.

I′-bēam, *n.* A beam the cross-section of which is shaped like the letter I.

I-bē′ri-ăn, *n.* 1. One of the primitive inhabitants of Spain. The Basques are supposed to be representatives of the ancient Spanish Iberians.

2. The language of the ancient Iberians, of which modern Basque is supposed to be the representative.

I-bē′ri-ăn, *a.* [L. *Iberia*, *Hiberia*; Gr. *Ibēria*, Spain, from *Ibēres*, the inhabitants of Spain.] Relating to Iberia in Europe, which formerly included Spain, Portugal, and a part of France.

I-bē′ri-ăn, *a.* [L. *Iberia*, Iberia, from *Iberes*; Gr. *Ibēres*, the ancient inhabitants of Iberia, in Asia.] Relating to ancient Asiatic Iberia, now Georgia in Transcaucasia.

I-bē′ris, *n.* [Gr. *ibēris*, a kind of pepperwort, from *Ibēria*, Iberia, Spain.] A genus of cruciferous plants, consisting of annual, perennial, and shrubby species, mostly natives of the Mediterranean region and of the East. Several species are cultivated under the name of *candytuft*.

ī′bex, *n.* [L., a kind of goat.] A species of wild goat, inhabiting the Alps, Pyrenees, Apennines, etc. The male is redbrown in summer and graybrown in winter. The female is earthy-brown and ashy. The young is gray. The horns of the male are flat and bent backward, with two longitudinal ridges at the sides, crossed by numerous transverse knots. The best-known species is the Alpine *ibex* or steinbok, *Capra ibex*.

Ibex (*Capra ibex*).

i-bī′dem, *adv.* [L.] In the same place; usually in the contracted form *ib.* or *ibid.*

ī′bis, *n.* [L., from Gr. *ibis*, the ibis.]

1. A genus of grallatorial birds allied to the storks, one of whose most remarkable species is the *Ibis æthiopica*, found throughout Africa. It is about the size of a common fowl, with head and neck bare, and white plumage, the primaries of the wings being tipped with black and the secondaries being bright black, glossed with green and violet. There are several other species.

2. [i—] Any bird of the genus or of closely related genera.

Sacred Ibis (*Ibis æthiopica*).

-ible. A suffix from L. *-ibilis*, used with adjectives that have not *a-* stems to signify capable of, worthy of, given to: as, exig*ible*, expans*ible*.

ī-bō′ga-in, ī-bō′ga-ine, *n.* An alkaloid obtained from a shrub of Central Africa. Sometimes used as a substitute for cocaine.

-iç. [ME. *-ik*; L. *-icus*; Gr. *-ikos*.] An adjective suffix, used with words of Latin and Greek origin to signify dealing with or connected with; as, scientif*ic*, philanthrop*ic*; also used with nouns; as, mus*ic*, log*ic*. It is used in chemistry to denote a higher valence than the suffix *-ous*; as, mercur*ic* chlorid, $HgCl_2$; mercur*ous* chlorid, HgCl. It sometimes has the meaning of pertaining to or relating to; as, borac*ic*, calc*ic*.

i-caç′ō, *n.* [Sp.] The cocoa-plum.

-içal. [L. *-icalis*, formed of *-icus*, -ic, and *-alis*, -al.] A compound adjective suffix, signifying like, of, or belonging to, and usually equivalent to *-ic*; as, hyster*ic*, hyster*ical*. In some cases they differ; as, polit*ic*, polit*ical*. When a noun ends in *-ic*, the adjective derived from it regularly ends in *-al*; as, mus*ic*, mus*ical*; crit*ic*, crit*ical*. Adverbs formed from adjectives in *-ic*, but which may have *-ical*, add *-al*, before *-ly*; as, intrins*ic*, intrins*ically*.

I-çā′ri-ăn, *a.* [L. *Icarius*; Gr. *Ikarios*, relating to *Icarus*, the son of Dædalus, who fled on wings to escape the resentment of Minos, but the sun melted the wax that cemented his wings and he drowned in the Ægean Sea.]

1. Of, like, or belonging to Icarus; hence, adventurous; foolhardy; flying too high for safety.

2. Of, like, or belonging to any place named Icaria, as (a) a deme of Attica; (b) an island near Samos, now Nikaria; (c) a fictitious community described by Etienne Cabet in a romance, Voyage en Icarie.

3. Of, like, or belonging to the communistic principles of, or to any of the settlements founded upon the principles of Cabet.

I-çā′ri-ăn, *n.* A native or resident of Icaria or of an Icarian settlement; a follower of the communist Cabet.

ice, *n.* [ME. *ise*, *is*, *ys*; AS. *is*, ice.]

1. Water congealed or in a solid state.

2. Icing; frosting, as for cakes.

3. Any frozen sweet or dessert, as cream, fruit juices, etc.; water-ice; ice-cream.

Bay ice; ice formed in bays or other inlets of the sea.

Ice age; in geology, the glacial epoch.

To break the ice; see under *Break*.

ice, *v.t.*; iced (īst), *pt.*, *pp.*; icing, *ppr.* 1. To cover with ice; to convert into ice.

2. To cover with icing; to frost.

3. To chill; to freeze.

-ice. [ME. *-ice*, *-ise*, *-is*; OFr. *-ice*; L. *-itius*, masc., *-itia*, f., *-itium*, neut.] A suffix of Latin origin, appearing in such words as just*ice*, coward*ice*.

ice′-an″ċhŏr, *n.* Nautically, an anchor with one arm, used for securing vessels to floes of ice.

ice′-ax, *n.* A form of ax used by mountain-climbers to cut steps in ice.

ice′bērg, *n.* A lofty floating mass of ice, generally one which has been detached from the seaward termination of a glacier; ice of great thickness and height in a floating state. Such

Iceberg.

masses are found in both frigid zones and sometimes float a considerable distance toward the equator.

ice′bīrd, *n.* A sea-bird of arctic regions; especially, the dovekie or little auk.

ice′=bliṅk, *n.* A bright yellowish-white tint near the horizon, reflected from the snow-covered surface of ice in arctic regions, and observed before the ice itself is seen.

ice′=bōat, *n.* 1. A strong boat, propelled by steam, used to break a passage through ice.

2. A framework mounted on runners and fitted with a mast etc., for sailing on the surface of ice.

īce′bound, *a.* Surrounded or obstructed by ice; frozen in; as, an *icebound* ship or bay.

īce′=box, *n.* 1. A refrigerator; an ice-chest.

2. A box or compartment, as in a refrigerator, for containing ice.

īce′=built (-bilt), *a.* Built of or loaded with ice.

īce′=chest, *n.* A refrigerator.

īce′=ċrēam′, *n.* A table delicacy composed of cream or a creamy mixture flavored and congealed, usually by a freezing-mixture of ice and salt, while being stirred to insure uniformity of consistency.

iced (īst), *a.* 1. Covered or cooled with or as with ice; congealed; frozen.

2. Frosted; coated with frosting or icing.

īce′=drops, *n.pl.* In botany, transparent processes resembling icicles.

īce′fạll, *n.* 1. The fall of masses of ice from an iceberg or glacier.

2. A glacier. [Rare.]

īce′=fiēld, *n.* An extensive flat mass of floating ice.

īce′=flōat, *n.* An ice-floe.

īce′=flōe, *n.* A great mass or sheet of floating ice.

īce′=glāzed, *a.* Glazed or incrusted with ice.

īce′=house, *n.* A storehouse designed for the preservation of ice during warm weather.

Ice′lănd-ēr, *n.* [ME. *Island*; Ice. *Island*, Iceland; *iss*, ice, and *land*, land.] A native of Iceland.

Ice-lan′diç, *a.* Pertaining to Iceland, to its people, or to their customs and speech.

Ice-lan′diç, *n.* The language of the people of Iceland.

Ice′lănd=moss, *n.* In botany, a species of lichen, *Cetraria Islandica*, found in the arctic regions and upon lofty mountains, used in Iceland as a food and as a medicine.

Ice′lănd=spär, *n.* Calcareous spar, in laminated masses, easily divisible into rhombs, perfectly similar to the primitive rhomb; used in optics for its strong double refractive power.

īce′=mạ-chīne″, *n.* A machine for making ice by artificial means.

īce′măn, *n.* 1. A man who is skilled in traveling upon or climbing over ice, as an Alpine climber.

2. One engaged in the industry of cutting and packing ice; a dealer in ice; one who delivers ice to consumers.

īce′=mas″tēr, *n.* One who has charge of a whaler or other ship in the ice, or who sails a ship through the ice of the Arctic Ocean; called also *ice-pilot*.

īce′=pack, *n.* A large expanse of broken floating ice.

īce′=pā″pēr, *n.* Transparent gelatin in thin sheets, used in copying and transferring writing and designs; also called *papier glacé*.

īce′=pick, *n.* An implement for breaking ice.

īce′=pī″lŏt, *n.* An ice-master.

īce′=pitch″ēr, *n.* A pitcher for containing ice-water.

īce′=plant, *n.* In botany, a plant, *Mesembryanthemum crystallinum*, having its leaves sprinkled with pellucid watery vesicles which shine like pieces of ice, and frequently cultivated; native of Greece, the Canary Islands, and the Cape, in the Canaries, large quantities of it are collected and burned, the ashes being sent to Spain for use in glassmaking; called also *dew-plant*.

īce′=plow, *n.* A sort of plow for cutting grooves in ice in ponds, lakes, etc., with a view to its removal, or to open a passage for boats.

īce′=pōul″tice (-pōl″), *n.* In medicine, a poultice made by filling a bladder or sack with pounded ice for application to hernial tumors and the like.

īce′quāke, *n.* The rending crash which precedes and forewarns of the breaking of floes of ice; sometimes, a shock following a collision between large bodies of ice or the falling of the fragments of a glacier.

ī-cē′ry-ȧ, *n.* In zoölogy, a scale-insect of the genus *Icerya*, infesting the orange-plant.

īce′=sạw, *n.* A large saw used for cutting through the ice to relieve ships when frozen up, or for cutting blocks of ice for storage, sometimes with a heavy weight attached for the purpose of giving the descending stroke.

īce′=spā, *n.* A variety of feldspar, the crystals of which resemble ice.

īce′=storm, *n.* A rain-storm, the drops of which are congealed as soon as they touch any object, as the branch of a tree.

īce′=tā″ble, *n.* A broad expanse of ice.

Ice-saw at work.

īce′=tongṣ, *n.pl.* Large iron nippers for handling ice, particularly when it is being delivered from a wagon.

īce′=wạ″tēr, *n.* 1. Water from melted ice.

2. Water cooled by ice; iced water.

ich, iche, *pron.*, old forms of the personal pronoun *I.* [Obs.]

ich, *v.t.* To eke. [Obs.]

ī′chi-bọọ, ī′chi-bū, *n.* [Japan. *ichiboo, ichibu, itzibu*, a silver coin; *ichi*, one, and *bu*, a division, the name of a coin.] See *Itzibu*.

Iç̣h-neū′mi-ȧ, *n.* [Gr. *ichneumōn*, the ichneumon.] A subgenus of *Herpestes*, distinguished from the true ichneumons by having longer limbs and hairy soles.

iç̣h-neū′mŏn, *n.* [L., from Gr. *ichneumōn*, the ichneumon, lit., a tracker, from *ichneuein*, to track out, hunt after, from *ichnos*, a track or footstep.]

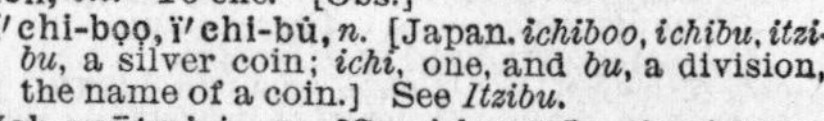

Egyptian Ichneumon (*Herpestes ichneumon*).

1. A digitigrade carnivorous animal of the genus *Herpestes*, family *Viverridæ*, resembling the weasel tribe both in form and in habits, in length about eighteen inches from the snout to the root of the tail. It inhabits Egypt and feeds on the eggs of the crocodile, on snakes, rats, lizards, mice, and various small animals.

2. One of a family of hymenopterous insects whose larvæ are parasitic on other insects.

iç̣h-neū′mŏn=flȳ, *n.* Same as *Ichneumon*, 2.

Iç̣h-neū-mon′i-dæ, *n.pl.* [Gr. *ichneumōn*, the ichneumon, and *eidos*, form.] A family of hymenopterous insects, the genera and species of which are very numerous, over 3000 species existing, it is said, in Europe alone; the ichneumon-flies. The perfect insects feed solely on the juices of flowers. Some of them have a long ovipositor, which is used to insert the eggs into the bodies of those caterpillars which live beneath the bark or in the crevices of wood; others, which have the ovipositor short, place their eggs in or upon the bodies of caterpillars of easier access; and others again in the nests of wasps, where they devour the young.

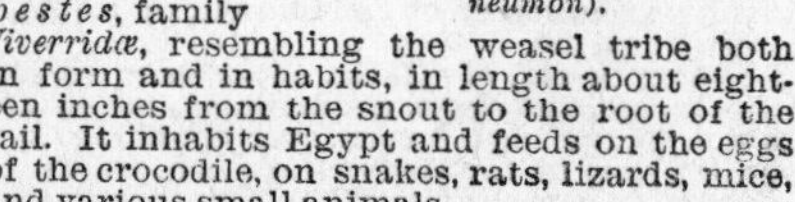

Rhyssa persuasoria (one of the Ichneumon-flies).

iç̣h-neū-mon′i-dăn, *a.* Relating to the *Ichneumonidæ*.

iç̣h-neū-mon′i-dēṣ, *n.pl.* The members of the family *Ichneumonidæ*.

iç̣h-neū′mous, *a.* Relating to or resembling an ichneumon-fly; parasitic.

iç̣h′nīte, *n.* [Gr. *ichnos*, a footprint.] In geology, a fossil footprint; often used in composition; as, ornith*ichnite*, bird footprint; sauroid*ichnite*, saurian footprint; tetrapod*ichnite*, the footprint of a four-footed animal, as a batrachian reptile.

iç̣hno-. A combining form from Gr. *ichnos*, a footprint, used in paleontology, etc., to signify a track, footprint, trace; as, *ichno*lite.

iç̣h′nō-grȧph, *n.* In drawing, a plan, as of a building; a ground-plan.

iç̣h-nō-graph′iç, iç̣h-nō-graph′iç-ăl, *a.* Pertaining to ichnography; describing a ground-plot.

iç̣h-nog′rȧ-phy, *n.* [L. *ichnographia*; Gr. *ichnographia*, a tracing out, a ground-plan; *ichnos*, a track, plan, and *graphein*, to write.] In drawing, a plan; a horizontal section of a building or other object, showing its true dimensions according to a geometric scale; also, the art of making ichnographs.

iç̣h′nō-līte, *n.* [*Ichno-*, and Gr. *lithos*, a stone.] A stone retaining the impression of a footmark of a fossil animal.

iç̣h″nō-li-thol′ō-ġy, *n.* [*Ichno-*, and Gr. *lithos*, a stone, and *-logia*, from *legein*, to speak.] Ichnology.

iç̣h-nō-loġ′iç-ăl, *a.* Of or relating to ichnology.

iç̣h-nol′ō-ġy, *n.* [*Ichno-*, and Gr. *-logia*, from *legein*, to speak.] That branch of geology which treats of the fossil footmarks of animals.

ī′ç̣hōr, *n.* [Gr. *ichōr*, the blood of the gods, juice, the serum of blood.]

1. In mythology, an ethereal fluid that supplied the place of blood in the veins of the gods of the Greeks and Romans.

> Of course his perspiration was but *ichor*,
> Or some such other spiritual liquor.—Byron.

2. Colorless matter flowing from an ulcer.

ī′ç̣hor-ous, *a.* Like ichor; thin; watery; serous.

ī-ç̣hor-rhæ′mi-ȧ, *n.* [Gr. *ichōr*, juice, ichor, *rhein*, to flow, and *haima*, blood.] In pathology, an infected condition of the blood due to the presence of ichorous matter.

iç̣h′thi-din, *n.* [Gr. *ichthys*, a fish, and *-id*, and *-in*.] A nitrogenous compound found in the yolk of the immature eggs of cyprinoid fishes.

iç̣h′thin, *n.* [Gr. *ichthys*, a fish, and *-in*.] In physiological chemistry, a substance closely allied to albumen, present in the yolk of the eggs of cartilaginous fishes.

iç̣h′thū-lin, *n.* [Gr. *ichthys*, a fish, and *hylē*, matter, and *-in*.] In chemistry, an albuminous compound, a constituent of the yolks of young eggs of salmon and allied fishes.

iç̣h′thus, *n.* Same as *Ichthys*.

iç̣h′thy-iç, *a.* [Gr. *ichthys*, a fish.] Pertaining to fishes; having the character of a fish.

iç̣hthyo-, iç̣hthy-. Combining forms from Gr. *ichthyo-*, from *ichthys*, a fish; used in zoölogy, geology, etc., to signify a fish, or fishlike; as, *ichthyo*latry, *ichythyo*morphous.

iç̣h′thy-ō-çol, iç̣h″thy-ō-çol′lȧ, *n.* [L. *ichthyocolla*; Gr. *ichthyokolla*, fish-glue; *ichthys*, a fish, and *kolla*, glue.] Fish-glue; isinglass; a glue prepared from the sounds of fish.

iç̣h″thy-ō-çop′rō-līte, *n.* [*Ichthyo-*, and Gr. *kopros*, dung, and *lithos*, a stone.] In geology, the fossil excrement of fishes.

iç̣h″thy-ō-dor′ū-līte, *n.* [*Ichthyo-*, and Gr. *dory*, a spear, and *lithos*, a stone.] The fossil dorsal spine of certain fishes.

iç̣h-thy-og′rȧ-phy, *n.* [*Ichthyo-*, and Gr. *graphein*, to write.] A treatise on fishes.

iç̣h′thy-oid, iç̣h-thy-oid′ăl, *a.* [Gr. *ichthys*, a fish, and *eidos*, form.] A term applied to saurians having many of the characteristics of a fish.

iç̣h′thy-ol, *n.* [*Ichthy-*, and L. *oleum*, oil.] An oleaginous compound derived from a bituminous mineral embodying a deposit of fossil fishes; used in medicine.

iç̣h-thy-ol′ȧ-try, *n.* [*Ichthyo-*, and Gr. *latreia*, worship.] Worship of fishes; also, worship of an ichthyomorphic image.

iç̣h′thy-ō-līte, *n.* [*Ichthyo-*, and Gr. *lithos*, a stone.] Fossil fish, or the figure or impression of a fish in rock.

iç̣h″thy-ō-loġ′iç, iç̣h″thy-ō-loġ′iç-ăl, *a.* Pertaining to ichthyology.

iç̣h-thy-ol′ō-ġist, *n.* One versed in ichthyology.

iç̣h-thy-ol′ō-ġy, *n.* [*Ichthyo-*, and Gr. *-logia*, from *legein*, to speak.] The science of fishes, or that part of zoölogy which treats of fishes, their structure, form, and classification, their habits, uses, etc.

iç̣h′thy-ō-man-cy, *n.* [*Ichthyo-*, and Gr. *manteia*, a prophesying.] Divination by the heads and entrails of fishes.

iç̣h′thy-ō-mọrph, *n.*; *pl.* **iç̣h″thy-ō-mọr′phȧ**. [*Ichthyo-*, and Gr. *morphē*, form.] A triton, salamander, or other urodele.

iç̣h″thy-ō-mọr′phiç, iç̣h″thy-ō-mọr′phous, *a.* [*Ichthyo-*, and Gr. *morphē*, form.]

1. Having the shape of a fish, as certain gods of ancient Assyria and Syria.

2. In zoölogy, resembling a fish in form and structure; ichthyopsid.

iç̣h-thy-oph′ȧ-ġist, *n.* One who eats or subsists on fish.

iç̣h-thy-oph′ȧ-gous, *a.* [Gr. *ichthyophagos*, eating fish; *ichthys*, a fish, and *phagein*, to eat.] Eating or subsisting on fish.

iç̣h′thy-oph-ȧ-ġy, *n.* The practice of eating fish.

iç̣h″thy-oph-thal′mīte, *n.* [*Ichthy-*, and Gr. *ophthalmos*, an eye, and *-ite*.] In mineralogy, fish-eye stone; apophyllite.

Iç̣h″thy-oph-thī′rȧ, *n.pl.* [*Ichthyo-*, and Gr. *phtheir*, a louse.] In zoölogy, an order of crustaceans embracing numerous species that are parasitic on fishes; fish-lice.

iç̣h-thy-op′sid, *a.* and *n.* I. *a.* Pertaining to or resembling the *Ichthyopsida*.

II. *n.* One of the *Ichthyopsida*.

Iç̣h-thy-op′si-dȧ, *n.pl.* [*Ichthy-*, and Gr. *opsis*, appearance, and *-ida*.] The primary division of *Vertebrata* comprising fishes and amphibians.

Iç̣h-thy-op-tē-ryġ′i-ȧ, *n. pl.* [*Ichthyo-*, and Gr. *pteryx*, *pterygos*, a wing.] In paleontology, an order of extinct reptiles of the Mesozoic; ichthyosaurs.

Iç̣h-thy-ọr′nis, *n.* [*Ichthy-*, and Gr. *ornis*, a bird.] An extinct genus of birds with socketed teeth and biconcave vertebræ, found in America in beds of Cretaceous rocks. [See illus. p. 832.]

ich-thy-or′ni-thēs, *n.pl.* [*Ichthy-*, and Gr. *ornis*, *ornithos*, a bird.] In ornithology, a group of extinct birds with teeth and biconcave vertebræ, of which *Ichthyornis* is the typical genus.

ich″thy-or-nith′ic, ich-thy-or′ni-thoid, *a.* Relating to or having the characteristics of both fishes and birds.

ich′thy-ō-saur, *n.* A saurian with some characteristics of a fish; one of the order *Ichthyosauria.*

Fig. 1. *Ichthyornis dispar*, restored. Fig. 2. Right jaw, inner view; half natural size.

ich″thy-ō-sau′ri-ā, *n.pl.* [*Ichthyo-*, and Gr. *sauros*, a lizard.] In paleontology, an order of gigantic reptiles now extinct, shaped somewhat like a whale, with very large head and no obvious neck, having paddle-like flippers, short biconcave vertebræ and an extended caudal extremity; called also *Ichthyopterygia*, *Ichthyosaura*, and *Ichthyosauri.*

ich″thy-ō-sau′ri-ăn, *a.* and *n.* I. *a.* Relating to the *Ichthyosauria.*

II. *n.* Any member of the *Ichthyosauria.*

Ich″thy-ō-sau′rus, *n.* 1. The typical genus of *Ichthyosauria.*

2. [i—] Any species of this genus; an ichthyosaur.

ich-thy-ō′sis, *n.* [Gr. *ichthys*, a fish, and *-osis.*] A disease of the skin, which renders it thick, hard, and scaly.

ich-thy-ot′ō-mist, *n.* One who is versed in ichthyotomy.

ich-thy-ot′ō-my, *n.* [*Ichthyo-*, and Gr. *tomē*, a cutting, from *temnein*, to cut.] The anatomical structure or the science of the anatomy of fishes.

ich′thys, *n.* [Gr. *ichthys*, a fish.] A word found on many seals, rings, urns, tombstones, etc., belonging to the early times of Christianity, and supposed to have a mystical meaning, from each character forming an initial letter of the words, Ἰησοῦς Χριστός, Θεοῦ Υἱός, Σωτήρ; *Iēsous Christos, Theou Hyios, Sōtēr*; that is, Jesus Christ, the Son of God, the Saviour.

-ician. [Fr. *-icien*; LL. *-icianus.*] A compound suffix used in forming nouns from adjectives in *-ic*, or nouns in *-ic*, *-ics*; as, mus*ician*, phy*sician.*

ī′ci-cle, *n.* [ME. *iseickle*, *isikel*, *hysehykylle*; AS. *isgicel*, an icicle; *is*, ice, and *gicel*, an icicle.] A pendent mass of ice, formed by the freezing of water or other fluid as it drops; as, the *icicles* formed on the eaves of a house.

ī′ci-cled (-kld), *a.* Studded with icicles.

ī′ci-ly, *adv.* In a cold manner; unsympathetically.

ī′ci-ness, *n.* 1. The state of being icy or of being very cold.

2. The state of generating ice.

ī′cing, *n.* A covering of concreted sugar, as on confections.

-icity. A suffix from L. *-icitas*, employed to form nouns from adjectives in *-ic*; as, publ*icity*, from publ*ic*; electr*icity*, from electr*ic*, etc.

ī′con, *n.*; *pl.* ī′cō-nēs or ī′cons. [L., from Gr. *eikōn*, an image, figure, likeness.] An image or representation, as in the Greek church an image of Christ or of a saint; in geometry or in scientific bookmaking, an illustrative engraving, diagram, or picture.

ī-con′ic, ī-con′ic-ăl, *a.* [L. *iconicus*; Gr. *eikonikos*, copied from life, from *eikōn*, a figure, likeness.] Relating to or resembling an icon or image of any kind; as, an *iconic* statue; an *iconic* diagram.

ī′cŏn-ism, *n.* [L. *iconismus*; Gr. *eikonismos*, delineation, from *eikonizein*, to delineate, mold into form.] A figure or representation, or the making of such a figure.

ī′cŏn-īze, *v.t.* [Gr. *eikonizein*, to mold into form, from *eikōn*, a figure, likeness.] To make an icon; to represent by an icon. [Rare.]

icono-. A combining form from L. *icon*; Gr. *eikōn*, a figure, image, used to signify a figure, image, likeness; as, *icono*dule, *icono*graph.

ī-con′ō-clasm, *n.* [*Icono-*, and Gr. *klān*, to break.]

1. The act of breaking or destroying images, as of idolaters; especially, the destruction of objects of veneration, as pictures and images in churches.

2. The act of exposing superstitions, delusions, or shams; the act of attacking cherished beliefs, or the spirit leading to such attack.

ī-con′ō-clast, *n.* [*Icono-*, and Gr. *klān*, to break.]

1. A breaker or destroyer of images; a person determinedly hostile to the worship of images.

2. Any destroyer or exposer of shams, superstitions, or impositions; one who makes attacks upon cherished beliefs.

ī-con-ō-clas′tic, *a.* Breaking images; exposing superstitions or shams; of or characteristic of iconoclasm or iconoclasts; as, *iconoclastic* zeal.

ī-con′ō-dūle, ī-con′ō-dū-list, *n.* [*Icono-*, and Gr. *douleia*, servitude, from *douleuein*, to be subject to, to serve.] A worshiper of images.

ī-con′ō-grăph, *n.* [*Icono-*, and Gr. *graphein*, to write.] An illustrative image.

ī-cō-nog′rā-phēr, *n.* One skilled in iconography.

ī-con-ō-graph′ic, ī-con-ō-graph′ic-ăl, *a.* Of or belonging to iconography.

ī-con-og′rā-phy, *n.* [Gr. *eikonographia*, a sketch, description, from *eikonographos*, a portrait painter; *eikōn*, a likeness, image, and *graphein*, to write, draw.]

1. That branch of knowledge which treats of the representation of objects by means of images or statues, busts, paintings, mosaic works, engravings on gems or metals, and the like.

2. The art of pictorial representation.

3. A series or collection of images.

ī-con-ol′ā-tēr, *n.* [*Icono-*, and Gr. *latreus*, a worshiper, from *latreuein*, to worship.] One who worships images.

ī-cō-nol′ā-try, *n.* [*Icono-*, and Gr. *latreia*, worship.] The worship of images as symbols, in contradistinction to idolatry.

ī-con-ol′ō-gy, *n.* [*Icono-*, and Gr. *-logia*, from *legein*, to speak.]

1. The doctrine of images or emblematical representations and of their worship.

2. Representation by icons or symbols.

ī-cō-nom′ā-chy, *n.* [Gr. *eikonomachia*, a war against the images; *eikōn*, an image, and *machē*, a battle.] Active opposition to icons or other sacred images; iconoclasm.

ī-cō-nom′ic-ăl, *a.* Iconoclastic. [Obs.]

ī-cō-noph′ī-list, *n.* [*Icono-*, and Gr. *philos*, loving.] A collector or connoisseur of prints, engravings, etc.

ī-cō-nos′tā-sis, *n.* [L.Gr. *eiknostasis*; Gr. *eikōn*, an image, and *stasis*, a standing.] In the Greek church, the high screen, corresponding to the altar-rails of the Western church, which separates the bema and sacristy from the remainder of the church.

icos-, icosa-. Combining forms derived from Gr. *eikosi*, twenty, used in mathematics, botany, etc., to signify twenty; as, *icos*ahedron, *icos*andria.

ī-cō-sā-hē′drăl, *a.* [*Icosa-*, and Gr. *hedra*, a seat, base.] Having twenty faces.

ī-cō-sā-hē′drŏn, *n.* [Gr. *eikosaedron*, a body with twenty sides; *eikosi*, twenty, and *hedra*, a side, base.] A solid of twenty faces.

Regular icosahedron; a regular solid, consisting of twenty equal and similar triangular pyramids whose vertices meet in the center of a sphere supposed to circumscribe it.

I-cō-san′dri-ā, *n.pl.* [*Icos-*, and Gr. *anēr*, *andros*, a male.] In the Linnean system of botany, a class of plants having twenty or more stamens inserted in the calyx.

ī-cō-san′drous, ī-cō-san′dri-ăn, *a.* Pertaining to the *Icosandria*; having twenty or more stamens inserted in the calyx.

Icosandria—Cherry-blossom.

ī″cō-si-tet-rā-hē′drŏn, *n.* [Gr. *eikosi*, twenty, *tettares*, four, and *hedra*, a seat, base.] In crystallography, a solid having twenty-four trapeziform faces.

-ics. A suffix formed from L. neut. pl. *-ica*; Gr. *-ika*, used to denote an art or science; as, mathemat*ics*, mechan*ics*. Such words are plural in form but singular in meaning, the plural form being in imitation of the Greek. In some cases both a plural in *-ics*, and a singular in *-ic*, are found; as, esthet*ics*, esthet*ic*; metaphys*ics*, metaphys*ic*, and in such cases the tendency is to restrict the plural to the science and the singular to the philosophy of the subject.

Ic-tē′ri-ā, *n.* [Gr. *ikteros*, jaundice, a yellow bird, the sight of which was said to cure the jaundice.] A genus of birds generally included in the family *Turdidæ* or thrushes; the chattering flycatchers or yellow-breasted chats of North America.

Chattering Flycatcher (*Icteria viridis*).

ic-ter′ic, *a.* [L. *ictericus*; Gr. *ikterikos*, jaundiced, from *ikteros*, jaundice.]

1. Affected with jaundice.

2. Good in the cure of jaundice.

ic-ter′ic, *n.* A remedy for jaundice.

ic-ter′ic-ăl, *a.* Same as *Icteric.*

ic′tēr-id, *n.* A bird of the genus *Icteria.*

ic′tēr-ine, *a.* Pertaining to the *Icteria*; yellow in coloration, as a bird.

ic-tēr-i′tious (-rish′us), **ic-ter′i-tous**, *a.* [L. *icterus*; Gr. *ikteros*, jaundice.] Yellow; having the color of skin affected by the jaundice.

ic′tēr-oid, *a.* [Gr. *ikteros*, jaundice, and *eidos*, form.] Icteritious; also, icterine.

ic′te-rus, *n.* [L., from Gr. *ikteros*, jaundice.]

1. A yellowness assumed by some plants, especially wheat, in continued cold wet weather.

2. In pathology, the jaundice.

ic′tic, *a.* [L. *ictus*, a blow.] Of, like, or due to a blow; striking; abrupt. [Rare.]

ic′tus, *n.* [L., a blow, stroke, in prosody a beating time, from *ictus*, pp. of *icere*, to strike, hit, beat.]

1. In medicine, a stroke; a beat; a sudden attack, as (a) a paralytic stroke; (b) the beat of the pulse; (c) a sting of an insect.

2. In music and prosody, the stress or accent marking the rhythm; the intensity of delivery which distinguishes one syllable or note from others.

ī′cy, *a.*; *comp.* icier; *superl.* iciest. [AS. *isig*, from *is*, ice, and *-ig*, *-y.*]

1. Of, like, belonging to, or abounding in ice; cold; frigid; chilling.

2. Destitute of affection or passion.

3. Indifferent; unaffected.

ī′cy-pēarled, *a.* Studded with spangles of ice.

I′d. A contracted form of *I would* or *I had.*

id, *n.* Same as *Nerfling.*

-id. [L. *-idus*, a suffix used to form adjectives from verbs in *-ēre*, or *-ere*, or from nouns, as *stupidus*, stupid, from *stupere*, to act stupidly; *albidus*, whitish, from *alba*, white.] A suffix used with adjectives of Latin origin, or nouns derived from adjectives; as, liqu*id*, ac*id*, ar*id*, etc.; also used in chemistry as a formative suffix, sometimes spelled *-ide*, with names of elements to form names of compounds; as, chlor*id*, from chlorin.

-id. A termination of nouns derived from Latin or Greek feminine nouns in *-is* or *-es*; as, hybr*id*, from Gr. *hybris*, wantonness, hydat*id*, from Gr. *hydatis*, a drop of water; also used in zoölogy as a suffix for nouns derived from Latin nouns in *-idæ*; as, congr*id*, from Congr*idæ.*

-ida. A suffix used in zoölogy as a termination of names of groups of animals.

-idæ. A patronymic suffix from Gr. *-idēs*, pl. *-idai*, used in words of Greek origin to denote that those to whose name the suffix is added are descendants of a certain person or family; as, the Atr*idæ* were the descendants of Atreus; also used in zoölogy as a suffix to the stem name of a genus, to denote the family; as, Columb*idæ*, from Columbæ; Iguan*idæ*, from Iguana, etc.

I-dæ′ăn, *a.* [L. *Idæus*; Gr. *Idaios*, from *Idē*, Mount Ida.] Relating to Mount Ida, not far from Troy.

I-dā′li-ăn, *a.* [L. *Idalius*, from *Idalium*; Gr. *Idalion*, Idalia.] Inhabiting or relating to the town of Idalia in Cyprus, which was sacred to the goddess Venus (Aphrodite).

ī′dănt, *n.* [Formed from *id.* used as an abbrev. of *idioplasma.*] In biology, one of Weismann's groups of pangens; a chromosome.

-ide. See first *-id.*

ide, *n.* [Norw. *id*, small-fry.] A fish of the carp family, *Leuciscus idus.*

ī-dē′ā, *n.* [L. *idea*; Gr. *idea*, a form, the look or appearance of a thing as opposed to its reality, from *idein*, to see.]

1. That which is seen; hence, form, image, model of anything in the mind; that which is held or comprehended by the understanding or intellectual faculties.

> I have used the word *idea* to express whatever is meant by phantasm, notion, species, or whatever it is which the mind can be employed about in thinking. —Locke.

2. Notion, conception, thought, opinion, belief, and even purpose or intention; as, I had no *idea* it was so late; I have an *idea* that he will come to-morrow; he had an *idea* of going to Washington; he hadn't an *idea* in his head.

3. An opinion; a proposition; as, these decisions are incompatible with the *idea* that the principles are derived from the civil law.

4. The object of thought, or the notice which the mind takes of its perceptions; a notion of external things which our organs make us acquainted with originally; a contraction, motion, or configuration of the fibers which constitute the immediate organ of sense.

5. The reflex perception of objects, after the original perception or impression has been felt by the mind.

> Plato believed that there are eternal forms of all possible things which exist without matter; and to those eternal and immaterial forms he gave the name of *ideas*. In the Platonic sense, *ideas* were the patterns according to which the Deity fashioned the phenomenal or ectypal world. —Sir W. Hamilton.

Syn.—Image, impression, conception.

ī-dē′aed, ī-dē′a-d, *a.* Possessed of an idea; inordinately imbued with an idea; as, a one-*ideaed* person.

ī-dē′ăl, *n.* A conception embodying perfection; an object which corresponds with such a conception; as, one's *ideal* of happy life.

Beau ideal; an imaginary object without fault; a flawless pattern, model, example, or standard.

ī-dē′ăl, *a.* [Fr. *ideal*; LL. *idealis*, existing in idea, ideal, from L. *idea*, an idea.]

1. Existing in idea; intellectual; mental; as, *ideal* knowledge.

2. Visionary; existing in fancy or imagination only; as, *ideal* good.

3. Considering ideas as images, phantasms, or forms in the mind; as, the *ideal* theory or philosophy.

4. Having the requirements of a fanciful standard; as, an *ideal* painting.

5. In mathematics, having no real existence.

Syn.—Fanciful, unreal, imaginary, perfect, visionary.

ī-dē′ă-less, *a.* Destitute of ideas.

ī-dē′ăl-işm, *n.* 1. The system or theory that makes everything to consist in ideas and denies the existence of material bodies.

2. The quality or condition of being ideal.

3. The concept of, desire for, or pursuit of the ideal.

4. The vesting of persons or things with ideal character or form; the antonym of *realism*.

ī-dē′ăl-ist, *n.* 1. One who holds the doctrine of idealism.

2. One who speculates in the ideal; a dreamer of daydreams.

ī-dē-ăl-is′tiç, *a.* Related to the idealists; pursuing and indulging idealism.

ī-dē-al′i-ty, *n.*; *pl.* **ī-dē-al′i-tieş.** 1. The quality of being ideal.

2. The state of an idealist.

3. In phrenology, the capacity for the conception of ideas.

ī-dē″ăl-i-zā′tion, *n.* 1. The act of forming in idea.

2. In the fine arts, the act of giving flattering portrayal to preferred points or objects in a representation; specialization.

ī-dē′ăl-īze, *v.i.*; idealized, *pt., pp.*; idealizing, *ppr.* To form ideas; specifically, in the fine arts, to portray a natural object in an ideal form.

ī-dē′ăl-īze, *v.t.* To apply an ideal concept to; as, to *idealize* a face in painting by minimizing its defects and magnifying its excellences.

ī-dē′ăl-ī-zẽr, *n.* One who indulges in ideals; one who applies ideals to real objects.

ī-dē′ăl-ly, *adv.* Intellectually; mentally; in idea.

ī-dē-ă-log′iç, *a.* Same as *Ideological*.

ī-dē′ă-logue (-log), *n.* Same as *Ideologue*.

ī-dē′āte, *a.* and *n.* [*Idea* and *-ate*.]

I. *a.* In philosophy, having origin in or connected with an idea.

II. *n.* The object of idealization, whether real or merely conceived.

ī-dē′āte, *v.t.* 1. To form in idea; to fancy. [Rare.]

2. To grasp in detail so as to retain in memory. [Rare.]

ī-dē-ā′tion, *n.* The mental process by which objects are apprehended and fixed in the mind.

ī-dē-ā′tion-ăl, *a.* Relating to the formation of ideas; ideative.

ī-dē′ă-tive, *a.* Same as *Ideational*.

ī′dem. [L.] The same; the last cited; usually abbreviated to *id.*

ī-den′tiç, *a.* Identical. [Rare.]

ī-den′tiç-ăl, *a.* [LL. *identicus*, the same, from L. *identidem*, repeatedly, from *idem*, the same.]

1. The same; not different; as, the *identical* person; an *identical* note.

2. The same in meaning, but different in expression; as, an *identical* proposition.

Identical equation; in algebra, an equation which may be satisfied by giving any values whatever to the literal quantities.

Identical note; in diplomacy, a formal communication the terms of which are concurred in by two or more powers, each of which despatches a copy to the power which it is sought to influence by such action.

ī-den′tiç-ăl-ly, *adv.* In an identical manner; with actual sameness.

ī-den′tiç-ăl-ness, *n.* Sameness.

ī-den-ti-fī′ă-ble, *a.* Capable of being identified.

ī-den″ti-fi-çā′tion, *n.* The act of making or proving to be the same; identity.

ī-den′ti-fȳ, *v.t.*; identified, *pt., pp.*; identifying, *ppr.* [LL. *identicus*, the same, and L. *-ficare*, from *facere*, to make.]

1. To ascertain or prove to be the same; as, *identify* stolen property; to *identify* the dead.

2. To make to be the same; to unite or combine in such a manner as to make one interest, purpose, or intention; to treat as having the same use; to consider as the same in effect; as, it is wise to *identify* oneself with the people.

3. In natural history, to decide the place of a specimen in classification.

ī-den′ti-fȳ, *v.i.* To become the same; to coalesce in interest, purpose, use, effect, etc.

ī-den′tişm, *n.* In metaphysics, the doctrine of Schelling, making subject and object identical; also called *doctrine of identity*.

ī-den′tist, *n.* In medicine, one who declares as identical diseases that are generally believed to be distinct.

ī-den′ti-ty, *n.* [LL. *identitas*, sameness, from *identicus*, the same, from L. *identidem*, repeatedly, from *idem*, the same.]

1. Sameness, as distinguished from similitude and diversity; as, the *identity* of persons, or personal *identity*.

2. The state of being the same and not other; as, the *identity* of a person or of stolen property.

3. In mathematics, sameness in value, as in the members of an identical equation.

ideo-. A combining form from Gr. *idea*, a form, idea, used to signify an idea or thought; as, *ideo*gram, *ideo*plasty.

ī″dē-ō-ġen′iç-ăl, *a.* Relating to the origin of ideas.

ī-dē-oġ′e-ny, *n.* [*Ideo-*, and Gr. *-geneia*, from *gignesthai*, to become.] The source or the discussion and science of the source of ideas.

ī′dē-ō-gram, *n.* Same as *Ideograph*.

ī′dē-ō-grȧph, *n.* [*Ideo-*, and Gr. *graphein*, to write.] A pictorial representation of a thought; a hieroglyph; a character which suggests the idea of a subject.

ī″dē-ō-graph′iç, ī″dē-ō-graph′iç-ăl, *a.* Representing ideas independently of sounds or of their names; hieroglyphic.

ī″dē-ō-graph′iç-ăl-ly, *adv.* In an ideographic manner.

ī″dē-ō-graph′içs, *n.* The method of writing with symbolic characters.

ī-dē-og′rȧ-phy, *n.* [*Ideo-*, and Gr. *-graphia*, from *graphein*, to write.] The representation of ideas directly through symbolic characters, as in stenography.

ī″dē-ō-log′iç-ăl, *a.* Pertaining to ideology.

ī″dē-ol′ō-ġist, *n.* One who treats of ideas or who supports the theory of ideology.

ī-dē′ō-logue (-log), *n.* [Fr. *idéologue*, from Gr. *idea*, an idea, and *logos*, a description.] An ideologist.

ī-dē-ol′ō-ġy, *n.* [Fr. *idéologie*; Gr. *idea*, an idea, and *-logia*, from *legein*, to speak.]

1. A treatise on ideas; the doctrine that ideas are derived exclusively through sensation.

2. The science of mind.

ī″dē-ō-mō′tion, *n.* [*Ideo-*, and L. *motus*, motion.] In physiology, motion having its origin in the force of an idea independently of the will or of reflex action.

ī″dē-ō-mō′tŏr, *a.* [*Ideo-*, and L. *motor*, a mover.] Pertaining to ideomotion.

ī″dē-ō-plas′ty, *n.* [*Ideo-*, and Gr. *plastos*, formed, molded, from *plassein*, to form.] The power of imagination.

ī″dē-ō-prax′ist, *n.* [*Ideo-*, and Gr. *praxis*, a doing, from *prassein*, to do.] One bent on carrying out an idea.

ideş, *n.pl.* [L. *īdūs*, pl. the ides.] In the ancient Roman calendar, the eighth day after the nones, that is, the fifteenth day of March, May, July, and October, and the thirteenth day of the other months.

idio-. A prefix from Gr. *idios*, one's own, used in botany, zoölogy, medicine, etc., to signify one's own, private, peculiar, personal, distinct; as, *idio*cracy, *idio*graph, *idio*neurosis.

id″i-ō-bi-ol′ō-ġy, *n.* [*Idio-*, and Gr. *bios*, life, and *-logia*, from *legein*, to speak.] The science of the functions of a particular organ.

id′i-ō-blast, *n.* [*Idio-*, and Gr. *blastos*, a bud, offshoot.] In botany, a distinctive cell, showing wide divergency from the surrounding cells, as a resin-cell in pine.

id″i-ō-çrā′sis, *n.* Same as *Idiocrasy*.

id-i-oç′rȧ-sy, *n.* [Gr. *idiokrasia*, a peculiar temperament; *idios*, one's own, and *krasis*, a mixture, temperament.] Peculiarity of constitution; that temperament or state of constitution which is peculiar to a person.

id″i-ō-çrat′iç, id″i-ō-çrat′iç-ăl, *a.* Peculiar in constitution.

id′i-ō-cy, *n.* [Gr. *idiōteia*, one's private or peculiar business, uncouthness, want of education, from *idiōtēs*, a private person, an ignorant or ill-informed person.] The nature or condition of being an idiot; a natural defect in understanding.

id″i-ō-çy-cloph′ȧ-nous, *a.* [*Idio-*, and *kyklos*, a circle, and *-phanēs*, from *phainesthai*, to appear.] Same as *Idiophanous*.

id″i-ō-ē-lec′triç, *a.* [*Idio-*, and Gr. *ēlektron*, amber.] In physics, having electricity as a natural quality; developing electricity under friction; the opposite of *anelectric*.

id′i-ō-grȧph, *n.* [*Idio-*, and Gr. *graphein*, to write.] A characteristic signature or writing; one's own private mark.

id″i-ō-graph′iç, id″i-ō-graph′iç-ăl, *a.* Belonging to, resembling, or containing an idiograph or idiographs.

id-i-ol′ȧ-try, *n.* [*Idio-*, and Gr. *latreia*, worship.] Worship of one's own personality; inordinate self-esteem.

id-i-ol′ō-ġişm, *n.* [*Idio-*, and Gr. *logos*, discourse, speech, from *legein*, to speak.] In medicine, peculiarity of speech, usually arising from some affection of the brain.

id′i-ŏm, *n.* [LL. *idioma*; Gr. *idiōma*, a peculiarity, a peculiar phraseology, an idiom, from *idiousthai*, to make one's own, from *idios*, one's own, private, peculiar.]

1. A mode of expression peculiar to a language; peculiarity of expression or phraseology; in the plural, forms of speech or phraseology peculiar to a nation or a language.

> And to just *idioms* fix our doubtful speech.
> —Prior.

2. The genius or peculiar cast of a language.

> He followed the Latin language, but did not comply with the *idiom* of ours. —Dryden.

3. Dialect.

Syn.—Diction, dialect.—The *idioms* of a language belong to its very structure; its *dialects* are varieties of expression ingrafted upon it in different localities or by different professions.

id″i-ō-mat′iç, id″i-ō-mat′iç-ăl, *a.* [Gr. *idiōmatikos*, peculiar, characteristic, from *idiōma*, a peculiarity, an idiom.] Peculiar to a language; pertaining to the particular genius or modes of expression which belong to a language; as, an *idiomatic* phrase.

id″i-ō-mat′iç-ăl-ly, *adv.* According to the idiom of a language.

id″i-ō-mor′phiç, *a.* [*Idio-*, and Gr. *morphē*, form.]

1. Having a form peculiar to itself.

2. In lithology, retaining characteristic form against influences tending to change it.

id″i-ō-mor′phous, *a.* 1. Same as *Idiomorphic*.

2. In crystallography, having the constituents of a rock characteristically and normally crystalline.

id″i-ō-mus′çū-lăr, *a.* [*Idio-*, and L. *musculus*, a muscle.] In physiology, relating to muscular action, especially to a temporary contraction of the muscle upon being struck by a dull implement transverse to its fibers.

id″i-ō-neū-rō′sis, *n.* [*Idio-* and Gr. *neuron*, a nerve.] In medicine, neurosis arising from disorder in the nerves remote from the nerve-centers.

id″i-ō-pȧ-thet′iç, *a.* Same as *Idiopathic*.

id″i-ō-path′iç, id″i-ō-path′iç-ăl, *a.* Relating to idiopathy.

id-i-op′ȧ-thy, *n.* [Gr. *idiopatheia*, feeling for oneself alone, from *idios*, one's own, peculiar, and *pathos*, feeling, suffering.] An independent disease, neither induced by nor related to another disease.

id-i-oph′ȧ-nous, *a.* [*Idio-*, and Gr. *-phanēs*, from *phainesthai*, to appear.] Designating a form of crystal in which axial interference figures are apparent without resort to the use of a polariscope.

id′i-ō-plaşm, *n.* Same as *Idioplasma*.

id″i-ō-plaş′mȧ, *n.* [*Idio-*, and Gr. *plasma*, a thing formed, from *plassein*, to form.] In biology, the active and characteristic part of cell protoplasm, in contradistinction to the *nutritive plasma*; germ-plasm.

id″i-ō-rē-pul′sive, *a.* [*Idio-*, and L. *repulsus*, pp. of *repellere*, to drive back, repel.] Repulsive by itself; as, the *idiorepulsive* power of heat.

id′i-ō-sōme, *n.* [*Idio-*, and Gr. *sōma*, the body.] In biology, a quickening unit of idioplasma which imparts the hereditary characteristics.

id″i-ō-stat′iç, *a.* [*Idio-*, and Gr. *statikos*, static, from *histanai*, to cause to stand.] In electricity, pertaining to a method, or designating a form of electrometer, by which measurements in difference of potential are made without the employment of auxiliary electrification.

id″i-ō-syn′çrȧ-sy, *n.*; *pl.* **id″i-ō-syn′çrȧ-sieş.** [Gr. *idiosynkrasia*; *idios*, one's own, peculiar, and *synkrasis*, a mixing together, tempering, from *synkerannynai*, to mix together; *syn*, together, and *kerannynai*, to mix.] A peculiarity of constitution and susceptibility occasioning certain peculiarities of effect from the impress of extraneous influences or agencies; a constitutional peculiarity of temperament which distinguishes an individual; a species of eccentricity; idiocrasy.

id″i-ō-syn-çrat′iç, id″i-ō-syn-çrat′iç-ăl, *a.* Having the characteristics of or affected by idiosyncrasy.

id′i-ŏt, *n.* [OFr. *idiot*, an idiot; L. *idiota*, an uneducated, ignorant, common person; Gr. *idiōtēs*, a private citizen, one without professional knowledge; an inexperienced and ignorant common person; from *idiousthai*, to make one's own, from *idios*, one's own, peculiar.]

1. A natural fool, or fool from his birth; a human being destitute of reason, or the ordinary intellectual powers of man.

2. A foolish person; one unwise; an epithet applied in reproach to a dull or silly person.

3. An uneducated or ignorant person. [Obs.]

4. A private citizen. [Obs.]

id′i-ŏt-cy, *n.* Idiocy. [Rare.]

id″i-ō-thal′ȧ-mous, *a.* In botany, designating certain lichens having some part, as the fruit, different in color from the thallus.

id″i-ō-thẽr′miç, *a.* [*Idio-*, and Gr. *thermē*, heat.] Heated by itself; requiring no external agent of heat; self-heating.

id-i-ot′iç, id-i-ot′iç-ăl, *a.* [Gr. *idiōtikos*, private, peculiar, rude, from *idiōtēs*, a private citizen, an unlettered, rude person.]

1. Illiterate. [Obs.]

2. Like an idiot; foolish.

id-i-ot′iç-ăl-ly, *adv.* After the manner of an idiot.

id-i-ot′i-çon, *n.*; *pl.* **id-i-ot′i-çȧ.** [Gr. *idiōtikos*, masc., *idiōtikon*, neut., private, peculiar to oneself.] A dictionary of a particular dialect, or of the words and phrases peculiar to one part of a country. [Rare.]

id′i-ŏt-ish, *a.* Idiotic.

id′i-ŏt-işm, *n.* [L. *idiotismus*; Gr. *idiōtismos*, the manner of a common person, a common or vulgar way of speaking, from *idiōtizein*, to use common language, from *idiōtēs*, a private person, from *idios*, one's own, peculiar.]

1. An idiom; a peculiarity of expression; a mode of expression peculiar to a language; a peculiarity in the structure of words and phrases.

> Scholars sometimes give terminations and *idiotisms*, suitable to their native language, to words newly invented. —Hale.

2. Idiocy.

id′i-ŏt-ize, *v.i.* To become stupid. [Rare.]

id′i-ŏt-ry, *n.* [Rare.] See *Idiocy.*

id′i-ō-tȳpe, *n.* [*Idio-*, and Gr. *typos*, type.] In chemistry, a substance that is typical of a class; one of a series having the same characteristics.

id″i-ō-typ′iç, *a.* Having the character of an idiotype.

ī′dle, *a.*; *comp.* idler; *superl.* idlest [ME. *idel*; AS. *idel*, useless, vain, empty.]

1. Not engaged in any occupation or employment; unoccupied; inactive; doing nothing.

> Why stand ye here all the day *idle?* —Matt. xx. 6.

2. Slothful; given to rest and ease; averse to labor or employment; lazy; as, an *idle* man; an *idle* fellow.

3. Affording leisure; vacant; not occupied; as, *idle* time; *idle* hours.

4. Remaining unused; unemployed.

> The *idle* spear and shield were high up hung. —Milton.

5. Producing no effect; useless; vain; ineffectual; fruitless; as, *idle* rage.

> Down their *idle* weapons dropped.—Milton.

6. Unfruitful; barren.

7. Trifling; of no importance; irrelevant; as, an *idle* story; an *idle* reason.

Syn.—Unoccupied, unemployed, vacant, inactive, sluggish, useless, ineffectual, futile, frivolous, vain, trifling, unprofitable, unimportant.

ī′dle, *v.i.*; idled, *pt.*, *pp.*; idling, *ppr.* [ME. *idlen*; AS. *idlian*, to become useless, from *idel*, idle, useless.] To lose or spend time in inaction or without being employed in business.

ī′dle, *v.t.* To waste; usually with *away*; as, to *idle away* time.

> If you have but an hour, will you improve that hour instead of *idling* it *away?* —Chesterfield.

ī′dle-head″ed (-hed″), *a.* 1. Foolish; unreasonable.

2. Delirious; infatuated.

ī′dle-ness, *n.* [ME. *idelnesse*; AS. *idelnes*, from *idel*, idle.] The state or condition of being idle.

ī′dle-pāt″ed, *a.* Idle-headed; stupid. [Obs.]

ī′d′ẽr, *n.* 1. One who does nothing; one who spends his time in inaction, or without being engaged in business; a lazy person; a sluggard.

2. Nautically, a person on board a ship who, because liable to constant day duty, is not required to keep night-watch.

3. In mechanics, an idle-wheel.

ī′dleş-by (-dlz-), *n.* An idle or lazy person. [Obs.]

ī′dless, ī′dlesse, *n.* A poetical term for *idleness*, now obsolescent.

ī′dle-wheel (-hwēl), *n.* In machinery, (a) a wheel placed between two others to transfer motion from one axis to another without change of direction. If A and B were in contact they would revolve in opposite directions; but in consequence of the intermediate axis of C they revolve in the same direction, and without any change of the velocity-ratio of the pair; (b) a pulley used otherwise than to communicate motion, as to take the slack of a loose belt.

Idle-wheel.

ī′dly, *adv.* [ME. *idelliche*; AS. *idellice*, from *idel*, idle.] In an idle manner; lazily; sluggishly; foolishly; uselessly.

id′ō-çrāse, *n.* Same as *Vesuvianite.*

ī′dŏl, *n.* [OFr. *idole*; L. *idolum*, an image, form, specter, apparition; Gr. *eidōlon*, an image, a phantom, from *eidenai*, to know, middle *eidesthai*, to appear.]

1. An image, form, or representation, usually of a man or other animal, consecrated as an object of worship; a pagan deity. Idols are usually statues or images carved out of wood or stone, or formed of metals, particularly silver or gold.

> The gods of the nations are *idols.*—Ps. xcvi. 5.

2. An image or effigy of anything. [Obs.]

3. An object of adoration or devotion; a person or thing worshiped as a god.

> An *idol* is anything which usurps the place of God in the hearts of his rational creatures. —Miller.

4. A fallacy; an erroneous opinion or idea; an idolon.

ī-dō′lȧ, *n.*, pl. of *idolon.*

ī-dō-las′tẽr, ī-dō-las′tre, *n.* [Obs.] Same as *Idolater.*

ī-dol′ȧ-tẽr, *n.* [OFr. *idolatre*; LL. *idololatres*; Gr. *eidōlolatrēs*, an idol-worshiper; *eidōlon*, an image, an idol, and *latris*, one hired to serve, a servant, from *latron*, pay, hire.]

1. A worshiper of idols; one who pays divine honors to images, statues, or representations of anything; one who worships as a deity that which is not God.

2. An adorer; a great admirer.

ī-dol′ȧ-tress, *n.* A female worshiper of idols.

ī-dō-lat′riç-ăl, *a.* Tending to idolatry. [Obs.]

ī-dol′ȧ-trize, *v.i.*; idolatrized, *pt.*, *pp.*; idolatrizing, *ppr.* To worship idols.

ī-dol′ȧ-trize, *v.t.* To adore; to worship.

ī-dol′ȧ-trous, *a.* 1. Pertaining to idolatry; partaking of the nature of idolatry, or of the worship of false gods; consisting in the worship of idols; as, *idolatrous* worship.

2. Consisting in or partaking of an excessive attachment or reverence; as, an *idolatrous* veneration for antiquity.

ī-dol′ȧ-trous-ly, *adv.* In an idolatrous manner; with excessive reverence.

ī-dol′ȧ-try, *n.*; *pl.* **ī-dol′ȧ-trieş.** [OFr. *idolatrie*; LL. *idolatria*; Gr. *eidōlolatreia*, idolatry; *eidōlon*, an idol, and *latreia*, service.]

1. The worship of idols, images, or anything made by hands; the act of paying divine homage and reverence to any created object.

2. Excessive attachment or veneration for anything; admiration which borders on adoration.

ī′dŏl-ish, *a.* Idolatrous. [Obs.]

ī′dŏl-işm, *n.* The worship of idols. [Obs.]

ī′dŏl-ist, *n.* A worshiper of images or idols. [Obs.]

ī′dŏl-ize, *v.t.*; idolized, *pt.*, *pp.*; idolizing, *ppr.*

1. To worship as an idol; to make an idol of; as, the Egyptians *idolized* the ibis.

2. To love to excess; to love or reverence to adoration; as, to *idolize* gold; to *idolize* children; to *idolize* a hero.

ī′dŏl-ize, *v.i.* To practise idolatry.

ī′dŏl-i-zẽr, *n.* One who idolizes or loves to reverence.

ī-dol′ō-çlast, *n.* [Gr. *eidōlon*, an idol, and *klān*, to break.] An idol-breaker; an iconoclast.

ī-dol-ō-graph′iç-ăl, *a.* [Gr. *eidōlon*, an idol, and *graphein*, to write.] Describing or treating of idols. [Rare.]

ī-dō′lon, ī-dō′lum, *n.*; *pl.* **ī-dō′lȧ.** [L. *idolum*; Gr. *eidōlon*, an image, phantom.]

1. An image or idol of any kind.

2. A mental image; a false idea; a fallacy; a phantom; a specter.

ī′dŏl-ous, *a.* Idolatrous; heathenish. [Obs.]

ī-dō′nē-ous, *a.* [L. *idoneus*, fit, proper.] Fit; suitable; proper; convenient; adequate. [Obs.]

id-ọr′găn, *n.* [Gr. *idea*, an idea and *organon*, an organ.] In biology, an elementary organism ranking below the *Metazoa*; a plastid.

id′ri-ȧ-lin, id′ri-ȧ-line, *n.* A bituminous substance obtained from idrialite.

id′ri-ȧ-līte, *n.* [*Idria*, a town in Austria, and *-lite.*] An opaque greenish or brownish-black mineral obtained from the quicksilver mines of Idria, Austria.

ī-drō′sis, *n.* Same as *Hidrosis.*

Id-ū-mē′ăn, *a.* and *n.* [L. *Idumæus*; Gr. *Idoumaios*, from *Idoumaia*; Heb. *Edōm*, Edom, lit., red.]

I. *a.* Of or pertaining to Idumæa or Edom, an ancient kingdom in western Asia.

II. *n.* A native or inhabitant of ancient Idumæa; an Edomite.

ī′dyl, ī′dyll, *n.* [L. *idyllium*; Gr. *eidyllion*, a short descriptive poem, mostly on pastoral subjects; *eidos*, form, figure, image, and *-yllion*, dim. suffix.]

1. In literature, (a) a short poem or composition in a poetical style, of which the object, or at least the necessary accompaniment, is a vivid and simple representation of ordinary objects in pastoral nature or of scenes or events of pastoral life; as, the *idyls* of Theocritus; (b) a longer poem of narrative or descriptive character written in a highly finished style; as, Tennyson's *Idylls* of the King.

2. In music, a sentimental or pastoral composition, generally instrumental.

ī-dyl′liç, ī-dyl′li-çăl, *a.* Of or pertaining to an idyl; suitable, or fit for an idyl.

-ieṛ. [ME. *-ier*, *-yer*, *-iere*, from *-ere*; AS. *-ere*, the suffix added to verbs to form nouns of the agent, preceded by *i*, the formative of weak verbs in ME. *-ien*, AS. *-ian.*] A suffix added to verbs to form nouns indicating the agent; as, glaz*ier*, from glaze; braz*ier*, from braze, etc.

-ier. See third *-er.*

if, *conj.* [ME. *if*, *ef*; AS. *gif*, if.]

1. In case that; granting that; supposing that; allowing that.

> *If* thou be the Son of God, command that these stones be made bread. —Matt. iv. 3.

2. Whether or not.

> She doubts *if* two and two make four.—Prior.

3. Although; as, I am innocent, *if* appearances are against me.

ī′faith′. Indeed; truly.

i-fecks′, *interj.* An exclamation equivalent to *i′faith.* [Obs.]

-iferous. See *-ferous.*

I-fū′rin. *n.* In Celtic mythology, the Hades of the ancient Gauls, where the wicked were tortured by being chained in the lairs of dragons, subjected to incessant distillation of poisons, exposed to serpents and savage beasts, etc.

-ify. See *-fy.*

ig-ȧ-sū′riç, *a.* Contained in or obtained from nux vomica, or St. Ignatius's bean.

ig-ȧ-sū′rin, *n.* [Malay *igasura*, the *Strychnos* bean, nux vomica.] An alkaloid obtained from St. Ignatius's bean, or nux vomica.

ig′lo͝o, *n.* 1. The name given by the Eskimos to a hut made of snow.

2. The excavation which a seal makes in the snow over its breathing-hole, for the protection of its young.

Igloo or Seal's House—shown in section.

ig-nä′rō, *n.* [It., from L. *ignarus*, ignorant.] A blockhead. [Obs.]

Ig-nā′tiăn, *a.* Pertaining to St. Ignatius, one of the Christian fathers, who suffered martyrdom about A. D. 107.

ig″nē-ō-ȧ′quē-ous (-kwē-), *a.* [L. *igneus*, of fire, and *aqua*, water.] In geology, pertaining to or formed by the combined action of fire and water.

ig′nē-ous, *a.* [L. *igneus*, of fire, fiery, from *ignis*, fire.]

1. Pertaining to or consisting of fire; containing fire; having the nature of fire; resembling fire.

2. In geology, proceeding from the action of fire; as, lavas and basalt are *igneous* rocks.

ig-nes′cent, *a.* [L. *ignescens* (*-entis*), ppr. of *ignescere*, to take fire, to burn, from *ignis*, fire.] Emitting sparks of fire when struck with steel; scintillating; as, *ignescent* stones.

ig-nes′cent, *n.* A stone or mineral that gives out sparks when struck with steel or iron.

> Many other stones, besides this class of *ignescents*, produce real scintillation when struck against steel. —Fourcroy.

ig′nēş fat′ū-ī, pl. of *ignis fatuus.*

igni-. A combining form from L. *ignis*, fire, used to signify fire; as, *igni*ferous.

ig-nic′ō-list, *n.* [*Igni-*, and L. *colere*, to worship.] A fire-worshiper. [Rare.]

ig-nif′ẽr-ous, *a.* [*Igni-*, and L. *ferre*, to bear.] Producing fire.

ig-nif′lū-ous, *a.* Flowing with fire. [Obs.]

ig′ni-fy, *v.t.* [*Igni-*, and L. *facere*, to make.] To form into fire. [Rare.]

ig-nig′e-nous, *a.* [L. *ignigenus*, producing fire; *ignis*, fire, and *-genus*, from *gignere*, to produce.] Produced by fire.

ig-nip′ō-tent, *a.* [L. *ignipotens* (*-entis*), ruler of fire; *ignis*, fire, and *potens*, powerful.] Presiding over fire.

ig-ni-punc′tūre, *n.* [*Igni-*, and L. *punctura*, a puncture.] In surgery, puncture with a heated needle or stylus.

ig′nis fat′ū-us; *pl.* **ig′nēş fat′ū-ī.** [L. *ignis*, fire, and *fatuus*, foolish.] A phosphorescent light that appears in the night over marshy grounds, supposed to be occasioned by the decomposition of animal or vegetable substances, or by some inflammable gas; popularly called *will-o'-the-wisp, corpse-candle*, and *Jack-o'-lantern.*

ig-nite', *v.t.*; ignited, *pt., pp.*; igniting, *ppr.* [L. *ignitus*, pp. of *ignire*, to set on fire, from *ignis*, fire.]

1. To kindle or set on fire.

2. To heat intensely; to make incandescent; to render luminous or red by heat; as, to *ignite* charcoal or iron.

ig-nite', *v.i.* To take fire; to become red with heat.

ig-nīt'i-ble, *a.* Capable of being ignited.

ig-ni'tiŏn (-nish'un), *n.* [Fr. *ignition*, from L. *ignire*, to set on fire.]

1. The act of kindling or setting on fire.

2. The act or operation of communicating fire or heat, till the substance becomes red or incandescent.

3. The state of being kindled or ignited.

4. A means of igniting; detonating powder or similar material. [Rare.]

ig-nīt'ŏr, *n.* [L. *ignitus*, pp. of *ignire*, to set on fire.] One who or that which ignites, as a device to explode a shell or torpedo.

ig-niv'ō-mous, *a.* [LL. *ignivomus*; L. *ignis*, fire, and *vomere*, to vomit.] Vomiting fire; as, an *ignivomous* mountain. [Rare.]

ig-nō-bil'i-ty, *n.* The state or quality of being ignoble; ignobleness.

ig-nō'ble, *a.* [Fr. *ignoble*; L. *ignobilis*, unknown, obscure; *in-* priv., and *nobilis*, known.]

1. Of low birth or family; not noble; not illustrious.

2. Base; not honorable, elevated, or generous; unworthy; mean; as, an *ignoble* motive.

3. Inferior in kind; especially, in falconry, applied to the short-winged falcons.

Syn.—Degraded, reproachful, scandalous, infamous, degenerate, mean, base, dishonorable, humble, plebeian, lowly.

ig-nō'ble, *v.t.* To render ignoble; to degrade. [Obs.]

ig-nō'ble-ness, *n.* The state or quality of being ignoble; want of dignity; meanness.

ig-nō'bly, *adv.* In an ignoble manner.

ig-nō-min'i-ous, *a.* [L. *ignominiosus*, disgraceful, shameful, from *ignominia*, disgrace.]

1. Incurring ignominy or disgrace; cowardly; of mean character; shameful; infamous.

2. Despicable; worthy of ignominy or contempt.

Syn.—Shameful, scandalous, dishonorable, infamous.

ig-nō-min'i-ous-ly, *adv.* In an ignominious manner; disgracefully; shamefully.

ig'nō-min-y, *n.*; *pl.* **ig'nō-min-ies**. [Fr. *ignominie*; L. *ignominia*, disgrace, dishonor; *in-* priv., and *nomen*, name, renown, reputation.]

1. Public disgrace under the imputation of dishonorable motives or conduct; shame; reproach; dishonor; infamy.

> Their generals have been received with honor after their defeat; yours with *ignominy* after conquest. —Addison.

2. An act deserving disgrace; a source or cause of disgrace.

Syn.—Infamy, opprobrium, disgrace.

ig'nō-my, *n.* [Obs.] Same as *Ignominy.*

ig-nō-rā'mus, *n.* [L., lit., we take no notice; first pers. pl. pres. ind. act. of *ignorare*, to take no notice, to be ignorant.]

1. In law, the indorsement formerly made by the grand jury upon a bill presented to them for inquiry, when the evidence was insufficient to support the charges, by virtue of which indorsement all proceedings were stopped and the defendant discharged.

2. An ignorant person; a vain pretender to knowledge.

ig'nō-rănce, *n.* [OFr. *ignorance*; L. *ignorantia*, want of knowledge, from *ignorans (-antis)*, ppr. of *ignorare*, to be ignorant.] The state of being ignorant; want, absence, or destitution of knowledge in general or in relation to a particular subject.

ig'nō-rănt, *a.* [OFr. *ignorant*; L. *ignorans (-antis)*, ppr. of *ignorare*, to lack knowledge, be ignorant.]

1. Destitute of knowledge; uninstructed or uninformed; untaught; unenlightened.

> So foolish was I, and *ignorant*: I was as a beast before thee. —Ps. lxxiii. 22.

2. Unacquainted with; unconscious.

> *Ignorant* of guilt, I fear not shame.—Dryden.

3. Manifesting want of knowledge; caused by ignorance; as, *ignorant* remarks.

4. Done without knowledge as being of the kind mentioned; unwittingly committed. [Obs.]

Syn.—Illiterate, unlearned, unlettered, uninformed, untaught, benighted, uneducated, unenlightened.—*Ignorant* denotes want of knowledge, either as to a single subject or to information in general; *illiterate* refers to an ignorance of letters, or of knowledge acquired by reading and study.

ig'nō-rănt, *n.* A person untaught or uninformed; one unlettered or unskilled. [Obs.]

ig'nō-rănt-ism, *n.* Same as *Obscurantism.*

ig'nō-rănt-ist, *n.* Same as *Obscurant.*

ig'nō-rănt-ly, *adv.* In an ignorant manner; without knowledge, instruction, or information.

ig-nō-rā'tion, *n.* [L. *ignoratio (-onis)*, ignorance, from *ignorare*, to be ignorant.] The want of precise and accurate discrimination between objects of thought.

Ignoration of the elench; in logic, a fallacy which consists in avoiding the point at issue either inadvertently or purposely.

ig-nōre', *v.t.*; ignored, *pt., pp.*; ignoring, *ppr.* [Fr. *ignorer*; L. *ignorane*, to have no knowledge of, to ignore, from *ignarus*, not knowing; *in-* priv., and *gnarus*, knowing.]

1. To be ignorant of. [Obs.]

2. To pass over or by without notice; to act as if one were unacquainted with; to shut the eyes to; to leave out of account; to disregard; as, to *ignore* facts.

3. To reject, as false or ungrounded; used with reference to the grand jury when it rejects a bill because there is not sufficient evidence to make a presentment.

ig-nōre'ment, *n.* The act of ignoring, or state of being ignored.

Igorrote (ē"gor-rō'ta,) *n.* A native savage of Luzon, Philippine Islands.

i-guä'nȧ, *n.* [Sp., from the native Haytian name.] A large lizard native to the warmer parts of America, of the genus *Iguana* or related genera. It is of a green color, having a body and tail covered with small imbricated scales; the ridge of the back garnished with a row of elevated, compressed, and pointed scales; under the throat a depressed and depending dewlap, the edge of which is attached to a cartilaginous appendage of the hyoid bone, and having the head covered with scaly plates. Its flesh is valued as food.

Common Iguana (*Iguana tuberculata*).

i-guä'ni-ăn, *a.* Pertaining to the iguana.

i-guä'nid, *n.* One of the *Iguanidæ.*

I-guä'ni-dæ, *n.pl.* [Sp. *iguana*, the iguana, and *-idæ.*] A family of lacertilian reptiles of which the *Iguana* is the type genus.

I-guä'nō-don, *n.* [Sp. *iguana*, and Gr. *odous, odontos*, tooth; so called from the resemblance of its teeth to those of the iguana.] A genus of extinct fossil lizards of great size, belonging to the order *Dinosauria.* They are described as having pelvic bones similar to those of a bird, especially in the elongation and slenderness of the ischium, large hind legs with three-toed feet capable of supporting the entire body, and teeth large and broad, transversely ridged and implanted in sockets, but not ankylosed to the jaw.

Remains of Iguanodon.

1. Right side of lower jaw. 2. *a*, Two upper molars, external aspect; *b*, do. inner aspect; *c*, external aspect of mature lower molar; *d*, inner aspect of do. 3. Fang. 4. Horn.

i-guä'nō-dont, *a.* Resembling or relating to the *Iguanodon.*

i-guä-nō-dont'oid, *a.* [Sp. *iguana*, the iguana, and Gr. *odous, odontos*, tooth, and *eidos*, form.] Of, pertaining to, or resembling the iguana or family *Iguanidæ.*

i-guä'noid, *a.* and *n.* [Sp. *iguana*, the iguana, and Gr. *eidos*, form.]

I. *a.* Same as *Iguanian.*

II. *n.* Any member of the *Iguanidæ.*

ĭh-läng'ĭh-läng', *n.* [Malay.] A perfume derived from the flowers of the East Indian tree *Cananga odorata*; spelled also *ylang-ylang.*

ih-räm', *n.* [Ar., from *harama*, to forbid.]

1. The dress worn by Mohammedan pilgrims to Mecca, consisting, for men, of two scarfs, one folded round the loins and the other thrown over the neck and shoulders; for women, of a cloak enveloping the whole person.

2. The state of a pilgrim when he assumes this garb and performs the required pilgrimage.

I. H. S. An abbreviation usually considered as standing for *Iesus Hominum Salvator*, Jesus the Saviour of men, or for *In Hac (cruce) Salus*, in this (cross) is salvation; but it was originally ΙΗΣ, the first three, or perhaps the first two and the last letters of ΊΗΣΟΥΣ (*Iēsous*), the Greek form of *Jesus.*

ik, *pron.* I. [Obs.]

ī'kŏn, *n.* A sacred figure of the Greek church; also written *icon.*

il-. [L. *il-*, assimilated form of *in-*.] An assimilated form used before *l* of the prefix *in-*, signifying in, to; also sometimes used with intensive force.

il-. [L. *il-*, assimilated form of *in-*.] An assimilated form before *l* of the prefix *in-*, used with negative or privative force.

-il, -ile. [ME. *-il, -ile, -yl, -yle*, from L. *-ilis.*] A suffix added to the infinitive stems of Latin verbs or to the past participle stems in *-s-*, or *-t-*, to form adjectives or nouns derived from them; as, doc*ile*, from L. doc*ilis*, teachable, from *docere*, to teach, and *-ilis*; miss*ile*, from L. miss*ilis*, that which may be thrown, a missile, from *missus*, pp. of *mittere*, to send, and *-ilis.*

ile, *n.* An ear of corn. [Obs.]

ile, *n.* An aisle. [Obs.]

ile, *n.* An isle. [Obs.]

il'ē-aç, *a.* Same as *Iliac.*

il-ē-ī'tis, *n.* [L. *ilium*, generally in pl. *ilia*, the flank, and *-itis.*] An inflamed condition of the ileum.

ileo-. A combining form from L. *ileum, ilium*, pl. *ilia*, the groin or flank, used in medicine and anatomy to signify the ileum; as, *ileo*typhus, *ileo*colic.

il"ē-ō-cæ'çăl, *a.* Pertaining to the ileum and cæcum.

Ileocæcal valve; a double fold of mucous membrane preventing passage from the large to the small intestine.

il"ē-ō-çol'iç, *a.* [*Ileo-*, and L. *colon*, the colon.] Of or relating to the ileum and the colon.

il-ē-os'tō-my, *n.* [*Ileo-*, and Gr. *stoma*, mouth, opening.] In surgery, incision of the ileum.

il"ē-ō-tȳ'phus, *n.* [*Ileo-*, and Gr. *typhos*, stupor, the stupor arising from fever.] Typhoid fever.

il'ē-um, *n.* [L. *ileum*, or *ilium*, usually in pl. *ilia*, the flank, groin, from Gr. *eilein*, to roll, twist.] In anatomy, the lower three-fifths of the small intestine, so called from the convolutions or peristaltic motions.

il'ē-us, *n.* [L. *ileos*; Gr. *eileos*, colic, from *eilein*, to twist, turn, roll.]

1. In pathology, colic.

2. In anatomy, the ileum.

Ilex, *n.* [L., the holm-oak.]

1. A genus of evergreen trees and shrubs of the holly tribe. It comprehends about 150 species, many of which are natives of Central America, others occurring throughout the tropical and temperate regions of the globe. One of the most remarkable is *Ilex Aquifolium*, the common holly.

2. [i—] A tree or shrub of this genus.

il'i-ȧ, *n.*, pl. of *ilium.*

Il'i-aç, *a.* Relating to Ilium, or Troy.

il'i-aç, *a.* [Fr. *iliaque*, from L. *ileum, ilium*, pl. *ilia*, the groin, flank.]

1. Pertaining to the ileum or lower bowels. [Obs.]

2. Pertaining to the ilium or flank-bone.

Iliac region; the side of the abdomen between the ribs and the hips.

Iliac arteries; the arteries formed by the bifurcation of the aorta, near the last lumbar vertebra. They divide into the external iliac and internal or hypogastric arteries.

Il'i-ăd, *n.* [L. *Ilias (-adis)*, Gr. *Ilias (-ados)*, the Iliad, from *Ilios, Ilion*, Ilium, a poetical name for Troy, from its founder *Ilus*, the son of Tros.] An epic poem in the Greek language, in twenty-four books, generally regarded as composed by Homer. The main or primary episodes of this poem are the wrath of Achilles and the circumstances resulting from it. Some critics maintain that the Iliad is not one homogeneous poem, but a series of ballads or rhapsodies on different episodes of the Trojan war either by one author (Homer) or by different poets, united somewhat loosely into a sort of coherent poem.

i-lic'iç, *a.* [L. *ilex, ilicis*, the holm-oak.] Of, obtained from, or relating to the holly and plants of the same genus.

il'i-cin, il'i-cine, *n.* [L. *ilex, ilicis*, the holm-oak, and *-in, -ine.*] A nonazotized vegetable compound constituting the bitter principle of *Ilex Aquifolium.* It forms brownish-yellow crystals, bitter and febrifuge.

Il-i-cin'ē-æ, *n.pl.* [L. *ilex, ilicis*, the holm-oak, and *-in-*, and *-eæ.*] The *Aquifoliaceæ*, or holly family of plants.

ilio-. A combining form from L. *ilium, ileum*, pl. *ilia*, the flank; used in medicine, anatomy, etc., to signify the ilium, flank, or groin; as, *ilio*psoas, *ilio*lumbar.

il"i-ō-cæ'çăl, *a.* Ileocæcal.

il"i-ō-fem'ō-răl, *a.* [*Ilio-*, and L. *femur*, the thigh.] Of or indicating the ilium and the femur.

il"i-ō-lum'băr, *a.* [*Ilio-*, and L. *lumbus*, the loin.] Of or indicating the ilium and the lumbar regions.

il"i-ō-psō'ăs, *n.* [*Ilio-*, and Gr. *psoa*, the muscle of the loins.] The great flexor muscle of the hip, constituting the iliac and great psoas muscles, by some anatomists designated as distinct.

il′i-um, *n.*; *pl.* **il′i-ȧ.** In anatomy, the upper part of the hip-bone; the flank-bone.

i-lix-an′thin, *n.* [L. *ilex*, the holm-oak, and Gr. *xanthos*, yellow, and *-in.*] A substance found in the leaves of holly. It forms a yellow dye on cloth prepared with alumina or iron mordants.

ilk, *n.* [ME. *ilke*; AS. *ilc*, the same.] The same; also written *ilka, ilke.*

Of that ilk; a phrase denoting that a person's surname and title are the same; as, Grant *of that ilk*, that is, Grant of Grant.

ilk, il′kȧ, *a.* Each. [Scot.]

il-kōn′, il-kōon′, *pron.* Each one. [Obs.]

ill, *a.* [ME. *ille*; Ice. *illr*, ill.]

1. Bad or evil; contrary to good, in a physical or moral sense; unfavorable; disagreeable; baneful; wicked; wrong; iniquitous; as, an *ill* wind; *ill* news; *ill* health; *ill* will; *ill* humor; he sets an *ill* example.

2. Diseased; disordered; sick or indisposed; as, the man is *ill* of a fever.

3. Rude; unpolished; not proper; not legitimate; as, *ill* breeding; *ill* manners.

That's an *ill* phrase. —Shak.

4. Wanting in skill; inexpert; as, *ill* at remembering.

Ill at ease; disquieted; anxious; troubled; restless.

Ill blood; hatred; hostility; unfriendliness; enmity.

Ill will; enmity; often wrongly written as a compound.

Syn.—Bad, iniquitous, evil, wicked, sick, ailing, indisposed, poorly.

ill, *n.* 1. Wickedness; depravity; evil.

Strong virtue, like strong nature, struggles still,
Exerts itself, and then throws off the *ill.* —Dryden.

2. Misfortune; calamity; evil; disease; pain; whatever annoys or impairs happiness, or prevents success.

ill, *adv.* [ME. *ille*; Ice. *illa*, ill, badly.]

1. In an ill manner; badly; unfavorably; unfortunately.

Ill fares the land, to hastening ills a prey,
Where wealth accumulates and men decay. —Goldsmith.

2. Not easily; with pain or difficulty; as, he is *ill* able to sustain the burden.

Ill, prefixed to participles of the present or the past tense, or to adjectives having the form of past participles, forms many compound words the meaning of which is generally obvious; as, *ill*-fated, *ill*-humored, *ill*-timed, etc.

il-lab′ile, *a.* Not liable to fall or err; infallible. [Obs.]

il-lȧ-bil′i-ty, *n.* The quality of being illabile. [Obs.]

il-lac′ẽr-ȧ-ble, *a.* [L. *illacerabilis*; *in-* priv., and *lacerare*, to tear.] That cannot be torn or lacerated.

il-lac′ry-mȧ-ble, *a.* [L. *illacrimabilis*; *in-* priv., and *lacrimabilis*, worthy of tears, from *lacrimare*, to weep.] Incapable of weeping. [Obs.]

il-laps′ȧ-ble, *a.* Not capable of lapsing; incapable of error. [Rare.]

il-lapse′, *n.* [L. *illapsus*, a falling or flowing into, properly pp. of *illabi*, to fall or flow into; *in*, into, and *labi*, to slip, fall.] A gliding in; an immission or entrance of one thing into another; a falling on; a sudden attack.

il-lapse′, *v.i.* [L. *illapsus*, pp. of *illabi*, to fall or flow into.] To fall, pass, or glide; usually followed by *into.* [Rare.]

il-lā′quē-ȧ-ble (-kwē-), *a.* Capable of being ensnared or illaqueated. [Rare.]

il-lā′quē-āte, *v.t.* [L. *illaqueatus*, pp. of *illaqueare*, to ensnare; *in*, into, and *laqueare*, to snare, from *laqueus*, a snare.] To ensnare; to entrap; to entangle; to catch. [Rare.]

il-lā-quē-ā′tion, *n.* 1. The act of ensnaring. [Rare.]

2. A snare; a noose; a trap. [Rare.]

il-lā′tion, *n.* [LL. *illatio* (*-onis*), a carrying in, an inference, from *illatus*, pp. of *inferre*, to carry in; *in*, into, and *ferre*, to carry.]

1. The act of inferring from premises or reasons; inference.

2. That which is inferred; an inference; a deduction; a conclusion.

Inconsequent *illations* from a false conception of things. —Sir T. Browne.

3. In liturgics, (a) the bringing in of the elements of the eucharist and placing them on the altar; (b) in the Mozarabic liturgy, the eucharistic prelude.

il′lȧ-tive, *a.* [L. *illativus*, from *illatus*, pp. of *inferre*, to carry in; *in*, into, and *ferre*, to bear.]

1. Relating to illation; that may be inferred; as, an *illative* consequence.

2. That denotes an inference; as, an *illative* word, like *then* and *therefore.*

Illative conversion; in logic, that conversion or transposition in which the truth of the converse follows from the truth of the proposition given; thus, the proposition "Religion is the truest wisdom," becomes, by *illative conversion*, "The truest wisdom is religion."

Illative sense; the faculty of the human mind whereby it forms a final judgment upon the validity of an inference.

il′lȧ-tive, *n.* That which denotes illation or inference; an illative particle.

il′lȧ-tive-ly, *adv.* By inference.

il-lạud′ȧ-ble, *a.* [L. *illaudabilis*, not praiseworthy; *in-* priv., and *laudabilis*, praiseworthy.] Not laudable; not worthy of approbation or commendation; blameworthy; worthy of censure or dispraise.

il-lạud′ȧ-bly, *adv.* In an illaudable manner.

il-lȧ-war′rȧ-pälm (-päm), *n.* [So called from *Illawarra*, a district of Australia in which it grows.] An Australian palm, *Ptychosperma Cunninghamii* or *Seaforthia elegans*; it is sometimes cultivated.

ill′-bōd″ing, *a.* Inauspicious; unfavorable.

ill′-bred, *a.* Not well bred; rude; unpolished; impolite.

ill′-dis-pōṣed′, *a.* Not well disposed.

il-lec-ē-brā′cē-æ, *n.pl.* [L. *illecebra*, a charm.] A small natural order of exogenous plants, chiefly consisting of herbaceous weeds, found in the temperate parts of the world. The typical genus is *Illecebrum*, and the order is sometimes called *Paronychiaceæ.*

il-lec-ē-brā′tion, *n.* Enticement; allurement. [Rare.]

il-lec′ē-brous, *a.* Alluring; full of allurement. [Obs.]

il′leck, *n.* [Etym. uncertain.] The gemmous dragonet, *Callionymus lyra.*

il-lē′găl, *a.* [L. *in-* priv., and *legalis*, lawful.] Not legal; unlawful; contrary to law; illicit; as, an *illegal* act; *illegal* trade; *illegal* relations.

il-lē-gal′i-ty, *n.*; *pl.* **il-lē-gal′i-tieṣ.** The condition, quality, or character of being illegal; unlawfulness; as, the *illegality* of trespass or of false imprisonment.

il-lē′găl-īze, *v.t.*; illegalized, *pt.*, *pp.*; illegalizing, *ppr.* To render illegal or unlawful.

il-lē′găl-ly, *adv.* In an illegal manner; unlawfully; as, a man *illegally* imprisoned.

il-lē′găl-ness, *n.* Illegality.

il-leg-i-bil′i-ty, *n.* The state or quality of being illegible.

il-leg′i-ble, *a.* [L. *in-* priv., and LL. *legibilis*, legible.] Incapable of being read; obscure or defaced so that the words cannot be known.

il-leg′i-ble-ness, *n.* Illegibility.

il-leg′i-bly, *adv.* In an illegible manner; as, a letter written *illegibly.*

il-lē-git′i-mȧ-cy, *n.* The condition or character of being illegitimate.

il-lē-git′i-māte, *a.* 1. Unlawfully begotten; born out of wedlock; bastard; as, an *illegitimate* child.

2. Not in conformity with law; not regular or authorized.

3. Not legitimately deduced; illogical; as, an *illegitimate* inference.

4. Not authorized by good usage; as, an *illegitimate* word.

Illegitimate fertilization; in botany, in dimorphic plants, the fertilization of a female plant of one form by the pollen from a male plant of the same form.

il-lē-git′i-māte, *v.t.*; illegitimated, *pt.*, *pp.*; illegitimating, *ppr.* To render illegitimate; to prove to be born out of wedlock; to bastardize.

The marriage should only be dissolved for the future, without *illegitimating* the issue. —Burnet.

il-lē-git′i-māte-ly, *adv.* In an illegitimate manner; unlawfully.

il-lē-git-i-mā′tion, *n.* 1. The act of illegitimating or the state of being illegitimate; bastardy; illegitimacy.

2. Want of genuineness; spuriousness. [Obs.]

il-lē-git′i-mȧ-tīze, *v.t.*; illegitimatized, *pt.*, *pp.*; illegitimatizing, *ppr.* To render illegitimate; to illegitimate.

il-lē′sive, *a.* [L. *in-* priv., and *læsus*, pp. of *lædere*, to injure.] Harmless. [Rare.]

il-lev′i-ȧ-ble, *a.* Incapable of being levied or collected.

ill′-fā′vōred, *a.* Ugly; ill-looking; wanting beauty; deformed.

Ill-favored and lean-fleshed. —Gen. xli. 3.

ill′-fā′vōred-ly, *adv.* 1. With deformity.

2. Roughly; rudely. [Obs.]

ill′-fā′vōred-ness, *n.* The state of being ill-favored.

il-lib′ẽr-ăl, *a.* [L. *illiberalis*, unworthy of a freeman, ignoble; *in-* priv., and *liberalis*, belonging to freedom, generous, liberal, from *liber*, free.]

1. Not liberal; not free or generous.

2. Not catholic; of a contracted mind; narrow.

3. Not pure; not well authorized or elegant; as, *illiberal* words in Latin. [Rare.]

il-lib′ẽr-ăl-iṣm, *n.* Same as *Illiberality.*

il-lib-ẽr-al′i-ty, *n.* 1. Narrowness of mind; contractedness; meanness; want of catholic opinions.

2. Parsimony; want of munificence.

il-lib′ẽr-ăl-īze, *v.t.*; illiberalized, *pt.*, *pp.*; illiberalizing, *ppr.* To make illiberal.

il-lib′ẽr-ăl-ly, *adv.* Ungenerously; uncandidly; uncharitably; disingenuously; parsimoniously.

il-lib′ẽr-ăl-ness, *n.* Illiberality.

il-lic′it, *a.* [L. *illicitus*, not allowed; *in-* priv., and *licitus*, pp. of *licere*, to allow, permit.] Not permitted or allowed; prohibited; unlawful; as, an *illicit* trade; *illicit* intercourse or connection.

il-lic′it-ly, *adv.* In an illicit manner.

il-lic′it-ness, *n.* Unlawfulness.

il-lic′it-ous, *a.* Unlawful. [Rare.]

il-lic′i-um, *n.* [From L. *illicere*, to allure, charm.] In botany, a genus of the magnolia family of trees and shrubs whose fruit is used as a spice and whose seeds yield a fragrant oil used in flavoring cordials, being nearly the same as oil of anise.

Chinese Anise (*Illicium anisatum*).

il-light′en, *v.t.* To enlighten. [Obs.]

il-lim′it-ȧ-ble, *a.* Incapable of being limited or bounded; as, the *illimitable* void.

Syn.—Boundless, unlimited, vast, infinite, unbounded, immeasurable, limitless.

il-lim′it-ȧ-ble-ness, *n.* The state of being illimitable.

il-lim′it-ȧ-bly, *adv.* 1. Without possibility of being bounded.

2. Without limits.

il-lim-it-ā′tion, *n.* [L. *in-* priv., and *limitatio* (*-onis*), limitation.] The state of being illimitable.

il-lim′it-ed, *a.* Unbounded; interminable.

il-lim′it-ed-ness, *n.* Boundlessness; the state of being without limits or restriction.

il-li-ni′tion (-nish′un), *n.* [L. *illinere*, to smear, spread on; *in*, on, and *linere*, to smear, spread.]

1. A thin crust of some extraneous substance formed on minerals. [Rare.]

2. A rubbing in of ointment or liniment; also, that which is rubbed in. [Rare.]

Il-li-nois′ (-noi′), *n. sing.* and *pl.* [A name given by the French explorers, from *Illini*, the native name of the tribe, lit., men, and Fr. *-ois.*] An Indian tribe formerly occupying the territory now included in the state of this name.

Il-li-nois′ăn (-noi′), *a.* and *n.* I. *a.* Of or pertaining to the state of Illinois, bordering on Lake Michigan.

II. *n.* A native or citizen of Illinois.

il-li-quā′tion, *n.* [L. *in*, in, and *liquatio* (*-onis*), a melting, from *liquare*, to melt.] The process of liquefying any substance in a solvent.

il-liq′uid (-lik′wid), *a.* [L. *in-* priv., and *liquidus*, liquid.] In law, not established by any documentary evidence.

ill′ish, *a.* Slightly ill. [Rare.]

il-li′ṣion (-lizh′un), *n.* [LL. *illisio* (*-onis*), from L. *illisus*, pp. of *illidere*, to strike against; *in*, on, against, and *lædere*, to strike.] A dashing against or into.

il-lit′ẽr-ȧ-cy, *n.* 1. The state of being untaught or unlearned; want of a knowledge of letters; ignorance; inability to read and write.

2. A literary expression showing ignorance. [Rare.]

il-lit′ẽr-ăl, *a.* Not literal. [Rare.]

il-lit′ẽr-āte, *a.* [L. *illiteratus*, unlettered, uneducated; *in-* priv., and *litteratus*, marked with letters, educated, from *littera*, a letter.]

1. Unlettered; ignorant of letters or books; uninstructed in science; as, an *illiterate* man, nation, or tribe.

2. Specifically, unable to read.

il-lit′ẽr-āte, *n.* A person who is illiterate.

il-lit′ẽr-āte-ly, *adv.* Ignorantly.

il-lit′ẽr-āte-ness, *n.* Want of learning; ignorance of letters, books, or science.

il-lit′ẽr-ȧ-tūre, *n.* Want of learning; illiteracy. [Rare.]

ill′-judged′, *a.* Injudicious.

ill′-lived, *a.* Living wickedly. [Obs.]

ill′-look′ing, *a.* Having a bad look; homely.

ill′-man′nered, *a.* Rude; not polite.

ill′-nā′tūred, *a.* Habitually bad-tempered; snappish.

ill′-nā′tūred-ly, *adv.* In an ill-natured manner.

ill′-nā′tūred-ness, *n.* The quality of being ill-natured.

ill′ness, *n.* 1. Badness; unfavorableness; as, the *illness* of the weather. [Obs.]

2. Disease; indisposition; sickness; as, he has recovered from his *illness.*

3. Wickedness; iniquity. [Obs.]

Syn.—Disease, disorder, distemper, indisposition, malady, sickness, ailment.

il-lō-çal′i-ty, *n.* The quality of not being located.

il-loġ′iç-ăl, *a.* 1. Ignorant or negligent of the rules of logic or correct reasoning; as, an *illogical* disputant.

2. Contrary to the rules of logic or sound reasoning; as, an *illogical* inference.

il-loġ′iç-ăl-ly, *adv.* In a manner contrary to the rules of correct reasoning.

il-loġ′iç-ăl-ness, *n.* Contrariety to sound reasoning.

ill′=ō′mened, *a.* Having unlucky omens.

il-lor′i-çāte, *a.* In zoölogy, without a protecting cover or lorica.

ill′=stärred′, *a.* Fated to be unfortunate.

ill′=tem′pēred, *a.* Of bad temper; morose; crabbed; sour; peevish; fretful.

ill′=timed′, *a.* Done or said at an unsuitable time; inopportune.

ill″trēat′, *v.t.*; illtreated, *pt., pp.*; illtreating, *ppr.* To treat unkindly or with injustice; to wrong; to abuse.

il-lū′ci-dāte, *v.t.* [Obs.] See *Elucidate*.

il-lūde′, *v.t.* [OFr. *illuder*; L. *illudere*, to play with, to make sport of; *in*, in, on, and *ludere*, to play.] To play upon by artifice; to deceive; to mock. [Rare.]

il-lūme′, *v.t.*; illumed, *pt., pp.*; illuming, *ppr.* [OFr. *illumer*; L. *illuminare*, to light up; *in*, on, and *luminare*, to light.] To illumine; to illuminate; used chiefly in poetry.

il-lū′mi-nȧ-ble, *a.* [LL. *illuminabilis*, from L. *illuminare*, to light up.] Capable of being illuminated.

il-lū′mi-nănt, *n.* That which illuminates or affords light; as, the candle was formerly the chief *illuminant*.

il-lū′mi-nănt, *a.* [L. *illuminans (-antis)*, ppr. of *illuminare*, to light up, illuminate.] Illuminating; giving or producing light.

il-lū′mi-nā-ry, *a.* Pertaining to illumination; illuminative.

il-lū′mi-nāte, *v.t.*; illuminated, *pt., pp.*; illuminating, *ppr.* [L. *illuminatus*, pp. of *illuminare*, to light up; *in*, on, and *luminare*, to light, from *lumen*, *luminis*, a light.]

1. To throw light on; to supply with light; to make luminous, in a literal or figurative sense; to enlighten; as, to *illuminate* a hall; to *illuminate* the mind.

2. To adorn with many lights; to light up profusely; as, the town was *illuminated* in honor of his arrival.

3. To adorn with ornamented letters, pictures, designs, etc.; as, to *illuminate* manuscripts or pages.

Syn.—Enlighten, illumine.—*Illuminate* and *enlighten* both denote the communication of light; the former in the natural, the latter in the moral sense. *Illumine* is a poetic variation of *illuminate*.

il-lū′mi-nāte, *v.i.* To make a display by means of lights, as on a festive occasion; as, the people of the city were anxious to *illuminate*.

il-lū′mi-nāte, *a.* Enlightened; illuminated; made bright. [Rare.]

il-lū′mi-nāte, *n.* One pretending to extraordinary knowledge or skill; one of the illuminati.

il-lū-mi-nā′tī, *n.pl.* [L., pl. of *illuminatus*, pp. of *illuminare*, to light up.]

1. In church history, persons who had received baptism, in which ceremony they were given a lighted taper, as a symbol of the faith and grace they had received by that sacrament.

2. [I—] Certain heretics, as the Alumbrados, who sprang up in Spain about the year 1575, and who afterward appeared in France. Their principal doctrine was that, by mental prayer, they had attained to so perfect a state as to have no need of ordinances, sacraments, and good works.

3. [I—] The members of a secret society founded in 1776 by Adam Weishaupt, professor of law at Ingolstadt in Bavaria. Its professed object was the attainment of a higher degree of virtue and morality than that reached in ordinary society. It was suppressed by the Bavarian government in 1785. Called also the *Order of the Illuminati*.

4. Persons who affect to possess extraordinary knowledge or enlightenment; chiefly a satirical use.

il-lū-mi-nā′tion, *n.* [OFr. *illumination*; LL. *Illuminatio (-onis)*, from L. *illuminare*, to light up, illuminate.]

1. The act of illuminating or the state of being illuminated; a decorating or adorning with festal lights; as, the *illumination* of a building.

2. That which gives light; brightness.

The sun is an *illumination* created.—Raleigh.

3. The amount of light received from a luminous source; as, the intensity of *illumination*.

4. Enlightenment of the mind; imparted knowledge.

5. The belief of the illuminati; extravagant admiration of enlightenment or knowledge.

6. The decoration of a manuscript or pages with colored drawings, figures, letters, etc., as done in the middle ages.

il-lū′mi-nȧ-tiṣm, *n.* Same as *Illuminism*.

il-lū′mi-nā-tive, *a.* Having the power of giving light; illustrative.

il-lū′mi-nā-tŏr, *n.* [LL. *illuminator*, from L. *illuminare*, to light up, illuminate.]

1. One who or that which illuminates or gives light, as (a) a lamp fitted with a lens for use in surgery; (b) an electric bulb used in surgery to examine cavities and passages; (c) the mirror or lens in optical instruments designed to reflect light upon an object or a particular part of an object.

2. One who illuminates manuscripts, pages, etc.

il-lū′mine, *v.t.*; illumined, *pt., pp.*; illumining, *ppr.* [Fr. *illuminer*; L. *illuminare*, to light up; *in*, in, and *luminare*, to light, from *lumen*, a light.] To illuminate; to enlighten; to throw light upon, in a literal or figurative sense.

il-lū-mi-nee′, *n.* [Fr. *illuminé*; L. *illuminatus*, pp. of *illuminare*, to light up, illuminate.] One of the Illuminati.

il-lū′mi-nēr, *n.* One who illuminates. [Rare.]

il-lū′mi-niṣm, *n.* The principles of the Illuminati.

il-lū-mi-nis′tiç, *a.* Relating to the Illuminati or to illuminism.

il-lū′mi-nīze, *v.t.*; illuminized, *pt., pp.*; illuminizing, *ppr.* To initiate into the doctrines or principles of the Illuminati.

il-lū′mi-nous, *a.* Bright; clear. [Rare.]

il′lū-pi, *n.* [E. Ind.] A tree, *Bassia longifolia* of the star-apple family, the bark, leaves, and juice of which are reputed to possess medicinal properties.

il-lūre′, *v.t.* To lure; to allure; to entice; to deceive. [Obs.]

il-lū′ṣiŏn, *n.* [L. *illusio (-onis)*, a mocking, jeering, from *illusus*, pp. of *illudere*, to mock, play with; *in*, on, and *ludere*, to play.]

1. The act of deceiving or imposing upon; deception; mockery.

This world is all a fleeting show,
For man's *illusion* given. —Moore.

2. That which deceives; an unreal vision presented to the bodily or mental eye; a deceptive appearance; a false show.

3. In psychology, an erroneous perception caused by a misinterpretation or exaggeration of a true perception; distinguished from *delusion* and *hallucination*.

4. A kind of tulle, used for veils, dresses, etc.; it is usually made of silk.

Syn.—Chimera, deception, delusion, fallacy.

il-lū′ṣiŏn-ȧ-ble, *a.* Liable to be deluded or deceived. [Rare.]

il-lū′ṣiŏn-ist, *n.* One given to illusion.

il-lū′sive, *a.* [L. *illusus*, pp. of *illudere*, to mock.] Deceiving by false show; deceitful; false.

il-lū′sive-ly, *adv.* In an illusive manner.

il-lū′sive-ness, *n.* Deception; false show; the quality of being illusive.

il-lū′sō-ry, *a.* [LL. *illusor*, a mocker, from L. *illusus*, pp. of *illudere*, to mock, illude.] Deceiving or intending to deceive, as by false appearances; fallacious.

Illusory creations of imagination.—J. Caird.

il-lus′trȧ-ble, *a.* Capable of being illustrated; admitting of illustration. [Rare.]

il-lus′trāte (*or* il′us-), *v.t.*; illustrated, *pt., pp.*; illustrating, *ppr.* [L. *illustratus*, pp. of *illustrare*, to light up, illuminate, from *illustris*, clear, bright, lustrous.]

1. To make clear, bright, or luminous. [Rare.]

2. To explain or elucidate; to make clear or intelligible; as, to *illustrate* a passage of Scripture by comments.

3. To ornament or elucidate by means of pictures, drawings, etc.; as, to *illustrate* a book.

4. To make celebrated or eminent; to glorify; to make illustrious. [Rare.]

il-lus′trāte, *a.* Famous; renowned; illustrious. [Obs.]

il-lus-trā′tion, *n.* 1. The act of illustrating; the act of rendering clear or obvious; explanation; elucidation.

2. The state of being illustrated.

3. That which illustrates, as a comparison or example intended to explain or make obvious; an engraving, picture, or the like, intended to ornament a book or elucidate the text.

4. Distinction. [Rare.]

il-lus′trȧ-tive, *a.* 1. Tending to illustrate, elucidate, explain, or exemplify; as, an argument or simile *illustrative* of a subject.

2. Tending to make glorious or illustrious; honorific. [Obs.]

il-lus′trȧ-tive-ly, *adv.* By way of illustration or elucidation.

il-lus′trā-tŏr (*or* il′us-), *n.* [LL. *illustrator*, an enlightener, from L. *illustrare*, to light up, illustrate.] One who illustrates.

il-lus′trȧ-tō-ry, *a.* Serving to illustrate.

il-lus′tri-ous, *a.* [L. *illustris*, clear, conspicuous, distinguished; *in*, in, and *lux*, *lucis*, light.]

1. Possessing luster or brilliancy; luminous; bright; shining. [Obs.]

2. Distinguished by greatness, nobleness, etc.; conspicuous; renowned; eminent; as, an *illustrious* general or magistrate; an *illustrious* prince.

3. Conferring luster or honor; brilliant; renowned.

Illustrious acts high raptures do infuse. —Waller.

Syn.—Renowned, glorious, brilliant, eminent, distinguished, celebrated, conspicuous, noble, famous.

il-lus′tri-ous-ly, *adv.* In an illustrious manner.

il-lus′tri-ous-ness, *n.* The state or quality of being illustrious; greatness; grandeur; glory.

il-lus′trous, *a.* Lacking luster. [Obs.]

il-lū-tā′tion, *n.* [L. *in*, in, and *lutum*, mud.] The act of bathing in mud or the sediment of a mineral spring.

il-lux-ū′ri-ous, *a.* Not luxurious. [Rare.]

ill′=will′, *n.* See *Ill will* under *Ill*, a.

ill′=wish′ēr, *n.* One who wishes ill to another.

il′ly, *adv.* In an ill manner; ill. The word is not in common or good use, *ill* being preferred.

il′men-īte, *n.* [Named from the *Ilmen* Mountains, where the mineral was first found.] An isomorph of hematite, found as a mineral oxid of iron and titanium.

il′vȧ-īte, *n.* [L. *Ilva*, Elba, and *-ite*.] In mineralogy, a black crystallized mineral composed of iron, calcium, and silica, found on the island of Elba; called also *lievrite* and *yenite*.

I′m. A contraction for *I am*.

im-. [L. *im-*, assimilated form of *in-*.] An assimilated form of *in-*, used before labials for the sake of euphony, signifying in, to, or sometimes with an intensive, negative, or privative force.

im-. An assimilated form of the prefix *in-*, from ME. *in-*, AS. *in-*, meaning in, into, used before labials for the sake of euphony.

im′āġe, *n.* [OFr. *image*; L. *imago (-inis)*, an imitation, copy, image.]

1. A representation or similitude of any person or thing, made of a material substance, however formed; as, an *image* wrought out of stone, wood, or wax, or on canvas or paper.

Its minted coins,
Now stamped with the *image* of good Queen Bess,
And now of a bloody Mary. —Hood.

2. An idol; the representation of any person or thing that is an object of worship.

3. Any copy, representation, or likeness; as, the child is the *image* of its mother.

4. Semblance; show; appearance.

The face of things a frightful *image* bears. —Dryden.

5. An idea; a representation of anything to the mind; a conception; a picture drawn by fancy.

Can we conceive
Image of aught delightful, soft, or great?
—Prior.

6. In rhetoric, a term loosely used, but which generally denotes a metaphor dilated and rendered a more complete picture by the assemblage of various ideas through which the same metaphor continues to run, yet not sufficiently expanded to form an allegory.

Images are of great use to give weight, magnificence, and strength to a discourse.
—London Encyc.

7. In optics, (a) the locus of all the pencils of converging or diverging rays emanating from every point of an object and received on a surface; (b) any likeness of an object produced by refraction or reflection, whether enlarged or diminished, erect or inverted, virtual or real.

Real image; in optics, an image that may be projected upon a screen; that is, formed by the rays themselves proceeding from an object.

Virtual image; in optics, an image that cannot be projected upon a screen; that is, formed by a prolongation of the rays which proceed from an object.

im′āġe, *v.t.*; imaged, *pt., pp.*; imaging, *ppr.*

1. To represent or form an image of; as, mountains *imaged* in the peaceful lake.

2. To form a likeness of in the mind by the fancy or by recollection; to imagine.

And *image* charms he must behold no more.
—Pope.

im′āġe-ȧ-ble, *a.* That may be imaged. [Rare.]

im′āġe=break″ēr, *n.* One who breaks images; an iconoclast.

im′āġe=grāv″ēr, *n.* A carver or sculptor.

im′āġe-less, *a.* Having no image.

im′ȧ-ġēr, *n.* One who forms images, material or mental. [Rare.]

im′āġe-ry, *n.* [OFr. *imagerie*, from L. *imago (-inis)*, an image.]

1. The work of one who makes representations, pictures, or statues.

Rich carvings, portraitures, and *imagery*. —Dryden.

2. Show; appearance.

What can thy *imagery* of sorrow mean? —Prior.

3. Forms of the fancy; false ideas; imaginary phantasms.

The *imagery* of a melancholic fancy. —Atterbury.

4. In rhetoric, representations in writing or speaking; lively descriptions which impress the images of things on the mind; figures in discourse.

I wish there may be in this poem any instance of good *imagery*. —Dryden.

5. Form; likeness. [Obs.]

im′āge-wor″ship, *n.* 1. The worship of images in their symbolical relation to that which they represent, as distinguished from the worship of images themselves.

2. The worship of images; idolatry.

im-ag′i-nȧ-ble, *a.* [Fr. *imaginable*; LL. *imaginabilis*, from L. *imaginari*, to imagine.] Capable of being imagined or conceived; as, the point is proved with all *imaginable* clearness.

im-ag′i-nȧ-ble-ness, *n.* The state of being imaginable.

im-ag′i-nȧ-bly, *adv.* In an imaginable manner.

im-ag′i-nȧl, *a.* [LL. *imaginalis*, figurative, from L. *imago (-inis)*, a figure, image.]

1. Noted for or given to imagination, imaginative.

2. Addicted to the intermingling of rhetorical figures in discourse.

3. In zoölogy, of or relating to the imago.

Imaginal disks; in zoölogy, the hypodermic cells retained by certain larvæ after separation from the eggs, out of which wings and legs are duly formed.

im-ag′i-nănt, *a.* Imagining; conceiving. [Obs.]

im-ag′i-nănt, *n.* One who is given to imagination or the forming of strange ideas. [Obs.]

im-ag′i-nā-ri-ly, *adv.* In an imaginary or fanciful manner, in imagination; ideally.

im-ag′i-nā-ri-ness, *n.* The state of being fancied or imaginary; the state of being unreal while pictured as real.

im-ag′i-nā-ry, *a.* [L. *imaginarius*, seeming, fancied, existing in imagination, from *imago (-inis)*, an image.] Existing only in imagination or fancy; visionary; fancied; not real.

Imaginary ills and fancied tortures.—Addison.

Imaginary quantity or *expression*; in mathematics, an algebraic expression or symbol having no assignable arithmetical or numerical meaning or interpretation; the even root of a negative quantity; as, $\sqrt{-a}$; $\sqrt[4]{-2}$. Called also *impossible quantity* or *expression*.

Syn.—Unreal, ideal, fanciful, chimerical, visionary.

im-ag′i-nā-ry, *n.*; *pl.* **im-ag′i-nā-ries**. In algebra, an imaginary quantity or expression.

im-ag-i-nā′tion, *n.* [L. *imaginatio (-onis)*, imagination, from *imaginari*, to imagine, from *imago (-inis)*, an image.]

1. The power or faculty of the mind by which it conceives and forms ideas of things communicated to it by the organs of sense. Imagination, in its proper sense, according to Reid, signifies a lively conception of objects of sight. It is distinguished from conception as a part from a whole. "The business of conception," says Stewart, "is to present us with an exact transcript of what we have felt or perceived. But we have also a power of modifying our conceptions, by combining the parts of different ones so as to form new wholes of our own creation. I shall employ the word *imagination* to express this power. I apprehend this to be the proper sense of the word, if imagination be the power which gives birth to the productions of the poet and the painter." Imagination might be defined as the will working on the materials of memory; not satisfied with following the order prescribed by nature or suggested by accident, it selects the parts of different conceptions or objects of memory to form a whole more pleasing, more elevated, more sublime, more terrible, or more awful than has ever been presented in the ordinary course of nature. The term is often employed in a narrow acceptation as synonymous with *fancy*, which properly is only a lower or slighter development of the imaginative faculty. In its widest signification, however, imagination is coextensive with *invention*, furnishing the writer with whatever is most happy and appropriate in language, or vivid and forcible in thought.

The power of the mind to decompose its conceptions, and to recombine the elements of them at its pleasure, is called its faculty of *imagination*. —Taylor.

2. Image in the mind; conception; idea.

Sometimes despair darkens all her *imaginations*. —Sir P. Sidney.

3. Contrivance; scheme; device; plot.

Thou hast seen all their vengeance and all their *imaginations* against me.—Lam. iii. 60.

4. An unsolid or fanciful opinion.

We are apt to think that space, in itself, is actually boundless; to which *imagination* the idea of space of itself leads us.—Locke.

im-ag-i-nā′tion-ăl, *a.* Imaginative.

im-ag-i-nā′tion-ăl-iṣm, *n.* A state of the mind in which the imagination rules.

im-ag′i-nā-tive, *a.* [OFr. *imaginatif*, from L. *imaginatus*, pp. of *imaginari*, to imagine.]

1. Forming images; endowed with imagination; as, the *imaginative* faculty.

2. Owing existence to or characterized by imagination; used generally in the highest sense of the word; as, *imaginative* art; *imaginative* genius.

Syn.—Creative, conceptive, ideal, poetical, romantic, inventive, original.

im-ag′i-nā-tive-ly, *adv.* In a fanciful or imaginative manner.

im-ag′i-nā-tive-ness, *n.* The state of being imaginative.

im-ag′ine, *v.t.*; imagined, *pt.*, *pp.*; imagining, *ppr.* [ME. *imaginen*; OFr. *imaginer*, *ymaginer*; L. *imaginari*, to picture to oneself, fancy, imagine, from *imago (-inis)*, a likeness, image.]

1. To form a notion or idea of in the mind; to fancy.

2. To conceive in thought; to think.

3. To contrive in purpose; to scheme; to devise.

How long will ye *imagine* mischief against a man? —Ps. lxii. 3.

Syn.—Apprehend, conceive, deem, opine.

im-ag′ine, *v.i.* 1. To conceive; to suppose; to fancy; to have a notion or idea; as, this has happened, I cannot *imagine* how.

2. To form conceptions; to exercise imagination.

im-ag′in-ẽr, *n.* One who forms ideas; one who imagines.

im′āg-ing, *n.* The forming of an image.

im-ag′in-ous, *a.* Fanciful or imaginative.

im′-a-gism, *n.* The art of creating mental images or pictures.

im′-a-gist, *a.* An artist who creates vivid mental pictures without closely adhering to the accepted canons of his art.

i-mā′gō, *n.*; *pl.* **i-mā′gōeṣ**. [L. *imago (-inis)*, an image, likeness.]

1. A perfect insect, which, being no longer disguised or confined, or in any respect imperfect, is become a true representative, or image of its species, and is qualified to fulfil the laws of nature in propagating its kind.

2. In a general sense, an image.

i-mäm′, i-mäum′, *n.* [Ar. *imam*, a guide, chief, leader, from *amma*, to walk before, preside.]

1. A minister or priest who performs the regular service of the mosque among the Mohammedans; generally, one who has precedence in war or prayer, sometimes also in science and literature.

2. A Mohammedan prince who, assuming to be a successor to Mohammed, unites in his person supreme spiritual and temporal power; as, the *imam* of Muscat. The sultan of Turkey, as chief of all ecclesiastical affairs, has the title, which is or has been borne by some other Mussulman princes.

Imam of a Mosque.

i-mā′ret, *n.* [Turk.] A hostelry for the free accommodation of Mohammedan pilgrims.

im-bälm′ (-bäm′), *v.t.* [Rare.] Same as *Embalm*.

im-ban′, *v.t.* [*In* and *ban*.] To put a ban upon; to excommunicate.

im-band′, *v.t.*; imbanded, *pt.*, *pp.*; imbanding, *ppr.* To form into a band or bands.

im′ban′nẽred, *a.* Furnished with banners.

im-bär-kā′tion, *n.* [Obs.] Same as *Embarkation*.

im-bärk′ment, *n.* [Obs.] Same as *Embarkment*.

im-bärn′, *v.t.*; imbarned, *pt.*, *pp.*; imbarning, *ppr.* To put in a barn, as to store. [Obs.]

A fair harvest, well in and *imbarned*. —Herbert.

im-bāse′, *v.t.* [Obs.] See *Embase*.

im-bas′tȧrd-īze, *v.t.* [Obs.] See *Embastardize*.

im-bāthe′, *v.t.* [Obs.] Same as *Embathe*.

im-bat′tle, *v.t.* To furnish with battlements; usually spelled *embattle*.

im-bat′tled, *a.* Same as *Embattled*.

im-bāy′, *v.t.* [Obs.] See *Embay*.

im′bē-cile, *a.* [OFr. *imbecile*; L. *imbecillis*, *imbecillus*, feeble, weak.]

1. Weak; feeble; destitute of strength; impotent. [Rare.]

We in a manner were got out of God's possession; were in respect to him become *imbecile* and lost. —Barrow.

2. Mentally feeble; fatuous; with mental faculties greatly impaired.

Syn.—Stupid, feeble-minded, idiotic.—An *imbecile* person often changes his views and vacillates in his purposes. A *stupid* person is very persistent in his opinions and resolves, both of which, however, are senseless.

im′bē-cile, *n.* One who is imbecile.

im′bē-cile, *v.t.* To weaken. [Obs.]

im-bē-cil′i-tāte, *v.t.*; imbecilitated, *pt.*, *pp.*; imbecilitating, *ppr.* To weaken; to render feeble.

im-bē-cil′i-ty, *n.* [OFr. *imbecilete*; L. *imbecilitas (-atis)*, weakness, feebleness of mind or body, from *imbecillis*, *imbecillus*, weak, feeble.]

1. Want of strength; weakness; feebleness of body or of mind.

Cruelty argues not only a depravedness of nature, but also a meanness of courage and *imbecility* of mind. —Sir W. Temple.

2. Impotence of body. [Obs.]

im-bed′, *v.t.* 1. Same as *Embed*.

2. In microscopy, to incase in paraffin, as material which has previously been infiltrated preparatory to being sectioned on the microtome.

im-bel′lic, *a.* [L. *in-* priv., and *bellicus*, warlike.] Not warlike or martial. [Rare.]

im-bench′ing, *n.* A raised work like a bench.

im′bẽr-goose, *n.* A loon; the ember-goose.

im-bez′zle, *v.t.* [Obs.] Same as *Embezzle*.

im-bibe′, *v.t.*; imbibed, *pt.*, *pp.*; imbibing, *ppr.* [L. *imbibere*, to drink in; *in*, in, and *bibere*, to drink.]

1. To drink in; to absorb; as, a sponge *imbibes* moisture.

2. To receive or admit into the mind and retain; as, to *imbibe* principles; to *imbibe* errors.

3. To imbue. [Obs.]

im-bib′ẽr, *n.* One who or that which imbibes.

im-bi-bi′tiŏn (-bish′un), *n.* The act of imbibing.

im-bit′tẽr, *v.t.* [Obs.] See *Embitter*.

im-bit′tẽr-ment, *n.* [Obs.] See *Embitterment*.

im-blāze′, *v.t.* [Obs.] See *Emblaze*.

im-blā′zŏn, *v.t.* To emblazon. [Obs.]

im-bod′y, *v.t.* and *v.i.* Same as *Embody*.

im-boil′, *v.t.* and *v.i.* [Obs.] See *Emboil*.

im-bōld′en, *v.t.* [Obs.] Same as *Embolden*.

im-bon′i-ty, *n.* [LL. *imbonitas*, want of goodness, inconvenience; L. *in-* priv., and *bonitas*, goodness, from *bonus*, good.] Deficiency in goodness.

im-bọr′dẽr, *v.t.* [Obs.] See *Emborder*.

im-bosh′, *n.* Foam on a quarry. [Obs.]

im-bosk′, *v.t.* [It. *imboscare*; *im-*, in, and *bosco*, a wood.] To conceal, as in bushes; to hide.

im-bosk′, *v.i.* To lie concealed.

im-boṣ′ŏm, *v.t.* Same as *Embosom*.

im-boss′, *v.t.* [Obs.] See first *Emboss*.

im-bos′ture, *n.* An embossed ornament. [Obs.]

im-bōw′, *v.t.* Same as *Embow*.

im-bow′el, im-bow′el-ẽr, etc. See *Embowel*, etc.

im-bow′ẽr, *v.i.* and *v.t.* See *Embower*.

im-box′, *v.t.* To embox.

im-brāce′, im-brāce′ment, etc. [Obs.] See *Embrace*, etc.

im-brāid′, *v.t.* [Obs.] See *Embraid*.

im-bran′gle, *v.t.* Same as *Embrangle*.

im-breed′, *v.t.* [Obs.] See *Inbreed*.

im′bri-çāte, im′bri-çā-ted, *a.* [L. *imbricatus*, pp. of *imbricare*, to cover with gutter tiles, to form like a roof or gutter tile, from L. *imbrex (-icis)*, a gutter tile, from *imber*, rain.]

1. Bent or hollowed like a roof or gutter tile.

2. In botany, lying over each other in regular order, like tiles on a roof, as the scales on the cup of some acorns; overlapping each other at the margins, without any involution, as leaves in the bud.

Imbricate Bud.

3. In decoration, overlapping, or represented as if overlapping; as, an *imbricated* pattern.

im′bri-çāte, *v.t.*; imbricated, *pt.*, *pp.*; imbricating, *ppr.* To place so as to overlap, or to make appear overlapped.

im-bri-çā′tion, *n.* 1. The state of being imbricate; particularly a real or apparent overlapping, as of shingles.

2. In masonry, a structure, as tiling, wall, or the like, laid so as to break joints.

3. A concavity like that of a gutter tile.

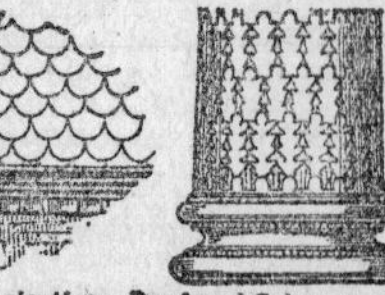

Imbrication—Roof and Column.

im′bri-cā-tive, *a.* Same as first *Imbricate.*

im-brō-cā′dō, *n.* [*Im-*, in or on, and Sp. *brocado*, brocade.] Cloth of gold or of silver.

im-brōc-cā′tȧ, im-brō-cā′tȧ, *n.* In fencing, a kind of thrust. [Obs.]

im-brogl′iō (-brōl′yō), *n.* [It., confusion, from *imbrogliare*, to confuse.]

1. An intricate, complicated plot, as in a drama.

2. A misunderstanding; a perplexing state of affairs.

im-brown′, *v.t.* [Obs.] See *Embrown.*

im-brūe′, *v.t.*; imbrued, *pt., pp.*; imbruing, *ppr.* [ME. *imbrowen*; OFr. *embruer*, to give to drink; L. *in-*, in, and *bibere*, to drink.]

1. To wet or moisten; to soak; to drench in a fluid, especially in blood.

Whose arrows in my blood their wings *imbrue.* —Sandys.

2. To soak into.

im-brū′ment, *n.* The act of imbruing; the condition of being imbrued.

im-brūte′, *v.t.*; imbruted, *pt., pp.*; imbruting, *ppr.* To degrade to the state of a brute; to reduce to brutality.

And mix with bestial slime
This essence to incarnate and *imbrute.*
—Milton.

im-brūte′, *v.i.* To sink to the state of a brute.

im-brūte′ment, *n.* The act of degrading to the level of a brute; the state of being thus degraded.

im-būe′, *v.t.*; imbued, *pt., pp.*; imbuing, *ppr.* [OFr. *imbuer*; L. *imbuere*, to wet, soak.]

1. To tinge deeply; to dye; as, to *imbue* cloth.

2. To tincture deeply; to cause to imbibe; as, to *imbue* the minds of youth with good principles.

im-būe′ment, *n.* The act of imbuing or the state of being imbued.

im-bŭrse′, *v.t.* [L. *in-*, in, and *bursa*, a purse.] To supply money, or to stock with money. [Obs.]

im-bŭrse′ment, *n.* 1. The act of supplying money. [Obs.]

2. Money laid up in stock. [Obs.]

im-bū′tiọn, *n.* The act of imbuing. [Obs.]

i-mes′ȧ-tin, *n.* [*Im*ide and *isatin.*] A crystalline substance, $C_8H_6N_2O$, formed by the action of ammonia on a boiling solution of isatin in alcohol.

im′ide, im′id, *n.* [Variant of *amide.*] A compound in which, in the ammonia ingredient, two atoms of hydrogen have been replaced by a divalent acid radical.

im′i-dō-. A combining form from *imide*, used in chemistry to denote substances which contain the radical NH, called the imido-group.

im′i-dō-ac′id, *n.* An organic acid formed by the union of one or more acid radicals with a compound of the imido-group, in which the hydrogen is replaceable.

im″i-tȧ-bil′i-ty, *n.* The quality of being imitable.

im′i-tȧ-ble, *a.* [Fr. *imitable*; L. *imitabilis*, from *imitari*, to imitate.]

1. Capable of being imitated or copied.

2. Worthy of imitation. [Rare.]

im′i-tȧ-ble-ness, *n.* The quality of being imitable.

im′i-tăn-cy, *n.* The inclination to imitate. [Rare.]

im′i-tāte, *v.t.*; imitated, *pt., pp.*; imitating, *ppr.* [L. *imitatus*, pp. of *imitari*, to imitate.]

1. To follow in manners; to copy in form, color, or quality; to reproduce in semblance of character, action, color, etc.

2. In biology, to assume the appearance of (something else in nature) for the purpose of concealment or security from attack.

Syn.—Copy, follow, mimic, ape, mock.

im-i-tā′tion, *n.* [L. *imitatio (-onis)*, imitation, from *imitari*, to imitate.]

1. The act of imitating.

Poetry is an act of *imitation*, that is to say, a representation, counterfeiting, or figuring forth. —Sidney.

2. That which is made or produced as a copy; likeness; resemblance.

Both these arts are not only true *imitations* of nature, but of the best nature. —Dryden.

3. In music, the repetition of essentially the same melodic idea, as different degrees of the scale, by different parts or voices in a polyphonic composition.

4. In biology, the act or quality of assuming a form like that of something else in nature, for the purpose of concealment or security from attack.

im-i-tā′tion-ăl, *a.* Relating to imitation. [Rare.]

im′i-tā-tive, *a.* [L. *imitatus*, pp. of *imitari*, to imitate.]

1. Inclined to imitate or follow in manner; as, man is an *imitative* being.

2. Aiming at resemblance; employed in the art of creating resemblances; as, painting is an *imitative* art.

3. Formed after a model, pattern, or original.

This temple, less in form, with equal grace,
Was *imitative* of the first in Thrace.—Dryden.

4. In biology, designating an animal which makes use of imitation, as for concealment.

im′i-tā-tive, *n.* In grammar, a verb whose enunciation imitates its meaning, as babble. [Rare.]

im′i-tā-tive-ly, *adv.* In an imitative manner.

im′i-tā-tọr, *n.* [L. *imitator*, from *imitari*, to imitate.] One who or that which imitates.

im′i-tā-tọr-ship, *n.* The office or state of an imitator.

im′i-tā-tress, *n.* A female imitator.

im′i-tā-trix, *n.* Same as *Imitatress.*

im-mac′ū-lāte, *a.* [ME. *immaculate*; L. *immaculatus*, unspotted; *in-* priv., and *maculatus*, pp. of *maculare*, to spot, soil.] Spotless; pure; unstained; undefiled; without blemish; as, *immaculate* reputation; *immaculate* thoughts; our Saviour has set us an example of an *immaculate* life and conversation.

Immaculate conception; a doctrine of the Roman Catholic church, that the Virgin Mary was conceived without original sin, proclaimed as a dogma by Pope Pius IX. in 1854.

im-mac′ū-lāte-ly, *adv.* With spotless purity.

im-mac′ū-lāte-ness, *n.* The quality or state of being immaculate; spotless purity.

im-māiled′, *a.* Wearing mail or armor.

im-mal′lē-ȧ-ble, *a.* Not malleable; that cannot be extended by hammering.

im-man′ȧ-cle, *v.t.* To put manacles on; to fetter or confine; to restrain from free action.

im-mȧ-nā′tion, *n.* [L. *in*, into, and *manatus*, pp. of *manare*, to flow.] A flowing or entering in.

im-māne, *a.* [L. *immanis*, great, large.] Vast; huge; very great; formidable; monstrous. [Rare.]

im-māne′ly, *adv.* Monstrously; cruelly.

im′mȧ-nence, im′mȧ-nen-cy, *n.* The state or condition of being immanent; the quality of dwelling within; as, the divine *immanence.*

im′mȧ-nent, *a.* [LL. *immanens (-entis)*, ppr. of *immanere*, to remain in or near; L. *in*, in, and *manere*, to remain.] Inherent; intrinsic; internal; indwelling; permanently and continuously inseparable from; opposed to *emanant* or *transitive*; subjective, as opposed to objective.

Im-mā′nēṣ, *n.pl.* [L., pl. of *immanis*, monstrous.] A group of gigantic, recently extinct birds of New Zealand.

im-man′i-fest, *a.* Hidden; not visible. [Obs.]

im-man′i-ty, *n.* [L. *immanitas*, hugeness, cruelty, from *immanis*, vast, huge.] Barbarity; savageness; the condition of being monstrous or cruel. [Obs.]

im-man′tle, *v.t.* To cover, as with a cloak or mantle.

Im-man′ū-el, Em-man′ū-el, *n.* [LL. *Emmanuel*; Gr. *Emmanouēl*; Heb. *Immanuel*, lit., God with us; *im*, with, *anu*, us, and *el*, God.] God with us; a name given to the Saviour.

They shall call his name *Emmanuel.*
—Matt. i. 23.

im-mär-ces′ci-ble, *a.* [LL. *immarcescibilis*, unfading; L. *in-* priv., and *marcescere*, to wither, fade.] Unfading; enduring. [Obs.]

im-mär-ces′ci-bly, *adv.* In an unfading manner. [Obs.]

im-mär′gin-āte, *a.* Without margin or border.

im-mär′tiăl, *a.* Not martial; not warlike. [Obs.]

im-mȧsk′, *v.t.* To cover, as with a mask; to disguise. [Rare.]

im-match′ȧ-ble, *a.* That cannot be matched; peerless.

im-mȧ-tē′ri-ăl, *a.* 1. Not material; not consisting of matter; incorporeal; as, *immaterial* spirits; the mind or soul is *immaterial.*

2. Unimportant; without weight; not material; of no essential consequence.

Syn.—Incorporeal, spiritual, unsubstantial, inconsequential, unimportant.

im-mȧ-tē′ri-ăl-iṣm, *n.* 1. The doctrine of the existence or state of immaterial substances or spiritual beings.

2. In philosophy, the doctrine of idealism; the belief that no material world exists, and that everything is reducible to mind and ideas.

im-mȧ-tē′ri-ăl-ist, *n.* One who professes immateriality or the doctrine of immaterialism.

im-mȧ-tē-ri-al′i-ty, *n.* The quality of being immaterial, or not consisting of matter; destitution of matter; as, the *immateriality* of the soul.

im-mȧ-tē′ri-ăl-īze, *v.t.*; immaterialized, *pt., pp.*; immaterializing, *ppr.* To make immaterial; to transform to an incorporeal state.

im-mȧ-tē′ri-ăl-ly, *adv.* 1. In an immaterial manner; in a manner not depending on matter; opposed to *materially.*

2. In an unimportant degree.

im-mȧ-tē′ri-ăl-ness, *n.* The state of being immaterial; immateriality.

im-mȧ-tē′ri-āte, *a.* Not consisting of matter; incorporeal; immaterial. [Obs.]

im-mȧ-tūre′, *a.* [L. *immaturus*, unripe; *in-* priv., and *maturus*, ripe.]

1. Not mature or ripe; unripe; that has not arrived at a complete state; not perfect; as, *immature* fruit; *immature* plans or counsels.

2. Hasty; too early; coming before the natural time. [Rare.]

im-mȧ-tūred′, *a.* Immature.

im-mȧ-tūre′ly, *adv.* In an immature manner; too soon; before ripeness or completion.

im-mȧ-tūre′ness, *n.* The state of being immature; unripeness; incompleteness.

im-mȧ-tū′ri-ty, *n.* [L. *immaturitas*, from *immaturus*, unripe, immature.] The state or quality of being unripe or incomplete.

im″mē-ȧ-bil′i-ty, *n.* [L. *in-* priv., and *meabilis*, passable, from *meare*, to go.] The quality of preventing the passage of fluids into or through a medium; impermeability.

im-meaṣ″ūr-ȧ-bil′i-ty (-mezh″), *n.* The quality of being immeasurable; infinitude.

im-meaṣ′ūr-ȧ-ble, *a.* That cannot be measured; immense; indefinitely extensive; as, an *immeasurable* distance or space; an *immeasurable* abyss.

im-meaṣ′ūr-ȧ-ble-ness, *n.* The state of being immeasurable.

im-meaṣ′ūr-ȧ-bly, *adv.* To an extent not to be measured; beyond all measure.

im-meaṣ′ūred, *a.* Exceeding common measure. [Rare.]

im-mē-chan′ic-ăl, *a.* Not consonant to the laws of mechanics. [Obs.]

im-mē-chan′ic-ăl-ly, *adv.* In a manner contrary to the laws of mechanics. [Obs.]

im-mē′di-ȧ-cy, *n.* Power of acting without dependence; the quality of direct relation; opposed to *mediacy.*

im-mē′di-āte, *a.* [L. *in-* priv., and LL. *mediatus*, pp. of *mediare*, to divide in the middle, from L. *medius*, middle.]

1. Proximate; without a medium or without the intervention of another cause or means; producing effect by direct agency.

2. Instant; present; without the intervention of time; as, we must have an *immediate* supply of bread; *immediate* duty.

3. Having no appreciable space intervening; nearest; as, *immediate* locality.

Syn.—Proximate, contiguous, present, direct, instant, next, close.

im-mē′di-āte-ly, *adv.* 1. In an immediate manner; without the intervention of any other cause or event; opposed to *mediately.*

The transfer, whether accepted *immediately* by himself, or mediately by his agent, vests in him the property. —Anon.

2. Instantly; at the present time; without delay or the intervention of time; as, he was healed *immediately.*

Syn.—Directly, instantly, forthwith, instanter, at once, straightway, right away, right off.

im-mē′di-āte-ness, *n.* The state of being immediate; presence with regard to time; exemption from second or intervening causes.

im-mē′di-ȧ-tiṣm, *n.* The quality or state of being immediate; immediateness.

im-med′i-cȧ-ble, *a.* [L. *immedicabilis*; *in-* priv., and *medicabilis*, curable.] Not to be healed; incurable.

im-mē-lō′di-ous, *a.* Not melodious.

im-mem′ō-rȧ-ble, *a.* Not to be remembered; not worth remembering.

im-mē-mō′ri-ăl, *a.* Beyond memory; of time so remote that the beginning cannot be remembered, traced, or ascertained.

im-mē-mō′ri-ăl-ly, *adv.* In an immemorial manner; beyond memory.

im-mense′, *a.* [Fr. *immense*; L. *immensus*, vast, unmeasured; *in-* priv., and *mensus*, pp. of *metiri*, to measure.]

1. Unlimited; unbounded; infinite.

O goodness infinite! goodness *immense!* —Milton.

2. Vast in extent; very great in extension or in volume; as, an *immense* distance or an *immense* mountain.

3. Entertaining; remarkable for any excellence whatever; as, the picnic was *immense.* [Slang.]

Syn.—Huge, gigantic, enormous, colossal, great, mammoth, stupendous, prodigious, vast, immeasurable, boundless.

im-mense′ly, *adv.* Infinitely; without limits or measure; vastly; very greatly.

im-mense′ness, *n.* Unbounded extent or greatness.

im-men′si-ty, *n.* [L. *immensitas (-atis)*, from *immensus*, unmeasurable.]

1. The state or quality of being immense; unlimited extension; an extent not to be measured; infinity.

By the power we find in ourselves of repeating, as often as we will, any idea of space, we get the idea of *immensity.* —Locke.

2. Vastness in extent or bulk; greatness.

im-men′sive, *a.* [Obs.] See *Immense.*

im-men″sū-rȧ-bil′i-ty (-shū-), *n.* The quality of being immensurable.

im-men′sū-rȧ-ble (-shū-), *a.* [LL. *immensurabilis*; L. *in-* priv., and LL. *mensurabilis*, measurable, from L. *mensura*, a measure.] Not to be measured; immeasurable.

The law of nature—a term of *immensurable* extent. —Ward.

im-men′sū-rāte, *a.* Unmeasured. [Rare.]

im-mẽrd′, *v.t.*; immerded, *pt.*, *pp.*; immerding, *ppr.* [Fr. *emmerder*; L. *in*, on, and *merda*, dung.] To conceal or cover with merd or dung. [Rare.]

im-mẽrge′, *v.t.*; immerged, *pt.*, *pp.*; immerging, *ppr.* [L. *immergere*; *in*, into, and *mergere*, to dip, plunge.] To plunge into or under a fluid; to immerse.

im-mẽrge′, *v.i.* To disappear; to become invisible by immersion into a shadow, as a satellite in the shadow of a planet.

im-mer′it, *n.* Want of worth. [Obs.]

im-mer′it-ed, *a.* Unmerited. [Obs.]

im-mer′it-ous, *a.* Undeserving. [Obs.]

im-mẽrs′ȧ-ble, *a.* Capable of being immersed.

im-mẽrse′, *v.t.*; immersed, *pt.*, *pp.*; immersing, *ppr.* [L. *immersus*, pp. of *immergere*, to dip, plunge into; *in*, into, and *mergere*, to dip, plunge.]

1. To put under water or other fluid; to plunge; to dip.

2. To baptize by putting the body under water.

3. To sink or cover deep; to cover wholly; as, to be *immersed* in a wood.

4. To plunge; to overwhelm; to involve; to engage deeply; as, to *immerse* in business or cares.

im-mẽrse′, *a.* Buried; covered; sunk deep.

im-mẽrsed′ (-mẽrst′), *a.* 1. Covered by a fluid; plunged; deeply engaged; concealed by entering into any medium, as into the light of the sun or the shadow of the earth.

2. In botany, (a) growing under water; (b) covered by the other organs or parts.

im-mẽrs′i-ble, *a.* [*In-* priv., and L. *mersus*, pp. of *mergere*, to plunge.] That cannot be immersed or covered in a fluid.

im-mẽrs′i-ble, *a.* Same as *Immersable*.

im-mẽr′sion, *n.* [LL. *immersio (-onis)*, from L. *immergere*, to dip or plunge into; *in*, into, and *mergere*, to dip, plunge.]

1. The act of immersing or of plunging into a fluid till covered.

2. A method of Christian baptism by submerging the entire person.

3. The state of being overwhelmed or deeply engaged; as, an *immersion* in the affairs of life.

4. In astronomy, the disappearance of a celestial body by entering into any medium, as into the light of the sun or the shadow of the earth; opposed to *emersion*.

5. In microscopy, the process of using a liquid medium between the objective and the object.

Immersion lens; in microscopy, an ordinary objective of short focal distance arranged so that when in use a body of liquid having an index of refraction equal to that of glass occupies a space between it and the cover-glass of the slide holding the object.

im-mẽr′sion-ist, *n.* In theology, one who believes and teaches that no baptism but that by immersion is valid.

im-mesh′, *v.t.*; immeshed (-mesht′), *pt.*, *pp.*; immeshing, *ppr.* To entangle in the meshes of a net or in a web; as, the fly is completely *immeshed*.

im-mē-thod′iç-ăl, *a.* Having no method; without systematic arrangement; without order or regularity; confused.

im-mē-thod′iç-ăl-ly, *adv.* Without order or regularity; irregularly.

im-mē-thod′iç-ăl-ness, *n.* Want of method; confusion.

im-meth′ŏd-īze, *v.t.* To destroy methodical arrangement of; to throw into confusion. [Rare.]

im-met′riç-ăl, *a.* Without meter; limping in meter. [Rare.]

im-mew′, *v.t.* [Obs.] Same as *Emmew*.

im′mi-grănt, *n.* [L. *immigrans (-antis)*, ppr. of *immigrare*, to go or remove into, to immigrate.] A person who removes into a country for the purpose of permanent residence.

im′mi-grāte, *v.i.*; immigrated, *pt.*, *pp.*; immigrating, *ppr.* [L. *immigratus*, pp. of *immigrare*, to go or remove into; *in*, into, and *migrare*, to remove.] To move into a country for the purpose of permanent residence.

im-mi-grā′tion, *n.* [L. *immigrare*, to immigrate.] The passing or moving into a country for the purpose of permanent residence.

im′mi-nence, *n.* [L. *imminentia*, from *imminens (-entis)*, ppr. of *imminere*, to project over, overhang, threaten.] A condition of danger; a threatening; a condition in which something may happen at any time.

im′mi-nent, *a.* [L. *imminens (-entis)*, ppr. of *imminere*, to project over, overhang, threaten; *in*, on, and *minere*, to project.]

1. Hanging over; projecting from above. [Obs.]

2. Appearing as if about to happen; fraught with danger, real or imaginary; threatening; as, *imminent* judgments, evils, or death.

Syn.—Impending, threatening, menacing.—*Imminent* is the strongest; it denotes that something is ready to fall on the instant; *impending* denotes that something hangs suspended over us, and may so remain indefinitely; *threatening* supposes some danger in prospect, but more remote.

im′mi-nent-ly, *adv.* In an imminent manner; threateningly.

im-min′gle, *v.t.*; immingled, *pt.*, *pp.*; immingling, *ppr.* To mingle; to mix; to unite promiscuously. [Rare.]

im-mi-nū′tion, *n.* A lessening; diminution; decrease. [Obs.]

im-mis-ci-bil′i-ty, *n.* Incapability of mingling or being mixed.

im-mis′ci-ble, *a.* [L. *in-* priv., and LL. *miscibilis*, mixable, from L. *miscere*, to mix.] Not capable of being mixed; as, oil and water are *immiscible*.

im-mis′sion (-mish′un), *n.* [L. *immissio (-onis)*, a letting in, from *immissus*, pp. of *immittere*, to let or send into; *in*, into, and *mittere*, to send.] The act of sending or thrusting in; injection.

im-mit′, *v.t.* [L. *immittere*, to send or let in.] To send in; to inject. [Rare.]

im-mit′i-gȧ-ble, *a.* Not mitigable; incapable of being mitigated or appeased.

im-mit′i-gȧ-bly, *adv.* In an immitigable manner.

im-mix′, *v.t.* To mix; to mingle. [Rare.]

im-mix′ȧ-ble, *a.* Not capable of being mixed.

im-mixed′ (-mixt′), *a.* Unmixed. [Obs.]

im-mix′tūre, *n.* Freedom from mixture. [Obs.]

im-mō′bile, *a.* [L. *immobilis*, immovable; *in-* priv., and *mobilis*, movable.] Not mobile; incapable of being moved; immovable; fixed; stable.

im-mō-bil′i-ty, *n.* [L. *immobilitas*, from *immobilis*, immovable; *in-* priv., and *mobilis*, movable, from *movere*, to move.] The state or character of being immobile.

im-mō-bi-li-zā′tion, *n.* The condition of being immobile.

im-mō′bi-līze, *v.t.*; immobilized, *pt.*, *pp.*; immobilizing, *ppr.* 1. To render immovable, as a limb by bandaging.

2. To cause to become incapable of being mobilized, as an army corps.

im-mō′ble, *a.* [Obs.] See *Immobile*.

im-mod′ẽr-āte, *a.* [L. *immoderatus*, unrestrained, without measure; *in-* priv., and *moderatus*, pp. of *moderari*, to restrain, measure.] Exceeding just or usual bounds; not confined to reasonable limits; excessive; extravagant; unreasonable; as, *immoderate* demands; *immoderate* passions; *immoderate* use.

Syn.—Inordinate, excessive, intemperate, exorbitant, extravagant, unreasonable.

im-mod′ẽr-āte-ly, *adv.* In an immoderate manner; excessively; unreasonably.

im-mod′ẽr-āte-ness, *n.* Excess; extravagance; lack of moderation.

im-mod-ẽr-ā′tion, *n.* Excess; want of moderation.

im-mod′est, *a.* [L. *immodestus*, unrestrained; *in-* priv., and *modestus*, restrained, modest.]

1. Not limited to due bounds; immoderate; exorbitant; unreasonable.

2. Wanting in the reserve or restraint which decency requires, wanting in decency; unchaste; lewd; obscene; as, *immodest* words, thoughts, people, etc.

Syn.—Indecent, indelicate, lewd, indecorous, impudent, gross, shameless, unchaste.

im-mod′est-ly, *adv.* In an immodest manner.

im-mod′es-ty, *n.* [L. *immodestia*; *in-* priv., and *modestia*, modesty.] Want of modesty; indecency; want of chastity; want of delicacy or decent reserve.

im′mō-lāte, *v.t.*; immolated, *pt.*, *pp.*; immolating, *ppr.* [L. *immolatus*, pp. of *immolare*, to sprinkle a victim with sacrificial meal; *in*, on, and *mola*, meal.] To sacrifice; to kill, as a sacrificial victim; to offer in sacrifice.

im-mō-lā′tion, *n.* 1. The act of immolating or the state of being immolated.

2. That which is immolated.

im′mō-lā-tŏr, *n.* One who offers in sacrifice.

im-mōld′, im-mōuld′, *v.t.* To mold into shape. [Obs.]

im-mō′ment, *a.* Trifling. [Obs.]

im-mō-men′tous, *a.* Unimportant; not momentous. [Obs.]

im-mor′ăl, *a.* [L. *in-* priv., and *moralis*, moral.] Inconsistent with rectitude; contrary to the moral or divine law; wicked; unjust; dishonest; vicious; dissolute; licentious.

A flatterer of vice is an *immoral* man. —Johnson.

Syn.—Depraved, wicked, lewd, licentious, vicious, dissolute, profligate, obscene, unchaste.

im-mō-ral′i-ty, *n.*; *pl.* **im-mō-ral′i-tieş.** 1. The quality or character of being immoral.

2. An immoral act or practice.

im-mor′ăl-ly, *adv.* In an immoral manner; in violation of morality.

im-mō-rig′ẽr-ous, *a.* Rude; uncivil; disobedient. [Obs.]

im-mō-rig′ẽr-ous-ness, *n.* Rudeness; disobedience. [Obs.]

im-mọr′tăl, *a.* [L. *immortalis*, undying, imperishable; *in-* priv., and *mortalis*, mortal.]

1. Not mortal; exempt from liability to death; having unlimited existence; undying; as, an *immortal* soul.

Unto the King eternal, *immortal*, invisible. —1 Tim. i. 17.

2. Connected with or terminating in immortality; never to cease; as, *immortal* hopes.

3. Destined to live in all ages of this world; imperishable; as, *immortal* fame.

4. Exceedingly great; excessive. [Obs.]

Syn.—Imperishable, incorruptible, eternal, deathless, sempiternal, indissoluble, everlasting, perpetual, endless, undying.

im-mọr′tăl, *n.* One who is immortal or exempt from death or annihilation; often applied, in the plural, to the gods of classical mythology.

The Forty Immortals; the members of the French Academy.

im-mọr′tăl-ist, *n.* One who holds that the soul is immortal.

im-mọr-tal′i-ty, *n.* [L. *immortalitas*, from *immortalis*, immortal.]

1. The condition or quality of being immortal; exemption from death and annihilation; unending existence.

2. Exemption from oblivion; perpetuity; as, the *immortality* of fame.

im-mọr″tăl-i-zā′tion, *n.* The act of immortalizing, or the state of being immortalized.

im-mọr′tăl-īze, *v.t.*; immortalized, *pt.*, *pp.*; immortalizing, *ppr.* 1. To render immortal; to give never-ending life to.

2. To exempt from oblivion; to perpetuate.

I look for streams *immortalized* in song. —Addison.

im-mọr′tăl-īze, *v.i.* To become immortal. [Rare.]

im-mọr′tăl-ly, *adv.* In an immortal manner; with exemption from death.

im-mọr-telle′, *n.*; *pl.* **im-mọr-telleş′.** [Fr., f. of *immortel*, undying.] Any flower commonly called *everlasting*, or a wreath made of such flowers. [See *Everlasting*, n. 2.]

im-mọr″ti-fi-çā′tion, *n.* Want of mortification or subjection of the passions. [Obs.]

im-mō′tile, *a.* Not motile; stationary; not capable of moving.

im-mōv-ȧ-bil′i-ty, *n.* The condition or quality of being immovable; steadfastness.

im-mōv′ȧ-ble, *a.* 1. Incapable of being moved; fast; firmly fixed; as, an *immovable* foundation.

2. Not to be moved from a purpose; steadfast; fixed; that cannot be induced to change or alter; as, a man who remains *immovable*.

3. That cannot be altered or shaken; unalterable; unchangeable; as, an *immovable* purpose or resolution.

4. That cannot be affected; not impressible; not susceptible of compassion or tender feelings; unfeeling.

5. In law, fixed; not liable to be removed; permanent in place; as, an *immovable* estate.

Immovable feast; see under *Feast*.

im-mōv′ȧ-ble, *n.* That which cannot be moved; specifically, in law, land and whatever is adherent thereto, as trees, buildings and their accessories, etc.

im-mōv′ȧ-ble-ness, *n.* The quality of being immovable.

im-mōv′ȧ-bly, *adv.* In an immovable manner; unalterably; unchangeably.

im-mund′, *a.* Unclean. [Obs.]

im-mun-dic′i-ty, *n.* Uncleanness. [Obs.]

im-mūne′, *a.* [L. *immunis*, free from public service, exempt; *in-* priv., and *munis*, ready to serve, *munus*, duty, burden, tax.] Exempt; protected by inoculation; as, *immune* from contagion.

im-mū′ni-ty, *n.*; *pl.* **im-mū′ni-tieş.** [L. *immunitas (-atis)*, freedom from public service, from *immunis*, free from public service.]

1. Freedom or exemption from obligation in any respect; exemption from any charge, duty, office, tax, or imposition; a particular privilege; as, the *immunities* of the free cities of Germany; the *immunities* of the clergy.

2. Freedom; as, *immunity* from error.

Syn.—Exemption, freedom, relief.

im′mū-nīze, *v.t.*; immunized, *pt.*, *pp.*; immunizing, *ppr.* To give immunity to; to render immune.

im-mūre′, *v.t.*; immured, *pt.*, *pp.*; immuring, *ppr.* [OFr. *emmurrer*; L. *in*, in, and *murus*, a wall.]

1. To inclose within walls; to shut up; to confine.

Thou wert *immured*, restrained, captivated, bound. —Shak.

2. To wall; to surround with walls. [Obs.]

im-mūre′, *n.* A wall; an inclosure. [Obs.]

im-mūre′ment, *n.* The act of immuring or the state of being immured; imprisonment.

im-mū′sic-ăl, *a.* Unmusical.

im-mū-tà-bil′i-ty, *n.* [L. *immutabilitas*, from *immutabilis*, unchangeable.] The quality of being immutable; unchangeableness; immutableness; invariableness.

im-mū′tà-ble, *a.* [L. *immutabilis*; *in-* priv., and *mutabilis*, changeable.] Unchangeable; invariable; unalterable; not capable or susceptible of change.

That by two *immutable* things, in which it was impossible for God to lie.—Heb. vi. 18.

im-mū′tà-ble-ness, *n.* Unchangeableness; immutability.

im-mū′tà-bly, *adv.* Unchangeably; unalterably; invariably; in an immutable manner.

im-mū′tāte, *a.* Unchanged. [Obs.]

im-mū-tā′tion, *n.* Change; mutation. [Obs.]

im-mūte′, *v.t.* To change or alter. [Obs.]

im′ōu-pine, *n.* [Prob. from native name.] In botany, a tree of the yew family, *Dacrydium cupressinum*, growing in New Zealand and having dense, heavy red wood.

imp, *n.* [ME. *impe*; AS. *impe*, a scion, shoot, twig.]

1. A son; offspring; progeny. [Obs.]

A lad of life, an *imp* of fame. —Shak.

2. A minor or puny devil; a little devil.

3. A mischievous child. [Colloq.]

4. Something fastened on, as by splicing, in order to repair, fill out, or lengthen, as a feather in a broken or deficient wing of a falcon. [Obs.]

5. A graft; a scion; a slip. [Obs.]

imp, *v.t.*; imped, *pt.*, *pp.*; imping, *ppr.* [ME. *impen*, from AS. *impe*, a scion, shoot.]

1. To graft. [Obs.]

2. To lengthen; to extend or enlarge by something inserted or added; originally used by falconers, who repaired a hawk's wing by adding feathers.

Imp out our drooping country's broken wings. —Shak.

im-pā′cà-ble, *a.* Not to be appeased or quieted. [Obs.]

im-pā′cà-bly, *adv.* In an impacable manner. [Obs.]

im-pack′ment, *n.* The state of being packed or compressed. [Rare.]

im-pact′, *v.t.*; impacted, *pt.*, *pp.*; impacting, *ppr.* [OFr. *impacter*, to press close together; L. *impactus*, pp. of *impingere*, to strike or thrust against, to strike together.] To drive close; to press or drive firmly together.

im′pact, *n.* The single instantaneous blow or stroke communicated from one body in motion to another either in motion or at rest; a forcible momentary touch, contact, or impression; the act of coming into forcible contact; collision.

im-pac′tion, *n.* [L. *impactio* (*-onis*), a striking against, from *impingere*, to thrust against or strike.] The act of impacting; the condition of being impacted, wedged, or closely fixed.

im-pāint′, *v.t.* To paint; to adorn with colors. [Rare.]

im-pāir′, *v.t.*; impaired, *pt.*, *pp.*; impairing, *ppr.* [ME. *empairen*; OFr. *empeirer*, to make worse; L. *in-*, intens., and *pejorare*, to make worse, from *pejor*, worse.] To make worse; to diminish in quantity, value, or excellence; to lessen in power; to weaken; to enfeeble; as, the constitution is *impaired* by intemperance, by infirmity, and by age.

Syn.—Weaken, injure, enfeeble, enervate, cripple.

im-pāir′, *v.i.* To become worn out; to deteriorate. [Obs.]

im′pāir, *a.* Unsuitable; unequal; unworthy. [Obs.]

im-pāir′, *n.* Diminution; decrease; injury. [Obs.]

im-pāir′ẽr, *n.* One who or that which impairs.

im-pāir′ment, *n.* Diminution; decrease; injury; deterioration; the act of injuring.

im-pal′à-tà-ble, *a.* Unpalatable. [Rare.]

im-pāle′, *v.t.*; impaled, *pt.*, *pp.*; impaling, *ppr.* [Fr. *empaler*, to impale; L. *in*, on, and *palus*, a pole, stake.]

1. To fix on a stake; to put to death by fixing on an upright, sharp stake.

2. To inclose with stakes, posts, or palisades.

3. In heraldry, to join palewise, as coats of arms.

im-pāle′ment, *n.* 1. The act of inclosing or surrounding with stakes; also, the space impaled.

2. A punishment once used by the Turks and other nations, which consisted in thrusting a stake through the body, and leaving the victim to a lingering death.

Impalement. Impalement.

3. In heraldry, the division of a shield palewise, especially for placing the arms of two persons side by side.

im-pal′là, *n.* [Native name.] The pallah, or roodebok, a South African deer.

im-pal′lid, *v.t.* To make pallid or pale. [Obs.]

im-pälm′ (-päm′), *v.t.* To grasp; to take in the hand. [Obs.]

im-pal-pà-bil′i-ty, *n.* The quality of being impalpable or not perceptible by the touch.

im-pal′pà-ble, *a.* [L. *in*, not, and *palpare*, to touch.]

1. Not to be felt; that cannot be perceived by the touch; as, an *impalpable* powder, so fine no grit can be felt.

2. Intangible; not readily grasped by the mind; incomprehensible; unsubstantial.

im-pal′pà-bly, *adv.* In a manner not to be felt.

im-pal′sy, *v.t.* To strike with palsy; to paralyze.

im-pā′nāte, *a.* [L. *in*, in, and *panis*, bread.] Embodied in bread.

im-pā′nāte, *v.t.* To embody in bread.

im-pà-nā′tion, *n.* The supposed real presence and union of Christ's material body and blood with the substance of bread and wine in the eucharist.

im′pà-nā-tŏr, *n.* [LL., from L. *in*, in, and *panis*, bread.] One who believes in impanation.

im-pan′el, *v.t.*; impaneled *or* impanelled, *pt.*, *pp.*; impaneling *or* impanelling, *ppr.* 1. To write or enter upon a panel, as a list of names for jury service.

2. To swear in jurors drawn from a panel. Also written *impannel*.

im-pan′el-ment, *n.* A listing upon a panel, or the state of being so listed; also written *impannelment*.

im-par′à-dise, *v.t.*; imparadised, *pt.*, *pp.*; imparadising, *ppr.* To put in a place of supreme felicity; to make perfectly happy.

im-par′ăl-leled, *a.* Unparalleled. [Obs.]

im-pär′dŏn-à-ble, *a.* Unpardonable. [Obs.]

im-par-i-dig′i-tāte, *a.* [L. *impar*, unequal, and *digitus*, finger.] Odd-toed; odd-fingered; perissodactyl; with an uneven number of digits on a foot or hand.

im-par-i-pin′nāte, *a.* [L. *impar*, unequal, and *pinnatus*, feathered.] Pinnate and terminated by a single leaflet; oddly pinnate.

im-par″i-syl-lab′ic, *a.* [L. *impar*, unequal, and *syllaba*, a syllable.] Having an unequal number of syllables in various cases; as, *timor*, *timoris*, is an *imparisyllabic* Latin noun.

im-par′i-ty, *n.* [L. *impar*, unequal.]

1. Inequality; disproportion; difference of degree, rank, or excellence; incongruity.

2. Oddness; indivisibility into equal parts. [Obs.]

Imparipinnate Leaf of *Robinia*.

im-pärk′, *v.t.*; imparked, *pt.*, *pp.*; imparking, *ppr.* To inclose for a park; to sever from a common; hence, figuratively, to inclose, as animals.

im-pärl′, *v.i.*; imparled, *pt.*, *pp.*; imparling, *ppr.* [OFr. *emparler*, to talk.]

1. To hold mutual discourse. [Obs.]

2. In law, to have license to settle a lawsuit amicably; to have delay for mutual adjustment.

im-pär′lănce, *n.* [OFr. *emparlance*, from *emparler*, to talk.]

1. In law, the license or privilege of a defendant, granted on motion, to have delay of trial, to see if he can settle the matter amicably by talking with the plaintiff.

2. The continuance of a cause till another day, or from day to day.

im-pär-sŏn-nee′, *a.* [LL. *impersonatus*; L. *in*, in, and *persona*, person.] Presented, instituted, and inducted into a rectory, and in full possession, as a clergyman. [Eng.]

im-pär-sŏn-nee′, *n.* A clergyman imparsonnee.

im-pärt′, *v.t.*; imparted, *pt.*, *pp.*; imparting, *ppr.* [OFr. *empartir*; L. *impertire*, to share with another; *in*, in, and *partire*, to part, divide.]

1. To bestow upon another a share or portion of (anything); to give, grant, or communicate; to make known; as, to *impart* a message; to *impart* honor or favor.

2. To give; to confer upon; as, salt *imparts* a yellow tinge to the Bunsen flame; gymnastics *impart* strength to the body.

Syn.—Share, give, disclose, divulge, communicate, reveal, confer, tell.

im-pärt′, *v.i.* 1. To bestow a share.

2. To consult. [Rare.]

im-pärt′ănce, *n.* Communication of a share; grant.

im-pär-tā′tion, *n.* The act of imparting; the property or object imparted.

im-pärt′ẽr, *n.* One who imparts. [Rare.]

im-pär′tiăl (-shăl), *a.* [L. *in-* priv., and LL. *partialis*, partial, from L. *pars*, *partis*, part.] Not partial; not biased in favor of one party more than another; indifferent; unprejudiced; disinterested; equitable; just; fair.

im-pär′tiăl-ist, *n.* One who is impartial. [Rare.]

im-pär-ti-al′i-ty (-shi-al′), *n.* Indifference of opinion or judgment; freedom from bias in favor of one side or party more than another; disinterestedness; equitableness; justice.

im-pär′tiăl-ly, *adv.* In an impartial manner; without bias of judgment.

im-pär′tiăl-ness, *n.* The state of being impartial.

im-pärt-i-bil′i-ty, *n.* The quality of not being subject to partition.

im-pärt-i-bil′i-ty, *n.* The quality of being capable of communication.

im-pärt′i-ble, *a.* [L. *impartibilis*; *in-* priv., and *partibilis*, partible, from *pars*, *partis*, a part.] Not partible or subject to partition; that cannot be parted.

im-pärt′i-ble, *a.* [L. *in*, in, and *partire*, to divide.] Capable of being imparted, communicated, or bestowed.

im-pärt′ment, *n.* The act of imparting; also, the thing imparted.

im-pass′à-ble, *a.* That cannot be passed; not admitting a passage; as, an *impassable* road, mountain, or gulf.

im-pass′à-ble-ness, *n.* The state of being impassable.

im-pass′à-bly, *adv.* In a manner or degree that prevents passing or the power of passing.

im-pas-si-bil′i-ty, *n.* [LL. *impassibilitas*, from *impassibilis*, not capable of passion, impassible.] The state or quality of being insensible to suffering; stolidness.

im-pas′si-ble, *a.* [LL. *impassibilis*, not capable of passion; L. *in-* priv., and *passibilis*, able to suffer, from *passus*, pp. of *pati*, to suffer, endure.]

1. Incapable of pain, passion, or suffering; that cannot be affected with pain or uneasiness.

2. Apathetic; not revealing emotion or passion.

im-pas′si-ble-ness, *n.* The state of being impassible.

im-pas′sion (-pash′un), *v.t.*; impassioned, *pt.*, *pp.*; impassioning, *ppr.* [L. *in-*, intens., and *passio* (*-onis*), passion, from *passus*, pp. of *pati*, to suffer.] To move or affect strongly with passion.

im-pas′siŏn-à-ble, *a.* Easily excited to anger; susceptible of strong emotion.

im-pas′siŏn-āte, *v.t.*; impassionated, *pt.*, *pp.*; impassionating, *ppr.* [LL. *impassionatus*, strongly affected; L. *in-*, intens., and *passio* (*-onis*), passion.] To affect powerfully; to arouse deep feeling in.

im-pas′siŏn-āte, *a.* Strongly affected. [Obs.]

im-pas′siŏn-āte, *a.* [L. *in-* priv., and LL. *passionatus*, passionate, from L. *passio* (*-onis*), passion.] Without passion or feeling. [Obs.]

im-pas′sioned (-pash′und), *a.* Actuated or moved by passion; animated; excited; expressive of passion or ardor; as, an *impassioned* speaker or address.

im-pas′sive, *a.* 1. Not susceptible of pain or suffering; as, the *impassive* clay.

2. Not expressing emotions; apathetic; as, an *impassive* face.

im-pas′sive-ly, *adv.* In an impassive manner.

im-pas′sive-ness, *n.* The state or quality of being impassive.

im-pas-siv′i-ty, *n.* Impassiveness.

im-pas-tā′tion, *n.* 1. The act of making into paste.

2. That which is made into paste; a union or mixture of different substances by means of cements which are capable of resisting the action of fire or air.

im-pāste′, *v.t.*; impasted, *pt.*, *pp.*; impasting, *ppr.* 1. To knead; to make into paste.

2. In painting, to lay on the colors of, thick and bold.

im-pas′tō, *n.* [It., from *impastare*, to cover with paste.] In painting, the laying on of thick and opaque pigments, in relief, to produce an effect of strength and solidity.

im-pat′i-ble, *a.* [L. *impatabilis*; *in-* priv., and *pati*, to suffer.]

1. Intolerable; that cannot be borne. [Obs.]

2. Apathetic; without feeling.

im-pā′tience (-shens), *n.* [OFr. *impacience*; L. *impatientia*, impatience, from *impatiens* (*-entis*), impatient.]

1. Uneasiness under pain or suffering; want of patience; petulance; fretfulness.

2. Restless desire for change; restlessness due to delays, opposition, or the absence of expected good.

im-pā′tien-cy, *n.* [Obs.] See *Impatience*.

Im-pā′ti-ens (*or* -shi-enz), *n.* [L. *impatiens* (*-entis*), not enduring, impatient.] A genus of herbs of the *Geraniaceæ* or geranium family. When the ripe seed capsules are touched, they spring open forcibly, scattering the seeds, whence the name of the genus and the popular terms, touch-me-not and snapweed, also called jewelweed and balsam, *Impatiens balsamina* being the well known lady's-slipper or garden balsam.

im-pā′tient (-shent), *a.* [OFr. *impacient*; L.

impatiens (*-entis*), not enduring or suffering, impatient; *in-* priv., and *patiens* (*-entis*), enduring, patient, ppr. of *pati*, to suffer, endure.]

1. Without patience; uneasy or fretful; not enduring evil, opposition, or delay; intolerant; hasty; eager; restless; as, *impatient* at the delay; *impatient* of restraint; *impatient* for a friend's arrival; *impatient* under evils.

2. Showing or caused by impatience; as, an *impatient* remark.

3. Not to be borne; intolerable. [Obs.]

Syn.—Eager, restless, uneasy, fretful, hasty, peevish, petulant, irritated.

im-pā′tient, *n.* One who is restless under suffering. [Rare.]

im-pā′tient-ly, *adv.* In an impatient manner; with uneasiness or restlessness; as, to bear disappointment *impatiently*.

im-pat″rŏn-i-zā′tion, *n.* Absolute seigniory or possession; also, the act of bestowing such possession. [Rare.]

im-pat′rŏn-īze, *v.t.*; impatronized, *pt., pp.*; impatronizing, *ppr.* To place in power or authority, as in a benefice. [Rare.]

im-pāve′, *v.t.* To incorporate in a pavement, as a figure in mosaic. [Rare.]

im-pav′id, *a.* [L. *impavidus*, fearless; *in-* priv., and *pavidus*, fearing.] Having no fear. [Rare.]

im-pav′id-ly, *adv.* Without fear; intrepidly. [Rare.]

im-pạwn′, *v.t.*; impawned, *pt., pp.*; impawning, *ppr.* To pawn; to pledge; to deposit as security.

im-pēach′, *v.t.*; impeached (-pēcht), *pt., pp.*; impeaching, *ppr.* [ME. *empechen*; OFr. *empescher*, to hinder; LL. *impedicare*, to fetter, to catch, entangle; L. *in*, in, and *pedica*, a fetter, from *pes*, *pedis*, foot.]

1. To hinder; to impede. [Obs.]

2. To call to account; to charge with impropriety; to accuse; as, to *impeach* one's motives or conduct.

3. Specifically, to charge with a crime or misdemeanor; to make charges of maladministration against (a public officer) before a competent tribunal; as, to *impeach* a judge.

4. In law, to call in question the reliability of, as a witness or commercial paper.

Syn.—Arraign, accuse, indict, discredit, censure, charge with, blame.

im-pēach′, *n.* Hindrance. [Obs.]

im-pēach′ȧ-ble, *a.* Liable to accusation; chargeable with a crime; accusable; censurable.

im-pēach′ẽr, *n.* An accuser; one who calls in question.

im-pēach′ment, *n.* [OFr. *empeschement*, hindrance, from *empescher*, to hinder.]

1. Hindrance; obstruction. [Obs.]

2. Censure; accusation; a calling in question the purity of motives or the rectitude of conduct; as, this declaration is no *impeachment* of his motives or of his judgment.

3. An accusation or charge brought against a public officer for maladministration of his office. In the United States, it is the right of the House of Representatives to impeach, and of the Senate to try and determine an impeachment of, the chief executive. In Great Britain the corresponding houses have analogous functions.

Articles of impeachment; see under *Article*.

Impeachment of waste; in law, an action to restrain a tenant from wasting the property of the owner or to compel him to pay for injury done by waste.

im-pēarl′, *v.t.*; impearled (-pẽrld), *pt., pp.*; impearling, *ppr.* 1. To form in the resemblance of pearls.

> Dewdrops which the sun
> *Impearls* on every leaf, and every flower.
> —Milton.

2. To decorate with pearls, or with anything resembling pearls.

> The dews of the morning *impearl* every thorn.
> —Digby.

im-peç-çȧ-bil′i-ty, *n.* The quality of not being liable to sin; exemption from sin, error, or offense.

im-peç′çȧ-ble, *a.* [LL. *impeccabilis*; L. *in-* priv., and *peccare*, to sin.] Not liable to sin; not subject to sin; exempt from the possibility of sinning; as, no mere man is *impeccable*.

im-peç′çȧ-ble, *n.* A sinless person; one of a religious sect professing absolute freedom from sin.

im-peç′çăn-cy, *n.* Freedom from sin; impeccability.

im-peç-çănt, *a.* [L. *in-* priv., and *peccans* (*-antis*), ppr. of *peccare*, to sin.] Exempt from sinning; impeccable.

im-pē-cū-ni-os′i-ty, *n.* The state of being impecunious or moneyless.

im-pē-cū′ni-ous, *a.* [L. *in-* priv., and *pecunia*, money.] Out of money; generally penniless; poor.

im-pē′dănce, *n.* Obstruction; resistance; in electricity, increased resistance, as in an alternating current, due to induction.

im-pēde′, *v.t.*; impeded, *pt., pp.*; impeding, *ppr.* [L. *impedire*, to entangle, ensnare, lit., to hold the feet; *in*, in, and *pes*, *pedis*, foot.] To hinder; to stop in progress; to obstruct; as, to *impede* the progress of troops.

Syn.—Hinder, obstruct, check, delay, prevent, embarrass, retard, fetter, hamper.

im-ped′i-ble, *a.* That may be impeded. [Rare.]

im-ped′i-ment, *n.* [L. *impedimentum*, a hindrance, from *impedire*, to hinder, impede.] That which hinders progress or motion; hindrance; obstruction; obstacle; as, bad roads are *impediments* in marching and traveling; idleness and dissipation are *impediments* to improvement.

Impediment in speech; any defect preventing perfect articulation.

Syn.—Obstacle, difficulty, hindrance.—An *impediment* literally strikes against our feet, and we remove it; an *obstacle* rises up before us in our path, and we surmount it; a *difficulty* sets before us something hard to be done, and we encounter it and overcome it; a *hindrance* holds us back for a time, but we break away from it.

im-ped′i-ment, *v.t.* To impede. [Obs.]

im-ped-i-men′tȧ, *n.pl.* [L., pl. of *impedimentum*, baggage, a hindrance.] Things which impede or hinder the progress of armies or travelers, such as baggage, provisions, implements, etc.

im-ped-i-men′tăl, *a.* Hindering; obstructing.

im′pē-dīte, *a.* Hindered. [Rare.]

im′pē-dīte, *v.t.* To impede. [Obs.]

im-pē-di′tion (-dish′un), *n.* A hindering. [Obs.]

im-ped′i-tive, *a.* [L. *impeditus*, pp. of *impedire*, to hinder.] Causing hindrance.

im-pel′, *v.t.*; impelled, *pt., pp.*; impelling, *ppr.* [L. *impellere*, to drive, push, or strike against, to drive on; *in*, on, and *pellere*, to drive.] To drive or urge forward; to press on; to incite to action, or to move forward, by the application of physical force, or moral suasion, or necessity; as, a ball is *impelled* by the force of powder; a man may be *impelled* by hunger; motives of policy *impel* nations to confederate.

Syn.—Actuate, drive, force, push, move, instigate, incite, urge, press, induce.

im-pel′lent, *a.* [L. *impellens* (*-entis*), ppr. of *impellere*, to drive on, impel.] Having the quality of impelling.

im-pel′lent, *n.* A power or force that drives forward; motive or impulsive power.

im-pel′lẽr, *n.* One who or that which impels.

im-pen′, *v.t.*; impenned, *pt., pp.*; impenning, *ppr.* To pen; to shut or inclose in a narrow place.

im-pend′, *v.i.*; impended, *pt., pp.*; impending, *ppr.* [L. *impendere*, to overhang, threaten; *in*, on, and *pendere*, to hang.] To hang over; to be suspended above; to threaten; as, a dark cloud *impends* over the land.

> Destruction sure o'er all your heads *impends*.
> —Pope.

im-pend′, *v.t.* To threaten. [Rare.]

im-pend′ence, im-pend′en-cy, *n.* The state of hanging over; near approach; a menacing attitude.

im-pend′ent, *a.* [L. *impendens* (*-entis*), ppr. of *impendere*, to overhang, impend.] Hanging over; imminent; threatening; pressing closely; as, an *impendent* evil.

im-pend′ing, *a.* Hanging over; approaching near; threatening.

Syn.—Imminent, threatening, menacing.

im-pen″ē-trȧ-bil′i-ty, *n.* 1. The quality of being impenetrable.

2. In physics, that property of matter by virtue of which but one body can occupy the same space at the same time.

3. Insusceptibility of intellectual impression; stupidity.

im-pen′ē-trȧ-ble, *a.* [L. *impenetrabilis*; *in-* priv., and *penetrabilis*, penetrable.]

1. That cannot be penetrated or pierced; not admitting the passage of other bodies; as, an *impenetrable* shield.

2. Not to be affected or moved; not admitting impressions on the mind; as, *impenetrable* to admonitions.

3. In physics, excluding all other matter from the same space at the same time.

im-pen′ē-trȧ-ble-ness, *n.* Impenetrability.

im-pen′ē-trȧ-bly, *adv.* In an impenetrable manner.

im-pen′i-tence, *n.* Want of penitence or repentance; absence of contrition or sorrow for sin; hardness of heart; as, final *impenitence* dooms the sinner to inevitable punishment.

> He will advance from one degree of *impenitence* to another. —Rogers.

im-pen′i-ten-cy, *n.* Same as *Impenitence*.

im-pen′i-tent, *a.* [LL. *impœnitens*; L. *in-* priv., and *pœnitens* (*-entis*), ppr. of *pœnitere*, to repent, from *pœna*, punishment.] Not penitent; not repenting of sin; not contrite; obdurate; of a hard heart.

im-pen′i-tent, *n.* One who does not repent; a hardened sinner.

im-pen′i-tent-ly, *adv.* Without repentance or contrition for sin; obdurately.

im-pen′nāte, *a.* [L. *in-* priv., and *pennatus*, winged.] Without feathers or wings; specifically, characterized by short wings covered with feathers resembling scales.

im-pen′nāte, *n.* An impennate bird, as the penguin.

Im-pen′nēş, *n.pl.* [L. *in-* priv., and *penna*, a feather, wing.] The penguin group of birds, unable to fly because of the absence of quills in their wings.

im-pen′nous, *a.* [L. *in-* priv., and *penna*, a wing.] In zoölogy, having no wings; said of invertebrates. [Obs.]

im-pēo′ple (-pē′), *v.t.* See *Empeople*.

im′pe-rănt, *a.* [L. *imperans* (*-antis*), ppr. of *imperare*, to command.] Commanding. [Obs.]

im′pe-rāte, *a.* Done by impulse or direction of the mind. [Obs.]

im-per-ȧ-tī′văl, *a.* In grammar, relating to the imperative mode.

im-per′ȧ-tive, *a.* [L. *imperativus*, commanding, from *imperare*, to command, order; *in*, in, on, and *parare*, to prepare, order.]

1. Commanding; authoritative; expressive of command; containing positive command; as, the orders are *imperative*.

2. Not to be avoided or evaded; that must be obeyed; obligatory; binding; as, an *imperative* task.

3. In grammar, designating the commanding, entreating, or hortative form of the verb, called the *imperative* mode.

Syn.—Urgent, irresistible, dictatorial, inexorable, peremptory, compulsory, obligatory, mandatory.

im-per′ȧ-tive, *n.* 1. An obligation.

2. In grammar, a mode or a word in the imperative form.

3. In philosophy, a relieving of conscience; an excitant of the moral sense.

The categorical imperative; in the philosophy of Kant, the unconditional command of conscience, obedience to which fulfils the universal law of action for all men.

im-per′ȧ-tive-ly, *adv.* With command; authoritatively.

im-pē-rā′tŏr, *n.* [L., from *imperare*, to command.]

1. Among the Romans, (a) during the earlier republic, the title given a victorious general; (b) later, one holding the imperium or power of chief military command; a commander; (c) during the empire, the official title of the supreme ruler or emperor as commander-in-chief of the armies; emperor.

2. [I—] In zoölogy, a genus of gasteropods.

Im-per-ȧ-tō′ri-ȧ, *n.* [L., f. of *imperatorius*, pertaining to a general or commander, from *imperator*, a commander.] A genus of plants, nearly identical with *Peucedanum*, having clustered flowers.

im-per-ȧ-tō′ri-ăl, *a.* [L. *imperatorius*, from *imperator*, a commander.]

1. Commanding.

2. Relating to an emperor or to his office.

im-per-ȧ-tō′ri-ăn, *a.* Imperatorial. [Rare.]

im-per′ȧ-tō-ry, *a.* Same as *Imperatorial*.

im-pẽr-çeiv′ȧ-ble, *a.* Imperceptible. [Rare.]

im-pẽr-çeiv′ȧ-ble-ness, *n.* Imperceptibleness. [Rare.]

im-pẽr-çēived′, *a.* Same as *Unperceived*.

im-pẽr-cep-ti-bil′i-ty, *n.* The quality of not being perceptible.

im-pẽr-cep′ti-ble, *a.* [LL. *imperceptibilis*; L. *in-* priv., and *perceptibilis*, perceptible.] Not to be perceived; not to be known or discovered by the senses; undiscernible; not easily seen or observed; as, *imperceptible* increase by growth.

im-pẽr-cep′ti-ble-ness, *n.* The quality of being imperceptible.

im-pẽr-cep′ti-bly, *adv.* In a manner not to be perceived.

im-pẽr-cep′tion, *n.* The absence of perception.

im-pẽr-cep′tive, *a.* Without ability to perceive.

im-pẽr-cip′i-ent, *a.* Not perceiving or not having power to perceive.

im-pẽr-di-bil′i-ty, *n.* The state or quality of being imperdible. [Obs.]

im-pẽr′di-ble, *a.* Not destructible or easily lost. [Obs.]

im-pẽr′di-bly, *adv.* In an indestructible manner. [Obs.]

im-pẽr′fect, *a.* [L. *imperfectus*, unfinished; *in-* priv., and *perfectus*, finished, pp. of *perficere*, to finish.] Not finished; not complete; defective; not entire, sound, or whole; wanting a part; impaired; blemished; as, an *imperfect* plant.

Imperfect arch; in architecture, an arch whose curve is less than that of a semicircumference.

Imperfect cadence; see under *Cadence*.

Imperfect consonance; in music, a combination of tones whose ratio of vibration is not so simple as those of the fourth or fifth; as, a *consonance* of the third and the sixth is *imperfect*.

Imperfect flower; wanting either stamens or pistils.

Imperfect interval; in music, an interval

which does not contain its complement of simple sounds.

Imperfect number; a number which is not equal to the sum of its aliquot parts or divisors.

Imperfect obligation; a self-imposed obligation; one that the law cannot enforce.

Imperfect tense; in grammar, the form of a verb that denotes an action in time past, but not finished.

im-pẽr′fect, *n.* In grammar, an imperfect tense.

im-pẽr′fect, *v.t.* To render imperfect. [Obs.]

im-pẽr-fec-ti-bil′i-ty, *n.* The state of being imperfectible.

im-pẽr-fec′ti-ble, *a.* Incapable of being perfected.

im-pẽr-fec′tion, *n.* [OFr. *imperfection*; LL. *imperfectio (-onis)*, imperfection, from L. *imperfectus*, imperfect.] Defect; fault; the want of a part or of something necessary to complete a thing; the state of being imperfect.

Syn.—Blemish, fault, immaturity, incompleteness, failing, deficiency, weakness, frailty.

im-pẽr′fect-ly, *adv.* In an imperfect manner or degree; not fully; not entirely; not completely; not in the best manner; not without fault or failure.

im-pẽr′fect-ness, *n.* The state of being imperfect.

im-pẽr′fō-rȧ-ble, *a.* Incapable of being perforated or bored through.

Im-pẽr-fō-rā′tȧ, *n.pl.* In zoölogy, a division of foraminifers whose exoskeletons are without perforations; opposed to *Perforata*.

im-pẽr′fō-rāte, im-pẽr′fō-rā-ted, *a.* [L. *in-* priv., and *perforatus*, pp. of *perforare*, to perforate.] Not perforated or pierced; having no opening.

im-pẽr-fō-rā′tion, *n.* The state of being imperforate.

im-pē′ri-ăl, *a.* [OFr. *imperial*; L. *imperialis*, pertaining to an empire or emperor, from *imperium*, an empire, command, from *imperare*, to command.]

1. Pertaining to an empire or to an emperor; as, an *imperial* government, authority, or edict.

2. Of supreme or unquestioned authority.

3. Worthy of an emperor; hence, of great excellence.

4. In architecture, designating a form of dome or roof, as used in Moorish buildings.

Imperial chamber; the sovereign court of the former German empire.

Imperial city; formerly, a city in Germany having no head but the emperor; also applied to the city of Rome.

Imperial diet; an assembly of all the states of the German empire.

Imperial guard; a name given to the royal guard of the first Napoleon.

Imperial weights and measures; a system of weights and measures based on a standard legalized by the English Parliament.

im-pē′ri-ăl, *n.* 1. In architecture, a kind of dome, which, viewed in profile, is pointed toward the top and widens as it descends, as in Moorish buildings; an imperial dome.

2. A tuft of hair on a man's chin under the lower lip.

3. Anything of unusual size, such as a large decanter, etc.

4. (a) A part of the top of a carriage for carrying luggage; (b) an outside seat on a French diligence.

5. An elegant fabric used in the middle ages, of now unknown material, often enriched with gold.

6. A Russian coin of the eighteenth century, made of gold and worth about eight dollars.

7. A game at cards in the time of Henry VIII. of England.

Imperial Dome, Christchurch College, Oxford.

im-pē′ri-ăl-iṣm, *n.* 1. Imperial state or authority; the system of government by an emperor; the spirit of empire.

2. A national policy of territorial expansion, or growth by the acquisition of foreign territory; so called by its opponents.

im-pē′ri-ăl-ist, *n.* A subject or soldier of an emperor; an advocate and promoter of an imperial form of government.

im-pē′ri-ăl-ite, *n.* A powerful explosive, made chiefly of ammonia, nitrate of potash and aluminum powder. It is not affected by cold or heat, not subject to the action of water, and is proof against accidental explosion.

im-pē-ri-al′i-ty, *n.* 1. Imperial power.

2. The right of an emperor to a share of the produce of mines; an imperial privilege or prerogative.

im-pē′ri-ăl-īze, *v.t.*; imperialized, *pt.*, *pp.*; imperializing, *ppr.* To bring into the condition of an empire; to endow with imperial qualities or characteristics.

im-pē′ri-ăl-ly, *adv.* In an imperial manner.

im-pē′ri-ăl-ty, *n.* Imperial power. [Rare.]

im-per′il, *v.t.*; imperiled *or* imperilled, *pt.*, *pp.*; imperiling *or* imperilling, *ppr.* To bring into danger.

im-per′il-ment, *n.* The act of endangering; jeopardy; danger; imperiling.

im-pē′ri-ous, *a.* [L. *imperiosus*, full of command, powerful, from *imperium*, command.]

1. Authoritative; commanding with rightful authority.

2. Dictatorial; haughty; overbearing; arrogant; domineering; as, an *imperious* tyrant; indicating an *imperious* temper; not to be opposed by obstacles; as, a man of a vast and *imperious* mind.

3. Commanding; urgent; pressing; as, *imperious* love; *imperious* circumstances; *imperious* appetite.

Syn.—Lordly, domineering, commanding, haughty, imperative, overbearing, tyrannical. —One who is *imperious* exercises his authority in a manner highly offensive for its spirit and tone; one who is *lordly* assumes a lofty air in order to display his importance; one who is *domineering* gives orders in a way to make others feel their inferiority.

im-pē′ri-ous-ly, *adv.* 1. With arrogance of command; with a haughty air of authority; in a domineering manner.

2. With urgency or force not to be opposed.

im-pē′ri-ous-ness, *n.* 1. Authority; air of command.

2. Arrogance of command; haughtiness.

im-per-ish-ȧ-bil′i-ty, *n.* The quality of being imperishable.

im-per′ish-ȧ-ble, *a.* Not subject to decay; not liable to perish; indestructible; enduring permanently; as, an *imperishable* monument; *imperishable* renown.

im-per′ish-ȧ-ble-ness, *n.* The quality of being imperishable.

im-per′ish-ȧ-bly, *adv.* So as not to be liable to decay.

im-pē′ri-um, *n.* [L., from *imperare*, to command.]

1. In ancient Rome, the authority conferred upon a chief military commander.

2. An empire with all its belongings, implying absolute dominion.

3. In law, one of the highest powers belonging to an executive; the power to employ all the forces of the state in carrying out its laws.

Imperium in imperio; a power within a power; an empire within an empire; a state within a state.

im-per′i-wigged (-wigd), *a.* Wearing a wig-like ornament of false hair; having a periwig on the head.

im-pẽr′mȧ-nence, *n.* Want of permanence or continued duration.

im-pẽr′mȧ-nen-cy, *n.* Same as *Impermanence*.

im-pẽr′mȧ-nent, *a.* Not permanent; not enduring.

im-pẽr″mē-ȧ-bil′i-ty, *n.* The quality in bodies of not permitting a fluid to pass through them.

im-pẽr′mē-ȧ-ble, *a.* Not permitting a fluid to pass through; as, india-rubber is *impermeable* to water.

im-pẽr′mē-ȧ-ble-ness, *n.* The state of being impermeable.

im-pẽr′mē-ȧ-bly, *adv.* In an impermeable manner.

im-pẽr-mis′si-ble, *a.* Not to be permitted; that cannot be granted or allowed.

im-pẽr-sc̦rū′tȧ-ble, *a.* That cannot be searched out. [Obs.]

im-pẽr-sc̦rū′tȧ-ble-ness, *n.* The state of not being capable of scrutiny. [Obs.]

im-pẽr′sŏn-ăl, *a.* [L. *in-* priv., and *personalis*, personal.] Without personality; not personal.

Impersonal verb; in grammar, a verb used without a definite subject, as *it rains*.

im-pẽr′sŏn-ăl, *n.* 1. Anything lacking personality.

2. An impersonal verb.

im-pẽr-sŏn-al′i-ty, *n.* Want or indistinctness of personality; the quality of being impersonal.

im-pẽr′sŏn-ăl-ly, *adv.* In an impersonal manner; not personally.

im-pẽr′sŏn-āte, *v.t.*; impersonated, *pt.*, *pp.*; impersonating, *ppr.* [L. *in*, in, and *persona*, a person.]

1. To invest with the bodily substance of a living being; to make a person of.

2. To invest with the qualities of a person; to personify.

3. To assume the personal characteristics and actions of, as in dramatic representation.

im-pẽr-sŏn-ā′tion, *n.* The act of impersonating, or state of being invested with personality.

im-pẽr′sŏn-ā-tŏr, *n.* One who impersonates.

im-pẽr-son″i-fi-c̦ā′tion, *n.* Impersonation.

im-pẽr-son′i-fȳ, *v.t.* To impersonate; to personify. [Rare.]

im-pẽr-spi-c̦ū′i-ty, *n.* Want of perspicuity or clearness to the mind. [Rare.]

im-pẽr-spic̦′ū-ous, *a.* [L. *imperspicuus*; *in-* priv., and *perspicuus*, clear.] Not perspicuous; not clear; obscure. [Rare.]

im-pẽr-suād′ȧ-ble (-swād′), *a.* Not open to persuasion. [Rare.]

im-pẽr-suād′ȧ-ble-ness, *n.* The state of being impersuadable. [Rare.]

im-pẽr-suā-si-bil′i-ty (-swā-), *n.* The quality of being impersuasible.

im-pẽr-suā′si-ble, *a.* Not to be moved by persuasion; not yielding to arguments. [Rare.]

im-pẽr′ti-nence, *n.* [LL. *impertinentia*, from L. *impertinens (-entis)*, not belonging or pertaining.]

1. The state or condition of being impertinent; inappropriateness; irrelevance.

2. That which is not pertinent; that which does not belong to the subject in hand; that which is out of place or irrelevant; specifically, in law, that which is irrelevant and consequently objectionable.

3. Rudeness; improper intrusion; interference by word or conduct which is not consistent with the age or station of the person.

> We should avoid the vexation and *impertinence* of pedants. —Swift.

4. A trifle; a thing of little or no value.

> There are many subtle *impertinences* learnt in schools. —Watts.

im-pẽr′ti-nen-cy, *n.* Same as *Impertinence*.

im-pẽr′ti-nent, *a.* [L. *impertinens (-entis)*, not belonging or pertaining; *in-* priv., and *pertinens (-entis)*, ppr. of *pertinere*, to belong, pertain; *per*, through, and *tenere*, to hold.]

1. Not pertaining to the matter in hand; of no weight; having no bearing on the subject; as, an *impertinent* remark.

2. Rude; intrusive; meddling with that with which one has no concern; as, an *impertinent* coxcomb.

3. Trifling; foolish; negligent of the present purpose. [Rare.]

Syn.—Officious, impudent, insolent, intrusive, irrelevant, meddling.—A person is *officious* who obtrudes his assistance where it is not needed; he is *impertinent* when he intermeddles in things with which he has no concern.

im-pẽr′ti-nent, *n.* An intruder; a meddler; one who interferes in what does not belong to him.

im-pẽr′ti-nent-ly, *adv.* In an impertinent manner; officiously; intrusively; rudely.

im-pẽr-tran-si-bil′i-ty, *n.* The quality of being impertransible. [Rare.]

im-pẽr-tran′si-ble, *a.* [L. *in-* priv., and *pertransire*, to pass through; *per*, through, and *transire*, to pass.] Not to be passed through. [Rare.]

im-pẽr-tŭrb-ȧ-bil′i-ty, *n.* The quality of being imperturbable.

im-pẽr-tŭrb′ȧ-ble, *a.* [LL. *imperturbabilis*; L. *in-* priv., and *perturbare*, to throw into confusion, disturb; *per*, through, and *turbare*, to disturb.] That cannot be disturbed or agitated; permanently quiet.

im-pẽr-tŭr-bā′tion, *n.* Freedom from agitation of mind; calmness. [Obs.]

im-pẽr-tŭrbed′, *a.* Unperturbed or not disconcerted. [Obs.]

im-pẽr-vi-ȧ-bil′i-ty, *n.* The quality of being impervious. [Rare.]

im-pẽr′vi-ȧ-ble, *a.* Impervious. [Rare.]

im-pẽr′vi-ȧ-ble-ness, *n.* Imperviousness.

im-pẽr′vi-ous, *a.* [L. *impervius*, impassable; *in-* priv., and *pervius*, passable, from *per*, through, and *via*, way.] Not to be penetrated or passed through; impenetrable; impermeable; as, an *impervious* shield; an *impervious* forest; paper is *impervious* to light.

im-pẽr′vi-ous-ly, *adv.* In an impervious manner.

im-pẽr′vi-ous-ness, *n.* The state or condition of being impervious.

im′pẽr-y, *n.* [Obs.] See *Empery*.

im-pest′, *v.t.* To affect with a pest. [Obs.]

im-pes′tẽr, *v.t.* To vex; to tease; to pester. [Obs.]

im-pē-tig′i-nous, *a.* [L. *impetigo*, a ringworm.] Of the nature of impetigo.

im-pē-tī′gō, *n.* [L., from *impetere*, to rush upon, attack.] A cutaneous eruption consisting of clustering pustules which are yellow and febrile and which terminate in a scaly crust, intersected by cracks.

im′pē-trȧ-ble, *a.* 1. That may be obtained by petition. [Obs.]

2. Persuasive. [Obs.]

im′pē-trāte, *v.t.* [L. *impetratus*, pp. of *impetrare*, to accomplish, gain by request; *in-*, intens., and *patrare*, to accomplish.] To obtain by request or entreaty. [Obs.]

im-pē-trā′tion, *n.* [OFr. *impetracion*; L. *impetratio (-onis)*, from *impetrare*, to get, obtain.]

1. The act of obtaining by prayer or petition. [Obs.]

2. In old English law, the preobtaining of benefices from the Church of Rome, which

belonged to the disposal of the king and other lay patrons of the realm.

im′pē-trā-tive, *a.* Obtaining; tending to obtain by entreaty. [Obs.]

im′pē-trā-tō-ry, *a.* Beseeching; containing entreaty. [Obs.]

im-pet-ū-os′i-ty, *n.* [LL. *impetuositas*, from L. *impetuosus*, impetuous.] The state or quality of being impetuous; fury; violence; vehemence; furiousness of temper.

im-pet′ū-ous, *a.* [L. *impetuosus*, from *impetus*, a rushing upon, from *impetere*, to rush upon; *in*, in, upon, and *petere*, to seek.]

1. Rushing with great force and violence; moving rapidly; furious; forcible; fierce; raging; as, an *impetuous* wind; an *impetuous* torrent.

2. Vehement of mind; fierce; hasty; passionate; violent; as, a man of *impetuous* temper.

Syn.—Rushing, hasty, precipitate, impulsive, vehement, rash, fiery, passionate, fierce.

im-pet′ū-ous-ly, *adv.* With impetuosity.

im-pet′ū-ous-ness, *n.* The state of being impetuous.

im′pē-tus, *n.* [L., a rushing upon, from *impetere*, to rush upon.]

1. Force of motion; the force with which a body is driven or impelled; momentum; impulse; stimulus.

2. In gunnery, the altitude through which a heavy body must fall to acquire a velocity equal to that with which a ball is discharged from a piece.

im′pey-ăn pheaṣ′ănt (-fez′). A bird, *Lophophorus impeyanus*, found in the colder portions of India. The male is particularly handsome, having a crest and spangled iridescent plumage.

im′phee, *n.* [African.] A sugar-cane, *Holcus saccharatus*, found in Africa, resembling the sorghum of the United States.

im-pic′tūre, *v.t.* [Obs.] See *Picture*.

im-pic′tūred, *a.* Painted; impressed. [Obs.]

im-piērce′, *v.t.* To pierce. [Obs.]

im-piērce′ȧ-ble, *a.* Not to be pierced or penetrated. [Obs.]

im-pī′e-ty, *n.*; *pl.* **im-pī′e-tieṣ.** [L. *impietas*, impiety, from *impius*, impious; *in-* priv., and *pius*, pious.]

1. The state or condition of being impious; irreverence toward God.

2. An impious or irreverent act; as, guilty of numerous *impieties*.

3. A general lack of reverence toward things usually held sacred; undutifulness; as, filial *impiety*.

im-pig′nō-rāte, *v.t.* To pledge or pawn. [Obs.]

im-pig-nō-rā′tiŏn, *n.* The act of pawning or the condition of being pawned. [Obs.]

imp′ing, *n.* [Verbal noun of *imp*, v.]

1. A graft; the act of grafting.

2. In falconry, repair of a hawk's feathers or wing.

im-pinġe′, *v.i.*; impinged, *pt.*, *pp.*; impinging, *ppr.* [L. *impingere*, to drive into, to thrust, strike at; *in*, in, and *pingere*, to strike.] To fall against; to strike; to dash against; to clash upon; with *on*, *upon*, or *against*.

> The cause of reflection is not the *impinging* of light *on* the solid or impervious parts of bodies. —Newton.

im-pinġe′ment, *n.* The act of impinging.

im-pin′ġent, *a.* Impinging.

im-piñ′guāte, *v.t.* To fatten; to make fat. [Obs.]

im-piñ-guā′tion, *n.* The process of fattening; a fattened state or condition. [Obs.]

im′pi-ous, *a.* [L. *impius*, without respect or love for the gods, one's parents, or native land; *in-* priv., and *pius*, devout, reverential.]

1. Not pious; wanting piety; irreverent toward the Supreme Being; irreligious; profane.

> When vice prevails and *impious* men bear sway. —Addison.

2. Proceeding from or manifesting irreverence; as, an *impious* deed; *impious* writings.

im′pi-ous-ly, *adv.* In an impious manner; profanely; wickedly.

im′pi-ous-ness, *n.* Impiety; the condition of being impious.

im′pīre, *n.* A corrupt form of *umpire*. [Obs.]

imp′ish, *a.* Having the qualities of an imp.

imp′ish-ly, *adv.* In an impish manner.

im-pit′ē-ous, *a.* Pitiless. [Obs.]

im-plā-ċȧ-bil′i-ty, *n.* [LL. *implacabilitas*, from L. *implacabilis*, implacable.] The quality of being implacable; inexorableness.

im-plā′ċȧ-ble, *a.* [L. *implacabilis*, unappeasable; *in-* priv., and *placabilis*, appeasable, from *placere*, to appease.]

1. Not placable; not to be appeased; that cannot be pacified; inexorable; as, an *implacable* prince; *implacable* malice.

2. Not to be relieved or assuaged. [Rare.]

Syn.—Irreconcilable, unappeasable, relentless, inexorable, vindictive, pitiless, unforgiving.

im-plā′ċȧ-ble-ness, *n.* Implacability.

im-plā′ċȧ-bly, *adv.* In an implacable manner or degree.

im-plāce′ment, *n.* See *Emplacement*.

im-plā-cen′tăl, *a.* Not having a placenta; pertaining to or characteristic of the *Implacentalia*.

im-plā-cen′tăl, *n.* A mammal destitute of a placenta.

im″plā-cen-tā′li-ȧ, *n.pl.* [L. *in-* priv., and *placenta*, a cake (in anat., placenta), and *-alia*.] A section or group of mammals not having the placenta developed. It includes the marsupials and monotremes.

im″plā-cen-tā′tȧ, *n.pl.* See *Implacentalia*.

im-plā-cen′tāte, *a.* See *Implacental*.

im-plant′, *v.t.*; implanted, *pt.*, *pp.*; implanting, *ppr.* [LL. *implantare*, to plant in, to invest; L. *in*, in, and *plantare*, to plant.] To set, plant, or infix, for the purpose of growth; to ingraft; to inculcate; to instil; as, to *implant* the seeds of virtue or the principles of knowledge in the minds of youth.

im-plan-tā′tion, *n.* The act of implanting, inculcating, or instilling.

im-plāte′, *v.t.* To plate; to cover or protect with plates. [Rare.]

im-plau-ṣi-bil′i-ty, *n.* The quality of being implausible or not specious; want of plausibility.

im-plau′ṣi-ble, *a.* Not plausible; not wearing the appearance of truth or credibility, and not likely to be believed.

im-plau′ṣi-ble-ness, *n.* Implausibility.

im-plau′ṣi-bly, *adv.* In an implausible manner.

im-plēach′, *v.t.* To interweave. [Obs.]

im-plēad′, *v.t.*; impleaded, *pt.*, *pp.*; impleading, *ppr.* [ME. *empleden*; OFr. *emplaidier*, to plead, pursue at law; *en-*, in, and *plaidier*, *pledier*, to plead.]

1. To institute and prosecute a suit against in court; to sue at law.

2. To accuse; to arraign; to impeach.

im-plēad′, *v.i.* To institute legal proceedings; to sue.

im-plēad′ȧ-ble, *a.* Not to be pleaded against or evaded. [Rare.]

im-plēad′ẽr, *n.* One who impleads or prosecutes another; an accuser.

im-plēaṣ′ing, *a.* Unpleasing. [Obs.]

im-pledġe′, *v.t.* To pawn. [Rare.]

im′plē-ment, *n.* [LL. *implementum*, a filling up, from L. *implere*, to fill up; *in*, in, and *plere*, to fill.] Whatever may supply a want; especially, an instrument, tool, utensil, vessel, or the like; as, the *implements* of trade or of husbandry.

im′plē-ment, *v.t.*; implemented, *pt.*, *pp.*; implementing, *ppr.* 1. To fulfil or satisfy the conditions of; to accomplish.

> The chief mechanical requisites of the barometer are *implemented* in such an instrument as the following. —Prof. Nichol.

2. To fulfil or perform; to carry into effect or execution; as, to *implement* a bargain or contract. [Scot.]

3. To provide or equip with implements.

im-plē-men′tăl, *a.* Pertaining to or in any way connected with implements; characterized by the use of implements.

im-plē′tion, *n.* [LL. *impletio* (*-onis*), from L. *impletus*, pp. of *implere*, to fill up.]

1. The act of filling; the state of being full.

2. That which fills up; filling.

im′plex, *a.* Infolded; intricate; entangled; complicated. [Rare.]

im′plex, *n.* In mathematics, a doubly infinite system of surfaces.

im-plex′iŏn (-plek′shun), *n.* [L. *implexio* (*-onis*), an entwining, from *implexus*, pp. of *implectere*, to entwine; *in*, in, and *plectere*, to twist.] The act of infolding or involving; the state of being involved; involution. [Rare.]

im-plex′ous, *a.* In botany, entangled; interwoven; interlaced.

im-plī′ȧ-ble, *a.* Not pliable.

im′pli-cāte, *v.t.*; implicated, *pt.*, *pp.*; implicating, *ppr.* [L. *implicatus*, pp. of *implicare*, to infold, involve; *in*, in, and *plicare*, to fold.]

1. To infold; to involve; to entangle.

2. To involve; to bring into connection with; to show or prove to be connected or concerned; as, the evidence did not *implicate* the accused person in the conspiracy; to be *implicated* in a plot.

Syn.—Entangle, involve.

im-pli-cā′tion, *n.* [L. *implicatio* (*-onis*), an entwining, infolding, from *implicare*, to infold, implicate.]

1. The act of implicating or the state of being implicated; involution; entanglement.

> Three principal causes of firmness are, the grossness, the quiet contact, and the *implication* of component parts. —Boyle.

2. An implying; that which is implied but not expressed; a deduction; an inference.

im′pli-cā-tive, *a.* Tending to implicate.

im′pli-cā-tive-ly, *adv.* By implication.

im-plic′it, *a.* [L. *implicitus*, pp. of *implicare*, to infold, entwine; *in*, in, and *plicare*, to fold.]

1. Infolded; entangled; complicated. [Obs.]

2. Implied; tacitly comprised; fairly to be understood, though not expressed in words; as, an *implicit* contract or agreement.

3. Resting on another; trusting in the word or authority of another, without doubt or reserve; as, *implicit* trust or confidence; *implicit* obedience.

Implicit function; see under *Function*.

im-plic′it-ly, *adv.* 1. By implication or influence; impliedly.

2. In an implicit manner; with unreserved confidence; unhesitatingly; undoubtingly.

> Too imperfect an instrument to be relied on *implicitly*. —Herschel.

im-plic′it-ness, *n.* The state of being implicit; the state of trusting without reserve.

im-plic′i-ty, *n.* [Obs.] See *Implicitness*.

im-plīed′, *a.* Contained in substance or essence, or by fair inference, but not actually expressed; deducible by inference or implication.

im-plī′ed-ly, *adv.* By implication or inference.

im-plōde′, *v.t.*; imploded, *pt.*, *pp.*; imploding, *ppr.* [Formed by substituting *im-* for *ex-* in *explode*.] In phonetics, to enunciate implosively; as, an *imploded* letter.

im-plō′dent, *n.* In phonetics, a sound made by implosion.

im-plō-rā′tion, *n.* [L. *imploratio* (*-onis*), from *implorare*, to implore.] Earnest supplication; the act of imploring.

im′plō-rā-tōr, *n.* One who implores. [Obs.]

im-plōr′ȧ-tō-ry, *a.* Earnestly imploring; supplicating. [Rare.]

im-plōre′, *v.t.*; implored, *pt.*, *pp.*; imploring, *ppr.* [L. *implorare*, to beseech, entreat; *in-*, intens., and *plorare*, to cry out, weep.]

1. To call upon in supplication; to beseech; to pray to earnestly; to petition with urgency; to entreat.

> *Imploring* all the gods that reign above. —Pope.

2. To ask for earnestly; to beg or pray for; to beseech; as, to *implore* forgiveness.

Syn.—Beseech, supplicate, entreat, request, pray, petition, beg.

im-plōre′, *v.i.* To entreat; to beg.

im-plōre′, *n.* Earnest supplication. [Obs.]

im-plōr′ẽr, *n.* One who implores.

im-plōr′ing-ly, *adv.* In an imploring manner.

im-plō′ṣion, *n.* [Formed by substituting *im-* for *ex-* in *explosion*.]

1. A sudden bursting inward; opposed to *explosion*.

2. In phonetics, a compression of the air in the mouth at the moment of uttering certain consonants, as *p* or *k*.

im-plō′sive, *a.* Produced by implosion.

im-plō′sive, *n.* A sound produced by implosion.

im-plō′sive-ly, *adv.* By implosion; in an implosive manner.

im-plūmed′, *a.* Having no plumes or feathers. [Rare.]

im-plunġe′, *v.t.* [Obs.] See *Emplunge*.

im-plū′vi-um, *n.*; *pl.* **im-plū′vi-ȧ.** [L. *impluvium* or *inpluvium*, from *impluere*, to rain into; *in*, in, and *pluere*, to rain.] In ancient Roman architecture, a basin in the middle of the atrium or entrance-hall, below the compluvium or open space in the roof, to receive the rain.

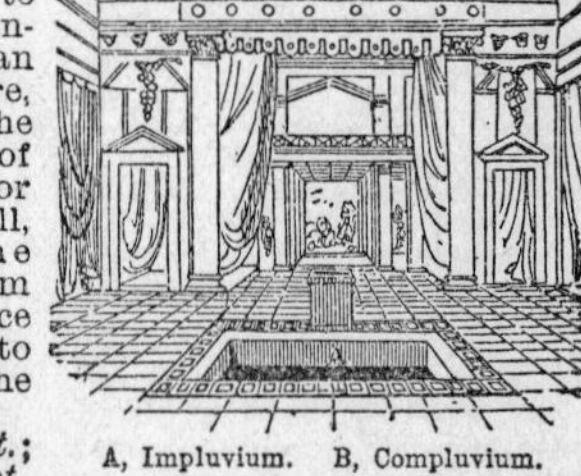

A, Impluvium. B, Compluvium.

im-plȳ′, *v.t.*; implied, *pt.*, *pp.*; implying, *ppr.* [L. *implicare*, to involve, entangle, infold; *in*, in, and *plicare*, to fold.]

1. To infold or involve; to wrap up. [Obs.]

2. To involve or contain in substance or essence, or by fair inference, or by construction of law, when not expressed in words; to signify; to contain by implication.

> Where a malicious act is proved, a malicious intention is *implied*. —Sherlock.

3. To ascribe; to refer. [Obs.]

Syn.—Signify, denote, include, betoken, mean, involve.

im-poi′ṣŏn, *v.t.* [Obs.] See *Empoison*.

im-poi′ṣŏn-ment, *n.* [Obs.] See *Empoisonment*.

im-pō′lăr-i-ly, im-pō′lăr-ly, *adv.* Not according to the direction of the poles. [Obs.]

im-pol′i-cy, *n.* Inexpedience; unsuitableness to the end proposed; bad policy.

im-pō-līte′, *a.* [L. *impolitus*, unpolished; *in-* priv., and *politus*, pp. of *polire*, to polish.] Not of polished manners; uncivil; rude in manners.

im-pō-līte′ly, *adv.* Uncivilly; in an impolite manner.

im-pō-līte′ness, *n.* Incivility; want of good manners.

im-pol′i-tiç, *a.* Not politic; unwise; imprudent; wanting in tact; not expedient; as, an *impolitic* measure; an *impolitic* diplomat.

im-pō-lit′i-çăl, *a.* Impolitic. [Obs.]

im-pō-lit′i-çăl-ly, *adv.* Impoliticly. [Obs.]

im-pol′i-tiç-ly, *adv.* Not wisely; not with due prudence; in a manner to injure interests.

im-pol′i-tiç-ness, *n.* The state or quality of being impolitic.

im-pon″dẽr-ȧ-bil′i-ty, *n.* Lack of sensible weight; the quality of being imponderable.

im-pon′dẽr-ȧ-ble, *a.* Not having sensible weight.

im-pon′dẽr-ȧ-ble, *n.* [*In-* priv., and LL. *ponderabilis*, that may be weighed.] In physics, anything supposed to have no weight; used formerly to designate heat, light, electricity, and magnetism when considered as fluids; sometimes applied to ether and to spiritual or mental phenomena or agencies.

im-pon′dẽr-ȧ-ble-ness, *n.* The state or quality of being imponderable.

im-pon′dẽr-ous, *a.* Imponderable. [Obs.]

im-pon′dẽr-ous-ness, *n.* The state of being imponderous. [Obs.]

im-pōne′, *v.t.* [L. *imponere*, to put or lay on; *in*, on, and *ponere*, to put.]

1. To stake; to wager. [Obs.]

2. To impose. [Scot.]

im-pọọf′, *n.* A South African animal, the eland; called also *impoofo*.

im-pọọn′, *n.* [S. African.] In zoölogy, the duykerbok.

im-pọọr′, *v.t.* To impoverish. [Obs.]

im-pō-ros′i-ty, *n.* Want of porosity; closeness of texture; compactness excluding pores.

im-pōr′ous, *a.* Solid; without pores; very close or compact in texture.

im-pōrt′, *v.t.*; imported, *pt.*, *pp.*; importing, *ppr.* [L. *importare*, to bring in, introduce, bring about; *in*, in, and *portare*, to carry.]

1. To bring from a foreign country into one's own country; as, we *import* wines from France.

2. To bring in or introduce into; as, to *import* vigor into one's style.

3. To bear or convey as signification or meaning; to mean; to signify; to imply; as, the term clearly *imports* a thorough understanding.

4. To be of weight, moment, or consequence to; to have a bearing on.

> If I endure it, what *imports* it you?—Dryden.

Syn.—Mean, signify, imply, interest, convey, concern, indicate.

im-pōrt′, *v.i.* To have meaning or significance.

im′pōrt, *n.* 1. That which is imported or brought into a country from another country or state; generally in the plural.

2. That which is borne or conveyed by words, actions, or circumstances; meaning; signification; the sense which words are intended to convey to the understanding or which they bear in sound interpretation.

3. Importance; weight; consequence.

im-pōrt′ȧ-ble, *a.* Capable of being imported.

im-pōrt′ȧ-ble, *a.* [ME. *importable*; LL. *importabilis*, that cannot be borne; L. *in-* priv., and *portabilis*, that can be borne.] Intolerable; unendurable. [Obs.]

im-pōrt′ȧ-ble-ness, *n.* The state of being intolerable. [Obs.]

im-pọr′tănce, *n.* [LL. *importantia*, importance, from L. *importans (-antis)*, ppr. of *importare*, to bring in; *in*, in, and *portare*, to bring.]

1. That quality of anything by which it may affect a measure, interest, or result; weight; consequence; a bearing on some interest; as, the education of youth is of great *importance* to a free government.

2. Weight or consequence in self-estimation; dignity; social standing; also, pompousness.

3. The thing implied; import; meaning. [Obs.]

4. An important matter; also, urgency; importunity. [Obs.]

Syn.—Consequence, weight, moment.—*Importance* is what things have in themselves; *consequence* is the *importance* of a thing from its consequences; *weight* implies a positively great degree of *importance*; *moment* is that *importance* which a thing has from the power in itself to produce effects, or to determine interests.

im-pọr′tăn-cy, *n.* Importance. [Obs.]

im-pọr′tănt, *a.* [LL. *importans (-antis)*, momentous, important, properly ppr. of L. *importare*, to bring in, introduce.]

1. Weighty; momentous; grave; of great consequence; having a bearing on some interest, measure, or result, by which good or ill may be produced.

2. Pompous; pretentious; as, an *important* manner.

3. Bearing on; forcible; importunate. [Obs.]

Syn.—Significant, relevant, considerable, dignified, influential, weighty, momentous, material, grave, essential.

im-pọr′tănt-ly, *adv.* In an important manner.

im-pōr-tā′tion, *n.* [L. *importare*, to bring in, import.]

1. The act or practice of importing, or of bringing from another country or state; opposed to *exportation*.

2. A person or thing imported; an import.

3. Conveyance. [Obs.]

im-pōrt′ẽr, *n.* One who imports; a merchant, corporation, etc., that brings goods from another country.

im′pōrt-less, *a.* Of no weight or import. [Obs.]

im-pọr′tū-nȧ-ble, *a.* Unendurable; burdensome. [Obs.]

im-pọr′tū-nȧ-cy, *n.* The act of importuning; persistent solicitation; also, the quality of being importunate.

im-pọr′tū-nāte, *a.* [LL. *importunatus*, pp. of *importunari*, to vex, be troublesome, from L. *importunus*, troublesome.]

1. Pressing or urging in request or demand; urgent and pertinacious in solicitation; as, an *importunate* suitor or petitioner; an *importunate* demand.

2. Causing vexation. [Obs.]

im-pọr′tū-nāte-ly, *adv.* In an importunate manner.

im-pọr′tū-nāte-ness, *n.* The state or quality of being importunate.

im-pọr′tū-nā-tŏr, *n.* One who importunes. [Obs.]

im-pọr-tūne′, *a.* Importunate; inopportune; vexatious. [Obs.]

im-pọr-tūne′, *v.t.*; importuned, *pt.*, *pp.*; importuning, *ppr.* [Fr. *importuner*; LL. *importunari*, to be troublesome, vex, from L. *importunus*, without access, troublesome; *in-* priv., and *portus*, a harbor.]

1. To request with urgency; to press with solicitation; to urge with frequent or unceasing application; hence, to vex; to annoy.

2. To import; to imply. [Obs.]

im-pọr-tūne′, *v.i.* To make demands; to solicit with pertinacity.

im-pọr-tūne′ly, *adv.* With importunity. [Obs.]

im-pọr-tū′nẽr, *n.* One who importunes.

im-pọr-tū′ni-ty, *n.*; *pl.* **im-pọr-tū′ni-tieş.** [Fr. *importunité*; L. *importunitas*, unfitness, unsuitableness, from *importunus*, unfit, troublesome.]

1. Pressing solicitation; urgent request; application for a claim or favor which is urged with troublesome frequency or pertinacity.

2. Unseasonableness. [Obs.]

im-pōr′tū-ous, *a.* [L. *importuosus*; *in-* priv., and *portuosus*, abounding in harbors, from *portus*, a harbor.] Without a port, haven, or harbor. [Rare.]

im-pōş′ȧ-ble, *a.* That may be imposed or laid on.

im-pōş′ȧ-ble-ness, *n.* The state of being imposable.

im-pōşe′, *v.t.*; imposed, *pt.*, *pp.*; imposing, *ppr.* [Fr. *imposer*; L. *imponere*, to lay or put on; *in*, on, and *ponere*, to put, place.]

1. To lay on; to set on; to put; to place or deposit; as, to *impose* the hands in the ceremony of ordination or of confirmation.

> It was here that Xerxes *imposed* a stupendous bridge of boats. —Gibbon.

2. To lay, as a burden, tax, toll, duty, penalty, command, law, restriction, and the like; to levy; hence, to lay on or place over, as something burdensome or hateful or regarded as such; as, the legislature *imposes* taxes for the support of government; to *impose* a governor on a colony.

3. To fix on; to impute. [Rare.]

4. To obtrude fallaciously; to palm off; as, he *imposed* the ring upon her as gold.

5. To subject by way of punishment. [Obs.]

> *Impose* me to what penance your invention
> Can lay upon my sin. —Shak.

6. In printing, to arrange, as pages of type on an imposing-stone and fasten in a chase.

im-pōşe′, *v.i.* To practise deception or to take an improper advantage; to lay a burden; with *on* or *upon*; as, to *impose upon* a person's ignorance or generosity; he has *imposed on* me.

im-pōşe′, *n.* Command; injunction. [Obs.]

im-pōşe′ment, *n.* Imposition. [Obs.]

im-pōş′ẽr, *n.* One who imposes; one who enjoins.

im-pōş′ing, *a.* Commanding; adapted to impress forcibly; as, an *imposing* air or manner.

im-pōş′ing-ly, *adv.* In an imposing manner.

im-pōş′ing-ness, *n.* The condition of being imposing.

im-pōş′ing-stōne, *n.* In printing, a smooth level stone or plate of metal on which pages or columns of type are imposed or forms made up.

im-pō-şi′tion (-zish′un), *n.* [Fr. *imposition*; L. *impositio (-onis)*, a laying upon, application, from *impositus*, pp. of *imponere*, to lay or put upon, impose.]

1. The act of imposing; (a) the act of laying, putting, or placing on; (b) the act of levying, enjoining, inflicting, and the like; as, the *imposition* of taxes; (c) in printing, the act of arranging the pages of a sheet upon the imposing-stone, adjusting the spaces between them, and fastening them into a chase.

2. That which is laid on, levied, inflicted, enjoined, and the like, as a burden, tax, duty, command, law, restriction, and the like.

3. The act of laying on hands in the church ceremonies of ordination, confirmation, etc.

4. A trick or deception put or laid on others; a fraud; a delusion; an imposture.

5. In schools, an exercise enjoined on students as a punishment.

im-pos-si-bil′i-ty, *n.* [LL. *impossibilitas*, from L. *impossibilis*, impossible.]

1. The state or quality of being impossible.

2. That which is impossible.

im-pos′si-ble, *a.* [OFr. *impossible*; L. *impossibilis*, not possible; *in-* priv., and *possibilis*, possible, from *posse*, to be able.]

1. Not possible; not capable of being or of being done, thought, endured, or the like; that cannot be or that cannot be done by the means at command or in the nature of the case.

2. In law, rendered incapable of being accomplished only by the act of God or of a public enemy or by the operation of law.

3. Colloquially in a French use, very odd or absurd; so remarkable as not to be considered possible, or to be imagined; as, an *impossible* cousin; an *impossible* gown.

Impossible quantity; see under *Imaginary*.

im-pos′si-ble, *n.* An impossibility. [Obs.]

im-pos′si-bly, *adv.* Not possibly.

im′pōst, *n.* [OFr. *impost*, a tax (Fr. *impost*, an impost in architecture); LL. *impositus*, a tax, from L. *impositus*, pp. of *imponere*, to lay upon, impose.]

1. Any tax or tribute imposed by authority; particularly, a duty or tax laid by government on goods imported, and paid or secured by the importer at the time of importation.

2. In architecture, the point where an arch rests on a wall or column, usually marked by horizontal moldings, though sometimes these are absent, especially in Gothic architecture.

A A, Shafted Impost, Austrey Church, Warwickshire.

im-post-hū′māte, etc. See *Impostumate*, etc.

im-pos′tŏr, *n.* [LL. *impostor*, a deceiver; L. *impositor*, one who deceives by imposing or applying a name, from *impositus*, pp. of *imponere*, to put upon, impose.] One who imposes on others, a person who assumes a character for the purpose of deception; a deceiver under a false character.

im-pos′tŏr-ship, *n.* The station or part of an impostor.

im-pos′tress, im-pos′trix, *n.* A female impostor. [Rare.]

im-pos′trous, *a.* [Obs.] See *Imposturous*.

im-pos′tū-māte, im-post′hū-māte, *v.i.* and *v.t.* [*Impostume* and *ate*.]

I. *v.i.* To form an abscess; to gather. [Obs.]

II. *v.t.* To affect with an impostume or abscess. [Obs.]

im-pos′tū-māte, im-post′hū-māte, *a.* Of the character of an abscess; affected with an abscess. [Obs.]

im-pos-tū-mā′tion, im-post-hū-mā′tion, *n.* The act of forming an abscess; also, an abscess; an impostume. [Obs.]

im-pos′tūme, im-post′hūme, *n.* [OFr. *empostume*, corruption of *apostume*, an apostem, abscess, from L. *apostema*; Gr. *apostēma*, an abscess; *apo*, from, and *histanai*, to stand.] An abscess; a collection of pus or purulent matter in any part of an animal body. [Obs.]

im-pos′tūme, im-post′hūme, *v.t.* and *v.i.* [Obs.] Same as *Impostumate*.

im-pos′tūr-āġe, *n.* Imposition; imposture. [Obs.]

im-pos′tūre, *n.* [LL. *impostura*, deceit, from L. *impositus*, pp. of *imponere*, to impose upon; *in*, upon, and *ponere*, to put.] Deception practised under a false or assumed character; fraud or imposition practised by a false pretender.

Syn.—Deception, cheat, imposition, fraud.

im-pos′tūred, *a.* Deceptive; deceitful; imposturous. [Obs.]

im-pos′tūr-ous, *a.* Having the characteristics of an imposture; deceptive; deceitful.

im-pos′tūr-y, *n.* Imposture. [Obs.]

im′pō-tence, *n.* [OFr. *impotence*; L. *impotentia*, want of power, inability; from *impotens (-entis)*, feeble, weak, impotent.]

1. Want of strength or power, physical, intellectual, or moral; weakness; feebleness; inability; defect of power to perform anything.

2. Inability to beget.

im′pō-ten-cy, *n.* Same as *Impotence*.

im′pō-tent, *a.* [OFr. *impotent*; L. *impotens (-entis)*, weak, feeble; *in-* priv., and *potens (-entis)*, powerful, ppr. of *posse*, to be able.]

1. Weak; feeble; wanting strength or power; unable by nature, or disabled by disease or accident, to perform any act.

2. Wanting the power of propagation, as males.

3. Wanting the power of restraint; not having the command over; as, *impotent* of tongue.

Syn.—Weak, powerless, useless, feeble, helpless, nerveless, enfeebled.

im′pō-tent, *n.* One who is feeble, infirm, or languishing under disease; especially, a male sexually enfeebled. [Rare.]

im′pō-tent-ly, *adv.* Weakly; without power.

im-pound′, *v.t.*; impounded, *pt., pp.*; impounding, *ppr.* To put, shut, or confine in a pound or close pen; as, to *impound* unruly or stray horses, cattle, etc.

im-pound′āġe, *n.* 1. The act of impounding or the state of being impounded.

2. The fine imposed for impounding.

im-pound′ēr, *n.* One who impounds.

im-pov′ēr-ish, *v.t.*; impoverished, *pt., pp.*; impoverishing, *ppr.* [OFr. *enpoverir*, to make poor; L. *in*, in, and *pauper*, poor.]

1. To make poor; to reduce to poverty or indigence.

2. To exhaust the strength, richness, or fertility of; to cause to deteriorate.

im-pov′ēr-ish-ēr, *n.* One who or that which impoverishes.

im-pov′ēr-ish-ly, *adv.* So as to impoverish.

im-pov′ēr-ish-ment, *n.* [OFr. *empoverissement*, from *empovrir* to make poor, impoverish.] A reducing to poverty; exhaustion of richness; the act of impoverishing or state of being impoverished.

im-pow′ēr, *v.t.* Same as *Empower.*

im-prac″ti-cȧ-bil′i-ty, *n.* 1. The state or quality of being impracticable.

2. Untractableness; stubbornness.

im-prac′ti-cȧ-ble, *a.* 1. Incapable of accomplishment; not feasible; as, it is *impracticable* for a man to lift a ton by his own unassisted strength.

2. Intractable; unmanageable; stubborn.

3. Incapable of being used; unfit; unserviceable.

Syn.—Impossible.—A thing is *impracticable* when it cannot be accomplished by any human means at present possessed; a thing is *impossible* when the laws of nature forbid it.

im-prac′ti-cȧ-ble-ness, *n.* Impracticability.

im-prac′ti-cȧ-bly, *adv.* In a manner or degree not practicable.

> Morality not *impracticably* rigid.—Johnson.

im-prac′ti-cȧl, *a.* Lacking practicality. [Rare.]

im′prē-cāte, *v.t.*; imprecated, *pt., pp.*; imprecating, *ppr.* [L. *imprecatus*, pp. of *imprecari*, to invoke, pray to; *in*, upon, and *precari*, to pray, from *prex (-ecis)*, a prayer.] To invoke, as an evil on any one; to pray that a curse or calamity may befall (one); to curse.

im-prē-cā′tion, *n.* [L. *imprecatio (-onis)*, an invoking of evil, a curse, from *imprecari*, to imprecate.] The act of imprecating, or invoking evil on any one; a prayer that a curse or calamity may befall some one; a curse.

Syn.—Curse, malediction, anathema, execration.

im′prē-cȧ-tō-ry, *a.* Containing a prayer for evil to befall a person.

im-prē-ci′sion (-sizh′un), *n.* Want of precision or exactness; defect of accuracy. [Rare.]

im-pregn′ (-prēn′), *v.t.* To impregnate. [Obs.]

im-preg-nȧ-bil′i-ty, *n.* The quality of being impregnable.

im-preg′nȧ-ble, *a.* [OFr. *imprenable*; *in-* priv., and *prenable*, able to be taken, from *prendre*, L. *prehendere*, to take, seize.]

1. Not to be stormed or taken by assault; that cannot be reduced by force; able to resist attack; as, an *impregnable* fortress.

2. Not to be moved, impressed, or shaken; invincible.

> The man's affection remains wholly unconcerned and *impregnable*. —South.

im-preg′nȧ-ble, *a.* In biology, capable of being made pregnant.

im-preg′nȧ-ble-ness, *n.* Impregnability.

im-preg′nȧ-bly, *adv.* In a manner to resist penetration or assault; in a manner to defy force; as, a place *impregnably* fortified.

im-preg′nănt, *a.* and *n.* [LL. *imprægnans (-antis)*, ppr. of *imprægnare*, to impregnate.]

I. *a.* Impregnating. [Obs.]

II. *n.* Any impregnating agent. [Rare.]

im-preg′nănt, *a.* [L. *in-* priv., and *prægnans (-antis)*, pregnant.] Not fertilized or made pregnant. [Rare.]

im-preg′nāte, *v.t.*; impregnated, *pt., pp.*; impregnating, *ppr.* [LL. *imprægnatus*, pp. of *imprægnare*, to make pregnant; L. *in*, in, and *prægnans (-antis)*, pregnant.]

1. To fertilize or make pregnant.

2. To cause to become permeated with; to imbue; as, winds *impregnated* with disease germs.

3. To infuse particles into; to communicate the virtues of another substance to, as in pharmacy, by mixture, digestion, etc.

im-preg′nāte, *v.i.* To become pregnant. [Rare.]

im-preg′nāte, *a.* Impregnated; rendered prolific or fruitful.

im-preg-nā′tion, *n.* 1. The act of impregnating; the state of becoming impregnated.

2. The substance that impregnates or fills.

3. Complete saturation.

4. In biology, sexual generation arising from the union of a spermatozoön with a female germ-cell to produce a new organism.

5. In geology, a mineral deposit somewhat resembling a true vein.

im-prē-jū′di-cāte, *a.* Not prejudiced; impartial. [Obs.]

im-prē′nȧ-ble, *a.* Impregnable. [Obs.]

im-prep-ȧ-rā′tion, *n.* Want of preparation, unreadiness. [Obs.]

im-pre′sȧ, *n.* [It.] A personal device, as on a seal, bookplate, etc.

im-pre-sä′ri-ō, *n.* [It., from *impresa*, an enterprise.] One who manages or conducts a company of musical artists.

im-prē-scrip-ti-bil′i-ty, *n.* The state of being imprescriptible.

im-prē-scrip′ti-ble, *a.* Incapable of being lost or impaired by disuse or by the claims of another founded on prescription.

im-prē-scrip′ti-bly, *adv.* In an imprescriptible manner.

im-prēse′, *n.* Same as *Impresa.*

im-press′, *v.t.*; impressed, *pt., pp.*; impressing, *ppr.* [ME. *impressen*; OFr. *empresser*, to impress; L. *impressus*, pp. of *imprimere*, to press into or upon, stamp, impress; *in*, on, upon, and *premere*, to press.]

1. To mark; to make an indentation or impression in; as, to *impress* a step in the snow.

2. To make an impression of; to make use of pressure in making a copy or reproduction of; to imprint.

3. To have a mental influence upon; to affect forcibly; as, she *impressed* him favorably.

4. To fix deeply; as, to *impress* truth on the mind, or facts on the memory.

im-press′, *v.i.* To be stamped. [Obs.]

im′press, *n.* [LL. *impressus*, a pressing upon, from L. *impressus*, pp. of *imprimere*, to press upon, impress.]

1. A mark or indentation by pressure.

2. The figure or image of anything made by pressure; stamp; likeness.

3. A mark of distinction; stamp; character.

> God leaves us this general *impress* or character on the works of creation, that they were very good. —South.

4. An impresa.

im-press′, *v.t.* 1. To compel to enter into public service, as seamen or soldiers.

2. To seize for public service; as, to *impress* provisions, money, etc.

im′press, *n.* Same as *Impressment.*

im-pressed′ (-prest′), *a.* 1. Stamped into; printed upon by pressing or stamping.

2. In biology, sunk below the general surface as if stamped, or marked with sunken lines, areas, etc.

im-press′-gang, *n.* [Obs.] See *Press-gang.*

im-press-i-bil′i-ty, *n.* The quality of being impressible.

im-press′i-ble, *a.* Capable of being impressed.

im-press′i-ble-ness, *n.* Impressibility.

im-press′i-bly, *adv.* In a manner to make impression.

im-pres′sion (-presh′un), *n.* [OFr. *impression*; L. *impressio (-onis)*, a pressing into or upon, an attack, impression, from *impressus*, pp. of *imprimere*, to press on or into, to impress.]

1. The act of impressing; the state of being impressed.

2. A mark, indentation, etc., produced by pressure.

3. Slight, indistinct remembrance; as, I have an *impression* that the fact was stated to me.

4. Effect or influence on the organs of sense, arising from contact with an external object; the object as perceived and remembered.

5. Effect produced on the mind, conscience, feelings, sentiments, and the like.

> We speak of moral *impressions*, religious *impressions*, *impressions* of sublimity and beauty. —Fleming.

6. Sensible result of an influence exerted from without; effect of a battle or the like.

> Such a defeat . . . may surely endure a comparison with any of the bravest *impressions* in ancient times. —Wotton.

7. Appearance; phenomenon; agency; power. [Obs.]

8. In printing, a copy taken by pressure from type, from an engraved plate, and the like; hence, the copies of a work taken at one time; an edition.

9. In painting, the first coat or ground color; also, a coat to prevent rust, as on a steam-pipe.

Proof impression; in engraving, an impression taken prior to finishing a block or plate, for the purpose of criticism and final correction.

im-pres″siŏn-ȧ-bil′i-ty, *n.* The quality of being impressionable.

im-pres′siŏn-ȧ-ble, *a.* Susceptible of impression; capable of being impressed.

im-pres′siŏn-ȧ-ble-ness, *n.* Impressionability. [Rare.]

im-pres′siŏn-ism, *n.* A method of representation in art, using a strong and vigorous style of treatment of a subject, with the idea of representing the first effects upon the senses of the delineator.

im-pres′siŏn-ist, *n.* One who in painting or writing yields to first and striking impressions; a devotee of impressionism.

im-pres-siŏn-is′tic, *a.* Relating to or characterized by impressionism.

im-pres′siŏn-less, *a.* Not susceptible; incapable of being impressed.

im-press′ive, *a.* 1. Making or tending to make an impression; having the power of affecting, or of exciting attention and feeling; adapted to affect the senses or the conscience; as, an *impressive* discourse; an *impressive* scene.

2. Capable of being impressed; susceptible. [Rare.]

Syn.—Forcible, solemn, affecting, imposing, important.

im-press′ive-ly, *adv.* In an impressive manner.

im-press′ive-ness, *n.* The quality of being impressive.

im-press′ment, *n.* The act of impressing; the state of being impressed; specifically, compulsion to serve, as in an army, navy, corps, etc.

im-press′ŏr, *n.* One who or that which impresses.

im-pres′sūre, *n.* The mark made by pressure; indentation; dent; impression. [Obs.]

im′prest, *n.* [ME. *in presto*, in ready money; LL. *imprӕstitum*; L. *in*, in, and *prӕsto*, at hand, ready.] A kind of earnest-money; loan; money advanced. [Eng.]

Imprest accountant; in English law, a person to whom imprest is given for disbursement.

im-prest′, *v.t.*; imprested, *pt., pp.*; impresting, *ppr.* To advance on loan. [Eng.]

im-prev′ȧ-lence, im-prev′ȧ-len-cy, *n.* Incapability of prevailing. [Rare.]

im-prē-vent-ȧ-bil′i-ty, *n.* The quality of being impreventable.

im-prē-vent′ȧ-ble, *a.* Incapable of being prevented.

im-pri-mā′tur, *n.* [L., lit., let it be pressed upon, or printed, 3rd pers. sing. pres. subj. pass. of *imprimere*, to press upon.]

1. Official license to issue a book or other printed matter.

2. License in general; sanction.

im-prim′ēr-y, *n.* A print; impression; a printing-house; art of printing. [Obs.]

im-prim′ing, *n.* First effort in an undertaking. [Obs.]

im-pri′mis, *adv.* [L., for *in primis*, lit., among the first; *in*, among, and *primis*, abl. pl. of *primus*, first.] In the first place; first in order.

im-print′, *v.t.*; imprinted, *pt., pp.*; imprinting, *ppr.* [ME. *emprinten*; OFr. *empreinter*, to stamp, imprint.]

1. To impress; to mark by pressure; as, a character or device *imprinted* on wax or cloth.

2. To stamp, as letters and words on paper by means of types; to print.

3. To fix on the mind or memory; to impress; as, let your father's admonitions and instructions be *imprinted* on your mind.

im′print, *n.* [OFr. *empreinte*, an imprint, from *empreint*, pp. of *empreindre*, to impress, stamp, from L. *imprimere*, to press upon, impress.]

1. An impression.

2. The name of the publisher of a book, newspaper, etc., often with the place of publication, printed on a title-page or elsewhere.

im-priṣ′ŏn, *v.t.* [ME. *imprisonen*; OFr. *emprisonner*, to imprison; *en-*, in, and *prison*, a prison.]

1. To put into a prison; to confine in a prison or jail, or to arrest and detain in custody in any place.

2. To confine; to shut up; to restrain from escape; to deprive of the liberty to move from place to place; as, to be *imprisoned* in a cell.

im-priṣ′ŏn-ēr, *n.* One who imprisons another.

im-priṣ′ŏn-ment, *n.* 1. The act of putting and confining in prison; the act of arresting and detaining in custody.

2. Confinement in a place; restraint of liberty to go from place to place at pleasure.

False imprisonment; the arrest and imprisonment of a person without warrant or cause, or contrary to law; or the unlawful detaining of a person in custody.

im-prob-ȧ-bil′i-ty, *n.* The quality of being improbable, or not likely to be true; unlikelihood.

im-prob′ȧ-ble, *a.* [L. *improbabilis*, not deserving of approbation; *in-* priv., and *probabilis*, deserving of approval, from *probare*, to approve.] Not likely to be true; not to be expected under the circumstances of the case.

im-prob′ȧ-ble-ness, *n.* The state of being improbable; improbability.

im-prob′ȧ-bly, *adv.* In a manner not likely to be true.

im′prō-bāte, *v.t.* [L. *improbatus*, pp. of *improbare*, to disapprove; *in-* priv., and *probare*, to approve.] To disallow; not to approve. [Rare.]

im-prō-bā′tion, *n.* [L. *improbatio* (*-onis*), from *improbatus*, pp. of *improbare*, to disapprove.]

1. The act of disapproving.

2. In Scots law, the act of disproving the legality or authenticity of a forged document.

im′prō-bā-tive, *a.* Relating to or of the character of improbation.

im′prō-bā-tō-ry, *a.* Same as *Improbative*.

im-prŏb′i-ty, *n.* [L. *improbitas* (*-atis*), badness, wickedness, from *improbus*, bad; *in-* priv., and *probus*, good.] Want of integrity or rectitude of principle; dishonesty; as, a man of known *improbity* is always suspected and usually despised.

im-prō-fi′cience (-fish′ens), *n.* Improficiency.

im-prō-fi′cien-cy (-fish′en-), *n.* Want of proficiency.

im-prof′it-ȧ-ble, *a.* Unprofitable. [Obs.]

im-prō-gress′ive, *a.* Not progressive. [Rare.]

im-prō-gress′ive-ly, *adv.* Not progressively. [Rare.]

im-prō-lif′ic, *a.* Not prolific; unfruitful. [Obs.]

im-prō-lif′ic-āte, *v.t.* To impregnate; to fecundate. [Obs.]

im-prompt′, *a.* [L. *impromptus*; *in-* priv., and *promptus*, ready, prepared.] Lacking promptness; not prepared. [Rare.]

im-promp′tū, *adv.* or *a.* [L. *in promptu*, in readiness; *in*, in, and *promptu*, abl. of *promptus*, readiness, from *promptus*, brought out, ready, prompt.] Offhand; without previous study; as, a verse uttered or written *impromptu*; an *impromptu* reply.

im-promp′tū, *n.* 1. A piece made offhand, at the moment, or without previous study; an extemporaneous composition, speech, or remark.

2. A musical composition evolved and played on the spur of the moment.

im-prop′ẽr, *a.* [ME. *improper*; OFr. *impropre*; L. *improprius*, not proper; *in-* priv., and *proprius*, one's own, proper.]

1. Not proper, suitable, or adapted to its end; unfit; as, an *improper* proceeding.

2. Not in accordance with recognized rules or customs; as, *improper* behavior of a child.

3. Not according to recognized laws of nature or the formulas of science; as, an *improper* fraction; *improper* development.

Improper diphthong; see under *Diphthong*.

Improper feud; in English law, a feud or title held by original grant, and not received as a reward for military service.

Improper fraction; see under *Fraction*.

im-prop′ẽr, *v.t.* To impropriate. [Obs.]

im-prop-ẽr-ā′tion, *n.* The act of reproaching. [Obs.]

im-prō-pē′ri-ȧ, *n.pl.* [LL., pl. of *improperium*, a reproach, from L. *improperare*, to reproach.] The reproaches; musical responses sung in Roman Catholic churches on Good Friday instead of the usual mass, intended to recall the reproaches of the Saviour to his disciples.

im-prop′ẽr-ly, *adv.* Not properly.

im-prop′ẽr-ty, *n.* [Obs.] See *Impropriety*.

im-prō-pi′tious (-pish′us), *a.* Not propitious unpropitious. [Obs.]

im-prō-pōr′tiŏn-ȧ-ble, *a.* Not proportionable. [Obs.]

im-prō-pōr′tiŏn-āte, *a.* Not proportionate; not adjusted. [Obs.]

im-prō′pri-āte, *v.t.*; impropriated, *pt., pp.*; impropriating, *ppr.* [LL. *impropriatus*, pp. of *impropriare*, to take as one's own; *in*, in, and *proprius*, one's own.]

1. To appropriate to private use; to take to oneself; as, to *impropriate* thanks to oneself. [Obs.]

2. To place the profits of ecclesiastical property in the hands of a layman. [Eng.]

im-prō′pri-āte, *v.i.* To act the part of an impropriator. [Obs.]

im-prō′pri-āte, *a.* Devolved into the hands of a layman.

im-prō-pri-ā′tion, *n.* 1. The act of putting an ecclesiastical benefice into the hands of a layman. [Eng.]

2. The benefice impropriated.

im-prō′pri-ā-tŏr, *n.* A layman who has possession of the lands of the church, or an ecclesiastical living. [Eng.]

im-prō-pri-ā′trix, *n.* A woman who takes to her own use or who acts as an impropriator.

im-prō-pri′e-ty, *n.* [Fr. *impropriété*; L. *improprietas* (*-atis*), impropriety, from *improprius*, improper.]

1. Unfitness; unsuitableness to character, time, place, or circumstances; as, *impropriety* of behavior or manners.

2. Inaccuracy in language; a word or phrase not according with the established usages or principles of speaking or writing.

> Many gross *improprieties*, however authorized by practice, ought to be discarded. —Swift.

im-pros-per′i-ty, *n.* Lack of success or prosperity. [Obs.]

im-pros′pẽr-ous, *a.* [L. *improsper*, not fortunate; *in-* priv., and *prosper*, fortunate.] Not prosperous. [Obs.]

im-pros′pẽr-ous-ly, *adv.* Unsuccessfully; unprosperously; unfortunately. [Obs.]

im-pros′pẽr-ous-ness, *n.* Ill success; want of prosperity. [Obs.]

im-prōv-ȧ-bil′i-ty, *n.* The state or quality of being capable of improvement; susceptibility of being made better.

im-prōv′ȧ-ble, *a.* 1. Susceptible of improvement; capable of growing or being made better; that may be advanced in good qualities.

> I have a fine spread of *improvable* lands. —Addison.

2. That may be used to advantage, or for the increase of anything valuable.

> The essays of weaker heads afford *improvable* hints to better. —Browne.

im-prōv′ȧ-ble-ness, *n.* Susceptibility of improvement or of being used to advantage.

im-prōv′ȧ-bly, *adv.* In a manner that admits of improvement.

im-prōve′, *v.t.*; improved, *pt., pp.*; improving, *ppr.* [*In-*, intens., and OFr. *prover*, to test, to show to be sufficient, from L. *probare*, to approve, from *probus*, good.]

1. To make better; to advance in value or good qualities; as, a good education *improves* the mind and the manners.

2. To use or employ to good purpose; to make productive; to turn to profitable account; to use for advantage; to employ for advancing interest, reputation, or happiness.

> True policy, as well as good faith, in my opinion, binds us to *improve* the occasion. —Washington.

3. To apply to practical purposes; as, to *improve* a discourse, or the doctrines stated and proved in a sermon.

Syn.—Correct, amend, mend, meliorate, heighten, advance.

im-prōve′, *v.i.* 1. To grow better or wiser; to advance in goodness, knowledge, wisdom, or other excellence; as, we are pleased to see our children *improve* in knowledge or strength.

> We take care to *improve* in our frugality and diligence. —Atterbury.

2. To advance in bad qualities; to grow worse. [Rare.]

> Domitian *improved* in cruelty. —Milner.

3. To increase; to be enhanced; to rise; as, the price of cotton *improves*, or is *improved*.

To improve on or *upon*; to make useful additions or amendments to; to bring nearer to perfection; as, *to improve on* the mode of manufacture.

im-prōve′ment, *n.* 1. Advancement in worth, learning, wisdom, skill, or other excellence; as, the *improvement* of the mind by cultivation; *improvement* in classical learning, science, or mechanical skill; *improvement* in music.

2. Melioration; a making or growing better, or more valuable; as, the *improvement* of the roads; the *improvement* of the breed of horses or cattle.

3. A valuable addition; excellence added, or a change for the better; sometimes with *on* or *to*; as, an *improvement* was made *to* the house by the addition of a veranda.

4. In patent law, an additional device or a change of form or of composition in something already patented.

5. Advance or progress from any state to a better.

6. Instruction; growth in knowledge or refinement; edification.

> I look upon your city as the best place of *improvement*. —South.

7. Use or employment to beneficial purposes; a turning to good account; as, the *improvement* of natural advantages, or spiritual privileges.

8. Practical application; as, the *improvement* of the doctrines of a sermon.

9. In the plural, the properties added to a farm or to a lot or plot of ground, such as houses, fences, drains, wells, etc.

Syn.—Betterment, melioration, amendment, advancement, enhancement, progress, proficiency.

im-prōv′ẽr, *n.* Any agent that effects improvement.

im-prō-vid′ed, *a.* Unforeseen; unexpected; not provided against. [Obs.]

im-prov′i-dence, *n.* [LL. *improvidentia*; L. *in-* priv., and *providus*, foresighted.] Want of providence or forecast; neglect of foresight, or of the measures which foresight might dictate for safety or advantage.

Syn.—Negligence, prodigality, carelessness, shiftlessness, wastefulness.

im-prov′i-dent, *a.* [L. *in-* priv., and *providus*, foresighted.] Wanting forecast; not foreseeing what will be necessary or convenient, or neglecting the measures which foresight would dictate; wanting care to make provision for future exigencies.

Syn.—Wasteful, negligent, shiftless, prodigal.

im-prov-i-den′tiăl-ly (-shăl-), *adv.* [Rare.] See *Improvidently*.

im-prov′i-dent-ly, *adv.* Without foresight or forecast; without care to provide for future wants.

im-prōv′ing, *a.* Growing better; tending to advance in good qualities; as, an *improving* rotation of crops.

Improving lease; in Scots law, a kind of lease or extension of lease granted to a tenant as an inducement for him to improve the leased premises.

im-prōv′ing-ly, *adv.* In an improving manner.

im-prov′i-sāte, *a.* Unpremeditated.

im-prov′i-sāte, *v.t.* and *v.i.* To produce impromptu; to extemporize. [Rare.]

im-prov-i-sā′tiŏn, *n.* The act of writing poetry or performing music extemporaneously, or the result of such act.

im-prō-vis′ȧ-tīze, *v.t.* and *v.i.* Same as *Improvisate*.

im-prov′i-sā-tŏr, *n.* One who composes impromptu.

im-prō-vï-ṣȧ-tō′re, *n.* [It. *improvvisatore*.] One who makes rimes, short poems, etc., extemporaneously.

im-prov-ï-ṣȧ-tō′ri-ăl, *a.* Pertaining to impromptu composition.

im-prov′i-ṣȧ-tō-ry, *a.* Relating to extemporary composition of rimes; improvisatorial.

im-prō-vï-ṣȧ-trï′ce (-chā), *n.* A woman who writes poetry, sings, or performs on a musical instrument extemporaneously.

im-prō-vïṣe′, *v.t.*; improvised, *pt., pp.*; improvising, *ppr.* [Fr. *improviser*, to improvise, from L. *improvisus*, unforeseen; *in-* priv., and *provisus*, pp. of *providere*, to foresee, anticipate.] To produce anything on the spur of the moment, usually in music or verse; to adapt one article to the use of another.

im-prō-vïṣe′, *v.i.* To speak extemporaneously, especially in verse, or to compose and execute music impromptu.

im-prō-vïṣ′ẽr, *n.* One who composes on the spur of the moment.

im-prō-vi′ṣion (-vizh′un), *n.* Want of forecast; improvidence. [Obs.]

im-prō-vï′ṣō, *a.* [L., on a sudden, abl. of *improvisus*, unforeseen; *in-* priv., and *provisus*, foreseen.] Impromptu; not previously prepared.

im-prov-vï-ṣȧ-tō′re, *n.* [It.] Same as *Improvisatore*.

im-prov-vï-ṣȧ-trï′ce (-chā), *n.* [It.] A female improviser; spelled also *improvisatrice*.

im-prụ′dence, *n.* [L. *imprudentia*, rashness, want of foresight, from *imprudens* (*-entis*), without foresight, imprudent.] Lack of prudence; indiscretion; want of caution, circumspection, or a due regard to the consequences of words to be uttered, or actions to be performed, or their probable effects on the interest, safety, reputation, or happiness of oneself or others; heedlessness; inconsiderateness; rashness.

im-prụ′dent, *a.* [L. *imprudens* (*-entis*), without foresight, imprudent; *in-* priv., and *prudens* (*-entis*), prudent.] Wanting prudence or discretion; indiscreet; injudicious; not attentive to the consequences of words or actions; rash; heedless.

im-prụ′dent-ly, *adv.* Without the exercise of prudence; indiscreetly.

im-pū′bẽr-ăl, *a.* [L. *impubes* (*-eris*); *in-* priv., and *pubes* (*-eris*), grown up.] Below the age of puberty; not mature.

im-pū′bẽr-ty, *n.* The state prior to that of puberty.

im′pū-dence, *n.* [OFr. *impudence*; L. *impudentia*, shamelessness, from *impudens* (*-entis*), shameless.] Shamelessness; want of modesty; effrontery; assurance, accompanied with a disregard of the opinions of others.

> Those clear truths, that either their own evidence forces us to admit, or common experience makes it *impudence* to deny. —Locke.

Syn.—Effrontery, sauciness, boldness, insolence, immodesty.—*Impudence* refers more especially to the feelings; *effrontery* to some gross and public exhibition of shamelessness; *sauciness* to a sudden outbreak of *impudence*.

im′pū-den-cy, *n.* Impudence.

im′pū-dent, *a.* [ME. *impudent*; L. *impudens* (*-entis*), shameless; *in-* priv., and *pudens* (*-entis*), ashamed.] Shameless; wanting modesty; bold, with contempt of others; saucy.

> When we behold an angel, not to fear
> Is to be *impudent*. —Dryden.

Syn.—Audacious, brazen, saucy, impertinent, insolent, pert, forward, rude.

im′pū-dent-ly, *adv.* Shamelessly; with inappropriate or unbecoming assurance.

> At once assail
> With open mouths, and *impudently* rail.
> —Sandys.

im-pū-dic′i-ty, *n.* [L. *impudicitia*, immodesty; *in-* priv., and *pudicus*, modest.] Immodesty.

im-pūgn′ (-pūn′), *v.t.*; impugned, *pt.*, *pp.*; impugning, *ppr.* [OFr. *impugner*; L. *impugnare*, to attack, assail; *in*, on, against, and *pugnare*, to fight.] To oppose; to attack by words or arguments; to contradict; to insinuate against; to cast reflections, as upon one's motives.

> The truth hereof I will not rashly *impugn*, or overboldly affirm. —Peacham.

im-pūgn′à-ble, *a.* Open to attack; questionable as to sincerity or honesty; that may be justly impugned.

im-pug-nā′tion, *n.* Opposition. [Obs.]

im-pūgn′ēr (-pūn′), *n.* One who opposes or contradicts; one given to impugning.

im-pūgn′ment, *n.* The act of making a charge or attack; also, the attack itself.

im-pū′is-sānce, *n.* [Fr.] Impotence; weakness; want of power or authority.

im-pū′is-sănt, *a.* [Fr.] Weak impotent.

im′pulse, *n.* [L. *impulsus*, a pushing against, a shock, impulse, from *impulsus*, pp. of *impellere*, to push or strike against; *in-*, against, and *pellere*, to push, strike.]

1. Force communicated instantaneously; the effect of a sudden or momentary force; the act of communicating such a force.

2. Influence acting on the mind; motive.

> These were my natural *impulses* for the undertaking. —Dryden.

3. Force of mind impelling to action; as, a man of generous *impulses*.

4. In mechanics, the action of a force upon or against a body momentarily to give it motion.

Syn.—Incentive, push, incitement, force, influence, instigation, feeling, sudden thought, motive.

im-pulse′, *v.t.* To impel; to incite.

im-pul′sion, *n.* [L. *impulsio* (*-onis*), a pushing against, from *impulsus*, pp. of *impellere*, to push against, impel.]

1. The act of driving against or impelling; the sudden or momentary agency of a body in motion on another body.

2. Influence on the mind; impulse.

im-pul′sive, *a.* 1. Having the power of driving or impelling; moving; impellent.

> Poor men! poor papers! We and they
> Do some *impulsive* force obey. —Prior.

2. Actuated by impulse; as, an *impulsive* young man.

3. In mechanics, said of forces that act instantaneously or by impulse; not continuous.

im-pul′sive, *n.* That which gives an impulse.

im-pul′sive-ly, *adv.* With force; by impulse.

im-pul′sive-ness, *n.* The state of having impulsive energy.

im-pul′sŏr, *n.* [L. *impulsor*, from *impellere*, to impel.] Any agent of impulsion. [Rare.]

im-punc̄′tāte, *a.* Without pits, spots, or holes.

im-punc̄′tū-ăl, *a.* Not punctual. [Rare.]

im-punc̄-tū-al′i-ty, *n.* Neglect of punctuality. [Rare.]

im-pūne′, *a.* [L. *impunis.*] Not yet punished. [Rare.]

im-pū′ni-bly, *adv.* Without punishment. [Obs.]

im-pū′ni-ty, *n.* [L. *impunitas*, from *impunis*, free from punishment; *in-* priv., and *pœna*, punishment.] Exemption from punishment, penalty, injury, or loss; as, no person should be permitted to violate the laws with *impunity*; some ferocious animals are not to be encountered with *impunity*.

im-pū-rā′tion, *n.* The act of rendering impure; impurity. [Obs.]

im-pūre′, *a.* [L. *impurus*; *in-* priv., and *purus*, pure.]

1. Not pure; foul; feculent; tinctured; mixed or impregnated with extraneous substances; adulterated; as, *impure* water or air; *impure* salt or milk.

2. Unchaste; lewd; unclean; obscene; as, *impure* actions or language.

3. Defiled by sin or guilt; unholy, as persons.

4. Unclean; not purified according to the ceremonial law of Moses.

5. In language, not conformable to the best authority; violating the idioms of a language; as, *impure* French; *impure* English.

Syn.—Adulterated, dirty, filthy, coarse, gross, ribald, immodest, vulgar.

im-pūre′, *v.t.* To render foul; to defile. [Obs.]

im-pūre′ly, *adv.* In an impure manner; with impurity.

im-pūre′ness, *n.* [L. *impuritas*, from *impurus*, impure; *in-* priv., and *purus*, pure.] The state of being impure.

im-pū′ri-ty, *n.*; *pl.* **im-pū′ri-ties.** 1. Want of purity; foulness; feculence; as, the *impurity* of water, of air, of liquors, or of any species of earth or metal.

2. Any foul matter.

3. Unchastity; lewdness.

> The foul *impurities* that reigned among the monkish clergy. —Atterbury.

im-pŭr′ple, *v.t.* Same as *Empurple.*

im-pūt-à-bil′i-ty, *n.* The quality of being attributable.

im-pūt′à-ble, *a.* 1. That may be imputed or charged to a person; chargeable; attributable; as, crimes and errors are *imputable* to those who commit them.

2. Accusable; chargeable with a fault. [Rare.]

im-pūt′à-ble-ness, *n.* The state of being imputable.

im-pūt′à-bly, *adv.* In an imputable manner.

im-pū-tā′tion, *n.* [LL. *imputatio* (*-onis*), a charge, an account, from L. *imputatus*, pp. of *imputare*, to charge, impute.]

1. The act of imputing or charging; attribution; as, the *imputation* of crimes or faults to the true authors of them; we are liable to the *imputation* of numerous errors.

2. Charge or attribution of evil; censure; reproach; as, the sly *imputations* of an enemy.

> Let us be careful to guard ourselves against these groundless *imputations* of our enemies, and to rise above them. —Addison.

3. Hint; slight notice; intimation.

4. In theology, the charging to the account of one something which properly belonged to another; or the attributing of personal guilt and its appropriate consequences to one or more persons on account of the offense of another, or a similar attribution of righteousness or merit and its consequences; as, to lay by *imputation* the sin of Adam on his posterity.

im-pūt′à-tive, *a.* [LL. *imputativus*, charging, accusatory, from L. *imputare*, to charge, impute.] That may be imputed; transmitted by imputation.

im-pūt′à-tive-ly, *adv.* By imputation.

im-pūte′, *v.t.*; imputed, *pt.*, *pp.*; imputing, *ppr.* [Fr. *imputer*; L. *imputare*, to set to the account of, impute; *in*, in, to, and *putare*, to estimate, charge, think.]

1. To charge; to attribute; to set to the account of; as, to *impute* crimes, faults, blame, etc., to guilty persons; to *impute* misfortune to imprudence.

2. In theology, to attribute on account of another; to place to one's account.

3. To reckon; to consider; to regard. [Rare.]

Syn.—Count, reckon, attribute, ascribe, charge.

im-pūt′ēr, *n.* One that imputes or attributes.

im-pū-tres′ci-ble, *a.* Not subject to putrefaction or corruption.

im′righ, im′rich, *n.* [Gael. *eanraich*, soup.] In Scotland, a kind of broth or soup made from parts of the beef.

in-. [ME. *in-*, *en-*; OFr. *in-*, *en-*; L. *in-*, from prep. *in*, in, within.] A prefix signifying in, into, within, on, toward; as, *in*augurate, *in*carnate, *in*candescent, etc.; sometimes used merely with intensive force; as, *in*ebriate, *in*vigilate. *In-* is assimilated to *il-* before *l-*, *im-* before a labial, and *ir-* before *r*.

in-. A prefix from L. *in-*, having a privative or negative force; as, *in*consistent, *in*convenient, *in*capable, etc. Also written *il-*, *im-*, and *ir-*, for the sake of euphony.

in-. A prefix from ME. *in-*, AS. *in-*, in, and always signifying in, into, within, etc. The prefix *in-* of Anglo-Saxon origin never has a merely intensive force, as the prefix *in-* of Latin origin. Also written *il-*, *im-*, or *ir-*, for the sake of euphony.

in, *v.t.* To bring in, as a harvest; to put into an inclosure or under cover. [Obs.]

in, *prep.* [ME. *in*, *yn*; AS. *in*, in; with the simple form of *in* there became merged the ME. *inne*, from AS. *inne*, in, within.]

1. A word denoting, generally, location or confinement within limits, beyond which is *out*; as, one cannot be *in* and *out* of a house at the same time.

2. Concerning place: within; among; within the boundaries of; as, *in* the city; *in* the crowd.

3. Concerning time: at; during; at the end of; as, *in* the beginning; *in* two hours; due *in* sixty days.

4. Concerning being: within the possession of; as, he has *in* him the elements of success.

5. Concerning action: on the way; undergoing the process of; as, he spent much time *in* making up his mind; time was lost *in* going and coming.

6. Concerning state, condition, etc.: in the condition of; of the nature of, etc.; as, *in* prosperity; written *in* verse; *in* distress, etc.

7. Concerning matter, method, form, etc.: of; consisting of; made of; with; as, painted *in* oil; a model *in* plaster.

8. Concerning extent, view, use, etc.: within the province of; with reference to; as, *in* biology; *in* ecclesiastical law; faulty *in* diction.

9. Concerning quantity, number, amount, etc.: embraced by; to the sum of; as, there are ten dimes *in* a dollar; fined *in* the sum of one hundred dollars.

10. Concerning means, etc.: by; through; with; by means of; as, *in* walking one finds good exercise; *in* talking he betrayed his ignorance; *in* the cotton-gin the world gained a valuable adjunct to advancement.

11. Concerning cause, origin, source, occasion, etc.: on account of; by reason of; by virtue of; as, *in* the name of all that is good; he glories *in* his ancestry; *in* union there is strength.

12. On; upon; engaged with; in accordance with; as, *in* a dream he beheld a form; *in* the stroke of the clock he read his doom; *in* all conscience you ought to desist; fowls multiply *in* the earth.

In as much as or *inasmuch as*; in view of the fact that; because; considering the fact that; since.

In that; because; for the reason that; in view of the fact that.

In the abstract; viewed with respect to essential features; omitting concomitant conditions and details.

In the concrete; viewed as things are and in their practical relations to each other.

In the name of; (a) by the authority of; as, *in the name of* the people of the United States; (b) regarding the obligation to; as, *in the name of* goodness, what are you doing?

To be in for it; (a) to be pledged in favor of its support, as a political measure or a business transaction; (b) to be threatened with something disagreeable from which there is no means of escape.

To be in it; to be intimately associated with some feat or function; to be one of two or more in a contest; generally in the negative; as, the contest was sharp, but he was simply *not in it*. [Slang.]

To be in with; to be associated with in a confidential way.

in, *adv.* [ME. *in*, *inne*; AS. *in*, *inne*, *innan*, in, within.]

1. In or within (some place, position, or condition expressed or implied); as, the lady is not *in*; the ship is *in*.

2. Into some place or state (implying motion); as, come *in* (into the house); the train has come *in* (into the station).

3. In law, a term used to express the nature of a privilege; as, a tenant is *in* by the lease.

4. In seamen's language, furled; as, the sails are *in*.

To be in; to be at home and willing to receive; as, Mrs. Brown *is in*.

To come in; see under *Come*.

in, *n.* 1. A person who is favored or approved, especially one who holds a public office or belongs to a successful party; used in the plural; as, an *in* or one of the *ins*.

2. A nook or corner, as in a building or garden with many intricate passages and secluded places; mostly in the plural; as, I know the *ins* and outs of the place.

Ins and outs; secluded places and misleading passages.

-in, -ine. [ME. *-in*, *-ine*; OFr. *-in*, *-ine*; L. *-inus*, *-ina*, *-inum*; Gr. *-inos*, *-inē*, *-inon*.] A suffix having the significance of pertaining to or like, added to nouns of Latin and Greek origin to form adjectives; as, aquil*ine*, from L. *aquilinus*, like an eagle, from *aquila*, an eagle; equ*ine*, from L. *equinus*, like a horse, from *equus*, a horse; sometimes used to form nouns from adjectives thus formed; as, div*ine*, n., from div*ine*, adj., from L. *divinus*, like a god, from *divus*, a god.

-in, -ine. [ME. *-in*, *-ine*; L. *-ina*, a suffix of f. abstract nouns.] A suffix used to form nouns from the infinitives of Latin verbs, from derivatives, or from undetermined roots; as, rap*ine*, L. *rapina*, from *rapere*, to seize; medic*ine*, L. *medicina*, from *medicus*, a physician, etc.

-in, -ine. [L. *-ina*, Gr. *-inē*, f. of L. *-inus*, Gr. *-inos*, a suffix of abstract nouns.] A suffix used to form feminine nouns from masculine, as hero*ine*, from *hero*; used in chemistry and mineralogy to form names of some elements; as, fluor*in*, iod*ine*, and names of derivatives; as, beryl*line*, ethyl*in*.

-ina. A suffix from L. *-ina*, f. of *-inus*, used in Spanish, Portuguese, Italian, Latin, and Latinized words; as, vag*ina*, far*ina*, etc.; used especially in Latinized feminine generic and specific names; as, Tell*ina*.

-ina. A suffix from L. *-ina*, neut. pl. of the adjective suffix *-inus*, used in Latin or Latinized names of groups of animals.

in-à-bil′i-ty, *n.* [Compare L. *inhabilis*, unfit, unable; *in-* priv., and *habilis*, fit, able.]

1. The state of being unable; lack of sufficient power, strength, or means to accomplish a desirable end; as, *inability* to purchase a farm, or to fit out a ship.

2. Want of moral or of intellectual strength or force; as, *inability* to discover what is right;

inability to comprehend a mathematical demonstration.

Syn.—Weakness, powerlessness, disability, incapacity, helplessness, impotence, incapability, incompetence.

in-ā'ble, *v.t.* [Obs.] See *Enable.*

in-ā'ble-ment, *n.* [Obs.] See *Enablement.*

in-ab'sti-nence, *n.* Want of abstinence; a partaking; indulgence of appetite; as, the *inabstinence* of Eve. [Rare.]

in-ab-stract'ed, *a.* Not abstracted. [Obs.]

in-à-bū'sive-ly, *adv.* Without abuse. [Obs.]

in-ac-cess-i-bil'i-ty, *n.* The quality or state of being inaccessible, or not to be reached.

in-ac-cess'i-ble, *a.* [LL. *inaccessibilis*, unapproachable; *in-* priv., and *accessibilis*, approachable, from L. *accessus*, an approach, access.] Not to be reached; not to be obtained, attained, or approached; forbidding access; as, an *inaccessible* rock; an *inaccessible* prince.

in-ac-cess'i-ble-ness, *n.* Inaccessibility.

in-ac-cess'i-bly, *adv.* In an inaccessible manner; unapproachably.

in-ac-cord'ănt, *a.* Not in accordance; disagreeing; lacking harmony.

in-ac'cū-rà-cy, *n.* Want of accuracy or exactness; mistake; fault; defect; error; as, an *inaccuracy* in writing, in typesetting, or in a calculation.

in-ac'cū-rāte, *a.* Not accurate; not exact or correct; not according to truth; erroneous; as, an *inaccurate* statement, copy, or transcript.

Syn.—Incorrect, erroneous, inexact, faulty, defective, blundering, loose.

in-ac'cū-rāte-ly, *adv.* In an inaccurate manner; not according to truth; incorrectly; erroneously.

in-ac-quaint'ănce (-kwānt'), *n.* Unacquaintance.

in-ac-qui-es'cent (-kwi-), *a.* Not acquiescing.

in-ac'tion, *n.* Want of action; forbearance of labor; idleness; rest.

in-ac'tive, *a.* [L. *in-* priv., and *activus*, active.]

1. Not active; inert; having no power to move; incapable of action; as, matter is of itself *inactive.*

2. Not diligent or industrious; not busy; idle; also, habitually idle; indolent; sluggish; as, an *inactive* official.

3. Inoperative; producing no effect; said of a chemical agent or medicine.

Syn.—Idle, inert, lazy, slothful, sluggish, dull, passive.

in-ac'tive-ly, *adv.* In an inactive manner; idly; sluggishly; without motion, labor, or employment.

in-ac-tiv'i-ty, *n.* 1. Inertness; as, the *inactivity* of matter.

2. Idleness or habitual idleness; want of action or exertion; sluggishness.

in-ac'tōse, *n.* A sugar derived from certain plants; so called because it is optically inactive.

in-ac'tū-āte, *v.t.* To put in action. [Obs.]

in-ac-tū-ā'tion, *n.* Operation. [Obs.]

in-ad-ap-tā'tion, *n.* A state of not being adapted or fitted.

in-ad'ē-quā-cy (-kwā-), *n.* The quality of being unequal or insufficient for a purpose; incompleteness; defectiveness; as, the *inadequacy* of ideas.

in-ad'ē-quāte, *a.* 1. Not equal to the purpose; insufficient to effect the object; unequal; as, *inadequate* power, strength, or resources.

2. Incomplete; defective; not just; as, *inadequate* representation or description.

in-ad'ē-quāte-ly, *adv.* Not fully or sufficiently; not completely.

in-ad'ē-quāte-ness, *n.* The state of being inadequate; inadequacy; inequality; incompleteness.

in-ad-ē-quā'tion, *n.* Want of exact correspondence. [Obs.]

in-ad-hēr'ent, *a.* 1. Free; not adhering.

2. In botany, a term applied to any organ that is free or not attached to any other, as a calyx when perfectly detached from the ovary.

in-ad-hē'sion (-zhun), *n.* Want of adhesion.

in-ad-mis-si-bil'i-ty, *n.* The quality of being inadmissible, or not proper to be received; as, the *inadmissibility* of an argument, or of evidence in court.

in-ad-mis'si-ble, *a.* Not admissible; not proper to be admitted, allowed, or received; as, *inadmissible* testimony; an *inadmissible* proposition.

in-ad-mis'si-bly, *adv.* In a manner not admissible.

in-ad'ū-nāte, *a.* [*In-*, not, and L. *adunatus*, pp. of *adunare*, to make into one.] With the arms free above the first radials, as certain crinoids.

in-ad-vẽrt'ence, *n.* 1. The condition of being inadvertent; inattention; negligence; heedlessness; as, many mistakes and some misfortunes arise from *inadvertence.*

2. The effect of inattention; any oversight, mistake, or fault which proceeds from negligence.

Syn.—Oversight, negligence, inattention, carelessness.

in-ad-vẽrt'en-cy, *n.* Inadvertence.

in-ad-vẽrt'ent, *a.* Not turning the mind to; heedless; careless; negligent.

in-ad-vẽrt'ent-ly, *adv.* Heedlessly; carelessly; from want of attention; inconsiderately.

in-ad-vis'à-ble, *a.* Not proper to be advised; inexpedient.

in-ad-vis'à-ble-ness, *n.* The state of being inadvisable.

-inæ. A suffix from L. *-inæ*, f. pl. of *-inus*, used in forming Latinized names of subfamilies of animals, as Elephant*inæ*, Equ*inæ*, etc. Words thus formed are properly adjectives in the feminine plural, with *bestiæ*, beasts, understood.

in-af-fà-bil'i-ty, *n.* Reservedness in conversation; lack of sociability.

in-af'fà-ble, *a.* Not affable; reserved.

in-af-fec-tā'tion, *n.* Lack of affected manner. [Rare.]

in-af-fect'ed, *a.* Unaffected. [Obs.]

in-āid'à-ble, *a.* That cannot be assisted. [Rare.]

in-aj'à-pälm (-päm), *n.* Same as *Jagua-palm.*

in-āl"ien-à-bil'i-ty (-yen-), *n.* The quality of being nontransferable.

in-āl'ien-à-ble, *a.* Not alienable; that cannot be legally or justly alienated or transferred to another; as, a minor's *inalienable* estate.

in-āl'ien-à-ble-ness, *n.* The state of being inalienable.

in-āl'ien-à-bly, *adv.* In a manner that forbids alienation; as, rights *inalienably* vested.

in-al-i-men'tăl, *a.* Affording no nourishment.

in-al"tẽr-à-bil'i-ty, *n.* The quality of not being alterable or changeable.

in-al'tẽr-à-ble, *a.* That cannot or may not be altered or changed; unalterable.

in-al'tẽr-à-ble-ness, *n.* The state of being unalterable.

in-al'tẽr-à-bly, *adv.* In an unalterable manner.

in-ā'mi-à-ble, *a.* Unamiable. [Obs.]

in-ā'mi-à-ble-ness, *n.* Unamiableness. [Obs.]

in-à-mis'si-ble, *a.* [LL. *inamissibilis*; L. *in-* priv., and *amissus*, pp. of *amittere*, to lose.] Not to be lost. [Rare.]

in-à-mis'si-ble-ness, *n.* The state of not being liable to be lost.

in-à-mō-rä'tà, *n.* [It., f. of *inamorato*, a lover.] A woman beloved; a sweetheart.

in-am'ō-rāte, *a.* [L. *in*, in, and *amor*, love.] Inflamed with love. [Rare.]

in-am'ō-rāte-ly, *adv.* In an enamored manner. [Rare.]

in-à-mō-rä'tō, *n.* [It., from LL. *inamoratus*, pp. of *inamorare*, to cause to love, from L. *in*, in, and *amor*, love.] A male in love; a lover.

in-à-möv'à-ble, *a.* Not subject to removal. [Rare.]

in'=and=in', *adv.* 1. From animals of the same stock that are closely related; as, to breed *in-and-in.*

2. With constant interaction.

in'=and=in', *n.* An old gambling game with dice.

in-āne', *a.* [L. *inanis*, empty.] Empty; void; characterless; senseless; foolish; silly; without substance.

in-āne', *n.* A void space; a space beyond the confines of the world.

in-āne'ly, *adv.* In an inane manner; senselessly.

in-nan'gà, *n.* [New Zealand.] A small fish, *Retropinna richardsoni*, found in the fresh waters of New Zealand.

in-an'gū-lăr, *a.* Not angular. [Obs.]

in-à-nil'ō-quent, *a.* [L. *inanis*, empty, and *loquens (-entis)*, ppr. of *loqui*, to speak, talk.] Inaniloquous.

in-à-nil'ō-quous (-kwus), *a.* [L. *inanis*, empty, and *loqui*, to talk.] Talkative; given to senseless loquacity.

in-an'i-māte, *v.t.* [LL. *inimatus*, pp. of *inimare*, to put life in; L. *in*, in, and *anima*, life.] To animate. [Obs.]

in-an'i-māte, *a.* [L. *inanimatus*; *in-* priv., and *anima*, life.] Destitute of animation or life; inert; dull; spiritless; inactive; dead; as, stones and earth are *inanimate* substances; an *inanimate* body.

in-an'i-mā-ted, *a.* Destitute of life; without animation.

in-an'i-māte-ness, *n.* The condition of being without life; dullness; want of spirit.

in-an-i-mā'tion, *n.* Inanimateness. [Rare.]

in-an-i-mā'tion, *n.* The act of animating by the infusion of life. [Obs.]

in-à-ni'ti-āte (-nish'i-), *v.t.* To reduce to a state of inanition; to exhaust as by starving. [Rare.]

in-à-ni-ti-ā'tion (-nish-i-ā'), *n.* Inane condition; exhaustion. [Rare.]

in-à-ni'tion (-nish'un), *n.* [Fr. *inanition*; LL. *inanitio (-onis)*, emptiness, from L. *inanitus*, pp. of *inanire*, to empty, from *inanis*, empty, void.] Emptiness; want of fullness; an inane condition; as, *inanition* of body or of the vessels; hence, exhaustion from fasting; starving or lack of nourishment through disorder of some organ.

in-an'i-ty, *n.*; *pl.* **in-an'i-ties.** [Fr. *inanité*; L. *inanitas*, emptiness, from *inanis*, empty.]

1. Emptiness; void space; vacuity.

2. Lack of sense; foolishness; frivolousness.

3. An inane action or pursuit; a silly thing.

in-an'thẽr-āte, *a.* In botany, having no anthers; with sterile filaments.

in-ap'à-thy, *n.* A condition without apathy. [Rare.]

in-ap-pēal'à-ble, *a.* That cannot be appealed.

in-ap-pēas'à-ble, *a.* Not admitting of appeasement.

in-ap-pel-là-bil'i-ty, *n.* The quality of being beyond the power of appeal.

in-ap-pel'là-ble, *a.* Beyond the power of appeal; settled finally.

in-ap'pē-tence, *n.* [Fr. *inappétence*; L. *in-* priv., and *appetentia*, appetite.] Want of appetence, or of a disposition to seek, select, or imbibe nutriment; want of desire or inclination.

in-ap'pē-ten-cy, *n.* Same as *Inappetence.*

in-ap"pli-cà-bil'i-ty, *n.* The quality of not being applicable; unfitness.

in-ap'pli-cà-ble, *a.* Not applicable; that cannot be applied; not suited or suitable to the purpose; as, the argument or the testimony is *inapplicable* to the case.

in-ap'pli-cà-ble-ness, *n.* The condition of being inapplicable.

in-ap'pli-cà-bly, *adv.* In a manner not suited to the purpose.

in-ap-pli-cā'tion, *n.* Want of application; want of attention or assiduity; negligence; indolence; neglect of study or industry.

in-ap'pō-site, *a.* Not apposite; not fit or suitable; not pertinent; as, an *inapposite* argument.

in-ap'pō-site-ly, *adv.* Not pertinently; not suitably.

in-ap-prē'ci-à-ble (-shi-à-), *a.* [LL. *inappretiabilis*; L. *in-* priv., and LL. *appretiare*, to value at a price; L. *ad*, to, and *pretium*, a price.] Not to be appreciated; that cannot be duly valued; that cannot be estimated.

in-ap-prē-ci-ā'tion (-shi-), *n.* Lack of just valuation.

in-ap-prē'ci-ā-tive, *a.* Wanting in just valuation; unappreciative.

in-ap-prē-hen'si-ble, *a.* [LL. *inapprehensibilis*; L. *in-* priv., and LL. *apprehensibilis*, apprehensible, from L. *apprehendere*, to take hold of, apprehend.] Not intelligible; that cannot be apprehended.

in-ap-prē-hen'sion, *n.* Lack of ability to grasp; dullness; stupidity.

in-ap-prē-hen'sive, *a.* Not apprehensive; regardless.

in-ap-prōach'à-ble, *a.* Not to be approached; inaccessible; excelling.

in-ap-prōach'à-bly, *adv.* So as not to be approached.

in-ap-prō'pri-āte, *a.* Not appropriate; unsuited; not proper; not belonging to or fitted for.

in-ap-prō'pri-āte-ly, *adv.* Not appropriately.

in-ap-prō'pri-āte-ness, *n.* Unsuitableness.

in-apt', *a.* Unapt; not apt; awkward; as, an *inapt* scholar or workman.

in-apt'i-tūde, *n.* Want of aptitude; unfitness; unsuitableness.

in-apt'ly, *adv.* Unfitly; unsuitably.

in-apt'ness, *n.* Unfitness.

in-ā'quāte, *a.* [L. *inaquatus*, pp. of *inaquare*, to turn into water; *in*, into, and *aqua*, water.] Embodied in water or transformed into water. [Rare.]

in-à-quā'tion, *n.* The state of being inaquate. [Rare.]

in-ar'à-ble, *a.* Not arable; not capable of being plowed or tilled.

in-ärch', *v.t.*; inarched (-ärcht'), *pt.*, *pp.*; inarching, *ppr.* To graft by approach; to graft by uniting a scion to a stock without separating it from its parent tree.

in-ärch'ing, *n.* A method of ingrafting by which a scion, without being separated from its parent tree, is joined to a stock standing near.

Inarching.

in-ärm', *v.t.* To encircle with the arms; to hug. [Rare.]

in-är-tic'ū-lāte, *a.* [LL. *inarticulatus*, not articulate; L. *in-* priv., and *articulatus*, pp. of *articulare*, to divide into joints, articulate.]

1. Not uttered with articulation or junction of the organs of speech; not articulate; not distinct, or with distinction of syllables; as, the sounds uttered by birds and beasts are, for the most part, *inarticulate.*

2. In zoölogy, not jointed or articulated.

3. Without ability to articulate.

in-är-tic'ū-lā-ted, *a.* In zoölogy, (a) not jointed; (b) having an inarticulate or hingeless shell.

in-är-tic'ū-lāte-ly, *adv.* Not with distinct syllables; indistinctly.

in-är-tic'ū-lāte-ness, *n.* Indistinctness of utterance by animal voices; want of distinct articulation.

in-är-tic-ū-lā'tion, *n.* Indistinctness of sounds in speaking.

in-är-ti-fi'ciăl (-fish'ăl), *a.* Not done by art;

not made or performed by the rules of art; formed without art; as, an *inartificial* style of composition.

in-är-ti-fi′ciăl-ly, *adv.* Without art; in an artless manner; contrary to the rules of art.

in-är-ti-fi′ciăl-ness, *n.* The state of being artless. [Rare.]

in-är-tis′tiç, *a.* Offensive to the æsthetic sense.

in-är-tis′tiç-ăl, *a.* Inartistic.

in-är-tis′tiç-ăl-ly, *adv.* Not artistically.

in-aṣ-much′, *adv.* Such being the case or fact; seeing; used only with *as* following; as, *inasmuch as* ye have done it unto one of these, ye have done it unto me.

in-at-ten′tion, *n.* 1. Want of attention; failure to fix the mind steadily on an object; heedlessness; neglect.

> Novel lays attract our ravished ears,
> But old the mind with *inattention* hears.
> —Pope.

2. A failure of courtesy; an act of neglect.

Syn.—Inadvertence.—We miss seeing a thing through *inadvertence* when we do not look at it; through *inattention* when we give no heed to it, though directly before us. The latter is therefore the stronger.

in-at-ten′tive, *a.* Not fixing the mind on; heedless; careless; negligent; regardless; as, an *inattentive* spectator or hearer; an *inattentive* habit.

Syn.—Heedless, unmindful, unobservant, absent-minded.

in-at-ten′tive-ly, *adv.* Without attention; carelessly; heedlessly.

in-at-ten′tive-ness, *n.* The condition of being heedless.

in-ąu-di-bil′i-ty, *n.* The quality of being inaudible.

in-ąu′di-ble, *a.* [LL. *inaudibilis*, not audible; L. *in-* priv., and *audire*, to hear.]

1. That cannot be heard; as, an *inaudible* voice or sound.

2. Making no sound; as, the *inaudible* foot of time. [Obs.]

Syn.—Low, suppressed, stifled, muffled, still, soundless, silent.

in-ąu′di-ble-ness, *n.* The condition of being inaudible.

in-ąu′di-bly, *adv.* In an inaudible manner.

in-ąu′gūr, *v.t.* [Obs.] See *Inaugurate.*

in-ąu′gū-răl, *a.* Pertaining to inauguration or to the ceremonies of inauguration, especially to the address delivered by the officer inaugurated.

in-ąu′gū-răl, *n.* An inaugural address; as, the *inaugural* delivered by a president of the United States upon the occasion of his accession to office.

in-ąu′gū-rāte, *a.* Invested with office.

in-ąu′gū-rāte, *v.t.*; inaugurated, *pt., pp.*; inaugurating, *ppr.* [L. *inauguratus*, pp. of *inaugurare*, to practise augury, to take the omens, to consecrate a place or a person by augury; *in*, in, and *augur*, an augur.]

1. To introduce or induct into an office with solemnity or suitable ceremonies; to invest with an office in a formal manner.

2. To initiate formally or ceremoniously, as some important public movement or campaign; as, to *inaugurate* a reform in the methods of transportation.

3. To ceremoniously open for use, as some important public work, a building, a park, or a bridge.

in-ąu-gū-rā′tion, *n.* [LL. *inauguratio (-onis)*, a beginning, from L. *inaugurare*, to consecrate, to inaugurate.]

1. The act of inducting into office with solemnity; investiture with office by appropriate ceremonies.

2. The formal or ceremonious institution of an important movement.

in-ąu′gū-rā-tŏr, *n.* One who inaugurates.

in-ąu′gū-rā-tō-ry, *a.* Suited to induction into office; pertaining to inauguration; as, *inauguratory* gratulations.

in-ąu′rāte, *v.t.* [L. *inauratus*, pp. of *inaurare*, to cover with gold; *in*, on, and *aurare*, to cover with gold, from *aurum*, gold.] To embellish with gold or with gold-leaf. [Obs.]

in-ąu′rāte, *a.* 1. Embellished with gold or with gold-leaf. [Obs.]

2. In biology, having a metallic luster resembling gold; specifically describing features of the *Coleoptera.*

in-au-rā′tion, *n.* The act or process of gilding or covering with gold.

in-ąus′pi-çāte, *a.* Ill-omened. [Obs.]

in-ąus-pi′cious (-pish′us), *a.* Ill-omened; unfortunate; unlucky; evil; unfavorable; as, the counsels of a bad man have an *inauspicious* influence on society.

in-ąus-pi′cious-ly, *adv.* With ill omens; unfortunately; unfavorably.

in-ąus-pi′cious-ness, *n.* Unluckiness; unfavorableness.

in-bärge′, *v.t.* and *v.i.* To embark. [Obs.]

in-bēam′ing, *n.* The entrance of light. [Obs.]

in-bē′ing, *n.* Inherence; inherent existence; inseparableness.

in-bind′, *v.t.* To inclose by binding. [Obs.]

in′blōwn, *a.* Having been blown into. [Obs.]

in′bōard, *a.* 1. Carried or stowed within the hold of a ship or other vessel; as, an *inboard* cargo.

2. In mechanics, inward; as, the stroke of a piston toward the steam-chest is the *inboard* stroke.

3. Not projecting over the rail or bulwarks; as, an *inboard* sail.

in′bōard, *adv.* 1. Within the hold of a vessel.

2. Within the rail or bulwarks of a ship; as, haul the sail *inboard.*

in′bond, *a.* In architecture, a term applied to a brick or stone laid lengthwise across a wall; opposed to *outbond*, where the brick or stone is laid with its length parallel to the face of the wall. An *inbond* and *outbond* wall is one where the bricks or stones are laid alternately across and in the direction of the face of the wall.

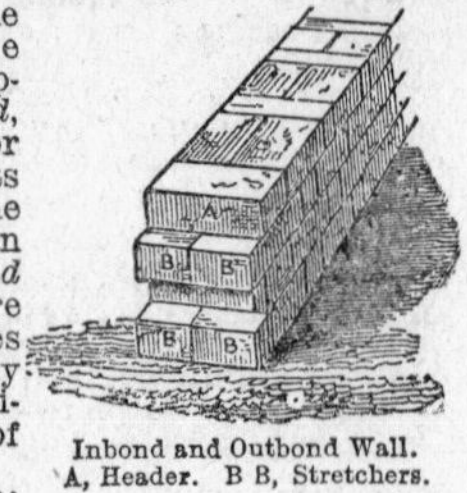

Inbond and Outbond Wall.
A, Header. B B, Stretchers.

in′bōrn, *a.* Innate; implanted by nature; as, *inborn* passions; *inborn* worth.

in′breāk, *n.* A break into or inward; opposed to *outbreak.* [Rare.]

in′breāk-ing, *n.* The act of breaking in. [Rare.]

in-brēathe′, *v.t.*; inbreathed, *pt., pp.*; inbreathing, *ppr.* 1. To infuse by breathing.

2. To inspire; opposed to *exhale.*

in′bred, *a.* Bred within; innate; natural; as, *inbred* worth; *inbred* affection.

in-breed′, *v.t.*; inbred, *pt., pp.*; inbreeding, *ppr.*

1. To produce or generate within.

2. To breed from animals of the same parentage; to breed in-and-in.

in′bŭrn-ing, *a.* Burning fiercely within or from within; said of the passions; as, *inburning* rage, fury, wrath, hatred, zeal, etc.

in′bŭrnt, *a.* Burned in, or as if burned in; impressed beyond effacement.

in′bŭrst, *n.* A sudden and violent rushing in; opposed to *outburst.*

in′by, in′bye, *adv.* Inward in direction; specifically, toward the inner part of a mine; away from the entrance; opposed to *outby.*

inç, *n.* [Japan.] A Japanese unit of linear measure equal to nineteen decimeters.

In′cá, *n.* [Sp. and Port., from Peruv. *inca.*]

1. The title given by the natives of Peru to their kings and to the princes of the blood before the conquest of that country by the Spaniards.

2. [I—] A member of the dominant tribe in Peru before the Spanish conquest.

in-çāge′, *v.t.* Same as *Encage.*

in-çal″çū-lȧ-bil′i-ty, *n.* The quality of being beyond calculation.

in-çal′çū-lȧ-ble, *a.* That cannot be calculated; beyond calculation.

in-çal′çū-lȧ-ble-ness, *n.* The quality of being beyond calculation.

in-çal′çū-lȧ-bly, *adv.* In a degree beyond calculation.

in-çȧ-les′cence, *n.* A growing warm; incipient or increasing heat.

in-çȧ-les′cen-cy, *n.* Incalescence.

in-çȧ-les′cent, *a.* [L. *incalescens (-entis)*, ppr. of *incalescere*, to grow warm or hot; *in-*, intens., and *calescere*, to become warm.] Growing warm; increasing in heat.

in-çam-ẽr-ā′tion, *n.* [L. *in*, in, and *camera*, chamber.] The act or process of uniting lands, revenues, or other rights to the pope's domain.

In′çăn, *a.* Relating to the Incas or ruling tribe in Peru previous to the Spanish conquest.

in-çan-des′cence, *n.* [L. *incandescere*, to become warm or hot, to glow; *in-*, intens., and *candescere*, to kindle, glow, from *candere*, to be of a glittering whiteness, from *canus*, white.] A white heat; the glowing whiteness of a body caused by intense heat; as, a metal is heated to *incandescence.*

in-çan-des′cent, *a.* [L. *incandescens (-entis)*, ppr. of *incandescere*, to become warm or hot, to glow.] White or glowing with heat; shining; brilliant.

Incandescent lamp; a lamp consisting of a transparent or translucent vacuum-bulb containing a filament rendered incandescent by resistance to an electric current passing through it.

in-çȧ-nes′cent, *a.* [L. *incanescens (-entis)*, ppr. of *incanescere*, to become gray; *in*, in, and *canescere*, to become gray, from *canus*, white, hoary.] Growing white or gray.

in-çā′nous, *a.* [L. *incanus*, quite gray, hoary; *in*, in, and *canus*, white, hoary.] In botany, covered with soft white hairs; said of leaves or stems.

in-çan-tā′tion, *n.* [LL. *incantatio (-onis)*, from L. *incantare*, to chant a magic formula; *in*, in, and *cantare*, to sing, chant.] The act of enchanting; enchantment; the act of using certain formulas of words and ceremonies for the purpose of raising spirits; also, the formulas of words in such ceremonies.

in-çant′ȧ-tō-ry, *a.* Dealing by enchantment; magical.

in-çant′ing, *a.* Enchanting. [Obs.]

in-çan′tŏn, *v.t.*; incantoned, *pt., pp.*; incantoning, *ppr.* To form a canton of or to unite with cantons already formed.

in-çā-pȧ-bil′i-ty, *n.* 1. The quality of being incapable; natural incapacity or want of power; as, the *incapability* of a child to comprehend logical syllogisms.

2. Want of legal qualifications or of legal power; as, the *incapability* of holding an office.

in-çā′pȧ-ble, *a.* [Fr. *incapable*; LL. *incapabilis*, incapable; L. *in-* priv., and LL. *capabilis*, capable, from L. *capere*, to take.]

1. Wanting capacity sufficient; not having room sufficient to contain or hold; followed by *of*; as, a vessel is *incapable of* containing or holding more than a certain quantity of liquor.

2. Wanting natural power or capacity to learn, know, understand, or comprehend; as, an idiot is *incapable* of learning to read.

3. Wanting power equal to any purpose.

> Is not your father grown *incapable*
> Of reasonable affairs? —Shak.

4. Wanting disposition; as, he is *incapable* of a dishonorable act.

5. Unqualified or disqualified in a legal sense; not having the legal or constitutional qualifications, as, a man not thirty-five years of age is unqualified and therefore *incapable* of holding the office of president of the United States; a man convicted on impeachment is disqualified, and therefore *incapable* of holding any office of honor or profit under the government.

Syn.—Unqualified, unable, unfitted, weak, incompetent, feeble, disqualified, insufficient.—*Incapable* properly denotes a want of passive power, the power of receiving, and is applicable particularly to the mind; *unable* denotes the want of active power, or power of performing, and is applicable to the body or mind.

in-çā′pȧ-ble, *n.* 1. An incapable person, mentally, morally, or physically.

2. In military customs, an epithet of reproach for an officer who has been cashiered.

in-çā′pȧ-bly, *adv.* In an incapable manner.

in-çȧ-pā′cious, *a.* [LL. *incapax (-acis)*, incapable; L. *in-* priv., and *capax (-acis)*, capable, capacious.] Not capacious; not large or spacious; narrow; of small content; as, an *incapacious* soul.

in-çȧ-pā′cious-ness, *n.* Narrowness; want of containing space.

in-çȧ-pac′i-tāte, *v.t.*; incapacitated, *pt., pp.*; incapacitating, *ppr.* 1. To deprive of capacity or natural power of learning, knowing, understanding, or performing; as, old age and infirmity often *incapacitate* men for holding the office of a judge.

2. To render or make incapable; as, infancy *incapacitates* a child for learning algebra.

3. To disqualify; to deprive of legal or constitutional requisites; as, conviction of a crime *incapacitates* one or testifying in court.

in-çȧ-pac-i-tā′tion, *n.* The act by which one is incapacitated, or the state of one who is incapacitated.

in-çȧ-pac′i-ty, *n.*; *pl.* **in-çȧ-pac′i-tieṣ.** 1. Want of capacity, intellectual power, or the power of receiving, containing, or understanding; as, the *incapacity* in children to comprehend difficult propositions in logic or metaphysics, and *incapacity* in men to comprehend the nature of spiritual beings.

2. Want of qualification or legal requisites; disqualification; disability by deprivation of power; as, the *incapacity* of a convict to give testimony in a court of law or of a minor to make contracts.

in-çap′sū-lāte, *v.t.* To encapsulate.

in-çap′sū-lāte, *a.* [L. *in*, in, and *capsula*, a box.] Shut up in a capsule or cyst.

in-çap-sū-lā′tion, *n.* The act of confining in a capsule or the state of being thus confined.

in-çär′cẽr-āte, *v.t.*; incarcerated, *pt., pp.*; incarcerating, *ppr.* [LL. *incarceratus*, pp. of *incarcerare*, to imprison; L. *in*, in, and *carcer*, a prison.]

1. To imprison; to confine in a jail.

2. To confine; to shut up or inclose.

Incarcerated hernia; in medicine, a form of hernia in which it is difficult to reduce constriction.

in-çär′cẽr-āte, *a.* Imprisoned; confined.

in-çär-cẽr-ā′tion, *n.* 1. The act of imprisoning or confining; imprisonment; confinement.

2. In surgery, constriction about the neck of a hernial sac; also, strangulation.

in-çär′cẽr-ā-tŏr, *n.* An imprisoner.

in-çärn′, *v.t.* To cover with flesh; to invest with flesh. [Obs.]

in-çärn′, *v.i.* To put on flesh; to become fleshy. [Obs.]

in-çär′nȧ-dine, *a.* Flesh-colored; of a carnation color; pale red. [Obs.]

in-çär′nȧ-dine, *v.t.* To dye red or flesh-color. [Rare.]

in-çär′nănt, *a.* Flesh-producing; wound-healing.

in-çär′nāte, *a.* [LL. *incarnatus*, pp. of *incarnari*, to be made flesh; L. *in*, in, and *caro*, *carnis*, flesh.]

1. Invested with flesh; embodied in flesh; as, the *incarnate* Son of God.

2. Of a red color; flesh-colored. [Obs.]

in-çär′nāte, *v.t.*; incarnated, *pt.*, *pp.*; incarnating, *ppr.* To clothe with flesh; to embody in flesh.

in-çär′nāte, *v.i.* To grow flesh, as in the healing of a wound. [Rare.]

in-çär-nā′tion, *n.* [OFr. *incarnatiun*; LL. *incarnatio (-onis)*, from *incarnari*, to be made flesh; L. *in*, in, and *caro*, *carnis*, flesh.]

1. The act of clothing with flesh.

2. The act of assuming flesh, or of taking a human body and the nature of man; as, the *incarnation* of the Son of God.

3. In surgery, the process of healing wounds and filling the part with new flesh.

4. An embodiment in fleshly form of some principle, virtue, vice, or trait; as, the *incarnation* of good humor, of honor, of greed, of perfection; a personification; an appearance in the flesh, as of the ghost of a departed person.

5. The color of a rose. [Obs.]

in-çär′nȧ-tive, *a.* and *n.* I. *a.* Causing new flesh to grow; healing.

II. *n.* A medicine that tends to promote the growth of new flesh and to assist nature in the healing of wounds.

in-çär″ni-fi-çā′tion, *n.* The act of producing incarnation, or the state thus produced.

in-çāse′, *v.t.*; incased, *pt.*, *pp.*; incasing, *ppr.* 1. To inclose in a case.

2. To cover around with something solid.

Also written *encase*.

in-çāse′ment, *n.* An inclosing with a case; also, the case, or inclosing substance itself; spelled also *encasement*.

in-çȧsk′, *v.t.*; incasked, *pt.*, *pp.*; incasking, *ppr.* To cover with or as with a casque.

in-ças′tel-lā-ted, *a.* [LL. *incastellatus*; L. *in*, in, and *castellum*, a castle.] Confined or inclosed in a castle.

in-çȧs′telled (-teld), *a.* 1. Incastellated.

2. In farriery, having a dry and contracted hoof, causing pain and lameness.

in-çat-ē-nā′tion, *n.* [LL. *incatenatio (-onis)*, from *incatenare*, to chain together; L. *in*, in, and *catena*, a chain.] The act of linking together.

in-çau′tion, *n.* The want of caution.

in-çau′tious, *a.* Not cautious; unwary; not circumspect; heedless; not attending to the circumstances on which safety and interest depend; as, *incautious* youth.

in-çau′tious-ly, *adv.* Unwarily; heedlessly; without due circumspection.

in-çau′tious-ness, *n.* Want of caution; unwariness; want of foresight.

in′çȧ-vā-ted, *a.* [L. *incavatus*, pp. of *incavare*, to make hollow; *in*, in, and *cavus*, hollow.] Made hollow; bent round or in.

in-çȧ-vā′tion, *n.* 1. The act of making hollow.

2. A hollow made.

in-çāved′, *a.* Shut up in a cave.

in-çav′ẽrned, *a.* Shut up in a cavern, or as if in a cavern.

in-çēd′ing-ly, *adv.* With majesty. [Rare.]

in-çē-leb′ri-ty, *n.* [L. *in-* priv., and *celeber*, famous.] Lack of distinction. [Rare.]

in-çend′, *v.t.* [L. *incendere*, to set on fire; *in*, on, in, and *candere*, to shine, glow, burn.] To inflame; to excite.

in-çen′di-ȧ-riṣm, *n.* The act or practice of maliciously setting fire to buildings.

in-çen′di-ā-ry, *n.*; *pl.* **in-çen′di-ā-rieṣ.** [L. *incendiarius*, setting on fire, an incendiary, from *incendium*, a fire, from *incendere*, to burn.]

1. A person who maliciously sets fire to a building, etc.; one who is guilty of arson.

2. A person who excites or inflames factions and promotes quarrels.

> Several cities of Greece drove them out as *incendiaries*. —Bentley.

in-çen′di-ā-ry, *a.* 1. Pertaining to the malicious burning of property; as, an *incendiary* purpose.

2. Tending to excite or inflame factions, sedition, or quarrel.

Incendiary shell; a shell loaded with combustibles and discharged for the purpose of setting fire to buildings, shipping, etc.

in-çen′di-ous, *a.* Promoting faction or contention. [Obs.]

in-çen′di-ous-ly, *adv.* In a manner tending to promote contention. [Obs.]

in-çen′sănt, *a.* Enraged; ferocious; in heraldry, describing the attitude of an animal, as a lion or a boar, filled with rage.

in-çen-sā′tion, *n.* Incense offering. [Rare.]

in-çense′, *v.t.*; incensed (-senst), *pt.*, *pp.*; incensing, *ppr.* [L. *incensus*, pp. of *incendere*, to set on fire, inflame; *in*, in, on, and *candere*, to shine, glow, burn.]

1. To set fire to. [Obs.]

2. To enkindle or inflame to violent anger; to excite angry passions in; to provoke; to irritate; to exasperate.

> How could my pious son thy power *incense*? —Dryden.

in′çense, *v.t.* and *v.i.* I. *v.t.* 1. To perfume with incense.

2. To make offering of incense. [Obs.]

II. *v.i.* To burn or offer incense.

in′çense, *n.* [ME. *encens*; OFr. *encens*; LL. *incensum*, incense, neut. of L. *incensus*, pp. of *incendere*, to set on fire, inflame.]

1. Perfume exhaled by fire; the odors of spices and gums burned in religious rites, or as an offering to some deity.

> A thick cloud of *incense* went up. —Ezek. viii. 11.

2. The materials burned for making perfumes; in the Jewish offerings, a mixture of sweet spices, stacte, onycha, galbanum, and the gum of the frankincense-tree.

3. Any agreeable odor or exhalation.

> See, Nature hastes her earliest wreaths to bring,
> With all the *incense* of the breathing spring. —Pope.

4. Figuratively, praise; admiration; adoration; high regard; as, to court the *incense* of flattery.

Cayenne incense; see *Conima*.

in′çense-breath″ing, *a.* Exhaling sweet odors, as of incense.

in-çensed′ (-senst′), *a.* 1. Inflamed to violent anger; exasperated.

2. In heraldry, depicted as in a rage.

in-çense′ment, *n.* Violent irritation of the passions; heat; exasperation.

in-çen′sẽr, *n.* One who incenses, inflames, excites, or exasperates.

in-çen′sion, *n.* [L. *incensio (-onis)*, from *incensus*, pp. of *incendere*, to set on fire.] The act of kindling; the state of being on fire.

in-çen′sive, *a.* Tending to excite or provoke.

in-çen′sŏr, *n.* [LL., from L. *incendere*, to set on fire.] A kindler of anger; an inflamer of the angry passions.

in-çen′sō-ry, *n.* The vessel in which incense is burnt and offered. [Obs.]

in-çen′sụr-ȧ-ble (-shụr-), *a.* Not censurable.

in-çen′sụr-ȧ-bly, *adv.* In a manner not admitting of censure.

in-çen′tive, *a.* [LL. *incentivus*, serving to incite; (L., that strikes up or sets the tune), from L. *incentus*, pp. of *incinere*, to sound an instrument, to sing; *in*, in, on, and *canere*, to sing.]

1. Having power to arouse, encourage, or stimulate.

2. Setting on fire; causing to burn. [Obs.]

in-çen′tive, *n.* That which moves the mind or operates on the passions; that which incites or has a tendency to incite to determination or action; that which prompts to good or ill; motive; spur; as, the love of money and the desire of promotion are two most powerful *incentives* to action.

in-çen′tive-ly, *adv.* Incitingly; encouragingly.

in-çept′, *v.i.*; incepted, *pt.*, *pp.*; incepting, *ppr.* [L. *inceptus*, pp. of *incipere*, to take up, to begin; *in*, in, on, and *capere*, to take.] To make a beginning; to enter upon; specifically, to become qualified for a degree in a university; to take a master's degree.

in-çept′, *v.t.* To receive; to grasp; to enter upon; to make a beginning of. [Rare.]

in-çep′tion, *n.* [L. *inceptio (-onis)*, from *inceptus*, pp. of *incipere*, to begin, lit., to take up.]

1. Beginning; outset; commencement.

2. The act of receiving. [Rare.]

3. The ceremony of taking the degree of M. A.

in-çep′tive, *a.* [L. *inceptus*, pp. of *incipere*, to begin.]

1. Beginning; noting beginning; inchoative; as, an *inceptive* verb, which expresses the beginning of an action.

2. In mathematics, generative as from a source; as, a point is *inceptive* of a line, a line *inceptive* of a surface, etc. [Rare.]

in-çep′tive, *n.* An inchoative word or phrase.

in-çep′tive-ly, *adv.* In an inceptive manner.

in-çep′tŏr, *n.* [LL. *inceptor*, from L. *inceptus*, pp. of *incipere*, to begin.]

1. A beginner; one in the rudiments.

2. One about to take the M. A. degree at an English university.

in-çẽr-ā′tion, *n.* [L. *inceratus*, pp. of *incerare*, to cover with wax.] The act of covering with wax. [Rare.]

in-çer′ȧ-tive, *a.* Cleaving to, like wax. [Rare.]

in-çẽr′tain (-tin), *a.* Uncertain; doubtful. [Obs.]

in-çẽr′tain-ly, *adv.* Doubtfully. [Obs.]

in-çẽr′tain-ty, *n.* Uncertainty; doubt. [Obs.]

in-çẽr′ti-tūde, *n.* [Fr. *incertitude*; LL. *incertitudo (-inis)*, uncertainty, from L. *incertus*, uncertain; *in-* priv., and *certus*, certain.]

1. Uncertainty; doubtfulness; doubt.

2. Obscurity.

in-çẽr′tum, *n.* [L., neut. of *incertus*, uncertain.] Rubblework; masonry of rough stones irregularly laid; generally in an adjective sense, in the phrase *opus incertum*.

in-çes′sȧ-ble, *a.* Unceasing; continual. [Obs.]

in-çes′sȧ-bly, *adv.* Continually; unceasingly. [Obs.]

in-çes′săn-cy, *n.* Unintermitted continuance; unceasingness. [Obs.]

in-çes′sănt, *a.* [LL. *incessans (-antis)*; L. *in-* priv., and *cessans (-antis)*, ppr. of *cessare*, to cease.] Unceasing; unintermitted; uninterrupted; continual; as, *incessant* rains; *incessant* clamors.

in-çes′sănt-ly, *adv.* Without ceasing; continually.

Syn.—Unceasingly, uninterruptedly.—*Incessantly* signifies without ceasing, but may be applied to things which admit of certain intervals; *unceasingly* signifies never ceasing.

in′çest, *n.* [OFr. *inceste*; L. *incestum*, unchastity, incest, neut. of *incestus*, unclean, unchaste; *in-* priv., and *castus*, chaste.] The crime of cohabitation or sexual commerce between persons related within the degrees wherein marriage is prohibited by the law of a country.

Spiritual incest; (a) in old church law, cohabitation committed between persons who had a spiritual alliance by means of baptism or confirmation; (b) the act of holding two benefices, by a vicar or other beneficiary, the one depending on the collation of the other.

in-çes′tū-ous, *a.* [LL. *incestuosus*, from L. *incestus*, unclean, unchaste.]

1. Guilty of incest; as, an *incestuous* person.

2. Involving the crime of incest; as, an *incestuous* connection.

in-çes′tū-ous-ly, *adv.* In an incestuous manner.

in-çes′tū-ous-ness, *n.* The state or quality of being incestuous.

inch, *n.* [ME. *inche*, *ynche*; AS. *ynce*, *ince*, an inch, from L. *uncia*, a twelfth part, an inch, an ounce.]

1. An English unit of linear measure equal to the thirty-sixth part of a yard or 2.54 centimeters.

2. An indefinitely small measure or distance.

> I'll not budge an *inch*, boy. —Shak.

By inches; by exceedingly small consecutive movements; as, we made progress against the current *by inches*.

Inches of pressure; in mechanics, a measure of pressure upon some liquid, as a column of mercury in the tube of a barometer or manometer.

Miners' inch; same as *Water-inch*.

inch, *n.* [Gael. *innis*, island.] An island.

inch, *a.* Being an inch in any dimension; as, an *inch* board; a three-*inch* nail.

inch, *v.t.*; inched (incht), *pt.*, *pp.*; inching, *ppr.* 1. To drive or deal out by inches or small degrees. [Rare.]

2. To divide into spaces an inch in width or length.

inch, *v.i.* To move slowly, by inches or as if by inches; as, to *inch* along.

in-chăm′bẽr, *v.t.*; inchambered, *pt.*, *pp.*; inchambering, *ppr.* To lodge in a chamber. [Obs.]

in-chānġe-ȧ-bil′i-ty, *n.* The quality of being unchangeable. [Obs.]

in-chȧnt′, *v.t.* [Obs.] See *Enchant*.

in-char′i-tȧ-ble, *a.* Uncharitable. [Obs.]

in-char′i-ty, *n.* Lack of charity. [Obs.]

in-chāse′, *v.t.* Same as *Enchase*.

in-chas′ti-ty, *n.* Lewdness; impurity; unchastity. [Obs.]

inched (incht), *a.* 1. Measured into inches; as, an *inched* rule.

2. Being or having a length of (a certain number of) inches; as, a four-*inched* blade; usually written four-*inch*, etc.

in-chest′, *v.t.* To put into a chest. [Obs.]

inch′i-pin, *n.* [Obs.] See *Inchpin*.

inch′mēal, *adv.* By the inch; a little at a time; slowly.

inch′mēal, *n.* A piece an inch long.

By inchmeal; by small degrees.

in′chō-āte, *v.t.* To begin. [Obs.]

in′chō-āte, *a.* [L. *inchoatus*, pp. of *inchoare*, to begin.] Begun; commenced, but only partially in operation or existence; in existence in an elementary form; incipient; elementary; rudimentary; as, an *inchoate* idea; an *inchoate* social organism.

in′chō-āte-ly, *adv.* Incipiently.

in-chō-ā′tion, *n.* [LL. *inchoatio (-onis)*, from L. *inchoare*, to begin.] The act of beginning; commencement; inception.

in-chō′ȧ-tive, *a.* [LL. *inchoativus*, from L. *inchoatus*, pp. of *inchoare*, to begin.] Denoting a beginning; incipient; inceptive; as, an *inchoative* verb, otherwise called *inceptive*.

inch′pin, *n.* A deer's sweetbread. [Obs.]

inch′wŏrm, *n.* A larva of various geometrid moths; the measuring-worm.

in-cic′ū-rȧ-ble, *a.* [L. *in-* priv., and *cicurare*, to tame, from *cicur*, tame.] Incapable of being tamed. [Rare.]

in-cīde′, *v.t.* To cut; to remove, as by drugs. [Obs.]

in′ci-dence, *n.* [Fr. *incidence*; LL. *incidentia*, a falling upon, from L. *incidens* (*-entis*), ppr. of *incidere*, to fall upon.]

1. Literally, a falling on; hence, an accident or casualty. [Obs.]

2. In physics, the direction in which a ray of light or heat falls on any surface.

Angle of incidence; the angle which a ray of light, falling on any surface, makes with a perpendicular to that surface.

Line of incidence; the line in the direction of which a ray meets a surface.

A B, line of incidence. A B H, angle of incidence.

in′ci-dĕn-cy, *n.* [Obs.] See *Incidence*.

in′ci-dent, *a.* [Fr. *incident*; L. *incidens* (*-entis*), ppr. of *incidere*, to fall upon; *in*, on, and *cadere*, to fall.]

1. Falling on; as, an *incident* ray.

2. Casual; fortuitous; coming or happening occasionally, or not in the usual course of things, or not according to expectation or in connection with the main design; as, the mishaps *incident* to human life.

3. Happening; apt to happen; as, misfortunes *incident* to the poor.

4. In law, appertaining to or following the chief or principal; as, a payment *incident* as a fee of office.

Incident proposition; in logic, a subordinate proposition, introduced merely as explanatory and not affecting the meaning of the main proposition; as, my friend, *whom I met on the train*, invited me to call and see him at his home.

in′ci-dent, *n.* 1. That which falls out or takes place; an event; casualty.

2. That which happens aside from the main design; an episode or subordinate action.

> No person, no *incident* in a play but must be of use to carry on the main design. —Dryden.

3. In law, something necessarily appertaining to and depending on another, which is termed the principal.

Syn.—Circumstance, event, contingency, fact, episode, happening, occurrence.

in-ci-den′tăl, *n.* An incident; something which is incidental; specifically, in the plural, minor expenses.

in-ci-den′tăl, *a.* 1. Happening without regularity; coming without design; casual; accidental; as, an *incidental* conversation.

2. Not necessary to the chief purpose; occasional; as, *incidental* business.

Syn.—Casual, accidental, contingent.—*Accidental* is opposed to what is designed or planned; *incidental* to what is premeditated; *casual* to what is constant and regular; *contingent* to what is definite and fixed. A meeting may be *accidental*, an expression *incidental*, a look, expression, etc., *casual*, an expense or circumstance *contingent*.

in-ci-den′tăl-ly, *adv.* 1. Casually; without intention; accidentally; as, I was *incidentally* present when the conversation took place.

2. Beside the main design; collaterally.

in-ci-den′tăl-ness, *n.* The condition of being incidental.

in′ci-dent-ly, *adv.* Incidentally. [Obs.]

in-cin′ẽr-ȧ-ble, *a.* That may be reduced to ashes by burning.

in-cin′ẽr-āte, *a.* Wholly consumed. [Obs.]

in-cin′ẽr-āte, *v.t.*; incinerated, *pt.*, *pp.*; incinerating, *ppr.* [LL. *incineratus*, pp. of *incinerare*, to burn to ashes; L. *in*, in, to, and *cinis* (*-eris*), ashes.] To burn to ashes; to consume; to cremate.

in-cin-ẽr-ā′tion, *n.* The act of reducing to ashes by combustion.

in-cip′i-ence, in-cip′i-en-cy, *n.* A beginning; commencement; first stage.

in-cip′i-ent, *a.* [L. *incipiens* (*-entis*), ppr. of *incipere*, to begin, lit., to take up; L. *in*, in, on, and *capere*, to take.] Beginning; commencing; as, the *incipient* stage of a fever.

in-cip′i-ent-ly, *adv.* In an incipient manner.

in-cir′cle, *v.t.* Same as *Encircle*.

in-cir′clet, *n.* [Obs.] Same as *Encirclet*.

in-cir-cum-scrip′ti-ble, *a.* That cannot be circumscribed or limited.

in-cir-cum-scrip′tion, *n.* The state of being limitless.

in-cir-cum-spect′, *a.* Lacking in circumspection.

in-cir-cum-spec′tion, *n.* Want of circumspection; heedlessness.

in-cīse′, *v.t.*; incised, *pt.*, *pp.*; incising, *ppr.* [Fr. *inciser*; L. *incisus*, pp. of *incidere*, to cut into; *in*, into, and *cædere*, to cut.]

1. To cut into; to carve; to engrave.

2. To cut or gash with a sharp instrument.

in-cīsed′, *a.* 1. Cut or engraved; made by cutting; as, an *incised* wound.

2. In botany, as if cut into deeply; with sharp angles between the lobes; as, an *incised* leaf or petal.

in-cīse′ly, *adv.* In the manner of incisions or notches. [Rare.]

in-ci′sion (-sizh′un), *n.* [Fr. *incision*; L. *incisio* (*-onis*), lit., a cutting into, used only in sense of division, cesura, from *incisus*, pp. of *incidere*, to cut into, incise.]

1. A cutting; the act of cutting into a substance.

2. A cut; a gash; a separation in the surface of any substance, made by a sharp instrument.

3. Separation of viscid matter by medicines. [Obs.]

in-cī′sive, *a.* [Fr. *incisif*, from L. *incisus*, pp. of *incidere*, to cut into.] Having the quality of cutting; hence, figuratively, sharp; penetrating; acute.

Incisive teeth; in animals, the fore teeth; the cutters or incisors.

in-cī′sŏr, *n.* [L. *incisus*, pp. of *incidere*, to cut into.] A cutter; a fore tooth which cuts, bites, or separates.

in-cī′sŏr, *a.* Incisorial; pertaining to the incisors or incisorial teeth.

in-ci-sō′ri-ăl, *a.* Having sharp edges fitted for cutting; as, the *incisorial* teeth.

in-cī′sō-ry, *a.* Having the quality of cutting.

in-cis′ūre (-sizh′), *n.* [L. *incisura*.] A cut; a place opened by cutting; an incision.

in-cī′tănt, *n.* [L. *incitans* (*-antis*), ppr. of *incitare*, to incite.] That which excites action; an inciting cause.

in-ci-tā′tion, *n.* [L. *incitatio* (*-onis*), from *incitare*, to incite.]

1. The act of inciting or moving to action; incitement.

2. Incitement; incentive; motive; that which excites to action.

in-cit′ȧ-tive, *n.* An inciting agent. [Rare.]

in-cīte′, *v.t.*; incited, *pt.*, *pp.*; inciting, *ppr.* [Fr. *inciter*; L. *incitare*, to arouse, set in motion, hasten, incite; *in*, in, on, and *citare*, to set in motion, urge.] To move to action by persuasion or motives presented; to stir up; to rouse; to spur on; as, to *incite* foes to combat.

Syn.—Stimulate, instigate, goad, arouse, animate, encourage, spur, urge, move.

in-cīte′ment, *n.* [L. *incitamentum*, an incentive, from *incitare*, to incite.]

1. Instigation.

2. That which incites the mind or moves to action; motive; incentive; impulse.

> From the long records of a distant age,
> Derive *incitements* to renew thy rage.—Pope.

3. The act of instigating.

in-cīt′ẽr, *n.* He who or that which incites or moves to action.

in-cīt′ing-ly, *adv.* So as to excite to action.

in-cī-tō-mō′tŏr, *a.* [L. *incitus*, pp. of *incitare*, to incite, and LL. *motor*, a mover, from L. *motus*, pp. of *movere*, to move.] In physiology, originating in the nerve-centers and inciting the muscles to action, as distinguished from *excitomotor*, originating in the muscles and producing reflex action; producing direct muscular action.

in-ci-tō-mō′to-ry, *a.* Same as *Incitomotor*.

in-civ′il, *a.* Uncivil. [Obs.]

in-ci-vil′i-ty, *n.*; *pl.* **in-ci-vil′i-ties.** [LL. *incivilitas*, from L. *incivilis*, uncivil; *in-* priv., and *civilis*, civil.]

1. Want of courtesy; rudeness of manners; impoliteness.

2. Any act of rudeness or ill-breeding.

3. Total lack of civilization. [Rare.]

Syn.—Rudeness, discourtesy, impoliteness, disrespect, unmannerliness.

in-civ″i-li-zā′tion, *n.* The state of being without civilization.

in-civ′il-ly, *adv.* Uncivilly; rudely.

in-civ′ism, *n.* [Fr. *incivisme*, lack of devotion to the existing government; L. *in-* priv., and *civis*, a citizen.] Want of civism; want of love for one's country, or of patriotism. [Rare.]

in-clȧ-mā′tion, *n.* [L. *inclamatio*.] A crying out. [Obs.]

in-clȧsp′, *v.t.* See *Enclasp*.

in-clau′dent, *a.* Failing to close, as a flower.

in′clȧ-vā-ted, *a.* [LL. *inclavatus*, pp. of *inclavare*, to fasten with a nail; L. *in*, in, and *clavare* to fasten with a nail, from *clavus*, a nail.] Set fast fixed.

in-clāve′, *a.* [L. *in*, in, and *clavus*, a nail.] In heraldry, shaped or cut into like a series of dovetails.

in′cle, *n.* Same as *Inkle*.

in-clem′en-cy, *n.* [L. *inclementia*, from *inclemens*, harsh, inclement.]

1. Want of clemency; want of mildness of temper; unmercifulness; harshness.

2. Roughness; storminess; severity; rigor; as, we were detained by the *inclemency* of the weather.

in-clem′ent, *a.* [L. *inclemens* (*-entis*), harsh, rude; *in-* priv., and *clemens* (*-entis*), kind.]

1. Destitute of a mild and kind temper; unmerciful; harsh; as, an *inclement* person.

2. Rough; stormy; rainy; rigorously cold; as, *inclement* weather; an *inclement* sky.

Syn.—Harsh, tyrannical, cruel, unmerciful, severe, stormy, rough, rigorous, unkind, forbidding.

in-clem′ent-ly, *adv.* In an inclement manner.

in-clīn′ȧ-ble, *a.* [L. *inclinabilis*, from *inclinare*, to lean upon, incline.]

1. Leaning; tending; as, a tower *inclinable* to fall.

2. Having a leaning in disposition; somewhat disposed; as, a mind *inclinable* to truth.

in-clīn′ȧ-ble-ness, *n.* The state of being inclinable; inclination.

in-cli-nā′tion, *n.* [ME. *inclinacioun*; L. *inclinatio* (*-onis*), a leaning, inclining, bending, from *inclinare*, to lean upon, incline.]

1. A leaning; any deviation of a body or line from an upright position or given direction; as, the *inclination* of the head in bowing.

2. In geometry, the angle made by two lines or planes which meet, or which would meet if produced; as, the *inclination* of the axis of the earth to the plane of the ecliptic.

3. A leaning of the mind or will; propensity; a disposition more favorable to one thing than to another; as, men have a natural *inclination* to pleasure.

> A mere *inclination* to a thing is not properly a willing of that thing. —South.

4. The dip of the magnetic needle, or its tendency to incline toward the earth; also, the angle made by the needle with the horizon.

5. The act of decanting liquors by stooping or inclining the vessel.

6. A person liked or preferred. [Obs.]

Inclination of an orbit; in astronomy, the angle which the plane of an orbit makes with the plane of the ecliptic, as, the *inclination of the orbit* of the earth is 23° 27′.

Syn.—Leaning, slope, tendency, disposition, proneness, aptness, predilection, bias, bent, attachment, affection, liking, wish.

in-cli-nā′tion-cŏm″păss, *n.* See *Dipping-compass*.

in-clīn′ȧ-tō-ri-ly, *adv.* Obliquely; with inclination.

in-clīn-ȧ-tō′ri-um, *n.* An inclination-compass.

in-clīn′ȧ-tō-ry, *a.* Disposed to incline or lean.

in-clīne′, *v.i.*; inclined, *pt.*, *pp.*; inclining, *ppr.* [ME. *inclinen*; OFr. *incliner*; L. *inclinare*, to bend down, lean; *in*, on, to, and *clinare*, to lean.]

1. To deviate from a direction which is regarded as normal; to bend down; to lean; to tend; as, converging lines *incline* toward each other; a road *inclines* to the north or south.

2. To be disposed; to have some wish or desire; to tend, as toward an opinion, course of action, etc.

> Their hearts *inclined* to follow Abimelech. —Jud. ix. 3.

in-clīne′, *v.t.* 1. To cause to deviate from a line, position, or direction; to give a leaning to; to direct; as, *incline* the column or post to the east.

2. To give a tendency or propension to; to turn; to dispose.

> *Incline* my heart unto thy testimonies. —Ps. cxix. 36.

3. To bend; to cause to stoop or bow; as, to *incline* the head or the body in acts of reverence or civility.

in-clīne′, *n.* [ME. *encline*; OFr. *enclin*, an incline, from *encliner*, to incline.] Anything that inclines, as an inclined plane, a sloping road, etc.

in-clīned′, *a.* 1. Having a leaning or tendency; disposed.

2. In botany, curved with the convex side up.

Inclined plane; in mechanics, a plane inclined to the horizon, or forming with a horizontal plane any angle whatever excepting a right angle. The figure A B C represents an inclined plane; A C is the plane properly so called; C B is the height of the plane, B A its base, and B A C the angle of inclination or elevation.

Inclined Plane.

in-clīn′ẽr, *n.* One who or that which inclines; specifically, an inclined dial.

in-clīn′ing, *a.* Inclined; leaning; causing to lean; in botany, same as *inclined*.

in-clīn′ing, *n.* 1. Tendency; as, he has an *inclining* toward music.

2. An inclination toward belief or doctrine; hence, a party or side. [Rare.]

in-cli-nom′e-tẽr, *n.* [L. *inclinare*, to incline, and *metrum*, a measure.]

1. In magnetism, an inclination-compass.

2. In civil engineering, a device for ascertaining the inclination of an embankment, declivity, etc.

in-çlip′, *v.t.* To enclasp; to inclose; to surround. [Rare.]

in-çlois′tẽr, *v.t.*; incloistered, *pt.*, *pp.*; incloistering, *ppr.* To shut up or confine in a cloister.

in-çlōṣe′, *v.t.*; inclosed, *pt.*, *pp.*; inclosing, *ppr.* [ME. *enclosen*; OFr. *enclos*, pp. of *enclore*, to inclose; L. *inclusus*, pp. of *includere*, to inclose; *in*, in, and *claudere*, to shut.]

1. To surround; to shut in; to confine on all sides; as, to *inclose* a field with a fence.

2. To separate from common grounds by a fence; as, to *inclose* lands.

3. To include; to shut or confine; as, to *inclose* trinkets in a box.

4. To environ; to encompass.

5. To cover with a wrapper or envelope; to cover under seal; as, to *inclose* a letter or a bill.

in-çlōṣ′ẽr, *n.* One who or that which incloses; one who separates land from common grounds by a fence.

in-çlō′ṣūre (-zhūr), *n.* 1. The act of inclosing; the state of being inclosed.

2. The separation of land from common ground into distinct possessions by a fence.

3. The appropriation of things common.

4. That which incloses; a barrier or fence.

5. A space inclosed or fenced; a space comprehended within certain limits; ground inclosed or separated from common land.

6. That which is inclosed or contained in an envelope, as a paper.

in-çloud′, *v.t.*; inclouded, *pt.*, *pp.*; inclouding, *ppr.* To darken; to obscure.

in-çlụde′, *v.t.*; included, *pt.*, *pp.*; including, *ppr.* [ME. *includen*; L. *includere*, to shut in, include; *in*, in, and *claudere*, to shut, close.]

1. To confine within; to hold; to contain; as, the shell of a nut *includes* the kernel; a pearl is *included* in a shell.

2. To comprise; to comprehend; to contain; as, the history of England necessarily *includes* a portion of that of France; the word duty *includes* what we owe to God, to our fellow-men, and to ourselves; it *includes* also a tax payable to the government.

3. To close up; to make an end of. [Obs.]

Syn.—Comprise, comprehend, embrace, inclose.—*Comprise, comprehend*, and *embrace* have regard to the aggregate value, quantity, or extent; *include*, to the individual things which form the whole; a yard is *inclosed* by a wall; particular goods are *included* in a reckoning; the kernel of a nut is *inclosed* in a shell; morality, as well as faith, is *included* in Christian perfection.

in-çlụd′ed, *a.* Contained; comprehended.

Included stamens; in botany, short stamens not projecting beyond the margin of the corolla.

in-çlụd′i-ble, *a.* Capable of being among the things embraced.

in-çlụ′sȧ, *n.pl.* [L., neut. pl. of *inclusus*, pp. of *includere*, to shut in, include.] In zoölogy, a tribe, division, or family of bivalvular mollusks characterized by having the mantle open anteriorly, including shipworms, clams, razor-clams, etc.

in-çlụ′ṣion (-zhun), *n.* [L. *inclusio* (*-onis*), a shutting up, from *inclusus*, pp. of *includere*, to shut in, include.]

1. The act of including; also, the state of being included; comprehension; the opposite of *exclusion*.

2. In mineralogy, any foreign matter, whether solid or liquid, inclosed within the mass of a mineral or crystal.

in-çlụ′sive, *a.* [L. *inclusus*, pp. of *includere*, to shut in, include.]

1. Inclosing; encircling.

2. Comprehending the limits named; as, from Monday to Saturday *inclusive*, that is, taking in both Monday and Saturday; the opposite of *exclusive*.

in-çlụ′sive-ly, *adv.* Comprehending the things mentioned; as, Monday to Saturday *inclusively*.

in-çōach′, *v.t.*; incoached, *pt.*, *pp.*; incoaching, *ppr.* To inclose in a coach. [Rare.]

in-çō-açt′, *a.* Unconstrained. [Obs.]

in-çō-açt′ed, *a.* Incoact. [Obs.]

in-çō-ag′ū-lȧ-ble, *a.* That cannot be coagulated or concreted.

in-çō-ȧ-les′cence, *n.* The condition or quality of not uniting or blending.

in-çoçt′ed, *a.* Uncooked; not to be digested. [Obs.]

in-çō-ẽr′ci-ble, *a.* 1. Not to be coerced or compelled; that cannot be forced.

2. In physics, (a) above the critical point of liquefaction by pressure; said of gases; (b) capable of passing through solids; said of radiant energy.

in-çō-ex-ist′ence, *n.* The state of not existing together. [Obs.]

in-çog.′, *a.*, *n.*, and *adv.* Incognito.

in-çog′i-tȧ-ble, *a.* [L. *incogitabilis*, thoughtless, unthinkable; *in-* priv., and *cogitabilis*, thinkable, from *cogitare*, to think.] That may not be thought of or apprehended.

in-çog′i-tănce, in-çog′i-tăn-cy, *n.* [L. *incogitantia*, thoughtlessness, from *incogitans* (*-antis*), thoughtless, unthinking.] Want of thought, or want of the power of thinking.

in-çog′i-tănt, *a.* [L. *incogitans* (*-antis*), unthinking, thoughtless; *in-* priv., and *cogitans* (*-antis*), ppr. of *cogitare*, to think.] Not thinking; thoughtless. [Rare.]

in-çog′i-tănt-ly, *adv.* Without consideration; thoughtlessly.

in-çog′i-tā-tive, *a.* Not thinking; wanting the power of thought; as, a vegetable is an *incogitative* being.

in-çog-i-tā-tiv′i-ty, *n.* The quality of being without the power of thought.

in-çog′ni-tȧ, *n.*, feminine form of *incognito*.

in-çog′ni-tănt, *a.* Illiterate; stupid. [Obs.]

in-çog′ni-tō, *adv.* [It.] In disguise; as, he travels *incognito*.

in-çog′ni-tō, *a.* [It., from L. *incognitus*, unknown; *in-* priv., and *cognitus*, pp. of *cognoscere*, to know.] Pertaining to a disguise in person or in character; as, his is an *incognito* character.

in-çog′ni-tō, *n.* The state or condition of being incognito; also, any person in this state; a man who assumes a costume and manner that tend to conceal his identity. Sometimes abbreviated to *incog*.

in-çog′ni-zȧ-ble, *a.* That cannot be recognized, known, or distinguished.

in-çog′ni-zănce, *n.* The quality of not cognizing or understanding.

in-çog′ni-zănt, *a.* Not knowing; having no power to apprehend; ignorant.

in-çog-nos-ci-bil′i-ty, *n.* The quality of being incognizable.

in-çog-nos′ci-ble, *a.* [L. *incognoscibilis*, not to be known; *in-* priv., and *cognoscibilis*, to be known, from *cognoscere*, to know.] Same as *Incognizable*.

in-çō-hēr′ence, *n.* 1. Want of coherence; want of cohesion or adherence; looseness or unconnected state of parts, as of a powder.

2. Want of connection; incongruity; inconsistency; want of agreement or dependence of one part on another; as, the *incoherence* of arguments, facts, or principles.

3. That which is not coherent.

in-çō-hēr′en-cy, *n.* Incoherence.

in-çō-hēr′ent, *a.* 1. Wanting cohesion; loose; unconnected; not fixed to each other; as, grains of sand are *incoherent*.

2. Wanting coherence or agreement; incongruous; inconsistent; having no dependence of one part on another; as, the thoughts of a dreaming man, and the language of a madman, are *incoherent*.

Syn.—Unconnected, incongruous, inconsequential, loose, inconsistent.

in-çō-hēr-en-tif′iç, *a.* Giving rise to incoherence. [Rare.]

in-çō-hēr′ent-ly, *adv.* Inconsistently; without coherence of parts; as, to talk *incoherently*.

in-çō-hēr′ent-ness, *n.* The state of being incoherent.

in-çō-in′ci-dence, *n.* Want of coincidence or agreement. [Rare.]

in-çō-in′ci-dent, *a.* Not coincident; not agreeing in time, place, or principle.

in-çō-lū′mi-ty, *n.* Safety; security. [Obs.]

in-çŏm′bẽr, *v.t.* [Obs.] Same as *Encumber*.

in-çom-bīne′, *v.i.* To fail to agree; to be incapable of effecting a combination. [Obs.]

in-çom-bīn′ing, *a.* Not combining or uniting; disagreeing; differing.

in-çŏm-bus-ti-bil′i-ty, *n.* The quality of being incapable of being burned or consumed.

in-çŏm-bus′ti-ble, *a.* Not to be burned, decomposed, or consumed by fire; as, asbestos is an *incombustible* substance.

in-çŏm-bus′ti-ble-ness, *n.* Incombustibility; the state of being incombustible.

in-çŏm-bus′ti-bly, *adv.* So as to resist combustion.

in′çŏme, *n.* [ME. *income*; AS. *in*, in, and *cuman*, to come.]

1. That gain which proceeds from labor, business, or property of any kind; the produce of a farm; the rent of houses; the proceeds of professional business; the profits of commerce or of occupation; the interest of money or stock in funds; revenue; salary; generally applied to the gain of private persons; as, the annual *income* of a gentleman.

2. A coming in; admission; introduction. [Obs.]

3. Whatever comes into the mind as a stimulant or inspiration, producing zeal, courage, hope, etc. [Rare.]

4. In physiology, whatever elements come in to build up the body; nutritious food; opposed to *output*.

Income bond; see under *Bond*.

Income tax; a tax laid upon a person's profits or income over and above a specified sum. The levying and collecting of such a tax has been made constitutional by amendment XVI to the Constitution.

in′çŏm-ẽr, *n.* 1. One coming into a country or organization, as an immigrant or a new member.

2. In England, one who takes the place of another as a tenant.

in′çŏm-ing, *a.* 1. Coming in; filling up; opposed to *outgoing*.

2. Taking possession or coming into a firm or company, as a new tenant or a new member.

3. Being next in turn; ensuing. [Scot.]

in′çŏm-ing, *n.* 1. The act of arriving; as, the *incoming* of a train.

2. Whatever comes in; often in the plural; as, the *incoming* exceeds the outgoing. [Rare.]

in-çom′i-ty, *n.* Lack of courtesy, civility, or good manners. [Rare.]

in″çŏm-men″sū-rȧ-bil′i-ty, *n.* The condition respecting two or more quantities when no quantity but unity will be an aliquot part of both or of all.

in-çŏm-men′sū-rȧ-ble, *a.* Having no common aliquot part or divisor; said of two or more lines, magnitudes, or quantities; as, seven and eleven are *incommensurable* numbers.

in-çŏm-men′sū-rȧ-ble, *n.* One of two or more incommensurable quantities.

in-çŏm-men′sū-rȧ-ble-ness, *n.* The state of being incommensurable.

in-çŏm-men′sū-rȧ-bly, *adv.* So as to be incommensurable.

in-çŏm-men′sū-rāte, *a.* 1. Not admitting of a common measure.

2. Not of equal measure or extent; not adequate; as, our means are *incommensurate* to our wants.

in-çŏm-men′sū-rāte-ly, *adv.* Not in equal or due measure or proportion.

in-çŏm-men′sū-rāte-ness, *n.* The condition or quality of being incommensurate.

in-çŏm-mis′ci-ble, *a.* [LL. *incommiscibilis*; L. *in-* priv., and LL. *commiscibilis*, mixable, from L. *commiscere*, to mix.] That cannot be mixed.

in-çŏm-mix′tūre, *n.* A state of being unmixed.

in-çom′mō-dāte, *v.t.* To incommode. [Obs.]

in-çom-mō-dā′tion, *n.* The state of being incommodated. [Obs.]

in-çŏm-mōde′, *v.t.*; incommoded, *pt.*, *pp.*; incommoding, *ppr.* [Fr. *incommoder*; L. *incommodare*, to inconvenience, from *incommodus*, inconvenient; *in-* priv., and *commodus*, convenient.] To give inconvenience to; to give trouble to; to disturb or molest.

Syn.—Disturb, molest, trouble, vex, inconvenience.

in-çŏm-mōde′, *a.* and *n.* I. *a.* Unsuitable; troublesome; inconvenient. [Obs.]

II. *n.* Anything that is troublesome or inconvenient. [Obs.]

in-çŏm-mōde′ment, *n.* Inconvenience. [Obs.]

in-çŏm-mō′di-ous, *a.* Inconvenient; not affording ease or advantage; unsuitable; giving trouble without much injury; as, an *incommodious* house.

in-çŏm-mō′di-ous-ly, *adv.* In a manner to create inconvenience; inconveniently; unsuitably.

in-çŏm-mō′di-ous-ness, *n.* Inconvenience; unsuitableness.

in-çŏm-mod′i-ty, *n.* Inconvenience; trouble. [Obs.]

in-çŏm-mū″ni-çȧ-bil′i-ty, *n.* The quality of not being communicable, or capable of being imparted to another.

in-çŏm-mū′ni-çȧ-ble, *a.* [LL. *incommunicabilis*; L. *in-* priv., and *communicare*, to communicate.] That cannot be communicated or imparted to others.

in-çŏm-mū′ni-çȧ-ble-ness, *n.* Incommunicability.

in-çŏm-mū′ni-çȧ-bly, *adv.* In a manner not to be imparted or communicated.

in-çŏm-mū′ni-çā-ted, *a.* Not imparted. [Obs.]

in-çŏm-mū′ni-çā-ting, *a.* Having no communion or intercourse with each other. [Obs.]

in-çŏm-mū′ni-çā-tive, *a.* 1. Not communicative; not free or apt to impart to others in conversation.

2. Not disposed to hold communion, fellowship, or intercourse with.

The Chinese—an *incommunicative* nation.
—Buchanan.

in-çŏm-mū′ni-çȧ-tive-ly, *adv.* Not communicatively.

in-çŏm-mū′ni-çȧ-tive-ness, *n.* The quality of being incommunicative.

in-çŏm-mūt-ȧ-bil′i-ty, *n.* The quality of being incommutable.

in-çŏm-mūt′ȧ-ble, *a.* [L. *incommutabilis*; *in-* priv., and *commutabilis*, changeable.] Not to be exchanged or commuted with another.

in-çŏm-mūt′ȧ-ble-ness, *n.* Incommutability.

in-çŏm-mūt′ȧ-bly, *adv.* Without reciprocal change.

in-çŏm-paçt′, in-çŏm-paçt′ed, *a.* Not compact; not having the parts firmly united; not solid.

in-çom′pȧ-rȧ-ble, *a.* [L. *incomparabilis*, that cannot be equaled; *in-* priv., and *comparabilis*, comparable.] That admits of no comparison with others; having no equal.

Her words do show her wit *incomparable*. —Shak.

Syn.—Matchless, unique, consummate, transcendent, inapproachable, unequaled, peerless.

in-com′pȧ-rȧ-ble-ness, *n.* Excellence beyond comparison.

in-com′pȧ-rȧ-bly, *adv.* Beyond comparison; without competition.

in-cŏm-pāred′, *a.* Not matched; peerless. [Obs.]

in-cŏm′păss, *v.t.* Same as *Encompass.*

in-cŏm-pas′sion, *n.* Want of compassion. [Obs.]

in-cŏm-pas′sion-āte, *a.* Void of compassion or pity; destitute of tenderness.

in-cŏm-pas′sion-āte-ly, *adv.* Without pity or tenderness.

in-cŏm-pas′sion-āte-ness, *n.* Want of pity.

in-cŏm-pat-i-bil′i-ty, *n.* Inconsistency; that quality or state of a thing which renders it impossible that it should be consistent with something else; as, there is a permanent *incompatibility* between truth and falsehood.

in-cŏm-pat′i-ble, *a.* 1. Inconsistent; that cannot subsist with something else; as, truth and falsehood are essentially *incompatible*, as are virtue and vice.

2. Irreconcilably different or disagreeing; incongruous; as, *incompatible* tempers.

3. Legally or constitutionally inconsistent; that cannot be united in the same person, without violating the law or constitution; as, the offices of a legislator and of a judge are *incompatible*, as they cannot be held at the same time by the same person.

4. In chemistry, a term applied to salts and other substances, which cannot exist together in solution without natural decomposition.

Incompatible terms; in logic, terms which do not admit of combination in thought, as in the phrase, thunderous silence.

in-cŏm-pat′i-ble, *n.* In medicine and in chemistry, usually in the plural, substances that cannot be used together because of either some affinity or some mutually repellent properties.

in-cŏm-pat′i-ble-ness, *n.* The quality, property, or state of being incompatible; incompatibility.

in-cŏm-pat′i-bly, *adv.* Inconsistently; incongruously.

in-com′pē-tence, *n.* 1. Inability or disqualification of any kind, intellectual, moral, or physical; as, *incompetence* of idiots; *incompetence* of bodily strength; *incompetence* of moral distinction; *incompetence* of a witness.

2. Inadequacy of means.

in-com′pē-ten-cy, *n.* Same as *Incompetence.*

in-com′pē-tent, *a.* [LL. *incompetens* (*-entis*), insufficient; *in-* priv., and *competens*, able, sufficient, competent.] Wanting adequate powers of mind or suitable faculties to perform a given function; as, *incompetent* to solve a problem, to diagnose a disease, to expound a law, to refute an argument, to fill an office, to give testimony, to decide a question; not competent; not having the requisite qualification.

Syn.—Disqualified, inefficient, unsuited, unfit, unable, incapable.—*Incompetent* denotes a want of the requisite qualifications for performing a given act; *incapable* denotes want of power, either natural or moral.

in-com′pē-tent-ly, *adv.* Insufficiently; inadequately; not suitably; in an incompetent manner.

in-cŏm-pet-i-bil′i-ty, *n.* [Obs.] Same as *Incompatibility.*

in-cŏm-pet′i-ble, *a.* [Obs.] Same as *Incompatible.*

in-cŏm-plēte′, *a.* [LL. *incompletus*; L. *in-* priv., and *completus*, complete.]

1. Not finished; as, the building is *incomplete.*

2. Imperfect; defective.

3. In botany, lacking any of the floral parts, whether of calyx, corolla, stamens, or pistils.

Incomplete equation; in algebra, an equation lacking one or more terms containing the unknown quantity with a power lower than the highest in that equation; as, $x^3-3r^2x+2ar^2=0$.

in-cŏm-plēte′ly, *adv.* In an unfinished manner; not completely.

in-cŏm-plēte′ness, *n.* An unfinished state; the lack of completeness.

in-cŏm-plē′tion, *n.* The quality of incompleteness.

in-com′plex, *a.* Not complex; uncompounded; simple.

in-cŏm-plī′ȧ-ble, *a.* Not compliable.

in-cŏm-plī′ănce, *n.* Defect of compliance; refusal to comply; noncompliance; untractableness.

in-cŏm-plī′ănt, *a.* Unyielding to request or solicitation; not disposed to comply.

in-cŏm-plī′ănt-ly, *adv.* Not compliantly.

in-cŏm-pōsed′, *a.* Disordered; disturbed. [Obs.]

in-cŏm-pōs′ed-ly, *adv.* Not composedly. [Obs.]

in-cŏm-pōs′ed-ness, *n.* Want of composure. [Obs.]

in-cŏm-pos′ite, *a.* [L. *incompositus*, not well put together; *in-* priv., and *compositus*, pp. of *componere*, to put together.] Uncompounded; simple; not composite.

in-cŏm-pos-si-bil′i-ty, *n.* The quality of not being possible but by the negation or destruction of something; inconsistency with something. [Obs.]

in-cŏm-pos′si-ble, *a.* Not possible to be or subsist with something else. [Obs.]

in-com-prē-hense′, *a.* Not to be comprehended. [Obs.]

in-com-prē-hen-si-bil′i-ty, *n.* [LL. *incomprehensibilitas*, from L. *incomprehensibilis*, that may not be laid hold of, incomprehensible.] The quality of being incomprehensible, or beyond the reach of human intellect; inconceivableness.

in-com-prē-hen′si-ble, *a.* [ME. *incomprehensibele*; OFr. *incomprehensible*; L. *incomprehensibilis*, that cannot be seized, taken, or comprehended; *in-* priv., and *comprehensibilis*, comprehensible.]

1. That cannot be comprehended or understood; that is beyond the reach of human intellect; inconceivable; as, the nature of spiritual being is *incomprehensible.*

2. Not to be contained within bounds. [Rare.]

in-com-prē-hen′si-ble-ness, *n.* Incomprehensibility.

in-com-prē-hen′si-bly, *adv.* In a manner which the human mind cannot comprehend or understand; inconceivably.

in-com-prē-hen′sion, *n.* Want of comprehension or understanding.

in-com-prē-hen′sive, *a.* Not comprehensive; not broadly inclusive; restricted.

in-com-prē-hen′sive-ly, *adv.* In an incomprehensive manner; in a limited manner.

in-com-prē-hen′sive-ness, *n.* That quality which makes a thing incomprehensible.

in-cŏm-press-i-bil′i-ty, *n.* The quality of resisting compression, or of being incapable of reduction by force into a smaller compass.

in-cŏm-press′i-ble, *a.* Not to be compressed; not capable of being reduced by force into a smaller compass; resisting compression; as, water is not, as was once supposed, wholly *incompressible.*

in-cŏm-press′i-ble-ness, *n.* That quality which makes an object incompressible.

in-cŏm-pūt′ȧ-ble, *a.* That cannot be computed.

in-con-cēal′ȧ-ble, *a.* Not concealable; not to be kept secret or out of sight.

in-con-cēiv′ȧ-ble, *a.* 1. That cannot be conceived by the mind; incomprehensible; as, it is *inconceivable* to us how the will acts in producing muscular motion.

2. That cannot be understood.

in-con-cēiv′ȧ-ble-ness, *n.* The quality of being inconceivable; incomprehensibility.

in-con-cēiv′ȧ-bly, *adv.* In a manner beyond comprehension, or beyond the reach of human intellect.

in-con-cep′ti-ble, *a.* Inconceivable. [Rare.]

in-con-cẽrn′ing, *a.* Trivial; of little moment. [Obs.]

in-cŏn-cinn′, in-cŏn-cinne′, *a.* [Obs.] Same as *Inconcinnous.*

in-cŏn-cin′ni-ty, *n.* [L. *inconcinnitas*, inelegance, from *inconcinnus*, inelegant; *in-* priv., and *concinnus*, elegant, graceful.] Unsuitableness; want of proportion.

in-cŏn-cin′nous, *a.* Incongruous; unsuitable; disagreeing; not to be reconciled. [Obs.]

in-con-clūd′ent, *a.* Not inferring a conclusion or consequence. [Obs.]

in-con-clūd′ing, *a.* Inferring no consequence. [Obs.]

in-con-clū′sive, *a.* Not producing a conclusion; not closing, concluding, or settling a point in debate, or a doubtful question; as, an argument or evidence is *inconclusive* when it does not exhibit the truth of a disputed case in such a manner as to satisfy the mind and put an end to debate or doubt.

in-con-clū′sive-ly, *adv.* Without such evidence as to determine the understanding in regard to truth or falsehood.

in-con-clū′sive-ness, *n.* The state or quality of being inconclusive.

in-con-coct′, *a.* Inconcocted. [Obs.]

in-con-coct′ed, *a.* Not fully digested; not matured; unripened. [Obs.]

in-con-coc′tion, *n.* The state of being indigested; unripeness; immaturity. [Obs.]

in-con′crēte, *a.* [LL. *inconcretus*, not concrete; L. *in-* priv., and *concretus*, concrete.] Lacking concrete characteristics.

in-con-cũr′ring, *a.* Not concurring; not agreeing. [Rare.]

in-con-cus′si-ble, *a.* [L. *in-* priv., and LL. *concussibilis*, that can be shaken, from L. *concussus*, pp. of *concutere*, to shake.] That cannot be shaken.

in-con-den-sȧ-bil′i-ty, *n.* The quality of being noncondensable; written also *incondensibility.*

in-con-den′sȧ-ble, *a.* 1. Not capable of condensation; that cannot be made more dense or compact.

2. Not to be converted from a state of vapor to a liquid.

Written also *incondensible.*

in-con′dite, *a.* [L. *inconditus*, without order, irregular; *in-* priv., and *conditus*, put together.] Rude; unpolished; irregular. [Rare.]

in-con-di′tion-ăl, *a.* Without any condition, exception, or limitation; absolute. [Obs.]

in-con-di′tion-āte, *a.* Not limited or restrained by conditions; absolute. [Obs.]

in-con-fọrm′, *a.* That will not conform. [Obs.]

in-con-fọrm′ȧ-ble, *a.* Not conformable. [Obs.]

in-con-fọrm′i-ty, *n.* Want of conformity; nonconformity; noncompliance with the practice of others, or with the requisitions of law, rule, or custom. [Obs.]

in-con-fūsed′, *a.* Not confused; distinct. [Obs.]

in-con-fū′sion, *n.* Distinctness; lack of confusion. [Obs.]

in-con-fūt′ȧ-ble, *a.* That cannot be confuted.

in-con-fūt′ȧ-bly, *adv.* Unanswerably. [Obs.]

in-con-ġēal′ȧ-ble, *a.* Not susceptible of being frozen.

in-con-ġēal′ȧ-ble-ness, *n.* The quality of being noncongealable.

in-con-ġēn′iăl, *a.* Not congenial; not of a like nature; unsuitable.

in-con-ġē-ni-al′i-ty, *n.* Unlikeness of nature; unsuitableness.

in-cŏn′grụ-ence, *n.* [LL. *incongruentia*, inconsistency, from L. *incongruens* (*-entis*), inconsistent; *in-* priv., and *congruens*, consistent.] Want of congruence, adaptation, or agreement; incongruity.

in-cŏn′grụ-ent, *a.* 1. Unsuitable; incongruous.

2. In anatomy, not agreeing in conformation; as, *incongruent* surfaces in a joint.

in-con-grụ′i-ty, *n.* 1. Want of congruity; impropriety; inconsistency; absurdity; unsuitableness of one thing to another; as, the levity of youth in a grave divine is deemed an *incongruity* between manners and profession.

2. Disagreement of parts; want of symmetry. [Obs.]

in-cŏn′grụ-ous, *a.* [L. *incongruus*, inconsistent; *in-* priv., and *congruus*, consistent.]

1. Not congruous; unsuitable; not fitting; inconsistent; improper; as. the dress of a seaman on a judge would be deemed *incongruous* with his character and station.

2. Composed of parts out of harmony or agreement; as, an *incongruous* speech.

Incongruous numbers; in arithmetic, two numbers whose difference is not a multiple of a third number; as, sixteen and twenty-three are *incongruous* with respect to five.

Syn.—Inconsistent, inappropriate, incompatible, unsuitable, disagreeing, inharmonious.

in-cŏn′grụ-ous-ly, *adv.* Unsuitably; unfitly; improperly.

in-cŏn′grụ-ous-ness, *n.* The state or quality of being incongruous.

in-con-nect′ed, *a.* Without connection. [Obs.]

in-con-nec′tion, *n.* Want of connection; loose, disjointed state.

in-con-nex′ed-ly, *adv.* Without connection. [Obs.]

in-con-nū′ (*or Fr. pron.* an-kon-nü′), *n.* [Fr., unknown.] In ichthyology, a name given to the salmon of the Mackenzie River, *Stenodus mackenzii*, by the travelers who first found it.

in-con′scion-ȧ-ble (-shun-), *a.* Having no sense of good and evil; unconscionable. [Obs.]

in-con′scious (-shus), *a.* [Obs.] See *Unconscious.*

in-con-sec′ū-tive-ness, *n.* The state of not succeeding in regular order.

in-con′sē-quence, *n.* [L. *inconsequentia*, from *inconsequens* (*-entis*), inconsequent.] Want of just inference; inconclusiveness; lacking logical sequence.

in-con′sē-quent, *a.* [L. *inconsequens* (*-entis*), not consequent; *in-* priv., and *consequens* (*-entis*), ppr. of *consequi*, to follow after.] Not following from the premises; without regular inference; as, an *inconsequent* deduction or argument.

in-con-sē-quen′tiăl, *a.* 1. Not regularly following from the premises.

2. Not of consequence; not of importance; of little moment.

in-con-sē-quen-ti-al′i-ty, *n.* State of being of no consequence.

in-con-sē-quen′tiăl-ly, *adv.* Without regular sequence or deduction.

in-con′sē-quent-ness, *n.* The state or quality of being inconsequent.

in-con-sid′ẽr-ȧ-ble, *a.* Not worthy of consideration or notice; unimportant; small; trivial; as, an *inconsiderable* distance.

in-con-sid′ẽr-ȧ-ble-ness, *n.* Small importance.

in-con-sid′ẽr-ȧ-bly, *adv.* In a small degree; to a small amount; very little.

in-con-sid′ẽr-ȧ-cy, *n.* Thoughtlessness; want of consideration. [Obs.]

in-con-sid′ẽr-āte, *a.* [L. *inconsideratus*, not considerate; *in-* priv., and *consideratus*, pp. of *considerare*, to look at carefully, to consider.]

1. Not considerate; not attending to the circumstances which regard safety or propriety;

hasty; rash; imprudent; careless; thoughtless; heedless; inattentive; as, the young are generally *inconsiderate*.

2. Proceeding from heedlessness; rash; as, *inconsiderate* conduct.

3. Of little importance. [Obs.]

in-çon-sid′ẽr-āte-ly, *adv.* Without due consideration or regard to consequences; heedlessly; carelessly; rashly; imprudently.

in-çon-sid′ẽr-āte-ness, *n.* Want of due regard to consequences; carelessness; thoughtlessness; inadvertence; inattention; imprudence.

in-çon-sid-ẽr-ā′tion, *n.* [LL. *inconsideratio* (*-onis*); L. *in-* priv., and *consideratio* (*-onis*), consideration, from *considerare*, to consider.] Want of due consideration; want of thought; inattention to consequences.

in-çon-sist′ence, *n.* Inconsistency.

in-çon-sist′en-cy, *n.* 1. Such opposition or disagreement as that one proposition infers the negation of the other; such contrariety between things that both cannot subsist together.

> There is a perfect *inconsistency* between that which is of debt and that which is of free gift. —South.

2. Absurdity in argument or narration; argument or narrative where one part destroys the other; self-contradiction.

3. Incongruity; want of agreement or uniformity; as, the *inconsistency* of a man with himself.

4. Unsteadiness; changeableness.

in-çon-sist′ent, *a.* 1. Incompatible; incongruous; not suitable; as, loud laughter in grave company is *inconsistent* with good breeding.

2. Not consistent; contrary, so that one infers the negation or destruction of the other, or so that the truth of one proves the other to be false; as, two covenants, one that a man shall have an estate in fee and the other that he shall hold it for years, are *inconsistent*.

3. Not uniform; being contrary at different times; as, men are sometimes *inconsistent* with themselves.

Syn.—Incongruous, incompatible, incoherent, disagreeing.—Things are *incongruous* when they are not suited to each other, so that their union is unbecoming; *inconsistent* when they are opposed to each other, so as to render it improper or wrong; *incompatible* when they cannot coexist, and it is therefore impossible to unite them. *Inconsistent* refers either to the actions or sentiments of men; *incongruous* to the modes and qualities of things; *incoherent* to speech or thoughts.

in-çon-sist′ent-ly, *adv.* In an inconsistent manner; with absurdity; incongruously; with self-contradiction; without steadiness or uniformity.

in-çon-sist′ent-ness, *n.* Inconsistency. [Obs.]

in-çon-sist′ing, *a.* Inconsistent. [Obs.]

in-çon-sōl′ȧ-ble, *a.* [L. *inconsolabilis*, inconsolable; *in-* priv., and *consolabilis*, consolable, from *consolari*, to console.] Not to be consoled; grieved beyond susceptibility of comfort.

Syn.—Cheerless, joyless, spiritless, melancholy, gloomy, disconsolate, comfortless, forlorn, heartsick.

in-çon-sōl′ȧ-ble-ness, *n.* The quality or state of being inconsolable.

in-çon-sōl′ȧ-bly, *adv.* In a manner or degree that does not admit of consolation.

in-çon′sō-nănce, *n.* Disagreement of sounds; discordance of any kind.

in-çon′sō-năn-cy, *n.* Inconsonance.

in-çon′sō-nănt, *a.* [LL. *inconsonans* (*-antis*), unsuitable; L. *in-* priv., and *consonans* (*-antis*), ppr. of *consonare*, to sound together, to agree.] Not agreeing; inconsistent; discordant.

in-çon′sō-nănt-ly, *adv.* Inconsistently; discordantly.

in-çon-spiç′ū-ous, *a.* [LL. *inconspicuus*; L. *in-* priv., and *conspicuus*, conspicuous.] Not discernible; scarcely to be perceived by the sight; not conspicuous.

in-çon-spiç′ū-ous-ly, *adv.* In an inconspicuous manner.

in-çon-spiç′ū-ous-ness, *n.* The state of being inconspicuous.

in-çon′stănce, *n.* Inconstancy.

in-çon′stăn-cy, *n.* [OFr. *inconstance*; L. *inconstantia*, inconstancy, from *inconstans* (*-antis*), inconstant.]

1. Mutability or instability of temper or affection; unsteadiness; fickleness.

2. Want of uniformity; dissimilitude.

in-çon′stănt, *a.* [OFr. *inconstante*; L. *inconstans* (*-antis*); *in-* priv., and *constans* (*-antis*), constant, ppr. of *constare*, to stand, halt.]

1. Mutable; subject to change of opinion, inclination, or purpose; not firm in resolution; unsteady; fickle; as, *inconstant* in love or friendship.

2. Mutable; changeable; variable; as, *inconstant* climate.

Syn.—Changeable, fluctuating, variable, mutable, unsteady, unstable, unsettled, vacillating.

in-çon′stănt-ly, *adv.* In an inconstant manner; not steadily.

in-çon-sūm′ȧ-ble, *a.* Not to be consumed; that cannot be wasted.

in-çon-sūm′ȧ-bly, *adv.* So as not to be consumable.

in-çon-sum′māte, *a.* [LL. *inconsummatus*, unfinished; L. *in-* priv., and *consummatus*, pp. of *consummare*, to accomplish, finish.] Not consummate; not finished; not complete.

in-çon-sum′māte-ness, *n.* State of being incomplete.

in-çon-sump′ti-ble, *a.* Not to be spent, wasted, or destroyed. [Obs.]

in-çon-tam′i-nāte, *a.* [L. *incontaminatus*; *in-* priv., and *contaminatus*, pp. of *contaminare*, to defile, contaminate.] Not contaminated.

in-çon-tam′i-nāte-ness, *n.* Uncorrupted state.

in-çon-ten-tā′tion, *n.* Discontentment. [Obs.]

in-çon-test-ȧ-bil′i-ty, *n.* The quality that renders incontestable.

in-çon-test′ȧ-ble, *a.* Not contestable; not to be disputed; not admitting debate; too clear to be controverted; incontrovertible; as, *incontestable* evidence, truth, or facts.

Syn.—Indisputable, unquestionable, unassailable, impregnable, incontrovertible, irrefutable.

in-çon-test′ȧ-ble-ness, *n.* The state or quality that renders incontestable.

in-çon-test′ȧ-bly, *adv.* In a manner to preclude debate; indisputably; incontrovertibly; indubitably.

in-çon-test′ed, *a.* Same as *Uncontested*.

in-çon-tig′ū-ous, *a.* [LL. *incontiguus*, that cannot be touched; L. *in-* priv., and *contiguus*, touching.] Not contiguous; not adjoining; not touching; separate.

in-çon-tig′ū-ous-ly, *adv.* Not contiguously; separately.

in-çon′ti-nence, *n.* [OFr. *incontinence*; L. *incontinentia*, lack of self-control, from *incontinens* (*-entis*), not containing, intemperate; *in-* priv., and *continere*, to contain.]

1. Want of restraint of the passions or appetites; free or uncontrolled indulgence of the passions or appetites; want of restraint of the sexual appetite; free or illegal indulgence of lust; lewdness.

2. In medicine, the inability of any of the animal organs to restrain discharges of their contents, so that the discharges are involuntary; as, *incontinence* of urine.

in-çon′ti-nen-cy, *n.* Incontinence.

in-çon′ti-nent, *a.* 1. Not restraining the passions or appetites, particularly the sexual appetite; indulging lust without restraint, or in violation of law; unchaste; lewd.

2. Unable to restrain discharges.

in-çon′ti-nent, *n.* One who is unchaste.

in-çon′ti-nent, *adv.* [Obs.] See *Incontinently*.

in-çon′ti-nent-ly, *adv.* 1. Without due restraint of the passions or appetites; unchastely.

2. Immediately; without delay.

in-çon-traçt′ed, *a.* Not contracted; not shortened. [Obs.]

in-çon-trōl′lȧ-ble, *a.* Not to be controlled; that cannot be restrained or governed; uncontrollable.

in-çon-trōl′lȧ-bly, *adv.* In a manner that admits of no control; uncontrollably.

in-çon-trō-vẽr-ti-bil′i-ty, *n.* The quality of being incontrovertible.

in-çon-trō-vẽr′ti-ble, *a.* Indisputable; too clear or certain to admit of dispute.

in-çon-trō-vẽr′ti-ble-ness, *n.* The condition of being incontrovertible.

in-çon-trō-vẽr′ti-bly, *adv.* In a manner or degree that precludes debate or controversy.

in-çon-vēn′ience, *n.* [OFr. *inconvenience*; LL. *inconvenientia*, inconvenience, inconsistency, from L. *inconveniens* (*-entis*), unsuitable, inconvenient.]

1. Unfitness; unsuitableness; inexpedience.

2. That which gives trouble or uneasiness, disadvantage; disturbance; impediment; as, the greatest *inconvenience* of life is the want of money.

in-çon-vēn′ience, *v.t.*; inconvenienced (-yenst), *pt.*, *pp.*; inconveniencing, *ppr.* To make inconvenient; to hinder.

Syn.—Annoy, molest, trouble, disturb, embarrass.—We *inconvenience* by omitting such things as might be convenient; we *annoy* or *molest* by doing that which is positively painful; we are *inconvenienced* by what is temporary; we are *annoyed* by that which is either temporary or durable; we are *molested* by that which is weighty and oppressive.

in-çon-vēn′ien-cy, *n.* Inconvenience.

in-çon-vēn′ient, *a.* [OFr. *inconvenient*; L. *inconveniens* (*-entis*), unsuitable, inconsistent; *in-* priv., and *conveniens* (*-entis*), ppr. of *convenire*, to come together, fit, accord.] Incommodious; unsuitable; disadvantageous; giving trouble or uneasiness; increasing the difficulty of progress or success; as, an *inconvenient* dress or garment; an *inconvenient* arrangement.

in-çon-vēn′ient-ly, *adv.* Unsuitably; incommodiously; in a manner to give trouble; unseasonably.

in-çon-vẽrs′ȧ-ble, *a.* Not inclined to free conversation; incommunicative; unsocial; reserved.

in-çon′vẽr-sănt, *a.* Not conversant; not familiar; not versed.

in-çon-vẽrt′ed, *a.* Not converted. [Rare.]

in-çon-vẽrt-i-bil′i-ty, *n.* The quality of not being changeable or convertible into something else; as, the *inconvertibility* of bank-notes or other currency into gold or silver.

in-çon-vẽrt′i-ble, *a.* [LL. *inconvertibilis*; L. *in-* priv., and LL. *convertibilis*, convertible, from L. *convertere*, to turn about, change.] Not convertible; that cannot be transmuted or changed into something else; as, one metal is *inconvertible* into another.

in-çon-vẽrt′i-ble-ness, *n.* The state of being inconvertible.

in-çon-vẽrt′i-bly, *adv.* In an inconvertible manner.

in-çon-vin′ci-ble, *a.* Not convincible; that cannot be convinced; not capable of conviction.

in-çon-vin′ci-bly, *adv.* In a manner not admitting of conviction.

in-çō′ny, *a.* Unlearned; artless. [Obs.]

in-çō-ọr′di-nāte, *a.* Lacking coördination.

in-çō-ọr-di-nā′tion, *n.* The state of being incoördinate.

Incoördination of muscular movement; in physiology, irregularity of movement, caused by loss of control.

in-çor′ō-nāte, *a.* [L. *in*, on, and *coronare*, to crown, from *corona*, a crown.] Invested with a crown. [Rare.]

in-çor′pō-răl, *a.* Not consisting of matter or body; immaterial. [Obs.]

in-çor-pō-ral′i-ty, *n.* The quality of being incorporeal; immateriality. [Obs.]

in-çor′pō-răl-ly, *adv.* Without matter or a body; immaterially. [Obs.]

in-çor′pō-rāte, *a.* [L. *in-* priv., and *corporatus*, pp. of *corporare*, to form into a body, from *corpus*, a body.]

1. Not consisting of matter; not having a material body; incorporeal.

2. Not incorporated; not having the character of a corporate body.

in-çor′pō-rāte, *a.* Made one body; associated as a corporation.

in-çor′pō-rāte, *v.t.*; incorporated, *pt.*, *pp.*; incorporating, *ppr.* [L. *incorporatus*, pp. of *incorporare*, to unite in a body, embody; *in*, in, and *corporare*, to form into a body, from *corpus*, a body.]

1. In pharmacy, to mix (different ingredients) in one mass or body; to reduce (dry substances) to the consistence o paste by the admixture of a fluid, as in making pills, etc.

2. To mix and embody, as one substance in another; as, to *incorporate* copper with silver.

3. To unite; to blend; to work into another mass or body; as, to *incorporate* plagiarisms into one's own composition.

4. To unite; to make a part of, as another government or empire; as, the Romans *incorporated* conquered countries into their government.

5. To embody; to give a material form to.

6. To form into a legal body or body politic; to constitute a body, composed of one or more individuals, wit the quality of perpetual existence or succession, unles limited by the act of incorporation; as, to *incorporate* the inhabitants of a city, town, or parish.

in-çor′pō-rāte, *v.i.* To unite so as to make a part of another body; to be mixed or blended; to be worked in; usually followed by *with*; as, paints *incorporate with* oil.

in-çor′pō-rā-ted, *a.* Mixed or united in one body; associated in the same political body; united in a legal body.

in-çor-pō-rā′tion, *n.* [OFr. *incorporation*; LL. *incorporatio* (*-onis*), an incorporating, embodying, from L. *incorporare*, to embody, incorporate.]

1. The act of incorporating.

2. Union of different ingredients in one mass.

3. Association in the same political body; as, the *incorporation* of conquered countries into the Roman republic.

4. In law, the formation of a legal or political body by the union of individuals, constituting an artificial person; also, the body thus incorporated.

in-çor′pō-rā-tive, *a.* Having the capacity and the tendency to incorporate; specifically, in philology, applied to certain languages, such as the Basque and those of the North American Indians, which have a tendency to incorporate with a word such modifiers as express common relations and actions. [Compare *polysynthetic*.]

in-çor′pō-rā-tŏr, *n.* One of a number of persons incorporating a company; a charter member of a corporation.

in-çor-pō′rē-ăl, *a.* [L. *incorporeus*, without a

body; *in-* priv., and *corporeus*, corporeal, from *corpus*, a body.]

1. Not consisting of matter; not having a material body; immaterial; as, spirits are deemed *incorporeal* substances.

2. In law, having no existence except in the eye of the law; not tangible; not seizable; as, an *incorporeal* hereditament.

Incorporeal hereditament; see under *Hereditament*.

in-cor-pō'rē-ăl-ism, *n.* 1. Belief in an incorporeal existence.

2. Incorporeal existence; immateriality.

in-cor-pō'rē-ăl-ist, *n.* A believer in an incorporeal existence.

in-cor-pō-rē-al'i-ty, *n.* Immateriality; incorporealism.

in-cor-pō'rē-ăl-ly, *adv.* Without body; immaterially.

in-cor-pō-rē'i-ty, *n.* The quality of being incorporeal; immateriality.

in-corpse', *v.t.* To incorporate. [Obs.]

in-cor-rect', *a.* [L. *incorrectus*, uncorrected, unimproved; *in-* priv., and *correctus*, pp. of *corrigere*, to correct, improve.]

1. Not correct; not exact; not according to a copy or model, or to established rules; inaccurate; faulty.

> The piece, you think, is *incorrect.* —Pope.

2. Not according to truth; inaccurate; as, an *incorrect* statement, narration, or calculation.

3. Not according to law or morality.

in-cor-rec'tion, *n.* Want of correction. [Obs.]

in-cor-rect'ly, *adv.* Not in accordance with truth or other standard; inaccurately; not exactly; as, a writing *incorrectly* copied; testimony *incorrectly* stated.

in-cor-rect'ness, *n.* Want of conformity to truth or to a standard; inaccuracy.

in-cor-re-spond'ence, *n.* Failure to correspond; want of agreement.

in-cor-re-spond'en-cy, *n.* Incorrespondence.

in-cor-re-spond'ing, *a.* Not corresponding.

in-cor"ri-ġi-bil'i-ty, *n.* The quality of being bad, erroneous, or depraved beyond correction; hopeless depravity in persons and hopeless error in things.

in-cor'ri-ġi-ble, *a.* [LL. *incorrigibilis*, from L. *in-* priv., and LL. *corrigibilis*, corrigible, from L. *corrigere*, to correct.] Not capable of correction or amendment; not to be reformed or redeemed; as, *incorrigible* error; *incorrigible* drunkards.

in-cor'ri-ġi-ble, *n.* One who is bad beyond hope of correction or reform.

in-cor'ri-ġi-ble-ness, *n.* Incorrigibility.

in-cor'ri-ġi-bly, *adv.* To a degree of depravity beyond all means of amendment.

in-cor-rōd'i-ble, *a.* That cannot be corroded.

in-cor-rupt', *a.* [L. *incorruptus*, uninjured; *in-* priv., and *corruptus*, pp. of *corrumpere*, to break up, destroy, corrupt.] Not corrupt; not marred, impaired, or spoiled; not defiled or depraved; pure; sound; untainted; above the power of bribes.

in-cor-rupt'ed, *a.* Incorrupt. [Obs.]

in-cor-rupt-i-bil'i-ty, *n.* The quality of being incapable of decay or of being corrupted.

in-cor-rupt'i-ble, *a.* [ME. *incorruptible*; OFr. *incorruptible*; LL. *incorruptibilis*, incorruptible; L. *in-* priv., and LL. *corruptibilis*, corruptible, from L. *corrumpere*, to destroy, corrupt.]

1. That cannot corrupt or decay; not admitting of corruption; as, gold is *incorruptible*; spirits are supposed to be *incorruptible*.

> Our bodies shall be changed into *incorruptible* and immortal substances. —Wake.

2. That cannot be bribed; inflexibly just and upright.

In-cor-rupt'i-ble, *n.* A member of a religious sect in the sixth century, which held the doctrine that Christ suffered only in appearance, as his body was incorruptible and therefore could not feel hunger, distress, or pain.

in-cor-rupt'i-ble-ness, *n.* The quality of being incorruptible or not liable to decay.

in-cor-rupt'i-bly, *adv.* So as not to admit of corruption or decay.

in-cor-rup'tion, *n.* [LL. *incorruptio (-onis)*, from L. *incorruptus*, not corrupt; *in-* priv., and *corruptus*, pp. of *corrumpere*, to destroy, corrupt.] Incapability of being corrupted.

> It is sown in corruption; it is raised in *incorruption.* —1 Cor. xv. 42.

in-cor-rup'tive, *a.* Not liable to corruption or decay. [Rare.]

in-cor-rupt'ly, *adv.* Purely; without yielding to corrupt influence.

in-cor-rupt'ness, *n.* 1. Exemption from decay or corruption.

2. Purity of mind or manners; probity; integrity; honesty.

in-cras'sāte, *v.t.*; incrassated, *pt.*, *pp.*; incrassating, *ppr.* [LL. *incrassatus*, pp. of *incrassare*, to make thick; L. *in*, in, and *crassare*, to thicken, from *crassus*, thick.]

1. To make thick or thicker; to thicken.

2. In pharmacy, to make (fluids) thicker by the mixture of other substances less fluid, or by evaporating the thinner parts.

in-cras'sāte, *v.i.* To become thick or thicker.

> Acids dissolve or attenuate; alkalis precipitate or *incrassate.* —Newton.

in-cras'sāte, *a.* 1. In botany, thickened or becoming thicker.

2. Enlarged; gradually swelling out toward the tip; said of the antennæ of insects.

in-cras'sā-ted, *a.* Made thick or thicker; incrassate.

in-cras-sā'tion, *n.* The act of thickening or the state of becoming thick or thicker.

in-cras'sȧ-tive, *a.* Having the quality of thickening.

in-cras'sȧ-tive, *n.* That which has the power to thicken.

in-crēas'ȧ-ble, *a.* That may be increased.

in-crēas'ȧ-ble-ness, *n.* The state or condition of being increasable.

in-crēase', *v.i.*; increased, *pt.*, *pp.*; increasing, *ppr.* [ME. *increassen*; OFr. *encreistre*; L. *increscere*, to increase; *in*, in, on, and *crescere*, to grow.] To become greater in bulk, quantity, number, value, or degree; to grow; to augment; as, plants *increase* in size by growing; population *increases* in number; property *increases* in value; a fever *increases* in violence; the moon *increases* in phase, etc.

Increasing function; in mathematics, a function whose value increases with that of a variable.

Syn.—Enlarge, swell, heighten, dilate, enhance, augment, grow, expand, spread.—*Enlarge* implies a widening of extent; *increase* an accession in point of size, number, strength, etc.

in-crēase', *v.t.* To augment or make greater in bulk, quantity, number, value, or degree; as, to *increase* wealth; to *increase* value.

in'crēase, *n.* 1. Augmentation; a growing larger in extent, quantity, number, or value.

> Of the *increase* of his government and peace, there shall be no end. —Isa. ix. 7.

2. The result of augmentation; profit; interest; produce; that which is added to the original stock.

> Take thou no usury of him or *increase*; but fear thy God. —Lev. xxv. 36.

3. Progeny; issue; offspring.

> All the *increase* of thine house shall die in the flower of their age. —1 Sam. ii. 33.

4. Generation. [Obs.]

5. The waxing, as of the moon.

> Seeds, hair, nails, hedges, and herbs will grow soonest, if set or cut in the *increase* of the moon. —Bacon.

Syn.—Addition, accession, augmentation, gain, accretion, enlargement, increment, extension, growth.—*Addition* is the artificial mode of making two things into one; the *increase* is the result; *addition* is an intentional mode of *increasing*; *accession* is an accidental mode; *augmentation* is a mode of *increasing*, not merely in quantity or number, but also in value or in the essential ingredient of a thing.

in-crēase'ful, *a.* Abundant in produce. [Rare.]

in-crēase'ment, *n.* The state of increasing; enlargement. [Rare.]

in-crēas'ẽr, *n.* Any agent of augmentation.

in'crēase-twist, *n.* Same as *Gaining-twist*.

in-crēas'ing-ly, *adv.* In the way of growing; growingly.

in-crē-āte', *v.t.* To create within. [Rare.]

in'crē-āte, in'crē-ā-ted, *a.* Uncreated. [Rare.]

in-cred-i-bil'i-ty, *n.* The quality of surpassing belief; also, anything too extraordinary to admit of belief.

in-cred'i-ble, *a.* [L. *incredibilis*; *in-* priv., and *credibilis*, credible, from *credere*, to believe.] That cannot be believed; not to be credited; too extraordinary and improbable to admit of belief.

> Why should it be thought a thing *incredible* with you, that God should raise the dead? —Acts xxvi. 8.

Syn.—Unbelievable, fabulous, unverified, mythical.

in-cred'i-ble-ness, *n.* Incredibility.

in-cred'i-bly, *adv.* In a manner to preclude belief.

in-cred'it-ed, *a.* Not believed. [Obs.]

in-crē-dū'li-ty, *n.* [L. *incredulitas (-atis)*, from *incredulus*, unbelieving; *in-* priv., and *credulus*, believing.] The quality of not believing; indisposition to believe; a withholding or refusal of belief.

> Of every species of *incredulity*, religious unbelief is infinitely the most irrational. —Buckminster.

in-cred'ū-lous, *a.* 1. Not believing; indisposed to admit the truth of what is related; refusing or withholding belief.

2. Suggesting want of belief; as, an *incredulous* smile.

3. Not warranting belief. [Rare.]

in-cred'ū-lous-ly, *adv.* In a manner not disposed to believe.

in-cred'ū-lous-ness, *n.* Incredulity.

in-crem'ȧ-ble, *a.* [OFr. *incremable*; L. *in-* priv., and LL. *cremabilis*, combustible, from L. *cremare*, to burn.] That cannot be burnt.

in'crē-māte, *v.t.* Same as *Cremate*.

in-crē-mā'tion, *n.* Same as *Cremation*.

in'crē-ment, *n.* [L. *incrementum*, growth, increase, from *increscere*, to increase; *in*, in, on, and *crescere*, to grow.]

1. Increase; a growing in bulk, quantity, number, value, or amount; augmentation.

2. Produce; production.

3. Matter added; increase.

4. In mathematics, the finite increase of a variable quantity.

5. In rhetoric, a climacteric period.

6. In heraldry, the condition of the waxing moon; represented by a crescent.

Infinitesimal increment; in mathematics, the variation considered in differential calculus.

Method of increments; in mathematics, the method of finite differences in contradistinction to that of fluxions.

in-crē-men'tăl, *a.* In biology, relating to the marks of increment in growth; as, the *incremental* lines in the growth of a tree, a shell, a tooth, etc.

in'crē-pāte, *v.t.* To chide; to rebuke. [Obs.]

in-crē-pā'tion, *n.* A chiding or rebuking; rebuke; reprehension. [Obs.]

in-cres'cence, *n.* An increase by successive additions, as in the growing of a plant.

in-cres'cent, *a.* [L. *increscens (-entis)*, ppr. of *increscere*, to increase; *in*, in, on, and *crescere*, to grow.]

1. Increasing; growing; augmenting; swelling.

2. In heraldry, said of the new moon, with its horns pointing toward the dexter side.

The Moon increscent.

in-crest', *v.t.* [Obs.] See *Crest*.

in-crim'i-nāte, *v.t.*; incriminated, *pt.*, *pp.*; incriminating, *ppr.* [LL. *incriminatus*, pp. of *incriminare*, to accuse of crime; L. *in*, in, on, and *criminare*, to accuse, from *crimen (-inis)*, a crime.] To accuse; to charge with a crime or fault.

in-crim-i-nā'tion, *n.* The act of making criminal.

in-crim'i-nȧ-tō-ry, *a.* Evidencing or fixing criminality; as, *incriminatory* testimony.

in-croy-ȧ'ble, *n.* [Fr., lit., incredible.] A French dandy.

in-crū-en'tăl, *a.* Unbloody; not attended with blood. [Obs.]

in-crust', *v.t.*; incrusted, *pt.*, *pp.*; incrusting, *ppr.* [OFr. *encrouster*; L. *incrustare*, to cover with a coat or rind; *in*, in, on, and *crusta*, a crust.]

1. To cover with a crust or with a hard coat; to form a crust on the surface of; as, iron *incrusted* with oxid or rust; a vessel *incrusted* with salt.

2. In the arts, to lay in or upon, as mosaic or enamel.

in-crus'tāte, *v.t.* To incrust. [Rare.]

in-crus-tā'tion, *n.* [LL. *incrustatio (-onis)*, from L. *incrustare*, to incrust.]

1. A crust or coat of anything on the surface of a body; also, the process of coating.

2. A covering or inlaying of marble, mosaic, enamel, or other substance.

in-crust'ment, *n.* Incrustation.

in-crys'tăl-lī-zȧ-ble, *a.* That will not crystallize; that cannot be formed into crystals; uncrystallizable.

in'cū-bāte, *v.i.*; incubated, *pt.*, *pp.*; incubating, *ppr.* [L. *incubatus*, pp. of *incubare*, to lie in or upon; *in*, in, on, and *cubare*, to lie.] To sit, as on eggs for hatching.

in'cū-bāte, *v.t.* To produce from an egg by sitting; to hatch out.

in-cū-bā'tion, *n.* [L. *incubatio (-onis)*, a lying upon eggs, a brooding, from *incubare*, to lie in or upon; *in*, in, on, and *cubare*, to lie, recline.]

1. The act of sitting on eggs for the purpose of hatching young.

2. In pathology, the development of the germs of a disease.

3. Among the ancient Greeks, the act of sleeping in a sacred place to receive revelations from a god in a vision or dream.

Period of incubation; in pathology, the time elapsing from exposure to a disease till symptoms appear.

in'cū-bā-tive, *a.* Pertaining to the process of hatching out or developing.

in'cū-bā-tōr, *n.* [LL. *incubator*, one who lies in a place, from L. *incubare*, to lie upon or in.]

1. Any agent which incubates or hatches out.

2. Specifically, a machine or apparatus constructed and used for hatching out eggs by subjecting them to artificial heat.

3. Any animal that sits upon its eggs to hatch them.

4. In biology, a device for developing germs.

5. An appliance for treating young infants, especially the prematurely born.

in-cū′bȧ-tō-ry, *a.* Pertaining to the process of incubation or to the means of incubating; as, the *incubatory* pouch of an ascidian.

in-cūbe′, *v.t.* To establish securely, as if set in a cube. [Obs.]

in-cū′bi-tūre, *n.* Incubation. [Obs.]

in′cū-bous, *a.* [L. *incubare*, to lie upon.] In botany, having the leaves arranged tile-like, the apex of one overlying the base of the next, and so on.

in′cū-bus, *n.*; *pl.* **in′cū-bus-es** or **in′cū-bī.** [LL., nightmare, a demon supposed to be the cause of nightmare, from L. *incubare*, to lie upon; *in*, in, upon, and *cubare*, to lie.]

1. The nightmare; suffocative anhelation, with a sense of external pressure upon the chest, often seeming to be that of some hideous monster, and with tremor or violent struggle; most commonly occurring during sleep, though sometimes during wakefulness.

2. A demon; an imaginary being or fairy; a lascivious being who was supposed to consort with women in their sleep; the counterpart of *succubus*.

3. Figuratively, any oppressive hindrance to favorable action, physical or mental.

in′cū-dăl, *a.* In anatomy, relating to one of the small bones (incus) in the middle ear.

in-cul′cāte, *v.t.*; inculcated, *pt.*, *pp.*; inculcating, *ppr.* [L. *inculcatus*, pp. of *inculcare*, to tread in, tread down; *in*, in, on, and *calcare*, to trample under foot, from *calx*, *calcis*, heel.] To impress by frequent admonitions; to teach and enforce by frequent repetitions; to urge on the mind; as, our Saviour *inculcates* on his followers humility and forgiveness of injuries.

Syn.—Impress, urge, enforce, infuse, instil, implant, press, teach.

in-cul-cā′tion, *n.* The action of impressing by repeated admonitions.

in-cul′cā-tŏr, *n.* One who impresses by frequent admonition.

in-culk′, *v.t.* [Obs.] See *Inculcate*.

in-culp′, *v.t.* To inculpate. [Obs.]

in-cul′pȧ-ble, *a.* [LL. *inculpabilis*, unblamable; L. *in-* priv., and *culpabilis*, blamable, from *culpa*, fault.] Without fault; unblamable; that cannot be accused.

in-cul′pȧ-ble-ness, *n.* Unblamableness.

in-cul′pȧ-bly, *adv.* Unblamably; without blame.

in-cul′pāte, *v.t.*; inculpated, *pt.*, *pp.*; inculpating, *ppr.* [LL. *inculpatus*, pp. of *inculpare*, to bring in fault; L. *in*, in, on, and *culpa*, fault, blame.] To blame; to censure; to charge with and furnish proof of guilt.

in-cul-pā′tion, *n.* Blame; censure.

in-cul′pȧ-tō-ry, *a.* Imputing blame.

in-cult′, *a.* [L. *incultus*, uncultivated; *in-* priv., and *cultus*, pp. of *colere*, to till, cultivate.] Untilled; uncultivated.

in-cul′ti-vā-ted, *a.* Not cultivated; uncultivated.

in-cul-ti-vā′tion, *n.* Neglect or want of cultivation.

in-cul′tūre, *n.* Want or neglect of cultivation. [Obs.]

in-cum′ben-cy, *n.* 1. A lying or resting on something.

2. The state of holding or being in possession of a benefice, or of an office.

> There is no test of the tenure but *incumbency* on the part of the king. —E. Everett.

in-cum′bent, *a.* [L. *incumbens* (*-entis*), ppr. of *incumbere*, to lay oneself upon, recline or rest upon; *in*, on, and *cubare*, to lie down.]

1. Lying or resting on.

> And when to move the *incumbent* load they try. —Addison.

2. In botany, leaning on or resting against; as, *incumbent* stamens or anthers.

3. Lying on, as duty or obligation; imposed and emphatically urging or pressing to performance; used with *upon* or *on*; as, the duties *incumbent upon* a minister.

> All men, truly zealous, will perform those good works which are *incumbent on* all Christians. —Sprat.

4. In ornithology, said of the hind toe of a bird when it is on a level with the front toes, so that in walking its entire length touches the ground.

Syn.—Pressing, binding, coercive, urgent, devolving, obligatory.

in-cum′bent, *n.* The person who is in present possession of a benefice, or of any office.

in-cum′bent-ly, *adv.* In an incumbent manner.

in-cum′bẽr, *v.t.* Same as *Encumber*.

in-cum-bi′tion (-bish′un), *n.* The act of sitting or lying in close contact. [Rare.]

in-cum′brănce, *n.* See *Encumbrance*.

in-cum′brăn-cẽr, *n.* See *Encumbrancer*.

in-cum′brous, *a.* Cumbersome; troublesome. [Obs.]

in-cū-nab′ū-lum, *n.*; *pl.* **in-cū-nab′ū-lȧ.** [L. *incunabula*, neut. pl., swaddling-clothes, a cradle, origin, beginning; *in*, in, and *cunabula*, neut. pl., a cradle, dim. of *cunæ*, f. pl., a cradle.]

1. An object connected with the place of origin of a thing, as a cradle with the origin of a person; hence, the earliest home.

2. In ornithology, a place where birds breed.

3. In bibliography, a book printed in the earliest days of the art of printing, prior to the year 1500; used chiefly in the plural.

in-cŭr′, *v.t.*; incurred, *pt.*, *pp.*; incurring, *ppr.* [L. *incurrere*, to run into, or toward, attack; *in*, in, toward, and *currere*, to run.]

1. Literally, to run against; hence, to become liable to; to become subject to; as, a thief *incurs* the punishment of the law by the act of stealing, before he is convicted.

2. To bring on; as, to *incur* a debt; to *incur* guilt; to *incur* the displeasure of God; to *incur* blame or censure.

in-cŭr′, *v.i.* To happen; to go or come. [Obs.]

in-cŭr-ȧ-bil′i-ty, *n.* The state of being incurable; impossibility of cure; insusceptibility of cure or remedy.

in-cŭr′ȧ-ble, *a.* [OFr. *incurable*; LL. *incurabilis*, incurable; L. *in-* priv., and LL. *curabilis*, curable, from L. *curare*, to care for, to cure.]

1. That cannot be cured; not admitting of cure; beyond the power of skill or medicine; as, an *incurable* disease.

2. Not admitting remedy or correction; irremediable; remediless; as, *incurable* evils.

Syn.—Irremediable, irredeemable, remediless, irreparable, immedicable.

in-cŭr′ȧ-ble, *n.* A person diseased beyond the reach of cure.

in-cŭr′ȧ-ble-ness, *n.* The state of not admitting cure or remedy.

in-cŭr′ȧ-bly, *adv.* In a manner or degree that renders cure impracticable.

in-cū-ri-os′i-ty, *n.* Same as *Incuriousness*.

in-cū′ri-ous, *a.* [L. *incuriosus*, careless; *in-* priv., and *curiosus*, careful.] Destitute of curiosity; not curious or inquisitive; inattentive.

in-cū′ri-ous-ly, *adv.* Without inquisitiveness.

in-cū′ri-ous-ness, *n.* Want of curiosity or inquisitiveness.

in-cŭr′rence, *n.* The act of bringing on or subjecting oneself to; as, the *incurrence* of guilt.

in-cŭr′rent, *a.* [L. *incurrens* (*-entis*), ppr. of *incurrere*, to run into or upon; *in*, into, and *currere*, to run.] Characterized by running into; as, an *incurrent* flow of water into a river or a lagoon; an *incurrent* flow of blood into the heart.

in-cŭr′sion, *n.* [L. *incursio* (*-onis*), from *incurrere*, to run against or into.]

1. A running into; hence, an entering into a territory with hostile ntention; an inroad; applied to the expeditions of small parties or detachments of an enemy's army entering a territory for attack, plunder, or destruction of a post or magazine.

2. Attack; occurrence; as, sins of daily *incursion*. [Obs.]

in-cŭr′sive, *a.* Hostile; making an attack or incursion.

in-cŭr′tain, *v.t.* [Obs.] See *Curtain*.

in-cŭr′vāte, *v.t.*; incurvated, *pt.*, *pp.*; incurvating, *ppr.* [L. *incurvatus*, pp. of *incurvare*, to bend in, curve in; *in*, in, and *curvare*, to bend, curve.] To bend; to crook; to turn from a right line or straight course.

in-cŭr′vāte, *a.* Curved inward or upward.

in-cŭr-vā′tion, *n.* 1. The act of bending.

2. The state of being bent or turned from a rectilinear course; curvature; crookedness.

3. The act of bowing or bending the body in respect or reverence.

in-cŭrve′, *v.t.*; incurved, *pt.*, *pp.*; incurving, *ppr.* To bend; to make crooked.

in′cŭrve, *n.* In baseball, a curve given by the pitcher to a ball so that in passing it approaches the body of the batsman from the right or from the left.

in-cŭrved′, *a.* Bent; bent or curved inward.

in-cŭr′vi-ty, *n.* A state of being bent or crooked; crookedness; a bending inward.

in′cus, *n.* [L., an anvil, from *incusus*, pp. of *incudere*, to forge, strike upon.]

1. A blacksmith's anvil.

2. In anatomy, (a) a small bone in the middle ear, named from its resemblance to the shape of a blacksmith's anvil; (b) the middle part of the mastax of a rotifer.

in-cūse′, *a.* Made by stamping, as a figure on a coin.

in-cūse′, *v.t.*; incused, *pt.*, *pp.*; incusing, *ppr.* [L. *incusus*, pp. of *incudere*, to forge with a hammer, lit., to pound upon; *in*, in, on, and *cudere*, to strike, hit.] To make an impression in by stamping, as in a coin.

in′cut, *a.* Inserted by cutting in; applied, in printing, to notes placed in reserved spaces in the text instead of in the margin or at the bottom of the page.

in-cūte′, *v.t.* [Obs.] See *Incuse*.

in-cyst′, *v.t.* Same as *Encyst*.

in-cyst′ed, *a.* Same as *Encysted*.

Ind, *n.* A poetic abbreviation of *India*.

in′dȧ-gāte, *v.t.* To seek or search out. [Obs.]

in-dȧ-gā′tion, *n.* The act of searching; search; inquiry; examination. [Obs.]

in′dȧ-gā-tive, *a.* Of a searching character; inquiring. [Obs.]

in′dȧ-gā-tŏr, *n.* A searcher; one who seeks or inquires with diligence. [Obs.]

in-dam′āge, *v.t.* [Obs.] See *Endamage*.

in-dam′āged, *a.* Undamaged. [Obs.]

in-därt′, *v.t.*; indarted, *pt.*, *pp.*; indarting, *ppr.* To dart in; to thrust or strike in.

in′dȧ-zōl, *n.* [*Ind*ol, and *az*ote.] A crystalline nitrogenous compound, $C_7H_6N_2$, formed from a diazo-derivative of cinnamic acid by heating.

inde, *a.* Sky-blue. [Obs.]

in-dēar′, *v.t.* [Obs.] See *Endear*.

in-debt′ (-det′), *v.t.* To bring into debt; obsolete except in past participle, *indebted*.

in-debt′ed, *a.* [ME. *endetted*, from LL. *indebitatus*, pp. of *indebitare*, to charge with debt; L. *in*, in, and *debitum*, debt.]

1. Being in debt; having incurred a debt; held or obliged to pay; as, A is *indebted* to B in a large sum.

2. Obliged by something received, for which restitution or gratitude is due; as, we are *indebted* to our parents for their care of us in infancy and youth.

in-debt′ed-ness, *n.* The state of being indebted.

in-debt′ment, *n.* The state of being indebted.

in-dē′cence, *n.* [Obs.] See *Indecency*.

in-dē′cen-cy, *n.*; *pl.* **in-dē′cen-cies.** [Fr. *indecence*; L. *indecentia*, unbecomingness, indecency; from *indecens* (*-entis*), unbecoming, indecent; *in-* priv., and *decens* (*-entis*), decent.]

1. The state of being vulgar; wanting in modesty; obscenity in speech or in manner.

2. That which is not decent.

in-dē′cent, *a.* [L. *indecens* (*-entis*), unbecoming, indecent; *in-* priv., and *decens* (*-entis*), ppr. of *decet*, it becomes.] Not decent.

Syn.—Immodest, filthy, obscene, nasty, impure, foul, shameless, indecorous, unchaste, lewd.

in-dē′cent-ly, *adv.* In a manner to offend modesty or delicacy.

in-dē-cid′ū-āte, *a.* In biology, not deciduate as to the placenta; also, destitute (as in some mammals) of a decidua.

in-dē-cid′ū-ous, *a.* [L. *in-* priv., and *deciduus*, falling.] Not falling, as the leaves of a tree in autumn; lasting; evergreen.

in-dec′i-mȧ-ble, *a.* Not liable to the payment of tithes.

in-dē-ci′phẽr-ȧ-ble, *a.* That cannot be deciphered.

in-dē-ci′phẽr-ȧ-bly, *adv.* In a manner not decipherable.

in-dē-ci′sion (-sizh′un), *n.* Want of decision; want of settled purpose or of firmness in the determination of the will; a wavering of mind; irresolution.

in-dē-ci′sive, *a.* 1. Not decisive; not bringing to a final close or ultimate issue; as, an *indecisive* battle or engagement; an argument *indecisive* of the question.

2. Unsettled; wavering; vacillating; hesitating; as, an *indecisive* state of mind; an *indecisive* character.

in-dē-ci′sive-ly, *adv.* Without decision.

in-dē-ci′sive-ness, *n.* The state of being undecided; unsettled state; state of not being brought to a final issue.

in-dē-clin′ȧ-ble, *n.* A word that is not declinable.

in-dē-clin′ȧ-ble, *a.* [L. *indeclinabilis*, unchangeable, indeclinable; *in-* priv., and *declinabilis*, declinable.] Not declinable; not varied by terminations; as, *pondo*, in Latin, is an *indeclinable* noun.

in-dē-clin′ȧ-bly, *adv.* Without variation. In grammar, without change in endings.

in-dē-com-pōs′ȧ-ble, *a.* Not capable of decomposition, or of being resolved into the primary constituent elements.

in-dē-com-pōs′ȧ-ble-ness, *n.* Incapableness of decomposition.

in-dē-cō′rous (or in-dek′ō-), *a.* [LL. *indecorosus*; L. *indecorus*, unbecoming, inappropriate; *in-* priv., *decorus*, seemly, becoming, decorous.] Unbecoming; violating good manners; contrary to the established rules of good breeding, or to the forms of respect which age and station require.

in-dē-cō′rous-ly, *adv.* In an unbecoming manner.

in-dē-cō′rous-ness, *n.* Violation of good manners in words or behavior.

in-dē-cō′rum, *n.* [L., neut. of *indecorus*, unbecoming, indecorous.]

1. Impropriety of behavior; that in behavior or manners which violates the established rules of civility, or the duties of respect which age or station requires; an unbecoming action.

2. Any action in violation of the usages of good society.

in-deed′, *adv.* [ME. *indede*, in deed, in fact.] In

reality; in truth; in fact; used (a) emphatically; as, *indeed* he did enjoy it; (b) to denote a concession or admission; as, not so strong, *indeed*, but more active; (c) to denote surprise; as, *indeed!* I was not aware of it; (d) interrogatively, for the purpose of obtaining confirmation; as, *indeed?* did it actually occur? The two elements of the word are sometimes separated by *very*, making the statement more emphatic.

And *in very deed* for this cause have I raised thee up, for to shew in thee my power. —Ex. ix. 16.

in-dē-fat″i-gȧ-bil′i-ty, *n.* The state or quality of being indefatigable; persistency.

in-dē-fat′i-gȧ-ble, *a.* [L. *indefatigabilis*, that cannot be tired out; *in-* priv., and *defatigare*, to tire out, weary.] Not defatigable; incapable of being fatigued; not easily exhausted; not yielding to fatigue; unremitting in labor or effort; as, *indefatigable* exertions; *indefatigable* attendance or perseverance.

Upborne with *indefatigable* wings.—Milton.

Syn.—Untiring, unwearied, assiduous, persistent, sedulous, unremitting, persevering.

in-dē-fat′i-gȧ-ble-ness, *n.* Indefatigability.

in-dē-fat′i-gȧ-bly, *adv.* Without weariness; without yielding to fatigue.

in-dē-fat-i-gā′tion, *n.* Unweariedness. [Obs.]

in-dē-fēa-ṣi-bil′i-ty, *n.* The quality or state of being indefeasible; as, the *indefeasibility* of a title.

in-dē-fēa′ṣi-ble, *a.* Not defeasible; not to be defeated; not to be made void; as, an *indefeasible* estate.

in-dē-fēa′ṣi-ble-ness, *n.* Same as *Indefeasibility.*

in-dē-fēa′ṣi-bly, *adv.* In a manner not to be defeated or made void; in an indefeasible manner.

in-dē-fec̦t-i-bil′i-ty, *n.* The quality of being indefectible.

in-dē-fec̦t′i-ble, *a.* Unfailing; not defectible; not liable to defect, failure, or decay.

in-dē-fec̦t′ive, *a.* Not defective; perfect; complete.

in-dē-fēi′ṣi-ble, *a.* Indefeasible. [Obs.]

in-dē-fen-si-bil′i-ty, *n.* The quality or state of being indefensible.

in-dē-fen′si-ble, *a.* Not defensible; incapable of being defended, maintained, or justified; as, a military post may be *indefensible*; *indefensible* conduct.

in-dē-fen′si-ble-ness, *n.* Indefensibility.

in-dē-fen′si-bly, *adv.* In an indefensible manner.

in-dē-fen′sive, *a.* Having no defense. [Obs.]

in-dē-fi′cien-cy (-fish′en-), *n.* The quality of not being deficient. [Obs.]

in-dē-fi′cient, *a.* Not deficient. [Obs.]

in-dē-fin′ȧ-ble, *a.* Not definable; incapable of being defined; not susceptible of definition; inexplicable.

in-dē-fin′ȧ-bly, *adv.* So as not to be capable of definition; in an indefinable manner.

in-def′i-nite, *a.* [L. *indefinitus*, indefinite; *in-* priv., and *definitus*, pp. of *definire*, to limit, define.]

1. Not limited or defined; not determinate; not precise or certain; vague; as, an *indefinite* time; an *indefinite* number.

2. Having no certain limits; unlimited; as, *indefinite* space.

Though it is not infinite, it may be *indefinite.* —Spectator.

3. In botany, too numerous to be easily enumerated; uncertain; indeterminate; applied to the parts of a flower.

Indefinite article; see *Article*, n. 7.

Indefinite inflorescence; an inflorescence not terminated by a flower, the terminal bud going on to grow and continuing the stem indefinitely; called also *indeterminate inflorescence.*

Indefinite proposition; in logic, a proposition which has for its subject a common term without any sign to indicate distribution or nondistribution, as man is mortal.

Indefinite term; in logic, a privative or negative term, in respect of its not defining or marking out an object by a positive attribute, as an unorganized being.

Syn.—Unlimited, undefined, indeterminate, inexact, vague, uncertain, indistinct.

in-def′i-nite-ly, *adv.* In an indefinite manner; without any settled limitation; not precisely; not with certainty or precision; as, to use a word *indefinitely.*

in-def′i-nite-ness, *n.* The quality of being indefinite, undefined, unlimited, or not precise and certain.

in-dē-fin′i-tūde, *n.* 1. Indefiniteness; want of precision.

2. Number or quantity not limited by human understanding, though finite. [Obs.]

in-dē-his′cence, *n.* In botany, the property of being indehiscent.

in-dē-his′cent, *a.* In botany, not opening spontaneously at maturity, as a capsule.

in-del-ē-bil′i-ty, in-del′e-ble, etc. See *Indelibility*, etc.

in-dē-lec̦′tȧ-ble, *a.* Not delectable; unpleasant; unamiable.

in-dē-lib′ẽr-āte, *a.* Not deliberate; done or performed without deliberation or consideration; sudden; unpremeditated.

in-dē-lib′ẽr-ā-ted, *a.* Unpremeditated. [Obs.]

in-dē-lib′ẽr-āte-ly, *adv.* Without deliberation or premeditation.

in-dē-lib-ẽr-ā′tion, *n.* Want of deliberation.

in-del-i-bil′i-ty, in-del-ē-bil′i-ty, *n.* The quality of being indelible.

in-del′i-ble, in-del′e-ble, *a.* [L. *indelibilis*, imperishable; *in-* priv., and *delibilis*, perishable, from *delere*, to destroy.]

1. Not to be blotted out; incapable of being effaced or obliterated; as, *indelible* letters; *indelible* colors; an *indelible* impression on the mind.

2. Not to be annulled. [Rare.]

Syn.—Ineffaceable, persistent, permanent.

in-del′i-ble-ness, in-del′e-ble-ness, *n.* The quality of being indelible.

in-del′i-bly, in-del′e-bly, *adv.* In a manner not to be blotted out or effaced.

in-del′i-c̦ȧ-cy, *n.*; *pl.* **in-del′i-c̦ȧ-cieṣ.** The condition or quality of being indelicate; want of delicacy; rudeness; coarseness of manners or language; that which is offensive to refined taste or purity of mind.

in-del′i-c̦āte, *a.* Not delicate; wanting delicacy; offensive to good manners or to purity of mind; as, an *indelicate* expression; *indelicate* behavior; *indelicate* customs.

Syn.—Impolite, indecorous, unrefined, rude, immodest, unbecoming, coarse.

in-del′i-c̦āte-ly, *adv.* In an indelicate manner; indecently; unbecomingly.

in-dem″ni-fi-c̦ā′tion, *n.* 1. The act of indemnifying or securing against loss, damage, or penalty.

2. That which indemnifies; reimbursement.

in-dem′ni-fȳ, *v.t.*; indemnified, *pt.*, *pp.*; indemnifying, *ppr.* [L *indemnis*, unhurt, and *facere*, to make.]

1. To save harmless; to secure against loss, damage, or penalty.

2. To make good to; to reimburse; to compensate.

in-dem-ni-tee′, *n.* A person who receives or is to receive an indemnity.

in-dem′ni-tŏr, *n.* A person who indemnifies.

in-dem′ni-ty, *n.*; *pl.* **in-dem′ni-tieṣ.** [Fr. *indemnité*; LL *indemnitas*, security from loss or damage, from L. *indemnis*, unhurt; *in-* priv., and *damnum*, a hurt, damage.]

1. Security given against damage, loss, or injury; exemption from punishment.

2. Indemnification; compensation for loss, damage, or injury sustained; reimbursement.

They were told to expect, upon the fall of Walpole, a large and lucrative *indemnity* for their pretended wrongs.—Lord Mahon.

Act of indemnity; an act or decree for the protection or relief of a person, especially a public officer, who, by reason of having violated the law in some particular, is liable to a penalty.

in-dē-mon-strȧ-bil′i-ty, *n.* The condition or quality of being indemonstrable.

in-dē-mon′strȧ-ble, *a.* Not demonstrable; incapable of being demonstrated.

in-dē-mon′strȧ-ble-ness, *n.* The state of being indemonstrable.

in-den-i-zā′tion, *n.* Endenization.

in-den′īze, *v.t.* To endenize. [Obs.]

in-den′i-zen, *v.t.* Same as *Endenizen.*

in-dent′, *v.t.*; indented, *pt.*, *pp.*; indenting, *ppr.*; [LL. *indentare*, to notch, to make jagged like a row of teeth; L. *in*, in, and *dens*, *dentis*, a tooth.]

1. To notch; to jag; to cut into points or inequalities, like a row of teeth; as, to *indent* the edge of paper.

2. To bind out or apprentice by indenture or contract; as, to *indent* a young man to a shoemaker; to *indent* a servant.

3. To make a dent in; to dent.

The few last lines the parasol *indented* into the tablecloth. —Dickens.

4. In printing, to begin, as a line, farther in from the margin of the paper than the rest of the paragraph.

in-dent′, *v.i.* 1. To be cut or notched.

2. To contract; to bargain or covenant.

3. To run or wind in and out; to move in a zigzag course; to double. [Obs.]

in-dent′, *n.* 1. A cut or notch in the margin of anything, or a recess like a notch.

2. A stamp; an impression. [Obs.]

3. A certificate or indented certificate issued by the government of the United States at the close of the Revolution, for the principal or interest of the public debt.

4. In India, an order on the commissariat for supplies.

5. An indenture; an article of agreement.

in-den-tā′tion, *n.* 1. The act of indenting or the state of being indented.

2. A notch; a cut in the margin of anything.

3. A dent or depression.

4. In printing, same as *indention.*

in-dent′ed, *a.* 1. Cut in the edge into points like teeth; notched; as, an *indented* paper; an *indented* molding.

Indented Molding.

2. Indentured; as, an *indented* apprentice or servant.

3. In heraldry, notched like a saw; serrated.

4. In zoölogy, having variegated marginal colors.

in-dent′ed-ly, *adv.* With indentations.

in-den-tee′, *a.* In heraldry, having indents not joined to each other, but set apart.

Indentee, borderwise.

in-den-til′ly, *a.* In heraldry, having long indents, somewhat resembling piles conjoined; as, a fesse *indentilly* at the bottom.

in-dent′ing, *n.* An impression like that made by a tooth.

in-den′tion, *n.* 1. A depression; a dent.

2. In printing, the setting of a line or series of lines, as the first line of a paragraph, farther in from the margin than others.

Hanging indention; in printing, a uniform indention of every line of a paragraph except the first, which is of full width and overhangs the others.

Indentilly.

in-dent′ment, *n.* Indenture. [Obs.]

in-den′tūre, *n.* [OFr. *endenture*; LL. *indentura*, an indenture, from *indentare*, to indent; L. *in*, in, toward, and *dens*, *dentis*, tooth.]

1. The act of indenting or the state of being indented; indentation.

2. In law, a deed or written agreement between two or more parties. Indentures were formerly duplicates, laid together and indented or cut in a waving line, so that the two papers or parchments corresponded to each other. But indenting is often neglected, while the writings or counterparts retain the name of *indentures.*

in-den′tūre, *v.t.*; indentured, *pt.*, *pp.*; indenturing, *ppr.* 1. To bind by indentures; as, to *indenture* an apprentice.

2. To indent; to wrinkle; to furrow. [Obs.]

Though age may creep on, and *indenture* the brow. —Woty.

in-den′tūre, *v.i.* To run in a zigzag course; to double in running. [Obs.]

in-dē-pend′ence, *n.* 1. The state of being independent; complete exemption from dependence upon others; self-maintenance; self-government.

Let fortune do her worst, whatever she makes us lose, as long as she never makes us lose our honesty and our *independence.*—Pope.

2. That which renders one independent; property or income sufficient to make one independent of others.

Declaration of Independence; the declaration of the Congress of the United States of America, on July 4, 1776, by which they formally renounced their subjection to the government of Great Britain.

Independence day; see under *Day.*

in-dē-pend′en-cy, *n.* 1. Independence.

2. In theology, the principles of the religious body called Independents.

in-dē-pend′ent, *a.* [L. *in-* priv., and *dependens* (*-entis*), ppr. of *dependere*, to depend upon, lit., to hang down from.]

1. Not dependent; not relying on others; not subject to the control of others; not subordinate.

A dry but *independent* crust. —Cowper.

2. Affording the means of independence; as, an *independent* estate.

3. Not subject to bias or influence; not obsequious; self-directing; as, a man of an *independent* mind.

4. Free; easy; self-commanding; bold; unconstrained; as, an *independent* air or manner.

5. Separate from; exclusive.

A gradual change is also more beneficial, *independent* of its being more safe. —Brougham.

6. [I—] Pertaining to the Independents or Congregationalists.

7. In politics, not connected with any party; not obligated to vote for any particular party.

8. In mathematics, applied to a quantity or function that does not depend upon another for its value.

Syn.—Free, separate, unrestricted, exempt, unconstrained, uncontrolled, clear.

in-dē-pend′ent, *n.* 1. One who maintains that every congregation of Christians is a complete church, subject to no superior authority, and competent to perform every act of government in ecclesiastical affairs; in England, a Congregationalist.

2. [i—] In politics, one not associated with, or constrained to support, any particular party.

in-dē-pend′ent-ism, *n.* Same as *Independency,* 2.

in-dē-pend′ent-ly, *adv.* In an independent manner; without regard to connection with other things.

in-dep′rȧ-vāte, *a.* Undepraved. [Obs.]

in-dep′rē-ċȧ-ble, *a.* Incapable of being deprecated.

in-dep-rē-hen′si-ble, *a.* That cannot be found out.

in-dē-prīv′ȧ-ble, *a.* Incapable of being deprived; incapable of being taken away.

in-dē-scrīb′ȧ-ble, *a.* Not describable; incapable of being described.

Syn.—Inexplicable, inexpressible, ineffable, unutterable.

in-dē-scrīb′ȧ-bly, *adv.* In an indescribable manner.

in-dē-scrip′tive, *a.* Not descriptive or containing just description.

in-dē-sērt′, *n.* Want of merit or worth. [Rare.]

in-des′i-nent, *a.* [L. *in-* priv., and *desinens* (*-entis*), ppr. of *desinere,* to cease.] Not ceasing; perpetual. [Rare.]

in-des′i-nent-ly, *adv.* Without cessation. [Rare.]

in-dē-ṣīr′ȧ-ble, *a.* Undesirable.

in-dē-struċ-ti-bil′i-ty, *n.* The quality or condition of being indestructible.

in-dē-struċ′ti-ble, *a.* Not destructible; incapable of being destroyed.

in-dē-struċ′ti-ble-ness, *n.* Indestructibility.

in-dē-struċ′ti-bly, *adv.* In an indestructible manner.

in-dē-tēr′mi-nȧ-ble, *a.* [LL. *indeterminabilis,* that cannot be defined; L. *in-* priv., and LL. *determinabilis,* that can be defined, from L. *determinare,* to define, limit.]

1. That cannot be determined, ascertained, or fixed.

2. Not to be determined or ended. [Rare.]

in-dē-tēr′mi-nȧ-ble-ness, *n.* The quality of being indeterminable.

in-dē-tēr′mi-nȧ-bly, *adv.* In an indeterminable manner.

in-dē-tēr′mi-nāte, *a.* [LL. *indeterminatus;* L. *in-* priv., and *determinatus,* pp. of *determinare,* to define, determine.] Not determinate; not settled or fixed; uncertain; not precise; indefinite; as, an *indeterminate* number of years.

Indeterminate analysis; a branch of algebra in which there is always given a greater number of unknown quantities than of independent equations, by reason of which the number of solutions is indefinite.

Indeterminate coefficients; in mathematics, a method of analysis invented by Descartes, the principle of which consists in this, that if we have an equation of this form:

$$A+Bx+Cx^2+Dx^3+\text{etc.}=0,$$

in which the coefficients A, B, C are constant, and x a variable which may be supposed as small as we please, each of these coefficients, taken separately, is necessarily equal to 0.

Indeterminate inflorescence; same as *Indefinite inflorescence* under *Indefinite.*

Indeterminate problem; in mathematics, a problem which admits of an infinite number of solutions, or one in which there are fewer imposed conditions than there are unknown or required results.

Indeterminate quantity; in mathematics, a quantity which has no fixed value, but which may be varied in accordance with any proposed condition.

Indeterminate series; in mathematics, a series whose terms proceed by the powers of an indeterminate quantity.

in-dē-tēr′mi-nāte-ly, *adv.* In an indeterminate manner; indefinitely.

in-dē-tēr′mi-nāte-ness, *n.* Indefiniteness; want of certain limits; want of precision.

in-dē-tēr-mi-nā′tion, *n.* 1. Want of determination; an unsettled or wavering state, as of the mind.

2. Want of fixed or stated direction.

in-dē-tēr′mined, *a.* Undetermined; unsettled; unfixed.

in-dē-tēr′min-iṣm, *n.* In metaphysics, the doctrine that the will is not wholly governed by motives, but has a certain freedom of action; opposed to *determinism.*

in-dē-vōte′, *a.* Not devout. [Obs.]

in-dē-vōt′ed, *a.* Not devoted. [Obs.]

in-dē-vō′tion, *n.* Want of devotion; absence of devout affections.

in-dē-vout′, *a.* Irreligious; not having devout affections.

in-dē-vout′ly, *adv.* Without devotion.

in′dex, *n.; pl.* **in′dex-eṣ** or **in′di-cēṣ.** [L. *index, indicis,* an informer, discoverer, that which points out, a title, index, from *indicare,* to point out, indicate; *in,* in, to, and *dicare,* to declare.]

1. That which points out; that which shows or manifests.

2. The hand, bar, or needle that points to anything, as the hour of the day, the road to a place, etc.; in printing, the picture of a hand (☞) directing special attention to a statement.

3. A table of the contents of a book; a table of references in alphabetical order.

4. In anatomy, the forefinger or pointing-finger.

5. In arithmetic and algebra, the figure or letter which shows to what power any quantity is involved; the exponent.

6. In music, a direct.

7. [I—] In the Roman Catholic church, the Index Expurgatorius.

Dental index; in craniometry, the ratio between the distance from basion to nasion and the distance from the anterior surface of the first premolar to the posterior surface of the last molar.

Index Expurgatorius; in the Roman Catholic church, a catalogue of books that may not be read unless the objectionable parts have been expurgated.

Index of a logarithm; the characteristic or integral part of a logarithm, which precedes it and is always one less than the number of integral figures in the given number.

Index of refraction; in optics, the ratio of the sine of the angle of incidence to the sine of the angle of refraction when light is transmitted through a refracting substance.

Index Prohibitorum; in the Roman Catholic church, a catalogue of books the reading of which is unreservedly prohibited.

Index rerum; an alphabetical index of topics, memoranda, occurrences, etc., kept for the purpose of ready reference.

in′dex, *v.t.;* indexed (-dext), *pt., pp.;* indexing, *ppr.* To provide with an index or table of references; to place in an index; as, to *index* a book.

in′dex-ēr, *n.* One who makes an index.

in′dex-er″rŏr, *n.* In physical measurements, a constant error arising from the inaccurate adjustment of the index before taking measurements, to be added to or deducted from (as the case may be) all readings taken.

in′dex-fin″gēr, *n.* The forefinger.

in′dex-glȧss, *n.* The mirror attached to the index of a quadrant or a sextant.

in′dex-hand, *n.* A pointer attached to the mechanism of a watch, clock, or any instrument having a dial or graduated arc or scale for measuring.

in-dex′iċ-ăl, *a.* Having the form of an index; pertaining to an index.

in-dex′iċ-ăl-ly, *adv.* In the manner of an index.

in′dex-plāte, *n.* In mechanics, a circular steel plate with holes in it, used for graduating circles or for subdividing wheels for gear-cutting; called also *division-plate.*

in-dex-ter′i-ty, *n.* Want of dexterity or readiness in the use of the hands; clumsiness; awkwardness.

In′di-ȧ, *a.* [L. *India;* Gr. *India,* India, from *Indos,* the Indus river.] Pertaining to India; Indian; made in or connected with India; attributive use of the name of an Asiatic country.

India ink; a kind of ink or paint for water-color work, made in China and Japan from fine lampblack and gelatin, perfumed and pressed into cakes or sticks; called also *China ink.*

India matting; a kind of matting made in China and India of grass and reeds.

India paper; a soft thin paper of a light buff color, made in China, Japan, etc., and used for taking the first or finest impressions of engravings.

India proof; a proof taken from an engraved block or plate upon India paper.

India silk; a thin silk fabric woven like cambric.

in-dī′ȧ-dem, *v.t.* To place or set in a diadem; to adorn a diadem with; as, to *indiadem* a precious stone. [Rare.]

In′di-ȧ-măn, *n.; pl.* **In′di-ȧ-men.** A large ship employed in the India trade.

In′di-ăn, *n.* 1. One of the aborigines of North or South America; so named by Columbus and others who regarded the lands in the New World discovered by them as part of the Indies.

2. An East Indian native or inhabitant.

In′di-ăn, *a.* [LL. *Indianus,* from L. *India;* Gr. *India,* India, from *Indos,* L. *Indus,* the Indus river, from Sans. *sindhu,* a river.] Pertaining to India, to either of the Indies, East or West, or to the aborigines of America.

Indian architecture; the architecture peculiar to India or Hindustan, comprehending a variety of styles, as the Buddhist, the Jain, the Dravidian, the northern Hindu, the Chalukyan, the modern Hindu or Mohammedan, etc. Among the most remarkable of the works of Indian architecture are the rock-cut temples, such as at Ellora. In decoration there is no trace of what may be called order. Among the

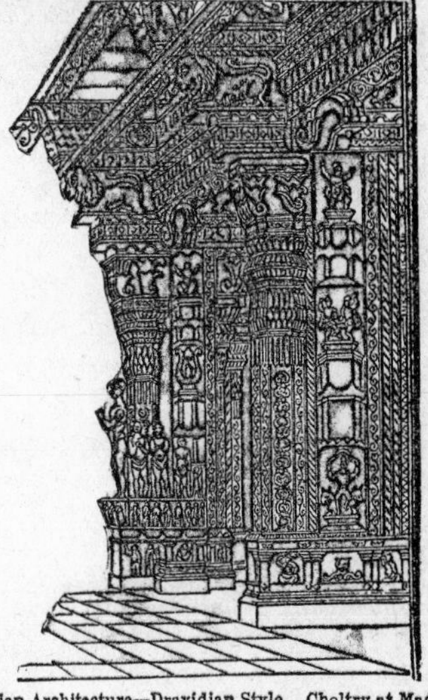

Indian Architecture—Dravidian Style. Choltry at Madura.

larger masses of decorations for support, sculptured elephants and lions frequently occur, as may be seen by the accompanying illustration of a portion of the choltry or pillared hall at Madura.

Indian bay; in botany, *Persea Indica,* a plant of the same genus as the Carolina red bay.

Indian bean; in botany, a name of the catalpa; so called from the shape of its pods.

Indian berry; in botany, *Anamirta paniculata,* of the moonseed family.

Indian bread; (a) same as *Cassava;* (b) corn bread.

Indian clubs; a pair of wooden clubs used in exercising the arms.

Indian cordage; a kind of rope made from the fiber of the husk of the cocoanut.

Indian corn; see under *Corn.*

Indian cress; in botany, the nasturtium, *Tropæolum majus.*

Indian cucumber; in botany, a plant of the lily family, *Medeola Virginiana,* having a tuberous white horizontal rootstock with the taste of a cucumber.

Indian currant; in botany, a shrub, *Symphoricarpus vulgaris,* of the honeysuckle family, bearing small dark-red berries resembling currants.

Indian fig; see under *Fig.*

Indian file; see under *File.*

Indian fire; a composition of sulphur, niter, and arsenic sulphid, giving a brilliant white light and used in fireworks.

Indian grass; in botany, a kind of coarse grass, *Chrysopogon nutans,* resembling broom-corn and yielding seeds which are sometimes used as a substitute for chocolate.

Indian hemp; in botany, a plant, *Apocynum cannabinum,* of the dogbane family, characterized by its milky acrid juice and the toughness of its bark.

Indian jalap; a jalap made from the *Ipomæa Turpethum* of East India.

Indian mallow; a plant, *Abutilon Avicennæ,* of the mallow family, with soft velvety leaves and small orange-yellow flowers.

Indian meal; corn-meal.

Indian-meal moth; same as *Meal-moth.*

Indian millet; a tall grass, *Sorghum vulgare,* a variety of which is used for making syrup and sugar.

Indian ox; same as *Zebu.*

Indian paint; the juice of the *Sanguinaria Canadensis,* or bloodroot.

Indian paper; same as *India paper.*

Indian physic; in botany, a plant of the rose family, embracing two species, *Gillenia trifoliata,* or Bowman's-root, and *Gillenia stipulacea,* or American ipecac.

Indian pink; in botany, (a) a plant (*Ipomæa Quamoclit*) of the *Convolvulaceæ,* native in tropical America but now generally naturalized, characterized by its red or crimson flowers; the cypress-vine; (b) the China pink, *Dianthus Chinensis,* characterized by large toothed petals of various colors.

Indian pipe; in botany, a plant (*Monotropa uniflora*) of the heath family, growing in dark rich woods, and characterized by a waxy-white stem and leaves and a single nodding flower of five petals and ten stamens.

Indian plantain; in botany, any one of the species of *Cacalia,* a plant of the composite family, native in rich soils and bearing corymbose heads of white or whitish flowers.

Indian poke; in botany, a plant (*Veratrum viride*) of the lily family, having yellowish-green flowers turning greener with age; the American white hellebore.

Indian pudding; a steamed pudding made of Indian meal, molasses, milk, etc., highly esteemed in New England.

Indian red; a red pigment found in natural soils but now made artificially of the red oxid of iron; called also *Persian red* from its having been at first imported from Persia.

Indian reed; same as *Indian shot*.

Indian rice; in botany, *Zizania aquatica*, or water-oats, a tall and reed-like grass whose seeds were used by American Indians for food.

Indian shot; in botany, a plant (*Canna Indica*) of the arrowroot family, cultivated for the beauty of its flowers and foliage; named from its hard shot-like seeds.

Fruit of *Canna Indica* (Indian Shot).

Indian soap; in botany, any tree of the genus *Sapindus* (*sapo Indus*, Indian soap), the fruit of which is used as a substitute for soap; the soapberry tree.

Indian summer; a period of the autumn season in the United States characterized by a dry hazy atmosphere and the absence of violent winds.

Indian tobacco; in botany, the *Lobelia inflata*, a plant common in fields in North America.

Indian turnip; in botany, a plant (*Arisæma triphyllum*) of the order *Araceæ*, commonly called jack-in-the-pulpit, whose farinaceous corm contains an intensely pungent juice.

Indian wheat; see *Indian corn* under *Corn*.

Indian yellow; a pigment of a deep yellow color said to be derived from the urine of herbivorous animals.

In″di-ăn-eer′, *n*. An Indiaman. [Rare.]

In′di-ăn-ist, *n*. A specialist in the history and languages of India.

in′di-ăn-ite, *n*. A doubtful mineral of the feldspar family, found in the gangue of corundum.

In″di-ăn-ol′ō-gist, *n*. [LL. *Indianus*, Indian, and Gr. *logos*, a description, from *legein*, to speak.] A specialist in the language and customs of the North American Indian.

in′di-ă-rub″bẽr, *n*. An elastic substance obtained by the inspissation of the juicy exudations from various trees of the tropical regions; gum elastic; caoutchouc.

India-rubber tree; any tree whose exudations yield india-rubber; specifically, the *Ficus elastica* of the East Indies, widely cultivated for the beauty of its thick, smooth, bright green, glossy leaves.

In′dic, *a*. Relating to India or to its people, languages, customs, etc.

in′dic-ăl, *a*. Pertaining to indexes. [Rare.]

in′di-căn, *n*. [From L. *indicum*, indigo, and *-an*.]

1. In chemistry, a syrupy substance ($C_{26}H_{31}NO_{17}$) obtained from several indigo-bearing plants and upon decomposition yielding natural indigo.

2. In physiological chemistry, a substance ($C_8H_6NSO_4K$) contained in urine and other animal liquids and convertible into indigo; potassium indoxyl sulphate.

in′di-cănt, *a*. [L. *indicans* (*-antis*), ppr. of *indicare*, to point out, indicate.] Pointing out what is to be done for the cure of disease.

in′di-cănt, *n*. Anything that points out or indicates, as a remedy for a disease.

in′di-cāte, *v.t.*; indicated, *pt.*, *pp.*; indicating, *ppr.* [L. *indicatus*, pp. of *indicare*, to show, indicate; *in*, in, to, and *dicare*, to point out, declare.]

1. To show; to point out; to discover; to direct the mind to a knowledge of something not seen, or something that will probably occur in future; as, fermentation *indicates* a certain degree of heat in a liquor.

2. To tell; to disclose.

3. In medicine, to show or manifest by symptoms; to point to as the proper remedies; as, great prostration of strength *indicates* the use of stimulants.

4. In machinery, to test; as, to *indicate* the capacity of a fire-engine or a dynamo.

Syn.—Designate, denote, show, mark, reveal, evidence, manifest, disclose, mark, tell, testify.

in′di-cā-ted, *a*. Manifested by an indicator.

Indicated horse-power; see under *Horse-power*.

in-di-cā′tion, *n*. [L. *indicatio* (*-onis*), from *indicare*, to point out, indicate.]

1. The act of pointing out.

2. Mark; token; sign; symptom; whatever serves to discover what is not before known, or otherwise obvious.

> The frequent stops they make in the most convenient places are plain *indications* of their weariness. —Addison.

3. In medicine, any symptom or occurrence in a disease, which serves to direct to suitable remedies.

4. Discovery made; intelligence given.

5. Explanation; display. [Obs.]

in-dic′ā-tive, *a*. [LL. *indicativus*; L. *indicare*, to point out, indicate.]

1. Showing; giving intimation or knowledge of something not visible or obvious; as, reserve is not always *indicative* of modesty; it may be *indicative* of prudence.

2. In grammar, designating the mode or form of the verb that indicates, that is, which affirms or denies; as, he writes; he is writing; they run; has the mail arrived?

3. In the fine arts, suggestive or symbolic, as representing an army by a soldier in arms or a nation by its flag.

in-dic′ā-tive, *n*. In grammar, the indicating or declaring mode.

in-dic′ā-tive-ly, *adv*. In a manner to show or signify.

in′di-cā-tōr, *n*. [LL. *indicator*, one who points out, from L. *indicare*, to point out, indicate.]

1. He who or that which shows or points out.

2. In machinery, any device or apparatus used to indicate pressure, speed, energy, rate of output, chemical characteristic, direction of wind, etc.

3. An instrument which registers the pressure in the cylinder of a steam-engine at every instant during the stroke of the piston, the pressure being admitted to the instrument and exerted upon a piston with a lever-index supplied with a stylus which rests against a sheet of paper or a card wrapped upon a rotating hollow cylinder.

Richard's Indicator.

4. An instrument attached to a telegraph line which indicates a message by means of a hand and a dial or face containing letters and symbols.

5. A steam-gauge attached to the boiler of a steam-engine to indicate at all times the state of tension of the steam being used.

Telegraph Indicator.

6. An attachment to machinery for counting and recording revolutions or strokes; as, an *indicator* of the number of strokes of a pump, or the number of rotations of a bicycle wheel.

7. In microscopy, a pointer or index attached to or near the eyepiece for the purpose of locating an object in the field.

8. In chemistry, any substance or device for indicating the character of a substance, as litmus for determining acidity or alkalinity.

9. In ornithology, the name of a bird and of its genus. [See *Honey-guide*.]

Indicator telegraph; a telegraph whose signals consist in movements of a needle over the face of a dial-plate.

in′di-cā-tōr-cärd, *n*. A card which contains the record made by an indicator of pressure in the cylinder of a steam-engine. [See *Indicator*, 3.]

in′di-cā-tōr-dī′ā-gram, *n*. See *Indicator-card*.

in′di-cā-tō-ry, *a*. Showing; serving to show or make known.

in-di-cā′trix, *n*. 1. In geometry, a curve made by a surface intersecting a plane infinitesimally near to and parallel with a tangent plane.

2. In crystallography, an ellipsoid assumed for the purpose of determining the optical structure of a crystal.

in-di-cā′vit, *n*. [L., lit., he has shown, 3rd pers. sing. perf. ind. act. of *indicare*, to show, indicate.] In English law, a writ of prohibition which lies for the patron of a church whose incumbent is sued in the spiritual court by another clergyman, for tithes amounting to a fourth part of the profits of the advowson. —Blackstone.

in′dice, *n*. [Obs.] See *Index*.

in′di-cēs, *n.*, pl. of *index*; used in mathematics and physical science.

in-di′ci-ă (-dish′i-), *n.pl.* [L., pl. of *indicium*, a notice, mark, disclosure, discovery, from *index* (*-icis*), an informer, sign, mark.] In law, marks which serve to point out, show, or discriminate.

in-dic′i-ble, *a*. That cannot be spoken or expressed. [Obs.]

in-dig′ō-lite, *n*. [Gr. *indikon*, indigo, and *lithos*, stone.] In mineralogy, a variety of shorl or tourmalin, of an indigo-blue color, sometimes with a tinge of azure or green.

in-dict′ (-dīte′), *v.t.*; indicted, *pt.*, *pp.*; indicting, *ppr.* [OFr. *enditer*, to accuse, point out, from L. *indicare*, to declare, proclaim, freq. of *indicere*, to declare, accuse; *in*, in, and *dicere*, to speak.]

1. In law, to accuse or charge with a crime or misdemeanor, in writing, by a grand jury under oath; as, to *indict* a person for the crime of murder. It is the peculiar province of a grand jury to *indict*, as it is of a house of representatives to *impeach*.

2. An obsolete form of *indite*.

3. To announce in public. [Obs.]

in-dict′ā-ble (-dīt′), *a*. 1. That may be indicted; as, an *indictable* offender.

2. Subject to be presented by a grand jury; subject to indictment; as, an *indictable* offense.

in-dict-ee′, *n*. A person indicted.

in-dict′ẽr, *n*. One who indicts.

in-dic′tion, *n*. [LL. *indictio* (*-onis*), a space of fifteen years; L., a proclamation of the imposition of a tax, from *indicere*, to declare, proclaim.]

1. Declaration; proclamation.

2. In chronology, a cycle of fifteen years, instituted by Constantine the Great; originally a period of taxation. Constantine, having reduced the time which the Romans were obliged to serve in the army to fifteen years, imposed a tax or tribute at the end of that term, to pay the troops discharged. This practice introduced the keeping of accounts by this period. But, as it is said, in honor of the great victory of Constantine over Mezentius, September 24, A. D. 312, by which Christianity was more effectually established, the council of Nice ordained that accounts of years should no longer be kept by Olympiads, but that the indiction should be used as the point from which to reckon and date years. This was begun January 1, A. D. 313.

in-dic′tive, *a*. [LL. *indictivus*, from L. *indictus*, pp. of *indicere*, to declare.] Proclaimed; declared.

in-dict′ment (-dīte′), *n*. 1. In law, a written accusation or formal charge of a crime or misdemeanor, preferred to a court by a grand jury under oath; also, the paper or parchment containing the accusation of a grand jury.

2. The condition of being indicted; as, the prisoner is under *indictment* for murder.

3. Any formal charge of crime.

Bill of indictment; see under *Bill*.

in-dict′ŏr, *n*. In law, the person who presents an indictment.

In′dieṣ, *n.pl.* All the countries bearing the name of India or Indies; the East and West Indies.

in-dif′fẽr-ence, *n*. [Fr. *indifférence*; L. *indifferentia*, from *indifferens* (*-entis*), indifferent, careless.]

1. Equipoise; neutrality of mind between different persons or things; a state in which the mind is not inclined to one side more than to the other; as, to view a contest of parties with *indifference*.

2. Impartiality; freedom from prejudice, prepossession, or bias; as, to read a book on controverted points with *indifference*.

3. Mediocrity.

4. A state in which there is no difference, or in which no moral or physical reason preponderates; as, the *indifference* of things in themselves.

Syn.—Insensibility, apathy, unconcern, disinterestedness, impartiality, lukewarmness.—*Indifference* is a partial state of the mind; *insensibility* and *apathy* are general states; *indifference* is either acquired or accidental; *insensibility* is either produced or natural; *apathy* is natural.

in-dif′fẽr-en-cy, *n*. Same as *Indifference*.

in-dif′fẽr-ent, *a*. [OFr. *indifferent*; L. *indifferens* (*-entis*), indifferent, careless; *in-* priv., and *differens* (*-entis*), different, ppr. of *differre*, to carry asunder, to differ; *dis-*, apart, and *ferre*, to carry.]

1. Neutral; not inclined to one side, party, or thing more than to another.

> Cato knows neither of them,
> *Indifferent* in his choice to sleep or die.
> —Addison.

2. Unconcerned; feeling no interest, anxiety, or care respecting anything; as, it seems to be impossible that a rational being should be *indifferent* to the means of obtaining endless happiness.

> It was a remarkable law of Solon, that any person, who, in the commotions of the republic, remained neuter, or an *indifferent* spectator of the contending parties, should be condemned to perpetual banishment. —Addison.

3. Having no influence or preponderating weight; having no difference that gives a preference; as, it is *indifferent* which road we take.

4. In law, impartial; disinterested; without prejudice; as, an *indifferent* judge, juror, or arbitrator.

5. Passable; of a middling state or quality; neither good nor very bad; as, *indifferent* writing or paper.

Indifferent tissue; in anatomy, tissue in a primitive condition, not yet having developed into any characteristic form; embryonic tissue.

Syn.—Neutral, unconcerned, apathetic, disinterested, regardless.

in-dif′fẽr-ent, *adv.* [Obs.] See *Indifferently.*

in-dif′fẽr-ent-iṣm, *n.* 1. The state of being indifferent.

2. The attitude of mind which perceives or acknowledges no difference between the true and the false in religion or philosophy; a kind of agnosticism.

3. In metaphysics, the doctrine of absolute identity.

4. In the Roman Catholic church, a heresy in any one who is indifferent to a creed, while insisting on morality.

in-dif′fẽr-ent-ist, *n.* Generally, one who is indifferent; specifically, a believer in and advocate of the doctrines of indifferentism.

in-dif′fẽr-ent-ly, *adv.* 1. Without distinction or preference; as, to offer pardon *indifferently* to all.

2. Equally; impartially; without favor, prejudice, or bias.

3. In a neutral state; without concern; without wish or aversion.

> Set honor in one eye and death i' the other,
> And I will look on death *indifferently.*—Shak.

4. Not well; tolerably; passably; as, *indifferently* well; to be *indifferently* entertained.

in-di-fụl′vin, *n.* [L. *indicum*, indigo, and *fulvus*, of a reddish yellow.] In chemistry, a reddish-yellow resin derived from indican.

in-di-fus′cin, *n.* [L. *indicum*, indigo, and *fuscus*, dusky, and *-in.*] In chemistry, a dusky compound, $C_{24}H_{20}N_2O_9$, derived from indican.

in′di-ġeen, *n.* Same as *Idigene.*

in′di-ġence, *n.* [Fr. *indigence*; L. *indigentia*, need, want, from *indigens* (*-entis*), needy, ppr. of *indigere*, to need; Old L. *indu*; L. *in*, in, and *egere*, to need.] Want of estate, or means of comfortable subsistence; penury; poverty; as, many of the human race live in *indigence.*

Syn.—Poverty, want, need, penury, destitution, privation.—*Poverty* is generic, denoting a deficiency in the means of living; *indigence* is stronger, implying an absence of the necessaries of life. *Want* and *need* are applied usually to temporary conditions, but are sometimes used in a more abstract sense, as a state of *want* or of *need*, being then identical with *poverty.*

in′di-ġen-cy, *n.* Same as *Indigence.*

in′di-ġēne, *n.* [L. *indigena*, a native.] One born in a country; a native animal or plant.

in-diġ′e-nous, *a.* [LL. *indigenus*; L. *indigena*, born in a country, native, from Old L. *indu*; L. *in*, within, and *gignere*, to bear, produce.] Native; born in a country; produced naturally in a country or climate; not exotic; as, corn and cotton are *indigenous* in North America.

Syn.—Original, native, aboriginal.

in′di-ġent, *a.* [Fr. *indigent*; L. *indigens* (*-entis*), in need; Old L. *indu*; L. *in*, in, and *egere*, to need.]

1. Destitute of property or means of comfortable subsistence; needy; poor.

> Charity consists in relieving the *indigent.*
> —Addison.

2. Not possessing; being without. [Obs.]

in′di-ġent-ly, *adv.* In an indigent, destitute manner.

in-di-ġest′, *n.* A crude mass. [Obs.]

in-di-ġest′, *a.* Without organization; not matured or digested; chaotic. [Obs.]

in-di-ġest′ed, *a.* [L. *indigestus*, unarranged, without order; *in-* priv., and *digestus*, pp. of *digerere*, to distribute, arrange.]

1. Not digested; not changed or prepared for nourishing the body; undigested; crude.

2. Not separated into distinct classes or orders, or into proper form; not regularly disposed and arranged; not methodized; not reduced to due form; crude; as, an *indigested* scheme.

3. Not prepared by heat; uncooked.

4. In medicine, not brought to suppuration, as the contents of an abscess or boil; not in a condition ready for healing; as, an *indigested* wound.

in-di-ġest′ed-ness, *n.* The condition or quality of not being digested; unfitness.

in-di-ġest-i-bil′i-ty, *n.* The condition or quality of not being digestible; crudeness; unfitness.

in-di-ġest′i-ble, *a.* [Fr. *indigestible*; LL. *indigestibilis*; L. *in-* priv., and LL. *digestibilis*, digestible, from L. *digerere*, to arrange, digest.]

1. Not digestible; not easily digested.

2. Not to be received or patiently endured; intolerable; incomprehensible; as, an *indigestible* story.

> Such a torrent of *indigestible* similes.
> —Wharton.

in-di-ġest′i-ble-ness, *n.* Indigestibility.

in-di-ġest′i-bly, *adv.* Not digestibly.

in-di-ġes′tion (-chun), *n.* [LL. *indigestio* (*-onis*); L. *in-* priv., and LL. *digestio* (*-onis*), digestion, from L. *digestus*, pp. of *digerere*, to arrange, digest.] Want of digestion; incapability of or difficulty in digesting food; dyspepsia.

in-di-ġest′ive, *a.* Dyspeptic; afflicted with indigestion.

in-diġ′i-tāte, *v.i.* To communicate ideas by the fingers; to show or compute by the fingers. [Obs.]

in-diġ′i-tāte, *v.t.* To point out with the finger. [Obs.]

in-diġ-i-tā′tion, *n.* The act of pointing out with the finger; indication. [Obs.]

in-di-glū′cin, *n.* [Gr. *indikon*, indigo, and *glykys*, sweet.] A sugar-like compound, $C_6H_{10}O_6$, obtained from indican.

in-dīgn′ (-dīn′), *a.* Unworthy; disgraceful. [Obs.]

in-dig′nănce, *n.* Indignation. [Obs.]

in-dig′năn-cy, *n.* Indignation. [Obs.]

in-dig′nănt, *a.* [L. *indignans* (*-antis*), ppr. of *indignari*, to consider as unworthy or improper, to be displeased at; *in-* priv., and *dignari*, to deem worthy, from *dignus*, worthy.] Affected with indignation; feeling the mingled emotions of anger and scorn or contempt, as when a person is exasperated by a mean action; incensed.

> Sought, with an *indignant* mien, counsel of her country's gods. —Cowper.

Syn.—Incensed, exasperated, provoked, irate.

in-dig′nănt-ly, *adv.* In an indignant manner.

in-dig-nā′tion, *n.* [OFr. *indignation*; L. *indignatio* (*-onis*), displeasure, indignation, from *indignari*, to consider as unworthy, to be indignant.]

1. Anger or extreme anger mingled with contempt, disgust, or abhorrence, caused by disapprobation of something mean, disgraceful, or unjust.

> And when the ten heard it, they were moved with *indignation* against the two brethren.
> —Matt. xx. 24.

2. The effects of anger as manifested in judgment or punishment.

> O, let them (the heavens) hurl down their *indignation.* —Shak.

Indignation meeting; a public meeting convened for the purpose of giving formal expression to indignation against something done or proposed to be done.

Syn.—Anger, resentment, wrath, ire, displeasure, scorn, fury.

in-dig′ni-fȳ, *v.t.* To treat disdainfully, unbecomingly, or unworthily. [Obs.]

in-dig′ni-ty, *n.*; *pl.* **in-dig′ni-tieṣ.** [L. *indignitas*, unworthiness, vileness, unbecoming behavior, from *indignus*, unworthy; *in-* priv., and *dignus*, worthy.] Unmerited contemptuous conduct toward another; any action toward another which manifests contempt for him; contumely; incivility or injury, accompanied with insult.

Syn.—Insult, affront, disrespect, contumely, dishonor.

in-dīgn′ly (-dīn′), *adv.* Unworthily. [Obs.]

in′di-gō, *n.*; *pl.* **in′di-gōeṣ.** [Sp. *indigo*; L. *indicum*, indigo; Gr. *indikon* (supply *pharmakon*, dye), indigo, lit., Indian dye, from *Indikos*, Indian, from *India*, India.]

1. A deep blue, or violet-blue; one of the seven primary colors.

2. A blue pigment, $C_{16}H_{10}N_2O_2$, formed by the decomposition of the indican contained in various leguminous plants of the genus *Indigofera.* The plant is bruised and fermented in vats of water, during which it deposits a blue powder, which is collected and dried in the form of the cubic cakes seen in commerce. In this state it has an intensely blue color and earthy fracture, the kind most esteemed being that which, when rubbed by a hard body, assumes a fine copper-red polish. Indigo is extensively used as a blue dye.

Bastard indigo; see *False indigo* (a).

Chinese indigo; a cruciferous plant, *Isatis indigotica*, of North China.

Egyptian indigo; a leguminous plant, *Tephrosia Apollinea*, a native of Egypt. It is narcotic, and yields a fine blue dye. The leaves are occasionally mixed with Alexandrian senna, and the plant is commonly cultivated in Nubia for its indigo.

False indigo; (a) *Amorpha fruticosa*, an American shrub of the bean family; (b) an American plant, *Baptisia australis*, of the bean family; called also *wild indigo* and *blue false indigo.*

Indigo blue; the blue coloring-matter, $C_{16}H_{10}N_2O_2$, of indigo; it forms fine right rhombic prisms, which have a blue color and a metallic luster; called also *indigotin.*

Indigo brown; a brown resinous substance obtained by treating an aqueous solution of indican with heat and acid.

Indigo carmine; a dyestuff obtained by treating indigo with sulphuric acid.

Indigo white; a compound, $C_{16}H_{12}N_2O_2$, obtained by subjecting commercial indigo to the action of reducing agents, such as alkaline fluids containing sulphate of iron, or a mixture of grape-sugar, alcohol, and strong soda lye; called also *indigogen.*

in′di-gō-ber″ry, *n.* The fruit of *Randia aculeata*, a rubiaceous shrub of the West Indies, yielding a blue dye.

in′di-gō-bird, *n.* A North American finch, *Cyanospiza* or *Passerina cyanea*, of a deep blue color; it is a sweet singer and a favorite cage-bird.

in′di-gō-cop″pẽr, *n.* Covellin.

in-di-gof′e-rȧ, *n.* [*Indigo*, and L. *ferre*, to bear.] A large genus of leguminous plants, including about 220 species, indigenous in the warmer parts of Asia, Africa, and America. Some of the species yield indigo.

in′di-gō-ġen, in′di-gō-ġēne, *n.* Same as *Indigo white* under *Indigo.*

in-dig′ō-lite (*or* in′di-), *n.* Same as *Indicolite.*

in-di-gom′e-tẽr, *n.* [*Indigo*, and Gr. *metron*, a measure.] An instrument for showing the strength of an indigo solution.

in-di-gom′e-try, *n.* The art or method of determining the coloring power of indigo.

in′di-gō-plant, *n.* A plant of the genus *Indigofera*, from which indigo is obtained. The species most commonly cultivated under this name is *Indigofera tinctoria*, a native of the East Indies and other parts of Asia, and grown in many parts of Africa and America. It is a shrubby plant about three or four feet high, with narrow pinnate leaves and long narrow pods. The West Indian indigo is *Indigofera Anil*, a short-podded plant, native of the West Indies and the warmer parts of America, and cultivated in Asia and Africa. Both are extensively grown for making indigo.

Indigo-plant (*Indigofera tinctoria*).

in′di-gō-snāke, *n.* The gopher-snake, *Spilotes couperi.*

in′di-gō-tāte, *n.* [*Indigotic* and *-ate.*] A compound of indigotic acid with a salifiable base or metallic oxid; as, *indigotate* of ammonia; *indigotate* of mercury.

in-di-got′iç, *a.* [*Indigotin* and *-ic.*]

1. Pertaining to or obtained from indigotin.

2. In botany, very deep blue.

Indigotic acid; an acid obtained by boiling indigo in dilute nitric acid; called also *nitrosalicylic* or *anilic acid.*

in′di-gō-tin, *n.* See *Indigo blue* under *Indigo.*

in-dig-rụ′bin, *n.* See *Urrhodin.*

in-di-hū′min, *n.* [L. *indicum*, indigo, and *humus*, earth, soil, and *-in.*] Same as *Indigo brown* under *Indigo.*

in-dil′ȧ-tō-ry, *a.* Not dilatory or slow. [Obs.]

in-dil′i-ġence, *n.* Lack of diligence. [Obs.]

in-dil′i-ġent, *a.* Not diligent; idle; slothful. [Obs.]

in-dil′i-ġent-ly, *adv.* Without diligence. [Obs.]

in-di-min′ish-ȧ-ble, *a.* Not diminishable. [Obs.]

in′din, *n.* [*Indigo* and *-in.*] A crystalline substance, $C_{16}H_{10}N_2O_2$, of a rose color, isomeric with indigo blue.

in-di-reçt′, *a.* [L. *indirectus*; *in-* priv., and *directus*, straight, pp. of *dirigere*, to make straight, mark out.]

1. Not straight or rectilinear; deviating from a direct line or course; circuitous; as, an *indirect* route.

2. Not tending to a purpose by the shortest or plainest course, or by obvious means, but obliquely or consequentially; by remote means; as, an *indirect* accusation; an *indirect* attack; an *indirect* answer or proposal.

3. Not fair or honest; not open; equivocal; tending to mislead or deceive.

> *Indirect* dealing will be discovered one time or other. —Tillotson.

4. Not resulting directly or immediately from a cause, but following consequentially and remotely; not direct in descent or derivation; as, *indirect* claims; an *indirect* inheritance.

Indirect claims; claims for damages, not direct but consequential.

Indirect demonstration; see under *Demonstration.*

Indirect discourse; in grammar, the form of a quotation in which the words are altered; thus, "he said that he would be there" is indirect discourse; "he said, I will be there" is direct discourse; in Latin, *oratio obliqua* and *oratio recta*, respectively.

Indirect evidence; in law, inferential or circumstantial evidence.

Indirect tax; a tax which falls in reality upon some other person than the immediate subject of it.

in-di-reç′tion, *n.* Oblique course or means; dishonest practice.

in-di-reçt′ly, *adv.* In an indirect manner; not in a straight line or course; obliquely; not by direct means; not in express terms; unfairly.

> Your crown and kingdom *indirectly* held.
> —Shak.

in-di-rect′ness, *n.* The condition or quality of being indirect; obliquity; devious course; unfairness; dishonesty.

in-di-rē′tin, *n.* See *Indigo brown* under *Indigo.*

in-di-rū′bin, *n.* [L. *indicum*, indigo, and *ruber*, red, and *-in.*] An isomer of indigo blue, C_8H_5NO, obtained by the decomposition of indican.

in-dis-cern′i-ble (-zern′), *a.* Imperceptible; not discoverable.

in-dis-cern′i-ble-ness, *n.* Incapability of being discerned.

in-dis-cern′i-bly, *adv.* In an indiscernible manner.

in-dis-cerp-i-bil′i-ty, *n.* The quality of being indiscerpible. [Obs.]

in-dis-cerp′i-ble, *a.* Not discerpible; not separable into parts. [Obs.]

in-dis-cerp′i-ble-ness, *n.* Indiscerpibility. [Obs.]

in-dis-cerp′i-bly, *adv.* In an indiscerpible manner. [Obs.]

in-dis-cerp-ti-bil′i-ty, *n.* Indiscerpibility. [Obs.]

in-dis-cerp′ti-ble, *a.* Indiscerpible. [Obs.]

in-dis-cerp′ti-ble-ness, *n.* Indiscerpibleness. [Obs.]

in-dis-cerp′ti-bly, *adv.* Indiscerpibly. [Obs.]

in-dis′ci-plin-a-ble, *a.* Undisciplinable.

in-dis′ci-pline, *n.* Want of discipline or instruction.

in-dis-cov′er-a-ble, *a.* Undiscoverable.

in-dis-cov′er-y, *n.* Want of discovery. [Obs.]

in-dis-creet′, *a.* Not discreet; wanting in discretion; imprudent; inconsiderate; injudicious.

Syn.—Injudicious, inconsiderate, rash, imprudent, hasty, unwise.

in-dis-creet′ly, *adv.* Not discreetly.

in-dis-creet′ness, *n.* Indiscretion.

in-dis-crete′, *a.* [L. *indiscretus*, not separated, undistinguished; *in-* priv., and *discretus*, pp. of *discernere*, to separate, distinguish.] Not discrete or separated.

in-dis-cre′tion (-kresh′un), *n.* 1. Want of discretion; the state or quality of being indiscreet.

2. An indiscreet action; indiscreet deportment.

Syn.—Imprudence, rashness, mistake.

in-dis-crim′i-nate, *a.* Not discriminate; undistinguishing; not making any distinction; lacking discrimination; indistinguishable; confused; promiscuous.

> The *indiscriminate* defense of right and wrong. —Junius.

in-dis-crim′i-nate-ly, *adv.* Without distinction; in confusion.

in-dis-crim′i-nā-ting, *a.* Not making any distinction.

in-dis-crim′i-nā-ting-ly, *adv.* In an indiscriminating manner.

in-dis-crim-i-nā′tion, *n.* Want of discrimination.

in-dis-crim′i-nā-tive, *a.* Making no distinction.

in-dis-cussed′, *a.* Not discussed. [Obs.]

in-dis-pen-sa-bil′i-ty, *n.* Indispensableness.

in-dis-pen′sa-ble, *a.* 1. Incapable of being dispensed with; not to be omitted, remitted, or spared; absolutely necessary or requisite; as, air and water are *indispensable* to life.

2. Inevitable. [Obs.]

3. Not subject to exemption; not admitting of a dispensation. [Obs.]

Syn.—Essential, necessary, requisite, needful, fundamental.

in-dis-pen′sa-ble-ness, *n.* The state or quality of being absolutely necessary or indispensable.

in-dis-pen′sa-bly, *adv.* In an indispensable manner.

in-dis-persed′, *a.* Not dispersed. [Obs.]

in-dis-pōse′, *v.t.*; indisposed, *pt., pp.*; indisposing, *ppr.* [Fr. *indisposer*, to indispose; L. *in-* priv., and *disponere*, to distribute, dispose.]

1. To disincline; to render averse or unfavorable.

> They may sometimes *indispose* and irritate the reader. —M. Arnold.

2. To render unfit; to disqualify.

3. To affect with indisposition or illness; to disorder; to make somewhat ill.

> It made him rather *indisposed* than sick. —Walton.

in-dis-pōs′ed-ness, *n.* The condition or quality of being indisposed.

in-dis-pō-si′tion (-zish′un), *n.* [LL. *indispositio* (*-onis*), inappropriateness; L. *in-* priv., and *dispositio* (*-onis*), arrangement, disposition.]

1. The state of being indisposed or disinclined; aversion; dislike.

> A general *indisposition* toward believing. —Atterbury.

2. Slight disorder of the normal functions of the body; tendency to sickness.

3. Want of tendency or natural appetency or affinity; as, the *indisposition* of two substances to combine.

in-dis″pū-ta-bil′i-ty, *n.* Indisputableness.

in-dis′pū-ta-ble, *a.* [LL. *indisputabilis*; L. *in-* priv., and *disputabilis*, disputable, from *disputare*, to dispute.] Incapable of being disputed; incontrovertible; incontestable; too evident to admit of dispute.

Syn.—Incontrovertible, indubitable, undeniable, unquestionable, incontestable, undoubted, positive, certain.

in-dis′pū-ta-ble-ness, *n.* The state or quality of being indisputable.

in-dis′pū-ta-bly, *adv.* Unquestionably.

in-dis-pūt′ed, *a.* Undisputed.

in-dis′si-pa-ble, *a.* Incapable of being dissipated.

in-dis″sō-lū-bil′i-ty, *n.* [Fr. *indissolubilité.*] The quality of being indissoluble.

in-dis′sō-lū-ble, *a.* [L. *indissolubilis*; *in-* priv., and *dissolubilis*, dissoluble, from *dissolvere*, to dissolve.]

1. Not capable of being dissolved, melted, or liquefied; as, few substances are absolutely *indissoluble* by heat, but many are *indissoluble* in water.

2. Not to be broken or rightfully violated; perpetually binding or obligatory; as, an *indissoluble* league or covenant.

in-dis′sō-lū-ble-ness, *n.* Indissolubility.

in-dis′sō-lū-bly, *adv.* In an indissoluble manner.

> On they move
> *Indissolubly* firm. —Milton.

in-dis-solv′a-ble, *a.* Indissoluble; incapable of being dissolved; perpetually firm and binding.

in-dis-solv′a-ble-ness, *n.* Indissolubility.

in-dis′tan-cy, *n.* Want of distance or separation. [Obs.]

in-dis-tinct′, *a.* [L. *indistinctus*, obscure, indistinct; *in-* priv., and *distinctus*, pp. of *distinguere*, to point out, distinguish.]

1. Not distinct or distinguishable; not separate in such a manner as to be perceptible by itself.

> *Indistinct* as water is in water. —Shak.

2. Imperfect; faint; obscure; not clear; blurred; as, an *indistinct* vision; an *indistinct* view.

Syn.—Confused, indefinite, indistinguishable, obscure, vague, ambiguous.

in-dis-tinc′ti-ble, *a.* Indistinguishable. [Obs.]

in-dis-tinc′tion, *n.* Want of distinction; confusion; uncertainty; want of distinguishableness.

> The *indistinction* of many of the same name . . . hath made some doubt. —Browne.

in-dis-tinc′tive, *a.* Not distinctive; commonplace.

in-dis-tinc′tive-ness, *n.* Commonness.

in-dis-tinct′ly, *adv.* Without distinction or separation; not clearly; dimly; obscurely.

in-dis-tinct′ness, *n.* The condition of being dim, obscure, confused, or indefinite; as, *indistinctness* of letters upon a printed page.

in-dis-tin′guish-a-ble, *a.* Not to be distinguished or separated.

in-dis-tin′guish-a-bly, *adv.* Indistinctly; indefinitely.

in-dis-tin′guished (-gwisht), *a.* Indefinite. [Rare.]

in-dis-tin′guish-ing, *a.* Making no difference; as, *indistinguishing* liberalities. [Obs.]

in-dis-turb′ance, *n.* Freedom from disturbance; calmness; repose; tranquillity.

in-ditch′, *v.t.* To bury in a ditch. [Obs.]

in-dite′, *v.t.*; indited, *pt., pp.*; inditing, *ppr.* [OFr. *enditer, inditer*, to write, accuse, from L. *indictare*, to declare, accuse, freq. of *indicere*, to declare; *in*, in, and *dicere*, to say, speak.] To compose; to write; to commit to words in writing; to be the author of.

in-dite′, *v.i.* To compose.

in-dite′ment, *n.* The act of inditing.

in-dit′er, *n.* One who indites.

in′di-um, *n.* [L. *indicum*, indigo.] A metallic element resembling zinc, characterized by two indigo-blue lines in its spectrum; it is malleable and readily fusible.

in-di-vert′i-ble, *a.* Incapable of being diverted; not to be turned aside. [Rare.]

in-di-vid′a-ble, *a.* Not capable of division. [Rare.]

in-di-vid′ed, *a.* Undivided. [Rare.]

in-di-vid′ū-al, *a.* [LL. *individualis*; L. *individuus*, indivisible, inseparable; *in-* priv., and *dividuus*, divisible, from *dividere*, to divide.]

1. Not divided, or not to be divided; single; one; as, an *individual* man or city.

2. Pertaining to one only; characteristic; distinctive; as, *individual* labor or exertions; *individual* traits of character.

Syn.—Identical, single, particular, indivisible.

in-di-vid′ū-al, *n.* 1. A single person, being, or thing of any kind; a single entity; one of a class.

2. In biology, a single organism in existence separate from the parent; one of a kind, whether partially or fully developed, as the entire product of a fertilized egg or ovule, or the bud of a plant.

in-di-vid′ū-al-ism, *n.* 1. The state of individual interest, or attachment to the interest of individuals in preference to the common interest of society.

2. The quality that characterizes every individual.

3. That doctrine or theory of government which recognizes the independence of the individual in every relation of life, as opposed to collectivism and paternalism; the theory of anarchism.

in-di-vid-ū-al-is′tic, *a.* Having the quality of individualism; relating to the individual.

in-di-vid-ū-al′i-ty, *n.* 1. Separate or distinct existence; a state of oneness.

2. Personality; that quality in the character of an individual which is the resultant of all his characteristics; as, he has a marked *individuality.*

in-di-vid″ū-al-i-zā′tion, *n.* The act of individualizing; the state of being individualized.

in-di-vid′ū-al-ize, *v.t.*; individualized (-īzd), *pt., pp.*; individualizing, *ppr.* To distinguish; to select or mark as an individual, or to distinguish the peculiar properties of (a person) from others.

in-di-vid′ū-al-ī-zer, *n.* Whoever or whatever individualizes.

in-di-vid′ū-al-ly, *adv.* 1. Separately; by itself; to the exclusion of others; as, ten men will unitedly accomplish what one of them *individually* cannot perform.

2. Inseparably; incommunicably.

> Omniscience—an attribute *individually* proper to the Godhead. —Hakewill.

in-di-vid′ū-āte, *a.* Undivided. [Obs.]

in-di-vid′ū-āte, *v.t.*; individuated, *pt., pt.*; individuating, *ppr.* [LL. *individuatus*, pp. of *individuare*, to make individual, from L. *individuus*, individual.] To make single; to distinguish from others; to individualize.

> Life is *individuated* into infinite numbers, that have their distinct sense and pleasure. —More.

in-di-vid-ū-ā′tion, *n.* 1. The act of making individual.

2. The state of being separated into individuals.

in-di-vid′ū-ā-tor, *n.* Whoever or whatever individuates.

in″di-vi-dū′i-ty, *n.* Separate existence; distinct entity. [Rare.]

in-di-vin′i-ty, *n.* Want of divine power. [Obs.]

in-di-vis-i-bil′i-ty, *n.* The state or property of being indivisible.

in-di-vis′i-ble, *a.* [LL. *indivisibilis*; L. *in-* priv., and LL. *divisibilis*, divisible, from L. *dividere*, to divide.] That cannot be divided, separated, or broken; not separable into parts.

in-di-vis′i-ble, *n.* 1. An individual; anything that cannot be divided; as, an atom has been assumed to be an *indivisible.*

2. In geometry, an infinitesimally small quantity, assumed to be without value and therefore indivisible.

Method of indivisibles; a method invented and used in the seventeenth century and founded upon the supposition that all magnitudes are made up of an infinite number of equal parts any one of which might be neglected without affecting a result.

in-di-vis′i-ble-ness, *n.* Indivisibility.

in-di-vis′i-bly, *adv.* So as not to be capable of division.

in-di-vi′sion, *n.* A state of being not divided. [Rare.]

Indo-. A combining form from L. *Indus*; Gr. *Indos*, Indian, from *India*, India, used in geography, ethnology, etc., to signify concerning or pertaining to India; as, *Indo*-European.

in-dō-an′i-lin, in-dō-an′i-line, *n.* [*Indigo*, and *anilin.*] In chemistry, any one of a series of artificial substitutes for indigo.

In′dō-Brit′on, *n.* A person born in India, whose parents are natives of Great Britain.

In′dō-Chī′na, *n.* The part of India beyond the Ganges; Farther India.

In′dō-Chī-nēse′, *a.* Pertaining to that part of India which lies beyond the River Ganges, or to the people of that country called Indo-China.

in-doc-i-bil′i-ty, *n.* [LL. *indocibilitas*, from *indocibilis*, unteachable; L. *in-* priv., and LL. *docibilis*, teachable, from L. *docere*, to teach.] The quality of being unteachable.

in-doc′i-ble, *a.* 1. Unteachable; not capable of being taught, or not easily instructed; dull in intellect.

2. Intractable, as a beast.

in-doc′i-ble-ness, *n.* Indocility.

in-doc′ile (*or* -dō′cile), *a.* [L. *indocilis*, not teachable; *in-* priv., and *docilis*, teachable, from *docere*, to teach.]

1. Not teachable; not easily instructed; dull.

2. Intractable, as a beast.

in-dō-cil′i-ty, *n.* [LL. *indocilitas (-atis)*, from L. *indocilis*, unteachable.]
1. Unteachableness; dullness of intellect.
2. Intractableness, as of a beast.

in-dog′tri-nāte, *v.t.*; indoctrinated, *pt.*, *pp.*; indoctrinating, *ppr.* [L. *in*, in, and *doctrinare*, to teach, from *doctrina*, learning.] To teach; to instruct in rudiments or principles; to imbue with a doctrine.

in-dog-tri-nā′tion, *n.* Instruction in the rudiments and principles of any science; information.

In′dō-Eng′lish, *a.* Relating to English people who live or were born in India.

In′dō-Eū-rō-pē′ăn, *a.* A word used to designate the languages, or the people speaking the languages, which took their origin in India and spread westward over Europe; Aryan.

In′dō-Eū-rō-pē′ăn, *n.* One belonging to an Indo-European race.

in′dō-ġēne, *n.* [*Indigo* and *-gen.*] The complex radical, C_8H_7NO, found in indigo.

in-dog′e-nid, in-dog′e-nide, *n.* One of the derivatives of indogen.

In′dō-Gĕr-man′ig, *a.* 1. Same as *Indo-European.*
2. Relating to the Teutonic languages derived from the Aryan.

in′dō-in, *n.* A substance of artificial formation resembling indigo.

in′dol, *n.* [*Indigo* and phen*ol*.] In chemistry, a substance, C_8H_7N, found in indigo, in the intestinal canal of herbivorous animals, and in human excrement.

in′dō-lence, *n.* [L. *indolentia*, freedom from pain; *in-* priv., and *dolens (-entis)*, ppr. of *dolere*, to feel pain.]
1. Freedom from pain or discomfort of body or of mind. [Obs.]
2. Habitual idleness; indisposition to labor; laziness; inaction, or want of exertion of body or mind, proceeding from love of ease or aversion to toil.

in′dō-len-cy, *n.* Indolence. [Obs.]

in′dō-lent, *a.* [L. *in-* priv., and *dolens (-entis)*, ppr. of *dolere*, to feel pain, grieve.]
1. Habitually idle or indisposed to labor; lazy; listless; sluggish; indulging in ease; inactive; idle; as, an *indolent* person; an *indolent* life.
2. Free from pain; as, an *indolent* tumor.

in′dō-lent-ly, *adv.* In habitual idleness and ease; without action, activity, or exertion; lazily.

in′dō-lēs, *n.* [L., an inborn or native quality, from Old L. *indu*, within.] Natural bent; characteristic qualities and temperament. [Rare.]

in′dō-lin, in′dō-line, *n.* [*Indigo* and phen*ol*, and *-in.*] In chemistry, a compound crystalline substance, $C_{16}H_{14}N_2$, a polymer of indol.

in-dom′ȧ-ble, *a.* [Obs.] See *Indomitable.*

in-dom′i-tȧ-ble, *a.* [L. *in-* priv., and *domitare*, freq. of *domere*, to tame, subdue.] That cannot be subdued; irrepressible; untamable; as, *indomitable* courage or will.

in-dom′ite, *a.* Not subdued; in a savage state. [Obs.]

in-domp′tȧ-ble, *a.* Not to be subdued. [Obs.]

In-dō-nē′si-ăn, *a.* [Gr. *Indos*, Indian, and *nēsos*, island.] In anthropology, of or related to the people of the Polynesian islands exhibiting the characteristics of the Caucasian race, as distinguished from those of the Malay tribes.

In-dō-nē′si-ăn, *n.* Any Indonesian person.

in′dōor, *a.* Carried on, performed, contemplated, originated, etc., within doors; as, *indoor* occupations; *indoor* baseball, etc.

in′dōors, *adv.* Into, inside, or within a building or house; as, come *indoors*; he is employed *indoors*.

in-dō-phē′nol, *n.* One of a series of dyestuffs used for coloring wool and cotton blue, a product of coal-tar, producing colors fast to light and bleaching-powders, but easily destroyed by acids.

in-dors′ȧ-ble, *a.* That may be indorsed, assigned, and made payable to order; transferable by indorsement.

in-dor-sā′tion, *n.* [Obs.] See *Indorsement.*

in-dorse′, en-dorse′, *v.t.*; indorsed, endorsed (-dorst), *pt.*, *pp.*; indorsing, endorsing, *ppr.* [LL. *indorsare*, to place on the back, to indorse; L. *in*, on, upon, and *dorsum*, the back.]
1. To write on the back of, as a paper or written instrument; as, to *indorse* a note or check; to *indorse* a receipt or assignment on a bill or note.
2. To assign by writing an order on the back of a note or bill; to assign or transfer by indorsement; as, the note was *indorsed* to the bank.
3. To give sanction or currency to; as, to *indorse* a statement or the opinions of another.
4. In law and commerce, to become surety for, by writing the name or names upon the back of a note or obligation of any kind; to become a guarantor for the payment of, as money, or the fulfilment of, as a contract.
To indorse in blank; to write a name only on a note or bill, leaving a blank to be filled by the holder.
Syn.—Sanction, approve, subscribe, accept, guarantee, O. K.

in-dorsed′ (-dorst′), *a.* Written on the back; assigned; sanctioned.

in-dor-see′, *n.* The person to whom a note or bill is indorsed, or assigned by indorsement.

in-dorse′ment, *n.* 1. The act of writing on the back of a note, bill, or other written instrument.
2. That which is written on the back of a note, bill, or other paper, as a name, an order for payment, the return of an officer, or the verdict of a grand jury.
3. Sanction or support given; as, the *indorsement* of a rumor.

in-dors′ẽr, *n.* The person who indorses or writes his name on the back of a note or bill of exchange, and who, by this act, as the case may be, makes himself liable to pay the note or bill.

in-dors′ŏr, *n.* An indorser.

in-dow′, *v.t.* [Obs.] See *Endow.*

in-dow′ment, *n.* [Obs.] See *Endowment.*

in-dox′yl, *n.* [*Indigo* and hydr*oxyl*.] In chemistry, an oily nitrogenous substance, C_8H_7NO.

in-dox-yl′ig, *a.* Related to indoxyl.

In′drȧ, *n.* [Sans.] A Hindu deity originally representing the sky or heavens, and worshiped in the Vedic period as the supreme god, though he afterward assumed a subordinate place in the Indian pantheon. He is represented in various ways in painting and sculpture, especially with four arms and hands, and riding on an elephant.

Indra.—Coleman's "Hindu Mythology."

in′drȧft, in′draught (-drȧft), *n.* 1. An inflow, as of water or air.

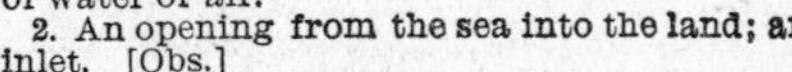

2. An opening from the sea into the land; an inlet. [Obs.]

in′drawn, *a.* Drawn in.

in-drench′, *v.t.* To overwhelm with water; to drown; to drench. [Obs.]

in′dri, *n.* [Malagasy *indri*, man of the woods.] A very short-tailed animal of the lemur family, *Indris laniger*, a native of the island of Madagascar.

Indri (*Indris laniger*).

in-dū′bi-ous, *a.* 1. Not dubious or doubtful; certain.
2. Not doubting; unsuspecting; as, *indubious* confidence.

in-dū′bi-tȧ-ble, *a.* [L. *indubitabilis*; *in-* priv., and *dubitabilis*, doubtful, from *dubitare*, to doubt.] Not to be doubted; unquestionable; evident; apparently certain; too plain to admit of doubt.
Syn.—Unquestionable, indisputable, undeniable, incontrovertible, irrefragable.

in-dū′bi-tȧ-ble, *n.* Any indubitable statement or proposition.

in-dū′bi-tȧ-ble-ness, *n.* State of being indubitable.

in-dū′bi-tȧ-bly, *adv.* Undoubtedly; unquestionably; in a manner to remove all doubt.

in-dū′bi-tāte, *a.* Not questioned; evident; certain. [Obs.]

in-dū′bi-tāte, *v.t.* To call in question; to surround with doubt. [Obs.]

in-dūce′, *v.t.*; induced (-dūst), *pt.*, *pp.*; inducing, *ppr.* [ME. *enducen*; L. *inducere*, to lead or bring in; *in*, in, and *ducere*, to lead.]
1. To lead, as by persuasion or argument; to prevail on; to incite; to influence by motives.
2. To produce; to bring on; to cause; as, a fever *induced* by extreme fatigue.
3. To introduce; to bring into view. [Obs.]
4. To put or draw on; to place upon. [Obs.]
5. In logic, to reach (a general conclusion) by inference from a number of individual cases.
6. In physics, to influence without direct contact; as, a magnet *induces* magnetism in iron when in proximity to it.
Syn.—Actuate, cause, incite, influence, instigate, persuade.

in-dūced′, *a.* Caused; brought on; caused by induction.
Induced current; in electricity, a current produced in a conductor by a variation in the intensity of the magnetic field through which it passes.

in-dūce′ment, *n.* 1. Motive; anything that leads the mind to will or to act; any argument, reason, or fact that tends to persuade or influence the mind; an influence that leads to action.

> If this *inducement* move her not to love,
> Send her a letter of thy noble deeds. —Shak.

2. In law, a statement of facts introducing other material facts.
3. The act of inducing.
Syn.—Cause, incitement, motive, reason.

in-dū′cẽr, *n.* One who or that which induces, persuades, or influences.

in-dū′ci-ble, *a.* 1. That may be moved to action.
2. Capable of being inferred by induction; derivable.

in-duct′, *v.t.*; inducted, *pt.*, *pp.*; inducting, *ppr.* [L. *inductus*, pp. of *inducere*, to lead or bring in; *in*, in, and *ducere*, to lead.]
1. To bring in or introduce; to initiate.
2. To introduce, as to a benefice or office; to put in actual possession of an office with the customary forms and ceremonies.

in-dug′tănce, *n.* 1. The act of causing or the power to cause induction.
2. In self-induction, the increase of electrical energy by induction; the coefficient of self-induction.

in-dug′tē-ous, *a.* In electricity, made to assume polarity or change of polarity by the agency of induction.

in-dug′tile, *a.* Not capable of being drawn into threads, as a metal; not ductile.

in-dug-til′i-ty, *n.* The quality of being inductile.

in-dug′tion, *n.* [OFr. *induction*; L. *inductio (-onis)*, a leading or bringing into, an introducing.]
1. The act of inducting or bringing in; introduction; entrance; initiation.
2. Specifically, the introduction of a person into an office with the customary forms and ceremonies; especially, the introduction of a clergyman into a benefice, or the giving possession of an ecclesiastical living.
3. An introduction or preface; an introductory scene in a play; a preamble or prologue. [Obs.]
4. Beginning: commencement. [Obs.]
5. In logic, the process of reasoning or drawing a conclusion from particular cases; also, the inference drawn from such reasoning.
6. In mathematics, the inference of some general truth from the investigation of particular cases, each of which is dependent upon that preceding.
7. In physics, the influence exerted by a body possessing electrical or magnetic properties upon a neighboring body, without apparent communication.
Electrodynamic induction; the generation of an electric current in a conductor by the influence of another current.
Electromagnetic induction; the generation of an electric current by the influence of a magnet or the production of magnetic polarity by a current.
Electrostatic induction; the development of an electrical charge in a body by the influence of a statical charge in another body, the induced charge being of opposite character to the inducing charge.
Magnetic induction; magnetization induced in a magnetizable substance when brought into a magnetic field.
Mutual induction; induction which two adjacent circuits produce on each other, due either to variations in the strength of the current in the circuits, or to variations in the distance between the circuits.
Syn.—Deduction.—In *induction* we observe a sufficient number of individual facts, and, on the ground of analogy, extend what is true of them to others of the same class, thus arriving at general principles or laws. In *deduction* we begin with a general truth, and seek to connect it with some individual case by means of a middle term or class of objects known to be equally connected with both. Thus we bring down the general into the individual, affirming of the latter the distinctive qualities of the former.

in-dug′tion-ăl, *a.* Pertaining to induction; inductive.

in-dug′tion-bal″ănce, *n.* An electrical apparatus for the detection of the presence of a metallic substance by the aid of induced currents. It consists essentially of two primary coils of wire placed in the circuit of a battery and microphone. Two small secondary coils are placed near them in the circuit of a telephone, and when the currents induced in them exactly neutralize or balance each other, no sound is heard in the telephone. Should the balance be disturbed as by the introduction of a piece of metal, the telephone is made to emit a sound.

in-duc′tion-bridge, *n.* A form of induction-balance for measuring the value of electric resistances.

in-duc′tion-coil, *n.* In electricity, an apparatus for producing currents by induction and for utilizing them. It consists essentially of two coils wound on a hollow cylinder, within which is a core formed of a bar of soft iron or a bundle of soft iron wires. One of the coils, called the *primary coil*, is connected with the battery by means of an arrangement for establishing and breaking connection with it, so as to produce temporary currents; the other, the secondary *coil*, is wound round the first, but carefully insulated from it, and in it is generated a current by induction every time the current begins or stops in the primary coil. Called also *Ruhmkorff coil* and *inductorium*.

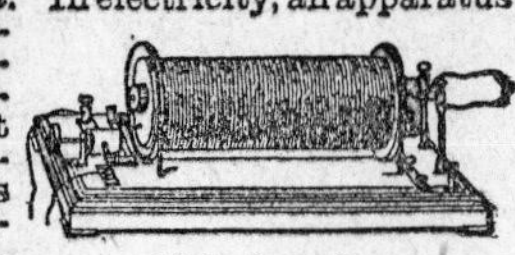
Induction-coil.

in-duc′tion-pipe, *n.* The pipe in a steam-engine through which the live steam passes to the cylinder.

in-duc′tion-port, *n.* In a steam-engine, the port which is open for the admission of steam into the cylinder.

in-duc′tion-valve, *n.* The valve in a steam-engine which directs the admission of steam into the cylinder.

in-duc′tive, *a.* [LL. *inductivus*, leading to] inferences, serving to induce.]

1. Leading or drawing; inducing; with *to*. [Rare.]

2. Tending to induce or cause. [Rare.]

3. Leading to inferences; proceeding by induction; as, *inductive* reasoning.

4. In electricity, (a) able to produce electricity by induction; as, *inductive* force; (b) operating by induction; as, an *inductive* electrical machine; (c) facilitating induction; susceptible of being acted on by induction; as, certain substances have a great *inductive* capacity.

Inductive philosophy; science based on induction or investigation.

Inductive sciences; those sciences which are based upon induction, or which admit of inductive reasoning, as botany, astronomy, chemistry, zoölogy, etc.

in-duc′tive-ly, *adv.* By induction or inference.

in-duc-tiv′i-ty, *n.* In electricity, inductive capacity; capacity for induction.

in-duc-tom′e-tẽr, *n.* [L. *inductio (-onis)*, induction, and *metrum*, a measure.] An instrument for measuring the degree or rate of electrical induction, or for comparing the specific inductive capacities of various substances.

in-duc′tŏr, *n.* [L., one who stirs up, a chastiser, lit., one who leads or brings in.]

1. The person who inducts another into an office or benefice.

2. In electricity, any portion of an electrical machine or apparatus which acts inductively on another; also, a part so acted upon.

in-duc-tō′ri-um, *n.* Same as *Induction-coil*.

in-duc′tō-scōpe, *n.* [L. *inductio (-onis)*, induction, and Gr. *skopein*, to view.] In electricity, an instrument for detecting magnetic or electric induction.

in-duc′tric, *a.* In electricity, acting on other bodies by induction, as an electrified body; relating to induction.

in-duc′tric-ăl, *a.* Same as *Inductric*.

in-due′, *v.t.*; indued, *pt., pp.*; induing, *ppr.* [L. *induere*, to put on, to dress oneself, from Old L. *indu*, L. *in*, in, on.]

1. To put on, as an article of dress. [Obs.]

2. To clothe; to furnish; to endow; a variant of *endue*.

> *Indued* with intellectual sense and souls. —Shak.

in-due′ment, *n.* Same as *Enduement*.

in-dulge′, *v.t.*; indulged, *pt., pp.*; indulging, *ppr.* [L. *indulgere*, to be kind or indulgent to.]

1. To gratify by compliance; to humor; to withhold restraint from; to yield to the desire or wishes of; as, to *indulge* a child.

2. To grant not of right, but as a favor; to grant in compliance with a wish or desire.

3. To give free course to; to yield to; as, to *indulge* a habit.

Syn.—Gratify, pamper, favor, humor, please.

in-dulge′, *v.i.* To yield to the gratification or practice of a habit without restraint or control; to be indulgent; with *in*; as, to *indulge in* sin.

> Most men are more willing to *indulge in* easy vices, than to practise laborious virtues. —Johnson.

in-dulge′ment, *n.* Indulgence. [Rare.]

in-dul′gence, *n.* [ME. *indulgence*; L. *indulgentia*, indulgence, gentleness, from *indulgens (-entis)*, ppr. of *indulgere*, to indulge.]

1. The act of indulging; forbearance of restraint or control.

> By this *indulgence* of men in their sins. —Stillingfleet.

2. Gratification; favor granted; liberality.

> If all these gracious *indulgences* are without effect on us, we must perish in our folly. —Rogers.

3. In the Roman Catholic church, remission, by church authority, to a repentant sinner, of the canonical penance attached to certain sins in this life, and also of the temporal punishment which would await the impenitent in purgatory.

in-dul′gen-cy, *n.* Indulgence.

in-dul′gent, *a.* [L. *indulgens(-entis)*, ppr. of *indulgere*, to indulge.] Yielding to the wishes, desires, humor, or appetites of those under one's care; compliant; not restraining or opposing; mild; favorable; not severe; gratifying; favoring.

Syn.—Compliant, forbearing, tender, tolerant, lenient.

in-dul-gen′tiăl (-shăl), *a.* Relating to the indulgences of the Roman Catholic church.

in-dul′gent-ly, *adv.* In an indulgent manner; with compliance; mildly; favorably; not severely.

in-dul′gẽr, *n.* One who indulges.

in-dul′gi-āte, *v.t.* To indulge. [Obs.]

in′dū-line, *n.* [Prob. from *indigo*, and *aniline*.] Any one of various coal-tar dyestuffs made by different processes but possessing similar dyeing properties. They all yield dark, dull blue colors resembling indigo.

in-dult′, *n.* [LL. *indultum*, an indulgence, neut. of L. *indultus*, pp. of *indulgere*, to indulge.]

1. In the Roman Catholic church, an indulgence; a privilege granted by the pope to certain persons, of doing or obtaining something contrary to the established rule or law of the church.

2. In Spain, a duty, tax, or custom formerly paid to the king on imported goods.

in-dul′tō, *n.* See *Indult*.

in′dū-ment, *n.* See *Indumentum*.

in-dū-men′tum, *n.* [L., a garment, from *induere*, to put on.]

1. In ornithology, plumage.

2. In botany, any hairy covering.

in-dū′pli-cāte, *a.* [L. *in*, in, on, and *duplicatus*, pp. of *duplicare*, to double, from *duplex*, double.] In botany, (a) having the edges bent abruptly toward the axis; said of the parts of the calyx or corolla in estivation; (b) having the edges rolled inward and then arranged about the axis without overlapping; said of leaves in vernation.

in-dū-pli-cā′tion, *n.* The state of being induplicate; anything induplicate.

in-dū′pli-cā-tive, *a.* Same as *Induplicate*.

in-dūr′ănce, *n.* [Obs.] Same as *Endurance*.

in-dū-ras′cent, *a.* In botany, hardening by degrees, as the permanent petioles of a tragacanth-bush. [Obs.]

in′dū-rāte, *a.* Hardened; obdurate; unfeeling; indurated.

in′dū-rāte, *v.t.*; indurated, *pt., pp.*; indurating, *ppr.* [L. *induratus*, pp. of *indurare*, to make hard; *in*, in, and *durare*, to harden, from *durus*, hard.]

1. To make hard; as, extreme heat *indurates* clay; some fossils are *indurated* by exposure to the air.

2. To make unfeeling; to deprive of sensibility; to render obdurate.

in′dū-rāte, *v.i.* To grow hard; to harden or become hard; as, clay *indurates* by drying and by extreme heat.

in′dū-rā-ted, *a.* Hardened; made obdurate.

in-dū-rā′tion, *n.* 1. The act of hardening, or the process of growing hard; the state of being indurated or of having become hard.

2. Hardness of heart; obduracy.

in-dū′si-ȧ, *n.*, pl. of *indusium*.

in-dū′si-ăl, *a.* [From L. *indusium*, a covering.] Composed of or containing the petrified cases of the larvæ of certain insects.

Indusial limestone; in geology, a fresh-water limestone found in Auvergne, France, supposed to be composed of the agglomerated indusia or cases of the larvæ of caddis-flies.

in-dū′si-āte, *a.* In botany, having an indusium.

in-dū′si-ā-ted, *a.* Indusiate.

in-dū′si-um, *n.*; *pl.* **in-dū′si-ȧ**. [L., a garment, from *induere*, to put on.]

1. In botany, (a) a collection of hairs united so as to form a sort of cup, inclosing the stigma of a flower; (b) the covering of the tuft of capsules or spore-cases in ferns.

G, Indusium.

2. In entomology, the case or covering of a larva.

3. In anatomy, the amnion.

4. In Roman antiquity, a general name for a garment worn by both men and women.

in-dus′tri-ăl, *n.* 1. A person engaged in an industrial pursuit.

2. A security based upon the value of the property of an industrial or manufacturing corporation.

in-dus′tri-ăl, *a.* [LL. *industrialis*, from L. *industria*, industry.] Pertaining to, involving, or characterized by industry; pertaining to those manufacturing or other operations through which marketable commodities are produced; as, *industrial* arts; *industrial* operations.

Industrial accession; in Scots law, the addition made to the value of a subject by human art or labor exercised thereon.

Industrial exhibition; an exhibition of industrial products.

Industrial school; a school for teaching one or more branches of industry; also, a school for educating neglected children, reclaiming them from evil habits, and training them to habits of industry.

in-dus′tri-ăl-işm, *n.* Devotion to or employment in industrial pursuits; also, the principles involved in such pursuits.

in-dus′tri-ăl-ist, *a.* Characterized by industry.

in-dus′tri-ăl-ly, *adv.* With reference to industry; in an industrial manner.

in-dus′tri-ous, *a.* [L. *industriosus*, active, diligent, from *industria*, diligence, industry.]

1. Given to industry; diligent in business; assiduous; laborious; not slothful or idle.

> Frugal and *industrious* men are commonly friendly to the established government. —Temple.

2. Diligent in a particular pursuit or to a particular end; not remiss or slack; as, an *industrious* fault-finder.

Syn.—Busy, active, diligent, laborious, sedulous.

in-dus′tri-ous-ly, *adv.* In an industrious manner.

in-dus′tri-ous-ness, *n.* The quality of being industrious.

in′dus-try, *n.*; *pl.* **in′dus-tries**. [Fr. *industrie*; L. *industria*, diligence, industry, assiduity, from *industrius*, active, industrious.]

1. Habitual diligence in any employment, either bodily or mental; steady attention to business; assiduity; opposed to *sloth* and *idleness*.

2. Any department of productive activity; particularly, a distinct established business or trade; as, the mining *industry*; the iron *industry*.

3. Any kind of labor employed in production.

Syn.—Activity, diligence, sedulousness, assiduity, laboriousness.

in-dū′tive, *a.* [L. *indutus*, pp. of *induere*, to cover.] In botany, having the usual integumentary covering; applied to seeds. [Rare.]

in-dū′vi-æ, *n.pl.* [L., garments, clothing, from *induere*, to put on.] The withered leaves which remain on the stems of some plants in consequence of not being joined to them by articulations which allow of their falling off.

in-dū′vi-āte, *a.* In botany, covered with induviæ.

in′dwell, *v.t.* and *v.i.*; indwelt, *pt., pp.*; indwelling, *ppr.* To dwell in; to abide within.

in′dwell-ẽr, *n.* An inhabitant.

in′dwell-ing, *a.* Dwelling within; remaining, as in the heart; as, *indwelling* sin.

in′dwell-ing, *n.* Residence within, as in the heart or soul.

-ine, variant form of the suffix *-in*.

in-ēarth′, *v.t.* To put into the earth; to inter. [Rare.]

in-ē′bri-ȧ-cy, *n.* The habit of becoming intoxicated.

in-ē′bri-ănt, *a.* [L. *inebrians (-antis)*, ppr. of *inebriare*, to intoxicate.] Intoxicating.

in-ē′bri-ănt, *n.* Anything that intoxicates, as alcohol.

in-ē′bri-āte, *v.t.*; inebriated, *pt., pp.*; inebriating, *ppr.* [L. *inebriatus*, pp. of *inebriare*, to intoxicate; *in-*, intens., and *ebriare*, to make drunk, from *ebrius*, drunk.]

1. To make drunk; to intoxicate.

2. To disorder the senses of; to stupefy.

in-ē′bri-āte, *v.i.* To become intoxicated. [Obs.]

in-ē′bri-āte, *n.* A habitual drunkard.

in-ē′bri-āte, *a.* Intoxicated; drunk.

in-ē-bri-ā′tion, *n.* Drunkenness; intoxication; the state of being inebriated; also used figuratively.

in-ē-bri′e-ty, *n.* Drunkenness; intoxication.

in-ē′bri-ous, *a.* [L. *in-*, intens., and *ebrius*, drunk.] Drunk or partly drunk; producing intoxication. [Rare.]

in-ed-i-bil′i-ty, *n.* The state or quality of being inedible.

in-ed′i-ble, *a.* Unfit for food.

in-ed′it-ed, *a.* Unpublished; not edited; as, an *inedited* manuscript.

In-ed″ū-cȧ-bil′i-ȧ, *n.pl.* [L. *in-* priv., and *educare*, to bring up, educate.] A series of mammals having a comparatively small cerebrum. The series includes rodents, edentates, etc.

in-ed″ū-cȧ-bil′i-ăn, *a.* Pertaining to the *Ineducabilia*.

in-ed″ū-cȧ-bil′i-ăn, *n.* One of the *Ineducabilia*.

i-nēe′ (-nā′), *n.* A poison for arrows used by natives of the Gaboon country.

in-ef-fā-bil′i-ty, *n.* Unspeakableness; the condition or quality of being ineffable.

in-ef′fā-ble, *a.* [L. *ineffabilis*; *in-* priv., and *effabilis*, utterable, from *effari*, to speak out, to utter.] Unspeakable; unutterable; that cannot be expressed in words; as, the *ineffable* joys of heaven.

Syn.—Inexpressible, inconceivable, unsurpassable, indescribable, exquisite, perfect.

in-ef′fā-ble-ness, *n.* Unspeakableness; the quality of being ineffable.

in-ef′fā-bly, *adv.* Unspeakably; in a manner not to be expressed in words.

in-ef-fāce′ȧ-ble, *a.* That cannot be effaced.

in-ef-fāce′ȧ-bly, *adv.* So as not to be effaceable.

in-ef-feçt′i-ble, *a.* Impracticable. [Rare.]

in-ef-feçt′ive, *a.* Not effective; not producing any effect, or the effect intended; inefficient; useless.

in-ef-feçt′ive-ly, *adv.* Without effect; inefficiently.

in-ef-feçt′ive-ness, *n.* The quality of being ineffective.

in-ef-feç′tū-ăl, *a.* Not producing the proper effect, or not able to produce the effect; inefficient; weak; as, an *ineffectual* remedy.

Syn.—Fruitless, useless, vain, idle, unavailing, abortive, ineffective.

in-ef-feç-tū-al′i-ty, *n.* Ineffectualness; the quality of being ineffectual. [Rare.]

in-ef-feç′tū-ăl-ly, *adv.* Without effect; in vain.

in-ef-feç′tū-ăl-ness, *n.* Want of effect, or of power to produce it; inefficacy.

in-ef-fẽr-ves′cence, *n.* Want of effervescence; a state of not effervescing.

in-ef-fẽr-ves′cent, *a.* Not effervescing, or not susceptible of effervescence.

in-ef-fẽr-ves-ci-bil′i-ty, *n.* The quality of being ineffervescible.

in-ef-fẽr-ves′ci-ble, *a.* Not capable of effervescence.

in-ef-fi-cā′cious, *a.* Not efficacious; not having power to produce the effect desired, or the proper effect; of inadequate power or force.

in-ef-fi-cā′cious-ly, *adv.* Without efficacy or effect.

in-ef-fi-cā′cious-ness, *n.* Want of power to produce the effect, or want of effect; inefficacy.

in-ef′fi-cȧ-cy, *n.* [LL. *inefficacia*, from L. *inefficax* (*-acis*), ineffectual, inefficacious.]

1. Want of power to produce the desired or proper effect; inefficiency; as, the *inefficacy* of medicines or of means.

2. Ineffectualness; failure of effect.

in-ef-fi′cien-cy (-fish′en-), *n.* Want of power or exertion of power to produce the effect; inefficacy; incapacity.

in-ef-fi′cient, *a.* 1. Not efficient; not producing the effect; inefficacious.

2. Not active; effecting nothing; as, an *inefficient* force.

in-ef-fi′cient-ly, *adv.* Ineffectually; without effect.

in-ē-lab′ō-rāte, *a.* Not elaborate; not wrought with care; unfinished as to details.

in-ē-las′tiç, *a.* Not elastic; wanting elasticity; unelastic.

in-ē-las-tiç′i-ty, *n.* The absence of elasticity; the want of elastic power.

in-el′ē-gănce, *n.* Want of elegance; want of beauty or polish in language, composition, or manners; want of symmetry or ornament in building; want of delicacy in coloring, etc.

in-el′ē-găn-cy, *n.* Inelegance.

in-el′ē-gănt, *a.* Not elegant; deficient in that which good taste requires.

in-el′ē-gănt-ly, *adv.* In an inelegant or unbecoming manner; coarsely; roughly.

in-el″i-ġi-bil′i-ty, *n.* 1. Incapacity for election to an office.

2. The state or quality of not being eligible.

in-el′i-ġi-ble, *a.* [LL. *ineligibilis*, that cannot be chosen; L. *in-* priv., and *eligere*, to choose.]

1. Not eligible for election to an office.

2. Not worthy to be chosen or preferred; not expedient.

in-el′i-ġi-bly, *adv.* In an ineligible manner.

in-el′ō-quent, *a.* Not eloquent; not persuasive.

in-el′ō-quent-ly, *adv.* Without eloquence.

in-ē-luç′tȧ-ble, *a.* [L. *ineluctabilis*; *in-* priv., and *eluctabilis*, that may be resisted by struggling, from *eluctari*, to struggle.] Not to be resisted by struggling; not to be overcome; not to be surmounted.

in-ē-lūd′i-ble, *a.* That cannot be eluded or escaped; imminent.

in-em′bry-ō-nāte, *a.* Not formed in embryo.

in-ē-nar′rȧ-ble, *a.* That cannot be narrated or told. [Obs.]

in-en′chy-mȧ, *n.* [L. *in*, in, and Gr. *enchyma*, an infusion.] In botany, a kind of fibrocellular tissue in which the cells appear to be spiral.

in-e-nū′clē-ȧ-ble, *a.* [L. *in-* priv., and *enucleatus*, pp. of *enucleare*, to enucleate; *e*, out, and *nucleus*, a kernel.] That cannot be removed without cutting; as, an *inenucleable* tumor.

in-ept′, *a.* [L. *ineptus*, unsuitable, stupid; *in-* priv., and *aptus*, suitable, fit.]

1. Not apt or fit; unfit; unsuitable.

2. Improper; unbecoming; foolish.

In-ep′ti, *n.pl.* [L., pl. of *ineptus*, stupid, inept.] A group of birds typified by the dodo.

in-ept′i-tūde, *n.* Unfitness; inaptitude; unsuitableness; want of fitness or skill.

in-ept′ly, *adv.* Unfitly; unsuitably; foolishly.

in-ept′ness, *n.* Unfitness; lack of aptitude.

in-ē′quȧ-ble (*or* -ek′), *a.* Not equable; wanting in uniformity; as, an *inequable* climate.

in-ē′quăl, *a.* Unequal; uneven; various. [Rare.]

in-ē-qual′i-ty, *n.*; *pl.* **in-ē-qual′i-tieṣ.** [L. *inæqualitas* (*-atis*), unlikeness.]

1. Difference or want of equality in degree, quantity, length, or quality of any kind; the state of not having equal measure, degree, dimensions, or amount; as, an *inequality* in size or stature.

2. Unevenness; want of levelness; the alternate rising and falling of a surface; as, the *inequalities* of the surface of the earth, or of a marble slab.

3. Disproportion to any office or purpose; inadequacy; incompetency; as, the *inequality* of terrestrial things to the wants of a rational soul.

4. Diversity; want of uniformity in different times or places; as, the *inequality* of air or temperature.

5. Difference of rank, station, or condition.

6. In astronomy, an irregularity or deviation in the motion of a planet or satellite from its uniform mean motion; also, the extent of such deviation.

7. In algebra, the expression of two unequal quantities with the sign of inequality between them, the angle being toward the symbol of the smaller quantity; as, the *inequality* $2<5$ (read, two less than five); $a>b$ (read, *a* greater than *b*).

in-ē-quā′tion, *n.* Same as *Inequality*, 7.

in-ē-qui-dis′tănt, *a.* Not being equally distant.

in-ē-qui-lat′ẽr-ăl, *a.* 1. Having unequal sides; not equilateral.

2. In conchology, lacking equality in the anterior and posterior parts of the valve, as in the mussel and oyster.

in-ē-qui-lō′bāte, *a.* In biology, having lobes differing in size or lacking symmetry.

in-eq′ui-tȧ-ble, *a.* Not equitable; not just.

in-eq′ui-tāte, *v.t.* To ride horseback into, upon, or over. [Obs.]

in-eq′ui-ty, *n.* A lack of the quality of equity or fairness.

in-ē′qui-valve, *a.* Having unequal valves, as the shell of an oyster.

in-ē-qui-val′vū-lăr, *a.* Inequivalve.

in-ē-rad′i-cȧ-ble, *a.* Incapable of being eradicated.

in-ē-rad′i-cȧ-bly, *adv.* So as not to be eradicable.

in-ē-rās′ȧ-ble, *a.* Incapable of being erased.

in-ẽr-ġet′iç, *a.* Having no energy. [Rare.]

in-ẽr-ġet′iç-ăl, *a.* Inergetic. [Rare.]

in-ẽr-ġet′iç-ăl-ly, *adv.* Without energy. [Rare.]

in-ẽrm′, *a.* [L. *inermis*, unarmed; *in-* priv., and *arma*, arms.] In botany, unarmed; destitute of prickles or thorns, as a leaf.

in-ẽr′mis, *a.* Same as *Inerm.*

in-ẽr′mous, *a.* Same as *Inerm.*

in-ẽr-rȧ-bil′i-ty, *n.* Exemption from error or from the possibility of erring; infallibility.

in-ẽr′rȧ-ble, *a.* [LL. *inerrabilis*; L. *in-* priv., and *errare*, to wander, err.] Exempt from error or mistake; infallible.

in-ẽr′rȧ-ble-ness, *n.* Exemption from error; inerrability.

in-ẽr′rȧ-bly, *adv.* With security from error; infallibly.

in-ẽr′răn-cy, *n.* The quality of being without error.

in-ẽr′rănt, *a.* Without error; not liable to err; as to the Bible, absolutely errorless.

in-er-rat′iç, *a.* Not erratic or wandering; fixed.

in-ẽrr′ing-ly, *adv.* Without error, mistake, or deviation.

in-ẽrt′, *a.* [L. *iners* (*-ertis*), without skill or art, idle; *in-* priv., and *ars*, *artis*, skill, art.]

1. Destitute of the power of moving itself, or of active resistance to motion; as, matter is *inert.*

2. Dull; sluggish; indisposed to move or act.

3. Incapable of producing an effect.

Syn.—Inactive, sluggish, powerless, lazy, slothful, lifeless, passive.—A man may be *inactive* from mere want of stimulus to effort, but one who is *inert* has something in his constitution or his habits which operates like a weight holding him back from exertion. *Sluggish* is still stronger, implying some defect of temperament which directly impedes action.

in-ẽr′tiȧ (-shȧ), *n.* [L. *inertia*, want of art or skill, ignorance, from *iners* (*-ertis*), unskillful, inert.]

1. A property of matter by which it tends to preserve a state of rest when still, and of uniform rectilinear motion when moving.

2. Inertness; indisposition to move.

3. In medicine, torpidity; want of energy, as of the uterus when it ceases to contract in parturition.

in-ẽr′tiăl, *a.* Pertaining to inertia.

in-ẽr′tion, *n.* Want of activity; want of action or exertion. [Rare.]

in-ẽrt′i-tūde, *n.* Inertness. [Rare.]

in-ẽrt′ly, *adv.* Without activity; sluggishly.

in-ẽrt′ness, *n.* 1. The state or quality of being inert.

2. Want of activity or exertion; habitual indisposition, action, or motion; sluggishness.

in-er′ū-dīte, *a.* [L. *ineruditus*; *in-* priv., and *eruditus*, polished.] Without erudition.

in-es-çap′ȧ-ble, *a.* Not admitting of escape.

in-es′çāte, *v.t.* To bait; to lay a bait for. [Obs.]

in-es-çā′tion, *n.* The act of baiting. [Obs.]

in-es-çutch′eŏn, *n.* In heraldry, a miniature escutcheon borne upon a shield or escutcheon.

Inescutcheon.

in es′sē. [L. *in*, in, and *esse*, to be.] In being; actually existing; distinguished from *in posse*, which denotes that a thing is not, but may be.

in-es-sen′tiăl, *a.* Not essential; unessential; without essence.

in-es′ti-mȧ-ble, *a.* [OFr. *inestimable*; L. *inæstimabilis*, not worthy to be esteemed; *in-* priv., and *æstimabilis*, worthy of estimation, from *æstimare*, to value, esteem.]

1. Not to be estimated or computed; as, an *inestimable* sum of money.

2. Too valuable or excellent to be rated; above all price; as, *inestimable* rights; the privileges of American citizens, civil and religious, are *inestimable.*

in-es′ti-mȧ-bly, *adv.* In a manner not to be estimated or rated.

in-ē-vā′ṣi-ble, *a.* Not to be evaded.

in-ev′i-dence, *n.* Want of evidence; obscurity. [Obs.]

in-ev′i-dent, *a.* Not evident; not clear or obvious; obscure.

in-ev″i-tȧ-bil′i-ty, *n.* Impossibility to be avoided; certainty to happen.

in-ev′i-tȧ-ble, *a.* [L. *inevitabilis*; *in-* priv., and *evitabilis*, avoidable, from *evitare*, to shun, avoid.] Not to be avoided; admitting of no escape or evasion; as, to die is the *inevitable* lot of man; we are all subjected to many *inevitable* calamities.

Syn.—Certain, unavoidable, necessary.

in-ev′i-tȧ-ble-ness, *n.* The state of being unavoidable.

in-ev′i-tȧ-bly, *adv.* Without possibility of escape or evasion; unavoidably; certainly.

in-ex-açt′ (-egz-), *a.* Not exact; not precisely correct or true.

in-ex-açt′i-tūde, *n.* The state of being inexact.

in-ex-açt′ly, *adv.* Without exactness; not accurately.

in-ex-açt′ness (-egz-), *n.* Incorrectness; want of precision.

in-ex-cit-ȧ-bil′i-ty, *n.* The quality or condition that excludes the possibility of being excited.

in-ex-cit′ȧ-ble, *a.* Not susceptible of excitement; dull; lifeless; torpid.

in-ex-çūṣ′ȧ-ble, *a.* [L. *inexcusabilis*; *in-* priv., and *excusabilis*, excusable, from *excusare*, to excuse.] Not to be excused or justified; as, *inexcusable* folly.

Syn.—Unpardonable, indefensible, unjustifiable.

in-ex-çūṣ′ȧ-ble-ness, *n.* The quality of being inexcusable.

in-ex-çūṣ′ȧ-bly, *adv.* With a degree of guilt or folly beyond excuse or justification.

in-ex′ē-crȧ-ble, *a.* Execrable in the highest degree; used only once, by Shakspere.

in-ex-ē-çūt′ȧ-ble, *a.* That cannot be executed or performed.

in-ex-ē-çū′tion, *n.* Neglect of execution; nonperformance; as, the *inexecution* of a treaty.

in-ex-ẽr′tion (-egz-), *n.* Want of effort; defect of action.

in-ex-hāl′ȧ-ble (-eks-), *a.* Not to be exhaled or evaporated; not evaporable.

in-ex-hạust′ed (-egz-), *a.* Unexhausted. [Obs.]

in-ex-hạust′ed-ly, *adv.* So as to be unexhausted.

in-ex-hạust-i-bil′i-ty, *n.* Inexhaustibleness.

in-ex-hạust′i-ble, *a.* Not to be exhausted or emptied; unfailing; as, an *inexhaustible* supply of water.

Syn.—Unfailing, unwearied, indefatigable, perennial, illimitable.

in-ex-hạust′i-ble-ness, *n.* The state of being inexhaustible.

in-ex-hạust′i-bly, *adv.* In an inexhaustible manner.

in-ex-hạust′ive, *a.* Not to be exhausted or spent.

in-ex-ist′ (-egz-), *v.i.* To exist within something else; to be inherent. [Rare.]

in-ex-ist′ănt, *a.* Having no existence. [Obs.]

in-ex-ist′ence, *n.* Want of being or existence.

in-ex-ist′ence, *n.* Existence within; inherence. [Rare.]

in-ex-ist′en-cy, *n.* Inherence. [Rare.]

in-ex-ist′ent, *a.* Not having being; not existing.

in-ex-ist′ent, *a.* Existing within; inherent.

in-ex″ō-rȧ-bil′i-ty (-eks″), *n.* The quality of being inexorable or unyielding to entreaty.

in-ex′ō-rȧ-ble, *a.* [L. *inexorabilis*; *in-* priv., and *exorabilis*, easily entreated, from *exorare*, to entreat, persuade.] Not to be persuaded or moved by entreaty or prayer; as, an *inexorable* tyrant; an *inexorable* judge.

Syn.—Unrelenting, immovable, unchangeable, unyielding, incompassionate, inflexible, implacable, relentless.

in-ex′ō-rȧ-ble-ness, *n.* The quality of being inexorable.

in-ex′ō-rȧ-bly, *adv.* In an inexorable manner.

in-ex-pan′si-ble, *a.* Not expansible.

in-ex-pect′ȧ-ble, *a.* That cannot be expected.

in-ex-pect′ănt, *a.* Without expectation.

in-ex-pec-tā′tion, *n.* State of having no expectation.

in-ex-pect′ed, *a.* Not expected. [Obs.]

in-ex-pect′ed-ly, *adv.* In an unexpected manner. [Obs.]

in-ex-pect′ed-ness, *n.* Want of expectation. [Obs.]

in-ex-pē′di-ence, *n.* Inexpediency.

in-ex-pē′di-en-cy, *n.* Want of fitness; unsuitableness to the purpose; as, the *inexpediency* of a measure is to be determined by the prospect of its advancing the purpose intended.

in-ex-pē′di-ent, *a.* Not expedient; not tending to promote a purpose; unsuitable; as, whatever tends to retard or defeat success is *inexpedient*; what is expedient at one time may be *inexpedient* at another.

Syn.—Improper, inconvenient, unfit, unsuitable, inappropriate, inadvisable, impolitic.

in-ex-pē′di-ent-ly, *adv.* Not expediently; unfitly.

in-ex-pens′ive, *a.* Not expensive.

in-ex-pē′ri-ence, *n.* [LL. *inexperientia*; L. *in-* priv., and *experientia*, experience, from *experiens* (*-entis*), ppr. of *experiri*, to try.] Want of experience or experimental knowledge; as, the *inexperience* of youth.

in-ex-pē′ri-enced (-enst), *a.* Not having experience; unskilled.

in-ex-pērt′, *a.* [L. *inexpertus*; *in-* priv., and *expertus*, pp. of *experiri*, to try.]

1. Not expert; not skilled.

2. Lacking in experience. [Obs.]

in-ex-pērt′ness, *n.* Want of expertness.

in-ex′pi-ȧ-ble, *a.* [L. *inexpiabilis*; *in-* priv., and *expiare*, to atone, expiate.]

1. Admitting of no atonement or satisfaction; as, an *inexpiable* crime or offense.

2. Not to be mollified or appeased by atonement; as, *inexpiable* hate.

in-ex′pi-ȧ-ble-ness, *n.* The quality or state of being beyond the reach of atonement.

in-ex′pi-ȧ-bly, *adv.* To a degree that admits of no atonement.

in-ex′pi-āte, *a.* Without expiation; not having been expiated. [Obs.]

in-ex-plāin′ȧ-ble, *a.* That cannot be explained; inexplicable.

in-ex′plē-ȧ-bly, *adv.* Insatiably. [Obs.]

in-ex″pli-cȧ-bil′i-ty, *n.* The quality or state of being inexplicable.

in-ex′pli-cȧ-ble, *a.* [L. *inexplicabilis*; *in-* priv., and *explicabilis*, explainable, from *explicare*, to set forth, explain.] Not capable of being rendered plain and intelligible; as, an *inexplicable* mystery.

in-ex′pli-cȧ-ble-ness, *n.* The state of being inexplicable.

in-ex′pli-cȧ-bly, *adv.* In a manner not explainable.

in-ex-plic′it, *a.* Not explicit; not clear in statement.

in-ex-plōr′ȧ-ble, *a.* That cannot be explored, searched, or discovered.

in-ex-plō′sive, *a.* That will not explode; not of the nature of an explosive.

in-ex-pō′ṣūre (-zhūr), *n.* The state of not being exposed.

in-ex-press′i-ble, *a.* Not to be expressed in words; not to be uttered; unspeakable; unutterable; as, *inexpressible* grief, joy, or pleasure.

in-ex-press′i-bleṣ, *n.pl.* Euphemistic slang for *breeches* or *trousers*.

in-ex-press′i-bly, *adv.* In a manner or degree not to be told or expressed in words; unspeakably; unutterably.

in-ex-press′ive, *a.* 1. Inexpressible. [Rare.]

2. Not tending to express; not expressing; without expression; as, an *inexpressive* face.

in-ex-press′ive-ness, *n.* The state of being inexpressive.

in-ex-pug′nȧ-ble (*or* -pūn′ȧ-), *a.* [L. *inexpugnabilis*; *in-* priv., and *expugnabilis*, that may be subdued by force, from *expugnare*, to subdue by force.] Not to be subdued by force; not to be taken by assault; impregnable.

in-ex-pug′nȧ-bly, *adv.* So as not to be subdued by force.

in-ex-sū′pēr-ȧ-ble, *a.* [L. *inexsuperabilis*; *in-* priv., and *exsuperabilis*, surmountable.] Not to be passed over or surmounted; that cannot be overcome.

in-ex-tend′ed, *a.* Having no extension.

in-ex-ten′si-ble, *a.* Without the property of extension; as, an *inextensible* thread.

in-ex-ten′sion, *n.* Want of extension; unextended state.

in-ex-tēr′mi-nȧ-ble, *a.* That cannot be exterminated.

in-ex-tinct′, *a.* Not quenched; not extinct.

in-ex-tin′gui-ble, *a.* [Obs.] See *Inextinguishable*.

in-ex-tin′guish-ȧ-ble, *a.* That cannot be extinguished; unquenchable; as, *inextinguishable* flame, thirst, or desire.

in-ex-tin′guish-ȧ-bly, *adv.* In such a manner as to render inextinguishable; unquenchably.

in-ex-tir′pȧ-ble, *a.* [L. *inextirpabilis*; *in-* priv., and *extirpare*, to root out, extirpate.] That cannot be extirpated; not to be uprooted.

in-ex′tri-cȧ-ble, *a.* [L. *inextricabilis*, *in-* priv., and *extricare*, to disentangle, extricate.] Not to be disentangled or untied; not to be freed from intricacy or perplexity; as, an *inextricable* maze or difficulty.

in-ex′tri-cȧ-ble-ness, *n.* The state of being inextricable.

in-ex′tri-cȧ-bly, *adv.* To a degree of perplexity not to be disentangled.

in-eye′ (-ī′), *v.t.*; ineyed (-īd′), *pt., pp.*; ineyeing, *ppr.* To propagate by budding; to bud.

in-fab′ri-cā-ted, *a.* Not fabricated; unwrought; in a natural state. [Obs.]

in-fal′li-bil-ist, *n.* A believer in the dogma of papal infallibility.

in-fal-li-bil′i-ty, *n.* The quality of being infallible or incapable of error or mistake; entire exemption from liability to error; inerrability.

Papal infallibility; in the Roman Catholic church, the dogma that the pope, as the supreme pontiff, is divinely guarded from error when speaking officially on matters of faith or of morals; the dogma was promulgated by the Vatican Council in July, 1870.

in-fal′li-ble, *a.* [LL. *infallibilis*; L. *in-* priv., and LL. *fallibilis*, fallible, from L. *fallere*, to deceive, err.]

1. Not fallible; not capable of erring; entirely exempt from liability to mistake; inerrable.

2. Not liable to fail or to deceive confidence; certain; as, *infallible* evidence.

3. In the Roman Catholic church, not liable to error in propounding doctrines of faith or morals; said of the pope.

in-fal′li-ble-ness, *n.* Infallibility.

in-fal′li-bly, *adv.* Without possibility of erring.

in-fāme′, *v.t.* To defame. [Obs.]

in′fȧ-mīze, *v.t.* To make infamous. [Rare.]

in′fȧ-mous, *a.* [OFr. *infameux*; LL. *infamosus*, L. *infamis*, of evil report; *in-* priv., and *fama*, report, fame.]

1. Of ill fame; having a reputation of the worst kind; publicly branded with odium for vice or guilt; base; scandalous; notoriously vile; as, an *infamous* liar.

2. Odious; detestable; held in abhorrence; causing or producing infamy; as, an *infamous* crime.

Infamous crime; in law, a crime or offense which renders the offender liable to infamous punishment, such as capital punishment or incarceration in the penitentiary.

Syn.—Wicked, heinous, disgraceful, shameful, execrable, ignominious.

in′fȧ-mous-ly, *adv.* In a manner or degree to render infamous; scandalously; disgracefully; shamefully.

in′fȧ-mous-ness, *n.* The quality that renders infamous.

in′fȧ-my, *n.*; *pl.* **in′fȧ-mieṣ.** [L. *infamia*, ill fame, from *infamis*, of ill report, infamous; *in-* priv., and *fama*, fame.]

1. Total loss of reputation; public disgrace; as, avoid the crimes and vices which expose men to *infamy*.

2. Infamous character; extreme baseness; depravity; qualities notoriously bad and scandalous; as, the *infamy* of an action.

3. In law, that loss of character or public disgrace which a convict incurs, and by which a person is rendered incapable of being a witness or juror.

Syn.—Ignominy, opprobrium.—*Infamy* is that which attaches either to the person or to the thing; *ignominy* is thrown upon the person; and *opprobrium* is thrown upon the agent rather than the action. *Infamy* causes either the person or thing to be ill spoken of; *ignominy* causes the name and the person to be held in contempt; *opprobrium* causes the person to be spoken of in severe terms of reproach.

in′făn-cy, *n.* [L. *infantia*, inability to speak, infancy, from *infans* (*-antis*), speechless, an infant; *in-* priv., and *fari*, to speak.]

1. The first part of life, beginning at birth; popularly regarded as the time of teething, or about two years.

2. In law, the entire period of life anterior to the time of becoming legally responsible; minority.

3. Figuratively, the first stage of anything; as, the *infancy* of a nation, language, art, etc.

in-fan′dous, *a.* Odious beyond the power of expression. [Obs.]

in-fang′thef, *n.* [AS. *infangenetheóf*; *infangen*, pp. of *infon*, to seize, and *theóf*, a thief.] In old English law, the right of a lord of the manor to deal with acts of petty larceny, etc., committed within his jurisdiction. [Obs.]

in′fănt, *n.* [L. *infans*, *infantis*, adj. not speaking, n. a child, infant; *in-* priv., and *fans*, *fantis*, ppr. of *fari*, to speak.]

1. One in infancy; a babe; a child during the first period of life.

2. In law, one who is not of full age; specifically, one who is under twenty-one years of age; a minor.

in′fănt, *a.* 1. Pertaining to infancy; as, *infant* food.

2. Young; tender; not mature; as, an *infant* bud; *infant* industries.

3. Minor; as, an *infant* child.

in′fănt, *v.t.* To originate. [Obs.]

in-fan′tȧ, *n.* [Sp. and Port., f. of *infante*, a child, infant.] In Spain and Portugal, any princess of the royal blood.

in-fan′te, *n.* [Sp. and Port., an infant, a child.] In Spain and Portugal, any son of the sovereign; any prince of the royal family.

in′fănt-hood, *n.* The state or period of infancy. [Rare.]

in-fan′ti-cī-dăl, *a.* Pertaining to child-murder.

in-fan′ti-cīde, *n.* [LL. *infanticidium*, the killing of an infant; L. *infans* (*-antis*), an infant, and *cædere*, to kill.] The intentional killing of an infant; child-murder.

in-fan′ti-cīde, *n.* [LL. *infanticida*, one who kills an infant.] One who kills an infant.

in′făn-tile, *a.* [L. *infantilis*, belonging to an infant, from *infans* (*-antis*), an infant.]

1. Pertaining to infancy; childish.

2. In physical geography, designating an early stage of development in a period succeeding a change of level caused by uplift.

Infantile paralysis; an acute, contagious disease, more common in children than adults, characterized by inflammation of the gray matter of the spinal cord and causing motor paralysis as well as permanent deformities.

in′făn-tīne, *a.* Pertaining to infants or to young children.

in′fănt-like, *a.* Like an infant.

in′fănt-ly, *a.* Like a child. [Obs.]

in′făn-try, *n.* [Fr. *infanterie*; Sp. *infanteria*, infantry, from Sp. and Port. *infante*, a very young person, a knight's page, foot-soldier, from L. *infans* (*-antis*), a child, infant.]

1. Children collectively. [Obs.]

2. In military affairs, foot-soldiers as distinguished from cavalry, artillery, etc.

in′făn-try-măn, *n.*; *pl.* **in′făn-try-men.** A soldier of infantry; a foot-soldier.

in-fārce′, *v.t.* To stuff; to puff out. [Obs.]

in-fārct′, *n.* [L. *infartus*, pp. of *infarcire*, to stuff; *in*, in, and *farcire*, to stuff.] The substance which produces, or the morbid condition produced by, infarction.

in-fārct′ed, *a.* Affected by infarction; having obstruction in some organ; as, an *infarcted* artery.

in-fārc′tion, *n.* The act of stuffing or filling; constipation.

in-fash′iŏn-ȧ-ble, *a.* Unfashionable. [Obs.]

in-fat′i-gȧ-ble, *a.* Indefatigable. [Obs.]

in-fat′ū-āte, *v.t.*; infatuated, *pt., pp.*; infatuating, *ppr.* [L. *infatuatus*, pp. of *infatuare*, to make a fool of; *in-*, intens., and *fatuus*, foolish.]

1. To make foolish; to affect with folly; to weaken the intellectual powers of or to deprive of sound judgment; as, whom the gods intend to destroy they first *infatuate*.

2. To inspire with an extravagant or foolish passion too obstinate to be controlled by reason; as, to be *infatuated* with love of gaming.

in-fat′ū-āte, *a.* Infatuated.

in-fat′ū-ā-ted, *a.* Affected with folly.

in-fat′ū-ā-ting, *a.* Affecting with folly.

in-fat-ū-ā′tion, *n.* [LL. *infatuatio* (*-onis*), from L. *infatuare*, to infatuate.]

1. The act of affecting with folly.

2. The state of mind when it is infatuated, or that which produces such a state of mind.

Syn.—Folly, madness, intoxication, foolishness, unreason.

in-faust′, *a.* [L. *infaustus*, unlucky, unfortunate; *in-* priv., and *faustus*, propitious.] Not propitious. [Rare.]

in-faust′ing, *n.* The act of making unlucky. [Obs.]

in-fēa-si-bil′i-ty, *n.* Impracticability; the quality of not being feasible.

in-fēa′ṣi-ble, *a.* Not to be done; that cannot be accomplished; impracticable.

in-fect′, *v.t.*; infected, *pt., pp.*; infecting, *ppr.* [OFr. *infecter*; L. *infectus*, pp. of *inficere*, to put or dip into, to tinge, stain; *in*, in, and *facere*, to do, to make.]

1. To taint with disease; as, persons in health are *infected* by the contagion of typhoid fever.

2. To taint or affect, as with morbid or noxious matter; as, to *infect* a lancet or clothing.

3. To communicate bad qualities to; to

corrupt; to taint by the communication of anything noxious or pernicious; as, a government *infected* by corruption.

4. In law, to contaminate with illegality.

Syn.—Defile, pollute, poison, vitiate, corrupt.

in-feçt′, *a.* Infected. [Obs.]

in-feçt′ẽr, *n.* One who or that which infects.

in-feçt′i-ble, *a.* That may be polluted by infection.

in-feç′tion, *n.* [LL. *infectio* (*-onis*), a dyeing, from L. *infectus*, pp. of *inficere*, to dip in, tinge, infect.]

1. The act or process of infecting.

2. The thing which infects; in medicine, any infecting agency, such as effluvia, miasmatic vapors, etc.

3. That which taints, poisons, or corrupts by communication from one to another; as, the *infection* of error or of evil example.

4. In law, contamination by illegality, as in cases of contraband goods.

5. Communication of like qualities, conditions, etc.

Mankind are gay or serious by *infection*. —Johnson.

6. The condition of an infected person; as, the *infection* may be serious enough to threaten life.

Syn.—Contagion.—We consider *contagion* as to the manner of spreading from one body to another; we consider *infection* as to the act of its working itself into the system. Whatever acts by *contagion* acts immediately by direct personal contact; whatever acts by *infection* acts gradually and indirectly or through the medium of a third body, as clothes or the air when *infected*. The word *contagion* is, therefore, properly applied only to particular diseases, but *infection* may be applied to every disease which is communicable from one subject to another. Whatever, therefore, is *contagious* is also *infectious*, but not vice versa.

in-feç′tious, *a.* 1. Having qualities that may taint, or communicate disease to; as, an *infectious* fever; *infectious* air.

2. Corrupting; tending to taint by communication; as, *infectious* vices or manners.

3. In law, contaminating with illegality; exposing to seizure and forfeiture.

4. Capable of being communicated by near approach.

Grief, as well as joy, is *infectious*.—Kames.

in-feç′tious-ly, *adv.* By infection.

in-feç′tious-ness, *n.* The quality of being infectious, or capable of communicating disease or taint from one to another.

in-feçt′ive, *a.* [L. *infectivus*, for dyeing, from *infectus*, pp. of *inficere*, to dye, infect.] Having the quality of communicating disease or taint from one to another.

in-feç′und, *a.* Unfruitful; not producing young; barren. [Obs.]

in-fe-çun′di-ty, *n.* [L. *infecunditas*, from *infecundus*, unfruitful; *in-* priv., and *fecundus*, fruitful.] Unfruitfulness; barrenness.

in-fe-çun′dous, *a.* Sterile; not producing offspring. [Obs.]

in-fee′ble, *v.t.* [Obs.] See *Enfeeble*.

in-feft′ment, *n.* In Scots law, the act of giving symbolic possession of heritable property.

in-fē-lic′i-tous, *a.* Not felicitous; unhappy; inapt.

in-fē-lic′i-ty, *n.*; *pl.* **in-fē-lic′i-ties.** 1. Unhappiness; misery; misfortune.

2. Unfortunate state; unfavorableness; as, the *infelicity* of the times or of the occasion.

3. An awkward mode of expression.

in-fē-lō′ni-ous, *a.* Lacking the character of felony.

in-felt′, *a.* Deeply felt; affecting the emotions.

in-feo-dā′tion (-fū-), *n.* Same as *Infeudation*.

in-feoff′ (-fef′), *v.t.* [Obs.] See *Enfeoff*.

in-feoff′ment, in-feof′ment, *n.* [Obs.] See *Enfeoffment*.

in-fẽr′, *v.t.*; inferred, *pt.*, *pp.*; inferring, *ppr.* [L. *inferre*, to bring or carry in, to infer; *in*, in, and *ferre*, to bring, carry.]

1. To bring on; to induce. [Obs.]

2. To deduce; to draw or derive, as a fact or consequence; as, from the past we *infer* that certain conditions have existed.

3. To offer; to produce. [Obs.]

in-fẽr′ȧ-ble, *a.* That may be inferred or deduced from premises; written also *inferrible*.

in′fẽr-ence, *n.* [LL. *inferentia*, an inference, from L. *inferre*, to bring in, to infer.]

1. The act of inferring.

Unjust and mistaken in the method of *inference*. —Glanvill.

2. A truth or proposition drawn from another which is admitted or supposed to be true; a conclusion.

Syn.—Conclusion, deduction.—*Conclusion* signifies the winding up of all arguments and reasoning. *Deduction* signifies the bringing or drawing one thing from another. A *conclusion* is full and decisive; an *inference* is partial and indecisive; a *conclusion* leaves the mind in no doubt or hesitation; it puts a stop to all further reasoning; *inferences* are special *conclusions* from particular circumstances; they serve as links in the chain of reasoning. *Conclusion* in the technical sense is the concluding proposition of a syllogism, drawn from the two others, which are called the premises.

in-fẽr-en′tiăl (-shăl), *a.* Deduced or deducible by inference.

in-fẽr-en′tiăl-ly, *adv.* By way of inference.

in-fē′ri-æ, *n.pl.* [L., from *inferi*, those inhabiting the infernal regions, the dead, from *inferus*, below.] Sacrifices offered by the ancients to the souls of deceased heroes or friends.

in-fē′ri-ŏr, *a.* [L. *inferior*, lower, inferior, comp. of *inferus*, low, below.]

1. Lower in station, excellence or value; subordinate; as, a poem of *inferior* merit; cloth of *inferior* quality or price.

2. Subordinate; lower in rank; as, an *inferior* officer.

3. In botany, growing below some other organ; used especially with reference to the position of the ovary when it seems to lie below the calyx.

Inferior Ovary.

4. In astronomy, (a) situated or occuring between the earth and the sun; as, the *inferior* planets; an *inferior* conjunction of Mercury and Venus; (b) lying below the horizon; as, the *inferior* part of a meridian.

5. In music, of a lower pitch.

6. In printing, standing below other type in the same line; as, the *inferior* characters of a chemical formula.

Inferior valve, in zoölogy, the valve of an adherent bivalve by which it is united to other substances.

in-fē′ri-ŏr, *n.* A person who is inferior to another, or lower in station or rank, intellect, importance, etc.

A person gets more by obliging his *inferior* than by disdaining him. —South.

in-fē-ri-or′i-ty, *n.* [LL. *inferioritas*, from L. *inferior*, lower, inferior.] The state of being inferior; as, the *inferiority* of rank, of office, of talents, of age, of worth.

A deep sense of our great *inferiority*. —Boyle.

in-fē′ri-ŏr-ly, *adv.* In an inferior manner, or on the inferior part.

in-fẽr′năl, *a.* [ME. *infernal*; OFr. *enfernal*; LL. *infernalis*, pertaining to the lower regions, from *infernus*, underground, lower, infernal, from *inferus*, below.]

1. Pertaining to the lower regions, or regions of the dead, the Tartarus of the ancients.

The Elysian fields, the *infernal* monarchy. —Garth.

2. Pertaining to or resembling hell; inhabiting hell; suitable or appropriate to hell or its inhabitants; hellish; diabolical; very wicked and detestable; as, *infernal* conduct.

Infernal machine; a machine or apparatus, generally of an explosive nature, contrived for the purposes of assassination or other mischief.

Infernal stone (*lapis infernalis*); a name formerly given to lunar caustic, as also to caustic potash.

Syn.—Hellish, fiendish, devilish, malicious, diabolical.

in-fẽr′năl, *n.* An inhabitant of hell, or of the lower regions.

in-fẽr′năl-ly, *adv.* In an infernal manner; diabolically; wickedly.

in-fẽr′nō, *n.* [It., hell, from L. *infernus*, below, infernal.] Hell; the infernal regions.

infero-. A combining form from L. *inferus*, below, used to signify low, below, underneath; as, *infero*lateral, *infero*median.

in″fe-rō-an-tē′ri-ŏr, *a.* [*Infero-*, and L. *anterior*, toward the front.] Situated below and in front.

in′fe-rō-branch, *n.* One of the *Inferobranchiata*.

in″fe-rō-bran′chi-ȧ, *n.pl.* Same as *Inferobranchiata*.

in″fe-rō-bran′chi-ăn, *n.* An inferobranch.

in″fe-rō-bran-chi-ā′tȧ, *n.pl.* [*Infero-*, and L. *branchiæ*, gills.] An order of nudibranchiate gasteropods, which have their branchiæ, instead of being placed on the back, arranged in the form of two long series of leaflets on the two sides of the body, under the advanced border of the mantle.

in″fe-rō-bran′chi-āte, *a.* Pertaining to or characteristic of the *Inferobranchiata*.

in″fe-rō-lat′ẽr-ăl, *a.* [*Infero-*, and L. *latus* (*-eris*), side.] Situated below and to one side.

in″fe-rō-mē′di-ăn, *a.* [*Infero-*, and L. *medianus*, situated in the middle, from *medius*, middle.] Situated in the middle of the under side.

in″fe-rō-pos-tē′ri-ŏr, *a.* [*Infero-*, and L. *posterior*, behind, comp. of *posterus*, next, following.] Situated below and behind.

in-fẽr′ri-ble, *a.* Inferable.

in-fẽr′tile, *a.* [LL. *infertilis*; L. *in-* priv., and *fertilis*, fertile.] Not fertile; not fruitful or productive; barren; as, an *infertile* soil.

in-fẽr′tile-ly, *adv.* In an unproductive manner.

in-fẽr-til′i-ty, *n.* Unfruitfulness; unproductiveness; barrenness; as, the *infertility* of land.

in-fest′, *v.t.*; infested, *pt.*, *pp.*; infesting, *ppr.* [OFr. *infester*; L. *infestare*, to attack, disturb, trouble, from *infestus*, hostile.] To trouble greatly; to disturb; to annoy; to harass; to prowl around with a mischievous intent; as, flies *infest* horses and cattle; small parties of the enemy *infest* the coast.

in-fest′, *a.* Mischievous. [Obs.]

in-fes-tā′tion, *n.* The act of infesting; molestation; annoyance.

in-fest′ẽr, *n.* One who or that which infests.

in-fest′ẽred, *a.* Rankling; inveterate. [Obs.]

in-fest′ive, *a.* Having no mirth; cheerless; forlorn. [Rare.]

in-fes-tiv′i-ty, *n.* Want of festivity, or of cheerfulness and mirth. [Rare.]

in-fes′tū-ous, *a.* Mischievous. [Obs.]

in-feū-dā′tion, *n.* [LL. *infeudatio* (*-onis*), from *infeudare*, to put one in possession in fee; L. *in*, in, and LL. *feudum*, a feud, fee, from O.H.G. *fihu*, cattle.]

1. In feudal law, the act of putting one in possession of an estate in fee.

2. The granting of tithes to laymen.

in-fib-ū-lā′tion, *n.* [L. *infibulare*, to fasten with a clasp or buckle; *in*, in, and *fibula*, a clasp, buckle.]

1. The act of clasping or confining with or as with a buckle or padlock.

2. The attachment of a ring, clasp, buckle, or the like, to the organs of generation so as to prevent copulation.

in′fi-del, *a.* [L. *infidelis*, unfaithful (LL., unbelieving); *in-* priv., and *fidelis*, faithful.] Unbelieving; disbelieving the inspiration of the Scriptures, or the divine institution of Christianity.

Infidel contempt of holy writ. —Cowper.

in′fi-del, *n.* A disbeliever; a skeptic in reference to some particular religious doctrine or belief; one who disbelieves or refuses to believe the inspiration of the Scriptures and the divine origin of Christianity; a freethinker.

Syn.—Unbeliever, freethinker, deist, atheist, skeptic.—A *freethinker* is now only another name for an *infidel*. An *unbeliever* is not necessarily a disbeliever or *infidel*, because he may still be inquiring after evidence to satisfy his mind. A *deist* believes in one God and a divine providence, but rejects revelation. An *atheist* denies the being of God. A *skeptic* is one whose faith in the reliability of evidence is weakened or destroyed, so that religion, to the same extent, has no practical hold on his mind.

in-fi-del′i-ty, *n.*; *pl.* **in-fi-del′i-ties.** [Fr. *infidélité*; L. *infidelitas*, faithlessness, infidelity, from *infidelis*, unfaithful; *in-* priv., and *fidelis*, faithful.]

1. Want of faith or belief; a withholding of credit.

2. Disbelief of the inspiration of the Scriptures, or the divine origin of Christianity; unbelief.

3. Unfaithfulness, particularly in married persons; a violation of the marriage covenant by adultery.

4. Breach of trust, treachery; deceit; as, the *infidelity* of a friend or a servant.

in′fiēld, *n.* 1. The diamond of the baseball field; the space ninety feet square within the baselines.

2. Land kept continually under crop; distinguished from outfield. [Scot.]

in-fiēld′, *v.t.* To inclose, as a piece of land. [Rare.]

in-file′, *v.t.* To place in a file; to arrange in a file or rank. [Obs.]

in′fill, *v.t.* To fill in.

in′fill-ing, *n.* Filling; that which fills in.

in-film′, *v.t.* To cover with or as with a film.

in-fil′tẽr, *v.t.* and *v.i.*; infiltered, *pt.*, *pp.*; infiltering, *ppr.* To filter or sift in.

in-fil′trāte, *v.i.*; infiltrated, *pt.*, *pp.*; infiltrating, *ppr.* To enter by penetrating the pores or interstices of a substance.

in-fil′trāte, *v.t.* To pass through slowly; to percolate.

in-fil-trā′tion, *n.* 1. The act or process of infiltrating.

2. That which infiltrates; the substance which has entered the pores or cavities of a body.

3. In pathology, the entrance into the tissue-spaces or into the tissue-elements of some abnormal substance or of a normal substance in excess.

in-fil′trȧ-tive, *a.* Pertaining to infiltration.

in′fi-nite, *a.* [ME. *infinite*; L. *infinitus*, boundless, unlimited; *in-* priv., and *finitus*, pp. of *finire*, to limit, bound.]

1. Without limits; unbounded; boundless; not circumscribed; applied to time or space.

An *infinite* standard of right. —Dr. Caird.

2. Indefinitely large; immense; boundless; vast; exceedingly great in excellence, degree, capacity, and the like.

Infinite riches in a little room. —Marlowe.

3. In mathematics, designating quantities which are greater than any assignable quantity.

4. In music, having no finale; capable of being repeated to infinity; said of perpetual fugues.

Infinite decimal; a decimal which is interminate, or which may be carried to infinity; thus, if the diameter of a circle be 1, the circumference is 3.14159265, etc., carried to infinity.

Infinite series; a series the terms of which go on increasing or diminishing without coming to an end.

Syn.—Unlimited, boundless, illimitable, immeasurable, interminable, eternal, countless, unbounded.

in′fi-nite, *n.* 1. Anything infinite; infinity.

2. In mathematics, an infinite quantity.

3. [I—] The Infinite Being; God.

4. An infinite or incalculable number.

Arithmetic of infinites; a term applied by Dr. Wallis to a method invented by him for the summation of infinite series.

in′fi-nite-ly, *adv.* 1. Without bounds or limits; as, an *infinitely* large number.

2. Extremely; greatly; to a great extent or degree.

in′fi-nite-ness, *n.* The state of being infinite; immensity; greatness; infinity.

in″fin-i-tes′i-măl, *a.* [L. *infinitus*, infinite.] Infinitely small; less than any assignable quantity.

in″fin-i-tes′i-măl, *n.* In mathematics, an infinitely small quantity; that which is less than any assignable quantity.

in″fin-i-tes′i-măl-ly, *adv.* By infinitesimals; in infinitely small quantities.

in-fin-i-ti′văl, *a.* In grammar, pertaining to the infinitive.

in-fin′i-tive, *a.* [LL. *infinitivus*, unlimited, undefined, from L. *infinitus*, infinite.] In grammar, unlimited; applied to the mode of the verb which expresses the action of the verb, without limitation of person or number.

in-fin′i-tive, *n.* In grammar, that form by which the action of a verb is expressed without regard to person or number; in English, sometimes designated by *to*; as, *to go*; the infinitive mode.

in-fin′i-tive-ly, *adv.* In grammar, in the manner of an infinitive mode.

in-fi-nī′tō, *a.* [It.] In music, perpetual, as a canon whose end leads back to the beginning.

in-fin′i-tūde, *n.* [L. *infinitus*, infinite.]

1. Infinity; infiniteness; the quality or state of being without limits.

2. Immensity; greatness; infinity.

3. Boundless number.

in-fin′i-tū-ple, *a.* Multiplied an infinite number of times. [Rare.]

in-fin′i-ty, *n.*; *pl.* **in-fin′i-tieṣ.** [L. *infinitas*, boundlessness, endlessness, from *infinitus*, infinite, boundless.]

1. Unlimited extent of time, space, or quantity; boundlessness.

2. Immensity; indefinite extent; as, the *infinity* of God's wisdom.

3. Endless or indefinite number; as, an *infinity* of beauties.

4. In geometry, the part of space infinitely distant from a fixed part.

in-fīrm′, *a.* [OFr. *infirm*; L. *infirmus*, weak, not strong; *in-* priv., and *firmus*, strong.]

1. Not firm or sound; weak; feeble; as, an *infirm* body; an *infirm* constitution.

2. Weak of mind; irresolute; as, *infirm* of purpose.

3. Not solid or stable.

Syn.—Decrepit, weak, imbecile, debilitated, feeble, vacillating, wavering.

in-fīrm′, *v.t.* To weaken. [Obs.]

in-fīr-mā′ri-an, *n.* One who helps in an infirmary or has charge of it; especially, one who has charge of an infirmary in a monastery.

in-fīrm′ȧ-ry, *n.*; *pl.* **in-fīrm′ȧ-rieṣ.** [OFr. *enfermerie*; LL. *infirmarium*, a hospital or infirmary, from L. *infirmus*, weak, infirm.] A hospital or place where the sick and wounded are lodged and nursed, sometimes for a very small fee or free of charge.

in-fīrm′ȧ-tive, *a.* Weakening; annulling, or tending to make void. [Obs.]

in-fīrm′ȧ-tō-ry, *n.* An infirmary. [Obs.]

in-fīrm′i-ty, *n.*; *pl.* **in-fīrm′i-tieṣ.** [ME. *infirmite*; OFr. *enfermete*; L. *infirmitas*, weakness, infirmity, from *infirmus*, weak, infirm.]

1. The state of being infirm; especially an unsound or unhealthy state of the body; weakness; feebleness.

2. A weakness; failing; fault; foible.

A friend should bear his friend's *infirmities*. —Shak.

Syn.—Feebleness, debility, imperfection, failing, foible, weakness.

in-fīrm′ly, *adv.* In an infirm manner.

in-fīrm′ness, *n.* Weakness; feebleness; unsoundness.

in-fix′, *v.t.*; infixed (-fixt′), *pt.*, *pp.*; infixing, *ppr.* [OFr. *infixer*; L. *infixus*, pp. of *infigere*, to fix, to thrust or drive in; *in*, in, and *figere*, to fix, fasten.]

1. To fix by piercing or thrusting in; as, to *infix* a sting, spear, or dart.

2. To implant or fix, as principles, thoughts, or instructions; as, to *infix* good principles in the mind, or ideas in the memory.

3. In grammar, to insert as an infix.

in′fix, *n.* 1. Something infixed. [Rare.]

2. In grammar, an element somewhat of the character of a suffix or prefix, but inserted in the body of a word.

in-flāme′, *v.t.*; inflamed, *pt.*, *pp.*; inflaming, *ppr.* [ME. *enflawmen*; OFr. *enflammer*; L. *inflammare*, to set on fire, to kindle; *in*, in, and *flamma*, a flame.]

1. To set on fire; to kindle; to cause to burn with a flame.

2. To excite or increase, as passion or appetite; to irritate; to anger; to exasperate; to excite to violent action; as, to *inflame* love; to *inflame* the populace.

3. In medicine, to set up inflammation in; as, to *inflame* a sore; to *inflame* the eyes.

4. To increase; to augment; to exaggerate. [Obs.]

Syn.—Anger, arouse, kindle, excite, incense, provoke, irritate.

in-flāme′, *v.i.* To grow hot, angry, or painful.

in-flāmed′, *a.* 1. Set on fire; enkindled; heated; provoked; exasperated.

2. In heraldry, applied to anything blazoned or decorated with flames; as, a bend *inflamed.*

in-flām′ẽr, *n.* The person or thing that inflames.

in-flam-mȧ-bil′i-ty, *n.* Susceptibility of taking fire.

in-flam′mȧ-ble, *a.* 1. Readily set on fire; easily enkindled; susceptible of combustion; as, *inflammable* oils or spirits.

2. Easily angered or excited; irascible.

Inflammable air; in chemistry, a name formerly applied to hydrogen.

in-flam′mȧ-ble-ness, *n.* Inflammability.

in-flam′mȧ-bly, *adv.* In an inflammable manner.

in-flam-mā′tion, *n.* [Fr. *inflammation*; L. *inflammatio* (*-onis*), a kindling, setting on fire, from *inflammare*, to set on fire, inflame.]

1. The act of setting on fire or inflaming; the state of being inflamed.

2. Violent excitement; heat; animosity; turbulence; as, an *inflammation* of the body politic or of parties.

3. In medicine, a redness and swelling of any part of an animal body, attended with heat, pain, and febrile symptoms.

in-flam′mȧ-tive, *a.* Inflammatory.

in-flam′mȧ-tō-ry, *a.* [L. *inflammare*, to inflame.]

1. Inflaming; tending to kindle or excite.

2. In medicine, accompanied by preternatural heat and excitement of arterial action; as, an *inflammatory* fever or disease.

3. Tending to excite anger, animosity, tumult, or sedition; as, *inflammatory* libels, writings, speeches, or publications.

in-flāt′ȧ-ble, *a.* Susceptible to inflation.

in-flāte′, *v.t.*; inflated, *pt.*, *pp.*; inflating, *ppr.* [L. *inflatus*, pp. of *inflare*, to blow into, inflate; *in*, in, and *flare*, to blow.]

1. To swell or distend by injecting air or gas; to expand; as, to *inflate* a bladder; to *inflate* the lungs.

2. To swell; to puff up; to elate; as, to *inflate* one with pride or vanity.

3. To increase or swell unduly; as, to *inflate* the currency.

in-flāte′, *v.i.* To distend; to swell out.

in-flāte′, *a.* Inflated.

in-flāt′ed, *a.* 1. Swollen or distended with gas or air, as a bladder.

2. Puffed up; turgid; pompous; bombastic; as, *inflated* with conceit.

3. In botany, hollow and distended, as a perianth or pericarp.

in-flāt′ẽr, *n.* One who or that which inflates; specifically, one who inflates or advances prices.

in-flāt′ing-ly, *adv.* In a manner tending to inflate.

in-flā′tion, *n.* [L. *inflatio* (*-onis*), from *inflare*, to blow into, inflate.]

1. The act of inflating or the condition of being inflated.

2. The state of being puffed up, as with vanity; conceit.

3. Undue expansion or an overissue of currency.

in-flā′tion-ist, *n.* In United States politics, an advocate of an increased issue of paper money.

in-flā′tus, *n.* [L., from *inflatus*, pp. of *inflare*, to blow into, to inflate.] A blowing or breathing into; hence, inspiration.

in-fleçt′, *v.t.*; inflected, *pt.*, *pp.*; inflecting, *ppr.* [L. *inflectere*, to bend, inflect; *in*, in, and *flectere*, to bend.]

1. To bend; to turn from a direct line or course.

Are not the rays of the sun reflected, refracted, and *inflected* by one and the same principle? —Newton.

2. In grammar, to vary, as a noun or a verb, in terminations; to decline, as a noun or adjective, or to conjugate, as a verb.

3. To modulate, as the voice.

in-fleçt′ed, *a.* 1. Bent or turned from a direct line or course.

2. In biology, bent inward or downward.

3. In grammar, changed in form and function by inflection.

Inflected cycloid; see *Cycloid.*

in-fleç′tion, in-flex′ion (-flek′shun), *n.* [L. *inflexio* (*-onis*), a bending, swaying, from *inflexus*, pp. of *inflectere*, to bend, inflect.]

1. The act of turning from a direct line, or the condition of being so turned; a bend or curve.

2. Modulation of the voice in speaking; any change in the pitch or tone of the voice in singing.

3. In grammar, the variation of nouns, etc., by declension, and of verbs by conjugation.

4. In optics, same as *diffraction.*

Point of inflection; in geometry, the point on opposite sides of which a curve bends in contrary ways.

in-fleç′tion-ăl, *a.* 1. Pertaining to or having inflection.

2. In grammar, inflective.

in-fleç′tion-less, *a.* Without inflection.

in-fleçt′ive, *a.* 1. Having the power of bending; as, the *inflective* quality of the air.

2. In grammar, characterized by variation in form to distinguish case, gender, etc.

Inflective language; a language composed largely of words of inflective character.

in-flesh′, *v.t.* Same as *Enflesh.*

in-flex′, *v.t.*; inflexed (-flext′), *pt.*, *pp.*; inflexing, *ppr.* [L. *inflexus*, pp. of *inflectere*, to turn or bend, inflect.] To bend; to curve; to flex.

in-flexed′, *a.* 1. Turned; bent; bent inward.

2. In botany, abruptly turned inward; said of the petals of a flower when bent toward the axis.

in-flex-i-bil′i-ty, *n.* The quality of being inflexible, or not capable of being bent; unyielding stiffness; obstinacy of will or temper; firmness of purpose; unbending pertinacity.

in-flex′i-ble, *a.* [L. *inflexibilis*, that cannot be bent; *in-* priv., and *flexibilis*, that can be bent, flexible, from *flectere*, to bend.]

1. Unbending; rigid; as, an *inflexible* oak.

2. Firm in purpose; not to be prevailed on; incapable of being turned; as, a man of upright and *inflexible* temper.

3. Not to be changed or altered; as, nature's *inflexible* laws.

in-flex′i-ble-ness, *n.* Inflexibility.

in-flex′i-bly, *adv.* In an inflexible manner.

in-flex′ion, *n.* Inflection.

in-flex′ive, *a.* Same as *Inflective.*

in-flex′ūre, *n.* An inflection; a bend.

in-fliçt′, *v.t.*; inflicted, *pt.*, *pp.*; inflicting, *ppr.* [L. *inflictus*, pp. of *infligere*, to strike or beat against, to strike on; *in*, on, against, and *fligere*, to strike.] To lay on; to throw or send on; to apply forcibly; to cause to be borne, felt, or suffered; as, to *inflict* punishment on an offender.

in-fliçt′ẽr, *n.* One who inflicts.

in-fliç′tion, *n.* [LL. *inflictio* (*-onis*), from L. *inflictus*, pp. of *infligere*, to strike on or against, to inflict.]

1. The act of inflicting; as, the *infliction* of punishment.

2. The punishment applied; that which is inflicted.

in-fliçt′ive, *a.* Tending or able to inflict.

in-flō-res′cence, *n.* [LL. *inflorescens* (*-entis*), ppr. of *inflorescere*, to begin to blossom; L. *in*, in, and *florescere*, incept. of *florere*, to blossom.]

1. In botany, a mode of flowering, or the manner in which flowers are supported on their footstalks, or disposed relatively to each other.

2. A flowering; the unfolding of blossoms.

in-flōw′, *v.i.*; inflowed, *pt.*, *pp.*; inflowing, *ppr.* To flow from without toward a center or interior; opposed to *outflow.*

in′flōw, *n.* That which flows in; also, the act of flowing in.

in-flow′ẽr-ing, *n.* The process of extracting the aroma of flowers for use in the making of perfumery.

in′flū-ence, *n.* [ME. *influence*; OFr. *influance*; LL. *influentia*, a flowing in, from L. *influens* (*-entis*), ppr. of *influere*, to flow in; *in*, in, and *fluere*, to flow.]

1. An influx. [Obs.]

2. In astrology, a supposed power proceeding from the celestial bodies, and operating on the affairs of men.

3. Agency or power serving to affect, modify, or sway in some way; ability or power sufficient to produce some effect; sway; bias; as,

the *influence* of heat in making crops grow; the *influence* of good advice or example on a person.

4. Power or authority arising from elevated station, wealth, and the like; acknowledged ascendancy.

5. In physics, induction.

Syn.—Power, control, sway, authority, supremacy, weight.

in′flū-ence, *v.t.*; influenced, *pt.*, *pp.*; influencing, *ppr.* To exercise influence on; to modify or affect in some way; to act on; to bias; to sway; as, the sun *influences* the tides; to *influence* a person by fears or hopes.

in′flū-en-cẽr, *n.* One who or that which influences.

in-flū-en′cive, *a.* Having influencing qualities or properties.

in′flū-ent, *a.* [OFr. *influent*, influential, lit., flowing in, from L. *influens* (*-entis*), ppr. of *influere* to flow in.]

1. Flowing in.

2. Having influence. [Obs.]

in-flū-en′tiăl (-shăl), *a.* Exerting influence; possessing power or influence.

Syn.—Potent, powerful, efficacious, forcible, persuasive, controlling, guiding, considerable, authoritative, leading.

in-flū-en′tiăl-ly, *adv.* In an influential manner; so as to incline, move, or direct.

in-flū-en′ză, *n.* [It. *influenza*, influenza, lit., an influence, so called because formerly attributed by astrologers to the influence of the stars, from LL. *influentia*, an influence, lit., a flowing in, from L. *influens* (*-entis*), ppr. of *influere*, to flow in.] In pathology, an epidemic affection characterized by catarrhal inflammation of the mucous membrane of the respiratory passages, accompanied by mucopurulent discharge, fever, pain in the muscles, and prostration.

in′flux, *n.* [L. *influxus*, a flowing in, properly pp. of *influere*, to flow in; *in*, in, and *fluere*, to flow.]

1. The act of flowing in; as, an *influx* of light or of air.

2. Infusion; intromission.

3. Influence; power. [Obs.]

4. A coming in; introduction; importation in abundance; as, a great *influx* of goods into a country.

in-flux′iŏn (-fluk′shun), *n.* Infusion; intromission. [Rare.]

in-flux′ious, *a.* Influential. [Obs.]

in-flux′ive, *a.* Having influence; having a tendency to flow in. [Rare.]

in-flux′ive-ly, *adv.* By influxion. [Rare.]

in-fōld′, *v.t.*; infolded, *pt.*, *pp.*; infolding, *ppr.*

1. To involve; to wrap up or inwrap; to inclose.

2. To clasp with the arms; to embrace.

in-fōld′ment, *n.* The act of infolding; the state of being infolded.

in-fō′li-āte, *v.t.* To cover or overspread with leaves. [Rare.]

in-fọrm′, *v.t.*; informed, *pt.*, *pp.*; informing, *ppr.* [ME. *informen*; OFr. *enformer*; L. *informare*, to shape, fashion, represent, instruct; *in*, in, and *formare*, to form, from *forma*, form, shape.]

1. To animate; to give form or shape to; to give life to; to actuate by vital powers.

> Let others better mold the running mass
> Of metals, and *inform* the breathing brass.
> —Dryden.

2. To instruct; to tell to; to acquaint; to communicate knowledge to; to make known to; usually followed by *of*; as, before we judge we should be well *informed of* the facts.

3. To communicate a knowledge of facts to by way of accusation. [Rare.]

Syn.—Acquaint, apprise, disclose, impart, instruct, notify, tell, teach, enlighten.

in-fọrm′, *v.i.* 1. To take shape; to become manifest.

2. To give intelligence; usually with *against* or *on*.

in-fọrm′, *a.* Without regular form; shapeless; ugly. [Obs.]

in-fọrm′ăl, *a.* [L. *in-* priv., and *forma*, form.]

1. Not formal; not in the regular or usual form; not in the usual manner; not according to custom; not in accordance with official, conventional, or customary forms; without ceremony; as, *informal* proceedings; an *informal* visit.

2. Irregular or deranged in mind. [Obs.]

in-fọr-mal′i-ty, *n.*; *pl.* **in-fọr-mal′i-tieṣ.**

1. The condition of being informal; lack of customary form.

2. An informal affair, or action.

in-fọrm′ăl-ly, *adv.* In an irregular or informal manner; without the usual forms.

in-fọrm′ănt, *n.* [L. *informans* (*-antis*), ppr. of *informare*, to inform.]

1. One who informs or instructs.

2. One who offers an accusation. [Obs.]

Syn.—Informer.—An *informer* is one who, for selfish ends, volunteers accusations with a view to have others punished; an *informant* is one who simply acquaints us with something we had not known before.

in-fọr-mā′tion, *n.* [OFr. *information*; L. *informatio* (*-onis*), a representation, an outline, sketch, from *informare*, to give form to, to represent, inform.]

1. Intelligence; notice; news or advice communicated by word or writing.

2. Knowledge derived from reading or instruction.

> He should get some *information* in the subject he intends to handle. —Swift.

3. Knowledge derived from the senses, or from the operation of the intellectual faculties.

> The active *informations* of the intellect.
> —South.

4. Communication of facts for the purpose of accusation; a charge or accusation exhibited to a magistrate or court.

5. In law, a procedure on the part of a public officer without indictment by a grand jury.

Syn.—Intelligence, notice, advice, counsel, instruction, news.

in-fọrm′ā-tive, *a.* 1. Having power to animate.

2. Instructive.

in-fọrm′ā-tō-ry, *a.* Having the quality of furnishing information.

in-fọrmed′, *a.* Ill-formed; misshapen. [Obs.]

Informed stars; stars not grouped into a constellation.

in-fọrm′ẽr, *n.* 1. One who animates or informs.

2. One who communicates to a magistrate a knowledge of the violations of law; one who prosecutes any person who offends against the law.

3. One who informs; an informant.

Common informer; formerly, one who made a business of giving information of violations of law, for the purpose of obtaining a portion of the fine imposed.

in-fọr′mi-dȧ-ble, *a.* Not formidable. [Obs.]

in-fọrm′i-ty, *n.* [LL. *informitas*, unshapeliness; L. *informis*, unshapely; *in-* priv., and *forma*, shape.] Want of regular form; shapelessness.

in-fọrm′ous, *a.* Of no regular form or figure; shapeless. [Obs.]

in-fọr′tū-nāte, *a.* [Obs.] See *Unfortunate.*

in-fọr′tū-nāte-ly, *adv.* [Obs.] See *Unfortunately.*

in-fọr′tūne, *n.* [OFr. *infortune*; L. *infortunium*, misfortune, punishment; *in-* priv., and *fortuna*, chance, fortune.]

1. Misfortune. [Obs.]

2. In astrology, any one of the planets, Saturn, Mars, or Mercury, believed to be of evil influence.

in-fọr′tūned, *a.* [Obs.] See *Unfortunate.*

in-found′, *v.t.* To infuse. [Obs.]

in′frȧ. [L. *infra*, adv. and prep., on the under side, below, underneath, contr. of *infera*, abl. f. of *inferus*, below, beneath.] A preposition and adverb of Latin origin signifying below, beneath, used especially in Latin phrases.

infra-. A prefix from Latin *infra*, adv. and prep., below, beneath; used in anatomy, botany, zoölogy, etc., to signify below, beneath, underneath; as, *infra*median, *infra*hyoid.

in″frȧ-ax′il-lā-ry, *a.* [*Infra-*, and L. *axilla*, axil.]

1. In botany, below the axil.

2. In zoölogy, below the axilla.

in-frȧ-brań′chi-ăl, *a.* [*Infra-*, and L. *branchiæ*, gills.] Situated beneath the gills.

in-frȧ-bug′găl, *a.* [*Infra-*, and L. *bucca*, the cheek, mouth.] Below the buccal mass of a mollusk; as, an *infrabuccal* nerve.

in-fraçt′, *a.* Unbroken. [Obs.]

in-fraçt′, *v.t.*; infracted, *pt.*, *pp.*; infracting, *ppr.* [L. *infractus*, pp. of *infringere*, to break off, break, bruise.] To break; to abandon; to violate. [Rare.]

in-fraçt′ed, *a.* In zoölogy, bent inward; geniculate.

in-fraçt′i-ble, *a.* Breakable. [Rare.]

in-frac′tion, *n.* [L. *infractio* (*-onis*), a breaking to pieces, from *infractus*, pp. of *infringere*, to break off, break; *in*, in, and *frangere*, to break.] The act of breaking; breach; violation; nonobservance; as, an *infraction* of a treaty, compact, agreement, or law.

in-fraçt′ŏr, *n.* One who violates an agreement.

in-frā′grănt, *a.* Not fragrant.

in-frȧ-hȳ′oid, *a.* [*Infra-*, and Gr. *hyoeidēs*, hyoid.] Beneath the hyoid.

in-frȧ-lā′bi-ăl, *a.* [*Infra-*, and L. *labia*, a lip.] Beneath the lower lip; as, *infralabial* scales.

in-frȧ-lap-sā′ri-ăn, *a.* and *n.* I. *a.* Pertaining to the Infralapsarians, or to their doctrine.

II. *n.* [I—] One of that class of Calvinists who consider the decree of election as contemplating the apostasy as past, and the elect when chosen as being in a fallen and guilty state; opposed to *Supralapsarian.*

in″frȧ-lap-sā′ri-ăn-iṣm, *n.* The doctrine of the Infralapsarians.

in-frȧ-mär′gin-ăl, *a.* [*Infra-*, and L. *margo* (*-inis*), border, margin.]

1. Below the outer edge or margin, as of the convolutions of the brain.

2. In entomology, posterior to a marginal cell.

in-frȧ-max′il-lā-ry, *a.* [*Infra-*, and L. *maxilla*, jaw.] In anatomy, situated under the jaw; belonging to the lower jaw.

in-frȧ-mē′di-ăn, *a.* [*Infra-*, and L. *medius*, middle.] Relating to a belt at the bottom of the sea, varying in depth from three hundred to six hundred feet.

in-frȧ-mun′dāne, *a.* [*Infra-*, and L. *mundus*, the world.] Lying or being beneath the world.

in-fran′chiṣe, *v.t.* Same as *Enfranchise.*

in-fran′chiṣe-ment, *n.* Same as *Enfranchisement.*

in-fran-ġi-bil′i-ty, *n.* The condition of being infrangible.

in-fran′ġi-ble, *a.* [Fr. *infrangible*; L. *in-* priv., and *frangere*, to break.]

1. Not to be broken or separated into parts; as, *infrangible* atoms.

2. Not to be violated; as, an *infrangible* vow.

in-fran′ġi-ble-ness, *n.* Infrangibility.

in-frȧ-oc′ū-lăr, *a.* [*Infra-*, and L. *oculus*, eye.] In zoölogy, placed beneath the eyes; said of the antennæ of certain insects.

in-frȧ-ō′răl, *a.* [*Infra-*, and L. *os*, *oris*, the mouth.] In zoölogy, placed beneath the mouth.

in-frȧ-ọr′bit-ăl, *a.* [*Infra-*, and L. *orbita*, orbit.] In anatomy, located beneath or at the under part of the orbit of the eye.

in-frȧ-pōṣe′, *v.t.* To put below or beneath. [Rare.]

in-frȧ-pō-ṣi′tion (-zish′un), *n.* [*Infra-*, and L. *positio* (*-onis*), position.] A situation underneath.

in′frȧ-red, *a.* [*Infra-*, and E. *red.*] In physics, pertaining to invisible solar rays falling outside the red end of the visible solar spectrum.

in-frȧ-scap′ū-lăr, *a.* [*Infra-*, and L. *scapula*, the shoulder-blade.] In anatomy, situated beneath the shoulder-blade; subscapular.

in-frȧ-spi′năl, *a.* Same as *Infraspinous.*

in-frȧ-spi′nāte, *a.* Same as *Infraspinous.*

in-frȧ-spi′nous, *a.* [*Infra-*, and L. *spina*, the spine.] In anatomy, located under the spine, especially that of the scapula; as, the *infraspinous* fossa of the shoulder-blade.

in″frȧ-stȧ-pē′di-ăl, *a.* and *n.* [*Infra-*, and LL. *stapes*, stirrup.]

I. *a.* Of or pertaining to the columella of the ear.

II. *n.* An infrastapedial bone.

in-frȧ-stẽr′năl, *a.* [*Infra-*, and Gr. *sternon*, the breast.] Beneath the sternum or breastbone.

in-frȧ-stip′ū-lăr, *a.* [*Infra-*, and L. *stipula*, stalk.] In botany, growing beneath the stipules.

in-frȧ-tem′pō-răl, *a.* [*Infra-*, and L. *tempora*, the temples.] In anatomy, below the temporal bone.

in-frȧ-ter-ri-tō′ri-ăl, *a.* [*Infra-*, and LL. *territorialis*, territorial, from L. *territorium*, territory.] Within the boundaries of a state or territory.

in-frȧ-troch′lē-ăr, *a.* [*Infra-*, and L. *trochlea*, a pulley.] In anatomy, lying beneath a trochlea; as, the *infratrochlear* nerve.

in-frē′quence (-kwens), *n.* [Rare.] Same as *Infrequency.*

in-frē′quen-cy, *n.* [L. *infrequentia*, a small number, scantiness, from *infrequens* (*-entis*), rare, infrequent.]

1. Uncommonness; rareness; the state of being infrequent.

2. The state of being unfrequented. [Obs.]

in-frē′quent, *a.* [L. *infrequens* (*-entis*), rare, uncommon, unusual; *in-* priv., and *frequens* (*-entis*), frequent, repeated.] Rare; uncommon; seldom happening or occurring.

in-frē′quent-ly, *adv.* Not frequently.

in-friġ′i-dāte, *v.t.* To chill; to make cold. [Obs.]

in-friġ-i-dā′tion, *n.* The act of making cold. [Obs.]

in-fringe′, *v.t.*; infringed, *pt.*, *pp.*; infringing, *ppr.* [L. *infringere*, to break off, break, impair, violate; *in*, in, and *frangere*, to break.]

1. To break; to violate; to transgress; to neglect to fulfil or obey; as, to *infringe* a law.

2. To destroy or hinder; as, to *infringe* efficacy. [Obs.]

in-fringe′, *v.i.* 1. To break or violate a law.

2. To trespass or encroach; followed by *on* or *upon*; as, to *infringe upon* one's rights.

Syn.—Violate, transgress, encroach, infract, intrude, invade, trespass.

in-fringe′ment, *n.* The act of violating; breach; violation; nonfulfilment; as, the *infringement* of an agreement or law; the *infringement* of a patent or copyright.

in-frin′ġẽr, *n.* One who infringes; a violator.

in-fruc′tū-ōse, *a.* Same as *Infructuous.*

in-fruc′tū-ous, *a.* [L. *infructuosus*; *in-* priv. and *fructuosus*, fruitful.] Not productive; not fruitful.

in-frū′găl, *a.* Not frugal; prodigal.

in-frū-ġif′ẽr-ous, *a.* [L. *in-* priv., and *frugifer*, bearing fruit.] Not bearing fruit.

in′fū-cāte, *v.t.* To stain; to paint; to daub. [Obs.]

in-fū-çā′tion, *n.* The act of staining, painting, or daubing, especially the face. [Obs.]

in′fū-lȧ, *n.*; *pl.* **in′fū-læ.** [L., a band, bandage, fillet.]

1. Among the ancient Romans, a kind of headdress consisting of a woolen band, generally white, worn by priests and vestal virgins as a sign of their calling, by emperors and the higher magistrates on solemn occasions, and by those seeking protection or sanctuary. It was also placed upon the head of a sacrificial victim.

Infula, from statue of Isis in the Vatican.

2. In the early Christian church, the head-covering of a priest; latterly, a pendent ornament at the back of a miter.

in′fū-māte, *v.t.*; infumated, *pt., pp.*; infumating, *ppr.* [L. *infumatus*, pp. of *infumare*, to smoke; *in*, in, on, and *fumare*, to smoke; from *fumus*, smoke.] To cure or dry by subjecting to smoke.

in′fū-māte, *a.* In entomology, having a brownish-black color as if from infumating.

in′fū-mā-ted, *a.* Same as *Infumate.*

in-fū-mā′tion, *n.* The process of infumating; the act of drying in smoke.

in-fūmed′, *a.* Dried in smoke.

in-fun-dib′ū-lăr, *a.* Same as *Infundibuliform.*

in-fun-dib-ū-lā′tȧ, *n.pl.* [L. *infundibulum*, a funnel.] In zoölogy, an order or group of polyzoans characterized by having infundibulate cell-mouths.

in-fun-dib′ū-lāte, *a.* 1. Having an infundibulum; pertaining to the *Infundibulata.*

2. Same as *Infundibuliform.*

in-fun-dib′ū-li-fọrm, *a.* [L. *infundibulum*, a funnel, and *forma*, form.]

1. Having the shape of a funnel.

2. In botany, having the shape of a funnel, as the corolla of a flower; monopetalous, having an inversely conical border rising from a tube, as in the stramonium or the morning-glory.

Infundibuliform Corolla of the Stramonium.

in-fun-dib′ū-lum, *n.* [L., a funnel, from *infundere*, to pour into; *in*, in, and *fundere*, to pour.]

1. In anatomy, a funnel-shaped organ, as the dilated ends of the bronchial tubes.

2. In zoölogy, a funnel-shaped organ or passage, as the siphon of a cephalopod, the gastric cavity of a ctenophore, or the oviduct of a bird.

in-fū′nēr-ăl, *v.t.* To bury with funeral ceremonies. [Obs.]

in-fŭr-çā′tion, *n.* [L. *in*, in, and *furca*, a fork.] A forked divergence or expansion.

in-fū′ri-āte, *a.* [LL. *infuriatus*, pp. of *infuriare*, to enrage; L. *in*, in, and *furiare*, to enrage, from *furia*, rage, anger.] Enraged; mad; raging; furious; exasperated.

in-fū′ri-āte, *v.t.*; infuriated, *pt., pp.*; infuriating, *ppr.* To render furious or mad; to enrage.

in-fus′cāte, *a.* Clouded, darkened, or tinged with a brownish color, as the tip of an insect's wing.

in-fus′cāte, *v.t.*; infuscated, *pt., pp.*; infuscating, *ppr.* [L. *infuscatus*, pp. of *infuscare*, to darken, to obscure; *in*, in, on, and *fuscare*, to make dark, from *fuscus*, dark.] To darken; to make black.

in-fus′cā-ted, *a.* Darkened; blackened.

in-fus-cā′tion, *n.* The act of darkening or blackening.

in-fūṣe′, *v.t.*; infused (-fūzd), *pt., pp.*; infusing, *ppr.* [ME. *enfusen*, from L. *infusus*, pp. of *infundere*, to pour in; *in*, in, and *fundere*, to pour.]

1. To pour in, as a liquid.

2. To instil, as principles or qualities.

3. To introduce; as, to *infuse* Gallicisms into composition.

4. To steep in liquor without boiling, for the purpose of extracting the qualities of.

5. To diffuse. [Obs.]

in-fūṣe′, *n.* Infusion. [Obs.]

in-fūṣ′ēr, *n.* One who or that which infuses.

in-fū-ṣi-bil′i-ty, *n.* Incapability of being fused or dissolved.

in-fū-ṣi-bil′i-ty, *n.* Capability of being infused, or poured in and mingled.

in-fū′ṣi-ble, *a.* [L. *infusus*, pp. of *infundere*, to infuse.] Capable of being infused; as, good principles are *infusible* into the minds of youth.

in-fū′ṣi-ble, *a.* [L. *in-* priv., and *fusus*, pp. of *fundere*, to pour in.] Not fusible; incapable of fusion; that cannot be dissolved or melted.

in-fū′ṣi-ble-neṣs, *n.* Infusibility.

in-fū′ṣion (-zhun), *n.* [L. *infusio (-onis)*, a pouring in, from *infusus*, pp. of *infundere*, to pour in, infuse.]

1. The act of pouring in or instilling; instillation; as, the *infusion* of good principles into the mind; the *infusion* of ardor or zeal.

2. Suggestion; whisper. [Obs.]

3. The process of steeping in a liquid, an operation by which the qualities of plants, etc., may be extracted without boiling.

4. The liquid in which plants, etc., are steeped, and which is impregnated with their virtues or qualities; as, an *infusion* of tea.

in-fū′ṣion-iṣm, *n.* The doctrine that the soul is a part of the divine element, and preëxistent to the body, into which it is infused with the breath of life; opposed to *creationism* and *traducianism.*

in-fū′sive, *a.* Having the power of infusion.

In-fū-sō′ri-ȧ, *n.pl.* [From L. *infusus*, pp. of *infundere*, to pour in, infuse.] Microscopic animals inhabiting water and liquids of various kinds, and having no organs of motion except extremely minute organs called cilia; a class of the *Protozoa.*

Magnified Drop of Water, showing Infusoria, etc.

in-fū-sō′ri-ăl, *a.* Pertaining to the *Infusoria*; composed of or containing *Infusoria.* *Infusorial earth*; in geology, a deposit occurring in a formation once the bed of a lake, pond, or quiet bay, and consisting chiefly of the frustules of diatoms. It is a porous, dust-like earth, and is used for polishing metal and as an absorbent in the manufacture of explosives.

in-fū-sō′ri-ăn, *n.* In zoölogy, one of the infusorial animals.

in-fū-sō′ri-fọrm, *a.* [L. *infusus*, pp. of *infundere*, to pour in, and *forma*, form.] Resembling an infusorian in shape; said of certain larvæ.

in-fū′sō-ry, *a.* Infusorial.

in-fū′sō-ry, *n.*; *pl.* **in-fū′sō-rieṣ.** An individual infusorian.

-ing. [ME. *-ing*, *-yng*; AS. *-ung*.] A suffix added to verbs to form verbal nouns expressing action or being; as, dredg*ing*, build*ing*, etc.

-ing. [ME. *-ing*, *-yng*, originally *-end*, *-and*, *-ind*, from AS. *-ende*, suffix of ppr. of verbs.] A suffix used to form the present participle of verbs; as, walk*ing*, sleep*ing*, etc.; participles thus formed readily become adjectives and such adjectives become nouns of agent.

-ing. [ME. *-ing*; AS. *-ing*.] A suffix used in nouns denoting origin, having the force of a patronymic; especially used in proper names; as, Birl*ing*, the son of Birl. By the addition of AS. *ham*, home, many local names were formed; as, Nott*ingham*. It is sometimes used with a diminutive force, equivalent to *-ling*; as, far*thing*, tith*ing*, etc.

-ing. A suffix from AS. *ing*, a meadow; used in local names; as, Wapp*ing*, Dork*ing*, etc.

ing, *n.* [ME. *ing*; AS. *ing*, a meadow.] A pasture or meadow. [Prov. Eng.]

iṅ′găn, iṅ′gun, *n.* An onion. [Dial.]

in-gan-nā′tion, *n.* Cheat; fraud. [Obs.]

in′gāte, *n.* 1. Entrance; passage in. [Obs.]

2. In founding, the opening through which metal is poured into a mold.

in-gath′ēr-ing, *n.* The act or business of collecting and securing the fruits of the earth; harvest; as, the feast of *ingathering.*

in-gel′ȧ-ble, *a.* [L. *in-* priv., and *gelare*, to freeze.] That cannot be congealed.

in-ġem′i-nāte, *a.* [L. *ingeminatus*, pp. of *ingeminare*, to redouble, repeat; *in*, in, to, and *geminare*, to double.] Redoubled; repeated.

in-ġem′i-nāte, *v.t.*; ingeminated, *pt., pp.*; ingeminating, *ppr.* To redouble or repeat.

in-ġem-i-nā′tion, *n.* Repetition; reduplication.

in-ġē′nȧ, *n.* In zoölogy, the gorilla.

in-ġen′dēr, *v.t.* and *v.i.* Same as *Engender.*

in-ġen-ēr-ȧ-bil′i-ty, *n.* Incapacity of being engendered.

in-ġen′ēr-ȧ-ble, *a.* [L. *in-* priv., and *generare*, to generate.] That cannot be engendered or produced.

in-ġen′ēr-ȧ-bly, *adv.* Not in a generable manner.

in-ġen′ēr-āte, *a.* [L. *ingeneratus*, pp. of *ingenerare*, to generate within; *in*, in, and *generare*, to generate.] Generated within; inborn; innate; inbred; as, *ingenerate* powers of body.

in-ġen′ēr-āte, *v.t.*; ingenerated, *pt., pp.*; ingenerating, *ppr.* To generate or produce within. [Rare.]

in-ġen-ēr-ā′tion, *n.* The act of generating within.

in-ġē′ni-āte, *v.t.* and *v.i.* To originate, plan, devise, etc. [Obs.]

in′ġē-nie, *n.* Same as *Ingeny.*

in-ġē′ni-ō, *n.* [Sp., an engine, a sugar-mill.] A mill; works; an engine, etc., used in the manufacture of sugar; a sugar-plantation. [Cuba.]

in-ġē-ni-os′i-ty, *n.* The quality of being cunning or skilful.

in-ġēn′ious, *a.* [L. *ingeniosus*, of good capacity, gifted with genius, ingenious, from *ingenium*, innate or natural quality, inclination, ability; *in*, in, and *gignere*, to produce.]

1. Possessed of genius, or the faculty of invention; hence, skilful or prompt to invent; having an aptitude to contrive, or to form new combinations of ideas; as, an *ingenious* author; an *ingenious* mechanic.

2. Proceeding from genius or ingenuity; of curious design, structure, or mechanism; as, an *ingenious* performance of any kind; an *ingenious* scheme or plan; an *ingenious* model or machine; *ingenious* fabric; *ingenious* contrivance.

3. Witty; well formed; well adapted; as, an *ingenious* reply.

Syn.—Inventive, talented, witty, skilful, clever, resourceful.

in-ġēn′ious-ly, *adv.* In an ingenious manner.

in-ġēn′ious-ness, *n.* The quality of being ingenious; ingenuity; as, the *ingeniousness* of an author.

in-ġen′it, *a.* Same as *Ingenite.*

in-ġen′ite, *a.* [L. *ingenitus*, pp. of *ingignere*, to implant; *in*, in, and *gignere*, to produce.] Innate; inborn; inbred; native; ingenerate.

iṅ-ġé-nüe′ (aṅ-zhā-nü′), *n.* [Fr., f. of *ingénu*; L. *ingenuus*, ingenuous.] A girl or young woman who is ingenuous; a person who displays candid simplicity; specifically, such a character represented on the stage.

in-ġē-nū′i-ty, *n.* [L. *ingenuitas*, the condition of a freeborn man, a mode of thinking worthy of a freeman, from *ingenuus*, native, freeborn; *in*, in, and *gignere*, to produce.]

1. The quality or power of ready invention; quickness or acuteness in combining ideas, or in forming new combinations; ingeniousness; skill; as, how many machines for saving labor has the *ingenuity* of men devised and constructed!

2. Curiousness in design, the effect of ingenuity; as, the *ingenuity* of a plan or of mechanism.

3. Openness of heart; fairness; candor. [Obs.]

in-ġen′ū-ous, *a.* [L. *ingenuus*, native, inborn, freeborn, noble, frank, from *ingignere*, to ingenerate; *in*, in, and *gignere*, to produce.]

1. Open; frank; fair; candid; free from reserve, disguise, equivocation, or dissimulation; as, an *ingenuous* mind; an *ingenuous* man; an *ingenuous* declaration or confession.

2. Noble; generous; as, an *ingenuous* ardor or zeal; *ingenuous* detestation of falsehood.

3. Of honorable extraction; freeborn; as, *ingenuous* blood or birth. [Rare.]

Syn.—Open, frank, artless.—One who is *open* speaks out at once what is uppermost in his mind; one who is *frank*, from a natural boldness or dislike of self-restraint; one who is *ingenuous* is actuated by candor and love of truth, which makes him willing to confess his faults and make known his sentiments without reserve.

in-ġen′ū-ous-ly, *adv.* Openly; fairly; candidly; without reserve or dissimulation.

in-ġen′ū-ous-ness, *n.* 1. Openness of heart; frankness; fairness; freedom from reserve or dissimulation; as, to confess our faults with *ingenuousness.*

2. The state of being open, frank, honest.

in′ġē-ny, *n.* Wit; ingenuity. [Obs.]

in-ġēr′mi-nāte, *v.t.*; ingerminated, *pt., pp.*; ingerminating, *ppr.* To germinate; to cause to grow from the germ.

in-ġest′, *v.t.*; ingested, *pt., pp.*; ingesting, *ppr.* [L. *ingestus*, pp. of *ingerere*, to carry, throw on, put into; *in*, into, and *gerere*, to carry, bear.] To throw into the stomach.

in-ġes′tȧ, *n.pl.* [L., neut. pl. of *ingestus*, pp. of *ingerere*, to carry or put in, to ingest.] Things taken into the body through the medium of the stomach; the opposite of *egesta.*

in-ġes′tion (-chun), *n.* [LL. *ingestio (-onis)*, an uttering, from L. *ingestus*, pp. of *ingerere*, to carry or pour in, to ingest.] The act of throwing or taking into the stomach; as, the *ingestion* of milk or other food.

in-ġes′tive, *a.* In physiology, of or relating to ingestion; capable of taking into the body through the medium of the stomach; the opposite of *egestive.*

iṅ-ghä′lȧ, *n.* [S. African.] In zoölogy, the South African rietbok, *Eleotragus arundinaceus.*

Ing′hăm-ite, *n.* In church history, a person who embraced the doctrine and practices inaugurated by Benjamin Ingham, who in the eighteenth century founded a sect with a creed partaking of Methodism and Moravianism.

in-gīrt′, *v.t.* Same as *Engirt.*

in-gīrt′, *a.* Engirdled.

iṅ′gle, *n.* 1. Flame; blaze. [Obs.]

2. A fire or fireplace. [Scot.]

3. A term of endearment; a darling; also, a paramour. [Obs.]

iṅ′gle, *v.t.* To wheedle; to coax. [Obs.]

iṅ′gle-nook, *n.* A chimney-corner. [Scot.]

iṅ′gle-side, *n.* A fireside; called also *inglecheek.* [Scot.]

in-glō′bāte, *a.* [L. *in*, in, and *globus*, a circle, sphere.] Formed or shaped into a globe; said of nebulous matter collected into globular form by the force of gravity.

in-glōbe′, *v.t.* To put into globular form; to fix firmly, as within a globe. [Obs.]

in-glō′ri-ous, *a.* 1. Not glorious; not bringing honor or glory; not accompanied with fame or celebrity; humble; as, an *inglorious* life of ease.

2. Shameful; disgraceful; as, he charged his troops with *inglorious* flight.

in-glō′ri-ous-ly, *adv.* In an inglorious manner; dishonorably; with shame.

in-glō′ri-ous-ness, *n.* The state of being inglorious or without celebrity.

in-glut′, *v.t.* [Rare.] See *Englut.*

in-glū′vi-ăl, *a.* In zoölogy, relating to ingluvies.

in-glū′vi-ēṣ, *n.* [L., a maw, crop, prob. from *in*, in, and *glutire*, to swallow.] In zoölogy, an enlargement of a digestive tube, as the craw or crop of a bird or the paunch of a ruminant.

in-glū′vin, *n.* [L. *ingluvies*, maw, crop, and *-in.*] In medicine, a peptic preparation from the inner coating of a fowl's gizzard, used as a remedy for dyspepsia.

in-glū′vi-ous, *a.* Given to excessive eating. [Obs.]

in-gorge′, *v.t.* and *v.i.* Same as *Engorge.*

in′gŏt, *n.* [ME. *ingot*, lit., that which is poured in, a mold for molten metal, from AS. *in*, in, and *geōtan*, to pour.]

1. A mass or wedge of gold, silver, or other fusible metal, cast in a mold; a mass of unwrought metal.

2. A mold for an ingot. [Obs.]

in′gŏt-i″ron (-ūrn), *n.* Decarbonized pig iron; Bessemer steel.

in′gŏt-mōld, *n.* A mold for casting ingots.

in-grāce′, *v.t.* [Obs.] See *Ingratiate.*

in-grā′cious (-shus), *a.* [Obs.] See *Ungracious.*

in-grȧff′, *v.t.* [Obs.] See *Ingraft.*

in-grȧft′, *v.t.*; ingrafted, *pt.*, *pp.*; ingrafting, *ppr.* 1. To insert, as a scion of one tree or plant into another, for propagation; as, to *ingraft* the scion of an apple-tree on a pear-tree as its stock; to *ingraft* a peach on a plum.

2. To propagate by incision and the insertion of a bud.

3. To insert or introduce (something foreign) into that which is native; to make a part of.

4. To set or fix deep and firm; to implant.

in-grȧf-tā′tion, *n.* [Rare.] Same as *Ingraftment.*

in-grȧft′ēr, *n.* A person who ingrafts.

in-grȧft′ment, *n.* 1. The act of ingrafting.

2. The thing ingrafted.

in′grāin, *a.* 1. Dyed in the yarn before weaving and fulling; as, *ingrain* carpet.

2. Dyed with grain, or the bodies of a kind of scale-insect. [Obs.]

Ingrain carpet; a carpet made of ingrain material, either worsted or cotton, and woven in either two or three plies or interwoven webs.

in-grāin′, *v.t.*; ingrained, *pt.*, *pp.*; ingraining, *ppr.* 1. To dye in the grain, or before manufacture; to dye with a permanent color.

2. To work into the natural texture; to impregnate the whole matter or substance; to imbue the entire being; as, stubbornness seems to be *ingrained* in the man.

in′grāin, *n.* A fabric or yarn that has been ingrained.

in-gram-mat′i-cism, *n.* [L. *in-* priv., and *grammatica*, grammar.] A form or expression in which some law of grammar has been violated.

in-grap′ple, *v.t.* and *v.i.* [Obs.] See *Grapple.*

in′grāte, *a.* [OFr. *ingrat*; L. *ingratus*, unpleasant, disagreeable, ungrateful; *in-* priv., and *gratus*, grateful, pleasing.] Ungrateful; unthankful.

in′grāte, *n.* An ungrateful person.

in-grāte′fụl, *a.* 1. Ungrateful; unthankful.

2. Displeasing to the senses; as, *ingrateful* food; an *ingrateful* odor. [Obs.]

in-grāte′fụl-ly, *adv.* Ungratefully.

in-grāte′fụl-ness, *n.* Ungratefulness.

in′grāte-ly, *adv.* In the manner of an ingrate. [Obs.]

in-grā′ti-āte (-shi-), *v.t.*; ingratiated, *pt.*, *pp.*; ingratiating, *ppr.* [L. *in*, in, and *gratia*, favor, agreeableness.]

1. To introduce or commend to another's good-will, confidence, or kindness; used reflexively and usually followed by *with* before the person whose favor is sought; as, he endeavored to *ingratiate* himself *with* me.

2. To recommend; to render easy. [Obs.]

in-grat′i-tūde, *n.* [LL. *ingratitudo (-inis)*, from L. *ingratus*, ungrateful; *in-* priv., and *gratus*, grateful.] Want of gratitude or sentiments of kindness for favors received; insensibility to favors and indisposition to repay them; unthankfulness.

> *Ingratitude* is abhorred both by God and man. —L'Estrange.

in-grāve′, *v.t.* To engrave. [Rare.]

in-grāve′, *v.t.* To bury. [Obs.]

in-grȧ-ves′cent, *a.* [L. *ingravescens (-entis)*, ppr. of *ingravescere*, to grow heavier; *in-*, intens., and *gravescere*, to grow heavy, from *gravis*, heavy.] In pathology, increasing in severity; as, *ingravescent* apoplexy.

in-grav′i-dāte, *v.t.* To impregnate. [Obs.]

in-grav-i-dā′tion, *n.* The act of ingravidating or impregnating, or the state of being pregnant or impregnated. [Obs.]

in-grēat′, *v.t.* To make great. [Obs.]

in-grē′di-ence, *n.* 1. Ingrediency. [Obs.]

2. An ingredient. [Obs.]

in-grē′di-en-cy, *n.* The quality or condition of being an ingredient.

in-grē′di-ent, *n.* [Fr. *ingrédient*, an ingredient, from L. *ingrediens (-entis)*, ppr. of *ingredi*, to step or go into, to enter in, to engage in; *in*, into, and *gradi*, to go.] That which enters into a compound, or is a component part of any compound or mixture.

> The chief *ingredients* of the national conception of greatness. —Lecky.

Syn.—Element, component, constituent.

in-grē′di-ent, *a.* Forming an ingredient; constituent. [Obs.]

in′gress, *n.* [ME. *ingress*, from L. *ingressus*, pp. of *ingredi*, to step or go into, to enter in; *in*, into, and *gradi*, to go.]

1. Entrance; as, the *ingress* of air into the lungs.

2. Power of entrance; means of entering; as, all *ingress* was prohibited.

3. In astronomy, (a) the entrance of the moon into the shadow of the earth in eclipses; (b) the sun's entrance into a sign.

in-gress′, *v.i.* To go in or enter. [Rare.]

in-gres′sion (-gresh′un), *n.* [L. *ingressio (-onis)*, a going into, entering, from *ingressus*, pp. of *ingredi*, to go into, to enter.] The act of entering; entrance.

in-griēve′, *v.t.* To make more grievous. [Obs.]

in-grọọve′, *v.t.* To groove in; to join or fix, as in a groove.

in-grŏss′, *v.t.* To engross. [Obs.]

in′grōw-ing, *a.* Growing in.

Ingrowing nail; an overlapping of the nail by the flesh from pressure, attended with ulceration.

in′grōwth, *n.* Inward growth; that which grows inward.

in′guen (-gwen), *n.* [L.] The groin.

in-guilt′y (-gilt′), *a.* Guiltless. [Obs.]

in′gui-năl, *a.* [L. *inguinalis*, from *inguen (-inis)*, the groin.] Pertaining to the groin; as, the *inguinal* glands.

in-gulf′, *v.t.* See *Engulf.*

in-gulf′ment, *n.* See *Engulfment.*

in-gŭr′gi-tāte, *v.t.*; ingurgitated, *pt.*, *pp.*; ingurgitating, *ppr.* [L. *ingurgitatus*, pp. of *ingurgitare*, to pour in like a flood, to gormandize; *in*, in, and *gurges (-itis)*, an abyss, gulf.]

1. To swallow greedily or in great quantity.

2. To engulf.

in-gŭr′gi-tāte, *v.i.* To drink much; to swill.

in-gŭr-gi-tā′tion, *n.* [LL. *ingurgitatio (-onis)*, from L. *ingurgitare*, to gormandize.]

1. The act of swallowing greedily, or in great quantity.

2. That which is so swallowed.

in-gust′ȧ-ble, *a.* [L. *ingustabilis*; *in-* priv., and *gustabilis*, tastable, from *gustare*, to taste.] That cannot be tasted; insipid; tasteless.

in-hab′ile, *a.* [L. *inhabilis*, unmanageable, unwieldy; *in-* priv., and *habilis*, manageable, fit, proper, from *habere*, to have.]

1. Not apt or fit; unfit; not convenient; as, *inhabile* matter. [Obs.]

2. Unskilled; unready; unqualified; used of persons. [Obs.]

in-hȧ-bil′i-ty, *n.* Unaptness; unfitness; want of skill. [Obs.]

in-hab′it, *v.t.*; inhabited, *pt.*, *pp.*; inhabiting, *ppr.* [ME. *inhabiten*; OFr. *inhabiter*; L. *inhabitare*, to dwell in, inhabit; *in*, in, and *habitare*, to dwell.] To live or dwell in; to occupy as a place of settled residence; as, wild beasts *inhabit* the forest; men *inhabit* cities and houses.

Syn.—Dwell, occupy, sojourn, stay, remain, abide, reside.

in-hab′it, *v.i.* To dwell; to live; to abide. [Poet.]

in-hab′it-ȧ-ble, *a.* [LL. *inhabitabilis*, inhabitable, from L. *inhabitare*, to inhabit.] Habitable; capable of being inhabited, or of affording habitation.

in-hab′it-ȧ-ble, *a.* Not habitable. [Obs.]

in-hab′it-ănce, in-hab′it-ăn-cy, *n.* 1. Residence; the condition of being inhabited; occupancy.

2. In law, a permanent residence in a town, city, county, etc.; domiciliation.

in-hab′it-ănt, *n.* [OFr. *inhabitant*, an inhabitant, from L. *inhabitans (-antis)*, ppr. of *inhabitare*, to dwell within, to inhabit.]

1. A dweller; one who dwells or resides permanently in a place, or who has a fixed residence, as distinguished from an occasional lodger or visitor; as, an *inhabitant* of a house, town, or state.

2. In law, one who has a legal settlement in a town, city, or parish.

in-hab′i-tāte, *v.t.* To inhabit. [Obs.]

in-hab-i-tā′tion, *n.* [LL. *inhabitatio (-onis)*, a dwelling, from L. *inhabitare*, to dwell within, to inhabit.]

1. The act of inhabiting, or the state of being inhabited.

2. Abode; place of dwelling. [Obs.]

3. Population; whole mass of inhabitants. [Obs.]

in-hab′it-ȧ-tive, *a.* Pertaining to inhabitation.

in-hab′it-ȧ-tive-ness, *n.* Inhabitiveness.

in-hab′it-ed, *a.* Uninhabited. [Obs.]

in-hab′it-ed, *a.* Having inhabitants; populated; as, a densely *inhabited* county.

in-hab′it-ēr, in-hab′it-ŏr, *n.* An inhabitant. [Rare.]

in-hab′it-ive-ness, *n.* In phrenology, a desire or natural inclination to reside permanently in a place or abode; love of country or home.

in-hab′it-ress, *n.* A female inhabitant. [Rare.]

in-hāl′ănt, *n.* An inhaler; something to be inhaled.

in-hāl′ănt, *a.* [L. *inhalans (-antis)*, ppr. of *inhalare*, to breathe in, inhale.] That inhales; inhaling; as, the *inhalant* end of a duct.

in-hȧ-lā′tion, *n.* 1. The act of inhaling; inspiration.

2. That which is inhaled; specifically, in pharmacy, a preparation in the form of a vapor intended to be inhaled.

in-hāle′, *v.t.*; inhaled, *pt.*, *pp.*; inhaling, *ppr.* [L. *inhalare*, to breathe in, inhale; *in*, in, and *halare*, to breathe.] To draw into the lungs; to inspire; as, to *inhale* air; opposed to *exhale.*

> Martin was walking forth to *inhale* the fresh breeze of the evening. —Arbuthnot.

in-hāl′ent, *a.* Inhalant.

in-hāl′ēr, *n.* 1. One who inhales.

2. In medicine, an apparatus for inhaling vapors and volatile substances, as steam of hot water, vapor of chloroform, iodine, etc.

3. An apparatus to enable a person to breathe without injury in a deleterious atmosphere; a respirator, as that used by persons of delicate lungs to prevent damp or cold air from entering the lungs, or that used by cutlers and others who have to breathe in an atmosphere full of metallic dust.

4. A breathing-device employed by divers.

in-hănce′, *v.t.* Same as *Enhance.*

in-hănce′ment, *n.* Enhancement.

in-hār-mon′ic, *a.* Not harmonic; discordant.

in-hār-mon′ic-ăl, *a.* Inharmonic.

in-hār-mō′ni-ous, *a.* 1. Not harmonious; unmusical; discordant.

2. Disagreeing; conflicting; wanting in harmony.

in-hār-mō′ni-ous-ly, *adv.* Without harmony; discordantly.

in-hār-mō′ni-ous-ness, *n.* The quality or state of being inharmonious; discord.

in-hār′mō-ny, *n.* Want of harmony; discord. [Rare.]

in′haul, *n.* An inhauler.

in′haul-ēr, *n.* Among seamen, a rope employed to haul in the jib-boom.

in-hēarse′, *v.t.*; inhearsed, *pt.*, *pp.*; inhearsing, *ppr.* To put or place in a hearse.

in-hēre′, *v.i.*; inhered, *pt.*, *pp.*; inhering, *ppr.* [L. *inhærere*, to stick in, to adhere, or cleave to; *in*, in, and *hærere*, to stick.] To exist or be fixed in; to be an inseparable part of something to be a member, adjunct, or quality of something; to be inherent.

in-hēr′ence, *n.* The state of inhering or of being inherent; existence in something.

in-hēr′en-cy, *n.* Inherence.

in-hēr′ent, *a.* [L. *inhærens (-entis)*, ppr. of *inhærere*, to stick in or to, to inhere.] Existing in something else, so as to be inseparable from it; innate; naturally pertaining to; as, the *inherent* qualities of the magnet; the *inherent* right of men to life, liberty, and protection.

> A most *inherent* baseness. —Shak.

Syn.—Inbred, inborn, innate, natural, inseparable, indwelling.

in-hēr′ent-ly, *adv.* By inherence.

in-her′it, *v.t.*; inherited, *pt.*, *pp.*; inheriting, *ppr.* [ME. *inheriten*, *enheriten*; OFr. *inheriter*, *enheriter*, to inherit, from LL. *inhereditare*, to appoint as heir, to inherit; L. *in*, in, and *heres (-edis)*, an heir.]

1. In law, to take by descent from an ancestor; to take by succession, as the representative of the former possessor; to receive, as a right or title descendible by law from an ancestor at his decease; as, the heir *inherits* the lands or real estate of his father; the eldest son of the nobleman *inherits* his father's title; the eldest son of a king *inherits* the crown.

2. To receive from a progenitor as part of one's nature; as, a man *inherits* his constitution.

3. To possess; to enjoy; to take as a possession, by gift or divine appropriation; to own.

4. To place in possession of. [Obs.]

in-her′it, *v.i.* To take or have as an inheritance, possession, or property; to come into possession, as an heir or successor; to take the position of heir or heirs.

Thou shalt not *inherit* in our father's house. —Jud. xi. 2.

in-hėr″it-à-bil′i-ty, *n.* The quality of being inheritable or descendible to heirs.

in-hėr′it-à-ble, *a.* [OFr. *inheritable, enheritable,* from *inheriter,* LL. *inhereditare,* to inherit.]

1. Capable of being inherited; transmissible or descendible from the ancestor to the heir by course of law; as, an *inheritable* estate or title. —Blackstone.

2. Capable of being transmitted from the parent to the child; as, *inheritable* qualities or infirmities.

3. Capable of taking by inheritance, or of receiving by descent.

By attainder the blood of the person attainted is so corrupted as to be rendered no longer *inheritable.* —Blackstone.

in-hėr′it-à-bly, *adv.* By inheritance.

in-hėr′it-ănce, *n.* [OFr. *enheritance,* an inheriting, from *enheriter,* LL. *inhereditare,* to inherit.]

1. The act of inheriting; as, the *inheritance* of property; the *inheritance* of disease.

2. That which is or may be inherited; a heritage; as, he enjoyed a large *inheritance.*

3. A permanent possession; a possession received by gift or without purchase.

4. Possession; ownership; acquisition. [Obs.]

5. In law, an estate acquired by operation of law, by an heir, in the property of an ancestor, upon the latter's death; properly used in reference to real property.

in-hėr′it-ŏr, *n.* An heir; one who inherits or may inherit.

in-hėr′it-ress, *n.* An heiress.

in-hėr′it-rix, *n.* An inheritress.

in-hẽrse′, *v.t.* [Obs.] See *Inhearse.*

in-hē′ṣion (-zhun), *n.* [LL. *inhæsio* (*-onis*), a clinging or fixing to, from L. *inhæsus,* pp. of *inhærere,* to stick in, inhere; *in,* in, and *hærere,* to stick.] Inherence; the state of existing or being fixed in something.

in-hi-ā′tion, *n.* A gaping after; eager desire. [Rare.]

in-hib′it, *v.t.*; inhibited, *pt., pp.*; inhibiting, *ppr.* [L. *inhibitus,* pp. of *inhibere,* to hold back, restrain, curb; *in,* in, on, and *habere,* to have, to hold.]

1. To restrain; to hinder; to check or repress.

2. To forbid; to prohibit; to interdict.

in-hib′i-tŏr, *n.* 1. One who or that which inhibits; specifically, in Scots law, a person who takes out inhibition, as against a wife or debtor.

2. In medicine, that which causes inhibitory action; especially, an inhibitory nerve.

in-hi-bi′tion (-bish′un), *n.* [L. *inhibitio* (*-onis*), a restraining, a holding back, from *inhibere,* to hold back, to restrain.]

1. Prohibition; restraint; embargo; the act of inhibiting, or the state of being inhibited.

2. In law, a writ to forbid or inhibit a judge from further proceedings in a cause pending before him; commonly, a writ issuing from a higher ecclesiastical court to an inferior one, on appeal. —Cowell.

3. In physiology, the checking or restraining of the action of an organ.

in-hib′i-tive, *a.* Inhibitory.

in-hib′i-tŏr, *n.* See *Inhibiter.*

in-hib′i-tō-ry, *a.* Checking; restraining; pertaining to inhibition.

Inhibitory nerves; nerves the stimulation of which inhibits or lessens the activity of an organ.

in-hīve′, *v.t.* To put into a hive; to hive.

in-hōld′, *v.t.* To have inherent; to contain in itself. [Obs.]

in-hōld′ẽr, *n.* An inhabitant. [Obs.]

in-hōōp′, *v.t.* To confine or inclose in or as in a hoop. [Rare.]

in-hos′pi-tà-ble, *a.* 1. Not hospitable; not disposed to entertain strangers gratuitously; declining to entertain guests, or entertaining them with reluctance; as, an *inhospitable* person or people.

2. Affording no conveniences, subsistence, or shelter; as, *inhospitable* deserts.

in-hos′pi-tà-ble-ness, *n.* The quality of being inhospitable.

in-hos′pi-tà-bly, *adv.* In an inhospitable manner.

in-hos-pi-tal′i-ty, *n.* Inhospitableness.

in-hū′măn, *a.* [L. *inhumanus,* rude, savage, barbarous, inhuman; *in-* priv., and *humanus,* human.]

1. Destitute of the kindness and tenderness that belong to a human being; cruel; barbarous; savage; unfeeling; as, an *inhuman* person or people.

2. Marked with cruelty; as, an *inhuman* act.

Syn.—Cruel, savage, barbarous, unfeeling, pitiless, ruthless.

in-hū-man′i-ty, *n.*; *pl.* **in-hū-man′i-ties.** [L. *inhumanitas* (*-atis*), inhuman conduct, savageness, incivility, from *inhumanus,* barbarous, inhuman.] The quality or state of being inhuman; barbarity; cruelty.

Syn.—Unkindness, cruelty, barbarity, brutality.

in-hū′măn-ly, *adv.* In an inhuman manner.

in-hū′māte, *v.t.* To inhume.

in-hū-mā′tion, *n.* 1. The act of burying; interment.

2. In old chemistry, a method of digesting substances by burying the vessel containing them in warm earth or dung.

in-hūme′, *v.t.*; inhumed (-hūmd), *pt., pp.*; inhuming, *ppr.* [L. *inhumare,* to bury in the earth, to inter; *in,* in, and *humus,* earth, ground.]

1. To bury; to inter, to deposit in the earth, as a dead body.

2. To surround with soil for medicinal or chemical purposes.

-ini. [Masc. pl. of L. *-inus.*] A suffix used to form Latinized names of some groups in zoölogy; as, Acanthurini.

in′i-ȧ, *n.* [S. Am. native name.] A dolphin found in the fresh waters of South America.

Inia boliviensis.

in′i-ăl, *a.* In anatomy, relating to the inion.

in-im-ag′in-à-ble, *a.* Unimaginable; inconceivable. [Rare.]

in-im′i-căl, *a.* [LL. *inimicalis,* hostile, unfriendly, from L. *inimicus,* hostile, an enemy; *in-* priv., and *amicus,* a friend.]

1. Unfriendly; having the disposition or temper of an enemy; applied to private enmity, as *hostile* is to public.

2. Adverse; hurtful; repugnant.

Syn.—Adverse, unfriendly, harmful, contrary, hostile, opposed, repugnant.

in-im-i-cal′i-ty, *n.* Unfriendliness. [Rare.]

in-im′i-căl-ly, *adv.* In an unfriendly manner.

in-im-i-ci′tious (-sish′us), *a.* Not friendly. [Rare.]

in-im′i-cous, *a.* Harmful. [Obs.]

in-im″i-tà-bil′i-ty, *n.* The quality of being incapable of imitation.

in-im′i-tà-ble, *a.* [L. *inimitabilis,* not to be imitated; *in-* priv., and *imitabilis,* imitable, from *imitare,* to imitate.] Not to be imitated or copied; surpassing imitation; as, *inimitable* beauty or excellence; *inimitable* description.

in-im′i-tà-ble-ness, *n.* Matchlessness; inimitability.

in-im′i-tà-bly, *adv.* In a manner not to be imitated; to a degree beyond imitation.

in′iŏn (-yun), *n.* An onion. [Dial.]

in′i-on, *n.* [Gr. *inion,* the back of the head, from *is, inos,* a sinew, muscle, lit., strength.] In anatomy, the median protuberance of the occipital.

in-iq′ui-tous (-ik′wi-), *a.* Unjust; wicked; as, an *iniquitous* bargain; an *iniquitous* proceeding.

Syn.—Wicked, nefarious.—*Wicked* is generic; *iniquitous* is stronger, denoting a violation of the rights of others, usually by fraud or circumvention; *nefarious* is still stronger, implying a breach of the most sacred obligations.

in-iq′ui-tous-ly, *adv.* Unjustly; wickedly.

in-iq′ui-ty (-ik′wi-), *n.* [ME. *iniquite;* OFr. *iniquiteit;* L. *iniquitas* (*-atis*), unevenness, inequality, injustice, from *iniquus,* unequal; *in-* priv., and *æquus,* level, equal.]

1. Injustice; unrighteousness; a deviation from rectitude; lack of equity; as, the *iniquity* of war; the *iniquity* of the opium traffic.

2. A particular deviation from rectitude; a sin or crime; wickedness; any act of injustice.

in-ī′quous, *a.* Unjust. [Obs.]

in-ir″ri-tà-bil′i-ty, *n.* The quality of being irritable.

in-ir′ri-tà-ble, *a.* Not irritable; not susceptible of irritation; said especially of muscles.

in-ir′ri-tā-tive, *a.* Not accompanied with excitement; as, an *inirritative* fever.

in-isle′ (-īle′), *v.t.* To surround; to encircle. [Obs.]

in-i′tiăl (-ish′ăl), *a.* [L. *initialis,* pertaining to the beginning, initial, from *initium,* a beginning, from *inire,* to go into, to enter upon, begin; *in,* into, in, and *ire,* to go.]

1. Beginning; placed at the beginning; as, the *initial* letters of a name.

2. Incipient; as, the *initial* symptoms of a disease.

Initial compression; in gun-making, the compression of the metal in a gun-barrel, produced by the shrinking of heated bands placed around it.

Initial tension; the strain upon any part of a structure or mechanism which is inherent in the structure itself and not from outside.

in-i′tiăl, *v.t.* To designate by using an initial or initials; to place one's initials upon.

in-i′tiăl, *n.* The first letter of a name.

in-i′tiăl-ly, *adv.* In an incipient degree; in the beginning.

in-i′ti-āte (-ish′i-), *v.t.*; initiated, *pt., pp.*; initiating, *ppr.* [LL. *initiatus,* pp. of *initiare,* to enter upon, to begin (L., to initiate), from L. *initium,* a beginning.]

1. To instruct in rudiments or principles; to introduce into any society or order by instructing the candidate in its principles or ceremonies; as, to *initiate* a person into the mysteries of freemasonry.

2. To begin upon; to originate; as, to *initiate* a movement for reform.

Syn.—Begin, commence, start, install, induct, inaugurate.

in-i′ti-āte, *v.i.* To do the first act; to perform the first rite. [Rare.]

in-i′ti-āte, *a.* 1. Unpractised. [Obs.]

2. Begun; commenced; instructed in first principles.

Initiate tenant by courtesy; in law, a tenant who becomes so by the birth of a child, but whose estate is not consummated till the death of the wife. —Blackstone.

in-i′ti-āte, *n.* One who is initiated.

in-i-ti-ā′tion (-ish-i-), *n.* [Fr. *initiation;* L. *initiatio* (*-onis*), an initiation, a taking part in sacred rites, from *initiare,* to initiate.]

1. The act or process of introducing one into a society, business, study, etc., by instructing him in its principles, rules, or ceremonies.

2. Admission by application of ceremonies or use of symbols; as, the *initiation* of a person into the visible church by baptism.

in-i′ti-à-tive, *a.* Serving to initiate; relating to initiation.

in-i′ti-à-tive, *n.* 1. An introductory act or step; the first active procedure in any enterprise; a beginning; as, he took the *initiative.*

2. The power of commencing; the power of taking the lead or of originating. In legislative assemblies constituted so as to comprise more than one chamber, or more than one distinct and coördinate power, that branch to which belongs of right the power to propose measures of a particular class is said to have the *initiative* with respect to those measures.

in-i′ti-ā-tŏr, *n.* [LL. *initiator,* from *initiare,* to begin (L., to initiate).] One who initiates.

in-i′ti-à-tō-ry, *a.* 1. Of or pertaining to or suitable for a beginning or introduction; introductory; as, an *initiatory* step.

2. Initiating or serving to initiate; introducing by instruction, or by the use and application of symbols or ceremonies.

Two *initiatory* rites of the same general import cannot exist together.—J. M. Mason.

in-i′ti-à-tō-ry, *n.* An introductory rite. [Rare.]

in-i′ti-à-trix, *n.* [LL., f. of *initiator,* a beginner, initiator.] A female initiator.

in-i′tion (-ish′un), *n.* A beginning. [Obs.]

in-ject′, *v.t.*; injected, *pt., pp.*; injecting, *ppr.* [Fr. *injecter,* from L. *injectus,* pp. of *injicere,* to throw, cast, or put in; *in,* in, and *jacere,* to throw.]

1. To throw or force in; to dart in; as, to *inject* cold water into the condenser of an engine; to *inject* fluids into the tissues of the body; to *inject* an anodyne with a hypodermic syringe.

2. To cast or throw on. [Obs.]

3. Figuratively, to throw in; to instil; to offer or propose along with or in the midst of matter under consideration; to interject; as, he *injected* an objectionable amendment to the bill.

4. In anatomy, to fill, as the vessels of an organ with a fluid; to treat by injection.

in-jec′tion, *n.* [L. *injectio* (*-onis*), a throwing or casting into, a laying on, from *injectus,* pp. of *inicere,* to throw or cast into, to inject.]

1. The act of injecting; applied particularly to the forcible throwing in of a liquid or aeriform body, by means of a syringe, pump, etc.

2. The substance injected, as a liquid medicine thrown into the body by a syringe or pipe; a clyster.

3. In anatomy, the act of filling the vessels or cavities of a body with a substance; also, the act of introducing a substance into a body as a preliminary to dissection.

4. In medicine, the introduction of an enema; also, the enema introduced.

5. The throwing of cold water into the condenser of a steam-engine to produce a vacuum; also, the water thrown into the condenser for such a purpose; injection-water.

in-jec′tion-cock, *n.* The cock in a steam-engine by which cold water is admitted into a condenser.

in-jec′tion-en″gine, *n.* A steam-engine in which the steam is condensed by a jet of cold water thrown into the condenser.

in-jec′tion-pipe, *n.* A pipe through which water is injected into the condenser of a steam-engine, to condense the steam.

in-jec′tion-valve, *n.* The valve in a steam-engine through which cold water is admitted into the condenser.

in-jec′tion-wa″tẽr, *n.* The water injected into the condenser of a steam-engine to condense the steam.

in-jeç′tŏr, *n.* [From L. *injectus*, pp. of *injicere*, to inject.] One who or that which injects; specifically, an apparatus for supplying the boilers of steam-engines, especially the boilers of locomotive engines, with water.

in-jel′ly, *v.t.* To bury in jelly. [Rare.]

in-join′, *v.t.* [Obs.] See *Enjoin.*

in-joint′, *v.t.* To unjoint. [Obs.]

in-joint′, *v.t.* To unite, as with joints; to join. [Rare.]

in-jū-çun′di-ty, *n.* Unpleasantness; disagreeableness. [Obs.]

in-jū′di-çȧ-ble, *a.* Not cognizable by a judge. [Obs.]

in-jū-di′ciăl (-dish′ăl), *a.* Not according to the forms of law. [Rare.]

in-jū-di′cious, *a.* 1. Not judicious; void of judgment; acting without judgment; lacking discretion; unwise; as, an *injudicious* person.

2. Not according to sound judgment or discretion; unwise; as, an *injudicious* measure.

Syn.—Unwise, indiscreet, hasty, imprudent, rash, undiscerning, ill-advised.

in-jū-di′cious-ly, *adv.* In an injudicious manner; unwisely.

in-jū-di′cious-ness, *n.* The quality of being injudicious or unwise.

in-junç′tion, *n.* [LL. *injunctio* (*-onis*), a command, order, from L. *injunctus*, pp. of *injungere*, to command, order, enjoin, lit., to join or fasten into; *in*, into, and *jungere*, to join.]

1. The act of enjoining or directing; direction.

2. That which is enjoined; a command; an order; a precept.

3. In law, a writ or process granted by a court of equity, and in some cases under statutes by a court of law, whereby a party is required to do or to refrain from doing certain acts, according to the exigency of the writ.

4. An obligation. [Obs.]

Syn.—Command, order, precept, behest, mandate.

in′jūre, *v.t.*; injured, *pt., pp.*; injuring, *ppr.* [OFr. *injurier*; L. *injuriari*, to injure, from *injuria*, an injury, wrong; *in-* priv., and *jus, juris*, right, law.] To do harm to; to hurt; to damage in any way; to impair the goodness, excellence, value, or strength of, etc.; to hurt physically; to slander; to depreciate; to tarnish; to impair or diminish, as happiness; to wrong; to do an injury or injustice to; to give pain to, as sensibility or feeling; to grieve; to impair, as the intellect or mind.

> When have I *injur'd* thee? when done thee wrong? —Shak.

Syn.—Damage, impair, deteriorate, hurt, harm, spoil, abuse, wrong.

in′jūr-ēr, *n.* One who or that which injures or harms.

in-jū′ri-ȧ, *n.*; *pl.* **in-jū′ri-æ**. [L.] In law, a legal wrong; an act or omission of which the law takes cognizance as a wrong.

in-jū′ri-ous, *a.* [Fr. *injurieux*; L. *injuriosus*, harmful, unjust, injurious, from *injuria*, a wrong, injury.]

1. Tending to injure in any sense; of a harmful character; hurtful; detrimental; as, deeds or acts *injurious* to health, morals, property, happiness, etc.

2. Insolent; insulting; overbearing.

> *Injurious* duke, that threat'st where is no cause. —Shak.

Syn.—Hurtful, deleterious, prejudicial, noxious, detrimental, baneful, pernicious, mischievous, damaging.

in-jū′ri-ous-ly, *adv.* In an injurious manner; wrongfully; hurtfully; mischievously.

in-jū′ri-ous-ness, *n.* The quality of being injurious or hurtful; injury.

in′jū-ry, *n.*; *pl.* **in′jū-rieș.** [ME. *injurie*; OFr. *injure*; L. *injuria*, wrong, an injury, an unjust act, from *injuriosus*, acting unjustly; *in-* priv., and *jus, juris*, right, justice.]

1. That which injures, harms, or hurts; that which occasions loss, detriment, or mischief; damage incurred; mischief; hurt; wrong; evil.

> Many times we do *injury* to a cause by dwelling upon trifling arguments. —Watts.

2. Calumny; abuse. [Obs.]

Syn.—Damage, hurt, harm, mischief, detriment, wrong, impairment.—*Damage* is that injury to a thing which occasions loss to a person or a diminution of value to a thing. *Hurt* is the injury which destroys the soundness or integrity of things; *harm* is the smallest kind of injury, which may simply produce inconvenience or trouble; *mischief* is a great injury, which more or less disturbs the order and consistency of things.

in-just′, *a.* Unjust. [Obs.]

in-jus′tice, *n.* [Fr. *injustice*; L. *injustia*, injustice, from *injustus*, not just; *in-* priv., and *justus*, just.] Want of justice or equity; violation of another's rights; iniquity; wrong.

> Whose conscience with *injustice* is corrupted. —Shak.

Syn.—Injury, unfairness, grievance, wrong, iniquity.

iṅk, *n.* [ME. *inke, ynke*; OFr. *enque*; LL. *encaustum*; L.Gr. *enkauston*, a purple or red ink, from *enkaustos*, burnt in, from *enkaiein*, to burn in; *en*, in, and *kaiein*, to burn.]

1. A colored liquid used for writing, or a viscous substance used in printing. Common black writing-ink is generally made of an infusion of galls, copperas, and gum arabic. Sulphate of copper is occasionally added to ink, but is rather injurious than otherwise.

2. A pigment, as India ink.

3. The black fluid of a cuttlefish.

China ink; see *India ink* under *India.*

Diamond ink; a solution of hydrofluoric acid used for engraving on glass.

Indelible ink; an ink that makes a mark which cannot easily be made to disappear by washing or use; called also *marking-ink.*

Invisible ink; sympathetic ink.

Lithographic ink; an ink used for writing on stone or for transferring autographically from paper to stone. It is a composition of virgin wax, dry white soap, tallow or lard, shellac, mastic, and lampblack.

Permanent ink; indelible ink.

Sympathetic ink; a liquid used in writing, which exhibits no color or appearance till some means are used, such as holding it to the fire, or rubbing something over it. Solutions of cobalt thus become blue or green, lemon juice turns brown, and a very dilute sulphuric acid blackens; called also *invisible ink.*

iṅk, *v.t.*; inked (iṅkt), *pt., pp.*; inking, *ppr.* 1. To daub or coat with ink.

2. To color with ink.

iṅk, *n.* 1. In falconry, the neck of a bird.

2. The socket of a mill-spindle.

iṅk′-bag, *n.* A bladder-shaped sac, found in some dibranchiate cephalopods, containing a black and viscid fluid resembling ink, by ejecting which, in case of danger, the animals are enabled to render the surrounding water opaque and thus conceal themselves. This fluid is to some extent used in drawing under the name of *sepia*, from the genus which first supplied it for commerce; called also *ink-gland* and *ink-sac.*

iṅk′ber″ry, *n.* 1. A shrub, *Ilex glabra*, of the holly family, growing on the eastern coast of North America. It produces small black berries.

2. The indigo-berry, *Randia aculeata*, of the West Indies.

iṅk′ber″ry-weed, *n.* The pokeweed, *Phytolacca decandra.*

iṅk′ēr, *n.* In a printing-press, a large roller which applies the ink to the form.

iṅk′fish, *n.* A calamary.

iṅk′-foun″tain (-tin), *n.* An inking-trough.

iṅk′horn, *n.* A small vessel used to hold ink on a writing-table or desk, or for carrying it about the person; a portable case for writing-instruments, originally made of horn or other material.

iṅk′horn, *a.* Affected; pedantic. [Obs.]

iṅk′horn-ișm, *n.* An affected, pedantic, or bombastic expression. [Obs.]

iṅk′i-ness, *n.* The state or quality of being inky.

iṅk′ing-rōll″ēr, *n.* In a printing-press, a soft, elastic roller made of glue, molasses, etc., used to supply the form with ink.

iṅk′ing-trough (-trof), *n.* A kind of trough from which an inking-roller receives its supply of ink; also called *ink-fountain.*

iṅ′kle, *n.* [ME. *lingel*; OFr. *ligneul*, dim. of *ligne*, a thread, from L. *lineola*, a thread, dim. of *linea*, a line; the *l* was probably taken for Fr. *le*, the, *l*, before a vowel.] A kind of broad linen tape.

iṅ′kle, *v.t.* To have a hint of; to guess. [Prov. Eng.]

iṅ′kling, *n.* 1. A hint; an intimation.

2. Inclination; desire. [Obs.]

iṅk′-mush″rōom, *n.* A mushroom, *Coprinus atrumentarius*, which yields a fluid resembling ink.

in′kneed (-nēd), *a.* Knock-kneed.

in-knit′ (-nit′), *v.t.*; inknitted, *pt., pp.*; inknitting, *ppr.* To knit in.

in-knot′ (-not′), *v.t.*; inknotted, *pt., pp.*; inknotting, *ppr.* To bind, as with a knot.

iṅk′-nut, *n.* The fruit of several species of *Terminalia*, as *Terminalia Bellerica, Terminalia Chebula*, etc., used in making ink and in dyeing black. [See *Myrobalan.*]

iṅk′-plant, *n.* In botany, (a) a shrub of New Zealand, *Coriaria thymifolia*, the juice of the fruit of which forms a black ink; (b) a shrub, *Coriaria myrtifolia*, of Europe, which yields a black dyestuff.

iṅk′-pow″dēr, *n.* A powder which when dissolved will make ink.

iṅk′-rōot, *n.* The marsh-rosemary or sea-lavender, *Statice Limonium.*

iṅk′stand, *n.* A vessel for holding ink; also, a receptacle to contain ink, pens, and other materials used in writing.

iṅk′stōne, *n.* A kind of small, round stone, of a white, red, gray, yellow, or black color, containing a quantity of native vitriol or sulphate of iron, used in making ink.

iṅk′-well, *n.* A cuplike receptacle used to contain ink.

iṅk′-writ″ēr, *n.* An instrument which makes a record in ink, used in telegraphy.

iṅk′y, *a.* Consisting of ink; containing ink; resembling ink; black; smeared with ink.

in-lāce′, *v.t.* See *Enlace.*

in-lag′ȧ-ry, *n.* [AS. *in*, in, and *lagu*, law.] In old English law, the restitution of an outlawed person to the protection of the law. [Obs.]

in-lȧ-gā′tion, *n.* [Obs.] See *Inlagary.*

in-lāid′, *v.*, past tense and past participle of *inlay.*

in′lănd, *n.* The interior part of a country.

in′lănd, *a.* 1. Interior; remote from the sea or ocean; as, an *inland* town or lake.

2. Carried on within a country; domestic; not foreign; as, *inland* trade or transportation; *inland* navigation.

3. Confined to a country; drawn and payable in the same country; as, an *inland* bill of exchange, distinguished from a *foreign* bill, which is drawn in one country on a person living in another.

in′lănd, *adv.* In or towards the interior of a country.

in′lănd-ēr, *n.* One who lives in the interior of a country, or at a distance from the sea.

in-land′ish, *a.* Inland. [Obs.]

in-lap′i-dāte, *v.t.* [L. *in*, in, into, and *lapis* (*-idis*), a stone.] To convert into a stony substance; to petrify. [Obs.]

in-lärd′, *v.t.* [Obs.] See *Enlard.*

in-lạw′, *v.t.* In old English law, to clear of outlawry or attainder; to grant the protection of the law to.

in′lāy, *n.* Pieces of wood, ivory, etc., inlaid or prepared for inlaying; that which is inlaid, as for ornamentation.

in-lāy′, *v.t.*; inlaid, *pt., pp.*; inlaying, *ppr.* To lay, place, or insert in; to diversify with decorative materials inserted into a groundwork or substratum; to decorate with insertions.

in-lāy′ēr, *n.* The person who inlays, or whose occupation it is to inlay.

in-lāy′ing, *n.* The art or operation of diversifying or ornamenting a groundwork by inserting decorative materials.

in-lēague′ (-lēg′), *v.t.* [Obs.] See *Enleague.*

in-lēa′guēr, *v.t.* and *v.i.* To beleaguer. [Obs.]

in′let, *n.* 1. A passage or opening by which an inclosed place may be entered; place of ingress; entrance.

> Doors and windows, *inlets* of men and of light, I couple together. —Wotton.

2. A small bay or recess, as in the shore of a sea or lake; a creek.

3. Any material or substance inserted or inlaid.

in′li-ēr, *n.* In geology, a portion of one formation completely surrounded by another formation that rests upon it; opposed to *outlier.*

in-light′en (-līt′), *v.t.* [Obs.] See *Enlighten.*

in-list′, *v.t.* and *v.i.* [Obs.] See *Enlist.*

in-list′ment, *n.* [Obs.] See *Enlistment.*

in-live′, *v.t.* [Obs.] See *Enlive.*

in-lock′, *v.t.* [Obs.] See *Lock.*

in lō′cō. [L.] In the place; in the right or specified place.

in′look, *n.* Introspection.

in-lū′mine, *v.t.* [Obs.] See *Illumine.*

in′ly, *a.* Internal; interior; secret. [Obs.]

in′ly, *adv.* Internally; within; in the heart.

in′māte, *n.* A person who lodges or dwells in a place with another; an occupant of any place; often used of the occupants of hospitals, asylums, prisons, etc.

in′māte, *a.* Admitted as a dweller; resident. [Rare.]

in′māte-cy, *n.* The state of being an inmate. [Obs.]

in′mēats, *n.pl.* 1. The entrails.

2. The inner parts of an animal used for food, as the liver, kidneys, heart, etc.

in mē′di-as rēș. [L.] Into the midst of things.

in-mesh′, *v.t.* Same as *Immesh.*

in-mew′, *v.t.* [Obs.] See *Emmew.*

in′mōst, *a.* Deepest within; remotest from the surface or external part; as, the *inmost* regions of the earth; also used figuratively.

inn, *n.* [ME. *inn*; AS. *inn*, a house, chamber, inn, from *in, inn*, in, within.]

1. A house; a dwelling; hence, a habitation; an abode. [Obs.]

2. A house for the lodging and entertainment of travelers; a tavern; a hostelry; a public house.

3. The town residence of a person of quality; as, Leicester *Inn.* [Obs., Eng.]

Inns of chancery; in London, colleges in which young students formerly began their law studies. These are now occupied chiefly by attorneys, solicitors, etc.

Inns of court; colleges or corporate societies

in London, to one of which all barristers and students for the bar must belong; also, the buildings belonging to such societies.

inn, *v.i.* To take up lodging; to lodge. [Obs.]

inn, *v.t.* To house; to lodge and entertain. [Obs.]

in′nāte (*or* -nāt′), *a.* [L. *innatus*, innate, properly pp. of *innasci*, to be born in, to originate in; *in*, in, and *nasci*, to be born.]

1. Inborn; native; natural; as, *innate* affection; an *innate* desire.

2. In metaphysics, derived from the constitution of the mind, as contrasted with what is derived from experience; intuitive.

3. In botany, (a) growing upon anything by one end, as an anther which is joined by its base to the apex of a filament; (b) originating within the substance of the plant.

Innate ideas; ideas which are held to be inborn and to belong to the mind from birth, as the idea of God or of immortality.

Syn.—Inborn, inherent, native, inbred, radical.

in-nāte′, *v.t.* To bring or call into existence; to inform. [Obs.]

in′nāte-ly (*or* -nāt′), *adv.* Naturally.

in′nāte-ness, *n.* The quality of being innate.

in-nā′tive, *a.* Native or natural. [Rare.]

in-nav′i-gȧ-ble, *a.* [L. *innavigabilis*; *in-* priv., and *navigabilis*, navigable, from *navigare*, to navigate.] Unnavigable; impassable by ships or vessels.

in-nav′i-gȧ-bly, *adv.* So as not to be navigable.

inne (in), *adv.* and *prep.* In. [Obs.]

in′nẽr, *a.* [ME. *inner*; AS. *innera*, inner, comp. of *inne*, within, in.]

1. Interior; farther inward; as, an *inner* chamber; the *inner* court of a temple or palace.

2. Interior; internal; not outward; as, to refresh the *inner* man.

3. Not obvious; dark; esoteric; as, an *inner* meaning.

4. In zoölogy, closer to the median line.

Inner house; the name given to the chambers in which the first and second divisions of the Court of Session hold their sittings in Edinburgh, Scotland; applied also to the divisions themselves.

Inner jib; see under *Jib*.

Inner part or *voice*; in music, a part between the highest and lowest; as, contralto and tenor are *inner parts* in a musical production which comprises soprano and bass.

in′nẽr, *n.* In marksmanship, that part of a target between the center and the outer; also, a shot which strikes that part.

in′nẽr-ly, *adv.* More within. [Obs.]

in′nẽr-mōst, *a.* Furthest inward; most remote from the outward part.

in′nẽr-mōst-ly, *adv.* In the innermost part. [Rare.]

in-nẽr′vāte, *v.t.*; innervated, *pt.*, *pp.*; innervating, *ppr.* [L. *in*, in, and *nervus*, nerve.] To supply with nerves; to give nervous influence to; to innerve.

in-nẽr-vā′tion, *n.* [LL. *innervis*, nerveless; L. *in-* priv., and *nervus*, nerve.] A state of nervelessness.

in-nẽr-vā′tion, *n.* [L. *in*, in, and *nervus*, nerve.]

1. The act of innervating; the act of innerving; specifically, in physiology, the function of the nervous system; nervous excitement; special activity excited in any part of the nervous system.

2. In anatomy, the arrangement or disposition of nerves in the animal body or any of its parts.

in-nẽrve′, *v.t.*; innerved, *pt.*, *pp.*; innerving, *ppr.* To give nerve to; to invigorate; to strengthen.

inn′hōld-ẽr, *n.* A person who keeps an inn or house for the entertainment of travelers.

in′ning, *n.* [ME. *inninge*; AS. *innung*, a putting or getting in, verbal n. of *innian*, to get in, put in.]

1. The ingathering, as of grain. [Obs.]

2. The time during which a person or party is in action or power; specifically, (a) in cricket, baseball, etc., the time or turn for batting, either of an individual player or of the whole side; sometimes in the plural; (b) the time during which a person or party is in office.

3. Land recovered from the sea.

in′nis, *n.* Same as *Ennis*.

in-ni′ten-cy, *n.* [L. *innitens* (*-entis*), ppr. of *inniti*, to lean or rest upon.] A resting upon; pressure. [Obs.]

in-nix′ion (-nik′shun), *n.* Incumbency; a resting upon. [Obs.]

inn′keep-ẽr, *n.* The keeper of an inn; an innholder; a taverner.

in′nō-cence, *n.* [OFr. *innocence*; L. *innocentia*, harmlessness, integrity, from *innocens* (*-entis*), harmless, innocent.]

1. Freedom from any quality that can injure; innoxiousness; harmlessness; as, the *innocence* of bread as diet.

2. Freedom from wrong in a moral sense; purity of heart and life; unimpaired integrity; as, the *innocence* of a child.

3. Freedom from the guilt of a particular crime or sin; guiltlessness; as, the prisoner may prove his *innocence*.

4. The state of being lawfully conveyed to a belligerent, or of not being contraband; as, the *innocence* of a cargo, or of merchandise.

5. Simplicity; mental imbecility; ignorance; idiocy; silliness.

6. A plant, *Houstonia cœrulea*; the bluet.

Syn.—Innocuousness, harmlessness, inoffensiveness, guilelessness, guiltlessness, simplicity, purity, sinlessness.

in′nō-cen-cy, *n.* The quality or condition of being innocent; innocence; an act of innocence.

in′nō-cent, *a.* [OFr. *innocent*; L. *innocens* (*-entis*), innocent, harmless; *in-* priv., and *nocens* (*-entis*), ppr. of *nocere*, to do wrong to.]

1. Not injurious; free from qualities that can injure; harmless; innoxious; as, an *innocent* medicine or remedy.

2. Free from guilt in a moral sense; not tainted with sin; pure; upright.

> A weak, poor, *innocent* lamb. —Shak.

3. Free from the guilt of a particular crime or evil action; as, the man is *innocent* of the crime charged in the indictment.

4. Lawful; permitted; as, an *innocent* trade.

5. Not contraband; not subject to forfeiture; as, *innocent* goods carried to a belligerent nation.

6. Artless; ignorant; imbecile; idiotic.

7. Pretty; modest; as, an *innocent* flower; an *innocent* little girl.

Syn.—Blameless, pure, undefiled, faultless, guiltless, innocuous, immaculate, sinless, spotless, virtuous.

in′nō-cent, *n.* 1. One free from guilt or sin; an innocent person.

2. A simple person; a natural; an idiot; a simpleton.

3. Same as *Innocence*, 6.

Innocents' Day; see *Childermas-day*.

in′nō-cent-ly, *adv.* In an innocent manner; harmlessly; guilelessly.

in-nō-cū′i-ty, *n.* The state or quality of being innocuous; innocuousness.

in-noc′ū-ous, *a.* [L. *innocuus*, harmless; *in-* priv., and *nocere*, to harm, injure.] Harmless; producing no ill effect; innocent.

Syn.—Harmless, inoffensive, innoxious.

in-noc′ū-ous-ly, *adv.* In an innocuous manner; without harm; without injurious effects.

in-noc′ū-ous-ness, *n.* The state or quality of being innocuous; harmlessness.

in′nō-dāte, *v.t.* To bind up or fasten, as in a knot. [Obs.]

in-nom′i-nȧ-ble, *a.* Not to be named. [Rare.]

in-nom′i-nāte, *a.* [LL. *innominatus*, unnamed; L. *in-* priv., and *nominatus*, pp. of *nominare*, to name.]

1. Having no name; anonymous. [Rare.]

2. In anatomy, a term applied to many parts in lieu of more specific names; as, the *innominate* artery, vein, gland, etc.

Innominate bone; one of the two bones to which the posterior limbs are attached and which form the pelvic basin; the innominatum.

Innominate contracts; in Roman law, contracts difficult to classify.

in-nom-i-nā′tum, *n.*; *pl.* **in-nom-i-nā′tȧ**, [Neut. of LL. *innominatus*, unnamed, innominate.]

1. The innominate bone.

2. A term used to designate a thing or things unclassified, as antiques, curios, etc.

in′nō-vāte, *v.t.*; innovated, *pt.*, *pp.*; innovating, *ppr.* [L. *innovatus*, pp. of *innovare*, to renew; *in*, in, and *novare*, to alter, to make new, from *novus*, new.]

1. To change or alter by introducing something new; to remodel. [Obs.]

2. To bring in something new; to introduce as a novelty.

in′nō-vāte, *v.i.* To introduce novelties; to make changes in anything established; as, it is often dangerous to *innovate* on the customs of a nation.

in-nō-vā′tion, *n.* [LL. *innovatio* (*-onis*), from L. *innovatus*, pp. of *innovare*, to renew, to innovate.]

1. The act of innovating or effecting a change in the established order; introduction of something new.

2. The change made by innovating; any custom, manner, etc., newly introduced.

3. In bryology, a new shoot or a new annual growth upon an old stem.

4. In Scots law, the renewal of an obligation to pay.

in-nō-vā′tion-ist, *n.* One who advocates innovations; a believer in changes for experiment.

in′nō-vā-tive, *a.* Having a tendency to innovate.

in′nō-vā-tōr, *n.* One who introduces novelties, or who makes changes by introducing something new.

in-nox′ious (-nok′shus), *a.* [L. *innoxius*, harmless; *in-* priv., and *noxius*, harmful.]

1. Free from mischievous qualities; innocent; harmless; as, an *innoxious* drug.

2. Free from crime; pure; innocent.

in-nox′ious-ly, *adv.* In an innoxious manner.

in-nox′ious-ness, *n.* Harmlessness.

in′nū-āte, *v.t.* To insinuate. [Obs.]

in-nū′bi-lous, *a.* Free from clouds. [Obs.]

in-nū-en′dō, *n.* [L., abl. of gerund of *innuere*, to nod to, to intimate, hint.]

1. An oblique hint; a remote intimation or reference to a person or thing not named.

2. In law, a word used to point out the application of some injurious remark to the person aimed at.

3. In rhetoric, insinuation; a form of expression incriminating a person without directly naming him.

Syn.—Insinuation.—An *innuendo* supposes a representation so framed as to point distinctly at something beyond which is injurious to the character; an *insinuation* consists in artfully winding into the mind imputations of an injurious nature without making any direct charge.

in′nū-ent, *a.* Significant. [Obs.]

In′nū-it, **In′ū-it**, *n.* [Eskimo, lit., the people.] The native name of the Eskimo.

in-nū″mẽr-ȧ-bil′i-ty, *n.* State of being innumerable.

in-nū′mẽr-ȧ-ble, *a.* [OFr. *innumerable*; L. *innumerabilis*, countless, without number; *in-* priv., and *numerabilis*, that can be numbered, from *numerare*, to number.] Not to be counted; that cannot be enumerated or numbered for multitude; of a very great number.

in-nū′mẽr-ȧ-ble-ness, *n.* Innumerability.

in-nū′mẽr-ȧ-bly, *adv.* Without number.

in-nū′mẽr-ous, *a.* [L. *innumerus*; *in-* priv., and *numerus*, number.] Too many to be counted or numbered; innumerable. [Rare.]

in-nū-tri′tion (-trish′un), *n.* Want of nutrition; failure of nourishment.

in-nū-tri′tious (-trish′us), *a.* Not nutritious; not supplying nourishment; not nourishing.

in-nū′tri-tive, *a.* Not nourishing.

-ino. A suffix from Sp., Port., and It., *-ino*, from L. *-inus*, used in several English nouns, such as alb*ino*, bamb*ino*, etc.

in-ō-bē′di-ence, *n.* [Obs.] See *Disobedience*.

in-ō-bē′di-ent, *a.* [Obs.] See *Disobedient*.

in-ō-bē′di-ent-ly, *adv.* [Obs.] See *Disobediently*.

in-ob-ṣẽrv′ȧ-ble, *a.* That cannot be seen, perceived, or observed.

in-ob-ṣẽrv′ănce, *n.* Want of observance; neglect of observing; disobedience.

in-ob-ṣẽrv′ăn-cy, *n.* The habit of not observing.

in-ob-ṣẽrv′ănt, *a.* [LL. *inobservans* (*-antis*), not observant, inattentive; L. *in-* priv., and *observans* (*-antis*), ppr. of *observare*, to observe.] Not taking notice.

in-ob-ṣẽrv′ănt-ly, *adv.* Without heed or observation.

in-ob-ṣẽr-vā′tion, *n.* Neglect or want of observation. [Rare.]

in-ob-trū′sive, *a.* Not obtrusive.

in-ob-trū′sive-ly, *adv.* Unobtrusively.

in-ob-trū′sive-ness, *n.* A quality of being not obtrusive.

in-ō-cär′pin, *n.* In chemistry, a red coloring-matter found in the juice of the *Inocarpus edulis*, a tree of Tahiti.

In-ō-cär′pus, *n.* [Gr. *is*, *inos*, a fiber, nerve, and *karpos*, fruit.] A genus of the bean family, including the *Inocarpus edulis* or Otaheite chestnut, whose seeds are edible and also produce a red dye.

in-oc-cū-pā′tion, *n.* Want of occupation.

In-ō-cer′ȧ-mus, *n.* [Gr. *is*, *inos*, a fiber, sinew, muscle, and *keramos*, a tile, shell.] In paleontology, a genus of bivalvular mollusks whose fossils are found in Cretaceous rocks.

in-oc″ū-lȧ-bil′i-ty, *n.* The state of being inoculable.

in-oc′ū-lȧ-ble, *a.* 1. That may be inoculated.

2. That may communicate disease by inoculation.

in-oc′ū-lăr, *a.* [L. *in*, in, and *oculus*, eye.] In entomology, inserted in the inner margin of the compound eye; said of the antennæ of certain insects, as the *Cerambycidæ*.

in-oc′ū-lāte, *v.t.*; inoculated, *pt.*, *pp.*; inoculating, *ppr.* [L. *inoculatus*, pp. of *inoculare*, to ingraft an eye or bud from one plant to another, to inoculate; *in*, in, and *oculus*, an eye, bud.]

1. To insert a bud in, as for the purpose of growth on a new stock.

2. In medicine, to communicate, as a disease, to a person by inserting infectious matter in the skin or flesh; as, to *inoculate* a person with the virus of smallpox.

3. Figuratively, to imbue; to infect; to corrupt; as, to *inoculate* treason.

in-oc′ū-lāte, *v.i.* 1. To propagate by budding.

2. To impart a disease by inoculation.

in-oc-ū-lā′tion, *n.* [L. *inoculatio* (*-onis*), an ingrafting, inoculation, from *inoculatus*, pp. of *inoculare*, to ingraft, inoculate.]

1. The act or practice of propagating by budding.

2. In medicine, the act or practice of communicating a disease to a person in health, by inserting contagious matter in his skin or flesh.

This term was formerly limited to the communication of smallpox.

3. The imparting of evil knowledge or vice to the mind.

in-oc′ū-lā-tŏr, *n.* [L. *inoculator*, an ingrafter, from *inoculare*, to ingraft, inoculate.] A person who inoculates; one who propagates plants or diseases by inoculation.

in-ō′di-āte, *v.t.* To make hateful. [Obs.]

in-ō′dŏr-āte, *a.* Having no odor. [Obs.]

in-ō′dŏr-ous, *a.* [L. *inodorus*; *in-* priv., and *odor*, a smell.] Having no smell; odorless.

in-ō′dŏr-ous-ness, *n.* The condition or quality of being inodorous.

in-of-fen′sive, *a.* 1. Giving no offense or provocation; causing no uneasiness or disturbance; as, an *inoffensive* man; an *inoffensive* sight.

2. Harmless; doing no injury or mischief.

Thy *inoffensive* satires never bite. —Dryden.

3. Not obstructing; presenting no hindrance. [Rare.]

in-of-fen′sive-ly, *adv.* In an inoffensive manner.

in-of-fen′sive-ness, *n.* The quality of being inoffensive.

in-of-fi′ciăl (-fish′ăl), *a.* Not official; not sanctioned by authority; unofficial; as, an *inofficial* communication; *inofficial* intelligence.

Pinckney and Marshall would not make *inofficial* visits to discuss official business. —Pickering.

Syn.—Unauthorized, unwarranted, informal, irregular, unofficial.

in-of-fi′ciăl-ly, *adv.* Without the usual forms, or not in the official character.

in-of-fi′cious, *a.* [LL. *inofficiosus*, regardless of duty, harmful; L. *in-* priv., and *officiosus*, obliging, dutiful, from *officium*, duty.]

1. In law, unkind; regardless of natural obligation; contrary to natural duty; as, an *inofficious* testament or will. —Blackstone.

2. Not civil or attentive. [Obs.]

in-of-fi′cious-ly, *adv.* Not officiously.

in′ō-gen, *n.* [Gr. *is*, *inos*, a fiber, nerve, and *-genēs*, producing.] A hypothetical substance believed to occur in muscular tissue and to undergo decomposition during contraction.

in-ō-gen′iç, *a.* Pertaining to inogen.

in-op-ĕr-ā′tion, *n.* Agency; influence; production of effects. [Obs.]

in-op′ĕr-ā-tive, *a.* Not operative; not active; having no operation; producing no effect; as, laws rendered *inoperative* by neglect; *inoperative* remedies.

in-ō-pĕr′çū-lăr, *a.* See *Inoperculate.*

in-ō-pĕr′çū-lāte, *a.* [L. *in-* priv., and *operculatus*, covered, from *operculum*, a cover, lid.]

1. In botany, without an operculum or lid.

2. In zoölogy, having no operculum, as a snail.

in-ō-pĕr′çū-lā-ted, *a.* Inoperculate.

in-ō-pin′ȧ-ble, *a.* Not to be expected or supposed. [Obs.]

in-op′i-nāte, *a.* Not expected. [Obs.]

in-op-pŏr-tūne′, *a.* [L. *inopportunus*, unsuitable, inconvenient; *in-* priv., and *opportunus*, suitable.] Not opportune; inconvenient; unseasonable; as, an *inopportune* statement.

in-op-pŏr-tūne′ly, *adv.* Unseasonably; at an inconvenient time.

in-op-pŏr-tūne′ness, *n.* The quality of being inopportune.

in-op-pŏr-tū′ni-ty, *n.* Unseasonableness; inopportuneness.

in-op-press′ive, *a.* Not oppressive; not burdensome.

in-op′ū-lent, *a.* Not opulent; not wealthy; not affluent or rich.

in-ọr′di-nȧ-cy, *n.* Deviation from order or rule prescribed; irregularity; disorder; excess; want of moderation; as, the *inordinacy* of desire or other passion.

in-ọr′di-nāte, *a.* [L. *inordinatus*, not arranged, out of order; *in-* priv., and *ordinatus*, pp. of *ordinare*, to arrange, put in order, from *ordo* (*-inis*), order.] Irregular; disorderly; excessive; immoderate; not limited to rules prescribed; as, an *inordinate* love of the world.

Inordinate proportion; in mathematics, a proportion in which the order of the terms is irregular.

Syn.—Excessive, immoderate, undue, intemperate, overmuch.

in-ọr′di-nāte-ly, *adv.* Irregularly; excessively; immoderately.

in-ọr′di-nāte-ness, *n.* Inordinacy.

in-ọr-di-nā′tion, *n.* Irregularity; deviation from rule or right. [Obs.]

in-ọr-gan′iç, *a.* Devoid of organs; not formed with the organs of life; unorganized; not organic; as, the *inorganic* matter that forms the earth's surface.

in-ọr-gan′iç-ăl, *a.* Inorganic.

in-ọr-gan′iç-ăl-ly, *adv.* Without organs or organization.

in-ọr-gan′i-ty, *n.* The quality or state of being inorganic. [Obs.]

in-ọr′găn-ī-zȧ-ble, *a.* Not organizable.

in-ọr″găn-i-zā′tion, *n.* The state of being unorganized; absence of organization.

in-ọr′găn-ized, *a.* Not having organic structure; devoid of organs.

in-ọr-thog′rȧ-phy, *n.* Incorrect orthography.

in-os′çū-lāte, *v.i.*; inosculated, *pt.*, *pp.*; inosculating, *ppr.* [L. *in*, in, on, and *osculum*, dim. of *os*, mouth.]

1. To unite by apposition or contact; to unite, as two vessels of the body at their extremities; to anastomose.

2. To run together; to intercommunicate.

in-os′çū-lāte, *v.t.* To unite, as two vessels in an animal body.

in-os-çū-lā′tion, *n.* Same as *Anastomosis.*

in-os′iç, *a.* [Gr. *is*, *inos*, strength, force, nerve, and *-ic*.] In chemistry, pertaining to inosite.

Inosic acid; an acid contained in the mother-liquor of the preparation of creatine from flesh-juice.

in-ō-sin′iç, *a.* Inosic.

in′ō-sīte, *n.* [*Inosic* and *-ite*.] In chemistry, muscle-sugar; a saccharine substance occurring in muscles, rarely in urine; called also *phaseomannite.*

in-ox′i-dī-zȧ-ble, *a.* Not admitting of oxidation.

in-ox′i-dīze, *v.t.*; inoxidized, *pt.*, *pp.*; inoxidizing, *ppr.* To prevent, or preserve from, oxidation.

in′-pȧ-rab″ō-lȧ, *n.* An inscribed parabola.

in pŏr-pet′ū-um. [L.] In perpetuity; forever.

in′-pol″y-gon, *n.* An inscribed polygon.

in pos′se. [L. *in*, in, and *posse*, to be able. In possibility of being.

in prō′pri-ȧ pēr-sō′nȧ. [L.] In one's own person.

in-quạr-tā′tion (-kwạr-), *n.* Quartation.

in′quest, *n.* [ME. *enquest*; OFr. *enqueste*; L. *inquisita*, something inquired or sought for, an inquest, properly f. of *inquisitus*, pp. of *inquirere*, to inquire into, inquire.]

1. In law, (a) a judicial inquiry, especially one held before a jury; (b) the jury itself; particularly, a coroner's jury, assembled to inquire into the cause of a sudden death.

2. Inquiry; search. [Rare.]

Inquest of office; an inquiry made by the sheriff, coroner, or escheator, concerning any matter that entitles the crown or the state to the possession of lands or tenements, goods or chattels; it is made by a jury of no determinate number.

in-quī′et, *v.t.* To disturb; to trouble. [Obs.]

in-quī-e-tā′tion, *n.* Disturbance. [Obs.]

in-quī′et-ness, *n.* Inquietude. [Obs.]

in-quī′e-tūde, *n.* [Fr. *inquiétude*; LL. *inquietudo*, uneasiness, from L. *inquietus*, restless, unquiet; *in-* priv., and *quietus*, quiet.] Disturbed state; want of quiet; restlessness; uneasiness, either of body or mind; disquietude.

in′qui-line, *n.* [L. *inquilinus*, an alien, one living in a place not his own, from *incola*, an inhabitant, from *incolere*, to inhabit; *in*, in, and *colere*, to dwell.] An animal that lives in an abode properly belonging to another, as certain insects that live in galls made by the true gall-insects.

in′qui-line, *a.* Like an inquiline in character.

in′qui-nāte, *v.t.* To defile; to pollute; to contaminate. [Obs.]

in-qui-nā′tion, *n.* The act of defiling, or state of being defiled; pollution; corruption. [Obs.]

in-quīr′ȧ-ble, *a.* Capable of being inquired into; subject to inquisition or inquest.

in-quīr′ănce, en-quīr′ănce, *n.* Inquiry. [Obs.]

in-qui-rā′tion, *n.* Inquiry. [Prov. Eng.]

in-quīre′, *v.i.*; inquired, *pt.*, *pp.*; inquiring, *ppr.* [L. *inquirere*, to seek after, search for, inquire; *in*, into, and *quærere*, to seek. Also *enquire.*]

1. To ask a question; to seek for truth or information by asking questions.

We will call the damsel and *inquire.* —Gen. xxiv. 57.

2. To seek for truth by argument or the discussion of questions, or by investigation.

Syn.—Ask, solicit, question, request, seek, demand, interrogate.

in-quīre′, *v.t.* 1. To ask about; to seek knowledge of by asking; as, he *inquired* the way.

2. To call or name. [Obs.]

in-quīr′ent, *a.* Making inquiry. [Obs.]

in-quīr′ĕr, *n.* One who inquires; one who searches or examines; an investigator.

in-quīr′ing, *a.* Given to inquiry; disposed to investigate causes; as, an *inquiring* mind.

in-quīr′ing-ly, *adv.* By way of inquiry.

in-quīr′y, *n.*; *pl.* **in-quīr′ieṣ.** 1. The act of inquiring; a seeking for information by asking questions; interrogation.

2. Search for truth, information, or knowledge; examination into facts or principles.

Writ of inquiry; a judicial process addressed to the sheriff of the county in which the venue in the action is laid, stating the former proceedings in the action, and commanding the sheriff that by the oath of twelve honest and lawful men of his county he diligently inquire what damages the plaintiff has sustained, and return the inquisition into court.

Syn.—Interrogation, question, asking, investigation, search, examination, research, scrutiny, exploration.

in-quiṣ′i-ble, *a.* Admitting of judicial inquiry. [Obs.]

in-qui-ṣi′tion (-zish′un), *n.* [L. *inquisitio* (*-onis*), a seeking or searching for, an inquiring into, from *inquisitus*, pp. of *inquirere*, to seek for, inquire into.]

1. Inquiry; examination; investigation; the act of inquiring.

2. In law, (a) judicial inquiry; official examination; inquest; (b) the verdict of a jury.

3. [I—] In the Roman Catholic church, a court or tribunal for the examination and punishment of heretics. It was fully established in 1235 by Pope Gregory IX. It still nominally exists, but its rigor is entirely mitigated, its action being confined to the examination of books and the trial of ecclesiastical offenses.

in-qui-ṣi′tion, *v.t.* To inquire into; to investigate. [Obs.]

in-qui-ṣi′tion-ăl, *a.* 1. Pertaining to inquisition; inquisitorial.

2. [I—] Relating to the Inquisition.

in-qui-ṣi′tion-ā-ry, *a.* Inquisitional. [Rare.]

in-quiṣ′i-tive, *a.* [OFr. *inquisitif*, inquisitive, from L. *inquisitus*, pp. of *inquirere*, to inquire into, to inquire.]

1. Addicted to inquiry; inclined to seek information; curious.

The whole neighborhood grew *inquisitive* after my name and character. —Addison.

2. Inclined to seek knowledge by discussion, investigation, observation, etc.; given to research.

A young, *inquisitive*, and sprightly genius. —Watts.

Syn.—Curious, prying.—*Curious* denotes a feeling, and *inquisitive* a habit. We are *curious* when we desire to learn something new; we are *inquisitive* when we set ourselves to gain it by inquiry or research. *Prying* implies *inquisitiveness* when carried to an extreme, and is more commonly used in a bad sense, as indicating a desire to penetrate into the secrets of others.

in-quiṣ′i-tive, *n.* A person who is inquisitive; one curious in research.

in-quiṣ′i-tive-ly, *adv.* In an inquisitive manner; with curiosity to obtain information; with scrutiny.

in-quiṣ′i-tive-ness, *n.* The disposition to obtain information by questioning others, or by researches into facts, causes, or principles; curiosity to learn what is not known; the character of being inquisitive.

in-quiṣ′i-tŏr, *n.* [L. *inquisitor*, a searcher, examiner, a police agent, from *inquisitus*, pp. of *inquirere*, to search for, inquire.]

1. One who inquires; particularly, one whose official duty it is to inquire and examine.

2. [I—] A member of the Court of Inquisition.

3. An inquisitive or curious person. [Obs.]

in-quiṣ-i-tō′ri-ăl, *a.* 1. Pertaining to inquisition; making strict or searching inquiry; as, *inquisitorial* power.

2. Pertaining to the Court of Inquisition or resembling its practices.

in-quiṣ-i-tō′ri-ăl-ly, *adv.* In an inquisitorial manner.

in-quiṣ-i-tō′ri-ous, *a.* Making strict inquiry. [Obs.]

in-quiṣ-i-tū′ri-ent, *a.* Given to inquisition, or making strict inquiry; inquisitorial. [Obs.]

in-rac′i-nāte, *v.t.*; inracinated, *pt.*, *pp.*; inracinating, *ppr.* [Fr. *inraciner*, from L. *in*, in, and OFr. *racine*, a root.] To root; to implant.

in-rāil′, *v.t.* [Obs.] See *Enrail.*

in-reg′is-tĕr, *v.t.* [Obs.] See *Enregister.*

in′rō, *n.* [Japan. from Chinese *yin*, a seal, and *lūng*, basket.] A small set of lacquered receptacles forming a flattened cylinder, carried at the girdle by the Japanese, and used to hold perfumes, medicines, and other articles of convenience.

in′rōad, *n.* The entrance of an enemy into a country with purposes of hostility; a sudden or desultory incursion or invasion; encroachment; irruption.

Syn.—Invasion, irruption, raid, incursion.

in-rōad′, *v.t.* and *v.i.* To make inroad into; to invade. [Obs.]

in-rōll′, *v.t.* [Obs.] See *Enroll.*

in′rush, *n.* A rushing in.

in-rush′, *v.i.* To rush in. [Obs.]

In-sab-bȧ-tā′ti, *n.pl.* [LL.] The Waldenses; so called from their peculiar shoes or sabots.

in-sāfe′ty, *n.* Want of safety; insecurity. [Obs.]

in-sal′i-vāte, *v.t.*; insalivated, *pt.*, *pp.*; insalivating, *ppr.* To mix with the saliva, as food.

in-sal-i-vā′tion, *n.* The mixture of the food with saliva during mastication.

in-sȧ-lū′bri-ous, *a.* Not salubrious; not healthful; unwholesome; as, an *insalubrious* air or climate.

in-sȧ-lū′bri-ty, *n.* Want of salubrity; unhealthfulness; unwholesomeness; as, the *insalubrity* of air.

in-sal′ū-tā-ry, *a.* [LL. *insalutaris*, not salutary; L. *in-* priv., and *salutaris*, healthful, salutary.]
1. Not salutary; not favorable to health.
2. Not tending to safety; productive of evil.

in-san-ȧ-bil′i-ty, *n.* State of being incurable.

in-san′ȧ-ble, *a.* [L. *insanabilis*; *in-* priv., and *sanabilis*, curable, from *sanus*, sound.] Incurable; that cannot be healed.

in-san′ȧ-ble-ness, *n.* Insanability.

in-san′ȧ-bly, *adv.* Incurably.

in-sāne′, *a.* [L. *insanus*, unsound in mind, mad, insane; *in-* priv., and *sanus*, sound.]
1. Unsound in mind or intellect; mad; deranged in mind; delirious; distracted.
2. Used by or appropriated to insane persons; as, an *insane* hospital.
3. Making mad; causing madness; as, the *insane* root. [Obs.]
4. Figuratively, resulting from insanity; as, an *insane* proposition.
Used substantively for persons not sane; as, a hospital for *the insane*.

in-sāne′ly, *adv.* Madly; foolishly; without reason.

in-sāne′ness, *n.* Insanity; madness.

in-sā′ni-āte, *v.t.* To madden. [Obs.]

in-sā′nie (-ni), *n.* Madness. [Obs.]

in-san′i-tā-ry, *a.* Unhealthy.

in-san-i-tā′tion, *n.* Lack of sanitation.

in-san′i-ty, *n.* [L. *insanitas* (*-atis*), unsoundness, unhealthiness, insanity, from *insanus*, unsound, insane.]
1. Any degree of persistent mental derangement as distinguished from such temporary delirium or wandering as is produced by disease, drugs, or injuries; unsoundness of intellect; madness.
2. In law, such mental unsoundness as frees a person from criminal responsibility, or such as renders a person incapable of making a valid contract, conveyance, or will, or of conducting his own affairs. Criminal responsibility depends upon the ability and freedom of the individual to choose between right and wrong in any particular case. In certain cases, the individual knows what is right and wrong but has an irresistible morbid impulse which renders choice impossible, as in kleptomania. This has been held by some authorities to constitute legal irresponsibility. In contracts, insanity is the incapacity to give a rational assent to the kind of contract in question, and in wills, is the inability to make a rational choice as to the disposition of property. The tendency is to enlarge the scope of the word.

Syn.—Lunacy, madness, derangement, alienation, aberration, mania, delirium, frenzy, monomania, dementia, paranoia.—*Insanity* is the generic term for all such diseases; *lunacy* has now an equal extent of meaning, though formerly used to denote periodical *insanity*; *madness* has the same extent, though originally referring to the rage created by the disease; *derangement, aberration, alienation*, are popular terms for *insanity*; *delirium, mania*, and *frenzy* denote excited states of the disease; *dementia* denotes the loss of mental power; *monomania* is *insanity* upon a single subject; *paranoia* is dementia with delusions.

in-sā′pō-ry, *a.* [L. *in-* priv., and *sapor*, taste, flavor, from *sapere*, to taste.] Without taste; lacking flavor. [Rare.]

in-sā-tiȧ-bil′i-ty (-shȧ-), *n.* [LL. *insatiabilitas*, from L. *insatiabilis*, insatiable.] Greediness of appetite that cannot be satisfied or appeased.

in-sā′tiȧ-ble, *a.* [L. *insatiabilis*, that cannot be satisfied; *in-* priv., and *satiare*, to satiate, satisfy.] Incapable of being satisfied or appeased; very greedy; as, an *insatiable* appetite or desire.

Syn.—Voracious, unappeasable, omnivorous, ravenous, rapacious, greedy.

in-sā′tiȧ-ble-ness, *n.* Insatiability.

in-sā′tiȧ-bly, *adv.* With greediness not to be satisfied.

in-sā′ti-āte, *a.* [LL. *insatiatus*, not satisfied; L. *in-* priv., and *satiatus*, pp. of *satiare*, to satiate, satisfy.] Insatiable.

in-sā′ti-āte-ly, *adv.* Insatiably.

in-sā′ti-āte-ness, *n.* The state of being unsatisfied.

in-sȧ-ti′e-ty, *n.* [L. *insatietas*; *in-* priv., and *satietas*, satiety.] Insatiableness.

in-sat-is-fac′tion, *n.* Want of satisfaction. [Obs.]

in-sat′ū-rȧ-ble, *a.* Not to be saturated, filled, or glutted.

in′science (-shens), *n.* Ignorance; want of knowledge. [Obs.]

in′scient (-shent), *a.* Without knowledge. [Obs.]

in′scient, *a.* [L. *in*, in, and *sciens* (*-entis*), ppr. of *scire*, to know.] Possessed of insight; discerning. [Rare.]

in-sconce′, *v.t.* [Obs.] See *Ensconce*.

in-scrīb′ȧ-ble, *a.* That may be inscribed.

in-scrīb′ȧ-ble-ness, *n.* State of being inscribable.

in-scribe′, *v.t.*; inscribed, *pt.*, *pp.*; inscribing, *ppr.* [L. *inscribere*, to write in, to write upon; *in*, in, on, and *scribere*, to write.]
1. To write on; to engrave on; as, to *inscribe* a line or verse on a monument.
2. To imprint on; to impress; as, to *inscribe* anything on the mind or memory.
3. To assign or address to; to commend to by a short address; as, to *inscribe* a book to a friend.
4. To mark with letters, characters, or words; to enter by writing; to *inscribe* a stone with a name; to *inscribe* one's name on a list or document.
5. To draw (a geometrical figure) within another so as to touch it at every possible point without intersecting it.

in-scrībed′, *a.* In entomology, marked or figured as though by written characters.

in-scrīb′ẽr, *n.* One who inscribes.

in-scrip′tion, *n.* [L. *inscriptio* (*-onis*), an inscription, title, lit., a writing upon, from *inscriptus*, pp. of *inscribere*, to write upon.]
1. The act of writing or engraving upon.
2. Something written or engraved; any character, word, or sentence written or engraved on a solid substance for duration, especially in raised or incised letters; as, *inscriptions* on monuments, called epitaphs, on pillars, etc.
3. An address of a book to a friend or patron, less formal than a dedication.
4. Words or letters in a straight line across a medal or coin, as distinguished from a legend, which is usually curved.
5. Lettering on an engraving or etching.
6. An entry upon a list, register, etc.; as, the *inscription* on a document.
7. In civil law, the agreement of a plaintiff or accuser to assume a penalty if the defendant is not convicted.

in-scrip′tive, *a.* Of the nature of an inscription.

in-scrōll′, *v.t.* To write on a scroll. [Rare.]

in-scrū-tȧ-bil′i-ty, *n.* The quality of being inscrutable.

in-scrū′tȧ-ble, *a.* [LL. *inscrutabilis*, inscrutable; L. *in-* priv., and *scrutari*, to search carefully, examine.] Not capable of being searched into and understood by inquiry or study; incapable of being discovered, comprehended, or accounted for; obscure; mysterious.

in-scrū′tȧ-ble-ness, *n.* Inscrutability.

in-scrū′tȧ-bly, *adv.* In an inscrutable manner.

in-sculp′, *v.t.* To engrave; to carve. [Obs.]

in-sculpt′, *a.* [L. *insculptus*, pp. of *insculpere*, to cut or carve in or upon, to engrave; *in*, in, on, and *sculpere*, to carve.] Imbedded and growing in rocks; said of certain lichens which flourish upon rocks.

in-sculp′tion, *n.* Inscription. [Obs.]

in-sculp′tūre, *n.* An engraving; sculpture.

in-sculp′tūred, *a.* Engraved.

in-sēam′, *v.t.*; inseamed, *pt.*, *pp.*; inseaming, *ppr.* To impress or mark with a seam or cicatrix. [Poet.]

in-search′ (-sẽrch′), *v.t.* To make search. [Obs.]

in-sec′ȧ-ble, *a.* [L. *insecabilis*; *in-* priv., and *secabilis*, able to be cut, from *secare*, to cut.] That cannot be divided by a cutting instrument; indivisible.

in′sect, *n.* [L. *insectum*, an insect, properly neut. of *insectus*, pp. of *insecare*, to cut into; *in*, into, and *secare*, to cut, divide; so called because the bodies of some insects seem to be cut or divided into segments.]

Figure showing the Parts of Insects.
Coleopter (*Cicindela campestris*). *a*, Head. *b*, Thorax. *c*, Abdomen. *d d*, Elytra. *e e*, Wings. *f f*, Antennæ.

1. One of a class of invertebrate animals of the division *Arthropoda*, distinguished from the other classes of the division by the fact that the three divisions of the body—the head, thorax, and abdomen—are always distinct from one another. There are never more than three pairs of legs in the adult, and these are all borne upon the thorax; respiration is effected by means of air-tubes or tracheæ, and in most insects two pairs of wings are developed from the back of the second and third segments of the thorax. The integument is more or less hardened by the deposition of chitin in it. The head is composed of several segments amalgamated together, and carries a pair of jointed feelers or antennæ, a pair of eyes, usually compound, and the appendages of the mouth. The thorax is composed of three segments, also amalgamated, but generally pretty easily recognized. Insects have been divided into three sections—*Ametabola, Hemimetabola*, and *Holometabola*, according as they remain always the same or undergo an incomplete or complete metamorphosis.
2. A member of the class *Insecta*.
3. Loosely, various small invertebrates.
4. Anything small or contemptible.

in′sect, *a.* Small; mean; contemptible.

In-sec′tȧ, *n.pl.* [L., pl. of *insectum*, an insect.] A class of *Arthropoda* generally understood to include the *Hexapoda* and the *Myriapoda*, but sometimes restricted to the *Hexapoda* or six-legged insects.

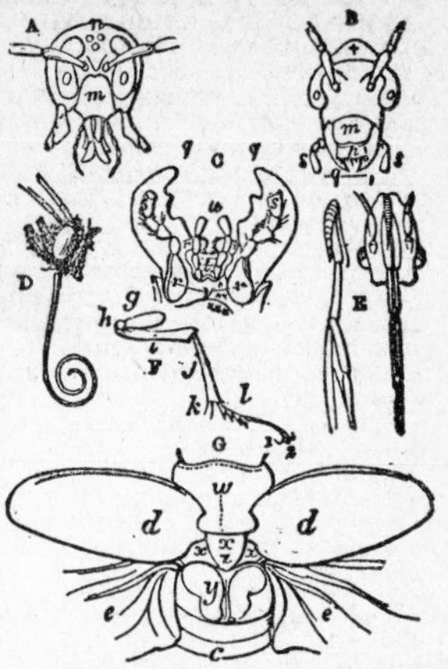

in-sec-tā′ri-um, *n.* A place for the propagation and study of insects.

in′sec-tā-ry, *n.* Same as *Insectarium*.

in-sec-tā′tŏr, *n.* A persecutor. [Obs.]

in′sect-ed, *a.* Divided into segments like an insect. [Obs.]

in-sec-ti-cī′dăl, *a.* [L. *insectum*, an insect, and *cædere*, to kill.] Possessing properties destructive to insects, as an insect-powder.

in-sec′ti-cīde, *n.* Any substance or preparation used in the extermination of insects.

Figure showing the Parts of Insects.
A, B, C, Mandibulate Mouth. A, Head of Hornet, and upper side of mouth. *m*, Clypeus. *n*, Ocelli, stemmata, or simple eyes. *o*, Compound eyes. B, Head of Beetle, and C, under side of mouth of Beetle. +, Vertex. *m*, Clypeus. *o*, Eyes. *p*, Labrum or upper lip. *q*, Mandibles or upper jaws. *r*, Maxillæ or lower jaws. *s*, Maxillary palpi. *t*, Labium or under lip. *u*, Labial palpi. *v*, Mentum or chin, consisting of three parts—x, Mentum; xx, Stipes; xxx, Jugulum.—D and E, Haustellate Mouths. D, Spiral mouth or sucker of a Butterfly, called also Antlia. E, Straight sucker of a Plant-bug (*Pentatoma*), called Haustellum.—F, Leg of Stag-beetle. *g*, Coxa. *h*, Trochanter. *i*, Femur. *j*, Tibia. *k*, Calcaria or spurs. *l*, Tarsus, which in this instance is pentamerous, or consisting of five pieces. 1. Ungues or hooks. 2. Pulvillus or cushion.—G, Thorax of Stag-beetle. *c*, Abdomen. *d d*, Elytra. *e e*, Wings. *w*, Prothorax—upper side, pronotum; under side, prosternum. *x*, Mesothorax—upper side, mesonotum; under side, mesosternum. *y*, Metathorax—upper side, metanotum; under side, metasternum. *z*, Scutellum.

in-sec′ti-fūge, *n.* Any preparation that will drive away insects.

in-sec′tile, *a.* Having the nature of insects.

in-sec′tion, *n.* A cutting in; incisure; incision.

In-sec-tiv′ō-rȧ, *n.pl.* [L. *insectum*, an insect, and *vorare*, to devour.]
1. An order of mammals which live to a great extent on insects, having the molar teeth set with sharp, conical cusps. They are usually of small size, and many of them live underground, hibernating for some months. The shrew, hedgehog, and mole are familiar examples.
2. A family of bats that feed upon insects.

in-sec′ti-vōre, *n.* A member of the *Insectivora*.

in-sec-tiv′ō-rous, *a.* Feeding or subsisting on insects.

in-sec-tol′ō-gẽr, *n.* [Obs.] See *Entomologist*.

in-sec-tol′ō-gy, *n.* [Obs.] See *Entomology*.

in′sect-pow′dẽr, *n.* A powder used in destroying insects; particularly, a powder made from the dried flowers of certain species of plants belonging to the genus *Pyrethrum*.

in-sē-cūre′, *a.* 1. Not secure; not safe; not confident of safety.
2. Not safe; not effectually guarded or protected; unsafe; exposed to danger or loss.

in-sē-cūre′ly, *adv.* Without security or safety; without certainty.

in-sē-cūre′ness, *n.* The state of being insecure.

in-sē-cū′ri-ty, *n.* 1. Want of safety, or want of confidence in safety; as, seamen in a tempest must be conscious of their *insecurity*.
2. Uncertainty; want of safety; danger; hazard; liability to destruction or loss; as, the *insecurity* of a building exposed to fire.

in-sē-cū′tion, *n.* Pursuit. [Obs.]

in-sem′i-nāte, *v.t.* To sow; to impregnate. [Obs.]

in-sem-i-nā′tion, *n.* The act of sowing or impregnating. [Obs.]

in-sen′sāte, *a.* Destitute of sense; stupid; foolish; wanting sensibility.

in-sen′sāte-ly, *adv.* In a stupid or foolish manner.

in-sen′sāte-ness, *n.* The state of being insensate or insensible; want of sense; stupidity; foolishness.

in-sense′, *v.t.*; insensed, *pt.*, *pp.*; insensing, *ppr.* To cause to perceive or understand. [Prov. Eng.]

in-sen-si-bil′i-ty, *n.* 1. Want of sensibility, or the power of feeling or perceiving.
2. Want of the power to be moved or affected;

want of tenderness or susceptibility of emotion and passion.

3. Dullness; stupidity; torpor.

Syn.—Apathy, immobility, indifference, stoicism, stupidity, unfeelingness.

in-sen'si-ble, *a.* [LL. *insensibilis*, that cannot be felt, unable to feel; L. *in-* priv., and *sensibilis*, perceptible by the senses, from *sensus*, sense, perception.]

1. Imperceptible; that cannot be felt or perceived; as, the motion of the earth is *insensible* to the eye.

2. Destitute of the power of feeling or perceiving; wanting corporeal sensibility.

3. Not susceptible of emotion or passion; void of feeling; wanting tenderness; as, to be *insensible* to the sufferings of our fellow-men.

4. Void of sense or meaning; as, *insensible* words. [Obs.]

Syn.—Dull, hard, impassive, indifferent, unfeeling, senseless.

in-sen'si-ble-ness, *n.* Inability to perceive; want of sensibility.

in-sen'si-bly, *adv.* 1. Imperceptibly; in a manner not to be felt or preceived by the senses.

The hills rise *insensibly*. —Addison.

2. By slow degrees; gradually; as, men often slide *insensibly* into vicious habits.

in-sen'si-tive, *a.* Lacking sensitiveness.

in-sen'sū-ous (-shū-), *a.* Free from sensuousness; not appealing to the senses.

in-sen'tient (-shent), *a.* Not having perception or the power of perception.

in-sep-ȧ-rȧ-bil'i-ty, *n.* [LL. *inseparabilitas*, from L. *inseparabilis*, inseparable.] The quality of being inseparable, or incapable of disjunction.

in-sep'ȧ-rȧ-ble, *a.* [L. *inseparabilis*; *in-* priv., and *separabilis*, separable, from *separare*, to separate.] That cannot be separated or disjoined; not to be parted; as, there is an *inseparable* connection between vice and suffering or punishment.

in-sep'ȧ-rȧ-ble-ness, *n.* Inseparability.

in-sep'ȧ-rȧ-bly, *adv.* In a manner that prevents separation; with indissoluble union.

in-sep'ȧ-rāte, *a.* Not separate.

in-sep'ȧ-rāte-ly, *adv.* So as not to be separated. [Obs.]

in-sērt', *v.t.*; inserted, *pt.*, *pp.*; inserting, *ppr.* [L. *insertus*, pp. of *inserere*, to put or thrust in, to introduce, to insert; *in*, into, and *serere*, to join.] To thrust in; hence, to set in or among; as, to *insert* an advertisement in a paper.

in-sērt'ed, *a.* In botany, attached or set in or upon some part; as, the stamens are *inserted* in or upon the calyx.

in-sērt'ing, *n.* 1. A setting in.

2. Anything set in or to be set in, as lace, etc., in a garment. [Rare.]

in-sēr'tion, *n.* [LL. *insertio (-onis)*, a putting or thrusting in, from L. *insertus*, pp. of *inserere*, to put or thrust in, to insert.]

1. The act of setting or placing in or among other things; as, the *insertion* of passages in writings.

2. The manner in which one part is inserted in, or adheres to, another; as, the *insertion* of muscles, tendons, etc., in parts of the body.

3. The thing inserted; especially, (a) an additional passage in a manuscript; (b) a band of lace or embroidery set in a fabric for purposes of ornament.

4. In botany, the place or mode of attachment of an organ to its support.

Epigynous insertion; an insertion on the summit of the ovary.

Hypogynous insertion; an insertion beneath the ovary.

Perigynous insertion; an insertion upon the calyx surrounding the ovary.

Epigynous Insertion.

Hypogynous Insertion.

Perigynous Insertion.

in-sērve', *v.t.* To be of use to. [Obs.]

in-sērv'i-ent, *a.* Conducive. [Obs.]

in-ses'sion (-sesh'un), *n.* [LL. *insessio (-onis)*, a sitting on, from L. *insessus*, pp. of *insidere*, to sit upon; *in*, on, upon, and *sedere*, to sit.]

1. The act of seating oneself; specifically, the sitting in a bath. [Rare.]

2. The thing sat in or upon, as a bath-tub. [Rare.]

in-ses'sŏr, *n.* A bird that perches; one of the *Insessores*.

In-ses-sō'rēs, *n.pl.* An order of birds originally embracing those which perched, including most of the song-birds.

in-ses-sō'ri-ăl, *a.* Perching; applied to those birds whose feet are formed for grasping.

in-set', *v.t.*; inset, *pt.*, *pp.*; insetting, *ppr.* [ME. *insetten*; AS. *insettan*, to set in, to appoint; *in*, in, and *settan*, to set.] To infix or implant.

in'set, *n.* 1. An extra leaf folded or bound in a book, pamphlet, or newspaper, as a plate or a map.

2. A flowing in, as of the tide.

3. In founding, the opening admitting the metal into a mold.

in-sev'ēr-ȧ-ble, *a.* That cannot be severed.

in-shād'ed, *a.* Marked with different shades.

in'shāve, *n.* In mechanics, an edge-tool or plane for smoothing concave surfaces, especially of barrels, casks, etc.

in-shēathe', *v.t.*; insheathed, *pt. pp.*; insheathing, *ppr.* To inclose in a sheath or as in a sheath; as, to *insheathe* a sword; spelled also *ensheathe*.

in-shell', *v.t.* To hide in a shell. [Obs.]

in-shel'tēr, *v.t.* To shelter. [Obs.]

in-ship', *v.t.* To ship; to embark. [Obs.]

in'shōre', *adv.* Near or toward the shore; to the shore side.

in'shōre, *a.* Placed along and near the shore as opposed to being a considerable distance seaward; as, *inshore* sailing, fishing, etc.

in-shrine', *v.t.* Same as *Enshrine*.

in-sic-cā'tion, *n.* [L. *in*, in, and *siccatus*, pp. of *siccare*, to dry.] The act of drying in.

in'side, *n.* The interior part of a thing; opposed to *outside*.

Patent inside or *patent outside*; a newspaper sheet printed on one side only and furnished to publishers in country towns, who print upon the other side such matter as pertains to their respective localities.

in'side, *a.* Situated within; inclosed; separated from the outside; pertaining to the interior of anything; as, the *inside* passengers of a coach; the *inside* decorations of a building.

Inside calipers; in mechanics, calipers adapted to the taking of inside measurements, as the diameter of a hollow cylinder.

Inside finish; in architecture, a term so general as to include everything that goes to complete a building, except the principal walls and the special decorations.

Inside track; in a circular or oval race-course, the track lying nearest to the concave edge; the shortest track; hence, to have the *inside track* is to have the advantage of others.

in'side, *adv.* Within (either space or time); as, all is quiet *inside*; the train will leave *inside* of an hour.

in'sīde, *prep.* Into; in; within; as, he went *inside* the house for safety; the letter is *inside* the book.

in-sid'i-āte, *v.t.* To lie in ambush for. [Obs.]

in-sid'i-ā-tŏr, *n.* One who lies in ambush. [Obs.]

in-sid'i-ous, *a.* [L. *insidiosus*, deceitful, sly, treacherous, lit., lying in wait, from *insidiæ*, an ambush, plot, from *insidere*, to sit in or upon, to lie in wait for; *in*, in, and *sedere*, to sit.]

1. Lying in wait; hence, watching an opportunity to ensnare or entrap; deceitful; sly; treacherous.

2. Intended to entrap; as, *insidious* arts.

Insidious disease; in medicine, a disease whose existence and progress are not marked by any decided symptoms, but which may suddenly develop with serious results.

Syn.—Artful, crafty, cunning, deceitful, intriguing, tricky, wily, guileful, foxy, designing, deceptive.

in-sid'i-ous-ly, *adv.* In an insidious manner; deceitfully; treacherously; with malicious artifice or stratagem.

in-sid'i-ous-ness, *n.* A watching for an opportunity to ensnare; deceitfulness; treachery.

in'sight (-sīt), *n.* 1. Sight or view of the interior of anything; deep inspection or view; introspection; thorough knowledge or skill; mental vision; as, an *insight* into political methods.

2. The power to perceive readily and thoroughly and to make clear and correct deductions; intuition.

Syn.—Discernment, inspection, introspection, acumen, perspicacity, shrewdness, keenness, penetration, cleverness.

in-sig'ni-ȧ, *n.pl.* [L. *insigne*, pl. *insignia*, a sign, decoration, badge of honor, neut. of *insignis*, distinguished by a mark, striking, eminent; *in*, in, and *signum*, a mark, sign.]

1. Badges or distinguishing marks of office or honor; as, the *insignia* of an order of knighthood.

2. Marks, signs, or visible impressions by which anything is known or distinguished.

in-sig-nif'i-cănce, *n.* 1. The quality or state of being insignificant; want of significance or meaning; as, the *insignificance* of words or phrases.

2. Unimportance; want of force or effect; as, the *insignificance* of human art.

3. Want of influence or consideration; meanness.

in-sig-nif'i-căn-cy, *n.* Same as *Insignificance*.

in-sig-nif'i-cănt, *a.* 1. Not significant; void of signification; destitute of meaning; as, *insignificant* words.

2. Answering no purpose; having no weight or effect; unimportant; as, *insignificant* rites.

3. Without weight of character; mean; contemptible; as, an *insignificant* fellow.

Syn.—Immaterial, inconsiderate, trivial, unimportant, small, irrelevant, paltry.

in-sig-nif'i-cănt-ly, *adv.* In an insignificant manner; without meaning; without importance or effect; to no purpose.

in-sig-nif'i-cȧ-tive, *a.* [LL. *insignificativus*; L. *in-* priv., and *significativus*, significative, from L. *significatus*, pp. of *significare*, to mean, signify.] Not expressing by external signs; not significative. [Rare.]

in-sign'ment (-sīn'), *n.* A token, mark, or explanation. [Obs.]

in-sim'ū-lāte, *v.t.* To accuse. [Obs.]

in-sin-cēre', *a.* [L. *insincerus*, not pure, adulterated; *in-* priv., and *sincerus*, pure, real, genuine.]

1. Not sincere; dissembling; hypocritical; false; deceitful.

To be always polite, you must be sometimes *insincere*. —Charles Reade.

2. Imperfect; unsound. [Obs.]

Syn.—Disingenuous, dissembling, false, deceptive, hypocritical, deceitful.

in-sin-cēre'ly, *adv.* Without sincerity; hypocritically.

in-sin-cer'i-ty, *n.*; *pl.* **in-sin-cer'i-ties.** The quality of being insincere; dissimulation; want of sincerity or of being in reality what one appears to be; hypocrisy; deceitfulness; hollowness.

In condemnation of the fashionable *insincerities* of his day. —A. Dobson.

in-sin'ew, *v.t.* To strengthen; to give vigor to. [Obs.]

in-sin'ū-ănt, *a.* Insinuating. [Obs.]

in-sin'ū-āte, *v.t.*; insinuated, *pt.*, *pp.*; insinuating, *ppr.* [L. *insinuatus*, pp. of *insinuare*, to introduce by windings and turnings, to insinuate, to work one's way into; *in*, in, and *sinus*, a curved surface, a fold, a bay, a bosom.]

1. To introduce gently, as by a devious course or narrow passage; as, water *insinuates* itself into the crevices of rocks.

2. To push or worm into favor; to introduce by slow, gentle, or artful means.

He *insinuated* himself into the very good grace of the Duke of Buckingham. —Clarendon.

3. To hint; to suggest by remote allusion.

And all the fictions bards pursue,
Do but *insinuate* what's true. —Swift.

4. To instil; to infuse gently; to introduce artfully.

All the arts of rhetoric, besides order and clearness, are for nothing else but to *insinuate* wrong ideas. —Locke.

Syn.—Hint, intimate, suggest.

in-sin'ū-āte, *v.i.* 1. To creep in; to wind in; to flow in; to enter gently, slowly, or imperceptibly, as into crevices.

2. To gain on the affections by gentle or artful means, or by imperceptible degrees; to ingratiate oneself.

in-sin'ū-ā-ting, *a.* Creeping or winding in; flowing in; tending to enter gently; insensibly winning favor and confidence.

His sly, polite, *insinuating* style. —Pope.

in-sin'ū-ā-ting-ly, *adv.* By insinuation; in an insinuating manner.

in-sin-ū-ā'tion, *n.* [L. *insinuatio (-onis)*, an insinuation, from *insinuare*, to insinuate.]

1. The act of insinuating; a creeping or winding in; a flowing in.

2. The act of gaining favor or affection by gentle or artful means.

3. The art or power of pleasing and stealing on the affections.

He had a natural *insinuation* and address, which made him acceptable in the best company. —Clarendon.

4. That which is insinuated; a hint; a suggestion or intimation by distant allusion; as, slander may be conveyed by *insinuations*.

Syn.—Innuendo, hint, suggestion, intimation, implication.

in-sin'ū-ā-tive, *a.* 1. Stealing on the affections; ingratiating.

Popular or *insinuative* carriage of himself. —Bacon.

2. Making insinuations; hinting; insinuating; as, *insinuative* comments.

in-sin'ū-ā-tŏr, *n.* One who insinuates or hints.

in-sin'ū-ā-tō-ry, *a.* Of an insinuating nature.

in-sip'id, *a.* [LL. *insipidus*, tasteless; L. *in-* priv., and *sapidus*, savory, from *sapere*, to taste.]

1. Tasteless; destitute of taste; wanting the

qualities which affect the organs of taste; vapid; flat in taste; as, *insipid* liquor; *insipid* fruit.

2. Wanting spirit, life, or animation; lacking in the power of exciting emotion; flat; dull; heavy; as, an *insipid* composition.

> His wife a faded beauty of the baths,
> *Insipid* as the queen upon a card.—Tennyson.

Syn.—Tasteless, vapid, uninteresting, characterless, flavorless, flat, lifeless, stale.

in-si-pid′i-ty, *n.* [Fr. *insipidité.*]

1. Want of taste, or the power of exciting sensation in the tongue.

2. Want of life or spirit.

in-sip′id-ly, *adv.* Without taste; without spirit or life; without enjoyment.

in-sip′id-ness, *n.* The state of being insipid.

in-sip′i-ence, *n.* [OFr. *insipience*; L. *insipientia*, lack of wisdom, from *insipiens* (*-entis*), unwise, foolish; *in-* priv., and *sapiens* (*-entis*), wise.] Want of wisdom; folly; foolishness; want of understanding. [Rare.]

in-sip′i-ent, *a.* [L. *insipiens* (*-entis*); *in-* priv., and *sapiens* (*-entis*), wise.] Unwise. [Rare.]

in-sip′i-ent, *n.* An unwise person. [Rare.]

in-sist′, *v.i.*; insisted, *pt., pp.*; insisting, *ppr.* [Fr. *insister*; L. *insistere*, to stand or tread upon, to pursue or follow diligently, persist; *in*, in, on, and *sistere*, to stand, to cause to stand.]

1. To stand or rest on or upon. [Rare.]

2. To dwell upon with emphasis in discourse; to take a decided stand; as, to *insist* upon fair dealing; to *insist* upon the payment of a debt.

Syn.—Stand, persist, demand, maintain, contend, urge, require.

in-sist′ence, *n.* The act of insisting.

in-sist′ent, *a.* [L. *insistens* (*-entis*), ppr. of *insistere*, to stand upon, to insist.]

1. Standing or resting on; as, an *insistent* wall. [Rare.]

2. Urgent; pressing; persistent.

3. Standing out conspicuously; graphic; intense.

4. In zoölogy, said of the hind toe of a bird when inserted so that it bends downward and merely touches the ground; the correlative of *incumbent.*

in-sist′ent-ly, *adv.* With insistence.

in-sis′tūre, *n.* A dwelling or standing on; fixedness. [Obs.]

in-si′ti-en-cy (-sish′i-), *n.* Freedom from thirst. [Obs.]

in-si′tion (-sish′un), *n.* [L. *insitio* (*-onis*), an ingrafting, from *insitus*, pp. of *inserere*, to ingraft, implant; *in*, in, and *serere*, to sow.] The insertion of a scion in a stock; ingraftment.

in si′tū. [L. *in*, in, and *situ*, abl. of *situs*, position, site.] In its original situation or bed; specifically, designating a rock or a fossil which has remained in the place where it was formed or deposited, as distinguished from a boulder or a fossil that has drifted.

in-snāre′, *v.t.* See *Ensnare.*

in-snār′ẽr, *n.* See *Ensnarer.*

in-snärl′, *v.t.* [Obs.] See *Ensnarl.*

in-sō-bri′ē-ty, *n.* Want of sobriety; intemperance; drunkenness.

in-sō-ciȧ-bil′i-ty (-shiȧ-), *n.* The quality of being not sociable; the lack of sociability. [Rare.]

in-sō′ciȧ-ble (-shiȧ-), *a.* 1. Not inclined to unite in social converse; not given to conversation; unsociable; taciturn. [Obs.]

2. That cannot be joined or connected. [Obs.]

in-sō′ciȧ-bly, *adv.* Not sociably. [Obs.]

in-sō′ci-āte (-shi-), *a.* Unconnected; alone; without an associate. [Obs.]

in′sō-lāte, *v.t.*; insolated, *pt., pp.*; insolating, *ppr.* [L. *insolatus*, pp. of *insolare*, to expose to the sun; *in*, in, and *sol* (*solis*), sun.] To dry in the sun's rays; to expose to the heat of the sun; to ripen or prepare by exposure to the sun.

in-sō-lā′tion, *n.* [L. *insolatio* (*-onis*), from *insolare*, to expose to the sun, to insolate.]

1. The act or process of exposing to the rays of the sun for drying or maturing, as fruits, drugs, etc., or for rendering acid, as vinegar.

2. In medicine, (a) disease produced by the action of the sun's rays; (b) treatment for disease by exposure to the sun's rays; a sun-bath.

3. In botany, a disease of plants, resulting from exposure to the rays of the sun.

in′sōle, *n.* The part of the sole of a boot or shoe next to the foot; sometimes a separate piece inserted for the purpose of securing warmth or ease.

in′sō-lence, *n.* [OFr. *insolence*; L. *insolentia*, a want of custom or use, want of moderation, excess, pride, from *insolens* (*-entis*), insolent.]

1. Pride or haughtiness manifested in contemptuous and overbearing treatment of others; impudence.

> Flown with *insolence* and wine. —Milton.

2. The act of behaving insolently; as, his *insolence* is unbearable.

3. The quality of being unusual. [Obs.]

Syn.—Impudence, arrogance, boldness, insult, sauciness, disrespectfulness, impertinence.

in′sō-lence, *v.t.* To treat with haughty contempt. [Obs.]

in′sō-len-cy, *n.* [Rare.] See *Insolence.*

in′sō-lent, *a.* [OFr. *insolent*; L. *insolens* (*-entis*), contrary to custom, excessive, haughty; *in-* priv., and *solens* (*-entis*), ppr. of *solere*, to be accustomed.]

1. Showing haughty disregard of others; overbearing; domineering; as, an *insolent* master.

2. Proceeding from insolence; insulting; as, *insolent* words or behavior.

3. Unwonted; unusual. [Obs.]

Syn.—Saucy, impertinent, impudent, rude, arrogant, overbearing.

in′sō-lent-ly, *adv.* With contemptuous pride; haughtily; rudely; saucily.

in-sō-lid′i-ty, *n.* Want of solidity; weakness. [Rare.]

in-sol-ū-bil′i-ty, *n.* [LL. *insolubilitas*, from L. *insolubilis*, that cannot be loosed, insoluble.]

1. The quality of not being soluble or dissolvable, particularly in a fluid; as, the *insolubility* of carbon.

2. Inexplicability, as of a line of conduct or of a mathematical problem.

in-sol′ū-ble, *a.* [OFr. *insoluble*; L. *insolubilis*, that cannot be loosed; *in-* priv., and *solvere*, to loosen.]

1. That cannot be dissolved, particularly by a liquid; as, a substance is *insoluble* in water when its parts will not separate and unite with that fluid.

2. Not to be solved or explained; not be resolved; as, an *insoluble* doubt or difficulty.

3. That cannot be separated into parts or loosened; hence, of great strength. [Obs.]

in-sol′ū-ble-ness, *n.* Insolubility.

in-solv′ȧ-ble, *a.* 1. Not to be cleared of difficulty or uncertainty; not to be solved or explained; as, an *insolvable* problem or difficulty.

2. That cannot be paid or discharged.

3. Incapable of being loosed.

in-sol′ven-cy, *n.* 1. Inability of a person to pay all his debts; the state of lacking property sufficient for such payment; the state of being bankrupt; bankruptcy; failure of resources; as, a merchant's *insolvency.*

2. Insufficiency to discharge all debts of the owner; as, the *insolvency* of an estate.

in-sol′vent, *a.* [L. *in-* priv., and *solvens* (*-entis*), ppr. of *solvere*, to loosen, dissolve, pay.]

1. Not having money, goods, or estate sufficient to pay all debts; as, an *insolvent* debtor.

2. Not sufficient to pay all the debts of the owner; as, an *insolvent* estate.

3. Relating to insolvency; as, *insolvent* law.

Insolvent law; see *Bankrupt law* under *Bankrupt.*

Syn.—Bankrupt, ruined, penniless, beggared.

in-sol′vent, *n.* A debtor unable to pay his debts.

in-som′ni-ȧ, *n.* [L., from *insomnis*, sleepless; *in-* priv., and *somnus*, sleep.] In pathology, chronic sleeplessness.

in-som′ni-ous, *a.* [L. *insomniosus*, from *insomnia*, sleeplessness, insomnia.] Troubled with dreams; restless in sleep.

in-som′nō-lence, *n.* The condition characterized by insomnia.

in′sō-much′, *adv.* So that; to that degree; followed by *that*, formerly by *as.*

> Simonides was an excellent poet, *insomuch that* he made his fortune by it.—L'Estrange.

in-sō-nō′rous, *a.* Unmelodious.

in sooth. [Obs.] See *Sooth*, n.

in-söu′ci-ānce (*or Fr. pron.* aṅ-sö-syoṅs′), *n.* [Fr., from *insouciant*, careless.] Gay heedlessness; light-hearted unconcern.

in-söu′ci-ānt (*or Fr. pron.* aṅ-sö-syoṅ′), *a.* [Fr., gay, careless; *in-* priv., and *souciant*, ppr. of *soucier*, to regard, to care, from *souci*, care.] Gay and unconcerned.

in-soul′, *v.t.* To put a soul into; hence, to place the affections on. [Obs.]

in′span, *v.t.* and *v.i.*; inspanned, *pt., pp.*; inspanning, *ppr.* [D. *inspannen*, to yoke or harness; *in*, in, and *spannen*, to fasten, join, tie.] To hitch up; to harness horses, mules, or oxen to a wagon. [S. Africa.]

in-spect′, *v.t.*; inspected, *pt., pp.*; inspecting, *ppr.* [L. *inspectare*, to look at, observe, freq. of *inspicere*, to look into, examine; *in*, in, at, and *specere*, to look at, behold.]

1. To look on; to view or oversee for the purpose of examination.

2. To look into; to view and examine, officially or critically, for the purpose of ascertaining the quality or condition of; as, to *inspect* potash; to *inspect* arms; to *inspect* the workmanship of a building, a bridge, a road, etc.

in-spect′, *n.* Close examination. [Obs.]

in-spec′tion, *n.* [OFr. *inspection*; L. *inspectio* (*-onis*), a looking into, inspection, from *inspectus*, pp. of *inspicere*, to look into, inspect.]

1. A looking on or into; examination; close or careful survey; as, the divine *inspection* of the affairs of the world.

2. Official view; a careful viewing and examining to ascertain quality or condition; as, the *inspection* of pork; the *inspection* of troops.

Trial by inspection; in old English law, the trial of a case by a judge alone, without jury.

in-spect′ive, *a.* Inspecting; admitting of inspection or subject to inspection.

in-spect′ŏr, *n.* [L. *inspector*, one who inspects or views, from *inspectus*, pp. of *inspicere*, to view, inspect.]

1. One who has a care for or oversees; as, an *inspector* of health; an *inspector* of the press.

2. A superintendent; one to whose care the excution of any work is committed, for the purpose of seeing it faithfully performed; as, a paving *inspector.*

3. A military officer whose duty it is to inspect troops and examine their arms, etc.; also, a similar officer of a civil organization; as, an *inspector* of police.

in-spect′ŏr-āte, *n.* The office of an inspector; also, a district in charge of an inspector.

in-spect′ŏr-gen′ẽr-ăl, *n.* An officer having general charge of a system of inspection; as, the *inspector-general* of the United States army; the supervising *inspector-general* of steam-vessels.

in-spec-tō′ri-ăl, *a.* Relating to an inspector or to his duties.

in-spect′ŏr-ship, *n.* The office or the jurisdiction of an inspector.

in-spẽrse′, *v.t.* To sprinkle upon. [Obs.]

in-spẽr′sion, *n.* The act of sprinkling on. [Obs.]

in-spex′i-mus, *n.* [L., we have inspected, 1st pers. pl. perf. ind. act. of *inspicere*, to examine, inspect.] In England, the first word of ancient charters, confirming a grant made by a former king; hence, a royal grant.

in-sphēre′, *v.t.* See *Ensphere.*

in-spir′ȧ-ble, *a.* That may be inspired or drawn into the lungs, as air or vapors.

in-spi-rā′tion, *n.* [OFr. *inspiration*; LL. *inspiratio* (*-onis*), inspiration, from L. *inspiratus*, pp. of *inspirare*, to blow or breathe into or upon, to inspire.]

1. The act of drawing air into the lungs; the inhaling of air; a part of respiration, and opposed to *expiration.*

2. The act of breathing into anything; an awakening of the mind or senses.

3. In Christian theology, the supernatural influence by which prophets, apostles, and sacred writers were qualified to set forth divine truth without any mixture of error; or the communication of the divine will to the understanding by suggestions or impressions on the mind, which leave no room to doubt the reality of their supernatural origin.

> All Scripture is given by *inspiration* of God.
> —2 Tim. iii. 16.

4. The infusion or communication of ideas or poetic spirit by a superior being or supposed presiding power; as, the *inspiration* of Homer or of other poets.

5. A highly exciting influence; as, the *inspiration* of the scene.

Plenary inspiration; in theology, inspiration that is perfect in the utterance of the inspired word.

Verbal inspiration; in theology, inspiration that attaches to the very words used in voicing the inspired message.

in-spi-rā′tion-ăl, *a.* Relating to inspiration.

in-spi-rā′tion-ist, *n.* One who believes in inspiration, especially of the Holy Scriptures; a believer in supernatural influences.

in′spi-rā-tŏr, *n.* [LL. *inspirator*, one who inspires, from L. *inspiratus*, pp. of *inspirare*, to blow into or upon, to inspire.] In a steam-engine, a kind of injector in which the water is first raised by a jet of steam and then injected into the boiler under pressure.

in-spir′ȧ-tō-ry, *a.* Relating to inspiration or the act and process of inhalation.

in-spire′, *v.t.*; inspired, *pt., pp.*; inspiring, *ppr.* [ME. *inspiren*; OFr. *inspirer*; L. *inspirare*, to blow into or upon, to breathe into; *in*, in, on, and *spirare*, to breathe.]

1. To breathe into.

> Ye nine, descend and sing,
> The breathing instruments *inspire.* —Pope.

2. To infuse by breathing.

3. To infuse into the mind; as, to *inspire* with new life.

4. To infuse or suggest ideas or monitions supernaturally; to communicate divine instructions to the mind; as, the prophets were *inspired.*

5. To infuse ideas or poetic spirit.

6. To draw into the lungs; as, to *inspire* and expire the air with difficulty.

Syn.—Animate, cheer, enliven, exhilarate, encourage, incite.

in-spire′, *v.i.* To draw in breath; to inhale air into the lungs; opposed to *expire.*

in-spired′, *a.* 1. Breathed in; inhaled; infused.

2. Informed or directed by supernatural influence.

3. Produced under inspiration; as, the *inspired* writings.

in-spīr′ẽr, *n.* He who inspires; any agent of inspiration.

in-spīr′ing, *a.* Infusing spirit or courage; animating.

in-spir′it, *v.t.*; inspirited, *pt., pp.*; inspiriting, *ppr.* To infuse or excite spirit in; to enliven; to animate; to give new life to; to encourage; to invigorate.

in-spis′sănt, *a.* [L. *in*, in, to, and *spissans* (*-antis*), ppr. of *spissare*, to thicken.] Tending to thicken a liquid; as, the *inspissant* agency of evaporation upon sugar-water.

in-spis′sănt, *n.* Anything that produces an inspissant effect upon a liquid, as evaporation.

in-spis′sāte, *v.t.*; inspissated, *pt., pp.*; inspissating, *ppr.* [LL. *inspissatus*, thick; L. *in*, in, and *spissatus*, pp. of *spissare*, to thicken, from *spissus*, thick.] To thicken, as liquids; to bring to greater consistence by evaporating the thinner parts, etc.

in-spis′sāte, *a.* Thick; thickened by evaporation.

in-spis-sā′tion, *n.* The act or operation of rendering a liquid substance thicker by evaporation, etc.

inst. Contraction for *instant*, used in correspondence, etc., for the current or present month; as, he wrote me on the 10th *inst.*, that is, on the 10th day of the present month.

in-stȧ-bil′i-ty, *n.* [L. *instabilitas* (*-atis*), want of stability, from *instabilis*, unsteady, unstable; *in-* priv., and *stabilis*, steady stable.]

1. Want of stability; want of firmness in purpose; inconstancy; fickleness; mutability of opinion or conduct; as, *instability* is the characteristi o' weak minds.

2. Changeableness; mutability; as, the *instability* of laws, plans, or measures.

in-stā′ble, *a.* 1. Inconstant; prone to change or recede from a purpose; mutable; unstable.

2. Not steady or fixed; changeable.

in-stā′ble-ness, *n.* Unstableness; mutability; instability.

in-stąll′, *v.t.*; installed, *pt., pp.*; installing, *ppr.* [Fr. *installer*; LL. *installare*, to put in a place or seat; L. *in*, in, and LL. *stallum*, from O.H.G. *stal*, a place, seat, stall.]

1. To set, place, or instate in an office, rank, or order; to invest with any charge, office, or rank, with the customary ceremonies; as, to *install* a clergyman or the president of a college.

2. To set in or give a place to for use or service; as, to *install* a road when finished for public use.

in-stăl-lā′tion, *n.* [Fr. *installation*; LL. *installatio* (*-onis*), from *installare*, to put in a place or seat, to install.]

1. The act of giving possession of an office, rank, or order, with the customary ceremonies.

2. The act of introducing and opening for operation a completed plant of machinery, apparatus, etc.

in-stąl′ment, in-stąll′ment, *n.* 1. The act of installing, or giving possession of an office with the usual ceremonies or solemnities.

2. The seat in which one is placed. [Obs.]

3. A part of a sum of money paid, or to be paid, at a stated period. In contracts, it is not unusual to agree that the money shall be paid by *instalments*.

in-stamp′, *v.t.* To enstamp. [Obs.]

in′stănce, *n.* [OFr. *instance*; LL. *instantia*, an objection, instance, from L. *instantia*, a standing upon or near, a being present, from *instans* (*-antis*), ppr. of *instare*, to stand upon, press upon; *in*, in, on, and *stare*, to stand.]

1. Urgency; a pressing; solicitation; importunity; application; as, the request was granted at the *instance* of the defendant's advocate.

2. Example; a case occurring; a case offered; as, Washington furnished a remarkable *instance* of patriotism.

> Suppose the earth should be removed nearer to the sun, and revolve, for *instance*, in the orbit of Mercury; the whole ocean would boil with heat. —Bentley.

3. Time; occasion; occurrence; as, in the first *instance*.

4. Motive; influence. [Obs.]

5. The process of a suit. [Obs.]

Causes of instance; in law, such causes as proceed at the request or solicitation of some party.

Court of first instance; the first court which tries a case.

For instance; for example; by way of illustration.

Instance court; in English law, a branch of the court of admiralty distinct from the prize-court.

Syn.—Entreaty, request, prompting, persuasion, example, solicitation, case, illustration, exemplification, occurrence, point, precedence.

in′stănce, *v.t.*; instanced (-stănst), *pt., pp.*; instancing, *ppr.* To mention as an example or case; as, he *instanced* the event of Cæsar's death.

in′stănce, *v.i.* To give or offer an example or case. [Obs.]

in′stăn-cy, *n.* [Obs.] See *Instance.*

in′stănt, *a.* [OFr. *instant*, from L. *instans* (*-antis*), pressing, urgent, ppr. of *instare*, to stand upon or near, to press; *in*, in, upon, and *stare*, to stand.]

1. Pressing; urgent; importunate; earnest; as, *instant* in prayer.

2. Immediate; without intervening time; present.

> Impending death is thine, and *instant* doom. —Prior.

3. Quick; making no delay; as, the *instant* flight of an arrow.

4. Present; current; as, on the 10th of July *instant.*

in′stănt, *n.* A point in duration; a moment; a part of duration in which we perceive no succession, or a part that occupies the time of a single thought.

in′stănt, *adv.* Without delay. [Poet.]

in″stăn-tȧ-nē′i-ty, *n.* Unpremeditated production; the quality of occupying the least conceivable part of time.

in-stăn-tā′nē-ous, *a.* 1. Done in an instant; occurring or acting without any perceptible succession; very speedily; as, the passage of electricity seems to be *instantaneous.*

2. Referring to or defining a particular instant; as, *instantaneous* retardation, acceleration, position, etc.

Instantaneous axis of rotation; in kinematics, the line, in a body having both rotary and translatory motion, which for the instant is stationary.

Instantaneous center of rotation; in kinematics, the point, in a plane figure having both rotary and translatory motion, which for the instan: i: stationary.

in-stăn-tā′nē-ous-ly, *adv.* In an instant; in a moment; without any perceptible lapse of time.

in-stăn-tā′nē-ous-ness, *n.* The quality of being done in an instant.

in-stan′tẽr, *adv.* [L., earnestly, pressingly, from *instans* (*-antis*), urgent, pressing, instant.] Immediately; at the present time; without delay; as, the party was compelled to plead *instanter.*

in′stănt-ly, *adv.* 1. Immediately; without any intervening time; at the moment; as, lightning often kills *instantly.*

2. With urgent importunity.

in-stär′, *v.t.* To set or adorn as with stars or brilliants; to embellish as if with stars. [Rare.]

in-stāte′, *v.t.*; instated, *pt., pp.*; instating, *ppr.*

1. To set or place; to establish, as in a rank or condition; as, to *instate* a person in greatness or in favor.

2. To invest. [Obs.]

in-stąu′rāte, *v.t.* [L. *instauratus*, pp. of *instaurare*, to renew, repeat.] To reform or restore in composition or appearance. [Rare.]

in-stąu-rā′tion, *n.* [L. *instauratio* (*-onis*), a renewing, repetition, from *instauratus*, pp. of *instaurare*, to renew, repeat.] Renewal; repair; reëstablishment; the restoration of a thing to its former state, after decay, lapse, or dilapidation.

in′stąu-rā-tŏr, *n.* One who renovates or restores to a former condition. [Rare.]

in-stąure′, *v.t.* [Obs.] Same as *Instaurate.*

in-stead′ (-sted′), *adv.* 1. In the place or room; followed by *of.*

> Let thistles grow *instead of* wheat. —Job xxxi. 40.

2. As an equivalent (sometimes without *of*); as, he rejected the black and took the white *instead.*

in-steep′, *v.t.* To steep or soak; to drench; to macerate in moisture. [Rare.]

in′step, *n.* 1. The upper side of the foot adjacent to the ankle.

2. In the horse and animals with legs of similar anatomy, the front part of the hind leg reaching from the ham to the pastern.

in′sti-gāte, *v.t.*; instigated, *pt., pp.*; instigating, *ppr.* [L. *instigatus*, pp. of *instigare*, to prick or goad on, to stimulate.] To incite; to set on; to provoke; to urge; as, to *instigate* one to evil; to *instigate* to a crime.

Syn.—Provoke, incite, tempt, impel, encourage, stimulate, induce, egg on.

in′sti-gā-ting-ly, *adv.* Incitingly; temptingly.

in-sti-gā′tion, *n.* [L. *instigatio* (*-onis*), from *instigare*, to goad, to instigate.] Incitement; temptation, particularly, to wrongdoing.

in′sti-gā-tŏr, *n.* One who or that which instigates.

in-stil′, in-still′, *v.t.*; instilled, *pt., pp.*; instilling, *ppr.* [Fr. *instiller*; L. *instillare*, to pour in by drops, to instil; *in*, in, and *stillare*, to drop, from *stilla*, a drop.]

1. To infuse by drops.

2. To infuse slowly, by small quantities, or insidiously; as, to *instil* good principles into the mind.

Syn.—Implant, inculcate, infuse, insinuate.

in-stil-lā′tion, *n.* [L. *instillatio* (*-onis*), from *instillare*, to pour in by drops, to instil.]

1. The act of infusing by drops or by small quantities.

2. The act of infusing slowly into the mind.

3. That which is instilled or infused.

in′stil-lā-tŏr, *n.* One who instils. [Rare.]

in-stil′lȧ-tō-ry, *a.* Relating to instillation. [Rare.]

in-still′ẽr, *n.* One who or that which instils.

in-stil′ment, in-still′ment, *n.* The act of instilling; anything instilled.

in-stim′ū-lāte, *v.t.* To stimulate; to excite. [Obs.]

in-stim-ū-lā′tion, *n.* The act of stimulating, inciting, or urging forward. [Obs.]

in′stinct, *n.* [L. *instinctus*, instigation, impulse, properly pp. of *instinguere*, to impel, instigate; as, in, and *stinguere*, to prick.]

1. Certain power or disposition by which, independent of instruction or experience, without deliberation, and without having any end in view, animals are unerringly directed to do spontaneously whatever is necessary for the preservation of the individual or the continuation of the kind; as, in the human species, the *instinct* of sucking, exerted immediately after birth; in the lower animals, the *instinct* of depositing their eggs in situations most favorable for hatching.

2. A natural bent or qualification for some specialty; as, he is a gentleman by *instinct*. Instinct in this sense is, in part at least, the result of training and habit.

in-stinct′, *a.* Moved; animated; excited; as, *instinct* with spirit.

in-stinct′, *v.t.* To stamp upon, as if to endow with instinct. [Obs.]

in-stinc′tion, *n.* Instinct. [Obs.]

in-stinc′tive, *a.* Prompted by instinct; spontaneous; acting without reasoning, deliberation, instruction, or experience; determined by natural impulse or propensity.

Syn.—Natural, voluntary, spontaneous, intuitive, impulsive, inborn, automatic.

in-stinc′tive-ly, *adv.* By force of instinct; without reasoning, instruction, or experience; by natural impulse.

in-stinc-tiv′i-ty, *n.* The quality of being led by instinct. [Rare.]

in-stip′ū-lāte, *a.* Same as *Exstipulate.*

in′sti-tŏr, *n.* [L., a broker, agent, huckster, from *institus*, pp. of *insistere*, to stand or tread upon, pursue, follow; *in*, in, on, and *sistere*, to stand.] In civil law, a person in charge of the business of another.

in-sti-tō′ri-ăl, *a.* Pertaining to an institor, or to his office and duties.

in′sti-tūte, *a.* Established; settled. [Obs.]

in′sti-tūte, *v.t.*; instituted, *pt., pp.*; instituting, *ppr.* [L. *institutus*, pp. of *instituere*, to set up, erect, construct; *in*, in, on, and *statuere*, to cause to stand, set up, place.]

1. To establish; to appoint; to enact; to form and prescribe; as, to *institute* laws; to *institute* rules and regulations.

2. To ground or establish in principles; to educate. [Obs.]

3. Specifically, in ecclesiastical use, to invest with the spiritual part of a benefice, or the care of souls.

in′sti-tūte, *n.* [L. *institutum*, an arrangement, plan, intention.]

1. Established law; settled order; a precept, maxim, or principle.

2. [*pl.*] A book of elements or principles; particularly a work containing the principles of the Roman law.

3. In Scots law, the first of a number of persons succeeding to an estate.

4. A literary and philosophical society; an organization for instruction in, and the promotion of, some branch of learning; as, an art *institute*; mechanics' *institute.*

Institutes of medicine; schools for the study of medicine theoretically.

Teachers' institute; in the common schools of the United States, a stated assembling of the teachers of a township or of a county, under the direction of the county superintendent, for the purpose of mutual help in methods of teaching and in the management of schools, by means of lectures, lessons, and examinations; called also *county institute* or *township institute.*

Syn.—Establishment, training-school, training-college, academy, seminary.

in-sti-tū′tion, *n.* [L. *institutio* (*-onis*), a disposition, arrangement, establishment.]

1. The act of establishing; establishment; that which is appointed, prescribed, or founded by authority, and intended to be permanent.

2. An organized society, established either by law or by the authority of individuals, for promoting any object, public or social; as, a

literary *institution*; a benevolent or charitable *institution*.

3. A system of the elements or rules of any art or science. [Obs.]

4. Education; instruction. [Obs.]

5. Specifically, in ecclesiastical use, the act or ceremony of investing a clergyman with the spiritual part of a benefice, by which the care of souls is committed to his charge.

in-sti-tū′tion-ăl, *a.* 1. Enjoined; instituted by authority.

2. Elementary.

3. Of, relating, or pertaining to an institution.

in-sti-tū′tion-ā-ry, *a.* Elemental; containing the first principles or doctrines; institutional.

in′sti-tū-tist, *n.* A writer of institutes or elementary rules and instructions. [Rare.]

in′sti-tū-tive, *a.* 1. That establishes; having the power to establish.

2. Established; depending on institution.

in′sti-tū-tive-ly, *adv.* According to the laws or customs of an institution.

in′sti-tū-tŏr, *n.* [L., a founder; establisher, from *institutus*, pp. of *instituere*, to set up, erect, institute.]

1. One who establishes; one who enacts laws, rites, and ceremonies, and enjoins the observance of them.

2. One who founds an order, sect, society, or scheme, for the promotion of a public or social object.

3. An instructor; one who educates; as, an *institutor* of youth. [Obs.]

4. In the Anglican church, a presbyter appointed by the bishop to institute a rector or assistant minister in a parish church.

in-stop′, *v.t.* To stop; to close; to fasten. [Obs.]

in-stōre′, *v.t.* [Obs.] Same as *Enstore*.

in-strat′i-fied, *a.* Stratified within something else; interstratified.

in-struct′, *v.t.*; instructed, *pt.*, *pp.*; instructing, *ppr.* [L. *instructus*, pp. of *instruere*, to pile upon, put in order, erect, prepare, teach, instruct; *in*, in, upon, and *struere*, to pile up, arrange, build.]

1. To teach; to inform the mind; to educate; to impart knowledge to.

2. To direct; to enjoin; to persuade; to admonish; to command.

> She, being before *instructed* by her mother, said, Give me here the head of John the Baptist in a charger. —Matt. xiv. 8.

3. To model; to form; to prepare. [Obs.]

Syn.—Direct, educate, teach, train, inform.

in-struct′, *a.* Supplied; trained. [Obs.]

in-struct′ẽr, *n.* An instructor.

in-struct′i-ble, *a.* That may be instructed.

in-struc′tion, *n.* [LL. *instructio* (*-onis*), instruction; L. *instructio* (*-onis*), a constructing, erecting.]

1. The act of teaching or informing; information.

2. Precepts conveying knowledge.

> Receive my *instruction*, and not silver. —Prov. viii. 10.

3. Direction; order; command; mandate.

in-struct′ive, *a.* Conveying knowledge; serving to instruct or inform.

in-struct′ive-ly, *adv.* So as to afford instruction.

in-struct′ive-ness, *n.* Power of instructing.

in-struct′ŏr, *n.* [LL., from L. *instructor*, one who prepares.] A teacher; a person who imparts knowledge to another by precept or information.

in-struct′ress, *n.* A female who instructs; a preceptress; a tutoress.

in′strū-ment, *n.* [L. *instrumentum*, a tool or tools, implement, stock in trade, furniture, dress, from *instruere*, to furnish, equip; *in*, in, and *struere*, to pile up, arrange.]

1. A tool; that by which work is performed or anything is effected; an aid in producing an effect; an agent; as, swords, muskets, and cannon are *instruments* of destruction.

2. One who or that which is subservient to the execution of a plan or purpose, or to the production of any effect; means used to accomplish a purpose.

> The bold are but the *instruments* of the wise. —Dryden.

3. Any mechanical contrivance constructed for yielding musical sounds, as an organ, piano, violin, or flute.

4. In law, a writing containing the terms of a contract, as a deed of conveyance, a grant, a patent, an indenture, etc.; a writing by which some fact is recorded for evidence, or some right conveyed.

in-strū-men′tăl, *a.* 1. Conducive, as an instrument or means, to some end; contributing aid; serving to promote or effect an object; helpful; as, the press has been *instrumental* in extending the bounds of knowledge.

2. Pertaining to instruments; made by or for instruments; as, *instrumental* music, distinguished from *vocal* music.

3. In grammar, designating the case of means or instrument, which existed in Sanskrit as a separate case, but the functions of which in Latin are performed by the ablative and in Greek and Anglo-Saxon by the dative.

Instrumental errors; errors due to the inaccuracy of instruments used in making measurements or tests.

in-strū-men′tăl-ist, *n.* In music, one who performs upon an instrument, as distinguished from a *vocalist*.

in″strū-men-tal′i-ty, *n.*; *pl.* **in″strū-men-tal′i-ties.** The condition of being an instrument; subordinate or auxiliary agency; agency of anything, as means to an end; as, the *instrumentality* of the law.

in-strū-men′tăl-ly, *adv.* 1. By way or means of an instrument; in the nature of an instrument, as means to an end.

2. With instruments of music.

in-strū-men′tăl-ness, *n.* Usefulness, as of means to an end; instrumentality. [Rare.]

in-strū-men-tā′tion, *n.* 1. The act of employing as an instrument.

2. In music, the arrangement of music for a combined number of instruments; also, the art or manner of playing on an instrument; execution; as, his *instrumentation* was defective.

in′strū-men-tist, *n.* Same as *Instrumentalist*.

in-stȳle′, *v.t.* To call; to denominate. [Obs.]

in-suav′i-ty (-swav′), *n.* Lack of pleasing qualities. [Obs.]

in-sub-jec′tion, *n.* State of disobedience to government.

in-sub-mis′sion (-mish′un), *n.* Lack of submission; disobedience.

in-sub-ọr′di-nāte, *a.* Not submitting to authority.

in-sub-ọr-di-nā′tion, *n.* Want of subordination; disorder; disobedience to lawful authority.

in-sub-stan′tiăl, *a.* Unsubstantial; not real.

in-sub-stan-ti-al′i-ty (-shi-), *n.* Lack of substantiality or reality.

in-suc-cā′tion, *n.* [L. *insucatus*, pp. of *insucare*, *insuccare*, to soak in; *in*, in, and *sucus*, *succus*, juice.] The act of soaking or moistening; maceration; solution in the juice of herbs. [Obs.]

in-suc-cess′, *n.* Lack of success. [Rare.]

in-sūe′, *v.i.* Same as *Ensue*.

in′suē-tūde (-swē-), *n.* [L. *insuetudo*, from *insuetus*, unaccustomed to.] The state of being out of use; unusualness. [Rare.]

in-suf′fẽr-ȧ-ble, *a.* 1. Intolerable; that cannot be borne or endured; as, *insufferable* heat, cold, or pain.

2. That cannot be permitted or tolerated; as, our wrongs are *insufferable*.

3. Detestable; contemptible; disgusting beyond endurance; as, *insufferable* writings.

Syn.—Intolerable, unpermissible, unallowable, unendurable, unbearable.

in-suf′fẽr-ȧ-bly, *adv.* To a degree beyond endurance; as, a blaze *insufferably* bright; a person *insufferably* proud.

in-suf-fi′cience (-fish′ens), *n.* Want of sufficiency. [Rare.]

in-suf-fi′cien-cy, *n.* Want of sufficiency; deficiency; inadequacy of power or skill; inability; incapacity; incompetency; as, the *insufficiency* of a man for an office; *insufficiency* of food.

in-suf-fi′cient (-fish′ent), *a.* [LL. *insufficiens* (*-entis*); *in-* priv., and *sufficiens* (*-entis*), sufficient.]

1. Not sufficient; inadequate to any need, use, or purpose; as, the provisions are *insufficient* in quantity and defective in quality.

2. Wanting in strength, power, ability, or skill; incapable; unfit; as, a person *insufficient* to discharge the duties of an office.

Syn.—Inadequate, incommensurate, short, scanty.

in-suf-fi′cient-ly, *adv.* With want of sufficiency; with want of proper ability or skill; inadequately.

in-suf′flāte, *v.t.*; insufflated, *pt.*, *pp.*; insufflating, *ppr.* [LL. *insufflatus*, pp. of *insufflare*, to blow or breathe into; L. *in*, in, and *sufflare*, to blow from below; *sub*, under, and *flare*, to blow.]

1. To blow (a substance) into the cavity of a body; especially, to breathe into the lungs of a person suffering from asphyxiation.

2. To blow or breathe upon; as, to *insufflate* a neophyte.

in-suf-flā′tion, *n.* 1. The act of breathing on or into.

2. The act of blowing a substance into a cavity of the body.

3. The breathing upon persons in a church sacrament as a symbol of new life breathed into them.

in-sūit-ȧ-bil′i-ty, *n.* Lack of suitability. [Obs.]

in-sūit′ȧ-ble, *a.* Unsuitable. [Obs.]

in′sū-lȧ, *n.*; *pl.* **in′sū-læ.** [L., an island.]

1. In anatomy, the lobule of the Sylvian fissure, a group of radiating cerebral convolutions lying beneath the frontal, parietal, and temporal lobes; also called *island of Reil*.

2. In Roman archæology, a consolidated block of buildings surrounded by four streets, as found in the excavations of Pompeii.

in′sū-lăr, *a.* [L. *insularis*, from *insula*, an island.]

1. Belonging to an island; surrounded by water; as, an *insular* situation; *insular* people.

2. Figuratively, of narrow views; illiberal; uncultured; as, his ideas of government are *insular*.

3. In medicine, characterizing isolated patches or masses, as of hard tissue dispersed through the spinal cord in locomotor ataxia.

in′sū-lăr, *n.* One who resides on an island. [Rare.]

in-sū-lar′i-ty, *n.* 1. The state of being insular.

2. Narrowness; lack of liberality in opinion; prejudice.

in′sū-lăr-ly, *adv.* In an insular manner.

in′sū-lā-ry, *a.* [Obs.] See *Insular*.

in′sū-lāte, *a.* Situated alone; in zoölogy, designating marks isolated from others of a similar character.

in′sū-lāte, *v.t.*; insulated, *pt.*, *pp.*; insulating, *ppr.* [LL. *insulatus*, made like an island, pp. of *insulare*, to make like an island, from L. *insula*, an island.]

1. To place in a detached situation, or in a state to have no communication with surrounding objects.

2. In electricity and thermotics, to place, as electrified or heated bodies, by means of nonconductors, in such a situation that the electricity or heat is prevented from escaping.

3. To make an island of.

Insulating stool; a stool having legs of a nonconducting material so that a person or object placed upon it is insulated.

in′sū-lā-ted, *a.* 1. Standing by itself; not being contiguous to other bodies; as, an *insulated* house or column.

2. In electricity and thermotics, placed, by means of nonconductors, so that electricity or heat is prevented from passing.

3. In astronomy, so far separated that gravitational force may be regarded as nil.

Insulated wire; wire covered with some insulating substance, such as silk, paraffined cotton, etc.

in-sū-lā′tion, *n.* 1. The act of insulating; the state of being detached from other objects.

2. In electricity and thermotics, the placing of bodies, by means of nonconductors, in such a situation that electricity or heat is prevented from passing; the state of being thus placed.

3. Material of a nonconducting character used for insulating.

in′sū-lā-tŏr, *n.* 1. Any insulating agent or apparatus.

2. In electricity and thermotics, the substance or body that insulates, or interrupts the communication of electricity or heat to surrounding objects; a nonconductor.

SECTIONS.

Insulator.

in′sū-lite, *n.* In electricity, a material used for the purpose of insulating.

in′sū-lous, *a.* [LL. *insulosus*, full of islands, from L. *insula*, an island.] Abounding in islands. [Rare.]

in-sulse′, *a.* [L. *insulsus*, unsalted, insipid; *in-* priv., and *salsus*, pp. of *salere*, to salt.] Dull; insipid. [Obs.]

in-sul′si-ty, *n.* The quality of being insulse. [Obs.]

in′sult, *n.* [LL. *insultus*, an insult, lit., a leaping upon, from L. *insultus*, pp. of *insilire*, to leap upon, to insult.]

1. The act of leaping on anything. [Obs.]

2. Any gross abuse offered to another, either by words or actions; any act or speech of insolence or contempt.

> The ruthless sneer that *insult* adds to grief. —Savage.

Syn.—Abuse, affront, contempt, indignity, insolence, outrage.

in-sult′, *v.t.*; insulted, *pt.*, *pp.*; insulting, *ppr.* [Fr. *insulter*; L. *insultare*, to leap or spring upon, to behave insolently; freq. of *insilire*, to leap upon, to insult; *in*, in, on, and *salire*, to leap.]

1. To attack or leap on. [Obs.]

2. To treat with gross abuse, insolence, or contempt, by words or actions; as, to call a man a coward or a liar, or to sneer at him, is to *insult* him.

in-sult′, *v.i.* 1. To spring; to leap. [Obs.]

2. To conduct oneself in an insolent manner; to triumph insultingly. [Rare.]

in-sult′ȧ-ble, *a.* Capable of being insulted; easily offended. [Rare.]

in-sult′ănce, *n.* Insolence; offense. [Obs.]

in-sult′ănt, *a.* [L. *insultans* (*-antis*), ppr. of *insultare*, to leap upon, insult.] Tending to insult. [Rare.]

in-sul-tā′tion, *n.* 1. The act of insulting or offending. [Obs.]

2. Insolent triumph or exultation. [Obs.]

in-sult′ẽr, *n.* One who insults or affronts.

in-sult'ing, *a.* Characterized by insolence or insult; of an offending nature; derogatory; abusive.

Syn.—Contemptuous, impertinent, insolent, rude.

in-sult'ing-ly, *adv.* In an insulting manner; with insolent contempt; with contemptuous triumph.

in-sult'ment, *n.* The act of insulting. [Obs.]

in-sūme', *v.t.* [L. *insumere*; *in*, in, and *sumere*, to take.] To take in. [Obs.]

in-sū"pēr-ȧ-bil'i-ty, *n.* The quality of being insuperable.

in-sū'pēr-ȧ-ble, *a.* [L. *insuperabilis*; *in-* priv., and *superabilis*, that may be surmounted, from *superare*, to overcome, surpass.] Incapable of being overcome or surmounted; insurmountable; as, *insuperable* difficulties, objections, or obstacles.

in-sū'pēr-ȧ-ble-ness, *n.* The quality of being insuperable or insurmountable.

in-sū'pēr-ȧ-bly, *adv.* In a manner or degree not to be overcome; insurmountably.

in-sup-pōrt'ȧ-ble, *a.* [LL. *insupportabilis*; L. *in-* priv., and *supportare*, to carry on, convey.] That cannot be borne or endured; insufferable; intolerable; as, *insupportable* pain.

Syn.—Unbearable, intolerable, insufferable, unendurable.

in-sup-pōrt'ȧ-ble-ness, *n.* The quality of being insupportable; insufferableness; the state of being beyond endurance.

in-sup-pōrt'ȧ-bly, *adv.* In a manner or degree that cannot be supported.

in-sup-pōṣ'ȧ-ble, *a.* Inconceivable; not supposable.

in-sup-press'i-ble, *a.* Not to be suppressed or concealed.

in-sup-press'i-bly, *adv.* In a manner or degree that cannot be suppressed.

in-sup-press'ive, *a.* Not tending to suppress. [Obs.]

in-sūr'ȧ-ble (-shūr'), *a.* That may be insured against loss or damage; proper to be insured.

Insurable interest; a right to or equity in a given property sufficient to legalize insurance thereon.

in-sūr'ănce, *n.* 1. The act of insuring or assuring against loss or damage; or a contract by which one engages, for a stipulated consideration or premium, to make up a loss which another may sustain from specified causes.

2. The premium paid for insuring property or life.

3. The amount of contingent indemnity specified in the policy.

4. A pledge, as of betrothal. [Obs.]

Accident insurance; insurance against personal disability resultant from accident.

Endowment insurance; life-insurance, in which the face of the policy is payable either upon the death of the assured or at the expiration of a term of years—usually ten or twenty—if the assured be then living.

Fire insurance; see *Fire-insurance*.

Fraternal insurance; life-insurance based upon a coöperative plan; usually having lodge features as an adjunct.

Insurance agent; a representative of an insurance company, authorized to transact certain business, as soliciting risks, issuing policies, etc.

Insurance commissioner; a state official who has supervision of insurance companies doing business in his state.

Insurance policy; the contract of insurance between the insurer and insured.

Life insurance; see *Life-insurance*.

Old-line insurance company; in life-insurance, a company which sets aside the reserve required by the laws of the various states in which it does business. The premiums and policy values are based upon standard mortality tables, while the premium rate is fixed and cannot be raised during the life of the contract; opposed to assessment or variable premium companies. The term is not specifically applied to fire-insurance companies.

in-sūr'ăn-cēr, *n.* An underwriter. [Obs.]

in-sūr'ănt, *n.* One insured; the assured.

in-sūre', *v.t.*; insured, *pt.*, *pp.*; insuring, *ppr.* [ME. *insuren, ensuren*; OFr. *enseurer*, to assure; *en*, in, and *seur*, sure.]

1. To make sure or secure; as, to *insure* safety to any one.

2. To contract or covenant, for a consideration, to secure against loss; to engage to indemnify for any specified loss at a stipulated rate, the total amount paid being called the premium.

in-sūre', *v.i.* To underwrite; to practise making insurance; as, this company *insures* at three per cent.

in-sūred' (-shūrd'), *n.* One who has insurance, either on his life or property; the assured.

in-sūr'ēr, *n.* One who insures; the person who contracts to pay the losses of another for a premium; an underwriter.

in-sūr'ġen-cy, in-sūr'ġence, *n.* The state of being insurgent; an uprising.

in-sūr'ġent, *a.* [L. *insurgens (-entis)*, ppr. of *insurgere*, to rise up, rise up against; *in*, in, upon, and *surgere*, to rise.] Rising in opposition to lawful civil or political authority; insubordinate; as, *insurgent* provinces.

in-sūr'ġent, *n.* A person who rises in opposition to civil or political authority; one who openly and actively resists the execution of laws; a belligerent.

in-sūr-mount'ȧ-bil-i-ty, *n.* The quality of being insurmountable; insurmountableness.

in-sūr-mount'ȧ-ble, *a.* Insuperable; that cannot be surmounted or overcome; as, an *insurmountable* difficulty, obstacle, or impediment.

in-sūr-mount'ȧ-ble-ness, *n.* Insurmountability.

in-sūr-mount'ȧ-bly, *adv.* In a manner or degree not to be overcome.

in-sūr-rect', *v.i.* To rise up in insurrection. [Colloq.]

in-sūr-rec'tion, *n.* [L. *insurrectus*, pp. of *insurgere*, to rise up, rise up against; *in*, in, upon, and *surgere*, to rise.]

1. A rising against civil or political authority; the open and active opposition of a number of persons to the execution of law in a city or state.

> It is found that this city of old time hath made *insurrection* against kings.
> —Ezra iv. 19.

2. A rising in mass to oppose an enemy. [Obs.]

Syn.—Sedition, revolt, rebellion.—*Sedition* is the raising of commotion in a state without aiming at open violence against the laws; *insurrection* is a rising up of individuals to prevent the execution of law, by force of arms; *revolt* is a casting off the authority of a government with a view to put it down by force; *rebellion* is an extended *insurrection* and *revolt*.

in-sūr-rec'tion-ăl, *a.* Pertaining to insurrection; consisting in insurrection.

in-sūr-rec'tion-ȧ-ry, *a.* Pertaining or suitable to insurrection.

in-sūr-rec'tion-ist, *n.* One who favors or takes part in insurrection; an insurgent.

in-sus-cep-ti-bil'i-ty, *n.* Want of susceptibility, or capacity to feel or perceive.

in-sus-cep'ti-ble, *a.* Not susceptible; not capable of being moved, affected, or impressed; as, a limb *insusceptible* of pain; a heart *insusceptible* of pity.

in-sus-cep'ti-bly, *adv.* Not susceptibly.

in-sus-cep'tive, *a.* Without susceptibility. [Rare.]

in-sū-sūr-rā'tion, *n.* [LL. *insusurratio*; L. *in*, in, and *susurrare*, to whisper.] The act of whispering into something, as the ear; insinuation. [Obs.]

in-swāthe', *v.t.*; inswathed, *pt.*, *pp.*; inswathing, *ppr.* To inwrap; to infold by wrapping.

in-tact', *a.* [L. *intactus*, untouched, uninjured; *in-* priv., and *tactus*, pp. of *tangere*, to touch.] Untouched; undisturbed; unchanged; undamaged; remaining complete.

in-tac'tȧ-ble, *a.* Not perceptible to the touch; also spelled *intactible*.

in-tagl'iā-ted (-tal'yā-), *a.* Engraved or stamped in, especially as an intaglio.

in-tagl'iō (-tal'yō), *n.*; *pl.* **in-tagl'iōs** or **in-tagl'i (-yē).** [It., from *intagliare*, to cut in, engrave.] A cutting or engraving, usually in a stone or gem, in which the figure is sunk below the surface; also, the gem thus engraved; opposite of *cameo*.

in-tāil', *v.t.* See *Entail*.

in'tāke, *n.* 1. What is taken in; opposite of *output*; as, the *intake* of a manufactory or a farm.

2. The point at which a tubular or cylindrical body begins to narrow.

3. The influx-point of a tube or pipe; as, the *intake* of a water-tunnel.

in-tam'i-nā-ted, *a.* [L. *intaminatus*, unsullied, undefiled.] Not contaminated. [Obs.]

in-tan-gi-bil'i-ty, *n.* The quality of being intangible.

in-tan'gi-ble, *a.* That cannot or may not be touched; not perceptible to the touch.

> A corporation is an artificial, invisible, *intangible* being.
> —Marshall.

in-tan'gi-ble-ness, *n.* Intangibility.

in-tan'gi-bly, *adv.* So as to be intangible.

in-tāst'ȧ-ble, *a.* Tasteless. [Rare.]

in'tē-ġēr, *n.* [L. *integer*, untouched, whole, entire; *in-* priv., and *tangere*, to touch.] The whole of anything; particularly, in arithmetic, a whole number, in contradistinction to a fraction.

Complex integer; the sum of a real and an imaginary integer.

in"tē-grȧ-bil'i-ty, *n.* The quality of being integrable.

in'tē-grȧ-ble, *a.* In mathematics, capable of being integrated, as a function or equation.

in'tē-grăl, *a.* [LL. *integralis*, from L. *integer*, untouched, whole, entire.]

1. Whole; entire; wanting nothing; complete as an entity.

2. Making part of a whole, or necessary to make a whole.

3. In mathematics, (a) not fractional; (b) of, relating, or pertaining to integration.

Integral calculus; see *Calculus*.

in'tē-grăl, *n.* 1. A whole; an entire thing; an individual.

2. In mathematics, the function or sum of any proposed differential quantity; denoted by the symbol $\int$.

Elliptic integral; an integral which expresses the length of an elliptical arc.

in-tē-gral'i-ty, *n.* Entireness. [Obs.]

in'tē-grăl-ly, *adv.* Wholly; completely.

in'tē-grănt, *a.* [L. *integrans (-antis)*, ppr. of *integrare*, to make whole, renew.] Making part of a whole; necessary to constitute an entire thing; integral.

Integrant parts or *particles*; the smallest particles into which a body can be divided by mechanical means.

in'tē-grāte, *v.t.*; integrated, *pt.*, *pp.*; integrating, *ppr.* [L. *integratus*, pp. of *integrare*, to make whole, renew, from *integer*, untouched, whole, entire.]

1. To renew; to restore; to perfect; to make a thing entire.

2. To indicate the sum total of; as, an anemometer *integrates* the entire force of the wind.

3. In mathematics, to find the integral of a differential expression.

in-tē-grā'tion, *n.* 1. The act of making entire.

2. In mathematics, the operation of finding the integral.

in-tē-grā'tŏr, *n.* One who or that which integrates; specifically an instrument for measuring irregular areas or giving mean values.

in"te-gri-pal'li-āte, *a.* See *Integropalliate*.

in-teg'ri-ty, *n.* [L. *integritas*, wholeness, soundness, from *integer*, untouched, whole, entire.]

1. Wholeness; entireness; unbroken state; as, the constitution guarantees to each state the *integrity* of its territories.

2. The entire, unimpaired state of anything, particularly of the mind; moral soundness or purity; incorruptness; uprightness; honesty. It comprehends the whole moral character, but has a special reference to uprightness in mutual dealings, transfers of property, and agencies for others.

> The moral grandeur of independent *integrity* is the sublimest thing in nature.
> —Buckminster.

3. Purity; genuine, unadulterated, unimpaired state; as, the *integrity* of language.

in"te-grō-pal'li-āte, *a.* In conchology, having the pallial line integral or unbroken by notches.

in-teg-ū-mā'tion, *n.* That part of physiology which treats of the integuments of animals and plants.

in-teg'ū-ment, *n.* [L. *integumentum*, a covering, from *integere*, to cover; *in*, in, upon, and *tegere*, to cover.] That which naturally invests or covers another thing; especially, in anatomy, a covering which invests the body, as the skin, or a membrane that invests a particular part.

in-teg-ū-men'tȧ-ry, *a.* Belonging to or composed of integuments.

in-teg"ū-men-tā'tion, *n.* The operation of covering or inclosing with integuments; also, the condition of being so covered, or the covering itself.

in'tel-lect, *n.* [L. *intellectus*, a perceiving, understanding, from *intellegere*, *intelligere*, to perceive, understand; *inter*, between, among, and *legere*, to gather, pick, choose.]

1. That faculty of the human soul or mind which receives or comprehends the ideas communicated to it by the senses, or by perception, or by other means; the faculty of thinking; the understanding.

2. Collective intelligence; as, the *intellect* of the period.

in'tel-lect-ed, *a.* Being possessed of intellectual powers. [Rare.]

in-tel-lec'tion, *n.* [L. *intellectio (-onis)*, from *intellegere, intelligere*, to perceive, understand.] The act of understanding; simple apprehension of ideas.

in-tel-lec'tive, *a.* 1. Having power to understand.

2. Produced by the understanding

3. Capable of being perceived by the understanding, not by the senses.

in-tel-lec'tive-ly, *adv.* In an intellective manner.

in-tel-lec'tū-ăl, *a.* [LL. *intellectualis*, pertaining to the understanding, from L. *intellectus*, perception, understanding, intellect.]

1. Relating to the intellect or understanding; belonging to the mind; performed by the understanding; mental; as, *intellectual* powers or operations.

2. Ideal; perceived by the intellect; existing in the understanding; as, an *intellectual* scene.

3. Having the power of understanding; as, an *intellectual* being.

4. Relating to the understanding; treating of the mind; as, *intellectual* philosophy.

Syn.—Mental, metaphysical, psychological, inventive, learned, cultured.

in-tel-leç'tū-ăl, *n.* The intellect or understanding. [Rare.]

in-tel-leç'tū-ăl-işm, *n.* 1. Intellectuality.

2. In philosophy, the doctrine that all knowledge is derived from the intellect.

in-tel-leç'tū-ăl-ist, *n.* 1. One who overrates the understanding. [Rare.]

2. In philosophy, a believer in the doctrine of intellectualism.

in-tel-leç-tū-al'i-ty, *n.* [LL. *intellectualitas,* from *intellectualis,* pertaining to the understanding, from L. *intellectus,* perception.] The state of intellectual power.

in-tel-leç'tū-ăl-īze, *v.t.* 1. To discuss intellectually.

2. To attribute intellectual characteristics to; to endow with an intellect or intellectual significance.

in-tel-leç'tū-ăl-ly, *adv.* By means of the intellect.

in-tel'li-ġence, *n.* [OFr. *intelligence;* L. *intelligentia,* perception, discernment, from *intelligens (-entis),* ppr. of *intelligere,* to perceive, understand.]

1. The quality of knowing or understanding.

2. Knowledge; wisdom; perception; as, a person of *intelligence.*

3. Ability to understand or comprehend.

4. Notice; information communicated by any means or contrivance.

5. Familiar terms of acquaintance; intercourse.

He lived rather in a fair *intelligence* than any friendship with the favorites.—Clarendon.

6. A spiritual being; as, a created *intelligence.*

Intelligence office; an office where information may be obtained, particularly, respecting servants to be hired, or situations to be obtained.

Syn.—Advice, intellect, instruction, news, report.

in-tel'li-ġen-cēr, *n.* One who sends or conveys intelligence; one who gives notice of private or distant transactions; a messenger; formerly much used as a title for newspapers.

in-tel'li-ġen-cy, *n.* Intelligence. [Obs.]

in-tel'li-ġent, *a.* [L. *intelligens (-entis),* ppr. of *intellegere,* to perceive, understand; *inter,* between, and *legere,* to gather, choose.]

1. Endowed with the faculty of understanding or reason; as, man is an *intelligent* being.

2. Knowing; understanding; well informed; sensible; having intelligence; skilled; as, an *intelligent* officer; an *intelligent* young man; an *intelligent* architect.

3. Giving information. [Obs.]

in-tel-li-ġen'tiăl, *a.* 1. Consisting of intelligence or unbodied mind.

Food alike those pure
Intelligential substances require. —Milton.

2. Pertaining to the intelligence; intellectual; exercising understanding.

3. Conveying intelligence.

in-tel-li-ġen'ti-ā-ry (-shi-), *n.* An intelligencer. [Obs.]

in-tel'li-ġent-ly, *adv.* In an intelligent manner.

in-tel''li-ġi-bil'i-ty, *n.* The quality or state of being intelligible; the possibility of being understood.

in-tel'li-ġi-ble, *a.* [L. *intelligibilis, intellegibilis,* from *intellegere,* to perceive, understand.] That may be understood or comprehended; comprehensible; as, an *intelligible* account.

in-tel'li-ġi-ble-ness, *n.* Intelligibility.

in-tel'li-ġi-bly, *adv.* In a manner to be understood; clearly; plainly; as, to write or speak *intelligibly.*

in-tem'ẽr-āte, in-tem'ẽr-ā-ted, *a.* [L. *intemeratus,* undefiled.] Pure; undefiled. [Obs.]

in-tem'ẽr-āte-ness, *n.* The state of being unpolluted. [Obs.]

in-tem'pẽr-ȧ-ment, *n.* A bad state or constitution; as, the *intemperament* of an ulcerated part. [Rare.]

in-tem'pẽr-ănce, *n.* [L. *intemperantia,* from *intemperans (-antis),* without self-restraint, extravagant, intemperate.]

1. Want of moderation or due restraint; excess in any kind of action or indulgence; any exertion of body or mind or any indulgence of appetites or passions which is injurious to the person or contrary to morality; as, *intemperance* in study or in labor, in eating or drinking, or in any other gratification.

2. Habitual indulgence in intoxicating liquors, with or without intoxication.

Should a foreign army land on our shores, to levy such a tax upon us as *intemperance* levies, no mortal power could resist the swelling tide of indignation that would overwhelm it. —L. Beecher.

in-tem'pẽr-ăn-cy, *n.* [Obs.] See *Intemperance.*

in-tem'pẽr-ănt, *a.* [Obs.] See *Intemperate.*

in-tem'pẽr-ănt, *n.* A drunkard.

in-tem'pẽr-āte, *a.* [L. *intemperatus; in-* priv., and *temperatus,* tempered, moderate, pp. of *temperare,* to combine in due proportion, qualify, from *tempus,* a portion or period of time.]

1. Not moderate or restrained within due limits; indulging to excess any appetite or passion, either habitually or in a particular instance; immoderate in enjoyment or exertion.

2. Addicted to an excessive or habitual use of intoxicating liquors.

3. Passionate; ungovernable; excessive; exceeding the convenient mean or degree; as, an *intemperate* climate; *intemperate* action.

in-tem'pẽr-āte, *v.t.* To disorder. [Obs.]

in-tem'pẽr-āte-ly, *adv.* With excessive indulgence of appetite or passion; with undue exertion; immoderately; excessively.

in-tem'pẽr-āte-ness, *n.* 1. Want of moderation; excessive degree of indulgence; as, the *intemperateness* of appetite or passion.

2. Immoderate degree of any quality in the weather, as in cold, heat, or storms.

in-tem'pẽr-ȧ-tūre, *n.* Excess. [Obs.]

in-tem-pes'tive, *a.* [L. *intempestivus; in-* priv., and *tempestivus,* timely, seasonable.] Untimely. [Obs.]

in-tem-pes'tive-ly, *adv.* Unseasonably. [Obs.]

in-tem-pes-tiv'i-ty, *n.* Untimeliness. [Obs.]

in-ten'ȧ-ble, *a.* 1. That cannot be held or maintained; that is not defensible; as, an *intenable* opinion; an *intenable* fortress.

2. Incapable of containing.

in-tend', *v.t.;* intended, *pt., pp.;* intending, *ppr.* [L. *intendere,* to stretch out, aim at; *in,* in, at, and *tendere,* to stretch.]

1. To stretch; to strain; to extend; to distend. [Obs.]

2. To fix the mind on, as something to be accomplished; to be intent upon; to mean; to purpose; to contemplate; often followed by an infinitive or a clause introduced by *that;* as, I *intend* to go; they *intend that* she shall remain.

For they *intended* evil against thee.
—Ps. xxi. 11.

3. To regard; to fix the mind on; to attend; to take care of. [Obs.]

4. To feign; to pretend. [Obs.]

5. To fashion; to design; to conceive. [Obs.]

6. To bend; to direct. [Rare.]

7. To enforce; to make intense; to intensify. [Obs.]

8. To signify; to have reference to; as, I *intended* nothing by the remark.

Syn.—Contemplate, design, plan, purpose.

in-tend'ănce, *n.* [Fr.] The control of any public business; superintendence.

in-tend'ăn-cy, *n.* The office or employment of an intendant or the district committed to his charge.

in-tend'ănt, *n.* [Fr., from L. *intendens (-entis),* ppr. of *intendere,* to stretch out, aim at, exert oneself, intend.] One who has the charge, oversight, direction, or management of some public business; a superintendent; used as a title of public officers in France and some other countries; as, an *intendant* of marine; an *intendant* of finance.

in-tend'ed, *a.* 1. Designed; purposed; as, the insult was *intended.*

2. Stretched; made intense. [Obs.]

in-tend'ed, *n.* The person to whom one is engaged to be married; with a possessive pronoun; as, she is my *intended.* [Colloq.]

in-tend'ed-ly, *adv.* With purpose or intention; by design; intentionally. [Rare.]

in-tend'ẽr, *n.* One who intends.

in-tend'i-ment, *n.* Attention; understanding; consideration. [Obs.]

in-tend'ment, *n.* [OFr. *entendement;* LL. *intendimentum,* attention, purpose, understanding, from L. *intendere,* to intend.]

1. Intention; design. [Obs.]

2. In law, the true meaning of a law or of any legal instrument.

3. Intelligence. [Obs.]

in-ten'ẽr-āte, *v.t.* [L. *in,* in, and *tener,* soft, tender.] To make tender; to soften. [Rare.]

in-ten'ẽr-āte, *a.* Made tender; tender; soft; intenerated. [Obs.]

in-ten-ẽr-ā'tion, *n.* The act of intenerating or making soft or tender. [Rare.]

in-ten'sāte, *v.t.* To make intense, or more intense. [Rare.]

in-ten-sā'tion, *n.* The act of intensating.

in-ten'sȧ-tive, *a.* Intensifying. [Rare.]

in-tense', *a.* [L. *intensus,* pp. of *intendere,* to stretch, intend.]

1. Strained; stretched; hence, very close; strict; as, *intense* study or application; *intense* thought.

2. Extreme in degree; ardent; severe; vehement.

3. Deep, as in color or tone.

in-tense'ly, *adv.* 1. To an extreme degree; extremely; as, a furnace *intensely* heated; weather *intensely* cold.

2. Attentively; earnestly. [Obs.]

in-tense'ness, *n.* 1. The state of being strained or stretched; intensity; as, the *intenseness* of a cord.

2. The state of being raised or concentrated to a great degree; extreme violence; as, the *intenseness* of heat or cold.

3. Extreme closeness or application; as, the *intenseness* of study or thought.

in-ten''si-fi-cā'tion, *n.* The act of intensifying or the result of making intense.

in-ten'si-fī-ẽr, *n.* 1. One who or that which intensifies.

2. In photography, any solution or appliance for intensifying the lights or shadows in a picture.

3. In physics, an apparatus for intensifying the pressure upon a mass of confined fluid.

in-ten'si-fȳ, *v.t.;* intensified, *pt., pp.;* intensifying, *ppr.* [L. *intensus,* intense, and *-ficare,* from *facere,* to make.]

1. To render intense or more intense.

2. In photography, to bring out more fully, as the lights and shadows in a picture.

in-ten'si-fȳ, *v.i.* To become intense or more intense; to act with increased vigor or force.

in-ten'sion, *n.* [L. *intensio (-onis),* from *intensus,* pp. of *intendere,* to stretch out, intend.]

1. A straining, stretching, or bending; the state of being strained; as, the *intension* of a musical string.

2. Increase of power or energy of any quality.

3. In logic, the collective content of a proposition.

in-ten'si-ty, *n.* 1. The state of being strained or stretched; intenseness, as of a musical string; the state of being raised to a great degree; extreme violence; as, the *intensity* of heat; extreme closeness; as, *intensity* of application.

2. In physics, the degree of energy in any acting force, as in traction or compression.

3. In photography, the degree of light or shadow in a picture.

4. In psychology, the degree of mental activity; the embodiment of emotion and feeling.

Syn.—Tension, force, strain, concentration, attention, eagerness, ardor, energy.

in-ten'sive, *a.* 1. Stretched or admitting of extension.

2. Intent; unremitted; assiduous; as, *intensive* circumspection.

3. Serving to give force or emphasis; as, an *intensive* particle or prefix.

4. In grammar, designating a word or particle used to give additional force to an expression.

in-ten'sive, *n.* That which gives point or emphasis, as an intensive word or particle; whatever intensifies.

in-ten'sive-ly, *adv.* By increase of degree; in a manner to give force.

in-ten'sive-ness, *n.* The condition or quality of being intensive.

in-tent', *a.* [L. *intensus,* pp. of *intendere,* to stretch, intend.] Having the mind concentrated; sedulously applied; anxiously diligent; generally used with *on* or *upon;* as, *intent upon* evil.

Be *intent* and solicitous to take up the meaning of the speaker. —Watts.

in-tent', *n.* The act of focusing the mind on an object; aim; intention; purpose.

To all intents and purposes; in all senses; whatever may be or may have been designed.

He was miserable *to all intents and purposes.*
—L'Estrange.

in-ten-tā'tion, *n.* [Obs.] See *Intention.*

in-ten'tion, *n.* [L. *intentio (-onis),* a stretching out, exertion, purpose, from *intendere,* to stretch out, intend.]

1. A stretching or bending of the mind, as toward an object; hence, uncommon exertion of the intellectual faculties; closeness of application; fixedness of attention; earnestness.

Intention is manifest when the mind, with great earnestness, and of choice, fixes its view on any idea, considers it on every side, and will not be called off by the ordinary solicitation of other ideas. —Locke.

2. Design; purpose; the fixed direction of the mind to a particular object; a determination to act in a particular manner; as, it is my *intention* to proceed to Paris.

3. End or aim; the object to be accomplished.

4. The state of being strained. [Obs.]

5. In logic, a concept or general apprehension gathered from other concepts as objects.

First intention; in logic, a first or general concept, as of an object as a whole.

Second intention; in logic, a conception gained by generalizing from the first conception.

To heal by first intention; in surgery, to unite without suppuration, the parts being kept in close contact by bandages while the exterior cicatrizes.

To heal by second intention; in surgery, to unite when suppuration intervenes before the restoration of the parts.

in-ten'tion-ăl, *a.* Intended; designed; done

with design or purpose; as, the act was *intentional*, not accidental.

Syn.—Purposed, designed, deliberate, intended, contemplated, premeditated, studied.

in-ten-tion-al′i-ty, *n.* The quality of being intentional; aim; design.

in-ten′tion-ăl-ly, *adv.* By design; of purpose; not casually.

in-ten′tioned, *a.* Having plans or intentions; used chiefly in composition; as, ill-*intentioned.*

in-ten′tive, *a.* Attentive; having the mind closely applied. [Obs.]

in-ten′tive-ly, *adv.* Closely; with close application. [Obs.]

in-ten′tive-ness, *n.* Closeness of attention or application of mind. [Obs.]

in-tent′ly, *adv.* With close attention or application; with eagerness or earnestness; as, to have the mind *intently* directed to an object, or the eyes *intently* fixed.

in-tent′ness, *n.* The state of being intent; close application; constant employment of the mind.

inter-. [ME. *enter-, inter-*; OFr. *entre-, inter-*; L. *inter-*, from *inter*, prep. between, among, during; *in*, in, within, and *-ter*, a comp. suffix.] A prefix signifying between, among, during; as, *inter*flow, *inter*change.

in-tẽr′, *v.t.*; interred, *pt., pp.*; interring, *ppr.* [OFr. *enterrer*; LL. *interrare*, to put in the earth, L. *in*, in, and *terra*, earth.] To place in the earth and cover over, as a dead body; to inhume; to bury.

in-tẽr-açt′, *v.i.* To act mutually; to perform reciprocal acts.

in-tẽr-açt′, *n.* Intermediate employment or time; a short piece between acts.

in-tẽr-aç′tion, *n.* Intermediate or mutual action.

in-tẽr-ad′di-tive, *a.* Added between; interpolated, as a word or phrase in a sentence.

in-tẽr-ā′ġen-cy, *n.* An intervening or intermediate agency.

in-tẽr-ā′ġent, *n.* An intermediate agent.

in′tẽr-ạll, *n.* An entrail. [Obs.]

in″tẽr-al-vē′ō-lăr, *a.* [L. *inter*, between, and *alveolus*, a small cavity or hollow.]

1. In anatomy, lying between cells or cavities, especially of the lungs.

2. In zoölogy, between the alveoli; as, the *interalveolar* muscles of a sea-urchin.

in-tẽr-am-bū-lā′çrăl, *a.* Relating to the interambulacra.

in-tẽr-am-bū-lā′çrum, *n.*; *pl.* **in-tẽr-am-bū-lā′çrȧ.** [*Inter-*, and L. *ambulacrum*, an alley or covered way.] In zoölogy, a zone between two ambulacra in echinoderms.

in-tẽr-am′ni-ăn, *a.* [LL. *interamnus*; *inter*, between, and *amnis*, river.] Situated between rivers.

in-tẽr-an′i-māte, *v.t.* To animate mutually. [Obs.]

in-tẽr-ăr-bō-rā′tion, *n.* The interlacing or mingling of the branches of trees. [Obs.]

in″tẽr-ăr-tiç′ū-lăr, *a.* In anatomy, being between the joints or articulating parts of bones.

in″tẽr-ȧ-tom′iç, *a.* In physics and chemistry, relating to spaces between atoms.

in-tẽr-ạu′liç, *a.* [L. *inter*, between, and *aula*, a hall.] Existing or carried on between sovereigns or courts. [Rare.]

in″tẽr-ạu-riç′ū-lăr, *a.* In anatomy, situated between the auricles.

in-tẽr-ax′ăl, *a.* Relating to an interaxis.

in-tẽr-ax′il-lā-ry, *a.* In botany, between the axils of leaves.

in-tẽr-ax′is, *n.*; *pl.* **in-tẽr-ax′ēṣ.** [L. *inter*, between, and *axis*, axis.] In architecture, the space between axes.

in″tẽr-bas-tā′tion, *n.* Patchwork. [Obs.]

in-tẽr-bed′ded, *a.* In geology, interstratified; interleaved.

in-tẽr-braçh′i-ăl, *a.* [L. *inter*, between, and *bracchium*, or *brachium*, arm.] In zoölogy, situated between brachia, as in the starfish.

in-tẽr-brāin′, *n.* In anatomy, the thalamencephalon or diencephalon.

in-tẽr-bran′çhi-ăl, *a.* In zoölogy, situated between the branchiæ or gills, as in fishes.

in-tẽr-breed′, *v.t.* and *v.i.* To breed by crossing one species or variety of animals or plants with another; to crossbreed.

in-tẽr′çȧ-lăr, *a.* Intercalary.

in-tẽr′çȧ-lā-ry, *a.* [L. *intercalarius, intercalaris*, that is inserted, from *intercalare*, to intercalate.]

1. Inserted or introduced in the midst of others; applied particularly to the odd day in leap-year.

2. Added or inserted; introduced; as, *intercalary* lines.

Intercalary day; (a) in chronology, one of the days inserted in the calendar to establish conformity, as the additional day in February of a leap-year; (b) in medicine, one of the days in the course of a disease, in which the patient is free from critical symptoms.

in-tẽr′çȧ-lāte, *v.t.*; intercalated, *pt., pp.*; intercalating, *ppr.* [L. *intercalatus*, pp. of *intercalare*, to insert; *inter*, between, and *calare*, to call proclaim.] To insert; specifically, (a) in chronology, to insert in the calendar, as an intercalary day; (b) in geology, to insert, as a layer of rock between two other layers.

in-tẽr-çȧ-lā′tion, *n.* 1. The introducing of any portion of time into a calendar.

2. The insertion of anything among other things, as, in geology, the insertion of a stratum between other layers.

in″tẽr-çȧ-rot′iç, in″tẽr-çȧ-rot′id, *a.* In anatomy, between the outer and inner carotid arteries.

in-tẽr-çăr′păl, *a.* In anatomy, situated between the bones of the wrist.

in-tẽr-çav′ẽrn-ous, *a.* In anatomy, relating to or connected with the cavernous sinuses of the brain.

in-tẽr-çēde′, *v.i.*; interceded, *pt., pp.*; interceding, *ppr.* [L. *intercedere*, to go or come between, interpose; *inter*, between, and *cedere*, to go.]

1. To pass between; to intervene.

> He supposes that a vast period *interceded* between that origination and the age in which he lived. —Hale.

2. To mediate; to interpose; to make intercession; to act between parties with a view to reconcile those who differ or contend; usually followed by *with*.

3. To plead in favor of another.

Syn.—Interpose, mediate, interfere, intermeddle.—One *intercedes* between parties that are unequal, in favor of that party which is threatened with punishment; one *interposes* between parties that are equal; one *intercedes* by means of persuasion; one *interposes* by an exercise of authority.

in-tẽr-çēde′, *v.t.* To place between. [Obs.]

in-tẽr-çēd′ence, *n.* The act of mediating, interposing, or interceding.

in-tẽr-çēd′ent, *a.* [L. *intercedens (-entis)*, ppr. of *intercedere*, to go or come between.] Passing between; mediating; pleading for. [Rare.]

in-tẽr-çēd′ent-ly, *adv.* In an intercedent manner.

in-tẽr-çēd′ẽr, *n.* One who intercedes or interposes between parties to effect a reconciliation; a mediator; an intercessor.

in-tẽr-çel′lū-lăr, *a.* Lying between the cells or elementary structures, as of plants.

in-tẽr-çen′trăl, *a.* Between or connecting centers; pertaining to an intercentrum.

Intercentral nerves; in physiology, nerves which convey impulses from nerve-center to nerve-center, as distinguished from nerves which transmit impulses between surface points and nerve-centers.

a a, Intercellular Spaces.

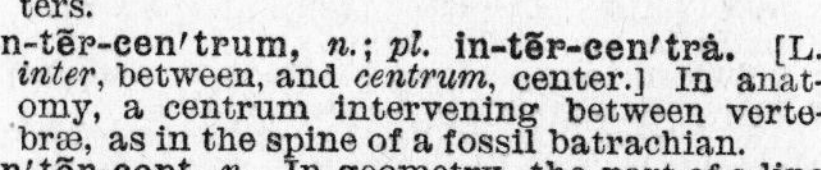

in-tẽr-çen′trum, *n.*; *pl.* **in-tẽr-çen′trȧ.** [L. *inter*, between, and *centrum*, center.] In anatomy, a centrum intervening between vertebræ, as in the spine of a fossil batrachian.

in′tẽr-çept, *n.* In geometry, the part of a line intercepted.

in-tẽr-çept′, *v.t.*; intercepted, *pt., pp.*; intercepting, *ppr.* [L. *interceptus*, pp. of *intercipere*, to take between, interrupt; *inter*, between, and *capere*, to take.]

1. To obstruct; to stop in progress; as, to *intercept* rays of light; to *intercept* the current of a river or a course of proceedings; to take or seize on by the way; to stop on its passage; as, to *intercept* a letter; the prince was *intercepted* at Rome; the convoy was *intercepted* by a detachment of the enemy.

2. To stop, as a course or passing; as, to *intercept* a journey; to interrupt or cut off progress toward.

> While storms vindictive *intercept* the shore. —Pope.

3. In mathematics, to take, include, or comprehend between.

in-tẽr-çept′ẽr, *n.* One who or that which intercepts.

in-tẽr-çep′tion, *n.* The act of seizing on its passage; a stopping; obstruction, as of a course or proceeding; hindrance.

in-tẽr-çept′ive, *a.* Intercepting or likely to intercept.

in-tẽr-çes′sion (-sesh′un), *n.* [L. *intercessio*, from *intercedere*, to come or go between, intercede.] The act of interceding; mediation; interposition between parties at variance with a view to reconciliation; prayer or solicitation to one party in favor of another, sometimes against another.

> Your *intercession* now is needless grown;
> Retire, and let me speak with her alone. —Dryden.

in-tẽr-çes′sion-ăl, *a.* Containing or pertaining to intercession or entreaty.

in-tẽr-çes′sion-āte, *v.t.* To implore. [Obs.]

in-tẽr-çes′sŏr, *n.* 1. A mediator; one who interposes between parties at variance, with a view to reconcile them; one who pleads in behalf of another.

2. Ecclesiastically, a bishop who during a vacancy of the see administers the bishopric till a successor is elected.

in″tẽr-çes-sō′ri-ăl, *a.* Pertaining to an intercessor.

in-tẽr-çes′sō-ry, *a.* Containing intercession; interceding.

in-tẽr-çhāin′, *v.t.*; interchained, *pt., pp.*; interchaining, *ppr.* To chain; to link together.

in′tẽr-çhānġe, *n.* 1. Mutual change, each giving and receiving; exchange; permutation of commodities; barter; as, the *interchange* of commodities between New York and Havana.

2. Alternate succession; as, the *interchange* of light and darkness.

3. A mutual giving and receiving; reciprocation; as, an *interchange* of civilities or kind offices.

in-tẽr-çhānġe′, *v.t.*; interchanged, *pt., pp.*; interchanging, *ppr.* [ME. *enterchangen*; OFr. *entrechangier*; *entre-*, between, and *changier, changer*, to change.]

1. To change by putting each of in the place of the other; to give and take mutually; to exchange; to reciprocate; as, to *interchange* places; to *interchange* cares or duties.

2. To succeed alternately or to cause alternation.

in-tẽr-çhānġe′, *v.i.* To change in a reciprocal manner.

in-tẽr-çhānġe-ȧ-bil′i-ty, *n.* The state of being interchangeable.

in-tẽr-çhānġe′ȧ-ble, *a.* 1. That may be interchanged; that may be given and taken mutually.

2. Following each other in alternate succession; as, the four *interchangeable* seasons.

in-tẽr-çhānġe′ȧ-ble-ness, *n.* Interchangeability.

in-tẽr-çhānġe′ȧ-bly, *adv.* Alternately; by reciprocation; in a manner in which each gives and receives.

Interchangeably Posed.

in-tẽr-çhānġe′ment, *n.* Exchange; mutual transfer. [Obs.]

in-tẽr-çhap′tẽr, *n.* An interpolated chapter.

in-tẽr′ci-dence, *n.* A happening between. [Obs.]

in-tẽr′ci-dent, *a.* [L. *intercidens (-entis)*, ppr. of *intercidere*, to fall between; *inter*, between, and *cadere*, to fall.] Falling or coming between. [Obs.]

in-tẽr-çip′i-ent, *a.* [L. *intercipiens (-entis)*, ppr. of *intercipere*, to take between, intercept.] Intercepting; seizing by the way; stopping.

in-tẽr-çip′i-ent, *n.* One who or that which intercepts or stops.

in-tẽr-ci′ṣion (-sizh′un), *n.* [LL. *intercisio (-onis)*, a cutting through; L. *inter*, between, and *cædere*, to cut.] Interruption by cutting off. [Rare.]

in-tẽr-çit′i-zen-ship, *n.* The right secured to the citizens of different states to enjoy mutual civic rights and privileges.

in-tẽr-çlav′i-çle, *n.* In anatomy and zoölogy, a membrane-bone lying between and sometimes uniting the clavicles of certain animals, as the frog, the turtle, and the ornithorhynchus.

in″tẽr-çlȧ-viç′ū-lăr, *a.* In zoölogy, situated between the clavicles; relating to the interclavicle.

in-tẽr-çlōṣe′, *v.t.* To shut in; to surround. [Obs.]

in-tẽr-çloud′, *v.t.* To surround with clouds; to obscure. [Rare.]

in-tẽr-çlūde′, *v.t.* [L. *intercludere*; *inter*, between, and *claudere*, to shut, close.] To shut from a place or course by something intervening; to intercept; to cut off; to interrupt.

in-tẽr-çlū′ṣion, *n.* [L. *interclusio (-onis)*, from *intercludere*, to shut off, shut in.] An obstruction by shutting off.

in″tẽr-çol-lē′ġi-āte, *a.* Between or among colleges; as, an *intercollegiate* oratorical contest; *intercollegiate* football.

in-tẽr-çol′line, *a.* [L. *inter*, between, and *collis*, a hill.] Between hills, especially between the cones of volcanoes. [Rare.]

in″tẽr-çō-lō′ni-ăl, *a.* Between colonies; having to do with the mutual relations of colonies; as, *intercolonial* commerce.

in″tẽr-çō-lō′ni-ăl-ly, *adv.* As between colonies.

in-tẽr-çō-lum′năr, *a.* Between columns; as, an *intercolumnar* statue.

Ionic Intercolumniation. A, Areostyle. B, Coupled columns. C, Diastyle. D, Eustyle.

in″tẽr-çō-lum-ni-ā′tion, *n.* [L.

intercolumnium; *inter*, between, and *columna*, a column.] In architecture, the art or method of dividing the space between two columns measured at the lower part of their shafts. Vitruvius enumerates five varieties of intercolumniation, and assigns to them definite proportions expressed in measures of the inferior diameter of the column; as the pycnostyle, of one diameter and a half; the systyle, of two diameters; the diastyle, of three diameters; the areostyle, of four or sometimes five diameters; and the eustyle, of two and a quarter diameters.

in-tēr-çom′bat, *n.* A fight. [Obs.]

in-tēr-çōm′ing, *a.* Coming between. [Obs.]

in-tēr-çom′mōn, *v.i.* 1. To feed at the same table. [Obs.]

2. In English law, to graze cattle in a common pasture; to use a common with others, or to possess or enjoy the right of feeding in common.

> Common because of vicinage is where the inhabitants of two townships contiguous to each other have usually *intercommoned* with one another. —Blackstone.

in-tēr-çom′mōn-āge, *n.* Mutual commonage.

in-tēr-çom′mōn-ēr, *n.* One privileged to intercommon.

in″tēr-çŏm-mūne′, *v.i.* 1. To hold mutual communication.

2. To converse. [Scot.]

in″tēr-çŏm-mū′ni-ça-ble, *a.* That may be mutually communicated.

in″tēr-çŏm-mū′ni-çāte, *v.i.*; intercommunicated, *pt., pp.*; intercommunicating, *ppr.* To communicate mutually; to hold mutual communication.

in″tēr-çŏm-mū-ni-çā′tion, *n.* Reciprocal communication.

in″tēr-çŏm-mūn′iŏn, *n.* Mutual communion; as, an *intercommunion* of deities.

in″tēr-çŏm-mū′ni-ty, *n.* A mutual communication or community.

in″tēr-çŏm-par′i-sŏn, *n.* Mutual or common comparison.

in-tēr-çon′dy-lăr, *a.* Intercondyloid.

in-tēr-çon′dy-loid, *a.* In anatomy, lying between condyles.

in″tēr-çŏn-neçt′, *v.t.* To give mutual connection to.

in″tēr-çŏn-neç′tion, *n.* Mutual union.

in-tēr-çon-ti-nen′tăl, *a.* Denoting a relation between continents.

in″tēr-çŏn-vērt′i-ble, *a.* Mutually exchangeable.

in-tēr-ços′tăl, *a.* [L. *inter*, between, and *costa*, a rib.] Placed or lying between the ribs; as, an *intercostal* muscle, artery, or vein.

in′tēr-çōurse, *n.* [ME. *entercourse*; OFr. *entrecors, intercours*; L. *intercursus*, a running between, intervention, from *intercurrere*, to run between; *inter*, between, and *currere*, to run.] Connection by reciprocal action or dealings, as between persons or nations; interchange of thought and feeling; communication; commerce; association; communion; as, to have much *intercourse* together.

Sexual intercourse; coition.

Syn.—Correspondence, dealing, intercommunication, intimacy, connection, commerce.

in-tēr-çross′, *v.i.* and *v.t.*; intercrossed (-krost), *pt., pp.*; intercrossing, *ppr.* I. *v.i.* To intersect.

II. *v.t.* In biology, to fertilize by a different variety of plant or animal.

in′tēr-çross, *n.* An instance of cross-fertilization; the act or process of intercrossing.

in-tēr-çrū′răl, *a.* In anatomy, between the crura or peduncles of the brain; also, pertaining to the crural area of the lower jaw of an animal.

in-tēr-çul′tūr-ăl, *a.* In agriculture, (a) designating the culture of one crop with another at the same time and upon the same ground, as of corn and beans; (b) relating to cultivation by stirring the soil lying between individual plants, as in the cultivation of corn with a hoe or with a cultivator.

in-tēr-çūr′, *v.i.* To intervene; to come in the meantime. [Obs.]

in-tēr-çur′rence, *n.* A passing or running between.

in-tēr-çur′rent, *a.* and *n.* [L. *intercurrens (-entis)*, ppr. of *intercurrere*, to run between; *inter*, between, and *currere*, to run.]

I. *a.* 1. Running between or among; intervening.

2. In medicine, used of diseases which occur at any time of the year, or of a disease which starts up during the course of another disease.

II. *n.* Something happening between; an intervention. [Obs.]

in-tēr-çū-tā′nē-ous, *a.* Being within or under the skin.

in-tēr-dash′, *v.t.* To dash at intervals; to intersperse. [Rare.]

in′tēr-dēal, *n.* Mutual dealing; traffic. [Obs.]

in-tēr-den′tăl, *a.* 1. Between the teeth, as of an animal or a toothed wheel.

2. Vocalized between the upper and lower teeth, as certain consonants.

in-tēr-den′til, in-tēr-den′tel, *n.* In architecture, the space between two dentils.

in″tēr-dē-pend′ence, *n.* Mutual dependence.

in″tēr-dē-pend′en-cy, *n.* Mutual reliance or dependence.

in″tēr-dē-pend′ent, *a.* Mutually dependent.

in-tēr-diçt′, *v.t.*; interdicted, *pt., pp.*; interdicting, *ppr.* [L. *interdictus*, pp. of *interdicere*, to speak between, to forbid, prohibit; *inter*, between, and *dicere*, to speak, say.]

1. To forbid; to prohibit; as, our intercourse with foreign nations was *interdicted*.

2. In ecclesiastical usage, to cut off from the enjoyment of communion with a church.

> An archbishop may not only excommunicate and *interdict* his suffragans, but his vicar-general may do the same. —Ayliffe.

3. To prohibit the execution of, as a law.

in′tēr-diçt, *n.* [L. *interdictum*, a prohibition.]

1. Prohibition; a prohibiting order or decree.

2. In the Roman Catholic church, formerly, a prohibition of the pope, by which persons or localities were denied the privileges of the church.

3. In civil law, an order which forbids specified action until a final decision is reached; an order of a court similar to an injunction.

in-tēr-diç′tion, *n.* 1. The act of interdicting; prohibition; a prohibiting decree; a curse.

2. A judicial order of a restraining nature placed on a person of unsound mind in order to preserve his legal rights.

in-tēr-diçt′ive, *a.* Having power to prohibit.

in-tēr-diçt′ō-ry, *a.* Serving to prohibit.

in-tēr-dig′i-tăl, *a.* Between the digits, as the web or membrane between the toes.

in-tēr-dig′i-tāte, *v.t.* To interlock; to interweave. [Rare.]

in-tēr-dig′i-tāte, *v.i.*; interdigitated, *pt., pp.*; interdigitating, *ppr.* [L. *inter*, between, and *digitus*, finger.] To commingle; to be put together in the manner of interlocking fingers.

in-tēr-dig-i-tā′tion, *n.* An interdigital space; the condition of being interdigitated; the process of interdigitating.

in′tēr-dōme, *n.* A space between two shells of a domelike structure.

in′tēr-dūçe, *n.* In carpentry, an intertie.

in-tēr-ē-pim′ēr-ăl, *a.* Situated between epimera.

in-tēr-ē-qui-noç′tiăl, *a.* Coming between the equinoxes.

> Summer and winter I have called *interequinoctial* intervals. —Belfour.

in′tēr-ess, *v.t.* To interest. [Obs.]

in′tēr-ess, *n.* Interest. [Obs.]

in′tēr-est, *v.t.*: interested, *pt., pp.*; interesting, *ppr.* 1. To gain the attention of; to give a share in to excite interest in; to engage; to induce to take part; as, to *interest* an audience; to *interest* a person in an undertaking.

2. To concern; to affect; to excite emotion or passion in, usually in favor of, but sometimes against, a person or thing.

3. To permit to share. [Obs.]

in′tēr-est, *n.* [ME. *interest*; OFr. *interest*, interest, concern, prejudice, from L. *interest*, it concerns, it is to the advantage, 3rd pers. sing. of *interesse*, to be between.]

1. A feeling of concern, as in something which promises profit or enjoyment, or opportunity for profit or enjoyment.

2. Welfare, personal or public; advantage; good; as, private *interest*; public *interest*.

> Divisions hinder the common *interest* and public good. —Temple.

3. Share; portion; part; participation in value; as, he has an *interest* in a manufactory of cotton goods.

4. Any surplus advantage.

> With all speed,
> You shall have your desires with *interest*.
> —Shak.

5. Premium paid for the use of money; the profit per cent derived from money loaned or property used by another person, or from debts remaining unpaid.

6. The capital invested and the commerce carried on in any particular industry; as, the mining *interests*.

Compound interest; that interest which arises from the principal with the interest added at stated times, as quarterly, yearly, etc.; interest on interest.

Simple interest; that interest which arises from the principal sum only.

Syn.—Concern, business, advantage, profit, attention, curiosity, behalf, share.

in′tēr-est-ed, *a.* 1. Affected; moved; having the passions excited; as, one *interested* by a story.

2. Having an interest; concerned, as in a cause or in consequences; liable to be affected; as, an *interested* witness.

in′tēr-est-ed-ly, *adv.* In an interested manner.

in′tēr-est-ed-ness, *n.* The condition of being interested.

in′tēr-est-ing, *a.* Engaging the attention or curiosity; exciting or adapted to excite emotions or passions; as, an *interesting* story.

in′tēr-est-ing-ly, *adv.* In an interesting manner.

in′tēr-est-ing-ness, *n.* The quality of being interesting.

in-tēr-fā′ciăl (-shăl), *a.* Included between two faces; as, an *interfacial* angle is formed by the meeting of two planes.

in″tēr-fas-ciç′ū-lăr, *a.* In anatomy and botany, located between fascicles.

in-tēr-fem′ō-răl, *a.* In anatomy, between the femora; as, the *interfemoral* membrane of a bat.

in-tēr-fen-es-trā′tion, *n.* In architecture, the process or art of arranging windows with special regard to the spaces between them.

in-tēr-fēr′ănt, *n.* One of the parties to a suit for interference in the Patent Office of the United States.

in-tēr-fēre′, *v.i.*; interfered, *pt., pp.*; interfering, *ppr.* [ME. *enterferen*; OFr. *entreferir*, to exchange blows; L. *inter*, between, among, and *ferire*, to strike.]

1. To interpose; to intermeddle; to enter into or take a part in the concerns of others.

2. To clash; to come in collision; to be in opposition; as, the claims of two nations may *interfere*.

3. In farriery, to strike the hoof or shoe of one hoof against the fetlock of the opposite leg, and break the skin or injure the flesh.

4. In physics, to act reciprocally upon each other so as to modify the effect of each by augmenting, diminishing, or nullifying it; said of waves of light, heat, sound, and the like.

5. In patent law, to encroach upon the claim of a patentee by using his principle of construction or composition.

6. In games in which a ball is used, as (a) in lawn-tennis, to offer an obstruction to the flight of the ball, as the branch of a tree or the body of a spectator; (b) in baseball, to obstruct a runner in his course between bases; (c) in football, to act defensively in guarding the player who has the ball; also, to unlawfully hinder the snapper-back or the player who is about to make a fair catch.

in-tēr-fēr′ence, *n.* 1. Interposition; an intermeddling; mediation.

2. A clashing or collision.

3. In physics, the mutual action of waves of any kind, as of water, sound, heat, or light, upon each other, by which in certain circumstances the vibrations and their effects are diminished or neutralized.

4. In patent law, some claim conflicting with a patent already granted or pending.

5. In football, (a) the act of the players who protect and assist in the progress of the man on their own side who attempts to advance the ball; (b) any hindrance offered to the snapper-back before the ball is put in play; (c) the act of unlawfully obstructing a player making a fair catch.

6. In baseball, an obstruction to a runner between bases.

7. In lawn-tennis, the intervention of anything out of the ordinary to the flight of the ball, as the branch of a near-by tree or the body of a spectator.

in″tēr-fē-ren′tiăl, *a.* In physics, pertaining to results obtained by interference.

in-tēr-fēr′ēr, *n.* One who or that which interferes.

in-tēr-fī′lăr, *a.* [L. *inter*, between, and *filum*, a thread.] In biology, existing or situated between the fibrils of a reticulum.

in-tēr-flōw′, *v.i.* To flow in or between. [Rare.]

in-tēr′flū-ent, in-tēr′flū-ous, *a.* Flowing between, among, or together.

in-tēr-fōld′ed, *a.* Folded or clasped together.

> With hands *interfolded*. —Longfellow.

in-tēr-fō-li-ā′ceous, *a.* [L. *inter*, between, and *folium*, a leaf.] In botany, being between opposite leaves, but placed alternately with them; as, *interfoliaceous* flowers or peduncles.

in-tēr-fō′li-āte, *v.t.* [Obs.] See *Interleave*.

in-tēr-fret′ted, *a.* In heraldry, interlaced; applied to any bearings linked together, one within the other, as keys interlaced in the bows, or one linked into the other.

in-tēr-ful′gent, *a.* [L. *interfulgens (-entis)*, ppr. of *interfulgere*, to shine between; *inter*, between, and *fulgere*, to shine.] Shining between.

in-tēr-fūse′, *v.t.*; interfused, *pt., pp.*; interfusing, *ppr.* [L. *interfusus*, pp. of *interfundere*, to pour between, among; *inter*, between, among, and *fundere*, to pour.]

1. To cause to flow together; hence, to infuse and diffuse; to intermix.

2. To cause to mingle; to permeate. [Rare.]

in-tēr-fūse′, *v.i.* To mingle and associate by fusion.

in-tēr-fū′sion, *n.* The act of interfusing; a mixing together.

in-tēr-glā′ciăl (-shăl), *a.* In geology, formed

or occurring between two periods of glacial action.

in-tẽr-glob′ū-lăr, *a.* In anatomy, lying between globules, as the minute spaces in certain tissues.

in-tẽr-grāde′, *n.* An intermediate form in a graded series.

in-tẽr-grāde′, *v.i.* To gradually approach a similarity of form.

in-tẽr-grāve′, *v.t.*; intergraved, *pt.*, *pp.*; intergraving, *ppr.* To grave or mark between; also, to engrave or carve in every other space.

in-tẽr-hē′măl, in-tẽr-hæ′măl, *a.* and *n.* I. *a.* In anatomy, situated between the hemal processes or spines.

II. *n.* An interhemal bone or spine.

in-tẽr-hȳ′ăl, *a.* and *n.* I. *a.* Relating to the space in the hyoid arch.

II. *n.* A bone or cartilage situated within the hyoid arch.

in′tẽr-im, *n.* [L., in the meantime, meanwhile.]

1. An intermediate period; intervening time; as, in the *interim.*

2. In history, one of the provisional arrangements of Emperor Charles V. to establish a truce or interval of peace between the Protestant and the Roman Catholic parties of Germany in the sixteenth century.

in-tē′ri-ŏr, *a.* [L. *interior*, inner, comp., from *inter*, between, within.]

1. Internal; being within; opposed to *exterior*; as, the *interior* ornaments; the *interior* surface of a hollow ball; the *interior* parts of the earth.

> Aiming, belike, at your *interior* hatred,
> That in your outward action shows itself.
> —Shak.

2. Inland; at some distance from the limits; as, the *interior* parts of a country, state, or kingdom.

Interior angles; see *Internal angles* under *Angle.*

Interior planets; in astronomy, the planets between the earth's orbit and the sun; also called *inferior planets.*

Interior screw; a screw cut on the interior surface of anything hollow, as a nut or tap-hole.

in-tē′ri-ŏr, *n.* 1. The internal part of a thing; the inside.

2. The inland part of a country.

3. The name given in some countries, as the United States, to the department of government having charge of home affairs; the home department; as, the secretary of the *Interior.*

Department of the Interior; see *Department*, 4.

in-tē-ri-or′i-ty, *n.* The condition or state of being interior or inside.

in-tē′ri-ŏr-ly, *adv.* Internally; inwardly; on the inside.

in-tẽr-jā′cence, in-tẽr-jā′cen-cy, *n.* A lying between; a being between; intervention; as, the *interjacency* of the Mississippi between Illinois and Iowa.

in-tẽr-jā′cent, *a.* [L. *interjacens* (*-entis*), ppr. of *interjacere*, to lie between; *inter*, between, and *jacere*, to lie.] Lying or being between; intervening; as, *interjacent* islands.

in-tẽr-jaç′ū-lāte, *v.t.* To ejaculate so as to interrupt conversation.

in-tẽr-jan′gle, *v.i.*; interjangled, *pt.*, *pp.*; interjangling, *ppr.* To make a dissonant, harsh noise one with another.

in-tẽr-ject′, *v.t.*; interjected, *pt.*, *pp.*; interjecting, *ppr.* [L. *interjectus*, pp. of *interjicere*, *interjacere*, to throw between; *inter*, between, and *jacere*, to throw.] To throw between; to throw in between other things; to insert; as, to *interject* a remark.

in-tẽr-ject′, *v.i.* To interpose; to come between or among. [Rare.]

in-tẽr-jec′tion, *n.* [L. *interjectio* (*-onis*), a throwing or placing between, interjection, from *interjicere*, to interject.]

1. The act of throwing between.

2. A word, in speaking or writing, thrown in between words connected in construction, to express some emotion or passion, as exclamations of joy, grief, astonishment, etc.; as, those were delightful days, but, *alas*, they are no more.

in-tẽr-jec′tion-ăl, *a.* Thrown in between other words or phrases; as, an *interjectional* remark.

in-tẽr-jec′tion-ăl-īze, *v.t.* To introduce or use as an interjection. [Rare.]

in-tẽr-jec′tion-ăl-ly, *adv.* In an interjectional manner; as an interjection.

in-tẽr-jec′tion-ā-ry, *a.* Same as *Interjectional.*

in-tẽr-join′, *v.t.* To join mutually; to unite. [Rare.]

in′tẽr-joist, *n.* In carpentry, (a) the space or interval between two joists; (b) a heavy middle joist or crossbeam.

in-tẽr-junc′tion, *n.* A mutual joining together.

in-tẽr-knit′ (-nit′), *v.t.*; interknitted *or* interknit, *pt.*, *pp.*; interknitting, *ppr.* To knit together; to join closely.

in-tẽr-knōw′ (-nō′), *v.t.* To know mutually. [Obs.]

in-tẽr-knowl′edge (-nol′ej), *n.* Mutual knowledge. [Obs.]

in-tẽr-lāce′, *v.t.*; interlaced (-lāst), *pt.*, *pp.*; interlacing, *ppr.* To intermix; to put or insert, as one thing within another; to interweave.

in-tẽr-lāce′, *v.i.* To become entangled or interwoven; to intertwine; as, ornamentations that *interlace.*

Interlacing arches; in architecture, arches so joined that they seem to interlace.

Interlacing Arches, Norwich Cathedral.

in-tẽr-lāce′ment, *n.* 1. The act of intermixture or insertion within.

2. An interlacing; that which is interlaced.

in-tẽr-lam′el-lăr, in-tẽr-lam′i-năr, *a.* In anatomy, placed between lamellæ or laminæ.

in-tẽr-lam′i-nā-ted, *a.* Placed between or containing laminæ or plates; inclosed by laminæ.

in-tẽr-lam-i-nā′tion, *n.* The condition of being interlaminated.

in′tẽr-lapse, *n.* The lapse or flow of time between two events. [Rare.]

in-tẽr-lärd′, *v.t.*; interlarded, *pt.*, *pp.*; interlarding, *ppr.* 1. To mix, as fat with lean. [Obs.]

2. To mix; to diversify by mixture; to insert between; to interpolate; as, to *interlard* an address with invectives.

in-tẽr-lāy′, *v.t.*; interlaid, *pt.*, *pp.*; interlaying, *ppr.* To lay between or among.

in′tẽr-lēaf, *n.*; *pl.* **in′tẽr-lēaves.** A leaf inserted between other leaves of a book; a blank leaf inserted.

in-tẽr-lēave′, *v.t.*; interleaved, *pt.*, *pp.*; interleaving, *ppr.* To insert a leaf in; to insert a blank leaf or blank leaves in or between, as in a book.

in-tẽr-lēaved′, *a.* 1. Inserted between leaves, or having blank leaves inserted between other leaves.

2. In geology, interbedded.

in-tẽr-lī′bel, *v.t.* To libel reciprocally.

in-tẽr-line′, *v.t.*; interlined, *pt.*, *pp.*; interlining, *ppr.* 1. To write in alternate lines; as, to *interline* Latin and English.

2. To insert between lines already written or printed, for the purpose of adding to or correcting what is written.

in-tẽr-lin′ē-ăl, *a.* Between lines.

in-tẽr-lin′ē-ăr, *a.* [LL. *interlinearis*; L. *inter*, between, and *linea*, a line.] Placed between lines previously written or printed; having interpolated lines.

in-tẽr-lin′ē-ăr-ly, *adv.* In an interlinear manner; by interlineation.

in-tẽr-lin′ē-ā-ry, *n.* and *a.* I. *n.* A book having insertions between the lines. [Rare.]

II. *a.* Interlinear.

in-tẽr-lin-ē-ā′tion, *n.* 1. The act of inserting words or lines between lines previously written or printed.

2. The words, passage, or line inserted between lines previously written or printed.

in-tẽr-lin′ing, *n.* 1. Correction or alteration by writing between the lines.

2. An intermediate lining, as of a garment.

in-tẽr-link′, *v.t.*; interlinked (-linkt), *pt.*, *pp.*; interlinking, *ppr.* To connect by uniting links; to join mutually by a link.

in′tẽr-link, *n.* An intermediate link.

in-tẽr-lō′bāte, *a.* In geology, located between or adjacent to mounds of glacial deposit.

in-tẽr-lob′ū-lăr, *a.* In anatomy, lying between lobes or between lobules, as in a gland.

in″tẽr-lō-cā′tion, *n.* A placing between; interposition.

in-tẽr-lock′, *v.t.*; interlocked, *pt.*, *pp.*; interlocking, *ppr.* To join together by reciprocal action; to clasp together; as, to *interlock* hands in walking.

in-tẽr-lock′, *v.i.* To embrace, communicate with, or flow into one another; to interlace firmly.

Interlocking system of signals; in operating railroad trains, a system by which the setting of a required signal is secured by a mechanism which locks all the switches in the system, leaving open the one indicated by the signal.

in′tẽr-lock, *n.* The condition of being interlocked; as, their hands lingered in loving *interlock.*

in″tẽr-lō-cū′tion, *n.* [L. *interlocutio* (*-onis*), from *interloqui*, to speak between, interrupt; *inter*, between, and *loqui*, to speak.]

1. Dialogue; conference; interchange of speech.

2. In law, an intermediate act or decree before final decision; an intermediate argument.

in-tẽr-loc′ū-tŏr, *n.* 1. One who speaks in dialogue or takes part in a conversation.

2. In Scots law, an interlocutory judgment or sentence.

3. A propounder of questions; specifically, the middleman in negro minstrelsy.

in-tẽr-loc′ū-tō-ry, *a.* 1. Consisting of dialogue; having the nature of dialogue.

2. In law, intermediate; not final or definitive.

in-tẽr-loc′ū-tō-ry, *n.* Something interpolated in a discussion or conversation.

in-tẽr-loc′ū-tress, in-tẽr-loc′ū-trice, *n.* A female interlocutor.

in-tẽr-lōpe′, *v.i.*; interloped (-lōpt), *pt.*, *pp.*; interloping, *ppr.* 1. To run between parties and intercept the advantage that one should gain from the other; to traffic without a proper license; to forestall.

2. To intrude where one has no business or right.

in′tẽr-lō-pẽr, *n.* [D. *enterlooper*, a coasting-vessel, smuggler; Fr. *entre*, between, and D. *loopen*, to run.] One who interlopes; an intruder.

in-tẽr-lū′cāte, *v.t.* To let light through, as by cutting away branches of trees. [Obs.]

in″tẽr-lū-cā′tion, *n.* The act of thinning a wood to let in light. [Obs.]

in-tẽr-lū′cent, *a.* [L. *interlucens* (*-entis*), ppr. of *interlucere*, to shine between; *inter*, between, and *lucere*, to shine, from *lux*, light.] Shining between.

in′tẽr-lūde, *n.* [OFr. *entrelude*; LL. *interludium*; L. *inter*, between, and *ludus*, play.]

1. A short entertainment exhibited on the stage between the acts of a play, or between the play and the afterpiece.

2. The first name given to regular dramatic compositions in England, from the time they superseded the miracle and mystery plays till the period of the Elizabethan drama.

3. In music, a short instrumental piece played between the stanzas of a song or hymn or between the acts of a drama.

in′tẽr-lū-ded, *a.* Inserted or made as an interlude.

in′tẽr-lū-dẽr, *n.* One who performs in an interlude.

in-tẽr-lū′en-cy, *n.* [L. *interluens* (*-entis*), ppr. of *interluere*, to flow between; *inter*, between, and *luere*, to wash.] A flowing between; water interposed. [Rare.]

in-tẽr-lū′năr, in-tẽr-lū′nȧ-ry, *a.* [L. *inter*, between, and *luna*, moon.] Belonging to the time when the moon, at or near its conjunction with the sun, is invisible.

in″tẽr-man-dib′ū-lăr, *a.* In anatomy, situated between the mandibles or rami of the lower jaw.

in-tẽr-mar′riage (-rij), *n.* Marriage between those of two families, nations, tribes, etc.

in-tẽr-mar′ry, *v.i.*; intermarried, *pt.*, *pp.*; intermarrying, *ppr.* To become connected by marriage, as two families, ranks, tribes, or the like.

in″tẽr-max-il′lȧ, *n.*; *pl.* **in″tẽr-max-il′læ.** In anatomy, the anterior part of the upper jawbone; the premaxilla.

in-tẽr-max′il-lā-ry, *a.* and *n.* I. *a.* Situated between the upper jawbones.

II. *n.* Same as *Intermaxilla.*

in′tẽr-mēan, *n.* Interact; something done in the meantime. [Obs.]

in″tẽr-mē-ā′tion, *n.* [L. *intermeare*, to pass through or between.] A flowing between. [Obs.]

in-tẽr-med′dle, *v.i.*; intermeddled, *pt.*, *pp.*; intermeddling, *ppr.* To meddle in the affairs of others, in which one has no concern; to meddle officiously; to interpose or interfere improperly; to intermix.

in-tẽr-med′dle, *v.t.* To mix together; to cause to mingle. [Obs.]

in-tẽr-med′dlẽr, *n.* One who interposes officiously; one who meddles or intrudes into business in which he has no right.

in-tẽr-med′dle-sŏme, *a.* Prone to intermeddle; meddlesome.

in-tẽr-med′dle-sŏme-ness, *n.* The quality of being intermeddlesome.

in-tẽr-med′dling, *n.* Officious interposition.

in-tẽr-mēde′, *n.* [Fr., from L. *inter*, between, and *medius*, middle.] An interlude; a short musical dramatic piece, usually of a burlesque character; called also *intermezzo.*

in-tẽr-mē′di-ā-cy, *n.* The condition of being intermediate; interposition; intervention.

in-tẽr-mē′di-æ, *n.pl.* [F. pl. of L. *intermedius*, intermedial.] In ornithology, the middle pair of quill-feathers in the tail of a bird.

in-tẽr-mē′di-ăl, *a.* [L. *intermedius*; *inter*, between, and *medius*, middle.] Lying between; intervening; intervenient.

in-tẽr-mē′di-ăn, *a.* Intermediate.

in-tẽr-mē′di-ā-ry, *a.* and *n.* I. *a.* Lying between; as, an *intermediary* project; intermediate.

II. *n.* Something that intervenes; an interagent.

in-tẽr-mē′di-āte, *a.* [LL. *intermediatus*, pp. of *intermediare*, to come between, from L. *intermedius*, that is between; *inter*, between, and *medius*, middle.] Lying or being in the middle place or degree between two extremes; intervening; interposed; as, an *intermediate* space between hills or rivers; *intermediate* colors.

Intermediate state; in theology, the condition of disembodied spirits between death and the day of judgment.

Intermediate terms; in mathematics, the terms of a progression or proportion between the first and last, which are called the extremes; thus in the proportion 2:4::6:12, four and six are the intermediate terms.

Syn.—Intervening, included, interposed, comprised, middle, moderate, interjacent.

in-tēr-mē′di-āte, *v.i.* To intermeddle; to intervene.

in-tēr-mē′di-āte-ly, *adv.* By way of intervention.

in-tēr-mē-di-ā′tion, *n.* Intervention; the act of intermediating.

in-tēr-mē-di-ā′tŏr, *n.* One who mediates.

in-tēr-mē′di-ous, *a.* Intermediate. [Rare.]

in-tēr-mē′di-um, *n.*; *pl.* **in-tēr-mē′di-ȧ.** [L. *intermedium*, neut. of *intermedius*, that is between; *inter*, between, and *medius*, middle.]

1. Intermediate space. [Rare.]

2. An intervening agent.

3. In anatomy and zoölogy, a median carpal or tarsal bone in some of the lower animals, corresponding nearly to the lunar and the astragalus in mammals.

in-tēr-mell′, *v.t.* and *v.i.* [OFr. *entremeller*, *entremesler*, to intermix.] To intermix or intermeddle. [Obs.]

in-tēr-mem′brăl, *a.* In anatomy, designating relations between the members or limbs; as, *intermembral* similarities or *intermembral* dissimilarities.

in-tēr′ment, *n.* [ME. *enterment*; OFr. *enterrement*; LL. *interramentum*, burial, from *interrare*, to put in the earth; L. *in*, in, and *terra*, earth.] The act of depositing a dead body in the earth; burial; sepulture.

in-tēr-men′tion, *v.t.* To mention among other things; to include. [Obs.]

in-tēr-meṣ-en-ter′iç, *a.* In biology, between the layers of the mesentery or between mesenteries; as, *intermesenteric* spaces.

in-tēr-met-ȧ-cär′păl, *a.* In anatomy, situated between bones of the metacarpus.

in-tēr-met-ȧ-tär′săl, *a.* In anatomy, situated between bones of the metatarsus.

in-tēr-mew′ (-mū′), *v.i.* [*Inter-*, and OFr. *muer*, from L. *mutare*, to change.] In falconry, to shed the feathers while confined.

in-tēr-mez′zō (-med′), *n.* See *Intermede.*

in-tēr-mi′çāte, *v.i.* [L. *intermicatus*, pp. of *intermicare*; *inter*, between, and *micare*, to gleam, glitter.] To shine or glitter between or in the midst of something, as light through foliage. [Rare.]

in-tēr-mi-çā′tion, *n.* A shining between or among. [Rare.]

in-tēr-mi-grā′tion, *n.* Reciprocal migration; removal from one country to another by men or tribes which take the place each of the other. [Rare.]

in-tēr′mi-nȧ-ble, *a.* Boundless; endless; admitting no limit; as, *interminable* space or duration; *interminable* sufferings.

in-tēr′mi-nȧ-ble-ness, *n.* The state of being endless.

in-tēr′mi-nāte, *a.* [L. *interminatus*; *in-* priv., and *terminatus*, pp. of *terminare*, to bound.] Unbounded; unlimited; endless; as, *interminate* sleep.

in-tēr′mi-nāte, *v.t.* To menace. [Obs.]

in-tēr′mi-nā-ted, *a.* Without end. [Obs.]

in″tēr-mi-nā′tion, *n.* [L. *interminatus*, pp. of *interminari*, to threaten; *inter*, between, and *minari*, to threaten.] A menace or threat. [Obs.]

in-tēr-mine′, *v.t.* To cut through or across with mines. [Obs.]

in-tēr-min′gle, *v.t.*; intermingled, *pt.*, *pp.*; intermingling, *ppr.* To mingle or mix together; to put together indiscriminately.

in-tēr-min′gle, *v.i.* To be mixed or incorporated.

in′tēr-miṣe, *n.* Interference; interruption; intervention. [Obs.]

in-tēr-mis′sion (-mish′un), *n.* [L. *intermissio* (*-onis*), a breaking off, interruption, from *intermissus*, pp. of *intermittere*, to interrupt, discontinue; *inter*, between, and *mittere*, to send.]

1. Cessation for a time; pause; intermediate stop; as, to labor without *intermission*.

2. Intervenient time.

3. Temporary cessation or subsidence, as of a fever; the space of time between the paroxysms of a disease.

4. The state of being neglected; disuse, as of words. [Obs.]

Syn.—Interlude, interruption, recess, cessation.

in-tēr-mis′sive, *a.* Coming by fits, or after temporary cessations; not continual.

in-tēr-mit′, *v.t.*; intermitted, *pt.*, *pp.*; intermitting, *ppr.* [L. *intermittere*, to interrupt, discontinue; *inter*, between, and *mittere*, to send.] To cause to cease for a time; to interrupt; to suspend.

Syn.—Abate, suspend, discontinue.

in-tēr-mit′, *v.i.* To cease for a time; to go away at intervals, as a fever.

in-tēr-mit′tent, *n.* A disease which entirely subsides or ceases at certain intervals, as in fever and ague.

in-tēr-mit′tent, *a.* Ceasing at intervals; as, an *intermittent* fever.

Intermittent current; in electricity, a current flowing and ceasing to flow at intervals, thus resulting in the alternate presence and absence of electricity from a circuit.

Intermittent fever; in medicine, a fever characterized by more or less regular abatement and recurrence, as malarial fevers, of which ague is a type.

Intermittent gearing; in machinery, a device which receives and imparts motion intermittently.

Intermittent spring; a spring that flows intermittently because supplied from an elevated source with which it has a siphon-like connection.

in-tēr-mit′tent-ly, in-tēr-mit′ting-ly, *adv.* With intermissions; at intervals.

in-tēr-mix′, *v.t.*; intermixed (-mixt′), *pt.*, *pp.*; intermixing, *ppr.* To mix together; to put together so as to intermingle.

in-tēr-mix′, *v.i.* To be mixed together; to be intermingled.

in-tēr-mix′ed-ly, *adv.* In a mixed or intermingled way.

in-tēr-mix′tūre, *n.* 1. A mass formed by mixture; a mass of ingredients mixed.

2. Admixture; something additional mingled in a mass.

In this height of impiety there wanted not an *intermixture* of levity and folly. —Bacon.

in″tēr-mō-bil′i-ty, *n.* The quality of being capable of moving among each other, as the particles of fluids.

in″tēr-mō-dil′liŏn (-yun), *n.* In architecture, the space between two modillions.

in″tēr-mō-leg′ū-lăr, *a.* Designating or relating to the spaces or areas existing between and among molecules.

in-tēr-mon′tāne, *a.* [L. *inter*, between, and *mons*, *montis*, a mountain.] Between mountains; as, *intermontane* soil.

in-tēr-mun′dāne, *a.* [L. *inter*, between, and *mundus*, world.] Being between worlds, or between orb and orb.

in-tēr-mun′di-ăn, *a.* Intermundane.

in-tēr-mū′răl, *a.* [L. *intermuralis*; *inter*, between, and *murus*, wall.] Lying between walls.

in-tēr-mūre′, *v.t.* To surround with walls; to wall in. [Obs.]

in-tēr-mus′cū-lăr, *a.* Between the muscles.

in-tēr-mū-tā′tion, *n.* [LL. *intermutare*, to interchange; L. *inter*, between, and *mutare*, to change.] Interchange; mutual or reciprocal change.

in-tēr-mū′tū-ăl, *a.* Mutual. [Obs.]

in-tēr-mū′tū-ăl-ly, *adv.* Mutually. [Obs.]

in-tērn′, *a.* [Fr. *interne*; L. *internus*, inward, internal.] Internal. [Rare.]

in-tērn′, *n.* [Fr. *interne*, from L. *internus*, inward, internal.] An inmate; especially, a resident hospital physician who takes the place of the attending physician in his absence.

in-tērn′, *v.t.* To confine within a particular place; especially, to cause to remain in an interior place, without permission to leave it, as a body of troops.

in-tēr′năl, *a.* [L. *internus*, within, inward, from *inter*, between, from *in*, in, within.]

1. Inward; interior; being within any limit or surface; not external; as, the *internal* parts of a body, of a bone, of the earth, etc.

2. Pertaining to the mind or thoughts; pertaining to one's inner being.

3. Intrinsic; real. [Rare.]

4. Belonging to itself or its own affairs or interests; said of a country; domestic; opposed to *foreign*; as, *internal* trade; *internal* troubles or dissensions; *internal* war.

5. Derived from or dependent on the object itself; inherent; as, *internal* forces; *internal* evidence.

6. In anatomy, situated within or on the inside; situated near the mesial plane.

Internal angles; see under *Angle.*

Internal gear; in machinery, a wheel whose cogs are on the internal perimeter.

Internal revenue; see under *Revenue.*

Internal work; see under *Work.*

in-tēr-nal′i-ty, *n.* The quality or state of being internal; interiority; inwardness.

in-tēr′năl-ly, *adv.* 1. Inwardly; within; in or at the interior; beneath the surface.

2. Mentally; intellectually; spiritually.

3. Respecting internal affairs.

in-tēr-nā′ṣăl, *a.* In anatomy, situated between the nasal passages.

in-tēr-na′tion-ăl (-nash′un-), *a.* 1. Pertaining to or mutually affecting two or more nations; regulating the mutual intercourse between different nations; as, *international* law; *international* relations.

2. [I—] Of or pertaining to the society called the International.

International code; in nautical parlance, a common system of maritime signaling by means of flags and balls, now adopted by commercial nations generally, in order to facilitate communication between vessels at sea or between vessels at sea and stations on shore.

International copyright; see under *Copyright.*

International law; the law of nations; those maxims or rules which independent political societies or states observe, or ought to observe, in their conduct toward one another. International law embraces the principles that should regulate the conduct of states toward each other, the principles that should regulate the rights and obligations of private parties, arising out of the conduct of states to each other, and the principles that should regulate the rights and obligations of private parties when they are affected by the separate internal codes of distinct nations.

Private international law; international law which deals with the private relations and rights of persons of different nationalities.

In-tēr-na′tion-ăl, *n.* 1. The recognized contraction for a society of which the full title was the International Workingmen's Association, founded in London in 1864 for the purpose of advancing the interests of the working classes of all nations.

2. A member of this association.

in-tēr-na′tion-ăl-iṣm, *n.* 1. The principles, doctrine, or theory advocated by the Internationalists.

2. [i—] The principles of international rights and interests.

in-tēr-na′tion-ăl-ist, *n.* 1. One who advocates or upholds the principles of international law.

2. [I—] A member of the International, or an advocate of its principles.

in-tēr-na′tion-ăl-ize, *v.t.*; internationalized, *pt.*, *pp.*; internationalizing, *ppr.* To make international; to cause to affect the mutual relations of two or more countries; as, to *internationalize* a war.

in-tēr-na′tion-ăl-ly, *adv.* In an international manner; so as to affect the mutual relations or interests of nations; from an international point of view.

in-tērne′, *n.* Same as *Intern.*

in-tēr-nē′ciā-ry (-shȧ-), *a.* Internecine. [Rare.]

in-tēr-nec′i-năl, *a.* Internecine. [Rare.]

in-tēr-nē′cine, *a.* [L. *internecinus*, for *internecivus*, deadly, murderous, from *internecare*, to kill, destroy; *inter*, between, and *necare*, to kill.] Mutually destructive; deadly; accompanied with much slaughter.

in-tēr-nē′cion, *n.* [L. *internecare*, to kill, slaughter.] Mutual slaughter or destruction. [Obs.]

in-tēr-nē′cive, *a.* Internecine. [Rare.]

in-tēr-neç′tion, *n.* Mutual connection. [Obs.]

in-tēr-neū′răl, *a.* In anatomy, situated between the neural processes or spines.

in-tēr-neū′răl, *n.* An interneural process.

in-tēr′ni-ty, *n.* [L. *internus*, inner, internal.] The state of being internal. [Rare.]

in-tērn′ment, *n.* The state of being interned, or confined in a particular locality.

in-tēr-nō′dăl, *a.* 1. Intervening between nodes or joints.

2. In botany, of or pertaining to an internode; pertaining to or characterizing the intermediate space of a stem or branch between the nodes.

in′tēr-nōde, *n.* [L. *internodium*; *inter*, between, and *nodus*, a knot, joint.]

1. In botany, the space between two nodes or points of the stem from which the leaves arise.

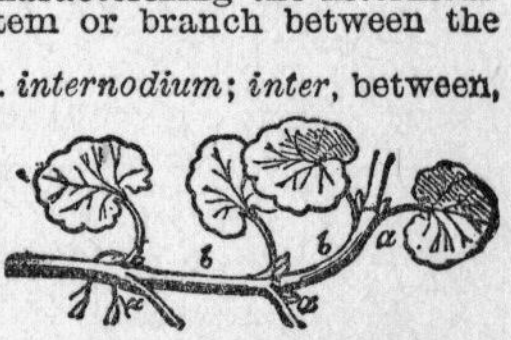

a, Nodes or joints. *b*, Internodes.

2. In anatomy, a part between two nodes or joints; especially, a phalanx.

in-tēr-nō′di-ăl, *a.* Internodal. [Rare.]

in-tēr-nō′di-um, *n.* In anatomy, an internode; a phalanx.

in-tēr-nō-mē′di-ăl, *a.* Internomedian.

in-tēr-nō-mē′di-ăn, *a.* [L. *internus*, inward, internal, and *medianus*, middle.] In entomology, situated between the median and internal vein.

in′tēr nōs. [L.] Between ourselves.

in-tēr-nun′ciăl (-shăl), *a.* 1. Of or belonging to an internuncio or his office.

2. In physiology, pertaining to, resembling, or possessing the function of the nervous system as communicating between different parts of the body.

in-tēr-nun′ciess (-shes), *n.* A female messenger. [Rare.]

in-tēr-nun′ci-ō (-shi-), *n.* [It. *internuncio*; L. *internuncius*, *internuntius*, a messenger between two parties; *inter*, between, and *nuncius*, *nuntius*, a messenger.]

1. A messenger between two parties. [Rare.]

2. An envoy of the pope, sent to small states

and republics, distinguished from the nuncio who represents the pope at the courts of emperors, kings, etc.

in-tẽr-nun′ci-ō-ship, *n.* The rank or office of an internuncio.

in-tẽr-nun′ci-us, *n.* Same as *Internuncio.*

in-tẽr-ō-cē-an′iç (-shi-), *a.* Between oceans; uniting oceans; as, an *interoceanic* railroad or canal.

in-tẽr-oç′ū-lăr, *a.* Situated between the eyes, as the antennæ of some insects.

in″tẽr-ō-pẽr′çle, *n.* See *Interoperculum.*

in″tẽr-ō-pẽr′çū-lăr, *a.* and *n.* I. *a.* Pertaining to an interoperculum.

II. *n.* See *Interoperculum.*

in″tẽr-ō-pẽr′çū-lum, *n.*; *pl.* **in-tẽr-ō-pẽr′çū-lȧ.** [L. *inter*, between, and *operculum*, a cover, lid.] One of the four parts of the gill-cover of fishes. It lies behind the angle of the jaw, below the preoperculum.

in-tẽr-op′tiç, *a.* [L. *inter*, between, and Gr. *optikos*, optic.] In herpetology, applied to a lobe of the brain between the optic lobes.

in-tẽr-ọr′bit-ăl, *a.* Situated between the orbits of the eyes.

in-tẽr-os′çū-lănt, *a.* [L. *inter*, between, and *osculans* (*-antis*), ppr. of *osculari*, to kiss.] Connecting two objects or classes; applied to a variety connecting two species, a species two genera, a genus two families, etc.

in-tẽr-os′çū-lāte, *v.i.*; interosculated, *pt.*, *pp.*; interosculating, *ppr.* To connect two different objects or classes; to be interosculant.

in-tẽr-os-çū-lā′tion, *n.* The act of interosculating or the state of being interosculant.

in-tẽr-os′sē-ăl, *a.* Interosseous.

in-tẽr-os′sē-ous, *a.* [L. *inter*, between, and *os*, *ossis*, a bone.] Situated between bones; as, an *interosseous* ligament.

in-tẽr-pāle′, *v.t.* 1. To place pales between; to divide by means of pales.

2. To interlace. [Rare.]

in′tẽr-pȧ-rī′ē-tăl, *a.* and *n.* I. *a.* In anatomy, situated between the parietal bones.

II. *n.* An interparietal bone or cartilage.

in′tẽr-pąuṣe, *n.* A stop or pause between; a temporary cessation. [Rare.]

in-tẽr-pēal′, *v.t.* [Obs.] See *Interpel.*

in″tẽr-pē-dun′çū-lăr, *a.* In anatomy, situated between the cerebral or cerebellar peduncles.

in-tẽr-pel′, *v.t.* [L. *interpellare*, to interrupt.] To interfere with; to intercede with; to break in upon. [Obs.]

in-tẽr-pel′lănt, *a.* and *n.* I. *a.* Causing interruption.

II. *n.* One who interrupts.

in-tẽr-pel′lāte, *v.t.*; interpellated, *pt.*, *pp.*; interpellating, *ppr.* [L. *interpellatus*, pp. of *interpellare*, to interrupt in speaking; *inter*, between, and *pellere*, to drive, urge.] To question; to address a question to; especially, to question publicly and formally; used originally in connection with legislative proceedings in France; as, to *interpellate* the minister of finance.

in″tẽr-pel-lā′tion, *n.* 1. The act of interrupting or interfering; interruption.

2. The act of interposing; interposition; intercession.

3. A summons; a citation.

4. A question put by a member of a legislative assembly to a minister or member of the government.

in-tẽr-pen′ē-trāte, *v.t.*; interpenetrated, *pt.*, *pp.*; interpenetrating, *ppr.* To penetrate between; to penetrate mutually so as to effect a union.

in-tẽr-pen′ē-trāte, *v.i.* To penetrate between or within bodies; to penetrate mutually.

in-tẽr-pen-ē-trā′tion, *n.* The act of interpenetrating; the act of penetrating between or within bodies; interior or mutual penetration; in architecture, a scheme of continuous moldings.

in-tẽr-pen′ē-trā-tive, *a.* Penetrating between or within other bodies; mutually penetrative.

in-tẽr-pet′ăl-ā-ry, *a.* In botany, between petals.

in-tẽr-pet′i-ō-lăr, *a.* Being between petioles.

in″tẽr-phȧ-lan′ġē-ăl, *a.* In anatomy, situated between two successive phalanges of a finger or toe.

in′tẽr-pi-las″tẽr, *n.* In architecture, the interval between two pilasters.

in-tẽr-plāce′, *v.t.* To place between or among. [Rare.]

in-tẽr-plan′et-ā-ry, *a.* Situated or existing between the planets; as, *interplanetary* space.

in′tẽr-plāy, *n.* Reciprocal action or influence.

in-tẽr-plēad′, *v.i.* In law, to plead or discuss a point incidental to a cause before the principal cause is tried.

in-tẽr-plēad′ẽr, *n.* 1. One who interpleads.

2. In law, the discussion or pleading of a point incidentally happening, as it were, between, or in the middle of a case, before the principal cause is determined. Interpleader is allowed that the defendant may not be charged to two severally where no fault is in him, as, where one party brings detinue against the defendant upon a bailment of goods, and another against him upon trover, there shall be interpleader to ascertain who has right to his action.

in-tẽr-pledġe′, *v.t.* To give and take as a mutual pledge. [Rare.]

in-tẽr-point′, *v.t.* To point; to distinguish by stops or marks; to punctuate. [Rare.]

in-tẽr′pō-lȧ-ble, *a.* Capable of being interpolated or inserted; suitable for interpolation.

in-tẽr′pō-lā-ry, *a.* In mathematics, pertaining to interpolation.

in-tẽr′pō-lāte, *v.t.*; interpolated, *pt.*, *pp.*; interpolating, *ppr.* [L. *interpolatus*, pp. of *interpolare*, to polish, dress up, corrupt, from *interpolis*, altered by furbishing, repaired; *inter*, between, and *polire*, to polish.]

1. To carry on with intermissions; to interrupt or discontinue for a time. [Obs.]

2. To foist in; to insert, as a spurious word or passage in a document or book; to add a spurious word or passage to.

3. To alter or corrupt by the insertion or introduction of foreign matter; especially, to corrupt or vitiate, as a book or text, by the interpolation of words or passages spurious or foreign to the subject.

4. In mathematics and physics, to introduce, in order to complete a partial series of numbers or observations (one or more intermediate terms), in accordance with the law of the series; to make the necessary interpolations in; as, to *interpolate* a number or a table of numbers.

5. To interpose; to place between.

in-tẽr-pō-lā′tion, *n.* [L. *interpolatio* (*-onis*), an alteration, furbishing, from *interpolare*, to alter, interpolate.]

1. The act of interpolating; the act of foisting a word or passage into a manuscript or book; the act of altering or vitiating by the insertion of new or foreign matter.

2. That which is interpolated; a spurious word or passage inserted in a text.

3. In mathematics and physics, the operation of finding terms between any two consecutive terms of a series, which shall conform to the law of the series.

in-tẽr′pō-lā-tŏr, *n.* [LL.] One who interpolates; one who foists into a book or manuscript spurious words or passages; one who, without authority, adds something to genuine writings.

in-tẽr-pōne′, *v.t.* [L. *interponere*; *inter*, between, and *ponere*, to set, place.] To set or insert between; to interpose. [Obs.]

in-tẽr-pō′nent, *n.* One who or that which interpones or interposes.

in-tẽr-pōr′tăl, *a.* Occurring or carried on between ports, especially ports of the same country; as, *interportal* trade.

in-tẽr-pōṣ′ăl, *n.* The act of interposing; interposition.

in-tẽr-pōṣe′, *v.t.*; interposed, *pt.*, *pp.*; interposing, *ppr.* [OFr. *interposer*; L. *interponere*; *inter*, between, and *ponere*, to place.]

1. To place between; as, to *interpose* a body between the eye and a light.

2. To place between or among; to thrust in; to intrude; to present, as an obstruction, interruption, or inconvenience, or for succor, relief, or the adjustment of differences; as, the emperor *interposed* his aid or services to reconcile the contending parties; to *interpose* a question.

in-tẽr-pōṣe′, *v.i.* 1. To step in between parties at variance, to mediate; as, the prince *interposed* and made peace.

2. To put in or make a remark by way of interruption.

3. To intervene; to stand or come between.

Syn.—Intermeddle, interfere, intercede, mediate, meddle, intervene.

in′tẽr-pōṣe, *n.* Interposal. [Obs.]

in-tẽr-pōṣ′ẽr, *n.* One who interposes or comes between others: a mediator or agent between parties.

in-tẽr-poṣ′it, *n.* [L. *interpositus*, from *interponere*, to place between; *inter*, between, and *ponere*, to place.] A place of deposit between one commercial city or country and another.

in-tẽr-pō-ṣi′tion (-zish′un), *n.* [L. *interpositio* (*-onis*), from *interponere*, to place or set between.]

1. A being, placing, or coming between; intervention.

2. Intervenient agency; agency between parties; mediation.

3. That which is interposed.

in-tẽr-pō′ṣūre (-zhūr), *n.* Interposition. [Obs.]

in-tẽr′pret, *v.t.*; interpreted, *pt.*, *pp.*; interpreting, *ppr.* [ME. *interpreten*; OFr. *interpreter*; L. *interpretari*, to explain, expound, from *interpres* (*-etis*), an agent between two parties, a broker, negotiator, interpreter.]

1. To explain the meaning of; to expound; to translate, as from an unknown or foreign language into one known; to explain or unfold the intent, meaning, or reasons of; to make clear; to free from obscurity or mystery; to make intelligible; to decipher; as, to *interpret* the French language to an American; to *interpret* a dream; to *interpret* a passage of Scripture.

2. To represent artistically; to portray or make clear by representation; as, an actor *interprets* a character in a drama; a musician *interprets* a piece of music.

3. To assume the meaning of; to explain to oneself; to construe; as, his statement was not correctly *interpreted.*

Syn.—Expound, explain, translate, decipher, construe, unravel, unfold, solve, elucidate.

in-tẽr′pret, *v.i.* To explain; to act as an interpreter; to make an interpretation.

in-tẽr′pret-ȧ-ble, *a.* Capable of being interpreted or explained.

in-tẽr′prē-tȧ-ment, *n.* Interpretation. [Obs.]

in-tẽr-prē-tā′tion, *n.* [L. *interpretatio* (*-onis*), an explanation, from *interpretari*, to explain, interpret.]

1. The act of interpreting, expounding, or explaining what is unintelligible, not understood, or not obvious; translation; explanation; exposition; as, the *interpretation* of a difficult passage in an author; the *interpretation* of dreams or prophecy.

Interpretation will misquote our looks.—Shak.

2. The sense given by an interpreter; exposition; construction; as, the remark admitted of many *interpretations.*

3. Artistic representation or rendering of a character or musical work according to one's idea of it.

Syn.—Construction, explanation, version, elucidation, translation, rendition, solution, exposition.

in-tẽr′prē-tā-tive, *a.* 1. Designed or fitted to explain; explaining; explanatory.

2. Constructive; inferential.

in-tẽr′prē-tā-tive-ly, *adv.* So as to interpret or give ground for interpretation; in an interpretative manner.

in-tẽr′pret-ẽr, *n.* [OFr. *interpreteur*; LL. *interpretator*, from L. *interpretari*, to explain, expound.] One who or that which interprets; one who explains or expounds; an expositor; a translator; especially, one who explains what a speaker says in a language not understood by the person addressed.

in-tẽr′prē-tive, *a.* Interpretative. [Rare.]

in-tẽr-pū′biç, *a.* In anatomy, situated between the pubic bones.

in-tẽr-punç′tion, *n.* [L. *interpunctio* (*-onis*), from *interpungere*, to place points between words; *inter*, between, and *pungere*, to point.] The placing of points between sentences or parts of a sentence; punctuation.

in-tẽr-rā′di-ăl, *a.* [L. *inter*, between, and *radius*, a ray.] Situated between the radii or rays.

in-tẽr-rā′di-ăl, *n.* A part situated between rays.

in-tẽr-rā′di-ăl-ly, *adv.* Between rays.

in-tẽr-rā′di-um, *n.*; *pl.* **in-tẽr-rā′di-ȧ.** An area between ambulacra.

in-tẽr-rā′di-us, *n.*, *pl.* **in-tẽr-rā′di-ī.** In zoology, an interradial process or part.

in-tẽr-rā′măl, *a.* [L. *inter*, between, and *ramus*, a branch.] In zoölogy, situated between the rami or branches of the lower jaw.

in-tẽr-ram′i-çọrn, *n.* [L. *inter*, between, and *ramus*, a branch, and *cornu*, a horn.] A horny part of the bill situated between the rami of the lower mandible of some birds.

in″tẽr-rē-cēive′, *v.t.* To receive between or within. [Rare.]

in-tẽr-rē′găl, *a.* Among kings. [Rare.]

in-tẽr-rē′gen-cy, *n.* An interregnum. [Obs.]

in-tẽr-rē′gent, *n.* One who governs during an interregnum; a regent.

in-tẽr-reg′num, *n.* [L. *interregnum*; *inter*, between, and *regnum*, reign, rule.]

1. The time during which a throne is vacant between the death or abdication of a ruler and the accession of his successor, or between the cessation of one government and the establishment of another.

2. Any period of abeyance.

in′tẽr-reign (-rān), *n.* [Fr. *interrègne*, from L. *interregnum*, an interregnum.] An interregnum. [Obs.]

in″tẽr-rē-lāte′, *v.t.* To cause to become reciprocally related. [Rare.]

in″tẽr-rē-lā′tion, *n.* Reciprocal relation.

in-tẽr-rē′năl, *a.* and *n.* [L. *inter*, between, and *renalis*, from *renes*, the kidneys.]

I. *a.* Located between the kidneys.

II. *n.* The interrenal body, an organ of certain fishes.

in″tẽr-rē-pel′lent, *a.* Mutually repellent. [Rare.]

in-tẽr′rẽr, *n.* One who inters or buries.

in′tẽr-rex, *n.*; *pl.* **in′tẽr-rex-eṣ** or **in-tẽr-rē′ġēṣ.** [L., from *inter*, between, and *rex*, *regis*, a king.] Among the Romans, a regent; a magistrate who governed during an interregnum.

in-ter′rō-gāte, *v.t.*; interrogated, *pt.*, *pp.*; interrogating, *ppr.* [L. *interrogatus*, pp. of *interrogare*, to question, ask; *inter*, between, and *rogare*, to ask.] To question; to examine

by asking questions; as, to *interrogate* a witness.
Syn.—Ask, examine, inquire of, question, interview.

in-ter′rō-gāte, *v.i.* To ask questions.

in-ter′rō-gāte, *n.* A question; an interrogation. [Obs.]

in-ter″rō-gā-tee′, *n.* One who is interrogated. [Rare.]

in-ter-rō-gā′tion, *n.* 1. The act of questioning; examination by questions.

2. A question put; an inquiry.

3. An interrogation-point.

in-ter-rō-gā′tion-point, *n.* A note, mark, or sign (?) indicating that the sentence immediately preceding it is a question. In Spanish, an interrogation-point is placed before as well as after a question, in the former position inverted.

in-tĕr-rog′ȧ-tive, *a.* [L. *interrogativus*, from *interrogare*, to question, ask, interrogate.] Denoting a question; expressed in the form of a question; as, an *interrogative* phrase or sentence; an *interrogative* sign.

in-tĕr-rog′ȧ-tive, *n.* In grammar, a word used in asking questions; as, *who? what? which? why?*

in-tĕr-rog′ȧ-tive-ly, *adv.* In the form of a question; in an interrogative manner.

in-ter′rō-gā-tŏr, *n.* One who interrogates or asks questions.

in-tĕr-rog′ȧ-tō-ry, *n.*; *pl.* **in-tĕr-rog′ȧ-tō-ries.** A question; an inquiry; a query; specifically, in law, a question asked in writing.

in-tĕr-rog′ȧ-tō-ry, *a.* [LL. *interrogatorius*, consisting of questions, from L. *interrogare*, to question, ask.] Containing a question; expressing a question; as, an *interrogatory* sentence.

in-tĕr-rupt′, *v.t.*; interrupted, *pt.*, *pp.*; interrupting, *ppr.* [L. *interruptus*, pp. of *interrumpere*, to break apart, break off; *inter*, between, and *rumpere*, to break.] To cause a break in; to stop or hinder by breaking in upon the course or progress of; to break the current or motion of; to cause a delay or intermission in; as, to *interrupt* a speaker by asking a question; to *interrupt* a conversation; the meeting was *interrupted* by frequent cheering.

> Do not *interrupt* me in my course. —Shak.

in-tĕr-rupt′, *a.* Irregular; interrupted. [Obs.]

in-tĕr-rupt′ed, *a.* 1. Broken; intermitted.

2. In botany, said of compound leaves, when the principal leaflets are divided by intervals of smaller ones; applied also to spikes of flowers, when the larger spikes are divided by a series of smaller ones.

in-tĕr-rupt′ed-ly, *adv.* With breaks or interruptions.

Interruptedly pinnate; see *Abruptly pinnate* under *Pinnate.*

in-tĕr-rupt′ĕr, *n.* One who or that which interrupts; specifically, in electricity, any device for interrupting or breaking an electrical circuit.

in-tĕr-rup′tion, *n.* [L. *interruptio (-onis)*, an interrupting, from *interruptus*, pp. of *interrumpere*, to break off, interrupt.]

1. The act of interrupting or breaking in upon.

2. The state of being interrupted; interposition.

3. Obstruction or hindrance caused by a breaking in upon any course, current, progress, or motion, stoppage; as, the author met with many *interruptions* in the execution of his work.

4. Cessation; intermission; interval.

> Amidst the *interruptions* of his sorrow. —Addison.

in-tĕr-rupt′ive, *a.* Tending to interrupt.

in-tĕr-rupt′ive-ly, *adv.* By interruption.

in-tĕr-scap′ū-lăr, *a.* [L. *inter*, between, and *scapulæ*, the shoulder-blades.]

1. Situated between the shoulder-blades.

2. In zoölogy, pertaining to the part between the scapulæ or shoulder-blades; as, an *interscapular* feather.

in-tĕr-scap′ū-lăr, *n.* In zoölogy, an interscapular feather.

in-tĕr-scap′ū-lā-ry, *a.* Interscapular.

in-tĕr-scap′ū-lum, *n.*; *pl.* **in-tĕr-scap′ū-lȧ.** In ornithology, the part of the back between the scapulæ.

in-tĕr-scend′ent, *a.* [L. *inter*, between, and *scandens (-entis)*, ppr. of *scandere*, to climb.] In algebra, having radicals as exponents; as, an *interscendent* expression.

in-tĕr-scind′, *v.t.* [L. *interscindere*, to cut off, separate; *inter*, between, and *scindere*, to cut.] To cut in two. [Obs.]

in-tĕr-scrībe′, *v.t.* To write between; to interline. [Obs.]

in-tĕr-sē′cant, *a.* Dividing into parts; crossing. [Rare.]

in-tĕr-sect′, *v.t.*; intersected, *pt.*, *pp.*; intersecting, *ppr.* [L. *intersectus*, pp. of *intersecare*, to cut between, cut off; *inter*, between, and *secare*, to cut.] To cut or cross mutually; to divide into parts; to cut into or between; as, the ecliptic *intersects* the equator.

in-tĕr-sect′, *v.i.* To meet and cross each other; to cut into each other; as, the point where two lines *intersect.*

in-tĕr-sec′tion, *n.* 1. The act or state of intersecting.

2. In geometry, the point or line in which a line or surface cuts another.

in-tĕr-sec′tion-ăl, *a.* Relating to or formed by an intersection or intersections.

in″tĕr-seg′men-tăl, *a.* In zoölogy, located between or uniting segments.

in-tĕr-sem′i-nāte, *v.t.* [L. *interseminatus*, pp. of *interseminare*; *inter*, between, and *seminare*, to sow.] To sow between or among. [Rare.]

in-tĕr-sep′tăl, *a.* Situated between septa or between pairs of septa.

in-tĕr-sĕrt′, *v.t.* [L. *intersertus*, pp. of *interserere*, to place between; *inter*, between, and *serere*, to join, weave.] To insert; to set or put in between other things. [Obs.]

in-tĕr-sĕr′tion, *n.* The act of interserting; anything interserted. [Obs.]

in-tĕr-set′, *v.t.* To set or put between. [Rare.]

in-tĕr-shock′, *v.t.* To shock mutually. [Rare.]

in″tĕr-si-dē′rē-ăl, *a.* Situated between or among the stars; interstellar.

in-tĕr-sō′ciăl (-shăl), *a.* Relating to intercourse or association; having mutual relations or intercourse; social.

in-tĕr-som′ni-ous, *a.* [L. *inter*, between, and *somnus*, sleep.] Occurring in an interval of wakefulness. [Rare.]

in′tĕr-spāce, *n.* An intervening space.

in-tĕr-spē-cif′ic, *a.* Between species.

in′tĕr-speech, *n.* A speech interposed between others. [Rare.]

in-tĕr-spĕrse′, *v.t.*; interspersed (-sperst′), *pt.*, *pp.*; interspersing, *ppr.* [L. *interspersus*, pp. of *interspergere*, to scatter between; *inter*, between, and *spargere*, to scatter.]

1. To scatter here and there among other things; as, to *intersperse* shrubs among trees.

2. To diversify by scattering or disposing various objects here and there.

in-tĕr-spĕr′sion, *n.* The act of interspersing, scattering, or placing here and there.

in-tĕr-spic′ū-lăr, *a.* Between or among spicules.

in-ter-spī′năl, *a.* In anatomy, lying between the processes of the spine, as muscles, nerves, etc.

in″tĕr-spi-nā′lis, *n.*; *pl.* **in″tĕr-spi-nā′lēs.** One of several muscles placed between the spinous processes of the contiguous vertebræ.

in-tĕr-spī′nous, *a.* Interspinal.

in″tĕr-spi-rā′tion, *n.* Inspiration between; occasional inspiration; a breathing-spell. [Obs.]

in″tĕr-stȧ-pē′di-ăl, *a.* and *n.* I. *a.* Between the stapes and the mediostapedial, as a columnlike part of the ear.

II. *n.* An interstapedial part.

in′tĕr-stāte, *a.* Existing or carried on between states; pertaining to the reciprocal relations of states; as, *interstate* trade.

Interstate Commerce Commission; see under *Commission.*

in-tĕr-stel′lăr, *a.* [L. *inter*, between, and *stella*, star.] Situated between or among the stars.

in-tĕr-stel′lȧ-ry, *a.* Interstellar.

in-tĕr-stĕr′năl, *a.* 1. In anatomy, situated between the sternal segments.

2. In zoölogy, situated between the sternites of an arthropodal animal.

in-tĕr′stice, *n.* [Fr. *interstice*, from L. *interstitium*, a space between; *inter*, between, and *sistere*, to set, from *stare*, to stand.]

1. A space which intervenes between one thing and another; especially, a narrow or small space between things close together, or between the component parts of a body; a chink; a crevice or cranny.

2. An interval of time; specifically, an interval which canon law in the Roman Catholic church requires between promotions from lower to higher degrees of orders.

in-tĕr′sticed (-stist), *a.* Having interstices or spaces between; situated at intervals.

in-tĕr-stinc′tive, *a.* Distinguishing. [Obs.]

in-tĕr-sti′tiăl (-stish′ul), *a.* [L. *interstitium*, a space between, and *-al*.]

1. Pertaining to or containing interstices; intermediate.

2. Situated between the tissues; occupying the interspaces or interstices of a part.

in-tĕr-sti′tion, *n.* A period of time; an interval. [Obs.]

in-tĕr-strat″i-fi-cā′tion, *n.* In geology, the state of being stratified between other strata; also, that which is so stratified.

in-tĕr-strat′i-fied, *a.* Stratified among or between other bodies.

in-tĕr-strat′i-fȳ, *v.t.*; interstratified, *pt.*, *pp.*; interstratifying, *ppr.* In geology, to cause to occupy a position among or between other strata.

in-tĕr-strat′i-fȳ, *v.i.* To assume a position between or among other strata.

in′tĕr-strēam, *a.* Between streams; as, an *interstream* range of hills.

in-tĕr-tạlk′ (-tạk′), *v.i.* To exchange conversation; to converse. [Obs.]

in-tĕr-tan′gle, *v.t.* To intertwist; to entangle.

in-tĕr-tär′săl, *a.* Situated or occurring between the tarsal bones.

in-tĕr-tĕr′găl, *a.* [L. *inter*, between, and *tergum*, back.] Situated between the terga or tergites of an arthropod.

in-tĕr-tex′, *v.t.* [L. *intertexere*, to interweave.] To interweave; to intertwine. [Obs.]

in-tĕr-tex′tūre, *n.* The act of interweaving, or the state of things interwoven; that which is interwoven.

in″tĕr-thō-rac′ic, *a.* Situated within the thorax.

in-tĕr-tid′ăl, *a.* Living between high-water mark and low-water mark, as the limpet.

in′tĕr-tie, *n.* A short piece of timber used in roofing, and in timber-framing generally, to bind upright posts together.

in-tĕr-tis′sūed (-tish′ūd), *a.* [Obs.] See *Entertissued.*

in-tĕr-traf′fic, *n.* Traffic between two or more persons or places; mutual trade.

in″tĕr-tran-spic′ū-ous, *a.* Transpicuous within or between. [Rare.]

in-tĕr-trans-vĕr-sā′lis, *n.*; *pl.* **in-tĕr-trans-vĕr-sā′lēs.** [L. *inter*, between, and *transversus*, transverse.] In anatomy, one of a number of short bundles of muscular fibers extending between the transverse processes of contiguous vertebræ.

in-tĕr-trans-vĕr-sā′ri-us, *n.*; *pl.* **in-tĕr-trans-vĕr-sā′ri-ī.** See *Intertransversalis.*

in″tĕr-trans-vĕrse′, *a.* In anatomy, connecting the transverse processes of contiguous vertebræ.

in″tĕr-trans-vĕr′sus, *n.*; *pl.* **in″tĕr-trans-vĕr′si.** See *Intertransversalis.*

in-tĕr-trīb′ăl, *a.* Existing or carried on between tribes; as, *intertribal* slavery.

in-tĕr-trī′gō, *n.* [L. *intertrigo*; *inter*, between, and *terere*, to rub.] In pathology, an eruption of the skin produced by friction of adjacent parts.

in-tĕr-trō-chan-ter′ic, *a.* In anatomy, situated between the trochanters.

in-tĕr-trop′ic-ăl, *a.* Situated between the tropics.

in-tĕr-tū′bū-lăr, *a.* Lying between tubes; as, the *intertubular* cells.

in-tĕr-twīne′, *v.t.*; intertwined, *pt.*, *pp.*; intertwining, *ppr.* To unite by twining or twisting one with another; to interlace.

in-tĕr-twīne′, *v.i.* To twine together; to be interwoven or interlaced.

in′tĕr-twīne, *n.* A mutual or reciprocal twining or winding. [Rare.]

in-tĕr-twin′ing-ly, *adv.* By intertwining or being intertwined.

in-tĕr-twist′, *v.t.*; intertwisted, *pt.*, *pp.*; intertwisting, *ppr.* To twist one with another; to twist together.

in-tĕr-twist′ing-ly, *adv.* By intertwisting or being intertwisted.

in-tĕr-un′gū-lăr, *a.* Located between ungulæ.

in-tĕr-un′gū-lāte, *a.* Interungular.

in-ter-ur′ban, *a.* [L. *inter*, between, and *urbs*, city.] Between cities, applied generally to rail ways.

in′tĕr-văl, *n.* [L. *intervallum*, a space between, pause, lit., space between two palisades, or walls; *inter*, between, and *vallum*, a palisade, wall.]

1. A space between things; a void space intervening between any two objects; as, an *interval* between two houses or walls.

2. Space of time between any two points or events, or between the return of like conditions; as, the *interval* between two wars; an *interval* in fever.

3. In music, the difference in pitch between two tones.

4. In logic, a proposition. [Rare.]

5. An intervale.

At intervals; from time to time; intermittently.

Augmented interval; in music, an interval lengthened by a semitone or half a step.

Syn.—Interim, gap, intermission, cessation.

in′tĕr-vāle, *n.* [A variant of *interval.*] A tract of low ground between hills or along the banks of rivers; also called *interval.* [Local, U. S.]

in-tĕr-val′lic, *a.* In music, pertaining to intervals.

in-tĕr-val′lum, *n.* An interval. [Obs.]

in-tĕr-vā′ry, *v.i.* To alter; to vary. [Obs.]

in-tĕr-vei̤ned′, *a.* Intersected with or as with veins.

in-tĕr-vēne′, *v.i.*; intervened, *pt.*, *pp.*; intervening, *ppr.* [L. *intervenire*, to come between; *inter*, between, and *venire*, to come.]

1. To come or be between persons or things; to be situated between places; as, hills *intervene* between two valleys.

2. To come or happen between points of time or events.

3. To interpose, as between parties at variance; as, he would have been injured had his brother not *intervened.*

4. In law, to interpose and become a party to a suit pending between other parties.

in-tẽr-vēne′, *v.t.* To divide; to come between. [Rare.]

in-tẽr-vēn′ẽr, *n.* One who intervenes; specifically, in law, a third person who intervenes in a suit to which he was not originally a party.

in-tẽr-vēn′ience (-yens), *n.* The act of coming between; interposition; intervention. [Rare.]

in-tẽr-vēn′ien-cy, *n.* Intervenience. [Rare.]

in-tẽr-vēn′ient, *a.* Coming or being between; intercedent; interposed. [Rare.]

in-tẽr-vē′ni-um, *n.* [L. *intervenium*, the space between veins; *inter*, between, and *vena*, a vein.] In botany, the space or area occupied by parenchyma between the veins of leaves.

in-tẽr-vent′, *v.t.* [L. *interventus*, pp. of *intervenire*, to come between; *inter*, between, and *venire*, to come.] To obstruct or thwart. [Obs.]

in-tẽr-vēn′tion, *n.* [L. *interventio (-onis)*, from *intervenire*, to come between; *inter*, between, and *venire*, to come.]

1. A state of coming or being between; interposition; as, light is not interrupted by the *intervention* of a transparent body.

2. Agency of persons between persons; interposition; mediation; any interference that may affect the interests of others; as, the *intervention* of a foreign power.

3. In law, the act by which a third party interposes and becomes a party to a suit pending between other parties.

4. In medicine, the act of interfering with the course of a disease for therapeutic purposes.

in-tẽr-ven′tion-ist, *n.* One who advocates or practises intervention in medicine.

in-tẽr-ven′tŏr, *n.* [L. *interventor*, one who comes in, a visitor (LL., an intercessor), from *interventus*, pp. of *intervenire*, to come between.] A mediator; a person anciently designated by a church to reconcile parties and unite them in the choice of officers.

in″tẽr-ven-tric′ū-lăr, *a.* Situated between the ventricles.

in-tẽr-ven′ūe, *n.* Interposition. [Obs.]

in-tẽr-ven′ū-lăr, *a.* [L. *inter*, between, and *vena*, a vein.] Lying between the veins of an insect's wing.

in-tẽr-vẽrt′, *v.t.* [L. *intervertere*, to turn aside.] To turn to another course or to another use. [Obs.]

in-tẽr-vẽr′tē-brăl, *a.* Being between the vertebræ.

in-tẽr-vẽr′tē-brăl-ly, *adv.* In an intervertebral position.

in′tẽr-view (-vū), *n.* [OFr. *entrevue*, from *entrevoir*, to meet, visit; *entre*, L. *inter*, between, and *voir*, L. *videre*, to see.]

1. A conference held for the purpose of discussing some important subject; a meeting for the mutual communication of thoughts; as, the parties had an *interview* and adjusted their differences.

2. A conversation held for the purpose of obtaining the opinions of a person for publication.

in′tẽr-view, *v.t.* To hold an interview with; to question for the purpose of eliciting information for publication.

in′tẽr-view-ẽr, *n.* One who interviews; one who elicits information for publication.

in′tẽr-view-ing, *n.* The act or practice of holding interviews.

in-tẽr-vis′i-ble, *a.* In surveying, an epithet applied to stations which are mutually visible, or can be seen the one from the other.

in-tẽr-vis′it, *v.i.* To interchange visits. [Rare.]

in-tẽr-vī′tăl, *a.* [L. *inter*, between, and *vita*, life.] Between two lives; pertaining to the intermediate state between death and the resurrection. [Rare.]

in″tẽr-vō-cal′ic, *a.* [L. *inter*, between, and *vocalis*, a vowel.] Denoting a letter situated between two vowels.

in″tẽr-vō-lū′tion, *n.* Same as *Convolution.*

in-tẽr-volve′, *v.t.*; intervolved, *pt., pp.*; intervolving, *ppr.* [L. *inter*, between, and *volvere*, to roll.] To involve or wind one within another.

in-tẽr-wēave′, *v.t.*; interwove, *pt.*; interwoven, *pp.*; interweaving, *ppr.* 1. To weave together; to intermix or unite in texture or construction; as, threads of silk and cotton *interwoven.*

2. To intermingle; to insert together as though woven; as, to *interweave* truth with falsehood.

in-tẽr-wish′, *v.t.* To wish mutually to each other. [Obs.]

in-tẽr-wŏrk′ing, *n.* The act of working together.

in-tẽr-wōve′, *v.*, past tense of *interweave.*

in-tẽr-wōv′en, *v.*, past participle of *interweave.*

in-tẽr-wrēathe′ (-rēth′), *v.t.* To weave into a wreath. [Rare.]

in-tes′tȧ-ble, *a.* [L. *intestabilis*, disqualified from witnessing or making a will; *in-* priv., and *testabilis*, from *testari*, to be a witness, make one's will.] Not capable of making a will; legally unqualified or disqualified to make a testament; as, a person unqualified for want of discretion, or disqualified by loss of reason, is *intestable.*

in-tes′tȧ-cy, *n.* The state of dying without making a will or disposing of one's effects.

in-tes′tāte, *a.* 1. Not having made a valid will; as, when a man dies *intestate*, his estate is committed for settlement to administrators.

2. Not devised; not disposed of by will; as, an *intestate* estate.

in-tes′tāte, *n.* [L. *intestatus*, having made no will; *in-* priv., and *testatus*, pp. of *testari*, to make a will.] A person who dies without making a valid will.

in-tes′ti-năl, *a.* Pertaining to the intestines of an animal body; as, the *intestinal* tube or canal.

Intestinal canal; the part of the alimentary canal between the stomach and the anus.

Intestinal worm; any worm that lives in the intestines of an animal.

in-tes′tine, *a.* [L. *intestinus*, inward, internal (neut. pl., *intestina*, entrails), from *intus*, within, from *in*, in.]

1. Internal; inward; opposed to *external.*

2. Internal with regard to a state or country; domestic; not foreign; as, *intestine* feuds; *intestine* war; *intestine* enemies.

3. Depending upon the subjective character of a being or thing.

4. Shut up within something; contained; innate. [Obs.]

in-tes′tine, *n.* [L. *intestinum*, a gut, an intestine, properly neut. sing. of *intestinus*, inward, internal, from *intus*, within.]

1. The canal or tube extending, with convolutions, from the right orifice of the stomach to the anus.

2. [*pl.*] The bowels; entrails; the organs of the abdomen; the viscera.

Large intestine; in human anatomy, the lower portion of the bowel, which is shorter, broader, and less convoluted than the small intestine, from which it is separated by the ileocæcal valve. It is about five feet long, terminating at the anus. Its three parts are the cæcum, the colon, and the rectum.

Small intestine; in human anatomy, the upper part of the bowel, which is narrow and very convoluted, being about twenty feet long. The process of digestion is completed in its three parts, the duodenum, the jejunum, and the ileum.

Human Stomach and Intestinal Tube.

a, Stomach. *b* to *d*, Small intestine. *b*, Duodenum. *c*, Jejunum with convolutions. *d*, Ileum with convolutions. *e* to *g*, Large intestine. *e*, Cæcum. *ff*, Colon. *g*, Rectum.

in′text, *n.* [L. *intextus*, pp. of *intexere*, to interweave.] The text or contents of a book. [Rare.]

in-tex′tine, *n.* [L. *intus*, within, and *exter*, on the outside, and *-ine.*] In botany, that membrane of the pollen-grain which is situated next to the extine or outermost membrane.

in-tex′tūred, *a.* Inwrought; woven in.

in-thirst′, *v.t.* To make thirsty. [Obs.]

in-thrąll′, in-thrąl′, *v.t.* Same as *Enthrall.*

in-thrąl′ment, in-thrąll′ment, *n.* See *Enthralment.*

in-thrōne′, *v.t.* Same as *Enthrone.*

in-thrŏng′, *v.i.* To crowd or throng together. [Rare.]

in-thrō-ni-zā′tion, *n.* Same as *Enthronization.*

in-thrŏn′īze, *v.t.* To enthrone.

in-tīce′, *v.t.* [Obs.] See *Entice.*

in′ti-mȧ, *n.*; *pl.* **in′ti-mæ**. [F. of L. *intimus*, inmost, superl. of *intus*, within.] In zoölogy, the innermost coat or layer of an organ or a part.

in′ti-mȧ-cy, *n.*; *pl.* **in′ti-mȧ-cieṣ**. Close familiarity or fellowship; nearness in friendship.

in′ti-māte, *a.* [L. *intimus*, inmost, superl. of *intus*, within.]

1. Inmost; inward; internal; as, *intimate* impulse.

2. Of the inmost mind; inward; as, *intimate* religious beliefs.

3. Approximating closely; familiar; near; as, *intimate* relation of parts.

4. Close in friendship or acquaintance; having familiar and friendly intercourse; as, an *intimate* friend.

5. Personal; as, one's *intimate* affairs.

in′ti-māte, *n.* A familiar friend or associate; one to whom the thoughts of another are intrusted without reserve.

in′ti-māte, *v.t.*; intimated, *pt., pp.*; intimating, *ppr.* [L. *intimatus*, pp. of *intimare*, to bring or press into, announce, from *intimus*, inmost, innermost, superl. of *intus*, within.]

1. To hint; to suggest obscurely, indirectly, or not very plainly; to give slight notice of.

2. To announce. [Obs.]

in′ti-māte-ly, *adv.* In an intimate manner.

in-ti-mā′tion, *n.* [L. *intimatio (-onis)*, from *intimare*, to announce.]

1. The act of intimating.

2. Proclamation; announcement.

3. A hint; an obscure or indirect suggestion or notice; a declaration or remark communicating imperfect information; as, he left us without any previous *intimation* of his intention.

in′time, *a.* Internal; intimate. [Obs.]

in-tim′i-dāte, *v.t.*; intimidated, *pt., pp.*; intimidating, *ppr.* [LL. *intimidatus*, pp. of *intimidare*, to make afraid; L. *in*, in, and *timidus*, afraid, fearful.] To make fearful; to inspire with fear; to dishearten; to abash; as, guilt *intimidates* the brave.

in-tim-i-dā′tion, *n.* The act of making fearful; the state of being abashed.

in-tim′i-dȧ-tō-ry, *a.* Causing or tending to cause intimidation.

in-tinc′tion, *n.* [LL. *intinctio (-onis)*, a dipping in, baptizing, from L. *intingere*, to dip in; *in*, in, and *tingere*, to tinge, dye.]

1. In the Greek church, a method or practice of administering both elements of the eucharist at the same time, by dipping the bread or wafer into the wine before passing it.

2. The act or process of dyeing. [Obs.]

in-tinc-tiv′i-ty, *n.* [L. *in-* priv., and *tinctus*, pp. of *tingere*, to dye, tinge.] Want of the quality of coloring or tingeing other bodies.

in′tine, *n.* [L. *intus*, within, and *-ine.*] A thin, transparent membrane forming the innermost layer of the coat of a pollen-grain.

in-tīre′, *a.* [Obs.] See *Entire.*

in-tīre′ly, *adv.* [Obs.] See *Entirely.*

in-tī′tle, *v.t.* [Obs.] See *Entitle.*

in-tit′ūle, *v.t.*; intituled, *pt., pp.*; intituling, *ppr.* [Fr. *intituler*; LL. *intitulare*, to entitle; L. *in*, in, on, and *titulus*, title.]

1. To entitle; to bestow a valid right upon.

2. To give a title to, as a book.

in′tō, *prep.* [ME. *into*; AS. *in tō*, in to; *in*, in, and *tō*, to.]

1. In and to; from the outside to the inside of. The instances in which this preposition is used may be divided into two great classes: (a) those in which it expresses motion or direction toward the inside of, whether literally or figuratively; and (b) those in which it expresses a change of condition. In both cases it is used after both transitive and intransitive verbs. The verbs after which it is used in the instances belonging to class (a) are such as fall, go, come, dart, flee, throw, look (as, to look *into* a letter or book), show (as, to show *into* a room), infuse (as, to infuse animation *into* a narrative), put, force, urge, etc. Those after which it is used in the instances belonging to class (b) are such as fall (as, to fall *into* a fever), change, transmute, convert, grow (as, the boy had grown *into* a young man), relax (as, to relax *into* good humor), etc. Sometimes verbs that are usually intransitive become changed into transitives when so used with *into*; as, to talk a man *into* submission; to reason oneself *into* false feelings. Sometimes the uses classed as (a) and (b) very nearly coincide.

2. Within; implying a lack or inadequacy; as, the string was a foot long *into* an inch. [Local, U. S.]

3. In; as, he has been *into* jail for a year. [Vulgar.]

in-tol″ẽr-ȧ-bil′i-ty, *n.* The state or quality of being intolerable or unbearable; intolerableness.

in-tol′ẽr-ȧ-ble, *a.* [OFr. *intolerable*; L. *intolerabilis*, that cannot be borne; *in-* priv., and *tolerabilis*, tolerable, from *tolerare*, to bear, endure.]

1. Not to be borne; that cannot be endured; as, *intolerable* pain.

2. Insufferable; not to be allowed; as, *intolerable* laziness.

in-tol′ẽr-ȧ-ble-ness, *n.* The quality of being intolerable.

in-tol′ẽr-ȧ-bly, *adv.* To a degree beyond endurance; as, *intolerably* cold; *intolerably* abusive.

in-tol′ẽr-ănce, *n.* 1. Want of capacity to endure.

2. Want of toleration; want of forbearance; unwillingness to tolerate contrary opinions or beliefs; as, *intolerance* toward a religious sect.

in-tol′ẽr-ăn-cy, *n.* Same as *Intolerance.*

in-tol′ẽr-ănt, *a.* [L. *intolerans (-antis)*; *in-* priv., and *tolerans (-antis)*, ppr. of *tolerare*, to bear, endure.]

1. Not enduring; not able to endure; as, *intolerant* of excesses.

2. Not enduring difference of opinion or of methods of practice; refusing to tolerate others in the enjoyment of their opinions, rights, and worship.

in-tol′ẽr-ănt, *n.* One who does not favor toleration.

in-tol′ẽr-ănt-ly, *adv.* In an intolerant manner.

in-tol′ẽr-ā-ted, *a.* Not endured; not tolerated.

in-tol′ẽr-ā-ting, *a.* [Rare.] See *Intolerant.*

in-tol-ẽr-ā′tion, *n.* Intolerance; refusal to tolerate others in their opinions or worship.

in-tömb′ (-tömʹ), *v.t.* [Obs.] See *Entomb.*

in-tömb′ment, *n.* [Obs.] See *Entombment.*

in-tō′nä-çō, *n.* [It., roughcast, plaster, from *intonacare*, to coat with plaster; *in*, on, and *tonica*, from L. *tunica*, a robe, tunic.] The preparatory or ground coat of plaster in fresco-painting.

in′tō-nāte, *v.i.*; intonated, *pt.*, *pp.*; intonating, *ppr.* [LL. *intonatus*, pp. of *intonare*, to sing according to tone; L. *in*, in, and *tonus*, tone.] To sound the notes of the musical scale; to practise solmization.

in′tō-nāte, *v.t.* To pronounce in a musical manner; to intone.

in′tō-nāte, *v.i.* [L. *intonatus*, pp. of *intonare*, to thunder, resound; *in*, in, and *tonare*, to thunder.] To thunder. [Obs.]

in-tō-nā′tion, *n.* 1. In music, the act of sounding with the voice the notes of the scale, or any other given order of musical tones.

2. The manner of sounding or tuning the notes of a musical scale; as, correct *intonation* is the first requisite in a singer.

3. The modulation of the voice in a musical manner, as in reading the liturgy; the act of intoning the church service.

in-tō-nā′tion, *n.* Thunder. [Obs.]

in-tōne′, *v.i.*; intoned, *pt.*, *pp.*; intoning, *ppr.* To utter a note, or a deep, protracted sound.

Ass *intones* to ass. —Pope.

in-tōne′, *v.t.* [LL. *intonare*, to sing according to tone, intone; L. *in*, in, and *tonus*, tone.] To recite in a monotonous manner; to modulate, as the tones of the voice in speaking; as, an artistically *intoned* address.

in-tor′sion, *n.* See *Intortion.*

in-tort′, *v.t.*; intorted, *pt.*, *pp.*; intorting, *ppr.* To twist; to wreathe; to wind; to wring.

in-tor′tion, *n.* [L. *intortio* (*-onis*), a curling, twisting, from *intortus*, pp. of *intorquere*, to curl, twist.] A winding, bending, or twisting, in any particular direction; in botany, the bending or twining of any part of a plant toward one side or the other, or in any direction from the vertical.

in tō′tō. [L.] Wholly; entirely.

in-tox′i-çănt, *n.* Anything that intoxicates, as whisky, wine, etc.

in-tox′i-çāte, *v.t.*; intoxicated, *pt.*, *pp.*; intoxicating, *ppr.* [L. *intoxicatus*, pp. of *intoxicare*, to poison, drug; *in*, in, and *toxicum*, poison.]

1. To inebriate; to make drunk, as with spirituous liquor.

2. To excite the spirits to a kind of delirium; to elate to enthusiasm, frenzy, or madness; as, *intoxicated* with zeal.

in-tox′i-çāte, *a.* Inebriated; drunk.

in-tox′i-çā-ted-ness, *n.* The state of intoxication.

in-tox′i-çā-ting, *a.* Having qualities or properties which produce intoxication; as, *intoxicating* liquors.

in-tox-i-çā′tion, *n.* 1. Inebriation; inebriety; drunkenness; overindulgence in alcoholic liquor; the act of making drunk.

2. A highly excited state of the nerves, producing frenzy.

3. A spirituous or narcotic poisoning.

intra-. A prefix or combining form from L. *intra-*, from *intra*, prep. and adv., within, from *in*, in, signifying in, within, interior; as, *intra*carpellary, *intra*cranial.

in-trȧ-çap′sū-lăr, *a.* In biology, contained within a capsule.

in-trȧ-çär′di-aç, *a.* [*Intra-*, and Gr. *kardia*, heart.] In anatomy, within the heart.

in-trȧ-çär′pel-lā-ry, *a.* In botany, within the carpel.

in-trȧ-cel′lū-lăr, *a.* Situated or occurring within a cell.

in-trȧ-çol′iç, *a.* Existing within the colon.

in-trȧ-çrā′ni-ăl, *a.* [*Intra-*, and L. *cranium*, the skull.] Situated inside the skull.

in-traçt-ȧ-bil′i-ty, *n.* The state or quality of being intractable.

in-traçt′ȧ-ble, *a.* [L. *intractabilis*, not to be handled, unmanageable; *in-* priv., and *tractabilis*, from *tractare*, to handle, manage.] Not to be governed or managed; violent; stubborn; obstinate; refractory; not to be taught; indocile; as, an *intractable* temper.

Syn.—Obstinate, stubborn, ungovernable, unmanageable, untoward.

in-traçt′ȧ-ble-ness, *n.* Intractability.

in-traçt′ȧ-bly, *adv.* In an intractable manner.

in-traçt′ile, *a.* Not capable of extension; not tractile.

in-trȧ-cyst′iç, *a.* Occurring or locked within a cyst.

in-trä′dȧ, *n.* [It. *intrata*, an entrance.] In music, a prelude.

in-trā′dōs, *n.* [Fr., from L. *intra*, within and *dorsum*, the back.] In architecture, the interior and lower line or curve of an arch.

in-trȧ-fō-li-ā′ceous, *a.* [*Intra-*, and L. *folium*, leaf.] In botany, growing on the inside or in front of a leaf; as, *intrafoliaceous* stipules.

in-trȧ-fū′şion (-zhun), *n.* [*Intra-*, and L. *fusio* (*-onis*), a pouring, from *fundere*, to pour.] The process of introducing a fluid into a bloodvessel of a living subject.

in-trȧ-lob′ū-lăr, *a.* Located in a lobule.

in-trȧ-mär′ġin-ăl, *a.* Within the margin; as, the *intramarginal* vein in the leaves of some of the plants belonging to the myrtle tribe.

in-trȧ-mẽr-çū′ri-ăl, *a.* Situated within the orbit of the planet Mercury.

in-trȧ-mō-leç′ū-lăr, *a.* Situated or exerted within a molecule.

in-trȧ-mun′dāne, *a.* [*Intra-*, and L. *mundus*, world.] Situated or occurring within the material world. [See *Extramundane.*]

in-trȧ-mū′răl, *a.* [*Intra-*, and L. *murus*, wall.]

1. Located within the walls of a city; within the corporate limits.

2. Occurring or located within the walls of an organ; as, *intramural* inflammation.

in-tran-quil′li-ty, *n.* Unquietness; inquietude; want of rest.

in-trans′çȧ-lent, *a.* [L. *in-* priv., and *trans*, across, through, and *calescens* (*-entis*), ppr. of *calescere*, to grow hot.] Not pervious to heat.

in-trans-gress′i-ble, *a.* Not transgressible.

in-trăn′şient (-shent), *a.* Not transient.

in-tran-şi-ġeant′ (*or* aṅ-troṅ-zē-zhoṅ′), *a.* [Fr.] Irreconcilable; applied to artists of the highly impressionistic school.

in-trans′i-ġent, *a.* [Sp. *intransigente*, from L. *in-* priv., and *transigens* (*-entis*), ppr. of *transigere*, to come to a settlement.] Uncompromising.

in-trans′i-ġent-ist, *n.* 1. A member of the irreconcilables, or extreme radicals of Spain (1873).

2. A member of a socialistic party in France.

in-tran′si-tive, *a.* [LL. *intransitivus*, not transitive; L. *in-* priv., and *transitivus*, passing over, from *transire*, to go or pass over; *trans*, across, and *ire*, to go.]

1. In grammar, a term applied to verbs expressing an action or state that is limited to the subject, or in other words, which do not express an action that passes over to or operates upon an object; as, I walk; I run; I sleep. It is also applied in a wider sense to verbs that are used without an expressed object though they may be really transitive in meaning; as, *build* in the sentence, "they *build* without stopping;" or *intoxicate* in "this liquor *intoxicates.*" Some purely intransitive verbs become transitive by the addition of a preposition and may be used in the passive; as, he *laughs*; he *laughs at* him; he is *laughed at.* Some may take a noun of kindred meaning as object; as, he *sleeps a sleep*; he *runs a race.*

2. Not transitive, as in logic or mathematics.

in-tran′si-tive, *n.* A verb not transitive.

in-tran′si-tive-ly, *adv.* Without an object following; in the manner of an intransitive verb.

in tran′si-tū. [L., from *in*, in, and *transitu*, abl. of *transitus*, passage.] In transit; while being conveyed.

in-trans-mis′si-ble, *a.* Incapable of transmission.

in-trans-mū-tȧ-bil′i-ty, *n.* The quality of not being transmutable.

in-trans-mū′tȧ-ble, *a.* Incapable of being transmuted or changed into another substance.

in′trănt, *a.* and *n.* Same as *Entrant.*

in-trȧ-nū′çlē-ăr, *a.* Situated in a nucleus.

in-trȧ-oç′ū-lăr, *a.* [*Intra-*, and L. *oculus*, eye.] Situated in the eye.

in-trap′, *v.t.* Same as *Entrap.*

in-trȧ-pā-rī′e-tăl, *a.* [*Intra-*, and L. *paries* (*-etis*), a wall.]

1. Located or occurring within walls; private; as, an *intraparietal* hanging.

2. Within the parietal lobe of a brain.

in-trȧ-pet′i-ō-lăr, *a.* [*Intra-*, and L. *petiolus*, a little stalk.] In botany, (a) denoting a pair of stipules at the base of a petiole united by those margins which are next the petiole, and thus seeming to form a single stipule between the petiole and the stem or branch; (b) situated within a petiole.

Intrapetiolar.

in-trȧ-tel-lū′riç, *a.* [*Intra-*, and L. *tellus* (*-uris*), the earth.] Located or formed within the earth; as, the *intratelluric* components of volcanic rocks.

in-trȧ-ter-ri-tō′ri-ăl, *a.* Situated within a territory.

in″trȧ-thō-raç′iç, *a.* Situated within the thorax.

in-trȧ-trop′iç-ăl, *a.* Situated within the tropics.

in-trȧ-ū′tẽr-ine, *a.* Occurring within the uterus.

in-trȧ-valv′ū-lăr, *a.* Located between valves.

in-trȧ-vē′nous, *a.* Situated within the veins.

in″trȧ-ven-triç′ū-lăr, *a.* Within ventricles.

in-treaş′ūre (-trezh′ūr), *v.t.* To lay up, as in a treasury. [Obs.]

in-trēat′, *v.t.* Same as *Entreat.*

in-trēat′ȧ-ble, *a.* Not entreatable. [Obs.]

in-trēat′ănce, *n.* Entreaty. [Obs.]

in-trēat′ful, *a.* Full of entreaty.

in-trench′, *v.t.* 1. To dig or cut a trench around a place, as in fortification; to fortify with a ditch and parapet; as, the army *intrenched* their camp, or they were *intrenched.*

2. To furrow; to make hollows in.

in-trench′, *v.i.* To invade; to encroach; to enter on and take possession of that which belongs to another.

in-trench′ănt, *a.* Not to be divided or wounded [Obs.]

in-trench′ment, *n.* 1. The act or process of intrenching or the condition of being intrenched.

2. In fortification, a defensive work consisting usually of a trench or ditch and a parapet, the latter constructed of the earth excavated in making the ditch.

Intrenchment. A B C, Banquette. C D E F, Parapet. K G H I, Ditch. G, Scarp. H I, Counterscarp.

3. Any defense or protection.

4. Invasion; infringement.

in-trep′id, *a.* [L. *intrepidus*; *in-* priv., and *trepidus*, alarmed, anxious, shaken.] Not trembling or shaking with fear; hence, fearless; bold; brave; undaunted; as, an *intrepid* soldier.

in-trē-pid′i-ty, *n.* Fearlessness; fearless bravery in danger; undaunted courage or boldness.

in-trep′id-ly, *adv.* Without trembling or shrinking from danger; fearlessly; daringly; resolutely.

in′tri-çȧ-ble, *a.* Entangling. [Obs.]

in′tri-çȧ-çy, *n.*; *pl.* **in′tri-çȧ-cieş.** The state of being entangled; perplexity; involution; complication; as, the *intricacy* of a knot; the *intricacy* of a cause in controversy; the *intricacy* of a plot.

Syn.—Complication, complexity, involution, perplexity.

in′tri-çāte, *a.* Entangled; involved; perplexed; complicated; obscure; as, *intricate* plots, accounts, etc.

Syn.—Complex, complicated.—A thing is *complex* when it is made up of parts; it is *complicated* when those parts are so many or so arranged as to make it difficult to grasp them; it is *intricate* when it has numerous windings and confused involutions which it is hard to follow out.

in′tri-çāte, *v.t.* [L. *intricatus*, pp. of *intricare*, to entangle, perplex, embarrass; *in*, in, and *tricæ*, vexations, perplexities.] To perplex; to make obscure. [Obs.]

in′tri-çāte-ly, *adv.* With perplexity or intricacy.

in′tri-çāte-ness, *n.* The state of being involved; involution; complication; perplexity.

in-tri-çā′tion, *n.* Entanglement. [Obs.]

in-trïgue′ (-trēg′), *n.* [Fr. *intrigue*, from *intriguer*, to plot, intrigue.]

1. A plot or scheme of a complicated nature, intended to effect some purpose by secret artifices.

2. The plot of a play or romance; a complicated scheme of designs, actions, and events.

3. A secret understanding or commerce of forbidden love between two persons of different sexes.

4. Intricacy; complication. [Obs.]

in-trïgue′, *v.i.* [Fr. *intriguer*; OFr. *intriguer*, from L. *intricare*, to entangle, perplex, embarrass.]

1. To form a plot or scheme, usually complicated, and intended to effect some purpose by secret artifices; as, the courtier *intrigues* with the minister.

2. To carry on forbidden love.

in-trïgue′, *v.t.* 1. To perplex; to render intricate. [Obs.]

2. To scheme for.

in-trïgu′ẽr (-trēg′), *n.* One who intrigues.

in-trïgu′ẽr-y, *n.* Intriguing arts.

in-trïgu′ing-ly, *adv.* After the manner of an intrigue.

in-trinse′, *a.* Drawn tight; ensnared. [Obs.]

in-trin′siç, *a.* [L. *intrinsecus*, on the inside, inwardly; *intra*, within, and *secus*, otherwise, beside.]

1. Inward; internal; hence, true; genuine; real; essential; inherent; not apparent or accidental; as, the *intrinsic* value of gold or silver; the *intrinsic* merit of an action.

2. In anatomy, comprised entirely within a certain limb or organ; opposed to *extrinsic.*

Intrinsic energy; the energy or force latent in any mechanism or form of matter; actual present power.

Intrinsic value; actual value as distinguished from trade value; value as measured by ability to satisfy the needs or desires of living organisms, especially the human. High intrinsic value may be consistent with little or no value as a commercial commodity.

Syn.—Real, genuine, native, inward, internal, true.

in-trin′siç, *n.* Something genuine. [Obs.]

in-trin′siç-ăl, *a.* 1. Intrinsic.

2. Familiar. [Obs.]

in-trin-si-çal′i-ty, *n.* Genuineness.

in-trin′siç-ăl-ly, *adv.* Internally; in the nature; really; truly.

A lie is a thing absolutely and *intrinsically* evil. —South.

in-trin′siç-ăl-ness, *n.* Intrinsicality.

in-trin′si-çāte, *a.* Intricate. [Obs.]

intro-. [L. *intro-*, from *intro*, prep., within, inward.] A prefix signifying within, into, in; as, *intro*duce, *intro*spect.

in-trō-ces′sion (-sesh′un), *n.* A depression, or sinking of parts inward.

in-trō-dūce′, *v.t.*; introduced (-dūst), *pt., pp.*; introducing, *ppr.* [L. *introducere*, to lead or bring in; *intro*, within, in, and *ducere*, to lead.]

1. To lead or bring in; to conduct or usher into a place; as, to *introduce* a person into a drawing-room.

2. To conduct and make known; to bring to be acquainted; as, to *introduce* a stranger to a person.

3. To bring into notice or practice; as, to *introduce* a new fashion.

4. To produce; to cause to exist; as, to *introduce* habits in children. [Obs.]

5. To begin; to open to notice; as, he *introduced* the subject with a long preface.

6. To insert, as a probe.

Syn.—Preface, present, usher in.

in-trō-dūce′ment, *n.* Introduction. [Obs.]

in-trō-dū′cẽr, *n.* Whoever or whatever introduces.

in-trō-duçt′, *v.t.* To introduce. [Obs.]

in-trō-duç′tion, *n.* [L. *introductio (-onis)*, a leading or bringing in, introduction, from *introducere*, to lead or bring in, introduce.]

1. The act of introducing or inserting.

2. The act of making persons known to each other; as, the *introduction* of strangers.

3. The part of a book which precedes the main work; a preface or preliminary discourse.

4. A treatise, generally more or less elementary, on any branch of study; a treatise introductory to more elaborate works on the same subject; as, an *introduction* to botany.

5. In music, a preliminary strain which is intended to prefigure the subsequent theme.

Syn.—Induction, importation, presentation, insertion, commencement, preliminary, preface, initiative, preamble, prelude.

in-trō-duç′tive, *a.* Serving to introduce; serving as the means to bring forward something.

in-trō-duç′tive-ly, *adv.* In a manner serving to introduce.

in-trō-duç′tŏr, *n.* An introducer. [Obs.]

in-trō-duç′tō-ri-ly, *adv.* By way of introduction.

in-trō-duç′tō-ry, *a.* [LL. *introductorius*, from L. *introductus*, pp of *introducere*, to introduce.] Serving to introduce something else; prefatory; preliminary; as, *introductory* remarks; an *introductory* discourse.

Syn.—Prefatory, preliminary.

in-trō-duç′tress, *n.* A female who introduces.

in-trō-fleç′tion, *n.* [*Intro-*, and L. *flexio (-onis)*, a bending, from *flectere*, to bend.] The condition of being introflexed.

in-trō-flexed′ (-flekst′), *a.* Flexed or bent inward.

in-trō-flex′iŏn (-flek′shun), *n.* See *Introflection.*

in-trō-gres′sion (-gresh′un), *n.* [L. *introgressus*, pp. of *introgredi*, to go in; *intro*, within, and *gradi*, to go.] Entrance.

in-trō′it, *n.* [L. *introitus*, a going in, entrance, from *introire*; *intro*, within, and *ire*, to go.]

1. In the Roman Catholic church, the entrance or beginning of the mass; a passage of Scripture sung or chanted when the priest enters within the rails of the altar.

2. Any musical composition designed for opening church services.

in-trō-mis′sion (-mish′un), *n.* 1. The act of sending in; insertion.

2. The act of admitting.

3. In Scots law, an intermeddling with the effects of another.

in-trō-mit′, *v.t.*; intromitted, *pt., pp.*; intromitting, *ppr.* [L. *intromittere*, to send in; *intro*, within, and *mittere*, to send.]

1. To send in; to let in; to admit.

2. To allow to enter; to be the medium or entrance for; as, glass in the window *intromits* light without cold into a room.

in-trō-mit′, *v.i.* In Scots law, to intermeddle with the effects of another.

in-trō-mit′tent, *a.* [L. *intromittens (-entis)*, ppr. of *intromittere*, to send in.] Conveying within; furnishing admission; as, an *intromittent* instrument; an *intromittent* organ.

in-trō-mit′tẽr, *n.* One who intromits.

in-trō-pres′sion (-presh′un), *n.* Internal pressure. [Rare.]

in″trō-rē-çep′tion, *n.* The act of admitting into or within.

in-trorse′, *a.* [L. *introrsus*, *introrsum*, toward the inside, contr. of *introversus*; *intro*, within, and *versus*, turned.] Turned inward; a term describing the direction of bodies, to denote their being turned toward the axis to which they appertain; thus, in most plants the anthers are introrse, their valves being turned toward the style. The cut shows the introrse anthers of the common grapevine, *Vitis vinifera.*

Introrse Anthers.

in-trō-speçt′, *v.t.* [L. *introspectare*, freq. of *introspicere*, to look within; *intro*, within, and *spicere*, to look.] To look into or within; to view the inside of.

in-trō-speç′tion, *n.* A view of the inside or interior; self-examination.

I was forced to make an *introspection* into mine own mind. —Dryden.

in-trō-speç′tion-ist, *n.* One who uses introspective methods in psychical research.

in-trō-speç′tive, *a.* Inspecting within; seeing inwardly; characterized by introspection.

in-trō-sūme′, *v.t.* [*Intro-*, and L. *sumere*, to take.] To suck in; to absorb.

in″trō-sus-çep′tion, *n.* [*Intro-*, and L. *susceptio (-onis)*, from *suscipere*, to take up or in.]

1. The act of taking in; absorption.

2. In medicine, same as *intussusception.*

in-trō-vē̄n′ient (-yent), *a.* [L. *introveniens (-entis)*, ppr. of *introvenire*, to come in, [e]nter; *intro*, within, and *venire*, to com[e].] Comi[n]g in or between; entering. [Rare.]

in-trō-vẽr′[sio]n, *n.* The act of turning inward.

in-trō-vẽrt′, *v.t.*; introverted, *pt., pp.*; introverting, *ppr.* [L. *introvertere*; *intro*, within, and *vertere*, to turn.]

1. To turn inward.

2. In zoölogy, to sheathe one part or organ of within another; to invert.

in′trō-vẽrt, *n.* An organ that has been or is capable of being introverted.

in-trūde′, *v.i.*; intruded, *pt., pp.*; intruding, *ppr.* [L. *intrudere*, to thrust in; *in*, in, and *trudere*, to thrust, push.]

1. To thrust oneself in; to come or go in without invitation or welcome; to enter, as into company, against the will of the company or the host; as, to *intrude* on families at unseasonable hours.

2. To encroach; to enter or force oneself in without permission; as, to *intrude* on the lands of another.

in-trūde′, *v.t.* 1. To thrust in or upon, without right or welcome.

2. To force or cast in. [Obs.]

3. In geology, to cause to penetrate, as into fissures or between the layers of rocks.

in-trūd′ẽr, *n.* One who intrudes; one who thrusts himself in, or enters where he has no right or is not welcome.

They were all strangers and *intruders*. —Locke.

in-trūd′ress, *n.* A woman who intrudes.

in-trunk′, *v.t.* To inclose as in a trunk or case. [Rare.]

in-trūse′, *a.* [L. *intrusus*, pp. of *intrudere*, to thrust in.] In botany, growing inward.

in-trū′ṣion, *n.* [LL. *intrusio (-onis)*, a thrusting in, from L. *intrudere*; *in*, in, and *trudere*, to thrust, push.]

1. The act of thrusting in, or of entering into a place or state without invitation, right, or welcome.

Why this *intrusion?*
Were not my orders that I should be private? —Addison.

2. In geology, the penetrating of one rock, while in a melted state, into the cavities of other rocks.

3. In law, an unlawful entry into lands and tenements void of a possessor by a person who has no right to the same.

in-trū′ṣion-ăl, *a.* Pertaining to intrusion.

in-trū′ṣion-ist, *n.* One who intrudes; especially, one who favors the settlement of a pastor in a church or congregation contrary to the will of the people or without their consent.

in-trū′sive, *a.* Thrusting in or entering without right or welcome; apt to intrude.

Intrusive rocks; rocks which have been forced, while in a melted state, into the cavities of other rocks.

in-trū′sive-ly, *adv.* Without welcome or invitation.

in-trū′sive-ness, *n.* The act of entering without permission or invitation.

in-trust′, *v.t.*; intrusted, *pt., pp.*; intrusting, *ppr.* To deliver in trust; to confide to the care of; to commit to (another) with confidence in his fidelity; as, to *intrust* a clerk with one's money or goods, or to *intrust* money or goods to a clerk; also written *entrust.*

Syn.—Commit, confide, consign.

in-tū-bā′tion, *n.* In medicine, the insertion of a tube in an organ to keep it from closing in certain diseases.

in′tū-it, *v.t.* and *v.i.* [L. *intuitus*, pp. of *intueri*, to look on, consider; *in*, in, on, and *tueri*, to look.] To know instinctively; to acquire knowledge by direct perception or comprehension.

in-tū-i′tion (-ish′un), *n.* [LL. *intuitio (-onis)*, a regarding, looking at, from L. *intueri*, to consider, look on.]

1. The act by which the mind perceives the agreement or disagreement of two ideas, or the truth of things, immediately, or the moment they are presented, without the intervention of other ideas, or without reasoning and deduction.

2. A first or primary truth; a truth that cannot be acquired by but is assumed in experience.

3. A looking on; a sight or view; hence, a regard to; an aim. [Obs.]

Syn.—Instinct, apprehension, recognition, insight.

in-tū-i′tiŏn-ăl, *a.* Pertaining to intuition.

in-tū-i′tiŏn-ăl-iṣm, *n.* In metaphysics, the doctrine that the perception of truth is from intuition.

in-tū-i′tiŏn-ăl-ist, *n.* One who believes in intuitionalism.

in-tū-i′tiŏn-iṣm, *n.* Same as *Intuitionalism.*

in-tū-i′tiŏn-ist, *n.* Same as *Intuitionalist.*

in-tū′i-tive, *a.* [LL. *intuitivus*, from L. *intueri*, to look on, consider; *in*, in, on, and *tueri*, to look at, regard.]

1. Perceived by the mind immediately, without the intervention of argument or testimony; exhibiting truth to the mind on bare inspection; as, *intuitive* evidence.

2. Received or obtained by intuition or simple inspection; as, *intuitive* judgment or knowledge.

3. Seeing clearly; as, an *intuitive* view; *intuitive* vision.

4. Having the power of discovering truth without reasoning.

in-tū′i-tive-ly, *adv.* By immediate perception; without reasoning; as, to perceive truth *intuitively.*

in-tū′i-tiv-iṣm, *n.* The doctrine that primary ethical principles are intuitive in the normal mind.

in-tū-mesce′, *v.i.*; intumesced (-mest), *pt., pp.*; intumescing, *ppr.* [L. *intumescere*, to swell up; *in*, in, on, and *tumescere*, incept. of *tumere*, to swell.] To swell; to enlarge or expand with or as with heat.

in-tū-mes′cence, *n.* 1. The act of swelling.

2. A swell; a swelling with bubbles; a rising and enlarging; a tumid state.

in-tū-mes′cent, *a.* Expanding.

in-tū-mū-lā-ted, *a.* [LL. *intumulatus*, pp. of *intumulare*, to bury; L. *in-* priv., and *tumulus*, a tomb.] Not interred; unburied. [Obs.]

in-tūne′, *v.t.* Same as *Intone.*

in-tũr′bid-āte, *v.t.*; inturbidated, *pt., pp.*; inturbidating, *ppr.* [L. *in*, in, and *turbidus*, full of confusion, muddy, thick.] To render turbid, dark, or confused. [Rare.]

in-tũr-ġes′cence, *n.* A swelling; the act of swelling or state of being swelled.

in′tūse, *n.* A bruise. [Obs.]

in″tus-sus-çep′ted, *a.* Received into; introverted.

in″tus-sus-çep′tion, *n.* [L. *intus*, within, and *susceptio (-onis)*, a taking up, from *suscipere*, to take up; *sub*, under, and *capere*, to take.]

1. The passing of one part within another.

2. In medicine, the falling of one part of an intestine into another.

3. In physiology, the process of nutrition of living tissues by the absorption of food particles from the blood; interstitial growth.

4. In botany, the theory that the growth of cell-walls is by the intercalation of new molecules between those forming the original material.

in-twīne′, *v.t.* See *Entwine.*

in-twist′, *v.t.* Same as *Entwist.*

in-ū-en′dō, *n.* Same as *Innuendo.*

In′ū-lȧ, *n.* [L., prob. a corruption of Gr. *helenion*, elecampane.] A genus of perennial herbs of the natural order *Compositæ*, containing about sixty species, natives of the temperate regions of Europe, Asia, and Africa. They have yellow flowers, the heads, which are sometimes very large, growing either singly or more frequently in terminal corymbs or panicles.

in′ū-lin, *n.* A peculiar vegetable principle, $C_6H_{10}O_5$, which is spontaneously deposited from a decoction of the roots of the *Inula Helenium.* It is a white powder, and in its chemical properties appears intermediate between gum and starch.

in′ū-loid, *n.* A substance similar to inulin found in the unripe buds of several plants of the order *Compositæ.*

in-um′brāte, *v.t.* [L. *inumbratus*, pp. of *inumbrare*, to cast a shadow upon; *in*, in, on, and *umbra*, a shadow.] To obscure; to shade. [Obs.]

in-uñç′ted, *a.* Anointed. [Obs.]

in-uṉc′tion, *n.* [L. *inunctio* (*-onis*), from *inungere*, to anoint, spread on; *in*, in, on, and *ungere*, to smear, anoint.] The action of anointing; unction.

in-uṉc-tū-os′i-ty, *n.* Want of unctuosity; destitution of greasiness or oiliness which is perceptible to the touch; as, the *inunctuosity* of porcelain clay.

in-un′dȧnt, *a.* Overflowing. [Rare.]

in-un′dāte, *v.t.*; inundated, *pt.*, *pp.*; inundating, *ppr.* [L. *inundatus*, pp. of *inundare*, to overflow; *in*, in, on, and *undare*, to move in waves, to flood, from *unda*, a wave.]

1. To overflow; to deluge; to spread over with a flood; as, the lowlands along the Mississippi are *inundated* almost every spring.

2. To fill with an overflowing abundance or superfluity; as, the country was once *inundated* with bills of credit.

in-un-dā′tion, *n.* [L. *inundatio* (*-onis*), from *inundare*, to overflow, inundate.]

1. The act of inundating, or the state of being inundated; an overflow of water or other fluid; a flood; a rising and spreading of water over low grounds; as, Holland has frequently suffered by *inundations* of the sea.

2. An overspreading of any kind; an overflowing or superfluous abundance; as, an *inundation* of poor literature.

in-un-dẽr-stand′ing, *a.* Void of understanding. [Obs.]

in-ũr-bāne′, *a.* [L. *inurbanus*; *in-* priv., and *urbanus*, civil, polite, from *urbs*, a city.] Uncivil; discourteous; unpolished.

in-ũr-bāne′ly, *adv.* Without urbanity.

in-ũr-bāne′ness, *n.* Incivility.

in-ũr-ban′i-ty, *n.* Incivility; rude, unpolished manners or deportment; want of courteousness.

in-ūre′, *v.t.*; inured, *pt.*, *pp.*; inuring, *ppr.* [*In-*, and ME. *ure*; OFr. *eure*, *ovre*; L. *opera*, work.]

1. To habituate; to accustom; to apply in use or practice till use gives little or no pain or inconvenience, or makes little impression; to harden; to destroy the sensibility of.

> We may *inure* ourselves by custom to bear the extremities of weather without injury.
> —Addison.

2. To establish in use. [Obs.]

in-ūre′, *v.i.* To pass in use; to take or have effect; to be applied; to serve to the use or benefit of; as, a gift of land *inures* to the heirs of the grantee, or it *inures* to their benefit.

in-ūre′ment, *n.* The act of inuring; practice; habit; custom; frequency.

in-ũrn′, *v.t.*; inurned, *pt.*, *pp.*; inurning, *ppr.* To put in an urn; to bury; to inter; to entomb. [Rare.]

-inus. [L. *-inus*, a suffix forming adjectives and nouns thence derived.] A suffix of Latin origin used in Latinized generic and specific names; as, Lup*inus*.

in-ū′ṣi-tāte, *a.* [L. *inusitatus*, unused, uncommon.] Unused or uncommon. [Rare.]

in-ū-ṣi-tā′tion, *n.* Neglect of use; disuse. [Rare.]

in-ust′, *a.* Burnt in. [Obs.]

in-us′tion (-chun), *n.* The act of burning in; a branding; the act of marking by burning. [Obs.]

in-ū′tile, *a.* Unprofitable; useless. [Obs.]

in-ū-til′i-ty, *n.* [L. *inutilitas*, uselessness, from *inutilis*, useless; *in-* priv., and *utilis*, useful.]

1. Uselessness; the quality of being unprofitable; unprofitableness; as, the *inutility* of vain speculations and visionary projects.

2. Anything that is useless or unprofitable. [Rare.]

in-ut′tẽr-ȧ-ble, *a.* That cannot be uttered.

in vac′ū-ō. [L.] In a vacuum or empty space.

in-vāde′, *v.t.*; invaded, *pt.*, *pp.*; invading, *ppr.* [L. *invadere*, to come or go in; *in*, in, and *vadere*, to come or go.]

1. To go into; to enter. [Obs.]

2. To enter, as an army, with hostile intentions; to enter, as an enemy, with a view to conquest or plunder; to attack; as, the French armies *invaded* Holland in 1795.

3. To attack; to infringe; to encroach on; to fall on; to seize; to violate; as, the king *invaded* the rights and privileges of the people; consumption *invades* the bronchial system.

in-vād′ẽr, *n.* One who enters the territory of another with a view to war, conquest, or plunder; an assailant; an encroacher; an intruder; one who infringes the rights of another.

in-vaġ′i-nāte, *v.t.*; invaginated, *pt.*, *pp.*; invaginating, *ppr.* [L. *in*, in, and *vagina*, a sheath.] To insert or receive, as into a sheath; to introvert.

in-vaġ′i-nāte, in-vaġ-i-nā′ted, *a.* Sheathed; received as into a sheath.

in-vaġ-i-nā′tion, *n.* 1. The act of invaginating or sheathing; in biology, the condition of a sheathed or invaginated part; intussusception.

2. That which is invaginated.

in-vȧ-les′cence, *n.* [L. *invalescere*, to become strong.] Strength; health. [Obs.]

in-val-ē-tū′di-nā-ry, *a.* Wanting health. [Obs.]

in-val′id, *a.* [L. *invalidus*, not strong, weak; *in-* priv., and *validus*, strong, from *valere*, to be strong.]

1. Weak; of no force, weight, or cogency.

2. In law, having no force, effect, or efficacy; void; null; as, an *invalid* contract or agreement.

in′vȧ-lid, *a.* Weak; sickly; infirm.

in′vȧ-lid, *n.* A person who is weak and infirm; a person sickly or indisposed; a person who is wounded, maimed, or otherwise disabled for active service; a soldier or seaman worn out in service.

in′vȧ-lid (*or* -lēd), *v.t.*; invalided, *pt.*, *pp.*; invaliding, *ppr.* 1. To enroll on the list of invalids in the military or naval service; to give leave of absence to, on account of sickness.

2. To render infirm; chiefly used in the past participle; as, an ancient and *invalided* mariner.

in-val′i-dāte, *v.t.*; invalidated, *pt.*, *pp.*; invalidating, *ppr.* To weaken or lessen the force of; to destroy the strength or validity of; to render of no force or effect; as, to *invalidate* an agreement or a contract; to *invalidate* an argument.

in-val-i-dā′tion, *n.* The act of invalidating or of rendering invalid.

in′vȧ-līde, *n.* An invalid. [Obs.]

in′vȧ-lid-iṣm, *n.* The condition of being an invalid; sickness.

in-vȧ-lid′i-ty, *n.* [LL. *invaliditas*, want of health, from L. *invalidus*, weak, invalid.]

1. Weakness. [Obs.]

2. Want of cogency; want of legal force or efficacy; as, the *invalidity* of an agreement or of a will.

in-val′id-ness, *n.* Invalidity; as, the *invalidness* of reasoning.

in-val′ŏr-ous, *a.* Without valor; cowardly; timid.

in-val′ū-ȧ-ble, *a.* Precious above estimation; so valuable that its worth cannot be estimated; inestimable.

in-val′ū-ȧ-bly, *adv.* Inestimably.

in-val′ūed, *a.* Inestimable; invaluable. [Rare.]

in-vā″ri-ȧ-bil′i-ty, *n.* The quality of being invariable; immutability.

in-vā′ri-ȧ-ble, *n.* In mathematics, an invariant; a constant.

in-vā′ri-ȧ-ble, *a.* Constant; in the same state; immutable; unalterable; unchangeable; that does not vary; always uniform.

in-vā′ri-ȧ-ble-ness, *n.* Constancy of state, condition, or quality; immutability; unchangeableness.

in-vā′ri-ȧ-bly, *adv.* Constantly; uniformly; without alteration or change; as, we are bound to pursue *invariably* the path of duty.

in-vā′ri-ănce, *n.* In mathematics, the property of remaining invariable after the process of linear transformation.

in-vā′ri-ănt, *n.* A function of the coefficients of a quantic, such that if the quantic is subjected to the process of linear transformation, the corresponding function of the new coefficients is equivalent to the original function multiplied by some power of the modulus of transformation.

in-vā′ried, *a.* Unvaried; not changing or altering.

in-vā′ṣion (-zhun), *n.* [LL. *invasio* (*-onis*), from L. *invadere*, to go in; *in*, in, and *vadere*, to go or come.]

1. A hostile entrance into the possessions of another; especially, the entrance of a hostile army into a country for the purpose of conquest or plunder or to attack a military force.

2. An attack on the rights of another; infringement or violation.

3. Attack of a disease or anything pernicious; as, the *invasion* of a plague.

4. The act of invading, encroaching, or trespassing.

Syn.—Incursion, irruption, inroad.—*Invasion* is generic, denoting a forcible entrance; *incursion* signifies a hasty and sudden *invasion*; *irruption* denotes a particularly violent *invasion*; *inroad* includes the idea of *invasion* with a design to occupy.

in-vā′sive, *a.* [LL. *invasivus*, from L. *invasus*, pp. of *invadere*, to invade.] Entering on another's possessions with hostile designs; aggressive; encroaching; tending to invade.

A Chief Invecked.

in-veck′ée (-ā), *a.* [Etym. doubtful.] In heraldry, double-arched; said of a line or the edge of an ordinary bent into curves.

in-vect′, *v.i.* To inveigh. [Obs.]

in-vec′ted, *a.* [L. *invectus*, pp. of *invehere*, to bring in, to penetrate.] In heraldry, the reverse of *engrailed*; having all the points turning inward to the ordinary, with the small semicircles outward to the field.

A Pale Invected.

in-vec′tion, *n.* Invective. [Obs.]

in-vec′tive, *n.* [L. *invectivus*, scolding, abusive, from *invectus*, pp. of *invehere*, to bring in, attack, scold; *in*, in, to, and *vehere*, to carry.] A railing speech or expression; an utterance or writing intended to cast opprobrium, censure, or reproach on another; a harsh or reproachful accusation; followed by *against*; as, he uttered severe *invectives against* the unfortunate general.

in-vec′tive, *a.* Satirical; abusive; railing.

in-vec′tive-ly, *adv.* Satirically; abusively.

in-veigh′ (-vā′), *v.i.*; inveighed, *pt.*, *pp.*; inveighing, *ppr.* [L. *invehere*, to bring in, or to attack with words, scold; *in*, in, to, and *vehere*, to carry.] To exclaim or rail against; to utter censorious and bitter language against any one; to reproach; with *against*; as, men *inveigh against* the follies of fashion.

in-veigh′ẽr (-vā′), *n.* One who inveighs or rails; a railer.

in-vēi′gle (-vē′), *v.t.*; inveigled, *pt.*, *pp.*; inveigling, *ppr.* [Prob. a corruption of OFr. *aveugler*, to blind, delude, from LL. *aboculus*, blind; L. *ab*, from, and *oculus*, eye.] To lead astray; to entice; to seduce; to wheedle; to persuade to something evil by deceptive arts or flattery.

in-vēi′gle-ment, *n.* The act of inveigling; seduction to evil; enticement.

in-vēi′glẽr, *n.* One who entices or draws into any design by arts and flattery.

in-veil′, *v.t.*; inveiled, *pt.*, *pp.*; inveiling, *ppr.* To cover or conceal, as with a veil.

> Her eyes *inveiled* with sorrow's clouds.
> —W. Browne.

in-vend-i-bil′i-ty, *n.* The state or quality of being invendible.

in-vend′i-ble, *a.* Not vendible or salable.

in-ven′ŏm, *v.t.* [Obs.] See *Envenom*.

in-vent′, *v.t.*; invented, *pt.*, *pp.*; inventing, *ppr.* [ME. *inventen*; OFr. *inventer*, from L. *inventus*, pp. of *invenire*, to come upon, meet with, discover; *in*, in, to, and *venire*, to come.]

1. To light on; to meet with.

2. To find out, as something new; to devise, as something not before known; to contrive and produce, as something that did not before exist; to discover; to originate; as, to *invent* a new instrument of music.

3. To forge; to fabricate; to contrive falsely; as, to *invent* falsehoods.

Syn.—Devise, discover, fabricate, feign.

in-vent′ẽr, *n.* [Obs.] See *Inventor*.

in-vent′fụl, *a.* Full of invention. [Obs.]

in-vent′i-ble, *a.* That can be invented.

in-vent′i-ble-ness, *n.* The state of being inventible.

in-ven′tion, *n.* [L. *inventio* (*-onis*), a discovery, invention, from *inventus*, pp. of *invenire*, to come upon, discover.]

1. The action or operation of finding out something new; the contrivance of that which did not before exist; as, the *invention* of wireless telegraphy.

2. That which is invented.

3. Forgery; fiction; as, fables are the *inventions* of ingenious men.

4. The power of inventing; that skill or ingenuity which is or may be employed in contriving anything new; as, a man of *invention*.

in-ven′tious, *a.* [Obs.] See *Inventive*.

in-vent′ive, *a.* 1. Of or pertaining to invention.

2. Able to invent; quick at contrivance; ready at expedients; as, an *inventive* genius.

in-vent′ive-ly, *adv.* By the power of invention.

in-vent′ive-ness, *n.* The faculty of inventing.

in-vent′ŏr, *n.* [L. *inventor*, a discoverer, inventor, from *invenire*, to find, discover.] One who finds out something new; one who contrives and produces anything not before existing; a contriver.

in-ven-tō′ri-ȧl, *a.* Of or pertaining to an inventory.

in-ven-tō′ri-ăl-ly, *adv.* In the manner of an inventory.

in′ven-tō-ry, *n.*; *pl.* **in′ven-tō-ries.** [LL. *inventorium*, a list, inventory, from L. *inventus*, pp. of *invenire*, to come upon, discover.] A detailed and descriptive list of articles, with or without valuation, and including such special information as may be deemed necessary; specifically, such a list of the goods of a merchant, of an insolvent estate, or of a deceased person.

in′ven-tō-ry, *v.t.* To make an inventory of; to make a list, catalogue, or schedule of; as, to *inventory* a stock of books.

in-vent′ress, *n.* A female who invents.

in-vē-rac′i-ty, *n.* Lack of veracity.

in-ver″i-si-mil′i-tūde, *n.* Want of verisimilitude; improbability.

in-vẽrse′ (*or* in′vẽrs), *a.* [L. *inversus*, pp. of *invertere*, to turn about; *in*, in, to, toward, and *vertere*, to turn.]

1. Inverted; reciprocal; opposed in relation; turned end for end.

2. In mathematics, opposite in nature and effect; said of any two operations which, when both are performed in succession upon a quantity, leave the quantity with its original value; as, addition is *inverse* to subtraction.

Inverse or *reciprocal ratio*; the ratio of the reciprocals of two quantities.

Inverse or *reciprocal proportion*; an equality between a direct ratio and a reciprocal ratio; thus, 4 : 2 :: ¼ : ½, or 4 : 2 :: 3 : 6, *inversely*.

in′vẽrse, *n*. That which is opposed; that which is opposite in effect.

in-vẽrse′ly, *adv*. In an inverted order or manner, as when one quantity is greater or less according as another is less or greater.

in-vẽr′sion, *n*. [L. *inversio* (*-onis*), from *invertere*, to turn about.]

1. The act of inverting or the state of being inverted; change of order, so that the last becomes first and the first last; a turning or change of the natural order of things.

2. Change of places, so that each takes the place of the other; as, the *inversion* of companies in military tactics.

3. A turning backward; a contrary method of operation; as, problems in arithmetic are often proved by *inversion*, as division by multiplication, and multiplication by division.

4. In geometry, a change in the order of the terms of a proportion, so that the second takes the place of the first, and the fourth of the third.

5. In grammar, a change of the natural order of words.

6. In music, the change of position either of a theme or of a chord.

7. In rhetoric, the use of an opponent's arguments to strengthen one's own cause.

8. In geology, the apparent reversion of the regular order of succession of layers of strata.

9. In chemistry, the change made in the properties of certain carbohydrates by decomposition caused by the action of a ferment or acid; as, the *inversion* of cane-sugar into grape-sugar and fruit-sugar.

in-vẽrt′, *v.t.*; inverted, *pt.*, *pp.*; inverting, *ppr.* [L. *invertere*, to turn about; *in*, in, to, toward, and *vertere*, to turn.]

1. To turn into a contrary direction; to turn upside down; to reverse; to place in a contrary order or method; as, to *invert* the rules of justice; to *invert* the order of words.

2. In music, to change the order of, as the notes which form a chord, or the parts which compose harmony.

3. To divert; to turn into another channel. [Obs.]

4. In chemistry, to decompose by inversion; to subject to inversion.

in-vẽrt′, *v.i.* To be subjected to chemical inversion.

in′vẽrt, *n*. 1. In masonry, an inverted arch, especially as in the floor of the lock-chamber of a canal or the bottom of a sewer.

2. In telegraphy, an inverted insulator.

in-vẽr′tē-brăl, *a*. Destitute of a vertebral column, as some animals.

In-vẽr-tē-brā′tȧ, *n.pl.* [L. *in-* priv., and *vertebratus*, vertebrate, from *vertebra*, a joint, especially of the spine.] One of the two great divisions of the animal kingdom (the other being the *Vertebrata*), including all animals destitute of vertebræ or a backbone.

in-vẽr′tē-brāte, *n*. An animal having no vertebral column, or spinal bone.

in-vẽr′tē-brāte, in-vẽr′tē-brā-ted, *a*. 1. Destitute of a backbone or vertebral chain.

2. Figuratively, lacking strength, as if from want of backbone.

in-vẽrt′ed, *a*. Turned to a contrary direction; changed in order; inverse; reversed; specifically, (a) in heraldry, turned the wrong way; as, wings when the points are downward are termed *inverted*, being contrary to their usual position; also called *invertant*; (b) in botany, placed in a position different from the normal one, as many seeds; (c) in geology, lying apparently in inverse or reverse order, as beds and strata which have been upheaved and folded back on each other by the intrusion of igneous rocks.

Eagle Displayed, Wings Inverted.

Inverted arch; in architecture, an arch with its intrados below the axis or springing-line, and of which therefore the lowest stone is the keystone.

in-vẽrt′ed-ly, *adv*. In a contrary or reversed order.

in-vẽrt′i-ble, *a*. [L. *in*, in, on, and *vertere*, to turn.]

1. Susceptible of being turned upside down.

2. Capable of being changed chemically by inversion.

in-vest′, *v.t.*; invested, *pt.*, *pp.*; investing, *ppr.* [Fr. *investir*; L. *investire*, to clothe, cover; *in*, in, and *vestire*, to clothe, from *vestis*, clothing.]

1. To clothe; to dress; to put garments on; to array; usually followed by *with* or *in* before the thing put on; as, to *invest* one *with* a mantle or robe.

2. To clothe with office or authority; to place in possession of an office, rank, or dignity; as, to *invest* a person with a civil office or with an ecclesiastical dignity.

3. To endow; to adorn; to grace; to endue by attribution; as, womanhood *invested* with beauty.

4. To inclose; to surround, especially with hostile intent; to block up, so as to intercept succors of men and provisions and prevent escape; to lay siege to; as, to *invest* a town.

5. To confer; to give. [Obs.]

6. To lay out, as money in the purchase of some kind of property, usually of a permanent nature; with *in*; as, to *invest* money *in* bank-stock; to *invest* it *in* lands or goods.

Syn.—Confer, endow, endue.

in-vest′, *v.i.* To make an investment; as, to *invest* in railway shares.

in-vest′ient (-yent), *a*. Covering; clothing. [Obs.]

in-ves′ti-gȧ-ble, *a*. That may be investigated or searched out; discoverable by rational search or disquisition; as, the causes or reasons of things are sometimes *investigable*.

in-ves′ti-gāte, *v.t.*; investigated, *pt.*, *pp.*; investigating, *ppr.* [L. *investigatus*, pp. of *investigare*, to trace out, search into; *in*, in, and *vestigare*, to track, from *vestigium*, a track, foot-track.] To search into; to inquire and examine into with care and accuracy; to find out by careful disquisition; as, to *investigate* the powers and forces of nature; to *investigate* the conduct of an agent.

in-ves-ti-gā′tion, *n*. The act or process of searching minutely for truth, facts, or principles; a careful inquiry to find out what is unknown, either in the physical or moral world, either by observation and experiment, or by argument and discussion; as, the *investigations* of the scientist; the *investigations* of a district attorney.

Syn.—Examination, inquiry, inquisition, research, search, scrutiny.

in-ves′ti-gā-tive, *a*. Curious and deliberate in researches; willing to investigate.

in-ves′ti-gā-tŏr, *n*. One who investigates.

in-vest′i-tūre, *n*. [Fr. *investiture*; LL. *investitura*, from L. *investire*, to clothe, cover; *in*, in, and *vestire*, to clothe, from *vestis*, clothing.]

1. The act of investing; the act of giving possession; the right of giving possession of any manor, office, honor, or benefice; livery of seizin.

2. That which invests or clothes; investment; clothing; covering.

in-vest′ive, *a*. Clothing; encircling.

in-vest′ment, *n*. 1. The act of investing; specifically, (a) the act of surrounding, blocking up, or besieging by an armed force; (b) the laying out of money in the purchase of some species of property; (c) in law, investiture.

2. The property in which one invests; also, the capital invested.

3. That which invests or clothes; dress; vestment.

in-vest′ŏr, *n*. One who invests.

in-ves′tūre, *n*. Investment; investiture. [Obs.]

in-ves′tūre, *v.t.* To invest; to clothe. [Obs.]

in-vet′ẽr-ȧ-cy, *n*. Firmness or deep-rooted obstinacy of any quality or state acquired by time or long continuance; as, the *inveteracy* of custom and habit; usually in a bad sense; as, the *inveteracy* of error.

in-vet′ẽr-āte, *v.t.* [L. *inveteratus*, pp. of *inveterare*, to keep a thing until it is old (in pass. to become old); *in*, in, and *vetus* (*-eris*), old.] To fix and settle by long continuance. [Obs.]

in-vet′ẽr-āte, *a*. 1. Deep-rooted; firmly established by long continuance; obstinate; used of evils; as, an *inveterate* disease; an *inveterate* abuse.

2. Having habits fixed by long continuance; used of persons; as, an *inveterate* toper.

3. Violent; obstinate; as, *inveterate* malice.

4. Old; long-established.

Syn.—Confirmed, established, deep-rooted.

in-vet′ẽr-āte-ly, *adv*. In an inveterate manner.

in-vet′ẽr-āte-ness, *n*. Inveteracy.

in-vet-ẽr-ā′tion, *n*. The act of establishing or confirming by long continuance.

in-vexed′ (-vekst′), *a*. [LL. *invexus*, equivalent to L. *convexus*, arched, vaulted.] In heraldry, arched or inarched.

Chief Invexed.

in-vict′, *a*. Unconquered; indomitable. [Obs.]

in-vid′i-ous, *a*. [L. *invidiosus*, from *invidia*, envy, ill will, from *invidere*, to look askance at.]

1. Envious; malignant; due to or expressing ill will.

2. Likely to incur ill will or hatred, or to provoke envy; hateful; as, *invidious* preferences.

3. Enviable; desirable. [Obs.]

Syn.—Envious, hateful, odious.

in-vid′i-ous-ly, *adv*. In an invidious manner.

in-vid′i-ous-ness, *n*. The quality of being invidious.

in-viġ′i-lănce, in-viġ′i-lăn-cy, *n*. Want of vigilance.

in-viġ′i-lāte, *v.i.* [L. *invigilatus*, pp. of *invigilare*, to watch diligently.] To watch diligently.

in-vig′ŏr, *v.t.* To invigorate. [Obs.]

in-vig′ŏr-āte, *v.t.*; invigorated, *pt.*, *pp.*; invigorating, *ppr.* [L. *in*, in, and *vigor*, strength, courage.] To give vigor to; to strengthen; to animate; to give life and energy to.

in-vig-ŏr-ā′tion, *n*. The act of invigorating, or state of being invigorated.

in-vile′, *v.t.* [LL. *invilare*; L. *in*, in, and *vilis*, vile, worthless.] To make vile. [Obs.]

in-vil′lāġed, *a*. Turned into a village. [Obs.]

in-vin-ci-bil′i-ty, *n*. Invincibleness.

in-vin′ci-ble, *a*. [L. *invincibilis*; *in-* priv., and *vincibilis*, conquerable, from *vincere*, to conquer, defeat.] Not to be conquered or subdued; that cannot be overcome; unconquerable; insuperable; as, an *invincible* army or objection.

in-vin′ci-ble-ness, *n*. The quality of being unconquerable; insuperableness.

in-vin′ci-bly, *adv*. Unconquerably; insuperably.

in-vī″ō-lȧ-bil′i-ty, *n*. Same as *Inviolableness*.

in-vī′ō-lȧ-ble, *a*. [L. *inviolabilis*, imperishable, indestructible; *in-* priv., and *violabilis*, from *violare*, to treat with violence, dishonor.]

1. Not to be violated; that ought not to be injured, broken, polluted, or treated with irreverence; as, a sacred place, an agreement, or promise should be considered *inviolable*.

2. Not susceptible of hurt or wound.

in-vī′ō-lȧ-ble-ness, *n*. The quality or state of being inviolable.

in-vī′ō-lȧ-bly, *adv*. So as to remain inviolate.

in-vī′ō-lȧ-cy, *n*. The quality of being inviolate.

in-vī′ō-lāte, *a*. [L. *inviolatus*; *in-* priv., and *violatus*, pp. of *violare*, to treat with violence, injure.] Unhurt; uninjured; unbroken; unprofaned; inviolable.

in-vī′ō-lā-ted, *a*. Inviolate. [Obs.]

in-vī′ō-lāte-ly, *adv*. Inviolably.

in-vī′ō-lāte-ness, *n*. The quality of being inviolate.

in′vi-ous, *a*. [L. *invius*; *in-* priv., and *via*, way, road.] Impassable; untrodden. [Rare.]

in′vi-ous-ness, *n*. State of being invious. [Rare.]

in-vir′ile, *a*. [L. *in-* priv., and *virilis*, belonging to man, from *vir*, a man.] Wanting in virility.

in-vi-ril′i-ty, *n*. Absence of manhood; departure from manly character.

in-vis′ċāte, *v.t.* To lime; to catch with or as with birdlime. [Obs.]

in-vis′cẽr-āte, *v.t.* To root or implant deeply. [Obs.]

in-vis′cẽr-āte, *a*. Implanted deeply. [Obs.]

in-viṣ-i-bil′i-ty, *n*. The state of being invisible.

in-viṣ′i-ble, *a*. [L. *invisibilis*; *in-* priv., and *visibilis*, visible, from *videre*, to see.] That cannot be seen; imperceptible by the sight.

Invisible green; a shade of green so dark as scarcely to be distinguishable from black.

In-viṣ′i-ble, *n*. 1. A Rosicrucian, from the secret methods of his organization.

2. A heretic of the sixteenth century, who denied the visibility of the church.

The Invisible; the Supreme Being.

in-viṣ′i-ble-ness, *n*. Invisibility.

in-viṣ′i-bly, *adv*. In an invisible manner.

in-vi′ṣion, *n*. Want of vision or the power of seeing. [Obs.]

in-vi-tā′tion, *n*. [L. *invitatio* (*-onis*), from *invitare*, to invite, ask.]

1. The act of inviting; solicitation to do or to come; the requesting of a person's company, as to visit or to dine.

2. A written, printed, or spoken message requesting one's presence.

3. Temptation; enticement; attraction.

in-vī′tȧ-tō-ry, *a*. Pertaining to or containing invitation; as, the *invitatory* or ninety-fifth Psalm, "O come, let us sing unto the Lord."

in-vī′tȧ-tō-ry, *n.*; *pl.* **in-vī′tȧ-tō-rieṣ**. [LL. *invitatorius*, inviting, from L. *invitator*, one who invites, from *invitare*, to invite.] A formula of invitation in a religious service, as the antiphon to the invitatory psalm in the Roman Catholic church.

in-vīte′, *v.t.*; invited, *pt.*, *pp.*; inviting, *ppr.* [Fr. *inviter*, from L. *invitare*, to ask, treat as a guest, entertain.]

1. To ask to do some act or to go to some place; to request the company of; as, to *invite* one to dine or sup; to *invite* friends to a wedding.

2. To present temptations or allurements to; to allure; to attract; to tempt to come; to give or offer favorable chance or opening for; as, an open door *invites* a thief.

in-vīte′, *v.i.* To extend invitation.

in′vīte, *n*. Invitation. [Obs. or Colloq.]

in-vīte′ment, *n*. Invitation. [Obs.]

in-vīt′ẽr, *n*. One who invites.

in-vi′ti-āte (-vish′i-), *a*. Not vitiated; pure; undefiled.

in-vīt′ing, *a*. Alluring; enticing; attractive; as an *inviting* spot.

in-vīt′ing-ly, *adv*. In an inviting manner.

in-vīt′ing-ness, *n*. The quality of being inviting.

in-vit′ri-fī-ȧ-ble, *a.* That cannot be vitrified.

in′vō-cāte, *v.t.* To invoke. [Obs.]

in-vō-cā′tion, *n.* 1. The act of addressing in prayer; the form or act of calling for the assistance or presence of any being, particularly of some divinity; as, the *invocation* of the Muses.

2. A judicial call, demand, or order; as, the *invocation* of papers or evidence into a court.

in′vō-cā-tō-ry, *a.* Making invocation; invoking.

in′voice, *n.* [Fr. *envois*, things sent, goods forwarded, pl. of *envoi*, a sending, conveyance, from *envoyer*, to send; *en-* (L. *in*, in), and *voyer*, to travel, from L. *via*, way.]

1. In commerce, a written account of the particulars of merchandise shipped or sent to a purchaser, consignee, factor, etc., with the value or prices and charges annexed.

2. A definite quantity of merchandise received or sent.

in′voice, *v.t.*; invoiced (-voist), *pt.*, *pp.*; invoicing, *ppr.* To make a written account or invoice of, as goods or property with their prices; to list in an invoice.

in-vōke′, *v.t.*; invoked (-vokt), *pt.*, *pp.*; invoking, *ppr.* [L. *invocare*, to call upon; *in*, in, on, and *vocare*, to call.]

1. To address in prayer; to call on for assistance or protection; as, to *invoke* the Supreme Being.

2. In law, to demand judicially.

in-vol′ū-cel, *n.* [Dim. from *involucre.*] The secondary involucre of small bracts surrounding one of the umbellules of an umbelliferous flower, or the florets of a capitulum.

in-vō-lū′cel-lāte, *a.* Having involucels.

in-vō-lū-cel′lum, *n.* Same as *Involucel.*

in-vō-lū′crăl, *a.* Of or like an involucre.

in-vō-lū′crāte, in-vō-lū′crā-ted, *a.* Involucred.

in-vō-lū′cre (-kẽr), *n.* [L. *involucrum*, a wrapper, case, envelope, from *involvere*, to roll up, wrap up; *in*, in, and *volvere*, to roll.]

1. In botany, (a) any collection of bracts round a cluster of flowers; (b) the covering of the sori of ferns.

2. In anatomy, a membrane which surrounds or incloses a part, as the pericardium.

Hemlock Plant.
a, Involucre. *b b*, Involucels.

3. In zoölogy, an involucrum.

in-vō-lū′cred (-kẽrd), *a.* Having an involucre, as umbels.

in-vō-lū′cret, *n.* An involucel.

in-vō-lū′crum, *n.*; *pl.* **in-vō-lū′crȧ.** 1. In botany, an involucre.

2. In zoölogy, a sheath inclosing the base of a cnida.

in-vol′un-tā-ri-ly, *adv.* Not by choice; not spontaneously; in an involuntary manner.

in-vol′un-tā-ri-ness, *n.* Want of choice or will; the state or quality of being involuntary.

in-vol′un-tā-ry, *a.* [LL. *involuntarius*; L. *in-* priv., and *voluntarius*, willing, from *voluntas*, will, choice, from the root of *velle*, to will.]

1. Independent of will or choice; as, the motion of the heart is *involuntary*, but not against the will.

2. Not proceeding from choice; not done willingly; unwilling; unintentional; opposed to the will; as, *involuntary* submission to a master.

in′vō-lūte, *n.* In geometry, the curve traced by any point of a flexible and inextensible string when the latter is unwrapped, under tension, from a given curve.

in′vō-lūte, in′vō-lū-ted, *a.* [L. *involutus*, pp. of *involvere*, to roll up, wrap up; *in*, in, and *volvere*, to roll.]

1. In botany, rolled spirally inward; as, *involuted* foliation or vernation is when the leaves within the bud have their edges rolled spirally inward.

2. In conchology, turned inward at the margin, as the outer lip in the *Cyprea.*

3. Involved; complicated.

in-vō-lū′tion, *n.* [LL. *involutio* (-*onis*), a rolling up, from L. *involutus*, pp. of *involvere*, to roll up.]

1. The action of involving or infolding.

2. The state of being entangled or involved; complexity; also, a complication.

3. In grammar, the insertion of one or more clauses or members of a sentence between the subject and the verb; involved or complicated grammatical construction.

4. In arithmetic and algebra, the raising of a quantity to any power assigned; the multiplication of a quantity into itself a given number of times.

5. In geometry, a series of elements associated in conjugate pairs and forming a continuous line.

6. In medicine, the retrogression of a distended organ to its normal condition, as the uterus after gestation.

7. That which encloses, covers or involves anything. [Obs.]

in-volve′, *v.t.*; involved, *pt.*, *pp.*; involving, *ppr.* [L. *involvere*, to roll up, wrap up; *in*, in, and *volvere*, to roll.]

1. To envelop in anything which exists on all sides; to cover with or as with surrounding matter; as, to *involve* in darkness or obscurity.

2. To include by rational or logical construction; to imply; to comprise, as a logical consequence.

3. To entwist; to entangle; to entwine; to draw in by way of connection; to implicate; as, to *involve* a friend in one's ruin.

4. To inwrap; to infold; to complicate or make intricate; as, *involved* folds; an *involved* phrase.

5. In mathematics, to raise a quantity to any assigned power; to multiply a quantity by itself a given number of times.

Syn.—Embarrass, entangle, implicate, imply.—That is *implied* which is to be understood from the words used or the circumstances of the case, though not set forth in form. *Involve* goes beyond the mere interpretation of things into their necessary relations; and hence, if one thing *involves* another, it so contains it that the two must go together by an indissoluble connection.

in-volved′, *a.* 1. In heraldry, enveloped.

2. In conchology, involute.

in-volv′ed-ness, *n.* The state or quality of being involved.

in-volve′ment, *n.* The act of involving; the state of being involved.

in-vul′gär, *v.t.* To make vulgar. [Obs.]

in-vul′gär, *a.* Not vulgar. [Obs.]

in-vul″nẽr-ȧ-bil′i-ty, *n.* The quality or state of being invulnerable, or secure from injury.

in-vul′nẽr-ȧ-ble, *a.* [L. *invulnerabilis*; *in-* priv., and *vulnerare*, to wound, from *vulnus* (-*eris*), a wound.]

1. That cannot be wounded; incapable of receiving injury.

2. Unassailable, as an argument; able to reply to all arguments; proof against overthrow.

in-vul′nẽr-ȧ-ble-ness, *n.* Invulnerability.

in-vul′nẽr-āte, *a.* Uninjured. [Obs.]

in-wall′, *v.t.*; inwalled, *pt.*, *pp.*; inwalling, *ppr.* To inclose or fortify with or as with a wall.

in′wall, *n.* An interior wall, particularly the lining wall of a blast-furnace.

in′wărd, *n.* 1. That which is inside; the viscera; generally in the plural.

2. [*pl.*] Mental endowments; ingenuity; genius. [Obs.]

3. A familiar; an intimate. [Obs.]

in′wărd, *a.* [ME. *inward*; AS. *inneweard*; *inne*, in, and *-weard*, -ward.]

1. Internal; interior; placed or being within; as, the *inward* structure of the body.

2. Intimate; domestic; familiar. [Obs.]

3. Seated in the mind or soul.

in′wărd, in′wărds, *adv.* [ME. *inward*; AS *inweard*, inward; *in*, in, and *-weard*, -ward. The suffix *-s* is an adverbial genit. ending.]

1. Toward the inside, center, or interior; as, to bend a thing *inward.*

2. Into the mind or thoughts.

> Celestial light shine *inward.* —Milton.

in′wărd-ly, *adv.* 1. In the inner parts; internally.

2. In the mind or heart; privately; secretly.

3. Toward the center; inward.

4. Familiarly; intimately. [Obs.]

in′wărd-ness, *n.* 1. Intimacy; familiarity. [Obs.]

2. Internal state; real nature or meaning.

3. The state or quality of being inward or of belonging to the inner life.

in′wărds, *adv.* See *Inward.*

in-wēave′, *v.t.*; inwove, *pt.*; inwoven, *pp.*; inweaving, *ppr.* To weave together; to intermix or intertwine by weaving.

in-wheel′ (-hwēl′), *v.t.* To encircle. [Rare.]

in′wit, *n.* Mind; understanding; conscience. [Obs.]

in-with′, *prep.* Within. [Obs.]

in-wood′, *v.t.* To hide in woods. [Obs.]

in-wŏrk′, *v.t.*; inworked, *pt.*, *pp.*; inworking, *ppr.* To work in or into.

in-wōrn′, *a.* Worn or wrought in or into.

in-wōve′, *v.*, past tense of *inweave.*

in-wōv′en, *v.*, past participle of *inweave.*

in-wrap′, en-wrap′, *v.t.*; inwrapped, enwrapped, *pt.*, *pp.*; inwrapping, enwrapping, *ppr.* 1. To infold; to cover by wrapping.

2. To involve in difficulty or perplexity; to perplex. [Rare.]

in-wrēathe′ (-rēth′), *v.t.*; inwreathed, *pt.*, *pp.* inwreathing, *ppr.* To surround or encompass with or as with a wreath; spelled also *enwreathe.*

in-wrought′ (-ra̤t′), *a.* Wrought or worked in or among other things; adorned with figures.

ī′ō, *interj.* A cry of pleasure or triumph.

Ī′ō, *n.* [Gr. *Iō*, the daughter of Inachus, loved by Zeus and, when changed into a heifer, tormented by a gadfly sent by Hera.]

1. The innermost moon of Jupiter.

2. [i—] A large, showy, yellow moth, *Hyperchiria io*, having a bright, pink-and-blue, eye-like spot on each hind wing.

3. [i—] The peacock-butterfly, *Vanessa io.*

ī′ō-dăl, *n.* [*Iod*ine and *al*cohol.] An oleaginous liquid, CI_3COH, obtained from the action of alcohol and nitric acid on iodine.

ī′ō-dāte, *n.* [*Iodic* and *-ate.*] Any compound of iodic acid with a base.

i-od-hȳ′drin, *n.* [*Iod*ine and chlor*hydrin.*] A compound formed by replacing one or more hydroxyl groups in glycerin by iodine.

ī-od′ic, *a.* [*Iod*ine and *-ic*]. Of or containing iodine.

Iodic acid; an acid, HIO_3, occurring as a white solid with a sour, astringent taste.

ī′ō-dide, *n.* [*Iod*ine and *-ide.*] A compound of iodine with a metal or radical more electropositive than itself; as, *iodide* of sodium.

ī′ō-dine (*or* -dīn), *n.* [Gr. *iōdēs*, violet-like; *ion*, a violet, and *eidos*, form.] A nonmetallic elementary solid substance, constituting one of the group of halogens. It exists in the water of the ocean and mineral springs, in marine molluscous animals, and in seaweeds, from the ashes of which it is chiefly procured. Its color is bluish-black or grayish-black, of a metallic luster. It is fusible at 225° Fahr., the color of its vapor being a beautiful violet, whence its name.

Iodine green; a green pigment derived from coal-tar.

Iodine scarlet; red mercuric iodide used as a pigment.

Iodine yellow; lead iodide used as a pigment.

ī′ō-dism, *n.* A pathological condition caused by iodine or its compounds used in excess.

ī′ō-dīze, *v.t.*; iodized, *pt.*, *pp.*; iodizing, *ppr.* To treat with or subject to the action of iodine.

ī′ō-di-zẽr, *n.* One who or that which iodizes.

iodo-, iod-. Combining forms from Gr. *iōdēs*, violet-like; used in chemistry to denote the presence of iodine; as, *iodo*quinine.

ī-od′ō-fọrm, *n.* [*Iodo* and *form*yl.] A yellow compound, CHI_3, produced by the action of iodine and potash on ethyl alcohol. It is used as an antiseptic and has a characteristic smell.

ī″ō-dō-hȳ′dric, *a.* Same as *Hydriodic.*

ī′ō-dol, *n.* [*Iod-* and pyr*rol.*] A crystalline antiseptic compound, C_4I_4NH, having a yellowish-brown color.

ī″ō-dō-met′ric, *a.* [*Iodo-*, and Gr. *metron*, a measure.] Of or relating to titration by the use of a standard iodine solution.

ī″ō-dō-qui′nine, *n.* [*Iodo-* and *quinine.*] The iodide of quinine.

ī-od′ū-ret, *n.* An iodide. [Obs.]

i-od′y-rite, *n.* [*Iod-*, and Gr. *argyros*, silver, and *-ite.*] A yellowish mineral iodide of silver.

ī′ō-lite, *n.* [Gr. *ion*, a violet, and *lithos*, stone.] A silicate of magnesium, aluminium, and iron, a mineral of a violet-blue color, with a shade of purple or black; called also *dichroite*, because the tints along the two axes are unlike, *cordierite*, and *water-sapphire.*

ī′on, *n.* [Gr. *iōn*, ppr. of *ienai*, to go.] One of the elements or radicals into which an electrolyte or compound undergoing electrolytic dissociation becomes divided; an anion or a cation.

I-ō′ni-ăn, *n.* and *a.* I. *n.* A member of the Ionic branch of the Greek race.

II. *a.* Of or belonging to the Ionians or to Ionia.

I-on′ic, *n.* The Ionic dialect, foot, verse, or type.

I-on′ic, *a.* Of, belonging to, or resembling Ionia, the Ionian Greeks, or their art, language, or civilization.

Ionic dialect; one of the three main divisions of ancient Greek, the Æolic and Doric being the other two. The epic or Old Ionic is the language of Homer and Hesiod; the New Ionic is that of Herodotus; the Attic or the Ionic dialect of Attica is that of Aristophanes, Plato, and Sophocles.

Ionic foot; a metrical foot of four syllables, the *greater Ionic* having two longs and two shorts, the *lesser Ionic* two shorts and two longs.

Ionic Order.

Ionic order; one of the three Greek orders of architecture, the distinguishing characteristic being the volute of its capital. The shaft, including the base, which is half a diameter, and the capital to the bottom of the volute, is about nine diameters high, and usually fluted in twenty-four flutes. It is more slender than the Doric and Tuscan, but less slender than the Corinthian and Composite. The Attic base is used in the best examples.

Ionic type; a style of type-face.

This line is set in Ionic.

I-ō-nid'i-um, *n.* [Gr. *ion*, a violet, and *eidos*, resemblance.] A large genus of subtropical American plants of the violet family; the root of the white ipecacuanha, *Ionidium Ipecacuanha*, is used as an emetic.

ī'ō-quá, *n.* Same as *Hiaqua.*

ī-ō'tȧ, *n.* [Gr.] Primarily the name of the Greek letter ι, often indicated by a sort of dot under another letter (as ῳ); hence, a very small quantity; a tittle; a jot.

Iota subscript; in Greek grammar, iota when silent written beneath α, η, or ω, with which it forms a diphthong, as ᾳ, ῃ, ῳ.

ī-ō'tȧ-cism, *n.* [LL. *iotacismus*; Gr. *iōtakismos*, too much use of iota, from *iōta*, iota.] The use of the sound of iota, that of long *e* in English, in pronouncing the Greek vowels and diphthongs ει, η, ῃ, οι, υ, and υι.

I O U. In England, a paper having on it these letters, signifying *I owe you*, followed by a sum, and duly signed, considered equally binding in honor with a promissory note.

I'ō-wȧs, *n.pl.* A division of the Sioux tribe of North American Indians.

ip'ē-çaç, *n.* Ipecacuanha.

American ipecac; a plant of the genus *Gillenia.*

ip-ē-çaç-ū-an'hȧ (-ȧ), *n.* [Port. *ipecacuanha*, from native name.] An emetic substance, of a nauseous odor and repulsive bitterish taste, the dried root of plants of the order *Rubiaceæ* growing in South America. The best is yielded by the *Cephaelis Ipecacuanha*, a small shrubby plant.

Ipecacuanha Plant (*Cephaelis Ipecacuanha*).

ip'ō-çras, *n.* Hippocras. [Obs.]

Ip-ō-mœ'ȧ, *n.* [Gr. *ips*, *ipos*, a worm, and *homoios*, like.] A large genus of plants of the order *Convolvulaceæ*, consisting of twining prostrate, or rarely low and erect, herbs, with entire, lobed, or divided leaves, and usually large showy flowers. The genus includes the jalap, the sweet potato, and the morning-glory.

ip-ō-mœ'iç, *a.* Of, like, or derived from the plants of the genus *Ipomœa*; as, *ipomœic* acid.

ir-. The form of the prefix *in-* used before *r*.

ī'rȧ-çund, *a.* [L. *iracundus*, from *ira*, anger, wrath.] Angry; irritable; passionate.

i-rä'de, *n.* [Turk.] A decree issued by the sultan of Turkey.

I-rän', *n.* [Per. *Īrān*, Persia.] The official name of the kingdom of Persia.

I-rā'ni-ăn, *a.* Of or belonging to Persia.

I-rā'ni-ăn, *n.* 1. A native of Persia.

2. The Iranian language or group of languages.

I-ran'iç, *a.* Same as *Iranian.*

ī-ras-ci-bil'i-ty, *n.* The quality of being irascible.

ī-ras'ci-ble, *a.* [LL. *irascibilis*, from L. *irasci*, to be angry, from *ira*, anger.] Very easily provoked or inflamed to anger or wrath; irritable; as, an *irascible* temper.

Syn.—Angry, fiery, hasty, choleric.

ī-ras'ci-ble-ness, *n.* Irascibility.

ī-ras'ci-bly, *adv.* In an irascible manner.

-rāte', *a.* [L. *iratus*, angry, from *irasci*, to be angry, from *ira*, anger.] Ireful; angry; enraged; incensed; wrathful.

īre, *n.* [OFr. *ire*, from L. *ira*, anger, wrath.] Anger; wrath; keen resentment.

Syn.—Fury, rage, resentment.

īre'fụl, *a.* Angry; wroth; furious with anger.

īre'fụl-ly, *adv.* In an angry manner.

īre'fụl-ness, *n.* The state or quality of being ireful.

ī'rē-närch, *n.* [LL. *irenarcha*, *irenarches*; Gr. *eirēnarchēs*; *eirēnē*, peace, and *archein*, to govern, rule.] A peace-officer of the Eastern or Greek empire.

ī-ren'iç, ī-ren'iç-ăl, *a.* Pacific; desirous of peace.

ī-ren'i-con, *n.*; *pl.* **ī-ren'i-cȧ.** [Gr. *eirēnikon*, neut. of *eirēnikos*, of or for peace, from *eirēnē*, peace.]

1. A proposition, scheme, or arrangement designed for peace, especially in the church.

2. [*pl.*] In the Greek church, the petition for peace with which the liturgy begins.

ī-ren'içs, *n.* That branch of theology treating upon the means of securing Christian unity or harmony; opposed to *polemics.*

ī'ri-ăn, *a.* Relating to the iris of the eye. [Rare.]

I'ri-cism, *n.* [Rare.] Same as *Irishism.*

I-ri-dā'cē-æ, *n.pl.* [Gr. *iris* (*-idos*), a rainbow.] An order of endogenous plants, usually with equitant leaves, including the crocus, gladiolus, and iris; also called *Irideæ.*

ir-i-dā'ceous, *a.* Of or pertaining to the order *Iridaceæ.*

ī'ri-dăl, *a.* [Gr. *iris* (*-idos*), a rainbow.] Belonging to or resembling the rainbow or the iris.

ir-i-deç'tō-my, *n.* [Gr. *iris* (*-idos*), the iris, rainbow, and *ektomē*, a cutting out; *ek*, out, and *temnein*, to cut.] A surgical operation in which a portion of the iris is removed to form an artificial pupil.

ir"i-dē-rē'mi-ȧ, *n.* [Gr. *iris* (*-idos*), the iris, and *erēmia*, solitude, desolation.] Partial or total absence of the iris.

ī'ri-dēṣ, *n.*, Latin pl. of *iris.*

ir-i-des'cence, *n.* Exhibition of colors like those of the rainbow; prismatic coloration.

ir-i-des'cent, *a.* [Gr. *iris* (*-idos*), a rainbow, and *-escent.*] Having colors like the rainbow; prismatic.

ī-rid'i-ăn, *a.* Pertaining to the iris of the eye.

ī-rid'i-ā-ted, *a.* Same as *Iridescent.*

ī-rid'iç, *a.* Relating to the iris of the eye.

ī-rid'iç, *a.* Of or containing iridium having the higher valence.

ī-rid'i-ous, *a.* Of or containing iridium having the lower valence.

ī-rid'i-sçōpe, *n.* A device for viewing the interior of the eye; spelled also *iridioscope.*

ī-rid'i-um, *n.* [From Gr. *iris* (*-idos*), a rainbow; so called because of the changing color of some of its salts.] A metal of a whitish color, not malleable, found in the ore of platinum, and in a native alloy with osmium.

ir'i-dize, *v.t.*; iridized, *pt.*, *pp.*; iridizing, *ppr.*

1. To cause to become iridescent, as glass.

2. To apply iridium to, as the point of a gold pen.

ī-rid'ō-lin, ī-rid'ō-line, *n.* [*Irid*escent, and L. *oleum*, oil, and *-ine.*] An oily fluid, $C_{10}H_9N$, derived from coal-tar.

ir-i-doş'mi-um, ir-i-doş'mine, *n.* A native osmite of iridium, in which the iridium is more or less replaced by platinum, rhodium, and ruthenium. It occurs commonly in irregular flattened grains, and, being harder than common platinum, is used for the points of gold pens.

ī'ris, *n.*; *pl.* **ī'ris-eṣ** or **ī'ri-dēṣ.** [L. *iris*; Gr. *iris*, rainbow.]

1. The rainbow; personified in mythology as a maiden acting as the messenger of the gods.

2. Any appearance resembling the rainbow, as the solar spectrum or any iridescence.

3. In anatomy, a colored muscular curtain stretched vertically in the midst of the aqueous humor of the eye and perforated by a circular opening called the pupil.

4. [I—] In botany, an extensive genus of plants of the order *Iridaceæ*, including the fleur-de-lis, and the orris; popularly known as the *flags*; also, [i—] any plant of the genus.

Yellow Iris or Fleur-de-lis (*Iris Pseudacorus*).

5. [I—] In astronomy, the seventh asteroid, discovered in 1847.

6. In entomology, the inmost circle of color in an ocellus.

ī'ris-ā-ted, *a.* Iridescent; irised.

ī'ri-sçōpe, *n.* A plate of polished black glass which exhibits iridescent colors. Soap is smeared over its surface and rubbed off with a chamois-skin; when the breath is blown upon the plate through a tube colored rings are formed.

ī'rised (-rist), *a.* Having colors like those of the rainbow.

I'rish, *n. sing.* and *pl.* [ME. *Irish*, *Irysh*; AS. *Irisc*, from *Iras*, the Irish, from Ir. *Eire*, *Erin*, Ireland.]

1. [*pl.*] The people of Ireland or their descendants.

2. The language of the Irish people; the Irish brogue.

3. A game similar to backgammon. [Obs.]

I'rish, *a.* 1. Of, relating to, or produced in Ireland; of or belonging to the people of Ireland or to their language.

2. Erse. [Obs.]

Irish moss; carrageen.

Irish stew; a stew of vegetables and meat in small pieces.

I'rish-işm, *n.* An Irish mode of expression.

I'rish-măn, *n.*; *pl.* **I'rish-men.** A man of the Irish race.

I'rish-ry, *n.* The people of Ireland.

ī-rī'tis, *n.* Inflammation of the iris.

irk, *v.t.* [ME. *irken*, *yrken*, *erken*, to tire, become tired, from Sw. *yrka*, to urge, press upon.] To weary; to give pain to; used only impersonally; as, it *irks* me, it gives me uneasiness.

irk'sōme, *a.* Wearisome; tedious; tiresome; giving uneasiness; troublesome by long continuance or repetition; as, *irksome* hours; *irksome* toil.

irk'sōme-ly, *adv.* In an irksome manner.

irk'sōme-ness, *n.* Tediousness; wearisomeness.

ī'ron (-ūrn), *v.t.*; ironed, *pt.*, *pp.*; ironing, *ppr.*

1. To smooth with an instrument of iron.

2. To shackle with irons; to fetter or handcuff.

3. To furnish or arm with iron.

ī'ron, *n.* [ME. *iron*, *iren*; AS. *iren*, *isen*, *isern*, iron.]

1. The commonest and most useful of all the metals. *Cast-iron* contains about 3.5 per cent of carbon, *wrought iron* about 0.4 per cent; intermediate between the two stands *steel*, which contains about 1 per cent of carbon, and possesses properties that render it perhaps the most important form in which this metal is employed, the range of its application extending from the minute and delicate balance-spring of a watch to the large and ponderous war vessel.

2. An instrument or utensil made of iron; as, a flat*iron*; a grid*iron.*

3. Figuratively, strength; power; as, a man of *iron.*

4. [*pl.*] Fetters; chains; manacles; handcuffs.

Bar iron; weld iron or wrought iron in bars.

Black iron; untinned cast or wrought iron.

Gray iron; cast-iron containing graphite.

Magnetic iron; magnetite.

Malleable iron; weld iron or wrought iron.

Meteoric iron; iron, usually alloyed with nickel and cobalt, found in meteorites.

Pig iron; iron cast in pigs or oblong masses.

Russia iron; a hard, glossy variety of sheet iron which does not rust readily.

Specular iron; crystalline hematite.

To be in irons; (a) to be bound with fetters; (b) to be unmanageable, as a sailing vessel, when, on being brought up head to the wind, she fails to fill away on a tack.

To have too many irons in the fire; to have more things to do than can be properly cared for.

To strike while the iron is hot; to be prompt in taking advantage of circumstances.

Weld iron; iron intermediate in percentage of carbon between cast and wrought iron.

White iron; a whitish crystalline variety of cast-iron.

Wrought iron; a soft, ductile, tough, and malleable iron containing a very low percentage of carbon. It will not temper and cannot be easily fused.

ī'ron, *a.* 1. Made of iron; consisting of iron; as, an *iron* gate; an *iron* bar; *iron* dust.

2. Resembling iron in some respect, either really or metaphorically: (a) harsh; rude; severe; miserable; as, *iron* years of wars; (b) binding fast; not to be broken; as, death's *iron* sleep; (c) hard of understanding; dull; as, *iron*-witted fools; (d) capable of great endurance; firm; robust; as, an *iron* constitution; (e) not to be bent; inflexible; as, an *iron* will; (f) having the color of iron; as, *iron*-gray.

Iron age; (a) in mythology, the last, wickedest, and most unlovely of the ages into which the world's history was divided by ancient writers, and in general, any rude, cruel, or degraded period; as, the *iron age* of Roman literature followed the fall of the Western empire; (b) that period in civilization in which iron implements begun to be used, although stone and bronze implements may still be found in use with them.

Iron crown; an antique crown of gold set with jewels, made originally for the Lombard kings, which was supposed to confer the right of sovereignty over all Italy on the wearer. It inclosed within its round an iron circlet forged, as was claimed, from one of the nails used in the crucifixion of Christ.

Iron Crown of Lombardy, in Monza Cathedral.

Order of the Iron Cross; an order founded by Frederick William III., of Prussia, in 1813 and reorganized in 1870 by William I. The decoration is a black cross patté of iron hung on a white-bordered black ribbon.

ī'ron-bärk-tree, *n.* One of various trees of Australia, having hard, durable wood, as the *Eucalyptus resinifera.*

Ironbark-tree (*Eucalyptus resinifera*).

ī'ron-bound, *a.* 1. Bound with iron.

2. Faced with rocks; rugged; as, an *ironbound* coast.

3. Unyielding; unalterable; as, *ironbound* laws.

ī'ron-cāsed (-kāst), *a.* Encased in iron; ironclad.

ī'ron-clad, *a.* 1. Clad in iron, as a vessel.

2. Rigorous; exacting, as rules. [Colloq.]

ī'ron-clad, *n.* A vessel sheathed with a defensive covering of iron or steel plates; an armored war-ship. [See illus. p. 896.]

ī′ron=clāy, *n.* Clay mixed with iron ore.
ī′ron-ẽr, *n.* A person or thing that irons.
ī′ron=fist″ed, *a.* Close-fisted; penurious.
ī′ron=flint, *n.* Ferruginous quartz.
ī′ron=found″ẽr, *n.* One who makes iron castings.
ī′ron=found″ry, *n.* The place where iron castings are made.
ī′ron=fũr″nāce, *n.* Any furnace used in connection with the smelting or working of iron.
ī′ron=glȧnce, *n.* Hematite.
ī′ron=grāy, *a.* and *n.* I. *a.* Of a gray hue approaching the color of freshly fractured iron.
II. *n.* A hue of gray approaching the color of freshly fractured iron; also, an iron-gray horse.

A, Iron plating. B, Teak backing. C, Ship's side.

ī′ron=hat, *n.* A headpiece of metal, made generally in the form here shown, worn during the twelfth to the seventeenth centuries.

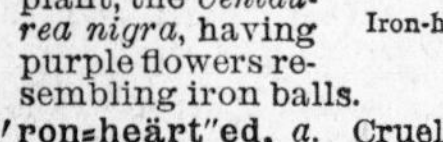
Iron-hats (time of Charles I. and Cromwell).

ī′ron-heads, *n.* A plant, the *Centaurea nigra*, having purple flowers resembling iron balls.
ī′ron=heãrt″ed, *a.* Cruel; merciless; pitiless.
ī-ron′iç, *a.* Ironical.
ī-ron′iç-ăl, *a.* [Gr. *eirōnikos*, from *eirōneia*, dissimulation, irony.]
1. Relating to or containing irony; expressing one thing and meaning another.
2. Addicted to irony; using irony.
ī-ron′iç-ăl-ly, *adv.* In an ironical manner.
ī-ron′iç-ăl-ness, *n.* The quality of being ironical.
ī′ron-ing, *n.* 1. A smoothing with an iron.
2. The articles ironed.
ī′ron-ing=bōard, *n.* A board upon which articles are laid for ironing.
ī′ron-ish, *a.* Like iron; as, an *ironish* taste.
ī′ron-ist, *n.* One who deals in irony. [Obs.]
ī′ron=liq″uŏr (-lik″ẽr), *n.* Acetate of iron, used as a mordant by dyers.
ī′ron-man, *n.* 1. A maker of or dealer in iron.
2. A spinning-mule.
3. A machine for cutting coal.
ī′ron-mȧs″tẽr, *n.* One who manufactures or deals largely in iron.
ī′ron=mōld, *n.* A spot on cloth made by iron-rust.
ī′ron-mŏn″gẽr, *n.* A dealer in iron wares.
ī′ron-mŏn″gẽr-y, *n.* Articles made of iron; hardware.
ī′ron=py-rī″tēs, *n.* Crystalline sulphid of iron.
ī′ron=sand, *n.* Granular iron ore.
ī′ron=sçāle, *n.* The scale formed on the surface of white-hot iron by oxidation.
ī′ron=shrub, *n.* St. Martin's herb.
ī′ron=sick, *a.* Having the bolts and nails so much corroded or eaten with rust as to become leaky; said of a vessel.
ī′ron-side, *n.* Same as *Ironsides.*
ī′ron=sīd″ed, *a.* Having sides of iron or of the firmness of iron; figuratively, rough; unfeeling.
ī′ron-sīdes, *n. sing.* and *pl.* One of Oliver Cromwell's veteran troopers; a soldier noted for rough hardihood.
ī′ron-smith, *n.* 1. A worker in iron; an artisan who makes and repairs utensils of iron; a blacksmith.
2. A bird having a note like the sounds made by a smith; the *Megalæma faber* of the island of Hainan.
ī′ron-stōne, *n.* An ore of iron, containing clay.
Ironstone china; a species of hard, white pottery.
ī′ron=tree, *n.* Any one of a number of hard-wood trees, as *Ixora ferrea.*
ī′ron-wãre, *n.* Hardware; ware made of iron.
ī′ron-wood, *n.* The flattop.
ī′ron-wood, *n.* Any one of many trees having very hard, firm, tough, strong, or heavy wood, as some species of trees of the genus *Sideroxylon*, so called from their hardness. Also the *Ostrya Virginica*, sometimes called hop-hornbeam, a tree of the United States. *Diospyros Ebenum*, the ebony, is also named ironwood, as are the *Metrosideros vera* of Java, and the *Mesua ferrea* of Hindustan. The wood of *Vepris undulata* is called white ironwood at the Cape of Good Hope, and that of *Olea laurifolia*, black ironwood.
ī′ron-wŏrk, *n.* The parts of a building, vessel, carriage, etc., which consist of iron; anything made of iron.
ī′ron-wŏrks, *n. sing.* and *pl.* An establishment where iron is manufactured, wrought, or cast into ironwork.
ī′ron-wŏrt, *n.* 1. A plant of the genus *Sideritis.*
2. One of the hemp-nettles, *Galeopsis Tetrahit* or *Galeopsis Ladanum.*
ī′ron-y (-ŭrn-), *a.* 1. Made or consisting of iron; partaking of iron; as, *irony* chains; *irony* particles.
2. Resembling iron; hard.
ī′ron-y, *n.*; *pl.* **ī′ron-ies.** [Fr. *ironie*; L. *ironia*; Gr. *eirōneia*, dissimulation, irony, from *eirōn*, a dissembler in speech, from *eirein*, to speak.]
1. A kind of ridicule which exposes the errors or faults of others by seeming to adopt, approve, or defend them; as, Nero was a very virtuous prince; a statement of the exact opposite of what is meant.
2. Pretended ignorance, with the intention of irritating or perplexing an opponent in a dispute.
Syn.—Burlesque, ridicule, sarcasm, satire.
Ir-ō-quois′ (-kwoi′), *n.* [Fr. form of native Indian name.] Any one of the North American Indians composing the confederacy of the Five Nations made up of Mohawks, Senecas, Oneidas, Onondagas, and Cayugas, of central New York, later augmented by a sixth tribe, the Tuscaroras; any Indian of the Iroquois stock of American Indians.
Ir-ō-quois′, *a.* Pertaining to the Indians of the Five Nations, or to their language, customs, and manners; relating to the stock from which sprang the men of the Five Nations.
ī′rous, *a.* Apt to be angry. [Obs.]
irp, *a.* Grimacing or contorting. [Obs.]
irp, irpe, *n.* [Origin doubtful.] A smirk of the face; a twisting of the body. [Obs.]
ir-rā′di-ănce, ir-rā′di-ăn-cy, *n.* 1. Emission of rays of light on an object.
2. Beams of light emitted; luster; splendor.
ir-rā′di-ănt, *a.* Emitting rays of light.
ir-rā′di-āte, *v.t.*; irradiated, *pt.*, *pp.*; irradiating, *ppr.* [L. *irradiatus*, pp. of *irradiare*, to beam upon, illumine; *in*, in, on, and *radiare*, to beam.]
1. To illuminate; to brighten; to make splendid; to adorn with luster.
2. To enlighten intellectually; to illuminate; as, to *irradiate* the mind.
3. To animate by heat or light.
4. To diffuse.
ir-rā′di-āte, *v.i.* To emit rays; to shine.
ir-rā′di-āte, *a.* Adorned with brightness, or with anything shining.
ir-rā-di-ā′tion, *n.* 1. The act of emitting beams of light.
2. Illumination; brightness.
3. Intellectual light.
4. In physics, an apparent enlargement of the area of a highly luminous body or of a white body on a black background; as, a white disk on a black background appears larger than a black disk on a white background, both being of equal size and at an equal distance.
ir-rad′i-cāte, *v.t.* [L. *in*, in, and *radicare*, to take root, from *radix* (-*icis*), a root.] To root deeply. [Rare.]
ir-ra′tion-ăl (-rash′un-ăl), *a.* [L. *irrationalis*; *in-* priv., and *rationalis*, reasonable, from *ratio* (-*onis*), the process of thinking, reason.]
1. Not rational; void of reason or understanding; as, brutes are *irrational* animals.
2. Not according to the dictates of reason; contrary to reason; absurd; as, to act in an *irrational* manner.
3. In mathematics, not being expressible by either an integral or a fractional number, as the square root of two and of other numbers.
Syn.—Foolish, absurd, preposterous.—*Irrational* signifies contrary to reason and is employed to express the want of the faculty itself or a deficiency in the exercise of it; *foolish* signifies the perversion of this faculty; *absurd* signifies that to which one would turn a deaf ear; *preposterous* expresses that which is unnatural and contrary to common sense.
ir-ra-tion-al′i-ty, *n.* Want of reason or the powers of understanding.
ir-ra′tion-ăl-ly, *adv.* Without reason; in a manner contrary to reason; absurdly.
ir-ra′tion-ăl-ness, *n.* Irrationality.
ir-rē-but′tȧ-ble, *a.* Not to be rebutted.
ir-rē-cep′tive, *a.* Having no inclination to receive.
ir-rē-çlāim′ȧ-ble, *a.* Not to be reclaimed; not able to be recalled from error or vice.
ir-rē-çlāim′ȧ-bly, *adv.* So as not to admit of being reclaimed.
ir-reç-ŏg-ni′tion (-nish′un), *n.* A want of recognition.
ir-reç′ŏg-ni-zȧ-ble, *a.* Unrecognizable.
ir-reç-ŏn-cī-lȧ-bil′i-ty, *n.* Impossibility of being reconciled.
ir-reç′ŏn-cī-lȧ-ble, *a.* 1. Not to be recalled to amity or a state of friendship and kindness; retaining enmity that cannot be appeased or subdued; as, an *irreconcilable* enemy or faction.
2. Not capable of being made to agree or be consistent; incongruous; incompatible; as, *irreconcilable* absurdities.
ir-reç′ŏn-cī-lȧ-ble-ness, *n.* The quality of being irreconcilable; incongruity; incompatibility.
ir-reç′ŏn-cī-lȧ-bly, *adv.* In a manner that precludes reconciliation.
ir-reç′ŏn-cīle, *v.t.* To prevent from being reconciled. [Obs.]
ir-reç′ŏn-cīle-ment, *n.* Want of reconciliation; disagreement.
ir-reç-ŏn-cil-i-ā′tion, *n.* Want of reconciliation.
ir-rē-çord′ȧ-ble, *a.* Not to be recorded.
ir-rē-çov′ẽr-ȧ-ble, *a.* Not to be recovered, regained, or remedied; as, an *irrecoverable* loss.
ir-rē-çov′ẽr-ȧ-ble-ness, *n.* The state of being irrecoverable.
ir-rē-çov′ẽr-ȧ-bly, *adv.* Beyond recovery.
ir-rē-çū′pẽr-ȧ-ble, *a.* [LL. *irrecuperabilis*, irrecoverable; L. *in-* priv., and *recuperare*, to recover, recuperate.] Irrecoverable.
ir-rē-çū′pẽr-ȧ-bly, *adv.* Irrecoverably.
ir-rē-çūred′, *a.* Not curable. [Obs.]
ir-rē-çū′ṣȧ-ble, *a.* [LL. *irrecusabilis*; L. *in-* priv., and LL. *recusabilis*, that should be rejected, from L. *recusare*, to refuse.] Not liable to exception or rejection.
ir-rē-deem-ȧ-bil′i-ty, *n.* Irredeemableness.
ir-rē-deem′ȧ-ble, *a.* 1. That cannot be redeemed; as, an *irredeemable* sinner.
2. Not subject to be paid at pleasure; as, *irredeemable* debts; *irredeemable* certificates or stock.
ir-rē-deem′ȧ-ble-ness, *n.* The quality of being nonredeemable.
ir-rē-deem′ȧ-bly, *adv.* So as not to be redeemed.
ir-rē-den′tiṣm, *n.* The platform of the Irredentists, a political party of Italy formed in 1878 for the purpose of joining to that country other regions populated by Italians but ruled by other governments.
Ir-rē-den′tist, *n.* [It. *irredentista*, from *irredento*, unredeemed, from L. *in-* priv., and *redemptus*, pp. of *redimere*, to redeem.] One of those favoring and attempting to bring about irredentism.
ir-rē-dū-ci-bil′i-ty, *n.* The quality that renders irreducible.
ir-rē-dū′ci-ble, *a.* 1. Not to be reduced; not to be brought to a desired state; not to be changed to a different state.
2. In mathematics, not capable of reduction to a simpler form.
Irreducible case; in algebra, a particular case in the solution of a cubic equation, in which the formula commonly employed contains an imaginary quantity, and therefore fails in its application.
ir-rē-dū′ci-ble-ness, *n.* The quality of being irreducible.
ir-rē-dū′ci-bly, *adv.* In a manner not reducible.
ir-rē-flec′tion, *n.* Want or absence of reflection.
ir-rē-flect′ive, *a.* Lacking the quality of reflection.
ir-rē-form′ȧ-ble, *a.* Not to be reformed; beyond the possibility of reformation.
ir-ref″rȧ-gȧ-bil′i-ty, *n.* The quality of being irrefragable or incapable of refutation.
ir-ref′rȧ-gȧ-ble, *a.* Not refragable; incapable of being refuted or overthrown; incontestable; undeniable; as, an *irrefragable* argument; *irrefragable* reason or evidence.
ir-ref′rȧ-gȧ-ble-ness, *n.* Irrefragability.
ir-ref′rȧ-gȧ-bly, *adv.* In an irrefragable manner.
ir-rē-fran-gi-bil′i-ty, *n.* 1. The quality that forbids a thing being broken or violated.
2. In optics, the quality that forbids change of direction, as in a ray of light.
ir-rē-fran′gi-ble, *a.* 1. In optics, not capable of being refracted, as light passing from one medium to another of different density.
2. Not refrangible; not to be broken or violated.
ir-rē-fran′gi-ble-ness, *n.* Irrefrangibility.
ir-rē-fūt′ȧ-ble, *a.* [LL. *irrefutabilis*; L. *in-* priv., and *refutare*, to refute.] Not to be refuted or disproved.
ir-rē-fūt′ȧ-ble-ness, *n.* The state or quality of being irrefutable.
ir-rē-fūt′ȧ-bly, *adv.* Beyond the possibility of refutation.
ir-rē-ġen′ẽr-ȧ-cy, *n.* Unregeneracy.
ir-rē-ġen-ẽr-ā′tion, *n.* An unregenerate state. [Obs.]
ir-reg′ū-lăr, *a.* [LL. *irregularis*, not regular; L. *in-* priv., and *regularis*, pertaining to rules, from *regula*, a rule.] Not regular; (a) not according to common form or rules; as, an *irregular* building or fortification; (b) not according to established principles or customs; deviating from usage; as, the *irregular* proceedings of a legislative body; (c) not conformable to nature or the usual operation of natural laws; as, an *irregular* action of the heart and arteries; (d) not according to the rules of art; immethodical; as, *irregular* verse; an *irregular* discourse; (e) not in conformity to laws human or divine; deviating from the rules of moral rectitude; vicious; as, *irregular* conduct or propensities; (f) not straight; as, an *irregular* line or course; (g) not uniform; as, *irregular*

motion; (h) in grammar, deviating from the common form in respect to the inflectional terminations; (i) in geometry, applied to a figure, whether plane or solid, whose sides as well as angles are not all equal and similar among themselves; (j) in music, applied to a cadence which does not end upon the tonic chord; (k) in botany, not having the parts of the same size or form, or arranged with symmetry; as, the petals of a labiate flower are *irregular*.

Syn.—Immethodical, unsystematic, anomalous, erratic, devious, eccentric, crooked, unsettled, variable, changeable, mutable, desultory, disorderly, wild, immoderate, intemperate, inordinate, vicious.

ir-reg′ū-lăr, *n.* One not conforming to settled rule; especially, a soldier unconnected with regular service.

ir-reg′ū-lăr-ist, *n.* One who is irregular. [Obs.]

ir-reg-ū-lar′i-ty, *n.*; *pl.* **ir-reg-ū-lar′i-ties.** 1. The state of being irregular; deviation from a straight line or from any common or established rule; deviation from method or order; as, the *irregularity* of proceedings.

2. That which is irregular or forms a deviation; a part exhibiting a divergence from the rest; action or conduct deviating from law human or divine or from moral rectitude.

ir-reg′ū-lăr-ly, *adv.* In an irregular manner; without rule, method, or order.

ir-reg′ū-lāte, *v.t.* To make irregular; to disorder. [Obs.]

ir-reg′ū-lous, *a.* Licentious; lawless; irregular. [Obs.]

ir-rē-ject′ȧ-ble, *a.* That may not be rejected.

ir-rē-laps′ȧ-ble, *a.* Not relapsable; incapable of falling back; permanent.

ir′rē-lāte, *a.* Not related; wanting connection.

ir-rē-lā′tion, *n.* The condition of being unrelated; lack of relation.

ir-rel′ȧ-tive, *a.* 1. Not relative; unconnected.

2. In music, having no tones in common; as, *irrelative* chords.

Irrelative repetition; in biology, the repetition of parts which are unrelated to each other but which have the same functions.

ir-rel′ȧ-tive-ly, *adv.* Unconnectedly.

ir-rel′ē-văn-cy, ir-rel′ē-vănce, *n.* Inapplicability; the quality of not being applicable or of not serving to aid and support; as, the *irrelevancy* of an argument or of testimony to a case in question.

ir-rel′ē-vănt, *a.* Not relevant; not applicable or pertinent; not serving to support.

ir-rel′ē-vănt-ly, *adv.* Without being to the purpose.

ir-rē-liēv′ȧ-ble, *a.* Not admitting relief.

ir-rē-lig′iŏn, *n.* Want of religion or contempt of it; impiety.

ir-rē-lig′iŏn-ist, *n.* One who is destitute of religious principles.

ir-rē-lig′ious, *a.* [LL. *irreligiosus*; L. *in-* priv., and *religiosus*, religious, from *religio (-onis)*, religion.]

1. Destitute of religious principles; impious; ungodly.

2. Contrary to religion; profane; wicked; as, an *irreligious* speech; *irreligious* conduct.

Syn.—Profane, impious, ungodly, wicked.

ir-rē-lig′ious-ly, *adv.* With impiety; wickedly.

ir-rē-lig′ious-ness, *n.* Want of religious principles or practices; ungodliness.

ir-rē′mē-ȧ-ble, *a.* Admitting no return; as, an *irremeable* way. [Obs.]

ir-rē-mē′di-ȧ-ble, *a.* [L. *irremediabilis*, incurable; *in-* priv., and *remediabilis*, curable, from *remedium*, a cure.]

1. Not to be remedied; that cannot be cured; as, an *irremediable* disease or evil.

2. Not to be corrected or redressed; as, *irremediable* error or mischief.

ir-rē-mē′di-ȧ-ble-ness, *n.* The state of being irremediable.

ir-rē-mē′di-ȧ-bly, *adv.* In a manner or degree that precludes remedy, cure, or correction.

ir-rē-mis′si-ble, *a.* [LL. *irremissibilis*; L. *in-* priv., and LL. *remissibilis*, pardonable, from L. *remittere*, to pardon.] Not to be pardoned; that cannot be forgiven or remitted.

ir-rē-mis′si-ble-ness, *n.* The quality of being unpardonable.

ir-rē-mis′si-bly, *adv.* So as not to be pardoned.

ir-rē-mis′sion (-mish′un), *n.* The act of refusing or delaying to remit or pardon; the act of withholding remission or pardon.

ir-rē-mis′sive, *a.* Not remitting.

ir-rē-mit′tȧ-ble, *a.* Irremissible; unpardonable.

ir-rē-mŏv-ȧ-bil′i-ty, *n.* The quality or state of being irremovable.

ir-rē-mŏv′ȧ-ble, *a.* That cannot be moved or changed.

ir-rē-mŏv′ȧ-bly, *adv.* So as not to admit of removal.

ir-rē-mŏv′ăl, *n.* Absence of removal.

ir-rē-mū′nēr-ȧ-ble, *a.* That cannot be rewarded.

ir-rē-nowned′, *a.* Not renowned. [Obs.]

ir-rep″ȧ-rȧ-bil′i-ty, *n.* The quality or state of being irreparable.

ir-rep′ȧ-rȧ-ble, *a.* [L. *in-* priv., and *reparabilis*, that can be repaired or regained.]

1. That cannot be repaired or mended; as, an *irreparable* breach.

2. That cannot be recovered or regained; as, an *irreparable* loss.

ir-rep′ȧ-rȧ-ble-ness, *n.* The state of being irreparable.

ir-rep′ȧ-rȧ-bly, *adv.* In a manner or degree that precludes recovery or repair.

ir-rē-pēal-ȧ-bil′i-ty, *n.* The quality of being irrepealable.

ir-rē-pēal′ȧ-ble, *a.* That cannot be legally repealed or annulled.

ir-rē-pēal′ȧ-ble-ness, *n.* Irrepealability.

ir-rē-pēal′ȧ-bly, *adv.* Beyond repeal.

ir-rē-pent′ănce, *n.* Want of repentance; impenitence.

ir-rē-plev′i-ȧ-ble, ir-rē-plev′i-sȧ-ble, *a.* That cannot be replevied.

ir-rep-rē-hen′si-ble, *a.* Not reprehensible; not to be blamed or censured; free from fault.

ir-rep-rē-hen′si-ble-ness, *n.* The quality of being irreprehensible.

ir-rep-rē-hen′si-bly, *adv.* In a manner not to incur blame; without blame.

ir-rep-rē-ṣent′ȧ-ble, *a.* Not to be represented; that cannot be figured or represented by any image.

ir-rē-press′i-ble, *a.* That cannot be repressed.

Syn.—Unrepressible, ungovernable, uncontrollable, insuppressible, free, unconfined, excitable.

ir-rē-press′i-bly, *adv.* In a manner or degree that cannot be repressed.

ir-rē-prōach′ȧ-ble, *a.* That cannot be justly reproached; free from blame; upright; innocent.

ir-rē-prōach′ȧ-ble-ness, *n.* The quality or state of being irreproachable.

ir-rē-prōach′ȧ-bly, *adv.* In a manner not to deserve reproach; blamelessly; as, conduct *irreproachably* upright.

ir-rē-prŏv′ȧ-ble, *a.* That cannot be justly reproved; blameless; upright.

ir-rē-prŏv′ȧ-ble-ness, *n.* The quality of being irreprovable.

ir-rē-prŏv′ȧ-bly, *adv.* So as not to be liable to reproof or blame.

ir-rep-ti′tious (-tish′us), *a.* [L. *irreptus*, pp. of *irrepere*, to creep in.] Secretly introduced; surreptitious. [Rare.]

ir-rep′ū-tȧ-ble, *a.* Not reputable; disreputable. [Obs.]

ir-rē-ṣil′i-ent, *a.* [L. *in-* priv., and *resiliens (-entis)*, ppr. of *resilire*, to spring back.] Not resilient; inelastic.

ir-rē-ṣist′ănce, *n.* Forbearance to resist; nonresistance; passive submission.

ir-rē-ṣist-i-bil′i-ty, *n.* The quality of being irresistible; power or force beyond resistance or opposition.

ir-rē-ṣist′i-ble, *a.* That cannot be successfully resisted or opposed; superior to opposition.

ir-rē-ṣist′i-ble-ness, *n.* Irresistibility.

ir-rē-ṣist′i-bly, *adv.* With a power that cannot be successfully resisted or opposed.

ir-rē-ṣist′less, *a.* That cannot be resisted. [Obs.]

ir-reṣ′ō-lū-ble, *a.* 1. Not to be dissolved; incapable of dissolution.

2. That cannot be relieved. [Obs.]

ir-reṣ′ō-lū-ble-ness, *n.* The quality of being indissoluble; resistance to separation of parts by heat.

ir-reṣ′ō-lūte, *a.* Not firm or constant in purpose; not decided; not determined; wavering; given to doubt.

ir-reṣ′ō-lūte-ly, *adv.* Without firmness of mind; without decision.

ir-reṣ′ō-lūte-ness, *n.* Want of firm determination or purpose; vacillation of mind.

ir-reṣ-ō-lū′tion, *n.* Want of resolution; want of decision in purpose; a fluctuation of mind, as in doubt, or between hope and fear; indecision; vacillation.

ir-rē-ṣolv-ȧ-bil′i-ty, *n.* The state or quality of not being resolvable.

ir-rē-ṣolv′ȧ-ble, *a.* That cannot be resolved; irresoluble.

ir-rē-ṣolv′ȧ-ble-ness, *n.* Irresolvability.

ir-rē-ṣolv′ed-ly, *adv.* Without settled determination.

ir-rē-spec′tive, *a.* 1. Not having regard to; unbiased; independent; with *of*; as, *irrespective of* consequences.

2. Not regarding circumstances.

> According to this doctrine, it must be resolved wholly into the absolute, *irrespective* will of God. —Bacon.

ir-rē-spec′tive-ly, *adv.* Without regard to; not taking circumstances into consideration.

ir-res′pi-rȧ-ble, *a.* Unfit for respiration; not having the qualities which support animal life; as, *irrespirable* air.

ir-rē-spon-si-bil′i-ty, *n.* Want of responsibility.

ir-rē-spon′si-ble, *a.* 1. Not responsible; not liable or able to answer for consequences; not answerable.

2. Not to be relied upon or trusted.

Syn.—Unbound, not answerable, excusable, lawless, arbitrary, unreliable.

ir-rē-spon′si-bly, *adv.* So as not to be responsible.

ir-rē-spon′sive, *a.* Unable or disinclined to respond; not responsive.

ir-rē-sus′ci-tȧ-ble, *a.* [L. *in-* priv., and *resuscitare*, to revive.] Not capable of being revived.

ir-rē-sus′ci-tȧ-bly, *adv.* So as not to be resuscitable.

ir-rē-ten′tion, *n.* Forgetfulness; lack of retention.

ir-rē-ten′tive, *a.* Not retentive or apt to retain.

ir-rē-trāce′ȧ-ble, *a.* That cannot be retraced.

ir-rē-tract′ile, *a.* 1. Without power of retraction.

2. Without ductility. [Rare.]

ir-rē-triēv′ȧ-ble, *a.* Not to be recovered or repaired; irrecoverable; irreparable; as, an *irretrievable* loss.

ir-rē-triēv′ȧ-ble-ness, *n.* The state of being irretrievable.

ir-rē-triēv′ȧ-bly, *adv.* Irreparably; irrecoverably; in a manner not to be regained.

ir-rē-tŭrn′ȧ-ble, *a.* Not to be returned.

ir-rē-vēal′ȧ-ble, *a.* That may not be revealed.

ir-rē-vēal′ȧ-bly, *adv.* So as not to be revealable.

ir-rev′ēr-ence, *n.* [L. *irreverentia*, irreverence, from *irreverens (-entis)*, irreverent.] Want of reverence or of veneration; want of a due regard for the authority and character of a superior; as, *irreverence* toward God.

ir-rev′ēr-end, *a.* [Obs.] See *Irreverent.*

ir-rev′ēr-ent, *a.* [L. *irreverens (-entis)*, irreverent; *in-* priv., and *reverens (-entis)*, ppr. of *revereri*, to stand in awe of.] Wanting in reverence and veneration.

ir-rev′ēr-ent-ly, *adv.* Without reverence.

ir-rē-vērs-i-bil′i-ty, *n.* The quality of being irreversible.

ir-rē-vērs′i-ble, *a.* 1. Incapable of being reversed; that cannot be recalled, repealed, or annulled; as, an *irreversible* decree or sentence.

2. In machinery, not reversible; incapable of turning or moving in an opposite direction, as a wheel or a crank.

ir-rē-vērs′i-ble-ness, *n.* Irreversibility.

ir-rē-vērs′i-bly, *adv.* In a manner which precludes a reversal or repeal.

ir-rev″ō-cȧ-bil′i-ty, *n.* The state of being irrevocable.

ir-rev′ō-cȧ-ble, *a.* [L. *irrevocabilis*; *in-* priv., and *revocabilis*, revocable, from *revocare*, to call back.] Not to be recalled or revoked; that cannot be reversed, repealed, or annulled; as, an *irrevocable* decree, sentence, edict, or doom.

ir-rev′ō-cȧ-ble-ness, *n.* Irrevocability.

ir-rev′ō-cȧ-bly, *adv.* Beyond recall; in a manner precluding repeal.

ir-rē-vōk′ȧ-ble, *a.* Not to be recalled; irrevocable. [Rare.]

ir-rev′ō-lū-ble, *a.* That has no revolution. [Rare.]

ir-rhē-tor′ic-ăl, *a.* Not rhetorical; unpersuasive.

ir′ri-gȧ-ble, *a.* That can be irrigated; as, an *irrigable* region.

ir′ri-gāte, *v.t.*; irrigated, *pt.*, *pp.*; irrigating, *ppr.* [L. *irrigatus*, pp. of *irrigare*, to bring water to or upon; *in*, in, to, upon, and *rigare*, to water, moisten.]

1. To water; to wet; to moisten.

2. To moisten, as land, by causing a stream to flow upon it and spread over it.

ir-ri-gā′tion, *n.* [L. *irrigatio (-onis)*, from *irrigare*, to irrigate.]

1. The act of watering or moistening.

2. In agriculture, the operation of causing water to flow over lands for nourishing plants.

ir′ri-gā-tŏr, *n.* Any agent of irrigation, especially a watering-cart, a watering-pot, or a sprayer.

ir-rig′ū-ous, *a.* 1. Watered; watery; moist.

2. Penetrating as water that irrigates; overspreading or pervading. [Obs.]

ir-riṣ′i-ble, *a.* Not risible; incapable of laughter. [Rare.]

ir-ri′ṣion, *n.* Same as *Derision.*

ir″ri-tȧ-bil′i-ty, *n.* [L. *irritabilitas (-atis)*, from *irritabilis*, irritable.]

1. Susceptibility of excitement; the quality of being easily irritated or exasperated; as, *irritability* of temper.

2. In physiology, a healthful vital susceptibility to the influence of natural, medicinal, and mechanical agents, and the power of responding in a normal manner, both by sensations and by actions; said especially of the muscles.

3. In medicine, a morbid condition of an organ with excessive susceptibility to stimulating influence.

4. In botany, that quality in certain plants by which they exhibit motion on the application of stimuli.

ir′ri-tȧ-ble, *a.* [L. *irritabilis*, from *irritare*, to irritate.]

1. Susceptible of excitement.

2. Very susceptible to anger or passion; easily inflamed or exasperated; as, an *irritable* temper.

3. In physiology, susceptible to irritation; endowed with irritability.

4. In medicine, excessively sensitive to the influence of irritants or stimuli.

ir′ri-tȧ-ble-ness, *n.* Irritability.

ir′ri-tȧ-bly, *adv.* In an irritable manner.

ir′ri-tăn-cy, *n.* 1. The state of being irritant.

2. In Scots law, the state of being irritant or of no force, or of being null and void.

ir′ri-tănt, *n.* 1. Anything that excites or irritates.

2. In physiology and medicine, any chemical, mechanical, or electrical agent which causes irritation or consequent inflammation, as a plaster, friction, or poison.

ir′ri-tănt, *a.* [L. *irritans (-antis)*, ppr. of *irritare*, to irritate.] Irritating; specifically, producing pain, heat, or tension; producing inflammation; as, an *irritant* poison.

ir′ri-tănt, *a.* [LL. *irritans (-antis)*, ppr. of *irritare*, to make void; from L. *irritus*, void, invalid.] In Scots law, working forfeiture; rendering void; as, an *irritant* clause. [Rare.]

ir′ri-tāte, *v.t.*; irritated, *pt., pp.*; irritating, *ppr.* [L. *irritatus*, pp. of *irritare*, to excite, stimulate, irritate.]

1. In medicine, to excite heat and redness in, as by friction; to inflame; to fret; as, to *irritate* a wounded part by a coarse bandage.

2. To excite to anger; to provoke; to tease; to exasperate; as, a tyrant *irritates* his subjects.

3. To increase action or violence in; to heighten excitement in.

4. In physiology, to produce irritation in; to stimulate.

Syn.—Provoke, exasperate.—Whatever comes across our feelings *irritates*; whatever excites anger *provokes*; whatever raises anger to a high point *exasperates*.

ir′ri-tāte, *v.t.* In Scots law, to render null and void. [Obs.]

ir′ri-tāte, *a.* Excited; heightened. [Obs.]

ir-ri-tā′tion, *n.* 1. The act of irritating or the state of being irritated; excitement, usually but not necessarily of a disagreeable kind; especially, excitement of anger; provocation; exasperation; anger.

2. In physiology, the change or action which takes place in the muscles or organs of sense when a nerve or nerves are affected by the application of external bodies; specifically, the operation of exciting muscular fiber to contraction by artificial stimulation; as, the muscle was made to contract by *irritation* of the nerve.

3. In medicine and pathology, the state of a tissue or organ in which there is an excess of vital movement; the discomfort set up in an organ by the presence of something unsuitable to its function or structure, or in the entire body by some local injury or internal disease.

ir′ri-tā-tive, *a.* 1. Serving to excite or irritate.

2. Accompanied with or produced by increased action or irritation; as, an *irritative* fever.

ir′ri-tȧ-tō-ry, *a.* Exciting; producing irritation. [Rare.]

ir′rō-rāte, *v.t.* To moisten with dew. [Obs.]

ir′rō-rāte, *a.* In zoölogy, marked with small dew-like spots, as the wings of some butterflies.

ir-rō-rā′tion, *n.* The act of bedewing; the state of being moistened with dew. [Obs.]

ir-rō-tā′tion-ăl, *a.* In physics, without rotation; said of the movement of parts of a liquid.

ir-rụ′bric-ăl, *a.* Opposed to the rubric; nonrubrical.

ir′rụ-gāte, *v.t.* [L. *irrugatus*, pp. of *irrugare*; *in*, in, on, and *rugare*, to wrinkle.] To render rugose; to wrinkle. [Obs.]

ir-rupt′ed, *a.* Broken with violence.

ir-rup′tion, *n.* [L. *irruptio (-onis)*, from *irrumpere*, to break in, burst in; *in*, in, and *rumpere*, to break, burst.]

1. A bursting in; a breaking or sudden violent rushing into.

2. A sudden invasion or incursion; a sudden, violent inroad, or entrance of invaders, as into a place or country; as, the *irruption* of the allies into Pekin.

Syn.—Incursion, inroad, raid, foray.

ir-rup′tive, *a.* Rushing in or upon.

Ir′ving-īte, *n.* One of a religious denomination named after Edward Irving (1792-1834), a Scotch minister and promulgator of mystical doctrines relative to the organization of the Christian church and the strict observance of ritualistic practices.

is-. See *Iso-*.

iṣ, *v.i.* [AS. *is*. It represents Goth. *ist*, L. *est*, Gr. *esti*, and Sans. *asti*, is.] The third person singular present indicative of *be*; sometimes used in the future; as, to-morrow *is* Christmas.

iṣ′ȧ-bel, iṣ′ȧ-belle, *n.* [Fr. *Isabelle*, a woman's name. Said to be so called from *Isabella* of Austria, who vowed she would not change her linen until Ostend was taken. The city held out from 1601 to 1604, and her linen became of a dingy hue.] A brownish-yellow color with a shade of brownish-red; called also *isabel-color*.

iṣ′ȧ-bel-īte, *n.* [*Isabelle*, a woman's name, and *-ite*.] A variety of angel-fish.

iṣ-ȧ-bel′lȧ-mọth, *n.* An American moth, *Pyrrharctia isabella*.

iṣ-ȧ-bel′lȧ-wood, *n.* In botany, an American tree of the genus *Persea*; the red bay.

iṣ-ȧ-bel′line, *a.* Of the color of isabel.

ī-sab-nor′măl, *n.* See *Isoabnormal*.

ī-sȧ-del′phous (-fus), *a.* [*Is-*, and Gr. *adelphos*, a brother.] In botany, a term applied to a diadelphous flower in which the separate bundles of stamens are equal in number or alike in appearance.

ī′sȧ-gōge, *n.* [Gr. *eisagōgē*, an introduction, from *eisagein*, to lead in, introduce.] An introduction, as to a book or to the works of an author.

ī-sȧ-gog′iç, ī-sȧ-gog′iç-ăl, *a.* [L. *isagogicus*; Gr. *eisagōgikos*, introductory, from *eisagōgē*, an introduction, from *eisagein*, to lead in; *eis*, in, and *agein*, to lead.] Introductory; particularly, introductory to biblical study.

ī-sȧ-gog′içs, *n.* That department of theological study introductory to exegesis or the interpretation of Scripture.

ī′sȧ-gon, *n.* [Gr. *isos*, equal, and *gōnia*, an angle.] In geometry, a figure whose angles are equal.

ī-san′drous, *a.* [*Is-*, and Gr. *anēr*, *andros*, a man, male.] In botany, designating a flower having similar stamens and of the same number as the divisions of the corolla.

ī-san′thēr-ous, *a.* [*Is-*, and Gr. *anthēros*, flowery, from *anthos* a flower.] In botany, designating a flower with equal anthers. [Rare.]

ī-san′thous, *a.* [*Is-*, and Gr. *anthos*, a flower.] In botany, designating a plant with regular flowers.

is-ap-os-tol′iç, *a.* [*Is-*, and Gr. *apostolikos*, apostolic, from *apostolos*, one sent away, a messenger.] Of equal authority with the apostles; specifically said of certain bishops of the Greek church and of others distinguished for their faith.

ī-sat′iç, ī-sȧ-tin′iç, *a.* Derived from or relating to isatin; as, *isatic* acid.

ī′sȧ-tid, ī′sȧ-tide, *n.* A substance obtained by reducing isatin; written also *isathyd*.

ī′sȧ-tin, *n.* [*Isatis* and *-in*.] A compound, $C_8H_5NO_2$, obtained by oxidizing indigo; it forms hyacinth-red or reddish-orange crystals of a brilliant luster; written also *isatine*.

I′sȧ-tis, *n.* [L. *isatis*; Gr. *isatis*, a kind of plant, used in healing wounds, woad.] In botany, a genus of herbs of the order *Cruciferæ*; *Isatis tinctoria* or dyer's woad is cultivated as a dye-plant.

is-çhē′mi-ȧ, is-çhæ′mi-ȧ, *n.* [Gr. *ischaimos*, quenching blood; *ischein*, to hold, and *haima*, blood.] In pathology, a suppression of the flow of blood, arising from various causes, producing local anemia.

is-çhē′miç, *a.* Relating to ischemia or local anemia.

is′çhi-ȧ, *n.*, pl. of *ischium*.

is-çhi-ad′iç, *a.* See *Ischiatic*.

is′çhi-ăl, *a.* [Gr. *ischion*, the hip-joint.] Ischiatic.

is-çhi-al′gi-ȧ, *n.* Same as *Sciatica*.

is-çhi-at′iç, *a.* [Gr. *ischion*, the hip, hip-joint, and *-atic*.] Pertaining to the ischium or hip; ischiadic; ischial.

Ischiatic callosity; one of the small areas of hairless bright-colored skin on the hips and buttocks of certain species of monkeys.

ischio-. A combining form from Gr. *ischion*, hip, hip-joint, used in anatomy, medicine, etc., to denote relation to the hip or hip-joint.

is″çhi-ō-çap′sū-lăr, *a.* [*Ischio-*, and L. *capsula*, a capsule, case.] In anatomy, relating to the ischium and the capsular ligament of the hip-joint.

is″çhi-ō-çē′rīte, *n.* [*Ischio-*, and Gr. *keras*, horn, and *-ite*.] In zoölogy, the third segment in a developed antenna of a crustacean.

is′çhi-on, *n.* Same as *Ischium*.

is-çhi-op′ō-dīte, *n.* [*Ischio-*, and Gr. *pous*, *podos*, foot.] In zoölogy, the third segment in a developed endopodite of a crustacean.

is″çhi-ō-reç′tăl, *a.* In anatomy, between or connecting the ischium and the rectum.

is′çhi-um, *n.*; *pl.* **is′çhi-ȧ.** [Gr. *ischion*, the hip, hip-joint.]

1. In anatomy, the posterior and inferior part of the pelvic arch in vertebrates; the lowermost of the three portions forming the os innominatum in the fetus; the lowermost part of the hip-bone in adults.

2. In zoölogy, same as *ischiopodite*.

is-çhū-ret′iç, *a.* and *n.* I. *a.* Efficacious in the treatment of ischuria.

II. *n.* A medicine for the relief of ischuria; a diuretic.

is-çhū′ri-ȧ, is′çhū-ry, *n.* [LL. *ischuria*; Gr. *ischouria*, retention of urine, from *ischourein*; *ischein*, to hold, and *ouron*, urine.] A stoppage or suppression of urine.

-ise. See *-ize*.

ī-sen-ēr′giç, *a.* [*Is-*, and Gr. *energeia*, action, energy.] In physics, relating to or having equal energy.

ī-sen-trop′iç, *a.* [*Is-*, and Gr. *entropē*, a turning about; *en*, in, and *trepein*, to turn.] In physics, equal in entropy.

Isentropic lines; the connecting lines between points of equal entropy.

ī-seth-ī-on′iç, *a.* [*Is-* and *ethionic*.] Pertaining to or resembling an oily acid derived from sulphuric acid.

-ish. [ME. *-ish*, *-issh*, *-isch*; AS. *-isc*.] A suffix used to form adjectives from nouns and adjectives. When added to nouns to form adjectives it gives the signification of being like or having the nature of that which is represented by the noun; as, bear*ish*, owl*ish*, wolf*ish*. When added to adjectives to form adjectives it gives a diminutive force often expressed by *rather*; as, blu*ish*, whit*ish*. It is also used as the regular formative of patrial adjectives from the proper nouns of a country or people; as, Dan*ish*, Greek*ish*.

-ish. [ME. *-ishen*, *-ischen*, *-issen*; OFr. *-iss-*, *-is-*, the ending of some parts of verbs, as ppr. of *finir*, to finish, from L. *-escere*, *-iscere*, an ending of incept. verbs.] A verb suffix appearing in verbs of French origin or verbs similarly formed; as, furn*ish*, fin*ish*, pun*ish*.

Ish′mā-el-īte, *n.* 1. A descendant of Ishmael.

2. An Ismailian.

3. One resembling Ishmael, whose hand was against every man and every man's hand against him; one at war with society.

> Jos's tents and pilau were pleasant to this little *Ishmaelite*. —Thackeray.

Ish′mā-el-ī-tish, *a.* Like Ishmael; partaking of the nature of an Ishmaelite.

ish-pin′gō, *n.* [Prob. from native name.] In botany, a South American tree of the genus *Nectandra*; called also *Santa Fé cinnamon*.

Ī′si-aç, *a.* [L. *Isiacus*; Gr. *Isiakos*, from *Isis*, Isis.] Relating to the female deity Isis.

ī′si-çle, *n.* [Obs.] See *Icicle*.

Is-i-dō′ri-ăn, *a.* Relating to St. Isidore, archbishop of Seville during the seventh century.

ī′ṣin-glȧss, *n.* [Prob. a corruption of M.D. *huizenblas*, lit., sturgeon-bladder; *huizen*, a sturgeon, and *blas*, a bladder.]

1. A pure gelatin made chiefly from the air bladders of sturgeons.

2. A name sometimes given to mica.

Ī′sis, *n.* [L., from Gr. *Isis*, the goddess **Isis**.] One of the chief deities of Egyptian mythology. She was regarded as the sister or sister-wife of Osiris and the mother of Horus. She was worshiped by the Egyptians as the being who had first civilized them. Among the higher and more philosophical theologians she was made the symbol of pantheistic divinity.

Isis.

Is′lăm, *n.* [Ar. *islām*, obedience to the will of God, submission, the orthodox faith.] The religion of Mohammed; also, the whole body of those who profess it throughout the world.

Is′lăm-iṣm, *n.* The true faith, according to the Mohammedans; Mohammedanism.

Is′lăm-īte, *n.* A Mohammedan; a Moslem.

Is-lăm-it′iç, *a.* Pertaining to Islam; Mohammedan.

Is′lăm-īze, *v.i.* and *v.t.*; Islamized, *pt., pp.*; Islamizing, *ppr.* To conform to Islamism; to Mohammedanize.

is′lănd (ī′), *n.* [ME. *iland*, *yland*; AS. *igland*, *iglond*, *iland*; *ig*, island and *land*, land. The *s* was inserted in the sixteenth century because of confusion with *isle*.]

1. A tract of land surrounded by water, whether of the sea, a river, or a lake; in contradistinction to *mainland* or *continent*.

2. Anything resembling an island, as a large mass of floating ice.

Islands of the Blessed; in Greek mythology, the Happy Islands, supposed to lie westward in the ocean, whither after death the souls of the virtuous were transported.

is′lănd, *v.t.*; islanded, *pt., pp.*; islanding, *ppr.*

1. To cause to become or appear like an island or islands; to isolate by surrounding, as with water.

2. To dot, as with islands.

is′lănd-ēr, *n.* An inhabitant of an island.

is'land-y (ī'), *a.* Relating to islands or to an island.
2. Having islands; abounding in islands; as, an *islandy* sea.

is'lāy, *n.* An evergreen shrub, *Prunus ilicifolia*, which bears a small pleasant-flavored plum.

isle (il), *n.* [Obs.] See *Aisle.*

isle, *n.* [ME. *ile, yle, isle*; OFr. *ile, isle*, from L. *insula*, an island.] An island or islet; chiefly in poetic use; as, the Emerald *Isle.*

isle, *v.t.* Same as *Island.*

is'let (ī'), *n.* [OFr. *islet*, dim. of *isle*, an island, from L. *insula*, an island.]
1. A little island.
2. Anything resembling a little island, as a mark on the wing of an insect or on a leaf or flower.

-ism. [L. *-ismus*; Gr. *-ismos.*] A suffix implying doctrine, theory, principle, system, or practice of; abstract idea of that signified by the word to which it is subjoined; as, monothe*ism*, spiritual*ism*, republican*ism*, mesmer*ism*, Presbyterian*ism*, libertin*ism*.

ism, *n.* [From its common use as a suffix in words signifying doctrine or theory, etc.] A doctrine or theory, but more especially a pretentious or absurd one; a crotchety or visionary speculation; generally used contemptuously; as, away with your *isms* and ologies.

Is-mā-il'i-ăn, Is-mā-ē'li-ăn, *n.* A member of the Mohammedan sect which maintained that Ismail, and not Moussa, ought to be Imam. In the tenth century they formed a secret society, from which sprang the Assassins. Written also *Ismaelite.*

Iso-, is-. Combining forms from Gr. *isos*, equal, used in zoölogy, botany, chemistry, etc., to signify equality, identity, or the same numerical value; as, *iso*dactylous, *iso*dulcite, *iso*cyanic, *iso*gnathous.

ī"sō-ab-nor'măl, *n.* [*Iso-*, and L. *abnormis*, deviating from a rule.] In meteorology, a line passing through those points of the earth's surface where the variation of temperature from the normal for a certain period is the same; written also *isabnormal.*

ī'sō-bär, *n.* [*Iso-*, and Gr. *baros*, weight.] In physical geography, a line drawn on a map to connect those places on the surface of the globe at which the mean height of the barometer at sea-level is the same; written also *isobare.*

ī-sō-bar'iç, *a.* Indicating equal weight; specifically, relating to equal atmospheric pressure or to isobars.

ī'sō-bär-ism, *n.* Equality or similarity of weight or pressure.

ī-sō-bar-ō-met'riç, *a.* [*Iso-*, and Gr. *baros*, weight, and *metron*, a measure.] Denoting equality in atmospheric pressure.

ī-sō-bath'y-thĕrm, *n.* [*Iso-*, and Gr. *bathys*, deep, and *thermē*, heat.] In physical geography, a line connecting points on the surface of the earth beneath which the temperature is constant at a given depth; a line on a map or chart representing the line described.

ī-sō-bath-y-thĕr'miç, *a.* Pertaining to an isobathytherm.

ī'sō-bront, *n.* [*Iso-*, and Gr. *brontē*, thunder.] A line passing through those points on the surface of the earth at which a clap of thunder is heard at the same time; the line on a chart representing the line described.

ī-sō-ceph'a-lism, *n.* [*Iso-*, and Gr. *kephalē*, head.] The designing of bas-reliefs in such a manner as to keep the heads of human figures at the same distance from the ground, regardless of size or position.

ī-sō-ceph'ā-ly, *n.* The practice of isocephalism.

ī-sō-cĕr'căl, *a.* [*Iso-*, and Gr. *kerkos*, tail.] In ichthyology, having the caudal vertebræ extended in a straight line, not bent upward, and the caudal fin equally developed above and below.

ī-sō-cĕr'cy, *n.* The state of having the caudal vertebræ isocercal.

ī'sō-chasm, *n.* [*Iso-*, and Gr. *chasma*, a gap, gulf.] In physical geography, a line passing through those points on the earth's surface at which the frequency of the occurrence of auroral displays is the same.

ī-sō-chas'miç, *a.* Pertaining to agreement in frequency of auroral displays.

ī-sō-chī'măl, ī-sō-chei'măl, *a.* Of the same mean winter temperature; written also *isochimenal, isochimonal,* and *isocheimonal.*

ī'sō-chīme, ī'sō-cheim, *n.* [*Iso-*, and Gr. *cheima*, winter.] In physical geography, a line drawn through places on the earth's surface which have the same mean winter temperature; the line on a chart representing the line described. Written also *isochimene.*

ī'sō-chor, *n.* [*Iso-*, and Gr. *chōra*, space, room, country.] A line on a thermodynamic diagram representing the variations in pressure of a constant volume of gas varying in temperature.

ī-sō-chor'iç, *a.* Pertaining to an isochor.

ī-sō-chrō-mat'iç, *a.* [*Iso-*, and Gr. *chrōma* (*-atos*), color.]
1. Having the same color; said of lines or curves of the same tint formed by biaxial crystals subjected to polarized light.
2. In photography, same as *orthochromatic.*

ī-soch'rō-năl, ī-sō-chron'iç, *a.* [*Iso-*, and Gr. *chronos*, time.] Equal in time; done in equal time; as, *isochronal* vibrations.

ī-soch'rō-nism, *n.* The quality which renders isochronous.

ī-soch'rō-non, *n.* [Gr. *isochronon*, properly neut. of *isochronos*, equal in time; *isos*, equal, and *chronos*, time.] An equal timekeeper; a clock designed to keep perfectly accurate time.

ī-soch'rō-nous, *a.* Same as *Isochronal.*

ī-soch'rō-ous, *a.* [Gr. *isochroos*, like-colored; *isos*, equal, and *chroa*, color.] In botany, being of equal color throughout.

ī-sō-clī'năl, *a.* In geology, of equal inclination or dip.
Isoclinal lines; in magnetism, curves connecting those places in the two hemispheres where the dip of the magnetic needle is equal.

ī'sō-clīne, *n.* [*Iso-*, and Gr. *klinein*, to slope, incline.] In geology, any fold of stratified rocks in which the two parts are parallel or have the same dip, as in certain mountain rocks.

ī-sō-clin'iç, *a.* Same as *Isoclinal.*

ī-sō-crȳ'măl, *a.* Pertaining to or having the nature of an isocryme.

ī'sō-crȳme, *n.* [*Iso-*, and Gr. *krymos*, cold.] In physical geography, a line drawn on maps showing the places having the same mean temperature during the coldest months of the year.

ī-sō-crȳm'iç, *a.* Same as *Isocrymal.*

ī-sō-cȳ-an'iç, *a.* [*Iso-* and *cyanic.*] Pertaining to isocyanic acid.
Isocyanic acid; a volatile colorless unisolated liquid compound isomeric with cyanic acid.

ī-sō-cȳ'ă-nide, *n.* Same as *Carbamine.*

ī-sō-cȳ-ā-nū'riç, *a.* Fulminuric.

ī-sō-dac'tyl-ous, *a.* [*Iso-*, and Gr. *daktylos*, a digit.] In zoölogy, having all the toes alike, especially in length.

ī-sō-dī-ā-bat'iç, *a.* [*Iso-*, and Gr. *diabatikos*, able to pass through, from *diabainein*, to pass through.] In physics, designating isothermal curves representing variations in the pressure and density of a body, the quantity of heat received or given out being constant.

ī-sō-dī-ă-met'riç, *a.* [*Iso-*, and Gr. *diametros*, diameter.]
1. In crystallography, having equal development in the directions of the lateral axes.
2. In botany, uniform in diameter; said of cells or organs.

ī-sod'i-cŏn, *n.*; *pl.* **ī-sod'i-cā.** [L.Gr. *eisodikon*, neut. of *eisodikos*, pertaining to the entrance, from Gr. *eisodos*, entrance; *eis*, into, and *hodos*, way.] In the Greek church, a brief anthem sung during the entrance and passage of an officiating priest through the church to the chancel.

ī"sō-dī-mor'phiç, *a.* See *Isodimorphous.*

ī"sō-dī-mor'phism, *n.* [*Iso-*, and Gr. *dimorphos*, two-formed; *dis*, twice, and *morphē*, form.] A similarity of crystalline form between the crystals of two dimorphous groups.

ī"sō-dī-mor'phus, *a.* Possessing the characteristics of isodimorphism.

ī-sod'ō-mon, ī-sod'ō-mum, *n.* [Gr. *isodomon*, properly neut. of *isodomos*, built alike; *isos*, equal, and *demein*, to build.] In Grecian architecture, a construction in which the parts are of equal thickness and equal length.

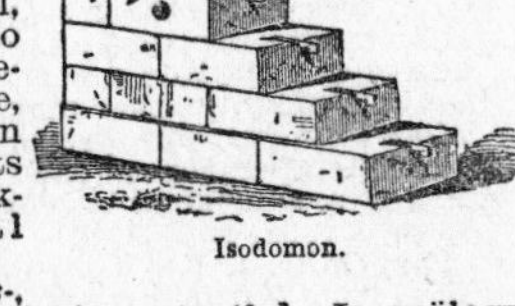
Isodomon.

ī'sō-dont, *a.* [*Iso-*, and Gr. *odous*, *odontos*, a tooth.] In zoölogy, having all the teeth alike or of the same class.

ī-sō-dul'cīte, *n.* [*Iso-* and *dulcite.*] A crystalline compound resembling sugar, derived from glucose.

ī"sō-dȳ-nam'iç, *a.* [*Iso-*, and Gr. *dynamis*, power, force.] Having or relating to equal power or force.
Isodynamic foods; foods equal in heat-producing qualities.
Isodynamic lines; in magnetism, lines connecting those places on the earth's surface where the intensity of terrestrial magnetism is equal.

ī"sō-dȳ-nam'iç, *n.* An isodynamic line.

ī-sō-dȳ'nă-mous, *a.* [Gr. *isodynamos*; *isos*, equal, and *dynamis*, power.] Having equal force; of equal size.

I-sō-ē-tā'cē-æ, *n. pl.* [L. *isoetes*, a houseleek, from Gr. *isoetēs*, in evergreen plant, lit. equal in years; *isos*, equal, and *etos*, a year, and *-aceæ*]. An order of vascular cryptogamous aquatic plants, including but one genus; *Isoetes*, or quillwort.

ī-sō-ē-tā'ceous, *a.* Belonging or pertaining to the order *Isoetaceæ.*

I-sō'ē-tæ-æ, *n.pl.* Same as *Isoetaceæ.*

I-sō'ē-tēs, *n.* The only known genus of *Isoetaceæ.*

ī-sog'ā-mous, *a.* Having the characteristics of isogamy.

ī-sog'ā-my, *n.* [*Iso-*, and Gr. *gamos*, marriage.] In botany, the union of two similar conjugating protoplasmic bodies indistinguishable as to sex. [See *Oögamy.*]

ī-sō-gē'ō-thĕrm, *n.* [*Iso-*, and Gr. *gē*, earth, and *thermē*, heat.] In physical geography, an imaginary line under the earth's surface passing through points having the same mean temperature.

ī-sō-gē-ō-thĕr'măl, *a.* Relating to or having the characteristics of an isogeotherm.

ī-sō-gē-ō-thĕr'miç, *a.* Isogeothermal.

ī-sog'nă-thous, *a.* [*Iso-*, and Gr. *gnathos*, jaw.] In odontology, having like molar teeth in both the upper and the lower jaw.

ī-sog'ō-năl, *a.* Equiangular.

ī-sō-gon'iç, *a.* [Gr. *isogōnios*, having equal angles; *isos*, equal, and *gōnia*, an angle.] Having equal angles.
Isogonic lines; in magnetism, lines connecting those places on the globe at which the deviation of the magnetic needle from the meridian or true north is the same.

ī-sō-gon'iç, *a.* In biology, pertaining to isogonism.

ī-sō-gō'ni-ō-stat, *n.* [Gr. *isogōnios*, having equal angles, and *statos*, verbal adj. of *histanai*, to stand.] A contrivance for regulating the motion of prisms, as in a spectroscope.

ī-sog'ō-nism, *n.* [*Iso-*, and Gr. *gonos*, an offspring.] In biology, the production of like reproductive parts from dissimilar stocks, as in certain hydroids; the quality of having like offspring.

ī-sō-graph'iç, *a.* Pertaining to isography.

ī-sog'ră-phy, *n.* [*Iso-*, and Gr. *graphein*, to write.] The imitation of handwriting.

ī-sog'y-nous, *a.* [*Iso-*, and Gr. *gynē*, a female.] In botany, having the pistils or the parts of a compound ovary agreeing in number with the sepals.

ī-sō-hal'sine, *n.* [*Iso-*, and Gr. *hals*, salt, and *-ine.*] In physical geography, a line passing through those points in the ocean at which the salinity of the water is equal.

ī-sō-hȳ'e-tăl, ī-sō-hȳ'e-tōse, *a.* and *n.* [*Iso-*, and Gr. *hyetos*, rain.]
I. *a.* Pertaining to lines connecting those places on the surface of the globe where the quantity of rain which falls annually is the same.
II. *n.* An isohyetal line.

ī'sō-lă-ble (*or* is'ō-), *a.* [*Isol*ate and *-able.*] That can be isolated; specifically, in chemistry, capable of being obtained pure, or uncombined with any other substance.

ī'sō-lāte (*or* is'ō-), *v.t.*; isolated, *pt.*, *pp.*; isolating, *ppr.* [It. *isolato*, pp. of *isolare*, to isolate, from *isola*, L. *insula*, an island.]
1. To set aside; to place apart; to insulate; often used reflexively; as, he *isolated* himself from all society.
2. In electricity, same as *insulate.*
3. In chemistry, to obtain free from all its combinations.

ī'sō-lā-ted, *a.* 1. Standing detached from others of a like kind; placed by itself, or alone.
2. In electricity, same as *insulated.*
3. In chemistry, pure; freed from combination.

ī'sō-lā-ted-ly, *adv.* In an isolated manner.

ī-sō-lā'tion, *n.* The state of being isolated or alone.

ī'sō-lā-tŏr, *n.* A person or thing that isolates.

ī-sol'ō-gous, *a.* [*Iso-*, and Gr. *logos*, proportion, ratio.] In chemistry, having similar differences in composition, as in the compounds C_2H_6, C_2H_4, C_2H_2, etc.

ī'sō-logue (-log), *n.* In chemistry, one of a series of isologous compounds, C_2H_4.

ī-sō-mas'ti-gāte, *a.* [*Iso-*, and Gr. *mastix* (*-igos*), a whip.] In biology, having like flagella, especially as to size and form.

ī'sō-mĕr, *n.* [Gr. *isomerēs*, having equal parts; *isos*, equal, and *meros*, part.] In chemistry, a compound which is one of an isomeric group.

ī'sō-mēre, *n.* [Gr. *isomerēs*, having equal parts.] In zoölogy, some part, as a limb or the segment of a limb, of an animal, having a homologous part in some other animal.

ī-sō-mer'iç, ī-sō-mer'iç-ăl, *a.* [*Isomer*ous and *-ic.*]
1. In chemistry, having the same percentage composition, but showing different properties.
2. In zoölogy, relating to an isomere.

ī-sō-mer'iç-ăl-ly, *adv.* In an isomeric manner.

ī-som'ĕr-ide, *n.* [Rare.] Same as *Isomer.*

ī-som'ĕr-ism, *n.* [*Isomer*ous and *-ism.*] In chemistry, identity of elements and proportions with diversity of properties; the state, property, or quality of being isomeric.

ī-sō-mer-ō-mor'phism, *n.* [*Iso-*, and Gr. *meros*, part, and *morphē*, form.] In crystallography, isomorphism between substances having the same atomic proportions.

ī-som′ẽr-ous, *a.* [Gr. *isomerēs*, having equal parts; *isos*, equal, and *meros*, part.]

1. In botany, having the same number of parts; said of the whorls of a flower.

2. In chemistry, designating isomorphism subsisting between substances of like composition.

ī-sō-met′riç, ī-sō-met′riç-ăl, *a.* [Gr. *isometros*, of equal measure; *isos*, equal, and *metron*, measure.]

1. Pertaining to equality of measure.

2. In crystallography, monometric; tessular.

Isometric lines; lines drawn on a thermodynamical diagram to represent the varying relations of the temperature and pressure of a gas whose volume remains constant.

Isometric projection; a method of drawing plans of machines, etc., whereby the elevation and ground-plan are represented in one view.

ī-sō-met′rō-grȧph, *n.* [*Iso-*, and Gr. *metron*, a measure, and *graphein*, to write.] A contrivance for drawing equidistant parallel lines.

ī′sō-morph, *n.* [*Iso-*, and Gr. *morphē*, form.]

1. In biology, an organism resembling another but not morphologically identical.

2. Any isomorphic substance.

ī-sō-mor′phiç, *a.* 1. Isomorphous.

2. In biology, having the same or a similar form.

ī-sō-mor′phişm, *n.* A similarity of crystalline form, as (a) between substances of like composition or atomic proportions, as arsenic acid and phosphorous acid, each containing five equivalents of oxygen; (b) between compounds of unlike composition or atomic proportions, as the metal arsenic and oxid of iron, the rhombohedral angle of the former being 85° 41′, of the latter 86° 4′. The first of these is sometimes distinguished as *isonomic isomorphism*; the second as *heteronomic isomorphism*.

ī-sō-mor′phous, *a.* [*Iso-*, and Gr. *morphē*, form.] Having isomorphism; isomorphic.

ī″sō-mȳ-ā′ri-ăn, *a.* [*Iso-*, and Gr. *mys*, *myos*, muscle, and *-arian*.] In conchology, having the two adductor muscles alike, or nearly so, in size and form.

ī-sō-nan′drȧ, *n.* [*Iso-*, and Gr. *anēr*, *andros*, a man, male.] A genus of East Indian trees including a species from which gutta-percha is obtained.

ī″sō-nē-phel′iç, *a.* [*Iso-*, and Gr. *nephelē*, a cloud.] In physical geography, designating equality in the prevalence of cloudiness during a stated period, as a year or a decade, at any given place.

ī-sō-niç′ō-tine, *n.* A crystalline compound isomeric with nicotine.

ī-sō-niç-ō-tin′iç, *a.* Pertaining to isonicotine.

ī-sō-nom′iç, *a.* Equal in law, right, or privilege.

ī-son′ō-my, *n.* [Gr. *isonomia*, equality of rights; *isos*, equal, and *nomos*, distribution, custom, law.] Equal law; equal distribution of rights and privileges.

ī′sō-nym, *n.* See *Paronym.*

ī-sō-nym′iç, *a.* See *Paronymic.*

ī-sop′ȧ-thy, *n.* [*Iso-*, and Gr. *pathos*, suffering, disease.] In medicine, (a) the theory that diseases are cured by the products of the diseases themselves, as that smallpox is cured by homeopathic doses of variolous matter; the cure of disease by the virus of the disease; (b) the theory that a diseased organ is cured by eating the same organ of a healthy animal.

ī-sō-per-i-met′riç-ăl, *a.* [*Iso-*, and Gr. *peri*, around, and *metron*, a measure.] In geometry, having equal boundaries; as, *isoperimetrical* figures or bodies.

ī″sō-per-im′e-try, *n.* In geometry, the science of measuring isoperimetrical figures.

ī-sō-pet′ȧ-lous, *a.* [*Iso-*, and Gr. *petalon*, a leaf, petal.] In botany, having all the petals alike.

ī″sō-pi-es′tiç, *a.* Same as *Isobaric.*

ī-sō-pleū′rȧ, *n.pl.* [Gr. *isopleuros*, having equal sides; *isos*, equal, and *pleura*, side.] A subdivision of gasteropods including those which are bilaterally symmetrical.

ī′sō-pod, *a.* and *n.* I. *a.* Pertaining to the *Isopoda.*

II. *n.* A crustacean of the order *Isopoda.*

ī-sop′ō-dȧ, *n.pl.* [*Iso-*, and Gr. *pous*, *podos*, a foot.] An order of arthrostracous crustaceans having seven pairs of similarly formed legs.

Isopoda.
1. *Bopyrus squillarum.* Sedentary section.
2. *Cymodocea lamarcki.* Natatory section.
3. *Oniscus asellus.* Cursorial section.
a, Head. *b*, Thorax. *c*, Abdomen.

ī-sō-pod′i-form, *a.* Formed like an isopod.

ī-sop′ō-dous, *a.* See *Isopod.*

ī-sō-pog′ō-nous, *a.* [*Iso-*, and Gr. *pōgōn*, beard.] In zoölogy, being symmetrically and equally barbed; said of a feather.

ī-sō-pol′i-ty, *n.* [Gr. *isopoliteia*, from *isopolitēs*, a citizen with equal civil rights; *isos*, equal, and *politēs*, a citizen.] Mutual civil and political rights as secured to the citizens of different states.

ī-sō-pyç′niç, *a.* and *n.* [*Iso-*, and Gr. *pyknos*, dense, solid.]

I. *a.* In physics, relating to or exhibiting equality of density, as in a body at different points; as, an *isopycnic* line.

II. *n.* Any isopycnic surface; an isopycnic line.

ī-sor′cin, *n.* [*Iso-* and *orcin.*] In chemistry, a crystalline compound produced by artificial means, metameric with orcin; also called *cresorcinol*, *cresorcin.*

ī-sor-rop′iç, *a.* [*Iso-*, and Gr. *rhopē*, downward inclination.] In mathematics, designating a line connecting points in a plane for which the value of a function remains constant.

ī-sos′cē-lēş, *a.* [L. *isosceles*; Gr. *isoskelēs*, with equal legs; *isos*, equal, and *skelos*, a leg.] Having two equal legs or sides; as, an *isosceles* triangle.

Isosceles Triangle.

ī-sō-seis′măl, *a.* and *n.* [*Iso-*, and Gr. *seismos*, a shaking, an earthquake.]

I. *a.* Pertaining to equality of disturbance by an earthquake.

II. *n.* A line connecting points on the surface of the earth equally affected by an earthquake; also, such a line marked on a map or chart.

ī-sō-seis′miç, *a.* Same as *Isoseismal.*

ī-sō-spon′dy-lī, *n.pl.* [*Iso-*, and Gr. *spondylos*, vertebra.] A large order of fishes including those having all the vertebræ essentially similar, embracing most malacopterygian fishes, such as the salmon, the herring, etc.

ī-sō-spon′dy-lous, *a.* Of or pertaining to the *Isospondyli.*

ī′sō-spōre, *n.* [*Iso-*, and Gr. *sporos*, seed.]

1. A zygospore.

2. A plant which produces only one kind of spore.

ī-sō-spor′iç, *a.* Same as *Homosporous.*

ī-sō-stat′iç, *a.* [*Iso-*, and Gr. *statikos*, causing to stand, from *histanai*, to stand.] Stationary; stable on account of equal pressure in all directions; said of a liquid at rest.

ī-sō-stem′ō-nous, *a.* [*Iso-*, and Gr. *stēmōn*, thread.] In botany, having as many stamens as pistils.

ī-sō-stem′ō-ny, *n.* The condition of being isostemonous.

ī″sō-sul-phō-çȳ′ȧ-nāte, *n.* In chemistry, a salt resulting from the action of isosulphocyanic acid on certain bases.

ī″sō-sul-phō-çȳ-an′iç, *a.* Pertaining to a colorless acid isomeric with the sulphacid, HSCN.

ī′sō-tel-y, *n.* [Gr. *isoteleia*, equality of taxation, from *isotelēs*, paying alike; *isos*, equal, and *telos*, tax.] Equality in taxation; a condition of certain aliens of ancient Athens who were granted the privileges and immunities of citizens; immunity from the disadvantages of being an alien.

ī-soth′ẽr-ăl, *a.* [*Iso-*, and Gr. *theros*, summer.] Having the same mean summer temperature.

ī′sō-thēre, *n.* A line passing through places having the same mean summer temperature.

ī′sō-thẽrm, *n.* [*Iso-*, and Gr. *thermē*, heat.] In physical geography, a line passing through such points on the earth's surface as have the same temperature; also, a line on a map or chart representing the line described, as one of the lines on a daily weather-map.

Mean isotherm; one prepared by taking the average temperature at each place of observation for a considerable length of time, as a month, a year, or a decade.

ī-sō-thẽr′măl, *a.* Having equal degrees of heat.

Isothermal line; a line passing through places of equal mean temperature; an isotherm.

Isothermal zones; spaces on opposite sides of the equator having the same mean temperature or bounded by corresponding isothermal lines.

ī-sō-thẽr′mō-bath, *n.* [*Iso-*, and Gr. *thermē*, heat, and *bathos*, depth.] In physical geography, a line connecting such points of equal temperature as are included within a fixed vertical section of the ocean.

ī-sō-thẽr-mō-bath′iç, *a.* Pertaining to an isothermobath.

ī-soth-ẽr-ŏm′brōse, *a.* [*Iso-*, and Gr. *theros*, summer, and *ombros*, rain.] Designating a line or lines connecting places on the surface of the earth where the same quantity of rain falls during the summer.

ī-sō-ton′iç, *a.* [Gr. *isotonos*, having equal accent or tone; *isos*, equal, and *tonos*, accent, tone.] Having equal tones.

Isotonic system; in music, intervals in which each concord is alike tempered and in which there are twelve equal semitones.

ī-sō-tri-mor′phişm, *n.* [*Iso-*, and Gr. *tris*, thrice, and *morphē*, form, and *-ism.*] In crystallography, a similarity of crystalline form between the members of two trimorphous groups.

ī″sō-trī-mor′phous, *a.* Characterized by isotrimorphism.

ī-sō-trop′iç, *a.* [*Iso-*, and Gr. *tropē*, a turning, from *trepein*, to turn.] In physics, having the same properties, as elasticity, diathermance, conductivity, etc., in like degree in all directions.

ī-sot′rō-pişm, *n.* See *Isotropy.*

ī-sot′rō-pous, *a.* Same as *Isotropic.*

ī-sot′rō-py, *n.* The state or quality of being isotropic.

ī′sō-tȳpe, *n.* [Gr. *isotypos*, shaped alike; *isos*, equal, and *typos*, impression, form, type.] In zoögeography and phytogeography, an organism represented by a species, genus, or family in different parts of the world.

ī-sō-ū′riç, *a.* [*Iso-* and *uric.*] Pertaining to an odorless, tasteless compound isomeric with uric acid.

ī-sō-zō′oid, *n.* [*Iso-*, and Gr. *zōon*, an animal, and *eidos*, form.] A zoöid resembling the parent.

is′pȧ-ghụl, *n.* [E. Ind.] An East Indian species of plantain, *Plantago Ispaghula*, bearing seeds much used in the preparation of a native drink.

I′-spȳ′, *n.* A child's game, hide-and-seek.

Is′rā-el-īte, *n.* [LL. *Israëlita*; Gr. *Israēlitēs*, a descendant of Israel, from *Israēl*; Heb. *Yisrāēl*, Israel, Jacob, lit., champion of God; *sārāh*, to fight, and *ēl*, God.] A descendant of Israel or Jacob; a Jew.

Is″rā-el-it′iç, *a.* Pertaining to Israel; Jewish.

Iş″rā-el-ī′tish, *a.* Of or belonging to the Israelites or to the Israelitic race.

is′sū-ȧ-ble (ish′ū-), *a.* 1. That may be issued.

2. Pertaining to an issue or issues; that admits of issue being taken upon it; in which issues are made up; as, an *issuable* plea; an *issuable* term.

Issuable plea; a plea upon which a plaintiff may take issue and go to trial upon the merits.

is′sū-ȧ-bly, *adv.* In an issuable manner.

is′sū-ănce, *n.* The act of sending or putting out.

is′sū-ănt, *a.* Coming out of; in heraldry, denoting a bearing, usually in the form of an animal emerging.

Lion Issuant.

is′sūe (ish′ū), *n.* [ME. *issue*, *issu*, *isshue*; OFr. *issue*, *eissue*, a going out, outlet, from *issu*, pp. of *issir*, *eisser*, to go out, from L. *exire*; *ex*, out, and *ire*, to go.]

1. The act of passing or flowing out; a moving out of any inclosed place; egress; as, an *issue* of blood from a wound.

2. A sending out; as, the *issue* of an order from a commanding officer or from a court; the *issue* of money from a treasury.

3. Event; consequence; end or ultimate result; as, the *issue* was favorable.

4. Progeny; a child or children; offspring; as, a man dies without *issue.*

5. Produce of the earth or profits of land; as, the *issues*, rents, etc., of an estate.

6. In surgery, a duct made in some part of an animal body to promote discharges.

7. Evacuation; discharge; a flux or running.

8. In law, the close or result of pleadings; the point of matter depending in suit, on which the parties join and put the case to trial.

9. A giving out from a repository; delivery; as, an *issue* of rations or provisions from a store; an *issue* of ammunition from a magazine.

At issue; opposing; disagreeing; in contention.

Bank of issue; see under *Bank.*

Collateral issue; see under *Collateral.*

To join issue, to take issue; to join in a contest; said of two parties who take up a positive and negative position respectively on a point in debate.

is′sūe, *v.i.*; issued, *pt.*, *pp.*; issuing, *ppr.* 1. To pass or flow out; to run out; to proceed, as from a source; as, water *issues* from springs; blood *issues* from wounds; light *issues* from the sun.

2. To go out; to rush out; as, troops *issued* from the town, and attacked the besiegers.

3. To proceed, as progeny; to be descended; to spring.

4. To be produced; to arise; to grow or accrue; as, rents and profits *issuing* from land.

5. In legal pleadings, to come to a point in fact or law on which the parties join and rest the decision of the cause.

6. To close; to end.

Syn. — Break out, emanate, flow, proceed, emerge, rise, spring.

is′sūe, *v.t.* 1. To send out; to put into circulation; as, to *issue* money from a treasury or notes from a bank.

2. To send out; to deliver from authority; as, to *issue* an order from the department of war; to *issue* a writ.

3. To deliver for use; as, to *issue* provisions from a store.

is′sūe-less, *a.* Having no issue or progeny.

is′sūe-pēa, *n.* In surgery, any small, round body inserted in an issue to irritate and thus to relieve it of pus.

is′sū-ẽr, *n.* One who issues or emits.

-ist. [L. *-ista, -istes;* Gr. *-istēs*, a termination denoting the agent, from verbs in *-izein.*] A noun suffix of words of Greek origin or those similarly formed, denoting the agent or doer, one who practises, or a believer in; as, evangel*ist*, pian*ist*, abolition*ist*, theor*ist*. The suffix *-ist* corresponds to *-er*, and frequently interchanges with it.

is′t. A contraction of *is it*.

isth′mi-ăn (ist′ *or* is′), *a.* 1. Pertaining to an isthmus.

2. [I—] Pertaining to the Isthmus of Corinth.

Isthmian games; one of the four great festivals of Greece; so called because celebrated on the Isthmus of Corinth.

isth′mi-āte, *a.* In zoölogy, having a narrow part between two broader parts.

isth′mus (ist′ *or* is′), *n.* [L. *isthmus;* Gr. *isthmos*, a neck, narrow passage, an isthmus.] A neck or narrow strip of land by which two larger bodies of land are connected, or by which a peninsula is united to the mainland; as, the *isthmus* of Panama connects North and South America.

-istic. [From *-ist*, and *-ic.*] An adjective termination added to nouns in *-ist;* as, lingu*istic*, eulog*istic*, euphu*istic*.

-istical. Same as *-istic*.

is′tle, *n.* [Mex.] A species of strong coarse fiber furnished by one of several tropical American plants, especially by *Bromelia sylvestris* and *Agave rigida;* called also *pita, silkgrass*, and *Tampico fiber*.

ī-sū′ret, *n.* [*Is-* and *-uret.*] A white crystalline basic compound of nitrogenous character, isomeric with urea.

it, *pron.* [ME. *it, hit;* AS. *hit*, neut. of *he*, he.]

1. The neuter singular form of the third-person pronoun, corresponding to the masculine and feminine forms *he* and *she* and having the plural forms *they, their, them;* used (a) to represent anything regarded as having no sex and in situations where sex is not specified; as, water is transparent when *it* is pure; the bird has a tuft of feathers on *its* head; the child loves *its* toys; (b) impersonally, with no definite antecedent; as, *it* snows; (c) to represent a clause or statement; as, *it* is well known that wood is combustible; *it* is best to be sincere; (d) to intensify the meaning of an intransitive verb; as, to rough *it;* to go *it*.

2. In children's play, the one whose lot is to be or to do some particular thing; as, you are *it*.

ī′tá-cism, *n.* The modern pronunciation of the Greek *ēta* (η), preferred by the followers of Reuchlin to the *etacism* of the followers of Erasmus.

ī′tá-cist, *n.* One who prefers itacism to etacism.

it-á-col′ū-mīte, *n.* [From *Itacolumi*, a mountain in Brazil, and *-ite.*] A laminated talcose sandstone, in connection with which the diamond is generally found.

it-á-con′iç, *a.* [From *aconitic*, by a transposition of the letters.] Pertaining to an acid, $C_5H_6O_4$, obtained from various organic substances.

it′á-kā-wood, *n.* The wood of a leguminous tree of British Guiana.

It′á-lá, *n.* [Properly f. of L. *Italus*, Italian.] A very old Latin version of the Scriptures.

I-tal′iăn, *a.* and *n.* [L. *Italus*, Italian.]

I. *a.* Pertaining to Italy.

II. *n.* A native of Italy; also, the language of Italy or the Italians.

Italian cloth; see *Farmer's satin* under *Farmer*.

Italian juice; a kind of licorice.

I-tal′iăn-āte, *v.t.* To render Italian, or conformable to Italian customs; to Italianize. [Rare.]

I-tal′iăn-āte, *a.* Italianized; applied to fantastic affectation of fashions borrowed from Italy.

I-tal′iăn-iṣm, *n.* An Italian expression, manner, or custom.

I-tal′iăn-īze, *v.i.;* Italianized, *pt., pp.;* Italianizing, *ppr.* To play the Italian; to speak Italian.

I-tal′iăn-īze, *v.t.* To render Italian; to give an Italian color or character to.

I-tal′iç, *a.* [L. *Italicus*, Italian, from *Italia*, Italy.] Relating to Italy.

i-tal′iç, *n.* In printing, a style of type with inclined letters; also used adjectively.

I-tal′i-ciṣm, *n.* 1. Same as *Italianism*.

2. [i—] In printing, the use of italics.

i-tal′i-cīze, *v.t.;* italicized, *pt., pp.;* italicizing, *ppr.* To print in italic characters; in copy for the printer, to underscore with a single line to indicate what is to be printed in italics.

I-tal′i-ot, I-tal′i-ōte, *a.* and *n.* [Gr. *Italiōtēs*, from *Italia*, Italy.]

I. *a.* Pertaining to the Greek residents of Italy.

II. *n.* A Greek resident of Italy.

ī′tá-pälm (-päm), *n.* In botany, a tall, valuable palm, *Mauritia flexuosa*, growing in the Amazon and Orinoco regions and furnishing the natives with food, drink, and fiber.

itch, *n.* 1. A cutaneous disease of the human skin, appearing in small, watery pustules, accompanied by an uneasiness or irritation, and due to the presence within the epidermis of a species of mite, *Sarcoptes scabiei*.

2. The sensation in the skin occasioned by this disease.

3. A constant teasing desire; as, an *itch* for praise; an *itch* for scribbling.

4. Any irritating sensation of the epidermis.

Baker's itch; see under *Baker*.

Barber's itch; see under *Barber*.

Bricklayer's itch; a form of eczema caused by the action of lime on the epidermis.

itch, *v.i.;* itched (icht), *pt., pp.;* itching, *ppr.* [ME. *icchen, iken, giken;* AS. *giccan*, to itch.]

1. To feel a peculiar and unpleasant irritation of the skin, which inclines the person to scratch the part.

2. To have a constant desire or teasing inclination; as, to *itch* after honors.

An itching palm; an avaricious disposition; an inordinate love of money.

itch′i-ness, *n.* The state or quality of being itchy.

itch′less, *a.* Free from the itch or its sensation.

itch′-mīte, *n.* A microscopic articulated insect, *Sarcoptes scabiei*, of the class *Arachnida*, which produces itch in man.

itch′y, *a.* Infected with the itch or its sensation.

-ite. [L. *-itus, -ita, -itum*, pp. ending of verbs of 2nd, 3rd, and 4th conjugations.] A suffix of some adjectives and nouns from adjectives, and also of some verbs derived from Latin; as, exquis*ite*, oppos*ite*, un*ite*, requis*ite*.

-ite. [Fr. *-ite;* L. *-ita, -ites;* Gr. *-itēs*, f. *-itis.*] A suffix denoting resemblance to, similarity, adherence to or descent from, nativity; specifically, in chemistry, denoting a salt of an acid having the termination *-ous*. It is also a common suffix in anatomy, biology, mineralogy, etc.

ī′tem, *adv.* [L. *item*, also.] Also; a word used when something is to be added.

ī′tem, *n.* 1. An article; a separate particular in an account; as, the account consists of many *items*.

2. A hint; an innuendo. [Obs.]

3. A short paragraph or reading-notice in a newspaper or other periodical; as, an *item* about a fire.

ī′tem, *v.t.* To make a note or memorandum of. [Obs.]

ī′tem-īze, *v.t.;* itemized, *pt., pp.;* itemizing, *ppr.* To state in items; to set down or describe by particulars; as, I will *itemize* the bill.

ī′tẽr, *n.* [L., a going, way, from *ire*, to go.] A journey; in anatomy, a passage or duct, especially the tubular cavity between the third and fourth ventricles of the brain; the aqueduct of Sylvius.

it′ẽr-á-ble, *a.* Capable of being repeated. [Obs.]

it′ẽr-ánce, *n.* [Obs.] See *Iteration*.

it′ẽr-ánt, *a.* [L. *iterans (-antis)*, ppr. of *iterare*, to do a thing a second time, to repeat, from *iterum*, again.] Repeating; as, an *iterant* echo.

it′ẽr-āte, *v.t.;* iterated, *pt., pp.;* iterating, *ppr.* [L. *iteratus*, pp. of *iterare*, to repeat, from *iterum*, again.] To repeat; to utter or do a second time; as, to *iterate* advice or admonition; to *iterate* a trespass.

it′ẽr-āte-ly, *adv.* By means of repetition or iteration.

it-ẽr-ā′tion, *n.* [L. *iteratio (-onis)*, from *iterare*, to repeat.] Repetition; recital or performance a second time.

it′ẽr-á-tive, *a.* Repeating.

it′ẽr-á-tive-ly, *adv.* In an iterative manner.

Ith′á-căn, *a.* Relating to the island of Ithaca.

Ith-á-cen′si-ăn, *a.* Ithacan.

I-thū′ri-el′s-spēar, *n.* [So called from *Ithuriel's spear*, in Milton's Paradise Lost, which caused everything it touched to assume its proper shape.] A liliaceous plant of northern California, *Brodiæa laxa*.

ith-y-phal′liç, *a.* [L. *ithyphallicus;* Gr. *ithyphallikos*, from *ithyphallos*, a phallus; *ithys*, straight, erect, and *phallos*, a phallus.]

1. Grossly vile or indecent; obscene; lascivious; lustful.

2. In prosody, descriptive of a verse which consists of a trochaic tripody; so named because sung in phallic celebrations.

ī-tin′ẽr-á-cy, *n.* The practice of itinerating.

ī-tin′ẽr-ăn-cy, *n.* 1. A passing from place to place.

2. The traveling from place to place in the discharge of duty; as, the *itinerancy* of a judge, a commercial traveler, or a preacher.

ī-tin′ẽr-ănt, *a.* [LL. *itinerans (-antis)*, ppr. of *itinerari*, to travel, go on a journey.] Passing or traveling about a country; wandering; not settled; as, an *itinerant* preacher.

ī-tin′ẽr-ănt, *n.* One who travels from place to place, particularly a preacher; one who is unsettled.

ī-tin′ẽr-ănt-ly, *adv.* In an unsettled or wandering manner.

ī-tin′ẽr-ā-ry, *n.;* *pl.* **ī-tin′ẽr-ā-rieṣ.** [LL. *itinerarium*, an account of a journey, a road-book, neut. of *itinerarius*, pertaining to a journey.] An account of travels; a register of places and their distances; as, the *itinerary* of a circuit judge.

ī-tin′ẽr-ā-ry, *a.* Traveling; passing from place to place; done on a journey.

ī-tin′ẽr-āte, *v.i.;* itinerated, *pt., pp.;* itinerating, *ppr.* [LL. *itineratus*, pp. of *itinerari*, to go on a journey, travel, from L. *iter*, a going, journey.] To travel from place to place, particularly for the purpose of preaching, lecturing, etc.; to wander without a settled habitation.

-ition. [L. *-itio (-onis)*, a termination for nouns from pp. in *-itus.*] A suffix used with many abstract and concrete nouns of Latin origin; as, exped*ition*, fru*ition*, erud*ition*, requis*ition*. [See first *-ite*, and *-tion.*]

-itious. [*-ition* and *-ous.*] A termination for adjectives associated with nouns in *-ition;* as, exped*itious*.

-itis. [L. *-itis;* Gr. *-itis*, originally an adj. suffix, signifying of the nature of.] A suffix used in medicine to denote inflammation; as, bronch*itis*, arthr*itis*, enter*itis*.

-itive. A compound adjective suffix from Latin *-itivus*, found in adjectives derived from the pp. suffix *-itus;* as, defin*itive*, infin*itive*, fug*itive*.

its, *pron.*, possessive form of *it*.

it-self′, *pron.* The neuter reciprocal pronoun applied to things; as, the thing is good in *itself;* it stands by *itself*.

it′tri-á, *n.* Same as *Yttria*.

it′tri-um, *n.* Same as *Yttrium*.

-ity. [Fr. *-ite;* L. *-itas*, acc. *-itatem*, formed from *-i-* and *-tas.*] A suffix used to form nouns from adjectives of Latin origin, or those similarly formed; as, frugal*ity*, nobil*ity*, joll*ity*, etc.

it′zi-bū, *n.* An old Japanese coin; spelled also *itzeboo, itzebu*, and *itchebu*.

ī-ū′li-dăn, *n.* A myriapod of the family *Iulidæ*.

I-ū′lus, *n.* [L. *iulus;* Gr. *ioulos*, down, a catkin, centipede.] A genus of *Myriapoda*, order *Chilognatha* or *Diplopoda*, a semicylindrical form, with moniliform antennæ and two articulated palpi. The common gallyworm, *Iulus terrestris*, is the type of the genus.

Iulus plicatus or Milleped.

I've. A contraction of *I have*. [Colloq.]

-ive. [L. *-ivus, -iva*, f., *-ivum* neut.] An adjective suffix signifying related to, belonging to, of the nature of; as, collect*ive*, act*ive*, correct*ive*.

ī′vied (-vid), *a.* Covered with ivy.

ī′vō-rīde, *n.* [*Ivory* and *-ide.*] An artificial imitation of ivory.

ī′vō-ry, *n.;* *pl.* **ī′vō-rieṣ.** [ME. *ivory, ivorie;* OFr. *ivurie;* Pr. *evori, bori;* LL. *eboreum*, from L. *ebur, eboris*, ivory.]

1. The substance forming the tusk of the elephant, a hard, solid, fine-grained form of dentine of a white color. It is highly prized and much used in the manufacture of articles of virtu, billiard balls, etc.

2. A piece of carved ivory; an ivory figure.

3 [*pl.*] The teeth. [Slang.]

Vegetable ivory; see *Ivory-nut*.

ī′vō-ry, *a.* 1. Consisting of ivory; made of ivory; as, an *ivory* comb.

2. White, hard, or smooth, like ivory; as, an *ivory* cheek.

ī′vō-ry-bill, *n.* A large woodpecker, *Campophilus principalis*, found in the Gulf states, and characterized by a hard white bill, resembling ivory.

ī′vō-ry-gull, *n.* A small white gull, *Larus eburneus*, of the arctic regions.

ī′vō-ry-nut, *n.* The nut of a species of palm, *Phytelephas macrocarpa*, often as large as a hen's egg, consisting of a close-grained and very hard substance resembling the finest ivory in texture and color and often wrought into ornamental work; called also *vegetable ivory*.

ī′vō-ry-pälm (-päm), *n.* The tree which produces the ivory-nut.

ī′vō-ry-shell, *n.* A univalve shell of a species of *Eburna*.

ī′vō-ry-tȳpe, *n.* In photography, a picture having the appearance of being made in natural colors upon ivory.

ī′vy, *n.* [ME. *ivy;* AS. *ifig*, ivy.] An epiphytic climbing plant, *Hedera Helix*, which creeps along the ground, or, if it finds support, rises on trees or buildings, often climbing to a great height.

> Direct the clasping *ivy* where to climb.
> —Milton.

American ivy; see under *American*.

Boston ivy; same as *Japanese ivy*.

English ivy; the common European ivy, *Hedera Helix.*

German ivy; a species of groundsel, *Senecio mikanioides.*

Japanese ivy; a climbing plant, *Ampelopsis tricuspidata*, identical with Boston ivy and very closely related to the Virginia creeper.

Kenilworth ivy; a European trailing plant of the figwort family, *Linaria Cymbalaria.*

Mexican ivy; a tropical climbing plant, *Cobœa scandens*, having large purple flowers.

West Indian ivy; a climbing plant, *Marcgravia umbellata.*

ī'vy-bind"weed, *n.* The black bindweed, *Polygonum Convolvulus.*

ī'vy-bush, *n.* 1. The mountain-laurel or calico-bush, *Kalmia latifolia.*

2. In England, a branch of the common ivy hung over a door to express good cheer.

ī'vy-man"tled, *a.* Covered with ivy.

ī'vy-owl, *n.* The brown or tawny owl of Europe, *Syrnium aluco.*

ī'vy-tod, *n.* An ivy plant or bush.

ī'vy-tree, *n.* A New Zealand evergreen tree, *Panax Colensoi.*

i-wis', y-wis', *adv.* Truly. [Obs.]

Ix'i-ȧ, *n.* [Gr. *ixos*, birdlime; so called because of the viscid nature of some of the species.] An extensive genus of Cape bulbs of the order *Iridaceæ*, occupying a high place among ornamental plants. They have narrow sword-shaped leaves and slender simple or branched stems, bearing spikes of large showy various-colored flowers.

Ix-ō'dēṣ, *n.* [Gr. *ixōdēs*, like birdlime, sticky; *ixos*, birdlime, and *eidos*, form.] A genus of parasitic insects including several species of tick.

ix-ō'di-ăn, *n.* One of the *Ixodes.*

Ix-ō'rȧ, *n.* [From *Iswara*, a Hind. divinity to whom flowers are offered, from Sans. *icvara*, master, lord.] An extensive genus of rubiaceous tropical shrubs and small trees, chiefly of the Old World.

ix'tle, ix'tli, *n.* Same as *Istle.*

I'yär, *n.* [Heb.] A Hebrew month; Zif.

iz'ăr, *n.* 1. A garment worn by Mohammedans.

2. [I—] A star in the constellation Boötes.

iz'ărd, *n.* [Fr. *isard*, an izard.] A kind of chamois.

-ize. [Fr. *-ise*; LL. *-izare*, from Gr. *-izein.*] A suffix forming verbs from adjectives and nouns, and signifying to do, to make, or to be the thing denoted by the noun or adjective; as, to Attic*ize*, to act or speak like an Athenian; apolog*ize*, civil*ize*. The suffix *-ize* is a variant of *-ise.*

Iz'ē-dĭ, *n.* One of a sect in Mesopotamia and neighboring regions, who are said to worship the devil; also written *Yezdi, Yezidi.*

Iz'ē-diṣm, *n.* The religion professed by the Izedis.

iz'zärd, *n.* Same as *Izard.*

iz'zărd, *n.* [Prob. corruption of *s hard.*] Old name for the last letter of the English alphabet.

J

J (jā). The tenth letter in the English alphabet, and the seventh consonant. The sound of this letter coincides exactly with that of *g* in *genius*. It is therefore classed as a palatal, and is the voiced sound corresponding to the breathed sound *ch* (as in *church*). The sound does not occur in Anglo-Saxon, and was introduced through the French. The French *j* now, however, has a different sound. As a character it was formerly used interchangeably with *i*, both letters having originally the same sound; and after the *j* sound came to be common in English *i* was often written where this sound must have been pronounced. The separation of these two letters is of comparatively recent date, being brought about through the influence of the Dutch printers.

J, j, *as a symbol.* In medical prescriptions, *j* is equivalent to the Roman *i*, or one, being used at the end of a number, as, *iij, vij.*

In thermodynamics, *J* denotes the mechanical equivalent of heat.

As an abbreviation, *J.* stands for Julius, Judge, Justice, etc.

jäal-gōat, *n.* [*Jaal*, African name.] An Abyssinian wild goat or ibex, *Capra jaala*; sometimes known as *beden.*

jab, *v.t.*; jabbed, *pt., pp.*; jabbing, *ppr.* To poke; to punch; to thrust; to stab; as, to *jab* an enemy with a pike. [Scot. and Colloq., U. S.]

jab, *n.* 1. A punch; a thrust; a poke; a stab.

2. A blow in boxing given by straightening the arm suddenly; a thrusting blow.

jab'bẽr, *v.t.*; jabbered, *pt., pp.*; jabbering, *ppr.* [Compare Ice. *gabba*, to mock.] To pronounce or utter indistinctly or rapidly; as, to *jabber* a foreign language.

jab'bẽr, *v.i.* To talk rapidly or indistinctly; to chatter; to gabble.

jab'bẽr, *n.* Rapid talk with indistinct utterance of words.

jab'bẽr-ẽr, *n.* One who talks rapidly, indistinctly, or unintelligibly.

jab'bẽr-ing-ly, *adv.* In a confused or jabbering manner.

jab'bẽr-ment, *n.* Idle prate. [Obs.]

jab'bẽr-nowl, *n.* Same as *Jobbernoll.*

jab'i-rŭ, *n.* [Braz. name.] A bird, *Mycteria americana*, of subtropical America, closely resembling the stork.

jab-ō-ran'di, *n.* [Braz.] A powerful drug obtained from the leaves and root of a plant belonging to the order *Rutaceæ*; also, the plant itself.

jab'ō-rine, *n.* [*Jabor*andi and *-ine.*] One of the alkaloids obtained from jaborandi leaves, similar in properties to atropin.

jȧ-bōt' (zhȧ-bō'), *n.* [Fr.] 1. A kind of ruffle or frill used as an ornament for the front of a woman's bodice.

2. Formerly, a ruffle on a man's shirt-front.

jȧ-çăl' (hȧ-kăl'), *n.* In Mexico and the southwestern part of the United States, a rude hut built of logs and daubed with mud.

jaç'ȧ-mär, *n.* [S. Am.] A brilliant tropical American bird resembling the kingfisher, having a long slender bill.

jaç'ȧ-nä, *n.* [Braz. name *jaçanā.*] Any one of several grallatorial birds, as *Parra jacana*, characterized by spurred wings, long legs, and long, spreading toes, by means of which they are able to walk upon the floating leaves of aquatic plants.

Jaç-ȧ-ran'dȧ, *n.* [Braz.] 1. A genus of bignoniaceous trees of which the rosewood is the best-known example.

2. [j—] A tree of this genus; also, certain trees of other genera resembling the rosewood.

jaç'ȧ-re, *n.* [Port. *jacaré*, from Braz. name.] A Brazilian alligator having a ridge from eye to eye, fleshy eyelids, the cervical distinct from the dorsal scutes, and small webs on the feet.

Long-tailed Jacana (*Parra sinensis*).

jac'chus, *n.* [L. *Jacchus*; Gr. *Iakchos*, a name of Bacchus.] A kind of marmoset.

jac'ō-net, *n.* Same as *Jaconet.*

jā'cent, *a.* [L. *jacens* (*-entis*), ppr. of *jacere*, to lie.] Lying at length. [Rare.]

jā'cinth, *n.* Same as *Hyacinth.*

jac-i-tä'rȧ-pälm, *n.* [S. Am. *jacitara*, and Eng. *palm.*] A South American palm with hooked spines at the extremities of its leaves, valued for its excellent fiber; the *Desmoncus macroacanthus.*

jack, *v.t.*; jacked, *pt., pp.*; jacking, *ppr.* To raise with a jack.

jack, *v.i.* To hunt or fish with a jack-lamp.

jack, *n.* [ME. *Jacke, Jake*; OFr. *Jaque, Jaques*; LL. *Jacobus*; Gr. *Iakōbos*, from Heb. *Ya'aqōb*, Jacob, lit., seizing by the heel, a supplanter. From the nickname being used for a servant or boy who made himself generally useful, it is applied to lifting-instruments.]

1. [J—] A nickname for Jacob, Jacques, or John, especially the latter.

2. A sailor.

3. A saucy or impertinent fellow; an upstart; a boor; a clown.

4. In playing-cards, a knave.

5. Any machine, device, or contrivance which serves as a convenient assistant, as (a) a portable machine for raising great weights through a small space, consisting of a system of screws operated by a handcrank; in the illustration, *a* is the handcrank; *b*, the movable upright upon which the load is placed; *c*, the screw-wheel; *d*, the claw which prevents the upright from rotating; *e, f*, the supports of the motor screw; (b) a jack-frame; (c) a jack-plane; (d) a jack-crosstree; (e) a jack-lamp; (f) a spring-clip electrical connector; (g) a device for turning logs; (h) a saw-buck; (i) a bootjack.

Lifting-jack.

6. In navigation, a small flag containing the canton of a national flag displayed on the jack-staff; as, the American *jack*; the British *jack.*

7. A drinking-vessel holding less than a pint. [Prov. Eng.]

8. One of several fishes, notably the pike, the pike-perch, and the Californian rockfish.

9. Of birds, the jackdaw; the jack-curlew; the jacobin-pigeon.

10. The automaton that strikes the hours on a clock.

11. A seal or its impression. [Slang.]

12. A male animal; especially, a male ass.

13. A small Newfoundland schooner-rigged fishing-vessel.

Builders' jack; a seat or support of some kind used to hold a workman while repairing a building.

Hydraulic jack; a lifting-jack in which the power is obtained by the action of a force-pump upon a liquid confined in a cylinder.

Jack in the green; a chimney-sweep dressed about with foliage for the procession on the first day of May. [Eng.]

Jack in office; an official who assumes an air of offensive authority.

Jack Ketch; a hangman; a public executioner. [Eng.]

Jack of all trades; a person who can turn his hand to any kind of business.

Jack of the dust; in the United States navy an enlisted man who assists a petty officer or yeoman in handling the ship's stores.

Jack on both sides; a trimmer; a person who is first with one party and then with the opposite one.

Yellow Jack; yellow fever. [Slang.]

jack, *n.* [OFr. *jaque, jacque*; prob. from the proper name, *Jaque, Jacque.*] A kind of military coat quilted and covered with leather, worn over a coat of mail.

Jack.

jack, *n.* In botany, same as *jack-tree.*

jack, *n.* A kind of pitcher made of waxed leather; a black-jack.

jack, *n.* A Jacqueminot rose.

jack'ȧ-dan'dy, *n.* A little, foppish, impertinent fellow.

jack'ạl, *n.* [OFr. *jackal, jakal*; Ar. *jaqāl*, from Per. *shaghāl*, a jackal.]

1. In zoölogy, an animal of the genus *Canis*, a native of Asia and Africa, of a cowardly nature and nocturnal habits, preying on poultry and various small animals, and feeding largely on carrion.

Jackal (*Canis aureus*).

2. Any one who does menial work in the interests of another.

Jack'ȧ-Lent', *n.* See *Jack-o'-Lent.*

jack'ạls-kōst', *n.* [*Jackal*, and G. *kost*, food. In botany, a fungus-like plant, *Hydnora Africana*, parasitic on the roots of other plants bearing a large, sessile, partially-buried flower it is roasted and eaten by the African natives

jack'ȧ-nāpes, *n.* [For *Jack o' apes*, Jack o apes, one who exhibited apes.]

1. A monkey; an ape. [Obs.]

2. A coxcomb; an impertinent or mischievous fellow.

A young upstart *jackanapes.* —Arbuthnot.

3. In mining, the small pulleys guiding the cable of a kind of hoist with a vertical drum.

jack'=ärch, *n.* An arch of the thickness of one brick.

jack'ȧ-roo, *n.* [Australian.] A tenderfoot; a greenhorn.

jack'ass, *n.* 1. The male of the ass; a jack; a donkey.

2. A dolt; a blockhead.

3. Among sailors, a hawse-bag.

jack'ass=deer, *n.* A large African antelope, *Kobus singsing*.

jack'ass=pen"guin, *n.* The common penguin; so called from its cry.

jack'ass=rab"bit, *n.* Same as *Jack-rabbit*.

jack'=at=a=pinch, *n.* One who is substituted for another in case of an emergency.

jack'=at=the=hedge, *n.* A plant of the madder family, *Galium Aparine*; goose-grass or cleavers.

jack'=back, *n.* 1. In brewing, a vessel below the copper which receives the infusion of malt and hops therefrom, and which has a perforated bottom to strain off the hops.

2. In vinegar-making, a vat for holding the cold wort.

jack'=bird, *n.* A small European thrush, the fieldfare.

jack'=block, *n.* A block used in sending top-gallantmasts up and down.

jack'=boot, *n.* A kind of large boot reaching up over the knee, and used as a sort of defensive armor for the leg, introduced in the seventeenth century; also, a similar boot, as that worn by fishermen.

Jack-boot. Seventeenth century.

jack'=by=the=hedge', *n.* In botany, one of several species of plants growing under hedges, especially a species of the cruciferous genus *Sisymbrium*, known as hedge-mustard.

jack'=chain, *n.* A chain formerly used on the wheels of a jack, having links made from a single piece of wire twisted into the shape of the figure 8.

jack'=cross"tree, *n.* In a ship, a crossbar of iron at the head of a topgallant-mast to support the royal mast and to spread the royal shrouds.

jack'=cur"lew (-lö), *n.* In zoölogy, either the European whimbrel, *Numenius phæopus*, or the lesser American or Hudsonian curlew, *Numenius hudsonicus*.

jack'daw, *n.* In zoölogy, (a) a bird, *Corvus monedula*, frequenting deserted chimneys, old towers, and ruins, in flocks, where it builds its nest; (b) a large long-tailed blackbird, *Quiscalus major*, of the family *Agelæidæ*, the boat-tailed grackle.

Jackdaw (*Corvus monedula*).

jack-een', *n.* A drunken, profligate fellow. [Ireland.]

jack'et, *n.* [OFr. *jaquette*. dim. of *jaque*, a coat of mail, a jack.]

1. A short, close garment extending downward to the hips; a short coat.

2. An outer case of cloth, felt, wood, steam, water, or other substance, generally used to prevent the radiation of heat; as, the felt *jacket* of a steam-boiler.

3. A garment lined with cork to support the wearer while swimming; a cork-jacket.

4. An envelope for official papers with space for various indorsements. [U. S.]

5. The skin of a potato; as, potatoes boiled in their *jackets*. [Colloq.]

To line one's jacket; to eat a hearty meal.

jack'et, *v.t.*; jacketed, *pt.*, *pp.*; jacketing, *ppr.* 1 To cover with a jacket, as a steam-boiler.

2. To give a beating to; to thrash. [Colloq.]

jack'et-ed, *a.* Wearing a jacket.

jack'et-ing, *n.* The materials, as felt, cloth, etc., from which a jacket is made; the jacket itself.

jack'=frame, *n.* In spinning, a contrivance for twisting the slivers after they have passed through the drawing-rollers.

jack'=fruit, *n.* The fruit borne by the jack-tree.

jack'=hare, *n.* The male of any species of hare.

jack'=in=a=box', **jack'=in=the=box'**, *n.* A name common to various things, as (a) a plant of the genus *Hernandia*, which bears a large nut that rattles in its pericarp when shaken; (b) a large wooden male screw turning in a female one, which forms the upper part of a strong wooden box shaped like the frustum of a pyramid; used, by means of levers passing through holes in it, as a press in packing, and for other purposes; (c) a kind of toy consisting of a box out of which a figure springs when the lid flies open; (d) a gambling sport in which a stick is placed upright in a hole with an article on the top of it, which is pitched at with sticks; if the article on the top, when struck, falls clear of the hole, the thrower wins; (e) a jack-frame.

jack'=in=the=bush', *n.* In botany, (a) jack-by-the-hedge; (b) a crassulaceous English weed of the genus *Cotyledon*; (c) a tropical shrub.

jack'=in=the=pul'pit, *n.* See *Indian turnip* under *Indian*.

jack'knife (-nīf), *n.* A large, strong clasp-knife for the pocket; a pocketknife larger than a penknife.

jack'=lamp, *n.* 1. A light used in hunting or fishing at night.

2. A Davy lamp with a cylinder of glass surrounding the gauze. [Eng.]

jack'=lan"tern, *n.* A jack-lamp; also, a Jack-o'-lantern.

jack'man, *n.*; *pl.* **jack'men**. One who wears a jack; especially, a military retainer.

jack'=of=the=but'ter-y, *n.* A plant, the mossy stonecrop.

jack'=of=the=clock', *n.* See *Jack*, n. 10.

Jack'=o'=lan'tern, *n.* [Abbrev. of *Jack of* (or *with*) *the lantern*.]

1. An ignis fatuus; a meteoric light that appears in low, moist lands.

2. A kind of lantern often made by children, especially on Hallowe'en. It is made of a pumpkin cut to resemble a face and lighted by a candle within. [U. S.]

jack'=pine, *n.* The gray pine, *Pinus Banksiana*, a low shrub of the northern United States and Canada.

jack'=plane, *n.* A carpenter's plane about eighteen inches long, used for coarse work.

jack'=pot, *n.* In the game of draw-poker, a form of play agreed upon by the players, in which all of them ante an equal amount at the same time, the ante being repeated until some player can open the betting with a pair of jacks or better; also, the pool or pot formed in this style of play; as, to play a *jack-pot* or *jack-pots*; to open a *jack-pot*.

jack'pud"ding, *n.* A merry-andrew; a buffoon.

jack'=rab"bit, *n.* Any one of several species of large hares, of the genus *Lepus*, remarkable for the length of their ears and legs, and found on the western prairies of the United States.

jack'=raft"er, *n.* In architecture, any short rafter necessitated in the construction of a roof, as in a hip-roof.

jack'=sal"mon (-sam"), *n.* A fresh-water fish of the genus *Stizostedium*; a wall-eyed pike or pike-perch.

jack'=sauce, *n.* A saucy fellow. [Obs.]

jack'saw, *n.* In zoölogy, the merganser; so called from its sharply serrated bill. [Prov. Eng.]

jack'screw, *n.* A lifting-jack operated by the turning of a screw.

jack'=shaft, *n.* In mechanics, a shaft receiving its motion from the main shaft; an intermediate shaft.

jack'=sink"er, *n.* In a knitting-machine, an attachment for depressing the threads to be caught by the hooked needles.

jack'slave, *n.* An inferior or menial servant. [Obs.]

jack'smith, *n.* A smith who makes jacks.

jack'snipe, *n.* In zoölogy, one of several snipes, (a) the common American snipe, *Gallinago wilsoni*; (b) the pectoral sandpiper, *Tringa maculata*; (c) the English snipe, *Gallinago gallinula*; (d) the dunlin, *Tringa alpina*.

Jack-sō'ni-ȧ, *n.* [Named after Mr. G. *Jackson*, an English botanist.] A genus of Australian shrubs of the order *Leguminosæ*, the chief characteristic of which is the absence of leaves, their places being taken by spinelike branches.

Jack-sō'ni-an, *a.* In United States history and politics, pertaining to Andrew Jackson, the seventh president of the United States, or to the political principles which he represented.

Jack'son's=broom, *n.* In botany, the dogwood, *Jacksonia scoparia*.

jack'=staff, *n.* The staff on the bowsprit or forepart of a vessel on which the union jack is flown.

jack'stay, *n.* One of a set of ropes, iron rods, or strips of wood attached to the yard for bending a squaresail to.

jack'stone, *n.* [A form of *chack*, *chuck*, and *stone*.]

1. One of five stones or metal pieces used in playing the game of jackstones, usually having six arms, each at right angles to four others.

2. [*pl.*] A child's game in which jackstones are tossed into the air and caught in various ways.

jack'straw, *n.* 1. A figure or effigy of a man, made of straw; hence, a man without any substance or means; a dependent.

2. One of the straws or strips of metal, etc., used in playing jackstraws.

3. [*pl.*] A game in which straws, strips of wood, metal, ivory, or the like are dropped in a pile, from which the players must with a small hook remove each one singly without moving or touching any other.

jack'=tim"ber, *n.* In architecture, a timber in a bay which, being intercepted by some other piece, is shorter than the rest.

jack'=tow"el, *n.* A coarse towel hanging from a roller for general use.

jack'=tree, *n.* An East Indian tree, *Artocarpus integrifolia*, bearing fruit of great size, called jack-fruit, the seeds of which are roasted and eaten; called also *jack*.

jack'wood, *n.* The wood of the jack-tree, used in carpentry and in cabinetwork.

jack'y, *n.*; *pl.* **jack'ies**. [Dim. of *Jack*.] A sailor.

jack'y, *n.* English gin. [Prov. Eng.]

jack'=yard, *n.* A spar extended above the gaff in order to allow greater spread to a topsail.

Jā'cob, *n.* [LL. *Jacobus*; Gr. *Iakōbos*; Heb. *Ya'aqōb*, Jacob, lit., one who seizes by the heel, a supplanter.]

1. A patriarch of the Hebrews, son of Isaac and Rebecca, brother of Esau; Israel.

2. [j—] The starling.

jac-ō-bæ'ȧ, *n.* In botany, the ragwort of Europe, *Senecio Jacobæa*.

jac-ō-bæ'ȧ=lil'y, *n.* A bulbous Mexican amaryllis, *Sprekelia formosissima*, which has a single large blossom, resembling a deep-red lily.

Jac-ō-bē'an, **Jȧ-cō'bi-an**, *a.* In architecture, relating to the later style of Elizabethan architecture, from its prevailing in the age of James I. It differed from pure Elizabethan chiefly in having a greater admixture of debased Italian forms.

Jacobean Architecture.

Jȧ-cō'bi-an, *n.* A determinant composed of the first derivatives of *n* functions of *n* variables; invented by K. G. J. Jacobi.

Jac'ō-bin, *n.* [OFr. *Jacobin*, from LL. *Jacobinus*, from *Jacobus*, Jacob, James.]

1. A black or Dominican friar, so called from these friars having first established themselves in Paris in the Rue St. Jacques (St. James street).

2. A member of a club of violent republicans in France during the revolution of 1789, who held secret meetings in a monastery of the Jacobin monks, in which measures were concerted to direct the proceedings of the National Assembly.

3. One who opposes government in a secret and unlawful manner or by violent means; a turbulent demagogue.

4. [j—] A variety of pigeon whose neck-feathers form a hood.

Jac'ō-bin, *a.* Same as *Jacobinic*.

Jac'ō-bine (-bin), *n.* Same as *Jacobin*.

Jac-ō-bin'ic, **Jac-ō-bin'ic-al**, *a.* Of, pertaining to, or resembling the Jacobins of France; turbulent; discontented with government; holding democratic principles.

Jac-ō-bin'ic-al-ly, *adv.* In a manner resembling the Jacobins.

Jac'ō-bin-ism, *n.* Unreasonable or violent opposition to legitimate government; an attempt to overthrow or change government by irregular means.

Jac'ō-bin-ize, *v.t.*; Jacobinized, *pt.*, *pp.*; Jacobinizing, *ppr.* To taint with Jacobinism.

Jac'ō-bite, *n.* [LL. *Jacobus*; Gr. *Iakōbos*, Jacob, James.]

1. A partizan or adherent of James II., king of England, after he abdicated the throne, and of his descendants.

2. One of a sect of Christians in Syria and Mesopotamia; so named from Jacob Baradzi, their leader, in the sixth century.

Jac'ō-bite, *a.* Pertaining to the Jacobites.

Jac-ō-bit'ic, *a.* Relating to Jacobitism.

Jac-ō-bit'ic-al, *a.* Belonging to the Jacobites.

Jac-ō-bit'ic-al-ly, *adv.* After the spirit or manner of the Jacobites.

Jac'ō-bit-ism, *n.* The principles of the partizans of James II.

Jā'cob's=lad'der, *n.* 1. A seaman's rope ladder with rounds of wood.

2. A garden herb, *Polemonium cæruleum*, whose leaves and blue blossoms are arranged in a way fancied to resemble a ladder.

3. The ladder seen in a vision by Jacob, as described in the Old Testament.

Jā'cob's=staff, *n.* 1. A pilgrim's staff.

2. A staff concealing a dagger.

3. A cross-staff; a kind of astrolabe.

4. The single staff used by surveyors to support a compass.

jȧ-cō′bus, *n.* A gold coin of England in the reign of James I., of the value of about six dollars.

Jac′ō-net, *n.* [Fr. *jaconas*, jaconet.] A light soft muslin of an open texture, used for dresses, neckwear, etc.

Jaç-quärd′ (-kärd′), *a.* Of or invented by Jos. Marie Jacquard of Lyons, France.

Jacque′mĭ-nŏt (-nō; *Fr. pron.* zhȧk-me-nō′), *n.* A deep-red remontant rose; named in honor of General Jacqueminot of France.

Jacque-rie′ (zhȧk-rē′), *n.* [Fr.] An insurrection of peasants; originally, the revolt of the peasants against the nobles of Picardy, France, in 1358.

jac′tăn-cy, *n.* A boasting. [Obs.]

jac-tā′tion, *n.* [L. *jactatio* (*-onis*), a throwing, vaunting, boasting, from *jactare*, to shake, agitate, boast.]

1. A tossing or agitation of the body, as in bed or for exercise; restlessness.

2. The throwing of missiles.

3. The act of bragging.

jac-ti-tā′tion, *n.* [LL. *jactitatio* (*-onis*), from L. *jactitare*, to bring forward in public, utter, freq. of *jactare*, to throw, shake, discuss.]

1. In medicine, same as *jactation*, 1.

2. In law, false statements or claims causing injury or loss to another.

Jactitation of marriage; in canon law, a false claim of being married to another.

jac′ū-lȧ-ble, *a.* Capable of being thrown. [Obs.]

jac′ū-lāte, *v.t.* To dart; to hurl; to launch. [Obs.]

jac-ū-lā′tion, *n.* The act of darting, throwing, or launching, as missile weapons. [Obs.]

jac′ū-lā-tŏr, *n.* 1. The archer-fish.

2. One who hurls or darts. [Obs.]

jac′ū-lȧ-tō-ry, *a.* Darting or throwing out suddenly, or suddenly thrown out; ejaculatory.

jad, *v.t.* To cut a pit or hole, as in coal or stone, in order to blast or wedge off a mass.

jāde, *n.* [Fr. *jade*; Sp. *jade*, jade, from *piedra de yjada*, stone of the side; so called because the stone was supposed to cure pain in the side.] Any of various ornamental green or white stones, especially a silicate of calcium and magnesium, tough and compact, and of a resinous or oily aspect when polished.

jāde, *n.* [ME. *jade*, a jade; Ice. *jalda*, a mare.]

1. A worn-out or tired horse; a worthless mare.

Tired as a *jade* in overloaden cart.—Sidney.

2. A worthless or disreputable person; now used especially of a vicious or impudent woman; a wench; a hussy.

3. A young woman; used in irony or jestingly.

jāde, *v.t.* and *v.i.*; jaded, *pt.*, *pp.*; jading, *ppr.* I. *v.t.* To act toward as toward a jade; to weary with long-continued repetition of the same act or effort; to fatigue; to tire out; to abuse.

II. *v.i.* To become weary or exhausted; to lose spirit.

jāde′ite, *n.* A silicate of sodium and aluminium, usually called *jade*.

jād′ẽr-y, *n.* The tricks of a jade.

jād′ish, *a.* 1. Vicious; like a jade; applied to a horse.

2. Unchaste; applied to a woman.

jæ′gẽr (yā′), *n.* Same as *Jäger*.

jag, *v.t.*; jagged, *pt.*, *pp.*; jagging, *ppr.* [ME. *jaggen*, *joggen*, to cut, jab, from Gael. *gag*, a notch, cleft.]

1. To notch; to cut into notches or teeth like those of a saw.

2. To jab, prick, or pierce, as with a sharp point. [Scot.]

jag, *n.* [ME. *jagge*, a projecting point; Gael. *gag*, a notch, cleft.]

1. A notch or denticulation; a cleft or division; a tooth; a ragged or zigzag edge; a sharp or rough point; a dag.

2. A stab; a jab. [Scot.]

3. A piece torn or broken off; a small fragment.

jag, *n.* 1. A small load, as for one horse.

2. Sufficient liquor to cause intoxication; hence, a state of intoxication. [Slang.]

They have the habit of adding whisky, or rum, and thus acquire a regular *jag*.
—N. Y. Sun, Dec. 27, 1903.

3. A fare of fish. [Local, U. S.]

4. A wallet; a saddlebag. [Scot.]

jag, *v.t.* To carry in a small load, as hay. [Colloq.]

Jag-ăn-nat′hȧ, *n.* [Hind. *Jagannāth*; Sans. *Jagannatha*, lit., ruler of men and beasts; *jagat*, all that moves, and *natha*, ruler, protector.] Lord of the earth; a title given to Krishna, one of the incarnations of Vishnu; hence a celebrated idol of Krishna in the temple at Puri, in Orissa, India. A huge wooden-wheeled car is used to bear this idol about in annual festivals and under this car fanatical pilgrims are said to have cast themselves as sacrifices; commonly spelled *Juggernaut*.

jag′=bōlt, *n.* A bolt barbed to resist withdrawal.

jä′gẽr (yā′), *n.* [G., a hunter, rifleman.]

1. In the German army, one of a body of sharpshooters; a rifleman.

2. A species of gull which secures its food by forcing other species to surrender their prey; especially, a skua of the genus *Stercorarius*.

jagg, *n.* Same as second *Jag*.

jag′ged, *a.* Notched; uneven; cleft; divided.

jag′ged-ly, *adv.* In a jagged manner; so as to be jagged.

jag′ged-ness, *n.* The state of being denticulated or jagged; unevenness.

jag′gẽr, *n.* One who or that which jags.

jag′gẽr, *n.* 1. One who carries a jag or wallet; a peddler. [Scot.]

2. A teamster. [Prov. Eng.]

jag′gẽr-y, *n.* [Anglo-Ind., from Sans. *çarkara*, sugar.] In India, dark, coarse sugar made of the juice of palms.

jag′ging=ī″ron (-ūrn), *n.* A wheel with a notched or jagged edge for decorating pastry, etc.

jag′gy, *a.* Set with teeth; denticulated; jagged.

jä-ghir′, jä-ghīre′, *n.* [Per. *jāgīr*, *jāigīr*; *jā*, *jāy*, a place, and *gīr*, a seizing, taking.] A district of land, or the product thereof, assigned by the East Indian government to an individual, commonly for the support of some public establishment, particularly of a military nature.

jä′ghīr-där, *n.* A person holding a jaghir.

jä′guȧ=pälm (-päm), *n.* [Sp. *jagua*, from native name.] A large Brazilian palm, the woody spathes of which harden when dry and are used as baskets, etc., by the natives.

jȧ-guär′ (-gwär′ *or* jag′ū-är), *n.* [Braz. *jaguara*, a jaguar.] A carnivorous animal, *Felis onca*, the largest and most formidable feline quadruped of America. It is marked with large dark spots in the form of circles, with a dark spot or pupil in the center of each. It is almost as large as the true tiger, and preys on all sorts of animals, up to horses and oxen. It rarely attacks man unless hard pressed by hunger or driven to bay.

Jaguar (*Felis onca*).

jȧ-guȧ-ron′di, *n.* [Native name.] A South American carnivorous animal, *Felis jaguarondi*, resembling a very large brown cat.

Jäh, *n.* Same as *Jehovah*.

jȧ″häd′, *n.* Same as *Jihad*.

Jäh′vęh (*or* yä′), *n.* Jehovah.

Jäh′vist, *n.* Same as *Jehovist*.

Jäh-vis′tic, *a.* Same as *Jehovistic*.

jāil, *n.* [ME. *jaile*, *gaile*, *gayhol*; OFr. *jaiole*, *jaole*, *gaole*, a cage, prison; LL. *gabiola*, dim. of *gabia*, a cage, prob. from L. *cavea*, a cage, coop.] A prison; a building or place for the confinement of persons arrested or of those restrained of personal liberty by act of law. Also written *gaol*.

Jail liberties or *limits*; the bounds limiting the personal freedom of a prisoner for debt who has given bond.

jāil, *v.t.*; jailed, *pt.*, *pp.*; jailing, *ppr.* To shut up in a jail; to imprison.

jāil′bīrd, *n.* A prisoner; one who has been confined in prison.

jāil′=dē-liv″ẽr-y, *n.* 1. The trial of all persons detained in a prison.

2. The forcible escape of prisoners from a jail.

jāil′ẽr, *n.* The keeper of a prison.

jāil′=fē″vẽr, *n.* Typhus fever, frequent in unsanitary jails.

Jāin, Jāi′nȧ, *n.* [Hind. *Jaina*, from *jina*, victorious.] One of a Hindu religious sect, which, from the wealth and influence of its members, forms an important division of the Indian population. Their religion is known as Jainism. They deny the divine origin and infallible authority of the Vedas, reverence certain holy mortals, and manifest extreme tenderness for animal life.

Jāin′ism, *n.* The religious principles and system of the Jains.

jai-rōu′ (yī-), *n.* Same as *Ahu*.

jak, *n.* Same as *Jack-tree*.

jākes, *n.* A privy. [Obs.]

jākes′=färm″ẽr, *n.* One who cleaned privies; a scavenger. [Obs.]

jä′kie, *n.* [S. Am.] A tropical American frog whose tadpole surpasses the adult in size.

jak′ō, *n.* The gray African parrot, *Psittacus erithacus*.

jak′wood, *n.* Same as *Jackwood*.

jal′ăp, *n.* [Sp. *jalapa*, from *Jalapa*, a city in Mexico from which it is imported.] The root of the climbing plant *Ipomœa purga*; also, a medicinal preparation of purgative properties, derived from the root.

False jalap; the root of the *Mirabilis jalapa*, the four-o'clock.

Jalap Plant (*Ipomœa purga*).

Indian jalap; see under *Indian*.

jȧ-lap′ic, *a.* Pertaining to jalap.

jal′ȧ-pin, *n.* [*Jalap* and *-in*.] A resin which is the purgative principle of the roots and tubers of jalap and some other plants of the convolvulaceous order.

jȧ-lōu-sie′ (zhȧ-), *n.* [Fr., jealousy, envy, a latticed window.] A Venetian blind.

jȧ-lōu-sied′, *a.* Having jalousies.

jam, *n.* In mining, same as *jamb*.

jam, *n.* [Prob. from *jam*, to press, squeeze, compare Ar. *jāmid*, ice, jelly, from *jamada*, to thicken, freeze.] A conserve or preserve made by cooking fruit with sugar to a thick pulp.

jam, *n.* [Per. and Hind. *jāmah*, raiment, robe.] A kind of frock for children.

jam, *n.* A crush; a crowd; a number of persons or things so tightly crowded together as to make movement impossible; also, the force, pressure, or stress of such a crowd; as, a *jam* of logs; crushed by the *jam*.

jam, *v.t.*; jammed, *pt.*, *pp.*; jamming, *ppr.* [Formerly, *jamb*, as if squeezed between *jambs* or from *cham*, *champ*, to chew, tread heavily.]

1. To press; to crowd; to wedge in; to squeeze tight; hence, to pinch; to crush.

2. To tread hard or make firm by treading, as land by cattle. [Prov. Eng.]

Jammed on the wind; very closehauled as a ship.

jam′ȧ-där, *n.* See *Jemidar*.

Jȧ-māi′cȧ, *n.* One of the islands of the West Indies, belonging to Great Britain.

Jamaica ginger; the white ginger grown in the West Indies; the drug prepared from it is a common stimulant and antispasmodic.

Jamaica rose; one of several tropical American shrubs of the order *Melastomaceæ*, as *Blakea trinervis*.

Jȧ-māi′căn, *a.* and *n.* I. *a.* Pertaining to Jamaica.

II. *n.* An inhabitant of Jamaica.

jȧ-māi′cine, jȧ-māi′cin, *n.* [From *Jamaica*.] An alkaloid obtained from the *Andira inermis*, the cabbage-tree of the West Indies.

jamb (jam), *n.* [ME. *jambe*, *jamne*; OFr. *jambe*, a leg, shank, pier, side post of a door, from LL. *gamba*, a hoof.]

1. In architecture, a side or vertical piece of any opening or aperture in a wall, such as a door, window, or chimney.

2. In mining, a mass of mineral or stone in a quarry or pit, standing upright, more or less distinct from adjoining parts.

3. A leg. [Obs.]

A, Jamb of Doorway.

jamb, *v.t.* To jam. [Obs.]

jambe, *n.* [OFr., leg.] Armor for the legs. [Obs.]

jam′beaus (-bō), **jam′beux** (-bū), *n.pl.* [OFr. *jambe*, leg.] Armor for the legs; spelled also *jambers*, *giambeux*. [Obs.]

jam-bee′, *n.* A kind of fashionable cane. [Obs.]

jam-bō-lä′nȧ, *n.* [E. Ind.] A tropical, fruit-bearing tree of the genus *Eugenia*; also, a medicine derived from its seeds or bark.

jam′bōne, *n.* In euchre, a variation in the play of lone hands by which they must be exposed, face up, on the table, and so played, the player to the left having the privilege of calling the first card to be played. Five tricks score eight points; a euchre of a jambone scores two points. [Slang.]

jam′bọọ, *n.* Same as *Jambu*.

jam′bọọl, *n.* Same as *Jambolana*.

jam-bō-ran′di, *n.* Same as *Jaborandi*.

jam-bō-ree′, *n.* 1. A wild spree or carousal. [Slang.]

2. In euchre, a variation by which the player holding the five highest trumps may show them and score sixteen points without playing out the hand. [Slang.]

jamb′=shȧft, *n.* A slender column near or a part of the jamb of a door or window.

jam′bū, *n.* [E. Ind.] An East Indian shrub, *Eugenia Jambos*; the rose-apple tree.

jam′bul, *n.* Same as *Jambolana*.

jam-dä′ni, *n.* [Hind. *jāmdānī*, a flowered muslin fabric; *jāma*, a garment, robe, and *dānī*.

bountiful, liberal.] An East Indian **cloth** flowered in the loom.
Jāme′sŏn-ite, *n.* [Named after Prof. *Jameson*, of Edinburgh.] A steel-gray ore of antimony and lead.
Jāmeṣ′town weed. Same as *Jimson-weed.*
jam′=nut, *n.* Same as *Check-nut.*
jam′pan, *n.* [E. Ind.] In the East Indies, a sedan-chair supported between two bamboo poles, and borne by four men.
jam′rō-ṣāde, *n.* [From the E. Ind. name, *jambos*, the rose-apple, influenced by L. *rosa*, rose.] The fruit of the jambu; the rose-apple.
jam′=weld, *n.* Same as *Butt-weld.*
jan, *n.* Same as *Jann.*
jan′ȧ-pȧ, jan′ȧ-pum, *n.* Bengal hemp. [See *Hemp.*]
jañ′çȧ=tree, *n.* [W. Ind. *janca*, and E. *tree.*] An evergreen tree of the genus *Amyris*, native to the West Indies.
jāne, *n.* [ME. *jane*, from LL. *Janua*; L. *Genua*, Genoa.]
1. A coin of Genoa.
2. A twilled cotton cloth. [See *Jean.*]
jāne′=ŏf=āpes′, *n.* [ME. *Jane*; OFr. *Jeanne*; LL. *Joanna*, f. of *Joannes*, John.] A pert girl; the female counterpart of *jackanapes.*
jan-gä′dȧ, *n.* [Sp. and Port.] A South American form of catamaran.
jañ′gle, *v.i.*; jangled, *pt., pp.*; jangling, *ppr.* [ME. *janglen, jangelen*; OFr. *jangler, gangler*, to jangle, prattle, wrangle.]
1. To quarrel; to altercate; to bicker; to wrangle.
2. To make a discordant sound; to jabber.
jañ′gle, *v.t.* To cause to sound discordantly.
jañ′gle, *n.* Babble; discordant sound; contention.
jañ′glẽr, *n.* A noisy fellow; a babbler.
jañ′glẽr-ess, *n.* A woman who jangles. [Obs.]
jañ′glẽr-y, *n.* Chatter; jangling. [Obs.]
jañ′gling, *n.* Babble; wrangling; discord.
jañ′gly, *a.* Discordant in sound.
jan′is-sā-ry, *n.* Same as *Janizary.*
jan′i-tŏr, *n.* [L., a doorkeeper, from *janua*, door.] A doorkeeper; a porter; the care-taker of a building.
jan′i-tress, *n.* A female janitor.
jan′i-trix, *n.* 1. A female janitor or doorkeeper.
2. In anatomy, the portal vein; the vena portæ. [Obs.]
jan′i-zär, *n.* A janizary. [Obs.]
jan-i-zā′ri-ăn, *a.* Pertaining to the janizaries or their government.
jan′i-zā-ry, *n.*; *pl.* **jan′i-zā-rieṣ.** [OFr. *jannissaire*, from Turk. *yeñicheri*, lit., new troops or soldiers.] Formerly, a soldier of the Turkish foot-guards, a body of infantry who finally became turbulent, and, rising in arms against the sultan, were attacked, defeated, and destroyed in Constantinople, in June, 1826.
jañ′kẽr, *n.* A pole mounted on two wheels, used in Scotland for transporting logs of wood.
jann, *n. sing.* and *pl.* [Per. *jān*, soul, spirit.] A demon of the lowest order in the Mohammedan mythology; the jinn collectively.
Jan′sen-iṣm, *n.* The doctrine of Jansen in regard to free will and grace.
Jan′sen-ist, *n.* A follower of Cornelius Jansen, a Roman Catholic bishop of Ypres, in Flanders, who denied free will, and held to irresistible grace and limited atonement.
jant, *v.i.* Same as *Jaunt.*
Jan′thi-nȧ, *n.* A genus of gasteropods; the *Ianthina.*
jan′ti-ly, *adv.* Same as *Jauntily.*
jan′ti-ness, *n.* Same as *Jauntiness.*
jan′ty, *a.* Same as *Jaunty.*
Jan′ū-ā-ry, *n.* [L. *Januarius* (supply *mensis*, month), the month of Janus, from *Janus*, Janus, to whom the month of January was sacred.] The first month of the year, containing thirty-one days; abbreviated *Jan.*
Jā′nus, *n.* [L.] A Latin deity, represented with two faces looking in opposite directions; his temple, at Rome, was never closed except in a time of universal peace.
Jā′nus=clọth, *n.* A double-faced cloth having faces which differ in color.
Jā′nus=fāced (-fāst), *a.* Having two faces; two-faced; deceitful.
Jā′nus=head″ed (-hed″), *a.* Double-headed.
Jap, *n.* A Japanese. [Colloq.]
jap′ȧ-lūre, *n.* A lizard of the genus *Japalura*, found in Asia.
jȧ-pan′, *n.* 1. Work varnished and figured in the manner practised by the natives of Japan.
2. A liquid resembling lacquer or varnish made by boiling shellac or a similar resin with linseed-oil and other ingredients and thinning the product with turpentine.
3. Any of various black varnishes.
4. A japanned black cane. [Obs.]
jȧ-pan′, *v.t.*; japanned, *pt., pp.*; japanning, *ppr.* To cover with or as with japan.
Jȧ-pan′, *a.* [Chinese *Jih-pun*, lit., sunrise; *jih*, sun, and *pun*, origin.] Of or pertaining to Japan; Japanese.
Japan allspice; a Japanese shrub, *Chimonanthus fragrans.*
Japan black; a jet-black varnish or lacquer, usually made of asphaltum, linseed-oil, and turpentine; called also *japan, japan lacquer*, and *Brunswick black.*
Japan clover; a plant of the bean family, *Lespedeza striata*, introduced into southern United States from Japan or China, and of much value for fodder.
Japan earth; catechu.
Jap-ȧ-nēse′, *n. sing.* and *pl.* A native of Japan; the language of the inhabitants of Japan.
Jap-ȧ-nēse′, *a.* Pertaining to Japan or its inhabitants.
jȧ-panned′, *a.* Varnished with or as with japan.
jȧ-pan′nẽr, *n.* 1. One who japans.
2. A shoeblack. [Rare.]
jȧ-pan′ning, *n.* The art of varnishing and drawing figures on wood or other material, in the manner practised by the Japanese.
Jȧ-pan′nish, *a.* Characteristic of the Japanese or their work. [Rare.]
jāpe, *v.i.* [ME. *japen*; OFr. *japer*, to jest.] To jest. [Obs.]
jāpe, *v.t.* To cheat. [Obs.]
jāpe, *n.* A jest; a trick; a gibe; a joke.
jāp′ẽr, *n.* A jester. [Obs.]
jāp′ẽr-y, *n.* Buffoonery. [Obs.]
Jā′pheth-īte, *n.* A Japhetite.
Jȧ-phet′iç, *a.* Pertaining to or descended from Japheth, the eldest son of Noah; as, the *Japhetic* nations.
Jā′phet-īte, *n.* One of Japheth's descendants.
jȧ-pon′i-çȧ, *n.* [From *Japan.*] Any of various Japanese plants having the specific name *Japonica*; especially, (a) *Camellia Japonica*; (b) *Pyrus Japonica.*
jȧ-quï′mȧ (-kē′), *n.* [Sp. *jáquima.*] The headstall of a bridle or halter.
jär, *n.* [ME. *char*; AS. *cyrr*, a turn.] The state of a door partly open; literally, a turn; now used only in the phrases *on a jar, on the jar*, that is, on the turn; ajar.
jär, *v.i.*; jarred (järd), *pt., pp.*; jarring, *ppr.* [Compare ME. *charken*, to creak; AS. *ceorian*, to murmur.]
1. To produce a short rattle or tremulous sound; to strike or sound discordantly; to be discordant; as, a *jarring* noise.
2. To clash; to act in opposition; to be inconsistent.
3. To have or receive a short quivering, shaking, or jolting motion, as from a fall or shock.
4. To vibrate regularly; to tick; to beat. [Obs.]
jär, *v.t.* 1. To shake; to cause to tremble; to cause a short, tremulous motion in a thing.
2. To make inharmonious. [Rare.]
3. To roughen.
4. To mark, as by beats or ticks. [Obs.]
jär, *n.* 1. A rattling vibration; a shake; a quiver; a sudden, tremulous or jolting motion; as, a trembling *jar.*
2. A harsh sound; discord.
3. Clash of interest or opinions; collision; discord; debate.
4. A beat; a tick, as of a pendulum. [Obs.]
5. [*pl.*] In well-drilling, a device which, on the up-stroke, lifts the drill with a sudden jerk in order to loosen it if caught.
jär, *n.* [OFr. *jare*; Sp. *jarra*, a jar, pitcher, from Per. *jarrah*, a jar, earthen water-vessel.]
1. A vessel with a large body and broad mouth, made of earthenware or glass.
2. The quantity held by a jar; as, a *jar* of oil.
Leyden jar; see *Leyden.*
jär-ȧ-rä′çȧ, *n.* [Braz.] A species of serpent of South America, of a dusky, brownish color, variegated with red and black spots; it is very poisonous.
jär′ble, *v.t.* To bemire. [Prov. Eng.]
järde, *n.* [Fr.] A callous tumor on the leg of a horse, below the bend of the ham on the outside.
jär-di-nière′ (zhär-dē-nyâr′), *n.* [Fr., a flower-stand, a female gardener.]
1. A holder for plants or flowers, as (a) a decorative vessel to hold a common flower-pot; (b) a jar or vase to hold flowers for table decoration; (c) a stand for flower-pots.
2. A lappet or pendant in a form of woman's headdress of the eighteenth century.
jär′dŏn, *n.* A jarde.
jär′fly̆, *n.* A cicada.
jär′gle, *v.i.* To emit a harsh or shrill sound. [Obs.]
jär′gŏn, *n.* [OFr. *jargon, gergon*, gibberish.]
1. Confused, unintelligible talk or language; gabble; gibberish.
2. The dialect resulting from the mixture of discordant languages; as, the Chinook *jargon.*
3. The cant, lingo, or slang of a trade, profession, art, etc.; as, the *jargon* of law.
jär′gŏn, *n.* [Fr. *jargon*; It. *giargone*, a sort of yellow diamond; perhaps from Per. *zargūn*, gold-colored; *zar*, gold, and *gūn*, color.] A mineral; a variety of zircon.
jär′gŏn, *v.i.*; jargoned, *pt., pp.*; jargoning, *ppr.* [Fr. *jargonner*, from *jargon*, gibberish.] To talk gibberish or jargon; to gabble.
jär-gō-nelle′, *n.* [Fr., dim. of *jargon*, the mineral.] A variety of pear.
jär-gon′iç, *a.* Pertaining to the mineral jargon.
jär′gŏn-ist, *n.* One who uses jargon.
jär′gọọn, *n.* See second *Jargon.*
järl (yärl), *n.* [Scand.] A nobleman; a chief or leader; hence, as a title, an earl.
jär′nut, *n.* [Dan. *jordnöd*, earthnut.] The pignut or earthnut.
jȧ-rọọl′, *n.* [E. Ind.] A valuable timber-tree found in tropical Asia.
jȧ-rō′sīte, *n.* [Named from Barranco *Jaroso*, in Spain.] A yellowish hydrous sulphate of potassium and iron.
jär′=owl, *n.* The goatsucker.
jär′räh, *n.* [Australian.] A tree, *Eucalyptus marginata*, of Australia, having a close-grained, heavy, red wood not attacked by the teredo, termites, or other common destructive organisms; also, the wood of the tree, resembling mahogany.
jär′ring-ly, *adv.* In a jarring or discordant manner.
jär′vel, *v.t.* Same as *Jarble.*
jär′vey, jär′vy, *n.* A hackney-coach, or one who drives a hackney-coach. [Eng. Slang.]
jā′ṣey, *n.* A wig, made of or like Jersey yarn.
jas′hawk, *n.* [A corruption of *eyas hawk.*] A young hawk.
jas′mine, jas′min, *n.* [Fr. *jasmin*; Sp. *jazmin*; Ar. *yāsmin*; Per. *yāsmin*, jasmine.]
1. Any species of the genus *Jasminum.* The common white jasmine, *Jasminum officinale*, is a climbing shrub, growing, on supports, 15 to 20 feet high; also called *jessamine.*

Common White Jasmine.

2. Any of various other plants similar to the true jasmine; as, the cape *jasmine*; the yellow or false *jasmine*, etc.
American jasmine; the *Ipomœa* or *Quamoclit coccinea*, the so-called red morning-glory of southern United States.
Cape jasmine; the *Gardenia florida*, a Chinese shrub, having white or cream-colored flowers.
False jasmine; the yellow jasmine.
French jasmine; the *Calotropis procera*, a shrub from which yercum or madar fiber is obtained.
Red jasmine; the *Plumeria rubra*, the source of the odor frangipani.
Yellow jasmine; the *Gelsemium sempervirens*, a shrub having showy, fragrant, yellow flowers.
jas′mine=tree, *n.* The red jasmine.
Jas-mi′num, *n.* A genus of the order *Oleaceæ*, whose species are cultivated for their flowers or fragrant oils.
jasp, *n.* Jasper. [Obs.]
jas′pȧ-chāte, *n.* Agate jasper. [Obs.]
jȧs-pé′ (zhȧs-pā′), *a.* [Fr.] In ceramics, streaked and mottled in imitation of jasper.
jas′pẽr, *n.* [ME. *jasper, jaspr*; OFr. *jaspre, jaspe*; L. *iaspis*; Gr. *iaspis*, a green-colored precious stone.] An opaque, impure variety of quartz, of red, yellow, and also of some dull colors, breaking with a smooth surface. When the colors are in stripes or bands, it is called *banded* or *striped jasper*; when it has layers of chalcedony, it is called *agate jasper.*
jas′pẽr-ā-ted, *a.* Mixed with jasper; containing particles of jasper; as, *jasperated* agate.
jas′pẽr-īte, *n.* Same as *Jasper.*
jas′pẽr-īze, *v.t.*; jasperized, *pt., pp.*; jasperizing, *ppr.* To cause to become or become like jasper; as, to *jasperize* wood.
jas′pẽr=ō″păl, *n.* A kind of opal containing yellow iron oxid, which gives the appearance of yellow jasper.
jas′pẽr=wāre, *n.* A white porcelain bisque or variety of terra-cotta invented and used by Josiah Wedgwood, particularly for cameo effects.
jas′pẽr-y, *a.* Having the qualities of jasper.
jas-pid′ē-ăn, jas-pid′ē-ous, *a.* Like jasper; consisting of or containing jasper.
jas′pi-līte, *n.* A silicious jaspoid rock.
jas′poid, *a.* [Gr. *iaspis*, jasper, and *eidos*, form.] Resembling jasper.
jasp-ō′nyx, *n.* [L. *iasponyx*; Gr. *iasponyx*, *iaspis*, jasper, and *onyx*, onyx.] A jasper having layers of contrasting color like an onyx.
jat-ȧ-man′si, *n.* The East Indian true spikenard, *Nardostachys Jatamansi.*
Jat″ē-ō-rhi′zȧ, *n.* [Gr. *iatēr* or *iatros*, a physician, and *rhiza*, a root.] A genus of climbing plants of Africa containing *Jateorhiza Calumba* which yields columbo.
Jat′rō-phȧ, *n.* [Gr. *iatros, iatēr*, a physician, and *trophē*, nourishment, food.] A genus of

woody plants of the order *Euphorbiaceæ*, found in the tropical parts of America.

jaun'ty, *a.*; *comp.* jauntier; *superl.* jauntiest. [From Fr. *gentil*, genteel.]

1. Gay and easy in manner; airy; sprightly; affecting elegance; showy; as, he walked along with quite a *jaunty* air.

2. Genteel. [Obs.]

Jä'vå, *n.* 1. A large variety of coffee-bean, originally from the island of Java; now, commercially, any similar berry, as a Sumatra variety, Maracaibo, etc.

2. A domestic fowl of a breed originated in the United States.

Java almond; the kanari.

Java cat; the musang or coffee-rat.

Java sparrow; the *Padda oryzivora*, a Javanese finch, common as a cage-bird.

Jav-å-nee'-seeds, *n.pl.* Same as *Ajowan*.

Jav-å-nēse', *a.* and *n.* I. *a.* Pertaining to the island of Java or its inhabitants.

II. *n. sing.* or *pl.* An inhabitant of Java or its inhabitants collectively; also, their language.

jav'el, *n.* A low fellow; a vagabond. [Obs.]

jav'el, *v.t.* To wet or bemire. [Obs.]

jave'lin, *n.* [OFr. *javelin*, m., *javeline*, f.; akin to Sp. *jabalina*; Arm. *gavlin*, *gavlod*, a javelin, from *gavl*, the fork of a tree.] A sort of light spear having the shaft of wood, pointed with steel.

jave'lin, *v.t.* To strike or wound with or as with a javelin. [Rare.]

jave-lin-ïēr', *n.* [OFr.] A soldier whose weapons are javelins.

jave'lin-snāke, *n.* Same as *Dartsnake*.

Jå-velle' wą'tēr. Same as *Eau de Javelle* under *Eau*.

jąw, *n.* [A modification of *chaw*, or *chew*, under the influence of Fr. *joue*, jaw.]

1. Either of the two parts or structures which together constitute the framework of the mouth; also, a bone or the bones collectively constituting the skeleton of such a part; a mandible; a maxilla.

2. Any mouth-part, as in an invertebrate, similar in function or position to the jaw of a vertebrate.

3. Anything resembling a jaw in form or use; especially, (a) one of two relatively movable members used to hold, cut, or crush an article placed between them; as, the *jaws* of a wrench; (b) the side of a frame of a machine holding a journal-box in place; a housing; (c) the hollowed inner end of a boom or gaff reaching part way around a mast.

4. Petulant loquacity; babble; scolding; wrangling; abusive clamor. [Slang.]

jąw, *v.t.* and *v.i.*; jawed, *pt.*, *pp.*; jawing, *ppr.* I. *v.t.* To abuse by scolding. [Colloq.]

II. *v.i.* To scold; to clamor. [Colloq.]

jąw'-bit, *n.* A bar which connects the two car-truck pedestals.

jąw'bōne, *n.* A bone of a jaw, particularly of a lower jaw.

jå-troph'ic, *a.* Of or resembling the seeds of species of the genus *Jatropha*.

jäunce, *v.t.* and *v.i.* [Obs.] Same as *Jounce*.

jäun'dice, *v.t.*; jaundiced, *pt.*, *pp.*; jaundicing, *ppr.* 1. To affect with jaundice.

2. To affect with prejudice or envy.

jäun'dice, *n.* [ME. *jaundys*, *jandis*; OFr. *jaunisse*, jaundice, yellows, from *jaune*, yellow.]

1. A disease, in its most common form characterized by suppression and alteration of the liver functions, yellowness of the eyes, skin, and urine, whiteness of the discharges from the intestines, uneasiness referred to the region of the stomach, loss of appetite, and general languor and lassitude.

2. A feeling or emotion disordering the judgment, as jealousy, envy, and the like.

Blue jaundice; a disordered circulation manifesting itself in a bluish discoloration of the skin; cyanosis.

jäun'dice-ber"ry, jäun'dice-tree, *n.* The barberry.

jäunt, *v.i.*; jaunted, *pt.*, *pp.*; jaunting, *ppr.* [Compare Scot. *jaunder*, to ramble.]

1. To ramble here and there; to make an excursion.

2. To ride about in a jaunting-car.

3. To jounce. [Obs.]

jäunt, *v.t.* To shake, to jolt. [Obs.]

jäunt, *n.* 1. An excursion; a ramble; a short journey.

2. A shaking up or jolting. [Obs.]

Syn.—Excursion, ramble, trip.

jäun'ti-ly, *adv.* Briskly; airily; gaily.

jäun'ti-ness, *n.* The quality of being jaunty; airiness; sprightliness.

jäun'ting-cär, *n.* A vehicle used in Ireland in which the passengers ride back to back on folding-down seats placed at right angles to the axle, the occupants having their feet near the ground.

jąw'-break"ēr, *n.* A word not easily pronounced. [Slang.]

jąwed, *a.* Having jaws; usually in compounds; as, square-*jawed*.

jąw'fąll, *n.* A lowering of the jaw; hence, depression; discouragement.

jąw'fąll"en, *a.* Crestfallen; discouraged. [Rare.]

jąw'foot, *n.* Same as *Maxilliped*.

jąw'ing, *n.* A scolding. [Colloq.]

jąw'less, *a* Having no jaws.

jąwn, *v.i.* To yawn. [Obs.]

jąw'-rōpe, *n.* The rope with which the jaws of a gaff are fastened to the mast.

jąw'-tooth, *n.* A tooth in the back part of the jaw; a molar.

jąw'y, *a.* Relating to the jaws.

jāy, *n.* [ME. *jay*; OFr. *jay*, *gay*, *gai*, a jay, from *gai*, gay; so called from its gay plumage.]

European Jay (*Garrulus glandarius*).

1. A bird of the family *Corvidæ*, having the tail wedge-shaped, rather long, and the feathers of the forehead erectile. The European jay, *Garrulus glandarius*, has, to some extent, the faculty of imitating the voices of other birds. The American jay, or blue jay, *Cyanocitta cristata*, is a beautiful bird, of very brilliant plumage, and ornamented with a crest of light blue or purple feathers.

2. A greenhorn; a stupid, awkward, or inexperienced person; a country lout. [Slang.]

3. An actor of small ability. [Slang.]

4. A loud or gaudy woman. [Obs.]

jāy'et, *n.* Jet. [Obs.]

jāy'hąwk"ēr, *n.* 1. A tarantula or spider, especially one of the genus *Mygale*.

2. A member of one of the bands of marauding guerrillas, who roved through Kansas and neighboring states during the Civil War.

3. A native of the state of Kansas. [Colloq.]

jāy'-thrush, *n.* An Asiatic thrushlike bird of the family *Crateropodidæ*.

jā'zel, *n.* A gem of an azure-blue color. [Obs.]

jaz'ēr-ănt, *n.* See *Jesserant*.

jazz band, *n.* A band eccentrically composed which usually plays rag-time music. From a self-styled Jazz Band composed of drums, trombone, cornet, clarinet, cymbals and piano.

jeal'ous (jel'), *a.* [ME. *jelous*, *gelous*; OFr. *jalous*, from LL. *zelosus*, full of zeal, from L. *zelus*; Gr. *zēlos*, zeal, emulation.]

1. Suspicious; apprehensive of rivalry; uneasy through fear that another has withdrawn or may withdraw from one the affections of a person he loves, or enjoys some good which he desires to obtain; followed by *of*, and applied both to the object of love and to the rival.

2. Careful in protecting; watchful; solicitous; as, *jealous* of one's reputation.

3. Zealous; commonly with *for*.

4. Doubtful. [Obs.]

Syn.—Envious, covetous, invidious, suspicious.

jeal'ous-hood, *n.* Jealousy. [Obs.]

jeal'ous-ly, *adv.* With jealousy.

jeal'ous-ness, *n.* The quality of being jealous.

jeal'ous-y, *n.*; *pl.* **jeal'ous-ieș.** [ME. *jelousie*, *gelousy*; OFr. *gelosie*, *jalousie*, from *jalous*, jealous.] The state or quality of being jealous.

Jēameș, *n.* [A colloq. form of *James*.] A liveried servant; a footman. [Slang.]

jēan, *n.* [Prob. from LL. *Janua*; L. *Genua*, Genoa.] A twilled cotton cloth; commonly used in the plural; as, a suit of *jeans*.

Satin jean; jean woven smooth and glossy.

jēarș, *n.pl.* On shipboard, same as *jeers*.

jēat, *n.* Jet. [Obs.]

jed'ding-ax, *n.* A cavel.

jee, *v.t.* and *v.i.* To gee.

jeel, *n.* Same as *Jhil*.

jeer, *n.* Tackle used to raise or lower yards; usually in the plural.

jeer, *n.* Railing language; a scoff; a taunt; a biting jest; a gibe; mockery; derision; ridicule with scorn.

jeer, *v.t.* and *v.i.*; jeered, *pt.*, *pp.*; jeering, *ppr.* [D. *scheeren*, *gekscheeren*, to jeer, mock, from the phrase *den gek scheeren*, to shear the fool.]

I. *v.t.* To treat with scoffs or derision; to deride; to mock.

II. *v.i.* To utter jeers; to scoff; to gibe.

jeer'ēr, *n.* A scoffer; a railer; a scorner; a mocker.

jeer'ing-ly, *adv.* With jeers or derision.

Jef-fēr-sō'ni-å, *n.* [Named after Thomas *Jefferson*.] A genus of herbaceous plants of the family *Berberidaceæ*.

Jef'fēr-sō'ni-ăn, *a.* Pertaining to Thomas Jefferson or his political doctrines.

jef'fēr-sŏn-īte, *n.* [Named after Thomas *Jefferson*.] A variety of augite containing zinc, of a dark olive-green color passing into brown.

jeg, *n.* A jig or templet.

Jē-hō'våh, *n.* [Heb. *Yehōwāh* or *Yahōwāh*, which is composed of YHWH, the four original consonants and the vowel-points of *Adōnāi*, Lord. What the original vowels were is unknown. The vowel-points of *Adōnāi* were substituted for the original vowels by the later Jews because they regarded the name as too sacred for utterance. The name is of unknown origin and meaning.] Lord; the specific name of God considered as the special deity of the Hebrews; usually rendered *the LORD*, in English translations of the Old Testament.

Jē-hō'vist, *n.* 1. One who maintains that the vowel-points annexed to the word *Jehovah*, in Hebrew, are the proper vowels of the word, and express the true pronunciation; opposed to the *Adonist*, who holds that the points annexed to the word *Jehovah* are the vowels of the word *Adonai*.

2. The writer, or writers, who wrote those portions of the Pentateuch in which the name *Jehovah* is used; in distinction from the writers of passages which contain *Elohim*.

Jē-hō-vis'tic, *a.* 1. Pertaining to Jehovah.

2. Using the word Jehovah for God; distinguished from *Elohistic*.

jē'hū, *n.* [In allusion to *Jehu*, son of Nimshi, in 2 Kings ix. 20.]

1. A driver; especially, a reckless driver. [Colloq.]

2. A coachman. [Colloq.]

jē-jū'năl, *a.* Relating to the jejunum.

jē-jūne', *a.* [L. *jejunus*, empty, dry, barren.]

1. Wanting; empty; vacant.

2. Dry; barren; wanting interesting matter; as, a *jejune* narrative.

jē-jūne'ly, *adv.* In a jejune, barren manner.

jē-jūne'ness, *n.* The quality of being jejune.

jē-jū'ni-ty, *n.* Jejuneness.

jē-jū'num, *n.* [L. *jejunus*, empty, dry, barren.] The portion of the intestines generally found empty in a post-mortem examination. It is the part between the duodenum and the ileum.

jel'ēr-ang, *n.* [Native name.] A large squirrel of Java and Asia; the Java squirrel.

jell, *v.i.* To become jelly. [Colloq.]

jel'li-cō, *n.* [Corruption of *Angelica*.]

1. A herb of the parsley family, *Angelica sylvestris*.

2. The water-parsnip of St. Helena, *Sium Helenium*, the uncooked stems of which are used as food.

jel'lied, *a.* Brought to the consistency of jelly; sweet or delicious as jelly.

jel'ly, *n.*; *pl.* **jel'lieș.** [Formerly *gelly*, from ME. *gely*, *gele*; OFr. *gelee*, a frost, jelly, properly f. pp. of *geler*, from L. *gelare*, to freeze.]

1. The inspissated juice of fruit, boiled with sugar.

2. Something of the consistency of jelly; a transparent substance, obtained from animal substances by decoction.

Jelly powder; an explosive compound of collodion and nitroglycerin which has the appearance of jelly.

jel'ly, *v.t.* and *v.i.*; jellied, *pt.*, *pp.*; jellying, *ppr.* I. *v.t.* To cause to become jelly or like jelly.

II. *v.i.* To assume the consistency of jelly.

jel'ly-bag, *n.* A bag for straining jelly.

jel'ly-fish, *n.* Any of various free-swimming hydrozoans having a gelatinous structure. [See *Acalephæ*.]

jel'ly-plant, *n.* A seaweed of Austrália used for making jelly.

jem'i-där, *n.* [Hind. and Per. *jamādār*, a chief or leader, officer of police, a native subaltern officer.] A native officer in the Anglo-Indian army having the rank of lieutenant.

Jem'läh goat. The thar.

jem'mi-ness, *n.* Spruceness. [Eng. Slang.]

jem'my, *a.* Spruce. [Eng. Slang.]

jem'my, *n.*; *pl.* **jem'mieș.** [A particular use of *Jemmy*, *Jimmy*, dim. from *James*; compare *jack*, a mechanical device.]

1. A short stout crowbar used by housebreakers for opening doors; a jimmy.

2. A baked sheep's head. [Eng. Slang.]

je-nē'quen (-ken), *n.* Same as *Heniquen*.

jē'nite, *n.* Same as *Yenite*.

Jen'kinș, *n.* One who runs after and toadies to prominent people, especially with the intention of publishing small talk about them. [Colloq.]

jen'net, *n.* [OFr. *genette*; Sp. *ginete*, a nag, originally a mounted soldier; Ar. *Zenāta*, a tribe of Barbary celebrated for its cavalry.] A small Spanish horse.

jen'net-ing, *n.* [Said to be corrupted from *juneating*, an apple ripe in June.] A species of early apple.

jen'ny, *n.*; *pl.* **jen'nieș.** 1. A female, as of a bird; used in composition, as in *jenny*-jay, *jenny*-wren, etc.

2. Specifically, (a) a wren; (b) a female ass.

3. A spinning-jenny.

jen'ny-wren (-ren), *n.* A plant, *Geranium Robertianum*, the herb-robert.

jent'ling, *n.* A fish, the blue chub of the Danube.

jeof'āil (jef'āl), *n.* [Fr. *j'ai failli*, I have failed.] An oversight in pleading or other proceeding at law; also, the acknowledgment of a mistake.

jeop′ärd (jep′), *v.t.* To hazard; to put in danger; to expose to loss or injury.

jeop′ärd-ẽr, *n.* One who puts to hazard.

jeop′ärd-ize, *v.t.*; jeopardized (-dizd), *pt., pp.*; jeopardizing, *ppr.* To expose to loss or injury; to jeopard.

jeop′ärd-ous, *a.* Exposed to danger; perilous; hazardous.

jeop′ärd-ous-ly, *adv.* With risk.

jeop′ärd-y, *n.* [ME. *jepardie, jeopardie*; OFr. *jeu parti*, lit., a divided game, a game in which the chances are even; LL. *jocus partitus*, an even chance, an alternative; L. *jocus*, a joke, play, game, and *partire*, to divide.] Exposure to death, loss, or injury; hazard; danger; peril.

jeop′ärd-y, *v.t.* Same as *Jeopardize*.

jē-quir′i-ty, *n.* [Prob. from native name.] The Indian licorice, *Abrus precatorius*, or its seed, known as the *jequirity bean*.

jẽr-bō′ȧ, *n.* [Ar. *yarbū*, an oblique, descending muscle; so called in allusion to the strong muscles of its hind legs.] Any rodent quadruped of the genus *Dipus*, particularly *Dipus ægypticus*, having long hind legs, short fore legs, and a long tail. Its method of locomotion is by long leaps.

Egyptian Jerboa (*Dipus ægypticus*).

Jerboa mouse; a kangaroo-rat.

Jerboa kangaroo; a small marsupial of Australia.

jer-eed′, *n.* [Turk. *jerīd*, from Ar. *jerīd, jarīd*, a rod, shaft, javelin of a horseman.] A wooden javelin, about five feet long, used in Persia and Turkey in mock fights.

jer-ē-mī′ad, jer-ē-mī′ade, *n.* [From *Jeremiah*, the prophet.] Lamentation; a tale of grief, sorrow, or complaint.

jẽr′fal″çŏn (-fa̤′kn *or* -fal′kŏn), *n.* Same as *Gerfalcon*.

jẽr′fär, *n.* [Prob. from Ar. *jarafah*, shad.] A fish of the genus *Gymnarchus*, found in the River Nile.

jẽr′guẽr (-gẽr), *n.* See first *Jerker*.

jer-īd′, *n.* Same as *Jereed*.

jẽrk, *v.t.* To cure by drying strips over a fire or in sunshine; as, to *jerk* venison.

jẽrk, *v.t.*; jerked, *pt., pp.*; jerking, *ppr.* [Etym. uncertain.]

1. To give a sudden start to, as by pulling or twitching; as, to *jerk* the rein of a bridle.

2. To cast or give motion to by a quick thrust of the arm from a position near the body; as, to *jerk* a stone across a pond.

3. To produce sudden and violent motion in; as, the sudden start of an engine *jerks* the cars.

4. To whip or strike. [Obs.]

jẽrk, *v.i.* 1. To make a sudden motion; to give a start; to move with a start or starts.

2. To mock; to insult; to sneer at.

jẽrk, *n.* 1. A short, sudden movement, as by pulling, twitching, or plucking; a spasmodic motion.

2. A sudden spring; a leap; a bound.

3. [*pl.*] Spasmodic motions of the face or body, often produced by intense religious excitement.

jẽrk, jẽrk′y, *n.* Meat that has been preserved by jerking; jerked meat.

jẽrk, jẽrque, *v.t.* [It. *cercare* (*pron.* cher-kä′re), to search.] In the customhouse, to search, as a vessel, for unentered goods. [Eng.]

jẽrk′ẽr, jẽr′quẽr, *n.* An officer of the customs who searches vessels for unentered goods. [Colloq., Eng.]

jẽrk′ẽr, *n.* 1. One who strikes with a smart, quick blow. [Obs.]

2. One who or that which jerks.

3. A North American fish, the hornyhead or river-chub.

jẽr′kin, *n.* [O.D. *jurk*, a frock, and dim. *kin*.]

1. A jacket; a short coat; a close waistcoat.

2. A kind of hawk, the male of the gerfalcon.

jẽrk′ing-ly, *adv.* In a jerking manner; with or by jerks.

jẽr′kin-head, *n.* In architecture, the end of a roof when it is formed into a shape intermediate between a gable and a hip, the gable rising about halfway to the ridge, so as to have a truncated shape, and the roof being hipped or inclined backward from this level.

Jerkinhead Roof.

jẽrk′y, *a.*; *comp.* jerkier; *superl.* jerkiest. Moving or advancing by jerks and starts.

jẽrk′y, *n.* Jerked meat.

jẽr-moọn′ăl, *n.* A species of snow-partridge found in the Himalayas.

Jē-ron′y-mīte, *n.* A member of one of the religious orders named after St. Jerome.

jer-ō-pig′i-ȧ, *n.* Same as *Geropigia*.

jẽr′quẽr (-kẽr), *n.* See first *Jerker*.

jer′ry=build″ẽr (-bild″), *n.* [Prob. from name *Jerry*.] One who builds cheap, unsubstantial buildings of inferior materials. [Colloq., Eng.]

jer′ry-built, *a.* Built hurriedly and of inferior materials. [Colloq., Eng.]

Jẽr′ṣey, *n.* [From *Jersey*, one of the Channel Islands.]

1. The finest of wool separated from the rest; combed wool; also, fine yarn of wool.

2. [j—] A tightly fitting elastic jacket for women.

3. A breed of cattle noted for the richness of their milk.

Jersey cudweed; Jersey livelong, a composite plant growing in the island of Jersey, of the genus *Gnaphalium*.

jer-ū-pig′i-ȧ, *n.* Same as *Geropigia*.

Jē-rṳ′sȧ-lem, *n.* [Gr. *Hierousalēm*; Heb. *Yerūshālaim*, Jerusalem.] The great city and capital of the Jewish nation; the holy city; the city of David.

Jerusalem artichoke; see under *Artichoke*.

Jerusalem cherry; a plant, or its fruit, a bright red globular berry resembling a cherry, belonging to the family *Solanaceæ*.

Jerusalem oak; the popular name of a very common aromatic weed of the goosefoot family.

Jerusalem pony; an ass.

The New Jerusalem; heaven as revealed in the Apocalypse; the city not made with hands, eternal in the heavens.

jẽr′vīne, jẽr′vin, *n.* [Sp. *jerva*, the poison of the *Veratrum*, and *-ine*.] An alkaloid obtained from the root of *Veratrum album*, or white hellebore.

jess, *n.* [ME. *ges*; OFr. *ges, giez, gets*; LL. *jactus*, a jess, so called from its use in letting a hawk fly, from L. *jactus*, a throw, cast.]

1. A short strap of leather or other material tied round the legs of a hawk, by which it is held on the fist.

2. A ribbon that hung down from a garland or crown in falconry.

jes′sȧ-mine, jes′sȧ-min, *n.* Same as *Jasmine*.

jes′sănt, *a.* [Corruption of *issuant*.] In heraldry, shooting forth, as vegetables spring or shoot out.

Jessant de lis; in heraldry, the head of a leopard having a fleur-de-lis passing through it.

Jessant de lis.

jes′sē, *n.* 1. A large brass candlestick branched into many sconces, hanging down in the middle of a church or choir, suggesting the genealogy of Jesse, whence the name.

2. Any branching device showing the genealogy of Christ, as in painting, sculpture, or stained glass.

Jesse window; in architecture, a window containing as its subject a genealogical tree of Jesse, either painted on the glass or carved on the mullions.

jessed (jest), *a.* In heraldry, having jesses on, as a hawk.

jes′sẽr-ănt, jes′sẽr-äunt, *n.* [ME. *jesseraunt, jasserant*; OFr. *gesseron, jazeran*, a chain-mail shirt, necklace, bracelet.] A frock of twisted or linked mail without sleeves, somewhat lighter than the hauberk. [Obs.]

jest, *n.* [ME. *geste, jeste*; OFr. *geste*, an exploit, tale of exploits.]

1. A joke; something ludicrous uttered and meant only to excite laughter.

2. The object of laughter or sport; a laughingstock; as, titles are *jests*.

3. A mask. [Obs.]

4. A deed; an action. [Obs.]

jest, *v.i.*; jested, *pt., pp.*; jesting, *ppr.* 1. To divert or make merry by words or actions; to joke.

2. To speak in sport; to say what is not true merely for diversion.

3. To play a part in a mask. [Obs.]

jest′=book, *n.* A book made up of jokes and humorous anecdotes.

jest′ẽr, *n.* 1. A person given to jesting, sportive talk, and merry pranks; a joker.

2. A buffoon; a merry-andrew; a person formerly retained by princes to make sport for them.

jest′fụl, *a.* Given to jesting; full of jokes.

jest′ing, *a.* Joking; talking for diversion or merriment.

jest′ing, *n.* A joking; concise wit; the act of jesting or of making a jest.

jest′ing-ly, *adv.* In a jocose manner; not in earnest.

jest′ing=stock, *n.* A laughingstock; a butt for ridicule. [Rare.]

Jeṣ′ū-āte, *n.* [It. *Gesuato*, from *Gesù*, Jesus.] A member of a religious order founded by Colombini in 1367 and abolished by Pope Clement IX. in 1668.

Jeṣ′ū-at-ess, *n.* A member of a religious order of women, now extinct, founded in 1387 by Blessed Catharine Colombini of Siena.

Jester.

Jeṣ′ū-it, *n.* [Fr. *Jesuite*, from L. *Jesus* or *Jesus*, Jesus, and *-ite*.]

1. One of the Company or Society of Jesus, a religious order founded by Ignatius Loyola in 1534, and approved by Pope Paul III in 1540. The popular conception that the order is organized on a military plan is partly correct; the General at the head is chosen for life and is vested with full administrative authority, subject, however, to the Roman Pontiff and the Constitutions of the Society, which he can suspend temporarily, but not change. The supreme power, however, is in the General Congregation, a body elected by these members of the Society who are professed of four vows. There are two general classes of members, laymen and priests, with six grades of training and advancement; the novice, the approved scholastic, the formed temporal coadjutor, the formed spiritual coadjutor, the professed of three vows, and the professed of four vows. After the first period of probation lasting two years, the vows of poverty, chastity and obedience are assumed; the fourth vow of the professed is that of special obedience to the Roman Pontiff in regard to missions. The power of the Society lies in its submission to legitimate authority; but by its enemies it has been unjustly alleged to be unscrupulous in intrigue and deceptive in purpose, tending to the subversion of legitimate government. On account of this calumny the word jesuitical has become synonymous with intriguing and deceptive.

2. A crafty person; an intriguer.

Jesuits' bark; Peruvian bark; the bark of certain species of *Cinchona*.

Jesuits' drops; friars' balsam.

Jesuits' nut; the water-chestnut.

Jesuits' powder; powdered Peruvian bark.

Jesuits' tea; a Chilean shrub of the genus *Ilex* or its leaves, used as a tea.

Jeṣ′ū-it-ess, *n.* A party name applied to a member of a religious congregation for women, founded in 1609 by Mary Ward, suppressed in 1630, and reëstablished in 1703 as "The Institute of Mary."

Jeṣ-ū-it′iç-ăl, Jeṣ-ū-it′iç, *a.* 1. Pertaining to the Jesuits or their principles and arts.

2. [j—] Designing; cunning; deceitful.

jeṣ-ū-it′iç-ăl-ly, *adv.* Craftily.

Jeṣ′ū-it-iṣm, *n.* 1. The arts, principles, and practices of the Jesuits.

2. [j—] Cunning; deceit; hypocrisy; prevarication; deceptive practices to effect a purpose.

Jeṣ″ū-it-oç′rȧ-cy, *n.* Jesuitical government; also, the entire body of Jesuits, as in a country. [Rare.]

Jeṣ′ū-it-ry, *n.* Jesuitism.

Jē′ṣus, *n.* [L. *Iesūs*; Gr. *Iēsous*; from Heb. *Yeshū'a*, contr. of *Yehōshū'a*, a name signifying help of Jehovah; *Yāh*, Jehovah, and *hōshīa*, to help.]

1. A name, the Greek form of *Joshua*.

2. The Saviour; being the personal name usually used in conjunction with the official title Christ.

3. An emblem of Christ; restrictedly, a painting or other representation of the crucifixion. [Obs.]

The Society of Jesus; see *Jesuit*.

jet, *n.* Device; fashion. [Obs.]

jet, *n.* [ME. *jet, geete*; OFr. *jet*; L. *gagates*; Gr. *gagatēs*, jet, from *Gagas*, a town and river of Lycia in Asia Minor.]

1. In mineralogy, a variety of lignite, of a very compact texture and velvet-black color, susceptible of a good polish and glossy in its fracture, which is conchoidal or undulating, used in the manufacture of toys, buttons, mourning jewels, etc.

2. A color suggested by jet; a deep black.

jet, *a.* Made of jet; having the color of jet; as, *jet* beads; *jet*-black.

jet, *n.* [ME. *jet, jette, get*; OFr. *get, giet, ject*, a throw, cast, gush, spurt, from L. *jactus*, a throw, cast, properly pp. of *jacere*, to throw.]

1. A spouting or shooting forth in a narrow stream; that which so spouts or shoots forth, as, a *jet* of gas, oil, or water; also, the device for making a jet, as in a gas-fixture or a fountain; as, a gas-*jet*.

2. In metal-casting, a hole or channel for admitting metal into a mold; also, a kind of bur

left on a casting at the point where the metal is poured into the mold.

3. An overhanging part; as, a *jet* in a wall or in a cliff.

jet, *v.t.*; jetted, *pt.*, *pp.*; jetting, *ppr.* To spurt or throw out in a stream; as, the water was *jetted* to form spray.

jet, *v.i.* 1. To shoot forward; to shoot out; to project; to jut; to intrude.

2. To strut; to throw or toss the body in haughtiness. [Obs.]

3. To jerk; to jolt; to be shaken. [Obs.]

jet′=black, *a.* Of the deepest black, resembling jet in color.

jet d'eau′ (zhȧ dō′). [Fr., a jet of water.] A spout for delivering water, as in a fountain; an upward jet of water.

jet′e-rus, *n.* In botany, a yellow tint of plants naturally green.

jet′ŏn, *n.* See *Jetton.*

jet′săm, jet′sŏm, *n.* [OFr. *getaison, gettaison,* a throwing, jetsam, from L. *jactatio* (*-onis*), a throwing, from *jactare,* to throw, hurl.]

1. In maritime law, the throwing of goods overboard in order to lighten a ship in a storm; jettison.

2. The goods thus thrown away. [See *Flotsam.*]

> *Jetsam* is where goods are cast into the sea, and there sink and remain under water; *flotsam* is where they continue swimming; *ligan* is where they are sunk in the sea, but tied to a cork or buoy. —Blackstone.

jet′teau (-tō), *n.* [Obs.] See *Jet d'eau.*

jet′tee, *n.* A projection in a building. [Obs. See *Jetty.*]

jet′tẽr, *n.* [ME. *jettour, jectour*; OFr. *jettour, jetteur,* from L. *jactator,* a boaster.] A spruce fellow; one who struts. [Obs.]

jet′ti-sŏn, *n.* In law, the act of throwing goods overboard for the purpose of easing a ship.

jet′ti-sŏn, *v.t.*; jettisoned, *pt.*, *pp.*; jettisoning, *ppr.* To throw overboard, as merchandise, for the purpose of easing a ship.

jet′tŏn, *n.* [Fr. *jeton,* a throw, counter, from *jeter,* to throw, cast.] A small metal counter used in some games of cards.

jet′ty, *n.*; *pl.* **jet′tieṣ.** [OFr. *jetee, jettee, getee,* a cast, jetty, jutty, from *jetter, jeter,* to throw.]

1. A small pier.

2. A projection into a river for narrowing it and raising the water, or for causing it to carry out gathering sediment and thus to deepen its channel.

3. A projecting portion of a building; especially a portion that projects so as to overhang the wall below, as in the upper stories of frame houses, or in bay-windows.

jet′ty, *a.* Made of jet, or black as jet.

jet′ty, *v.t.* and *v.i.*; jettied, *pt.*, *pp.*; jettying, *ppr.* I. *v.t.* To furnish with a jetty; as, to *jetty* the mouth of a river.

II. *v.i.* To jut; to extend out or over.

jet′ty-head (-hed), *n.* The projecting part of a jetty or of a wharf; the front of a wharf whose side forms one of the cheeks of a dock.

jeu d'es-prit′ (zhū de-sprē′). [Fr., lit., a play of spirit.] A witticism; a play of wit.

jeu-nesse′ do-rée′ (zhū-nes′ dō-rā′). [Fr.] The rich spendthrift youth of a community; specifically, in France, the fashionable set of the reactionary party in 1794.

Jew (jū), *n.* [ME. *Jew, Giw*; OFr. *Jeu, Geu*; L. *Judæus*; Gr. *Ioudaios,* a Jew, an inhabitant of Judea, from *Ioudaia,* Judea, from Heb. *Yehūdāh,* Judah.] A Hebrew or Israelite; any descendant of Jacob.

Jew's frankincense; a resin obtained from the plant *Styrax officinale.*

Jew's pitch; bitumen.

The Wandering Jew; a legendary personage who, for some slight or indignity to the Saviour while on his way to the cross, was condemned to wander over the earth until Christ shall come again.

jew, *v.t.* and *v.i.*; jewed, *pt.*, *pp.*; jewing, *ppr.* I. *v.t.* To cheat in trade; as, to *jew* one out of a horse. [Colloq.]

II. *v.i.* To practise cheating in trade; as, he is said to *jew.* [Colloq.]

To jew down; to lower the price of; to persuade or to induce (a seller) to take less, as for a coat or a hat.

jew′bait″ẽr, *n.* A person who wantonly abuses or persecutes Jews.

jew′bush, *n.* A West Indian plant, *Pedilanthus tithymaloides,* notable for its drastic and emetic qualities.

Jew′=crōw, *n.* The hooded crow; the chough.

jew′el, *n.* [ME. *jewel, juel, jowel*; OFr. *jouel, joel,* a jewel, dim. of *joie, goie,* joy, pleasure, from L. *gaudium,* joy.]

1. An ornament of dress in which precious stones form a principal part.

2. A precious stone.

3. A name expressive of fondness; as, a mother calls her child her *jewel.*

4. A piece of glass, stone, or crystal shaped and fitted to a watch as a bearing for a pivot.

jew′el, *v.t.*; jeweled *or* jewelled, *pt.*, *pp.*; jeweling *or* jewelling, *ppr.* To fit or adorn with jewels; as, a watch *jeweled* in nine holes.

jew′el=block, *n.* In a ship, one of two small blocks suspended from the extremities of a yardarm to lead the studdingsail halyards through.

jew′el-ẽr, *n.* [ME. *jueler*; OFr. *joieleor,* from *joel, jouel,* a jewel.] One who makes or deals in jewels and other ornaments; written also *jeweller.*

jew′el=house, *n.* The place where the royal ornaments are deposited. [Eng.]

jew′el=līke, *a.* Brilliant as a jewel.

jew′el-ry, jew′el-lẽr-y, *n.* 1. Jewels in general.

2. The jeweler's art. [Rare.]

jew′el-weed, *n.* An American plant, *Impatiens fulva* or *Impatiens pallida.*

Jew′ess, *n.* A Hebrew woman.

jew′fish, *n.* One of several fishes, including *Promicrops guasa* and *Megalops atlanticus,* the tarpon, of the Atlantic coast, and the black sea-bass of the Californian coast.

jew′ing, *n.* [*Jew* and *-ing,* in allusion to the curved characteristic of the Jewish nose.] A curvature in the beak or in the wattles of a bird.

jew′iṣe, *n.* See *Juise.*

Jew′ish, *a.* Of or relating to the Jews or Hebrews, their customs, or their history; Israelitish.

Jew′ish-ly, *adv.* In the manner of the Jews.

Jew′ish-ness, *n.* The state of being Jewish.

Jew′ry, *n.* [OFr. *juerie,* from *Jeu,* a Jew.]

1. Judea; also, a district inhabited by Jews, whence the name of a street in London.

2. The Jewish people collectively.

Jew′ṣ=ap″ple, *n.* See *Eggplant.*

Jew′ṣ=ēar, *n.* The popular name of a fungus, *Hirneola Auricula-Judæ,* bearing some resemblance to the human ear.

jewṣ″=härp, *n.* [So called from the use of the harp by the Jews.]

1. An instrument of music usually made of iron and played by placing against the slightly separated front teeth its two parallel jaws, between which a steel tongue is made to vibrate by striking its free bent end with the finger, the sound made being modulated by varying the shape and size of the cavity of the mouth.

2. Among seamen, a form of fastening by which a cable is attached to the anchor-ring.

Jews′=mal″lōw, *n.* A plant, a species of *Corchorus.*

Jewṣ″=stōne, Jew′stōne, *n.* The club-shaped spine of a fossil echinus.

Jews′=thorn, *n.* Same as *Christ's-thorn.*

Jez′e-bel, *n.* [From *Jezebel,* the wife of Ahab (1 Kings xvi. 31).] An impudent, daring, vicious woman.

jhā′răl, *n.* [Native name.] The thar, a wild mountain goat of India, *Capra jemlaica.*

jhīl, jheel, *n.* [Hind.] In India, a pool or lagoon left after an inundation and covered or surrounded with a rank growth of plants.

jib, *n.* [So called because easily shifted from side to side or *jibbed.*]

1. The foremost sail of a ship, being a large, triangular staysail extended from the outer end of the jib-boom toward the foretopmast-head.

2. The projecting beam or arm of a crane, from which the pulleys and weights are suspended.

Inner jib; the after of two jibs which take the place of one large jib on a boom; distinguished from the *outer jib,* which is the forward jib of the two.

The cut of one's jib; one's personal appearance.

jib, *v.i.*; jibbed, *pt.*, *pp.*; jibbing, *ppr.* [ME. *regibben,* to kick back; OFr. *regiber,* to wince, kick; prob. of Scand. origin.] To pull against the bit, as a horse; to move restively sideways or backward; written also *jibb.*

jib′bẽr, *n.* One who jibs; a horse that jibs.

jib′=bōom, *n.* A spar run out from the extremity of the bowsprit of a ship, and serving as a continuation of it; beyond it is sometimes extended the flying-jib boom.

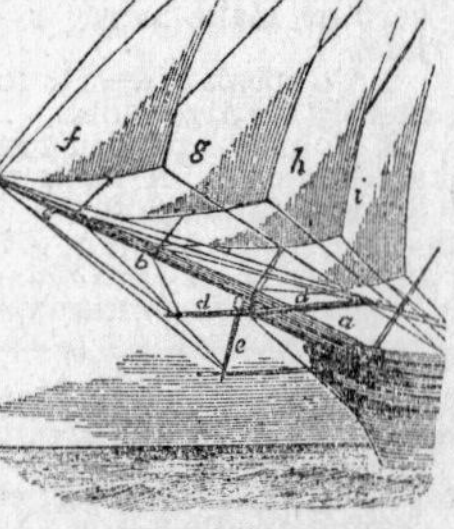

Stem of Ship.

a, Bowsprit. *b,* Jib-boom. *c,* Flying-jib boom. *d,* Spritsail yard. *e,* Martingale. *f,* Flying jib. *g,* Jib. *h,* Foretopmast staysail. *i,* Fore staysail.

jib′dōor (-dōr), *n.* A door which stands flush with the wall, without dressing or moldings.

jibe, *v.t.* and *v.i.*; jibed, *pt.*, *pp.*; jibing, *ppr.* [Dan. *gibbe,* to jib, jibe, compare Sw. dial. *jippa,* to jerk.]

I. *v.t.* In navigation, to shift from one side of a vessel to the other; as, to *jibe* the boom; formerly *jib.*

II. *v.i.* 1. In navigation, to tack without going about; to shift a sail from one side to the other.

2. To agree one with another; to work together in harmony. [Colloq.]

jib′=head (-hed), *n.* In navigation, a piece of iron fastened to the end of a shortened jib.

jib′=head″ẽr, *n.* A topsail that has the shape of a jib.

jib′=top″sāil (*or* -sl), *n.* A small jib set between the mast and the boom, flying from the extremity of the flying-jib boom.

jif′fy, *n.*; *pl.* **jif′fieṣ.** A very short time; an instant; as, I will be there in a *jiffy.*

jig, *n.* [OFr. *gigue, gige,* a fiddle, a kind of dance; M.H.G. *gige,* a fiddle.]

1. A kind of light dance; also, the music suitable to such a dance, which is usually performed by a single dancer.

2. In angling, a device consisting of a hook or system of hooks attached to a bright piece of metal, the movement of which attracts fishes, which may be caught by a sudden jerk on the line attached.

3. In mechanics, (a) a kind of pattern or guide made of steel to secure uniformity in cutting, drilling, etc.; as, a drilling-*jig*; a punching-*jig*; (b) a contrivance for operating a saw used in light work; (c) a device for drilling wells by means of an elastic pole for lifting the drill; (d) in mining, a device for separating ore.

4. A sportive trick or practical joke. [Obs.]

5. A kind of social entertainment consisting of recitation, rime, and song. [Obs.]

jig, *v.t.*; jigged, *pt.*, *pp.*; jigging, *ppr.* 1. To play or sing in jig-time.

2. To deceive; to delude; to cheat; to defraud.

3. In metal-working, to make by the use of a jigging-machine.

4. In mining, to separate (metalliferous ore) from the refuse by means of a sieve constructed and placed for this purpose.

5. To catch with a jig; as, to *jig* a fish.

6. To produce vertical reciprocating motion in.

7. To drill with a spring-pole jig; as, to *jig* a well. [See *Jig,* n. 3, c.]

jig, *v.i.* [OFr. *giguer,* from *gigue,* a fiddle, a kind of dance.]

1. To dance a jig.

2. To skip as if dancing a jig.

3. To use a jig in catching fish.

jig′=drill″ing, *n.* Drilling by the use of a jig, so as to secure accuracy of dimension or of position.

jig′=fīl″ing, *n.* Filing by the use of a jig, so as to secure exactness of dimension.

jig′gẽr, *n.* 1. Any one of many mechanical devices or structures, as (a) in navigation, a machine consisting of a rope about five feet long with a block at one end and a sheave at the other, used to hold on the cable when it is heaved into the ship by the revolution of the windlass, and for other purposes; (b) a potter's wheel, by which earthenware vessels are shaped by a rapid motion; (c) a small square sail on a mast and boom at the stern of a boat; (d) a separator of ore; (e) a leather-graining device; (f) a warehouse crane; (g) a hook for coupling cars in a coal-mine; (h) a bridge used in playing billiards; (i) a drawing-knife used by a cooper; (j) the index of an electrical indicator used on 'Change, or the indicator itself.

2. A small fishing-boat formerly used about Cape Cod, sloop-rigged and holding about four persons.

3. A one-horse street-railway car with a box for receiving fares.

4. A small metal cup or measure, used in mixing drinks.

5. A drink of whisky. [Slang.]

6. One who or that which jigs.

jig′gẽr, *n.* 1. The common name of the chigoe or chigre, *Pulex penetrans.*

2. A harvest-tick.

jig′gẽr=māst, *n.* The aftmost mast of a four-masted ship; also, the small stern-mast of a yawl.

jig′ging, *n.* In mining, the process of separating ore with a jigger.

jig′ging=mȧ-chine″, *n.* 1. A machine for separating ore by jigging.

2. A machine having a tool for cutting or for boring, the action of which is controlled by a jig.

jig′gish, *a.* 1. Of, pertaining to, resembling, or suitable to a jig.

2. Frolicsome; playful.

jig′jog, *a.* Having or pertaining to a jolting motion.

jig′jog, *n.* A jolting motion; a jog; a push.

jig′=māk″ẽr, *n.* One who makes or plays jigs.

jig′=pin, *n.* A pin used by miners to hold the turn-beams and prevent them from turning.

jig'=saw, *n.* A small reciprocating saw used in scrollwork or openwork; a scroll-saw.

ji-häd', *n.* [Ar.] Among Mohammedans, a holy war waged against infidels or disbelievers in the prophet.

jill, *n.* [ME. *Jille, Gille*, abbrev. of *Jillian, Gillian*, forms of *Julian, Julyan*, a feminine name commonly applied to a girl or young woman, as *Jack* was to a boy or young man.]
1. A young woman; a sweetheart.
2. A female ferret.

jill'=flirt, *n.* A light, wanton woman.

jilt, *n.* One who discards a lover capriciously or wantonly.

jilt, *v.t.*; jilted, *pt., pp.*; jilting, *ppr.* To encourage and then frustrate one's hopes; to trick in love; as, to *jilt* a lover.

jilt, *v.i.* To play the jilt; to practise deception in love; to discard lovers.

jim'crack, *n.* See *Gimcrack*.

jim'=crōw, *n.* 1. In machinery, a strong iron frame with a screw for holding and straightening or bending iron rails or bars.
2. In mining, a crowbar with a claw at one end.

Jim Crōw. [The title of one of the early negro minstrel songs, taken as typical of the negro race.]
1. One of the negro race.
2. A planing-machine having a reversible cutting-tool.

jim'my, *n.*; *pl.* **jim'mies.** A burglar's tool used to break open doors and windows; a small crowbar.

jimp, *a.* Neat; handsome; slender in form. [North Eng. and Scot.]

jim'sŏn=weed, *n.* [A corruption of Jamestown weed; so called because it is said to have grown upon heaps of ballast and other rubbish discharged from vessels at Jamestown, Virginia.] A poisonous weed, *Datura Stramonium*, the thorn-apple; called also *jimpson, jimpson-weed*, and *Jamestown weed.*

jin, *n.* See *Jinn.*

jin'gal, *n.* [Hind. *jangāl*, a large musket, a swivel.] A large musket mounted as a swivel-gun, used in warfare by the Chinese and other Asiatics.

jin'gle, *v.i.*; jingled, *pt., pp.*; jingling, *ppr.* [ME. *gingelen, ginglen*, to jingle, akin to *chink.*] To sound with a fine, sharp rattle; to clink; as, *jingling* chains or bells.

jin'gle, *v.t.* To cause to give a sharp sound, as a little bell, or as pieces of metal.

The bells she *jingled*, and the whistle blew. —Pope.

jin'gle, *n.* 1. A rattling or clinking sound, as of little bells or pieces of metal.
2. Correspondence of sound in rimes.
3. Anything that makes a jingling sound, as a little bell or rattle.
4. A one-horse public conveyance used in the south of Ireland.
Syn.—Rime, chime, tinkle, clink.

jin'glẽr, *n.* One who or that which jingles.

jin'gle=shell, *n.* A bivalve shell; the gold-shell.

jin'gling, *n.* A sharp, fine, rattling sound, as of little bells.

jin'gō, *n.* [Used in the oath "by jingo," which is probably from the Basque *Jinkoa, Jeinkoa*, abbrev. of *Jaungoicoa, Jangoikoa*, God, lit., the lord of the high. The word was introduced by Gipsies or soldiers.]
1. An expletive used as a mild oath, with *by.*
2. A person clamorous for war, or a warlike or aggressive policy; originally one of those who maintained that Great Britain should actively support the Turks in the Turco-Russian war of 1877-78; from the words of a song then popular:

We don't want to fight, but, by *jingo*, if we do,
We've got the ships, we've got the men, we've got the money, too.

jin'gō, *a.* Belonging or relating to jingoes; as, a *jingo* policy; *jingo* bluster.

jin'gō-ism, *n.* The principles and policy of jingoes.

jink, *v.t.*; jinked, *pt., pp.*; jinking, *ppr.* To elude by moving nimbly; to dodge; to cheat. [Scot.]

jink, *v.i.* 1. To move nimbly; to dodge.
2. To take all the tricks in some card-games, as in forty-five and spoilfive.

jink, *n.* 1. A quick illusory turn; the act of eluding another.
2. The act of winning a game of spoilfive or forty-five by taking all five tricks.

jinn, *n.*, pl. of *jinnee.*

jin'nee, *n.*; *pl.* **jinn.** [Ar. *jinn*, pl. *jinniy*, a kind of demon.] In Mohammedan mythology, one of a race of genii, spirits, or demons, fabled to have been created some thousands of years before Adam, having supernatural powers, able to assume various forms, and to befriend or work mischief on mankind.

jin'ny=rōad, *n.* In mining, an inclined railroad which loaded cars descend by their own weight and by such descent cause empty cars to ascend.

jin-rik'i-sha, *n.* [Japan., from *jin*, a man, *riki*, power, and *sha*, carriage.] A Japanese two-wheeled vehicle with springs and a hood, drawn

Jinriksha.

by a native, sometimes by two; used by travelers; spelled also *jinricksha* and *jinriksha.*

jinx, *n.* Any person or thing that is supposed to bring bad luck. [Slang.]

jip'pō, *n.* [Fr. *jupon*, a kind of skirt.] A waistcoat or kind of stays for women's wear. [Obs.]

jit'ney, *n.* 1. Five cents; a nickel. [Slang.]
2. A motor vehicle other than a street-car, carrying passengers for a small fare, usually five cents, between fixed points, though not running on a regular time schedule. [Colloq.]

Jiu Jit'sū. See under *Training.*

jō, *n.* A sweetheart or lover of either sex.

job, *n.* [ME. *jobbe*, a portion, lump.]
1. A piece of work; anything to be done, whether of more or less importance; as, the mechanic has many small *jobs* on hand.
2. An undertaking with a view to profit; a public transaction done for private profit.
3. Employment; position; situation; as, he has a good *job.*
4. A sudden stab with a pointed instrument; a jab.
5. An incident or occurrence. [Colloq.]
6. A scheme; as, to put up a *job.* [Colloq.]
By the job; at a stated price for a certain piece of work.

job, *a.* Of a miscellaneous character.
Job lot; a miscellaneous assortment of articles bought or sold together.

job, *v.t.*; jobbed, *pt., pp.*; jobbing, *ppr.* [A variant of *jab*, from ME. *jobben*, to peck with the bill; prob. from Ir. and Gael. *gob*, the beak or bill of a bird.]
1. To strike or stab with a sharp instrument.
2. To drive in, as a sharp-pointed instrument.
3. To scheme or plot against; to injure in an underhanded way; as, to *job* a public official. [Slang.]

job, *v.t.* 1. To let out in separate portions, as work, among different contractors or workmen.
2. To let out or hire; as, to *job* horses.
3. To buy in large quantities and sell in smaller lots; as, to *job* cotton; to *job* cigars.

job, *v.i.* 1. To deal in the public stocks; to buy and sell, as a broker.
2. To work at chance work; to undertake employment of a menial kind.
3. To do work so as to make it subserve one's private ends; to pervert public service to private advantage.

Judges *job*, and bishops bite the town.—Pope.

Jōb, *n.* The title of one of the books of the Bible; also, the hero of that book, regarded as the type of patience.
Job's comforter; a person who, while pretending to sympathize with one, really adds to one's afflictions by administering rebukes.
Job's news; bad news.

jō-bā'tion, *n.* A scolding; a long, tedious reproof. [Colloq.]

job'bẽr, *n.* 1. One who does small jobs; one who works at chance work.
2. A dealer in the public stocks or funds; a stockjobber. [Eng.]
3. One who purchases goods from importers or wholesale dealers and sells to retailers.
4. One who renders the discharge of public duty subservient to private ends; an intriguer who turns public work to his own or his friends' advantage; hence, one who performs low or dirty work in office, politics, or intrigue.

job'bẽr-noll, *n.* A loggerhead; a blockhead. [Obs.]

job'bẽr-y, *n.* The act or practice of jobbing; unfair and underhand means used to procure some private end; the act of turning public matters to private advantage.

job'bing, *a.* Pertaining to jobbery.
Jobbing house; a mercantile establishment that buys in quantity from the importer or manufacturer and sells in smaller lots to the retailer.

Jōb's'=tēars, *n.* A variety of grass, *Coix Lacryma*, or its hard, bony seeds, which are used for beads.

jō'cănt-ry, *n.* The art or practice of jesting. [Obs.]

jock, *v.t.* and *v.i.* To jolt. [Prov. Eng.]

jock'ey, *n.* [From *Jocky, Jockie*, the northern Eng. and Scot. pronunciation of *Jacky*, dim. of *Jack*, a name applied to boy-servants, grooms, etc.]
1. One who rides a horse in a race.
2. A dealer in horses; one who makes it his business to buy and sell horses for gain.
3. A cheat; one who deceives or takes undue advantage in trade.
4. See *Jockey-pulley.*

jock'ey, *v.t.*; jockeyed, *pt., pp.*; jockeying, *ppr.*
1. To play the jockey to; to cheat; to trick; to deceive in trade.
2. To jostle by riding against.

jock'ey, *v.i.* To cheat; to act the jockey.

jock'ey=box, *n.* A box beneath the driver's seat in a wagon, for carrying small articles.

jock'ey=club, *n.* A club or association of persons interested in horse-racing, etc.

jock'ey=gēar, *n.* The gear connected with an apparatus for paying out submarine cables.

jock'ey=grȧss, *n.* Quaking-grass, *Briza media.* [Prov. Eng.]

jock'ey-ing, *n.* The act of one who jockeys; hence, trickery.

jock'ey-ism, *n.* The practice of jockeys.

jock'ey=pad, *n.* A pad on a saddle for the knee.

jock'ey=pul"ley, *n.* A small wheel which revolves on the rim of a larger grooved wheel, used to prevent a rope or hawser from slipping out of the groove.

jock'ey-ship, *n.* The art or practice of riding horses in races; horsemanship.

jock'ey=wheel (-hwēl), *n.* See *Jockey-pulley.*

jō-cōse', *a.* [L. *jocosus*, from *jocus*, a joke, jest.]
1. Given to jokes and jesting; merry; waggish; said of persons.
2. Containing a joke; of the nature of a joke; sportive; merry; as, a *jocose* or comical air.
Syn.—Facetious, jocular, merry, humorous waggish, witty, comical, droll.

jō-cōse'ly, *adv.* In a jocose manner; in jest; for sport or game; waggishly.

jō-cōse'ness, *n.* The quality of being jocose; waggery; merriment.

jō-cō-sē'ri-ous, *a.* [L. *jocus*, a joke, jest, and *serius*, serious.] Partaking of mirth and seriousness; serio-comic.

jō-cos'i-ty, *n.* 1. Jocularity; merriment; waggery.
2. A jocose act or saying; a joke. [Rare.]

joc'ū-lăr, *a.* [L. *jocularis*, from *jocus*, a joke jest.]
1. Jocose; waggish; merry; given to jesting; said of persons.
2. Containing jokes; sportive; not serious; as, a *jocular* expression or style.

joc-ū-lar'i-ty, *n.* Merriment; jesting.

joc'ū-lăr-ly, *adv.* In jest; for sport or mirth.

joc'ū-lā-ry, *a.* Jocular. [Obs.]

joc'ū-lā-tŏr, *n.*; *pl.* **joc"ū-lā-tō'rēs.** [L., from *joculari*, to joke, jest, from *jocus*, a joke, jest.] A professional jester; also, a minstrel.

joc'ū-lā-tō-ry, *a.* Droll. [Obs.]

joc'und, *a.* [LL. *jocundus*; L. *jucundus*, pleasant, agreeable, originally helpful, from *juvare*, to help.] Merry; gay; airy; lively; sportive.
Syn.—Gay, light-hearted, lively, merry, vivacious, mirthful, sprightly, sportive, cheerful.

jō-cun'di-ty, *n.* The state of being jocund or merry; gaiety.

joc'und-ly, *adv.* In a jocund manner; merrily; gaily.

joc'und-ness, *n.* Jocundity.

jō'del (yō'), *v.* and *n.* Same as *Yodel.*

jōe, *n.* 1. A fourpenny-piece; so named after Joseph Hume, M. P., at whose instance the coin was issued in 1836. [Eng. Slang.]
2. [J—] A stale joke. [Same as *Joe Miller.*]
3. A lobster less than ten inches long, and which according to law is not large enough to be sold. [Local, U. S.]

jōe, *n.* [Abbrev. of *Johannes.*] A coin. [See *Johannes.*]

Jōe Mil'lẽr. [After *Joe* or *Joseph Miller*, an English comic actor, whose name was attached to a jest-book published in 1739, the year after his death.] An old jest; a stale joke; also a jest-book. [Colloq.]

Jōe'=Mil'lẽr-ism, *n.* The art or practice of making, reciting, or retailing jests; the repetition of stale or flat jokes; an old jest.

Jōe'=Mil'lẽr-ize, *v.t.* To give a jesting or jocular character to; to mingle with stale jokes.

jōe-pȳe'=weed, *n.* A tall American plant, *Eupatorium purpureum*, of the aster family, bearing purple flowers; called also *trumpetweed.*

jō'ey, *n.* [Dim of *Joe*, an abbrev. of *Joseph.*]
1. In coal-mining, a workman whose duty is to set the timber in a stall or working while coal is being raised. [Eng. Slang.]
2. A coin; a joe. [Eng. Slang.]
3. In Australia, a young kangaroo.

jog, *v.t.*; jogged, *pt., pp.*; jogging, *ppr.* [ME. *joggen*, from W. *gogi*, to shake, agitate.]
1. To push or shake with the elbow or hand;

to push so as to give notice or excite attention; to nudge.

Sudden I *jogged* Ulysses. —Pope.

2. To remind; to stimulate or excite gently; to suggest to; as, to *jog* one's memory.

3. To cause to jog or move slowly; as, to *jog* a horse.

jog, *v.i.* To move by jogs or small shocks, like those of a slow trot; to walk or travel idly, heavily, or slowly; usually followed by *along* or *on*.

Thus they *jog on*, still tricking, never thriving. —Dryden.

jog, *n.* 1. A push; a slight shake; a nudge; a shake or push intended to give notice or awaken attention.

2. A rub; an obstruction; irregularity of motion; a jolt.

3. In machinery, a square notch.

4. Any break in a line; a depression in a surface.

jog′gẽr, *n.* 1. One who jogs or moves heavily and slowly.

2. One who jogs or gives a sudden push.

jog′gle, *v.t.*; joggled, *pt.*, *pp.*; joggling, *ppr.* [Freq. of *jog*.]

1. To shake slightly; to give a sudden but slight push to; to jostle.

2. In carpentry, to unite by notches and teeth in order to prevent sliding apart.

jog′gle, *v.i.* To move with unsteady, wavering motion; to totter; to shake.

jog′gle, *n.* 1. In architecture, a joint of stones or other bodies, so constructed as to prevent them sliding past each other by any force acting perpendicularly to the pressure or pressures by which they are held together; a joint held in place by means of teeth and notches.

a a, Joggle-joints. u, The last Joggle.

2. A shoulder on a truss-post supporting the lower ends of a strut or brace.

3. A jog; a jolt.

jog′gle-bēam, *n.* A built beam the parts of which are united by teeth fitting into notches.

jog′gle-joint, *n.* See *Joggle*, n. 1.

jog′gle-piēce, *n.* The upright member in the middle of a truss; a king-post.

jog′gle-pōst, *n.* 1. A post having shoulders to receive the feet of struts.

2. A post built of pieces of timber held together by teeth fitting into notches.

jog′gle-truss, *n.* A hanging-post truss with one post.

jog′gle-wŏrk, *n.* In masonry, work in which the courses are secured by joggling.

jog′-trot, *n.* A slow motion on horseback; hence, a slow routine mode of performing daily duty to which one pertinaciously adheres.

jog′-trot, *a.* Easy-going; monotonous; humdrum.

Jō-han′nē-ăn, *a.* [LL. *Johannes*, *Joannes*, John.] Of or pertaining to the apostle John, or the book of the New Testament written by him; written also *Johannine*.

jō-han′nēs, jō-an′nēs, *n.* [LL. *Johannes*, *Joannes*, John.] A Portuguese gold coin of the value of eight dollars, named from the figure of King John, which it bore.

Jō-han′nine, *a.* Johannean.

Jō-han′nis-bẽr-gẽr, *n.* [G., so called from Schloss *Johannisberg*, on the Rhine, where it is produced.] A Rhenish wine of very fine quality.

jō-han′nite, *n.* [LL. *Johannes*, John.]

1. A mineral of an emerald or apple-green color, a hydrous sulphate of the protoxid of uranium.

2. [J—] A member of the Knights Hospitalers of St. John of Jerusalem.

John (jon), *n.* [LL. *Johannes*, *Joannes*; Gr. *Iōannēs*, from Heb. *Yōhānān*, John, lit., Jehovah hath been gracious.] A proper name of a male person.

John Bull; see under *Bull*.

John Doe; in law, a name formerly given to the fictitious lessee of the plaintiff in the mixed action of ejectment, that of the fictitious defendant being *Richard Roe*.

John′ā-drēamṣ, *n.* A dreamy, idle fellow. [Obs.]

john′-ap″ple, *n.* A sort of apple good for use when other fruit is spent, as it long retains its freshness.

John′-Bull′iṣm, *n.* Anything typical of the character of the English people.

John Chi′nă-măn. A Chinaman; the Chinese generally.

john′-crōw′, *n.* The local name in Jamaica for the turkey-buzzard.

John-dō′ry, John-dō′ree, *n.* See second *Dory*.

John′i-ăn, *n.* A member or graduate of St. John's College, of Cambridge, England.

john′ny, *n.*; *pl.* **john′nieṣ.** 1. [J—] A diminutive of the name John; a nickname given to the Confederates by the Union soldiers during the Civil War.

2. A kind of penguin, *Pygoscelis tæniata*.

3. A cottoid fish, *Oligocottus maculosus*. [Local, U. S.]

4. A variety of darter, *Etheostoma nigrum*. [Local, U. S.]

john′ny-çāke, *n.* A cake made of the meal of Indian corn, mixed with milk or water, and baked.

john′ny-jump-up′, *n.* A species of pansy, *Viola tricolor*; also, the bird-foot violet, *Viola pedata*. [Local, U. S.]

John′ny-rạw′, *n.* A beginner; a novice. [Slang.]

John′ny-vẽrde′, *n.* A serranoid fish of California, *Paralabrax nebulifer*.

john′-pạw, *n.* A serranoid fish, *Epinephelus drummond-hayi*, found along the coast of the Gulf of Mexico.

John-sŏn-ese′, *n.* The style or language of Dr. Samuel Johnson, or an imitation of it; a pompous, inflated style, especially affecting words of classical origin.

John′sŏn gråss. A kind of grass, *Sorghum Halepense*, highly prized for fodder; called also *Arabian* or *evergreen millet*, *Cuba grass*, and *Means grass*; named after William Johnson, who introduced it into Alabama from South Carolina.

John-sō′ni-ăn, *a.* Relating to Dr. Samuel Johnson, his writings, or his style.

John-sō′ni-ăn-iṣm, *n.* A word, idiom, or habit peculiar to Dr. Samuel Johnson, or a style resembling his.

John′sŏn-iṣm, *n.* Johnsonianism.

John′ṣ′-wŏrt, *n.* See *St.-John's-wort* under *Saint*.

john′-tō-whit′, *n.* A species of greenlet, *Vireo olivaceus*.

join, *v.t.*; joined, *pt.*, *pp.*; joining, *ppr.* [ME. *joynen*, *joignen*; OFr. *joindre*, *juindre*, from L. *jungere*, to yoke, bind together.]

1. To connect or bring together, in a literal or figurative sense; to place in contiguity; to couple; to combine; to associate.

What therefore God hath *joined* together, let not man put asunder. —Matt. xix. 6.

2. To associate or unite with; to become connected with; as, to *join* a society; to *join* an army.

And *joins* the sacred senate of the skies. —Pope.

3. To engage in; to take part in; as, to *join* battle; to *join* issue.

4. To command; to enjoin. [Obs.]

5. To be contiguous to; to adjoin. [Colloq.]

Syn.—Combine, append, unite, add, connect, attach, annex, couple.

join, *v.i.* 1. To be contiguous, close, or in contact; to form a union.

2. To unite; to league; to confederate.

The rougher voices of the men *joined* in the song. —William Morris.

3. To meet in hostile encounter; to join battle. [Obs.]

join, *n.* A joint; a place or point of contact or connection.

join′ănt, *a.* [OFr. *joignant*, ppr. of *joindre*, to join.]

1. Adjoining. [Obs.]

2. In heraldry, conjoined.

join′dẽr, *n.* 1. A joining. [Obs.]

2. In law, (a) the coupling or joining of two things in a suit or action against another; (b) the coupling of two or more persons together as defendants; (c) the acceptance by a party in an action of the challenge laid down in his adversary's demurrer or last pleading.

join′ẽr, *n.* 1. One who joins; specifically, one whose occupation is to construct things by joining pieces of wood by means of glue, framing, or nails; appropriately and usually, a mechanic who does the woodwork for the interior and exterior finishings of buildings, ships, etc.

2. In woodworking, a machine for sawing, planing, chamfering, etc.

join′ẽr-y, *n.* 1. The art or occupation of a joiner.

2. The work of a joiner.

join′hand, *n.* Writing in which letters are joined in words, as distinguished from writing in single letters. [Obs.]

joint, *n.* [OFr. *joint*, *joinct*; LL. *juncta*, a joining, joint, connection, from L. *junctus*, pp. of *jungere*, to yoke, join.]

1. The place or part in which two things are joined or united; the mode of connection of two things with the contiguous parts connected, whether the parts are movable or stationary; juncture; articulation; hinge.

A scaly gauntlet now with *joints* of steel, Must glove this hand. —Shak.

2. In anatomy, an articulation; also, an internode; a part between two nodes.

3. In botany, an articulation.

4. One of the pieces of the carcass of an animal as cut off by a butcher; as, a *joint* of beef.

5. Any place where low practices are indulged in, as a resort for opium-smokers. [Colloq.]

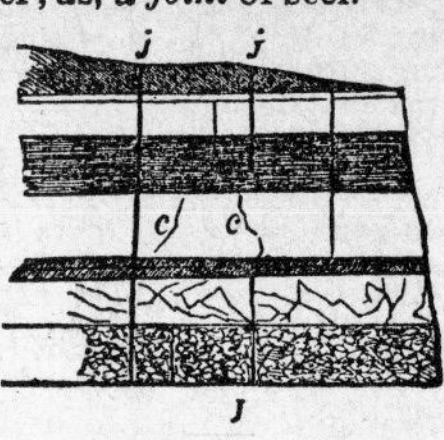
jj, Joints. cc, Cracks.

6. In architecture, the surface of contact between two bodies that are held firmly together by means of cement, mortar, etc., or by a superincumbent weight; as, the *joint* between two stones.

7. In geology, a natural fissure or line of parting traversing rocks in a straight and well-determined line, often at right angles to the planes of stratification.

8. In joinery, the place where one piece of timber is united to another; also, the mode in which the pieces are united.

Out of joint; dislocated, as when the head of a bone is displaced from its socket; hence, figuratively, confused; disordered.

Universal joint; in mechanics, an arrangement by which one part of a machine may be made to move freely in all directions in relation to another. A familiar example is afforded by the well-known ball-and-socket joint, which consists of a solid working into a hollow sphere.

joint, *a.* 1. Shared by two or more; held jointly; as, *joint* property.

2. United in action, relation, or interest; acting together; as, a *joint* heir; *joint* debtors; *joint* owners.

3. United, combined; acting in concert; as, *joint* force; *joint* efforts; *joint* vigor.

Joint and several; united in obligation, debt, etc., in such a manner that individually or collectively all are chargeable.

Joint resolution; see under *Resolution*.

Joint rule; see under *Rule*.

Joint tenancy; in law, a tenure of estate by unity of interest, title, time, and possession.

Joint tenant; in law, one who holds an estate by joint tenancy.

joint, *v.t.*; jointed, *pt.*, *pp.*; jointing, *ppr.* 1. To join; to unite.

2. To form in joints or articulations; to articulate.

3. To plane and prepare the edges, as of a board to be closely joined to another.

4. To divide or cut into joints or pieces; to separate the joints of; to disjoint.

joint, *v.i.* To unite, as by joints or parts fitting into each other; as, stones cut so as to *joint* into each other.

joint′-chāir, *n.* In railways, the chair at the joining of two rail-ends.

joint′-çlāy, *n.* A clay which when dried breaks up into angular blocks.

joint′-coup″ling (-kup″), *n.* A form of universal joint for coupling sections of shafting.

joint′ed, *a.* Provided with joints; formed with knots or nodes; as, a *jointed* stem.

joint′ed-ly, *adv.* By joints.

joint′ẽr, *n.* 1. One who or that which joints; specifically, (a) a long plane used by carpenters and joiners to straighten the edges of boards, timbers, etc., that are to be joined to other pieces; (b) a tool or a machine used by coopers for jointing staves.

2. In masonry, a bent piece of iron inserted into a wall to strengthen a joint.

joint′-fïr, *n.* 1. Any plant of the natural order *Gnetaceæ*.

2. Any coniferous plant of the family *Taxaceæ*.

joint′-gråss, *n.* 1. A grass, *Paspalum distichum*, growing in southern United States.

2. Any one of several species of the genus *Equisetum*. [Prov. Eng.]

3. The yellow bedstraw or goose-grass, *Galium verum*. [Prov. Eng.]

joint′-hinge, *n.* Same as *Strap-hinge*.

joint′ing, *n.* The act or process of making a joint; a joint.

joint′ing-mä-çhïne″, *n.* A planing-machine used in making furniture, pianos, etc.

joint′ing-plāne, *n.* 1. A plane with a long stock used to true the edges of boards or staves which are to be accurately fitted together.

2. A small additional share on a plow.

joint′ing-rüle, *n.* A straight rule about six feet long, used by bricklayers in marking with white paint along each joint of the brickwork.

joint′less, *a.* Having no joint; rigid; stiff.

joint′ly, *adv.* Together; unitedly; in concert.

joint′-oil, *n.* Same as *Synovia*.

joint′-pīpe, *n.* A short section of pipe forming a connection between two lengths.

joint′-pli″ẽrs, *n.pl.* A pair of pliers adapted for securing the points of compasses and other instruments; also, pliers by which the hinging of watch-cases is effected.

joint'ress, *n.* A woman who has a jointure. [Rare.]

joint'=snāke, *n.* Same as *Glass-snake.*

joint'=splice, *n.* A reinforced splice for securing firmly two parts of anything.

joint'=stock, *a.* Pertaining to stock held in company.

Joint-stock company; an association of a number of individuals for the purpose of carrying on some business or undertaking in which the shares of each member are transferable without the consent of the other partners.

joint'stool, *n.* 1. A stool made with jointed parts; a folding stool.

2. A block holding up the ends of parts which belong in apposition, as railway rails, ways of vessels, etc.

join'tūre, *n.* [OFr. *jointure, joincture,* from L. *junctura,* a joining, from *jungere,* to join.]

1. In law, an estate in lands or tenements, settled on a woman in consideration of marriage, and which she is to enjoy after her husband's decease.

2. A joining; junction. [Obs.]

join'tūre, *v.t.*; jointured, *pt., pp.*; jointuring, *ppr.* To settle a jointure upon.

join'tūre-less, *a.* Having no jointure.

join'tūr-ess, *n.* A jointress.

joint'weed, *n.* 1. An American plant, *Polygonella articulata,* having racemes with many joints.

2. A species of the genus *Equisetum.*

3. The mare's-tail, *Hippuris vulgaris.*

joint'=wire, *n.* The tubular wire, sections of which form the joints of watch-cases, lockets, etc.

joint'=wŏrm, *n.* The larva of a hymenopterous insect of the genus *Isosoma,* as *Isosoma hordei,* which infests the stalks of wheat and other grain in some parts of America, often doing much damage.

joint'y, *a.* Full of joints.

joist, *n.* [ME. *giste, gyste,* a joist, beam; OFr. *giste,* a bed, couch, beam, from *gesir,* to lie, from L. *jacere,* to lie.] In architecture, one of the pieces of timber to which the boards of a floor or the laths of a ceiling are nailed, and which rest on the walls or on girders, and sometimes on both. Joists are laid horizontally in parallel equidistant rows.

Joists.
1. A A, Joists. B, Floor boards. 2. C, Trimming-joist. 3. D D, Binding-joists. E E, Bridging-joists. B, Floor boards.

joist, *v.t.*; joisted, *pt., pp.*; joisting, *ppr.* To fit or furnish with joists.

jōke, *n.* [L. *jocus,* a joke, jest.]

1. A jest; something said for the sake of exciting a laugh; something witty or sportive; raillery.

2. An illusion; something not real, or to no purpose; what is not in earnest or actually meant.

Inclose whole downs in walls, 'tis all a *joke!* —Pope.

In joke; in jest; for the sake of raising a laugh; not in earnest.

Practical joke; see under *Practical.*

jōke, *v.t.*; joked (jōkt), *pt., pp.*; joking, *ppr.* To rally; to cast jokes at; to make merry with; as, to *joke* a man about his age.

jōke, *v.i.* To jest; to be merry in words or actions.

Syn.—Banter, jest, rally, tease.

jōk'ēr, *n.* 1. One who jokes; a jester; a merry fellow.

2. In some games at cards, an extra card added to the pack, which is always the highest trump; it is frequently used in the game of euchre.

jōk'ing-ly, *adv.* In a joking manner.

jōk'ish, *a.* Jocular; given to joking.

jōle, *n.* and *v.* Same as *Jowl.*

jol'if, *a.* Jolly. [Obs.]

jōll, *n.* and *v.* See *Jowl.*

jol-li-fi-cā'tion, *n.* A scene or occasion of merriment; noisy festivity; merrymaking. [Colloq.]

jol'li-ly, *adv.* In a jolly manner.

jol'li-ment, *n.* Mirth; merriment. [Obs.]

jol'li-ness, *n.* The quality or state of being jolly.

jol'li-ty, *n.* [OFr. *jolite,* from *joli,* jolly.] Noisy mirth; gaiety; merriment; festivity.

All now was turned to *jollity* and game. —Milton.

Syn.—Festivity, gaiety, frolic, hilarity, joviality, merriment, mirth.

jol'lŏp, *n.* The gobble of a turkey. [Prov. Eng.]

jol'ly, *a.*; *comp.* jollier; *superl.* jolliest. [OFr. *jolif, joli,* gay, joyful, merry, prob. from Ice. *jol,* the feast of Christmas.]

1. Merry; gay; lively; full of life and mirth; jovial; as, a *jolly* crew.

2. Expressing mirth or inspiring it; exciting mirth and gaiety; characterized by mirth; as, a *jolly* trip.

3. Of fine appearance; handsome. [Obs.]

4. Great; uncommon. [Eng. Slang.]

5. Brave; courageous. [Obs.]

Syn.—Gay, mirthful, jovial, lively, merry, sportive, sprightly.

jol'ly, *v.t.*; jollied, *pt., pp.*; jollying, *ppr.* 1. To endeavor to make jolly or cheerful in order to gain the good will of; to make good-natured; sometimes with *up* or *along*; as, to *jolly* the schoolmaster; to *jolly along* an office-seeker. [Slang.]

2. To joke; to poke fun at; to tease; as, they *jollied* him so much that he became angry. [Slang.]

jol'ly, *v.i.* To rejoice; to be pleased. [Obs.]

jol'ly, *adv.* Exceedingly; very; as, *jolly* good; *jolly* drunk. [Eng. Slang.]

jol'ly=bōat, *n.* A small clincher-built boat belonging to a ship. It is smaller than a cutter, being about 4 feet beam to 12 feet in length. It has a bluff bow and wide transom, and is used for general miscellaneous work.

jol'ly-head (-hed), *n.* A state of jollity. [Obs.]

jol'ly-tāil, *n.* A Tasmanian fish of the genus *Galaxias.*

jōlt, *v.t.*; jolted, *pt., pp.*; jolting, *ppr.* [Prob. from *jole, joll, jowl,* to knock the head against anything.] To shake with sudden jerks, as in a carriage on rough ground, or on a high-trotting horse.

Jolted and commended in a stagecoach. —Tatler.

jōlt, *v.i.* To shake with short, abrupt risings and fallings, as a carriage moving on rough ground; as, the wagon *jolts.*

jōlt, *n.* A shock or shake by a sudden jerk, as in a carriage.

jōlt'ēr, *n.* One who or that which jolts.

jōlt'ēr-head, *n.* See *Jolthead.*

jōlt'head (-hed), *n.* A dunce; a blockhead.

jōlt'ing-ly, *adv.* In a jolting manner.

jōlt'y, *a.* Having a jolting motion. [Colloq.]

Jō'năh, *n.* Any one whose presence is regarded as the cause of ill luck, especially on shipboard; in allusion to the Biblical story of Jonah, the Hebrew prophet who was thrown overboard as one who jeopardized the lives of those on board the ship.

Jō'năh=crab, *n.* A crab, *Cancer borealis,* found along the Atlantic coast of the United States.

jon'ȧ-thăn, *n.* A device with which smokers light their pipes. [Prov. Eng.]

Brother Jonathan; see under *Brother.*

jond'lȧ, *n.* [E. Ind.] The Indian millet.

jon'glēur, *n.* [OFr. *jongleur,* a juggler.] In France and England during the middle ages, a strolling minstrel who sang songs, usually of his own composition; also, a juggler; a mountebank.

jon'quil (-kwil), *n.* [Fr. *jonquille,* from L. *juncus,* a rush.]

1. A plant of the genus *Narcissus,* chiefly *Narcissus Jonquilla*; the rush-leafed daffodil. *Narcissus odorus* is the sweet-scented jonquil.

2. A light-yellow color of certain porcelains.

Jonquil (*Narcissus Jonquilla*).

jon'quille (-kwil), *n.* Same as *Jonquil.*

jook, *v.i.* See *Jouk.*

jō'pim, *n.* [Prob. from native name.] An American icteroid bird of the genus *Cassicus.*

jō'răm, *n.* Same as *Jorum.*

jor'dăn, *n.* 1. Originally, a bottle in which a pilgrim brought home water from the river Jordan.

2. A kind of pot or vessel formerly used by alchemists, in shape not unlike a soda-water bottle, only that the neck was wider. [Obs.]

3. A chamber-pot. [Obs.]

jor'dăn-ite, *n.* [Named after Dr. *Jordan,* of Prussia.] An orthorhombic mineral, occurring in the dolomite of the Binnenthal, Switzerland, in fine crystals. It is a sulphid of arsenic and lead.

jor-nä'dä (hor-), *n.* [Sp., a journey.]

1. A day's travel.

2. The Mexican name for a long stretch of desert land.

jō'rum, *n.* A large bowl or vessel for drinking; also, the quantity of liquor contained in such a vessel. [Colloq.]

jō'sĕph, *n.* [Prob. from *Joseph's* "coat of many colors" (Gen. xxxvii. 3).] A riding-coat or habit for women, with buttons down to the skirts, in use in the eighteenth century.

Jō'sĕph's=cōat, *n.* A variety of border-plants, *Amarantus tricolor.*

Jō'sĕph's=flow"ēr, *n.* The goat's-beard, *Tragopogon pratensis,* a composite plant of Europe.

Josh'ū-ȧ=tree, *n.* A tree, *Yucca brevifolia,* found in some desert altitudes of southwestern United States.

joss, *n.* [Chinese, a corruption of Port. *deos,* L. *deus,* God.] A Chinese god or idol.

jos'sȧ, *interj.* An old word of command to horses, probably equivalent to *whoa,* or *stand still.*

joss'=house, *n.* A Chinese temple or place for idolatrous worship; sometimes applied by the Chinese to a Christian church.

joss'=stick, *n.* A small reed, covered with the dust of fragrant woods, and burned before idols in China.

jos'tle (-l), *v.t.*; jostled, *pt., pp.*; jostling, *ppr.* [Freq. from ME. *justen*; OFr. *juster, joster,* to come together, tilt.] To run against and shake; to crowd against so as to render unsteady; to elbow; to hustle.

jos'tle, *v.i.* To hustle; to shove about, as in a crowd; to be shoved about.

jos'tle, *n.* A pushing against; crowding; hustling.

jos'tle-ment, *n.* The act of jostling or crowding against. [Rare.]

jot, *n.* [LL. *iota*; Gr. *iōta,* ι, the smallest letter in the Greek alphabet, something small.] An iota; a point; a tittle; the least quantity assignable.

One *jot* or one tittle shall in no wise pass from the law. —Matt. v. 18.

jot, *v.t.*; jotted, *pt., pp.*; jotting, *ppr.* To set down quickly, as in hasty writing; to make a memorandum or brief note of; usually with *down.*

jot'tēr, *n.* 1. One who jots down notes or memoranda.

2. The book in which notes or memoranda are made.

jot'ting, *n.* A memorandum; a brief note.

jöu'bärb, *n.* [Fr. *joubarbe,* from L. *Jovis barba,* Jupiter's beard.] The houseleek.

jöugs, *n.* [OFr. *joug,* from L. *jugum,* a yoke.] An instrument of punishment formerly used in Scotland, consisting of an iron collar which surrounded the neck of the criminal, and was fastened to a wall or tree by an iron chain.

Jougs.

jöu'i-sănce, jöu'is-sănce, *n.* [Fr.] Jollity; merriment. [Obs.]

jöuk, *v.i.* To perch; to roost. [Obs.]

jöuk, jook, *v.i.* To bend or incline the body forward with a quick motion in order to avoid a stroke or any injury; to dodge; to duck. [Scot.]

jöuk'ēr-y, jook'ēr-y, *n.* Trickery; jugglery. [Scot.]

joule, *n.* [Named after J. P. *Joule,* an English physicist.] In the C. G. S. system, a unit of electrical energy or work which is equivalent to the work done in raising the potential of one coulomb of electricity one volt, or in maintaining for one second a current of one ampere against a resistance of one ohm; a volt-coulomb. One joule is equivalent to 10,000,000 ergs or .73732 foot-pound.

Joule's equivalent; see *Mechanical equivalent of heat* under *Equivalent.*

joule'mē"tēr, *n.* A meter in which the joule is employed as the unit of energy.

jounce, *v.t.* and *v.i.* To jolt; to shake, especially by rough-riding.

jounce, *n.* A jolt; a shake.

jöur'năl, *a.* Daily; quotidian; diurnal. [Obs.]

jöur'năl, *n.* [OFr. *journal, jornal, jurnal,* daily, a journal, from L. *diurnalis,* daily, from *dies,* day.]

1. A diary; an account of daily transactions and events, or the book containing such account; any record of a series of transactions; specifically, (a) in bookkeeping, a book in which every particular article or charge is entered under each day's date; (b) in nautical parlance, a daily register of the ship's course and distance, the winds, weather, and other conditions or circumstances; (c) a newspaper or other periodical published daily; any publication issued at successive periods, containing a report of passing events; (d) a record of the daily proceedings of a legislative assembly.

2. In machinery, that part of a shaft which rests in the bearings.

3. A day's work; a journey. [Obs.]

jöur'năl, *v.t.*; journaled *or* journalled, *pt., pp.*; journaling *or* journalling, *ppr.* To adjust or insert, as a shaft, in a journal-box or bearing.

jöur'năl=beâr"ing, *n.* A journal-box.

jöur'năl=box, *n.* In machinery, the carrier of a journal; the box on which the journal of a shaft, axle, or pin bears and moves.

jöur'năl-ism, *n.* 1. The keeping of a journal. [Rare.]

2. The business, occupation, or profession of

publishing, writing for, or conducting a journal; the profession of a journalist.

jour'năl-ist, *n.* 1. The writer of a journal or diary.

2. One who conducts or writes for a public journal; an editor, correspondent, critic, or reporter of a newspaper; a newspaper man.

jour-năl-is'tic, *a.* Pertaining to journals, journalism, or journalists; as, *journalistic* literature.

jour'năl-ize, *v.t.*; journalized, *pt., pp.*; journalizing, *ppr.* To enter in a journal or diary; to set down a daily account of, as events or transactions.

jour'năl-ize, *v.i.* To contribute to or aid in conducting a journal.

jour'ney, *n.* [ME. *journee, jorney*; OFr. *journee, jornee*; LL. *diurnata*, a day's journey, day's work, from L. *diurnus*, daily.]

1. A day's work or travel. [Obs.]

2. Travel from one place to another; passage; as, a *journey* from London to Paris; a tiresome *journey*.

3. Figuratively, passage through life.

Syn.—Tour, excursion, pilgrimage, travel, trip, voyage.—*Journey* suggests the idea of a somewhat prolonged traveling for a specific object, leading a person to pass directly from one point to another. In a *tour* we take a roundabout course from place to place, more commonly for pleasure, though sometimes on business. An *excursion* is never on business, but always for pleasure, health, etc. In a *pilgrimage* we travel to a place hallowed by our religious affections, or by some train of interesting associations.

jour'ney, *v.i.*; journeyed, *pt., pp.*; journeying, *ppr.* To travel from place to place; to leave home and travel for a distance.

Abram *journeyed*, going on still toward the south. —Gen. xii. 9.

jour'ney-bāt"ed, *a.* Fatigued or worn out with a journey. [Obs.]

jour'ney-ēr, *n.* One who journeys.

jour'ney-măn, *n.*; *pl.* **jour'ney-men.** Originally, a man hired to work by the day; now, a mechanic or workman who has served his apprenticeship, and is so supposed to have learned his trade.

jour'ney-wŏrk, *n.* 1. Work done by the day. [Obs.]

2. Work done for hire by a journeyman.

joust (just), *n.* and *v.* See *Just.*

joust'ēr, *n.* See *Juster.*

Jōve, *n.* [L. *Jovis*, genit. of *Jupiter*, Jupiter.]

1. The chief of the Roman divinities; Jupiter.

2. The planet Jupiter. [Rare.]

3. In alchemy, the metal tin. [Obs.]

Bird of Jove; the eagle.

Jōve's'-fruit, *n.* An American shrub, *Lindera melissæfolius*, a species of wild allspice.

Jōve's'-nuts, *n.pl.* Acorns. [Prov. Eng.]

jō'vi-ăl, *a.* 1. Pertaining to the god Jove or to the planet Jupiter.

2. Under the influence of Jupiter, the planet. [Obs.]

3. [j—] Gay; merry; joyous; jolly; characterized by gaiety; as, a *jovial* youth; a *jovial* throng; a *jovial* disposition.

4. [j—] In alchemy, pertaining to the metal tin. [Obs.]

jō'vi-ăl-ist, *n.* One who lives a jovial life.

jō-vi-al'i-ty, *n.* The state or quality of being jovial; merriment; festivity.

jō'vi-ăl-ize, *v.t.*; jovialized, *pt., pp.*; jovializing, *ppr.* To cause to be jovial or gay.

jō'vi-ăl-ly, *adv.* In a jovial manner; merrily; gaily.

jō'vi-ăl-ness, *n.* Joviality; gaiety.

jō'vi-ăl-ty, *n.* Joviality. [Rare.]

Jō'vi-ăn, *a.* Pertaining to Jove, the god, or to the planet Jupiter.

jō-vi-cen'tric, *a.* [L. *Jovis*, genit. of *Jupiter*, or *Juppiter*, Jupiter, and *centrum*, center.] In astronomy, having relation to Jupiter as a center.

jō'vi-lābe, *n.* [L. *Jovis*, of Jupiter, and *-labe*, as in *astrolabe*.] In astronomy, an instrument for ascertaining the situations of the satellites of the planet Jupiter.

Jō-vin'ián-ist, *n.* A follower of Jovinian, a monk of the fourth century, who denied the virginity of Mary and denounced asceticism.

jōwl (*or* joul), *n.* [A corruption of *chol, chaul*, which is a corruption of *chavel*, from AS. *ceafl*, jaw.] The cheek; especially, the cheek or head of a pig or fish, cooked for food.

Cheek by jowl; see under *Cheek.*

jōwl, jōll, *v.t.* To strike, as with the head; to butt. [Obs.]

jōwl, jōll, *v.i.* To scold; to jaw. [Obs.]

jōwl'ēr, *n.* A dog with heavy jaws, as a beagle, hound, or other hunting-dog.

jow'tēr, *n.* One who hawks fish about the country on horseback. [Local, Eng.]

joy, *n.* [ME. *joye, joie*; OFr. *joie, joye*, joy, pleasure, from LL. *gaudia*, f., joy, a jewel, from L. *gaudium*, joy.]

1. The passion or emotion excited by the acquisition or expectation of good; that excitement of pleasurable feeling which is caused by success, good fortune, etc., or by a rational prospect of possessing what we love or desire; gladness; exultation; exhilaration of spirits.

Joy is a delight of the mind, from the consideration of the present or assured approaching possession of a good. —Locke.

2. Gaiety; mirth; festivity. [Obs.]

3. The cause of joy or happiness.

For ye are our glory and *joy*.—1 Thess. ii. 20.

Syn.—Delight, gladness, rapture, ecstasy, happiness, exultation.

joy, *v.i.*; joyed, *pt., pp.*; joying, *ppr.* To rejoice; to be glad; to exult.

I will *joy* in the God of my salvation. —Hab. iii. 18.

joy, *v.t.* 1. To give joy to; to congratulate. [Obs.]

2. To gladden; to exhilarate. [Obs.]

3. To enjoy; to have or possess with pleasure, or have pleasure in the possession of. [Obs.]

joy'ănce, *n.* Gaiety; festivity; rejoicing. [Rare.]

joy'ăn-cy, *n.* Joyance. [Rare.]

joy'-bells, *n.pl.* Bells rung on a festive occasion.

joy'ful, *a.* Full of joy; very glad; exulting.

joy'ful-ly, *adv.* In a joyful manner; with joy; gladly.

joy'ful-ness, *n.* The state of being joyful; gladness; joy.

joy'less, *a.* 1. Destitute of joy; wanting joy.

2. Giving no joy or pleasure.

joy'less-ly, *adv.* In a joyless manner; without joy.

joy'less-ness, *n.* The state of being joyless.

joy'ous, *a.* [OFr. *joyous*, from *joie*, joy.]

1. Glad; gay; merry; joyful.

2. Giving or inspiring joy.

joy'ous-ly, *adv.* In a joyous manner; with joy or gladness.

joy'ous-ness, *n.* The state of being joyous.

joy-rīd'ēr, *n.* One who takes his employer's automobile without permission and uses it for his own pleasure. Hence, one who drives an automobile recklessly.

joy'sŏme, *a.* Causing joy or gladness. [Rare.]

jub, *n.* A bottle or vessel for holding liquor. [Obs.]

jū'bȧ, *n.*; *pl.* **jū'bæ.** [L., a mane.]

1. An animal's mane.

2. In botany, a loose panicle, like that of many grasses.

jū'bȧ, *n.* [Negro.] A negro dance accompanied by the onlookers, who clap their hands, stamp their feet, slap their knees or thighs, and sing a refrain in which the word *juba* is repeated again and again.

jū'bȧ, *n.* [Prob. from native name.] A species of snake found in Cuba.

One of the Cuban snakes is the *juba*. —"Our Islands and their People," vol. I.

Jū'bȧ's-bush, Jū'bȧ's-brush, *n.* An American plant, *Iresine celosioides*, of the amaranth family.

jū'bāte, *a.* [L. *jubatus*, from *juba*, a mane.] Having a mane; fringed with long hair like a mane.

jub'bȧh, *n.* [Hind.] A sort of gown with wide sleeves, worn by the more respectable class of Mohammedans.

jū'bē (*or* zhū-bā'), *n.* [Fr., from L. *jube*, 2nd pers. sing. imper. of *jubere*, to bid, command.]

1. The rood-loft or gallery in a cathedral or church, over the entrance to the choir.

2. An ambo. [Rare.]

jubh'ȧ, *n.* See *Jubbah.*

jū'bi-lănce, *n.* Jubilation; gladness.

jū'bi-lănt, *a.* [L. *jubilans* (*-antis*), ppr. of *jubilare*, to shout for joy.] Uttering songs of triumph; rejoicing; shouting with joy.

While the bright pomp ascended *jubilant*. —Milton.

Syn.—Joyous, triumphant, exultant.

jū'bi-lănt-ly, *adv.* In a jubilant manner.

jū'bi-lăr, *a.* Relating to or having the character of a jubilee. [Obs.]

Jū-bi-lā'tē, *n.* [L., 2nd pers. pl. imper. act. of *jubilare*, to shout for joy, rejoice.]

1. The third Sunday after Easter; so called because in the primitive church divine service began with the words of the 66th Psalm, *Jubilate Deo.*

2. The 100th Psalm; so called from the first word in the Latin version.

jū'bi-lāte, *v.i.* [L. *jubilatus*, pp. of *jubilare*, to shout for joy, from *jubilum*, a wild cry.] To rejoice; to exult.

jū-bi-lā'tion, *n.* The act of exulting; rejoicing.

jū'bi-lee, *n.* [ME. *jubilee*; OFr. *jubile*; LL. *jubilæus*; Gr. *iōbēlaios*, from Heb. *yōbēl*, the blast of a trumpet, the sabbatical year which was announced by the blast of a trumpet.]

1. Among the ancient Jews, every fiftieth year, following an interval of seven sabbaths of years, at which time all slaves of Hebrew blood were liberated, and all lands, which had been alienated during the whole period, reverted to their former owners.

2. A season of great public rejoicing; any occasion of joy or rejoicing.

3. In the Roman Catholic church, a feast first instituted in the year 1300 by Boniface VIII., who proposed that it should be celebrated at the commencement of each succeeding century. The period was afterward reduced to fifty, and later to thirty-three years. Paul II. finally reduced it to twenty-five years, and since his time there has been no alteration. The jubilee is a year of indulgence in which remission from the penal consequences of sin may be obtained by those who comply with certain conditions and perform certain acts.

4. The fiftieth anniversary of some event of public interest and importance, or the year of such anniversary; as, the *jubilee* of the reign of Queen Victoria.

5. A state of joy or delight. [Rare.]

jū'bi-list, *n.* One who participates in the celebration of a jubilee.

jū-cun'di-ty, *n.* Pleasantness; agreeableness. [Obs.]

Jū'dȧh-īte, *n.* A member of the tribe of Judah; a member of the kingdom of Judah; a Jew.

Jū-dā'ic, *a.* [L. *Judaicus*; Gr. *Ioudeikos*, from *Ioudaia*, Judea.] Pertaining to the Jews.

Jū-dā'ic-ăl, *a.* Judaic.

Jū-dā'ic-ăl-ly, *adv.* After the Jewish manner.

Jū'dā-ism, *n.* [LL. *Judaismus*; Gr. *Ioudaismos*, Judaism, from *Ioudaizein*, to Judaize.]

1. The religious doctrines and rites of the Jews, as enjoined in the laws of Moses.

2. Conformity to the Jewish rites and ceremonies.

Jū'dā-ist, *n.* An adherent of Judaism.

Jū-dā-is'tic, *a.* Relating to Judaism.

Jū-dā-is'tic-ăl-ly, *adv.* In a Judaistic manner.

Jū-dā-i-zā'tion, *n.* The act of Judaizing; a conforming to the Jewish religion or ritual.

Jū'dā-ize, *v.i.*; Judaized, *pt., pp.*; Judaizing, *ppr.* [LL. *Judaizare*; Gr. *Ioudaizein*, to live or act like Jews, from *Ioudaios*, a Jew.] To conform to the religious doctrines and rites of the Jews; to affect the manners or customs of the Jews.

Jū'dā-ize, *v.t.* To bring into conformity with the manners, customs, or rites of the Jews; as, to *Judaize* the Christian Sabbath.

Jū'dā-i-zēr, *n.* 1. One who conforms to Judaism.

2. In the early church, a Jew who accepted Christianity but adhered to the Mosaic law.

Jū'dăs, *n.* [LL. *Judas*; Gr. *Ioudas*, from Heb. *Yehūdah*, Judah.]

1. The apostle who betrayed Christ.

2. A treacherous person; one who betrays under the semblance of friendship.

3. [j—] Same as *Judas-hole.*

Jū'dăs-cŏl"ŏred, *a.* Red; applied to hair, from the notion that Judas had red hair.

There's treachery in that *Judas-colored* beard. —Dryden.

jū'dăs-hōle, *n.* A small trap or peephole in a door.

Jū'dăs-līght, *n.* An imitation of a paschal candle, made of wood.

Jū'dăs-tree, *n.* [So called because Judas is said to have hanged himself on a tree of this kind.]

1. A leguminous tree, *Cercis Siliquastrum*, of Europe, bearing handsome rose-colored flowers.

2. The redbud of America, *Cercis Canadensis.*

3. The elder, *Sambucus nigra.*

California Judas-tree; the redbud, *Cercis occidentalis.*

jud'cock, jud'dŏck, *n.* See *Jacksnipe.*

Jū-dē'ăn, Jū-dæ'ăn, *a.* and *n.* [L. *Judæus*; Gr. *Ioudaios*, a Jew, of or pertaining to Judea, from *Ioudaia*, Judea.]

I. *a.* Relating to Judea.

II. *n.* A native or inhabitant of Judea; a Jew.

judge, *n.* [OFr. *juge*, from L. *judex* (*-icis*), a judge, one who declares the law; *jus*, the law, and *dicere*, to say, declare.]

1. A public officer invested with authority to hear and determine causes, civil and criminal, and to administer justice between parties in courts held for the purpose.

2. One who has skill, science, or experience sufficient to decide upon the merits, value, or quality of anything; a connoisseur; a critic.

3. A person appointed to decide in any contest between two or more parties; as, a *judge* at a county fair; a *judge* at a yacht race.

4. A ruler or governor of the ancient Israelites.

5. [J—*pl.*] The name of the seventh book of the Old Testament; the Book of Judges.

Judge advocate; see under *Advocate.*

Syn.—Umpire, arbitrator, referee.—A *judge*, in the legal sense, is a magistrate appointed to determine questions of law. An *umpire* is a person selected to decide between two or more who contend for a prize An *arbitrator* is one chosen to allot to two contestants their portion of a claim, usually on grounds of equity and common sense. A *referee* is one to whom a case is referred for final adjustment.

judge, *v.i.*; judged, *pt.*, *pp.*; judging, *ppr.* [ME. *jugen*; OFr. *juger*, from L. *judicare*, to judge, declare the law, from *judex* (*-icis*), a judge.]

1. To compare facts or ideas and perceive their agreement or disagreement, and thus to distinguish truth from falsehood.

2. To form an opinion; to bring to issue the reasoning or deliberations of the mind.

3. To hear and determine causes on trial; to pass sentence.

judge, *v.t.* 1. To hear and determine; to examine and decide; as, to *judge* a case in dispute.

2. To try; to examine and pass sentence on.

3. Rightly to understand and discern.

He that is spiritual *judgeth* all things. —1 Cor. ii. 15.

4. To esteem; to think; to reckon.

If ye have *judged* me to be faithful to the Lord. —Acts xvi. 15.

5. To rule or govern. [Obs.]

judg'ẽr, *n.* One who judges or passes sentence.

judge'ship, *n.* The office of a judge.

judg'ment, judge'ment, *n.* [ME. *juggement*; OFr. *jugement*; LL. *judicamentum*, a judgment, from L. *judicare*, to judge.]

1. The act of judging; the act or process of the mind in comparing its ideas to find their agreement or disagreement, and to ascertain truth; the process of examining facts and arguments to ascertain propriety and justice; the process of examining the relations between one proposition and another.

2. The faculty of the mind by which man is enabled to compare ideas and ascertain the relations of terms and propositions; as, a man of sound *judgment*.

3. In law, the sentence or doom pronounced in any cause, civil or criminal, by the judge or court by which it is tried.

4. Opinion; notion; as, in my *judgment*, the case is hopeless.

5. Determination; decision; as, let reason govern us in the formation of our *judgment* of things proposed to our inquiry.

6. In philosophy, the comparison of two of the simple notions which are the subjects of simple apprehension and pronouncing that they agree or disagree with each other.

7. A calamity regarded as inflicted by God for the punishment of sinners.

8. The final trial of the human race, when God will decide the fate of every individual and award sentence according to justice.

Arrest of judgment; see under *Arrest*.

Judgment of God; formerly, extraordinary trials of secret crimes, as by arms and single combat, by ordeal or hot plowshares, etc., it being imagined that God would work miracles to vindicate innocence.

Syn.—Discernment, discrimination, penetration, sagacity, decision.

judg'ment-day, *n.* In theology, the last day, or the day when final judgment will be pronounced on the subjects of God's moral government.

judg'ment-debt (-det), *n.* In law, a debt secured to the creditor by a judge's order and in respect of which he can at any time attach the debtor's goods and chattels.

judg'ment-hall, *n.* The hall where courts are held.

judg'ment-seat, *n.* 1. The seat or bench on which judges sit in court.

2. A court; a tribunal.

jū'di-cȧ-ble, *a.* That may be tried and judged.

jū'di-cȧ-tive, *a.* Having power to judge.

jū'di-cȧ-tō-ry, *a.* Dispensing justice; pertaining to judicial jurisdiction and administration.

jū'di-cȧ-tō-ry, *n.*; *pl.* **jū'di-cȧ-tō-ries**. 1. A court of justice; a tribunal.

2. Distribution of justice.

jū'di-cȧ-tūre, *n.* [Fr. *judicature*; LL. *judicatura*, from L. *judicare*, to judge.]

1. The power of distributing justice by legal trial and determination.

2. A court of justice; a judicatory.

3. The territory over which the power of a court extends; also, the jurisdiction of a court.

jū-di'cial (-dish'ăl), *a.* 1. Pertaining or appropriate to courts of justice or to a judge thereof; as, *judicial* power.

2. Practised or employed in the administration of justice; as, *judicial* proceedings.

3. Proceeding from, issued, or ordered by a court of justice; as, a *judicial* writ; a *judicial* sale.

4. Inflicted as a penalty or in judgment; as, a *judicial* punishment.

5. Enacted by statute or established by constituted authority.

6. In astrology, giving judgments regarding future events.

7. Judicious. [Obs.]

jū-di'cial-ly, *adv.* In a judicial manner; after a judicial form.

jū-di'cia-ry (-dish'ȧ-ry *or* -i-ā-ry), *a.* [L. *judiciarius*, pertaining to a court of justice, from *judicium*, judgment, a court of justice, from *judex* (*-icis*), a judge.]

1. Passing judgment or sentence.

2. Pertaining to the courts of judicature or legal tribunals.

jū-di'cia-ry, *n.* That branch of government which is concerned in the trial and determination of controversies between parties and of criminal prosecutions; the system of courts of justice in a government; the judges collectively.

jū-di'cious (-dish'us), *a.* [LL. *judiciosus*, prudent, judicious, from L. *judicium*, judgment.]

1. According to sound judgment; possessing sound judgment; wise; directed by reason and wisdom; as, a *judicious* magistrate; a *judicious* historian.

2. Judicial. [Obs.]

Syn.—Wise, sagacious, expedient, sensible, prudent, discreet, well-judged, well-advised, politic, discerning, thoughtful.

jū-di'cious-ly, *adv.* In a judicious manner; wisely.

jū-di'cious-ness, *n.* The quality of being judicious.

jug, *n.* [Perhaps connected with *Jug* or *Judge*, familiar nicknames of *Judith*, and equivalent to *Joan* or *Jenny*. *Jack* and *Jill* were also used as names of drinking-vessels.]

1. A vessel, usually of earthenware, glass, or metal, with a swelling body and narrow mouth, used for holding and conveying liquids.

2. A jail or prison; a lockup or calaboose. [Slang.]

jug, *v.i.*; jugged, *pt.*, *pp.*; jugging, *ppr.* To utter a sound resembling this word, as certain birds do, especially the nightingale.

jug, *v.i.* To come closely together, as birds in nestling.

jug, *v.t.* 1. To pour into a jug; to heat in a jug.

2. To shut up or imprison. [Slang.]

jū'găl, *a.* [L. *jugalis*, pertaining to a yoke, matrimonial, from *jugum*, a yoke.]

1. Pertaining to the cheek-bone or to the region of the cheek-bone.

2. Having reference to a yoke, or to marriage. [Obs.]

jū'găl, *n.* In anatomy, the malar or cheek-bone.

jū-gā'tȧ, *n.pl.* Two heads represented together on a coin or medal.

jū'gāte, *a.* [L. *jugatus*, pp. of *jugare*, to yoke, connect, from *jugum*, a yoke.]

1. In botany, coupled together, as the pairs of leaflets in compound leaves.

2. In numismatics, joined or overlapping, as two heads on a coin.

jū'gā-ted, *a.* Same as *Jugate*.

juge, *n.* and *v.* [Obs.] See *Judge*.

juge'ment, *n.* [Obs.] See *Judgment*.

jū'ge-rum, *n.*; *pl.* **jū'ge-rȧ**. [L.] In Roman land-measurement, a piece of land two hundred and forty feet in length by one hundred and twenty feet in breadth.

jug'gẽr, *n.* [E. Ind.] An East Indian falcon, *Falco jugger*; written also *juggur* and *lugger*.

Jug'gẽr-naut, *n.* [Sans. *Jagannatha*, lit., lord of the world.]

1. The popular name of the Hindu idol Jagannatha, under the wheels of whose car worshipers have been said to hurl themselves as sacrifices.

2. Anything, as an idea, custom, fashion, and the like, to which one either devotes himself or is blindly or ruthlessly sacrificed.

jug'gle, *n.* A trick by legerdemain; an imposture; a deception.

jug'gle, *n.* A square-ended block of timber cut to a certain length.

jug'gle, *v.i.*; juggled, *pt.*, *pp.*; juggling, *ppr.* [ME. *juglen*, *jogelen*; OFr. *jogler*, to juggle, play false, from L. *joculari*, to jest, joke, from *joculus*, dim. of *jocus*, a joke, jest.]

1. To play tricks requiring great dexterity; to practise sleight of hand.

2. To practise artifice or imposture.

jug'gle, *v.t.* To deceive by trick or artifice; as, to *juggle* one into a false position.

Syn.—Conjure, cheat, bamboozle, shuffle, trick, beguile, circumvent, swindle, overreach, mystify, mislead.

jug'glẽr, *n.* One who juggles; also, a cheat; a deceiver; a trickish fellow.

jug'glẽr-ess, *n.* A woman who juggles.

jug'glẽr-y, *n.*; *pl.* **jug'glẽr-ies**. Legerdemain.

jug'gling, *n.* 1. The art or practice of exhibiting tricks of skill or legerdemain.

2. Trickery; deceit.

jug'gling-ly, *adv.* In a deceptive manner.

juggs, *n.pl.* See *Jougs*.

Jū-glan-dā'cē-æ, *n.pl.* [L. *juglans* (*-andis*), a walnut, walnut-tree, and *-aceæ*.] The walnut family, a natural order of exogenous plants found chiefly in North America. They are trees with alternate pinnate stipulate leaves, and unisexual flowers, the males in catkins, the females in terminal clusters or loose racemes.

jū-glan-dā'ceous, *a.* Of or pertaining to the *Juglandaceæ*.

jug'lan-din, jug'lan-dine, *n.* [L. *juglans* (*-andis*), a walnut, walnut-tree, and *-in*, *-ine*.] In chemistry, (a) a compound derived from the juice of walnut-shells, which is used medicinally as an alterative and also as a hair-dye; (b) an alkaloid found in the leaves of *Juglans regia*.

Jū'glăns, *n.* [L., a walnut, walnut-tree.] In botany, a genus of trees in which are included the true European walnut and the black walnut and butternut of America.

jū'glōne, *n.* [L. *juglans*, the walnut, and *-one*.] A crystalline substance, $C_{10}H_6O_3$, obtained from the walnut; called also *nucin*.

Jū'gō-Slăv (yū'), *n.* One of the southern Slavs or Serbs, the race including the Bulgarians, Serbo-Croatians and Slovenes.

jū'gū-lȧ, *n.*, pl. of *jugulum*.

jū'gū-lăr, *a.* [L. *jugulum*, the collar-bone, the neck, throat, dim. of *jugum*, a yoke.]

1. In anatomy, pertaining to the neck or throat.

2. Relating to the jugular vein or to the jugulum of a bird.

3. In zoölogy, characterizing the ventral fins of a fish when situated anterior to the pectoral fins, as beneath the throat.

Jugular vein; in anatomy, one of the trunk veins of the neck.

jū'gū-lăr, *n.* 1. A jugular vein.

2. A member of the group *Jugulares*.

Jū-gū-lā'rēs, *n.pl.* [L. *jugularis*, jugular, from *jugulum*, the collar-bone, neck, throat.] A division of fishes the general character of which is that the ventral fins are placed anterior to the pectoral.

Jugulares. *v*, Ventral fin. *p*, Pectoral fin.

jū'gū-lāte, *v.t.* To kill by cutting the throat of. [Rare.]

jū-gū-lā'tion, *n.* [LL. *jugulatio* (*-onis*), from *jugulare*, to cut the throat of, kill, from *jugulum*, the throat.] In medicine, the sudden arrest of a disease by timely and judicious treatment.

jū'gū-lum, *n.*; *pl.* **jū'gū-lȧ**. [L.] In ornithology, the lower section of the throat; also, an analogous part in an invertebrate.

jū'gum, *n.*; *pl.* **jū'gȧ**. [L., a yoke, crossbeam, ridge.]

1. In botany, one of the elevated portions by which the carpels of umbelliferous plants are traversed; also, paired leaflets in a compound leaf.

2. In zoölogy, a backward-extending lobe near the inner marginal base of the anterior wing of an insect.

jūice (jūs), *n.* [ME. *juis*, *juce*, *jus*; OFr. *jus*, from L. *jus*, broth, soup, juice.]

1. The fluid part of an animal body.

2. [*pl.*] All the fluid constituents of the body.

3. The sap or watery part of a plant or fruit.

jūice, *v.t.* To moisten. [Obs.]

jūice'less, *a.* Destitute of juice; dry; without moisture; not juicy.

jūi'ci-ness, *n.* The state of abounding with juice; succulence in plants.

jūi'cy, *a.*; *comp.* juicier; *superl.* juiciest. Abounding with juice; moist; succulent.

jū-işe', *n.* Judgment; justice. [Obs.]

jū'jūbe, *n.* [Fr., from L. *zizyphum*; Gr. *zizyphon*, from Per. *zizafun*, *zayzafun*, *zizfun*, the jujube-tree.]

1. The name of a plant and of its fruit, which is pulpy and resembles a small plum; the *Zizyphus jujuba*, a native of the East Indies, formerly used in pectoral decoctions.

2. Any of other species of *Zizyphus*.

3. A confection resembling the inspissated juice of a jujube in taste.

jūke, *n.* A bird's neck. [Prov. Eng.]

jūke, *v.i.* Same as *Jouk*.

jū-lā'ceous, *a.* [L. *julus*, a catkin, and *-aceous*.] In botany, like a catkin in character or appearance; bearing catkins; amentaceous.

jū'lep, *n.* [Fr. *julep*; Sp. *julepe*; Ar. *jūlāb*; Per. *jūlāb*, *gūlāb*, julep, rose-water; *gūl*, rose, and *āb*, water.]

1. In pharmacy, a medicine composed of some proper liquor and a syrup of sugar, serving as a vehicle to other forms of medicine.

2. An American drink composed of spirituous liquor, as brandy or whisky, sugar, pounded ice, and a seasoning of mint; called *mint-julep*.

Jūl'iăn, *a.* [L. *Julianus*, from *Julius*, Julius.] Of or pertaining to Julius Cæsar.

Julian calendar; the calendar as regulated by Julius Cæsar, giving every fourth year 366 days, the other years having 365 days each.

Julian epoch; the epoch of the commencement of the Julian calendar, which began in the forty-sixth year before Christ.

Julian period; a period consisting of 7980 Julian years. The number 7980 is formed by the continual multiplication of the three numbers 28, 19, and 15; that is, of the cycle of the sun, the cycle of the moon, and the indiction. The first year of the Christian era had 10 for its number in the cycle of the sun, 2 in the cycle of the moon, and 4 in the indiction. Now, the only number less than 7980 which, on being divided successively by 28, 19, and 15, leaves the respective remainders 10, 2, and 4, is 4714. Hence the first year of the Christian era corresponded with the year 4714 of the Julian period.

Julian year; the year, as regulated by Julius Cæsar, which continued to be used in England till 1752, when the Gregorian year, or new style, was adopted.

Jū́l′iăn-ist, *n.* One of a section of the early Coptic church, who held the body of Christ to be incorruptible; so called from Julian of Halicarnassus, their leader.

jū-li-enne′ (-en′), *n.* [Named after *Julien*, a French caterer of Boston.] A clear soup containing shredded vegetables.

jū′li-fŏrm, *a.* [L. *julus*, a catkin, and *forma*, form.] In botany, having the shape of a julus. [Rare.]

jū′lus, *n.*; *pl.* **jū′lī.** [L. *julus*, from Gr. *ioulos*, down, a catkin, centipede.] In botany, a catkin or ament.

Jū-lȳ′, *n.* The seventh month of the Gregorian year, during which the sun enters the sign Leo; it has thirty-one days.

Jū-lȳ′-flow″ẽr, *n.* The gillyflower, *Dianthus Caryophyllus.*

jū′märt, *n.* [Fr.] The fabled offspring of a bull and a mare.

jum′ble, *v.t.*; jumbled, *pt., pp.*; jumbling, *ppr.* [Freq. from *jump.*] To mix in a confused mass; to put or throw together without order; often followed by *together* or *up*; as, to *jumble together* passages of Scripture.

jum′ble, *v.i.* To meet, mix, or unite in a confused manner.

jum′ble, *n.* 1. A confused mixture, mass, or collection; disorder.

2. A small cake shaped like a ring.

jum′ble-bēad, *n.* A seed of the wild licorice, used in India for stringing as a bead.

jum′ble-ment, *n.* Confused mixture. [Obs.]

jum′blẽr, *n.* One who mixes things in confusion.

jum′bling-ly, *adv.* In a confused manner.

jum′bō, *n.* [So called from *Jumbo*, the largest captive elephant known.] Anything of unusual size; as, a *jumbo* of a building. [Colloq.]

jūme, *n.* [S. Am.] A South American plant which is unusually rich in carbonate of soda.

jū′ment, *n.* [Fr.] A beast of burden. [Obs.]

jump, *v.i.*; jumped (jumt), *pt., pp.*; jumping, *ppr.* [ME. *jumpen*; Sw. dial. *gumpa*, to spring, jump.]

1. To throw oneself in any direction by lifting the feet wholly from the ground and again alighting upon them; to leap; to spring; to bound.

2. To bound; to pass from object to object; to jolt.

3. To agree; to tally; to coincide.

In some sort it *jumps* with my humor.—Shak.

To jump at; to embrace or accept with eagerness; to catch at; as, *to jump at* an opportunity. [Colloq.]

jump, *v.t.* 1. To pass by a leap; to pass over eagerly or hastily; as, to *jump* a stream.

2. To cause to leap; as, to *jump* a horse over a fence.

3. To take possession of by stealth; as, to *jump* a miner's claim.

4. To elude; to run away to escape (an obligation); as, to *jump* one's bail or surety; in time of war, to *jump* a bounty.

5. In blacksmithing, to unite by a butt-weld.

6. To bore or drill with a jumper.

7. To skip over, to neglect; as, to *jump* pages in reading.

8. To jeopardize; to hazard. [Obs.]

To jump a claim; in the United States and Australia, to endeavor to obtain possession of, as the claim or land which has been taken up and occupied by a settler or squatter in a new country, the first occupant, by squatter law and custom, being entitled to the first claim on the land.

To jump one's bail; to abscond, thereby forfeiting one's bail-bonds. [Slang, U. S.]

jump, *n.* 1. The act of jumping; a leap; a spring; a bound.

2. The distance covered by a leap; hence, an omission; a passing over.

3. In geology, a dislocation of a stratum or vein.

4. In construction, an abrupt rise in a level course of brickwork or masonry to accommodate the work to the inequality of the ground.

5. A risk; a venture; a hazard. [Obs.]

Our fortune lies upon this *jump.* —Shak.

From the jump; from the beginning.

jump, *n.* [Prob. from Fr. *jupe*, a long petticoat or skirt.]

1. A kind of loose or limber stays or waistcoat formerly worn by women.

2. A short loose coat worn by men.

jump, *a.* and *adv.* I. *a.* Exact; matched. [Obs.]

II. *adv.* Exactly; as, *jump* at the dead of night. [Obs.]

jump′ẽr, *n.* 1. One who or that which jumps.

2. A long iron chisel pointed with steel used by masons and miners for boring holes in stones and rocks, as in cases when they are to be split or blasted by an explosive.

3. A maggot or larva of the cheese-fly, *Piophila casei.*

4. One of a sect of fanatics among the Calvinistic Methodists and others in Wales, from their violent agitations and motions during the time of divine worship.

5. A kind of sled which consists of a box placed on runners, each of which is in one piece, with a pole forming a thill.

6. A spring which controls the motion of the star-wheel of a watch; also, a pawl to prevent reverse motion of a ratchet-wheel of a repeating timepiece.

7. One who attempts to seize a land or mining claim already held by another.

jump′ẽr, *n.* [Compare *jump*, a coat.]

1. A kind of loose coat made of coarse goods and worn by workmen.

2. A fur jacket worn in the arctic regions.

jum′pẽr-stāy, *n.* In navigation, an additional stay for holding a yard or boom more securely in heavy weather.

jump′ing, *n.* The act of leaping or springing.

Jumping bean; same as *Jumping seed.*

Jumping deer; an American species of deer known also as the *black-tailed deer*; the muledeer.

Jumping hare; a South African rodent with very long tail and hind legs.

Jumping louse; a plant-louse of the family *Psyllidæ.*

Jumping mouse; see *Deer-mouse.*

Jumping mullet; a food-fish, *Mugil albula.*

Jumping rat; (a) a jumping mouse; (b) any rodent of the family *Dipodidæ.*

Jumping seed; the seed of a Mexican plant of the genus *Euphorbia*, which is inhabited by the larva of a tortricid moth, the movements of which cause the seed to roll and tumble about.

Jumping shrew; a shrewlike insectivore of the genus *Macroscelides.*

Jumping spider; a saltigrade spider which does not spin a web but captures its prey by leaping upon it.

jump′ing-jack, *n.* A toy made in imitation of the human figure whose jointed limbs are made to move by means of strings.

jump′-joint, *n.* A butt-joint; a joint made without lapping.

jump′-sēat, *n.* A folding carriage-seat; a carriage equipped with such a seat.

jump′-weld, *n.* A butt-weld.

Jun-cā′cē-æ, *n.pl.* [L. *juncus*, a rush, and *-aceæ.*] In botany, an order of monocotyledonous plants; the rush family.

jun-cā′ceous, *a.* Of or pertaining to the *Juncaceæ.*

jun′cāte, *n.* [Obs.] See *Junket.*

jun′cite, *n.* [L. *juncus*, a rush, and *-ite.*] In geology, a striated, grooved, and tapering rushlike fragment of a leaf occurring in the Devonian formation.

Jun′cō, *n.* [Origin obscure.] In zoölogy, a North American genus of the finch family; the snowbirds.

jun′cous, *a.* [L. *juncosus*, full of rushes, from *juncus*, a rush.] Of or pertaining to the order *Juncaceæ.*

junc′tion, *n.* [L. *junctio (-onis)*, from *jungere*, to join.]

1. The act or operation of joining; as, the *junction* of two armies or detachments.

2. Union; coalition; combination.

3. The place or point of union or meeting; especially, the crossing-place of two or more railroads.

junc′tion-plāte, *n.* A piece of boiler-plate used for uniting two plates which make a butt joint.

junc′ture, *n.* [L. *junctura*, from *jungere*, to join.]

1. A joining; union; amity; as, the *juncture* of hearts. [Obs.]

2. The line or point at which two bodies are joined; a joint; an articulation.

3. A point of time; a point rendered critical or important by a concurrence of circumstances.

Jun′cus, *n.* [L., a rush.] The type genus of the order *Juncaceæ* or rush family.

Jūne, *n.* [L. *Junius* (supply *mensis*, month), June, from *Junius*, a Roman gentile name.] The sixth month of the year, in which the sun enters the sign Cancer; it contains thirty days.

jū′nēat-ing, *n.* See *Jenneting.*

Jūne′ber″ry, *n.* A small North American tree, *Amelanchier Canadensis*, which bears a berry of pleasant flavor; also, its fruit or berry; called also *shad-bush* and *service-berry.*

Jūne′-bug, *n.* 1. In the northern part of the United States, any large brown beetle of the genus *Lachnosterna.*

2. In the southern part of the United States, a large greenish lamellicorn beetle of the genus *Allorhina.*

Jūne′-grȧss, *n.* The blue grass of Kentucky; *Poa pratensis.*

Jun-gẽr-man′ni-ȧ, *n.* [Named after *Jungermann*, a German botanist.] In botany, the type genus of the order *Jungermanniaceæ.*

Jun-gẽr-man-ni-ā′cē-æ, *n.pl.* [*Jungermannia* and *-aceæ.*] An order of cellular cryptogams; the scale-mosses.

jun-gẽr-man-ni-ā′ceous, *a.* Of or pertaining to the order *Jungermanniaceæ.*

jun′gle, *n.* [Hind. *jangal*, a desert, forest, jungle, from Sans. *jaṅgala*, dry, desert.] A dense tropical thicket of rank vegetation, including trees, grasses, reeds, vines, and the like; also, the land covered by such a growth; as, to be lost in the *jungle.*

jun′gle-bēar, *n.* The sloth-bear of India.

jun′gle-ben″dy, *n.* An East Indian tree, *Tetrameles nudiflora*; called also *weenong.*

jun′gle-cock, *n.* See *Jungle-fowl.*

jun′gle-fē″vẽr, *n.* A malarial fever prevalent in the jungle districts of India and Africa; called also *hill-fever.*

jun′gle-fowl, *n.* 1. Any one of several species of wild fowl of the genus *Gallus*, found in India, especially *Gallus sonnerati.*

2. An Australian wild fowl, as *Megapodius tumulus.*

jun′gle-nail, *n.* An East Indian leguminous tree, *Acacia tomentosa.*

jun′gle-sheep, *n.* A small East Indian deer; the muntjac.

jun′gly, *a.* Consisting of jungles; abounding with jungles.

jūn′iŏr, *a.* [L., contr. of *juvenior*, compar. of *juvenis*, young.]

1. Younger; not as old as another; as, a *junior* partner in a company. It is applied to the younger of two persons bearing the same name in one family or town, and opposed to *elder* or *senior*; as, John Doe, *junior.*

2. Noting the third year of the four-year collegiate course in American colleges, or the first year in certain seminaries; pertaining to the last year or class but one.

3. Inferior in rank or more recent in office; as, a *junior* captain or *junior* counsel.

4. Pertaining to youth or an earlier time in one's life.

jūn′iŏr, *n.* 1. A person younger than another.

The fools, my *juniors* by a year. —Swift.

2. One in the junior year of his collegiate course.

jū′ni-pẽr, *n.* [L. *juniperus*, juniper, properly youth-producing; *juvenis*, young, and *parere*, to produce.] A coniferous tree of the genus *Juniperus*, closely allied to the cedar, yielding a rich aromatic juice and a valuable oil which is used in flavoring gin and for other purposes, its wood also being valued for cabinetwork.

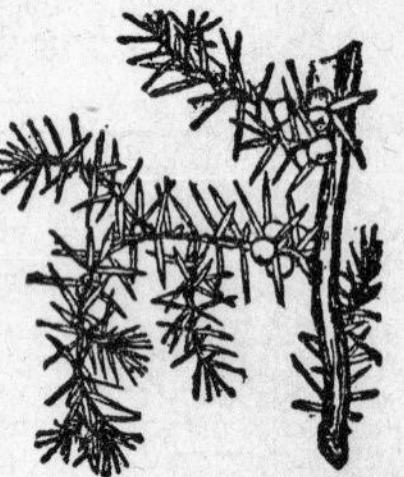
Juniper (*Juniperus communis*).

jū′ni-pẽr-in, *n.* A black or yellow resinous extract of juniper-berries.

jū′ni-pẽr-ite, *n.* [L. *juniperus*, juniper, and *-ite.*] A fossil tree related to the juniper.

Jū-nip′e-rus, *n.* [L., juniper.] A genus of evergreen trees and shrubs of the family *Coniferæ.*

jū′ni-pẽr-wŏrm, *n.* The larva of a moth, *Drepanodes varus*, which lives upon the leaves of the juniper.

junk, *n.*, a variant of *chunk.*

junk, *n.* [ME. *jonke*; OFr. *jonc*, a rush; Port. *junco*, junk, a rush; L. *juncus*, a rush; so called from rushes being used to weave ropes.]

1. Among seamen, a collection of old cable or old cordage, used for making points, gaskets, mats, etc.; when untwisted and picked to pieces, it forms oakum for filling the seams of ships.

2. Scraps of old metal, paper, glass, and other refuse, taken collectively.

3. Salt beef supplied to vessels for long voyages; so called from its resembling old ropes' ends in hardness and toughness.

The purser's *junk* had become tough. —Dickens.

4. The mass of cellular tissue in the head of a sperm-whale, containing oil and spermaceti.

junk, *n.* [Sp. and Port. *junco*, from Malay *ajong*; Chinese *chw′an, chw′en*, a ship, boat, junk.] A flat-bottomed ship used in China and Japan, often of large dimensions, with a high forecastle and poop, and ordinarily with three masts of considerable height, each mast being in one piece.

junk′=bot″tle, *n.* A thick strong bottle, usually made of stout green glass.

junk′=deal″ẽr, *n.* The proprietor of a junk-shop; one who buys and sells junk.

jun′kẽr, *n.* [G., contr. of *jung herr*; *jung*, young, and *herr*, master, lord, proprietor.]

1. A young German aristocrat, especially one of a military family.

2. [J—] A member of the Prussian aristocratic party of which Bismarck was formerly the leader.

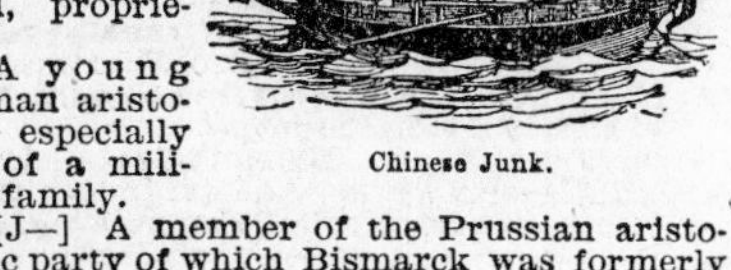

Chinese Junk.

Jun′kẽr-iṣm, *n.* The policy of the aristocratic party in Prussia.

jun′ket, *n.* [Formerly also *juncate*, from It. *giuncata*, a sweetmeat, cream-cheese, from L. *juncus*, a rush; so called because brought to market on rushes.]

1. A kind of custard of curds, cream, and sugar.

2. Any kind of delicate food.

3. A feast; a picnic; a gay entertainment of any kind; specifically, in United States politics, a tour of public officials, ostensibly on public business, but having the character of a picnic.

jun′ket, *v.i.*; junketed, *pt. pp.*; junketing, *ppr.* To feast; to banquet; to take part in a gay entertainment; to picnic.

jun′ket, *v.t.* To furnish with entertainment; to give a feast to.

jun′ket-ing, *n.* A festivity; a gay entertainment of any kind; a picnic.

junk′=hook, *n.* A hook used on board a whaling-vessel for hoisting blubber on deck.

junk′=ring, *n.* In steam-engines, a ring fitting into a groove round a piston to keep it steam-tight.

junk′=shop, *n.* A shop where junk, such as old metal, bottles, rags, etc., is bought and sold.

junk′=vat, *n.* In tanning, a tank or vat for containing the spent tan-liquor.

junk′=wäd, *n.* A wad used in testing muzzle-loading cannon.

Jū′nō, *n.* [L.] 1. In Roman mythology, the queen of heaven, sister and wife of Jupiter, and next to him the highest divinity.

2. In astronomy, one of the small planets or asteroids which revolve round the sun between the orbits of Mars and Jupiter.

Jū-nō′ni-ăn, *a.* Pertaining to or having the characteristics of Juno; proud; haughty.

jun′tȧ, *n.* [Sp., from L. *juncta*, f. of *junctus*, pp. of *jungere*, to join.]

1. A meeting; a council; specifically, a grand council of state in Spain.

Juno, from the Capitoline Museum.

2. In Spanish-speaking countries, a deliberative representative assembly or committee; as, the Panama *junta* of 1903; the Filipino *junta* of 1898.

jun′tō, *n.* [An erroneous form of *junta*.]

1. A select council or assembly, which deliberates in secret on any affair of government.

2. A cabal; a meeting for secret deliberation and intrigue for party purposes; a faction; as, the *junto* of English ministers in the reign of William III.

jup′är-dle, jup′är-tie, *n.* [Obs.] See *Jeopardy*.

jū′pȧ-ti=pälm (-päm), *n.* [*Jupati*, S. Am. name, and E. *palm*.] A Brazilian palm, *Raphia tædigera*, whose enormous leaves and leaf-stalks are used by the natives for a variety of purposes.

jūpe, *n.* See *Jupon*.

Jū′pi-tẽr, *n.* [L. *Juppiter* or *Jupiter*, from Old L. *Jovis*, Jove, and *pater*, father.]

1. The chief divinity of the Romans; Jove; the equivalent of the Greek Zeus. As the deity presiding over the sky, he was considered as the originator of all atmospheric changes.

2. One of the superior planets, remarkable for its brightness; it is the largest body of the solar system except the sun itself.

Jū′pi-tẽr′ṣ=bēard, *n.* 1. An evergreen plant, *Anthyllis Barba-Jovis*.

2. The houseleek.

3. A European perennial herb, *Centranthus ruber*.

Jū′pi-tẽr′ṣ=flow″ẽr, *n.* The pink, genus *Dianthus*.

Jū′pi-tẽr′ṣ=nut, *n.* The European walnut, of the genus *Juglans*.

Jū′pi-tẽr′ṣ=staff, *n.* The common mullen, *Verbascum Thapsus*.

jū-pon′, jūp-pon′, *n.* [Fr. *jupon*, from *jupe*; Sp. *juba*; Ar. *jubbah*, *al-jubbah*, a garment so called.]

1. In ancient armor, a tight-fitting military garment without sleeves, worn over the armor and descending just below the hips.

2. A petticoat.

Jupiter, from an antique statue.

Jū′rȧ, *n.* In geology, the Jurassic period or formation.

jū′răl, *a.* [L. *jus*, *juris*, right, law, and *-al*.] Pertaining to natural or absolute rights as defined by jurisprudence.

jū″rȧ-men-tä′dō, *n.* A Filipino Mohammedan who takes a solemn oath before a priest that he will die killing Christians.

jū-rȧ-men′tum, *n.* [L.] An oath.

jū′rănt, *n.* [Fr. *jurant*, ppr. of *jurer*, to swear.] One who is under oath.

Jū-ras′siç, *a.* and *n.* I. *a.* 1. Pertaining to the Jura Mountains, lying between France and Switzerland.

2. Of or pertaining to the geological period known as the Jurassic.

II. *n.* In geology, the middle Mesozoic period.

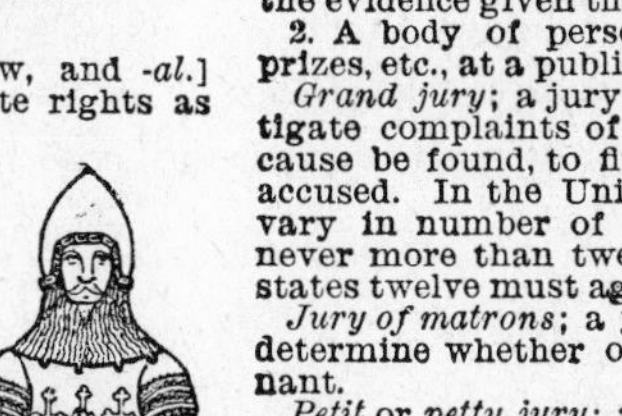

Jupon.

jū′rat, *n.* [Fr. *jurat*, from LL. *juratus*, lit., one sworn, from L. *juratus*, pp. of *jurare*, to swear.]

1. In England, a magistrate in some corporations; an alderman; an assistant to a bailiff.

> Jersey has a bailiff and twelve sworn *jurats* to govern the island. —Craig.

2. In law, the memorandum of the time when, the place where, and the person before whom an affidavit is sworn.

jū′rȧ-tō-ry, *a.* [LL. *juratorius*, from L. *jurator*, a sworn witness, from *jurare*, to swear.] Comprising an oath; as, *juratory* caution.

jur-diç′ci-oun (-un), *n.* [Obs.] See *Jurisdiction*.

jūr′dŏn, *n.* [Obs.] See *Jordan*.

jū′rel, *n.* [Sp.] A food-fish of the genus *Caranx*, found along the southern coast of the United States.

jū-rid′iç, *a.* Juridical. [Rare.]

jū-rid′i-çăl, *a.* [L. *juridicus*, from *jus*, *juris*, law, and *dicare*, point out, declare.]

1. Acting in the distribution of justice; pertaining to a judge.

2. Used in courts of law or tribunals of justice.

Juridical days; those days on which courts are in session.

jū-rid′i-çăl-ly, *adv.* According to forms of law, or proceedings in tribunals of justice; with legal authority.

jū-ris-çon′sult, *n.* [L. *jurisconsultus*; *jus*, *juris*, law, and *consultus*, pp. of *consulere*, to consult.] A man learned in the law; a counselor-at-law; one versed in civil law; a jurist.

jū-ris-diç′tion, *n.* [L. *jurisdictio* (*-onis*), *juris dictio*, administration of the law; *jus*, *juris*, right, law, and *dictio* (*-onis*), from *dicere*, to speak, declare.]

1. The legal power or authority of doing justice in cases of complaint; the power of executing the laws and distributing justice; as, certain suits or actions, or the cognizance of certain crimes, are within the *jurisdiction* of a court, that is, within the limits of its authority or commission.

2. The power or right of exercising authority.

3. The district or limit within which power may be exercised.

jū-ris-diç′tion-ăl, *a.* Pertaining to jurisdiction.

jū-ris-diç′tive, *a.* Having jurisdiction.

jū-ris-prū′dence, *n.* [L. *jurisprudentia*; *jus*, *juris*, right, law, and *prudentia*, a foreseeing, knowledge, skill.] The science of law; the knowledge of the laws, customs, and rights of men in a state or community, necessary for the due administration of justice.

Medical jurisprudence; forensic medicine.

jū-ris-prū′dent, *n.* An expert in jurisprudence.

jū-ris-prū′dent, *a.* Understanding law.

jū-ris-prū-den′tiăl, *a.* Pertaining to jurisprudence.

jū′rist, *n.* [Fr. *juriste*; LL. *jurista*, from L. *jus*, *juris*, right, law.] A man who professes the science of law; one versed in the law, particularly in the civil law; an author of legal treatises.

jū-ris′tiç, jū-ris′tiç-ăl, *a.* Pertaining to a jurist; juridical; legal.

jū′rŏr, *n.* [ME. *jurour*; OFr. *jureur*, *jureor*, from L. *jurator*, a swearer, one who takes an oath, from *jurare*, to swear.]

1. One who serves on a jury; a juryman.

2. One of a body of men selected to adjudge prizes, etc., at a public exhibition.

jū′ry, *n.*; *pl.* **jū′rieṣ**. [OFr. *juree*, an oath, judicial inquest, from LL. *jurata*, a jury, a sworn body of men, properly f. pp. of L. *jurare*, to swear, to take an oath, from *jus*, *juris*, law.]

1. In law, a number of qualified persons, selected in the manner prescribed by law, impaneled and sworn to inquire into and try any matter of fact, and to declare the truth on the evidence given them in the case.

2. A body of persons selected to adjudge prizes, etc., at a public exhibition.

Grand jury; a jury which is called to investigate complaints of criminal offenses and, if cause be found, to find true bills against the accused. In the United States, grand juries vary in number of members but there are never more than twenty-three and in all the states twelve must agree to an indictment.

Jury of matrons; a jury of women chosen to determine whether or not a woman is pregnant.

Petit or *petty jury*; a jury consisting usually of twelve men, selected in court to try issues of fact.

Special jury; a jury called for a particular purpose, as a jury of a certain class or trade called to determine a question relating to their occupation or profession.

jū′ry, *a.* [Prob. from *jury*, n., and due to sailors' humor.] Temporary; makeshift; used in composition; as, a *jury*-mast.

jū′ry=box, *n.* The place in a court where the jury sit.

jū′ry=leg, *n.* An artificial leg. [Slang.]

jū′ry-măn, *n.*; *pl.* **jū′ry-men.** One who is impaneled on a jury, or who serves as a juror.

jū′ry=mȧst, *n.* A mast erected in a ship temporarily, to supply the place of one carried away.

jū′ry=rigged (-rigd), *a.* Rigged in a temporary manner.

jū′ry=rud″dẽr, *n.* A temporary sort of rudder used when an accident has befallen the original one.

jus′si, *n.* [A Manila word.] A fine vegetable fiber used in making women's garments in the Philippines.

just, *a.* [OFr. *juste*; L. *justus*, lawful, rightful, proper, from *jus*, right, law.]

1. Upright; honest; having principles of rectitude; conforming to principles of rectitude in social conduct; righteous.

2. Equitable in the distribution of justice; impartial; fair.

3. Conformed to fact; exact; accurate; precise; neither too much nor too little; neither more nor less; as, *just* expressions or representations; a *just* description.

4. In music, not tempered; correct or pure harmonically; in exact tune.

Syn.—Exact, honest, impartial, precise, proper, upright.

just, *adv.* 1. Close or closely; near or nearly in place; as, he stood *just* by the speaker, and heard what he said.

2. Exactly or nearly in time; almost; immediately; as, *just* at that moment he arose.

3. Narrowly; barely; only; as, he *just* escaped.

4. Exactly; nicely; accurately; as, *just* a fit; *just* three inches.

just, joust (just *or* jŭst), *n.* A mock encounter on horseback; a combat in which the combatants pushed with lances and swords; in the days of chivalry, a tilt; one of the sports of a tournament.

just, joust, *v.i.* [ME. *justen*, *justien*; OFr. *juster*, *joster*, *jouster*, from LL. *juxtare*, to come together, approach, tilt, from L. *juxta*, close to, hard by.] To engage in mock fight on horseback; to tilt.

jūste=au=çorps (zhūst-ō-kor), *n.* [Fr., close to the body.] A close body-coat, similar to, if not identical with, the jupon.

just′ẽr, *n.* One who participates in a just.

jus′tice, *n.* [Fr., from L. *justitia*, justice, from *justus*, lawful, rightful, just, from *jus*, law, right.]

1. The virtue which consists in giving to every one what is his due; practical conformity to the principles of rectitude, in the dealings of

men with each other; honesty; integrity in commerce or mutual intercourse.

2. Impartiality; equal distribution of right in expressing opinions; fair representation of facts.

3. Equity; agreeableness to right; as, he proved the *justice* of his claim.

4. Vindictive retribution; merited punishment; as, sooner or later, *justice* overtakes the criminal.

5. Right; application of equity; as, his arm will do him *justice*.

6. A person commissioned to hold court, or to try and decide controversies and administer justice to individuals; as, the chief *justice* of the Supreme Court.

Justice of the peace; an inferior magistrate having the power to try minor cases and discharge certain other legal functions within a specified district.

Syn.—Equity, law, impartiality, fairness, right, reasonableness, propriety, uprightness, desert, integrity.

jus′tice, *v.t.* To administer justice. [Obs.]

jus′tice-à-ble, *a.* Liable to judicial trial. [Obs.]

jus′tice-hood, *n.* Justiceship. [Rare.]

jus′tice-ment, *n.* Judicial procedure. [Obs.]

jus′ti-cēr, *n.* An administrator of justice. [Obs.]

jus′tice-ship, *n.* The office or dignity of a justice.

jus-ti′ci-à-ble (-tish′i-), *a.* Proper to be examined in a court of justice. [Obs.]

jus-ti′ci-ăr (-tish′i-), *n.* Same as *Justiciary*.

jus-ti′ci-ā-ry (-tish′i-ā-),*n.*; *pl.* **jus-ti′ci-ā-ries.**

1. An administrator of justice.

2. In early English history, an officer whose functions were the administration of both government and justice.

3. One who boasts of his own justice. [Obs.]

jus-ti′ci-ā-ry, *a.* Of a justiciary; legal.

jus′ti-çō, jus′ti-çōat, *n.* Same as *Juste-au-corps*.

jus′ti-fī-à-ble, *a.* That may be justified, vindicated, or defended.

jus′ti-fī-à-ble-ness, *n.* The quality of being justifiable.

jus′ti-fī-à-bly, *adv.* In a justifiable manner.

jus″ti-fi-cā′tion, *n.* 1. The act of justifying; a showing to be just or conformable to law, rectitude, or propriety; vindication; defense.

2. In law, (a) the showing of a sufficient reason in court why a defendant did what he is called to answer; (b) proof of qualification as bailor or surety, as by showing ownership of enough property.

3. In theology, remission of sin, and absolution from guilt and punishment; an act of free grace by which God pardons the sinner, and accepts him as righteous, on account of the atonement of Christ.

4. The act of arranging, fitting, or making uniform, as lines of type.

jus′tif-i-çà-tive, *a.* Justifying; vindicatory.

jus′ti-fi-çā-tŏr, *n.* One who justifies.

jus-tif′i-çà-tō-ry, *a.* Vindicatory; defensory.

jus′ti-fī-ēr, *n.* 1. One who justifies; one who vindicates, supports, or defends.

2. One who or that which justifies lines of type, as an automatic attachment to a typesetting machine.

3. In type-founding, one who adjusts matrices for use in a mold.

jus′ti-fȳ, *v.t.*; justified, *pt.*, *pp.*; justifying, *ppr.* [ME. *justifien*; OFr. *justifier*; LL. *justificare*, to act justly toward, to justify; L. *justus*, just, and *-ficare*, from *facere*, to do, make.]

1. To prove or show to be just, or conformable to law, right, justice, propriety, or duty; to defend or maintain; to vindicate as right.

2. To declare free from guilt or blame; to absolve; to clear.

3. In theology, to pardon and clear from guilt; to treat as just, though guilty and deserving punishment; to pardon.

4. To make exact; to cause to fit, as the parts of a complex object; to adjust, as the words in lines in printing, by proper use of spaces.

5. To prove by evidence; to verify; to establish; as, to *justify* the truth of an observation; to *justify* one's qualification as surety.

Syn.—Excuse, defend, warrant, maintain, vindicate.

jus′ti-fȳ, *v.i.* 1. In printing, to agree; to suit; to conform exactly; to form an even surface or true line with something else.

2. In law, to prove the sufficiency of bail or sureties in point of property.

Jus-tin′i-ăn, *a.* Of or pertaining to the code of laws arranged by the Roman emperor Justinian.

jus′tle (-l), *n.* A jostle. [Obs.]

jus′tle, *v.t.* and *v.i.* To jostle. [Rare.]

just′ly, *adv.* In a just manner; fairly; accurately.

just′ness, *n.* 1. Accuracy; exactness; conformity to truth; as, the *justness* of a description.

2. The quality of being just; justice; reasonableness; equity; as, the *justness* of a cause.

jut, *v.i.* [A variant of *jet*.]

1. To extend forward; to project beyond the main body; as, the *jutting* part of a building.

2. To butt; to strike. [Obs.]

jut, *n.* A shooting forward; a projection.

jūte, *n.* [Hind. *jūt*; Sans. *jūta*, matted hair, *jaṭā*, matted hair, fibrous roots.]

1. A fibrous substance resembling hemp, obtained from the East Indian plants, *Corchorus olitorius* and *Corchorus capsularis*. It is much used in the manufacture of bagging, carpets, etc.

2. A plant which yields the fiber.

American jute; a fiber resembling the jute of East India but obtained from the velvetleaf, *Abutilon Avicennæ*.

Jute (*Corchorus capsularis*).

Jūte, *n.* One of a tribe of Low Germans who originally lived in Jutland and who accompanied the Angles and Saxons in their invasion of England in the fifth century.

Jut′lănd-ēr, *n.* An inhabitant of Jutland.

Jut′lănd-ish, *a.* Belonging to or like Jutland or the Jutlanders.

jut′ting-ly, *adv.* Projectingly.

jut′ty, *v.t.* and *v.i.* To jut; to extend beyond. [Obs.]

jut′ty, *n.* A projection in a building; also, a pier or mole; a jetty. [Obs.]

jut′=win″dōw, *n.* A window that projects from the line of a building; a bay-window.

jū′ve-năl, *n.* A youth. [Obs.]

jū-ve-nes′cence, *n.* A growing young.

jū-ve-nes′cent, *a.* [Rare.] Becoming young.

jū′ve-nile, *a.* [L. *juvenilis*, from *juvenis*, young.]

1. Young; youthful; as, *juvenile* years of age.

2. Pertaining or suited to youth; as, *juvenile* sports.

Syn.—Youthful, young, infantine, boyish, girlish, early, immature, adolescent, pubescent.

jū′ve-nile, *n.* A youth; also, a book for the young.

jū′ve-nile-ness, *n.* Juvenility. [Rare.]

jū-ve-nil′i-ty, *n.* 1. Youthfulness.

2. Collectively, the manners, customs, or crudities of youth.

jū′vi-à, *n.* The tree on which brazil-nuts grow, *Bertholletia excelsa*.

jụ-wăn′sà, *n.* The camel's-thorn.

jū-wīṣe′, *n.* [Obs.] Same as *Juise*.

jux′tà-pōṣe, *v.t.*; juxtaposed, *pt.*, *pp.*; juxtaposing, *ppr.* To place side by side.

jux-tà-poṣ′it, *v.t.* To juxtapose. [Rare.]

jux″tà-pō-ṣi′tion, *n.* A placing or being placed in nearness or contiguity; the state of being side by side.

jym′ōld, *n.* [Obs.] Same as *Gimbal*.

jyn′tee, *n.* [E. Ind.] An East Indian leguminous plant, *Sesbania Ægyptiaca*, which furnishes charcoal for use in making gunpowder.

K

K (kā). The eleventh letter and eighth consonant of the English alphabet. It came into the English through the Latin and Greek from the Phenician alphabet, where it was eleventh in order. The form and sound came from the Greek and early Latin. It was little used during the classical period, *c* being substituted for it, and on this account it did not descend to the Romanic languages and seldom appeared in them except in some foreign words. It was seldom used in Anglo-Saxon, the *k* sound being represented by *c*. During the Middle English period, from the thirteenth century on, it came to be used to represent the *k* sound where *c* would be ambiguous. In the middle and at the end of a word, *ck* represents *k*, as in *back*, *dicker*. Before *n*, *k* is silent, as in *knife*, *knight*, *knee*. *K* has but one sound and is classed as a guttural, or back-palatal. Etymologically, it is most closely related to *c*, *g*, and *h*.

K, k, *as a symbol*. In the Roman notation, *K* represents the number 250; *K̄*, 250,000. [Obs.]

In chemistry, *K* stands for *potassium*.

As an abbreviation, *k* stands for carat; *K* for king, kings, knight, etc.

Kä-ā′bà, Çà-ā′bà, *n.* [Ar. *ka'bah*, a square building, from *ka'b*, a cube.] A cube-shaped flat-roofed shrine in the great mosque at Mecca, toward which all Mohammedans turn when they pray. It contains the sacred black stone which is said to have descended from heaven and which is fastened in the wall at a convenient height to receive the kisses of pilgrims.

kāa′mà, *n.* Same as *Caama*.

kab′à-là, *n.* Same as *Cabala*.

kà-bas′sōu, çà-bas′sōu, *n.* [S. Am. name.] An armadillo of the genus *Xenurus*; specifically, the twelve-banded armadillo.

kà-bob′, *n.* and *v.t.* Same as *Cabob*.

kà-bọọk′, *n.* In Ceylon, a kind of building-stone which becomes very hard after being quarried; written also *cabook*.

Kà-bȳle′, *n.* [Fr. *Kabyle*; Ar. *Qabāil*, properly pl. of *qabīla*, a tribe, horde.]

1. In ethnology, a member of a Berber race in Algiers and Tunis.

2. A dialect among the Berbers, spoken by the Kabyles.

kad′dēr, *n.* A caddow.

kä′di (*or* kā′), *n.* [Turk. *kadi*, *kazi*; Ar. *qadi*, a judge, magistrate, from *qaday*, to judge.] Among the Moslems, a judge; written also *cadi*.

kä-di-les′kēr, *n.* A Turkish judge of superior rank whose jurisdiction was formerly military as well as civil.

kà-fāl′, *n.* [Ar.] A tree yielding aromatic resin and wood.

Kaf′fīr, *n.* and *a.* See *Kafir*.

kaf′fle, *n.* Same as *Coffle*.

kä′fī-là, *n.* [Ar. *qāfila*, a caravan.] A pack-train of camels; spelled also *caffila*, *cafilah*, *kafilah*.

Kaf′īr, *n.* [Ar. *kāfir*, an unbeliever, infidel.]

1. Among Mohammedans, an infidel, a term of reproach applied to Christians and pagans.

2. In ethnology, a member of one of the races of South Africa of which the Zulus are best known, characterized by athletic bodies, tufted woolly hair, bronze complexions, and acute intellect.

3. The language of the Kafirs; sometimes called *Zulu-Kafir*.

4. A member of a race inhabiting the mountainous country north and east of Afghanistan.

Kaf′īr, *a.* Relating to the Kafirs, their language or their customs; written also *Caffer*, *Caffre*, *Kaffer*, *Kaffre*.

Kaf′īr=bọọm, *n.* In botany, a leguminous tree of South Africa, of the genus *Erythrina*.

Kaf′īr=bread (-bred), *n.* The pith from the stem of a tree in South Africa, used by the natives for food; also, the tree itself, *Encephalartos Caffer*.

Kaf′īr=çorn, *n.* Indian millet.

kaf′tà, *n.* [Ar.] The leaves of a celastraceous shrub, *Catha edulis*, of Arabia, used in making a beverage.

kaf′tăn, *n.* Same as *Caftan*.

kä′gō, *n.* [Japan.] In Japan, a chair made of basketwork and slung from a pole to be borne by two men in carrying a traveler; written also *cango*.

kä′gū, *n.* [Native name.] A wading bird of New Caledonia distinguished by its long erectile nuchal crest and for its being the only representative of its family, the *Rhinochetidæ*; written also *kagou*.

kä-gū-ăn′, *n.* Same as *Flying-lemur*.

kà-hä′ni, *n.* In the Levant, a kind of attorney or notary public.

kä-hau′, *n.* [Native name, so called from its cry.] In zoölogy, the proboscis-monkey, *Nasalis larvatus*, of Borneo, remarkable for the great length of its nose.

kä″hi-kä-tē′ȧ, *n.* [Maori name.] A tall coniferous tree of New Zealand, *Podocarpus dacrydioides*, whose fruit is used as food by the natives. Colonists call it *white pine*. Written also *kai-katea*, *kakikatea*, and *kakaterro*.

kai′-ap″ple, *n.* Same as *Kei-apple*.

kāil, *n.* Same as *Kale*.

kāils, *n.pl.* [ME. *kayle*; D. *kegel*, a pin, ninepin; G. *kegel*; Dan. *kegle*, a cone, ninepin.] An old English game played by rolling iron balls among nine holes made in the ground; also applied to various early games in which ninepins were used; spelled also *kayles*.

kāi-mȧ-kam′, *n.* [Turk. *kāimakām*, from Ar. *qāim-makām*, a lieutenant, from *qāim*, firm, fixed, and *makām*, a deputy.] In Turkey, an officer of the rank of lieutenant-colonel in the army, or of lieutenant-governor in the civil service.

kāin, *n.* In Scotland, a duty paid in kind by a tenant to his landlord, as poultry, eggs, butter, etc.

kaī′nite, *n.* [Gr. *kainos*, new, recent, and *-ite*.] In mineralogy, a compound salt used for fertilizing soils, found in salt-mines at Stassfurt, Germany.

Kaī-nō-zō′iç, *a.* Same as *Cænozoic*.

kä-ïque′ (-ēk′), *n.* Same as *Caique*.

kaī′rin, kaī′rine, *n.* [Perhaps from Gr. *kairos*, the right time, and *-in*, *-ine*.] In chemistry, a bitter crystalline substance used in medicine as an antipyretic; hydrochlorid of kairolin.

kaī′rō-lin, kaī′rō-line, *n.* [*Kairin*, and L. *oleum*, oil.] In chemistry, an oily compound, $C_{10}H_{13}N$, used as a febrifuge.

Kaī′sēr, *n.* [G. from L. *Cæsar*, Cæsar.]

1. The German form of Cæsar, the title of a long line of Roman emperors, and until recent times the title of the ruler of the German empire; as, *Kaiser* Wilhelm.

2. [k—] An emperor; one in supreme authority.

kaī′sēr-ship, *n.* The office or functions of a kaiser; a rulership.

kȧ-jụ-gä′rụ, *n.* [Malay.] The aromatic wood of a Malayan tree, *Gonystylus Miquelianus*.

kä′kȧ, *n.* [Maori.] A parrot of New Zealand of the genus *Nestor*; specifically, the brown parrot, *Nestor meridionalis*.

kä-kȧ-pō′, *n.* [Maori.] The owl-parrot or night-kaka, *Strigops habroptilus*, a small parrot having the habits of an owl; called also *night-parrot* and *ground-parrot*, the latter because of its occupying a hole in the ground during the day.

kak-ȧ-ral′i, *n.* [S. Am.] A large tree common in British Guiana, *Lecythis Ollaria*, the wood of which is very durable in salt water, resisting the depredations of sea-worms and barnacles; written also *kakaralli*.

kȧ-kē-mō′nō, *n.* [Japan.] In Japanese fine art, a picture painted in transparent colors upon a strip or scroll of silk, gauze, or paper, and mounted on rollers for hanging upon a wall; distinguished from *makimono*, a hand-scroll.

kä′kī, *n.* [Japan.] A Japanese or Chinese tree, *Diospyros Kaki*, bearing fruit about as large as an apple and resembling a date or persimmon.

kak-is-toç′rȧ-cy, *n.*; *pl.* **kak-is-toç′rȧ-cieṣ** [Gr. *kakistos*, superl. of *kakos*, bad, and *-kratia*, from *kratein*, to rule.] Dominance of the worst men in the state; opposed to *aristocracy*.

kak′ō-dyl, kak′ō-dyle, *n.* Same as *Cacodyl*.

kȧ-kox′ēne, kȧ-kox′īne, *n.* Same as *Cacoxene*.

kā′lan, *n.* A fur-bearing animal, *Enhydris marina*, of the North Pacific coast, closely allied to the common otter and much valued for the quality of its fur; called also *sea-otter*.

kä-lȧ-sie′, *n.* in zoölogy, a monkey, *Semnopithecus rubicundus*, of Borneo, belonging to the family of sacred monkeys and characterized by a tuft of long hair on its head.

kāle, kāil, *n.* [Scot. *kale*, *kail*; Gael. *cal*, cabbage; AS. *cawl*, *cawel*, from L. *caulis*, a cabbage stalk, cabbage, stalk or stem of a plant.]

1. A kind of cabbage, having the leaves generally curled or wrinkled, but not formed into a close, round head; loosely, in Scotland, any kind of cabbage or greens.

2. A kind of broth made in Scotland with kale and other vegetables; by extension, a dinner. [Scot.]

kȧ-leeġe′, *n.* [E. Ind. *kalij*.] Any one of several species of pugnacious drumming pheasants of India; spelled also *kalij* and *caliage*.

kȧ-leī′dō-grȧph, *n.* [Gr. *kalos*, beautiful, *eidos*, form, and *graphein*, to write.] An instrument for projecting the figures of a kaleidoscope upon a screen.

kȧ-leī′dō-phōne, kȧ-leī′dō-phon, *n.* [Gr. *kalos*, beautiful, and *eidos*, form, and *phōnē*, sound.] An instrument for i llustrating the phenomena of sound-waves; written also *caleidophone*.

kȧ-leī′dō-sçōpe, *n.* [Gr. *kalos*, beautiful, and *eidos*, form, and *skopein*, to view.] An optical instrument which, by an arrangement of reflecting surfaces, exhibits an infinite variety of beautiful colors and symmetrical forms of its contents; an invention of Sir David Brewster about 1815.

kȧ-leī-dō-sçop′iç, *a.* Resembling the figures in a kaleidoscope; going through many and varied changes in form.

kȧ-leī-dō-sçop′iç-ăl, *a.* Kaleidoscopic.

kal′en-dăr, *n.* Same as *Calendar*.

kal-en-dā′ri-ăl, *a.* Same as *Calendarial*.

kal′en-dēr, *n.* Same as *Calender*.

kal′endṣ, *n.pl.* Same as *Calends*.

kāle′-tūr″nip, *n.* A kind of cabbage, *Brassica oleracea*, developing into a turnip form just above the ground; a turnip-cabbage; kohlrabi.

kāle′-yärd, *n.* A kitchen-garden; a cabbage-garden. [Scot.]

kā′lī, *n.* [Ar. *qali*, from *qalay*, to fry.] A plant, *Salsola Kali*, the saltwort or glasswort, the ashes of which are used in making glass.

Kä′lī, *n.* [Sans. *kālī*.] In Hindu mythology, the goddess of destruction.

kä′lī, *n.* [Per. *kālī*, a large carpet.] Among the Persians, a very large ruglike carpet with long nap, placed in the middle of a room; distinguished from a carpet without nap.

kā′lif, *n.* Same as *Calif*.

kā′li-fọrm, *a.* [Ar. *qali*, saltwort, and L. *forma*, form.] Having the form of saltwort.

kȧ-liġ′e-nous, *a.* [Ar. *qali*, saltwort, and Gr. *-genēs*, producing.] Having the property of forming an alkali when oxidized; as, potassium and sodium are *kaligenous* metals.

kā′li-nīte, *n.* [G. *kali*, potash, *-n-*, and *-ite*.] In mineralogy, native alum.

kā′li-um, *n.* [From Ar. *qali*, saltwort.] A chemical name for potassium, and the source of its symbol K.

kal′ki, *n.* [Sans.] The tenth incarnation of Vishnu.

Kal′mi-ȧ, *n.* [Named after Peter *Kalm*, a Swedish botanist.] A genus of evergreen shrubs, natives of North America, chiefly of the Appalachian region; various species are called *calico-bush*, *laurel*, *mountain-laurel*.

Kal′muck, *n.* [Russ. *Kalmuik′*.]

1. One of a branch of Mongolians inhabiting the western part of China.

2. The language of the Kalmucks.

3. [k—] A kind of shaggy cloth resembling bearskin; also, a coarse cotton cloth made in Persia.

kȧ-long′, *n.* [E. Ind.] A fox-bat; specifically, the *Pteropus edulis*.

kȧ-loy′ēr, *n.* Same as *Caloyer*.

kal′pȧ, *n.* [Sans.] In Hindu chronology, a cycle; one of the ages of the world from creation to destruction; 4,320,000,000 years.

kal′pis, *n.* [Gr. *kalpis*, a pitcher, urn.] In Grecian archæology, a kind of vase or pitcher with three handles.

kal′sō-mīne, *n.* and *v.t.* Same as *Calcimine*.

Kä′mȧ, *n.* [Sans. *kāma*, love, the god of love.] The Hindu god of love.

kȧ-mā′lȧ, *n.* See *Kamila*.

kam′ȧs, kam′ȧss, *n.* Same as *Camass*.

kȧ-mas′si, *n.* [S. African.] In botany, a small tree, *Gonioma Kamassi*, of the dogbane family; also, its yellow wood, which is used in fancy woodwork.

kam-bā′lȧ, *n.* [E. Ind.] A tree, *Sonneratia apetala*, growing in the delta of the Ganges and belonging to the myrtle family; also, its hard red wood, used in building and in making boxes for packing.

Kam-chat′kăn, *n.* A native of Kamchatka, a peninsula in northeastern Russia; also, the language of the Kamchatkans.

kāme, *n.* A ridge formed by glacial drift; a low mound or hill composed of sand, gravel, etc. [Scot.]

kȧ-mees′, *n.* Same as *Kamis*.

kä-me-räd′, (rät′), *n.* [Ger.] Comrade. The word of surrender used by the German soldier in the World War.

kä′mī, *n.* [Japan.] A Japanese title belonging primarily to the celestial gods who formed the first mythological dynasty, then extended to the terrestrial gods of the second dynasty, and then to the long line of spiritual princes who are still represented by the mikado.

kȧ-mī′chī, *n.* In Zoölogy, the *Palamedea cornuta*, a bird of South America, larger than the common goose, remarkable for having its wings armed with two strong spurs, and for having a long, slender, horn-like appendage growing from the skin of its head; called the *horned screamer*. Written also *kamachi* and *kamechi*.

kȧ-mī′lȧ, *n.* [Hind. *kamīla* or *kamelā*.] The orange-colored down obtained from the capsules of the tree *Mallotus Philippinensis*; it is used as a dyestuff, and in medicine as a vermifuge.

kȧ-mīs′, *n.* [Ar. *qamīs*, a shirt.] A loose, shirt-like overgarment worn by Mohammedans.

kamp-tū′li-çon, *n.* [Gr. *kamptos*, flexible, and *oulos*, thick, close-pressed.] A warm, soft, and elastic kind of floor-cloth composed of india-rubber, gutta-percha, and ground cork.

kȧm′sin, *n.* Same as *Khamsin*.

kȧ-nä′kȧ, *n.* [Hawaiian, a man.] A native of the Sandwich Islands; a Hawaiian; also, any South Sea islander; written also *Kanacha*, *Kanaker*, and *Kanak*.

kȧ-nä′ri, *n.* [Javanese.] A tree of the East Indies, *Canarium commune*, known as the Java almond, the seeds of which yield the valuable kanari-oil, used as an illuminant.

kan′chil, *n.* [E. Ind.] An agile and cunning little deer of Java and adjacent islands; specifically, the *Tragulus pygmæus*.

kand, *n.* See *Cand*.

Kan-dē′li-ȧ, *n.* [From *kandel*, the Malabar name.] In botany, a genus of trees of East India whose bark is used in dyeing red and for tanning.

kañ-gȧ-rọọ′, *n.* [Native Australian name.] A large marsupial animal of Australia and adjacent islands characterized by a small head, neck, and shoulders, the body increasing in thickness to the rump. The forelegs are very short, useless in walking, but used for digging, bringing food to the mouth, etc. The hind legs, which are long, are used in moving, particularly in leaping. There are several kinds of kangaroo, designated as tree-kangaroo, rock-kangaroo, brush kangaroo, etc. They are gregarious, inoffensive, and timid, except when brought to bay.

Kangaroo (*Macropus ualabatus*)

kañ-gȧ-rọọ′-ap″ple, *n.* The yellow edible fruit of the solanaceous plant, *Solanum aviculare*, of Tasmania and Australia; also, the plant itself.

kañ-gȧ-rọọ′-bee″tle, *n.* A beetle with large hind legs, of the genus *Sagra*.

kañ-gȧ-rọọ′-grȧss, *n.* A perennial forage grass of Australia.

kañ-gȧ-rọọ′-hāre, *n.* A small Australian hare-like kangaroo.

kañ-gȧ-rọọ′-hound, *n.* A kind of greyhound used for hunting kangaroos in Australia.

kañ-gȧ-rọọ′-mouse, *n.* A mouse of North America resembling the kangaroo in its manner of leaping; the jumping mouse.

kañ-gȧ-rọọ′-rat, *n.* 1. A small Australian kangaroo.

2. A rodent of southern United States and Mexico.

kañ-gȧ-rọọ′-thorn, *n.* A prickly plant, *Acacia armata*, of Australia, used for making hedges.

kañ-gȧ-rọọ′-vīne, *n.* A climbing plant of Australia, *Cissus Baudiniana*; called also *kangaroogrape*.

Kan′sas, *n.pl.*; sing. **Kan′sȧ.** In ethnology, a tribe of North American Indians formerly occupying the territory of Kansas.

Kant′i-ăn, *a.* Relating to the German philosopher Immanuel Kant or to his works and doctrines; resembling or conforming to the philosophy of Kant.

Kant′i-ăn, *n.* A disciple of Kant.

Kant′i-ăn-iṣm, *n.* The doctrines or theory of the philosopher Kant.

Kant′iṣm, *n.* Kantianism.

Kant′ist, *n.* A disciple or follower of Kant.

kan′try, *n.* Same as *Cantred*.

kā′ō-lin, *n.* [Chinese *kaoling*, high ridge, the name of a hill where it is found.] A variety of clay used for making porcelain, proceeding from the decomposition of the mineral feldspar; any species of porcelain clay.

kā-ō-lin-i-zā′tion, *n.* The process of changing feldspar into kaolin.

kā′ō-lin-īze, *v.t.*; kaolinized, *pt.*, *pp.*; kaolinizing, *ppr.* To change into kaolin, as feldspar.

kȧ-pel′le, *n.* [G.] A chapel; in music, the choir or orchestra, or both combined; any musical establishment, especially orchestral.

kȧ-pell′meis″tēr, *n.* [G. *kapelle*, chapel, chapel-choir, and *meister*, master.]

1. In music, the conductor or director of a musical establishment or of a band of musicians.

2. Any bandmaster.

Written also *capellmeister*.

kap-nog′rȧ-phy, *n.* Drawing by means of smoke; specifically, the production of pictures in a coating of carbon deposited by a flame.

kap′nō-mär, kap′nō-mọr, *n.* Same as *Capnomor*.

kȧ-pok′, *n.* [E. Ind.] The silklike covering of the seeds of *Eriodendron anfractuosum*, a tree of the East and West Indies related to the cotton-plant; it is an article of commerce and used for stuffing cushions, pillows, etc.

kar′ȧ-gan, *n.* [Russ. *karagan′*.] A little fox, *Vulpes karagan*, of Tartary; written also *karagane*.

Kā′rȧ-işm, *n.* The teachings and beliefs of the Karaites.

Kā′rȧ-īte, *n.* [Heb. *karaīm*, readers, from *kara*, to read.] One of a sect of Jews who adhere to scriptural as contrasted with oral teaching, denying the authority of the Talmud as binding.

kar′ăt, *n.* Same as *Carat.*

kȧ-rā′tȧs, *n.* [S. Am.] 1. In botany, a plant of the West Indies and South America, *Nidularium Karatas*, of the pineapple family, yielding a valuable fiber; called also *silk-grass.*

2. [K—] A genus of tropical American plants of the order *Bromeliaceæ*, several species of which are cultivated for ornament.

kȧ-rat′tō, *n.* Same as *Keratto.*

kar′ăt-tree, *n.* A leguminous tree of Abyssinia, *Erythrina Abyssinica*, whose small, firm, and equal-sized beans are reputed to have formed the standard for the carat.

kar′i-tē, *n.* Same as *Shea-tree.*

kär′mȧ, *n.* [Sans.] 1. In Hindu religion, the aggregate effect of one's acts in this life as determining his status in the next.

2. In theosophy, (a) the theory of unavoidable consequence, or the doctrine of necessity; (b) the consequences following one's own actions in respect to matters over which he may exercise choice or volition.

Kär-mā′thi-ăn, *n.* One of a heretical Mohammedan sect founded in the ninth century by Karmat, who regarded the Koran as merely allegorical, rejected all revelation, fasting, and prayer, and advocated and practised communism to the fullest extent.

kärn, *n.* [Corn., a cairn; compare Gael. *carn*, a heap.] In Cornish mining, a heap of rocks, or a solid rock resembling a heap.

kā′rŏb, *n.* Among goldsmiths, the twenty-fourth part of a grain.

kȧ-rọọ′, *n.* [S. African.] In the physical geography of South Africa, a table-land rendered unproductive through lack of moisture, the soil being of a fertile nature but becoming hard and barren.

kȧ-ross′, *n.* [S. African.] Among the natives of South Africa, a rude ruglike cloak made of skins in the form of a square and worn over the shoulders; written also *carosse.*

kär′phō-līte, *n.* [Gr. *karphos*, dry stalk, straw, and *lithos*, stone.] In mineralogy, a yellow fibrous mineral found in the Schlackenwald tin-mines, a hydrated silicate of alumina and manganese; written also *carpholite.*

kȧr-rọọ′, *n.* See *Karoo.*

kär′sten-īte, *n.* Same as *Anhydrite.*

kär′vel, *n.* [Obs.] See *Caravel.*

kar-y-as′tẽr, *n.* [Gr. *karyon*, a nut, and *astēr*, a star.] A starlike group of filaments in a nucleus at a certain stage of karyokinesis.

karyo-. A combining form from Gr. *karyon*, a nut, used in biology to denote a nucleus; as, *karyo*lymph, *karyo*plasm.

kar″y-ō-ki-nē′sis, *n.* [*Karyo-*, and Gr. *kinēsis*, movement, change.] In embryology, a series of complicated nuclear changes taking place before the division of a cell.

kar″y-ō-ki-net′iç, *a.* In embryology, of the nature of or relating to karyokinesis; as, *karyokinetic* division of cells as distinguished from *karyostenotic* division.

kar′y-ō-lymph, *n.* [*Karyo-*, and L. *lympha*, water.] In embryology, the more liquid portion of a nucleus, surrounding and holding the denser parts.

kar-y-om′i-tōme, *n.* [*Karyo-*, and Gr. *tomē*, a cutting, from *temnein*, to cut.] In biology, the reticular structure in a nucleus.

kar′y-ō-plaşm, *n.* [*Karyo-*, and Gr. *plasma*, anything formed, from *plassein*, to form, mold.] In embryology, the plasmic part of a nucleus; called also *nucleoplasm.*

kar″y-ō-stē-nō′sis, *n.* [*Karyo-*, and Gr. *stenōsis*, a stretching, narrowing, from *stenos*, narrow.] In embryology, the division of a cell by direct process, not preceded by karyokinetic changes.

kar″y-ō-stē-not′iç, *a.* Pertaining to or resulting from karyostenosis.

kar″y-ō-thē′cȧ, *n.* [*Karyo-*, and Gr. *thēkē*, a case, box.] In embryology, the nuclear wall or coat.

Kȧ-sack′, *n.* Same as *Cossack.*

kas′sū, *n.* [E. Ind.] An astringent substance extracted from the betel-nut.

kat, *n.* In ancient Egypt, the principal unit of weight, equivalent to about 150 grains.

kat-ȧ-bol′iç, *a.* Same as *Catabolic.*

kȧ-tab′ō-lişm, *n.* Same as *Catabolism.*

kat′ȧ-stāte, *n.* Same as *Catastate.*

kat-ȧ-tō′ni-ȧ, *n.* [Gr. *kata*, down, and *tonos*, tone, tension.] In medicine, a kind of melancholia accompanied by periods of mania.

kat-ȧ-tō′ni-aç, *n.* One who is afflicted with katatonia.

kat′ȧ-tȳp-y, *n.* A method in modern photography, so called from the catalytic action of the chemicals used.

kāte, *n.* The European mountain-finch, *Fringilla montifringilla.* [Local, Eng.]

kat″e-leç-trot′ō-nus, *n.* Same as *Catelectrotonus.*

kath′ē-tăl, *a.* Same as *Cathetal.*

kath-ē-tom′e-tẽr, *n.* Same as *Cathetometer.*

kath′ō-dăl, *a.* Same as *Cathodal.*

kath′ōde, *n.* Same as *Cathode.*

ka′ti-pō, *n.* The native name of a venomous spider in New Zealand.

kat-ti-mun′dọọ, *n.* Same as *Cattimandoo.*

kā′ty-did, *n.* A large insect, of a greenish color, belonging to the order *Orthoptera*; the *Cyrtophyllum concavum*, characterized by producing a stridulous note with its wings, sounding much like the combination *ka-ty-did*; whence the name.

kä′ụ-ri, *n.* [Maori.] In botany, a tall coniferous tree, *Agathis australis*, the finest forest-tree of New Zealand, valuable for its timber and for the gum or resin which it yields; spelled also *cowdi, cowdie, cowrie, kaurie, kowrie*, etc.

kä′ụ-ri-gum, *n.* The resin which exudes from the kauri-pine and which is used in making varnish; called also *kauri-resin* and *cowdie-gum.*

kä′ụ-ri-pīne, *n.* The kauri.

kä′vȧ, *n.* [Polynesian.] In botany, (a) a plant of Polynesia, *Macropiper latifolium*, having a root which yields an intoxicating beverage; (b) the beverage itself; written also *ava, cava, kawa, awa.*

kȧ-vass′, *n.* Same as *Cavass.*

kạw, *v.i.* Same as *Caw.*

kȧ-wä′kȧ, *n.* [New Zealand.] The New Zealand arbor-vitæ, *Thuja Doniana*, prized for its hard resinous wood.

kạwn (kan), *n.* Same as *Khan.*

kāy, *n.* See *Cay.*

kā′yä, *n.* [Chinese.] A timber-tree of China, the *Torreya grandis* of the *Coniferæ.*

kāy′ak, *n.* [Native Eskimo name.] In navigation, a small boat or canoe made of skins and used by inhabitants of the arctic regions in fishing; written also *kaiak, kajak, kayack.*

kāy′ak-ẽr, *n.* One who uses a kayak, especially in fishing.

kāyleş, *n.pl.* Same as *Kails.*

kāy′nărd, *n.* Same as *Caynard.*

kȧ-zä′, *n.* [Turk. *qaza*, a judging, decree.] A subdivision of an administrative district in Turkey, analogous to a canton or a county.

kaz′ărd-ly, *a.* Unlucky; liable to accident.

kä″zi-ăs-kiẽr′, *n.* [Turk.] In Turkey, either of two officers of the ulema, one serving in Asia and the other in Europe.

kȧ-zọọ′, *n.* [Prob. coined.] A rude musical toy made of a tube in which a strip of catgut is stretched so as to vibrate sympathetically when one sings or hums into the tube.

kē′ȧ, *n.* [Australian.] A flesh-eating parrot of the mountainous regions of New Zealand.

kēarn, *n.* [Obs.] See first *Kern.*

keb, *n.* A tick or sheep-louse. [Scot.]

keb′lăh, *n.* See *Kiblah.*

kech′il, *n.* [Obs.] Same as *Kichel.*

keck, *v.i.* [Compare G. *köken*, to vomit.] To heave the stomach; to retch, as in an effort to vomit. [Rare.]

keck, *n.* 1. A retching or heaving of the stomach. [Rare.]

2. Any umbelliferous plant with a hollow stem. [Prov. Eng.]

keç′kle, *v.t.*; keckled, *pt., pp.*; keckling, *ppr.* [A variant of *kinkle.*] Nautically, to treat or cover, as a chain, cable, or the like, with a substance or covering so as to prevent wear.

keç′kle, *v.i.* To cackle. [Scot.]

keç′kling, *n.* [Verbal n. of *keckle*, v.t.] Material used for wrapping ropes or cables.

keç′klish, *a.* Sick at the stomach; having a desire to vomit.

keck′sy, *n.* Same as *Kex.*

keck′y, *a.* Resembling a keck, or hollow-stemmed plant.

kedġe, *v.t.*; kedged, *pt., pp.*; kedging, *ppr.* [Compare Sw. dial. *keka*, to tug, drag oneself slowly forward.] To warp, as a ship; to move by means of a kedge, as in a river.

kedġe, *n.* A small anchor with an iron stock, used to keep a ship steady when riding in a harbor or river.

kedġe, *a.* [ME. *kydge, kygge*; Ice. *kykr*, contr. of *kvikr*, quick.] Brisk; lively.

kedġ′ẽr, *n.* [From *kedge.*] A small anchor used in a river.

kedġ′ẽr, *n.* A fisherman; one who deals in or peddles fish. [Prov. Eng.]

ked′lock, *n.* Charlock. [Prov. Eng.]

kee, *n.*, plural of *cow.* [Prov. Eng.]

keech, *n.* A mass or lump, as of fat rolled together. [Obs.]

keek, *v.i.* To peep; to look pryingly. [Scot.]

keel, *n.* [Partly from AS. *ceōl, ciōl*, a ship, and partly Ice. *kjölr*, a keel of a ship.]

1. The principal timber in a ship, extending from stem to stern at the bottom and supporting the whole frame; in iron vessels, a combination of plates corresponding to this timber.

2. A low, flat-bottomed vessel, used on the Tyne to convey coal from Newcastle for loading the colliers. [Eng.]

3. A ship.

4. In botany, the lower pair of petals of a papilionaceous flower; in zoology, a ridgelike process.

5. In aeronautics, a vertical plane or planes fixed above or below the body of a flying-machine for the purpose of giving stability.

A, Main keel. B, False keel. C, Keelson. D, Stemson. F, Gripe.

False keel; a strong, thick piece of timber bolted to the bottom of the keel, to preserve it from injury.

On an even keel; in a level or horizontal position.

keel, *v.i.*; keeled, *pt., pp.*; keeling, *ppr.* To turn bottom side up; to upset; used with *over*; as, the boat, or the man, *keeled over.* [Colloq.]

keel, *v.t.* To plow with a keel; to navigate.

keel, *v.t.* [ME. *kelen*; AS. *celan*, to cool, from *col*, cool.] To cool; as, to *keel* the pot. [Obs.]

keel′āġe, *n.* Duty paid for a ship entering a port; also, the right to demand such a duty.

a, Keel. bb, Alæ or wings. c, Vexillum.

keel′-bōat, *n.* A boat without sails, decked over, and built with a keel, used for transporting freight on rivers and canals.

keeled, *a.* 1. In botany, carinated; having a longitudinal prominence on the back; as, a *keeled* leaf, calyx, or nectary.

2. In zoölogy, having a ridge along the median line; as, a *keeled* bone or scale.

keel′ẽr, *n.* One who navigates a keel; a keelman. [Eng.]

keel′ẽr, *n.* A shallow tub.

keel′fat, *n.* [AS. *celan*, to cool, and *fæt*, a vat.] A cooler; a vessel in which liquor is set for cooling.

keel′hạul, *v.t.*; keelhauled, *pt., pp.*; keelhauling, *ppr.* To haul under the keel of a ship, a punishment formerly inflicted in various navies for certain offenses.

keel′ing, *n.* [ME. *keling*; compare Ice. *keila*, Sw. *kolja*, a cod.] A kind of small cod, of which stockfish is made.

kee′li-vīne, *n.* In Scotland, the name of a pencil made of either red or black lead; called also *keelyvine pen.*

keel′măn, *n.* Same as first *Keeler.*

keel′-piēce, *n.* One of the pieces composing a keel.

keel′rāke, *v.t.* Same as *Keelhaul.*

keelş, *n.pl.* Same as *Kails.*

keel′sŏn, *n.* [From Sw. *kölsvin*; Norw. *kjölsvill*, keelson; *kjöl*, keel, and *svill*, sill.] A piece of timber in a ship, laid on the middle of the floor-timbers over the keel, fastened with long bolts and clinched, thus binding the floor-timbers to the keel; in iron vessels, plates constructed and combined to correspond to this timber.

Cross keelson; a strong timber laid transverse to the keelson to give support to heavy machinery, as engines, boilers, etc.

keel′vat, *n.* Same as *Keelfat.*

keen, *a.*; *comp.* keener; *superl.* keenest. [ME. *kene*; AS. *cene, cyne*, bold, wise, clever, from *cunnan*, to be able.]

1. Eager; vehement; as, hungry curs too *keen* at the sport.

2. Eager; sharp; as, a *keen* appetite.

3. Sharp; having a very fine edge; as, a *keen* razor, or a razor with a *keen* edge.

4. Piercing; penetrating; severe; applied to cold or to wind; as, a *keen* wind; the cold is very *keen.*

5. Bitter; piercing; acrimonious; as, *keen* satire or sarcasm.

6. Acute of mind; sharp; penetrating; as, a man of *keen* intellect.

keen, *n.* [Ir. *caoine*, a wail for the dead.] A piercing lamentation made over a corpse. [Irish.]

keen, *v.i.* To make a loud lamentation on the death of a person. [Irish.]

keen, *v.t.* To sharpen. [Rare.]

keen′ly, *adv.* In a keen manner.

keen′ness, *n.* The state or quality of being keen.

Syn.—Eagerness, earnestness, asperity, acumen, sharpness.

keep, *v.t.*; kept, *pt., pp.*; keeping, *ppr.* [ME. *kepen, kipen*; AS. *cepan*, to keep, observe, await.]

1. To hold; to retain in one's power or possession; not to lose or part with; as, to *keep* a house or a farm; to *keep* anything in the memory, mind, or heart.

2. To have in custody for security or preservation; as, to *keep* valuables in a vault.

3. To preserve; to retain.

4. To hold or restrain from departure; to detain.

5. To tend; to feed; to pasture; as, to *keep* a flock of sheep or a herd of cattle in a yard or in a field.

6. To preserve in any tenor or state.

Keep the constitution sound. —Addison.

7. To regard; to attend to; as, the stars in heaven he *keeps*.

8. To practise; to do or perform; to obey; to observe in practice; not to neglect or violate; as, to *keep* the laws of God.

9. To fulfil; to perform; as, to *keep* one's word, promise, or covenant.

10. To practise; to use habitually; as, to *keep* bad hours.

11. To observe or solemnize.

Ye shall *keep* it a feast to the Lord. —Ex. xii. 14.

12. To board; to maintain; to supply with necessaries of life; as, the men are *kept* at a moderate price per week.

13. To maintain; not to intermit; as, to *keep* watch or guard.

14. To hold in one's own bosom; to confine to one's own knowledge; not to disclose or communicate to others; not to betray; as, to *keep* a secret.

15. To have in pay; as, to *keep* a servant.

16. To make the necessary entries in; as, to *keep* the books of a firm.

To keep a stiff upper lip; to put on a bold front; to refuse to be discouraged under difficulties.

To keep back; (a) to conceal; as, I will *keep* nothing *back*, but will tell all I know; (b) to hold back, to restrain; as, *to keep back* the encroachment of a flood.

To keep company; see under *Company*.

To keep down; (a) to prevent from rising or becoming too eager; to subject to discipline; (b) in the fine arts, to modify a prominence or a too intense coloring, so that an important but less prominent feature may receive due attention.

To keep good hours; see under *Hour*.

To keep house; see under *House*.

To keep one's hand in; to retain one's skill or dexterity by regular practice.

To keep one's own counsel; see under *Counsel*.

To keep open house; see under *House*.

To keep school; to attend to all the duties incumbent upon an instructor or preceptor.

To keep term; in university-life, to remain during the entire term; in English law, to observe all requirements necessary for admission to the bar.

To keep the peace; in law, to prevent breaches of the law and of good order.

To keep touch; see under *Touch*.

To keep under; to keep in a subordinate state or position; to treat oppressively.

To keep up; to prevent from drooping or failing; to sustain; as, *to keep up* the price of a commodity or one's financial standing.

Syn.—Retain, preserve.—*Retain* denotes that we *keep* or *hold* things, as against influences which might deprive us of them; *preserve* denotes that we *keep* a thing against agencies which might lead to its being destroyed or broken in upon.

keep, *v.i.* 1. To remain in any state; as, to *keep* at a distance; to *keep* aloft; to *keep* near; to *keep* in the house; to *keep* before or behind; to *keep* in favor; to *keep* out of company or out of reach; in popular language, used with a present participle to express continuous action; as, he *keeps* moving.

2. To last; to endure; not to perish or be impaired; as, apples that *keep* well.

3. To lodge; to dwell; to reside for a time. [Rare.]

Knock at study, where, they say, he *keeps*. —Shak.

4. To be in session; as, school does not *keep* to-day. [Colloq.]

5. To take care; to be alert; to watch. [Obs.]

To keep from; to abstain; to refrain.

To keep in with, to remain on good terms with.

To keep on; to go forward; to proceed; to continue to advance.

To keep to; to adhere strictly; not to neglect or deviate from; as, *to keep to* old customs; *to keep to* a rule; *to keep to* one's word or promise.

To keep up; to remain unsubdued; not to be confined to one's bed.

keep, *n.* 1. Custody; guard; care or keeping; the act of keeping; as, the *keep* of a horse.

2. The state of being kept; case; condition; as, in good *keep*.

3. Guardianship; restraint.

4. A stronghold in the middle of a castle, the last resort in a siege; in old castles, the dungeon.

5. That which is kept. [Obs.]

6. The support or means by which anything is kept; as, one who is not worth his *keep*.

For keeps; for good; used in children's games, particularly marbles.

keep'ẽr, *n.* 1. One who keeps; one who holds or has possession of anything.

2. One who retains in custody; one who has the care of a prison and the custody of prisoners.

3. One who has the care of a park or other inclosure, or the custody of beasts; as, the *keeper* of a park, a pound, or of sheep.

4. That which keeps, retains, or holds anything in place, as a locknut, ring, clamp, etc.

5. Anything that is capable of preservation, as fruit.

6. One who remains behind or stays closely; as, she was always a close home-*keeper*.

Keeper of a magnet; an armature of soft iron connecting the poles of a magnet when not in use to prevent diminution of magnetism.

Keeper of the forest; in English law, an officer whose duty was to look after the interests of the forests.

Keeper of the great seal; in England, a high officer of state in charge of the great seal of state, an office now administered by the lord chancellor.

Keeper of the king's conscience; in England, the lord chancellor in his ecclesiastical capacity.

Keeper of the privy seal; in England, an officer who passes upon all documents prior to their being stamped with the great seal; a privy councilor.

keep'ẽr-ship, *n.* The office of a keeper.

keep'ing, *n.* 1. Custody; guard; preservation.

2. Subsistence; feed; fodder; as, the cattle have good *keeping*.

3. Just proportion; conformity; congruity; consistency; as, these subjects are in *keeping* with each other.

keep'ing-rọọm, *n.* A common parlor or sitting-room in which a family generally live. [Local, U. S.]

keep'-rọọm, *n.* A room for keepsakes. [Local, U. S.]

keep'sāke, *n.* Anything kept, or given to be kept, for the sake of the giver; a token of friendship.

keesh, *n.* Same as *Kish*.

keeve, *n.* [AS. *cyfe*, a tub or vat.] One of various kinds of tubs, as a brewer's mash-tub.

keeve, *v.t.*; keeved, *pt.*, *pp.*; keeving, *ppr.* 1. To set in a keeve for fermentation.

2. To tip up, as a cart. [Prov. Eng.]

keev'ẽr, *n.* A keeve.

kef'fē-kil, *n.* Same as *Kiefekil*.

kef'fi-eh, *n.* [Ar.] A kind of kerchief worn as a headdress by some of the tribes on the Asiatic deserts, particularly the Bedouins.

keg, *n.* [Ice. *kaggi*; Sw. and Norw. *kagge*, a keg, a heap.] A small cask or barrel.

kei'-ap"ple, *n.* [S. African *kei* or *kai*, and E. *apple*.] A South African shrub, *Dovyalis Caffra*, used for hedges and bearing an edible fruit; written also *kai-apple*.

keil'hau-ite, *n.* [Named after Prof. *Keilhau* of Norway.] A Norwegian mineral related in form to titanite, containing iron, yttrium, and aluminium.

kēir, *n.* [Ice. *ker*, a tub.] In bleaching, a vat containing the alkaline liquor used in the process; written also *kier*.

keit-lō'ȧ, *n.* [S. African.] A species of rhinoceros, *Rhinoceros keitloa*, native of South Africa, having two horns nearly equal in length.

keld, *a.* [Obs.] See *Kelled*.

kēle, *v.t.* [Obs.] See fourth *Keel*.

kē'lis, *n.* [Gr. *kēlē*, a tumor.] In pathology, a tumorous affection of the skin; white leprosy.

kelk, *v.t.* To beat soundly. [Rare.]

kelk, *n.* [Prob. from Gael. and Ir. *clach*, a stone.] A blow; also, a large stone. [Prov. Eng.]

kell, *n.* [Obs.] See *Kale*, 2.

kell, *n.* [ME. *calle*, *kalle*; OFr. *cale*, a kind of cap.] One of various membranes or substances resembling network, as a caul, a chrysalis, etc.

kelled, *a.* Having a caul-like covering; having the parts united by a thin membrane. [Obs.]

kē'loid, *a.* [Gr. *kēlē*, a tumor, and *eidos*, form.] Tumorous; in medicine, relating to a kind of hard irregular tumor of the skin of a fibrous growth and usually occurring at the site of a scar.

kē'loid, *n.* A keloid tumor.

kē-lō-tō'mi-ȧ, kē-lot'ō-my, *n.* Same as *Celotomy*.

kelp, *n.* [Origin unknown.]

1. Collectively, large seaweeds used in the manufacture of commercial kelp; specifically, *Macrocystis pyrifera*, a large seaweed of the Pacific coast.

2. A substance consisting of burnt seaweeds, used in the manufacture of carbonate of soda.

kelp'-crab, *n.* A spider-crab having the color of the seaweeds among which it makes its home.

kelp'fish, *n.* One of several fishes living among seaweeds, especially the food-fish *Heterostichus rostratus*.

kel'pie, kel'py, *n.* An imaginary spirit of the waters, in the form of a horse, vulgarly believed to warn, by preternatural noises and lights, those who are to be drowned in that neighborhood. [Scot.]

kelp'-pig"eŏn, *n.* A sea-bird of the antarctic islands related to the plovers, characterized by white plumage and a sheathed bill.

kelp'-salm"ŏn (-sam"), *n.* The rock-bass of the American Pacific coast.

kelp'wŏrt, *n.* A kind of glasswort; a seaweed yielding kelp.

kel'py, *n.* Same as *Kelpie*.

kel'sŏn, *n.* Same as *Keelson*.

Kelt, *n.* Same as *Celt*.

kelt, *n.* Same as *Kilt*.

kelt, *n.* In Scotland, the name given to a salmon spent by spawning; a foul fish.

kelt, *n.* A rough black woolen cloth. [Scot.]

kel'tẽr, *n.* See *Kilter*.

Kelt'ic, *a.* Same as *Celtic*.

kemb (kem), *v.t.* To comb. [Obs.]

kem'ē-lin, *n.* A tub; a brewer's vessel; written also *kimnel*. [Obs.]

kemp, *n.* [ME. *kempe*, *campe*, rough, shaggy.] The coarse hairs mingled with the fur of some animals; spelled also *kempty*.

kemps, *n.pl.* The long stems bearing the flowers of the English plantain.

kempt, *v.*, past participle of *kemb*.

kemp'ty, *n.* Same as *Kemp*.

ken, *v.t.*; kenned, *pt.*, *pp.*; kenning, *ppr.* [ME. *kennen*; Ice. *kenna*, to know; AS. *cennan*, caus. of *cunnan*, to know.]

1. To see at a distance; to descry. [Scot.]

2. To know; to understand. [Poet.]

ken, *v.i.* To look round. [Obs.]

ken, *n.* View; reach of sight.

ken, *n.* [Perhaps an abbrev. of *kennel*.] A lodge for low or disreputable characters; as, a sporting-*ken*. [Slang, Eng.]

kench, *n.* A box or receptacle for curing fish or green hides by salting; also, the contents of such a box.

ken'dăl, *n.* A kind of coarse cloth made of wool.

Kendal green; in coloring cloth, a color obtained by the use of dyer's-weed; a green cloth made at Kendal, England.

Ken-nē'dy-ȧ, *n.* [Named after Lewis *Kennedy*, an English gardener.] A genus of leguminous Australian plants cultivated in conservatories for their handsome flowers.

ken'nel, *n.* [ME. *kenel*, *kenell*; LL. *canile*, a house for a dog, kennel, from L. *canis*, a dog.]

1. A house or cot for dogs, or for a pack of hounds.

2. A pack of hounds, or their cry.

3. The hole of a fox or other beast; a haunt.

ken'nel, *n.* [ME. *canel*; OFr. *canel*, *chanel*, a channel.] The gutter of a street; a little canal or channel.

ken'nel, *v.i.*; kenneled *or* kennelled, *pt.*, *pp.*; kenneling *or* kennelling, *ppr.* To lodge; to lie; to dwell, as a dog or a fox.

ken'nel, *v.t.* To keep or confine in a kennel.

ken'nel-cōal, *n.* Same as *Cannel-coal*.

ken'ning, *n.* View; sight; range of vision; limit of vision on the sea.

kē'nō, *n.* [Fr. *quine*, five winners, from L. *quini*, five each, from *quinque*, five.] A game of chance played with numbered balls and cards

ken-ō-ġen'e-sis, *n.* [Gr. *kenos*, empty, and *genesis*, generation.] In biology, a kind of evolution of an embryo in which it takes on characteristics differing from the parent type; evolution modified or vitiated by conditions of environment; opposed to *palingenesis*.

ken"ō-ġē-net'ic, *a.* Relating to kenogenesis; as, *kenogenetic* evolution.

ke-nō'sis, *n.* [Gr. *kenōsis*, an emptying, from *kenos*, empty; compare Phil. ii. 6, 7.] In theology, the doctrine that Christ renounced his godhood in the incarnation.

ke-not'ic, *a.* Relating to kenosis.

ken'spec-kle, *a.* Recognizable by distinguishing marks; conspicuously marked. [Prov. Eng. and Scot.]

kent, *n.* A pole; especially, a vaulting-pole. [Scot.]

kent, *v.t.* and *v.i.* To punt or propel, as a boat. [Scot.]

Kent bū'gle. A key-bugle; named after the Duke of Kent.

ken'tle, *n.* See *Quintal*.

kent'ledge, *n.* In seamen's language, pigs of iron for ballast laid on the floor of a ship.

ken'trō-līte, *n.* [Gr. *kentron*, a point, center, and *lithos*, stone.] In mineralogy, a lead and manganese silicate, occurring in Chile in sharp-pointed crystals.

Ken-tuck'y, *n.* One of the United States, having the Ohio River for its northern boundary.

Kentucky blue-grass; see *Blue-grass*.

Kentucky coffee-tree; in botany, a leguminous tree yielding a hard disklike bean which has been used as a substitute for coffee; the *Gymnocladus Canadensis*.

keph'ȧ-lin, *n.* [Gr. *kephalē* and *-in*.] In chemistry, a substance found in the tissues of the brain, containing nitrogen and phosphorus.

keph'ir, *n.* [Caucasian.] A kind of kumiss or

fermented milk, used as a food by the inhabitants of the northern Caucasus.

keph'ir-grains, *n.pl.* The masses of fungi and bacteria placed in milk to produce kephir

kep'i, *n.* [Fr.] A kind of cap with a circular flat top and a horizontal vizor, first worn by French troops in Algiers.

kept, *v.*, past tense and past participle of *keep*.

kē-ram'ic, *a.* Same as *Ceramic*.

kē-ram'ics, *n.* Same as *Ceramics*.

kē-rä'nä, *n.* [Per.] In music, a Persian trumpet.

kē-rär'gy-rite, *n.* Same as *Cerargyrite*.

ker'ä-sin, *n.* Same as *Cerasin*.

ker'ä-sine, *a.* Same as *Cerasine*.

ker'ä-tin, *n.* Same as *Ceratin*.

ker-ä-ti'tis, *n.* Same as *Ceratitis*.

kerato-. See *Cerat-*.

ker'ä-tōde, *n.* Same as *Ceratode*.

ker-ä-tog'e-nous, *a.* Same as *Ceratogenous*.

ker'ä-tōme, *n.* Same as *Ceratome*.

ker"ä-tō-nyx'is, *n.* Same as *Ceratonyxis*.

ker'ä-tō-phyte, *n.* Same as *Ceratophyte*.

Ker-ä-tō'sä, *n.* Same as *Ceratospongiæ*.

ker'ä-tōse, *n.* Same as *Ceratose*.

ker'ä-tōse, *a.* Same as *Ceratose*.

ker-at'tō, *n.* A West Indian plant, *Agave keratto*, from which a valuable fiber is obtained.

kē-rau'lō-phon, *n.* [Gr. *keras*, a horn, and *aulos*, a flute, pipe, and *phōnē*, voice, sound.] In organ-building, a stop giving a light, smooth, reedy tone.

kē-rau'nō-graph, *n.* [Gr. *keraunos*, a thunderbolt, and *graphein*, to write, register.] A mark or impress left upon a body by lightning.

kē-rau-nō-phō'bi-ä, *n.* [Gr. *keraunos*, thunderbolt, and *-phobia*, from *phobos*, fear.] Fear of thunder.

kērb, *n.* Same as *Curb*.

kērb'stōne, *n.* Same as *Curbstone*.

kēr'chēr, *n.* A square of linen worn on the head by a woman. [Obs.]

kēr'chēred, *a.* Wearing a kercher. [Obs.]

kēr'chief (-chif), *n.* [ME. *kerchef*, *curcheff*, *courchef*, *coverchief*; OFr. *covrechef*, *couvrechef*, a kerchief; *covrir*, to cover, and *chef*, *chief*, head.]

1. A headdress; a cloth to cover the head.

2. A piece of cloth used in dress; the word is now seldom used except in its compounds hand*kerchief* and neck*erchief*.

kēr'chiefed, *a.* Dressed; hooded; covered; having a kerchief. [Rare.]

kērf, *n.* [ME. *kerf*, *kyrf*; AS. *cyrf*, a cutting, from *ceorfan*, to cut.]

1. The cut of an ax, a saw, or other instrument; the notch or slit made in wood by cutting.

2. A stroke with a weapon. [Obs.]

3. A layer of hay or turf. [Prov. Eng.]

kērfed, *a.* Having cuts or slits; as, a *kerfed* beam.

kē'rite, *n.* [Gr. *kēros*, wax, and *-ite*.] A compound made of tar and other substances, used for insulating electric wires.

kērl, *n.* Same as *Carl*.

kēr'mes, *n.* [Ar. and Per. *qirmiz*, kermes, crimson; from Sans. *krimija*, produced by a worm; *krimi*, a worm, and the root of *jan*, to produce.]

1. A dyestuff composed of the dead bodies of the females of the scale-insect *Coccus ilicis*; spelled also *chermes*.

2. [K—] A genus of *Coccinæ* or scale-insects.

3. An oak-tree on which the insect *Coccus ilicis* feeds; the kermes-oak.

kēr'me-site, *n.* [*Kermes* and *-ite*.] In mineralogy, a very hard mineral containing antimony and sulphur (Sb_2S_2O), and of a bright cherry-red color, crystallizing in the monoclinic system.

kēr'mes-min"ēr-ăl, *n.* An orange-red amorphous trisulphid of antimony.

kēr'mess, **kir'mess**, **kēr'mis**, *n.* [D. and Flem. *kermis*, *kerkmis*; M.D. *kermisse*, *kerckmiss*, a church festival, lit., church mass.]

1. An annual outdoor festival held in the Low Countries of Europe and in French Flanders, characterized by feasting, dancing, clownish processions, and other forms of amusement.

2. In the United States, a form of entertainment, usually for the benefit of some charity, in which the participants appear in costume, the fashions and sports of the Flemish kermess being imitated.

kērn, *n.* [ME. *kerne*; Ir. *ceatharnach*, a soldier.]

1. A foot-soldier of the ancient militia of Ireland and the Scottish Highlands, belonging to the lowest grade; hence, a churl; a boor; a bumpkin.

2. In English law, an idle person or vagabond.

kērn, *n.* Same as *Quern*.

kērn, *n.* [Variant of *corn*.]

1. Same as *Kernel*.

2. In harvesting, the last sheaf reaped.

3. The ingathering of the harvest.

4. In printing, that part of a type which hangs over the body or shank, as in some italic letters.

kērn, *v.i.*; kerned, *pt.*, *pp.*; kerning, *ppr.* [ME. *kernen*, *kurnen*, *curnen*, to form corns, sow with corn, from *corn*, corn.]

1. To harden, as corn in ripening.

2. To take the form of corns; to granulate.

kērn, *v.t.* [Perhaps from L. *crena*, a notch.] In type-founding, to form with a kern.

kērn'-bā"by, *n.* An image dressed with corn and carried before reapers to their harvest-home; called also *harvest-queen*. [Prov. Eng.]

kērned, *a.* In printing, having a part overhanging the shank; said of type, especially the letters *f* and *j*.

kēr'nel, *n.* [ME. *kirnel*, *kyrnel*; AS. *cyrnel*, a little corn or grain, dim. of *corn*, a corn.]

1. The edible substance contained in the shell of a nut.

2. Anything included in a shell, husk, or integument; a grain of corn; as, a *kernel* of wheat or oats.

3. The seed of pulpy fruit; as, the *kernel* of an apple.

4. The central part of anything; a small mass around which other matter is concreted; a nucleus.

5. A hard concretion in the flesh.

6. The essential part of anything; the essence; as, the *kernel* of an argument.

kēr'nel, *v.i.*; kerneled, kernelled, *pt.*, *pp.*; kerneling, kernelling, *ppr.* To harden or ripen into kernels, as the seeds of plants.

kēr'neled, *a.* Having a kernel.

kēr'nel-ly, *a.* Full of kernels; resembling kernels.

kērn'ish, *a.* Having the characteristics of a kern or boorish person. [Obs.]

ker'ō-lite, *n.* Same as *Cerolite*.

ker'ō-sēne, *n.* [Gr. *kēros*, wax, and *-ene*.] A volatile oil distilled from petroleum and other hydrocarbons and extensively used as an illuminant and for other purposes; called also *coal-oil*.

Ker'ri-ä, *n.* [Named after John B. *Ker*, an English botanist.] In botany, a genus of plants of the rose family, native in Japan and cultivated throughout the world for its handsome yellow flowers; the *Kerria Japonica* is the best-known species.

kērs, **kērse**, *n.* [Obs.] See *Cress*.

kēr'sey, *n.* [So called from *Kersey*, a village in Suffolk, England, once a seat of wool manufacture.] A kind of coarse woolen cloth; a coarse stuff made for centuries in England and used for garments.

kēr'sey-mēre, *n.* [A corruption of *cassimere*.] A twilled woolen cloth; cashmere.

kēr-sey-nette' (-net'), *n.* Same as *Cassinette*.

kērve, *v.t.* To carve. [Obs.]

kērv'ēr, *n.* A carver. [Obs.]

kē'sär, *n.*, obsolete variant of *kaiser*.

kes'lop, *n.* The dried fourth stomach of a calf; rennet; called also *keeslip*. [Prov. Eng.]

Kestrel (*Falco tinnunculus*).

kess, **kesse**, *v.t.* [Obs.] See *Kiss*.

kest, *v.*, obsolete past tense of *cast*.

kes'trel, *n.* [OFr. *quercerelle*, *cercerelle*, *crescerelle*, a kestrel, from L. *querquedula*, a kind of teal.] A bird of the genus *Falco*, or hawk kind; called also *stannel* and *windhover*. It builds in hollow oaks, and feeds on mice, insects, and small birds.

ket, *n.* Carrion; filth of any kind. [Prov. Eng.]

ketch, *n.* [Fr. *caiche*, *caique*; Turk. *qāiq*, *qaïq*, a boat, skiff.] A vessel with two masts, usually from 100 to 250 tons burden; they were formerly much used as yachts or as bomb-vessels, in the latter case being called *bomb-ketches*.

Ketch.

ketch, *v.t.* [Obs.] See *Catch*.

ketch'up, *n.* Catchup.

kē'tin, **kē'tine**, *n.* In chemistry, an unstable organic oily base, $C_8H_8O_2$, with an aromatic odor, obtained by the reduction of certain compounds of the ketones.

ket'mi-ä, *n.* [Etym. unknown.] A plant of the genus *Hibiscus*; written also *ketmie*.

Bladder ketmia; named from its inflated bladdery calyx; the *Hibiscus Trionum*; called also *flower-of-an-hour*.

kē'tōl, *n.* [*Ket*one and ind*ol*.] In chemistry, one of a series of nitrogenous substances related to indol.

kē'tōne, *n.* [An arbitrary variation of *acetone*.] In chemistry, one of a series of compounds containing the group CO combined with two alkyl radicals. Ketones are mostly volatile liquids insoluble in water.

kē-ton'ic, *a.* Related to a ketone.

ket'tle, *n.* [ME. *ketel*, *kettyl*; AS. *cetel*, *cytel*, from L. *catillus*, dim. of *catinus*, a deep vessel, bowl, pot.]

1. A vessel of iron or other metal, of various shapes, with or without a cover, used for heating and boiling water or other liquids.

2. Figuratively, any cavity or depression resembling a kettle, as (a) a deep rounded-out hole at the bottom of a river; (b) in geology, a cavity in solid rock made through erosion or other causes; as, the *kettle* of the Sierra Nevada.

ket'tle-drum, *n.* 1. A drum made of a brass or copper vessel like a kettle, covered with parchment.

1. Patent Kettledrum. 2. Ordinary Kettledrum.

ket'tle-drum"mēr, *n.* One who beats the kettledrum.

ket'tle-hōle, *n.* In geology, a kettle-shaped concavity in rock, sand, gravel, or any part of the natural formation of the earth.

ket'tle-pins, *n.pl.* Ninepins; skittles. [Obs.]

kē-tū'pä, *n.* [Javanese.] 1. In zoölogy, a Javanese eared owl.

2. [K—] A genus of fish-eating owls of India, characterized by large ear-tufts and including three species, among which is the Indian fish-owl, *Ketupa ceylonensis*.

Keu'pēr (koi'), *n.* [G.] In geology, a division of the Triassic in Europe, especially in Germany, where its formations abound in rock-salt and gypsum.

kev'el, *n.* 1. See *Cavel*, 3.

kev'el, *n.* [Prob. native name.] A North African gazel.

kev'el-head (-hed), *n.* In navigation, the end or projecting part of a timber used as a cavel.

kev'ēr, *v.t.* and *v.i.* [Obs.] See *Cover*.

kev'ēr-chef, *n.* [Obs.] See *Kerchief*.

kewie or **keewee** or **kievi**. In the vernacular of the Royal Flying Corps, a member of the Corps who does not fly, in allusion to a flightless bird of Australia. Such members, officers and men, attend to supply and repair work.

kex, *n.* [ME. *kex*, *kix*; W. *cecys*, pl., dry stalks, hemlock.]

1. A hollow stalk.

2. A husk no longer useful, as the larval covering of an insect.

key, *n.* [ME. *keye*, *keie*, *kay*; AS. *cæg*, *cæge*, a key.]

1. A fastener; that which fastens, as a piece of wood in the frame of a building or in a chain.

2. An instrument for shutting or opening a lock by pushing the bolt one way or the other.

3. An instrument by which something is screwed or turned; as, the *key* of a watch or other timepiece.

4. In a musical instrument, a lever or bar by which the instrument is played on with the finger.

5. In music, the fundamental note or tone to which the whole piece is accommodated and with which it usually begins and always ends; the diatonic scale founded on this note.

6. An index, or that which serves to explain a cipher; as, a *key* to a diagram or drawing.

7. A ledge of rocks near the surface of the water; a cay.

8. The indehiscent husk of a winged fruit, as of the ash, maple, elm, etc.

9. A circumstance or fact leading to discovery or explanation; as, a *key* to a mystery

10. In architecture, a binding piece, as a pin, a wedge, or a last board in a floor or in wainscoting.

11. In masonry, a sustaining stone or brick in an arch or the plastering forced between laths.

12. Any part of apparatus or machinery by which it is operated; as, the *key* of a telegraphic transmitter, of a type-writing machine, etc.

13. A quay or wharf.

Analytical key; in science, an orderly arrangement of groups, orders, families, etc., with their characteristics, in such a way as to facilitate the placing of an individual; as, an *analytical key* to the orders of plants.

Power of the keys; in church government, a power claimed to be derived from the Saviour's words to Peter: I will give unto thee the keys of the kingdom of heaven, and whatsoever thou shalt bind on earth shall be bound in heaven; and whatsoever thou shalt loose on earth shall be loosed in heaven. [Matt. xvi. 19.]

kēy, *v.t.*; keyed, *pt.*, *pp.*; keying, *ppr.* To bind or fasten with a key; to tighten.

To key up; (a) in music, to give greater tension to and hence higher pitch, as in tuning the string of a violin or of a guitar; (b) in architecture, to raise by means of a wedge or key, as in elevating a wall or an arch that has sunk by settling.

kēy'āge, *n.* Money paid for the use of a key or quay.

kēy'-bed, *n.* A groove or slot cut into metal for receiving a key, as in a shaft carrying a pulley, to prevent slipping or turning of the shaft in the pulley.

kēy'bōard, *n.* A board or frame, including the keys arranged upon it, which forms a part of an instrument operated by means of keys;

kēy'-bōlt, *n.* A bolt held in place by a key passed through a hole near the end of the bolt.

kēy'-bū"gle, *n.* A kind of bugle having six keys and a compass of about two octaves; also called *Kent-bugle*.

Key-bugle.

kēy'-cōld, *a.* Cold as an iron key; lifeless. [Obs.]

kēyed, *a.* 1. Furnished with keys; as, a *keyed* instrument.

2. Set to key, as a tune.

kēy'-fruit, *n.* Same as *Samara*.

kēy'hōle, *n.* 1. A hole or aperture in a door or lock for receiving a key.

2. In carpentry, a hole or slot in timbers designed for joining with a key or wedge; an aperture for receiving a key.

kēy'hōle-guärd, *n.* A cover for a keyhole when the key is not inserted.

kēy'hōle-lim"pet, *n.* In zoölogy, a limpet with a hole at the apex of its shell; one of the *Fissurellidæ*.

kēy'hōle-saw, *n.* A handsaw with a narrow stiff blade used in following sharp curves; a compass-saw.

kēy'hōle-ūr"chin, *n.* In zoölogy, one of several species of sea-urchins with holes in their disks resembling keyholes.

kēy'nōte, *n.* 1. In music, the fundamental tone of a key or of a composition or passage of music.

2. The leading fact or thought in discourse or discussion; as, the *keynote* of the address.

kēy'sēat, *n.* A key-bed.

kēy'stōne, *n.* 1. The stone on the top or middle of an arch or vault, which, being wider at the top than at the bottom, enters like a wedge and binds the work; sometimes made projecting, and ornamented.

A, Keystone in Plan of Groin.

2. In a system, that which holds the several parts together; the supporting fact or principle.

3. The first stone in chromolithography.

Keystone state; in the United States, Pennsylvania; so called because of its central location in the chain of original states.

kēy'-stōne, *n.* In music, the fundamental tone of any given key; as, the tone of G is the *keytone* in the key of G.

kēy'wāy, *n.* A key-bed or keyseat.

khāir'-trēe, *n.* [E. Ind.] An oriental leguminous tree, *Acacia Catechu*, producing the catechu of commerce.

khä'ki, *n.* [E. Ind. *khākī*, dusty, dust-colored, from *khāk*, dust, earth.] A heavy light-brown cotton cloth used for uniforming soldiers in warm climates; collectively, uniforms made of this cloth, as, soldiers in *khaki*.

khä'lif, khä'liff, *n.* Same as *Calif*.

khäm'sīn, *n.* [Ar. *khamsīn*, from *khamsīn*, fifty, fiftieth.] A very warm and dry wind blowing over Egypt from the Sahara region for about fifty days in the spring season.

khän, *n.* [Turk. and Per. *khān*, a prince; of Tatar origin.] Originally, the title of a king, governor, or prince; now applied to various dignitaries in Oriental countries, as a prince in Tatar countries, a nomadic chief in Persia, and any Hindu of distinction in India; one of the titles of the sultan of Turkey.

khan, *n.* [Turk. *khān*; Per. *khāna*, a house, dwelling.] An Eastern inn or caravansary; written also *kawn* and *kane*.

khan'ate (*or* kän'), *n.* The dominion or jurisdiction of a khan.

khan'jee, *n.* [Hind. *khangī*, *khanagī*; Per. *khānagī*, from *khāna*, house.] The keeper of an Eastern caravansary.

khän'sȧ-mäh, khän'su-mȧ, *n.* [Hind. *khānsāmān*.] Among East Indians, an indoor servant, as a steward or butler.

khä-nŭm', *n.* [Turk. *khānim*, f. of *khān*, lord.] The feminine of *khan*; a woman of distinction in Tatar countries.

Khä'yȧ, *n.* [From native name in Senegambia.] A genus of mahogany-like trees growing in tropical Africa and furnishing the so-called Senegal mahogany.

Interior of a Khan.

khe-dīve', *n.* [Turk. *khidīv*, from Per. *khidīw*, *khadīw*, lord, great prince, king.] The title of the ruler of Egypt.

khen'nȧ, *n.* Same as *Henna*.

khit'mut-gär (kit'), *n.* [Hind. *khidmatgār*, a servant, butler; *khidmat*, attendance, service, and *-gār*, denoting agent.] A Mohammedan waiter at table; a table-servant.

Khlis'tie, *n.* [Russ., from *khlestatĭ*, *khlūistatĭ*, to whip, lash, from *khlvistŭ*, a whip, switch.] A religious sect in Russia; called also *People of God* and *Danielites*, the latter from the name of the founder of the sect, which practises flagellation, celibacy, and total abstinence from intoxicants; written also *Khlisti*.

khō'läh, *n.* [E. Ind.] The golden-gray jackal, *Canis aureus*, of southern Asia.

khōl'sun, *n.* [Hind.] The wild mountain-dog; the dhole.

khut'bȧh, *n.* [Ar. *khutba*, *khotba*, an address.] A Mohammedan formal address and prayer delivered at the beginning of the midday service in a mosque every Friday.

kī-ȧ-boo'çȧ-wood, *n.* [E. Ind. *kiabooca*, and E. *wood*.] A wood used in ornamental work, taken from the knots of the *Pterocarpus Indicus*, a leguminous tree of the Malayan islands and New Guinea; spelled also *kyaboca-wood*.

kī-ack', *n.* [Burmese.] A Burmese temple of Buddha.

kī-äng', *n.* [Chinese.] The dziggetai.

kib'ble, *v.t.* To bruise. [Prov. Eng.]

kib'ble, *n.* A bucket for hoisting from a well or mine; written also *kibbal*. [Prov. Eng.]

kib'blings, *n.pl.* Parts of fishes cut into small pieces for bait. [U. S. and Newfoundland.]

kibe, *n.* [W. *cibi*, a chilblain.] A chap or crack in the flesh occasioned by cold; an ulcerated chilblain, as in the heels.

kībed, *a.* Chapped; cracked with cold; affected with chilblains; as, *kibed* heels.

ki-bit'kȧ, *n.* [Russ.] 1. A Tatar vehicle, consisting of a frame of wood rounded at top, covered with felt, and placed on wheels, serving as a kind of movable habitation.

2. Among the Kirghiz, a kind of round-topped tent.

Kibitka or Kirghiz Tent.—From Zaleski.

kib'läh, *n.* [Ar. *qibla*, that which is opposite, the south, from *qabala*, to be opposite.] The direction toward the Kaaba in the great mosque at Mecca, toward which the Mohammedan turns when he prays; written also *keblah*.

kib'ling, *n.* See *Caplin*.

kib'y, *a.* Affected with kibes.

kich'el, kitch'el, *n.* A small cake. [Obs.]

kick, *v.t.*; kicked, *pt.*, *pp.*; kicking, *ppr.* [ME. *kiken*; W. *cicio*, to kick.]

1. To strike with the foot; as, a horse *kicks* a groom; a man *kicks* a dog.

2. To retroact; to force back; as, the gun was overloaded and *kicked* him severely.

3. In printing, to impel (a job-press) by means of the treadle.

4. Figuratively, to start or stir; with *up*; as, to *kick up* a row.

To kick up a dust; see under *Dust*.

kick, *v.i.* 1. To practise striking with the foot or feet; as, a horse accustomed to *kick*.

2. To thrust out the foot or feet with violence, as in resistance, anger, or contempt; to manifest opposition.

3. To recoil, as a firearm on being discharged; as, a light gun *kicks*.

4. To offer objection; to express dissatisfaction; as, the employees *kicked* at the requirement. [Slang.]

To kick against the pricks; to kick, as an ox, against the goad of the driver; hence, to offer useless resistance to a superior force.

To kick over the traces; to resist control; to manifest insubordination. [Colloq.]

kick, *n.* 1. A blow with the foot or feet; a striking or thrust of the foot.

2. The recoil of a firearm upon being discharged.

3. Open resistance to any requirement. [Slang.]

4. In molding, a projection upon a mold to form a depression in the thing molded; also, the depression itself; as, the *kick* in the bottom of a bottle.

5. The proper thing, as in fashion or style; said of dress, conduct, or speech. [Slang, Eng.]

6. The part of the blade of a pocketknife that acts as a stop in closing.

kick'ȧ-ble, *a.* That may be or ought to be kicked.

Kick-ȧ-po͝os', *n.pl.* In ethnology, a tribe of American Indians once occupying a region along the Illinois River; a branch of the Algonkins.

kick'ēr, *n.* One who or that which kicks.

kick'-off, *n.* In football, the act of putting the ball in play by a kick from the center of the field.

kick'shaw, *n.* [Properly *kickshaws*, a corruption of Fr. *quelque chose*, something.]

1. Something fantastical or uncommon, or something that has no particular name.

2. A dish so changed by cooking that it can scarcely be known; an unsubstantial delicacy.

kick'shōe, *n.* A kickshaw. [Rare.]

kick'sy-wick'sy, *n.* A wife; in a humorous or contemptuous sense.

kick'sy-wick'sy, *a.* Capricious; ludicrously restless.

kick'up, *n.* 1. A row or commotion.

2. A river-steamer with a propelling wheel at the stern.

3. A bird of the genus *Seiurus*, named from its manner of jerking its tail.

kid, *n.* [ME. *kid*, *kide*, *kydde*; Ice. *kidh*; compare Dan. and Sw. *kid*, O.H.G. *kizzi*, *chitzi*, a kid.]

1. A young goat.

2. A young roe deer.

3. A small wooden tub or vessel; applied, among seamen, to one in which they receive their food.

4. A child. [Slang.]

5. The leather made from the skin of a young goat, or an imitation of it made of various other skins.

6. [*pl.*] Gloves made of the skin of a young goat, or of an imitation of it; as, to wear buff *kids*.

kid, *a.* Made of the leather called kid; as, a *kid* glove.

kid, *v.i.*; kidded, *pt.*, *pp.*; kidding, *ppr.* To bring forth a young goat.

kid, *v.t.* To banter, mislead, or hoax. [Slang.]

kid, *n.* [W. *cidys*, fagots.] A bundle of heath and furze. [Prov. Eng.]

kid, *v.t.* To make into a bundle, as fagots, etc. [Prov. Eng.]

kid'daw, *n.* [Corn.] A web-footed fowl; called also *guillemot*.

kid'dēr, *n.* 1. Formerly, a grain merchant or engrosser.

2. A huckster. [Prov. Eng.]

Kid'dēr-min-stēr, *n.* A two-ply carpet made at Kidderminster, England.

kid'di-ēr, *n.* A kidder. [Obs.]

kid'dle, *n.* [OFr. *quidel*, a kiddle; Arm. *kidel*, a net at the mouth of a stream.] A kind of weir in a river, for catching fish.

kid'dōw, *n.* Same as *Kiddaw*.

kid'dy, *v.t.* Same as *Kid*.

kid'dy, *n.* [Dim. of *kid*.] A child; a kid.

kid'dy-ish, *a.* Playful; frolicsome. [Slang.]

kid'-fox, *n.* The young of a fox.

kid'ling, *n.* [Sw. *kidling*; *kid*, a kid, and dim. *-ling*.] A young kid.

kid'nap, *v.t.* [*Kid*, a child, and *nap*, a variant of *nab*, to snatch.] To forcibly abduct or steal, as a human being, whether man, woman, or child; to seize and forcibly carry away, as a person from one country or jurisdiction to another, or into slavery.

kid'nap-ēr, kid'nap-pēr, *n.* One who steals or forcibly carries away a human being; a man-stealer.

kid'nap-ing, kid'nap-ping, *n.* The act of forcibly abducting a human being.

kid'ney (-ni), *n.* [ME. *kidney*, *kidenei*, a corruption of *kidneer*, *kidnere*; *kid*, from Ice. *kvidhr*, AS. *cwith*, belly, womb, and *neer*, from Ice. *nyra*, kidney.]

1. In anatomy, one of two oblong, flattened, bean-shaped glands, situated on either side of the lumbar vertebræ, surrounded with fatty tissue. They are of a reddish-brown color, and secrete the urine. Each

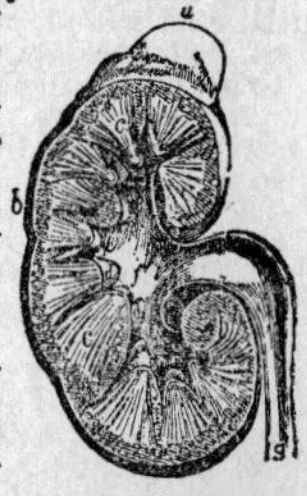

Section of Human Kidney.
a, Suprarenal capsule. *b*, Vascular or cortical portion of kidney. *c c*, Tubular portion, consisting of cones. *d d*, Two of the papillæ, projecting into their corresponding calyces. *e e e*, The three infundibula. *f*, Pelvis. *g*, Ureter.

kidney consists of a cortical or outer part, and a medullary or central portion. The gland is essentially composed of numerous minute tubes, which are straight in the outer and convoluted in the central part. The tubes are lined with cells, and the cells separate the urine from the blood brought to the kidney, the urine passing in drops into the pelvis or cavity of the organ, and thence through the ureter into the bladder.

2. Sort; kind; character; disposition; temper.

There are millions in the world of this man's *kidney*. —L'Estrange.

3. [*pl.*] The inward impulses; the reins.

4. Anything resembling a kidney in shape or otherwise, as a potato.

5. A cant term for a waiting-servant. [Obs.]

Floating kidney; see *Wandering kidney* under *Wandering*.

kid'ney-bean, *n.* A sort of bean, so named from its resemblance to the kidney; the *Phaseolus vulgaris*, or common pole-bean of gardens.

kid'ney-cot"ton, *n.* A South American species of cotton, *Gossypium religiosum*, taking its name from the shape of its seed-groups.

Kidney-shaped leaf.

kid'ney-form, *a.* Same as *Kidney-shaped*.

kid'ney-link, *n.* A link used in harness to connect the pole-chain with the horse's hames or collar.

kid'ney-ōre, *n.* In mineralogy, a kind of iron ore which occurs in reniform masses.

kid'ney-shāped, *a.* Having the form of a kidney; kidney-form.

kid'ney-vetch, *n.* A leguminous plant, *Anthyllis vulneraria*, once used as a remedy in disorders of the kidneys.

kid'ney-wŏrt, *n.* 1. A plant, *Cotyledon Umbilicus*; called also *pennywort* and *navelwort*.

2. The star-saxifrage.

kie, *n.pl.* Kine. [Scot.]

kie'fe-kil, *n.* [Per. *keff*, foam, scum, and *gil*, clay, mud.] Meerschaum; spelled also *keffekil*.

kie'-kie, *n.* [New Zealand.] The native name of a plant, *Freycinetia Banksii*, of the screw-pine family.

kiēr, *n.* Same as *Keir*.

kie'ṣel-gụ̈hr, *n.* [G., from *kiesel*, flint, flint-stone, and *guhr*, an earthy sediment deposited in water.] Diatomaceous earth used in making dynamite.

kie'ṣēr-ite, *n.* [Named after Prof. *Kieser* of Jena.] A mineral occurring in the salt-mines at Stassfurt, Saxony, and used in making Epsom salts.

kiēve, *n.* Same as *Keeve*.

kike, *v.t.* [Obs.] See *Kick*.

ki-kụ'el-oil, *n.* [E. Ind. *kikuek*, and E. *oil*.] A vegetable fat from the seeds of an Oriental tree, *Salvadora Persica*, used in the arts and as a food.

kil-, kill-. [Celt., from L. *cella*, a cell.] A common element in Celtic names of places, signifying cell, church, churchyard, burying-place; as, *Kil*kenny, *Kil*bride, etc.

kil'dēr-kin, *n.* [ME. *kylderkin*, *kinderkin*, a corruption of M.D. *kindekin*, a small barrel, lit., a little child; *kind*, child, and dim. *-kin*.] A small barrel; a liquid measure containing two firkins, or 18 gallons; written also *kinderkin*.

kil'ērg, *n.* [Gr. *chilioi*, a thousand, and *ergon*, work.] In mechanics, a unit of work equal to one thousand ergs.

kill, *n.* [D. *kil*, a channel; Ice. *kill*; Norw. *kil*, a channel, inlet.] A channel or a stream; used chiefly in composition of place-names in regions settled by the Dutch; as, Schuyl*kill*, Cats*kill*, etc.

kill, *n.* In hunting, a killing; also, the thing killed; as, the hunters made a good *kill*, which they brought in with them.

kill, *v.t.*; killed, *pt.*, *pp.*; killing, *ppr.* [ME. *killen*, *kyllen*, *cullen*, to strike, cut, from Ice. *kolla*, to hit on the head, injure, from *kollr*, head.]

1. To deprive of life, animal or vegetable, in any manner or by any means; to put to death; to slay.

2. To butcher; to slaughter for food; as, to *kill* an ox.

3. To quell; to appease; to calm; to still; as, in nautical language, a shower of rain *kills* the wind.

4. To destroy the effect of; to neutralize; to render useless; as, to *kill* a legislative measure; an acid *kills* an alkali.

5. In printing, to mark as dead matter; to delete; as, to *kill* a paragraph in type.

6. To fascinate by means of personal charms or gayness of attire; as, to *kill* with a glance; dressed to *kill*.

To kill time; to give attention to that which is not important for the sole purpose of preventing ennui or the weariness of idleness.

Syn.—Murder, assassinate.—To *kill* does not necessarily mean any more than to deprive of life. To *murder* is to *kill* with malicious forethought and intention. To *assassinate* is to *murder* suddenly and by stealth.

kil'lăs, *n.* [Corn.] The name of clay-slate among the Cornish miners.

kill'dee, kill'deer, *n.* A small bird of America, so called from its voice or note, *Ægialites vocifera*, a species of plover.

kill'ēr, *n.* 1. One who deprives of life; that which kills.

2. A kind of whale, *Orca gladiator*, a very ravenous feeder.

kil-lesse', *n.* A coulisse. [Prov. Eng.]

kil'li-fish, *n.* [D. *kil*, channel, and E. *fish*.] Any one of several small striped fish living in brackish or fresh water, mostly of the genus *Fundulus*.

kil'li-grew, *n.* [Corn.] A crow with red feet and beak.

kil"li-ki-nick', *n.* Same as *Kinnikinick*.

kill'ing, *a.* 1. Depriving of life; quelling; overcoming; destroying; as, a *killing* frost.

2. Irresistible; overpowering; as, the *killing* glances of a coquette.

kill'ing, *n.* 1. The act of slaying or depriving of life.

2. In sporting slang, a large winning or series of winnings by a better; as, to make a *killing* at the races.

kill'ing-ly, *adv.* In a killing manner; fatally.

kil'li-nite, *n.* A mineral, a variety of spodumene, found at Killiney, in Ireland.

kill'joy, *n.* A destroyer of joy; an agent of gloom or low spirits.

kil'lŏck, *n.* 1. A sharp arm, as of a pickax; the fluke of an anchor. [Scot.]

2. A light anchor sometimes made by inclosing a stone in a frame of wood; spelled also *killick*, *killeck*. [U. S.]

kil'lōw, *n.* [A corruption of *colly* or *collow*.] An earth of a blackish or deep-blue color.

kil'mà-gōre, *n.* In zoölogy, a species of parrot-fish.

kiln (kil), *n.* [ME. *kylne*, *kulne*; AS. *cyln*, *cylene*, a kiln, drying-house, from L. *culina*, a kitchen.]

1. A large stove or oven; a structure of brick or stone which may be heated for the purpose of hardening, burning, or drying anything; as, a *kiln* for baking or hardening earthenware or porcelain; a *kiln* for drying grain, meal, or lumber.

2. A pile of brick constructed for burning and hardening; a brickkiln.

kiln'-drȳ (kil'), *v.t.*; kiln-dried, *pt.*, *pp.*; kiln-drying, *ppr.* To dry in a kiln; as, to *kiln-dry* meal or grain.

kiln'-hōle, *n.* The opening of a drying-oven or kiln.

kilo-. A combining form from Gr. *chilioi*, thousand, used in the metric system, physics, etc., to signify a thousand; as, *kilo*gram, *kilo*dyne.

ki'lō, *n.* A kilogram.

kil'ō-dȳne, *n.* [*Kilo-*, and Gr. *dynamis*, power.] In physics, a unit of force equivalent to one thousand dynes.

kil'ō-gram, *n.* [*Kilo-*, and Gr. *gramma*, a weight.] A unit of weight equivalent to 1,000 grams, or 2.2 pounds; written also *kilogramme*.

kil'ō-gram-mē-tēr, *n.* In mechanics, a unit of work accomplished in raising a kilogram through a meter against the force of gravity.

kil'ō-li-tēr, *n.* [*Kilo-*, and Gr. *litra*, a pound.] A measure of capacity equivalent to 1,000 liters.

kil'ō-mē-tēr, *n.* [*Kilo-*, and Gr. *metron*, a measure.] A linear unit of measure equivalent to 1,000 meters, or about five-eighths of a mile.

kil'ō-stēre, *n.* [*Kilo-*, and Gr. *stereos*, solid.] A cubic measure equivalent to 1,000 cubic meters.

kil'ō-wätt, *n.* [*Kilo-*, and E. *watt*.] In electricity, a unit of work or activity equivalent to 1,000 watts.

kilt, *n.* [Compare Ice. *kilting*, a skirt. Old Gael. *cealt*, clothes.] A kind of short heavy petticoat, reaching from the waist to the knees, worn by men in the Highlands of Scotland, and widely imitated in children's dress. In the original Highland dress it was the portion of the belted plaid hanging below the waist, and is retained as part of the uniform of the distinctive Highland regiments of the British army.

kilt, *v.t.* [Dan. *kilte*, *kiltre*, to tuck up, truss up; Ice. *kjalta*, the lap.] To tuck up; to truss up, as the clothes. [Scot.]

kilt, *v.*, obsolete past participle of *kill*.

kilt'ed, *a.* Dressed in a kilt; made after the manner of a kilt as to plaiting, tucking, etc.; as, a *kilted* Highlander, a *kilted* costume.

kil'tēr, *n.* [Compare Dan. *kilte*, *kiltre*, to tuck up, truss up.] Orderly arrangement; proper disposition; as, to be out of *kilter*; spelled also *kelter*.

kilt'ing, *n.* In dressmaking, work done in plaits overlapping each other so as to produce about triple thickness when completed.

kim'bō, *a.* [Perhaps from W. *cam*, crooked, and E. *bow*.] Crooked; arched; bent; as, a *kimbo* handle. [Rare.]

Kim-mē'ri-ăn, *n.* and *a.* Same as *Cimmerian*.

kim'nel, *n.* A large tub for general household use. [Obs.]

ki-mō'nō, *n.* [Japan.] In Japanese costume, a kind of loose overgarment fastened with a sash, the upper part folding across the breast.

Kim'ri, Kim'ry, *n.pl.* Same as *Cymry*.

-kin. [ME. *-kin*, prob. from D. *-ken*, a dim. suffix.] A diminutive suffix attached to nouns; as, lamb*kin*, cat*kin*.

kin, *n.* [ME. *kin*, *kyn*, *kun*; AS. *cynn*, *cyn*, kin, kind, akin to AS. *cennan*, to beget; L. *genus*, race, kind, *gignere*, to beget; Gr. *gignesthai*, to be born; Sans. root *jan*, to beget.]

1. Relation, properly by consanguinity or blood, but used for relation by affinity or marriage; kindred; relationship; as, the father, mother, and the *kin* beside.

2. The same generic class; a thing related.

And the ear-deafening voice of the oracle,
Kin to Jove's thunder. —Shak.

kin, *a.* Of the same nature; kindred; congenial.

kin-æ-sod'ic, *a.* Same as *Kinesodic*.

kin-æs-thē'si-à (-es-), *n.* [Gr. *kinein*, to move, and *aisthēsis*, perception.] The sense of muscular motion or of muscular force exerted.

kin-æs-thē'sis, *n.* Kinæsthesia.

kin-æs-thet'ic, *a.* Relating to kinæsthesia or the muscular sense.

kin'āt, *a.* [*Kin*ic and *-ate*.] In chemistry, any salt formed by the action of kinic acid.

kin'cob, *n.* [Anglo-Ind., from Hind. *kimkhwab*.] A kind of silk or silk and cotton fabric brocaded with silver or gold, made in India; spelled also *kinkhab*.

kīnd, *a.* [ME. *kinde*, *kynde*, *kunde*; AS. *gecynde*, *cynde*, natural, inborn, native, from root of *cennan*, to bring forth.]

1. Disposed to do good to others, and to make them happy by granting their requests, supplying their wants, or assisting them in distress; having tenderness or goodness of nature; benevolent; benignant.

Be ye *kind* one to another, tender-hearted. —Eph. iv. 32.

2. Proceeding from tenderness or goodness of heart; benevolent; as, a *kind* act; a *kind* return of favors.

3. Of a gentle and teachable disposition, as a horse in harness or under the saddle.

Syn.—Tender, affectionate, well-disposed, courteous, tender-hearted.

kīnd, *n.* [ME. *kinde*, *kynde*, *kunde*; AS. *gecynde*, *cynde*, natural, inborn, native, properly pp. from root of *cennan*, to bring forth.]

1. Race; genus; generic class; as, in man*kind* or human *kind*.

2. Sort, in a sense more loose than genus; as, there are several *kinds* of eloquence and of style, many *kinds* of music, many *kinds* of government, various *kinds* of architecture, or of painting, various *kinds* of soil, etc.

3. Natural state; produce or commodity, as distinguished from money; as, taxes paid in *kind*.

In kind; with something of the same kind or of the most convenient kind as to pay rent of land in grain or vegetables.

Kind of, often abbreviated to *kind o'* or corrupted to *kinder*; a colloquial expression in the United States equivalent to *somewhat*, *approximately*, etc.; as, the weather is *kind o'* hazy; he acted *kind o'* gentlemanly.

Syn.—Class, race, kin, sort, genus.

kin'dēr-gär"ten, *n.* [G., lit., garden of children; *kinder*, genit. pl. of *kind*, a child, and *garten*, garden.] A special school for very young children, in which instruction is adapted to the natural desires and capacities of the children by means of objects, songs, games, etc.

kin'dēr-gärt"nēr, *n.* An advocate of the kindergarten or a teacher in a kindergarten.

kīnd'-heärt"ed, *a.* Having much kindness of nature.

kīnd'-heärt"ed-ness, *n.* The quality of having a kind heart.

kin'dle, *v.t.*; kindled, *pt.*, *pp.*; kindling, *ppr.* [ME. *kindlen*, *kyndlen*, to set on fire, from Ice. *kyndill*, a candle, torch; L. *candela*, a candle.]

1. To set on fire; to cause to burn with flame; to light; as, to *kindle* a fire.

2. To inflame, as the passions; to exasperate; to rouse; to provoke; to excite to action; to heat; to fire; to animate; as, to *kindle* anger or wrath; to *kindle* resentment.

So is a contentious man to *kindle* strife. —Prov. xxvi. 21.

kin'dle, *v.i.* 1. To take fire; to begin to burn with flame; as, fuel and fire, well laid, will *kindle* without a bellows.

2. To begin to rage, or be violently excited; to be roused or exasperated.

It shall *kindle* in the thickest of the forest. —Isa. ix. 18.

kin'dlēr, *n.* One who or that which kindles or sets on fire.

kīnd'less, *a.* Destitute of kindness; unnatural. [Obs.]

kīnd'li-ness, *n.* The state or quality of being kind; affection; benignity.

kin'dling, *n.* 1. The act of inflaming or causing to kindle.

2. In the plural, materials for starting a fire.

kind′ly, *a.*; *comp.* kindlier; *superl.* kindliest. 1. Homogeneal; congenial; kindred; of the same nature; natural; fit.

2. Mild; bland; softening; as, *kindly* showers.

3. Favorable; assisting; favoring; as, *kindly* showers; *kindly* aid.

kind′ly, *adv.* With good will; with a disposition to make others happy or to oblige; benevolently; favorably.

kind′ness, *n.* 1. Good will; benevolence; that temper or disposition which delights in contributing to the happiness of others.

2. An act of good will; beneficence; any act of benevolence which promotes the happiness or welfare of others.

kin′dred, *n.* [ME. *kinrede, kynrede, kynredyn,* kinship; AS. *cynn,* kin, and *-ræden,* state, or condition.] Individuals related by consanguinity or by marriage; kinsfolk.

Syn.—Relationship, affinity, consanguinity.—*Relationship* is a state less general than *kindred* but more extended than either *affinity* or *consanguinity*; it applies to particular families only, but to all of the same family, whether closely or distantly related. *Affinity* denotes a close *relationship,* whether of an artificial or of a natural kind; *consanguinity* denotes descent from the same parents in a direct line; *kindred* may embrace all mankind, or refer to particular families or communities.

kin′dred, *a.* Related; congenial; of the like nature or properties; as, *kindred* souls; *kindred* skies.

kine, *n.,* pl. of *cow.* [Obs. or Poet.]

kine, *n.* [Gr. *kinein,* to move.] In physics, a name proposed for the c. g. s. unit of velocity.

kin′ē-ma-cōl″ŏr, *n.* A method of producing moving pictures in the original colors by employing revolving color screens.

kin-ē-mat′iç, *a.* In physics, relating to kinematics.

Kinematic curve; in mechanics, any curve described by a point in a piece of a machine in motion as distinguished from a mathematical curve.

kin-ē-mat′iç-ăl, *a.* Kinematic.

kin-ē-mat′içs, *n.* [Gr. *kinēma* (*-atos*), movement, from *kinein,* to move.] In physics, that branch which treats of motion in all its relations and modifications, irrespective of causes.

kin-ē-mat′ō-grȧph (-gräf), *n.* [Gr. *kinēma* (*-atos*), movement, and *graphein,* to write.] In physics, an apparatus for taking a series of instantaneous photographs or for exhibiting such photographs upon a screen, showing a moving picture.

kīne′pox, *n.* Same as *Cowpox.*

kin′ē-sçōpe, *n.* Same as *Kinetoscope.*

kin-ē-sī-at′riçs, *n.* [Gr. *kinēsis,* motion, and *iatrikos,* pertaining to medicine, from *iatros,* a physician.] In medicine, muscular exercise as a remedy for disease; the movement-cure; also called *kinesipathy.*

kin-ē-si-ol′ō-ġy, *n.* [Gr. *kinēsis,* motion, movement, and *logia* from *legein,* to speak.] In medicine, the science which aims to prevent or to cure disease by means of movements in the parts of the body.

kin-ē-sip′ȧ-thy, *n.* [Gr. *kinēsis,* movement, and *pathos,* suffering.] Kinesitherapy; kinesiatrics.

kin-ē-si-ther′ȧ-py, *n.* [Gr. *kinēsis,* movement, and *therapeia,* cure.] In therapeutics, the movement-cure; kinesipathy; kinesiatrics.

kin-ē-sod′iç, *a.* [Gr. *kinēsis,* movement, and *hodos,* way.] Conveying impulses of motion; particularly relating to the nerves of the spinal cord.

kin-es-thē′si-ȧ, kin-es-thē′sis, *n.* Same as *Kinæsthesia.*

kin-es-thet′iç, *a.* Same as *Kinæsthetic.*

ki-net′iç, *a.* [Gr. *kinētikos,* putting in motion, from *kinētos,* verbal adj. of *kinein,* to move.] In physics, having to do with motion; producing motion or arising from motion; as, *kinetic* energy, the opposite of potential energy or energy of position.

Kinetic energy; the energy of motion; the capacity of a moving body to do work.

Kinetic theory of gases; in physics, a theory that explains the phenomena of gases by assuming that every particle of a gas is continually in motion and endeavoring to fly away from other particles in the same aggregation and that the velocity of these particles depends upon their thermal condition.

ki-net′içs, *n.* In physics, that branch of dynamics which treats of matter in motion, as opposed to *statics.*

ki-nē-tō-ġen′e-sis, *n.* [Gr. *kinētos,* verbal adj. of *kinein,* to move, and *genesis,* birth.] In biology the genesis of organic structures by purely kinetic operations; the doctrine that animal tissues are produced by movements of the animal.

ki-nē′tō-grȧph, *n.* [Gr. *kinētos,* verbal adj. of *kinein,* to move, and *graphein,* to write.] A kinematograph.

ki-nē′tō-phōne, *n.* [Gr. *kinētos,* verbal adj. of *kinein,* to move, and *phonē,* sound.] An invention of Edison, consisting of synchronizing apparatus combined with the phonograph and projecting kinetoscope, so arranged and operated as to reproduce simultaneously sound and motion previously recorded and photographed, such reproduction being popularly known as a *talking moving picture.*

ki-nē-tō-phō′nō-grȧph, *n.* An instrument in which a phonograph is combined with a kinetograph.

ki-nē′tō-sçōpe, *n.* [Gr. *kinētos,* verbal adj. of *kinein,* to move, and *skopein,* to view.]

1. An instrument for illustrating various combinations of kinematic curves.

2. A machine for producing a picture with moving figures.

king, *v.t.* To place on a throne; to make a king of; to elevate to a kingdom. [Rare.]

king, *n.* [ME. *king, kyng*; AS. *cyng,* a contr. of *cyning,* a king; from *cynn,* a race, tribe, kin, and *-ing,* a patronymic suffix.]

1. The chief magistrate or sovereign of a nation; a man invested with supreme authority over a nation, tribe, or country; a monarch, usually inheriting his title and authority.

2. Any one holding a very high position or rank; as, a *king* of industry.

3. In games, (a) a card next in rank to the ace; (b) the principal piece in the game of chess; (c) a crowned piece in the game of checkers.

4. In the plural, the name of the eleventh and twelfth books in the Old Testament.

Apostolic king; see under *Apostolic.*

King bird of paradise; of the several birds of paradise, the *Cicinnurus regius.*

King Charles spaniel; a small spaniel with long drooping ears and long wavy hair.

King Cole; a mythical king, of fame in nursery-books.

King Cotton; in southern United States, a popular personification of the staple product in the days of negro slavery.

King of terrors; death.

King of Yvetot; (a) a king in name only, from the insignificant size and political importance of Yvetot, a seigniory near Rouen, France; (b) in modern use, one who assumes great honors without the means to support them.

King's, or *queen's, counsel*; in English law, lawyers appointed or designated to plead for the crown, but not against it without special permission.

The king's English; correct English language, approved by the best speakers and writers.

King's, or *queen's, evidence*; see under *Evidence.*

King's evil; see *Evil,* n. 3.

King's scholar; in England, a scholar supported by a royal fund or one in a royally endowed school.

King's yellow; yellow orpiment.

Syn.—Prince, sovereign, master, ruler, autocrat, potentate.

king′=at=ärms′, *n.* In Great Britain, any one of the three members of the official board of Heralds' College; the chief is entitled Garter, the second in rank is called Clarencieux, and the third Norroy; also one of the heraldic officials having jurisdiction over Scotland, Ireland, and Wales, known respectively as Lyon, Ulster, and Bath or Gloucester.

king′bird, *n.* In zoölogy, a flycatcher of the *Tyrannidæ* common in southern United States, where it is called *bee-bird* or *bee-martin*; *Tyrannus carolinensis.*

king′bōlt, *n.* In a wagon or carriage, the vertical bolt that connects the hind part of the running-gear with the front axle and serves as a pivot.

king′=cärd, *n.* In whist, the highest card that has not been played.

king′=conch, *n.* A large and handsome univalve shell of the West Indies.

king′=crab, *n.* 1. The horseshoe crab, *Limulus polyphemus,* of the Atlantic Ocean.

2. The *Maia squinado,* or thornback crab.

King-crab (*Limulus polyphemus*).

king′craft, *n.* The craft of kings; the art of governing.

king′=crōw, *n.* A species of shrike, *Dicrurus macrocercus.*

king′cup, *n.* The buttercup, *Ranunculus bulbosus,* a species of crowfoot.

king′=dev″il, *n.* In botany, a weed of the composite family, a pest to farmers, introduced from Europe; the *Hieracium prœaltum.*

king′dŏm, *n.* [ME. *kingdom, kyngdom*; AS. *cyningdom*; *cyning,* king, and *-dom,* jurisdiction.]

1. The territory or country subject to a king; the territory under the dominion of a king or monarch.

2. The office and state of a king.

3. In natural history, a division; as, the animal, vegetable, and mineral *kingdoms.*

4. A region; a tract; the place where anything prevails and holds sway; as, the watery *kingdom.*

Animal kingdom; see under *Animal.*

Kingdom of God; (a) all creation; (b) the entire spiritual realm of which God is the Supreme Ruler; (c) the kinghood of God.

Mineral kingdom; see under *Mineral.*

United kingdom; see under *United.*

Vegetable kingdom; see under *Vegetable.*

king′dōmed, *a.* Having the authority and dignity of a king; furnished with a kingdom.

king′=duck, *n.* A beautiful eider-duck, *Somateria spectabilis,* of the arctic regions.

king′=ēa″gle, *n.* The imperial Roman eagle, *Aquila heliaca,* of Asia and southern Europe.

king′=fērn, *n.* The royal fern, *Osmunda regalis,* common in swamps and wet woods.

king′fish, *n.* One of several excellent food-fishes, among which is *Menticirrus nebulosus,* of the Atlantic coast.

king′fish″ēr, *n.* A bird of the genus *Ceryle,* which preys on fish; notably the spotted kingfisher, *Ceryle guttata,* of Asia, and the belted kingfisher, *Ceryle alcyon,* of the United States.

Spotted Kingfisher (*Ceryle guttata*).

king′=hāke, *n.* A fish, *Phycis regius.*

king′hood, *n.* State of being a king.

king′hunt″ēr, *n.* A bird of the kingfisher kind without aquatic habits.

king′less, *a.* Having no king.

king′let, *n.* [*King* and dim. *-let.*]

1. A king of no importance; a petty sovereign.

2. The golden-crested wren, *Regulus cristatus.*

king′li-hood, *n.* Kingliness; royal dignity.

king′li-ness, *n.* State of being kingly.

king′ling, *n.* A little king; a kinglet.

king′ly, *a.* 1. Belonging to a king; suitable to a king; as, a *kingly* couch.

2. Royal; sovereign; monarchical; as, a *kingly* government.

3. Noble; august; splendid; becoming a king; as, *kingly* magnificence.

king′ly, *adv.* With an air of royalty; with a superior dignity.

Syn.—Regal, royal, imperial, sovereign, splendid, monarchical, powerful.

king′māk″ēr, *n.* One who wields powerful influence in the enthronement of a king; in English history, said of Richard Nevil, Earl of Warwick.

king′=mul″let, *n.* See *Goatfish,* 2.

king′nut, *n.* The shellbark hickory; also, its fruit.

king′=ŏr″tō-lăn, *n.* The marsh-hen, *Rallus elegans.*

king′=pen″guin, *n.* The great penguin, *Aptenodytes pennanti*; also, other species of *Aptenodytes.*

king′=pin, *n.* 1. In bowling, the pin which stands at the front apex when the pins are set in place.

2. The leader in an enterprise or company. [Colloq.]

king′=plant, *n.* In botany, a cultivated orchid from Java, the *Anæctochilus setaceus,* characterized by yellow lines on its purplish-brown leaves.

king′=pōst, *n.* In carpentry, a beam in the frame of a roof rising from the tie-beam to the ridge.

A, The King-post. B, Tiebeam. CC, Struts or Braces.

king′=rāil, *n.* The marsh-hen.

king′=rod, *n.* In architecture, an iron rod used as a king-post.

king′=rōll″ēr, *n.* In a sugar-mill, the middle or principal roller employed in crushing the cane to extract its juice.

king′=salm″ŏn (-sam″ŏn), *n.* In zoölogy, the *Oncorhynchus quinnat* of the Columbia and other rivers of the Pacific slope, the most valuable species of the genus; also called *quinnat.*

King's Bench. Formerly a high court or tribunal in England, so called because the king used to sit there in person; the supreme court of common law, consisting of a chief justice and four other justices.

king's′=cush″iŏn (-un), *n.* A seat made by two persons, each clasping one of his own wrists and then with the free hand clasping the free wrist of the other. [Prov. Eng.]

king′ship, *n.* Royalty; the state, office, or dignity of a king.

king'-snāke, *n.* In zoölogy, a large harmless spotted snake of southern United States, which kills and eats other snakes; the *Ophibolus getulus.*

king's'-spēar, *n.* In botany, *Asphodelus albus*, the white asphodel, a liliaceous plant.

king'stŏn, *n.* The angel-fish, *Squatina angelus.*

king'-tō"dy, *n.* In zoölogy, a small tropical fly-catching bird with a broad fan-shaped red crest bordered with black.

king'-truss, *n.* In carpentry, a truss having a king-post for strength and support.

king'-tȳ"rănt, *n.* Same as *Kingbird.*

king'-vul"tūre, *n.* In zoölogy, the *Sarcorhampus papa*, of the intertropical regions of America, belonging to the family *Cathartidæ*; named from its dominance over other vultures, not allowing them to eat until it has finished its repast.

king'wood, *n.* In botany, a Brazilian wood used much in cabinetwork and in turning on account of its streakings of violet tints; a species of *Dalbergia* of the family *Leguminosæ*; called also *violet-wood.*

kī'nic (*or* kin'), *a.* [Fr. *kinique*, from *kina*, an abbrev. of *quinquina*, cinchona.] Pertaining to cinchona; cinchonic.

Kinic acid; a vegetable acid, $C_7H_{12}O_6$, contained in the bark of the cinchona and in some other vegetable substances.

kiṅk, *n.* [Norw. and Sw. *kink*, a twist or curl in a rope.]

1. The twist of a rope or thread occasioned by a spontaneous winding when doubled, as when hard-twisted ropes or threads wind about each other; a tangle, loop, or curl; as, pack-thread will curl up, running into loops or *kinks.*

2. Figuratively, an inexplicable mental attitude or condition; an unreasonable belief or assertion. [Colloq.]

kiṅk, *v.i.*; kinked (kiṅkt), *pt., pp.*; kinking, *ppr.* To form kinks; to twist spontaneously; as, the yarn *kinks.*

kiṅk, *v.t.* To form a kink or kinks in; as, to *kink* a rope by twisting and releasing.

kiṅk, *n.* A fit of coughing; a convulsive fit of laughter. [Scot.]

kiṅ'kà-jöu, *n.* [From native name.] A plantigrade, carnivorous mammal living in South America, about as large as a full-grown cat, having a prehensile tail, the *Cercoleptes caudivolvulus.*

kiṅk'çough (-kọf), *n.* The whooping-cough. [Scot. or Prov. Eng.]

kiṅk'hōst, kiṅk'hạust, *n.* Same as *Kinkcough.*

kiṅ'kle, *n.* A fit of coughing; a kink.

kiṅ'kle, *v.i.*; kinkled, *pt., pp.*; kinkling, *ppr.* [Freq. of *kink*, to form kinks.] To form kinks.

kiṅk'y, *a.* 1. Kinked; having kinks; as, *kinky* beard or hair.

2. Figuratively, whimsical; given to eccentric notions; full of crotchets.

kin"ni-ki-nick', kin"ni-ki-niç', *n.* [Am. Ind., lit., a mixture.]

1. The dried bark or leaves of plants, as sumac, willow, etc., used for smoking by the aborigines of America.

2. A species of cornel, *Cornus sericea*, whose bark was used by American Indians for smoking; also, the astringent leaves of the bearberry, *Arctostaphylos Uva-ursi.*

kī'nō, *n.* [E. Ind.] An astringent extract obtained as a gum from various tropical trees; a kind of catechu.

kin'ō-drōme, *n.* [Gr. *kinō* (Doric), moving, and *dromos*, a course, running.] A form of apparatus for projecting life-motion pictures upon a screen.

ki-nof'lū-ous, *a.* [*Kino*, and L. *fluere*, to flow.] In botany, yielding the gum kino by exudation.

ki-nol'ō-ġy, *n.* [Gr *kinein*, to move, and *-logia*, from *legein*, to speak.] In physics, the branch relating to bodies in motion. [Rare.]

kī'nōne, *n.* Same as *Quinone.*

kin'red, kin'rede, *n.* [Obs.] See *Kindred.*

kins'fōlk (-fōk), *n.* Relations; kindred; persons of the same family.

kin'ship, *n.* Relationship; generic affinity.

kins'măn, *n.*; *pl.* **kins'men.** A man of the same race or family; one related by blood; loosely, one related by marriage.

kins'măn-ship, *n.* Relationship.

kins'wom"ăn (-woom"), *n.*; *pl.* **kins'wom"en** (-wim"). A female relation.

kint'ledge, *n.* Same as *Kentledge.*

kī-osk', *n.* [Fr. *kiosque*; Turk. *kushk*; Per. *kushk*, a palace, pavilion, portico.] A Turkish open summerhouse supported by pillars.

Kiosk in the Serai Bournon, Constantinople.

Ki'ō-wāys, *n.pl.*; *sing.* **Ki'ō-wāy.** In ethnology, a tribe of American aborigines.

kip, *n.* [Prob., that which is snatched or pulled off, from ME. *kippen*; Ice. *kippa*, to pull, snatch.]

1. The untanned skin of a calf not younger than about six weeks.

2. The untanned skin of any individual of a breed of very small cattle.

3. The leather made from such skins.

kīpe, *n.* [AS. *cypa*, a basket.] A kind of basket made of osier for catching fish. [Prov. Eng.]

kip'pēr, *n.* [D. *kippen*, to catch, seize.]

1. A salmon unfit to be taken, or one caught and detained in fresh water.

2. A herring that is kippered or one used for kippering.

kip'pēr, *v.t.*; kippered, *pt., pp.*; kippering, *ppr.* To prepare (a fish) by splitting, cleaning, drying, and rubbing with salt and pepper; as, to *kipper* herring for the market. [Scot.]

kip'pēr, *a.* 1. Gay; chipper; saucy; full of spirit.

2. In zoölogy, having a drooping or hooked lower jaw, as that of a male salmon after spawning. [Prov. Eng.]

kip'pēr-nut, *n.* Any one of several kinds of nuts or seeds growing underground.

kip'pēr-time, *n.* In old English law, a period during which it was unlawful to take salmon from the Thames between Henley and Gravesend, extending from May 3 to May 12.

kip'skin, *n.* Leather prepared from the skin of young cattle, intermediate between calfskin and cowhide.

kīrk, *n.* [ME. *kirke*; AS. *cyrc, cyric*, a church.]

1. A church or house built for worship. [Scot. and Northern Eng.]

2. Specifically, the Church of Scotland; as, the *kirk* and state. [Scot.]

kīrked (kīrkt), *a.* [Obs.] See *Crooked.*

kīrk'măn, *n.*; *pl.* **kīrk'men.** 1. A member or adherent of the Church of Scotland. [Scot.]

2. A preacher or officer of a kirk. [Scot.]

kīrk'yärd, *n.* A graveyard attached to church premises; a churchyard. [Scot.]

kīr'mes, kīr'mess, *n.* Same as *Kermess.*

kirsch'was"sēr (-vos"), *n.* [G., from *kirsche*, cherry, and *wasser*, water.] A distilled liquor, obtained by fermenting a small black cherry.

kīr'tle, *n.* [ME. *kirtel, kyrtel*; AS. *cyrtel*, a kirtle.] An upper garment; a gown; a petticoat; a short jacket; a mantle; an article of dress in former use, the shape and style of which varied at different times.

kīr'tled, *a.* Wearing a kirtle.

ki-rum'bō, *n.* [Malagasy.] A bird of Madagascar belonging to the *Leptosomidæ*, the only representative of its family.

kī'sel, *n.* [Russ. *kiselu*, sour jelly.] A kind of jelly used in Slavic countries, made from the juice of certain fruits mixed with flour and water.

kish, *n.* [G. *kies*, gravel, pyrites.] A substance resembling graphite, consisting of carbon and manganese, found in some iron-smelting furnaces.

kis'kà-tom, *n.* The American Indian name for the hickory-nut.

Kis'leū, *n.* Same as *Chisleu.*

kis'met, *n.* [Turk. *qismet*; Ar. *qisma*, from *qasama*, to divide.] Portion; doom; appointed lot; fate; predetermined fortune.

kiss, *v.t.*; kissed (kist), *pt., pp.*; kissing, *ppr.* [ME. *kissen, kyssen*; AS. *cyssan*, to kiss, from *coss*, a kiss.]

1. To salute or caress with the lips; to touch or press with the lips, often with a slight sound or smack of the lips; as, to *kiss* a lady's hand; to *kiss* the book.

2. To touch gently.

> When the sweet wind did gently *kiss* the trees. —Shak.

3. To touch by interference, as balls in the game of billiards.

To kiss away; to lose by neglect on account of too much gallantry and fondling.

To kiss hands; to perform a courtesy to a superior by kissing the hand, as on state occasions.

To kiss the dust; to fall in combat.

To kiss the rod; to accept punishment submissively as being just.

kiss, *v.i.* 1. To greet a person by kissing as a mark of friendship.

2. To meet with a slight impact; to barely touch.

kiss, *n.* [ME. *kiss, kyss, cuss*, from AS. *coss*, a kiss.]

1. A salute or caress given with the lips; a common token of affection.

2. A small piece of confectionery; a sweetmeat.

3. A gentle touch of interference, as of balls in billiards.

Kiss of peace; in the early church, and yet with some Christian people, a kiss as a token of Christian love and confidence, a manifestation of peace or the absence of any ill will.

kiss'ēr, *n.* One who kisses.

kiss'ing-bug, *n.* A small black hemipterous insect, *Melanolestes picipes*, with a long sharp beak; also, one of several other insects which make incisions in the lips, causing painful sores by poisoning.

kiss'ing-çŏm"fit, *n.* Perfumed sugarplums to sweeten the breath.

kiss'ing-çrust, *n.* In cookery, the edge of crust that hangs from a loaf and touches another while baking.

kiss'ing-hand, *n.* In zoölogy, the two-toed anteater, *Cyclothurus didactylus.*

kiss'-mē, *n.* 1. In botany, the *Viola tricolor*, or wild pansy.

2. A short open bonnet once worn by women.

kist, *n.* A chest. [Obs.]

kist, *n.* [E. Ind.] In the East Indies, a stated payment, as for rent, taxes, etc.

kist'vāen, *n.* Same as *Cist*, 2.

kī'sutch, *n.* The native Kamchatkan name of a salmon, *Oncorhyncus kisutch*, of the northern Pacific coasts; also called *silver salmon, white salmon*, and *whitefish.*

kit, *n.* [D. *kit*, a beaker; M.D. *kitte*, a beaker, a large drinking-vessel made of staves and hoops.]

1. A large bottle or drinking-vessel. [Rare.]

2. A kind of fish-basket; also, a milk-pail.

3. A kind of wooden tub, used in packing various commodities; as, a *kit* of mackerel.

kit, *n.* [Abbrev. of *kitten.*] A small cat; a kitten.

kit, *n.* [AS. *cytere*, a gittern.] A small fiddle.

kit, *n.* 1. The whole; particularly applied to a soldier's complement of necessaries, a mechanic's outfit of tools, etc.

2. A family; a brood; a variant of *kith.*

The whole kit or *all the kit*; the entire lot; the assemblage; used in contempt of persons; as, I hate *the whole kit* of them.

Kit'çat, *a.* A term designating a club in London, to which Addison and Steele belonged; so called from Christopher (Kit) Cat, a pastry-cook, who served the club with mutton-pies; [k—] applied to portraits a little less than half-length in size, because such portraits of members were placed in the rooms of the Kit-cat club.

kit'çat, *n.* A portrait resembling in size those of the members of the Kitcat club.

kit'çat-rōll, *n.* In agriculture, a roller for ground, larger in the middle than at the ends.

kitch'en, *n.* [ME. *kitchen, kichen, kechen, cochine*; AS. *cycen, cycene*, from L. *coquina*, a kitchen, cooking-room, from *coquere*, to cook.]

1. A cookroom; the room of a house appropriated to cookery.

2. In ships, the galley or caboose.

Kitchen cabinet; see under *Cabinet.*

kitch'en, *v.t.* To feed or supply with food from a kitchen. [Obs.]

kitch'en-ēr, *n.* 1. One who cooks or assists in the kitchen.

2. An elaborate range or cook-stove.

kitch'en-ette", *n.* A small kitchen.

kitch'en-gär"den, *n.* A garden or piece of ground appropriated to the raising of vegetables for the table.

kitch'en-māid, *n.* A female servant whose business is to clean the kitchen and utensils of cookery, or, in general, to do the work of a kitchen.

kitch'en-mid"den, *n.* [Dan. *kjökkenmödding*, a shell mound, refuse heap, lit., kitchen refuse.] In archæology, a heap of refuse supposed to have accumulated around the dwelling of early man, consisting of shells, bones, bits of rude crockery, etc., such as are found in Europe and in North America.

kitch'en-ry, *n.* The belongings of a kitchen. [Obs.]

kite, *n.* [ME. *kite, kete*; AS. *cyta*, a kite (a kind of bird).]

1. A bird of the family *Milvinæ*, a subfamily of *Falconidæ*, characterized by a gliding motion when flying, and usually by a forked tail.

Kite (*Milvus ictinus*).

2. A name of reproach, denoting rapacity.

3. A light frame of wood covered with paper constructed for flying in the air, as for the amusement of boys; so called from its hovering in the air like the bird kite.

4. In navigation, a small sail carried in a light breeze.

5. In commerce, negotiable paper of doubtful

value, floated for the purpose of raising money or sustaining credit.

6. In geometry, a quadrilateral which by a diagonal may be divided into two symmetrical triangles.

7. The flatfish. [Prov. Eng.]

Electrical kite; a silk kite first used by Franklin, giving direct electrical communication with the upper atmosphere, by which he established the identity of lightning and electricity.

Flying kites; see under *Flying.*

kite, *v.i.*; kited, *pt.*, *pp.*; kiting, *ppr.* To raise money by issuing questionable paper. [Colloq.]

kīte′-fal″cŏn (fa″), *n.* In zoölogy, a falcon resembling a kite, of the genus *Avicida* or *Baza.*

kīte′flī-ẽr, *n.* In commerce, one who issues questionable paper. [Colloq.]

kīte′flȳ-ing, *n.* The act of flying a kite, or of transacting business by kiting.

kith, *n.* [ME. *kith, kyth, cuth*; AS. *cyth, cyththe*, knowledge, relationship, native land, from *cuth*, known, pp. of *cunnan*, to know.] Acquaintance or relation. [Obs.]

Kith and kin; one's own acquaintances and kinsfolk.

kith′ȧ-rȧ, *n.* Same as *Cithara.*

kithe, *v.t.* and *v.i.* [AS. *cythan*, to make known.] To recognize or to be recognized; written also *kythe.*

kit′ish, *a.* Resembling a kite.

kit′kat, *n.* Same as *Kitcat.*

kit′ling, *n.* [Ice. *ketlingr*, a kitten.]

1. A whelp; a cub.

2. A kitten. [Scot. and Prov. Eng.]

kit′mut-gär, *n.* Same as *Khitmutgar.*

kit′ten, *n.* [Dim. from *cat.*] A young cat; the young of any animal of the cat tribe.

kit′ten, *v.i.*; kittened, *pt.*, *pp.*; kittening, *ppr.* To bring forth young, as a cat.

kit′ten-ish, *a.* Like a kitten in disposition and action; disposed to play; frolicsome.

kit′tle, *n.* Same as *Kitty.*

kit′ti-wāke, *n.* [So called from its cry.] A three-toed gull, *Rissa tridactyla*, of the *Laridæ* family, having a white and pearl-gray body with black-tipped wings; it is found along the coasts of the North Atlantic and Arctic Oceans.

kit′tle, *v.t.* [ME. *kitelen*; AS. *citelian*, to tickle.] To tickle. [Prov. Eng. and Scot.]

kit′tle, *a.* Ticklish; skittish. [Prov. Eng. and Scot.]

kit′tlish, *a.* Ticklish; difficult to manage.

kit-tül′, *n.* [Cingalese.] A rope-making fiber from the *Caryota urens*, an Asiatic palm; spelled also *kittool.*

kit′ty, *n.* [Dim. from *cat.*] A pet name for a kitten.

kit′ty, *n.* In gaming, a certain part of a pool set apart for the payment of expenses of the game.

kit′ty, *n.* A kittiwake.

kit′ty-sol, *n.* [Port. *quitasol*, an umbrella; *quitar*, to remit, hinder, and *sol*, sun.] A parasol made of bamboo and paper, as a Chinese umbrella or parasol.

kive, *n.* Same as *Keeve.*

kiv′ẽr, *v.t.* [Obs.] See *Cover.*

kī′vi, kī′vi-kī′vi, *n.* Same as *Kiwi.*

kī′wi, *n.* In zoölogy, a nocturnal wingless bird of Australia; the *Apteryx australis*; named from its cry.

kī′wi-kī′wi, *n.* Same as *Kiwi.*

Klä′măth (-măt), *n.* One of the Indians living on the reservation at Lake Klamath, California; also called *Clamat* and *Hamati.*

klang, *n.* [G.] In music, a tone made by a combination of the fundamental with its overtones.

klang-fär′be, *n.* Timbre.

kleene′bok, *n.* [D., from *kleen*, little, and *bok*, buck.] A small timid antelope (*Cephalophus pygmæus*) of South Africa; called also *pygmy antelope* and *guevi.*

Klein-hō′vi-ȧ, *n.* [Named after M. *Kleinhof*, a German botanist.] In botany, a genus of trees in the East Indies having only one species (*hospita*), characterized by its five-parted bladdery fruit-bearing structure.

klep-tō-mā′ni-ȧ, *n.* Same as *Cleptomania.*

klep-tō-mā′ni-ac, *n.* Same as *Cleptomaniac.*

klick, *v.i.* Same as *Click.*

klick, *n.* Same as *Click.*

klick′et, *n.* [OFr. *cliquet*, the latch of a door.] In fortification, a small gate for passage through a palisade.

klink′stōne, *n.* See *Phonolite.*

klī-nom′e-tẽr, *n.* Same as *Clinometer.*

klī′nō-stat, *n.* Same as *Clinostat.*

klip, *n.* [S. African D.] In South Africa, a steep rock or cliff.

klip′das, *n.* [D. *klipdas*; *klip*, a cliff, and *das*, a badger.] A small ungulate mammal, *Hyrax capensis*, bearing some resemblance to a rabbit; called also *rock-rabbit* and *rock-badger.*

klipp′fish, *n.* Same as *Clippfish.*

klip′spring″ẽr, *n.* [S. African D., from *klip*, a cliff, and *springer*, springer.] A South African antelope, *Oreotragus saltatrix*, resembling the chamois in habits.

kloof, *n.* [S. African D.] In South Africa, a gulch, gorge, or ravine.

klō-pē-mā′ni-ȧ, *n.* Cleptomania. [Rare.]

knab (nab), *v.t.* [Obs.] See *Nab.*

knab′ble, *v.i.* [Obs.] See *Nibble.*

knack (nak), *n.* [ME. *knakke*; D. *knak*; G. *knack*; W. *cnec*, a knock, crack, snap.]

1. A snap; a crack. [Obs.]

2. A trick or device.

3. Readiness or ability in some slight operation; habitual facility of performance; dexterity; adroitness; as, a *knack* at remarks.

4. A toy. [Obs.]

knack, *v.i.* 1. To crack; to make a sharp, abrupt noise. [Obs.]

2. To speak in an affected manner. [Prov. Eng.]

knack′ȧ-wāy, *n.* [Corruption of *anaqua*, the Sp. Am. name.] A tree, *Ehretia elliptica*, of Texas and Mexico, having hard close-grained wood and bearing edible fruit; native name *anaqua* or *anagua.*

knack′ẽr, *n.* 1. A maker of knacks, toys, or small work.

2. A rope-maker or horse-collar-maker. [Obs.]

3. One who buys worn-out horses for slaughter and cuts them up for dog's meat. [Eng.]

knack′ẽr, *n.* One of the pieces held between the fingers for making a clacking, as in some classes of music; a bone; a clacker.

knack′ish, *a.* Trickish. [Obs.]

knack′ish-ness, *n.* Artifice; trickishness. [Obs.]

knack′-kneed, *a.* [Obs.] See *Knock-kneed.*

knack′y, *a.* Having special aptitude. [Prov. Eng.]

knag (nag), *n.* [ME. *knagg*; L.G. *knagge*, a knob, thick piece; Dan. *knage*, a knot in wood.]

1. A knot in wood or a protuberant knot; a wart; a peg for hanging things on. [Prov. Eng.]

2. The shoot of a deer's horns.

3. A rugged hilltop. [Prov. Eng.]

knag′ged, *a.* Knotted; decorated with tufts or knots, as a dress.

knag′gi-ness, *n.* The state of being knaggy or knotty.

knag′gy, *a.* Knotty; full of knots; rough with knots; hence, rough in temper.

knap (nap), *n.* [ME. *knap*, from AS. *cnæp*, *cnæpp*, top, knob, button.] A protuberance; a swelling; hence, a mound or rise of ground; a knob.

knap, *v.i.*; knapped (napt), *pt.*, *pp.*; knapping, *ppr.* To make a short, sharp sound.

knap, *v.t.* [D. *knappen*, to crack, crush.]

1. To bite; to bite off; to break short. [Obs.]

2. To strike with a loud noise. [Obs.]

knap, *n.* A short, sharp noise, as of a smart blow. [Obs.]

knap′bot″tle, *n.* A plant, *Silene inflata.*

knap′pẽr, *n.* One who uses a knapping-hammer.

knap′ping, *n.* Breaking stones for macadamizing.

knap′ping-ham″mẽr, *n.* A road-maker's hammer for breaking stones.

knap′pish, *a.* Snappish. [Obs.]

knap′ple, *v.i.* To break off with an abrupt, sharp noise. [Obs.]

knap′py, *a.* Having many knaps or swellings. [Obs.]

knap′sack, *n.* [D. *knapzak*, from *knappen*, to snap, eat, and *zak*, sack.] A case of leather or of canvas for containing clothing, borne on the back by soldiers, travelers, etc.

knap′weed, *n.* A plant, *Centaurea nigra*; called also *knobweed* and *bullweed.*

knär (när), *n.* [O.D. *knorre*, a knot on a tree.]

1. A knot of wood. [Obs.]

2. A rock. [Obs.]

3. A short, heavy man. [Obs.]

knärl, *n.* Same as *Gnarl.*

knärled, *a.* Knotted; gnarled.

knärred, *a.* Having knars or knots; gnarled; knotty.

knär′ry, *a.* Knotty. [Obs.]

knāve (nāv), *n.* [ME. *knave, cnave*; AS. *cnafa*, a boy.]

1. A boy; a man-child. [Obs.]

2. A servant. [Obs.]

3. A false, deceitful fellow; a dishonest man or boy.

4. A playing-card with a picture of a soldier or servant on it; a jack.

Knave bairn; a male child. [Scot.]

Syn.—Rascal, rogue, scoundrel, villain.

knāv′er-y, *n.* 1. Dishonesty; deception in traffic; trick; petty villainy; fraud.

2. Mischievous tricks or practices. [Obs.]

knāv′ish, *a.* 1. Dishonest; fraudulent; as, a *knavish* fellow, or a *knavish* trick or transaction.

2. Waggish; mischievous.

Syn.—Dishonest, fraudulent, villainous.

knāv′ish-ly, *adv.* 1. Dishonestly; fraudulently.

2. Waggishly; mischievously.

knāv′ish-ness, *n.* The quality or habit of knavery; dishonesty.

knaw, *v.t.* [Obs.] See *Gnaw.*

knaw′el, *n.* [Compare G. *knauel, knäuel*, a clue, ball of thread.] A plant, *Scleranthus annuus*, of the pink family, growing in waste, gravelly soil, having awl-shaped leaves and small greenish flowers.

knēad (nēd), *v.t.*; kneaded, *pt.*, *pp.*; kneading, *ppr.* [ME. *kneden*; AS. *cnedan*, to knead.]

1. To work and press into a mass, usually with the hands; to work into a well-mixed mass, as the materials of bread, cake, or paste; as, to *knead* dough.

2. To treat by working and pressing as if kneading dough, as in massage.

knēad′ȧ-ble, *a.* In a proper condition for kneading.

knēad′ẽr, *n.* A person who kneads, or a machine for kneading.

knēad′ing-ly, *adv.* In the manner of working and mixing.

knēad′ing-trough (-trof), *n.* A trough or vessel in which dough is worked and mixed.

kneb′el-ite, *n.* [Named after Major von *Knebel.*] In mineralogy, a brittle silicate of manganese and iron.

kneck, *n.* [Etym. doubtful.] In navigation, the twisting motion of a rope or cable while running out.

knee (nē), *n.* [ME. *kne, knee, know, cneowe*; AS. *cneów*, knee.]

1. In anatomy, the articulation of the thigh and leg bones in mankind; in the horse, cow, and allied animals, the joint corresponding with the carpal or tarsal joint in man.

2. A piece of timber or metal cut or cast with an angle somewhat in the shape of the human knee when bent; as, in shipbuilding, the *knees* are timbers having two branches or arms and used to connect the beams of a ship with her sides or timbers.

3. In a tree, the upward projection of the base of the root, as in the cypress and other trees.

4. Any kneelike formation or structure, natural or mechanical.

5. Reverence signified by genuflection.

Housemaid's knee; see under *Housemaid.*

To bow the knee; to express reverence or offer worship.

knee, *v.t.* To supplicate by kneeling. [Obs.]

knee′-boss, *n.* A protection for the knee, consisting of a metal or leathern cap strapped over the kneejoint.

knee′-breech″eṣ (-brich″), *n.pl.* Breeches terminating just below the knee with a snug fit; knickerbockers.

knee′brush, *n.* In zoölogy, (a) the bunch of hair on the knee of an animal, as an antelope; (b) the bunch of fine hairs or bristles on the leg of a bee whereby it carries pollen.

knee′cap, *n.* 1. In anatomy, the patella.

2. A knee-boss.

knee′-crook″ing, *a.* Obsequious.

kneed, *a.* 1. Having knees; used in composition; as, in*kneed*, weak-*kneed.*

2. In botany, geniculated; forming an obtuse angle at the joints, like the knee when a little bent.

knee′-deep, *a.* 1. Rising to the knees; as, water or snow *knee-deep.*

2. Sunk to the knees; as, wading *knee-deep* in water.

knee′-high (-hī), *a.* Rising to the knees; as, water *knee-high.*

Knee-high to a grasshopper; very small in stature. [Humorous, U. S.]

knee′hol″ly, *n.* Butcher's-broom, a plant of the genus *Ruscus.*

knee′hōlm, *n.* Kneeholly.

knee′joint, *n.* 1. The joint which connects the thigh and leg bones. It is a complex articulation, consisting of an angular ginglymus or hinge joint, formed by the condyles of the femur, the upper extremity of the tibia, and the posterior surface of the patella.

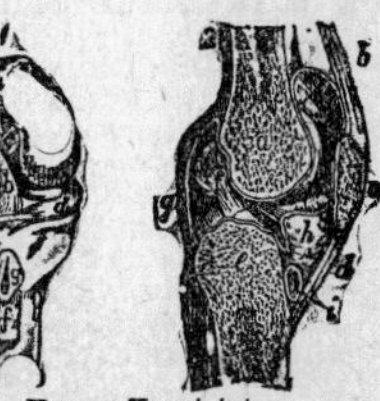

Human Kneejoint.

1. Right Kneejoint laid open from the front, to show the internal ligaments. *a*, Cartilaginous surface of lower extremity of the femur, with its two condyles. *b*, Anterior crucial ligament. *c*, Posterior do. *d*, Internal semilunar fibrocartilage. *e*, External fibrocartilage. *f*, Part of the ligament of the patella turned down. *g*, Bursa situated between the ligament of the patella and head of the tibia laid open.

2. Longitudinal Section of the Left Kneejoint. *a*, Cancellous structure of lower part of femur. *b*, Tendon of extensor muscles of leg. *c*, Patella. *d*, Ligament of the patella. *e*, Cancellous structure of head of tibia. *f*, Anterior crucial ligament. *g*, Posterior ligament. *h*, Mass of fat projecting into the cavity of the joint below the patella. *i*, Bursa.

2. In machinery, a toggle-joint.

knee′joint″ed, *a.* In botany, kneed; geniculated; having an obtuse angle at the joint.

kneel (nēl), *v.i.*; knelt *or* kneeled, *pt.*, *pp.*; kneeling, *ppr.* [ME. *knelen*, *cneolien*, to kneel, from AS. *cneów*, knee.] To bend a knee and rest upon it; also, to bend both knees and rest upon them; as, to *kneel* in reverence or homage.

kneel′ẽr, *n.* One who kneels or who worships by kneeling.

kneel′ing-ly, *adv.* In a kneeling position.
knee′pan, *n.* The kneecap; patella.
knee′piēce, *n.* In building, a piece shaped like a knee, as in a rafter.
knee′=tim″bēr, *n.* Timber suitable for making knees, either by natural growth or by bending.
knee′=trib″ūte, *n.* Tribute paid by kneeling; worship or obeisance by genuflection. [Obs.]
knee′=wŏr″ship, *n.* Worship rendered by bending the knee.
knell (nel), *n.* [ME. *knel, knul*; AS. *cnyll*, a loud noise, from *cnyllan*, to beat noisily.] The stroke of a bell; hence, the sound caused by striking a bell; the sound of a bell rung at a funeral; a tolling.
knell, *v.i.*; knelled, *pt., pp.*; knelling, *ppr.* To sound as a token of departure.
knell, *v.t.* [ME. *knellen, knyllen*; AS. *cnyllan*, to knock, to beat noisily.] To call by the sounding of a bell.
knelt, *v.*, past tense and past participle of *kneel.*
knew (nū), *v.*, past tense of *know.*
knib, *n.* and *v.* Same as *Nib.*
knick′ēr (nik′), *n.* [D. *knikker*, marble, from *knikken*, to knock.] A small marble used by boys in play, made of clay rolled into a sphere, baked, and oiled.
Knick′ēr-bock-ēr, *n.* [A name given by Washington Irving to the typical New York Dutch settler.] A citizen of New York descended from a Dutch settler of that state.
knick′ēr-bock-ērs, *n.pl.* [So called in allusion to the style worn by the Dutch in the 17th century.] A kind of loose breeches, terminating just below the knees; knee-breeches.
knick′knack (-nak), *n.* [A reduplication of *knack*, a trick, toy.] A trifle or toy; any small article more for ornament than for use.
knick′knack-ȧ-tō-ry, *n.* A house or room for a collection of knickknacks; also, the collection itself.
knick′knack-ēr-y, *n.* Articles classified as knickknacks.
knife (nīf), *n.*; *pl.* **knīves.** [ME. *knif, knyf*; AS. *cnif*, a knife.]
1. An instrument for cutting, having a blade or blades relatively short, and means for grasping and using with the hand.
2. A cutting-part of an instrument or machine.
3. A sword. [Obs.]
War to the knife; unceasing strife; combat to end in death; mortal conflict.
knife, *v.t.*; knifed, *pt., pp.*; knifing, *ppr.* To stab with or as with a knife.
knife′=bär, *n.* The bar holding the knives in a harvester.
knife′bōard, *n.* In a kitchen, a board on which knives are cleaned.
knife′=edge, *n.* In mechanics, a piece of steel with a sharp edge used in bearings for pendulums and balances
Knife-edge file; a file having one sharp edge.
knife′=gräss, *n.* A plant, *Scleria latifolia*, of tropical America, with very sharp-edged leaves.
knight (nīt), *n.* [ME. *knight, kniht, cniht*; AS. *cniht*, a boy, youth, attendant.]
1. A youth; a young man. [Obs.]
2. A soldier or follower.
3. A champion; one devoted especially to the service of another as a defender or avenger.
4. In feudal times, a man armored and bearing arms, devoted to the maintenance of virtue and integrity and to the protection of all in distress, having sworn to lead a blameless life.
5. In Great Britain, one who for merit or distinguished service in any line has had the dignity of knighthood conferred upon him,
6. In the game of chess, a piece bearing the head of a horse.
Knight bachelor; in England, a knight of low order, not being eligible to any titular order, such as that of the Bath, etc.
Knight banneret; see *Banneret*, 2.
Knight errant; see *Errant*, a. 1.
Knight of industry; a person who lives by cheating, trickery, and theft.
Knights of Labor; an organization of workingmen in the United States, founded for the protection of the interests of all classes of working people.
Knight of Malta; one of an order of knights who founded a hospital for pilgrims at Jerusalem, which was afterward removed to Malta; called also *knight of St. John of Jerusalem.*
Knights of Pythias; a secret fraternal order founded in Washington in 1864, in the interest of sociability and charity.
Knight of the post; a person who had been dubbed at the whipping-post; a person who could be hired to give false testimony; an acknowledged rascal.
Knights of the Round Table; a mythical order of knights said to have been established by Arthur, a legendary king of Britain, and to have gathered at a round table as signifying equality of rank.
Knight Templar; one of the order of Freemasons having a ritual founded upon the ancient order of Knights Templars.
knight, *v.t.*; knighted, *pt., pp.*; knighting, *ppr.* To dub or create a knight; to raise to the honor of knighthood.
knight′āge, *n.* The entire body of knights, or the knights collectively of a country or district; as, the *knightage* of the empire.
knight′=er′rănt-ry, *n.* The practice of wandering in quest of adventures; the manners of wandering knights.
knight′=er-rat′iç, *a.* Relating to knight-errantry or to the functions of a knight.
knight′head (-hed), *n.* In shipbuilding, a bollard timber, one of two pieces of timber rising just within the stem, one on each side of the bowsprit, to secure its inner end; also, one of two strong frames of timber which inclose and support the ends of the windlass.
knight′hood, *n.* 1. The character or dignity of a knight.
2. An order, honor, or degree of ancient nobility, conferred as a reward of valor or merit.
3. Knights collectively.

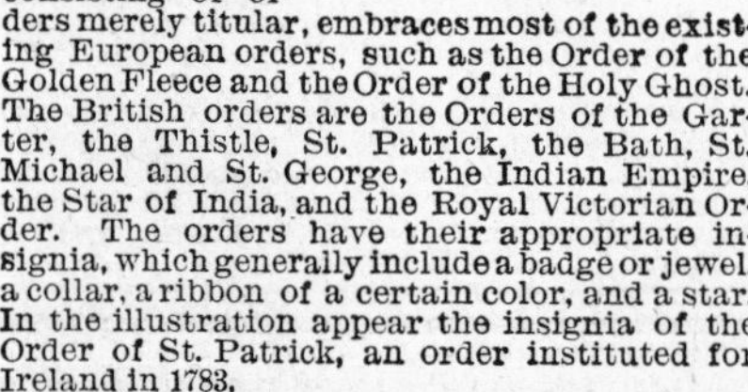
Star, Jewel, and Collar of the Order of St. Patrick.

Order of Knighthood; an organized and duly constituted body of knights. The orders of knighthood are of two classes: either they are associations or fraternities, possessing property and rights of their own as independent bodies, or they are merely honorary associations established by sovereigns within their respective dominions. To the former class belonged the three celebrated religious orders founded during the crusades: Templars, Hospitalers, and Teutonic Knights. The other class, consisting of orders merely titular, embraces most of the existing European orders, such as the Order of the Golden Fleece and the Order of the Holy Ghost. The British orders are the Orders of the Garter, the Thistle, St. Patrick, the Bath, St. Michael and St. George, the Indian Empire, the Star of India, and the Royal Victorian Order. The orders have their appropriate insignia, which generally include a badge or jewel, a collar, a ribbon of a certain color, and a star. In the illustration appear the insignia of the Order of St. Patrick, an order instituted for Ireland in 1783.
Knight′i-ȧ, *n.* [Named after Thomas A. *Knight*, an English horticulturist.] A genus of plants, belonging to the order *Proteaceæ*, of Australia and adjacent regions; only three species are known, the wood of one, the *Knightia excelsa* of New Zealand, being highly prized for ornamental work and for furniture; called *rewarewa* and *New Zealand oak.*
knight′less, *a.* Unbecoming a knight. [Obs.]
knight′li-ness, *n.* Duties of a knight; the state of being knightly or chivalrous.
knight′ly, *a.*; *comp.* knightlier; *superl.* knightliest. Pertaining to a knight; becoming a knight; as, a *knightly* combat.
knight′ly, *adv.* In a manner becoming a knight.
knight′=sērv″ice, *n.* In English feudal law, a tenure of lands held by knights on condition of performing military service, every possessor of a knight's fee, or estate, originally of twenty pounds' annual value, being obliged to attend the king in his wars.
knights′wŏrt, *n.* In botany, a plant of Great Britain having leaves like the blade of a sword.
Knip-hō′fi-ȧ (nip-), *n.* [Named after Prof. J. H. *Kniphof*, of Erfurt, Germany.] A genus of South African plants called torch-lilies, distinguished for the beauty of their spiked flowers; the *Tritoma* of florists.
knit (nit), *v.t.*; knitted *or* knit, *pt., pp.*; knitting, *ppr.* [ME. *knitten, knutten*; AS. *cnyttan*, to knit, from *cnotta*, a knot.]
1. To unite, as threads by needles; to connect in a kind of network; as, to *knit* a stocking.
2. To unite closely; as, let our hearts be *knitted* together in love.
3. To join or cause to grow together; as, to *knit* the bones.
4. To tie; to fasten. [Rare.]
5. To draw together; to contract; as, to *knit* the brows.
knit, *v.i.* 1. To unite or interweave by needles.
2. To unite closely; to grow together; as, broken bones will in time *knit* and become sound.
knit, *n.* 1. Union by knitting; texture.
2. The kind of stitch used in knitting; as, a smooth or a ribbed *knit.*
3. Among miners, a little piece of galena, or lead ore; used mostly in the plural. [Prov. Eng.]
knit′back, *n.* In botany, *Symphytum officinale*, or common comfrey; named on account of its healing properties.
knitch, *n.* A fagot or burden of wood. [Prov. Eng.]
knitch′et, *n.* A knitch.
knit′stēr, *n.* A female knitter. [Prov. Eng.]
knit′tȧ-ble, *a.* That may be knitted.
knit′tēr, *n.* One who or that which knits.
knit′ting, *n.* 1. The formation of network by knitting-needles or machinery.
2. The network thus formed.
To attend to one's knitting; to attend assiduously to one's occupation in order to succeed; as, to say to one disposed to idle, *attend to your knitting.*
knit′ting=çāse, *n.* A case or sheath fastened to the dress to support one of the needles while knitting.
knit′ting=mȧ-çhīne″, *n.* A machine for knitting.
knit′ting=nee″dle, *n.* A long needle, usually made of steel, used for knitting.
knit′ting=sheath, *n.* An instrument with a small perforation to receive the end of the needle in knitting; a knitting-case.
knit′tle, *n.* [*Knit* and dim. *-le.*]
1. A string that gathers or draws together a purse. [Prov. Eng.]
2. A small line used in ships to sling hammocks, etc.
knīves, *n.*, plural of *knife.*
knob (nob), *n.* [A later form of *knop.*]
1. A hard protuberance; a hard swelling or rising; a bunch; as, a *knob* in the flesh or on a bone.
2. A round ball at the end of or forming a part of anything; as, the *knob* of a lock.
3. In southern and western United States, a rounded hill or mountain.
4. In glass-making, the bulb in the center of a table of glass when cut for use.
5. In architecture, a boss; a rounded ornament at the intersection of the ribs of a groined arch.
knob, *v.i.* To develop into knobs. [Obs.]
knob, *v.t.* To produce or to form a knob or knobs on.
knobbed, *a.* Supplied with a knob or knobs; terminating in a knob; as, *knobbed* antennæ.
knob′bēr, *n.* A male animal of the deer kind in its second year.
knob′bi-ness, *n.* The quality of having knobs, or of being full of protuberances.
knob′bing, *n.* In quarrying stone, the act of knocking off the prominent protuberances from a block.
knob′ble, *v.t.*; knobbled, *pt., pp.*; knobbling, *ppr.* [Freq. of *knob.*] To produce a knob, as in stonecutting.
knob′blēr, *n.* A knobber.
knob′by, *a.*; *comp.* knobbier; *superl.* knobbiest.
1. Full of knobs or hard protuberances; hard.
2. Having knobs or abrupt mounds; abounding in rounded hills; as, a *knobby* section of country.
3. Heady; obstinate. [Obs.]
knob′ker″rie, *n.* [S. African.] In South Africa, a stick with a round head on one end, used by Kafirs for striking or for throwing; also spelled *knobkerry.*
knob′stick, *n.* 1. A knobbed stick.
2. In England, a person who refuses to join a trade-union or who withdraws therefrom; equivalent to *scab* in United States.
knob′weed, *n.* Same as *Knapweed.*
knock, *v.i.*; knocked (nokt), *pt., pp.*; knocking, *ppr.* [ME. *knocken*; AS. *cnucian*, to knock, beat; prob. imitative of the sound.]
1. To strike or beat with something thick or heavy; as, to *knock* with a club or with the fist; to *knock* at the door.
2. To drive or be driven against; to strike against; to clash; as, one heavy body *knocks* against another.
3. To criticize captiously; to oppose; to find fault; also *v.t.* and *n.* [Colloq.]
To knock about; to go from place to place, usually receiving rough treatment; to saunter about without definite aim. [Colloq.]
To knock off; to quit; to cease working.
To knock under; to yield; to submit; to acknowledge to be conquered; an expression borrowed from the practice of *knocking under* the table when conquered.
knock, *v.t.* 1. To strike; to drive against; as, to *knock* the head against a post.
2. To strike a door for admittance; to rap.
To knock down; to strike down; to fell; to prostrate by a blow or by blows; as, *to knock down* an ox; also, to disconnect the parts of

machinery or furniture for convenience in shipping.

To knock off; to force off by beating; to assign to a bidder by a blow on the counter.

To knock on the head; to kill by a blow or by blows.

To knock out; (a) to force out by a blow or by blows; as, *to knock out* the brains; (b) in prize-fighting, to render incapable of continuing the fight, by a blow or series of blows; to beat thoroughly; to disable.

To knock up; to arouse by knocking; also, to beat out; to fatigue till unable to do more; as, the men were entirely *knocked up*.

knock, *n.* 1. A blow; a stroke with something thick or heavy.

2. A stroke on a door intended as a request for admittance; a rap.

knock′ȧ-bout, *n.* 1. In navigation, a kind of small sailboat for errands.

2. A man employed for doing odd jobs.

3. A farmer's light vehicle for making quick trips around the farm and in the neighborhood.

knock′ȧ-wāy, *n.* Same as *Knackaway*.

knock′down, *a.* Having power to fell or to silence; as, a *knockdown* blow or argument; made so as to be easily taken apart.

knock′down, *n.* Prostration by a blow or as if by a blow.

knock′ẽr, *n.* 1. One who or that which knocks.

2. An instrument or kind of hammer, fastened to a door to be used in seeking for admittance.

3. A person who captiously criticizes; a grumbler; one who assails the character or reputation of another in an underhanded way. [Slang.]

knock′ing, *n.* A beating; a rap; repeated rappings.

knock′ings, *n.pl.* 1. In mining, the larger pieces of ore from a blast or a sieve.

2. The chips of stone knocked off by a stonemason.

knock′-knee (-nē), *n.* In medicine, a malformation or deformity by reason of which the knees interfere in walking; opposite of *bowleg*.

knock′-kneed, *a.* Affected by knock-knee; opposite of *bow-legged*.

knock′out, *a.* Causing prostration; disabling; as, a *knockout* blow.

Knockout drops; a powerful narcotic in the form of a liquid, administered usually in a beverage, and employed for the purpose of stupefying a victim preparatory to robbing him. [Slang.]

knock′stōne, *n.* In mining, a heavy flat stone or a metal plate upon which ore is broken into small pieces for smelting.

knōll (nōl), *v.t.*; knolled, *pt., pp.*; knolling, *ppr.* [AS. *cnyllan*, to beat or strike.] To ring, as a bell for a funeral.

knōll, *v.i.* To sound, as a bell.

knōll, *n.* [ME. *knol*; AS. *cnol*, *cnoll*, a top, summit; compare W. *cnol*, dim. of Gael. *cnoc*, a hill, knoll.] The top or crown of a hill; a little round hill or mount; a small elevation of earth.

knōll, *n.* The ringing of a bell; as, the curfew *knoll*.

knōll′ẽr, *n.* One who tolls a bell. [Obs.]

knop (nop), *n.* [ME. *knop*, *knoppe*; compare D. *knop*, a knob, bud.]

1. A knob; a tufted top; a bud; a bunch; a button.

2. In architecture, a knob; a bunch of some kind, as of foliage, in high relief.

Knop-and-flower pattern; in Persian pottery, a decorative pattern in which a knob of flowers in high relief has a low-relief background of delicately painted flowers.

knopped (nopt), *a.* Having knops or knobs; fastened as with buttons. [Obs.]

knop′pẽr, *n.* [G. *knopper*, a gallnut.] A kind of gall formed by the puncture of insects on the unripe acorns of the oak, and used in tanning and dyeing.

knop′weed, *n.* Same as *Knapweed*.

knor, *n.* [Obs.] See *Nur*.

knosp, *n.* [G. *knospe*, a bud.] In architecture, a knop.

knot (not), *n.* [ME. *knotte*; AS. *cnotta*, a knot.]

1. The complication of threads made by knitting; a tie; a union of cords, etc., by interweaving or interlacing; as, a *knot* difficult to be untied.

Knots.
1. Diamond-knot. 2. Figure-of-eight knot. 3. Overhand-knot. 4. Bowline-knot.

2. Any figure the lines of which frequently intersect each other; as, a *knot* in gardening.

3. A bond of association or union; as, the nuptial *knot*.

4. The part of a tree where a branch shoots.

5. The protuberant joint of a plant.

6. A cluster; a collection; a group; as, a *knot* of ladies; a *knot* of figures in painting.

7. Difficulty; intricacy; something not easily solved.

8. A bird of the genus *Tringa*; a sandpiper.

9. An epaulet.

10. A nautical mile, varying with the latitude, but fixed in the United States navy at 6,080.27 feet, in the English navy at 6,080 feet.

Syn.—Bond, connection, tie, snarl, tangle, bunch, collection, perplexity.

knot, *v.t.*; knotted, *pt., pp.*; knotting, *ppr.* 1. To complicate or tie in a knot or knots; to form a knot in.

2. To entangle; to perplex. [Rare.]

3. To unite closely.

knot, *v.i.* 1. To form knots or joints, as in plants.

2. To knit knots for fringe.

knot′ber″ry, *n.* A plant of the genus *Rubus*, having knotted stems.

knot′grȧss, *n.* The name of several species of plants, so denominated from the joints of the stem; specifically, *Polygonum aviculare*, of the buckwheat family; called also *knotweed*, *goose-grass*, and *doorweed*. An infusion of this plant was once supposed to be efficacious in stopping the growth of an animal body, whence Shakspere calls it *hindering knotgrass*.

knot′less, *a.* Free from knots; without knots.

knot′ted, *a.* 1. Full of knots; having knots; as, the *knotted* oak.

2. Having intersecting figures.

3. In geology, a term applied to rocks characterized by small, detached points, chiefly composed of mica, less decomposable than the mass of the rock, and forming knots in relief on the weathered surface.

Knotted pillar; in architecture, a pillar of the Romanesque style carved in such a way as to appear knotted in the middle.

Knotted Pillar.

knot′ti-ness, *n.* 1. Fullness of knots; the quality of having many knots or swellings.

2. Difficulty of solution; intricacy.

knot′ty, *a.*; *comp.* knottier; *superl.* knottiest. 1. Full of knots; having many knots; as, *knotty* timber.

2. Hard; rugged; as, a *knotty* head.

3. Difficult; intricate; perplexing; as, a *knotty* question or point.

knot′weed, *n.* Same as *Knotgrass*.

knot′wŏrt, *n.* In botany, any plant of the genus *Illecebrum*.

knout (nout), *n.* [Fr. *knout*; Russ. *knutŭ*, a whip scourge; compare Ice. *knutr*, a knot.] An instrument of punishment formerly used in Russia, often consisting of a strap of leather half an inch wide with one end fastened to a handle and the other holding a ring to which was attached some instrument that would cut the skin and mangle the flesh of the victim when it was applied to his bare back.

knout, *v.t.*; knouted *pt., pp.*; knouting, *ppr.* To inflict punishment upon with the knout.

knōw (nō), *v.t.*; knew, *pt.*; knowing, *ppr.*; known, *pp.* [ME. *knowen*, *knawen*; AS. *cnawan*, to know; akin to L. *gnoscere*, *noscere*, Gr. *gignōskein*, to know, Sans. root *jnā*, to know.]

1. To perceive with certainty; to understand clearly; to have a clear and certain perception of, as truth, fact, or anything that actually exists; as, to *know* the difference between fire and water.

2. To distinguish; as, to *know* one man from another; we *know* a fixed star from a planet by its twinkling.

3. To recognize by recollection, remembrance, representation, or description; as, to *know* a person after a long absence; to *know* a man by having seen his portrait or by having heard him described.

4. In Scripture, to have sexual commerce with.

I know not what; an expression implying an indefinite collection of facts or deeds; as, the boy is up to *I know not what* schemes of deviltry.

Not to know beans when the bag is open; to be dull of apprehension; to be slow to comprehend; to be unsophisticated; to be liable to be cheated.

Not to know B from a bull's foot; to be absolutely ignorant, illiterate, and stupid.

To know a hawk from a handsaw (*hernshaw*); to have wonderful power of discrimination. [Ironical.]

To know the ropes; to be acquainted with all the details of any business or procedure. [Colloq.]

To know what's what; to know all about anything; to be proof against trickery. [Colloq.]

knōw (nō), *v.i.* [ME. *knowen*, *knawen*; AS. *cnawan*, to know.]

1. To have clear and certain perception; not to be doubtful; sometimes with *of*.

> If any man will do his will, he shall *know of* the doctrine, whether it be of God, or whether I speak of myself. —John vii. 17.

2. To be informed.

> Sir John must not *know* of it. —Shak.

3. To take cognizance; to examine.

> *Know* of your youth—examine well your blood. —Shak.

I want to know; a colloquial expression of surprise equivalent to *it seems impossible*.

Not that I know of; if it is so, I am not aware of the fact; not to my knowledge.

knōw′ȧ-ble, *a.* That may be known; that may be discovered, understood, or ascertained.

knōw′ȧ-ble-ness, *n.* The quality of being within the reach of (one's) knowledge.

knōw′-ȧll, *n.* One who makes a pretense of knowing everything; one who will undertake to give information to any one on any subject; used ironically. [Colloq.]

knōw′ẽr, *n.* One who knows.

knōw′ing, *a.* 1. Skilful; well-informed; well-instructed; as, a *knowing* man.

2. Shrewd; cunning; possessing the art of deceiving.

Syn.—Shrewd, astute, discerning, sharp, acute, sagacious, penetrating, proficient, skilful, intelligent, experienced, well-informed, accomplished.

knōw′ing, *n.* Knowledge; means of obtaining knowledge.

knōw′ing-ly, *adv.* With knowledge; designedly; as, he would not *knowingly* offend.

knōw′ing-ness, *n.* The quality of having knowledge or of being shrewd or artful.

knowl′eche, *n.* [Obs.] See *Knowledge*.

knowl′edge (nol′ej), *n.* [ME. *knowlege*, *knowleche*, knowledge; *knowen*, to know, and *-leche*, *-leke*, from Ice. *-leikr*, *-leiki*, a suffix used in forming abstract nouns.]

1. A clear and certain perception of that which exists, or of truth and fact; the perception of the connection and agreement, or disagreement and repugnance, of our ideas.

2. Learning; illumination of mind.

> Ignorance is the curse of God,
> *Knowledge* the wing wherewith we fly to heaven. —Shak.

3. Skill; as, a *knowledge* of seamanship.

4. Acquaintance with any fact or person; as, I have no *knowledge* of the man or thing.

5. Cognizance; recognition.

6. Information, power of knowing.

7. Sexual intercourse, usually with *carnal*.

Syn.—Learning, skill, erudition, understanding, information, lore.

knowl′edge, *v.t.* [Obs.] See *Acknowledge*.

Knōwl-tō′ni-ȧ, *n.* [Named after Thomas *Knowlton*, an English botanist.] A genus of herbaceous plants belonging to the order *Ranunculaceæ*, natives of the Cape of Good Hope.

knōwn, *v.*, past participle of *know*.

Knōw′-nŏth″ing, *n.* A member of the American party. [See *American party* under *American*.]

Knōw′nŏth-ing-ism, *n.* The principles and doctrines of the Know-nothing or American party.

knub (nub), *n.* [A variant of *knob*.] A knob; also, the refuse or husklike envelope of a silk-cocoon.

knub, *v.t.* To beat; to strike with the knuckles. [Obs.]

knuc′kle (nuk′l), *n.* [ME. *knokel*, *knokil*; compare G. *knöchel*; D. *knokkel*, a joint, knuckle.]

1. The joint of a finger, particularly when protuberant by the closing of the fingers.

2. The kneejoint of a calf; as, a *knuckle* of veal.

3. The joint of a plant. [Obs.]

4. In mechanics, (a) the part or parts of a hinge carrying the hinge-pin; (b) a part of an automatic car-coupler.

5. [*pl.*] A metal covering for the knuckles of the hand, to protect them and to aid in giving an effective blow; also called *brass knuckles*; used by robbers.

Knuckle of veal; the part of a leg of veal containing the knuckle-joint.

knuc′kle, *v.i.*; knuckled, *pt., pp.*; knuckling, *ppr.* To yield; to submit in contest to an antagonist.

To knuckle down, to, or *under*; to yield to, as an opponent; to give up in a contest.

knuc′kle, *v.t.* To strike with brass knuckles; to beat with the fist. [Rare.]

knuc′kled, *a.* Jointed. [Obs.]

knuff (nuf), *n.* A lout; a clown. [Obs.]

knūr, **knūrr**, *n.* [Compare O.D. *knorre*; G. *knorren*, a lump, knot; Sw. dial. *knur*, *knurra*, a knob, knot.] Same as *Nur*.

knūrl, *n.* [A dim. of *knur*.]

1. A part of wood knotted in the grain; a curly knob or projection.

2. A crossgrained person; a hunchback. [Prov. Eng. and Scot.]

knūrl, *v.t.* [Obs.] See *Nurl*.

knūrled, *a.* 1. Full of knots; gnarled. [Prov. Eng.]

2. Made small and distorted by shrinking.

knūrl′y, *a.* Full of knots; hard; hard to break or split.

knūr′ry, *a.* Full of knots. [Obs.]

kō′ȧ, *n.* [Hawaiian.] A leguminous Hawaiian tree, *Acacia Koa*, its wavy-grained wood being used for cabinetwork and its bark for tanning.

kō-ä′lȧ, *n.* [Native name.] A marsupial animal, *Phascolarctos cinereus*, of Australia, somewhat resembling a bear.

kob, *n.* [African.] Any one of many species of African antelope belonging to the genus *Kobus.*

kō′bȧ, *n.* A kob.

kō′bȧlt, *n.* Same as *Cobalt.*

kō′bel-līte, *n.* [Named after Franz von *Kobell*, a German mineralogist.] A mineral containing sulphur, antimony, bismuth, and lead.

kō′bold, *n.* [G., from M.H.G. *kobolt*, fairy.] In Germany, a kind of elemental spirit; a gnome.

Kō′chi-ȧ, *n.* [Named after W. D. J. *Koch*, a German botanist.] A genus of plants belonging to the goosefoot family and embracing about thirty species.

kō′dak, *n.* [A trade name.] A portable camera, often folding, using films.

kō′el, *n.* [Prakrit *koelo*, from Sans. *kokila*, a cuckoo.] A parasitic cuckoo of the East Indies.

Kœl-reu-tē′ri-ȧ (kel-), *n.* [Named after Prof. Joseph G. *Kölreuter*, a German naturalist.] A genus of small Chinese trees of the soapberry family, cultivated for their handsome leaves, flowers, and bladdery fruit.

koff, *n.* [D. *kof*, a two-masted sailing vessel.] A small two-masted Dutch vessel, used for fishing.

koft′gä-ri, *n.* [Hind. *koftgari*; *kofta*, pounded, and *-gari*, doing, making.] Ornamental metalwork of steel inlaid with gold, made in India.

Kōh-i-nọọr′, *n.* [Per. *koh-i-nūr*, lit., mountain of light.] A famous diamond of India, belonging to the British crown, weighing over one hundred carats; also spelled *Kohinur.*

kōhl, *n.* [Ar. *al-koh'l*; *al-*, the, and *koh'l*, a fine powder of antimony used to paint the eyebrows.] An antimonial powder for darkening the orbits of the eyes.

kōhl-rä′bi, *n.* [G.] A kind of cabbage with a consolidated head; called also *kale-turnip.*

Kō-lä′ri-ăn, *n.* In ethnology, an aboriginal linguistic stock of India.

kō-mec′e-ras, *n.* [Gr. *komē*, hair, and *keras*, horn.] A kind of horn formed of highly compacted hairs and shed annually, as in the pronghorn of America; also written *komoceras.*

kō-ni-ol′ō-ġy, *n.* [Gr. *konia*, dust, and *-logia*, from *legein*, to speak.] The science treating of the germs and particles of dust floating in the atmosphere.

kon′i-scōpe, *n.* [Gr. *konia*, dust, and *skopein*, to view.] In meteorology, an instrument for examining and determining the quantity of floating particles in the atmosphere.

kō′nite, *n.* Same as *Conite.*

kọọ-chăh′bee, *n.* [Am. Ind.] A food collected on borders of salt lakes by Indians in the western part of the United States, consisting of the larvæ of certain dipterous insects.

kọọ′dọọ, *n.* [African.] The striped antelope, *Strepsiceros kudu*, of Africa; written also *koodo, kudu.*

kọọ-lō-kam′bȧ, *n.* [Native name.] An anthropoid ape of equatorial Africa.

kọọn′ti, *n.* Same as *Coontie.*

kọọr′bash, *n.* [Ar. *kurbāj*, from Turk. *qirbāch*, a whip, scourge.] A whip made of heavy rawhide, as of a hippopotamus or rhinoceros, used in Africa.

Kọọrd, *n.* Same as *Kurd.*

Kọọrd′ish, *a.* Same as *Kurdish.*

kop, *n.* [S. African D., from D. *kop*, a head.] In South Africa, a mountain or headland.

kō′peck, kō′pek, *n.* Same as *Copeck.*

kop′je (-i), *n.* [S. African D.] A hill or hillock; a hill with a steep side and a flat top; a diminutive kop.

Kō′răn (*or* kō-rän′), *n.* [Ar. *qurān, qorān* (written with article *al-*, the), book, reading, from *qarā*, to read.] The Mohammedan book of faith; Alkoran, said to contain the revelations of Allah, or God, to Mohammed.

Kos-te-letz′ky-ȧ, *n.* [Named after V. F. *Kosteletzky*, a Bohemian botanist.] A genus of the mallow family, resembling *Hibiscus*, except that the cells of the ovary are one-seeded; eight species are known.

kō-tow′ (*or* -tō′), *n.* [Chinese *k'ow t'ow*, lit., knocking the head.] A bow or salaam made by knocking the forehead on the ground, practised by the Chinese in courtesy to their superiors.

kō-tow′, *v.i.*; kotowed, *pt., pp.*; kotowing, *ppr.* To salute by knocking the head against the ground.

kot′wạl, *n.* Same as *Cutwal.*

köu′lăn, *n.* Same as *Dziggetai.*

köu′miss, köu′mys, *n.* Same as *Kumiss.*

köus′sō, *n.* Same as *Cusso.*

kow′rie-pine′, *n.* Same as *Kauri.*

kōw-tow′ (*or* -tō′), *n.* and *v.i.* Same as *Kotow.*

krȧ, *n.* [E. Ind.] An ape with a long tail, native of India and Sumatra, *Macacus cynomolgus.*

krääl (*or* krạl), *n.* [S. African D., a village pen, inclosure, prob. from Port. *curral*, a pen or inclosure for cattle.]

1. In South Africa, a stockaded village.

2. A corral for elephants. [Ceylon.]

3. A pen in which Cuban fishers deposit sponges prior to curing them for market. It

krāit, *n.* [E. Ind.] A cobra-like poisonous snake, *Bungarus cœruleus*, of India.

krä′ken, *n.* [Dan. *kraken*; Norw. *krake*, a fabled sea-monster, prob. from O.Sw. *krake*, the stump or stem of a tree, which the monster was supposed to resemble.] A mythical sea-monster of the Scandinavian coast; a sea-serpent.

krȧ-kō′wi-ȧk, *n.* [From *Krakow*, a city in Austria.] The name of a spirited Polish dance.

krä′mȧ, *n.* [Gr. *krama*, a mixture, from *kra*, the root of *kerannynai*, to mix.] In the Greek and other churches, a mixture of water and wine used in the eucharist.

Krā-mē′ri-ȧ, *n.* [Named after J. G. H. and W. H. *Kramer*, German botanists.] In botany, a genus of bushy, many-stemmed shrubs of South America, belonging to the order *Polygalaceæ*, among which is the *Krameria triandra*, which yields the ratany used in medicine.

Krā-mer′ic, *a.* [Named after J. G. H. and W. H. *Kramer*, German botanists.] Pertaining to or derived from ratany.

Krameric acid; in chemistry, an astringent compound crystalline substance derived from the root of *Krameria triandra.*

krang, *n.* [D. *kreng*, a carcass.] The body of a whale stripped of its blubber; spelled also *kreng.*

krang′ing-hook, *n.* In whaling, a hook used for holding the mass of blubber until it is cut loose.

krȧntz, *n.* [S. African D., from D. *krans*, a garland, cornice.] In South Africa, a precipitous elevation; a high steep cliff.

krạu-rō′sis, *n.* [Gr. *krauros*, dry, brittle, and *-osis.*] In pathology, a disease marked by a dry and shriveled condition of the skin or mucous membrane.

krē-at′iç, *a.* Same as *Creatic.*

krē′ȧ-tine, krē′ȧ-tin, *n.* Same as *Creatine.*

krē-at′i-nine, krē-at′i-nin, *n.* Same as *Creatinine.*

kreel, *n.* Same as *Creel.*

krem′lin, *n.* [Fr. *kremlin*, from Russ. *kremlĭ*, a citadel, fortress.] In Russia, the citadel of a town or city; specifically, the citadel of Moscow, including the palace and other public buildings.

kremṣ, *n.* [So called from *Krems*, a town in Austria.] Hydrated carbonate of lead; white lead; also called *Kremnitz white.*

kreng, *n.* Same as *Krang.*

kren′nēr-īte, *n.* [Named after Prof. J. A. *Krenner*, of Budapest.] In mineralogy, a telluride of silver and gold occurring in Transylvania.

kreut′zēr (kroit′sēr), *n.* [G., from *kreuz*, a cross; so called because the type of the coin was a cross.] An Austrian copper coin, the hundredth part of a florin and of the value of about one-half of a cent; also, formerly, a German coin.

kriēg′spiēl, *n.* [G., from *krieg*, war, and *spiel*, a game.] A military game played on a map by students of the art of war.

kri′ō-sphinx, *n.* Same as *Criosphinx.*

kriṣ, *n.* Same as *Creese.*

Krish′nȧ, *n.* [Sans., from *krishna*, black.] In modern Hindu mythology, an incarnation of Vishnu.

Krishna.

kri′tärch-y, *n.* [Gr. *kritēs*, a judge, and *archē*, rule.] Government by judges, as by the judges of Israel. [Rare.]

krō′ne (-nȧ), *n.*; *pl.* **krō′nēr.** [Dan., lit., a crown.] A Scandinavian coin worth about twenty-seven cents; also, an Austrian coin, one half of a florin, worth about twenty-four cents.

Krọọ, *n.* [African.] One of a tribe of negroes on the western coast of Africa, employed as seamen on account of their strength and skill; spelled also *Kru.*

Krọọ′măn, *n.*; *pl.* **Krọọ′men.** A Kroo.

krü′gite, *n.* [Named after *Krug* von Nidda, a mining director of Germany.] In mineralogy, a polyhalite occurring in Stassfurt, Germany.

krul′lēr, *n.* Same as *Cruller.*

krümm′họrn, *n.* [G., from *krumm*, crooked and *horn*, horn.] In music, an instrument resembling a clarinet, formerly in use; also, a reed-stop of an organ, called also *clarinet-stop, cromorna*, and *cremona.*

Krupp gun. See under *Gun.*

krȳ′ō-līte, krȳ′ō-lith, *n.* Same as *Cryolite.*

krȳ-om′e-tēr, *n.* [Gr. *kryos*, cold, and *metron*, a measure.] In physics, an instrument for measuring temperatures below the freezing-point of water.

kryp′tŏn, *n.* [Gr. *krypton*, properly neut. of *kryptos*, hidden, from *kryptein*, to hide.] A chemical element existing in the atmosphere.

kṣär (zär), *n.* [Obs.] See *Czar.*

Kshȧ′tri-yȧ, *n.* [Sans., from *kshatra*, rule, authority.] Among Hindus, the second caste, or a member of that caste.

kū′dos, *n.* [Gr. *kydos*, glory, fame.] Fame; honor; glory; renown; estimation; credit, as for an achievement; chiefly in humorous use.

kụ′dụ, *n.* Same as *Koodoo.*

Kū′fiç, *a.* and *n.* Same as *Cufic.*

kụ-kang′, *n.* [Javanese.] In zoölogy, *Nycticebus javanicus*, the slow lemur of Java.

Kū′klux, *n.* One of the Kuklux Klan.

Kū′klux Klan. [A name derived from Gr. *kyklos*, circle, and E. *clan.*] In the history of the United States, a lawless secret combination of men in the South after the close of the Civil War, who sought to repress the freedmen and their friends by intimidation, expulsion, and murder, usually operating in disguise at night.

kụ′lăn, *n.* [Per.] The dziggetai.

kụl-tür′, *n.* Culture. The English use of the word reflects the belief that Germans employ it to express political ideas and national program together with other elements which through the Great War they endeavored to impress upon an unwilling world.

kụ′miss, *n.* [Russ. *kumuisŭ*, from Tatar *kumiz*, fermented mares' milk.]

1. Fermented mares' milk, a beverage used in the Orient.

2. An artificial imitation of fermented mares' milk, used dietetically in Western countries; written also *kumyss.*

kum′mel (küm′), *n.* [G. *kümmel*, caraway.] A cordial flavored with caraway, cumin, or fennel, made in the Baltic provinces of Russia and in Germany.

kum′mēr-bund, *n.* Same as *Cummerbund.*

kum′quät (-kwät), *n.* Same as *Cumquat.*

kụn′dȧh-oil, *n.* [*Kundah*, native name in Guinea, and E. *oil.*] An oil obtained from the seeds of a species of *Carapa*, a genus of tropical trees.

kụnz′īte, *n.* A beautiful mineral of a rich lilac color recently discovered in S. California and named after Dr. S. C. Kunz. Really a variety of spodumene, with which it corresponds in every respect except color, the latter mineral always occurring in large white crystals.

Kụrd, *n.* [Turk. and Ar. *Kurd.*] In ethnology, a member of an Aryan race in Persia and Turkey; spelled also *Koord.*

Kụrd′ish, *a.* Relating to the Kurds; designating the language or dialect of the Kurds; spelled also *Koordish.*

Kụ-ril′i-ăn, *a.* and *n.* I. *a.* Relating to the Kurils, a chain of islands in the North Pacific.

II. *n.* A native of the Kuril Islands.

Kụ-rō-shi′wō, *n.* [Japan., from *kuro*, black, and *shiwo*, tide.] In physical geography, the Japanese name for the great oceanic current that sweeps the shores of Japan and running north and east mingles with the waters of the Alaskan coast; the Black Current, Japan Current, or Gulf Stream of Japan; also spelled *Kurosiwo.*

kụr′säal, *n.* [G., from *kur*, cure, and *saal*, a hall.] A public room for guests at a watering-place in Germany.

Kụsh-it′iç, *a.* Same as *Cushite.*

kus′kus, *n.* Same as *Cuscus.*

kụs′si-ēr, *n.* [Turk.] In music, a drumlike Turkish instrument with strings stretched across its head.

kutch, *n.* In goldbeating, the leaves of parchment between which the sheets of gold are placed for beating; also spelled *cutch.*

kutch, *n.* Catechu.

kutch′ẽr-ry, *n.* Same as *Cutchery.*

kuwä-zō′kụ (kwä-), *n.* [Japan.] The noble class in Japan; also, one of this class; spelled also *kwazoku* and *kuazoku.*

kvass, *n.* [Russ. *kvasŭ*, a kind of beer.] A mild beer made in Russia; called also *quass.*

kwä-zō′kụ, *n.* See *Kuwazoku.*

kȳ′ack, *n.* Same as *Kayak.*

kȳ′ȧ-nīte, *n.* Same as *Cyanite.*

kȳ′ăn-īze, *v.t.*; kyanized, *pt., pp.*; kyanizing, *ppr.* [Named after J. H. *Kyan*, the inventor of the process.] To treat with a solution of chlorid of mercury, as wood, for preserving it; also spelled *kyanise.*

kȳ′ȧ-nol, *n.* [Gr. *kyanos*, blue, and *-ol.*] In chemistry, same as *aniline.*

kȳ-an′ō-phyl, *n.* Same as *Cyanophyl.*

kyd, *v.*, obsolete past tense of *kithe.*

kye, *n.pl.* Kine. [Obs.]

kȳ-es′thē-in, *n.* [Perhaps from Gr. *kyein*, to be pregnant, and *esthēs*, a garment.] A pellicle forming on certain stagnant urines.

kȳke, *v.i.* [Obs.] Same as *Keek.*

kȳ′lōe, *n.*; *pl.* **kȳ′lōeṣ.** [Gael.] One of the Hebridean or Scotch-Highland cattle.

kȳ′mō-grȧph, *n.* [Gr. *kyma*, a wave, and *graphein*, to write.] In physiology, an instrument for graphically recording variations in delicate forces, especially for noting variations in the pressure of the blood in circulation; called also *kymographion.*

kȳ-mō-grȧph′iç, *a.* Relating to a kymograph or to the use of it; as, a *kymographic* test.

Kym′riç, *a.* Same as *Cymric.*

Kym′ry, *n.* Same as *Cymry.*

Kyr′i-ē, *n.*; *pl.* **Kyr′i-ēṣ.** [Gr. *Kyrie eleēson*, Lord, have mercy.] A portion of the mass, or the music set to it; the Kyrie eleïson.

Kyrie eleïson; a responsive phrase in a liturgy, meaning *Lord, have mercy.*

Kyr-i-elle′ (-el′), *n.* Any form of litany opening with the Kyrie eleïson.

kyr′i-ō-lex-y, *n.* [Gr. *kyriolexia*; *kyrios*, authorized, regular, and *lexis*, speaking.] Expression in plain as opposed to figurative language. [Rare.]

kyr-i-ō-log′iç, kyr-i-ō-log′iç-ăl, *a.* Same as *Cyriologic.*

kȳthe, *v.t.* and *v.i.* [Obs.] Same as *Kithe.*

kȳ-tō-plaṣ′mȧ, *n.* [Gr. *kytos*, a hollow vessel, and *plasma*, a thing molded.] Cytoplasm; protoplasm.

L

L (el). The twelfth letter of the English alphabet, usually denominated a semivowel or a liquid. It came into the English through the Latin and Greek, from Phenician. It is formed by placing the tip of the tongue against the gum that incloses the roots of the upper teeth, and allowing the breath to escape by the sides of the tongue. *L* has only one sound in English, as in *like, canal.* At the end of monosyllables it is often doubled, as in *fall, full, tell, bell*, but not after diphthongs and digraphs, as *foul, fool, prowl, growl, foal*, etc. Etymologically, *l* is related to *r, u*, and *d*; as, L. *peregrinus*, Eng. *pilgrim*; L. *bellus*, Fr. *beau*, Eng. *beautiful*; Gr. *Odysseus*, L. *Ulysses*; Gr. *dakry*, L. *lacrima*, tear.

L, l, *as a symbol.* In the Roman notation, *L* represents the number 50; *L̄*, 50,000.

In chemistry, *L* stands for lithium.

As an abbreviation, *L* or *l* stands for Latin, Liberal, logarithm, lake, etc.

L, *n.* 1. A wing or ell of a building giving it the shape of the letter L.

2. Any common object, as a piece of pipe, when L-shaped.

L, *n.* [Contr. of *el*evated.] An elevated railway; also used adjectively; as, an *L* train.

lä, *n.* [It.] In vocal music, the name of the sixth tone of the scale. [See *Solmization.*]

lä, *interj.* [AS. *la*, interj.] An expression of mild surprise. [Colloq.]

läa′gēr, *n.* [D., from *leger*, a camp.] In South Africa, the camp of an army, etc., surrounded by wagons and impedimenta as a defense.

läa′gēr, *v.t.* To arrange or distribute so as to form a defensive inclosure or laager. [S. African.]

lab, *v.t.* and *v.i.* To blab. [Obs.]

lab, *n.* A blabber; a tattler. [Obs.]

Lab′ȧ-dist, *n.* A follower of Jean de Labadie, who held that God can and does deceive men, that the observance of the Sabbath is a matter of indifference, and other peculiar opinions.

lab′ȧ-rum, *n.* [LL.] 1. The standard borne before the Emperor Constantine after his conversion to Christianity.

2. A banner of like form borne in the Roman Catholic church in ecclesiastical processions.

3. A moral guide or standard.

Labarum.—Medal of Constantine.

lab′dȧ-num, *n.* Same as *Ladanum.*

lab-ē-fac′tion, *n.* [L. *labefactus*, pp. of *labefacere*, to cause to totter or fall.] A weakening or loosening; a falling; decay; downfall; ruin; also written *labefactation.* [Rare.]

lab′ē-fȳ, *v.t.* To weaken or impair. [Rare.]

lā′bel, *n.* [ME. *label*; OFr. *label*, a rag, strip, tatter, from O.H.G. *lappa*, a rag, shred.]

1. A tassel or ribbon-like pendant hanging from a headdress or helmet. [Obs.]

2. A narrow slip, as of silk, paper, or parchment, containing a name or title and affixed to anything, denoting its contents; as, the *labels* affixed to the vessels of an apothecary.

Label of three points.

3. Any paper annexed to a will by way of addition, as a codicil.

4. In heraldry, a fillet with pendants.

5. A long, thin, brass rule, with a small sight at one end, and a center-hole at the other, commonly used with a tangent line on the edge of a circumferentor, to take altitudes.

6. In architecture, same as *dripstone*, n. 1.

lā′bel, *v.t.*; labeled, labelled, *pt., pp.*; labeling, labelling, *ppr.* 1. To affix a label to; to classify; to designate.

2. In architecture, to furnish with a label or dripstone.

lā′bel-ēr, lā′bel-lēr, *n.* One who affixes labels.

lā-bel′lum, *n.*; *pl.* **lā-bel′lȧ.** [L., dim. of *labrum*, a lip.]

1. In botany, one of the parts of an orchidaceous corolla, usually of fantastic shape.

2. In zoölogy, (a) a subsidiary labrum; (b) a swollen termination of the proboscis of certain dipterous insects.

Flower of *Orchis maculata.* L, Labellum.

lā′bent, *a.* [L. *labens* (*-entis*), ppr. of *labi*, to fall, slip.] Sliding; gliding. [Rare.]

lā′bi-ȧ, *n.*, pl. of *labium.*

lā′bi-ăl, *a.* [LL. *labialis*, pertaining to the lips, from L. *labium*, the lip.]

1. Pertaining to the lips; formed by the lips; as, a *labial* articulation. Thus *b, p*, and *m* are *labial* articulations.

2. In zoölogy, pertaining to the liplike organ of an insect.

3. In music, designating tones produced by a liplike structure, as in the organ-pipe.

4. In anatomy, relating to or associated with the lip or lips; as, a *labial* vein, artery, or gland.

lā′bi-ăl, *n.* 1. A letter or character representing an articulation of the lips; as, *b, f, m, p, v.*

2. In music, a pipe with a liplike structure for producing sound, as an organ-pipe.

3. In zoölogy, an appendage upon or closely associated with the mouth; as, the *labials* of a snake, a fish, etc.

lā′bi-ăl-iṣm, *n.* The tendency to labialize, or the quality of being labial.

lā″bi-ăl-i-zā′tion, *n.* The act of labializing.

lā′bi-ăl-ize, *v.t.*; labialized, *pt., pp.*; labializing, *ppr.* In phonetics, to render labial; to cause to utter by the use of the lips.

lā′bi-ăl-ly, *adv.* In a labial manner; by the lips.

Lā-bi-ā′tæ, *n.pl.* [L. *labium*, the lip, and *-atæ.*] The mint family, embracing herbaceous aromatic plants with square stems, opposite simple leaves, and two-lipped corollas, with either four didynamous or only two stamens, the ovary four-parted.

lā′bi-āte, *a.* [L. *labium*, lip.]

1. Having lips or parts resembling lips.

2. In botany, (a) having an irregular monopetalous corolla with a wide mouth, divided into two or more segments arranged in two opposite divisions or lips; (b) having the characteristics of the *Labiatæ.*

Labiate Corolla.

lā′bi-āte, *n.* One of the *Labiatæ.*

lā′bi-ā-ted, *a.* Labiate.

lā-bi-ā-ti-flō′răl, *a.* [L. *labium*, lip, and *flos, floris*, a flower.] Having flowers with labiate corollas like those of the *Labiatæ.*

lā-bi-ā-ti-flō′rous, *a.* Labiatifloral.

lab-i-dom′e-tēr, *n.* [Gr. *labis* (*-idos*), forceps, and *metron*, a measure.] In obstetrics, a graduated instrument for ascertaining the diameter of the head of a fetus.

lā′bile, *a.* [L. *labilis*, liable to slip, from *labi*, to slip, fall.]

1. Liable to err, fall, or apostatize. [Obs.]

2. In chemistry, liable to disintegration by reaction.

lā-bil′i-ty, *n.* The condition or quality of being labile; liability. [Rare.]

lā-bim′e-tēr, *n.* Same as *Labidometer.*

lā″bi-ō-den′tăl, *a.* [L. *labium*, a lip, and *dens, dentis*, a tooth.] Formed or pronounced by the coöperation of the lips and teeth, as *f* and *v.*

lā″bi-ō-den′tăl, *n.* A labiodental sound, as that of the letter *f* or *v*; also, the letter representing such a sound.

lā″bi-ō-nā′ṣăl, *a.* [L. *labium*, lip, and *nasus*, nose.] Formed or uttered by the coöperation of the lips and the nose.

lā′bi-ōse, *a.* In botany, of the nature or appearance of a labiate.

lā′bi-palp, *n.* [L. *labium*, lip, and *palpare*, to stroke, touch softly.] In zoölogy, one of the feelers connected with the lip or labrum.

lā-bi-pal′pus, *n.* A labipalp.

lā′bis, *n.* [L.Gr. *labis*, a spoon; Gr. *labis*, a handle, holder, forceps, from *lambanein*, to take.] In the Greek church, a spoonlike implement for administering the eucharist where the bread and wine are served together.

lā′bi-um, *n.*; *pl.* **lā′bi-ȧ.** [L., a lip.]

1. A lip or something like a lip.

2. The liplike structure of an organ-pipe.

3. In zoölogy, the under lip of an insect or the inner margin of the shell of a mollusk.

4. In botany, the inferior lip of a labiate flower.

lab′lab, *n.* In the East Indies, a name commonly applied to the Egyptian bean, *Dolichos Lablab*, but embracing several other leguminous plants.

lā′bŏr, lā′bŏur, *n.* [ME. *labour*; OFr. *labor*; L. *labor*, labor, exertion, hardship, pain.]

1. Exertion of muscular strength; bodily exertion which occasions weariness; particularly, the exertion of the limbs in occupations by which subsistence is obtained, as in agriculture and manufactures, in distinction from exertions of strength in play or amusements; toilsome work; pains; travail; as, after the *labors* of the day rest is sweet.

2. Intellectual exertion; application of the mind which occasions weariness; as, the *labor* of compiling and writing a history.

3. Exertion of mental powers united with bodily employment; as, the *labors* of a Christian minister.

4. Work done or to be done; that which requires wearisome exertion.

5. Travail; the pangs and efforts of childbirth.

6. Workingmen collectively; as, the joint interests of *labor* and capital; a *labor* union.

7. In mining, a place worked; especially, in the plural, a place where work is proceeding at different points and on different levels.

Labor day; in the United States, a legal holiday in most of the states in recognition of the dignity of labor, usually the first Monday in September.

Syn.—Drudgery, exertion, effort, pains, painstaking, task, toil, travail, undertaking, work.

lā′bŏr, *v.i.*; labored, *pt., pp.*; laboring, *ppr.* [ME. *labouren*; OFr. *laborer*; L. *laborare*, to labor, strive, toil, from *labor*, toil, exertion, labor.]

1. To exert muscular strength; to act or move with painful effort, particularly in servile occupations; to work; to toil.

> Six days shalt thou *labor*, and do all thy work. —Ex. xx. 9.

2. To exert one's powers of body or mind, or both, in the prosecution of any design; to strive; to take pains.

3. To move irregularly with little progress; to pitch and roll heavily, as a ship in a turbulent sea.

4. To be in travail; to suffer the pangs of childbirth.

To labor under; to be afflicted with; to be burdened or distressed with; as, *to labor under* a disease or an affliction.

lā′bŏr, *v.t.* 1. To cause to work; to weary with exercise.

2. To work at; to till; to cultivate. [Rare.]

> The most excellent lands are lying fallow, or only *labored* by children. —Tooke.

3. To prosecute with effort; to urge; as, to *labor* a point or argument.

4. To form or fabricate with exertion; as, to *labor* arms for Troy.

5. To beat; to belabor. [Obs.]

lab′ō-rănt, *n.* A chemist. [Obs.]

lab′ō-rȧ-tō-ry, *n.* [LL. *laboratorium*, a workshop or place to labor, from L. *laborare*, to labor.]

1. A house or place where operations and experiments in chemistry, pharmacy, pyrotechny, etc., are performed.

2. A place where work is performed, or anything is prepared for use; as, the stomach may be called the grand *laboratory* of the human body, the liver the *laboratory* of the bile, etc.

3. An establishment for the manufacture of fuses, rockets, primers, etc., for military use.

lā′bŏred, *a.* Bearing marks of constraint in execution; as, a *labored* style.

lā′bŏred-ly, *adv.* In a labored manner; with the expenditure of labor.

lā′bŏr-ēr, *n.* [ME. *laborer, labourer*; OFr. *laboreor, laborier*; LL. *laborator, laborarius*, a laborer, from L. *laborare*, to labor, from *labor*, labor, toil.] One who labors in a toilsome occupation; a man who does work that requires little skill, as distinguished from an *artisan* or *mechanic*.

lā′bŏr-ing, *a.* 1. Performing work that requires no apprenticeship or professional skill; as, a *laboring* man.

2. Undergoing suffering or painful experience.

Laboring oar; the oar which requires the most strength or exertion, or on which most depends.

lā-bō′ri-ous, *a.* [L. *laboriosus*, from *labor*, labor.]

1. Using exertion; employing labor; diligent in work or service; assiduous; as, a *laborious* husbandman or mechanic; a *laborious* minister or pastor.

2. Requiring labor; toilsome; tiresome; not easy; as, *laborious* duties or services.

Syn.—Assiduous, diligent, painstaking, indefatigable, arduous, burdensome, toilsome, wearisome, industrious, hard-working, active, difficult, tedious.

lā-bō′ri-ous-ly, *adv.* With labor, toil, or difficulty.

lā-bō′ri-ous-ness, *n.* 1. The quality of being laborious, or attended with toil; toilsomeness; difficulty.

2. Diligence; assiduity.

lā′bŏr-less, *a.* Not laborious; not requiring labor; without labor.

lā′bŏr-ous, *a.* [Obs.] Same as *Laborious*.

lā′bŏr-sāv″ing, *a.* Saving labor; adapted to supersede or diminish the labor of men; as, a *labor-saving* machine.

lā′bŏr-sōme, *a.* 1. Made with great labor and diligence. [Obs.]

2. Given to rolling and pitching in a storm; said of ships.

lā′brȧ, *n.*, pl. of *labrum*.

Lab-rȧ-dọr′, *n.* [Sp. *labrador*, a laborer, peasant; so called because the aborigines were strong and capable of hard labor.] A part of British America on the North Atlantic coast.

Labrador duck; an extinct or nearly extinct species of sea-duck, *Camptolæmus Labradorius*, formerly found on the coast of New England.

Labrador feldspar; same as *Labradorite*.

Labrador tea; the name given to two species of evergreen shrub, *Ledum palustre* and *Ledum latifolium*, possessing properties which warrant their use in British America as a substitute for tea, and in Scandinavia as a substitute for hops.

lab′rȧ-dọr-ite, *n.* Labrador spar, a beautiful variety of opalescent feldspar, the finest specimens of which come from Labrador.

lā′bret, *n.* [L. *labrum*, lip.] An ornament worn on the lip by various savage tribes.

Lab′ri-dæ, *n.* [L. *labrum*, lip.] A family of acanthopterygian fishes of which the *Labrus* is the type genus.

lā′broid, *a.* and *n.* I. *a.* Of, pertaining to, or resembling the *Labridæ*.

II. *n.* A fish of the family *Labridæ*.

lā′brōse, *a.* [L. *labrosus*, from *labrum*, lip.] Having thick lips.

lā′brum, *n.*; *pl.* L. **lā′brȧ,** Eng. **lā′brums.** [L., a lip, edge, margin.]

1. A lip or rim, as of a bowl.

2. The upper lip, or what corresponds to an upper lip, in insects and crustaceans; also, the rim of a molluscan shell.

Lā′brus, *n.* [L. *labrum*, lip; so called from the thick, fleshy lips.] A genus of fishes typical of the *Labridæ*.

lȧ-bŭr′nic, *a.* Pertaining to or obtained from the plant laburnum.

lȧ-bŭr′nine, *n.* [*Laburnum* and *-ine*.] A poisonous crystalline compound ($C_{20}H_{27}N_3O$), found in the immature seed of the laburnum.

lȧ-bŭr′num, *n.* [L.] A tree of the genus *Cytisus*, a native of the Alps and much cultivated on account of its hard, dark, polishable wood, which is much in demand among cabinetmakers.

lab′y-rinth, *n.* [L. *labyrinthus*; Gr. *labyrinthos*, a labyrinth, from *laura, labra*, an alley, lane.]

1. Among the ancients, an edifice or place full of intricacies, or formed with winding passages, which rendered it difficult to find the way from the interior to the entrance. The most remarkable of these edifices were the Egyptian and the Cretan labyrinths.

2. A maze; an inexplicable difficulty; any arrangement characterized by great complexity.

3. In anatomy, that part of the internal ear behind the cavity of the tympanum or drum; the inner ear.

4. In metallurgy, a series of troughs in a stamping-mill, through which water passes for washing pulverized ore.

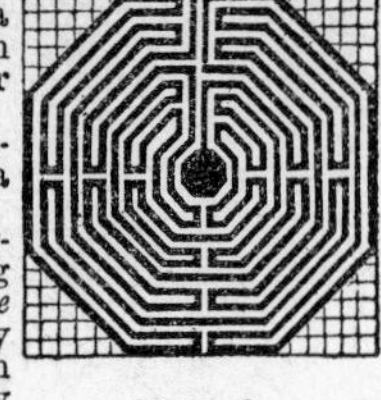
Labyrinth.

5. In architecture, a design in the tiling of a floor.

Syn.—Maze.—A *labyrinth* denotes anything extremely intricate; *maze* denotes the perplexity and confusion into which the mind is thrown by unexpected or inexplicable events.

lab-y-rin′thăl, *a.* Same as *Labyrinthian*.

lab-y-rin′thi-ăn, *a.* Winding; intricate; perplexing.

lab-y-rin′thi-branch, *n.* [Gr. *labyrinthos*, a labyrinth, and *branchia*, gills.] One of the order of *Labyrinthici*.

lab-y-rin′thiç, *a.* Like a labyrinth; labyrinthine.

lab-y-rin′thiç-ăl, *a.* Labyrinthic.

Lab-y-rin′thi-cī, *n.pl.* An order of fishes furnished with a labyrinthine gill-chamber whereby they retain water sufficient to allow them to live in the air, travel about on the land, and even climb trees.

lab-y-rin′thi-fọrm, *a.* [L. *labyrinthus*, a labyrinth, and *forma*, form.]

1. Having the form of a labyrinth; intricate.

2. Having labyrinthine gills, as the *Labyrinthici*.

lab-y-rin′thine, *a.* Pertaining to or like a labyrinth.

Lab-y-rin′thō-don, *n.* [Gr. *labyrinthos*, a labyrinth, and *odous, odontos*, tooth.] A genus of gigantic fossil amphibians, having a peculiar labyrinthine structure of teeth and furnished with bonelike scales on the under side of the body.

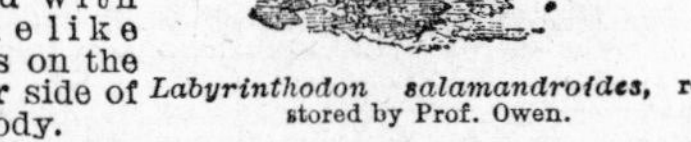
Labyrinthodon salamandroides, restored by Prof. Owen.

lab-y-rin′thō-dont, *a.* Having the characteristics of the *Labyrinthodonta*, especially in the structure of the teeth.

lab-y-rin′thō-dont, *n.* A member of the *Labyrinthodonta*.

Lab-y-rin-thō-don′tȧ, *n.pl.* [Gr. *labyrinthos*, a labyrinth, and *odous, odontos*, tooth.] An order of fossil amphibia of Paleozoic times, of which *Labyrinthodon* is a typical genus.

laç, lakh, *n.* [Sans. *laksha*, a hundred thousand.] In the East Indies, the sum of 100,000, especially in counting money; as, a *lac* of rupees; also used for a large, indefinite quantity.

laç, *n.* [Per. *lak*, lac; Sans. *lākshā*, the lac-insect, from *laksha*, a hundred thousand, a great number; so called from the great number of insects in a nest.] A resinous substance deposited upon trees by exudation from the female of a scale-insect as a protection to its eggs and larvæ. While still attached to twigs and dried, it is called *stick-lac*; when dissolved out and separated from the twigs it is called *seed-lac*, and when strained through a cloth and dried it constitutes *shell-lac*, or the *shellac* of commerce. Lac is used extensively in making varnishes, lacquers, sealing-wax, stiffening for hat-bodies, dyes, etc.

laç′cāte, *a.* In botany, appearing as if having been varnished or lacquered; said of leaves.

laç′ciç, *a.* [*Lac* and *-ic*.] Relating to or produced by or from lac. [Rare.]

laç′cine, laç′cin, *n.* [*Lac* and *-in*.] A substance derived from lac, brittle, yellow, and translucent, insoluble except in caustic potash and in sulphuric acid.

laç′cō-lite, laç′cō-lith, *n.* [Gr. *lakkos*, a pit, and *lithos*, stone.] In geology, an injected mass of igneous rock material, much thicker in the center than at the margin, lying between layers of sedimentary rock and giving the upper layer the shape of a mound or knoll.

laç-cō-lith′iç, *a.* Relating to or having the form of a laccolith.

laç′-dȳe, *n.* Dye extracted from stick-lac, resembling cochineal in color.

lāce, *n.* [ME. *las*; OFr. *las, laqs*, a snare, string, cord; L. *laqueus*, a noose, snare, trap.]

1. A fabric composed of threads interwoven into a net, and worked on a pillow with spindles or pins.

2. A string; a cord; as, a shoe-*lace*; a corset-*lace*.

3. A snare; a gin. [Obs.]

4. Spirits added to coffee or other beverage. [Obs.]

Alençon lace; a needle point-lace first made at Alençon, France, in the seventeenth century, of fine quality and very durable.

Antwerp lace; a bobbin lace resembling Alençon lace.

Brussels lace; see under *Brussels*.

Gold lace and *silver lace*; see under *Gold* and *Silver*.

Honiton lace; a lace made at Honiton, England, remarkable for the beauty of its figures.

Mechlin lace; a lace which has the bobbin ground and designs outlined by a narrow but very distinct flat cord or band.

Point lace; a lace made entirely with a needle by delicate stitching, chiefly in the buttonhole stitch.

Torchon lace; a kind of coarse bobbin lace made of soft and rather loosely-twisted threads by the peasants of Europe.

Valenciennes lace; a very rich bobbin lace, each piece being made throughout, ground and pattern, by the same person and with the same thread, the pattern being worked in the net.

lāce, *v.t.*; laced (lāst), *pt., pp.*; lacing, *ppr.* 1. To fasten with a string through eyelet holes; to fasten by using a cord passing through or under; to intertwine.

2. To adorn with lace; as, cloth *laced* with silver.

3. To beat; to lash; to make stripes on.

I'll *lace* your coat for ye. —L'Estrange.

4. In old slang, to add spirits to coffee or other beverage.

lāce, *v.i.* To be fastened with a lace; as, the boot *laces* in front.

lāce′bärk, *n.* A West Indian shrub, *Lagetta lintearia*, having a lace-like inner bark.

lāced, *a.* Fastened with a lace or string; also, ornamented with lace.

Laced coffee; coffee with spirits in it.

Laced mutton; a prostitute. [Obs.]

Laced stocking; a strong stocking with laces for binding weak legs.

Lac″e-dæ-mō′ni-ăn, *a.* [L. *Lacedæmonius*; Gr. *Lakedaimonios*, Lacedæmonian, from *Lakedaimōn*, Sparta, Lacedæmon, Laconia.] Belonging or pertaining to Lacedæmon or Sparta, the principal city of the Peloponnesus.

Lac″e-dæ-mō′ni-ăn, *n.* A native or a citizen of Lacedæmon; a Spartan.

lāce′-fērn, *n.* An American fern, *Cheilanthes gracillima*.

lāce′leaf, *n.* Same as *Latticeleaf*.

lāce′-liz″ärd, *n.* A large water-lizard, *Varanus giganteus*, of Australia.

lāce′măn, *n.* A man who deals in lace.

lāce′-pā″pēr, *n.* Paper cut or stamped out in figures resembling those of lace.

lāce′-piece, *n.* In shipbuilding, the piece supporting the beak.

lāce′-pil″lōw, *n.* A pillow or cushion used for holding the work and material in making lace.

lac′ēr-ȧ-ble, *a.* That may be torn.

lac′ēr-āte, *v.t.*; lacerated, *pt., pp.*; lacerating, *ppr.* [L. *laceratus*, pp. of *lacerare*, to tear, lacerate, from *lacer*, mangled, lacerated.]

1. To tear; to rend; to separate by violence or tearing; as, to *lacerate* the flesh.

2. Figuratively, to cause pain to, as if by tearing.

lac′ēr-āte, lac′ēr-ā-ted, *a.* 1. Rent; torn.

2. In botany and zoölogy, having the edge variously cut into irregular segments; as, a *lacerate* leaf or organ.

lac-ēr-ā′tion, *n.* [L. *laceratio* (*-onis*), from *lacerare*, to tear, mangle.]

1. The act of tearing or rending.

2. The breach made by rending.

lac′ēr-ȧ-tive, *a.* Tearing; having the power to tear; as, *lacerative* humors.

lā′cērt, *n.* A muscle. [Obs.]

Lȧ-cēr′tȧ, *n.* [L. *lacertus* or *lacerta*, a lizard.]

1. In zoölogy, a large genus of lizards, slender of form, with a long, slender tail and nonimbricated scales.

2. In astronomy, the Lizard, a small northern constellation.

lȧ-cēr′tȧ, *n.* [L. *lacertus*, the arm.] A fathom. [Obs.]

lȧ-cēr′ti-ăn (-shi-ăn), *a.* and *n.* I. *a.* Lizard-like.

II. *n.* A lizard.

Lac-ēr-til′i-ȧ, *n.pl.* [L. *lacerta*, a lizard.] An order of reptiles, including the lizards proper, the slowworms, monitors, iguanas, chameleons, and geckos. With the exception of the *Helodermatidæ*, they are not venomous.

lac-ēr-til′i-ăn, *a.* and *n.* I. *a.* Of, pertaining to, or having the characteristics of the *Lacertilia*; saurian.

II. *n.* One of the *Lacertilia*; a saurian.

lȧ-cēr′ti-loid, *a.* [L. *lacerta*, a lizard, and Gr. *eidos*, form.] Lizard-like.

lȧ-cēr′tine, *a.* Same as *Lacertian* and *Lacertiloid*.

Lacertine work; a style of ornamentation used in ancient Celtic manuscripts.

lȧ-cẽr′tus, *n.*; *pl.* **lȧ-cẽr′tī.** [L. *lacertus*, the arm, pl. *lacerti*, muscle, strength.] In anatomy, a bundle of muscles.

lāce′wing, *n.* A neuropterous insect of the family *Hemerobiidæ*, and especially of the genus *Chrysopa*.

lach′eṣ, *n.* [OFr. *lachesse*, negligence, laxness, from *lache*, lax, negligent.] Negligence; inexcusable delay; specifically, in law, remissness in asserting or enforcing a right; a delay which justifies the court in refusing relief.

Lach′e-sis, *n.* [L., from Gr. *lachesis*, lit., lot, fate, from *lanchanein*, to obtain by lot or fate, to happen.] In classical mythology, that one of the three Parcæ or Fates who measured out the span of mortal life, and so presided over the future.

lach′ry-măl, lach′ry-mōse, etc. Same as *Lacrymal, Lacrymose*, etc.

lā′cing, *n.* 1. The act of binding, fastening, securing, or tightening with a cord, thong, or lace; specifically, the drawing or wearing of one's stays or corsets too tight; as, athletics have driven *lacing* out of fashion.

2. A cord used in drawing tight or fastening; laces in general; specifically, (a) in bookbinding, the cords which pass through holes pierced in the boards of the book, binding them to the back; (b) in nautical language, the cord or rope used to fasten two parts of a sail or awning together or to bind them to yard, boom, or gaff; (c) in machinery, a thong or narrow strip of leather by which belts are joined; a belt-lace.

3. In bridge-building, a system of braces which connect the bars of a truss, without crossing each other.

4. In shipbuilding, a piece of compass or knee-timber fayed to the back of the figure and the knee of the head.

5. In ornithology, a border of a feather, which differs in color from the web; also, the resultant coloration of the plumage, considered collectively.

6. In mathematics, a complex of three or more bands so arranged that they cannot be separated without breaking, although no two are interlinked.

lȧ-cin′i-ȧ, *n.*; *pl.* **lȧ-cin′i-æ.** [L., the lappet or hem of a garment.]

1. In botany, one of the straps or tags forming the fringe on the outer portion of the blade of the petals of certain flowers; also, one of the incisions making this fringe.

2. In entomology, the blade or apex of the maxilla of an insect.

lȧ-cin′i-āte, lȧ-cin′i-ā-ted, *a.* [L. *lacinia*, a hem.]

1. Adorned with fringes.

2. In botany, jagged; said of leaves, petals, bracts, etc.

3. In zoölogy, lacerate; resembling fringe; slashed irregularly into narrow lobes or segments.

lȧ-cin′i-form, *a.* [L. *lacinia*, a hem, and *forma*, form.] In botany and zoölogy, laciniate in form; resembling fringe.

lac-i-nī′o-lȧ, *n.*; *pl.* **lac-i-nī′o-læ.** [Dim. of *lacinia*.] A minute lacinia.

lȧ-cin′i-ō-lāte, *a.* [*Laciniola* and *-ate*.] In botany, finely fringed; having many small laciniæ.

lȧ-cin′i-ōse, *a.* Same as *Laciniate*.

lȧ-cin′ū-lȧ, *n.*; *pl.* **lȧ-cin′ū-læ.** [Dim. from L. *lacinia*, a flap, hem.] In botany, (a) a minute lacinia; (b) the abruptly inflexed acumen or point of each of the petals of an umbelliferous flower.

lȧ-cin′ū-lāte, *a.* In botany, (a) having minute laciniæ; (b) having lacinulæ, as the petals of umbelliferous flowers.

Lac-i-stē′mȧ, *n.* [Gr. *lakis*, a rent, and *stēma*, a stamen.] The only genus of the order *Lacistemaceæ*.

Lac″i-stē-mā′cē-æ, *n.pl.* [*Lacistema* and *-aceæ*.] A small order of monochlamydeous exogenous shrubs, allied to the *Euphorbiaceæ*. The flowers are in catkins, the fruit a three-valved capsule.

lack, *n.* [ME. *lak*, *lac*, defect, want; compare D. *lak*, a stain; Ice. *lakr*, lacking, defective.]

1. Want; destitution; need; failure.

> He that gathered little had no *lack*.
> —Ex. xvi. 18.

2. Absence; the state of being away. [Obs.]

3. Blame; rebuke; censure. [Obs.]

4. A fault; an offense; a blemish, especially a moral blemish; a defect in character. [Obs.]

lack, *v.t.*; lacked, *pt.*, *pp.*; lacking, *ppr.* [ME. *lakken*, to lack, blame; compare D. *laken*, to blame, O.D. *læcken*, to fail.]

1. To want; to be destitute of; not to have or possess.

> If any of you *lack* wisdom, let him ask of God.
> —James i. 5.

2. To blame; to reproach; to detract. [Prov. Eng.]

3. To beat. [Prov. Eng.]

4. To suffer the absence or deprivation of; to miss. [Obs.]

lack, *v.i.* 1. To be in want.

> The young lions do *lack* and suffer hunger.
> —Ps. xxxiv. 10

2. To be wanting; to be deficient; to fail.

> Peradventure there shall *lack* five of the fifty righteous. —Gen. xviii. 28.

lack, *v.t.* In nautical language, to pierce the hull of (a ship) with shot. [Rare.]

lack, *interj.* An exclamation of sorrow or regret; alas! usually preceded by *good*.

lack-ȧ-dāi′ṣi-c̦ăl, *a.* Affectedly pensive; languid; listless.

lack-ȧ-dāi′ṣi-c̦ăl-ly, *adv.* In a lackadaisical manner.

lack′ȧ-dāi-ṣy, *a.* Same as *Lackadaisical*.

lack′ȧ-dāi-ṣy, *interj.* A ludicrous form of *lackaday*.

lack′ȧ-dāy, *interj.* An exclamation of sorrow or regret; alas the day!

lack′brāin, *n.* A witless person; one without much understanding.

lack′ẽr, *n.* One who lacks.

lack′ẽr, *n.* and *v.* Same as *Lacquer*.

lack′ey, *n.* [OFr. *laquay*, a lackey, also a soldier; Sp. *lacayo*, a lackey, footman; compare Ar. *luka*, worthless, servile, Pr. *lacai*, a gormand.]

1. An attending servant; a footboy or footman; hence, any servile follower.

2. A lackey-moth.

lack′ey, *v.t.*; lackeyed, *pt.*, *pp.*; lackeying, *ppr.* To attend as or as if a lackey; to attend servilely.

lack′ey, *v.i.* To act as lackey or footboy; to pay servile attendance.

lack′ey-cat′ẽr-pil-lăr, *n.* The larva of a lackey-moth, which is striped with various colors and sometimes very destructive. They live on trees under a web; hence are also called *tent-caterpillars*.

lack′ey-mọth, *n.* A bombycid moth of the genus *Clisiocampa*, especially *Clisiocampa neustria*, so called because the fore-wings, which are striped, are supposed to resemble a lackey's livery. It is a common European moth.

lack′lus″tẽr, *a.* and *n.* I. *a.* Wanting luster; dull, as the eyes.

II. *n.* A want of luster or brightness; that which lacks luster or brightness.

lac̦′moid, *n.* [*Lacmus* and *-oid*.] A violet-blue coal-tar color used in dyeing.

lac̦′mus, *n.* [D. *lakmoes*, lacmus; *lak*, lac, and *moes*, pulp.] Same as *Litmus*.

Lȧ-cō′ni-ăn, *a.* and *n.* [L. *Laconia*, Laconia, Sparta, from *Laco (-onis)*; Gr. *Lakōn*, a Spartan.]

I. *a.* Of or pertaining to Laconia in ancient Greece, or to its inhabitants; Spartan; Lacedæmonian.

II. *n.* A native or inhabitant of Laconia; a Spartan; a Lacedæmonian.

Lȧ-c̦on′ic̦, *a.* [L. *Laconicus*; Gr. *Lakōnikos*, pertaining to Laconia, Laconian, from *Lakōn*, an inhabitant of Laconia, a Laconian or Spartan.]

1. Same as *Laconian*. [Rare.]

2. [l—] Short; brief; pithy; sententious; expressing much in few words, after the manner of the Laconians; as, a *laconic* phrase.

3. [l—] Having the characteristics of the Laconians; inexorable; stern; harsh; severe. [Rare.]

Syn.—Concise, pithy, short, brief, curt, epigrammatic, terse.—*Laconic* implies few words; *concise*, only the necessary words.

lȧ-c̦on′ic̦, *n.* 1. Laconicism; a brief, pithy mode of expression. [Rare.]

2. A brief, pithy expression; a laconism; used chiefly in the plural; as, he spoke in *laconics*.

3. In ancient prosody, a reversed dactyl having four measures and catalectic with a spondee instead of the penultimate anapest.

lȧ-c̦on′i-c̦ȧ, *n.*, pl. of *laconicum*.

lȧ-c̦on′ic̦-ăl, *a.* [Rare.] Same as *Laconic*.

lȧ-c̦on′ic̦-ăl-ly, *adv.* In a laconic manner; briefly; concisely; as, a sentiment *laconically* expressed.

lȧ-c̦on′i-c̦iṣm, *n.* 1. A laconic or concise, pithy mode of expression; laconism.

2. A laconic or concise, pithy phrase; a laconism.

lȧ-c̦on′i-c̦um, *n.*; *pl.* **lȧ-c̦on′i-c̦ȧ.** [L.] In Roman antiquity, a vapor-bath; a chamber either in a bathing-establishment or separate, heated by hot air; so called because the Laconians used such a dry bath as less weakening than one of water.

lac̦′ō-niṣm, *n.* [Gr. *Lakōnismos*, the imitation of the Lacedæmonians or Spartans in manners, dress, etc., from *Lakōnizein*, to imitate the Lacedæmonians, to speak laconically, to laconize.]

1. A concise style.

2. A brief, sententious phrase or expression.

lac̦′ō-nīze, *v.i.*; laconized, *pt.*, *pp.*; laconizing, *ppr.* To imitate the Laconians in their thrift, frugality, austerity of life or pithiness of expression.

lac̦′quẽr (-ẽr), *n.* [Fr. *lacre*, from *laca*, gum lac, from Per. *lak*, lac.]

1. An opaque varnish much used for woodwork and metal-work, a solution of shellac in alcohol being the chief or sole ingredient, except coloring matter.

2. Wooden articles ornamented by a coating of lacquer and often inlaid with figures and ornaments of gold, silver, bronze, mother-of-pearl, ivory, and other materials. Such ware is extensively made in China and Japan, especially in Japan. Also called *lacquer-work* and *lacquer-ware*.

3. Decorative work which is varnished after being painted to give the effect of enamel.

4. A varnish obtained from the Japanese varnish-tree, *Rhus vernicifera*, by making incisions in the bark.

lac̦′quẽr, *v.t.* To varnish; to smear over with lacquer; to decorate with lacquer.

lac̦′quẽr-ẽr, *n.* One who lacquers; a lacquer-maker.

lac̦′quẽr-ing, *n.* The act of putting on lacquer; also, the covering of lacquer or varnish put on.

lac̦′quẽr-tree, *n.* A tree, *Rhus vernicifera*, of the cashew family.

lȧ-c̦rĭ-mō′ṣō, *a.* Same as *Lagrimoso*.

lȧ-c̦rọsse′ (-krọs′), *n.* [Fr. *la crosse*; *la*, the, and *crosse*, a crutch, hockey-stick, cross.] A game of ball originated by the North American Indians. It is a favorite field-sport in Canada, and is also played in England and the United States. The point of the game is to drive or carry the ball with the crosse between and past two goal-posts at the opponents' end of the field.

Crosse or Bat used in Game of Lacrosse.

lȧ-c̦rọsse′-stick, *n.* The racket used in playing the game of lacrosse.

lac̦′ry-mȧ-ble, *a.* Lamentable; mournful; tearful. [Obs.]

lac̦′ry-măl, *a.* [LL. *lacrimalis*, of or pertaining to tears, from L. *lacrima*, a tear.] In anatomy and physiology, of or pertaining to tears; generating, secreting, or conveying tears; as, the *lacrymal* gland or canal.

lac̦′ry-măl, *n.* 1. A membrane-bone of the face in vertebrates. In man, it is wholly within the orbit of the eye on the inner side. Also called *lacrymal bone*, *lacrymale*, *os tarsale*, *os lacrymale*, and *os unguis*.

2. Same as *Lacrymatory*.

3. [*pl.*] A humorous word for tears or a fit of weeping.

lac̦-ry-mā′lē, *n.*; *pl.* **lac̦-ry-mā′li-ȧ.** Same as *Lacrymal*, n. 1.

lac̦′ry-mā-ry, *a.* [L. *lacrima*, or *lacryma*, a tear.] Holding or intended to hold tears; lacrymal.

lac̦′ry-māte, *v.i.* To weep. [Rare.]

lac̦-ry-mā′tion, *n.* [L. *lacrimatio (-onis)*, a weeping, from *lacrimare*, to weep, from *lacrima*, a tear.] The act of shedding tears; an emission of tears; weeping.

lac̦′ry-mȧ-tō-ry, *n.* [LL. *lacrimatorium*, properly neut. of *lacrimatorius*, of or pertaining to tears, from L. *lacrima*, a tear.] One of a class of glass vessels or phials found in sepulchers of the ancients, in which it has been supposed the tears of a deceased person's friends were collected and preserved with the ashes. Also called *lacrymal*.

Lacrymatories, from specimens in British Museum.

lac̦′ry-mi-form, *a.* [L. *lacrima*, a tear, and *forma*, form.] In botany and zoölogy, shaped like a tear or a drop; guttiform.

lac̦′ry-mōse, *a.* [L. *lacrimosus*, full of tears, tearful, from *lacrima*, a tear.]

1. Shedding tears; addicted to shedding tears; appearing as if shedding tears; tearful.

2. Of a tearful quality; exhibiting or producing tearfulness; mournful; lugubrious; often used in sarcasm; as, a *lacrymose* woman; a *lacrymose* tone.

lac̦′ry-mōse-ly, *adv.* In a lacrymose manner.

lac̦′tāge, *n.* [OFr. *laictage*, a diet of milk, from *laict*; L. *lac*, *lactis*, milk.] The produce of animals yielding milk; milk and the products manufactured from it.

lac̦′tam, *n.* [*Lactone* and *amido*.] One of a series of anhydrids of an amido-acid.

lac-tam'ic, *a.* Pertaining to an amic acid, $C_3H_7NO_2$, derived from lactic acid.

lac-tam'ide, *n.* [*Lactic* and *amide*.] A colorless, crystalline substance, $C_3H_7NO_2$, formed by the union of lactide and ammonia.

lac'tānt, *a.* [L. *lactans* (*-antis*), ppr. of *lactare*, to contain milk, to give suck, from *lac*, *lactis*, milk.] Suckling; giving suck.

lac'tā-rēne, lac'tā-rine, *n.* A preparation of milk-casein used in calico-printing.

lac'tā-ry, *n.* A dairy-house. [Rare.]

lac'tā-ry, *a.* Milky; full of white juice like milk. [Obs.]

lac'tāte, *n.* [L. *lac*, *lactis*, milk, and *-ate*.] A salt of lactic acid.

lac'tāte, *v.i.*; lactated, *pt.*, *pp.*; lactating, *ppr.* [L. *lactatus*, pp. of *lactare*, to contain milk, to give suck, from *lac*, *lactis*, milk.]

1. To cause the secretion of milk.
2. To give suck to the young.

lac'tāte, *v.t.* To convert into milk; to make milk-like.

lac-tā'tion, *n.* 1. The act of giving suck or the time of suckling.

2. In medicine, the function of secreting and excreting milk.

lac'tē-ăl, *a.* [L. *lacteus*, milky, from *lac*, *lactis*, milk.]

1. Pertaining to milk.
2. Conveying chyle; as, a *lacteal* vessel.

lac'tē-ăl, *n.* In anatomy, one of numerous minute tubes which absorb or take up the chyle or milk-like fluid from the alimentary canal and convey it to the thoracic duct.

lac'tē-ăl-ly, *adv.* Milkily; in the manner of milk.

lac'tē-ăn, *a.* [L. *lacteus*, milky, and *-an*.]

1. Milky; containing or resembling milk.
2. Lacteal; conveying chyle.

lac'tē-in, *n.* [L. *lacteus*, milky, and *-in*.] Milk solidified by evaporation.

lac'tē-ous, *a.* [L. *lacteus*, from *lac*, *lactis*, milk.]

1. Milky; resembling milk.
2. Lacteal; conveying chyle; as, a *lacteous* vessel.

lac'tē-ous-ly, *adv.* Milkily; lacteally; in a lacteous manner.

lac-tes'cence, *n.* 1. The state of being lactescent; milkiness or milky color.

2. In botany, milkiness; the liquor which flows abundantly from a plant, when wounded, commonly white, but sometimes yellow or red.

lac-tes'cent, *a.* [L. *lactescens* (*-entis*), ppr. of *lactescere*, to turn into milk, incept. of *lactare*, to be milky, from *lac*, *lactis*, milk.]

1. Becoming milky; resembling milk.
2. In botany, producing milk or a juice resembling milk, as the milkweed.

lacti-, lacto-. Combining forms from L. *lac*, *lactis*, milk, used in chemistry, botany, etc., to signify milk, or like milk; as, *lacti*florous, *lacto*-albumin.

lac'tic, *a.* [L. *lac*, *lactis*, milk, and *-ic*.] Of the nature of, pertaining to, or procured from milk.

Lactic acid; an intensely sour, syrupy compound, $C_3H_6O_3$, most common in sour milk, but also found in the fermentation of several vegetable juices and in the putrefaction of some animal matters, particularly in human urine. It is colorless and odorless, forms well-defined salts, and coagulates milk.

Lactic ferment; the cause of the process of lactic fermentation. [See under *Fermentation*.]

lac'tide, *n.* [L. *lac*, *lactis*, milk, and *-ide*.] A volatile substance, $C_6H_8O_4$, which is one of the products of the dry distillation of lactic acid.

lac-tif'ēr-ous, *a.* [LL. *lactifer*, from L. *lac*, *lactis*, milk, and *ferre*, to bear.]

1. Bearing or conveying milk or white juice; as, a *lactiferous* duct.
2. Producing a thick, milky juice, as a plant.

lac-tif'ic, lac-tif'ic-ăl, *a.* [*Lacti-*, and L. *facere*, to make.] Producing milk.

lac-ti-flō'rous, *a.* Bearing flowers of milk-white color.

lac-tif'ū-găl, *a.* Serving or tending to check the secretion of milk; having the properties and powers of a lactifuge.

lac'ti-fūge, *n.* [*Lacti-*, and L. *fugare*, to put to flight, from *fugere*, to flee.] A medicine which checks the secretion of milk.

lac-tim'id, lac-tim'ide, *n.* [*Lactic* and *imid*, or *amide*.] A white crystalline substance obtained by heating lactamic and hydrochloric acids together.

lac'tine, lac'tin, *n.* [L. *lac*, *lactis*, milk, and *-ine*, *-in*.] Same as *Lactose*.

lacto-. See *Lacti*.

lac"tō-al-bū'min, *n.* [*Lacto-*, and L. *albumen*, whiteness, from *albus*, white.] The albumin found in milk.

lac-tō-bū-ty-rom'e-tēr, *n.* [*Lacto-*, and L. *butyrum*, butter, and *metrum*, a measure.] A device for ascertaining the percentage of butter fat in a given quantity of milk.

lac'tō-cēle, *n.* [*Lacto-*, and Gr. *kēlē*, a tumor.] In pathology, a tumor containing milk or a fluid resembling it; also called *galactocele*.

lac'tō-crite, lac'tō-crit, *n.* [*Lacto-*, and Gr. *kritēs*, a judge.] An apparatus used in creameries for ascertaining the proportion of fatty substance or butter in a sample of milk.

lac"tō-den-sim'e-tēr, *n.* [*Lacto-*, and L. *densus*, thick, dense, and *metrum*, a measure.] A hydrometer so constructed as to show the density of milk and the proportion of cream removed from it.

lac'tō-lith, *n.* [*Lacto-*, and Gr. *lithos*, a stone.] One of the products of skimmed milk, made by solidifying it until a substance resembling stone is produced, used much the same as celluloid; called also *milkstone*.

lac-tom'e-tēr, *n.* [*Lacto-*, and Gr. *metron*, a measure.] An instrument for ascertaining the different qualities of milk; also called *galactometer*.

lac'tōne, *n.* [L. *lac*, *lactis*, milk, and *-one*.] A colorless, volatile liquid ($C_5H_8O_2$) possessing an aromatic odor and produced, along with lactide, by the dry distillation of lactic acid.

lac-tō-prō'tē-in, *n.* [*Lacto-*, and Gr. *prōtos*, first, and *-in*.] A specific proteid component of milk, as casein.

lac'tō-ry, *a.* [Obs.] Same as *Lactiferous*.

lac'tō-scōpe, *n.* [*Lacto-*, and Gr. *skopein*, to view.] An instrument for determining the opacity of milk, that its cream content may be estimated.

lac'tōse, *n.* [L. *lac*, *lactis*, milk, and *-ose*.] Milk-sugar, $C_{12}H_{22}O_{11}$, obtained by evaporating whey, filtering through animal charcoal, and crystallizing. It is used in food and medicine. Also called *galactine* and *lactine*.

lac-tō-sū'ri-ȧ, *n.* [*Lacto-*, and Gr. *ouron*, urine.] In pathology, the presence of lactose or milk-sugar in the urine.

Lac-tū'cȧ, *n.* [L., lettuce.] A genus of liguliflorous herbs of the aster family, to which the lettuce, *Lactuca sativa*, belongs.

lac-tū-cā'ri-um, *n.* [L. *lactuca*, lettuce.] The inspissated juice of the common lettuce, sometimes used as a substitute for opium.

lac-tū'cic, *a.* Of, pertaining to, or derived from lettuce.

Lactucic acid; an acid obtained from the strong-scented lettuce, *Lactuca virosa*, and bearing some resemblance to oxalic acid.

lac-tū'cin, lac-tū'cine, *n.* [L. *lactuca*, lettuce, and *-in*, *-ine*.] One of the essential ingredients of lactucarium, a bitter, crystalline substance with a neutral reaction.

lac-tū'cōne, *n.* [L. *lactuca*, lettuce, and *-one*.] In chemistry, a tasteless substance, white and crystalline, obtained from lactucarium, of which it is an essential ingredient, by the action of boiling alcohol.

lac-tū-ram'ic, *a.* [*Lactic* and *urea* and *-amic*.] Of, pertaining to, or derived from lactic acid and urea.

lac'tyl, *n.* [*Lactic*, and *-yl*.] In chemistry, a lactic acid anhydrid.

lȧ-cū'nȧ, *n.*; *pl.* **lȧ-cū'næ.** [L., a ditch, hole, cavity, pool, from *lacus*, a hollow, tank, lake.]

1. A small opening; a small pit or depression; a small blank space.
2. In botany, (a) one of the small hollows or pits on the upper surface of a lichen's thallus; (b) an internal organ or air-cell found in the midst of a plant's cellular tissue.
3. In anatomy, one of a multitude of follicles in the mucous membranes, as in those of the urethra.
4. In physiology, one of the spaces left among the tissues of the lower animals and serving in place of vessels for the circulation of the fluids of the body.

lȧ-cū'năl, lȧ-cū'năr, *a.* Pertaining to or having lacunæ.

lȧ-cū'năr, *n.*; *pl.* **lȧ-cū'nărs** or **lac-ū-nā'ri-ȧ.** [L., a panel-ceiling, from *lacuna*, a hollow, pit.]

1. In architecture, the ceiling or under surface of any part, when it consists of compartments sunk or hollowed, without spaces or bands between the panels.
2. One of the sunken panels in a ceiling or a soffit.

Ceiling with Lacunars, Buckingham Palace.

lac'ū-nā-ry, *a.* Pertaining to a lacuna; lacunal.

lȧ-cūne', *n.* [Fr., from L. *lacuna*, a hollow.] A lacuna; a gap; a defect. [Rare.]

lac-ū-nette' (-net'), *n.* [Fr., dim. of *lacune*, a lacuna.] In fortifications, a small ditch; a moat; a foss.

lac'ū-nōse, lȧ-cū'nous, *a.* [L. *lacunosus*, full of holes, from *lacuna*, a hollow, cavity.] In biology, furrowed or pitted; abounding in cavities or lacunæ; as, a *lacunose* leaf; a *lacunose* elytra of a beetle.

lac-ū-nō-sō-rū'gōse, *a.* In botany, having deep irregular pits or furrows, as a peach-stone.

lȧ-cū'nū-lōse, *a.* Having minute lacunæ.

lȧ-cus'tri-ăn, *a.* and *n.* I. *a.* Same as *Lacustrine*.

II. *n.* A lake-dweller.

lȧ-cus'trine, lȧ-cus'trăl, *a.* [L. *lacus*, a lake.]

1. Of or pertaining to a lake.
2. In biology, living or growing in a lake.

Lacustrine deposits; in geology, deposits of silt, peat, etc., formed at the bottom of lakes. They frequently consist of a series of strata arranged in regular order, one above another.

Lacustrine dwelling or *habitation*; same as *Lake-dwelling*.

lac'wŏrk, *n.* Japanese lacquer.

lā'cy, lā'cey, *a.* Lacelike; of the appearance of lace.

lad, *n.* [ME. *ladde*, of Celtic origin; compare, Ir. *lath*, a youth, AS. *leód*, a man.]

1. A young man, or boy; a stripling.
2. A male lover or sweetheart, correlative to *lass*. [Scot.]
3. A male servant. [Obs.]

lad, *v.*, obsolete past tense and past participle of *lead*.

lad'ȧ-num, *n.* [L. *ladanum*; Gr. *lēdanon*, gum, ladanum, from *lēdon*, the mastic, a shrub; Per. *lādan*, a shrub; compare *laudanum*.] A resinous gum which exudes from a shrub, *Cistus ladaniferus*, which grows in Spain and Portugal, or from *Cistus Creticus* of Oriental countries. It is dark-colored, has a pleasant odor, and is of the consistency of a soft plaster. It was formerly in great demand as a stomachic and to apply externally, but is now little used. Also called *labdanum*, *laudanum*, *gum ladanum*, *gum labdanum*, and *gum ledon*.

lad'de, *v.*, obsolete past tense of *lead*.

lad'dēr, *n.* [ME. *laddere*; AS. *hlæder*, *hlædder*, a ladder.]

1. A frame of wood, metal, or rope, consisting of two side-pieces, connected by rounds or rungs inserted in them at suitable distances and thus forming steps by which persons may ascend a building, etc.
2. Figuratively, anything by which a person ascends or rises; means of ascending.

> Lowliness is young ambition's *ladder*. —Shak.

Accommodation ladder; see under *Accommodation*.

lad'dēr-bee"tle, *n.* A beetle, *Chrysomela scalaris*, very common in America. It lives and feeds upon leaves, and has silvery-white fore wings striped with green.

lad'dēr-shell, *n.* Any marine shell of the genus *Scalaria*; so called because of the conspicuous transverse ribs, which are thought to resemble the rounds of a ladder; a wentletrap.

lad'die, *n.* A lad or young man; a lover. [Scot.]

lāde, *v.t.*; laded, *pt.*; lading, *ppr.*; laden *or* laded, *pp.* [ME. *laden*; AS. *hladan*, to heap, pile on, load, draw.]

1. To load; to put on or in, as a burden or freight; as, to *lade* a ship with cotton; to *lade* a horse or other beast with corn.
2. To dip; to throw in or out, as a fluid, with a ladle or dipper; as, to *lade* water out of a tub or into a cistern.
3. Figuratively, to oppress; usually in the past participle.

> Come unto me, all ye that labor and are heavy *laden*. —Matt. xi. 28.

4. To admit (water), as a sinking ship. [Obs.]

lāde, *v.i.* 1. To draw water. [Obs.]

2. To leak.

lāde, *n.* [ME. *lode*; AS. *lad*, a way, course, path.]

1. The mouth of a river. [Obs.]
2. A watercourse; a mill-race; a drain. [Prov. Eng. and Scot.]

lāde'măn, *n.* [ME. *lodeman*; AS. *ladman*, a leader, guide; *lad*, way, path, course, and *man*, man.]

1. One who has charge of a packhorse.
2. A servant employed by a miller to return to the owners their quantities of meal when ground. [Scot.]

lād'en, *v.*, past participle of *lade*.

lā'died, *a.* Ladylike. [Obs.]

lā'di-fȳ, *v.t.* To render ladylike; to make a lady of; to give the title or style of lady to. [Obs.]

Lȧ-dïn', *n.* [Rheto-Romanic *ladin*; L. *Latinus*, Latin.] A dialect of the Rheto-Romanic language used in the southeastern part of Switzerland and the upper part of the Tyrol.

lād'ing, *n.* [ME. *lading*; AS. *hladung*, a drawing, loading, from *hladan*, to load, draw.]

1. The act of loading.
2. That which constitutes a load or cargo; freight; burden; as, the *lading* of a ship.

Lȧ-dï'nō, *n.*; *pl.* **Lȧ-dï'nōs.** [Sp., from L. *Latinus*, Latin.]

1. The old language of Spain; the ancient Castilian language.

2. A jargon of Spanish and Portuguese, spoken by Jews in Turkey and other places.

3. In Central America, a mestizo; a half-breed of white and Indian parentage.

lad′kin, *n.* A little lad; a youth. [Rare.]

lā′dle, *n.* [ME. *ladel*; AS. *hlædel*, a ladle, from *hladan*, to draw water, to lade.]

1. A utensil somewhat like a spoon with a long handle, used for lading or dipping.

2. The receptacle of a mill-wheel, which receives the water which moves it.

3. In gunnery, (a) an instrument for drawing the charge of a cannon; (b) a ring provided with one or more handles for carrying shot.

4. In founding, an iron vessel, often with two handles, in which liquid metal is carried from the furnace to the mold.

lā′dle, *v.t.*; ladled, *pt.*, *pp.*; ladling, *ppr.* To lift or dip out with a ladle; as, to *ladle* out soup.

lā′dle-fụl, *n.* The quantity contained in a ladle.

lā′dle-wood, *n.* A small South African tree, *Cassine Colpoon*, with very hard, beautifully veined wood which is valuable for carving and in cabinetwork.

lȧ-drōne′, *n.* [Sp. *ladron*, from L. *latro (-onis)*, a mercenary soldier, a servant, a freebooter, a robber.] Originally, a soldier who fought for money; a mercenary; now, a pirate; a robber; a rogue; a thief.

lā′dy, *n.* [ME. *lavedi*, *levedy*; AS. *hlæfdige*, a lady, mistress, prob. f. of *hlaford*, lord.]

1. A woman of distinction, correlative to *lord*; the proper title of any woman whose husband is above the rank of a baronet or knight, or who is the daughter of a nobleman not lower than an earl, though often the wife of a baronet or a knight is called by this title. [Eng.]

2. A term applied by courtesy to any woman; one of the fair sex; specifically, a woman of good breeding, education, and refinement of mind; the correlative to *gentleman*.

3. A wife; a spouse, considered with direct reference to the husband; as, John Johnson and *lady*. This use was once quite common, but is now considered in bad taste.

4. Mistress; the woman who presides or has authority over a household, estate, or family.

5. In the days of chivalry, the woman to whom a knight or squire paid his homage and in whose honor he entered the lists; as, he wore his *lady's* colors on his sleeve.

6. The calcareous apparatus in a lobster's stomach, in which its food is reduced to a pulp.

Ladies' man; a man who is fond of the society of ladies and pays them marked attentions; a gallant.

Lady in waiting; a lady of rank who is a member of the royal household and in attendance on a queen.

Lady of the manor; a lady who is the head of a manor or the wife of the lord of the manor.

Leading lady; the actress of a theatrical company who plays the leading female rôle.

Our Lady; the Virgin Mary.

lā′dy=ạl″tạr, *n.* The altar of a lady-chapel.

lā′dy=bee″tle, *n.* Same as *Ladybird*.

lā′dy-bīrd, *n.* [Bird of Our Lady, the Virgin Mary.] A small insect of the family *Coccinellidæ* and order *Coleoptera*. Various species are extremely common on trees and plants in gardens. Their larvæ are very useful on account of the number of plant-lice which they destroy. They receive their name from their graceful form and delicate coloring; also called *ladybug*, *ladyclock*, *ladycow*, *lady-beetle*, and *ladyfly*.

lā′dy-bug, *n.* Same as *Ladybird*.

lā′dy=chap″el, *n.* In Roman Catholic churches, a chapel dedicated to the Virgin Mary. It is usually behind the high altar at the eastern end of the church, but is sometimes a separate building.

lā′dy-çlock, *n.* Same as *Ladybird*.

lā′dy=çōurt, *n.* The court of a lady of the manor.

lā′dy-çow, *n.* Same as *Ladybird*.

lā′dy=çrab, *n.* The commonest edible crab of the United States, *Callinectes hastatus*, found in great numbers on the Atlantic coast. The name is also applied to several other species of crab.

Lā′dy=dāy, *n.* The day of the annunciation of the Virgin Mary, March 25. It is one of the immovable festivals of the Anglican church.

lā′dy=fẽrn, *n.* A species of polypodiaceous fern, the *Asplenium Filix-fœmina*, widely distributed. It has bipinnate or tripinnate fronds of delicate texture, and of a remarkably elegant plumy structure.

lā′dy-fin″gẽr, *n.* Same as *Lady's-finger*.

lā′dy-fish, *n.* 1. A brilliant, silvery-colored fish, *Albula vulpes*, abundant in the warmer waters of both the Atlantic and Pacific. It is of but little value as food.

2. A brilliant labroid fish, *Harpe rufa*, common along the West Indian and Florida coasts; also called *Spanish ladyfish* and *doncella*.

3. The saury, *Scomberesox saurus*; so called in Florida.

lā′dy-flȳ, *n.* Same as *Ladybird*.

lā′dy-hood, *n.* The state or condition of being a lady; the character, personality, quality, rank, etc., of a lady.

lā′dy=kill″ẽr, *n.* A man who is supposed to have great powers of fascination over women; a beau who attracts the admiration of women. [Slang.]

lā′dy=kill″ing, *n.* The arts practised by a lady-killer; excessive gallantry. [Slang.]

lā′dy-kin, *n.* A little lady; used by Elizabethan writers as a term of endearment for the Virgin Mary.

lā′dy-līke, *a.* 1. Like a lady in any respect; genteel; well-bred; refined; delicate.

2. As applied to men, affected; effeminate.

> Spruce *ladylike* preachers. —Jer. Taylor.

lā′dy-līke-ness, *n.* The condition or quality of being ladylike.

lā′dy-lŏve, *n.* A sweetheart.

lā′dy=măss, *n.* A mass in honor of the Virgin Mary.

lā′dy's=bed′strạw, *n.* In botany, (a) a plant, *Galium verum*; (b) an East Indian evergreen shrub of the genus *Pharnaceum*.

lā′dy's=bow″ẽr, *n.* The only British species of virgin's-bower, or clematis, *Clematis Vitalba*.

lā′dy's=çloth, *n.* A smooth, heavy woolen cloth, resembling broadcloth but of lighter weight.

lā′dy's=çōmb (-kōm), *n.* See *Venus's-comb*.

lā′dy's=çush″iŏn, *n.* A plant, *Saxifraga hypnoides*; the name is also applied to *Armeria vulgaris*.

lā′dy's=ēar′drops, *n.* The fuchsia.

lā′dy's=fin″gẽr, *n.* 1. A variety of apple.

2. A variety of potato, white and delicately flavored and so called because resembling somewhat a finger in shape.

3. [*pl.*] The kidney-vetch, *Anthyllis vulneraria*.

4. One of the gills, branchiæ, or hairy appendages attached to the base of a lobster's leg.

5. A kind of delicate sponge-cake, so called because about the size and shape of a finger.

lā′dy's=gär″tẽrs, *n.* Ribbon-grass.

lā′dy's=glōve, *n.* The purple foxglove, *Digitalis purpurea*.

lā′dy's=gown, *n.* In Scots law, a gift sometimes made by a purchaser to a vendor's wife on her renouncing her life-rent in her husband's estate.

lā′dy's=hāir, *n.* The quaking-grass, *Briza media*.

lā′dy-ship, *n.* The condition or rank of a lady; employed as a title preceded by *her* or *your*; as, *her ladyship* was not at the ball.

lā′dy's=lā′çes, *n.* Any species of dodder.

lā′dy's=māid, *n.* A woman-servant who attends a lady, especially one who assists her at her toilet.

lā′dy's=man″tle, *n.* The popular name of *Alchemilla vulgaris*, an old-world herb.

lā′dy's=sēal, *n.* A plant, *Tamus communis*; also called *black bryony*.

lā′dy's=slip″pẽr, *n.* 1. Any orchid of the genus *Cypripedium*; so called because the labellum is supposed to resemble a slipper.

2. The garden-balsam, *Impatiens balsamina*; the local name of various other plants. [U. S.]

lā′dy's=smock, *n.* A cruciferous plant, *Cardamine pratensis*; also called *lady-smock* and *cuckooflower*.

lā′dy's=thim″ble, *n.* The harebell, *Campanula rotundifolia*.

lā′dy's=thumb (-thum), *n.* The common persicaria, *Polygonum Persicaria*; it is an annual weed with oblong spikes of reddish flowers and tapering leaves with a dark spot in the center.

lā′dy's=tress″es, lā′dy's=trā″çes, *n.* Any orchid of the genus *Spiranthes*; so called because the spikes of white spirally-arranged flowers are thought to resemble braided hair.

Læ′laps, *n.* [L., the name of a dog mentioned by Ovid in his Metamorphoses, from Gr. *lailaps*, a tempest, storm.]

1. In zoölogy, a genus of huge dinosaurian reptiles, carnivorous and rapacious. Some species resembled the kangaroo and grew to a height of eighteen feet.

2. [l—] Any species of the genus *Lælaps*.

laem′mẽr-gei-ẽr, laem′mẽr-geȳ-ẽr, *n.* Same as *Lammergeier*.

læ-mod′i-pod, *a.* and *n.* I. *a.* Pertaining to or having the characteristics of the *Læmodipoda*.

II. *n.* One of the *Læmodipoda*.

Læ-mō-dip′ō-dȧ, *n.pl.* [Gr. *laimos*, the throat, and *dipous (-podos)*, two-footed; *dis*, double, and *pous*, *podos*, foot.] An order of marine sessile-eyed crustaceans which have the anterior pair of feet attached to the cephalic segment. They have no branchiæ appended to the posterior extremity. The females have a kind of pouch under the second and third segments, in which the ova are carried. The whale-louse, *Cyamus*, and *Caprella* are examples.

læ-mō-dip′ō-dăn, *a.* and *n.* Same as *Læmodipod*.

læ-mō-dip′ō-di-fọrm, *a.* [Gr. *laimos*, throat, and *dipous (-podos)*, two-footed, and L. *forma*, form.] In entomology, resembling the *Læmodipoda* in form; said of certain larvæ as the walking-sticks or *Phasmidæ*.

læ-mō-dip′ō-dous, *a.* Same as *Læmodipod*.

læ″mō-pȧ-ral′y-sis, *n.* [Gr. *laimos*, the throat, and *paralysis*, paralysis.] Paralysis of the esophagus or gullet.

læ″mō-stē-nō′sis, *n.* [Gr. *laimos*, throat, and *stenōsis*, a straitening.] Stricture of the esophagus or gullet.

læ-ō-trop′iç, læ-ot′rō-pous, *a.* [Gr. *laios*, left, and *tropos*, a turning.] Sinistral; turned or turning to the left; opposed to *dexiotropic* and *dexiotropous*.

Læ-tā′re, *n.* The fourth Sunday in Lent; so called because the ancient Christian church began its service on that day with *Lætare, sterilis*, or *Lætare, Jerusalem*, Rejoice, barren one, or Rejoice, Jerusalem; also called *Mid-Lent Sunday*.

læv′i-gāte, *a.* Same as *Levigate*.

læv-ō-glū′çōse, *n.* Same as *Levoglucose*.

læ-vō-gȳ′rāte, *a.* Same as *Levogyrate*.

læ-vō-rō′tȧ-tō-ry, *a.* Same as *Levorotatory*.

læv′ū-lōse, *n.* Same as *Levulose*.

lȧ-fȧ-yette′, *n.* 1. A sciænoid fish, *Liostomus xanthurus*, of the northern part of the United States; so called because it first became well known during the last visit of Lafayette to the United States in 1824. Also called *spot*, *oldwife*, and *goody*.

2. The dollar-fish, *Stromateus triacanthus*; also called *butterfish* and *harvest-fish*.

lafe, *n.* The lave. [Obs.]

laft, laf′te, *v.*, obsolete past tense of *leave*.

lag, *a.* [Celtic origin, compare W. *llag*, slack, sluggish, Gael. and Ir. *lag*, weak, feeble.]

1. Coming after or behind; slow; sluggish; tardy. [Obs.]

2. Last; long delayed; as, the *lag* end.

3. Of the poorest quality, as if made last, and hence of refuse. [Obs.]

lag, *n.* 1. One who or that which comes behind or last. [Obs.]

2. The lowest class; the rump; the fag-end. [Obs.]

3. In mechanics, the quantity of retardation of some movement; as, the *lag* of an engine's slide-valve.

4. In machinery, one of the strips which form the outer covering of a drum, cylinder, steam-boiler, etc.

5. An old convict. [Australia.]

6. A graylag goose.

lag, *v.i.*; lagged, *pt.*, *pp.*; lagging, *ppr.* To walk or move slowly; to loiter; to stay behind.

> I shall not *lag* behind. —Milton.

Syn.—Loiter, linger, delay, retard, saunter, tarry.

lag, *v.t.* 1. To slacken. [Obs.]

2. To bring into the hands of justice; to cause to be punished for a crime. [Slang.]

3. To clothe, as a steam-boiler, to prevent radiation of heat.

lā′găn, *n.* Same as *Ligan*.

lȧ-gär′tō, *n.* An alligator. [Obs.]

lȧ-ġē′nȧ, *n.*; *pl.* **lȧ-ġē′næ.** [L. *lagena*, *lagœna*, *lagona*; Gr. *lagēnos*, *lagynos*, a flagon, a flask.]

1. In Roman antiquity, an amphora.

2. A vase shaped like a bottle, of Oriental or unfamiliar ware.

3. The saccular extremity of the cochlea in birds and reptiles.

Laġ-ē-nā′ri-ȧ, *n.* [L. *lagena*, a bottle.] A genus of plants of the order *Cucurbitaceæ*. There is only one species, *Lagenaria vulgaris*, which occurs throughout tropical and subtropical Asia and Africa.

lȧ-ġē′ni-fọrm, *a.* [L. *lagena*, a flask, and *forma*, form.] In botany and zoölogy, flask-shaped; of the form of a Florentine vase.

lä′gẽr, *n.* Same as *Lager-beer*.

lä′gẽr=beer, *n.* [G. *lagerbier*, lit., store-beer; *lager*, storehouse, a place for storing things, and *bier*, beer.] A popular German beer, so called from its being stored for some months before use. It is now largely manufactured in the United States and elsewhere.

Lā-gẽr-strœ′mi-ȧ, *n.* [Named after Magnus von *Lagerström*, a Swedish merchant.] A genus of polypetalous, lythraceous trees and shrubs, comprising twenty-one known species. They are native to tropical Asia, Africa, Australia, and Madagascar. Some species, as the crape-myrtle or Indian lilac, are cultivated on account of their beauty.

lä′gẽr=wine, *n.* [G. *lagerwein*; *lager*, a storehouse, and *wein*, wine.] Bottled wine that has been kept in the cellar until quite old.

lag′gärd, *a.* and *n.* I. *a.* Slow; sluggish; backward.

II. *n.* One who lags; a loiterer.

lag′gẽr, *n.* A loiterer; an idler; a laggard.

lag′ging, *n.* 1. The planking laid on the ribs of the centering of a tunnel to carry the brick or stone work.

2. In machinery, the covering of a steam-boiler, and the like, to prevent the radiation of heat; also called *deading*.

3. A lining of strips of wood, used to support the roof of a mine.

lag′ging-ly, *adv.* Loiteringly; tardily.

lag′ly, *adv.* In a lagging manner. [Prov. Eng.]

la-gnappe′, la-gniappe′ (lan-yap′), *n.* [Etym. doubtful.] In Louisiana, a small gift or present added to a purchase by a tradesman as a favor to customers.

lago-. A combining form from Gr. *lagōs, lagos*, a hare, used in zoölogy, anatomy, etc., to signify a hare or harelike; as, *lago*stoma, *lago*mys.

lag′ō-mọrph, *n.* One of the *Lagomorpha.*

Lag-ō-mọr′phȧ, *n.pl.* [*Lago-*, and Gr. *morphē*, form, shape.] A suborder of rodents, including the hare, rabbit, pika, etc.; also called *Duplicidentata.*

Lȧ-gō′mys, *n.* [*Lago-*, and Gr. *mys*, a mouse.] A genus of rodent animals, of the family *Lagomyidæ*, forming a link between the hare and the rat. They differ from the hares proper in having moderate-sized ears, legs nearly equal, and no tail. The American species is known as the pika or little chief hare.

lȧ-gọọn′, *n.* [It. and Sp. *laguna*, from L. *lacuna*, a ditch, pool, from *lacus*, lake.]

1. A shallow lake or creek connected with the sea or a river.

2. The sheet of water surrounded by an atoll or coral island.

lȧ-gọọn′=is″lănd (-ī), **lȧ-gọọn′=reef**, *n.* An atoll.

lag-oph-thal′mi-ȧ, lag-oph-thal′mus (-of-), *n.* [*Lago-*, and Gr. *ophthalmos*, the eye.] The continued abnormal retraction of the upper eyelid which prevents its covering the eyeball during sleep; so called from the supposition that this is the natural condition of the eye of the hare when asleep.

lag-oph-thal′mic, *a.* Pertaining to or affected with lagophthalmia.

lȧ-gō′pō-dous, *a.* [Gr. *lagōpous* (*-podos*); *lagōs*, a hare, and *pous, podos*, foot.] In zoölogy, harefooted; having the feet furry or feathery.

lȧ-gō′pous, *a.* [Gr. *lagōpous*, hare-footed.] In botany, hare-footed; having a covering of soft, long hairs and so resembling the foot of a hare.

lȧ-gos′tō-mȧ, *n.* [*Lago-*, and Gr. *stoma*, mouth.] Harelip.

lȧ-got′iç, *a.* [*Lago-*, and Gr. *ous, ōtos*, the ear.] Having ears like a rabbit.

lä-grï-mō′sō, *a.* [It., from L. *lacrimosus*, tearful, mournful, from *lacrima*, a tear.] In music, denoting or indicating passages to be rendered in a mournful or pathetic manner; also written *lacrimoso.*

Läg′thing (-ting), *n.* [Norw. *lagthing, lagting*; *lag*, company, society, law, and *thing, ting*, parliament.] In Norway, the upper house of the parliament or Storthing.

lȧ-güne′, *n.* Same as *Lagoon.*

lā′iç, *a.* [LL. *laicus*; Gr. *laikos*, of or belonging to the people, from *laos*, the people.] Belonging to the laity or people, in distinction from the clergy.

lā′iç, *n.* A layman.

lā′iç-ăl, *a.* Laic. [Rare.]

lā-iç-al′i-ty, *n.* The state or quality of being laic.

lā′iç-ăl-ly, *adv.* In a laic manner.

lā″i-ci-zā′tion, *n.* The act of laicizing; removal from clerical rank or power.

lā′i-cize, *v.t.*; laicized, *pt., pp.*; laicizing, *ppr.* To render lay or laic; to deprive of clerical rank or power.

lāid, *v.*, past tense and past participle of *lay.*

lāid, *a.* 1. Prostrate; thrown or put down.

2. Pressed.

Laid paper; paper which is marked with parallel lines or water marks from the wires on which the pulp was laid in the process of making; opposed to *wove paper*, which is laid on flannels or felts instead of wires.

Laid up; stored away; dismantled and out of use, as a ship; hence, colloquially, so wearied or ill as to be confined to one's home or bed.

lāid′ly, *a.* Unsightly; extremely ugly. [Scot.]

lāin, *v.*, past participle of *lie.*

lāin′ẽr, lāin′ēre, *n.* [Obs.] Same as *Lannier.*

lāir, *n.* [ME. *leir*; AS. *leger*, a bed, couch, place of rest, from *licgan*, to lie.]

1. A place of rest; a bed or couch; now used only of the den or resting or hiding place of a wild beast.

2. A pasture; a field; the ground. [Obs.]

3. A litter, as of rabbits. [Obs.]

4. In Scotland, a portion of a burying-ground affording space sufficient for one or more graves.

lāird, *n.* A lord; a landed proprietor. [Scot.]

lāird′ship, *n.* The estate of a laird; the rank of a laird. [Scot.]

lais′ser=faire′, lais′sez=faire′ (lā′sā-fār′), *n.* [Fr., to let alone, or let act; L. *laxare*, to relax, and *facere*, to do, act.] A letting alone; noninterference, applied to that policy of government which allows the people to govern themselves as much as possible, and without much interference from their rulers.

lā′i-ty, *n.* [LL. *laïcus*; Gr. *laïkos*, belonging to the people, from *laos*, the people.]

1. The people, as distinguished from the clergy; the body of the people not in orders.

2. People outside of any profession, as distinguished from those belonging to it.

3. The state of a layman, or of not being in orders. [Obs.]

lāke, *n.* [Fr. *laque*; Per. *lāk*, lake, from *lak*, lac.] A compound of aluminous earth with coloring matter of certain animal and vegetable substances. Sometimes the term *lake* is indiscriminately applied to all compounds of alumina and coloring matter.

lāke, *v.i.* To play; to sport. [Prov. Eng.]

lāke, *n.* A kind of fine, white linen, used chiefly for shirts. [Obs.]

lāke, *n.* [ME. *lake*; AS. *lacu*, a lake, pool; L. *lacus*, a hollow, a basin, tub, pool, lake.]

1. A large sheet or body of water, wholly surrounded by land, and having no immediate communication with other bodies of water.

2. A small body of water, wholly or in part artificial, as an ornament of a park, etc.

Lake poet; one of the poets of the Lake school.

Lake school; the name originally given by the Edinburgh Review in derision to a class of English poets who, at the beginning of the nineteenth century, endeavored to substitute a simple and natural taste for the classicism of Pope and Addison; so called from their residence in the lake district.

The Great Lakes; see under *Great.*

lāke′=dwell″ẽr, *n.* One who lives in a lake-dwelling.

lāke′=dwell″ing, *n.* A dwelling built on small islands in lakes, or on platforms supported by piles near the shores of lakes; especially, such a dwelling erected in prehistoric times.

Lake-dwellings restored.—From Troyon.

lāke′=fē″vẽr, *n.* Malaria. [Local, U. S.]

lāke′=flȳ, *n.* 1. A dayfly, *Ephemera simulans*, which swarms on the Great Lakes in the latter part of the summer. [U. S.]

2. A midge of the genus *Chironomus.*

lāke′=her″ring, *n.* A variety of the cisco, *Coregonus artedi.*

lāke′let, *n.* A small lake.

lāke′=shad, *n.* One of several inferior food-fishes, as suckers, found in the Great Lakes.

lāke′=stūr″geŏn, *n.* A food-fish, *Acipenser rubicundus*, of the Great Lakes and Mississippi River.

lāke′=trout, *n.* 1. A salmonoid fish, *Salmo purpuratus*, the Rocky Mountain or Yellowstone trout.

2. The Mackinaw trout, *Salvelinus namaycush.*

lāke′weed, *n.* The common smartweed or water-pepper, *Polygonum Hydropiper.*

lāke′=whit″ing, *n.* The whitefish, *Coregonus labradoricus.*

lākh, *n.* [Hind. *lak*; Sans. *lākshā*, a hundred thousand.] A lac; one hundred thousand.

lā′kin, *n.* A plaything; a toy. [Prov. Eng.]

lā′kin, *n.* A diminutive of *lady* and a contraction of *ladykin.*

lak′ke, *n.* and *v.* [Obs.] Same as *Lack.*

lāk′y, *a.* Of, pertaining to, or like a lake.

lāk′y, *a.* Transparent; applied to blood lacking in red corpuscles.

Lal′lăn, *a.* and *n.* [Dial. for *lowland.*]

I. *a.* Of, pertaining to, or belonging to the Lowlands of Scotland. [Scot.]

II. *n.* The dialect of the Lowlands of Scotland.

lal-lā′tion, *n.* [Fr., from L. *lallare*, to sing a lullaby.] An imperfect pronunciation of the letter *r*, which makes it sound like *l.*

lā′lō, *n.* [African.] Same as *Baobab.*

lȧ-lop′ȧ-thy, *n.* [Gr. *lalein*, to talk, and *pathos*, suffering.] Any defect of the organs of speech or disturbance of the function of language.

lam, *v.t.*; lammed, *pt., pp.*; lamming, *ppr.* [Ice. *lemja*, to beat.] To beat. [Colloq.]

lä′mȧ, *n.* In zoölogy, same as *llama.*

lä′mȧ, *n.* [Tibetan *blama*, a chief, high priest.] A priest or ecclesiastic belonging to that variety of Buddhism which is known as Lamaism, and prevails in Tibet and Mongolia. There are several grades of lamas, both male and female, of whom the *dalai-lama* and the *tesho-lama* are regarded as supreme pontiffs.

Lama of Tibet.

Grand Lama; the *dalai-lama*; so called by Europeans.

lä′mȧ-iç, *a.* Pertaining to or made up of lamas.

Lä′mȧ-iṣm, *n.* A variety of Buddhism, chiefly prevailing in Tibet and Mongolia; so called from the lamas or priests belonging to it. The highest object of worship is Buddha, who is regarded as the founder of the religion, and the first in rank among the saints.

Lä′mȧ-ist, Lä′mȧ-ite, *n.* One who believes in Lamaism.

Lä-mȧ-is′tiç, *a.* Of or pertaining to Lamaism; lamaic.

lȧ-man′tin, *n.* Same as *Manatee.*

Lȧ-märck′i-an, *a.* Of or pertaining to Lamarck, the French naturalist.

Lȧ-märck′i-ăn-iṣm, *n.* Same as *Lamarckism.*

Lȧ-märck′iṣm, *n.* In biology, the theory of evolution propounded by Lamarck, a distinguished French naturalist, early in the nineteenth century. It teaches that all life has been differentiated from a primitive and simple form.

lä′mȧ-ser-y, *n.* [Tibetan *blama*, a chief, lama, and Per. *sarāi*, an inn.] A Buddhist monastery or nunnery in Tibet or Mongolia, corresponding to an abbey or priory and having a chief lama in charge.

lamb (lam), *n.* [ME. *lamb*; AS. *lamb, lomb*, lamb.]

1. The young of the sheep kind.

2. One who is like a lamb in being innocent and gentle.

3. One who is so unsophisticated as to be deceived or fleeced with ease; one who is inexperienced in business and is beguiled into making losing investments. [Slang.]

The Lamb or *the Lamb of God*; in Scripture, the Saviour, Jesus Christ, who was typified by the paschal lamb.

> Behold *the Lamb of God*, which taketh away the sin of the world. —John i. 29.

lamb, *v.i.*; lambed, *pt., pp.*; lambing, *ppr.* To bring forth young, as sheep.

lamb′āle, *n.* A feast at the time of shearing lambs. [Eng.]

lam-bāste′, *v.t.*; lambasted, *pt., pp.*; lambasting, *ppr.* To beat or thrash severely. [Slang.]

lam′bȧ-tive, *a.* and *n.* I. *a.* Taken by licking. [Obs.]

II. *n.* A medicine taken by licking with the tongue. [Obs.]

lamb′dȧ, *n.* [Gr. *lambda*, lambda.]

1. The eleventh letter of the Greek alphabet, corresponding to the English *l.*

2. In craniology, the junction of the sagittal and lambdoid sutures.

lamb′dȧ-ciṣm, *n.* [LL. *lambdacismus*; Gr. *lambdakismos*, a lambdacism, from *lambdakizein*, to pronounce *l* imperfectly, from *lambda*, lambda, the letter *l.*]

1. A too frequent repetition of the letter *l* in speaking or writing, as in Martial's line: *Sol et luna luce lucent alba, leni, lactea.*

2. A faulty pronunciation of *ll*, as when the tongue is pressed against the palate and produces a sound similar to *lli* in *million.*

3. An imperfect pronunciation of the letter *r*, which is made to sound like *l*; lallation. The defect is common among children and Chinese.

lamb′doid, lamb-doid′ăl, *a.* [Gr. *lambda*, the letter Λ, lambda, and *eidos*, form.] Resembling in shape the Greek capital letter *lambda*; specifically applied, in craniology, to the suture between the occipital and parietal bones.

lam′ben-cy, *n.* The state or quality of being lambent; that which is lambent.

lam′bent, *a.* [L. *lambens* (*-entis*), ppr. of *lambere*, to lick, lap.]

1. Licking. [Rare.]

2. Touching lightly or running over, as if licking; gleaming; twinkling; flickering.

> A great *lambent* planet was shining in the northern sky. —W. Black.

lamb′kill, *n.* The sheep-laurel, *Kalmia angustifolia*, so called because it poisons sheep.

lamb′kin, *n.* A small lamb.

lamb′like, *a.* Like a lamb; gentle; humble; meek; mild; innocent; unassuming; as, a *lamblike* temper.

lam′boys, *n.pl.* [OFr. *lambeau*, a shred, flap.] In medieval armor, the imitation in steel of the plaited skirts or bases worn over the thighs. They were worn especially in Germany in the earlier part of the sixteenth century.

1. Lamboys (time of Henry VIII.). 2. Lamboys from a German suit (early sixteenth century).

lam′bre-quin (-kin), *n.* [Fr., the coverings or trappings of a helmet, a mantle, scallop.]

1. In medieval armor, a sort of scarf worn over the helmet, as an ornament or for protection.

2. In upholstery, a piece of cloth, leather, lace, etc., forming a sort of curtain for the upper part of an opening, as a door, window, or arch, or an ornamental drapery of a mantel, etc.

3. In heraldry, the mantelet.

4. In decorative art, imitation of a lambrequin design, as in certain Chinese vases which display a solid color above and an edge of jagged or ornamented outline below.

lamb′skin, *n.* 1. The skin of a lamb dressed with the fleece on, and sometimes colored, used for ornament in dress, for mats, etc.

2. The skin of a lamb from which the fleece has been removed to prepare it for being made into gloves, etc.

3. Woolen cloth made to resemble the dressed skin of a lamb.

lamb′skin-net, *n.* Same as *Lansquenet*, 2.

lamb's′-let″tuce (-is), *n.* Same as *Corn-salad.*

lamb's′-quar″tērs (-kwar″), *n.* A European weed, *Atriplex patula*; also, an American weed, white goosefoot.

lamb's′-wool, *n.* 1. Wool obtained from lambs.

2. Ale mixed with sugar, nutmeg, and the pulp of roasted apples.

> The *lamb's-wool*, even in the opinion of my wife, who was a connoisseur, was excellent.
> —Goldsmith.

lāme, *n.* In armor, a metal plate. [Obs.]

lāme, *a.*; *comp.* lamer; *superl.* lamest. [ME. *lame*; AS. *lama*, lame.]

1. Crippled or disabled by natural defect of or injury to limb or limbs; limping; halting; moving with difficulty or pain; as, a *lame* man or horse.

2. Unsound from natural defect or injury; crippled; as, a *lame* back or arm.

3. Figuratively, imperfect; not satisfactory or convincing; hobbling; lacking in smoothness; as, a *lame* excuse; *lame* verses.

> The prose is fustian, and the numbers *lame.*
> —Dryden.

Lame duck; a bankrupt; a defaulter on the stock exchange. [Slang.]

Syn.—Weak, faltering, hobbling, hesitating, ineffective, impotent, crippled, halt, defective, imperfect.

lāme, *v.t.*; lamed, *pt.*, *pp.*; laming, *ppr.* To make lame; to cripple or disable; to render imperfect and unsound; as, to *lame* an arm or a leg.

lam′el, *n.* Same as *Lamella.*

lȧ-mel′lȧ, *n.*; *pl.* **lȧ-mel′læ.** [L., a small or thin plate, from *lamina*, a thin piece of metal or wood.] A thin plate or scale; specifically, in zoölogy, one of the thin plates or scales which compose certain shells, or of which the gills of certain mollusks, as the oyster, are composed; in botany, (a) one of the gills forming the hymenium of an agaric; (b) one of the foliaceous erect scales appended to the corolla of many plants.

lam′el-lăr, *a.* Composed of thin plates, layers, or scales; disposed in thin plates or scales.

lam′el-lăr-ly, *adv.* In thin plates or scales.

lam′el-lăr-stel′lāte, *a.* In mineralogy, formed of lamellæ arranged in the form of a star.

lam′el-lāte, lam′el-lā-ted, *a.* Formed in thin plates or scales, or covered with them; furnished with lamellæ or little plates.

lamelli-, lamello-. Combining forms from L. *lamella*, a small or thin plate, used in zoölogy to signify resemblance to a thin plate or leaf; as, *Lamelli*branchiata.

lȧ-mel′li-branch, *a.* and *n.* I. *a.* Having lamellate gills; of, pertaining to, or having the characteristics of the *Lamellibranchiata.*

II. *n.* One of the *Lamellibranchiata.*

Lȧ-mel-li-bran-chi-ā′tȧ, Lȧ-mel-li-bran′chi-ȧ, *n.pl.* [*Lamelli-*, and L. *branchiæ*, gills.] A class of *Mollusca*, containing all the true or ordinary bivalve mollusks, as oysters, clams, etc. They have no distinct head or cephalic eyes. The valves of the shell articulate over the back, and are opened by an elastic ligament and closed by one or two adductor muscles. They are so called from the fact that respiration is effected by two pairs of lamellated gills. Synonymous names are *Acephala, Bivalvia, Conchifera, Cormopoda*, and *Pelecypoda.*

lȧ-mel-li-bran′chi-āte, *a.* and *n.* Same as *Lamellibranch.*

lȧ-mel′li-corn, *n.* One of the *Lamellicornia.*

lȧ-mel′li-corn, lȧ-mel-li-cor′nāte, *a.* [*Lamelli-*, and L. *cornu*, horn.]

1. Having or composed of lamellæ, as an insect's antennæ.

2. Having lamellate antennæ; of or pertaining to the *Lamellicornia.*

Lȧ-mel-li-cor′nēs, *n.pl.* [Obs.] Same as *Lamellicornia.*

Lȧ-mel-li-cor′ni-ȧ, *n.pl.* [*Lamelli-*, and L. *cornu*, horn.] A suborder of pentamerous *Coleoptera* (beetles) in which the antennæ are inserted into a deep cavity under the lateral margin of the head. The antennæ are short, and the last three joints are platelike and disposed somewhat like the teeth of a comb. This suborder is very numerous, including the dungbeetles, stag-beetles, cockchafers, etc. Some of the species feed on vegetables and others on decomposed vegetable matter.

lam-el-lif′ēr-ous, *a.* [*Lamelli-*, and L. *ferre*, to bear.] Having lamellæ or a structure composed of thin layers; having a foliated structure.

lȧ-mel′li-form, *a.* [*Lamelli-*, and L. *forma*, form.] Having the form of a plate or scale; lamellar.

lȧ-mel′li-ped, *a.* and *n.* [*Lamelli-*, and L. *pes*, *pedis*, foot.]

I. *a.* Having a flattened foot in the shape of a lamella, as some mollusks.

II. *n.* A mollusk having a lamelliform foot.

lȧ-mel-li-ros′tēr, *n.* A lamellirostral bird.

lȧ-mel-li-ros′trăl, *a.* and *n.* I. *a.* Having a lamellose bill; of or pertaining to the *Lamellirostres.*

II. *n.* One of the *Lamellirostres.*

Lȧ-mel-li-ros′trēs, *n.pl.* [*Lamelli-*, and L. *rostrum*, a beak.] A family of natatorial birds, characterized by having the beak flattened and covered with a soft skin. The margins of the beak are furnished with numerous lamellæ or dental plates, arranged in a regular series. The family comprises the ducks, geese, swans, flamingos, etc.

lam′el-lōse, *a.* Having lamellæ; covered with lamellæ.

lāme′ly, *adv.* In a lame manner; imperfectly.

lāme′ness, *n.* The state of being lame; imperfection; weakness.

lȧ-ment′, *v.i.*; lamented, *pt.*, *pp.*; lamenting, *ppr.* [Fr. *lamenter*; L. *lamentari*, to mourn, lament, from *lamentum*, a mourning, wailing.] To mourn; to grieve; to weep or wail; to express sorrow.

> Jeremiah *lamented* for Josiah.
> —2 Chron. xxxv 25.

lȧ-ment′, *v.t.* To bewail; to mourn for; to bemoan; to deplore.

Syn.—Bemoan, bewail, complain, grieve, deplore, mourn, regret.

lȧ-ment′, *n.* [L. *lamentum*, a mourning, wailing.]

1. Grief or sorrow expressed in complaints or cries; lamentation; a weeping.

> Torment, and loud *lament*, and furious rage.
> —Milton.

2. An elegy or mournful ballad.

lam′en-tȧ-ble, *a.* [L. *lamentabilis*, from *lamentari*, to mourn, lament.]

1. To be lamented; exciting or deserving sorrow; as, a *lamentable* state of morals.

2. Mournful; expressing grief or sorrow; as, a *lamentable* speech.

3. Miserable; pitiful; low; poor.

lam′en-tȧ-ble-ness, *n.* The state of being lamentable.

lam′en-tȧ-bly, *adv.* In a lamentable manner.

lam-en-tā′tion, *n.* [OFr. *lamentation*; L. *lamentatio (-onis)*, a weeping, lamenting, from *lamentari*, to weep, lament.]

1. Expression of sorrow; cries of grief; the act of bewailing.

2. [L—*pl.*] The shorter title of the Lamentations of Jeremiah, one of the lyrical, poetical books of the Old Testament; generally accredited by scholars to Jeremiah and so called because it bewails the destruction of Jerusalem by the Chaldeans.

3. [*pl.*] In the Roman Catholic church, the music to which are sung parts of the Lamentations of Jeremiah, in the Tenebræ.

lȧ-ment′ed, *a.* Bewailed; mourned for.

lȧ-ment′ēr, *n.* One who mourns, or cries out with sorrow.

lȧ-ment′ing, *n.* A mourning; lamentation.

lȧ-ment′ing-ly, *adv.* In lamenting manner; with lamentation.

lȧ-met′tȧ, *n.* [It., dim. of *lama*, a plate of metal, from L. *lamina*, a thin piece of metal, wood, marble, etc.] Gold, silver, or brass wire or foil.

lā′mi-ȧ, *n.* [L. *lamia*; Gr. *lamia*, a female demon.]

1. In Greek and Roman mythology, a female demon or vampire who fed on the flesh and blood of children and youths whom she enticed; a witch; a hag.

2. [L—] A genus of longicorn beetles belonging to the family *Cerambycidæ*, and living in decaying willows, etc. The male of *Lamia ædilis* has the antennæ four times as long as the body.

lam′i-nȧ, *n.*; *pl.* **lam′i-næ.** [L. *lamina*, a thin plate of metal, wood, or marble.]

1. A thin plate or scale; a layer or coat lying over another; applied to the plates of minerals, bones, etc.

2. In anatomy, a bone, or part of a bone, resembling a thin plate, such as the cribriform plate of the ethmoid bone.

3. In botany, (a) the border, or the upper, broad, or spreading part of the petal in a polypetalous corolla; (b) the part of a leaf which is an expansion of the parenchyma of the petiole. It is traversed by veins.

4. In ornithology, one of the thin flat scales or plates, serving as one of the processes of a feather's vane.

5. In geology, the thinnest distinct layer or sheet into which a stratified rock can be divided.

lam″i-nȧ-bil′i-ty, *n.* The state of being laminable.

lam′i-nȧ-ble, *a.* Capable of being formed into thin plates.

lam′i-năr, lam′i-năl, *a.* Arranged in or composed of plates; consisting of thin plates or layers.

Lam-i-nā′ri-ȧ, *n.* [L. *lamina*, a thin plate.] A genus of dark-spored seaweeds, belonging to the order *Laminariaceæ.*

Lam-i-nā-ri-ā′cē-æ, *n.pl.* [*Laminaria* and *-aceæ.*] One of the orders into which the *Algæ* are divided.

lam-i-nā′ri-ăn, *a.* Of or pertaining to the genus *Laminaria*; specifically, noting that belt or zone of marine life which extends from low-water mark to a depth of from forty to ninety feet, and in which the *Laminariaceæ* are found.

lam′i-nȧ-rite, *n.* [*Laminaria* and *-ite.*] A broad-leaved fossil alga, found in the upper secondary and tertiary formations.

lam′i-nā-ry, *a.* Laminar.

lam′i-nāte, *v.t.*; laminated, *pt.*, *pp.*; laminating, *ppr.* [LL. *laminatus*, pp. of *laminare*, to flatten into a thin plate, from L. *lamina*, a thin plate.]

1. To make into a lamina; to pound or beat out thin. [Rare.]

2. To separate or split up into thin plates or layers.

lam′i-nāte, *v.i.* To become divided or separated into laminæ.

lam′i-nāte, lam′i-nā-ted, *a.* Plated; consisting of plates, scales, or layers, one over another.

lam-i-nā′tion, *n.* The act of laminating or the state of being laminated; specifically, in geology, a division of rocks into very thin plates or laminæ, similar to stratification.

lam-i-nif′ēr-ous, *a.* [L. *lamina*, a thin plate, and *ferre*, to bear.] Having a structure consisting of laminæ, or layers.

lam′i-ni-form, *a.* [L. *lamina*, a thin plate, and *forma*, form.] Having the form of a lamina; laminar.

lam″i-ni-plan′tăr, *a.* [L. *lamina*, a thin plate, and *planta*, sole.] In ornithology, having laminate tarsi; having two lateral laminæ which meet in a sharp ridge and cover the back of the tarsus, as in most singing birds except the larks.

lam-i-ni′tis, *n.* In farriery, the founder; inflammation of the laminæ or interstitial tissue of a horse's foot.

lam′i-nōse, *a.* Laminiform.

lām′ish, *a.* Somewhat lame.

lamm, *v.t.* Same as *Lam.*

Lam′măs, *n.* [ME. *lammasse*; AS. *hlammæsse*, for *hlafmæsse*, lit., loaf-mass, bread-feast; *hlaf*, loaf, and *mæsse*, mass, festival.]

1. Formerly, in England, the festival of the wheat-harvest or loaf-mass, held on the first day of August, corresponding to the twelfth day of the month in the modern calendar. It was a continuation of a similar festival of pagan times.

2. In Great Britain, the first of August, which is quarter-day in Scotland, and in England half-quarter day or cross-quarters. Also called *Lammas-day.*

3. In the Roman Catholic church, the feast of Peter's Chains, which falls on the first day of August and commemorates the imprisonment and miraculous deliverance of the Apostle Peter.

Lam′măs-dāy, *n.* Same as *Lammas*, 2.

Lam′măs-land, *n.* Cultivated land under the control of individual owners until harvest, which is about Lammastide, when it is thrown open for common pasturage until sowing time.

Lam′măs-tīde, *n.* The time or season of Lammas.

lam′mēr-gei-ēr, laem′mēr-gei-ēr (lam′), *n.* [G. *lämmergeier*; *lämmer*, pl. of *lamm*, a lamb, and *geier*, a vulture.] The bearded vulture, a bird of prey, *Gypaëtos barbatus*, family *Vulturidæ*, forming a link between

Lammergeier or Bearded Vulture (*Gypaëtos barbatus*).

the vultures and the eagles. It inhabits the Swiss and German Alps, as well as the higher mountains of Asia and Africa, and is the largest European bird of prey, measuring upward of four feet from beak to tail, and nine or ten in the expanse of its wings. Besides eating carrion, it preys on living chamois, lambs, kids, hares, and such animals, but it does not disdain rats, mice, and other small quadrupeds. Written also *lammergeir*, *lemmergeyer*, *laemmergeyer*.

lam′my, lam′mie, *n.* A thick, warm, quilted frock or jumper worn as an outer garment by sailors in severe weather.

Lam-nuñ′gui-à, *n.pl.* [L. *lamina*, a scale, and *unguis*, a nail.] Same as *Hyracoidea*.

lamp, *v.t.* To supply light to; to illuminate. [Rare.]

lamp, *v.i.* To shine. [Rare.]

lamp, *n.* A thin plate or lamina. [Obs.]

lamp, *n.* [ME. *lampe*; OFr. *lampe*; L. *lampas* (*-adis*); Gr. *lampas* (*-ados*), a lamp, torch, light, from *lampein*, to shine.]

1. A vessel for containing oil or other liquid inflammable substance, to be burned by means of a wick; any contrivance for producing artificial light, whether by means of an inflammable liquid or of gas or electricity.

2. Anything suggesting the light of a lamp, whether in appearance or use; anything possessing or communicating light, real or metaphorical.

> Thy gentle eyes send forth a quickening spirit,
> And feed the dying *lamp* of life within me.
> —Rowe.

Aphlogistic lamp; a lamp in which a coil of platinum wire is kept in continued ignition by incandescence without flame.

Arc lamp; see under *Arc*.

Argand lamp; see under *Argand*.

Dobereiner's lamp; a hydrogen lamp for producing an instantaneous light by throwing a jet of hydrogen gas upon spongy platinum. The metal is at once heated to luminosity, and by the aid of the oxygen in the atmosphere, sets fire to the hydrogen. It was invented in 1824 by Prof. Dobereiner, of Jena.

Flameless lamp; same as *Aphlogistic lamp*.

Fresnel lamp; a lamp surrounded by a Fresnel lens.

Safety lamp; a lamp for lighting coal mines, without exposing workmen to the explosion of inflammable air.

Student lamp or *student's lamp*; a lamp having an Argand burner supplied by a reservoir, self-flowing and connected with the burner by a lateral tube. The burner has a tall, slender chimney and shade, and the whole is usually adjustable in height.

lam′pad, *n.* A lamp, torch, or candlestick. [Rare.]

lam′pà-dā-ry, *n.* [LL. *lampadarius*; L.Gr. *lampadarios*, from Gr. *lampas* (*-ados*), a torch, a lamp.] In the Greek church, an officer who carries a lighted taper before the patriarch in processions and has charge of the church lamps.

lam-pà-ded′rō-my, *n.* [Gr. *lampadēdromia*; *lampas* (*-ados*), a torch, lamp, and *dromos*, race.] In Greek antiquity, a torch-race, in which each contestant carried a lighted torch, the victor being the one who reached the goal first, with his torch unextinguished.

lam-pad′ē-phōre, *n.* [Gr. *lampadēphoros*, a torch-bearer; *lampas* (*-ados*), a torch, lamp, and *pherein*, to carry.] In Greek antiquity, one who ran as a contestant in a lampadedromy.

lam-pad-ē-phō′ri-à, *n.* [Gr. *lampadēphoria*, the carrying of torches; from *lampas* (*-ados*), a torch, and *pherein*, to carry.] In Greek antiquity, a lampadedromy in honor of a fire-god, as Prometheus or Hephæstus (Vulcan).

lam-pà-doph′ō-ros, lam′pà-dist, *n.* Same as *Lampadephore*.

lam-pad′ō-man-cy, *n.* [Gr. *lampas* (*-ados*), a lamp, and *manteia*, divination.] An ancient method of divination by means of the flame of a lamp or torch.

lam′pà-drōme, *n.* Same as *Lampadedromy*.

lam′pȧs, *n.* [OFr., from *lampas*, the throat.] In farriery, a swelling of the fleshy lining of the roof of the mouth immediately behind the fore teeth in the horse, which soon subsides if left to itself; also called *lampers*.

lam′pāte, *n.* A compound salt, composed of lampic acid and a base. [Obs.]

lamp′black, *n.* A fine soot consisting of particles of carbon, pure or almost pure, and formed by the condensation of the smoke of burning oil, pitch, or resinous substances. It is used in the manufacture of paints and inks.

lamp′-bŭrn″ẽr, *n.* That part of a lamp within which the wick burns.

lamp′-chim″ney, *n.* A funnel of glass or other material used to incase the flame of a lamp.

lam′pẽr-eel, *n.* 1. A lamprey.

2. The mutton-fish or eel-pout, *Zoarces anguillaris*.

lam′pẽrn, *n.* The river-lamprey, *Petromyzon fluviatilis*.

lam′pẽrs, *n.* Same as *Lampas*.

lamp′-fly, *n.* A firefly. [Rare.]

lamp′-hour (-our), *n.* In electricity, the current necessary to keep one light burning one hour.

lam′pic, *a.* Of, pertaining to, caused by, or derived from a lamp or flame.

Lampic acid; a volatile compound of acetic acid, modified by a peculiar hydrocarbon. It is obtained by the combustion of ether by means of a lamp furnished with a coil of platinum wire.

lamp′ing, *a.* Shining; bright; brilliant; sparkling. [Obs.]

lam′pi-ŏn, *n.* [Fr., from *lampe*, a lamp.] A small lamp used for illuminations.

> At the French Chancellerie, they had six more *lampions* in their illumination, than ours had. —Thackeray.

lamp′-jack, *n.* A hood or covering placed over the lamp-chimney or vent of a railroad-car, to protect the light from wind and rain.

lamp′less, *a.* Having no lamp or light; hence figuratively, dull of perception; not bright mentally.

lamp′light, *n.* Light from a lamp; artificial light.

lamp′light″ẽr, *n.* 1. One who lights lamps, especially street-lamps, or that by which they are lighted.

2. The calico bass. [Local, U. S.]

lam-pōōn′, *n.* [Fr. *lampon*, originally a drinking-song, from *lamper*, to drink.] A personal satire in writing; abuse or censure of a malicious nature and written to reproach and vex rather than to reform.

Syn.—Satire, invective.—The appropriate object of *satire* is found in the vices and follies of the times. It is usually general, and designed to expose and reform. A *lampoon* is a bitter personal satire, dictated by malignant feelings, and intended only to distress and degrade.

lam-pōōn′, *v.t.*; lampooned, *pt.*, *pp.*; lampooning, *ppr.* To abuse with personal censure; to reproach in written satire; to write a lampoon about.

lam-pōōn′ẽr, *n.* One who abuses with personal satire; the writer of a lampoon.

> The squibs are those who are called libelers, *lampooners*, and pamphleteers. —Tatler.

lam-pōōn′ry, *n.* Abuse in lampoons.

lamp′-pōst, *n.* A pillar or similar support for a lamp or gaslight used in outdoor lighting.

lam′preel, *n.* A lamper-eel; a lamprey. [Obs.]

lam′prel, *n.* A lamprey of a certain age. [Obs.]

lam′prey, *n.* [ME. *lampreie*; OFr. *lamproie*; LL. *lampreda*, *lampetra*, a lamprey, lit., lick-rock, so called from their habit of clinging to rocks with their mouths; L. *lambere*, to lick, and *petra*, a rock.] The popular name of several species of *Petromyzon*, a genus of marsipobranchiate, eel-like, scaleless fishes which inhabit both fresh and salt water. The mouth is in the form of a sucker, lined with strong teeth and cutting-plates, and the river-lampreys are often seen clinging to stones by it. The marine or sea-lamprey, *Petromyzon marinus*, is sometimes found so large as to weigh four or five pounds. The river-lamprey or lampern, *Petromyzon fluviatilis*, is a smaller species, and abounds in the fresh-water lakes and rivers of northern countries. Lampreys attach themselves to other fishes and eat their way into them.

Sea-lamprey (*Petromyzon marinus*).

lam′prŏn, *n.* [Obs.] Same as *Lamprey*.

lam′prō-phȳre, *n.* [Gr. *lampros*, bright, and *porphyreos*, purple.] In geology, fine-grained, dark-colored rocks occurring in dikes in strata of the Paleozoic age.

lam-prō-phyr′ic, *a.* Of the nature of, composed of, or pertaining to lamprophyre.

Lamp′sà-nà, *n.* Same as *Lapsana*.

lamp′-shāde, *n.* A shade or screen placed above the flame of a lamp to mellow or intercept it. It may have a dark exterior and a reflecting interior substance.

lamp′-shell, *n.* A mollusk of the class *Brachiopoda*.

lamp′wick, *n.* 1. The wick of a lamp.

2. A cultivated evergreen shrub, *Phlomis Lychnites*, of the mint family, native to the southern part of Europe. It derives its name from the fact that its leaves are said to have been used as lampwicks.

lam-pȳ′rid, *a.* and *n.* Same as *Lampyrine*.

Lam-pyr′i-dæ, *n.pl.* A family of coleopterous insects of the section *Malacodermi*. The insects of this family have five joints to all the tarsi, flexible elytra, the body usually elongated and somewhat depressed. Many are phosphorescent, as the firefly, glowworm, etc. The type of the family is the genus *Lampyris*.

lam-pȳ′rine, *a.* and *n.* I. *a.* Of or pertaining to the *Lampyridæ*.

II. *n.* One of the *Lampyridæ*.

Lam-pȳ′ris, *n.* [L. *lampyris*; Gr. *lampyris*, or *lampouris*, a glowworm, from *lampouros*, bright-tailed, having a shining tail; *lampein*, to shine, and *ouron*, tail.] The type genus of the *Lampyridæ*.

lä′nà, *n.* A close-grained and tough wood obtained from *Genipa Americana*, a South American and West Indian tree of the order *Rubiaceæ*. The fruit, called genipap, yields a pigment which, under the name of lana-dye, the Indians use to stain their faces and persons.

lan′ärk-īte, *n.* A greenish-white translucent and transparent mineral, formed principally of lead sulphate (Pb_2SO_5) and found in quantities in Lanarkshire, Scotland; hence its name.

lā′nà-ry, *n.* A store-place for wool. [Obs.]

lā′nāte, lā′nā-ted, *a.* [L. *lanatus*, woolly, from *lana*, wool.] Woolly; covered with a substance like curled hairs; as, a *lanated* leaf or stem.

Lañ-cas-tē′ri-ăn, *a.* Relating to the educational system introduced into some English primary schools at the end of the eighteenth century by John Lancaster; it included teaching by upper pupils. [Rare.]

Lañ-cas′tri-ăn, *a.* and *n.* I. *a.* In English history, of or pertaining to the royal house of Lancaster, descended from John of Gaunt, fourth son of Edward III.

II. *n.* In English history, a supporter of the house of Lancaster in its claim to the throne as against the house of York, especially in the Wars of the Roses, 1455–85.

lànce, *n.* [ME. *launce*; OFr. *lance*; L. *lancea*, a light spear, lance.]

1. An offensive weapon consisting of a long wooden shaft with a sharp-pointed head of steel or other metal, used in war by both ancient and modern nations; a spear. The ancient lances were thrown from the hand like the javelin. The lance used in certain modern cavalry regiments has a shaft of ash or beech wood, in some cases about sixteen feet long, with a steel point eight or ten inches in length, adorned by a small pennon.

2. A soldier armed with a lance; a lancer.

3. Any long spear; applied to weapons of savages, etc.

4. A lancet used by physicians and surgeons.

5. An iron rod used to hold a founding-core in place when a shell is being cast in the mold.

6. The rammer long used with muzzle-loading guns.

7. A small paper case filled with colored-fire composition, used to mark out the outlines of figures in large pyrotechnical displays.

8. A spear with which a whale is killed, after being harpooned.

Free lance; in the middle ages, a mercenary soldier; hence, one who writes, speaks, etc., with comparative freedom from control.

Holy lance; in the Greek church, a knife with a blade resembling a lance and a handle shaped like a cross, with which the holy bread is cut for the eucharist; also called *holy spear*.

To break a lance; see under *Break*.

lànce, *v.t.*; lanced, *pt.*, *pp.*; lancing, *ppr.* 1. To pierce with a lance, or with a sharp-pointed instrument.

> Seized the due victim, and with fury *lanced*
> Her back. —Dryden.

2. To pierce or cut; to open with a lancet; as, to *lance* a vein or an abscess.

3. To throw in the manner of a lance; to hurl. [Obs.]

lànce′-buck″et, *n.* A rest for the butt of a lance, attached to a cavalryman's stirrup-leather.

lànce′-cor″pō-răl, *n.* An infantryman having the temporary rank of corporal.

lànce′fish, *n.* The English sand-lance, a long, slender sea-fish of the genus *Ammodytes*.

lànce′gāy, *n.* A kind of slender spear or javelin, tipped with iron. [Obs.]

lànce′-knight (-nit), *n.* A foot-soldier; a lansquenet.

lànce′let, *n.* A small fish of very anomalous structure, the *Amphioxus lanceolatus* or *Branchiostoma lanceolatum*.

lànce′ly, *a.* Suitable to a lance. [Obs.]

lan′cē-ō-lăr, *a.* In botany, tapering toward each end.

lan′cē-ō-lāte, lan′cē-ō-lā-ted, *a.* [L. *lanceola*, dim. of *lancea*, a lance.] Shaped like a lance; oblong and gradually tapering toward the outer extremity; as, a *lanceolate* leaf.

Lanceolate Leaf.

lànce-pe-sāde′, *n.* [Fr. *lancepessade*, a lance-corporal; It. *lancia spezzata*, a broken lance or demilance.] An officer under the corporal; specifically, in the sixteenth and seventeenth centuries, a trooper who had been unhorsed or had had his lance broken, and who was serving temporarily as a subordinate officer; a lance-corporal.

lan'cẽr, *n.* [OFr. *lanceor*, from *lance*, a lance.]

1. One who lances; one who carries a lance.

2. A lancet. [Obs.]

3. [*pl.*] A form of quadrille; also, music composed for such a dance.

lance'-snāke, *n.* Same as *Fer-de-lance.*

lan'cet, *n.* [ME. *launcet*; OFr. *lancete*, dim. of *lance*, a lance.]

1. A surgical instrument, sharp-pointed and two-edged, used in operations, as in opening tumors, abscesses, etc.

2. In architecture, a lancet-window or lancet-arch.

lan'cet-ärch, *n.* An arch whose head is shaped like the point of a lancet; generally used in lancet-windows.

lan'cet-fish, *n.* 1. A fish of the family *Teuthididæ* or *Acanthuridæ*; also called *barber-fish*, *doctor-fish*, and *surgeon-fish.*

2. A large, voracious fish, of the *Alepidosauridæ*, having large teeth shaped like lances. It is found in deep seas.

lan'cet-win'dōw, *n.* A high and narrow window pointed like a lancet. Lancet-windows are a marked characteristic of the early English style of Gothic architecture, and are in a great degree peculiar to England and Scotland. They are often double or triple, and sometimes five are placed together.

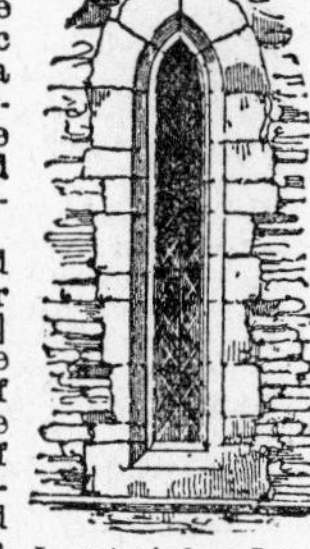
Lancet-window, Comberton.

lance'wood, *n.* [So named from its being suitable for making the shafts of lances.] The popular name of the wood of several trees of the order *Anonaceæ*, as of the *Oxandra virgata*, a native of Jamaica, or *Duguetia quitarensis*, a native of Cuba and Guiana, which possesses in a high degree the qualities of toughness and elasticity.

lanch, *v.* and *n.*, variant spelling of *launch.*

lan'ciẽrs, *n.pl.* See *Lancer*, 3.

lan-cif'ẽr-ous, *a.* [L. *lancea*, a lance, and *ferre*, to bear.] Bearing a lance. [Rare.]

lan'ci-fọrm, *a.* [L. *lancea*, a lance, and *forma*, form.] Having the form of a lance.

lan'ci-nāte, *v.t.*; lancinated, *pt.*, *pp.*; lancinating, *ppr.* [L. *lancinatus*, pp. of *lancinare*, to tear.] To tear; to lacerate.

lan-ci-nā'tion, *n.* A tearing; laceration.

land, *n.* Urine. [Obs.]

land, *n.* [ME. *land*; AS. *land*, land.]

1. Earth; the solid matter which constitutes the fixed part of the surface of the globe, in distinction from the sea or other waters, which constitute the fluid or movable part; as, the earth is composed of *land* and water.

2. Any part of the earth's surface, as distinguished from other parts; any country, region, or tract of land, considered as the home of a person or people, characterized by peculiarities of formation, vegetation, etc., or interesting by reason of its history, etc.; as, my native *land*; Bible *lands*; the *land* of the midnight sun.

Go, view the *land*, even Jericho.—Josh. ii. 1.

3. A continent, as opposed to an island.

4. Ground; soil, or the superficial part of the earth in respect to its nature or quality; as, good *land*; poor *land*; moist or dry *land.*

5. In law, real estate; any ground which can be held as individual property, considered as extending indefinitely upward and downward and including all upon it whether by nature, as trees, water, etc., or by hand of man, as houses, barns, etc.; as, a traitor forfeits all his *lands* and tenements.

6. The inhabitants of a country or region; a nation or people.

These answers, in the silent night received,
The king himself divulged; the *land* believed.
—Dryden.

7. The ground left unplowed between furrows.

8. The smooth part of any surface which is grooved or marked with indentations, as the part of a rifle between the grooves, the surface of a millstone between two furrows, or the lap of the strakes in a clinker-built boat.

Bad lands; tracts of land in the western part of the United States, particularly in South Dakota, consisting of horizontal strata void of vegetation and broken by erosion into fantastic superficial forms. The name *mauvaises terres*, bad lands, originated with the French Jesuit explorers.

Land ho; a cry used by sailors to signal the sight of land.

Land of Nod; sleep; slumber.

Land or *house of bondage*; in biblical history, Egypt; hence, any place of oppression or persecution.

Land o' the leal; place of the faithful or blessed; heaven. [Scot.]

The Holy Land; Judea or Palestine, so called because the scene of the events narrated in the Bible and the region where Jesus Christ was born and lived.

To make the land or *to make land*; in nautical language, to discover land from the sea, as the ship approaches it.

To set the land; to see by the compass how the shore bears from the ship.

To shut in the land; to lose sight of the land by the intervention of a point or promontory.

land, *v.t.*; landed, *pt.*, *pp.*; landing, *ppr.* [ME. *landen*; AS. *lendan*, to land, from *land*, land.]

1. To set on shore; to disembark; to debark; as, to *land* troops from a ship or boat; to *land* goods.

2. To catch; to capture; as, to *land* a fish or prisoner.

3. To bring to or put in a certain place or condition; used literally or figuratively; as, we were *landed* in difficulties.

land, *v.i.* 1. To go on shore from a ship or boat; to disembark.

2. To arrive; to reach; as, I *landed* at his house.

land'-ā"ġent, *n.* A real-estate agent.

lan'dam-man, *n.* [G., from *land*, land, country, and *ammann*, for *amtmann*, bailiff, magistrate.]

1. A chief magistrate in some of the Swiss cantons.

2. The president of the diet of the Helvetic republic.

lan'dau, *n.* A kind of coach or carriage having two seats facing each other and a top in two sections which may be opened and thrown back; so called from Landau, a town in Germany, where first made.

lan-dau-let', *n.* A small landau or one with only one seat.

land'-blink, *n.* A peculiar atmospheric brightness perceived in the arctic regions on approaching land covered with snow. It is more yellow than ice-blink.

land'-bōat, *n.* A vehicle with wheels designed to be propelled by means of sails.

land'-breeze, *n.* A current of air setting from the land toward the sea.

land'-chāin, *n.* A surveyor's chain.

land'-crab, *n.* A crustacean whose habits are terrestrial, as distinguished from one whose habits are aquatic; particularly, one of the species of *Gecarcinus*, which lives much on land and only visits the sea to deposit its eggs. It is found in the higher parts of Jamaica, and often proves very destructive to the sugar plantations.

land'-croc"ō-dīle, *n.* A monitor-lizard or sand-monitor, *Psammosaurus arenarius.*

land'-damn (-dam), *v.t.* To banish from the land. [Obs.]

land'drost, *n.* [D., from *land*, land, and *drost*, an officer, magistrate.] In South Africa, a local official who acts as a chief magistrate.

lande, *n.* [Fr., from OFr. *laund*, a heath, waste.] A heath; a heathy or sandy plain incapable of bearing cereals; specifically applied, in the plural, to extensive areas in France stretching from the mouth of the Garonne along the Bay of Biscay and inward toward Bordeaux.

land'ed, *a.* 1. Having an estate in land; as, a *landed* gentleman.

2. Consisting in real estate or land; as, *landed* security; *landed* property.

land'ẽr, *n.* 1. One who lands or makes a landing.

2. One who lands or sets on land; especially, in mining, the one who attends at the mouth of the pit to receive the kibble or bucket in which ore is brought to the surface.

land'fall, *n.* 1. A sudden transference of property in land by the death of its owner.

2. In nautical language, the first land sighted after a voyage.

land'-fish, *n.* Any one out of his natural element, as a fish would be out of water; any one acting contrary to his usual character.

He's grown a very *land-fish*, languageless, a monster. —Shak.

land'flōod (-flud), *n.* An overflowing of land by water; an inundation.

land'-fōrce, *n.* A military force, army, or body of troops serving on land, as distinguished from a naval force.

land'grāve, *n.* [G. *landgraf*; *land*, land, and *graf*, a count.] A title taken by some German counts in the twelfth century, to distinguish themselves from the inferior counts under their jurisdiction. Three of them were princes of the empire.

land-grā'vi-āte, *n.* The territory held by a landgrave, or his office, jurisdiction, or authority.

land'grā-vīne, *n.* The wife of a landgrave; any woman equal in rank to a landgrave.

land'hōld-ẽr, *n.* A holder, owner, or proprietor of land.

land'-īce, *n.* A field or floe of ice stretching along the land which lies between two headlands.

land'ing, *n.* [ME. *londyng*; AS. *lending*, a landing, verbal n. of *lendan*, to go on shore, land.]

1. The act of going or setting on shore from a vessel.

2. A place for going or setting on shore; a wharf; a dock; a pier.

3. In architecture, the part of a staircase which is level, without steps, connecting one flight with another.

land'ing, *a.* Pertaining to that which lands, in any sense of the word.

land'ing-chär"ġes, *n.pl.* Charges to be paid on goods landed; also, fees for landing goods.

land'ing-net, *n.* A small hoop-net used by anglers to land the fish they have taken.

land'ing-plāce, *n.* A place for the landing of persons or goods from a vessel, or for alighting or resting.

land'ing-rātes, *n.pl.* Same as *Landing-charges.*

land'ing-skāte, *n.* One of the runners in an aeroplane alighting gear.

land'ing-stāġe, *n.* A platform or float attached to a wharf and so constructed that it accords with the tide, thus facilitating the landing of goods or passengers from vessels.

land'ing-sũr-vey"ŏr, *n.* In Great Britain, an officer of the customs who appoints and superintends the landing-waiters.

land'ing-wāit"ẽr, *n.* Same as *Coast-waiter.*

land'lā-dy, *n.* 1. A woman who has tenants renting from her.

2. The mistress of an inn, a boarding-house, or a lodging-house.

3. The wife of a landlord or proprietor.

land'lēap"ẽr, *n.* A vagabond or vagrant; one who has no settled habitation, and frequently removes from one place or country to another.

land'-leech, *n.* A terrestrial leech of the genus *Hæmodipsa.* It is found in great numbers in Ceylon, especially in the rainy season, is about an inch long and very slender, and is a great pest to man and beast.

land'less, *a.* [AS. *landleas*; *land*, land, and *-leas* -less.] Destitute of land; having no property in land.

land'lock, *v.t.* To inclose or encompass by land. [Obs.]

land'locked (-lokt), *a.* 1. Encompassed or nearly encompassed by land; surrounded and protected by land, as a harbor.

2. Inhabiting landlocked waters; shut off from the sea, applied especially to fishes which naturally seek the sea after spawning; as, a *landlocked* salmon.

land'lō"pẽr, *n.* [D. *landlooper*; *land*, land, and *loopen*, to run.] A landleaper.

land'lō"ping, *a.* Wandering about; vagrant; vagabond.

land'lọrd, *n.* [ME. *londelorde*; AS. *landhlaford*; *land*, land, and *hlaford*, lord.]

1. The lord of a manor or of land; the owner of land who has tenants under him; the holder of a tenement, to whom a rent is paid.

2. The master of an inn, tavern, or lodging-house; a host.

The jolly *landlord*. —Addison.

land'lọrd-ism, *n.* The conduct or opinions characteristic of landlords; the authority of a landlord; specifically, the political and ethical doctrine of the superiority of the landed interests.

land'lọrd-ry, *n.* The state of a landlord. [Obs.]

land'lōup"ẽr, *n.* Same as *Landloper.*

land'lōup"ing, *a.* Same as *Landloping.*

land'lub"bẽr, *n.* A landsman; one who is awkward or inexperienced on a ship; a raw seaman; used by sailors in ridicule or contempt.

A navy which is not manned is no navy. A navy which is recruited mainly from *landlubbers* is hardly better.—Saturday Review.

land'măn, *n.*; *pl.* **land'men.** 1. A man who lives or serves on land; opposed to *seaman.*

2. In English law, a tenant; a terre-tenant.

3. One who owns land. [Scot.]

land'märk, *n.* [AS. *landmearc*; *land*, land, and *mearc*, mark.]

1. A mark to designate the boundary of land; any mark or fixed object, as a marked tree, a stone, a ditch, or a heap of stones, by which the limits of a farm, a town, or other portion of territory may be known and preserved.

2. Any prominent object marking a locality, oftentimes one of historical interest; any elevated object on land that serves as a guide to seamen.

3. Figuratively, anything which marks the stage of advancement at which anything capable of development has arrived at a given period; any phenomenon or striking event; anything which marks the end of one system or state of things and the introduction of a new system or state; as, *landmarks* of history, science, or art.

land'-meas̱"ūre (-mezh"ūr), *n.* Measurement of land; also, a table of square measure by which land is measured.

land′-ọf″fice, *n.* In the United States and the British colonies, an office in which the sales of new land are registered, warrants are issued for the location of land, and other business respecting unsettled land is transacted.

Lan-dol′phi-ȧ, *n.* [Named after Capt. *Landolph* of the French navy.] A genus of climbing shrubs of the order *Apocynaceæ*. They have opposite, veiny leaves, large flowers of yellow or white in terminal cymes, and bear a large berry. There are seventeen known species, native to South Africa and Madagascar. *Landolphia florida* and *Landolphia Kirkii* are valued for the rubber they yield.

land′ōwn″ẽr, *n.* One who owns land or real-estate.

land′ōwn″ẽr-ship, *n.* The state of being an owner or proprietor of land.

land′ōwn″ing, *a.* and *n.* I. *a.* Of or pertaining to landowners; possessing land; as, the *landowning* interests.

II. *n.* The owning of land.

land′-pike, *n.* 1. The sauger, *Stizostedion canadense.*

2. An American batrachian having a naked skin, limbs, and a tail, as a menopome, hellbender, or axolotl.

land′-plas″tẽr, *n.* Rock-gypsum used as a fertilizer after being ground to a powder.

land′-pọọr, *a.* Financially embarrassed through holding much land which does not yield a profit.

land′-rāil, *n.* 1. The European corncrake, *Crex pratensis.*

2. An Australian rail, *Hypotænidia philippensis.*

land′reeve, *n.* A subordinate officer on an extensive estate, who acts as an assistant to the steward.

land′sçāpe, *n.* [AS. *landscipe*; *land*, land, and *-scipe*, -ship, a suffix denoting art, etc.]

1. A portion of land or territory which the eye can comprehend in a single view, including mountains, rivers, lakes, and whatever the land contains.

2. A picture, exhibiting the form of a district of country as far as the eye can reach, or a particular extent of land and the objects it contains or its various scenery; also, such pictures collectively as distinguished from marine pictures or portraits or those wherein figures are prominent.

land′sçāpe-gär″den-ẽr, *n.* One who lays out grounds and arranges trees, shrubbery, etc., in such a manner as to produce the most pleasing effect.

land′sçāp-ist, *n.* One who paints landscapes.

land′-sçrip, *n.* A certificate given to a person who has purchased public land in the United States, that he has paid his purchase-money to the proper officer.

land′-shärk, *n.* 1. A swindler who makes sailors his victims, while they are on shore.

2. A shrewd speculator in land; a land-grabber.

land′-sīde, *n.* The flat side of a plow which is away from the furrow and presses against the unplowed land.

land′skip, *n.* [Obs.] Same as *Landscape.*

land′-slat″ẽr, *n.* A crustacean that exists on land; a sow-bug.

land′slīde, *n.* A portion of a hill or mountain, which slips or slides down; the sliding down of a considerable tract of land from a mountain; as, *landslides* are not infrequent in Switzerland.

land′slip, *n.* A landslide.

lands′măn, *n.*; *pl.* **lands′men.** 1. One who lives on the land; opposed to *seaman.*

2. In nautical language, a sailor on board a ship who has not before been at sea.

3. A fellow-countryman. [Rare.]

land′-snāil, *n.* Any one of several species of snails that live on land.

land′-spout, *n.* A variety of waterspout that occurs during a tornado.

land′-spring, *n.* A spring of water which overflows only after heavy rains. [Eng.]

land′-stew″ȧrd, *n.* One who is in charge of a landed estate.

Lănds′thing (läns′ting), *n.* [Dan., from *land* (poss. *lands*), land, and *thing*, parliament.] The upper house of the parliament or Rigsdag of Denmark. It is composed of sixty-six members, twelve of whom, by appointment of the crown, hold their places for life while the others serve for a term of eight years, and are elected by delegates representing those of the fifty-four districts which have the necessary property qualifications to secure them representation.

land′strāit, land′streight (-strāt), *n.* A narrow strip of land. [Obs.]

länd′stụrm (länt′), *n.* [G., lit., landstorm.] A local militia of Germany, which is never called from its own district but in case of actual invasion. It comprises that portion of the reserve too old for the landwehr. Switzerland and Austria have forces of the same nature.

Länd′täg (länt′), *n.* [G., lit., land diet or day; *land*, land, and *tag*, day, diet.]

1. In Germany, a parliament of a country included in the empire, as Prussia, Saxony, Bavaria, etc.

2. The parliament of a province of Austria-Hungary, as Bohemia or Moravia.

land′-tax, *n.* A tax assessed on land and buildings.

land′-tọr″toise (-tis), *n.* Any tortoise that exists almost entirely on land; a testudine; also called *land-turtle.*

land′-tŭrn, *n.* A land-breeze.

land′-tŭr″tle, *n.* A land-tortoise.

land′-ŭr″chin, *n.* A hedgehog.

land′-wāit″ẽr, *n.* Same as *Coast-waiter.*

land′wȧrd, land′wȧrds, *adv.* Toward the land.

land′wȧrd, *a.* 1. Lying toward the land, or toward the interior, or away from the seacoast.

2. Situated in or forming part of the country, as opposed to the town; rural. [Scot.]

land′-wär″rănt, *n.* In the United States, a security or title authorizing a person to enter on a tract of public land.

länd′wehr (länt′vār), *n.* [G., from *land*, country, and *wehr*, defense, from *wehren*, to defend, ward off.] That portion of the military force of some continental nations which in time of peace follow their ordinary occupations, excepting when called out for occasional training.

land′-whin (-hwin), *n.* In botany, the rest-harrow, *Ononis arvensis.*

land′-wind, *n.* A wind blowing from the land.

lāne, *n.* [ME. *lane*, *lone*; AS. *lane*, a lane.]

1. A narrow way or passage, as between hedges or buildings; a narrow street; an alley; a narrow pass.

> The leafy *lanes* behind the down.—Tennyson.

2. Any opening resembling such a passage, as between lines of people standing on each side; a navigable opening in ice.

lāne, *a.* Alone. [Scot.]

My, thy, his (or *him*) *lane*; myself, thyself, himself alone.

Our, your, their lanes; ourselves, yourselves, themselves alone. *Lane* is shortened for *alane*, alone, and these usages arose by corruption from the older expressions *me lane*, etc.

lang, *a.*, *adv.*, and *v.*, a Scotch dialectal form of *long.*

lan̄-gä′hȧ, *n.* [Malagasy.] A wood-snake or tree-serpent, *Xiphorhynchus langaha*, native to Madagascar. It is less than three feet long and has a fleshy, scale-covered projection of the snout.

lan̄-gȧ-rey′, *n.* A wood-swallow or swallow-shrike, native to Australia.

lan̄′gāte, *n.* [Etym. doubtful.] In surgery, a linen roller or bandage.

läng′dăk, *n.* A wolf, *Canis pallipes*, native to India.

lan̄′gour, *n.* and *v.* [Obs.] Same as *Languor.*

lan̄′grel, lan̄′grāge, *n.* A kind of shot formerly used at sea for tearing sails and rigging, and thus disabling an enemy's ship. It consisted of bolts, nails, and other pieces of iron fastened together [Obs.]

lan̄′gret, *n.* A kind of false dice, so loaded that certain numbers come up more readily and frequently than others. [Obs.]

lan̄′gridge, *n.* Same as *Langrel.*

Langs-dọrf′fi-ȧ, *n.* [Named after G. H. von *Langsdorff*, a German traveler and scientist.] A genus of herbs of the order *Balanophoreæ*, having only one species, *Langsdorffia hypogæa*, native to the tropics of South America. It is thick, waxy, and yellow and has purple flowers which are either diœcious or monœcious.

lang′syne′, *adv.* Long ago; long since. [Scot.]

lang′syne′, *n.* [Scot., from *lang*, long, and *syne*, since.] The past; the days of long ago. [Scot.]

> A friend, in short, of the happy *langsyne.*
> —Lord Lytton.

lang-tẽr-ȧ-lọọ′, *n.* Same as *Lanterloo.*

lan̄′guāge (-gwāj), *n.* [ME. *langage*; OFr. *langage*; L. *lingua*, a tongue, language, lit., the tongue.]

1. Human speech; the expression of ideas by words or significant articulate sounds, for the communication of thoughts. Language consists in the utterance of sounds which usage has made the representatives of ideas. When two or more persons customarily annex the same sounds to the same ideas, the expression of these sounds by one person communicates his ideas to another. This is the primary sense of language, the use of which is to communicate the thoughts of one person to another through the organs of hearing. Articulate sounds are represented by letters, marks, or characters, which form words.

2. A particular set of articulate sounds used in the expression of thoughts; the aggregate of the words employed by any community for intercommunication; as, the English *language*; the Greek *language.*

3. Words or expressions appropriate to or especially employed in any branch of knowledge; as, the *language* of chemistry.

4. Style; manner of expression, either by speech or writing.

> Others for *language* all their care express.
> —Pope.

5. The inarticulate sounds by which irrational animals express their feelings and wants.

6. The expression of thought in any way, articulate or inarticulate, conventional or unconventional; as, the *language* of signs; the *language* of flowers, etc.

> The *language* of the eyes frequently supplies the place of that of the tongue. —Crabb.

7. A nation, as distinguished by the speech of its people. [Obs.]

Syn.—Speech, tongue, idiom, dialect.—*Language* is generic, denoting any mode of conveying ideas; *speech* is the *language* of articulate sounds; *tongue* is the *language* of a particular people; *idiom* denotes the forms of construction peculiar to a *language*; *dialects* are varieties of expression which spring up in different parts of a country, or in different professions, etc.

lan̄′guāge, *v.t.*; languaged, *pt.*, *pp.*; languaging, *ppr.* To express in language; to put into words.

lan̄′guāged, *a.* 1. Having a language.

2. Skilled in language or learned in several languages.

lan̄′guāge-less, *a.* Wanting speech or language.

lan̄′guāge-mȧs″tẽr, *n.* One whose profession is to teach languages. [Rare.]

lan̄gued, *a.* [Fr. *langue*, a tongue.] In heraldry, having a tongue; applied to beasts and birds when bearing a tongue of a different tincture from themselves.

län̄gue d'oc (läng dok). The independent Romance dialect spoken in Provence in the middle ages, from its word for *yes* being *oc*, a form of the Latin *hoc*, this.

län̄gue d'oui (läng dwē). The language of the north of France in the middle ages; so named from its word for *yes* (*oui*) It developed into modern French.

lȧn-guen′te (-gwen′), *adv.* [It.] In music, in a languishing manner.

lan̄-gues′cent, *a.* Growing languid or tired. [Rare.]

lan̄′guet (-get), *n.* [Fr. *languette*, dim. of *langue*; L. *lingua*, tongue.] Anything in the shape of a tongue; specifically, (a) on the hilt of a sword, a small hinged piece of metal, which overlaps the scabbard; (b) in zoölogy, one of the series of small tongue-like processes along the median line of the pharyngeal cavity or branchial sac of an ascidian; (c) in entomology, same as *languette*, 2 (a); (d) in music, same as *languette*, 3.

lan̄-guette′ (-get′), *n.* [Fr., dim. of *langue*, tongue.]

1. A kind of hood, much worn by women in the seventeenth century.

2. In zoölogy, (a) the tonguelet or ligula of an insect; (b) the organ of a mollusk which secretes the byssus.

3. In music, (a) a key of a wind-instrument (b) the slip or tongue of a reed in a harmonium or reed-organ.

lan̄′guid (-gwid), *a.* [L. *languidus*, from *languere*, to be faint or listless.]

1. Flagging; drooping; feeble; weak; heavy; dull; indisposed to exertion; as, the body is *languid* after excessive action, which exhausts its powers.

2. Slow; as, *languid* motion.

3. Dull; heartless; without animation.

> And fire their *languid* souls with Cato's virtue.
> —Addison.

Syn.—Drooping, dull, exhausted, faint, weak.

lan̄′guid-ly, *adv.* In a languid manner; weakly; slowly; listlessly.

lan̄′guid-ness, *n.* The state or condition of being languid; slowness; listlessness; languor.

lan̄′guish, *v.i.*; languished, *pt.*, *pp.*; languishing, *ppr.* [ME. *languishen*; OFr. *languir*; L. *languescere*, to grow weak, incept. of *languere*, to be faint or weary, to languish.]

1. To lose strength or animation; to be or become dull, feeble, or spiritless; to pine; to be or to grow heavy; as, to *languish* under disease or after excessive exertion.

2. To wither; to fade; to lose the vegetating power.

> For the fields of Heshbon *languish.*—Isa. xvi. 8.

3. To act in a languid manner; to affect a languid or pathetic expression as indicative of a tender or consuming affection.

lan̄′guish, *v.t.* To cause to droop or pine. [Obs.]

lan̄′guish, *n.* The act of pining; also, a soft and tender look or appearance.

lan̄′guish-ẽr, *n.* One who languishes or pines.

lan̄′guish-ing, *a.* 1. Becoming or being feeble; losing strength; pining; withering; fading.

2. Having a soft and tender look or appearance: as, a *languishing* eye.

lan′guish-ing-ly, *adv.* In a languishing manner.

lan′guish-ment, *n.* 1. The state of languishing or pining.

2. A languid expression, especially one assumed to indicate a tender affection; pensiveness.

lan′guish-ness, *n.* Languor; languidness. [Obs.]

lan′guŏr (-gẽr *or* -gwẽr), *n.* [ME. *langour*; OFr. *langueur*; L. *languor*, faintness, feebleness, from *languere*, to be faint or weary.]

1. Feebleness, heaviness; dullness; lassitude of body; that state of the body which is induced by exhaustion of strength.

2. Dullness of the intellectual faculty; listlessness.

3. An agreeable listless or dreamy state; voluptuous indolence; softness; laxity.

4. In vegetable pathology, that condition of plants in which, from unwholesome food, bad drainage, ungenial subsoil, and the like, they fall into a state of premature decrepitude.

Syn.—Feebleness, weakness, faintness, weariness, dullness, heaviness, lassitude, listlessness.

lan′guŏr, *v.i.* To languish. [Obs.]

lan′guŏr-ous, *a.* Characterized by or suggesting languor; inducing or tending to induce languor; seductive; as, *languorous* eyes.

lan′gŭr, *n.* See *Entellus.*

lan′gūre, *v.* and *n.* [Obs.] Same as *Languor.*

lan′gyȧ, *n.* [E. Ind.] A walking-fish, native to the East Indies.

lan′iărd (-yẽrd), *n.* Same as *Lanyard.*

lā-ni-ar′i-fọrm, *a.* [L. *laniare*, to tear, rend, and *forma*, shape.] Shaped like the laniaries or canine teeth of the *Carnivora.*

lā′ni-ā-ry, *n.* 1. Shambles; a place of slaughter.

2. A canine or dogtooth.

lā′ni-ā-ry, *a.* [L. *laniarius*, pertaining to a butcher, from *lanius*, a butcher, from *laniare*, to tear, rend.] Lacerating or tearing; applied especially to the canine teeth, when fully developed.

lā′ni-āte, *v.t.* [L. *laniatus*, pp. of *laniare*, to tear, rend.] To tear in pieces. [Rare.]

lā-ni-ā′tion, *n.* A tearing in pieces. [Rare.]

lan′iẽr (-yẽr), *n.* [Obs.] Same as *Lannier.*

lan′iẽr, *n.* Same as *Lanner.*

lȧ-nif′ẽr-ous, *a.* [L. *lanifer*; *lana*, wool, and *ferre*, to bear.] Bearing or producing wool. [Rare.]

lȧ-nif′iç-ăl, *a.* Working in wool. [Obs.]

lan′i-fice, *n.* A woolen fabric. [Obs.]

lȧ-nig′ẽr-ous, *a.* [L. *laniger*; *lana*, wool, and *gerere*, to produce.] Bearing or producing wool.

Lȧ-ni′i-dæ, *n.pl.* [*Lanius* and *-idæ.*] A family of insessorial or perching birds, in which the bill is abruptly hooked at the end; the shrikes. They are insectivorous, but some even prey on small birds and mammals.

Lȧ-ni-ī′næ, *n.pl.* [*Lanius* and *-inæ.*] A subfamily of the *Laniidæ*, having the bill short and the tooth very prominent. It contains the typical genus *Lanius.*

lā′ni-oid, *a.* Of or pertaining to the *Laniidæ.*

Lā′ni-us, *n.* [L. *lanius*, a butcher.] The typical genus of the *Laniidæ*; the shrikes; the butcher-birds.

lank, *a.*; *comp.* lanker; *superl.* lankest. [ME. *lank*; AS. *hlanc*, lank, slim.]

1. Slim; lean; attenuated; gaunt; as, his *lank* figure.

2. Loose or lax and easily yielding to pressure; not distended; not stiff or firm by distention; not plump; as, a *lank* purse.

3. Straight, flat, and long; as, *lank* hair.

4. Languid; drooping. [Obs.]

lank, *v.t.* and *v.i.* To make or become lank or lean. [Rare.]

lank′ly, *adv.* In a lank manner.

lank′ness, lank′i-ness, *n.* The state or quality of being lank; gauntness; leanness.

lank′y, *a.* Somewhat lank or lean.

lan′nẽr, *n.* [OFr. *lanier*, a kind of falcon or hawk, from L. *laniarius*, of or pertaining to a butcher, from *lanius*, a butcher.] A species of falcon or hawk, *Falco laniarius*, especially the female of the species, found in the south and east of Europe.

lan′nẽr-et, *n.* [Dim. of *lanner.*] The male of the lanner.

lan′niẽr, *n.* A strap or thong of leather; also written *lanier.* [Obs.]

lan′ō-lin, *n.* [L. *lana*, wool, and *oleum*, oil.] A substance extracted from the natural grease of wool and used as the basis of ointments.

lā′nōse, *a.* [L. *lanosus*, from *lana*, wool.] Resembling wool, woolly.

lan′sȧ, lan′seh, *n.* [E. Ind.] The fruit of *Lansium domesticum.*

Lan′si-um, *n.* [*Lansa* or *lanseh*, the E. Ind. name.] A genus of trees belonging to the order *Meliaceæ.* It comprises two or three species, natives of India, the most important of which is *Lansium domesticum*, the large yellowish fruit of which is highly esteemed, and eaten either fresh or prepared in various ways.

lans′que-net (-ke-), *n.* [Fr., from G. *landsknecht*, a foot-soldier; *land*, land, and *knecht*, a boy, servant.]

1. Originally, a German feudal soldier, or one of the infantry first raised by the Emperor Maximilian; a soldier of fortune.

2. A game at cards much played among or introduced by the lansquenets; also called *lambskinnet.*

lant, *n.* [AS. *hland*, urine.] Urine, especially when stale, used as a detergent in scouring wool.

lant, *n.* Same as *Lanterloo.*

lant, *n.* The sand-eel. [Prov. Eng.]

Lan-tā′nȧ, *n.* A genus of plants belonging to the order *Verbenaceæ*, containing about forty or fifty species. These are mostly natives of tropical and sub-tropical America. *Lantana macrophylla* is employed in infusions as a stimulant, and *Lantana pseudo-thea* as a substitute for tea.

lan′tẽr-lo͞o, *n.* A game at cards, now called *loo*, sometimes *lant.*

lan′tẽrn, *n.* [ME. *lanterne*; Fr. *lanterne*; L. *lanterna*; Gr. *lamptēr*, a lantern, a light, a stand or grate for lighting, from *lampein*, to shine.]

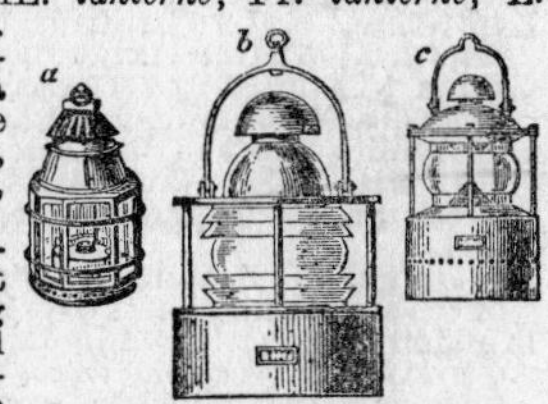

Ship's Lanterns.
a, Octagon. *b*, Masthead. *c*, Signal.

1. A case inclosing a light and protecting it from wind and rain, sometimes portable and sometimes fixed.

2. In architecture, (a) an erection on the top of a dome, on the roof of an apartment, or in similar situations, to give light, to promote ventilation, or to serve as a sort of ornament; (b) a tower which has the whole or a considerable portion of the interior open to view from the ground, and is lighted by an upper tier of windows.

Lantern, Boston Church, Lincolnshire.

3. A square cage of carpentry placed over the ridge of a corridor or gallery, between two rows of stores, to illuminate them, as in many public arcades.

4. The upper part of a lighthouse, where the light is shown.

5. In machinery, same as *lantern-wheel.*

6. In founding, a short core with holes bored in it, used in making hollow castings.

Chinese lantern; a lantern made of thin paper, usually variously colored, much used in illuminations.

Dark lantern; a lantern with a single opening, which may be closed so as to conceal the light.

Lantern of Aristotle or *Aristotle's lantern*; the oral skeleton and soft parts of the sea-urchin, the most highly complex dentary structure to be found in the *Echinoidea.* It has twenty important parts, including five teeth, five alveoli, five rotulæ, and five radii.

Magic lantern; see under *Magic.*

lan′tẽrn, *v.t.*; lanterned, *pt.*, *pp.*; lanterning, *ppr.* 1. To furnish or equip with a lantern or light; as, to *lantern* a lighthouse.

2. To kill by hanging to a lamp-post; frequently done during the French Revolution.

lan′tẽrn-ċar″ri-ẽr, *n.* Same as *Lantern-fly.*

lan′tẽrn-fish, *n.* The smooth sole. [Prov. Eng.]

lan′tẽrn-flȳ, *n.* Any insect of the family *Fulgoridæ*, so called because supposed to be phosphorescent and to emit a strong light in the darkness.

Lantern-fly (*Fulgora lanternaria*).

lan′tẽrn-jack, *n.* The ignis fatuus.

lan′tẽrn-jạwed, *a.* Having lantern-jaws or a long, thin visage.

lan′tẽrn-jạws, *n.pl.* Long, thin jaws; hence, a thin visage.

lan′tẽrn-pin″ion (-yun), *n.* See *Lantern-wheel.*

lan′tẽrn-shell, *n.* The shell of any bivalve of the genus *Anatina.*

lan′tẽrn-wheel (-hwēl), *n.* In machinery, a kind of pinion or small gear-wheel having, instead of leaves, cylindrical teeth or bars called trundles, or spindles, on which the teeth of the main wheel act. The ends of the trundles being

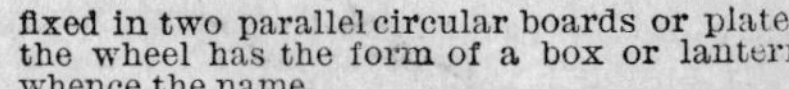

fixed in two parallel circular boards or plates, the wheel has the form of a box or lantern, whence the name.

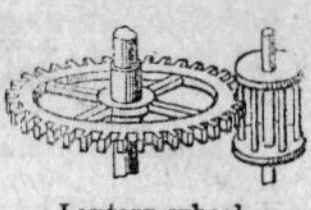
Lantern-wheel.

lan′thȧ-nite, *n.* [*Lanthanum* and *-ite.*] In mineralogy, a rare basic carbonate of lanthanum, found in tabular white, grayish-white, or pink crystals.

lan′thȧ-num, lan-thā′ni-um, *n.* [Gr. *lanthanein*, to conceal.] A rare metal discovered by Mosander, associated with didymium in the oxid of cerium, and so named from its properties being concealed by those of cerium.

lan′thō-pine, *n.* [Gr. *lanthanein*, to conceal, and *opion*, poppy-juice.] A white crystalline alkaloid extracted in small quantities from opium.

lan′thọrn, *n.* [Obs.] Same as *Lantern.*

lȧ-nū′gi-nous, lȧ-nū′gi-nōse, *a.* [L. *lanuginosus*, from *lanugo* (*-inis*), down, from *lana*, wool.] Downy; covered with down, or fine, soft hair.

lȧ-nū′gō, *n.* [L., down, from *lana*, wool.] In anatomy, the coat of delicate, downy hairs with which the human fetus is covered for some time before birth and which is shed in the womb or soon after birth.

lan′yȧrd, lan′iȧrd, *n.* [OFr. *laniere*, a thong, strap.]

1. A short piece of rope for fastening something in ships; as, the *lanyards* of the gun-ports, of the buoy, of the cat-hook, etc.; especially used to extend the shrouds and stays of the masts by connection with the deadeyes, etc.

2. In military language, a piece of cord having a small hook at one end and used in firing cannon of old-fashioned makes, with a friction-tube.

lan′yẽr, *n.* [Obs.] Same as *Lannier.*

Lā-oc′ō-on, *n.* [L., from Gr. *Laokoōn*, Laocoön.]

1. In Greek mythology, a priest of Apollo or Neptune during the Trojan war, who with his two sons was crushed to death in the folds of two enormous serpents.

The Group of the Laocoön.

2. One of the most famous groups of sculpture in the world and a rare example of ancient art, depicting the death of Laocoön and his two sons by the serpents.

Lā-od-i-cē′ăn, *a.*

1. Of or pertaining to Laodicea, an ancient city of Phrygia Major, or to its inhabitants.

2. Like the Christians of Laodicea; lukewarm in religion.

Lā-od-i-cē′ăn, *n.* [L. *Laodicea*; Gr. *Laodikei*, Laodicea.]

1. A native or inhabitant of Laodicea.

2. One who resembles the Christians of Laodicea; a lukewarm, unenthusiastic Christian.

lap, *n.* [ME. *lappe*; AS. *læppa*, the edge or flap of a garment, the lap.]

1. The loose part of a coat; the lower part of a garment that plays loosely. [Obs.]

2. The part of clothes that lies on the knees when a person sits down; especially, this part of the wearing apparel or of an apron, as used to catch or hold something.

3. The part of the body below the waist on which, when sitting, something may be held; that part of the body covered by the front part of a garment's skirt or by an apron, especially when sitting, and used with reference to nursing, caressing, or cherishing; as, she held the baby in her *lap.*

4. Figuratively, anything which supports, cherishes, or fosters; a retreat; a shelter; as, in the *lap* of luxury; the *lap* of the valley.

lap, *v.t.*; lapped, *pt.*, *pp.*; lapping, *ppr.* [ME. *lappen*, *wlappen*, prob. another form of *wrappen*, to wrap.]

1. To fold; to bend and lay over or on; as, to *lap* a piece of cloth.

2. To wrap or twist round.

I *lapped* a slender thread about the paper.
—Newton.

3. To infold; to involve; to wrap.

As *lapped* in thought I used to lie
And gaze into the summer sky.—Longfellow.

4. To lay one thing partly above another: to overlap or cause to overlap; as, to *lap* boards or shingles.

5. To polish or cut with a lap; as, to *lap* a gem.

lap, *v.i.* To be spread or laid; to be turned over a part of something else; to overlap.

lap, *n.* 1. The part of one body which lies on and covers a part of another; as, the *lap* of a slate in roofing.

2. A piece of brass, lead, or other soft metal, usually in the form of a rotating disk, used to hold a cutting or polishing powder in cutting glass, gems, and the like, or in polishing cutlery, etc.

3. A roll or sliver of cotton, wool, or the like, for feeding the cards of a carding-machine.

4. In a steam-engine, the distance the slide-valve moves to or from the cylinder after the closing of the steam-passage.

5. In certain games played with cards, as euchre, the points won in addition to those necessary for winning the game, and the carrying of them over to the score of the next game.

6. In races, one circuit of the track along which the competitors have to go a certain number of times to complete a specified distance; as, six *laps* to the mile.

lap, *v.i.* [ME. *lappen*; AS. *lapian*, to lick, lap.]

1. To take up liquor or food with the tongue; to feed or drink by licking.

2. To make a sound like that produced by taking up water by the tongue.

Waters *lapping* on the crag. —Tennyson.

lap, *v.t.* To take into the mouth with the tongue; to lick up; as, a cat *laps* milk.

lap, *n.* 1. An action or sound suggestive of lapping; a licking up.

2. That which is lapped or licked up, as soup. [Slang.]

lap, *v.t.* To repose or rest in a lap, or as if in a lap; as, to *lap* one's head.

Lap-ȧ-ġē′ri-ȧ, *n.* [Named after Josephine de *la Pagerie*, the Empress Josephine.] A genus of Chilean plants of the lily family.

lap′ȧ-rō-cēle, *n.* [Gr. *lapara*, the loins, and *kēlē*, tumor.] In pathology, a lumbar hernia.

lap-ȧ-rot′ō-my, *n.* [Gr. *lapara*, the loins, and *tomē*, a cutting.] In surgery, an incision into the cavity of the abdomen.

lap′bōard, *n.* A small, thin board, usually shaped so as to fit the body while held on the lap, used by tailors, cobblers, etc., in place of a table.

lap′dog, *n.* A small dog fondled in the lap.

lȧ-pel′, *n.* That part of a garment which is made to lap or fold over; as, the *lapels* of a coat.

lap′el-hout, *n.* Same as *Ladlewood*.

lȧ-pelled′, *a.* Furnished with lapels.

lap′ful, *n.* As much as the lap can contain.

lap′i-cide, *n.* A stonecutter. [Obs.]

lap-i-dā′ri-ăn, *a.* Same as *Lapidary*.

lap-i-dā′ri-ous, *a.* [L. *lapidarius*, from *lapis* (*-idis*), a stone.] Stony; consisting of stones. [Rare.]

lap′i-dȧ-rist, *n.* An expert in precious stones; a connoisseur of gems; a lapidist.

lap′i-dā-ry, *n.*; *pl.* **lap′i-dā-rieṣ.** [L. *lapidarius*, of or belonging to stones, from *lapis* (*-idis*), a stone.]

1. An artificer who cuts, polishes, and engraves precious stones.

2. A dealer in precious stones.

3. A virtuoso skilled in the nature and kinds of gems or precious stones. [Rare.]

lap′i-dā-ry, *a.* 1. Of or pertaining to a stone or stones; pertaining to the art of polishing and engraving precious stones.

2. Inscribed upon stone; of or pertaining to inscriptions on stone; monumental; as, *lapidary* lettering.

Lapidary style; in literature, the style appropriate for monumental and other inscriptions.

lap′i-dāte, *v.t.* To stone. [Obs.]

lap-i-dā′tion, *n.* [L. *lapidatio* (*-onis*), from *lapidare*, to stone.] The act of stoning a person to death.

lȧ-pid′ē-ous, *a.* Stony; of the nature of stone; as, *lapideous* matter.

lap′i-dēṣ, *n.*, pl. of *lapis*.

lap-i-des′cence, *n.* Petrifaction; a substance formed by petrifaction. [Obs.]

lap-i-des′cent, *a.* Growing or turning to stone; petrifying. [Obs.]

lap-i-des′cent, *n.* [L. *lapidescens* (*-entis*), ppr. of *lapidescere*, to become stone, from *lapis* (*-idis*), a stone.] Any substance which has the quality of petrifying a body, or converting it to stone. [Obs.]

lap-i-dif′iç, lap-i-dif′iç-ăl, *a.* [L. *lapis* (*-idis*), a stone, and *facere*, to make.] Forming or converting into stone.

lȧ-pid″i-fi-cā′tion, *n.* Petrifaction; the act or process of changing or converting into stone.

lȧ-pid′i-fȳ, *v.t.*; lapidified, *pt.*, *pp.*; lapidifying, *ppr.* [L. *lapis* (*-idis*), a stone, and *facere*, to make.] To form into stone.

lȧ-pid′i-fȳ, *v.i.* To turn into stone; to become stone.

lap′i-dist, *n.* A connoisseur of gems or lapidary work.

lap′i-dōse, *a.* [L. *lapidosus*, stony, from *lapis* (*-idis*), a stone.]

1. Stony. [Obs.]

2. In botany, growing in stony places.

lap-il-lā′tion, *n.* [L. *lapillus*, dim. of *lapis* (*-idis*), a stone.] The state of being or act of making stony.

lȧ-pil′li-fōrm, *a.* [L. *lapillus*, a small stone, and *forma*, form.] Formed like small stones.

lȧ-pil′lus, *n.*; *pl.* **lȧ-pil′li.** [L., dim. of *lapis* (*-idis*), a stone.]

1. A small stone; specifically, in the plural, volcanic ashes which are composed of angular stony or slaggy particles, varying in size from that of a pea to that of a walnut.

2. In anatomy, an otolith.

lā′pis, *n.*; *pl.* **lap′i-dēṣ.** [L., a stone.] A stone; used only in Latin phrases.

Lapis causticus; caustic potash.

Lapis infernalis; fused nitrate of silver; lunar caustic.

Lapis lazuli; azure-stone, an aluminous mineral, of a rich blue color, resembling the blue carbonate of copper.

Lapis Lydius; touchstone; basanite; a variety of silicious slate.

Lapis ollaris; soapstone or potstone or talc; a hydrated silicate of magnesia.

Lap′ith, *n.*; *pl.* **Lap′i-thæ, Lap′iths.** One of the Lapithæ.

Lap′i-thæ, *n.pl.* [L., from Gr. *Lapithai*, the Lapithæ.] In Greek mythology, a race of warriors, who inhabited Thessaly, and were said to be descended from Lapithes, who was a son of Apollo. Most of the legends told of them deal with their wars with the Centaurs, and Greek artists frequently depicted these conflicts.

lap′-joint, *n.* A joint in which the edge of one of the component parts overlaps the other.

lap′-joint″ed, *a.* Having joints formed by edges overlapping, as by the edges of plates overlapping, as in steam-boilers, iron ships, etc.

Lap′lănd-ẽr, *n.* A native of Lapland; a Lapp.

Lap′lănd-ish, *a.* Pertaining to Lapland or the Laplanders.

lap′ling, *n.* One who indulges in ease and sensual delights; a term of contempt.

Lapp, *n.* [Sw. *Lapp*, a Lapp; of Laplandish origin.] One of the race from which Lapland takes its name, though it forms only a portion of the population.

lap-pā′ceous, *a.* [L. *lappaceus*, from *lappa*, a bur.] In botany, of, pertaining to, or resembling a bur.

lap′pẽr, *n.* One who laps or takes up food or drink with the tongue.

lap′pẽr, *n.* 1. One who laps, wraps, folds, or uses a lap; as, a cloth *lapper*; a lapidary.

2. In textile manufacturing, a machine which receives the dressed fiber and forms it into a lap or fleece.

lap′pet, *n.* [Dim. of *lap*, a fold.]

1. A little lap or flap, especially one on a coat or headdress as an ornament.

2. In ornithology, a wattle.

3. An English book-name for certain bombycid moths, as *Lasiocampa quercifolia* or *Lasiocampa ilicifolia*.

lap′pet, *v.t.* To ornament with a lappet. [Rare.]

lap′pet-moth, *n.* Same as *Lappet*, 3.

Lap′piç, *a.* and *n.* Same as *Lappish*.

lap′ping, *n.* 1. The act of wrapping or folding.

2. That which is lapped; a flap or pendant.

3. A kind of blanket or wrapper used on a calico-printing machine.

4. The act or process of forming a lap-joint or of placing the edge of one material above that of another.

5. In textile manufacturing, the act or process of forming a lap or fleece of fibrous material for a carding-machine.

lap′ping-en″ġine, *n.* In metal-working, a machine which doubles over the two laps which are to be welded.

lap′ping-mȧ-çhïne″, *n.* Same as second *Lapper*, 2.

Lap′pish, *a.* and *n.* I. *a.* Of or pertaining to Lapland or the Lapps.

II. *n.* The language of the Lapps, which is related to the Finnic.

Lap-pō′ni-ăn, *a.* Same as *Lappish*.

laps′ȧ-ble, *a.* Capable of lapsing, falling, or relapsing.

Lap′sȧ-nȧ, *n.* [L. *lapsana*; Gr. *lapsanē*, the charlock, or nipplewort.] A genus of plants of the order *Compositæ*, containing three or four species, natives of the northern hemisphere in the Old World. One species, *Lapsana communis*, is the nipplewort.

lapse, *n.* [L. *lapsus*, a falling, properly pp. of *labi*, to slip, fall.]

1. The act of lapsing, gliding, slipping, or gradually falling; an unnoticed passing away; as, the *lapse* of a stream; the *lapse* of time.

2. A slip; an error; a fault; a failing in duty; a slight deviation from truth or rectitude; as, a *lapse* in style or propriety.

3. In English ecclesiastical law, the slip or omission of a patron to present a clerk to a benefice within six months after it becomes void. In this case, the benefice is said to be lapsed, or in lapse.

4. In law, the termination or defeat of a right or interest through failure to comply with conditions.

5. In theology, apostasy.

lapse, *v.i.*; lapsed, *pt.*, *pp.*; lapsing, *ppr.* [L. *lapsare*, to slip, stumble, freq. of *labi*, to slip, fall.]

1. To glide; to pass slowly, silently, or by degrees.

2. To slide or slip in moral conduct; to fail in duty; to deviate from rectitude; to commit a fault.

3. To fail; specifically, in law, to become ineffectual or void.

4. To fall or pass from one proprietor to another, by the omission or negligence of the patron, etc.

lapse, *v.t.* 1. To let slip; to suffer to become vacant. [Rare.]

2. To surprise in a fault; to apprehend; to overtake. [Obs.]

Lap′sī, *n.pl.* [L., masc. pl. of *lapsus*, pp. of *labi*, to fall.] Among the early Christians, those who deserted their faith when persecuted.

laps′i-ble, *a.* Same as *Lapsable*.

lap′sid″ed, *a.* Same as *Lopsided*.

lap′stōne, *n.* A stone on which shoemakers beat leather, and held on the knees.

lap′strēak, lap′strāke, *a.* Constructed of boards overlapping one another at the edges; clincher-built.

Lȧ-pū′tăn, *a.* Pertaining to Laputa, the imaginary island which is spoken of as the home of absurd dreamers in Swift's Gulliver's Travels; hence, chimerical; ridiculous.

lap′wing, *n.* [ME. *lapwing*, for *lapwink*; AS. *hleápewince*, the lapwing; *hleápan*, to leap, and *wince*, probably from *wincan*, to wink.] One of a genus of birds belonging to the family *Charadriidæ* (plovers), differing from the plovers chiefly in having a hind toe, and in the nasal grooves being prolonged over two-thirds of the beak. The common lapwing, *Vanellus cristatus*, a well-known bird in England, is about the size of a pigeon; it is often called the *pewit* from its peculiar cry. Its eggs are esteemed a great luxury.

Lapwing (*Vanellus cristatus*).

lap′wōrk, *n.* Metal work in which one part laps over another.

laq′uay (lak′y), *n.* A lackey. [Obs.]

lā′quē-ăr (-kwē-), *n.* [L.] In architecture, a ceiling divided into sunk compartments with beams or spaces between.

laq′uē-ā-ry (-wē-), *a.* [L. *laqueus*, a noose.] Using a noose in a combat. [Obs.]

Lär, *n.*; *pl.* **Lā′rēṣ** or **Lärṣ.** [L. *Lar*, pl. *Lares*; Old L. *Lases*, Lares.]

1. In Roman mythology, one of the gods of the household.

2. A cherished household possession.

lȧ-rā′ri-um, *n.*; *pl.* **lȧ-rā′ri-ȧ.** [L.] In Roman antiquity, the shrine of the Lares or household gods.

lär′bōard, *n.* [ME. *laddebord*, the larboard, lit., prob. the lading-side; AS. *hladan*, to lade, and *bord*, side.] The port side of a vessel; the left-hand side as a person on deck faces toward the bow. *Port* has been officially substituted for *larboard* to avoid possible confusion in sound with *starboard*.

lär′bōard, *a.* Situated on or relating to the left-hand side of a ship; port; as, the *larboard* anchor.

lär′ce-nẽr, lär′ce-nist, *n.* One guilty of larceny; a thief.

lär′ce-nous, *a.* Having the quality of larceny; thievish.

lär′ce-ny, *n.* [OFr. *larrecin*; L. *latrocinium*, robbery, from *latrocinari*, to rob, plunder, from *latro* (*-onis*), a freebooter, mercenary soldier, hired servant, robber.] Theft; the act of taking and carrying away the goods or personal property of another feloniously. *Larceny* is of two kinds: *simple larceny*, or theft, not accompanied with any atrocious circumstance; and *mixed* or *compound larceny*, which includes in it the aggravation of taking from one's house or person, as in burglary or robbery.

Grand and *petit* or *petty larceny*; theft of goods exceeding twelve pence in value was *grand larceny* at English common law; theft of goods less than twelve pence in value was *petit larceny*, a distinction now abolished in England; in the United States, the distinguishing amount varies from $25 to $50.

lärch, *n.* [OFr. *larege*, *larice*; L. *larix* (*-icis*); Gr. *larix* (*-ikos*), the larch.] Any tree of the genus *Larix*, as *Larix Americana*, the black larch or tamarack of North America, a conifer whose deciduous needles are borne in clusters or fascicles upon graceful drooping branches. *Larix Europæa* is the European larch, having bark of use medicinally. *Larix occidentalis* is the western larch of Washington and Oregon.

lärch′en, *a.* Of or relating to the larch.

lärd, *n.* [ME. *larde*; OFr. *lard*, bacon, pig's fat, the blubber of whales, from L. *lardum*, the fat of bacon.]

1. The fat of swine, after being melted and separated from the flesh.

2. Bacon; the flesh of swine. [Obs.]

Leaf lard; lard rendered from the internal masses or leaves of fat surrounding a hog's kidneys, etc.; also, the leaves before rendering.

lärd, *v.t.* [Fr. *larder*, from *lard*, bacon.]

1. To stuff with bacon or pork; to interlard; to garnish with lardons; to place strips of pork or bacon in, as in a roast of beef.

2. To mix with something by way of improvement; to garnish.

3. To grease; to baste; to cover with fat or lard.

4. To fatten; to enrich. [Obs.]

lärd, *v.i.* To grow fat. [Obs.]

lär-dȧ-cē′in, *n.* [*Lardaceous* and *-in.*] An albuminoid product occurring in certain degenerations, as in infiltrations of the pancreas, spleen, liver, etc.

lär-dā′ceous, *a.* 1. Of the nature of lard or lardacein.

2. Affected with amyloid degeneration.

lärd′ẽr, *n.* [ME. *larder*; OFr. *lardier*, a larder, a tub for bacon; LL. *lardarium*, a room for meats, from L. *lardum*, the fat of bacon, lard.] A room where meat and other articles of food are kept; a pantry; provisions.

lärd′ẽr-bee″tle, *n.* The bacon-beetle.

lärd′ẽr-ẽr, *n.* One who has charge of the larder.

lärd′ẽr-y, *n.* A larder. [Obs.]

lärd′-oil, *n.* An oil derived from lard used as an illuminant and lubricant, and also in making soap.

lär′dŏn, lär-do͞on′, *n.* [Fr. *lardon*, from *lard*, bacon, pig's fat.] A strip of bacon or pork used in larding.

lärd′ry, *n.* A larder. [Obs.]

lärd′y, *a.* Like lard; covered with or containing lard.

lāre, *n.* 1. Soil; pasture; litter. [Obs.]

2. Lore; counsel. [Obs.]

lāre, *v.t.* To feed. [Obs.]

Lā′rēs, *n.*, pl. of *Lar.*

lär-gä-men′te, *adv.* [It., from *largo*, large.] With a broad, slow, full movement.

lärġe, *a.* [OFr. *large*; L. *largus*, abundant, copious, plentiful, large.]

1. Of more than the average size, extent, range, dimensions, bulk, capacity, quantity, number, etc., relative to other things of the same kind, or in general; great; big; bulky; extensive; ample; abundant; copious; plentiful; populous; as, a *large* body, surface, measure, city, contract, etc.

2. Embracing many objects; liberal; many-sided; comprehensive; as, a *large* mind.

3. Generous; noble; as, a *large* heart.

4. At sea, blowing in a favorable direction; said of the wind.

5. Free; unrestrained; licentious; boisterous. [Obs.]

6. Free; unencumbered. [Obs.]

7. Lavish; prodigal. [Obs.]

At large; (a) without restraint or confinement; as, to go *at large*; (b) diffusely; fully; to the full extent; as, to discourse on a subject *at large*; (c) not confined to a particular district; for the entire state; as, a congressman, or an elector, *at large.*

Syn.—Big, great, bulky, huge, extensive, wide, spacious, colossal, gigantic, grand, immense, massive, vast, capacious, comprehensive, ample, abundant, plentiful, populous, copious, diffuse, liberal.

lärġe, *adv.* 1. With a favorable wind.

2. Freely; fully. [Obs.]

lärġe, *n.* Formerly, a musical note equal to four breves.

lärġe′-ā″cred (-kẽrd), *a.* Having much land.

lärġe′-hand″ed, *a.* 1. Having large hands; rapacious; grasping; greedy.

2. Generous; liberal; free-handed.

lärġe′-heärt″ed, *a.* Having a large heart or liberal disposition; generous; liberal; magnanimous.

lärġe′-heärt″ed-ness, *n.* Largeness of heart; liberality.

lärġe′ly, *adv.* In a large manner.

lärġe′ness, *n.* The quality or condition of being large; greatness; amplitude; extensiveness; comprehensiveness; applied to any conceivable thing.

lär′ġess, *n.* [OFr. *largesse*, a bounty, from L. *largiri*, to give bountifully, from *largus*, abundant, large.] A present; a gift or donation; a bounty bestowed; a liberal bestowment.

lär′ġesse, *n.* Same as *Largess.*

lär′ġet, *n.* A billet of iron cut in size for rolling into a sheet.

lär-ghet′tō, *a.* and *n.* [It., somewhat slow, from *largo*, large, bulky; L. *largus*, large.] A musical term indicating a movement intermediate between largo and andante.

lär-ġif′i-căl, *a.* Benevolent; generous; liberal. [Obs.]

lär-ġif′lū-ous, *a.* Flowing copiously. [Obs.]

lär-ġil′ō-quent (-kwent), *a.* [Obs.] Same as *Grandiloquent.*

lär′ġish, *a.* Somewhat large. [Rare.]

lär-ġi′tion (-jish′un), *n.* The bestowment of a largess or gift. [Obs.]

lär′gō, *a.* and *n.* [It., large, slow, from L. *largus*, large.] A musical term directing slow movement; *largo* is one degree quicker than *grave*, and two degrees quicker than *adagio*. A quaver in *largo* is equal to a minim in *presto.*

lar′i-at, *n.* [Sp. *la reata*; *la*, the, and *reata*, a rope.] A strong slender cord or cable carried by a plainsman and used for picketing his horse to keep him from straying while grazing; a lasso. [Western U. S.]

lar′i-at, *v.t.*; lariated, *pt.*, *pp.*; lariating, *ppr.* To fasten with a lariat; to picket for grazing; to catch with a lariat. [Western U. S.]

Lar′i-dæ, *n.pl.* [LL. *larus*; Gr. *laros*, a ravenous sea-bird, and *-idæ.*] A family of aquatic birds; the gull family.

lā′rine, *a.* Of or pertaining to the *Laridæ*, or gull family.

Lā′rix, *n.* [L. *larix*, the larch.] A genus of coniferous trees with deciduous leaves; the larches.

lar-ix-in′ic, *a.* Related to or derived from the larch; as, *larixinic* acid.

lärk, *n.* [ME. *larke*; AS. *laferce*, *lauerce*, a lark.] A small passerine bird of the family *Alaudidæ*, the species being mostly migratory birds of Europe, Asia, and Africa. The skylark of Europe, *Alauda arvensis*, which rises high in the air and sings with a very clear and sweet note, is considered a table delicacy. It appears occasionally in the western hemisphere.

Skylark (*Alauda arvensis*).

lärk, *n.* A sport or occasion of merriment; a frolic; a merry adventure; as, to go on a *lark.* [Colloq.]

lärk, *v.i.* 1. To catch larks.

2. To make sport; to sport; to frolic. [Colloq.]

lärk′-bun″ting, *n.* A bird of the family *Fringillidæ* inhabiting the western plains of the United States.

lärk′ẽr, *n.* A catcher of larks; also, one who frolics.

lärk′-finch, *n.* See *Lark-sparrow.*

lärk′like, *a.* Resembling a lark in manners.

lärk's′-heel, *n.* A flower called Indian cress, *Tropæolum majus*; the nasturtium.

lärk′-spar″rōw, *n.* A fringilloid bird, *Chondestes grammica*, of the Mississippi valley and western United States; the lark-finch.

lärk′spŭr, *n.* A plant whose flower is somewhat showy and furnished with a long-spurred calyx; a plant of the genus *Delphinium.*

lärme, *n.* [Fr., a tear, from L. *lacrima*, a tear.] A design resembling a tear-drop; used in lace patterns and in heraldry.

lär′mi-ẽr, *n.* [Fr., from *larme*, a tear or drop.]

1. The flat, jutting part of a cornice; literally, the dropper; the eaves or drip of a house; the corona.

2. The lacrymal sinus in deer and antelope; the tearpit.

lā′roid, *a.* [Gr. *laros*, a ravenous sea-bird, and *eidos*, form.] Like or resembling the gull family *Laridæ.*

lar′ri-kin, *n.* [Colloq., Eng.; said to have been first used for *larking*, by James Dalton, a Melbourne police-sergeant of Irish birth.] In Australia, a boisterous, rude, ill-bred rowdy; a hoodlum.

lar′ri-kin-iṣm, *n.* The quality of a larrikin; rowdyism; extreme rudeness. [Australian.]

lar′rup, *v.t.*; larruped (-rupt), *pt.*, *pp.*; larruping, *ppr.* [Etym. doubtful; compare D. *larpen*, to thresh; *larp*, a whip.] To thrash or beat soundly. [Slang.]

lar′ry, *n.* Same as *Lorry.*

lar′um, *n.* [For *alarum.*] Alarm; a noise giving notice of danger. [See *Alarm.*]

lär′vȧ, *n.*; *pl.* **lär′væ.** [L. *larva*, a ghost, specter.] Any insect from the time it leaves the egg until it reaches the pupa state; the early form of any animal when unlike its mature form.

Loeven's larva; the larva of a marine worm, *Polygordius*, discovered and so named before the adult was known; called after S. F. Loeven, a Swedish zoölogist.

lär′văl, *a.* Belonging to a larva.

Lär-vā′li-ȧ, *n.pl.* [L. *larvalis*, pertaining to a ghost, from *larva*, ghost.] A division of tunicates, so named because they retain certain larval features through life.

lär-vā′ri-um, *n.*; *pl.* **lär-vā′ri-ȧ** or **lär-vā′ri-ums.** A shelter for larvæ, as the web of the caterpillar; also, a box or case for the artificial rearing of insects.

lär′vāte, lär′vā-ted, *a.* [L. *larva*, a ghost, specter.] Masked; clothed as with a mask; obscure; difficult to find; in medicine, said of some diseases when diagnosis is difficult.

lärve, *n.* and *a.* I. *n.* A larva. [Rare.]

II. *a.* Larval. [Rare.]

lärvi-. A combining form from L. *larva*, a ghost, specter, mask, used in zoölogy to signify larva; as, *larvi*gerous.

lär′vi-fọrm, *a.* [*Larvi-*, and L. *forma*, form.] Having the form or condition of a larva.

lär-viġ′ẽr-ous, *a.* [*Larvi-*, and L. *gerere*, to produce.] Bearing the larval skin in the pupa state; said of the pupa of dipterous insects.

lär-vip′ȧ-rous, *a.* [*Larvi-*, and L. *parere*, to bring forth.] Producing, instead of an egg, the living larva; said of some insects.

lär-viv′ō-rous, *a.* [*Larvi-*, and L. *vorare*, to devour.] Subsisting upon the larvæ of insects; as, *larvivorous* birds.

lā′ry, *n.* [L. *larus*; Gr. *laros*, a ravenous sea-bird, the gull.] The guillemot, a sea-bird related to the auks.

laryng-. See *Laryngo.*

lȧ-ryn′ġē-ăl, *a.* Pertaining to the larynx.

lȧ-ryn′ġē-ăn, *a.* Same as *Laryngeal.*

lar-yn-ġec′tō-my, *n.* [*Laryng-*, and Gr. *ektomē*, a cutting out; *ek*, out, and *tomē*, a cutting, from *temnein*, to cut.] The operation of cutting away a part of the larynx.

lar-yn-ġis′mus, *n.* [Gr. *laryngismos*, a croaking, from *laryngizein*, to shout, croak, from *larynx*, the larynx.] An affection producing spasmodic action of the glottal muscles, occasioning involuntary closing of the glottis.

lar-yn-ġī′tis, *n.* [Gr. *larynx*, *laryngos*, the larynx, and *-itis.*] An inflammation of the larynx of any sort.

laryngo-, laryng-. Combining forms from Gr. *larynx*, *laryngos*, the larynx; used in medical and surgical terms to signify of or pertaining to the larynx or throat; as, *laryngo*tomy, *laryngo*logy.

lȧ-ryn-gō-loġ′ic-ăl, *a.* Pertaining to the science of laryngology.

lar-yn-gol′ō-ġist, *n.* An expert in the science of laryngology.

lar-yn-gol′ō-ġy, *n.* [*Laryngo-*, and Gr. *-logia*, from *legein*, to speak.] That department of pathology which has to do with diseases of the larynx, including a knowledge of the structure, action, and functions of the larynx.

lar-yn-goph′ō-ny, *n.* [*Laryngo-*, and Gr. *phōnē*, voice.] The sound heard through the stethoscope when placed over the larynx while the patient is speaking.

lȧ-ryn′gō-scōpe, *n.* [*Laryngo-*, and Gr. *skopein*, to view.] An instrument for examining the larynx by means of mirrors reflecting light upon it.

lȧ-ryn-gō-scop′ic, *a.* Of or pertaining to the examination of the larynx by means of the laryngoscope.

lar-yn-gos′cō-pist, *n.* An expert in the use of the laryngoscope.

lar-yn-gos′cō-py, *n.* The science or practice of making examinations with the laryngoscope.

lȧ-ryn′gō-tōme, *n.* An instrument used in laryngotomy.

lar-yn-got′ō-my, *n.* [*Laryngo-*, and Gr. *tomē*, a cutting, from *temnein*, to cut.] The operation of cutting into the larynx; the making of an incision into the larynx for assisting respiration when obstructed, or for removing foreign bodies.

lȧ-ryn-gō-trā′chē-ăl, *a.* [*Laryngo-*, and Gr. *tracheia*, the trachea.] Of or pertaining to both the larynx and the trachea; as, the *laryngotracheal* cartilage.

lȧ-ryn-gō-trā-chē-ot′ō-my, *n.* [*Laryngo-*, and Gr. *tracheia*, the trachea, and *tomē*, a cutting.] The operation performed to relieve obstructed breathing by cutting into the larynx and the upper part of the trachea.

lar′ynx, *n.* [Gr. *larynx*, *laryngos*, the larynx, the upper part of the windpipe, throat, gullet.] In anatomy, the upper part of the windpipe or trachea, a cartilaginous cavity, which modulates the voice in speaking and singing, containing the vocal cords and connected with the pharynx by means of the glottis, which in mammals is covered by a lid called the epiglottis, preventing solid substances from entering the trachea. Its various parts, anatomically considered, are extremely complex and intricate. Fig. 1 above

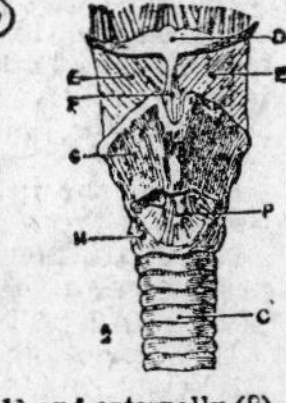

Larynx internally (1) and externally (2).

shows, A, the larynx internally, B being the epiglottis, C C the trachea, and D the esophagus or gullet. In fig. 2, C is the trachea, D the hyoid bone, E E the thyrohyoid membrane, F the thyrohyoid ligament, G the thyroid cartilage, H the cricoid cartilage, P the cricothyroid ligament.

las, *n.* A lace. [Obs.]

las, *a.* and *adv.* Less. [Obs.]

las-çär′, *n.* [Hind. *lashkar*, an inferior artilleryman, a regimental servant, a native sailor; Per. *lashkarī*, belonging to the army, a soldier, from *lashkar*, the army.] In the East Indies, a term applied to native sailors, many of whom are employed on European vessels; also, a native employed about camps and arsenals of foreigners; a camp-follower.

las-civ′i-en-cy, *n.* Lasciviousness; wantonness. [Obs.]

las-civ′i-ent, *a.* Lascivious. [Obs.]

las-civ′i-ous, *a.* [L. *lascivus*, wanton, from *laxus*, loose, open.]

1. Loose; wanton; lewd; lustful; as, *lascivious* men; *lascivious* desires; *lascivious* eyes.

2. Soft; wanton; luxurious; tending to voluptuousness.

las-civ′i-ous-ly, *adv.* Loosely; wantonly; lewdly.

las-civ′i-ous-ness, *n.* 1. Looseness; irregular indulgence of animal desires; wantonness; lustfulness.

2. Tendency to excite lust and promote irregular indulgences.

Las-ẽr-pi′ti-um (-pish′i-), *n.* [L. *laserpicium*, laserwort.] A genus of umbelliferous perennial herbs native to the Old World, having medicinal roots.

lā′sẽr-wŏrt, *n.* The plant *Laserpitium latifolium*, or any other plant of the same genus.

lash, *n.* [ME. *lashe*, the flexible part of a whip; compare G. *lasche*, a flap, D. *lasch*, a joint, seam; prob. from L. *laxus*, loose.]

1. The thong or braided cord at the point of a whip; any thong, cord, or the like for flogging; a whip; a scourge.

2. A stroke with a whip or anything pliant and tough.

3. A stroke of satire; a sarcasm; an expression or retort that cuts or gives pain.

4. An eyelash.

5. A leash or snare. [Obs.]

6. In weaving, a leash.

lash, *v.t.*; lashed (lasht), *pt.*, *pp.*; lashing, *ppr.* 1. To strike with a lash or anything pliant; to whip or scourge; to beat, as with something loose; to dash against.

> And big waves *lash* the frighted shores.
> —Prior.

2. To tie or bind with a rope or cord; to secure or fasten by a string; as, to *lash* anything to a mast or to a yard; to *lash* a trunk on a coach.

3. To satirize; to censure with severity; as, to *lash* vice.

lash, *v.i.* 1. To ply the whip; to strike.

2. To break forth, as a flame. [Obs.]

lash′ẽr, *n.* 1. One who lashes.

2. A lashing; a cord used as a fastening.

3. The fatherlasher, a kind of fish.

lash′ẽr, *n.* Sluggish water above a dam; hence, a dam or weir.

lash′ing, *n.* 1. A piece of rope for binding or making fast one thing to another.

2. Castigation; chastisement.

3. [*pl.*] Abundance; profusion; as *lashings* of drink. [Ir. or Scot.]

lā-si-an′thous, *a.* [Gr. *lasios*, shaggy, woolly, and *anthos*, a flower.] Having flowers covered with a woolly growth.

lask, *v.i.* To sail large, or with a quartering wind, that is, with a wind about 45° abaft the beam. [Obs.]

lask, *n.* Diarrhea; flux. [Obs.]

las′ket, *n.* [Compare Sw. *laska*, to stitch, Dan. *laske*, to join, *lask*, a scarf; perhaps from L. *laxus*, loose.] A loop to fasten a bonnet to the foot of a sail.

lȧss, *n.* [ME. *lasse*; of Celtic origin; compare W. *llodes*, f. of *llawd*, a lad.]

1. A young woman; a girl.

2. A female sweetheart. [Scot.]

lasse, *a.* and *adv.* Less. [Obs.]

las′sie, *n.* A young or small lass. [Scot.]

las′si-tūde, *n.* [L. *lassitudo* (*-inis*), faintness, weariness, from *lassus*, faint, weary.] Languor of body or mind; indisposition to exertion resulting from fatigue or due to morbid conditions; dullness; heaviness; weariness.

lȧss′lọrn, *a.* Forsaken by a lass or sweetheart.

las′sō, *n.*; *pl.* **las′sōş** or **las′sōeş.** [Port. *laço*; L. *laqueus*, a noose, snare, trap.] A rope or leather line, with a running noose, used for catching horses and cattle.

las′sō, *v.t.*; lassoed, *pt.*, *pp.*; lassoing, *ppr.* To catch or take by using a lasso.

las′sō-cell, *n.* A thread-cell or stinging-cell of certain cœlenterates from which a long thread may be cast to sting or poison; a cnida or nettling-cell.

lȧst, *n.* [AS. *hlæst*, a load, from *hladan*, to load, lade.]

1. A load; hence, a certain weight or measure, generally estimated at 4,000 pounds, but varying as to different articles. A last of codfish, white herrings, meal, or ashes is twelve barrels; a last of corn is eighty bushels; of gunpowder, twenty-four barrels; of red herrings, twenty cades; of hides, twelve dozen; of leather, twenty dickers; of pitch or tar, fourteen barrels; of wool, twelve sacks; of flax or feathers, 1,700 pounds. [Rare.]

2. A ship's cargo.

lȧst, *n.* [ME. *last*, *lest*; AS. *last*, *læst*, a footstep, track, *læst*, a boot, *læste*, a last.] A mold or form of the human foot, made of wood, on which shoes are formed.

lȧst, *v.t.* To fit to or shape with a last; as, to *last* a shoe.

lȧst, *a.* [ME. *last*, *latst*, contr. of *latest*, superl. of *late*, from AS. *læt*, slow, late.]

1. Coming after or following all others in order of place or time; latest; hindmost; closing; final; as, the *last* hour of the day; the *last* page of a book.

2. Next before the present; as, *last* week.

3. Utmost; above all else in importance; as, the *last* degree of perfection.

4. Lowest; meanest; least; as, the *last* prize.

5. Most unlikely (to possess a certain character, quality, or disposition); as, the *last* man to do such a thing.

Syn.—Latest, final, ultimate.—*Last* and *ultimate* respect the order of succession; *latest*, the order of time; *final* respects the completion of an object. What is *last* or *ultimate* is succeeded by nothing else; what is *latest* is succeeded by no great interval of time; what is *final* requires to be succeeded by nothing else.

lȧst, *n.* The conclusion; end; as, true to the *last*.

At last; finally; implying difficulty or delay.

lȧst, *v.i.*; lasted, *pt.*, *pp.*; lasting, *ppr.* [ME. *lasten*; AS. *læstan*, to accomplish, follow, perform, endure, lit., to follow closely in track, from *last*, a track, footprint.]

1. To continue in time; to endure; to remain in existence; as, the services *lasted* an hour.

2. To continue unimpaired; not to decay or perish; as, select for winter the best apples to *last*.

3. To hold out; to continue unconsumed; as, the ship had water on board to *last* a week.

lȧst, *adv.* 1. Following all else in time or place; as, news told *last*.

2. At the time next before the present; as, I saw him *last* in the depot.

3. In conclusion; finally.

lȧst, *n.* Endurance; stamina; as, there is not much *last* in him.

lȧst′āge, *n.* [ME. *last*; AS. *hlæst*, a load.]

1. The lading of a ship; ballast.

2. Space to stow goods.

3. A duty (a) on goods sold by the last; (b) on the right to carry goods about at will; (c) for freight or transportation. [Obs.]

lȧste, *v.*, obsolete past tense of *last*.

lȧst′ẽr, *n.* One who or that which shapes parts of boots or shoes on a last.

lȧst′ing, *n.* 1. A stout worsted fabric used for shoe-uppers, etc.; everlasting.

2. Endurance.

lȧst′ing, *a.* Continuing in time; enduring; durable; permanent.

Syn.—Permanent, durable, perpetual.—*Lasting* is more commonly applied to things abstract, which from their very nature endure; *permanent*, chiefly to things established and designed to remain unchanged; *durable*, to material substances or fabrics, so far as they resist agencies which tend to destroy them; *perpetual*, to motion not subject to interruption.

lȧst′ing-ly, *adv.* Durably; with continuance.

lȧst′ing-ness, *n.* Durability; the quality or state of long continuance.

lȧst′ly, *adv.* 1. In the last place.

2. In the conclusion; at last; finally. [Rare.]

lat, *v.*, obsolete form of *let*.

lät, *n.* [Hind.] An isolated column, common in Indian architecture, used for inscriptions, to bear a statue, or as a flagstaff.

lat, *a.* 1. Wet; unseasonable, as weather. [Prov. Eng.]

2. Slow; tedious. [Prov. Eng.]

lat-ȧ-kī′ȧ, *n.* A fine variety of Turkish tobacco, so named from Latakia (anciently Laodicea), near which it is produced.

Lȧ-tā′ni-ȧ, *n.* [*Latania*, the native name of a species in the Isle of Bourbon.] A genus of fan-palms, native to the Mascarene Islands.

latch, *v.t.*; latched (lacht), *pt.*, *pp.*; latching, *ppr.* [ME. *latchen*; AS. *læccan*, to seize, catch hold of.]

1. To fasten with a latch; to fasten.

2. To seize. [Obs.]

latch, *n.* [ME. *lacche*, from *lacchen*, to fasten, latch.]

1. A device of iron or wood used to fasten a door or gate; the simplest form is a pivoted bar falling into a slot and raised by pulling a string; the commonest form is a spring-bolt withdrawn by turning a knob.

2. A fish-line clamp.

3. A lasket.

4. See second *Fly*, n. 5.

On the latch; fastened only by a latch; inviting entrance.

latch′et, *n.* [ME. *lachet*; OFr. *lacet*, dim. of *las*, a string, lace.] A shoestring; a leather strap used to fasten on a sandal.

latch′ing, *n.* A lasket.

latch′kēy, *n.* A key for a latch; especially, a small key for a spring night-latch.

latch′string, *n.* A string passed through a hole in the door and used to lift up the more primitive kind of latch.

lāte, *a.*; *comp.* later; *superl.* latest. [ME. *lat*; AS. *læt*, slow, tardy, late.]

1. Coming after the usual time; slow; tardy; long delayed; as, a *late* spring; a *late* summer; the crops or harvest will be *late*.

2. Far advanced toward the end or close; as, a *late* hour of the day; he began at a *late* period of his life.

3. Being last or recently in any place, office, or character; as, the *late* ministry; the *late* administration.

4. Existing not long ago, but now dead, decayed, or departed; as, the *late* president; the *late* archbishop.

5. Not long past; happening not long ago; recent; as, the *late* rains; we have received *late* intelligence.

lāte, *adv.* 1. After the usual time, or the time appointed; after delay; as, he arrived *late*.

2. After the proper or usual season; as, this year the fruits ripen *late*.

3. Not long ago; lately.

> And round them throng
> With leaps and bounds the *late* imprisoned young.
> —Pope.

4. Far in the night, day, week, or other particular period; as, to lie abed *late*; to sit up *late* at night.

Of late; in time not long past, or near the present; as, the practice is *of late* uncommon.

Too late; after the proper time; not in due time; as, we arrived *too late* to see the procession.

lȧ-teen′, *a.* [Fr. *latine*, f. of *latin*, Latin (for *voile latine*, Latin sail), from L. *Latinus*, Latin.] Of or relating to a kind of rig used in certain small boats on the Mediterranean; literally, Latin.

Lateen sail; a triangular sail, extended by a long yard and slung about one quarter the distance from the lower end, which is brought down at the tack, while the other end is elevated at an angle of about 45°; a *lateen yard* is the yard of such a sail.

Felucca with Lateen Sails.

lāte′ly, *adv.* Not long ago; recently.

lā′tence, *n.* Latency.

lā′ten-cy, *n.* The state of being concealed; abstruseness.

lāte′ness, *n.* The quality or condition of being tardy, or of coming after the usual time.

lā′tent, *a.* [L. *latens* (*-entis*), ppr. of *latere*, to lie hidden or concealed, to lurk.] Hidden; concealed; secret; not seen; not visible or apparent; as, *latent* reasons; *latent* springs of action.

Latent ambiguity; doubt as to the meaning of a legal instrument, arising not from the document itself, but from extrinsic causes; as, a legacy to James Jones of Tor becomes ambiguous when it appears that there are two men of that name in Tor. Doubt caused by the wording of the instrument itself, and obvious upon reading it, is *patent ambiguity*.

Latent heat; heat producing a change in the molecular structure of a body without altering the temperature, as in the conversion of a liquid into the gaseous state.

Latent period; (a) the time during which a disease exists in the system before its symptoms become manifest; (b) a period of arrested activity in the development of an ovum; (c) the period of unseen changes in muscle or nerve before contraction of a muscle.

lā′tent-ly, *adv.* In a latent manner.

lā′tẽr, *n.*; *pl.* **lat′e-rēş.** [L.] A tile; a brick.

lāt′ẽr, *adv.* Hereafter; afterward; as, I will tell you *later*.

lat′e-rȧ, *n.*, pl. of *latus*.

lat′ẽr-ad, *adv.* [L. *latus* (*-eris*), the side, and *ad*, to, toward.] From the median plane; toward a side.

lat′ẽr-ăl, *a.* [L. *lateralis*, from *latus* (*-eris*), a side.] Pertaining to the side; hence, (a) directed toward a side; as, a *lateral* view; (b) placed at either side of the median plane; as, *lateral* ventricles; (c) situated on the side of (the hinge of a bivalve shell); as, a *lateral* tooth; (d) borne on the side, as distinguished from *medial* or *terminal*; as, *lateral* nerves; (e) operating on the side, or crosswise of the length; as, *lateral* strain.

Lateral line; in fishes, a longitudinal line consisting of a row of tubes or ducts of excretory glands generally marked by a difference in structure or color of the skin.

lat′ẽr-ăl, *n.* Anything growing on, projecting from, or situated at a side; as, the *laterals* of a grapevine (shoots from leaf axils).

lat-ẽr-al′i-ty, *n.* The quality of having distinct sides.

lat′ẽr-ăl-ly, *adv.* By the side; sidewise; in the direction of the side.

Lat′ẽr-ăn, *n.* One of the churches at Rome, built originally by Constantine the Great, and dedicated to St. John of Lateran. It is the episcopal church of the pope, and the principal church of Rome. The ecclesiastical councils called *Lateran councils* are held in the annexed palace.

lāt′ẽred, *a.* Unpunctual; dilatory. [Obs.]

lateri-. A combining form from L. *latus* (*-eris*), side, used in botany, zoölogy, etc., to signify on the side, or toward the side; as, *lateri*grade, *lateri*folious.

lat-ẽr-i′ceous (-ish′us), *a.* [L. *latericius*, made of bricks, from *later* (*-eris*), a brick.] Brick-colored; like brick; as, the *latericeous* sediment in urine.

lat″ẽr-i-fō′li-ous, *a.* [*Lateri-*, and L. *folium*, a leaf.] In botany, growing on the side of a leaf at the base; as, a *laterifolious* flower.

lat′ẽr-i-grāde, *a.* [*Lateri-*, and L. *gradi*, to step.] Progressing sidewise, as certain crabs.

lat′ẽr-i-grāde, *n.* An animal that progresses sidewise, especially one of a family of spiders which run sidewise and backward.

lat′ẽr-ite, *n.* [L. *later* (*-eris*), a brick, tile.] A red, argillaceous, ferruginous rock of India and other tropical countries.

lat-ẽr-it′iç, *a.* Of or pertaining to laterite.

lat-ẽr-i′tious (-ish′us), *a.* Same as *Latericeous*.

Lā′tēş, *n.* [Gr. *latos*, a fish of the Nile.] A genus of fishes found in the Nile, the Ganges, etc. They are of the perch family and are much used as food.

lȧ-tes′cence, *n.* The condition of becoming latent or obscure; partial obscurity.

lȧ-tes′cent, *a.* [L. *latescens* (*-entis*), ppr. of *latescere*, to lie hidden, incept. of *latere*, to lurk, lie hidden.] Withdrawing into obscurity.

lāte′wāke, *n.* [Obs.] Same as *Likewake*.

lāte′wãrd, *a.* and *adv.* Somewhat late; backward. [Obs.]

lā′tex, *n.* [L., a liquid, water, wine.] The milky fluid secreted by some plants and exuding when leaves or stems are broken; thus, opium is the dried *latex* of the poppy.

lȧth, *n.* [ME. *lathe*; AS. *lætt*, a narrow strip of wood, lath.]

1. A thin, narrow strip of wood, nailed to the rafters, studs, etc., of a building, to support the tiles, plaster, or other covering.

2. The bow portion of a crossbow. [Obs.]

lȧth, *v.t.* To cover or line with laths.

lȧth′=brick, *n.* A long brick used in malt-drying kilns.

lāthe, *n.* A granary; a barn. [Obs.]

lāthe, *n.* [AS. *læth*, *leth*, a district.] In Anglo-Saxon England, a district or division of a county; now used only of the five parts of the county of Kent.

lāthe, *n.* [Ice. *lödh*, pl. *ladhar*, a lathe.]

1. A machine by which an article may be shaped or polished by being rotated before a tool pressed against its surface.

2. That part of a loom in which the reed is fixed, and by the movements of which the weft-threads are laid parallel to each other, shot after shot, in the process of weaving; a lay; a batten.

lath′ẽr, *v.i.*; lathered, *pt.*, *pp.*; lathering, *ppr.* To form a foam with water and soap; to become froth or frothy matter.

lath′ẽr, *v.t.* [AS. *lethrian*, to smear, lather, anoint, from *leáthor*, lather.] To spread over with lather.

lath′ẽr, *n.* [AS. *leáthor*, niter, lather.]

1. Foam or froth made by soap moistened with water.

2. Foam or froth from profuse sweat, as of a horse.

lath′ẽr, *v.t.* To beat; to leather. [Colloq.]

lathe′rēeve, lath′rēeve, *n.* The reeve of a lathe or county district.

lȧth′ing, *n.* A covering or lining of laths for walls, etc.; the act of covering with laths.

lȧth′=nāil, *n.* A small nail used in lathing.

lȧth′=pot, *n.* A closed lobster trap made of laths.

lȧth′wŏrk, *n.* Lathing.

lȧth′y, *a.* Thin as a lath; long and slender.

lath′y-riṣm, *n.* Paraplegia, etc., caused by eating the seeds of *Lathyrus Cicera*.

lati-. A combining form from L. *latus*, broad, used in zoölogy, botany, etc., to signify wide, broad; as, *lati*foliate, *lati*pennate.

Lā′tiăn (-shăn), *a.* Of or relating to Latium, one of the countries of early Italy; Latin. [Rare.]

lȧ-tib′ū-līze, *v.i.* [L. *latibulum*, a hiding-place.] To retire into a den, burrow, or cavity, and lie dormant in winter; to retreat and lie hidden.

lȧ-tib′ū-lum, *n.*; *pl.* **lȧ-tib′ū-lȧ**. [L., from *latere*, to lurk.] A secret place of hiding; a lair or den.

lat-i-cif′ẽr-ous, *a.* [L. *latex* (*-icis*), a liquid, and *ferre*, to bear.] In botany, bearing the latex, as certain vessels of plants.

lat′i-çlāve, *n.* [L. *laticlavus*; *latus*, broad, and *clavus*, a stripe.] A distinctive badge worn by Roman senators, supposed to have been a broad stripe of purple on the fore part of the tunic.

lat-i-ços′tāte, *a.* [*Lati-*, and L. *costatus*, ribbed, from *costa*, a rib.] Broad-ribbed.

lat-i-den′tāte, *a.* [*Lati-*, and L. *dentatus*, toothed, from *dens*, *dentis*, a tooth.] Broad-toothed.

lat-i-fō′li-āte, lat-i-fō′li-ous, *a.* Broad-leaved.

lat-i-fun′di-um, *n.*; *pl.* **lat-i-fun′di-ȧ**. [L., from *latus*, broad and *fundus*, estate.] In Roman history, a considerable landed property.

lat′i-gō, *n.* [Sp. *látigo*, a thong.] A strap with which a saddle-girth is adjusted.

lat′i-mẽr, *n.* One having a knowledge of Latin; hence, an interpreter. [Obs.]

Lat′in, *n.* 1. The language of the ancient Romans.

2. One of the people inhabiting Latium; hence, one speaking the Latin language; a Roman.

3. A member of one of the modern peoples whose language is derived from that of the ancient Romans, as the Spanish, Italians, Portuguese, etc.

4. In Turkey, a person of foreign ancestry of the Roman Catholic church.

5. A Roman Catholic; so used by Greek Catholics and Oriental Christians.

6. An exercise in schools, consisting in turning another language into Latin. [Obs.]

Lat′in, *a.* [ME. *Latin*, *Latyn*; OFr. *latin*; L. *Latinus*, Latin, of or pertaining to Latium, from *Latium*, a country in Italy.]

1. Pertaining to the Latins, a people of Latium, in Italy; Roman; as, the *Latin* language.

2. Of or in the language of the Romans; as, *Latin* inscriptions.

3. Of or relating to modern peoples or languages akin to the ancient Romans.

4. Of or related to Western as distinguished from the Greek or Eastern Christian faiths; Roman Catholic; as, the *Latin* church; *Latin* Christianity.

Lat′in, *v.t.* To express in Latin. [Obs.]

Lat′in, *v.i.* To use Latin. [Obs.]

Lat′in=Ȧ-mer′i-căn, *a.* Of or relating to those countries in North or South America whose governing people are of the Latin races; also, relating to the Latin peoples of such countries.

Lat′in=Ȧ-mer′i-căn, *n.* A native of a Latin-American country, whose ancestry is of the Latin races.

Lat′in-ẽr, *n.* One skilled in Latin; an interpreter. [Obs.]

Lat′in-iṣm, *n.* A form of expression characteristic of Latin; an idiom of Latin.

Lat′in-ist, *n.* One skilled in Latin.

Lat′in-is-tiç, *a.* Resembling the Latin idiom.

Lat′in-i-tas″tẽr, *n.* One who has a fragmentary or superficial knowledge of Latin. [Rare.]

Lȧ-tin′i-ty, *n.* [L. *latinitas* (*-atis*), from *Latinus*, Latin, and *-aster*.] Purity of the Latin style or idiom; the Latin tongue.

Lat′in-i-zā-tion, *n.* The act of rendering into Latin.

Lat′in-īze, *v.t.* [LL. *latinizare*, to translate into Latin, from L. *Latinus*, Latin.] To give to (foreign words) Latin terminations and make them Latin.

Lat′in-īze, *v.i.* To use words or phrases borrowed from the Latin.

Lat′in-ly, *adv.* In good Latin style. [Obs.]

lā′tion, *n.* Conveyance; transportation. [Obs.]

lat-i-pen′nāte, lat-i-pen′nine, *a.* [*Lati-*, and L. *pennatus*, winged, from *penna*, a wing.] Having broad wings.

lat-i-ros′trăl, lat-i-ros′trous, *a.* Having a broad beak, as a bird.

Lat-i-ros′trēş, *n.pl.* [*Lati-*, and L. *rostrum*, a beak.] A class of singing birds having wide bills.

lat-i-sep′tāte, *a.* [*Lati-*, and L. *sæptum*, *septum*, a partition.] In botany, having a broad partition, as some cruciferous fruits.

lāt′ish, *a.* Somewhat late.

lat-i-stẽr′năl, *a.* [*Lati-*, and Gr. *sternon*, the breast, chest.] In zoölogy, having a broad sternum.

lat′i-tăn-cy, *n.* The state of lying concealed; the state of lurking. [Obs.]

lat′i-tănt, *a.* Lurking; concealed. [Obs.]

lat′i-tat, *n.* [L., he lurks, 3rd pers. sing. pres. ind. of *latitare*, to lurk, freq. of *latere*, to hide, lurk.] In old English law, a writ by which a person was summoned in the King's Bench to answer, as supposing he lay concealed.

lat-i-tā′tion, *n.* A lying in concealment. [Obs.]

lat′i-tūde, *n.* OFr. *latitude*; L. *latitudo* (*-inis*), breadth, width, extent, latitude.]

1. Breadth; extent from side to side. [Obs.]

2. Extent; room; space. [Obs.]

3. In astronomy, the distance of a heavenly body from the ecliptic.

4. In geography, the distance of any place on the globe, north or south of the equator, measured in degrees.

5. Extent of meaning or construction; indefinite acceptation; as, the words will not bear this *latitude* of construction.

6. Extent of deviation from a settled point; freedom from rules or limits; laxity.

lat-i-tū′di-năl, *a.* Pertaining to latitude; in the direction of latitude.

lat-i-tū-di-nā′ri-ăn, *n.* [L. *latitudo* (*-inis*), breadth.]

1. One who is moderate in his notions, or not restrained by precise settled limits in opinion; one who indulges freedom in thinking.

2. In the Church of England, formerly, one who denied or doubted the divine right or origin of episcopacy, though he admitted its expediency.

3. In theology, one who departs in opinion from the strict principles of orthodoxy; or one who indulges an undue latitude of thinking and interpretation.

lat-i-tū-di-nā′ri-ăn, *a.* Not restrained; not confined by precise limits; thinking or acting at large; lax in religious principles or views; as, *latitudinarian* opinions or doctrines.

lat-i-tū-di-nā′ri-ăn-iṣm, *n.* Undue freedom or laxness of opinion, particularly in theology.

lat-i-tū′di-nous, *a.* Having large extent.

lat′on, lat′öun, *n.* Latten. [Obs.]

lā′trănt, *a.* Barking. [Obs.]

lā′trāte, *v.i.* To bark as a dog. [Obs.]

lȧ-trā′tion, *n.* A barking. [Obs.]

lȧ-treū′tiç-ăl, *a.* [Gr. *latreuein*, to serve, to work for hire, from *latris*, a hired servant.]

1. Helping or ministering; filling the office of a servant for hire. [Rare.]

2. Of or relating to latria. [Rare]

lȧ-trī′ȧ, *n.* [LL. *latria*; Gr. *latreia*, service, worship, from *latreuein*, to work for hire, to serve, worship, from *latris*, a hired servant.] The highest kind of worship, or that paid to God; distinguished by Roman Catholics from *dulia*, or the inferior worship paid to saints.

lȧ-trīne′, *n.* [L. *latrina*, a bath, privy, contr. of *lavatrina*, a bath, from *lavare*, to wash.] A water-closet, particularly one used in a camp, factory, etc.

lȧ-trōbe′, *n.* [Named after its inventor, I. *Latrobe*, of Baltimore.] A stove placed in a fireplace and used to heat both by radiation and by hot air; known also as the *Baltimore heater*.

Lat-rō-cin′i-um, *n.* [L., the military service of a mercenary, from *latro* (*-onis*), a hired servant, a robber.] A council of the early Christian church held at Ephesus A. D. 449, notable for the violent and turbulent character of its proceedings, hence its name.

lat′ten, *n.* [OFr. *laton*, brass hammered into thin plates, from G. *latte*, a thin plate, a lath.]

1. In the middle ages, a fine kind of brass used for crosses, candlesticks, etc.

2. Sheet tin; iron plate covered with tin; any thin sheet metal.

Black latten; plates of milled brass.

Roll latten; sheet brass polished on both sides.

White latten; a mixture of copper, zinc, and tin in thin sheets.

lat′tẽr, *a.* [ME. *later*, *lætter*, comp. of *lat*; AS. *læt*, late.]

1. Coming or happening after something else; opposed to *former*; as, the former and *latter* rain; former or *latter* harvest.

2. Mentioned the last of two.

> The difference between reason and revelation —and in what sense the *latter* is superior. —Watts.

3. Modern; lately done or past; as, in these *latter* days.

Lat′tẽr=day Sāint. A Mormon.

lat′tẽr-kin, *n.* A glazing tool, used particularly on leaden latticework.

lat′tẽr-ly, *adv.* Of late; in time not long past.

lat′tẽr-măth, *n.* The latter mowing; aftermath. [Rare.]

lat′tice (-tis), *n.* [OFr. *lattis*, a lattice, from *latte*; AS. *lætt*, a lath.]

1. Any work of wood, metal, etc., made by crossing laths, rods, or bars,

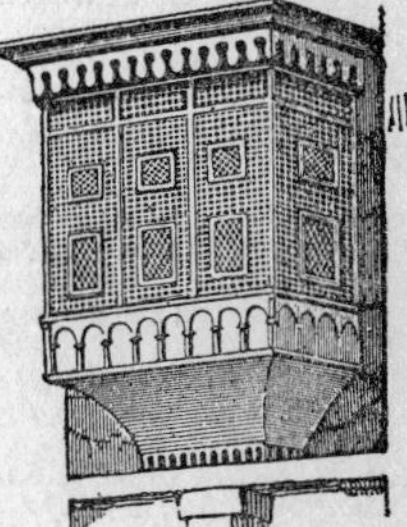
Lattice-window, Cairo.

and forming a network; as, the *lattice* of a window.

2. Anything made of or covered with strips interwoven so as to form a sort of network, as a window.

3. In heraldry, a bearing of crossbars, vertical and horizontal.

lat′tice, *v.t.*; latticed, *pt.*, *pp.*; latticing, *ppr.* 1. To form with crossbars and openwork.

2. To furnish with a lattice.

lat′tice-lēaf, *n.* A plant, *Ouvirandra fenestralis*, with leaves like latticework, found in Madagascar and belonging to the pondweed family.

Latticeleaf (*Ouvirandra fenestralis*).

lat′tice=win″dōw, *n.* A window inclosed by or covered with lattice.

lat′tice-wŏrk, *n.* 1. Lattice.

2. Embroidery in imitation of a lattice.

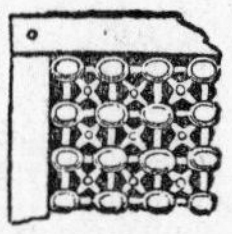

Latticework, from a window in Cairo.

lat′ti-cing, *n.* 1. Making or placing a lattice.

2. A series of cross-timbers or cross-irons placed as braces to the regular supports of a bridge.

lȧt-tï-ci′ni-ō (-chï′), *n.* [It., from L. *lacticinium*, milk food, from *lac*, *lactis*, milk.] A milky-white glass worked into decorative designs.

lā′tus, *n.*; *pl.* **lat′e-rȧ.** [L.] A side.

Latus rectum; the parameter of a conic section.

lạud (lạd), *n.* [L. *laus*, *laudis*, praise, commendation, glory, fame, esteem.]

1. Praise; commendation; honorable mention.

2. That part of divine worship which consists in praise.

3. Music or singing in honor of any one.

4. [*pl.*] In the Roman Catholic church, the prayers formerly used at daybreak, between those of matins and prime.

lạud, *v.t.* [ME. *lauden*; L. *laudare*, to praise, from *laus*, *laudis*, praise, glory.] To praise in words alone, or with words and singing; to extol.

lạud-ȧ-bil′i-ty, *n.* Laudableness; commendability.

lạud′ȧ-ble, *a.* [L. *laudabilis*, from *laudare*, to praise.]

1. Praiseworthy; commendable; as, *laudable* motives; *laudable* actions.

2. Healthy; salubrious; normal; as, *laudable* juices of the body.

Syn.—Praiseworthy, commendable.—What is *laudable* is entitled to encouragement and general approbation; what is *praiseworthy* obtains the respect of men; what is *commendable* is not equally important with the former two; it entitles one only to a temporary or partial expression of good will and approbation.

lạud′ȧ-ble-ness, *n.* The quality of deserving praise; praiseworthiness.

lạud′ȧ-bly, *adv.* In a manner deserving praise.

lạu′dȧ-nine, *n.* An alkaloid derived from opium.

lạu′dȧ-num, *n.* [L. *ladanum*, ladanum.]

1. Tincture of opium.

2. Ladanum.

lạu-dā′tion, *n.* [L. *laudatio* (*-onis*), from *laudare*, to praise.] Praise; commendation.

lạud′ȧ-tive, *n.* A panegyric. [Obs.]

lạud′ȧ-tive, *a.* Eulogistic; laudatory.

lạud′ȧ-tō-ry, *a.* Containing praise; tending to praise.

lạud′ȧ-tō-ry, *n.* That which contains praise.

lạud′ẽr, *n.* One who praises.

läugh (läf), *v.i.*; laughed (läft), *pt.*, *pp.*; laughing, *ppr.* [ME. *laughen*; AS. *hlehhan*, *hlihhan*, to laugh; of imitative origin.]

1. To make the noise and exhibit the features characteristic of mirth, joy, or derision, in the human species.

2. To be gay; to appear gay, cheerful, pleasant, lively, or brilliant.

> Then *laughs* the childish year with flowerets crowned. —Dryden.

3. To ridicule; to treat with some degree of contempt;—used with *at*; as, he *laughed at* the idea.

To laugh in the sleeve; to laugh to oneself and secretly while outwardly serious.

To laugh out of the other side of the mouth; to weep or become dejected after a period of excessive elation.

läugh, *v.t.* 1. To ridicule or deride; to produce an effect upon by laughter; with *out*; as, to *laugh* one *out* of a plan.

2. To utter laughingly; to express with laughter.

läugh, *n.* An expression of mirth, satisfaction, or derision, peculiar to the human species; hence, merriment; as, he has the *laugh* now.

läugh′ȧ-ble, *a.* Capable of exciting laughter; as, a *laughable* story; a *laughable* scene.

läugh′ȧ-ble-ness, *n.* The quality of being laughable.

läugh′ȧ-bly, *adv.* In a manner to excite laughter.

läugh′ẽr, *n.* 1. One who laughs or is fond of merriment.

> The *laughers* are much the majority.—Pope.

2. One of a breed of pigeons; so called from their cry.

läugh′ing, *a.* Expressing or uttering laughter.

Laughing falcon; a hawk of the genus *Herpetotheres*. [S. Am.]

Laughing goose; in zoölogy, the white-fronted goose, *Anser albifrons*.

Laughing gull; *Larus atricilla*, the black-headed gull of eastern United States; also, *Xema ridibundus*, the black-headed European gull.

Laughing hyena; the spotted hyena.

Laughing owl; a New Zealand owl, *Sceloglaux albifacies*, said to be nearly extinct.

läugh′ing=bïrd, *n.* *Gecinus viridis*, the yaffle or green woodpecker.

läugh′ing=gas, *n.* Nitrous oxid, N_2O, so called from the exhilaration and laughter ordinarily produced when it is inhaled.

läugh′ing=jack″ȧss, *n.* A bird, *Dacelo gigas*, the large kingfisher of Australia.

läugh′ing-ly, *adv.* In a merry way; with laughter.

läugh′ing-stock, *n.* An object of ridicule; a butt of sport.

läugh′tẽr, *n.* [ME. *laughter*, *lauhter*; AS. *hleahtor*, laughter, from *hlehhan*, to laugh.] An expression of mirth, manifested chiefly in certain convulsive and partly involuntary actions of the muscles of respiration, by means of which the air, being expelled from the chest in a series of jerks, produces a succession of short abrupt sounds, certain movements of the muscles of the face, and often of other parts of the body also taking place; also, any expression of merriment, derision, etc., perceivable in the countenance, as in the eyes.

Syn.—Merriment, glee, derision, ridicule, cachinnation, contempt.

läugh′tẽr-less, *a.* Without laughing.

läugh′wŏr-thy, *a.* Deserving to be laughed at.

lạu′mont-ïte, *n.* Efflorescent zeolite; so called from Laumont, its discoverer.

läunce, *n.* Balance. [Obs.]

läunce, *n.* A lance. [Obs.]

läunce, *n.* The lant or sand-eel.

läunce′gāy, *n.* A lancegay. [Obs.]

läunch, *v.t.*; launched, *pt.*, *pp.*; launching, *ppr.* [ME. *lanchen*, *launchen*; OFr. *lanchier*, *lancier*, to throw, hurl as a lance, from *lance*; L. *lancea*, a lance.]

1. To move or to cause to slide from the land into the water; as, to *launch* a ship.

2. To put out into or as into another sphere of duty, another field of activity, or the like; as, to *launch* one on the world.

3. To cast or hurl, as a lance; to send flying; to propel; as, to *launch* the shafts of invective.

4. To pierce or cut with or as with a lance; to lance. [Obs.]

5. To drop suddenly into place, as a topmast on a fid.

6. To cause to move by pressure, as casks, etc.

läunch, *v.i.* 1. To move or glide forward, as a ship into the water.

2. To enter upon a field of activity or the like; to begin; as, to *launch* into a controversy.

läunch, *n.* 1. The act of launching.

2. The sliding or movement of a ship from the land into the water, on ways prepared for the purpose.

3. The largest boat carried by a man-of-war.

4. An open boat of any size driven by steam, electricity, naphtha, etc.

5. A trap for eels. [Prov. Eng.]

6. A stab; a cut. [Obs.]

lạund, *n.* A lawn; a glade. [Obs.]

läun′dẽr, *n.* [ME. *launder*, from *lavander*, a washerwoman; OFr. *lavandier*; LL. *lavandarius*, masc., *lavandaria*, f., a washer, from L. *lavare*, to wash.]

1. A washerwoman. [Obs.]

2. In mining, a long and hollow trough, used to receive the powdered ore from the box where it is crushed.

läun′dẽr, *v.t.* 1. To wash; to wash and iron.

2. To wet; also, to cover with a thin coating, as a metal.

läun′dẽr-ẽr, *n.* One who follows the business of washing clothes.

läun′dress, *n.* A washerwoman; a female whose employment is to wash clothes.

läun′dress, *v.i.* To serve as laundress. [Obs.]

läun′dry, *n.*; *pl.* **läun′dries.** [ME. *lavendrie*, from *lavander*, a washerwoman, from OFr. *lavandier*; LL. *lavandarius*, masc., *lavandaria*, f., a washer, from L. *lavandus*, gerundive of *lavare*, to wash.]

1. A washing. [Obs.]

2. A place where clothes are laundered.

lạu′rȧ, *n.* [Gr. *laura*, an alley, lane, a narrow passage between houses.] Formerly, and especially in the Levant, a collection of cells or hermitages where the monks did not live in community, but were governed by the same superior.

Lạu-rā′cē-æ, *n.pl.* [L. *laurus*, the laurel, and *-aceæ*.] An order or family of apetalous aromatic plants. Cinnamon, cassia, sassafras, and camphor are products of the order. The best-known species is the *Laurus nobilis*, or sweet-bay.

lạu-rā′ceous, *a.* Of or pertaining to the order *Lauraceæ*.

lạu′rē-āte, *a.* [L. *laureatus*, from *laurea*, the laurel-tree, from *laurus*, laurel.] Decked or invested with laurel; wearing a laurel wreath; as, *laureate* brows.

lạu′rē-āte, *n.* 1. A person crowned with laurel.

2. The poet given the official title of laureate by the sovereign of Great Britain. Formerly, he was an officer of the king's household, whose business was to compose an ode annually for the king's birthday and for the new year. It is said this title was first given in the time of Edward IV.

3. A student crowned with laurel, when receiving a degree in rhetoric and poetry.

lạu′rē-āte, *v.t.* To honor with a degree in a university and a present of a wreath of laurel.

lạu′rē-āte-ship, *n.* The office of a laureate.

lạu-rē-ā′tion, *n.* Formerly, the act of conferring a degree in a university together with a wreath of laurel.

lạu′rel, *n.* [ME. *loral*, *laurer*; OFr. *laurier*; L. *laurus*, the bay-tree, laurel.]

1. Any shrub of the genus *Laurus*, especially the sweet-bay, *Laurus nobilis*, a native of the north of Africa and south of Europe, cultivated for the aromatic fragrance of its evergreen leaves. In ancient times, heroes and scholars were crowned with bay leaves and berries, whence the terms *baccalaureus* and *laureate*.

Laurel (*Laurus nobilis*).

2. Any of various similar shrubs, as *Prunus Lauro-Cerasus*, the cherry-laurel, *Daphne Laureola*, the spurge-laurel, *Kalmia latifolia*, the mountain-laurel, and *Rhododendron maximum*, the great laurel or rosebay.

3. A crown or wreath of laurel, as a mark of honor, fame, or distinction; hence, honor, glory; usually in the plural; as, to win *laurels*.

4. A gold coin of the reign of James I., struck in 1619, so called from the head of the king being crowned with laurel.

lạu′reled (-reld), *a.* Crowned or decorated with laurel or with a laurel wreath; laureate.

lạu′rel=wạ″tẽr, *n.* A sedative narcotic water distilled from cherry-laurel leaves.

Lạu-ren′tiăn (-shăn), *a.* 1. Relating to or adjacent to the St. Lawrence River; as, the *Laurentian* hills.

2. Of or pertaining to Lorenzo dei Medici or to the library in Florence founded by Pope Clement VII. and named in honor of Lorenzo.

3. Relating to the Laurentian.

Lạu-ren′tiăn, *n.* A series of crystalline rocks of the Archæan epoch, found in the region of the Great Lakes.

lạu′res-tine, *n.* [L. *laurus*, the laurel, and *tinus*, a plant.] *Viburnum Tinus*, an evergreen shrub of the south of Europe.

lạu′ret, *n.* [Obs.] Same as *Laurel*, 4.

lạu′riç, *a.* [L. *laurus*, laurel.] Of or derived from *Laurus nobilis*, the laurel or bay.

Lauric acid; $C_{12}H_{24}O_2$, a compound obtained from several sources, particularly from the laurel.

lạu-rif′ẽr-ous, *a.* [L. *laurus*, laurel, and *ferre*, to bear.] Producing or bringing laurel.

lạu′rin, *n.* [L. *laurus*, laurel, and *-in*.] A fatty, acrid, crystalline substance contained in the berries of the laurel.

lạu′ri-nōl, *n.* [*Laurin* and *-ol*.] Camphor.

lạu′ri-ol, *n.* The spurge-laurel. [Obs.]

lạu′ri-ŏn-ïte, *n.* [So called from *Laurion*, Greece, where it is found.] A prismatic hydroxychlorid of lead found in lead slags in the vicinity of Laurion, Greece.

lạu′rïte, *n.* [From *Laura*, a woman's name.] A crystalline sulphid of ruthenium and osmium found in platinum mines in Borneo and also in Oregon.

lạu′rōne, *n.* A crystalline derivative of lauric acid.

Lạu′rus, *n.* [L., the laurel or bay-tree.] A genus of the *Lauraceæ*, which includes the bay-tree.

laus, *a.* Loose. [Obs.]

lä′vȧ, *n.* [It. *lava*, a stream, lava, from *lavare*; L. *lavare*, to wash.]

1. A mass or stream of melted minerals or stony matter which bursts or is thrown from the mouth or sides of a volcano.

2. The same matter when cool and hardened.

lȧ-vā′bō, *n.* [L., lit., I shall wash, 1st pers. sing. fut. ind. act. of *lavare*, to wash.]

1. A washing of the hands of the celebrant of the eucharist after the offertory.

2. A kind of large basin in a monastery; also, the room in which such a basin was located.

lāv′ăge, *n.* [L. *lavare*, to wash.] A washing; specifically, the cleansing of the walls of the stomach by injections.

Lȧ-van′dū-lȧ, *n.* [LL. *lavandula*, *lavendula*, lavender; It. *lavanda*, lavender, from L. *lavare*, to wash.] A genus of perennial shrubs and plants of which lavender, *Lavandula vera*, is the type.

lav′ȧ-ret, *n.* [Fr.] A species of whitefish found in Europe.

lä-vat′ic, *a.* Resembling or composed of lava.

lȧ-vā′tion, *n.* A washing or cleansing. [Obs.]

lav′ȧ-tō-ry, *n.* [LL. *lavatorium*, a place for bathing, from *lavator*, a clothes-washer, from L. *lavare*, to wash.]

1. A place for washing; a toilet-room.

2. A wash or lotion for a diseased part.

3. A place where gold is obtained by washing.

4. A vessel for washing.

lav′ȧ-tō-ry, *a.* Cleansing by washing.

lav′ȧ-tūre, *n.* A wash; a lotion. [Obs.]

lāve, *v.t.*; laved, *pt.*, *pp.*; laving, *ppr.* [ME. *laven*; OFr. *laver*; L. *lavare*, to bathe, wash.] To wash; to bathe; especially, with flowing water.

lāve, *v.i.* To bathe; to wash oneself.

lāve, *v.t.* To throw up or out; to lade out. [Obs.]

lāve, *v.i.* To droop; to be pendent. [Obs.]

lāve, *n.* [ME. *lave*, *lafe*; AS. *laf*, the remainder.] The remainder; others. [Scot.]

lāve′-eared, *a.* Having pendent ears. [Obs.]

lȧ-veer′, *v.i.* Nautically, to tack. [Obs.]

lāve′ment, *n.* [Fr.] 1. A washing or bathing. [Obs.]

2. A clyster. [Obs.]

lav′en-dẽr, *n.* [ME. *lavendre*; It. *lavanda*, lavender, a washing, from *lavare*, L. *lavare*, to wash; so called because used in washing.]

1. An aromatic plant, *Lavandula vera*; also applied to other species of *Lavandula*.

2. The color of the blossoms of lavender; a pale lilac.

Lavender (*Lavandula Spica*).

lav′en-dẽr-cot′tŏn, *n.* A small shrub with wiry twigs covered with a hoary pubescence; called also *ground-cypress*.

lav′en-dẽr-thrift, *n.* The marsh-rosemary or sea-lavender.

lav′en-dẽr-wa″tẽr, *n.* A perfume of spirits of wine, essential oil of lavender, ambergris, etc.

lāv′ẽr, *n.* [ME. *laver*, *lavour*; OFr. *lavor*, *lavur*; LL. *lavatorium*; a place for bathing, from L. *lavare*, to wash.]

1. A vessel for washing; a large basin; in Scripture, a basin placed in the court of the Jewish tabernacle, where officiating priests washed their hands and feet, and the entrails of sacrifices.

2. That which cleanses or laves.

lāv′ẽr, *n.* One who washes or laves. [Obs.]

lā′vẽr, *n.* [L., a water-plant.] The fronds or leaves of certain marine plants, or the same prepared as food.

lav′ẽr-ock, *n.* The lark. [Scot.]

lä′vic, *a.* Resembling lava; lavatic.

lav′ish, *a.* [ME. *lavage*, from *laven*; AS. *laflan*, to pour out, sprinkle water.]

1. Prodigal; expending or bestowing with profusion; profuse; as, *lavish* of expense.

2. Wild; unrestrained; excessive.

lav′ish, *v.t.*; lavished (-isht), *pt.*, *pp.*; lavishing, *ppr.* 1. To expend or bestow with profusion; as, to *lavish* praise or encomiums.

2. To waste; to expend without necessity or use; to squander; as, to *lavish* money on vices.

lav′ish-ẽr, *n.* A prodigal; a profuse person.

lav′ish-ly, *adv.* In a lavish manner.

lav′ish-ment, *n.* The act of expending lavishly.

lav′ish-ness, *n.* Profusion; prodigality.

lȧ-vol′tȧ, **lȧ-volt′**, *n.* [It. *la volta*, the turn.] An old dance somewhat resembling a waltz. [Obs.]

lȧ-vol′te-tēre, *n.* One who dances the lavolta. [Obs.]

lāv′ŏur, *n.* [Obs.] Same as *Laver*, n. 1.

lav′rock, *n.* A laverock. [Obs.]

law, **laws**, *interj.* [A corruption of *Lord*; or same as *la!*] An exclamation common among uneducated people, expressing astonishment.

law, **lawe**, *v.t.* To cut off the claws and balls of, as of a dog's fore feet; to mutilate the feet of, as a dog.

law, **lawe**, *a.* Low. [Obs.]

law, *n.* A hill or mound. [Scot.]

law, *n.* [ME. *lawe*, *laghe*; AS. *lagu*, law, that which is laid or fixed, from *licgan*, to lie.]

1. A general rule of action or conduct established or enforced by a sovereign authority; as, a *law* of Cæsar; a *law* of God. Specifically, (a) any rule of civil conduct which will be recognized and enforced by the supreme judicial decision, whether established in a national or state constitution, by a lawmaking body in statutes, treaties, ordinances, etc., by the rulings of courts, or by common usage; as, a *law* in Ohio; a *law* of the land; (b) a statute, act, decree, ordinance, etc., as distinguished from a constitution; as, a *law* in conformity to the constitution.

2. In a collective sense, the aggregate or entire body of established rules, in any matter; specifically, (a) the general rules of conduct with respect to rights and property, which will be enforced by the sovereign authority in any community or state, either by punishment for infraction, by interference to prevent disobedience, or by the restoration of things to the position in which they were before disobedience; as, civil *law*; criminal *law*; (b) the body of rules personified; as, the prisoner is in the hands of the *law*; (c) legal procedure; litigation; as, to go to *law*; (d) legal science; jurisprudence, as, to study *law*; (e) the profession of a lawyer; as, to practise *law*; (f) common law procedure or rules, as distinguished from those of equity; as, a case both at *law* and in equity; (g) any rules agreed upon or recognized as binding between states, groups, or individuals; as, international *law*; commercial *law*; *laws* of etiquette or of a game; (h) a rule of conduct established by the ethical or religious nature of man; as, a moral *law*; a sacred *law*; (i) in the Bible, the books of Moses or the Mosaic code, as distinguished from the rest of the Old Testament, or from the New Testament; as, the *law* and the prophets; the *law* and the gospel.

3. In mathematics, the rule by which or the order in which any operation proceeds; as, the *law* of the generation of a curve.

4. In physics or philosophy, (a) the constant relation that exists between any phenomenon and its cause; the method of the phenomena of the universe; an order in nature by which certain results follow certain causes; as, the *law* of gravitation; a *law* of nature; (b) a formula which denotes the constant mode of operation of a force or agent; as, Boyle's *law*.

Syn.—Act, canon, code, command, commandment, common law, decree, edict, enactment, formula, injunction, mandate, order, ordinance, principle, regulation, rule, statute.—*Law* is the general term signifying a rule laid down or established, whether by custom or as the expression of the will of a person or power able to enforce its demands. *Law* implies a penalty or inconvenience for disobedience, and also generality of application as distinguished from a special *command*. A *canon*, *order*, *regulation*, or *rule* is a regular established method of procedure or action; as, *canons* of the church; naval *orders*; school *regulations*; office *rules*. A *code* is an entire system of rules or laws. A *command*, *commandment*, or *mandate* is a specific act of authority; as, a parent's *command*; the *mandate* of a court. *Common law* is the entire body of rules of conduct established by long usage and the decisions of law courts. A *decree* or an *edict* is a law or decision given by a sovereign power; as, an *edict* of Cæsar; a *decree* of the court. An *act*, *enactment*, or *statute* is a specific law enacted by the lawmaking body of a state, while an *ordinance* is usually a municipal regulation, though also used in a general sense. These are *law* only if they do not conflict with the organic *law* or constitution. *Injunction* is a general term, though specifically applied to an *order* of a court of equity. A *formula* is a conventional form or a set *rule*.

Avogadro's law; in physics, the law that at any given temperature and pressure the number of molecules in any volume is the same for all gases.

Bode's law; in astronomy, the law that the relative distances of the planets from the sun are indicated approximately by the series 4, 7, 10, 16, 28, etc.; a series formed by adding 4 to each term of the series 0, 3, 6, 12, 24, etc. Neptune is an exception.

Boyle's law; in physics, the law of compressibility of gases, viz.: the temperature remaining the same, the volume of a given quantity of a gas is inversely as the pressure which it bears.

Canon law; in the Roman Catholic church, a collection of laws or rules compiled from canons of church councils, papal decrees and decretals, and other rules of discipline. In the Church of England, the canon law consists of canons decided upon by synods or adopted from foreign sources by custom.

Charles's law; in physics, the law that all gases have the same coefficient of expansion; i. e., the volume or the pressure of all gases varies directly as the change in temperature.

Civil law; (a) the law recognized and enforced as controlling the rights and conduct of the citizens of any state; (b) specifically, the system of Roman law which forms the base of the legal systems of all the nations of continental Europe. It is also the basis of the Louisiana code.

Commercial law, or *law merchant*; the customs observed by merchants and other business men in their dealings with each other, now part of the common law recognized and enforced by the courts.

Common law; (a) in general, the laws pertaining to an entire state or community; (b) especially, that system of unwritten law which forms the basis of the English legal system. Its source is the long continued usages or customs recognized as certain, reasonable, and compulsory, enforced by the interpretations and decisions of courts.

Gresham's law; in political economy, the law that if two forms of currency of unequal intrinsic value are given the same legal value in any country, the form of greater intrinsic value will be hoarded or exported, and thus will cease to circulate, or will be held at a premium; the rule that "bad money drives out good." Named after Sir Thos. Gresham, master of the mint under Queen Elizabeth.

Grimm's law; see *Grimm*.

Kepler's laws; in astronomy, the three laws which denote the method of planetary motions. (1) The orbits of the planets about the sun are ellipses, of each of which the sun occupies one focus. (2) The area described by the radius vector of a planet is the same for equal periods of time. (3) The squares of the periods of revolution about the sun of the several planets are in the proportion of the cubes of their mean solar distances.

Law French; the Norman dialect, or old French, used in all legal proceedings from the time of William the Conqueror to that of Edward III., and still employed in certain formal state proceedings.

Law language; (a) the precise, technical, and formal style of expression used in legal documents; (b) law French; (c) law Latin.

Law Latin; a corrupt form of Latin used in legal documents and certain medieval statutes.

Law merchant; commercial law.

Law of nations; international law.

Law of nature; (a) a physical law; (b) that portion of morality which supplies the more important and universal rules for the governance of the outward acts of mankind.

Laws of honor; see under *Honor*.

Laws of motion; in physics, the laws relating to bodies in motion; sometimes called *Newton's laws*. (1) Every body continues in its state of rest or of uniform motion in a straight line, except as it is compelled by force to change that state. (2) Change of motion takes place in the direction of the straight line in which an applied force acts and is directly proportional to the amount of that force. (3) Every action has an equal and contrary reaction; i.e., the mutual actions of two bodies on each other are always forces equal in amount and opposite in direction.

Lenz's law; in physics, the law that induced currents are always such as, by their direction or action, to oppose the inducing cause. Named after H. F. E. Lenz.

Mariotte's law; same as *Boyle's law*.

Maritime or *marine law*; the system of law which relates to marine affairs generally, including navigation, ships, seamen, and the transportation of persons and property by sea.

Martial law; the military rules and regulations by which the municipal law is superseded in time of war or during public emergencies; established and enforced by the officer in charge in accordance with military law and the usages of war.

Military law; the system of rules and regulations which govern a nation's military forces; not to be confused with *martial law*, which controls all persons within its jurisdiction, civilians as well as soldiers.

Moral law; (a) that system of rules of human action which has its origin in a general sense of the members of any community of what is right and wrong, and which derives its authority from the general disapprobation of acts contrary to its principles; (b) the decalogue and moral maxims of the Mosaic law.

Municipal law; a system of rules of human action established by the governmental power of a state.

Ohm's law; in physics, the law that the strength of an electric current is equal to its electromotive force divided by the circuit resistance. Named after G. S. Ohm.

Periodic law; in chemistry, the law that at regular intervals in the table of chemical elements arranged according to their atomic weights, elements will be found to have similar chemical and physical properties; or, as expressed by Mendelejeff, the scientist who developed the law, the properties of chemical elements are periodic functions of the atomic weights.

Roman law; same as *Civil law*, (b).

Statute law; municipal law as defined by statutory enactments.

Sumptuary laws; laws restricting or regulating wages, expenditures of individuals, prices of merchandise, etc., especially such as relate to extravagance, and those concerning the sale of liquors.

Verner's law; in philology, the law that the original *k, p, s, t*, became *g, b, z* or *r*, and *d*, respectively, in the old Teutonic, if the accent fell on any other than the preceding syllable. Proposed by Karl Verner to account for exceptions to Grimm's law.

Wager of law; a species of trial formerly used in England, in which the defendant gave security that he would, on a certain day, make his law; that is, make oath that he owed nothing to the plaintiff, and would produce eleven of his neighbors as compurgators, who should swear that they believed in their consciences that he had sworn the truth.

law′-ȧ-bīd″ing, *a.* Observant of the law; obeying the law; as, *law-abiding* citizens.

law′-bīnd″ing, *n.* The style of light-brown leather binding peculiar to law-books; called also *law-calf*.

law′-book, *n.* A book containing laws or relating to laws.

law′break″ẽr, *n.* One who violates the law.

law′-bŭr″rōws, *n.* In Scots law, a writ or document in the name of the sovereign, commanding a person to give security against offering violence to another.

law′-cạlf (-käf), *n.* See *Law-binding*.

law′dāy, *n.* 1. A day of open court.

2. A leet or sheriff's court. [Obs.]

3. The last day upon which a debt secured by a mortgage could be paid and the debtor be secure from forfeiture.

law′fụl, *a.* 1. Agreeable to law; conformable to law; allowed by law; legitimate.

2. Constituted by law; rightful; as, the *lawful* owner of lands.

law′fụl-ly, *adv.* Legally; without violating law.

law′fụl-ness, *n.* The quality of being conformable to law; legality.

law′giv″ẽr, *n.* One who makes or enacts a law.

law′giv″ing, *a.* Making or enacting laws.

law′ing, *n.* 1. Expeditation; the act of cutting off the claws and balls of the forefeet of mastiffs, to prevent them from running after deer.

2. Litigation. [Colloq.]

3. A tavern-bill. [Scot.]

law′less, *a.* 1. Not subject to law; unrestrained by law; as, a *lawless* tyrant; *lawless* men.

2. Contrary to law; illegal; unauthorized.

3. Not subject to the laws of nature; uncontrolled.

law′less-ly, *adv.* In a manner contrary to law.

law′less-ness, *n.* The quality or state of being unrestrained by law; disorder.

law′māk″ẽr, *n.* One who enacts laws.

law′mŏn″gẽr, *n.* A low mean lawyer; a pettifogger.

lawn, *n.* [ME. *launde*; OFr. *lande*, a heath; of Celtic origin; compare W. *llan*, a lawn.] An open space among or between woods; a space of ground covered with grass, generally in front of or around a house or mansion.

lawn, *a.* Made of lawn.

lawn, *n.* [Prob. from *Laon*, a town in France.] A thin, fine muslin or cambric. It is used in the sleeves of an Anglican bishop's gown, and hence denotes his office.

A saint in crape is twice a saint in *lawn*.
—Pope.

lawn′-mōw″ẽr, *n.* A machine used by hand or horse-power for cutting grass on lawns.

lawn ten′nis. A kind of tennis usually played out of doors on a smooth surface, as on a lawn. [See under *Tennis*.]

lawn′y, *a.* Like a lawn; having a lawn.

lawn′y, *a.* Made of or resembling lawn.

law′ren-cīte, *n.* [Named after J. *Lawrence* Smith, an American mineralogist.] A native ferrous chlorid sometimes found in meteorites.

Law-sō′ni-ȧ, *n.* [Named after Dr. John *Lawson*.] A genus of Eastern shrubs containing only one species, the henna-plant, *Lawsonia inermis*, bearing white flowers. Henna, a reddish dyestuff, is obtained from the leaves.

law′suit, *n.* A suit in law, equity, or admiralty.

law′yẽr, *n.* [From *law* and *-yer, -ier*.]

1. One versed in the laws, or a practitioner of law; one whose profession is to institute suits in courts of law, to give legal advice, and to prosecute or defend the cause of clients. This is a general term, comprehending attorneys, counselors, solicitors, barristers, sergeants, and advocates.

2. In zoölogy, (a) the black-necked stilt; (b) the burbot; (c) the bowfin.

3. The thorny stem of a bramble or brier. [Eng.]

law′yẽr-like, law′yẽr-ly, *a.* Like or appropriate to a lawyer.

lax, *a.*; *comp.* laxer; *superl.* laxest. [L. *laxus*, slack, loose, open.]

1. Slack; loose; flabby; soft; not tense, firm, or rigid; as, *lax* muscles; a *lax* cord.

2. Not strict or rigorous; as, *lax* control.

3. Not rigidly exact; loose; vague; as, *lax* interpretation.

4. Loose; relaxed; as, *lax* intestines.

5. In botany, open; loose; said of panicles.

lax, *n.* Diarrhea.

lax-ā′tion, *n.* The act of loosening or slackening; the state of being loosened or slackened.

lax′ȧ-tive, *a.* [Fr. *laxatif*; L. *laxativus*, mitigating, loosening, from *laxare*, to loosen, from *laxus*, loose.] Having the power or quality of loosening or opening the intestines and relieving from constipation.

lax′ȧ-tive, *n.* A medicine that relaxes the intestines and relieves from costiveness.

lax′ȧ-tive-ness, *n.* The quality of relaxing.

lax-ā′tŏr, *n.*; *pl.* **lax-ȧ-tō′rēs.** [From L. *laxatus*, pp. of *laxare*, to loosen.] In anatomy, a part, especially a muscle, which loosens or relaxes.

lax-i-flō′rous, *a.* [L. *laxus*, loose, and *flos*, *floris*, a flower.] In botany, having the flowers loose or scattered.

lax′i-ty, *n.* [Fr. *laxité*; L. *laxitas* (*-atis*), looseness, from *laxus*, loose, slack.] Looseness; slackness; want of exactness or precision.

lax′ly, *adv.* Loosely; without exactness.

lax′ness, *n.* Looseness; softness; laxity.

lāy, *v.*, past tense of *lie*.

lāy, *v.t.*; laid, *pt.*, *pp.*; laying, *ppr.* [ME. *leyen*, *leien*; AS. *lecgan*, to cause to lie, to lay, from *licgan*, to lie.]

1. To cause to lie; to put or place; to impose; to deposit; to apply; as, to *lay* a book on a table; to *lay* one's hand to the plow; to *lay* a tax on land; to *lay* blame on one; to *lay* claim; to *lay* an indictment in a certain county.

2. To cause to lie prostrate; hence, to strike down; to overthrow; as, he *laid* his foe at his feet; the storm *laid* the town in ruins.

3. To cause to lie regularly, or in the desired position; to place in order; to arrange in the proper places; as, to *lay* brick; to *lay* a gun; to *lay* the table for a meal; to *lay* new type in a printer's case; to *lay* pages for a form.

4. To make or construct by placing the parts in position; literally, as, to *lay* a foundation, or figuratively, as, to *lay* plans, snares, schemes, etc.

5. To cause to lie so as not to rise; to allay; to suppress; to quiet; to still; as, to *lay* the dust; to *lay* a ghost; to *lay* a wind.

6. To place or cause to be in a state, condition, or position indicated by a qualifying word or phrase; as, to *lay* away, down, in, out, etc.

7. To spread on a surface; to cover (a surface) with; as, to *lay* plaster; to *lay* a cloth with braid.

8. To play at hazard; to wage; to stake; as, to *lay* a wager; to *lay* a dollar.

9. To bring forth; to extrude; as, to *lay* eggs.

To lay a course; to proceed in a certain direction without tacking; to take a straight course.

To lay away; (a) to place aside for keeping; (b) to discard; to lay aside.

To lay before; to present for consideration.

To lay by; to lay away.

To lay down; (a) to resign, as an office; (b) to deposit, as a pledge; (c) to offer, assert, or declare, as a principle or a command; (d) to preserve; to lay by, as salt meats or provisions; (e) to draft, as a plan or diagram.

To lay in; (a) to get and lay aside; to store; (b) to put in; to enter; as, *to lay in* a claim.

To lay it on; to act lavishly or extravagantly.

To lay off, (a) to put off or aside, as a burden; (b) to turn, as the bow of a boat or vessel from any point; (c) to discharge or dismiss temporarily, as employees; (d) to draw on paper, as a chart; (e) to transfer (the plans of a ship) from the paper to the full size on the floor of the molding-loft.

To lay on; to apply with force, as blows.

To lay open; to open; to make bare; to expose; to reveal; to make an opening in.

To lay out; (a) to expend; as, *to lay out* money; (b) to plan; to arrange after a plan; as, *to lay out* a garden; (c) to dress in grave-clothes and place in a suitable posture; as, *to lay out* a corpse; (d) to exert; as, *to lay out* one's strength; (e) to knock down or disable; in this sense slang.

To lay the land; to cause the land to seem lower by sailing from it.

To lay to; (a) to apply with vigor; (b) to attack; (c) to impute; to charge with; (d) to check the motion of (a ship) and cause her to become stationary.

To lay up; (a) to store for future use; (b) to confine to a bed or room; (c) to dismantle and put out of use, as a ship.

To lay waste; to devastate, make desolate, or ravage.

lāy, *v.i.* 1. To produce and give forth eggs, as hens.

2. In nautical language, to go to a station or to assume a position; as, to *lay* aft; to *lay* aloft.

3. To put up a wager; to make a bet.

To lay about one; to deliver blows on all sides.

To lay for; to make ready to assault or capture. [Slang.]

To lay in for; to make overtures for; to engage or secure the possession of. [Obs.]

To lay out; to purpose; to intend; as, he *lays out* to make a journey.

lāy, *n.* 1. That which lies or is laid; a row; a stratum; a layer; one rank in a series reckoned upward; as, a *lay* of wood.

2. The way anything is laid; the arrangement, contour, situation, or relative position; as, the *lay* of the land; the *lay* of a rope, that is, the manner in which the strands are arranged.

3. A bet; a wager. [Obs.]

4. A scheme; a plan; as, what's your *lay?* [Slang.]

5. Profit; gain; especially, in the United States, a share of the proceeds of an undertaking or enterprise; as, the *lay* of a sealing or whaling voyage.

6. Station; rank. [Obs.]

7. A certain quantity of thread or yarn; a lea.

8. In a loom, the lathe or batten.

lāy, *n.* The laity. [Obs.]

lāy, *a.* [OFr. *lai*; LL. *laicus*, the laity; Gr. *laïkos*, belonging to the people or laity, from *laos*, the people.]

1. Pertaining to the laity or people in contradistinction to the clergy; as, a *lay* speaker.

2. Not derived from, or allied with a profession or the special profession or work in discussion; as, a *lay* opinion as to the law.

Lay baptism, baptism administered by one of the laity.

Lay brother; a layman; one received under religious vows into a monastery, but not in holy orders.

Lay clerk; a layman who leads the responses, etc., in a church service.

lāy, *n.* A lea; meadow. [Obs.]

lāy, *n.* 1. Faith; religious creed. [Obs.]

2. A vow; pledge. [Obs.]

3. A law. [Obs.]

lāy, *n.* [ME. *laye*, *lai*; OFr. *lai*, *lais*, a song; prob. of Celtic origin.] A song; a ballad; a lyric; as, an amorous *lay*; the *lay* of the lark.

lāy′-dāy, *n.* 1. One of the days allowed to a person chartering a vessel, in which to load or unload the cargo.

2. One of the days for which insurance premiums may be deducted, as when a ship is in port with no fires.

lāy′ẽr, *v.t.* In gardening, to propagate by bending the shoot of a living stem into the soil, the shoot striking root while being fed by the parent plant.

lāy′ẽr, *n.* 1. One who or that which lays.

2. That which is laid on any surface; a stratum; a bed; a thickness or fold spread over another; as, a *layer* of clay or sand.

Layer.

3. A welt; a strip to give extra strength.

4. A shoot or twig of a plant, not detached from the stock, laid under ground for propagation.

5. An oyster-bed made artificially.

Crookes layer; see *Crookes*.

lāy′ẽr-out, *n.* One who expends money.

lāy-ette′ (-et′), *n.* [Fr.] 1. An entire outfit prepared for a newborn babe, as the cradle, blankets, clothing, etc.

2. A triangular tray used to convey powder about in powdermills.

lāy′-fig″ūre, *n.* 1. A figure made of wood or cork, in imitation of the human body. It can be placed in any position or attitude, and serves, when clothed, as a model for drapery, etc.

2. Any person acting as a mere puppet for another.

lāy′ing, *n.* 1. The first coat on laths of plasterer's two-coat work.

Lay-figure.

2. The act or period of laying eggs; the eggs laid.

lāy'lănd, *n.* Lealand; fallow ground. [Obs.]

lāy'măn, *n.*; *pl.* **lāy'men.** 1. One not a clergyman; one of the laity or people, distinct from the clergy; a man who is not a member of a profession, in distinction from one who is.

2. A figure used by painters; a lay-figure.

lāy'nēr, *n.* A lannier; a whiplash. [Obs.]

lāy'out, *n.* 1. The manner in which something is or is to be laid out; a plan; arrangement.

2. Something laid out, provided, or prepared; a display; an outfit; a spread; specifically, in faro, the cards of a suit fastened in two rows on the table.

3. The space inclosed or passed over by a seine.

lāy'-rāce, *n.* A shuttle-race.

lāy'ship, *n.* The state of being a layman. [Obs.]

lāy'stall, *n.* 1. A heap of dung, or a place where dung is laid. [Obs.]

2. A shelter for milch cows or market cattle.

lā'zăr, *n.* [ME. *lazar, lazer*; OFr. *lazar*; LL. *lazarus*, a leper, from L. *Lazarus*; Gr. *Lazaros*, Lazarus, the beggar spoken of in the parable, Luke xvi. 19–31, from Heb. *El'āzār*, lit., he whom God helps.] A person infected with nauseous and pestilential disease; especially, a leper.

laz-ȧ-ret'tō, laz-ȧ-ret', *n.* [It. *lazzeretto*, from *lazzaro*, a leper.]

1. A hospital or pesthouse for the reception of diseased persons, particularly for those affected with diseases of a contagious nature; hence, a place of quarantine.

2. The storeroom of a ship, usually near the stern.

lā'zăr-house, *n.* A lazaretto.

Laz'ȧ-rist, Laz'ȧ-rīte, *n.* A member of an order of missionaries in the Roman Catholic church, established in 1624, and deriving their name from the priory of St. Lazarus, in Paris, which was their headquarters.

lā'zăr-like, *a.* Full of sores; leprous.

lā'zăr-ly, *a.* Lazarlike.

laz-ȧ-rō'nī, *n.pl.*, incorrect spelling for *lazzaroni*.

lā'zăr-wŏrt, *n.* Laserwort.

lāze, *v.i.* To live in idleness. [Colloq.]

lāze, *v.t.* To waste in sloth. [Colloq.]

lā'zi-ly, *adv.* In a lazy manner; sluggishly.

lā'zi-ness, *n.* The state or quality of being lazy; indisposition to action or exertion; indolence.

laz'ū-lī, *n.* [LL. *lazulus*; Ar. *lāzward*; Per. *lajhward*, azure.] Lapis lazuli.

laz'ū-li-finch, *n.* A bird of brillant blue coloring, *Passerina amœna*, common to western North America.

laz'ū-līte, *n.* [LL. *lazulus*, azure, and *-ite*.] A mineral of a light indigo-blue color, occurring in small masses, or in oblique, four-sided prisms. It is hydrous aluminium-iron-magnesium phosphate.

lā'zy, *a.* [OFr. *lasche*, loose, sluggish, slack; L. *laxus*, loose, open, lax.]

1. Disinclined to action or exertion; naturally or habitually slothful; sluggish; indolent; averse to labor.

2. Slow; moving slowly or sluggishly; as, a *lazy* stream.

3. Wicked or vicious. [Obs. or Prov. Eng.]

lā'zy-back, *n.* A bar attached to a seat, as in a carriage, to support one's back.

lā'zy-bōnes, *n.* One who is lazy. [Colloq.]

lā'zy-tongs, *n.pl.* A mechanical device in the form of extensible tongs by which objects at a distance may be grasped.

Lazy-tongs.

laz-zȧ-rō'nī, *n.pl.* In Naples, the poor who live chiefly by begging or have no permanent homes; so called from the hospital of St. Lazarus, which serves as their refuge.

lē, *n.* A li; a measure or coin of China.

-le. [ME. *-le, -el*; AS. *-ol, -ul*, or *-el*.] A suffix for nouns and adjectives of English or Anglo-Saxon origin; as, cock*le*, fick*le*, etc. So far as is known the suffix has no significance.

-le. [ME. *-le, -el*; OFr. *-el, -le, -al*, from L. *-ellus, -ilis, -alis*, respectively.] A suffix with no apparent significance used in nouns and adjectives of Latin origin; as, batt*le*, bott*le*, etc.

-le. A suffix, variant of ME. *-eren*, AS. *-erian*, used in frequentative verbs; as, babb*le*, pratt*le*, etc.

lēa, *a.* Untilled; fallow, as land. [Obs.]

lēa, *n.* A scythe. [Obs.]

lēa, *n.* [ME. *ley, lay*; AS. *leáh*, a meadow, pasture, lea.] A meadow or sward land.

lēa, *n.* [ME. *leyen*; AS. *lecgan*, to lay.]

1. A measure of yarn; a certain quantity of thread or worsted.

2. One of the alternating sets of warp threads in a loom.

lēach, *n.* Same as third *Leech*.

lēach, *v.t.*; leached (lēcht), *pt., pp.*; leaching, *ppr.* [AS. *leccan*, to wet, moisten.]

1. To wash, as ashes, by percolation, or causing water to pass through them, and thus to separate from them the alkali.

2. To drain by percolation; as, to *leach* lye.

lēach, *v.i.* 1. To lose soluble matter by percolation; as, ashes *leach*.

2. To drain out in percolating; as, lye *leaches* out.

lēach, *n.* [Compare AS. *leáh*, lye.]

1. A quantity of wood ashes, through which water passes, and thus imbibes the alkali.

2. A vat in which ashes are leached.

3. The operation of leaching.

4. The material resulting from leaching.

lēach, *n.* A leech; a physician. [Obs.]

lēach'-tub, *n.* A vessel in which ashes are leached.

lēach'y, *a.* Incapable of retaining water; porous, as a gravelly soil.

lead (led), *n.* [ME. *leed*; AS. *leád*, lead.]

1. A metal having a specific gravity of about 11.36 and an atomic weight of 205.35. It is soft, malleable, easily fused, and when freshly broken has a bluish-white color. It is used extensively for water-pipes, bullets, shot, etc., and in alloys, as pewter and type-metal.

2. A plummet of lead, used in sounding at sea.

3. A thin plate of type-metal or brass, used to separate lines in printing.

4. The small cylinder of graphite in a lead-pencil.

5. White lead.

6. [*pl.*] Sheets of lead used as a roof covering; also, a roof thus covered.

Kremnitz lead; white lead.

Red lead; a vivid red oxid of lead, Pb_3O_4, used as a pigment.

Sugar of lead; lead acetate.

White lead; a pigment containing about three parts of lead carbonate to one part of hydrated lead oxid.

lead (led), *v.t.*; leaded, *pt., pp.*; leading, *ppr.*

1. To fit, cover, or weight with lead.

2. In printing, to insert metal strips between (lines of type).

3. In pottery, to glaze with an ore of lead.

lead, *v.i.* To become filled with lead, as a rifle groove.

lēad (lēd), *v.t.*; led, *pt., pp.*; leading, *ppr.* [ME. *leden*; AS. *lǣdan*, to lead, from *līdhan*, to go, glide on.]

1. To guide by the hand; as, to *lead* a child.

2. To guide or conduct by showing the way; to direct; as, the Israelites were *led* by a pillar of cloud by day.

3. To conduct, as a chief or commander, implying authority; to direct and govern; as, a general *leads* his troops to battle and to victory.

4. To precede; to introduce by going first.

5. To hold the first place in rank or dignity among; as, the violins were *led* by so-and-so.

6. To show the method of attaining an object; to direct, as in an investigation; as, self-examination may *lead* us to a knowledge of ourselves.

7. In card-playing, to commence a round or trick with; as, he *leads* hearts; he *led* the ace of trumps.

8. To draw; to entice; to allure; as, the love of pleasure *leads* men into vices.

9. To induce; to prevail on; to influence.

10. To pass; to spend; as, to *lead* a life of gaiety, or a solitary life.

11. To cause to pass; to cause to spend; to cause to endure; in a bad sense.

> You remember the life he *led* his wife and daughter. —Dickens.

To lead astray; to lead from the right path; to seduce.

Syn.—Conduct, guide, precede, induce, commence, inaugurate, convey, persuade, direct, influence.

lēad, *v.i.* 1. To go before and show the way.

2. To have precedence or preëminence; as, to *lead* in an orchestra; said of the principal first violin.

3. To have a position of authority as commander or director.

4. To conduct; to bring; to draw; to induce; as, gaming *leads* to other vices.

5. In card-playing, to play the first card of a round or trick.

To lead off or *out*; to begin.

lēad, *n.* 1. Precedence; a going before; guidance; as, let the general take the *lead*.

2. The right of playing the first card in a round or trick; the suit or card so played.

3. A lane or navigable opening in a field of ice.

4. In mining, a lode.

5. In engineering, the average distance of travel requisite to remove the earth of an excavation to form an embankment.

6. A lade.

7. In a steam-engine, the width of opening of a steam-port.

8. In electricity, (a) a conductor; (b) the angular distance between the contact points of the brushes of a dynamo and the line bisecting the field.

Syn.—Priority, precedence, preëminence, initiative, guidance, control.

lēad, *n.* A caldron. [Obs.]

lead'ed (led'), *a.* 1. Fitted or provided with lead.

2. Separated by leads, as lines in printing.

lead'en, *a.* 1. Made of lead.

2. Figuratively, having one or more of the qualities of lead; blue-gray, heavy, dull, or sluggish; as, a *leaden* sky; a *leaden* weight, face, gait, etc.

lēad'ēr, *n.* [ME. *leder*; AS. *lǣdere*, a leader, from *lǣdan*, to lead.]

1. One who leads in any capacity, as chief, commander, conductor of a band, etc.

2. Anything that leads, as (a) the first horse in a tandem; (b) the driving wheel in gearing; (c) a conducting pipe; (d) the leading editorial in a newspaper; (e) in mining, a small vein that leads to a rich lode; (f) in navigation, a guide block to receive ropes; (g) in printing, a row of dots, etc., to guide the eye across the page; (h) an article sold at a special figure; (i) a tendon; a sinew.

lēad'ēr-ship, *n.* The state of being a leader.

lead'hill-īte (led'), *n.* In mineralogy, a sulphato-carbonate of lead, found at Leadhills, Scotland.

lead'ing (led'), *n.* 1. Work made of lead, as a roof, or as the cames in certain windows.

2. A clogging of the grooves of a rifle with bullet lead.

lēad'ing, *a.* 1. Guiding; conducting; preceding; drawing; alluring; as, a *leading* article at a store, that is, something sold very cheap to attract custom.

2. Chief; principal; capital; most influential; as, a *leading* motive.

3. Showing the way by going first; constituting a precedent.

Leading case; in law, a reported case which is considered to determine the law upon the points in question.

Leading question; a question so worded as to suggest the answer desired.

lēad'ing, *n.* 1. The act of guiding or being foremost.

2. A hinting; suggestion. [Obs.]

3. A spiritual guidance or direction.

lead'-line (led'), *n.* Nautically, a line used in taking soundings, having marks at interval for noting depths.

lēad'măn, *n.* One who leads a dance. [Obs.]

lead'-mill (led'), *n.* 1. A grinding wheel of lead used in gem-cutting.

2. A mill in which white lead is ground.

lead'-ō"chēr (-kēr), *n.* Massicot.

lead'-pen"cil, *n.* A graphite pencil, commonly with a case of wood.

lead'-plant, *n.* A small leguminous shrub, *Amorpha canescens*, found chiefly in regions containing lead ore.

lead'-screw (-skrū), *n.* In a lathe, the screw which gives longitudinal motion to the slide-rest.

leads'măn, *n.* The sailor who takes soundings by heaving the lead.

lead'-tree, *n.* 1. A leguminous tree, *Leucæna glauca*, of the American tropics.

2. The treelike crystallization of lead obtained by hanging zinc in a lead acetate solution.

lead'wŏrt, *n.* A herbaceous plant, *Plumbago Europæa*, or any other plant of the same genus.

lead'y, *a.* Of the color of lead.

lēaf, *n.*; *pl.* **lēaves.** [ME. *leef*; AS. *leáf*, a leaf.]

1. One of the green deciduous parts of a plant by which the sap is elaborated or fitted for the nourishment of the plant by being exposed to air and light on its extensive surface. A fully developed leaf generally consists of two parts, an expanded part, called the *blade*, and a stalk supporting that part, called the *petiole* or *leaf-stalk*. Leaves generally consist of vascular tissue in the veins or ribs, with cellular tissue or parenchyma filling up the interstices, and an epidermis over all. Some leaves, however, as those of the mosses, are entirely cellular.

2. Something resembling a leaf in any of its properties, as (a) a very thin plate of metal, as gold leaf; (b) a single unfolded sheet of paper or one of the divisions of a folded sheet, as in a book; (c) a movable part of a flat body, as of a fire-screen, window shutter, table, etc.; (d) a hat flap or brim; (e) an ornament in the form of a plant leaf; (f) a separate layer of fat, as about a hog's kidneys; (g) a pinion tooth; (h) in zoölogy, a part or organ resembling a leaf.

To turn over a new leaf; to adopt a new and better line of conduct.

lēaf, *v.i.*; leafed, *pt., pp.*; leafing, *ppr.* To shoot out leaves; to produce leaves.

lēaf'āge, *n.* Foliage.

lēaf'-bee"tle, *n.* Any beetle of the *Chrysomelidæ*, as the common potato-beetle, which feeds on potato leaves.

lēaf'-blight, *n.* A disease due to parasitic fungi affecting chiefly the leaves of trees.

lēaf'-bridge, *n.* A drawbridge having a leaf on each side, which rises and falls, or platform on each side, which rises and falls.

leaf′-bud, *n.* A bud from which leaves only are produced.

lēaf′-but′tẽr-flȳ, *n.* A butterfly which in appearance and color resembles a leaf, as those of the genus *Kallima* of Asia.

lēaf′-crump″lẽr, *n.* A moth having larvæ which crumple leaves together to make nests; especially, a member of the genus *Phycis*.

lēaf′cup, *n.* A coarse weed of North America belonging to the genus *Polymnia*.

lēaf′-cut″tẽr, *n.* A wild bee, usually of the genus *Megachile*, which cuts out small portions of leaves for a lining to its nest.

lēaf′-fat, *n.* The fat which lies in leaves or layers within the body of an animal.

lēaf′-flēa, *n.* A kind of psyllid or plant-louse.

lēaf′-frog, *n.* A tree-frog of the genus *Phyllomedusa*.

lēaf′-green, *n.* Chlorophyl.

lēaf′-hop″pẽr, *n.* An insect of the family *Jassidæ*, very destructive to vegetation.

lēaf′i-ness, *n.* The state of having leaves.

lēaf′-in″sect, *n.* An insect of the family *Phasmidæ*, whose wings, etc., are leaf-shaped.

lēaf′less, *a.* Destitute of leaves; as, a *leafless* tree.

lēaf′less-ness, *n.* Destitution of leaves.

lēaf′let, *n.* 1. A little leaf; a small sheet of printed matter.

2. In botany, one of the divisions of a compound leaf; a foliole.

3. In zoölogy, any part expanded like a leaf.

lēaf′-louse, *n.* An aphid; a plant-louse.

lēaf′-met″ăl, *n.* Metal, as bronze, resembling silver or gold, prepared for use in thin sheets.

lēaf′-min″ẽr, *n.* An insect larva which feeds between the two surfaces of a leaf.

lēaf′-mōld, *n.* Soil composed of decayed leaves.

lēaf′-nōse, *n.* A leaf-nosed bat.

lēaf′-nōsed, *a.* Having the snout provided with leaflike appendages, as certain bats.

lēaf′-notch″ẽr, *n.* A beetle of Florida, *Artipus floridanus*, which cuts into the edges of orange leaves.

lēaf′-rōll″ẽr, *n.* An insect larva which rolls up leaves to make its nest.

lēaf′-sight (-sīt), *n.* A sight for a gun, hinged so as to be lifted vertically.

lēaf′stạlk, *n.* The stalk or petiole of a leaf.

lēaf′-valve, *n.* A flap-valve; a hinged valve.

lēaf′-wäsp, *n.* A sawfly.

lēaf′y, *a.* Full of leaves; having leaves.

lēague (lēg), *n.* [ME. *lege*; OFr. *legue*; LL. *lega*, *leuca*, a Gallic mile; of Celtic origin.] A unit of length. The marine league is a distance of three geographical miles or one-twentieth of an equatorial degree. The league as a land measure varies from 12,750 to 24,250 feet, in England being about three statute miles.

lēague, *n.* [ME. *lege*; OFr. *ligue*; LL. *liga*, *lega*, an alliance or league, from L. *ligare*, to bind.] An alliance between persons, parties, or states for mutual aid or for executing any design in concert.

lēague, *v.i.*; leagued, *pt.*, *pp.*; leaguing, *ppr.* To unite or join in a league; to confederate.

lēague, *v.t.* To cause to unite for a common purpose.

lēa′guẽr (-gẽr), *v.t.* To beleaguer. [Obs.]

lēa′guẽr, *n.* One who joins in a league.

lēa′guẽr, *n.* [D. *leger*, a bed, couch, camp.] A siege; a siege-camp.

lēa′guẽr-ẽr, *n.* A besieger. [Obs.]

lēak, *n.* [D. *lek*; Ice. *lekr*; Dan. *læk*, leaky, a leak; AS. *hlec*, full of cracks.]

1. A crack or hole that admits a fluid, or permits a fluid to escape where it should not.

2. The oozing or passing of a fluid through a crack or aperture either into anything, as a ship, or out of anything, as a cask.

3. An escape of electricity because of crossed or grounded wires, poor insulation, etc.

To spring a leak; to open or crack so as to let a fluid in or out; to begin to leak.

lēak, *a.* Leaky. [Obs.]

lēak, *v.t.*; leaked (lēkt), *pt.*, *pp.*; leaking, *ppr.* [ME. *leken*; compare D. *lekken*, Dan. *lække*, to leak, Ice. *leka*, to drip; AS. *leccan*, to wet.] To let (a fluid, light, etc.) into or out of a vessel, etc., by an accidental opening; as, the balloon *leaks* gas.

lēak, *v.i.* 1. To let anything into or out of a vessel, etc., by an unintentional aperture; as, the sand-box *leaks*.

2. To pass in or out of a receptacle undesignedly; as, the grain *leaks* out of the sack.

To leak out; to find vent; to escape privately from confinement or secrecy, as a fact or report.

lēak′āge, *n.* 1. A leaking.

2. The quantity of fluid, electricity, light, etc., that enters or issues by leaking.

3. In commerce, an allowance of a certain rate per cent for the leaking of casks, etc.

lēak′āge-cŏn-duc″tŏr, *n.* A conductor arranged to dispose of leakage in electric circuits; usually, a heavy grounded wire.

lēak′i-ness, *n.* A leaky condition.

lēak′y, *a.*; *comp.* leakier; *superl.* leakiest. 1. Allowing the entrance or escape of a fluid, light, etc.; having one or more leaks; as, a *leaky* camera, cask, etc.

2. Apt to disclose secrets; tattling. [Colloq.]

lēal, *a.* [ME. *leel*; OFr. *leial*, faithful, loyal, from L. *legalis*, legal.] Faithful; true; sometimes used in poetry. [Prov. Eng. or Scot.]

Land of the leal; paradise. [Scot.]

lēa′land, *n.* Fallow land. [Obs.]

lēam, *n.* and *v.* Gleam. [Obs.]

lēam, *n.* A lime; a string to lead a dog. [Obs.]

lēam′ẽr, *n.* A limmer or limehound. [Obs.]

lēan, *v.i.*; leaned *or* leant (lent), *pt.*, *pp.*; leaning, *ppr.* [ME. *lenen*; AS. *hlinian*, to lean.]

1. To deviate or move from a straight or perpendicular line; or to be in a position thus deviating; as, a column *leans* to the north or to the east.

2. To incline in sentiment, conduct, or opinions; with *to* or *toward*.

3. To bend or incline so as to rest on something; as, to *lean* on the arm of another.

Syn.—Incline, rest, support, tend, bend, depend, hang, repose, confide, slope.

lēan, *v.t.* [ME. *lenen*; AS. *hlænan*, to cause to lean.] To incline; to cause to lean.

lēan, *v.t.* To conceal. [Obs.]

lēan, *a.*; *comp.* leaner; *superl.* leanest. [ME. *lene*; AS. *hlæne*, meager, lean.]

1. Wanting flesh; meager; not fat; as, a *lean* animal; *lean* meat.

2. Not rich; destitute of good qualities; bare; barren; as, *lean* earth; a *lean* discourse.

3. In printing, unprofitable; requiring extra time or labor without extra compensation; as, *lean* work.

Syn.—Meager, lank, emaciated, shriveled, thin, skinny, scanty, slender.

lēan, *n.* 1. Flesh which consists of muscle without fat.

2. In printing, unprofitable matter.

lēan′-fāced, *a.* Having a thin face; specifically, among printers, applied to type which has little breadth in proportion to height.

lēan′ing, *n.* Tendency; inclination.

lēan′ly, *adv.* Without fat; meagerly.

lēan′ness, *n.* The quality or state of being lean.

leant (lent), *v.*, past tense and past participle of *lean*.

lēan′-tō″, *n.* and *a.* I. *n.* A building having its rafters supported by leaning on another building, a wall, etc.; a penthouse.

II. *a.* Having the upper ends of the rafters supported by leaning on or against a wall, etc.

lēan′-wit″ted, *a.* Having scanty wit or shrewdness.

lēan′y, *a.* Lean. [Obs.]

lēap, *v.i.*; leaped (lept) *or* leapt, *pt.*, *pp.*; leaping, *ppr.* [ME. *lepen*; AS. *hleápan*, to leap.]

1. To spring or rise from any support by a self-given impulse; to jump; to vault; as, a man *leaps* over a fence or *leaps* upon a horse.

2. To spring or move suddenly; to bound; to move as by a leap; as, one's blood *leaps*.

lēap, *v.t.* 1. To pass over by leaping; to spring or bound from one side to the other of; as, to *leap* a wall.

2. To cause to vault or jump; as, to *leap* a horse over a wall.

3. To cover; to serve; said of the male of certain animals.

lēap, *n.* A basket or wicker fish-snare. [Obs.]

lēap, *n.* [ME. *leep*; AS. *hlyp*, a leap, from *hleápan*, to leap.]

1. A jump; a spring; a bound; the act of leaping.

2. The space passed over at a bound.

3. A point from which one has leaped; as, Lover's *Leap*.

4. The act of the male of beasts in covering or serving.

5. In music, the passing from a note to another at a distance of two or more diatonic intervals.

6. In mining, a fault.

lēap′ẽr, *n.* One who or that which leaps; specifically, (a) a salmon, from its leaping; (b) a hook used to untwist old rope.

lēap′frog, *n.* A play among boys, in which one stoops down and another leaps over him by placing his hands on the shoulders of the former.

lēap′fụl, *n.* A basketful. [Obs.]

lēap′ing-house, *n.* A brothel. [Obs.]

lēap′ing-ly, *adv.* By leaps.

lēap′-yēar, *n.* A bissextile; a year containing 366 days; every fourth year, which *leaps* over a day more than a common year, a day being added to February, except years divisible by 100, of which only those divisible by 400 are leap-years.

lēar, *n.* Lore. [Obs.]

lēar, *n.* A leer, or annealing oven.

lēar, *v.t.* and *v.i.* To teach; also, to learn. [Obs.]

lēar, *a.* Empty. [Obs.]

lēarn, *v.t.*; learned *or* learnt, *pt.*, *pp.*; learning, *ppr.* [ME. *lernen*, *leornen*; AS. *leornian*, to learn.]

1. To gain knowledge of; to acquire information concerning, by instruction, by study, by observation, by experience, or in any other way; to acquire skill in (anything); as, to *learn* the news, or a lesson; to *learn* instrumental music.

2. Formerly, to teach; but this use is now obsolete among careful writers and speakers.

lēarn, *v.i.* To gain or receive knowledge, instruction, or skill; as, he *learns* easily.

lēarn′ȧ-ble, *a.* Capable of being learned.

lēarn′ed, *a.* 1. Versed in literature, science, or the arts; erudite; as, a *learned* writer.

2. Exhibiting or characterized by learning or erudition; scholastic; as, a *learned* discussion.

lēarn′ed-ly, *adv.* With learning or erudition.

lēarn′ed-ness, *n.* The condition of being learned.

lēarn′ẽr, *n.* [ME. *lernere*; AS. *leornere*, from *leornian*, to learn.] One who is learning; a pupil.

lēarn′ing, *n.* [ME. *lernyng*; AS. *leornung*, the act of learning, verbal n. of *leornian*, to learn.]

1. The act of gaining knowledge or skill.

2. Education; acquired knowledge in any special subject, especially in science or literature, as the result of study or instruction; erudition; as, a judge of great *learning* in the law.

lēarnt, *v.*, past tense and past participle of *learn*.

lēas′ȧ-ble, *a.* Capable of being leased.

lēase (lēs), *n.* [OFr. *lais*, *lays*, *lees*, a thing left by will, a lease, from *laisier*, to let go, to lease.]

1. A demise or letting of lands, tenements, or hereditaments to another for life, for a term of years, or at will, for a rent or compensation reserved.

2. The contract for such letting.

3. Any tenure by grant or permission; the time of tenure; an allotted time of possession; as, the *lease* of life.

Lease and release; in England, a former method of conveying a freehold estate; a purchaser, having first received a *lease* and possession, became capable of receiving a deed (*release*) for the freehold.

lēase, *v.t.*; leased, *pt.*, *pp.*; leasing, *ppr.* [OFr. *laisier*, *leisseir*, to lease, let out; L. *laxare*, to loosen, relax, from *laxus*, loose.]

1. To let; to demise; to grant the temporary possession of (lands, tenements, or hereditaments) to another for a rent reserved; as, A *leased* to B his land in Dale.

2. To hold by lease; as, B *leased* the land from A.

lēaṣe, *v.i.* To glean; to gather what harvesters have left. [Obs.]

lēase′hōld, *a.* Held by lease; as, a *leasehold* tenement.

lēase′hōld, *n.* A tenure held by lease.

lēase′hōld-ẽr, *n.* A tenant under a lease.

lēaṣ′ẽr, *n.* A gleaner. [Obs.]

lēas′ẽr, *n.* A liar. [Obs.]

lēash, *n.* [ME. *leesshe*, *lese*, *lees*; OFr. *lesse*; LL. *laxa*, a loose cord, a thong, snare, properly f. of L. *laxus*, loose.]

1. A thong of leather, or long line, by which a falconer holds his hawk, or a courser his dog.

2. Among sportsmen, a brace and a half; tierce; three; three creatures of any kind, especially greyhounds, foxes, bucks, and hares.

3. In the harness of a loom, a thread or wire holding a loop through which a warp thread passes and is lifted and guided in weaving.

lēash, *v.t.*; leashed (lēsht), *pt.*, *pp.*; leashing, *ppr.* To bind with a leash; to hold by a string.

lēaṣ′ing, *n.* [ME. *leesing*; AS. *leásung*, the act of lying, verbal n. of *leásian*, to tell a lie, from *leás*, false.] Falsehood; lies. [Obs.]

Leasing making; in Scots law, the uttering of anything libelous against the sovereign, his court, or his family.

lēa′sōw, *n.* A pasture. [Obs.]

lēast, *a.* [ME. *leste*, *lest*; AS. *læst*, least, contr. of *læsast*, superl. of *læs*, less.] Smallest; little beyond others, either in size or degree; as, the *least* insect; the *least* mercy.

At least or *at the least*; at the lowest estimate; to say no more; at any rate; as, there were ten *at least*.

In the least; in the slightest degree, manner, etc., at all.

Least squares; in mathematics, a method of finding the probable error in assuming a mean of a number of varying observations of a phenomenon; the rule being that the most probable result is the one which makes the sum of the squares of the errors the least possible.

lēast, *a.*, superl. of *little*.

lēast, *adv.* In the smallest or lowest degree; in a degree below all others; as, to reward those who *least* deserve it.

lēast, *conj.* Lest. [Obs.]

lēast′wāyṣ, lēast′wīṣe, *adv.* At least. [Colloq.]

lēa′ṣy, *a.* Thin; flimsy. [Obs.]

lēat, *n.* [AS. *lædan*, to lead.] An artificial trench to conduct water, as to a mill; a flume.

leath′ẽr (leth′), *n.* [ME *lether*; AS. *lether*, leather.]

1. The skin of an animal, dressed and prepared for use.

2. Dressed hides in general.

3. Skin; in an ironical sense.

leath'ẽr, *a.* Leathern; consisting of leather; as, *leather* belting.
leath'ẽr, *v.t;* leathered, *pt., pp.*; leathering, *ppr.* To beat, as with a thong of leather. [Colloq.]
leath'ẽr-back, *n.* A turtle, *Dermochelys coriacea*, having a carapace resembling leather.
leath'ẽr-bōard, *n.* A composition of paper, leather scraps, etc., used to imitate sole leather.
leath'ẽr-cärp, *n.* A carp having few or no scales.
leath'ẽr-cōat, *n.* Anything having a tough skin or rind; especially, an apple, the golden russet.
leath-ẽr-ette' (-et'), *n.* Imitation leather.
leath'ẽr-flow"ẽr, *n.* A vine, *Clematis Viorna*, having purple blossoms of a leathery texture.
leath'ẽr-head (-hed), *n.* 1. The friar-bird.
2. A blockhead; a dull-witted fellow.
leath'ẽr-ing, *n.* 1. A flogging. [Colloq.]
2. On shipboard, leather used on spars, etc., to prevent chafing.
leath'ẽr-jack"et, *n.* 1. The hickory-eucalyptus, or any of various similar trees.
2. Any of various fishes, as (a) the trigger-fish (genus *Balistes*) of the Atlantic; (b) an allied fish (genus *Monacanthus*) of Australian waters; (c) *Oligoplites saurus*, a fish of tropical seas.
leath'ẽr-lēaf, *n.* A small evergreen shrub, *Cassandra calyculata*, with leathery leaves.
leath'ẽr-mouthed (-moutht), *a.* Having the mouth without teeth and of a leathery smoothness and toughness.
leath'ẽrn, *a.* Made of leather.
leath'ẽr-oid, *n.* A leather-like material composed of vegetable fibers chemically treated.
leath'ẽr-plant, *n.* In New Zealand, any plant of the genus *Celmisia*.
leath'ẽr-side, *n.* A minnow, *Tigoma tænia*.
leath'ẽr-wood, *n.* A small shrub, *Dirca palustris*, of North America, having a tough leathery bark; moosewood.
leath'ẽr-y, *a.* Resembling leather.
lēave (lēv), *v.t.*; left, *pt., pp.*; leaving, *ppr.* [ME. *leeven, leven*; AS. *læfan*, to leave, from *laf*, a heritage, something left or remaining.]
1. To withdraw or depart from; to quit for a longer or shorter time indefinitely; as, to *leave* home.
2. To forsake; to desert; to abandon; to relinquish; as, to *leave* one's old beliefs.
3. To cease to do; to desist from; to forbear; usually with *off*; as, *leave off* crying.
4. To suffer to remain; not to take or remove; as, to *leave* fruit on a tree.
5. To deliver; to place; as, to *leave* a note.
6. To have remaining at death; as, to *leave* a good name.
7. To refer: to commit for decision; as, to *leave* a case with the jury.
lēave, *v.i.* 1. To cease; to desist; usually with *off*; as, where did I *leave off?*
2. To go; to depart; as, he *leaves* at ten.
lēave, *v.i.*; leaved, *pt., pp.*; leaving, *ppr.* To leaf; to shoot out leaves.
lēave, *n.* [ME. *leve, leef*; AS. *leáf*, permission, license.]
1. Permission; allowance; license; liberty granted by which restraint or illegality is removed; especially, permission to go or to be gone.
2. Farewell; adieu; a formal parting; chiefly in the phrase *to take leave*.
Syn.—Liberty, permission, license.—*Leave* denotes that he who obtains it may decide whether to use it or not; *liberty*, that all obstructions in the way of his using it are removed and set aside. *Permission* implies a formal consent given by one who had the right to refuse it. *License* denotes that this consent extends to a mode of acting for which special permission is required.
lēave, *v.t.* [ME. *leven*; AS. *lyfan, lefan*, to allow, permit.] To allow; to permit; to let; to give leave to; as, I *leave* you to guess the rest.
lēave, *v.t.* To raise; to levy. [Obs.]
lēaved, *a.* Having a leaf or leaves; made or furnished with leaves or folds; as, a broad-*leaved* plant.
lēave'less, *a.* Destitute of leaves. [Obs.]
lēave'less, *a.* Without leave. [Rare.]
leav'en (lev'n), *n.* [ME. *levain, levein*; OFr. *levain*; LL. *levamen*, leaven L. *levamen*, an alleviation, mitigation, solace, from *levare*, to make light, relieve, lift up, raise.]
1. Sour dough, which, mixed with other dough or paste, produces fermentation in it and renders it light; hence, any substance causing fermentation, as yeast.
2. Anything which makes a general change in a mass; as, the *leaven* of discontent.
leav'en, *v.t.*; leavened, *pt., pp.*; leavening, *ppr.* 1. To excite fermentation in; to raise and make light, as dough or paste.

A little leaven *leaveneth* the whole lump. —1 Cor. v. 6.

2. To taint; to imbue.
leav'en-ing, *n.* That which leavens.
leav'en-ous, *a.* Containing leaven; tainted.
lēav-ẽr, *n.* One who leaves or relinquishes.
lēaves, *n.*, pl. of *leaf*.
lēav'i-ness, *n.* Leafiness. [Obs.]
lēav'ings, *n.pl.* Things left; remnants; refuse.
lēav'y, *a.* Full of leaves; leafy. [Obs.]
leb'ăn, *n.* [Ar. *leban*.] Artificially soured milk used as food or drink by the Arabs; also written *leben, lebban*.
le-ġä'mȧ, *n.* The hartbeest.
lē-can'ō-man-cy, *n.* [Gr. *lekanomanteia*; *lekanē*, a dish, pan, and *manteia*, divination.] Divination by throwing three stones into water in a basin and invoking the aid of a demon.
Leç-ȧ-nō'rȧ, *n.* [Gr. *lekanē*, a dish; so called from the form of the shields.] A genus of lichens of the order *Parmeliaceæ*, resembling *Lecidea*, but distinguished by the border being formed from the thallus. Several of the species furnish dyes.
leç-ȧ-nō'rie, *a.* [*Lecanora* and *-ic*.] In chemistry, derived from lichens of the genus *Lecanora*; as *lecanoric* acid, called also *lecanorin*.
leç-ȧ-nō'rin, *n.* [*Lecanora* and *-in*.] An acid derived from lichens, forming salts called *lecanorates*.
lech, *v.t.* To lick. [Obs.]
lē-chē', *n.* [S. African.] A water-buck of South Africa.
lech'ẽr, *n.* [ME. *letchour*; OFr. *lecheor, lecheur*, a glutton, a lewd man, from *lecher*, to lick, to indulge in lust.] A man given to lewdness or to excessive indulgence of lust.
lech'ẽr, *v.i.* To practise lewdness. [Obs.]
lech'ẽr-ẽr, *n.* One given to lechery.
lech'ẽr-ous, *a.* [ME. *lecherous*, from OFr. *lecherie*, lewdness, lechery.]
1. Addicted to lewdness; prone to indulge lust; lustful; lewd; as, a *lecherous* man.
2. Provoking lust; as, a *lecherous* novel.
lech'ẽr-ous-ly, *adv.* Lustfully; lewdly.
lech'ẽr-ous-ness, *n.* The state or quality of being lecherous.
lech'ẽr-y, *n.* [OFr. *lecherie, lescherie*, from *lecher*, to lick, to indulge in lust.] Lewdness; free indulgence of lust.
lec'i-thin, *n.* [Gr. *lekithos*, the yolk of an egg, and *-in*.] A complex nitrogenous fat, phosphorized and colorless, contained in nerve and brain tissues, in leucocytes, in egg-yolk, etc.
leç'tẽrn, leç'tũrn, *n.* [ME. *lectorn, letteron*; OFr. *lettrin*; LL. *lectrinum, lectrum*, a pulpit, a reading-desk, from Gr. *lektron*, a couch, bed, a support for books.] A reading-desk in some churches; specifically, a desk from which lections or lessons are read or chanted.

Lectern, Yeovil, Somersetshire.

leç'ti-cȧ, *n.*; *pl.* **leç'ti-cæ.** [L.] In Roman history, a form of litter or palanquin.
leç'tion, *n.* [L. *lectio* (*-onis*), a gathering, selecting, reading, from *lectus*, pp. of *legere*, to gather, select, read.]
1. A difference or variety in copies of a manuscript or book; a reading.
2. A portion of Scripture read in divine service.
leç'tiōn-ā-ry, *n.* The Roman Catholic service-book, containing portions of Scripture.
leç-ti-stẽr'ni-um, *n.*; *pl.* **leç-ti-stẽr'ni-ȧ.** [L., from *lectus*, couch, and *sternere*, to spread.] Among the ancient Greeks and Romans, a feast and sacrifice, at which were images of the gods reclining upon couches at the table.
leç'tŏr, *n.* [L., a reader, from *lectus*, pp. of *legere*, to read.] A person designated to read parts of the Bible in church services; one of the minor orders leading to the priesthood.
leç'tress, *n.* A female reader.
leç'tū-ăl, *a.* [LL. *lectualis*, pertaining to a bed, from L. *lectus*, bed.] Relating to extended confinement in bed.
leç'tūre, *n.* [LL. *lectura*, a reading, lecture, properly f. of L. *lecturus*, fut. p. of *legere*, to read.]
1. A discourse read or pronounced on any subject; usually a formal or methodical discourse, intended for instruction; as, a *lecture* on philosophy; a *lecture* on travel.
2. A reading; the act or practice of reading. [Obs.]
3. A reprimand; a formal reproof.
4. In English universities, a rehearsal of a lesson.
leç'tūre, *v.t.*; lectured, *pt., pp.*; lecturing, *ppr.* 1. To instruct by discourses.
2. To speak to dogmatically or authoritatively; to reprove; as, to *lecture* one for his faults.
3. To influence by a lecture or reprimand; as, *lecture* him into the notion.
leç'tūre, *v.i.* To read or deliver a lecture.
leç'tūr-ẽr, *n.* One who lectures; a professor or an instructor who delivers formal discourses.
leç'tūre-ship, *n.* The office of a lecturer.
leç'tũrn, *n.* See *Lectern*.
Leç'y-this, *n.* [LL. *lecythus*; Gr. *lēkythos*, an oil-flask; so named from the shape of the seed-vessels.] A genus of large tropical trees of the order *Myrtaceæ*.
leç'y-thus, *n.*; *pl.* **leç'y-thī.** [LL., from Gr. *lēkythos*, an oil-vase.] In Grecian archæology, a tall narrow-necked earthenware vase for oil or perfume.
led, *v.*, past tense and past participle of *lead*.
led, *a.* Under control; as, a *led* farm, that is, one not occupied by the owner or lessee.
Led captain; a henchman; an obsequious follower. [Obs.]
Led horse; a spare horse; a pack-horse.
led'dy, *n.* Lady. [Dial.]
led'en, led'den, *n.* Language; voice. [Obs.]
ledġe (lej), *n.* [From the same root as AS. *licgan*, to lie; of Scand. origin, compare Sw. *lagg*, Ice. *lögg*, the rim of a cask.]
1. A shelf or shelflike projection; a ridge or projecting part; a reef; especially, (a) in architecture, a horizontal rectangular molding; (b) in mining, a lode or metalliferous quartz vein; (c) in a snip, a part of the deck-frame.
2. A bar for a gate. [Prov. Eng.]
ledġed, *a.* Having or resembling a ledge.
ledġe'ment, *n.* See *Ledgment*.
ledġ'ẽr, *n.* [Compare D. *legger*, a layer, day-book, from O.D. *leggen*, to lie, from same root as AS. *licgan*, to lie.]
1. The principal book of accounts in business records, so arranged as to show the debits and credits of each account.
2. A slab, beam, or the like made to lie stationary, as (a) in a scaffolding, a horizontal timber supporting the putlogs; (b) a slab of stone placed horizontally upon a tomb or grave; (c) the wall under a lode; (d) ledger-bait.
3. A resident ambassador or agent. [Obs.]
ledġ'ẽr-bāit, *n.* Bait used on a line kept in one stationary position.
ledġ'ẽr-blāde, *n.* In a machine for shearing cloth, the fixed blade against which the moving blades work.
ledġ'ẽr-taç"kle, *n.* Fishing-tackle having the end of the line touching bottom.
ledġ'ment, *n.* 1. A horizontal course of moldings.
2. The development, on a plane, of a curved surface.
ledġ'ment-tā"ble, *n.* That part of a plinth which projects.
ledġ'y, *a.* Having many ledges.
Lē'dum, *n.* [Gr. *lēdon*, ladanum.] A genus of small white-flowered shrubs of the tribe *Rhodoreæ*, having fragrant leaves and commonly known as Labrador tea. *Ledum palustre*, or wild rosemary, furnishes an essential oil called Ledum oil.
lee, *v.i.* To lie; to tell lies. [Scot. and Dial.]
lee, *n.*; *pl.* **lees.** [ME. *lie*, pl. *lies*; OFr. *lie*; LL. *lia*, pl. *liæ*, lees, dregs.] The sediment found in the bottom of liquor vessels; dregs; usually in the plural.
lee, *n.* [ME. *lee, le*; AS. *hleó, hleów*, a shelter, protection.]
1. A calm or sheltered place; a place defended from the wind; hence, shelter.
2. The side or quarter toward which the wind blows, as opposed to that from which it proceeds.
Under the lee; in nautical language, on that side, or in a position, sheltered from the wind; as, *under the lee* of a ship or a breakwater.
lee, *a.* 1. Of or relating to the side or quarter sheltered from the wind; opposed to *weather*; as, on the *lee* bow.
2. In geology, of or relating to the side (of glaciated rocks) facing away from the point whence the glacier moved.
Lee shore; the shore under the lee of a ship.
Lee tide; a tide running in the direction in which the wind blows.
lee'bōard, *n.* A long flat piece of wood attached to each side of a flat-bottomed vessel (as a Dutch galiot)

Dutch Galiot, with Leeboards.

by a bolt on which it traverses. When close-hauled the one on the lee side is let down, and reaching below the keel, when the ship is listed over by the wind, prevents her from drifting fast to leeward.

leech, *v.t.* and *v.i.* Same as *Leach.*

leech, *n.* See fourth *Leach.*

leech, *n.* [Ice. *lik*, a leech-line.] The sloping or vertical edge of a sail; in fore-and-aft sails, the after edge, in distinction from the fore edge or *luff*.

leech, *n.* [ME. *leeche*; AS. *læce*, a physician, prob. from *lac*, medicine.] A physician; a doctor. [Obs.]

leech, *v.t.* To heal; to treat, as a physician. [Obs.]

leech, *n.* [ME. *leche*; AS. *læce*, a leech, from *læce*, a physician.]

1. A blood-sucking aquatic worm of the genus *Hirudo* or allied genera. The mouth is furnished with three small white teeth, serrated along the edges, to enable the animal to inflict its peculiar triradiate wound. *Hirudo medicinalis* is used in medicine to draw blood. Hence, any device for drawing blood.

2. Figuratively, one who holds on and, as it were, draws his victim's blood or wealth.

leech, *v.t.* To bleed with a leech.

leech′craft, *n.* The art of healing. [Obs.]

leech′-eat″ẽr, *n.* A plover of Egypt, the crocodile-bird.

lee-chee′, *n.* Same as *Lichi.*

leech′-line, *n.* A rope which hauls a sail to its yard.

leech′-rōpe, *n.* The part of the boltrope that has the leech of a sail attached to it.

leed, *n.* A lead or caldron. [Obs.]

leef, *adv.* Lief. [Obs.]

lee′-gāuge, *n.* A position on the lee side; said of one vessel with reference to another.

leek, *n.* [ME. *leek*; AS. *leác*, a leek.] A plant, *Allium Porrum*, with a bulbous cylindrical root and flat leaves, allied to and resembling an onion.

Wild leek; an American plant, *Allium tricoccum.*

lee′lāne, *adv.* All alone. [Scot.]

leem, leeme, lēme, *v.* and *n.* See first *Leam.*

leep, *v.*, obsolete past tense of *leap.*

leer, *a.* Empty; frivolous; trifling; riderless, as a horse. [Obs.]

leer, *n.* [ME. *lere*; AS. *hleór*, the cheek, face.]

1. The cheek; the face; the complexion. [Obs.]

2. A peculiar facial expression, consisting chiefly in a side-glance of the eye, conveying an idea of evil or insolence.

leer, *v.i.*; leered, *pt., pp.*; leering, *ppr.* To have an expression of face suggesting insolence or evil passion; to look obliquely.

leer, *v.t.* To allure; to entice with a leer.

leer, *n.* An oven for annealing glass.

leer, *v.t.* To learn. [Obs.]

leer, *n.* Braid; tape. [Obs.]

leer, *a.* Left; as, a hat-brim turned up on the *leer* side. [Obs.]

leer′ing-ly, *adv.* With an oblique look or smile.

lees, *n.* A leash. [Obs.]

leese, *v.t.* To lose. [Obs.]

leese, *v.t.* To hurt. [Obs.]

leet, *n.* [AS. *læth*, a territorial division.]

1. In Great Britain, a court; the court-leet.

2. The local extent of a court-leet's jurisdiction.

3. The day for holding a court-leet.

leet, *v.*, obsolete past tense of *let.*

leet, *n.* [Ice. *leiti*, a share, a part.]

1. A share; a lot.

2. A list, as of persons eligible to an office.

leet, *n.* The pollack, a fish.

leet, *n.* A leat; a flume. [Obs.]

leet, *v.i.* To feign; to let on. [Prov. Eng.]

leet′-āle, *n.* The dinner at a court-leet.

leet′măn, *n.*; *pl.* **leet′men.** A man subject to the jurisdiction of a court-leet. [Obs.]

lee′wăn, *n.*, a variant spelling for *lewan.*

lee′wărd (*or* lū′ẽrd), *n.* The lee.

lee′wărd, *adv* Toward the lee.

lee′wărd, *a.* Lee; having the same direction as the wind; the reverse of *windward.*

lee′wărd-ly, *a.* Not able to sail close-hauled without making great leeway.

lee′wāy, *n.* 1. The leeward drift of a ship.

2. The angle the line of a ship's keel makes with her course.

3. Figuratively, retrogression; deviation from a direct course.

To have or *give leeway*; to have or give room for operations; as, this *gives* much *leeway* for speculation.

lēfe, *n.* One loved; a friend. [Obs.]

left, *v.*, past tense and past participle of *leave.*

left, *a.* [ME. *left, lift*; AS. *lyft, left*, weak, worthless.]

1. Of or belonging to that side of one's body which is toward the rising sun as one faces to the south; opposed to *right.*

2. Being, or located on the left-hand side. The left bank of a river is that which is on the left hand of a person who faces downstream.

left, *adv.* To or toward the left.

left, *n.* 1. The side opposite to the right.

2. In European politics, that party whose legislative representatives sit to the left of the presiding officer when in assembly; the radical or liberal party; as, a member of the *Left.*

Over the left (*shoulder*); not at all; a colloquial phrase indicating negation of a statement; as, yes, I like it—*over the left.*

left′-hand, *a.* 1. Situated on one's left side.

2. Having direction or position toward the left hand, as a screw whose threads turn from right to left as they recede.

3. Unfavorable; unlucky. [Obs.]

left′-hand″ed, *a.* 1. Having the left hand or arm more strong or dexterous than the right.

2. Unlucky; clumsy; insincere; as, a *left-handed* compliment.

3. Moving from right to left; opposite to the motion of the clock's hands.

left′-hand″ed-ness, left′-hand″i-ness, *n.* 1. Habitual use of the left hand; ability to use the left hand with more ease and strength than the right.

2. By a false figure of speech, awkwardness.

left′-off, *a.* Cast aside.

left′wărd, *adv.* Toward the left.

lē′fụl, *a.* [Obs.] Same as *Leveful.*

leg, *n.* [ME. *leg*, pl. *legges*; Ice. *leggr*, a leg, hollow bone.]

1. One of the limbs of man or of an animal, used in supporting the body, and in walking and running; properly, that part of the limb from the knee to the foot, but in a more general sense, the whole limb, including the thigh, the leg, and the foot.

Bones of the Human Leg.

A, Femur 1, Head, 2, Neck; 3, Shaft; 4, External condyle, 5, Internal do. B, Patella. 1, Apex of the bone; 2, Surface of articulation with external condyle of the femur; 3, Do. with internal condyle. C, Fibula 6, Shaft; 9, Lower extremity, the external malleolus; 10, Upper extremity. D, Tibia. 1, Spinous process; 2, Inner tuberosity; 3, Outer do.; 4, Tubercle; 5, Shaft; 7, Internal surface of shaft; the sharp border between 5 and 7 the crest of tibia; 8, Internal malleolus.

2. Something like a leg; as, a stove-*leg*; the *leg* of a table.

3. Any clothing which covers a lower limb separately, either wholly or in part.

4. A blackleg. [Eng. Slang.]

5. The distance traversed by a ship on one tack.

6. The water-leg of a steam-boiler, a downward projection which often surrounds part of the furnace.

7. The case of a grain-elevator bucket-belt.

8. In cricket, a player who stands back of, and usually somewhat to the left of, the batter.

A good leg; in navigation, a course close to the one desired, when tacking.

Legs of a hyperbola, parabola, etc.; the branches.

Legs of a triangle; the sides of a triangle; seldom used unless one of the sides is first distinguished by some appropriate term; as, the hypotenuse and two *legs* of a right-angled triangle.

On one's last legs; about to fall, die, collapse, or fail.

To have legs; to have momentum or speed.

To make a leg; to bow; from the practice of drawing the right leg backward.

To stand on one's own legs; to support oneself; to trust to one's own strength or efforts without aid.

leg, *v.i.* 1. To bow. [Obs.]

2. To run; sometimes with *it*; as, to *leg it.* [Colloq.]

leg′ȧ-cy, *n.*; *pl.* **leg′ȧ-cies.** [OFr. *legacie*; L. *legatum*, a bequest, legacy, from *legatus*, pp. of *legare*, to bequeath.]

1. A bequest; a particular thing or certain sum of money given by last will or testament; hence, anything obtained from a predecessor or ancestor; as, a *legacy* of power.

2. A commission. [Obs.]

Legacy duty; a tax on inheritances.

leg′ȧ-cy-hunt″ẽr, *n.* One who flatters and courts for legacies.

le-gȧ-de′rō, *n.* [Sp. Am., from Sp. *legar*, L. *ligare*, to bind, tie.] A broad leather stirrup-strap.

lē′găl, *a.* [Fr. *légal*; L. *legalis*, legal, from *lex, legis*, law.]

1. Lawful; according or conformable to law; created or permitted by law; pertaining to law; judicial; as, a *legal* business; *legal* incapacity; *legal* decisions.

2. Pertaining to, under the control of, or remediable by law as distinguished from equity; as, *legal* assets.

3. In theology, according to the law of works, as distinguished from free grace.

Legal tender; (a) currency that the law permits one to offer and requires another to accept, in payment of a debt; (b) a formal offer of anything in accordance with a contract, or to satisfy an obligation.

lē′găl-ism, *n.* Close conformity to law.

lē′găl-ist, *n.* One who advocates legalism.

lē-gal′i-ty, *n.* [Fr. *légalité*; LL. *legalitas*, lawfulness, from L. *legalis*, legal.]

1. Lawfulness; conformity to law.

2. In theology, reliance on works for salvation.

lē″găl-i-zā′tion, *n.* The process of legalizing.

lē′găl-īze, *v.t.*; legalized, *pt., pp.*; legalizing, *ppr.*

1. To make lawful; to render conformable to law; to authorize; to sanction; to give the authority of law to.

2. To apply (the Scriptures) as a legalist.

lē′găl-ly, *adv.* Lawfully; according to law; in a legal manner.

leg′ăn-tine, *a.* [Obs.] Same as *Legatine.*

leg′ȧ-tȧ-ry, *n.* [L. *legatarius*, from *legatum*, a legacy.] A legatee.

leg′āte, *n.* [Fr. *légat*; L. *legatus*, a legate, deputy, properly pp. of *legare*, to appoint, choose, to send as an ambassador, from *lex, legis*, law.]

1. An ambassador or envoy.

2. The pope's ambassador to a foreign prince or state; a cardinal or bishop sent as the pope's representative or commissioner to a sovereign power.

3. In Roman history, an assistant to a general or governor of a province; an ambassador from or to the Roman emperor.

leg-ȧ-tee′, *n.* [L. *legatus*, pp. of *legare*, to bequeath.] One to whom a legacy is bequeathed.

leg′āte-ship, *n.* The office of a legate.

leg′ȧ-tine, *a.* 1. Pertaining to a legate; as, *legatine* power.

2. Made by or proceeding from a legate; as, a *legatine* constitution.

lē-gā′tion, *n.* [Fr. *légation*; L. *legatio* (*-onis*), an embassy, from *legatus*, pp. of *legare*, to send as ambassador.]

1. An embassy; a deputation; the person or persons sent as envoys or ambassadors to a foreign court.

2. The official residence of a foreign diplomat, or his place of business.

3. The act of commissioning a person to act for another or others.

le-gä′tō, *adv.* [It., pp. of *legare*; L. *ligare*, to tie, bind.] In music, in a close, smooth, gliding manner; opposed to *staccato.*

le-gä′tō, *a.* Smooth; gliding; connected; as, a *legato* movement.

le-gä′tō, *n.* A legato style or passage.

leg-ȧ-tọr′, *n.* [L., from *legatus*, pp. of *legare*, to bequeath.] A testator. [Rare.]

le-gȧ-tū′rȧ, *n.* [It.] In music, a ligature; a syncopation, brace, or tie.

leg′ȧ-tūre, *n.* Legateship. [Obs.]

leg′-bāil, *n.* Escape from custody.

To give leg-bail; to elude arrest or imprisonment by flight.

lege, *v.t.* To allege. [Obs.]

lege′ment, *n.* [Obs.] Same as *Ledgment.*

leg′end (*or* lē′jend), *n.* [OFr. *legende*, LL. *legenda*, a story, legend, neut. pl. of L. *legendus*, gerundive of *legere*, to read.]

1. Any unauthentic narrative handed down by tradition and having a basis in fact; a tradition. Originally, a chronicle or register of the lives of saints, formerly read at matins, and in the refectories of religious houses.

2. Fictitious or nonhistorical narrative; fiction; fable; myth.

3. An inscription; specifically, (a) the motto of a coat of arms; (b) the explanatory reading below an engraving or drawing or on a monument, etc.

4. Music written to express a story without words.

5. A book; a list; a roll. [Obs.]

leg′end, *v.t.* To tell or narrate as a legend. [Rare.]

lē-gen′dȧ, *n.pl.* [LL., neut. pl. of L. *legendus*, gerundive of *legere*, to read.] Things which are to be read, as distinct from *credenda*, things which are to be believed.

leg′end-ā-ry, *a.* Consisting of legends; fabulous.

leg′end-ā-ry, *n.* A book of legends; a relater of legends.

leg′ẽr, *n.* 1. Anything that lies in a place. [Obs.]

2. A ledger.

3. A resident representative or envoy. [Obs.]

leg′ẽr, *a.* Resident; as, a *leger* ambassador. [Obs.]

leg′ẽr, *a.* [OFr. *legier*, from L. *levis*, light.] Fine; light; slender.

Leger line; in music, a line added above or below the staff of five lines, when more lines than five are wanted.

Leger lines.

leg″ẽr-dē-māin′, *n.* [Fr., light of hand; *leger*, from L. *levis*, light, *de*, from L. *de*, of, from, and *main*, from L. *manus*, hand.] Sleight of hand, a deceptive performance which depends on dexterity of hand; a trick performed with such art and adroitness that the manner or art eludes observation.

leġ″ẽr-dē-māin′ist, *n.* One skilled in legerdemain; a prestidigitator.

lē-ġẽr′i-ty, *n.* Lightness; nimbleness. [Obs.]

legge, *v.t.* To lay; to allay. [Obs.]

leg′ged (*or* legd), *a.* Having legs; used in composition; as, a two-*legged* animal.

leġ-ġiä′drō, leġ-ġie′rō, *a.* and *adv.* [It.] I. *a.* In music, brisk; gay; light; graceful.

II. *adv.* Gaily; briskly; lightly.

leg′ging, leg′gin, *n.* A cover for the leg, like a long gaiter; a garment that incloses the leg.

leg′gy, *a.* Having long, thin, or numerous legs.

leg′hŏrn, *n.* 1. A fine plaiting made from a certain kind of wheat straw, used in making hats, etc.; so named because chiefly exported from Leghorn, Italy.

2. A hat or bonnet of such plaiting.

3. [L—] An excellent breed of domestic fowls.

Leg′hŏrn, *a.* Of or relating to Leghorn, a city of Italy; relating to or made of Leghorn straw, a variety of wheat straw.

leġ-i-bil′i-ty, *n.* Legibleness; the quality or state of being legible.

leġ′i-ble, *a.* [LL. *legibilis*, from L. *legere*, to read.]

1. That may be read; distinct; easily deciphered; as, a *legible* manuscript.

2. That may be discovered or understood by visible marks or indications.

leġ′i-ble-ness, *n.* Quality of being legible.

leġ′i-bly, *adv.* In a legible way.

lē-ġif′iç, *a.* [L. *lex, legis*, law, and *facere*, to make.] Of or pertaining to legislating. [Rare.]

lē′ġi-ō, *n.* [L.] In zoölogy, a legion.

lē′ġiŏn (-jun), *n.* [OFr. *legion*; L. *legio* (*-onis*), a legion, from *legere*, to choose, select.]

1. In Roman history, a military body consisting of from three to six thousand foot soldiers besides from three to seven hundred cavalry. Each legion of six thousand was divided into ten cohorts of three maniples each, and each maniple into two centuries.

2. Hence, a military force; an army.

3. A great number; a host; a multitude.

4. In zoölogy, a subdivision of a class higher in rank than an order.

Legion of honor; an order instituted in France by Napoleon Bonaparte, as a reward of merit, both civil and military.

lē′ġiŏn, *v.t.* To form or arrange into a legion.

lē′ġiŏn-ā-ry, *a.* [L. *legionarius*, of or pertaining to a legion, from *legio* (*-onis*), a legion.]

1. Relating to or consisting of a legion or legions; as, a *legionary* force.

2. Containing a great number; as, a *legionary* body of errors.

lē′ġiŏn-ā-ry, *n.* One of a legion.

lē′ġiŏn-ry, *n.* A body of legions. [Obs.]

leġ′is-lāte, *v.i.*; legislated, *pt., pp.*; legislating, *ppr.* To make or enact a law or laws.

leġ′is-lāte, *v.t.* To effect or affect by legislation; as, to *legislate* an office into being.

leġ-is-lā′tion, *n.* [L. *legis latio* (*-onis*); *lex, legis*, law, and *latio* (*-onis*), a bringing, proposing, from *latus*, pp. of *ferre*, to bring.] The act of passing a law or laws; enacting of laws; also, the laws enacted.

leġ′is-lā-tive, *a.* 1. Giving or enacting laws; as, a *legislative* body.

2. Capable of enacting laws; as, *legislative* power.

3. Pertaining to the enacting of laws; suitable to laws; as, the *legislative* style.

leġ′is-lā-tive-ly, *adv.* By legislation.

leġ′is-lā-tŏr, *n.* [L. *legis lator*, or *legum lator*, a lawgiver; *legis*, genit. sing., *legum*, genit. pl. of *lex*, law, and *lator*, a mover or proposer of a law, from *latus*, pp. of *ferre*, to bring.] A lawgiver; one who makes laws, or is a member of a legislature.

leġ″is-lā-tō′ri-ăl, *a.* 1. Of or relating to a legislator, a legislature, or legislation.

2. Having legislative power; lawmaking.

leġ′is-lā-tŏr-ship, *n.* The office of a legislator.

leġ′is-lā-tress, leġ′is-lā-trix, *n.* A female who makes laws.

leġ′is-lā-tūre, *n.* [L. *lex, legis*, law, and LL. *latura*, a bringing, carrying, from L. *latus*, pp. of *ferre*, to bring, bear.]

1. The body of men in a state or kingdom invested with power to make and repeal laws; the supreme lawmaking power of a state.

2. Legislative power. [Rare.]

lē′ġist, *n.* [OFr. *legiste*; LL. *legista*, one skilled in the law, from *lex, legis*, law.] A person versed in the laws; a lawyer.

lē-ġit′im, *n.* Same as *Legitime*.

lē-ġit′i-mȧ-cy, *n.* 1. Accordance with law; lawfulness; genuineness; regular sequence or deduction; as, the *legitimacy* of a government or of a conclusion.

2. Lawfulness of birth; opposed to *bastardy*.

lē-ġit′i-māte, *a.* [LL. *legitimatus*, pp. of *legitimare*, to make lawful, from L. *legitimus*, lawful, from *lex, legis*, law.]

1. Lawful; in accordance with established law; regular; as, a *legitimate* government.

2. Genuine; real; not false or spurious.

3. Lawfully begotten or born; born in wedlock.

4. Following by regular sequence; in accordance with established principles.

lē-ġit′i-māte, *v.t.*; legitimated, *pt., pp.*; legitimating, *ppr.* [LL. *legitimatus*, pp. of *legitimare*, to make lawful, from L. *legitimus*, lawful, from *lex, legis*, law.]

1. To make lawful.

2. To render legitimate; to invest with the rights of a legitimate child, as one who is illegitimate.

lē-ġit′i-māte-ly, *adv.* Lawfully; genuinely.

lē-ġit′i-māte-ness, *n.* Legality; genuineness.

lē-ġit-i-mā′tion, *n.* 1. The act of rendering legitimate.

2. Lawful birth. [Rare.]

lē-ġit′i-mȧ-tist, *n.* Same as *Legitimist*.

lē-ġit′i-mȧ-tīze, *v.t.* To make legitimate.

leġ′i-time, *n.* [Fr. *légitime*; L. *legitimus*, fixed or allowed by law, legitimate, from *lex, legis*, law.] In civil law, that portion of a man's estate of which he cannot disinherit his children.

lē-ġit′i-miṣm, *n.* The doctrine or theory of the Legitimists.

lē-ġit′i-mist, *n.* [Fr. *légitimiste*, from L. *legitimus*, legitimate, from *lex, legis*, law.]

1. One who upholds legitimate authority.

2. [L—] In France, an adherent of the elder branch of the Bourbon family, descendants of Louis XIV.

3. [L—] In Spain, a Carlist.

leg′less, *a.* Without legs.

leg′let, *n.* An ornamental leg-band.

lē-guän′, *n.* [Braz. *leguana*.] An iguana.

lē-gū-lē′iăn, *a.* and *n.* [L. *leguleius*, a pettifogging lawyer.]

I. *a.* Pettifogging. [Rare.]

II. *n.* A pettifogger. [Rare.]

leg′ūme (*or* lē-gūm′), *n.* [Fr. *légume*; L. *legumen*, pulse, any leguminous plant, lit., anything that may be gathered, from *legere*, to gather.]

1. In botany, a seed-vessel of two valves, in which the seeds are fixed to one suture only. In the latter circumstance, it differs from a siliqua, in which the seeds are attached to both sutures. In popular use, a legume is called a *pod* or a *cod*; as, pea-*pod* or peas*cod*.

2. [*pl.*] Pulse; the fruit borne by *Leguminosæ*, as peas, beans, lentils, etc.

lē-gū′men, *n.* Same as *Legume*.

lē-gū′min, *n.* [*Legumen* and *-in*.] A caseinlike proteid found in legumes.

Lē-gū-mi-nō′sæ, *n.pl.* [L. *legumen* (*-inis*), any leguminous plant.] One of the largest and most important orders of plants, including about seven thousand species, dispersed throughout the world. They are trees, shrubs, or herbs, usually with alternate, pinnate, compound leaves, and axillary or terminal one or many flowered peduncles of often showy flowers, succeeded by a leguminous fruit. Three suborders are recognized: *Papilionaceæ*, *Cæsalpinieæ*, and *Mimoseæ*. It contains the peas, beans, lentils, clover, vetches, indigo, etc.

le-gū-min-ō-ther′ȧ-py, *n.* [*Legumen*+*therapy*.] A scientific vegetable diet whereby the exact physiological and temperamental relations of each vegetable to the human system are carefully determined.

lē-gū′mi-nōse, *a.* Leguminous.

lē-gū′mi-nous, *a.* [L. *legumen* (*-inis*), any leguminous plant, pulse.]

1. Pertaining to or consisting of pulse.

2. In botany, having the seed contained in a legume.

lei, *n.*, pl. of *leu*.

lei′ġẽr, *n.* A ledger or resident envoy. [Obs.]

Lei-ō-phyl′lum, *n.* [Gr. *leios*, smooth, and *phyllon*, leaf.] A genus of the *Ericaceæ*, of which *Leiophyllum buxifolium*, the sand-myrtle, is the only known species.

lei-ot′ri-chăn, *a.* Relating to the Leiotrichi.

Lei-ot′ri-chī, *n.pl.* [Gr. *leios*, smooth, and *thrix, trichos*, hair.] Smooth-haired people; a division of mankind characterized by smoothness of the hair, the other division being *Ulotrichi*, crisp or woolly haired people.

lei-ot′ri-chous, *a.* Of or belonging to the Leiotrichi; having smooth hair.

lei-pō′ȧ, *n.* [Prob. from Gr. *leipein*, to leave, and *ōa*, pl. of *ōon*, an egg; also thought to be from native name.] The native pheasant of Western Australia, which does not sit on its eggs, but builds mounds of sand and weeds in which the eggs are hatched by the heat produced by decomposition of the weeds; called also *mound-bird*.

lei-pō-thym′iç, *a.* Same as *Lipothymic*.

leis′tẽr, lis′tẽr, *n.* [Ice. *ljóstr*, a salmon-spear.] A spear, generally three-pronged and barbed, for taking fish. [Scot.]

lei′ṣūr-ȧ-ble (-zhūr-), *a.* Leisure; leisurely. [Rare.]

lei′ṣūr-ȧ-bly, *adv.* At leisure. [Rare.]

lei′ṣūre (*or* lezh′ūr), *n.* [ME. *leiser, leyser*; OFr. *leisir*, leisure, permission, from *leisir*, L. *licere*, to be permitted.]

1. Freedom from occupation or business; idle time; time free from employment.

2. Time at one's disposal; convenience.

At leisure; disengaged; having spare time.

lei′ṣūre, *a.* Unoccupied; not employed in any necessary occupation; as, *leisure* moments.

lei′ṣūred, *a.* Having much leisure.

lei′ṣūre-ly, *a.* Not hasty; deliberate; slow.

lei′ṣūre-ly, *adv.* At leisure; deliberately; slowly.

leit′mō-tif″, *n.* [G., lit., leading motive.] In music, a distinguishing theme or melodic phrase indicating an idea, quality, sentiment, or person, as in the operas of Wagner.

lek′y-thŏs, *n.* [Gr. *lēkythos*, an oil-vase.] A lecythus or flask.

lē′măn, *n.* A sweetheart; a gallant or a mistress. [Obs.]

lēme, *n.* A leam or gleam. [Obs.]

lēme, *v.i.* To shine. [Obs.]

lem′mȧ, *n.*; *pl.* **lem′mȧ-tȧ.** [L., a theme, subject; Gr. *lēmma*, anything received, an assumption, from *lambanein*, to take, assume.]

1. In mathematics, a preliminary proposition demonstrated for the purpose of being used in the demonstration of some other proposition.

2. In logic, formerly, a premise, especially a hypothetical major premise.

3. A theme; a subject or thesis. [Rare.]

4. A membrane; a sheath, as that of the germinal vesicle; also used in composition; as, sarco*lemma*.

lem′ming, *n.* [Norw., prob. from *lemja*, to maim, strike, beat.] A rodent of the genus *Myodes* or of the genus *Cuniculus*. Those of Norway are about the size of a water-rat, those of Lapland and Siberia scarcely larger than a field-mouse. The common or European lemming is very prolific, and vast hordes periodically migrate from the mountains to the sea, destroying all vegetation in their path.

Common Lemming (*Myodes lemmus*).

Lem′nȧ, *n.* [Gr. *lemna*, a water-plant.] A genus of aquatic plants of the *Lemnaceæ* or duckweed tribe. They consist of small floating fronds, almost destitute of vascular tissue. The very minute flowers are produced from the edge of the frond. They are known by the common name of *duckmeat* or *duckweed*.

Lem-nā′cē-æ, *n.pl.* An order of monocotyledons, of which *Lemna* is the typical genus.

Lem′ni-ăn, *a.* [L. *Lemnius*; Gr. *Lēmnios*, Lemnian, from *Lēmnos*, the isle of Lemnos.] Of or relating to the isle of Lemnos.

Lemnian earth; sphragide or cimolite, a kind of astringent, medicinal earth, of a fatty consistence and reddish color; a kind of clay used as fuller's earth.

Lemnian ruddle; a kind of red chalk found in the isle of Lemnos.

lem-nis′ċāte, *n.* [L. *lemniscatus*, adorned with pendent ribbons, from *lemniscus*, a ribbon.] In geometry, the name of a curve in the form of the figure 8, forming the locus of the base of a perpendicular drawn from the center to the tangent to an equilateral hyperbola.

lem-nis′ċus, *n.*; *pl.* **lem-nis′ci.** [L., a ribbon adorning a victor's wreath; Gr. *lēmniskos*, a woolen fillet or band, from *lēnos*, wool.]

1. A various-colored woolen fillet or ribbon pendent at the back part of the head, from diadems, crowns, etc., and likewise attached to prizes as a mark of additional honor.

Ancient Lemniscus.

2. One of the minute ribbon-shaped appendages of the generative pores of some entozoans.

3. A band of longitudinal nerve-fibers at the base of the brain in the pons and crura; called also *fillet*.

lem′ŏn, *n.* [Fr. *limon*; LL. *limo* (*-onis*); Ar. *līmūn*, a lemon.]

1. The fruit of a tree belonging to the genus *Citrus*, which furnishes a cooling acid juice.

2. The tree that bears this fruit.

Essential salt of lemon; binoxalate of potash, used for removing ink-stains from linen.

lem-ŏn-āde′, *n.* A popular drink made of water, lemon juice, and sugar.

lem′ŏn-bird, *n.* The linnet. [Prov. Eng.]

lem′ŏn-grass, *n.* A fragrant East Indian grass, *Andropogon Schœnanthus*, and other allied species which yield a fragrant oil, used in perfumery.

lem′ŏn-juice, *n.* The juice of the lemon. It is somewhat opaque and extremely sour, owing its acidity to citric and malic acids.

lem′ŏn-squash, *n.* A drink of lemon-juice, sugar, and soda water. [Eng.]

lem′ŏn-vẽr-bē″nȧ, *n.* A shrub, *Lippia citriodora*, having leaves with an odor like that of a lemon.

lē′mūr, *n.* [L. *lemur*, found only in pl. *lemures*, ghost, specter; so called from its nocturnal habits.] One of a family of small, nocturnal, quadrumanous mammals, closely allied to monkeys, but somewhat resembling the fox in their elongated pointed head and sharp projecting muzzle. They inhabit Madagascar and the East Indian islands.

Red Lemur (*Lemur ruber*).

lem′ū-rēs̤, *n.pl.* [L.] In ancient Rome, the spirits of the evil dead or those who died an unnatural death and hence found no rest in the grave; ghosts; goblins.

Lē-mū′ri-ȧ, *n.* A continent in the Indian Ocean, thought to have existed formerly as the center from which the lemurs were distributed.

lem′ū-rid, *a.* and *n.* See *Lemuroid.*

lē-mū′ri-dous, lem′ū-rine, *a.* Lemuroid.

lem′ū-roid, *a.* Relating to or resembling lemurs; of or relating to the *Lemuroidea.*

lem′ū-roid, *n.* One of the *Lemuroidea.*

Lem-ū-roi′dē-ȧ, *n.pl.* A suborder of primates akin to the monkeys, and including lemurs, or *Prosimiæ.*

lē′nȧ, *n.* A procuress. [Obs.]

Lē-naī′ȧ, *n.pl.* [Gr. *Lēnaia*, from *lēnaios*, belonging to the wine-press, from *lēnos*, the wine-press.] One of a series of festivals in honor of Dionysus, celebrated at Athens in January and accompanied by orgies in which women were the principal participants.

lend, *v.t.*; lent, *pt.*, *pp.*; lending, *ppr.* [ME. *lenen*; AS. *lænan*, to lend, from *lan*, *læn*, a loan.]

1. To grant to another for temporary use, on the express or implied condition that the thing shall be returned, or its equivalent in kind; as, to *lend* a book, a sum of money, or a loaf of bread.

2. To grant for temporary use, on condition of receiving a compensation at certain periods for the use of the thing, and an ultimate return of the thing, or its full value; as, money is *lent* at interest.

3. To afford; to grant; to furnish, in general; as, to *lend* assistance; to *lend* an ear to a discourse.

lend, *v.i.* To grant a loan; to make a business of lending.

lend′ȧ-ble, *a.* That may be lent.

lend′ẽr, *n.* [ME. *lendare*, *lenere*; AS. *lænere*, a lender, from *lænan*, to lend.]

1. One who lends.

2. One who makes a trade of putting money to interest; a money-lender.

lend′ing, *n.* The act of loaning; a loan.

lends̤, *n.pl.* Loins. [Obs.]

lē′nē, *a.* [L. *lenis*, smooth.] Smooth; unaspirated, as a mute consonant.

lē′nē, *n.* The smooth breathing; any unaspirated consonant.

lēne, *v.t.* To lend. [Obs.]

length, *n.* [ME. *lengthe*; AS. *length*, length, from *lang*, long.]

1. The quality or condition of being long; as, the giraffe's neck is noted for its *length.*

2. Extension; extent of anything material from end to end; the distance from end to end of the principal axis of any figure; as, the *length* of a house, board, etc., as distinguished from *breadth* and *thickness.*

3. Distance along a line without reference to its position or space relations; linear extent; as, the *length* of a spiral; the *length* of a railway.

4. Duration; continuance; extent of time; as, the *length* of his visit; the *length* of a sound.

5. In orthoepy and prosody, (a) quantity; the time used in uttering a vowel or syllable; (b) the relative quality of a vowel as short or long in pronunciation; (c) in accented verse, the relative quality of a syllable as accented or unaccented.

6. In music, relative duration of a note as compared with a standard.

7. Reach; extent; power of range; as, the *length* of one's powers; at arm's *length*; what *lengths* of passion.

8. A portion of space; a certain extent; a thing, distance, or extent of time of known amount, used specifically as a measure; as, a *length* of hose; a *length* of fence; a race won by a *length* (of the horse, boat, etc., which was racing); in an actor's part, 42 lines is a *length*; in archery, the *length* is the space from archer to target; etc.

To go to all lengths; to use every means.

length, *v.t.* To lengthen. [Obs.]

length′en, *v.t.*; lengthened, *pt.*, *pp.*; lengthening, *ppr.* 1. To extend in length; to make longer; to elongate; as, to *lengthen* a line.

2. To draw out or extend in time; to protract; to continue in duration; as, to *lengthen* life.

3. To draw out in pronunciation; as, to *lengthen* a sound or a syllable.

length′en, *v.i.* To grow longer; to extend in length; as, the days *lengthen* with spring.

length′fụl, *a.* Of great length. [Obs.]

length′i-ly, *adv.* In a lengthy manner.

length′i-ness, *n.* The quality of being lengthy.

length′wāy̤s, *adv.* Same as *Lengthwise.*

length′wīṣe, *adv.* In the direction of the length.

length′y, *a.* Being long or immoderately long; not short; not brief; as, a *lengthy* sermon.

lē′ni-ence, *n.* Same as *Leniency.*

lē′ni-en-cy, *n.* Clemency; lenity.

lē′ni-ent, *n.* In medicine, an emollient; alenitive. [Obs.]

lē′ni-ent, *a.* [L. *leniens* (*-entis*), ppr. of *lenire*, to soften, alleviate, from *lenis*, soft, mild.]

1. Softening; assuasive; relaxing; emollient. [Rare.]

2. Indulgent; merciful; not severe or harsh; mild; as, a *lenient* disposition.

lē′ni-ent-ly, *adv.* In a lenient way.

len′i-fȳ, *v.t.* To assuage; to mitigate. [Obs.]

len′i-ment, *n.* A liniment; an alleviative. [Obs.]

len′i-tive, *a.* [L. *lenitus*, pp. of *lenire*, to soften, assuage.] Assuasive; emollient; palliative.

len′i-tive, *n.* 1. A medicine or application for easing pain; a laxative.

2. A palliative; that which abates passion.

len′i-tive-ness, *n.* Quality or state of being lenitive.

len′i-ty, *n.* [OFr. *lenite*; L. *lenitas* (*-atis*), smoothness, softness, from *lenis*, smooth, soft, mild.] Mildness of temper; softness; tenderness; mercy.

Len-nō-ā′cē-æ, *n.pl.* [Etym. unknown.] A family of fleshy parasitic plants, devoid of chlorophyl, having small flowers and two-celled fruit.

lē′nō, *n.* [Corruption of Fr. *linon*, lawn.] A thin cotton gauze used for window-shades, etc.

lē-noc′i-nănt, *a.* Given to lewdness. [Obs.]

lens̤, *n.* [L. *lens*, a lentil, which resembles a double-convex lens.]

1. A piece of glass or other transparent substance, having two surfaces, of which one at least is curved, usually spherical. The most common forms are those used for optical purposes to cause rays of light to converge or diverge. Other forms of radiant energy may be similarly affected by suitable devices, as electricity, by a lens of pitch or paraffin. Lenses are double-convex, or convex on both sides; double-concave, or concave on both sides; plano-convex or plano-concave, with one side plane and the other convex or concave; concavo-convex, or convex on one side and concave on the other. If the convexity be greater than the concavity, or if the two surfaces would meet if produced, the lens is called a *meniscus*; and if the concavity be greater than the convexity, the lens is termed *concavo-convex.*

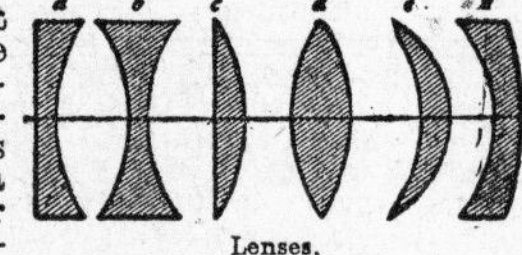

Lenses.
a, Plano-concave; *b*, Concavo-concave; *c*, Plano-convex; *d*, Convexo-convex; *e*, Meniscus; *f*, Concavo-convex.

2. Specifically, in anatomy, a double-convex body in the eye, behind the iris, serving to form images on the retina; the crystalline lens.

3. [L—] In botany, a genus of the *Leguminosæ*, of which the lentil is a species.

lens̤′-cap, *n.* A cover fitting into or over the end of the tube in which a lens is mounted.

lent, *v.*, past tense and past participle of *lend.*

lent, *a.* Slow; mild. [Obs.]

Lent, *n.* [ME. *lenten*; AS. *lencten*, the spring, from *lang*, long; so called from the lengthening of the days in the spring.] A fast of forty days, observed by the Roman Catholic and other churches in commemoration of the fast of Christ. It begins at Ash Wednesday and continues till Easter, Sundays not being included.

len-tä-men′te, *adv.* [It.] In music, slowly.

len-tän′dō, *a.* [It., ppr. of *lentare*, to make slow, from *lento*, L. *lentus*, slow, sluggish.] Rallentando; gradually becoming slower.

lent′en, *n.* Spring; Lent. [Obs.]

lent′en, *a.* Pertaining to Lent; used in Lent; sparing; as, a *lenten* entertainment.

lent′en-tide, *n.* The lenten season.

Len-tib-ū-lā-ri-ā′cē-æ, *n.pl.* [L. *lens*, *lentis*, a lentil, and *tubulus*, a small pipe.] A small order of aquatic or subaquatic herbs; the bladderworts.

len′ti-cel, *n.* [Fr. *lenticelle*, dim. of *lenticule*, lens-shaped, from L. *lens*, *lentis*, lentil.]

1. In botany, a lenticular cluster of cells in the periderm of plants, considered a breathing pore.

2. A lenticular gland.

len-ti-cel′lāte, *a.* Having lenticels.

len-ti-celle′, *n.* [Fr.] A lenticel.

len-tiç′ū-lȧ, *n.*; *pl.* **len-tiç′ū-læ.** [L. *lenticula*, a lentil, a vessel shaped like a lentil, a freckle, from *lens*, *lentis*, a lentil.]

1. In pathology, a freckle.

2. In optics, a small-sized lens.

3. In botany, a lenticel.

len-tiç′ū-lăr, *a.* [L. *lenticularis*, from *lenticula*, a lentil.] Resembling a lentil; having the form of a double-convex lens; lentiform.

len-tiç′ū-lăr-ly, *adv.* With a curve; like a lens.

len′ti-fọrm, *a.* [L. *lens*, *lentis*, a lentil, and *forma*, form.] Of the form of a double-convex lens.

len-tiġ′i-nōse, *a.* [LL. *lentiginosus*, freckled, from L. *lentigo* (*-inis*), a freckly eruption, from *lens*, *lentis*, a lentil.] Speckled with dots like freckles.

len-tiġ′i-nous, *a.* Lentiginose.

len-tī′gō, *n.* [L., a spot like a lentil, a freckle, from *lens*, *lentis*, a lentil.] A freckle.

len′til, *n.* [ME. *lentil*; OFr. *lentille*; L. *lenticula*, dim. of *lens*, *lentis*, a lentil.]

1. An annual plant, *Lens esculenta*, belonging to the papilionaceous division of the order *Leguminosæ*. It is an annual plant, rising with weak stalks about eighteen inches. The seeds, which are contained in a pod, are round, flat, and a little convex in the middle. It is cultivated for fodder and for its seeds.

2. In the rectifying of alcohol, a lens-shaped bulb in the condenser.

len′tille, *n.* [Fr.] A lens-shaped rock-mass.

len′tisk, len-tis′çus, *n.* [ME. *lentiske*; L. *lentiscus*, or *lentiscum*, the mastic-tree.] The mastic-tree.

len′ti-tūde, *n.* Slowness. [Obs.]

len′tō, *a.* and *adv.* [It.] In music, slow; slowly.

len′toid, *a.* [L. *lens*, *lentis*, a lentil, and Gr. *eidos*, form.] Shaped like a lentil or double-convex lens.

len′tŏr, len′tŏur, *n.* 1. Tenacity; viscosity. [Obs.]

2. Slowness; delay; sluggishness. [Obs.]

len′tous, *a.* Viscid; viscous; tenacious. [Obs.]

l'en-voy′, l'en-voi′ (len- *or Fr. pron.* loṅ-vwä′), *n.* [OFr., lit., the sending; *le*, the, and *envoi*, a sending.]

1. A few detached words or verses at the end of a piece, to convey the moral, or to address the poem to a particular person.

2. An ending; a consequence.

Lē′ō, *n.* [L., a lion, the constellation Leo.]

1. In astronomy, the fifth sign of the zodiac.

2. A constellation east of Cancer in which is the bright star Regulus.

Leo Minor; a constellation smaller than Leo, between it and the Great Bear.

lē′od, *n.* People; a nation. [Obs.]

lē′ŏn, *n.* A lion. [Obs.]

lē′ŏnced (-ŏnst), *a.* In heraldry, same as *lionced.*

Lē-ō-nēse′ (*or* -nēz′), *a.* [Sp. *Leonés*, from *León*, Leon.] Pertaining to Leon, a province in Spain.

Lē-ō-nese′, *n. sing.* and *pl.* A person or persons born or living in Leon.

Lē′ō-nid, *n.*; *pl.* **Lē-on′i-dēs̤.** One of a group of meteors observed in the month of November each year, but occurring with extreme profusion about three times in a century; so called because they seem to radiate from the constellation Leo.

lē′ō-nine (*or* -nīne), *n.* A counterfeit copper coin of the reign of Edward I., worth about a halfpenny, coined abroad and smuggled into England; so called from bearing the figure of a lion.

lē′ō-nine, *a.* [OFr. *leonin*; L. *leoninus*, like a lion, from *leo* (*-onis*), a lion.]

1. Belonging to or resembling a lion, or partaking of his qualities; as, *leonine* fierceness or rapacity.

2. Consisting of hexameters or of hexameters and pentameters in which the final syllable rimes with one in the middle of the line.

lē′ō-nine-ly, *adv.* In the manner of a lion.

lē-on-ti′ȧ-sis, *n.* [Gr., from *leōn* (*-ontos*), a lion, and *-iasis.*] A variety of leprosy or elephantiasis in which the head and face resemble those of a lion.

Lē-on′ti-cē, *n.* [L., the wild chervil; Gr. *leontikē*, the coltsfoot, from *leōn* (*-ontos*), a lion.] A genus of herbs of the barberry family, native to Asia.

Lē-on′tō-don, *n.* [Gr. *leōn* (*-ontos*), a lion, and *odous*, *odontos*, tooth.] A genus of the *Compositæ. Leontodon autumnale* is the fall dandelion.

Lē-on-tō-pō′di-um, *n.* [Gr. *leōn* (*-ontos*), a lion, and *pous*, *podos*, foot.] A genus of the *Compositæ*, including the edelweiss.

Leopard (*Felis pardus*).

leop′ărd (lep′), *n.* [ME. *lepard*,

lepart, leopard; OFr. *leopard*; L. *leopardus*; Gr. *leopardos* or *leontopardos*, the leopard; *leōn* (*-ontos*), a lion, and *pardos*, a pard, panther.]

1. A carnivorous mammal, *Felis pardus*, the pard or panther. Its color is a yellowish fawn with clusters of small black spots on head, back, and sides, merging into white below the body. There is also a black variety.

2. Any similar animal, as the chetah or hunting-leopard; the jaguar; the cougar, etc.

3. A gold coin of Edward III. of England, intended for use in France, and having on one side a lion leopardé.

leop′ărd=çat, *n.* A small spotted cat of Asia, Africa, and the East Indies; also, the ocelot of America.

leop-ăr-dé′ (-dā′), *a.* [Fr.] In heraldry, passant gardant.

leop′ărd-ess, *n.* A female leopard.

leop′ărd=fish, *n.* The lesser wolf-fish.

leop′ărd=flow″ẽr, *n.* A Chinese plant.

leop′ărd=frog, *n.* The common frog of America.

leop′ărd=mär″mot, *n.* A gopher or spermophile.

leop′ărd=moth, *n.* A common spotted moth, *Zeuzera pyrina*, of Europe.

leop′ărd-wood, *n.* The spotted wood of *Brosimum Aubletii*, a tropical tree; called also *snakewood* and *letterwood*.

lep, *v.*, obsolete past tense of *leap*.

lep′ȧ-dīte, *n.* [Gr. *lepas* (*-ados*), a limpet, and *-ite*.] An aptychus.

lep′ȧ-doid, *n.* [Gr. *lepas* (*-ados*), a limpet, and *eidos*, form.] A goose-mussel.

lep′ăl, *n.* [L. *lepis*; Gr. *lepis*, a scale.] A sterile stamen transformed into a scale.

Lē′pas, *n.* [L. *lepas* (*-adis*); Gr. *lepas* (*-ados*), a limpet, from *lepas*, a bare rock.] A genus of cirripeds of which the barnacle, *Lepas anatifera*, is an example.

lep′ẽr, *n.* [ME. *lepre*; OFr. *liepre*; L. *lepra* or *lepræ*; Gr. *lepra*, leprosy, from *lepros*, rough, scaly; *lepos*, a scale, from *lepein*, to peel or bark.] One affected with leprosy.

lep′ẽred (-ẽrd), *a.* Stricken with leprosy.

lep′ẽr-īze, *v.t.* To taint with leprosy.

lep′ẽr-ous, *a.* Same as *Leprous*.

lep′id, *a.* Pleasant; jocose. [Obs.]

lep′i-dīne, *n.* [*Lepidium* and *-ine*.] An oily compound obtained by distilling cinchonine.

Lē-pid′i-um, *n.* [L. *lepidium*, from Gr. *lepidion*, a plant, prob. pepperwort, dim. of *lepis* (*-idos*), a scale; so called from the form of the little pouches.] A genus of plants of the mustard family; the peppergrasses.

lepido-. A combining form from Gr. *lepis* (*-idos*), a scale, husk, used in botany, zoölogy, etc., to signify scaly; as, *lepido*dendron, *lepido*siren.

lep″i-dō-den′droid, *a.* [*Lepido-*, and Gr. *dendron*, a tree, and *eidos*, form.] Pertaining to lepidodendrons.

lep″i-dō-den′drŏn, *n.* [*Lepido-*, and Gr. *dendron*, a tree.] A fossil tree of the genus *Lepidodendron*, occurring in the coal formations; so named from the scaly appearance of the stem, produced by the separation of the leaf stalks.

lep″i-dō-gā′noid, *n.* [*Lepido-*, and Gr. *ganos*, brightness, and *eidos*, form.] One of an order of ganoid fishes with scales.

lep′i-dō-līte, *n.* [*Lepido-*, and Gr. *lithos*, stone.] A species of mica presenting a lilac or rose-violet color; it usually occurs in masses consisting of small scales.

lep-i-dom′ē-lāne, *n.* [*Lepido-*, and Gr. *melas* (*-anos*), black.] A scaly black iron-potash mica.

lep-i-dop′tẽr, *n.* One of the *Lepidoptera*.

Lep-i-dop′tē-rȧ, *n.pl.* [*Lepido-*, and Gr. *pteron*, a wing.] An order of insects having four membranaceous wings, covered with fine imbricate scales, like powder, as the butterfly.

Lepidoptera.

1. Butterfly — *Hipparchia galathea*, marbled white butterfly. 2. Hawk-moth or sphinx—*Macroglossa stellatarum*, humming-bird hawk-moth. 3. Moth—*Abraxas grossulariata*, magpie-moth. 4. Palpi and spiral mouth of butterfly. 5. Antennæ—*a*, Butterfly's; *b*, Sphinx's; *c*, Moth's. 6. Portion of wing of cabbage-butterfly, with part of the scales removed. 7. Scales of do. magnified.

lep-i-dop′tẽr-ist, *n.* A student of the *Lepidoptera*.

lep-i-dop′tẽr-ous, *a.* Belonging to the order of *Lepidoptera*.

Lep″i-dō-sau′ri-ȧ, *n.pl.* [*Lepido-*, and Gr. *sauros*, a lizard.] A group of reptiles among which are serpents and lizards.

lep″i-dō-sī′ren, *n.* [*Lepido-*, and L. *siren*; Gr. *seirēn*, a siren.] An eel-like fish with both gills and lungs, found in Africa and South America.

lep′i-dōte, lep′i-dō-ted, *a.* [Gr. *lepidōtos*, covered with scales, from *lepidoun*, to make scaly, from *lepis* (*-idos*), a scale.] With a coat of scurfy scales.

Lepidosiren Annectens.

Le-pis′mȧ, *n.* [Gr. *lepisma*, peel, anything peeled off, from *lepizein*, to husk, peel, from *lepis* (*-idos*), a husk scale.] A genus of insects with a long, flat body covered with scales; the bristletails.

le-pis′moid, *a.* [Gr. *lepisma*, peel, and *eidos*, appearance.] Relating to the *Lepisma*.

lep′ō-cȳte, le-poc′y-tȧ, *n.* [Gr. *lepos*, a husk, scale, and *kytos*, a hollow.] An organism with a cell-membrane.

lep′ō-rīne (*or* rin), *a.* [L. *leporinus*, from *lepus* (*-oris*), a hare.] Pertaining to or having the qualities of the hare.

lē′prȧ, *n.* [L., from Gr. *lepra*, leprosy.] Leprosy.

lep′rōse, *a.* Having scurfy or leprous scales.

lē-pros′i-ty, *n.* The condition of being leprous.

lep′rō-sy, *n.* [OFr. *leprosie*; L.Gr. *leprōsis*; Gr. *lepra*, leprosy, from *lepros*, scaly, from *lepos*, a scale, from *lepein*, to peel, strip.] A foul cutaneous disease, appearing in dry, white, thin, scurfy scabs, attended with violent itching. It sometimes covers the whole body. One species of it is called *elephantiasis*.

lep′rous, *a.* [OFr. *leprous, lepros*; LL. *leprosus*, from L. *lepra*; Gr. *lepra*, leprosy.]

1. Infected with or pertaining to leprosy.

2. Covered with scales; leprose.

lep′rous-ly, *adv.* In a leprous manner.

lep′rous-ness, *n.* The state of being leprous.

lep′ry, *n.* Leprosy. [Obs.]

lep-tan′drȧ, *n.* [Gr. *leptos*, fine, delicate, and *anēr*, *andros*, man, male.] The rhizome of *Veronica Virginica*.

lep-tan′drin, *n.* [*Leptandra* and *-in*.] A glucoside derived from leptandra, having cathartic properties.

lep′ti-form, *a.* [Gr. *leptos*, fine, delicate, and L. *forma*, form.] Shaped like a leptus.

lepto-. A combining form from Gr. *leptos*, thin, fine, small, used in botany, zoölogy, etc., to signify thin, fine, narrow; as, *lepto*cephaly, *lepto*meninx.

Lep-tō-căr′di-ȧ, *n.pl.* Same as *Leptocardii*.

lep-tō-căr′di-ăn, *a.* Of or like the *Leptocardii*.

Lep-tō-căr′di-ī, *n.pl.* [*Lepto-*, and Gr. *kardia*, heart.] A group of *Vertebrata* in which skull, brain, heart, limbs, and jaws are wanting. The blood is colorless, the mouth longitudinal, and the notochord persistent in place of a backbone. There are about six known species, including *Amphioxus*.

lep″tō-cē-phal′iç, *a.* Characterized by leptocephaly.

lep-tō-ceph′ȧ-ly, *n.* [*Lepto-*, and Gr. *kephalē*, head.] Extreme narrowness of skull.

lep-tō-daç′tyl, *a.* and *n.* [*Lepto-*, and Gr. *daktylos*, finger or toe.]

I. *a.* Having slim fingers or toes.

II. *n.* An animal having slim fingers or toes.

lep-tō-daç′tyl-ous, *a.* Leptodactyl.

lep-tol′ō-ġy, *n.* [Gr. *leptologia*, minute description, quibbling; *leptos*, fine, and *-logia*, from *legein*, to speak.] A minute and tedious discourse on trifling things.

lep′tōme, *n.* [Gr. *leptos*, fine, thin, slender.] The fibrous portion or phloem of a fibrovascular bundle.

lep″tō-mē-nin′ġēş, *n.pl.* [*Lepto-*, and Gr. *mēninx*, *mēningos*, a membrane.] In anatomy, the arachnoid and the pia mater.

lep-tō-men-in-ġī′tis, *n.* Inflammation of the leptomeninx.

lep-tō-mē′ninx, *n.*; *pl.* **lep″tō-mē-nin′ġēş.** [*Lepto-*, and Gr. *mēninx*, *mēningos*, a membrane.] The pia mater or the arachnoid or both.

lep′ton, *n.*; *pl.* **lep′tȧ.** [Gr. *lepton*, a small coin, properly neut. of *leptos*, thin, fine, small.]

1. An ancient Greek coin of small value.

2. A modern Greek copper coin worth about one-fifth of a cent.

lep′tō-rhīne (-rīn *or* -rin), *a.* [*Lepto-*, and Gr. *rhis*, *rhinos*, nose.] With narrow nasal bones.

Lep-tō-spẽr′mum, *n.* [*Lepto-*, and Gr. *sperma*, seed.] A genus of the *Myrtaceæ*, having about twenty-five species, mostly Australian.

lep″tō-spō-ran′ġi-āte, *a.* [*Lepto-*, and Gr. *spora*, a seed, and *angeion*, a vessel.] Having sporangia which are each developed from a single cell of the epidermis, as in most ferns.

Lep-tos′trȧ-çȧ, *n.pl.* [*Lepto-*, and Gr. *ostrakon*, a shell.] An order of bivalve crustaceans including the genus *Nebalia*.

lep′tō-thrix, *n.* [*Lepto-*, and Gr. *thrix*, hair.] A bacterium in which the slender, hairlike cells continue joined end to end after fission.

lep′tus, *n.* [Gr. *leptos*, thin, fine, slender, delicate.] A form of larva having six legs, as in the harvest-mites.

lep′ty-nīte, *n.* [Gr. *leptynein*, to make thin, from *leptos*, thin, slender, and *-ite*.] Granulite, a granular rock.

lēre, *n.* Learning; lesson; lore. [Obs.]

lēre, *v.t.* and *v.i.* To learn; to teach. [Obs.]

lēre, *a.* Empty. [Obs.]

lēre, *n.* Skin; flesh. [Obs.]

lēr′ed, *a.* Learned. [Obs.]

Lẽr-næ′ȧ, *n.* [L., f. of *Lernæus*; Gr. *Lernaios*, Lernæan, from *Lerna* or *Lernē*, Lerne, a district in Argolis; so called in reference to the Lernæan hydra.] A genus of parasitic suctorial crustaceans; the typical genus of the fish-lice family.

lẽr-næ′ăn, lẽr-nē′ăn, *n.* A member of the *Lernæa* or of the *Lernæidæ*, minute crustaceans parasitic on fishes.

lẽr-næ′oid, *a.* Resembling the lernæans.

lē′rōt, *n.* [Fr.] The garden-dormouse.

lẽrp, *n.* [Australian.] A sweet secretion of a kind of plant-louse found on certain eucalyptus leaves.

les, *n.* A leash. [Obs.]

Les′bi-ăn, *a.* [L. *Lesbius*; Gr. *Lesbios*, from *Lesbos*, the isle of Lesbos.]

1. Belonging or pertaining to Lesbos, the ancient name of an island in the Ægean sea, now called Mytilene.

2. [l—] Erotic; debauched; in reference to the character of the people and their poetry.

lēşe, *v.t.* To loose; to release. [Obs.]

lēşe′=maj′es-ty, *n.* [Fr. *lèse-majesté*; LL. *læsa majestas*, high treason; L. *læsa*, f. of *læsus*, pp. of *lædere*, to hurt, injure, and *majestas*, majesty.] Treason.

lē′şion, *n.* [Fr. *lésion*; L. *læsio* (*-onis*), a hurt, injury, from *læsus*, pp. of *lædere*, to harm, injure.]

1. A hurt, wound, or injury.

2. In medicine, a morbid alteration in structure or function of any organ or tissue.

3. In civil law, an injury sustained by one who fails to receive a just equivalent for what he has given in a contract.

less, *a.*, comp. of *little*. [ME. *lesse*, *lasse*; AS. *læssa*, smaller, inferior, less.] Smaller; inferior; not so large, so much, or so great; as, *less* in size or value; this is *less* than that. Frequently the qualified noun is omitted; as, some had more, some *less* (goods, etc.).

less, *adv.* [ME. *lesse*, *les*; AS. *læs*, less.] Not so much; in a smaller or lower degree; as, *less* bright; *less* careful.

less, *v.t.* To make less. [Obs.]

less, *conj.* Unless. [Obs.]

-less. [ME. *-les*, *-leas*; AS. *-leās*, from *leās*, free, loose.] A suffix used to form, from nouns, adjectives signifying without or devoid of the quality denoted by the noun to which it is added; as, love*less*, law*less*, head*less*, etc.

les-see′, *n.* [OFr. *lessé*, pp. of *lesser*, to let, from L. *laxare*, to loosen.] The person to whom a lease is given, or who takes an estate by lease.

less′en, *v.t.*; lessened, *pt.*, *pp.*; lessening, *ppr.*

1. To make less; to diminish; to reduce in bulk, size, quantity, number, or amount; to make smaller; as, to *lessen* a kingdom or its population.

2. To diminish in degree, state, or quality; as, awkward manners tend to *lessen* our respect for men.

3. To degrade; to reduce in dignity.

less′en, *v.i.* 1. To become less; to shrink; to contract in bulk, quantity, number, or amount; to be diminished; as, the apparent magnitude of objects *lessens* as we recede from them.

2. To become less in degree, quality, or intensity; to decrease.

less′en-ẽr, *n.* One who or that which makes less.

less′ẽr, *a.* Less; smaller; minor; as, the *lesser* prophets.

less′ẽr, *adv.* Less. [Obs.]

les′seş, *n.pl.* The dung of the wild boar, bear, or wolf. [Obs.]

les′sŏn, *n.* [ME. *lessoun*; OFr. *leçon*, a lesson, from L. *lectio* (*-onis*), a reading, from *lectus*, pp. of *legere*, to read.]

1. Anything read or recited to a teacher by a pupil or learner, or such a portion of a book or the like as is assigned by a preceptor to a pupil to be learned at one time; something to be learned.

2. Instruction conveyed to a pupil at one time; as, to receive twelve *lessons* in music; a half-hour *lesson* on the piano.

3. Anything learned or that may be learned from experience; doctrine; precept; moral.

4. A portion of Scripture read in divine service; as, here endeth the first *lesson*.

5. Severe lecture; reproof; rebuke.

6. A musical composition written as an exercise for an instrument; exercise; étude.

les′sŏn, *v.t.*; lessoned, *pt.*, *pp.*; lessoning, *ppr.* To teach; to instruct.

les′sŏr, *n.* [OFr., from *lesser*, to lease.] One who leases; the person who lets to a tenant or gives a lease.

lest, *conj.* [ME. *leste*, *les the*, lest; AS. *thy læs the*,

the less that; *thy*, instrumental of *thæt*, the, that, and *læs*, less, and *the*, that, conj.]

1. That . . . not; in order that . . . not; as, take care *lest* you stumble; that is, take heed *that* you stumble *not*.

2. That; for fear that; with expressions indicating fear or anxiety; as, she worried *lest* he should forget.

lest, *n.* Lust; desire. [Obs.]

lest, *v.i.* To listen. [Obs.]

lest, *a.* Least; last. [Obs.]

-let. [OFr. *-let*, masc., *-lette*, f., dim.; *-el*, from L. *-ellus*, and *-et*.] A suffix forming derivatives from French and English nouns, with a diminutive force; as, rivu*let*, brace*let*, stream*let*.

let, *n.* 1. A hindrance; obstacle; impediment; delay; used commonly only in the phrase, *without let or hindrance*.

2. In lawn tennis, a stroke, as in serving, in which the ball touches the net in going over.

let, *v.i.* To forbear; to delay; to hinder. [Obs.]

let, *v.t.* [ME. *letten*; AS. *lettan*, to delay, hinder, from *læt*, late, slow.] To retard; to hinder; to impede. [Obs.]

let, *v.t.*; let, *pt.*, *pp.*; letting, *ppr.* [ME. *leten*, *laten*; AS. *lætan*, to let, allow, permit.]

1. To permit; to allow; to suffer; to give leave or power to by a positive act, or negatively, to withhold restraint from; not to prevent; followed by the infinitive without *to*, or by expressions in which the verb is entirely omitted; as, *let* me pass; *let* water (flow) into the tank; *let* me (be or act) alone.

2. In the imperative, followed by the infinitive without *to*, it expresses (a) with the first person plural, exhortation or entreaty; as, *let* us go; (b) with the third person, permission, concession, desire, or command; as, *let* him go; *let* them understand the order.

3. To lease; to grant possession and use for a compensation; as, to *let* an estate for a year; to *let* a room; often followed by *out*; as, to *let out* a farm.

4. To cause; to make; followed by the infinitive without *to*; as, he *let* the arrow fly; *let* make a feast; *let* cry after him; *let* do tell. [Rare.]

Let her go, let her rip; allow it to go or continue regardless of consequences. [Slang.]

To let blood; to cause to bleed.

To let down; (a) to lower; to permit to descend; (b) to allow to be withdrawn, as milk; said of a cow; (c) to soften the temper of, as steel.

To let in; (a) to admit; (b) to swindle; to cheat; (c) to inlay or insert, as a piece into a place prepared.

To let out; (a) to suffer to escape, as an animal; (b) to extend or loosen, as the folds of a garment; (c) to lease or let for hire; (d) to divulge, as a secret.

let, *v.i.* 1. To be leased; as, the flats *let* quickly.

2. To allow to be done, or to occur; in phrases.

To let on; (a) to tell; to divulge; as, never *let on*; (b) to pretend; to feign. [Colloq.]

To let up; to abate; to cease; as, the rain will soon *let up*. [Colloq.]

letch, *n.* A leach; a leach-tub.

letch, *v.t.* and *v.i.* Same as *Leach*.

letch, *n.* Passion; ardent desire. [Obs. or Prov. Eng.]

letch'y, *a.* Leachy; porous. [Obs.]

lete, *v.t.* To let or leave. [Obs.]

let'en, *v.*, obsolete past participle of *let*.

lē'thăl, *a.* [L. *letalis* or *lethalis*, from *letum* or *lethum*, death.] Deadly; mortal; fatal.

leth'ăl, *n.* [Lauric, *eth*er, and *al*cohol.] A white, crystalline higher alcohol derived from spermaceti.

lē-thal'i-ty, *n.* Mortality. [Rare.]

lē-thär'gic, lē-thär'gic-ăl, *a.* [L. *lethargicus*; Gr. *lēthargikos*, drowsy, slothful, from *lēthargos*, forgetful, from *lēthē*, forgetfulness.] Relating to, like, causing, or subject to lethargy; drowsy; dull; heavy; apathetic.

lē-thär'gic-ăl-ly, *adv.* In a lethargic manner.

lē-thär'gic-ăl-ness, lē-thär'gic-ness, *n.* Sluggishness.

leth'ăr-gize, *v.t.* To cause to be lethargic. [Rare.]

leth'ăr-gy, *n.* [ME. *letharge*; OFr. *letharge*; LL. *lethargia*; Gr. *lēthargia*, sleepiness, from *lēthargos*, forgetful; *lēthē*, forgetfulness, and *algos*, pain.]

1. Preternatural sleepiness; morbid drowsiness; continued or profound sleep, from which a person can scarcely be awakened; stupor; torpor.

2. Dullness; inaction; inattention; apathy.

leth'ăr-gy, *v.t.* To lethargize. [Obs.]

Lē'thē, *n.* [L., from Gr. *lēthē*, forgetfulness, oblivion.]

1. In Greek mythology, oblivion personified as the daughter of Eris.

2. In later mythology, one of the rivers of the lower world, whose waters caused those who drank of them to forget all their former life.

3. Oblivion; a draught causing oblivion.

4. Death. [Obs.]

Lē-thē'ăn, *a.* [L. *Lethæus*; Gr. *Lēthaios*, from *lēthē*, oblivion.] Of or like the waters of Lethe; inducing forgetfulness.

Lē'thē'd, *a.* Lethean; as if caused by Lethe. [Obs.]

lē"thē-ō-mā'ni-ȧ, *n.* [Gr. *lēthē*, forgetfulness, and *mania*, madness.] A mania for narcotics. [Rare.]

lē'thē-ŏn, *n.* Ethyl ether, used as an anæsthetic. [Obs.]

lē'thē-ŏn-ize, *v.t.* To anæsthetize with letheon. [Obs.]

lē-thif'ẽr-ous, *a.* Deadly; mortal; bringing death or destruction. [Obs.]

lē'thy, *a.* Lethean. [Obs.]

let'-off, *n.* A releasing device, especially that in a loom to let off the warp from the beam.

Lett, *n.* [Lettic *Latvi.*] A member of a division of the Lithuanian people who dwell in the western provinces of Russia.

let'ten, *a.* In law, leased; demised.

let'tẽr, *n.* One who lets, in any sense.

let'tẽr, *v.t.*; lettered, *pt.*, *pp.*; lettering, *ppr.* To inscribe, engrave, print, or otherwise form letters upon; to place an inscription upon.

let'tẽr, *n.* [ME. *lettre*, *letre*; OFr. *lettre*; L. *littera*, a letter of the alphabet, in pl. a letter, epistle.]

1. A mark or character used as the representative of a sound or of an articulation of the human organs of speech; one of the first elements of written language; one of the characters of an alphabet.

2. In printing, a type representing such a character; hence, collectively, type; also, a style of type face; as, a Gothic *letter*.

3. A written or printed message; an epistle; a communication made by visible characters from one person to another at a distance.

4. The exact or literal meaning; as, the *letter* of the law.

5. [*pl.*] Learning; erudition; literature; as, a man of *letters*; the field of *letters*.

6. [*pl.*] An official document granting certain rights or powers; as, *letters* patent; sometimes also in the singular; as, *letter* of attorney.

let'tẽr-căr"ri-ẽr, *n.* One who collects and delivers mail; a postman.

let'tẽred, *a.* 1. Literate; educated; versed in literature or science.

2. Belonging to learning; suiting letters.

3. Bearing an inscription or letters.

let'tẽr-ẽr, *n.* One who letters.

let'tẽr-found"ẽr, *n.* A type-founder.

let'tẽr-gram, *n.* A telegram of more than ordinary ten-word length, which is now sent at special rates.

let'tẽr-head (-hed), *n.* A heading printed on a sheet of paper for letters; also, a sheet with such a printed form.

let'tẽr-ing, *n.* 1. The act of impressing or marking with letters.

2. The letters impressed or marked; an inscription.

let'tẽr-less, *a.* Illiterate; unlettered.

let'tẽrn, *n.* Same as *Lectern*.

let'tẽr-pẽr"fect, *a.* Perfect to the letter in memorizing; said especially of actors.

let'tẽr-press, *n.* and *a.* I. *n.* Print; text; printed letters and words, as distinguished from illustrations.

II. *a.* Printed from type in contrast to matter printed from plates; as, *letterpress* printing.

let'tẽr-press, *n.* A press used to copy letters.

let'tẽr-ūre, *n.* Literature; scripture. [Obs.]

let'tẽr-wood, *n.* Same as *Leopardwood*.

let'tẽr-writ"ẽr, *n.* 1. One who writes letters; especially, one who makes a business of so doing.

2. A book giving forms and instructions for writing various kinds of letters

Let'tic, *n.* and *a.* I. *n.* Same as *Lettish*.

II. *a.* Of, pertaining to, or related to the Letts.

Let'tish, *a.* and *n.* I. *a.* Relating to the Letts as distinguished from other Lithuanians.

II. *n.* The language of the Letts, a branch of the Aryan family of languages closely allied to the Slavonic.

let'trūre, *n.* Literature. [Obs.]

lett'sŏm-ite, *n.* See *Cyanotrichite*.

let'tuce (-is), *n.* [ME. *letuce*; L. *lactuca*, lettuce, from *lac*, *lactis*, milk; so called from its milky juice.] The popular name of several species of *Lactuca*, some of which are used as salads. *Lactuca sativa* is the common salad lettuce; *Lactuca Scariola* is thought to be the variety from which the cultivated varieties are derived.

let'tuce-bīrd, *n.* The American goldfinch.

let'ū-ā-ry, *n.* An electuary. [Obs.]

let'-up, *n.* Cessation; intermission; as, there was no *let-up* to the pain. [Colloq.]

leu (lā), *n.*; *pl.* **lei** (lē). [Rumanian.] A Rumanian silver coin worth about nineteen United States cents.

leuc-. A combining form signifying white. [See *Leuco-*.]

Leū-cȧ-den'drŏn, *n.* [*Leuc-*, and Gr. *dendron*, tree.] A South African genus of shrubs and trees. *Leucadendron argenteum*, which has beautiful, silky, silvery leaves, is the silver-tree or witteboom of Cape Town.

leū-căn'i-line, *n.* [*Leuc-*, and Ar. *an-nīl*, *al-nīl*, the indigo-plant.] A white, crystalline coal-tar derivative yielding rosaniline when oxidized.

leū-cē'mi-ȧ, leū-cæ'mi-ȧ, *n.* [*Leuc-*, and Gr. *haima*, blood.] A disease marked by a great increase in the proportion of white blood-corpuscles, with enlargement of the spleen.

leū-chæ'mi-ȧ, *n.* Same as *Leucemia*.

leū'cic, *a.* Relating to or derived from leucin.

leū'cin, *n.* [Gr. *leukos*, white, and *-in*.] A white, crystalline compound occurring as a product of decomposition of animal substances, also during the pancreatic digestion of albuminoids.

leū'cīte, *n.* [Gr. *leukos*, white, and *-ite*.]

1. A mineral found in the volcanic rocks of Italy. It is a vitreous, crystalline silicate of potassium and aluminium.

2. In botany, same as *leucoplast*.

leū-cit'ic, *a.* Of or like leucite.

leū'ci-toid, *n.* [Gr. *leukos*, white, and *eidos*, form.] An icositetrahedron or trapezohedron; named from the crystalline form of leucite.

leuco-, leuc-. Combining forms from Gr. *leukos*, white, used in medicine, chemistry, botany, etc., to signify white or colorless, as *leucocyte*, *leucemia*.

leū'cō-blast, *n.* [*Leuco-*, and Gr. *blastos*, a bud, germ.] The germ-cell of a leucocyte.

leū'cō-cȳte, *n.* [*Leuco-*, and Gr. *kytos*, hollow.] A colorless, nucleated protoplasmic mass found in the blood, lymph, marrow, and other tissues, as the white blood-corpuscles; a phagocyte.

leū"cō-cy-thē'mi-ȧ, leū"cō-cy-thæ'mi-ȧ, *n.* Same as *Leucemia*.

leū-cō-cy-tō-gen'e-sis, *n.* [*Leuco-*, and Gr. *kytos*, a hollow, and *genesis*, generation.] The origin and growth of leucocytes.

leū"cō-cy-tō'sis, *n.* [*Leuco-*, and Gr. *kytos*, a hollow, and *-osis*.] A temporary increase in the quantity of white blood-corpuscles in the blood.

leū-cō-dẽr'mi-ȧ, leū-cō-dẽr'mȧ, *n.* [*Leuco-*, and Gr. *derma*, skin.] Deficiency of pigment in the skin; albinism.

leū-cō-ē-thi-op'ic, *a.* White and black; designating a white animal of a black species, or the albino of the negro race.

leū-cō-ē'thi-ops, *n.* [*Leuco-*, and Gr. *Aithiops*, an Ethiop, a negro.] An albino.

leū-cō'mȧ, *n.* [Gr. *leukōma*, anything whitened, a white spot in the eye, from *leukoun*, to whiten, from *leukos*, white.] A whitish cloudiness of the cornea.

leū-con'ic, *a.* [*Leuc-* and *croconic*.] Of or designating a whitish acid derivative of croconic acid.

leū-cō-nos'toc, *n.* [*Leuco-*, and G. *nostoch*, nostoc.] A form of bacterium characterized by the production of gelatinous masses.

leū-cop'ȧ-thy, *n.* [*Leuco-*, and Gr. *pathos*, affection.] Albinism; also, chlorosis.

leū'cō-phāne, *n.* [L.Gr. *leukophanēs*, of white or bright appearance; Gr. *leukos*, white, and *-phanēs*, from *phainesthai*, to appear.] A greenish-yellow fluosilicate of calcium, sodium, and beryllium.

leū-cō-phleg'mȧ-cy, *n.* [Gr. *leukophlegmatia*, the dropsy; *leukos*, white, and *phlegma*, phlegm.] A tendency to a dropsical condition.

leū"cō-phleg-mat'ic, *a.* Affected with leucophlegmacy.

leū'cō-phyl, *n.* [*Leuco-*, and Gr. *phyllon*, leaf.] A substance in the leaves of etiolated plants, which may become chlorophyl under the action of light.

leū-coph'yl-lous, *a.* Having white foliage.

leū'cō-plast, leū-cō-plas'tid, *n.* [*Leuco-*, and Gr. *plastos*, formed, verbal adj. of *plassein*, to form, mold.] A colorless granule forming a nucleus in the protoplasm of certain vegetable cells for the accumulation of starch.

leū-cop'y-rīte, *n.* A metal, almost silver-white in color, consisting mostly of arsenic and iron.

leū-cor-rhē'ȧ, leū-cor-rhœ'ȧ, *n.* [*Leuco-*, and Gr. *rhoia*, a flowing, from *rhein*, to flow.] The whites; a whitish mucous discharge from the vagina.

leū'cō-ryx, *n.* [*Leuco-*, and Gr. *oryx*, a kind of gazel.] A large North African species of antelope.

leū'cō-scōpe, *n.* [*Leuco-*, and Gr. *skopein*, to view.] An instrument used to test the ability of the eye to distinguish variations in color or intensity of light.

leū-cō'sis, *n.* [Gr. *leukōsis*, whiteness, from *leukoun*, to make white, from *leukos*, white.]

1. Albinism; morbid whitening of the skin.

2. The development of leucoma.

leū'cō-sphēre, *n.* [*Leuco-*, and Gr. *sphaira*, a sphere.] The inner portion of a solar corona. [Rare.]

leū-cō-tū'ric, *a.* Pertaining to or designating a white compound obtained from uric acid; as, *leucoturic* acid.

leū'cous, *a.* [Gr. *leukos*, bright, white.] Albinistic; abnormally white, as an albino.

leū-cox'ōne, *n.* [*Leuco-*, and Gr. *xenos*, a

stranger.] A white substance resulting from the decomposition of titanic iron.

lē′vănt, *a.* [Fr., rising, from L. *levans* (*-antis*), ppr. of *levare*, to raise, from *levis*, light.]

1. Eastern; from the east. [Obs.]

2. Rising; as in the phrase *levant and couchant*. [See under *Couchant*.]

Lē-vant′, *n.* [Fr., from LL. *levans* (*-antis*), the east, sunrise, from L. *levans* (*-antis*), ppr. of *levare*, to raise.]

1. The countries, or more especially the maritime parts of the countries, lying on the eastern portion of the Mediterranean and its contiguous waters, as Turkey, Syria, Asia Minor, Greece, and Egypt.

2. [l—] A levanter, an easterly wind.

3. [l—] Fine morocco leather.

lē′vănt, *n.* A spring of water. [Prov. Eng.]

lē-vant′, *v.i.* [Sp. *levantar*, to raise, lift up, to start, from L. *levare*, to raise.] To decamp; to run away; to abscond.

lē-vant′ēr, *n.* [Fr. *Levant*, the East, the Orient, the Levant.] A strong easterly wind in the Mediterranean.

lē-vant′ēr, *n.* One who runs away disgracefully.

Lē-vant′ine, *a.* Of, relating to, or from the Levant; Oriental.

Lē-vant′ine, *n.* [From Fr. *Levant*, the Levant.]

1. One born or living in the Levant.

2. [l—] A vessel of the Levant.

3. [l—] A strong cloth of silk whose opposite faces were of different shades. [Obs.]

lē-vā′rī fā′ci-as (-shi-). [L., lit., cause to be levied.] In law, a writ of execution formerly used, now superseded by the writ of *elegit*.

lē-vā′tion, *n.* The elevation of the host; elevation. [Obs.]

lē-vā′tŏr, *n.* [L., a raiser, lifter, from *levatus*, pp. of *levare*, to raise.]

1. In anatomy, a muscle that serves to raise some part, as the lip or the eyelid.

2. A surgical instrument used to raise a depressed part of the skull.

lēve, *v.t.* To believe. [Obs.]

lēve, *v.i.* To leave. [Obs.]

lēve, *v.i.* To live. [Obs.]

lēve, *n.* Leave; permission. [Obs.]

lēve, *a.* Dear; lief. [Obs.]

lev-ee′ (*or* lev′ē), *n.* [Fr. *lever*, arising, a morning reception, from *lever*; L. *levare*, to rise.]

1. The act or time of rising. [Obs.]

2. A morning reception held by a great personage; a morning assembly; hence, any reception or assemblage of visitors.

lev-ee′, *v.t.* To attend the levees of. [Obs.]

lev-ee′, *n.* [Fr. *levée*, a raising, embankment.]

1. A bank or causeway, particularly along a river, to prevent inundation; as, the *levees* along the Mississippi. [U. S.]

2. A wharf, pier, or other landing-place.

lev-ee′, *v.t.* and *v.i.*; leveed, *pt., pp.*; leveeing, *ppr.* I. *v.t.* To embank or provide with a levee or levees; as, to *levee* the river.

II. *v.i.* To engage in erecting levees.

lēve′fụl, *a.* Lawful; permissible. [Obs.]

lev′el, *n.* [ME. *level*, *livel*; OFr. *livel*; L. *libella*, a level, dim. of *libra*, a balance, level.]

1. A line or surface which is at all points parallel to the free surface of a liquid at rest; a line or surface perpendicular at all points to the line of action of gravity.

2. Loosely, a horizontal line or plane. This so-called *apparent level* is a tangent at the point of observation to the *level* of definition 1, or the *true level* which is curved to correspond with the shape of the earth.

3. A plain; a surface nearly horizontal.

4. The average distance or vertical altitude from the center of the earth; as, the *level* of the sea.

5. In a figurative sense, the degree of elevation of thought, action, morals, social standing, or the like; especially, equality of rank; as, he viewed it from a higher moral *level*; persons of the same social *level*.

6. The line of aim or direction, as of a gun.

7. A more or less horizontal passage or drift of a mine.

8. An instrument used to find the plane of the horizon or to determine the position of any object with reference to that plane.

Dead level; an unvarying level; hence, monotonous uniformity.

Level of the sea; the level surface midway between low water and high water of any of the oceans.

lev′el, *a.* 1. Even; flat; not having one part higher than another; having no inequalities; parallel with the free surface of a liquid at rest; as, a *level* surface.

2. Horizontal; not ascending or descending; as, a *level* floor; a *level* road.

3. Even with, of the same height, or on the same line or plane with something else; as, *level* with his ability; *level* with the brim.

4. Equal in rank or degree; as, *level* in value.

5. Even; uniform; unchanging; as, a *level* voice; a *level* hue.

6. Direct; straightforward; undeviating; as, a *level* story.

7. Balanced; steady; exhibiting sound judgment; as, a *level* head. [Colloq.]

8. Equipotential; being in a field of force at points of equal potential (gravitational, magnetic, electrical, etc.); said of lines and surfaces.

lev′el, *adv.* In a level or horizontal line; evenly; directly; steadily; as, aim it *level*.

lev′el, *v.t.*; leveled *or* levelled, *pt., pp.*; leveling *or* levelling, *ppr.* 1. To make horizontal.

2. To make even; to reduce or remove inequalities of surface in; as, to *level* a road.

3. To reduce to equality of position, condition, state, or degree; to bring to a level; to lay flat; to reduce or elevate to the same plane; as, to *level* social ranks; to *level* mountains.

4. To point in taking aim; to direct; to aim, as a gun.

5. To suit or adapt to a level or degree of intelligence, or the like; as, to *level* one's words to one's hearers.

6. To find the contours of with a leveling-instrument.

lev′el, *v.i.* 1. To aim; to point; to direct a weapon at the mark; to direct one's view, attention, purpose, or the like, toward an object.

2. To be aimed; to accord; to suit. [Rare.]

3. To take observations with a level.

4. To attempt to guess; to conjecture.

lev′el-ēr, *n.* 1. One who levels or makes even.

2. One who destroys, or attempts to destroy, distinctions and reduce to equality, as one of a political faction in England in the time of Cromwell.

3. A road-scraper.

4. A means of adjustment used to level a body, as a billiard table or the like.

lev′el-ing, *n.* 1. The reduction of uneven surfaces to a level or plane.

2. In surveying, the art or practice of finding a horizontal line, or of ascertaining the different elevations of objects on the surface of the earth.

lev′el-ing-in″strụ-ment, *n.* A surveying instrument consisting of a telescope with a spirit-level connected.

lev′el-ing-pōle, lev′el-ing-rod, *n.* Same as *Leveling-staff*.

lev′el-ing-staff, *n.* A graduated pole used in conjunction with a leveling-instrument to mark a level.

lev′el-ism, *n.* Socialism in so far as it advocates the abolition of social ranks.

lev′el-ly, *adv.* Evenly; sanely.

lev′el-ness, *n.* Level state or quality.

lev′en, *n.* Lightning. [Obs.]

lev′en, *n.* A lawn. [Scot.]

lev′ēr (*or* lē′vēr), *n.* [ME. *lever*, *levour*; OFr. *leveor*, a lifter, lever; L. *levator*, a lifter, from *levatus*, pp. of *levare*, to raise up, lift.]

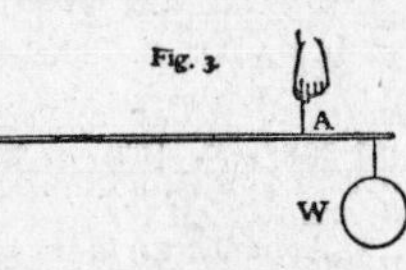

1. A bar or other rigid structure, turning on a support called the fulcrum, and used to overcome a certain resistance or weight at one point by means of a power applied at another point. Levers are divided into three classes; first, when the fulcrum is between the resistance and the power, as in a crowbar, scissors, and a steelyard; second, when the resistance is between the power and the fulcrum, as in nutcrackers, a wheelbarrow, and an oar; third, when the power is between the resistance and the fulcrum, as in sugar-tongs, a lathe-treadle, and the forearm. Fig. 1 represents a lever of the first class; fig. 2 one of the second class; fig. 3 one of the third class. In each, A is the power, W the resistance, and C the fulcrum.

2. Specifically, (a) in a steam-engine, a bar controlling the steam valves; (b) in firearms, a rod used to open and close a breech-loading gun; (c) in dentistry, a turnkey to extract the stump of a tooth; (d) in surgery, an arm of an obstetrical forceps; (e) in general, any bar used for leverage.

3. In a figurative sense, anything exerting or applying power.

Compound lever; a system of two or more simple levers acting upon one another.

Universal lever; a device securing rotary motion by the reciprocating action of a lever.

lev′ēr, *adv.* Rather. [Obs.]

lev′ēr, *a.*, comparative of *lief*. [Obs.]

lev′ēr-āġe, *n.* 1. Mechanical advantage gained by the use of a lever.

2. The method of applying a lever; the use of a lever.

3. Figuratively, advantage; power.

lev′ēr-et, *n.* [OFr. *levret*, dim. of *levre*; L. *lepus* (*-oris*), a hare.] A hare in the first year of its age.

lev′ēr-ock, *n.* A laverock; a lark. [Scot.]

lev′et, *n.* A blast of a trumpet as a morning call; reveille. [Obs.]

lev′i-à-ble, *a.* 1. That may be levied.

2. That may be seized under an execution.

lē-vī′à-than, *n.* [LL. *leviathan*; Heb. *livyāthān*, the leviathan.]

1. A large and powerful aquatic animal described in Job xli., and mentioned in other passages of Scripture; perhaps a crocodile, a whale, or a species of serpent.

2. Hence, anything of great size, usually marine, as a whale, a large ship, etc.

lev′i-ēr, *n.* One who levies.

lev′i-gā-ble, *a.* Susceptible of levigation.

lev′i-gāte, *a.* Made smooth; polished.

lev′i-gāte, *v.t.*; levigated, *pt., pp.*; levigating, *ppr.* [L. *levigatus*, pp. of *levigare*, to make smooth, polish, from *levis*, smooth.]

1. To rub or grind to a fine, impalpable powder, as by rubbing a moist substance between hard, flat surfaces.

2. To make smooth; to polish. [Obs.]

lev-i-gā′tion, *n.* [L. *levigatio* (*-onis*), a smoothing, from *levigatus*, pp. of *levigare*, to make smooth.] The act or operation of grinding or rubbing a substance to a fine, impalpable powder.

lev′in, *n.* Leven; lightning. [Obs.]

lev′in-ēr, *n.* A fleet hound. [Obs.]

lō′vīr, *n.* [L.] A brother of a husband.

lev′i-rāte, *n.* [L. *levir*, a husband's brother, brother-in-law.] A custom prescribed by the Mosaic code, according to which a woman whose husband died without issue was to be married by the husband's brother.

lev′i-rāte, lev-i-rat′iç-ăl, *a.* Of or relating to the levirate.

lev-i-rā′tion, *n.* Leviratical marriage.

Lev-i-ros′trēs, *n.pl.* [L. *levis*, light, and *rostrum*, beak.] A former group of birds which included parrots, toucans, hornbills, etc.

Lē-vis′ti-cum, *n.* [L. *ligusticum*, lovage.] A genus of the *Umbelliferæ*, having only one known species, the garden-lovage.

lev′i-tāte, *v.t.*; levitated, *pt., pp.*; levitating, *ppr.* [L. *levitas* (*-atis*), lightness, buoyancy, from *levis*, light.] To make light or buoyant and thus cause to rise and float in the air.

lev′i-tāte, *v.i.* To move contrary to or independently of the force of gravity; said of supposed spiritualistic phenomena.

lev-i-tā′tion, *n.* Lightness; buoyancy; act of making light.

Lē′vīte, *n.* [LL. *Levites*, *Levita*; Gr. *Levitēs*, a Levite, from Heb. *Levi*, Levi.]

1. One of the tribe or family of Levi; a descendant of Levi; particularly, an officer in the Jewish church, employed in manual service, as subordinate to the priests, the descendants of Aaron, who was also of the family of Levi.

2. In the early Christian church, a deacon.

3. A clergyman; a priest. [Rare.]

Lē-vit′iç-ăl, *a.* 1. Belonging to the Levites, or descendants of Levi; as, the *Levitical* law.

2. Priestly. [Rare.]

3. Of or relating to Leviticus, one of the books of the Bible.

Lē-vit′iç-ăl-ly, *adv.* After the manner of Levites.

Lē-vit′i-çus, *n.* [LL., pertaining to the Levites, from *Levites*, *Levita*, a Levite.] A canonical book of the Old Testament, containing the laws and regulations which relate to the priests and Levites among the Jews, or the body of the ceremonial law.

lev′i-ty, *n.* [L. *levitas* (*-atis*), lightness, gaiety, levity, from *levis*, light.]

1. Lightness; comparatively low specific gravity.

2. A hypothetical force contrary to gravity; also, a tendency to rise by the action of such force.

3. Lightness of temper or conduct; want of seriousness; disposition to trifle; volatility; frivolity; inconstancy.

4. Gaiety; mirth; cheerfulness.

levo-. A combining form from L. *lævus*, left, signifying pertaining to or toward the left; as, *levogyrate*.

lē-vō-glū′çōse, *n.* [*Levo-*, and Gr. *glykys*, sweet.] Levulose.

lē-vō-ġȳ′rāte, *a.* [*Levo-*, and L. *gyratus*, pp. of *gyrare*, to turn round in a circle.] Rotating the plane of polarization to the left.

lē-vō-rō-tā′tion, *n.* [*Levo-*, and L. *rotatus*, pp. of *rotare*, to turn.] Rotation of the plane of polarization to the left.

lē-vō-rō′tà-tō-ry, læ-vō-rō′tà-tō-ry, *a.* Levogyrate.

lev′ū-lin, *n.* [*Levul*ose and *-in.*] A carbohydrate similar to starch, derived from various tubers and yielding levulose upon decomposition.

lev-ū-lin′ic, *a.* Of or derived from levulin.

Levulinic acid; an acid derived from levulin, levulose, and the like; acetyl propionic acid.

lev-ū-lō′săn, *n.* An unfermentable derivative of levulose.

lev′ū-lōse, læv′ū-lōse, *n.* [L. *lævus*, left.] A sugar which is levogyrate. It is an isomer of dextrose and occurs with it in fruits, honey, invert sugar, and other substances, usually as a syrup. Called also *fruit-sugar*.

lev′y, *n.*; *pl.* **lev′ies**. [ME. *levy, levey*; OFr. *levee*, a raising, a raising of troops, of taxes, etc., from LL. *levata*, something raised, a tax, properly f. of L. *levatus*, pp. of *levare*, to raise.]

1. The act of raising, enlisting, levying, or collecting, especially for public service; as, a *levy* of troops.

2. Anything collected by a levy, as money for taxes.

Levy in mass; the act of levying for military service all the able-bodied men in a country.

lev′y, *v.t.*; levied, *pt., pp.*; levying, *ppr.* 1. To raise; to collect, as troops; to form, as an army, by enlistments, conscriptions, or other means.

2. To assess and collect by authority or force.

3. To give up or cease from; as, to *levy* a siege. [Obs.]

4. In law, to seize (property) under a writ of execution.

To levy a fine; to commence and carry on a suit for assuring the title to lands or tenements.

To levy war; to raise or begin war; to take arms for attack; to attack.

lev′y, *v.i.* To seize property in making a levy; to make a levy; usually with *on*; as to *levy on* goods and chattels.

lev′y, *n.* [Abbrev. of *eleven-penny bit*, or *elevenpence*.]

1. A small Spanish silver coin, a real, or eighth of a dollar, formerly current in eastern United States at eleven cents. [Obs.]

2. A bit; twelve and a half cents' value.

lev′yne, *n.* [Named after Mr. *Levy*, an English mineralogist.] A mineral hydrous silicate of calcium and aluminium.

lew, *a.* Tepid; lukewarm; weak. [Obs.]

lē′wăn, *n.* [Ar.] A kind of reception room in Oriental houses, usually having its floor raised above the court upon which it opens, and furnished with rugs and divans.

lewd (lūd), *a.* [ME. *lewde*; AS. *læwed*, unlearned, ignorant.]

1. Lustful; libidinous; licentious; dissolute; given to the unlawful indulgence of lust.

2. Exhibiting or proceeding from lust.

3. Vile; wicked; profligate. [Archaic.]

4. Ignorant; unlearned; lay; not clerical. [Obs.]

lewd′ly, *adv.* In a lewd manner.

lewd′ness, *n.* The state or quality of being lewd.

lewd′stẽr, *n.* One who is lewd. [Obs.]

lew′is, lew′is-sŏn, *n.* [So named by the architect who brought it to its present form, in honor of Louis XIV.]

1. An instrument of iron used in raising large stones by dovetailing one of its ends into an opening in the stone. In the cut, *a a* are first inserted and *b* wedged between them, all being held firm and attached to the lifting-ring *e*, by the bolt *c d*.

Lewis.

2. A variety of shears.

lew′is-hōle, *n.* A hole into which a lewis is to be fitted.

lex, *n.*; *pl.* **lē′gēs**. [L.] Law; used in legal phrases; as, *lex talionis*, the law of retaliation.

lex′ic-ăl, *a.* 1. Pertaining to a lexicon or lexicography.

2. Of or relating to the vocabulary of a language, as distinct from its grammar.

lex′ic-ăl-ly, *adv.* As regards words or vocabulary.

lex-i-cog′rȧ-phẽr, *n.* [L.Gr. *lexikographos*, one who writes a lexicon; Gr. *lexikon*, a lexicon, and *graphein*, to write.] A person who compiles a lexicon or dictionary.

lex″i-cō-graph′ic, lex″i-cō-graph′ic-ăl, *a.* Pertaining to the writing or compilation of a dictionary.

lex″i-cō-graph′ic-ăl-ly, *adv.* In a lexicographic manner.

lex-i-cog′rȧ-phist, *n.* A lexicographer.

lex-i-cog′rȧ-phy, *n.* [Gr. *lexikon*, a lexicon, and *graphein*, to write.]

1. The act of writing a lexicon or dictionary, or the occupation of composing dictionaries.

2. The principles on which dictionaries are, or should be, constructed; the art of compiling a dictionary.

lex-i-col′ō-gist, *n.* One skilled in lexicology; one who makes dictionaries or lexicons; a lexicographer.

lex-i-col′ō-gy, *n.* [Gr. *lexikon*, a lexicon, and *-logia*, from *legein*, to speak.] That science which treats of words, their derivation, meaning, form, and application.

lex′i-cŏn, *n.* [LL. *lexicon*; Gr. *lexikon*, a lexicon, properly neut. of *lexikos*, of or belonging to words, from *lexis*, a saying, phrase, word, from *legein*, to say, speak.] A dictionary; a vocabulary, or book containing an alphabetical arrangement of words in a language, with the definition of each; particularly, a vocabulary of Greek, Latin, or Hebrew.

lex′i-cŏn-ist, *n.* A writer of a lexicon. [Rare.]

lex-i-graph′ic, *a.* Relating to lexigraphy.

lex-ig′rȧ-phy, *n.* [Gr. *lexis*, a word, and *-graphia*, from *graphein*, to write.] The art or practice of defining words. [Rare.]

lex-i-phan′ic, *a.* [Gr. *lexiphanēs*, a phrasemonger; *lexis*, a phrase, word, and *phainein*, to show.] Relating to lexiphanicism; bombastic; turgid; inflated. [Obs.]

lex-i-phan′i-cism, *n.* The habit of using an inflated, pompous style in speaking or writing. [Obs.]

lex-i-phär′mic, *a.* Antidotal. [Obs.]

ley, *v.t.* To wager; to bet. [Obs.]

ley, *n.* Law. [Obs.]

lēy (lī), *n.* Lye. [Obs.]

lēy, *n.* A lea. [Obs.]

ley, *n.* [Sp., lit., law, from L. *lex, legis*, law.] Assay percentage; yield; quantity.

lēy, *a.* Fallow. [Obs.]

Ley′den jär. A glass jar coated inside and outside with tin-foil, to within a third of the top and usually having a metallic knob at the top connected with the inside coating. It is used as a condenser or accumulator of static electricity. Invented in *Leyden*, of Holland, and called also *Leyden phial* or *vial*.

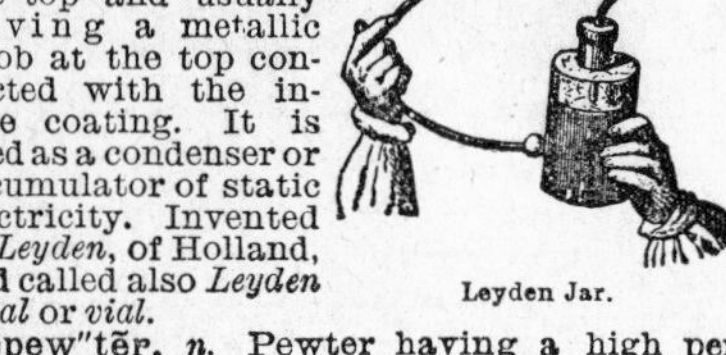

Leyden Jar.

ley′-pew″tẽr, *n.* Pewter having a high percentage of lead.

lēy′sẽr, *n.* Leisure. [Obs.]

lēze′-maj′es-ty, *n.* Same as *Lese-majesty*.

lhẽr′zō-līte, *n.* [*Lherz*, from Lake *Lherz*, and Gr. *lithos*, stone.] A crystalline rock containing pyroxene, chrysolite, diallage, and picotite, occurring in the vicinity of Lake Lherz in the French Pyrenees.

lī, *n.* [Chinese.] 1. A Chinese road measure equal to about 1,900 feet.

2. A Chinese measure of weight equal to one thousandth of a tael or about .6 grain.

3. A Chinese coin of bronze equal in value to the weight of a li of silver; a cash.

lī-ȧ-bil′i-ty, *n.*; *pl.* **lī-ȧ-bil′i-ties**. 1. The state of being bound or obliged in law or duty; responsibility; as, one's *liability* for the acts of an agent.

2. The state of being subject, exposed, or liable; susceptibility; as, one's *liability* to accidents or disease.

3. An obligation; that for which one is liable.

lī′ȧ-ble, *a.* [From Fr. *lier*; L. *ligare*, to bind.]

1. Bound; answerable; responsible in law or equity; as, *liable* for a debt.

2. Subject; exposed; open; applied to evils or things disagreeable; having such a character that one is able (to do or incur something undesirable); as, a physician is *liable* to contagion.

Syn.—Apt, likely.—*Apt* indicates a characteristic tendency; as, ether is *apt* to evaporate. *Likely* indicates a probability of some event good or bad occurring; as, so cold it is *likely* to freeze. *Liable* indicates the possibility of an unpleasant event; as, one is *liable* to fall even though not *likely*.

lī′ȧ-ble-ness, *n.* The quality or state of being liable.

lī′āge, *n.* Alliance; league. [Obs.]

lī-ăl-sŏn′, *n.* [Fr., a binding, a union, from L. *ligatio* (*-onis*), a binding, from *ligatus*, pp. of *ligare*, to bind.]

1. A bond; an entanglement; especially, an illicit sexual intimacy.

2. In cookery, a thickening, as of eggs, used to combine the components of a dish.

3. A French term signifying the connection or communication between various officers or between various units and officers.

4. In the French language, the practice of pronouncing a final consonant, usually silent, as if it were the initial of a succeeding word when such a word begins with a vowel or mute *h*, as in *les hommes*. In such cases, *s* and *x* take the sound of *z*, *d* of *t*, and *g* of *k*.

Liaison officer; a staff officer charged with the duty of linking together different units or armies.

li-ā′nȧ, li-āne′, *n.* [Fr. *liane*, a tropical creeper, from *lier*, to bind.] Any of the climbing and twining plants of tropical forests.

lī′ăr, *n.* [ME. *leigher, leghere*; AS. *leógere*, a liar, from *leógan*, to lie.] A person who knowingly utters falsehood, one who declares to another as a fact what he knows to be not true, and with an intention to deceive him.

Liärd (lyär), *n.* [Fr., from OFr. *liar, liard*, a small coin.] A former coin of France valued at one-fourth of a sou.

Lī′ăs, *n.* [Fr. *liais*, a hard freestone; Arm. *liach, leach*, a stone.] The geological series at the base of the Jurassic and above the Triassic; noted for the abundance of its fossils.

Lī-as′sic, *a.* Of or relating to the Lias.

Lī′ȧ-tris, *n.* [Etym. unknown.] A genus of the *Compositæ*, the species of which are known as *button-snakeroot* and *blazing-star*.

lib, *v.t.* To castrate. [Prov. Eng.]

lib, *n.* A basket. [Prov. Eng.]

lib′ȧ-ment, *n.* A libation. [Obs.]

lī′bănt, *a.* [L. *libans* (*-antis*), ppr. of *libare*, to taste, to sip.] Tasting or touching delicately. [Rare.]

lī′bāte, *v.t.* and *v.i.* I. *v.t.* To pour. [Rare.]

II. *v.i.* To perform a libation. [Rare.]

lī-bā′tion, *n.* [Fr. *libation*; L. *libatio* (*-onis*), a libation, from *libatus*, pp. of *libare*, to taste, pour out.]

1. The act of pouring a liquor, usually wine, either on the ground, or on a victim in sacrifice, in honor of some deity.

2. The wine or other liquor poured out in honor of a diety.

lī′bȧ-tō-ry, *a.* Of or relating to libation.

li-bā′vi-us, *n.* [Named after A. *Libavius*, a German chemist, who discovered it.] A volatile, fuming liquid, tin chlorid, $SnCl_4$.

lib′bȧrd, *n.* A leopard. [Obs.]

lib′bȧrd′s-bāne, *n.* A composite herb.

li-bec′ciō (-bech′ō), *n.* [It., from L. *Libs*; Gr. *Lips*, the southwest wind.] The southwest wind. [Obs.]

lī′bel, *v.t.*; libeled *or* libelled, *pt., pp.*; libeling *or* libelling, *ppr.* 1. To defame or expose to public hatred or contempt by a writing, picture, and the like; to lampoon.

2. In law, to file a libel against, as against a ship or its cargo.

lī′bel, *v.i.* To spread defamation; with *against*. [Obs.]

lī′bel, *n.* [OFr. *libel, libeau*, masc., *libele, libelle*, f.; L. *libellus*, a little book, tablet, note, writing, lampoon, dim. of *liber*, a book.]

1. In law, (a) anything written, printed, or expressed by a sign or picture, containing representations maliciously made or published, tending to bring a person into contempt, or expose him to public hatred and derision; (b) the document or writing setting forth the plaintiff's allegations and beginning suit in an admiralty or ecclesiastical court; (c) the crime of publishing a libel.

2. Defamation; traducement; anything having a tendency to lower reputation or to lead to disrepute; as, such a verdict is a *libel* on justice.

3. A lampoon. [Rare.]

lī′bel-ănt, *n.* Same as *Libellant*.

lī′bel-ẽr, lī′bel-lẽr, *n.* One who libels.

lī′bel-ist, *n.* A libeler. [Obs.]

li-bel′lȧ, *n.* [L.] A balance; also, a level. [Rare.]

lī′bel-lănt, *n.* [Fr., properly ppr. of *libeller*, to draw up a legal demand, to libel.] The person who brings a libel in an admiralty or ecclesiastical court.

lī′bel-lee, *n.* The party defendant in an admiralty suit.

li-bel′lū-lid, *n.* [L. *libellulus*, a very small book, dim. of *libellus*, a little book; so called from its resemblance to a book when flying.] A dragon-fly.

li-bel′lū-loid, *a.* Like a dragon-fly.

li-bel′lū-line, *a.* Libelluloid.

lī′bel-ous, lī′bel-lous, *a.* Like or containing a libel; defamatory.

lī′bel-ous-ly, *adv.* In a libelous manner.

lī′bẽr, *n.* [L., the inner bark of a tree, a book; so called because bark was used to write upon.]

1. In botany, the inner, newly-formed bark of an exogen, characterized by the presence of long, fibrous cells.

2. A book; used to distinguish volumes of a series, as in large reference works, public records, etc.

lib′ẽr-ăl, *a.* [ME. *liberal*; OFr. *liberal*; L. *liberalis*, of or pertaining to a freeman, befitting a freeman, noble, liberal.]

1. Of a free heart; free to give or bestow; munificent; bountiful; generous; giving largely; as, a *liberal* donor.

2. Generous; ample; large; as, a *liberal* donation.

3. Not selfish, narrow, bigoted, or contracted; catholic; enlarged; embracing other interests than one's own; as, *liberal* sentiments.

4. General; extensive; embracing literature and the sciences generally; as, a *liberal* education.

5. Free; not literal or strict; as, a *liberal* construction of law.

6. Not mean; not low in birth or mind.

7. Licentious; free to excess. [Obs.]

Liberal has *of* or *with* before the thing bestowed, *to* before the person or object on which anything is bestowed, and *in* before an expression of action; as, *liberal of* praise; *to* the poor; *in* translating.

Liberal party; a party claiming to advocate progress and reform.

lib′ẽr-ăl, *n.* 1. One who advocates greater freedom of thought or action; one who has liberal principles.

2. [L—] A member of a Liberal political party, as in Great Britain, Canada, etc.

lib′ẽr-ăl-iṣm, *n.* 1. The principles of liberals; especially in religion.

2. [L—] The principles and methods of a Liberal political party.

lib′ẽr-ăl-ist, *n.* A liberal.

lib″ẽr-ăl-is′tiç, *a.* Of or exhibiting liberalism.

lib-ẽr-al′i-ty, *n.*; *pl.* **lib-ẽr-al′i-tieṣ.** [OFr. *liberalite*; L. *liberalitas (-atis)*, a way of thinking or acting befitting a freeman, nobleness, generosity, liberality.]

1. Munificence; the quality of being liberal.

2. A particular act of generosity; a donation; a gratuity; usually in the plural; as, a prudent man is not impoverished by his *liberalities*.

3. Largeness of mind; catholicism; freedom of thought; impartiality.

lib″ẽr-ăl-i-zā′tion, *n.* The act of making liberal.

lib′ẽr-ăl-īze, *v.t.*; liberalized, *pt.*, *pp.*; liberalizing, *ppr.* To render liberal or catholic; to enlarge; to free from narrow views or prejudices.

lib′ẽr-ăl-ī-zẽr, *n.* One who or that which liberalizes or makes liberal.

lib′ẽr-ăl-ly, *adv.* In a liberal manner.

lib′ẽr-āte, *v.t.*; liberated, *pt.*, *pp.*; liberating, *ppr.* [L. *liberatus*, pp. of *liberare*, to set free, release, from *liber*, free.] To free; to release from restraint or bondage; to set at liberty.

lib-ẽr-ā′tion, *n.* [L. *liberatio (-onis)*, from *liberatus*, pp. of *liberare*, to set free, liberate.] The act of delivering from restraint or the state of being freed.

lib′ẽr-ā-tŏr, *n.* [L., from *liberatus*, pp. of *liberare*, to liberate.] One who liberates.

lib′ẽr-ȧ-tō-ry, *a.* Tending to set free. [Rare.]

lib″ẽr-ō-mō′tŏr, *a.* [L. *liberare*, to liberate, and *motor*, a mover.] Letting out motor energy.

lib-ẽr-tā′ri-ăn, *a.* Pertaining to the doctrine of free will, as opposed to the doctrine of necessity.

lib-ẽr-tā′ri-ăn, *n.* One who holds to free will.

lib-ẽr-tā′ri-ăn-iṣm, *n.* The principles or doctrines of libertarians.

lib′ẽr-ti-cīde, *n.* [L. *libertas (-atis)*, liberty, and *cædere*, to kill.]

1. Destruction of liberty.

2. A destroyer of liberty.

lib′ẽr-tin-āġe, *n.* Libertinism; license. [Rare.]

lib′ẽr-tine (-tin), *n.* [L. *libertinus*, of or belonging to the condition of a freedman, a freedman, from *libertus*, a freedman, from *liber*, free.]

1. Among the Romans, a freedman; a person manumitted from servitude, or the child of a freedman.

2. One unconfined; one free from restraint; one who indulges his desires without restraint; a rake; a debauchee.

3. [L—] A member of a pantheistic sect of the sixteenth century in Holland, who maintained that nothing is sinful but to those who think it sinful, and that perfect innocence is to live without doubt. They practised licentiousness and communism.

4. One of a sect of infidels and voluptuaries in Geneva, opposed to the reforms of Calvin.

5. In Scripture, a member of a certain synagogue of the Jews, as mentioned in Acts vi. 9.

lib′ẽr-tine, *a.* 1. Licentious; dissolute; not under the restraint of law or religion.

lib′ẽr-tin-iṣm, *n.* 1. State of a freedman. [Obs.]

2. Excessive freedom of opinion or practice; debauchery; lewdness.

lib′ẽr-ty, *n.* [OFr. *liberte*; L. *libertas (-atis)*, freedom, from *liber*, free.]

1. Freedom from restraint, in a general sense, applicable to the body, or to the will or mind; as, the body is at *liberty* when not confined; the will or mind is at *liberty* when not checked or controlled.

2. In philosophy, the ability of a rational mind to choose and decide in conformity to reason or motive; freedom of the will; exemption from compulsion or restraint in willing or volition.

3. Freedom from restraint abridged only so far as is necessary and expedient for the safety and interest of the society, state, or nation; civil liberty.

4. Privilege; exemption; right or immunity enjoyed by prescription or by grant; as, *liberty* to speak, to play, to go ashore.

5. A space in which one is permitted to pass without restraint, and beyond which he may not lawfully pass; with a plural; as, the *liberties* of a prison.

6. Freedom of action or speech beyond the ordinary bounds of civility or decorum.

7. A curvature in a horse's bit to allow room for the tongue.

At liberty; free from occupation, constraint, restraint, or use.

Civil liberty; see under *Civil.*

Liberty Bond; a U. S. government bond issued during the World War as security for the repayment of money loaned to the U. S. for war purposes.

Liberty Loan; one of several loans made by the people of the U. S. to their government during the World War, secured by government bonds.

Liberty Motor; a 12-cylinder gasoline motor capable of great speed used to equip all U. S. aeroplanes during the World War.

Liberty of the press; freedom from any restriction on the power to publish books; the free power of publishing what one pleases, subject only to punishment for abusing the privilege, or publishing what is mischievous to the public or injurious to individuals.

Religious liberty; the free right of adopting opinions on religious subjects, and of worshiping the Supreme Being according to the dictates of conscience.

li-beth′en-īte, *n.* A mineral, first found at Libethen, in Hungary, having an olive-green color, and consisting of basic copper phosphate.

li-bid′i-nist, *n.* One given to lewdness. [Rare.]

li-bid-i-nos′i-ty, *n.* Libidinousness.

li-bid′i-nous, *a.* [Fr. *libidineux*; L. *libidinosus*, *lubidinosus*, full of desire or passion, licentious, from *libido*, or *lubido (-inis)*, desire, pleasure, inclination, passion, wantonness, from *libet* or *lubet*, it pleases.] Lustful; lewd; exhibiting lasciviousness.

li-bid′i-nous-ly, *adv.* Lustfully; with lewd desire.

li-bid′i-nous-ness, *n.* The state or quality of being lustful; inordinate appetite for venereal pleasure.

lib′ken, lib′kin, *n.* Lodgings. [Old Slang.]

Lī′brȧ, *n.* [L., a balance, a Roman pound.]

1. The Balance; the seventh sign in the zodiac, which the sun enters at the autumnal equinox, in September.

2. A constellation of the southern heavens, once in the sign Libra, but now near Scorpio.

3. [l—; *pl.* lī′bræ.] A weight of Italy, Spain, and Portugal, derived from the Roman *libra* of 5,046 grains but having several values up to 7,363 grains.

lī-brā′ri-ăn, *n.* [L. *librarius*, adj., pertaining to books; n., a transcriber of books, a keeper of books, from *liber*, a book.]

1. The keeper or one who has the care of a library or collection of books.

2. One who transcribes or copies books. [Obs.]

lī-brā′ri-ăn-ship, *n.* The office of a librarian.

lī′brȧ-ry, *n.* [OFr. *librarie*, a bookcase, a bookseller's shop, library; L. *libraria*, a bookseller's shop (also, LL., a library), from *librarius*, belonging to books, from *liber*, a book.]

1. A collection of books belonging to a private person, public institution, or company.

2. An edifice or apartment for holding a collection of books.

Circulating library; a library from which books may be removed to be read elsewhere.

lī′brāte, *v.t.* and *v.i.* [L. *libratus*, pp. of *librare*, to weigh, balance, from *libra*, a balance.]

I. *v.t.* To poise; to balance; to hold in equipoise. [Rare.]

II. *v.i.* To move, as a balance; to be poised. [Rare.]

lī-brā′tion, *n.* [Fr., from L. *libratio (-onis)*, a balancing, from *libratus*, pp. of *librare*.

1. The act of balancing or oscillating; the state of being balanced; equipoise.

2. In astronomy, an oscillatory motion, either actual or only apparent, of a heavenly body to either side of its mean position.

Libration of the moon; changes in the disk of the moon, by which certain parts of it alternately appear and disappear. The moon always turns nearly the same face to the earth; but, by the libration in longitude, the parts near the eastern and western borders alternately appear and disappear; by the libration in latitude, the parts about the poles alternately appear and disappear; by the diurnal, or parallactic libration, more of the upper limb is brought into view at rising and setting.

lī′brȧ-tō-ry, *a.* Balancing; moving like a balance, as it tends to an equipoise; oscillating.

li-bret′tist, *n.* The composer of a libretto.

li-bret′tō, *n.* [It., dim. of *libro*, a book, from L. *liber*, a book.] The words of an opera, or a book containing them.

lī′bri-fọrm, *a.* [L. *liber*, the inner bark of a tree, and *forma*, form.] Like the liber of exogens.

Libriform cells; the tough, slender wood-cells of the inner bark.

Lib′y-ăn, *a.* and *n.* [L. *Libys*, or *Libycus*; Gr. *Libys*, Libyan, from *Libyē*, Libya.]

I. *a.* Relating to Libya, an old name for Africa; or, specifically, the northern part from the Atlantic to Egypt.

II. *n.* A Berber; an inhabitant of Libya.

līce, *n.*, pl. of *louse.*

lī′cens-ȧ-ble, *a.* Capable of being licensed.

lī′cense, *n.* [OFr. *licence*; L. *licentia*, freedom, liberty, license, from *licens (-entis)*, ppr. of *licere*, to be permitted.]

1. Leave; permission; authority or liberty given to do or forbear any act, especially one otherwise prohibited.

2. The paper containing such authority.

3. Excess of liberty; exorbitant freedom; freedom abused, or used in contempt of law or decorum.

4. Variation from fact or fixed rule for the purpose of poetical, rhetorical, or other effect.

lī′cense, *v.t.*; licensed (-senst), *pt.*, *pp.*; licensing, *ppr.* [Fr. *licencier*; LL. *licentiare*, to license, from L. *licentia*, license.] To permit by grant of authority; to remove legal restraint by a grant of permission; as, to *license* a man to keep a saloon.

lī′censed (-senst), *a.* Permitted by authority.

Licensed victualer; one having a license as innkeeper; particularly, one licensed to sell intoxicants.

lī-cen-see′, *n.* The holder of a license.

lī′cens-ẽr, lī′cens-ŏr, *n.* One who licenses.

lī′cen-sūre (-shūr), *n.* A licensing.

lī-cen′ti-āte (-shi-), *n.* [LL. *licentiatus*, pp. of *licentiare*, to license, from L. *licentia*, license.]

1. One who has a license to practise a profession; as, a *licentiate* in medicine or theology.

2. An independent friar, licensed to hear confessions and grant absolution anywhere. [Obs.]

3. One who takes liberties. [Obs.]

4. In Continental universities, a degree between the baccalaureate and the doctorate.

lī-cen′ti-āte, *v.t.* To give license to. [Obs.]

lī-cen′tious, *a.* [L. *licentiosus*, wanton, unrestrained, using license, from *licentia*, license.]

1. Using license; indulging freedom to excess; unrestrained by law; loose. [Rare.]

2. Exceeding the limits of law or propriety; wanton; unrestrained; lascivious.

Syn.—Voluptuous, dissolute, debauched, profligate, unbridled.

lī-cen′tious-ly, *adv.* In a licentious way.

lī-cen′tious-ness, *n.* A licentious state.

lich, *a.* Like; equal. [Obs.]

lich, *n.* A dead body; a corpse. [Obs.]

lī′ḉhen, *n.* [L. *lichen*; Gr. *leichēn*, a tree-moss, lichen, a lichen-like eruption on the skin, scurvy, prob. from *leichein*, to lick.]

1. One of a group of cellular cryptogamic plants without stem or leaves and consisting of a fungus parasitic upon an alga. They appear in the form of thin flat crusts, covering rocks and the barks of trees, or growing upon the ground, or in foliaceous expansions, or branched like a shrub in miniature, or sometimes only as a gelatinous mass or a powdery substance. They include the Iceland-moss and reindeer-moss, but are entirely distinct from the true mosses, *Musci*.

Lichen.
Reindeer-moss (*Cladonia rangiferina*).

2. In medicine, a papular cutaneous eruption, consisting of diffuse red pimples, which are attended usually with a troublesome tingling and pricking.

lī-ḉhen-ā′ceous, *a.* Of or like a lichen.

lī′ḉhened, *a.* Covered or coated with lichens.

lī-ḉhen′iç, *a.* Of, like, or derived from lichen; as, *lichenic* acid.

Lichenic acid; fumaric acid, derived from Iceland-moss.

lī-ḉhen-iç′ō-lous, *a.* [L. *lichen*, a lichen, and *colere*, to inhabit.] Inhabiting a lichen as a parasite.

lī-ḉhen′i-fọrm, *a.* [L. *lichen*, a lichen, and *forma*, form.] Formed like a lichen.

lī′ḉhen-in, *n.* A starch derived from Iceland-moss.

lī′ḉhen-iṣm, *n.* The condition of intimate union between algæ and fungi producing lichens.

lī″ḉhen-ō-graph′iç, lī″ḉhen-ō-graph′iç-ăl, *a.* Pertaining to lichenography.

lī-ḉhen-og′rȧ-phist, *n.* One who describes the lichens.

lī-ḉhen-og′rȧ-phy, *n.* [Gr. *leichēn*, a lichen, and *graphein*, to write.] The science which describes and classifies lichens.

lī′ḉhen-oid, *a.* [Gr. *leichēn*, a lichen, and *eidos*, form.] Like lichen or lichens.

lī-ḉhen-ol′ō-ġist, *n.* An expert in lichenology.

lī-ḉhen-ol′ō-ġy, *n.* [Gr. *leichēn*, a lichen, and *-logia*, from *legein*, to speak.] The science of lichens.

lī′ḉhen-ōse, *a.* Lichenous.

lī′ḉhen-ous, *a.* Of, like, or full of lichens.

lich′-fowl, *n.* [AS. *lic*, a body, and *fugol*, fowl.] The European goatsucker.

lich′=gāte, *n.* [AS. *lic*, a body, and *geat*, a gate.] A churchyard gate, with a porch under which a bier might stand while the introductory part of the service was read before proceeding to the church.

Lich-gate, Clifton Hampton, Oxfordshire.

lī′chī″, *n.* [Chinese.] A Chinese fruit having a sweet pulp enclosed in a thin, rough shell and containing a single brown seed; spelled also *litchi, leechee, lychee.*

lich′=owl, *n.* [AS. *lic*, a body, corpse, and *ule*, an owl.] A screech-owl, superstitiously supposed to forebode death.

licht, *v., n.*, and *a.* Light. [Scot.]

lich′wāke, *n.* [Obs.] Same as *Likewake.*

lich′wāle, *n.* The gromwell.

lich′wāy, *n.* [AS. *lic*, a corpse, and *weg*, way.] The path used in carrying a corpse to its grave. [Prov. Eng.]

lich′wŏrt, *n.* [AS. *lic*, a body, and *wyrt*, a plant.] The wall-pellitory.

lic′it, *a.* [L. *licitus*, lawful, permitted, properly pp. of *licere*, to be permitted.] Lawful.

lic′i-tā-tion, *n.* [L. *licitatio* (*-onis*), a bidding at sales, from *licitatus*, pp. of *licitari*, to bid, offer a price.] The act of offering at auction; especially, in law, such a sale of an indivisible property, the proceeds of which are divided among joint owners.

lic′it-ly, *adv.* Lawfully.

lic′it-ness, *n.* Lawfulness. [Rare.]

lick, *v.t.*; licked, *pt., pp.*; licking, *ppr.* [ME. *licken*; AS. *liccian*, to lick.]

1. To pass or draw the tongue over the surface of; as, a dog *licks* a wound.

2. To lap; to take in by the tongue; as, a dog or cat *licks* milk.

3. To strike repeatedly for punishment; to flog; to beat; to conquer. [Colloq.]

lick, *v.i.* 1. To move as in licking.

2. To be victor; as, he *licked.* [Colloq.]

To lick into shape; to bring into shape by gradual treatment.

lick, *n.* 1. A rubbing or drawing of the tongue over anything; hence, any stroke resembling that of a tongue; as, a *lick* with a paint-brush.

2. A light smear or stroke, as of color. [Colloq.]

3. A small amount; as much as can be taken up by the tongue at a stroke; as, a *lick* of sugar. [Colloq.]

4. A place where animals lick the ground for salt.

5. A blow; a slap. [Colloq.]

6. A stroke; as, four at one *lick.* [Colloq.]

7. [*pl.*] A beating. [Prov. Eng. and Scot.]

8. [*pl.*] Strokes; work; effort; as, he put in his best *licks.* [Colloq.]

lick′ẽr, *n.* 1. One who or that which licks.

2. In machinery, a lubricating device which laps up oil and conveys it to a bearing.

lick′ẽr=in, *n.* A drum in a carding machine, which conveys the fibers from the feed-rolls to the main carding cylinder.

lick′ẽr-ish, *a.* 1. Dainty; tempting the appetite; as, *lickerish* baits. [Obs.]

2. [Obs.] Same as *Lickerous.*

lick′ẽr-ish-ly, *adv.* Daintily. [Obs.]

lick′ẽr-ish-ness, *n.* Daintiness. [Obs.]

lick′ẽr-ous, *a.* 1. Fastidious; dainty. [Obs.]

2. Eager; greedy to swallow; eager to taste or enjoy; having a keen relish. [Obs.]

3. Lecherous; sensual; luxurious; lustful. [Obs.]

lick′ẽr-ous-ness, *n.* Keen desire; sensuality. [Obs.]

lick′et-y=cut′, lick′et-y=split′, *adv.* Recklessly; headlong; rapidly. [Slang.]

lick′ing, *n.* 1. A lapping with the tongue.

2. A flogging or castigation. [Colloq.]

lick′pen″ny, *n.* A greedy miser. [Scot.]

lick′=spig″ot, *n.* A tapster. [Obs.]

lick′spit″tle, *n.* A flatterer or parasite of the most abject character.

Licorice Plant (*Glycyrrhiza glabra*).

lic′ō-rice, *n.* [OFr. *licorice*; LL. *liguiritia*, corrupted from L. *glycyrrhiza*; Gr. *glykyrrhiza*, licorice; *glykys*, sweet, and *rhiza*, root.]

1. A perennial herbaceous plant of the genus *Glycyrrhiza* of the *Leguminosæ.*

2. The root of the licorice plant or its juice extracted and dried, usually in the form of small rolls known as stick-licorice.

3. Any of various plants having sweet roots, as (a) *Abrus precatorius*, or Indian licorice; (b) *Galium lanceolatum* or *Galium circæzans*, wild licorice.

lic′ō-rous, *a.* Same as *Lickerous.*

lic′our, *n.* Liquor [Obs.]

lic′tŏr, *n.* [L., from *ligare*, to bind, in allusion to the bundles of bound rods which he bore.] An officer among the Romans, who bore an ax and fasces as ensigns of his office. The duty of a lictor was to attend the chief magistrates when they appeared in public, to clear the way, and cause due respect to be paid to them, and also to apprehend and punish criminals.

lid, *n.* [ME. *lid*; AS. *hlid*, a lid, cover, from *hlidan*, to cover, conceal.]

1. A cover; that which shuts the opening of a vessel, box, or the like; as, the *lid* of a trunk or basket.

2. The cover of the eye; the eyelid.

3. One of the movable sides or boards of a book cover. [Colloq.]

4. In botany, the top portion of a pyxis; an operculum.

5. A coverlet. [Prov. Eng.]

6. A roof-timber supported by an upright in a coal-mine.

lid′ded, *a.* Provided with or covered by a lid.

lidge, *n.* [Obs.] Same as *Ledge.*

lid′less, *a.* Having no lid.

lie, *n.* [ME. *lie, lye*; AS. *lyge*, a lie, from *leógan*, to lie.]

1. A falsehood uttered in speech or act for the purpose of deception; an intentional violation of truth. Fiction, or a false statement or misrepresentation, not intended to deceive, mislead, or injure, as in fables, parables, and the like, is not a lie.

> It is wilful deceit that makes a *lie.* A man may act a *lie*, as by pointing his finger in a wrong direction, when a traveler inquires of him his road. —Paley.

2. That which deceives and disappoints confidence.

lie, *v.i.*; lied (lĭd), *pt., pp.*; lying, *ppr.* [ME. *lien, lyen*; AS. *leógan*, to lie, tell a falsehood.]

1. To utter falsehood with an intention to deceive, or with an immoral design; to say or do that which is designed to deceive another, when he has a right to know the truth, or when morality requires a just representation.

2. To cause an incorrect impression; to present a misleading appearance; as, figures frequently *lie.*

līe, *v.i.*; lay, *pt.*; lying, *ppr.*; lain, *pp.* [ME. *lien, lyen*; AS. *licgan*, to lie.]

1. To be in a horizontal position, or nearly so; to rest on anything lengthwise; to rest; to be prostrate; as, the fallen tree *lies* on the ground; he *lies* in his eternal resting-place.

2. To lay or place oneself in a horizontal or nearly horizontal position; often with *down*; as, to *lie down* upon a couch.

3. To be situated; as, Ireland *lies* west of England.

4. To sojourn; to lodge; to sleep.

5. To be; to rest; to abide; to remain; often followed by some word denoting a particular condition; as, to *lie* fallow; to *lie* open; to *lie* hid; to *lie* at the mercy of a creditor.

6. To depend; to have results determined; followed by *in*; as, our success *lies in* vigilance.

7. To be sustainable in law; to be capable of being maintained; as, an action *lies* against the tenant for waste.

To lie along; to lean over with a side wind, as a ship.

To lie along the land; to keep a course nearly parallel to the land.

To lie at one's heart; to be an object of affection, desire, or anxiety.

To lie by; (a) to be deposited or remaining with; as, he has the manuscript *lying by* him; (b) to rest; to intermit labor; as, we *lay by* during the heat of the day; (c) nautically, to remain near, as one ship to another at sea.

To lie hard or *heavy upon*; to press; to oppress; to burden.

To lie in; to be in childbed.

To lie (*in a person*); to be in the power of; to belong to.

To lie in the way; to be an obstacle or impediment.

To lie in wait; to wait for in concealment; to lie in ambush; to watch for an opportunity to attack or seize.

To lie on or *upon*; (a) to be a matter of obligation or duty to; as, it *lies on* the plaintiff to maintain his action; (b) to depend on.

To lie on hand; to be or remain in possession; to remain unsold or undisposed of.

To lie on one's hands; (a) to remain unsold; (b) not to require to be expended in employment; hence, to be tedious; as, men are sometimes at a loss to know how to employ the time that *lies on their hands.*

To lie on the head of; to come on; to fall to the share of; to be imputable to.

To lie over; (a) to remain unpaid after the time when payment is due, as a note in bank; (b) to be deferred to some future occasion, as a motion or resolution in a deliberative assembly.

To lie to; to be stationary, as a ship. A ship is said *to lie to* when her progress is checked, either by counterbracing the yards or taking in sail.

To lie to one's work; to exert all one's strength or powers in the performance of one's work.

To lie under; to be subject to; to suffer; to be oppressed by.

To lie with; (a) to lodge or sleep with; (b) to have carnal knowledge of; (c) to belong to.

> *Lie, lay.*—*Lay* is a transitive verb, and has for its preterit *laid*; as, he told me to *lay* it down, and I *laid* it down. *Lie* is intransitive, and has for its preterit *lay*; as, he told me to *lie* down, and I *lay* down. Some persons blunder by using *laid* for the preterit of *lie*; as, he told me to *lie* down, and I *laid* down. So persons often wrongly say, the ship *laid* at anchor; they *laid* by during the storm; the book *laid* on the shelf, etc. It is only necessary to remember, in all such cases, that *laid* is the preterit of *lay* and not of *lie*. This would save many respectable writers from a gross error which seems to be increasing among us. —Goodrich.

līe, *n.* 1. The relative position, situation, order, direction, arrangement, or the like; the lay.

2. A haunt, lair, or place frequented by an animal.

3. On a railroad, a side-track; a siding.

lië′bẽr-kuhn, *n.* [Named after J. N. *Lieberkühn*, its inventor.] An annular concave reflector around the object-glass of a microscope to focus light on the field.

Liē-bẽr-kuh′ni-ăn, *a.* Named or described by Johann Nathanael Lieberkühn (1711-56), a scientist of Berlin, as certain glands, crypts, or follicles of the small intestine.

lied (lēt), *n.*; *pl.* **lie′dẽr.** [G.] A German lyric poem; a song; a ballad.

lie′dẽr-kränz (-kränts), *n.* [G., from *lieder*, pl. of *lied*, a song, lay, and *kranz*, a garland, wreath.] A German vocal organization or glee-club, usually consisting of men only; a männerchor.

lie′dẽr-tä″fel, *n.* [G., from *lieder*, pl. of *lied*, a song, and *tafel*, a table.] A männerchor; a liederkranz; a German male vocal organization.

lie′=de=vin′ (-vañ′), *n.* [Fr., from *lie*, lees, *de*, of, and *vin*, wine.] Lees-of-wine, a dark-red color of certain porcelains, silks, etc.

liēf, *a.* [ME. *leef*; AS. *leóf*, dear, beloved.]

1. Dear; beloved. [Obs.]

2. Willing; inclined. [Obs.]

liēf, *n.* A darling; a loved one. [Obs.]

liēf, *adv.* Gladly; willingly; as, I had as *lief* go as not.

liēf, *n.* See *Lif.*

liēf′kin, *n.* A darling. [Obs.]

liēf′sōme, *a.* Agreeable. [Obs.]

liēge, *a.* [OFr. *lige, liege*, liege, free; LL. *ligius, legius*, unlimited, complete, liege; M.H.G. *ledic, ledec*, free, unhindered.]

1. Sovereign; bound by feudal laws to protection and justice, and having the counter right to loyal service; as, a *liege* lord.

2. Bound by feudal tenure to be faithful and loyal to a superior, as a vassal to his lord, serving him against all, not even excepting his sovereign; faithful; as, a *liege*man.

3. Of or relating to the feudal relations of vassal and superior; as, *liege* government.

liēge, *n.* 1. A vassal; a liegeman; a citizen.

2. A lord or superior; a sovereign

liēge′dŏm, *n.* Allegiance. [Rare.]

liēge′măn, *n.* A vassal. [Obs.]

liēge′=pous″tie, *n.* [OFr. *liege poustee*, free sovereignty; *liege*, free, and *poustie*, from L. *potestas*, power.] In Scots law, that state of health which gives a person full power to dispose, mortis causa or otherwise, of his heritable property.

liē′gẽr, *n.* A ledger, or resident ambassador. [Obs.]

lī′en, *v.*, obsolete past participle of third *lie.*

lī′en (*or* lēn), *n.* [Fr. *lien*; L. *ligamen*, a band, from *ligare*, to bind, tie.]

1. In law, a legal right or claim upon a specific property to have it applied on a debt, or to hold it until the debt is satisfied; as, a mechanic's *lien.*

2. A claim; a bond of obligation; a right to be paid.

lī′en, *n.*; *pl.* **lī′en-ēs.** [L.] The spleen.

lī-ē′năl, *a.* Splenic; relating to the spleen.

lī-en′cū-lus, *n.*; *pl.* **lī-en′cū-lī.** [A dim. from L. *lien*, the spleen.] A small body consisting of splenic tissue frequently found near the spleen.

lī-ē-nī′tis, *n.* [L. *lien*, the spleen, and *-itis*.] Splenitis.

lī″ē-nō=in-tes′ti-năl, *a.* Belonging to both spleen and intestine.

liēn′ŏr, *n.* One who holds a lien.

lī-en-tĕr′iç, *a.* [Gr. *leienteria*, the passing one's food without digesting; *leios*, smooth, and *enteron*, intestine.] Pertaining to a lientery.

lī′en-ter-y, *n.* A lax or diarrhea in which the aliments are discharged undigested, and with little alteration either in color or substance.

lī′ēr, *n.* One who lies down; one who rests or remains; as, a *lier* in wait or in ambush.

li-ērne′, *n.* [Fr., from *lier*; L. *ligare*, to bind.] A branch-rib between principal ribs in a groined arch.

lieū, *n.* [Fr., from L. *locus*, place.] Place; stead; now used only in a phrase, *in lieu of*, equivalent to *instead of*.

lieū-ten′ăn-cy, *n.* 1. The rank, office, or commission of a lieutenant.

2. The territory within a lieutenant's jurisdiction.

3. The collective body of lieutenants. [Obs.]

lieū-ten′ănt, *n.* [ME. *levetenant*; OFr. *lieutenant*; LL. *locum tenens (-entis)*, one holding the place of another; L. *locum*, acc. of *locus*, place, and *tenens (-entis)*, ppr. of *tenere*, to hold.]

1. An officer, civil or military, who supplies the place of a superior in his absence or under his orders, as (a) in an army, a commissioned officer next in rank below a captain; (b) in the United States navy, a commissioned officer next in rank below a lieutenant-commander; (c) in the British navy, a commissioned officer next in rank below a commander. In Great Britain and Ireland and the British possessions, the word is generally pronounced *lef-ten′ănt*, a form regarded in the United States as archaic.

2. Any one empowered to act for or represent another; a deputy.

lieū-ten′ănt=çō-lo′nel (-kēr′), *n.* An officer next in rank below a colonel.

lieū-ten′ănt=çŏm-mȧnd′ēr, *n.* A naval officer of the United States next in rank below a commander.

lieū-ten′ănt=ġen′ēr-ăl, *n.* A military officer next in rank below a general; in the army of the United States, the title has been conferred upon Washington, Scott (by brevet), Grant, Sherman, Sheridan, and others.

lieū-ten′ănt=gŏv′ērn-ŏr, *n.* An officer performing the duties of a governor in case of his absence, illness, disability, or death. In some British possessions and colonies, under a governor-general, the chief magistrate of a separate district is called a lieutenant-governor.

lieū-ten′ănt-ry, *n.* Lieutenancy. [Obs.]

lieū-ten′ănt-ship, *n.* Lieutenancy.

liev′ēr, *adv.* comp. of *lief*.

lif, *n.* [Ar.] A fiber obtained from the date-palm, used in making ropes, etc.

līfe, *n.*; *pl.* **līveṣ**. [ME. *lif*; AS. *lif*, life.]

1. The principle or power which is the source or controlling factor of the vital phenomena characteristic of organized beings; the essential vital element; hence, the aggregate properties by which an organism is capable of self-preservation and development by adapting itself to surrounding conditions; vitality; power of living; as, there is still *life* in the seed; to take one's *life*.

2. The state of an organism in which its organs are capable of performing their functions, or in which the performance of functions has not permanently ceased; animate existence; the condition of being alive.

3. The time during which any organism is alive, or any portion of that time; the time from birth or beginning of existence to death, or the period from any point in such existence to death; as, *life* is brief; a position for *life*.

4. The sum of the actions or phenomena exhibited by a living organism; vital phenomena.

Life is the continuous adjustment of internal relations to external relations.
—Herbert Spencer.

5. Hence, the outward manifestation of animate existence; the mode, manner, condition, character, or quality of living; the circumstances or general state of human existence; the course of human affairs; as, a strenuous *life*; a *life* of seclusion, sorrow, poverty, shame, etc.; *life* in a great city; a good *life*; high *life*; the *life* of a slave; daily *life*.

6. Living organisms in general or collectively; as, nature swarms with *life*.

7. That which makes alive, or causes growth and development; the animating or inspiring principle, force, energy, or idea; spirit; vigor; vivacity; animation. Hence, a person or thing regarded as the source of vigor, animation, spirit, or enjoyment; as, the blood is the *life*; his *life* ran from his veins; that thought was the *life* of the crusade; put new *life* into the business; she was the *life* of the party; his writings lack *life* and fire.

8. A vital point; as, the arrow reached its *life*.

9. The attainment or experience of enjoyment in the full and free use of the powers; also, eternal existence; eternal happiness in heaven.

10. The duration of existence, usefulness, or efficiency; the period within which anything has efficient force; as, the *life* of an engine, a rope, or a wheel; the *life* of an execution.

11. A person; persons collectively; as, another *life* lost.

12. A person as dear as one's existence; a darling; as, my *life*! my own!

13. A biography; as, a new *life* of Napoleon.

14. The living form; the real state or character; as, a picture from the *life*; true to *life*.

15. A life-insurance policy; also, a person as a subject for insurance. [Slang.]

līfe′=ar″rōw, *n.* An arrow shot from a gun to carry a line to a vessel needing help.

līfe′=as-sūr″ănce (-shūr″), *n.* See *Life-insurance*.

līfe′blood (-blud), *n.* 1. The blood necessary to life; vital blood.

2. That which gives strength and energy.

līfe′bōat, *n.* A boat constructed for preserving lives in cases of shipwreck or other destruction of a vessel. The festooned line in figure 1 shows the exterior life-line. In figure 2, A A are side air-cases; B B, relieving tubes through which any water that is shipped is got rid of; C C spaces beneath the deck placed longitudinally at the midship part of the boat, with cases packed with cork; *d*, scuttle for ventilation with pump fixed in it.

Lifeboat.
Fig. 1. Sheer plan. Fig. 2. Section amidships.

līfe′=çär, *n.* A car used to save persons or goods from a wreck. A rope is run from the shore to the vessel, and the car is drawn along this rope by cords.

līfe′=drop, *n.* A drop of lifeblood. [Rare.]

līfe′=es-tāte″, *n.* An estate limited to the duration of some one's life.

līfe′=ev-ēr-lȧst″ing, *n.* A plant of the genus *Gnaphalium*; cudweed.

līfe′fụl, *a.* Full of life; giving life.

līfe′=giv″ing, *a.* Giving life or spirit; having power to give life; inspiriting; invigorating.

līfe′=guärd, *n.* A guard of the life or person; a guard that attends a prince or other person.

līfe′hōld, *n.* Life-land.

līfe′=in-sūr″ănce (-shūr″), *n.* A contract for the payment of a certain sum of money upon the death of a specified person known as the insured.

līfe′=in″tēr-est, *n.* An interest or estate not of inheritance, held only during the life of a person or persons.

līfe′=land, *n.* Land held on a lease during the term of a life or lives.

līfe′less, *a.* [ME. *lifles*; AS. *lifleās*; *lif*, life, and *-leās*, -less.]

1. Dead; destitute of life; inanimated; as, *lifeless* matter; a *lifeless* body.

2. Destitute of power, force, vigor, or spirit; dull.

3. Showing no signs of life.

līfe′less-ly, *adv.* In a lifeless manner.

līfe′less-ness, *n.* Lifeless quality or state.

līfe′līke, *a.* Realistic; like the living thing.

līfe′=līne, *n.* Any line used to protect or rescue life, as (a) a line on a vessel for safety in rough weather; (b) a line on a lifeboat or buoy to support a person in the water; (c) a line at a bathing-beach for the safety of bathers; (d) a line shot out to a wreck by a life-saving crew.

līfe′lōde, *n.* Manner or means of living. [Obs.]

līfe′lŏng, *a.* Enduring or uninterrupted throughout life.

līfe′ly, *a.* Lively; lifelike. [Obs.]

līfe′māte, *n.* A mate for a lifetime.

līf′en, *v.t.* To enliven. [Obs.]

līfe′=plant, *n.* An evergreen of the genus *Bryophyllum* having leaves which develop buds, roots, and new plants when laid on moist ground.

līfe′=prē-sērv″ēr, *n.* 1. A belt, jacket, or other device sufficiently buoyant to support a person's body in water.

2. A billy, cane, revolver, or other defensive weapon. [Colloq.]

līfe′=rent, *n.* The rent of an estate for life.

līfe′=rock″et, *n.* A rocket used by life-savers to carry a line to a vessel.

līfe′=sāv″ing, *a.* Saving, or intended to save, life; as, a *life-saving* device.

Life-saving service; in the United States, an organization under the Treasury Department which maintains a series of stations equipped with crews and devices for saving the lives of persons shipwrecked near the shores of the ocean and the great lakes. Other countries have similar organizations maintained by private societies.

Figure wearing a Life-preserver.

līfe′-shot, *n.* A shot used to carry a line to a vessel in need of help.

līfe′-sīze, *a.* Of the size of the living original.

līfe′sŏme, *a.* Lively; gay; vivacious. [Rare.]

līfe′spring, *n.* The spring or source of life.

līfe′string, *n.* A hypothetical nerve or string essential to life; used in figures comparing life to a harp.

līfe′-tā″ble, *n.* A table showing the average number of people that attain various ages, out of a specified number of births.

līfe′tīme, *n.* The time that life continues.

līf′lōde, *n.* [Obs.] Same as *Lifelode*.

lift, *n.* [AS. *lyft*, the air, sky.] The sky; the heavens; the atmosphere. [Scot.]

lift, *v.t.*; lifted, *pt.*, *pp.*; lifting, *ppr.* [ME. *liften*, *lyften*, from Ice. *lypta*, to lift, to raise in the air, from *lopt*, the air.]

1. To move or raise against the force of gravitation; to elevate; as, to *lift* a load.

2. To raise in estimation, dignity, or rank; to elevate to a higher state, pitch, or degree; to exalt; as, his merits *lifted* him into notice.

3. To preserve in an elevated state; as, the mountain *lifts* its snow-capped peaks toward the sky.

4. To take away, as weight or pressure; as, to *lift* a weight from one's mind; to *lift* a note or debt.

5. To steal; to take and carry away, particularly cattle; as, to *lift* a fine herd. [Colloq.]

6. To bear; to support. [Obs.]

7. To raise; to collect. [Scot.]

To lift up; to raise; to elevate; especially, in the New Testament, to raise upon the cross.

lift, *v.i.* 1. To try to raise; to exert the strength for the purpose of raising or bearing.

2. To practise theft. [Obs.]

3. To rise or appear to rise or disappear in the air; as, a fog *lifts*; the sailors see the land *lift*.

4. To flutter or shake, as a sail of a ship when it is close to the wind.

lift, *n.* 1. The act of raising; as, the *lift* of the feet in walking or running.

2. Assistance in lifting, and hence assistance in general; as, give us a *lift*. [Colloq.]

3. A rise; a degree of elevation; as, the *lift* of a lock in canals; a short *lift*.

4. In nautical language, a rope from the masthead to the extremity of a yard, used to support the yard and raise the end when required.

5. The means by which anything lifts or is lifted, as (a) an elevator; (b) a hoisting apparatus; (c) a machine for exercising the muscles; (d) a handle.

6. That which is lifted; as, a heavy *lift*.

7. In horology, that period of the oscillation of a balance which gives the impulse.

8. A step in a cone-pulley.

9. In shoemaking, a thickness of leather in a heel.

10. A lift-gate.

11. A promotion; a raise. [Colloq.]

12. In aviation, the rising force of a flying apparatus.

lift′ȧ-ble, *a.* Capable of being lifted.

lift′-bridġe, *n.* A form of bridge in which a movable part may be lifted.

lift′ēr, *n.* One who or that which lifts or raises; (a) a thief; as, a cattle-*lifter*; (b) a latch-key; (c) an apparatus for lifting goods or persons; a lift; (d) in founding, a tool for dressing the mold; also, a device to hold the sand together in lifting the cope; (e) in the steam-engine, the arm on a lifting-rod that raises the puppet-valve; (f) a bucket-wheel used to lift paper pulp; (g) a device used to lift stove-lids.

lift′-gāte, *n.* A gate that must be raised to open it.

lift′ing=dāy, *n.* Monday or Tuesday after Easter. [Prov. Eng.]

lift′ing=dog, *n.* A clutch, pawl, or the like, used to lift another piece.

lift′ing=mȧ-çhine″, *n.* A health-lift.

lift′ing=rod, *n.* In a steam-engine, a rod receiving motion from the rock-shaft, and imparting motion to the lifter of a puppet-valve.

lift′ing=sāil, *n.* A sail tending to raise a ship's bow out of the water, as the jib.

lift′ing=set, *n.* A set or series of pumps used to lift water from a mine, by a series of lifts.

lift′-pump, *n.* A pump which raises a liquid only to its own top, and is not a force-pump.

lift′-ten″tēr, *n.* A windmill governor to control the speed of the vanes, or to regulate the space between millstones driven by the windmill.

lift′=wạll, *n.* A cross-wall in a lock of a canal.

lig, *v.i.* [Obs.] See third *Lie*.

lig′ȧ-ment, *n.* [Fr. *ligament*; L. *ligamentum*, a band, bandage, from *ligare*, to tie, bind.]

1. Anything that ties or unites one thing or part to another; a bond; a tie.
2. In anatomy, a strong, compact substance, serving to bind one bone to another, or to hold an organ in position; it is a white, solid, inelastic, tendinous substance, softer than cartilage, but harder than membrane.
3. In a bivalve shell, the elastic cuticular band uniting the valves at the hinges.

lig-ȧ-men′tăl, lig-ȧ-men′tous, *a.* Composing a ligament; of the nature of a ligament; binding; as, a strong *ligamentous* membrane.

lī′găn, *n.* [Contr. of L. *ligamen*, a band, tie, from *ligare*, to bind, fasten.] In law, goods sunk in the sea, but tied to a cork or buoy to locate them. [Compare *Flotsam* and *Jetsam.*]

lī′gāte, *v.t.* [L. *ligatus*, pp. of *ligare*, to bind, tie.] To bind with a bandage or ligature; to tie.

lī-gā′tion, *n.* [L. *ligatio* (*-onis*), a binding, from *ligatus*, pp. of *ligare*, to bind.] The act of binding, or state of being bound; especially, the tying of an artery in a surgical operation; also, the constriction thus produced.

lī-gā′tŏr, *n.* A surgical instrument used in ligation.

lig′ȧ-tūre, *n.* [Fr., from LL. *ligatura*, a band, from L. *ligare*, to bind.]
1. Anything that binds; a band or bandage.
2. The act of binding; as, by a strict *ligature* of the parts.
3. In music, a band or line connecting notes; a slur.
4. In printing, a double character, or a type consisting of two or more letters or characters united, as *fl, fi, ff, ffi, æ, œ*; also, the character employed to indicate connection of letters.
5. In medicine, the state of being bound; stiffness of a joint.
6. In surgery, a cord or string for tying the blood-vessels, particularly the arteries, to prevent hemorrhage; also, for removing tumors.
7. Impotence due to magic. [Obs.]

lig′ȧ-tūre, *v.t.* In surgery, to ligate.

lig′e, *v.t.* and *v.i.* To lie. [Obs.]

lī′geănce, *n.* Allegiance. [Obs.]

lige′ment, *n.* See *Ledgment*. [Obs.]

lig′ge, *v.i.* To recline; to lie. [Obs.]

lig′gẽr, *n.* [Prov. Eng.] 1. A horizontal scaffold-beam.
2. A plank pathway across a ditch.
3. A coverlet.
4. A fish-line with a float, used in fishing for pike.
5. The nether millstone.

līght, *n.* [ME. *light, liht*; AS. *leóht*, light, from the Teut. root *luh*, to be light.]
1. That form of motion or energy capable of affecting the organs of sight and thus rendering visible the objects from which it proceeds. The *undulatory theory* is that light results from rapid vibrations of the molecules of the luminous body; that these vibrations are transmitted through the ether as wavelike movements at the rate of over 186,400 miles per second; and that these movements act upon the nerves of the retina, causing the sensation of light. The *corpuscular* or *emission theory* of Newton supposed that luminous bodies threw off corpuscles or particles in straight lines. The *electromagnetic theory* considers light to be an electromagnetic wave disturbance.
2. The sensation caused by the action of certain wave-motions on the retina.
3. Anything that emits, or is a source of light, as a lamp, candle, taper, lighthouse, star, etc. Specifically, in fireworks, a piece giving a brilliant flame; as, a Bengal *light*.
4. A place that admits light; a window; a window-pane; as, a broken *light* in the sash.
5. The physical conditions constituting day; the dawn of day; space or area illuminated; hence, open view; visible state; public view or notice; as, rise with the *light*; new evidence brought to *light*.
6. The manner in which the light strikes upon a picture, statue, etc.; situation to be seen or viewed; hence, position or circumstances in which any matter is regarded or thought upon; as, the painting is in a good *light*; that puts matters in a different *light*.
7. The part of a picture supposed to be illuminated by the source of light of the subject, as opposed to *shade*.
8. Illumination of mind; instruction; knowledge; intelligence; as, I got some *light* from his letter.
9. Joy; felicity; heaven; a state of bliss.
10. In law, the right which one has to have the access of the sun's rays to his windows free from any obstruction on the part of his neighbors.

Northern lights; the aurora borealis.

Syn.—Luminosity, radiance, beam, gleam, phosphorescence, scintillation, coruscation, flash, brightness, brilliancy, effulgence, splendor, blaze, candle, lamp, lantern, explanation, instruction, illumination, understanding, interpretation, day, life.

līght (lit), *a.* [ME. *light, liht*; AS. *leóht, leht*, light, bright, from Teut. root *luh* in verbs signifying to be light.]
1. Bright; clear; not dark or obscure; as, the morning is *light*; the apartment is *light*.
2. In colors, white or whitish; pale; as, a *light* color; a *light* brown; a *light* complexion.

līght, *v.t.*; lighted *or* lit, *pt., pp.*; lighting, *ppr.* [ME. *lighten, lichten*; AS. *lyhtan, lihtan*, to shine, to make light, from *leóht*, bright, light.]
1. To kindle; to inflame; to set fire to; as, to *light* a candle or lamp; sometimes with *up*; as, to *light up* a brilliant flame.
2. To give light to; to illuminate; to fill or spread over with light; as, to *light* the streets of a city.
3. To accompany with a light; as, to *light* one home.

līght, *v.i.* 1. To ignite; to kindle; to catch fire; as, his cigar would not *light*.
2. To grow luminous or bright; to receive or exhibit light; as, the clouds *light* up at sunrise.

līght, *a.* [ME. *light, licht*; AS. *leóht, liht*, light.]
1. Having little weight; having relatively small weight; not heavy; as, a feather is *light* compared with lead or silver.
2. Not burdensome; easy to be lifted, borne, endured, performed, digested, or the like; as, a *light* burden; a *light* affliction; a *light* task; *light* food.
3. Not heavily armed, laden, or burdened; not encumbered; clear of impediments; as, *light* troops; the ship returned *light*.
4. Slight; trifling; not important; as, a *light* error; a *light* remark.
5. Not heavy in manner, movement, use, or result; having slight force; not intense or violent; moderate; delicate; easy; graceful; agile; as, a *light* wind or rain; a *light* touch; *light* sleep; *light* style; *light* of foot.
6. Without gravity; indulging in, exhibiting, or indicating levity; wanting in solidity; volatile; unsteady; frivolous; wanton; unchaste; as, a *light* mind; *light* conduct; a *light* wife.
7. Free from a burden of pain, care, or trouble; cheerful; gay; as, *light* of heart.
8. Having a feeling of lightness; dizzy; giddy; flighty; as, *light*-headed.
9. Not of legal weight; clipped; as, *light* coin.
10. Loose; easily pulverized; as, a *light* soil.
11. Not soggy; properly raised; spongy; as, *light* bread.
12. Containing little nutriment. [Rare.]
13. Used for light work. [Rare.]
14. Sickly; feeble. [Prov. Eng.]
15. Transitory; insubstantial. [Obs.]

Light eater; one who eats only a small amount of food.

Light sleeper; one who can be readily awakened.

To make light of; to treat as of little consequence; to slight; to disregard.

To set light by; to undervalue; to slight; to treat as of no importance; to despise.

Syn.—Imponderable, portable, buoyant, volatile, easy, active, unencumbered, empty, scanty, slight, gentle, delicate, unsteady, capricious, vain, frivolous, characterless, thoughtless, inadequate, unsubstantial, gay, bright, lively.

līght, *adv.* Lightly; cheaply; easily.

līght, *v.i.*; lighted *or* lit, *pt., pp.*; lighting, *ppr.* [ME. *lighten, lichten*; AS. *lihtan, lyhtan*, to dismount, to alight, originally to relieve of the rider's burden, to make light, from *leóht, liht*, light.]
1. To fall; to come by chance; to happen; with *on* or *upon*; as, to *light upon* a treasure.
2. To descend, as from a horse or carriage; to alight; with *down, off*, or *from*.

He *lighted down* from his chariot.
—2 Kings v. 21.

3. To settle; to rest; to stoop from flight; as, the bee *lights* on this flower and that.

To light out; to hurry away; to abscond. [Slang.]

līght, *v.t.* [ME. *lighten, lychten*; AS. *lihtan*, to make light, from *leóht*, light.]
1. To lighten. [Obs.]
2. To deliver, as in childbirth. [Prov. Eng.]

līght′ȧ-ble, *a.* Capable of being lighted.

līght′-ärmed, *a.* Armed with light weapons and equipped for active service.

līght′-ball, *n.* In military operations, a device to furnish light for one's own operations or to reveal the enemy's works; usually, a canvas bag or frame with a combustible preparation.

līght′-bar″rel, *n.* A barrel filled with combustibles, used to furnish light.

līght′-bōat, *n.* A light-ship.

līght′-box, *n.* A lightroom.

līght′brāin, *n.* A person of weak mind.

līght′-cōurse, *n.* A band of copper at the top of a sugar-clarifying pan, to keep the scum from boiling over.

līght′-dūes, *n.pl.* Dues or tolls charged upon shipping for lighthouse maintenance.

līght′en, *v.t.*; lightened, *pt., pp.*; lightening, *ppr.* [ME. *lightnen, lightenen*, to become light.]
1. To make light or clear; to dissipate darkness from; to fill with light; to illuminate; to enlighten; as, to *lighten* an apartment; to *lighten* the understanding.
2. To emit or send forth, as lightning or something resembling lightning; to flash. [Rare.]
3. To cause to become lighter in color.

līght′en, *v.i.* 1. To exhibit the phenomenon of lightning; to give out flashes; to flash.
2. To become more light; to grow less dark or gloomy; to clear; as, the sky *lightens*.

līght′en, *v.t.* 1. To make lighter; to reduce in weight; to make less heavy; as, to *lighten* a burden.
2. To make less burdensome; to alleviate, as toil.
3. To cheer; to exhilarate; to gladden.

līght′en, *v.i.* To grow lighter or less heavy.

līght′en, *v.i.* To light; to alight; to descend. [Obs.]

līght′en-ing, *n.* 1. Lightning. [Obs.]
2. Fulguration.
3. A becoming light or bright.

līght′ẽr, *n.* [D. *ligter*, from *ligt*, light.] A large, open, flat-bottomed barge, used in lightening or unloading and loading ships, etc.

līght′ẽr, *v.t.* and *v.i.* I. *v.t.* To transport by means of or as by a lighter; as, to *lighter* coal to a ship.
II. *v.i.* To be engaged in lightering goods.

līght′ẽr, *n.* 1. One who or that which lights; as, a spill, a cigar-*lighter*, etc.
2. [*pl.*] Blinders for a horse. [Obs.]

līght′ẽr-āge, *n.* 1. Conveyance by a lighter.
2. The act of removing a cargo by a lighter.
3. The cost of transportation by a lighter.

līght′ẽr-măn, *n.*; *pl.* **līght′ẽr-men.** A manager of or an employee on a lighter.

līght′ẽr-screw (-skrụ), *n.* A screw regulating the space between millstones.

līght′ẽr-stăff, *n.* A lever controlling the adjustment of the bridgetree of a grain-mill.

līght′-fin″gẽred, *a.* 1. Dexterous in taking and conveying away; addicted to petty thefts.
2. Having a light touch, as in piano-playing.

līght′-foot, līght′-foot″ed, *a.* Nimble in running or dancing; not heavy of tread.

līght′fụl, *a.* Bright; cheerful. [Rare.]

līght′fụl-ness, *n.* Brightness; cheerfulness. [Rare.]

līght′-hand″ed, *a.* 1. Light of touch.
2. Carrying little in one's hands.
3. Short-handed; lacking the regular number of hands or assistants, as a ship, factory, etc.

līght′-head″ed, *a.* Dizzy; delirious; giddy; volatile; frivolous; thoughtless; mentally unsteady or unsound.

līght′-head″ed-ness, *n.* The state of being light-headed.

līght′-heärt″ed, *a.* Free from grief or anxiety; gay; cheerful; merry.

līght′-heärt″ed-ly, *adv.* With a light heart.

līght′-heärt″ed-ness, *n.* The state of being free from care or grief; cheerfulness.

līght′-heeled, *a.* Lively in walking or running; brisk; swift.

līght′-hŏrse, *n.* Light-armed cavalry.

līght′-hŏrse″măn, *n.* A light-armed cavalryman.

līght′house, *n.* A tower or other lofty structure with a powerful light at top, erected at the entrance of a port or at some important point on a coast, and serving as a guide or warning of danger to navigators at night; a pharos. The old method of illuminating lighthouses was simply by means of a fire. Reflectors and lenses were not used till near the close of the eighteenth century. The apparatus for illumination now consists of an elaborate arrangement of glass lenses and prisms, with which reflectors may or may not be combined. The source of the light is gas, oil, or sometimes electricity.

līght′ing, *n.* [ME. *lihtinge*; AS. *lihtung*, verbal n. of *lihtan, leóhtan*, to make light, illuminate.]
1. Illumination; also, the act of growing light.
2. Ignition; as, the *lighting* of a match.
3. Same as *Annealing*.

līght′ing, *n.* The act of alighting.

līght′-ī″ron (-ūrn), *n.* A candle-holder or lamp-stand of iron. [Obs.]

līght′-keep″ẽr, *n.* One whose duty is to care for the light of a lighthouse or light-ship.

līght′-leg″ged (*or* -legd), *a.* Nimble; swift of foot.

līght′less, *a.* [AS. *leóhtleás*, without light; *leóht*, light, and *-leás*, -less.] Dark; having no light.

līght′ly, *adv.* [ME. *lightly, lihtliche*; AS. *leóhtlice*, lightly, from *leóhtlic*, light; *leóht*, light, and *-lic*, -ly.]
1. With little weight; not heavily or severely; as, to tread *lightly*; to punish *lightly*.
2. With lightness or levity; gaily; cheerfully.
3. For reasons of little weight.
4. Easily; readily; without difficulty.
5. Nimbly; with agility; quickly.
6. Wantonly; unchastely.
7. Usually. [Obs.]

līght′măn, *n.* A linkman or a light-keeper.

light′=mind″ed, *a.* Inconsiderate; volatile; unsteady; weak in mind.
light′=mind″ed-ness, *n.* The state or quality of being light-minded.
light′=mŏn″ey, *n.* Light-dues.
light′ness, *n.* The quality or state of being light in any sense; absence of heaviness or darkness; buoyancy; levity; ease; grace; cheerfulness.
light′ning, *n.* [From the verb *lighten.*]
1. A discharge of atmospheric electricity, accompanied by a vivid flash of light; the flash thus caused. It is commonly the discharge of electricity from one cloud to another, sometimes from a cloud to the earth.
2. A growing light or bright; a lightening; illumination; flashing.

In the golden *lightning*
Of the sunken sun. —Shelley.

light′ning, *n.* A lightening in weight. [Obs.]
light′ning=ar-rest″ẽr, *n.* A device to prevent injury to persons, instruments, or buildings from a lightning discharge conveyed along a wire; called also *lightning-protector.*
light′ning=bug, *n.* A firefly.
light′ning=rod, *n.* A pointed, insulated metallic rod erected to protect a building or vessel from lightning.

Lightning-rods. *a b e*, Various forms of Rods. *c d f*, Various forms of Tips. *g h i*, Various forms of Attachments.

light′=ō′=lōve″, *n.* 1. An old dance-tune.
2. A loose, wanton, or light woman.
light′rọom, *n.* 1. A room beside the magazine of a ship of war, having windows through which light can be supplied to the magazine without danger of an explosion.
2. The room in a lighthouse containing the illuminating apparatus; the lantern.
lights, *n.pl.* [So called from their being light.] The lungs, especially of an animal other than man.
light′=ship, *n.* A ship anchored and serving as a lighthouse in places where a fixed structure is impracticable.

Light-ship.

light′sŏme, *a.* 1. Luminous; not obscure. [Rare.]
2. Cheering; gay; exhilarating.
light′sŏme-ly, *adv.* In a lightsome way.
light′sŏme-ness, *n.* Luminousness; cheerfulness.
light′=struck, *a.* In photography, accidentally exposed to light; fogged by actinic rays.
light′=wāve, *n.* A wave in the ether of such length as to be capable of causing the sensation of light.
light′weight (-wāt), *a.* 1. Of less than a certain fixed weight; specifically, in boxing, between a featherweight and below a middleweight; weighing 133 pounds.
2. Of small importance.
light′=weight, *n.* A light-weight person, jockey, boxer, horse, etc.
light′=winged, *a.* Having light or fleet wings; quick to move; elusive.
light′=wit″ted, *a.* Of deficient intellect.
light′wood, *n.* 1. The knots and other resinous parts of pine-trees.
2. In Australia, a species of acacia; blackwood.
light′y, *a.* Illuminated. [Obs.]
lig-nal′ōes, *n.* Aloes-wood or agallochum.
lig′nȧ-tile, *a.* [L. *lignum*, wood.] Growing on wood.
lig′nē-ous, *a.* [L. *ligneus*, from *lignum*, wood.] Wooden; made of, consisting of, or resembling wood; woody.
lig-nes′cent, *a.* Partly woody.
lig′ni-cōle, *a.* Lignicoline.
lig-nic′ō-line, *a.* [L. *lignum*, wood, and *colere*, to inhabit.] Growing on wood.
lig-nif′ẽr-ous, *a.* [L. *lignifer*; *lignum*, wood, and *ferre*, to produce.] Yielding or producing wood.
lig″ni-fi-cā′tion, *n.* The process of becoming or of converting into wood.
lig′ni-fọrm, *a.* [L. *lignum*, wood, and *forma*, form.] Like wood; resembling wood.
lig′ni-fȳ, *v.t.* and *v.i.*; lignified, *pt., pp.*; lignifying, *ppr.* [L. *lignum*, wood, and *facere*, to make.] To convert into or to become wood.
lig′nin, *n.* [L. *lignum*, wood, and *-in.*] A substance closely allied to cellulose and forming the heaviest part of dried wood; as, a woody fiber consists of cellulose and *lignin.*
lig-ni-pẽr′dous, *a.* [L. *lignum*, wood, and *perdere*, to destroy.] Causing destruction to wood, as certain insects, mollusks, etc.
lig-nir′ē-ōse, *n.* A form of lignin slightly soluble in water.
lig′nīte, *n.* [L. *lignum*, wood, and *-ite.*] Fossil wood, wood-coal, or brown coal, a combustible substance mineralized to a certain degree, but retaining distinctly its woody texture. It holds a station intermediate between peat and coal. Beds of lignite occur chiefly in the upper Cretaceous and Tertiary formations.
lig-nit′ic, *a.* Containing lignite; resembling lignite.
Lignitic group; the Laramie group.
lig-ni-tif′ẽr-ous, *a.* Bearing lignite.
lig-niv′ō-rous, *a.* [L. *lignum*, wood, and *vorare*, to devour.] Devouring wood, as insect larvæ.
lig-nō-cer′ic, *a.* [L. *lignum*, wood, and *cera*, wax, and *-ic.*] Of or derived from the wax or distillate of wood.
Lignoceric acid; a substance derived from beech and other woods by distillation.
lig′nōne, *n.* [L. *lignum*, wood, and *-one.*] A form of lignin.
lig′nōse, *a.* and *n.* [L. *lignosus*, woody, from *lignum*, wood.]
I. *a.* Ligneous.
II. *n.* A nitroglycerin wood-fiber explosive; also, a form of lignin.
lig′nous, *a.* Ligneous.
lig′num, *n.* [L.] Wood, as distinguished from bark or soft tissues.
lig′num=rhō′di-um, *n.* [L. *lignum*, wood, and Gr. *rhodon*, a rose.] Rosewood.
lig′num=vī′tæ, *n.* [L. *lignum*, wood, and *vitæ*, genit. of *vita*, life.]
1. A tree, *Guaiacum officinale*, of tropical America, having a hard, solid, heavy wood, used for bowling-balls, pulleys, etc.
2. Any of several trees having similar wood, as *Acacia falcata* and *Eucalyptus polyanthema* of New South Wales, *Vitex lignum-vitæ* of Queensland, and *Sarcomphalus laurinus* of Jamaica, the bastard lignum-vitæ.
lig′rō-in, *n.* A trade name for the portion of petroleum whose boiling-point is slightly lower than safe kerosene.
lig′săm, *n.* [Obs.] Same as *Ligan.*
lig′ū-lȧ, *n.*; *pl.* **lig′ū-læ**. [L. *ligula* or *lingula*, dim. of *lingua*, tongue.]
1. In botany, same as *Ligule.*
2. In zoölogy, (a) the distal portion of an insect's labium, usually divided into the glossa and paraglossæ. In some insects, notably the bee, it serves as a proboscis; (b) a linguiform lobe of the lateral appendages of certain annelids.
3. In anatomy, a border of white nervous matter in the covering of the fourth cerebral ventricle.
lig′ū-lăr, *a.* Of, like, or consisting of ligulæ or ligules.
lig′ū-lāte, lig′ū-lā-ted, *a.* [L. *ligula*, a tongue, strap, and *-ate.*]
1. In botany, like a tongue or strap; strap-shaped.
2. Having a ligula or ligule.
lig′ūle, *n.* [L. *ligula* or *lingula*, a small tongue, tongue of a shoe, a strap.] In botany, a strap-like part, as (a) the strap-shaped petal of certain flowers of the *Compositæ*; (b) the membrane at the base of the lamina of a grass-leaf, as that of millet-grass, *Milium multiflorum*, shown in the figure; (c) an outgrowth on the inner side of certain petals, as in *Silene.*

L, Ligule.

Lig″ū-li-flō′ræ, *n.pl.* [L. *ligula*, a small tongue, a strap, and *flos*, *floris*, a flower.] In the *Compositæ*, a suborder having ligulate florets, including the lettuce, dandelion, hawkweed, chicory, etc.
lig″ū-li-flō′rous, *a.* Producing only ligulate florets; of or pertaining to the *Liguliforæ.*
li-gū′li-fọrm, *a.* [L. *ligula*, a small tongue, strap, and *forma*, form.] Flat and strap-like; ligulate.
lig′ū-loid, *a.* Resembling a strap, tongue, or ligula.
Li-guō′rist, *n.* One who follows the theological theories of St. Alfonso Maria da Liguori (1696–1787); a Redemptorist; called also *Liguorian.*
lig′ūre, *n.* [LL. *ligurius*, *lyncurius*, *lyncurion*; L. Gr. *linkourion*, *lingourion*, a kind of gem; prob. from Gr. *lynx*, *lynkos*, a lynx, and *ouron*, urine, from the belief that it was composed of the petrified urine of the lynx.] A precious stone, being one of the twelve in the breastplate of the Jewish high priest; possibly jacinth, opal, or amber.
Li-gū′ri-ăn, *a.* and *n.* [L. *Liguria*, Liguria, from *Ligus* or *Ligur* (*-uris*), a Ligurian.]
I. *a.* Belonging to Liguria, an ancient country lying between modern Marseilles and Genoa.
II. *n.* One of an ancient race, possibly pre-Aryan, inhabiting Liguria, conquered by the Romans.
Ligurian sea; the Gulf of Genoa.
Li-gus′ti-cum, *n.* [L., a plant native to Liguria, from *Ligusticus*, Ligurian, from *Ligus* or *Ligur*, a Ligurian.] A genus of the *Umbelliferæ*, characterized by the presence of oil-tubes in the fruit.
li-gus′trin, *n.* [*Ligustrum* and *-in.*] A bitter substance derived from *Ligustrum vulgare*, the privet.
Li-gus′trum, *n.* [L., the privet.] A genus of the *Oleaceæ*, including the common privet.
līk′ȧ-ble, *a.* Worthy of being liked.
līke, *n.* [ME. *like*, *lyke*; AS. *lic*, the body.] Body; person; form; also, a corpse. [Obs.]
līke, *a.*; *comp.* liker; *superl.* likest. [ME. *like*, *lyke*; AS. *gelic*, like, lit., having the same body; *ge-* together, and *lic*, body.]
1. Similar; of the same or nearly the same kind; having resemblance; as, for *like* uses.
2. Equal in quantity, number, or degree; equivalent; corresponding; as, *like* figures.
3. Probable; likely; as, he is *like* to die.
4. Equal or disposed to; moved by wish or judgment toward; as, do you feel *like* eating? [Colloq.]
Had like; came near; used with an infinitive; as, she *had like* to have fallen. [Colloq.]
līke, *adv.* 1. In the same or a similar way; in the manner of; equally; as, act *like* men; *like* as a father pitieth.
2. Likely; probably; as, *like* enough. [Colloq.]
3. As one may say; somewhat; as, he talked broken-*like.* [Colloq.]
līke, *n.* A person or thing resembling or equal to another; as, where can you find his *like.*
Such like; similar persons or things.
līke, *v.i.* To be likely; used only in the past tense; as, he *liked* to have had a fall. [Rare.]
līke, *v.t.* To liken. [Obs.]
līke, *v.t.*; liked (līkt), *pt., pp.*; liking, *ppr.* [ME. *liken*, *lyken*; AS. *lician*, *lican*, to like, to please, prob. from *lic*, form, body.]
1. To be pleased with; to approve; to have a liking for; to enjoy; as, to *like* a person, a book, or a food.
2. To please; to be agreeable. [Obs.]
līke, *v.i.* 1. To be pleased; to choose; as, do as you *like.*
2. To please; to be agreeable. [Obs.]
3. To thrive. [Prov. Eng.]
līke, *n.* A liking; as, *likes* and dislikes.
-like. A suffix from the adjective *like*, used with nouns to form adjectives denoting likeness or resemblance; as, war*like*, man*like.*
like′ȧ-ble, *a.* Same as *Likable.*
like′hood, *n.* Likelihood. [Rare.]
like′li-hood, *n.* 1. Probability; likeliness; as, there is little *likelihood* of success.
2. Likeness; indication; good appearance. [Obs.]
like′li-ness, *n.* The state or quality of being likely; likelihood; suitableness; resemblance.
like′ly, *a.*; *comp.* likelier; *superl.* likeliest. [ME. *likli*; AS. *geliclic*, from *gelic*, like.]
1. Having the appearance of truth; credible; probable; as, a *likely* story.
2. So situated as probably to adopt some line of action, or the like; as, I am *likely* to be from home to-morrow.
3. Suitable; well-adapted; convenient; as, a *likely* person for the place; a *likely* topic.
4. Such as may be liked; pleasing; agreeable; promising; good-looking; as, a *likely* lass.
5. Similar. [Obs.]
like′ly, *adv.* Probably.
like′=mind″ed, *a.* Having a like disposition; having similar purposes, motives, and desires.
līk′en, *v.t.*; likened, *pt., pp.*; likening, *ppr.* To compare; to represent as similar.
like′ness, *n.* [ME. *liknesse*; AS. *gelicnes*, resemblance, likeness, from *gelic*, like.]
1. Resemblance; similitude; similarity.
2. That which resembles something else; a copy; a portrait; a representation; guise.
līk′ẽr-ous, *a.* Lickerous; sensual. [Obs.]
like′wāke, *n.* A wake or watch with a corpse. [Obs.]
like′wīse, *adv.* In like manner; also; moreover; too.
lī′kin′, *n.* [Chinese, from *li*, the thousandth part of a tael, and *kin*, money.] In China, a special inland tax, formerly on all sales, now on merchandise in transit, collected at various barriers. Foreign goods are exempt on payment of a duty of 2½ per cent at the customs house.
līk′ing, *n.* 1. Inclination; desire; pleasure; preference due to being pleased with something; used with *for* or *to*; as, took a *liking to* him; no *liking for* music.
2. Bodily health or appearance. [Obs.]
On liking; on approval; on trial. [Prov. Eng.]
līk′ing, *a.* Good-looking; pleasing. [Obs.]
lī′lăc, *a.* Of a light-purple color.
lī′lăc, *n.* [Sp., from Ar. *lilāk*; Per. *lilaj* or *lilanj*

the lilac, the indigo-plant, from *nīlah*, or *nīl*, the indigo-plant, from Sans. *nīla*, dark-blue indigo.]

1. A shrub of the genus *Syringa*, a native of Persia. Several species are in cultivation for the beauty and fragrance of the blossoms.

2. A light-purple color with a tinge of pink.

lil′ȧ-cine, *n.* [*Lilac* and *-ine.*] A bitter substance derived from the lilac.

Lil-i-ā′cē-æ, *n.pl.* [From L. *lilium*, a lily, and *-aceæ.*] An order of endogens, including the true lilies, tulips, hyacinths, aloes, onions, New Zealand flax, and others, with a total of about 2,400 species.

lil-i-ā′ceous, *a.* [LL. *liliaceus*, pertaining to the lily, from L. *lilium*, a lily.] Like a lily; characteristic of the *Liliaceæ*.

lil′i-ăl, *a.* Resembling lilies.

lil′ied, *a.* Like or embellished with lilies.

lil′i-fọrm, *a.* [L. *lilium*, lily, and *forma*, form.] Shaped like a lily.

Lil′i-um, *n.* [L., a lily.] A genus of the *Liliaceæ* including the true lilies.

lill, *v.i.* To loll. [Obs.]

lill, *n.* 1. One of the holes of a wind-instrument. [Scot.]

2. A little pin.

Lil″li-bul-lē′rō, Lil″li-bŭr-lē′rō, *n.* Originally, a supposed watchword of the Irish Roman Catholics in their massacre of Protestants in 1641; also used as the name and refrain of a political song during the revolution of 1688 in England.

Lil-li-pū′tiăn, *a.* and *n.* I. *a.* Of or relating to Lilliput, the fictitious island of Gulliver's Travels, or to its people, six inches in height; hence, diminutive.

II. *n.* A resident in Lilliput; hence, a person of very small size; a dwarf.

lil′ly-pil-ly, *n.* A large hardwood tree, *Eugenia Smithii*, of Australia. Its white flowers are borne in terminal panicles and its bark is rich in tannin.

lilt, *v.t.*; lilted, *pt., pp.*; lilting, *ppr.* [Compare Norw. *lilla, lirla*, to sing in a high tone.] To utter, sing, or play with animation, gaiety, and rhythmic movement; as, a bird *lilts* out its song.

lilt, *v.i.* 1. To sing or play cheerfully.

2. To do anything dexterously. [Prov.]

lilt, *n.* 1. A melody with an animated rhythm; a merry, sprightly tune; hence, cadence; rhythm; animation of rhythm; as, to speak trippingly and with a *lilt*.

lil′y, *a.* Resembling a white lily; unsullied; pure.

lil′y, *n.*; *pl.* **lil′ieṣ**. [ME. *lilie*; AS. *lilie* or *lilige*; L. *lilium*; Gr. *leirion*, a lily.]

1. Any plant of the genus *Lilium*, or the flower of such a plant. There are many species, as the white lily, orange lily, tiger-lily, scarlet lily, etc., all herbaceous perennials with scaly bulbs, whence arise tall slender stems, with alternate or somewhat whorled leaves, and bearing upon their summit a number of erect or drooping flowers of great beauty and variety of colors, having a bell-like perianth of six distinct or slightly cohering segments.

2. Any of various other plants whose flowers resemble lilies, as the calla-lily, water-lily, pond-lily, etc.

White Lily (*Lilium candidum*).

3. In heraldry, a fleur-de-lis.

4. The north pole of a compass-needle, formerly marked with a fleur-de-lis.

African lily; a blue-flowered exotic plant, *Agapanthus umbellatus*.

lil′y-bee″tle, *n.* A small beetle, *Crioceris merdigera*, found upon the white lily.

lil′y-daf″fō-dil, *n.* A daffodil.

lil′y-en″cri-nīte, *n.* An encrinite or stone-lily.

lil′y-hand″ed, *a.* Having white, delicate hands.

lil′y-hȳ′ȧ-cinth, *n.* A bulbous perennial of the genus *Scilla*, having blue flowers.

lil′y-ī″ron (-ŭrn), *n.* A barbed removable head of a harpoon.

lil′y-liv″ẽred, *a.* White-livered; cowardly.

lil′y-ŏf-the-val′ley, *n.* A plant of the genus *Convallaria*, having two ovate lanceolate leaves and a raceme of pure white fragrant flowers.

Lily-of-the-Valley (*Convallaria majalis*).

lil′y-pad, *n.* A water-lily leaf floating on water.

lil′y-white (-hwīt), *a.* White as a lily.

lil′y-wŏrt, *n.* Any plant of the *Liliaceæ*.

lim, *n.* A limb. [Obs.]

Lī′mȧ, *n.* A city, the capital of Peru, in South America.

Lima bark; the bark of a species of *Cinchona*.

Lima bean; *Phaseolus lunatus*, a pole-bean or one of its flat seeds, highly esteemed as food.

Lima wood; same as *Brazil*, 1.

lī-mā′ceous, *a.* [L. *limax* (*-acis*), a snail, slug.] Of or like a slug.

lī-mac′i-fọrm, *a.* [L. *limax* (*-acis*), a slug, and *forma*, form.] Slug-shaped.

Lī-mȧ-cī′nȧ, *n.* [L. *limax* (*-acis*), a snail, slug, and *-ina.*]

1. A genus of gasteropods of the northern seas.

2. [l—] A member of the genus constituting a part of brit or whale-food.

lim′ȧ-çon, *n.* [Fr., a snail, from L. *limax* (*-acis*), a snail.]

1. A unicursal curve of the fourth order investigated and named by Pascal.

2. Any univalve shell. [Obs.]

lī-māil′, lī′māille, *n.* Metal filings. [Obs.]

lī′măn, *n.* [Fr. *limon*; L. *limus*, mud, slime.] Slime, especially at a river's mouth.

lī-mā′tion, *n.* [L. *limatus*, pp. of *limare*, to file, from *lima*, a file.] The act of filing or polishing. [Rare.]

lī′mȧ-tūre, *n.* [L. *limatura*, from *limare*, to file, from *lima*, a file.] Filing; also, filings. [Rare.]

Lī′max, *n.* [L., a snail, slug.] A genus of naked gasteropods; the slugs.

limb (lim), *n.* [ME. *lim*; AS. *lim*, a member of the body, a limb.]

1. An articulated part attached to the trunk of an animal; an arm, leg, wing, or one of a pair of fins; without a qualifying word, a leg.

2. The branch of a tree; applied only to a branch of some size, and not to a small twig.

3. A person or thing considered as a member or portion of some other thing; as, a *limb* of the devil.

4. A young scamp; an imp; a mischievous child. [Colloq.]

5. The part of a bow on either side of the handle or grip.

Limb of the law; a lawyer; also, any officer of the law.

limb, *v.t.*; limbed, *pt., pp.*; limbing, *ppr.* 1. To remove the limbs from; to dismember; as, to *limb* a chicken.

2. To put limbs upon. [Rare.]

limb, *n.* [Fr. *limbe*; L. *limbus*, border, hem, edge.]

1. In astronomy, the border or outermost edge of the sun or moon.

2. The graduated edge of a circle or arc.

3. In botany, (a) the border or upper spreading part of a monopetalous corolla, of a sepal, or of a petal; (b) a blade or lamina.

lim′bat, *n.* [Etym. doubtful.] In the island of Cyprus, a cool northwest wind blowing from about 8 A. M. for four hours or more.

lim′bāte, *a.* [LL. *limbatus*, edged, bordered, from L. *limbus*, edge, border.] Bordered, as a flower when one color is surrounded by an edging of another.

lim-bā′tion, *n.* In zoölogy, a border.

lim′beç, lim′beck, *n.* and *v.t.* I. *n.* An alembic; a still. [Obs.]

II. *v.t.* To strain or pass through a still. [Obs.]

limbed (limd), *a.* Having limbs; as, long-*limbed*.

lim′bẽr, *a.* [Compare Ice. *limpa*, weakness.] Easily bent; flexible; pliant; not stiff; as, *limber* joints.

Syn.—Supple, pliable, pliant, flexible, limp, lithe.

lim′bẽr, *v.t.* To render pliable; to make limber.

lim′bẽr, *n.* [Prob. from Ice. *limar*, limbs, boughs, pl. of *lim*, foliage, from *limr*, a branch, limb.]

1. The fore-part of the carriage of a field-gun, consisting of an ammunition-chest set on a frame supported by two wheels and an axle, with a shaft for the horses.

Limber of Gun-carriage.

2. A gutter parallel to the keel, to convey water to the pump-well of a vessel.

3. [*pl.*] Shafts; thills. [Prov. Eng.]

lim′bẽr, *v.t.* and *v.i.*; limbered, *pt., pp.*; limbering, *ppr.* I. *v.t.* To attach to the limber; as, to *limber* the gun.

II. *v.i.* To attach the limber to a gun; to limber up.

lim′bẽr-bōard, *n.* A plank cover to keep the limber of a vessel from becoming filled with dirt.

lim′bẽr-box, *n.* A limber-chest.

lim′bẽr-chāin, *n.* 1. A chain to keep the trail from becoming loose from the limber.

2. A chain in a ship's limber used to keep it clean; called also *limber-clearer*.

lim′bẽr-chest, *n.* The chest for ammunition on a limber.

lim′bẽr-ness, *n.* Limber quality or state.

lim′bẽr-strāke, *n.* The breadth of planking nearest to the keelson in a ship's hull.

limb′-gīr″dle, *n.* In anatomy, the bony girdle at the shoulders or hips of a vertebrate.

lim′bī, *n.*, pl. of *limbus*.

lim′biç, *a.* Of or constituting a limbus.

limb′less, *a.* Destitute of limbs.

limb′mēal, *adv.* Piecemeal. [Obs.]

lim′bō, *n.* [L. *limbo*, in phrase *in limbo*, in or on the border; *in*, in, on, and *limbo*, abl. of *limbus*, edge, border.]

1. In medieval theology, a region bordering on hell. The *limbus patrum* was a place for the souls of good men until the coming of Christ. The *limbus infantum* was a similar place for the souls of unbaptized infants. The term *limbo* has been applied by the poets to other supposed places on the outer borders of hell. Shakspere applies the term to hell itself; Ariosto makes it the place of all lost things; Milton, the paradise of fools.

2. Any place of restraint or confinement.

lim′bous, *a.* Bordered; having edges partly overlapping, as a suture.

lim′bus, *n.* [L., edge, border.]

1. Same as *Limbo*.

2. In anatomy, a margin; a border.

līme, *v.t.*; limed, *pt., pp.*; liming, *ppr.* [ME. *limen*; AS. *limian*, to smear with lime, from *lim*, lime.]

1. To treat in any way with lime; (a) to manure with lime; (b) to soak hides in limewater to loosen the hair; (c) to sprinkle with lime as a disinfectant; (d) to put lime into, to kill the fish; as, to *lime* a pond; (e) to smear with a viscous substance to catch birds or the like.

2. To entangle; to ensnare.

3. To cement. [Obs.]

līme, *n.* [Fr., from Per. *līmū*, a lemon, a citron.] A tree, *Citrus medica*, akin to the lemon; also, its acid fruit, smaller than the lemon, and with a characteristic flavor.

līme, *n.* A leam or leash. [Obs.]

līme, *n.* [A corruption of *line*, which is a corruption of *lind*, from AS. *lind*, linden.] The linden.

līme, *n.* [ME. *lim, lym*; AS. *lim*, cement, glue, lime; compare L. *limus*, mud.]

1. Birdlime; any viscous material.

2. Calcium oxid, obtained from chalk, marble, limestone, or sea-shells, by calcining. When this so-called *quicklime* is moistened, it evolves heat and slakes, forming *slaked lime*. If the moisture is derived entirely from the air, it becomes *air-slaked lime*.

Caustic lime; hydrate of calcium, slaked lime; sometimes, quicklime.

līme′-bŭrn″ẽr, *n.* One who burns limestone to lime.

līme′hound, *n.* A dog used to hunt the wild boar. [Obs.]

līme′-jụ̈ice, *n.* The juice of the fruit of the lime, used extensively as an antiscorbutic.

līme′kiln (-kil), *n.* A kiln or furnace in which lime is made by calcining limestone, shells, etc.

līme′-light, *n.* A calcium light.

Lī-men′ē-ăn, *a.* and *n.* I. *a.* Of or relating to Lima, Peru, or its people.

II. *n.* One born or living in Lima.

līme′-pit, *n.* A limestone quarry; also, a lime-kiln.

lim′ẽr, *n.* A limehound. [Obs.]

līme′-rod, *n.* A twig with birdlime smeared upon it; a snare; a trick.

lī′mēṣ, *n.*; *pl.* **lim′i-tēṣ**. [L., a cross-path, boundary, limit.]

1. In anatomy, either of two tracts in the brain at the point of attachment of the olfactory lobe; called respectively *limes cinerea* and *limes alba*.

2. In zoölogy, a boundary line; the line separating two parts.

līme′stōne, *n.* Rock composed entirely or chiefly of carbonate of calcium. When containing sand or silica, it is called *silicious*; containing clay, it is *argillaceous*; and containing carbonate of magnesium, it is *dolomitic*. When firm and crystalline, it is called *marble*.

līme′-twig, *n.* A lime-rod.

līme′twig, *v.t.*; limetwigged, *pt., pp.*; limetwigging, *ppr.* To place snares about; to entangle; to snare.

līme′wash, *v.t.* To whitewash.

līme′wa″tẽr, *n.* A saturated solution of lime in water, used as an antacid.

Lī-miç′ō-læ, *n.pl.* [L. *limus*, mud, slime, and *colere*, to inhabit.]

1. An order of waders, including most of those whose broods are able to run about as soon as hatched, as snipes, plovers, sandpipers, curlews, stilts, godwits, etc.

2. A group of aquatic worms having well-developed looped canals.

lī-miç′ō-line, *a.* and *n.* I. *a.* Living on the

shore or in mud; of or belonging to the *Limicolæ*.

II. *n.* One of the *Limicolæ*.

li-mic′ō-lous, *a.* Limicoline.

lim′i-năl, *a.* [L. *limen* (*-inis*), the threshold.] Of or belonging to the threshold, beginning, or first stage; inceptive; inchoative.

līm′i-ness, *n.* The condition of being limy.

līm′ing, *n.* Limewater, used in bleaching.

lim′it, *n.* [ME. *limite, lymyte*; OFr. *limite*; L. *limes* (*-itis*), a boundary line, limit, cross-path between two fields, a border.]

1. A point, line, surface, or other boundary which limits or terminates a thing; bound; edge; end; as, the *limits* of a field; the *limit* of life; the *limits* of thought, knowledge, or power.

2. Anything having bounds; a period; a space; region; as, divided into five *limits*.

3. In mathematics, (a) a definite point or boundary separating two continuous quantities, especially that point at which the independent variable of a function moves through infinity; usually said to be a determinate quantity or point to which a variable continuously approaches, and may come nearer than any given difference, but with which it can never coincide; (b) any of various points or values between which a function has real magnitudes.

4. A limb. [Obs.]

5. A term; a characteristic attribute. [Obs.]

lim′it, *v.t.* and *v.i.*; limited, *pt.*, *pp.*; limiting, *ppr.* [ME. *limiten*; OFr. *limiter*; L. *limitare*, to bound, limit, define, from *limes* (*-itis*), a boundary, limit.]

I. *v.t.* To bound; to set bounds to; to confine within bounds; to restrict; to restrain.

II. *v.i.* To exercise any function, as begging, within a definite district; as, a *limiting* friar.

lim′it-ȧ-ble, *a.* That may be limited.

lim-i-tā′nē-ous, *a.* Pertaining to bounds. [Obs.]

lim-i-tā′ri-ăn, *a.* and *n.* I. *a.* Having a tendency to limit.

II. *n.* In theology, one who maintains that only a limited portion of mankind are to be saved.

lim′i-tā-ry, *a.* [L. *limitaris*, on the border, from *limes* (*-itis*), border, limit.]

1. Limiting; marking or constituting a limit.

2. Limited; kept within limits.

lim′i-tā-ry, *n.* 1. A limit or boundary; a boundary region. [Obs.]

2. A limiter.

lim′i-tāte, *a.* [L. *limitatus*, pp. of *limitare*, to bound, limit.] Having a distinct boundary line.

lim-i-tā′tion, *n.* [L. *limitatio* (*-onis*), a bounding, limiting, from *limitatus*, pp. of *limitare*, to limit, bound, from *limes* (*-itis*), a limit.]

1. The act of restricting; the state of being restricted; restriction.

2. A restriction; a limit; a limiting circumstance, qualification, or condition; as, the *limitations* of our human powers.

3. In law, the period of time limited by statute after which an action cannot be maintained.

4. A limiter's precinct. [Obs.]

lim′it-ed, *a.* Restricted; bounded; kept within fixed limits; narrow.

Limited company; a company whose shareholders have a limited liability dependent on the amount of stock held.

Limited ticket; a railway ticket restricted as to the time or manner of use.

Limited train; a train restricted (a) as to the kind of tickets receivable, only first-class being good; (b) as to the running-time between terminals; (c) as to the number of cars per engine.

lim′it-ed, *n.* An express-train on which only first-class tickets will be accepted.

lim′it-ed-ly, *adv.* With limitation.

lim′it-ed-ness, *n.* The state of being limited.

lim′it-ẽr, *n.* 1. One who or that which limits or confines.

2. A friar licensed to beg within certain bounds, or whose duty was limited to a certain district.

lim′i-tēş, *n.*, pl. of *limes*.

lim′it-ive, *a.* Designed to limit.

lim′it-less, *a.* Having no limits; unbounded.

lim′it-ōur, *n.* Same as *Limiter*, 2.

li-miv′ō-rous, *a.* [L. *limus*, mud, and *vorare*, to devour.] Using mud for food.

lim′mȧ, *n.* [LL., from Gr. *leimma*, a remnant, remainder, from *leipein*, to leave.]

1. A semitone in Pythagorean music.

2. A time period in the rhythm of verse, equal to a short or mora, but having no corresponding syllable in the words; a pause; usually indicated by a ʌ derived from initial Λ or λ of the Greek name.

lim′mẽr, *n.* A man-rope beside a ladder. [Obs.]

lim′mẽr, *a.* and *n.* [Obs.] Same as *Limber*.

lim′mẽr, *n.* [ME. *limer*; OFr. *liemier*, a large dog, a dog held in leash, from *liem*; L. *ligamen*, a band, bandage.]

1. A limehound; hence, a mongrel.

2. A scoundrel; a jade. [Scot.]

limn (lim), *v.t.*; limned, *pt.*, *pp.*; limning, *ppr.* [ME. *limnen*, contr. of *luminen*, for *enluminen*; OFr. *enluminer*; L. *illuminare*, to make light.]

1. To draw or paint; portray; delineate.

2. To illuminate, as manuscripts. [Obs.]

limn, *v.i.* To paint, especially in water-colors.

Lim-næ′ȧ, *n.* [Gr. *limnaios*, marshy, of or from a marsh, from *limnē*, a stagnant lake, a marsh.] A genus of pond-snails common in inland waters.

lim-næ′mic, *a.* [Gr. *limnē*, a marsh, and *haima*, blood.] Caused by or having an abnormal susceptibility to malarial influences.

lim′nẽr, *n.* [OFr. *enlumineur*; LL. *illuminator*, an illuminator, limner.] An illuminator of books or parchments; a portrait-painter.

lim′ni-ad, *n.* [Gr. *limnē*, a pool, lake.] A water-nymph; a Naiad.

lim′ning, *n.* The act or art of drawing or painting; that which has been limned; a portrait.

lim-noph′i-lous, *a.* [Gr. *limnē*, a pool, and *philos*, loving.] Adapted to or inhabiting pools or ponds of fresh water.

li-mō′ni-ad, *n.* Same as *Limniad*.

li-mō′nin, *n.* [Fr. *limon*, lemon, and *-in*.] A bitter crystallizable matter found in the seeds of oranges, lemons, etc.

lī′mōn-īte, *n.* [Gr. *leimōn*, meadow, and *-ite*.] An iron ore, $H_6Fe_4O_9$, found in earthy, concretionary, and fibrous forms. Its brownish-yellow streak distinguishes it from hematite.

lī′mōse, *a.* Same as *Limous*.

li-mō′sis, *n.* [Gr. *limos*, hunger, and *-osis*.] An unnatural appetite, as in certain diseases.

li-mō-ther-ȧ-pī′ȧ, li-mō-ther′ȧ-py, *n.* [Gr. *limos*, hunger, and *therapeia*, service.] Reduction of the quantity of food, a form of medical treatment.

lī′mous, *a.* Muddy; slimy. [Obs.]

limousine (lē′mö-sēn), *n.* A close automobile body, with inside seats for two or more and an outside seat for the chauffeur, designed for elegance and comfort.

limp, *a.* [Prob. from AS. *lemphealt*, awkward, lame; compare Ice. *limpa*, limpness, weakness.] Lacking firmness or elasticity; flaccid; flabby; limber; hence, weak; vapid; spiritless.

limp, *n.* The act of limping; a halt.

limp, *v.i.*; limped (limpt), *pt.*, *pp.*; limping, *ppr.* [Compare O.H.G. *limphen*, to limp, to be weak.] To walk lamely; to halt.

limp, *n.* A wooden or iron scraper to scrape ore from a sieve.

limp′ẽr, *n.* One who limps.

lim′pet, *n.* [ME. *lempet*, a limpet, from AS. *lempedu*, a lamprey.]

1. A marine gasteropod having an open, conical shell not perforated at the apex, usually found adhering to intertidal rocks.

2. Any of various gasteropods having a shell like that of the true limpets.

lim′pid, *a.* [Fr. *limpide*; L. *limpidus*, clear, bright.] Characterized by clearness; clear; transparent; as, a *limpid* stream.

Syn.—Transparent, lucid, clear, crystal, translucent.

lim-pid′i-ty, *n.* [Fr. *limpidité*; LL. *limpiditas* (*-atis*), from L. *limpidus*, limpid.] The state of being limpid; limpidness.

lim′pid-ly, *adv.* In a limpid manner.

lim′pid-ness, *n.* The state or quality of being limpid; transparency; clearness.

lim′pin, *n.* A limpet. [Obs.]

limp′ing-ly, *adv.* In a limping or halting manner; lamely.

limp′i-tūde, *n.* Limpidness. [Obs.]

limp′kin, *n.* A courlan, *Aramus giganteus*, of the West Indies and Florida.

limp′ly, *adv.* In a limp manner.

limp′ness, *n.* The quality or condition of being limp.

limp′sy, *a.* Limp; flabby; flimsy. [Colloq.]

lī′mū, *n.* [Hawaiian.] Seaweed.

lim′ūle, *n.* A limulus.

lim′ū-loid, *n.* A limuloid crab.

lim′ū-loid, *a.* Pertaining to or characteristic of the genus *Limulus*.

Lim-ū-loi′dē-ȧ, *n.pl.* The *Xiphosura*.

Lim′ū-lus, *n.* [L. *limulus*, somewhat askance, dim. of *limus*, sidelong, askance.]

1. A genus of large crustaceans; the king-crabs or horseshoe crabs.

2. [l—] Any species of the genus *Limulus*.

līm′y, *a.* Containing, resembling, or covered with lime; having the qualities of lime.

lin, *v.t.* and *v.i.* To cease from; to cease. [Obs.]

lin, linn, *n.* The linden.

lin, linn, *n.* [Gael. *linne*, a pool, pond.] A pool or collection of water, particularly one above or below a fall of water.

lin, linn, *n.* [AS. *hlynn*, a torrent.]

1. A cataract or waterfall.

2. The face of a precipice; a shrubby ravine.

Li-nā′cē-æ, *n.pl.* See *Lineæ*.

li-nā′ceous, *a.* Pertaining or belonging to the *Linaceæ*.

lin′āge, *n.* Lineage. [Obs.]

lin-ȧ-lō′ȧ, *n.* [Mex.] The wood of a species of myrrh found in Mexico from which an oil is derived for use in perfumery.

lin′ȧ-ment, *n.* [L. *linamentum*, linen stuff, from *linum*, flax.] In surgery, lint; a tent for a wound.

Li-nā′ri-ȧ, *n.* [L. *linum*, flax, and *-aria*.] A genus of herbs of the family *Scrophularineæ*, embracing about 130 species. *Linaria vulgaris* is the toadflax.

li-när′ite, *n.* [Named from *Linares*, a town in Spain, and *-ite*.] A sky-blue, hydrous sulphate of lead and copper, crystallizing in the monoclinic system.

linch, *n.* [ME. *lynch*; AS. *hlinc*, a ridge of land.] A ledge, projection, cliff, terrace, ridge, or bank; a pathway on a steep bank; also, a hamlet. [Prov. Eng.]

linch, *v.i.* To prance about, as a horse in high mettle. [Prov. Eng.]

linch, *v.t.* To chastise. [Prov. Eng.]

linch′-hoop, *n.* A ring on the spindle of a carriage-axle, held in place by the linchpin.

lin′chi, *n.* A Chinese name for the esculent swallow.

linch′pin, *n.* [AS. *lynis*, the axletree, and *pinn*, pin.] A pin at the end of an axletree to prevent the wheel of a vehicle from sliding off.

Lin′cōln (-kun) **green**. A color originally made in Lincoln, England; also, a cloth of this color.

linc′tūre, *n.* [L. *linctus*, pp. of *lingere*, to lick.] A medicine to be taken by licking; a substance of the consistence of honey, used for coughs, etc.

linc′tus, *n.* See *Lincture*.

lind, *n.* [ME. *lind, lynde*; AS. *lind*, the linden.] The linden. [Obs.]

lin′den, *n.* [ME. *linden*; AS. *linden*, of the linden, from *lind*, the lind, linden.] Either of two trees, *Tilia Europæa*, or *Tilia Americana*, the latter sometimes taking the name of *basswood* and *bee-tree*.

lin′di-ȧ, *n.* [Etym. uncertain.] A rotifer in which the trochal disk is not present; also, [L—] a genus of such rotifers.

lin′di-form, *a.* Shaped like a lindia, as the larvæ of certain insects.

lin′dō, *n.* [Sp., Port., and It. *lindo*, beautiful, fine, elegant.] A tanager of the genus *Euphonia*.

līne, *n.* [ME. *lin*; AS. *lin*, linen, flax, from L. *linum*, flax.]

1. Linen. [Obs.]

2. The long and fine fiber of flax.

līne, *v.t.*; lined, *pt.*, *pp.*; lining, *ppr.* [ME. *linen*, to cover on the inside, prob. lit., to cover with linen, from *line*; AS. *lin*, linen.]

1. To cover on the inside; as, to *line* a garment with fur; to *line* a box with tin.

2. To put in the inside of; to stuff; as, to *line* a purse with money.

3. To place in a line by the side of; to arrange along the side of for security or defense; as, to *line* works with soldiers.

4. To impregnate; applied to animals.

Lined gold; gold backed by other metal.

līne, *v.t.* [Fr. *ligner*; L. *lineare*, to fasten to a straight line (LL., also, to draw lines upon), from *linea*, a line.]

1. To draw lines upon; to mark with lines or threadlike strokes; as, to *line* a writing-tablet.

2. To delineate; to draw; to paint. [Rare.]

3. To repeat line by line, as a hymn, before singing; an old custom.

4. To arrange, as a body of soldiers, so that they shall form an even line.

5. To measure, as land, with a line; to fix the boundaries of. [Scot.]

To line bees; to track wild bees to their nests by following them in the line of their flight.

līne, *n.* [ME. *line, lyne*, cord, snare, line, mark, from AS. *line*, cord, rope, influenced by OFr. *ligne*, a cord, line, mark, ultimately from L. *linea*, cord, rope, line, mark, properly f. of *lineus*, of flax, linen, from *linum*, flax.]

1. A string, cord, or rope used for some special purpose; as, a tow*line*, fishing-*line*, plumb-*line*, etc.

2. Anything which resembles a thread or string in tenuity and extension; a mark, as made with a pencil, pen, or graving-tool.

3. A marking or furrow upon the hands or face.

On his brow were graven *lines* austere.
—Byron.

4. Outline; contour; lineament; as, a ship of fine *lines*.

5. The course in which anything moves or aims to move; route; trend of action, occupation, thought, or the like; as, a *line* of travel; a *line* of policy; a *line* of business.

6. A short letter; a note; as, I received a *line* from my friend.

7. A straight row of letters or words between two margins; as, a page of fifty *lines*.

8. In geometry, that which has length, without breadth or thickness.

9. In poetry, a verse, or the words which form a certain number of feet, according to the measure.

10. A continued series or rank; a row; as, a *line* of battleships; a *line* of ramparts.

11. [*pl.*] The words of a part recited by an actor.
12. Boundary; limit; dividing mark.
13. A continuous or connected series, as of progeny or relations descending from a common progenitor; as, a *line* of kings; the male *line.*
14. A series of public conveyances, as coaches, steamers, and the like, passing between places with regularity; as, a *line* of ships to Australia; the American *Line.*
15. [*pl.*] The reins by which a horse is guided in driving.
16. The twelfth part of an inch, a measure of length.
17. The roadbed of a railway.
18. The wire connecting various telegraphic stations, and forming with them the circuit.
19. In nautical parlance, the equator; used with the definite article; as, to cross *the line.*
20. In Scripture, (a) a cord used for measuring land; (b) that which was marked off by a line; hence, condition; lot; (c) instruction; doctrine.

The *lines* are fallen unto me in pleasant places. —Ps. xvi. 6.

21. In music, one of the straight, parallel, and horizontal strokes constituting the staff.
22. In military language, (a) a rank of soldiers drawn up in an extended front; opposed to *column*; (b) the infantry of an army, as distinguished from cavalry, artillery, militia, volunteer corps, etc.; (c) a trench or rampart.
23. In machinery, the proper adjustment of parts in working order.
24. In commerce, (a) an order given to a traveling agent for goods; (b) the goods received upon such order; (c) any particular class of goods; as, a first-class *line* of shoes.
25. In higher geometry, a curve of the first order; a right line, axis, or ray.

Hard lines; an unfortunate condition.

Line of battle; the disposition of troops or battleships when or as when an engagement is anticipated.

Line-of-battle ship; see *Ship of the line* under *Ship.*

Line of beauty; in art, a line regarded as beautiful in itself, to which different artists have given different forms. It is frequently represented in the form of a very slender elongated letter *S.*

Line of defense; any continuous bulwark, whether natural or artificial, which serves as a means of defense against the attacks of an enemy.

Line of dip; in geology, a line in the plane of a stratum, or part of a stratum, perpendicular to its intersection with a horizontal plane; the line of greatest inclination of a stratum to the horizon.

Line of fire; the direction of artillery fire.

Line of force; (a) a straight line in the direction of the action of a force; (b) a curve so drawn in a field in which forces act, that it has the direction of the resultant of all the forces at every point.

Line of life; in palmistry, a line on the inside of the hand, curving about the base of the thumb, and supposed to denote the length of a person's life.

Line of march; the direction in which a body of troops marches; also, the arrangement of troops for marching.

Line of operations; a line of communication by which an army may reach its objective point.

Line of sight; the line passing through the breech and muzzle sights of a gun to the object sighted.

Mason and Dixon's line; the line bounding Pennsylvania on the south; formerly used to designate the boundary between the free and the slave states; so named after the two English astronomers who partly surveyed it in 1763-1767.

Right line; a straight line; the shortest line that can be drawn between two points.

Ship of the line; see under *Ship.*

Syn.—Cord, thread, length, outline, row, direction, course, succession, sequence.

Lin′ē-æ, *n.pl.* [L. *linum,* flax, and *-eæ.*] An order of exogens, the flax family, characterized by their regular flowers with imbricate glandular sepals. It embraces 15 genera and about 235 species, which are widely distributed.

lin′ē-āge, *n.* [ME. *linage*; OFr. *linage,* descent, lineage, from *ligne*; L. *linea,* a line.] Race; progeny; descent in a line from a common progenitor.

Cell lineage; in embryology, the theory that certain cells in the early cleavage of the ovum give rise to definite and regular successions of cells which are destined to form definite structures in the embryo. Recent investigation has strengthened the theory that differentiation of protoplasm takes place at a very early stage in development, even in the unsegmented egg.

lin′ē-ăl, *a.* [L. *linealis,* from *linea,* line.]

1. Composed of lines; delineated; as, *lineal* designs.
2. In a direct line from an ancestor; hereditary; opposed to *collateral*; as, *lineal* descent.
3. In the direction of a line; pertaining to a line; linear; as, *lineal* measure; in this sense usually written *linear.*
4. Allied by direct descent. [Obs.]

lin-ē-al′i-ty, *n.* The state of being lineal, or in the form of a line. [Rare.]

lin′ē-ăl-ly, *adv.* In a direct line; in a lineal manner; as, one *lineally* descended from William the Conqueror.

lin′ē-ȧ-ment, *n.* [L. *lineamentum,* line, feature, lineament, from *lineare,* to fashion to a straight line, from *linea,* a line.] Feature; form; contour; the outline or exterior of a body or figure, particularly of the face; chiefly used in the plural.

lin′ē-ăr, *a.* [L. *linearis,* pertaining to or consisting of lines, linear, from *linea,* a line.]

1. Pertaining to a line; consisting of lines; in a straight direction.
2. In botany, like a line; slender; of the same breadth throughout, except at the extremities; as, a *linear* leaf.

Linear differential equation; an equation of the first degree formed by equating to zero an expression understood to be a linear function of the dependent variable and its derivatives.

Linear equation; an equation of the first degree between two variables; so called because every such equation may be considered as representing a right line.

Linear measure; same as *Long measure* under *Measure.*

Linear numbers; in mathematics, such numbers as have relation to length only; such is a number which represents one side of a plane figure. If the plane figure is a square, the linear side is called a root.

Linear perspective; perspective which regards only the positions, magnitudes, and forms of the objects delineated; distinguished from *aerial perspective,* which also exhibits the variations of the light, shade, and color of objects, according to their different distances and the quantity of light which falls on them.

Linear problem; a problem that may be solved geometrically by the intersection of two right lines, or algebraically by an equation of the first degree.

Linear transformation; in algebra, a change of variables in which a function of the first degree takes the place of each variable changed.

lin′ē-ăr-ȧ-cūte′, *a.* [L. *linearis,* linear, and *acutus,* sharp-pointed, acute.] In botany, acuminate.

lin″ē-ăr-en′sāte, *a.* [L. *linearis,* linear, and *ensis,* sword.] In botany, having the form of a long, narrow sword.

lin-ē-ar′i-ty, *n.* The state of being linear.

lin′ē-ăr-ly, *adv.* In a linear manner; with lines.

lin′ē-ā-ry, *a.* Linear. [Obs.]

lin′ē-āte, *a.* [L. *lineatus,* pp. of *lineare,* to fashion to a straight line, from *linea,* a line.] Marked with lines; specifically, marked longitudinally with depressed parallel lines; as, a *lineate* leaf.

lin′ē-ā-ted, *a.* Lineate.

lin-ē-ā′tion, *n.* [L. *lineatio* (*-onis*), a drawing of a line, from *lineatus,* pp. of *lineare,* to fashion to a line.] Delineation; a marking by one or more lines.

lin′ē-ȧ-tūre, *n.* Anything which has outline. [Obs.]

line′=conch, *n.* A large gasteropod, *Fasciolaria distans,* of Florida and the West Indies, marked by several black revolving lines.

line′=en-grāv″ing, *n.* In art, (a) the process of engraving designs on metal by incised lines; (b) a plate engraved by such a process; (c) a print produced from such a plate.

line′măn, *n.*; *pl.* **line′men.** 1. A surveyor's assistant who carries the chain.
2. One employed to do the overhead work in placing in position the wires of a trolley, telegraph, or telephone line, or in repairing them.

lin′en, *n.* [ME. *linen, lynen*; AS. *linen,* made of flax, linen, from *lin,* flax.]

1. Cloth or thread woven from flax and sometimes from hemp; a name given to the different varieties of linen cloth, such as damask, cambric, shirting, lawn, diaper, etc.
2. Collectively, various articles which are made of linen or were formerly made exclusively of it, although they may now be made of cotton; as, *table-linen, bed-linen,* etc.; the name is also given by extension to underwear, especially the shirt.

Fossil linen; a variety of hornblende having flexible fibers.

lin′en, *a.* 1. Made of flax-fiber; as, *linen* cloth.
2. Resembling linen cloth; white; pale. [Rare.]

lin′en-drā″pẽr, *n.* One who deals in linen or goods made from linen.

lin′en-ẽr, *n.* A linen-draper. [Obs.]

lin′en=pat″tẽrn, *n.* A linen-scroll.

lin′en=prōv″ẽr, *n.* A small microscope used in the examination of linen fabrics.

lin′en=scrōll, *n.* In architecture, an ornament employed to fill panels; so called from its resemblance to the convolutions of a folded napkin. It belongs peculiarly to the latter part of the fifteenth and the beginning of the sixteenth centuries. The figure shows the scroll from a panel in Layer Marney Hall, Essex, England.

Linen-scroll.

lin′ē-ō-lāte, *a.* [LL. *lineola,* dim. of L. *linea,* a line, and *-ate.*] In zoölogy and botany, marked with minute lines.

lin′ē-ō-lā-ted, *a.* Lineolate.

lin″ē-ō-lin′ē-ăr, *a.* [L. *linea,* a line, and *linearis,* linear.] In mathematics, designating a function which is linear to each of two different variables or sets of variables.

lin′ẽr, *n.* 1. One who lines or makes linings, as in manufactures of various kinds.
2. Same as *Ship of the line* under *Ship.*
3. A vessel belonging to a steamship-line, which makes voyages to and from certain ports, usually on scheduled time; as, a Cunard *liner.*
4. In machinery, a thin piece inserted between parts to adjust them; a packing-piece.
5. The lining inside the cylinder of a steam-engine.
6. In marble-working, a long slab of stone to which pieces of marble are secured in order to be ground or polished.
7. In baseball, a ball so thrown, or struck with the bat, that it travels in a nearly straight horizontal line.

line′=rock″et, *n.* In pyrotechnics, a small rocket made to run along an extended wire or line.

lineṣ′măn, *n.*; *pl.* **lineṣ′men.** 1. A private of the line; a soldier of infantry.
2. In football, an official who, under the supervision of the referee, marks the distance gained or lost by the side having the ball and gives testimony regarding the infringement of rules, etc.

ling, *n.* [ME. *lenge, leenge,* from AS. *lang,* long.] A gadoid food-fish, *Molva vulgaris,* inhabiting the seas of northern Europe. When salted and dried it forms a considerable article of commerce. The name is also given to various other fishes, as (a) the American burbot; (b) a hake of the genus *Phycis*; (c) *Genypterus blacodes,* a New Zealand food-fish; (d) the cultus-cod, *Ophiodon elongatus*; (e) the cobia.

Ling (*Molva vulgaris*).

ling, *n.* A Chinese name for the native water-chestnut.

ling, *n.* [Ice. *lyng,* heath.] Common heather, *Calluna vulgaris.*

-ling. [ME. *-ling, -lyng*; AS. *-ling,* a suffix used with a diminutive force or to denote origin.] A suffix used with nouns to give generally a diminutive or depreciative force; as, gos*ling,* first*ling,* duck*ling,* dar*ling.*

liṅ′gȧ, *n.* See *Lingam.*

liṅ′gam, *n.* [Sans.] In Hindu mythology, the male organ of generation, worshiped as being representative of the god Siva or of the productive power of nature.

ling′=bird, *n.* The meadow-pipit, *Anthus pratensis.*

liṅ′gel, *n.* 1. A shoemaker's waxed thread. [Obs.]
2. A shoe-latchet. [Obs.]

lin′gence, *n.* A lincture. [Obs.]

liṅ′gẽr, *v.i.*; lingered, *pt., pp.*; lingering, *ppr.* [ME. *lengen,* to tarry; AS. *lengan,* to prolong, put off, from *lang,* long.] To delay; to loiter; to remain or wait long; to hesitate; to be slow in deciding; to be in suspense.

Perhaps thou *linger'st,* in deep thoughts detained. —Milton.

Syn.—Tarry, loiter, lag, hesitate, saunter, delay.—To *linger* is to stop altogether, or to move but slowly forward; to *tarry* is properly to suspend one's movement; to *loiter* is to move slowly and reluctantly; to *lag* is to move slower than others, to stop while they are going on.

liṅ′gẽr, *v.t.* 1. To spend in a wearisome or tedious manner; to drag; followed by *away* or *out*; as, he is but *lingering out* his allotted time.
2. To protract; to defer; to put off. [Obs.]

liṅ′gẽr-ẽr, *n.* One who lingers.

lin-ge-rie′ (*or Fr. pron.* lan-zhe-rē′), *n.* [Fr., from *linger,* a dealer in linen, from *linge,* L. *linum,* flax, linen.] Linen goods; particularly, the linen underclothing of women; used in a collective sense.

liñ′gẽr-ing, *a.* 1. Delaying; loitering.

2. Drawing out in time; remaining long; protracted; as, a *lingering* disease.

liñ′gẽr-ing-ly, *adv.* With delay; slowly; tediously.

liñ′get, *n.* See *Lingot.*

ling′ism, *n.* [Named after Peter H. *Ling*, a Swedish poet, the originator of the method.] A Swedish gymnastic treatment for obesity; kinesitherapy.

liñ′gle, liñ′gel, *n.* [L. *lingula*, dim. of *lingua*, tongue.] A tongue or thong of leather used as a lace for belts.

liñ′gō, *n.* [L. *lingua*, tongue, language.] Language; speech somewhat unintelligible; dialect. [Slang.]

liñ′gŏt, *n.* [OFr. *lingot*, prob. from L. *lingua*, tongue.]

1. A mass of metal cast in a mold; an ingot.

2. A mold in which an ingot is cast.

ling′thorn, *n.* A starfish found in European waters, *Luidia fragilissima.*

liñ′guȧ, *n.*; *pl.* **liñ′guæ**. [L.] The tongue; the central lobe of the ligula of insects which has the functions of a tongue.

Lingua Franca; a composite language made up of Italian and the various languages of western Asia, used in the Levant by foreign traders and natives of that region.

liñ-guā′cious, *a.* Talkative; loquacious. [Obs.]

liñ-guȧ-den′tăl, *a.* and *n.* [L. *lingua*, tongue, and *dens, dentis*, tooth.] Same as *Dentilingual.*

liñ′guăl, *a.* [L. *lingua*, the tongue.]

1. Pertaining to the tongue; as, the *lingual* nerves; the *lingual* muscle.

2. Pronounced chiefly by means of the tongue; as, a *lingual* consonant.

Lingual ribbon; in zoölogy, the radula or odontophore.

liñ′guăl, *n.* A letter pronounced chiefly by means of the tongue, as *t* or *d.*

liñ-gual′i-ty, *n.* The condition or quality of being lingual.

liñ′guăl-ly, *adv.* In a lingual manner.

Liñ-guat-ū-lī′nȧ, *n.pl.* [L. *linguatus*, tongued, from *lingua*, a tongue.] An order of parasitic vermiform arachnidans, found in the young state in the internal organs of various animals.

liñ-gui-den′tăl, *a.* and *n.* See *Dentilingual.*

liñ′gui-fọrm, *a.* [L. *lingua*, tongue, and *forma*, form.] Having the form or shape of the tongue.

liñ′guist, *n.* [L. *lingua*, the tongue.]

1. A person skilled in languages; a student of philology.

2. A master of language; a ready talker. [Obs.]

liñ-guis′tiç, *a.* Relating to language or linguistics; pertaining to the affinities of language.

liñ-guis′tiç-ăl, *a.* Linguistic.

liñ-guis′tiç-ăl-ly, *adv.* With respect to language or linguistics.

liñ-guis′tics, *n.* The science of languages, or of the origin, signification, and application of words; called also *comparative philology.*

liñ′gū-lȧ, *n.*; *pl.* **liñ′gū-læ**. [L., dim. of *lingua*, tongue.]

1. In anatomy, a process or part which is shaped like a tongue.

2. In zoölogy, any brachiopod of the genus *Lingula* or family *Lingulidæ.*

liñ′gū-lāte, *a.* [L. *lingulatus*, from *lingula*, dim. of *lingua*, tongue.] Ligulate; shaped like the tongue or a strap.

li-nig′ẽr-ous, *a.* [L. *liniger*, linen-wearing; *linum*, linen, flax, and *gerere*, to bear.] Bearing flax; producing linen.

lin′i-ment, *n.* [Fr., from LL. *linimentum*, a soft ointment, from L. *linere*, to smear.] In medicine, an oily liquid preparation intended for application to the skin, in cases of muscular affections, bruises, etc.

lī′nin, *n.* [L. *linum*, flax, and *-in.*]

1. In chemistry, the crystallizable bitter principle of *Linum catharticum*, or purging-flax.

2. In biology, parachromatin.

līn′ing, *n.* 1. The covering of the inner surface of anything, as of a garment or a box.

2. That which is within; the contents.

> The *lining* of his coffers. —Shak.

liñk, *n.* [Prob. corrupted from *lint, lunt*, a torch, from D. *lont*, a match.] A torch made of tow or hards, etc., and pitch.

liñk, *n.* [AS. *hlence*, a link.]

1. A single ring or division of a chain.

2. Anything doubled and closed like a link; as, a *link* of horsehair.

3. A chain; anything connecting; a bond; any single part of a connected series; used also figuratively; as, this argument is a *link* in the chain of reasoning.

4. A surveyor's measure of length, equal to 7.92 inches; the hundredth part of Gunter's chain.

5. In machinery, any connecting bar or rod which transmits motion, especially one with a bearing in each end.

6. The link-motion in a steam-engine.

7. A sausage; so called from sausages being made in a continuous chain. [Colloq.]

liñk, *v.t.*; linked, *pt.*, *pp.*; linking, *ppr.* To unite or connect by or as if by a link or links; to unite by something intervening; to unite in any way; to couple; to join.

> *Link* towns to towns with avenues of oak. —Pope.

liñk, *v.i.* To be or become connected; to be united in marriage.

liñk′āge, *n.* 1. The act of linking; the condition of being linked.

2. A series of links, as of pieces so fastened together as to turn about one another.

3. In chemistry, the system or manner of combining; applied to the combination of atoms or radicals in a molecule or compound.

liñk′=block, *n.* In a steam-engine, the movable sliding or die-block in a slot-link, to which the valve-rod is connected.

liñk′boy, *n.* A boy or man who carries a link or torch to light passengers.

liñk′măn, *n.* See *Linkboy.*

liñk′=mō″tion, *n.* Motion communicated by links; applied especially to a system of gearing for working the valves of locomotive, marine, and similar engines. In the accompanying cut,

Link-motion.

A is the rod by which the slide-valve is worked, and by which, accordingly, the admission of steam to the cylinder is regulated; B, the reversing-rod, which is fixed to a crossbar, one end of which is jointed by means of another rod to a runner, which slides up and down in the slit of the curved piece, and which is also jointed to the rod A. The curved piece is the link, and is jointed near the extremities to the rods of two eccentrics, an inner and an outer. When the engineer pushes forward the rod B, the runner is raised to the top of the link, and therefore follows the motions of the upper end of the link, and places the slide-valve rod under the control of the inner eccentric. When he pushes it back he similarly places the rod under the control of the outer eccentric, which reverses the engine.

liñks, *n.pl.* [AS. *hlinc*, hill, ridge.]

1. The crooks or windings of a river; the grounds lying along such windings; as, the *links* of the Forth. [Scot.]

2. A stretch of flat or slightly undulating ground on the seashore, often in part sandy and covered with bent-grass, furze, etc. [Scot.]

3. The grounds laid out for playing golf.

liñk′wọrk, *n.* 1. A term sometimes applied to the various rods, levers, and links connected with an engine slide-valve, sometimes to the coupling or connecting-rods of wheels and cranks.

2. A kind of fabric made by joining together links; a chain.

linn, *n.* See *Lin.*

Lin-næ′ȧ, *n.* [Named after *Linnæus*, a celebrated Swedish botanist.] A genus of plants of the natural order *Caprifoliaceæ*, containing but one species, *Linnæa borealis*, the twinflower.

lin-næ′ite, *n.* [*Linnæus* and *-ite.*] A sulphid of cobalt, crystallizing in the isometric system. It is of a pale steel-gray color.

linne (lin), *n.* Flax. [Obs.]

Lin-nē′ăn, Lin-næ′ăn, *a.* Pertaining to Linnæus, the Swedish botanist, or to his system of classification.

Linnean system; in botany, the system of classification deriving its name from Linnæus, who introduced it. It consists of twenty-four classes, founded principally on the number of the stamens, and their connection with each other, etc.; while the orders are classified mainly according to the number of styles or stigmas.

lin′net, *n.* [ME. *linet, lynet*; AS. *linete, linetwige*, a linnet, from *lin*, flax; so called from its feeding on the seed of flax and hemp.] One of several species of singing birds of the family *Fringillidæ*, especially *Linota cannabina.* In autumn and winter the plumage is brown; in the breeding season, the breast and head of both sexes become a crimson-red, varying only in degree. It is popularly known, according to its sex and the season of the year, as the *red linnet, gray linnet*, or *brown linnet.*

li-nō′lē-iç, *a.* [L. *linum*, flax, and *oleum*, oil, and *-ic.*] Pertaining to or derived from linseed-oil.

Linoleic acid; a yellow, oily compound contained in linseed-oil and other drying-oils.

li-nō′lē-in, *n.* [*Linoleic* and *-in.*] The glyceride of linoleic acid.

li-nō′lē-um, *n.* [L. *linum*, flax, and *oleum*, oil.]

1. A preparation of linseed-oil, rendered solid by some process of oxidation, and used as a substitute for india-rubber or gutta-percha.

2. A floor-cloth made by mixing linoleum with ground cork and pressing it upon canvas.

lin′ō-type, *n.* [L. *linea*, a line, and *typus*, a figure, image.]

1. A line of type cast in an unbroken strip.

2. A machine for casting stereotyped lines, used as a substitute for the slower hand-method of setting type.

li-nox′in, li-nox′yn, *n.* [*Lin*oleic and *ox*ygen and *-in.*] A substance obtained in a resinous state from linseed-oil through a process of oxidation.

lin′sang, *n.* [E. Ind.] An animal allied to the civet, found in the East Indies; *Prionodon gracilis* is the common linsang.

lin′seed, *n.* [ME. *linseede, linsede*; AS. *linsæd*; *lin*, flax, and *sæd*, seed.] Flaxseed.

lin′seed=cāke′, *n.* The solid mass or cake which remains when oil is expressed from flaxseed; called also *oil-cake.*

lin′seed=mēal′, *n.* Linseed-cake pulverized.

lin′seed=oil′, *n.* Oil obtained from flaxseed by pressure.

lin′sey, *n.* Linsey-woolsey.

lin′sey=wool′sey, *a.* [ME. *lynsy wolsye*, from *linsel*, linen, and *wolsye*, wool.] Made of linen and wool; hence, of different and unsuitable parts; ill-sorted.

lin′sey=wool′sey, *n.* 1. Stuff made of linen and wool, mixed.

2. Jargon; gibberish. [Obs.]

lin′stock, lint′stock, *n.* [D. *lontstok*; *lont*, a match used for firing a cannon, and *stock*, a stick.] A pointed staff with a crotch or fork at one end to hold a lighted match, used in firing cannon.

lint, *n.* [AS. *linet*, flax, hemp, from *lin*; L. *linum*, flax.]

1. Flax.

2. Linen scraped into a soft substance, and used for dressing wounds and sores.

3. Fluff; nap.

lint′=doc″tŏr, *n.* A device used in calico-printing to scrape off lint from the cylinder of the machine.

lin′tel, *n.* [ME. *lintel, lyntell*; OFr. *lintel*; LL. *lintellus*, the headpiece of a door or window, the lintel, from L. *limes (-itis)*, a border, boundary, limit.] In architecture, a horizontal piece of timber or stone over a door, window, or other opening, to support the superincumbent weight.

lin′tẽr, *n.* A corruption of *lean-to.*

lin′tie (-ti), *n.* The linnet. [Scot.]

lint′seed, *n.* Linseed. [Obs.]

lint′stock, *n.* See *Linstock.*

lint′whīte, *n.* [AS. *linetwige*, a linnet, from *lin*, flax.] The linnet. [Prov. Eng. and Scot.]

Lī′num, *n.* [L., flax, hemp.] A genus of herbs of the order *Lineæ*, including *Linum usitatissimum*, the common flax-plant.

lī″ō-my̆-ō′mȧ, *n.* [Gr. *leios*, smooth, and *mys*, a muscle, and *-oma.*] A tumor composed of unstriated or smooth muscular tissue.

lī′ŏn, *n.* [ME. *lion, lioun*; OFr. *lion*; L. *leo, leonis*; Gr. *leōn, leontos*, a lion.]

1. A quadruped of the genus *Felis*, *Felis leo*, the largest of all carnivorous animals, distinguished by its tawny or yellow color, a full flowing mane in the male, a tufted tail, and the disappearance of the feline markings in both sexes before they arrive at maturity. Of the African lion there are several varieties, as the Barbary, Gambian, Senegal, and Cape lions. The Asiatic varieties are generally distinguished as the Bengal, the Persian or Arabian, and the maneless lion of Gujarat.

Head of Gambian Lion (*Felis leo gambianus*).

2. [L.—] In astronomy, the constellation or sign of the zodiac, Leo.

3. An object of interest and curiosity; especially, a conspicuous person much sought by society or the public in general; as, the *lion* of the day; to visit the *lions* of a place.

Head of Maneless Lion (*Felis leo goojratensis.*)

American lion, mountain lion; the cougar.

Lion's provider; (a) a popular name for the jackal; (b) any humble friend or follower who acts as a tool, sycophant, or foil to another.

Lion's share; the whole or an unreasonably large share of anything.

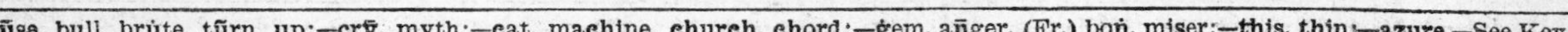

To put one's head into the lion's mouth; to put oneself into a position of great danger.

lī′ŏn-ănt, *n.* The ant-lion.

lī′ŏnced, lē′ŏnced (-ŏnst), *a.* In heraldry, adorned with lions' heads, as a cross the ends of which terminate in lions' heads.

lī′ŏn-cel, lī′ŏn-celle, *n.* [OFr. *lioncel*, dim. of *lion*, a lion.] In heraldry, a young lion used as a bearing in a coat of arms.

lī′ŏn-dog, *n.* A variety of dog which has a flowing mane.

lī′ŏn-el, *n.* [OFr. *lionel*, dim. of *lion*, a lion.]
1. A lion's whelp; a young lion.
2. In heraldry, a lioncel.

lī′ŏn-ess, *n.* [OFr. *lionnesse*, f. of *lion*, a lion.] The female of the lion.

lī′ŏn-et, *n.* A young or small lion.

lī′ŏn-heärt, *n.* One who has great courage.

lī′ŏn-heärt″ed, *a.* Having a lion's heart or courage; brave and magnanimous.

lī′ŏn-ism, *n.* The attracting of notice, as a lion; the treating of a person as an object of curiosity or as a celebrity.

lī′ŏn-īze, *v.t.*; lionized, *pt., pp.*; lionizing, *ppr.*
1. To treat as a lion or as an object of curiosity and interest.
2. To exhibit objects of curiosity to. [Rare.]

lī′ŏn-īze, *v.i.* To visit the lions or objects of interest or curiosity of a place.

lī′ŏn-like, *a.* Like a lion in strength or courage.

lī′ŏn-liz″ărd, *n.* A lizard, the basilisk.

lī′ŏn-ly, *a.* Like a lion; fierce. [Obs.]

lī′ŏn-mŏn″key, *n.* The marikina.

lī′ŏn's-ēar, *n.* 1. Any labiate plant of the genus *Leonotis*.
2. Any one of various composite plants of South America, of the genera *Culcitium* and *Espeletia*.

lī′ŏn's-foot, *n.* 1. Either of two composite plants, *Prenanthes alba* or *Prenanthes serpentaria*, of the United States.
2. The lady's-mantle, *Alchemilla vulgaris*; also, the edelweiss, *Leontopodium alpinum*.

lī′ŏn's-heärt, *n.* The false dragon's-head, *Physostegia Virginiana*.

lī′ŏn-ship, *n.* The state of being a lion.

lī′ŏn's-lēaf, *n.* A plant of the genus *Leontice*; especially, *Leontice Leontopetalum* of Europe.

lī′ŏn's-mouth, *n.* The snapdragon, *Antirrhinum majus*.

lī′ŏn's-tāil, *n.* Any labiate plant of the genus *Leonurus*, as *Leonurus Cardiaca*, the motherwort.

lī′ŏn's-tooth, *n.*; *pl.* **lī′ŏn's-teeth**. A composite plant of the genus *Leontodon*; the common dandelion.

lī′ŏn's-tŭr″nip, *n.* The tuberous root of the lion's-leaf.

li-ot′ri-chous, leī-ot′ri-chous, *a.* [Gr. *leios*, smooth, and *thrix*, *trichos*, hair.] In anthropology, having smooth hair.

lip, *n.* [ME. *lip*, *lyp*; AS. *lippa*, *lippe*, lip.]
1. One of the two edges or borders of the mouth; one of the two fleshy or muscular parts, composing the exterior of the mouth in man and many animals. In man the lips are organs of speech essential to certain articulations. Hence the lips, by a figure, denote the mouth, or all the organs of speech, and sometimes speech itself.
2. Anything resembling a lip; the edge or border of anything; as, the *lip* of a vessel; the *lips* of a wound.
3. In botany, (a) one of the two opposite divisions of a labiate corolla; (b) the lower petal of an orchid.
4. In zoölogy, any part or organ resembling a lip.
5. The blade of an auger which cuts the chip after it has been marked out by the spur.
6. Abusive talk; cheek. [Slang.]
7. A cuttoo-plate of a vehicle.
8. In music, the adjusting or power of adjusting one's lips to the mouthpiece of a wind-instrument.
To hang the lip; to be sulky.
To keep a stiff upper lip; see under *Keep*.
To make a lip; to drop the under lip in sullenness or contempt. [Rare.]
To shoot out the lip; in Scripture, to protrude the lip as a sign of scorn.

lip, *v.t.*; lipped, *pt., pp.*; lipping, *ppr.* 1. To touch with the lips; hence, to kiss.
2. To speak. [Rare.]
3. To clip; to trim. [Obs.]

lip, *v.i.* To shape one's lips to the mouthpiece of a wind-instrument.

li-pæ′mi-ȧ, *n.* [Gr. *lipos*, fat, and *haima*, blood.] The presence of an emulsion of fine oil-globules in the blood.

Li-päns′, *n.pl.*; *sing.* **Li-pän′**. A tribe of North American Indians originally inhabiting the region of the Rio Grande, Texas.

li-pā′ri-ăn, *n.* Any bombycid moth of the family *Liparididæ*.

Lip′ȧ-ris, *n.* [Gr. *liparos*, oily, shining, greasy, from *lipos*, fat.]
1. In botany, a genus of orchids, both terrestrial and epiphytic, comprising about 120 species, found in warm regions.
2. A genus of fishes; the suckers or sea-snails.

lip′ȧ-rīte, *n.* [Named after the *Lipari* Islands in the Mediterranean.] Rhyolite.

lip′ȧ-rō-cēle, *n.* [Gr. *liparos*, oily, and *kēlē*, a tumor.] See *Lipoma*.

lip′-cŏm″fŏrt, *n.* Consolation given by utterance of words only.

lip′-cŏm″fŏrt-ēr, *n.* One who consoles with empty words.

lip′-dē-vō″tion, *n.* Prayers uttered by the lips without the desires of the heart.

lip′-fērn, *n.* In botany, a fern of the genus *Cheilanthes*, having a liplike indusium.

lip′fish, *n.* A labroid fish; a wrasse.

lip′-good, *a.* Good in profession only.

li-phæ′mi-ȧ, *n.* [Gr. *lipein*, or *leipein*, to leave, and *haima*, blood.] An impoverished condition of the blood; deficiency of blood; also spelled *leiphæmia*.

lip′-head, *n.* A head of a bolt projecting on one side only.

lip′-hook, *n.* 1. In angling, the upper hook of a number attached to a line, which is passed through the lips of a live bait-fish.
2. A sort of grapnel used for towing a dead whale.

lip′iç, *a.* [Gr. *lipos*, fat.] Of, pertaining to, or derived from fat.
Lipic acid; a compound formerly supposed to be a distinct acid of the oxalic series, but now believed to be an impure succinic acid obtained by the action of nitric acid upon oleic or stearic acid.

li-pin′iç, *a.* Lipic.

lip′-lā″bŏr, *n.* Action of the lips without concurrence of the mind; words without sentiment.

lip′-lā-bō″ri-ous, *a.* Uttering words without sentiment; hypocritical.

lip′-lan″guāge, *n.* Oral or articulate language, as distinguished from that of signs or the fingers.

lip′less, *a.* Having no lips.

lip′let, *n.* A little lip.

lipo-. A combining form from Gr. *leipein*, pres., *lipein*, aor., to leave, lack, be wanting, used in zoölogy, medicine, etc., to signify lacking, destitute of, or without; as, *Lipo*branchia.

Lip-ō-brā′chi-ȧ, *n.pl.* [*Lipo-*, and L. *brachium*, arm.] A group of echinoderms having no arms, as the holothurians.

lip-ō-brā′chi-āte, *a.* Without arms or rays; specifically, pertaining to the *Lipobrachia*.

Lip-ō-bran′chi-ȧ, *n.pl.* [*Lipo-*, and Gr. *branchia*, gills.] A division of arachnidan arthropods comprising the weasel-spiders, false scorpions, harvestmen, and mites.

lip-ō-bran′chi-āte, *a.* Pertaining to the *Lipobranchia*.

Lip-ō-ceph′ȧ-lȧ, *n.pl.* The *Lamellibranchia* or bivalve mollusks.

lip-ō-ceph′ȧ-lous, *a.* Pertaining to the *Lipocephala*; headless; said of bivalve mollusks.

lip″ō-fi-brō′mȧ, *n.* [Gr. *lipos*, fat, and L. *fibra*, fiber, and *-oma*.] In pathology, a lipoma or fatty tumor largely composed of connective tissue; called also *adipofibroma*.

lip″ō-gas-trō′sis, *n.* [*Lipo-*, and Gr. *gastēr*, *gastros*, stomach, and *-osis*.] Absence of a stomach; in spongology, absence of the paragaster.

lip″ō-gas-trot′iç, *a.* Without a stomach; in spongology, characterized by lipogastrosis.

lip-ō-gen′e-sis, *n.* [Gr. *lipos*, fat, and *genesis*, generation.] The formation of fat.

li-pog′e-nous, *a.* Generating or tending to generate fat.

lip′ō-gram, *n.* [*Lipo-*, and Gr. *gramma*, a letter.] A writing that omits or dispenses with all words containing a particular letter of the alphabet, as the Odyssey of Tryphiodorus, in which there was no A in Book I., no B in Book II., etc.

lip″ō-gram-mat′iç, *a.* [Gr. *lipogrammatos*, or *leipogrammatos*, having a letter omitted; *leipein*, *lipein*, to leave, omit, and *gramma*, a letter.] Of or pertaining to lipograms; of the nature of a lipogram; as, *lipogrammatic* writings.

lip-ō-gram′mȧ-tism, *n.* The art or act of writing lipograms.

lip-ō-gram′mȧ-tist, *n.* A writer of lipograms.

li-pō′mȧ, *n.* [Gr. *lipos*, fat, and *-oma*.] In pathology, a fatty tumor.

li-pō-mȧ-tō′sis, *n.* [*Lipoma* (*t-*), and *-osis*.] In pathology, a general deposition of fat; obesity; fatty degeneration.

li-pom′ȧ-tous, *a.* Of the nature of a lipoma.

lip″ō-myx-ō′mȧ, *n.*; *pl.* **lip″ō-myx-ō′mȧ-tȧ**. [Gr. *lipos*, fat, and *myxa*, phlegm, mucus, and *-oma*.] In pathology, a myxoma combined with fatty tissue.

lip′ō-pod, *a.* and *n.* I. *a.* Pertaining to the *Lipopoda*.
II. *n.* One of the *Lipopoda*.

Li-pop′ō-dȧ, *n.pl.* [*Lipo-*, and Gr. *pous*, *podos*, foot.] In zoölogy, a division of rotifers having no feet, including the three orders, *Ploima*, *Bdelligrada*, and *Rhizota*.

Li-pos′tō-mȧ, *n.pl.* See *Lipostomata*.

Lī-pō-stō′mȧ-tȧ, *n.pl.* [*Lipo-*, and Gr. *stoma* (*-atos*), mouth.] A group of corticate protozoans having no mouth; the sporozoans.

lip-ō-stom′ȧ-tous, *a.* Pertaining to the *Lipostomata*; mouthless.

lip-ō-stō-mō′sis, *n.* Absence of a mouth; in spongology, absence of an oscule.

lip-ō-stō-mot′iç, *a.* Lacking a mouth; in spongology, destitute of an oscule.

li-pos′tō-mous, *a.* Lipostomatous.

li-pos′tō-my, *n.* [*Lipo-*, and Gr. *stoma*, mouth.] Imperfect development of the mouth.

li-pō-thym′i-ȧ, *n.* Same as *Lipothymy*.

li-pō-thym′iç, *a.* Lipothymous.

li-poth′y-mous, *a.* [Gr. *lipothymos*, fainting; *leipein*, *lipein*, to leave, and *thymos*, soul, life.] Given to swooning; fainting.

li-poth′y-my, *n.* In pathology, faintness; syncope.

lip′ō-tȳpe, *n.* [*Lipo-*, and Gr. *typos*, an impression, type.] In zoögeography, a type of animal life the absence of which is characteristic of a particular district or region.

Lip-ō-typh′lȧ, *n.pl.* [*Lipo-*, and Gr. *typhlos*, blind.] In mammalogy, a division of *Insectivora* destitute of a cæcum.

lip-ō-typ′iç, *a.* [*Lipo-*, and Gr. *typos*, impression, type.] Pertaining to a lipotype.

li-pox′e-nous, *a.* [*Lipo-*, and Gr. *xenos*, host, and *-ous*.] Designating certain parasitic fungi which desert their host and complete their development from the reserve previously taken from it.

lī-pox′e-ny, *n.* In botany, the abandoning of its host by a parasitic plant.

lipped (lipt), *a.* 1. Having lips; having a raised or rounded edge resembling the lip; often used in composition.
2. In botany, labiate.

lip′pēr, *n.* 1. A thin oblong-shaped piece of blubber for wiping up gurry from the deck of a whaler.
2. A large ladle with which the oil from the deck of a whaler is scooped up.

Lip′pi-ȧ, *n.* [Named after Augustus *Lippi*, a French physician and traveler.] In botany, a genus of shrubs of the vervain family, natives of the tropics, especially of America. *Lippia citriodora* is the lemon-scented verbena.

lip′pi-tūde, *n.* [L. *lippitudo*, from *lippus*, blear-eyed.] Soreness of the eyes; blearedness.

lip-pi-tū′dō, *n.* In pathology, the state of being blear-eyed, a condition marked by ulcerative marginal blepharitis.

lip′-plāte, *n.* The hypostome of a trilobite.

lip′py, *a.* Saucy; impudent. [Slang.]

lip′-rēad″ing, *n.* Interpreting the visible movements of the mouth and lips of a speaker, so as to understand the words he utters, no less accurately than if they were heard.

lip′-sälve (-säv), *n.* 1. A salve or ointment for the lips.
2. Figuratively, flattering speech. [Obs.]

lip″sȧ-nō-thē′cȧ, *n.* [Gr. *leipsanon*, a relic, remnant, from *leipein*, to leave, and *thēkē*, a chest, shrine.] A shrine for holding relics.

lipse, *v.i.* To lisp. [Obs.]

lip′-sērv″ice, *n.* Insincere service rendered by the lips.

lip′-wis″dŏm, *n.* Wisdom in talk or words but not in action or experience; theory dissociated from practice.

lip′-wŏrk, *n.* 1. See *Lip-labor*.
2. The act of kissing.

lip′yl, *n.* In old chemistry, a hypothetical radical, C_3H_4, of glycerin. [Obs.]

liq′uȧ-ble (-wȧ-), *a.* Capable of being liquefied or melted.

lī′quāte, *v.i.* To melt; to liquefy; to become dissolved. [Obs.]

lī′quāte, *v.t.*; liquated, *pt., pp.*; liquating, *ppr.* To melt; to liquefy; specifically, in metallurgy, to separate, as one metal from another less fusible, by applying just sufficient heat to melt the more easily liquefiable, so that it can be run off from the other.

li-quā′tion, *n.* [LL. *liquatio* (*-onis*), a melting.]
1. The act or operation of liquating or melting.
2. The condition or capacity of being melted; as, a substance congealed beyond *liquation*.
3. In metallurgy, the process of separating, by a regulated heat, an easily fusible metal from one less fusible; eliquation.

liq-uē-fā′cient, *n.* [L. *liquefaciens* (*-entis*), ppr. of *liquefacere*, to melt, dissolve.]
1. That which liquefies or tends to liquefy.
2. In medicine, an agent which augments the secretions and promotes the liquefying processes of the animal economy.

liq-uē-fac′tion, *n.* [LL. *liquefactio* (*-onis*), a melting.]
1. The act or operation of liquefying, melting, or dissolving; the conversion of a solid into a liquid by the sole agency of heat.
2. The state of being liquefied, melted, or dissolved.
3. The conversion of a gas or vapor into a liquid by cold or pressure; as, the *liquefaction* of air.

liq-uē-fac′tive, *a.* Pertaining to or causing liquefaction.

liq′uē-fī-à-ble, *a.* Capable of being liquefied, or changed from a solid to a liquid state.

liq′uē-fī-ẽr, *n.* One who or that which liquefies.

liq′uē-fȳ, *v.t.*; liquefied, *pt.*, *pp.*; liquefying, *ppr.* [L. *liquefieri*, to become liquid, pass. of *liquefacere*, to make liquid, melt, dissolve; *liquere*, to be fluid, or liquid, and *facere*, to make.] To melt; to dissolve; to convert from a solid or gaseous form to that of a liquid; and technically, to melt by the sole agency of heat.

liq′uē-fȳ, *v.i.* To become liquid.

li-ques′cence, li-ques′cen-cy, *n.* The condition or quality of being liquescent; aptness to melt.

li-ques′cent, *a.* [L. *liquescens* (*-entis*), ppr. of *liquescere*, to become liquid.] Melting; having a tendency to become liquid.

li-queur′ (-kẽr′), *n.* [Fr.] A drink compounded of alcohol, water, and sugar, flavored with an infusion or extract of some fruit, spice, or aromatic substance.

li-queur′, *v.t.*; liqueured, *pt.*, *pp.*; liqueuring, *ppr.* To treat or mix with liqueur, as wine.

liq′uid, *n.* 1. A substance whose parts are capable of moving freely among themselves on the least pressure, and which, therefore, retains no fixed form; a substance in a state of liquidity; a fluid not aeriform.

2. In grammar, a letter or sound pronounced with a slight contact of the organs of articulation; a letter with a smooth flowing sound; as, *l*, *m*, *n*, *r*.

Burnett's liquid; a solution of chlorid of zinc used as a preservative, disinfectant, and antiseptic.

liq′uid, *a.* [L. *liquidus*, liquid, fluid, from *liquere*, to be fluid or liquid.]

1. Composed of particles that move freely among each other on the slightest pressure; fluid; flowing, or capable of flowing; not fixed or solid.

2. Flowing smoothly or easily; sounding agreeably or smoothly to the ear; devoid of harshness; as, *liquid* melody.

3. Smooth; easy; pronounced easily, and with a slight contact of the organs of articulation; as, a *liquid* letter.

4. Clear; transparent; limpid.

The deep *liquid* blue of the sky.—Butterworth.

5. Tearful; suggestive of liquid; as, a *liquid* look.

Liquid air; air cooled and compressed to its critical temperature and pressure, by a reduction of volume to $\frac{1}{800}$. It is employed in many experiments and to a limited extent as a refrigerant.

Liquid assets; in banking, coin, bank-notes, and securities which can be instantly converted into cash.

Liquid debt; in Scots law, a debt, the amount of which is ascertained and constituted against the debtor, either by a written obligation or by the decree of a court.

Liquid measure; see under *Measure*.

Liquid securities; see *Liquid assets*.

liq′uid-à-ble, *a.* Capable of being liquidated.

Liq′uid-am″bär, *n.* [L. *liquidus*, liquid, and LL. *ambar*, amber.]

1. A genus of trees of the witch-hazel family, consisting of two species. *Liquidambar orientale* of Asia Minor yields a balsam known as liquid storax. The other species, *Liquidambar styraciflua*, is found in Mexico and the United States, and is known as the sweet-gum.

2. [l—] A tree of this genus.

3. [l—] The balsamic juice of these trees, used to some extent in medicine.

liq′uid-am″bẽr, *n.* See *Liquidambar*, 2.

liq′ui-dāte, *v.t.*; liquidated, *pt.*, *pp.*; liquidating, *ppr.* [LL. *liquidatus*, pp. of *liquidare*, to make liquid or clear, from L. *liquidus*, liquid.]

1. In law, (a) to clear off; to satisfy; to defray; to pay; to settle; as, to *liquidate* a debt; to *liquidate* a mortgage; (b) to adjust; to reduce to order or precision, as the affairs of a corporation that has failed.

2. To free from obscurity; to make plain or clear. [Rare.]

3. To make less harsh and offensive; as, to *liquidate* the harshness of sound.

4. To cause to become liquid. [Obs.]

Liquidated damages; in law, a certain fixed and ascertained sum, in contradistinction to a penalty which is both uncertain and unascertained.

liq-ui-dā′tion, *n.* The act of liquidating; the act of settling and adjusting debts, or ascertaining their amount or the balance of them due; the act or operation of winding up the affairs of a firm or company by settling with its debtors and creditors, apportioning the amount of each partner's or shareholder's profit and loss, etc.

To go into liquidation; to give attention solely, as a firm, to collecting its assets, paying its debts, etc., ceasing the solicitation of new business.

liq′ui-dā-tŏr, *n.* One who or that which liquidates or settles; specifically, in Great Britain, an officer appointed to conduct the winding-up of the affairs of a firm or company, to bring and defend actions and suits in its name, and to do all necessary acts on behalf of the firm or company.

li-quid′i-ty, *n.* [LL. *liquiditas* (*-atis*), from L. *liquidus*, fluid, liquid.]

1. The state or quality of being liquid.

2. The quality of being smooth, flowing, and agreeable; said of sound, music, and the like.

liq′uid-ize, *v.t.* To cause to become liquid. [Rare.]

liq′uid-ly, *adv.* In a liquid or flowing manner.

liq′uid-ness, *n.* The state or quality of being liquid; fluency.

liq′uŏr (lik′ẽr), *n.* [ME. *licour*, *lycour*; OFr. *licor*; L. *liquor*, fluidity, a liquor, from *liquere*, to be liquid or fluid.]

1. A liquid of any kind, as water, alcohol, sap, milk, blood, etc.

2. Any liquid containing alcohol or possessing intoxicating properties; especially, spirituous drink, as whisky, gin, etc., as distinguished from such beverages as wine or beer, that have undergone fermentation.

3. A term applied in pharmacy to any aqueous solution in the United States Pharmacopœia, which does not contain sugar and does not hold gaseous or very volatile matter in solution.

Liquor amnii; the fluid contained in the amniotic sac.

Liquor of flints; see under *Flint*.

Liquor of Libavius; see *Fuming Liquor of Libavius* under *Fuming*.

Liquor sanguinis; the blood-plasma.

Liquor silicum; see *Liquor of flints* under *Flint*.

liq′uŏr, *v.t.* 1. To furnish with liquor. [Rare.]

2. To oil; to grease. [Obs.]

liq′uŏr, *v.i.* To drink; especially, to drink spirits; frequently with *up*. [Slang.]

liq′uŏr-ice, *n.* See *Licorice*.

liq′uŏr-ish, *a.* [Obs.] See *Lickerish*.

liq′uŏr-ous, *a.* Lickerous. [Obs.]

liq′uŏr-thiēf, *n.* A tube let down through the bunghole of a cask to draw liquor therefrom; a sampling-tube.

lī′rà, *n.*; *pl.* **lī′re**. [It., from L. *libra*, a balance, pound.]

1. An Italian silver coin, divided into 100 centesimi, and in value equivalent to a French franc.

2. A Turkish gold coin worth $4.40.

li-rel′là, *n.* [Dim., from L. *lira*, a furrow.] In botany, a linear shield with a channel along the middle, characteristic of some lichens.

li-rel′lāte, *a.* Having the character of or resembling a lirella.

li-rel′li-fŏrm, *a.* Lirellate.

li-rel′line, *a.* Lirellate.

lir″i-ō-den′drin, *n.* In chemistry, a neutral, bitter, and partly volatile substance obtained from the tulip-tree, *Liriodendron Tulipifera*.

Lir″i-ō-den′drŏn, *n.* [Gr. *leirion*, a lily, and *dendron*, tree.]

1. A genus of North American trees of the magnolia family. *Liriodendron Tulipifera*, the tulip-tree, is the only species extant.

2. [l—] A tree of this genus.

lir′i-pipe, *n.* [Obs.] See *Liripipium*.

lir-i-pip′i-um, *n.* The ancient dress of a clergyman; in early times, probably a hood or tippet; later, a scarf or an appendage to the hood, consisting of long tails or tippets, passing around the neck, and hanging down to the feet, and often jagged.

lir′i-pọọp, *n.* [OFr. *liripipion*; LL. *liripipium*, said to be a corruption of *cleri ephippium*, lit., caparison of a cleric.]

1. A liripipium. [Obs.]

2. A degree of learning worthy the wearer of a liripoop; acuteness; smartness; a smart trick. [Obs.]

3. A silly person. [Obs.]

li-roc′ō-nite, *n.* [Gr. *leiros*, pale, and *konia* or *konis*, dust, powder.] A crystalline hydrated arseniate of copper, formerly found in various Cornish mines; it is of a sky-blue or verdigris-green color.

Lis′bŏn, *n.* 1. A kind of white or light-colored wine produced in the province of Estremadura, Portugal; so called from being shipped at Lisbon.

2. A kind of soft sugar. [Obs.]

lis′keărd-ite, *n.* [From *Liskeard*, in Cornwall, England, where it is found.] A mineral occurring in thin, fibrous crusts. It is a hydrous arseniate of aluminium and iron.

Lisle (lil) **thread** (thred). See under *Thread*.

lisne (lin), *n.* [Obs.] See *Lissen*.

lisp, *v.i.*; lisped (lispt), *pt.*, *pp.*; lisping, *ppr.* [ME. *lispen*, *lipsen*, from AS. *wlisp*, *wlips*, a stammering, lisping.]

1. To pronounce the sibilant letters *s* and *z* imperfectly, as by giving them the sound of *th* or *th*.

2. To speak imperfectly; to utter in a hesitating, modest way; to make feeble, tentative, or imperfect efforts at speaking.

I *lisp'd* in numbers, for the numbers came.
—Pope.

lisp, *v.t.* 1. To pronounce with a lisp or imperfectly.

2. To speak in a timid, secret, or confidential manner; as, to *lisp* treachery.

lisp, *n.* The habit or act of lisping, as in uttering an aspirated *th* for *s*, *th* for *z*.

lisp′ẽr, *n.* One who lisps.

lisp′ing-ly, *adv.* In a lisping manner; with a lisp.

liss, *v.t.* To free, as from care or pain; to ease; to abate. [Obs.]

liss, *n.* Abatement; relief; ease; happiness [Obs.]

lis′sen, *n.* A cleft. [Prov. Eng.]

Lis-sen-ceph′à-là, *n.pl.* [Gr. *lissos*, smooth, and *enkephalos*, brain.] A primary division of mammalia having smooth cerebral hemispheres which have few folds, the cerebellum and part of the olfactory nerves being exposed. The division comprises the *Chiroptera*, *Insectivora*, *Rodentia*, and *Edentata*.

lis-sen-ceph′à-lous, *a.* 1. Having a smooth brain.

2. Of or pertaining to the *Lissencephala*.

lis′sōme, *a.* Lithesome; limber; supple; flexible; light; lithe; nimble; active; also written *lissom*.

lis′sōme-ness, *n.* The state of being lissome or lithesome; flexibility; agility; lightness.

lis-sō-trich′i-ăn, *a.* Lissotrichous.

lis-sot′ri-chous, *a.* [Gr. *lissos*, smooth, and *thrix*, *trichos*, hair.] Having smooth hair; liotrichous; applied to men and animals.

list, *v.i.*; listed, *pt.*, *pp.*; listing, *ppr.* [ME. *listen*, *lysten*; AS. *lystan*, to please, from *lust*, pleasure, desire.]

1. To be inclined; to choose; to prefer.

The wind bloweth where it *listeth*.—John iii. 8.

2. In nautical parlance, to incline; to lean; to careen; as, the vessel *listed* to port.

list, *v.t.* 1. To cause to incline or careen, as a vessel when, owing to a storm encountered, the cargo has shifted to one side.

2. To gratify; to suit; to please. [Obs.]

list, *v.t.* [ME. *listen*, *lesten*; AS. *hlystan*, to listen, harken, from *hlyst*, hearing.] To harken to; to hear; to listen to; used chiefly in poetry.

list, *v.i.* To harken; to attend; to listen; chiefly poetical.

list, *n.* [OFr. *liste*, a roll, list, border, band, from M.H.G. *liste*, a border, strip, edge.] A roll or catalogue, that is, a row or line; a schedule; a record; a register; as, a *list* of names; a *list* of articles; a *list* of ratable estate.

Civil list; see under *Civil*.

Free list; (a) a list of articles exempt from customs duties; (b) a list of persons to whom is granted the privilege of attending a performance of any kind without payment.

Syn.—Enrolment, record, index, inventory, roll, schedule, invoice, register, catalogue.

list, *v.t.* To enroll; to insert in a list or catalogue; specifically, (a) to enroll or engage for the public service, as soldiers; to enlist; (b) to record or set down for taxation, as property.

list, *v.i.* To engage in the public service by enrolling one's name; to enlist.

list, *n.* [ME. *liste*, *lyste*; OFr. *liste*, *lisse*, *lice*, list; LL. *licia*, a barrier, pl. *liciæ*, barriers of a tournament, the lists, from L. *licium*, a thread, a small girdle; prob. on account of the ropes used as barriers.] A line inclosing or forming the extremity of a piece of ground, or field of combat; hence, in the plural, *lists*, the ground or field inclosed for a race or combat.

To enter the lists; to accept a challenge, or engage in contest.

list, *v.t.* To inclose for combat; as, to *list* a field.

list, *n.* [ME. *list*, *liste*; AS. *list*, a list or border of cloth.]

1. The border, edge, or selvage of cloth; a strip of cloth forming the border or edge, particularly of broadcloth, and serving to strengthen it; a strip of cloth; a fillet.

2. A limit or boundary; a border; chiefly a poetical use.

3. In architecture, a little square molding; a fillet; also called *listel*.

4. In tin-working, (a) a thin coat of tin applied preparatory to the thicker coat, in tinning iron plates; (b) a selvage of wire or tin formed on the under edge of tin-plates.

5. In rope-making, a woolen flap in the hands of a rope-maker, through which the yarn goes.

6. In carpentry, (a) the upper rail of a railing; (b) a narrow strip from the edge of a plank.

7. A stripe. [Obs.]

8. The lobe of the ear; the ear itself. [Obs.]

9. A close dense streak in heavy bread. [Prov. Eng.]

10. A ridge or border of earth formed by a lister, as in cultivating corn. [Local, U. S.]

list, *v.t.* 1. To sew together, as strips of cloth, so as to make a party-colored show, or to form a border.

2. To cover with list, or with strips of cloth; as, to *list* a door; hence, to mark as if with list; to streak.

3. To make (a ridge of earth) with a lister on each side of a row, as of corn. [Local, U. S.]

4. In cultivating cotton, to prepare (land) for the crop by making alternate beds and alleys with the hoe. [Local, U. S.]

5. In carpentry, to reduce in breadth, as a board, by cutting off the sapwood from the edge.

list, *n.* [ME. *list, lyst*; AS. *lust*, desire, pleasure.]

1. Wish; choice; desire; inclination; lust. [Obs.]

2. In nautical parlance, an inclination or a careening to one side; as, the ship has a *list* to port.

list'el, *n.* In architecture, a fillet; a list.

lis'ten (lis'n), *v.i.*; listened, *pt., pp.*; listening, *ppr.* [ME. *listnen, lustnen, listen*; AS. *hlystan*, to listen, to list, from *hlyst*, hearing.]

1. To harken; to give ear; to attend closely with a view to hear.

On the green bank I sat, and *listened* long. —Dryden.

2. To obey; to yield to advice; to follow admonition; as, to *listen* to warning.

Syn.—Attend, harken, heed, list.

lis'ten, *v.t.* To hear, to attend to. [Obs.]

lis'ten-ẽr, *n.* One who listens; a harkener.

list'ẽr, *n.* One who makes a list or roll.

lis'tẽr, *n.* Same as *Leister*

list'ẽr, *n.* [So called in reference to the ridges and furrows formed, from AS. *list*, a border of cloth; O.H.G., *lista*, a border.] An agricultural implement for making furrows, in which it plants and covers grain simultaneously; a double-moldboard plow.

Lis'te-rȧ, *n.* [Named after Martin *Lister*, an English physician and naturalist.] A genus of small terrestrial orchids, natives of Europe, northern Asia, and North America. [See *Twayblade*.]

Lis-tē'ri-ăn, *a.* Of or pertaining to Sir Joseph Lister, an English physician, or to his antiseptic method of surgery.

lis'tẽr-ine (*or* -ïne), *n.* [Named after Sir Joseph *Lister*, an English physician.] A proprietary antiseptic preparation.

Lis'tẽr-ism, *n.* A general name for the antiseptic and aseptic treatment of wounds according to the principles first enunciated by Lister, an English physician.

Lis'tẽr-īze, *v.t.*; Listerized, *pt., pp.*; Listerizing, *ppr.* To treat (wounds) by the antiseptic method introduced by Sir Joseph Lister.

list'ful, *a.* Attentive. [Obs.]

list'ing, *n.* 1 The act of cutting away the sapwood from the edge of a board; also, the edge thus cut away.

2. The selvage of cloth; list.

3. In agriculture, the throwing up of the soil into ridges. [Local, U. S.]

4. The act or process of listing, in any sense.

list'ing-plow, *n.* Same as third *Lister*.

list'less, *a.* 1. Indifferent to or taking no pleasure in what is passing; languid and indifferent; as, a *listless* hearer or spectator.

2. Characterized by inactivity and languor; inanimate; as, a *listless* attitude.

Syn.—Careless, heedless, languid, indifferent, spiritless, supine, indolent.

list'less-ly, *adv.* In a listless manner; without attention; heedlessly.

list'less-ness, *n.* The state of being listless; inattention; heedlessness; indifference to what is passing.

list'ly, *a.* Quick f hearing. [Prov. Eng.]

list'ly, *adv.* Easily; distinctly. [Prov. Eng.]

list'-pot, *n.* A heated pan with a small quantity of tin at the bottom, and the last of the series of five pans used in the manufacture of tin-plate.

list'wŏrk, *n.* Rough embroidery-work in which list is sewed upon a garment, edge to edge or overlapping.

lit, *v.*, past tense and past participle of *light*.

lit'ȧ-ny, *n.*; *pl.* **lit'ȧ-nieş**. [OFr. *letanie*; LL. *litania*; Gr. *litaneia*, an entreating prayer, from *litainein*, to pray, entreat, from *litesthai*, *lissesthai*, to pray, beg, from *litē*, a prayer.] A solemn form of supplicatory prayer used in public worship; specifically, in liturgies, a responsive form of prayer in certain churches, usually of a penitential character.

Lesser litany; (a) the petitions, *Lord, have mercy upon us*; *Christ, have mercy upon us*; *Lord, have mercy upon us*, sometimes repeated three times, as at the beginning of the mass or eucharist; (b) an abbreviated form of the litany in which some of the invocations and responses are omitted; used in the Protestant Episcopal church.

lit'ȧ-ny-desk, *n.* In the Anglican church, a portable desk placed in the center of the choir or the chancel, facing the communion table, and at which the minister kneels to recite the litany.

lit'ȧ-ny-stool, *n.* See *Litany-desk*.

Li'tchī (-chē), *n.* [Chinese, *lichi*.] A genus of trees of the soapberry family, containing but one species, *Litchi Chinensis* or *Nephelium Litchi*, which yields the lichi, an edible fruit.

-lite. [L. *-lithus*, from Gr. *lithos*, a stone.] A suffix used chiefly in names of minerals and rocks, signifying stone.

lite, *a.* and *n.* Little. [Obs.]

lī'tẽr, lī'tre, *n.* [Fr. *litre*, from Gr. *litra*, a pound.] In the metric system, a measure of capacity, being a cubic decimeter, equal to 61.026 cubic inches, or 1.056 quarts.

lit'ẽr-ȧ-cy, *n.* The condition of being literate.

lit'ẽr-ăl, *a.* [OFr. *literal*; LL. *litteralis, literalis*, belonging to letters, literal, from L. *littera* or *litera*, a letter.]

1. According to the letter of verbal expression; primitive; real; not figurative or metaphorical; as, the *literal* meaning of a phrase.

2. Following the letter or exact words; not free; as, a *literal* translation.

3. Consisting of or expressed by letters.

The *literal* notation of numbers was known to Europeans before the ciphers.—Johnson.

4. Disposed to give a strict construction; unimaginative; matter-of-fact; said of persons.

Literal contract; in law, a contract the entire evidence of which is in writing.

Literal equation; in mathematics, an equation in which letters are used to represent the known quantities.

lit'ẽr-ăl, *n.* Literal meaning. [Obs.]

lit'ẽr-ăl-işm, *n.* 1. That which accords with the letter; a mode of interpreting literally; the act of adhering to the letter.

2. In the fine arts, a disposition to represent exactly without treating in an ideal manner.

lit'ẽr-ăl-ist, *n.* 1. One who adheres to the letter or exact word; an interpreter according to the letter.

2. In the fine arts, one who represents exactly without regard to idealization.

lit-ẽr-al'i-ty, *n.* The quality of being literal; verbal or literal meaning.

lit''ẽr-ăl-i-zā'tion, *n.* The act of literalizing or rendering literal; the act of reducing to a literal meaning.

lit'ẽr-ăl-ize, *v.t*; literalized, *pt., pp.*; literalizing, *ppr.* To render literal; to conform or adhere to the letter; to interpret or put in practice according to the strict meaning of the words.

lit'ẽr-ăl-ī-zẽr, *n.* One who literalizes or interprets literally.

lit'ẽr-ăl-ly, *adv.* 1. According to the primary and natural import of the words; not figuratively; as, a man and his wife cannot be *literally* one flesh.

2. With close adherence to words; word by word; as, to quote a writer *literally*.

lit'ẽr-ăl-ness, *n.* The state or quality of being literal; literal import.

lit'ẽr-ȧ-ry, *a.* [L. *litterarius, literarius*, of or belonging to letters, from *littera, litera*, a letter.]

1. Pertaining to letters or literature; treating of or dealing with learning or learned men; as, a *literary* history; *literary* conversation.

2. Versed in letters or literature; engaged in literature; as, a *literary* man or woman.

Literary property; property consisting in written or printed compositions; also, the exclusive legal right to publish such compositions.

lit'ẽr-āte, *a.* [L. *litteratus*, or *literatus*, lettered, learned, from *littera* or *litera*, a letter, pl. learning.]

1. Learned; lettered; instructed; educated; opposed to *illiterate*.

2. Literary; pertaining to letters.

lit'ẽr-āte, *n.* 1. A literary man.

2. In England, one who has received an education in a college or university, but who has not graduated; especially, a candidate for holy orders who has not studied at a university.

lit-ē-rā'tī, *n.*, pl. of *literatus*.

lit-ē-rā'tim, *adv.* [LL., from L. *littera*, or *litera*, letter.] Letter for letter.

lit-ẽr-ā'tion, *n.* The act or process of representing by letters.

lit'ẽr-ȧ-tŏr, *n.* 1. A petty schoolmaster; a dabbler in learning.

2. A literary man; a man of literary culture; a man of letters.

lit'ẽr-ȧ-tūre, *n.* [OFr. *literature*; L. *litteratura*, or *literatura*, a writing, grammar, philology, learning, from *littera* or *litera*, a letter, pl. learning.]

1. Learning; acquaintance with letters or books.

2. The collective body of literary productions, embracing the entire results of knowledge and fancy preserved in writing; also, the whole body of literary productions or writings upon a given subject, or relative to a particular science or branch of knowledge; the collective literary productions of any country or period; as, the *literature* of geology; the *literature* of chess; Elizabethan *literature*; American *literature*.

3. The class of writings in which beauty of style or expression is a characteristic feature, as poetry, romance, history, biography, essays, etc., in contradistinction to scientific works, or those written expressly to impart knowledge; belles-lettres.

4. The literary profession; the profession of a man of letters.

Literature is a very bad crutch, but a very good walking-stick. —Lamb.

Syn.—Learning, erudition, belles-lettres.

lit'ẽr-ȧ-tūred, *a.* Learned; literate.

lit-ē-rā'tus, *n.*; *pl.* **lit-ē-rā'tī**. [L., learned, from *littera, litera*, a letter, pl. learning.] A man of letters or learning; a savant; used chiefly in the plural.

-lith. [L. *-lithus*, from Gr. *lithos*, a stone.] A suffix used chiefly in geology to signify stone; as, mono*lith*.

lith-. See *Litho-*.

lith, *n.* A joint of the human body; a member; a limb; a division. [Obs.]

lith'ȧ-gogue (-gog), *n.* [*Lith-*, and Gr. *agōgos*, a leading, guiding, from *agein*, to lead.] In medicine, any agent tending to expel calculi from the bladder.

lith'ȧ-gogue, *a.* In medicine, having the power of expelling stone from the bladder or kidneys.

lith'ȧ-nōde, *n.* [*Lith-* and *anode*.] A hard peroxid of lead employed in storage-batteries.

lith-an'thrax, *n.* [*Lith-*, and Gr. *anthrax*, coal.] Stone-coal, as distinguished from *xylanthrax*, or wood-coal.

lith'ärġe, *n.* [OFr. *litarge*; L. *lithargyrus*; Gr. *lithargyros*, the spume or foam of silver; *lithos*, stone, and *argyros*, silver] The yellow or reddish protoxid of lead partially fused. On cooling it passes into a mass consisting of small six-sided plates of a reddish-yellow color, and semitransparent. It is much used in assaying as a flux, and enters largely into the composition of the glaze of common earthenware.

lith'āte, *n.* [*Lith*ic and *-ate*.] A salt of lithic acid.

līthe, *a.* [ME *lithe, lythe*; AS. *lithe*, soft, pliant, gentle.]

1. Easily bent; pliant; flexible; limber; as, the elephant's *lithe* proboscis.

2. Mild; agreeable; gentle; calm. [Obs.]

līthe, *v.t.* and *v.i.* I. *v.t.* To soften; to mitigate. [Obs.]

II. *v.i.* To become soft or mild. [Obs.]

lithe, *v.t.* and *v.i.* I. *v.t.* To listen to; to give ear to. [Obs.]

II. *v.i.* To listen; to give ear. [Obs.]

līthe'ly, *adv.* In a lithe manner.

li-thē'mi-ȧ, li-thæ'mi-ȧ, *n.* [*Lith-*, and Gr. *haima*, blood.] In pathology, a diseased condition of the blood, due to the presence of an excess of uric acid.

li-thē'miç, *a.* Pertaining to or suffering from lithemia.

līthe'ness, *n.* Flexibility; limberness; the condition or quality of being lithe.

lī'thẽr, *a.* Bad; corrupt; wicked. [Obs.]

lī'thẽr, *a.* Pliant; flexible. [Obs.]

lī'thẽr-ly, *a.* Wicked; mischievous; idle; lazy. [Obs.]

lī'thẽr-ly, *adv.* Wickedly; badly; mischievously. [Obs.]

lī'thẽr-ness, *n.* Laziness; wickedness. [Obs.]

lī'thẽr-ness, *n* The condition or quality of being lither; flexibility. [Obs.]

līthe'sŏme, *a.* Pliant; limber; nimble; lissome.

līthe'sŏme-ness, *n.* The condition of being lithesome.

lith'i-ȧ, *n.* [Gr. *lithos*, a stone.] An oxid of lithium of a white color. It dissolves slowly in water, forming a hydrate of lithium.

li-thī'ȧ-sis, *n.* [Gr. *lithiasis*, from *lithos*, a stone.] In pathology, the formation of calculi in any part of the body, especially in the urinary passages.

lith'i-āte, *n.* See *Lithate*.

lith'iç, *a.* [Gr. *lithikos*, of or pertaining to stone, from *lithos*, a stone.]

1. Pertaining to or consisting of stone; as, *lithic* ornaments.

2. Pertaining to stone in the bladder; uric.

Lithic acid; see *Uric acid* under *Uric*.

lith'iç, *a.* Pertaining to the element lithium.

lith'iç, *n.* A medicine used in treating stone in the bladder.

lith''i-fi-çā'tion, *n.* [Gr. *lithos*, a stone, and L. *facere*, to make.] The conversion or consolidation of loose mineral or sand particles into stone.

lith-i-oph'i-līte, *n.* [Gr. *lithos*, a stone, and *philos*, loving, and *-ite*.] In mineralogy, a vitreous phosphate of lithium and manganese occurring in orthorhombic crystals. It is a variety of triphylite.

lith'is-tid, *a.* and *n.* I. *a.* Pertaining to the *Lithistida*.

II. *n.* A sponge of the division *Lithistida*.